MUNICIPAL YEAR BOOK

www.MunicipalYearBook.co.uk *2013 Edition*

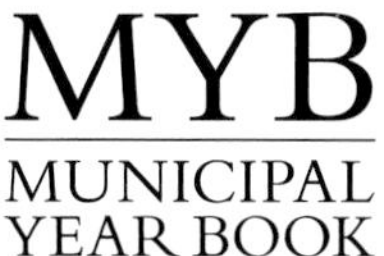

MYB
MUNICIPAL
YEAR BOOK

INFORMING LOCAL GOVERNMENT SINCE 1897

EDITOR Dean Wanless
ASSISTANT EDITOR Ali Lawrenson
EDITORIAL ASSISTANT Pete Stickland
EDITORIAL DIRECTOR Michael Burton
MANAGING DIRECTOR Graham Bond
MARKETING MANAGER Phaedra Rees

PUBLISHED BY: Hemming Information Services
A DIVISION OF HEMMING GROUP LTD
32 Vauxhall Bridge Road
t +44 (0)20 7973 6400
f +44 (0)20 7973 4794
e myb@hgluk.com

ISBN 978-0-7079-7127-8

Hemming Information Services is a division of Hemming Group Ltd.

Founded in 1893 with the launch of The MJ magazine, Hemming Group Ltd is a family owned company, specialising in the provision of business to business information.

Hemming Information Services deliver several print and online titles in the local government marketplace including: The Municipal Year Book, LocalGov.co.uk, The MJ, Surveyor, the Surveyor Highway Maintenance Yearbook, LAPV, TEC, and Governetz Public Property. Hemming Information Services also publishes a selection of private sector directories and magazines including the Retail Directory, Bridge Design and Engineering and Lingerie Buyer.

Other divisions of the Hemming Group include Hemming Conferences, which specialises in organising public sector conferences, and Brintex, the organisers of leading trade fairs such as the LGA Annual Conference and The London International Wine Trade Fair.

The Municipal Year Book was founded in 1897 by Sir Robert Donald, GBE, LLD

A member of the Directory & Database Publishers Association & The European Association of Directory Publishers

Letter from the editor

After a tumultuous couple of years for local government, things finally seem to be settling down a bit. After spending reviews, Icelandic banking and enormous budget cuts, the sector has responded with it's usual resilience by innovating to ensure that essential services continue to be provided in a timely and efficient fashion.

The major innovation that we've seen while compiling this year's Municial Year Book is the increasing number of officers that are shared by two or more authorities. The most exciting example of this new arrangement is the Tri-Borough arrangement between the London boroughs of Kensington and Chelsea, Hammersmith and Fulham and the City of Westminster. It is reported that the arrangement will result in savings of over £40 million by 2015 while still providing an excellent level of services. The chief executive of Kensington & Chelsea and Hammersmith & Fulham, Derek Myers, has very kindly written this year's foreword. I'm confident that you will find it as thought provoking as I did.

You will also notice that the Municipal Year Book has changed this year. While we continue to offer excellent information on all of the UK's local authorities, we have responded to feedback to provide more statistical information on the sector. You will find this in our new companion product The Municipal Year Book Compendium. I'm certain that you will find it a very useful resource.

Obviously it is impossible to compile a book of the Municipal Year Book's size and stature without the efforts of a great many people. My thanks go to the hundreds of local authority officers who take the time to ensure that the information that we hold is correct, we are very grateful for their contribution.

The editorial team of Ali Lawrenson and Pete Stickland have worked tirelessly to ensure that the Year Book is as accurate as ever.

The work put in by the editorial team would be pointless if the directory were not seen by the right people. Phaedra Rees and her marketing team do an excellent job to ensure that the Municipal Year Book is on the desks of professionals throughout the industry.

Managing data on a large scale always offers unique challenges and I must thank Malcolm Collins, for his constant alterations to our databases to ensure that our data is securely stored and easily edited, and Barry Halper and Harshen Shah, for making the data presentable both on paper and online.

I hope that you find the Municipal Year Book as useful as ever, and urge you to visit www.LocalGov.co.uk for both up-to-date news and the full Municipal Year Book data listings.

Dean Wanless

MANAGING EDITOR

Foreword

By Derek Myers - Chair Solace Management Board

The Municipal Year Book reminds us of change and continuity and this combination will serve us well as a short form summary of this period in local government's history.

We leave 2012 having had a memorable year in the life of the nation with the Olympics and Paralympics following the Jubilee celebrations. Never have so many flags flown.

The local government workforce may not have felt quite so celebratory, but an objective overview reveals a more balanced picture.

It is surely right that public services are efficient and run at the minimum cost necessary to secure quality, sustainable arrangements that hold the commitment of staff.

This is no new mission. None of our predecessors wanted to run inefficient services, but the optimisation of efficiency is illusive and definitions of target quality in delivery and even preferred outcomes remain open to debate and review.

I discern five observations of current local government practice that we might do well to recognise and reflect upon. We all aspire to be professionals and professionalism is at base, considered and documented practice. If we cannot guarantee to get it right, let us at least be able to describe why we do what we do.

The first feature I identify is political consensus about direction. The debate about budget reductions has been academic (about political and economic causation) and subtle (about extent and timing) but not polarised or stark.

Deficit deniers are rare; no-one thinks the NHS should not be protected, at least in part. There is no lobby saying local government deserved to stay as it was (or at least nobody paid any attention if it did). Budget driven change became a given.

My second observation is that The Prime Minister's big idea-Big Society- was not still born but is only growing slowly. 70,000 Olympic Games Makers may impress the world, but volunteering driven by vicarious excitement is not the same as regular, routine, local service that runs libraries, looks after the vulnerable or tidies parks.

Councils can claim to be at the heart of this leadership towards a new community spirit, yet I worry these new skills and new attitudes are still rarer than we admit. Do we really think 'amateurs' can do things as well as paid staff?

A third observation is that local government is now developing a serious track record in collaboration to reduce costs.

These new operating models – where my own two Councils are prominent – are to be celebrated because they are created locally – designed to fit local needs and preferences – yet all serve to protect the front line services that matter. Where councils collaborate new behaviours have to follow, including new habits and expectations for Councillors. But this is surely right if the once in a decade changes we are now making are that important.

This collaboration is between authorities and between authorities and other providers. Expect further fusions of structures as CCGs aggregate and some partner with councils.

The next test will be whether small councils might agree to voluntarily merge to form more viable councils. I predict this will not happen in 2013 but it will happen in the next five years.

My fourth observation has been the success of budget plans so far. There have been local controversies and perhaps in some areas quality may have been diluted in a way that may lead to later regrets, but largely the local decision-making has been painstaking and the execution exemplary. Of course jobs have gone, careers ended and family incomes trashed, but only where no other alternatives existed. The rate of redeployment and voluntary exits has properly minimised compulsory redundancies.

So if these have been the main features of change – what of continuity? A striking feature for me is that most of the forecasts that the range and breadth of the local government service offer are simply unsustainable have yet to translate into radical action. No local politicians have offered their communities a small state, stripped back, it's going to be very different now, vision as a policy preference, though no doubt some have regretfully described it as a consequence of 'Coalition Cuts'. Part of this perhaps reflects British innateconservatism, but partly it might reflect a genuine consensus that pretty much all of what local government does is worth doing and should not be discarded. Indeed the arrival of public health and likely some involvement in Universal Credit, produces areas for new ambition in 2013 and beyond.

And therefore my last area of continuity is the day by day, quiet service that is the lot of the majority of local government staff. No doubt grumbling about hyper-ambitious managers and out of touch councillors, hundreds of thousands of staff have continued to get on with business, helping their communities survive and with the best of work, thrive, week by week, year by year.

This service is only relative continuity. It exists in a context of management churn, continuous re-organisation and constantly changing job titles. Exactly the context where a good Year Book is invaluable.

MJ has been published since 1893 and the Year Book since 1897, We have a proud history in local government and I truly believe a confident future too, strengthened by our ability to adjust and re-invent ourselves and underpinned by the quiet professionalism of our staff, partners and allies.

Derek Myers

Derek Myers
Chair, SOLACE Management Board

User guide

MAIN COUNCIL CONTACT DETAILS

Under the council heading you will find the full council name followed by its main contact address. For Wales, Scotland and Northern Ireland the council's local language name is listed in brackets after the full council name.

The council type is indicated to the right of the council name.

Election Frequency

This shows the type and frequency of elections held by each authority. If elections are 'of whole council' this means elections are held every four years. If elections are 'held by thirds' then one third of the seats are elected each year for three years out of four. For details of the council's next election please see the General Information section at the back of Volume Two.

Members of the Council

The Municipal Year Book asks local authorities to indicate the Leader and Deputy Leader of the Council, the Chair / Mayor / Convenor / Sheriff / Provost and their deputies and the Group Leaders of the political parties represented on their council.

A full political breakdown can be found in each council entry at the end of the Members of the Council section.

Indices

An index for local authorities by type can be found at the end of the local authorities listings.

KEY TO POLITICAL PARTIES

ALL	Alliance Party
C	Conservative
CAP	Community Action Party
DUP	Democratic Unionist Party
GRN	Green
IND	Independent
INDNA	Independent (Non Aligned)
INDU	Independent Unionists
LAB	Labour
LIB	Liberal
LD	Liberal Democrat
NILAB	Northern Ireland Labour
O	Other
OFF	Official Unionist
PC	Plaid Cymru
PUP	Progressive Unionist Party
R	Ratepayer or Residents Association
RSP	Respect The Unity Coalition
SD	Social Democrat Party
SDLP	Social Democratic and Labour Party
SF	Sinn Féin
SNP	Scottish Nationalist Party
UKIP	UK Independence Party
UU	Ulster Unionists Party
VCNY	Vacancy
WP	Workers Party

User guide - Sample Entry

Below is an example entry from the Year Book. This provides a brief explanation of all the information contained within a local authority entry.

Authority type e.g. District Main contact details for local authority	**BLYTH VALLEY** D Blyth Valley Borough Council, Civic Centre, Blyth NE24 2BX **t** 01670 542000 **f** 01670 542102 **e** yourlink@blythvalley.gov.uk **www.blythvalley.gov.uk**
Useful information relating to council	FACTS & FIGURES **Police Authority:** Northumbria Police Authority **Election Frequency:** Elections are of whole council
Details of decision making officers	PRINCIPAL OFFICERS **Computer Management:** Mr N Arnold, IT Manager, Council Offices, Avenue Road, Seaton Delaval, Whitley Bay NE25 0DX **t** 01670 542000 **f** 01670 542390 **e** narnold@blythvalley.gov.uk
Total number of council members Full list of council members	MEMBERS OF THE COUNCIL (50) **Mayor:** Cobb, W (LAB - Cramlington East) 18 Village Road, Cramlington NE23 2AQ
Overall political composition of the council	POLITICAL COMPOSITION **LAB:** 34, **LD:** 10, **C:** 3, **IND:** 3
Details of political structure, listing cabinet members. Scrutiny chairs may be listed in brackets alongside the relevant portfolio.	CABINET **Total Cabinet Members:** 8 Leader and Strategic Policy: D Stephens
Details of Committee chairs. Scrutiny committees are marked with an (S).	COMMITTEE CHAIRS **Overview and Scrutiny (S):** S Dungworth

Contents

ABERDEEN CITY S

Aberdeen City Council, 5th Floor, St Nicholas House, Broad Street, Aberdeen AB10 1BX ☎ 0845 608 0910 🖷 01224 636181 ✉ shfindlay@aberdeencity.gov.uk 💻 www.aberdeencity.gov.uk

FACTS & FIGURES

Police Authority: Grampian Joint Police Board
Health Authority: NHS Grampian
Learning and Skills Council: Scotland
Parliamentary Constituencies: Aberdeen North, Aberdeen South, Gordon
EU Constituencies: Scotland
Election Frequency: Elections are of whole council
Twinning: Bulawayo (Zimbabwe); Clermont-Ferrand (France); Gomel (Belarus); Regensburg (Germany); Stavangar (Norway)

PRINCIPAL OFFICERS

Chief Executive: Ms Valerie Watts, Chief Executive, 2nd Floor, Old Town House, Broad Street, Aberdeen AB10 1FY ☎ 01224 522500 ✉ vwatts@aberdeencity.gov.uk

Assistant Chief Executive: Mr Ciaran Monaghan, Head of Service, 2nd Floor, Old Town House, Broad Street, Aberdeen AB10 1FY ☎ 01224 522293 🖷 01224 644346 ✉ cmonaghan@aberdeencity.gov.uk

Senior Management: Mr Stewart Carruth, Director of Corporate Governance, Business Hub 12, 2nd Floor West, Marischal College, Broad Street, Aberdeen AB10 1AB ☎ 01224 522550 🖷 01224 522568 ✉ scarruth@aberdeencity.gov.uk

Senior Management: Mr Pete Leonard, Director of Housing & Environment, Business Hub 12, 2nd Floor West, Marischal College, Broad Street, Aberdeen AB10 1AB ☎ 01224 346012 🖷 01224 523764 ✉ pleonard@aberdeencity.gov.uk

Senior Management: Mr Fred McBride, Director of Social Care & Wellbeing, Business Hub 12, 2nd Floor West, Marischal College, Broad Street, Aberdeen AB10 1AB ☎ 01224 523797 🖷 01224 346012 ✉ frmcbride@aberdeencity.gov.uk

Senior Management: Mr Gordon McIntosh, Director of Enterprise, Planning & Infrastructure, Business Hub 12, 2nd Floor West, Marischal College, Broad Street, Aberdeen AB10 1AB ☎ 01224 522941 🖷 01224 346012 ✉ gmcintosh@aberdeencity.gov.uk

Architect, Building / Property Services: Mr Hugh Murdoch, Head of Asset Management & Operations, Business Hub 10, 2nd Floor South, Marischal College, Broad Street, Aberdeen AB10 1AB ☎ 01224 523965 🖷 01224 523315 ✉ hughm@aberdeencity.gov.uk

Architect, Building / Property Services: Mr William Watson, Principal Architect, Crown House, 27 -29 Crown Street, Aberdeen AB11 6HA ☎ 01224 439215 🖷 01224 439216 ✉ williamwatson@aberdeencity.gov.uk

Best Value: Mr Paul Fleming, Head of Customer Service & Performance, Business Hub 17, 3rd Floor North, Marischal College, Broad Street, Aberdeen AB10 1AB ☎ 01224 523366 🖷 01224 522832 ✉ pfleming@aberdeencity.gov.uk

Building Control: Dr Margaret Bochel, Head of Planning & Sustainable Development, Business Hub 4, Ground Floor North, Marischal College, Broad Street, Aberdeen AB10 1AB ☎ 01224 523133 🖷 01224 523180 ✉ mbochel@aberdeencity.gov.uk

Building Control: Mr Gordon Spence, Building Standards Manager, Business Hub 4, Ground Floor North, Marischal College, Broad Street, Aberdeen AB10 1AB ☎ 01224 522436 🖷 01224 523180 ✉ gspence@aberdeencity.gov.uk

Children / Youth Services: Ms Susan Devlin, Head of Children's Services, Business Hub 8, 1st Floor North, Marischal College, Broad Street, Aberdeen AB10 1BX ☎ 01224 522110 🖷 01224 523195 ✉ sdevlin@aberdeencity.gov.uk

Children / Youth Services: Mr David Leng, Head of Schools & Educational Establishments, Business Hub 12, 2nd Floor North, Marischal College, Broad Street, Aberdeen AB10 1AB ☎ 01224 523517 🖷 01224 522022 ✉ dleng@aberdeencity.gov.uk

Civil Registration: Ms Gladys Nicol, Senior Registrar, Business Hub 3, Ground Floor South, Marischal College, Broad Street, Aberdeen AB10 1AB ☎ 01224 522617 ✉ gnicol@aberdeencity.gov.uk

PR / Communications: Ms Dawn Schultz, Senior IVSA Officer, Business Hub 10, 2nd Floor South, Marischal College, Broad Street, Aberdeen AB10 1AB ☎ 01224 522767 🖷 01224 523315 ✉ dschultz@aberdeencity.gov.uk

Community Planning: Mr Martin Murchie, Corporate Planning & Corporate Performance Manager, Business Hub 18, 4th Floor West, Marischal College, Broad Street, Aberdeen AB10 1AB ☎ 01224 522008 🖷 01224 522832 ✉ mmurchie@aberdeencity.gov.uk

Community Safety: Mr Neil Carnegie, Community Safety Manager, 3rd Floor, Old Town House, Broad Street, Aberdeen AB10 1AQ ☎ 01224 523945 ✉ ncarnegie@aberdeencity.gov.uk

Community Safety: Mr Donald Urquhart, Head of Housing & Community Safety, Business Hub 11, 2nd Floor West, Marischal College, Broad Street, Aberdeen AB10 1AB ☎ 01224 522119 🖷 01224 523764 ✉ dourquhart@aberdeencity.gov.uk

Community Safety: Mr Colin Walker, Anti-Social Behaviour Officer, 3rd Floor, Old Town House, Broad Street, Aberdeen AB10 1AQ ☎ 01224 523917 🖷 01224 623156 ✉ colinwalker@aberdeencity.gov.uk

Computer Management: Mr Paul Fleming, Head of Customer Service & Performance, Business Hub 17, 3rd Floor West, Marischal College, Broad Street, Aberdeen AB10 1AB ☎ 01224 523366 🖷 01224 522832 ✉ pfleming@aberdeencity.gov.uk

Computer Management: Ms Sandra Massey, IT Manager, Business Hub 17, 3rd Floor North, Marischal College, Broad Street, Aberdeen AB10 1AB ☎ 01224 522778 ✉ smassey@aberdeencity.gov.uk

LOCAL AUTHORITIES

Consumer Protection and Trading Standards: Ms Carole Jackson, Trading Standards & Commercial Premises Manager, Business Hub 15, 3rd Floor South, Marischal College, Broad Street, Aberdeen AB10 1AB ☎ 01224 522057 🖷 01224 523887 🖱 cjackson@aberdeencity.gov.uk

Contracts: Mr Craig Innes, Head of Procurement, ☎ 01224 665650 🖱 cinnes@aberdeencity.gov.uk

Corporate Services: Mr Stewart Carruth, Director of Corporate Governance, Business Hub 12, 2nd Floor West, Marischal College, Broad Street, Aberdeen AB10 1AB ☎ 01224 522550 🖷 01224 522568 🖱 scarruth@aberdeencity.gov.uk

Corporate Services: Mr Pete Leonard, Director of Housing & Environment, Business Hub 12, 2nd Floor West, Marischal College, Broad Street, Aberdeen AB10 1AB ☎ 01224 346012 🖷 01224 523764 🖱 pleonard@aberdeencity.gov.uk

Corporate Services: Mr Fred McBride, Director of Social Care & Wellbeing, Business Hub 12, 2nd Floor West, Marischal College, Broad Street, Aberdeen AB10 1AB ☎ 01224 523797 🖷 01224 346012 🖱 frmcbride@aberdeencity.gov.uk

Corporate Services: Mr Gordon McIntosh, Director of Enterprise, Planning & Infrastructure, Business Hub 12, 2nd Floor West, Marischal College, Broad Street, Aberdeen AB10 1AB ☎ 01224 522941 🖷 01224 346012 🖱 gmcintosh@aberdeencity.gov.uk

Customer Service: Mr Paul Fleming, Head of Customer Service & Performance, Business Hub 17, 3rd Floor North, Marischal College, Broad Street, Aberdeen AB10 1AB ☎ 01224 523366 🖷 01224 522832 🖱 pfleming@aberdeencity.gov.uk

Economic Development: Mr Gerry Brough, Project Director - Economic & Business Development, Business Hub 10, 2nd Floor South, Marischal College, Broad Street, Aberdeen AB10 1AB ☎ 01224 523197 🖷 01224 813315 🖱 gbrough@aberdeencity.gov.uk

Education: Mr David Leng, Head of Schools & Educational Establishments, Business Hub 12, 2nd Floor North, Marischal College, Broad Street, Aberdeen AB10 1AB ☎ 01224 523517 🖷 01224 522022 🖱 dleng@aberdeencity.gov.uk

Education: Mr Charlie Penman, Head of Educational Development, Policy & Performance, Business Hub 12, 2nd Floor North, Marischal College, Broad Street, Aberdeen AB10 1AB ☎ 01224 522375 🖷 01224 522022 🖱 cpenman@aberdeencity.gov.uk

E-Government: Mr Ian Watt, E-Government Manager, Business Hub 17, 3rd Floor North, Marischal College, Broad Street, Aberdeen AB10 1AB ☎ 01224 522830 🖷 01224 522771 🖱 ianw@aberdeencity.gov.uk

Electoral Registration: Mr Ian Milton, Assessor & Electoral Registration Officer, Grampian Valuation Joint Board, Woodhill House, Westburn Road, Aberdeen AB16 5GA ☎ 01224 664360 🖷 01224 664361 🖱 assessor@grampian-vjb.gov.uk

Emergency Planning: Mr David McIntosh, Emergency Planning Manager, 1 Queen's Gardens, Aberdeen AB15 4YD ☎ 01224 633030 🖷 01224 645647 🖱 dmcintosh@aberdeencity.gov.uk

Energy Management: Ms Mai Muhammad, Energy Manager, Business Hub 10, 2nd Floor South, Marischal College, Broad Street, Aberdeen AB10 1AB ☎ 01224 522383 🖱 mmuhammad@aberdeencity.gov.uk

Environmental / Technical Services: Mr Mark Reilly, Head of Environmental Services, Kittybrewster Depot, Powis Terrace, Aberdeen AB25 3RF ☎ 01224 523096 🖷 01224 487807 🖱 mareilly@aberdeencity.gov.uk

Environmental Health: Ms Carole Jackson, Trading Standards & Commercial Premises Manager, Business Hub 15, 3rd Floor South, Marischal College, Broad Street, Aberdeen AB10 1AB ☎ 01224 522057 🖷 01224 523887 🖱 cjackson@aberdeencity.gov.uk

Estates, Property & Valuation: Mr Michael Duncan, General Manager - Asset Management, Business Hub 10, 2nd Floor South, Marischal College, Broad Street, Aberdeen AB10 1AB ☎ 01224 522166 🖷 01224 813315 🖱 mjd@aberdeencity.gov.uk

European Liaison: Mr Yasa Ratnayeke, Manager - EU Policy & External Funding, Business Hub 10, 2nd Floor South, Marischal College, Broad Street, Aberdeen AB10 1AB ☎ 01224 523807 🖷 01224 813315 🖱 yratnayeke@aberdeencity.gov.uk

Events Manager: Ms Dawn Schultz, Senior IVSA Officer, Business Hub 10, 2nd Floor South, Marischal College, Broad Street, Aberdeen AB10 1AB ☎ 01224 522767 🖷 01224 523315 🖱 dschultz@aberdeencity.gov.uk

Facilities: Mr Simon Williams, Facilities Manager, Business Hub 10, 2nd Floor South, Marischal College, Broad Street, Aberdeen AB10 1AB ☎ 01224 522587 🖷 01224 813315 🖱 swilliams@aberdeencity.gov.uk

Finance and Treasurer: Mr Barry Jenkins, Head of Finance, Town House Extension, Broad Street, Aberdeen AB10 1AH ☎ 01224 522551 🖷 01224 632343 🖱 bajenkins@aberdeencity.gov.uk

Fleet Management: Mr Nigel Buchan, Fleet Services Manager, Kittybrewster Depot, Powis Terrace, Aberdeen AB25 3RF ☎ 01224 489317 🖷 01224 277728 🖱 nbuchan@aberdeencity.gov.uk

Grounds Maintenance: Mr Steven Shaw, Environmental Manager, Kittybrewster Depot, Powis Terrace, Aberdeen AB25 3RF ☎ 01224 489273 🖷 01224 489270 🖱 stevens@aberdeencity.gov.uk

Health and Safety: Mrs Mary Agnew, Health, Safety & Wellbeing Manager, Business Hub 18, 4th Floor West, Marischal College, Broad Street, Aberdeen AB10 1AB ☎ 01224 523088 🖷 01224 522257 🖱 magnew@aberdeencity.gov.uk

Highways: Mr Richard Blain, Roads Operations Manager, West Tullos Roads Depot, Craigshaw Drive, Aberdeen AB12 3AL ☎ 01224 241525 🖱 rblain@aberdeencity.gov.uk

Housing: Mr Donald Urquhart, Head of Housing & Community Safety, Business Hub 11, 2nd Floor West, Marischal College, Broad Street, Aberdeen AB10 1AB ☎ 01224 522119 🖷 01224 523764 ✉ dourquhart@aberdeencity.gov.uk

Housing Maintenance: Mr Ian Burrows, Property Manager, Ground Floor, Kittybrewster Depot, Powis Place, Aberdeen AB25 3RF ☎ 01224 489365 🖷 01224 487807 ✉ iburrows@aberdeencity.gov.uk

Legal: Ms Jane MacEachran, Head of Legal & Democratic Services, 1st Floor, Old Town House, Broad Street, Aberdeen AB10 1AQ ☎ 01224 522084 ✉ janem@aberdeencity.gov.uk

Leisure and Cultural Services: Ms Patricia Cassidy, Head of Communties, Culture & Sport, Business Hub 12, 2nd Floor North, Marischal College, Broad Street, Aberdeen AB10 1AB ☎ 01224 522473 🖷 01224 522022 ✉ pcassidy@aberdeencity.gov.uk

Licensing: Ms Jane MacEachran, Head of Legal & Democratic Services, 1st Floor, Old Town House, Broad Street, Aberdeen AB10 1AQ ☎ 01224 522084 ✉ janem@aberdeencity.gov.uk

Lifelong Learning: Ms Gail Woodcock, Service Manager - Communities, Business Hub 12, 2nd Floor North, Marischal College, Broad Street, Aberdeen AB10 1AB ☎ 01224 522732 ✉ gwoodcock@aberdeencity.gov.uk

Lighting: Mr Richard Blain, Roads Operations Manager, West Tullos Roads Depot, Craigshaw Drive, Aberdeen AB12 3AL ☎ 01224 241525 ✉ rblain@aberdeencity.gov.uk

Lottery Funding, Charity and Voluntary: Ms Susan McCorquodale, External Funding Officer, Business Hub 10, 2nd Floor South, Marischal College, Broad Street, Aberdeen AB10 1AB ☎ 01224 523373 🖷 01224 523315 ✉ smccorquodale@aberdeencity.gov.uk

Member Services: Mr Roderick MacBeath, Head of Democratic Services, 1st Floor, Town House, Broad Street, Aberdeen AB10 1AQ ☎ 01224 523054 🖷 01224 523768 ✉ rmacbeath@aberdeencity.gov.uk

Parking: Mr Neil Carnegie, Community Safety Manager, 3rd Floor, Old Town House, Broad Street, Aberdeen AB10 1AQ ☎ 01224 523945 ✉ ncarnegie@aberdeencity.gov.uk

Partnerships: Ms Jan Falconer, Projects, Partnerships & Funding Manager, Business Hub 18, 4th Floor West, Marischal College, Broad Street, Aberdeen AB10 1AB ☎ 01224 522662 🖷 01224 523315 ✉ jfalconer@aberdeen.gov.uk

Personnel / HR: Mr Ewan Sutherland, Head of Human Resources & Organisational Development, Business Hub 18, 4th Floor West, Marischal College, Broad Street, Aberdeen AB10 1AB ☎ 01224 522192 🖷 01224 522257 ✉ esutherland@aberdeencity.gov.uk

Planning: Dr Margaret Bochel, Head of Planning & Sustainable Development, Business Hub 4, Ground Floor North, Marischal College, Broad Street, Aberdeen AB10 1AB ☎ 01224 523133 🖷 01224 523180 ✉ mbochel@aberdeencity.gov.uk

Procurement: Mr Craig Innes, Head of Procurement, Woodhill House, Ashgrove Road, Aberdeen AB16 5GA ☎ 01224 665650 ✉ cinnes@aberdeencity.gov.uk

Public Libraries: Mr Neil Bruce, Service Manager - Culture & Sport, Business Hub 12, 2nd Floor North, Marischal College, Broad Street, Aberdeen AB10 1AB ☎ 01224 523144 🖷 01224 522022 ✉ neilbr@aberdeencity.gov.uk

Recycling & Waste Minimisation: Mr Angus Sefton, Waste Collection & Disposal Manager, 1st Floor, Kittybrewster Depot, Powis Terrace, Aberdeen AB25 3RF ☎ 01224 489354 🖷 01224 489270 ✉ asefton@aberdeencity.gov.uk

Regeneration: Mr John Quinn, Head of Service Regeneration & Housing Investment, Crown House, 27 - 29 Crown Street, Aberdeen AB11 6HA ☎ 01224 439202 🖷 01224 439216 ✉ jquinn@aberdeencity.gov.uk

Road Safety: Mr Andrew Smith, Traffic Engineering Manager, 1st Floor, 74 - 76 Spring Garden, Aberdeen AB25 1GN ☎ 01224 528056 ✉ andrews@aberdeencity.gov.uk

Social Services: Mr Fred McBride, Director of Social Care & Wellbeing, Business Hub 12, 2nd Floor West, Marischal College, Broad Street, Aberdeen AB10 1AB ☎ 01224 523797 🖷 01224 346012 ✉ frmcbride@aberdeencity.gov.uk

Social Services: Mrs Liz Taylor, Head of Older People & Rehabiliation Services, Business Hub 8, 1st Floor North, Marischal College, Broad Street, Aberdeen AB10 1AB ☎ 01224 522457 🖷 01224 523195 ✉ litaylor@aberdeencity.gov.uk

Social Services (Adult): Mr Tom Cowan, Head of Adult Services, Business Hub 8, 1st Floor North, Marischal College, Broad Street, Aberdeen AB10 1AB ☎ 01224 523162 🖷 01224 523195 ✉ tcowan@aberdencity.gov.uk

Social Services (Children): Ms Susan Devlin, Head of Children's Services, Business Hub 8, 1st Floor North, Marischal College, Broad Street, Aberdeen AB10 1AB ☎ 01224 522110 🖷 01224 523195 ✉ sdevlin@aberdeencity.gov.uk

Street Scene: Mr Steven Shaw, Environmental Manager, Kittybrewster Depot, Powis Terrace, Aberdeen AB25 2RF ☎ 01224 489273 🖷 01224 489270 ✉ stevens@aberdeencity.gov.uk

Sustainable Communities: Mr Will Napier, Programme Manager, Business Hub 13, 2nd Floor West, Marischal College, Broad Street, Aberdeen AB10 1AB ☎ 01224 522042 🖷 01224 636181 ✉ wnapier@aberdeencity.gov.uk

Sustainable Development: Dr Margaret Bochel, Head of Planning & Sustainable Development, Business Hub 4, 2nd Floor North, Marischal College, Broad Street, Aberdeen AB10 1AB ☎ 01224 523133 🖷 01224 523180 ✉ mbochel@aberdeencity.gov.uk

Tourism: Ms Dawn Schultz, Senior IVSA Officer, Business Hub 10, 2nd Floor South, Marischal College, Broad Street, Aberdeen AB10 1AB ☎ 01224 522767 🖷 01224 523315

✉ dschultz@aberdeencity.gov.uk

Town Centre: Mr Tom Moore, City Centre Manager, Business Hub 10, 2nd Floor South, Marischal College, Broad Street, Aberdeen AB10 1AB ☎ 01224 523444 🖷 01224 523315 ✉ tommoore@aberdeencity.gov.uk

Traffic Management: Mr Andrew Smith, Traffic Engineering Manager, 1st Floor, 74 - 76 Spring Garden, Aberdeen AB25 1GN ☎ 01224 528056 ✉ andrews@aberdeencity.gov.uk

Transport: Dr Margaret Bochel, Head of Planning & Sustainable Development, Business Hub 4, Ground Floor North, Marischal College, Broad Street, Aberdeen AB10 1AB ☎ 01224 523133 🖷 01224 523180 ✉ mbochel@aberdeencity.gov.uk

Transport Planner: Dr Margaret Bochel, Head of Planning & Sustainable Development, Business Hub 4, Ground Floor North, Marischal College, Broad Street, Aberdeen AB10 1AB ☎ 01224 523133 🖷 01224 523180 ✉ mbochel@aberdeencity.gov.uk

Waste Collection and Disposal: Mr Angus Sefton, Waste Collection & Disposal Manager, 1st Floor, Kittybrewster Depot, Powis Terrace, Aberdeen AB25 3RF ☎ 01224 489354 🖷 01224 489270 ✉ asefton@aberdeencity.gov.uk

Waste Management: Mr Peter Lawrence, Waste & Recycling Manager, 1st Floor, Kittybrewster Depot, Powis Terrace, Aberdeen AB25 3RF ☎ 01224 489331 🖷 01224 489270 ✉ plawrence@aberdeencity.gov.uk

MEMBERS OF THE COUNCIL (43)

***Lord Provost:* Adam**, George (LAB - Hilton / Stockethill)
gadam@aberdeencity.gov.uk
***Deputy Provost:* Reynolds**, John (LD - Bridge of Don)
jreynolds@aberdeencity.gov.uk
***Leader of the Council:* Crockett**, Barney (LAB - Dyce / Bucksburn / Danestone)
bcrockett@aberdeencity.gov.uk
***Deputy Leader of the Council:* Boulton**, Marie (IND - Lower Deeside)
mboulton@aberdeencity.gov.uk
Allan, Yvonne (LAB - Torry / Ferryhill)
yallan@aberdeencity.gov.uk
Blackman, Kirsty (SNP - Hilton / Stockethill)
kblackman@aberdeencity.gov.uk
Camerson, David (SNP - Kingswell / Sheddocksley)
dacameron@aberdeencity.gov.uk
Carle, Scott (LAB - Northfield)
sccarle@aberdeencity.gov.uk
Cooney, Neil (LAB - Kincorth / Loirston)
ncooney@aberdeencity.gov.uk
Corall, John (SNP - Hazlehead / Ashley / Queens Cross)
jcorall@aberdeencity.gov.uk
Cormie, Bill (SNP - Midstocket / Rosemount)
bcormie@aberdeencity.gov.uk
Delaney, Steve (LD - Kingswell / Sheddocksley)
sdelaney@aberdeencity.gov.uk
Dickson, Graham (SNP - Torry / Ferryhill)
gdickson@aberdeencity.gov.uk
Donelly, Alan (CON - Torry / Ferryhill)
adonnelly@aberdeencity.gov.uk
Dunbar, Jackie (SNP - Northfield)
jdunbar@aberdeencity.gov.uk
Dunbar, Lesley (LAB - Hilton / Stockethill)
Finlayson, Andrew (IND - Kincorth / Loirston)
Forsyth, Fraser (O - Midstocket / Rosemount)
fforsyth@aberdeencity.gov.uk
Graham, Gordon (LAB - Northfield)
ggraham@aberdeencity.gov.uk
Grant, Ross (LAB - Tillydrone / Seaton / Old Aberdeen)
rossgrant@aberdeencity.gov.uk
Greig, Martin (LD - Hazlehead / Ashley / Queens Cross)
mgreig@aberdeencity.gov.uk
Ironside, Len (LAB - Kingswell / Sheddocksley)
lironside@aberdeencity.gov.uk
Jaffrey, Muriel (SNP - Bridge of Don)
mjaffrey@aberdeencity.gov.uk
Kiddie, James (SNP - Torry / Ferryhill)
jkiddie@aberdeencity.gov.uk
Laing, Jenny (LAB - Midstocket / Rosemount)
jelaing@aberdeencity.gov.uk
Lawrence, Graeme (LAB - Dyce / Bucksburn / Danestone)
glawrence@aberdeencity.gov.uk
MacGregor, Neil (SNP - Dyce / Bucksburn / Danestone)
nmacgregor@aberdeencity.gov.uk
Malik, M. Tauqeer (LAB - Lower Deeside)
mmalik@aberdeencity.gov.uk
Malone, Aileen (LD - Lower Deeside)
amalone@aberdeencity.gov.uk
May, Andrew (SNP - George Street / Harbour)
andrewmay@aberdeencity.gov.uk
McCaig, Callum (SNP - Kincorth / Loirston)
cmccaig@aberdeencity.gov.uk
Milne, Ramsay (LAB - Tillydrone / Seaton / Old Aberdeen)
rmilne@aberdeencity.gov.uk
Morrison, Nathan (LAB - George Street / Harbour)
namorrison@aberdeencity.gov.uk
Morrison, Jean (LAB - George Street / Harbour)
jemorrison@aberdeencity.gov.uk
Noble, Jim (SNP - Tillydrone / Seaton / Old Aberdeen)
jimnoble@aberdeencity.gov.uk
Samarai, Gill (SNP - Dyce/Bucksburn/Danestone)
gsamarai@aberdeencity.gov.uk
Stewart, Jennifer (LD - Hazlehead / Ashley / Queens Cross)
jastewart@aberdeencity.gov.uk
Stuart, Sandy (SNP - Bridge of Don)
sandystuart@aberdeencity.gov.uk
Taylor, Angela (LAB - Airyhall / Broomhill / Garthdee)
angelataylor@aberdeencity.gov.uk
Thomson, Ross (O - Hazlehead / Ashley / Queens Cross)
rossthomson@aberdeencity.gov.uk
Townson, Gordon (SNP - Airyhall / Broomhill / Garthdee)
gtownson@aberdeencity.gov.uk
Young, Willie (LAB - Bridge of Don)
wyoung@aberdeencity.gov.uk
Yuill, Ian (LD - Airyhall / Broomhill / Garthdee)
iyuill@aberdeencity.gov.uk

POLITICAL COMPOSITION

LAB: 17, SNP: 15, LD: 6, O: 2, IND: 2, CON: 1

COMMITTEE CHAIRS

Adult Services Sub: Mr James Kiddie
Audit & Risk: Mr Barney Crockett
Budget Monitoring Board: Mr John Stewart
Budget Monitoring Board: Mr Kevin Stewart
Children's Services Sub: Mr Gordon Leslie

Corporate Policy & Performance: Ms Jennifer Stewart
Council: Mr Peter Stephen
Development Management Sub (Visits): Ms Katharine Dean
Development Management Sub: Ms Katharine Dean
Education, Culture & Sport: Mr Andrew May
Enterprise, Planning & Infrastructure: Ms Katharine Dean
Finance & Resources: Mr Kevin Stewart
Grampian Joint Police Board: Mr Martin Greig
Housing & Environment: Ms Aileen Malone
Licensing Board: Ms Muriel Jaffrey
Licensing: Mr John Reynolds
Local Licensing Forum: Mr Allan McIntosh (External)
Pensions Panel: Mr Neil Fletcher
Social Care & Wellbeing: Mr James Kiddie
Taxi Consultation Group: Mr John Reynolds
Urgent Business: Mr John Stewart

ABERDEENSHIRE S

Aberdeenshire Council, Woodhill House, Westburn Road, Aberdeen AB16 5GB ☎ 0845 608 1207 💻 www.aberdeenshire.gov.uk

FACTS & FIGURES

Police Authority: Grampian Joint Police Board
Health Authority: NHS Grampian
Learning and Skills Council: Scotland
Parliamentary Constituencies: Aberdeenshire West and Kincardine, Banff and Buchan, Gordon
EU Constituencies: Scotland
Election Frequency: Elections are of whole council

PRINCIPAL OFFICERS

Chief Executive: Mr Colin Mackenzie, Chief Executive, Woodhill House, Westburn Road, Aberdeen AB16 5GB ☎ 01224 665400 🖷 01224 665444 🖱 colin.mackenzie@aberdeenshire.gov.uk

Senior Management: Mr Stephen Archer, Director - Infrastructure Services, Woodhill House, Westburn Road, Aberdeen AB16 5GB ☎ 01224 664568 🖱 stephen.archer@aberdeenshire.gov.uk

Senior Management: Dr Christine Gore, Director - Corporate Services, Woodhill House, Westburn Road, Aberdeen AB16 5GB ☎ 01224 665510 🖷 01224 664888 🖱 christine.gore@aberdeenshire.gov.uk

Senior Management: Ms Maria Walker, Director - Education, Learning & Leisure, Woodhill House, Westburn Road, Aberdeen AB16 5GB ☎ 01224 668469 🖱 maria.walker@aberdeenshire.gov.uk

Senior Management: Ms Karen Wiles, Head of Legal & Governance, Woodhill House, Westburn Road, Aberdeen AB16 5GB ☎ 01224 665430 🖱 karen.wiles@aberdeenshire.gov.uk

Architect, Building / Property Services: Mr Allan Whyte, Head of Property & Facilities Management, Woodhill House, Westburn Road, Aberdeen AB16 5GB ☎ 01224 664500 🖷 01224 664470 🖱 allan.whyte@aberdeenshire.gov.uk

Building Control: Mr Robert Gray, Head of Planning & Building Standards, Woodhill House, Westburn Road, Aberdeen AB16 5GB ☎ 01224 664728 🖱 robert.gray@aberdeenshire.gov.uk

Catering Services: Mr Allan Doig, Catering Services Manager, Harlaw Road Depot, Harlaw Road, Inverurie AB51 4TE ☎ 01467 627500 🖱 allan.doig@aberdeenshire.gov.uk

Children / Youth Services: Mr Philip English, Head of Adult & Criminal Justice Services, Woodhill House, Westburn Road, Aberdeen AB16 5GB ☎ 01224 664940 🖷 01224 664992 🖱 philip.english@aberdeenshire.gov.uk

Civil Registration: Ms Karen Wiles, Head of Legal & Governance, Woodhill House, Westburn Road, Aberdeen AB16 5GB ☎ 01224 665430 🖱 karen.wiles@aberdeenshire.gov.uk

PR / Communications: Ms Kate Bond, Head of Customer Communication & Improvements, Woodhill House, Westburn Road, Aberdeen AB16 5GB ☎ 01224 664405 🖷 01224 665204 🖱 kate.bond@aberdeenshire.gov.uk

Community Planning: Mr Les Allan, Area Manager - Marr, Marr Area Office, School Road, Alford AB33 8TY ☎ 01975 564800 🖱 les.allan@aberdeenshire.gov.uk

Community Planning: Ms Margaret-Jane Cardno, Area Manager - Banff & Buchan, Banff and Buchan Area Office, St. Leonard's, Sandyhill Road, Banff AB45 1BH ☎ 01779 483200 🖱 margaret-jane.cardno@aberdeenshire.gov.uk

Community Planning: Ms Hazel McLaren, Policy Officer - Community Planning, School Road, Alford AB33 8TY ☎ 01975 564804 🖱 hazel.mclaren@aberdeenshire.gov.uk

Community Planning: Mr Douglas Milne, Area Manager - Garioch, Garioch Area Office, Gordon House, Blackhall Road, Inverurie AB51 3WB ☎ 01467 628201 🖱 douglas.milne@aberdeenshire.gov.uk

Community Planning: Mr William Munro, Area Manager - Kincardine & Mearns, Viewmount, Arduthie Road, Stonehaven AB3 2DQ ☎ 01569 768200 🖷 01569 767972 🖱 william.munro@aberdeenshire.gov.uk

Community Planning: Mr Keith Newton, Area Manager - Formartine, Formartine Area Office, 29 Bridge Street, Ellon AB41 9AA ☎ 01358 726402 🖱 keith.newton@aberdeenshire.gov.uk

Community Planning: Mr Chris White, Area Manager - Buchan, Buchan Area Office, Arbuthnot House, 62 Broad Street, Peterhead AB42 1DA ☎ 01779 483200 🖱 chris.white@aberdeenshire.gov.uk

Community Planning: Mrs Erin Wood, Policy Officer - Community Planning, Woodhill House, Westburn Road, Aberdeen AB16 5GB ☎ 01224 664316 🖷 01224 665444 🖱 erin.wood@aberdeenshire.gov.uk

Computer Management: Ms Nicola Graham, Head of ICT, Woodhill House, Westburn Road, Aberdeen AB16 5GB ☎ 01224 664287 🖷 01224 664001 🖱 nicola.graham@aberdeenshire.gov.uk

Consumer Protection and Trading Standards: Mr Ian Robertson, Head of Service - Protective Services & Waste Management, Mercat Cross, 36 Low Street, Banff AB45 1AY ☎ 01261 813271 🖷 01261 818649 ✉ ian.robertson@aberdeenshire.gov.uk

Contracts: Mr Craig Innes, Head of Central Procurement Services, Woodhill House, Westburn Road, Aberdeen AB16 5GB ☎ 01224 665650 ✉ craig.innes@aberdeenshire.gov.uk

Corporate Services: Dr Christine Gore, Director of Corporate Services, Woodhill House, Westburn Road, Aberdeen AB16 5GB ✉ christine.gore@aberdeenshire.gov.uk

Customer Service: Ms Morag Esson, Customer Services Manager, Woodhill House, Westburn Road, Aberdeen AB16 5GB ☎ 01224 664583 🖷 01224 664022 ✉ morag.esson@aberdeenshire.gov.uk

Economic Development: Ms Belinda Miller, Head of Economic Development, Woodhill House, Westburn Road, Aberdeen AB16 5GB ☎ 01224 664568 🖷 01224 664713 ✉ belinda.miller@abderdeenshire.gov.uk

Education: Mr Andrew Griffiths, Interim Head of Service - Education & Staff Development, Woodhill House, Westburn Road, Aberdeen AB16 5GB ☎ 01224 664568 ✉ andrew.griffiths@aberdeenshire.gov.uk

Education: Ms Heather Hamilton, Head of Service - Integration & Inclusion, Woodhill House, Westburn Road, Aberdeen AB16 5GB ☎ 01224 668469 ✉ heather.hamilton@aberdeenshire.gov.uk

Education: Ms Maria Walker, Director - Education, Learning & Leisure, Woodhill House, Westburn Road, Aberdeen AB16 5GB ☎ 01224 668469 ✉ maria.walker@aberdeenshire.gov.uk

Education: Mr Wilf Weir, Head of Service - Policy & Resources, Woodhill House, Westburn Road, Aberdeen AB16 5GB ☎ 01224 664568 ✉ wilf.weir@aberdeenshire.gov.uk

E-Government: Ms Nicola Graham, Head of ICT, Woodhill House, Westburn Road, Aberdeen AB16 5GB ☎ 01224 664287 🖷 01224 664001 ✉ nicola.graham@aberdeenshire.gov.uk

Electoral Registration: Mr Allan Bell, Senior Committee Officer/Elections Organiser, Woodhill House, Westburn Road, Aberdeen AB16 5GB ☎ 01224 665119 🖷 01224 664019 ✉ allan.bell@aberdeenshire.gov.uk

Emergency Planning: Mr David McIntosh, Emergency Planning Manager, 1 Queen's Gardens, Aberdeen AB15 4YD ☎ 01224 633030 🖷 01224 645647 ✉ david@grampian.epu.co.uk

Energy Management: Mr Allan Whyte, Head of Property & Facilities Management, Woodhill House, Westburn Road, Aberdeen AB16 5GB ☎ 01224 664500 🖷 01224 664470 ✉ allan.whyte@aberdeenshire.gov.uk

Environmental / Technical Services: Mr Stephen Archer, Director - Infrastructure Services, Woodhill House, Westburn Road, Aberdeen AB16 5GB ☎ 01224 664568 ✉ stephen.archer@aberdeenshire.gov.uk

Environmental Health: Mr Ian Robertson, Head of Service - Protective Services & Waste Management, Mercat Cross, 36 Low Street, Banff AB45 1AY ☎ 01261 813271 🖷 01261 818649 ✉ ian.robertson@aberdeenshire.gov.uk

Estates, Property & Valuation: Mr Gordon Daniels, Estates Manager, Woodhill House, Westburn Road, Aberdeen AB16 5GB ☎ 01224 664257 🖷 01224 664470 ✉ gordon.daniels@aberdeenshire.gov.uk

European Liaison: Mr Martin Brebner, European Programmes Executive, Woodhill House, Westburn Road, Aberdeen AB16 5GB ☎ 01224 665225 🖷 01224 664713 ✉ martin.brebner@aberdeenshire.gov.uk

Facilities: Mr Ray Walkinshaw, Facilities Manager, Woodhill House, Westburn Road, Aberdeen AB16 5GB ☎ 01224 664463 ✉ ray.walkinshaw@aberdeenshire.gov.uk

Facilities: Mr Allan Whyte, Head of Property & Facilities Management, Woodhill House, Westburn Road, Aberdeen AB16 5GB ☎ 01224 664500 🖷 01224 664470 ✉ allan.whyte@aberdeenshire.gov.uk

Finance and Treasurer: Mr Allan Wood, Head of Service - Finance, Woodhill House, Westburn Road, Aberdeen AB16 5GB ☎ 01224 664202 ✉ allan.wood@aberdeenshire.gov.uk

Fleet Management: Mr Ian Paisley, Fleet Manager, Inverurie Repair Depot, Harlow Way, Inverurie AB51 4TE ☎ 01467 627530 🖷 01467 624256 ✉ ian.paisley@aberdeenshire.gov.uk

Grounds Maintenance: Mr Philip McKay, Head of Roads & Landscape Services, T & I Operations, Harlow Way, Inverurie AB51 4SG ☎ 01467 627644 🖷 01467 624827 ✉ philip.mckay@aberdeenshire.gov.uk

Health and Safety: Ms Pamela Bruce, Principal Health & Safety Adviser, Woodhill House, Westburn Road, Aberdeen AB16 5GB ☎ 01224 664067 🖷 01224 665122 ✉ pamela.bruce@aberdeenshire.gov.uk

Highways: Mr Stephen Archer, Director - Infrastructure Services, Woodhill House, Westburn Road, Aberdeen AB16 5GB ☎ 01224 664568 ✉ stephen.archer@aberdeenshire.gov.uk

Home Energy Conservation: Mr David Cooper, Specialist Officer - Housing & Pollution, Planning and Environmental Services, Gordon House, Blackhall Road, Inverurie AB51 3WA ☎ 01467 628159 🖷 01467 628358 ✉ david.cooper@aberdeenshire.gov.uk

Housing: Mr Douglas Edwardson, Head of Housing, Woodhill House, Westburn Road, Aberdeen AB16 5GB ☎ 01224 664900 🖷 01224 664992 ✉ douglas.edwardson@aberdeenshire.gov.uk

Housing: Mr Ritchie Johnson, Director of Housing & Social Work, Woodhill House, Westburn Road, Aberdeen AB16 5GB ☎ 01224 665490 🖷 01224 664992 ✉ ritchie.johnson@aberdeenshire.gov.uk

Housing Maintenance: Mr Douglas Edwardson, Head of Housing, Woodhill House, Westburn Road, Aberdeen AB16 5GB ☎ 01224 664900 🖷 01224 664992 ✉ douglas.edwardson@aberdeenshire.gov.uk

Legal: Ms Karen Wiles, Head of Legal & Governance, Woodhill House, Westburn Road, Aberdeen AB16 5GB ☎ 01224 665430 ✉ karen.wiles@aberdeenshire.gov.uk

Leisure and Cultural Services: Mr John Harding, Head of Service - Lifelong Learning & Leisure, Woodhill House, Westburn Road, Aberdeen AB16 5GB ☎ 01224 664568 ✉ john.harding@aberdeenshire.gov.uk

Licensing: Ms Karen Wiles, Head of Legal & Governance, Woodhill House, Westburn Road, Aberdeen AB16 5GB ☎ 01224 665430 ✉ karen.wiles@aberdeenshire.gov.uk

Lifelong Learning: Mr John Harding, Head of Service - Lifelong Learning & Leisure, Woodhill House, Westburn Road, Aberdeen AB16 5GB ☎ 01224 664568 ✉ john.harding@aberdeenshire.gov.uk

Lighting: Mr Brian Strachan, Strategy/Lighting Officer, Harlaw Way, Inverurie AB51 5SG ☎ 01467 627626 🖷 01467 624827 ✉ brian.strachan@aberdeenshire.gov.uk

Lottery Funding, Charity and Voluntary: Mr Walter Taylor, Grants & Outdoor Activities Officer, Woodhill House, Westburn Road, Aberdeen AB16 5GB ☎ 01224 664237 🖷 01224 664615 ✉ walter.taylor@aberdeenshire.gov.uk

Parking: Mr Philip McKay, Head of Roads & Landscape Services, T & I Operations, Harlaw Way, Inverurie AB51 4SG ☎ 01467 627644 🖷 01467 624827 ✉ philip.mckay@aberdeenshire.gov.uk

Personnel / HR: Ms Laura Simpson, Head of HR & OD, Woodhill House, Westburn Road, Aberdeen AB16 5GB ☎ 01224 664021 ✉ laura.simpson@aberdeenshire.gov.uk

Planning: Mr Robert Gray, Head of Planning & Building Standards, Woodhill House, Westburn Road, Aberdeen AB16 5GB ☎ 01224 664728 ✉ robert.gray@aberdeenshire.gov.uk

Procurement: Mr Craig Innes, Head of Central Procurement Services, Woodhill House, Westburn Road, Aberdeen AB16 5GB ☎ 01224 665650 ✉ craig.innes@aberdeenshire.gov.uk

Public Libraries: Ms Helen Dewar, Principal Libraries Officer, Woodhill House, Westburn Road, Aberdeen AB16 5GB ☎ 01651 871210 ✉ helen.dewar@aberdeenshire.gov.uk

Recycling & Waste Minimisation: Mrs Pam Walker, Waste Management Officer, Unit 7, Harlaw Industrial Estate, Harlaw Way, Inverurie AB51 4SG ☎ 01467 628682 🖷 01467 625706 ✉ pam.walker@aberdeenshire.gov.uk

Regeneration: Mr Reid Hutchison, CED Co-ordinator, Woodhill House, Westburn Road, Aberdeen AB16 5GB ☎ 01358 726411 ✉ reid.hutchison@aberdeenshire.gov.uk

Road Safety: Mr Ewan Wallace, Head of Transportation, Woodhill House, Westburn Road, Aberdeen AB16 5GB ☎ 01224 664580 🖷 01224 662005 ✉ ewan.wallace@aberdeenshire.gov.uk

Social Services: Mr Ritchie Johnson, Director of Housing & Social Work, Woodhill House, Westburn Road, Aberdeen AB16 5GB ☎ 01224 665490 🖷 01224 664992 ✉ ritchie.johnson@aberdeenshire.gov.uk

Social Services (Adult): Mr Philip English, Head of Adult & Criminal Justice Services, Woodhill House, Westburn Road, Aberdeen AB16 5GB ☎ 01224 664940 🖷 01224 664992 ✉ philip.english@aberdeenshire.gov.uk

Social Services (Adult): Ms Patricia MacLachlan, Head of Service - Older People & Disabilities, Woodhill House, Westburn Road, Aberdeen AB16 5GB ☎ 01224 664940 ✉ patricia.maclachlan@aberdeenshire.gov.uk

Social Services (Children): Mr Robert Driscoll, Head of Child Services, Woodhill House, Westburn Road, Aberdeen AB16 5GB ☎ 01261 664940 ✉ robert.driscoll@aberdeenshire.gov.uk

Staff Training: Ms Laura Simpson, Head of HR & OD, Woodhill House, Westburn Road, Aberdeen AB16 5GB ☎ 01224 664021 ✉ laura.simpson@aberdeenshire.gov.uk

Street Scene: Mr Philip McKay, Head of Roads & Landscape Services, T & I Operations, Harlaw Way, Inverurie AB51 4SG ☎ 01467 627644 🖷 01467 624827 ✉ philip.mckay@aberdeenshire.gov.uk

Sustainable Development: Ms Anne Laird, Project & Performance Officer, Woodhill House, Westburn Road, Aberdeen AB16 5GB ☎ 01224 665528 🖷 01224 664615 ✉ anne.laird@aberdeenshire.gov.uk

Tourism: Ms Belinda Miller, Head of Economic Development, Woodhill House, Westburn Road, Aberdeen AB16 5GB ☎ 01224 664568 🖷 01224 664713 ✉ belinda.miller@abderdeenshire.gov.uk

Town Centre: Mr Bill Clark, Towns Programme Co-ordinator, Woodhill House, Westburn Road, Aberdeen AB16 5GB ☎ 07769 642360 ✉ bill.clark@aberdeenshire.gov.uk

Traffic Management: Mr Philip McKay, Head of Roads & Landscape Services, T & I Operations, Harlaw Way, Inverurie AB51 4SG ☎ 01467 627644 🖷 01467 624827 ✉ philip.mckay@aberdeenshire.gov.uk

Transport: Mr Ewan Wallace, Head of Transportation, Woodhill House, Westburn Road, Aberdeen AB16 5GB ☎ 01224 664580 🖷 01224 662005 ✉ ewan.wallace@aberdeenshire.gov.uk

Transport Planner: Mr Ewan Wallace, Head of Transportation, Woodhill House, Westburn Road, Aberdeen AB16 5GB ☎ 01224 664580 🖷 01224 662005 ✉ ewan.wallace@aberdeenshire.gov.uk

Waste Collection and Disposal: Mr Ian Robertson, Head of Service - Protective Services & Waste Management, Mercat Cross, 36 Low Street, Banff AB45 1AY ☎ 01261 813271

🖷 01261 818649 ✉ ian.robertson@aberdeenshire.gov.uk

Waste Management: Mr Ian Robertson, Head of Service - Protective Services & Waste Management, Mercat Cross, 36 Low Street, Banff AB45 1AY ☎ 01261 813271 🖷 01261 818649 ✉ ian.robertson@aberdeenshire.gov.uk

MEMBERS OF THE COUNCIL (67)

Leader of the Council: **Robertson**, Anne (LD - Turriff & District)
cllr.a.robertson@aberdeenshire.gov.uk
Agnew, Wendy (CON - Stonehaven & Lower Deeside)
cllr.w.agnew@aberdeenshire.gov.uk
Aitchison, David (SNP - Westhill & District)
cllr.d.aitchison@aberdeenshire.gov.uk
Allan, Anne (SNP - Peterhead North & Rattray)
cllr.a.m.allan@aberdeenshire.gov.uk
Allan, Amanda (SNP - Westhill & District)
cllr.a.j.allan@aberdeenshire.gov.uk
Argyle, Peter (LD - Aboyne, Upper Deeside & Donside)
cllr.p.argyle@aberdeenshire.gov.uk
Bellarby, Peter (LD - Stonehaven & Lower Deeside)
cllr.p.bellarby@aberdeenshire.gov.uk
Bews, Alistair (SNP - North Kincardine)
cllr.a.bews@aberdeenshire.gov.uk
Blackett, Geva (SNP - Aboyne, Upper Deeside & Donside)
cllr.g.blackett@aberdeenshire.gov.uk
Buchan, Charles (SNP - Fraserburgh & District)
cllr.c.buchan@aberdeenshire.gov.uk
Buchan, Alan (IND - Peterhead North & Rattray)
cllr.a.buchan@aberdeenshire.gov.uk
Carr, George (CON - Mearns)
cllr.g.carr@aberdeenshire.gov.uk
Chapman, Edie (CON - Central Buchan)
cllr.e.chapman@aberdeenshire.gov.uk
Clark, Graeme (SNP - Stonehaven & Lower Deeside)
cllr.g.clark@aberdeenshire.gov.uk
Clark, Karen (LD - Banchory & Mid-Deeside)
cllr.k.clark@aberdeenshire.gov.uk
Clark, Linda (SNP - Banchory & Mid-Deeside)
cllr.l.clark@aberdeenshire.gov.uk
Cowling, Richard (CON - Inverurie & District)
cllr.r.cowling@aberdeenshire.gov.uk
Cox, John (IND - Banff & District)
cllr.j.cox@aberdeenshire.gov.uk
Cullinane, Nan (LD - East Garioch)
cllr.n.cullinane@aberdeenshire.gov.uk
Davidson, Isobel (LD - Ellon & District)
cllr.i.davidson@aberdeenshire.gov.uk
Dick, Jean (SNP - Mearns)
cllr.j.dick@aberdeenshire.gov.uk
Duncan, Sandy (SNP - Turriff & District)
cllr.a.duncan@aberdeenshire.gov.uk
Duncan, John (CON - Troup)
cllr.j.duncan@aberdeenshire.gov.uk
Evison, Alison (LAB - North Kincardine)
cllr.a.evison@aberdeenshire.gov.uk
Farquhar, Katrina (CON - Aboyne, Upper Deeside & Donside)
cllr.k.farquhar@aberdeenshire.gov.uk
Findlater, Mark (IND - Troup)
cllr.m.findlater@aberdeenshire.gov.uk
Ford, Martin (SGP - East Garioch)
cllr.m.ford@aberdeenshire.gov.uk
Gardiner, Alan (IND - Peterhead North & Rattray)
cllr.a.gardiner@aberdeenshire.gov.uk
Gifford, Jim (CON - Mid-Formartine)
cllr.j.gifford@aberdeenshire.gov.uk
Grant, Allison (SNP - West Garioch)
cllr.a.grant@aberdeenshire.gov.uk
Gray, Ian (SNP - Banff & District)
cllr.i.gray@aberdeenshire.gov.uk
Hendry, Allan (SNP - Mid-Formartine)
cllr.a.hendry@aberdeenshire.gov.uk
Hood, Fergus (SNP - East Garioch)
cllr.f.hood@aberdeenshire.gov.uk
Howatson, Bill (LD - Mearns)
cllr.w.howatson@aberdeenshire.gov.uk
Ingleby, Moira (CON - Huntly, Strathbogie & Howe of Alford)
cllr.m.ingleby@aberdeenshire.gov.uk
Ingram, Jim (SNP - Central Buchan)
cllr.j.ingram@aberdeenshire.gov.uk
Johnston, Paul (IND - Mid-Formartine)
cllr.p.johnston@aberdeenshire.gov.uk
Kitts-Hayes, Martine (LD - Inverurie & District)
cllr.m.kitts-hayes@aberdeenshire.gov.uk
Latham, John (IND - Huntly, Strathbogie & Howe of Alford)
cllr.j.latham@aberdeenshire.gov.uk
Lonchay, Sheena (LD - West Garioch)
cllr.s.lonchay@aberdeenshire.gov.uk
Malone, Tom (IND - Peterhead South & Cruden)
cllr.t.malone@aberdeenshire.gov.uk
McKail, Ron (CON - Westhill & District)
cllr.r.mckail@aberdeenshire.gov.uk
McRae, Fiona (SNP - Peterhead North & Rattray)
cllr.f.mcrae@aberdeenshire.gov.uk
Merson, Rob (SNP - Ellon & District)
cllr.r.merson@aberdeenshire.gov.uk
Mollison, Ian (LD - North Kincardine)
cllr.i.mollison@aberdeenshire.gov.uk
Nelson, Carl (CON - North Kincardine)
cllr.c.nelson@aberdeenshire.gov.uk
Norrie, Alisan (IND - Turriff & District)
cllr.a.norrie@aberdeenshire.gov.uk
Oddie, Patricia (CON - West Garioch)
cllr.p.oddie@aberdeenshire.gov.uk
Owen, Gillian (CON - Ellon & District)
cllr.g.owen@aberdeenshire.gov.uk
Partridge, Hamish (SNP - Troup)
cllr.h.partridge@aberdeenshire.gov.uk
Pirie, Lenny (SNP - Central Buchan)
cllr.l.pirie@aberdeenshire.gov.uk
Pratt, Stuart (SNP - Peterhead South & Cruden)
cllr.s.pratt@aberdeenshire.gov.uk
Ross, Alastair (LD - Huntly, Strathbogie & Howe of Alford)
cllr.a.ross@aberdeenshire.gov.uk
Roy, Mike (CON - Banff & District)
cllr.m.roy@aberdeenshire.gov.uk
Shand, Cryle (SNP - Mid-Formartine)
cllr.c.shand@aberdeenshire.gov.uk
Smith, Stephen (SNP - Peterhead South & Cruden)
cllr.s.smith@aberdeenshire.gov.uk
Smith, Norman (IND - Central Buchan)
cllr.n.smith@aberdeenshire.gov.uk
Stewart, Dave (IND - Mearns)
cllr.d.stewart@aberdeenshire.gov.uk
Strathdee, Joanna (SNP - Huntly, Strathbogie & Howe of Alford)
cllr.j.strathdee@aberdeenshire.gov.uk
Stuart, Bryan (SNP - Inverurie & District)
cllr.b.stuart@aberdeenshire.gov.uk

Tait, Ian (IND - Fraserburgh & District)
cllr.i.tait@aberdeenshire.gov.uk
Thomson, Richard (SNP - Ellon & District)
cllr.r.thomson@aberdeenshire.gov.uk
Topping, Brian (SNP - Fraserburgh & District)
cllr.b.topping@aberdeenshire.gov.uk
Vernal, Hamish (SNP - Inverurie & District)
cllr.h.vernal@aberdeenshire.gov.uk
Walker, Iris (LD - Westhill & District)
cllr.i.walker@aberdeenshire.gov.uk
Watt, Michael (IND - Fraserburgh & District)
cllr.m.watt@aberdeenshire.gov.uk
Webster, Jill (CON - Banchory & Mid-Deeside)
cllr.j.webster@aberdeenshire.gov.uk

POLITICAL COMPOSITION
SNP: 27, CON: 14, IND: 12, LD: 12, SGP: 1, LAB: 1

COMMITTEE CHAIRS
Education, Learning & Leisure: Ms Isobel Davidson
Infrastructure Services: Mr Peter Argyle
Policy & Resources: Mr Jim Gifford
Scrutiny & Audit: Ms Gillian Owen
Social Work & Housing: Ms Karen Clark

ADUR D

Adur District Council, Civic Centre, Ham Road, Shoreham-by-Sea BN43 6PR ☎ 01273 263000 ✉ info@adur.gov.uk 💻 www.adur.gov.uk

FACTS & FIGURES
Police Authority: Sussex Police Authority
Health Authority: South East Coast Strategic Health Authority
Learning and Skills Council: South East
EU Constituencies: South East
Election Frequency: Elections are biennial
Twinning: Riom (France); Zywiec (Poland)

PRINCIPAL OFFICERS
Chief Executive: Mr Peter Latham, Chief Executive, Worthing Town Hall, Chapel Road, Worthing BN11 1HA ☎ 01903 221001; 01903 221001 ✉ peter.latham@adur-worthing.gov.uk

Senior Management: Mr Andrew Gardiner, Strategic Director, Worthing Town Hall, Chapel Road, Worthing BN11 1HA ☎ 01903 221301; 01903 221301 ✉ andrew.gardiner@adur-worthing.gov.uk

Senior Management: Mr John Mitchell, Strategic Director, Adur Civic Centre, Ham Road, Shoreham-by-Sea BN43 6PR ☎ 01273 263312; 01273 263312 ✉ john.mitchell@adur-worthing.gov.uk

Architect, Building / Property Services: Mr Cliff Harrison, Executive Head of Technical Services, Portland House, Richmond Road, Worthing BN11 1HS ☎ 01903 221370; 01903 221370 ✉ cliff.harrison@adur-worthing.gov.uk

Best Value: Mr Bill Parsons, Performance, Scrutiny & Communications, Worthing Town Hall, Chapel Road, Worthing BN11 1HA ☎ 01903 221005; 01903 221005
✉ bill.parsons@adur-worthing.gov.uk

Best Value: Mrs Carol Stephenson, Adur & Worthing Partnership Programme Manager, Civic Centre, Ham Road, Shoreham-by-Sea BN43 6PR ☎ 01273 263205
✉ carol.stephenson@adur-worthing.gov.uk

Building Control: Mr James Appleton, Executive Head of Planning, Regeneration & Wellbeing, Portland House, Richmond Road, Worthing BN11 1HS ☎ 01903 221333; 01903 221333
✉ james.appleton@adur-worthing.gov.uk

PR / Communications: Mrs Wendy Knight, Communications Manager, Worthing Town Hall, Chapel Road, Worthing BN11 1HA
☎ 01903 221017; 01903 221017
✉ wendy.knight@adur-worthing.gov.uk

Community Planning: Mr Paul Pennicott, Development Control Manager, Worthing Town Hall, Chapel Road, Worthing BN11 1HA
☎ 01903 221347
✉ paul.pennicott@adur-worthing.gov.uk

Community Safety: Mrs Jacqui Cooke, Safer Communities Manager, Worthing Town Hall, Chapel Road, Worthing BN11 1HA
☎ 08456 070999; 08456 070999
✉ jacqui.cooke@adur-worthing.gov.uk

Computer Management: Mr Mark Gawley, Head of IT Contract Services, Worthing Town Hall, Chapel Road, Worthing BN11 1HA
☎ 01903 221477; 01903 221477
✉ mark.gawley@adur-worthing.gov.uk

Contracts: Mr Cliff Harrison, Executive Head of Technical Services, Portland House, Richmond Road, Worthing BN11 1HS
☎ 01903 221370; 01903 221370
✉ cliff.harrison@adur-worthing.gov.uk

Corporate Services: Mr Andrew Gardiner, Strategic Director, Worthing Town Hall, Chapel Road, Worthing BN11 1HA
☎ 01903 221301; 01903 221301
✉ andrew.gardiner@adur-worthing.gov.uk

Customer Service: Mr Kevin Masters, Executive Head of Customer Services, Worthing Town Hall, Chapel Road, Worthing BN11 1HA ☎ 01903 221243; 01903 221243
✉ kevin.masters@adur-worthing.gov.uk

Direct Labour: Mr John Mitchell, Strategic Director, Worthing Town Hall, Chapel Road, Worthing BN11 1HA ☎ 01273 263312; 01273 263312 ✉ john.mitchell@adur-worthing.gov.uk

Economic Development: Ms Tina Barker, Economic Development Officer, Commerce Way, Lancing BN15 8TA ☎ 01273 263147
✉ tina.barker@adur-worthing.gov.uk

E-Government: Mr John Mitchell, Strategic Director, Worthing Town Hall, Chapel Road, Worthing BN11 1HA ☎ 01273 263312; 01273 263312 ✉ john.mitchell@adur-worthing.gov.uk

Electoral Registration: Ms Teresa Bryant, Electoral Services Manager, Worthing Town Hall, Chapel Road, Worthing BH11 1HA
☎ 01903 221474; 01903 221474
✉ teresa.bryant@adur-worthing.gov.uk

Emergency Planning: Mr Tony Lucas, Emergency Planning Officer, Worthing Town Hall, Chapel Road, Worthing BH11 1HA ☎ 01903 221025; 01903 221025 ✉ tony.lucas@adur-worthing.gov.uk

Energy Management: Mr Cliff Harrison, Executive Head of Technical Services, Portland House, Richmond Road, Worthing BN11 1HS ☎ 01903 221370; 01903 221370 ✉ cliff.harrison@adur-worthing.gov.uk

Environmental / Technical Services: Mr Cliff Harrison, Executive Head of Technical Services, Portland House, Richmond Road, Worthing BN11 1HS ☎ 01903 221370; 01903 221370 ✉ cliff.harrison@adur-worthing.gov.uk

Environmental Health: Mr James Elliot, Senior Environmental Health Officer, Adur Civic Centre, Ham Road, Shoreham-by-Sea BN43 6PR ☎ 01273 263032; 01273 263032 ✉ james.elliot@adur-worthing.gov.uk

Estates, Property & Valuation: Mr Cliff Harrison, Executive Head of Technical Services, Portland House, Richmond Road, Worthing BN11 1HS ☎ 01903 221370; 01903 221370 ✉ cliff.harrison@adur-worthing.gov.uk

Facilities: Mr Cliff Harrison, Executive Head of Technical Services, Portland House, Richmond Road, Worthing BN11 1HS ☎ 01903 221370; 01903 221370 ✉ cliff.harrison@adur-worthing.gov.uk

Finance and Treasurer: Mrs Sarah Gobey, Executive Head of Financial Services, Worthing Town Hall, Chapel Road, Worthing BN11 1HA ☎ 01903 221221; 01903 221221 ✉ sarah.gobey@adur-worthing.gov.uk

Fleet Management: Mr Kevin Masters, Executive Head of Customer Services, Worthing Town Hall, Chapel Road, Worthing BN11 1HA ☎ 01903 221243; 01903 221243 ✉ kevin.masters@adur-worthing.gov.uk

Grounds Maintenance: Mr Chris Bradley, Park Manager, Commerce Way, Lancing BN15 8TA ☎ 01273 263134 ✉ chris.bradley@adur-worthing.gov.uk

Health and Safety: Mr Lesley Dexter, Senior Corporate Safety Officer, Portland House, Richmond Road, Worthing BN11 1LF ☎ 01903 221357; 01903 221357 ✉ lesley.dexter@adur-worthing.gov.uk

Housing: Mr David Pannell, Executive Head of Adur Homes, Civic Centre, Ham Road, Shoreham-by-Sea BN43 6PR ☎ 01273 263358; 01273 263358 ✉ david.pannell@adur-worthing.gov.uk

Housing Maintenance: Mr David Pannell, Executive Head of Adur Homes, Civic Centre, Ham Road, Shoreham-by-Sea BN43 6PR ☎ 01273 263358; 01273 263358 ✉ david.pannell@adur-worthing.gov.uk

Legal: Mr Jeremy Cook, Executive Head of Corporate & Cultural Services, Worthing Town Hall, Chapel Road, Worthing BN11 1HA ☎ 01903 221028; 01903 221028 ✉ jeremy.cook@adur-worthing.gov.uk

Leisure and Cultural Services: Mr Jeremy Cook, Executive Head of Corporate & Cultural Services, Worthing Town Hall, Chapel Road, Worthing BN11 1HA ☎ 01903 221028; 01903 221028 ✉ jeremy.cook@adur-worthing.gov.uk

Licensing: Ms Theresa Cuerva, Licensing Officer, Adur Civic Centre, Ham Road, Shoreham-by-Sea BN43 6PR ☎ 01273 263193; 01273 263193 ✉ theresa.cuerva@adur-worthing.gov.uk

Lottery Funding, Charity and Voluntary: Ms Katie Neal, External Funding Officer, Worthing Town Hall, Chapel Road, Worthing BN11 1HA ☎ 01903 221283 ✉ katie.neal@worthing.gov.uk

Member Services: Mrs Julia Smith, Democratic Services Manager, Worthing Town Hall, Chapel Road, Worthing BN11 1HA ☎ 01903 221150; 01903 221150 ✉ julia.smith@adur-worthing.gov.uk

Parking: Ms Mandy Ainsworth, Parking Enforcement Officer, Worthing Town Hall, Chapel Road, Worthing BH11 1HA ☎ 01903 221089; 01903 221089 ✉ mandy.ainsworth@adur-worthing.gov.uk

Partnerships: Mr Peter Latham, Chief Executive, Worthing Town Hall, Chapel Road, Worthing BN11 1HA ☎ 01903 221001; 01903 221001 ✉ peter.latham@adur-worthing.gov.uk

Personnel / HR: Mr Jeremy Cook, Executive Head of Corporate & Cultural Services, Worthing Town Hall, Chapel Road, Worthing BN11 1HA ☎ 01903 221028; 01903 221028 ✉ jeremy.cook@adur-worthing.gov.uk

Personnel / HR: Mrs Tracy Darey, Human Resources Manager, Civic Centre, Ham Road, Shoreham-by-Sea BN43 6PR ☎ 01273 263063; 01273 263063 ✉ tracy.darey@adur-worthing.gov.uk

Planning: Mr James Appleton, Executive Head of Planning, Regeneration & Wellbeing, Portland House, Richmond Road, Worthing BN11 1HS ☎ 01903 221333; 01903 221333 ✉ james.appleton@adur-worthing.gov.uk

Procurement: Mr Bill Williamson, Procurement Officer, Portland House, Richmond Road, Worthing BN11 1HS ☎ 01903 221056; 01903 221056 ✉ bill.williamson@adur-worthing.gov.uk

Recycling & Waste Minimisation: Mr Kevin Masters, Executive Head of Customer Services, Worthing Town Hall, Chapel Road, Worthing BN11 1HA ☎ 01903 221243; 01903 221243 ✉ kevin.masters@adur-worthing.gov.uk

Regeneration: Mr James Appleton, Executive Head of Planning, Regeneration & Wellbeing, Portland House, Richmond Road, Worthing BN11 1HS ☎ 01903 221333; 01903 221333 ✉ james.appleton@adur-worthing.gov.uk

Staff Training: Ms Mo Belcher, Learning & Development Co-ordinator, Worthing Town Hall, Chapel Road, Worthing BN11 1HA ☎ 01903 221043; 01903 221043 ✉ mo.belcher@adur-worthing.gov.uk

Street Scene: Mr David Steadman, Adur Town Centres and Street Scene Co-ordinator, Civic Centre, Ham Road, Shoreham-by-Sea BN43 6PR ☎ 01273 263152; 01273 263152 🖷 01273 263131 ✉ david.steadman@adur.gov.uk

Sustainable Communities: Ms Colette Blackett, Planning Policy Manager, Civic Centre, Ham Road, Shoreham-by-Sea BN43 6PR ☎ 01273 263242; 01273 263242 ✉ colette.blackett@adur-worthing.gov.uk

Sustainable Development: Mr James Appleton, Executive Head of Planning, Regeneration & Wellbeing, Portland House, Richmond Road, Worthing BN11 1HS ☎ 01903 221333; 01903 221333 ✉ james.appleton@adur-worthing.gov.uk

Tourism: Ms Eileen Suchodolski, Tourist Information Centres Manager, Worthing Town Hall, Chapel Road, Worthing BN11 1HA ☎ 01903 239868 ✉ eileen.suchodolski@adur-worthing.gov.uk

Town Centre: Mr David Steadman, Adur Town Centre & Street Scene Co-ordinator, Civic Centre, Ham Road, Shoreham-by-Sea BN43 6PR ☎ 01273 263152; 01273 263152 ✉ david.steadman@adur-worthing.gov.uk

Waste Collection and Disposal: Mr Kevin Masters, Executive Head of Customer Services, Worthing Town Hall, Chapel Road, Worthing BN11 1HA ☎ 01903 221243; 01903 221243 ✉ kevin.masters@adur-worthing.gov.uk

Waste Management: Mr Kevin Masters, Executive Head of Customer Services, Worthing Town Hall, Chapel Road, Worthing BN11 1HA ☎ 01903 221243; 01903 221243 ✉ kevin.masters@adur-worthing.gov.uk

MEMBERS OF THE COUNCIL (29)

Leader of the Council: **Parkin**, Neil (CON - St Nicolas)
neil.parkin@adur.gov.uk
Albury, Carson (CON - Peveral)
carson.albury@adur.gov.uk
Albury, Carol (CON - Churchill)
carol.albury@adur.gov.uk
Barnes, Andrew (CON - Mash Barn)
andrew.barnes@adur-worthing.gov.uk
Beresford, Pat (CON - Churchill)
pat.beresford@adur.gov.uk
Boggis, Brian (CON - Peverel)
brian.boggis@adur.gov.uk
Bridges, Ann (CON - Widewater)
ann.bridges@adur.gov.uk
Burns, Darren (CON - Southlands)
darren.burns@adur.gov.uk
Burt, Richard (LD - Mash Barn)
richard.burt@adur.gov.uk
Coomber, Brian (CON - St Nicolas)
brian.coomber@adur.gov.uk
Dollemore, Keith (CON - Manor)
keith.dollemore@adur.gov.uk
Donaldson, David (CON - Eastbrook)
david.donaldson@adur-worthing.gov.uk
Dunn, Angus (CON - Hillside)
angus.dunn@adur.gov.uk
Evans, Emma (CON - Buckingham)
emma.evans@adur.gov.uk
Funnell, Jim (CON - Eastbrook)
jim.funnell@adur.gov.uk
Graysmark, Paul (CON - Southlands)
paul.graysmark@adur-worthing.gov.uk
Hamblin, Mary (CON - Widewater)
mary.hamblin@adur.gov.uk
Hedley-Barnes, Stephanie (CON - Manor)
stephanie.hedley-barnes@adur.gov.uk
Hotton, Rod (CON - St Mary's)
rod.hotton@adur.gov.uk
Kennard, Debbie (CON - Buckingham)
debbie.kennard@adur.gov.uk
Lewis, Fred (CON - Widewater)
fred.lewis@adur.gov.uk
McKinney, Liza (IND - Marine)
liza.mckinney@adur.gov.uk
Mear, Barry (LAB - Cokeham)
barry.mear@adur-worthing.gov.uk
Mendoza, Mike (CON - St Mary's)
mike.mendoza@adur.gov.uk
Metcalfe, Peter (CON - Southwick Green)
peter.metcalfe@adur.gov.uk
Mockridge, Janet (CON - Hillside)
janet.mockridge@adur.gov.uk
Searle, Julie (CON - Southwick Green)
julie.searle@adur.gov.uk
Simmons, David (CON - Cokeham)
david.simmons@adur.gov.uk
Stride, Ben (IND - Marine)
ben.stride@adur.gov.uk

POLITICAL COMPOSITION

CON: 25, IND: 2, LAB: 1, LD: 1

CABINET

Leader: Mr Neil Parkin
Customer Services: Ms Julie Searle
Environment: Mr Keith Dollemore
Health & Wellbeing: Mr David Simmons
Regeneration: Mr Jim Funnell
Resources: Mr Angus Dunn

COMMITTEE CHAIRS

Constitution & Audit: Mr Rod Hotton
Licensing: Mr Carson Albury
Overview & Scrutiny: Ms Liza McKinney
Planning: Mr Pat Beresford
Standards: Mr Anthony Case (External)

ALLERDALE — D

Allerdale Borough Council, Allerdale House, Workington CA14 3YJ ☎ 01900 702702 🖷 01900 702507 🖳 www.allerdale.gov.uk

FACTS & FIGURES

Police Authority: Cumbria Police Authority
Health Authority: North West Strategic Health Authority
Learning and Skills Council: North West
Parliamentary Constituencies: Penrith and The Border, Workington
EU Constituencies: North West
Election Frequency: Elections are of whole council

LOCAL AUTHORITIES

PRINCIPAL OFFICERS

Chief Executive: Mr Harry Dyke, Chief Executive, Allerdale House, Workington CA14 3YJ ☎ 01900 702578
🖱 harry.dyke@allerdale.gov.uk

Senior Management: Mr Ian Frost, Interim Strategic Manager, Allerdale House, Workington CA14 3YJ ☎ 01900 702526
🖱 ian.frost@allerdale.gov.uk

Senior Management: Mr Charles Holmes, Strategic Manager, Allerdale House, Workington CA14 3YJ ☎ 01900 702959
🖱 charles.holmes@allerdale.gov.uk

Architect, Building / Property Services: Mr Chris Rolle, Service Manager - Property & Parking, Allerdale House, Workington CA14 3YJ ☎ 01900 702754 🖱 chris.rolle@allerdale.gov.uk

Building Control: Mr Paul Shankland, Building Control Manager, Customer Contact Centre, Town Hall, Oxford Street, Workington CA14 2RS ☎ 01900 702517 🖷 01900 702783
🖱 paul.shankland@allerdale.gov.uk

Computer Management: Mr Michael Scott, IT Service Manager, Allerdale House, Workington CA14 3YJ ☎ 01900 702681
🖱 michael.scott@allerdale.gov.uk

E-Government: Mr Steven Brailey, Business Development Manager, Allerdale House, Workington CA14 3YJ
☎ 01900 702793 🖱 steven.brailey@allerdale.gov.uk

Environmental Health: Mr Peter Daley, Environmental Health Unit Manager, Allerdale House, Workington CA14 3YJ
☎ 01900 702786 🖷 01900 702507
🖱 peter.daley@allerdale.gov.uk

Estates, Property & Valuation: Ms Linda Doyle, Valuation Officer, Allerdale House, Workington CA14 3YJ ☎ 01900 702762
🖱 linda.doyle@allerdale.gov.uk

Licensing: Ms Gillian Collinson, Senior Land Charges & Licensing Officer, Allerdale House, Workington CA14 3YJ
☎ 01900 702692 🖷 01900 702698
🖱 gillian.collinson@allerdale.gov.uk

Parking: Mr Mike Rollo, Parking Operations Manager, Allerdale House, Workington CA14 3YJ ☎ 01900 702859
🖱 mike.rollo@allerdale.gov.uk

Recycling & Waste Minimisation: Mr Ernie Davidson, Assistant Manager - Contract, Allerdale House, Workington CA14 3YJ
☎ 01900 702803 🖱 ernie.davidson@allerdale.gov.uk

Regeneration: Ms Debbie Cosgrove, Manager - Economic Growth, Allerdale House, Workington CA14 3YJ
☎ 01900 702771
🖱 debbie.cosgrove@allerdale.gov.uk

MEMBERS OF THE COUNCIL (56)

***Mayor:* Armstrong**, Carole (LAB - Moss Bay Workington)
carole.armstrong@allerdale.gov.uk
***Deputy Mayor:* Bacon**, Bill (LAB - Moss Bay Workington)
bill.bacon@allerdale.gov.uk
***Leader of the Council:* Smith**, Alan (LAB - All Saints Cockermouth)
alan.smith@allerdale.gov.uk
***Deputy Leader of the Council:* Cannon**, Barbara (LAB - Moss Bay Workington)
barbara.cannon@allerdale.gov.uk
Armstrong, John (Binky) (ALL - Wigton)
binky.armstrong@allerdale.gov.uk
Bainbridge, Mary (LAB - St Michaels Workington)
mary.bainbridge@allerdale.gov.uk
Bales, Peter (LAB - Moorclose Workington)
peter.bales@allerdale.gov.uk
Cockburn, Nicky (IND - Broughton St Bridgets)
nicky.cockburn@allerdale.gov.uk
Colhoun, John (LAB - Ellen)
john.colhoun@allerdale.gov.uk
Cowell, Joe (CON - Waver)
joe.cowell@allerdale.gov.uk
Crouch, John (LAB - Wigton)
john.crouch@allerdale.gov.uk
Davies, Len (LAB - All Saints Cockermouth)
len.davies@allerdale.gov.uk
Fairbairn, Duncan (ALL - Warnell)
duncan.fairbairn@allerdale.gov.uk
Fee, Trevor (IND - Seaton)
trevor.fee@allerdale.gov.uk
Finlay, Bill (IND - Aspatria)
bill.finlay@allerdale.gov.uk
Fryer, Mark (LAB - Stainburn)
mark.fryer@allerdale.gov.uk
Gainford, Miriam (ALL - Seaton)
miriam.gainford@allerdale.gov.uk
Garrard, Chris (ALL - Dalton)
chris.garrard@allerdale.gov.uk
Hansen, Konrad (LAB - St Johns Workington)
konrad.hansen@allerdale.gov.uk
Harrington, Hilary (IND - Harrington Workington)
hilary.harrington@allerdale.gov.uk
Heaslip, Michael (LAB - St Johns Workington)
michael.heaslip@allerdale.gov.uk
Heslop, Timothy (ALL - Derwent Valley)
tim.heslop@allerdale.gov.uk
Hodgson, Vaughan (CON - Marsh)
vaughan.hodgson@allerdale.gov.uk
Holding, Carl (LAB - St Michaels Workington)
carl.holding@allerdale.gov.uk
Holliday, Joe (LAB - St Johns Workington)
joe.holliday@allerdale.gov.uk
Jackson, Margaret (ALL - Christchurch Cockermouth)
margaret.jackson@allerdale.gov.uk
Jefferson, William (IND - Silloth)
william.jefferson@allerdale.gov.uk
Kemp, George (NP - Netherhall Maryport)
george.kemp@allerdale.gov.uk
Kemp, Denstone (LAB - Keswick)
denstone.kemp@allerdale.gov.uk
Kendall, Angela (LAB - Netherhall Maryport)
angela.kendall@allerdale.gov.uk
Kendall, Peter (LAB - Flimby)
peter.kendall@allerdale.gov.uk
Lister, Jim (ALL - Solway)
jim.lister@allerdale.gov.uk
Maguire, Lousie (LAB - Ellen)
louise.maguire@allerdale.gov.uk

Markley, Anthony (ALL - Holme)
anthony.markley@allerdale.gov.uk
McCarron-Holmes, Carni (LAB - Ewanrigg Maryport)
carni.mccarron-holmes@allerdale.gov.uk
Miskelly, Billy (LAB - St Michaels Workington)
billy.miskelly@allerdale.gov.uk
Moffat, Stuart (ALL - Wampool)
stuart.moffat@allerdale.gov.uk
Moore, Ashley (LAB - Ewanrigg Maryport)
ashley.moore@allerdale.gov.uk
Mounsey, Jacqueline (ALL - Wharrels)
jacqueline.mounsey@allerdale.gov.uk
Mumberson, Joseph (IND - Boltons)
joe.mumberson@alledale.gov.uk
Munby, Ronald (CON - Keswick)
ron.munby@allerdale.gov.uk
Nicholson, Eric (CON - Crummock)
eric.nicholson@allerdale.gov.uk
North, Tony (IND - Broughton St Bridgets)
tony.north@allerdale.gov.uk
Pugmire, Martin (LD - Keswick)
Rae, Marjorie (LAB - Harrington Workington)
marjorie.rae@allerdale.gov.uk
Robertson, Denis (IND - Moorclose Workington)
denis.robertson@allerdale.gov.uk
Scott, George (ALL - Wigton)
george.scott@allerdale.gov.uk
Smith, Christine (LAB - All Saints Cockermouth)
christine.smith@allerdale.gov.uk
Snaith, Margaret (IND - Silloth)
margaret.snaith@allerdale.gov.uk
Standage, Sam (CON - Christchurch Cockermouth)
sam.standage@allerdale.gov.uk
Tibble, Philip (LAB - Clifton)
philip.tibble@allerdale.gov.uk
Tibble, Celia (LAB - Seaton)
celia.tibble@allerdale.gov.uk
Wilson, David (IND - Aspatria)
david.wilson@allerdale.gov.uk
Wood, Martin (LAB - Ellenborough Maryport)
martin.wood@allerdale.gov.uk
Wood, Janice (LAB - Ellenborough Maryport)
janice.wood@allerdale.gov.uk
Wright, Joan (LAB - Moorclose Workington)
joan.wright@allerdale.gov.uk

POLITICAL COMPOSITION

LAB: 28, ALL: 11, IND: 10, CON: 5, LD: 1, NP: 1

CABINET

Leader: Mr Alan Smith
Deputy Leader / Budget & Asset Management: Ms Barbara Cannon
Customer & Regulatory Services: Mr Philip Tibble
Economic Growth: Mr Mark Fryer
Housing & Health: Mrs Carni McCarron-Holmes
Locality Services: Mr Michael Heaslip
Organisational Development: Mr Carl Holding

COMMITTEE CHAIRS

Audit: Mr Ashley Moore
Licensing: Mrs Angela Kendall
Scrutiny: Mr Trevor Fee

AMBER VALLEY — D

Amber Valley Borough Council, Po Box 17, Town Hall, Ripley DE5 3BT ☎ 01773 570222 🖷 01773 841616
enquiry@ambervalley.gov.uk 🖳 www.ambervalley.gov.uk

FACTS & FIGURES

Police Authority: Derbyshire Police Authority
Health Authority: East Midlands Strategic Health Authority
Learning and Skills Council: East Midlands
Parliamentary Constituencies: Amber Valley
EU Constituencies: East Midlands
Election Frequency: Elections are by thirds
Twinning: Blackstone Valley (Rhode Island, USA); Glogow (Poland)

PRINCIPAL OFFICERS

Chief Executive: Mr Peter Carney, Chief Executive, Town Hall, Market Place, Ripley DE5 3BT ☎ 01773 570222
peter.carney@ambervalley.gov.uk

Assistant Chief Executive: Mr John Grady, Assistant Chief Executive & Monitoring Officer, Town Hall, Market Place, Ripley DE5 3BT ☎ 01773 841630 john.grady@ambervalley.gov.uk

Architect, Building / Property Services: Mr Paul Benski, Principal Solicitor, Town Hall, Market Place, Ripley DE5 3BT ☎ 01773 841641 paul.benski@ambervalley.gov.uk

Best Value: Ms Susan Bamford, Assistant Director - Policy & Improvement, Town Hall, Ripley DE5 3BT ☎ 01773 841658
susan.bamford@ambervalley.gov.uk

Building Control: Mr Dave Chard, Building Control Manager, Town Hall, Market Place, Ripley DE5 3BT ☎ 01773 841513
dave.chard@ambervalley.gov.uk

PR / Communications: Mr Luke Barrett, Communications Manager, Town Hall, Market Place, Ripley DE5 3BT
☎ 01773 841655 luke.barrett@ambervalley.gov.uk

Community Planning: Mr Rob Thorley, Community Planning Manager, Town Hall, Market Place, Ripley DE5 3BT
☎ 01773 841582 rob.thorley@ambervalley.gov.uk

Community Safety: Ms Sally Price, Community Safety Officer, Town Hall, Market Place, Ripley DE5 3BT ☎ 01773 841652
sally.price@ambervalley.gov.uk

Computer Management: Mr Carl Marples, IT Operations & Support Manager, PO Box 1, Town Hall, Market Place, Ripley DE5 3BT ☎ 01773 841347 carl.marples@ambervalley.gov.uk

Corporate Services: Ms Susan Bamford, Assistant Director - Policy & Improvement, Town Hall, Market Place, Ripley DE5 3BT
☎ 01773 841658 susan.bamford@ambervalley.gov.uk

Customer Service: Ms Olive Green, Head of Customer Services & Exchequer, PO Box 1, Town Hall, Market Place, Ripley DE5 3BT
☎ 01773 841614 olive.green@ambervalley.gov.uk

Economic Development: Mr Stephen Jackson, Regeneration Manager, Town Hall, Market Place, Ripley DE5 3BT

☏ 01773 841520 ✉ stephen.jackson@ambervalley.gov.uk

E-Government: Mr Andy Wilde, Information Development Manager, PO Box 1, Town Hall, Market Place, Ripley DE5 3BT ☏ 01773 570222 ✉ andy.wilde@ambervalley.gov.uk

Electoral Registration: Mrs Pat Hardwick, Democratic Services Officer (Elections), Town Hall, Market Place, Ripley DE5 3BT ☏ 01773 841631 ✉ pat.hardwick@ambervalley.gov.uk

Emergency Planning: Mr Peter Carney, Chief Executive, Town Hall, Market Place, Ripley DE5 3BT ☏ 01773 570222 ✉ peter.carney@ambervalley.gov.uk

Energy Management: Mrs Sharon Hampson, Facilities & Energy Co-ordinator, Town Hall, Market Place, Ripley DE5 3BT ☏ 01773 841563 ✉ sharon.hampson@ambervalley.gov.uk

Environmental / Technical Services: Mr Julian Townsend, Executive Director - Environmental Services, Town Hall, Market Place, Ripley DE5 3BT ☏ 01773 841316 ✉ julian.townsend@ambervalley.gov.uk

Environmental Health: Mr Julian Townsend, Executive Director - Environmental Services, Town Hall, Market Place, Ripley DE5 3BT ☏ 01773 841316 ✉ julian.townsend@ambervalley.gov.uk

Estates, Property & Valuation: Mr Melvyn Boot, Senior Surveyor, Town Hall, Market Place, Ripley DE5 3BT ☏ 01773 841562 ✉ melvyn.boot@ambervalley.gov.uk

Events Manager: Ms Joanne Bamford, Tourism & Culture Co-ordinator, Town Hall, Market Place, Ripley DE5 3BT ☏ 01773 841485 ✉ joanne.bamford@ambervalley.gov.uk

Facilities: Mrs Sharon Hampson, Facilities & Energy Co-ordinator, Town Hall, Market Place, Ripley DE5 3BT ☏ 01773 841563 ✉ sharon.hampson@ambervalley.gov.uk

Finance and Treasurer: Ms Sylvia Delahay, Executive Director - Financial Services, PO Box 1, Town Hall, Market Place, Ripley DE5 3BT ☏ 01773 841610 ✉ sylvia.delahay@ambervalley.gov.uk

Fleet Management: Mr Shane Staley, Fleet Officer, Town Hall, Market Place, Ripley DE5 3BT ☏ 01773 841491 ✉ shane.staley@ambervalley.gov.uk

Grounds Maintenance: Mr Simon Gladwin, Assistant Director - Landscape Services, Town Hall, Market Place, Ripley DE5 3BT ☏ 0173 841415 ✉ simon.gladwin@ambervalley.gov.uk

Health and Safety: Mr Brian Shore, Health & Safety Officer, Town Hall, Market Place, Ripley DE5 3BT ☏ 01773 841668 ✉ brian.shore@ambervalley.gov.uk

Home Energy Conservation: Ms Joanne Walker, Energy Officer, Town Hall, Market Place, Ripley DE5 3BT ☏ 01773 841332 ✉ joanne.walker@ambervalley.gov.uk

Housing: Mr David Arkle, Housing Manager, Town Hall, Market Place, Ripley DE5 3BT ☏ 01773 841334 ✉ david.arkle@ambervalley.gov.uk

Local Area Agreement: Mr Peter Carney, Chief Executive, Town Hall, Market Place, Ripley DE5 3BT ☏ 01773 570222 ✉ peter.carney@ambervalley.gov.uk

Legal: Mr Paul Benski, Principal Solicitor, Town Hall, Market Place, Ripley DE5 3BT ☏ 01773 841641 ✉ paul.benski@ambervalley.gov.uk

Leisure and Cultural Services: Mr Kirk Monk, Assistant Director - Well-Being, Town Hall, Market Place, Ripley DE5 3BT ☏ 01773 841646 ✉ kirk.monk@ambervalley.gov.uk

Licensing: Ms Heather Adams, Licensing Manager, Town Hall, Market Place, Ripley DE5 3BT ☏ 01773 841602 ✉ heather.adams@ambervalley.gov.uk

Lottery Funding, Charity and Voluntary: Mrs Wendy Burridge, Funding Officer, Town Hall, Market Place, Ripley DE5 3BT ☏ 01773 841493 ✉ wendy.burridge@ambervalley.gov.uk

Member Services: Mr John Grady, Assistant Chief Executive & Monitoring Officer, Town Hall, Market Place, Ripley DE5 3BT ☏ 01773 841630 ✉ john.grady@ambervalley.gov.uk

Parking: Ms Pam Leigh, Parking Contracts Officer, Town Hall, Market Place, Ripley DE5 3BT ☏ 01773 841437 ✉ pam.leigh@ambervalley.gov.uk

Partnerships: Mr Peter Carney, Chief Executive, Town Hall, Market Place, Ripley DE5 3BT ☏ 01773 570222 ✉ peter.carney@ambervalley.gov.uk

Personnel / HR: Ms Susan Bamford, Assistant Director - Policy & Improvement, Town Hall, Ripley DE5 3BT ☏ 01773 841658 ✉ susan.bamford@ambervalley.gov.uk

Planning: Ms Clare Thornton, Development Manager, Town Hall, Market Place, Ripley DE5 3BT ☏ 01773 841551 ✉ clare.thornton@ambervalley.gov.uk

Procurement: Mr John Grady, Assistant Chief Executive & Monitoring Officer, Town Hall, Market Place, Ripley DE5 3BT ☏ 01773 841630 ✉ john.grady@ambervalley.gov.uk

Recycling & Waste Minimisation: Ms Theresa Barnes, Principal Waste Performance & Recycling Officer, Town Hall, Market Place, Ripley DE5 3BT ☏ 01773 841323 ✉ theresa.barnes@ambervalley.gov.uk

Regeneration: Mr Stephen Jackson, Regeneration Manager, Town Hall, Market Place, Ripley DE5 3BT ☏ 01773 841520 ✉ stephen.jackson@ambervalley.gov.uk

Staff Training: Mr Ian Shepherd, Learning & Development Manager, Town Hall, Market Place, Ripley DE5 3BT ☏ 01773 841665 ✉ ian.shepherd@ambervalley.gov.uk

Street Scene: Mrs Sharon Thomas, Landscape Development Manager, Town Hall, Market Place, Ripley DE5 3BT ☏ 01773 841570 ✉ sharon.thomas@ambervalley.gov.uk

Sustainable Communities: Mr Derek Stafford, Assistant

Director - Planning & Regeneration, Town Hall, Market Place, Ripley DE5 3BT ☎ 01773 841581 ✉ derek.stafford@ambervalley.gov.uk

Sustainable Development: Mr Ian Shaw, Environment Manager, Town Hall, Market Place, Ripley DE5 3BT ☎ 01773 841324 ✉ ian.shaw@ambervalley.gov.uk

Tourism: Ms Joanne Bamford, Tourism & Culture Co-ordinator, Town Hall, Market Place, Ripley DE5 3BT ☎ 01773 841485 ✉ joanne.bamford@ambervalley.gov.uk

Town Centre: Mr Simon Gladwin, Assistant Director - Landscape Services, Town Hall, Market Place, Ripley DE5 3BT ☎ 0173 841415 ✉ simon.gladwin@ambervalley.gov.uk

Waste Collection and Disposal: Mr Ian Shaw, Environment Manager, Town Hall, Ripley DE5 3BT ☎ 01773 841324 ✉ ian.shaw@ambervalley.gov.uk

Waste Management: Mr Ian Shaw, Environment Manager, Town Hall, Ripley DE5 3BT ☎ 01773 841324 ✉ ian.shaw@ambervalley.gov.uk

Children's Play Areas: Mr Simon Gladwin, Assistant Director - Landscape Services, Town Hall, Market Place, Ripley DE5 3BT ☎ 0173 841415 ✉ simon.gladwin@ambervalley.gov.uk

MEMBERS OF THE COUNCIL (46)

***Leader of the Council:* Bradford**, Stuart (CON - Duffield)
cllr.stuart.bradford@ambervalley.gov.uk
***Deputy Leader of the Council:* Bowley**, Liz (CON - Ripley)
cllr.liz.bowley@ambervalley.gov.uk
***Group Leader:* Jones**, Paul (LAB - Heanor West)
cllr.paul.jones@ambervalley.gov.uk
Ainstrop, Barrie (LAB - Heanor East)
cllr.barrie.aistrop@ambervalley.gov.uk
Anderson, Jim (CON - Belper South)
cllr.jim.anderson@ambervalley.gov.uk
Arnold, Peter (CON - Belper South)
cllr.peter.arnold@ambervalley.gov.uk
Bennett, Marlene (LAB - Alfreton)
cllr.marlene.bennett@ambervalley.gov.uk
Blake, Michael (IND - N/A)
Bull, Norman (CON - Kilburn, Denby & Holbrook)
cllr.norman.bull@ambervalley.gov.uk
Buttery, Kevin (CON - Kilburn, Denby & Holbrook)
cllr.kevin.buttery@ambervalley.gov.uk
Cox, Alan (CON - Belper North)
cllr.alan.cox@ambervalley.gov.uk
Cox, Lyndsay (LAB - Ripley & Marehay)
cllr.lyndsay.cox@ambervalley.gov.uk
Cox, Jackie (CON - Belper East)
cllr.jackie.cox@ambervalley.gov.uk
Dolman, Gail (LAB - Alfreton)
cllr.gail.dolman@ambervalley.gov.uk
Emmas-Williams, Christopher (LAB - Codnor & Waingroves)
cllr.chris.emmas-williams@ambervalley.gov.uk
Gee, Gareth (CON - Crich)
cllr.gareth.gee@ambervalley.gov.uk
Gemmell, Jean (CON - Kilburn, Denby & Holbrook)
cllr.jean.gemmell@ambervalley.gov.uk
Gent, Maurice (LAB - Heage & Ambergate)
cllr.maurice.gent@ambervalley.gov.uk
Gration, Brian (LAB - Langley Mill & Aldercar)
cllr.brian.gration@ambervalley.gov.uk
Hamilton, Eileen (LAB - Langley Mill & Aldercar)
cllr.eileen.hamilton@ambervalley.gov.uk
Hayes, Stephen (CON - Swanwick)
cllr.stephen.hayes@ambervalley.gov.uk
Hill, Phil (LAB - Heanor East)
Holmes, Tony (LAB - Ripley)
cllr.tony.holmes@ambervalley.gov.uk
Janes, Bob (LAB - Heanor West)
Joynes, Stuart (CON - Ripley)
cllr.stuart.joynes@ambervalley.gov.uk
King, Allen (CON - Swanwick)
cllr.allen.king@ambervalley.gov.uk
Longdon, Alan (LAB - Heanor & Loscoe)
cllr.alan.longdon@ambervalley.gov.uk
Lyttle, Brian (LAB - Somercotes)
cllr.brian.lyttle@ambervalley.gov.uk
Makin, Peter (CON - Belper Central)
cllr.peter.makin@ambervalley.gov.uk
McCabe, John (LAB - Somercotes)
cllr.john.mccabe@ambervalley.gov.uk
Moon, Bob (LAB - Heanor & Loscoe)
cllr.bob.moon@ambervalley.gov.uk
Nelson, John (CON - Belper Central)
cllr.john.nelson@ambervalley.gov.uk
Orton, Jane (CON - South West Parishes)
cllr.jane.orton@ambervalley.gov.uk
Parkes, George (LAB - Codnor & Waingroves)
cllr.george.parkes@ambervalley.gov.uk
Parkinson, Kevin (CON - Shipley Park, Horsley & Horsley Woodhouse)
cllr.kevin.parkinson@ambervalley.gov.uk
Robertson, Mark (CON - Belper North)
cllr.mark.robertson@ambervalley.gov.uk
Short, Christopher (CON - Duffield)
cllr.chris.short@ambervalley.gov.uk
Smith, Paul (LAB - Ironville & Riddings)
cllr.paul.smith@ambervalley.gov.uk
Stevenson, Alex (CON - Shipley Park, Horsley & Horsley Woodhouse)
cllr.alex.stevenson@ambervalley.gov.uk
Taylor, David (CON - Alport)
cllr.david.taylor@ambervalley.gov.uk
Thorpe, Valerie (CON - Wingfield)
cllr.valerie.thorpe@ambervalley.gov.uk
Tomlinson, Martin (CON - Belper East)
cllr.martin.tomlinson@ambervalley.gov.uk
Walker, Roy (LAB - Ironville & Riddings)
cllr.roy.walker@ambervalley.gov.uk
Walker, John (LAB - Alfreton)
cllr.john.walker@ambervalley.gov.uk
Ward, Angela (CON - Heage & Ambergate)
cllr.angela.ward@ambervalley.gov.uk
Wilson, Mick (LAB - Ripley & Marehay)
cllr.mick.wilson@ambervalley.gov.uk

POLITICAL COMPOSITION

CON: 24, LAB: 21, IND: 1

CABINET

Leader / Policy, Corporate & Financial Matters: Mr Stuart Bradford
Deputy Leader / People & Change: Mrs Liz Bowley

LOCAL AUTHORITIES

Active & Healthier Places to Live: Mr Christopher Short
Decent & Affordable Places to Live: Mr Norman Bull
Developing Places to Live: Mr Stephen Hayes
Green & Thriving Places to Live: Mr Jack Brown

COMMITTEE CHAIRS

Appeals Board: Mrs Valerie Thorpe
Governance & Audit Board: Mr Alan Cox
Licensing Board: Mr Allen King
Planning Board: Mr Jim Anderson
Scrutiny: Mr Martin Tomlinson
Standards: Mr Ken Newton (External)

ANGUS S

Angus Council, Council Headquarters, The Cross, Forfar DD8 1BX ☎ 01307 461460 🖷 01307 461874 ✉ chiefexec@angus.gov.uk
💻 www.angus.gov.uk

FACTS & FIGURES

Police Authority: Tayside Joint Police Board
Health Authority: NHS Tayside
Learning and Skills Council: Scotland
Parliamentary Constituencies: Angus, Dundee West
EU Constituencies: Scotland
Election Frequency: Elections are of whole council

PRINCIPAL OFFICERS

Chief Executive: Mr Richard Stiff, Chief Executive, Council Headquarters, The Cross, Forfar DD8 1BX ☎ 01307 476100 🖷 01370 476140 ✉ stiffr@angus.gov.uk

Assistant Chief Executive: Mr Hugh Robertson, Assistant Chief Executive, Angus House, Orchardbank Business Park, Forfar DD8 1AP ☎ 01307 476111 🖷 01307 476140 ✉ robertsonh@angus.gov.uk

Architect, Building / Property Services: Mr John Pearson, Head of Property Services, Bruce House, Wellgate, Arbroath DD11 3TP ☎ 01241 435054 🖷 01241 435038 ✉ pearsonjw@angus.gov.uk

Building Control: Mr Iain Mitchell, Senior Service Manager, County Buildings, Market Street, Forfar DD8 3LG ☎ 01307 473290 🖷 01307 461895 ✉ mitchelli@angus.gov.uk

Catering Services: Ms Fiona Dawson, Catering Advisor, Angus House, Orchardbank Business Park, Forfar DD8 1AE ☎ 01307 461460 ✉ dawsonf@angus.gov.uk

Children / Youth Services: Dr Robert Peat, Director of Social Work & Health, St Margaret's House, Orchard Loan, Orchardbank Business Park, Forfar DD8 1WS ☎ 01307 474839 🖷 01307 474899 ✉ peatr@angus.gov.uk

Civil Registration: Ms Carolyn MacPherson, Chief Registrar, 69-71 High Street, Arbroath DD11 1AN ☎ 01241 874805 🖷 01241 874805 ✉ macphersonc@angus.gov.uk

PR / Communications: Ms Moira Naulty, Public Relations Manager, Angus House, Orchardbank Business Park, Forfar DD8 1AX ☎ 01307 476090 🖷 01307 476140 ✉ naultym@angus.gov.uk

Community Planning: Ms Vivien Smith, Senior Service Manager, Angus House, Orchardbank Business Park, Forfar DD8 1AX ☎ 01307 476105 🖷 01307 476140 ✉ smithv@angus.gov.uk

Community Safety: Mr Bob Myles, Community Safety Manager, Sheriff Court Annexe, Market Street, Forfar DD8 3WF ☎ 01307 477470 🖷 01307 462590 ✉ mylesb@angus.gov.uk

Computer Management: Mr Neil Munro, Head of IT, Angus House, Orchardbank Business Park, Forfar DD8 1BX ☎ 01307 476444 🖷 01307 476401 ✉ munrons@angus.gov.uk

Consumer Protection and Trading Standards: Mr David Valentine, Head of Economic Development & ECP, County Buildings, Market Street, Forfar DD8 3LG ☎ 01307 473358 🖷 01307 467357 ✉ valentined@angus.gov.uk

Corporate Services: Mr Colin McMahon, Director of Corporate Services, Angus House, Orchardbank Business Park, Forfar DD8 1AF ☎ 01307 476200 🖷 01307 476216 ✉ mcmahonc@angus.gov.uk

Economic Development: Mr David Valentine, Head of Economic Development & ECP, Infrastructure Services, County Buildings, Forfar DD8 3WD ☎ 01307 473358 🖷 01307 467357 ✉ valentined@angus.gov.uk

Education: Mr Neil Logue, Director of Education, Council Headquarters, The Cross, Forfar DD8 1BX

Electoral Registration: Mrs Shona Cameron, Projects & Elections Officer, Angus House, Orchardbank Business Park, Forfar DD8 1AN ☎ 01307 476226 🖷 01307 476299 ✉ cameronsd@angus.gov.uk

Emergency Planning: Ms Jacqui Semple, Civil Contingencies Manager, Angus House, Orchardbank Business Park, Forfar DD8 1AX ☎ 01307 476123 🖷 01307 476140 ✉ semplej@angus.gov.uk

Energy Management: Mr John Pearson, Head of Property Services, Bruce House, Wellgate, Arbroath DD11 3TP ☎ 01241 435054 🖷 01241 435038 ✉ pearsonjw@angus.gov.uk

Environmental / Technical Services: Mr Duncan Inglis, Head of Environmental Management, Ravenswood, New Road, Forfar DD8 2ZX ☎ 01307 473803 🖷 01307 474799 ✉ inglisdf@angus.gov.uk

Environmental Health: Mr David Valentine, Head of Economic Development & ECP, Infrastructure Services, County Buildings, Forfar DD8 3WD ☎ 01307 473358 🖷 01307 467357 ✉ valentined@angus.gov.uk

Estates, Property & Valuation: Mr Neil MacKenzie, Principal Estates Manager, Bruce House, Wellgate, Arbroath DD11 3TP ☎ 01307 435037 ✉ mackenzien@angus.gov.uk

European Liaison: Ms Alison Smith, Senior External Funding Officer, County Buildings, Market Street, Forfar DD8 3WD ☎ 01307 473222 🖷 01307 467357 ✉ smithaj@angus.gov.uk

Events Manager: Ms Jacqui Semple, Civil Contingencies Manager, Angus House, Orchardbank Business Park, Forfar DD8 1AX ☎ 01307 476123 🖷 01307 476140 ✉ semplej@angus.gov.uk

Finance and Treasurer: Mr Ian Lorimer, Head of Finance, Angus House, Orchardbank Business Park, Forfar DD8 1AF ☎ 01307 476222 🖷 01307 476216 ✉ lorimeri@angus.gov.uk

Health and Safety: Mr Charles McGlade, Safety Manager, Angus House, Orchardbank Business Park, Forfar DD8 1AP ☎ 01307 476119 🖷 01307 476140 ✉ mcgladec@angus.gov.uk

Highways: Mr Jeff Green, Head of Roads, Council Headquarters, County Buildings, Market Street, Forfar DD8 1BX ☎ 01307 473289 🖷 01307 473388 ✉ greenjw@angus.gov.uk

Home Energy Conservation: Mr Bob Berry, Service Manager (Technical), William Wallace House, Orchard Loan, Orchardbank Business Park, Forfar DD8 1WH ☎ 01307 474795 🖷 01307 474799 ✉ berrybh@angus.gov.uk

Housing: Mr Ron Ashton, Director of Neighbourhood Services, William Wallace House, Orchard Loan, Orchardbank Business Park, Forfar DD8 1WH ☎ 01307 474710 🖷 01307 474799 ✉ AshtonR@angus.gov.uk

Housing: Mr Alan McKeown, Head of Housing, William Wallace House, Orchard Loan, Orchardbank Buiness Park, Forfar DD8 1WH ☎ 01307 474779 🖷 01307 474799 ✉ mckeowna@angus.gov.uk

Housing Maintenance: Mr Ron Ashton, Director of Neighbourhood Services, William Wallace House, Orchard Loan, Orchardbank Business Park, Forfar DD8 1WH ☎ 01307 474710 🖷 01307 474799 ✉ AshtonR@angus.gov.uk

Legal: Mrs Sheona Hunter, Head of Law & Administration, Angus House, Orchardbank Business Park, Forfar DD8 1AN ☎ 01307 476262 🖷 01307 476299 ✉ hunters@angus.gov.uk

Leisure and Cultural Services: Mr Ron Ashton, Director of Neighbourhood Services, William Wallace House, Orchard Loan, Orchardbank Business Park, Forfar DD8 1WH ☎ 01307 474710 🖷 01307 474799 ✉ AshtonR@angus.gov.uk

Licensing: Mrs Sheona Hunter, Head of Law & Administration, Angus House, Orchardbank Business Park, Forfar DD8 1AN ☎ 01307 476262 🖷 01307 476299 ✉ hunters@angus.gov.uk

Lifelong Learning: Mr Neil Logue, Director of Education, Council Headquarters, The Cross, Forfar DD8 1BX

Lottery Funding, Charity and Voluntary: Ms Alison Smith, Senior External Funding Officer, County Buildings, Market Street, Forfar DD8 3WD ☎ 01307 473222 🖷 01307 467357 ✉ smithaj@angus.gov.uk

Member Services: Mr Gary Miller, Chief Executive's Support Manager, Angus House, Orchardbank Business Park, Forfar DD8 1AX ☎ 01307 476099 🖷 01307 476140 ✉ millerg@angus.gsx.gov.uk

Parking: Mr Jeff Green, Head of Roads, Council Headquarters, County Buildings, Market Street, Forfar DD8 1BX ☎ 01307 473289 🖷 01307 473388 ✉ greenjw@angus.gov.uk

Personnel / HR: Mr Hugh Robertson, Assistant Chief Executive, Chief Executive's Department, Angus House, Orchardbank Business Park, Forfar DD8 1AP ☎ 01307 476111 🖷 01307 476140

Planning: Mr George Chree, Head of Planning & Transport, County Buildings, Market Street, Forfar DD8 3LG ☎ 01307 473292 ✉ chreegw@angus.gov.uk

Procurement: Mr Mark Allan, Procurement Manager, Angus House, Orchardbank Business Park, Forfar DD8 1AF ☎ 01307 476195 🖷 01307 476216 ✉ allanm@angus.gov.uk

Public Libraries: Mr Norman Atkinson, Senior Service Manager, William Wallace House, Orchard Loan, Forfar DD8 1WH ☎ 01307 474713 🖷 01307 462590 ✉ atkinsonnk@angus.gov.uk

Recycling & Waste Minimisation: Mr Duncan Inglis, Head of Environmental Management, Neighbourhood Services, Ravenswood, New Road, Forfar DD8 2ZX ☎ 01307 473803 🖷 01307 474799 ✉ inglisdf@angus.gov.uk

Road Safety: Mr Jeff Green, Head of Roads, Council Headquarters, County Buildings, Market Street, Forfar DD8 1BX ☎ 01307 473289 🖷 01307 473388 ✉ greenjw@angus.gov.uk

Social Services: Dr Robert Peat, Director of Social Work & Health, St Margaret's House, Orchard Loan, Orchardbank Business Park, Forfar DD8 1WS ☎ 01307 474839 🖷 01307 474899 ✉ peatr@angus.gov.uk

Social Services (Adult): Ms Lorraine Young, Senior Manager - Community Care Services, St Margaret's House, Orchardbank Business Park, Forfar DD8 1WS ☎ 01307 474840 🖷 01307 474899 ✉ youngl@angus.gov.uk

Social Services (Children): Mr Tim Armstrong, Senior Manager, Ravenswood, New Road, Forfar DD8 2ZG ☎ 01307 462405 🖷 01307 461261 ✉ armstrongt@angus.gov.uk

Staff Training: Mr Ken Ritchie, Senior Service Manager (Personnel), Angus House, Orchardbank Business Park, Forfar DD8 1AP ☎ 01307 476091 🖷 01307 476410 ✉ ritchiek@angus.gov.uk

Street Scene: Mr Jeff Green, Head of Roads, Council Headquarters, County Buildings, Market Street, Forfar DD8 1BX ☎ 01307 473289 🖷 01307 473388 ✉ greenjw@angus.gov.uk

Sustainable Development: Mr George Chree, Head of Planning & Transport, County Buildings, Market Street, Forfar DD8 3LG ☎ 01307 473292 ✉ chreegw@angus.gov.uk

Tourism: Mr David Valentine, Head of Economic Development & ECP, Infrastructure Services, County Buildings, Forfar DD8 3WD ☎ 01307 473358 🖷 01307 467357 ✉ valentined@angus.gov.uk

Traffic Management: Mr Graham Harris, Traffic Manager, County Buildings, Market Street, Forfar DD8 3WR

☎ 01307 473283 🖷 01307 473388

Transport: Mr George Chree, Head of Planning & Transport, County Buildings, Market Street, Forfar DD8 3LG ☎ 01307 473292 ✉ chreegw@angus.gov.uk

Transport Planner: Mr George Chree, Head of Planning & Transport, County Buildings, Market Street, Forfar DD8 3LG ☎ 01307 473292 ✉ chreegw@angus.gov.uk

Waste Collection and Disposal: Mr Duncan Inglis, Head of Environmental Management, Ravenswood, New Road, Forfar DD8 2ZX ☎ 01307 473803 🖷 01307 474799 ✉ inglisdf@angus.gov.uk

Waste Management: Mr Duncan Inglis, Head of Environmental Management, Ravenswood, New Road, Forfar DD8 2ZX ☎ 01307 473803 🖷 01307 474799 ✉ inglisdf@angus.gov.uk

MEMBERS OF THE COUNCIL (29)

Bowles, Bill (IND - Carnoustie & District)
cllrbowles@angus.gov.uk
Boyd, Brian (IND - Carnoustie & District)
cllrboyd@angus.gov.uk
Brown, Colin (IND - Forfar & District)
cllrbrown@angus.gov.uk
Devine, Lynne (SNP - Forfar & District)
cllrdevine@angus.gov.uk
Duff, Bill (SNP - Montrose & District)
cllrduff@anugs.gov.uk
Evans, Mairi (SNP - Brechin & Edzell)
cllrevans@angus.gov.uk
Fairweather, David (IND - Arbroath West & Letham)
cllrfairweather@angus.gov.uk
Fotheringham, Craig (CON - Monifieth & Sidlaw)
cllrfotheringham@angus.gov.uk
Gaul, Iain (SNP - Kirriemuir & Dean)
cllrgaul@angus.gov.uk
Gaul, Jeanette (SNP - Kirriemuir & Dean)
cllrgaulje@angus.gov.uk
Geddes, Martyn (CON - Arbroath East & Lunan)
cllrgeddes@angus.gov.uk
Hands, Sheila (SNP - Monifieth & Sidlaw)
cllrhands@angus.gov.uk
Houston, Jim (SNP - Brechin & Edzell)
cllrhouston@angus.gov.uk
King, Alex (SNP - Arbroath West & Letham)
cllrking@angus.gov.uk
Lumgair, David (CON - Arbroath West & Letham)
cllrlumgair@angus.gov.uk
May, David (LD - Montrose & District)
cllrmay@angus.gov.uk
McLaren, Ian (IND - Forfar & District)
cllrmclaren@angus.gov.uk
Middleton, Glennis (SNP - Forfar & District)
Morrison, Donald (SNP - Arbroath East & Lunan)
cllrmorrison@angus.gov.uk
Murray, Rob (SNP - Monifieth & Sidlaw)
cllrmurray@angus.gov.uk
Myles, Bob (IND - Brechin & Edzell)
cllrmyles@angus.gov.uk
Oswald, Helen (SNP - Carnoustie & District)
cllroswald@angus.gov.uk
Proctor, Ronnie (CON - Kirriemuir & Dean)
cllrproctor@angus.gov.uk
Salmond, Mark (IND - Montrose & District)
cllrsalmond@angus.gov.uk
Smith, Ewan (SNP - Arbroath West & Letham)
cllrsmith@angus.gov.uk
Spink, Bob (IND - Arbroath East & Lunan)
cllrspink@angus.gov.uk
Thomson, Margaret (LAB - Monifieth & Sidlaw)
cllrthomson@angus.gov.uk
Valentine, Paul (SNP - Montrose & District)
cllrvalentine@angus.gov.uk
Welsh, Sheena (SNP - Arbroath East & Lunan)
cllrwelsh@angus.gov.uk

POLITICAL COMPOSITION

SNP: 15, IND: 8, CON: 4, LAB: 1, LD: 1

COMMITTEE CHAIRS

Civic Licensing: Mr Alex King
Corporate Services: Mr Alex King
Development Standards: Mr Rob Murray
Education: Ms Sheena Welsh
Infrastructure Services: Ms Mairi Evans
Neighbourhood Services: Mr Donald Morrison
Social Work & Health: Mrs Glennis Middleton
Strategic Policy: Mr Iain Gaul

ANTRIM — N

Antrim Borough Council, Antrim Civic Offices, 50 Stiles Way, Antrim BT41 2UB ☎ 028 9446 3113 🖷 028 9446 3113 ✉ corporate@antrim.gov.uk 🖳 www.antrim.gov.uk

FACTS & FIGURES

Police Authority: Northern Ireland Policing Board
Health Authority: Health & Social Care Board
Learning and Skills Council: Northern Ireland
Parliamentary Constituencies: Antrim South
EU Constituencies: Northern Ireland
Election Frequency: Elections are of whole council

PRINCIPAL OFFICERS

Chief Executive: Mr David McCammick, Clerk of the Council & Chief Executive, Antrim Civic Offices, 50 Stiles Way, Antrim BT41 2UB ☎ 028 9446 3113 🖷 028 9448 1324 ✉ david.mccammick@antrim.gov.uk

Deputy Chief Executive: Mrs Catherine McFarland, Director of Corporate & Regulatory Services, Antrim Civic Offices, 50 Stiles Way, Antrim BT41 2UB ☎ 028 9446 3113 🖷 028 9448 1324 ✉ catherine.mcfarland@antrim.gov.uk

Access Officer / Social Services (Disability): Mr Reggie Hillen, Assistant Director - Property Services, Antrim Civic Offices, 50 Stiles Way, Antrim BT41 2UB ☎ 028 9446 3113 🖷 028 9448 1324 ✉ reggie.hillen@antrim.gov.uk

Architect, Building / Property Services: Mr Reggie Hillen, Assistant Director - Property Services, Antrim Civic Offices, 50 Stiles Way, Antrim BT41 2UB ☎ 028 9446 3113 🖷 028 9448 1324 ✉ reggie.hillen@antrim.gov.uk

Building Control: Ms Bronagh Doonan, Assistant Director -

Building Control, Antrim Civic Offices, 50 Stiles Way, Antrim BT41 2UB ☎ 028 9446 3113 🖷 028 9448 1324 🖰 bronagh.doonan@antrim.gov.uk

Civil Registration: Ms Liz Johnston, Assistant Director - Administration, Antrim Civic Centre, 50 Stiles Way, Antrim BT41 2UB ☎ 028 9446 3113 🖷 028 9448 1324 🖰 liz.johnston@antrim.gov.uk

PR / Communications: Mrs Elish Martin, Public Relations Officer, Antrim Civic Centre, 50 Stiles Way, Antrim BT41 2UB ☎ 028 9446 3113 🖷 028 9448 1324 🖰 elish.martin@antrim.gov.uk

Community Safety: Ms Alison Allen, Partnership Manager, Antrim Civic Offices, 50 Stiles Way, Antrim BT41 2UB ☎ 028 9446 3113 🖰 alison.allen@antrim.gov.uk

Computer Management: Mr John Balmer, Assistant Director - Finance, Antrim Civic Offices, 50 Stiles Way, Antrim BT41 2UB ☎ 028 9446 3113 🖷 028 9448 1324 🖰 john.balmer@antrim.gov.uk

Consumer Protection and Trading Standards: Mr Ian Suiter, Assistant Director - Environmental Health, Antrim Civic Offices, 50 Stiles Way, Antrim BT41 2UB ☎ 028 9446 3113 🖷 028 9448 1324 🖰 ian.suiter@antrim.gov.uk

Contracts: Mr Kevin Logan, Procurement Officer, Antrim Civic Offices, 50 Stiles Way, Antrim BT41 2UB ☎ 028 9446 3113 🖷 028 9448 1324 🖰 kevin.logan@antrim.gov.uk

Corporate Services: Mrs Catherine McFarland, Director of Corporate & Regulatory Services, Antrim Civic Offices, 50 Stiles Way, Antrim BT41 2UB ☎ 028 9446 3113 🖷 028 9448 1324 🖰 catherine.mcfarland@antrim.gov.uk

Customer Service: Ms Liz Johnston, Assistant Director - Administration, Antrim Civic Centre, 50 Stiles Way, Antrim BT41 2UB ☎ 028 9446 3113 🖷 028 9448 1324 🖰 liz.johnston@antrim.gov.uk

Direct Labour: Mr Paul Holly, Assistant Director - Operational Services, Antrim Civic Offices, 50 Stiles Way, Antrim BT41 2UB ☎ 028 9446 3113 🖷 028 9448 1324 🖰 paul.holly@antrim.gov.uk

Economic Development: Mr Paul Kelly, Development Director, Antrim Civic Offices, 50 Stiles Way, Antrim BT41 2UB ☎ 028 9446 3113 🖷 028 9442 8059 🖰 paul.kelly@antrim.gov.uk

E-Government: Mr John Balmer, Assistant Director - Finance, Antrim Civic Offices, 50 Stiles Way, Antrim BT41 2UB ☎ 028 9446 3113 🖷 028 9448 1324 🖰 john.balmer@antrim.gov.uk

Electoral Registration: Ms Liz Johnston, Assistant Director - Administration, Antrim Civic Centre, 50 Stiles Way, Antrim BT41 2UB ☎ 028 9446 3113 🖷 028 9448 1324 🖰 liz.johnston@antrim.gov.uk

Emergency Planning: Mr David McCammick, Clerk of the Council & Chief Executive, Antrim Civic Offices, 50 Stiles Way, Antrim BT41 2UB ☎ 028 9446 3113 🖷 028 9448 1324 🖰 david.mccammick@antrim.gov.uk

Energy Management: Mr Paul Holly, Assistant Director - Operational Services, Antrim Civic Offices, 50 Stiles Way, Antrim BT41 2UB ☎ 028 9446 3113 🖷 028 9448 1324 🖰 paul.holly@antrim.gov.uk

Environmental / Technical Services: Mr Paul Holly, Assistant Director - Operational Services, Antrim Civic Offices, 50 Stiles Way, Antrim BT41 2UB ☎ 028 9446 3113 🖷 028 9448 1324 🖰 paul.holly@antrim.gov.uk

Environmental Health: Mr Ian Suiter, Assistant Director - Environmental Health, Antrim Civic Offices, 50 Stiles Way, Antrim BT41 2UB ☎ 028 9446 3113 🖷 028 9448 1324 🖰 ian.suiter@antrim.gov.uk

Estates, Property & Valuation: Ms Liz Johnston, Assistant Director - Administration, Antrim Civic Centre, 50 Stiles Way, Antrim BT41 2UB ☎ 028 9446 3113 🖷 028 9448 1324 🖰 liz.johnston@antrim.gov.uk

Events Manager: Mrs Elish Martin, Public Relations Officer, Antrim Civic Offices, 50 Stiles Way, Antrim BT41 2UB ☎ 028 9446 3113 🖷 028 9448 1324 🖰 elish.martin@antrim.gov.uk

Facilities: Mr Graham Reid, Facilities Manager, Antrim Civic Offices, 50 Stiles Way, Antrim BT41 2UB ☎ 028 9446 3113 🖷 028 9448 1324 🖰 graham.reid@antrim.gov.uk

Finance and Treasurer: Mrs Catherine McFarland, Director of Corporate & Regulatory Services, Antrim Civic Offices, 50 Stiles Way, Antrim BT41 2UB ☎ 028 9446 3113 🖷 028 9448 1324 🖰 catherine.mcfarland@antrim.gov.uk

Fleet Management: Mr Paul Holly, Assistant Director - Operational Services, Antrim Civic Offices, 50 Stiles Way, Antrim BT41 2UB ☎ 028 9446 3113 🖷 028 9448 1324 🖰 paul.holly@antrim.gov.uk

Grounds Maintenance: Mr Reggie Hillen, Assistant Director - Property Services, Antrim Civic Offices, 50 Stiles Way, Antrim BT41 2UB ☎ 028 9446 3113 🖷 028 9448 1324 🖰 reggie.hillen@antrim.gov.uk

Health and Safety: Mrs Diane Irwin, Health & Safety Well-Being Advisor, Antrim Civic Offices, 50 Stiles Way, Antrim BT41 2UB ☎ 028 9446 3113 🖷 028 9446 1324 🖰 diane.irwin@antrim.gov.uk

Home Energy Conservation: Ms Alison Briggs, Health & Well-Being Manager, Antrim Civic Offices, 50 Stiles Way, Antrim BT41 2UB ☎ 028 9446 3113 🖷 028 9448 1324 🖰 alison.briggs@antrim.gov.uk

Legal: Ms Liz Johnston, Assistant Director - Administration, Antrim Civic Centre, 50 Stiles Way, Antrim BT41 2UB ☎ 028 9446 3113 🖷 028 9448 1324 🖰 liz.johnston@antrim.gov.uk

Leisure and Cultural Services: Ms Geraldine Girvan, Director - Development, Leisure & Borough Services, Antrim Civic Offices, 50 Stiles Way, Antrim BT41 2UB ☎ 028 9446 3113 🖷 028 9448 1324 🖰 geraldine.girvan@antrim.gov.uk

Leisure and Cultural Services: Mr Ivor McMullan, Assistant

Director - Culture & Community Services, Antrim Civic Offices, 50 Stiles Way, Antrim BT41 2UB ☎ 028 9446 3113 ✉ ivor.mcmullan@antrim.gov.uk

Licensing: Mr Fergus Mackay, Regulatory Services Manager, Antrim Civic Centre, 50 Stiles Way, Antrim BT41 2UB ☎ 028 9446 3113 🖷 028 9448 1324 ✉ fergus.mackay@antrim.gov.uk

Lifelong Learning: Mr Stuart Wilson, People Development Manager, Antrim Civic Centre, 50 Stiles Way, Antrim BT41 2UB ☎ 028 9446 3113 🖷 028 9448 1324 ✉ stuart.wilson@antrim.gov.uk

Lottery Funding, Charity and Voluntary: Mr Ivor McMullan, Assistant Director - Culture & Community Services, Antrim Civic Offices, 50 Stiles Way, Antrim BT41 2UB ☎ 028 9446 3113 ✉ ivor.mcmullan@antrim.gov.uk

Member Services: Mrs Catherine McFarland, Director of Corporate & Regulatory Services, Antrim Civic Offices, 50 Stiles Way, Antrim BT41 2UB ☎ 028 9446 3113 🖷 028 9448 1324 ✉ catherine.mcfarland@antrim.gov.uk

Personnel / HR: Mrs Elaine Magee, Assistant Director - Human Resources, Antrim Civic Offices, 50 Stiles Way, Antrim BT41 2UB ☎ 028 9446 3113 🖷 028 9448 1324 ✉ elaine.magee@antrim.gov.uk

Planning: Mr Alastair Law, Planning Officer, Antrim Civic Centre, 50 Stiles Way, Antrim BT41 2UB ☎ 028 9446 3113 ✉ alastair.law@antrim.gov.uk

Procurement: Mr Kevin Logan, Procurement Officer, Antrim Civic Offices, 50 Stiles Way, Antrim BT41 2UB ☎ 028 9446 3113 🖷 028 9448 1324 ✉ kevin.logan@antrim.gov.uk

Recycling & Waste Minimisation: Mr Paul Holly, Assistant Director - Operational Services, Antrim Civic Offices, 50 Stiles Way, Antrim BT41 2UB ☎ 028 9446 3113 🖷 028 9448 1324 ✉ paul.holly@antrim.gov.uk

Staff Training: Mr Stuart Wilson, People Development Manager, Antrim Civic Centre, 50 Stiles Way, Antrim BT41 2UB ☎ 028 9446 3113 🖷 028 9448 1324 ✉ stuart.wilson@antrim.gov.uk

Street Scene: Mr Paul Holly, Assistant Director - Operational Services, Antrim Civic Offices, 50 Stiles Way, Antrim BT41 2UB ☎ 028 9446 3113 🖷 028 9448 1324 ✉ paul.holly@antrim.gov.uk

Sustainable Communities: Mr Paul Kelly, Development Director, Antrim Civic Offices, 50 Stiles Way, Antrim BT41 2UB ☎ 028 9446 3113 🖷 028 9442 8059 ✉ paul.kelly@antrim.gov.uk

Sustainable Development: Mr Paul Holly, Assistant Director - Operational Services, Antrim Civic Offices, 50 Stiles Way, Antrim BT41 2UB ☎ 028 9446 3113 🖷 028 9448 1324 ✉ paul.holly@antrim.gov.uk

Tourism: Mr Paul Kelly, Development Director, Antrim Civic Offices, 50 Stiles Way, Antrim BT41 2UB ☎ 028 9446 3113 🖷 028 9442 8059 ✉ paul.kelly@antrim.gov.uk

Town Centre: Mr Paul Kelly, Development Director, Antrim Civic Offices, 50 Stiles Way, Antrim BT41 2UB ☎ 028 9446 3113 🖷 028 9442 8059 ✉ paul.kelly@antrim.gov.uk

Waste Collection and Disposal: Mr Paul Holly, Assistant Director - Operational Services, Antrim Civic Offices, 50 Stiles Way, Antrim BT41 2UB ☎ 028 9446 3113 🖷 028 9448 1324 ✉ paul.holly@antrim.gov.uk

Waste Collection and Disposal: Mr Peter Jones, Cleansing Manager, Antrim Civic Offices, 50 Stiles Way, Antrim BT41 2UB ☎ 028 9448 1308 🖷 028 9448 1324 ✉ peter.jones@antrim.gov.uk

Waste Management: Mr Paul Holly, Assistant Director - Operational Services, Antrim Civic Offices, 50 Stiles Way, Antrim BT41 2UB ☎ 028 9446 3113 🖷 028 9448 1324 ✉ paul.holly@antrim.gov.uk

Children's Play Areas: Mr Ivor McMullan, Assistant Director - Culture & Community Services, Antrim Civic Offices, 50 Stiles Way, Antrim BT41 2UB ☎ 028 9446 3113 ✉ ivor.mcmullan@antrim.gov.uk

MEMBERS OF THE COUNCIL (19)

***Mayor:* Michael**, Paul (UUP - Antrim South East)
paul.michael@antrim.gov.uk

***Deputy Mayor:* Thompson**, Roy (DUP - Antrim South East)
minnie.aiken@antrim.gov.uk

Brady, Anthony (SF - Antrim North West)
anthony.brady@antrim.gov.uk

Brown, Pam (DUP - Antrim Town)
pam.brown@antrim.gov.uk

Burns, Thomas (SDLP - Antrim South East)
thomas.burns@antrim.gov.uk

Clarke, Trevor (DUP - Antrim North West)
trevor.clarke@antrim.gov.uk

Cochrane-Watson, Adrian (UUP - Antrim Town)
adrian.watson@antrim.gov.uk

Cushinan, Henry (SF - Antrim North West)
henry.cushinan@antrim.gov.uk

Dunlop, Samuel (DUP - Antrim South East)
sam.dunlop@antrim.gov.uk

Graham, Brian (DUP - Antrim Town)
brian.graham@antrim.gov.uk

Kelly, Neil (ALL - Antrim Town)
neil.kelly@antrim.gov.uk

Lawther, Alan (ALL - Antrim South East)
alan.lawther@antrim.gov.uk

Logue, Anne-Marie (SF - Antrim South East)
annemarie.logue@antrim.gov.uk

Loughran, Robert (SDLP - Antrim North West)
bobby.loughran@antrim.gov.uk

Maguire, Noel (SF - Antrim Town)
minnie.aiken@antrim.gov.uk

McMullan, Kieran (SDLP - Antrim Town)
kieran.mcmullan@antrim.gov.uk

Rea, Mervyn (UUP - Antrim South East)
mervyn.rea@antrim.gov.uk

Ritchie, Drew (UUP - Antrim Town)
drew.ritchie@antrim.gov.uk

Swann, Roderick (UUP - Antrim North West)
minnie.aiken@antrim.gov.uk

POLITICAL COMPOSITION

DUP: 5, UUP: 5, SF: 4, SDLP: 3, ALL: 2

COMMITTEE CHAIRS

Community Planning: Mr Thomas Burns
Development & Leisure Services: Mr Stephen Nicholl
Environment & Borough Services: Mr Mervyn Rea
Public Services: Mr Henry Cushinan
Resources: Mr Brian Graham

ARDS N

Ards Borough Council, 2 Church Street, Newtownards BT23 4AP
☎ 028 9182 4000 🖷 028 9181 9628 ✉ ards@ards-council.gov.uk
💻 www.ards-council.gov.uk

FACTS & FIGURES

Police Authority: Northern Ireland Policing Board
Health Authority: Eastern Health & Social Services Board
Learning and Skills Council: Northern Ireland
Parliamentary Constituencies: Down North, Strangford
EU Constituencies: Northern Ireland
Election Frequency: Elections are of whole council
Twinning: Kemi (Finland)
Peoria (Arizona, USA) - Sister City

PRINCIPAL OFFICERS

Chief Executive: Mr Ashley Boreland, Chief Executive, 2 Church Street, Newtownards BT23 4AP ☎ 028 9182 4004 🖷 028 9181 9628 ✉ ashley.boreland@ards-council.gov.uk

Senior Management: Mr David Clarke, Director of Corporate Services, 2 Church Street, Newtownards BT23 4AP ☎ 028 9182 4000 🖷 028 9181 9628 ✉ david.clarke@ards-council.gov.uk

Senior Management: Mr Derek McCallan, Director of Development, 2 Church Street, Newtownards BT23 4AP ☎ 028 9182 4065 🖷 028 9181 9628 ✉ derek.mccallan@ards-council.gov.uk

Senior Management: Mr John Rea, Director of Environmental Services, 2 Church Street, Newtownards BT23 4AP ☎ 028 9182 4000 🖷 028 9181 9628 ✉ john.rea@ards-council.gov.uk

Senior Management: Mr Archie Walls, Director of Leisure Services, 2 Church Street, Newtownards BT23 4AP ☎ 028 9182 4018 🖷 028 9181 9628 ✉ archie.walls@ards-council.gov.uk

Best Value: Mr Ashley Boreland, Chief Executive, 2 Church Street, Newtownards BT23 4AP ☎ 028 9182 4004 🖷 028 9181 9628 ✉ ashley.boreland@ards-council.gov.uk

Building Control: Mr Robert Shields, Chief Building Control Officer, 2 Church Street, Newtownards BT23 4AP ☎ 028 9182 4033 or 028 9182 4034 🖷 028 9181 9628 ✉ robert.shields@ards-council.gov.uk

Civil Registration: Mrs Heather Cannavan, Registrar, 2 Church Street, Newtownards BT23 4AP ☎ 028 9182 4003 🖷 028 9181 9628 ✉ registration@ards-council.gov.uk

PR / Communications: Ms Ursula Mezza, Public Relations Officer, 2 Church Street, Newtownards BT23 4AP ☎ 028 9182 4021 🖷 028 9181 9628 ✉ ursula.mezza@ards-council.gov.uk

Community Safety: Mrs Nicola Dorrian, Community Safety Manager, 2 Church Street, Newtownards BT23 4AP ☎ 028 9182 4047 🖷 028 9181 9628 ✉ nicola.dorrian@ards-council.gov.uk

Computer Management: Mr Colin White, Information Technology, 2 Church Street, Newtownards BT23 4AP ☎ 028 9182 4000

Consumer Protection and Trading Standards: Mr John Rea, Director of Environmental Services, 2 Church Street, Newtownards BT23 4AP ☎ 028 9182 4000 🖷 028 9181 9628 ✉ john.rea@ards-council.gov.uk

Corporate Services: Mr David Clarke, Director of Corporate Services, 2 Church Street, Newtownards BT23 4AP ☎ 028 9182 4000 🖷 028 9181 9628 ✉ david.clarke@ards-council.gov.uk

Customer Service: Ms Ursula Mezza, Public Relations Officer, 2 Church Street, Newtownards BT23 4AP ☎ 028 9182 4021 🖷 028 9181 9628 ✉ ursula.mezza@ards-council.gov.uk

Economic Development: Mr Derek McCallan, Director of Development, 2 Church Street, Newtownards BT23 4AP ☎ 028 9182 4065 🖷 028 9181 9628 ✉ derek.mccallan@ards-council.gov.uk

Emergency Planning: Mr Ashley Boreland, Chief Executive, 2 Church Street, Newtownards BT23 4AP ☎ 028 9182 4004 🖷 028 9181 9628 ✉ ashley.boreland@ards-council.gov.uk

Energy Management: Mr Ken Green, Energy Engineer, 2 Church Street, Newtownards BT23 4AP ☎ 028 9182 4000 🖷 028 9181 9628 ✉ ken.green@ards-council.gov.uk

Environmental / Technical Services: Mr John Rea, Director of Environmental Services, 2 Church Street, Newtownards BT23 4AP ☎ 028 9182 4000 🖷 028 9181 9628 ✉ john.rea@ards-council.gov.uk

Environmental Health: Mr John Rea, Director of Environmental Services, 2 Church Street, Newtownards BT23 4AP ☎ 028 9182 4000 🖷 028 9181 9628 ✉ john.rea@ards-council.gov.uk

Estates, Property & Valuation: Mr Ashley Boreland, Chief Executive, 2 Church Street, Newtownards BT23 4AP ☎ 028 9182 4004 🖷 028 9181 9628 ✉ ashley.boreland@ards-council.gov.uk

European Liaison: Mr Brian Dorrian, Project Officer, 2 Church Street, Newtownards BT23 4AP ☎ 028 9182 4020 🖷 028 9181 9628 ✉ brian.dorrian@ards-council.gov.uk

Events Manager: Ms Ursula Mezza, Public Relations Officer, 2 Church Street, Newtownards BT23 4AP ☎ 028 9182 4021 🖷 028 9181 9628 ✉ ursula.mezza@ards-council.gov.uk

Finance and Treasurer: Mr David Clarke, Director of Corporate Services, 2 Church Street, Newtownards BT23 4AP ☎ 028 9182 4000 🖷 028 9181 9628 ✉ david.clarke@ards-council.gov.uk

Grounds Maintenance: Mr John McConnell, Operations Manager: Parks & Cemeteries, 2 Church Street, Newtownards BT23 4AP ☎ 028 9182 4061 🖷 028 9181 9628 ✉ john.mcconnell@ards-council.gov.uk

Health and Safety: Mr Paul Hanley, Health and Safety Officer, 2 Church Street, Newtownards BT23 4AP ☎ 028 9182 4000 🖷 028 9181 9628 ✉ paul.hanley@ards-council.gov.uk

Legal: Mr Ashley Boreland, Chief Executive, 2 Church Street, Newtownards BT23 4AP ☎ 028 9182 4004 🖷 028 9181 9628 ✉ ashley.boreland@ards-council.gov.uk

Leisure and Cultural Services: Mr Archie Walls, Director of Leisure Services, 2 Church Street, Newtownards BT23 4AP ☎ 028 9182 4018 🖷 028 9181 9628 ✉ archie.walls@ards-council.gov.uk

Licensing: Mr Richard Brittain, Borough Inspector, 2 Church Street, Newtownards BT23 4AP ☎ 028 9182 4005 🖷 028 9181 9628 ✉ richard.brittain@ards-council.gov.uk

Member Services: Mrs Jeanette Wilson, Senior Committee Adminstrator, 2 Church Street, Newtownards BT23 4AP ☎ 028 9182 4000 🖷 028 9181 9628 ✉ jeanette.wilson@ards-council.gov.uk

Partnerships: Mr Ashley Boreland, Chief Executive, 2 Church Street, Newtownards BT23 4AP ☎ 028 9182 4004 🖷 028 9181 9628 ✉ ashley.boreland@ards-council.gov.uk

Personnel / HR: Mrs Rosemary McCullough, Human Resources Manager, 2 Church Street, Newtownards BT23 4AP ☎ 028 9182 4000 🖷 028 9181 9628 ✉ hrmanager@ards-council.gov.uk

Recycling & Waste Minimisation: Mr Nigel Martin, Waste Services Manager, 2 Church Street, Newtownards BT23 4AP ☎ 028 9182 4000 🖷 028 9181 9628 ✉ nigel.martin@ards-council.gov.uk

Regeneration: Mr Brian Dorrian, Acting Director of Development, 2 Church Street, Newtownards BT23 4AP ☎ 028 9182 4065 🖷 028 9181 9628 ✉ brian.dorrian@ards-council.gov.uk

Staff Training: Mrs Rosemary McCullough, Human Resources Manager, 2 Church Street, Newtownards BT23 4AP ☎ 028 9182 4000 🖷 028 9181 9628 ✉ hrmanager@ards-council.gov.uk

Tourism: Mrs Sharon Mahaffy, Tourism Development Officer, Tourist Information Centre, 31 Regent Street, Newtownards BT23 4AD ☎ 028 9182 6846 🖷 028 9182 6681 ✉ sharon.mahaffy@ards-council.gov.uk

Waste Collection and Disposal: Mr John Rea, Director of Environmental Services, 2 Church Street, Newtownards BT23 4AP ☎ 028 9182 4000 🖷 028 9181 9628 ✉ john.rea@ards-council.gov.uk

Waste Management: Mr John Rea, Director of Environmental Services, 2 Church Street, Newtownards BT23 4AP ☎ 028 9182 4000 🖷 028 9181 9628 ✉ john.rea@ards-council.gov.uk

MEMBERS OF THE COUNCIL (23)

***Mayor:* Oswald**, Mervyn (DUP - Ards West)
councillor.mervyn.oswald@ards-council.gov.uk
***Deputy Mayor:* Gregory**, Hamilton (DUP - Ards East)
alderman.hamilton.gregory@ards-council.gov.uk
***Alderman:* Elliott**, Colville (DUP - Ards East)
alderman.colville.elliot@ards-council.gov.uk
***Alderman:* Ferguson**, Ronald (UUP - Ards East)
ronald.ferguson@hotmail.co.uk
***Alderman:* Gibson**, Robert (DUP - Ards West)
alderman.robert.gibson@ards-council.gov.uk
***Alderman:* McCarthy**, Kieran (ALL - Ards Peninsula)
alderman.kieran.mccarthy@ards-council.gov.uk
Adair, Robert (DUP - Ards Peninsula)
councillor.robert.adair@ards-council.gov.uk
Armstrong-Cotter, Naomi (DUP - Newtownards)
councillor.naomi.armstrong@ards-council.gov.uk
Boyle, Joe (SDLP - Ards Peninsula)
councillor.joe.boyle@ards-council.gov.uk
Carson, Angus (UUP - Ards Peninsula)
councillor.angus.carson@ards-council.gov.uk
Cleland, Linda (ALL - Ards East)
linda.cleland@talktalk.net
Cummings, Trevor (DUP - Ards West)
councillor.trevor.cummings@ards-council.gov.uk
Fletcher, Jim (UUP - Ards West)
councillor.jim.fletcher@ards-council.gov.uk
Girvan, Deborah (ALL - Ards West)
councillor.deborah.girvan@ards-council.gov.uk
Hamilton, Tom (UUP - Newtownards)
cllr.tomhamilton@gmail.com
Kennedy, Colin (DUP - Ards Peninsula)
cllrcolinkennedy@mail.com
McDowell, Alan (ALL - Newtownards)
councillor.alan.mcdowell@ards-council.gov.uk
McIlveen, Stephen (DUP - Newtownards)
councillor.stephen.mcilveen@ards-council.gov.uk
Menagh, Jimmy (IND - Newtownards)
councillor.jimmy.menagh@ards-council.gov.uk
Smith, Philip (UUP - Ards West)
councillor.philip.smith@ards-council.gov.uk
Smith, Tom (DUP - Ards East)
tom@tomsmithdup.org
Smyth, David (UUP - Newtownards)
councillor.david.smyth@ards-council.gov.uk
Thompson, Eddie (DUP - Ards East)
councillor.eddie.thompson@ards-council.gov.uk

POLITICAL COMPOSITION

DUP: 11, UUP: 6, ALL: 4, IND: 1, SDLP: 1

COMMITTEE CHAIRS

Council Services: Mr Colville Elliott
Development: Mr Stephen McIlveen
External Affairs & Planning: Mr Tom Hamilton
Policy & Resources: Mr Angus Carson

ARGYLL & BUTE S

Argyll & Bute Council, (Comhairle Earra Ghaidheal agus Bhoid), Kilmory, Lochgilphead PA31 8RT ☎ 01546 602127 🖷 01546 604138 ✉ enquiries@argyll-bute.gov.uk 🖳 www.argyll-bute.gov.uk

FACTS & FIGURES

Police Authority: Strathclyde Police Authority
Health Authority: NHS Highland
Learning and Skills Council: Scotland
Parliamentary Constituencies: Argyll and Bute
EU Constituencies: Scotland
Election Frequency: Elections are of whole council
Twinning: Amberg (Germany); Sulzbach (Germany); Korcula (Croatia); Thouars (France); Gorey (Ireland)

PRINCIPAL OFFICERS

Chief Executive: Ms Sally Loudon, Chief Executive, Kilmory, Lochgilphead PA31 8RT ☎ 01546 604350 🖷 01546 604349 ✉ sally.loudon@argyll-bute.gov.uk

Architect, Building / Property Services: Mr Angus Gilmour, Head of Planning & Regulatory Services, Kilmory, Lochgilphead PA31 8RT ☎ 01546 604288 🖷 01546 604237 ✉ angus.gilmour@argyll-bute.gov.uk

Best Value: Ms Jane Fowler, Head of Improvement & HR, Kilmory, Lochgilphead PA31 8RT ☎ 01546 604466 ✉ jane.fowler@argyll-bute.gov.uk

Building Control: Mr Ross McLaughlin, Development Manager, Blairbadach House, Helensburgh G84 8ND ☎ 01546 604172 ✉ ross.mclaughlin@argyll-bute.gov.uk

Catering Services: Mr Malcolm MacFadyen, Head of Facility Services, Kilmory, Lochgilphead PA31 8RT ☎ 01546 604412 🖷 01546 604434 ✉ malcolm.macfadyen@argyll-bute.gov.uk

Civil Registration: Ms Shona Brechin, Area Registrar, Dalriada House, Lochgilphead PA31 8ST ☎ 01546 604515 🖷 01546 604530 ✉ shona.brechin@argyll-bute.gov.uk

PR / Communications: Ms Jo Smith, Communications Manager, Kilmory, Lochgilphead PA31 8RT ☎ 01546 604136 🖷 01546 604346 ✉ jo.smith@argyll-bute.gov.uk

Community Planning: Ms Eileen Wilson, Community Planning Manager, 25 West King Street, Helensburgh G84 8UW ☎ 01436 658726 ✉ eileen.wilson@argyll-bute.gov.uk

Community Safety: Mr Charles Reppke, Head of Governance & Law, Kilmory, Lochgilphead PA31 8RT ☎ 01546 604192 🖷 01546 604434 ✉ charles.reppke@argyll-bute.gov.uk

Computer Management: Ms Judy Orr, Head of Support & Customer Services, Witchburn Road, Campbeltown PA28 6JX ☎ 01586 555280 🖷 01586 553050 ✉ judy.orr@argyll-bute.gov.uk

Consumer Protection and Trading Standards: Mr Angus Gilmour, Head of Planning & Regulatory Services, Kilmory , Lochgilphead PA31 8RT ☎ 01546 604288 🖷 01546 604237 ✉ angus.gilmour@argyll-bute.gov.uk

Contracts: Ms Anne MacColl-Smith, Service Commissioning Manager, Kilmory, Lochgilphead PA31 8RT ☎ 01546 604194 🖷 01546 604434 ✉ anne.maccoll-smith@argyll-bute.gov.uk

Customer Service: Mr Douglas Hendry, Executive Director of Customer Services, Kilmory, Lochgilphead PA31 8RT ☎ 01546 604244 🖷 01546 604434 ✉ douglas.hendry@argyll-bute.gov.uk

Customer Service: Mrs Judy Orr, Head of Support & Customer Services, Witchburn Road, Campbeltown PA28 6JU ☎ 01586 555280 ✉ judy.orr@argyll-bute.gov.uk

Direct Labour: Mr Graham Brown, Operations Manager, Manse Brae, Lochgilphead PA31 8RD ☎ 01546 604687 🖷 01546 606443 ✉ graham.brown@argyll-bute.gov.uk

Economic Development: Mr Robert Pollock, Head of Economic Development, Kilmory, Lochgilphead PA31 8RT ☎ 01546 604115 🖷 01546 604237 ✉ robert.pollock@argyll-bute.gov.uk

Education: Mrs Carol Walker, Head of Education, Oban Education Office, Dalintart Drive, Oban PA34 4EF ☎ 01631 564908 🖷 01631 564615 ✉ carol.walker@argyll-bute.gov.uk

E-Government: Ms Judy Orr, Head of Support & Customer Services, Witchburn Road, Campbeltown PA28 6JX ☎ 01586 555280 🖷 01586 553050 ✉ judy.orr@argyll-bute.gov.uk

Electoral Registration: Mr Charles Reppke, Head of Governance & Law, Kilmory, Lochgilphead PA31 8RT ☎ 01546 604192 🖷 01546 604434 ✉ charles.reppke@argyll-bute.gov.uk

Emergency Planning: Ms Carol Keeley, Emergency Planning Officer, 25 West King Street, Helensburgh G84 8UW ☎ 01436 677819 🖷 01436 672531 ✉ carol.keeley@argyll-bute.gov.uk

Energy Management: Mr Paul Gillies, Energy Manager, Argyll House, Alexandra Parade, Dunoon PA23 8AJ ☎ 01369 708573 🖷 01369 708554 ✉ paul.gillies@argyll-bute.gov.uk

Environmental / Technical Services: Mr Angus Gilmour, Head of Planning & Regulatory Services, Kilmory , Lochgilphead PA31 8RT ☎ 01546 604288 🖷 01546 604237 ✉ angus.gilmour@argyll-bute.gov.uk

Environmental Health: Mr Angus Gilmour, Head of Planning & Regulatory Services, Kilmory , Lochgilphead PA31 8RT ☎ 01546 604288 🖷 01546 604237 ✉ angus.gilmour@argyll-bute.gov.uk

Estates, Property & Valuation: Mr Nicholas Allan, Strategic Assets Manager, Kilmory, Lochgilphead PA31 8RT ☎ 01436 658950 🖷 01436 658989 ✉ nick.allan@argyll-bute.gov.uk

European Liaison: Mr Robert Pollock, Head of Economic Development, Kilmory, Lochgilphead PA31 8RT ☎ 01546 604115 🖷 01546 604237 ✉ robert.pollock@argyll-bute.gov.uk

Facilities: Mr Malcolm MacFadyen, Head of Facility Services, Kilmory, Lochgilphead PA31 8RT ☎ 01546 604412

🖷 01546 604434 ✉ malcolm.macfadyen@argyll-bute.gov.uk

Finance and Treasurer: Mr Bruce West, Head of Strategic Finance, Kilmory, Lochgilphead PA31 8NN ☎ 01546 604220 🖷 01546 604411 ✉ bruce.west@argyll-bute.gov.uk

Fleet Management: Ms Moya Ingram, Strategic Transportation Manager, Kilmory, Lochgilphead PA31 8RT ☎ 01546 604190 🖷 01546 604386 ✉ moya.ingram@argyll-bute.gov.uk

Grounds Maintenance: Mr Callum Robertson, Assistant Operations Manager - Roads & Grounds, Manse Brae, Lochgilphead PA31 8RD ☎ 01546 604887 🖷 01546 606443 ✉ callum.robertson@argyll-bute.gov.uk

Health and Safety: Mr Logie Collins, Health & Safety Manager, Whitegate Offices, Lochgilphead PA31 8SY ☎ 01546 604014 🖷 01546 606692 ✉ logie.collins@argyll-bute.gov.uk

Housing: Mr Donald MacVicar, Head of Community & Culture, Kilmory, Lochgilphead PA31 8RT ☎ 01546 604364 🖷 01546 604434 ✉ donald.macvicar@argyll-bute.gov.uk

Housing Maintenance: Mr Donald MacVicar, Head of Community & Culture, Kilmory, Lochgilphead PA31 8RT ☎ 01546 604364 🖷 01546 604434 ✉ donald.macvicar@argyll-bute.gov.uk

Legal: Mr Charles Reppke, Head of Governance & Law, Kilmory, Lochgilphead PA31 8RT ☎ 01546 604192 🖷 01546 604434 ✉ charles.reppke@argyll-bute.gov.uk

Leisure and Cultural Services: Mr Donald MacVicar, Head of Community & Culture, Kilmory, Lochgilphead PA31 8RT ☎ 01546 604364 🖷 01546 604434 ✉ donald.macvicar@argyll-bute.gov.uk

Licensing: Mr Charles Reppke, Head of Governance & Law, Kilmory, Lochgilphead PA31 8RT ☎ 01546 604192 🖷 01546 604434 ✉ charles.reppke@argyll-bute.gov.uk

Lighting: Mr Ryan McGlynn, Technical Officer - Street Lighting, Manse Brae, Lochgilphead PA31 8RD ☎ 01546 604646 🖷 01546 606443 ✉ ryan.mcglynn@argyll-bute.gov.uk

Lottery Funding, Charity and Voluntary: Ms Arlene Cullum, Funding Officer, 25 West King Street, Helensburgh G84 8UW ☎ 07979 214501 ✉ arlene.cullum@argyll-bute.gov.uk

Member Services: Mr Charles Reppke, Head of Governance & Law, Kilmory, Lochgilphead PA31 8RT ☎ 01546 604192 🖷 01546 604434 ✉ charles.reppke@argyll-bute.gov.uk

Parking: Mr Neil Brown, Roads & Amenity Services Manager, Lorn House, Albany Street, Oban PA34 4AR ☎ 01631 569196 ✉ neil.brown@argyll-bute.gov.uk

Partnerships: Ms Eileen Wilson, Community Planning Manager, 25 West King Street, Helensburgh G84 8UW ☎ 01436 658726 ✉ eileen.wilson@argyll-bute.gov.uk

Personnel / HR: Ms Jane Fowler, Head of Improvement & HR, Kilmory, Lochgilphead PA31 8RT ☎ 01546 604466 ✉ jane.fowler@argyll-bute.gov.uk

Planning: Mr Angus Gilmour, Head of Planning & Regulatory Services, Kilmory , Lochgilphead PA31 8RT ☎ 01546 604288 🖷 01546 604237 ✉ angus.gilmour@argyll-bute.gov.uk

Procurement: Mr Alan Brough, Exchequer Services Manager, Kilmory, Lochgilphead PA31 8RT ☎ 01546 604146 ✉ alan.brough@argyll-bute.gov.uk

Public Libraries: Ms Pat McCann, Culture & Libraries Manager, West King Street Library, West King Street, Helensburgh G84 8GB ☎ 01436 658811 ✉ pat.mccann@argyll-bute.gov.uk

Recycling & Waste Minimisation: Mr Alan Millar, Assistant Operations Manager - Waste Management, Manse Brae, Lochgilphead PA31 8RD ☎ 01546 604628 🖷 01546 606443 ✉ alan.millar@argyll-bute.gov.uk

Regeneration: Mr Donald MacVicar, Head of Community & Culture, Kilmory, Lochgilphead PA31 8RT ☎ 01546 604364 🖷 01546 604434 ✉ donald.macvicar@argyll-bute.gov.uk

Road Safety: Mrs June Graham, Road Safety Officer, Kilmory, Lochgilphead PA31 8RT ☎ 01546 604182 🖷 01546 604386 ✉ june.graham@argyll-bute.gov.uk

Social Services: Ms Louise Long, Head of Children & Families, Kilmory, Lochgilphead PA31 8RT ☎ 01546 604256 🖷 01546 604434 ✉ louise.long@argyll-bute.gov.uk

Social Services: Mr Jim Robb, Head of Adult Services, Struan Lodge - Top Floor, Bencorrum Brae, Dunoon PA23 8HU ☎ 01369 708911 🖷 01369 708909 ✉ jim.robb@argyll-bute.gov.uk

Social Services: Mr Cleland Sneddon, Executive Director of Community Services, Kilmory, Lochgilphead PA31 8RT ☎ 01546 604168 🖷 01546 604434 ✉ cleland.sneddon@argyll-bute.gov.uk

Social Services (Adult): Mr Jim Robb, Head of Adult Services, Struan Lodge - Top Floor, Bencorrum Brae, Dunoon PA23 8HU ☎ 01369 708911 🖷 01369 708909 ✉ jim.robb@argyll-bute.gov.uk

Social Services (Children): Ms Louise Long, Head of Children & Families, Kilmory, Lochgilphead PA31 8RT ☎ 01546 604256 🖷 01546 604434 ✉ louise.long@argyll-bute.gov.uk

Staff Training: Ms Jane Fowler, Head of Improvement & HR, Kilmory, Lochgilphead PA31 8RT ☎ 01546 604466 ✉ jane.fowler@argyll-bute.gov.uk

Street Scene: Mr John Downie, Area Street Scene Manager, Manse Brae, Lochgilphead PA31 8RD ☎ 01546 604636 🖷 01546 606443 ✉ john.downie@argyll-bute.gov.uk

Sustainable Communities: Mr Robert Pollock, Head of Economic Development, Kilmory, Lochgilphead PA31 8RT ☎ 01546 604115 🖷 01546 604237 ✉ robert.pollock@argyll-bute.gov.uk

Sustainable Development: Mr Angus Gilmour, Head of Planning & Regulatory Services, Kilmory , Lochgilphead PA31 8RT ☎ 01546 604288 🖷 01546 604237 ✉ angus.gilmour@argyll-bute.gov.uk

Tourism: Mr Robert Pollock, Head of Economic Development, Kilmory, Lochgilphead PA31 8RT ☎ 01546 604115 🖷 01546 604237 ✉ robert.pollock@argyll-bute.gov.uk

Town Centre: Mr Robert Pollock, Head of Economic Development, Kilmory, Lochgilphead PA31 8RT ☎ 01546 604115 🖷 01546 604237 ✉ robert.pollock@argyll-bute.gov.uk

Traffic Management: Mr Martin Gannon, Roadspace Manager, Manse Brae, Lochgilphead PA31 8RD ☎ 01436 658850 ✉ martin.gannon@argyll-bute.gov.uk

Transport: Ms Moya Ingram, Strategic Transportation Manager, Kilmory, Lochgilphead PA31 8RT ☎ 01546 604190 🖷 01546 604386 ✉ moya.ingram@argyll-bute.gov.uk

Waste Collection and Disposal: Mr Tom Murphy, Area Street Scene Manager, Blairvedach House, Helensburgh G84 8ND ☎ 01436 658908 ✉ tom.murphy@argyll-bute.gov.uk

Waste Management: Mr Alan Millar, Assistant Operations Manager - Waste Management, Manse Brae, Lochgilphead PA31 8RD ☎ 01546 604628 🖷 01546 606443 ✉ alan.millar@argyll-bute.gov.uk

MEMBERS OF THE COUNCIL (36)

***Provost:* Strong**, Isobel (SNP - Isle of Bute)
isobel.strong@argyll-bute.gov.uk

***Deputy Provost:* Philand**, Douglas (IND - Mid Argyll)
dougie.philand@argyll-bute.gov.uk

***Leader of the Council:* McCuish**, Roddy (SNP - Oban South & Isles)
roderick.mccuish@argyll-bute.gov.uk

***Deputy Leader of the Council:* Semple**, John (SNP - South Kintyre)
john.semple@argyll-bute.gov.uk

Blair, William Gordon (SNP - Cowal)
williamgordon.blair@argyll-bute.gov.uk

Breslin, Michael (SNP - Dunoon)
michael.breslin@argyll-bute.gov.uk

Colville, Rory (LD - South Kintyre)
rory.colville@argyll-bute.gov.uk

Corry, Maurice (CON - Lomond North)
maurice.corry@argyll-bute.gov.uk

Currie, Robin (LD - Kintyre & the Islands)
robin.currie@argyll-bute.gov.uk

Dance, Vivien (IND - Helensburgh Central)
vivien.dance@argyll-bute.gov.uk

Devon, Mary-Jean (IND - Oban South & Isles)
mary-jean.devon@argyll-bute.gov.uk

Freeman, George (IND - Lomond North)
george.freeman@argyll-bute.gov.uk

Glen-Lee, Louise (SNP - Oban North & Lorn)
louise.glen-lee@argyll-bute.gov.uk

Hall, Fred (SNP - Oban South & Isles)
fred.hall@argyll-bute.gov.uk

Horn, Anne (SNP - Kintyre & the Islands)
anne.horn@argyll-bute.gov.uk

Kelly, Donald (CON - South Kintyre)
donald.kelly2@argyll-bute.gov.uk

Kinniburgh, David (CON - Helensburgh & Lomond South)
david.kinniburgh@argyll-bute.gov.uk

MacDonald, Iain Angus (IND - Oban North & Lorn)
iainangus.macdonald@argyll-bute.gov.uk

MacDougall, Alistair (IND - Oban South & Isles)
alistair.macdougall@argyll-bute.gov.uk

MacIntyre, Duncan (IND - Oban North & Lorn)
duncan.macintyre@argyll-bute.gov.uk

MacIntyre, Robert (IND - Lomond North)
robertgraham.macintyre@argyll-bute.gov.uk

MacIntyre, Robert (SNP - Isle of Bute)
robert.macintyre@argyll-bute.gov.uk

MacMillan, Donnie (IND - Mid Argyll)
donald.macmillan@argyll-bute.gov.uk

Marshall, Bruce (IND - Cowal)
bruce.marshall@argyll-bute.gov.uk

McAlpine, John (IND - Kintyre & the Islands)
john.mcalpine@argyll-bute.gov.uk

McNaughton, Alex (IND - Cowal)
alex.mcnaughton@argyll-bute.gov.uk

McQueen, James (IND - Dunoon)
james.mcqueen@argyll-bute.gov.uk

Morton, Aileen (LD - Helensburgh Central)
aileen.morton@argyll-bute.gov.uk

Morton, Ellen (LD - Helensburgh & Lomond South)
ellen.morton@argyll-bute.gov.uk

Mulvaney, Gary (CON - Helensburgh Central)
gary.mulvaney@argyll-bute.gov.uk

Robb, James (SNP - Helensburgh Central)
james.robb@argyll-bute.gov.uk

Robertson, Elaine (IND - Oban North & Lorn)
elaine.robertson@argyll-bute.gov.uk

Scoullar, Len (IND - Isle of Bute)
len.scoullar@argyll-bute.gov.uk

Taylor, Sandy (SNP - Mid Argyll)
sandy.taylor@argyll-bute.gov.uk

Trail, Richard (SNP - Helensburgh & Lomond South)
richard.trail@argyll-bute.gov.uk

Walsh, Dick (IND - Dunoon)
dick.walsh@argyll-bute.gov.uk

POLITICAL COMPOSITION

IND: 16, SNP: 12, CON: 4, LD: 4

CABINET

Leader of the Council: Mr Roddy McCuish
Deputy Leader: Mr John Semple
Adult Care & Learning Disabilities: Ms Anne Horn
Children & Families: Ms Mary-Jean Devon
Community, Culture, Customer & Communications: Ms Louise Glen-Lee
Education & Lifelong Learning: Mr Michael Breslin
Energy, Development, Infrastructure & Tourism: Mr John Semple
Housing: Mr George Freeman
Human Resources & Sport: Mr Douglas Philand
Planning & Regulatory Services: Mr Sandy Taylor
Roads & Amenity Services: Mr Donald Kelly
Strategic Finance & European Affairs: Mr James Robb

ARMAGH N

Armagh District Council, (Armagh City and District Council), Council Offices, The Palace Demesne, Armagh BT60 4EL ☎ 028 3752 9600 🖷 028 3752 9601 ✉ info@armagh.gov.uk 💻 www.armagh.gov.uk

FACTS & FIGURES

Police Authority: Northern Ireland Policing Board

Health Authority: Southern Health & Social Care Board
Learning and Skills Council: Northern Ireland
Parliamentary Constituencies: Newry and Armagh
EU Constituencies: Northern Ireland
Election Frequency: Elections are of whole council

PRINCIPAL OFFICERS

Chief Executive: Mr John Briggs, Clerk & Chief Executive, Council Offices, The Palace Demesne, Armagh BT60 4EL ☎ 028 3752 9697 🖷 028 3752 9604 ✉ john.briggs@armagh.gov.uk

Deputy Chief Executive: Miss Sharon O'Gorman, Strategic Director of Regeneration & Development, Council Offices, The Palace Demesne, Armagh BT60 4EL ☎ 028 3752 9642 🖷 028 3752 9631 ✉ sharon.o'gorman@armagh.gov.uk

Senior Management: Mrs Carol Corvan, Strategic Director of Corporate Services & Governance, Council Offices, The Palace Demesne, Armagh BT60 4EL ☎ 028 3752 9605 🖷 028 3752 9638 ✉ carol.corvan@armagh.gov.uk

Senior Management: Miss Sharon O'Gorman, Strategic Director of Regeneration & Development, Council Offices, The Palace Demesne, Armagh BT60 4EL ☎ 028 3752 9642 🖷 028 3752 9631 ✉ sharon.o'gorman@armagh.gov.uk

Building Control: Mr Jonathan Hayes, Building Control Manager, Council Offices, The Palace Demesne, Armagh BT60 4EL ☎ 028 3752 9616 🖷 028 3752 9617 ✉ jonathan.hayes@armagh.gov.uk

Civil Registration: Mrs Jennifer Coulter, Registrar of Births, Deaths & Marriages, Council Offices, The Palace Demesne, Armagh BT60 4EL ☎ 028 3752 9615 ✉ jennifer.coulter@armagh.gov.uk

PR / Communications: Ms Claire Shields, Communications Assistant, Council Offices, The Palace Demesne, Armagh BT60 4EL ☎ 028 3752 9636 ✉ claire.shields@armagh.gov.uk

Community Planning: Mr Godfrey McCartney, Community & Economic Development Manager, Council Offices, The Palace Demesne, Armagh BT60 4EL ☎ 028 3751 9632 🖷 028 2751 9631 ✉ godfrey.mccartney@armagh.gov.uk

Community Safety: Mr John Doyle, Community Safety Officer, Council Offices, The Palace Demesne, Armagh BT60 4EL ☎ 028 3752 9600 🖷 028 3752 9601 ✉ john.doyle@armagh.gov.uk

Computer Management: Mr Con Donnelly, Information Technology Officer, Council Offices, The Palace Demesne, Armagh BT60 4EL ☎ 028 3752 9600 🖷 028 3752 9601 ✉ con.donnelly@armagh.gov.uk

Consumer Protection and Trading Standards: Mr John Briggs, Clerk & Chief Executive, Council Offices, The Palace Demesne, Armagh BT60 4EL ☎ 028 3752 9697 🖷 028 3752 9604 ✉ john.briggs@armagh.gov.uk

Contracts: Mr Stephen Hyde, Head of Financial Services, Council Offices, The Palace Demesne, Armagh BT60 4EL ☎ 028 3752 9619 🖷 028 3752 9613 ✉ stephen.hyde@armagh.gov.uk

Corporate Services: Mrs Carol Corvan, Strategic Director of Corporate Services & Governance, Council Offices, The Palace Demesne, Armagh BT60 4EL ☎ 028 3752 9605 🖷 028 3752 9638 ✉ carol.corvan@armagh.gov.uk

Customer Service: Mr John Briggs, Clerk & Chief Executive, Council Offices, The Palace Demesne, Armagh BT60 4EL ☎ 028 3752 9697 🖷 028 3752 9604 ✉ john.briggs@armagh.gov.uk

Direct Labour: Mr David McKee, Deputy Director of Operational Services, Council Offices, The Palace Demesne, Armagh BT60 4EL ☎ 028 3752 9624 🖷 028 3752 9614 ✉ david.mckee@armagh.gov.uk

Economic Development: Miss Sharon O'Gorman, Strategic Director of Regeneration & Development, Council Offices, The Palace Demesne, Armagh BT60 4EL ☎ 028 3752 9642 🖷 028 3752 9631 ✉ sharon.o'gorman@armagh.gov.uk

E-Government: Mr John Briggs, Clerk & Chief Executive, Council Offices, The Palace Demesne, Armagh BT60 4EL ☎ 028 3752 9697 🖷 028 3752 9604 ✉ john.briggs@armagh.gov.uk

Electoral Registration: Mr John Briggs, Clerk & Chief Executive, Council Offices, The Palace Demesne, Armagh BT60 4EL ☎ 028 3752 9697 🖷 028 3752 9604 ✉ john.briggs@armagh.gov.uk

Emergency Planning: Mr John Briggs, Clerk & Chief Executive, Council Offices, The Palace Demesne, Armagh BT60 4EL ☎ 028 3752 9697 🖷 028 3752 9604 ✉ john.briggs@armagh.gov.uk

Energy Management: Mr Aidan Mallon, Finance Officer (Purchasing) Property Services Manager, Council Offices, The Palace Demesne, Armagh BT60 4EL ☎ 028 3752 9624 🖷 028 3752 9614 ✉ aidan.mallon@armagh.gov.uk

Environmental / Technical Services: Mr John Briggs, Clerk & Chief Executive, Council Offices, The Palace Demesne, Armagh BT60 4EL ☎ 028 3752 9697 🖷 028 3752 9604 ✉ john.briggs@armagh.gov.uk

Environmental Health: Mr Seamus Donaghy, Principal Environmental Health Officer, Council Offices, The Palace Demesne, Armagh BT60 4EL ☎ 028 3752 9616 🖷 028 3752 9617 ✉ seamus.donaghy@armagh.gov.uk

Estates, Property & Valuation: Mr Philip Beattie, Head of Estates, Council Offices, The Palace Demesne, Armagh BT60 4EL ☎ 028 3752 9600 ✉ philip.beattie@armagh.gov.uk

Estates, Property & Valuation: Mr Darren Heasty, Corporate Manager, Council Offices, The Palace Demesne, Armagh BT60 4EL ☎ 028 3752 9605 🖷 028 3752 9638 ✉ darren.heasty@armagh.gov.uk

European Liaison: Mr John Briggs, Clerk & Chief Executive, Council Offices, The Palace Demesne, Armagh BT60 4EL ☎ 028 3752 9697 🖷 028 3752 9604 ✉ john.briggs@armagh.gov.uk

Events Manager: Ms Gill Robb, Events, Council Offices, The Palace Demesne, Armagh BT60 4EL ☎ 028 3752 9600

Finance and Treasurer: Mr Stephen Hyde, Head of Financial Services, Council Offices, The Palace Demesne, Armagh BT60 4EL ☎ 028 3752 9619 🖷 028 3752 9613 🖰 stephen.hyde@armagh.gov.uk

Fleet Management: Mr David McKee, Deputy Director of Operational Services, Council Offices, The Palace Demesne, Armagh BT60 4EL ☎ 028 3752 9624 🖷 028 3752 9614 🖰 david.mckee@armagh.gov.uk

Grounds Maintenance: Mr David McKee, Deputy Director of Operational Services, Council Offices, The Palace Demesne, Armagh BT60 4EL ☎ 028 3752 9624 🖷 028 3752 9614 🖰 david.mckee@armagh.gov.uk

Health and Safety: Ms Linda Fitzsimmons, Principal Environmental Health Officer (Health & Safety), Southern Group Headquarters, Riverside House, Towerhill Complex, Armagh BT60 4EL ☎ 028 3751 5800 🖷 028 3751 5801 🖰 linda.fitzsimmons@sgehc.com

Legal: Mrs Carol Corvan, Strategic Director of Corporate Services & Governance, Council Offices, The Palace Demesne, Armagh BT60 4EL ☎ 028 3752 9605 🖷 028 3752 9638 🖰 carol.corvan@armagh.gov.uk

Leisure and Cultural Services: Mr Gerard Houlahan, Deputy Director of Recreation & Leisure, Council Offices, The Palace Demesne, Armagh BT60 4EL ☎ 028 3752 9636 🖷 028 3752 9601 🖰 gerard.houlahan@armagh.gov.uk

Licensing: Mr John Briggs, Clerk & Chief Executive, Council Offices, The Palace Demesne, Armagh BT60 4EL ☎ 028 3752 9697 🖷 028 3752 9604 🖰 john.briggs@armagh.gov.uk

Lottery Funding, Charity and Voluntary: Mr Godfrey McCartney, Community & Economic Development Manager, Council Offices, The Palace Demesne, Armagh BT60 4EL ☎ 028 3751 9632 🖷 028 2751 9631 🖰 godfrey.mccartney@armagh.gov.uk

Lottery Funding, Charity and Voluntary: Mrs Mary Toal, Community Regeneration Officer, Council Offices, The Palace Demesne, Armagh BT60 4EL ☎ 028 3752 9632 🖷 028 3752 9631 🖰 mary.toal@armagh.gov.uk

Member Services: Mrs Lynne Brown, Corporate Manager (Democratic Services), Council Offices, The Palace Demesne, Armagh BT60 4EL ☎ 028 3752 9603 🖷 028 3752 9604 🖰 lynne.brown@armagh.gov.uk

Personnel / HR: Mrs Carol Corvan, Strategic Director of Corporate Services & Governance, Council Offices, The Palace Demesne, Armagh BT60 4EL ☎ 028 3752 9605 🖷 028 3752 9638 🖰 carol.corvan@armagh.gov.uk

Procurement: Mr Adrian Faulkner, Procurement Officer, Council Offices, The Palace Demesne, Armagh BT60 4EL ☎ 028 3752 9605 🖷 028 3752 9638 🖰 carol.corvan@armagh.gov.uk

Recycling & Waste Minimisation: Ms Irene Kempton, Environmental Health Co-ordinator, Council Offices, The Palace Demesne, Armagh BT60 4EL ☎ 028 3752 9626 🖷 028 3752 9621 🖰 irene.kempton@armagh.gov.uk

Regeneration: Miss Sharon O'Gorman, Strategic Director of Regeneration & Development, Council Offices, The Palace Demesne, Armagh BT60 4EL ☎ 028 3752 9642 🖷 028 3752 9631 🖰 sharon.o'gorman@armagh.gov.uk

Staff Training: Mrs Aisling Knipe, HR Manager, Council Offices, The Palace Demesne, Armagh BT60 4EL ☎ 028 3752 9605 🖷 028 3752 9638 🖰 aisling.knipe@armagh.gov.uk

Street Scene: Mr David McKee, Deputy Director of Operational Services, Council Offices, The Palace Demesne, Armagh BT60 4EL ☎ 028 3752 9624 🖷 028 3752 9614 🖰 david.mckee@armagh.gov.uk

Sustainable Communities: Mr John Briggs, Clerk & Chief Executive, Council Offices, The Palace Demesne, Armagh BT60 4EL ☎ 028 3752 9697 🖷 028 3752 9604 🖰 john.briggs@armagh.gov.uk

Sustainable Development: Ms Irene Kempton, Environmental Health Co-ordinator, Council Offices, The Palace Demesne, Armagh BT60 4EL ☎ 028 3752 9626 🖷 028 3752 9621 🖰 irene.kempton@armagh.gov.uk

Tourism: Mr Brian Johnstone, Tourism Development Officer, Council Offices, The Palace Demesne, Armagh BT60 4EL ☎ 028 3752 9600 🖷 028 3752 9601 🖰 brian.johnston@armagh.gov.uk

Town Centre: Mrs Dawn Park, Urban Regeneration Officer, Council Offices, The Palace Demesne, Armagh BT60 4EL ☎ 028 3752 9642 🖷 028 3752 9631 🖰 dawn.park@armagh.gov.uk

Traffic Management: Mr David McKee, Deputy Director of Operational Services, Council Offices, The Palace Demesne, Armagh BT60 4EL ☎ 028 3752 9624 🖷 028 3752 9614 🖰 david.mckee@armagh.gov.uk

Transport: Mr David McKee, Deputy Director of Operational Services, Council Offices, The Palace Demesne, Armagh BT60 4EL ☎ 028 3752 9624 🖷 028 3752 9614 🖰 david.mckee@armagh.gov.uk

Transport Planner: Mr David McKee, Deputy Director of Operational Services, Council Offices, The Palace Demesne, Armagh BT60 4EL ☎ 028 3752 9624 🖷 028 3752 9614 🖰 david.mckee@armagh.gov.uk

Waste Collection and Disposal: Mr John Briggs, Clerk & Chief Executive, Council Offices, The Palace Demesne, Armagh BT60 4EL ☎ 028 3752 9697 🖷 028 3752 9604 🖰 john.briggs@armagh.gov.uk

Waste Collection and Disposal: Mr David McKee, Deputy Director of Operational Services, Council Offices, The Palace Demesne, Armagh BT60 4EL ☎ 028 3752 9624 🖷 028 3752

9614 david.mckee@armagh.gov.uk

Waste Management: Mr John Briggs, Clerk & Chief Executive, Council Offices, The Palace Demesne, Armagh BT60 4EL ☎ 028 3752 9697 🖷 028 3752 9604 john.briggs@armagh.gov.uk

MEMBERS OF THE COUNCIL (22)

***Mayor:* Donnelly**, Freda (DUP - Armagh City)
freda.donnelly@armagh.gov.uk
***Deputy Mayor:* Campbell**, Maella (SDLP - Armagh City)
mealla.campbell@armagh.gov.uk
Berry, Paul (IND - Cusher)
paul.berry@armagh.gov.uk
Campbell, John (SDLP - The Orchard)
john.campbell@armagh.gov.uk
Doyle, Mary (SF - Crossmore)
mary.doyle@armagh.gov.uk
Eagle, Mavis (UUP - Crossmore)
mavis.eagle@armagh.gov.uk
Haughey, Sharon (SDLP - Cusher)
sharon.haughey@armagh.gov.uk
Irwin, William (DUP - The Orchard)
william.irwin@armagh.gov.uk
Kennedy, Gordon (UUP - Cusher)
gordon.kennedy@armagh.gov.uk
Mallon, Gerald (SDLP - Crossmore)
gerald.mallon@armagh.gov.uk
McCartney, Roy (SF - Armagh City)
roy.mccartney@armagh.gov.uk
McNally, Darren (SF - Crossmore)
darren.mcnally@armagh.gov.uk
McRoberts, Sylvia (UUP - Armagh City)
sylvia.mcroberts@armagh.gov.uk
McWilliams, Terry (DUP - Cusher)
terry.mcwilliams@armagh.gov.uk
O'Hanlon, Thomas (SDLP - Crossmore)
thomas.o'hanlon@armagh.gov.uk
Rafferty, Cathy (SF - Armagh City)
info@armagh@sinn-fein.ie
Rollston, Joy (UUP - The Orchard)
joy.rollston@armagh.gov.uk
Sheridan, Noel (SF - Armagh City)
noel.sheridan@armagh.gov.uk
Speers, Jim (UUP - The Orchard)
jim.speers@armagh.gov.uk
Turner, Robert (UUP - Cusher)
robert.turner@armagh.gov.uk
White, Gerard (SF - The Orchard)
gerardpaul.white@armagh.gov.uk
Wilson, Gareth (DUP - Cusher)
gareth.wilson@armagh.gov.uk

POLITICAL COMPOSITION

SF: 6, UUP: 6, SDLP: 5, DUP: 4, IND: 1

ARUN D

Arun District Council, Arun Civic Centre, Maltravers Road, Littlehampton BN17 5LF ☎ 01903 737500 🖷 01903 730442 www.arun.gov.uk

FACTS & FIGURES

Police Authority: Sussex Police Authority
Health Authority: South East Coast Strategic Health Authority
Learning and Skills Council: South East
Parliamentary Constituencies: Arundel and South Downs, Bognor Regis and Littlehampton, Worthing West
EU Constituencies: South East
Election Frequency: Elections are of whole council
Twinning: Angmering: Ouistreham-riva-Bella (France); Bognor Regis: Trebbin (Germany); St. Maur-des-Fosses (France); Weil am Rhein (Germany); East Preston: Brou (France); Littlehampton: Chennevieres-sur-Marne (France); Durmersheim (Germany); Rustington: Los Altos (USA); Kunzell (Germany)

PRINCIPAL OFFICERS

Chief Executive: Mr Nigel Lynn, Chief Executive, Arun Civic Centre, Maltravers Road, Littlehampton BN17 5LF

Senior Management: Mr Brian Holland, Engineering Services Manager, Arun Civic Centre, Maltravers Road, Littlehampton BN17 5LF ☎ 01903 737815 brian.holland@arun.gov.uk

Senior Management: Mr Paul Warters, Head of Revenues & Benefits, Arun Civic Centre, Maltravers Road, Littlehampton BN17 5LF ☎ 01903 737515 🖷 01903 730442 paul.warters@arun.gov.uk

Best Value: Mr Paul Askew, Head of Improvement, Performance & Scrutiny, Arun Civic Centre, Maltravers Road, Littlehampton BN17 5LF ☎ 01903 737568 🖷 01903 730442 paul.askew@arun.gov.uk

Building Control: Mr James Henn, Head of Building Control, Arun Civic Centre, Maltravers Road, Littlehampton BN17 5LF ☎ 01903 737596 🖷 01903 716019 jim.henn@arun.gov.uk

PR / Communications: Ms Harriet Shelley, Public Relations Officer, Arun Civic Centre, Maltravers Road, Littlehampton BN17 5LF ☎ 01903 737606 🖷 01903 737707 harriet.shelley@arun.gov.uk

Community Planning: Mrs Jaqui Ball, Head of Strategy & Partnerships, Arun Civic Centre, Maltravers Road, Littlehampton BN17 5LF ☎ 01903 737602 🖷 01903 737707 jaqui.ball@arun.gov.uk

Community Safety: Mr Kevin Basford, Head of Environmental Amenities & Community Safety, Arun Civic Centre, Maltravers Road, Littlehampton BN17 5LF ☎ 01903 737706 🖷 01903 723936 kevin.basford@arun.gov.uk

Computer Management: Mr Brian Pople, Head of Technology, Arun Civic Centre, Maltravers Road, Littlehampton BN17 5LF ☎ 01903 737802 🖷 01903 730442 brian.pople@arun.gov.uk

Contracts: Mr Philip Pickard, Procurement Manager, Arun Civic Centre, Maltravers Road, Littlehampton BN17 5LF ☎ 01903 737677 🖷 01903 730442 philip.pickard@arun.gov.uk

Customer Service: Mrs Julie Pearce, Head of Customer Services, Arun Civic Centre, Maltravers Road, Littlehampton BN17 5LF ☎ 01903 737590 🖷 01903 716019 julie.pearce@arun.gov.uk

Economic Development: Mrs Jaqui Ball, Head of Strategy & Partnerships, Arun Civic Centre, Maltravers Road, Littlehampton BN17 5LF ☎ 01903 737602 🖷 01903 737707 jaqui.ball@arun.gov.uk

Economic Development: Mr Anthony Everitt, Senior Economic Development Officer, Arun Civic Centre, Maltravers Road, Littlehampton BN17 5LF ☎ 01903 737846 🖷 01903 737701 anthony.everitt@arun.gov.uk

E-Government: Mrs Maureen Chaffe, Head of Information Management, Arun Civic Centre, Maltravers Road, Littlehampton BN17 5LF ☎ 01903 737591 🖷 01903 730442 maureen.chaffe@arun.gov.uk

Electoral Registration: Mrs Liz Futcher, Head of Democratic Services, Arun Civic Centre, Maltravers Road, Littlehampton BN17 5LF ☎ 01903 737610 🖷 01903 730442 liz.futcher@arun.gov.uk

Emergency Planning: Mrs Philippa Dart, Head of Parks, Green Spaces & Emergency Planning, Town Hall, Clarence Road, Bognor Regis PO21 1LD ☎ 01903 737913 🖷 01903 737967 philippa.dart@arun.gov.uk

Energy Management: Mr Roger Wood, Chief Environmental Health Officer, Arun Civic Centre, Maltravers Road, Littlehampton BN17 5LF ☎ 01903 737671 🖷 01903 723936 roger.wood@arun.gov.uk

Environmental Health: Mr Roger Wood, Chief Environmental Health Officer, Arun Civic Centre, Maltravers Road, Littlehampton BN17 5LF ☎ 01903 737671 🖷 01903 723936 roger.wood@arun.gov.uk

Estates, Property & Valuation: Mr Nigel Horwill, Head of Surveying & Estates, Arun Civic Centre, Maltravers Road, Littlehampton BN17 5LF ☎ 01903 737788 🖷 01903 716019 nigel.horwill@arun.gov.uk

European Liaison: Mrs Jaqui Ball, Head of Strategy & Partnerships, Arun Civic Centre, Maltravers Road, Littlehampton BN17 5LF ☎ 01903 737602 🖷 01903 737707 jaqui.ball@arun.gov.uk

Events Manager: Mr Phil Graham, Marketing Events and Filming Officer, Arun Civic Centre, Maltravers Road, Littlehampton BN17 5LF ☎ 01903 737858 phil.graham@arun.gov.uk

Facilities: Mr Nigel Horwill, Head of Surveying & Estates, Arun Civic Centre, Maltravers Road, Littlehampton BN17 5LF ☎ 01903 737788 🖷 01903 716019 nigel.horwill@arun.gov.uk

Facilities: Mr Martin Stubbs, Facilities Manager, Arun Civic Centre, Maltravers Road, Littlehampton BN17 5LF ☎ 01903 737766 🖷 01903 716019 martin.stubbs@arun.gov.uk

Finance and Treasurer: Mr Nigel Croad, Corporate Resources Director, Arun Civic Centre, Maltravers Road, Littlehampton BN17 5LF ☎ 01903 737810 🖷 01903 730442 nigel.croad@arun.gov.uk

Finance and Treasurer: Mr Alan Peach, Head of Finance, Arun Civic Centre, Maltravers Road, Littlehampton BN17 5LF ☎ 01903 737558 🖷 01903 730747 alan.peach@arun.gov.uk

Grounds Maintenance: Mrs Philippa Dart, Head of Parks, Green Spaces & Emergency Planning, Town Hall, Clarence Road, Bognor Regis PO21 1LD ☎ 01903 737913 🖷 01903 737967 philippa.dart@arun.gov.uk

Health and Safety: Mr Roger Wood, Chief Environmental Health Officer, Arun Civic Centre, Maltravers Road, Littlehampton BN17 5LF ☎ 01903 737671 🖷 01903 723936 roger.wood@arun.gov.uk

Home Energy Conservation: Mr Roger Wood, Chief Environmental Health Officer, Arun Civic Centre, Maltravers Road, Littlehampton BN17 5LF ☎ 01903 737671 🖷 01903 723936 roger.wood@arun.gov.uk

Housing: Mr Frank Hickson, Head of Housing Management, Arun Civic Centre, Maltravers Road, Littlehampton BN17 5LF ☎ 01903 737718 🖷 01903 723431 frank.hickson@arun.gov.uk

Housing Maintenance: Mr Frank Hickson, Head of Housing Management, Arun Civic Centre, Maltravers Road, Littlehampton BN17 5LF ☎ 01903 737718 🖷 01903 723431 frank.hickson@arun.gov.uk

Legal: Mrs Wendy Ashenden-Bax, Solicitor to the Council, Arun Civic Centre, Maltravers Road, Littlehampton BN17 5LF ☎ 01903 737589 🖷 01903 716019 wendy.ashenden-bax@arun.gov.uk

Leisure and Cultural Services: Mrs Jaqui Ball, Head of Strategy & Partnerships, Arun Civic Centre, Maltravers Road, Littlehampton BN17 5LF ☎ 01903 737602 🖷 01903 737707 jaqui.ball@arun.gov.uk

Licensing: Mr Glenn James, Health, Safety & Licensing Officer, Arun Civic Centre, Maltravers Road, Littlehampton BN17 5LF ☎ 01903 737681 🖷 01903 733585 glenn.james@arun.gov.uk

Licensing: Mr Roger Wood, Chief Environmental Health Officer, Arun Civic Centre, Maltravers Road, Littlehampton BN17 5LF ☎ 01903 737671 🖷 01903 723936 roger.wood@arun.gov.uk

Lottery Funding, Charity and Voluntary: Mrs Jaqui Ball, Head of Strategy & Partnerships, Arun Civic Centre, Maltravers Road, Littlehampton BN17 5LF ☎ 01903 737602 🖷 01903 737707 jaqui.ball@arun.gov.uk

Member Services: Mrs Liz Futcher, Head of Democratic Services, Arun Civic Centre, Maltravers Road, Littlehampton BN17 5LF ☎ 01903 737610 🖷 01903 730442 liz.futcher@arun.gov.uk

Parking: Mr Calvin Baylis, Outdoor Services Manager, Arun Civic Centre, Maltravers Road, Littlehampton BN17 5LF ☎ 01903 737649 🖷 01903 716019 calvin.baylis@arun.gov.uk

Partnerships: Mrs Jaqui Ball, Head of Strategy & Partnerships, Arun Civic Centre, Maltravers Road, Littlehampton BN17 5LF ☎ 01903 737602 🖷 01903 737707 jaqui.ball@arun.gov.uk

Personnel / HR: Mrs Jackie Follis, Head of Human Resources, Arun Civic Centre, Maltravers Road, Littlehampton BN17 5LF ☎ 01903 737580 🖷 01903 713606 ✉ jackie.follis@arun.gov.uk

Planning: Mr Karl Roberts, Assistant Director of Planning & Housing Strategy, Arun Civic Centre, Maltravers Road, Littlehampton BN17 5LF ☎ 01903 737760 🖷 01903 716019 ✉ karl.roberts@arun.gov.uk

Procurement: Mr Philip Pickard, Procurement Manager, Arun Civic Centre, Maltravers Road, Littlehampton BN17 5LF ☎ 01903 737677 🖷 01903 730442 ✉ philip.pickard@arun.gov.uk

Recycling & Waste Minimisation: Mr Kevin Basford, Head of Environmental Amenities & Community Safety, Arun Civic Centre, Maltravers Road, Littlehampton BN17 5LF ☎ 01903 737706 🖷 01903 723936 ✉ kevin.basford@arun.gov.uk

Regeneration: Mrs Jaqui Ball, Head of Strategy & Partnerships, Arun Civic Centre, Maltravers Road, Littlehampton BN17 5LF ☎ 01903 737602 🖷 01903 737707 ✉ jaqui.ball@arun.gov.uk

Regeneration: Mr Anthony Everitt, Senior Economic Development Officer, Arun Civic Centre, Maltravers Road, Littlehampton BN17 5LF ☎ 01903 737846 🖷 01903 737701 ✉ anthony.everitt@arun.gov.uk

Staff Training: Mrs Jackie Follis, Head of Human Resources, Arun Civic Centre, Maltravers Road, Littlehampton BN17 5LF ☎ 01903 737580 🖷 01903 713606 ✉ jackie.follis@arun.gov.uk

Sustainable Communities: Mr Karl Roberts, Assistant Director of Planning & Housing Strategy, Arun Civic Centre, Maltravers Road, Littlehampton BN17 5LF ☎ 01903 737760 🖷 01903 716019 ✉ karl.roberts@arun.gov.uk

Sustainable Development: Mr Roger Wood, Chief Environmental Health Officer, Arun Civic Centre, Maltravers Road, Littlehampton BN17 5LF ☎ 01903 737671 🖷 01903 723936 ✉ roger.wood@arun.gov.uk

Tourism: Mrs Jaqui Ball, Head of Strategy & Partnerships, Arun Civic Centre, Maltravers Road, Littlehampton BN17 5LF ☎ 01903 737602 🖷 01903 737707 ✉ jaqui.ball@arun.gov.uk

Town Centre: Mrs Jaqui Ball, Head of Strategy & Partnerships, Arun Civic Centre, Maltravers Road, Littlehampton BN17 5LF ☎ 01903 737602 🖷 01903 737707 ✉ jaqui.ball@arun.gov.uk

Waste Collection and Disposal: Mr Kevin Basford, Head of Environmental Amenities & Community Safety, Arun Civic Centre, Maltravers Road, Littlehampton BN17 5LF ☎ 01903 737706 🖷 01903 723936 ✉ kevin.basford@arun.gov.uk

Waste Management: Mr Kevin Basford, Head of Environmental Amenities & Community Safety, Arun Civic Centre, Maltravers Road, Littlehampton BN17 5LF ☎ 01903 737706 🖷 01903 723936 ✉ kevin.basford@arun.gov.uk

Children's Play Areas: Mrs Philippa Dart, Head of Parks, Green Spaces & Emergency Planning, Town Hall, Clarence Road, Bognor Regis PO21 1LD ☎ 01903 737913 🖷 01903 737967 ✉ philippa.dart@arun.gov.uk

MEMBERS OF THE COUNCIL (55)

***Chair:* Smee**, Ann (CON - Bersted)
cllr.ann.smee@arun.gov.uk

***Vice-Chair:* Chapman**, Terence (CON - East Preston & Kingston)
cllr.terence.chapman@arun.gov.uk

***Leader of the Council:* Brown**, Gillian (CON - Aldwick East)
gillianannabrown@aol.com

***Deputy Leader of the Council:* Wensley**, Dudley (CON - Angmering)
cllr.dudley.wensley@arun.gov.uk

Ayling, Don (CON - Arundel)
cllr.don.ayling@arun.gov.uk

Bence, Trevor (CON - Pevensey (Bognor Regis))
cllr.trevor.bence@arun.gov.uk

Bicknell, Paul (CON - Angmering)
paul@bicknells.f2s.com

Bower, Philipa (CON - Rustington East)
philippa.bower@btconnect.com

Bower, Richard (CON - East Preston & Kingston)
r.bower@btconnect.com

Bowyer, Joyce (CON - Brookfield (Littlehampton))
joycebower@sky.com

Britton, David (CON - River (Littlehampton))
cllr.david.britton@arun.gov.uk

Brooks, James (IND - Marine (Bognor Regis))
cllr.jim.brooks@arun.gov.uk

Brown, Robin (CON - Aldwick East)
robinbrownassocs@aol.com

Brown, Leonard (CON - Pagham & Rose Green)

Caffyn, June (CON - Wick with Toddington)
june_caffyn@yahoo.co.uk

Charles, John (CON - Barnham)
cllr.john.charles@arun.gov.uk

Clayden, Mike (CON - Rustington West)
mjclayden@gmail.com

Cunard, Adam (CON - Bersted)
adam@bognorcinema.co.uk

Daniells, Sandra (CON - Orchard (Bognor Regis))
cllr.sandra.daniells@arun.gov.uk

Dendle, Paul (CON - Arundel)
pauldendle@aol.com

Dingemans, Norman (CON - Walberton)
normandingemans@aol.com

Edwards, David (CON - Hotham (Bognor Regis))
cllr.david.edwards@arun.gov.uk

Elkins, Roger (CON - Ferring)
cllr.roger.elkins@arun.gov.uk

Emberson, Carol (CON - Wick with Toddington)
cllr.carol.emberson@arun.gov.uk

English, Paul (CON - Felpham East)
paul@englishdynasty.com

Evans, Andrew (CON - Marine (Bognor Regis))
cllr.andrew.evans@arun.gov.uk

Gammon, Alan (CON - Brookfield (Littlehampton))
alan.gammon@yahoo.co.uk

Goad, Jean (CON - Barnham)
cllr.jean.goad@arun.gov.uk

Hall, Dawn (CON - Pagham & Rose Green)
cllr.dawn.hall@arun.gov.uk

Harrison, Florence (CON - Rustington West)
f.harrison456@btinternet.com

Haymes, Stephen (CON - Yapton)
cllr.stephen.haymes@arun.gov.uk
Hazlehurst, Julie (CON - Angmering)
cllr.julie.hazlehurst@arun.gov.uk
Hitchins, Phil (CON - Aldwick West)
cllr.phil.hitchins@arun.gov.uk
Holman, John (CON - Felpham East)
cllr.john.holman@arun.gov.uk
Jones, Peter (CON - Findon)
peterandjenjones242@btinternet.com
Maconachie, Dougal (CON - Barnham)
dougalmaconachie@yahoo.co.uk
Madeley, Gill (CON - Felpham West)
cllr.gill.madeley@arun.gov.uk
McDougall, Simon (LD - Bersted)
cllr.simon.mcdougall@arun.gov.uk
McIntyre, Angus (CON - Yapton)
angussmcintyre@gmail.com
Nash, Roger (LAB - Pevensey (Bognor Regis))
rnash10@hotmail.com
Neno, Emma (CON - Beach (Littlehampton))
emma@neno77.freeserve.co.uk
Northeast, Michael (LAB - Ham (Littlehampton))
cllr.mike.northeast@arun.gov.uk
Oakley, Barbara (CON - Middleton-on-Sea)
Oliver-Redgate, Colin (CON - Ferring)
cllr.colin.oliver-redgate@arun.gov.uk
Oppler, Francis (LD - Orchard (Bognor Regis))
francis.oppler@westsussex.gov.uk
Patel, Ashvin (CON - Pagham & Rose Green)
ashvinpatel@hotmail.co.uk
Pendleton, Jacky (CON - River (Littlehampton))
cllr.jacky.pendleton@arun.gov.uk
Squires, Tony (LAB - Ham (Littlehampton))
cllr.tony.squires@arun.gov.uk
Stainton, Elaine (CON - Felpham West)
cllr.elaine.stainton@arun.gov.uk
Steward, Ray (CON - Rustington West)
ray.steward@btinternet.com
Tyler, Graham (CON - Rustington East)
gtyler2@btinternet.com
Walsh, James (LD - Beach (Littlehampton))
james.walsh@westsussex.gov.uk
Warr, Jeanette (LD - Hotham (Bognor Regis))
jinny_chapman@uwclub.net
Wilde, Dennis (CON - East Preston & Kingston)
cllr.dennis.wilde@arun.gov.uk
Wotherspoon, Paul (CON - Middleton-on-Sea)

POLITICAL COMPOSITION

CON: 47, LD: 4, LAB: 3, IND: 1

CABINET

Leader / Strategy: Mrs Gillian Brown
Deputy / Corporate Governance: Mr Dudley Wensley
Community Development: Mr Paul Wotherspoon
Customer Services: Mr Norman Dingemans
Environmental Services: Mr Paul Dendle
Housing: Mr Roger Elkins
Planning & Economic Regeneration: Mr Richard Bower

COMMITTEE CHAIRS

Audit: Mrs Barbara Oakley
Development Control: Mrs Jacqui Maconachie
Licensing & Enforcement: Mr Graham Tyler
Overview Select (Scrutiny): Mr Terence Chapman
Standards: Mrs Katherine Vagg

ASHFIELD D

Ashfield District Council, Council Offices, Urban Road, Kirkby-in-Ashfield NG17 8DA ☎ 01623 450000 🖷 01623 457585 💻 www.ashfield-dc.gov.uk

FACTS & FIGURES

Police Authority: Nottinghamshire Police Authority
Health Authority: East Midlands Strategic Health Authority
Learning and Skills Council: East Midlands
Parliamentary Constituencies: Ashfield, Newark
EU Constituencies: East Midlands
Election Frequency: Elections are of whole council

PRINCIPAL OFFICERS

Chief Executive: Mr Philip Marshall, Chief Executive, Council Offices, Urban Road, Kirkby-in-Ashfield NG17 8DA
☎ 01623 457251 🖷 01623 457585
p.marshall@ashfield-dc.gov.uk

Deputy Chief Executive: Mr David Greenwood, Deputy Chief Executive (Resources), Council Offices, Urban Road, Kirkby-in-Ashfield NG17 8DA ☎ 01623 457201 🖷 01623 457585
d.greenwood@ashfield-dc.gov.uk

Assistant Chief Executive: Mrs Ruth Dennis, Assistant Chief Executive (Governance), Council Offices, Urban Road, Kirkby-in-Ashfield NG17 8DA ☎ 01623 457331
r.dennis@ashfield-dc.gov.uk

Architect, Building / Property Services: Ms Elaine Saxton, Building Services Manager, Council Offices, Urban Road, Kirkby-in-Ashfield NG17 8DA ☎ 01623 457360 🖷 01623 457590
e.p.saxton@ashfield-dc.gov.uk

Best Value: Mrs Joanne Wright, Corporate Performance Manager, Council Offices, Urban Road, Kirkby-in-Ashfield NG17 8DA ☎ 01623 457328 j.wright@ashfield-dc.gov.uk

Building Control: Mrs Christine Sarris, Planning & Building Control Manager, Council Offices, Urban Road, Kirkby-in-Ashfield NG17 8DA ☎ 01623 457375 c.m.sarris@ashfield-dc.gov.uk

Catering Services: Ms Elaine Saxton, Building Services Manager, Council Offices, Urban Road, Kirkby-in-Ashfield NG17 8DA ☎ 01623 457360 🖷 01623 457590
e.p.saxton@ashfield-dc.gov.uk

PR / Communications: Ms Carys Turner-Jones, Corporate Communications Manager, Ashfield District Council, Urban Road, Kirkby-in-Ashfield NG17 8DA ☎ 01623 457004
c.turner-jones@ashfield-dc.gov.uk

Community Planning: Mrs Lisa Bell, Principal Planning Officer, Council Offices, Urban Road, Kirkby-in-Ashfield NG17 8DA
☎ 01623 457385 l.bell@ashfield.gov.uk

Community Safety: Miss Rebecca Whitehead, Community

Protection Manager, Council Offices, Urban Road, Kirkby-in-Ashfield NG17 8DA ☎ 01623 457349 r.whitehead@ashfield-dc.gov.uk

Computer Management: Mr Andy Slate, ICT Manager, Council Offices, Urban Road, Kirkby-in-Ashfield NG17 8DA ☎ 01623 457555 a.slate@ashfield-dc.gov.uk

Contracts: Mr Bob Trusswell, Head - Procurement, Council Offices, Urban Road, Kirkby-in-Ashfield NG17 8DA ☎ 01246 242311 bob.trusswell@bolsover.gov.uk

Corporate Services: Mr Craig Bonar, Service Director - Corporate Services, Council Offices, Urban Road, Kirkby-in-Ashfield NG17 8DA ☎ 01623 457203 c.bonar@ashfield-dc.gov.uk

Customer Service: Mr Bill Nichols, Customer Services Manager, Council Offices, Urban Road, Kirkby-in-Ashfield NG17 8DA ☎ 01623 457509 b.nichols@ashfield-dc.gov.uk

Economic Development: Mr Paul Thomas, Regeneration Manager, Council Offices, Urban Road, Kirkby-in-Ashfield NG17 8DA ☎ 01623 457161 p.thomas@ashfield-dc.gov.uk

Electoral Registration: Mrs Diana Marshall, Electoral Services Manager, Council Offices, Urban Road, Kirkby-in-Ashfield NG17 8DA ☎ 01623 457314 🖷 01623 457585 d.marshall@ashfield-dc.gov.uk

Emergency Planning: Mr Mark Gasston, Corporate Safety Officer, Council Offices, Urban Road, Kirkby-in-Ashfield NG17 8DA ☎ 01623 457468 🖷 01623 457585 m.gasston@ashfield-dc.gov.uk

Energy Management: Ms Jenni French, Business Contingency & Sustainability Manager, Ashfield District Council, Urban Road, Kirkby-in-Ashfield NG17 8DA ☎ 01623 457370 j.french@ashfield-dc.gov.uk

Environmental Health: Mr Chris Booth, Environmental Health Manager, Council Offices, Urban Road, Kirkby-in-Ashfield NG17 8DA ☎ 01623 457228 c.booth@ashfield-dc.gov.uk

Estates, Property & Valuation: Mr Matthew Kirk, Estates Manager, Council Offices, Urban Road, Kirkby-in-Ashfield NG17 8DA ☎ 01623 457277 m.kirk@ashfield-dc.gov.uk

Facilities: Mr Neil Cotterill, Facilities Manager, Council Offices, Urban Road, Kirkby-in-Ashfield NG17 8DA ☎ 01623 457257 n.cotterill@ashfield-dc.gov.uk

Finance and Treasurer: Mr David Greenwood, Deputy Chief Executive (Resources), Council Offices, Urban Road, Kirkby-in-Ashfield NG17 8DA ☎ 01623 457201 🖷 01623 457585 d.greenwood@ashfield-dc.gov.uk

Fleet Management: Mr David White, Transport Services Manager, Council Offices, Urban Road, Kirkby-in-Ashfield NG17 8DA ☎ 01623 457883 d.c.white@ashfield-dc.gov.uk

Health and Safety: Mr Mark Gasston, Corporate Safety Officer, Council Offices, Urban Road, Kirkby-in-Ashfield NG17 8DA ☎ 01623 457468 🖷 01623 457585 m.gasston@ashfield-dc.gov.uk

Home Energy Conservation: Ms Jenni French, Business Contingency & Sustainability Manager, Ashfield District Council, Urban Road, Kirkby-in-Ashfield NG17 8DA ☎ 01623 457370 j.french@ashfield-dc.gov.uk

Housing: Mr Peter Kandola, Housing Strategy & Development Manager, Council Offices, Urban Road, Kirkby-in-Ashfield NG17 8DA ☎ 01623 457351 p.kandola@ashfield-dc.gov.uk

Housing Maintenance: Mr Paul Bingham, Assistant Director of Technical Services - Ashfield Homes, Ashfield Homes Ltd, Broadway, Brook Street, Sutton-in-Ashfield NG17 1AL ☎ 01623 608877 p.bingham@ashfield-dc.gov.uk

Legal: Mrs Ruth Dennis, Assistant Chief Executive (Governance), Council Offices, Urban Road, Kirkby-in-Ashfield NG17 8DA ☎ 01623 457331 r.dennis@ashfield-dc.gov.uk

Leisure and Cultural Services: Mrs Theresa Hodgkinson, Leisure & Community Development Manager, Council Offices, Urban Road, Kirkby-in-Ashfield NG17 8DA ☎ 01623 457588 t.hodgkinson@ashfield-dc.gov.uk

Licensing: Mr Chris Booth, Environmental Health Manager, Council Offices, Urban Road, Kirkby-in-Ashfield NG17 8DA ☎ 01623 457228 c.booth@ashfield-dc.gov.uk

Member Services: Mr Simon Oldham, Democratic Services Manager, Council Offices, Urban Road, Kirkby-in-Ashfield NG17 8DA ☎ 01623 457002 🖷 01623 457314 s.oldham@ashfield.gov.uk

Parking: Mr Neil Cotterill, Facilities Manager, Council Offices, Urban Road, Kirkby-in-Ashfield NG17 8DA ☎ 01623 457257 n.cotterill@ashfield-dc.gov.uk

Personnel / HR: Mrs Karen Barke, Senior HR Officer, Ashfield District Council, Urban Road, Kirkby-in-Ashfield NG17 8DA ☎ 01623 457455 k.barke@ashfield-dc.gov.uk

Planning: Mrs Christine Sarris, Planning & Building Control Manager, Council Offices, Urban Road, Kirkby-in-Ashfield NG17 8DA ☎ 01623 457375 c.m.sarris@ashfield-dc.gov.uk

Procurement: Mr Bob Trusswell, Head - Procurement, Council Offices, Urban Road, Kirkby-in-Ashfield NG17 8DA ☎ 01246 242311 bob.trusswell@bolsover.gov.uk

Recycling & Waste Minimisation: Mr Paul Rowbotham, Waste Operations Officer, Council Offices, Urban Road, Kirkby-in-Ashfield NG17 8DA ☎ 01623 457860 p.rowbotham@ashfield-dc.gov.uk

Regeneration: Mr Paul Thomas, Regeneration Manager, Council Offices, Urban Road, Kirkby-in-Ashfield NG17 8DA ☎ 01623 457161 p.thomas@ashfield-dc.gov.uk

Staff Training: Ms Jacqueline Mansell, Training Officer, Council

Offices, Urban Road, Kirkby-in-Ashfield NG17 8DA
☎ 01623 457359 🖷 01623 457585
✉ j.mansell@ashfield-dc.gov.uk

Street Scene: Miss Rebecca Whitehead, Community Protection Manager, Council Offices, Urban Road, Kirkby-in-Ashfield NG17 8DA ☎ 01623 457349 ✉ r.whitehead@ashfield-dc.gov.uk

Sustainable Development: Ms Jenni French, Business Contingency & Sustainability Manager, Ashfield District Council, Urban Road, Kirkby-in-Ashfield NG17 8DA ☎ 01623 457370 ✉ j.french@ashfield-dc.gov.uk

Town Centre: Mr Mark Armstrong, Town Centre Manager, Ashfield District Council, Urban Road, Kirkby-in-Ashfield NG17 8DA ☎ 01623 457159 ✉ m.armstrong@ashfield-dc.gov.uk

Transport: Mr David White, Transport Services Manager, Council Offices, Urban Road, Kirkby-in-Ashfield NG17 8DA
☎ 01623 457883 ✉ d.c.white@ashfield-dc.gov.uk

Waste Management: Mr Paul Rowbotham, Waste Management Manager, Council Offices, Urban Road, Kirkby-in-Ashfield NG17 8DA ☎ 01623 457931 ✉ p.rowbotham@ashfield-dc.gov.uk

MEMBERS OF THE COUNCIL (33)

***Chair:* Carroll**, Terence (LAB - Sutton East)
cllr.s.t.carroll
***Vice-Chair:* Barsby**, May (LAB - Sutton East)
cllr.m.a.barsby@ashfield-dc.gov.uk
***Leader of the Council:* Knight**, John (LAB - Kirkby West)
cllr.j.knight@ashfield-dc.gov.uk
***Deputy Leader of the Council:* Wilmott**, John (LAB - Hucknall North)
cllr.j.m.wilmott@ashfield-dc.gov.uk
Baron, Chris (LAB - Hucknall West)
cllr.c.baron@ashfield-dc.gov.uk
Barsby, Kier (LAB - Sutton East)
cllr.k.barsby@ashfield-dc.gov.uk
Brown, Tim (LAB - Sutton Central)
cllr.t.brown@ashfield-dc.gov.uk
Butler, Cheryl (LAB - Kirkby Central)
cllr.c.butler@ashfield-dc.gov.uk
Buttery, Ramon (IND - Sutton West)
cllr.r.buttery@ashfield-dc.gov.uk
Coppin, Mick (LAB - Sutton Central)
cllr.m.coppin@ashfield-dc.gov.uk
Davidson, Andrew (LAB - Kirkby West)
cllr.a.davidson@ashfield-dc.gov.uk
Davis, Don (LAB - Woodhouse)
cllr.d.davis@ashfield-dc.gov.uk
Gibbons, Linford (LAB - Kirkby East)
cllr.l.m.gibbons@ashfield-dc.gov.uk
Grundy, Jim (LAB - Hucknall West)
cllr.j.grundy@ashfield-dc.gov.uk
Hollis, Thomas (LD - Sutton North)
cllr.t.j.hollis@ashfield-dc.gov.uk
Keetley, Terence (LAB - Sutton West)
cllr.t.keetley@ashfield-dc.gov.uk
Kirkham, David (LAB - Sutton Central)
cllr.d.j.kirkham@ashfield-dc.gov.uk
Knight, Kenneth (LAB - Hucknall West)
cllr.k.knight@ashfield-dc.gov.uk
Locke, Trevor (LAB - Hucknall Central)
cllr.t.locke@ashfield-dc.gov.uk
Madden, Rachel (LD - Kirkby Central)
cllr.r.e.madden@ashfield-dc.gov.uk
Maxwell, Glenys (LAB - Sutton West)
cllr.g.c.maxwell@ashfield-dc.gov.uk
Mays, Elizabeth (LAB - Jacksdale)
cllr.e.mays@ashfield-dc.gov.uk
Morrison, Ian (LAB - Hucknall North)
cllr.l.morrison@ashfield-dc.gov.uk
Morrison, Keir (LAB - Hucknall East)
cllr.k.a.morrison@ashfield-dc.gov.uk
Morrison, Lachlan Stuart (LAB - Hucknall Central)
cllr.l.s.morrison@ashfield-dc.gov.uk
Nuttall, Warren (LAB - Kirkby East)
cllr.w.nuttall@ashfield-dc.gov.uk
Patrick, Margaret Ann (LD - Sutton North)
cllr.a.patrick@ashfield-dc.gov.uk
Sears-Piccavey, Robert (LD - Underwood)
cllr.r.sears-piccavey@ashfield-dc.gov.uk
Shaw, David (LAB - Hucknall East)
cllr.d.shaw@ashfield-dc.gov.uk
Smith, Helen (LD - Woodhouse)
cllr.h.smith@ashfield-dc.gov.uk
Turner, Gail (IND - Selston)
cllr.b.g.turner@ashfield-dc.gov.uk
Wilson, Samuel (IND - Selston)
cllr.s.wilson@ashfield-dc.gov.uk
Zadrozny, Jason (LD - Sutton North)
cllr.j.zadrozny@ashfield-dc.gov.uk

POLITICAL COMPOSITION

LAB: 24, LD: 6, IND: 3

CABINET

Leader: Mr John Knight
Deputy Leader / Economy & Partnerships: Mr John Wilmott
Customer & Corporate Services, Planning & Partnerships: Mr Chris Baron
Environment, Public Health & Community Protection: Mr Warren Nuttall
Finance: Mr Trevor Locke
Regeneration, Culture & Housing: Mr Terence Carroll

COMMITTEE CHAIRS

Appeals: Mrs Cheryl Butler
Audit: Mr Ramon Buttery
Licensing & Registration: Mrs Elizabeth Mays
Overview & Scrutiny: Mr David Kirkham
Planning: Ms Glenys Maxwell

ASHFORD — D

Ashford Borough Council, Civic Centre, Tannery Lane, Ashford TN23 1PL ☎ 01233 331111 🖷 01233 645654 🖳 www.ashford.gov.uk

FACTS & FIGURES

Police Authority: Kent Police Authority
Health Authority: South East Coast Strategic Health Authority
Learning and Skills Council: South East
Parliamentary Constituencies: Ashford
EU Constituencies: South East
Election Frequency: Elections are of whole council
Twinning: Bad Munstereifel (Germany); Fougeres (France); Hopewell (USA)

LOCAL AUTHORITIES

PRINCIPAL OFFICERS

Chief Executive: Mr John Bunnett, Chief Executive, Civic Centre, Tannery Lane, Ashford TN23 1PL ☎ 01233 330201 🖷 01233 330610 ✉ john.bunnett@ashford.gov.uk

Deputy Chief Executive: Mr Paul Naylor, Deputy Chief Executive, Civic Centre, Tannery Lane, Ashford TN23 1PL ☎ 01233 330436 🖷 01233 330610 ✉ paul.naylor@ashford.gov.uk

Architect, Building / Property Services: Mrs Tracey Kerly, Head of Customers, Homes & Property Services, Civic Centre, Tannery Lane, Ashford TN23 1PL ☎ 01233 330607 🖷 01233 330425 ✉ tracey.kerly@ashford.gov.uk

Building Control: Mr Tim Parrett, Business Manager & Head of Building Control, Civic Centre, Tannery Lane, Ashford TN23 1PL ☎ 01233 330275 🖷 01233 330682 ✉ tim.parrett@ashford.gov.uk

Children / Youth Services: Mrs Carol Morton, Youth Projects Co-ordinator, Civic Centre, Tannery Lane, Ashford TN23 1PL ☎ 01233 330290 ✉ carol.morton@ashford.gov.uk

PR / Communications: Mr Dean Spurrell, Communications & Marketing Manager, Civic Centre, Tannery Lane, Ashford TN23 1PL ☎ 01233 330647 🖷 01233 330610 ✉ dean.spurrell@ashford.gov.uk

Community Safety: Mr David Lloyd, Community Safety Manager, Ashford Community Safety Unit, Tufton Street, Ashford TN23 ☎ 01233 330891 🖷 01233 660747 ✉ david.lloyd@ashford.gov.uk

Computer Management: Mr Rob Neil, Head of Business Change & Technology, Civic Centre, Tannery Lane, Ashford TN23 1PL ☎ 01233 330850 ✉ rob.neil@ashford.gov.uk

Contracts: Mr Philip Bond, Street Scene & Open Spaces Manager, Civic Centre, Tannery Lane, Ashford TN23 1PL ☎ 01233 330346 🖷 01233 330620 ✉ philip.bond@ashford.gov.uk

Customer Service: Mrs Tracey Kerly, Head of Customers, Homes & Property Services, Civic Centre, Tannery Lane, Ashford TN23 1PL ☎ 01233 330607 🖷 01233 330425 ✉ tracey.kerly@ashford.gov.uk

Customer Service: Mrs Julie Rogers, Customer Service Manager/Joint Operations Manager Gateway, Civic Centre, Tannery Lane, Ashford TN23 1PL ☎ 01233 330856 🖷 01233 330425 ✉ julie.rogers@ashford.gov.uk

Economic Development: Mr Andrew Osborne, Economic Development Manager, Civic Centre, Tannery Lane, Ashford TN23 1PL ☎ 01233 330310 🖷 01233 330682 ✉ andrew.osborne@ashford.gov.uk

E-Government: Mr Rob Neil, Head of Business Change & Technology, Civic Centre, Tannery Lane, Ashford TN23 1PL ☎ 01233 330850 ✉ rob.neil@ashford.gov.uk

Electoral Registration: Mrs Valma Page, Senior Electoral Services Officer, Civic Centre, Tannery Lane, Ashford TN23 1PL ☎ 01233 330462 ✉ valma.page@ashford.gov.uk

Emergency Planning: Ms Della Fackrell, Resilience Partnership Manager, Civic Centre, Tannery Lane, Ashford TN23 1PL ☎ 01233 330389 ✉ della.fackrell@ashford.gov.uk

Environmental Health: Mr Paul Jackson, Head of Environmental Services, Civic Centre, Tannery Lane, Ashford TN23 1PL ☎ 01233 330518 🖷 01233 330620 ✉ paul.jackson@ashford.gov.uk

Estates, Property & Valuation: Mrs Tracey Kerly, Head of Customers, Homes & Property Services, Civic Centre, Tannery Lane, Ashford TN23 1PL ☎ 01233 330607 🖷 01233 330425 ✉ tracey.kerly@ashford.gov.uk

Facilities: Mr Peter Brooker, Building Facilities Officer, Civic Centre, Tannery Lane, Ashford TN23 1PL ☎ 01233 330514 ✉ peter.brooker@ashford.gov.uk

Finance and Treasurer: Mr Ben Lockwood, Finance Manager, Civic Centre, Tannery Lane, Ashford TN23 1PL ☎ 01233 330540 🖷 01233 330383 ✉ ben.lockwood@ashford.gov.uk

Finance and Treasurer: Mr Peter Purcell, Head of Revenue & Benefits, Civic Centre, Tannery Lane, Ashford TN23 1PL ☎ 01233 330562 ✉ peter.purcell@ashford.gov.uk

Fleet Management: Ms Michelle Pecci, Head of Personnel & Development, Civic Centre, Tannery Lane, Ashford TN23 1PL ☎ 01233 330602 🖷 01233 330610 ✉ michelle.pecci@ashford.gov.uk

Grounds Maintenance: Mr Philip Bond, Street Scene & Open Spaces Manager, Civic Centre, Tannery Lane, Ashford TN23 1PL ☎ 01233 330346 🖷 01233 330620 ✉ philip.bond@ashford.gov.uk

Grounds Maintenance: Mr Paul Jackson, Head of Environmental Services, Civic Centre, Tannery Lane, Ashford TN23 1PL ☎ 01233 330518 🖷 01233 330620 ✉ paul.jackson@ashford.gov.uk

Health and Safety: Mr Graham Stewart, Internal Health & Safety Officer, Civic Centre, Tannery Lane, Ashford TN23 1PL ☎ 01233 330397 🖷 01233 330469 ✉ graham.stewart@ashford.gov.uk

Home Energy Conservation: Ms Sharon Williams, Housing Operations Manager, Civic Centre, Tannery Lane, Ashford TN23 1PL ☎ 01233 330803 🖷 01233 330425 ✉ sharon.williams@ashford.gov.uk

Housing: Mrs Tracey Kerly, Head of Customers, Homes & Property Services, Civic Centre, Tannery Lane, Ashford TN23 1PL ☎ 01233 330607 🖷 01233 330425 ✉ tracey.kerly@ashford.gov.uk

Housing Maintenance: Mr Chris Tillin, Planned Maintenance Manager, Civic Centre, Tannery Lane, Ashford TN23 1PL ☎ 01233 330483 🖷 01233 330425 ✉ chris.tillin@ashford.gov.uk

Legal: Mr Terry Mortimer, Head of Legal & Democratic Services, Civic Centre, Tannery Lane, Ashford TN23 1PL ☎ 01233 330210 🖷 01233 330649 ✉ terry.mortimer@ashford.gov.uk

Leisure and Cultural Services: Mr Mark Carty, Head of Cultural & Project Services, Civic Centre, Tannery Lane, Ashford TN23 1PL ☎ 01233 330477 ✉ mark.carty@ashford.gov.uk

Licensing: Mr James Hann, Licensing Manager, Civic Centre, Tannery Lane, Ashford TN23 1PL ☎ 01233 330721 🖷 01233 330469 ✉ james.hann@ashford.gov.uk

Lottery Funding, Charity and Voluntary: Ms Michelle Byrne, Funding & Partnerships Officer, Civic Centre, Tannery Lane, Ashford TN23 1PL ☎ 01233 330485 🖷 01233 330620 ✉ michelle.byrne@ashford.gov.uk

Member Services: Mr Keith Fearon, Member Services & Scrutiny Manager, Civic Centre, Tannery Lane, Ashford TN23 1PL ☎ 01233 330564 🖷 01233 330537 ✉ keith.fearon@ashford.gov.uk

Parking: Mr Ray Wilkinson, Engineering Services Manager, Civic Centre, Tannery Lane, Ashford TN23 1PL ☎ 01233 330299 🖷 01233 330639 ✉ ray.wilkinson@ashford.gov.uk

Personnel / HR: Ms Michelle Pecci, Head of Personnel & Development, Civic Centre, Tannery Lane, Ashford TN23 1PL ☎ 01233 330602 🖷 01233 330610 ✉ michelle.pecci@ashford.gov.uk

Planning: Mr Richard Alderton, Head of Planning & Development, Civic Centre, Tannery Lane, Ashford TN23 1PL ☎ 01233 330239 🖷 01233 330682 ✉ richard.alderton@ashford.gov.uk

Regeneration: Ms Michelle Byrne, Funding & Partnerships Officer, Civic Centre, Tannery Lane, Ashford TN23 1PL ☎ 01233 330485 🖷 01233 330620 ✉ michelle.byrne@ashford.gov.uk

Staff Training: Ms Michelle Pecci, Head of Personnel & Development, Civic Centre, Tannery Lane, Ashford TN23 1PL ☎ 01233 330602 🖷 01233 330610 ✉ michelle.pecci@ashford.gov.uk

Street Scene: Mr Philip Bond, Street Scene & Open Spaces Manager, Civic Centre, Tannery Lane, Ashford TN23 1PL ☎ 01233 330346 🖷 01233 330620 ✉ philip.bond@ashford.gov.uk

Tourism: Miss Sarah Barber, Tourism & Heritage Manager, Civic Centre, Tannery Lane, Ashford TN23 1PL ☎ 01233 330345 🖷 01233 330620 ✉ sarah.barber@ashford.gov.uk

Town Centre: Ms Viv Kenny, Town Centre Co-ordinator, 2nd Floor, Ashford House, County Square Shopping Centre, Ashford TN23 1QG ☎ 01233 664410 🖷 01233 662345

Waste Collection and Disposal: Mr Philip Bond, Street Scene & Open Spaces Manager, Civic Centre, Tannery Lane, Ashford TN23 1PL ☎ 01233 330346 🖷 01233 330620 ✉ philip.bond@ashford.gov.uk

Waste Management: Mr Philip Bond, Street Scene & Open Spaces Manager, Civic Centre, Tannery Lane, Ashford TN23 1PL ☎ 01233 330346 🖷 01233 330620 ✉ philip.bond@ashford.gov.uk

MEMBERS OF THE COUNCIL (43)

***Mayor:* Davidson**, Robert (LD - North Willesborough (Ashford))
bob.davidson11@googlemail.com

***Deputy Mayor:* Smith**, David (IND - South Willesborough (Ashford))
david.smith@ashford.gov.uk

***Leader of the Council:* Wood**, Peter (CON - Saxon Shore)
peter.wood@ashford.gov.uk

***Deputy Leader of the Council:* Clarkson**, Gerry (CON - Charing)
gerrydclarkson@aol.com

***Group Leader:* Davison**, Peter (O - Weald South)
peter.davison22@btinternet.com

***Group Leader:* Yeo**, Harriet (LAB - Norman (Ashford))
harriet.yeo@ashford.gov.uk

Adby, Jeremy (LD - Victoria (Ashford))
jeremy.adby@btinternet.com

Adley, David (LAB - Aylesford Green (Ashford))
david.adley@ashford.gov.uk

Apps, Howard (CON - Victoria (Ashford))

Bartlett, Paul (CON - Weald East)
paul.bartlett@ashford.gov.uk

Bell, Neil (CON - Biddenden)
neilbell@solutionprovider.co.uk

Bell, Clair (CON - Weald Central)
clairbell@solutionprovider.co.uk

Bennett, Mike (CON - Rolvenden & Tenterden West)
mikebennettkm@tiscali.co.uk

Blanford, Jessamy (CON - Great Chart with Singleton North)
jessamy.blandford@ashford.gov.uk

Buchanan, Andrew (CON - Bybrook (Ashford))
andrewjohnbuchanan@hotmail.com

Burgess, Michael (CON - Isle of Oxney)
michael.burgess@ashford.gov.uk

Chilton, Brendan (LAB - Stanhope (Ashford))

Clark, Chris (LAB - Beaver (Ashford))
chris.clark@ashford.gov.uk

Claughton, Michael (CON - Bockhanger (Ashford))
michael.claughton@ashford.gov.uk

Clokie, Paul (CON - Tenterden North)
paul.clokie@ashford.gov.uk

Davey, Jane (IND - Highfield (Ashford))
janedavey123@btinternet.com

Dyer, Geraldine (CON - Weald North)

Feacey, Peter (CON - Godinton (Ashford))
peter.feacey@ashford.gov.uk

French, Matthew (CON - Stour (Ashford))
cllrfrench@hotmail.co.uk

Galpin, Graham (CON - Stour (Ashford))

Heyes, Bernard (CON - Godinton (Ashford))
bernardjdheys@talktalk.net

Heyes, Tina (CON - Park Farm North)
tinaheyes@btinternet.com

Hicks, Aline (CON - Weald South)
aline.hicks@ashford.gov.uk

Hodgkinson, Amanda (CON - Singleton South)
amanda.hodgkinson@ashford.gov.uk

Howard, William (CON - Saxon Shore)
william.howard@ashford.gov.uk

Link, John (CON - St. Michaels)

Marriott, Doug (CON - Downs North)
marriottuk@aol.com

Martin, Marion (CON - Little Burton Farm (Ashford))

Michael, Winston (IND - Boughton Aluph & Eastwell)

Mortimer, Andrew (IND - North Willesborough (Ashford))
andrew.mortimer@ashford.gov.uk

Robey, David (CON - Downs West Ward)
david.roebry@virgin.net

Rutter, Rebecca (LAB - Beaver (Ashford))
rebecca.rutter@ashford.gov.uk

Shorter, Neil (CON - Washford)
njshorter@btinternet.com
Sims, Philip (IND - Kennington (Ashford))
Taylor, Robert (CON - Weald Central)
robert.taylor@ashford.gov.uk
Wedgbury, Jim (CON - Park Farm South)
jimwedgbury@aol.com
Wright, Steven (CON - Wye)
steve.wright.wye@gmail.com

POLITICAL COMPOSITION
CON: 29, IND: 5, LAB: 5, LD: 2, O: 1, Vacant: 1

CABINET
Leader: Mr Peter Wood
Deputy Leader: Mr Gerry Clarkson
Core Services: Mr Robert Taylor
Culture & Recreation: Mr Bernard Heyes
Housing & Customer Services: Mrs Aline Hicks
Youth & Sport: Mr William Howard

COMMITTEE CHAIRS
Appointments: Mr Peter Wood
Audit: Mr Paul Clokie
Licensing and Health & Safety: Mr Peter Feacey
Overview & Scrutiny: Mr Jeremy Adby
Planning: Mr David Robey

AYLESBURY VALE D

Aylesbury Vale District Council, Council Offices, The Gateway, Gatehouse Road, Aylesbury HP19 8FF ☎ 01296 585858 🖷 01296 336977 💻 www.aylesburyvaledc.gov.uk

FACTS & FIGURES
Police Authority: Thames Valley Police Authority
Health Authority: South Central Strategic Health Authority
Learning and Skills Council: South East
Parliamentary Constituencies: Aylesbury, Buckingham
EU Constituencies: South East
Election Frequency: Elections are of whole council
Twinning: Aylesbury: Bourgen Bresse; Buckingham: Joinville (France); Stoke Mandeville: Aubigny (France); Wendover: Liffre (France); Winslow: Cours-la-Ville (France)

PRINCIPAL OFFICERS
Chief Executive: Mr Andrew Grant, Chief Executive, The Gateway, Gatehouse Road, Aylesbury HP19 8FF ☎ 01296 585001 ✉ agrant@aylesburyvaledc.gov.uk

Deputy Chief Executive: Mr Jon McGinty, Deputy Chief Executive, Council Offices, The Gateway, Gatehouse Road, Aylesbury HP19 8FF ☎ 01296 585051 ✉ jmcginty@aylesburyvaledc.gov.uk

Senior Management: Ms Tracey Aldworth, Director, The Gateway, Gatehouse Road, Aylesbury HP19 8FF ☎ 01296 585003 ✉ taldworth@aylesburyvaledc.gov.uk

Senior Management: Mr Matthew Partridge, Director, Council Offices, The Gateway, Gatehouse Road, Aylesbury HP19 8FF ☎ 01296 585585 🖷 01296 398804 ✉ mpartridge@aylesburyvaledc.gov.uk

Architect, Building / Property Services: Miss Alison Watkinson, Property Services Manager, Council Offices, The Gateway, Gatehouse Road, Aylesbury HP19 8FF ☎ 01296 585822

Building Control: Mr Adam Heeley, Building Control & Access Manager, The Gateway, Gatehouse Road, Aylesbury HP19 8FF ☎ 01296 585459

PR / Communications: Miss Teresa Lane, Head of Communications, Marketing & Town Centre Management, The Gateway, Gatehouse Road, Aylesbury HP19 8FF ☎ 01296 585006 🖷 01296 336977 ✉ tlane@aylesburyvaledc.gov.uk

Community Safety: Ms Kay Aitken, Community Safety Officer, The Gateway, Gatehouse Road, Aylesbury HP19 8FF ☎ 01296 585005 🖷 01296 336977

Computer Management: Mr Alan Evans, Head of IT Services, The Gateway, Gatehouse, Aylesbury HP19 8FF ☎ 01296 585767 ✉ aevans@aylesburyvaledc.gov.uk

Contracts: Mr Alan Drew, Contracts Services Officer, Pembroke Road, Aylesbury HP20 1DG ☎ 01296 585021 ✉ adrew@aylesburyvaledc.gov.uk

Customer Service: Ms Lesley Yates, Customer Care, Customer Service Centre, 66 High Street, Aylesbury HP20 1SD ☎ 01296 585665 ✉ lyates@aylesburyvaledc.gov.uk

Direct Labour: Mr Andy Wilkins, Operations Manager, Pembroke Road, Aylesbury HP20 1DG ☎ 01296 585303 ✉ awilkins@aylesburyvaledc.gov.uk

Economic Development: Mr Mark Wathan, Economic Development Manager, The Gateway, Gatehouse Road, Aylesbury HP19 8FF ☎ 01296 585064 ✉ mwathan@aylesburyvaledc.gov.uk

E-Government: Mr Alan Evans, Head of IT Services, The Gateway, Gatehouse Road, Aylesbury HP19 8FF ☎ 01296 585767 ✉ aevans@aylesburyvaledc.gov.uk

Electoral Registration: Mr Chris Sheard, Electoral Registration Officer, The Gateway, Gatehouse Road, Aylesbury HP19 8FF ☎ 01296 585050

Emergency Planning: Mr David Thomas, Corporate Health & Safety Advisor, The Gateway, Gatehouse Road, Aylesbury HP19 8FF ☎ 01296 585158 ✉ dthomas@aylesburyvaledc.gov.uk

Energy Management: Mr Alan Asbury, Sustainability Team Leader, The Gateway, Gatehouse Road, Aylesbury HP19 8FF ☎ 01296 585858 ✉ aasbury@aylesburyvaledc.gov.uk

Environmental / Technical Services: Mr Robert Smart, Environment Officer, The Gateway, Gatehouse Road, Aylesbury HP19 8FF ☎ 01296 585147 ✉ rsmart@aylesburyvaledc.gov.uk

Environmental Health: Mr Richard Hiscock, Environmental Support Manager, The Gateway, Gatehouse Road, Aylesbury HP19 8FF ☎ 01296 585156 ✉ rhiscock@aylesburyvaledc.gov.uk

Estates, Property & Valuation: Mrs Joanna Swift, Head of Legal & Estates, Council Offices, The Gateway, Gatehouse Road, Aylesbury HP19 8FF ☎ 01296 585024; 01296 585024 🖷 01296 585585 ✉ jswift@aylesburyvaledc.gov.uk

Events Manager: Ms Sophia Fulchini, Conference Centre Manager, The Gateway, Gatehouse Road, Aylesbury HP19 8FF ☎ 01296 585969 ✉ sfulchini@aylesburyvaledc.gov.uk

Facilities: Ms Jane Heywood, Facilities Manager, The Gateway, Gatehouse Road, Aylesbury HP19 8FF ☎ 01296 585191 ✉ sfulchini@aylesburyvaledc.gov.uk

Finance and Treasurer: Mr Membery, Head of Revenues & Benefits, The Gateway, Gatehouse Road, Aylesbury HP19 8FF ☎ 01296 585259 ✉ jmembery@aylesburyvaledc.gov.uk

Finance and Treasurer: Mr Andrew Small, Director, The Gateway, Gatehouse Road, Aylesbury HP19 8FF ☎ 01296 585507 ✉ asmall@aylesburyvaledc.gov.uk

Grounds Maintenance: Mrs Lesley Davies, Leisure Services Manager, The Gateway, Gatehouse Road, Aylesbury HP19 8FF ☎ 01296 585504 ✉ ldavies@aylesburyvaledc.gov.uk

Health and Safety: Mr David Thomas, Corporate Health & Safety Advisor, The Gateway, Gatehouse Road, Aylesbury HP19 8FF ☎ 01296 585158 ✉ dthomas@aylesburyvaledc.gov.uk

Home Energy Conservation: Mr Robert Smart, Environment Officer, The Gateway, Gatehouse Road, Aylesbury HP19 8FF ☎ 01296 585147 ✉ rsmart@aylesburyvaledc.gov.uk

Housing: Mr Roy Brooks, Housing Needs & Advice Manager, The Gateway, Gatehouse Road, Aylesbury HP19 8FF ☎ 01296 585171 ✉ housingneeds@aylesburyvaledc.gov.uk

Housing: Ms Anna Gordon, Strategic Housing Manager, The Gateway, Gatehouse Road, Aylesbury HP19 8FF ☎ 01296 585171 ✉ agordon@aylesburyvaledc.gov.uk

Legal: Mrs Joanna Swift, Head of Legal & Estates, Council Offices, The Gateway, Gatehouse Road, Aylesbury HP19 8FF ☎ 01296 585024; 01296 585024 🖷 01296 585585 ✉ jswift@aylesburyvaledc.gov.uk; jswift@aylesburyvaledc.gov.uk

Leisure and Cultural Services: Mrs Lesley Davies, Leisure Services Manager, The Gateway, Gatehouse Road, Aylesbury HP19 8FF ☎ 01296 585504 ✉ ldavies@aylesburyvaledc.gov.uk

Licensing: Mr Peter Seal, Licensing Officer, The Gateway, Gatehouse Road, Aylesbury HP19 8FF ☎ 01296 585083 ✉ pseal@aylesburyvaledc.gov.uk

Lottery Funding, Charity and Voluntary: Ms Lynne Maddocks, Community Engagement Officer, The Gateway, Gatehouse Road, Aylesbury HP19 8FF ✉ lmaddocks@aylesburyvaledc.gov.uk

Member Services: Mr Les White, Head of Administration, Council Offices, The Gateway, Gatehouse Road, Aylesbury HP19 8FF ☎ 01296 585048 🖷 01296 488887 ✉ lwhite@aylesburyvaledc.gov.uk

Parking: Mr Stephen Harding, Parking Manager, The Gateway, Gatehouse Road, Aylesbury HP19 8FF ☎ 01296 585381 ✉ sharding@aylesburyvaledc.gov.uk

Personnel / HR: Ms Ann Kiceluk, Head of People & Payroll, Corporate Health & Safety and Business Transformation, The Gateway, Gatehouse Road, Aylesbury HP19 8FF ☎ 01296 585103 🖷 01296 488887 ✉ akiceluk@aylesburyvaledc.gov.uk

Planning: Mr John Byrne, Head of Planning Services, The Gateway, Gatehouse Road, Aylesbury HP19 8FF ☎ 01296 585678 ✉ jbyrne@aylesburyvaledc.gov.uk

Procurement: Ms Sarah Deyes, Procurement Strategy Officer, The Gateway, Gatehouse Road, Aylesbury HP19 8FF ☎ 01296 585871 ✉ sdeyes@aylesburyvaledc.gov.uk

Recycling & Waste Minimisation: Mr Alan Asbury, Sustainability Team Leader, The Gateway, Gatehouse Road, Aylesbury HP19 8FF ☎ 01296 585858 ✉ aasbury@aylesburyvaledc.gov.uk

Staff Training: Ms Vivien Hoare, Training Administrator, The Gateway, Gatehouse Road, Aylesbury HP19 8FF ☎ 01296 585015 ✉ vhoare@aylesburyvaledc.gov.uk

Sustainable Communities: Mrs Stephanie Moffat, Community Engagement Manager, The Gateway, Gatehouse Road, Aylesbury HP19 8FF ☎ 01296 585295 ✉ smoffat@aylesburyvaledc.gov.uk

Tourism: Mr Ian Barham, Bucks 2012 Manager, The Gateway, Gatehouse Road, Aylesbury HP19 8FF ☎ 01296 585184 ✉ ibarham@aylesburyvaledc.gov.uk

Town Centre: Ms Diana Fawcett, Town Centre Manager, The Gateway, Gatehouse Road, Aylesbury HP19 8FF ☎ 01296 396370 ✉ dfawcett@aylesburyvaledc.gov.uk

Transport: Mr Barry Waters, Transport Manager, New Century House, 18 Pembroke Road, Stocklake Industrial Estate, Aylesbury HP20 1DG ☎ 01296 585514 🖷 01296 397325

Waste Collection and Disposal: Mr Andy Wilkins, Operations Manager, Pembroke Road, Aylesbury HP20 1DG ☎ 01296 585303 ✉ awilkins@aylesburyvaledc.gov.uk

Waste Management: Mr Pete Randall, Refuse Manager, Pembroke Road, Aylesbury HP20 1DG ☎ 01296 585858

Children's Play Areas: Mr Phil Black, Community Development Manager, The Gateway, Gatehouse Road, Aylesbury HP19 8FF ☎ 01296 585183 ✉ pblack@aylesburyvaledc.gov.uk

MEMBERS OF THE COUNCIL (59)

***Chair:* Isham**, Derrick (CON - Buckingham North)
dri@talk21.com

***Vice-Chair:* Rand**, Michael (CON - Brill)
mrand@aylesburyvaledc.gov.uk

***Leader of the Council:* Cartwright**, John (CON - Grendon Underwood)
jcartwright@aylesburyvaledc.gov.uk

***Deputy Leader of the Council:* Edmonds**, Michael (CON - Long Crendon)
medmonds@aylesburyvaledc.gov.uk

LOCAL AUTHORITIES

Adams, Chris (UKIP - Quarrendon)
cadams@aylesburyvaledc.gov.uk
Bell, Michael (LAB - Southcourt)
mbeall@aylesburyvaledc.gov.uk
Blake, Neil (CON - Great Brickhill)
nblake@aylesburyvaledc.gov.uk
Blake, Janet (CON - Stewkley)
jblake@aylesburyvaledc.gov.uk
Bloom, Jenny (CON - Bedgrove)
jbloom@aylesburyvaledc.gov.uk
Bond, Ashley (CON - Weedon)
abond@aylesburyvaledc.gov.uk
Bowles, Steve (CON - Wendover)
sbowles@aylesburyvaledc.gov.uk
Brandis, Judy (CON - Haddenham)
jbrandis@aylesburyvaledc.gov.uk
Cashman, Corry (LD - Cheddington)
c.cashman@zen.co.uk
Chapple, Sue (CON - Mandeville & Elm Farm)
schapple@aylesburyvaledc.gov.uk
Chilver, John (CON - Steeple Claydon)
jchilver@aylesburyvaledc.gov.uk
Cooper, Peter (IND - Wingrave)
pcooper@aylesburyvaledc.gov.uk
Davies, Avril (LD - Pitstone)
acdavies@buckscc.gov.uk
Douglas-Bate, Andrew (CON - Haddenham)
adouglas-bate@aylesburyvaledc.gov.uk
Fealey, Patrick (CON - Tingewick)
pfealey@aylesburyvaledc.gov.uk
Foster, Brian (CON - Haddenham)
bfoster@aylesburyvaledc.gov.uk
Glover, Netta (CON - Wing)
nglover@aylesburyvaledc.gov.uk
Hawkett, Mike (CON - Long Crendon)
mhawkett@aylesburyvaledc.gov.uk
Hughes, Paul (LD - Coldharbour)
phughes@aylesburyvaledc.gov.uk
Hunter-Watts, Tom (CON - Bedgrove)
tom.hunterwatts@gmail.com
Hussain, Tuffail (LD - Gatehouse)
thussain@aylesburyvaledc.gov.uk
Huxley, Andy (UKIP - Quarrendon)
ahuxley@aylesburyvaledc.gov.uk
Jarvis, Stuart (LD - Gatehouse)
sjarvis@aylesburyvaledc.gov.uk
Kennell, Steven (LD - Walton Court & Hawkslade)
skennell@aylesburyvaledc.gov.uk
Khan, Raj (LD - Elmhurst & Watermead)
rkhan@buckscc.gov.uk
Lambert, Steven (LD - Coldharbour)
slambert@aylesburyvaledc.gov.uk
Lewis, Pearl (CON - Luffield Abbey)
plewis@aylesburyvaledc.gov.uk
Mills, Timothy (CON - Buckingham North)
tmills@aylesburyvaledc.gov.uk
Monger, Llew (LD - Winslow)
lmonger@aylesburyvaledc.gov.uk
Mordue, Howard (CON - Buckingham South)
hmordue@aylesburyvaledc.gov.uk
Paternoster, Carole (CON - Aston Clinton)
cpaternoster@aylesburyvaledc.gov.uk
Patrick, Steve (LD - Oakfield)
spatrick@aylesburyvaledc.gov.uk
Pearce, Pam (IND - Newton Longville)
ppearce@aylesburyvaledc.gov.uk
Phipps, Jackie (CON - Marsh Gibbon)
jphipps@aylesburyvaledc.gov.uk
Polhill, Sue (CON - Quainton)
spolhill@aylesburyvaledc.gov.uk
Poll, Chris (CON - Edlesborough)
cpoll@aylesburyvaledc.gov.uk
Renshell, Susan (CON - Winslow)
srenshaell@aylesburyvaledc.gov.uk
Reynolds, Glenda (LD - Oakfield)
greynolds@aylesburyvaledc.gov.uk
Richards, Chris (CON - Wendover)
crichards@aylesburyvaledc.gov.uk
Roberts, Freda (LD - Southcourt)
froberts@buckscc.gov.uk
Roberts, Brian (CON - Mandeville & Elm Farm)
cllrbroberts@aylesburyvaledc.gov.uk
Russel, Barbara (CON - Aylesbury Central)
russelbarbara19@gmail.com
Smith, Lisa (LD - Elmhurst & Watermead)
lsmith@aylesburyvaledc.gov.uk
Smith, Mike (LD - Coldharbour)
msmith2@aylesburyvaledc.gov.uk
Stanier Bt, Beville (CON - Great Horwood)
bstanier@aylesburyvaledc.gov.uk
Strachan, Peter (CON - Wendover)
pstrachan@aylesburyvaledc.gov.uk
Stuchbury, Robin (LAB - Buckingham South)
stuchbury@dsl.pipex.com
Takodora, Ranjula (LD - Walton Court & Hawkslade)
rtakodora@aylesburyvaledc.gov.uk
Thompson, David (CON - Aston Clinton)
dthompson@aylesburyvaledc.gov.uk
Tyndall, Brian (CON - Mandeville & Elm Farm)
btyndall@aylesburyvaledc.gov.uk
Vick, David (LD - Waddesdon)
dvick@aylesburyvaledc.gov.uk
Ward, Julie (LD - Bierton)
jward@aylesburyvaledc.gov.uk
Ward, Alan (CON - Elmhurst & Watermead)
award@aylesburyvaledc.gov.uk
Winn, Mark (CON - Bedgrove)
mwinn@aylesburyvaledc.gov.uk
Yerby, Phil (CON - Aston Clinton)
pyerby@aylesburyvaledc.gov.uk

POLITICAL COMPOSITION

CON: 36, LD: 17, UKIP: 2, IND: 2, LAB: 2

CABINET

Leader: Mr John Cartwright
Deputy Leader /
Economic Development: Mr Michael Edmonds
Civic Amenities: Mr Brian Roberts
Community Matters: Ms Pam Pearce
Environment & Health: Sir Beville Stanier
Leisure: Mr David Thompson
Planned Development, Design & Conservation: Ms Sue Polhill
Resources: Mr Neil Blake
Strategic Planning: Mrs Carole Paternoster

BABERGH D

Babergh District Council, Council Offices, Corks Lane, Hadleigh, Ipswich IP7 6SJ ☎ 01473 822801 🖷 01473 825742 💻 www.babergh.gov.uk

FACTS & FIGURES

Police Authority: Suffolk Police Authority
Health Authority: East of England Strategic Health Authority
Learning and Skills Council: Eastern
EU Constituencies: Eastern
Election Frequency: Elections are of whole council
Twinning: Boxford: Boxford (USA); East Bergholt: Barbizon (France); Hadleigh: Rousies (France) and Schoorl (Netherlands); Sudbury: Hoxter (Germany); Clermont (France)

PRINCIPAL OFFICERS

Chief Executive: Ms Charlie Adan, Chief Executive, Council Offices, Corks Lane, Hadleigh, Ipswich IP7 6SJ ☎ 01473 825710 🖷 01473 825742 ✉ charlie.adan@babergh.gov.uk

Deputy Chief Executive: Mr Mike Hammond, Interim Transformation Director, Council Offices, Corks Lane, Hadleigh, Ipswich IP7 6SJ ☎ 01473 825750 🖷 01473 825742 ✉ mike.hammond@babergh.gov.uk

Senior Management: Ms Lindsay Barker, Strategic Director (Place), Council Offices, Corks Lane, Hadleigh, Ipswich IP7 6SJ ☎ 01473 825211 🖷 01473 825742 ✉ lindsay.barker@babergh.gov.uk

Senior Management: Mr Mike Evans, Strategic Director (People), Council Offices, Corks Lane, Hadleigh, Ipswich IP7 6SJ ☎ 01473 825212 🖷 01473 825742 ✉ mike.evans@babergh.gov.uk

Senior Management: Mr Andrew Hunkin, Strategic Director (Corporate), Council Offices, Corks Lane, Hadleigh IP7 6SJ ☎ 01473 825820 🖷 01473 823742 ✉ andrew.hunkin@babergh.gov.uk

Architect, Building / Property Services: Mr Ben Hancock, Building Services Manager, Council Offices, Corks Lane, Hadleigh IP7 6SJ ☎ 01473 825785 🖷 01473 825770 ✉ ben.hancock@babergh.gov.uk

Best Value: Mr Peter Quirk, Head of Corporate Organisation, Council Offices, Corks Lane, Hadleigh, Ipswich IP7 6SJ ☎ 01473 825829 🖷 01473 823742 ✉ peter.quirk@babergh.gov.uk

Building Control: Mr Gary Starling, Building Control Partnership Manager, Council Offices, Corks Lane, Hadleigh IP7 6SJ ☎ 01473 825856 🖷 01473 825708 ✉ gary.starling@babergh.gov.uk

PR / Communications: Mr Paul Simon, Communications & PR Manager, Council Offices, Corks Lane, Hadleigh IP7 6SJ ☎ 01473 826634 🖷 01473 825742 ✉ paul.simon@babergh.gov.uk

Community Safety: Mr Paul Little, Community Safety & Leisure Manager, Council Offices, Corks Lane, Hadleigh, Ipswich IP7 6SJ ☎ 01473 826679 🖷 01473 825770 ✉ paul.little@babergh.gov.uk

Computer Management: Mr Kevin Peck, Technical Support Manager, Council Offices, Corks Lane, Hadleigh, Ipswich IP7 6SJ ☎ 01473 825824 🖷 01473 823594 ✉ kevin.peck@babergh.gov.uk

Contracts: Ms Tracey Farthing, Procurement Manager, Council Offices, Corks Lane, Hadleigh, Ipswich IP7 6SJ ☎ 01473 825715 🖷 01473 825770 ✉ tracey.farthing@babergh.gov.uk

Corporate Services: Mr Andrew Hunkin, Strategic Director (Corporate), Council Offices, Corks Lane, Hadleigh IP7 6SJ ☎ 01473 825820 🖷 01473 823742 ✉ andrew.hunkin@babergh.gov.uk

Customer Service: Mrs Dawn Williams, Access Manager, Council Offices, Corks Lane, Hadleigh, Ipswich IP7 6SJ ☎ 01473 825189 🖷 01473 825724 ✉ dawn.williams@babergh.gov.uk

Economic Development: Mrs Sue Dawes, Economic Development Technical Officer, Council Offices, Corks Lane, Hadleigh, Ipswich IP7 6SJ ☎ 01473 825868 🖷 01473 825708 ✉ sue.dawes@babergh.gov.uk

E-Government: Mr Carl Reeder, Information & Project Manager, Council Offices, Corks Lane, Hadleigh, Ipswich IP7 6SJ ☎ 01473 826659 🖷 01473 823594 ✉ carl.reeder@babergh.gov.uk

Electoral Registration: Mr Ray Amesbury, Senior Democratic Services Manager, Council Offices, Corks Lane, Hadleigh IP7 6SJ ☎ 01473 825891 🖷 01473 825742 ✉ ray.amesbury@babergh.gov.uk

Emergency Planning: Mr Steve Pinion, District Emergency Planning Officer, Council Offices, Corks Lane, Hadleigh, Ipswich IP7 6SJ ☎ 07920139293 ✉ steve.pinion@babergh.gov.uk

Energy Management: Mr Ben Hancock, Building Services Manager, Council Offices, Corks Lane, Hadleigh IP7 6SJ ☎ 01473 825785 🖷 01473 825770 ✉ ben.hancock@babergh.gov.uk

Environmental / Technical Services: Mr Ryan Jones, Head of Contract & Asset Management, Council Offices, Corks Lane, Hadleigh IP7 6SJ ☎ 01473 825787 🖷 01473 825770 ✉ ryan.jones@babergh.gov.uk

Environmental Health: Mr Chris Fry, Head of Environment, Council Offices, Corks Lane, Hadleigh, Ipswich IP7 6SJ ☎ 01473 826649 🖷 01473 825742 ✉ chris.fry@babergh.gov.uk

Estates, Property & Valuation: Mr Ryan Jones, Head of Contract & Asset Management, Council Offices, Corks Lane, Hadleigh IP7 6SJ ☎ 01473 825787 🖷 01473 825770 ✉ ryan.jones@babergh.gov.uk

European Liaison: Mrs Sue Dawes, Economic Development Technical Officer, Council Offices, Corks Lane, Hadleigh, Ipswich IP7 6SJ ☎ 01473 825868 🖷 01473 825708 ✉ sue.dawes@babergh.gov.uk

Finance and Treasurer: Mrs Katherine Steel, Head of Corporate Resources, Council Offices, Corks Lane, Hadleigh, Ipswich IP7 6SJ ☎ 01473 826649 🖷 01473 825742 ✉ katherine.steel@babergh.gov.uk

Housing: Mr Martin King, Head of Housing, Council Offices, 131 High Street, Needham Market IP6 8DL ☎ 01449 724769 ✉ martin.king@midsuffolk.gov.uk

Housing Maintenance: Mr Ryan Jones, Head of Contract & Asset Management, Council Offices, Corks Lane, Hadleigh IP7 6SJ ☎ 01473 825787 🖷 01473 825770 ✉ ryan.jones@babergh.gov.uk

Legal: Ms Kathryn Saward, Solicitor to the Council, Council Offices, Corks Lane, Hadleigh IP7 6SJ ☎ 01473 825729 ✉ kathryn.saward@babergh.gov.uk

Leisure and Cultural Services: Mr Jonathan Free, Head of Communities, Council Offices, Corks Lane, Hadleigh, Ipswich IP7 6SJ ☎ 01473 826649 🖷 01473 825742 ✉ jonathan.free@babergh.gov.uk

Licensing: Mr Lee Carvell, Licensing Officer, Council Offices, Corks Lane, Hadleigh IP7 6SJ ☎ 01473 825719 🖷 01473 825742 ✉ lee.carvell@babergh.gov.uk

Member Services: Mr Steve Ellwood, Democratic Services Manager, Council Offices, Corks Lane, Hadleigh IP7 6SJ ☎ 01473 825876 🖷 01473 825742 ✉ steve.ellwood@babergh.gov.uk

Parking: Mr Ryan Jones, Head of Contract & Asset Management, Council Offices, Corks Lane, Hadleigh IP7 6SJ ☎ 01473 825787 🖷 01473 825770 ✉ ryan.jones@babergh.gov.uk

Partnerships: Mr Jonathan Free, Head of Communities, Council Offices, Corks Lane, Hadleigh, Ipswich IP7 6SJ ☎ 01473 826649 🖷 01473 825742 ✉ jonathan.free@babergh.gov.uk

Personnel / HR: Mrs Jeanette Bray, HR & OD Manager, Council Offices, Corks Lane, Hadleigh IP7 6SJ ☎ 01473 825744 🖷 01473 825742 ✉ jeanette.bray@babergh.gov.uk

Planning: Mr Nicholas Ward, Chief Planning Control Officer, Council Offices, Corks Lane, Hadleigh, Ipswich IP7 6SJ ☎ 01473 825851 🖷 01473 825708 ✉ nicholas.ward@babergh.gov.uk

Procurement: Ms Tracey Farthing, Procurement Manager, Council Offices, Corks Lane, Hadleigh, Ipswich IP7 6SJ ☎ 01473 825715 🖷 01473 825770 ✉ tracey.farthing@babergh.gov.uk

Recycling & Waste Minimisation: Mr Chris Fry, Head of Environment, Council Offices, Corks Lane, Hadleigh, Ipswich IP7 6SJ ☎ 01473 826649 🖷 01473 825742 ✉ chris.fry@babergh.gov.uk

Staff Training: Mrs Jo Knight, Human Resources Officer, Council Offices, Corks Lane, Hadleigh, Ipswich IP7 6SJ ☎ 01473 825804 🖷 01473 825742 ✉ jo.knight@babergh.gov.uk

Sustainable Communities: Mr Jonathan Free, Head of Communities, Council Offices, Corks Lane, Hadleigh, Ipswich IP7 6SJ ☎ 01473 826649 🖷 01473 825742 ✉ jonathan.free@babergh.gov.uk

Sustainable Development: Mr Chris Fry, Head of Environment, Council Offices, Corks Lane, Hadleigh, Ipswich IP7 6SJ ☎ 01473 826649 🖷 01473 825742 ✉ chris.fry@babergh.gov.uk

Tourism: Mr Peter Burrows, Head of Economy, Council Offices, Corks Lane, Hadleigh, Ipswich IP7 6SJ ☎ 01473 826649 🖷 01743 825742 ✉ peter.burrows@babergh.gov.uk

Tourism: Mrs Helen Cutting, Tourism Officer, Council Offices, 131 High Street, Needham Market IP6 8DL ☎ 01449 724636 ✉ helen.cutting@midsuffolk.gov.uk

Waste Collection and Disposal: Mr Chris Morton, Joint Client Manager, Mid Suffolk District Council, 131 High Street, Needham Market, Ipswich IP6 8DL ☎ 01449 778645 ✉ chris.morton@midsuffolk.gov.uk

Waste Management: Mr Chris Fry, Head of Environment, Council Offices, Corks Lane, Hadleigh, Ipswich IP7 6SJ ☎ 01473 826649 🖷 01473 825742 ✉ chris.fry@babergh.gov.uk

Children's Play Areas: Mr Jonathan Free, Head of Communities, Council Offices, Corks Lane, Hadleigh, Ipswich IP7 6SJ ☎ 01473 826649 🖷 01473 825742 ✉ jonathan.free@babergh.gov.uk

MEMBERS OF THE COUNCIL (43)

***Chair:* Ridley**, Nick (CON - Brook)
nick.ridley@babergh.gov.uk

***Vice-Chair:* Long**, James (IND - Chadacre)
james.long@babergh.gov.uk

***Group Leader:* Bavington**, Tony (LAB - Great Cornard)
tony.bavington@babergh.gov.uk

***Group Leader:* Carpendale**, Sue (LD - Mid Samford)
sue.carpendale@babergh.gov.uk

***Group Leader:* Jenkins**, Jennifer (CON - Leavenheath)
jennifer.jenkins@babergh.gov.uk

***Group Leader:* Wigglesworth**, Sue (IND - Lower Brett)
sue.wigglesworth@babergh.gov.uk

Antill, Jenny (CON - Waldingfield)
jenny.antill@babergh.gov.uk

Arthey, Clive (O - North Cosford)
clive.arthey@babergh.gov.uk

Bamford, Michael (LD - Dodnash)
michael.bamford@babergh.gov.uk

Barrett, Simon (CON - Sudbury South)
simon.barrett@babergh.gov.uk

Beer, Peter (CON - Great Cornard (South))
peter.beer@babergh.gov.uk

Bennett, Nigel (LD - Sudbury (South))
nigel.bennett@babergh.gov.uk

Burgoyne, Peter (CON - Pinewood)
peter.burgoyne@babergh.gov.uk

Busby, David (LD - Pinewood)
david.busby@babergh.gov.uk

Cave, Richard (CON - Nayland)
richard.cave@babergh.gov.uk

Deacon, John (LD - Berners)
john.deacon@babergh.gov.uk

Grandon, Kathryn (CON - Hadleigh South)
kathryn.grandon@babergh.gov.uk

Grutchfield, David (LD - Hadleigh South)
david.grutchfield@babergh.gov.uk

Hinton, John (CON - Dodnash)
john.hinton@babergh.gov.uk

Holbrook, Peter (CON - Bures St Mary)
peter.holbrook@babergh.gov.uk
Hurren, Bryn (LD - Boxford)
bryn.hurren@babergh.gov.uk
Jones, Peter (IND - Brook)
peter.jones@babergh.gov.uk
Keane, Desmond (CON - Brett Vale)
desmond.keane@babergh.gov.uk
Kemp, Richard (IND - Long Melford)
richard.kemp@babergh.gov.uk
Kendall, Dawn (CON - South Cosford)
dawn.kendall@babergh.gov.uk
Lawrenson, Frank (CON - Waldingfield)
frank.lawrenson@babergh.gov.uk
Macmaster, Neil (LAB - Great Cornard North)
neil.mcmaster@babergh.gov.uk
Munson, Mary (LD - Hadleigh (South))
mary.munson@babergh.gov.uk
Newman, Mark (CON - Great Cornard (South))
mark.newman@babergh.gov.uk
Norman, Andrea (IND - Lavenham)
jack.nunn@babergh.gov.uk
Nunn, John (IND - Long Melford)
john.nunn@babergh.gov.uk
Osbourne, Adrian (CON - Sudbury (East))
adrian.osborne@babergh.gov.uk
Owen, Jack (LAB - Sudbury East)
jack.owen@babergh.gov.uk
Pollard, Kathy (LD - Mid Samford)
kathy.pollard@babergh.gov.uk
Riley, Brian (CON - Hadleigh (North))
brian.riley@babergh.gov.uk
Roberts, Tony (LD - Berners)
tony.roberts@babergh.gov.uk
Rose, David (IND - Holbrook)
david.rose@babergh.gov.uk
Sayers, John (CON - Sudbury (North))
john.sayers@babergh.gov.uk
Smith, Ray (CON - Sudbury (North))
ray.smith@babergh.gov.uk
Thake, Rex (LD - Glemsford & Stanstead)
rex.thake@babergh.gov.uk
Ward, Trot (LD - Alton)
trot.ward@babergh.gov.uk
Wood, David (LD - Alton)
david.wood@babergh.gov.uk
Young, Len (IND - Glemsford & Stanstead)
len.young@babergh.gov.uk

POLITICAL COMPOSITION

CON: 18, LD: 13, IND: 8, LAB: 3, O: 1

COMMITTEE CHAIRS

Development: Mr Peter Beer
Licensing & Appeals: Mr Peter Holbrook
Overview & Scrutiny (Community Services): Mr James Long
Standards: Mr P Down (External)

BALLYMENA N

Ballymena Borough Council, Ardeevin, 80 Galgorm Road, Ballymena BT42 1AB ☎ 028 2566 0300 🖷 028 2566 0400
info@ballymena.gov.uk
www.ballymena.gov.uk

FACTS & FIGURES

Police Authority: Northern Ireland Policing Board
Health Authority: Health & Social Care Board
Learning and Skills Council: Northern Ireland
Parliamentary Constituencies: Antrim North
EU Constituencies: Northern Ireland
Election Frequency: Elections are of whole council

PRINCIPAL OFFICERS

Chief Executive: Mrs Anne Donaghy, Town Clerk & Chief Executive, Ardeevin, 80 Galgorm Road, Ballymena BT42 1AB ☎ 028 2566 0300 🖷 028 2563 1277 anne.donaghy@ballymena.gov.uk

Deputy Chief Executive: Mr Ronnie McBride, Deputy Town Clerk & Chief Executive, Ardeevin, 80 Galgorm Road, Ballymena BT42 1AB ☎ 028 2566 0300 🖷 028 2566 0400 ronnie.mcbride@ballymena.gov.uk

Deputy Chief Executive: Mr Rodger McKnight, Deputy Town Clerk & Chief Executive, Ardeevin, 80 Galgorm Road, Ballymena BT42 1AB ☎ 028 2566 0300 🖷 028 2566 0400 rodger.mcknight@ballymena.gov.uk

Access Officer / Social Services (Disability): Mr Ronnie McBride, Deputy Town Clerk & Chief Executive, Ardeevin, 80 Galgorm Road, Ballymena BT42 1AB ☎ 028 2566 0300 🖷 028 2566 0400 ronnie.mcbride@ballymena.gov.uk

Best Value: Mr Greg Dornan, Corporate Policy Officer, Ardeevin, 80 Galgorm Road, Ballymena BT42 1AB ☎ 028 2566 0300 🖷 028 2566 0400 greg.dornan@ballymena.gov.uk

Best Value: Mr Rodger McKnight, Deputy Town Clerk & Chief Executive, Ardeevin, 80 Galgorm Road, Ballymena BT42 1AB ☎ 028 2566 0300 🖷 028 2566 0400 rodger.mcknight@ballymena.gov.uk

Building Control: Mr Trevor Kyle, Assistant Chief Building Control Officer, Ardeevin, 80 Galgorm Road, Ballymena BT42 1AB ☎ 028 2566 0300 🖷 028 2566 0400 trevor.kyle@ballymena.gov.uk

Catering Services: Mrs Cecilia McWhirter, Catering Manager, The Braid Museum and Arts Centre, 1-29 Bridge Street, Ballymena BT43 5EJ ☎ 028 2563 5953 cecilia.mcwhirter@ballymena.gov.uk

Civil Registration: Mrs Rhonda McIlroy, Registrar, Ardeevin, 80 Galgorm Road, Ballymena BT42 1AB ☎ 028 2566 0352 🖷 028 2566 0400 rhonda.mcilroy@ballymena.gov.uk

PR / Communications: Mr Ronnie McBride, Deputy Town Clerk & Chief Executive, Ardeevin, 80 Galgorm Road, Ballymena BT42 1AB ☎ 028 2566 0300 🖷 028 2566 0400 ronnie.mcbride@ballymena.gov.uk

Community Planning: Mr Ronnie McBride, Deputy Town Clerk & Chief Executive, Ardeevin, 80 Galgorm Road, Ballymena BT42 1AB ☎ 028 2566 0300 🖷 028 2566 0400 ronnie.mcbride@ballymena.gov.uk

Community Safety: Ms Karen Moore, Community Safety Officer, 4 Wellington Court, Ballymena BT43 6EQ ☎ 028 2563 3930 karen.moore@ballymena.gov.uk

Computer Management: Mrs Sandra Cole, Finance & Estate Services, Ardeevin, 80 Galgorm Road, Ballymena BT42 1AB ☎ 028 2566 0300 Fax 028 2566 0400 sandra.cole@ballymena.gov.uk

Consumer Protection and Trading Standards: Ms Nicola McCall, Deputy Chief Environmental Health Officer, Ardeevin, 80 Galgorm Road, Ballymena BT42 1AB ☎ 028 2566 0300 Fax 028 2566 0400 nicola.mccall@ballymena.gov.uk

Contracts: Mr Rodger McKnight, Deputy Town Clerk & Chief Executive, Ardeevin, 80 Galgorm Road, Ballymena BT42 1AB ☎ 028 2566 0300 Fax 028 2566 0400 rodger.mcknight@ballymena.gov.uk

Direct Labour: Mr Rodger McKnight, Deputy Town Clerk & Chief Executive, Ardeevin, 80 Galgorm Road, Ballymena BT42 1AB ☎ 028 2566 0300 Fax 028 2566 0400 rodger.mcknight@ballymena.gov.uk

Economic Development: Mr Aidan Donnelly, Assistant Director - Development, Leisure & Cultural Services, Ardeevin, 80 Galgorm Road, Ballymena BT42 1AB ☎ 028 2566 0300 Fax 028 2566 0400 aidan.donnelly@ballymena.gov.uk

E-Government: Mrs Sandra Cole, Finance & Estate Services, Ardeevin, 80 Galgorm Road, Ballymena BT42 1AB ☎ 028 2566 0300 Fax 028 2566 0400 sandra.cole@ballymena.gov.uk

Emergency Planning: Mr Perry Donaldson, Acting Director, 58 Cardonaghy Road, Ballymena BT42 1JE ☎ 028 2587 9519 pdonaldson@ngs-ni.org.uk

Energy Management: Mr Ronnie McBride, Deputy Town Clerk & Chief Executive, Ardeevin, 80 Galgorm Road, Ballymena BT42 1AB ☎ 028 2566 0300 Fax 028 2566 0400 ronnie.mcbride@ballymena.gov.uk

Environmental / Technical Services: Mr Rodger McKnight, Deputy Town Clerk & Chief Executive, Ardeevin, 80 Galgorm Road, Ballymena BT42 1AB ☎ 028 2566 0300 Fax 028 2566 0400 rodger.mcknight@ballymena.gov.uk

Environmental Health: Ms Nicola McCall, Deputy Chief Environmental Health Officer, Ardeevin, 80 Galgorm Road, Ballymena BT42 1AB ☎ 028 2566 0300 Fax 028 2566 0400 nicola.mccall@ballymena.gov.uk

Estates, Property & Valuation: Mrs Sandra Cole, Finance & Estate Services, Ardeevin, 80 Galgorm Road, Ballymena BT42 1AB ☎ 028 2566 0300 Fax 028 2566 0400 sandra.cole@ballymena.gov.uk

European Liaison: Mr Aidan Donnelly, Assistant Director - Development, Leisure & Cultural Services, Ardeevin, 80 Galgorm Road, Ballymena BT42 1AB ☎ 028 2566 0300 Fax 028 2566 0400 aidan.donnelly@ballymena.gov.uk

Facilities: Mr Rodger McKnight, Deputy Town Clerk & Chief Executive, Ardeevin, 80 Galgorm Road, Ballymena BT42 1AB ☎ 028 2566 0300 Fax 028 2566 0400 rodger.mcknight@ballymena.gov.uk

Finance and Treasurer: Mrs Sandra Cole, Finance & Estate Services, Ardeevin, 80 Galgorm Road, Ballymena BT42 1AB ☎ 028 2566 0300 Fax 028 2566 0400 sandra.cole@ballymena.gov.uk

Fleet Management: Mrs Sandra Cole, Finance & Estate Services, Ardeevin, 80 Galgorm Road, Ballymena BT42 1AB ☎ 028 2566 0300 Fax 028 2566 0400 sandra.cole@ballymena.gov.uk

Grounds Maintenance: Mr Ronnie McBride, Deputy Town Clerk & Chief Executive, Ardeevin, 80 Galgorm Road, Ballymena BT42 1AB ☎ 028 2566 0300 Fax 028 2566 0400 ronnie.mcbride@ballymena.gov.uk

Health and Safety: Mr Aidan Toner, Health & Safety Officer, Ardeevin, 80 Galgorm Road, Ballymena BT42 1AB ☎ 028 2566 0300 Fax 028 2566 0400 aidan.toner@ballymena.gov.uk

Home Energy Conservation: Mr Clive Kyle, Assistant Director - Development, Leisure & Cultural Services, Ardeevin, 80 Galgorm Road, Ballymena BT42 1AB ☎ 028 2566 0300 Fax 028 2566 0400 clive.kyle@ballymena.gov.uk

Leisure and Cultural Services: Mr Ronnie McBride, Deputy Town Clerk & Chief Executive, Ardeevin, 80 Galgorm Road, Ballymena BT42 1AB ☎ 028 2566 0300 Fax 028 2566 0400 ronnie.mcbride@ballymena.gov.uk

Lottery Funding, Charity and Voluntary: Mr Aidan Donnelly, Assistant Director - Development, Leisure & Cultural Services, Ardeevin, 80 Galgorm Road, Ballymena BT42 1AB ☎ 028 2566 0300 Fax 028 2566 0400 aidan.donnelly@ballymena.gov.uk

Member Services: Ms Rhonda Craig, Administrator for Member Services, Ardeevin, 80 Galgorm Road, Ballymena BT42 1AB ☎ 028 2566 0300 Fax 028 2566 0400 rhonda.craig@ballymena.gov.uk

Member Services: Ms Catherine Livingstone, Mayor's Secretary, Ardeevin, 80 Galgorm Road, Ballymena BT42 1AB ☎ 028 2566 0359 Fax 028 2566 0400 mayor.secretary@ballymena.gov.uk

Partnerships: Mr Rodger McKnight, Deputy Town Clerk & Chief Executive, Ardeevin, 80 Galgorm Road, Ballymena BT42 1AB ☎ 028 2566 0300 Fax 028 2566 0400 rodger.mcknight@ballymena.gov.uk

Personnel / HR: Mr Rodger McKnight, Deputy Town Clerk & Chief Executive, Ardeevin, 80 Galgorm Road, Ballymena BT42 1AB ☎ 028 2566 0300 Fax 028 2566 0400 rodger.mcknight@ballymena.gov.uk

Procurement: Mr Samuel Faulkner, Reprographics / Purchasing Officer, Ardeevin, 80 Galgorm Road, Ballymena BT42 1AB ☎ 028 2566 0300 Fax 028 2566 0400 samuel.faulkner@ballymena.gov.uk

Recycling & Waste Minimisation: Mr Rodger McKnight, Deputy Town Clerk & Chief Executive, Ardeevin, 80 Galgorm Road, Ballymena BT42 1AB ☎ 028 2566 0300 🖷 028 2566 0400 rodger.mcknight@ballymena.gov.uk

Regeneration: Mr Aidan Donnelly, Assistant Director - Development, Leisure & Cultural Services, Ardeevin, 80 Galgorm Road, Ballymena BT42 1AB ☎ 028 2566 0300 🖷 028 2566 0400 aidan.donnelly@ballymena.gov.uk

Staff Training: Mr Rodger McKnight, Deputy Town Clerk & Chief Executive, Ardeevin, 80 Galgorm Road, Ballymena BT42 1AB ☎ 028 2566 0300 🖷 028 2566 0400 rodger.mcknight@ballymena.gov.uk

Street Scene: Mr John Hood, Works Superintendent, Ardeevin, 80 Galgorm Road, Ballymena BT42 1AB ☎ 028 2566 0300 john.hood@ballymena.gov.uk

Sustainable Development: Mr Ronnie McBride, Deputy Town Clerk & Chief Executive, Ardeevin, 80 Galgorm Road, Ballymena BT42 1AB ☎ 028 2566 0300 🖷 028 2566 0400 ronnie.mcbride@ballymena.gov.uk

Tourism: Mrs Christine Butler, Tourist Officer, Tourist Information Centre, The Braid, 1-29 Bridge Street, Ballymena BT43 5EJ ☎ 028 2563 5900 🖷 028 2563 5903 christine.butler@ballymena.gov.uk

Town Centre: Mr Sean Trainor, Economic & Tourism Development Manager, Economic Development Unit, 2 Wellington Court, Ballymena BT42 1AB ☎ 028 2563 3930 🖷 028 2563 9785 sean.trainor@ballymena.gov.uk

Transport: Mr Rodger McKnight, Deputy Town Clerk & Chief Executive, Ardeevin, 80 Galgorm Road, Ballymena BT42 1AB ☎ 028 2566 0300 🖷 028 2566 0400 rodger.mcknight@ballymena.gov.uk

Transport Planner: Mr Sean Trainor, Economic & Tourism Development Manager, Economic Development Unit, 2 Wellington Court, Ballymena BT42 1AB ☎ 028 2563 3930 🖷 028 2563 9785 sean.trainor@ballymena.gov.uk

Waste Collection and Disposal: Mr Rodger McKnight, Deputy Town Clerk & Chief Executive, Ardeevin, 80 Galgorm Road, Ballymena BT42 1AB ☎ 028 2566 0300 🖷 028 2566 0400 rodger.mcknight@ballymena.gov.uk

Waste Management: Mr Rodger McKnight, Deputy Town Clerk & Chief Executive, Ardeevin, 80 Galgorm Road, Ballymena BT42 1AB ☎ 028 2566 0300 🖷 028 2566 0400 rodger.mcknight@ballymena.gov.uk

MEMBERS OF THE COUNCIL (24)

***Alderman:* Cherry**, R J (UUP - Braid)
cr.cherry@ballymena.gov.uk
***Alderman:* Clarke**, M (DUP - Ballymena South)
ald.clarke@ballymena.gov.uk
***Alderman:* Hanna**, S J (DUP - Braid)
ald.hanna@ballymena.gov.uk
***Alderman:* Henry**, James (IND - Ballymena North)
james-henry@btconnect.com
***Alderman:* McAvoy**, P J (SDLP - Ballymena North)
ald.mcavoy@ballymena.gov.uk
***Alderman:* Mills**, Maurice (DUP - Ballymena North)
cr.mills@ballymena.gov.uk
Adger, E (DUP - Ballymena South)
cr.adger@ballymena.gov.uk
Carson, J (DUP - Ballymena North)
cr.carson@ballymena.gov.uk
Clyde, S E (DUP - Braid)
beth.clyde@ballymena.gov.uk
Currie, J (UUP - Ballymena South)
ald.currie@ballymena.gov.uk
Digney, Monica (SF - Bannside)
digney_monica@hotmail.com
Dunlop, Jayne (ALL - Ballymena North)
cr.dunlop@ballymena.gov.uk
Frew, P R (DUP - Braid)
cr.frew@ballymena.gov.uk
Gillespie, R (O - Bannside)
ald.gillespie@ballymena.gov.uk
Henry, B (DUP - Bannside)
billy.henry@ballymena.gov.uk
Maguire, P. D (SF - Braid)
pauldmaguire@btinternet.com
McClean, J (UUP - Ballymena North)
ja.mcclean@virgin.net
McNeilly, W R (UUP - Bannside)
cr.mcneilly@ballymena.gov.uk
Nicholl, T (DUP - Bannside)
crt.nicholl@ballymena.gov.uk
Nicholl, H (DUP - Ballymena South)
crh.nicholl@ballymena.gov.uk
O'Loan, D (SDLP - Ballymena South)
declanoloan@gmail.com
Robinson, D (DUP - Ballymena South)
cr.robinson@ballymena.gov.uk
Tweed, D A (O - Ballymena South)
cr.tweed@ballymena.gov.uk
Wales, A (DUP - Ballymena North)
cr.wales@ballymena.gov.uk

POLITICAL COMPOSITION

DUP: 12, UUP: 4, O: 2, SF: 2, SDLP: 2, IND: 1, ALL: 1

BALLYMONEY N

Ballymoney Borough Council, Riada House, 14 Charles Street, Ballymoney BT53 6DZ ☎ 028 2766 0200 🖷 028 2766 0222
info@ballymoney.gov.uk
www.ballymoney.gov.uk

FACTS & FIGURES

Police Authority: Northern Ireland Policing Board
Health Authority: Health & Social Care Board
Learning and Skills Council: Northern Ireland
Parliamentary Constituencies: Antrim North
EU Constituencies: Northern Ireland
Election Frequency: Elections are of whole council
Twinning: Douglas, Isle of Man; Vanves (France);

PRINCIPAL OFFICERS

Chief Executive: Mr John Dempsey, Chief Executive, Riada House, 14 Charles Street, Ballymoney BT53 6DZ ☎ 028 2766

0237 🖷 028 2766 0222 ✉ john.dempsey@ballymoney.gov.uk

Senior Management: Ms Iris McCleery, Director of Central & Leisure Services, Riada House, 14 Charles Street, Ballymoney BT53 6DZ ☎ 028 2766 0200 🖷 028 2766 0222 ✉ iris.mccleery@ballymoney.gov.uk

Best Value: Mr John Dempsey, Chief Executive, Riada House, 14 Charles Street, Ballymoney BT53 6DZ ☎ 028 2766 0237 🖷 028 2766 0222 ✉ john.dempsey@ballymoney.gov.uk

Building Control: Mr William Campbell, Head of Building Control, Riada House, 14 Charles Street, Ballymoney BT53 6DZ ☎ 028 2766 0224 ✉ william.campbell@ballymoney.gov.uk

Civil Registration: Mrs Janet McCaughey, Registrar, Riada House, 14 Charles Street, Ballymoney BT53 6DZ ☎ 028 2766 0206 🖷 028 2766 0222 ✉ janet.mccaughey@ballymoney.gov.uk

PR / Communications: Mrs Liz Johnston, Head of Corporate & Development Services, Riada House, 14 Charles Street, Ballymoney BT53 6DZ ☎ 028 2766 0244 🖷 028 2766 3852 ✉ liz.johnston@ballymoney.gov.uk

Community Safety: Mrs Cathy Watson, Community Safety Officer, Riada House, 14 Charles Street, Ballymoney BT53 6DZ ☎ 028 2766 0255 🖷 028 2766 0222 ✉ communitysafety@ballymoney.gov.uk

Computer Management: Mr David Wright, Head of Finance & IT, Riada House, 14 Charles Street, Ballymoney BT53 6DZ ☎ 028 2766 0211 🖷 028 2766 0222 ✉ david.wright@ballymoney.gov.uk

Consumer Protection and Trading Standards: Mr John Michael, Director of Borough Services, Riada House, 14 Charles Street, Ballymoney BT53 6DZ ☎ 028 2766 0257 🖷 028 2766 0222 ✉ john.michael@ballymoney.gov.uk

Corporate Services: Mrs Liz Johnston, Head of Corporate & Development Services, Riada House, 14 Charles Street, Ballymoney BT53 6DZ ☎ 028 2766 0244 🖷 028 2766 3852 ✉ liz.johnston@ballymoney.gov.uk

Economic Development: Mrs Margaret Doole, Development Officer, Riada House, 14 Charles Street, Ballymoney BT53 6DZ ☎ 028 2766 0253 🖷 028 2766 0222 ✉ margaret.doole@ballymoney.gov.uk

E-Government: Ms Iris McCleery, Director of Central & Leisure Services, Riada House, 14 Charles Street, Ballymoney BT53 6DZ ☎ 028 2766 0200 🖷 028 2766 0222 ✉ iris.mccleery@ballymoney.gov.uk

Emergency Planning: Mr John Michael, Director of Borough Services, Riada House, 14 Charles Street, Ballymoney BT53 6DZ ☎ 028 2766 0257 🖷 028 2766 0222 ✉ john.michael@ballymoney.gov.uk

Energy Management: Mr Gareth Doyle, Head of Amenities, Riada House, 14 Charles Street, Ballymoney BT53 6DZ ☎ 028 2766 0231 🖷 028 2766 0222 ✉ gareth.doyle@ballymoney.gov.uk

Environmental / Technical Services: Mr Nigel McKeown, Head of Environmental Services, Riada House, 14 Charles Street, Ballymoney BT53 6DZ ☎ 028 2766 0200 ✉ nigel.mckeown@ballymoney.gov.uk

Environmental / Technical Services: Mr John Michael, Director of Borough Services, Riada House, 14 Charles Street, Ballymoney BT53 6DZ ☎ 028 2766 0257 🖷 028 2766 0222 ✉ john.michael@ballymoney.gov.uk

Environmental Health: Mr John Michael, Director of Borough Services, Riada House, 14 Charles Street, Ballymoney BT53 6DZ ☎ 028 2766 0257 🖷 028 2766 0222 ✉ john.michael@ballymoney.gov.uk

Estates, Property & Valuation: Mr William Campbell, Head of Building Control, Riada House, 14 Charles Street, Ballymoney BT53 6DZ ☎ 028 2766 0224 ✉ william.campbell@ballymoney.gov.uk

Finance and Treasurer: Ms Iris McCleery, Director of Central & Leisure Services, Riada House, 14 Charles Street, Ballymoney BT53 6DZ ☎ 028 2766 0200 🖷 028 2766 0222 ✉ iris.mccleery@ballymoney.gov.uk

Grounds Maintenance: Mr Gareth Doyle, Head of Amenities, Riada House, 14 Charles Street, Ballymoney BT53 6DZ ☎ 028 2766 0231 🖷 028 2766 0222 ✉ gareth.doyle@ballymoney.gov.uk

Health and Safety: Mr John Michael, Director of Borough Services, Riada House, 14 Charles Street, Ballymoney BT53 6DZ ☎ 028 2766 0257 🖷 028 2766 0222 ✉ john.michael@ballymoney.gov.uk

Leisure and Cultural Services: Mr Paul Lyness, Head of Leisure Services, Riada House, 14 Charles Street, Ballymoney BT53 6DZ ☎ 028 2766 0260 ✉ paul.lyness@ballymoney.gov.uk

Leisure and Cultural Services: Ms Iris McCleery, Director of Central & Leisure Services, Riada House, 14 Charles Street, Ballymoney BT53 6DZ ☎ 028 2766 0200 🖷 028 2766 0222 ✉ iris.mccleery@ballymoney.gov.uk

Licensing: Mr John Michael, Director of Borough Services, Riada House, 14 Charles Street, Ballymoney BT53 6DZ ☎ 028 2766 0257 🖷 028 2766 0222 ✉ john.michael@ballymoney.gov.uk

Member Services: Mrs Liz Johnston, Head of Corporate & Development Services, Riada House, 14 Charles Street, Ballymoney BT53 6DZ ☎ 028 2766 0244 🖷 028 2766 3852 ✉ liz.johnston@ballymoney.gov.uk

Partnerships: Mrs Liz Johnston, Head of Corporate & Development Services, Riada House, 14 Charles Street, Ballymoney BT53 6DZ ☎ 028 2766 0244 🖷 028 2766 3852 ✉ liz.johnston@ballymoney.gov.uk

Personnel / HR: Miss Joan Kinnaird, Head of Human Resources, Riada House, 14 Charles Street, Ballymoney BT53 6DZ ☎ 028 2766 0202 🖷 028 2766 0222 ✉ joan.kinnaird@ballymoney.gov.uk

Procurement: Ms Iris McCleery, Director of Central & Leisure

Services, Riada House, 14 Charles Street, Ballymoney BT53 6DZ ☎ 028 2766 0200 🖷 028 2766 0222 iris.mccleery@ballymoney.gov.uk

Recycling & Waste Minimisation: Mr John Michael, Director of Borough Services, Riada House, 14 Charles Street, Ballymoney BT53 6DZ ☎ 028 2766 0257 🖷 028 2766 0222 john.michael@ballymoney.gov.uk

Road Safety: Miss Joan Kinnaird, Head of Human Resources, Riada House, 14 Charles Street, Ballymoney BT53 6DZ ☎ 028 2766 0202 🖷 028 2766 0222 joan.kinnaird@ballymoney.gov.uk

Staff Training: Miss Joan Kinnaird, Head of Human Resources, Riada House, 14 Charles Street, Ballymoney BT53 6DZ ☎ 028 2766 0202 🖷 028 2766 0222 joan.kinnaird@ballymoney.gov.uk

Street Scene: Mr John Michael, Director of Borough Services, Riada House, 14 Charles Street, Ballymoney BT53 6DZ ☎ 028 2766 0257 🖷 028 2766 0222 john.michael@ballymoney.gov.uk

Sustainable Development: Mr John Michael, Director of Borough Services, Riada House, 14 Charles Street, Ballymoney BT53 6DZ ☎ 028 2766 0257 🖷 028 2766 0222 john.michael@ballymoney.gov.uk

Tourism: Ms Iris McCleery, Director of Central & Leisure Services, Riada House, 14 Charles Street, Ballymoney BT53 6DZ ☎ 028 2766 0200 🖷 028 2766 0222 iris.mccleery@ballymoney.gov.uk

Town Centre: Mrs Joanne McLaughlin, Town Centre Project Officer, Riada House, 14 Charles Street, Ballymoney BT53 6DZ ☎ 028 2766 0238 🖷 028 2766 3852 tcm@ballymoney.gov.uk

Waste Collection and Disposal: Mr John Michael, Director of Borough Services, Riada House, 14 Charles Street, Ballymoney BT53 6DZ ☎ 028 2766 0257 🖷 028 2766 0222 john.michael@ballymoney.gov.uk

Waste Management: Mr John Michael, Director of Borough Services, Riada House, 14 Charles Street, Ballymoney BT53 6DZ ☎ 028 2766 0257 🖷 028 2766 0222 john.michael@ballymoney.gov.uk

MEMBERS OF THE COUNCIL (16)

***Mayor:* Stevenson**, Ian (DUP - Ballymoney Town)
ian.stevenson@ballymoney.gov.uk
***Deputy Mayor:* McKeown**, Thomas (UUP - Ballymoney Town)
thomas.mckeown@ballymoney.gov.uk
***Group Leader:* Blair**, William (O - Bunn Valley)
william.blair@ballymoney.gov.uk
***Group Leader:* Finlay**, John (DUP - Bann Valley)
john.finlay@ballymoney.gov.uk
***Group Leader:* McGuigan**, Philip (SF - Bann Valley)
philipmcguigan@hotmail.com
***Alderman:* Campbell**, Frank (DUP - Bushvale)
frank.campbell@ballymoney.gov.uk
***Alderman:* Connolly**, Harry (SDLP - Bushvale)
harry.connolly@btopenworld.com
***Alderman:* Cousley**, Cecil (DUP - Ballymoney Town)
cecil.cousley@ballymoney.gov.uk
***Alderman:* Kennedy**, William (DUP - Bushvale)
wtkennedy@btopenworld.com
Atkinson, Jason (DUP - Bunn Valley)
jason.atkinson@ballymoney.gov.uk
Cavlan, Anita (IND - Bushvale)
Halliday, Robert (DUP - Bann Valley)
McAfee, Roma (IND - Ballmoney Town)
McLaughlin, Cathal (SF - Bann Valley)
Robinson, Evelyne (DUP - Bushvale)
evelyne.robinson@ballymoney.gov.uk
Storey, Mervyn (DUP - Ballymoney Town)
mervynstorey@btconnect.com

POLITICAL COMPOSITION

DUP: 9, IND: 2, SF: 2, SDLP: 1, UUP: 1, O: 1

COMMITTEE CHAIRS

Corporate & Central Services: Mr Cecil Cousley
Development: Mr John Finlay
Health & Environment Services: Mrs Evelyne Robinson
Leisure & Amenities: Mr Frank Campbell

BANBRIDGE N

Banbridge District Council, Civic Building, Downshire Road, Banbridge BT32 3JY ☎ 028 4066 0600 🖷 028 4066 0601 info@banbridge.gov.uk www.banbridge.gov.uk

FACTS & FIGURES

Police Authority: Northern Ireland Policing Board
Health Authority: Southern Health & Social Care Board
Learning and Skills Council: Northern Ireland
Parliamentary Constituencies: Down South, Lagan Valley, Upper Bann
EU Constituencies: Northern Ireland
Election Frequency: Elections are of whole council
Twinning: Carlow (Ireland); Ruelle (France); Dromore: Drumore, Pennsylvania (USA)

PRINCIPAL OFFICERS

Chief Executive: Mr Liam Hannaway, Chief Executive, Civic Building, Downshire Road, Banbridge BT32 3JY ☎ 028 4066 0602 🖷 028 4066 0661 liam.hannaway@banbridge.gov.uk

Best Value: Mr Pat Cumiskey, Director of Corporate Services, Civic Building, Downshire Road, Banbridge BT32 3JY ☎ 028 4066 0600 🖷 028 4066 0601 pat.cumiskey@banbridge.gov.uk

Building Control: Mr Kevin Fitzsimons, Head of Building & Techical Services, Civic Building, Downshire Road, Banbridge BT32 3JY ☎ 028 4066 0603 🖷 028 4066 0601 kevin.fitzsimons@banbridge.gov.uk

Building Control: Mr David Lindsay, Director of Environmental Services, Civic Building, Downshire Road, Banbridge BT32 3JY ☎ 028 4066 0604 david.lindsay@banbridge.gov.uk

Civil Registration: Mrs Elaine Gilmour, Registrar, Civic Building, Downshire Road, Banbridge BT32 3JY ☎ 028 4066 0614 🖷 028 4066 0601 elaine.gilmour@banbridge.gov.uk

PR / Communications: Ms Sharon Harrison, Corporate

Marketing Officer, Civic Building, Downshire Road, Banbridge BT32 3JY ☎ 028 4066 0619 🖷 028 4066 0601 🖰 sharon.harrison@banbridge.gov.uk

Community Planning: Mrs Elaine Gillespie, Head of Community Planning, Civic Building, Downshire Road, Banbridge BT32 3JY ☎ 028 4066 0644 🖷 028 4066 0601 🖰 elaine.gillespie@banbridge.gov.uk

Community Safety: Mrs Rhonda Abraham, Community Safety Officer, Civic Building, Downshire Road, Banbridge BT32 3JY ☎ 028 4066 0609 🖷 028 4066 0601 🖰 rhonda.abraham@banbridge.gov.uk

Community Safety: Mrs Alison Beattie, Community Safety Officer, Civic Building, Downshire Road, Banbridge BT32 3JY ☎ 028 4066 0609 🖷 028 4066 0601 🖰 alison.beattie@banbridge.gov.uk

Community Safety: Mrs Pamela Matthews, Head of Community Services, Civic Building, Downshire Road, Banbridge BT32 3JY ☎ 028 4066 0605 🖰 pamela.matthews@banbridge.gov.uk

Consumer Protection and Trading Standards: Mrs Jill Boyd, Environmental Health Officer, Gate Lodge, Linenhall Street, Banbridge BT32 3EG ☎ 028 4066 0606 🖷 028 4066 0651 🖰 jill.boyd@banbridge.gov.uk

Corporate Services: Mr Pat Cumiskey, Director of Corporate Services, Civic Building, Downshire Road, Banbridge BT32 3JY ☎ 028 4066 0600 🖷 028 4066 0601 🖰 pat.cumiskey@banbridge.gov.uk

Economic Development: Ms Therese Rafferty, Head of Regeneration, Civic Building, Downshire Road, Banbridge BT32 3JY ☎ 028 4066 0609 🖷 028 4066 0601 🖰 therese.rafferty@banbridge.gov.uk

Emergency Planning: Mr Liam Hannaway, Chief Executive, Civic Building, Downshire Road, Banbridge BT32 3JY ☎ 028 4066 0602 🖷 028 4066 0661 🖰 liam.hannaway@banbridge.gov.uk

Energy Management: Mr Pat Cumiskey, Director of Corporate Services, Civic Building, Downshire Road, Banbridge BT32 3JY ☎ 028 4066 0600 🖷 028 4066 0601 🖰 pat.cumiskey@banbridge.gov.uk

Environmental / Technical Services: Mr David Lindsay, Director of Environmental Services, Civic Building, Downshire Road, Banbridge BT32 3JY ☎ 028 4066 0604 🖷 028 4066 0601 🖰 david.lindsay@banbridge.gov.uk

Environmental Health: Mr David Lindsay, Director of Environmental Services, Civic Building, Downshire Road, Banbridge BT32 3JY ☎ 028 4066 0604 🖷 028 4066 0601 🖰 david.lindsay@banbridge.gov.uk

Environmental Health: Mrs Gillian Topping, Head of Environmental Health, Civic Building, Downshire Road, Banbridge BT32 3JY ☎ 028 4066 0604 🖷 028 4066 0601 🖰 gillian.topping@banbridge.gov.uk

Events Manager: Mrs Danielle Fegan, Events Officer, Civic Building, Downshire Road, Banbridge BT32 3JY ☎ 028 4066 0605 🖰 danielle.fegan@banbridge.gov.uk

Facilities: Mrs Sharon Currans, Head of Human Resources, Civic Building, Downshire Road, Banbridge BT32 3JY ☎ 028 4066 0608 🖷 028 4066 0601 🖰 sharon.currans@banbridge.gov.uk

Finance and Treasurer: Mr Pat Cumiskey, Director of Corporate Services, Civic Building, Downshire Road, Banbridge BT32 3JY ☎ 028 4066 0600 🖷 028 4066 0601 🖰 pat.cumiskey@banbridge.gov.uk

Health and Safety: Mrs Jill Boyd, Environmental Health Officer, Gate Lodge, Linenhall Street, Banbridge BT32 3EG ☎ 028 4066 0606 🖷 028 4066 0651 🖰 jill.boyd@banbridge.gov.uk

Leisure and Cultural Services: Mr Ben Corr, Head of Leisure Services, Civic Building, Downshire Road, Banbridge BT32 3JY ☎ 028 4066 0605 🖰 ben.corr@banbridge.gov.uk

Leisure and Cultural Services: Mrs Catriona Regan, Director of Community & Enterprise Services, Civic Building, Downshire Road, Banbridge BT32 3JY ☎ 028 4066 0605 🖷 028 4066 0601 🖰 catriona.regan@banbridge.gov.uk

Member Services: Mrs Dawn McDowell, Head of Member Services, Civic Building, Downshire Road, Banbridge BT32 3JY ☎ 028 4066 0602 🖷 028 4066 0661 🖰 dawn.mcdowell@banbridge.gov.uk

Personnel / HR: Mrs Sharon Currans, Head of Human Resources, Civic Building, Downshire Road, Banbridge BT32 3JY ☎ 028 4066 0608 🖷 028 4066 0601 🖰 sharon.currans@banbridge.gov.uk

Procurement: Mr Pat Cumiskey, Director of Corporate Services, Civic Building, Downshire Road, Banbridge BT32 3JY ☎ 028 4066 0600 🖷 028 4066 0601 🖰 pat.cumiskey@banbridge.gov.uk

Recycling & Waste Minimisation: Mr David Lindsay, Director of Environmental Services, Civic Building, Downshire Road, Banbridge BT32 3JY ☎ 028 4066 0604 🖷 028 4066 0601 🖰 david.lindsay@banbridge.gov.uk

Regeneration: Ms Therese Rafferty, Head of Regeneration, Civic Building, Downshire Road, Banbridge BT32 3JY ☎ 028 4066 0609 🖷 028 4066 0601 🖰 therese.rafferty@banbridge.gov.uk

Staff Training: Mrs Sharon Currans, Head of Human Resources, Civic Building, Downshire Road, Banbridge BT32 3JY ☎ 028 4066 0608 🖷 028 4066 0601 🖰 sharon.currans@banbridge.gov.uk

Sustainable Communities: Mrs Pamela Matthews, Head of Community Services, Civic Building, Downshire Road, Banbridge BT32 3JY ☎ 028 4066 0605 🖰 pamela.matthews@banbridge.gov.uk

Sustainable Development: Mr David Lindsay, Director of Environmental Services, Civic Building, Downshire Road, Banbridge BT32 3JY ☎ 028 4066 0604 🖷 028 4066 0601

david.lindsay@banbridge.gov.uk

Tourism: Mr John Douglas, Tourist Officer, Civic Building, Downshire Road, Banbridge BT32 3JY ☎ 028 4066 0609 🖷 028 4066 0601 john.douglas@banbridge.gov.uk

Town Centre: Mrs Mechelle Brown, Town Centre Manager, Civic Building, Downshire Road, Banbridge BT32 3JY ☎ 028 4066 2668 🖷 028 4066 0601 mb@banbridgetowncentre.com

Waste Collection and Disposal: Mr David Lindsay, Director of Environmental Services, Civic Building, Downshire Road, Banbridge BT32 3JY ☎ 028 4066 0604 🖷 028 4066 0601 david.lindsay@banbridge.gov.uk

Waste Management: Mr David Lindsay, Director of Environmental Services, Civic Building, Downshire Road, Banbridge BT32 3JY ☎ 028 4066 0604 🖷 028 4066 0601 david.lindsay@banbridge.gov.uk

MEMBERS OF THE COUNCIL (17)
***Chair:* Baird**, Joan (UUP - Banbridge)
Barr, Glenn (UUP - knockiveagh)
Black, Carol (UUP - Dromore)
Burns, Ian (UUP - Banbridge)
Curran, Brendan (SF - Knockiveagh)
Doyle, Seamus (SDLP - Knockiveagh)
Gamble, Hazel (DUP - Dromore)
Gribben, Paul (SF - Dromore)
Hamilton, Marie (SDLP - Banbridge)
Hanna, John (UUP - Knockiveagh)
Herron, David (DUP - Knockiveagh)
Ingram, Elizabeth (UUP - Knockiveagh)
McCrum, Junior (DUP - Banbridge)
McElroy, Jim (DUP - Banbridge)
McQuaid, Sheila (ALL - Banbridge)
Mercer, Olive (UUP - Dromore)
Rankin, Paul (DUP - Dromore)

POLITICAL COMPOSITION
UUP: 7, DUP: 5, SF: 2, SDLP: 2, ALL: 1

BARKING & DAGENHAM L

Barking & Dagenham London Borough Council, Civic Centre, Dagenham RM10 7BN ☎ 020 8215 3000 🖷 020 8227 5184; 020 8227 2806 3000direct@lbbd.gov.uk www.lbbd.gov.uk

FACTS & FIGURES
Police Authority: Metropolitan Police Authority
Health Authority: NHS London
Learning and Skills Council: London
Parliamentary Constituencies: Barking, Dagenham and Rainham
EU Constituencies: London
Election Frequency: Elections are of whole council
Twinning: Witten (Germany)

PRINCIPAL OFFICERS
Chief Executive: Mr Graham Farrant, Chief Executive, Civic Offices, New Road, Grays RM17 6SL ☎ 01375 652652 gfarrant@thurrock.gov.uk

Senior Management: Ms Anne Bristow, Corporate Director - Adult & Community Services, Barking Town Hall, 1 Town Square, Barking IG11 7LU ☎ 020 8227 2300 anne.bristow@lbbd.gov.uk

Senior Management: Ms Tracie Evans, Corporate Director - Finance & Commercial Services, Town Hall, 1 Town Square, Barking IG11 7LU ☎ 020 8227 2932 tracie.evans@lbbd.gov.uk

Senior Management: Ms Helen Jenner, Corporate Director - Children's Services, Town Hall, 1 Town Square, Barking IG11 7LU ☎ 020 8227 5800 🖷 020 8227 3274 helen.jenner@lbbd.gov.uk

Senior Management: Mr Ken Jones, Divisional Director Housing Strategy, Town Hall, 1 Town Square, Barking IG11 7LU ☎ 020 8227 5703 ken.jones@lbbd.gov.uk

Senior Management: Ms Stella Manzie, Chief Executive, Barking Town Hall, 1 Town Square, Barking IG11 7LU ☎ 020 8227 2789 🖷 020 8227 3274 stella.manzie@lbbd.gov.uk

Architect, Building / Property Services: Ms Julie Bateman, Development Manager, Civic Centre, Dagenham RM10 7BN ☎ 020 8227 3849 julie.bateman@lbbd.gov.uk

Building Control: Mr Daniel Pope, Group Manager - Development & Planning, Civic Centre, Dagenham RM10 7BN ☎ 020 8227 3933 daniel.pope@lbbd.gov.uk

Catering Services: Ms Maureen Lowes, Catering Services Manager, Town Hall, 1 Town Square, Barking IG11 7LU ☎ 020 8227 5505 🖷 020 8227 5562 maureen.lowes@lbbd.gov.uk

Children / Youth Services: Ms Meena Kishinani, Divisional Director - Strategic Commissioning & Safeguarding, Town Hall, 1 Town Square, Barking IG11 7LU ☎ 020 8227 3507 🖷 020 8227 3274 meena.kishinani@lbbd.gov.uk

Civil Registration: Ms Cheryl Davis, Superintendent Registrar, Civic Centre, Dagenham RM10 7BN ☎ 020 8270 4742 cheryl.davis@lbbd.gov.uk

Community Planning: Mr Amir Rashid, Group Manager Performance & Innovation, Civic Centre, Dagenham RM10 7BN ☎ 020 8227 2317 amir.rashid@lbbd.gov.uk

Community Safety: Ms Glynis Rogers, Corporate Director - Community Safety and Public Protection, Civic Centre, Dagenham RM10 7BN ☎ 020 8227 2827 glynis.rogers@lbbd.gov.uk

Computer Management: Ms Katherine Maddock-Lyon, Divisional Director - Customer Strategy, ICT & Transformation, Barking Town Hall, 1 Town Square, Barking IG11 7LU ☎ 020 8227 5730 katherine.maddock-lyon@lbbd.gov.uk

Consumer Protection and Trading Standards: Mr Darren Henaghan, Corporate Director - Customer Services, Barking Town Hall, 1 Town Square, Barking IG11 7LU ☎ 020 8227 5660 🖷 020 8227 2608 darren.henaghan@lbbd.gov.uk

Consumer Protection and Trading Standards: Mr Chris Martin,

Divisional Director - Children's Complex Needs & Social Care, Town Hall, 1 Town Square, Barking IG11 7LU ☎ 020 8227 2233 ✉ chris.martin@lbbd.gov.uk

Customer Service: Mr Robin Payne, Divisional Director - Environment, Civic Centre, Dagenham RM10 7BN ☎ 020 8227 5730 ✉ robin.payne@lbbd.gov.uk

Education: Ms Jane Hargreaves, Divisional Director - Education, Roycraft House, 15 Linton Road, Barking IG11 7LU ☎ 020 8227 2686 ✉ jane.hargreaves@lbbd.gov.uk

Education: Ms Helen Jenner, Corporate Director - Children's Services, Town Hall, 1 Town Square, Barking IG11 7LU ☎ 020 8227 5800 🖷 020 8227 3274 ✉ helen.jenner@lbbd.gov.uk

E-Government: Ms Katherine Maddock-Lyon, Divisional Director - Customer Strategy, ICT & Transformation, Barking Town Hall, 1 Town Square, Barking IG11 7LU ☎ 020 8227 5730 ✉ katherine.maddock-lyon@lbbd.gov.uk

Electoral Registration: Mr John Dawe, Group Manager - Democratic Services, Room 195, Civic Centre, Dagenham RM10 7BN ☎ 020 8227 2135 🖷 020 8227 2171 ✉ john.dawe@lbbd.gov.uk

Emergency Planning: Mr Danny Caine, Head - Emergency Planning, Civic Centre, Dagenham RM10 7BN ☎ 020 8227 3363 ✉ danny.caine@Lbbd.gov.uk

Environmental / Technical Services: Ms Sue Lees, Divisional Director - Asset Management & Capital Delivery, Town Hall, 1 Town Square, Barking IG11 7LU ☎ 0845 313 3932 🖷 020 8227 3231 ✉ sue.lees@elevateeastlondon.co.uk

Environmental Health: Mr Darren Henaghan, Corporate Director - Customer Services, Town Hall, 1 Town Square, Barking IG11 7LU ☎ 020 8227 5660 🖷 020 8227 2608 ✉ darren.henaghan@lbbd.gov.uk

Estates, Property & Valuation: Mr Kevin Sullivan, Group Manager - Asset Management, Town Hall, Barking IG11 7LU ☎ 020 8724 3258 ✉ kevin.sullivan@lbbd.gov.uk

Events Manager: Ms Janice Hunte, Events Manager, Maritime House, Barking IG11 8HG ☎ 020 8227 3093 ✉ janice.hunte@lbbd.gov.uk

Facilities: Ms Sue Lees, Divisional Director - Asset Management & Capital Delivery, Town Hall, 1 Town Square, Barking IG11 7LU ☎ 0845 313 3932 🖷 020 8227 3231 ✉ sue.lees@elevateeastlondon.co.uk

Fleet Management: Mr Peter Jackman, Fleet Manager, Frizland Depot, Frizlands Lane, Dagenham RM10 7HX ☎ 020 8227 2610 🖷 020 8227 2221 ✉ peter.jackman@lbbd.gov.uk

Health and Safety: Mr Gary Frost, Manager - Health, Safety & Wellbeing, Civic Centre, Dagenham RM10 7BN ☎ 020 8227 3073 🖷 020 8227 2806 ✉ gary.frost@lbbd.gov.uk

Housing: Mr James Goddard, Group Manager - Housing Strategy, Roycroft House, Linton Road, Barking IG11 8HE ☎ 020 8724 8238 ✉ james.goddard@lbbd.gov.uk

Housing Maintenance: Mr Rob Wood, Group Manager - Repairs & Maintenance, Pondfield House, 100 Wantz Road, Dagenham RM10 8PP ☎ 020 8724 8831 🖷 020 8984 4051 ✉ rob.wood@lbbd.gov.uk

Local Area Agreement: Mr Timothy Pearce, Customer Strategy, Civic Centre, Dagenham RM10 7BN ☎ 020 8227 5003 ✉ timothy.pearce@lbbd.gov.uk

Legal: Ms Tasnim Shawkat, Divisional Director - Legal & Democratic Services, Room 152, Civic Centre, Dagenham RM10 7BN ☎ 020 8227 2114 🖷 020 8227 2279 ✉ tasmin.shawkat@lbbd.gov.uk

Leisure and Cultural Services: Mr Paul Hogan, Divisional Director - Culture & Sport, Maritime House, Barking IG11 8HG ☎ 020 8227 3576 ✉ paul.hogan@lbbd.gov.uk

Licensing: Ms Sajida Majid, Licensing Officer, Roycraft House, Linton Road, Barking IG11 8HE ☎ 020 8724 5677 🖷 020 8227 5699 ✉ sajida.majid@lbbd.gov.uk

Member Services: Ms Belinda Lee, PA to the Leader, Civic Centre, Dagenham RM10 7BN ☎ 020 8724 8448 ✉ belinda.lee@lbbd.gov.uk

Personnel / HR: Mr Martin Rayson, Divisional Director - Human Resources & OD, Town Hall, 1 Town Square, Barking IG11 7LU ☎ 020 8227 3113 ✉ martin.rayson@lbbd.gov.uk

Planning: Mr Jeremy Grint, Divisional Director - Regeneration, Barking Town Hall, Barking IG11 7LU ☎ 020 8227 2443 🖷 020 8227 5326 ✉ jeremy.grint@lbbd.gov.uk

Recycling & Waste Minimisation: Mr Abdul Jallow, Waste Strategy & Recycling Manager, Frizlands Depot, Frizlands Lane, Dagenham RM10 7HX ☎ 020 8227 2657 🖷 020 8227 2221 ✉ abdul.jallow@lbbd.gov.uk

Regeneration: Mr Jeremy Grint, Divisional Director - Regeneration, Barking Town Hall, 1 Town Square, Barking IG11 7LU ☎ 020 8227 2443 🖷 020 8227 5326 ✉ jeremy.grint@lbbd.gov.uk

Social Services: Ms Anne Bristow, Corporate Director - Adult & Community Services, Barking Town Hall, 1 Town Square, Barking IG11 7LU ☎ 020 8227 2300 ✉ anne.bristow@lbbd.gov.uk

Social Services: Mr David Horne, Joint Director - NELFT, The Hedgecock Centre, Upney Lane, Barking IG11 9LX ☎ 0300 555 1201 ✉ david.horne@lbbd.gov.uk

Social Services: Ms Christine Pryor, Divisional Director - Targeted Support, Bridge House, 150 London Road, Barking IG11 8BB ☎ 020 8227 5552 ✉ christine.pryor@lbbd.gov.uk

Social Services (Adult): Ms Karen Ahmed, Divisional Director - Adult Commissioning, Town Hall, 1 Town Square, Barking IG11 7LU ☎ 020 8227 2331 ✉ karen.ahmed@lbbd.gov.uk

Social Services (Adult): Mr Bruce Morris, Divisional Director - Adult Social Care, Town Hall, 1 Town Square, Barking IG11 7LU ☎ 020 8227 2749 ✉ bruce.morris@lbbd.gov.uk

Social Services (Children): Ms Helen Jenner, Corporate Director - Children's Services, Town Hall, 1 Town Square, Barking IG11 7LU ☎ 020 8227 5800 🖷 020 8227 3274 ✉ helen.jenner@lbbd.gov.uk

Sustainable Communities: Mr Jeremy Grint, Divisional Director - Regeneration, Barking Town Hall, 1 Town Square, Barking IG11 7LU ☎ 020 8227 2443 🖷 020 8227 5326 ✉ jeremy.grint@lbbd.gov.uk

Sustainable Development: Mr Jeremy Grint, Divisional Director - Regeneration, Barking Town Hall, 1 Town Square, Barking IG11 7LU ☎ 020 8227 2443 🖷 020 8227 5326 ✉ jeremy.grint@lbbd.gov.uk

Town Centre: Mr Ralph Cook, Manager - Market Contracts, 53a East Street, Barking IG11 8EN ☎ 020 8227 6015 🖷 020 8270 6048 ✉ ralph.cook@lbbd.gov.uk

Transport: Ms Ruth Du-Lieu, Group Manager - Waste & Street Scene Strategy, Frizlands Depot, Frizlands Lane, Dagenham RM10 7BN ☎ 020 8227 2641 🖷 020 8227 2221 ✉ ruth.dulieu@lbbd.gov.uk

Transport Planner: Mr Jeremy Grint, Divisional Director - Regeneration, Barking Town Hall, 1 Town Square, Barking IG11 7LU ☎ 020 8227 2443 🖷 020 8227 5326 ✉ jeremy.grint@lbbd.gov.uk

Waste Collection and Disposal: Mr Abdul Jallow, Waste Strategy & Recycling Manager, Frizlands Depot, Frizlands Lane, Dagenham RM10 7HX ☎ 020 8227 2657 🖷 020 8227 2221 ✉ abdul.jallow@lbbd.gov.uk

Waste Management: Mr Abdul Jallow, Waste Strategy & Recycling Manager, Frizlands Depot, Frizlands Lane, Dagenham RM10 7HX ☎ 020 8227 2657 🖷 020 8227 2221 ✉ abdul.jallow@lbbd.gov.uk

MEMBERS OF THE COUNCIL (51)

***Mayor:* Ramsay**, Tony (LAB - Eastbrook)
tony.ramsay@lbbd.gov.uk
***Deputy Chair:* Davis**, John (LAB - Alibon)
john.davis@lbbd.gov.uk
***Leader of the Council:* Smith**, Liam (LAB - River)
leader@lbbd.gov.uk
Alasia, Sanchia (LAB - Alibon)
sanchia.alasia@lbbd.gov.uk
Alexander, Jeannette (LAB - Eastbury)
jeannette.alexander@lbbd.gov.uk
Asraf, Saima (LAB - Gascoigne)
saima.ashraf@lbbd.gov.uk
Baldwin, Ralph (CON - Mayesbrook)
ralph.baldwin@lbbd.gov.uk
Barratt, George (IND - Mayesbrook)
george.barratt@lbbd.gov.uk
Bremmer, Simon (LAB - Goresbrook)
Burgon, Pam (LAB - Eastbrook)
pam.burgon2@lbbd.gov.uk
Butt, Laila (LAB - Abbey)
laila.butt@lbbd.gov.uk
Carpenter, Evelyn (LAB - Becontree)
evelyn.carpenter@lbbd.gov.uk
Channer, Josephine (LAB - Thames)
josephine.channer@lbbd.gov.uk
Clee, Jim (LAB - Goresbrook)
jim.clee@lbbd.gov.uk
Collins, Herbert (LAB - Parsloes)
herbert.collins@lbbd.gov.uk
Douglas, Rob (LAB - Becontree)
rob.douglas@lbbd.gov.uk
Gafoor Aziz, Abdul (LAB - Gascoigne)
abdul.gafooraziz@lbbd.gov.uk
Geddes, Cameron (LAB - Thames)
cameron.geddes2@lbbd.gov.uk
Gill, Rocky (LAB - Longbridge)
rocky.gill@lbbd.gov.uk
Gill, Nirmal (LAB - Longbridge)
nirmal.gill@lbbd.gov.uk
Hunt, Dee (LAB - Mayesbrook)
dee.hunt@lbbd.gov.uk
Hussain, Manzoor (LAB - Abbey)
manzoor.hussain@lbbd.gov.uk
Jamu, Inder (LAB - River)
indersingh.jamu@lbbd.gov.uk
Jamu, Amardeep (LAB - Whalebone)
amardeep.jamu@lbbd.gov.uk
Kangethe, Elizabeth (LAB - Parsloes)
elizabeth.kangethe@lbbd.gov.uk
Keller, Eileen (LAB - River)
eileen.keller2@lbbd.gov.uk
Letchford, Graham (LAB - Goresbrook)
graham.letchford@lbbd.gov.uk
McCarthy, Mick (LAB - Eastbrook)
mick.mccarthy@lbbd.gov.uk
McDermott, James (LAB - Eastbury)
james.mcdermott@lbbd.gov.uk
McKenzie, Milton (LAB - Chadwell Heath)
milton.mckenzie@lbbd.gov.uk
Miles, Dave (LAB - Heath)
dave.miles2@lbbd.gov.uk
Mullane, Margaret (LAB - Village)
margaret.mullane@lbbd.gov.uk
Obasohan, Emmanuel (LAB - Valence)
emmanuel.obasohan@lbbd.gov.uk
Ogungbose, James (LAB - Becontree)
james.ogungbose@lbbd.gov.uk
Perry, Tony (LAB - Whalebone)
tony.perry@lbbd.gov.uk
Poulton, Barry (LAB - Thames)
barry.poulton@lbbd.gov.uk
Rai, Hardial (LAB - Eastbury)
hardialsingh.rai@lbbd.gov.uk
Reason, Linda (LAB - Heath)
linda.reason2@lbbd.gov.uk
Rice, Lynda (LAB - Longbridge)
lynda.rice@lbbd.gov.uk
Rice, Chris (LAB - Parsloes)
chris.rice@lbbd.gov.uk
Rodwell, Darren (LAB - Alibon)
darren.rodwell@lbbd.gov.uk
Saeed, Tariq (LAB - Abbey)
tariq.saeed@lbbd.gov.uk
Salam, Abdus (LAB - Valence)
abdus.salam@lbbd.gov.uk

Tarry, Sam (LAB - Chadwell Heath)
sam.tarry@lbbd.gov.uk
Twomey, Dominic (LAB - Gascoigne)
dominic.twomey@lbbd.gov.uk
Vincent, Gerald (LAB - Heath)
gerald.vincent@lbbd.gov.uk
Wade, Jeff (LAB - Chadwell Heath)
jeff.wade@lbbd.gov.uk
Waker, Lee (LAB - Village)
lee.waker@lbbd.gov.uk
Waker, Philip (LAB - Village)
philip.waker@lbbd.gov.uk
White, John (LAB - Whalebone)
john.white@lbbd.gov.uk
Worby, Maureen (LAB - Valence)
maureen.worby@lbbd.gov.uk

POLITICAL COMPOSITION
LAB: 49, CON: 1, IND: 1

CABINET
Leader: Mr Liam Smith
Deputy Leader: Mr Rocky Gill
Crime, Justice & Communities: Mrs Jeannette Alexander
Culture, Leisure & Sport: Mr Herbert Collins
Customer Services & Human Resources: Mr John White
Environment: Mr Mick McCarthy
Finance & Education: Mr Rocky Gill
Health: Ms Maureen Worby
Housing: Mr Philip Waker
Regeneration: Mr Cameron Geddes

COMMITTEE CHAIRS
Assembly: Mr Nirmal Gill
Barking & Dagenham Partership: Ms Maureen Worby
Children's Services: Mr Graham Letchford
Development Control Board: Mr Inder Jamu
Health & Adult Services: Ms Sanchia Alasia
Licensing & Regulatory Board: Mr Lee Waker
Living & Working: Ms Josephine Channer
Pensions: Mr Rocky Gill
Personnel Board: Mrs Pam Burgon
Public Accounts & Audit: Mr Amardeep Jamu
Safer & Stronger Community: Ms Margaret Mullane

BARNET — L

London Borough of Barnet, (London Borough of Barnet), Building 4, North London Business Park, Oakleigh Road South, London N11 1NP ☎ 020 8359 2000 🖷 0871 911 6188 ✉ first.contact@barnet.gov.uk 💻 www.barnet.gov.uk

FACTS & FIGURES
Police Authority: Metropolitan Police Authority
Health Authority: NHS London
Learning and Skills Council: London
Parliamentary Constituencies: Chipping Barnet, Finchley and Golders Green, Hendon
EU Constituencies: London
Election Frequency: Elections are of whole council
Twinning: Chaville and Le Raincy (France); Jinja (Uganda); Montclair, New Jersey (USA); Morphou (Cyprus); Ramat Gan (Israel); Siegen-Wittgenstein (Germany); Tempelhof-Schoneberg (Germany)

PRINCIPAL OFFICERS
Chief Executive: Mr Nick Walkley, Chief Executive, Building 2, North London Business Park, Oakleigh Road South, New Southgate, London N11 1NP ✉ nick.walkley@barnet.gov.uk

Deputy Chief Executive: Mr Andrew Travers, Deputy Chief Executive, Building 2, North London Business Park, Oakleigh Road South, New Southgate, London N11 1NP ✉ andrew.travers@barnet.gov.uk

Assistant Chief Executive: Ms Julie Taylor, Assistant Chief Executive, Building 2, North London Business Park, Oakleigh Road South, New Southgate, London N11 1NP ✉ julie.taylor@barnet.gov.uk

Senior Management: Mr Craig Cooper, Commercial Director, Building 4, North London Business Park, Oakleigh Road South, New Southgate, London N11 1NP ✉ craig.cooper@barnet.gov.uk

Senior Management: Ms Kate Kennally, Director of Adult Social Care & Health, Building 4, North London Business Park, Oakleigh Road South, New Southgate, London N11 1NP ✉ kate.kennally@barnet.gov.uk

Senior Management: Mr Jeff Lustig, Director of Corporate Governance & Monitoring Officer, Building 4, North London Business Park, Oakleigh Road South, New Southgate, London N11 1NP ✉ jeff.lustig@barnet.gov.uk

Senior Management: Mr Robert McCulloch-Graham, Director of Children's Services, Building 4, North London Business Park, Oakleigh Road South, New Southgate, London N11 1NP ✉ robert.mcculloch-graham@barnet.gov.uk

Senior Management: Ms Pam Wharfe, Interim Director of Planning & Environment, Building 4, North London Business Park, Oakleigh Road South, New Southgate, London N11 1NP ✉ pamela.wharfe@barnet.gov.uk

Catering Services: Ms Teresa Goodall, Catering Services Manager, Building 4, North London Business Park, Oakleigh Road South, New Southgate, London N11 1NP ✉ teresa.goodall@barnet.gov.uk

Children / Youth Services: Ms Ann Graham, Assistant Director - Children's Social Care, Building 4, North London Business Park, Oakleigh Road South, New Southgate, London N11 1NP ✉ ann.graham@barnet.gov.uk

Children / Youth Services: Mr Jay Mercer, Deputy Director - Safeguarding, Prevention & Partnership, Building 4, North London Business Park, Oakleigh Road South, New Southgate, London N11 1NP ✉ jay.mercer@barnet.gov.uk

Children / Youth Services: Mr Mick Quigley, Assistant Director - Schools & Learning, Building 4, North London Business Park, Oakleigh Road South, New Southgate, London N11 1NP ✉ mick.quigley@barnet.gov.uk

Children / Youth Services: Ms Valerie White, Assistant Director - Policy, Performance & Planning, Building 4, North London Business Park, Oakleigh Road South, New Southgate, London N11 1NP 🖱 val.white@barnet.gov.uk

Civil Registration: Mr Mark Rimmer, Head of Registration, Barnet Register Office, 182 Burnt Oak Broadway, Edgware HA8 0AU 🖱 mark.rimmer@barnet.gov.uk

PR / Communications: Mr Chris Palmer, Assistant Director - Communications, Building 4, North London Business Park, Oakleigh Road South, London N11 1NP 🖱 chris.palmer@barnet.gov.uk

Computer Management: Mr Andrew Gee, Head of I.S. Service Delivery, Building 4, North London Business Park, Oakleigh Road South, London N11 1NP 🖱 andrew.gee@barnet.gov.uk

Consumer Protection and Trading Standards: Ms Emma Phasey, Trading Standards / Licensing Manager, Building 4, North London Business Park, Oakleigh Road South, New Southgate, London N11 1NP 🖱 emma.phasey@barnet.gov.uk

Corporate Services: Mr Tom Pike, Head of Corporate Performance, Building 2, North London Business Park, Oakleigh Road South, New Southgate, London N11 1NP 🖱 tom.pike@barnet.gov.uk

Customer Service: Mrs Lauren Doody, Head of Customer Services & Libraries, Building 4, North London Business Park, Oakleigh Road South, London N11 1NP 🖱 lauren.doody@barnet.gov.uk

Customer Service: Mr Bill Murphy, Assistant Director - Customer Services & Libraries, Building 2, North London Business Park, Oakleigh Road South, New Southgate, London N11 1NP 🖱 bill.murphy@barnet.gov.uk

Education: Mr Mick Quigley, Assistant Director - Schools & Learning, Building 4, North London Business Park, Oakleigh Road South, New Southgate, London N11 1NP 🖱 mick.quigley@barnet.gov.uk

Electoral Registration: Mr Jeff Lustig, Director of Corporate Governance, Building 4, North London Business Park, Oakleigh Road South, London N11 1NP 🖱 jeff.lustig@barnet.gov.uk

Environmental Health: Mr Rick Mason, Assistant Director - Environmental Health, Building 4, North London Business Park, Oakleigh Road South, London N11 1NP 🖱 rick.mason@barnet.gov.uk

Facilities: Mr Jeff Mazzoni, Facilities Manager, Building 2, North London Business Park, Oakleigh Road South, New Southgate, London N11 1NP 🖱 jeff.mazzoni@barnet.gov.uk

Finance and Treasurer: Ms Maria Christofi, Assistant Director - Financial Services, Building 4, North London Business Park, Oakleigh Road South, New Southgate, London N11 1NP 🖱 maria.christofi@barnet.gov.uk

Finance and Treasurer: Mr John Hooton, Assistant Director - Strategic Finance, Building 4, North London Business Park, Oakleigh Road South, London N11 1NP 🖱 john.hooton@barnet.gov.uk

Finance and Treasurer: Ms Maryellen Salter, Assistant Director - Audit & Risk Management, Building 4, North London Business Park, Oakleigh Road South, London N11 1NP 🖱 maryellen.salter@barnet.gov.uk

Fleet Management: Mr Declan Hoare, Assistant Director - Highways & Transport, Building 4, North London Business Park, Oakleigh Road South, London N11 1NP 🖱 declan.hoare@barnet.gov.uk

Fleet Management: Mr Bernard McGreevy, Transport Services, Mill Hill Depot, Bittacy Hill, Mill Hill, London NW7 1BL 🖱 bernard.mcgreevy@barnet.gov.uk

Grounds Maintenance: Mrs Lynn Bishop, Assistant Director - Environment, Building 4, North London Business Park, Oakleigh Road South, London N11 1NP 🖱 lynn.bishop@barnet.gov.uk

Health and Safety: Mr Mike Koumi, Head of Health, Safety & Wellbeing, Building 4, North London Business Park, Oakleigh Road South, London N11 1NP 🖱 mike.houmi@barnet.gov.uk

Highways: Mr Declan Hoare, Assistant Director - Highways & Transport, Building 4, North London Business Park, Oakleigh Road South, London N11 1NP 🖱 declan.hoare@barnet.gov.uk

Housing: Mr Martin Cowie, Assistant Director - Planning & Development, Building 4, North London Business Park, Oakleigh Road South, London N11 1NP 🖱 martin.cowie@barnet.gov.uk

Housing: Mr Andy Milne, Assistant Director - Housing, Building 4, North London Business Park, Oakleigh Road South, London N11 1NP 🖱 andy.milne@barnet.gov.uk

Housing: Ms Lucy Shomali, Assistant Director - Strategic Planning & Regeneration, Building 4, North London Business Park, Oakleigh Road South, London N11 1NP 🖱 lucy.shomali@barnet.gov.uk

Local Area Agreement: Mr Andrew Nathan, Policy & Partnerships Group Manager, Building 4, North London Business Park, Oakleigh Road South, London N11 1NP 🖱 andrew.nathan@barnet.gov.uk

Legal: Ms Margaret Martinus, Assistant Director - Legal, Building 4, North London Business Park, Oakleigh Road South, New Southgate, London N11 1NP 🖱 margaret.martinus@barnet.gov.uk

Licensing: Ms Emma Phasey, Trading Standards / Licensing Manager, Building 4, North London Business Park, Oakleigh Road South, New Southgate, London N11 1NP 🖱 emma.phasey@barnet.gov.uk

Lottery Funding, Charity and Voluntary: Mr Ken Argent, Grants Manager, Building 4, North London Business Park, Oakleigh Road South, New Southgate, London N11 1NP 🖱 ken.argent@barnet.gov.uk

Member Services: Ms Victoria Blyth, Openness & Transparency Manager, Building 4, North London Business Park, Oakleigh Road South, London N11 1NP victoria.blyth@barnet.gov.uk

Member Services: Mrs Aysen Giritli, Head of Governance, Building 4, North London Business Park, Oakleigh Road South, London N11 1NP aysen.giritli@barnet.gov.uk

Parking: Mr Declan Hoare, Assistant Director - Highways & Transport, Building 4, North London Business Park, Oakleigh Road South, London N11 1NP declan.hoare@barnet.gov.uk

Personnel / HR: Ms Jacquie McGeachie, Assistant Director - Human Resources, Building 4, North London Business Park, Oakleigh Road South, New Southgate, London N11 1NP jacquie.mcgeachie@barnet.gov.uk

Personnel / HR: Mrs Sarah Murphy-Brookman, Head of BP & EE Engagement, Building 4, North London Business Park, Oakleigh Road South, New Southgate, London N11 1NP sarah.murphy-brookman@barnet.gov.uk

Planning: Mr Martin Cowie, Head of Planning & Development Management, Building 4, North London Business Park, Oakleigh Road South, London N11 1NP martin.cowie@barnet.gov.uk

Procurement: Ms Lesley Meekes, Head of Procurement, Building 4, North London Business Park, Oakleigh Road South, London N11 1NP lesley.meekes@barnet.gov.uk

Public Libraries: Mrs Lauren Doody, Head of Customer Services & Libraries, Building 4, North London Business Park, Oakleigh Road South, London N11 1NP lauren.doody@barnet.gov.uk

Recycling & Waste Minimisation: Mrs Lynn Bishop, Assistant Director - Environment, Building 4, North London Business Park, Oakleigh Road South, London N11 1NP lynn.bishop@barnet.gov.uk

Regeneration: Ms Lucy Shomali, Assistant Director - Strategic Planning & Regeneration, Building 4, North London Business Park, Oakleigh Road South, London N11 1NP lucy.shomali@barnet.gov.uk

Road Safety: Ms Lisa Wright, Principal Engineer - Traffic Management & Schools, Building 4, North London Business Park, Oakleigh Road South, New Southgate, London N11 1NP lisa.wright@barnet.gov.uk

Social Services (Adult): Mr Mathew Kendall, Assistant Director - Transformation & Resources, Building 4, North London Business Park, Oakleigh Road South, New Southgate, London N11 1NP mathew.kendall@barnet.gov.uk

Social Services (Adult): Ms Kate Kennally, Director of Adult Social Care & Health, Building 4, North London Business Park, Oakleigh Road South, New Southgate, London N11 1NP kate.kennally@barnet.gov.uk

Social Services (Adult): Mr Jim Wilson, Deputy Director - Adult Social Care & Health, Building 4, North London Business Park, Oakleigh Road South, London N11 1NP jim.wilson@barnet.gov.uk

Social Services (Children): Ms Ann Graham, Assistant Director - Children's Social Care, Building 4, North London Business Park, Oakleigh Road South, New Southgate, London N11 1NP ann.graham@barnet.gov.uk

Social Services (Children): Mr Jay Mercer, Deputy Director - Safeguarding, Prevention & Partnership, Building 4, North London Business Park, Oakleigh Road South, New Southgate, London N11 1NP jay.mercer@barnet.gov.uk

Social Services (Children): Mr Mick Quigley, Assistant Director - Schools & Learning, Building 4, North London Business Park, Oakleigh Road South, New Southgate, London N11 1NP mick.quigley@barnet.gov.uk

Street Scene: Mrs Lynn Bishop, Assistant Director - Environment, Building 4, North London Business Park, Oakleigh Road South, London N11 1NP lynn.bishop@barnet.gov.uk

Sustainable Development: Mr Michael Lai, ESM Waste Strategy, Building 4, North London Business Park, Oakleigh Road South, New Southgate, London N11 1NP michael.lai@barnet.gov.uk

Traffic Management: Mr Declan Hoare, Assistant Director - Highways & Transport, Building 4, North London Business Park, Oakleigh Road South, London N11 1NP declan.hoare@barnet.gov.uk

Waste Collection and Disposal: Mrs Lynn Bishop, Assistant Director - Environment, Building 4, North London Business Park, Oakleigh Road South, London N11 1NP lynn.bishop@barnet.gov.uk

Waste Management: Mrs Nicola Cross, Environmental Services Manager (Waste Strategy), Building 4, North London Business Park, Oakleigh Road South, New Southgate, London N11 1NP nicola.cross@barnet.gov.uk

MEMBERS OF THE COUNCIL (62)

Leader of the Council: **Cornelius**, Richard (CON - Totteridge)
cllr.r.cornelius@barnet.gov.uk

Group Leader: **Cohen**, Jack (LD - Childs Hill)
cllr.j.cohen@barnet.gov.uk

Braun, Maureen (CON - Hendon)
cllr.m.braun@barnet.gov.uk

Brodkin, Alex (LAB - Burnt Oak)
cllr.a.brodkin@barnet.gov.uk

Campbell, Anita (LAB - Underhill)
cllr.a.campbell@barnet.gov.uk

Coakley Webb, Pauline (LAB - Coppetts)
cllr.p.coakleywebb@barnet.gov.uk

Cohen, Dean (CON - Golders Green)
cllr.d.cohen@barnet.gov.uk

Cohen, Melvin (CON - Golders Green)
cllr.m.cohen@barnet.gov.uk

Coleman, Brian (CON - Totteridge)
cllr.b.coleman@barnet.gov.uk

Cooke, Geof (LAB - Woodhouse)
cllr.g.cooke@barnet.gov.uk

Cornelius, Alison (CON - Totteridge)

cllr.a.cornelius@barnet.gov.uk
Davey, Tom (CON - Hale)
cllr.t.davey@barnet.gov.uk
Evangeli, Barry (CON - East Barnet)
cllr.b.evangeli@barnet.gov.uk
Farrier, Claire (LAB - Burnt Oak)
cllr.c.farrier@barnet.gov.uk
Finn, Anthony (CON - Hendon)
cllr.a.finn@barnet.gov.uk
Gordon, Brian (CON - Hale)
cllr.b.gordon@barnet.gov.uk
Greenspan, Eva (CON - Finchley Church End)
cllr.e.greenspan@barnet.gov.uk
Harper, Andrew (CON - Garden Suburb)
cllr.a.harper@barnet.gov.uk
Hart, Helena (CON - Edgware)
cllr.h.hart@barnet.gov.uk
Hart, John (CON - Mill Hill)
cllr.j.hart@barnet.gov.uk
Houston, Ross (LAB - West Finchley)
cllr.r.houston@barnet.gov.uk
Hutton, Anne (LAB - Woodhouse)
cllr.a.hutton@barnet.gov.uk
Johnson, Julie (LAB - West Hendon)
cllr.j.johnson@barnet.gov.uk
Johnson, Geoffrey (LAB - Colindale)
cllr.g.johnson@barnet.gov.uk
Khatri, Sury (CON - Mill Hill)
cllr.s.khatri@barnet.gov.uk
Longstaff, David (CON - High Barnet)
cllr.d.longstaff@barnet.gov.uk
Marshall, John (CON - Garden Suburb)
cllr.j.marshall@barnet.gov.uk|
McGuirk, Kathy (LAB - West Finchley)
cllr.k.mcguirk@barnet.gov.uk
Mittra, Arjun (LAB - East Finchley)
cllr.a.mittra@barnet.gov.uk
Moore, Alison (LAB - East Finchley)
cllr.a.moore@barnet.gov.uk
Old, Graham (CON - Finchley Church End)
cllr.g.old@barnet.gov.uk
O-Macauley, Charlie (LAB - Burnt Oak)
cllr.c.omacauley@barnet.gov.uk
Palmer, Susette (LD - Childs Hill)
cllr.s.palmer@barnet.gov.uk
Palmer, Monroe (LD - Childs Hill)
cllr.m.palmer@barnet.gov.uk
Perry, Bridget (CON - High Barnet)
cllr.b.perry@barnet.gov.uk
Prentice, Wendy (CON - High Barnet)
cllr.w.prentice@barnet.gov.uk
Rajput, Sachin (CON - Oakleigh)
cllr.s.rajput@barnet.gov.uk
Rams, Robert (CON - East Barnet)
cllr.r.rams@barnet.gov.uk
Rawlings, Barry (LAB - Coppetts)
cllr.b.rawlings@barnet.gov.uk
Rayner, Hugh (CON - Hale)
cllr.h.rayner@barnet.gov.uk
Rogers, Colin (LAB - East Finchley)
cllr.c.rogers@barnet.gov.uk
Rutter, Lisa (CON - Brunswick Park)
cllr.l.rutter@barnet.gov.uk
Salinger, Kate (CON - Coppetts)
cllr.c.salinger@barnet.gov.uk
Salinger, Brian (CON - Oakleigh)
cllr.b.salinger@barnet.gov.uk
Sargeant, Gill (LAB - Colindale)
cllr.g.sargent.barnet.gov.uk
Scannell, Joan (CON - Edgware)
cllr.j.scannell@barnet.gov.uk
Schama, Brian (CON - Mill Hill)
cllr.b.schama@barnet.gov.uk
Schneiderman, Alan (LAB - Woodhouse)
cllr.a.schneiderman@barnet.gov.uk
Seal, Daniel (CON - Garden Suburb)
cllr.d.seal@barnet.gov.uk
Shooter, Mark (CON - Hendon)
cllr.m.shooter@barnet.gov.uk
Slocombe, Agnes (LAB - West Hendon)
cllr.a.slocombe@barnet.gov.uk
Sodha, Ansuya (LAB - West Hendon)
cllr.a.sodha@barnet.gov.uk
Sowerby, Stephen (CON - Oakleigh)
cllr.s.sowerby@barnet.gov.uk
Strongolou, Andrew (CON - Underhill)
cclr.a.strongolou@barnet.gov.uk
Tambourides, Andreas (CON - Brunswick Park)
cllr.a.tambourides@barnet.gov.uk
Tambourides, Joanna (CON - East Barnet)
cllr.j.tambourides@barnet.gov.uk
Thomas, Daniel (CON - Finchley Church End)
cllr.d.thomas@barnet.gov.uk
Thompstone, Reuben (CON - Golders Green)
cllr.r.thompstone@barnet.gov.uk
Tierney, Jim (LAB - West Finchley)
cllr.j.tierney@barnet.gov.uk
Turner, Rowan (CON - Underhill)
cllr.r.turner@barnet.gov.uk
Yawitch, Darell (CON - Edgware)
cllr.d.yawitch@barnet.gov.uk
Zubairi, Zakia (LAB - Colindale)
cllr.z.zubari@barnet.gov.uk

POLITICAL COMPOSITION

CON: 38, LAB: 21, LD: 3

CABINET

Leader: Mr Richard Cornelius
Vice-Chairman: Mr Daniel Thomas

COMMITTEE CHAIRS

Appeals: Ms Eva Greenspan
Audit: Mr Monroe Palmer
Barnet Partnership Board: Mr Richard Cornelius
Budget & Performance Overview & Scrutiny Committee: Mr Brian Coleman
Business Management Overview & Scrutiny: Mr Hugh Rayner
Cabinet Resources: Mr Daniel Thomas
Chipping Barnett Residents Forum: Mrs Kate Salinger
Corporate Health & Safety Joint Negotiation Consultation: Mr Sury Khatri
General Functions: Ms Joan Scannell
Health & Well Being Board: Ms Helena Hart
Health Overview & Scrutiny: Ms Alison Cornelius
Licensing: Mr Andreas Tambourides
Pension Fund: Mr Anthony Finn
Planning & Environment Committee: Ms Wendy Prentice

Remuneration: Mr Richard Cornelius
Safeguarding Overview & Scrutiny: Ms Bridget Perry
Special Committee: Mr Melvin Cohen

BARNSLEY M

Barnsley Metropolitan Borough Council, Town Hall, Church Street, Barnsley S70 2TA ☎ 01226 770770 🖷 01226 773099 ✉ townhall@barnsley.gov.uk 💻 www.barnsley.gov.uk

FACTS & FIGURES

Police Authority: South Yorkshire Police Authority
Health Authority: NHS Yorkshire & the Humber
Learning and Skills Council: Yorkshire and the Humber
Parliamentary Constituencies: Barnsley Central, Barnsley East
EU Constituencies: Yorkshire and the Humber
Election Frequency: Elections are by thirds
Twinning: Gorlovka (Ukraine); Schwabisch Gmund (Germany)

PRINCIPAL OFFICERS

Chief Executive: Mr Steve Pick, Acting Chief Executive, Corporate Management Team, Westgate Plaza One, Barnsley S70 9FH ☎ 01226 773101 🖷 01226 772499 ✉ stevepick@barnsley.gov.uk

Deputy Chief Executive: Ms Frances Foster, Acting Executive Director of Finance & Property, Corporate Management Team, Westgate Plaza One, PO Box 609, Barnsley S70 9FH ☎ 01226 773163 🖷 01226 772499 ✉ francesfoster@barnsley.gov.uk

Assistant Chief Executive: Ms Julia Bell, Assistant Chief Executive (Human Resources), Gateway Plaza, PO Box 634, Barnsley S70 9GG ☎ 01226 773304 ✉ juliabell@barnsley.gov.uk

Senior Management: Mr Martin Farran, Executive Director of Adults' Social Services, Westgate Plaza One, PO Box 609, Barnsley S70 9FH ☎ 01226 772301 ✉ martinfarran@barnsley.gov.uk

Senior Management: Ms Frances Foster, Acting Executive Director of Finance & Property, Corporate Management Team, Westgate Plaza One, PO Box 609, Barnsley S70 9FH ☎ 01226 773163 🖷 01226 772499 ✉ francesfoster@barnsley.gov.uk

Senior Management: Mr Andrew Frosdick, Borough Secretary, Westgate Plaza One, PO Box 609, Barnsley S70 9FH ☎ 01226 773001 🖷 01226 772499 ✉ andrewfrosdick@barnsley.gov.uk

Senior Management: Ms Ann Gosse, Executive Director of Development, Environment & Culture, Westgate Plaza One, PO Box 609, Barnsley S70 9FH ☎ 01226 772001 🖷 01226 772499 ✉ anngosse@barnsley.gov.uk

Senior Management: Ms Judith Harwood, Executive Director of Children & Young People, Corporate Management Team, Westgate Plaza One, PO Box 609, Barnsley S70 9FH ☎ 01226 773602 🖷 01226 772499 ✉ judithharwood@barnsley.gov.uk

Access Officer / Social Services (Disability): Mr Martin Farran, Executive Director of Adults' Social Services, Westgate Plaza One, PO Box 609, Barnsley S70 9FH ☎ 01226 772301 ✉ martinfarran@barnsley.gov.uk

Architect, Building / Property Services: Mr Steve Pick, Acting Chief Executive, Corporate Management Team, Westgate Plaza One, Barnsley S70 9FH ☎ 01226 773101 🖷 01226 772499 ✉ stevepick@barnsley.gov.uk

Building Control: Mr Stephen Moralee, Assistant Director - Planning & Regulatory Services, Westgate Plaza One, PO Box 609, Barnsley S70 9FH ☎ 01226 772601 ✉ stephenmoralee@barnsley.gov.uk

Catering Services: Ms Frances Foster, Acting Executive Director of Finance & Property, Corporate Management Team, Westgate Plaza One, PO Box 609, Barnsley S70 9FH ☎ 01226 773163 🖷 01226 772499 ✉ francesfoster@barnsley.gov.uk

Children / Youth Services: Mr Richard Lohan, Assistant Director - Children, Family & Wellbeing Services, Berneslai Close, Barnsley S70 2HS ☎ 01226 774509 ✉ richardlohan@barnsley.gov.uk

Civil Registration: Mr Andrew Frosdick, Borough Secretary, Westgate Plaza One, PO Box 609, Barnsley S70 9FH ☎ 01226 773001 🖷 01226 772499 ✉ andrewfrosdick@barnsley.gov.uk

PR / Communications: Mr Bob Williams, Head of Corporate Communications, Gateway Plaza, PO Box 634, Barnsley S70 9GG ☎ 01226 773401 🖷 01226 773305 ✉ bobwilliams@barnsley.gov.uk

Community Planning: Mr Andrew Frosdick, Borough Secretary, Westgate Plaza One, PO Box 609, Barnsley S70 9FH ☎ 01226 773001 🖷 01226 772499 ✉ andrewfrosdick@barnsley.gov.uk

Community Safety: Mr Paul Brannen, Assistant Director - Community Safety Services, Beevor Court 2, PO Box 609, Barnsley S71 1 ☎ 01226 776477 ✉ paulbrannen@barnsley.gov.uk

Computer Management: Ms Frances Foster, Acting Executive Director of Finance & Property, Corporate Management Team, Westgate Plaza One, PO Box 609, Barnsley S70 9FH ☎ 01226 773163 🖷 01226 772499 ✉ francesfoster@barnsley.gov.uk

Consumer Protection and Trading Standards: Mr Stephen Moralee, Assistant Director - Planning & Regulatory Services, Westgate Plaza One, PO Box 609, Barnsley S70 9FH ☎ 01226 772601 ✉ stephenmoralee@barnsley.gov.uk

Corporate Services: Mr Shaun Jones, Assistant Executive Head of Performance, Gateway Plaza, PO Box 634, Barnsley S70 9GG ☎ 01226 773401 ✉ shaunjones@barnsley.gov.uk

Corporate Services: Mr Steve Pick, Acting Chief Executive, Corporate Management Team, Westgate Plaza One, Barnsley S70 9FH ☎ 01226 773101 🖷 01226 772499 ✉ stevepick@barnsley.gov.uk

Economic Development: Ms Carol Cooper-Smith, Assistant Director - Economy, Culture & Housing, Westgate Plaza One, PO Box 609, Barnsley S70 9FH ☎ 01226 787538 🖷 01226 772499 ✉ carolcooper-smith@barnsley.gov.uk

Education: Ms Judith Harwood, Executive Director of Children & Young People, Corporate Management Team, Westgate Plaza One, PO Box 609, Barnsley S70 9FH ☎ 01226 773602 🖷 01226 772499 ✉ judithharwood@barnsley.gov.uk

E-Government: Ms Frances Foster, Acting Executive Director of Finance & Property, Corporate Management Team, Westgate Plaza One, PO Box 609, Barnsley S70 9FH ☎ 01226 773163 🖷 01226 772499 ✉ francesfoster@barnsley.gov.uk

Electoral Registration: Mr Andrew Frosdick, Borough Secretary, Westgate Plaza One, PO Box 609, Barnsley S70 9FH ☎ 01226 773001 🖷 01226 772499 ✉ andrewfrosdick@barnsley.gov.uk

Emergency Planning: Mr Doug Cartwright, Head of Corporate Health, Safety & Emergencies, Gateway Plaza, PO Box 634, Barnsley S70 9GG ☎ 01226 772257 ✉ dougcartwright@barnsley.gov.uk

Energy Management: Ms Frances Foster, Acting Executive Director of Finance & Property, Corporate Management Team, Westgate Plaza One, PO Box 609, Barnsley S70 9FH ☎ 01226 773163 🖷 01226 772499 ✉ francesfoster@barnsley.gov.uk

Environmental / Technical Services: Ms Ann Gosse, Executive Director of Development, Environment & Culture, Westgate Plaza One, PO Box 609, Barnsley S70 9FH ☎ 01226 772001 🖷 01226 772499 ✉ anngosse@barnsley.gov.uk

Environmental Health: Ms Ann Gosse, Executive Director of Development, Environment & Culture, Westgate Plaza One, PO Box 609, Barnsley S70 9FH ☎ 01226 772001 🖷 01226 772499 ✉ anngosse@barnsley.gov.uk

Estates, Property & Valuation: Ms Frances Foster, Acting Executive Director of Finance & Property, Corporate Management Team, Westgate Plaza One, PO Box 609, Barnsley S70 9FH ☎ 01226 773163 🖷 01226 772499 ✉ francesfoster@barnsley.gov.uk

European Liaison: Ms Eleanor Dearle, Project Co-ordinator, Westgate Plaza One, Barnsley S70 9FH ☎ 01226 773825 ✉ eleanordearle@barnsley.gov.uk

Events Manager: Ms Helen Ball, Head of Culture & Creative Industries, Westgate Plaza One, PO Box 609, Barnsley S70 9FH ☎ 01226 787506 ✉ helenball@barnsley.gov.uk

Facilities: Mr Steve Pick, Acting Chief Executive, Corporate Management Team, Westgate Plaza One, Barnsley S70 9FH ☎ 01226 773101 🖷 01226 772499 ✉ stevepick@barnsley.gov.uk

Finance and Treasurer: Ms Frances Foster, Acting Executive Director of Finance & Property, Corporate Management Team, Westgate Plaza One, PO Box 609, Barnsley S70 9FH ☎ 01226 773163 🖷 01226 772499 ✉ francesfoster@barnsley.gov.uk

Fleet Management: Mr Darren Richardson, Assistant Director - Environmental Services, Westgate Plaza One, PO Box 609, Barnsley S70 9FH ☎ 01226 772063 ✉ darrenrichardson@barnsley.gov.uk

Grounds Maintenance: Mr Derek Williams, Assistant Director - Neighbourhood Services (Customer & Neighbourhood Services), Westgate Plaza One, PO Box 609, Barnsley S70 9FH ☎ 01226 774369 ✉ derekwilliams@barnsley.gov.uk

Health and Safety: Ms Julia Bell, Assistant Chief Executive (Human Resources), Gateway Plaza, PO Box 634, Barnsley S70 9GG ☎ 01226 773304 ✉ juliabell@barnsley.gov.uk

Highways: Mr Darren Richardson, Assistant Director - Environmental Services, Westgate Plaza One, PO Box 609, Barnsley S70 9FH ☎ 01226 772063 ✉ darrenrichardson@barnsley.gov.uk

Home Energy Conservation: Ms Frances Foster, Acting Executive Director of Finance & Property, Corporate Management Team, Westgate Plaza One, PO Box 609, Barnsley S70 9FH ☎ 01226 773163 🖷 01226 772499 ✉ francesfoster@barnsley.gov.uk

Housing: Mr Steve Jagger, Assistant Director - Strategy, Growth & Regeneration, Westgate Plaza One, Barnsley S70 9FH ☎ 01226 772774 ✉ stevejagger@barnsley.gov.uk

Housing Maintenance: Mr Steve Jagger, Assistant Director - Strategy, Growth & Regeneration, Westgate Plaza One, Barnsley S70 9FH ☎ 01226 772774 ✉ stevejagger@barnsley.gov.uk

Local Area Agreement: Mr Shaun Jones, Assistant Executive Head of Performance, Gateway Plaza, PO Box 634, Barnsley S70 9GG ☎ 01226 773401 ✉ shaunjones@barnsley.gov.uk

Legal: Mr Andrew Frosdick, Borough Secretary, Westgate Plaza One, PO Box 609, Barnsley S70 9FH ☎ 01226 773001 🖷 01226 772499 ✉ andrewfrosdick@barnsley.gov.uk

Leisure and Cultural Services: Ms Helen Ball, Head of Culture & Creative Industries, Westgate Plaza One, PO Box 609, Barnsley S70 9FH ☎ 01226 787506 ✉ helenball@barnsley.gov.uk

Leisure and Cultural Services: Ms Ann Gosse, Executive Director of Development, Environment & Culture, Westgate Plaza One, PO Box 609, Barnsley S70 9FH ☎ 01226 772001 🖷 01226 772499 ✉ anngosse@barnsley.gov.uk

Licensing: Mr Stephen Moralee, Assistant Director - Planning & Regulatory Services, Westgate Plaza One, PO Box 609, Barnsley S70 9FH ☎ 01226 772601 ✉ stephenmoralee@barnsley.gov.uk

Lifelong Learning: Ms Judith Harwood, Executive Director of Children & Young People, Corporate Management Team, Westgate Plaza One, PO Box 609, Barnsley S70 9FH ☎ 01226 773602 🖷 01226 772499 ✉ judithharwood@barnsley.gov.uk

Lighting: Mr Darren Richardson, Assistant Director - Environmental Services, Westgate Plaza One, PO Box 609, Barnsley S70 9FH ☎ 01226 772063 ✉ darrenrichardson@barnsley.gov.uk

Member Services: Mr Andrew Frosdick, Borough Secretary, Westgate Plaza One, PO Box 609, Barnsley S70 9FH ☎ 01226 773001 🖷 01226 772499 ✉ andrewfrosdick@barnsley.gov.uk

Parking: Mr Darren Richardson, Assistant Director - Environmental Services, Westgate Plaza One, PO Box 609, Barnsley S70 9FH ☎ 01226 772063 🖱 darrenrichardson@barnsley.gov.uk

Partnerships: Mr Andrew Frosdick, Borough Secretary, Westgate Plaza One, PO Box 609, Barnsley S70 9FH ☎ 01226 773001 🖷 01226 772499 🖱 andrewfrosdick@barnsley.gov.uk

Personnel / HR: Ms Julia Bell, Assistant Chief Executive (Human Resources), Gateway Plaza, PO Box 634, Barnsley S70 9GG ☎ 01226 773304 🖱 juliabell@barnsley.gov.uk

Planning: Mr Stephen Moralee, Assistant Director - Planning & Regulatory Services, Westgate Plaza One, PO Box 609, Barnsley S70 9FH ☎ 01226 772601 🖱 stephenmoralee@barnsley.gov.uk

Procurement: Ms Frances Foster, Acting Executive Director of Finance & Property, Corporate Management Team, Westgate Plaza One, PO Box 609, Barnsley S70 9FH ☎ 01226 773163 🖷 01226 772499 🖱 francesfoster@barnsley.gov.uk

Public Libraries: Mr Derek Williams, Assistant Director - Neighbourhood Services (Customer & Neighbourhood Services), Westgate Plaza One, PO Box 609, Barnsley S70 9FH ☎ 01226 774369 🖱 derekwilliams@barnsley.gov.uk

Regeneration: Ms Ann Gosse, Executive Director of Development, Environment & Culture, Westgate Plaza One, PO Box 609, Barnsley S70 9FH ☎ 01226 772001 🖷 01226 772499 🖱 anngosse@barnsley.gov.uk

Road Safety: Mr Darren Richardson, Assistant Director - Environmental Services, Westgate Plaza One, PO Box 609, Barnsley S70 9FH ☎ 01226 772063 🖱 darrenrichardson@barnsley.gov.uk

Social Services: Mr Martin Farran, Executive Director of Adults' Social Services, Westgate Plaza One, PO Box 609, Barnsley S70 9FH ☎ 01226 772301 🖱 martinfarran@barnsley.gov.uk

Social Services (Adult): Mr Martin Farran, Executive Director of Adults' Social Services, Westgate Plaza One, PO Box 609, Barnsley S70 9FH ☎ 01226 772301 🖱 martinfarran@barnsley.gov.uk

Social Services (Children): Mr Richard Lohan, Assistant Director - Children, Family & Wellbeing Services, Berneslai Close, Barnsley S70 2HS ☎ 01226 774509 🖱 richardlohan@barnsley.gov.uk

Staff Training: Ms Julia Bell, Assistant Chief Executive (Human Resources), Gateway Plaza, PO Box 634, Barnsley S70 9GG ☎ 01226 773304 🖱 juliabell@barnsley.gov.uk

Street Scene: Mr Stephen Moralee, Assistant Director - Planning & Regulatory Services, Westgate Plaza One, PO Box 609, Barnsley S70 9FH ☎ 01226 772601 🖱 stephenmoralee@barnsley.gov.uk

Sustainable Communities: Ms Ann Gosse, Executive Director of Development, Environment & Culture, Westgate Plaza One, PO Box 609, Barnsley S70 9FH ☎ 01226 772001 🖷 01226 772499 🖱 anngosse@barnsley.gov.uk

Sustainable Development: Mr Stephen Moralee, Assistant Director - Planning & Regulatory Services, Westgate Plaza One, PO Box 609, Barnsley S70 9FH ☎ 01226 772601 🖱 stephenmoralee@barnsley.gov.uk

Tourism: Ms Helen Ball, Head of Culture & Creative Industries, Westgate Plaza One, PO Box 609, Barnsley S70 9FH ☎ 01226 787506 🖱 helenball@barnsley.gov.uk

Town Centre: Ms Helen Ball, Head of Culture & Creative Industries, Westgate Plaza One, PO Box 609, Barnsley S70 9FH ☎ 01226 787506 🖱 helenball@barnsley.gov.uk

Traffic Management: Mr Darren Richardson, Assistant Director - Environmental Services, Westgate Plaza One, PO Box 609, Barnsley S70 9FH ☎ 01226 772063 🖱 darrenrichardson@barnsley.gov.uk

Transport: Mr Stephen Moralee, Assistant Director - Planning & Regulatory Services, Westgate Plaza One, PO Box 609, Barnsley S70 9FH ☎ 01226 772601 🖱 stephenmoralee@barnsley.gov.uk

Transport Planner: Mr Stephen Moralee, Assistant Director - Planning & Regulatory Services, Westgate Plaza One, PO Box 609, Barnsley S70 9FH ☎ 01226 772601 🖱 stephenmoralee@barnsley.gov.uk

Waste Collection and Disposal: Mr Darren Richardson, Assistant Director - Environmental Services, Westgate Plaza One, PO Box 609, Barnsley S70 9FH ☎ 01226 772063 🖱 darrenrichardson@barnsley.gov.uk

Waste Management: Mr Darren Richardson, Assistant Director - Environmental Services, Westgate Plaza One, PO Box 609, Barnsley S70 9FH ☎ 01226 772063 🖱 darrenrichardson@barnsley.gov.uk

MEMBERS OF THE COUNCIL (63)

***Mayor:* Higginbottom**, Dorothy (LAB - North East)
CllrDorothyHigginbottom@barnsley.gov.uk
***Deputy Mayor:* Dyson**, Karen (LAB - Stairfoot)
CllrKarenDyson@barnsley.gov.uk
***Leader of the Council:* Houghton**, Stephen (LAB - Cudworth)
cllrstephenhoughton@barnsley.gov.uk
***Deputy Leader of the Council:* Andrews**, James (LAB - Rockingham)
CllrJamesAndrews@barnsley.gov.uk
Barlow, Betty (LAB - Worsbrough)
CllrBettyBarlow@barnsley.gov.uk
Barnard, Robert (CON - Penistone East)
CllrRobertBarnard@barnsley.gov.uk
Birkinshaw, Phillip (IND - Dodworth)
CllrPhillipBirkinshaw@barnsley.gov.uk
Birkinshaw, Doug (LAB - Central)
Cllrdougbirkinshaw@barnsley.gov.uk
Brook, Sharron (LAB - Dearne South)
CllrSharronBrook@barnsley.gov.uk
Bruff, Margaret (LAB - Central)
CllrMargaretBruff@barnsley.gov.uk
Burgess, Linda (LAB - Darton West)

CllrLindaBurgess@barnsley.gov.uk
Carr, Gill (IND - Worsbrough)
CllrGillCarr@barnsley.gov.uk
Carr, Jack (IND - Dodworth)
CllrJackCarr@barnsley.gov.uk
Cave, Alice (LAB - Darton West)
CllrAliceCave@barnsley.gov.uk
Cheetham, Tracey (LAB - Royston)
Cheetham, Tim (LAB - Royston)
CllrTimCheetham@barnsley.gov.uk
Cherryholme, Anita (LAB - Old Town)
cllranitacherryholme@barnsley.gov.uk
Clarke, John (LAB - Worsbrough)
CllrJohnClarke@barnsley.gov.uk
Davies, Phil (LAB - Old Town)
cllrphildavies@barnsley.gov.uk
Duerden, Lesley (LAB - Darton East)
cllrlesleyduerden@barnsley.gov.uk
Dures, Emma (LAB - Rockingham)
cllremmadures@barnsley.gov.uk
Dyson, Martin (LAB - Central)
cllrmartindyson@barnsley.gov.uk
Ennis, Jeff (LAB - North East)
cllrjeffennis@barnsley.gov.uk
Franklin, Robert (LAB - Hoyland Milton)
CllrRobinFranklin@barnsley.gov.uk
Gardiner, Alan (LAB - Dearne North)
CllrAlanGardiner@barnsley.gov.uk
Green, Donna (LAB - Kingstone)
cllrdonnagreen@barnsley.gov.uk
Green, Steve (LAB - Monk Bretton)
cllrstevegreen@barnsley.gov.uk
Hancock, Janice (LAB - Dearne North)
CllrJaniceHancocl@barnsley.gov.uk
Hand-Davis, Paul (CON - Penistone East)
CllrPaulHand-Davis@barnsley.gov.uk
Hayward, Joseph (LAB - Cudworth)
cllrjoehayward@barnsley.gov.uk
Howard, Sharon (LAB - Darton West)
CllrSharonHoward@barnsley.gov.uk
Johnson, Wayne (LAB - Stairfoot)
cllrwaynejohnson@barnsley.gov.uk
Key, Brian (LAB - Darfield)
cllrbriankey@barnsely.gov.uk
Kyte, Graham (LAB - Royston)
CllrGrahamKyte@barnsley.gov.uk
Lamb, Chris (LAB - Rockingham)
cllrchrislamb@barnsley.gov.uk
Leech, Dave (LAB - St. Helen's)
cllrdavidleech@barnsley.gov.uk
Lofts, Penny (LAB - Old Town)
CllrPennyLofts@barnsley.gov.uk
Markham, Pauline (LAB - Darfield)
CllrPaulineMarkham@barnsley.gov.uk
Mathers, Brian (LAB - Stairfoot)
cllrbrianmathers@barnsley.gov.uk
Miller, Roy (LAB - Darton East)
CllrRoyMiller@barnsley.gov.uk
Millner, Andrew (CON - Penistone West)
CllrAndrewMillner@barnsley.gov.uk
Mitchell, Kath (LAB - Kingstone)
CllrKathMitchell@barnsley.gov.uk
Morgan, Margaret (LAB - Wombwell)
cllrmargaretmorgan@barnsley.gov.uk
Noble, May (LAB - Dearne South)
CllrMayNoble@barnsley.gov.uk
North, Dave (IND - North East)
CllrDaveNorth@barnsley.gov.uk
Perrin, Brian (IND - Dodworth)
CllrBrianPerrin@barnsley.gov.uk
Platts, Jenny (LAB - St. Helen's)
CllrJennyPlatts@barnsley.gov.uk
Richardson, Kenneth (LAB - Monk Bretton)
cllrkenrichardson@barnsley.gov.uk
Rusby, Ann (CON - Penistone West)
cllrannrusby@barnsley.gov.uk
Sheard, Tom (LAB - Kingstone)
cllrtomsheard@barnsley.gov.uk
Sheard, Margaret (LAB - Monk Bretton)
CllrMargaretSheard@barnsley.gov.uk
Shepherd, Tim (LAB - Hoyland Milton)
cllrtimshepherd@barnsley.gov.uk
Sixsmith, Ralph (LAB - Dearne South)
cllrralphsixsmith@barnsley.gov.uk
Spence, Harry (NP - Darton East)
CllrHarrySpence@barnsley.gov.uk
Starling, Peter (LAB - Penistone West)
cllrpeterstarling@barnsley.gov.uk
Stowe, Mick (LAB - Hoyland Milton)
cllrmickstowe@barnsely.gov.uk
Tattersall, Sarah (LAB - St Helen's)
cllrsarahtattersall@barnsley.gov.uk
Ward, Caroline (LAB - Darfield)
cllrcaolinesaunders@barnsely.gov.uk
Wilde, Denise (LAB - Wombwell)
CllrDeniseWilde@barnsley.gov.uk
Wilson, John (CON - Penistone East)
CllrJohnWilson@barnsley.gov.uk
Worton, Jennifer (LAB - Dearne North)
CllrJenniferWorton@barnsley.gov.uk
Wraith, Charlie (LAB - Cudworth)
CllrCharlesWraith@barnsley.gov.uk
Wraith, Richard (LAB - Wombwell)
CllrRichardWraith@barnsley.gov.uk

POLITICAL COMPOSITION

LAB: 52, CON: 5, IND: 5, NP: 1

CABINET

Leader: Mr Stephen Houghton
Deputy Leader: Mr James Andrews
Adults & Communities: Ms Jenny Platts
Children, Young People & Families: Mr Tim Cheetham
Corporate Services: Mr Alan Gardiner
Development, Environment & Culture: Mr Roy Miller

COMMITTEE CHAIRS

Appeals & Awards Regulatory Board: Mr Brian Mathers
Audit: Mr Joseph Hayward
Community Well-Being: Ms Margaret Bruff
Economy & Skills: Mr Richard Wraith
General Licensing Regulatory Board: Mr Charlie Wraith
Personal & Family Well-Being: Ms Jennifer Worton
Physical Sustainability: Mr Graham Kyte
Planning Regulatory Board: Ms Denise Wilde
Statutory Licensing Regulatory Board: Mr Charlie Wraith

BARROW-IN-FURNESS D

Barrow-in-Furness Borough Council, (Barrow Borough Council), Town Hall, Duke Street , Barrow-in-Furness LA14 2LD ☎ 01229 876300 🖷 01229 876317 🖳 www.barrowbc.gov.uk

FACTS & FIGURES

Police Authority: Cumbria Police Authority
Health Authority: North West Strategic Health Authority
Learning and Skills Council: North West
Parliamentary Constituencies: Barrow and Furness
EU Constituencies: North West
Election Frequency: Elections are by thirds

PRINCIPAL OFFICERS

Senior Management: Mr Jeff Bright, Deputy Executive Director, Town Hall, Barrow-in-Furness LA14 2LD ☎ 01229 876334 🖷 01229 876317 🖰 jbright@barrowbc.gov.uk

Senior Management: Mr Phil Huck, Executive Director, Town Hall, Duke Street , Barrow-in-Furness LA14 2LD ☎ 01229 876503 🖷 01229 876317 🖰 philhuck@barrowbc.gov.uk

Access Officer / Social Services (Disability): Mr Kevan Morrison, Principal Building Control Surveyor, Town Hall, Duke Street, Barrow-in-Furness LA14 2LD ☎ 01229 876481 🖷 01229 876317 🖰 kcmorrison@barrowbc.gov.uk

Architect, Building / Property Services: Mr Brian Vickers, Building Surveyor, Town Hall, Duke Street , Barrow-in-Furness LA14 2LD ☎ 01229 876358 🖷 01229 876317 🖰 bvickers@barrowbc.gov.uk

Best Value: Mr John Penfold, Policy Review Officer, Town Hall, Duke Street, Barrow-in-Furness LA14 2LD ☎ 01229 876344 🖷 01229 876317 🖰 jpenfold@barrowbc.gov.uk

Building Control: Mr Kevan Morrison, Principal Building Control Surveyor, Town Hall, Duke Street, Barrow-in-Furness LA14 2LD ☎ 01229 876481 🖷 01229 876317 🖰 kcmorrison@barrowbc.gov.uk

Community Planning: Mr Steve Solsby, Assistant Director - Regeneration & Built Environment, Town Hall, Duke Street , Barrow-in-Furness LA14 2LD ☎ 01229 876359 🖷 01229 876317 🖰 ssolsby@barrowbc.gov.uk

Community Safety: Ms Rebecca Rawlings, Community Safety Co-ordinator, Neighbourhood Management Office, 242-244 Dalton Road, Barrow-in-Furness LA14 1PN ☎ 01229 876475 🖰 rrawlings@barrowbc.gov.uk

Computer Management: Mr Jeff Bright, Deputy Executive Director, Town Hall, Duke Street , Barrow-in-Furness LA14 2LD ☎ 01229 876334 🖷 01229 876317 🖰 jbright@barrowbc.gov.uk

Contracts: Mr Richard Hennah, Technical Support Unit Manager, Town Hall, Duke Street , Barrow-in-Furness LA14 2LD ☎ 01229 876325 🖷 01229 876317 🖰 rhennah@barrowbc.gov.uk

Contracts: Mrs Margaret Wilson, Sports Contract Manager, Parks Leisure Centre, Greengate Street, Barrow-in-Furness LA13 9DT ☎ 01229 871146 🖷 01229 430224 🖰 mwilson@barrowbc.gov.uk

Corporate Services: Mr Jeff Bright, Deputy Executive Director, Town Hall, Barrow-in-Furness LA14 2LD ☎ 01229 876334 🖷 01229 876317 🖰 jbright@barrowbc.gov.uk

Customer Service: Ms Debbie Reid, Customer Relations Supervisor, Town Hall, Duke Street , Barrow-in-Furness LA14 2LD ☎ 01229 876446 🖷 01229 876446 🖰 dareid@barrowbc.gov.uk

Economic Development: Mr Steve Solsby, Assistant Director - Regeneration & Built Environment, Town Hall, Duke Street , Barrow-in-Furness LA14 2LD ☎ 01229 876359 🖷 01229 876317 🖰 ssolsby@barrowbc.gov.uk

Electoral Registration: Mr Jon Huck, Democratic Services Manager, Town Hall, Duke Street, Barrow-in-Furness LA14 2LD ☎ 01229 876312 🖷 ; 01229 876317 🖰 jwhuck@barrowbc.gov.uk

Electoral Registration: Mrs Judith Swarbrick, Electoral Registration Co-ordinator, Town Hall, Duke Street, Barrow-in-Furness LA14 2LD ☎ 01229 876318 🖷 01229 873617 🖰 jswarbrick@barrowbc.gov.uk

Emergency Planning: Mr Andy Buck, Health & Safety Advisor, Town Hall, Duke Street, Barrow-in-Furness LA14 2LD ☎ 01229 876509 🖷 01229 876317 🖰 abuck@barrowbc.gov.uk

Energy Management: Mr Richard Hennah, Technical Support Unit Manager, Town Hall, Duke Street , Barrow-in-Furness LA14 2LD ☎ 01229 876325 🖷 01229 876317 🖰 rhennah@barrowbc.gov.uk

Environmental / Technical Services: Mr Alan Barker, Streetcare Manager, Town Hall, Duke Street , Barrow-in-Furness LA14 2LD ☎ 01229 876412 🖷 01229 876317 🖰 abarker@barrowbc.gov.uk

Environmental Health: Mrs Anne Pearson, Environmental Health Manager, Town Hall, Duke Street , Barrow-in-Furness LA14 2LD ☎ 01229 876386 🖷 01229 876317 🖰 apearson@barrowbc.gov.uk

Estates, Property & Valuation: Mr David Joyce, Commercial Estates Manager, Town Hall, Duke Street , Barrow-in-Furness LA14 2LD ☎ 01229 876362 🖷 ; 01229 876317 🖰 djjoyce@barrowbc.gov.uk

European Liaison: Mr Steve Solsby, Assistant Director - Regeneration & Built Environment, Town Hall, Duke Street , Barrow-in-Furness LA14 2LD ☎ 01229 876359 🖷 01229 876317 🖰 ssolsby@barrowbc.gov.uk

Events Manager: Mrs Sandra Baines, Forum Venue Manager, The Forum, Duke Street, Barrow-in-Furness LA14 1HH ☎ 01229 876484 🖰 sbaines@barrowbc.gov.uk

Events Manager: Mrs Ann Taylforth, Town Centre & Festivals Manager, Town Hall, Duke Street , Barrow-in-Furness LA14 2LD ☎ 01229 876389 🖷 01229 876317 🖰 ataylforth@barrowbc.gov.uk

Facilities: Mr Richard Hennah, Technical Support Unit Manager, Town Hall, Duke Street , Barrow-in-Furness LA14 2LD ☎ 01229

876325 🖷 01229 876317 ✉ rhennah@barrowbc.gov.uk

Finance and Treasurer: Ms Susan Roberts, Borough Treasurer, Town Hall, Duke Street , Barrow-in-Furness LA14 2LD ☎ 01229 876433 🖷 01229 876317 ✉ smroberts@barrowbc.gov.uk

Grounds Maintenance: Mr Bill Brown, Parks & Playgrounds Manager, Town Hall, Duke Street, Barrow-in-Furness LA14 2LD ☎ 01229 876564 🖷 01229 876317 ✉ wrbrown@barrowbc.gov.uk

Health and Safety: Mr Andy Buck, Health & Safety Advisor, Town Hall, Duke Street, Barrow-in-Furness LA14 2LD ☎ 01229 876509 🖷 01229 876317 ✉ abuck@barrowbc.gov.uk

Home Energy Conservation: Mr Chris Jones, Housing Renewal Manager, Town Hall, Duke Street , Barrow-in-Furness LA14 2LD ☎ 01229 876351 🖷 01229 876317 ✉ cwjones@barrowbc.gov.uk

Housing: Mr Colin Garnett, Housing Manager, Housing Department, Cavendish House, 78 Duke Street, Barrow-in-Furness LA14 1RR ☎ 01229 876462 🖷 01229 876525 ✉ cgarnett@barrowbc.gov.uk

Housing Maintenance: Mr Les Davies, Housing Maintenance Manager, Housing Department, Cavendish House, 78 Duke Street, Barrow-in-Furness LA14 1RR ☎ 01229 876540 🖷 01229 876525 ✉ ldavies@barrowbc.gov.uk

Legal: Mrs Jane Holden, Corporate Services Officer, Town Hall, Duke Street, Barrow-in-Furness LA14 2LD ☎ 01229 876452 🖷 01229 876317 ✉ jmholden@barrowbc.gov.uk

Leisure and Cultural Services: Mrs Sandra Baines, Forum Venue Manager, The Forum, Duke Street, Barrow-in-Furness LA14 1HH ☎ 01229 876484 ✉ sbaines@barrowbc.gov.uk

Leisure and Cultural Services: Mr Keith Johnson, Assistant Director - Community Services, Town Hall, Duke Street , Barrow-in-Furness LA14 2LD ☎ 01229 876437 ✉ kjohnson@barrowbc.gov.uk

Leisure and Cultural Services: Ms Sabine Skae, Collections & Exhibitions Manager, The Dock Museum, North Road, Barrow-in-Furness LA14 2PW ☎ 01229 876401 🖷 01229 811361 ✉ sskae@barrowbc.gov.uk

Leisure and Cultural Services: Mrs Ann Taylforth, Town Centre & Festivals Manager, Town Hall, Duke Street , Barrow-in-Furness LA14 2LD ☎ 01229 876389 🖷 01229 876317 ✉ ataylforth@barrowbc.gov.uk

Leisure and Cultural Services: Mrs Margaret Wilson, Sports Contract Manager, Parks Leisure Centre, Greengate Street, Barrow-in-Furness LA13 9DT ☎ 01229 871146 🖷 01229 430224 ✉ mwilson@barrowbc.gov.uk

Licensing: Mrs Anne Pearson, Environmental Health Manager, Town Hall, Duke Street , Barrow-in-Furness LA14 2LD ☎ 01229 876386 🖷 01229 876317 ✉ apearson@barrowbc.gov.uk

Lottery Funding, Charity and Voluntary: Mr Keith Johnson, Assistant Director - Community Services, Town Hall, Duke Street, Barrow-in-Furness LA14 2LD ☎ 01229 876437 ✉ kjohnson@barrowbc.gov.uk

Member Services: Mr Jon Huck, Democratic Services Manager, Town Hall, Duke Street, Barrow-in-Furness LA14 2LD ☎ 01229 876312 🖷 ; 01229 876317 ✉ jwhuck@barrowbc.gov.uk

Parking: Mrs Caren Hindle, Parking Services Manager, Town Hall, Duke Street, Barrow-in-Furness LA14 2LD ☎ 01229 876565 🖷 01229 876317 ✉ cahindle@barrowbc.gov.uk

Personnel / HR: Miss Cathy Noade, Principal Personnel Officer, Town Hall, Duke Street , Barrow-in-Furness LA14 2LD ☎ 01229 876350 🖷 01229 876317 ✉ cnoade@barrowbc.gov.uk

Planning: Mr Jason Hipkiss, Planning Manager, Town Hall, Duke Street , Barrow-in-Furness LA14 2LD ☎ 01229 876377 🖷 01229 876317 ✉ jhipkiss@barrowbc.gov.uk

Procurement: Mr Richard Hennah, Technical Support Unit Manager, Town Hall, Duke Street , Barrow-in-Furness LA14 2LD ☎ 01229 876325 🖷 01229 876317 ✉ rhennah@barrowbc.gov.uk

Recycling & Waste Minimisation: Mr Peter Buckley, Recycling Officer, Town Hall, Duke Street , Barrow-in-Furness LA14 2LD ☎ 01229 876330 🖷 01229 876317 ✉ pbuckley@barrowbc.gov.uk

Regeneration: Mr Phil Huck, Executive Director, Town Hall, Duke Street , Barrow-in-Furness LA14 2LD ☎ 01229 876503 🖷 01229 876317 ✉ philhuck@barrowbc.gov.uk

Regeneration: Mr Steve Solsby, Assistant Director - Regeneration & Built Environment, Town Hall, Duke Street , Barrow-in-Furness LA14 2LD ☎ 01229 876359 🖷 01229 876317 ✉ ssolsby@barrowbc.gov.uk

Staff Training: Miss Cathy Noade, Principal Personnel Officer, Town Hall, Duke Street , Barrow-in-Furness LA14 2LD ☎ 01229 876350 🖷 01229 876317 ✉ cnoade@barrowbc.gov.uk

Street Scene: Mr Alan Barker, Streetcare Manager, Town Hall, Duke Street , Barrow-in-Furness LA14 2LD ☎ 01229 876412 🖷 01229 876317 ✉ abarker@barrowbc.gov.uk

Sustainable Communities: Mr Phil Huck, Executive Director, Town Hall, Duke Street , Barrow-in-Furness LA14 2LD ☎ 01229 876503 🖷 01229 876317 ✉ philhuck@barrowbc.gov.uk

Sustainable Development: Mr Phil Huck, Executive Director, Town Hall, Duke Street , Barrow-in-Furness LA14 2LD ☎ 01229 876503 🖷 01229 876317 ✉ philhuck@barrowbc.gov.uk

Tourism: Mrs Ann Taylforth, Town Centre & Festivals Manager, Town Hall, Duke Street, Barrow-in-Furness LA14 2LD ☎ 01229 876389 🖷 01229 876317 ✉ ataylforth@barrowbc.gov.uk

Town Centre: Mrs Ann Taylforth, Town Centre & Festivals Manager, Town Hall, Duke Street, Barrow-in-Furness LA14 2LD ☎ 01229 876389 🖷 01229 876317 ✉ ataylforth@barrowbc.gov.uk

Waste Collection and Disposal: Mr Alan Barker, Streetcare Manager, Town Hall, Duke Street , Barrow-in-Furness LA14 2LD

☎ 01229 876412 🖷 01229 876317 ✉ abarker@barrowbc.gov.uk

Waste Management: Mr Alan Barker, Streetcare Manager, Town Hall, Duke Street , Barrow-in-Furness LA14 2LD ☎ 01229 876412 🖷 01229 876317 ✉ abarker@barrowbc.gov.uk

Children's Play Areas: Mr Bill Brown, Parks & Playgrounds Manager, Town Hall, Duke Street, Barrow-in-Furness LA14 2LD ☎ 01229 876564 🖷 01229 876317 ✉ wrbrown@barrowbc.gov.uk

MEMBERS OF THE COUNCIL (36)

***Mayor:* Maddox**, Wendy (LAB - Dalton South)
wemaddox@barrowbc.gov.uk
***Deputy Mayor:* Thomson**, Colin (LAB - Walney South)
cthomson@barrowbc.gov.uk
***Leader of the Council:* Pidduck**, David (LAB - Hindpool)
dpidduck@barrowbc.gov.uk
***Group Leader:* Richardson**, J (CON - Hawcoat)
jrrichardson@barrowbc.gov.uk
Barlow, Desmond (LAB - Walney North)
dbarlow@barrowbc.gov.uk
Bell, D (LAB - Dalton North)
dbell@barrowbc.gov.uk
Biggins, Trevor (LAB - Central)
tabiggins@barrowbc.gov.uk
Burns, A (LAB - Hindpool)
aburns@barrowbc.gov.uk
Callister, Anthony (LAB - Walney North)
acallister@barrowbc.gov.uk
Cassidy, F (LAB - Walney South)
fcassidy@barrowbc.gov.uk
Derbyshire, M (LAB - Newbarns)
mderbyshire@barrowbc.gov.uk
Doughty, Barry (LAB - Dalton North)
bjdoughty@barrowbc.gov.uk
Garnett, Jeffrey, Harold (LAB - Risedale)
jhgarnett@barrowbc.gov.uk
Graham, L (LAB - Risedale)
lmgraham@barrowbc.gov.uk
Guselli, Ramon, John, Levio (Ray) (CON - Roosecote)
rjlguselli@barrowbc.gov.uk
Hamilton, K (LAB - Risedale)
krhamilton@barrowbc.gov.uk
Husband, Anita, Gwendoline (LAB - Walney North)
aghusband@barrowbc.gov.uk
Irwin, Mary, Teresa (LAB - Central)
mtirwin@barrowbc.gov.uk
Johnston, A (LAB - Barrow Island)
ajohnston@barrowbc.gov.uk
McClure, W (CON - Newbarns)
wmcclure@barrowbc.gov.uk
McClure, Rory (CON - Roosecote)
rmcclure@barrowbc.gov.uk
McKenna, L (LAB - Ormsgill)
lmckenna@barrowbc.gov.uk
Murphy, John (LAB - Newbarns)
jdmurphey@barrowdc.gov.uk
Murray, F (LAB - Dalton South)
fgmurray@barrowbc.gov.uk
Opie, S (LAB - Parkside)
sopie@barrowdc.gov.uk
Pemberton, A (CON - Hawcoat)
aipemberton@barrowbc.gov.uk
Pointer, Robert (LAB - Ormsgill)
rjpointer@barrowbc.gov.uk
Preston, H (LAB - Ormsgill)
hpreston@barrowbc.gov.uk
Roberts, David (CON - Hawcoat)
droberts@barrowbc.gov.uk
Seward, D (LAB - Parkside)
dmseward@barrowbc.gov.uk
Sweeney, Brendan (LAB - Parkside)
bsweeney@barrowbc.gov.uk
Thomson, Ann (LAB - Hindpool)
mathomson@barrowbc.gov.uk
Thurlow, A (LAB - Dalton North)
athurlow@barrowbc.gov.uk
Wall, H (LAB - Walney South)
hwall@barrowbc.gov.uk
Williams, Kenneth, Michael (CON - Roosecote)
kenwilliams@barrowbc.gov.uk
Wilson, E (LAB - Dalton South)
erwilson@barrowbc.gov.uk

POLITICAL COMPOSITION

LAB: 29, CON: 7

CABINET

Leader: Mr David Pidduck

COMMITTEE CHAIRS

Audit: Mrs A Burns
Corporate Services: Mrs A Burns
Executive: Mr David Pidduck
Licensing: Mr Anthony Callister
Overview & Scrutiny: Mr David Roberts
Planning: Ms Ann Thomson

BASILDON D

Basildon District Council, The Basildon Centre, St. Martin's Square, Basildon SS14 1DL ☎ 01268 533333 🖷 01268 294350 💻 www.basildon.gov.uk

FACTS & FIGURES

Police Authority: Essex Police Authority
Health Authority: East of England Strategic Health Authority
Learning and Skills Council: Eastern
Parliamentary Constituencies: Basildon and Billericay, Basildon South and Thurrock East
EU Constituencies: Eastern
Election Frequency: Elections are by thirds
Twinning: Heiligenhaus (Germany); Meaux (France)

PRINCIPAL OFFICERS

Chief Executive: Mr Bala Mahendran, Chief Executive, The Basildon Centre, St. Martins Square, Basildon SS14 1DL ☎ 01268 294560 🖷 01268 294747 ✉ bala.mahendran@basildon.gov.uk

Senior Management: Mr Mick Nice, Executive Director, The Basildon Centre, St. Martin's Square, Basildon SS14 1DL ☎ 01268 294615 🖷 01268 294241 ✉ mick.nice@basildon.gov.uk

Senior Management: Mr Chris White, Executive Director and Monitoring Officer, The Basildon Centre, St. Martin's Square, Basildon SS14 1DL ☎ 01268 294838 ✉ chris.white@basildon.gov.uk

Senior Management: Mr Ian Woolford, Interim Executive Director, The Basildon Centre, St. Martin's Square, Basildon SS14 1DL ☎ 01238 294602 🖷 01268 294241 ✉ ian.woolford@basildon.gov.uk

Architect, Building / Property Services: Mr Ken Baikie, Manager of Building Control, The Basildon Centre, St. Martin's Square, Basildon SS14 1DL ☎ 01268 294780 🖷 01268 294181 ✉ ken.baikie@basildon.gov.uk

Best Value: Mr Paul Burkinshaw, Manager of Policy, Performance & Review, The Basildon Centre, St. Martin's Square, Basildon SS14 1DL ☎ 01268 294422 🖷 01268 294599 ✉ paul.burkinshaw@basildon.gov.uk

Catering Services: Mr Paul Brace, Manager of Leisure & Countryside, The Basildon Centre, St. Martin's Square, Basildon SS14 1DL ☎ 01268 295452 🖷 01268 289844 ✉ paul.brace@basildon.gov.uk

Children / Youth Services: Ms Philippa Brent-Isherwood, Manager of Community Services, The Basildon Centre, St. Martin's Square, Basildon SS14 1DL ☎ 01268 294849 ✉ philippa.brent-isherwood@basildon.gov.uk

PR / Communications: Mr Cormac Smith, Head of Communications, The Basildon Centre, St. Martin's Square, Basildon SS14 1DL ☎ 01268 294765 ✉ cormac.smith@basildon.gov.uk

Community Planning: Ms Philippa Brent-Isherwood, Manager of Community Services, The Basildon Centre, St. Martin's Square, Basildon SS14 1DL ☎ 01268 294849 ✉ philippa.brent-isherwood@basildon.gov.uk

Community Safety: Ms Paula Mason, Community Safety Manager, The Basildon Centre, St. Martin's Square, Basildon SS14 1DL ☎ 01268 294764 🖷 01268 294324 ✉ paula.mason@basildon.gov.uk

Computer Management: Mr Lee Hession, Manager of Information Technology, The Basildon Centre, St. Martin's Square, Basildon SS14 1DL ☎ 01268 294029 🖷 01268 289844 ✉ lee.hession@basildon.gov.uk

Contracts: Mrs Lisa Hamilton, Manager of Legal & Corporate Governance, The Basildon Centre, St. Martin's Square, Basildon SS14 1DL ☎ 01268 294377 🖷 01268 294451 ✉ lisa.hamilton@basildon.gov.uk

Corporate Services: Miss Dawn French, Head of Corporate Services, The Basildon Centre, St. Martin's Square, Basildon SS14 1DL ☎ 01268 294858 🖷 ; 01268 294858 ✉ dawn.french@basildon.gov.uk

Corporate Services: Mr Chris White, Executive Director, The Basildon Centre, St. Martin's Square, Basildon SS14 1DL ☎ 01268 294838 ✉ chris.white@basildon.gov.uk

Customer Service: Mr Lee Washbrook, Manager of Customer Services & Office Facilities, The Basildon Centre, St. Martin's Square, Basildon SS14 1DL ☎ 01268 294064 ✉ lee.washbrook@basildon.gov.uk

Economic Development: Ms Gunilla Edwards, Economic Regeneration Officer, The Basildon Centre, St. Martin's Square, Basildon SS14 1DL ☎ 01268 294230 🖷 01268 294318 ✉ gunilla.edwards@basildon.gov.uk

Electoral Registration: Mr Paul Burkinshaw, Manager of Policy, Performance & Review, The Basildon Centre, St. Martin's Square, Basildon SS14 1DL ☎ 01268 294422 🖷 01268 294599 ✉ paul.burkinshaw@basildon.gov.uk

Emergency Planning: Mr Scott Logan, Head of Customer Services, The Basildon Centre, St. Martin's Square, Basildon SS14 1DL ☎ 01268 294777 🖷 01268 294662 ✉ scott.logan@basildon.gov.uk

Environmental Health: Mr Phil Easteal, Manager - Environmental Health & Community Safety, The Basildon Centre, St. Martin's Square, Basildon SS14 1DL ☎ 01268 294271 🖷 01268 294550 ✉ phil.easteal@basildon.gov.uk

Environmental Health: Mr Gerry Levelle, Head of Environment & Community, Church Walk House, Church Walk, Basildon SS14 1BY ☎ 01268 294617 🖷 01268 294662 ✉ gerry.levelle@basildon.gov.uk

Estates, Property & Valuation: Mr Ken Baikie, Manager of Building Control, The Basildon Centre, St. Martin's Square, Basildon SS14 1DL ☎ 01268 294780 🖷 01268 294181 ✉ ken.baikie@basildon.gov.uk

European Liaison: Ms Gunilla Edwards, Economic Regeneration Officer, The Basildon Centre, St. Martin's Square, Basildon SS14 1DL ☎ 01268 294230 🖷 01268 294318 ✉ gunilla.edwards@basildon.gov.uk

Facilities: Mr Lee Washbrook, Manager of Customer Services & Office Facilities, The Basildon Centre, St. Martin's Square, Basildon SS14 1DL ☎ 01268 294064 ✉ lee.washbrook@basildon.gov.uk

Finance and Treasurer: Mr Kieran Carrigan, Head of Resources, The Basildon Centre, St Martin's Square, Basildon SS14 1DL ☎ 01268 294614 🖷 01268 294662 ✉ kieran.carrigan@basildon.gov.uk

Fleet Management: Mr Stuart Noyce, Manager of Street Scene & Depot Services, Central Depot, Barleylands Road, Billericay CM11 2UF ☎ 01268 294880 🖷 01268 294968 ✉ stuart.noyce@basildon.gov.uk

Grounds Maintenance: Mr Gary Edwards, Head of Street Scene & Depot Services, Central Depot, Barleylands Road, Billericay CM11 2UF ☎ 01268 294900 🖷 01268 294968 ✉ gary.edwards@basildon.gov.uk

Health and Safety: Miss Dawn French, Head of Corporate Services, The Basildon Centre, St. Martin's Square, Basildon SS14 1DL ☎ 01268 294858 🖷 ; 01268 294858 ✉ dawn.french@basildon.gov.uk

Home Energy Conservation: Mr Graham Bannister, Principal Environmental Health Officer, The Basildon Centre, St. Martin's Square, Basildon SS14 1DL ☎ 01268 294272 🖷 01268 294550 ✉ graham.bannister@basildon.gov.uk

Housing: Mr Rab Fallon, Head of Housing Strategy & Client Services, The Basildon Centre, St. Martin's Square, Basildon SS14 1DL ☎ 01268 294012 🖷 01268 294518 ✉ rab.fallon@basildon.gov.uk

Housing Maintenance: Mr James Henderson, Property Services Business Manager, The Basildon Centre, St. Martin's Square, Basildon SS14 1DL ☎ 01268 295301 ✉ james.henderson@basildon.gov.uk

Legal: Mrs Lorraine Browne, Solicitor to the Council, The Basildon Centre, St. Martin's Square, Basildon SS14 1DL ☎ 01268 294461 🖷 01268 294451 ✉ lorraine.browne@basildon.gov.uk

Leisure and Cultural Services: Mr Paul Brace, Manager of Leisure & Countryside, Towngate Theatre, St Martin's Square, Basildon SS14 1DL ☎ 01268 465452 🖷 01268 465457 ✉ paul.brace@basildon.gov.uk

Leisure and Cultural Services: Mr Gary Edwards, Head of Street Scene & Depot Services, Central Depot, Barleylands Road, Billericay CM11 2UF ☎ 01268 294900 🖷 01268 294968 ✉ gary.edwards@basildon.gov.uk

Lottery Funding, Charity and Voluntary: Mrs Tracey Parry, Youth & Community Development Coordinator, The Basildon Centre, St. Martin's Square, Basildon SS14 1DL ☎ 01268 294052 🖷 01268 295206 ✉ tracey.parry@basildon.gov.uk

Member Services: Mr Paul Burkinshaw, Manager of Policy, Performance & Review, The Basildon Centre, St. Martin's Square, Basildon SS14 1DL ☎ 01268 294422 🖷 01268 294599 ✉ paul.burkinshaw@basildon.gov.uk

Parking: Mr Stuart Noyce, Manager of Street Scene & Depot Services, Central Depot, Barleylands Road, Billericay CM11 2UF ☎ 01268 294880 🖷 01268 294968 ✉ stuart.noyce@basildon.gov.uk

Partnerships: Mr Paul Burkinshaw, Manager of Policy, Performance & Review, The Basildon Centre, St. Martin's Square, Basildon SS14 1DL ☎ 01268 294422 🖷 01268 294599 ✉ paul.burkinshaw@basildon.gov.uk

Personnel / HR: Ms Caroline Nugent, Manager of Human Resources, The Basildon Centre, St. Martin's Square, Basildon SS14 1DL ☎ 01268 294190 ✉ caroline.nugent@basildon.gov.uk

Planning: Mr Clive Simpson, Manager of Planning Services, The Basildon Centre, St. Martin's Square, Basildon SS14 1DL ☎ 01268 294160 🖷 01268 294162 ✉ clive.simpson@basildon.gov.uk

Procurement: Mrs Lisa Hamilton, Manager of Legal & Corporate Governance, The Basildon Centre, St. Martin's Square, Basildon SS14 1DL ☎ 01268 294377 🖷 01268 294451 ✉ lisa.hamilton@basildon.gov.uk

Recycling & Waste Minimisation: Mr Gary Edwards, Head of Street Scene & Depot Services, Central Depot, Barleylands Road, Billericay CM11 2UF ☎ 01268 294900 🖷 01268 294968 ✉ gary.edwards@basildon.gov.uk

Regeneration: Mr Ken Baikie, Manager of Building Control, The Basildon Centre, St. Martin's Square, Basildon SS14 1DL ☎ 01268 294780 🖷 01268 294181 ✉ ken.baikie@basildon.gov.uk

Staff Training: Ms Caroline Nugent, Manager of Human Resources, The Basildon Centre, St. Martin's Square, Basildon SS14 1DL ☎ 01268 294190 ✉ caroline.nugent@basildon.gov.uk

Street Scene: Mr Gary Edwards, Head of Street Scene & Depot Services, Central Depot, Barleylands Road, Billericay CM11 2UF ☎ 01268 294900 🖷 01268 294968 ✉ gary.edwards@basildon.gov.uk

Sustainable Communities: Ms Philippa Brent-Isherwood, Manager of Community Services, The Basildon Centre, St. Martin's Square, Basildon SS14 1DL ☎ 01268 294849 ✉ philippa.brent-isherwood@basildon.gov.uk

Sustainable Development: Ms Philippa Brent-Isherwood, Manager of Community Services, The Basildon Centre, St. Martin's Square, Basildon SS14 1DL ☎ 01268 294849 ✉ philippa.brent-isherwood@basildon.gov.uk

Transport: Mr Stuart Noyce, Manager of Street Scene & Depot Services, Central Depot, Barleylands Road, Billericay CM11 2UF ☎ 01268 294880 🖷 01268 294968 ✉ stuart.noyce@basildon.gov.uk

Total Place: Mr Chris White, Executive Director, The Basildon Centre, St. Martin's Square, Basildon SS14 1DL ☎ 01268 294838 ✉ chris.white@basildon.gov.uk

Waste Collection and Disposal: Mr Gary Edwards, Head of Street Scene & Depot Services, Central Depot, Barleylands Road, Billericay CM11 2UF ☎ 01268 294900 🖷 01268 294968 ✉ gary.edwards@basildon.gov.uk

Waste Management: Mr Gary Edwards, Head of Street Scene & Depot Services, Central Depot, Barleylands Road, Billericay CM11 2UF ☎ 01268 294900 🖷 01268 294968 ✉ gary.edwards@basildon.gov.uk

Children's Play Areas: Mr Paul Brace, Manager of Leisure & Countryside, Towngate Theatre, St Martin's Square, Basildon SS14 1DL ☎ 01268 465452 🖷 01268 465457 ✉ paul.brace@basildon.gov.uk

MEMBERS OF THE COUNCIL (42)

***Mayor:* Larkin**, Maureen (CON - Pitsea South East)
mo.larkin@members.basildon.gov.uk

***Deputy Mayor:* Jackman**, Christopher (CON - Wickford Park)
chris.jackman@members.basildon.gov.uk

***Deputy Leader of the Council:* Turner**, Philip (CON - Billericay West)
phil.turner@members.basildon.gov.uk

***Group Leader:* Smith**, Nigel (LAB - Lee Chapel North)
nigel.smith@members.basildon.gov.uk

Group Leader: **Williams**, Geoffrey (LD - Nethermayne)
geoff.williams@members.basildon.gov.uk
Abrahall, D (CON - Pitsea South East)
david.abrahall@members.basildon.gov.uk
Allen, Stuart (CON - Crouch)
stuart.allen@members.basildon.gov.uk
Archer, Anthony (CON - Billericay East)
tony.archer@members.basildon.gov.uk
Archibald, Bill (LAB - Fryerns)
bill.archibald@members.basildon.gov.uk
Arnold, Paul (CON - Burstead)
paul.arnold@members.basildon.gov.uk
Ball, Anthony (CON - Wickford North)
tony.ball@members.basildon.gov.uk
Bennett, Alan (LAB - Lee Chapel North)
alan.bennett@members.basildon.gov.uk
Blake, Kevin (CON - Burstead)
kevin.blake@members.basildon.gov.uk
Bobbin, Keith (LAB - Pitsea North West)
keith.bobbin@members.basildon.gov.uk
Brown, Adele (LAB - Fryerns)
adele.brown@members.basildon.gov.uk
Buckley, Malcolm (CON - Wickford Castledon)
malcolm.buckley@members.basildon.gov.uk
Buckley, Sylvia (CON - Wickford Castledon)
sylvia.buckley@members.basildon.gov.uk
Callaghan, Gavin (LAB - Pitsea North West)
gavin.callaghan@members.basildon.gov.uk
Dadds, David (CON - Billericay East)
david.dadds@members.basildon.gov.uk
Davies, Allan (LAB - Fryerns)
allan.davies@members.basildon.gov.uk
Dornan, J (CON - Laindon Park)
john.dornan@members.basildon.gov.uk
Gordon, Lynda (LAB - Lee Chapel North)
lynda.gordon@members.basildon.gov.uk
Gordon, Andrew (LAB - Nethermayne)
andrew.gordon@members.basildon.gov.uk
Hedley, Anthony (CON - Billericay West)
anthony.hedley@members.basildon.gov.uk
Hillier, Sandra (CON - Langdon Hills)
sandra.hillier@members.basildon.gov.uk
Hillier, Stephen (CON - Langdon Hills)
stephen.hillier@members.basildon.gov.uk
Hyde, Jilly (CON - Laindon Park)
jilly.hyde@members.basildon.gov.uk
Lawrence, Daniel (CON - Billericay West)
daniel.lawrence@members.basildon.gov.uk
Livesey, R (CON - Pitsea North West)
ron.livesey@members.basildon.gov.uk
McGurran, Aidan (LAB - Pitsea South East)
aidan.mcgurran@members.basildon.gov.uk
Moore, Richard (CON - Burstead)
richard.moore@members.basildon.gov.uk
Morris, Carole (CON - Wickford North)
carole.morris@members.basildon.gov.uk
Morris, Donald (CON - Wickford Park)
don.morris@members.basildon.gov.uk
Mowe, Michael (CON - Wickford North)
michael.mowe@members.basildon.gov.uk
Munyambu, Daniel (IND - Vange)
daniel.munyambu@members.basildon.gov.uk
Rackley, Patricia (LAB - St Martin's)
rackleypat@btinternet.com
Rackley, Philip (LAB - St Martin's)
phil.rackley1@btopenworld.com
Sargent, Terri (CON - Crouch)
terri.sargent@members.basildon.gov.uk
Scarola, John (LAB - Laindon Park)
john.scarola@members.basildon.gov.uk
Sullivan, Stuart (CON - Billericay East)
stuart.sullivan@members.basildon.gov.uk
Taylor, Byron (LAB - Vange)
byron.taylor@members.basildon.gov.uk
Williams, Linda (LD - Nethermayne)
linda.williams@members.basildon.gov.uk

POLITICAL COMPOSITION
CON: 25, LAB: 14, LD: 2, IND: 1

CABINET
Leader: Mr Anthony Ball
Deputy Leader: Mr Philip Turner
Community: Mrs Terri Sargent
Leisure & Arts: Mr Kevin Blake
Planning: Mr Richard Moore
Regeneration & Community Safety: Mr Malcolm Buckley
Resources: Mr Stuart Sullivan

COMMITTEE CHAIRS
Appeals & General Purposes Committee: Mr Anthony Ball
Appointments: Mr Anthony Ball
Audit & Risk: Mr Donald Morris
Development Control & Traffic Management: Mr Anthony Hedley
Environment & Regeneration: Ms Sandra Hillier
Housing & Community: Mr David Dadds
Leisure & Community Services: Mrs Carole Morris
Licensing: Mr D Abrahall
Overview & Scrutiny: Mr Stephen Hillier

BASINGSTOKE & DEANE D

Basingstoke & Deane Borough Council, Civic Offices, London Road, Basingstoke RG21 4AH ☎ 01256 844844 🖷 01256 845200 💻 www.basingstoke.gov.uk

FACTS & FIGURES
Police Authority: Hampshire Police Authority
Health Authority: South Central Strategic Health Authority
Learning and Skills Council: South East
Parliamentary Constituencies: Basingstoke, Hampshire North West
EU Constituencies: South East
Election Frequency: Elections are by thirds
Twinning: Alencon (France); Braine-L'Alleud (Belgium); Euskirchen (Germany); Whitchurch and Overton: Neuvic (France)

PRINCIPAL OFFICERS
Chief Executive: Mr Tony Curtis, Chief Executive, Civic Offices, London Road, Basingstoke RG21 4AH ☎ 01256 845788 🖷 01256 845200 ✉ tony.curtis@basingstoke.gov.uk

Senior Management: Mrs Karen Brimacombe, Corporate Director, Civic Offices, London Road, Basingstoke RG21 4AH ☎ 01256 845789 🖷 01256 845200 ✉ karen.brimacombe@basingstoke.gov.uk

Senior Management: Mrs Dorcas Bunton, Corporate Director,

Civic Offices, London Road, Basingstoke RG21 4AH ☎ 01256 845797 🖷 01256 845200 ✉ dorcas.bunton@basingstoke.gov.uk

Access Officer / Social Services (Disability): Ms Tracey Cole, Head of Residents' Services, Civic Offices, London Road, Basingstoke RG21 4AH ☎ 01256 845759 🖷 01256 845200 ✉ tracey.cole@basingstoke.gov.uk

Architect, Building / Property Services: Ms Patricia Hughes, Head of Community Protection, Civic Offices, London Road, Basingstoke RG21 4AH ☎ 01256 845675 🖷 01256845200 ✉ patricia.hughes@basingstoke.gov.uk

Best Value: Mr David Robb, Head of Audit, Governance & Monitoring Officer, Civic Offices, London Road, Basingstoke RG21 4AH ☎ 01256 845315 🖷 01256 845200 ✉ david.robb@basingstoke.gov.uk

Building Control: Ms Tracey Cole, Head of Residents' Services, Civic Offices, London Road, Basingstoke RG21 4AH ☎ 01256 845759 🖷 01256 845200 ✉ tracey.cole@basingstoke.gov.uk

Catering Services: Ms Patricia Hughes, Head of Community Protection, Civic Offices, London Road, Basingstoke RG21 4AH ☎ 01256 845675 🖷 01256845200 ✉ patricia.hughes@basingstoke.gov.uk

PR / Communications: Mrs Sara Shepherd, Communications Manager, Civic Offices, London Road, Basingstoke RG21 4AH ☎ 01256 844844 ✉ sara.shepherd@basingstoke.gov.uk

Community Safety: Mr James Knight, Community Safety Manager, Civic Offices, London Road, Basingstoke RG21 4AH ☎ 01256 844844 ✉ james.knight@basingstoke.gov.uk

Contracts: Mrs Dorcas Bunton, Corporate Director, Civic Offices, London Road, Basingstoke RG21 4AH ☎ 01256 845797 🖷 01256 845200 ✉ dorcas.bunton@basingstoke.gov.uk

Corporate Services: Mrs Karen Brimacombe, Corporate Director, Civic Offices, London Road, Basingstoke RG21 4AH ☎ 01256 845789 🖷 01256 845200 ✉ karen.brimacombe@basingstoke.gov.uk

Economic Development: Mr Tony Curtis, Chief Executive, Civic Offices, London Road, Basingstoke RG21 4AH ☎ 01256 845788 🖷 01256 845200 ✉ tony.curtis@basingstoke.gov.uk

Electoral Registration: Mrs Dorcas Bunton, Corporate Director, Civic Offices, London Road, Basingstoke RG21 4AH ☎ 01256 845797 🖷 01256 845200 ✉ dorcas.bunton@basingstoke.gov.uk

Electoral Registration: Mr Wayne Dash, Electoral Services Team Leader, Civic Offices, London Road, Basingstoke RG21 4AH ☎ 01256 844844; 01256 844844 ✉ wayne.dash@basingstoke.gov.uk

Emergency Planning: Mr Tony Curtis, Chief Executive, Civic Offices, London Road, Basingstoke RG21 4AH ☎ 01256 845788 🖷 01256 845200 ✉ tony.curtis@basingstoke.gov.uk

Estates, Property & Valuation: Ms Patricia Hughes, Head of Community Protection, Civic Offices, London Road, Basingstoke RG21 4AH ☎ 01256 845675 🖷 01256845200 ✉ patricia.hughes@basingstoke.gov.uk

European Liaison: Mr Daniel Garnier, International Partnerships & Tourism Officer, Civic Offices, London Road, Basingstoke RG21 4AH ☎ 01256 845720 🖷 01256 845200 ✉ daniel.garnier@basingstoke.gov.uk

Events Manager: Mr Andrew Grove, Events Officer, Civic Offices, London Road, Basingstoke RG21 4AH ☎ 01256 845455 🖷 01256 845200 ✉ andrew.grove@basingstoke.gov.uk

Facilities: Ms Patricia Hughes, Head of Community Protection, Civic Offices, London Road, Basingstoke RG21 4AH ☎ 01256 845675 🖷 01256845200 ✉ patricia.hughes@basingstoke.gov.uk

Finance and Treasurer: Mr Kevin Jaquest, Head of Finance, Local Tax & Procurement, Civic Offices, London Road, Basingstoke RG21 4AH ☎ 01256 845513 🖷 01256 845200 ✉ kevin.jaquest@basingstoke.gov.uk

Fleet Management: Mr Steve Deverill, Insurance & Transport Officer, Civic Offices, London Road, Basingstoke RG21 4AH ☎ 01256 844446 🖷 01256 845200 ✉ steve.deverill@basingstoke.gov.uk

Grounds Maintenance: Mr Steve Featherstone, Environmental Care Operations Manager, Civic Offices, London Road, Basingstoke RG21 4AH ☎ 01256 845335 🖷 01256 845200 ✉ steve.featherstone@basingstoke.gov.uk

Health and Safety: Ms Lisa Kirkman, Interim Head of Service, Civic Offices, London Road, Basingstoke RG21 4AH ☎ 01256 845345 🖷 01256 845200 ✉ lisa.kirkman@basingstoke.gov.uk

Highways: Mr Tim Boschi, Head of Neighbourhood Development, Civic Offices, London Road, Basingstoke RG21 4AH ☎ 01256 845473 🖷 01256 845200 ✉ tim.boschi@basingstoke.gov.uk

Home Energy Conservation: Ms Claire Harper, Head of Environmental Care, Civic Offices, London Road, Basingstoke RG21 4AH ☎ 01256 845226 🖷 01256 845200 ✉ claire.harper@basingstoke.gov.uk

Housing: Ms Tracey Cole, Head of Residents' Services, Civic Offices, London Road, Basingstoke RG21 4AH ☎ 01256 845759 🖷 01256 845200 ✉ tracey.cole@basingstoke.gov.uk

Legal: Mr Chris Guy, Head of Legal, Democratic Services, Elections & Land Charges, Civic Offices, London Road, Basingstoke RG21 4AH ☎ 01256 845402 🖷 01256 845200 ✉ chris.guy@basingstoke.gov.uk

Leisure and Cultural Services: Ms Therese Lawlor, Head of Strategy & Innovation, Civic Offices, London Road, Basingstoke RG21 4AH ☎ 01256 845743 🖷 01256 845200 ✉ therese.lawlor@basingstoke.gov.uk

Licensing: Ms Lisa Kirkman, Interim Head of Service, Civic Offices, London Road, Basingstoke RG21 4AH ☎ 01256 845345 🖷 01256 845200 ✉ lisa.kirkman@basingstoke.gov.uk

Lifelong Learning: Mr Tim Boschi, Head of Neighbourhood Development, Civic Offices, London Road, Basingstoke RG21 4AH ☎ 01256 845473 🖷 01256 845200 ✉ tim.boschi@basingstoke.gov.uk

Lighting: Mr Tim Boschi, Head of Neighbourhood Development, Civic Offices, London Road, Basingstoke RG21 4AH ☎ 01256 845473 🖷 01256 845200 ✉ tim.boschi@basingstoke.gov.uk

Lottery Funding, Charity and Voluntary: Mr Tim Boschi, Head of Neighbourhood Development, Civic Offices, London Road, Basingstoke RG21 4AH ☎ 01256 845473 🖷 01256 845200 ✉ tim.boschi@basingstoke.gov.uk

Member Services: Mr Chris Guy, Head of Legal, Democratic Services, Elections & Land Charges, Civic Offices, London Road, Basingstoke RG21 4AH ☎ 01256 845402 🖷 01256 845200 ✉ chris.guy@basingstoke.gov.uk

Parking: Ms Lisa Kirkman, Interim Head of Service, Civic Offices, London Road, Basingstoke RG21 4AH ☎ 01256 845345 🖷 01256 845200 ✉ lisa.kirkman@basingstoke.gov.uk

Partnerships: Ms Therese Lawlor, Head of Strategy & Innovation, Civic Offices, London Road, Basingstoke RG21 4AH ☎ 01256 845743 🖷 01256 845200 ✉ therese.lawlor@basingstoke.gov.uk

Personnel / HR: Ms Shella Smith, Head of Personnel & Training, Civic Offices, London Road, Basingstoke RG21 4AH ☎ 01256 844844 🖷 01256 845200 ✉ shella.smith@basingstoke.gov.uk

Planning: Mr Giorgio Framalicco, Interim Head of Planning & Transport, Civic Offices, London Road, Basingstoke RG21 4AH ☎ 01256 845440 ✉ giorgio.framalicco@basingstoke.gov.uk

Procurement: Mr Kevin Jaquest, Head of Finance, Local Tax & Procurement, Civic Offices, London Road, Basingstoke RG21 4AH ☎ 01256 845513 🖷 01256 845200 ✉ kevin.jaquest@basingstoke.gov.uk

Recycling & Waste Minimisation: Ms Claire Harper, Head of Environmental Care, Civic Offices, London Road, Basingstoke RG21 4AH ☎ 01256 845226 🖷 01256 845200 ✉ claire.harper@basingstoke.gov.uk

Regeneration: Mr Tim Boschi, Head of Neighbourhood Development, Civic Offices, London Road, Basingstoke RG21 4AH ☎ 01256 845473 🖷 01256 845200 ✉ tim.boschi@basingstoke.gov.uk

Street Scene: Ms Claire Harper, Head of Environmental Care, Civic Offices, London Road, Basingstoke RG21 4AH ☎ 01256 845226 🖷 01256 845200 ✉ claire.harper@basingstoke.gov.uk

Sustainable Communities: Mrs Karen Brimacombe, Corporate Director, Civic Offices, London Road, Basingstoke RG21 4AH ☎ 01256 845789 🖷 01256 845200 ✉ karen.brimacombe@basingstoke.gov.uk

Sustainable Development: Mrs Karen Brimacombe, Corporate Director, Civic Offices, London Road, Basingstoke RG21 4AH ☎ 01256 845789 🖷 01256 845200 ✉ karen.brimacombe@basingstoke.gov.uk

Traffic Management: Mr Tim Boschi, Head of Neighbourhood Development, Civic Offices, London Road, Basingstoke RG21 4AH ☎ 01256 845473 🖷 01256 845200 ✉ tim.boschi@basingstoke.gov.uk

Transport: Mr Giorgio Framalicco, Interim Head of Planning & Transport, Civic Offices, London Road, Basingstoke RG21 4AH ☎ 01256 845440 ✉ giorgio.framalicco@basingstoke.gov.uk

Transport Planner: Mr Giorgio Framalicco, Interim Head of Planning & Transport, Civic Offices, London Road, Basingstoke RG21 4AH ☎ 01256 845440 ✉ giorgio.framalicco@basingstoke.gov.uk

Waste Collection and Disposal: Ms Claire Harper, Head of Environmental Care, Civic Offices, London Road, Basingstoke RG21 4AH ☎ 01256 845226 🖷 01256 845200 ✉ claire.harper@basingstoke.gov.uk

Waste Management: Ms Claire Harper, Head of Environmental Care, Civic Offices, London Road, Basingstoke RG21 4AH ☎ 01256 845226 🖷 01256 845200 ✉ claire.harper@basingstoke.gov.uk

MEMBERS OF THE COUNCIL (60)

***Mayor:* Biermann**, Martin (IND - Chineham)
cllr.martin.biermann@basingstoke.gov.uk

***Deputy Mayor:* Putty**, Dan (CON - Hatch Warren & Beggarwood)
cllr.dan.putty@basingstoke.gov.uk

Baker, Paula (LD - Overton, Laverstoke & Steventon)
cllr.paula.baker@basingstoke.gov.uk

Barnes, John (LD - Brighton Hill South)
cllr.john.branes@basingstoke.gov.uk

Bean, Rebecca (CON - Hatch Warren & Beggarwood)
cllr.rebecca.bean@basingstoke.gov.uk

Bound, Michael (LD - Baughurst & Tadley North)
cllr.michael.bound@basingstoke.gov.uk

Burgess, Rita (CON - Kempshott)
cllr.rita.burgess@basingstoke.gov.uk

Cherrett, Karen (CON - Rooksdown)
cllr.karen.cherrett@basingstoke.gov.uk

Court, Anne (CON - Kempshott)
cllr.anne.court@basingstoke.gov.uk

Cousens, Jack (LAB - Brookvale & Kings Furlong)
cllr.jack.cousens@basingstoke.gov.uk

Cubit, Onnalee (IND - Basing)
cllr.onnalee.cubitt@basingstoke.gov.uk

Day, Stephen (LD - Grove)
cllr.stephen.day@basingstoke.gov.uk

Donnell, Robert (CON - Winklebury)
cllr.robert.donnell@basingstoke.gov.uk

Dunlop, Eric (LD - Whitchurch)
cllr.eric.dunlop@basingstoke.gov.uk

Eachus, Hayley (CON - Kempshott)
cllr.hayley.eachus@basingstoke.gov.uk

Eyre, David (LAB - Brighton Hill South)
cllr.david.eyre@basingstoke.gov.uk

Finney, Andrew (CON - Oakley & North Waltham)
cllr.andrew.finney@basingstoke.gov.uk

Frankum, Paul (LAB - Popley West)
cllr.paul.frankum@basingstoke.gov.uk
Frankum, Jane (LAB - Popley West)
cllr.jane.frankum@basingstoke.gov.uk
Gardiner, Roger (CON - Pamber & Silchester)
cllr.roger.gardiner@basingstoke.gov.uk
Godesen, Sven (CON - Basing)
cllr.sven.godesen@basingstoke.gov.uk
Golding, Rob (CON - Oakley & North Waltham)
cllr.rob.goulding@basingstoke.gov.uk
Gurden, Brian (LD - Brighton Hill North)
cllr.brian.gurden@basingstoke.gov.uk
Harvey, Paul (LAB - Norden)
cllr.paul.harvey@basingstoke.gov.uk
Hood, George (LAB - Norden)
cllr.george.hood@basingstoke.gov.uk
Hussey, Ronald (LD - Grove)
cllr.ron.hussey@basingstoke.gov.uk
Izett, John (CON - Burghclere, Highclere & Bourne)
cllr.john.izett@basingstoke.gov.uk
James, Laura (LAB - Norden)
cllr.laura.james@basingstoke.gov.uk
James, Gavin (LD - Eastrop)
cllr.gavin.james@basingstoke.gov.uk
Jayawardena, Ranil (CON - Bramley & Sherfield)
cllr.ranil.jayawardena@basingstoke.gov.uk
Jones, Tony (LAB - Buckskin)
cllr.tony.jones@basingstoke.gov.uk
Keating, Sean (LAB - South Ham)
cllr.sean.keating@basingstoke.gov.uk
Leek, John (CON - Sherborne St John)
cllr.john.leek@basingstoke.gov.uk
Leeks, David (CON - Tadley South)
cllr.david.leeks@basingstoke.gov.uk
Marks, Stephen (CON - Basing)
cllr.stephen.marks@basingstoke.gov.uk
Miller, Paul (CON - Chineham)
cllr.paul.miller@basingstoke.gov.uk
Mitchell, Horace (CON - Burghclere, Highclere & Bourne)
cllr.horace.mitchell@basingstoke.gov.uk
Musson, Robert (CON - Tadley South)
cllr.robert.musson@basingstoke.gov.uk
Osselton, Cathy (CON - Kingsclere)
cllr.cathy.osselton@basingstoke.gov.uk
Parker, Stuart (LD - Eastrop)
cllr.stuart.parker@basingstoke.gov.uk
Peach, Steven (CON - Winklebury)
cllr.steven.peach@basingstoke.gov.uk
Potter, David (LAB - Popley East)
cllr.david.potter@basingstoke.gov.uk
Regan, Colin (LAB - South Ham)
cllr.colin.regan@basingstoke.gov.uk
Reid, Terri (CON - Hatch Warren & Beggarwood)
cllr.terri.reid@basingstoke.gov.uk
Round, Graham (CON - Baughurst & Tadley North)
cllr.graham.round@basingstoke.gov.uk
Ruffell, Mark (CON - Upton Grey & The Candovers)
cllr.mark.ruffell@basingstoke.gov.uk
Sanders, Clive (CON - East Woodhay)
cllr.clive.sanders@basingstoke.gov.uk
Shaw, John (LD - Brookvale & Kings Furlong)
cllr.john.shaw@basingstoke.gov.uk
Sherlock, Donald (CON - Kingsclere)
cllr.donald.sherlock@basingstoke.gov.uk
Still, Elaine (CON - Chineham)
cllr.elaine.still@basingstoke.gov.uk
Taylor, Diane (CON - Oakley & North Waltham)
cllr.diane.taylor@basingstoke.gov.uk
Taylor, Robert (CON - Buckskin)
cllr.robert.taylor@basingstoke.gov.uk
Tilbury, Ian (IND - Overton, Laverstoke & Steventon)
cllr.ian.tilbury@basingstoke.gov.uk
Tomblin, Chris (IND - Bramley & Sherfield)
cllr.chris.tomblin@basingstoke.gov.uk
Tucker, Marilyn (CON - Pamber & Silchester)
cllr.marilyn.tucker@basingstoke.gov.uk
Washbourne, Vivien (LAB - Popley East)
cllr.vivien.washbourne@basingstoke.gov.uk
Watts, Gary (LAB - South Ham)
cllr.gary.watts@basingstoke.gov.uk
Watts, Keith (LD - Whitchurch)
cllr.keith.watts@basingstoke.gov.uk
West, Stephen (CON - Tadley Central)
cllr.stephen.west@basingstoke.gov.uk
Wooldridge, Carolyn (LAB - Brighton Hill North)
cllr.carolyn.wooldridge@basingstoke.gov.uk

POLITICAL COMPOSITION
CON: 31, LAB: 14, LD: 11, IND: 4

CABINET
Leader: Mr Clive Sanders
Deputy Leader: Mr Ranil Jayawardena
Communities, Sport & Culture: Ms Elaine Still
Community Services: Ms Hayley Eachus
Economic Strategy & Development: Mr Andrew Finney
Environment & Climate Change: Mr Robert Donnell
Housing & Regeneration: Mr Rob Golding
Partnerships: Ms Cathy Osselton
Planning: Mr Donald Sherlock
Property & Finance: Mr John Izett

COMMITTEE CHAIRS
Audit Governance & Accounts: Ms Karen Cherrett
Community Wellbeing: Mr Robert Taylor
Development Control: Mr Horace Mitchell
Economic Prosperity & Performance: Mr Graham Round
Housing & Environment: Mr Stephen Marks
Human Resources: Mr Stephen West
Licensing: Ms Diane Taylor
Planning & Infrastructure: Mr Mark Ruffell

BASSETLAW D

Bassetlaw District Council, Queen's Buildings, Potter Street, Worksop S80 2AH ☎ 01909 533533 🖷 01909 501758
🖳 www.bassetlaw.gov.uk

FACTS & FIGURES
Police Authority: Nottinghamshire Police Authority
Health Authority: East Midlands Strategic Health Authority
Learning and Skills Council: East Midlands
Parliamentary Constituencies: Bassetlaw
EU Constituencies: East Midlands
Election Frequency: Elections are by thirds
Twinning: Aurillac / Arpajon (France); Farmers Branch (Texas, USA); Retford: Pfungstadt (Germany); Worksop: Garbsen (Germany)

PRINCIPAL OFFICERS

Chief Executive: Mr David Hunter, Chief Executive, Queen's Buildings, Potter Street, Worksop S80 2AH ☎ 01909 533533 🖷 01909 535498 ✉ david.hunter@bassetlaw.gov.uk

Senior Management: Mr Mark Ladyman, Director - Community Services, Queen's Buildings, Potter Street, Worksop S80 2AH ☎ 01909 533160 🖷 01909 535498 ✉ mark.ladyman@bassetlaw.gov.uk

Senior Management: Mr Neil Taylor, Director - Resources, Queen's Buildings, Potter Street, Worksop S80 2AH ☎ 01909 533221 🖷 01909 535498 ✉ neil.taylor@bassetlaw.gov.uk

Senior Management: Ms Ros Theakstone, Director - Corporate Services, Queen's Buildings, Potter Street, Worksop S80 2AH ☎ 01909 533160 🖷 01909 535498 ✉ ros.theakstone@bassetlaw.gov.uk

Access Officer / Social Services (Disability): Mr Malcolm Robson, Access Officer, Queen's Buildings, Potter Street, Worksop S80 2AH ☎ 01909 533195 🖷 01909 533400 ✉ malcolm.robson@bassetlaw.gov.uk

Architect, Building / Property Services: Mr John Unstead, Property Manager, Queen's Buildings, Worksop S80 2AH ☎ 01909 533706 🖷 01909 501246 ✉ john.unstead@bassetlaw.gov.uk

Best Value: Ms Gillian Blenkinsop, Corporate Development & Policy Manager, Queen's Buildings, Potter Street, Worksop S80 2AH ☎ 01909 533142 🖷 01909 501758 ✉ gillian.blenkinsop@bassetlaw.gov.uk

Building Control: Mrs Angela Edwards, Building Control Manager, Queen's Buildings, Potter Street, Worksop S80 2AH ☎ 01909 533130 🖷 01909 533400 ✉ building.control@bassetlaw.gov.uk

Building Control: Mr Robert Whatley, Principal Building Control Officer, Queen's Buildings, Potter Street, Worksop S80 2AH ☎ 01909 533130 🖷 01909 482622 ✉ bob.whatley@bassetlaw.gov.uk

PR / Communications: Mr Jonathan Brassington, Communications Manager, Queen's Buildings, Potter Street, Worksop S80 2AH ☎ 01909 533726 🖷 01909 501758 ✉ jonathan.brassington@bassetlaw.gov.uk

Community Planning: Ms Gillian Blenkinsop, Corporate Development & Policy Manager, Queen's Buildings, Potter Street, Worksop S80 2AH ☎ 01909 533142 🖷 01909 501758 ✉ gillian.blenkinsop@bassetlaw.gov.uk

Community Safety: Ms Gillian Blenkinsop, Corporate Development & Policy Manager, Queen's Buildings, Potter Street, Worksop S80 2AH ☎ 01909 533142 🖷 01909 501758 ✉ gillian.blenkinsop@bassetlaw.gov.uk

Computer Management: Mr Andrew Bramall, Strategic ICT Manager, Queen's Buildings, Potter Street, Worksop S80 2AH ☎ 01909 533122 🖷 01909 535506 ✉ andrew.bramall@bassetlaw.gov.uk

Contracts: Mr Bob Trusswell, Head - Procurement, Sherwood Lodge, Bolsover S44 6NF ☎ 01246 242311 ✉ bob.trusswell@bolsover.gov.uk

Contracts: Mrs Sandy Williams, Principal Procurement Manager, Queen's Buildings, Potter Street, Worksop S80 2AH ☎ 01909 533449 🖷 01909 501758 ✉ sandy.williams@bassetlaw.gov.uk

Corporate Services: Ms Ros Theakstone, Director - Corporate Services, Queen's Buildings, Potter Street, Worksop S80 2AH ☎ 01909 533160 🖷 01909 535498 ✉ ros.theakstone@bassetlaw.gov.uk

Customer Service: Mr Andrew Burton, Head - Revenues & Customer Services, Queen's Buildings, Potter Street, Worksop S80 2AH ☎ 01909 533238 🖷 01909 533700 ✉ andrew.burton@bassetlaw.gov.uk

Economic Development: Mr Robert Wilkinson, Economic Development Team Manager, Queen's Buildings, Potter Street, Worksop S80 2AH ☎ 01909 533230 🖷 01909 501246 ✉ robert.wilkinson@bassetlaw.gov.uk

E-Government: Mr Steve Brown, Senior Manager Support Services, Queen's Buildings, Potter Street, Worksop S80 2AH ☎ 01909 533767 🖷 01909 535498 ✉ steve.brown@bassetlaw.gov.uk

Electoral Registration: Mr Stephen Phillips, Election Officer, Queen's Buildings, Potter Street, Worksop S80 2AH ☎ 01909 533464 🖷 01909 501758 ✉ stephen.phillips@bassetlaw.gov.uk

Emergency Planning: Mr Jim Moran, Principal Safety Officer, Carlton Forest House, Hundred Acre Lane, Carlton Forest, Worksop S81 0TS ☎ 01909 534337 ✉ james.moran@bassetlaw.gov.uk

Energy Management: Miss Kerri Ellis, Sustainability Officer, Queen's Buildings, Potter Street, Worksop S80 2AH ☎ 01909 533211 🖷 01909 533486 ✉ kerri.ellis@bassetlaw.gov.uk

Environmental / Technical Services: Mr Mark Ladyman, Director - Community Services, Queen's Buildings, Potter Street, Worksop S80 2AH ☎ 01909 533160 🖷 01909 535498 ✉ mark.ladyman@bassetlaw.gov.uk

Environmental Health: Mrs Elizabeth Prime, Queen's Buildings, Potter Street, Worksop S80 2AH ☎ 01909 533219 🖷 01909 533397 ✉ elizabeth.prime@bassetlaw.gov.uk

Environmental Health: Mr Julian Proudman, Joint Principal Environmental Health Manager, Queen's Buildings, Potter Street, Worksop S80 2AH ☎ 01909 533219 🖷 01909 533397 ✉ julian.proudman@bassetlaw.gov.uk

Estates, Property & Valuation: Mr John Unstead, Property Manager, Queen's Buildings, Worksop S80 2AH ☎ 01909 533706 🖷 01909 501246 ✉ john.unstead@bassetlaw.gov.uk

Finance and Treasurer: Mr Mike Hill, Head - Finance &

Property, Queen's Buildings, Potter Street, Worksop S80 2AH ☎ 01909 533174 🖷 01909 501246 ✉ mike.hill@bassetlaw.gov.uk

Finance and Treasurer: Mr Neil Taylor, Director - Resources, Queen's Buildings, Potter Street, Worksop S80 2AH ☎ 01909 533221 🖷 01909 535498 ✉ neil.taylor@bassetlaw.gov.uk

Fleet Management: Mr Peter Jones, Operational Services Manager - Fleet & Admin Services, Hundred Acre Lane, Carlton Forest, Worksop S81 0TS ☎ 01909 534487 🖷 01909 730586 ✉ peter.jones@bassetlaw.gov.uk

Grounds Maintenance: Mr Keith Somers, Operational Services Manager - Parks, Open Spaces & Cemeteries, West House, Hundred Acre Lane, Carlton Forest, Worksop S81 0TS ☎ 01919 534420 ✉ keith.somers@bassetlaw.gov.uk

Health and Safety: Mr Jim Moran, Principal Safety Officer, Carlton Forest House, Hundred Acre Lane, Carlton Forest, Worksop S81 0TS ☎ 01909 534337 ✉ james.moran@bassetlaw.gov.uk

Home Energy Conservation: Mrs Wendy Piggott, Strategic Housing Development Manager, Queen's Buildings, Potter Street, Worksop S80 2AH ☎ 01909 533425 ✉ wendy.piggott@bassetlaw.gov.uk

Housing: Ms Claire Frost, Housing Strategy & Renewal Manager, Queen's Buildings, Potter Street, Worksop S80 2AH ☎ 01909 533857 ✉ claire.frost@bassetlaw.gov.uk

Legal: Mr Steve Brown, Senior Manager Support Services, Queen's Buildings, Potter Street, Worksop S80 2AH ☎ 01909 533767 🖷 01909 535498 ✉ steve.brown@bassetlaw.gov.uk

Leisure and Cultural Services: Mr Peter Clark, Leisure & Cultural Services Manager, 17b The Square, Retford DN22 6DB ☎ 01909 534507 🖷 01909 534529 ✉ peter.clark@bassetlaw.gov.uk

Licensing: Mr Stephen Wormald, Principal Solicitor - Licensing & Regulatory, Queen's Buildings, Potter Street, Worksop S80 2AH ☎ 01909 533160 🖷 01909 535498 ✉ stephen.wormald@bassetlaw.gov.uk

Lottery Funding, Charity and Voluntary: Mr Mike Hill, Head - Finance & Property, Queen's Buildings, Potter Street, Worksop S80 2AH ☎ 01909 533174 🖷 01909 501246 ✉ mike.hill@bassetlaw.gov.uk

Member Services: Ms Ros Theakstone, Director - Corporate Services, Queen's Buildings, Potter Street, Worksop S80 2AH ☎ 01909 533160 🖷 01909 535498 ✉ ros.theakstone@bassetlaw.gov.uk

Parking: Mr Richard Blagg, Town Centre Manager - Operational, Queen's Buildings, Potter Street, Worksop S80 2AH ☎ 01909 535104 🖷 01909 501246 ✉ richard.blagg@bassetlaw.gov.uk

Partnerships: Ms Ros Theakstone, Director - Corporate Services, Queen's Buildings, Potter Street, Worksop S80 2AH ☎ 01909 533160 🖷 01909 535498 ✉ ros.theakstone@bassetlaw.gov.uk

Personnel / HR: Mr Len Hull, Head - Human Resources, Queen's Buildings, Potter Street, Worksop S80 2AH ☎ 01909 534136 🖷 01909 533451 ✉ len.hull@bassetlaw.gov.uk

Planning: Mr David Armiger, Head - Community Prosperity, Queen's Buildings, Potter Street, Worksop S80 2AH ☎ 01909 533187 🖷 01909 533400 ✉ david.armiger@bassetlaw.gov.uk

Procurement: Mr Bob Trusswell, Head - Procurement, Sherwood Lodge, Bolsover S44 6NF ☎ 01246 242311 ✉ bob.trusswell@bolsover.gov.uk

Procurement: Mrs Sandy Williams, Principal Procurement Manager, Queen's Buildings, Potter Street, Worksop S80 2AH ☎ 01909 533449 🖷 01909 501758 ✉ sandy.williams@bassetlaw.gov.uk

Recycling & Waste Minimisation: Mr Tim Andrew, Operational Services Manager - Waste & Recyling, Hundred Acre Lane, Carlton Forest, Worksop S81 0TS ☎ 01909 534422 🖷 01909 730586 ✉ tim.andrew@bassetlaw.gov.uk

Recycling & Waste Minimisation: Mr Mark Ladyman, Director - Community Services, Queen's Buildings, Potter Street, Worksop S80 2AH ☎ 01909 533160 🖷 01909 535498 ✉ mark.ladyman@bassetlaw.gov.uk

Regeneration: Mr Robert Wilkinson, Economic Development Team Manager, Queen's Buildings, Potter Street, Worksop S80 2AH ☎ 01909 533230 🖷 01909 501246 ✉ robert.wilkinson@bassetlaw.gov.uk

Staff Training: Mrs Jenny Rodriguez, HR Business Partner - Learning & Development, Queen's Buildings, Potter Street, Worksop S80 2AH ☎ 01909 534134 ✉ jenny.rodriguez@bassetlaw.gov.uk

Street Scene: Mr Tim Andrew, Operational Services Manager - Waste & Recyling, Hundred Acre Lane, Carlton Forest, Worksop S81 0TS ☎ 01909 534422 🖷 01909 730586 ✉ tim.andrew@bassetlaw.gov.uk

Sustainable Communities: Mr Mark Ladyman, Director - Community Services, Queen's Buildings, Potter Street, Worksop S80 2AH ☎ 01909 533160 🖷 01909 535498 ✉ mark.ladyman@bassetlaw.gov.uk

Sustainable Communities: Ms Ros Theakstone, Director - Corporate Services, Queen's Buildings, Potter Street, Worksop S80 2AH ☎ 01909 533160 🖷 01909 535498 ✉ ros.theakstone@bassetlaw.gov.uk

Sustainable Development: Mr Mark Ladyman, Director - Community Services, Queen's Buildings, Potter Street, Worksop S80 2AH ☎ 01909 533160 🖷 01909 535498 ✉ mark.ladyman@bassetlaw.gov.uk

Tourism: Ms Sandra Withington, Development & Marketing Officer, Queen's Buildings, Potter Street, Worksop S80 2AH ☎ 01909 533533 🖷 01909 501246 ✉ sandra.withington@bassetlaw.gov.uk

Town Centre: Mr Richard Blagg, Town Centre Manager - Operational, Queen's Buildings, Potter Street, Worksop S80 2AH ☎ 01909 535104 🖷 01909 501246 ✉ richard.blagg@bassetlaw.gov.uk

Transport: Mr Peter Jones, Operational Services Manager - Fleet & Admin Services, Hundred Acre Lane, Carlton Forest, Worksop S81 0TS ☎ 01909 534487 🖷 01909 730586 ✉ peter.jones@bassetlaw.gov.uk

Waste Collection and Disposal: Mr Tim Andrew, Operational Services Manager - Waste & Recyling, Hundred Acre Lane, Carlton Forest, Worksop S81 0TS ☎ 01909 534422 🖷 01909 730586 ✉ tim.andrew@bassetlaw.gov.uk

Waste Collection and Disposal: Mr Mark Ladyman, Director - Community Services, Queen's Buildings, Potter Street, Worksop S80 2AH ☎ 01909 533160 🖷 01909 535498 ✉ mark.ladyman@bassetlaw.gov.uk

Waste Management: Mr Tim Andrew, Operational Services Manager - Waste & Recyling, Hundred Acre Lane, Carlton Forest, Worksop S81 0TS ☎ 01909 534422 🖷 01909 730586 ✉ tim.andrew@bassetlaw.gov.uk

Waste Management: Mr Mark Ladyman, Director - Community Services, Queen's Buildings, Potter Street, Worksop S80 2AH ☎ 01909 533160 🖷 01909 535498 ✉ mark.ladyman@bassetlaw.gov.uk

Children's Play Areas: Mr Peter Clark, Leisure & Cultural Services Manager, 17b The Square, Retford DN22 6DB ☎ 01909 534507 🖷 01909 534529 ✉ peter.clark@bassetlaw.gov.uk

MEMBERS OF THE COUNCIL (48)

***Chair:* Campbell**, Ian James (LAB - East Retford West)
ian.campbell@bassetlaw.gov.uk

***Leader of the Council:* Greaves**, Simon (LAB - Worksop North East)
simon.greaves@bassetlaw.gov.uk

***Deputy Leader of the Council:* Wynne**, Griffith (LAB - Worksop East)
griff.wynne@bassetlaw.gov.uk

***Group Leader:* Burton**, Hugh (IND - Sturton)
hugh.burton@bassetlaw.gov.uk

Barker, Bill (LAB - Worksop North)
bill.barker@bassetlaw.gov.uk

Battery, Ann (LAB - East Retford South)
ann.battery@bassetlaw.gov.uk

Bowles, Barry (CON - Blyth)
barry.bowles@bassetlaw.gov.uk

Brand, Hazel (IND - Misterton)
hazel.brand@bassetlaw.gov.uk

Carrington-Wilde, Robin Brian (LAB - Carlton)
robin.carrington-wilde@bassetlaw.gov.uk

Challinor, David (LAB - Harworth)
david.challinor@bassetlaw.gov.uk

Chambers, Alan (LAB - East Retford West)
alan.chambers@bassetlaw.gov.uk

Douglas, Pat (LAB - Welbeck)
patricia.douglas@bassetlaw.gov.uk

Entwistle, Clifford (LAB - Worksop East)
cliff.entwistle@bassetlaw.gov.uk

Evans, June (LAB - harworth)
june.evans@bassetlaw.gov.uk

Fielding, Sybil (LAB - Worksop North West)
sybil.fielding@bassetlaw.gov.uk

Freeman, Gillian (LAB - Langold)
gillian.freeman@bassetlaw.gov.uk

Gray, Michael (CON - Ranskill)
michael.gray@bassetlaw.gov.uk

Gregory, Michelle (LAB - East Retford North)
michelle.gregory@bassetlaw.gov.uk

Hart, Frank (LAB - Harworth)
frank.hart@bassetlaw.gov.uk

Hopkinson, Brian (LAB - Worksop South East)
brian.hopkinson@bassetlaw.gov.uk

Isard, Keith (CON - Tuxford & Trent)
keith.isard@bassetlaw.gov.uk

Isard, Shirley (CON - Tuxford & Trent)
shirley.isard@bassetlaw.gov.uk

Jones, Gwynneth (LAB - Worksop North)
gwynneth.jones@bassetlaw.gov.uk

Leigh, Rebecca (LAB - Worksop North East)
rebecca.leigh@bassetlaw.gov.uk

Leigh, Julie (LAB - Worksop South)
julie.leigh@bassetlaw.gov.uk

May, Sylvia (LAB - Worksop South)
sylvia.may@bassetlaw.gov.uk

Mumby, Adele (LAB - East Retford North)
adele.mumby@bassetlaw.gov.uk

Ogle, John (CON - East Markham)
john.ogle@bassetlaw.gov.uk

Oxby, Graham (LAB - East Retford North)
graham.oxby@bassetlaw.gov.uk

Palmer, Carol (LAB - East Retford East)
carol.palmer@bassetlaw.gov.uk

Pidwell, David George (LAB - Carlton)
david.pidwell@bassetlaw.gov.uk

Potts, Josie (LAB - Worksop South East)
josie.potts@bassetlaw.gov.uk

Potts, David (LAB - Worksop North)
david.potts@bassetlaw.gov.uk

Pressley, David (LAB - Worksop North West)
david.pressley@bassetlaw.gov.uk

Quigley, Margaret (CON - East Retford East)
wendy.quigley@bassetlaw.gov.uk

Rafferty, Tina (LAB - Carlton)
tina.rafferty@bassetlaw.gov.uk

Rhodes, Alan (LAB - Worksop North West)
alan.rhodes@bassetlaw.gov.uk

Rickells, Jeffery (CON - Rampton)
jeffery.rickells@bassetlaw.gov.uk

Sanger, Joan (IND - Beckingham)
joan.sanger@bassetlaw.gov.uk

Shephard, John (LAB - Worksop South East)
john.shephard@bassetlaw.gov.uk

Simpson, Annette (CON - Everton)
annette.simpson@bassetlaw.gov.uk

Storey, Michael (LAB - East Retford East)
michael.storey@bassetlaw.gov.uk

Sutton, kathleen (CON - Clayworth)
kath.sutton@bassetlaw.gov.uk

Taylor, Tracey (CON - Sutton)
tracey.taylor@bassetlaw.gov.uk

Toms, Shirley (LAB - Worksop North East)
shirley.toms@bassetlaw.gov.uk

Troop, Carolyn (LAB - East Retford South)

carolyn.troop@bassetlaw.gov.uk
Wanless, Christopher (CON - Worksop South)
chris.wanless@bassetlaw.gov.uk
White, Jo (LAB - Worksop East)
jo.white@bassetlaw.gov.uk

POLITICAL COMPOSITION

LAB: 34, CON: 11, IND: 3

CABINET

Leader: Mr Simon Greaves
Deputy Leader: Mr Griffith Wynne
Community Prosperity: Mr David Pressley
Environment & Leisure: Ms Julie Leigh
Finance & Property: Ms June Evans
Housing: Mr Alan Rhodes
Performance & Strategy: Mr Griffith Wynne
Planning: Mr David Pressley
Policy & Community Engagement: Mr Simon Greaves

COMMITTEE CHAIRS

Appointments: Mr Simon Greaves
Audit & Risk: Mr Robin Brian Carrington-Wilde
Licensing: Ms Josie Potts
Overview & Scrutiny: Mr John Shephard
Planning: Mr David Pressley

BATH & NORTH EAST SOMERSET U

Bath & North East Somerset Council, Guildhall, High Street, Bath BA1 5AW ☎ 01225 477000 🖷 01225 477499 cis@bathnes.gov.uk 🖳 www.bathnes.gov.uk

FACTS & FIGURES

Police Authority: Avon & Somerset Police Authority
Health Authority: NHS South West
Learning and Skills Council: South West
Parliamentary Constituencies: Bath
EU Constituencies: South West
Election Frequency: Elections are of whole council

PRINCIPAL OFFICERS

Chief Executive: Dr Jo Farrar, Chief Executive, Guildhall, High Street, Bath BA1 5AW ☎ 01225 477400 🖷 01225 477062 jo_farrar@bathnes.gov.uk

Senior Management: Mr Ashley Ayre, Divisional Director - Children, YP & Family Support Services, Guildhall, High Street, Bath BA1 1LA ☎ 01225 394200 🖷 01225 394011 ashley_ayre@bathnes.gov.uk

Senior Management: Mr Glen Chipp, Strategic Director - Place, Riverside, Temple Street, Keynsham, Bristol BS31 1LA ☎ 01225 394567 🖷 01225 396523 glen_chipp@bathnes.gov.uk

Senior Management: Mr Andrew Pate, Strategic Director - Resources, Guildhall, High Street, Bath BA1 5AW ☎ 01225 477300 🖷 01225 477377 andrew_pate@bathnes.gov.uk

Architect, Building / Property Services: Mr Tom McBain, Divisional Director - Property & Facilities, Northgate House, Upper Borough Walls, Bath BA1 1RG ☎ 01225 477806 🖷 01225 477108 tom_mcbain@bathnes.gov.uk

Building Control: Mr David Trigwell, Divisional Director - Planning & Transport Development, Riverside, Temple Street, Keynsham BS31 1LA ☎ 01225 477702 🖷 01225 394199 david_trigwell@bathnes.gov.uk

Catering Services: Mr Tom McBain, Divisional Director - Property & Facilities, Northgate House, Upper Borough Walls, Bath BA1 1RG ☎ 01225 477806 🖷 01225 477108 tom_mcbain@bathnes.gov.uk

Children / Youth Services: Mr Maurice Lindsay, Divisional Director - Children, YP & Family Support Services, Riverside, Temple Street, Keynsham, Bristol BS31 1LA ☎ 01225 396289 🖷 01225 396115 maurice_lindsay@bathnes.gov.uk

Civil Registration: Mr Vernon Hitchman, Divisional Director - Legal & Democratic Services, Riverside, Temple Street, Keynsham BS31 1LA ☎ 01225 395171 🖷 01225 394043 vernon_hitchman@bathnes.gov.uk

PR / Communications: Mr David Thompson, Divisional Director - Improvement & Performance, Guildhall, High Street, Bath BA1 5AW ☎ 01225 394368 🖷 01225 394298 dave_thompson@bathnes.gov.uk

Community Planning: Mr David Tethewey, Divisional Director - Policy and Partnerships, Guildhall, High Street, Bath BA1 5AW ☎ 01225 477300 🖷 01225 396353 david_trethewey@bathnes.gov.uk

Community Safety: Mr David Tethewey, Divisional Director - Policy and Partnerships, Guildhall, High Street, Bath BA1 5AW ☎ 01225 477300 🖷 01225 396353 david_trethewey@bathnes.gov.uk

Computer Management: Mrs Angela Parratt, Head - Transformation, Guildhall, High Street, Bath BA1 5AW ☎ 01225 476576 🖷 01225 477377 angela_parratt@bathnes.gov.uk

Consumer Protection and Trading Standards: Mr Matthew Smith, Divisional Director - Environmental Services, Royal Victoria Park Nursery, Marlborough Lane, Bath BA1 2LZ ☎ 01225 396888 🖷 01225 480072 matthew_smith@bathnes.gov.uk

Contracts: Mr Jeff Wring, Head - Risk & Assurance, Guildhall, High Street, Bath BA1 5AW ☎ 01225 477323 jeff_wring@bathnes.gov.uk

Corporate Services: Mr Tim Richens, Divisional Director - Finance, Guildhall, High Street, Bath BA1 5AW ☎ 01225 477468 🖷 01225 477377 tim_richens@bathnes.gov.uk

Customer Service: Mr Ian Savigar, Divisional Director - Customer Services, Lewis House, Manvers Street, Bath BA1 1JG ☎ 01225 477327 ian_savigar@bathnes.gov.uk

Direct Labour: Mr Matthew Smith, Divisional Director - Environmental Services, Royal Victoria Park Nursery, Marlborough Lane, Bath BA1 2LZ ☎ 01225 396888 🖷 01225 480072 matthew_smith@bathnes.gov.uk

Economic Development: Mr John Wilkinson, Development Manager, 10 Palace Mews, Bath BA1 2NH ☎ 01225 396593 john_Wilkinson@bathnes.gov.uk

Education: Mr Tony Parker, Divisional Director, Riverside, Temple Street, Keynsham, Bristol BS31 1LA ☎ 01225 394197 tony_parker@bathnes.gov.uk

Electoral Registration: Mr Vernon Hitchman, Divisional Director - Legal & Democratic Services, Riverside, Temple Street, Keynsham BS31 1LA ☎ 01225 395171 🖷 01225 394043 vernon_hitchman@bathnes.gov.uk

Emergency Planning: Mr Jeff Wring, Head - Risk & Assurance, Guildhall, High Street, Bath BA1 5AW ☎ 01225 477323 jeff_wring@bathnes.gov.uk

Energy Management: Mr Tom McBain, Divisional Director - Property & Facilities, Northgate House, Upper Borough Walls, Bath BA1 1RG ☎ 01225 477806 🖷 01225 477108 tom_mcbain@bathnes.gov.uk

Environmental / Technical Services: Mr Matthew Smith, Divisional Director - Environmental Services, Royal Victoria Park Nursery, Marlborough Lane, Bath BA1 2LZ ☎ 01225 396888 🖷 01225 480072 matthew_smith@bathnes.gov.uk

Environmental Health: Mr Matthew Smith, Divisional Director - Environmental Services, Royal Victoria Park Nursery, Marlborough Lane, Bath BA1 2LZ ☎ 01225 396888 🖷 01225 480072 matthew_smith@bathnes.gov.uk

Estates, Property & Valuation: Mr Tom McBain, Divisional Director - Property & Facilities, Northgate House, Upper Borough Walls, Bath BA1 1RG ☎ 01225 477806 🖷 01225 477108 tom_mcbain@bathnes.gov.uk

Events Manager: Mr David Lawrence, Divisional Director - Tourism, Leisure & Culture, Abbey Chambers, Abbey Green, Bath BA1 1NJ ☎ 01225 395385 david_lawrence@bathnes.gov.uk

Facilities: Mr Tom McBain, Divisional Director - Property & Facilities, Northgate House, Upper Borough Walls, Bath BA1 1RG ☎ 01225 477806 🖷 01225 477108 tom_mcbain@bathnes.gov.uk

Finance and Treasurer: Mr Tim Richens, Divisional Director - Finance, Guildhall, High Street, Bath BA1 5AW ☎ 01225 477468 🖷 01225 477377 tim_richens@bathnes.gov.uk

Fleet Management: Mr Matthew Smith, Divisional Director - Environmental Services, Royal Victoria Park Nursery, Marlborough Lane, Bath BA1 2LZ ☎ 01225 396888 🖷 01225 480072 matthew_smith@bathnes.gov.uk

Grounds Maintenance: Mr Matthew Smith, Divisional Director - Environmental Services, Royal Victoria Park Nursery, Marlborough Lane, Bath BA1 2LZ ☎ 01225 396888 🖷 01225 480072 matthew_smith@bathnes.gov.uk

Health and Safety: Mr William Harding, Head - Human Resources, Riverside, Temple Street, Keynsham, Bristol BS31 1LA ☎ 01225 477203 🖷 01225 477423 william_harding@bathnes.gov.uk

Highways: Mr David Trigwell, Divisional Director - Planning & Transport Development, Lewis House, PO BOX 5006, Bath BA1 1`JG ☎ 01225 477702 🖷 01225 394199 david_trigwell@bathnes.gov.uk

Home Energy Conservation: Mrs Jane Shayler, Programme Director - Non-Acute Health, Social Care and Housing, St Martin's Hospital, Clara Cross Lane, Midford Road, Bath BA2 5RP ☎ 01225 396120 🖷 01225 396268 jane_shayler@bathnes.gov.uk

Housing: Mrs Jane Shayler, Programme Director - Non-Acute Health, Social Care and Housing, St Martin's Hospital, Clara Cross Lane, Midford Road, Bath BA2 5RP ☎ 01225 396120 🖷 01225 396268 jane_shayler@bathnes.gov.uk

Local Area Agreement: Mr David Tretheway, Divisional Director - Policy & Partnerships, Lewis House, Manvers Street, Bath BA11 1JG ☎ 01225 396353 david_trethewey@bathnes.gov.uk

Legal: Mr Vernon Hitchman, Divisional Director - Legal & Democratic Services, Riverside, Temple Street, Keynsham BS31 1LA ☎ 01225 395171 🖷 01225 394043 vernon_hitchman@bathnes.gov.uk

Leisure and Cultural Services: Mr David Lawrence, Divisional Director - Tourism, Leisure & Culture, Abbey Chambers, Abbey Green, Bath BA1 1NJ ☎ 01225 395385 david_lawrence@bathnes.gov.uk

Licensing: Mr Matthew Smith, Divisional Director - Environmental Services, Royal Victoria Park Nursery, Marlborough Lane, Bath BA1 2LZ ☎ 01225 396888 🖷 01225 480072 matthew_smith@bathnes.gov.uk

Lifelong Learning: Mr Jeremy Smalley, Divisional Director- Development & Regeneration, Riverside, Temple Street, Keynsham, Bristol BS31 1LA ☎ 01225 477822 jeremy_smalley@bathnes.gov.uk

Lighting: Mr Matthew Smith, Divisional Director - Environmental Services, Royal Victoria Park Nursery, Marlborough Lane, Bath BA1 2LZ ☎ 01225 396888 🖷 01225 480072 matthew_smith@bathnes.gov.uk

Lottery Funding, Charity and Voluntary: Mr David Tretheway, Divisional Director - Policy & Partnerships, Lewis House, Manvers Street, Bath BA11 1JG ☎ 01225 396353 david_trethewey@bathnes.gov.uk

Member Services: Mr Vernon Hitchman, Divisional Director - Legal & Democratic Services, Riverside, Temple Street, Keynsham BS31 1LA ☎ 01225 395171 🖷 01225 394043 vernon_hitchman@bathnes.gov.uk

Parking: Mr Matthew Smith, Divisional Director - Environmental Services, Royal Victoria Park Nursery, Marlborough Lane, Bath BA1 2LZ ☎ 01225 396888 🖷 01225 480072 matthew_smith@bathnes.gov.uk

LOCAL AUTHORITIES

Partnerships: Mr David Tretheway, Divisional Director - Policy & Partnerships, Lewis House, Manvers Street, Bath BA11 1JG ☎ 01225 396353 ✉ david_trethewey@bathnes.gov.uk

Personnel / HR: Mr William Harding, Head - Human Resources, Riverside, Temple Street, Keynsham, Bristol BS31 1LA ☎ 01225 477203 🖷 01225 477423 ✉ william_harding@bathnes.gov.uk

Planning: Mr David Trigwell, Divisional Director - Planning & Transport Development, Lewis House, PO BOX 5006, Bath BA1 1JG ☎ 01225 477702 🖷 01225 394199 ✉ david_trigwell@bathnes.gov.uk

Procurement: Mr Jeff Wring, Head - Risk & Assurance, Guildhall, High Street, Bath BA1 5AW ☎ 01225 477323 ✉ jeff_wring@bathnes.gov.uk

Public Libraries: Mr David Lawrence, Divisional Director - Tourism, Leisure & Culture, Guildhall, High Street, Bath BA1 5AW ☎ 01225 395385 ✉ david_lawrence@bathnes.gov.uk

Recycling & Waste Minimisation: Mr Matthew Smith, Divisional Director - Environmental Services, Royal Victoria Park Nursery, Marlborough Lane, Bath BA1 2LZ ☎ 01225 396888 🖷 01225 480072 ✉ matthew_smith@bathnes.gov.uk

Regeneration: Mr Derek Quilter, Divisional Director - Project Management, 10 Palace Mews, Bath BA1 2NH ☎ 01225 477739 ✉ derek_quilter@bathnes.gov.uk

Road Safety: Mr David Trigwell, Divisional Director - Planning & Transport Development, Riverside, Temple Street, Keynsham BS31 1LA ☎ 01225 477702 🖷 01225 394199 ✉ david_trigwell@bathnes.gov.uk

Social Services: Mr Maurice Lindsay, Divisional Director - Children, YP & Family Support Services, Riverside, Temple Street, Keynsham, Bristol BS31 1LA ☎ 01225 396289 🖷 01225 396115 ✉ maurice_lindsay@bathnes.gov.uk

Social Services (Adult): Mrs Jane Shayler, Programme Director - Non-Acute Health, Social Care and Housing, St Martin's Hospital, Clara Cross Lane, Midford Road, Bath BA2 5RP ☎ 01225 396120 🖷 01225 396268 ✉ jane_shayler@bathnes.gov.uk

Social Services (Children): Mr Maurice Lindsay, Divisional Director - Children, YP & Family Support Services, Riverside, Temple Street, Keynsham, Bristol BS31 1LA ☎ 01225 396289 🖷 01225 396115 ✉ maurice_lindsay@bathnes.gov.uk

Staff Training: Mr William Harding, Head - Human Resources, Riverside, Temple Street, Keynsham, Bristol BS31 1LA ☎ 01225 477203 🖷 01225 477423 ✉ william_harding@bathnes.gov.uk

Street Scene: Mr Matthew Smith, Divisional Director - Environmental Services, Royal Victoria Park Nursery, Marlborough Lane, Bath BA1 2LZ ☎ 01225 396888 🖷 01225 480072 ✉ matthew_smith@bathnes.gov.uk

Sustainable Communities: Mr David Tretheway, Divisional Director - Policy & Partnerships, Lewis House, Manvers Street, Bath BA11 1JG ☎ 01225 396353 ✉ david_trethewey@bathnes.gov.uk

Sustainable Development: Mr David Tretheway, Divisional Director - Policy & Partnerships, Lewis House, Manvers Street, Bath BA11 1JG ☎ 01225 396353 ✉ david_trethewey@bathnes.gov.uk

Tourism: Mr David Lawrence, Divisional Director - Tourism, Leisure & Culture, Guildhall, High Street, Bath BA1 5AW ☎ 01225 395385 ✉ david_lawrence@bathnes.gov.uk

Town Centre: Mr Matthew Smith, Divisional Director - Environmental Services, Royal Victoria Park Nursery, Marlborough Lane, Bath BA1 2LZ ☎ 01225 396888 🖷 01225 480072 ✉ matthew_smith@bathnes.gov.uk

Traffic Management: Mr David Trigwell, Divisional Director - Planning & Transport Development, Trimbridge House, Trim Street, Bath BA1 2DP ☎ 01225 477702 🖷 01225 394199 ✉ david_trigwell@bathnes.gov.uk

Transport: Mr David Trigwell, Divisional Director - Planning & Transport Development, Trimbridge House, Trim Street, Bath BA1 2DP ☎ 01225 477702 🖷 01225 394199 ✉ david_trigwell@bathnes.gov.uk

Transport Planner: Mr David Trigwell, Divisional Director - Planning & Transport Development, Trimbridge House, Trim Street, Bath BA1 2DP ☎ 01225 477702 🖷 01225 394199 ✉ david_trigwell@bathnes.gov.uk

Total Place: Mr David Tretheway, Divisional Director - Policy & Partnerships, Lewis House, Manvers Street, Bath BA11 1JG ☎ 01225 396353 ✉ david_trethewey@bathnes.gov.uk

Waste Collection and Disposal: Mr Matthew Smith, Divisional Director - Environmental Services, Royal Victoria Park Nursery, Marlborough Lane, Bath BA1 2LZ ☎ 01225 396888 🖷 01225 480072 ✉ matthew_smith@bathnes.gov.uk

Waste Management: Mr Matthew Smith, Divisional Director - Environmental Services, Royal Victoria Park Nursery, Marlborough Lane, Bath BA1 2LZ ☎ 01225 396888 🖷 01225 480072 ✉ matthew_smith@bathnes.gov.uk

Children's Play Areas: Mr Matthew Smith, Divisional Director - Environmental Services, Royal Victoria Park Nursery, Marlborough Lane, Bath BA1 2LZ ☎ 01225 396888 🖷 01225 480072 ✉ matthew_smith@bathnes.gov.uk

MEMBERS OF THE COUNCIL (65)

***Chair:* Appleyard**, Rob (LAB - Westfield)
rob_appleyarrd@bathnes.gov.uk

***Leader of the Council:* Crossley**, Paul (LD - Southdown)
paul_crossley@bathnes.gov.uk

***Deputy Leader of the Council:* Hartley**, Nathan (LD - Peasedown)
nathan_hartley@msn.com

Allen, Simon (LD - Radstock)
simon.neslibdems@btinternet.com

Anketell-Jones, Patrick (CON - Lansdown)
patrick_aneketell-jones@bathnes.gov.uk

Ball, Timothy (LD - Twerton)
tim_ball@bathnes.gov.uk
Ball, Sharon (LD - Westmoreland)
sg.ball@blueyonder.co.uk
Barrett, Colin (CON - Weston)
barrettsofbath@yahoo.co.uk
Batt, Gabriel (CON - Bathavon North)
gabriel_batt@bathnes.gov.uk
Beath, Cherry (LD - Combe Down)
cherry_beath@bathnes.gov.uk
Bellotti, David (LD - Lyncombe)
dbellotti@btinternet.com
Bevan, Sarah (LD - Peasedown)
sarah_bevan@bathnes.gov.uk
Blankley, Matthew (CON - Saltford)
matthew_blankley@bathnes.gov.uk
Brett, Lisa (LD - Walcot)
lisa_brett@bathnes.gov.uk
Bull, John (LAB - Paulton)
john_bull@bathnes.gov.uk
Butters, Neil (LD - Bathavon South)
cllrneilbutters@aol.com
Chalker, Bryan (CON - Lambridge)
bryan_chalker@bathnes.gov.uk
Clarke, Anthony (CON - Lansdown)
anthony_clarke@bathnes.gov.uk
Coombes, Nicholas (LD - Bathwick)
nicholas_coombes@bathnes.gov.uk
Curran, Gerry (LD - Twerton)
gerry_curran@bathnes.gov.uk
Davis, Sally (CON - Farmborough)
sally_davis@bathnes.gov.uk
Deacon, Douglas (IND - Timsbury)
douglas_deacon@bathnes.gov.uk
Dixon, David (LD - Oldfield)
david_dixon@bathnes.gov.uk
Edwards, Peter (CON - Publow & Whitchurch)
peter_edwards@bathnes.gov.uk
Evans, Michael (CON - Midsomer Norton North)
michael_evans@bathnes.gov.uk
Fox, Paul (LD - Walcot)
paul_fox2@bathnes.gov.uk
Furse, Andrew (LD - Kingsmead)
andrew_furse@bathnes.gov.uk
Gerrish, Charles (CON - Keynsham North)
charles_gerrish@bathnes.gov.uk
Gilchrist, Ian (LD - Widcombe)
ian_gilchrist@bathnes.gov.uk
Haeberling, Francine (CON - Saltford)
francine_haeberling@bathnes.gov.uk
Hale, Alan (CON - Keynsham South)
alan_hale@bathnes.gov.uk
Hall, Katie (LD - Lyncombe)
katiehall.bath@gmail.com
Hanney, Malcom (CON - Chew Valley North)
mchanney1@aol.com
Hardman, Liz (LAB - Paulton)
liz_hardman@bathnes.gov.uk
Hedges, Stephen (LD - Odd Down)
steve_hedges@bathnes.gov.uk
Jackson, Eleanor (LAB - Radstock)
eleanor_jackson@bathnes.gov.uk
Kew, Les (CON - High Littleton)
les_kew@bathnes.gov.uk
Laming, Dave (IND - Lambridge)
dave_laming@bathnes.gov.uk
Lees, Malcolm (IND - Weston)
mlees@bathinsurance.co.uk
Longstaff, Marie (CON - Keynsham East)
marie_brewer@bathnes.gov.uk
Macrae, Barry (CON - Midsomer Norton North)
barry_macrae@bathnes.gov.uk
Martin, David (LD - Bathwick)
david_martin@bathnes.gov.uk
Morgan-Brinkhurst, Loraine (LD - Newbridge)
lorraine_brinkhurst@bathnes.gov.uk
Moss, Robin (LAB - Westfield)
robin_moss@bathnes.gov.uk
Myers, Paul (CON - Midsomer Norton Redfield)
paul_myers@bathnes.gov.uk
Nicol, Douglas (LD - Kingsmead)
douglas_nicol@bathnes.gov.uk
Organ, Bryan (CON - Keynsham East)
bryan_organ@bathnes.gov.uk
Player, June (IND - Westmoreland)
june_player@bathnes.gov.uk
Pritchard, Victor (CON - Chew Valley South)
vic_pritchard@bathnes.gov.uk
Rigby, Manda (LD - Abbey)
manda_rigby@bathnes.gov.uk
Roberts, Nigel (LD - Odd Down)
nigelroberts@clara.co.uk
Roberts, Caroline (LD - Newbridge)
cmroberts@clara.co.uk
Romero, Dine (LD - Southdown)
dine_romero@bathnes.gov.uk
Sandry, Will (LD - Oldfield)
willsandry@blueyonder.co.uk
Simmons, Brian (CON - Keynsham North)
brian_simmons@bathnes.gov.uk
Simmons, Kate (CON - Keynsham South)
kate_simmons@bathnes.gov.uk
Sparks, Jeremy (LD - Clutton)
jeremy_sparks@bathnes.gov.uk
Stevens, Ben (LD - Widcombe)
ben_stevens@bathnes.gov.uk
Symonds, Roger (LD - Combe Down)
rogersymonds@me.com
Veal, Martin (CON - Bathavon North)
martin_veal@bathnes.gov.uk
Veale, David (CON - Bathavon West)
david_veale@bathnes.gov.uk
Ward, Geoff (CON - Bathavon North)
geoff_ward@bathnes.gov.uk
Warren, Tim (CON - Mendip)
tim@warrenequestrian.co.uk
Watt, Christopher (CON - Midsomer Norton Redfield)
chris.watt@cognisantresearch.com
Webber, Brian (CON - Abbey)
brian_webber@bathnes.gov.uk

POLITICAL COMPOSITION
LD: 29, CON: 27, LAB: 5, IND: 4

CABINET
Leader: Mr Paul Crossley
Deputy Leader: Mr Nathan Hartley
Community Resources: Mr David Bellotti
Early Years, Children & Youth: Mr Nathan Hartley

Homes & Planning: Mr Timothy Ball
Neighbourhoods: Mr David Dixon
Sustainable Development: Mrs Cherry Beath
Transport: Mr Roger Symonds
Wellbeing: Mr Simon Allen

COMMITTEE CHAIRS

Avon Pension Fund: Mr Paul Fox
Bath & North East Somerset Local Strategic Partnership Board: Mr Paul Crossley
Corporate Audit Committee: Mr Andrew Furse
Development Control: Mr Gerry Curran
Early Years, Children & Youth Policy Development: Ms Sally Davis
Economic & Community Development: Mr Robin Moss
Employement: Mr Colin Barrett
Housing & Major Projects Policy Development: Dr Eleanor Jackson
Licensing: Ms Sarah Bevan
Planning, Transport & Environment Policy Development: Mrs Marie Longstaff
Regulatory: Mr Nicholas Coombes
Resources Policy Development: Mr John Bull
Standards: Ms Susan Toland
Wellbeing Policy Development: Mr Victor Pritchard

BEDFORD U

Bedford Borough Council, Town Hall, St. Paul's Square, Bedford MK40 1SJ ☎ 01234 267422 🖷 01234 221606 ✉ enquiries@bedford.gov.uk 💻 www.bedford.gov.uk

FACTS & FIGURES

Police Authority: Bedfordshire Police Authority
Health Authority: East of England Strategic Health Authority
Learning and Skills Council: Eastern
Parliamentary Constituencies: Bedford
EU Constituencies: Eastern
Election Frequency: Elections are by thirds
Twinning: Bedford: Bamberg (Germany); Rovigo (Italy); Great Barford: Wollstein (Germany)

PRINCIPAL OFFICERS

Chief Executive: Mr Philip Simpkins, Chief Executive, Borough Hall, Cauldwell Street, Bedford MK42 9AP ☎ 01234 718202 🖷 01234 718201 ✉ philip.simpkins@bedford.gov.uk

Access Officer / Social Services (Disability): Mr Stuart O'Dell, Access Officer, Planning Services, Town Hall, St Pauls Square, Bedford MK40 1SJ ☎ 01234 221762 🖷 01234 325671 ✉ stuart.odell@bedford.gov.uk

Architect, Building / Property Services: Mr Malcolm Parker, Business Manager (Consultancy), Bedford Design Group, Riverside House, Horne Lane, Bedford MK40 1PY ☎ 01234 221692 🖷 01234 221716 ✉ malcolm.parker@bedford.gov.uk

Best Value: Mr Jashpal Mann, Corporate Performance & Policy Manager, Borough Hall, Cauldwell Street, Bedford MK42 9AP ☎ 01234 228380 ✉ jashpal.mann@bedford.gov.uk

Building Control: Mr Richard Martin, Building Control Manager, Riverside House, Home Lane, Bedford MK40 1PY ☎ 01234 221759 🖷 01234 221760 ✉ richard.martin@bedford.gov.uk

Catering Services: Mr Adrian Piper, Head of Property Services, Borough Hall, Cauldwell Street, Bedford MK42 9AP ☎ 01234 718248 ✉ adrian.piper@bedford.gov.uk

Children / Youth Services: Mr Chris Hilliard, Executive Director for Children's Services, Schools & Families, Borough Hall, Cauldwell Street, Bedford MK42 9AP ☎ 01234 276371 ✉ chris.hilliard@bedford.gov.uk

Civil Registration: Mr Keith Simmons, Head of Registration & Records, Borough Hall, Cauldwell Street, Bedford MK42 9AP ☎ 01234 221676 🖷 01234 221837 ✉ keith.simmons@bedford.gov.uk

PR / Communications: Mr Keiron Fletcher, Senior Communications Officer, Borough Hall, Cauldwell Street, Bedford MK42 9AP ☎ 01234 276277 ✉ keiron.fletcher@bedford.gov.uk

Community Planning: Mr Stewart Briggs, Executive Director of Environment & Sustainable Communities, Borough Hall, Cauldwell Street, Bedford MK42 9AP ☎ 01234 228283 ✉ stewart.briggs@bedford.gov.uk

Community Safety: Mr Stephen Tomlin, Assistant Director (Environment & Community), Room B107, Riverside House, Bedford MK40 1SJ ☎ 01234 221745 ✉ stephen.tomlin@bedford.gov.uk

Computer Management: Mr Lawrence McArdle, Head of IT Services, Borough Hall, Cauldwell Street, Bedford MK42 9AP ☎ 01234 276221 🖷 01234 227406 ✉ lawrence.mcardle@bedford.gov.uk

Consumer Protection and Trading Standards: Mr Craig Austin, Assistant Director (Regulatory Services), Town Hall, St. Paul's Square, Bedford MK40 1SJ ☎ 01234 227356 ✉ craig.austin@bedford.gov.uk

Contracts: Mr Mike Nacey, Procurement & Review Manager, Borough Hall, Cauldwell Street, Bedford MK42 9AP ☎ 01234 228150 ✉ mike.nacey@bedford.gov.uk

Corporate Services: Mr Trevor Roff, Executive Director for Finance & Corporate Services, Borough Hall, Cauldwell Street, Bedford MK42 9AP ☎ 01234 718208 🖷 01234 718205 ✉ trevor.roff@bedford.gov.uk

Customer Service: Mr Lee Phanco, Assistant Director of Finance (Revenues, Benefits & Risk), Borough Hall, Cauldwell Street, Bedford MK40 1SJ ☎ 01234 718358 ✉ lee.phanco@bedford.gov.uk

Economic Development: Mr Mark Oakley, Head of Economic Development, Borough Hall, Cauldwell Street, Bedford MK42 9AP ☎ 01234 221730 ✉ mark.oakley@bedford.gov.uk

Education: Mr Brian Glover, Assistant Director - Chief Education Officer, Borough Hall, Cauldwell Street, Bedford MK42 9AP

☎ 01234 276658 🖰 brian.glover@bedford.gov.uk

E-Government: Mr Lawrence McArdle, Head of IT Services, Borough Hall, Cauldwell Street, Bedford MK42 9AP ☎ 01234 276221 📠 01234 227406 🖰 lawrence.mcardle@bedford.gov.uk

Electoral Registration: Mr Keith Simmons, Head of Registration & Records, Town Hall, St. Paul's Square, Bedford MK40 1SJ ☎ 01234 221676 📠 01234 221837 🖰 keith.simmons@bedford.gov.uk

Emergency Planning: Mr Craig Austin, Assistant Director (Regulatory Services), Town Hall, St. Paul's Square, Bedford MK40 1SJ ☎ 01234 227356 🖰 craig.austin@bedford.gov.uk

Energy Management: Mr Stephen Tomlin, Assistant Director (Environment & Community), Room B107, Riverside House, Bedford MK40 1SJ ☎ 01234 221745 🖰 stephen.tomlin@bedford.gov.uk

Environmental / Technical Services: Mr Craig Austin, Assistant Director (Regulatory Services), Town Hall, St. Paul's Square, Bedford MK40 1SJ ☎ 01234 227356 🖰 craig.austin@bedford.gov.uk

Environmental Health: Mr Craig Austin, Assistant Director (Regulatory Services), Town Hall, St. Paul's Square, Bedford MK40 1SJ ☎ 01234 227356 🖰 craig.austin@bedford.gov.uk

Estates, Property & Valuation: Mr Adrian Piper, Head of Property Services, Borough Hall, Cauldwell Street, Bedford MK42 9AP ☎ 01234 718248 🖰 adrian.piper@bedford.gov.uk

Events Manager: Mr Andy Pidgen, Events & Marketing Manager, Town Hall, Bedford MK40 1SJ ☎ 01234 227392 🖰 andy.pidgen@bedford.gov.uk

Facilities: Mr Adrian Piper, Head of Property Services, Borough Hall, Cauldwell Street, Bedford MK42 9AP ☎ 01234 718248 🖰 adrian.piper@bedford.gov.uk

Finance and Treasurer: Mr Trevor Roff, Executive Director for Finance & Corporate Services, Borough Hall, Cauldwell Street, Bedford MK42 9AP ☎ 01234 718208 📠 01234 718205 🖰 trevor.roff@bedford.gov.uk

Fleet Management: Mr Chris Pettifer, Head of Transport Operations, Borough Hall, Cauldwell Street, Bedford MK42 9AP ☎ 01234 228881 🖰 chris.pettifer@bedford.gov.uk

Grounds Maintenance: Mr Stephen Tomlin, Assistant Director (Environment & Community), Room B107, Riverside House, Bedford MK40 1SJ ☎ 01234 221745 🖰 stephen.tomlin@bedford.gov.uk

Health and Safety: Mr Craig Austin, Assistant Director (Regulatory Services), Town Hall, St. Paul's Square, Bedford MK40 1SJ ☎ 01234 227356 🖰 craig.austin@bedford.gov.uk

Highways: Mr Glenn Barcham, Assistant Director Highways & Transport, Town Hall, St. Paul's Square, Bedford MK40 1SJ ☎ 01234 228075 🖰 glenn.barcham@bedford.gov.uk

Highways: Mr Brian Hayward, Head of Highways, Town Hall, St. Paul's Square, Bedford MK40 1SJ ☎ 01234 228012

Home Energy Conservation: Mr James Shearman, Corporate Carbon & Energy Manager, Borough Hall, Cauldwell Street, Bedford MK42 9AP ☎ 01234 718286 🖰 james.shearman@bedford.gov.uk

Housing: Mr Paul Rowland, Assistant Director of Planning & Housing, Town Hall, St. Paul's Square, Bedford MK40 1SJ ☎ 01234 221720 🖰 paul.rowland@bedford.gov.uk

Housing: Mr Simon White, Assistant Director (Commissioning & Business Support), Borough Hall, Cauldwell Street, Bedford MK42 9AP 🖰 simon.white@bedford.gov.uk

Local Area Agreement: Mr Mark Minion, Head of Partnerships & Community Engagement, Borough Hall, Cauldwell Street, Bedford MK42 9AP ☎ 01234 228078 🖰 mark.minion@bedford.gov.uk

Legal: Ms Sue Drummond, Head of Leisure & Culture, Borough Hall, Cauldwell Street, Bedford MK42 9AP 🖰 sue.drummond@bedford.gov.uk

Legal: Mr Michael Gough, Assistant Chief Executive (Governance), Borough Hall, Cauldwell Street, Bedford MK42 9AP ☎ 01234 718206 📠 01234 718666 🖰 michael.gough@bedford.gov.uk

Leisure and Cultural Services: Ms Sue Drummond, Head of Leisure & Culture, Borough Hall, Cauldwell Street, Bedford MK42 9AP 🖰 sue.drummond@bedford.gov.uk

Licensing: Mr Keith Simmons, Head of Registration & Records, Town Hall, St. Paul's Square, Bedford MK40 1SJ ☎ 01234 221676 📠 01234 221837 🖰 keith.simmons@bedford.gov.uk

Lifelong Learning: Mr Frank Toner, Executive Director for Adult Services, Borough Hall, Cauldwell Street, Bedford MK42 9AP ☎ 01234 228620 🖰 frank.toner@bedford.gov.uk

Lighting: Mr Darryl Hall, Project Engineer (Electrical), Riverside House, Town Hall, St Paul's Square, Bedford MKo 1SJ ☎ 01234 221702 🖰 darryl.hall@bedford.gov.uk

Lottery Funding, Charity and Voluntary: Ms Susan Audin, Head of Revenues & Benefits, Town Hall, St. Paul's Square, Bedford MK40 1SJ

Member Services: Mrs Linda Stevens, Head of Member Services, Borough Hall, Cauldwell Street, Bedford MK42 9AP ☎ 01234 228294 🖰 linda.stevens@bedford.gov.uk

Parking: Mr Stewart Briggs, Executive Director of Environment & Sustainable Communities, Borough Hall, Cauldwell Street, Bedford MK42 9AP ☎ 01234 228283 🖰 stewart.briggs@bedford.gov.uk

Partnerships: Mr Mark Minion, Head of Partnerships & Community Engagement, Borough Hall, Cauldwell Street, Bedford MK42 9AP ☎ 01234 228078 🖰 mark.minion@bedford.gov.uk

Personnel / HR: Mr Martin Williams, Assistant Chief Executive (HR/OD), Borough Hall, Cauldwell Street, Bedford MK42 9AP ☎ 01234 276038 ✉ martin.williams@bedford.gov.uk

Planning: Mr Paul Rowland, Assistant Director of Planning & Housing, Town Hall, St. Paul's Square, Bedford MK40 1SJ ☎ 01234 221720 ✉ paul.rowland@bedford.gov.uk

Procurement: Mr Mike Nacey, Procurement & Review Manager, Borough Hall, Cauldwell Street, Bedford MK42 9AP ☎ 01234 228150 ✉ mike.nacey@bedford.gov.uk

Public Libraries: Mrs Jenny Poad, Head of Libraries, Bedford Central Library, Harpur Street, Bedford MK40 1PG ☎ 01234 718158 ✉ jenny.poad@bedford.gov.uk

Recycling & Waste Minimisation: Mr Stewart Briggs, Executive Director of Environment & Sustainable Communities, Borough Hall, Cauldwell Street, Bedford MK42 9AP ☎ 01234 228283 ✉ stewart.briggs@bedford.gov.uk

Regeneration: Mr Mark Oakley, Head of Economic Development, Borough Hall, Cauldwell Street, Bedford MK42 9AP ☎ 01234 221730 ✉ mark.oakley@bedford.gov.uk

Road Safety: Mr Glenn Barcham, Assistant Director Highways & Transport, Borough Hall, Cauldwell Street, Bedford MK42 9AP ☎ 01234 228075 ✉ glenn.barcham@bedford.gov.uk

Social Services (Adult): Mr Frank Toner, Executive Director for Adult Services, Borough Hall, Cauldwell Street, Bedford MK42 9AP ☎ 01234 228620 ✉ frank.toner@bedford.gov.uk

Social Services (Children): Mr Simon Westwood, Assistant Director (Vulnerable Children & Children's Social Care), Borough Hall, Cauldwell Street, Bedford MK42 9AP ☎ 01234 228683 ✉ simon.westwood@bedford.gov.uk

Staff Training: Mrs Alison Lowe, Head of Learning & Development, Borough Hall, Cauldwell Street, Bedford MK42 9AP ☎ 01234 228358 ✉ alison.lowe@bedford.gov.uk

Street Scene: Mr Stewart Briggs, Executive Director of Environment & Sustainable Communities, Borough Hall, Cauldwell Street, Bedford MK42 9AP ☎ 01234 228283 ✉ stewart.briggs@bedford.gov.uk

Sustainable Communities: Mrs Joanne Broughton, Sustainable Development Officer, Town Hall, St. Paul's Square, Bedford MK40 1SJ ☎ 01234 227365 🖷 01234 221710 ✉ joanne.broughton@bedford.gov.uk

Sustainable Development: Mr Stephen Tomlin, Assistant Director (Environment & Community), Town Hall, St. Paul's Square, Bedford MK40 1SJ ☎ 01234 221745 ✉ stephen.tomlin@bedford.gov.uk

Tourism: Mr Mark Oakley, Head of Economic Development, Borough Hall, Cauldwell Street, Bedford MK42 9AP ☎ 01234 221730 ✉ mark.oakley@bedford.gov.uk

Town Centre: Mr Mark Oakley, Head of Economic Development, Borough Hall, Cauldwell Street, Bedford MK42 9AP ☎ 01234 221730 ✉ mark.oakley@bedford.gov.uk

Traffic Management: Mr Glenn Barcham, Assistant Director Highways & Transport, Town Hall, St. Paul's Square, Bedford MK40 1SJ ☎ 01234 228075 ✉ glenn.barcham@bedford.gov.uk

Traffic Management: Mr Brian Hayward, Head of Highways, Town Hall, St. Paul's Square, Bedford MK40 1SJ ☎ 01234 228012

Transport: Mr Glenn Barcham, Assistant Director Highways & Transport, Borough Hall, Cauldwell Street, Bedford MK42 9AP ☎ 01234 228075 ✉ glenn.barcham@bedford.gov.uk

Transport: Mr Chris Pettifer, Head of Transport Operations, Town Hall, St. Paul's Square, Bedford MK40 1SJ ☎ 01234 228881 ✉ chris.pettifer@bedford.gov.uk

Transport Planner: Mr Glenn Barcham, Assistant Director Highways & Transport, Borough Hall, Cauldwell Street, Bedford MK42 9AP ☎ 01234 228075 ✉ glenn.barcham@bedford.gov.uk

Waste Collection and Disposal: Mr Stewart Briggs, Executive Director of Environment & Sustainable Communities, Borough Hall, Cauldwell Street, Bedford MK42 9AP ☎ 01234 228283 ✉ stewart.briggs@bedford.gov.uk

Waste Management: Mr Stewart Briggs, Executive Director of Environment & Sustainable Communities, Borough Hall, Cauldwell Street, Bedford MK42 9AP ☎ 01234 228283 ✉ stewart.briggs@bedford.gov.uk

MEMBERS OF THE COUNCIL (41)

***Deputy Mayor:* Royden**, Charles (LD - Brickhill)
CharlesRoyden@gmail.com
***Deputy Speaker:* Smith**, Mark (CON - Kempston Rural)
mark.smith792@googlemail.com
***Group Leader:* Clifton**, Ian (IND - Riseley)
ian.clifton@bedford.gov.uk
***Group Leader:* Ellis**, Carole (CON - Great Barford)
carolebarford@aol.com
***Group Leader:* Sawyer**, David (LD - De Parys)
sawyerbedford@hotmail.com
Adams, Kristy (CON - Newnham)
kristy.adams@bedford.gov.uk
Atkins, Colleen (LAB - Harpur)
colleenatkins@ntlworld.com
Bagchi, Apu (IND - Castle)
apu.bagchi@bedford.gov.uk
Charles, Randolph (LAB - Cauldwell)
randolph.charles@bedford.gov.uk
Coombes, Graeme (CON - Wilshamstead)
Fensome, Caroline (CON - Castle)
caroline.fensome@bedford.gov.uk
Foster, Alison (CON - Harrold)
afield_foster@btinternet.com
Gambold, Jon (CON - Bromham & Biddenham)
jonathan.gambold@btinternet.com
Gerard, Anita (LD - Kingsbrook)
anitagerard.kb@gmail.com
Gillard, Sylvia (LD - Goldington)
cllrsylvia.gillard@bedford.gov.uk
Headley, Michael (LD - Putnoe)

michael@mheadley.co.uk
Hill, Tim (LD - Elstow)
tim.hill@bedford.gov.uk
Hodgson, Dave (LD -)
dave.hodgson@bedford.gov.uk
Holland, Sarah-Jayne (LD - Eastcotts)
sarahjayne.holland@bedford.gov.uk
Hunt, Shan (LAB - Kempston North)
shanhunt@ntlworld.com
Hunt, Will (LAB - Kempston West)
willhunt@ntlworld.com
King, Louise (LAB - Harpur)
louise.king@bedford.gov.uk
Masud, Mohammed (LAB - Queens Park)
mohammed.masud@bedford.gov.uk
McMurdo, Doug (IND - Sharnbrook)
doug.mcmurdo@bedford.gov.uk
Meader, Carl (LAB - Kempston South)
carl.meader@bedford.gov.uk
Merryman, Philip (LD - Goldington)
philip.merryman@bedford.gov.uk
Mingay, John (CON - Newnham)
john.mingay@bedford.gov.uk
Moon, Stephen (CON - Great Barford)
shmoon@tiscali.co.uk
Nawaz, Mohammed (LAB - Kempston Central & East)
mohammed.nawaz@bedford.gov.uk
Oliver, Susan (LAB - Cauldwell)
s.j.oliver@ntlworld.com
Olney, Patricia (IND - Oakley)
pat.olney@btopenworld.com
Prescod, Paul (LD - Wootton)
paul.prescod@bedford.gov.uk
Rider, Wendy (LD - Brickhill)
wendyrider41@gmail.com
Rigby, Roger (CON - Bromham & Biddenham)
roger.rigby110@googlemail.com
Saunders, James (LAB - Kingsbrook)
james.saunders@bedford.gov.uk
Smith, Sallyanne (LD - Putnoe)
sallyanne_69@btinternet.com
Valentine, James (LAB - Kempston Central & East)
james.valentine@bedford.gov.uk
Vann, Henry (LD - De Parys)
henry.vann@bedford.gov.uk
Walker, Jane (CON - Clapham)
Jane@Janewalker.co.uk
Wootton, Tom (CON - Wyboston)
tom.wootton@bedford.gov.uk
Yasin, Mohammad (LAB - Queens Park)
mohammad.yasin@bedford.gov.uk

POLITICAL COMPOSITION

LD: 13, LAB: 12, CON: 12, IND: 4

CABINET

Leader: Mr Dave Hodgson
Deputy Mayor: Mr Charles Royden
Adult Services & Community Wellbeing: Ms Colleen Atkins
Children's Social Care: Ms Susan Oliver
Community & Regulatory Services: Ms Sarah-Jayne Holland
Economic Development, Rural Affairs & Partnerships: Mr Dave Hodgson
Education: Mr David Sawyer
Environment & Transport: Mr Charles Royden
Finance & Asset Management: Mr Michael Headley
Leisure & Culture: Mr Doug McMurdo
Revenues, Benefits, Customer Services & ICT: Mrs Shan Hunt

COMMITTEE CHAIRS

Admissions: Mr David Sawyer
Appointments: Mr Dave Hodgson
Executive: Mr Dave Hodgson
Planning: Mrs Anita Gerard
Sustainability: Mr Charles Royden

BELFAST CITY — N

Belfast City Council, City Hall, Belfast BT1 5GS ☎ 028 9032 0202 🖷 028 9072 6424; 028 9072 6424
✉ corporatecommunications@belfastcity.gov.uk
🖳 www.belfastcity.gov.uk

FACTS & FIGURES

Police Authority: Northern Ireland Policing Board
Health Authority: Eastern Health & Social Services Board
Learning and Skills Council: Northern Ireland
Parliamentary Constituencies: Belfast East, Belfast North, Belfast South, Belfast West
EU Constituencies: Northern Ireland
Election Frequency: Elections are of whole council

PRINCIPAL OFFICERS

Chief Executive: Mr Peter McNaney, Chief Executive & Town Clerk, City Hall, Belfast BT1 5GS ☎ 028 9032 0202 🖷 028 9027 0232 ✉ mcnaneyp@belfastcity.gov.uk

Assistant Chief Executive: Mr Ciaran Quigley, Town Solicitor & Assistant Chief Executive, City Hall, Belfast BT1 5GS ☎ 028 9027 0239 🖷 ; 028 9050 2099 ✉ quigleyc@belfastcity.gov.uk

Senior Management: Mr John McGrillen, Director - Development, Cecil Ward Building, 4-10 Linenhall Street, Belfast BT2 8BP ☎ 028 9027 0485 🖷 028 9027 0496 ✉ mcgrillenj@belfastcity.gov.uk

Senior Management: Mr Ciaran Quigley, Town Solicitor & Assistant Chief Executive, City Hall, Belfast BT1 5GS ☎ 028 9027 0239 🖷 ; 028 9050 2099 ✉ quigleyc@belfastcity.gov.uk

Architect, Building / Property Services: Mr George Wright, Head - Facilities Management, Duncrue Complex, Duncrue Road, Belfast BT3 9BP ☎ 028 9037 3034 🖷 ; 028 9037 3042 ✉ wrightg@belfastcity.gov.uk

Building Control: Mr Trevor Martin, Head - Building Control, 5th Floor, 9 Lanyon Place, Belfast BT1 3LP ☎ 028 9027 0283 🖷 028 9043 8805 ✉ martint@belfastcity.gov.uk

Catering Services: Ms Gail Maguire, Restaurant & Catering Manager, Cecil Ward Building, 4-10 Linenhall Street, Belfast BT2 8BP ☎ 028 9027 0326 🖷 028 9027 0490 ✉ maguireg@belfastcity.gov.uk

Civil Registration: Mrs Vivienne Fullerton, Registrar, City Hall, Belfast BT1 5GS ☎ 028 9027 0274 🖷 028 9027 0520

☞ fullertonv@belfastcity.gov.uk

Civil Registration: Miss Aileen Tyney, Registrar, City Hall, Belfast BT1 5GS ☎ 028 9027 0274 🖷 028 9027 0520 ☞ tyneya@belfast.gov.uk

PR / Communications: Mr Eamon Deeny, Head - Corporate Communications, City Hall, Belfast BT1 5GS ☎ 028 9027 0664 🖷 028 9072 6424 ☞ deenye@belfastcity.gov.uk

Community Safety: Mr Stevie Lavery, Safer City Manager, Cecil Ward Building, 4-10 Linenhall Street, Belfast BT2 8BP ☎ 028 9027 0469 🖷 028 9027 0422

Computer Management: Mr Paul Gribben, Head - ISB, 22-38 Gloucester Street, Belfast BT1 4LS ☎ 028 9024 4832 🖷 028 9027 0717 ☞ gribbenp@belfastcity.gov.uk

Computer Management: Mr David Kelly, IS Portfolio Manager, 22-38 Gloucester Street, Belfast BT1 4LS ☎ 028 9024 4832 🖷 028 9027 0717 ☞ kellyd@belfastcity.gov.uk

Corporate Services: Mr Andrew Wilson, Head - Audit, Governance & Risk, 24-26 Adelaide Street, Belfast BT2 8GD ☎ 028 9027 0513 ☞ wilsona@belfastcity.gov.uk

Economic Development: Ms Shirley McCay, Head - Economic Initiatives, Cecil Ward Building, 4-10 Linenhall Street, Belfast BT2 8BP ☎ 028 9027 0529 🖷 ; 028 9027 0325 ☞ mccays@belfastcity.gov.uk

E-Government: Mr Paul Gribben, Head - ISB, 22-38 Gloucester Street, Belfast BT1 4LS ☎ 028 9024 4832 🖷 028 9027 0717 ☞ gribbenp@belfastcity.gov.uk

E-Government: Mr David Kelly, IS Portfolio Manager, 22-38 Gloucester Street, Belfast BT1 4LS ☎ 028 9024 4832 🖷 028 9027 0717 ☞ kellyd@belfastcity.gov.uk

Emergency Planning: Mr David Neill, Emergency Planning Officer, Cecil Ward Building, 4-10 Linenhall Street, Belfast BT2 8BP ☎ 028 9027 0734 🖷 028 9027 0399 ☞ neilld@belfastcity.gov.uk

Energy Management: Mr George Wright, Head - Facilities Management, Duncrue Complex, Duncrue Road, Belfast BT3 9BP ☎ 028 9037 3034 🖷 ; 028 9037 3042 ☞ wrightg@belfastcity.gov.uk

Environmental / Technical Services: Ms Suzanne Wylie, Director - Health & Environmental Services, Cecil Ward Building, 4-10 Linenhall Street, Belfast BT2 8BP ☎ 028 9027 0299 🖷 028 9024 0396 ☞ wylies@belfastcity.gov.uk

Environmental Health: Ms Siobhan Toland, Head - Environmental Health, Cecil Ward Building, 4-10 Linenhall Street, Belfast BT2 8BP ☎ 028 9027 0304 🖷 ; 028 9027 0422 ☞ tolands@belfastcity.gov.uk

Environmental Health: Ms Suzanne Wylie, Director - Health & Environmental Services, Cecil Ward Building, 4-10 Linenhall Street, Belfast BT2 8BP ☎ 028 9027 0299 🖷 028 9024 0396 ☞ wylies@belfastcity.gov.uk

Estates, Property & Valuation: Ms Cathy Reynolds, Estates Manager, Adelaide Exchange, 24-26 Adelaide Street, Belfast BT2 8GD ☎ 028 9027 0386 🖷 028 9027 0590 ☞ reynoldsc@belfastcity.gov.uk

European Liaison: Ms Laura Leonard, European Manager, Cecil Ward Building, 4-10 Linenhall Street, Belfast BT2 8BP ☎ 028 9027 0317 🖷 ; 028 9027 0325 ☞ leonardl@belfastcity.gov.uk

Events Manager: Mr Gerry Copeland, Events Manager, Cecil Ward Building, 4-10 Linenhall Street, Belfast BT2 8BP ☎ 028 9027 0341 🖷 ; 028 9027 0325 ☞ copelandg@belfastcity.gov.uk

Facilities: Mr George Wright, Head - Facilities Management, 2nd Floor Adelaide Exchange, 24-26 Adelaide Street, Belfast BT2 8GD ☎ 028 9037 3034 🖷 ; 028 9037 3042 ☞ wrightg@belfastcity.gov.uk

Finance and Treasurer: Mr R Cregan, Head - Finance & Performance, Adelaide Exchange, 24-26 Adelaide Street, Belfast BT2 8GD ☎ 028 9050 0532 🖷 028 9072 6418 ☞ creganr@belfastcity.gov.uk

Fleet Management: Mr Gerry Fleming, Fleet Manager, Fleet Management Unit, Duncrue Complex, Duncrue Road, Belfast BT3 9BP ☎ 028 9037 3024 🖷 028 9027 0503 ☞ flemingg@belfastcity.gov.uk

Grounds Maintenance: Mr Andrew Hassard, Director - Parks & Leisure Services, Adelaide Exchange, 24-26 Adelaide Street, Belfast BT2 8GD ☎ 028 9027 0327 🖷 028 9023 7080 ☞ hassarda@belfastcity.gov.uk

Health and Safety: Ms Emma Eaton, Corporate Health & Safety Manager, Cecil Ward Building, 4-10 Linenhall Street, Belfast BT2 8BP ☎ 028 9027 0581 🖷 028 9027 0518 ☞ eatone@belfastcity.gov.uk

Legal: Mr Ciaran Quigley, Town Solicitor & Assistant Chief Executive, City Hall, Belfast BT1 5GS ① 028 9027 0239 🖷 028 9050 2099 ☞ quigleyc@belfastcity.gov.uk

Leisure and Cultural Services: Mr Andrew Hassard, Director - Parks & Leisure Services, Adelaide Exchange, 2nd Floor, 24-26 Adelaide Street, Belfast BT2 8GD ☎ 028 9027 0327 🖷 028 9023 7080 ☞ hassarda@belfastcity.gov.uk

Member Services: Mr Steven McCrory, Democratic Services Manager, City Hall, Belfast BT1 5GS ☎ 028 9027 0382 ☞ mccrorys@belfastcity.gov.uk

Partnerships: Mr Eamon Deeny, Head - Corporate Communications, City Hall, Belfast BT1 5GS ☎ 028 9027 0664 🖷 028 9072 6424 ☞ deenye@belfastcity.gov.uk

Personnel / HR: Ms Jill Minne, Head - Human Resources, Cecil Ward Building, 4-10 Linenhall Street, Belfast BT2 8BP ☎ 028 9027 0395 🖷 028 9027 0534 ☞ minnj@belfastcity.gov.uk

Procurement: Ms Valerie Cupples, Procurement Manager, Adelaide Exchange, 24-26 Adelaide Street, Belfast BT2 8GD ☎ 028 9027 0269 🖷 ; 028 9027 0590 ✉ cupplesv@belfastcity.gov.uk

Recycling & Waste Minimisation: Mr Tim Walker, Head - Waste Service, Cecil Ward Building, 4-10 Linenhall Street, Belfast BT2 8BP ☎ 028 9032 0202 🖷 028 9033 0900 ✉ walkert@belfastcity.gov.uk

Regeneration: Ms Shirley McCay, Head - Economic Initiatives, Cecil Ward Building, 4-10 Linenhall Street, Belfast BT2 8BP ☎ 028 9027 0529 🖷 ; 028 9027 0325 ✉ mccays@belfastcity.gov.uk

Regeneration: Mr John McGrillen, Director - Development, Cecil Ward Building, 4-10 Linenhall Street, Belfast BT2 8BP ☎ 028 9027 0485 🖷 028 9027 0496 ✉ mcgrillenj@belfastcity.gov.uk

Staff Training: Ms Catherine Christy, Principal HR Advisor - Development, Cecil Ward Building, 4-10 Linenhall Street, Belfast BT2 8BP ☎ 028 9027 0571 🖷 028 9027 0534 ✉ christyc@belfastcity.gov.uk

Street Scene: Mr S Skimin, Head - Cleansing Services, 5th Floor, 9 Lanyon Place, Belfast BT7 3LP ☎ 028 9037 3021 ✉ skimins@belfastcity.gov.uk

Sustainable Development: Mr Alastair Curran, Sustainable Development Manager, Cecil Ward Building, 4-10 Linenhall Street, Belfast BT2 8BP ☎ 028 9050 0544 🖷 ; 028 9027 0399 ✉ currana@belfastcity.gov.uk

Tourism: Ms K Sweeney, Tourism, Culture & Arts Manager, Cecil Ward Building, 4-10 Linenhall Street, Belfast BT2 8BP ☎ 028 9027 0228 🖷 028 9027 3025 ✉ sweeneyk@belfastcity.gov.uk

Waste Collection and Disposal: Mr Tim Walker, Head - Waste Service, Cecil Ward Building, 4-10 Linenhall Street, Belfast BT2 8BP ☎ 028 9032 0202 🖷 028 9033 0900 ✉ walkert@belfastcity.gov.uk

Waste Management: Mr Tim Walker, Head - Waste Service, Cecil Ward Building, 4-10 Linenhall Street, Belfast BT2 8BP ☎ 028 9032 0202 🖷 028 9033 0900 ✉ walkert@belfastcity.gov.uk

MEMBERS OF THE COUNCIL (51)

***Deputy Lord Mayor:* Cunningham**, Tierna (SF - Castle)
tiernac77@gmail.com
***High Sheriff:* Campbell**, May (DUP - Pottinger)
***Mayor:* Robinson**, Gavin (DUP - Pottinger)
robinsong@belfastcity.gov.uk
***Alderman:* Browne**, David (UUP - Castle)
d.browne@ntlworld.com
***Alderman:* Ekin**, Thomas (ALL - Balmoral)
tom@weaverscourt.com
***Alderman:* Humphrey**, William (DUP - Court)
williamhy@dup-belfast.co.uk
***Alderman:* McCoubrey**, Frank (IND - Court)
frankmccoubrey1@hotmail.co.uk
***Alderman:* Newton**, Robin (DUP - Victoria)
carole.newton@hotmail.com
***Alderman:* Patterson**, Ruth (DUP - Balmoral)
***Alderman:* Rodgers**, Jim (UUP - Victoria)
rodgersj@belfastcity.gov.uk
***Alderman:* Smyth**, Hugh (PUP - Court)
***Alderman:* Stalford**, Christopher (DUP - Laganbank)
Christopher_stalford@yahoo.com
***Alderman:* Stoker**, Robert (UUP - Balmoral)
stokerb@belfastcity.gov.uk
Attwood, Tim (SDLP - Upper Falls)
attwoodt@belfastcity.gov.uk
Austin, Janice (SF - Lower Falls)
Campbell, Mary Ellen (SF - Castle)
maryellencampbell@hotmail.com
Convery, Patrick (SDLP - Castle)
converyp@belfastcity.gov.uk
Corr, Steven (SF - Lower Falls)
corrs@belfastcity.gov.uk
Curran, Catherine (ALL - Laganbank)
catherine.curran@allianceparty.org
Garrett, Matt (SF - Upper Falls)
garrettm@belfastcity.gov.uk
Groves, Emma (SF - Upper Falls)
empgroves@msn.com
Haire, Tom (DUP - Victoria)
hairet@belfastcity.gov.uk
Hanna, Claire (SDLP - Balmoral)
hannac@belfastcity.gov.uk
Hargey, Deirdre (SF - Laganbank)
sandebelfast@sinn-fein.ie
Hartley, Tom (SF - Lower Falls)
Hartley_tom@hotmail.com
Hendron, Marie (ALL - Pottinger)
marie.hendron@allianceparty.org
Hussey, John (DUP - Victoria)
husseyj@belfastcity.gov.uk
Jones, Mervyn (ALL - Victoria)
mervynjones54@yahoo.co.uk
Keenan, Colin (SDLP - Lower Falls)
keenancolin@belfast.gov.uk
Kelly, Bernie (SDLP - Balmoral)
bkelly@utvinternet.com
Kingston, Brian (DUP - Court)
kingstonb@belfastcity.gov.uk
Kyle, John (PUP - Pottinger)
kylej@belfastcity.gov.uk
Lavery, Danny (SF - Oldpark)
Mac Giolla Mhin, Caoimhin (SF - Upper Falls)
caoimhinmgm@yahoo.com
Mallon, Nichola (SDLP - Oldpark)
mallonn@belfastcity.gov.uk
Maskey, Conor (SF - Oldpark)
conormaskey@hotmail.com
McCabe, Gerard (SF - Oldpark)
McCarthy, Patrick (SDLP - Laganbank)
mccarthyp@belfastcity.gov.uk
McKee, Gareth (DUP - Oldpark)
gareth@dup-belfast.co.uk
McNamee, Laura (ALL - Victoria)
laura.mcnamee@allianceparty.org
McVeigh, Jim (SF - Lower Falls)
mcveighjames@belfastcity.gov.uk
Mullan, Kate (SDLP - Laganbank)
mullankate@belfastcity.gov.uk

Newton, Adam (DUP - Pottinger)
adam.newton@live.co.uk
O Donnghaile, Niall (SF - Pottinger)
niallodonnghaile@gmail.com
O Muilleoir, Mairtin (SF - Balmoral)
mairtin@newbelfast.com
O'Neill, Gerard (SF - Upper Falls)
Patterson, Lynda (DUP - Castle)
lydia@dup-belfast.co.uk
Reynolds, Lee (DUP - Oldpark)
reynoldsl@belfastcity.gov.uk
Spence, Guy (DUP - Castle)
spenceg@belfastcity.gov.uk
Thompson, Naomi (DUP - Court)
naomi@dup-belfast.co.uk
Webb, Andrew (ALL - Victoria)
andrew.webb@allianceparty.org

POLITICAL COMPOSITION

SF: 16, DUP: 15, SDLP: 8, ALL: 6, UUP: 3, PUP: 2, IND: 1

COMMITTEE CHAIRS

Development Committee: Mr Christopher Stalford
Health & Environmental Services: Mr Patrick McCarthy
Licensing: Mr Thomas Ekin
Parks & Leisure: Mr Steven Corr
Strategic Policy & Resources: Ms Deirdre Hargey
Town Planning: Ms Lynda Patterson

BEXLEY L

London Borough of Bexley, (The London Borough of Bexley), Bexley Civic Offices, Broadway, Bexleyheath DA6 7LB ☎ 020 8303 7777 🖷 020 8301 2661 ✉ customer.services@bexley.gov.uk 💻 www.bexley.gov.uk

FACTS & FIGURES

Police Authority: Metropolitan Police Authority
Health Authority: NHS London
Learning and Skills Council: South East
Parliamentary Constituencies: Bexleyheath & Crayford, Erith and Thamesmead, Old Bexley and Sidcup
EU Constituencies: South East
Election Frequency: Elections are of whole council
Twinning: Evry (France); Neheim-Husten (Germany)

PRINCIPAL OFFICERS

Chief Executive: Mr Will Tuckley, Chief Executive, Bexley Civic Offices, Broadway, Bexleyheath DA6 7LB ☎ 020 3045 3232 🖷 020 8294 6024 ✉ will.tuckley@bexley.gov.uk

Senior Management: Mr Peter Ellershaw, Director of Environment & Wellbeing, Bexley Civic Offices, Broadway, Bexleyheath DA6 7LB ☎ 020 3045 5706 🖷 020 3045 5448 ✉ peter.ellershaw@bexley.gov.uk

Senior Management: Mrs Fola Ikpehai, Head of Strategy 2014 Review Team, Bexley Civic Offices, Broadway, Bexleyheath DA6 7LB ☎ 020 3045 3553 🖷 020 8294 6094 ✉ fola.ikpehai@bexley.gov.uk

Senior Management: Mr Terry Pearce, Financial Resources Manager, Bexley Civic Offices, Broadway, Bexleyheath DA6 7LB ☎ 020 3045 5145 🖷 020 8303 4987 ✉ terry.pearce@bexley.gov.uk

Access Officer / Social Services (Disability): Mr Mark Charters, Director of Education & Social Care, Bexley Civic Offices, Broadway, Bexleyheath DA6 7LB ☎ ; 020 3045 4090 🖷 020 8836 8300 ✉ mark.charters@bexley.gov.uk

Access Officer / Social Services (Disability): Prof Vinod Kumar Khanna, Chief Executive Inspire Community Trust, 20 Whitehall Lane, Erith DA8 2DH ☎ ; 020 3045 5312 🖷 01322 345416 ✉ vinod.kumar@bexley.gov.uk

Best Value: Mr Trevor Wentworth, Surveying Services Manager, Bexley Civic Offices, Broadway, Bexleyheath DA6 7LB ☎ 020 3045 5757 🖷 020 8308 7959 ✉ trevor.wentworth@bexley.gov.uk

Building Control: Mr Adrian Cole, Head of Building Services, Bexley Civic Offices, Broadway, Bexleyheath DA6 7LB ☎ 020 3045 5802 🖷 020 8308 7897 ✉ adrian.cole@bexley.gov.uk

Catering Services: Ms Helen Sellick, Facilities Senior Contract Officer, Bexley Civic Offices, Broadway, Bexleyheath DA6 7LB ☎ ; 020 3045 3639 ✉ helen.sellick@bexley.gov.uk

PR / Communications: Mr John Ferry, Communications Manager, Bexley Civic Offices, Broadway, Bexleyheath DA6 7LB ☎ ; 020 3045 4867 🖷 ; 020 3045 5444 ✉ john.ferry@bexley.gov.uk

Community Planning: Ms Maureen Holkham, Deputy Director - Corporate Policy & Communications, Bexley Civic Offices, Broadway, Bexleyheath DA6 7LB ☎ 020 3045 3608 🖷 020 8294 6863 ✉ maureen.holkham@bexley,gov.uk

Community Safety: Mr Mark Usher, Community Safety Co-ordinator, Bexley Civic Offices, Broadway, Bexleyheath DA6 7LB ☎ ; 020 3045 3580 🖷 020 8294 6226 ✉ mark.usher@bexley.gov.uk

Computer Management: Mr Tony Allen, Deputy Director (ICT), Bexley Civic Offices, Broadway, Bexleyheath DA6 7LB ☎ 020 3045 4904 🖷 ; 020 3045 5444 ✉ tony.allen@bexley.gov.uk

Consumer Protection and Trading Standards: Mr David Bryce-Smith, Deputy Director - Development, Housing & Community, Bexley Civic Offices, Broadway, Bexleyheath DA6 7LB ☎ 020 3045 5718 🖷 020 8308 7897 ✉ david.brycesmith@bexley.gov.uk

Contracts: Mr Michael Frizoni, Deputy Director - Public Realm Management, Footscray Offices, Maidstone road, Sidcup DA14 5HS ☎ 020 3045 4625 ✉ mike.frizoni@bexley.gov.uk

Corporate Services: Mr Steve Hobdell, Development Control Admin & Systems Manager, Bexley Civic Offices, Broadway, Bexleyheath DA6 7LB ☎ 020 3045 5740 🖷 020 8308 7897 ✉ steve.hobdell@bexley.gov.uk

Customer Service: Mr Graham Ward, Deputy Director Customer Relations, Bexley Civic Offices, Broadway, Bexleyheath DA6 7LB

☎ 020 3045 4622 🖷 020 8294 6796
🖱 graham.ward@bexley.gov.uk

Economic Development: Mr Tim Walby, Economic Development Officer, Bexley Civic Offices, Broadway, Bexleyheath DA6 7LB ☎ ; 020 3045 5723 🖷 020 8308 7887 🖱 tim.walby@bexley.gov.uk

Electoral Registration: Ms Clare Oakley, Electoral Services Manager, Bexley Civic Offices, Broadway, Bexleyheath DA6 7LB ☎ 020 3045 3649 🖱 clare.oakley@bexley.gov.uk

Emergency Planning: Mr Tony Plowright, Emergency Planning & Business Continuity Manager, Bexley Civic Offices, Broadway, Bexleyheath DA6 7LB ☎ 020 3045 4623 🖷 020 8309 4040 🖱 tony.plowright@bexley.gov.uk

Energy Management: Mr Kevin Murphy, Head of Housing Services, Bexley Civic Offices, Broadway, Bexleyheath DA6 7LB ☎ 020 3045 5623 🖷 020 8308 1300 🖱 kevin.murphy@bexley.gov.uk

Environmental / Technical Services: Mr Peter Ellershaw, Director of Environment & Wellbeing, Bexley Civic Offices, Broadway, Bexleyheath DA6 7LB ☎ 020 3045 5706 🖷 020 3045 5448 🖱 peter.ellershaw@bexley.gov.uk

Environmental Health: Mr David Bryce-Smith, Deputy Director - Development, Housing & Community, Bexley Civic Offices, Broadway, Bexleyheath DA6 7LB ☎ 020 3045 5718 🖷 020 8308 7897 🖱 david.brycesmith@bexley.gov.uk

Estates, Property & Valuation: Ms Suzanne Jackson, Head of Property & Facilities, Bexley Civic Offices, Broadway, Bexleyheath DA6 7LB ☎ 020 3045 4830 🖷 020 8294 6995 🖱 suzanne.jackson@bexley.gov.uk

Events Manager: Ms Saskia Delman, Arts Manager, Footscray Offices, Maidstone road, Sidcup DA14 5HS ☎ ; 020 3045 4555 🖱 saskia.delman@bexley.gov.uk

Facilities: Mr Graham Raven, Facilities Services Manager, Bexley Civic Offices, Broadway, Bexleyheath DA6 7LB ☎ 020 3045 3640 🖷 020 8294 6125 🖱 graham.raven@bexley.gov.uk

Finance and Treasurer: Mr Mike Ellsmore, Director of Finance & Resources, Bexley Civic Offices, Broadway, Bexleyheath DA6 7LB ☎ 020 3045 4955 🖷 020 8294 6299 🖱 mike.ellsmore@bexley.gov.uk

Finance and Treasurer: Mr John Peters, Deputy Director of Finance, Bexley Civic Offices, Broadway, Bexleyheath DA6 7LB ☎ 020 3045 4954 🖷 080 8294 6333 🖱 john.peters@bexley.gov.uk

Grounds Maintenance: Mr Michael Frizoni, Deputy Director - Public Realm Management, Footscray Offices, Maidstone road, Sidcup DA14 5HS ☎ 020 3045 4625 🖱 mike.frizoni@bexley.gov.uk

Health and Safety: Mr Clive Cain, Head of Community Safety Services, 2A Hadlow Road, Sidcup DA14 4AF ☎ ; 020 3045 5633 🖷 020 8308 1300 🖱 clive.cain@bexley.gov.uk

Highways: Mr Michael Frizoni, Deputy Director - Public Realm Management, Footscray Offices, Maidstone road, Sidcup DA14 5HS ☎ 020 3045 4625 🖱 mike.frizoni@bexley.gov.uk

Home Energy Conservation: Mr Kevin Murphy, Head of Housing Services, Bexley Civic Offices, Broadway, Bexleyheath DA6 7LB ☎ 020 3045 5623 🖷 020 8308 1300 🖱 kevin.murphy@bexley.gov.uk

Local Area Agreement: Mrs Fola Ikpehai, Head of Strategy 2014 Review Team, Bexley Civic Offices, Broadway, Bexleyheath DA6 7LB ☎ 020 3045 3553 🖷 020 8294 6094 🖱 fola.ikpehai@bexley.gov.uk

Legal: Mr Akin Alabi, Head of Legal Services & Monitoring Officer, Bexley Civic Offices, Broadway, Bexleyheath DA6 7LB ☎ 020 3045 3922 🖷 020 8294 6071 🖱 akin.alabi@bexley.gov.uk

Leisure and Cultural Services: Ms Toni Ainge, Deputy Director Cultural Services, Bexley Civic Offices, Broadway, Bexleyheath DA6 7LB ☎ ; 020 3045 4879 🖷 020 8294 6778 🖱 antonia.ainge@bexley.gov.uk

Licensing: Mr David Bryce-Smith, Deputy Director - Development, Housing & Community, Bexley Civic Offices, Broadway, Bexleyheath DA6 7LB ☎ 020 3045 5718 🖷 020 8308 7897 🖱 david.brycesmith@bexley.gov.uk

Lighting: Mr Michael Frizoni, Deputy Director - Public Realm Management, Bexley Civic Offices, Broadway, Bexleyheath DA6 7LB ☎ 020 3045 4625 🖱 mike.frizoni@bexley.gov.uk

Parking: Ms Tina Brooks, Head of Traffic & Parking Services, Bexley Civic Offices, Broadway, Bexleyheath DA6 7LB ☎ 020 3045 3934 🖷 020 8294 6891 🖱 tina.brooks@bexley.gov.uk

Partnerships: Mrs Fola Ikpehai, Head of Strategy 2014 Review Team, Bexley Civic Offices, Broadway, Bexleyheath DA6 7LB ☎ 020 3045 3553 🖷 020 8294 6094 🖱 fola.ikpehai@bexley.gov.uk

Personnel / HR: Mr Nick Hollier, Deputy Director - HR & Corporate Support, Hill View, Hill View Drive, Welling DA16 3RY ☎ 020 3045 4091 🖷 020 8836 8063 🖱 nick.hollier@bexley.gov.uk

Procurement: Mr Taraq Bashir, Deputy Director - Property, Procurement & Commissioning, Bexley Civic Offices, Broadway, Bexleyheath DA6 7LB ☎ 020 3045 4957 🖱 taraq.bashit@bexley.gov.uk

Procurement: Mr Mike Ellsmore, Director of Finance & Resources, Bexley Civic Offices, Broadway, Bexleyheath DA6 7LB ☎ 020 3045 4955 🖷 020 8294 6299 🖱 mike.ellsmore@bexley.gov.uk

Public Libraries: Ms Judith Mitlin, Head of Libraries, Heritage & Archives, Footscray Offices, Maidstone road, Sidcup DA14 5HS ☎ 020 3045 4531 🖷 020 8309 4152 🖱 judith.mitlin@bexley,gov,uk

Public Libraries: Mr Hugh Paton, Development Manager (Libraries), Footscray Offices, Maidstone Road, Sidcup DA14 5HS ☎ ; 020 3045 4534 🖷 020 8309 4152

hugh.paton@bexley.gov.uk

Recycling & Waste Minimisation: Mr Michael Frizoni, Deputy Director - Public Realm Management, Footscray Offices, Maidstone road, Sidcup DA14 5HS ☎ 020 3045 4625 mike.frizoni@bexley.gov.uk

Regeneration: Ms Jane Richardson, Deputy Director - Strategic Planning & Regeneration, Hill View, Hill View Drive, Welling DA16 3RS ☎ 020 3045 5775 🖷 020 8308 7887 jane.richardson@bexley.gov.uk

Road Safety: Mr Mark Bunting, Team Leader - Road Safety, Bexley Civic Offices, Broadway, Bexleyheath DA6 7LB ☎ 020 3045 5875 🖷 020 8308 7902 mark.bunting@bexley.gov.uk

Social Services: Mr Mark Charters, Director of Education & Social Care, Hill View, Hill View Drive, Welling DA16 3RY ☎ 020 3045 4090 🖷 020 8836 8300 mark.charters@bexley.gov.uk

Social Services (Adult): Mr Mark Charters, Director of Education & Social Care, Hill View, Hill View Drive, Welling DA16 3RY ☎ 020 3045 4090 🖷 020 8836 8300 mark.charters@bexley.gov.uk

Social Services (Children): Ms Sheila Murphy, Deputy Director - Social Care, Safeguarding & SEN, Hill View, Hill View Drive, Welling DA16 3RY ☎ 020 3045 4128 🖷 020 8836 8148 sheila.murphy@bexley.gov.uk

Social Services (Children): Miss Linda Tottman, Deputy Director - Family, Youth & Employment, Hill View, Hill View Drive, Welling DA16 3RY ☎ 020 3045 4129 🖷 020 8836 8148 linda.tottman@bexley.gov.uk

Staff Training: Mr Nick Hollier, Deputy Director - HR & Corporate Support, Hill View, Hill View Drive, Welling DA16 3RY ☎ 020 3045 4091 🖷 020 8836 8063 nick.hollier@bexley.gov.uk

Street Scene: Mr Tony Hughes, Head of Operational Services, Footscray Offices, Maidstone road, Sidcup DA14 5HS ☎ 020 3045 4512 tony.hughes@bexley.gov.uk

Sustainable Communities: Ms Susan Clark, Head of Development Control, Bexley Civic Offices, Broadway, Bexleyheath DA6 7LB ☎ 020 3045 5761 🖷 020 8308 7897 susan.clark@bexley.gov.uk

Tourism: Ms Toni Ainge, Deputy Director Cultural Services, Bexley Civic Offices, Broadway, Bexleyheath DA6 7LB ☎ 020 3045 4879 🖷 020 8294 6778 antonia.ainge@bexley.gov.uk

Town Centre: Mr Ian Payne, Town Centre Manager, c/o M&S, The Mall, Broadway, Bexleyheath DA6 7JN ☎ 020 8304 0775 ian.payne@bexley.gov.uk

Waste Collection and Disposal: Mr Michael Frizoni, Deputy Director - Public Realm Management, Bexley Civic Offices, Broadway, Bexleyheath DA6 7LB ☎ 020 3045 4625 mike.frizoni@bexley.gov.uk

Waste Management: Mr Michael Frizoni, Deputy Director - Public Realm Management, Bexley Civic Offices, Broadway, Bexleyheath DA6 7LB ☎ 020 3045 4625 mike.frizoni@bexley.gov.uk

Children's Play Areas: Mr Colin Rowland, Head of Parks & Open Spaces, Bexley Civic Offices, Broadway, Bexleyheath DA6 7LB ☎ ; 020 3045 3686 🖷 020 8294 6552 colin.rowland@bexley.gov.uk

MEMBERS OF THE COUNCIL (63)

***Mayor:* Sams**, Ray (CON - St Michael's)
councillor.ray.sams@bexley.gov.uk

***Leader of the Council:* O'Neill**, Teresa (CON - Brampton)
councillor.teresa.o'neill@bexley.gov.uk

***Deputy Leader of the Council:* Campbell**, Colin (CON - St Mary's)
councillor.colin.campbell@bexley.gov.uk

Allon, Kerry (CON - Belvedere)
councillor.kerry.allon@bexley.gov.uk

Ashmole, Roy (CON - Christchurch)
councillor.roy.ashmole@bexley.gov.uk

Bacon, Cheryl (CON - Cray Meadows)
councillor.cheryl.bacon@bexley.gov.uk

Bacon, Gareth (CON - Longlands)
councillor.gareth.bacon@bexley.gov.uk

Bailey, Linda (CON - Danson Park)
councillor.linda.bailey@bexley.gov.uk

Ball, Chris (LAB - Erith)
councillor.chris.ball@bexley.gov.uk

Bauer, Sandra (LAB - Thamesmead East)
councillor.sandra.bauer@bexley.gov.uk

Beckwith, Brian (CON - Blackfen & Lamorbey)
councillor.brian.beckwith@bexley.gov.uk

Beckwith, Aileen (CON - Sidcup)
councillor.aileen.beckwith@bexley.gov.uk

Betts, Nigel (CON - Falconwood & Welling)
councillor.nigel.betts@bexley.gov.uk

Bishop, Brian (CON - Colyers)
councillor.brian.bishop@bexley.gov.uk

Boateng, Edward (LAB - Erith)
councillor.edward.boateng@bexley.gov.uk

Borella, Stefano (LAB - North End)
councillor.stefano.borella@bexley.gov.uk

Cammish, Pat (CON - Blendon & Penhill)
councillor.pat.cammish@bexley.gov.uk

Camsey, Sybil (CON - Brampton)
councillor.sybil.camsey@bexley.gov.uk

Catterall, Peter (CON - Falconwood & Welling)
councillor.peter.catterall@bexley.gov.uk

Clark, Val (CON - Falconwood & Welling)
councillor.val.clark@bexley.gov.uk

Craske, Peter (CON - Blackfen & Lamorbey)
councillor.peter.craske@bexley.gov.uk

D'Amiral, Graham (CON - Blendon & Penhill)
councillor.graham.d'amiral@bexley.gov.uk

Davey, John (CON - Lesnes Abbey)
councillor.john.davey@bexley.gov.uk

Deadman, Alan (LAB - North End)
christina.ford@bexley.gov.uk

Downing, Ross (CON - Cray Meadows)
councillor.ross.downing@bexley.gov.uk

Downing, Alan (CON - St Mary's)
councillor.alan.downing@bexley.gov.uk

Evans, Jackie (CON - Sidcup)
councillor.jackie.evans@bexley.gov.uk
Fothergill, Maxine (CON - Colyers)
councillor.maxine.fothergill@bexley.gov.uk
Fuller, John (CON - Lesnes Abbey)
councillor.john.fuller@bexley.gov.uk
Gillespie, Richard (CON - Longlands)
councillor.richard.gillespie@bexley.gov.uk
Hall, Steven (CON - East Wickham)
councillor.steven.hall@bexley.gov.uk
Hunt, James (CON - East Wickham)
councillor.james.hunt@bexley.gov.uk
Hurt, Eleanor (CON - Lesnes Abbey)
councillor.eleanor.hurt@bexley.gov.uk
Hurt, David (CON - Barnehurst)
councillor.david.hurt@bexley.gov.uk
Langstead, Brenda (LAB - North End)
councillor.brenda.langstead@bexley.gov.uk
Lucia-Hennis, Geraldene (CON - Crayford)
councillor.geraldene.lucia-hennis@bexley.gov.uk
MacDonald, Gill (LAB - Belvedere)
councillor.gill.macdonald@bexley.gov.uk
Malik, Munir (LAB - Thamesmead East)
councillor.munir.malik@bexley.gov.uk
Marriner, Howard (CON - Barnehurst)
councillor.howard.marriner@bexley.gov.uk
Massey, Sharon (CON - Danson Park)
councillor.sharon.massey@bexley.gov.uk
Massey, Donald (CON - Cray Meadows)
councillor.donald.massey@bexley.gov.uk
Newman, Sean (LAB - Belvedere)
councillor.sean.newman@bexley.gov.uk
Newton, Caroline (CON - St Michael's)
councillor.caroline.newton@bexley.gov.uk
O'Hare, Nick (CON - Blendon & Penhill)
councillor.nick.o'hare@bexley.gov.uk
O'Neill, Margaret (LAB - Erith)
councillor.margaret.o'neill@bexley.gov.uk
Pallen, Eileen (CON - Crayford)
councillor.eileen.pallen@bexley.gov.uk
Perrior, Katie (CON - Blackfen & Lamorbey)
councillor.katie.perrior@bexley.gov.uk
Persaud, Harry (LAB - Thamesmead East)
christina.ford@bexley.gov.uk
Pollard, Joseph (CON - St Michael's)
councillor.joseph.pollard@bexley.gov.uk
Read, Philip (CON - Northumberland Heath)
councillor.philip.read@bexley.gov.uk
Reader, Peter (CON - Northumberland Heath)
councillor.peter.reader@bexley.gov.uk
Sawyer, Alex (CON - Northumberland Heath)
councillor.alex.sawyer@bexley.gov.uk
Seymour, Melvin (CON - Crayford)
councillor.melvin.seymour@bexley.gov.uk
Slaughter, Mike (CON - Longlands)
councillor.michael.slaughter@bexley.gov.uk
Slaughter, June (CON - Sidcup)
councillor.june.slaughter@bexley.gov.uk
Smith, Brad (CON - Christchurch)
councillor.brad.smith@bexley.gov.uk
Spencer, James (CON - Christchurch)
councillor.james.spencer@bexley.gov.uk
Tandy, Colin (CON - St Mary's)
councillor.colin.tandy@bexley.gov.uk
Tarrant, Michael (CON - East Wickham)
councillor.michael.tarrant@bexley.gov.uk
Taylor, Chris (CON - Colyers)
councillor.chris.taylor@bexley.gov.uk
Waters, John (CON - Danson Park)
councillor.john.waters@bexley.gov.uk
Wilkinson, John (CON - Brampton)
jane.foord-divers@bexley.gov.uk
Windle, Simon (CON - Barnehurst)
councillor.simon.windle@bexley.gov.uk

POLITICAL COMPOSITION
CON: 52, LAB: 11

CABINET
Leader: Ms Teresa O'Neill
Deputy Leader: Mr Colin Campbell
Adult's Services: Mr Chris Taylor
Children's Services: Ms Katie Perrior
Economic Development & Regeneration: Ms Linda Bailey
Education: Mr John Fuller
Environment: Mr Gareth Bacon
Finance & Corporate Services: Mr Colin Campbell
Leisure: Mr Donald Massey
Public: Ms Teresa O'Neill
Public Realm & Community Safety: Mr Peter Craske

COMMITTEE CHAIRS
Adult Services Overview: Ms Eileen Pallen
Appeals: Mr John Fuller
Audit: Mr Steven Hall
Bexley Community Safety Partnership: Ms Katie Perrior
Children's Services & Education Overview: Mr James Hunt
Constitution Review Panel: Ms Teresa O'Neill
Crime & Disorder Overview: Mr Alex Sawyer
Environment & Leisure Overview: Mr Melvin Seymour
Finance & Corporate Services Overview: Mr Philip Read
General Purposes: Ms Geraldene Lucia-Hennis
Governor Appointment: Ms Geraldene Lucia-Hennis
Health Overview: Mrs Ross Downing
Licensing: Mr Brad Smith
Pensions: Mr John Waters
Planning: Mr Peter Reader
Public Realm, Community Safety, Economic Development & Regeneration Overview: Ms Cheryl Bacon

BIRMINGHAM CITY M

Birmingham City Council, The Council House, Victoria Square, Birmingham B1 1BB ☎ 0121 303 9944
contact@birmingham.gov.uk www.birmingham.gov.uk

FACTS & FIGURES
Police Authority: West Midlands Police Authority
Health Authority: NHS West Midlands
Learning and Skills Council: West Midlands
Parliamentary Constituencies: Birmingham, Edgbaston, Birmingham, Erdington, Birmingham, Hall Green, Birmingham, Hodge Hill, Birmingham, Ladywood, Birmingham, Northfield, Birmingham, Perry Bar, Birmingham, Selly Oak, Birmingham, Yardley, Sutton Coldfield
EU Constituencies: West Midlands
Election Frequency: Elections are by thirds

LOCAL AUTHORITIES

Twinning: Chicago (USA); Frankfurt (Germany); Lyon (France); Johannesburg (South Africa); Leipzig (Germany); Milan (Italy); Guanzhou (China)

PRINCIPAL OFFICERS

Chief Executive: Mr Stephen Hughes, Chief Executive, The Council House, Victoria Square, Birmingham B1 1BB ☎ 0121 303 2000 🖷 0121 303 1309 ✉ stephen.hughes@birmingham.gov.uk

Senior Management: Dr Mirza Ahmad, Corporate Director - Governance & Monitoring Officer, The Council House, Victoria Square, Birmingham B1 1BB ☎ 0121 303 9991 ✉ mirza.ahmad@birmingham.gov.uk

Senior Management: Mr Mark Barrow, Strategic Director - Development, 1 Lancaster Circus, Queensway, Birmingham B1 1TR ☎ 0121 303 4223 ✉ mark.barrow@birmingham.gov.uk

Senior Management: Mr Peter Duxbury, Strategic Director - Children, Young People & Families, The Council House, Victoria Square, Birmingham B1 1BB

Senior Management: Ms Elaine Elkington, Strategic Director - Homes & Neighbourhoods, Louisa Ryland House, 44 Newhall Street, Birmingham B3 3PL ☎ 0121 303 3595 🖷 0121 303 4631 ✉ elaine.elkington@birmingham.gov.uk

Senior Management: Mr Peter Hay, Strategic Director - Adults & Communities, Louisa Ryland House, 44 Newhall Street, Birmingham B3 3PL ☎ 0121 303 2992 ✉ peter.hay@birmingham.gov.uk

Senior Management: Ms Sharon Lea, Strategic Director - Environment & Culture, House of Sport, 300 Broad Street, Birmingham B1 2DR ☎ 0121 303 2047 🖷 0121 464 0969 ✉ sharon.lea@birmingham.gov.uk

Access Officer / Social Services (Disability): Ms Cheryl Bates, Team Manager - Perry Barr & Ladywood Home Care Service, Louisa Ryland House, 44 Newhall Street, Birmingham B3 3PL ☎ 0121 303 0775 ✉ cheryl.bates@birmingham.gov.uk

Architect, Building / Property Services: Ms Helen Bonham, Head - Regeneration & Property Law, The Council House, Victoria Square, Birmingham B1 1BB ☎ 0121 3034287 ✉ helen.bonham@birmingham.gov.uk

Architect, Building / Property Services: Mr Peter Jones, Director - Property, PO BOX 16255, Birmingham B2 2WT ☎ 0121 303 3844 ✉ peter.jones@birmingham.gov.uk

Architect, Building / Property Services: Mr Roger Lloyd, Head - Regeneration & Property Law, The Council House, Victoria Square, Birmingham B1 1BB ☎ 0121 303 4287 ✉ roger.lloyd@birmingham.gov.uk

Building Control: Mr Trevor Haynes, Operational Director - Construction & FM Services, 1 Lancaster Circus, Queensway, Birmingham B1 1TU ☎ 0121 303 3069 ✉ trevor.haynes@acivico.co.uk

Children / Youth Services: Mr David Brown, Head - Education & Children's Services Law, The Council House, Victoria Square, Birmingham B1 1BB ☎ 0121 675 3428 ✉ david.brown@birmingham.gov.uk

Children / Youth Services: Ms Trisha Jervis, Head - Children's Services East & Charities & Trusts, The Council House, Victoria Square, Birmingham B1 1BB ☎ 0121 675 5425 ✉ trisha.jervis@birmingham.gov.uk

Community Planning: Mr Peter Hay, Strategic Director - Adults & Communities, Louisa Ryland House, 44 Newhall Street, Birmingham B3 3PL ☎ 0121 303 2992 ✉ peter.hay@birmingham.gov.uk

Community Safety: Mr Feizal Hajat, Head - Law, Housing & Community Safety Team, The Council House, Victoria Square, Birmingham B1 1BB ☎ 0121 464 3373 ✉ feizal.hajat@birmingham.gov.uk

Corporate Services: Mr Kevin Hubery, Head - Policy & Delivery, The Council House, Victoria Square, Birmingham B1 1BB ☎ 0121 303 4960 🖷 0121 464 6601 ✉ kevin.hubery.gov.uk

Corporate Services: Mr Jason Lowther, Director - Policy & Delivery, The Council House, Victoria Square, Birmingham B1 1BB ☎ 0121 303 4960 🖷 0121 464 6601 ✉ jason.lowther@birmingham.gov.uk

Corporate Services: Ms Wendy Terry, Head - Performace Improvement, The Council House, Victoria Square, Birmingham B1 1BB ☎ 0121 464 8121 ✉ wendy_terry@birmingham.gov.uk

Customer Service: Ms Georgina Foxwell, Head - Integrated Services, The Council House, Victoria Square, Birmingham B1 1BB ☎ 0121 675 9571 ✉ georgina.foxwell@birmingham.gov.uk

E-Government: Mr Raj Mack, Director - Digital Development & Communities, The Council House, Victoria Square, Birmingham B1 1BB ☎ 0121 464 5792 ✉ raj.mack@birmingham.gov.uk

Environmental / Technical Services: Ms Sharon Lea, Strategic Director - Environment & Culture, House of Sport, 300 Broad Street, Birmingham B1 2DR ☎ 0121 303 2047 🖷 0121 464 0969 ✉ sharon.lea@birmingham.gov.uk

Environmental Health: Mr Stuart Evans, Head - Environment, Development & Planning Team, The Council House, Victoria Square, Birmingham B1 1BB ☎ 0121 303 4868 ✉ stuart_j_evans@birmingham.gov.uk

Environmental Health: Mr John Wyn, Assistant Director - Housing, Development, Constituencies & Environment, The Council House, Victoria Square, Birmingham B1 1BB ☎ 0121 303 2036 ✉ john.wyn@birmingham.gov.uk

Events Manager: Mr Steve Hollingworth, Assistant Director - Sports & Events, 1st Floor Manor House, Moat Lane, Birmingham B5 5BD ☎ 0121 464 2024 ✉ steve.hollingworth@birmingham.gov.uk

Finance and Treasurer: Ms Alison Jarrett, Assistant Director - Finances Development Directorate, The Council House, Victoria

Square, Birmingham B1 1BB ☎ 0121 303 2950
alison.jarrett@birmingham.gov.uk

Finance and Treasurer: Mr Jon Warlow, Director - Corporate Finance, The Council House, Victoria Square, Birmingham B1 1BB ☎ 0121 303 2950 🖷 0121 303 1356
jon.warlow@birmingham.gov.uk

Fleet Management: Mr Matt Kelly, Assistant Director - Fleet & Waste Management (Operations), House of Sport, 300 Broad Street, Birmingham B1 2DR ☎ 0121 303 6171
matt.kelly@birmingham.gov.uk

Fleet Management: Mr Kevin Mitchell, Assitant Director - Fleet & Waste Management (Operations), House of Sport, 300 Broad Street, Birmingham B1 2DR ☎ 0121 675 0648
kevin.mitchell@birmingham.gov.uk

Fleet Management: Ms Chloe Tringham, Head - Fleet & Waste Management, House of Sport, 300 Broad Street, Birmingham B1 2DR ☎ 0121 675 0648 chloe.tringham@birmingham.gov.uk

Fleet Management: Mr Tommy Wallace, Director - Fleet & Waste Management, House of Sport, 300 Broad Street, Birmingham B1 2DR ☎ 0121 303 6171
tommy.wallace@birmingham.gov.uk

Highways: Mr John Blakemore, Director - Highways & Resilience, 1 Lancaster Circus, Birmingham B4 7DQ ☎ 0121 303 7329 🖷 0121 303 6451 john.blakemore@birmingham.gov.uk

Housing: Ms Lousie Collett, Service Director - Policy Commission, Louisa Ryland House, 44 Newhall Street, Birmingham B3 3PL ☎ 0121 303 6136
louise.collett@birmingham.gov.uk

Housing: Ms Elaine Elkington, Strategic Director - Homes & Neighbourhoods, Louisa Ryland House, 44 Newhall Street, Birmingham B3 3PL ☎ 0121 303 3595 🖷 0121 303 4631
elaine.elkington@birmingham.gov.uk

Housing: Ms Sheila Espen, Assistant Director - Head of Landlord Services, The Council House, Victoria Square, Birmingham B1 1BB ☎ 0121 303 7882
sheila.espen@birmingham.gov.uk

Housing: Mr John Wyn, Assistant Director - Housing, Development, Constituencies & Environment, The Council House, Victoria Square, Birmingham B1 1BB ☎ 0121 303 2036
john.wyn@birmingham.gov.uk

Housing Maintenance: Mr John Jamieson, Interim Assistant Director - Asset Management, The Council House, Victoria Square, Birmingham B1 1BB ☎ 0121 3066136
john.jamieson@birmingham.gov.uk

Legal: Dr Mirza Ahmad, Corporate Director - Governance & Monitoring Officer, The Council House, Victoria Square, Birmingham B1 1BB ☎ 0121 303 9991
mirza.ahmad@birmingham.gov.uk

Legal: Mr David Tatlow, Director - Democratic Services, The Council House, Victoria Square, Birmingham B1 1BB
☎ 0121 303 2151 david.tatlow@birmingham.gov.uk

Leisure and Cultural Services: Mr Brian Gambles, Assistant Director - Culture, Birmingham Museum & Art Gallery, Chamblerlain Square, Birmingham B3 3DH ☎ 0121 303 3372
brian.gambles@birmingham.gov.uk

Leisure and Cultural Services: Ms Sharon Lea, Strategic Director - Environment & Culture, House of Sport, 300 Broad Street, Birmingham B1 2DR ☎ 0121 303 2047 🖷 0121 464 0969
sharon.lea@birmingham.gov.uk

Lottery Funding, Charity and Voluntary: Ms Nimmi Patel, Head - Third Sector Partnerships, The Council House, Victoria Square, Birmingham B1 1BB ☎ 07774 337353
nimmi.patel@birmingham.gov.uk

Member Services: Mr Prakash Patel, Admin Manager - Committee & Services, The Council House, Victoria Square, Birmingham B1 1BB ☎ 0121 303 2018 🖷 0121 606 1672
prakesh.patel@birmingham.gov.uk

Parking: Mr Bob Wilde, Head - Parking & Services, The Council House, Victoria Square, Birmingham B1 1BB ☎ 0121 303 6421
bob.wilde@birmingham.gov.uk

Personnel / HR: Mr Andy Albon, Director - Equalities & Human Resources, The Council House, Victoria Square, Birmingham B1 1BB ☎ 0121 303 2265 🖷 0121 303 1311
andy.albon@birmingham.gov.uk

Personnel / HR: Dr Mashuq Ally, Assistant Director - Equality & Human Resources, The Council House, Victoria Square, Birmingham B1 1BB ☎ 0121 303 2627
mashuq.ally@birmingham.gov.uk

Personnel / HR: Mr Tarik Chawdry, Assistant Director - Human Resources, The Council House, Victoria Square, Birmingham B1 1BB ☎ 0121 303 2120 tarik.chawdry@birmingham.gov.uk

Personnel / HR: Mr Bill Fletcher, Assistant Director - Human Resources, The Council House, Victoria Square, Birmingham B1 1BB ☎ 0121 303 2271 🖷 0121 303 1311
bill.fletcher@birmingham.gov.uk

Procurement: Mr Rob Barker, Head - Service (Procurement), The Council House, Victoria Square, Birmingham B1 1BB
☎ 0121 303 3870 rob.barker@birmingham.gov.uk

Procurement: Mr Nigel Kletz, Assistant Director - Procurement, The Council House, Victoria Square, Birmingham B1 1BB
☎ 0121 303 6610 nigel.kletz@birmingham.gov.uk

Regeneration: Mr Mark Barrow, Strategic Director - Development, 1 Lancaster Circus, Queensway, Birmingham B1 1TR
☎ 0121 303 4223 mark.barrow@birmingham.gov.uk

Regeneration: Mr Azmat Mir, Head - Development & Regeneration, The Council House, Victoria Square, Birmingham B1 1BB ☎ 0121 303 3298 azmat.mir@birmingham.gov.uk

Regeneration: Mr Waheed Nazir, Director - Planning & Regeneration, 1 Lancaster Circus, Queensway, Birmingham B1 1R ☎ 0121 464 7735 waheed.nazir@birmingham.gov.uk

Regeneration: Mr Andrew Round, Head - City Centre Development, PO Box 28, 1 Lancaster Circus, Queensway, Birmingham B4 7DJ ☎ 0121 303 2676 andrew.round@birmingham.gov.uk

Social Services (Adult): Mr Peter Hay, Strategic Director - Adults & Communities, Louisa Ryland House, 44 Newhall Street, Birmingham B3 3PL ☎ 0121 303 2992 peter.hay@birmingham.gov.uk

Social Services (Adult): Mr Alan Lotinga, Service Director - Assessment & Support, The Council House, Victoria Square, Birmingham B1 1BB ☎ 0121 303 4917 alan.lotinga@birmingham.gov.uk

Social Services (Adult): Ms Charmaine Murray, Principal Solicitor - Legal & Democratic Services, The Council House, Victoria Square, Birmingham B1 1BB ☎ 0121 303 2857 charmaine.murray@birmingham.gov.uk

Social Services (Adult): Mr Jon Tomlinson, Service Director - Joint Commissioning, Louisa Ryland House, 44 Newhall Street, Birmingham B3 3PL ☎ 0121 675 8727 jon.tomlinson@birmingham.gov.uk

Social Services (Adult): Mr Steve Wise, Service Director - Specialist Care Services, The Council House, Victoria Square, Birmingham B1 1BB ☎ 0121 3032428 steve.wise@birmingham.gov.uk

Social Services (Children): Mr David Brown, Head - Education & Children's Services Law, The Council House, Victoria Square, Birmingham B1 1BB ☎ 0121 675 3428 david.brown@birmingham.gov.uk

Social Services (Children): Mr Peter Duxbury, Strategic Director - Children, Young People & Families, The Council House, Victoria Square, Birmingham B1 1BB

Social Services (Children): Ms Trisha Jervis, Head - Children's Services East & Charities & Trusts, The Council House, Victoria Square, Birmingham B1 1BB ☎ 0121 675 5425 trisha.jervis@birmingham.gov.uk

Street Scene: Mr Paul O'Day, Street Services Manager, 1 Lancaster Circus, Birmingham B4 7DQ ☎ 0121 303 7412 🖷 0121 303 6451 paul.o'day@birmingham.gov.uk

Traffic Management: Mr Kevin Hicks, Traffic Manager, 1 Lancaster Circus, Birmingham B4 7DQ ☎ 0121 303 7693 🖷 0121 303 6451 kevin.hicks@birmingham.gov.uk

Waste Management: Mr Matt Kelly, Assistant Director - Fleet & Waste Management (Operations), House of Sport, 300 Broad Street, Birmingham B1 2DR ☎ 0121 303 6171 matt.kelly@birmingham.gov.uk

Waste Management: Mr Kevin Mitchell, Assitant Director - Fleet & Waste Management (Operations), House of Sport, 300 Broad Street, Birmingham B1 2DR ☎ 0121 675 0648 kevin.mitchell@birmingham.gov.uk

Waste Management: Ms Chloe Tringham, Head - Fleet & Waste Management, House of Sport, 300 Broad Street, Birmingham B1 2DR ☎ 0121 675 0648 chloe.tringham@birmingham.gov.uk

Waste Management: Mr Tommy Wallace, Director - Fleet & Waste Management, House of Sport, 300 Broad Street, Birmingham B1 2DR ☎ 0121 303 6171 tommy.wallace@birmingham.gov.uk

Children's Play Areas: Ms Kami Folarin, Head - Community & Play Strategic Team, The Council House, Victoria Square, Birmingham B1 1BB ☎ 0121 3032640 kami.folarin@birmingham.gov.uk

MEMBERS OF THE COUNCIL (120)

***The Lord Mayor:* Lines**, John (CON - Bartley Green)
john.lines@birmingham.gov.uk
***Deputy Lord Mayor:* Ward**, Anita (LAB - Hodge Hill)
anita.ward@birmingham.gov.uk
***Leader of the Council:* Bore**, Albert (LAB - Ladywood)
albert.bore@birmingham.gov.uk
***Group Leader:* Tilsley**, Paul (LD - Sheldon)
paul.tilsley@birmingham.gov.uk
***Group Leader:* Whitby**, Mike (CON - Harborne)
mike.whitby@birmingham.gov.uk
Afzal, Muhammed (LAB - Aston)
muhammad.afzal@birmingham.gov.uk
Ahmed, Uzma (LAB - Bordesley Green)
uzma.ahmed@birmingham.gov.uk
Aikhlaq, Mohammed (LAB - Bordesley Green)
Alden, Deirdre (CON - Edgbaston)
deirdre.alden@birmingham.gov.uk
Alden, Robert (CON - Erdington)
robert.alden@birmingham.gov.uk
Ali, Nawaz (LAB - South Yardley)
nawaz.ali@birmingham.gov.uk
Ali, Tahir (LAB - Nechells)
tahir.ali@birmingham.gov.uk
Anderson, Sue (LD - Sheldon)
sue.anderson@birmingham.gov.uk
Atwal, Gurdial Singh (LAB - Handsworth Wood)
gurdialsingh.atwal@birmingham.gov.uk
Azim, Mohammed (LAB - Sparkbrook)
mohammed.azim@birmingham.gov.uk
Badley, Caroline (LAB - Quinton)
caroline.badley@birmingham.gov.uk
Barnett, Susan (LAB - Billesley)
susan.barnett@birmingham.gov.uk
Barrie, David (CON - Sutton New Hall)
david.barrie@birmingham.gov.uk
Barton, Vivienne (CON - Longbridge)
vivienne.barton@birmingham.gov.uk
Beauchamp, Bob (CON - Erdington)
bob.beauchamp@birmingham.gov.uk
Bedser, Steve (LAB - Kings Norton)
steve.bedser@birmingham.gov.uk
Bird, James (CON - Sutton New Hall)
james.bird@birmingham.gov.uk
Bowen, Iain (LD - Acocks Green)
iain.bowen@birmingham.gov.uk

Bowles, Barry (LAB - Hall Green)
barry.bowles@birmingham.gov.uk
Brew, Randal (CON - Northfield)
randal.brew@birmingham.gov.uk
Bridle, Marje (LAB - Shard End)
marje.bridle@birmingham.gov.uk
Brown, Mick (LAB - Tyburn Ward)
mick.brown@birmingham.gov.uk
Buchanan, Alexander (LAB - Billesley)
alex.buchanan@birmingham.gov.uk
Burden, Sam (LAB - Hall Green)
samburden1@gmail.com
Cartwright, Andy (LAB - Longbridge)
andy.cartwright@birmingham.gov.uk
Chatfield, Tristan (LAB - Oscott)
tristan.chatfield@birmingham.gov.uk
Clancy, John (LAB - Quinton)
john.clancy@birmingham.gov.uk
Clinton, Lynda (LAB - Tyburn)
lynda.clinton@birmingham.gov.uk
Collin, Lyn (CON - Sutton Vesey)
lyn.collin@birmingham.gov.uk
Cornish, Maureen (CON - Sutton Four Oaks)
maureen.cornish@birmingham.gov.uk
Corns, Reg (CON - Northfield)
reginald.corns@birmingham.gov.uk
Cotton, John (LAB - Shard End)
john.cotton@birmingham.gov.uk
Cruise, Ian (LAB - Longbridge)
ian.cruise@birmingham.gov.uk
Davis, Philip (LAB - Billesley)
phil.davis@birmingham.gov.uk
Delaney, Adrian (CON - Weoley)
adrian.delaney@birmingham.gov.uk
Douglas Osborn, Peter (CON - Weoley)
peter.douglasosborn@birmingham.gov.uk
Dring, Barbara (LAB - Oscott)
barbara.dring@birmingham.gov.uk
Eustace, Neil (LD - Stechford & Yardley North)
neil.eustace@birmingham.gov.uk
Evans, Jerry (LD - Springfield)
jerry.evans@birmingham.gov.uk
Evans, Tim (LAB - Hodge Hill)
tim.evans@birmingham.gov.uk
Fazal, Mohammed (LAB - Springfield)
mohammed.fazal@birmingham.gov.uk
Finnegan, Mick (LAB - Stockland Green)
mick.finnegan@birmingham.gov.uk
Freeman, Eddie (CON - Weoley)
eddie.freeman@birmingham.gov.uk
Gregson, Matthew (LAB - Quinton)
matthew.gregson@birmingham.gov.uk
Griffiths, Peter (LAB - Kings Norton)
peter.griffiths@birmingham.gov.uk
Grundy, Catharine (LAB - Kingstanding)
catharine.grundy@birmingham.gov.uk
Hamilton, Paulette (LAB - Handsworth Wood)
paulette.hamilton@birmingham.gov.uk
Hamilton, Karen (LD - Perry Barr)
karen.hamilton@birmingham.gov.uk
Hargreaves, Dorothy (LAB - Soho)
dorothy.hargreaves@birmingham.gov.uk
Hartley, Kath (LAB - Ladywood)
kath.hartley@birmingham.gov.uk
Hassall, Ray (LD - Perry Barr)
ray.hassall@birmingham.gov.uk

Hendricks, Ernest (LD - Moseley & Kings Heath)
ernie.hendricks@birmingham.gov.uk
Henley, Barry (LAB - Brandwood)
barry.henley@birmingham.gov.uk
Holbrook, Penny (LAB - Stockland Green)
pennyholbrook@hotmail.com
Hughes, Des (LAB - Kingstanding)
Hunt, Jon (LD - Perry Barr)
jon.hunt@birmingham.gov.uk
Hussain, Mahmood (LAB - Lozells & Handsworth)
mahmood.hussain@birmingham.gov.uk
Hutchings, James (CON - Edgbaston)
james.hutchings@birmingham.gov.uk
Huxtable, Timothy (CON - Bournville)
timothy.huxtable@birmingham.gov.uk
Idrees, Mohammed (LAB - Washwood Heath)
mohammed.idrees@birmingham.gov.uk
Iqbal, Zafar (LAB - South Yardley)
zafar@southyardley.co.uk
Islam, Ziaul (LAB - Aston)
ziaul.islam@birmingham.gov.uk
Jackson, Barbara (LD - Stechford & Yardley North)
barbara.jackson@birmingham.gov.uk
Jenkins, Meirion (CON - Sutton Four Oaks)
meirion.jenkins@birmingham.gov.uk
Jones, Carol (LD - Stechford & Yardley North)
carol.jones@birmingham.gov.uk
Jones, Josh (LAB - Stockland Green)
josh4stocklandgreen@yahoo.co.uk
Jones, Brigid (LAB - Selly Oak)
brigid.jones@birmingham.gov.uk
Kane, Peter (LAB - Kingstanding)
peter.kane@birmingham.gov.uk
Kauser, Nagina (LAB - Aston)
nagina.kauser@birmingham.gov.uk
Kennedy, Tony (LAB - Sparkbrook)
tony.kennedy@birmingham.gov.uk
Khan, Ansar Ali (LAB - Washwood Heath)
ansar.ali.khan@birmingham.gov.uk
Khan, Mariam (LAB - Washwood Heath)
mariam.khan@birmingham.gov.uk
Kooner, Narinder Kaur (LAB - Handsworth Wood)
narinderkaur.kooner@birmingham.gov.uk
Lal, Chaman (LAB - Soho)
chaman.lal@birmingham.gov.uk
Leddy, Mike (LAB - Brandwood)
mike.leddy@birmingham.gov.uk
Lines, Bruce (CON - Bartley Green)
bruce.lines@birmingham.gov.uk
Linnecor, Keith (LAB - Oscott)
keith.linnecor@birmingham.gov.uk
Mahmood, Majid (LAB - Hodge Hill)
majid.mahmood@birmingham.gov.uk
McCarthy, Karen (LAB - Selly Oak)
karen.mccarthy@birmingham.gov.uk
McKay, James (LAB - Harborne)
james.mckay@birmingham.gov.uk
Moore, Gareth (CON - Erdington)
gareth.moore@birmingham.gov.uk
Mosquito, Yvonne (LAB - Nechells)
yvonne.mosquito@birmingham.gov.uk
O'Reilly, Brett (LAB - Northfield)
brett.o'reilly@birmingham.gov.uk
O'Shea, John (LAB - Acocks Green)
john.o'shea@birmingham.gov.uk

Parkin, Phillip (CON - Sutton Trinity)
philip.parkin@birmingham.gov.uk
Pears, David (CON - Sutton Trinity)
david.pears@birmingham.gov.uk
Phillips, Eva (LAB - Brandwood)
eva.phillips@birmingham.gov.uk
Phillips, Jess (LAB - Longbridge)
jess.phillips@birmingham.gov.uk
Pocock, Rob (LAB - Sutton Vesey)
rob.pocock@birmingham.gov.uk
Quinn, Victoria (LAB - Sparkbrook)
victoria.quinn@birmingham.gov.uk
Quinnen, Hendrina (LAB - Lozells & East Handsworth)
hendrina.quinnen@birmingham.gov.uk
Radcliffe, David (LD - Selly Oak)
david.radcliffe@birmingham.gov.uk
Rashid, Chauhdry (LAB - Nechells)
chauhdry.rashid@birmingham.gov.uk
Rehman, Habib (LAB - Springfield)
habib.ul.rehman@birmingham.gov.uk
Rice, Carl (LAB - Ladywood)
carl.rice@birmingham.gov.uk
Roberts, Guy (CON - Sutton New Hall)
guy@newhallconservatives.org
Robinson, Fergus (CON - Edgbaston)
fergus.robinson@birmingham.gov.uk
Rudge, Alan (CON - Sutton Vesey)
alan.rudge@birmingham.gov.uk
Seabright, Valerie (LAB - Kings Norton)
valerie.seabright@birmingham.gov.uk
Sealey, Rob (CON - Bournville)
robert.sealey@birmingham.gov.uk
Shah, Shafique (LAB - Bordesley Green)
shafique.shah@birmingham.gov.uk
Sharpe, Mike (LAB - Tyburn)
mike.sharpe@birmingham.gov.uk
Smith, Paula (LD - Hall Green)
paula.d.smith@birmingham.gov.uk
Spence, Sybil (LAB - Soho)
sybil.spence@birmingham.gov.uk
Stacey, Stewart (LAB - Acocks Green)
stewart.stacey@birmingham.gov.uk
Straker-Welds, Martin (LAB - Moseley & Kings Heath)
martin.straker.welds@birmingham.gov.uk
Trickett, Lisa (LAB - Moseley & Kings Heath)
lisa.trickett@birmingham.gov.uk
Underwood, Anne (CON - Sutton Four Oaks)
anne.underwood@birmingham.gov.uk
Waddington, Margaret (CON - Sutton Trinity)
margaret.waddington@birmingham.gov.uk
Walkling, Phil (LAB - Bournville)
phil.walkling@birmingham.gov.uk
Ward, Ian (LAB - Shard End)
ian.ward@birmingham.gov.uk
Ward, Mike (LD - Sheldon)
mike.ward@birmingham.gov.uk
Williams, Elaine (LAB - Harborne)
elaine.v.williams@birmingham.gov.uk
Willis, David (LD - South Yardley)
david.willis@birmingham.gov.uk
Zaffar, Waseem (LAB - Lozells & East Handsworth)
waseem.zaffar@birmingham.gov.uk

POLITICAL COMPOSITION
LAB: 77, CON: 28, LD: 15

CABINET
Leader: Sir Albert Bore
Deputy Leader: Mr Ian Ward
Birmingham Economy & Jobs Overview: Mr Ian Cruise
Children & Family Services: Ms Brigid Jones
Development, Jobs & Skills: Mr Tahir Ali
Green Safe & Smart City: Mr James McKay
Health & Wellbeing: Mr Steve Bedser
Social Cohesion & Equalities: Mr John Cotton

COMMITTEE CHAIRS
Audit: Mr Phil Walkling
Commissioning, Contracting & Improvement: Mr Stewart Stacey
Council Business Management: Sir Albert Bore
Education & Vulnerable Children Overview: Ms Anita Ward
Employement & Human Resources: Mr Muhammed Afzal
Licensing & Public Protection: Ms Barbara Dring
Planning: Mr Mike Sharpe
Social Cohesion & Community Safety Overview: Mr Waseem Zaffar
Transport Connectivity & Sustainability Overview: Ms Victoria Quinn
Trusts & Charities: Ms Narinder Kaur Kooner

BLABY — D

Blaby District Council, Council Offices, Desford Road, Narborough LE19 2EP ☎ 0116 275 0555 🖷 0116 275 0368 ✉ customer.services@blaby.gov.uk 🖳 www.blaby.gov.uk

FACTS & FIGURES
Police Authority: Leicestershire Police Authority
Health Authority: East Midlands Strategic Health Authority
Learning and Skills Council: East Midlands
Parliamentary Constituencies: Charnwood, Leicestershire South
EU Constituencies: East Midlands
Election Frequency: Elections are of whole council

PRINCIPAL OFFICERS
Chief Executive: Mrs Sandra Whiles, Chief Executive, Council Offices, Desford Road, Narborough LE19 2EP ☎ 0116 272 7501 🖷 0116 272 7600 ✉ chief.executive@blaby.gov.uk

Deputy Chief Executive: Mr Jim Holden, Deputy Chief Executive & Section 51 Officer, Council Offices, Desford Road, Narborough LE19 2EP ☎ 0116 272 7502 🖷 0116 272 7600 ✉ jlh@blaby.gov.uk

Senior Management: Mr Steve Beard, Director, Council Offices, Desford Road, Narborough LE19 2EP ☎ 0116 272 7550 🖷 0116 272 7600 ✉ sab@blaby.gov.uk

Senior Management: Mrs Jane Toman, Director, Council Offices, Desford Road, Narborough LE19 2EP ☎ 0116 272 7576 🖷 0116 272 7600 ✉ jet2@blaby.gov.uk

Best Value: Mrs Alison Moran, Performance & Audit Manager, Council Offices, Desford Road, Narborough LE19 2EP ☎ 0116 272 7732 🖷 0116 272 7600

Building Control: Mr John Wells, Regulatory Services Group Manager, Council Offices, Desford Road, Narborough LE19 2EP ☎ 0116 272 7545 🖷 0116 275 0368 ✉ jtw@blaby.gov.uk

PR / Communications: Ms Julie Hutchinson, Communications Manager, Council Offices, Desford Road, Narborough LE19 2EP ☎ 0116 272 7648 🖷 0116 275 0368 ✉ jh3@blaby.gov.uk

Community Safety: Ms Amanda Quin, Head of Community Services Group Manager, Council Offices, Desford Road, Narborough LE19 2EP ☎ 0116 272 7595 🖷 0116 275 0368 ✉ agq@blaby.gov.uk

Computer Management: Mr Colin Jones, Corporate Services Group Manager, Council Offices, Desford Road, Narborough LE19 2EP ☎ 0116 272 7569 🖷 0116 275 0368 ✉ caj@blaby.gov.uk

Contracts: Ms Judith Warner, Legal Services Manager, Council Offices, Desford Road, Narborough LE19 2EP ☎ 0116 272 7641 🖷 0116 275 0368 ✉ ac1@blaby.gov.uk

Customer Service: Mr Colin Jones, Corporate Services Group Manager, Council Offices, Desford Road, Narborough LE19 2EP ☎ 0116 272 7569 🖷 0116 275 0368 ✉ caj@blaby.gov.uk

Economic Development: Mr Jim Holden, Deputy Chief Executive & Section 51 Officer, Council Offices, Desford Road, Narborough LE19 2EP ☎ 0116 272 7502 🖷 0116 272 7600 ✉ jlh@blaby.gov.uk

E-Government: Ms Julie Hutchinson, Communications Manager, Council Offices, Desford Road, Narborough LE19 2EP ☎ 0116 272 7648 🖷 0116 275 0368 ✉ jh3@blaby.gov.uk

Electoral Registration: Mr Neil Briggs, Customer Services & Electoral Services Manager, Council Offices, Desford Road, Narborough LE19 2EP ☎ 0116 272 7667 🖷 0116 275 0638 ✉ ndb@blaby.gov.uk

Emergency Planning: Mr John Wells, Regulatory Services Group Manager, Council Offices, Desford Road, Narborough LE19 2EP ☎ 0116 272 7545 🖷 0116 275 0368 ✉ jtw@blaby.gov.uk

Energy Management: Mr John Wells, Regulatory Services Group Manager, Council Offices, Desford Road, Narborough LE19 2EP ☎ 0116 272 7545 🖷 0116 275 0368 ✉ jtw@blaby.gov.uk

Environmental Health: Mr John Wells, Regulatory Services Group Manager, Council Offices, Desford Road, Narborough LE19 2EP ☎ 0116 272 7545 🖷 0116 275 0368 ✉ jtw@blaby.gov.uk

Finance and Treasurer: Ms Sarah Pennelli, Financial Services Group Manager, Council Offices, Desford Road, Narborough LE19 2EP ☎ 0116 272 7650 🖷 0116 275 0368 ✉ sp5@blaby.gov.uk

Fleet Management: Mr Kevin Pegg, Neighbourhood Services Group Manager, Council Offices, Desford Road, Narborough LE19 2EP ☎ 0161 272 7615 🖷 0116 275 0368 ✉ kp1@blaby.gov.uk

Grounds Maintenance: Mr Kevin Pegg, Neighbourhood Services Group Manager, Council Offices, Desford Road, Narborough LE19 2EP ☎ 0161 272 7615 🖷 0116 275 0368 ✉ kp1@blaby.gov.uk

Health and Safety: Mr Jon Thorpe, Corporate Health & Safety Advisor, Council Offices, Desford Road, Narborough LE19 2EP ☎ 0116 272 7571 🖷 0116 275 0368 ✉ tjt@blaby.gov.uk

Housing: Ms Amanda Quin, Head of Community Services Group Manager, Council Offices, Desford Road, Narborough LE19 2EP ☎ 0116 272 7595 🖷 0116 275 0368 ✉ agq@blaby.gov.uk

Legal: Ms Judith Warner, Legal Services Manager, Council Offices, Desford Road, Narborough LE19 2EP ☎ 0116 272 7641 🖷 0116 275 0368 ✉ ac1@blaby.gov.uk

Leisure and Cultural Services: Ms Amanda Quin, Head of Community Services Group Manager, Council Offices, Desford Road, Narborough LE19 2EP ☎ 0116 272 7595 🖷 0116 275 0368 ✉ agq@blaby.gov.uk

Licensing: Mr John Wells, Regulatory Services Group Manager, Council Offices, Desford Road, Narborough LE19 2EP ☎ 0116 272 7545 🖷 0116 275 0368 ✉ jtw@blaby.gov.uk

Lottery Funding, Charity and Voluntary: Ms Jill Stevenson, Domestic Violence Co-ordinator Outreach, Council Offices, Desford Road, Narborough LE19 2EP ☎ 0116 272 7582 🖷 0116 275 0368 ✉ jps@blaby.gov.uk

Member Services: Mr Neil Briggs, Customer Services & Electoral Services Manager, Council Offices, Desford Road, Narborough LE19 2EP ☎ 0116 272 7667 🖷 0116 275 0638 ✉ ndb@blaby.gov.uk

Parking: Mr John Wells, Regulatory Services Group Manager, Council Offices, Desford Road, Narborough LE19 2EP ☎ 0116 272 7545 🖷 0116 275 0368 ✉ jtw@blaby.gov.uk

Partnerships: Ms Jill Stevenson, Domestic Violence Co-ordinator Outreach, Council Offices, Desford Road, Narborough LE19 2EP ☎ 0116 272 7582 🖷 0116 275 0368 ✉ jps@blaby.gov.uk

Personnel / HR: Mrs Jane Toman, Director, Council Offices, Desford Road, Narborough LE19 2EP ☎ 0116 272 7576 🖷 0116 272 7600 ✉ jet2@blaby.gov.uk

Planning: Mr Andrew Senior, Development & Conservation Manager, Council Offices, Desford Road, Narborough LE19 2EP ☎ 0116 272 7519 🖷 0116 275 0368 ✉ aks@blaby.gov.uk

Procurement: Mr Jim Holden, Deputy Chief Executive & Section 51 Officer, Council Offices, Desford Road, Narborough LE19 2EP ☎ 0116 272 7502 🖷 0116 272 7600 ✉ jlh@blaby.gov.uk

Recycling & Waste Minimisation: Mr Kevin Pegg, Neighbourhood Services Group Manager, Council Offices, Desford Road, Narborough LE19 2EP ☎ 0161 272 7615 🖷 0116 275 0368 ✉ kp1@blaby.gov.uk

Staff Training: Mrs Sudha Dandikar, Training & Development Advisor, Council Offices, Desford Road, Narborough LE19 2EP ☎ 0116 272 7573 🖷 0116 275 0368 ✉ sd2@blaby.gov.uk

Sustainable Communities: Mrs Jane Toman, Director, Council Offices, Desford Road, Narborough LE19 2EP ☎ 0116 272 7576

🖷 0116 272 7600 ✉ jet2@blaby.gov.uk

Sustainable Development: Mr John Leach, Corporate Head of Policy & Partnerships, Council Offices, Desford Road, Narborough LE19 2EP ☎ 0116 272 7727 ✉ ajl@blaby.gov.uk

Tourism: Mr Jim Holden, Deputy Chief Executive & Section 51 Officer, Council Offices, Desford Road, Narborough LE19 2EP ☎ 0116 272 7502 🖷 0116 272 7600 ✉ jlh@blaby.gov.uk

Town Centre: Mr John Leach, Corporate Head of Policy & Partnerships, Council Offices, Desford Road, Narborough LE19 2EP ☎ 0116 272 7727 ✉ ajl@blaby.gov.uk

Waste Collection and Disposal: Mr Kevin Pegg, Neighbourhood Services Group Manager, Council Offices, Desford Road, Narborough LE19 2EP ☎ 0161 272 7615 🖷 0116 275 0368 ✉ kp1@blaby.gov.uk

Waste Management: Mr Kevin Pegg, Neighbourhood Services Group Manager, Council Offices, Desford Road, Narborough LE19 2EP ☎ 0161 272 7615 🖷 0116 275 0368 ✉ kp1@blaby.gov.uk

MEMBERS OF THE COUNCIL (38)

***Chair:* Blackwell**, J (CON - Enderby & St. John's)
cllr.blackwell@blaby.gov.uk
***Chair:* Garner**, B (CON - Narborough & Littlethorpe)
cllr.garner@blaby.gov.uk
***Vice-Chair:* Tanner**, A C (CON - Cosby with South Whetstone)
cllr.tanner@blaby.gov.uk
***Leader of the Council:* White**, E F (CON - Stanton & Flamville)
cllr.white@blaby.gov.uk
***Deputy Leader of the Council:* Hudson**, J O (CON - Fairestone)
cllr.hudson@blaby.gov.uk
Berrington, R J (LAB - Winstanley)
cllr.berrington@blaby.gov.uk
Breckon, L M (CON - Ellis)
cllr.breckon@blaby.gov.uk
Broomhead, M G (CON - Blaby South)
Clements, D R (CON - Forest)
cllr.clements@blaby.gov.uk
Coles, K D (CON - North Whetstone)
cllr.coles@blaby.gov.uk
Dickinson, J A (CON - Enderby & St. John's)
cllr.dickinson@blaby.gov.uk
Dolby, J A (CON - Forest)
cllr.dolby@blaby.gov.uk
Findlay, D J (CON - Countesthorpe)
Forey, J (CON - Cosby with South Whetstone)
cllr.forey@blaby.gov.uk
Fox, J M (LAB - Ravenhurst & Fosse)
cllr.jm.fox@blaby.gov.uk
Freer, D (CON - Croft Hill)
cllr.freer@blaby.gov.uk
Greenwood, A V (CON - North Whetstone)
cllr.greenwood@blaby.gov.uk
Hewson, I M (CON - Stanton & Flamville)
cllr.hewson@blaby.gov.uk
Jackson, F (CON - Pastures)
cllr.jackson@blaby.gov.uk
Jennings, D (CON - Countesthorpe)
cllr.jennings@blaby.gov.uk
Merrill, Christine (LD - Saxondale)
cllr.merrill@blaby.gov.uk
Moitt, P L (LAB - Ravenhurst & Fosse)
cllr.moitt@blaby.gov.uk
Moseley, A (LD - Blaby South)
cllr.moseley@blaby.gov.uk
Parkins, B M (CON - Fairstone)
cllr.parkins@blaby.gov.uk
Parsons, D R (CON - Muxloe)
cllr.d.parsons@blaby.gov.uk
Parsons, E (CON - Muxloe)
cllr.parsons@blaby.gov.uk
Richardson, T J (CON - Narborough & Littlethorpe)
cllr.richardson@blaby.gov.uk
Sanders, G (LAB - Winstanley)
cllr.sanders@blaby.gov.uk
Scott, S (CON - Stanton & Flamville)
cllr.scott@blaby.gov.uk
Smith, S (CON - Forest)
cllr.smith@blaby.gov.uk
Springthorpe, J (LD - Ellis)
cllr.springthorpe@blaby.gov.uk
Ward, R C (CON - Winstanley)
cllr.ward@blaby.gov.uk
Weatherstone, J L (CON - Countesthorpe)
Webster-Williams, E A (CON - Pastures)
cllr.webster-williams@blaby.gov.uk
Welsh, G L (LD - Saxondale)
cllr.welsh@blaby.gov.uk
Welsh, B J (LD - Saxondale)
cllr.b.welsh@blaby.gov.uk
Wright, B (LAB - Millfield)
cllr.wright@blaby.gov.uk
Wright, M A (CON - Normanton)
cllr.m.wright@blaby.gov.uk

POLITICAL COMPOSITION

CON: 28, LAB: 5, LD: 5

CABINET

Leader: Mr E F White
Deputy Leader: Mr J O Hudson
Chair of the Council: Mrs J Blackwell
Community Services: Mr D Jennings
Finance, Efficiency & Assets: Mr J O Hudson
Health, Improvement & Corporate Services: Mr D R Clements
Neighbourhood & Environmental Health Services: Mr F Jackson
Planning, Economic Development & Housing Strategy: Mrs J A Dickinson
Policy, Performance & Partnerships: Mr K D Coles

COMMITTEE CHAIRS

Appeals Against Dissmissals: Mrs J A Dickinson
Audit: Mr T J Richardson
Development Control: Ms S Scott
Investment Fund Panel: Mr T J Richardson
Licensing: Mr L M Breckon
Regulatory: Mr A C Tanner

BLACKBURN WITH DARWEN U

Blackburn with Darwen Borough Council, Town Hall, Blackburn BB1 7DY ☎ 01254 585585 🖷 01254 682201 ✉ blackburnwithdarwen@blackburn.gov.uk 💻 www.blackburn.gov.uk

FACTS & FIGURES

Police Authority: Lancashire Police Authority
Health Authority: North West Strategic Health Authority
Learning and Skills Council: North West
Parliamentary Constituencies: Blackburn, Rossendale and Darwen
EU Constituencies: North West
Election Frequency: Elections are by thirds
Twinning: Altena (Germany); Peronne (France)

PRINCIPAL OFFICERS

Deputy Chief Executive: Mr Harry Catherall, Deputy Chief Executive, Town Hall, Blackburn BB1 7DY ☎ 01254 585299 🖷 01254 697223 ✉ harry.catherall@blackburn.gov.uk

Senior Management: Mr Dominic Harrison, Director of Public Health, Town Hall, Blackburn BB1 7DY ☎ 01254 588920 ✉ dominic.harrison@bwd.nhs.uk

Senior Management: Mr Andrew Lightfoot, Managing Director, Local Government Services, Town Hall, Blackburn BB1 7DY ☎ 01254 585504 🖷 01254 697223 ✉ andrew.lightfoot@blackburn.gov.uk

Senior Management: Mr Roger Parr, Locality Director of Finance, Town Hall, Blackburn BB1 7DY ☎ 01254 282119 ✉ roger.parr@bwd.nhs.uk

Senior Management: Mr Jonathan Tew, Head of Policy, Town Hall, Blackburn BB1 7DY ☎ 01254 585320 ✉ jonathan.tew@blackburn.gov.uk

Architect, Building / Property Services: Mr Stuart Davey, Building Services Manager, Capita Symonds, Castleway House, 17 Preston New Road, Blackburn BB2 1AU ☎ 01254 273343 🖷 01254 273429 ✉ stuart.davey@capita.co.uk

Building Control: Mr Brian Bailey, Director of Regeneration, Town Hall, Blackburn BB1 7DY ☎ 01254 585360 ✉ brian.bailey@blackburn.gov.uk

Catering Services: Mr Neil Dagnall, Bar & Catering Manager, King Georges Hall, Northgate, Blackburn BB2 1AA ☎ 01254 503235 ✉ neil.dagnall@blackburn.gov.uk

Children / Youth Services: Ms Linda Clegg, Director of Safeguarding, The Exchange, Ainsworth Street, Blackburn BB1 6AD ☎ 01254 666430 ✉ linda.clegg@blackburn.gov.uk

Children / Youth Services: Ms Gladys Rhodes White, Director of Children's Services & Education, The Exchange, Ainsworth Street, Blackburn BB1 6AD ☎ 01254 666425 🖷 01254 666443 ✉ gladys.rhodes@blackburn.gov.uk

Civil Registration: Mr David Fairclough, Director of HR & Legal Services, Town Hall, Blackburn BB1 7DY ☎ 01254 585642 🖷 01254 585101 ✉ david.fairclough@blackburn.gov.uk

PR / Communications: Mr Marc Schmid, Head of Communications & Marketing, Town Hall, Blackburn BB1 7DY ☎ 01254 585480 ✉ marc.schmid@blackburn.gov.uk

PR / Communications: Mr Tom Stannard, Director of Policy & Communications, Town Hall, Blackburn BB1 7DY ☎ 01254 585305 🖷 01254 687223 ✉ tom.stannard@blackburn.gov.uk

Community Planning: Mr Sayyed Osman, Director of Environment, Neighbourhoods & Housing, Town Hall, Blackburn BB1 7DY ☎ 01254 585340 🖷 01254 265340 ✉ sayyed.osman@blackburn.gov.uk

Community Safety: Mr Mark Aspin, CSP Manager, Town Hall, Blackburn BB1 7DY ☎ 01254 585513 ✉ mark.aspin@blackburn.gov.uk

Computer Management: Mr Mike Zammit, Director of ITMG, Town Hall, Blackburn BB1 7DY ☎ 01254 585127 ✉ mike.zammit@blackburn.gov.uk

Consumer Protection and Trading Standards: Mr Chris Allen, Head of Public Protection & Interim Head of Fleet Transport, Davyfield Road, Davyfield, Blackburn BB1 2QY ☎ 01254 585041 🖷 01254 698312 ✉ christopher.allen@blackburn.gov.uk

Contracts: Mr David Fairclough, Director of HR & Legal Services, Town Hall, Blackburn BB1 7DY ☎ 01254 585642 🖷 01254 585101 ✉ david.fairclough@blackburn.gov.uk

Customer Service: Ms Elizabeth Hall, Director of Finance, Town Hall, Blackburn BB1 7DY ☎ 01254 585482 🖷 01254 663416 ✉ elizabeth.hall@blackburn.gov.uk

Economic Development: Mr Brian Bailey, Director of Regeneration, Town Hall, Blackburn BB1 7DY ☎ 01254 585360 ✉ brian.bailey@blackburn.gov.uk

Education: Mrs Lisa Bibby, Director of Education, The Exchange, Ainsworth Street, Blackburn BB1 6AD ☎ 01254 666433 ✉ lisa.bibby@blackburn.gov.uk

Education: Ms Gladys Rhodes White, Director of Children's Services & Education, East Wing, Floor 2, The Exchange, Ainsworth Street, Blackburn BB1 6AD ☎ 01254 666425 🖷 01254 666443 ✉ gladys.rhodes@blackburn.gov.uk

E-Government: Ms Denise Park, Strategic Director of Resources & Shared Services, Town Hall, Blackburn BB1 7DY ☎ 01254 585655 🖷 01254 697223 ✉ denise.park@blackburn.gov.uk

Electoral Registration: Mr Tom Stannard, Director of Policy & Communications, Town Hall, Blackburn BB1 7DY ☎ 01254 585305 🖷 01254 687223 ✉ tom.stannard@blackburn.gov.uk

Emergency Planning: Mr David Fairclough, Director of HR & Legal Services, Town Hall, Blackburn BB1 7DY ☎ 01254 585642 🖷 01254 585101 ✉ david.fairclough@blackburn.gov.uk

Environmental / Technical Services: Mr Sayyed Osman, Director of Environment, Neighbourhoods & Housing, Town Hall, Blackburn BB1 7DY ☎ 01254 585340 🖷 01254 265340 ✉ sayyed.osman@blackburn.gov.uk

Environmental Health: Mr Chris Allen, Head of Public Protection & Interim Head of Fleet Transport, Davyfield Road,

Davyfield, Blackburn BB1 2QY ☎ 01254 585041 🖷 01254 698312 🖰 christopher.allen@blackburn.gov.uk

European Liaison: Mr Sayyed Osman, Director of Environment, Neighbourhoods & Housing, Town Hall, Blackburn BB1 7DY ☎ 01254 585340 🖷 01254 265340 🖰 sayyed.osman@blackburn.gov.uk

Events Manager: Ms Anne Macksmith, Head of Culture & Entertainment, King George's Hall, Northgate, Blackburn BB2 1AA ☎ 01254 582579 Ext 210 🖰 anne.macksmith@blackburn.gov.uk

Facilities: Mr Steve Cox, Facilities Manager, C Floor, Tower Block, Town Hall, Blackburn BB1 7DY ☎ 01254 585497 🖷 01254 585101 🖰 steve.cox@blackburn.gov.uk

Finance and Treasurer: Ms Elizabeth Hall, Director of Finance, Town Hall, Blackburn BB1 7DY ☎ 01254 585482 🖷 01254 663416 🖰 elizabeth.hall@blackburn.gov.uk

Fleet Management: Mr Chris Allen, Head of Public Protection & Interim Head of Fleet Transport, Davyfield Road, Davyfield, Blackburn BB1 2QY ☎ 01254 585041 🖷 01254 698312 🖰 christopher.allen@blackburn.gov.uk

Grounds Maintenance: Mr Sayyed Osman, Director of Environment, Neighbourhoods & Housing, Town Hall, Blackburn BB1 7DY ☎ 01254 585340 🖷 01254 265340 🖰 sayyed.osman@blackburn.gov.uk

Health and Safety: Mr David Fairclough, Director of HR & Legal Services, Town Hall, Blackburn BB1 7DY ☎ 01254 585642 🖷 01254 585101 🖰 david.fairclough@blackburn.gov.uk

Highways: Mr Brian Bailey, Director of Regeneration, Town Hall, Blackburn BB1 7DY ☎ 01254 585360 🖰 brian.bailey@blackburn.gov.uk

Home Energy Conservation: Mr Stuart Pye, Home Improvement & Energy Solutions Manager, N Floor, Tower Block, Town Hall, Blackburn BB1 7DY ☎ 01254 588890 🖷 01254 588889 🖰 stuart.pye@blackburn.gov.uk

Housing: Mr Sayyed Osman, Director of Environment, Neighbourhoods & Housing, Town Hall, Blackburn BB1 7DY ☎ 01254 585340 🖷 01254 265340 🖰 sayyed.osman@blackburn.gov.uk

Local Area Agreement: Ms Philippa Cross, Policy & Performance Officer, Town Hall, Blackburn BB1 7DY ☎ 01254 585245 🖰 philippa.cross@blackburn.gov.uk

Legal: Mr David Fairclough, Director of HR & Legal Services, Town Hall, Blackburn BB1 7DY ☎ 01254 585642 🖷 01254 585101 🖰 david.fairclough@blackburn.gov.uk

Leisure and Cultural Services: Mr Martin Eden, Director of Culture, Leisure, Sport & Young People, Town Hall, Blackburn BB1 7DY ☎ 01254 585102 🖰 martin.eden@blackburn.gov.uk

Leisure and Cultural Services: Ms Claire Ramwell, Head of Service, Town Hall, Blackburn BB1 7DY ☎ 01254 587238 🖰 claire.ramwell@blackburn.gov.uk

Licensing: Mr Chris Allen, Head of Public Protection & Interim Head of Fleet Transport, Davyfield Road, Davyfield, Blackburn BB1 2QY ☎ 01254 585041 🖷 01254 698312 🖰 christopher.allen@blackburn.gov.uk

Lottery Funding, Charity and Voluntary: Mr Tom Stannard, Director of Policy & Communications, Town Hall, Blackburn BB1 7DY ☎ 01254 585305 🖷 01254 687223 🖰 tom.stannard@blackburn.gov.uk

Member Services: Mr Phil Llewllyn, Executive & Councillor Support Manager, Town Hall, Blackburn BB1 7DY ☎ 01254 585369 🖰 phil.llewellyn@blackburn.gov.uk

Partnerships: Mr Andrew Lightfoot, Managing Director, Local Government Services, Town Hall, Blackburn BB1 7DY ☎ 01254 585504 🖷 01254 697223 🖰 andrew.lightfoot@blackburn.gov.uk

Personnel / HR: Mr David Fairclough, Director of HR & Legal Services, Town Hall, Blackburn BB1 7DY ☎ 01254 585642 🖷 01254 585101 🖰 david.fairclough@blackburn.gov.uk

Planning: Mr Brian Bailey, Director of Regeneration, Town Hall, Blackburn BB1 7DY ☎ 01254 585360 🖰 brian.bailey@blackburn.gov.uk

Procurement: Mrs Sylvia Richardson, Head of Procurement, Town Hall, Blackburn BB1 7DY ☎ 01254 585296 🖰 sylvia.richardson@blackburn.gov.uk

Public Libraries: Ms Claire Ramwell, Head of Service, Town Hall, Blackburn BB1 7DY ☎ 01254 587238 🖰 claire.ramwell@blackburn.gov.uk

Recycling & Waste Minimisation: Mr Stuart Hammond, Environmental Sustainability Manager, Davyfield Road, Blackburn BB1 2LX ☎ 01254 585863 🖷 01254 585803 🖰 stuart.hammond@blackburn.gov.uk

Regeneration: Mr Brian Bailey, Director of Regeneration, Town Hall, Blackburn BB1 7DY ☎ 01254 585360 🖰 brian.bailey@blackburn.gov.uk

Social Services: Ms Sally McIvor, Director of Adult Services, Town Hall, Blackburn BB1 7DY ☎ 01254 585349 🖰 sally.mcivor@blackburn.gov.uk

Social Services (Adult): Ms Sally McIvor, Director of Adult Services, Town Hall, Blackburn BB1 7DY ☎ 01254 585349 🖰 sally.mcivor@blackburn.gov.uk

Social Services (Children): Ms Gladys Rhodes White, Director of Children's Services & Education, East Wing, Floor 2, The Exchange, Ainsworth Street, Blackburn BB1 6AD ☎ 01254 666425 🖷 01254 666443 🖰 gladys.rhodes@blackburn.gov.uk

Staff Training: Mr David Fairclough, Director of HR & Legal Services, Town Hall, Blackburn BB1 7DY ☎ 01254 585642 🖷 01254 585101 🖰 david.fairclough@blackburn.gov.uk

Street Scene: Mr Brian Bailey, Director of Regeneration, Town Hall, Blackburn BB1 7DY ☎ 01254 585360
✉ brian.bailey@blackburn.gov.uk

Tourism: Mr Brian Bailey, Director of Regeneration, Town Hall, Blackburn BB1 7DY ☎ 01254 585360
✉ brian.bailey@blackburn.gov.uk

Town Centre: Mr Brian Bailey, Director of Regeneration, Town Hall, Blackburn BB1 7DY ☎ 01254 585360
✉ brian.bailey@blackburn.gov.uk

Transport: Mr Mike Cliffe, Strategic Transport Manager, Davyfield Road, Davyfield, Blackburn BB1 1LX ☎ 01254 585310
✉ mike.cliffe@blackburn.gov.uk

Waste Collection and Disposal: Mr Tony Watson, Head of Environmental Services, Davyfield Road, Davyfield, Blackburn BB1 2QY ☎ 01254 585054 🖷 01254 265340
✉ tony.watson@blackburn.gov.uk

Waste Management: Mr Tony Watson, Head of Environmental Services, Davyfield Road, Davyfield, Blackburn BB1 2QY ☎ 01254 585054 🖷 01254 265340 ✉ tony.watson@blackburn.gov.uk

MEMBERS OF THE COUNCIL (64)

***Mayor:* Khan**, Zamir (LAB - Audley)
zamir.khan@blackburn.gov.uk
***Deputy Mayor:* Mulla**, Salim (LAB - Queen's Park)
salim.mulla@blackburn.gov.uk
***Group Leader:* Foster**, David (LD - Whitehall)
david.foster@blackburn.gov.uk
***Group Leader:* Lee**, Michael (CON - Beardwood with Lammack)
michael.lee@blackburn.gov.uk
Akhtar, Parwaiz (LAB - Bastwell)
parwaiz.akhtar@blackburn.gov.uk
Bateson, Maureen (LAB - Ewood)
maureen.bateson@blackburn.gov.uk
Brookfield, Stephanie (LAB - Earcroft)
stephanie.brookfield@blackburn.gov.uk
Browne, Paul (LD - Sudell)
paul.browne@blackburn.gov.uk
Connor, Frank (LAB - Marsh House)
f.connor@blackburn.gov.uk
Cottam, Alan (CON - Livesey with Pleasington)
alan.cottam@blackburn.gov.uk
Daley, Julie (CON - Beardwood with Lammack)
julie.daley@blackburn.gov.uk
Davies, Roy (LD - Sudell)
roy.davies@blackburn.gov.uk
Desai, Mustafa (LAB - Queen's Park)
mustafa.desai@blackburn.gov.uk
Entwistle, Eileen (LAB - Sudell)
eileen.entwhistle@blackburn.gov.uk
Evans, Tom (LAB - Marsh House)

Foster, Karimeh (LD - Whitehall)
karimeh.foster@blackburn.gov.uk
Gee, Denise (CON - Fernhurst)
denise.gee@blackburn.gov.uk
Groves, Jamie (LAB - Ewood)
jamie.groves@blackburn.gov.uk
Hardman, Derek (CON - Livesey with Pleasington)
derek.hardman@blackburn.gov.uk
Harling, David (LAB - Wensley Fold)
david.harling@blackburn.gov.uk
Hirst, James (CON - Beardwood with Lammack)
james.hirst@blackburn.gov.uk
Hollern, Kate (LAB - Wensley Fold)
kate.hollern@blackburn.gov.uk
Hollings, Pete (LAB - Sunnyhurst)
Humphrys, Anthony (LAB - Shadsworth with Whitebirk)
anthony.humphrys@blackburn.gov.uk
Hussain, Faryad (LAB - Queen's Park)
faryad.hussain@blackburn.gov.uk
Hussain, Iftakhar (LAB - Bastwell)
iftakhar.hussain@blackburn.gov.uk
Hussain, Shaukat (LAB - Bastwell)
Jan-Virmani, Yusuf (LAB - Audley)
yusuf.jan-virmani@blackburn.gov.uk
Johnson, Mike (LAB - Higher Croft)
m.johnson@blackburn.gov.uk
Kay, Andy (LAB - Higher Croft)
andy.kay@blackburn.gov.uk
Khan, Mohammed (LAB - Wensley Fold)
mohammed.khan@blackburn.gov.uk
Khonat, Suleman (LAB - Shear Brow)
suleman.khonat@blackburn.gov.uk
Khonat, Hanif (LAB - Shear Brow)
hanif.khonat@blackburn.gov.uk
Liddle, Sylvia (LAB - Roe Lee)
Mahmood, Arshid (LAB - Corporation Park)
arshid.mahmood@blackburn.gov.uk
Maxfield, Trevor (O - Earcroft)
trevor.maxfield@blackburn.gov.uk
McFall, Patricia (LAB - Little Harwood)
pat.mcfall@blackburn.gov.uk
Nuttall, Carl (LAB - Meadowhead)
carl.nuttall@blackburn.gov.uk
O' Keeffe, Ronald (LAB - Shadsworth with Whitebirk)
ronald.o'keeffe@blackburn.gov.uk
Oldfield, Florence (LAB - Ewood)
florence.oldfield@blackburn.gov.uk
Patel, Abdul (LAB - Little Harwood)
abdul.patel@blackburn.gov.uk
Pearson, John (CON - Livesey with Pleasington)
john.pearson@blackburn.gov.uk
Pearson, David (CON - Roe Lee)
david.pearson@blackburn.gov.uk
Rehman, Abdul (LAB - Corporation Park)
abdul.rehman@blackburn.gov.uk
Rigby, Colin (CON - North Turton with Tockholes)
colin.rigby@blackburn.gov.uk
Rigby, Jean (CON - North Turton with Tockholes)
jean.rigby@blackburn.gov.uk
Riley, Phil (LAB - Roe Lee)
phil.riley@blackburn.gov.uk
Shorrock, James (LAB - Shadsworth with Whitebirk)
james.shorrock@blackburn.gov.uk
Sidat, Salim (LAB - Audley)
salim.sidat@blackburn.gov.uk
Slater, Julie (CON - East Rural)
julie.slater@blackburn.gov.uk
Slater, John (CON - Fernhurst)
john.slater@blackburn.gov.uk
Slater, Jacqueline (CON - Fernhurst)
jacqueline.slater@blackburn.gov.uk
Smith, James (LAB - Mill Hill)
jim.smith@blackburn.gov.uk

Smith, Dave (LAB - Sunnyhurst)
david.smith@blackburn.gov.uk
Solkar, Shahabuddin (LAB - Shear Brow)
Shahabuddin.solkar@blackburn.gov.uk
Surve, Naushad (LAB - Little Harwood)
naushad.surve@blackburn.gov.uk
Talbot, Damian (LAB - Mill Hill)
damian.talbot@blackburn.gov.uk
Tapp, Konrad (CON - Meadowhead)
konrad.tapp@blackburn.gov.uk
Taylor, Brian (LAB - Sunnyhurst)
brian.taylor@blackburn.gov.uk
Thayne, Christopher (LD - Marsh House)
christopher.thayne@blackburn.gov.uk
Walsh, Dorothy (LAB - Higher Croft)
dorothy.walsh@blackburn.gov.uk
Walsh, Carol (LAB - Mill Hill)
Whalley, Ashley (LAB - Meadowhead)
Wright, John (LAB - Corporation Park)
john.wright@blackburn.gov.uk

POLITICAL COMPOSITION
LAB: 44, CON: 14, LD: 5, O: 1

CABINET
Leader: Ms Kate Hollern
Deputy Leader: Mr Andy Kay
Deputy Leader: Mr Mohammed Khan
Adult Social Care: Mr Mohammed Khan
Children's Services: Ms Maureen Bateson
Environmental Improvement & Sustainability: Mr Faryad Hussain
Housing: Mr Anthony Humphrys
Leisure & Culture: Mr Damian Talbot
Neighbourhoods & Customer Services: Mr Yusuf Jan-Virmani
Regeneration: Mr David Harling
Resources: Mr Andy Kay

COMMITTEE CHAIRS
Audit: Mr Salim Sidat
Children & Health: Mr Ronald O' Keeffe
Finance: Mr Zamir Khan
Licensing: Mr John Wright
Planning & Highways: Mr James Smith
Policy & Review: Mr Derek Hardman
Regeneration & Neighbourhoods Overview: Mr Naushad Surve
Standards: Mr Abdul Rehman

BLACKPOOL U

Blackpool Borough Council, Town Hall, Blackpool FY1 1AD
☏ 01253 477477 🖷 01253 477101 ✉ webmaster@blackpool.gov.uk
🖳 www.blackpool.gov.uk

FACTS & FIGURES
Police Authority: Lancashire Police Authority
Health Authority: North West Strategic Health Authority
Learning and Skills Council: North West
Parliamentary Constituencies: Blackpool North and Cleveleys, Blackpool South
EU Constituencies: North West
Election Frequency: Elections are of whole council

Twinning: Bottrop (Germany)

PRINCIPAL OFFICERS
Chief Executive: Mr Neil Jack, Chief Executive, PO Box 77, Town Hall, Blackpool FY1 1AD ☏ 01253 477000 🖷 01253 477003 ✉ neil.jack@blackpool.gov.uk

Assistant Chief Executive: Mr Alan Cavill, Assistant Chief Executive - Regeneration, Tourism & Culture, PO Box 77, Town Hall, Blackpool FY1 1AD ☏ 01253 477006 🖷 01253 477003 ✉ alan.cavill@blackpool.gov.uk

Assistant Chief Executive: Ms Carmel McKeogh, Assistant Chief Executive - Human Resources, Communication & Engagement, Progress House, Clifton Road, Blackpool FY4 4US ☏ 01253 477247 ✉ carmel.mckeogh@blackpool.gov.uk

Senior Management: Mr David Lund, Executive Director of Children, Adult & Family Services, Progress House, Clifton Road, Blackpool FY4 4US ☏ 01253 476501 🖷 01253 476523 ✉ david.lund@blackpool.gov.uk

Building Control: Mr David Clarke, Development Control Manager, PO Box 17, Town Hall, Blackpool FY1 1LZ ☏ 01253 476212 ✉ david.clarke@blackpool.gov.uk

Catering Services: Mr John Blackledge, Assistant Director - Leisure & Operational Services, Progress House, Clifton Road, Blackpool FY4 4US ☏ 01253 478400 ✉ john.blackledge@blackpool.gov.uk

Children / Youth Services: Ms Sue Harrison, Service Director - Learning, Schools & Communities, Progress House, Clifton Road, Blackpool FY4 4US ☏ 01253 476530 ✉ sue.harrison@blackpool.gov.uk

Children / Youth Services: Mr David Lund, Executive Director of Children, Adult & Family Services, Progress House, Clifton Road, Blackpool FY4 4US ☏ 01253 476501 🖷 01253 476523 ✉ david.lund@blackpool.gov.uk

Civil Registration: Mr Mark Towers, Head of Democratic Services, PO Box 1066, Town Hall, Blackpool FY1 1GB ☏ 01253 477127 ✉ mark.towers@blackpool.gov.uk

PR / Communications: Ms Suzanne Halliwell, Head of Communications, Town Hall, Blackpool FY1 1AD ☏ 01253 477133 ✉ suzanne.halliwell@blackpool.gov.uk

PR / Communications: Ms Carmel McKeogh, Assistant Chief Executive - Human Resources, Communication & Engagement, Progress House, Clifton Road, Blackpool FY4 4US ☏ 01253 477247 ✉ carmel.mckeogh@blackpool.gov.uk

Community Planning: Mr John Donnellon, Housing, Planning & Transport, Town Hall, Blackpool FY1 1AD

Community Safety: Mr Russ Weaver, Assistant Director - Neighbourhood Services, Layton Depot, Plymouth Road, Blackpool FY3 7HW ☏ 01253 478610 ✉ russ.weaver@blackpool.gov.uk

Computer Management: Mr Tony Doyle, Head of ICT, Blackpool Football Club, Bloomfield Road, Seasiders Way, Blackpool FY1 6JJ ☎ 01253 478834 ✉ tony.doyle@blackpool.gov.uk

Consumer Protection and Trading Standards: Mr Tim Coglan, Service Manager - Enforcement & Quality Standards, Progress House, Clifton Road, Blackpool FY4 4US ☎ 01253 478376 ✉ tim.coglan@blackpool.gov.uk

Contracts: Mr Trevor Rayner, Head of Procurement & Development, PO Box 4, Town Hall, Blackpool FY1 1AD ☎ 01253 478531 ✉ trevor.rayner@blackpool.gov.uk

Customer Service: Ms Marie McRoberts, Assistant Director - Revenues, Benefits & Customer First, Town Hall, Blackpool FY1 1AD ☎ 01253 478910 ✉ marie.mcroberts@blackpool.gov.uk

Education: Ms Charlotte Clarke, Head of School Improvement, Town Hall, Blackpool FY1 1AD ✉ charlotte.clarke@blackpool.gov.uk

Education: Mr David Lund, Executive Director of Children, Adult & Family Services, Progress House, Clifton Road, Blackpool FY4 4US ☎ 01253 476501 🖷 01253 476523 ✉ david.lund@blackpool.gov.uk

Electoral Registration: Mr Mark Towers, Head of Democratic Services, Town Hall, Blackpool FY1 1AD ☎ 01253 477127 ✉ mark.towers@blackpool.gov.uk

Emergency Planning: Mr Steve Thompson, Chief Financial Officer, PO Box 4, Town Hall, Blackpool FY1 1NA ☎ 01253 478505 ✉ steve.thompson@blackpool.gov.uk

Energy Management: Mr Andy Duckett, Principal Energy & Sustainability Surveyor, Westgate House, Squires Gate Lane, Blackpool FY4 2TS ☎ 01253 476083 ✉ andy.duckett@blackpool.gov.uk

Environmental Health: Mr Tim Coglan, Service Manager - Enforcement & Quality Standards, 125 Albert Road, Blackpool FY1 4PW ☎ 01253 478376 ✉ tim.coglan@blackpool.gov.uk

Estates, Property & Valuation: Mr Stephen Waterfield, Head of Strategic Asset & Estate Management, Town Hall, Blackpool FY1 1AD ✉ stephen.waterfield@blackpool.gov.uk

European Liaison: Mr Alan Cavill, Assistant Director of Enterprise & Business Development, PO Box 77, Town Hall, Blackpool FY1 1AD ☎ 01253 477006 🖷 01253 477003 ✉ alan.cavill@blackpool.gov.uk

Facilities: Mr Steve Thorley-Baines, Head of Facilities Management, Town Hall, Blackpool FY1 1AD ✉ steve.thorley-baines@blackpool.gov.uk

Finance and Treasurer: Mr Steve Thompson, Chief Financial Officer, PO Box 4, Town Hall, Blackpool FY1 1NA ☎ 01253 478505 ✉ steve.thompson@blackpool.gov.uk

Grounds Maintenance: Mr John Blackledge, Assistant Director - Leisure & Operational Services, Progress House, Clifton Road, Blackpool FY4 4US ☎ 01253 478400 ✉ john.blackledge@blackpool.gov.uk

Health and Safety: Mr Terry Hall, Head of Health & Safety, Town Hall, Blackpool FY1 1AD ☎ 01253 477264 ✉ terry.hall@blackpool.gov.uk

Highways: Mr Peter Cross, Head of Transportation, Town Hall, Blackpool FY1 1AD ☎ 01253 476160 ✉ peter.cross@blackpool.gov.uk

Home Energy Conservation: Mr Steve Matthews, Service Manager - Strategic Housing & Planning, Town Hall, Blackpool FY1 1AD ✉ steve.matthews@blackpool.gov.uk

Housing Maintenance: Mr Peter Jefferson, Chief Executive, Blackpool Coastal Housing, Progress House, Clifton Road, Blackpool FY4 4US ☎ 01253 477988 ✉ peter.jefferson@blackpool.gov.uk

Local Area Agreement: Mr Alan Cavill, Assistant Chief Executive - Regeneration, Tourism & Culture, PO Box 77, Town Hall, Blackpool FY1 1AD ☎ 01253 477006 🖷 01253 477003 ✉ alan.cavill@blackpool.gov.uk

Legal: Ms Christine Baines, Head of Legal Services, PO Box 11, Town Hall, Blackpool FY1 1NB ☎ 01253 477410 ✉ christine.baines@blackpool.gov.uk

Leisure and Cultural Services: Ms Polly Hamilton, Assistant Director - Cultural Services, Town Hall, Blackpool FY1 1AD ☎ 01253 476155 ✉ polly.hamilton@blackpool.gov.uk

Lottery Funding, Charity and Voluntary: Mr Steve Thompson, Chief Financial Officer, PO Box 4, Town Hall, Blackpool FY1 1NA ☎ 01253 478505 ✉ steve.thompson@blackpool.gov.uk

Member Services: Mr Mark Towers, Head of Democratic Services, Town Hall, Blackpool FY1 1AD ☎ 01253 477127 ✉ mark.towers@blackpool.gov.uk

Partnerships: Mr Philip Welsh, Head of Partnerships & Development, Town Hall, Blackpool FY1 1AD ✉ philip.welsh@blackpool.gov.uk

Personnel / HR: Ms Linda Dutton, Head of Organisation & Workforce Development, Town Hall, Blackpool FY1 1AD ✉ linda.dutton@blackpool.gov.uk

Planning: Mr Gary Johnston, Head of Development Management, Town Hall, Blackpool FY1 1AD ☎ 01253 476220 ✉ gary.johnston@blackpool.gov.uk

Procurement: Mr Trevor Rayner, Head of Procurement & Development, PO Box 4, Town Hall, Blackpool FY1 1AD ☎ 01253 478531 ✉ trevor.rayner@blackpool.gov.uk

Public Libraries: Ms Anne Ellis, Head of Libraries, Central Library, Queen Street, City Centre, Blackpool FY1 1PX ☎ 01253 478102 ✉ anne.ellis@blackpool.gov.uk

Recycling & Waste Minimisation: Mr Russ Weaver, Assistant

Director - Neighbourhood Services, Layton Depot, Plymouth Road, Blackpool FY3 7HW ☎ 01253 478610
✉ russ.weaver@blackpool.gov.uk

Regeneration: Mr Alan Cavill, Assistant Director of Enterprise & Business Development, PO Box 77, Town Hall, Blackpool FY1 1AD ☎ 01253 477006 📠 01253 477003
✉ alan.cavill@blackpool.gov.uk

Road Safety: Mr Peter Cross, Head of Transportation, Town Hall, Blackpool FY1 1AD ☎ 01253 476160
✉ peter.cross@blackpool.gov.uk

Social Services: Ms Janet Hambly, Service Director - Social Work & Safeguarding, Town Hall, Blackpool FY1 1AD
✉ janet.hambly@blackpool.gov.uk

Social Services (Adult): Ms Brenda Smith, Head of Adult Social Care, Progress House, Clifton Road, Blackpool FY4 4US
☎ 01253 476734 ✉ brenda.smith@blackpool.gov.uk

Social Services (Children): Ms Paula Swindlehurst, Head of Children's Social Care, Progress House, Clifton Road, Blackpool FY4 4US ☎ 01253 477655 ✉ paula.swindlehurst.gov.uk

Tourism: Mr Alan Cavill, Assistant Chief Executive - Regeneration, Tourism & Culture, PO Box 77, Town Hall, Blackpool FY1 1AD ☎ 01253 477006 📠 01253 477003
✉ alan.cavill@blackpool.gov.uk

Traffic Management: Mr Peter Cross, Head of Transportation, Town Hall, Blackpool FY1 1AD ☎ 01253 476160
✉ peter.cross@blackpool.gov.uk

Transport: Mr Peter Cross, Head of Transportation, Town Hall, Blackpool FY1 1AD ☎ 01253 476160
✉ peter.cross@blackpool.gov.uk

Transport Planner: Mr Peter Cross, Head of Transportation, Town Hall, Blackpool FY1 1AD ☎ 01253 476160
✉ peter.cross@blackpool.gov.uk

Waste Collection and Disposal: Mr James Kelly, Head of Integrated Transport & Waste Services, Town Hall, Blackpool FY1 1AD ✉ james.kelly@blackpool.gov.uk

Waste Management: Mr James Kelly, Head of Integrated Transport & Waste Services, Town Hall, Blackpool FY1 1AD
✉ james.kelly@blackpool.gov.uk

MEMBERS OF THE COUNCIL (42)

***Mayor:* Taylor**, Sylvia (LAB - Claremont)
cllr.sylvia.taylor@blackpool.gov.uk
Blackburn, Simon (LAB - Brunswick)
cllr.simon.blackburn@blackpool.gov.uk
Boughton, John (LAB - Layton)
cllr.john.boughton@blackpool.gov.uk
Brown, Tony (CON - Warbreck)
cllr.tony.brown@blackpool.gov.uk
Cain, Graham (LAB - Bloomfield)
cllr.graham.cain@blackpool.gov.uk
Callow, Maxine (CON - Norbreck)
cllr.maxine.callow@blackpool.gov.uk
Callow, Peter (CON - Norbreck)
cllr.peter.callow@blackpool.gov.uk
Campbell, Gillian (LAB - Park)
cllr.gillian.campbell@blackpool.gov.uk
Clapham, Donald (CON - Bispham)
cllr.don.clapham@blackpool.gov.uk
Coleman, Gary (LAB - Brunswick)
cllr.gary.coleman@blackpool.gov.uk
Coleman, Debbie (LAB - Marton)
cllr.debbie.coleman@blackpool.gov.uk
Collett, Eddie (LAB - Tyldesley)
cllr.eddie.collett@blackpool.gov.uk
Cox, Christian (CON - Squires Gate)
cllr.christian.cox@blackpool.gov.uk
Cross, Amy (LAB - Ingthorpe)
cllr.amy.cross@blackpool.gov.uk
Delves, Joyce (CON - Warbreck)
cllr.joyce.delves@blackpool.gov.uk
Doherty, Brian (LAB - Park)
cllr.brian.doherty@blackpool.gov.uk
Elmes, Jim (LAB - Marton)
cllr.jim.elmes@blackpool.gov.uk
Evans, Peter (CON - Stanley)
cllr.peter.evans@blackpool.gov.uk
Galley, Paul (CON - Anchorsholme)
cllr.paul.galley@blackpool.gov.uk
Green, Douglas (LD - Squires Gate)
cllr.douglas.green@blackpool.gov.uk
Greenhalgh, Joan (LAB - Clifton)
cllr.joan.greenhalgh@blackpool.gov.uk
Hardy, Norman (LAB - Hawes Side)
cllr.norman.hardy@blackpool.gov.uk
Haynes, Valerie (LAB - Hawes Side)
cllr.valerie.haynes@blackpool.gov.uk
Henderson, Lily (CON - Highfield)
cllr.lily.henderson@blackpool.gov.uk
Hutton, Adrian (LAB - Clifton)
cllr.adrian.hutton@blackpool.gov.uk
Jackson, Fred (LAB - Victoria)
cllr.fred.jackson@blackpool.gov.uk
Jones, John (LAB - Bloomfield)
cllr.john.jones@blackpool.gov.uk
Lee, Tony (CON - Waterloo)
cllr.tony.lee@blackpool.gov.uk
Matthews, Allan (LAB - Tyldesley)
cllr.allan.matthews@blackpool.gov.uk
Maughan, Chris (LAB - Highfield)
cllr.chris.maughan@blackpool.gov.uk
Mitchell, Henry (CON - Bispham)
cllr.henry.mitchell@blackpool.gov.uk
Mitchell, Martin (LAB - Layton)
cllr.martin.mitchell@blackpool.gov.uk
O'Hara, David (LAB - Waterloo)
cllr.david.ohara@blackpool.gov.uk
Owen, David (LAB - Victoria)
cllr.david.owen@blackpool.gov.uk
Riding, Sarah (LAB - Talbot)
cllr.sarah.riding@blackpool.gov.uk
Rowson, Kath (LAB - Ingthorpe)
cllr.kath.rowson@blackpool.gov.uk
Ryan, Chris (LAB - Greenlands)
cllr.chris.ryan@blackpool.gov.uk
Smith, Mark (LAB - Talbot)
cllr.mark.smith@blackpool.gov.uk

Stansfield, Andrew (CON - Stanley)
cllr.andrew.stansfield@blackpool.gov.uk
Taylor, Ivan (LAB - Claremont)
cllr.ivan.taylor@blackpool.gov.uk
Williams, Tony (CON - Anchorsholme)
cllr.tony.williams@blackpool.gov.uk
Wright, Christine (LAB - Greenlands)
cllr.christine.wright@blackpool.gov.uk

POLITICAL COMPOSITION
LAB: 28, CON: 13, LD: 1

CABINET
Leader: Mr Simon Blackburn
Deputy Leader: Mr Fred Jackson
Adult Social Care: Mrs Kath Rowson
Children's Social Care: Mr Simon Blackburn
Crime & Community Safety: Mr Eddie Collett
Equality & Diversity: Ms Sarah Riding
Health & Wellbeing: Mr Ivan Taylor
Housing: Ms Gillian Campbell
Regeneration & Urban Development: Mr Gary Coleman
Schools, Education & Children's Services: Ms Sarah Riding
Streets & Transport: Mr Fred Jackson
Tourism & Culture: Mr Graham Cain
Younger People: Ms Amy Cross

COMMITTEE CHAIRS
Appeals: Mr John Boughton
Finance & Audit: Mr Donald Clapham
Health Scrutiny: Mr Allan Matthews
Licensing: Mr Norman Hardy
Planning: Mr David Owen
Public Protection: Mr Norman Hardy

BLAENAU GWENT W

Blaenau Gwent County Borough Council, (Cyngor Bwrdeisdref Sirol Blaenau Gwent), Municipal Offices, Civic Centre, Ebbw Vale NP23 6XB ☎ 01495 350555 🖷 01495 301255
🖳 www.blaenau-gwent.gov.uk

FACTS & FIGURES
Police Authority: Gwent Police Authority
Learning and Skills Council: Wales
Parliamentary Constituencies: Blaenau Gwent
EU Constituencies: Wales
Election Frequency: Elections are of whole council

PRINCIPAL OFFICERS
Chief Executive: Mr David Waggett, Chief Executive, Municipal Offices, Civic Centre, Ebbw Vale NP23 6XB ☎ 01495 355001
david.waggett@blaenau-gwent.gov.uk

Senior Management: Mr Stuart Bees, Assistant Chief Finance Officer, Municipal Offices, Civic Centre, Ebbw Vale NP23 6XB
☎ 01495 355115 stuart.bees@blaenau-gwent.gov.uk

Senior Management: Ms Liz Majer, Director of Social Services, Anvil Court, Church Street, Abertillery NP13 1DB ☎ 01495 355261
🖷 01495 355285 liz.majer@blaenau-gwent.gov.uk

Senior Management: Mr John Parsons, Director of Environment & Regeneration, Municipal Offices, Civic Centre, Ebbw Vale NP23 6XB ☎ 01495 356088 🖷 01495 357770
john.parsons@blaenau-gwent.gov.uk

Access Officer / Social Services (Disability): Mr Alan Burkitt, Equalities Officer, Municipal Offices, Civic Centre, Ebbw Vale NP23 6XB ☎ 01495 355108 alan.burkitt@blaenau-gwent.gov.uk

Architect, Building / Property Services: Mr Clive Rogers, Chief Technical Services Officer, Baldwin House, Victoria Park, Ebbw Vale NP23 6ED ☎ 01495 355384

Best Value: Mrs Bernadette Elias, Head of Policy, Performance & Development, Municipal Offices, Civic Centre, Ebbw Vale NP23 6XB ☎ 01495 355016 🖷 01495 301255
bernadette.elias@blaenau-gwent.gov.uk

Building Control: Mr Roger Evans, Head of Building Control, Blaina District Office, High Street, Blaina, Blaenau NP13 3AG
☎ 01495 355520 roger.evans@blaenau-gwent.gov.uk

Catering Services: Mrs Hannah Meyrick, Head of Catering Services, Festival House, Victoria Business Park, Ebbw Vale, Blaenau NP23 8ER ☎ 01495 355456 🖷 01495 355330
hannah.meyrick@blaenau-gwent.gov.uk

Civil Registration: Mrs Sue Mitchell, Superintendent Registrar, Blaenau Gwent Register Office, Registration Suite, Bedwelty House, Morgan Street, Tredegar NP22 3XN ☎ 01495 353370
sue.mitchell@blaenau-gwent.gov.uk

PR / Communications: Ms Kelly Paterson, Corporate Communications & Marketing Manager, Municipal Offices, Civic Centre, Ebbw Vale NP23 6XB ☎ 01495 355113
kelly.paterson@blaenau-gwent.gov.uk

Community Planning: Mrs Bernadette Elias, Head of Policy, Performance & Development, Municipal Offices, Civic Centre, Ebbw Vale NP23 6XB ☎ 01495 355016 🖷 01495 301255
bernadette.elias@blaenau-gwent.gov.uk

Community Safety: Mrs Helena Hunt, Community Safety Officer, The Lodge, Bedwellty House, Morgan Street, Tredegar NP22 3XN ☎ 01495 356145

Computer Management: Mrs Linda Squire, Assistant Director Revenues, Benefits & ICT, Municipal Offices, Civic Centre, Ebbw Vale NP23 6XB ☎ 01495 355176 🖷 01495 355789
linda.squire@blaenau-gwent.gov.uk

Consumer Protection and Trading Standards: Mr Steve Jones, Head of Trading Standards & Licensing, District Office, 18 Beaufort Street, Ebbw Vale NP23 4AG ☎ 01495 350555
licensing@blaenau-gwent.gov.uk

Contracts: Mr John Parsons, Director of Environment & Regeneration, Municipal Offices, Civic Centre, Ebbw Vale NP23 6XB ☎ 01495 356088 🖷 01495 357770
john.parsons@blaenau-gwent.gov.uk

Corporate Services: Mrs Angela O'Leary, Corporate Support Manager, Municipal Offices, Civic Centre, Ebbw Vale NP23 6XB ☎ 01495 355090 🖷 ; 01495 357789 ✉ angela.oleary@blaenau-gwent.gov.uk

Direct Labour: Mr John Parsons, Director of Environment & Regeneration, Municipal Offices, Civic Centre, Ebbw Vale NP23 6XB ☎ 01495 356088 🖷 01495 357770 ✉ john.parsons@blaenau-gwent.gov.uk

Economic Development: Mr Gareth Jones, Chief Regeneration Officer, Business Resource Centre, Tafarnaubach Industrial Estate, Tredegar, NP22 3AA ☎ 01495 355502 ✉ gareth.jones@blaenau-gwent.gov.uk

Education: Mr Byron Jones, Learning Services Manager, Leisure Services & School Transformation, Anvil Court, Church Street, Abertillery NP13 1DB ☎ 01495 355608 🖷 01495 355900 ✉ byron.jones@blaenau-gwent.gov.uk

Education: Ms Sylvia Lindoe, Director of Education & Leisure, Central Depot, Barleyfields Industrial Estate, Brynmawr NP23 4YF ☎ 01495 355334 🖷 01495 355468 ✉ sylvia.lindoe@blaenau-gwent.gov.uk

Education: Mr Richard Parsons, Assistant Director - Achievement, Inclusion & Behaviour Support, Central Depot, Barleyfields Industrial Estate, Brynmawr NP23 4YF ☎ 01495 355452 🖷 01495 355468 ✉ richard.parsons@blaenau-gwent.gov.uk

Electoral Registration: Mrs Angela O'Leary, Corporate Support Manager, Municipal Offices, Civic Centre, Ebbw Vale NP23 6XB ☎ 01495 355090 🖷 ; 01495 357789 ✉ angela.oleary@blaenau-gwent.gov.uk

Emergency Planning: Mrs Deanne Griffiths, Principal Civil Contingencies Officer, Central Depot, Barleyfield Industrial Estate, Brynmawr NP23 4YF ☎ 01495 355568 🖷 01495 312357 ✉ deanne.griffiths@blaenau-gwent.gov.uk

Energy Management: Mr Matthew Lane, Senior Energy Officer, Baldwin House, Victoria Park, Abertillery NP23 8ED ☎ 01495 355562 ✉ matthew.lane@blaenau-gwent.gov.uk

Environmental / Technical Services: Mr Alan Reed, Chief Environmental Services Officer, Central Depot, Barleyfield Industrial Estate, Brynmawr NP23 4YF ☎ 01495 355612 🖷 01495 355475 ✉ alan.reed@blaenau-gwent.gov.uk

Environmental Health: Mr Dave Thompson, Head of Environmental Health, Blaina District Office, High Street, Blaina, Blaenau NP13 3XD ☎ 01495 355960 🖷 01495 335598 ✉ dave.thompson@blaenau-gwent.gov.uk

Estates, Property & Valuation: Mr Paul Miles, Valuation & Estates Officer, Municipal Offices, Civic Centre, Ebbw Vale NP23 6XB ☎ 01495 355030 🖷 01495 301255 ✉ paul.miles@blaenau-gwent.gov.uk

European Liaison: Mr Gareth Jones, Chief Regeneration Officer, Business Resource Centre, Tafarnaubach Industrial Estate, Tredegar, NP22 3AA ☎ 01495 355502 ✉ gareth.jones@blaenau-gwent.gov.uk

Events Manager: Mr Peter Henry, Venues & Events Officer, Beaufort Theatre, Beaufort Hill, Ebbw Vale NP23 5QQ ☎ 01495 354766 ✉ peter.henry@blaenau-gwent.gov.uk

Facilities: Mr Karl Hale, Sports Facilities Manager, Leisure Services & School Transformation, Anvil Court, Church Street, Abertillery NP13 1DB ☎ 01495 355322 🖷 01495 355900 ✉ karl.hale@blaenau-gwent.gov.uk

Facilities: Mr John Parsons, Director of Environment & Regeneration, Municipal Offices, Civic Centre, Ebbw Vale NP23 6XB ☎ 01495 356088 🖷 01495 357770 ✉ john.parsons@blaenau-gwent.gov.uk

Finance and Treasurer: Mr Dave McAuliffe, Chief Finance Officer, Municipal Offices, Civic Centre, Ebbw Vale NP23 6XB ☎ 01495 355005 🖷 01495 355788 ✉ dave.mcauliffe@blaenau-gwent.gov.uk

Fleet Management: Mr Neil Hughes, Fleet Manager, Central Depot, Barleyfields Industrial Estate, Nantyglo NP23 4YF ☎ 01495 355629 🖷 01495 301255 ✉ neil.hughes@blaenau-gwent.gov.uk

Grounds Maintenance: Mr Karl Hale, Sports Facilities Manager, Leisure Services & School Transformation, Anvil Court, Church Street, Abertillery NP13 1DB ☎ 01495 355322 🖷 01495 355900 ✉ karl.hale@blaenau-gwent.gov.uk

Health and Safety: Mr Jim Thomas, Health & Safety Manager, Municipal Offices, Civic Centre, Ebbw Vale NP23 6XB ☎ 01495 355035 🖷 01495 355245 ✉ jim.thomas@blaenau-gwent.gov.uk

Highways: Mr Alan Reed, Chief Environmental Services Officer, Central Depot, Barleyfield Industrial Estate, Brynmawr NP23 4YF ☎ 01495 355612 🖷 01495 355475 ✉ alan.reed@blaenau-gwent.gov.uk

Home Energy Conservation: Mr John Parsons, Director of Environment & Regeneration, Municipal Offices, Civic Centre, Ebbw Vale NP23 6XB ☎ 01495 356088 🖷 01495 357770 ✉ john.parsons@blaenau-gwent.gov.uk

Legal: Mr Dylan John, Chief Legal Officer, Municipal Offices, Civic Centre, Ebbw Vale NP23 6XB ☎ 01495 355012 🖷 01495 301255 ✉ dylan.john@blaenau-gwent.gov.uk

Leisure and Cultural Services: Mr Lynn Phillips, Assistant Director, Leisure Services & School Transformation, Anvil Court, Church Street, Abertillery NP13 1DB ☎ 01495 355603 🖷 01495 355900 ✉ lynn.phillips@blaenau-gwent.gov.uk

Licensing: Mr Steve Jones, Head of Trading Standards & Licensing, District Office, 18 Beaufort Street, Ebbw Vale NP23 4AG ☎ 01495 350555 ✉ licensing@blaenau-gwent.gov.uk

Licensing: Mr Dave Thompson, Head of Environmental Health, Blaina District Office, High Street, Blaina, Blaenau NP13 3XD ☎ 01495 355960 🖷 01495 335598

dave.thompson@blaenau-gwent.gov.uk

Lifelong Learning: Ms Sylvia Lindoe, Director of Education & Leisure, Central Depot, Barleyfields Industrial Estate, Brynmawr NP23 4YF ☎ 01495 355334 🖷 01495 355468 sylvia.lindoe@blaenau-gwent.gov.uk

Lighting: Mr Alan Reed, Chief Environmental Services Officer, Central Depot, Barleyfield Industrial Estate, Brynmawr NP23 4YF ☎ 01495 355612 🖷 01495 355475 alan.reed@blaenau-gwent.gov.uk

Lottery Funding, Charity and Voluntary: Mr John Parsons, Director of Environment & Regeneration, Municipal Offices, Civic Centre, Ebbw Vale NP23 6XB ☎ 01495 356088 🖷 01495 357770 john.parsons@blaenau-gwent.gov.uk

Member Services: Mrs Ceri Edwards Brown, Member Development Co-ordinator/Member Services, Municipal Offices, Civic Centre, Ebbw Vale NP23 6XB ☎ 01495 356139 ceri.edwardsbrown@blaenau-gwent.gov.uk

Partnerships: Ms Sharn Annett, Assistant Director - Department Business Management & Support (S.M.S.), Catering & Partnerships, Heart of the Valleys Children's Centre, High Street, Blaenau NP13 3BN ☎ 01495 354719 🖷 01495 291813 sharn.annett@blaenau-gwent.gov.uk

Personnel / HR: Mrs Chris Denmead, Head of Human Resources, Municipal Offices, Civic Centre, Ebbw Vale NP23 6XB ☎ 01495 355041 🖷 01495 355787 chris.denmead@blaenau-gwent.gov.uk

Planning: Mr Steve Smith, Head of Planning, Blaina District Office, High Street, Blaina, Blaenau NP13 3XD ☎ 01495 355510 🖷 01495 355598 steve.smith@blaenau-gwent.gov.uk

Procurement: Mr Lee Williams, Corporate Procurement Manager, Municipal Offices, Civic Centre, Ebbw Vale NP23 6XB ☎ 01495 355686 🖷 01495 301255 lee.williams@blaenau-gwent.gov.uk

Public Libraries: Mr Lynn Phillips, Assistant Director, Leisure Services & School Transformation, Anvil Court, Church Street, Abertillery NP13 1DB ☎ 01495 355603 🖷 01495 355900 lynn.phillips@blaenau-gwent.gov.uk

Recycling & Waste Minimisation: Mr Alan Reed, Chief Environmental Services Officer, Central Depot, Barleyfield Industrial Estate, Brynmawr NP23 4YF ☎ 01495 355612 🖷 01495 355475 alan.reed@blaenau-gwent.gov.uk

Regeneration: Mr Gareth Jones, Chief Regeneration Officer, Business Resource Centre, Tafarnaubach Industrial Estate, Tredegar, NP22 3AA ☎ 01495 355502 gareth.jones@blaenau-gwent.gov.uk

Road Safety: Mr John Parsons, Director of Environment & Regeneration, Municipal Offices, Civic Centre, Ebbw Vale NP23 6XB ☎ 01495 356088 🖷 01495 357770 john.parsons@blaenau-gwent.gov.uk

Social Services: Ms Liz Majer, Director of Social Services, Anvil Court, Church Street, Abertillery NP13 1DB ☎ 01495 355261 🖷 01495 355285 liz.majer@blaenau-gwent.gov.uk

Social Services (Adult): Mr Stephen Gillingham, Assistant Director - Adult Services, Anvil Court, Church Street, Abertillery NP13 1DB ☎ 01495 355383 🖷 01495 355285 stephen.gillingham@blaenau-gwent.gov.uk

Social Services (Children): Mr Nigel Brown, Assistant Director - Children's Services, Anvil Court, Church Street, Abertillery NP13 1DB ☎ ; 01495 355285 nigel.brown@blaenau-gwent.gov.uk

Staff Training: Mr Simon Green, Organisational Development Officer, Municipal Offices, Civic Centre, Ebbw Vale NP23 6XB ☎ 01495 355040 🖷 01495 355787 simon.green@blaenau-gwent.gov.uk

Sustainable Communities: Mr Mark Price, Head of Community Regeneration, Business Resource Centre, Tafarnaubach Industrial Estate, Tredegar NP22 3AA ☎ 01495 355812

Sustainable Development: Mr Gareth Jones, Chief Regeneration Officer, Business Resource Centre, Tafarnaubach Industrial Estate, Tredegar, NP22 3AA ☎ 01495 355502 gareth.jones@blaenau-gwent.gov.uk

Tourism: Mr Lynn Phillips, Assistant Director, Leisure Services & School Transformation, Anvil Court, Church Street, Abertillery NP13 1DB ☎ 01495 355603 🖷 01495 355900 lynn.phillips@blaenau-gwent.gov.uk

Town Centre: Ms Beth Cartwright, Town Centre Manager, Municipal Offices, Civic Centre, Ebbw Vale NP23 6XB ☎ 01495 355539

Town Centre: Ms Karin Lamb, Town Centre Manager, Municipal Offices, Civic Centre, Ebbw Vale NP23 6XB ☎ 07968 243128

Transport: Mr John Parsons, Director of Environment & Regeneration, Central Depot, Barleyfield Industrial Estate, Brynmawr NP23 4YF ☎ 01495 356088 🖷 01495 357770 john.parsons@blaenau-gwent.gov.uk

Transport Planner: Ms Sharn Annett, Assistant Director - Department Business Management & Support (S.M.S.), Catering & Partnerships, Heart of the Valleys Children's Centre, High Street, Blaenau NP13 3BN ☎ 01495 354719 🖷 01495 291813 sharn.annett@blaenau-gwent.gov.uk

Waste Collection and Disposal: Mr Alan Reed, Chief Environmental Services Officer, Central Depot, Barleyfield Industrial Estate, Brynmawr NP23 4YF ☎ 01495 355612 🖷 01495 355475 alan.reed@blaenau-gwent.gov.uk

Waste Management: Mr Alan Reed, Chief Environmental Services Officer, Central Depot, Barleyfield Industrial Estate, Brynmawr NP23 4YF ☎ 01495 355612 🖷 01495 355475 alan.reed@blaenau-gwent.gov.uk

Children's Play Areas: Mr Alun Watkins, Grounds Operations Manager, Leisure Services and School Transformation, Anvil Court, Church Street, Abertillery NP13 1DB ☎ 01495 355603

🖷 01495 355675 ✉ alun.watkins@blaenau-gwent.gov.uk

MEMBERS OF THE COUNCIL (42)

***Mayor:* Bartlett**, Graham (LAB - Cwmtillery)
***Deputy Mayor:* Lewis**, Mostyn (LAB - Ebbw Vale South)
mostyn.lewis@blaenau-gwent.gov.uk
***Leader of the Council:* McCarthy**, Hedley (LAB - Llanhilleth)
hedley.mccarthy@blaenau-gwent.gov.uk
***Deputy Leader of the Council:* Thomas**, Stephen (LAB - Tredegar Central & West)
stephen.thomas@blaenau-gwent.gov.uk
Baldwin, Peter (LAB - Nantyglo)
Bartlett, Mike (LAB - Llanhilleth)
mike.bartlett@blaenau-gwent.gov.uk
Bender, Keren (LAB - Cwm)
Bevan, Derrick (LAB - Cwm)
Brown, Kevin (IND - Brynmawr)
kevin.brown@blaenau-gwent.gov.uk
Chaplin, Keith (LAB - Abertillery)
Clements, Brian (LAB - Ebbw Vale South)
brian.clements@blaenau-gwent.gov.uk
Collier, Garth (IND - Blaina)
garth.collier@blaenau-gwent.gov.uk
Coughlin, Derek (LAB - Ebbw Vale North)
Cross, Malcolm (LAB - Sirhowy)
Dally, Malcolm (LAB - Nantyglo)
malcolmdally1@blaenau-gwent.gov.uk
Daniels, Nigel (INDNA - Abertillery)
nigel.daniels@blaenau-gwent.gov.uk
Hancock, Denzil (IND - Six Bells)
denzil.hancock@blaenau-gwent.gov.uk
Hayden, Keith (LAB - Georgetown)
keith.hayden@blaenau-gwent.gov.uk
Hobbs, Anita (LAB - Tredegar Central & West)
nita.hobbs@blaenau-gwent.gov.uk
Holland, Mark (LAB - Six Bells)
Hopkins, John (IND - Brynmawr)
john.hopkins@blaenau-gwent.gov.uk
Jones, Richard (LAB - Abertillery)
Lewis, Ann (LAB - Ebbw Vale North)
Mason, John (IND - Nantyglo)
john.mason@blaenau-gwent.gov.uk
McLlwee, Jim (LAB - Llanhilleth)
Meredith, Clive (IND - Badminton)
clive.meredith@blaenau-gwent.gov.uk
Morgan, Jennifer (LAB - Ebbw Vale North)
jennifer.morgan@blaenau-gwent.gov.uk
Morgan, John (LAB - Georgetown)
Owens, Dennis (LAB - Sirhowy)
dennis.owens@blaenau-gwent.gov.uk
Pagett, Bob (LAB - Blaina)
Rowberry, Diane (LAB - Sirhowy)
diane.rowberry@blaenau-gwent.gov.uk
Scully, Brian (LAB - Badminton)
brian.scully@blaenau-gwent.gov.uk
Sharrem, Tim (LAB - Cwntillery)
Sutton, Barrie (LAB - Brynmawr)
Thomas, Godfrey (IND - Beaufort)
godfrey.thomas@blaenua-gwent.gov.uk
Tidey, Christine (LAB - Cwmtillery)
Trollope, Haydn (LAB - Tredegar Central & West)
hayden.trollope@blaenau-gwent.gov.uk
White, David (IND - Beaufort)
Wilkshire, David (LAB - Rassau)
david.wilkshire@blaenau-gwent.gov.uk
Williams, William John (IND - Rassau)
john.williams@blaenau-gwent.gov.uk
Willis, Bernard (LAB - Tredegar Central & West)
bernard.willis@blaenau-gwent.gov.uk
Winnett, Lisa (LAB - Blaina)

POLITICAL COMPOSITION

LAB: 32, IND: 9, INDNA: 1

CABINET

Leader: Mr Hedley McCarthy
Deputy Leader: Mr Stephen Thomas
Environment & Community Safety: Mr Keith Hayden
Executive Business Manager: Mr Stephen Thomas
Governance: Mr Jim McLlwee
Highways & Transportation: Mr David White
Leisure & Young People: Mr David Wilkshire
Regeneration: Mr Brian Scully
Resources: Mr Barrie Sutton
Social Services: Ms Anita Hobbs
Work Transportation & Partnership: Mr Haydn Trollope

COMMITTEE CHAIRS

Audit: Mr Keith Hayden
Education & Leisure: Mr David Wilkshire
Planning: Mr Denzil Hancock

BOLSOVER — D

Bolsover District Council, Sherwood Lodge, Bolsover S44 6NF
☎ 01246 242424; 01246 242424 🖷 01246 242423; 01246 242424
✉ enquiries@bolsover.gov.uk 🖳 www.bolsover.gov.uk

FACTS & FIGURES

Police Authority: Derbyshire Police Authority
Health Authority: East Midlands Strategic Health Authority
Learning and Skills Council: East Midlands
Parliamentary Constituencies: Bolsover
EU Constituencies: East Midlands
Election Frequency: Elections are of whole council

PRINCIPAL OFFICERS

Chief Executive: Mr Wes Lumley, Joint Chief Executive Officer, Sherwood Lodge, Bolsover S44 6NF ☎ 01246 242462; 01246 242462 🖷 01246 242423; 01246 242423
✉ wes.lumley@bolsover.gov.uk

Senior Management: Mr Paul Hackett, Joint Director - Health & Wellbeing, Sherwood Lodge, Bolsover S44 6NF ☎ 01246 242566; 01246 242566 🖷 01246 242423; 01246 242423
✉ paul.hackett@ne-derbyshire.gov.uk

Senior Management: Mr Kevin Hopkinson, Joint Director - Development, Sherwood Lodge, Bolsover S44 6NF ☎ 01246 242585; 01246 242585 🖷 01246 242423; 01246 242423
✉ kevin.hopkinson@bolsover.gov.uk

Senior Management: Mr Bryan Mason, Joint Director - Corporate Resources, Sherwood Lodge, Bolsover S44 6NF
☎ 01246 242431 🖷 01246 242423

bryan.mason@ne-derbyshire.gov.uk

Senior Management: Mr Stuart Tomlinson, Joint Director - Neighbourhoods, Riverside Depot, Mansfield Road, Doe Lea, Chesterfield S44 5NY ☎ 01246 593099 🖷 01246 242423 stuart.tomlinson@bolsover.gov.uk

Architect, Building / Property Services: Mr Grant Galloway, Buildings & Contracts Manager, Sherwood Lodge, Bolsover S44 6NF ☎ 01246 242284 🖷 01246 242423 grant.galloway@bolsover.gov.uk

Architect, Building / Property Services: Mr Tim Robinson, Principal Building Surveyor, Sherwood Lodge, Bolsover S44 6NF ☎ 01246 242239 🖷 01246 242423 tim.robinson@bolsover.gov.uk

Best Value: Mrs Jane Foley, Joint Assistant Director - Strategy & Performance, Sherwood Lodge, Bolsover S44 6NF ☎ 01246 242343 🖷 01246 242423 jane.foley@bolsover.gov.uk

Best Value: Mr Robin Railly, Performance & Quality Officer, Sherwood Lodge, Bolsover S44 6NF ☎ 01246 242508 🖷 01246 242423 robin.railly@bolsover.gov.uk

Building Control: Mr Malcolm Clinton, Business Manager, Unit 2, Dunston Technology Park, Millennium Way, Dunston Road, Chesterfield S41 8ND ☎ 01246 345817 malcolm.clinton@ne-derbyshire.gov.uk

PR / Communications: Mr Scott Chambers, Communications Officer, Sherwood Lodge, Bolsover S44 6NF ☎ 01246 242323 🖷 01246 242423 scott.chambers@bolsover.gov.uk

Community Planning: Mrs Pam Brown, Partnership Co-ordinator, Sherwood Lodge, Bolsover S44 6NF ☎ 01246 242499 🖷 01246 242423 pam.brown@bolsover.gov.uk

Community Planning: Mr Wes Lumley, Joint Chief Executive Officer, Sherwood Lodge, Bolsover S44 6NF ☎ 01246 242462 🖷 01246 242423 wes.lumley@bolsover.gov.uk

Community Safety: Mr Stuart Tomlinson, Joint Director - Neighbourhoods, Riverside Depot, Mansfield Road, Doe Lea, Chesterfield S44 5NY ☎ 01246 593099 🖷 01246 242423; 01246 242423 stuart.tomlinson@bolsover.gov.uk

Computer Management: Mr Nick Blaney, Joint IT Services Manager, Sherwood Lodge, Bolsover S44 6NF ☎ 01246 217103 🖷 01246 242423 nick.blaney@ne-derbyshire.gov.uk

Contracts: Mr Bob Trusswell, Head - Procurement, Sherwood Lodge, Bolsover S44 6NF ☎ 01246 242311 bob.trusswell@bolsover.gov.uk

Corporate Services: Mrs Allison Westray-Chapman, Joint Assistant Director - Resources, Sherwood Lodge, Bolsover S44 6NF allison.westray-chapman@ne-derbyshire.gov.uk; allison.westray-chapman@ne-derbyshire.gov.uk

Customer Service: Mrs Allison Westray-Chapman, Joint Assistant Director - Resources, Sherwood Lodge, Bolsover S44 6NF allison.westray-chapman@ne-derbyshire.gov.uk; allison.westray-chapman@ne-derbyshire.gov.uk

Economic Development: Mr Dave Eccles, Joint Assistant Director - Regeneration, Sherwood Lodge, Bolsover S44 6NF ☎ 01246 242421; 01246 242421 🖷 01246 242423; 01246 242423 dave.eccles@bolsover.gov.uk

Electoral Registration: Mr Wes Lumley, Joint Chief Executive Officer, Sherwood Lodge, Bolsover S44 6NF ☎ 01246 242462; 01246 242462 🖷 01246 242423; 01246 242423 wes.lumley@bolsover.gov.uk

Emergency Planning: Mr Paul Hackett, Joint Director - Health & Wellbeing, Sherwood Lodge, Bolsover S44 6NF ☎ 01246 242566; 01246 242566 🖷 01246 242423; 01246 242423 paul.hackett@ne-derbyshire.gov.uk

Energy Management: Ms Natasha Potter, HIA Caseworker, Sherwood Lodge, Bolsover S44 6NF ☎ 01246 242281 natasha.potter@bolsover.gov.uk

Environmental / Technical Services: Mrs Gael Hepburn, Joint Assistant Director - Environmental Services, Sherwood Lodge, Bolsover S44 6NF ☎ 01246 242254; 01246 2422254 🖷 01246 242423; 01246 242423 gael.hepburn@ne-derbyshire.gov.uk

Environmental Health: Ms Sharon Gillott, Environmental Health Commercial Manager, Sherwood Lodge, Bolsover S44 6NF ☎ 01246 242283 🖷 01246 242423 sharon.gillott@bolsover.gov.uk

Estates, Property & Valuation: Mr Dave Eccles, Joint Assistant Director - Regeneration, Sherwood Lodge, Bolsover S44 6NF ☎ 01246 242421; 01246 242421 🖷 01246 242423 dave.eccles@bolsover.gov.uk

European Liaison: Mr Wes Lumley, Joint Chief Executive Officer, Sherwood Lodge, Bolsover S44 6NF ☎ 01246 242462; 01246 242462 🖷 01246 242423 wes.lumley@bolsover.gov.uk

Facilities: Mr Tim Robinson, Principal Building Surveyor, Sherwood Lodge, Bolsover S44 6NF ☎ 01246 242239 🖷 01246 242423 tim.robinson@bolsover.gov.uk

Finance and Treasurer: Mr Geoff Bagnell, Joint Assistant Director - Finance, Sherwood Lodge, Bolsover S44 6NF ☎ 01246 242420 geoff.bagnell@ne-derbyshire.gov.uk

Finance and Treasurer: Mr Bryan Mason, Joint Director - Corporate Resources, Sherwood Lodge, Bolsover S44 6NF ☎ 01246 242431 🖷 01246 242423 bryan.mason@ne-derbyshire.gov.uk

Grounds Maintenance: Mr Adrian Lowery, Street Services Manager, Riverside Depot, Doe Lea, Bolsover S44 5NY ☎ 01246 593044 🖷 01246 242423 adrian.lowery@bolsover.gov.uk

Health and Safety: Mrs Angela Grundy, Joint Assistant Director - Human Resources & Payroll, Sherwood Lodge, Bolsover S44

6NF ☎ 01246 242411 🖷 01246 242423
🖰 angela.grundy@ne-derbyshire.gov.uk

Housing: Mr Peter Campbell, Head - Housing, Sherwood Lodge, Bolsover S44 6NF ☎ 01246 242240 🖷 01246 242423
🖰 peter.campbell@bolsover.gov.uk

Housing Maintenance: Mr Peter Campbell, Head - Housing, Sherwood Lodge, Bolsover S44 6NF ☎ 01246 242240
🖷 01246 242423 🖰 peter.campbell@bolsover.gov.uk

Legal: Mrs Sarah Sternberg, Solicitor to the Council & Monitoring Officer, Sherwood Lodge, Bolsover S44 6NF ☎ 01246 242414
🖷 01246 242423 🖰 sarah.sternberg@bolsover.gov.uk

Leisure and Cultural Services: Mr Lee Hickin, Head - Leisure, Riverside Depot, Doe Lea, Bolsover S44 5NY ☎ 01246 593056; 01246 593056 🖷 01246 242423 🖰 lee.hickin@bolsover.gov.uk

Licensing: Mr Geoff Allcock, Enforcement Officer, Sherwood Lodge, Bolsover S44 6NF ☎ 01246 242417 🖷 01246 242423 🖰 geoff.allcock@bolsover.gov.uk

Member Services: Miss Kath Whittingham, Committee & Support Services Manager, Sherwood Lodge, Bolsover S44 6NF
☎ 01246 242422 🖷 01246 242423
🖰 kath.whittingham@bolsover.gov.uk

Partnerships: Mrs Pam Brown, Partnership Co-ordinator, Sherwood Lodge, Bolsover S44 6NF ☎ 01246 242499 🖷 01246 242423 🖰 pam.brown@bolsover.gov.uk

Personnel / HR: Mrs Angela Grundy, Joint Assistant Director - Human Resources & Payroll, Sherwood Lodge, Bolsover S44 6NF
☎ 01246 242411; 01246 242411 🖷 01246 242423
🖰 angela.grundy@ne-derbyshire.gov.uk

Planning: Mr James Arnold, Head - Planning & Environmental Health, Sherwood Lodge, Bolsover S44 6NF ☎ 01246 242254; 01246 242254 🖷 01246 242423 🖰 james.arnold@bolsover.gov.uk

Procurement: Mr Bob Trusswell, Head - Procurement, Sherwood Lodge, Bolsover S44 6NF ☎ 01246 242311
🖰 bob.trusswell@bolsover.gov.uk

Recycling & Waste Minimisation: Mr Adrian Lowery, Street Services Manager, Riverside Depot, Doe Lea, Bolsover S44 5NY
☎ 01246 593044 🖷 01246 242423
🖰 adrian.lowery@bolsover.gov.uk

Regeneration: Mr Dave Eccles, Joint Assistant Director - Regeneration, Sherwood Lodge, Bolsover S44 6NF ☎ 01246 242421; 01246 242421 🖷 01246 242423; 01246 242423
🖰 dave.eccles@bolsover.gov.uk; david.eccles@bolsover.gov.uk

Staff Training: Mrs Fran Ingram, Organisational Development Officer, Sherwood Lodge, Bolsover S44 6NF ☎ 01246 242412
🖷 01246 242423 🖰 fran.ingram@bolsover.gov.uk

Street Scene: Mr Adrian Lowery, Street Services Manager, Riverside Depot, Doe Lea, Bolsover S44 5NY ☎ 01246 593044
🖷 01246 242423 🖰 adrian.lowery@bolsover.gov.uk

Tourism: Mrs Theresa Garrod, Tourism Officer, Sherwood Lodge, Bolsover S44 6NF ☎ 01246 242324 🖷 01246 242423
🖰 theresa.garrod@bolsover.gov.uk

Waste Collection and Disposal: Mr Adrian Lowery, Street Services Manager, Riverside Depot, Doe Lea, Bolsover S44 5NY
☎ 01246 593044 🖷 01246 242423
🖰 adrian.lowery@bolsover.gov.uk

Waste Management: Mr Adrian Lowery, Street Services Manager, Riverside Depot, Doe Lea, Bolsover S44 5NY ☎ 01246 593044 🖷 01246 242423 🖰 adrian.lowery@bolsover.gov.uk

MEMBERS OF THE COUNCIL (37)

***Chair:* Walker**, Kenneth (LAB - Shirebrook Langwith)
ken.walker@bolsover.gov.uk
***Vice-Chair:* Dooley**, Mary (LAB - Pinxton)
mary.dooley@bolsover.gov.uk
***Leader of the Council:* Watts**, Eion (LAB - Barlborough)
eion.watts@bolsover.gov.uk
***Deputy Leader of the Council:* Tomlinson**, Alan (LAB - Blackwell)
alan.tomlinson@bolsover.gov.uk
***Group Leader:* Clifton**, James (IND - Elmton with Creswell)
jim.clifton@bolsover.gov.uk
***Group Leader:* Webster**, George (R - Whitwell)
george.webster@bolsover.gov.uk
Anderson, Andrew (LAB - Shirebrook South East)
andrew.anderson@bolsover.gov.uk
Bennett, Toni (LAB - Bolsover South)
toni.bennet@bolsover.gov.uk
Bowler, Rosemary (LAB - Bolsover West)
rose.bowler@bolsover.gov.uk
Bowman, Keith (LAB - Bolsover West)
keith.bowman@bolsover.gov.uk
Bowmer, Pauline (LAB - Pleasley)
pauline.bowmer@bolsover.gov.uk
Brooks, Ray (LAB - South Normanton West)
Connerton, Terry (LAB - Clowne North)
terry.connerton@bolsover.gov.uk
Cook, Terry (LAB - South Normanton East)
Cooper, Paul (LAB - Bolsover North West)
paul.cooper@bolsover.gov.uk
Crane, Malcolm (LAB - Scarcliffe)
malc.crane@bolsover.gov.uk
Fritchley, Stephen (LAB - Shirebrook North West)
steve.fritchley@bolsover.gov.uk
Gilmour, Hilary (LAB - Barlborough)
hilary.gilmour@bolsover.gov.uk
Hall, Eric (LAB - Bolsover South)
eric.hall@bolsover.gov.uk
Heffer, Ray (IND - Tibshelf)
ray.heffer@bolsover.gov.uk
Hendry, Brian (LAB - Clowne North)
brian.hendry@bolsover.gov.uk
Kelly, Dennis (LAB - Pinxton)
dennis.kelly@bolsover.gov.uk
Kerr, Duncan (GRN - Whitwell)
duncan.kerr@bolsover.gov.uk
McGregor, Duncan (LAB - Elmton with Creswell)
duncan.mcgregor@bolsover.gov.uk
Munks, Clare (LAB - Blackwell)
clare.munks@bolsover.gov.uk

Murray-Carr, Brian (LAB - Shirebrook East)
brian.murray-carr@bolsover.gov.uk
Parkin, Graham (LAB - South Normanton West)
graham.parking@bolsover.gov.uk
Peake, Sandra (LAB - Shirebrook South West)
sandra.peake@bolsover.gov.uk
Phelan, Joe (LAB - South Normanton East)
joe.phelan@bolsover.gov.uk
Reid, Karl (LAB - Clowne South)
karl.reid@bolsover.gov.uk
Rodda, Thomas (LAB - Bolsover North West)
tom.rodda@bolsover.gov.uk
Smith, James (LAB - Clowne South)
jim.smith@bolsover.gov.uk
Syrett, Ann (LAB - Pleasley)
ann.syrett@bolsover.gov.uk
Turner, Rita (LAB - Elmton with Creswell)
rita.turner@bolsover.gov.uk
Wallis, Susan (LAB - South Normanton West)
sue.wallis@bolsover.gov.uk
Watson, Deborah (IND - Tibshelf)
deborah.watson@bolsover.gov.uk
Wilson, Jen (LAB - Scarcliffe)
jennifer.wilson@bolsover.gov.uk

POLITICAL COMPOSITION
LAB: 32, IND: 3, R: 1, GRN: 1

CABINET
Leader: Mr Eion Watts
Deputy Leader: Mr Alan Tomlinson
Chair of the Council: Mr Kenneth Walker
Community Safety: Mr Brian Murray-Carr
Corporate Efficiencies: Mr Duncan McGregor
Environment: Mr Dennis Kelly
Housing Management: Mr Keith Bowman
Social Inclusion: Ms Ann Syrett

COMMITTEE CHAIRS
Improvement Scrutiny: Mrs Hilary Gilmour
Licensing: Mrs Toni Bennett
Planning: Mr Dennis Kelly
Safe & Inclusive Scrutiny: Mrs Mary Dooley
Scrutiny Management Board: Mrs Mary Dooley
Sustainable Communities Scrutiny: Mr Karl Reid

BOLTON M

Bolton Metropolitan Borough Council, Town Hall, Bolton BL1 1RU ☎ 01204 333333 🖷 01204 331042
firstname.surname@bolton.gov.uk
www.bolton.gov.uk

FACTS & FIGURES
Police Authority: Greater Manchester Police Authority
Health Authority: North West Strategic Health Authority
Learning and Skills Council: North West
Parliamentary Constituencies: Bolton North East, Bolton South East, Bolton West
EU Constituencies: North West
Election Frequency: Elections are by thirds
Twinning: Le Mans (France); Paderborn (Germany)

PRINCIPAL OFFICERS
Chief Executive: Mr Sean Harriss, Chief Executive, Town Hall, Bolton BL1 1RU ☎ 01204 331001 🖷 01204 381942
sean.harriss@bolton.gov.uk

Deputy Chief Executive: Mr Steve Arnfield, Deputy Chief Executive, Town Hall, Bolton BL1 1RU ☎ 01204 331502
🖷 01204 331521 steve.arnfield@bolton.gov.uk

Senior Management: Ms Lynne Ridsdale, Assistant Director - People & Transformation, Town Hall, Bolton BL1 1RU
☎ 01204 331201 lynne.ridsdale@bolton.gov.uk

Best Value: Ms Lynne Ridsdale, Assistant Director - People & Transformation, Town Hall, Bolton BL1 1RU ☎ 01204 331201
lynne.ridsdale@bolton.gov.uk

Catering Services: Ms Christine Forster, Head of Albert Halls Complex, Town Hall, Bolton BL1 1RU ☎ 01204 334305
christine.forster@bolton.gov.uk

Catering Services: Mrs Elaine Long, Head of Catering (Schools), Facilities Section, Environmental Services, Wellington House, Wellington Street, Bolton BL3 5DX ☎ 01204 336940
🖷 01204 336709 elaine.long@bolton.gov.uk

Children / Youth Services: Mr Chris McIver, Positive Activities - Head of Service, 5th Floor, Paderborn House, Civic Centre, Bolton BL1 1JW ☎ 01204 334107 🖷 01204 332243
chris.mciver@bolton.gov.uk

Civil Registration: Ms Helen Gorman, Borough Solicitor, Town Hall, Bolton BL1 1RU ☎ 01204 331314
helen.gorman@bolton.gov.uk

PR / Communications: Mr Andrew Donaldson, Assistant Director of Policy, Partnerships & Communication, Town Hall, Bolton BL1 1RU ☎ 01204 331001 🖷 01204 381942
andrew.donaldson@bolton.gov.uk

Community Planning: Mr Andrew Donaldson, Assistant Director of Policy, Partnerships & Communication, Town Hall, Bolton BL1 1RU ☎ 01204 331001 🖷 01204 381942
andrew.donaldson@bolton.gov.uk

Community Safety: Mr Nick Maher, Head of Community Safety Services, 1st Floor, Paderborn House, Bolton BL1 1JW
☎ 01204 331226 🖷 01204 338493 nick.maher@bolton.gov.uk

Computer Management: Ms Sue Johnson, Assistant Director - Financial Services & Corporate ICT, Town Hall, Bolton BL1 1RU
☎ 01204 331504 sue.johnson@bolton.gov.uk

Consumer Protection and Trading Standards: Mr Richard Lindley, Group Manager - Trading Standards & Consumer Protection, Castle Hill Centre, Castleton Street, Bolton BL2 2JW
☎ 01204 336585 🖷 01204 336599
richard.lindley@bolton.gov.uk

Corporate Services: Mr Steve Arnfield, Deputy Chief Executive, Town Hall, Bolton BL1 1RU ☎ 01204 331502 🖷 01204 331521
steve.arnfield@bolton.gov.uk

LOCAL AUTHORITIES

Customer Service: Mr John Rowlands, Assistant Director - Customer Services, 2nd Floor, Howell Croft House, Bolton BL1 1QY ☎ 01204 331506 ✉ john.rowlands@bolton.gov.uk

Economic Development: Mr Keith Davies, Director of Development & Regeneration, Wellsprings, Civic Centre, Bolton BL1 1US ☎ 01204 334002 📠 01204 362018 ✉ keith.davies@bolton.gov.uk

Education: Mrs Margaret Asquith, Director of Children's Services, Paderborn House, Bolton BL1 1JW ☎ 01204 332010 📠 01204 332228 ✉ margaret.asquith@bolton.gov.uk

E-Government: Ms Helen Gorman, Borough Solicitor, Town Hall, Bolton BL1 1RU ☎ 01204 331314 ✉ helen.gorman@bolton.gov.uk

Electoral Registration: Mr Andrew Donaldson, Assistant Director of Policy, Partnerships & Communication, Town Hall, Bolton BL1 1RU ☎ 01204 331001 📠 01204 381942 ✉ andrew.donaldson@bolton.gov.uk

Emergency Planning: Ms Janet Pollard, Head of Service Finance & Business Development, 3rd Floor, Wellsprings, Civic Centre, Bolton BL1 1US ☎ 01204 336710 ✉ janet.pollard@bolton.gov.uk

Energy Management: Ms Anne Mason, Energy Manager, Town Hall, Bolton BL1 1RU ☎ 01204 331351 ✉ anne.mason@bolton.gov.uk

Environmental / Technical Services: Mr Malcolm Cox, Director of Environmental Services, Wellsprings, Civic Centre, Bolton BL1 1US ☎ 01204 336711 ✉ malcolm.cox@bolton.gov.uk

Environmental Health: Mrs Linda Duckworth, Group Manager - Environmental Health & Food Control, Castle Hill Centre, Castleton Street, Bolton BL2 2JW ☎ 01204 336530 ✉ linda.duckworth@bolton.gov.uk

Estates, Property & Valuation: Mr Paul Brown, Chief Property Officer, Town Hall, Bolton BL1 1RU ☎ 01204 331350 ✉ joseph.brown@bolton.gov.uk

Events Manager: Ms Norma Rutherford, Communications & Marketing, Town Hall, Bolton BL1 1RU ☎ 01204 332000 ✉ norma.rutherford@bolton.gov.uk

Facilities: Ms Christine Quinn, Operational Facilities Manager, Ground Floor, Howell Croft House, Howell Croft North, Bolton BL1 1QY ☎ 01204 331362 ✉ chris.quinn@bolton.gov.uk

Finance and Treasurer: Mr Steve Arnfield, Deputy Chief Executive, Town Hall, Bolton BL1 1RU ☎ 01204 331502 📠 01204 331521 ✉ steve.arnfield@bolton.gov.uk

Finance and Treasurer: Ms Sue Johnson, Assistant Director - Financial Services & Corporate ICT, Town Hall, Bolton BL1 1RU ☎ 01204 331504 ✉ sue.johnson@bolton.gov.uk

Fleet Management: Ms Donna Ball, Assistant Director - Waste & Fleet Management, Town Hall, Bolton BL1 1RU ☎ 01204 336713 📠 01204 336889 ✉ donna.ball@bolton.gov.uk

Grounds Maintenance: Mr Bill Moran, Neighbourhood Services Manager, Milton House, Wellington Street, Bolton BL3 1DX ☎ 01204 336912 📠 01204 336709 ✉ bill.moran@bolton.gov.uk

Health and Safety: Mr Frank Warren, Principal Health & Safety Manager, Occupational Safety & Health Unit, 2nd Floor Paderborn House, Howell Croft North, Bolton BL1 1UA ☎ 01204 336776 ✉ frank.warren@bolton.gov.uk

Highways: Mr Stephen Young, Assistant Director Highways & Engineering, The Wellsprings, Civic Centre, Bolton BL1 1US ☎ 01204 336490 📠 01204 336709 ✉ stephen.young@bolton.gov.uk

Housing: Mr Tim Hill, Chief Planning & Housing Officer, Room 315 3rd Floor, Town Hall, Bolton BL1 1RU ☎ 01204 336004 📠 01204 336399 ✉ tim.hill@bolton.gov.uk

Legal: Ms Helen Gorman, Borough Solicitor, Town Hall, Bolton BL1 1RU ☎ 01204 331314 ✉ helen.gorman@bolton.gov.uk

Leisure and Cultural Services: Mrs Julie Spencer, Head of Libraries, Museums & Archives, 1st Floor, Le Mans Crescent, Bolton BL1 1SA ☎ 01204 332276 ✉ julie.spencer@bolton.gov.uk

Licensing: Ms Sarah Schofield, Assistant Director - Neighbourhood & Regulatory Services, 3rd Floor, Wellsprings, Civic Centre, Bolton BL1 1US ☎ 01204 336718 ✉ sarah.schofield@bolton.gov.uk

Lifelong Learning: Ms Sue Somerville, Adult Safeguard Learning Officer, Town Hall, Bolton BL1 1RU ☎ 01204 334187 ✉ sue.somerville@bolton.gov.uk

Lighting: Mr Paul Worthington, Principal Officer - Street Lighting Design, Ellesmere House, Ellesmere Street, Bolton BL3 5DT ☎ 01204 336455 ✉ paul.worthington@bolton.gov.uk

Lottery Funding, Charity and Voluntary: Mr Andrew Donaldson, Assistant Director of Policy, Partnerships & Communication, Town Hall, Bolton BL1 1RU ☎ 01204 331001 📠 01204 381942 ✉ andrew.donaldson@bolton.gov.uk

Member Services: Mr Andrew Donaldson, Assistant Director of Policy, Partnerships & Communication, Town Hall, Bolton BL1 1RU ☎ 01204 331001 📠 01204 381942 ✉ andrew.donaldson@bolton.gov.uk

Parking: Mr Ian Taylor, Head of Parking Services, Minerva House, Chorley Street, Bolton BL1 4AL ☎ 01204 336350 📠 01204 336397 ✉ ian.taylor@bolton.gov.uk

Partnerships: Mr Andrew Donaldson, Assistant Director of Policy, Partnerships & Communication, Town Hall, Bolton BL1 1RU ☎ 01204 331001 📠 01204 381942 ✉ andrew.donaldson@bolton.gov.uk

Personnel / HR: Ms Lynne Ridsdale, Assistant Director - People & Transformation, Town Hall, Bolton BL1 1RU ☎ 01204 331201 ✉ lynne.ridsdale@bolton.gov.uk

Planning: Mr Jon Berry, Strategic Development Manager, Town

Hall, Bolton BL1 1RU ☎ 01204 336042
✉ jonathan.berry@bolton.gov.uk

Planning: Mr Tim Hill, Chief Planning & Housing Officer, Town Hall, Bolton BL1 1RU ☎ 01204 336004 🖷 01204 336399
✉ tim.hill@bolton.gov.uk

Planning: Mr Brian Johnson, Development Manager - Planning, Town Hall, Bolton BL1 1RU ☎ 01204 336057
✉ brian.johnson@bolton.gov.uk

Procurement: Ms Sue Johnson, Assistant Director - Financial Services & Corporate ICT, Town Hall, Bolton BL1 1RU ☎ 01204 331504 ✉ sue.johnson@bolton.gov.uk

Public Libraries: Mrs Julie Spencer, Head of Libraries, Museums & Archives, Central Library, Le Mans Crescent, Bolton BL1 1SA ☎ 01204 332276 ✉ julie.spencer@bolton.gov.uk

Recycling & Waste Minimisation: Mr Mark Hoban, Neighbourhood Service Manager - Waste, Wellington House, Wellington Street, Bolton BL3 5DX ☎ 01204 336911 🖷 01204 336919 ✉ mark.hoban@bolton.gov.uk

Regeneration: Mr Keith Davies, Director of Development & Regeneration, 1st Floor, The Wellsprings, Civic Centre, Bolton BL1 1US ☎ 01204 334002 🖷 ; 01204 362018
✉ keith.davies@bolton.gov.uk

Road Safety: Mr John Davies, Senior Engineering Manager, 3rd Floor, Wellsprings, Civic Centre, Bolton BL1 1US ☎ 01204 336461 🖷 01204 336709 ✉ john.davies@bolton.gov.uk

Social Services: Mr John Rutherford, Director of Adult & Community Services, Le Mans Crescent, Bolton BL1 1SA ☎ 01204 337201 🖷 01204 337285
✉ john.rutherford@bolton.gov.uk

Social Services (Adult): Mr Andrew Kilpatrick, Chief Officer for Health & Social Care, Le Mans Crescent, Bolton BL1 1SA ☎ 01204 337205 🖷 01204 337288
✉ andrew.kilpatrick@bolton.gov.uk

Social Services (Adult): Mrs Ellen Miller, Assistant Director for Strategy & Commissioning, Le Mans Crescent, Bolton BL1 1SA ☎ 01204 337297 🖷 01204 337285 ✉ ellen.miller@bolton.gov.uk

Social Services (Children): Mr John Daly, Assistant Director - Staying Safe, Le Mans Crescent, Bolton BL1 1JW ☎ 01204 332130 🖷 01204 337288 ✉ john.daly@bolton.gov.uk

Staff Training: Ms Lynne Ridsdale, Assistant Director - People & Transformation, Town Hall, Bolton BL1 1RU ☎ 01204 331201
✉ lynne.ridsdale@bolton.gov.uk

Street Scene: Mr Bill Moran, Neighbourhood Services Manager, Milton House, Wellington Street, Bolton BL3 1DX ☎ 01204 336912 🖷 01204 336709 ✉ bill.moran@bolton.gov.uk

Sustainable Communities: Mr Andrew Donaldson, Assistant Director of Policy, Partnerships & Communication, Town Hall, Bolton BL1 1RU ☎ 01204 331001 🖷 01204 381942
✉ andrew.donaldson@bolton.gov.uk

Sustainable Development: Mr Simon Godley, Development Manager (Planning Strategy), 5th Floor, Town Hall, Bolton BL1 1RU ☎ 01204 336111 🖷 01204 336695
✉ simon.godley@bolton.gov.uk

Tourism: Mr Nick White, Head of Tourism, Town Hall, Bolton BL1 1RU ☎ 01204 334271 🖷 01204 336309
✉ nick.white@bolton.gov.uk

Town Centre: Ms Kathryn Carr, Head of Strategic Development, Town Hall, Bolton BL1 1RU ☎ 01204 336236 🖷 01204 336236
✉ kathryn.carr@bolton.gov.uk

Traffic Management: Mr John Davies, Senior Engineering Manager, 3rd Floor, Wellsprings, Civic Centre, Bolton BL1 1US ☎ 01204 336461 🖷 01204 336709 ✉ john.davies@bolton.gov.uk

Transport Planner: Mr John Davies, Senior Engineering Manager, 4th Floor, Wellsprings, Civic Centre, Bolton BL1 1US ☎ 01204 336461 🖷 01204 336709 ✉ john.davies@bolton.gov.uk

Waste Collection and Disposal: Mr Mark Hoban, Neighbourhood Service Manager - Waste, Wellington House, Wellington Street, Bolton BL3 5DX ☎ 01204 336911 🖷 01204 336919 ✉ mark.hoban@bolton.gov.uk

Waste Management: Mr Mark Hoban, Neighbourhood Service Manager - Waste, Wellington House, Wellington Street, Bolton BL3 5DX ☎ 01204 336911 🖷 01204 336919
✉ mark.hoban@bolton.gov.uk

MEMBERS OF THE COUNCIL (60)

***Mayor:* Harkin**, Guy (LAB - Crompton)
guy.harkin@bolton.gov.uk
***Deputy Mayor:* Spencer**, Noel (LAB - Farnworth)
noel.spencer@bolton.gov.uk
***Leader of the Council:* Morris**, Cliff (LAB - Halliwell)
cliff.morris@bolton.gov.uk
***Deputy Leader of the Council:* Thomas**, Linda (LAB - Halliwell)
linda.thomas@bolton.gov.uk
***Group Leader:* Greenhalgh**, David (CON - Bromley Cross)
david.greenhalgh@bolton.gov.uk
***Group Leader:* Hayes**, Roger (LD - Smithills)
roger.hayes@bolton.gov.uk
Adia, Ebrahim (LAB - Rumworth)
ebrahim.adia@bolton.gov.uk
Allen, Robert (CON - Heaton & Lostock)
robert.allen@bolton.gov.uk
Ashcroft, Phil (CON - Hulton)
phil.ashcroft@bolton.gov.uk
Ayub, Mohammed (LAB - Great Lever)
mohammed.ayub@bolton.gov.uk
Bashir-Ismail, Sufrana (LAB - Crompton)
sufrana.bashir-ismail@bolton.gov.uk
Burrows, Derek (LAB - Kearsley)
derek.burrows@bolton.gov.uk
Burrows, Carol (LAB - Kearsley)
carol.burrows@bolton.gov.uk
Byrne, Lynda (LAB - Breightmet)
lynda.byrne@bolton.gov.uk
Byrne, John (LAB - Breightmet)

john.bynre@bolton.gov.uk
Chadwick, David (LAB - Westhoughton South)
david.chadwick@bolton.gov.uk
Challender, Kate (LAB - Breightmet)
kate.challender@bolton.gov.uk
Clare, Margaret (LAB - Harper Green)
margaret.clare@bolton.gov.uk
Connell, Maureen (LAB - Little Lever & Darcy Lever)
maureen.connell@bolton.gov.uk
Connell, Anthony (LAB - Little Lever & Darcy Lever)
anthony.connell@bolton.gov.uk
Cox, Martin (CON - Westhoughton North & Chew Moor)
martyn.cox@bolton.gov.uk
Critchley, Norman (CON - Bromley Cross)
norman.critchley@bolton.gov.uk
Cunliffe, Ann (LAB - Horwich & Blackrod)
ann.cuncliffe@bolton.gov.uk
Darvesh, Hanif (LAB - Crompton)
hanif.darvesh@bolton.gov.uk
Dean, Mudasir (CON - Bradshaw)
mudasir.dean@bolton.gov.uk
Donaghy, Martin (LAB - Tonge with the Haulgh)
martin.donaghy@bolton.gov.uk
Evans, David (LAB - Little Lever & Darcy Lever)
david.evans@bolton.gov.uk
Fairclough, Hilary (CON - Astley Bridge)
hilary.fairclough@bolton.gov.uk
Francis, Michael (LAB - Harper Green)
michael.francis@bolton.gov.uk
Gillies, Jean (LAB - Farnworth)
jean.gillies@bolton.gov.uk
Hall, Walter (CON - Bradshaw)
walter.hall@bolton.gov.uk
Harkin, Sean (LAB - Westhoughton North & Chew Moor)
sean.harkin@bolton.gov.uk
Haslam, Stuart (CON - Bradshaw)
stuart.haslam@bolton.gov.uk
Ibrahim, Asif (LAB - Farmworth)
asif.ibrahim@bolton.gov.uk
Ibrahim, Ismail (LAB - Rumworth)
ismail.ibrahim@bolton.gov.uk
Iqbal, Mohammed (LAB - Great Lever)
mohammed.igbal@botlon.gov.uk
Irving, Liam (LAB - Kearsley)
liam.irving@bolton.gov.uk
Jones, Kevan (LAB - Westhoughton South)
kevan.jones@bolton.gov.uk
Kay, Rosa (LAB - Rumworth)
rosa.kay@bolton.gov.uk
Kell, Lindsey (LAB - Horwich and Blackrod (Two Towns))
linsey.kell@bolton.gov.uk
Kellett, Joyce (LAB - Horwich North East (Two Towns))
joyce.kellett@bolton.gov.uk
McKeon, Kevin (LAB - Horwich North East (Two Towns))
kevin.mckeon@bolton.gov.uk
Mistry, Champak (LAB - Harper Green)
champak.mistry@bolton.gov.uk
Morgan, Andrew (CON - Hulton)
andrew.morgan@bolton.gov.uk
Murray, Madeline (LAB - Great Lever)
madeline.murray@bolton.gov.uk
Peacock, Christopher (LAB - Westhoughton North & Chew Moor)
christopher.peacock@bolton.gov.uk
Peel, Nicholas (LAB - Tonge with the Haulgh)
nicholas.peel@bolton.gov.uk
Pickup, Stephen (LAB - Horwich and Blackrod (Two Towns))
stephen.pickup@bolton.gov.uk
Radlett, Anthony (LD - Smithills)
anthony.radlett@bolton.gov.uk
Rushton, Frank (CON - Heaton & Lostock)
frank.rushton@bolton.gov.uk
Shaw, Colin (CON - Heaton & Lostock)
colin.shaw@bolton.gov.uk
Sherrington, Elaine (LAB - Tonge with the Haulgh)
elaine.sherrington@bolton.gov.uk
Silvester, Richard (LAB - Horwich North East (Two Towns))
richard.silvester@bolton.gov.uk
Swarbrick, Carole (LD - Smithills)
carole.swarbrick@bolton.gov.uk
Walsh, Alan (CON - Hulton)
alan.walsh@bolton.gov.uk
Walsh, John (CON - Astley Bridge)
john.walsh@bolton.gov.uk
Watters, Anna-Marie (LAB - Westhoughton South)
anna-marie.watters@bolton.gov.uk
Wild, Paul (CON - Astley Bridge)
paul.wild@bolton.gov.uk
Wilkinson, Alan (CON - Bromley Cross)
alan.wilkinson@bolton.gov.uk
Zaman, Akhtar (LAB - Halliwell)
akhtar.zaman@bolton.gov.uk

POLITICAL COMPOSITION
LAB: 41, CON: 16, LD: 3

CABINET
Leader: Mr Cliff Morris
Deputy Leader: Mrs Linda Thomas
Adults: Mrs Maureen Connell
Cleaner, Greener, Safer: Mr Andrew Morgan
Community Safety & Police: Mr Derek Burrows
Economy, Housing & Skills: Mr John Byrne
Environment, Regulatory Services & Skills: Mr Nicholas Peel
Highways & Transport: Mr David Chadwick
Human Resources & Cohesion: Mr Ebrahim Adia
Looked After Children & Safeguarding: Ms Madeline Murray
Neighbourhood & Community Services: Mr Akhtar Zaman
Public Health: Mr Ismail Ibrahim
Schools & Early Years: Mr Kevin McKeon
Sport, Libraries, Youth & Culture: Mr Christopher Peacock
Waste & Recycling: Mrs Elaine Sherrington

COMMITTEE CHAIRS
Children's & Adult's Services Scrutiny: Mr Phil Ashcroft
Corporate Resources, Strategy & Policy Development Group: Mr Mohammed Iqbal
Economy, Housing & Skills Policy Development Group: Mr David Evans
Environmental Services Scrutiny: Cllr Norman Critchley
Health Overview & Scrutiny: Ms Joyce Kellett
Human Resources, Organisational Development & Diversity Policy Development Group: Mr Asif Ibrahim
Licensing & Environement Regulation: Mrs Rosa Kay
Neighbourhood & Community Services Policy Development Group: Mr Richard Silvester
Planning: Mr Anthony Connell

BOSTON D

Boston Borough Council, Municipal Buildings, West Street, Boston PE21 8QR ☎ 01205 314200 🖷 01205 364604 info@boston.gov.uk www.boston.gov.uk

FACTS & FIGURES

Police Authority: Lincolnshire Police Authority
Health Authority: East Midlands Strategic Health Authority
Learning and Skills Council: East Midlands
Parliamentary Constituencies: Boston and Skegness
EU Constituencies: East Midlands
Election Frequency: Elections are of whole council
Twinning: Laval (France)

PRINCIPAL OFFICERS

Chief Executive: Mr Richard Harbord, Chief Executive, Municipal Buildings, West Street, Boston PE21 8QR ☎ 01205 314200 🖷 01205 364604 richard.harbord@boston.gov.uk

Deputy Chief Executive: Mr Phil Drury, Strategic Director & Deputy Chief Executive, Municipal Buildings, West Street, Boston PE21 8QR ☎ 01205 314200 🖷 01205 364604 phil.drury@boston.gov.uk

Senior Management: Mr Robert Barlow, Deputy Chief Executive/Section 151 Officer, Municipal Buildings, West Street, Boston PE21 8QR ☎ 01205 314200; 01507 613413 🖷 01205 364604; 01507 329486 robert.barlow@boston.gov.uk

Architect, Building / Property Services: Mr Steve Lumb, Head of Planning & Strategy, Municipal Buildings, West Street, Boston PE21 8QR ☎ 01205 314200 🖷 01205 364604 steve.lumb@boston.gov.uk

Architect, Building / Property Services: Mr Gary Sargeant, Property & Technical Services Manager, Tedder Hall, Manby Park, Louth LN11 8UP ☎ 01507 613020 gary.sargeant@e-lindsey.gov.uk

Building Control: Mr Simon Sandland-Taylor, Head of Regulatory Services, Municipal Buildings, West Street, Boston PE21 8QR ☎ 01205 314200 🖷 01205 346604 simon.sandland-taylor@boston.gov.uk

PR / Communications: Mr Andrew Malkin, Communications Manager, Municipal Buildings, West Street, Boston PE21 8QR ☎ 01205 314308 🖷 01205 364604 andrew.malkin@boston.gov.uk

Community Safety: Mr Andy Fisher, Head of Housing, Property & Communities, Municipal Buildings, West Street, Boston PE21 8QR ☎ 01205 314200 🖷 01205 364604 andy.fisher@boston.gov.uk

Computer Management: Mr Peter Linfield, Head of Finance & IT, Municipal Buildings, West Street, Boston PE21 8QR ☎ 01205 314200 🖷 01205 364604 peter.linfield@boston.gov.uk

Customer Service: Ms Cherilyn Black, Head of Revenues & Benefits, Municipal Buildings, West Street, Boston PE21 8QR ☎ 01205 314200 🖷 01205 364604 cherilyn.black@boston.gov.uk

Direct Labour: Mr George Bernard, Head of Environmental Operations, Fen Road, Frampton Fen, Boston PE20 1RZ ☎ 01205 311112 george.bernard@boston.gov.uk

Economic Development: Mr Steve Lumb, Head of Planning & Strategy, Municipal Buildings, West Street, Boston PE21 8QR ☎ 01205 314200 🖷 01205 364604 steve.lumb@boston.gov.uk

E-Government: Mr Peter Linfield, Head of Finance & IT, Municipal Buildings, West Street, Boston PE21 8QR ☎ 01205 314200 🖷 01205 364604 peter.linfield@boston.gov.uk

Electoral Registration: Mrs Lorraine Bush, Democratic Services Manager, Municipal Buildings, West Street, Boston PE21 8QR ☎ 01205 314224 🖷 01205 364604 lorraine.bush@boston.gov.uk

Emergency Planning: Mr Simon Sandland-Taylor, Head of Regulatory Services, Municipal Buildings, West Street, Boston PE21 8QR ☎ 01205 314200 🖷 01205 346604 simon.sandland-taylor@boston.gov.uk

Energy Management: Mr Ian Farmer, Partnerships & Sustainability Manager, Municipal Buildings, West Street, Boston PE21 8QR ☎ 01205 314200 🖷 01205 364604 ian.farmer@boston.gov.uk

Environmental Health: Mr Simon Sandland-Taylor, Head of Regulatory Services, Municipal Buildings, West Street, Boston PE21 8QR ☎ 01205 314200 🖷 01205 346604 simon.sandland-taylor@boston.gov.uk

Estates, Property & Valuation: Mr Andy Fisher, Head of Housing, Property & Communities, Municipal Buildings, West Street, Boston PE21 8QR ☎ 01205 314200 🖷 01205 364604 andy.fisher@boston.gov.uk

Finance and Treasurer: Mr Robert Barlow, Deputy Chief Executive/Section 151 Officer, Municipal Buildings, West Street, Boston PE21 8QR ☎ 01205 314200; 01507 613413 🖷 01205 364604; 01507 329486 robert.barlow@boston.gov.uk

Grounds Maintenance: Mr George Bernard, Head of Environmental Operations, Fen Road, Frampton Fen, Boston PE20 1RZ ☎ 01205 311112 george.bernard@boston.gov.uk

Health and Safety: Ms Katharine Nundy, Head of Chief Executive's Office, Municipal Buildings, West Street, Boston PE21 8QR ☎ 01205 314274 🖷 01205 364604 katharine.nundy@boston.gov.uk

Housing: Mr Andy Fisher, Head of Housing, Property & Communities, Municipal Buildings, West Street, Boston PE21 8QR ☎ 01205 314200 🖷 01205 364604 andy.fisher@boston.gov.uk

Legal: Ms Eleanor Hoggart, Assistant Director- Legal Services Lincolnshire, Municipal Buildings, West Street, Boston PE21 8QR ☎ 01205 314200 🖷 01205 364604 eleanor.hoggart@lincolnshire.gov.uk

Leisure and Cultural Services: Mr Phil Drury, Strategic Director & Deputy Chief Executive, Municipal Buildings, West Street, Boston PE21 8QR ☎ 01205 314200 🖷 01205 364604

phil.drury@boston.gov.uk

Licensing: Ms Fiona White, Principal Licensing & Land Charges Officer, Municipal Buildings, West Street, Boston PE21 8QR ☎ 01205 314242 fiona.white@boston.gov.uk

Lottery Funding, Charity and Voluntary: Mr Andy Fisher, Head of Housing, Property & Communities, Municipal Buildings, West Street, Boston PE21 8QR ☎ 01205 314200 🖷 01205 364604 andy.fisher@boston.gov.uk

Member Services: Mrs Lorraine Bush, Democratic Services Manager, Municipal Buildings, West Street, Boston PE21 8QR ☎ 01205 314224 🖷 01205 364604 lorraine.bush@boston.gov.uk

Parking: Mr Steve Lumb, Head of Planning & Strategy, Municipal Buildings, West Street, Boston PE21 8QR ☎ 01205 314200 🖷 01205 364604 steve.lumb@boston.gov.uk

Partnerships: Mr Steve Lumb, Head of Planning & Strategy, Municipal Buildings, West Street, Boston PE21 8QR ☎ 01205 314200 🖷 01205 364604 steve.lumb@boston.gov.uk

Personnel / HR: Ms Katharine Nundy, Head of Chief Executive's Office, Municipal Buildings, West Street, Boston PE21 8QR ☎ 01205 314274 🖷 01205 364604 katharine.nundy@boston.gov.uk

Planning: Mr Steve Lumb, Head of Planning & Strategy, Municipal Buildings, West Street, Boston PE21 8QR ☎ 01205 314200 🖷 01205 364604 steve.lumb@boston.gov.uk

Procurement: Mr Peter Linfield, Head of Finance & IT, Municipal Buildings, West Street, Boston PE21 8QR ☎ 01205 314200 🖷 01205 364604 peter.linfield@boston.gov.uk

Recycling & Waste Minimisation: Mr George Bernard, Head of Environmental Operations, Fen Road, Frampton Fen, Boston PE20 1RZ ☎ 01205 311112 george.bernard@boston.gov.uk

Staff Training: Ms Katharine Nundy, Head of Chief Executive's Office, Municipal Buildings, West Street, Boston PE21 8QR ☎ 01205 314274 🖷 01205 364604 katharine.nundy@boston.gov.uk

Sustainable Communities: Mr Andy Fisher, Head of Housing, Property & Communities, Municipal Buildings, West Street, Boston PE21 8QR ☎ 01205 314200 🖷 01205 364604 andy.fisher@boston.gov.uk

Sustainable Development: Mr Steve Lumb, Head of Planning & Strategy, Municipal Buildings, West Street, Boston PE21 8QR ☎ 01205 314200 🖷 01205 364604 steve.lumb@boston.gov.uk

Tourism: Mr Phil Drury, Strategic Director & Deputy Chief Executive, Municipal Buildings, West Street, Boston PE21 8QR ☎ 01205 314200 🖷 01205 364604 phil.drury@boston.gov.uk

Town Centre: Mr Steve Lumb, Head of Planning & Strategy, Municipal Buildings, West Street, Boston PE21 8QR ☎ 01205 314200 🖷 01205 364604 steve.lumb@boston.gov.uk

Waste Collection and Disposal: Mr George Bernard, Head of Environmental Operations, Fen Road, Frampton Fen, Boston PE20 1RZ ☎ 01205 311112 george.bernard@boston.gov.uk

Waste Management: Mr George Bernard, Head of Environmental Operations, Fen Road, Frampton Fen, Boston PE20 1RZ ☎ 01205 311112 george.bernard@boston.gov.uk

MEMBERS OF THE COUNCIL (32)

***Mayor:* Brotherton**, Colin (CON - Kirton)
colin.brotherton@boston.gov.uk
***Deputy Mayor:* Lee**, Alan (IND - Kirton)
alan.lee@boston.gov.uk
***Group Leader:* Fountain**, Elliott (LD - Fenside)
elliott.fountain@boston.gov.uk
***Group Leader:* Kenny**, Paul (LAB - Skirbeck)
paul.kenny@boston.gov.uk
***Group Leader:* Staples**, Helen (IND - Fishtoft)
helen.staples@boston.gov.uk
Austin, Richard (IND - Wyberton)
richard.austin@boston.gov.uk
Austin, Alison (IND - South)
alison.austin@boston.gov.uk
Baker, Mark (CON - Pilgrim)
mark.baker@boston.gov.uk
Bedford, Peter (CON - Coastal)
peter.bedford@boston.gov.uk
Brookes, Michael (CON - Swineshead & Holland Fen)
michael.brookes@boston.gov.uk
Dennis, Maureen (CON - Old Leake & Wrangle)
maureen.dennis@boston.gov.uk
Gilbert, Mike (CON - Central)
mike.gilbert@boston.gov.uk
Gleeson, Paul (LAB - Skirbeck)
paul.gleeson@boston.gov.uk
Goodale, Paul (LAB - Staniland North)
paul.goodale@boston.gov.uk
Gunter, Yvonne (CON - Staniland South)
yvonne.gunter@boston.gov.uk
Knowles, James (CON - Wyberton)
james.knowles@boston.gov.uk
Leggott, Richard (IND - Swineshead & Holland Fen)
richard.leggott@boston.gov.uk
Mould, Paul (CON - Staniland South)
paul.mould@boston.gov.uk
Owens, David (IND - Fenside)
david.owens@boston.gov.uk
Pickett, Frank (CON - Old Leake & Wrangle)
frank.pickett@boston.gov.uk
Richmond, Derek (CON - North)
derek.richmond@boston.gov.uk
Rush, Brian (IND - Frampton & Holme)
brian.rush@boston.gov.uk
Samra, Gurdip (CON - North)
gurdip.samra@boston.gov.uk
Singleton McGuire, Raymond (CON - Costal)
raymond.singleton-mcguire@boston.gov.uk
Skinner, Judith Ann (CON - Fishtoft)
judith.skinner@boston.gov.uk
Smith, Gloria (CON - Skirbeck)
gloria.smith@boston.gov.uk
Snell, Ossy (IND - Fishtoft)
ossy.snell@boston.gov.uk
Spencer, Aaron (CON - Five Village)
aaron.spencer@boston.gov.uk

Taylor, Carol (IND - Witham)
carol.taylor@boston.gov.uk
Witts, David (IND - Five Village)
david.witts@boston.gov.uk
Woodcliffe, Stephen (CON - West)
stephen.woodcliffe@boston.gov.uk
Wright, Mary (CON - Witham)
mary.wright@boston.gov.uk

POLITICAL COMPOSITION
CON: 18, IND: 10, LAB: 3, LD: 1

CABINET
Leader: Mr Peter Bedford
Deputy Leader: Mr Michael Brookes
Deputy Leader: Mr Raymond Singleton McGuire
Building Control & Environmental Health: Mr Stephen Woodcliffe
Finance & Governance: Mr Raymond Singleton McGuire
Leisure Services, Parks & Ground Maintenance: Mrs Yvonne Gunter

COMMITTEE CHAIRS
Audit: Mr Richard Leggott
Corporate & Community Overview & Scrutiny: Mr Paul Kenny
Environment & Performance Overview & Scrutiny: Mr Brian Rush
Licensing, Regulatory & Appeals: Ms Gloria Smith
Planning: Mrs Mary Wright
Standards: Mr Dennis Bambridge (External)

BOURNEMOUTH U
Bournemouth Council, (Bournemouth Borough Counicl), Town Hall, Bourne Avenue, Bournemouth BH2 6DY ☎ 01202 451451 🖷 01202 451000 ✉ firstname.surname@bournemouth.gov.uk 💻 www.bournemouth.gov.uk

FACTS & FIGURES
Police Authority: Dorset Police Authority
Health Authority: NHS South West
Learning and Skills Council: South West
Parliamentary Constituencies: Bournemouth East, Bournemouth West
EU Constituencies: South West
Election Frequency: Elections are of whole council
Twinning: Lucerne (Switzerland); Netanya (Israel); Targu Mures (Romania)

PRINCIPAL OFFICERS
Chief Executive: Mr Tony Williams, Chief Executive, Town Hall, Bourne Avenue, Bournemouth BH2 6DY ☎ 01202 451130 🖷 01202 451000 ✉ tony.williams@bournemouth.gov.uk

Senior Management: Mr Roger Ball, Service Director - Technical Services, Town Hall Annexe, St. Stephen's Road, Bournemouth BH2 6EA ☎ 01202 451340 🖷 01202 451006 ✉ roger.ball@bournemouth.gov.uk

Senior Management: Ms Sue Bickler, Service Director - Partnership & Improvement, Town Hall, Bourne Avenue, Bournemouth BH2 6DY ☎ 01202 454966 🖷 01202 451000 ✉ sue.bickler@bournemouth.gov.uk

Senior Management: Ms Ivor Cawthorn, Service Director - Community Care, Town Hall, Bourne Avenue, Bournemouth BH2 6DY ☎ 01202 458703 🖷 01202 451000 ✉ ivor.cawthorn@bournemouth.gov.uk

Senior Management: Ms Kim Drake, Service Director - Children's Social Care, Town Hall, Bourne Avenue, Bournemouth BH2 6DY ☎ 01202 458721 🖷 01202 456105 ✉ kim.drake@bournemouth.gov.uk

Senior Management: Ms Eileen Dunnachie, Service Director - Adult & Community Support, Town Hall, Bourne Avenue, Bournemouth BH2 6DY ☎ 01202 458707 🖷 01202 451000 ✉ eileen.dunnachie@bournemouth.gov.uk

Senior Management: Ms Kay Errington, Service Director - Children's Learning & Engagement, Town Hall, Bourne Avenue, Bournemouth BH2 6DY ☎ 01202 456118 🖷 01202 456105 ✉ kay.errington@bournemouth.gov.uk

Senior Management: Ms Judith Geddes, Executive Director - Adult & Community Services, Town Hall, Bourne Avenue, Bournemouth BH2 6DY ☎ 01202 458702 🖷 01202 451000 ✉ judith.geddes@bournemouth.gov.uk

Senior Management: Mr Neil Goddard, Service Director - Children's Strategic Services, Town Hall, Bourne Avenue, Bournemouth BH2 6DY ☎ 01202 456136 🖷 01202 456105 ✉ neil.goddard@bournemouth.gov.uk

Senior Management: Mr Mike Holmes, Service Director - Planning & Transport, Town Hall Annexe, St. Stephen's Road, Bournemouth BH2 6EA ☎ 01202 451315 🖷 01202 451005 ✉ mike.holmes@bournemouth.gov.uk

Senior Management: Ms Jane Portman, Executive Director - Children & Families Services, Town Hall, Bourne Avenue, Bournemouth BH2 6DY ☎ 01202 456104 🖷 01202 451000 ✉ jane.portman@bournemouth.gov.uk

Senior Management: Ms Joy Postings, Service Director - Law & Governance, Town Hall, Bourne Avenue, Bournemouth BH2 6DY ☎ 01202 456953 🖷 01202 451000 ✉ joy.postings@bournemouth.gov.uk

Senior Management: Mr Mark Smith, Service Director - Tourism & Corporate Communications, Visitor Information Bureau, Westover Road, Bournemouth BH1 2BU ☎ 01202 451706 🖷 01202 451743 ✉ mark.smith@bournemouth.gov.uk

Senior Management: Mrs Liz Wilkinson, Executive Director for Finance & Section 151 Officer, Town Hall, Bourne Avenue, Bournemouth BH2 6DY ☎ 01202 451131 🖷 01202 451000 ✉ liz.wilkinson@bournemouth.gov.uk

Access Officer / Social Services (Disability): Ms Katie Carpenter, Access Surveyor, Town Hall Annexe, St. Stephen's Road, Bournemouth BH2 6EA ☎ 01202 454789 🖷 01202 451006 ✉ katie.carpenter@bournemouth.gov.uk

Architect, Building / Property Services: Mr Roger Ball, Service Director - Technical Services, Town Hall Annexe, St. Stephen's Road, Bournemouth BH2 6EA ☎ 01202 451340 🖷 01202 451006 ✉ roger.ball@bournemouth.gov.uk

Best Value: Ms Sue Bickler, Service Director - Information Culture & Community Learning, Town Hall, Bourne Avenue, Bournemouth BH2 6DY ☎ 01202 454966 🖷 01202 451000 ✉ sue.bickler@bournemouth.gov.uk

Catering Services: Mr Graham Waddington, Facilities Manager, Town Hall, Bournemouth BH2 6DY ☎ 01202 454884 ✉ graham.waddington@bournemouth.gov.uk

Children / Youth Services: Mr Neil Goddard, Service Director - Children's Strategic Services, Town Hall, Bourne Avenue, Bournemouth BH2 6DY ☎ 01202 456136 🖷 01202 456105 ✉ neil.goddard@bournemouth.gov.uk

Civil Registration: Ms Helen Rigg, Registration & Coroners Services Manager, Town Hall, Bourne Avenue, Bournemouth BH2 6DY ☎ 01202 454629 ✉ helen.rigg@bournemouth.gov.uk

PR / Communications: Ms Georgia Turner, Corporate Communications Manager, Town Hall, Bournemouth BH2 6DY ☎ 01202 451039 🖷 01202 451000 ✉ georgia.turner@bournemouth.gov.uk

Community Planning: Mr Lee Green, Environmental Strategy & Sustainability Manager, Town Hall, Bourne Avenue, Bournemouth BH2 6DY ☎ 01202 451144 🖷 01202 451000 ✉ lee.green@bournemouth.gov.uk

Community Safety: Ms Sue Bickler, Service Director - Information Culture & Community Learning, Town Hall, Bourne Avenue, Bournemouth BH2 6DY ☎ 01202 454966 🖷 01202 451000 ✉ sue.bickler@bournemouth.gov.uk

Community Safety: Mr Andrew Williams, Team Manager Safer & Stronger Communities, Town Hall, Bourne Avenue, Bournemouth BH2 6DY ☎ 01202 458240 🖷 01202 451000 ✉ andrew.williams@bournemouth.gov.uk

Computer Management: Mr Mark Baillie, ICT Manager, Town Hall, Bournemouth BH2 6DY ☎ 01202 451197 🖷 01202 451000 ✉ mark.baillie@bournemouth.gov.uk

Consumer Protection and Trading Standards: Mr Mike Edwards, Service Director - Environmental Health & Customer Services, Town Hall, Bourne Avenue, Bournemouth BH2 6DY ☎ 01202 451310 🖷 01202 451011 ✉ mike.edwards@bournemouth.gov.uk

Contracts: Ms Anna Bourne, Strategic Procurement Manager, Town Hall, Bourne Avenue, Bournemouth BH2 6DY ☎ 01202 458233 🖷 01202 451000 ✉ anna.bourne@bournemouth.gov.uk

Contracts: Ms Eileen Dunnachie, Service Director - Adult & Community Support, Town Hall, Bourne Avenue, Bournemouth BH2 6DY ☎ 01202 458707 🖷 01202 451000 ✉ eileen.dunnachie@bournemouth.gov.uk

Customer Service: Ms Maria O'Reilly, Strategic ICT Manager, Town Hall, Bourne Avenue, Bournemouth BH2 6DY ☎ 01202 454953 ✉ maria.o'reilly@bournemouth.gov.uk

Customer Service: Mr Stuart Walters, Customer Services Manager, Town Hall, Bourne Avenue, Bournemouth BH2 6DY ☎ 01202 454711 ✉ stuart.walters@bournemouth.gov.uk

Education: Ms Kay Errington, Service Director - Children's Learning & Engagement, Town Hall, Bourne Avenue, Bournemouth BH2 6DY ☎ 01202 456118 🖷 01202 456105 ✉ kay.errington@bournemouth.gov.uk

Education: Ms Jane Portman, Executive Director - Children & Families Services, Town Hall, Bourne Avenue, Bournemouth BH2 6DY ☎ 01202 456104 🖷 01202 451000 ✉ jane.portman@bournemouth.gov.uk

E-Government: Ms Maria O'Reilly, Strategic ICT Manager, Town Hall, Bourne Avenue, Bournemouth BH2 6DY ☎ 01202 454953 ✉ maria.o'reilly@bournemouth.gov.uk

Electoral Registration: Mr Matt Pitcher, Electoral Services Officer, Room 40, Town Hall, Bourne Avenue, Bournemouth BH2 6DY ☎ 01202 451122 🖷 01202 451003 ✉ matt.pitcher@bournemouth.gov.uk

Emergency Planning: Mr Keith Stuart, Emergency Planning Officer, Town Hall, Bourne Avenue, Bournemouth BH2 6DY ☎ 01202 451485 🖷 01202 451000 ✉ keith.stuart@bournemouth.gov.uk

Energy Management: Mr Roger Ball, Service Director - Technical Services, Town Hall Annexe, St. Stephen's Road, Bournemouth BH2 6EA ☎ 01202 451340 🖷 01202 451006 ✉ roger.ball@bournemouth.gov.uk

Environmental / Technical Services: Mr Roger Ball, Service Director - Technical Services, Town Hall Annexe, St. Stephen's Road, Bournemouth BH2 6EA ☎ 01202 451340 🖷 01202 451006 ✉ roger.ball@bournemouth.gov.uk

Environmental Health: Mr Mike Edwards, Service Director - Environmental Health & Customer Services, Town Hall, Bourne Avenue, Bournemouth BH2 6DY ☎ 01202 451310 🖷 01202 451011 ✉ mike.edwards@bournemouth.gov.uk

Estates, Property & Valuation: Mr Gary Platt, Property Services Manager, Town Hall Annexe, St. Stephen's Road, Bournemouth BH2 6EA ☎ 01202 451477 ✉ gary.platt@bournemouth.gov.uk

European Liaison: Ms Joanna Gozlan, International Officer, Town Hall Annexe, St. Stephen's Road, Bournemouth BH2 6EA ☎ 01202 454744 ✉ joanna.gozlan@bournemouth.gov.uk

Events Manager: Mr Jon Weaver, Marketing & Events Manager, Visitor Information Bureau, Westover Road, Bournemouth BH1 2BU ☎ 01202 451737 ✉ jon.weaver@bournemouth.gov.uk

Facilities: Mr Graham Waddington, Facilities Manager, Town Hall, Bournemouth BH2 6DY ☎ 01202 454884 ✉ graham.waddington@bournemouth.gov.uk

Finance and Treasurer: Mrs Liz Wilkinson, Executive Director for Finance & Section 151 Officer, Town Hall, Bourne Avenue, Bournemouth BH2 6DY ☎ 01202 451131 🖷 01202 451000 ✉ liz.wilkinson@bournemouth.gov.uk

Fleet Management: Mr Roger Ball, Service Director - Technical Services, Town Hall Annexe, St. Stephen's Road, Bournemouth BH2 6EA ☎ 01202 451340 🖷 01202 451006 ✉ roger.ball@bournemouth.gov.uk

Grounds Maintenance: Mr Michael Rowland, Green Spaces Project Officer, Queens Park Pavilion, Queens Park West Drive, Bournemouth BH8 9BY ☎ 01202 451632 ✉ michael.rowlands@bournemouth.gov.uk

Highways: Mr Ken Hobbs, Principal Traffic Engineer, Town Hall Annexe, St. Stephen's Road, Bournemouth BH2 6EA ☎ 01202 451388 🖷 01202 451005 ✉ ken.hobbs@bournemouth.gov.uk

Home Energy Conservation: Mr Mike Edwards, Service Director - Environmental Health & Customer Services, Town Hall, Bourne Avenue, Bournemouth BH2 6DY ☎ 01202 451310 🖷 01202 451011 ✉ mike.edwards@bournemouth.gov.uk

Housing: Ms Eileen Dunnachie, Service Director - Adult & Community Support, Town Hall, Bourne Avenue, Bournemouth BH2 6DY ☎ 01202 458707 🖷 01202 451000 ✉ eileen.dunnachie@bournemouth.gov.uk

Housing: Ms Lorraine Mealings, Strategic Housing Services Manager, Town Hall, Bourne Avenue, Bournemouth BH2 6DY ☎ 01202 458226 ✉ lorraine.mealings@bournemouth.gov.uk

Housing Maintenance: Mr Gary Josey, Service Director - Housing Landlord & Parks, Housing Technical Services, Unit 4, Dalling Road, Poole BH12 6DJ ☎ 01202 458301 ✉ gary.josey@bournemouth.gov.uk

Local Area Agreement: Ms Sue Bickler, Service Director - Partnership & Improvement, Town Hall, Bourne Avenue, Bournemouth BH2 6DY ☎ 01202 454966 🖷 01202 451000 ✉ sue.bickler@bournemouth.gov.uk

Legal: Ms Joy Postings, Service Director - Law & Governance, Town Hall, Bourne Avenue, Bournemouth BH2 6DY ☎ 01202 456953 🖷 01202 451000 ✉ joy.postings@bournemouth.gov.uk

Leisure and Cultural Services: Ms Judith Geddes, Executive Director - Adult & Community Services, Town Hall, Bourne Avenue, Bournemouth BH2 6DY ☎ 01202 458702 🖷 01202 451000 ✉ judith.geddes@bournemouth.gov.uk

Licensing: Mr Mike Edwards, Service Director - Environmental Health & Customer Services, Town Hall, Bourne Avenue, Bournemouth BH2 6DY ☎ 01202 451310 🖷 01202 451011 ✉ mike.edwards@bournemouth.gov.uk

Lifelong Learning: Ms Sue Bickler, Service Director - Information Culture & Community Learning, Town Hall, Bourne Avenue, Bournemouth BH2 6DY ☎ 01202 454966 🖷 01202 451000 ✉ sue.bickler@bournemouth.gov.uk

Lifelong Learning: Ms Jane Portman, Executive Director - Children & Families Services, Town Hall, Bourne Avenue, Bournemouth BH2 6DY ☎ 01202 456104 🖷 01202 451000 ✉ jane.portman@bournemouth.gov.uk

Lighting: Mr Roger Ball, Service Director - Technical Services, Technical Services, Town Hall Annexe, St Stephen's Road, Bournemouth BH2 6EA ☎ 01202 451340 🖷 01202 451006 ✉ roger.ball@bournemouth.gov.uk

Lottery Funding, Charity and Voluntary: Mr Gary Bentham, Community Liaison Officer, Town Hall, Bourne Avenue, Bournemouth BH2 6DY ☎ 01202 451165 🖷 01202 451000 ✉ gary.bentham@bournemouth.gov.uk

Member Services: Mr Kevin Neale, Democratic & Member Support Services Manager, Town Hall, Bourne Avenue, Bournemouth BH2 6DY ☎ 01202 454689 🖷 01202 454741 ✉ kevin.neale@bournemouth.gov.uk

Parking: Mr Barrie Clarke, Enforcement & Parking Manager, Enforcement and Parking Centre, 1st Floor, Parkway House, 28 Avenue Road, Bournemouth BH2 6DY ☎ 01202 451456 🖷 01202 451492 ✉ barrie.clarke@bournemouth.gov.uk

Partnerships: Ms Sue Bickler, Service Director - Information Culture & Community Learning, Town Hall, Bourne Avenue, Bournemouth BH2 6DY ☎ 01202 454966 🖷 01202 451000 ✉ sue.bickler@bournemouth.gov.uk

Personnel / HR: Mr Richard Saunders, Service Director HR & Organisational Development, Town Hall, Bournemouth BH2 6DY ☎ 01202 451129 ✉ richard.saunders@bournemouth.gov.uk

Planning: Mr Mike Holmes, Service Director - Planning & Transport, Town Hall Annexe, St. Stephen's Road, Bournemouth BH2 6EA ☎ 01202 451315 🖷 01202 451005 ✉ mike.holmes@bournemouth.gov.uk

Procurement: Ms Anna Bourne, Strategic Procurement Manager, Town Hall, Bourne Avenue, Bournemouth BH2 6DY ☎ 01202 458233 🖷 01202 451000 ✉ anna.bourne@bournemouth.gov.uk

Public Libraries: Ms Sue Bickler, Service Director - Information Culture & Community Learning, Town Hall, Bourne Avenue, Bournemouth BH2 6DY ☎ 01202 454966 🖷 01202 451000 ✉ sue.bickler@bournemouth.gov.uk

Recycling & Waste Minimisation: Mr Roger Ball, Service Director - Technical Services, Town Hall Annexe, St. Stephen's Road, Bournemouth BH2 6EA ☎ 01202 451340 🖷 01202 451006 ✉ roger.ball@bournemouth.gov.uk

Recycling & Waste Minimisation: Ms Emma Sadiwskyj-Frewer, Waste Minimisation & Recycling Manager, Southcote Road Depot, 103 Southcote Road, Bournemouth BH1 3SW ☎ 01202 451608 ✉ emma.sadiwskyj-frewer@bournemouth.gov.uk

Regeneration: Mr Phil Robinson, Policy, Conservation & Design Manager, Town Hall Annexe, St. Stephen's Road, Bournemouth BH2 6EA ☎ 01202 451320 ✉ phil.robinson@bournemouth.gov.uk

Road Safety: Mr John Satchwell, Road Safety Manager, Town Hall Annexe, St. Stephen's Road, Bournemouth BH2 6EA ☎ 01202 451461 ✉ john.satchwell@bournemouth.gov.uk

Social Services: Ms Ivor Cawthorn, Service Director - Community Care, Town Hall, Bourne Avenue, Bournemouth BH2 6DY ☎ 01202 458703 🖷 01202 451000 ✉ ivor.cawthorn@bournemouth.gov.uk

Social Services (Adult): Ms Eileen Dunnachie, Service Director - Adult & Community Support, Town Hall, Bourne Avenue, Bournemouth BH2 6DY ☎ 01202 458707 🖷 01202 451000 ✉ eileen.dunnachie@bournemouth.gov.uk

Social Services (Adult): Ms Judith Geddes, Executive Director - Adult & Community Services, Town Hall, Bourne Avenue, Bournemouth BH2 6DY ☎ 01202 458702 🖷 01202 451000 ✉ judith.geddes@bournemouth.gov.uk

Social Services (Children): Ms Kim Drake, Service Director - Children's Social Care, Town Hall, Bourne Avenue, Bournemouth BH2 6DY ☎ 01202 458721 🖷 01202 456105 ✉ kim.drake@bournemouth.gov.uk

Social Services (Children): Ms Jane Portman, Executive Director - Children & Families Services, Town Hall, Bourne Avenue, Bournemouth BH2 6DY ☎ 01202 456104 🖷 01202 451000 ✉ jane.portman@bournemouth.gov.uk

Staff Training: Mr Richard Saunders, Service Director HR & Organisational Development, Town Hall, Bournemouth BH2 6DY ☎ 01202 451129 ✉ richard.saunders@bournemouth.gov.uk

Street Scene: Mr Larry Austin, Street Services Manager, Southcote Road Depot, 103 Southcote Road, Bournemouth BH1 3SW ☎ 01202 451690 ✉ larry.austin@bournemouth.gov.uk

Sustainable Communities: Ms Eileen Dunnachie, Service Director - Adult & Community Support, Town Hall, Bourne Avenue, Bournemouth BH2 6DY ☎ 01202 458707 🖷 01202 451000 ✉ eileen.dunnachie@bournemouth.gov.uk

Sustainable Development: Mr Tony Williams, Chief Executive, Town Hall, Bourne Avenue, Bournemouth BH2 6DY ☎ 01202 451130 🖷 01202 451000 ✉ tony.williams@bournemouth.gov.uk

Tourism: Mr Mark Smith, Service Director - Tourism & Corporate Communications, Visitor Information Bureau, Westover Road, Bournemouth BH1 2BU ☎ 01202 451706 🖷 01202 451743 ✉ mark.smith@bournemouth.gov.uk

Town Centre: Mr Roger Parker, Town Centre Manager, Visitor Information Bureau, Westover Road, Bournemouth BH1 2BU ☎ 01202 454807 ✉ roger.parker@bournemouth.gov.uk

Traffic Management: Mr Ken Hobbs, Principal Traffic Engineer, Town Hall Annexe, St. Stephen's Road, Bournemouth BH2 6EA ☎ 01202 451388 🖷 01202 451005 ✉ ken.hobbs@bournemouth.gov.uk

Transport: Mr Mike Holmes, Service Director - Planning & Transport, Town Hall Annexe, St. Stephen's Road, Bournemouth BH2 6EA ☎ 01202 451315 🖷 01202 451005 ✉ mike.holmes@bournemouth.gov.uk

Total Place: Ms Judith Geddes, Executive Director - Adult & Community Services, Town Hall, Bourne Avenue, Bournemouth BH2 6DY ☎ 01202 458702 🖷 01202 451000 ✉ judith.geddes@bournemouth.gov.uk

Waste Collection and Disposal: Mr Reg Hutton, Head of Cleansing & Waste Operations, Technical Services Division, Southcote Road Depot, Southcote Road, Bournemouth BH1 3SW ☎ 01202 451643 🖷 01202 451084 ✉ reg.hutton@bournemouth.gov.uk

Waste Management: Mr Roger Ball, Service Director - Technical Services, Town Hall Annexe, St. Stephen's Road, Bournemouth BH2 6EA ☎ 01202 451340 🖷 01202 451006 ✉ roger.ball@bournemouth.gov.uk

MEMBERS OF THE COUNCIL (54)

***Mayor:* Stanley-Watts**, Philip (CON - Boscombe West)
philip.stanley-watts@bournemouth.gov.uk

***Deputy Mayor:* Rochester**, Christopher (CON - Boscombe East)
christopher.rochester@bournemouth.gov.uk

***Group Leader:* Ainge**, Carol (LD - Queens Park)
carol.ainge@bournemouth.gov.uk

Adams, John (CON - Strouden Park)
john.adams@bournemouth.gov.uk

Anderson, Mark (CON - Queens Park)
mark.anderson@bournemouth.gov.uk

Anderson, Sue (CON - Moordown)
sue.anderson@bournemouth.gov.uk

Angiolini, Amedeo (CON - Kinson North)
amedeo.angiolini@bournemouth.gov.uk

Bailey, Linda (CON - Boscombe East)
linda.bailey@bournemouth.gov.uk

Battistini, Mark (CON - Kinson North)
mark.battistini@bournemouth.gov.uk

Baxter, Beryl (LAB - Kinson South)
beryl.baxter@bournemouth.gov.uk

Beesley, John (CON - Westbourne & West Cliff)
john.beesley@bournemouth.gov.uk

Borthwick, Derek (CON - Throop & Muscliff)
derek.borthwich@bournemouth.gov.uk

Chapman, Robert (CON - Central)
robert.chapman@bournemouth.gov.uk

Chappell, Stephen (CON - Talbot & Branksome Woods)
stephen.chappell@bournemouth.gov.uk

Coope, Eddie (CON - East Southbourne & Tuckton)
eddie.coope@bournemouth.gov.uk

Cooper, Rod (CON - Wallisdown & Winton West)
rod.cooper@bournemouth.gov.uk

Crawford, Blair (CON - West Southbourne)
blair.crawford@bouremouth.gov.uk

Davie, Anniina (CON - Winton East)
anniina.davie@bournemouth.gov.uk

Davies, Malcolm (CON - East Southbourne & Tuckton)
malcolm.davies@bournemouth.gov.uk

D'Orton-Gibson, David (CON - Redhill & Northbourne)
david.dorton-gibson@bournemouth.gov.uk

Dunlop, Beverley (CON - Moordown)
beverley.dunlop@bournemouth.gov.uk

Edward, Johann (CON - Winton East)
johann.edward@bournemouth.gov.uk

Filer, Michael (CON - East Cliff & Springbourne)
michael.filer@bournemouth.gov.uk
Filer, Anne (CON - East Cliff & Springbourne)
anne.filer@bournemouth.gov.uk
Goldbart, Barry (CON - Westbourne & West Cliff)
barry.goldbart@bournemouth.gov.uk
Greene, Mike (CON - Central)
mike.greene@bournemouth.gov.uk
Greene, Nicola (CON - Wallisdown & Winton West)
nicola.greene@bournemouth.gov.uk
Gritt, Dennis (LAB - Kinson North)
dennis.gritt@bournemouth.gov.uk
Grower, Ben (LAB - Kinson South)
ben.grower@bournemouth.gov.uk
Johnson, Cheryl (CON - Queens Park)
cheryl.johnson@bournemouth.gov.uk
Kelly, Jane (CON - Boscombe West)
jane.kelly@bournemouth.gov.uk
Kelsey, David (CON - East Cliff & Springbourne)
david.kelsey@bournemouth.gov.uk
King, Nicholas (CON - Littledown & Ilford)
nick.king@bournemouth.gov.uk
Lancashire, Ian (CON - Moordown)
ian.lancashire@bournemouth.gov.uk
Lawton, Robert (CON - East Southbourne & Tuckton)
Levell, Susan (IND - Redhill & Northbourne)
susan.levell@bournemouth.gov.uk
Marley, Roger (CON - Kinson South)
roger.marley@bournemouth.gov.uk
Mayne, Chris (CON - West Southbourne)
chris.mayne@bournemouth.gov.uk
Montrose, Jane (CON - Littledown & Iford)
jane.montrose@bournemouth.gov.uk
Morgan, Andrew (CON - Talbot & Branksome Woods)
andrew.morgan@bournemouth.gov.uk
Phillips, Susan (CON - Wallisdown & Winton West)
susan.phillips@bournemouth.gov.uk
Price, Lynda (CON - Talbot & Branksome Woods)
lynda.price@bournemouth.gov.uk
Rey, Anne (IND - Throop & Muscliff)
anne.rey@bournemouth.gov.uk
Russell, Allister (CON - West Southbourne)
allister.russell@bournemouth.gov.uk
Smith, David (CON - Central)
david.smith@bournemouth.gov.uk
Stollard, Rae (CON - Westbourne & West Cliff)
rae.stollard@bournemouth.gov.uk
Stratton, Theo (CON - Winton East)
theo.stratton@bournemouth.gov.uk
Trickett, John (CON - Strouden Park)
john.trickett@bournemouth.gov.uk
Wakefield, Christopher (CON - Boscombe West)
christopher.wakefield@bournemouth.gov.uk
Weinhonig, Michael (CON - Strouden Park)
michael.weinhonig@bournemouth.gov.uk
West, Roger (LD - Redhill & Northbourne)
roger.west@bournemouth.gov.uk
Whittaker, Ronald (IND - Throop & Muscliff)
ronald.whittaker@bournemouth.gov.uk
Williams, Lawrence (CON - Littledown & Iford)
lawrence.williams@bournemouth.gov.uk
Wilson, John
(CON - Boscombe East)
john.wilson@bournemouth.gov.uk

POLITICAL COMPOSITION

CON: 46, IND: 3, LAB: 3, LD: 2

CABINET

Leader: Mr John Beesley
Deputy Leader: Mrs Nicola Greene
Adult Social Care: Mr Blair Crawford
Corporate Efficiency: Mrs Anne Filer
Corporate Policy Implementation: Mr Lawrence Williams
Education & Children's Services: Mrs Nicola Greene
Housing: Mr Robert Lawton
Partnerships & Regeneration: Ms Jane Kelly
Planning & Environment: Mr David Smith

COMMITTEE CHAIRS

Administration & Resources: Mr Mike Greene
Adult & Community: Mr Michael Weinhonig
Appeals: Mrs Jane Montrose
Audit & Governance: Mr Ben Grower
Children's Services: Mr Eddie Coope
Economy & Tourism: Mr Robert Chapman
Environment & Transport: Mr Mark Anderson
Health: Mr John Trickett
Licensing: Mr Andrew Morgan
Management Panel: Mr Nicholas King
Planning: Mr David Kelsey

BRACKNELL FOREST U

Bracknell Forest Borough Council, Easthampstead House, Town Square, Bracknell RG12 1AQ ☎ 01344 352000 🖷 01344 411875
💻 www.bracknell-forest.gov.uk

FACTS & FIGURES

Police Authority: Thames Valley Police Authority
Health Authority: South Central Strategic Health Authority
Learning and Skills Council: South East
Parliamentary Constituencies: Bracknell
EU Constituencies: South East
Election Frequency: Elections are of whole council
Twinning: Bracknell Town Council: Leverkusen (Germany)

PRINCIPAL OFFICERS

Chief Executive: Mr Timothy Wheadon, Chief Executive, Easthampstead House, Town Square, Bracknell RG12 1AQ ☎ 01344 352000 🖷 01344 352111
✉ timothy.wheadon@bracknell-forest.gov.uk

Deputy Chief Executive: Mrs Alison Sanders, Director - Corporate Services, Civic Offices, Easthampstead House, Town Square, Bracknell RG12 1AQ ☎ 01344 352000
✉ alison.sanders@bracknell-forest.gov.uk

Assistant Chief Executive: Mr Victor Nicholls, Assistant Chief Executive, Easthampstead House, Town Square, Bracknell RG12 1AQ ☎ 01344 352000 ✉ victor.nicholls@bracknell-forest.gov.uk

Senior Management: Dr Janette Karklins, Director - Children, Young People & Learning, Seymour House, 38 Broadway, Bracknell RG12 1AU ☎ 01344 352000
✉ janette.karklins@bracknell-forest.gov.uk

LOCAL AUTHORITIES

Senior Management: Mr Vincent Paliczka, Director - Environment, Culture & Communities, Time Square, 4th Floor Time Square South, Market Street, Bracknell RG12 1AU ☎ 01344 352000 ✉ vincent.paliczka@bracknell-forest.gov.uk

Senior Management: Mrs Alison Sanders, Director - Corporate Services, Easthampstead House, Town Square, Bracknell RG12 1AQ ☎ 01344 352000 ✉ alison.sanders@bracknell-forest.gov.uk

Access Officer / Social Services (Disability): Mrs Ann Groves, Urban Design Officer, Time Square, Market Street, Bracknell RG12 1JD ☎ 01344 352000 ✉ ann.groves@bracknell-forest.gov.uk

Architect, Building / Property Services: Mr Barry Francis, Chief Officer - Property, Easthampstead House, Town Square, Bracknell RG12 1AQ ☎ 01344 352000 🖷 01344 351260 ✉ barry.francis@bracknell-forest.gov.uk

Best Value: Mr Richard Beaumont, Head - Overview & Scrutiny, Easthampstead House, Town Square, Bracknell RG12 1AQ ☎ 01344 352000 ✉ richard.beaumont@bracknell-forest.gov.uk

Building Control: Mr David Constable, Senior Building Control Surveyor, Time Square, Market Street, Bracknell RG12 1JD ☎ 01344 352000 ✉ david.constable@bracknell-forest.gov.uk

Catering Services: Mr David Eagle, Contracts Monitoring Officer, Seymour House, 38 Broadway, Town Square, Bracknell RG12 1AU ☎ 01344 352000 ✉ david.eagle@bracknell-forest.gov.uk

Children / Youth Services: Mrs Lorna Hunt, Chief Officer - Children's Social Care, Time Square, Market Street, Bracknell RG12 1JD ☎ 01344 352000 ✉ lorna.hunt@bracknell-forest.gov.uk

Children / Youth Services: Dr Janette Karklins, Director - Children, Young People & Learning, Seymour House, 38 Broadway, Bracknell RG12 1AU ☎ 01344 352000 ✉ janette.karklins@bracknell-forest.gov.uk

Civil Registration: Mrs Ann Moore, Head - Democratic & Registration Services, Corporate Services, Easthampstead House, Town Square, Bracknell RG12 1AQ ☎ 01344 352000 ✉ ann.moore@bracknell-forest.gov.uk

PR / Communications: Mrs Gemma Morgan, Head - Communications & Marketing, Easthampstead House, Town Square, Bracknell RG12 1AQ ☎ 01344 352000 🖷 01344 352136 ✉ gemma.morgan@bracknell-forest.gov.uk

Community Planning: Mr Victor Nicholls, Assistant Chief Executive, Easthampstead House, Town Square, Bracknell RG12 1AQ ☎ 01344 352000 ✉ victor.nicholls@bracknell-forest.gov.uk

Community Safety: Mr Ian Boswell, Safer Communities Manager, Easthampstead House, Town Square, Bracknell RG12 1AQ ☎ 01344 352000 🖷 01344 351596 ✉ ian.boswell@bracknell-forest.gov.uk

Computer Management: Mr Pat Keane, Chief Officer - Information Services, Time Square, Market Street, Bracknell RG12 1JD ☎ 01344 352000 🖷 01344 352277 ✉ pat.keane@bracknell-forest.gov.uk

Consumer Protection and Trading Standards: Mr Robert Sexton, Trading Standards & Services Manager, Time Square, Market Street, Bracknell RG12 1JD ☎ 01344 352000 🖷 01344 353122 ✉ robert.sexton@bracknell-forest.gov.uk

Contracts: Mr Timothy Wheadon, Chief Executive, Easthampstead House, Town Square, Bracknell RG12 1AQ ☎ 01344 352000 🖷 01344 352111 ✉ timothy.wheadon@bracknell-forest.gov.uk

Corporate Services: Mrs Alison Sanders, Director - Corporate Services, Easthampstead House, Town Square, Bracknell RG12 1AQ ☎ 01344 352000 ✉ alison.sanders@bracknell-forest.gov.uk

Customer Service: Mrs Bobby Mulheir, Chief Officer - Customer Services, Easthampstead House, Town Square, Bracknell RG12 1AQ ☎ 01344 352000 ✉ bobby.mulheir@bracknell-forest.gov.uk

Economic Development: Mrs Jayne Mills, Economic Development Officer, Easthampstead House, Town Square, Bracknell RG12 1AQ ☎ 01344 352000 ✉ jayne.mills@bracknell-forest.gov.uk

Education: Dr Janette Karklins, Director - Children, Young People & Learning, Seymour House, 38 Broadway, Bracknell RG12 1AU ☎ 01344 352000 ✉ janette.karklins@bracknell-forest.gov.uk

E-Government: Mr Pat Keane, Chief Officer - Information Services, Time Square, Market Street, Bracknell RG12 1JD ☎ 01344 352000 🖷 01344 352277 ✉ pat.keane@bracknell-forest.gov.uk

Electoral Registration: Mrs Daphne Gray, Registration Services Manager, Easthampstead House, Town Square, Bracknell RG12 1AQ ☎ 01344 352000 ✉ daphne.gray@bracknell-forest.gov.uk

Emergency Planning: Mrs Louise Osborn, Emergency Planning Officer, The Central Depot, Old Bracknell Lane West, Bracknell Forest Borough Council, Bracknell RG12 7QT ☎ 01344 352000 ✉ louise.osborn@bracknell-forest.gov.uk

Energy Management: Mr Steven Milne, Energy Manager, Time Square, Market Street, Bracknell RG12 1JD ☎ 01344 352000 ✉ steven.milne@bracknell-forest.gov.uk

Environmental / Technical Services: Mr Vincent Paliczka, Director - Environment, Culture & Communities, Time Square, Market Street, Bracknell RG12 1JD ☎ 01344 352000 ✉ vincent.paliczka@bracknell-forest.gov.uk

Environmental Health: Mr Steve Loudoun, Chief Officer - Environment & Public Protection, Time Square, Market Street, Bracknell RG12 1JD ☎ 01344 352000 🖷 01344 353122 ✉ steve.loudoun@bracknell-forest.gov.uk

Estates, Property & Valuation: Mr Barry Francis, Chief Officer - Property, Easthampstead House, Town Square, Bracknell RG12 1AQ ☎ 01344 352000 🖷 01344 351260 ✉ barry.francis@bracknell-forest.gov.uk

Facilities: Mr David Elmes, Civic Facilities Manager, Easthampstead House, Town Square, Bracknell RG12 1AQ ☎ 01344 352000 ✉ david.elmes@bracknell-forest.gov.uk

Finance and Treasurer: Mr Alan Nash, Borough Treasurer, Easthampstead House, Town Square, Bracknell RG12 1AQ ☎ 01344 352000 🖷 01344352255 ✉ alan.nash@bracknell-forest.gov.uk

Fleet Management: Mr Damian James, Head - Transport Provision, The Central Depot, Old Bracknell Lane West, Bracknell Forest Borough Council, Bracknell RG12 7QT ✉ damian.james@bracknell-forest.gov.uk

Health and Safety: Mr Andy Anderson, Senior Health & Safety Advisor, Easthampstead House, Town Square, Bracknell RG12 1AQ ☎ 01344 352000 🖷 01344 353122 ✉ andy.anderson@bracknell-forest.gov.uk

Highways: Mr Steve Loudoun, Chief Officer - Environment & Public Protection, Time Square, Market Street, Bracknell RG12 1JD ☎ 01344 352000 🖷 01344 353122 ✉ steve.loudoun@bracknell-forest.gov.uk

Home Energy Conservation: Mrs Hazel Hill, Sustainable Energy Officer, Time Square, Market Street, Bracknell RG12 1JD ☎ 01344 352000 ✉ hazel.hill@bracknell-forest.gov.uk

Housing: Mr Simon Hendey, Chief Officer - Housing, Time Square, Market Street, Bracknell RG12 1JD ☎ 01344 352000 ✉ simon.hendey@bracknell-forest.gov.uk

Local Area Agreement: Mr Victor Nicholls, Assistant Chief Executive, Easthampstead House, Town Square, Bracknell RG12 1AQ ☎ 01344 352000 ✉ victor.nicholls@bracknell-forest.gov.uk

Legal: Mr Alex Jack, Borough Solicitor, Easthampstead House, Town Square, Bracknell RG12 1AQ ☎ 01344 352000 🖷 01344 352236 ✉ alex.jack@bracknell-forest.gov.uk

Leisure and Cultural Services: Mr Vincent Paliczka, Director - Environment, Culture & Communities, Time Square, Market Street, Bracknell RG12 1JD ☎ 01344 352000 ✉ vincent.paliczka@bracknell-forest.gov.uk

Licensing: Ms Laura Driscoll, Licensing Team Leader, Easthampstead House, Town Square, Bracknell RG12 1AQ ☎ 01344 352517 ✉ laura.driscoll@bracknell-forest.gov.uk

Lifelong Learning: Mrs Amanda Waters, Grow Our Own Project Manager, Seymour House, 38 Broadway, Bracknell RG12 1AU ☎ 01344 352000 ✉ amanda.waters@bracknell-forest.gov.uk

Lighting: Mr Steve Loudoun, Chief Officer - Environment & Public Protection, Time Square, Market Street, Bracknell RG12 1JD ☎ 01344 352000 🖷 01344 353122 ✉ steve.loudoun@bracknell-forest.gov.uk

Lottery Funding, Charity and Voluntary: Mr Victor Nicholls, Assistant Chief Executive, Easthampstead House, Town Square, Bracknell RG12 1AQ ☎ 01344 352000 ✉ victor.nicholls@bracknell-forest.gov.uk

Member Services: Mrs Kirsty Hunt, Senior Democratic Services Officer, Easthampstead House, Town Square, Bracknell RG12 1AQ ☎ 01344 352000 ✉ kirsty.hunt@bracknell-forest.gov.uk

Parking: Mr Roger Cook, Transport Development Manager, Time Square, Market Street, Bracknell RG12 1JD ☎ 01344 352000 ✉ roger.cook@bracknell-forest.gov.uk

Partnerships: Mrs Genny Webb, Head - Performance & Partnerships, Easthampstead House, Town Square, Bracknell RG12 1AQ ☎ 01344 352000 ✉ genny.webb@bracknell-forest.gov.uk

Personnel / HR: Mr Tony Madden, Chief Officer - Human Resources, Easthampstead House, Town Square, Bracknell RG12 1AQ ☎ 01344 352000 🖷 01344 352029 ✉ tony.madden@bracknell-forest.gov.uk

Planning: Mr Vincent Haines, Head - Planning & Building Control, Time Square, Market Street, Bracknell RG12 1JD ☎ 01344 352000 ✉ vincent.haines@bracknell-forest.gov.uk

Procurement: Mr Rob Atkins, Head - Procurement, Easthampstead House, Town Square, Bracknell RG12 1AQ ☎ 01344 352000 ✉ rob.atkins@bracknell-forest.gov.uk

Public Libraries: Ms Ruth Burgess, Head - Libraries, Time Square, Market Street, Bracknell RG12 1JD ☎ 01344 352000 🖷 01344 354100 ✉ ruth.burgess@bracknell-forest.gov.uk

Recycling & Waste Minimisation: Mrs Janet Dowlman, Waste & Recycling Manager, Time Square, Market Street, Bracknell RG12 1JD ☎ 01344 352000 🖷 01344 353122 ✉ janet.dowlman@bracknell-forest.gov.uk

Road Safety: Mr Roger Cook, Transport Development Manager, Time Square, Market Street, Bracknell RG12 1JD ☎ 01344 352000 ✉ roger.cook@bracknell-forest.gov.uk

Social Services: Mr Glyn Jones, Director - Adult Social Care, Health & Housing, Time Square, Market Street, Bracknell RG12 1JD ☎ 01344 352000 🖷 01344 351441 ✉ glyn.jones@bracknell-forest.gov.uk

Social Services (Adult): Mr Glyn Jones, Director - Adult Social Care, Health & Housing, Time Square, Market Street, Bracknell RG12 1JD ☎ 01344 352000 🖷 01344 351441 ✉ glyn.jones@bracknell-forest.gov.uk

Social Services (Children): Mrs Lorna Hunt, Chief Officer - Children's Social Care, Time Square, Market Street, Bracknell RG12 1JD ☎ 01344 352000 ✉ lorna.hunt@bracknell-forest.gov.uk

Staff Training: Mr Tony Madden, Chief Officer - Human Resources, Easthampstead House, Town Square, Bracknell RG12 1AQ ☎ 01344 352000 🖷 01344 352029 ✉ tony.madden@bracknell-forest.gov.uk

Street Scene: Mr Steve Loudoun, Chief Officer - Environment & Public Protection, Time Square, Market Street, Bracknell RG12 1JD ☎ 01344 352000 🖷 01344 353122 ✉ steve.loudoun@bracknell-forest.gov.uk

Sustainable Communities: Mr Simon Hendey, Chief Officer -

Housing, Time Square, Market Street, Bracknell RG12 1JD
☎ 01344 352000 ✉ simon.hendey@bracknell-forest.gov.uk

Tourism: Mr Vincent Paliczka, Director - Environment, Culture & Communities, Time Square, Market Street, Bracknell RG12 1JD
☎ 01344 352000 ✉ vincent.paliczka@bracknell-forest.gov.uk

Traffic Management: Mr Roger Cook, Transport Development Manager, Time Square, Market Street, Bracknell RG12 1JD
☎ 01344 352000 ✉ roger.cook@bracknell-forest.gov.uk

Transport: Mr Roger Cook, Transport Development Manager, Time Square, Market Street, Bracknell RG12 1JD ☎ 01344 352000
✉ roger.cook@bracknell-forest.gov.uk

Waste Collection and Disposal: Mrs Janet Dowlman, Waste & Recycling Manager, Time Square, Market Street, Bracknell RG12 1JD ☎ 01344 352000 🖷 01344 353122
✉ janet.dowlman@bracknell-forest.gov.uk

Waste Collection and Disposal: Mr Vincent Paliczka, Director - Environment, Culture & Communities, Time Square, Market Street, Bracknell RG12 1JD ☎ 01344 352000
✉ vincent.paliczka@bracknell-forest.gov.uk

Waste Management: Mr Vincent Paliczka, Director - Environment, Culture & Communities, Time Square, Market Street, Bracknell RG12 1JD ☎ 01344 352000
✉ vincent.paliczka@bracknell-forest.gov.uk

MEMBERS OF THE COUNCIL (42)

***Mayor:* McCracken**, Jennifer (CON - Great Hollands South)
jennie.mccracken@bracknell-forest.gov.uk
***Deputy Mayor:* Angell**, Jan (CON - Great Hollands South)
jan.angell@bracknell-forest.gov.uk
Allen, Nick (CON - College Town)
nick.allen@bracknell-forest.gov.uk
Angell, Bob (CON - Bullbrook)
robert.angell@bracknell-forest.gov.uk
Baily, Chas (CON - Hanworth)
chas.baily@bracknell-forest.gov.uk
Ballin, Mary (CON - Winkfield & Cranbourne)
mary.ballin@bracknell-forest.gov.uk
Barnard, Gareth (CON - Warfield Harvest Ride)
gareth.barnard@bracknell-forest.gov.uk
Barnard, Emma (CON - Wildridings & Central)
emma.barnard@bracknell-forest.gov.uk
Bettison, Paul (CON - Little Sandhurst)
paul.bettison@bracknell-forest.gov.uk
Birch, Gill (CON - Hanworth)
gill.birch@bracknell-forest.gov.uk
Birch, Dale (CON - Little Sandhurst)
dale.birch@bracknell-forest.gov.uk
Blatchford, Andy (CON - College Town)
andy.blatchford@bracknell-forest.gov.uk
Brossard, Michael (CON - Central Sandhurst)
michael.brossard@bracknell-forest.gov.uk
Brown, Tricia (LAB - Priestwood & Garth)
patricia.brown@bracknell-forest.gov.uk
Brunel-Walker, Marc (CON - Crown Wood)
marc.brunel-walker@bracknell-forest.gov.uk
Davison, Will (CON - Hanworth)
will.davison@bracknell-forest.gov.uk
Dudley, Colin (CON - Crown Wood)
colin.dudley@bracknell-forest.gov.uk
Finch, Alvin (CON - Priestwood & Garth)
alvin.finch@bracknell-forest.gov.uk
Finnie, Jim (CON - Crowthorne)
jim.finnie@bracknell-forest.gov.uk
Gbadebo, Michael (CON - Great Hollands North)
michael.gbadebo@bracknell-forest.gov.uk
Harrison, John (CON - Binfield with Warfield)
john.harrison@bracknell-forest.gov.uk
Hayes, Suki (CON - Crown Wood)
suki.hayes@bracknell-forest.gov.uk
Hayes, Dorothy (CON - Ascot)
dorothy.hayes@bracknell-forest.gov.uk
Heydon, Peter (CON - Old Bracknell)
peter.heydon@bracknell-forest.gov.uk
Kendall, Alan (CON - Winkfield & Cranbourne)
alan.kendall@bracknell-forest.gov.uk
Kensall, Trevor (CON - Harmans Water)
trevor.kensall@bracknell-forest.gov.uk
Leake, Ian (CON - Binfield with Warfield)
ian.leake@bracknell-forest.gov.uk
McCracken, Iain (CON - Old Bracknell)
iain.mccracken@bracknell-forest.gov.uk
McLean, Robert (CON - Warfield Harvest Ride)
robert.mclean@bracknell-forest.gov.uk
Miller, Kirsten (CON - Priestwood & Garth)
kirsten.miller@bracknell-forest.gov.uk
Pile, Shelagh (IND - Harmans Water)
shelagh.pile@bracknell-forest.gov.uk
Porter, John (CON - Owlsmoor)
john.porter@bracknell-forest.gov.uk
Sargeant, Michael (IND - Bullbrook)
michael.sargeant@bracknell-forest.gov.uk
Temperton, Mary (LAB - Great Hollands North)
mary.temperton@bracknell-forest.gov.uk
Thompson, Clifton (CON - Warfield Harvest Ride)
cliff.thompson@bracknell-forest.gov.uk
Turrell, Chris (CON - Harmans Water)
chris.turrell@bracknell-forest.gov.uk
Virgo, Tony (CON - Ascot)
tony.virgo@bracknell-forest.gov.uk
Wade, Bob (CON - Crowthorne)
bob.wade@bracknell-forest.gov.uk
Ward, Alan (CON - Central Sandhurst)
alan.ward@bracknell-forest.gov.uk
Whitbread, Denise (CON - Wildridings & Central)
Wilson, Brenda (CON - Binfield with Warfield)
brenda.wilson@bracknell-forest.gov.uk
Worrall, David (CON - Owlsmoor)
david.worrall@bracknell-forest.gov.uk

POLITICAL COMPOSITION

CON: 38, IND: 2, LAB: 2

CABINET

Leader: Mr Paul Bettison
Deputy Leader: Mr Dale Birch
Adult Services, Health & Housing: Mr Dale Birch
Children, Young People & Learning: Mr Gareth Barnard
Culture, Corporate Services & Public Protection: Mr Iain McCracken
Council Strategy & Community Cohesion: Mr Paul Bettison
Economic Development & Regeneration: Mr Marc Brunel-

Walker
Environment: Mrs Dorothy Hayes
Planning & Transport: Mrs Mary Ballin
Transformation & Finance: Mr Alan Ward

COMMITTEE CHAIRS

Access Advisory Panel: Mr Clifton Thompson
Adult Social Care & Housing Overview & Scrutiny: Mr Chris Turrell
Appeals: Mr Jim Finnie
Children & Young Peoples' Partnership: Mr Gareth Barnard
Education Governor Appointments: Mr Gareth Barnard
Employement: Mr Robert McLean
Environment, Culture & Communities Overview & Scrutiny: Mr Jim Finnie
Governance & Audit: Mr Alan Ward
Health Overview & Scrutiny: Mr Tony Virgo
Licensing & Safety: Mr Clifton Thompson
Overview & Scrutiny: Mr Ian Leake
Planning: Mr Colin Dudley
School & Children's Centre Performance: Mr Gareth Barnard
Town Centre Regeneration: Mr Marc Brunel-Walker

BRADFORD CITY M

Bradford City Council, City Hall, Channing Way, Bradford BD1 1HY ☎ 01274 431000 🖳 www.bradford.gov.uk

FACTS & FIGURES

Police Authority: West Yorkshire Police Authority
Health Authority: NHS Yorkshire & the Humber
Learning and Skills Council: Yorkshire and the Humber
Parliamentary Constituencies: Bradford East, Bradford South, Bradford West, Keighley, Shipley
EU Constituencies: Yorkshire and the Humber
Election Frequency: Elections are by thirds
Twinning: Galway (Republic of Ireland); Ilkley: Coutances (France); Keighley: Poix-du-Nord (France); Mirpur (Azad Kashmir); Monchengladbach (Germany); Roubaix (France); Shipley: Hamm (Germany); Skopje (Macedonia); Verviers (Belgium); Wilsden: Eppeville (France)

PRINCIPAL OFFICERS

Chief Executive: Mr Tony Reeves, Chief Executive, City Hall, Channing Way, Bradford BD1 1HY ☎ 01274 432001 🖷 01274 392718 ✉ tony.reeves@bradford.gov.uk

Senior Management: Ms Mary Weastell, Strategic Director - Business Support, City Hall, Channing Way, Bradford BD1 1HY ☎ 01274 434330 ✉ mary.weastell@bradford.gov.uk

Building Control: Mr Chris Eaton, Head - Building Control, City Hall, Channing Way, Bradford BD1 1HY ☎ 01274 433777 ✉ chris.eaton@bradford.gov.uk

Civil Registration: Ms Christina Smith, Superintendent Registrar, City Hall, Channing Way, Bradford BD1 1HY ☎ 01274 432151 ✉ christina.smith@bradford.gov.uk

PR / Communications: Ms Alison Milner, Assistant Director - Communications, City Hall, Channing Way, Bradford BD1 1HY ☎ 01274 432131 🖷 01274 432321 ✉ alison.milner@bradford.gov.uk

Computer Management: Mr James Drury, Assistant Director Council Change Program, City Hall, Channing Way, Bradford BD1 1HY ☎ 01274 432850 ✉ james.drury@bradford.gov.uk

Corporate Services: Ms Becky Hellard, Strategic Director - Finance, City Hall, Channing Way, Bradford BD1 1HY ☎ 01274 431000 🖷 01274 730337 ✉ becky.hellard@bradford.gov.uk

Customer Service: Ms Gail Burston, Strategic Manager - Customer Contact, Britannia House, Bradford BD1 1HX ☎ 01274 432839 ✉ gail.burston@bradford.gov.uk

Economic Development: Mr Mike Cowlam, Assistant Director - Economic Development Services & Property, Olicana House, 35 Chapel Street, Little Germany , Bradford BD1 5RE ☎ 01274 434223 🖷 01274 432516 ✉ mike.cowlam@bradford.gov.uk

Education: Ms Kath Tunstall, Strategic Director - Children's Services, City Hall, Bradford BD1 1HY ☎ 01274 431266 ✉ kath.tunstall@bradford.gov.uk

E-Government: Ms Becky Hellard, Strategic Director - Finance, City Hall, Channing Way, Bradford BD1 1HY ☎ 01274 431000 🖷 01274 730337 ✉ becky.hellard@bradford.gov.uk

Electoral Registration: Ms Susan Saunders, Electoral Services Manager, Ground Floor, City Hall, Channing Way, Bradford BD1 1HY ☎ 01274 432285 🖷 01274 432799 ✉ susan.saunders@bradford.gov.uk

Emergency Planning: Mr Mike Powell, Emergency Planning Manager, City Hall, Channing Way, Bradford BD1 1HY ☎ 01274 432011 🖷 01274 434910 ✉ mike.powell@bradford.gov.uk

Energy Management: Mr Ian Bairstow, Strategic Director - Environment & Sport, Harris Street Depot, Bradford BD1 5HU ☎ 01274 434748 🖷 01274 432832 ✉ ian.bairstow@bradford.gov.uk

Environmental / Technical Services: Mr Ian Bairstow, Strategic Director - Environment & Sport, Harris Street Depot, Bradford BD1 5HU ☎ 01274 434748 🖷 01274 432832 ✉ ian.bairstow@bradford.gov.uk

Environmental Health: Mr Ian Bairstow, Strategic Director - Environment & Sport, Harris Street Depot, Bradford BD1 5HU ☎ 01274 434748 🖷 01274 432832 ✉ ian.bairstow@bradford.gov.uk

Estates, Property & Valuation: Mr Barra Mac Ruairi, Strategic Director - Regeneration & Culture, 5th Floor, Jacobs Well, Bradford BD1 5RW ☎ 01274 433762 🖷 01274 434583 ✉ barra.macruairi@bradford.gov.uk

Events Manager: Ms Vanessa Mitchell, Manager - Major Programmes, Jacobs Well, Bradford BD1 5RW ☎ 01274 434783 🖷 01274 434676 ✉ vanessa.mitchell@bradford.gov.uk

Finance and Treasurer: Ms Becky Hellard, Strategic Director -

Finance, City Hall, Channing Way, Bradford BD1 1HY ☎ 01274 431000 🖷 01274 730337 ✉ becky.hellard@bradford.gov.uk

Health and Safety: Ms Susan Gee, Senior Occupational Saftey Officer, City Hall, Channing Way, Bradford BD1 1HY ☎ 01274 434246 ✉ susan.gee@bradford.gov.uk

Highways: Mr Julian Jackson, Assistant Director - Planning, Transportation & Highways, City Hall, Channing Way, Bradford BD1 1HY ☎ 01274 437419 ✉ julian.jackson@bradford.gov.uk

Housing: Mr David Shepherd, Assistant Director - Housing, Employment and Skills, City Hall, Channing Way, Bradford BD1 1HY ☎ 01274 434561 ✉ david.shepherd@bradford.gov.uk

Local Area Agreement: Ms Roz Hall, Assistant Director - Strategic Support, Argus Chambers, Britannia House, Bradford BD1 1HX ☎ 01274 433716 ✉ roz.hall@bradford.gov.uk

Legal: Ms Suzan Hemingway, City Solicitor, City Hall, Channing Way, Bradford BD1 1HY ☎ 01274 432496 🖷 01274 730337 ✉ suzan.hemingway@bradford.gov.uk

Licensing: Ms Tracy McLuckie, Manager - Local Land Charges & Licensing, City Hall, Channing Way, Bradford BD1 1HY ☎ 01274 432209 ✉ tracy.mcluckie@bradford.gov.uk

Lifelong Learning: Ms Kath Tunstall, Strategic Director - Children's Services, City Hall, Bradford BD1 1HY ☎ 01274 431266 ✉ kath.tunstall@bradford.gov.uk

Lighting: Mr Allun Preece, Principal Engineer, Flockton House , Flockton Road , Bradford BD4 7RY ☎ 01274 434019 🖷 01274 737722 ✉ allun.preece@bradford.gov.uk

Member Services: Ms Suzan Hemingway, City Solicitor, City Hall, Channing Way, Bradford BD1 1HY ☎ 01274 432496 🖷 01274 730337 ✉ suzan.hemingway@bradford.gov.uk

Parking: Mr Michael Ferguson, Manager - Business Service, City Hall, Channing Way, Bradford BD1 1HY ☎ 01274 434018 ✉ michael.ferguson@bradford.gov.uk

Personnel / HR: Mr Matt Burghardt, Assistant Director - Human Resources, City Exchange, 61 Hall Ings, Bradford BD1 5SG ☎ 01274 436135 🖷 01274 730337 ✉ matt.burghardt@bradford.gov.uk

Procurement: Ms Jill Cambell, Assistant Director, Procurement, City Hall, Channing Way, Bradford BD1 1HY ☎ 01274 431497 ✉ jill.cambell@bradford.gov.uk

Public Libraries: Ms Christine Dyson, Principle Head of Libraries, Archives & Information Service, City Hall, Channing Way, Bradford BD1 1HY ☎ 01274 433640 ✉ christine.dyson@bradford.gov.uk

Public Libraries: Ms Jackie Kitwood, Principle Head - Libraries, Archives & Information Service, City Hall, Channing Way, Bradford BD1 1HY ☎ 01274 433640 ✉ jackie.knitwood@bradford.gov.uk

Recycling & Waste Minimisation: Ms Edith Grooby, Recycling Officer & Waste Minimisation, City Hall, Channing Way, Bradford BD1 1HY ☎ ; 01274 432854 ✉ edith.grooby@bradford.gov.uk

Regeneration: Mr Mike Cowlam, Assistant Director - Economic Development Services & Property, Olicana House, 35 Chapel Street, Little Germany , Bradford BD1 5RE ☎ 01274 434223 🖷 01274 432516 ✉ mike.cowlam@bradford.gov.uk

Regeneration: Mr Barra Mac Ruairi, Strategic Director - Regeneration & Culture, 5th Floor, Jacobs Well, Bradford BD1 5RW ☎ 01274 433762 🖷 01274 434583 ✉ barra.macruairi@bradford.gov.uk

Social Services (Adult): Ms Janice Simpson, Interim Strategic Director - Adult Services, City Hall, Channing Way, Bradford BD1 1HY ☎ 01274 432900 ✉ janice.simpson@bradford.gov.uk

Social Services (Children): Ms Kath Tunstall, Strategic Director - Children's Services, City Hall, Bradford BD1 1HY ☎ 01274 431266 ✉ kath.tunstall@bradford.gov.uk

Street Scene: Mr Ian Bairstow, Strategic Director - Environment & Sport, Harris Street Depot, Bradford BD1 5HU ☎ 01274 434748 🖷 01274 432832 ✉ ian.bairstow@bradford.gov.uk

Tourism: Ms Jackie Bennett, Senior Marketing Officer - Tourism, City Hall, Channing Way, Bradford BD1 1HY ☎ ; 01274 431847 🖷 01274 434857 ✉ jackie.bennett@bradford.gov.uk

Town Centre: Ms Yvonne Crossley, Town Centre Manager, Shipley Town Hall, Shipley BD18 3EJ ☎ 01274 437136 🖷 01274 433763 ✉ yvonne.crossley@bradford.gov.uk

Traffic Management: Mr Julian Jackson, Assistant Director - Planning, Transportation & Highways, City Hall, Channing Way, Bradford BD1 1HY ☎ 01274 437419 ✉ julian.jackson@bradford.gov.uk

Transport: Mr Julian Jackson, Assistant Director - Planning, Transportation & Highways, City Hall, Channing Way, Bradford BD1 1HY ☎ 01274 437419 ✉ julian.jackson@bradford.gov.uk

Transport Planner: Mr Julian Jackson, Assistant Director - Planning, Transportation & Highways, City Hall, Channing Way, Bradford BD1 1HY ☎ 01274 433766 ✉ julian.jackson@bradford.gov.uk

Total Place: Ms Becky Hellard, Strategic Director - Finance, City Hall, Channing Way, Bradford BD1 1HY ☎ 01274 431000 🖷 01274 730337 ✉ becky.hellard@bradford.gov.uk

Waste Collection and Disposal: Mr Ian Bairstow, Strategic Director - Environment & Sport, Harris Street Depot, Bradford BD1 5HU ☎ 01274 434748 🖷 01274 432832 ✉ ian.bairstow@bradford.gov.uk

Waste Management: Mr Ian Bairstow, Strategic Director - Environment & Sport, Harris Street Depot, Bradford BD1 5HU ☎ 01274 434748 🖷 01274 432832 ✉ ian.bairstow@bradford.gov.uk

MEMBERS OF THE COUNCIL (91)

***Deputy Lord Mayor:* Gibbons**, Mike (CON - Ilkley)
mike.gibbons@bradford.gov.uk
***Mayor:* Smith**, Dale (CON - Wharfedale)
dale.smith@bradford.gov.uk
***Leader of the Council:* Green**, David (LAB - Wibsey)
david.green@bradford.gov.uk
Ahmed, Ishtiaq (RSP - Manningham)
ishtiaq.ahmed@bradford.gov.uk
Akthar, Kaneez (LAB - Keighley Central)
kaneez.akthar@bradford.gov.uk
Azam, Nazam (LAB - City)
nazam.azam@bradford.gov.uk
Berry, Ralph (LAB - Wibsey)
ralph.berry@bradford.gov.uk
Billheimer, Ruth (LAB - Eccleshill)
ruth.billheimer@bradford.gov.uk
Binney, Valerie (CON - Thornton & Allerton)
valerie.binney@bradford.gov.uk
Brown, Russell (CON - Worth Valley)
russell.brown@bradford.gov.uk
Collector, Rugayyah (RSP - City)
rugayyah.collector@bradford.gov.uk
Cooke, Simon (CON - Bingley Rural)
simon.cooke@bradford.gov.uk
Cromie, Paul (IND - Queensbury)
paul.cromie@bradford.gov.uk
Cromie, Lynda (IND - Queensbury)
lynda.cromie@bradford.gov.uk
Davies, Debbie (CON - Baildon)
debbie.davies@bradford.gov.uk
Dodds, Joanne (LAB - Great Horton)
joanne.dodds@bradford.gov.uk
Dredge, Keith (LAB - Keighley West)
keith.dredge@bradford.gov.uk
Eaton, Margaret (CON - Bingley Rural)
margaret.eaton@bradford.gov.uk
Ellis, Michael (CON - Bingley Rural)
michael.ellis@bradford.gov.uk
Engel, Sinead (LAB - Clayton & Fairweather Green)
sinead.engel@bradford.gov.uk
Farley, Adrian (LAB - Keighley West)
adrian.farley@bradford.gov.uk
Ferriby, Sarah (LAB - Wyke)
sarah.ferriby@bradford.gov.uk
Godward, John (LAB - Great Horton)
john.godward@bradford.gov.uk
Gray, David (LD - Bolton & Undercliffe)
david.gray@bradford.gov.uk
Greaves, Chris (IND - Wharfedale)
chris.greaves@bradford.gov.uk
Greenwood, Vanda (LAB - Windhill & Wrose)
vanda.greenwood@bradford.gov.uk
Griffiths, Alun (LD - Idle & Thackley)
alun.griffiths@bradford.gov.uk
Hall, John (LD - Windhill & Wrose)
john.hall@bradford.gov.uk
Hawkesworth, Anne (CON - Ilkley)
anne.hawkesworth@bradford.gov.uk
Heseltine, David (CON - Bingley)
david.heseltine@bradford.gov.uk
Hinchcliffe, Susan (LAB - Windhill & Wrose)
susan.hinchcliffe@bradford.gov.uk
Hussain, Imdad (IND - Heaton)
imdad.hussain@bradford.gov.uk
Hussain, Shabir (LAB - Manningham)
shabir.hussain@bradford.gov.uk
Hussain, Abid (LAB - Keighley Central)
cllr.abidhussain@bradford.gov.uk
Hussain, Hawarun (GRN - Shipley)
hawarun.hussain@bradford.gov.uk
Hussain, Arshad (LAB - Toller)
arshad.hussain@bradford.gov.uk
Hussain, Khadim (LAB - Keighley Central)
khadim.hussain@bradford.gov.uk
Hussain, Amir (LAB - Toller)
amir.hussain@bradford.gov.uk
Hussain, Imran (LAB - Toller)
cllr.imranhussain@bradford.gov.uk
Ikram, Naveeda (LAB - Little Horton)
naveeda.ikram@bradford.gov.uk
Jabar, Abdul (LAB - Great Horton)
abdul.jabar@bradford.gov.uk
Javed, Asama (LAB - Manningham)
asama.javed@bradford.gov.uk
Johnson, Michael (LAB - Tong)
michael.johnson@bradford.gov.uk
Karmani, Alyas (RSP - Little Horton)
alyas.karmani@bradford.gov.uk
Kelly, Michael (CON - Craven)
michael.kelly@bradford.gov.uk
Khaliq, Ghazanfer (LAB - Bradford Moor)
ghazanfer.khaliq@bradford.gov.uk
Khan, Imran (LAB - Bowling & Barkerend)
cllr.imrankhan@bradford.gov.uk
Khan, Sher (LAB - Little Horton)
sher.khan@bradford.gov.uk
Khan, Hassan (LAB - Bowling & Barkerend)
hassan.khan@bradford.gov.uk
Khan, Faisal (RSP - Bradford Moor)
cllr.faisalkhan@bradford.gov.uk
Lal, Shakeela (LAB - City)
shakeela.lal@bradfod.gov.uk
L'Amie, Roger (CON - Balidon)
roger.lamie@bradford.gov.uk
Lee, Doreen (LAB - Keighley East)
doreen.lee@bradford.gov.uk
Leeming, Tracey (LD - Bolton & Undercliffe)
tracey.leeming@bradford.gov.uk
Love, Martin (GRN - Shipley)
martin.love@bradford.gov.uk
Malik, Rizwan (LAB - Heaton)
rizwan.malik@bradford.gov.uk
Mallinson, Andrew (CON - Craven)
andrew.mallinson@bradford.gov.uk
McCabe, Michael (CON - Thornton & Allerton)
michael.mccabe@bradford.gov.uk
Middleton, Howard (LD - Bolton & Undercliffe)
howard.middleton@bradford.gov.uk
Miller, Glen (CON - Worth Valley)
glen.miller@bradford.gov.uk
Naylor, Adrian (IND - Craven)
adrian.naylor@bradford.gov.uk
Palmer, Matt (CON - Wharfedale)
matt.palmer@bradford.gov.uk
Pennington, John (CON - Bingley)
john.pennington@bradford.gov.uk
Poulsen, Rebecca (CON - Worth Valley)
rebecca.poulsen@bradford.gov.uk
Pullen, Steve (LAB - Keighley East)

steve.pullen@bradford.gov.uk
Reid, Geoff (LD - Eccleshill)
geoff.reid@bradford.gov.uk
Reid, Chris (LD - Idle & Thackley)
chris.reid@bradford.gov.uk
Robinson, David (LAB - Wyke)
cllr.davidrobinson@bradford.gov.uk
Ross-Shaw, Alexander (LAB - Windhil & Wrose)
alex.ross-shaw@bradford.gov.uk
Ruding, John (LAB - Tong)
john.ruding@bradford.gov.uk
Shabbir, Mohammad (RSP - Heaton)
mohammad.shabbir@bradford.gov.uk
Shafiq, Mohammed (LAB - Bradford Moor)
mohammed.shafiq@bradford.gov.uk
Shah, Zameer (CON - Bowling & Barkerend)
zameer.shah@bradford.gov.uk
Shaw, Mark (CON - Bingley)
mark.shaw@bradford.gov.uk
Slater, Val (LAB - Royds)
val.slater@bradford.gov.uk
Slater, Malcolm (LAB - Keighley East)
malcolm.slater@bradford.gov.uk
Smith, Lynne (LAB - Wibsey)
lynne.smith@bradford.gov.uk
Smith, Brian (CON - Ilkley)
martin.smith@bradford.gov.uk
Smithies, Jan (LAB - Keighley West)
jan.smithies@bradford.gov.uk
Sunderland, Jeanette (LD - Idle & Thackley)
jeanette.sunderland@bradford.gov.uk
Swallow, Michelle (LAB - Clayton & Fairweather Green)
michelle.swallow@bradford.gov.uk
Sykes, Malcolm (CON - Thornton & Allerton)
malcolm.sykes@bradford.gov.uk
Thirkill, Carol (LAB - Clayton & Fairweather Green)
carol.thirkill@bradford.gov.uk
Thornton, Gill (LAB - Royds)
gill.thornton@bradford.gov.uk
Thornton, Andrew (LAB - Royds)
andrew.thornton@bradford.gov.uk
Townend, Valerie (CON - Balidon)
val.townend@bradford.gov.uk
Wainwright, Alan (LAB - Tong)
alan.wainwright@bradford.gov.uk
Wallace, Dorothy (LD - Eccleshill)
ann.wallace@bradford.gov.uk
Walls, Michael (CON - Queensbury)
michael.walls@bradford.gov.uk
Warburton, David (LAB - Wyke)
david.warburton@bradford.gov.uk
Warnes, Kevin (GRN - Shipley)
kevin.warnes@bradford.gov.uk

POLITICAL COMPOSITION
LAB: 45, CON: 24, LD: 9, RSP: 5, IND: 5, GRN: 3

CABINET
Leader: Mr David Green
Deputy Leader: Mr Imran Hussain
Change Programme, Housing, Planning & Transport: Mrs Val Slater
Children & Young People's Services: Mr Ralph Berry
Employment, Skills & Culture: Ms Susan Hinchcliffe
Environment, Sport & Sustainability: Mr Andrew Thornton
Safer & Stronger Communities: Mr Imran Hussain

COMMITTEE CHAIRS
Area Planning: Mrs Doreen Lee
Children's Services: Mr Malcolm Sykes
Corporate Governance & Audit: Ms Lynne Smith
Corporate Overview & Scrutiny: Mr Rizwan Malik
Environment & Waste Management Overview & Services: Mr Martin Love
Health Overview & Scrutiny: Mr Mike Gibbons
Licensing: Mr John Ruding
Regeneration & Economy Overview & Scrutiny: Mr Andrew Mallinson
Regulatory & Appeals: Mr David Warburton
Social Care: Mr Roger L'Amie
Staffing: Mr David Green

BRAINTREE — D
Braintree District Council, Causeway House, Braintree CM7 9HB
☎ 01376 552525 🖷 01376 552626
webmaster@braintree.gov.uk 💻 www.braintree.gov.uk

FACTS & FIGURES
Police Authority: Essex Police Authority
Health Authority: East of England Strategic Health Authority
Learning and Skills Council: Eastern
Parliamentary Constituencies: Braintree, Witham
EU Constituencies: Eastern
Election Frequency: Elections are of whole council
Twinning: Braintree and Bocking: Pierrefitte (France); Earls Colne: Nonancourt (France); Gosfield: Chouze sur Loire (France); Halstead: Haubourdin (France); Panfield: St Symphorien-le-Chateau (France); Rayne: Verbene (France); Side Hedingham: Choisy au Bac (France); Witham: Waldbrol (Germany)

PRINCIPAL OFFICERS
Chief Executive: Mr Allan Reid, Chief Executive, Causeway House, Bocking End, Braintree CM7 9HB ☎ 01376 552525 🖷 01376 552626 allan.reid@braintree.gov.uk

Assistant Chief Executive: Ms Sharon Lowe, Assistant Chief Executive, Causeway House, Bocking End, Braintree CM7 9HB ☎ 01376 552525 🖷 01376 552626 sharon.lowe@braintree.gov.uk

Senior Management: Ms Nicola Beach, Corporate Director, Causeway House, Braintree CM7 9HB ☎ 01376 552525 🖷 01376 552626 nicola.beach@braintree.gov.uk

Senior Management: Mr Chris Fleetham, Corporate Director, Causeway House, Bocking End, Braintree CM7 9HB ☎ 01376 552525 🖷 01376 552626 chris.fleetham@braintree.gov.uk

Senior Management: Mr Jon Hayden, Corporate Director, Causeway House, Braintree CM7 9HB ☎ 01376 552525 🖷 01376 55266 jon.hayden@braintree.gov.uk

Architect, Building / Property Services: Mr Trevor Wilson, Head of Finance, Causeway House, Braintree CM7 9HB ☎ 01376 552525 🖷 01376 552626 trevor.wilson@braintree.gov.uk

Building Control: Mr Lee Crabb, Head of Environment, Causeway House, Braintree CM7 9HB ☎ 01376 552525 🖷 01376 552626 🖰 lee.crabb@braintree.gov.uk

PR / Communications: Miss Jackie Brown, Corporate Communications Officer, Causeway House, Braintree CM7 9HB ☎ 01376 557752 🖰 jackie.brown@braintree.gov.uk

PR / Communications: Ms Tania Roberge, Marketing & Communications Manager, Causeway House, Braintree CM7 9HB ☎ 01376 552525 🖷 01376 552626 🖰 tania.roberge@braintree.gov.uk

Community Planning: Mrs Charmaine Dean, Head of Community Services, Causeway House, Bocking End, Braintree CM7 9HB ☎ 01376 552525 🖷 01376 557726 🖰 charmaine.dean@braintree.gov.uk

Community Safety: Mrs Charmaine Dean, Head of Community Services, Causeway House, Bocking End, Braintree CM7 9HB ☎ 01376 552525 🖷 01376 557726 🖰 charmaine.dean@braintree.gov.uk

Computer Management: Ms Cherie Root, Customer & ICT Manager, Causeway House, Bocking End, Braintree CM7 9HB ☎ 01376 552525 🖷 01376 552626 🖰 cherie.root@braintree.gov.uk

Corporate Services: Ms Sharon Lowe, Assistant Chief Executive, Causeway House, Bocking End, Braintree CM7 9HB ☎ 01376 552525 🖷 01376 552626 🖰 sharon.lowe@braintree.gov.uk

Customer Service: Ms Cherie Root, Customer & ICT Manager, Causeway House, Bocking End, Braintree CM7 9HB ☎ 01376 552525 🖷 01376 552626 🖰 cherie.root@braintree.gov.uk

Economic Development: Mr Jon Hayden, Corporate Director, Causeway House, Braintree CM7 9HB ☎ 01376 552525 🖷 01376 55266 🖰 jon.hayden@braintree.gov.uk

Electoral Registration: Mr Steve Daynes, Electoral Registration Manager, Causeway House, Braintree CM7 9HB ☎ 01376 552525 🖷 01376 552626 🖰 steve.daynes@braintree.gov.uk

Emergency Planning: Ms Kathy Brown, Health, Safety & Emergency Manager, Causeway House, Bocking End, Braintree CM7 9BR ☎ 01376 557753 🖷 01376 552626 🖰 kathy.brown@braintree.gov.uk

Energy Management: Mr Mark Wilson, Climate Change Manager, Causeway House, Braintree CM7 9HB ☎ 01376 552525 🖷 01376 552626 🖰 mark.wilson@braintree.gov.uk

Environmental Health: Mr Lee Crabb, Head of Environment, Causeway House, Braintree CM7 9HB ☎ 01376 552525 🖷 01376 552626 🖰 lee.crabb@braintree.gov.uk

Estates, Property & Valuation: Mr Andrew Epsom, Asset & Property Manager, Causeway House, Bocking End, Braintree CM7 9HB ☎ 01376 552525 🖷 01376 552626 🖰 andrew.epsom@braintree.gov.uk

Facilities: Mr Andrew Epsom, Asset & Property Manager, Causeway House, Bocking End, Braintree CM7 9HB ☎ 01376 552525 🖷 01376 552626 🖰 andrew.epsom@braintree.gov.uk

Finance and Treasurer: Mr Chris Fleetham, Corporate Director, Causeway House, Bocking End, Braintree CM7 9HB ☎ 01376 552525 🖷 01376 552626 🖰 chris.fleetham@braintree.gov.uk

Fleet Management: Mr Nick Johnson, Waste & Transport Manager, Unit 4, Lakes Industrial Park, Lower Chapel Hill, Braintree CM7 3RU ☎ 01376 332300 🖷 01376 332525 🖰 nick.johnson@braintree.gov.uk

Grounds Maintenance: Mr Paul Partridge, Head of Operations, Causeway House, Bocking End, Braintree CM7 9HB ☎ 01376 552525 🖷 01376 552626 🖰 paul.partridge@braintree.gov.uk

Health and Safety: Ms Kathy Brown, Health, Safety & Emergency Manager, Causeway House, Bocking End, Braintree CM7 9BR ☎ 01376 557753 🖷 01376 552626 🖰 kathy.brown@braintree.gov.uk

Home Energy Conservation: Mr Mark Wilson, Climate Change Manager, Causeway House, Braintree CM7 9HB ☎ 01376 552525 🖷 01376 552626 🖰 mark.wilson@braintree.gov.uk

Housing: Ms Joanne Albini, Strategic Housing Services Manager, Causeway House, Braintree CM7 9HB ☎ 01376 557753 🖷 01376 552626 🖰 joanne.albini@braintree.gov.uk

Legal: Ms Sarah Stockings, Assistant Solicitor, Causeway House, Braintree CM7 9HB ☎ 01376 552525 🖷 01376 552626 🖰 sara.stockings@braintree.gov.uk

Leisure and Cultural Services: Mr Robert Rose, Museum Services Manager, Town Hall Centre, Market Place, Braintree CM7 3YG ☎ 01376 325266 🖰 robert.rose@braintree.gov.uk

Licensing: Mr Lee Crabb, Head of Environment, Causeway House, Braintree CM7 9HB ☎ 01376 552525 🖷 01376 552626 🖰 lee.crabb@braintree.gov.uk

Lifelong Learning: Ms Sam Jenkins, Learning & Development Consultant, Causeway House, Bocking End, Braintree CM7 9HB ☎ 01376 552525 🖷 01376 552626 🖰 sam.jenkins@braintree.gov.uk

Lottery Funding, Charity and Voluntary: Mrs Angela Verghese, External Funding & Voluntary Sector Development Manager, Causeway House, Braintree CM7 9HB ☎ 01376 552525 🖷 01376 557726 🖰 angela.verghese@braintree.gov.uk

Member Services: Mr Alastair Peace, Member Services Manager, Causeway House, Braintree CM7 9HB 🖰 alastair.peace@braintree.gov.uk

Personnel / HR: Ms Helen Krischock, HR Manager, Causeway House, Braintree CM7 9HB ☎ 01376 552525 🖷 01376 552626 🖰 helen.krischock@braintree.gov.uk

Planning: Mr Jon Hayden, Corporate Director, Causeway House,

Braintree CM7 9HB ☎ 01376 552525 🖷 01376 55266 ✉ jon.hayden@braintree.gov.uk

Planning: Ms Tessa Lambert, Development Control Manager, Causeway House, Braintree CM7 9HB ☎ 01376 552525 🖷 01376 552626 ✉ tessa.lambert@braintree.gov.uk

Procurement: Mr John Wickes, Procurement Manager, Causeway House, Bocking End, Braintree CM7 9HB ☎ 01376 552525 🖷 01376 557792 ✉ john.wickes@braintree.gov.uk

Recycling & Waste Minimisation: Mr Nick Johnson, Waste & Transport Manager, Unit 4, Lakes Industrial Park, Lower Chapel Hill, Braintree CM7 3RU ☎ 01376 332300 🖷 01376 332525 ✉ nick.johnson@braintree.gov.uk

Regeneration: Ms Alison Jennings, Regeneration Manager, Causeway House, Braintree CM7 9HB 🖷 01376 552626 ✉ alison.jennings@braintree.gov.uk

Staff Training: Ms Sam Jenkins, Learning & Development Consultant, Causeway House, Bocking End, Braintree CM7 9HB ☎ 01376 552525 🖷 01376 552626 ✉ sam.jenkins@braintree.gov.uk

Street Scene: Mr Paul Partridge, Head of Operations, Causeway House, Bocking End, Braintree CM7 9HB ☎ 01376 552525 🖷 01376 552626 ✉ paul.partridge@braintree.gov.uk

Sustainable Communities: Mr Jon Hayden, Corporate Director, Causeway House, Braintree CM7 9HB ☎ 01376 552525 🖷 01376 55266 ✉ jon.hayden@braintree.gov.uk

Sustainable Development: Mr Jon Hayden, Corporate Director, Causeway House, Braintree CM7 9HB ☎ 01376 552525 🖷 01376 55266 ✉ jon.hayden@braintree.gov.uk

Tourism: Mr Jon Hayden, Corporate Director, Causeway House, Braintree CM7 9HB ☎ 01376 552525 🖷 01376 55266 ✉ jon.hayden@braintree.gov.uk

Town Centre: Mr Jon Hayden, Corporate Director, Causeway House, Braintree CM7 9HB ☎ 01376 552525 🖷 01376 55266 ✉ jon.hayden@braintree.gov.uk

Transport: Mr Jon Hayden, Corporate Director, Causeway House, Braintree CM7 9HB ☎ 01376 552525 🖷 01376 55266 ✉ jon.hayden@braintree.gov.uk

Transport Planner: Mr Jon Hayden, Corporate Director, Causeway House, Braintree CM7 9HB ☎ 01376 552525 🖷 01376 55266 ✉ jon.hayden@braintree.gov.uk

Waste Collection and Disposal: Mr Nick Johnson, Waste & Transport Manager, Unit 4, Lakes Industrial Park, Lower Chapel Hill, Braintree CM7 3RU ☎ 01376 332300 🖷 01376 332525 ✉ nick.johnson@braintree.gov.uk

Waste Management: Ms Nicola Beach, Corporate Director, Causeway House, Braintree CM7 9HB ☎ 01376 552525 🖷 01376 552626 ✉ nicola.beach@braintree.gov.uk

MEMBERS OF THE COUNCIL (58)

***Group Leader:* Abbott**, James (GRN - Bradwell, Silver End & Rivenhall)
cllr.jabbott@braintree.gov.uk
***Group Leader:* Banthorpe**, Michael (CON - Rayne)
cllr.mbanthorpe@braintree.gov.uk
Allen, Julia (CON - Halstead St. Andrew's)
cllr.jallen@braintree.gov.uk
Barlow, Philip (LAB - Witham North)
cllr.pbarlow@braintree.gov.uk
Baugh, John (CON - Bocking South)
cllr.jbaugh@braintree.gov.uk
Beavis, Joanne (CON - Hedingham & Maplestead)
cllr.jbeavis@braintree.gov.uk
Bebb, David (CON - Hatfield Peverel)
cllr.dbebb@braintree.gov.uk
Bishop, Elwyn (LAB - Braintree East)
cllr.ebishop@braintree.gov.uk
Bolton, Robert (CON - Upper Colne)
cllr.rbolton@braintree.gov.uk
Butland, Graham (CON - Great Notley & Braintree West)
cllr.gbutland@braintree.gov.uk
Cadman, Chris (CON - Bumpstead)
cllr.ccadman@braintree.gov.uk
Canning, Stephen (CON - Bocking Blackwater)
cllr.scanning@braintree.gov.uk
Cunningham, Tom (CON - Black Notley & Terling)
cllr.tcunningham@braintree.gov.uk
Elliott, John (CON - Witham South)
cllr.jelliott@braintree.gov.uk
Evans, Robert (LAB - Witham North)
cllr.revans@braintree.gov.uk
Everard, Anthony (LAB - Bocking North)
cllr.aeverard@braintree.gov.uk
Finbow, John (CON - Three Fields)
cllr.jfinbow@braintree.gov.uk
Fincken, John (LAB - Halstead Trinity)
cllr.mfincken@braintree.gov.uk
Flint, Lynette (IND - Cressing & Stisted)
cllr.lflint@braintree.gov.uk
Foster, Tom (CON - Kelvedon)
cllr.tfoster@braintree.gov.uk
Galione, Margaret (CON - Black Notley & Terling)
cllr.mgalione@braintree.gov.uk
Gibson, Collette (LAB - Braintree East)
cllr.cgibson@braintree.gov.uk
Horner, Patrick (CON - Witham West)
cllr.phorner@braintree.gov.uk
Howell, Sandra (CON - Witham Chipping Hill & Central)
cllr.showell@braintree.gov.uk
Johnson, Hylton (CON - Hedingham & Maplestead)
cllr.hjohnson@braintree.gov.uk
Kirby, Stephen (CON - Halstead St. Andrew's)
cllr.skirby@braintree.gov.uk
Lager, Michael (CON - Witham Chipping Hill & Central)
cllr.mlager@braintree.gov.uk
Loius, Cheryl (CON - Witham West)
cllr.clouis@braintree.gov.uk
Louis, Derek (CON - Hatfield Peverel)
cllr.dlouis@braintree.gov.uk
Mann, David (LAB - Bocking North)
cllr.dmann@braintree.gov.uk

McKee, John (CON - Braintree Central)
cllr.jmckee@braintree.gov.uk
Mitchell, Robert (CON - Kelvedon)
cllr.rmitchell@braintree.gov.uk
Money, Janet (CON - Witham South)
cllr.jmoney@braintree.gov.uk
Newton, Patricia (CON - Coggeshall & North Feering)
cllr.ladynewton@braintree.gov.uk
O'Reilly-Cicconi, John (CON - Gosfield & Greenstead)
cllr.jo'reilly-cicconi@braintree.gov.uk
Parker, Iona (CON - Yeldham)
cllr.iparker@braintree.gov.uk
Pell, Jacqueline (R - Halstead Trinity)
cllr.jpell@braintree.gov.uk
Ramage, Ron (CON - Braintree Central)
cllr.rramage@braintree.gov.uk
Reid, David (CON - Three Fields)
cllr.dreid@braintree.gov.uk
Ricci, Francesco (CON - Great Notley & Braintree West)
cllr.fricci@braintree.gov.uk
Rice, Douglas (LAB - Braintree South)
cllr.drice@braintree.gov.uk
Rose, Bill (CON - Witham West)
cllr.wrose@braintree.gov.uk
Santomauro, Vanessa (CON - Bocking Blackwater)
cllr.vsantomauro@braintree.gov.uk
Scattergood, Wendy (CON - Hedingham & Maplestead)
cllr.wscattergood@braintree.gov.uk
Schmitt, Wendy (CON - Bocking Blackwater)
cllr.wschmitt@braintree.gov.uk
Shelton, Anthony (CON - Stour Valley South)
cllr.ashelton@braintree.gov.uk
Shepherd, Lene (CON - Braintree Central)
cllr.lshepherd@braintree.gov.uk
Siddall, Chris (CON - The Three Colnes)
cllr.csiddall@braintree.gov.uk
Spray, Gabrielle (CON - The Three Colnes)
cllr.gspray@braintree.gov.uk
Sutton, Jennie (CON - Halstead St. Andrew's)
cllr.jsutton@braintree.gov.uk
Swift, Julian (CON - Stour Valley North)
cllr.jswift@braintree.gov.uk
Tattersley, Peter (CON - Panfield)
cllr.ptattersley@braintree.gov.uk
Thompson, Corinne (CON - Witham South)
cllr.cthompson@braintree.co.uk
Thorogood, Moira (LAB - Bocking South)
cllr.mthorogood@braintree.gov.uk
Walters, Lyn (CON - Braintree South)
cllr.lwalters@braintree.gov.uk
Walters, Roger (CON - Great Notley & Braintree West)
cllr.rwalters@braintree.gov.uk
Wilson, Sue (CON - Coggeshall & North Feering)
cllr.swilson@braintree.gov.uk
Wright, Bob (GRN - Bradwell, Silver End & Rivenhall)
cllr.bwright@braintree.gov.uk

POLITICAL COMPOSITION
CON: 45, LAB: 9, GRN: 2, R: 1, IND: 1

CABINET
Leader: Mr Graham Butland
Deputy Leader: Mr Chris Siddall
Chair of the Council: Ms Janet Money
Communities: Mrs Joanne Beavis
Efficiency & Resources: Mr Chris Siddall
Enterprise, Housing & Development: Lady Patricia Newton
Environment: Mrs Wendy Schmitt
Vice Chairman: Ms Lynette Flint

COMMITTEE CHAIRS
Licensing: Mr Michael Banthorpe
Overview & Scrutiny: Dr Robert Evans
Planning: Mrs Wendy Scattergood

BRECKLAND — D
Breckland District Council, Elizabeth House, Walpole Loke, Dereham NR19 1EE ☎ 01362 656870 🖳 www.breckland.gov.uk

FACTS & FIGURES
Police Authority: Norfolk Police Authority
Health Authority: East of England Strategic Health Authority
Learning and Skills Council: Eastern
EU Constituencies: Eastern
Election Frequency: Elections are of whole council
Twinning: Attleborough: Nueil Les Aubiers (France); Dereham: Ruthen (Germany); Les Ulis (France); Swaffham: Couhe-Verac (France) and Hemmoor-Warstade (Germany); Thetford: Hurth (Germany) and Spijkenisse (Netherlands); Watton: Weeze (Germany)

PRINCIPAL OFFICERS
Chief Executive: Mr Terry Huggins, Chief Executive, Elizabeth House, Walpole Loke, Dereham NR19 1EE ☎ 01362 656870 ✉ chief.executive@breckland-sholland.gov.uk

Deputy Chief Executive: Mr Mark Stokes, Deputy Chief Executive, Elizabeth House, Walpole Loke, Dereham NR19 1EE ☎ 01362 656870 ✉ mark.stokes@breckland-sholland.gov.uk

Senior Management: Mr Mark Finch, Assistant Director - Finance, Elizabeth House, Walpole Loke, Dereham NR19 1EE ☎ 01362 656870 ✉ mark.finch@breckland-sholland.gov.uk

Senior Management: Ms Maxine O'Mahony, Director - Commissioning, Elizabeth House, Walpole Loke, Dereham NR19 1EE ☎ 01362 656870 ✉ maxine.omahony@breckland-sholland.gov.uk

Senior Management: Mrs Vicky Thomson, Assistant Director - Democratic Services, Elizabeth House, Walpole Loke, Dereham NR19 1EE ☎ 01362 656870 ✉ vicky.thomson@breckland-sholland.gov.uk

Senior Management: Mr Robert Walker, Assistant Director - Commissioning, Elizabeth House, Walpole Loke, Dereham NR19 1EE ☎ 01362 656870 ✉ robert.walker@breckland-sholland.gov.uk

Architect, Building / Property Services: Mr Stephen Udberg, Asset & Property Manager, Elizabeth House, Walpole Loke, Dereham NR19 1EE ☎ 01362 656870 ✉ steve.udberg@breckland-sholland.gov.uk

Building Control: Mr Phil Adams, Building Control Manager,

Elizabeth House, Walpole Loke, Dereham NR19 1EE
☎ 01362 656870 ✉ phillip.adams@breckland-sholland.gov.uk

PR / Communications: Mr Dominic Chessum, Senior Marketing & Communications Officer, Elizabeth House, Walpole Loke, Dereham NR19 1EE ☎ 01362 656870
✉ dominic.chessum@breckland-sholland.gov.uk

Computer Management: Mr Kevin Rump, ICT & Customer Manager, Elizabeth House, Walpole Loke, Dereham NR19 1EE
☎ 01362 656870 ✉ kevin.rump@breckland.gov.uk

Customer Service: Mr Kevin Rump, ICT & Customer Manager, Elizabeth House, Walpole Loke, Dereham NR19 1EE
☎ 01362 656870 ✉ kevin.rump@breckland.gov.uk;

Economic Development: Mr Mark Stanton, Economic Development Manager, Elizabeth House, Walpole Loke, Dereham NR19 1EE ☎ 01362 656870 🖷 01362 656360
✉ mark.stanton@breckland-sholland.gov.uk

E-Government: Mr Kevin Rump, ICT Project Manager, Elizabeth House, Walpole Loke, Dereham NR19 1EE ☎ 01362 656870
✉ kevin.rump@breckland.gov.uk

Electoral Registration: Mr Rory Ringer, Member Services Manager, Elizabeth House, Walpole Loke, Dereham NR19 1EE
☎ 01362 656870 ✉ rory.ringer@breckland.gov.uk

Emergency Planning: Mrs Teresa Cannon, Emergency Planning Officer, Elizabeth House, Walpole Loke, Dereham NR19 1EE
☎ 01362 656870 🖷 01362 693733
✉ teresa.cannon@breckland.gov.uk

Environmental Health: Mr Phil Adams, Building Control Manager, Elizabeth House, Walpole Loke, Dereham NR19 1EE
☎ 01362 656870 ✉ phillip.adams@breckland-sholland.gov.uk

Estates, Property & Valuation: Mrs Trisha Bailey, Commercial Property Manager, Elizabeth House, Walpole Loke, Dereham NR19 1EE ☎ 01362 656870 ✉ trisha.bailey@breckland.gov.uk

European Liaison: Mr Mark Stanton, Economic Development Manager, Elizabeth House, Walpole Loke, Dereham NR19 1EE
☎ 01362 656870 🖷 01362 656360
✉ mark.stanton@breckland-sholland.gov.uk

Finance and Treasurer: Mr Mark Finch, Assistant Director - Finance, Elizabeth House, Walpole Loke, Dereham NR19 1EE
☎ 01362 656870 ✉ mark.finch@breckland-sholland.gov.uk

Health and Safety: Mr Jeremy Hadaway, Technical Officer, Elizabeth House, Walpole Loke, Dereham NR19 1EE
☎ 01362 656870 ✉ jeremy.hadaway@breckland.gov.uk

Home Energy Conservation: Mr Gordon Partridge, Environmental Health Manager - Housing, Elizabeth House, Walpole Loke, Dereham NR19 1EE ☎ 01362 656870
🖷 01362 656353 ✉ gordon.partridge@breckland.gov.uk

Legal: Mr Michael Horn, Head - Legal Services, Elizabeth House, Walpole Loke, Dereham NR19 1EE ☎ 01362 656870
🖷 01362 690821 ✉ mike.horn@breckland.gov.uk

Licensing: Ms Fiona Inston, Licensing Manager, Elizabeth House, Walpole Loke, Dereham NR19 1EE ☎ 01362 656870
✉ fiona.inston@breckland.gov.uk

Lighting: Mr Anthony Wright, Building Services Manager, Elizabeth House, Walpole Loke, Dereham NR19 1EE
☎ 01362 656870 ✉ anthony.wright@breckland.gov.uk

Member Services: Mrs Vicky Thomson, Assistant Director - Democratic Services, Elizabeth House, Walpole Loke, Dereham NR19 1EE ☎ 01362 656870
✉ vicky.thomson@breckland-sholland.gov.uk

Personnel / HR: Mrs Natalie King, HR Manager, Elizabeth House, Walpole Loke, Dereham NR19 1EE ☎ 01362 656870 ✉ natalie.king@breckland-sholland.gov.uk

Planning: Mr Paul Jackson, Planning Manager, Elizabeth House, Walpole Loke, Dereham NR19 1EE ☎ 01362 656870
✉ paul.jackson@breckland-sholland.gov.uk

Procurement: Mrs Samantha Dancer, Policy & Performance Team Leader, Elizabeth House, Walpole Loke, Dereham NR19 1EE
☎ 01362 656870 ✉ sdancer@sholland.gov.uk

Regeneration: Mr Mark Stanton, Economic Development Manager, Elizabeth House, Walpole Loke, Dereham NR19 1EE
☎ 01362 656870 🖷 01362 656360
✉ mark.stanton@breckland-sholland.gov.uk

Staff Training: Ms Julia Thaxton, Training & Development Manager, Elizabeth House, Walpole Loke, Dereham NR19 1EE
☎ 01362 656896 ✉ julia.thaxton@breckland. gov.uk

Street Scene: Mrs Sarah Bruton, Environmental Services Manager, Elizabeth House, Walpole Loke, Dereham NR19 1EE
☎ 01362 656870 🖷 01362 699096
✉ sarah.bruton@breckland.gov.uk

MEMBERS OF THE COUNCIL (53)

***Chair:* Goreham**, Robin (LAB - Dereham - Central)
robin.goreham@breckland.gov.uk
***Vice-Chair:* Claussen**, Paul (CON - Two Rivers)
paul.claussen@breckland.gov.uk
***Leader of the Council:* Nunn**, William (CON - West Guiltcross)
william.nunn@breckland.gov.uk
***Group Leader:* Jermy**, Terry (LAB - Thetford - Saxon)
terry.jermy@breckland.gov.uk
Armes, Sylvia (LAB - Thetford - Saxon)
sylvia.armes@breckland.gov.uk
Askew, Stephen (CON - East Guiltcross)
stephen.askew@breckland.gov.uk
Bambridge, Gordon (CON - Eynsford)
gordon.bambridge@breckland.gov.uk
Borrett, Bill (CON - Upper Wensum)
bill.borrett@breckland.gov.uk
Bowes, Claire (CON - Watton)
claire.bowes@breckland.gov.uk
Byrne, Alexander (CON - Queens)
alexander.byrne@breckland.gov.uk
Carter, Trevor (CON - Hermitage)

trevor.carter@breckland.gov.uk
Carter, Charles (CON - Haggard de Toni)
charles.carter@breckland.gov.uk
Childerhouse, Robert (CON - Weeting)
robert.childerhouse@breckland.gov.uk
Clark, Carl (IND - Thetford - Abbey)
pastorbishop32@yahoo.com
Cowen, Philip (CON - Wayland)
philip.cowen@breckland.gov.uk
Darby, Paul (CON - Wissey)
paul.darby@breckland.gov.uk
Duffield, Richard (CON - Taverner)
richard.duffield@breckland.gov.uk
Duigan, Philip (CON - Dereham - Toftwood)
phillip.duigan@breckland.gov.uk
English, Bernard (CON - Mid Forest)
bernard.english@breckland.gov.uk
Fisher, Kay (CON - Harling & Heathlands)
karen.fisher@breckland.gov.uk
Gilbert, Keith (IND - Watton)
keith.gilbert@breckland.gov.uk
Gould, Elizabeth (CON - Springvale & Scarning)
elizabeth.gould@breckland.gov.uk
Green, Stuart (CON - Dereham - Humbletoft)
stuart.green@breckland.gov.uk
Irving, Diana (CON - Springvale & Scarning)
diana.irving@breckland.gov.uk
Joel, Adrian (CON - Buckenham)
adrian.joel@breckland.gov.uk
Jolly, Ellen (CON - Harling & Heathlands)
ellen.jolly@breckland.gov.uk
Jordan, Cliff (CON - Upper Yare)
cliff.jordan@breckland.gov.uk
Kiddle-Morris, Mark (CON - Launditch)
mark.kiddle-morris@breckland.gov.uk
Kybird, Robert (CON - Thetford - Guildhall)
robert.kybird@breckland.gov.uk
Lamb, Terry (IND - Thetford - Castle)
Martin, Keith (CON - Burgh & Haverscroft)
keith.martin@breckland.gov.uk
Matthews, Shirley (CON - Swaffham)
shirley.matthews@breckland.gov.uk
Millbank, Kate (CON - Dereham - Toftwood)
kate.millbank@breckland.gov.uk
Monument, Linda (CON - Dereham - Neatherd)
linda.monument@breckland.gov.uk
Monument, Thomas (CON - Dereham - Central)
thomas.monument@breckland.gov.uk
North, Jenny (CON - Queens)
jenny.north@breckland.gov.uk
Quadling, Pauline (IND - Thetford - Abbey)
pauline.quadling@breckland.gov.uk
Richmond, Robert (CON - Swanton Morley)
robert.richmond@breckland.gov.uk
Richmond, William (CON - Dereham - Neatherd)
william.richmond@breckland.gov.uk
Robinson, Mark (CON - Thetford - Saxon)
mark.robinson@breckland.gov.uk
Rogers, John (CON - Templar)
john.rogers@breckland.gov.uk
Rose, Brian (CON - Two Rivers)
brian.rose@breckland.gov.uk
Sharpe, Frank (CON - Swaffham)
frank.sharpe@breckland.gov.uk
Sherwood, Ian (CON - Swaffham)
ian.sherwood@breckland.gov.uk
Skull, Bryan (CON - Thetford - Guildhall)
bryan.skull@breckland.gov.uk
Smith, William (CON - All Saints)
william.smith@breckland.gov.uk
Spencer, Pamela (CON - Thetford - Guildhall)
pamela.spencer@breckland.gov.uk
Stasiak, Adrian (CON - Burgh & Haverscroft)
adrian.stasiak@breckland.gov.uk
Steward, Ann (CON - Conifer)
ann.steward@breckland.gov.uk
Turner, Lynda (CON - Shipdham)
lynda.turner@breckland.gov.uk
Wassell, Michael (CON - Watton)
michael.wassell@breckland.gov.uk
Wilkin, Nigel (CON - Necton)
nigel.wilkin@breckland.gov.uk
Williams JP, David (CON - Nar Valley)
david.williams@breckland.gov.uk

POLITICAL COMPOSITION

CON: 46, IND: 4, LAB: 3

CABINET

Leader: Mr William Nunn
Deputy Leader: Mr Michael Wassell
Assets & Strategic Development: Mr Mark Kiddle-Morris
Finance & Democratic Services: Mr Michael Wassell
Internal Services: Mr William Smith
Localism, Community & Environmental Services: Ms Lynda Turner
Planning & Environmental Services: Ms Elizabeth Gould
Performance & Business Development: Mr Ian Sherwood

COMMITTEE CHAIRS

Appeals: Mrs Linda Monument
Audit: Mr Cliff Jordan
General Purposes: Mr Philip Duigan
Licensing: Mr Gordon Bambridge
Overview & Scrutiny: Mr Philip Cowen
Planning: Mr Nigel Wilkin

BRENT L

Brent London Borough Council, (London Borough of Brent), Brent Town Hall, Forty Lane, Wembley HA9 9HD ☎ 020 8937 1234 ✉ customer.services@brent.gov.uk 🖳 www.brent.gov.uk

FACTS & FIGURES

Police Authority: Metropolitan Police Authority
Health Authority: NHS London
Learning and Skills Council: London
Parliamentary Constituencies: Brent Central, Brent North, Hampstead and Kilburn
EU Constituencies: London
Election Frequency: Elections are of whole council
Twinning: South Dublin County Council (Ireland)

PRINCIPAL OFFICERS

Chief Executive: Mr Gareth Daniel, Chief Executive, Brent Town Hall, Forty Lane, Wembley HA9 9HD ☎ 020 8937 1007 🖷 020 8937 1003 ✉ gareth.daniel@brent.gov.uk

Senior Management: Ms Sue Harper, Director - Environment & Neighbourhood Services, Brent House, 349-357 High Road, Wembley HA9 6BZ ☎ 020 8937 5192 🖷 020 8937 5010 ✉ sue.harper@brent.gov.uk

Senior Management: Mr Clive Heaphy, Director - Finance & Corporate Services, Brent Town Hall, Forty Lane, Wembley HA9 9HD ☎ 020 8937 1424 🖷 020 8937 1294 ✉ clive.heaphy@brent.gov.uk

Senior Management: Ms Fiona Ledden, Director - Legal & Procurement, Brent Town Hall, Forty Lane, Wembley HA9 9HD ☎ 020 8937 1292 🖷 020 8937 2164; 020 123 456 ✉ fiona.ledden@brent.gov.uk

Senior Management: Ms Toni McConville, Director - Customer & Community Engagement, Brent Town Hall, Forty Lane, Wembley HA9 9HD ☎ 020 8937 1079 🖷 020 8907 1105 ✉ toni.mcconville@brent.gov.uk

Senior Management: Mr Phil Newby, Brent Town Hall, Forty Lane, Wembley HA9 9HD ☎ 020 8937 1032 🖷 020 8937 1050 ✉ phil.newby@brent.gov.uk

Access Officer / Social Services (Disability): Mr David Dunkley, Head - Mental Health Service, 15 Brondesbury Road, Kilburn, London NW6 6BX ☎ 020 8937 4297 ✉ david.dunkley@brent.gov.uk

Architect, Building / Property Services: Mr Richard Ubertowski, Building Projects Manager, Brent Town Hall, Forty Lane, Wembley HA9 9HD ☎ 0208 937 1440 ✉ richard.ubertowski@brent.gov.uk

Best Value: Ms Cathy Tyson, Assistant Director - Corporate Policy, Brent Town Hall, Forty Lane, Wembley HA9 9HD ☎ 020 8937 1045 🖷 020 8937 1050 ✉ cathy.tyson@brent.gov.uk

Catering Services: Ms Meenal Shah, Acting Venues Manager, Brent Town Hall, Forty Lane, Wembley HA9 9HD ☎ 020 8937 6203 🖷 020 8937 1444 ✉ meenal.shah@brent.gov.uk

Children / Youth Services: Ms Angela Chiswell, Brent Town Hall, Forty Lane, Wembley HA9 9HD ☎ 020 8937 3667 ✉ angela.chiswell@brent.go.uk

Children / Youth Services: Dr Krutika Pau, Director - Children & Families, Chesterfield House, 9 Park Lane, Wembley HA9 7RH ☎ 020 8937 3126 🖷 020 8937 3073 ✉ krutika.pau@brent.gov.uk

Civil Registration: Mr Mark Rimmer, Head - Registration & Nationality Service, Brent Town Hall, Forty Lane, Wembley HA9 9HD ☎ 020 8937 1011 🖷 020 8937 1021 ✉ reg@brent.gov.uk

PR / Communications: Ms Toni McConville, Director - Customer & Community Engagement, Brent Town Hall, Forty Lane, Wembley HA9 9HD ☎ 020 8937 1079 🖷 020 8907 1105 ✉ toni.mcconville@brent.gov.uk

Community Safety: Ms Genny Renard, Interim Head - Community Safety Team, Brent Town Hall, Forty Lane, Wembley HA9 9HD ☎ 020 8937 1028 🖷 020 8937 1056 ✉ genny.renard@brent.gov.uk

Consumer Protection and Trading Standards: Mr Nagendar Bilon, Head - Consumer & Business Protection, Quality House, 249 Willesden Lane, London NW2 5JH ☎ 020 8937 5500 🖷 020 8937 5544 ✉ nagendar.bilon@brent.gov.uk

Contracts: Ms Deborah Down, Joint Head of Contracts - Legal Team, Brent Town Hall, Forty Lane, Wembley HA9 9HD ☎ 020 8937 1543 🖷 020 8937 1313 ✉ deborah.down@brent.gov.uk

Contracts: Ms Bridget Larsen, Joint Head of Contracts - Legal Team, Town Hall Annexe, Brent Town Hall, Forty Lane, Wembley Park HA9 9HD ☎ 020 8937 1486 ✉ bridget.larsen@brent.gov.uk

Customer Service: Ms Margaret Read, Assistant Director - Customer Services, Brent Town Hall, Forty Lane, Wembley HA9 9HD ☎ 020 8937 1521 🖷 020 8937 1202 ✉ margaret.read@brent.gov.uk

Economic Development: Mr Andrew Donald, Assistant Director - Regeneration, Brent House, High Road, Wembley HA9 9BZ ☎ 020 8937 1049 🖷 020 8937 1050 ✉ andrew.donald@brent.gov.uk

Education: Ms Carmen Coffey, Head - Pupil Parent Services, Chesterfield House, 9 Park Lane, Wembley HA9 7RW ☎ 020 8937 3033 ✉ carmen.coffey@brent.gov.uk

Education: Dr Krutika Pau, Director - Children & Families, Chesterfield House, 9 Park Lane, Wembley HA9 7RH ☎ 020 8937 3126 🖷 020 8937 3073 ✉ krutika.pau@brent.gov.uk

Electoral Registration: Mr Sean O'Sullivan, Electoral Services Manager, Brent Town Hall, Forty Lane, Wembley HA9 9HD ☎ 020 8937 1370 🖷 020 8937 1373 ✉ s.osullivan@brent.gov.uk

Emergency Planning: Mr Martyn Horne, Head - Emergency Planning & Control, Brent House, 349-357 High Road, Wembley HA9 6BZ ☎ 020 8937 5457 🖷 020 8937 5439 ✉ martyn.horne@brent.gov.uk

Environmental / Technical Services: Ms Sue Harper, Director - Environment & Neighbourhood Services, Brent House, 349-357 High Road, Wembley HA9 6BZ ☎ 020 8937 5192 🖷 020 8937 5010 ✉ sue.harper@brent.gov.uk

Environmental Health: Mr David Thrale, Head - Safer Streets & Protection, Brent House, 349-357 High Road, Wembley HA9 6BZ ☎ 020 8937 5164 🖷 020 8937 5150 ✉ david.thrale@brent.gov.uk

Estates, Property & Valuation: Mr Richard Barrett, Head - Property & Asset Management, Brent Town Hall Annexe, Forty Lane, Wembley HA9 9HD ☎ 020 8937 1334 ✉ richard.barrett@brent.gov.uk

European Liaison: Mr Andrew Donald, Assistant Director - Regeneration, Brent House, High Road, Wembley HA9 9BZ ☎ 020 8937 1049 🖷 020 8937 1050 ✉ andrew.donald@brent.gov.uk

Events Manager: Ms Meenal Shah, Acting Venues Manager, Brent Town Hall, Forty Lane, Wembley HA9 9HD ☎ 020 8937

6203 🖷 020 8937 1444 ✉ meenal.shah@brent.gov.uk

Facilities: Ms Meenal Shah, Acting Venues Manager, Brent Town Hall, Forty Lane, Wembley HA9 9HD ☎ 020 8937 6203 🖷 020 8937 1444 ✉ meenal.shah@brent.gov.uk

Facilities: Mr Keith Surrey, Head - Facilities & Business Management, Brent Town Hall, Forty Lane, Wembley HA9 9HD ☎ 020 8937 1437 ✉ keith.surrey@brent.gov.uk

Finance and Treasurer: Mr Mick Bowden, Deputy Director - Finance & Corporate Services, Brent Town Hall, Forty Lane, Wembley HA9 9HD ☎ 020 8937 1460 ✉ mick.bowden@brent.gov.uk

Finance and Treasurer: Mr Clive Heaphy, Director - Finance & Corporate Services, Brent Town Hall, Forty Lane, Wembley HA9 9HD ☎ 020 8937 1424 🖷 020 8937 1294 ✉ clive.heaphy@brent.gov.uk

Fleet Management: Mr Dave Shelley, Head - Passenger Transport, Hirst Hall, Tower Lane, GEC Estate, East Lane, Wembley HA9 7NB ☎ 020 8937 6720 🖷 020 8937 6759 ✉ david.shelley@brent.gov.uk

Highways: Mr Sandor Fazekas, Head - Highways, Brent House, 349-357 High Road, Wembley HA9 6BZ ☎ 020 8937 5113 🖷 020 8937 5129 ✉ sandor.fazekas@brent.gov.uk

Home Energy Conservation: Mr Perry Singh, Assistant Director - Housing Needs/Private Sector, Mahatma Gandhi House, 34 Wembley Hill Road, Wembley HA9 8AD ☎ 020 8937 2332 🖷 020 8937 2282 ✉ perry.singh@brent.gov.uk

Housing: Mr Saeed Hussein, Head - Private Housing Information Unit, Mahatma Gandhi House, 34 Wembley Hill Road, Wembley HA9 8AD ☎ 020 8937 1234 ✉ saeed.hussein@brent.gov.uk

Housing Maintenance: Mr Gerry Doherty, Chief Executive - BHP, Chancel House, Neasden Lane, London NW10 2UF ☎ 020 8937 2244 🖷 020 8937 2422 ✉ gerry.doherty@brent.gov.uk

Legal: Ms Fiona Ledden, Director - Legal & Procurement, Brent Town Hall, Forty Lane, Wembley HA9 9HD ☎ 020 8937 1292 🖷 020 8937 1313 ✉ fiona.ledden@brent.gov.uk

Leisure and Cultural Services: Ms Jenny Isaac, Assistant Director - Neighbourhoods, Brent House, 349-357 High Road, Wembley HA9 6BZ ☎ 020 8937 5001 🖷 020 8937 5010 ✉ jenny.isaac@brent.gov.uk

Leisure and Cultural Services: Mr Gerry Keifer, Head - Sports & Parks Service, Brent House, 349-357 High Road, Wembley HA9 6BZ ☎ 020 8937 1234 ✉ gerry.keifer@brent.gov.uk

Lifelong Learning: Ms Sue McKenzie, Head - Libraries, Arts & Heritage, Brent House, 349-357 High Road, Wembley HA9 6BZ ☎ 020 8937 3149 🖷 020 8937 3008 ✉ sue.mckenzie@brent.gov.uk

Member Services: Mr Peter Goss, Democratic Services Manager, Brent Town Hall, Forty Lane, Wembley HA9 9HD ☎ 020 8937 1353 🖷 020 8937 1360 ✉ peter.goss@brent.gov.uk

Member Services: Ms Fiona Ledden, Director - Legal & Procurement, Brent Town Hall, Forty Lane, Wembley HA9 9HD ☎ 020 8937 1292 🖷 020 8937 2164; 020 123 456 ✉ fiona.ledden@brent.gov.uk

Partnerships: Ms Cathy Tyson, Assistant Director - Corporate Policy, Brent Town Hall, Forty Lane, Wembley HA9 9HD ☎ 020 8937 1045 🖷 020 8937 1050 ✉ cathy.tyson@brent.gov.uk

Personnel / HR: Ms Tracey Connage, Assistant Director - People & Development, Brent Town Hall, Forty Lane, Wembley HA9 9HD ☎ 020 8937 1611 🖷 020 8937 6191 ✉ tracey.connage@brent.gov.uk

Planning: Mr Chris Walker, Chief Planner, Brent House, 349-357 High Road, Wembley HA9 6BZ ☎ 020 8937 5246 🖷 020 8937 5207 ✉ chris.walker@brent.gov.uk

Procurement: Ms Alison Matheson, Head - Procurement Strategy & Risk Management, Brent Town Hall Annexe, Forty Lane, Wembley HA9 9HD ☎ 020 8937 1363 🖷 020 8937 1179 ✉ alison.matheson@brent.gov.uk

Public Libraries: Ms Sue McKenzie, Head - Libraries, Arts & Heritage, Brent House, 349-357 High Road, Wembley HA9 6BZ ☎ 020 8937 3149 🖷 020 8937 3008 ✉ sue.mckenzie@brent.gov.uk

Recycling & Waste Minimisation: Mr Chris Whyte, Head - Recycling & Waste, Brent House, 349 - 357 High Road, Wembley HA9 9HD ☎ 020 8937 5342 🖷 020 8937 5090 ✉ chris.whyte@brent.gov.uk

Road Safety: Ms Debbie Fowler, Accident Prevention Manager, Brent Town Hall, Forty Lane, Wembley HA9 9HD ☎ 020 8903 8537 🖷 020 8903 7306 ✉ debbie.fowler@brent.gov.uk

Social Services: Ms Alison Elliott, Director - Adult Social Services, Mahatma Gandhi House, 34 Wembley Hill Road, Wembley HA9 8AD ☎ 020 8937 4230 ✉ alison.elliott@brent.gov.uk

Social Services (Adult): Ms Alison Elliott, Director - Adult Social Services, Mahatma Gandhi House, 34 Wembley Hill Road, Wembley HA9 8AD ☎ 020 8937 4230 ✉ alison.elliott@brent.gov.uk

Social Services (Children): Mr Graham Genoni, Assistant Director - Social Care, Chesterfield House, 9 Park Lane, Wembley HA9 7RJ ☎ 020 8937 4091 🖷 020 8937 3073 ✉ graham.genoni@brent.gov.uk

Staff Training: Ms Tracey Connage, Assistant Director - People & Development, Brent Town Hall, Forty Lane, Wembley HA9 9HD ☎ 020 8937 1611 🖷 020 8937 6191 ✉ tracey.connage@brent.gov.uk

Sustainable Communities: Ms Sue Harper, Director - Environment & Neighbourhood Services, Brent House, 349-357

High Road, Wembley HA9 6BZ ☎ 020 8937 5192 🖷 020 8937 5010 ✉ sue.harper@brent.gov.uk

Sustainable Development: Mr Michael Read, Assistant Director - Protection, Brent House, 349-357 High Road, Wembley HA9 6BX ☎ 020 8937 5302 🖷 020 8937 5010 ✉ michael.read@brent.gov.uk

Traffic Management: Mr Peter Boddy, Traffic Management Team Leader, Brent Town Hall, Forty Lane, Wembley HA9 9HD ☎ 020 8937 1234 ✉ peter.boddy@brent.gov.uk

Waste Collection and Disposal: Mr Neal St Lewis, Street Scene Manager, Brent House, 349-357 High Road, Wembley HA9 6BZ ☎ 020 8937 5079 🖷 020 8937 5090 ✉ neal.stlewis@brent.gov.uk

Waste Management: Mr Chris Whyte, Head - Recycling & Waste, Brent House, 349 - 357 High Road, Wembley HA9 9HD ☎ 020 8937 5342 🖷 020 8937 5090 ✉ chris.whyte@brent.gov.uk

MEMBERS OF THE COUNCIL (63)

***Mayor:* Adeyeye**, Michael (LAB - Queen's Park)
cllr.michael.adeyeye@brent.gov.uk
***Mayor:* Choudry**, Aslam (LAB - Dudden Hill)
cllr.aslam.choudry@brent.gov.uk
***Deputy Mayor:* Thomas**, Bobby (LAB - Kensal Green)
cllr.bobby.thomas@brent.gov.uk
***Group Leader:* Kansagra**, Suresh (CON - Kenton)
cllr.suresh.kansagra@brent.gov.uk
***Group Leader:* Lorber**, Paul (LD - Sudbury)
cllr.paul.lorber@brent.gov.uk
Aden, Abdi (LAB - Barnhill)
cllr.abdifatah.aden@brent.gov.uk
Al-Ebadi, Emad (LAB - Wembley Central)
cllr.emad.al-ebadi@brent.gov.uk
Allie, James (LD - Alperton)
cllr.james.allie@brent.gov.uk
Arnold, Mary (LAB - Kilburn)
cllr.mary.arnold@brent.gov.uk
Ashraf, Javaid (LD - Dollis Hill)
cllr.javaid.ashraf@brent.gov.uk
Bacchus, Joyce (LAB - Tokyngton)
cllr.joyce.bacchus@brent.gov.uk
Baker, Eddie (CON - Northwick Park)
cllr.eddie.baker@brent.gov.uk
Beck, Jack (LD - Dollis Hill)
cllr.jack.beck@brent.gov.uk
Beswick, Lincoln (LAB - Harlesden)
cllr.lincoln.beswick@brent.gov.uk
Brown, Daniel (LD - Alperton)
cllr.daniel.brown@brent.gov.uk
Butt, Muhammed (LAB - Tokyngton)
cllr.muhammed.butt@brent.gov.uk
Cheese, Barry (LD - Brondesbury Park)
cllr.barry.cheese@brent.gov.uk
Chohan, Bhagwanji (LAB - Alperton)
cllr.bhagwanji.chohan@brent.gov.uk
Choudhary, Shafique (LAB - Barnhill)
cllr.shafique.choudhary@brent.gov.uk
Clues, David (LD - Dudden Hill)
cllr.david.clues@brent.gov.uk
Colwill, Reg (CON - Kenton)
cllr.reg.colwill@brent.gov.uk
Crane, George (LAB - Fryent)
cllr.george.crane@brent.gov.uk
Cummins, Mark (LD - Brondesbury Park)
cllr.mark.cummins@brent.gov.uk
Daly, Mary (LAB - Sudbury)
cllr.mary.daly@brent.gov.uk
Denslow, James (LAB - Queen's Park)
cllr.james.denslow@brent.gov.uk
Gladbaum, Helga (LAB - Harlesden)
cllr.helga.gladbaum@brent.gov.uk
Green, Simon (LD - Queen's Park)
cllr.simon.green@brent.gov.uk
Harrison, Patricia (LAB - Preston)
cllr.patricia.harrison@brent.gov.uk
Hashmi, Sami (LD - Mapesbury)
cllr.sami.hashmi@brent.gov.uk
Hector, Claudia (LAB - Kensal Green)
cllr.claudia.hector@brent.gov.uk
Hirani, Krupesh (LAB - Dudden Hill)
cllr.krupesh.hirani@brent.gov.uk
Hopkins, Alison (LD - Dollis)
cllr.alison.hopkins@brent.gov.uk
Hossain, Jean (LAB - Preston)
cllr.jean.hossain@brent.gov.uk
Hunter, Ann (LD - Willesden Green)
cllr.ann.hunter@brent.gov.uk
John, Ann (LAB - Stonebridge)
cllr.ann.john@brent.gov.uk
Jones, Lesley (LAB - Willesden Green)
cllr.lesley.jones@brent.gov.uk
Kabir, Sandra (LAB - Queensbury)
cllr.sandra.kabir@brent.gov.uk
Kataria, Dhiraj (LAB - Welsh Harp)
cllr.dhiraj.kataria@brent.gov.uk
Leaman, Chris (LD - Mapesbury)
cllr.chris.leaman@brent.gov.uk
Long, Janice (LAB - Harlesden)
cllr.janice.long@brent.gov.uk
Mashari, Roxanne (LAB - Welsh Harp)
cllr.roxanne.mashari@brent.gov.uk
Matthews, Hayley (LD - Mapesbury)
cllr.hayley.matthews@brent.gov.uk
McLennan, Margaret (LAB - Northwick Park)
cllr.margaret.mclennan@brent.gov.uk
Mitchell Murray, Wilhelmina (LAB - Wembley Central)
cllr.wilhelmina.mitchellmurray@brent.gov.uk
Moher, Jim (LAB - Fryent)
cllr.jim.moher@brent.gov.uk
Moher, Ruth (LAB - Fryent)
cllr.ruth.moher@brent.gov.uk
Moloney, Colum (LAB - Stonebridge)
cllr.colum.moloney@brent.gov.uk
Naheerathan, Kana (LAB - Queensbury)
cllr.kana.naheerathan@brent.gov.uk
Ogunro, Benjamin (LAB - Kilburn)
cllr.benjamin.ogunro@brent.gov.uk
Oladapo, Tayo (LAB - Kilburn)
cllr.tayo.oladapo@brent.gov.uk
Patel, Harihar (CON - Northwick Park)
cllr.harihar.patel@brent.gov.uk
Patel, Bhiku (CON - Kenton)
cllr.bhiku.patel@brent.gov.uk
Patel, Chandubhai (LD - Sudbury)
cllr.chandubhai.patel@brent.gov.uk
Patel, Harshadbhai (CON - Preston)

cllr.harshadbhai.patel@brent.gov.uk
Patel, Ramesh (LAB - Queensbury)
cllr.ramesh.patel@brent.gov.uk
Pavey, Michael (LAB - Barnhill)
cllr.michael.pavey@brent.gov.uk
Powney, James (LAB - Kensal Green)
clr.james.powney@brent.gov.uk
Shaw, Carol (LD - Brondesbury Park)
cllr.carol.shaw@brent.gov.uk
Sheth, Ketan (LAB - Tokyngton)
cllr.ketan.sheth@brent.gov.uk
Sheth, Krupa (LAB - Wembley Central)
cllr.krupa.sheth@brent.gov.uk
Singh, Harbhajan (LAB - Welsh Harp)
cllr.harbhajan.singh@brent.gov.uk
Sneddon, Gavin (LD - Willesden Green)
cllr.gavin.sneddon@brent.gov.uk
Van Kalwala, Zaffar (LAB - Stonebridge)
cllr.zaffar.vankalwala@brent.gov.uk

POLITICAL COMPOSITION

LAB: 40, LD: 17, CON: 6

CABINET

Leader: Mr Muhammed Butt
Deputy Leader: Mrs Ruth Moher
Adults & Health: Mr Krupesh Hirani
Corporate Strategy & Policy Co-ordination: Mr Muhammed Butt
Crime & Public Safety: Mr Lincoln Beswick
Customers & Citizens: Ms Lesley Jones
Environment & Neighbourhoods: Mr James Powney
Finance & Corporate Services: Mrs Ruth Moher
Highways & Transportation: Mr Jim Moher
Housing: Ms Janice Long
Regeneration & Major Projects: Mr George Crane

COMMITTEE CHAIRS

Alcohol & Entertainment Licensing: Mrs Joyce Bacchus
Audit: Mr Stephen Wood (External)
Brent Pension Fund: Mr Shafique Choudhary
Budget & Finance Overview & Scrutiny: Mr James Allie
Children & Young People Overview & Scrutiny: Ms Roxanne Mashari
General Purposes: Mr Muhammed Butt
Health Partnerships Overview & Scrutiny: Ms Sandra Kabir
Partnerships & Place: Mr Zaffar Van Kalwala
Planning: Mr Ketan Sheth
Standards: Ms Angela Ruotolo (External)

BRENTWOOD D

Brentwood Borough Council, Town Hall, Ingrave Road, Brentwood CM15 8AY ☎ 01277 312500 🖷 01277 312743 ✉ enquiries@brentwood.gov.uk 💻 www.brentwood.gov.uk

FACTS & FIGURES

Police Authority: Essex Police Authority
Health Authority: East of England Strategic Health Authority
Learning and Skills Council: Eastern
Parliamentary Constituencies: Brentwood and Ongar
EU Constituencies: Eastern
Election Frequency: Elections are by thirds
Twinning: Montbazon (France); Roth LK (Germany); Sister City: City of Brentwood (TN, USA)

PRINCIPAL OFFICERS

Chief Executive: Mrs Alison Crowe, Managing Director, Town Hall, Ingrave Road, Brentwood CM15 8AY ☎ 01277 312648 🖷 01277 312743 ✉ alison.crowe@brentwood.gov.uk

Senior Management: Mr Steven Boyle, Head of Legal & Governance, Town Hall, Ingrave Road, Brentwood CM15 8AY ☎ 01277 312555 🖷 01277 312703 ✉ steve.boyle@brentwood.gov.uk

Senior Management: Ms Jo-Anne Ireland, Head of Corporate Finance, Town Hall, Ingrave Road, Brentwood CM15 8AY ☎ 01277 312712 🖷 01277 312743 ✉ jo-anne.ireland@brentwood.gov.uk

Senior Management: Mr Roy Ormsby, Head of Sustainable Communities & Public Places, Town Hall, Ingrave Road, Brentwood CM15 8AY ☎ 01277 312554 🖷 01277 312743 ✉ roy.ormsby@brentwood.gov.uk

Senior Management: Mr Brian Partridge, Director of Strategic & Corporate Services, Town Hall, Ingrave Road, Brentwood CM15 8AY ☎ 01277 312689 ✉ brian.partridge@brentwood.gov.uk

Senior Management: Mr Steve Summers, Business Improvement Executive Manager, Town Hall, Ingrave Road, Brentwood CM15 8AY ☎ 01277 312749 🖷 01277 312743 ✉ steve.summers@brentwood.gov.uk

Access Officer / Social Services (Disability): Mrs Jennifer Candler, Head of Planning, Town Hall, Ingrave Road, Brentwood CM15 8AY ✉ jennifer.candler@brentwood.gov.uk

Building Control: Mr Gary Price, Building Control Team Leader, Town Hall, Ingrave Road, Brentwood CM15 8AY ☎ 01277 312534 🖷 ; 01277 312743 ✉ gary.price@brentwood.gov.uk

Children / Youth Services: Ms Kim Anderson, Partnerships, Leisure & Funding Manager, Town Hall, Ingrave Road, Brentwood CM15 8AY ☎ 01277 312634 🖷 ; 01277 312743 ✉ kim.anderson@brentwood.gov.uk

PR / Communications: Miss Catherine Campling, Account Manager - Communications, Town Hall, Ingrave Road, Brentwood CM15 8AY ☎ 01277 312569 🖷 01277 312743 ✉ catherine.campling@brentwood.gov.uk

Community Planning: Ms Kate Gordon, Planning Policy Manager, Town Hall, Ingrave Road, Brentwood CM15 8AY ☎ 01277 312609 🖷 01277 312743 ✉ kate.gordon@brentwood.gov.uk

Community Safety: Ms Tracey Lilley, Anti-Social Behaviour Co-ordinator, Town Hall, Ingrave Road, Brentwood CM15 8AY ☎ 01277 312644 🖷 01277 312743 ✉ tracey.lilley@brentwood.gov.uk

Computer Management: Mr Tim Huggins, ICT Manager, Town Hall, Ingrave Road, Brentwood CM15 8AY ☎ 01277 312719

🖷 01277 312743 ⌂ tim.huggins@brentwood.gov.uk

Contracts: Mr Colin Heaps, Procurement Officer, Town Hall, Ingrave Road, Brentwood CM15 8AY ☎ 01277 312587 ⌂ colin.heaps@brentwood.gov.uk

Corporate Services: Mr Lee Taylor, Executive Office Manager, Town Hall, Ingrave Road, Brentwood CM15 8AY ☎ 01277 312740 🖷 01277 312743 ⌂ lee.taylor@brentwood.gov.uk

Customer Service: Mr Rick Steels, Revenues & Benefits Officer, Town Hall, Ingrave Road, Brentwood CM15 8AY ☎ 01277 312866 🖷 01277 312643 ⌂ rick.steels@brentwood.gov.uk

Direct Labour: Mr Darren Laver, Waste & Grounds Manager, Town Hall, Ingrave Road, Brentwood CM15 8AY ☎ 01277 312779 🖷 01277 312743 ⌂ darren.laver@brentwood.gov.uk

Economic Development: Ms Davina Fell, Business Development & Marketing Manager, Town Hall, Ingrave Road, Brentwood CM15 8AY ☎ 01277 312629 🖷 01277 312643 ⌂ davina.fell@brentwood.gov.uk

E-Government: Mr Tim Huggins, ICT Manager, Town Hall, Ingrave Road, Brentwood CM15 8AY ☎ 01277 312719 🖷 01277 312743 ⌂ tim.huggins@brentwood.gov.uk

Electoral Registration: Mrs Carole Tatton-Bennett, Electoral Services Manager, Town Hall, Ingrave Road, Brentwood CM15 8AY ☎ 01277 312709 🖷 01277 312743 ⌂ carole.tatton-bennett@brentwood.gov.uk

Emergency Planning: Mr Greg Campbell, Emergency Planning Officer, Town Hall, Ingrave Road, Brentwood CM15 8AY ☎ 01277 312527 🖷 01277 312743 ⌂ greg.campbell@brentwood.gov.uk

Environmental Health: Mr Ashley Culverwell, Head of Environmental Health & Enforcement, Town Hall, Ingrave Road, Brentwood CM15 8AY ☎ 01277 312504 🖷 01277 312526 ⌂ ashley.culverwell@brentwood.gov.uk

Events Manager: Ms Kim Anderson, Partnerships, Leisure & Funding Manager, Town Hall, Ingrave Road, Brentwood CM15 8AY ☎ 01277 312634 🖷 ; 01277 312743 ⌂ kim.anderson@brentwood.gov.uk

Fleet Management: Mr Colin Heaps, Procurement Officer, Town Hall, Ingrave Road, Brentwood CM15 8AY ☎ 01277 312587 🖷 01277 312743 ⌂ colin.heaps@brentwood.gov.uk

Grounds Maintenance: Mr Stuart Anderson, Open Space Strategy Coordinator, Town Hall, Ingrave Road, Brentwood CM15 8AY ☎ 01277 312654 🖷 01277 312743 ⌂ stuart.anderson@brentwood.gov.uk

Health and Safety: Mr Mark Stanbury, Team Environmental Health Officer, Town Hall, Ingrave Road, Brentwood CM15 8AY ☎ 01277 312510 🖷 01277 312743 ⌂ mark.stanbury@brentwood.gov.uk

Housing: Mr Malcolm Knights, Housing Services Manager, Town Hall, Ingrave Road, Brentwood CM15 8AY ☎ 01277 312586 🖷 01277 312643 ⌂ malcolm.knights@brentwood.gov.uk

Housing Maintenance: Mr Malcolm Knights, Housing Services Manager, Town Hall, Ingrave Road, Brentwood CM15 8AY ☎ 01277 312586 🖷 01277 312643 ⌂ malcolm.knights@brentwood.gov.uk

Legal: Mr Steven Boyle, Head of Legal & Governance, Town Hall, Ingrave Road, Brentwood CM15 8AY ☎ 01277 312555 🖷 01277 312703 ⌂ steve.boyle@brentwood.gov.uk

Leisure and Cultural Services: Ms Kim Anderson, Partnerships, Leisure & Funding Manager, Town Hall, Ingrave Road, Brentwood CM15 8AY ☎ 01277 312634 🖷 ; 01277 312743 ⌂ kim.anderson@brentwood.gov.uk

Licensing: Mr Simon Harvey, Principal Licensing Officer, Town Hall, Ingrave Road, Brentwood CM15 8AY ☎ 01277 312503 🖷 01277 312643 ⌂ simon.harvey@brentwood.gov.uk

Parking: Ms Carol Tomlin, Parking Manager, Town Hall, Ingrave Road, Brentwood CM15 8AY ☎ 01277 312583 🖷 ; 01277 312643 ⌂ carol.tomlin@brentwood.gov.uk

Personnel / HR: Mr Steve Summers, Business Improvement Executive Manager, Town Hall, Ingrave Road, Brentwood CM15 8AY ☎ 01277 312749 🖷 01277 312743 ⌂ steve.summers@brentwood.gov.uk

Procurement: Mr Colin Heaps, Procurement Officer, Town Hall, Ingrave Road, Brentwood CM15 8AY ☎ 01277 312587 ⌂ colin.heaps@brentwood.gov.uk

Recycling & Waste Minimisation: Mr Darren Laver, Waste & Grounds Manager, Town Hall, Ingrave Road, Brentwood CM15 8AY ☎ 01277 312779 🖷 01277 312743 ⌂ darren.laver@brentwood.gov.uk

Staff Training: Mr Steve Summers, Business Improvement Executive Manager, Town Hall, Ingrave Road, Brentwood CM15 8AY ☎ 01277 312749 🖷 01277 312743 ⌂ steve.summers@brentwood.gov.uk

Street Scene: Mr Roy Ormsby, Head of Sustainable Communities & Public Places, Town Hall, Ingrave Road, Brentwood CM15 8AY ☎ 01277 312554 🖷 01277 312743 ⌂ roy.ormsby@brentwood.gov.uk

Waste Collection and Disposal: Mr Darren Laver, Waste & Grounds Manager, Town Hall, Ingrave Road, Brentwood CM15 8AY ☎ 01277 312779 🖷 01277 312743 ⌂ darren.laver@brentwood.gov.uk

Waste Management: Mr Darren Laver, Waste & Grounds Manager, Town Hall, Ingrave Road, Brentwood CM15 8AY ☎ 01277 312779 🖷 01277 312743 ⌂ darren.laver@brentwood.gov.uk

Children's Play Areas: Mr Stuart Anderson, Open Space Strategy Coordinator, Town Hall, Ingrave Road, Brentwood CM15 8AY ☎ 01277 312654 🖷 01277 312743 ⌂ stuart.anderson@brentwood.gov.uk

MEMBERS OF THE COUNCIL (37)

***Mayor:* Coe**, Ann (CON - South Weald)
ann.coe@brentwood.gov.uk
***Deputy Mayor:* Henwood**, Madeline (CON - Tipps Cross)
madeline.henwood@brentwood.gov.uk
***Group Leader:* Kendall**, David (LD - Pilgrims Hatch)
david.kendall@brentwood.gov.uk
Aspinell, Barry (LD - Pilgrims Hatch)
barry.aspinell@brentwood.gov.uk
Baker, Phil (CON - Shenfield)
phil.baker@brentwood.gov.uk
Braid, Alan (CON - Hutton Central)
alan.braid@brentwood.gov.uk
Carter, Ross (LD - Brentwood North)
ross.carter@brentwood.gov.uk
Chilvers, Karen (LD - Brentwood West)
Clark, Graeme (LD - Shenfield)
graeme.clark@brentwood.gov.uk
Clarke, Nigel (CON - Brentwood West)
nigel.clarke@brentwood.gov.uk
Cornell, Claire (CON - Hutton East)
claire.cornell@brentwood.gov.uk
Davies, Vicky (LD - Pilgrims Hatch)
vicky.davies@brentwood.gov.uk
Golding, Linda (CON - Herongate & Ingave & West Horndon)
linda.golding@brentwood.gov.uk
Hirst, Roger (CON - Hutton South)
roger.hirst@brentwood.gov.uk
Hones, Noelle (CON - Ingatestone, Fryerning & Mountnessing)
noelle.hones@brentwood.gov.uk
Hossack, Chris (CON - Hutton East)
chris.hossack@brentwood.gov.uk
Keeble, Roger (IND - Tipps Cross)
roger.keeble@brentwood.gov.uk
Kerslake, John (CON - Hutton Central)
Lee, Lionel (CON - Shenfield)
lionel.lee@brentwood.gov.uk
Le-Surf, Mike (LAB - Brentwood South)
mike.le-surf@brentwood.gov.uk
Lewis, Cheralyn (CON - Brentwood South)
cheralyn.lewis@brentwood.gov.uk
Lloyd, William (CON - Warley)
william.lloyd@brentwood.gov.uk
McCheyne, Roger (CON - Brizes & Doddinghurst)
roger.mccheyne@brentwood.gov.uk
McKinlay, Louise (CON - Hutton North)
louise.mckinlay@brentwood.gov.uk
Morrissey, Julie (LAB - Brentwood South)
Murphy, Sheila (CON - Herongate, Ingrave & West Horndon)
Mynott, Philip (LD - Brentwood North)
philip.mynott@brentwood.gov.uk
Naylor, Ann (CON - Brizes & Doddinghurst)
ann.naylor@brentwood.gov.uk
Parker, Keith (CON - Brizes & Doddinghurst)
keith.parker@brentwood.gov.uk
Pound, Janet (CON - Warley)
jan.pound@brentwood.gov.uk
Quirk, Russell (CON - Hutton North)
russell.quirk@brentwood.gov.uk
Reed, Mark (CON - Hutton South)
mark.reed@brentwood.gov.uk
Russell, Will (CON - Brentwood West)
will.russell@brentwood.gov.uk
Sapwell, James (LD - Brentwood North)
james.sapwell@brentwood.gov.uk
Sleep, Tony (CON - Ingatestone, Fryerning & Mountnessing)
tony.sleep@brentwood.gov.uk
Sparling, Keith (CON - Ingatestone, Fryerning & Mountnessing)
keith.sparling@brentwood.gov.uk
Tee, David (CON - Warley)
david.tee@brentwood.gov.uk

POLITICAL COMPOSITION

CON: 26, LD: 8, LAB: 2, IND: 1

CABINET

Leader: Mrs Louise McKinlay
Deputy Leader: Mr Roger Hirst

COMMITTEE CHAIRS

Asset, Infrastructure & Localism: Mr Russell Quirk
Audit: Mr Chris Hossack
Environment: Mr Tony Sleep
Housing & Health: Ms Janet Pound
Overview & Scrutiny: Mr Barry Aspinell
Planning Development Control & Licensing: Mr Roger Hirst

BRIDGEND W

Bridgend County Borough Council, (Cyngor Bwrdeistref Sirol Pen-y-bont ar Ogwr), Civic Offices, Angel Street, Bridgend CF31 4WB ☎ 01656 643643 🖷 01656 668126
✉ talktous@bridgend.gov.uk 💻 www.bridgend.gov.uk

FACTS & FIGURES

Police Authority: South Wales Police Authority
Learning and Skills Council: Wales
Parliamentary Constituencies: Bridgend, Ogmore
EU Constituencies: Wales
Election Frequency: Elections are of whole council

PRINCIPAL OFFICERS

Chief Executive: Dr Jo Farrar, Chief Executive, Civic Offices, Angel Street, Bridgend CF31 4WB ☎ 01656 643643 🖷 01656 643215 ✉ jo.farrar@bridgend.gov.uk

Assistant Chief Executive: Mr Andrew Jolley, Assistant Chief Executive - Legal & Regulatory Services, Civic Offices, Angel Street, Bridgend CF31 4WB ☎ 01656 643106 🖷 01656 657899 ✉ andrew.jolley@bridgend.gov.uk

Assistant Chief Executive: Mr David MacGregor, Assistant Chief Executive, Civic Offices, Angel Street, Bridgend CF31 4WB ☎ 01656 643307 ✉ david.macgregor@bridgend.gov.uk

Architect, Building / Property Services: Mr Martin Keegan, Group Manager - Architectural Services, Morien House, Bennett Street, Bridgend Industrial Estate, Bridgend CF31 3SH ☎ 01656 644010 🖷 01656 646972 ✉ martin.keegan@bridgend.gov.uk

Best Value: Mr David MacGregor, Assistant Chief Executive, Civic Offices, Angel Street, Bridgend CF31 4WB ☎ 01656 643307 ✉ david.macgregor@bridgend.gov.uk

Best Value: Ms Yuan Shen, Corporate Improvement Manager, Civic Offices, Angel Street, Bridgend CF31 4WB ☎ 01656 643224 ✉ yuan.shen@bridgend.gov.uk

Building Control: Mr Brian Wallace, Building Control Manager, Civic Offices, Angel Street, Bridgend CF31 4WB ☎ 01656 643406 🖷 01656 668249 ✉ brian.wallace@bridgend.gov.uk

Catering Services: Ms Louise Kerton, Team Manager - Catering Services, Supplies Building, Waterton, Bridgend CF31 7YR ☎ 01656 664527 ✉ louise.kerton@bridgend.gov.uk

Children / Youth Services: Ms Hilary Anthony, Executive Director - Children, Sunnyside Offices, Sunnyside, Bridgend CF31 4AR ☎ 01656 642617 🖷 01656 642675 ✉ hilary.anthony@bridgend.gov.uk

Children / Youth Services: Mr Colin Turner, Head of Safeguarding & Family Support, Sunnyside Offices, Sunnyside, Bridgend CF31 4AR ☎ 01656 642314 🖷 01656 766162 ✉ colin.turner@bridgend.gov.uk

Civil Registration: Ms Lucy Bratcher, Superintendent Registrar, Register Office, Ty'r Ardd, Sunnyside, Bridgend CF31 4AR ☎ 01656 642391 🖷 01656 667529 ✉ lucy.bratcher@bridgend.gov.uk

PR / Communications: Ms Michelle Bower, Communications & Marketing Manager, Civic Offices, Angel Street, Bridgend CF31 4WB ☎ 01656 643648 🖷 01656 643215 ✉ michelle.bower@bridgend.gov.uk

Community Safety: Mr John Davies, Community Safety Team Leader, 3rd Floor, Derwen House, Court Road, Bridgend CF31 1BN ☎ 01656 679935 🖷 01656 679553 ✉ john.davies@bridgend.gov.uk

Computer Management: Mr David Sutherland, Head of ICT & Property Services, Sunnyside House, Sunnyside, Bridgend CF31 4AR ☎ 01656 642110 🖷 01656 642125 ✉ david.sutherland@bridgend.gov.uk

Consumer Protection and Trading Standards: Mr Lee Jones, Group Manager, Civic Offices, Angel Street, Bridgend CF31 4WB ☎ 01656 643259 ✉ lee.jones@bridgend.gov.uk

Contracts: Mr James Ferris, Head of Procurement, Raven's Court, Brewery Lane, Bridgend CF31 4AP ☎ 01656 664586 🖷 01656 664550 ✉ james.ferris@bridgend.gov.uk

Customer Service: Ms Beverley Davies, Customer Service Manager, Civic Offices, Angel Street, Bridgend CF31 4WB ☎ 01656 643333 ✉ beverley.davies@bridgend.gov.uk

Customer Service: Mr David Sutherland, Head of ICT & Property Services, Sunnyside House, Sunnyside, Bridgend CF31 4AR ☎ 01656 642110 🖷 01656 642125 ✉ david.sutherland@bridgend.gov.uk

Economic Development: Mr Ray Pearce, Manager Regeneration & Economic Development, Economic Development Unit, Innovation Centre, Bridgend Science Park, Bridgend CF31 3NA ☎ 01656 815311 🖷 01656 641714 ✉ ray.pearce@bridgend.gov.uk

Education: Ms Hilary Anthony, Executive Director - Children, Sunnyside Offices, Sunnyside, Bridgend CF31 4AR ☎ 01656 642617 🖷 01656 642675 ✉ hilary.anthony@bridgend.gov.uk

E-Government: Mr David Sutherland, Head of ICT & Property Services, Sunnyside House, Sunnyside, Bridgend CF31 4AR ☎ 01656 642110 🖷 01656 642125 ✉ david.sutherland@bridgend.gov.uk

Electoral Registration: Ms Eirwen Eves, Electoral Services Manager, Civic Offices, Angel Street, Bridgend CF31 4WB ☎ 01656 643146 🖷 01656 657704 ✉ eirwen.eves@bridgend.gov.uk

Emergency Planning: Mrs Julie Cooper, Principal Emergency Planning Officer, Civic Offices, Angel Street, Bridgend CF31 4WB ☎ 01656 643300 🖷 01656 643215 ✉ julie.cooper@bridgend.gov.uk

Energy Management: Ms Satwant Pryce, Head of Regeneration & Development, Civic Offices, Angel Street, Bridgend CF31 4WB ☎ 01656 643151 🖷 01656 643190 ✉ satwant.pryce@bridgend.gov.uk

Environmental / Technical Services: Mr Richard Fletcher, Head of Street Scene, Civic Offices, Angel Street, Bridgend CF31 4WB ☎ 01656 643403 ✉ richard.fletcher@bridgend.gov.uk

Environmental Health: Mr Philip Stanton, Service Manager, Civic Offices, Angel Street, Bridgend CF31 4WB ☎ 01656 643141 ✉ philip.stanton@bridgend.gov.uk

Estates, Property & Valuation: Ms Fiona Blick, Group Manager - Property Services, Raven's Court, Brewery Lane, Bridgend CF31 4AP ☎ 01656 642702 🖷 01656 660137 ✉ fiona.blick@bridgend.gov.uk

European Liaison: Mr Mark Halliwell, Manager - Regeneration Funding, Innovation Centre, Bridgend Science Park, Bridgend CF31 3NA ☎ 01656 815329 🖷 01656 768098 ✉ mark.halliwell@bridgend.gov.uk

Events Manager: Ms Emma Winkley, Marketing Team Leader, Civic Offices, Angel Street, Bridgend CF31 4WB ☎ 01656 642047 ✉ emma.winkley@bridgend.gov.uk

Facilities: Mr Gwyn Harding, Principal Facilities Manager, Raven's Court, Brewery Lane, Bridgend CF31 4AP ☎ 01656 643121 🖷 01656 657899 ✉ gwyn.harding@bridgend.gov.uk

Facilities: Mr David Sutherland, Head of ICT & Property Services, Sunnyside House, Sunnyside, Bridgend CF31 4AR ☎ 01656 642110 🖷 01656 642125 ✉ david.sutherland@bridgend.gov.uk

Finance and Treasurer: Mr David MacGregor, Assistant Chief Executive, Civic Offices, Angel Street, Bridgend CF31 4WB ☎ 01656 643307 ✉ david.macgregor@bridgend.gov.uk

Fleet Management: Mr Anthony Thomas, Chief Assistant - Fleet Services, Waterton Lane, Warterton, Bridgend CF31 3YP ☎ 01656 642844 🖷 01656 642869 ✉ anthony.thomas@bridgend.gov.uk

Grounds Maintenance: Mr Gareth Evans, Parks & Playing Fields Manager, Civic Offices, Angel Street, Bridgend CF31 4WB

☎ 01656 642720 🖷 01656 662150 ✉ gareth.evans@bridgend.gov.uk

Health and Safety: Ms Claire Howells, Heath & Safety Manager, Raven's Court, Brewery Lane, Bridgend CF31 4AP ☎ 01656 642872 🖷 01656 646966 ✉ claire.howells@bridgend.gov.uk

Highways: Mr Glyn Jenkins, Group Manager - Highways & Fleet, Morien House, Bennett Street, Bridgend Industrial Estate, Bridgend CF31 3SH ☎ 01656 642545 🖷 01656 642581 ✉ glyn.jenkins@bridgend.gov.uk

Home Energy Conservation: Ms Louise Fradd, Corporate Director - Communities, Civic Offices, Angel Street, Bridgend CF31 4WB ☎ 01656 643380 ✉ louise.fradd@bridgend.gov.uk

Housing: Ms Satwant Pryce, Head of Regeneration & Development, Civic Offices, Angel Street, Bridgend CF31 4WB ☎ 01656 643151 🖷 01656 643190 ✉ satwant.pryce@bridgend.gov.uk

Legal: Mr Andrew Jolley, Assistant Chief Executive - Legal & Regulatory Services, Civic Offices, Angel Street, Bridgend CF31 4WB ☎ 01656 643106 🖷 01656 657899 ✉ andrew.jolley@bridgend.gov.uk

Leisure and Cultural Services: Mr Mark Shephard, Head of Healthy Living, Sunnyside Offices, Sunnyside, Bridgend CF31 4AR ☎ 01656 642613 🖷 01656 642675 ✉ mark.shephard@bridgend.gov.uk

Licensing: Ms Yvonne Witchell, Licensing & Registration Officer, Civic Offices, Angel Street, Bridgend CF31 4WB ☎ 01656 643105 🖷 01656 657899 ✉ yvonne.witchell@bridgend.gov.uk

Lifelong Learning: Mr Richard Landy, Head of Learning, Sunnyside Offices, Sunnyside, Bridgend CF31 4AR ☎ 01656 642612 ✉ richard.landy@bridgend.gov.uk

Member Services: Mr Gary Jones, Democratic Services Manager, Civic Offices, Angel Street, Bridgend CF31 4WB ☎ 01656 643385 🖷 01656 643602 ✉ gary.jones@bridgend.gov.uk

Parking: Mr John Duddridge, Group Manager - Transportation & Engineering, Morien House, Bennett Street, Bridgend Industrial Estate, Bridgend CF31 4WB ☎ 01656 642535 🖷 01656 642581 ✉ john.duddridge@bridgend.gov.uk

Partnerships: Ms Hilary Anthony, Executive Director - Children, Sunnyside Offices, Sunnyside, Bridgend CF31 4AR ☎ 01656 642617 🖷 01656 642675 ✉ hilary.anthony@bridgend.gov.uk

Partnerships: Mr Trevor Guy, Head of Strategy Partnerships & Commissioning, Sunnyside, Bridgend CF31 4AR ☎ 01656 642615 ✉ trevor.guy@bridgend.gov.uk

Partnerships: Mr David MacGregor, Assistant Chief Executive, Civic Offices, Angel Street, Bridgend CF31 4WB ☎ 01656 643307 ✉ david.macgregor@bridgend.gov.uk

Partnerships: Ms Yuan Shen, Corporate Improvement Manager, Civic Offices, Angel Street, Bridgend CF31 4WB ☎ 01656 643224 ✉ yuan.shen@bridgend.gov.uk

Personnel / HR: Ms Sarah Kingsbury, Head of Human Resources & Organisational Development, Raven's Court, Brewery Lane, Bridgend CF31 4AP ☎ 01656 643209 🖷 01656 646966 ✉ sarah.kingsbury@bridgend.gov.uk

Planning: Ms Satwant Pryce, Head of Regeneration & Development, Civic Offices, Angel Street, Bridgend CF31 4WB ☎ 01656 643151 🖷 01656 643190 ✉ satwant.pryce@bridgend.gov.uk

Procurement: Mr James Ferris, Head of Procurement, Raven's Court, Brewery Lane, Bridgend CF31 4AP ☎ 01656 664586 🖷 01656 664550 ✉ james.ferris@bridgend.gov.uk

Recycling & Waste Minimisation: Mr Huw Jenkins, Group Manager - Street Works, Civic Offices, Angel Street, Bridgend CF31 4WB ☎ 01656 643416 🖷 01656 646972 ✉ huw.jenkins@bridgend.gov.uk

Regeneration: Ms Louise Fradd, Corporate Director - Communities, Civic Offices, Angel Street, Bridgend CF31 4WB ☎ 01656 643380 ✉ louise.fradd@bridgend.gov.uk

Regeneration: Ms Satwant Pryce, Head of Regeneration & Development, Civic Offices, Angel Street, Bridgend CF31 4WB ☎ 01656 643151 🖷 01656 643190 ✉ satwant.pryce@bridgend.gov.uk

Road Safety: Mr Trevor Taylor, Road Safety / Traffic Management Team Leader, Civic Offices, Angel Street, Bridgend CF31 4WB ☎ 01656 642587 ✉ trevor.taylor@bridgend.gov.uk

Social Services (Adult): Mrs Susan Cooper, Head of Adult Social Care, Sunnyside Offices, Sunnyside, Bridgend CF31 4AR ☎ 01656 642251 🖷 01656 766162 ✉ susan.cooper@bridgend.gov.uk

Social Services (Children): Mr Colin Turner, Head of Safeguarding & Family Support, Sunnyside Offices, Sunnyside, Bridgend CF31 4AR ☎ 01656 642314 🖷 01656 766162 ✉ colin.turner@bridgend.gov.uk

Street Scene: Mr Richard Fletcher, Head of Street Scene, Civic Offices, Angel Street, Bridgend CF31 4WB ☎ 01656 643403 ✉ richard.fletcher@bridgend.gov.uk

Street Scene: Ms Louise Fradd, Corporate Director - Communities, Civic Offices, Angel Street, Bridgend CF31 4WB ☎ 01656 643380 ✉ louise.fradd@bridgend.gov.uk

Street Scene: Mr Mike Toozer, Traffic Management & Road Safety Manager, Morien House, Bennett Street, Bridgend Industrial Estate, Bridgend CF31 3YR ☎ 01656 642524 🖷 01656 642581 ✉ mike.toozer@bridgend.gov.uk

Sustainable Communities: Mr Michael Jenkins, Principal Sustainable Development Officer, Civic Offices, Angel Street, Bridgend CF31 4WB ☎ 01656 643179 🖷 01656 643669 ✉ michael.jenkins@bridgend.gov.uk

Sustainable Development: Mr Michael Jenkins, Principal Sustainable Development Officer, Civic Offices, Angel Street, Bridgend CF31 4WB ☎ 01656 643179 🖷 01656 643669

michael.jenkins@bridgend.gov.uk

Tourism: Mr Andrew Lloyd-Hughes, Manager Countryside and Tourism, Innovation Centre, Bridgend Science Park, Bridgend CF31 3NA ☎ 01656 815334 🖷 01656 768757 Andrew.Lloyd-Hughes@bridgend.gov.uk

Tourism: Ms Satwant Pryce, Head of Regeneration & Development, Civic Offices, Angel Street, Bridgend CF31 4WB ☎ 01656 643151 🖷 01656 643190 satwant.pryce@bridgend.gov.uk

Town Centre: Mr Mike Toozer, Traffic Management & Road Safety Manager, Morien House, Bennett Street, Bridgend Industrial Estate, Bridgend CF31 3YR ☎ 01656 642524 🖷 01656 642581 mike.toozer@bridgend.gov.uk

Traffic Management: Mr Trevor Taylor, Traffic Management & Road Safety Team Leader, Morien House, Bennett Street, Bridgend Industrial Estate, Bridgend CF31 3SH ☎ 01656 642587 trevor.taylor@bridgend.gov.uk

Traffic Management: Mr Mike Toozer, Traffic Management & Road Safety Manager, Morien House, Bennett Street, Bridgend Industrial Estate, Bridgend CF31 3YR ☎ 01656 642524 🖷 01656 642581 mike.toozer@bridgend.gov.uk

Transport: Mr John Duddridge, Group Manager - Transportation & Engineering, Morien House, Bennett Street, Bridgend Industrial Estate, Bridgend CF31 3SH ☎ 01656 642535 🖷 01656 642581 john.duddridge@bridgend.gov.uk

Transport Planner: Mr Richard Metford, Policy, Development & Co-ordination Manager, Morien House, Bennett Street, Bridgend Industrial Estate, Bridgend CF31 3SH ☎ 01656 642520 richard.metford@bridgend.gov.uk

Waste Collection and Disposal: Mr Huw Jenkins, Group Manager - Street Works, Civic Offices, Angel Street, Bridgend CF31 4WB ☎ 01656 643416 🖷 01656 646972 huw.jenkins@bridgend.gov.uk

Waste Management: Mr Huw Jenkins, Group Manager - Street Works, Civic Offices, Angel Street, Bridgend CF31 4WB ☎ 01656 643416 🖷 01656 646972 huw.jenkins@bridgend.gov.uk

MEMBERS OF THE COUNCIL (53)

Aspey, Sean (IND - Porthcawl West Central)
cllr.sean.aspey@bridgend.gov.uk
Butcher, Megan (IND - Cornelly)
Cllr.Megan.Butcher@bridgend.gov.uk
Clarke, Norah (LD - Nottage)
Cllr.Norah.Clarke@bridgend.gov.uk
David, Huw (LAB - Cefn Cribwr)
Cllr.Huw.David@bridgend.gov.uk
Davies, Pamela (LAB - Bryntirion, Laleston & Merthyr Mawr)
cllr.pam.davies@bridgend.gov.uk
Davies, Gareth (LAB - Caerau)
cllr.wyn.davies@bridgend.gov.uk
Davies, Gerald (LD - Rest Bay)
Cllr.Gerald.Davies@bridgend.gov.uk
Dodd, Ella (IND - Coity)
Cllr.Ella.Dodd@bridgend.gv.uk
Edwards, Keith (LAB - Maesteg East)
Cllr.Keith.Edwards@bridgend.gov.uk
Ellis, Luke (LAB - Pyle)
cllr.luke.ellis@bridgend.gov.uk
Foley, Peter (IND - Morfa)
cllr.peter.foley@bridgend.gov.uk
Francis, Malcolm (LAB - Llangewydd & Brynhyfryd)
cllr.malcolm.francis@bridgend.gov.uk
Green, Cheryl (LD - Bryntirion, Laleston & Merthyr Mawr)
cllr.cheryl.green@bridgend.gov.uk
Gregory, Michael (LAB - Felindre)
Cllr.Mike.Gregory@bridgend.gov.uk
Hughes, Edith (LAB - Oldcastle)
Cllr.Edith.M.Hughes@bridgend.gov.uk
Hughes, Della (IND - Ogmore Vale)
cllr.della.hughes@bridgend.gov.uk
James, Pauline (LAB - Pyle)
cllr.pauline.james@bridgend.gov.uk
James, Malcolm (PC - Llangynwyd)
Cllr.Malcolm.James@bridgend.gov.uk
James, Clive (LAB - Pyle)
cllr.clive.james@bridgend.gov.uk
Jenkins, Reg (LAB - Pontycymer)
membersbcbc@bridgend.gov.uk
John, Phil (LAB - Caerau)
cllr.phil.john@bridgend.gov.uk
Jones, Craig (LAB - Brackla)
cllr.craig.l.jones@bridgend.gov.uk
Jones, Brian (IND - Porthcawl East Central)
cllr.brian.jones@bridgend.gov.uk
Jones, Cherie (LAB - Litchard)
cllr.cherie.jones@bridgend.gov.uk
Lewis, David (LAB - Pen-Y-Fai)
cllr.david.lewis@bridgend.gov.uk
McCarthy, John (LAB - Hendre)
cllr.john.mccarthy@bridgend.gov.uk
Morgan, Haydn (LAB - Morfa)
cllr.haydn.morgan@bridgend.gov.uk
Morgan, Lyn (LAB - Ynysawdre)
Cllr.Lyn.Morgan@bridgend.gov.uk
Nott, Melvyn (LAB - Sarn)
Cllr.MEJ.Nott@bridgend.gov.uk
Owen, David (IND - Nant-y-Moel)
cllr.david.owen@bridgend.gov.uk
Owen, Alexander (LAB - Penprysg)
cllr.alex.owen@bridgend.gov.uk
Penpraze, Patricia (LAB - Bryncoch)
Cllr.Patricia.Penpraze@bridgend.gov.uk
Phillips, Gareth (LAB - Oldcastle)
cllr.gareth.phillips@bridgend.gov.uk
Pugh, David (LAB - Blaengarw)
membersbcbc@bridgend.gov.uk
Rees, Christina (LAB - Newcastle)
cllr.christina.rees@bridgend.gov.uk
Reeves, Ceri (LAB - Maesteg West)
cllr.ceri.reeves@bridgend.gov.uk
Reeves, Mal (LAB - Maesteg East)
Cllr.Mal.Reeves@bridgend.gov.uk
Sage, David (LAB - Brackla)
Cllr.David.Sage@bridgend.gov.uk
Spanswick, John (LAB - Brackla)
Cllr.John.Spanswick@bridgend.gov.uk
Thomas, Gary (LAB - Bryncethin)
Cllr.Gary.Thomas@bridgend.gov.uk
Thomas, Marlene (LAB - Llangeinor)

Cllr.Marlene.Thomas@bridgend.gov.uk
Thomas, Ross (LAB - Maesteg West)
cllr.ross.thomas@bridgend.gov.uk
Tildesley, Jeff (IND - Cornelly)
Cllr.Jeff.Tildesley@bridgend.gov.uk
Townsend, Hailey (LAB - Brackla)
cllr.hailey.j.townsend@bridgend.gov.uk
Venables, Elaine (IND - Coychurch Lower)
cllr.elaine.venables@bridgend.gov.uk
Watts, Kenneth (CON - Newton)
cllr.ken.watts@bridgend.gov.uk
Westwood, Cleone (LAB - Cefn Glas)
Cllr.Cleone.Westwood@bridgend.gov.uk
White, Phillip (LAB - Caerau)
Cllr.Phil.White@bridgend.gov.uk
White, David (LAB - Newcastle)
cllr.david.white@bridgend.gov.uk
Williams, Richard (LAB - Hendre)
Cllr.Richard.Williams@bridgend.gov.uk
Williams, Hywel (LAB - Blackmill)
Cllr.Hywel.Williams@bridgend.gov.uk
Winter, Mel (IND - Aberkenfig)
membersbcbc@bridgend.gov.uk
Young, Richard (LAB - Pendre)
membersbcbc@bridgend.gov.uk

POLITICAL COMPOSITION
LAB: 38, IND: 10, LD: 3, PC: 1, CON: 1

CABINET
Leader: Mr Melvyn Nott
Deputy Leader: Mr Craig Jones
Children & Young People: Mr Huw David
Communities: Mr Phillip White
Resources: Mr Michael Gregory
Wellbeing: Mr Lyn Morgan

COMMITTEE CHAIRS
Appeals: Mr Reg Jenkins
Community Renewel & Environment Overview & Scrutiny: Mr John Spanswick
Community Safety & Governance Overview & Scrutiny: Mrs Norah Clarke
Corporate Resources & Improvement: Mr Mal Reeves
Democratic Services: Mr Jeff Tildesley
Development Control: Mr Hywel Williams
Health & Wellbeing Overview & Scrutiny: Mr Malcolm Francis

BRIGHTON & HOVE U

Brighton & Hove City Council, Kings House, Grand Avenue, Hove BN3 2LS ☎ 01273 290000
💻 www.brighton-hove.gov.uk

FACTS & FIGURES
Police Authority: Sussex Police Authority
Health Authority: South East Coast Strategic Health Authority
Learning and Skills Council: South East
Parliamentary Constituencies: Brighton, Kemptown, Brighton, Pavilion, Hove
EU Constituencies: South East
Election Frequency: Elections are of whole council

PRINCIPAL OFFICERS
Chief Executive: Mr John Barradell, Chief Executive, Kings House, Grand Avenue, Hove BN3 2LS ☎ 01273 291132 ✉ john.barradell@brighton-hove.gov.uk

Senior Management: Mr David Murray, Strategic Director - Communities, Kings House, Grand Avenue, Hove BN3 2LS ☎ 01273 290453 ✉ david.murray@brighton-hove.gov.uk

Senior Management: Mr Terry Parkin, Strategic Director of People, Kings House, Grand Avenue, Hove BN3 2LS ☎ 01273 290446 ✉ terry.parkin@brighton-hove.gov.uk

Senior Management: Mr Geoff Raw, Strategic Director - Place, Kings House, Grand Avenue, Hove BN3 2LS ☎ 01273 290453 ✉ geoff.raw@brighton-hove.gov.uk

Senior Management: Mr Charlie Stewart, Strategic Director - Resources, Kings House, Grand Avenue, Hove BN3 2LS ☎ 01273 290703 ✉ charlie.stewart@brighton-hove.gov.uk

Senior Management: Ms Catherine Vaughan, Director of Finance, King's House, Grand Avenue, Hove BN3 2LS ☎ 01273 291333 🖷 01273 292131 ✉ catherine.vaughan@brighton-hove.gov.uk

Access Officer / Social Services (Disability): Ms Diana Bernhardt, Lead Commissioner - Learning Disabilities, Kings House, Grand Avenue, Hove BN3 2LS ☎ 01273 292363 ✉ diana.bernhardt@brighton-hove.gov.uk

Architect, Building / Property Services: Mrs Angela Dymott, Head of Property Services, King's House, Grand Avenue, Hove BN3 2LS ☎ 01273 291450 🖷 01273 291467 ✉ angela.dymott@brighton-hove.gov.uk

Building Control: Mr Mike Sansom, Head of Building Control, Hove Town Hall, Norton Road, Hove BN3 3BE ☎ 01273 292188 🖷 01273 292075 ✉ mike.sansom@brighton-hove.gov.uk

Catering Services: Mrs Angela Dymott, Head of Property Services, King's House, Grand Avenue, Hove BN3 2LS ☎ 01273 291450 🖷 01273 291467 ✉ angela.dymott@brighton-hove.gov.uk

Civil Registration: Ms Valerie Pearce, Head of City Services, 4th Floor, Priory House, Bartholomew Square, Brighton BN1 1JR ☎ 01273 291850 🖷 01273 291862 ✉ valerie.pearce@brighton-hove.gov.uk

PR / Communications: Mr John Shewell, Head of Communications, Kings House, Grand Avenue, Hove BN3 2LS ☎ 01273 291039 🖷 01273 292855 ✉ john.shewell@brighton-hove.gov.uk

Community Planning: Mr Rob Dumbrill, Parks Development Manager, Kings House, Grand Avenue, Hove BN3 2LS ☎ 01273 292929 ✉ rob.dumbrill@brighton-hove.gov.uk

Community Planning: Mr Rob Fraser, Head of Planning Strategy, Kings House, Grand Avenue, Hove BN3 2LS ☎ 01273 295078 ✉ rob.fraser@brighton-hove.gov.uk

Community Safety: Ms Linda Beanlands, Commissoner Community Safety, 162 North Street, Brighton BN1 2LS ☎ 01273 291115 🖷 01273 292808 ✉ linda.beanlands@brighton-hove.gov.uk

Computer Management: Mr Paul Colbran, Head of ICT, Kings House, Grand Avenue, Hove BN3 2LS ☎ 01273 290283 ✉ paul.colbran@brighton-hove.gov.uk

Contracts: Ms Catherine Vaughan, Director of Finance, King's House, Grand Avenue, Hove BN3 2LS ☎ 01273 291333 🖷 01273 292131 ✉ catherine.vaughan@brighton-hove.gov.uk

Corporate Services: Mr Richard Tuset, Head of Policy & Performance, Kings House, Grand Avenue, Hove BN3 2LS ☎ 01273 295514 ✉ richard.tuset@brighton-hove.gov.uk

Corporate Services: Mr Ian Withers, Head of Audit & Business Risk, Kings House, Grand Avenue, Hove BN3 2LS ☎ 01273 291323 ✉ ian.withers@brighton-hove.gov.uk

Customer Service: Mr Terry Parkin, Strategic Director of People, Kings House, Grand Avenue, Hove BN3 2LS ☎ 01273 290446 ✉ terry.parkin@brighton-hove.gov.uk

Customer Service: Ms Valerie Pearce, Head of City Services, 4th Floor, Priory House, Bartholomew Square, Brighton BN1 1JR ☎ 01273 291850 🖷 01273 291862 ✉ valerie.pearce@brighton-hove.gov.uk

Economic Development: Ms Cheryl Finella, Economic Development Manager, Kings House, Grand Avenue, Hove BN3 2LS ☎ 01273 291095 ✉ cheryl.finella@brighton-hove.gov.uk

Economic Development: Ms Paula Murray, Commissioner - Culture, Kings House, Grand Avenue, Hove BN3 2LS ☎ 01273 292534 🖷 01273 292614 ✉ paula.murray@brighton-hove.gov.uk

Education: Ms Jo Lyons, Lead Commissoner of Schools, Skills & Learning, Kings House, Grand Avenue, Hove BN3 2LS ☎ 01273 293514 ✉ jo.lyons@brighton-hove.gov.uk

E-Government: Mr Paul Colbran, Head of ICT, Kings House, Grand Avenue, Hove BN3 2LS ☎ 01273 290283 ✉ paul.colbran@brighton-hove.gov.uk

Electoral Registration: Mr Paul Holloway, Head of Life Events & ES, Town Hall, Bartholomew Square, Brighton BN1 1JA ☎ 01273 292005 🖷 01273 291222 ✉ paul.holloway@brighton-hove.gov.uk

Emergency Planning: Mr Robin Humphries, Civil Contingencies Manager, Kings House, Grand Avenue, Hove BN3 2LS ☎ 01273 291313 🖷 01273 292362 ✉ robin.humphries@brighton-hove.gov.uk

Energy Management: Mrs Angela Dymott, Head of Property Services, King's House, Grand Avenue, Hove BN3 2LS ☎ 01273 291450 🖷 01273 291467 ✉ angela.dymott@brighton-hove.gov.uk

Environmental / Technical Services: Mr Geoff Raw, Strategic Director - Place, Kings House, Grand Avenue, Hove BN3 2LS ☎ 01273 290453 ✉ geoff.raw@brighton-hove.gov.uk

Environmental Health: Mr Tim Nichols, Head of Regulatory Services, Bartholemew House, Bartholemew Square, Brighton BN1 1JA ☎ 01273 292163 🖷 01273 292196 ✉ tim.nichols@brighton-hove.gov.uk

Estates, Property & Valuation: Mrs Angela Dymott, Head of Property Services, King's House, Grand Avenue, Hove BN3 2LS ☎ 01273 291450 🖷 01273 291467 ✉ angela.dymott@brighton-hove.gov.uk

Events Manager: Mr Ian Shurrock, Commissioner - Sports & Leisure, Kings House, Grand Avenue, Hove BN3 2LS ☎ 01273 292084 🖷 01273 292360 ✉ ian.shurrock@brighton-hove.gov.uk

Facilities: Mrs Angela Dymott, Head of Property Services, King's House, Grand Avenue, Hove BN3 2LS ☎ 01273 291450 🖷 01273 291467 ✉ angela.dymott@brighton-hove.gov.uk

Finance and Treasurer: Mr Nigel Manvell, Head of Financial Services, Kings House, Grand Avenue, Hove BN3 2LS ☎ 01273 293104 ✉ nigel.manvell@brighton-hove.gov.uk

Finance and Treasurer: Ms Catherine Vaughan, Director of Finance, King's House, Grand Avenue, Hove BN3 2LS ☎ 01273 291333 🖷 01273 292131 ✉ catherine.vaughan@brighton-hove.gov.uk

Fleet Management: Ms Gillian Marston, Head of City Infrastructure, Hollingdean Depot, Upper Hollingdean Road, Brighton BN1 7GA ☎ 01273 274701 🖷 01273 274666 ✉ gillian.marston@brighton-hove.gov.uk

Grounds Maintenance: Ms Gillian Marston, Head of City Infrastructure, Hollingdean Depot, Upper Hollingdean Road, Brighton BN1 7GA ☎ 01273 274701 🖷 01273 274666 ✉ gillian.marston@brighton-hove.gov.uk

Health and Safety: Ms Hilary Ellis, Head of Health & Safety, King's House, Grand Avenue, Hove BN3 2LS ☎ 01273 291305 ✉ hilary.ellis@brighton-hove.gov.uk

Highways: Mr Jeff Elliott, Highway & Traffic Manager, Kings House, Grand Avenue, Hove BN3 2LS ☎ 01273 292468 ✉ jeff.elliott@brighton-hove.gov.uk

Highways: Mr Mark Prior, Lead Commissioner City Regulation & Infastructure, Kings House, Grand Avenue, Hove BN3 2LS ☎ 01273 292095 ✉ mark.prior@brighton-hove.gov.uk

Home Energy Conservation: Mr Geoff Raw, Strategic Director - Place, Kings House, Grand Avenue, Hove BN3 2LS ☎ 01273 290453 ✉ geoff.raw@brighton-hove.gov.uk

Housing: Mr Jungal Sharma, Lead Commisoner - Housing, Kings House, Grand Avenue, Hove BN3 2LS ☎ 01273 293101 ✉ jungal.sharma@brighton-hove.gov.uk

Housing Maintenance: Mr Nick Hibberd, Head of Housing & Social Inclusion, Kings House, Grand Avenue, Hove BN3 2LS ☎ 01273 293020 🖷 01273 293709 ✉ nick.hibberd@brighton-hove.gov.uk

Local Area Agreement: Mr Richard Tuset, Head of Policy &

Performance, Kings House, Grand Avenue, Hove BN3 2LS ☎ 01273 295514 ✉ richard.tuset@brighton-hove.gov.uk

Legal: Mr Abraham Ghebre-Ghiorghis, Head of Legal & Democratic Services, Kings House, Grand Avenue, Hove BN3 2LS ☎ 01273 291500 🖷 01273 291454 ✉ abraham.ghebre-ghiorghis@brighton-hove.gov.uk

Leisure and Cultural Services: Mr Toby Kingsbury, Sports Facilities Manager, Kings House, Grand Avenue, Hove BN3 2LS ☎ 01273 292701 ✉ toby.kingsbury@brighton-hove.gov.uk

Leisure and Cultural Services: Mr Geoff Raw, Strategic Director - Place, Kings House, Grand Avenue, Hove BN3 2LS ☎ 01273 290453 ✉ geoff.raw@brighton-hove.gov.uk

Leisure and Cultural Services: Mr Ian Shurrock, Commissioner - Sports & Leisure, Kings House, Grand Avenue, Hove BN3 2LS ☎ 01273 292084 🖷 01273 292360 ✉ ian.shurrock@brighton-hove.gov.uk

Licensing: Mr Tim Nichols, Head of Regulatory Services, Bartholemew House, Bartholemew Square, Brighton BN1 1JA ☎ 01273 292163 🖷 01273 292196 ✉ tim.nichols@brighton-hove.gov.uk

Lifelong Learning: Ms Jo Lyons, Lead Commissoner of Schools, Skills & Learning, Kings House, Grand Avenue, Hove BN3 2LS ☎ 01273 293514 ✉ jo.lyons@brighton-hove.gov.uk

Lighting: Mr Geoff Raw, Strategic Director - Place, Kings House, Grand Avenue, Hove BN3 2LS ☎ 01273 290453 ✉ geoff.raw@brighton-hove.gov.uk

Member Services: Mr Mark Wall, Head of Democratic Services, King's House, Grand Avenue, Hove BN3 2LS ☎ 01273 291006 🖷 01273 291003 ✉ mark.wall@brighton-hove.gov.uk

Parking: Mr Geoff Raw, Strategic Director - Place, Kings House, Grand Avenue, Hove BN3 2LS ☎ 01273 290453 ✉ geoff.raw@brighton-hove.gov.uk

Partnerships: Mr Simon Newell, Head of Partnerships & External Relationships, Kings House, Grand Avenue, Hove BN3 2LS ☎ 01273 291128 ✉ simon.newell@brighton-hove.gov.uk

Partnerships: Mr Richard Tuset, Head of Policy & Performance, Kings House, Grand Avenue, Hove BN3 2LS ☎ 01273 295514 ✉ richard.tuset@brighton-hove.gov.uk

Personnel / HR: Ms Charlotte Thomas, Head of Human Resources & Organisational Development, Kings House, Grand Avenue, Hove BN3 2LS ☎ 01273 291290 ✉ charlotte.thomas@brighton-hove.gov.uk

Planning: Mr Martin Randall, Head of Planning & Public Protection, Hove Town Hall, Norton Road, Hove BN3 3BQ ☎ 01273 292257 🖷 01273 293330 ✉ martin.randall@brighton-hove.gov.uk

Procurement: Mr Mark Ireland, Head of Strategic Finance & Procurement, Kings House, Grand Avenue, Hove BN3 2LS ☎ 01273 291240 🖷 01273 292558 ✉ mark.ireland@brighton-hove.gov.uk

Public Libraries: Ms Sally McMahon, Head of Library Services, Pavilion Buildings, Brighton BN1 1UE ☎ 01273 296933 🖷 01273 292871 ✉ sally.mcmahon@brighton-hove.gov.uk

Recycling & Waste Minimisation: Ms Gillian Marston, Head of City Infrastructure, Hollingdean Depot, Upper Hollingdean Road, Brighton BN1 7GA ☎ 01273 274701 🖷 01273 274666 ✉ gillian.marston@brighton-hove.gov.uk

Regeneration: Ms Gillian Marston, Head of City Infrastructure, Hollingdean Depot, Upper Hollingdean Road, Brighton BN1 7GA ☎ 01273 274701 🖷 01273 274666 ✉ gillian.marston@brighton-hove.gov.uk

Road Safety: Mr Phil Clarke, Road Safety Manager, Hove Town Hall, Hove BN3 4AH ☎ 01273 293705 ✉ philip.clarke@brighton-hove.gov.uk

Social Services: Ms Denise D'Souza, Director of Adult Social Services / Lead Commissioner ASC & Health, Kings House, Grand Avenue, Hove BN3 2LS ☎ 01273 295048 🖷 01273 698312 ✉ denise.d'souza@brighton-hove.gov.uk

Social Services (Adult): Ms Denise D'Souza, Director of Adult Social Services / Lead Commissioner ASC & Health, Kings House, Grand Avenue, Hove BN3 2LS ☎ 01273 295048 🖷 01273 698312 ✉ denise.d'souza@brighton-hove.gov.uk

Social Services (Children): Mr Steve Barton, Lead Commissioner - Children, Youth & Families, Kings House, Grand Avenue, Hove BN3 2LS ☎ 01273 296105 ✉ steve.barton@brighton-hove.gov.uk

Social Services (Children): Ms Jo Lyons, Lead Commissoner of Schools, Skills & Learning, Kings House, Grand Avenue, Hove BN3 2LS ☎ 01273 293514 ✉ jo.lyons@brighton-hove.gov.uk

Sustainable Communities: Mr Thurstan Crockett, Head of Sustainability & Environmental Policy, King's House, Grand Avenue, Hove BN3 2LS ☎ 01273 292503 🖷 01273 293330 ✉ thurstan.crockett@brighton-hove.gov.uk

Sustainable Development: Mr Martin Randall, Head of Planning & Public Protection, Hove Town Hall, Norton Road, Hove BN3 3BQ ☎ 01273 292257 🖷 01273 293330 ✉ martin.randall@brighton-hove.gov.uk

Tourism: Mr Adam Bates, Head of Tourism & Leisure, Brighton Town Hall, Brighton BN1 1JR ☎ 01273 292633 🖷 01273 292614 ✉ adam.bates@brighton-hove.gov.uk

Traffic Management: Mr Mark Prior, Lead Commissioner City Regulation & Infastructure, Kings House, Grand Avenue, Hove BN3 2LS ☎ 01273 292095 ✉ mark.prior@brighton-hove.gov.uk

Transport Planner: Mr Austen Hunter, Head of Transport Operations, 6a Pavilion Buildings, Brighton BN1 1EE ☎ 01273 292245 ✉ austen.hunter@brighton-hove.gov.uk

Waste Collection and Disposal: Ms Gillian Marston, Head of City Infrastructure, Hollingdean Depot, Upper Hollingdean Road, Brighton BN1 7GA ☎ 01273 274701 🖷 01273 274666
✉ gillian.marston@brighton-hove.gov.uk

Waste Management: Ms Gillian Marston, Head of City Infrastructure, Hollingdean Depot, Upper Hollingdean Road, Brighton BN1 7GA ☎ 01273 274701 🖷 01273 274666
✉ gillian.marston@brighton-hove.gov.uk

MEMBERS OF THE COUNCIL (54)

***Mayor:* Randall**, Bill (GRN - Hanover & Elm Grove)
bill.randall@brighton-hove.gov.uk
***Deputy Mayor:* Meadows**, Anne (IND - Moulsecoomb & Bevendean)
anne.meadows@brighton-hove.gov.uk
***Group Leader:* Mitchell**, Gill (IND - East Brighton)
gill.mitchell@brighton-hove.gov.uk
Barnett, Dawn (CON - Hangleton & Knoll)
dawn.barnett@brighton-hove.gov.uk
Bennett, Jayne (CON - Hove Park)
jayne.bennett@brighton-hove.gov.uk
Bowden, Geoffrey (GRN - Queen's Park)
geoffrey.bowden@brighton-hove.gov.uk
Brown, Vanessa (CON - Hove Park)
vanessa.brown@brighton-hove.gov.uk
Buckley, Ruth (GRN - Goldsmid)
ruth.buckley@brighton-hove.gov.uk
Carden, Robert (IND - North Portslade)
bob.carden@brighton-hove.gov.uk
Cobb, Denise (CON - Westbourne)
denise.cobb@brighton-hove.gov.uk
Cox, Graham (CON - Westbourne)
graham.cox@brighton-hove.gov.uk
Davey, Ian (GRN - St. Peters & North Laine)
ian.davey@brighton-hove.gov.uk
Deane, Lizzie (GRN - St. Peter's & North Laine)
lizzie.deane@brighton-hove.gov.uk
Duncan, Ben (GRN - Queen's Park)
ben.duncan@brighton-hove.gov.uk
Farrow, Leigh (IND - Moulsecoomb & Bevendean)
leigh.farrow@brighton-hove.gov.uk
Fitch, Brian (IND - Hangleton & Knoll)
brian.fitch@brighton-hove.gov.uk
Follett, Matt (GRN - Hanover & Elm Grove)
matt.follett@brighton-hove.gov.uk
Gilbey, Penny (IND - North Portslade)
penny.gilbey@brighton-hove.gov.uk
Hamilton, Leslie (IND - South Portslade)
leslie.hamilton@brighton-hove.gov.uk
Hawtree, Christopher (GRN - Central Hove)
christopher.hawtree@brighton-hove.gov.uk
Hyde, Lynda (CON - Rottingdean Coastal)
lynda.hyde@brighton-hove.gov.uk
Janio, Tony (CON - Hangleton & Knoll)
tony.janio@brighton-hove.gov.uk
Jarrett, Rob (GRN - Goldsmid)
rob.jarrett@brighton-hove.gov.uk
Jones, Mike (GRN - Preston Park)
mike.jones@brighton-hove.gov.uk
Kennedy, Amy (GRN - Preston Park)
amy.kennedy@brighton-hove.gov.uk
Kitcat, Ania (GRN - Regency)
ania.kitcat@brighton-hove.gov.uk
Kitcat, Jason (GRN - Regency)
jason.kitcat@brighton-hove.gov.uk
Lepper, Jeane (IND - Hollingbury & Stanmer)
jeane.lepper@brighton-hove.gov.uk
Littman, Leo (GRN - Preston Park)
leo.littman@brighton-hove.gov.uk
MacCafferty, Phelim (GRN - Brunswick & Adelaide)
phelim.maccafferty@brighton-hove.gov.uk
Marsh, Mo (IND - Moulsecoomb & Bevendean)
mo.marsh@brighton-hove.gov.uk
Mears, Mary (CON - Rottingdean Coastal)
mary.mears@brighton-hove.gov.uk
Morgan, Warren (IND - East Brighton)
warren.morgan@brighton-hove.gov.uk
Norman, Ken (CON - Withdean)
ken.norman@brighton-hove.gov.uk
Norman, Ann (CON - Withdean)
ann.norman@brighton-hove.gov.uk
Peltzer Dunn, Garry (CON - Wish)
garry.peltzerdunn@brighton-hove.gov.uk
Philips, Alexandra (GRN - Goldsmid)
alex.phillips@brighton-hove.gov.uk
Pidgeon, Brian (CON - Patcham)
brian.pidgeon@brighton-hove.gov.uk
Pissaridou, Anne (IND - Wish)
anne.pissaridou@brighton-hove.gov.uk
Powell, Stephanie (GRN - Queen's Park)
stephanie.powell@brighton-hove.gov.uk
Robins, Alan (IND - South Portslade)
alan.robins@brighton-hove.gov.uk
Rufus, Sven (GRN - Hollingbury & Stanmer)
sven.rufus@brighton-hove.gov.uk
Shanks, Sue (GRN - Withdean)
sue.shanks@brighton-hove.gov.uk
Simson, Dee (CON - Woodingdean)
dee.simson@brighton-hove.gov.uk
Smith, David (CON - Rottingdean Coastal)
david.smith@brighton-hove.gov.uk
Summers, Christina (GRN - Hollingbury & Stanmer)
christina.summers@brighton-hove.gov.uk
Sykes, Ollie (GRN - Brunswick & Adelaide)
ollie.sykes@brighton-hove.gov.uk
Theobald, Geoffrey (CON - Patcham)
geoffrey.theobald@brighton-hove.gov.uk
Theobald, Carol (CON - Patcham)
carol.theobald@brighton-hove.gov.uk
Turton, Craig (IND - East Brighton)
craig.turton@brighton-hove.gov.uk
Wakefield, Liz (GRN - Hanover & Elm Grove)
liz.wakefield@brighton-hove.gov.uk
Wealls, Andrew (CON - Central Hove)
andrew.wealls@brighton-hove.gov.uk
Wells, Geoffrey (CON - Woodingdean)
geoffrey.wells@brighton-hove.gov.uk
West, Peter (GRN - St. Peters & North Laine)
pete.west@brighton-hove.gov.uk

POLITICAL COMPOSITION

GRN: 23, CON: 18, IND: 13

CABINET

Leader: Mr Jason Kitcat
Deputy Leader: Mr Phelim MacCafferty
Children & Young People: Ms Sue Shanks

Culture, Recreation & Tourism: Mr Geoffrey Bowden
Environment & Sustainability: Mr Peter West
Housing: Ms Liz Wakefield

COMMITTEE CHAIRS
Adult Care & Health: Mr Rob Jarrett
Children & Young People: Ms Sue Shanks
Economic Development & Culture: Mr Geoffrey Bowden
Health & Wellbeing Overview & Scrutiny: Mr Sven Rufus
Housing: Ms Liz Wakefield
Licensing: Ms Lizzie Deane
Overview & Scrutiny: Mr Warren Morgan
Planning: Mr Christopher Hawtree
Policy & Resources: Mr Jason Kitcat
Transport: Mr Ian Davey

BRISTOL CITY U
Bristol City Council, The Council House, College Green, Bristol BS1 5TR ☎ 0117 922 2000 🖷 0117 922 2024 💻 www.bristol.gov.uk

FACTS & FIGURES
Police Authority: Avon & Somerset Police Authority
Health Authority: NHS South West
Learning and Skills Council: South West
Parliamentary Constituencies: Bristol East, Bristol North West, Bristol South, Bristol West
EU Constituencies: South West
Election Frequency: Elections are by thirds
Twinning: Beira (Portugal), Bordeaux (France), Guangzhou (China), Hanover (Germany), Oporto (Portugal), Puerto Morazan (Nicaragua), Tbilisi (Georgia)

PRINCIPAL OFFICERS
Chief Executive: Ms Jan Ormondroyd, Chief Executive, The Council House, College Green, Bristol BS1 5TR ☎ 0117 922 4888 ✉ jan.ormondroyd@bristol.gov.uk

Senior Management: Mr Will Godfrey, Director of Corporate Services, The Council House, College Green, Bristol BS1 5TR ☎ 0117 922 4420 ✉ will.godfrey@bristol.gov.uk

Architect, Building / Property Services: Mr Alun Owen, Service Director - Major Projects, Brunel House, St George's Road, Bristol BS1 5UY ☎ 0117 903 7481 ✉ alun.owen@bristol.gov.uk

Best Value: Mr Russell Ward, Head of Partnership - Commissioning & Procurement, B Bond, Smeaton Road, Bristol BS1 6EE ☎ 0117 922 5485 ✉ russell.ward@bristol.gov.uk

Building Control: Mr Gary Collins, Service Manager - Development Services, Brunel House, St George's Road, Bristol BS1 5UY ☎ 0117 922 5485 ✉ gary.collins@bristol.gov.uk

Children / Youth Services: Ms Rose Richards, Head of Youth & Play Services, The Council House, College Green, Bristol BS1 5TR ☎ 0117 922 2000 ✉ rose.richards@bristol.gov.uk

Civil Registration: Ms Yvonne Dawes, Statutory Services Manager, The Council House, College Green, Bristol BS1 5TR ☎ 0117 922 3488 ✉ yvonne.dawes@bristol.gov.uk

Civil Registration: Ms Zillah Morris, Statutory Services Manager, The Council House, College Green, Bristol BS1 5TR ☎ 0117 922 3488 ✉ zillah.morris@bristol.gov.uk

PR / Communications: Mr Peter Holt, Service Director - Communications & Marketing, The Council House, College Green, Bristol BS1 5TR ☎ 0117 922 2657 ✉ peter.holt@bristol.gov.uk

Community Safety: Mr Stuart Pattison, Community Confidence Manager, Princess House, Bedminster, Bristol BS1 4AG ☎ 0117 914 2201 ✉ stuart.pattison@bristol.gov.uk

Computer Management: Mr Paul Arrigoni, Service Director - Business Change & ICT, The Council House, College Green, Bristol BS1 5TR ☎ 0117 922 2081 ✉ paul.arrigoni@bristol.gov.uk

Consumer Protection and Trading Standards: Mr Jonathan Miller, Regulatory Compliance Manager, Princess House, Bedminster, Bristol BS3 4AG ☎ 0117 922 2626 ✉ jonathan.miller@bristol.gov.uk

Economic Development: Mr Ian MacDougall, Service Manager - Economic Development, The Council House, College Green, Bristol BS1 5TR ☎ 0117 922 2928 ✉ investinbristol@bristol.gov.uk

Education: Mr Nick Batchelar, Service Director - Education, The Council House, College Green, Bristol BS1 5TR ☎ 0117 922 4836 ✉ nick.batchelar@bristol.gov.uk

Electoral Registration: Mr Stephen McNamara, Electoral Registration Officer, The Council House, College Green, Bristol BS1 5TR ☎ 0117 922 2839 ✉ stephen.mcnamara@bristol.gov.uk

Emergency Planning: Mr Simon Creed, Civil Protection Manager, The Council House, College Green, Bristol BS1 5TR ☎ 0117 922 3233 ✉ simon.creed@bristol.gov.uk

Energy Management: Mr Paul Isbell, Energy Manager, 5th Floor, B Bond Building, Smeaton Road, Bristol BS1 6EE ☎ 0117 922 4430 ✉ paul.isbell@bristol.gov.uk

Estates, Property & Valuation: Mr Peter Robinson, Service Director - Corporate Finance, The Council House, College Green, Bristol BS1 5TR ☎ 0117 922 2419 ✉ peter.robinson@bristol.gov.uk

European Liaison: Ms Mhairi Ambler, European & Regional Officer, The Council House, College Green, Bristol BS1 5TR ☎ 0117 922 3229 ✉ mhairi.ambler@bristol.gov.uk

Events Manager: Mr Simon Brown, Arts & Festivals Manager, The Council House, College Green, Bristol BS1 5TR ✉ simon.brown@bristol.gov.uk

Finance and Treasurer: Mr Peter Robinson, Service Director - Corporate Finance, The Council House, College Green, Bristol BS1 5TR ☎ 0117 922 2419 ✉ peter.robinson@bristol.gov.uk

Fleet Management: Mr Nick Gingell, Fleet Services Manager, Brislington Depot, Sandy Park Road, Bristol BS4 3NZ ☎ 0117 352 5611 ✉ nick.gingell@bristol.gov.uk

Highways: Mr Terry Bullock, Highways & Traffic Manager, Wilder House, Wilder Street, Bristol BS2 8PQ ☎ 0117 903 6843 ✉ terry.bullock@bristol.gov.uk

Housing: Mr Nick Hooper, Service Director - Strategic Housing, Brunel House, St George's Road, Bristol BS1 5UY ☎ 0117 922 4681 ✉ nick.hooper@bristol.gov.uk

Legal: Mr Stephen McNamara, Electoral Registration Officer, The Council House, College Green, Bristol BS1 5TR ☎ 0117 922 2839 ✉ stephen.mcnamara@bristol.gov.uk

Licensing: Mr Jonathan Martin, Regulatory Compliance Manager, Princess House, Princess Street, Bedminster, Bristol BS3 4AG ☎ 0117 922 2626 ✉ jonathan.martin@bristol.gov.uk

Lifelong Learning: Ms Jane Taylor, Service Manager - Communities & Adult Skills, The Park, Daventry Road, Bristol BS4 1DQ ☎ 0117 903 9752 ✉ jane.taylor@bristol.gov.uk

Lighting: Mr Adam Crowther, Traffic Signals & Lighting Manager, Wilder House, Wilder Street, Bristol BS2 8PH ☎ 0117 903 6854 ✉ adam.crowther@bristol.gov.uk

Member Services: Mr Ian Pagan, Service Manager - Democratic Services, The Council House, College Green, Bristol BS1 5TR ☎ 0117 922 2387 ✉ ian.pagan@bristol.gov.uk

Parking: Mr David Bunting, Parking Services Manager, Wilder House, Wilder Street, Bristol BS2 8PH ☎ 0117 922 3085 ✉ david.bunting@bristol.gov.uk

Personnel / HR: Mr Mark Williams, Service Manager - Corporate HR, The Council House, College Green, Bristol BS1 5TR ☎ 0117 922 4838 ✉ mark.williams@bristol.gov.uk

Planning: Ms Zoe Willcox, Service Director - Planning & Sustainable Development, Brunel House, St George's Road, Bristol BS1 5UY ☎ 0117 922 2942 ✉ zoe.willcox@bristol.gov.uk

Public Libraries: Ms Kate Murray, Service Manager - Libraries, Bristol Central Library, College Green, Bristol BS1 5TL ☎ 0117 352 1264 ✉ kate.murray@bristol.gov.uk

Recycling & Waste Minimisation: Ms Pam Jones, Service Manager - Operations, Brunel House, St George's Road, Bristol BS1 5UY ☎ 0117 922 3240 ✉ pam.jones@bristol.gov.uk

Road Safety: Mr Alistair Cox, Service Manager - City Transport, Transport Service, Brunel House, St George's Road, Bristol BS1 5UY ☎ 0117 922 2940 🖷 0117 903 6716 ✉ alistair.cox@bristol.gov.uk

Social Services: Ms Alison Comley, Interim Strategic Director - Health & Social Care, The Council House, College Green, Bristol BS1 5TR ☎ 0117 903 7860 ✉ alison.comley@bristol.gov.uk

Social Services (Adult): Ms Alison Comley, Interim Strategic Director - Health & Social Care, The Council House, College Green, Bristol BS1 5TR ☎ 0117 903 7860 ✉ alison.comley@bristol.gov.uk

Social Services (Children): Ms Annie Hudson, Strategic Director - Children, Young People & Skills, The Council House, College Green, Bristol BS1 5TR ☎ 0117 903 7960 ✉ annie.hudson@bristol.gov.uk

Sustainable Development: Mr Stephen Hilton, Service Director - Bristol Futures, The Council House, College Green, Bristol BS1 5TR ☎ 0117 922 2947 ✉ stephen.hilton@bristol.gov.uk

Tourism: Mr John Hallett, Chief Executive, Destination Bristol, 53 Queen Square, Bristol BS1 4LH ☎ 0117 946 2207 ✉ john.hallett@destinationbristol.co.uk

Town Centre: Mr Eric Dougall, Harbour Estates Officer, The Harbour Office, Underfall Yard, Bristol BS1 5TR ☎ 0117 903 1491 ✉ eric.dougall@bristol.gov.uk

Traffic Management: Mr Terry Bullock, Highways & Traffic Manager, Wilder House, Wilder Street, Bristol BS2 8PQ ☎ 0117 903 6843 ✉ terry.bullock@bristol.gov.uk

Transport: Mr Alistair Cox, Service Manager - City Transport, Transport Service, Brunel House, St George's Road, Bristol BS1 5UY ☎ 0117 922 2940 🖷 0117 903 6716 ✉ alistair.cox@bristol.gov.uk

Transport Planner: Mr Alistair Cox, Service Manager - City Transport, Transport Service, Brunel House, St George's Road, Bristol BS1 5UY ☎ 0117 922 2940 🖷 0117 903 6716 ✉ alistair.cox@bristol.gov.uk

Waste Collection and Disposal: Ms Tracey Morgan, Service Director - Environment & Leisure Services, Brunel House, St George's Road, Bristol BS1 5UY ☎ ; 0117 922 3183 ✉ tracey.morgan@bristol.gov.uk

Waste Management: Ms Tracey Morgan, Service Director - Environment & Leisure Services, Brunel House, St George's Road, Bristol BS1 5UY ☎ ; 0117 922 3183 ✉ tracey.morgan@bristol.gov.uk

MEMBERS OF THE COUNCIL (70)

***Leader of the Council:* Cook**, Simon (LD - Clifton East)
simon.cook@bristol.gov.uk
***Group Leader:* Green**, Tess (GRN - Southville)
tess.green@bristol.gov.uk
Abraham, Peter (CON - Stoke Bishop)
peter.abraham@bristol.gov.uk
Alexander, Lesley (CON - Frome Vale)
lesley.alexander@bristol.gov.uk
Ann, Cheryl (LD - Horfield)
cheryl.ann@bristol.gov.uk
Bailey, Mark (LD - Windmill Hill)
mark.bailey@bristol.gov.uk
Beynon, Sean (LAB - Southville)
sean.beynon@bristol.gov.uk
Blythe, Trevor (LD - Clifton)
trevor.blythe@bristol.gov.uk
Bradshaw, Mark (LAB - Bedminster)
mark.bradshaw@bristol.gov.uk
Brain, Mark (LAB - Hartcliffe)
mark.brain@bristol.gov.uk
Breckels, Fabian (LAB - St. George East)

fabian.breckels@bristol.gov.uk
Campion-Smith, Clare (LD - Henleaze)
clare.campion-smith@bristol.gov.uk
Choudhury, Faruk (LAB - Easton)
faruk.choudhury@bristol.gov.uk
Clark, Barry (LAB - Hengrove)
barry.clark@bristol.gov.uk
Comer, Steven (LD - Eastville)
steve.comer@bristol.gov.uk
Davies, Christopher (LD - Knowle)
christopher.davies@bristol.gov.uk
Doubell, Sylvia (LD - Hengrove)
sylvia.doubell@bristol.gov.uk
Eddy, Richard (CON - Bishopsworth)
richard.eddy@bristol.gov.uk
Emmett, Sean (LD - Lockleaze)
sean.emmett@bristol.gov.uk
Gollop, Geoffrey (CON - Westbury-on-Trym)
geoffrey.gollop@bristol.gov.uk
Goulandris, John (CON - Stoke Bishop)
john.goulandris@bristol.gov.uk
Hammond, Peter (LAB - St. George West)
peter.hammond@bristol.gov.uk
Hanby, Phil (LAB - Hillfields)
phil.hanby@bristol.gov.uk
Hance, Fi (LD - Redland)
fi.hance@bristol.gov.uk
Harrison, Neil (LD - Cotham)
neil.harrison@bristol.gov.uk
Hassell, Patrick (LD - Hillfields)
patrick.hassell@bristol.gov.uk
Havvock, Alf (LD - Windmill Hill)
alf.havvock@bristol.gov.uk
Hickman, Margaret (LAB - Lawrence Hill)
margaret.hickman@bristol.gov.uk
Holland, Helen (LAB - Whitchurch Park)
helen.holland@bristol.gov.uk
Hopkins, Gary (LD - Knowle)
gary.hopkins@bristol.gov.uk
Hoyt, Gus (GRN - Ashley)
gus.hoyt@bristol.gov.uk
Hugill, Brenda (LAB - Lawrence Hill)
brenda.hugill@bristol-city.gov.uk
Jackson, Christopher (LAB - Filwood)
christopher.jackson@bristol.gov.uk
Janke, Barbara (LD - Clifton)
barbara.janke@bristol.gov.uk
Jethwa, Jay (CON - Stockwood)
jay.jethwa@bristol.gov.uk
Kennedy-Hall, Siobhan (CON - Avonmouth)
siobhan.kennedy-hall@bristol.gov.uk
Kent, Tim (LD - Whitchurch Park)
tim.kent@bristol.gov.uk
Khan, Mahmadur (LAB - Eastville)
mahmadur.khan@bristol.gov.uk
Kiely, John (LD - Easton)
john.kiely@bristol.gov.uk
Knott, Beverley (LD - Bishopston)
bev.knott@bristol.gov.uk
Langley, Mike (LAB - Brislington East)
mike.langley@bristol.gov.uk
Leaman, Tim (LD - Kingsweston)
tim.leaman@bristol.gov.uk
Levy, Pete (LD - Horfield)
pete.levy@bristol.gov.uk
Lovell, Jeff (LAB - Filwood)
jeff.lovell@bristol.gov.uk
Main, Peter (LD - Brislington West)
peter.main@bristol.gov.uk
Martin, Christian (LD - Clifton East)
christian.martin@bristol.gov.uk
Massey, Brenda (LAB - Southmead)
brenda.massey@bristol.gov.uk
Morgan, Glenise (LD - Henleaze)
glenise.morgan@bristol.gov.uk
Morris, David (CON - Stockwood)
david.morris@bristol.gov.uk
Naysmith, Doug (LAB - Avonmouth)
doug.naysmith@bristol.gov.uk
Negus, Anthony (LD - Cotham)
anthony.negus@bristol.gov.uk
Norman, Jackie (LD - Brislington West)
jackie.norman@bristol.gov.uk
Pearce, Alex (CON - St. George East)
alex.pearce@bristol.gov.uk
Pickup, Derek (LAB - Hartcliffe)
derek.pickup@bristol.gov.uk
Poultney, Guy (LD - Lockleaze)
guy.poultney@bristol.gov.uk
Quartley, Kevin (CON - Bishopsworth)
kevin.quartley@bristol.gov.uk
Rayner, Simon (LD - Kingsweston)
simon.rayner@bristol.gov.uk
Rogers, Jon (LD - Ashley)
jon.rogers@bristol.gov.uk
Smith, Jenny (LAB - Southmead)
jenny.m.smith@dsl.pipex.com
Smith, Colin (LAB - Bedminster)
colin.smith@bristol.gov.uk
Stevenson, James (CON - Frome Vale)
james.stevenson@bristol.gov.uk
Stone, Ron (LAB - St. George West)
ron.stone@bristol.gov.uk
Townsend, Sylvia (LD - Redland)
sylvia.townsend@bristol.gov.uk
Watson, Alastair (CON - Westbury-on-Trym)
alastair.watson@bristol.gov.uk
Weston, Mark (CON - Henbury)
mark.weston@bristol.gov.uk
Willingham, David (LD - Bishopston)
david.willingham@bristol.gov.uk
Windows, Chris (CON - Henbury)
chris.windows@bristol.gov.uk
Wollacott, Mike (LAB - Brislington East)
mike.wollacott@bristol.gov.uk
Woodman, Alex (LD - Cabot)
alex.woodman@bristol.gov.uk
Wright, Mark (LD - Cabot)
mark.wright@bristol.gov.uk

POLITICAL COMPOSITION
LD: 32, LAB: 22, CON: 14, GRN: 2

CABINET
Leader: Mr Simon Cook
Deputy Leader: Dr Jon Rogers
Budget & Transport: Mr Tim Kent
Care & Health: Ms Glenise Morgan
Children & Young People: Ms Clare Campion-Smith

Corporate Employee Health & Safety Consultative: Mr Sean Emmett
Environment & Community Safety: Mr Gary Hopkins
Festivals & Community: Mr Guy Poultney
Housing, Property Services & Regeneration Executive: Mr Anthony Negus
Joint Employee Relations Board: Mr Sean Emmett
Resources: Dr Jon Rogers

COMMITTEE CHAIRS

Audit: Mr Mark Weston
Children's Services Scrutiny: Mr Alastair Watson
Community Cohesion & Safety Scrutiny: Mr Faruk Choudhury
Development Control: Mr Alex Woodman
Health & Adult Social Care Scrutiny: Ms Lesley Alexander
Human Resources: Mr Mike Wollacott
Overview & Scrutiny Management: Mr Derek Pickup
Public Safety & Protection: Mr David Morris
Resources: Mr Mark Brain
Sustainable Development & Transport Scrutiny: Mr Mark Bradshaw

BROADLAND D

Broadland District Council, Thorpe Lodge, 1 Yarmouth Road, Thorpe St. Andrew, Norwich NR7 0DU ☎ 01603 431133 🖷 01603 300087 ✉ reception@broadland.gov.uk 💻 www.broadland.gov.uk

FACTS & FIGURES

Police Authority: Norfolk Police Authority
Health Authority: East of England Strategic Health Authority
Learning and Skills Council: Eastern
Parliamentary Constituencies: Norwich North
EU Constituencies: Eastern
Election Frequency: Elections are of whole council

PRINCIPAL OFFICERS

Chief Executive: Mr Phil Kirby, Chief Executive, Thorpe Lodge, 1 Yarmouth Road, Thorpe St. Andrew, Norwich NR7 0DU ☎ 01603 430566 🖷 01603 430565 ✉ phil.kirby@broadland.gov.uk

Deputy Chief Executive: Mr Matthew Cross, Deputy Chief Executive, Thorpe Lodge, 1 Yarmouth Road, Thorpe St. Andrew, Norwich NR7 0DU ☎ 01603 430588 🖷 01603 430565 ✉ matthew.cross@broadland.gov.uk

Access Officer / Social Services (Disability): Mr Kevin Philcox, Director of CNC Building Control Services, Thorpe Lodge, 1 Yarmouth Road, Thorpe St. Andrew, Norwich NR7 0DU ☎ 01603 430552 🖷 01603 430578 ✉ kevin.philcox@broadland.gov.uk

Architect, Building / Property Services: Mr John Frary, Facilities Manager, Thorpe Lodge, 1 Yarmouth Road, Thorpe St. Andrew, Norwich NR7 0DU ☎ 01603 430416 🖷 01603 430614 ✉ john.frary@broadland.gov.uk

Building Control: Mr Richard Gawthorpe, Director of CNC Building Control Services, Thorpe Lodge, 1 Yarmouth Road, Thorpe St. Andrew, Norwich NR7 0DU ☎ 01603 430552 🖷 01603 430541 ✉ richard.gawthorpe@broadland.gov.uk

PR / Communications: Ms Angi Doy, Communications Manager, Thorpe Lodge, 1 Yarmouth Road, Thorpe St. Andrew, Norwich NR7 0DU ☎ 01603 430523 🖷 01603 430614 ✉ angi.doy@broadland.gov.uk

Community Planning: Ms Liz Mowl, Head of Policy, Thorpe Lodge, 1 Yarmouth Road, Thorpe St. Andrew, Norwich NR7 0DU ☎ 01603 430593 ✉ liz.mowl@broadland.gov.uk

Computer Management: Mr Stephen Fennell, Head of Corporate Resources, Thorpe Lodge, 1 Yarmouth Road, Thorpe St. Andrew, Norwich NR7 0DU ☎ 01603 430524 🖷 01603 430614 ✉ stephen.fennell@broadland.gov.uk

Corporate Services: Mr Martin Thrower, Head of Corporate Services & Monitoring Officer, Thorpe Lodge, 1 Yarmouth Road, Thorpe St. Andrew, Norwich NR7 0DU ☎ 01603 430546 🖷 01603 430591 ✉ martin.thrower@broadland.gov.uk

Customer Service: Ms Dee Young, Personnel & Customer Services Manager, Thorpe Lodge, 1 Yarmouth Road, Thorpe St. Andrew, Norwich NR7 0DU ☎ 01603 430526 ✉ dee.young@broadland.gov.uk

Economic Development: Mr Hamish Melville, Business Development Manager, Thorpe Lodge, 1 Yarmouth Road, Thorpe St. Andrew, Norwich NR7 0DU ☎ 01603 430611 🖷 01603 430614 ✉ hamish.melville@broadland.gov.uk

E-Government: Mr Matthew Cross, Deputy Chief Executive, Thorpe Lodge, 1 Yarmouth Road, Thorpe St. Andrew, Norwich NR7 0DU ☎ 01603 430588 🖷 01603 430565 ✉ matthew.cross@broadland.gov.uk

Electoral Registration: Mrs Ann Watkins, Electoral Services Manager, Thorpe Lodge, 1 Yarmouth Road, Thorpe St. Andrew, Norwich NR7 0DU ☎ 01603 430424 🖷 01603 430591 ✉ ann.watkins@broadland.gov.uk

Emergency Planning: Mr Simon Faraday Drake, Emergency Planning Manager, Thorpe Lodge, 1 Yarmouth Road, Thorpe St. Andrew, Norwich NR7 0DU ☎ 01603 430643 ✉ simon.faraday.drake@broadland.gov.uk

Energy Management: Ms Deborah Collis, Climate Change Officer, Thorpe Lodge, 1 Yarmouth Road, Thorpe St. Andrew, Norwich NR7 0DU ☎ 01603 430629 ✉ katie.hughes@broadland.gov.uk

Environmental / Technical Services: Mr Richard Block, Head of Environmental Services, Thorpe Lodge, 1 Yarmouth Road, Thorpe St. Andrew, Norwich NR7 0DU ☎ 01603 430535 🖷 01603 430616 ✉ richard.block@broadland.gov.uk

Environmental Health: Mr Richard Block, Head of Environmental Services, Thorpe Lodge, 1 Yarmouth Road, Thorpe St. Andrew, Norwich NR7 0DU ☎ 01603 430535 🖷 01603 430616 ✉ richard.block@broadland.gov.uk

European Liaison: Mr Chris Hill, Head of Business Development, Thorpe Lodge, 1 Yarmouth Road, Thorpe St. Andrew, Norwich NR7 0DU ☎ 01603 430613 🖷 01603 484102

chris.hill@broadland.gov.uk

Facilities: Mr John Frary, Facilities Manager, Thorpe Lodge, 1 Yarmouth Road, Thorpe St. Andrew, Norwich NR7 0DU ☎ 01603 430416 🖷 01603 430614 john.frary@broadland.gov.uk

Finance and Treasurer: Mrs Jill Penn, Head of Finance & Revenues Services / S151 Officer, Thorpe Lodge, 1 Yarmouth Road, Thorpe St. Andrew, Norwich NR7 0DU ☎ 01603 430589 🖷 01603 430537 jill.penn@broadland.gov.uk

Health and Safety: Mr John Frary, Facilities Manager, Thorpe Lodge, 1 Yarmouth Road, Thorpe St. Andrew, Norwich NR7 0DU ☎ 01603 430416 🖷 01603 430614 john.frary@broadland.gov.uk

Housing: Mrs Leigh Booth, Strategic Director & Chief Planner, Thorpe Lodge, 1 Yarmouth Road, Thorpe St. Andrew, Norwich NR7 0DU ☎ 01603 430566 🖷 01603 430565 leigh.booth@broadland.gov.uk

Legal: Mr Martin Thrower, Head of Corporate Services & Monitoring Officer, Thorpe Lodge, 1 Yarmouth Road, Thorpe St. Andrew, Norwich NR7 0DU ☎ 01603 430546 🖷 01603 430591 martin.thrower@broadland.gov.uk

Leisure and Cultural Services: Mr Chris Hill, Head of Business Development, Thorpe Lodge, 1 Yarmouth Road, Thorpe St. Andrew, Norwich NR7 0DU ☎ 01603 430613 🖷 01603 484102 chris.hill@broadland.gov.uk

Licensing: Mr Paul Hemnell, Environmental Enforcement Manager, Thorpe Lodge, 1 Yarmouth Road, Thorpe St. Andrew, Norwich NR7 0DU ☎ 01603 430577 🖷 01603 701859 paul.hemnell@broadland.gov.uk

Lifelong Learning: Mrs Sharon Money, Learning & Development Manager, 9 Hellesdon Park Road, Norwich NR6 5DR ☎ 01603 788950 🖷 01603 484102 sharon.money@broadland.gov.uk

Lighting: Mr Richard Block, Head of Environmental Services, Thorpe Lodge, 1 Yarmouth Road, Thorpe St. Andrew, Norwich NR7 0DU ☎ 01603 430535 🖷 01603 430616 richard.block@broadland.gov.uk

Lottery Funding, Charity and Voluntary: Ms Sally Hoare, Partnership & Funding Officer, Thorpe Lodge, 1 Yarmouth Road, Thorpe St. Andrew, Norwich NR7 0DU ☎ 01603 430620 🖷 01603 430592 sally.hoare@broadland.gov.uk

Member Services: Mr Martin Thrower, Head of Corporate Services & Monitoring Officer, Thorpe Lodge, 1 Yarmouth Road, Thorpe St. Andrew, Norwich NR7 0DU ☎ 01603 430546 🖷 01603 430591 martin.thrower@broadland.gov.uk

Partnerships: Ms Liz Mowl, Head of Policy, Thorpe Lodge, 1 Yarmouth Road, Thorpe St. Andrew, Norwich NR7 0DU ☎ 01603 430620 🖷 01603 430592 liz.mowl@broadland.gov.uk

Personnel / HR: Mr Stephen Fennell, Head of Corporate Resources, Thorpe Lodge, 1 Yarmouth Road, Thorpe St. Andrew, Norwich NR7 0DU ☎ 01603 430524 🖷 01603 430614 stephen.fennell@broadland.gov.uk

Planning: Mr Phil Courtier, Head of Development Management & Conservation, Thorpe Lodge, 1 Yarmouth Road, Thorpe St. Andrew, Norwich NR7 0DU ☎ 01603 430566 🖷 01603 430565 phil.courtier@broadland.gov.uk

Procurement: Mr Stephen Fennell, Head of Corporate Resources, Thorpe Lodge, 1 Yarmouth Road, Thorpe St. Andrew, Norwich NR7 0DU ☎ 01603 430524 🖷 01603 430614 stephen.fennell@broadland.gov.uk

Recycling & Waste Minimisation: Mr Richard Block, Head of Environmental Services, Thorpe Lodge, 1 Yarmouth Road, Thorpe St. Andrew, Norwich NR7 0DU ☎ 01603 430535 🖷 01603 430616 richard.block@broadland.gov.uk

Staff Training: Ms Dee Young, Personnel & Customer Services Manager, Thorpe Lodge, 1 Yarmouth Road, Thorpe St. Andrew, Norwich NR7 0DU ☎ 01603 430526 dee.young@broadland.gov.uk

Street Scene: Mr Peter Leggett, Street Scene Officer, Thorpe Lodge, 1 Yarmouth Road, Thorpe St. Andrew, Norwich NR7 0DU ☎ 01603 431133 peter.leggett@broadland.gov.uk

Sustainable Communities: Mr Phil Courtier, Head of Development Management & Conservation, Thorpe Lodge, 1 Yarmouth Road, Thorpe St. Andrew, Norwich NR7 0DU ☎ 01603 430566 🖷 01603 430565 phil.courtier@broadland.gov.uk

Sustainable Communities: Mr Phil Kirby, Chief Executive, Thorpe Lodge, 1 Yarmouth Road, Thorpe St. Andrew, Norwich NR7 0DU ☎ 01603 430566 🖷 01603 430565 phil.kirby@broadland.gov.uk

Sustainable Development: Ms Liz Mowl, Head of Policy, Thorpe Lodge, 1 Yarmouth Road, Thorpe St. Andrew, Norwich NR7 0DU ☎ 01603 430593 liz.mowl@broadland.gov.uk

Tourism: Mr Chris Hill, Head of Business Development, Thorpe Lodge, 1 Yarmouth Road, Thorpe St. Andrew, Norwich NR7 0DU ☎ 01603 430613 🖷 01603 484102 chris.hill@broadland.gov.uk

Tourism: Ms Kirstin Hughes, Tourism & Arts Development Officer, Thorpe Lodge, 1 Yarmouth Road, Thorpe St. Andrew, Norwich NR7 0DU ☎ 01603 430563 kirstin.hughes@broadland.gov.uk

Waste Collection and Disposal: Mr Richard Block, Head of Environmental Services, Thorpe Lodge, 1 Yarmouth Road, Thorpe St. Andrew, Norwich NR7 0DU ☎ 01603 430535 🖷 01603 430616 richard.block@broadland.gov.uk

Waste Management: Mr Richard Block, Head of Environmental Services, Thorpe Lodge, 1 Yarmouth Road, Thorpe St. Andrew, Norwich NR7 0DU ☎ 01603 430535 🖷 01603 430616 richard.block@broadland.gov.uk

MEMBERS OF THE COUNCIL (47)

***Chair:* Gurney**, Shelagh (CON - Hellesdon North West)
cllr.shelagh.gurney@broadland.gov.uk

***Vice-Chair:* Foulger**, Roger (CON - Drayton South)
cllr.roger.foulger@broadland.gov.uk
Adams, Tony (CON - Hellesdon South East)
cllr.tony.adams@broadland.gov.uk
Balcombe, Peter (LD - Hellesdon South East)
cllr.peter.balcombe@broadland.gov.uk
Bannock, Claudette (CON - Taverham South)
cllr.claudette.bannock@broadland.gov.uk
Bracey, John (CON - Sprowston East)
cllr.john.bracey@broadland.gov.uk
Bradley, Maggie (CON - Sprowston East)
cllr.maggie.bradley@broadland.gov.uk
Buck, Danny (CON - Hellesdon North West)
cllr.danny.buck@broadland.gov.uk
Buckle, Steve (LD - Wroxham)
cllr.steve.buckle@broadland.gov.uk
Carrick, Paul (CON - Hevingham)
cllr.paul.carrick@broadland.gov.uk
Carswell, James (CON - Blofield with South Walsham)
cllr.james.carswell@broadland.gov.uk
Clancy, Stuart (CON - Taverham South)
cllr.stuart.clancy@broadland.gov.uk
Cottingham, Joella (CON - Aylsham)
cllr.joella.cottingham@broadland.gov.uk
Couzens, Bill (LAB - Sprowston Central)
cllr.bill.couzens@broadland.gov.uk
Davis-Claydon, Kim (CON - Thorpe St Andrew South East)
cllr.kim.davis-claydon@broadland.gov.uk
Dunn, Stuart (CON - Old Catton & Sprowston West)
cllr.stuart.dunn@broadland.gov.uk
Emsell, Jonathan (CON - Thorpe St Andrew South East)
cllr.jonathan.emsell@broadland.gov.uk
Findlay, Paul (CON - Sprowston East)
cllr.paul.findlay@broadland.gov.uk
Fisher, John (CON - Thorpe St Andrew North West)
cllr.john.fisher@broadland.gov.uk
Graham, Ian (CON - Aylsham)
cllr.ian.graham@broadland.gov.uk
Green, Paul (CON - Blofield with South Walsham)
cllr.paul.green@broadland.gov.uk
Harrison, David (LD - Aylsham)
cllr.david.harrison@broadland.gov.uk
Hempsall, Lana (CON - Acle)
cllr.lana.hempsall@broadland.gov.uk
Joyce, James (LD - Eynesford)
cllr.james.joyce@broadland.gov.uk
Keeler, Joanne (CON - Horsford & Felthorpe)
cllr.joanne.keeler@broadland.gov.uk
Knowles, Robin (CON - Sprowston Central)
cllr.robin.knowles@broadland.gov.uk
Kular, Balvinder (LD - Spixworth with St Faiths)
cllr.balvinder.kular@broadland.gov.uk
Leggett, Kenneth (CON - Old Catton & Sprowston West)
cllr.ken.leggett@broadland.gov.uk
Mackie, Ian (CON - Thorpe St Andrew North West)
cllr.ian.mackie@broadland.gov.uk
Mallett, Alan (CON - Coltishall)
cllr.alan.mallett@broadland.gov.uk
Mancini-Boyle, Trudy (CON - Thorpe St Andrew South East)
cllr.trudy.mancini-boyle@broadland.gov.uk
McGilvray, Benjamin (LD - Wroxham)
cllr.ben.mcgilvray@broadland.gov.uk
Nash, Roger (CON - Drayton North)
cllr.roger.nash@broadland.gov.uk
Pettman, John (CON - Marshes)
cllr.john.pettman@broadland.gov.uk
Proctor, Andrew (CON - Brundall)
cllr.andrew.proctor@broadland.gov.uk
Rix, Barbara (LD - Buxton)
cllr.barbara.rix@broadland.gov.uk
Roper, Dan (LD - Spixworth with St Faiths)
cllr.dan.roper@broadland.gov.uk
Shaw, Nigel (CON - Thorpe St Andrew North West)
cllr.nigel.shaw@broadland.gov.uk
Snowling, Michael (CON - Brundall)
cllr.michael.snowling@broadland.gov.uk
Starling, Nicholas (LD - Taverham North)
cllr.nicholas.starling@broadland@gov.uk
Starling, John (LD - Horsford & Felthorpe)
cllr.john.starling@broadland.gov.uk
Thompson, David (CON - Old Catton & Sprowston West)
cllr.david.thompson@broadland.gov.uk
Vincent, Shaun (CON - Plumstead)
cllr.shaun.vincent@broadland.gov.uk
Ward, David (CON - Burlingham)
cllr.david.ward@broadland.gov.uk
Ward, Carole (LD - Taverham North)
cllr.carole.ward@broadland.gov.uk
Wheeler, Chris (LD - Reepham)
cllr.chris.wheeler@broadland.gov.uk
Woodbridge, Simon (CON - Great Witchingham)
cllr.simon.woodbridge@broadland.gov.uk

POLITICAL COMPOSITION
CON: 34, LD: 12, LAB: 1

CABINET
Leader: Mr Andrew Proctor
Deputy Leader: Mrs Joella Cottingham
Community & Housing: Mrs Joella Cottingham
Economic Development: Mr Stuart Clancy
Environmental Excellence: Mr John Fisher
Finance: Mr Paul Carrick
Operations & Resources: Mrs Kim Davis-Claydon
Policy: Mr Andrew Proctor

COMMITTEE CHAIRS
Appeals: Mr Michael Snowling
Appointments & Pay: Mrs Kim Davis-Claydon
Final Accounts: Mr Paul Carrick
Licensing: Mr Stuart Dunn
Overview & Scrutiny: Mr James Joyce
Planning: Mr Michael Snowling

BROMLEY L

Bromley London Borough Council, Civic Centre, Stockwell Close, Bromley BR1 3UH ☎ 020 8464 3333 💻 www.bromley.gov.uk

FACTS & FIGURES
Police Authority: Metropolitan Police Authority
Health Authority: NHS London
Learning and Skills Council: London
Parliamentary Constituencies: Beckenham, Bromley and Chislehurst, Orpington
EU Constituencies: London
Election Frequency: Elections are of whole council
Twinning: Neuwied (Germany)

PRINCIPAL OFFICERS

Chief Executive: Mr Doug Patterson, Chief Executive, Civic Centre, Stockwell Close, Bromley BR1 3UH ☎ 020 8313 4354 🖷 020 8313 4444 ✉ doug.patterson@bromley.gov.uk

Assistant Chief Executive: Mr Charles Obazuaye, Assistant Chief Executive: Human Resources, Civic Centre, Stockwell Close, Bromley BR1 3UH ☎ 020 8313 4355 🖷 020 8313 4444 ✉ charles.obazuaye@bromley.gov.uk

Senior Management: Mr Mark Bowen, Director of Resources, Civic Centre, Stockwell Close, Bromley BR1 3UH ☎ 020 8313 4355 🖷 020 8313 4444 ✉ mark.bowen@bromley.gov.uk

Senior Management: Mr Nigel Davies, Director of Environmental Services, Civic Centre, Stockwell Close, Bromley BR1 3UH ☎ 020 8313 4443 🖷 020 8313 4460 ✉ nigel.davies@bromley.gov.uk

Senior Management: Mr Marc Hume, Director of Renewal & Recreation, Civic Centre, Stockwell Close, Bromley BR1 3UH ☎ 020 8461 7557 🖷 020 8313 4460 ✉ marc.hume@bromley.gov.uk

Architect, Building / Property Services: Mr Bob McQuillan, Chief Planner, Civic Centre, Stockwell Close, Bromley BR1 3UH ☎ 020 8461 7718 🖷 020 8313 0095 ✉ bob.mcquillan@bromley.gov.uk

Best Value: Mr Chris Spellman, Assistant Director: Organisational Improvement, Civic Centre, Stockwell Close, Bromley BR1 3UH ☎ 020 8461 7942 🖷 020 8313 4418 ✉ chris.spellman@bromley.gov.uk

Building Control: Mr Steve Moore, Head of Building Control, Building Control, Civic Centre, Stockwell Close, Bromley BR1 3UH ☎ ; 020 8313 4315 🖷 020 8313 4604 ✉ steve.moore@bromley.gov.uk

Catering Services: Mrs Karen Stephen, Property Facilities Manager, Civic Centre, Stockwell Close, Bromley BR1 3UH ☎ 020 8313 4053 🖷 020 8313 4939 ✉ karen.stephen@bromley.gov.uk

Civil Registration: Ms Carol Andrews, Superintendent Registrar, Civic Centre, Stockwell Close, Bromley BR1 3UH ☎ 020 8313 7957 🖷 020 8313 4699 ✉ carol.andrews@bromley.gov.uk

Community Safety: Mr Colin Newman, Head of Community Safety, Civic Centre, Stockwell Close, Bromley BR1 3UH ☎ 020 8461 7915 🖷 020 8290 0608 ✉ colin.newman@bromley.gov.uk

Computer Management: Ms Sue Essler, Head of Information Systems, Civic Centre, Stockwell Close, Bromley BR1 3UH ☎ 020 8313 4273 ✉ sue.essler@bromley.gov.uk

Consumer Protection and Trading Standards: Mr Clive Davison, Assistant Director for Public Protection, Civic Centre, Stockwell Close, Bromley BR1 3UH ☎ 020 8313 4688 🖷 020 8313 4450 ✉ clive.davison@bromley.gov.uk

Contracts: Mr Dave Starling, Head of Corporate Procurement, Civic Centre, Stockwell Close, Bromley BR1 3UH ☎ 020 8313 4639 🖷 020 8313 4746 ✉ dave.starling@bromley.gov.uk

Corporate Services: Ms Julie Daly, Head of Safeguarding & Quality, Civic Centre, Stockwell Close, Bromley BR1 3UH ☎ 020 8313 4610 ✉ julie.daly@bromley.gov.uk

Corporate Services: Ms Valerie Jenkins, Head of HR Organisational Development, Civic Centre, Stockwell Close, Bromley BR1 3UH ☎ 020 8313 4380 🖷 020 8313 4241 ✉ val.jenkins@bromley.gov.uk

Customer Service: Mr Duncan Bridgewater, Head of Customer Services, Civic Centre, Stockwell Close, Bromley BR1 3UH ☎ 020 8313 7676 ✉ duncan.bridgewater@bromely.gov.uk

Economic Development: Mr Marc Hume, Director of Renewal & Recreation, Civic Centre, Stockwell Close, Bromley BR1 3UH ☎ 020 8461 7557 🖷 020 8313 4460 ✉ marc.hume@bromley.gov.uk

Electoral Registration: Mrs Carol Ling, Electoral Services Manager, Civic Centre, Stockwell Close, Bromley BR1 3UH ☎ 020 8313 4367 🖷 020 8313 4995 ✉ carol.ling@bromley.gov.uk

Emergency Planning: Mr Stephen Lewis, Emergency Planning Manager, Civic Centre, Stockwell Close, Bromley BR1 3UH ☎ 020 8313 4388 🖷 020 8313 4348 ✉ stephen.lewis@bromley.gov.uk

Energy Management: Mr Gerry Kelly, Property Energy Manager, Civic Centre, Stockwell Close, Bromley BR1 3UH ☎ 020 8313 4570 🖷 020 8313 4504 ✉ gerry.kelly@bromley.gov.uk

Environmental / Technical Services: Mr Peter Turvey, Head of Street Environment, Civic Centre, Stockwell Close, Bromley BR1 3UH ☎ 020 8313 4901 🖷 020 8313 4478 ✉ peter.turvey@bromley.gov.uk

Environmental Health: Mr Clive Davison, Assistant Director for Public Protection, Civic Centre, Stockwell Close, Bromley BR1 3UH ☎ 020 8313 4688 🖷 020 8313 4450 ✉ clive.davison@bromley.gov.uk

Events Manager: Mr Toby Smith, Parks Community & Infrastructure Manager, Civic Centre, Stockwell Close, Bromley BR1 3UH ☎ 020 8658 1593 🖷 020 8650 9880 ✉ toby.smith@bromley.gov.uk

Facilities: Mr Andrew Champion, Facilities & Support Services Manager, Civic Centre, Stockwell Close, Bromley BR1 3UH ☎ 020 8313 4394 🖷 020 8290 0608 ✉ andrew.champion@bromley.gov.uk

Finance and Treasurer: Mrs Lesley Moore, Head of Finance & Resources, Civic Centre, Stockwell Close, Bromley BR1 3UH ☎ 020 8313 4140 🖷 020 8313 4620 ✉ lesley.moore@bromley.gov.uk

Finance and Treasurer: Mr Peter Turner, Finance Director, Civic Centre, Stockwell Close, Bromley BR1 3UH ☎ 020 8313 4807 🖷 020 8313 4338 ✉ peter.turner@bromley.gov.uk

Fleet Management: Mr Gavin Moore, Head of Strategy Development & Services, Civic Centre, Stockwell Close, Bromley BR1 3UH ☎ 020 8313 4539 🖷 020 8461 7925 ✉ gavin.moore@bromley.gov.uk

Grounds Maintenance: Mr Patrick Phillips, Head of Parks & Green Spaces, Civic Centre, Stockwell Close, Bromley BR1 3UH ☎ 020 8313 4322 🖷 020 8313 9975 ✉ patrick.phillips@bromley.gov.uk

Health and Safety: Mrs Elaine Pilkington, Health & Safety Manager, Civic Centre, Stockwell Close, Bromley BR1 3UH ☎ 020 8313 4386 🖷 020 8313 4334 ✉ elaine.pilkington@bromley.gov.uk

Highways: Mr Paul Symonds, Assistant Director, Transport & Highways, Civic Centre, Stockwell Close, Bromley BR1 3UH ☎ 020 8313 4540 ✉ paul.symonds@bromley.gov.uk

Housing: Mr David Gibson, Assistant Director: Housing & Residential Services, Civic Centre, Stockwell Close, Bromley BR1 3UH ☎ 020 8313 4794 🖷 020 8313 4620 ✉ david.gibson@bromley.gov.uk

Legal: Mr Mark Bowen, Director of Resources, Civic Centre, Stockwell Close, Bromley BR1 3UH ☎ 020 8313 4355 🖷 020 8313 4444 ✉ mark.bowen@bromley.gov.uk

Leisure and Cultural Services: Mr Colin Brand, Assistant Director, Civic Centre, Stockwell Close, Bromley BR1 3UH ☎ 020 8313 4107 🖷 020 8461 7890 ✉ colin.brand@bromley.gov.uk

Licensing: Mr Paul Lehane, Food Safety, Occupational Safety & Licensing Manager, Civic Centre, Stockwell Close, Bromley BR1 3UH ☎ 020 8313 4216 🖷 020 8313 4450 ✉ paul.lehane@bromley.gov.uk

Lighting: Mr Garry Warner, Head of Highway Network Management/Traffic Manager, Civic Centre, Stockwell Close, Bromley BR1 3UH ☎ 020 8313 4929 🖷 020 8313 4312 ✉ garry.warner@bromley.gov.uk

Member Services: Mr Graham Walton, Head of Democratic Services, Civic Centre, Stockwell Close, Bromley BR1 3UH ☎ 020 8461 7743 🖷 020 8290 0608 ✉ graham.walton@bromley.gov.uk

Parking: Mr Benjamin Stephens, Head of Parking, Civic Centre, Stockwell Close, Bromley BR1 3UH ☎ 020 8313 4514 🖷 020 8313 4446 ✉ benjamin.stephens@bromley.gov.uk

Personnel / HR: Mr Charles Obazuaye, Assistant Chief Executive/Head of Human Resources, Civic Centre, Stockwell Close, Bromley BR1 3UH ☎ ; 020 8313 4355 🖷 020 8313 4444 ✉ charles.obazuaye@bromley.gov.uk

Planning: Mr Bob McQuillan, Chief Planner, Civic Centre, Stockwell Close, Bromley BR1 3UH ☎ 020 8461 7718 🖷 020 8313 0095 ✉ bob.mcquillan@bromley.gov.uk

Procurement: Mr Dave Starling, Head of Corporate Procurement, Civic Centre, Stockwell Close, Bromley BR1 3UH ☎ 020 8313 4639 🖷 020 8313 4746 ✉ dave.starling@bromley.gov.uk

Public Libraries: Mr Tim Woolgar, Library Operations & Commissioning Manager, Bromley Central Library, High Street, Bromley BR1 1EX ☎ 020 8461 7233 🖷 020 8461 7230 ✉ tim.woolgar@bromley.gov.uk

Recycling & Waste Minimisation: Mr John Woodruff, Head of Waste Services, Civic Centre, Stockwell Close, Bromley BR1 3UH ☎ 020 8313 4910 🖷 020 8313 4460 ✉ john.woodruff@bromley.gov.uk

Regeneration: Mr Marc Hume, Director of Renewal & Recreation, Civic Centre, Stockwell Close, Bromley BR1 3UH ☎ 020 8461 7557 🖷 020 8313 4460 ✉ marc.hume@bromley.gov.uk

Road Safety: Mr Angus Culverwell, Manager of Casualty Reduction & Sustainable Travel Unit Manager, Civic Centre, Stockwell Close, Bromley BR1 3UH ☎ 020 8313 4959 🖷 020 8313 1948 ✉ angus.culverwell@bromley.gov.uk

Social Services (Adult): Mr David Roberts, Assistant Director: Adult Care, Civic Centre, Stockwell Close, Bromley BR1 3UH ☎ 020 8313 4754 🖷 020 8313 4620 ✉ david.roberts@bromley.gov.uk

Social Services (Children): Ms Elaine Morgan, Youth Offending Team Manager, 8 Mason's Hill, Bromley BR2 9EY ☎ 020 8466 3080 🖷 020 8466 3099 ✉ elaine.morgan@bromley.gov.uk

Social Services (Children): Ms Kay Weiss, Assistant Director: Children & Families, Civic Centre, Stockwell Close, Bromley BR1 3UH ☎ 020 8313 4062 🖷 020 8313 4122 ✉ kay.weiss@bromley.gov.uk

Staff Training: Mr Charles Obazuaye, Assistant Chief Executive/Head of Human Resources, Civic Centre, Stockwell Close, Bromley BR1 3UH ☎ ; 020 8313 4355 🖷 020 8313 4444 ✉ charles.obazuaye@bromley.gov.uk

Street Scene: Mr Peter McCready, Head of Area Management, Civic Centre, Stockwell Close, Bromley BR1 3UH ☎ 020 8313 4942 🖷 020 8313 4478 ✉ peter.mccready@bromley.gov.uk

Sustainable Communities: Mr Marc Hume, Director of Renewal & Recreation, Civic Centre, Stockwell Close, Bromley BR1 3UH ☎ 020 8461 7557 🖷 020 8313 4460 ✉ marc.hume@bromley.gov.uk

Sustainable Development: Mr Marc Hume, Director of Renewal & Recreation, Civic Centre, Stockwell Close, Bromley BR1 3UH ☎ 020 8461 7557 🖷 020 8313 4460 ✉ marc.hume@bromley.gov.uk

Tourism: Ms Margaret Carr, Projects & Partnerships Manager, Civic Centre, Stockwell Close, Bromley BR1 3UH ☎ 020 8313 4463 🖷 020 8313 4571 ✉ margaret.carr@bromley.gov.uk

Town Centre: Mr Colin Brand, Assistant Director, Civic Centre, Stockwell Close, Bromley BR1 3UH ☎ 020 8313 4107 🖷 020 8461

7890 ✉ colin.brand@bromley.gov.uk

Traffic Management: Mr Dave Blackburn, Traffic Officer, Civic Centre, Stockwell Close, Bromley BR1 3UH ☎ 020 8313 4907 🖷 020 8313 4796 ✉ dave.blackburn@bromley.gov.uk

Transport: Mr Paul Chilton, Transport Operations Manager, Central Depot, Baths Road, Bromley BR2 9RB ☎ 020 8313 4849 🖷 020 8461 7689 ✉ paul.chilton@bromley.gov.uk

Waste Collection and Disposal: Mr John Woodruff, Head of Waste Services, Civic Centre, Stockwell Close, Bromley BR1 3UH ☎ 020 8313 4910 🖷 020 8313 4460 ✉ john.woodruff@bromley.gov.uk

Waste Management: Mr Paul Symonds, Assistant Director, Transport & Highways, Civic Centre, Stockwell Close, Bromley BR1 3UH ☎ 020 8313 4540 ✉ paul.symonds@bromley.gov.uk

MEMBERS OF THE COUNCIL (60)

***Mayor:* Turner**, Michael (CON - Plaistow & Sundridge)
michael.turner@bromley.gov.uk
***Deputy Mayor:* Payne**, Ian (CON - Chislehurst)
ian.payne@bromley.gov.uk
***Leader of the Council:* Carr**, Stephen (CON - Bromley Common & Keston)
stephen.carr@bromley.gov.uk
***Group Leader:* Getgood**, John (LAB - Penge & Cator)
john.getgood@bromley.gov.uk
***Group Leader:* Papworth**, Tom (LD - Crystal Palace)
tom.papworth@bromley.gov.uk
Adams, Reg (LD - Clock House)
reg.adams@bromley.gov.uk
Arthur, Graham (CON - Hayes & Coney Hall)
graham.arthur@bromley.gov.uk
Auld, Douglas (CON - Petts Wood & Knoll)
douglas.auld@bromley.gov.uk
Bance, Kathy (LAB - Penge & Cator)
katherine.bance@bromley.gov.uk
Beckley, Jane (CON - West Wickham)
jane.beckley@bromley.gov.uk
Benington, Julian (CON - Biggin Hill)
julian.benington@bromley.gov.uk
Bennett, Nicholas (CON - West Wickham)
md@kentrefurbishment.co.uk
Bennett, Ruth (CON - Bromley Common & Keston)
ruth.bennett@bromley.gov.uk
Bosshard, Eric (CON - Chislehurst)
eric.bosshard@bromley.gov.uk
Boughey, Katy (CON - Chislehurst)
katy.boughey@bromley.gov.uk
Buttinger, Lydia (CON - Orpington)
lydia.buttinger@bromley.gov.uk
Canvin, John (LD - Crystal Palace)
john.canvin@bromley.gov.uk
Charsley, Roger (CON - Mottingham & Chislehurst North)
roger.charsley@bromley.gov.uk
Dean, Peter (CON - Kelsey & Eden Park)
peter.dean@bromley.gov.uk
Dykes, Nicky (CON - Bromley Town)
nicky.dykes@bromley.gov.uk
Ellis, Judi (CON - Cray Valley West)
judith.ellis@bromley.gov.uk
Evans, Robert (CON - Farnborough & Crofton)
robert.evans@bromley.gov.uk
Fawthrop, Roxy (CON - Cray Valley East)
roxy.fawthrop@bromley.gov.uk
Fawthrop, Simon (CON - Petts Wood & Knoll)
simon.fawthrop@bromley.gov.uk
Fookes, Peter (LAB - Penge & Cator)
peter.fookes@bromley.gov.uk
Fortune, Peter (CON - Cray Valley East)
peter.fortune@bromley.gov.uk
Grainger, Julian (CON - Chelsfield & Pratts Bottom)
julian.grainger@bromley.gov.uk
Harmer, Will (CON - Bromley Town)
will.harmer@bromley.gov.uk
Harmer, Ellie (CON - Plaistow & Sundridge)
ellie.harmer@bromley.gov.uk
Hastings, David (CON - Bromley Town)
david.hastings@bromley.gov.uk
Humphrys, Brian (CON - West Wickham)
brian.humphrys@bromley.gov.uk
Huntington-Thresher, William (CON - Orpington)
william.huntington-thresher@bromley.gov.uk
Huntington-Thresher, Samaris (CON - Chelsfield & Pratts Bottom)
samaris.huntington-thresher@bromley.gov.uk
Ince, John (CON - Cray Valley West)
john.ince@bromley.gov.uk
Jackson, Russell (CON - Chelsfield & Pratts Bottom)
russell.jackson@bromley.gov.uk
Jeffreys, David (CON - Shortlands)
david.jeffreys@bromley.gov.uk
Joel, Charles (CON - Farnborough & Crofton)
charles.joel@bromley.gov.uk
Lymer, Kate (CON - Bickley)
kate.lymer@bromley.gov.uk
Lynch, Paul (CON - Kelsey & Eden Park)
paul.lynch@bromley.gov.uk
Manning, Anne (CON - Hayes & Coney Hall)
anne.manning@bromley.gov.uk
McBride, David (LD - Cray Valley East)
david.mcbride@bromley.gov.uk
Mellor, Russell (CON - Copers Cope)
russell.mellor@bromley.gov.uk
Michael, Alexa (CON - Bromley Common & Keston)
alexa.michael@bromley.gov.uk
Milner, Nick (CON - Clock House)
nick.milner@bromley.gov.uk
Morgan, Peter (CON - Plaistow & Sundridge)
peter.morgan@bromley.gov.uk
Noad, Ernest (CON - Shortlands)
ernest.noad@bromley.gov.uk
Norrie, Gordon (CON - Biggin Hill)
gordon.norrie@bromley.gov.uk
Owen, Tony (CON - Petts Wood & Knoll)
tony.owen@bromley.gov.uk
Phillips, Sarah (CON - Clock House)
sarah.phillips@bromley.gov.uk
Reddin, Neil (CON - Hayes & Coney Hall)
neil.reddin@bromley.gov.uk
Rideout, Catherine (CON - Bickley)
catherine.rideout@bromley.gov.uk
Rideout, Charles (CON - Mottingham & Chislehurst North)
charles.rideout@bromley.gov.uk
Scoates, Richard (CON - Darwin)
richard.scoates@bromley.gov.uk
Smith, Diane (CON - Kelsey & Eden Park)

diane.smith@bromley.gov.uk
Smith, Colin (CON - Bickley)
colin.smith@bromley.gov.uk
Stevens, Tim (CON - Farnborough & Crofton)
tim.stevens@bromley.gov.uk
Stranger, Harry (CON - Cray Valley West)
harry.stranger@bromley.gov.uk
Tickner, Michael (CON - Copers Cope)
michael.tickner@bromley.gov.uk
Tunnicliffe, Pauline (CON - Orpington)
pauline.tunnicliffe@bromley.gov.uk
Wells, Stephen (CON - Copers Cope)
stephen.wells@bromley.gov.uk

POLITICAL COMPOSITION
CON: 53, LD: 4, LAB: 3

CABINET
Leader: Mr Stephen Carr
Deputy Leader: Mr Colin Smith
Care Services: Mr Robert Evans
Education: Mr Stephen Wells
Environment: Mr Colin Smith
Public Protection & Safety: Mr Tim Stevens
Renewal & Recreation: Mr Peter Morgan
Resources & Public Health Matters: Mr Graham Arthur

COMMITTEE CHAIRS
Bromley Economic Partnership: Mr Peter Morgan
Care Services Policy Development & Scrutiny: Ms Judi Ellis
Development Control: Mr Peter Dean
Education Policy Development & Scrutiny: Mr Nicholas Bennett
Environmental Policy Development & Scrutiny: Mr William Huntington-Thresher
Executive & Resources Policy Development: Mr Eric Bosshard
General Purposes & Licensing: Mr Tony Owen
Pension Investment Sub: Mr Paul Lynch
Public Protection & Safety Policy Development & Scrutiny: Mr Douglas Auld
Renewal & Recreation Policy Development & Scrutiny: Ms Sarah Phillips

BROMSGROVE D

Bromsgrove District Council, The Council House, Burcot Lane, Bromsgrove B60 1AA ☎ 01527 881288; 01527 881288 (Customer Service Centre) 🖷 01527 881414 🖳 www.bromsgrove.gov.uk

FACTS & FIGURES
Police Authority: West Mercia Police Authority
Health Authority: NHS West Midlands
Learning and Skills Council: West Midlands
Parliamentary Constituencies: Bromsgrove
EU Constituencies: West Midlands
Election Frequency: Elections are of whole council
Twinning: Gronau (Germany)

PRINCIPAL OFFICERS
Chief Executive: Mr Kevin Dicks, Chief Executive, The Council House, Burcot Lane, Bromsgrove B60 1AA ☎ 01527 881400; 01527 64252 🖷 01527 881212; 01527 65216 ✉ k.dicks@bromsgroveandredditch.gov.uk

Deputy Chief Executive: Mrs Susan Hanley, Executive Director & Deputy Chief Executive, The Council House, Burcot Lane, Bromsgrove B60 1AA ☎ 01527 64252 Extn 3601; 01527 881483 🖷 01527 65216 ✉ s.hanley@bromsgroveandredditch.gov.uk

Senior Management: Mrs Susan Hanley, Executive Director & Deputy Chief Executive, Town Hall, Walter Stranz Square, Redditch B98 8AH ☎ 01527 64252 Extn 3601; 01527 881483 🖷 01527 65216 ✉ s.hanley@bromsgroveandredditch.gov.uk

Senior Management: Ms Jayne Pickering, Director of Finance & Corporate Resources, The Council House, Burcot Lane, Bromsgrove B60 1AA ☎ 01527 64252; 01527 881207 🖷 01527 65216 ✉ j.pickering@bromsgroveandredditch.gov.uk

Senior Management: Mr John Staniland, Executive Director of Planning, Regeneration, Regulatory & Housing, The Council House, Burcot Lane, Bromsgrove B60 1AA ☎ 01527 64252 Extn 3702; 01527 881202; 01527 534002 🖷 01527 65216 ✉ j.staniland@bromsgroveandredditch.gov.uk

Best Value: Ms Jayne Pickering, Director of Finance & Corporate Resources, Town Hall, Walter Stranz Square, Redditch B98 8AH ☎ 01527 64252; 01527 881207 🖷 01527 65216 ✉ j.pickering@bromsgroveandredditch.gov.uk

Building Control: Mr Adrian Wyre, Principle Building Control Surveyor, The Council House, Burcot Lane, Bromsgrove B60 1AA ☎ 01527 881350 🖷 01527 881313 ✉ a.wyre@bromsgrove.gov.uk

PR / Communications: Mrs Anne-Marie Darroch, Communications & Publicity Manager, The Council House, Burcot Lane, Bromsgrove B60 1AA ☎ 01527 881651; 01527 65252 🖷 01527 881212; 01527 65216 ✉ a.darroch@bromsgroveandredditch.gov.uk

Community Planning: Ms Angie Heighway, Head of Community Services, The Council House, Burcot Lane, Bromsgrove B60 1AA ☎ 01527 64252; 01527 881747 🖷 01527 65216 ✉ a.heighway@bromsgroveandredditch.gov.uk

Community Safety: Ms Angie Heighway, Head of Community Services, Town Hall, Walter Stranz Square, Redditch B98 8AH ☎ 01527 64252; 01527 881747 🖷 01527 65216 ✉ a.heighway@bromsgroveandredditch.gov.uk

Consumer Protection and Trading Standards: Mr Steve Jorden, Head of Regulatory Services, Wyatt House, Farrier Street, Worcester WR1 3BH ☎ 01527 64252; 01527 881466 🖷 01527 65216 ✉ s.jorden@redditchbc.gov.uk; s.jorden@worcsregservices.gov.uk

Contracts: Mr Alex Haslam, Procurement Officer, The Council House, Burcot Lane, Bromsgrove B60 1AA ☎ 01527 64252 ext. 3010; 01527 64252 🖷 01527 881414; 01527 65216 ✉ a.haslam@bromsgroveandredditch.gov.uk

Customer Service: Ms Amanda de Warr, Head of Customer Services, The Council House, Burcot Lane, Bromsgrove B60 1AA ☎ 01527 64252; 01527 881241 🖷 01527 65216

a.dewarr@bromsgroveandredditch.gov.uk

Direct Labour: Mr Guy Revans, Head of Environmental Services, The Council House, Burcot Lane, Bromsgrove B60 1AA ☎ 01527 64252; 01527 64252 ext. 3292 🖷 01527 65216 g.revans@bromsgroveandredditch.gov.uk

Economic Development: Mr Peter Michael, Economic Development Officer, The Council House, Burcot Lane, Bromsgrove B60 1AA ☎ 01527 881327 🖷 01527 881313 p.michael@bromsgrove.gov.uk

E-Government: Mrs Deb Poole, Head of Business Transformation, Town Hall, Walter Stranz Square, Redditch B98 8AH ☎ 01527 64252; 01527 64252 🖷 01527 65216 d.poole@bromsgroveandredditch.gov.uk

Electoral Registration: Mrs Susan Mould, Electoral Services Manager, The Council House, Burcot Lane, Bromsgrove B60 1AA ☎ 01527 881462; 01527 881462 🖷 01527 881414 s.mould@bromsgroveandredditch.gov.uk

Emergency Planning: Ms Ruth Bamford, Head of Planning & Regeneration Services, Town Hall, Walter Stranz Square, Redditch B98 8AH ☎ 01527 64252 Extn 3201; 01527 64252 ext. 3201 🖷 01527 65216 r.bamford@bromsgroveandredditch.gov.uk; r.bamford@bromsgroveandredditch.gov.uk

Emergency Planning: Mr Andrew Coel, Strategic Housing Manager, The Council House, Burcot Lane, Bromsgrove B60 1AA ☎ 01527 881270 🖷 01527 881414 a.coel@bromsgroveandredditch.gov.uk

Emergency Planning: Mr Richard Davis-Leech, North Worcestershire Civil Contingencies Resilience Manager, Civic Centre, New Street, Stourport-on-Severn DY13 8UJ ☎ 01562 732711 richard.davis-leech@wyreforestdc.gov.uk

Energy Management: Mr Alex Haslam, Procurement Officer, The Council House, Burcot Lane, Bromsgrove B60 1AA ☎ 01527 64252 ext. 3010 🖷 01527 881414; 01527 65216 a.haslam@bromsgroveandredditch.gov.uk

Environmental Health: Mr Steve Jorden, Head of Regulatory Services, Town Hall, Walter Stranz Square, Redditch B98 8AH ☎ 01527 64252; 01527 881466 🖷 01527 65216 s.jorden@redditchbc.gov.uk; s.jorden@worcsregservices.gov.uk

Estates, Property & Valuation: Mr Steve Martin, Facilities & Business Development Officer, The Council House, Burcot Lane, Bromsgrove B60 1AA ☎ 01527 881180 🖷 01527 881608 steve.martin@bromsgroveandredditch.gov.uk

European Liaison: Mr Peter Michael, Economic Development Officer, The Council House, Burcot Lane, Bromsgrove B60 1AA ☎ 01527 881327 🖷 01527 881313 p.michael@bromsgrove.gov.uk

Events Manager: Mr Hugh Moseley, Arts Development & Special Events Officer, The Council House, Burcot Lane, Bromsgrove B60 1AA ☎ 01527 881381 h.mosley@bromsgroveandredditch.gov.uk

Facilities: Mr Steve Martin, Facilities & Business Development Officer, Central Depot, Aston Road, Aston Fields, Bromsgrove B60 3EX ☎ 01527 881180 🖷 01527 881608 steve.martin@bromsgroveandredditch.gov.uk

Finance and Treasurer: Ms Jayne Pickering, Director of Finance & Corporate Resources, Town Hall, Walter Stranz Square, Redditch B98 8AH ☎ 01527 64252; 01527 881207 🖷 01527 65216 j.pickering@bromsgroveandredditch.gov.uk

Fleet Management: Mr Kevin Hirons, Environmental Business Development Manager, The Council House, Burcot Lane, Bromsgrove B60 1AA ☎ 01527 881705 k.hirons@bromsgroveandredditch.gov.uk

Health and Safety: Mrs Dawn Ibbitson, Health & Safety Advisor, The Council House, Burcot Lane, Bromsgrove B60 1AA ☎ 01527 881398 🖷 01527 881313 d.ibbitson@bromsgroveandredditch.gov.uk

Home Energy Conservation: Ms Ceridwen John, Climate Change Manager, c/o Central Depot, Aston Road, Aston Fields, Bromsgrove B60 3EX ☎ 01527 64252 ext. 3046 ceridwen.john@bromsgroveandredditch.gov.uk

Housing: Mr Andrew Coel, Strategic Housing Manager, The Council House, Burcot Lane, Bromsgrove B60 1AA ☎ 01527 881270 🖷 01527 881414 a.coel@bromsgroveandredditch.gov.uk

Legal: Mrs Claire Felton, Head of Legal, Equalities & Democratic Services, The Council House, Burcot Lane, Bromsgrove B60 1AA ☎ 01572 64252; 01527 881429 🖷 01527 65216; 01527 881414 c.felton@redditchbc.gov.uk; c.felton@bromsgroveandredditch.gov.uk

Leisure and Cultural Services: Mr John Godwin, Head of Leisure, The Council House, Burcot Lane, Bromsgrove B60 1AA ☎ 01527 64252; 01527 881762 🖷 01527 65216 j.godwin@bromsgroveandredditch.gov.uk

Licensing: Mrs Sue Garratt, Senior Licensing Practitioner, Wyatt House, Farrier Street, Worcester WR1 3BH ☎ 01527 64252 ext. 3032 sue.garratt@worcsregservices.gov.uk

Lottery Funding, Charity and Voluntary: Ms Jayne Pickering, Director of Finance & Corporate Resources, The Council House, Burcot Lane, Bromsgrove B60 1AA ☎ 01527 64252; 01527 881207 🖷 01527 65216 j.pickering@bromsgroveandredditch.gov.uk

Member Services: Ms Karen Firth, Committee Group Leader, The Council House, Burcot Lane, Bromsgrove B60 1AA ☎ 01527 881625 🖷 01527 881414 k.firth@bromsgroveandredditch.gov.uk

Partnerships: Mrs Rebecca Dunn, Policy Manager, Bromsgrove District Council, The Council House, Burcot Lane, Bromsgrove B66 1AA ☎ 01527 881616 r.dunn@bromsgroveandredditch.gov.uk

Personnel / HR: Ms Teresa Kristunas, Head of Finance & Corporate Resources, Town Hall, Walter Stranz Square, Redditch B98 8AH ☎ 01527 64252; 01527 64252 ext. 3295 🖷 01527 65216 t.kristunas@bromsgroveandredditch.gov.uk

LOCAL AUTHORITIES

Planning: Mr Dale Birch, Development Control Manager, The Council House, Burcot Lane, Bromsgrove B60 1AA ☎ 01527 881341 🖷 01527 881313 ✉ d.birch@bromsgroveandredditch.gov.uk

Procurement: Mr Alex Haslam, Procurement Officer, The Council House, Burcot Lane, Bromsgrove B60 1AA ☎ 01527 64252 ext. 3010; 01527 64252 🖷 01527 881414; 01527 65216 ✉ a.haslam@bromsgroveandredditch.gov.uk

Recycling & Waste Minimisation: Mr Guy Revans, Head of Environmental Services, Central Depot, Aston Road, Aston Fields, Bromsgrove B60 3EX ☎ 01527 64252; 01527 64252 ext. 3292 🖷 01527 65216 ✉ g.revans@bromsgroveandredditch.gov.uk

Regeneration: Mr John Staniland, Executive Director of Planning, Regeneration, Regulatory & Housing, The Council House, Burcot Lane, Bromsgrove B60 1AA ☎ 01527 64252 Extn 3702; 01527 881202 🖷 01527 65216 ✉ j.staniland@bromsgroveandredditch.gov.uk

Street Scene: Mr Guy Revans, Head of Environmental Services, Central Depot, Aston Road, Aston Fields, Bromsgrove B60 3EX ☎ 01527 64252; 01527 64252 ext. 3292 🖷 01527 65216 ✉ g.revans@bromsgroveandredditch.gov.uk

Sustainable Communities: Mr John Staniland, Executive Director of Planning, Regeneration, Regulatory & Housing, The Council House, Burcot Lane, Bromsgrove B60 1AA ☎ 01527 64252 Extn 3702; 01527 881202; 01527 534002 🖷 01527 65216 ✉ j.staniland@bromsgroveandredditch.gov.uk

Sustainable Development: Mr John Staniland, Executive Director of Planning, Regeneration, Regulatory & Housing, The Council House, Burcot Lane, Bromsgrove B60 1AA ☎ 01527 64252 Extn 3702; 01527 881202; 01527 534002 🖷 01527 65216 ✉ j.staniland@bromsgroveandredditch.gov.uk

Tourism: Mr John Godwin, Head of Leisure, The Council House, Burcot Lane, Bromsgrove B60 1AA ☎ 01527 64252; 01527 881762 🖷 01527 65216 ✉ j.godwin@bromsgroveandredditch.gov.uk

Town Centre: Mr Peter Michael, Economic Development Officer, The Council House, Burcot Lane, Bromsgrove B60 1AA ☎ 01527 881327 🖷 01527 881313 ✉ p.michael@bromsgrove.gov.uk

Waste Collection and Disposal: Mr Guy Revans, Head of Environmental Services, Central Depot, Aston Road, Aston Fields, Bromsgrove B60 3EX ☎ 01527 64252; 01527 64252 ext. 3292 🖷 01527 65216 ✉ g.revans@bromsgroveandredditch.gov.uk; g.revans@bromsgroveandredditch.gov.uk

Waste Management: Mr Guy Revans, Head of Environmental Services, Central Depot, Aston Road, Aston Fields, Bromsgrove B60 3EX ☎ 01527 64252; 01527 64252 ext. 3292 🖷 01527 65216 ✉ g.revans@bromsgroveandredditch.gov.uk

MEMBERS OF THE COUNCIL (39)

***Chair:* Griffiths**, J (CON - Alvechurch)
j.griffiths@bromsgrove.gov.uk
Baxter, S (R - Drakes Cross & Walkers Heath)
s.baxter@bromsgrove.gov.uk
Bloore, C (LAB - Sidemoor)
c.bloore@bromsgrove.gov.uk
Booth, Del (CON - Stoke Heath)
d.booth@bromsgrove.gov.uk
Boswell, J (CON - Furlongs)
j.boswell@bromsgrove.gov.uk
Boulter, J (CON - Wythall South)
j.boulter@bromsgrove.gov.uk
Brogan, J (CON - Catshill)
j.brogan@bromsgrove.gov.uk
Bullivant, M (CON - Hollywood & Majors Green)
m.bullivant@bromsgrove.gov.uk
Buxton, M (LAB - Whitford)
m.buxton@bromsgrove.gov.uk
Clarke, R (CON - Drakes Cross & Walkers Heath)
r.clarke@bromsgrove.gov.uk
Colella, S (CON - Hagley)
s.colella@bromsgrove.gov.uk
Cooper, B (CON - Marlbrock)
b.cooper@bromsgrove.gov.uk
Deeming, R (CON - Hillside)
r.deeming@bromsgrove.gov.uk
Dent, R (CON - St. Johns)
r.dent@bromsgrove.gov.uk
Dudley, S (CON - Hillside)
s.dudley@bromsgrove.gov.uk
Grant-Pearce, K (CON - Uffdown)
k.grant-pearce@bromsgrove.gov.uk
Harrison, P (CON - Alvechurch)
p.harrison@bromsgrove.gov.uk
Hollingworth, Roger (CON - Alvechurch)
r.hollingworth@bromsgrove.gov.uk
Jones, H (CON - Catshill)
h.jones@bromsgrove.gov.uk
Laight, R (CON - Slideslow)
r.laight@bromsgrove.gov.uk
Lammas, P (CON - Norton)
p.lammas@bromsgrove.gov.uk
Lewis, B (CON - Woodvale)
b.lewis@bromsgrove.gov.uk
Mallett, L (LAB - Whitford)
l.mallett@bromsgrove.gov.uk
McDonald, P (LAB - Waseley)
p.mcdonald@bromsgrove.gov.uk
McDonald, C (LAB - Beacon)
c.mcdonald@bromsgrove.gov.uk
Murray, E (LAB - Sidemoor)
e.murray@bromsgrove.gov.uk
Ruck, J (CON - Marlbrook)
j.ruck@bromsgrove.gov.uk
Scurrell, C (CON - Hagley)
c.scurrell@bromsgrove.gov.uk
Shannon, E (LAB - Charford)
e.shannon@bromsgrove.gov.uk
Shannon, S (LAB - Charford)
s.shannon@bromsgrove.gov.uk
Shannon, R (LAB - St. Johns)
r.shannon@bromsgrove.gov.uk
Sherrey, Margaret (CON - Furlongs)
m.sherry@bromsgrove.gov.uk
Spencer, C (CON - Slideslow)
c.spencer@bromsgrove.gov.uk
Taylor, C (CON - Linthurst)
k.taylor@bromsgrove.gov.uk
Tidmarsh, J (CON - Stoke Prior)
j.tidmarsh@bromsgrove.gov.uk

Turner, L (R - Hollywood & Majors Green)
l.turner@bromsgrove.gov.uk
Webb, Mike (CON - Norton)
m.webb@bromsgrove.gov.uk
Whittaker, Peter (CON - Tardebigge)
p.whittaker@bromsgrove.gov.uk
Wilson, C (LAB - Waseley)
c.wilson@bromsgrove.gov.uk

POLITICAL COMPOSITION

CON: 27, LAB: 10, R: 2

CABINET

Leader: Mr Roger Hollingworth
Deputy Leader: Mrs Margaret Sherrey
Business Transformation (Town Centre Regeneration & Special Projects): Dr Del Booth
Community Services, Older People, the Young & the Vulnerable: Mrs Margaret Sherrey
Finance, Partnerships & Economic Development: Mr Roger Hollingworth
Leisure, Cultural Services, Environmental Services & Emergency Planning: Mr Mike Webb
Planning, Regeneration, Regulatory Services & Strategic Housing: Mr C Taylor
Policy, Performance, Communications, Customer Services, Legal, Equalities, Democratic Services & Human Resources: Mr M Bullivant

COMMITTEE CHAIRS

Audit: Mr L Mallett
Licensing: Mrs R Dent
Overview & Scrutiny: Mr S Colella
Planning: Mr R Deeming

BROXBOURNE D

Broxbourne Borough Council, Borough Offices, Bishops' College, Churchgate, Cheshunt EN8 9XQ ☎ 01992 785555 🖷 01992 785578 ✉ enquiry@broxbourne.gov.uk
💻 www.broxbourne.gov.uk

FACTS & FIGURES

Police Authority: Hertfordshire Police Authority
Health Authority: East of England Strategic Health Authority
Learning and Skills Council: Eastern
Parliamentary Constituencies: Broxbourne
EU Constituencies: Eastern
Election Frequency: Elections are by thirds
Twinning: Borough: Sutera (Sicily); Cheshunt: Stains (France)

PRINCIPAL OFFICERS

Chief Executive: Mr Mike Walker, Chief Executive, Borough Offices, Bishops' College, Churchgate, Cheshunt EN8 9XQ ☎ 01992 785533 🖷 01992 626917 ✉ ceo@broxbourne.gov.uk

Building Control: Mr Keith Loxley, Head of Building Control, Borough Offices, Bishop's College, Churchgate, Cheshunt EN8 9NF ☎ 01922 785555 🖷 01922 785578 ✉ buildingcontrol@broxbourne.gov.uk

PR / Communications: Ms Angela Fieldhouse, Head of Communications, Borough Offices, Bishops' College, Churchgate, Cheshunt EN8 9XQ ☎ 01992 785531 🖷 01992 626917 ✉ press@broxbourne.gov.uk

Community Planning: Ms Rosie Sanderson, Head of Community Planning & Corporate Projects, Borough Offices, Bishops' College, Churchgate, Cheshunt EN8 9XQ ☎ 01992 785555 🖷 01992 626917 ✉ rs.projects@broxbourne.gov.uk

Community Safety: Mr Tony Cox, Community Safety/Town Centres Team Manager, Borough Offices, Bishops' College, Churchgate, Cheshunt EN8 9XQ ☎ 01992 785555 🖷 01992 785578 ✉ tc.memberservices@broxbourne.gov.uk

Computer Management: Mrs J Brook, Head of Computer Services, Borough Offices, Bishops' College, Churchgate, Cheshunt EN8 9XQ ☎ 01992 785555 🖷 01992 785578 ✉ ict.enquiries@broxbourne.gov.uk

Contracts: Mr Mike Walker, Chief Executive, Borough Offices, Bishops' College, Churchgate, Cheshunt EN8 9XQ ☎ 01992 785533 🖷 01992 626917 ✉ ceo@broxbourne.gov.uk

Direct Labour: Mr Peter Linkson, Head of Broxbourne Services, Borough Offices, Bishops' College, Churchgate, Cheshunt EN8 9XQ ☎ 01992 642240 🖷 01992 642216 ✉ broxserv@broxbourne.gov.uk

Economic Development: Mr Mike Walker, Chief Executive, Borough Offices, Bishops' College, Churchgate, Cheshunt EN8 9XQ ☎ 01992 785533 🖷 01992 626917 ✉ ceo@broxbourne.gov.uk

E-Government: Mrs J Brook, Head of Computer Services, Borough Offices, Bishops' College, Churchgate, Cheshunt EN8 9XQ ☎ 01992 785555 🖷 01992 785578 ✉ ict.enquiries@broxbourne.gov.uk

Electoral Registration: Mr Stephen Billington, Head of Support Services, Borough Offices, Bishops' College, Churchgate, Cheshunt EN8 9XQ ☎ 01992 785534 🖷 01992 785578 ✉ licensing@broxbourne.gov.uk

Emergency Planning: Mr Mike Walker, Chief Executive, Borough Offices, Bishops' College, Churchgate, Cheshunt EN8 9XQ ☎ 01992 785533 🖷 01992 626917 ✉ ceo@broxbourne.gov.uk

Environmental / Technical Services: Mr Jeffrey Stack, Director of Environmental Services, Borough Offices, Bishops' College, Churchgate, Cheshunt EN8 9XQ ☎ 01992 785555 🖷 01992 785578 ✉ des@broxbourne.gov.uk

Environmental Health: Mr Joe Ward, Head of Environmental Health Services, Borough Offices, Bishops' College, Churchgate, Cheshunt EN8 9XQ ☎ 01992 785555 🖷 01992 785578 ✉ envhealth@broxbourne.gov.uk

Estates, Property & Valuation: Mr Roland Childerhouse, Assistant Director (Property), Borough Offices, Bishops' College, Churchgate, Cheshunt EN8 9XQ ☎ 01992 785555 🖷 01992 785578

Facilities: Mr Patrick Cody, Facilities Manager, Borough Offices, Bishops' College, Churchgate, Cheshunt EN8 9XQ ☎ 01992 785555 🖷 01992 785578 ✉ pdc.facilities@broxbourne.gov.uk

Finance and Treasurer: Mrs S Beck, Head of Financial Services, Borough Offices, Bishops' College, Churchgate, Cheshunt EN8 9XQ ☎ 01992 785555

Finance and Treasurer: Ms Gillian Clelland, Director of Resources, Borough Offices, Bishops' College, Churchgate, Cheshunt EN8 9XQ ☎ 01992 785555 🖷 01992 626917 ✉ finance@broxbourne.gov.uk

Finance and Treasurer: Mrs L M Robinson, Head of Revenues & Exchequer, Borough Offices, Bishops' College, Churchgate, Cheshunt EN8 9XQ ☎ 01992 785555

Health and Safety: Mr Geoff Schooling, Health & Safety Manager, Civic Offices, Elstree Way, Borehamwood WD6 1WA ☎ 020 8207 2277; 020 8207 2277 ✉ geoff.schooling@hertsmere.gov.uk

Housing: Mr Stephen Tingley, Assistant Director (Housing & Community Care), Borough Offices, Bishops' College, Churchgate, Cheshunt EN8 9XQ ☎ 01992 785555 🖷 01992 785578 ✉ housingservices@broxbourne.gov.uk

Legal: Mr Gavin Miles, Head of Legal Services, Borough Offices, Bishops' College, Churchgate, Cheshunt EN8 9NF ☎ 01992 785555 🖷 01992 785578 ✉ legal@broxbourne.gov.uk

Licensing: Mr Stephen Billington, Head of Support Services, Borough Offices, Bishops' College, Churchgate, Cheshunt EN8 9XQ ☎ 01992 785534 🖷 01992 785578 ✉ licensing@broxbourne.gov.uk

Member Services: Mr Stephen Billington, Head of Support Services, Borough Offices, Bishops' College, Churchgate, Cheshunt EN8 9XQ ☎ 01992 785534 🖷 01992 785578 ✉ licensing@broxbourne.gov.uk

Personnel / HR: Mr Richard Pennell, Head of Personnel Services, Borough Offices, Bishops' College, Churchgate, Cheshunt EN8 9XG ☎ 01992 785536 🖷 01992 785578 ✉ personnel@broxbourne.gov.uk

Planning: Mr Peter Quaile, Principal Planning Officer, Borough Offices, Bishops' College, Churchgate, Cheshunt EN8 9XQ ☎ 01992 785560 🖷 01992 785578 ✉ planning@broxbourne.gov.uk

Procurement: Ms Rosie Sanderson, Head of Community Planning & Corporate Projects, Borough Offices, Bishops' College, Churchgate, Cheshunt EN8 9XQ ☎ 01992 785555 🖷 01992 626917 ✉ rs.projects@broxbourne.gov.uk

Recycling & Waste Minimisation: Mr Alf Cuffaro, Head of Environmental Contracts, Borough Offices, Bishops' College, Churchgate, Cheshunt EN8 9XQ ☎ 01992 785555 🖷 01992 785578 ✉ recycling@broxbourne.gov.uk

Staff Training: Mr Richard Pennell, Head of Personnel Services, Borough Offices, Bishops' College, Churchgate, Cheshunt EN8 9XG ☎ 01992 785536 🖷 01992 785578 ✉ personnel@broxbourne.gov.uk

Town Centre: Mr Tony Cox, Community Safety/Town Centres Team Manager, Borough Offices, Bishops' College, Churchgate, Cheshunt EN8 9XQ ☎ 01992 785555 🖷 01992 785578 ✉ tc.memberservices@broxbourne.gov.uk

Waste Collection and Disposal: Mr Alf Cuffaro, Head of Environmental Contracts, Borough Offices, Bishops' College, Churchgate, Cheshunt EN8 9XQ ☎ 01992 785555 🖷 01992 785578 ✉ recycling@broxbourne.gov.uk

MEMBERS OF THE COUNCIL (30)

***Mayor:* Rowland**, Eddy (CON - Broxbourne & Hoddesdon South)
cllr.e.rowland@broxbourne.gov.uk

***Deputy Mayor:* Perryman**, Bren (CON - Hoddesdon Town & Rye Park)
cllr.b.perryman@broxbourne.gov.uk

***Leader of the Council:* Mason**, Paul (CON - Broxbourne & Hoddesdon South)
cllr.p.mason@broxbourne.gov.uk

***Deputy Leader of the Council:* Hannam**, Ray (CON - Cheshunt North)
cllr.r.hannam@broxbourne.gov.uk

Aitken, Malcolm (LAB - Waltham Cross)
malcolm.a@broxbournelabour.org

Ayling, Ken (CON - Hoddesdon Town & Rye Park)
ken.ayling@ntlworld.com

Ball-Greenwood, Suzanne (CON - Flamstead End)

Bettiss, Yvonne (CON - Rosedale & Bury Green)
yvonnebettiss@btinternet.com

Bick, Bob (CON - Wormley & Turnford)
bobbick@btinternet.com

Brown, Keith (CON - Hoddesdon North)
keithbrown3@hotmail.com

Crump-Eynon, Carol (CON - Cheshunt South & Theobalds)
carolann.crump@sky.com

Evans, Justin (CON - Hoddesdon North)
justin.h.evans@gmail.com

Greensmyth, Martin (CON - Rosedale & Bury Green)
m.greensmyth@ntlworld.com

Hart, Nick (CON - Cheshunt North)
cllr.n.hart@broxbourne.gov.uk

Hart, Dolores (CON - Flamstead End)
dolores.hart@tesco.net

Harvey, Neil (LAB - Waltham Cross)
neil.h@broxbournelabour.org.uk

Hutchings, Tim (CON - Broxbourne & Hoddesdon South)
trhutchings59@gmail.com

Infantino, Antonio (CON - Hoddesdon Town & Rye Park)
tony@ainfantino.fsnet.co.uk

Iszatt, Mike (CON - Cheshunt North)
iszatt@live.com

Jackson, Hazel (CON - Rosedale & Bury Green)
hazeljackson@talktalk.net

McCormick, Cody (CON - Cheshunt South & Theobalds)
cllr.c.mccormick@broxbourne.gov.uk

Metcalf, James (CON - Wormley & Turnford)
jmetcalf@btinternet.com

Mills-Bishop, Mark (CON - Goffs Oak)
cllr.m.mills-bishop@broxbourne.gov.uk

Moule, Peter (CON - Goffs Oak)
peter@billmoule.co.uk
Nicholson, Gordon (CON - Wormley & Turnford)
cllr.g.nicholson@broxbourne.gov.uk
Pearce, Jeremy (CON - Goffs Oak)
cllr.j.pearce@broxbourne.gov.uk
Seeby, Paul (CON - Flamstead End)
cllr.p.seeby@broxbourne.gov.uk
Siracusa, Tony (CON - Cheshunt South & Theobalds)
cllr.t.siracusa@broxbourne.gov.uk
Watson, Michael (LAB - Waltham Cross)
michaelwatson4@hotmail.com
White, Lyn (CON - Hoddesdon North)
lyn.white@ntlworld.com

POLITICAL COMPOSITION

CON: 27, LAB: 3

CABINET

Leader: Mr Paul Mason
Deputy Leader: Mr Ray Hannam
Finance & Corporate Services: Mr Mark Mills-Bishop
Housing & Community Development: Mr Paul Seeby
Leisure & Recreation: Mrs Hazel Jackson
Planning & Regeneration: Mr James Metcalf
Public & Environmental Protection: Mr Ray Hannam

COMMITTEE CHAIRS

Planning & Regulatory: Mr Ken Ayling
Scrutiny: Mr Michael Watson

BROXTOWE D

Broxtowe Borough Council, Council Offices, Foster Avenue, Beeston NG9 1AB ☎ 0115 917 7777 🖷 0115 917 3030
💻 www.broxtowe.gov.uk

FACTS & FIGURES

Police Authority: Nottinghamshire Police Authority
Health Authority: East Midlands Strategic Health Authority
Learning and Skills Council: East Midlands
Parliamentary Constituencies: Ashfield, Broxtowe
EU Constituencies: East Midlands
Election Frequency: Elections are of whole council
Twinning: Gütersloh (Germany), Friendship Agreement with Myszkow, Poland.

PRINCIPAL OFFICERS

Chief Executive: Ms Ruth Hyde, Chief Executive, Town Hall, Foster Avenue, Beeston NG9 1AB ☎ 0115 917 3255
✉ ceo@broxtowe.gov.uk

Deputy Chief Executive: Mr Malcolm Staley, Deputy Chief Executive, Council Offices, Foster Avenue, Beeston NG9 1AB
☎ 0115 917 3232 🖷 0115 917 3131
✉ malcolm.staley@broxtowe.gov.uk

Senior Management: Mr Ted Czerniak, Director of Housing, Leisure & Culture, Council Offices, Foster Avenue, Beeston NG9 1AB ☎ 0115 917 3419 🖷 0115 917 3508
✉ ted.czerniak@broxtowe.gov.uk

Senior Management: Mr Malcolm Staley, Deputy Chief Executive, Council Offices, Foster Avenue, Beeston NG9 1AB
☎ 0115 917 3232 🖷 0115 917 3131
✉ malcolm.staley@broxtowe.gov.uk

Best Value: Mr Colin Lewis, Principal Performance Improvement & Equalities Manager, Council Offices, Foster Avenue, Beeston NG9 1AB ☎ 0115 917 3352 🖷 0115 917 3377
✉ colin.lewis@broxtowe.gov.uk

Building Control: Mr Andy Limb, Chief Building Control Officer, Council Offices, Foster Avenue, Beeston NG9 1AB
☎ 0115 917 3470 🖷 0115 917 3377 ✉ andy.limb@broxtowe.gov.uk

PR / Communications: Mrs Jackie Harwood, Corporate Communications Manager, Town Hall, Foster Avenue, Beeston NG9 1AB ☎ 0115 917 3743 ✉ jackie.harwood@broxtowe.gov.uk

Community Planning: Mrs Marice Hawley, Principal Community Development Officer, Council Offices, Foster Avenue, Beeston NG9 1AB ☎ 0115 917 3492 🖷 0115 917 3377
✉ marice.hawley@broxtowe.gov.uk

Community Safety: Mrs Marice Hawley, Principal Community Development Officer, Council Offices, Foster Avenue, Beeston NG9 1AB ☎ 0115 917 3492 🖷 0115 917 3377
✉ marice.hawley@broxtowe.gov.uk

Computer Management: Mr Kevin Powell, Head of ICT & Corporate Services, Town Hall, Foster Avenue, Beeston NG9 1AB
☎ 0115 917 3214 🖷 0115 917 3030
✉ kevin.powell@broxtowe.gov.uk

Contracts: Mr Mike Taylor, Director of Environment, Council Offices, Foster Avenue, Beeston NG9 1AB ☎ 0115 917 3627
🖷 0115 917 3600 ✉ mike.taylor@broxtowe.gov.uk

Customer Service: Mr Robert Williams, Customer Services Manager, Council Offices, Foster Avenue, Beeston NG9 1AB
☎ 0115 917 3940 ✉ robert.williams@broxtowe.gov.uk

Direct Labour: Mr John Delaney, Head of Built Environment, Council Offices, Foster Avenue, Beeston NG9 1AB ☎ 0115 917 3655 🖷 0115 917 3160 ✉ john.delaney@broxtowe.gov.uk

Economic Development: Mrs Marice Hawley, Principal Community Development Officer, Council Offices, Foster Avenue, Beeston NG9 1AB ☎ 0115 917 3492 🖷 0115 917 3377
✉ marice.hawley@broxtowe.gov.uk

E-Government: Mr Kevin Powell, Head of ICT & Corporate Services, Town Hall, Foster Avenue, Beeston NG9 1AB
☎ 0115 917 3214 🖷 0115 917 3030
✉ kevin.powell@broxtowe.gov.uk

Electoral Registration: Ms Ruth Hyde, Chief Executive, Town Hall, Foster Avenue, Beeston NG9 1AB ☎ 0115 917 3255
✉ ceo@broxtowe.gov.uk

Emergency Planning: Mr Steve Newton, Health & Safety Officer, Town Hall, Foster Avenue, Beeston NG9 1AB
☎ 0115 917 3330 🖷 0115 917 3030 ✉ steve.newton@broxtowe.gov.uk

LOCAL AUTHORITIES

Environmental / Technical Services: Mr Mike Taylor, Director of Environment, Council Offices, Foster Avenue, Beeston NG9 1AB ☎ 0115 917 3627 🖷 0115 917 3600 ✉ mike.taylor@broxtowe.gov.uk

Environmental Health: Mr Rob Westwood, Head of Regulatory Services, Council Offices, Foster Avenue, Beeston NG9 1AB ☎ 0115 917 3236 🖷 0115 917 3508 ✉ rob.westwood@broxtowe.gov.uk

Estates, Property & Valuation: Mr Steve Dance, Head of Planning & Building Control, Council Offices, Foster Avenue, Beeston NG9 1AB ☎ 0115 917 3495 🖷 0115 917 3377

Finance and Treasurer: Mr Malcolm Staley, Deputy Chief Executive, Council Offices, Foster Avenue, Beeston NG9 1AB ☎ 0115 917 3232 🖷 0115 917 3131 ✉ malcolm.staley@broxtowe.gov.uk

Grounds Maintenance: Mr Tim Crawford, Parks & Environment Manager, Council Offices, Foster Avenue, Beeston NG9 1AB ☎ 0115 917 3643 🖷 0115 917 3600 ✉ tim.crawford@broxtowe.gov.uk

Health and Safety: Mr Steve Newton, Health & Safety Officer, Town Hall, Foster Avenue, Beeston NG9 1AB ☎ 0115 917 3330 🖷 0115 917 3030 ✉ steve.newton@broxtowe.gov.uk

Highways: Mr John Delaney, Head of Built Environment, Council Offices, Foster Avenue, Beeston NG9 1AB ☎ 0115 917 3655 🖷 0115 917 3160 ✉ john.delaney@broxtowe.gov.uk

Housing: Mr Ted Czerniak, Director of Housing, Leisure & Culture, Council Offices, Foster Avenue, Beeston NG9 1AB ☎ 0115 917 3419 🖷 0115 917 3508 ✉ ted.czerniak@broxtowe.gov.uk

Housing Maintenance: Mr Gary Duckmanton, Building Maintenance Manager, Kimberley Depot, Eastwood Road, Kimberley, Nottingham NG16 2HX ☎ 0115 917 7777 🖷 0115 917 3106

Legal: Mr Simon Smith, Head of Legal Services & Monitoring, Council Offices, Foster Avenue, Beeston NG9 1AB ☎ 0115 917 3230 🖷 0115 917 3131 ✉ simon.smith@broxtowe.gov.uk

Leisure and Cultural Services: Mr Ashley Marriott, Head of Leisure & Culture, Council Offices, Foster Avenue, Beeston NG9 1AB ☎ 0115 917 3626 🖷 0115 917 3394 ✉ ashley.marriott@broxtowe.gov.uk

Licensing: Mr Simon Smith, Head of Legal Services & Monitoring, Council Offices, Foster Avenue, Beeston NG9 1AB ☎ 0115 917 3230 🖷 0115 917 3131 ✉ simon.smith@broxtowe.gov.uk

Lighting: Mr John Delaney, Head of Built Environment, Council Offices, Foster Avenue, Beeston NG9 1AB ☎ 0115 917 3655 🖷 0115 917 3160 ✉ john.delaney@broxtowe.gov.uk

Lottery Funding, Charity and Voluntary: Mr Ashley Marriott, Head of Leisure & Culture, Council Offices, Foster Avenue, Beeston NG9 1AB ☎ 0115 917 3626 🖷 0115 917 3394 ✉ ashley.marriott@broxtowe.gov.uk

Member Services: Mrs Sue Rodden, Head of Administrative Services, Council Offices, Foster Avenue, Beeston NG9 1AB ☎ 0115 917 3295 🖷 0115 917 3131 ✉ sue.rodden@broxtowe.gov.uk

Parking: Mr Mike Taylor, Director of Environment, Council Offices, Foster Avenue, Beeston NG9 1AB ☎ 0115 917 3627 🖷 0115 917 3600 ✉ mike.taylor@broxtowe.gov.uk

Partnerships: Ms Ruth Hyde, Chief Executive, Town Hall, Foster Avenue, Beeston NG9 1AB ☎ 0115 917 3255 ✉ ceo@broxtowe.gov.uk

Personnel / HR: Mrs Jane Lunn, Head of Human Resources, Town Hall, Foster Avenue, Beeston NG9 1AB ☎ 0115 917 3346 🖷 0115 917 3030 ✉ jane.lunn@broxtowe.gov.uk

Planning: Mr Steve Dance, Head of Planning & Building Control, Council Offices, Foster Avenue, Beeston NG9 1AB ☎ 0115 917 3495 🖷 0115 917 3377

Procurement: Mr Steve Cotterill, Procurement Officer, Council Offices, Foster Avenue, Beeston NG9 1AB ☎ 0115 917 3296 🖷 0115 917 3131 ✉ steve.cotterill@broxtowe.gov.uk

Recycling & Waste Minimisation: Mr Paul Wolverson, Waste & Recycling Officer, Kimberley Depot, Eastwood Road, Kimberley, Nottingham NG16 2HX ☎ 0115 917 3106 🖷 0115 917 3600 ✉ paul.wolverson@broxtowe.gov.uk

Regeneration: Mrs Marice Hawley, Principal Community Development Officer, Council Offices, Foster Avenue, Beeston NG9 1AB ☎ 0115 917 3492 🖷 0115 917 3377 ✉ marice.hawley@broxtowe.gov.uk

Staff Training: Mrs Julie Fish, Training Officer, Town Hall, Foster Avenue, Beeston NG9 1AB ☎ 0115 917 3365 🖷 0115 917 3030 ✉ julie.fish@broxtowe.gov.uk

Sustainable Communities: Mrs Marice Hawley, Principal Community Development Officer, Council Offices, Foster Avenue, Beeston NG9 1AB ☎ 0115 917 3492 🖷 0115 917 3377 ✉ marice.hawley@broxtowe.gov.uk

Sustainable Development: Mrs Marice Hawley, Principal Community Development Officer, Council Offices, Foster Avenue, Beeston NG9 1AB ☎ 0115 917 3492 🖷 0115 917 3377 ✉ marice.hawley@broxtowe.gov.uk

Tourism: Mrs Karen Webb, Cultural Services Manager, Durban House, Mansfield Road, Eastwood NG16 3DZ ☎ 01773 717353 🖷 01773 713509 ✉ karen.webb@broxtowe.gov.uk

Traffic Management: Mr Mike Taylor, Director of Environment, Council Offices, Foster Avenue, Beeston NG9 1AB ☎ 0115 917 3627 🖷 0115 917 3600 ✉ mike.taylor@broxtowe.gov.uk

Transport: Mr Alan Pye, Transport Manager, Kimberley Depot,

Eastwood Road, Kimberley, Nottingham NG16 2HX
☎ 0115 917 3049 🖷 0115 917 3106 ✉ alan.pye@broxtowe.gov.uk

Waste Collection and Disposal: Mr Paul Syson, Refuse and Cleansing Manager, Kimberley Depot, Eastwood Road, Kimberley, Nottingham NG16 2HX ☎ 0115 917 3062 🖷 0115 927 3106
✉ paul.syson@broxtowe.gov.uk

Waste Management: Mr Paul Wolverson, Waste & Recycling Officer, Kimberley Depot, Eastwood Road, Kimberley, Nottingham NG16 2HX ☎ 0115 917 3106 🖷 0115 917 3600
✉ paul.wolverson@broxtowe.gov.uk

MEMBERS OF THE COUNCIL (44)

Atherton, Eileen (CON - Chilwell West)
eileen.atherton@broxtowe.gov.uk
Bagshaw, Susan (LAB - Eastwood South)
susan.bagshaw@broxtowe.gov.uk
Bagshaw, David (LAB - Eastwood North & Greasley)
david.bagshaw@broxtowe.gov.uk
Ball, Lydia (CON - Awsworth)
lydia.ball@broxtowe.gov.uk
Barber, Steve (LAB - Beeston Rylands)
steve.barber@broxtowe.gov.uk
Booth, John (CON - Brinsley)
Briggs, Joan (CON - Chilwell East)
joan.briggs@broxtowe.gov.uk
Brindley, Tim (CON - Chilwell West)
tim.brindley@broxtowe.gov.uk
Brown, Mick (CON - Greasley (Giltbrook & Newthorpe))
mick.brown@broxtowe.gov.uk
Burnett, Derek (CON - Nuthall West & Greasley (Watnall))
derek.burnett@broxtowe.gov.uk
Carr, Stephen (LD - Beeston North)
steve.carr@broxtowe.gov.uk
Charlesworth, Bob (LD - Eastwood North & Greasley)
bob.charlesworth@broxtowe.gov.uk
Cooper, Andy (LAB - Cossall & Kimberley)
andy.cooper@broxtowe.gov.uk
Darby, Ray (LAB - Stapleford South West)
ray.darby@broxtowe.gov.uk
Ford, Anthony (CON - Toton & Chilwell Meadows)
tony.ford@broxtowe.gov.uk
Green, Nita (CON - Nuthall East & Strelley)
nita.green@broxtowe.gov.uk
Grindell, David (LD - Stapleford South East)
david.grindell@broxtowe.gov.uk
Handley, Margaret (CON - Greasley (Giltbrook & Newthorpe))
margaret.handley@broxtowe.gov.uk
Harvey, Graham (CON - Chilwell West)
graham.harvey@broxtowe.gov.uk
Hegyi, Marilyn (CON - Toton & Chilwell Meadows)
marilyn.hegyi@broxtowe.gov.uk
Heptinstall, Stanley (LD - Bramcote)
stan.heptinstall@broxtowe.gov.uk
Jackson, Richard (CON - Chilwell East)
richard.jackson@broxtowe.gov.uk
Kerry, Eric (CON - Attenborough)
eric.kerry@broxtowe.gov.uk
Khaled, Halimah (CON - Toton & Chilwell Meadows)
halimah.khaled@broxtowe.gov.uk
Lally, Lynda (LAB - Beeston Central)
lynda.lally@broxtowe.gov.uk
Lally, Patrick (LAB - Beeston Central)
pat.lally@broxtowe.gov.uk
Marshall, Greg (LAB - Beeston West)
greg.marshall@broxtowe.gov.uk
McGrath, John (LAB - Stapleford South West)
john.mcgrath@broxtowe.gov.uk
McGuckin, Mary (LAB - Cossall & Kimberley)
mary.mcguckin@broxtowe.gov.uk
Oates, Andrea (LAB - Beeston North)
andrea.oates@broxtowe.gov.uk
Owen, Jill (CON - Nuthall West & Greasley (Watnall))
jill.owen@broxtowe.gov.uk
Patrick, Janet (LAB - Beeston West)
janet.patrick@broxtowe.gov.uk
Prince, Frank (LAB - Beeston Rylands)
frank.prince@broxtowe.gov.uk
Radulovic, Milan (LAB - Eastwood South)
milan.radulovic@broxtowe.gov.uk
Rigby, Kenneth (LD - Trowell)
ken.rigby@broxtowe.gov.uk
Robb, Charles (LAB - Eastwood South)
charles.robb@broxtowe.gov.uk
Robinson, Richard (LAB - Cossall & Kimberley)
richard.robinson@broxtowe.gov.uk
Rowland, Stuart (CON - Greasley (Giltbrook & Newthorpe))
stuart.rowland@broxtowe.gov.uk
Simpson, Paul (CON - Nuthall East & Strelley)
paul.simpson@broxtowe.gov.uk
Tyler, Ian (LD - Bramcote)
ian.tyler@broxtowe.gov.uk
Watts, David (LD - Bramcote)
david.watts@broxtowe.gov.uk
White, Iris (LAB - Stapleford North)
iris.white@broxtowe.gov.uk
Williams, Jacky (LD - Stapleford South East)
jacky.williams@broxtowe.gov.uk
Wombwell, Brian (LD - Stapleford North)
brian.wombwell@broxtowe.gov.uk

POLITICAL COMPOSITION

CON: 18, LAB: 17, LD: 9

CABINET

Leader: Mr Milan Radulovic
Deputy Leader: Mr Patrick Lally
Arts, Culture & Leisure: Mr Richard Robinson
Economy & Regeneration: Mr David Watts
Environment: Mr Stanley Heptinstall
Housing: Mr Milan Radulovic
Resources: Mr Patrick Lally

COMMITTEE CHAIRS

Development Control: Mr Steve Barber
General Purposes & Audit: Mr Stephen Carr
Licensing & Appeals: Mrs Lynda Lally
Overview & Scrutiny: Mr Brian Wombwell
Standards: P Hamilton (External)

BUCKINGHAMSHIRE C

Buckinghamshire County Council, County Hall, Walton Street, Aylesbury HP20 1YU ☎ 01296 395000 🖳 www.buckscc.gov.uk

FACTS & FIGURES

Police Authority: Thames Valley Police Authority

LOCAL AUTHORITIES

Health Authority: South Central Strategic Health Authority
Learning and Skills Council: South East
EU Constituencies: South East
Election Frequency: Elections are of whole council
Twinning: Trier R. B. (Germany)

PRINCIPAL OFFICERS

Chief Executive: Mr Chris Williams, Chief Executive Officer, County Hall, Walton Street, Aylesbury HP20 1UY ☎ 01296 382201 🖷 01296 383441 ✉ cmwilliams@buckscc.gov.uk

Senior Management: Mr Trevor Boyd, Interim Strategic Director - Adults & Family Wellbeing, County Hall, Walton Street, Aylesbury HP20 1YU ☎ 01296 382074 ✉ tboyd@buckscc.gov.uk

Senior Management: Mr Neil Gibson, Strategic Director - Communities & Built Environment, County Hall, Walton Street, Aylesbury HP20 1YU ☎ 01296 383106 🖷 01296 382718 ✉ negibson@buckscc.gov.uk

Access Officer / Social Services (Disability): Ms Sarah Holding, School Relationship Manager, County Hall, Walton Street, Aylesbury HP20 1YU ☎ 01296 383038 ✉ sholding@buckscc.gov.uk

Best Value: Ms Sarah Ashmead, Corporate Manager (Policy & Performance), County Hall, Walton Street, Aylesbury HP20 1YU ☎ 01296 383986 ✉ sashmead@buckscc.gov.uk

Best Value: Ms Gillian Hibberd, Strategic Director - Resources & Business Transformation, County Hall, Walton Street, Aylesbury HP20 1YU ☎ 01296 383127 ✉ ghibberd@buckscc.gov.uk

Children / Youth Services: Mr Chris Munday, Division Director - Commissioning & Business Improvement, County Hall, Walton Street, Aylesbury HP20 1YU ☎ 01296 387849 ✉ ccmunday@buckscc.gov.uk

Children / Youth Services: Ms Laura Nankin, Head of Fair Access & Youth Provision, County Hall, Walton Street, Aylesbury HP20 1YU ☎ 01296 382078 ✉ lnankin@buckscc.gov.uk

Civil Registration: Mr Terry Carter, Trading Standards Manager, County Hall, Walton Street, Aylesbury HP20 1YU ☎ 01296 383934 ✉ tcarter@buckscc.gov.uk

PR / Communications: Ms Amanda Brooke-Webb, Service Director - Customer Services & Communication, County Hall, Walton Street, Aylesbury HP20 1YU ☎ 01296 387416 ✉ abwebb@buckscc.gov.uk

Computer Management: Ms Caroline Cooper, Chief Information Officer, IT Unit, County Hall, Walton Street, Aylesbury HP20 1YQ ☎ 01296 387084 🖷 01296 382655 ✉ cacooper@buckscc.gov.uk

Consumer Protection and Trading Standards: Mr Phil Dart, Service Director - Localities & Safer Communities, 5-7 Walton Street, Aylesbury HP20 1UY ☎ 01296 382398 🖷 01296 382017 ✉ pdart@buckscc.gov.uk

Contracts: Ms Tricia Hook, Senior Procurement Manager, County Hall, Walton Street, Aylesbury HP20 1YU ☎ 01296 383615 ✉ phook@buckscc.gov.uk

Education: Ms Sarah Holding, School Relationship Manager, County Hall, Walton Street, Aylesbury HP20 1YU ☎ 01296 383038 ✉ sholding@buckscc.gov.uk

Education: Mrs Sue Imbriano, Strategic Director - Children & Young People's Services, County Hall, Walton Street, Aylesbury HP20 1UZ ☎ 01296 383104 🖷 01296 383994 ✉ simbriano@buckscc.gov.uk

Electoral Registration: Mr Clive Parker, Democratic Services Manager & Deputy Monitoring Officer, Legal and Democratic Services, County Hall, Walton Street, Aylesbury HP20 1UA ☎ 01296 383685 🖷 01296 382538 ✉ cparker@buckscc.gov.uk

Emergency Planning: Mr Andrew Fyfe, Resilience Manager, County Hall, Walton Street, Aylesbury HP20 1YU ☎ 01296 382937 🖷 01296 383052 ✉ afyfe@buckscc.gov.uk

Environmental / Technical Services: Mr Neil Gibson, Strategic Director - Communities & Built Environment, County Hall, Walton Street, Aylesbury HP20 1YU ☎ 01296 383106 🖷 01296 382718 ✉ negibson@buckscc.gov.uk

Finance and Treasurer: Mr Richard Ambrose, Service Director - Finance & Commercial Services, County Hall, Walton Street, Aylesbury HP20 1YU ☎ 01296 383120 ✉ rambrose@buckscc.gov.uk

Health and Safety: Ms Karen Newman, Health & Safety Manager, County Hall, Walton Street, Aylesbury HP20 1UA ☎ 01296 382166 🖷 01296 382200 ✉ knewman@buckscc.gov.uk

Highways: Mr Neil Gibson, Strategic Director - Communities & Build Environment, County Hall, Walton Street, Aylesbury HP20 1YU ☎ 01296 383106 🖷 01296 382718 ✉ negibson@buckscc.gov.uk

Local Area Agreement: Ms Sarah Ashmead, Service Director - Corporate Manager (Policy & Performance), County Hall, Walton Street, Aylesbury HP20 1YU ☎ 01296 383986 ✉ sashmead@buckscc.gov.uk

Legal: Mrs Anne Davies, Service Director - Legal & Democratic Services, County Hall, Walton Street, Aylesbury HP20 1UA ☎ 01296 383650 🖷 01296 382421 ✉ adavies@buckscc.gov.uk

Leisure and Cultural Services: Ms Paula Buck, Service Director - Head of Culture & Learning, County Hall, Walton Street, Aylesbury HP20 1UZ ☎ 01296 382986 🖷 01296 382474 ✉ pbuck@buckscc.gov.uk

Lifelong Learning: Ms Paula Buck, Service Director - Head of Culture & Learning, County Hall, Walton Street, Aylesbury HP20 1UZ ☎ 01296 382986 🖷 01296 382474 ✉ pbuck@buckscc.gov.uk

Member Services: Mr Clive Parker, Democratic Services Manager & Deputy Monitoring Officer, Legal and Democratic Services, County Hall, Walton Street, Aylesbury HP20 1UA ☎ 01296 383685 🖷 01296 382538 ✉ cparker@buckscc.gov.uk

Personnel / HR: Ms Gillian Hibberd, Strategic Director - Resources & Business Transformation, County Hall, Walton Street, Aylesbury HP20 1YU ☎ 01296 383127 ghibberd@buckscc.gov.uk

Planning: Mr David Sutherland, Sustainability Service Business Manager, County Hall, Walton Street, Aylesbury HP20 1UY ☎ 01296 383003 🖷 01296 383003 dsutherland@buckscc.gov.uk

Public Libraries: Ms Amanda Brooke-Webb, Service Director - Customer Services & Communication, County Hall, Walton Street, Aylesbury HP20 1YU ☎ 01296 387416 abwebb@buckscc.gov.uk

Recycling & Waste Minimisation: Mr David Sutherland, Sustainability Service Business Manager, County Hall, Walton Street, Aylesbury HP20 1UY ☎ 01296 383003 🖷 01296 383003 dsutherland@buckscc.gov.uk

Social Services (Adult): Mr Trevor Boyd, Interim Strategic Director - Adults & Family Wellbeing, County Hall, Walton Street, Aylesbury HP20 1YU ☎ 01296 382074 tboyd@buckscc.gov.uk

Staff Training: Ms Gillian Hibberd, Strategic Director - Resources & Business Transformation, County Hall, Walton Street, Aylesbury HP20 1YU ☎ 01296 383127 ghibberd@buckscc.gov.uk

Sustainable Communities: Ms Sarah Ashmead, Service Director - Corporate Manager (Policy & Performance), County Hall, Walton Street, Aylesbury HP20 1YU ☎ 01296 383986 sashmead@buckscc.gov.uk

Sustainable Communities: Mr Neil Gibson, Strategic Director - Communities & Build Environment, County Hall, Walton Street, Aylesbury HP20 1YU ☎ 01296 383106 🖷 01296 382718 negibson@buckscc.gov.uk

Sustainable Development: Mrs Zoe Dixon, Environmental Co-ordinator, County Hall, Walton Street, Aylesbury HP20 1UZ ☎ 01296 382132 🖷 01296 382060 zdixon@buckscc.gov.uk

Traffic Management: Mr Neil Gibson, Strategic Director - Communities & Built Environment, County Hall, Walton Street, Aylesbury HP20 1YU ☎ 01296 383106 🖷 01296 382718 negibson@buckscc.gov.uk

Waste Management: Ms Gill Harding, Senior Manager, County Hall, Walton Street, Aylesbury HP20 1YU ☎ 01296 382853 🖷 01296 382732 gharding@buckscc.gov.uk

MEMBERS OF THE COUNCIL (57)

***Chair:* Clayton**, Marion (CON - Wendover & Halton)
mclayton@buckscc.gov.uk

***Deputy Chair:* Etholen**, Carl (CON - The Risboroughs)
cetholen@buckscc.gov.uk

Adams, Steven (CON - Amersham)
sadams@buckscc.gov.uk

Allen, Bruce (CON - Chalfont St Peter)
bgallen@buckscc.gov.uk

Anson, Doug (CON - Marlow)
danson@buckscc.gov.uk

Appleyard, Michael (CON - Thames)
mappleyard@buckscc.gov.uk

Aston, Margaret (CON - Haddenham)
maston@buckscc.gov.uk

Baldwin, Mary (LD - Aylesbury North)
mbaldwin@buckscc.gov.uk

Bhatti, Mohammad (CON - Chesham East)
mzbhatti@buckscc.gov.uk

Birchley, Patricia (CON - Chiltern Ridges)
pbirchley@buckscc.gov.uk

Brand, Michael (LD - Chesham North West)
mbrand@buckscc.gov.uk

Brown, Noel (CON - Chess Valley)
nbrown@buckscc.gov.uk

Busby, Adrian (CON - Beaconsfield)
ajbusby@buckscc.gov.uk

Butcher, Timothy (CON - The Chalfonts & Seer Green)
trbutcher@buckscc.gov.uk

Cadd, Hedley (CON - Buckingham South)
hcadd@buckscc.gov.uk

Carroll, David (CON - Hazlemere)
dcarroll@buckscc.gov.uk

Cartwright, Peter (CON - Ryemead, Tylers Green & Loudwater)
pcartwright@buckscc.gov.uk

Cartwright, John (CON - Grendon Underwood)
jcartwright@buckscc.gov.uk

Chapple, William (CON - Aston Clinton)
bchapple@buckscc.gov.uk

Clarke, Lesley (CON - Abbey)
lmclarke@buckscc.gov.uk

Colston, Michael (CON - Great Missenden)
mcolston@buckscc.gov.uk

Davies, Avril (LD - Ivinghoe)
acdavies@buckscc.gov.uk

Dhillon, Dev (CON - Taplow, Dorney & Lent Rise)
ddhillon@buckscc.gov.uk

Ditta, Chaudhary (LD - Bowerdean, Micklefield & Totteridge)
cditta@buckscc.gov.uk

Downes, Frank (CON - Stokenchurch, Radnage & West Wycombe)
fdownes@buckscc.gov.uk

Edmonds, Michael (CON - Bernwood)
medmonds@buckscc.gov.uk

Egleton, Trevor (CON - Stoke Poges & Farnham)
tegleton@buckscc.gov.uk

Glover, Netta (CON - Wing)
nglover@buckscc.gov.uk

Hardy, Peter (CON - Bulstrode)
phardy@buckscc.gov.uk

Hazell, Lin (CON - Burnham Beeches)
lhazell@buckscc.gov.uk

Hill, Alan (CON - Booker Cressex & Sands)
alhill@buckscc.gov.uk

Hussain, Niknam (LD - Aylesbury North)
nihussain@buckscc.gov.uk

Jennings, Brenda (CON - Great Brickhill)
bjennings@buckscc.gov.uk

Jones, Chester (LD - Aylesbury South East)
chjones@buckscc.gov.uk

Kennell, Steven (LD - Aylesbury West)
skennell@buckscc.gov.uk

Khan, Raj (LD - Aylesbury East)
rkhan@buckscc.gov.uk

Letheren, Valerie (CON - Terriers & Amersham Hill)

vletheren@buckscc.gov.uk
Lidgate, Bill (CON - Alderbourne)
blidgate@buckscc.gov.uk
Mallen, Wendy (CON - Downley, Disraeli, Oakridge & Castlefield)
wmallen@buckscc.gov.uk
Mohammed, Zahir (CON - Downley, Disraeli, Oakridge & Castlefield)
zamohammed@buckscc.gov.uk
Phillips, Martin (CON - Amersham)
mphillips@buckscc.gov.uk
Polhill, David (CON - Buckingham North)
dpolhill@buckscc.gov.uk
Puddefoot, Jenny (LD - Aylesbury East)
jpuddefoot@buckscc.gov.uk
Pushman, Richard (CON - Greater Hughenden)
rpushman@buckscc.gov.uk
Reed, Roger (CON - Gerrards Cross & Denham North)
roreed@buckscc.gov.uk
Roberts, Brian (CON - Aylesbury South)
broberts@buckscc.gov.uk
Roberts, Freda (LD - Aylesbury West)
froberts@buckscc.gov.uk
Rogerson, Paul (CON - Icknield & Bledlow)
progerson@buckscc.gov.uk
Rowlands, David (CON - Winslow)
drowlands@buckscc.gov.uk
Schofield, David (CON - Penn, Coleshill & Holmer Green)
dschofield@buckscc.gov.uk
Scott, Richard (CON - Marlow)
rjscott@buckscc.gov.uk
Shakespeare, David (CON - Ryemead, Tylers Green & Loudwater)
dshakespeare@buckscc.gov.uk
Tett, Martin (CON - The Chalfonts & Seer Green)
mtett@buckscc.gov.uk
Vigor-Hedderly, Ruth (CON - Iver)
rvhedderly@buckscc.gov.uk
Wassell, Julia (LD - Bowerdean, Micklefield & Totteridge)
jwassell@buckscc.gov.uk
Watson, David (CON - Thames)
dwatson@buckscc.gov.uk
Woollard, Robert (CON - Chiltern Valley)
rwollard@buckscc.gov.uk

POLITICAL COMPOSITION
CON: 46, LD: 11

CABINET
Leader: Mr Martin Tett
Deputy Leader: Mr Michael Appleyard
Children's Services: Mrs Valerie Letheren
Community Engagement: Mr Martin Phillips
Education & Skills: Mr Michael Appleyard
Environment: Mr Steven Adams
Finance & Resources: Mr Peter Cartwright
Health & Wellbeing: Mrs Patricia Birchley
Planning & Transportation: Mr Peter Hardy

COMMITTEE CHAIRS
Appeals & Complaints: Mrs Margaret Aston
Development Control: Mr David Polhill
Overview & Scrutiny: Mrs Lesley Clarke
Pension Fund: Mr Frank Downes
Regulatory & Audit: Mr Zahir Mohammed
Review of Care of Older People (in a Hospital Setting): Mr Richard Pushman

BURNLEY D
Burnley Borough Council, Town Hall, Manchester Road, Burnley BB11 9SA ☎ 01282 425011 🖷 01282 438772
enquiries@burnley.gov.uk www.burnley.gov.uk

FACTS & FIGURES
Police Authority: Lancashire Police Authority
Health Authority: North West Strategic Health Authority
Learning and Skills Council: North West
Parliamentary Constituencies: Burnley
EU Constituencies: North West
Election Frequency: Elections are by thirds
Twinning: Vitry sue Seine (France)

PRINCIPAL OFFICERS
Chief Executive: Mr Steve Rumbelow, Chief Executive, Town Hall, Manchester Road, Burnley BB11 9SA ☎ 01282 425011 srumbelow@burnley.gov.uk

Senior Management: Mr Nick Aves, Director of Resources, Town Hall, Manchester Road, Burnley BB11 9SA ☎ 01282 425011 🖷 01282 450594 naves@burnley.gov.uk

Senior Management: Mr Mick Cartledge, Director of Community Services, Town Hall, Manchester Road, Burnley BB11 9SA ☎ 01282 425011 mcartledge@burnley.gov.uk

Senior Management: Mr Mike Cook, Director of Housing & Regeneration, Town Hall, Manchester Road, Burnley BB11 9SA ☎ 01282 425011 mcook@burnley.gov.uk

Architect, Building / Property Services: Mr Nick Aves, Director of Resources, Town Hall, Manchester Road, Burnley BB11 9SA ☎ 01282 425011 🖷 01282 450594 naves@burnley.gov.uk

Best Value: Mr Chris Gay, Performance & Improvement Manager, Town Hall, Manchester Road, Burnley BB11 9SA ☎ 01282 425011 cgay@burnley.gov.uk

PR / Communications: Mr Mike Waite, Head of Corporate Engagement & Cohesion, Town Hall, Manchester Road, Burnley BB11 9SA ☎ 01282 425011 mwaite@burnley.gov.uk

Community Planning: Mr Mike Waite, Head of Corporate Engagement & Cohesion, Town Hall, Manchester Road, Burnley BB11 9SA ☎ 01282 425011 mwaite@burnley.gov.uk

Community Safety: Mr S McConnell, Community Safety Manager, 18/20 Nicholas Street, Burnley BB11 2AP ☎ 01282 425011 🖷 01282 477321 smcconnell@burnley.gov.uk

Computer Management: Mrs Sharon Hargraves, Customer Services Manager, Town Hall, Manchester Road, Burnley BB11 9SA ☎ 01282 425011 🖷 01282 664498 shargraves@burnley.gov.uk

Contracts: Mr Tom Forshaw, Head of Chief Executive's Office,

Town Hall, Manchester Road, Burnley BB11 9SA ☎ 01282 477260 ✉ tforshaw@burnley.gov.uk

Corporate Services: Mr Tom Forshaw, Head of Chief Executive's Office, Town Hall, Manchester Road, Burnley BB11 9SA ☎ 01282 477260 ✉ tforshaw@burnley.gov.uk

Customer Service: Mrs Sharon Hargraves, Customer Services Manager, Town Hall, Manchester Road, Burnley BB11 9SA ☎ 01282 425011 🖷 01282 664498 ✉ shargraves@burnley.gov.uk

Economic Development: Ms Kate Ingram, Head of Business Support & Regeneration, 1st Floor, Parker Lane Offices, Parker Lane, Burnley BB11 2DT ☎ 01282 477310 ✉ kingram@burnley.gov.uk

E-Government: Mrs Sharon Hargraves, Customer Services Manager, Town Hall, Manchester Road, Burnley BB11 9SA ☎ 01282 425011 🖷 01282 664498 ✉ shargraves@burnley.gov.uk

Electoral Registration: Mrs Alison Morville, Elections Officer, Town Hall, Manchester Road, Burnley BB11 9SA ☎ 01282 425011 ✉ amorville@burnley.gov.uk

Energy Management: Mr Phil Moore, Head of Finance, Town Hall, Manchester Road, Burnley BB11 9SA ☎ 01282 425011 ✉ pmoore@burnley.gov.uk

Estates, Property & Valuation: Mr Phil Moore, Head of Finance, Town Hall, Manchester Road, Burnley BB11 9SA ☎ 01282 425011 ✉ pmoore@burnley.gov.uk

European Liaison: Ms Kate Ingram, Head of Business Support & Regeneration, 1st Floor, Parker Lane Offices, Parker Lane, Burnley BB11 2DT ☎ 01282 477310 ✉ kingram@burnley.gov.uk

Events Manager: Mr Mike Waite, Head of Corporate Engagement & Cohesion, Town Hall, Manchester Road, Burnley BB11 9SA ☎ 01282 425011 ✉ mwaite@burnley.gov.uk

Facilities: Mr Colin Hill, Head of Markets, Market Hall, Curzon Street, Burnley BB11 2AP ☎ 01282 425011 🖷 01282 664665 ✉ chill@burnley.gov.uk

Finance and Treasurer: Mr Nick Aves, Director of Resources, Town Hall, Manchester Road, Burnley BB11 9SA ☎ 01282 425011 🖷 01282 450594 ✉ naves@burnley.gov.uk

Fleet Management: Mr M Rogers, Operations Manager, 93 Rossendale Road, Burnley BB11 5DD ☎ 01282 425011 🖷 01282 458904 ✉ mrogers@burnley.gov.uk

Grounds Maintenance: Mr Simon Goff, Head of Greenspaces & Amenities, 93 Rossendale Road, Burnley BB11 5DD ☎ 01282 425011 🖷 01282 458904 ✉ sgoff@burnley.gov.uk

Health and Safety: Mr D Lawrence, Health & Safety Adviser, Town Hall, Manchester Road, Burnley BB11 9SA ☎ 01282 425011; 01706 252655 🖷 01282 455464 ✉ davidlawrence@rossendalebc.gov.uk

Home Energy Conservation: Mr S Nutter, Project Officer, Parker Lane Offices, Parker Lane, Burnley BB11 2DT ☎ 01282 425011 🖷 01282 477266 ✉ snutter@burnley.gov.uk

Housing: Mr Paul Gatrell, Head of Housing & Development Control, Parker Lane Offices, Parker Lane, Burnley BB11 2DT ☎ 01282 425011 ✉ pgatrell@burnley.gov.uk

Legal: Mr David Wilcock, Head of People & Law, Town Hall, Manchester Road, Burnley BB11 9SA ☎ 01282 425011 🖷 01282 452536 ✉ dwilcock@burnley.gov.uk

Leisure and Cultural Services: Mr Gerard Vinton, Head of Leisure Services, St Peters Leisure Centre, Church Street, Burnley BB11 2DL ☎ 01282 425011 🖷 01282 458904 ✉ gvinton@burnley.gov.uk

Member Services: Mr Tom Forshaw, Head of Chief Executive's Office, Town Hall, Manchester Road, Burnley BB11 9SA ☎ 01282 477260 ✉ tforshaw@burnley.gov.uk

Parking: Mrs J Swift, Head of Street Scene, 18/20 Nicholas Street, Burnley BB11 2AP ☎ 01282 425011 🖷 01282 415194 ✉ jswift@burnley.gov.uk

Partnerships: Mr Tom Forshaw, Head of Chief Executive's Office, Town Hall, Manchester Road, Burnley BB11 9SA ☎ 01282 477260 ✉ tforshaw@burnley.gov.uk

Personnel / HR: Ms Heather Brennan, Head of Personnel, Town Hall, Manchester Road, Burnley BB11 9SA ☎ 01282 425011 🖷 01282 455464 ✉ hbrennan@burnley.gov.uk

Planning: Mr Paul Gatrell, Head of Housing & Development Control, Parker Lane Offices, Parker Lane, Burnley BB11 2DT ☎ 01282 425011 ✉ pgatrell@burnley.gov.uk

Procurement: Mr Tom Forshaw, Head of Chief Executive's Office, Town Hall, Manchester Road, Burnley BB11 1JA ☎ 01282 477260 ✉ tforshaw@burnley.gov.uk

Procurement: Mr Tom Forshaw, Head of Chief Executive's Office, Town Hall, Manchester Road, Burnley BB11 1JA ☎ 01282 477260 ✉ tforshaw@burnley.gov.uk

Recycling & Waste Minimisation: Mrs J Swift, Head of Street Scene, 18/20 Nicholas Street, Burnley BB11 2AP ☎ 01282 425011 🖷 01282 415194 ✉ jswift@burnley.gov.uk

Regeneration: Ms Kate Ingram, Head of Business Support & Regeneration, 1st Floor, Parker Lane Offices, Parker Lane, Burnley BB11 2DT ☎ 01282 477310 ✉ kingram@burnley.gov.uk

Staff Training: Ms Heather Brennan, Head of Personnel, Town Hall, Manchester Road, Burnley BB11 9SA ☎ 01282 425011 🖷 01282 455464 ✉ hbrennan@burnley.gov.uk

Street Scene: Mrs J Swift, Head of Street Scene, 18/20 Nicholas Street, Burnley BB11 2AP ☎ 01282 425011 🖷 01282 415194 ✉ jswift@burnley.gov.uk

Sustainable Communities: Mr Mike Cook, Director of Housing & Regeneration, Town Hall, Manchester Road, Burnley BB11 9SA

☎ 01282 425011 ✉ mcook@burnley.gov.uk

Sustainable Development: Mrs M Whewell, Policy & Environment Manager, 1st Floor, Contact Burnley, 9 Parker Lane, Burnley BB11 2BY ☎ 01282 425011 🖷 01282 477272 ✉ mwhewell@burnley.gov.uk

Tourism: Ms Jacqueline Whitaker, Visitor Economy Manager, 1st Floor, Parker Lane Offices, Parker Lane, Burnley BB11 2DT ☎ 01282 425011 ✉ j.whitaker@burnley.gov.uk

Town Centre: Mr Colin Hill, Head of Markets, Market Hall, Curzon Street, Burnley BB11 2AP ☎ 01282 425011 🖷 01282 664665 ✉ chill@burnley.gov.uk

Waste Collection and Disposal: Mrs J Swift, Head of Street Scene, 18/20 Nicholas Street, Burnley BB11 2AP ☎ 01282 425011 🖷 01282 415194 ✉ jswift@burnley.gov.uk

Waste Management: Mrs J Swift, Head of Street Scene, 18/20 Nicholas Street, Burnley BB11 2AP ☎ 01282 425011 🖷 01282 415194 ✉ jswift@burnley.gov.uk

MEMBERS OF THE COUNCIL (45)

***Mayor:* Bullas**, Charles (LD - Coalclough with Deerplay)
cbullas@burnley.gov.uk
***Deputy Mayor:* Cant**, Frank (LAB - Gawthorpe)
fcant@burnley.gov.uk
Baker, Howard (LAB - Trinity)
hbaker@burnley.gov.uk
Barker, Jonathan (LAB - Hapton with Park)
jbarker@burnley.gov.uk
Birtwistle, Gordon (LD - Coalclough with Deerplay)
gordon.bitwistle.mp@parliament.uk
Briggs, Charlie (LD - Gannow)
cbriggs@burnley.gov.uk
Brindle, Margaret (LD - Coalclough with Deerplay)
mbrindle@burnley.gov.uk
Brown, Jan (LD - Queensgate)
jbrown@burnley.gov.uk
Campbell, Paul (LAB - Rosehill with Burnley Wood)
pcampbell@burnley.gov.uk
Carmichael, Ida (CON - Whittlefield with Ightenhill)
icarmichael@burnley.gov.uk
Chaudhary, Saeed (LAB - Daneshouse with Stoneyholme)
schauldhary@burnley.gov.uk
Cooper, Julie (LAB - Bank Hall)
jcooper@burnley.gov.uk
Cunningham, Jean (LAB - Hapton with Park)
jcunningham@burnley.gov.uk
Fifield, John (LAB - Bank Hall)
jfifield@burnley.gov.uk
Foster, Bea (LAB - Rosegrove with Lowerhouse)
bfoster@burnley.gov.uk
Frayling, Gary (LAB - Bank Hall)
gfrayling@burnley.gov.uk
Frost, Roger (LD - Briercliffe)
rfrost@burnley.gov.uk
Greenwood, Joanne (LAB - Hapton with Park)
joannegreenwood@burnley.gov.uk
Harbour, John (LAB - Gawthorpe)
jharbour@burnley.gov.uk
Harrison, Tony (LAB - Brunshaw)
tharrison@burnley.gov.uk
Heginbotham, David (CON - Cliviger with Worsthorne)
dheginbotham@burnley.gov.uk
Hussain, Shah (LAB - Daneshouse with Stoneyholme)
shussain@burnley.gov.uk
Isherwood, Mathew (CON - Whittlefield with Ightenhill)
misherwood@burnley.gov.uk
Johnstone, Marcus (LAB - Rosegrove with Lowerhouse)
mjohnstone@burnley.gov.uk
Kelly, Anne (LD - Briercliffe)
annekelly@burnley.gov.uk
Kennedy, Tracy (LD - Rosehill with Burnley Wood)
tkennedy@burnley.gov.uk
Khan, Wajid (LAB - Daneshouse with Stoneyholme)
wajidkhan@burnley.gov.uk
Khan, Arif (LAB - Queensgate)
arifkhan@burnley.gov.uk
Knowles, Jennifer (LD - Queensgate)
jknowles@burnley.gov.uk
Lambert, Anthony (LAB - Trinity)
alambert@burnley.gov.uk
Large, Stephen (LAB - Lanehead)
slarge@burnley.gov.uk
Lishman, Margaret (LD - Briercliffe)
mlishman@burnley.gov.uk
McCann, Peter (LD - Lanehead)
pmccann@burnley.gov.uk
Monk, Elizabeth (LAB - Trinity)
emonk@burnley.gov.uk
Mottershead, Neil (LD - Gannow)
nmottershead@burnley.gov.uk
Newhouse, Andrew (CON - Cliviger with Wosthorne)
anewhouse@burnley.gov.uk
Pate, Lian (LAB - Brunshaw)
lpate@burnley.gov.uk
Porter, Tom (LD - Whittlefield with Ightenhill)
tporter@burnley.gov.uk
Reynolds, Paul (LAB - Rosegrove with Lowerhouse)
preynolds@burnley.gov.uk
Royle, Ann (LAB - Lanehead)
aroyle@burnley.gov.uk
Stringer, Betsy (LAB - Gannow)
bstringer@burnley.gov.uk
Sumner, Jeff (LD - Rosehill with Burnley Wood)
jsumner@burnley.gov.uk
Tatchell, Andrew (LAB - Gawthorpe)
atatchell@burnley.gov.uk
Towneley, Cosima (CON - Cliviger with Worsthorne)
mail@cositowneley.co.uk
Townsend, Mark (LAB - Brunshaw)
mtownsend@burnley.gov.uk

POLITICAL COMPOSITION

LAB: 26, LD: 14, CON: 5

CABINET

Leader: Ms Julie Cooper
Deputy leader: Mr Andrew Tatchell
Community Services: Mr Mark Townsend
Housing & Development: Mr Howard Baker
Leisure & Culture: Mr John Harbour
Regeneration & Economic Development: Mr Andrew Tatchell
Resources & Performance Management: Mr Mark Townsend

COMMITTEE CHAIRS

Audit: Mr Tony Harrison
Community Services Scrutiny: Ms Bea Foster
Development Control: Mr Frank Cant
Economic Regeneration Scrutiny: Ms Elizabeth Monk
Licensing: Mr Anthony Lambert
Resources Scrutiny: Ms Margaret Lishman
Standards: Ms Ann Royle

BURY M

Bury Metropolitan Borough Council, 3 Knowsley Place, Duke Street, Bury BL9 0EJ ☎ 0161 253 5000 🖷 0161 253 5119 info@bury.gov.uk 💻 www.bury.gov.uk

FACTS & FIGURES

Police Authority: Greater Manchester Police Authority
Health Authority: North West Strategic Health Authority
Learning and Skills Council: North West
Parliamentary Constituencies: Bury North, Bury South
EU Constituencies: North West
Election Frequency: Elections are by thirds
Twinning: Angouleme (France); Tulle (France); Schorndorf (Germany); Woodbury (NJ, USA); Datong (China)

PRINCIPAL OFFICERS

Chief Executive: Mr Mike Kelly, Chief Executive, Town Hall, Knowsley Street, Bury BL9 0SW ☎ 0161 253 5000 🖷 0161 253 5108 m.w.kelly@bury.gov.uk

Deputy Chief Executive: Mrs Ruth Fairhurst, Deputy Chief Executive, Town Hall, Knowsley Street, Bury BL9 0SW ☎ 0161 253 5955 🖷 0161 253 5972 r.e.fairhurst@bury.gov.uk

Architect, Building / Property Services: Mr Alex Holland, Head - Property & Asset Management, 3 Knowsley Place, Duke Street, Bury BL9 0EJ ☎ 0161 253 5992 a.holland@bury.gov.uk

Best Value: Mr David Hipkiss, Head - Risk Management, Town Hall, Knowsley Street, Bury BL9 0SW ☎ 0161 253 5084 d.hipkiss@bury.gov.uk

Building Control: Mr Rob Thorpe, Principal Building Control Officer, 3 Knowsley Place, Duke Street, Bury BL9 OEJ ☎ 0161 253 5289 🖷 0161 253 5290 r.c.thorpe@bury.gov.uk

Catering Services: Mr Charles Walton, Head - Civics & Leisure Catering, Unit 3, Bradley Fold Trading Estate, Bradley Fold Road, Bolton BL2 6RF ☎ 0161 253 5709 c.k.walton@bury.gov.uk

Children / Youth Services: Mr Mark Carriline, Executive Director - Children's Services, Athenaeum House, Market House, Bury BL9 0BN ☎ 0161 253 5603 🖷 0161 253 6093 m.carriline@bury.gov.uk

Children / Youth Services: Mr Gavin Emberton, Strategic Leader - Early Intervention, Athenaeum House, Market Street, Bury BL9 0BN ☎ 0161 253 5920 g.emberton@bury.gov.uk

Civil Registration: Mr Graeme Ramsden, Head - Registration, Town Hall, Knowsley Street, Bury BL9 0SW ☎ 0161 253 6027 🖷 0161 253 6028 g.h.ramsden@bury.gov.uk

PR / Communications: Mrs Katy Quinn, Corporate Communications Manager, Town Hall, Knowsley Street, Bury BL9 0SW ☎ 0161 253 5007 🖷 0161 253 5972 k.quinn@bury.gov.uk

Community Planning: Mr David Fowler, Head - Communities, Town Hall, Knowsley Street, Bury BL9 0SW ☎ 0161 253 6356 🖷 0161 253 5393 d.fowler@bury.gov.uk

Community Safety: Mr David Fowler, Head - Communities, Town Hall, Knowsley Street, Bury BL9 0SW ☎ 0161 253 6356 🖷 0161 253 5393 d.fowler@bury.gov.uk

Computer Management: Mr Stephen Denton, ICT Development & Programme Manager, Town Hall, Knowsley Street, Bury BL9 0SW ☎ 0161 253 6043 s.denton@bury.gov.uk

Consumer Protection and Trading Standards: Mr Tom Mitchell, Assistant Director - Planning, Environmental & Regulatory Services, 3 Knowsley Place, Duke Street, Bury BL9 0EJ ☎ 0161 253 5000 t.mitchell@bury.gov.uk

Corporate Services: Mrs Dionne Brandon, Head - Policy & Improvement, Town Hall, Knowsley Street, Bury BL9 0SW ☎ 0161 253 5125 d.brandon@bury.gov.uk

Corporate Services: Mrs Sue Hobson, Head - Business Support, Town Hall, Knowsley Street, Bury BL2 0SW ☎ 0161 253 5906 s.hobson@bury.gov.uk

Customer Service: Ms Kathleen Rowlands, Customer Contact Co-ordinator, 7 Whittaker Street, Radcliffe M26 2DT ☎ 0161 253 5124 k.rowlands@bury.gov.uk

Economic Development: Mr David Fowler, Head - Communities, Town Hall, Knowsley Street, Bury BL9 0SW ☎ 0161 253 6356 🖷 0161 253 5393 d.fowler@bury.gov.uk

Education: Mr Ian Chambers, Assistant Director - Learning, Athenaeum House, Market Street, Bury BL9 0BN ☎ 0161 253 5477 🖷 0161 253 6093 l.chambers@bury.gov.uk

Education: Ms Diana Sorrigan, Assistant Director - Business, Change & Redesign, 3 Knowsley Place, Duke Street, Bury BL9 0EJ ☎ 0161 253 5602 d.sorrigan@bury.gov.uk

E-Government: Mr Michael Owen, Executive Director - Resources, Town Hall, Knowsley Street, Bury BL9 0SW ☎ 0161 253 5000 🖷 0161 253 5070 m.a.owen@bury.gov.uk

Electoral Registration: Mr Warren Rafferty, Elections & Land Charges Officer, Town Hall, Knowsley Street, Bury BL9 0SW ☎ 0161 253 6018 🖷 0161 253 5248 w.j.rafferty@bury.gov.uk

Emergency Planning: Mr Mike Moore, Civil Contingency Co-ordinator, Town Hall, Knowsley Street, Bury BL9 0SW ☎ 0161 253 7732 m.moore@bury.gov.uk

Energy Management: Mr Ian Smith, Contract Administrator - South, 3 Knowsley Place, Duke Street, Bury BL9 0EJ ☎ 0161 253 5000 i.r.smith@bury.gov.uk

Environmental / Technical Services: Mr Neil Long, Assistant

Director - Operations, 3 Knowsley Place, Duke Street, Bury BL9 0EJ ☎ 0161 253 5735 ✉ n.s.long@bury.gov.uk

Environmental Health: Mr Tom Mitchell, Assistant Director - Planning, Environmental & Regulatory Services, 3 Knowsley Place, Duke Street, Bury BL9 0EJ ☎ 0161 253 5000 ✉ t.mitchell@bury.gov.uk

Estates, Property & Valuation: Mr Alex Holland, Head - Property & Asset Management, 3 Knowsley Place, Duke Street, Bury BL9 0EJ ☎ 0161 253 5992 ✉ a.holland@bury.gov.uk

European Liaison: Ms Tracey Flynn, Principal Strategy & Resources Officer, 3 Knowsley Place, Duke Street, Bury BL9 0EJ ☎ 0161 253 6040 ✉ t.flynn@bury.gov.uk

Events Manager: Mr Neil Long, Assistant Director - Operations, 3 Knowsley Place, Duke Street, Bury BL9 0EJ ☎ 0161 253 5735 ✉ n.s.long@bury.gov.uk

Facilities: Mr Neil Long, Assistant Director - Operations, 3 Knowsley Place, Duke Street, Bury BL9 0EJ ☎ 0161 253 5735 ✉ n.s.long@bury.gov.uk

Finance and Treasurer: Mr Steve Kenyon, Assistant Director - Finance & Efficiency, 3 Knowsley Place, Duke Street, Bury BL9 0EJ ☎ 0161 253 5237 ✉ s.kenyon@bury.gov.uk

Finance and Treasurer: Mr Michael Owen, Executive Director - Resources, Town Hall, Knowsley Street, Bury BL9 0SW ☎ 0161 253 5000 🖷 0161 253 5070 ✉ m.a.owen@bury.gov.uk

Fleet Management: Mr Stephen Fleming, Head - Transport Services & Workshop, Unit 34, Bradley Fold Trading Estate, Bradley Fold Road, Bolton BL2 6RF ☎ 0161 253 6624 🖷 0161 253 6130 ✉ s.j.fleming@bury.gov.uk

Grounds Maintenance: Mr Neil Long, Assistant Director - Operations, 3 Knowsley Place, Duke Street, Bury BL9 0EJ ☎ 0161 253 5735 ✉ n.s.long@bury.gov.uk

Health and Safety: Mr Alan Manchester, Principal Occupational Health. Safety & Emergency Planning, 3 Knowsley Place, Duke Street, Bury BL9 0EJ ☎ 0161 253 5143 🖷 0161 253 5137 ✉ a.manchester@bury.gov.uk

Highways: Mr Neil Long, Assistant Director - Operations, 3 Knowsley Place, Duke Street, Bury BL9 0EJ ☎ 0161 253 5735 ✉ n.s.long@bury.gov.uk

Home Energy Conservation: Mr Ian Smith, Contract Administrator - South, 3 Knowsley Place, Duke Street, Bury BL9 0EJ ☎ 0161 253 5000 ✉ i.r.smith@bury.gov.uk

Housing: Mrs Sharon McCambridge, Chief Executive - Six Town Housing, Point Blue, Moor Street, Bury BL9 5AQ ☎ 0161 686 8000 🖷 0161 764 5078 ✉ s.mccambridge@sixtownhousing.org

Housing Maintenance: Mr Wayne Campbell, Head - Repairs & Maintenance, 3 Knowsley Place, Duke Street, Bury BL9 0EJ ☎ 0161 253 5000 ✉ w.campbell@bury.gov.uk

Legal: Mrs Jayne Hammond, Assistant Director - Legal & Democratic Services, Town Hall, Knowsley Street, Bury BL9 0SW ☎ ; 0161 253 5237 🖷 0161 253 6091 ✉ j.m.hammond@bury.gov.uk

Leisure and Cultural Services: Mr Neil Long, Assistant Director - Operations, 3 Knowsley Place, Duke Street, Bury BL9 0EJ ☎ 0161 253 5735 ✉ n.s.long@bury.gov.uk

Leisure and Cultural Services: Ms Diana Sorrigan, Assistant Director - Business, Change & Redesign, 3 Knowsley Place, Duke Street, Bury BL9 0EJ ☎ 0161 253 5602 ✉ d.sorrigan@bury.gov.uk

Licensing: Mr Andrew Johnson, Head - Commercial & Lighting, 3 Knowsley Place, Duke Street, Bury BL9 0EJ ☎ 0161 253 5514 ✉ a.johnson@bury.gov.uk

Lifelong Learning: Ms Diana Sorrigan, Assistant Director - Business, Change & Redesign, 3 Knowsley Place, Duke Street, Bury BL9 0EJ ☎ 0161 253 5602 ✉ d.sorrigan@bury.gov.uk

Lighting: Mr Phil Hewitt, Principal Engineer - Street Lighting, Fernhill Depot, Todd Street, Bury BL9 5BJ ☎ 0161 253 5000 🖷 0161 763 6484 ✉ p.m.hewitt@bury.gov.uk

Lottery Funding, Charity and Voluntary: Mr Peter Harrington, Group Accountant, Town Hall, Knowsley Street, Bury BL9 0SW ☎ 0161 253 5045 🖷 0161 253 5112 ✉ p.harrington@bury.gov.uk

Member Services: Mr Chris Shilitto, Head - Democratic Services, Town Hall, Knowsley Street, Bury BL9 0SW ☎ 0161 253 5000 🖷 0161 253 5132 ✉ c.shilitto@bury.gov.uk

Parking: Mr John Foudy, Car Parking Manager, 3 Knowsley Place, Duke Street, Bury BL9 0EJ ☎ 0161 253 5445 ✉ j.foudy@bury.gov.uk

Partnerships: Mr David Fowler, Head - Communities, Town Hall, Knowsley Street, Bury BL9 0SW ☎ 0161 253 6356 🖷 0161 253 5393 ✉ d.fowler@bury.gov.uk

Personnel / HR: Mr Guy Berry, Director - Personnel, Town Hall, Knowsley Street, Bury BL9 0SW ☎ 0161 253 5160 🖷 0161 253 6091 ✉ g.berry@bury.gov.uk

Personnel / HR: Ms Tracey Johnson, Head - People, Strategy & Organisational Development, 3 Knowsley Place, Duke Street, Bury BL9 0EJ ☎ 0161 253 5151 ✉ t.johnson@bury.gov.uk

Planning: Mr Tom Mitchell, Assistant Director - Planning, Environmental & Regulatory Services, 3 Knowsley Place, Duke Street, Bury BL9 0EJ ☎ 0161 253 5000 ✉ t.mitchell@bury.gov.uk

Procurement: Mrs Sarah Janusz, Corporate Procurement Manager, Town Hall, Knowsley Street, Bury BL9 0SW ☎ 0161 253 6147 🖷 0161 253 5779 ✉ s.e.janusz@bury.gov.uk

Public Libraries: Ms Diana Sorrigan, Assistant Director - Business, Change & Redesign, 3 Knowsley Place, Duke Street, Bury BL9 0EJ ☎ 0161 253 5602 ✉ d.sorrigan@bury.gov.uk

Recycling & Waste Minimisation: Mr Glenn Stuart, Head - Waste Management, Unit 3, Bradley Fold Trading Estate, Bradley

Fold Road, Bolton BL2 6RF ☎ 0161 253 6621 🖷 0161 253 7473 ✉ g.stuart@bury.gov.uk

Road Safety: Ms Jan Brabin, Principal Road Safety Officer, 3 Knowsley Place, Duke Street, Bury BL9 0EJ ☎ 0161 253 5787 ✉ j.brabin@bury.gov.uk

Social Services (Adult): Mrs Linda Jackson, Assistant Director - Operations, Castle Buildings, Market Place, Bury BL9 0LT ☎ 0161 253 6033 🖷 0161 253 6961 ✉ l.a.jackson@bury.gov.uk

Social Services (Adult): Mrs Pat Jones-Greenhalgh, Executive Director - Adult Care Services, Castle Buildings, Market Place, Bury BL9 0LT ☎ 0161 253 5405 🖷 0161 253 6961 ✉ p.jones-greenhalgh@bury.gov.uk

Social Services (Children): Mr Mark Carriline, Executive Director - Children's Services, Athenaeum House, Market Street, Bury BL9 0BN ☎ 0161 253 5603 ✉ m.carriline@bury.gov.uk

Staff Training: Ms Tracey Johnson, Head - People, Strategy & Organisational Development, 3 Knowsley Place, Duke Street, Bury BL9 0EJ ☎ 0161 253 5151 ✉ t.johnson@bury.gov.uk

Sustainable Communities: Mr David Fowler, Head - Communities, Town Hall, Knowsley Street, Bury BL9 0SW ☎ 0161 253 6356 🖷 0161 253 5393 ✉ d.fowler@bury.gov.uk

Sustainable Development: Mr Paul Allen, Head - Planning, Policy & Projects, 3 Knowsley Place, Duke Street, Bury BL9 0EJ ☎ 0161 253 5284 ✉ p.n.allen@bury.gov.uk

Tourism: Ms Jill Youlton, Tourism Development Officer, 3 Knowsley Place, Duke Street, Bury BL9 0EJ ☎ 0161 253 6075 ✉ j.youlton@bury.gov.uk

Town Centre: Mrs Elizabeth Gillan, Unit Manager - Environment & Development Services, 3 Knowsley Place, Duke Street, Bury BL9 0EJ ☎ 0161 253 5000 ✉ e.gillan@bury.gov.uk

Traffic Management: Mr Ian Lord, Manager - Traffic Management & Road Safety Services, 3 Knowsley Place, Duke Street, Bury BL9 0EJ ☎ 0161 253 5783 ✉ i.c.lord@bury.gov.uk

Transport: Mr Stephen Fleming, Head - Transport Services & Workshop, Unit 34, Bradley Fold Trading Estate, Bradley Fold Road, Bolton BL2 6RF ☎ 0161 253 6624 🖷 0161 253 6130 ✉ s.j.fleming@bury.gov.uk

Waste Collection and Disposal: Mr Glenn Stuart, Head - Waste Management, Unit 3, Bradley Fold Trading Estate, Bradley Fold Road, Bolton BL2 6RF ☎ 0161 253 6621 🖷 0161 253 7473 ✉ g.stuart@bury.gov.uk

Waste Management: Mr Glenn Stuart, Head - Waste Management, Unit 3, Bradley Fold Trading Estate, Bradley Fold Road, Bolton BL2 6RF ☎ 0161 253 6621 🖷 0161 253 7473 ✉ g.stuart@bury.gov.uk

MEMBERS OF THE COUNCIL (51)

Leader of the Council: **Connolly**, Mike (LAB - East)
m.connolly@bury.gov.uk

Audin, Ken (LAB - Besses)
k.audin@bury.gov.uk

Audin, Ann (LAB - Unsworth)
a.audin@bury.gov.uk

Bailey, Matt (LAB - Radcliffe East)
M.Bailey@bury.gov.uk

Bailey, Daisy (LAB - Radcliffe East)
d.bailey@bury.gov.uk

Bayley, Noel (LAB - St Marys)
N.Bayley@bury.gov.uk

Bevan, Ian (CON - Ramsbottom)
i.bevan@bury.gov.uk

Bibby, Bob (CON - Church)
r.a.bibby@bury.gov.uk

Black, Jane (LAB - St Marys)
j.black@bury.gov.uk

Brigg, Sharon (LAB - Radcliffe North)
s.briggs@bury.gov.uk

Bury, Peter (LAB - Radcliffe North)
P.Bury@bury.gov.uk

Campbell, Gill (LAB - Holyrood)
G.Campbell@bury.gov.uk

Caserta, Robert (CON - Pilkington Park)
r.caserta@bury.gov.uk

Cassidy, Dorothy (LAB - Moorside)
D.M.Cassidy@bury.gov.uk

Columbine, Joanne (LAB - Ramsbottom)
J.Columbine@bury.gov.uk

Cummings, Tony (LAB - Radcliffe West)
a.j.cummings@bury.gov.uk

Fitzgerald, Elizabeth (LAB - Besses)
e.fitzgerald@bury.gov.uk

Fitzwalter, Luise (LAB - Ramsbottom)
l.fitzwalter@bury.gov.uk

Frith, James (LAB - Elton)
james.frith@bury.gov.uk

Garter, Simon (LAB - Tottington)

Gartside, Iain (CON - Tottington)
i.b.gartside@bury.gov.uk

Grimshaw, Joan (LAB - Unsworth)
j.grimshaw@bury.gov.uk

Gunther, Dorothy (CON - North Manor)
d.l.gunther@bury.gov.uk

Hankey, Michael (CON - Elton)
m.hankey@bury.gov.uk

Haroon, Shaheena (LAB - Redvales)
s.haroon@bury.gov.uk

Heneghan, Paddy (LAB - Holyrood)
p.heneghan@bury.gov.uk

Holt, Trevor (LAB - East)
t.holt@bury.gov.uk

Hussain, Khalid (CON - North Manor)
K.Hussain@bury.gov.uk

Isherwood, Anthony (LAB - Radcliffe West)
a.isherwood@bury.gov.uk

James, Michael (LAB - Sedgley)
M.A.James@bury.gov.uk

Jones, David (LAB - Unsworth)
david.jones@bury.gov.uk

Lewis, Jane (LAB - Radcliffe North)
j.lewis@bury.gov.uk

Matthews, Alan (LAB - Besses)
a.k.matthews@bury.gov.uk

O'Hanlon, Donal (LD - St Marys)
d.o'hanlon@bury.gov.uk

Parnell, Nick (LAB - Radcliffe East)
n.parnell@bury.gov.uk
Pickstone, Tim (LD - Holyrood)
t.d.pickstone@bury.gov.uk
Quinn, Alan (LD - Sedgley)
alan.quinn@bury.gov.uk
Rothwell, Keith (LAB - Moorside)
k.rothwell@bury.gov.uk
Shori, Rishi (LAB - Radcliffe West)
r.shori@bury.gov.uk
Simpson, Andrea (LAB - Sedgley)
a.simpson@bury.gov.uk
Smith, Stella (LAB - East)
stella.smith@bury.gov.uk
Smith, John (LAB - Redvales)
john.smith@bury.gov.uk
Southworth, Susan (LAB - Elton)
s.southworth@bury.gov.uk
Tarig, Tamoor (LAB - Redvales)
t.tarig@bury.gov.uk
Taylor, Jim (CON - North Manor)
j.w.h.taylor@bury.gov.uk
Vincent, Bernie (CON - Pilkington Park)
b.vincent@bury.gov.uk
Walker, Roy (CON - Church)
roy@edwardwalker.freeserve.co.uk
Walmsley, Sandra (LAB - Moorside)
sandra.walmsley@gov.uk
Walton, Jack (CON - Church)
j.f.walton@bury.gov.uk
Wiseman, Michelle (CON - Pilkington Park)
m.j.wiseman@bury.gov.uk
Wright, Yvonne (CON - Tottington)
y.s.wright@bury.gov.uk

POLITICAL COMPOSITION
LAB: 35, CON: 13, LD: 3

CABINET
Leader: Mr Mike Connolly
Deputy Leader: Mr John Smith
Adult Care, Health & Housing: Mr Rishi Shori
Children & Families: Mr Nick Parnell
Community Development: Ms Sandra Walmsley
Corporate Affairs: Mr John Smith
Finance & Resources: Mr Anthony Isherwood
Leisure, Tourism & Culture: Mrs Jane Lewis
Neighbourhood & Regeneration: Ms Gill Campbell

COMMITTEE CHAIRS
Audit: Mrs Ann Audin
Health Scrutiny: Mr Peter Bury
Human Resources & Appeals Panel: Mr Trevor Holt
Licensing & Safety Panel: Mr Matt Bailey
Overview & Scrutiny: Mr Michael Hankey
Planning Control: Mr Tony Cummings

CAERPHILLY W

Caerphilly County Borough Council, (Cyngor Bwrdeistref Sirol Caerffili), Penallta House, Tredomen Park, Ystrad Mynach, Hengoed CF82 7PG ☎ 01443 815588 🖷 01443 864443
info@caerphilly.gov.uk 💻 www.caerphilly.gov.uk

FACTS & FIGURES
Police Authority: Gwent Police Authority
Learning and Skills Council: Wales
Parliamentary Constituencies: Caerphilly, Islwyn
EU Constituencies: Wales
Election Frequency: Elections are by thirds
Twinning: Ludwigsburg (Germany); Pisek (Czech Republic)

PRINCIPAL OFFICERS
Chief Executive: Mr Anthony O'Sullivan, Chief Executive, Penallta House, Tredomen Park, Ystrad Mynach, Hengoed CF82 7PG ☎ 01443 864410 🖷 01495 235011
anthonyo'sullivan@caerphilly.gov.uk

Deputy Chief Executive: Mr Nigel Barnett, Deputy Chief Executive, Penallta House, Tredomen Park, Ystrad Mynach, Hengoed CF82 7PG ☎ 01443 864419 🖷 01443 864202
barnen@caerphilly.gov.uk

Senior Management: Mrs Sandra Aspinall, Director of Education & Leisure, Penallta House, Tredomen Park, Ystrad Mynach, Hengoed CF82 7PG ☎ 01443 864948 🖷 01443 864807
aspins@caerphilly.gov.uk

Senior Management: Mr Albert Heany, Corporate Director of Social Services, Penallta House, Tredomen Park, Ystrad Mynach, Hengoed CF82 7PG ☎ 01443 864560 🖷 01443 864513
heanea@caerphilly.gov.uk

Access Officer / Social Services (Disability): Mr Simon Dixon, Disabled Access Officer, Tredomen House, Tredomen Park, Ystrad Mynach, Hengoed CF82 7WF ☎ 01443 864085 🖷 01443 865550 dixons@caerphilly.gov.uk

Architect, Building / Property Services: Mr Colin Jones, Head of Performance & Property, Penallta House, Tredomen Park, Ystrad Mynach, Hengoed CF82 7PG ☎ 01443 864382 🖷 01443 864235 jonesrc@caerphilly.gov.uk

Best Value: Ms Nicole Scammel, Head of Corporate Finance, Ty Penallta, Tredomen Park, Ystrad Mynach, Hengoed CF82 7PG ☎ 01443 863022 🖷 01443 863347 scammn@caerphilly.gov.uk

Building Control: Mr Jason Lear, Team Leader - Building Control, Ty Pontllanfraith, Blackwood Road, Pontllanfraith, Blackwood NP12 2YW ☎ 01495 235091 learj@caerphilly.gov.uk

Catering Services: Ms Marcia Lewis, Head of Catering, Pontllanfraith House, Blackwood Road, Pontllanfraith, Blackwood NP12 2YW ☎ 01443 863174 lewism@caerphilly.gov.uk

Children / Youth Services: Mr Albert Heany, Corporate Director of Social Services, Penallta House, Tredomen Park, Ystrad Mynach, Hengoed CF82 7PG ☎ 01443 864560 🖷 01443 864513
heanea@caerphilly.gov.uk

Civil Registration: Ms Della Mahony, Superintendent Registrar, Penallta House, Tredomen Park, Ystrad Mynach, Hengoed CF82 7PG ☎ 01443 863074 🖷 01443 863385

PR / Communications: Ms Rosemary Mathews, Communications

Manager, Penallta House, Tredomen Park, Ystrad Mynach, Hengoed CF82 7PG ☎ 01443 864262 🖷 01443 864246 ✉ matthr@caerphilly.gov.uk

Community Planning: Mr Pat Mears, Chief Planning Officer, Council Offices, Pontllanfraith, Blackwood NP12 2YW ☎ 01495 235320 🖷 01495 235022 ✉ mearsp@caerphilly.gov.uk

Community Safety: Mr Rob Hartshorn, Head of Public Protection, Council Offices, Pontllanfraith, Blackwood NP12 2YW ☎ 01495 235315 🖷 01495 235018 ✉ hartsr@caerphilly.gov.uk

Computer Management: Mr Phillip Evans, Head of Information & Citizen Engagement, Penallta House, Tredomen Park, Ystrad Mynach, Hengoed CF82 7PG ☎ ; 01443 864005 🖷 01443 863488 ✉ evansps@caerphilly.gov.uk

Consumer Protection and Trading Standards: Mr Rob Hartshorn, Head of Public Protection, Council Offices, Pontllanfraith, Blackwood NP12 2YW ☎ 01495 235315 🖷 01495 235018 ✉ hartsr@caerphilly.gov.uk

Contracts: Ms Nicole Scammel, Head of Corporate Finance, Penallta House, Tredomen Park, Ystrad Mynach, Hengoed CF82 7PG ☎ 01443 863022 🖷 01443 863347 ✉ scammn@caerphilly.gov.uk

Corporate Services: Mr Nigel Barnett, Deputy Chief Executive, Penallta House, Tredomen Park, Ystrad Mynach, Hengoed CF82 7PG ☎ 01443 864419 🖷 01443 864202 ✉ barnen@caerphilly.gov.uk

Customer Service: Mr David Titley, Customer Services Manager, Ty Duffryn, Duffryn Business Park, Ystrad Mynach, Hengoed CF82 7TW ☎ ; 01443 864548 🖷 01443 866501 ✉ titled@caerphilly.gov.uk

Direct Labour: Mr Shaun Couzens, Head of Housing Services, Tir-y-berth Depot, New Road, Tir-y-berth, Hengoed CF82 8NR ☎ 01443 863282 🖷 01443 863401 ✉ couzens@caerphilly.gov.uk

Economic Development: Mr Pat Mears, Chief Planning Officer, Council Offices, Pontllanfraith, Blackwood NP12 2YW ☎ 01495 235320 🖷 01495 235022 ✉ mearsp@caerphilly.gov.uk

Education: Mrs Sandra Aspinall, Director of Education & Leisure, Penallta House, Tredomen Park, Ystrad Mynach, Hengoed CF82 7PG ☎ 01443 864948 🖷 01443 864807 ✉ aspins@caerphilly.gov.uk

E-Government: Mr Phillip Evans, Head of Information & Citizen Engagement, Penallta House, Tredomen Park, Ystrad Mynach, Hengoed CF82 7PG ☎ ; 01443 864005 🖷 ; 01443 863488 ✉ evansps@caerphilly.gov.uk

Electoral Registration: Mr Dave Beecham, Electoral Services Manager, Enterprise House, Tir y Berth Industrial Estate, New Road, Tir y Berth, Hengoed CF82 8AU ☎ 01443 864405 🖷 01443 864379 ✉ beechd@caerphilly.gov.uk

Emergency Planning: Ms Sheryl Andrews, Emergency Planning Manager, Pontllanfraith House, Blackwood Road, Pontllanfraith, Blackwood NP12 2YW ☎ 01495 235048 🖷 01443 864326 ✉ andres@caerphilly.gov.uk

Energy Management: Mr Colin Jones, Head of Performance & Property, Penallta House, Tredomen Park, Ystrad Mynach, Hengoed CF82 7PG ☎ 01443 864382 🖷 01443 864235 ✉ jonesrc@caerphilly.gov.uk

Environmental / Technical Services: Mr Anthony O'Sullivan, Chief Executive, Penallta House, Tredomen Park, Ystrad Mynach, Hengoed CF82 7PG ☎ 01443 864410 🖷 01495 235011 ✉ anthonyo'sullivan@caerphilly.gov.uk

Environmental Health: Mr Rob Hartshorn, Head of Public Protection, Council Offices, Pontllanfraith, Blackwood NP12 2YW ☎ 01495 235315 🖷 01495 235018 ✉ hartsr@caerphilly.gov.uk

Estates, Property & Valuation: Mr Colin Jones, Head of Performance & Property, Penallta House, Tredomen Park, Ystrad Mynach, Hengoed CF82 7PG ☎ 01443 864382 🖷 01443 864235 ✉ jonesrc@caerphilly.gov.uk

European Liaison: Ms Victoria Phillips, European Officer, Pontllanfraith House, Blackwood Road, Pontllanfraith, Blackwood NP12 2YW ☎ 01443 864416 🖷 01443 864310 ✉ phillv@caerphilly.gov.uk

Events Manager: Mr Paul Hudson, Senior Events & Marketing Officer, Tredomen Business & Technology Centre, Tredomen Business Park, Ystrad Mynach, Hengoed CF82 7FN ☎ 01443 866228 🖷 01443 864446 ✉ hudsop@caerphilly.gov.uk

Facilities: Mr Adrian Crabb, Senior Facilities Manager, Tredomen House, Tredomen Park, Ystrad Mynach, Hengoed CF82 7WF ☎ 01443 863307 🖷 01495 235550 ✉ crabba@caerphilly.gov.uk

Finance and Treasurer: Ms Nicole Scammel, Head of Corporate Finance, Penallta House, Tredomen Park, Ystrad Mynach, Hengoed CF82 7PG ☎ 01443 863022 🖷 01443 863347 ✉ scammn@caerphilly.gov.uk

Fleet Management: Ms Mary Powell, Fleet Manager, Tir-y-berth Depot, New Road, Tir-y-berth, Hengoed CF82 8NR ☎ 01495 235365 🖷 01495 233446 ✉ powelem@caerphilly.gov.uk

Grounds Maintenance: Mr Derek Price, Principal Parks & Open Spaces Officer, Council Offices, Pontllanfraith, Blackwood NP12 2YW ☎ 01495 235470 🖷 01495 235471 ✉ priced@caerphilly.gov.uk

Health and Safety: Ms Emma Townsend, Corporate Health & Safety Manager, Nelson Road, Tredomen, Ystrad Mynach, Hengoed CF82 7SF ☎ 01443 864280 🖷 01443 864343 ✉ townsenj@caerphilly.gov.uk

Highways: Mr Terry Shaw, Head of Engineering, Pontllanfraith, Blackwood Road, Pontllanfraith, Blackwood NP12 2YW ☎ 01495 235319 🖷 01495 235012 ✉ shawt@caerphilly.gov.uk

Home Energy Conservation: Mr Paul Rossiter, Energy & Water Conservation Officer, Woodfieldside Business Park, Penmaen Road, Pontllanfriath, Blackwood NP12 2DG ☎ 01495 235535

🖷 01495 235551 ✉ rossip@caerphilly.gov.uk

Housing: Mr Graham North, Public Sector Housing Manager, Pontllanfraith House, Blackwood House, Pontllanfraith, Blackwood NP12 2YW ☎ 01495 235296 ✉ northg@caerphilly.gov.uk

Housing Maintenance: Mr Shaun Couzens, Head of Housing Services, Tir y Berth Depot, New Road, Hengoed CF82 8NR ☎ 01443 863282 🖷 01443 863401 ✉ couzens@caerphilly.gov.uk

Legal: Mr Dan Perkins, Head of Legal Services & Monitoring Officer, Penallta House, Tredomen Park, Ystrad Mynach, Hengoed CF82 7PG ☎ 01443 863142 🖷 01443 863154 ✉ perkid@caerphilly.gov.uk

Leisure and Cultural Services: Mrs Sandra Aspinall, Director of Education & Leisure, Penallta House, Tredomen Park, Ystrad Mynach, Hengoed CF82 7PG ☎ 01443 864948 🖷 01443 864807 ✉ aspins@caerphilly.gov.uk

Licensing: Mr Paul Hotchkiss, Registration & Licensing Officer, Pontllanfraith Offices, Blackwood NP12 2PZ ☎ 01495 235099 🖷 01495 235016 ✉ hotchp@caerphilly.gov.uk

Lifelong Learning: Ms Keri Cole, Head of Lifelong Learning & Leisure, Penallta House, Tredomen Park, Ystrad Mynach, Hengoed CF82 7PG ☎ 01443 864891 ✉ colek@caerphilly.gov.uk

Lighting: Mr Terry Shaw, Head of Engineering, Council Offices, Pontllanfraith, Blackwood NP12 2YW ☎ 01495 235319 🖷 01495 235012 ✉ shawt@caerphilly.gov.uk

Lottery Funding, Charity and Voluntary: Mr Colin Jones, Head of Performance & Property, Tredomen House, Nelson Road, Tredomen, Ystrad Mynach, Hengoed CF82 7WF ☎ 01443 864382 🖷 01443 864235 ✉ jonesrc@caerphilly.gov.uk

Member Services: Mr Jonathan Jones, Member Services & Scrutiny Manager, Penallta House, Tredomen Park, Ystrad Mynach, Hengoed CF82 7PG ☎ 01443 864242 ✉ jonesj@caerphilly.gov.uk

Parking: Mr Terry Shaw, Head of Engineering, Council Offices, Pontllanfraith, Blackwood NP12 2YW ☎ 01495 235319 🖷 01495 235012 ✉ shawt@caerphilly.gov.uk

Partnerships: Mr Colin Jones, Head of Performance & Property, Penallta House, Tredomen Park, Ystrad Mynach, Hengoed CF82 7PG ☎ 01443 864382 🖷 01443 864235 ✉ jonesrc@caerphilly.gov.uk

Personnel / HR: Mr Gareth Hardacre, Head of People Management & Development, Penallta House, Tredomen Park, Ystrad Mynach, Hengoed CF82 7PG ☎ 01443 864309 🖷 01443 864389 ✉ hardag@caerphilly.gov.uk

Planning: Mr Pat Mears, Chief Planning Officer, Council Offices, Pontllanfraith, Blackwood NP12 2YW ☎ 01495 235320 🖷 01495 235022 ✉ mearsp@caerphilly.gov.uk

Procurement: Mrs Elizabeth Lucas, Head of Procurement, Penallta House, Tredomen Park, Ystrad Mynach, Hengoed CF82 7PG ☎ 01443 863160 🖷 01443 863167 ✉ lucasej@caerphilly.gov.uk

Public Libraries: Mr Gareth Evans, Business Development Manager, Penallta House, Tredomen Park, Ystrad Mynach, Hengoed CF82 7PG ☎ 01443 864033 ✉ evansg1@caerphilly.gov.uk

Recycling & Waste Minimisation: Mr Mark Williams, Head of Public Services, Council Offices, Pontllanfraith, Blackwood NP12 2YW ☎ 01495 235070 🖷 01495 235014 ✉ willias@caerphilly.gov.uk

Regeneration: Mrs Jan Bennett, Group Manager - Advisory Services, Tredomen House, Nelson Road, Tredomen, Ystrad Mynach, Hengoed CF82 7WF ☎ 01443 864340 🖷 01443 864372 ✉ bennej@caerphilly.gov.uk

Road Safety: Mr Terry Shaw, Head of Engineering, Council Offices, Pontllanfraith, Blackwood NP12 2YW ☎ 01495 235319 🖷 01495 235012 ✉ shawt@caerphilly.gov.uk

Social Services: Mr Albert Heany, Corporate Director of Social Services, Penallta House, Tredomen Park, Ystrad Mynach, Hengoed CF82 7PG ☎ 01443 864560 🖷 01443 864513 ✉ heanea@caerphilly.gov.uk

Social Services (Adult): Mr Dave Street, Assistant Director - Adult Services, Penallta House, Tredomen Park, Ystrad Mynach, Hengoed CF82 7PG ☎ 01443 864611 🖷 01443 864513 ✉ streed@caerphilly.gov.uk

Social Services (Children): Mr Andrew Jarreett, Assistant Director - Children's Services, Penallta House, Tredomen Park, Ystrad Mynach, Hengoed CF82 7PG ☎ 01443 864520 🖷 01443 864513 ✉ heanea@caerphilly.gov.uk

Staff Training: Ms Jane Haile, Training Manager, Tredomen House, Nelson Road, Tredomen, Ystrad Mynach, Hengoed CF82 7WF ☎ 01443 863410 🖷 01443 863101 ✉ hailej@caerphilly.gov.uk

Sustainable Communities: Mrs Jan Bennett, Group Manager - Advisory Services, Tredomen House, Nelson Road, Tredomen, Ystrad Mynach, Hengoed CF82 7WF ☎ 01443 864340 🖷 01443 864372 ✉ bennej@caerphilly.gov.uk

Sustainable Development: Mr Pat Mears, Chief Planning Officer, Council Offices, Pontllanfraith, Blackwood NP12 2YW ☎ 01495 235320 🖷 01495 235022 ✉ mearsp@caerphilly.gov.uk

Tourism: Mr Paul Hudson, Senior Events & Marketing Officer, Tredomen Business & Technology Centre, Tredomen Business Park, Ystrad Mynach, Hengoed CF82 7FN ☎ 01443 866228 🖷 01443 864446 ✉ hudsop@caerphilly.gov.uk

Town Centre: Mr Andrew Highway, Town Centre Development Manager, Tredomen Business and Technology Centre, Ystrad Mynach, Hengoed CF82 7FN ☎ 01443 866213 ✉ highwa@caerphilly.gov.uk

Traffic Management: Mr Terry Shaw, Head of Engineering,

Council Offices, Pontllanfraith, Blackwood NP12 2YW
☎ 01495 235319 🖷 01495 235012 ✉ shawt@caerphilly.gov.uk

Transport: Mr Clive Campbell, Transportation Engineering Manager, Council Offices, Pontllanfraith, Blackwood NP12 2YW
☎ 01495 235339 🖷 01495 235045 ✉ campbc@caerphilly.gov.uk

Transport Planner: Mr Clive Campbell, Transportation Engineering Manager, Council Offices, Pontllanfraith, Blackwood NP12 2YW ☎ 01495 235339 🖷 01495 235045
✉ campbc@caerphilly.gov.uk

Waste Collection and Disposal: Mr Mark Williams, Head of Public Services, Council Offices, Pontllanfraith, Blackwood NP12 2YW ☎ 01495 235070 🖷 01495 235014
✉ willias@caerphilly.gov.uk

Waste Management: Mr Mark Williams, Head of Public Services, Council Offices, Pontllanfraith, Blackwood NP12 2YW
☎ 01495 235070 🖷 01495 235014 ✉ willias@caerphilly.gov.uk

Children's Play Areas: Mr Derek Price, Principal Parks & Open Spaces Officer, Pontllanfraith House, Blackwood Road, Pontllanfraith, Blackwood NP12 2YW ☎ 01495 235470
🖷 01495 235471 ✉ priced@caerphilly.gov.uk

MEMBERS OF THE COUNCIL (73)

***Mayor:* Oliver**, Gaynor (LAB - Pontlottyn)
gaynoroliver@caerphilly.gov.uk
***Deputy Mayor:* Gray**, Michael (LAB - Crosskeys)
michaelgray@caerphilly.gov.uk
***Leader of the Council:* Andrews**, Harry (LAB - Gilfach)
harryandrews@caerphilly.gov.uk
***Deputy Leader of the Council:* Jones**, Gerald (LAB - New Tredegar)
geraldjones@caerphilly.gov.uk
***Deputy Leader of the Council:* Reynolds**, Keith (LAB - Aberbargoed)
keithreynolds@caerphilly.gov.uk
Ackerman, Lyn (PC - Newbridge)
lynackerman@caerphilly.gov.uk
Adams, Michael (LAB - Pontllanfraith)
michaeladams@caerphilly.gov.uk
Aldworth, Elizabeth (LAB - Bedwas, Trethomas & Machen)
lizaldworth@caerphilly.gov.uk
Angel, Alan (PC - Ystrad Mynach)
alanangel@caerphilly.gov.uk
Baker, Kath (PC - Newbridge)
kathbaker@caerphilly.gov.uk
Bevan, Gina (LAB - Moriah)
ginabevancaerphilly.gov.uk
Bevan, John (LAB - Moriah)
johnbevan@caerphilly.gov.uk
Bevan, Phil (PC - Morgan Jones)
philbevan@caerphilly.gov.uk
Binding, Lyndon (PC - Aber Valley)
lyndonbinding@caerphilly.gov.uk
Blackman, Anne (IND - Nelson)
anneblackman@caerphilly.gov.uk
Bolter, Dennis (PC - Hengoed)
dennisbolter@caerphilly.gov.uk
Carter, David (LAB - Bargoed)
davidcarter@caerphilly.gov.uk
Collins, Anne (PC - Penyrheol)
annecollins@caerphilly.gov.uk
Cook, Patrica (LAB - Blackwood)
patriciacook@caerphilly.gov.uk
Cuss, Carl (LAB - Twyn Carno)
carlcuss@caerphilly.gov.uk
David, Wynne (LAB - St Cattwg)
wynnedavid@caerphilly.gov.uk
David, Hefin (LAB - St Cattwg)
hefindavid@caerphilly.gov.uk
Davies, Tudor (LAB - Bargoed)
tudordavies@caerphilly.gov.uk
Davies, Huw (LAB - Penyrheol)
huwdavies@caerphilly.gov.uk
Davies, Ray (LAB - Bedwas, Trethomas & Machen)
raydavies@caerphilly.gov.uk
Dawson, Kevin (LAB - Pengam)
kevindawson@caerphilly.gov.uk
Dix, Nigel (LAB - Blackwood)
nigeldix@caerphilly.gov.uk
Durham, Colin (LAB - Ynysddu)
colindurham@caerphilly.gov.uk
Ellis, Diana (LAB - Blackwood)
dianaellis@caerphilly.gov.uk
Elsbury, Colin (PC - St Martins)
colinelsbury@caerphilly.gov.uk
Forehead, Elaine (LAB - St James)
elaineforehead@caerphilly.gov.uk
Forehead, Christine (LAB - St James)
christineforehead@caerphilly.gov.uk
Fussell, James (PC - St Martins)
jamesfussell@caerphilly.gov.uk
Gale, June (LAB - Bedwas, Trethomas & Machen)
junegalecaerphilly.gov.uk
Gardiner, Leon (LAB - Argoed)
leongardiner@caerphilly.gov.uk
George, Nigel (LAB - Risca East)
nigelgeorge@caerphilly.gov.uk
Gordon, Colin (LAB - Pontllanfraith)
colingordon@caerphilly.gov.uk
Gough, Rob (PC - Llanbradach)
robgough@caerphilly.gov.uk
Griffiths, Phyl (LAB - Risca West)
phyllisgriffiths@caerphilly.gov.uk
Hardacre, David (LAB - Darren Valley)
davidhardacre@caerphilly.gov.uk
Havard, Derek (LAB - Bedwas, Trethomas & Machen)
derekhavard@caerphilly.gov.uk
Hawker, Chris (LAB - Cefn Fforest)
chrishawker@caerphilly.gov.uk
Higgs, Alan (LAB - Aberbargoed)
alanhiggs@caerphilly.gov.uk
Hughes, Graham (LAB - St Cattwg)
grahamhughes@caerphilly.gov.uk
James, Ken (LAB - Abercarn)
kenjames@caerphilly.gov.uk
James, Martyn (PC - Ystrad Mynach)
martynjames@caerphilly.gov.uk
Jenkins, Stan (LAB - Risca East)
stanjenkins@caerphilly.gov.uk
Johnston, Gary (LAB - Newbridge)
garyjohnston@caerphilly.gov.uk
Jones, Barbara (LAB - St James)
barbarajones@caerphilly.gov.uk
Jones, Janet (LAB - Ynysddu)

janetjones@caerphilly.gov.uk
Kent, Stephen (PC - St Martins)
stephenkent@caerphilly.gov.uk
Kirby, Gez (LAB - Pontllanfraith)
gezkirby@caerphilly.gov.uk
Lewis, Andrew (LAB - Crumlin)
andrewlewis@caerphilly.gov.uk
Lloyd, Keith (PC - Crumlin)
keithlloyd@caerphilly.gov.uk
Mann, Colin (PC - Llanbradach)
colinmann@caerphilly.gov.uk
Morgan, Sean (LAB - Nelson)
seanmorgan@caerphilly.gov.uk
Passmore, Rhianon (LAB - Risca East)
rhianonpassmore@caerphilly.gov.uk
Poole, David (LAB - Pengam)
davidpoole@caerphilly.gov.uk
Preece, Denver (LAB - Abercarn)
denverpreece@caerphilly.gov.uk
Prew, Michael (PC - Morgan Jones)
michaelprew@caerphilly.gov.uk
Price, Dianne (LAB - Bargoed)
dianneprice@caerphilly.gov.uk
Pritchard, James (LAB - Morgan Jones)
jamespritchard@caerphilly.gov.uk
Pritchard, Judith (PC - Hengoed)
judithpritchard@caerphilly.gov.uk
Rees, Les (LAB - New Tredegar)
lesrees@caerphilly.gov.uk
Rees, Dave (O - Risca West)
daverees@caerphilly.gov.uk
Roberts, John (PC - Aber Valley)
johnroberts@caerphilly.gov.uk
Saralis, Roy (LAB - Penmaen)
roysaralis@caerphilly.gov.uk
Sargent, Margaret (PC - Penyrheol)
margaretsargent@caerphilly.gov.uk
Summers, Jean (LAB - Penmaen)
jeansummers@caerphilly.gov.uk
Taylor, John (PC - Aber Valley)
johntaylor@caerphilly.gov.uk
Whittle, Lindsay (PC - Penyrheol)
lindsaywhittle@caerphilly.gov.uk
Williams, Tom (LAB - Cefn Fforest)
tomwilliams@caerphilly.gov.uk
Woodyatt, Robin (LAB - Maesycwmmer)
robinwoodyatt@caerphilly.gov.uk

POLITICAL COMPOSITION

LAB: 51, PC: 20, IND: 1, O: 1

CABINET

Leader: Mr Harry Andrews
Deputy Leader / Housing: Mr Gerald Jones
Deputy Leader / Corporate Services: Mr Keith Reynolds
Community & Leisure Services: Mr David Poole
Education & Lifelong Learning: Mrs Rhianon Passmore
Highways, Transportation & Engineering: Mr Tom Williams
HR & Governance: Ms Christine Forehead
Performance & Asset Management: Mr David Hardacre
Regeneration, Planning & Sustainable Development: Mr Ken James
Social Services: Mr Robin Woodyatt

COMMITTEE CHAIRS

Appointment: Ms Christine Forehead
Health Social Care & Wellbeing Scrutiny: Miss Lyn Ackerman
Licensing: Mr John Bevan
Planning: Mr Stan Jenkins
Policy & Resources Scrutiny: Mr Hefin David
Regeneration & Environment Scrutiny: Mr Tudor Davies

CALDERDALE M

Calderdale Metropolitan Borough Council, Northgate House, Halifax HX1 1UN ☎ 0845 245 6000 🖷 01422 393102
🖳 www.calderdale.gov.uk

FACTS & FIGURES

Police Authority: West Yorkshire Police Authority
Health Authority: NHS Yorkshire & the Humber
Learning and Skills Council: Yorkshire and the Humber
Parliamentary Constituencies: Calder Valley, Halifax
EU Constituencies: Yorkshire and the Humber
Election Frequency: Elections are by thirds
Twinning: Brighouse: Ludenscheid (Germany); Elland: Riorges (France); Halifax: Aachen (Germany); Calderdale: Strakonice (Czech Rep), County Mayo (Ireland); Halifax (Canada); Hebden Bridge: St. Pol-sur-Ternoise (France); Todmorden: Bramsche (Germany); Roncq (France)

PRINCIPAL OFFICERS

Chief Executive: Mr Gordon Mitchell, Interim Chief Executive, Town Hall, Halifax HX1 1UJ ☎ 01422 393005 🖷 01422 393085 ✉ gordon.mitchell@calderdale.gov.uk

Senior Management: Mr Ian Gray, Director - Economy & Environment, Northgate House, Halifax HX1 1UN ☎ 01422 393006 🖷 01422 392205 ✉ ian.gray@calderdale.gov.uk

Senior Management: Ms Bev Maybury, Director - Adults, Health & Social Care, Park Road, Halifax HX1 2TU ☎ 01422 393800 🖷 01422 393848 ✉ bev.maybury@calderdale.gov.uk

Senior Management: Mr Stuart Smith, Director - Children & Young People, Northgate House, Halifax HX1 1UN ☎ 01422 392500 🖷 01422 392481 ✉ stuart.smith@calderdale.gov.uk

Senior Management: Mr Robin Tuddenham, Director - Communities, Westgate House, Halifax HX1 1PS ☎ 01422 393018 🖷 01422 393220 ✉ robin.tuddenham@calderdale.gov.uk

Access Officer / Social Services (Disability): Mr Mick Mellor, Head of Commissioning for Adult Services, Park House, Halifax HX1 2TU ☎ 01422 393864 ✉ mick.mellor@calderdale.gov.uk

Access Officer / Social Services (Disability): Mr Phil Shire, Head of Wellbeing & Social Care, Park Road, Halifax HX1 2TU ☎ 01422 393809 🖷 01422 393815 ✉ phil.shire@calderdale.gov.uk

Architect, Building / Property Services: Mr Dave Higgot, Team Leader - Building Maintenance, Westgate House, Halifax HX1 1PS ☎ 01422 392051 ✉ david.higgot@calderdale.gov.uk

Architect, Building / Property Services: Ms Geraldine Rushton, Disabilities Liaison Officer, Northgate House, Halifax HX1 1UN

☎ 01422 393077 🖷 01422 393136
✉ geraldine.rushton@calderdale.gov.uk

Building Control: Mr Mike Terry, Building Control Manager, Westgate House, Westgate, Halifax HX1 1PS ☎ 01422 392221 🖷 01422 392203 ✉ mike.terry@calderdale.gov.uk

Catering Services: Ms Lyn Plant, Catering Manager, Northgate House, Northgate, Halifax HX1 1UN ☎ 01422 392365 🖷 01422 392369 ✉ lyn.plant@calderdale.gov.uk

Children / Youth Services: Mr David Whalley, Head of Learning, Northgate House, Halifax HX1 1UN ☎ 01422 392716 🖷 01422 392481 ✉ david.whalley@calderdale.gov.uk

Civil Registration: Ms Sarah Richardson, Superintendent Registrar, Spring Hall Mansion, Huddersfield Road, Halifax HX3 0AQ ☎ 01422 284470 🖷 01422 284472 ✉ sarah.richardson@calderdale.gov.uk

PR / Communications: Mr Neil Beecham, Corporate Communications Officer, Westgate House, Westgate, Halifax HX1 1PS ☎ 01422 393100 🖷 01422 393136 ✉ neil.beecham@calderdale.gov.uk

Community Safety: Mr Derek Benn, Community Safety Manager & Resilience Manager, Northgate House, Northgate, Halifax HX1 1UN ☎ 01422 393130 🖷 01422 393183 ✉ derek.benn@calderdale.gov.uk

Computer Management: Mr Peter Hartley, Head of Business Change & Performance, Mulcture House, Mulcture Hall Road, Halifax HX1 1SP ☎ 01422 393400 🖷 01422 393427 ✉ peter.hartley@calderdale.gov.uk

Contracts: Ms Deborah Gaunt, Corporate Procurement Officer, Princess Buildings, Halifax HX1 1TP ☎ 01422 393176 🖷 01422 393526 ✉ deborah.gaunt@calderdale.gov.uk

Contracts: Ms Sian Rees, Head of Children's Trust, Northgate House, Halifax HX1 1UN ☎ 01422 392527 ✉ sian.rees@calderdale.gov.uk

Customer Service: Ms Ann Wardle, Head of Customer Services & Communications, Westgate House, Halifax HX1 1PS ☎ 01422 393201 🖷 01422 393220 ✉ ann.wardle@calderdale.gov.uk

Economic Development: Mr John Hodgson, Business & Economy Team Leader, Northgate House, Halifax HX1 1UN ☎ 01422 392235 🖷 01422 392260 ✉ john.hodgson@calderdale.gov.uk

Education: Ms Fiona Fitzpatrick, Head of Children's Social Care, Northgate House, Halifax HX1 1UN ☎ 01422 392722 ✉ fiona.fitzpatrick@calderdale.gov.uk

Electoral Registration: Ms Linda Clarkson, Principal Electoral Services Officer, Westgate House, Westgate, Halifax HX1 1PS ☎ 01422 393049 🖷 01422 393090 ✉ linda.clarkson@calderdale.gov.uk

Emergency Planning: Ms Amanda Webster, Senior Emergency Planning Advisor, Northgate House, Halifax HX1 1UN ☎ 01422 392870 🖷 01422 392879 ✉ amanda.webster@calderdale.gov.uk

Energy Management: Mr Phil Ratcliffe, Development Strategy Manager, Northgate House, Halifax HX1 1UN ☎ 01422 392255 🖷 01422 392076 ✉ phil.ratcliffe@calderdale.gov.uk

Environmental / Technical Services: Mr Peter Broadbent, Environmental Health Manager, Northgate House, Halifax HX1 1UN ☎ 01422 392345 ✉ peter.broadbent@calderdale.gov.uk

Environmental Health: Mr Peter Broadbent, Environmental Health Manager, Northgate House, Halifax HX1 1UN ☎ 01422 392345 ✉ peter.broadbent@calderdale.gov.uk

Estates, Property & Valuation: Mr Paul Fleming, Acting Land & Property Manager, Westgate House, Westgate, Halifax HX1 1PS ☎ 01422 392070 🖷 01422 392059 ✉ paul.fleming@calderdale.gov.uk

Events Manager: Mr Peter Vardy, Recreation Officer - Licensing & Events, The Piece Hall, Halifax HX1 1RE ☎ 01422 384796 ✉ peter.vardy@calderdale.gov.uk

Facilities: Ms Donna Bamforth, Facilities Manager, Westgate House, Westgate, Halifax HX1 1PX ☎ 01422 393027 🖷 01422 393073 ✉ donna.bamforth@alderdale.gov.uk

Finance and Treasurer: Mr Nigel Broadbent, Assistant Chief Finance Officer, Princess Buildings, Halifax HX1 1TP ☎ 01422 393872 ✉ nigel.broadbent@calderdale.gov.uk

Finance and Treasurer: Mr Pete Smith, Head of Finance, PO Box 51, Princess Buildings, Halifax HX1 1TP ☎ 01422 393535 🖷 01422 393533 ✉ pete.smith@calderdale.gov.uk

Fleet Management: Mr Paul Topham, Transport Manager, Regeneration and Development Directorate, Battinson Road Depot, Queen's Road, Halifax HX1 4PL ☎ ; 01422 264350 🖷 01422 264357 ✉ paul.topham@calderdale.gov.uk

Grounds Maintenance: Mr Andrew Pitts, Acting Head of Neighbourhoods & Community Engagement, Northgate House, Halifax HX1 1UN ☎ 01422 393264 ✉ andrew.pitts@calderdale.gov.uk

Health and Safety: Mr Martin Allingham, Principal Health & Safety Adviser, Northgate House, Halifax HX1 1UN ☎ 01422 393080 🖷 01422 353635 ✉ martin.allingham@calderdale.gov.uk

Highways: Ms Carolyn Walton, Highway Network Manager, Northgate House, Halifax HX1 1UN ☎ 01422 392167 ✉ carolyn.walton@calderdale.gov.uk

Home Energy Conservation: Mr David Parkin, Private Sector Housing Officer, Northgate House, Halifax HX1 1UN ☎ 01422 392585 🖷 ; 01422 392469 ✉ david.parkin@calderdale.gov.uk

Housing: Mr Mark Thompson, Head of Housing & Environment, Northgate House, Northgate, Halifax HX1 1UN ☎ 01422 392435 🖷 01422 392466 ✉ mark.thompson@calderdale.gov.uk

Housing Maintenance: Mr Mark Thompson, Head of Housing & Environment, Northgate House, Northgate, Halifax HX1 1UN ☎ 01422 392435 🖷 01422 392466 ✉ mark.thompson@calderdale.gov.uk

Local Area Agreement: Mr Alan Duncan, LSP & Partnerships Manager, Northgate House, Halifax HX1 1UN ☎ 01422 392207 ✉ alan.duncan@calderdale.gov.uk

Legal: Mr Ian Hughes, Head of Democratic & Partnership Services, Westgate House, Westgate, Halifax HX1 1PS ☎ 01422 393063 🖷 01422 393073 ✉ ian.hughes@calderdale.gov.uk

Leisure and Cultural Services: Mr Gary Borrows, Head of Cultural Services, Central Library, Northgate, Halifax HX1 1UN ☎ 01422 392600 🖷 01422 393220 ✉ gary.borrows@calderdale.gov.uk

Licensing: Ms Sarah Richardson, Registration & Licensing Services Manager, Westgate House, Westgate, Halifax HX1 1PS ☎ 01422 393043 🖷 01422 392147 ✉ sarah.richardson@calderdale.gov.uk

Lifelong Learning: Ms Eileen Fawcett, Head of Calderdale Adult Learning, Horton House, Horton Street, Halifax HX1 1PU ☎ 01422 392829 🖷 01422 392821 ✉ eileen.fawcett@calderdale.gov.uk

Lighting: Mr David Newton, Group Engineer (Works), Engineering Services, Huddersfield Road, Elland HX5 9JR ☎ 01422 392946 🖷 01422 392965 ✉ david.newton@calderdale.gov.uk

Lottery Funding, Charity and Voluntary: Ms Sarah Manfredi, Locality & Commissioning Manager, Westgate House, Westgate, Halifax HX1 1PS ☎ 01422 393271 ✉ sarah.manfredi@calderdale.gov.uk

Member Services: Mr Peter Burton, Democratic Services Manager, Town Hall, Halifax HX1 1UJ ☎ 01422 393011 🖷 01422 393073 ✉ peter.burton@calderdale.gov.uk

Parking: Ms Debbie Calcott, Parking Services Manager, Multure House, Halifax HX1 1SP ☎ 01422 392158 🖷 01422 392191 ✉ debbie.calcott@calderdale.gov.uk

Partnerships: Mr Andrew Pitts, Acting Head of Neighbourhoods & Community Engagement, Northgate House, Halifax HX1 1UN ☎ 01422 393264 ✉ andrew.pitts@calderdale.gov.uk

Personnel / HR: Mr John Walsh, Head of Human Resources, 3rd Floor, G Mill, Dean Clough, HX3 5AX ☎ 01422 288300 🖷 01422 288306 ✉ john.walsh@calderdale.gov.uk

Planning: Mr Geoff Willerton, Head of Planning & Highways, Northgate House, Halifax HX1 1UN ☎ 01422 392242 🖷 01422 392205 ✉ geoff.willerton@calderdale.gov.uk

Procurement: Ms Deborah Gaunt, Corporate Procurement Officer, Westgate House, Halifax HX1 1PS ☎ 01422 393176 🖷 01422 393526 ✉ deborah.gaunt@calderdale.gov.uk

Public Libraries: Mr Gary Borrows, Head of Cultural Services, Central Library, Northgate, Halifax HX1 1UN ☎ 01422 392600 🖷 01422 393220 ✉ gary.borrows@calderdale.gov.uk

Recycling & Waste Minimisation: Ms Heidi Wilson, Acting Waste Manager, Northgate House, Halifax HX1 1UN ☎ 01422 392406 🖷 01422 392399 ✉ heidi.wilson@calderdale.gov.uk

Regeneration: Mr David Moore, Head of Regeneration, Westgate House, Westgate, Halifax HX1 1PS ☎ 01422 392001 🖷 01422 392059 ✉ david.moore@calderdale.gov.uk

Road Safety: Ms Carolyn Walton, Highway Network Manager, Northgate House, Halifax HX1 1UN ☎ 01422 392167 ✉ carolyn.walton@calderdale.gov.uk

Social Services: Ms Fiona Fitzpatrick, Head of Children's Social Care, Northgate House, Halifax HX1 1UN ☎ 01422 392722 ✉ fiona.fitzpatrick@calderdale.gov.uk

Social Services: Ms Anne Scarborough, Head of Family Support, Northgate House, Halifax HX1 1UN ☎ 01422 392663 🖷 01422 392481 ✉ anne.scarborough@calderdale.gov.uk

Social Services: Mr Phil Shire, Head of Wellbeing & Social Care, Park Road, Halifax HX1 2TU ☎ 01422 393809 🖷 01422 393815 ✉ phil.shire@calderdale.gov.uk

Social Services (Children): Mr Stuart Smith, Director - Children & Young People, Northgate House, Halifax HX1 1UN ☎ 01422 392500 🖷 01422 392481 ✉ stuart.smith@calderdale.gov.uk

Staff Training: Mr Chris Nicholson, OD Projects Manager, 3 rd Floor, G Mill, Dean Clough, Halifax HX3 5AX ☎ 01422 288385 🖷 01422 288306 ✉ chris.nicholson@calderdale.gov.uk

Street Scene: Ms Amanda Firth, Acting Safer, Cleaner, Greener Manager, Spring Hall Mansion, Spring Hall, Halifax HX3 0AQ ☎ 01422 284441 🖷 01422 284421 ✉ amanda.firth@calderdale.gov.uk

Sustainable Communities: Mr Phil Ratcliffe, Development Strategy Manager, Northgate House, Halifax HX1 1UN ☎ 01422 392255 🖷 01422 392076 ✉ phil.ratcliffe@calderdale.gov.uk

Tourism: Ms Katie Kinsella, Tourism Manager, Westgate House, Halifax HX1 1PS ☎ 01422 392293 🖷 01422 393220 ✉ katie.kinsella@calderdale.gov.uk

Town Centre: Ms Michay Matthews, Town Centre Manager, The Town Centre Manager's Office, Second Floor, 4 Albion Street, Halifax HX1 1DU ☎ 01422 360035 🖷 01422 322960 ✉ enquiries@halifaxuk.co.uk

Traffic Management: Ms Carolyn Walton, Highway Network Manager, Northgate House, Halifax HX1 1UN ☎ 01422 392167 ✉ carolyn.walton@calderdale.gov.uk

Transport: Mr Paul Topham, Transport Manager, Regeneration and Development Directorate, Battinson Road Depot, Queen's Road, Halifax HX1 4PL ☎ ; 01422 264350 🖷 ; 01422 264357 ✉ paul.topham@calderdale.gov.uk

Transport Planner: Mr Paul Topham, Transport Manager, Regeneration and Development Directorate, Battinson Road Depot, Queen's Road, Halifax HX1 4PL ☎ 01422 264350 🖷 01422 264357 ✉ paul.topham@calderdale.gov.uk

Waste Collection and Disposal: Ms Heidi Wilson, Acting Waste Manager, Northgate House, Halifax HX1 1UN ☎ 01422 392406 🖷 01422 392399 ✉ heidi.wilson@calderdale.gov.uk

Waste Management: Ms Heidi Wilson, Acting Waste Manager, Northgate House, Halifax HX1 1UN ☎ 01422 392406 🖷 01422 392399 ✉ heidi.wilson@calderdale.gov.uk

Children's Play Areas: Ms Amanda Firth, Acting Safer, Cleaner, Greener Manager, Spring Hall Mansion, Spring Hall, Halifax HX3 0AQ ☎ 01422 284441 🖷 01422 284421 ✉ amanda.firth@calderdale.gov.uk

MEMBERS OF THE COUNCIL (50)

***Mayor:* Hardy**, John (CON - Skircoat)
councillor.jhardy@calderdale.gov.uk
***Deputy Mayor:* Beal**, Christine (CON - Rastrick)
councillor.cbeal@calderdale.gov.uk
***Leader of the Council:* Swift**, Tim (LAB - Town)
councillor.tswift@calderdale.gov.uk
***Deputy Leader of the Council:* Battye**, Janet (LD - Calder)
councillor.jbattye@calderdale.gov.uk
***Group Leader:* Baines**, Stephen (CON - Northowram & Shelf)
councillor.sbaines@calderdale.gov.uk
***Group Leader:* Stout**, Colin (IND - Brighouse)
councillor.cstout@calderdale.gov.uk
Ali, Ferman (LAB - Park)
councillor.fali@calderdale.gov.uk
Allen, Patricia (LD - Elland)
councillor.pallen@calderdale.gov.uk
Barret, Kay (CON - Ryburn)
councillor.kbarret@calderdale.gov.uk
Beacroft-Mitchell, John (LD - Luddendenfoot)
councillor.jbeacroft-mitchell@calderdale.gov.uk
Benton, Scott (CON - Brighouse)
councillor.sbenton@calderdale.gov.uk
Booth, Jayne (LAB - Todmorden)
councillor.jbooth@calderdale.gov.uk
Burton, Martin (LAB - Warley)
councillor.mburton@calderdale.gov.uk
Caffrey, Peter (CON - Northowram & Shelf)
councillor.pcaffrey@calderdale.gov.uk
Carter, Geraldine (CON - Ryburn)
councillor.gcarter@calderdale.gov.uk
Collins, Anne (LAB - Ovenden)
councillor.acollins@calderdale.gov.uk
Collins, Barry (LAB - Illingworth & Mixenden)
councillor.bcollins@calderdale.gov.uk
Draycott, David (LAB - Sowerby Bridge)
councillor.ddraycott@calderdale.gov.uk
Evans, Ashley (LD - Warley)
councillor.aevans@calderdale.gov.uk
Fekri, Nader (LD - Calder)
naderfekri@hotmail.com
Ford, John (CON - Elland)
councillor.jford@calderdale.gov.uk
Goldthorpe, Ruth (LD - Todmorden)
councillor.rgoldthorpe@calderdale.gov.uk
Hall, Graham (CON - Hipperholme & Lightcliffe)
councillor.ghall@calderdale.gov.uk
Hardy, David (LD - Elland)
councillor.dhardy@calderdale.gov.uk
James, Malcolm (LD - Greetland & Stainland)
councillor.mjames@calderdale.gov.uk
Kirton, David (CON - Hipperholme & Lightcliffe)
councillor.dkirton@calderdale.gov.uk
Lambert, Lisa (LAB - Illingworth & Mixenden)
councillor.llambert@calderdale.gov.uk
Lynn, Jenny (LAB - Park)
councillor.jlynn@calderdale.gov.uk
Marshall, Richard (CON - Luddendenfoot)
councillor.rmarshall@calderdale.gov.uk
Martin, Ann (LAB - Brighouse)
councillor.amartin@calderdale.gov.uk
McAllister, Ann (CON - Rastrick)
councillor.amcallister@calderdale.gov.uk
Metcalfe, Bob (LAB - Town)
councillor.bmetcalfe@calderdale.gov.uk
Nash, Pauline (LD - Skircoat)
councillor.pnash@calderdale.gov.uk
Peel, Martin (CON - Sowerby Bridge)
councillor.mpeel@calderdale.gov.uk
Pillai, Chris (CON - Rastrick)
Raistrick, Colin (IND - Hipperholme & Lightcliffe)
councillor.craistrick@calderdale.gov.uk
Rivron, Helen (LAB - Ovenden)
councillor.hrivron@calderdale.gov.uk
Shoukat, Faisal (LAB - Park)
councillor.fshoukat@calderdale.gov.uk
Smith, Bryan (LAB - Ovenden)
councillor.bsmith@calderdale.gov.uk
Sutherland, Daniel (LAB - Illingworth & Mixenden)
councillor.dsutherland@calderdale.gov.uk
Sweeney, Steve (LAB - Todmorden)
councillor.ssweeney@calderdale.gov.uk
Swift, Megan (LAB - Town)
councillor.mswift@calderdale.gov.uk
Taylor, Roger (CON - Northowram & Shelf)
coun.rogertaylor@btinternet.com
Thompson, Marcus (CON - Skircoat)
councillor.mthompson@calderdale.gov.uk
Thornber, Robert (CON - Ryburn)
councillor.rthornber@calderdale.gov.uk
Wardhaugh, Peter (LD - Greetland & Stainland)
councillor.pwardhaugh@calderdale.gov.uk
Wilkinson, Adam (LAB - Sowerby Bridge)
councillor.awilkinson@calderdale.gov.uk
Winterburn, Conrad (LD - Greetland & Stainland)
councillor.cwinterburn@calderdale.gov.uk
Young, Dave (LAB - Calder)
councillor.dyoung@calderdale.gov.uk
Young, Simon (LAB - Luddendenfoot)
email@simonyoung.info

POLITICAL COMPOSITION

LAB: 20, CON: 17, LD: 11, IND: 2

CABINET

Leader: Mr Tim Swift
Deputy Leader: Ms Janet Battye
Adults, Health & Social Care: Mr Bob Metcalfe
Children's Social Care: Ms Megan Swift
Communities: Ms Pauline Nash

Economy & Environment: Mr Barry Collins
Education & Lifelong Learning: Mr Ashley Evans
Performance & Resources: Mr Bryan Smith

COMMITTEE CHAIRS

Adults, Health & Social Care: Mrs Ruth Goldthorpe
Appeals: Mr David Hardy
Audit: Mr Peter Wardhaugh
Children & Young People Scrutiny: Mr Colin Raistrick
Communities Scrutiny: Ms Helen Rivron
Economy & Environment Scrutiny: Mr David Hardy
Employment: Mr Tim Swift
Governance & Business: Mr John Beacroft-Mitchell
Licensing & Regulatory: Mr Simon Young
Planning: Mr Daniel Sutherland
Use of Resources: Mr John Beacroft-Mitchell

CAMBRIDGE CITY D

Cambridge City Council, Lion House, Lion Yard, Cambridge CB2 3NA ☎ 01223 457000 🖷 01223 457009 💻 www.cambridge.gov.uk

FACTS & FIGURES

Police Authority: Cambridgeshire Police Authority
Health Authority: East of England Strategic Health Authority
Learning and Skills Council: Eastern
Parliamentary Constituencies: Cambridge, Cambridgeshire South
EU Constituencies: Eastern
Election Frequency: Elections are by thirds
Twinning: Heidelberg (Germany); Szeged (Hungary)

PRINCIPAL OFFICERS

Chief Executive: Ms Antoinette Jackson, Chief Executive, The Guildhall, Cambridge CB2 3QJ ☎ 01223 457003 🖷 01223 457009 ✉ antoinette.jackson@cambridge.gov.uk

Senior Management: Ms Liz Bisset, Director of Customer & Community Services, Hobson House, 44 St. Andrew's Street, Cambridge CB2 3AS ☎ 01223 457801 ✉ liz.bisset@cambridge.gov.uk

Senior Management: Mr David Horspool, Director of Resources, The Guildhall, Cambridge CB2 3QJ ☎ 01223 457007 ✉ david.horspool@cambridge.gov.uk

Senior Management: Mr Simon Payne, Director of Environment, Mill Road Depot, Mill Road, Cambridge CB1 2AZ ☎ 01223 458517; 🖷 01223 458249 ✉ simon.payne@cambridge.gov.uk

Access Officer / Social Services (Disability): Mr Mark Taylor, Disability Access Officer, The Guildhall, Cambridge CB2 3QJ ☎ 01223 457075 🖷 01223 457379 ✉ mark.taylor@cambridge.gov.uk

Architect, Building / Property Services: Mr Jim Stocker, Technical Services Manager, The Guildhall, Cambridge CB2 3QJ ☎ 01223 457351 🖷 01223 457359 ✉ jim.stocker@cambridge.gov.uk

Building Control: Mr Ian Boulton, Building Control Manager, The Guildhall, Cambridge CB2 3QJ ☎ 01223 457111 🖷 01223 457109 ✉ ian.boulton@cambridge.gov.uk

PR / Communications: Mr Ashley Perry, Corporate Marketing Manager, The Guildhall, Cambridge CB2 3QJ ☎ 01223 457064 🖷 01223 457009 ✉ ashley.perry@cambridge.gov.uk

Community Safety: Ms Lynda Kilkelly, Community Safety Manager, Hobson House, 44 St. Andrew's Street, Cambridge CB2 3AS ☎ 01223 457045 🖷 01223 457009 ✉ lynda.kilkelly@cambridge.gov.uk

Computer Management: Mr James Nightingale, Head of ICT Client Services, The Guildhall, Cambridge CB2 3QJ ☎ 01223 457461 🖷 01223 558501 ✉ james.nightingale@cambridge.gov.uk

Corporate Services: Mr Steve Crabtree, Head of Internal Audit, Lion House, Lion Yard, Cambridge CB2 3NA ☎ 01223 458181; 01223 458181 ✉ steve.crabtree@cambridge.gov.uk

Corporate Services: Mr Andrew Limb, Head of Corporate Strategy, The Guildhall, Cambridge CB2 3QJ ☎ 01223 457004 🖷 01223 457009 ✉ andrew.limb@cambridge.gov.uk

Customer Service: Mr Jonathan James, Head of Customer Services, Mandela House, 4 Regent Street, Cambridge CB2 1BY ☎ 01223 458601 ✉ jonathan.james@cambridge.gov.uk

Direct Labour: Mrs Toni Ainley, Head of Streets & Open Spaces, Mill Road Depot, Mill Road, Cambridge CB1 2AZ ☎ 01223 458201 🖷 01223 458249 ✉ toni.ainley@cambridge.gov.uk

Economic Development: Mr Simon Payne, Director of Environment, Mill Road Depot, Cambridge CB1 2AZ ☎ 01223 458517; 🖷 01223 458249 ✉ simon.payne@cambridge.gov.uk

Electoral Registration: Ms Vicky Breading, Electoral Services Manager, The Guildhall, Cambridge CB2 3QJ ☎ 01223 457057 🖷 01223 457079 ✉ vicky.breading@cambridge.gov.uk

Emergency Planning: Ms Antoinette Jackson, Chief Executive, The Guildhall, Cambridge CB2 3QJ ☎ 01223 457003 🖷 01223 457009 ✉ antoinette.jackson@cambridge.gov.uk

Energy Management: Mr Jim Stocker, Technical Services Manager, The Guildhall, Cambridge CB2 3QJ ☎ 01223 457351 🖷 01223 457359 ✉ jim.stocker@cambridge.gov.uk

Environmental Health: Mr Jas Lally, Head of Refuse & Environment, Mill Road Depot, Mill Road, Cambridge CB1 2AZ ☎ 01223 458572 ✉ jas.lally@cambridge.gov.uk

Finance and Treasurer: Mr John Frost, Head of Revenues, Mandela House, 4 Regent Street, Cambridge CB2 1BY ☎ 01223 457701 🖷 01223 457709 ✉ john.frost@cambridge.gov.uk

Finance and Treasurer: Mr David Horspool, Director of Resources, The Guildhall, Cambridge CB2 3QJ ☎ 01223 457007 ✉ david.horspool@cambridge.gov.uk

Finance and Treasurer: Ms Julia Minns, Head of Accountancy & Support Services, Lion House, Lion Yard, Cambridge CB2 3NA ☎ 01223 458134 🖷 01223 458129

julia.minns@cambridge.gov.uk

Fleet Management: Mr David Cox, Fleet Manager, Mill Road Depot, Mill Road, Cambridge CB1 2AZ ☎ 01223 458265 🖷 01223 458249 david.cox@cambridge.gov.uk

Grounds Maintenance: Mrs Toni Ainley, Head of Streets & Open Spaces, Mill Road Depot, Mill Road, Cambridge CB1 2AZ ☎ 01223 458201 🖷 01223 458249 toni.ainley@cambridge.gov.uk

Health and Safety: Mr Paul Parry, Health & Safety Manager, Mill Road Depot, Mill Road, Cambridge CB1 2AZ ☎ 01223 458033 🖷 01223 458249 paul.parry@cambridge.gov.uk

Home Energy Conservation: Mr Bob Hadfield, Head of Repairs & Maintenance, Mill Road Depot, Mill Road, Cambridge CB1 2AZ ☎ 01223 457831 🖷 01223 457979 bob.hadfield@cambridge.gov.uk

Housing: Ms Liz Bisset, Director of Customer & Community Services, Hobson House, 44 St. Andrew's Street, Cambridge CB2 3AS ☎ 01223 457801 liz.bisset@cambridge.gov.uk

Housing: Mr Robert Hollingsworth, Head of City Homes, City Homes North, 171 Arbury Road, Cambridge CB4 2YG ☎ 01223 458401 robert.hollingsworth@cambridge.gov.uk

Housing Maintenance: Mr Bob Hadfield, Head of Repairs & Maintenance, Mill Road Depot, Mill Road, Cambridge CB1 2AZ ☎ 01223 457831 🖷 01223 457979 bob.hadfield@cambridge.gov.uk

Legal: Mr Simon Pugh, Head of Legal Services, The Guildhall, Cambridge CB2 3QJ ☎ 01223 457401 🖷 01223 457409 simon.pugh@cambridge.gov.uk

Leisure and Cultural Services: Ms Debbie Kaye, Head of Arts & Recreation, Hobson House, 44 St Andrew's Street, Cambridge CB2 3AS ☎ 01223 458633 🖷 01223 457539 debbie.kaye@cambridge.gov.uk

Licensing: Mr Jas Lally, Head of Refuse & Environment, Mill Road Depot, Mill Road, Cambridge CB1 2AZ ☎ 01223 457881 🖷 01223 457909 jas.lally@cambridge.gov.uk

Lottery Funding, Charity and Voluntary: Mr Trevor Woollams, Head of Community Development, Mandela House, 4 Regent Street, Cambridge CB2 1BY ☎ 01223 457861 🖷 01223 457869 trevor.woollams@cambridge.gov.uk

Member Services: Mr Gary Clift, Head of Democratic Services, The Guildhall, Cambridge CB2 3QJ ☎ 01223 457011 gary.clift@cambridge.gov.uk

Member Services: Mr Alexander Finlayson, Administration Support Officer, The Guildhall, Cambridge CB2 3QJ ☎ 01223 457022 🖷 01223 457029 alexander.finlayson@cambridge.gov.uk

Parking: Mr Paul Necus, Head of Specialist Services, Mill Road Depot, Mill Road, Cambridge CB1 2AZ ☎ 01223 458510 paul.necus@cambridge.gov.uk

Personnel / HR: Ms Deborah Simpson, Head of Human Resources, Lion House, Lion Yard, Cambridge CB2 3NA ☎ 01223 458101 🖷 01223 458109 deborah.simpson@cambridge.gov.uk

Planning: Ms Patsy Dell, Head of Planning, The Guildhall, Cambridge CB2 3QJ ☎ 01223 457103 🖷 01223 457109 patsy.dell@cambridge.gov.uk

Procurement: Ms Debbie Quincey, Strategic Procurement Advisor, Lion House, Lion Yard, Cambridge CB2 3NA ☎ 01223 457400 🖷 01223 458129 debbie.quincey@cambridge.gov.uk

Recycling & Waste Minimisation: Ms Jen Robertson, Waste & Street Services Strategy Manager, Mill Road Depot, Mill Road, Cambridge CB1 2AZ ☎ 01223 458225 jen.robertson@cambridge.gov.uk

Staff Training: Ms Deborah Simpson, Head of Human Resources, Lion House, Lion Yard, Cambridge CB2 3NA ☎ 01223 458101 🖷 01223 458109 deborah.simpson@cambridge.gov.uk

Street Scene: Mrs Toni Ainley, Head of Streets & Open Spaces, Mill Road Depot, Mill Road, Cambridge CB1 2AZ ☎ 01223 458201 🖷 01223 458249 toni.ainley@cambridge.gov.uk

Tourism: Mrs Emma Thornton, Head of Tourism & City Centre Management, The Guildhall, Cambridge CB2 3QJ ☎ 01223 457464 emma.thornton@cambridge.gov.uk

Town Centre: Mrs Emma Thornton, Head of Tourism & City Centre Management, The Guildhall, Cambridge CB2 3QJ ☎ 01223 457464 emma.thornton@cambridge.gov.uk

Waste Collection and Disposal: Mr Jas Lally, Head of Refuse & Environment, Mill Road Depot, Mill Road, Cambridge CB1 2AZ ☎ 01223 458572 jas.lally@cambridge.gov.uk

Waste Management: Mr Jas Lally, Head of Environmental Services, Mill Road Depot, Mill Road, Cambridge CB1 2AZ ☎ 01223 458572 jas.lally@cambridge.gov.uk

MEMBERS OF THE COUNCIL (42)

***Mayor:* Stuart**, Sheila (LD - Trumpington)
sheilastuart17@gmail.com

***Deputy Mayor:* Saunders**, Paul (LD - Romsey)
lo_maximo@hotmail.com

***Leader of the Council:* Bick**, Tim (LD - Market)
tim.bick@btinternet.com

***Group Leader:* Hipkin**, John (IND - Castle)
castleindependent@gmail.com

Abbott, Margery (LAB - East Chesterton)
margery.abbott.labour@hotmail.co.uk

Ashton, Mark (LAB - Cherry Hinton)
mark.ashton@cambridge.gov.uk

Benstead, Jeremy (LAB - Coleridge)
j_benstead@live.co.uk

Bird, Gerri (LAB - East Chesterton)
gerribird@sky.com

Birtles, Sue (LAB - Queen Edith's)
sue.birtles@cambridge.gov.uk
Blackhurst, Andrew (LD - Trumpington)
andy.blackhurst@cambridge.gov.uk
Blencowe, Kevein (LAB - Petersfield)
kevin.blencowe@gmail.com
Boyce, Max (LD - West Chesterton)
maxboyce@cix.co.uk
Brierley, Simon (LD - Kings Hedges)
simon.brierley1@googlemail.com
Brown, Sarah (LD - Petersfield)
sarah.brown@cambridge.gov.uk
Cantrill, Rod (LD - Newnham)
rcantrill@millingtonadvisory.com
Dryden, Robert (LAB - Cherry Hinton)
robert.dryden@cambridge.gov.uk
Gawthrope, Nigel (LAB - Kings Hedges)
nigel.gawthrope@cambridge.gov.uk
Hart, Caroline (LAB - Abbey)
caroline.hart@cambridge.gov.uk
Herbert, Lewis (LAB - Coleridge)
lewis.herbert@cambridge.gov.uk
Johnson, Richard (LAB - Abbey)
richard.johnston@cambridge.gov.uk
Kerr, Susannah (LD - East Chesterton)
susannahfkerr@gmail.com
Kightley, Simon (LD - Castle)
simon.kightley@googlemail.com
Marchant-Daisley, Gail (LAB - Petersfield)
gail.marchant-daisley@cambridge.gov.uk
McPherson, Russell (LAB - Cherry Hinton)
russ.mcpherson@cambridge.gov.uk
Meftah, Shapour (CON - Trumpington)
shapour.meftah@cambridge.gov.uk
Moghadas, Zoe (LAB - Romsey)
zoe.moghadas@cambridge.gov.uk
O'Reilly, Carina (LAB - Arbury)
carinaoreilly@gmail.com
Owers, George (LAB - Coleridge)
george.owers@cambridge.gov.uk
Pippas, George (LD - Queen Edith's)
george.pippas@cambridge.gov.uk
Pitt, Mike (LD - West Chesterton)
mike@einval.com
Pogonowski, Adam (LAB - Abbey)
aepogonowski@gmail.com
Price, Kevin (LAB - Kings Hedges)
kevin.price@cambridge.gov.uk
Reid, Sian (LD - Newnham)
sianreid27@gmail.com
Reiner, Andrea (LD - Market)
andreareiner23@gmail.com
Rosenstiel, Colin (LD - Market)
rosenstiel@cix.co.uk
Smart, Catherine (LD - Romsey)
chlsmart@cix.co.uk
Smith, Julie (LD - Newnham)
julie.smith@cambridge.gov.uk
Swanson, Jean (LD - Queen Edith's)
jsswanson@ntlworld.com
Todd-Jones, Mike (LAB - Arbury)
mike.todd-jones@cambridge.gov.uk
Tucker, Philip (LD - Castle)
tuckerphilipa@btinternet.com
Tunnacliffe, Damien (LD - West Chesterton)
damientunnacliffe@yahoo.gov.uk
Ward, Tim (LD - Arbury)
tim@brettward.co.uk

POLITICAL COMPOSITION
LD: 21, LAB: 19, CON: 1, IND: 1

CABINET
Leader: Mr Tim Bick
Arts, Sports & Public Places: Mr Rod Cantrill
Community Development & Health: Mr Mike Pitt
Customer Services & Resources: Ms Julie Smith
Housing: Ms Catherine Smart

COMMITTEE CHAIRS
Civic Affairs: Mr Max Boyce
Community Services (Scrutiny): Ms Susannah Kerr
Environment (Scrutiny): Mr Simon Kightley
Housing Management Board: Mr Andrew Blackhurst
Licensing: Mr Colin Rosenstiel
Planning: Ms Sheila Stuart
Strategy & Resources (Scrutiny): Ms Sarah Brown

CAMBRIDGESHIRE C

Cambridgeshire County Council, Box ET 1021, Castle Court, Shire Hall, Castle Hill, Cambridge CB3 0AP ☎ 0345 045 5200
🖷 01223 717201 info@cambridgeshire.gov.uk
💻 www.cambridgeshire.gov.uk

FACTS & FIGURES
Police Authority: Cambridgeshire Police Authority
Health Authority: East of England Strategic Health Authority
Learning and Skills Council: Eastern
Parliamentary Constituencies: Huntingdon
EU Constituencies: Eastern
Election Frequency: Elections are of whole council
Twinning: Kreis Viersen (Germany)

PRINCIPAL OFFICERS
Chief Executive: Mr Mark Lloyd, Chief Executive, Box RES 1109, Shire Hall, Castle Hill, Cambridge CB3 0AP ☎ 01223 699188 🖷 01223 669188 mark.lloyd@cambridgeshire.gov.uk

Senior Management: Mr Nick Dawe, Corporate Director: Finance, Box RES 1006, Shire Hall, Castle Hill, Cambridge CB3 0AP ☎ 01223 699236 nick.dawe@cambridgeshire.gov.uk

Senior Management: Ms Pat Harding, Corporate Director: Customer Service & Transformation, Box CC 1306, Shire Hall, Castle Hill, Cambridge CB3 0AP ☎ 01223 699247 🖷 01223 699248 pat.harding@cambridgeshire.gov.uk

Senior Management: Mr Adrian Loades, Executive Director - Children & Young People's Services & Adult Social Care, CC 1001, Castle Court, Shire Hall, Cambridge CB3 0AP ☎ 01223 727993 adrian.loades@cambridgeshire.gov.uk

Senior Management: Mr Alex Plant, Executive Director - Environment Services, Box ET 1021, Castle Court, Shire Hall, Castle Hill, Cambridge CB3 0AP ☎ 01223 715660 alex.plant@cambridgeshire.gov.uk

Senior Management: Ms Christine Reed, Director of HR & OD, RES 1006, Shire Hall, Castle Hill, Cambridge CB3 0AP ☎ 01223 699246 ✉ christine.reed@cambridgeshire.gov.uk

Access Officer / Social Services (Disability): Mr Geoff Sherlock, Interim Service Director of Opperations, CC 1315, Castle Court, Shire Hall, Castle Hill, Cambridge CB3 0AP ☎ 01223 715672 ✉ geoff.sherlock@cambridgeshire.gov.uk

Architect, Building / Property Services: Mr Steve Alderton, Head of Property Commissioning, RES 1301, Shire Hall, Castle Hill, Cambridge CB3 0AP ☎ 01223 699072 ✉ steve.alderton@cambridgeshire.gov.uk

Architect, Building / Property Services: Mr Nick Dawe, Corporate Director: Finance, Box Res 1101, Castle Court, Shire Hall, Castle Hill, Cambridge CB3 0AP ☎ 01223 699236 ✉ nick.dawe@cambridgeshire.gov.uk

Best Value: Mr Simon Willson, Head of Regulation, Performance & Business Support, CC 1221, Shire Hall, Castle Hill, Cambridge CB3 0AP ☎ 01223 699162 ✉ simon.willson@cambridgeshire.gov.uk

Catering Services: Mr Andrew Carter, Contracts Catering Manager, Box ET 1021, Castle Court, Shire Hall, Castle Hill, Cambridge CB3 0AP ☎ ; 01354 750030 ✉ andrew.carter@cambridgeshire.gov.uk

Catering Services: Mr Richard Ware, Head of Catering & Cleaning Services, CC 1105, Castle Court, Shire Hall, Castle Hill, Cambridge CB3 0AP ☎ 01223 703509 ✉ richard.ware@cambridgeshire.gov.uk

Children / Youth Services: Ms Charlotte Black, Service Director: Children's Enhanced & Preventative Services, CC 1001, Castle Court, Shire Hall, Cambridge CB3 0AP ☎ 01223 727990 ✉ charlotte.black@cambridgeshire.gov.uk

Children / Youth Services: Ms Nicola Clemo, Director: Social Care, Children & Young People Services, CC 1001, Castle Court, Shire Hall, Cambridge CB3 0AP ☎ 01223 727989 🖷 01223 717307 ✉ nicola.clemo@cambridgeshire.gov.uk

Children / Youth Services: Ms Gayle Gorman, Service Director of Learning, CC 1001, Castle Court, Shire Hall, Cambridge CB3 0AP ☎ 01223 727988

Children / Youth Services: Mr Adrian Loades, Executive Director - Children & Young People's Services & Adult Social Care, CC 1001, Castle Court, Shire Hall, Cambridge CB3 0AP ☎ 01223 727993 ✉ adrian.loades@cambridgeshire.gov.uk

Civil Registration: Mr Jim Milne, Head of Registration & Coroners Service, IC/9A3, Huntingdon, Cambridge PE29 3PA ☎ 01223 715364 ✉ jim.milne@cambridgeshire.gov.uk

PR / Communications: Mr Mark Miller, Interim Head of Communications, Box RES 1101, Shire Hall, Castle Hill, Cambridge CB3 0AP ☎ 01223 699283 ✉ mark.miller@cambridgeshire.gov.uk

Community Planning: Mr Joseph Whelan, Head of Passenger Transport, CC 1212, Castle Court, Shire Hall, Castle Hill, Cambridge CB3 0AP ☎ 01223 715585 ✉ joseph.whelan@cambridgeshire.gov.uk

Community Safety: Mr Mike Davey, Service Director: Community Engagement Fenland, Fenland District Council, Fenland Hall, County Road, March PE15 8NQ ☎ 01223 699921 ✉ mike.davey@cambridgeshire.gov.uk

Community Safety: Dr Liz Robin, Director of Public Health, NHS Cambridgeshire Lockton House, Clarendon Road, Cambridge CB2 8FH ☎ 01223 725299 ✉ liz.robin@cambridgeshire.gov.uk

Computer Management: Ms Noelle Godfrey, Head of Information Technology, RES 1406, Babbage House, Shire Hall, Castle Hill, Cambridge CB3 0AP ☎ 01223 699011 ✉ noelle.godfrey@cambridgeshire.gov.uk

Consumer Protection and Trading Standards: Mr Leon Livermore, Head of Trading Standards, Box ET 4000, Sackville House, Sackville Way, Great Cambourne, Cambridge CB3 0AP ☎ 01954 284647 ✉ leon.livermore@cambridgeshire.gov.uk

Contracts: Mr Paul Rouse, Head of Procurement & Major ICT Projects, RES 1406, Babbage House, Shire Hall, Castle Hill, Cambridge CB3 0AP ☎ 01223 699153 ✉ paul.rouse@cambridgeshire.gov.uk

Corporate Services: Ms Christine Reed, Director of HR & OD, RES 1006, Shire Hall, Castle Hill, Cambridge CB3 0AP ☎ 01223 699246 ✉ christine.reed@cambridgeshire.gov.uk

Customer Service: Ms Pat Harding, Corporate Director: Customer Service & Transformation, Box CC 1306, Castle Court, Shire Hill, Castle Hall, Cambridge CB3 0AP ☎ 01223 699247 🖷 01223 699248 ✉ pat.harding@cambridgeshire.gov.uk

Customer Service: Ms Joanna Leung, Head of Service Transformation, RES 1405, Shire Hall, Castle Hill, Cambridge CB3 0AP ☎ 01223 699702 ✉ joanna.leung@cambridgeshire.gov.uk

Economic Development: Mr Guy Mills, Economic Development Manager, Economic Development Section, Box Res 1219, 42 Castle Street, Shire Hall, Castle Hill, Cambridge CB3 0AP ☎ 01223 699929 ✉ guy.mills@cambridgeshire.gov.uk

Education: Ms Gayle Gorman, Service Director of Learning, Box CC 1001, Castle Court, Shire Hall, Castle Hill, Cambridge CB3 0AP ☎ 01223 727988

Education: Mr Paul Springford, Head of Education ICT Services, 42 West Street, Godmanchester, Huntingdon PE29 2HJ ☎ 01480 376655 ✉ paul.springford@cambridgeshire.gov.uk

E-Government: Ms Noelle Godfrey, Head of Information Technology, RES 1406, Babbage House, Shire Hall, Castle Hill, Cambridge CB3 0AP ☎ 01223 699011 ✉ noelle.godfrey@cambridgeshire.gov.uk

Emergency Planning: Mr Stewart Thomas, Head of Emergency Planning, RES 1403, Shire Hall, Castle Hill, Cambridge CB3 0AP ☎ 01223 727944 ✉ stewart.thomas@cambridgeshire.gov.uk

Energy Management: Mr John Peacey, Energy Manager, Box RES 1406, Babbage House, Castle Park, Castle Hill, Cambridge CB3 0AT ✉ john.peacey@cambridgeshire.gov.uk

Environmental / Technical Services: Mr Alex Plant, Executive Director: Environment Services, Box ET 1021, Castle Court, Shire Hall, Castle Hill, Cambridge CB3 0AP ☎ 01223 715660 ✉ alex.plant@cambridgeshire.gov.uk

Estates, Property & Valuation: Mr David Nuttycombe, Head of Strategy & Estates, RES 1302, Shire Hall, Castle Hill, Cambridge CB3 0AP ☎ 01223 699081 ✉ david.nuttycombe@cambridgeshire.gov.uk

European Liaison: Mr David Arkell, Head of Innovation & Partnerships, CC1308, Castle Court, Shire Hall, Cambridge CB3 0AP ☎ 01223 715941 ✉ david.arkell@cambridgeshire.gov.uk

Finance and Treasurer: Mr Nick Dawe, Corporate Director: Finance, Box RES 1006, Shire Hall, Castle Hill, Cambridge CB3 0AP ☎ 01223 699236 ✉ nick.dawe@cambridgeshire.gov.uk

Finance and Treasurer: Ms Sarah Heywood, Head of Finance & Performance (CYPS), Shire Hall, Castle Hill, Cambridge CB3 0AP ☎ 01223 699714 ✉ sarah.heywood@cambridgeshire.gov.uk

Finance and Treasurer: Mr Ian Smith, Service Finance Manager, Shire Hall, Castle Hill, Cambridge CB3 0AP ☎ 01223 699807 ✉ ian.smith@cambridgeshire.gov.uk

Health and Safety: Mr Chris Young, Health & Safety Manager, RES 1413, Shire Hall, Castle Hill, Cambridge CB3 0AP ☎ 01223 699253 ✉ chris.young@cambridgeshire.gov.uk

Highways: Mr John Onslow, Service Director - Infrastructure Management & Operations, CC 1307, Shire Hall, Castle Hill, Cambridge CB3 0AP ☎ 01223 715663 ✉ john.onslow@cambridgeshire.gov.uk

Legal: Mr Quentin Baker, Director of Legal Services, Shire Hall, Castle Hill, Cambridge CB3 0AP ☎ 01223 727961 ✉ quentin.baker@cambridgeshire.gov.uk

Lighting: Mr Chris Sproston, Senior Lighting Engineer, Via ET 1031, Stanton House, Stanton Way, Huntingdon PE29 6XL ✉ chris.sproston@cambridgeshire.gov.uk

Lottery Funding, Charity and Voluntary: Mr Robert Sanderson, Senior Democratic Services Officer, Box Res 1102, Shire Hall, Castle Hill, Cambridge CB3 0AP ☎ 01223 699181 ✉ robert.sanderson@cambridgeshire.gov.uk

Member Services: Ms Wilma Wilkie, Head of Democratic & Members' Services, Shire Hall, Castle Hill, Cambridge CB3 0AP ☎ 01223 699183 ✉ wilma.wilkie@cambridgeshire.gov.uk

Personnel / HR: Ms Janet Bosworth, Head of Human Resources (CAS,ES,CD), Shire Hall, Castle Hill, Cambridge CB3 0AP ☎ 01223 699481 ✉ janet.bosworth@cambridgeshire.gov.uk

Personnel / HR: Ms Joyce Fenton, Head of Human Resources (CYPS), Shire Hall, Castle Hill, Cambridge CB3 0AP ☎ 01223 699634 ✉ joyce.fenton@cambridgeshire.gov.uk

Personnel / HR: Ms Jackie McCarter, Head of HR Policy & Business Services, Shire Hall, Castle Hill, Cambridge CB3 0AP ☎ 01223 699441 ✉ jackie.mccarter@cambridgeshire.gov.uk

Personnel / HR: Ms Christine Reed, Director of HR & OD, Box RES 1006, Shire Hall, Castle Hill, Cambridge CB3 0AP ☎ 01223 699246 ✉ christine.reed@cambridgeshire.gov.uk

Planning: Mr Graham Hughes, Director - Strategy & Development, Box CC 1307, Shire Hall, Castle Hill, Cambridge CB3 0AP ☎ 01223 715664 ✉ graham.hughes@cambridgeshire.gov.uk

Procurement: Ms Jean Fletcher, Head of Procurement (Social Care), Box CC 1006, Shire Hall, Castle Hill, Cambridge CB3 0AP ☎ ; 01223 729130 ✉ jean.fletcher@cambridgeshire.gov.uk

Public Libraries: Ms Christine May, Head of Libraries, Archives & Information, Box CC 1218, Shire Hall, Castle Hill, Cambridge CB3 0AP ☎ 01223 703521 ✉ christine.may@cambridgeshire.gov.uk

Recycling & Waste Minimisation: Mr Gifford Lewis, Head of Waste Management, Box CC 1215, Shire Hall, Castle Hill, Cambridge CB3 0AP ☎ 01223 715453 ✉ gifford.lewis@cambridgeshire.gov.uk

Road Safety: Mr David Frost, Head of Road Safety Services, CCC1309, Stanton House, Stanton Way, Huntingdon PE29 6XL ☎ ; 01480 375105 ✉ david.frost@cambridgeshire.gov.uk

Social Services: Ms Jean Fletcher, Head of Procurement (Social Care), Box CC 1006, Shire Hall, Castle Hill, Cambridge CB3 0AP ☎ ; 01223 729130 ✉ jean.fletcher@cambridgeshire.gov.uk

Social Services: Mr Adrian Loades, Executive Director - Children & Young People's Services & Adult Social Care, Box CC 1001, Shire Hall, Castle Hill, Cambridge CB3 0AP ☎ 01223 727993 ✉ adrian.loades@cambridgeshire.gov.uk

Social Services (Adult): Ms Claire Bruin, Service Director: Adult Social Care, Box CC1315, Castle Court, Shire Hall, Castle Hill, Cambridge CB3 0AP ☎ 01223 715665 ✉ claire.bruin@cambridgeshire.gov.uk

Social Services (Adult): Mr Adrian Loades, Executive Director - Children & Young People's Services & Adult Social Care, CC 1001, Castle Court, Shire Hall, Cambridge CB3 0AP ☎ 01223 727993 ✉ adrian.loades@cambridgeshire.gov.uk

Social Services (Children): Mr Adrian Loades, Executive Director - Children & Young People's Services & Adult Social Care, Box CC 1001, Shire Hall, Castle Hill, Cambridge CB3 0AP ☎ 01223 727993 ✉ adrian.loades@cambridgeshire.gov.uk

Staff Training: Mr Rob Parker, Organisational & Workforce Development Advisor, RES 1227, Shire Hall, Castle Hill, Cambridge CB3 0AP ☎ 01223 706337 ✉ rob.parker@cambridgeshire.gov.uk

Sustainable Communities: Mr Graham Hughes, Director - Strategy & Development, Box CC 1307, Shire Hall, Castle Hill, Cambridge CB3 0AP ☎ 01223 715664
✉ graham.hughes@cambridgeshire.gov.uk

Transport: Mr Chris Capps, Head of Transport Asset Management, Castle Park, Castle Hill, Cambridge CB3 0AT
☎ 01223 715640 ✉ chris.capps@cambridgeshire.gov.uk

Transport Planner: Mr Graham Hughes, Director - Strategy & Development, Box CC 1307, Shire Hall, Castle Hill, Cambridge CB3 0AP ☎ 01223 715664
✉ graham.hughes@cambridgeshire.gov.uk

MEMBERS OF THE COUNCIL (69)

***Chair:* Powley**, John (CON - Soham & Fordham Villages)
john.powley@cambridgeshire.gov.uk

***Vice-Chair:* Reynolds**, Kevin (CON - St Ives)
kevin.reynolds@cambridgeshire.gov.uk

***Leader of the Council:* Clarke**, Nick (CON - Fulbourn)
nick.clarke@cambridgeshire.gov.uk

***Deputy Leader of the Council:* McGuire**, Mac (CON - Norman Cross)
mac.mcguire@cambridgeshire.gov.uk

***Group Leader:* Bourke**, Kilian (LD - Romsey)
kilian.bourke@gmail.com

***Group Leader:* Sadiq**, Tariq (LAB - Coleridge)
tariq.sadiq@cambridgeshire.gov.uk

Austen, Sue (LD - Ely South & West)
sue.austen@cambridgeshire.gov.uk

Batchelor, John (LD - Linton)
john.batchelor@cambridgeshire.gov.uk

Bates, Ian (CON - The Hemingfords & Fenstanton)
ian.bates@cambridgeshire.gov.uk

Bell, Nigel (LD - Ely North & East)
nbell@waitrose.com

Brooks-Gordon, Belinda (LD - Castle)
b.brooks-gordon@bbk.ac.uk

Brown, Peter (CON - Huntingdon)
sirpeter.brown@cambridgeshire.gov.uk

Brown, Fred (CON - Littleport)
fred_brown@live.co.uk

Brown, David (CON - Burwell)
david.brown@cambridgeshire.gov.uk

Butcher, Ralph (CON - Whittlesey South)
butcher919@btinternet.com

Carter, Christine (LAB - Cherry Hinton)
christine.carter@cambridgeshire.gov.uk

Churchill, Kenneth (CON - Little Paxton & St Neots North)
ken.churchill@huntsdc.gov.uk

Clark, John (CON - March West)
johnclark786@btinternet.com

Count, Steve (CON - March North)
steve.count@cambridgeshire.gov.uk

Criswell, Steve (CON - Somersham & Earith)
steve.criswell@cambridgeshire.gov.uk

Curtis, Martin (CON - Whittlesey North)
martin.curtis@cambridgeshire.gov.uk

Downes, Peter (LD - Brampton & Kimbolton)
peter.downes@cambridgeshire.gov.uk

Dutton, Jeffery (CON - Godmanchester & Huntingdon East)
hdcdutton@gmail.com

Farrer, Bob (CON - St Neots Eaton Socon & Eynesbury)
bob.farrer@cambridgeshire.gov.uk

Guyatt, Nick (CON - Norman Cross)
nickguyatt@btinternet.com

Gymer, Sue (LD - Cottenham, Histon & Impington)
sue.gymer@cambridgeshire.gov.uk

Harper, Geoffrey (CON - Forty Foot)
geoffrey.harper@virgin.net

Harrison, Nichola (IND - Petersfield)
nharrison@freenetname.co.uk

Harty, David (CON - Little Paxton & St Neots North)
david.harty@cambridgeshire.gov.uk

Heathcock, Geoffrey (LD - Queen Edith's)
geoffrey.heathcock@cambridgeshire.gov.uk

Hoy, Samantha (CON - Wisbech North)
samantha.hoy@cambridgeshire.gov.uk

Hunt, William (CON - Haddenham)
william.hunt@cambridgeshire.gov.uk

Hutton, Catherine (CON - St Neots Eaton Socon & Eynesbury)
catherine.hutton14@gmail.com

Jenkins, David (LD - Cottenham, Histon & Impington)
ccc@davidjenkins.org.uk

Johnstone, Shona (CON - Willingham)
shona.johnstone@cambridgeshire.gov.uk

Kadic, Laine (CON - Huntingdon)
laine.kadic@cambridgeshire.gov.uk

Kenney, Gail (CON - Sawston)
gail.kenney@cambridgeshire.gov.uk

Kindersley, Sebastian (LD - Gamlingay)
skindersley@hotmail.com

King, Simon (CON - Wisbech South)
sking@fenland.gov.uk

Lucas, Victor (CON - Warboys & Upwood)
victor.lucas@cambridgeshire.gov.uk

Manning, Ian (LD - East Chesterton)
ian.manning@cambridgeshire.gov.uk

McGuire, Viv (CON - Sawtry & Ellington)
viv.mcguire@cambridgeshire.gov.uk

Melton, Alan (CON - Chatteris)
meltonalan@aol.com

Nethsingha, Lucy (LD - Newnham)
nethsingha@btinternet.com

Oliver, Linda (CON - Bassingbourn)
linda.oliver@cambridgeshire.gov.uk

Orgee, Tony (CON - Sawston)
tony.orgee@cambridgeshire.gov.uk

Palmer, James (CON - Soham & Fordham Villages)
jpp@oakhouse@gmail.com

Pegram, Roy (CON - St Ives)
roy.pegram@cambridgeshire.gov.uk

Pellew, Andy (LD - King's Hedges)
andy.pellew@gmail.com

Read, Philip (CON - Sutton)
philip.read@eastcambs.gov.uk

Reeve, Peter (UKIP - Ramsey)
reeve@ukip.org

Reynolds, John (CON - Bar Hill)
john.reynolds@cambridgeshire.gov.uk

Sales, Paul (LAB - Arbury)
cccpaul.sales@gmail.com

Sedgwick-Jell, Simon (GRN - Abbey)
simon.sedgwick-jell@cambridgeshire.gov.uk

Shepherd, Caroline (LD - Trumpington)
cllr.shepherd@gmail.com

Shuter, Mathew (CON - Woodditton)
mshuter@btinternet.com

Smith, Mandy (CON - Papworth & Swavesey)

mandysmith310@btinternet.com
Stone, Timothy (LD - Duxford)
timothy.stone@cambridgeshire.gov.uk
Tierney, Steve (CON - Roman Bank & Peckover)
cllr@stevetierney.org
Tuck, Jill (CON - Waldersey)
jill.tuck@cambridgeshire.gov.uk
van de Ven, Susan (LD - Melbourn)
susanvendeven@yahoo.co.uk
West, Richard (CON - Buckden, Gransden & The Offords)
richard.west@cambridgeshire.gov.uk
Whelan, Fiona (LD - Hardwick)
fewhelan@gmail.com
Whitebread, Sarah (LD - Market)
swhitebread@googlemail.com
Wilkins, Kevin (LD - West Chesterton)
kevin.wilkins303@gmail.com
Williamson, Michael (LD - Waterbeach)
michael.williamson@cambridgeshire.gov.uk
Wilson, Graham (LD - Godmanchester & Huntingdon East)
graham.wilson@cambridgeshire.gov.uk
Wilson, Lister (CON - Bourn)
lister@listerwilson.net
Yeulett, Frederick (CON - March East)
fred.yeulett@cambridgeshire.gov.uk

POLITICAL COMPOSITION

CON: 42, LD: 21, LAB: 3, GRN: 1, UKIP: 1, IND: 1

CABINET

Leader: Mr Nick Clarke
Deputy Leader / Community Engagement: Mr Mac McGuire
Children & Young People's Services: Mr David Brown
Community Infrastructure: Mr Tony Orgee
Enterprise: Mr Mathew Shuter
Growth & Planning: Mr Ian Bates
Health & Wellbeing: Mr Steve Tierney
Learning: Mr David Harty
Resources & Performance: Mr Steve Count

COMMITTEE CHAIRS

Adults, Wellbeing & Health Overview & Scrutiny: Mr Kevin Reynolds
Appointments & Renumeration: Mr Steve Count
Audit & Accounts: Mr Timothy Stone
Children & Young People Overview & Scrutiny: Mrs Shona Johnstone
Enterprise, Growth & Community Infrastructure Overview & Scrutiny: Mr Ralph Butcher
Resources & Performance Overview & Scrutiny: Mr Fred Brown

CAMDEN L

Camden London Borough Council, Town Hall, Judd Street, London WC1H 9JE ☎ 020 7974 4444 🖳 www.camden.gov.uk

FACTS & FIGURES

Police Authority: Metropolitan Police Authority
Health Authority: NHS London
Learning and Skills Council: London
Parliamentary Constituencies: Hampstead and Kilburn, Holborn and St. Pancras
EU Constituencies: London
Election Frequency: Elections are of whole council

PRINCIPAL OFFICERS

Chief Executive: Mr Mike Cooke, Chief Executive, Town Hall, Judd Street, London WC1H 9JE ☎ 020 7974 5686 🖷 020 7974 5998 ✉ mike.cooke@camden.gov.uk

Assistant Chief Executive: Ms Juliet Chua, Assistant Chief Executive, Town Hall, Judd Street, London WC1H 9JE ☎ 020 7974 5994 ✉ juliet.chua@camden.gov.uk

Assistant Chief Executive: Ms Sarah Mullen, Assistant Chief Executive, Town Hall, Judd Street, London WC1H 9JE ☎ 020 7974 5994 🖷 020 7974 6750 ✉ sarah.mullen@camden.gov.uk

Senior Management: Ms Rosemary Westbrook, Director of Housing, Adult Social Care & HR, Town Hall, Judd Street, London WC1H 9JE ✉ rosemary.westbrook@camden.gov.uk

Access Officer / Social Services (Disability): Ms Angela Neblett, Head Strategy & Comm/Mental Health/Subst Abuse, 2nd Floor Bidborough House, 38-50 Bidborough Street, London WC1H 9DB ☎ 020 7974 6717 ✉ angela.neblett@camden.gov.uk

Architect, Building / Property Services: Mr David Tullis, Head of Property Services, Town Hall Extension, Argyle Street, London WC1H 8NG ☎ 020 7974 1604 ✉ david.tullis@camden.gov.uk

Best Value: Ms Finneguela O'Brien, Head of Strategy & Performance, Town Hall, Judd Street, London WC1H 9JE ☎ 020 7974 5645 ✉ finneguela.o'brien@camden.gov.uk

Building Control: Mr Nasser Rad, Interim Head of Service - Building Control, Town Hall Extension, Argyle Street, London WC1H 8NL ☎ 020 7974 2387 ✉ nasser.rad@camden.gov.uk

Children / Youth Services: Ms Ann Baxter, Director of Children, Schools & Families, Upper 1st Floor, 218 Eversholt Street, London NW1 1BD ☎ 020 7974 1505 🖷 020 7974 4136 ✉ ann.baxter@camden.gov.uk

Civil Registration: Ms Jenni Grant, Superintendent Registrar, Town Hall, Judd Street, London WC1H 9JE ☎ 020 7974 1940 🖷 020 7974 5792 ✉ jenni.grant@camden.gov.uk

PR / Communications: Ms Kathryn Myers, Head of Communications, 3rd Floor, Town Hall, Judd Street, London WC1H 9JE ☎ 020 7974 6020 ✉ kathryn.myers@camden.gov.uk

PR / Communications: Mr Steve Shawcross, HASC Account Manager, Town Hall, Judd Street, London WC1H 9JE ☎ 020 7974 2464 ✉ steve.shawcross@camden.gov.uk

Community Planning: Ms Alison Griffin, Assistant Director - Communities, 6th Floor, Town Hall Extension, London WC1H 8EQ ☎ 020 7974 6960 ✉ alison.griffin@camden.gov.uk

Community Safety: Mr Tom Preest, Head of Community Safety Services, 302 Town Hall Extension, Argyle Street, London WC1H 8EQ ☎ 020 7974 3461 ✉ tom.preest@camden.gov.uk

Computer Management: Mr John Jackson, Assistant Director (Corporate ICT), Roy Shaw Centre, 3-5 Cressy Road, London NW3 2ND ☎ 020 7974 1529 ✉ john.jackson@camden.gov.uk

Consumer Protection and Trading Standards: Mr Jim Foudy, Head of Regulatory Services, 7th Floor, Town Hall Extension, Argyle Street, London WC1H 8EQ ☎ 020 7974 6962 🖷 020 7974 6940 ✉ jim.foudy@camden.gov.uk

Contracts: Mr Terry Brewer, Chief Procurement Officer, Town Hall Extension, Argyle Street, London WC1H 9JE ☎ 020 7974 5696 ✉ terry.brewer@camden.gov.uk

Contracts: Mr Garry Griffiths, Head of Joint Commissioning & Strategy, Bidborough House, 38-50 Bidborough Street, London WC1H 9BD ☎ 020 7974 2579 ✉ garry.griffiths@camden.gov.uk

Customer Service: Ms Fiona Dean, Director of Finance, Town Hall, Argyle Street, London WC1H 8NP ☎ 020 7974 4172 ✉ fiona.dean@camden.gov.uk

Economic Development: Ms Angela McKeever, Strategic Lead - Employment & Skills, 7th Floor, Town Hall Extension, Argyle Street, London WC1H 8EQ ☎ 020 7974 7211 ✉ angela.mckeever@camden.gov.uk

Education: Mr Michael Shew, Assistant Director - Achievement, 2nd Floor, Crowndale Court, 218 Eversholt Street, London NW1 1BD ☎ 020 7974 4273 ✉ michael.shew@camden.gov.uk

E-Government: Mr John Jackson, Assistant Director (Corporate ICT), 3rd Floor, Old Town Hall, Judd Street, London WC1H 8NJ ☎ 020 7974 1529 ✉ john.jackson@camden.gov.uk

Electoral Registration: Mr Richard Lefley, Elections Manager, Town Hall, Judd Street, London WC1H 9LZ ☎ 020 7974 6372 🖷 020 7974 6375 ✉ richard.lefley@camden.gov.uk

Emergency Planning: Ms Melissa Brackley, Head of Emergency Planning, 2nd floor, Medburn Centre, 136 Charlton Street, London NW1 1RX ☎ 020 7974 5643 🖷 020 7974 4374 ✉ melissa.brackley@camden.gov.uk

Emergency Planning: Mr Trevor Kings, Senior Emergency Planning & Business Continuity Coordinator, 2nd floor, Medburn Centre, 136 Charlton Street, London NW1 1RX ☎ 020 7974 3495 🖷 020 7974 4374 ✉ trevor.king@camden.gov.uk

Energy Management: Ms Julie Granger, Principle Energy Management Officer, 2nd Floor, Cockpit Yard, Northington Street, London WC1N 2NP ☎ 020 7974 3795 🖷 020 7974 3293 ✉ julie.granger@camden.gov.uk

Environmental / Technical Services: Mr Sam Monck, Assistant Director - Environment & Transport, 6th Floor, Town Hall Extension (Environment), Argyle Street, London WC1H 8EQ ☎ 020 7974 5602 ✉ sam.monck@camden.gov.uk

Environmental / Technical Services: Ms Rachel Stopard, Director of Culture & Environment, Town Hall, Argyle Street, London WC1H 8NP ☎ 020 7974 5621 🖷 020 7974 5556 ✉ rachel.stopard@camden.gov.uk

Environmental Health: Mr Ed Watson, Assistant Director - Regeneration & Planning, Town Hall, Argyle Street, London WC1H 8NP ☎ 020 7974 5622 ✉ ed.watson@camden.gov.uk

Environmental Health: Mr Andrew Woolmer, Private Sector Housing Team Manager, 33-35 Jamestown Road, London NW1 7DB ☎ 020 7974 2159 🖷 020 7974 6955 ✉ andrew.woolmer@camden.gov.uk

Estates, Property & Valuation: Mr David Tullis, Head of Property Services, Town Hall Extension, Argyle Street, London WC1H 8NG ☎ 020 7974 1604 ✉ david.tullis@camden.gov.uk

Facilities: Mr Richard Spear, Category Manager - FM & Capital, Crowndale Centre, 218 Eversholt Road, London NW1 1BD ☎ 020 7974 4337 🖷 020 7974 1649 ✉ richard.spear@camden.gov.uk

Finance and Treasurer: Mr Mike O'Donnell, Director of Finance, 7th Floor, Town Hall Extension, Argyle Street, London WC1H 8EQ ☎ 020 7974 5933 ✉ mike.o'donnell@camden.gov.uk

Finance and Treasurer: Mr Pat O'Neill, Head of Service Delivery, 1st Floor Block C, 33-35 Jamestown Road, London NW1 7DB ☎ 020 7974 3264 ✉ pat.o'neill@camden.gov.uk

Fleet Management: Mr Lew Price, Head of Transport, York Way Depot, 7 York Way, London N1 0BE ☎ 020 7974 6724 🖷 020 7974 3712 ✉ lew.price@camden.gov.uk

Grounds Maintenance: Ms Jessica Gibbons, Head of Parks & Open Spaces, 7th Floor, Town Hall Extension, Argyle Street, London WC1H 8EQ ☎ 020 7974 4226 ✉ jessica.gibbons@camden.gov.uk

Health and Safety: Ms Vivienne Broadhurst, Head of Assessment & Care Management, Bidborough House, 38-50 Bidborough Street, London WC1H 9DB ☎ 020 7974 6092 ✉ vivienne.broadhurst@camden.gov.uk

Health and Safety: Mr Matt Green, Health & Safety Manager, 3rd Floor, Town Hall Extension, Argyle Street, WC1H 8NP ☎ 020 7974 7845 ✉ matt.green@camden.gov.uk

Highways: Mr George Loureda, Head of Engineering, 7th Floor, Town Hall Extension, Argyle Street, London WC1H 8EQ ☎ 020 7974 6949 ✉ george.loureda@camden.gov.uk

Home Energy Conservation: Mr Oliver Myers, Head of Corporate Sustainability, Town Hall Extension, Argyle Street, London WC1H 8EQ ☎ 020 7974 6370 ✉ oliver.myers@camden.gov.uk

Housing: Mr David Padfield, AD Housing Management, Bidborough House, 38-50 Bidborough Street, London WC1H 9BF ☎ 020 7974 5816 ✉ david.padfield@camden.gov.uk

Housing: Mr Steve Platt, Head of Leaseholder Services, Medburn Centre, 136 Charlton Street, London NW1 1RX ☎ 020 7974 6313 ✉ steve.platt@camden.gov.uk

Housing: Ms Rosemary Westbrook, Director of Housing, Adult Social Care & HR, Town Hall, Judd Street, London WC1H 9JE

✉ rosemary.westbrook@camden.gov.uk

Housing Maintenance: Mr Ross Barber, Principal Building Surveyor, 1st Floor, Holmes Road Depot, 79 Holmes Road, London NW5 3AP ☎ 020 7974 6763 ✉ ross.barber@camden.gov.uk

Housing Maintenance: Mr Kim Wells, Head of Housing Repairs, 33-35 Jamestown Road, London NW1 7DB ☎ 020 7974 1746 🖷 020 7974 5371 ✉ kim.wells@camden.gov.uk

Local Area Agreement: Ms Finneguela O'Brien, Head of Strategy & Performance, Town Hall, Judd Street, London WC1H 9JE ☎ 020 7974 5645 ✉ finneguela.o'brien@camden.gov.uk

Local Area Agreement: Ms Louise Regan, Senior Policy Officer, Town Hall, Judd Street, London WC1H 9JE ☎ 0207 974 3200 ✉ Louise.Regan@camden.gov.uk

Legal: Mr Andrew Maughan, Head of Legal Services, Town Hall, Judd Street, London WC1H 9JE ☎ 020 7974 5656 ✉ andrew.maughan@camden.gov.uk

Leisure and Cultural Services: Ms Fiona Dean, Director of Finance, Town Hall, Argyle Street, London WC1H 8NP ☎ 020 7974 4172 ✉ fiona.dean@camden.gov.uk

Leisure and Cultural Services: Ms Caroline Jenkinson, Head of Arts & Tourism, 7th Floor, Town Hall Extension, Argyle Street, London WC1H 8EQ ☎ 020 7974 1685 ✉ caroline.jenkinson@camden.gov.uk

Leisure and Cultural Services: Mr Nigel Robinson, Head of Sport & Physical Activities, Town Hall Extension, Argyle Street, London WC1H 8EQ ☎ 020 7974 1614 ✉ nigel.robinson@camden.gov.uk

Leisure and Cultural Services: Ms Rachel Stopard, Director of Culture & Environment, Town Hall, Argyle Street, London WC1H 8NP ☎ 020 7974 5621 ✉ rachel.stopard@camden.gov.uk

Licensing: Mr Jim Foudy, Head of Regulatory Services, 7th Floor, Town Hall Extension, Argyle Street, London WC1H 8EQ ☎ 020 7974 6962 🖷 020 7974 6940 ✉ jim.foudy@camden.gov.uk

Lifelong Learning: Ms Jennie Lavis, Head of Adult Community Learning, Upper 1st Floor, 218 Eversholt Street, London NW1 1BD ☎ 020 7974 4525 ✉ jennie.lavis@camden.gov.uk

Lighting: Mr Martin Reading, Implementation & Maintenance Manager, Town Hall, Argyle Street, London WC1H 8NP ☎ 020 7974 2018 ✉ martin.reading@camden.gov.uk

Lottery Funding, Charity and Voluntary: Ms Alice Wallace, Head of Communities & Third Sector, 7th Floor, Town Hall Extension, Argyle Street, London WC1H 8EQ ☎ 020 7974 3428 ✉ alice.wallace@camden.gov.uk

Member Services: Ms Asha Paul, Head of Democratic Services, Town Hall, Judd Street, London WC1H 9JE ☎ 020 7974 5944 🖷 020 7974 5921 ✉ asha.paul@camden.gov.uk

Member Services: Ms Rhiannon Rees, Councillor Services Manager, Town Hall, Judd Street, London WC1H 9JE ☎ 020 7974 5730 ✉ rhiannon.rees@camden.gov.uk

Parking: Ms Nicolina Cooper, Head of Parking Services, 100 St Pancras Way, London NW1 9NF ☎ 020 7974 4678 ✉ nicolina.cooper@camden.gov.uk

Personnel / HR: Mr Dave Rodgers, People & Services Workstream Programme Manager, Town Hall, Argyle Street, London WC1H 8NP ☎ 020 7974 5873 ✉ dave.rodgers@camden.gov.uk

Planning: Mr Brian O'Donnell, Strategic Planning & Information Manager, 6th Floor, Town Hall Extension, London WC1H 8EQ ☎ 020 7974 5502 ✉ brian.o'donnell@camden.gov.uk

Planning: Mr Ed Watson, Assistant Director - Regeneration & Planning, Town Hall, Argyle Street, London WC1H 8NP ☎ 020 7974 5622 ✉ ed.watson@camden.gov.uk

Procurement: Mr Paul Deegan, Interim Head of Strategic Procurement, 2nd Floor, Town Hall Extension, Argyle Street, London WC1H 9JE ☎ 020 7974 5696 ✉ paul.deegan@camden.gov.uk

Public Libraries: Mr Mike Clarke, Head of Libraries, Information & Community Learning, 7th Floor, Town Hall Extension, Argyle Street, London WC1H 8EQ ☎ 020 7974 4058 🖷 020 7974 4801 ✉ mike.clarke@camden.gov.uk

Recycling & Waste Minimisation: Ms Ann Baker, Principal Environmental Services Officer, Recycling Centre, Regis Road, London NW5 3EW ☎ 020 7974 8998 🖷 020 7974 9374 ✉ ann.baker@camden.gov.uk

Regeneration: Ms Melissa Dillon, Head of Regeneration, Development & Sustainability, 1st Floor, 33-35 Jamestown Road, London NW1 7DB ☎ 020 7974 3100 ✉ melissa.dillon@camden.gov.uk

Road Safety: Mr Christopher Nicola, Team Manager, Town Hall Extension, Argyle Street, London WC1H 8EQ ☎ 020 7974 5619 ✉ christopher.nicola@camden.gov.uk

Social Services: Ms Lyn Romeo, Assistant Director - Adult Social Care, 2nd Floor, Bidborough House, 38-50 Bidborough Street, London WC1H 9DB ☎ 020 7974 1441 ✉ lyn.romeo@camden.gov.uk

Social Services (Children): Ms Anne Turner, Assistant Director - CSF, Crowndale Centre, 218-220 Eversholt Street, London NW1 1BD ☎ 020 7974 6641 ✉ anne.turner@camden.gov.uk

Staff Training: Ms Maria di-Sapia, Interim Assistant Director of HR, 3rd Floor, Town Hall Extension, Argyle Street, WC1H 8NP ☎ 020 7974 6109 🖷 020 7974 6980 ✉ maria.di-sapia@camden.gov.uk

Tourism: Ms Caroline Jenkinson, Head of Arts & Tourism, 7th Floor, Town Hall Extension, Argyle Street, London WC1H 8EQ ☎ 020 7974 1685 ✉ caroline.jenkinson@camden.gov.uk

Transport: Mr Lew Price, Head of Transport, York Way Depot, 7 York Way, London N1 0BE ☎ 020 7974 6724 🖷 020 7974 3712 ✉ lew.price@camden.gov.uk

Transport Planner: Ms Josephine Allman, Head of Passenger & Accessible Transport Services, 1st Floor, Bidborough House, 38-50 Bidborough Street, London WC1H 9DB ☎ 020 7974 5560 ✉ josephine.allman@camden.gov.uk

Waste Collection and Disposal: Mr Paul Dunphy, Head of Environment Services, Cockpit Yard, London WC1H 2NP ☎ 020 7974 2246 ✉ paul.dunphy@camden.gov.uk

MEMBERS OF THE COUNCIL (54)

***Mayor:* Johnson**, Heather (LAB - Regent's Park)
heather.johnson@camden.gov.uk
***Deputy Mayor:* Simpson**, Jonathan (LAB - King's Cross)
jonathan.simpson@camden.gov.uk
***Leader of the Council:* Hayward**, Sarah (LAB - King's Cross)
sarah.hayward@camden.gov.uk
***Deputy Leader of the Council:* Callaghan**, Patricia (LAB - Camden Town with Primrose Hill)
patricia.callaghan@camden.gov.uk
Ali, Nasim (LAB - Regent's Park)
nasim.ali@camden.gov.uk
Apak, Meric (LAB - Kentish Town)
meric.apak@camden.gov.uk
Birch, Sean (LAB - Gospel Oak)
sean.birch@camden.gov.uk
Blackwell, Theo (LAB - Gospel Oak)
theo.blackwell@camden.gov.uk
Bokth, Rahel (LD - Haverstock)
rahel.bokth@camden.gov.uk
Braithwaite, Paul (LD - Cantelowes)
paul.braithwaite@camden.gov.uk
Brayshaw, Peter (LAB - St Pancras & Somers Town)
peter.brayshaw@camden.gov.uk
Bryant, John (LD - West Hampstead)
john.bryant@camden.gov.uk
Bucknell, Jonny (CON - Belsize)
jonny.bucknell@camden.gov.uk
Chung, Linda (LD - Hampstead Town)
linda.chung@camden.gov.uk
De Souza, Maya (GRN - Highgate)
maya.desouza@camden.gov.uk
Eagling, Russell (LD - Fortune Green)
russell.eagling@camden.gov.uk
Eslamdoust, Maryam (LAB - Kilburn)
maryam.eslamdoust@camden.gov.uk
Fraser, Jill (LD - Haverstock)
jill.fraser@camden.gov.uk
Freeman, Roger (CON - Swiss Cottage)
roger.freeman@camden.gov.uk
Fulbrook, Julian (LAB - Holborn & Covent Garden)
julian.fulbrook@camden.gov.uk
Gardiner, Thomas (LD - Kilburn)
thomas.gardiner@camden.gov.uk
Gimson, Sally (LAB - Highgate)
sally.gimson@camden.gov.uk
Gould, Georgia (LAB - Kentish Town)
georgia.gould@camden.gov.uk
Hai, Abdul (LAB - King's Cross)
abdul.hai@camden.gov.uk
Harrison, Adam (LAB - Bloomsbury)
adam.harrison@camden.gov.uk
Headlam-Wells, Jenny (LAB - Kentish Town)
jenny.headlam-wells@camden.gov.uk
Jirira, Nancy (LD - Fortune Green)
nancy.jirira@camden.gov.uk
Jones, Phil (LAB - Cantelowes)
phil.jones@camden.gov.uk
Katz, Mike (LAB - Kilburn)
mike.katz@camden.gov.uk
Khatoon, Samata (LAB - St Pancras & Somers Town)
samata.khatoon@camden.gov.uk
Knight, Christopher (CON - Hampstead Town)
chris.knight@camden.gov.uk
Leach, Valerie (LAB - Highgate)
valerie.leach@camden.gov.uk
Leyland, Claire-Louise (CON - Belsize)
claire-louise.leyland@camden.gov.uk
Marshall, Andrew (CON - Swiss Cottage)
andrew.marshall@camden.gov.uk
Mason, Angela (LAB - Cantelowes)
angela.mason@camden.gov.uk
Mennear, Andrew (CON - Frognal & Fitzjohns)
andrew.mennear@camden.gov.uk
Moffitt, Keith (LD - West Hampstead)
keith.moffitt@camden.gov.uk
Naylor, Chris (LD - Camden Town with Primrose Hill)
chris.naylor@camden.gov.uk
Nuti, Milena (LAB - Bloomsbury)
milena.nuti@camden.gov.uk
Olad, Awale (LAB - Holborn & Covent Garden)
awale.olad@camden.gov.uk
Pietragnoli, Lazzaro (LAB - Camden Town with Primrose Hill)
lazzaro.pietragnoli@camden.gov.uk
Quadir, Abdul (LAB - Bloomsbury)
abdul.quadir@camden.gov.uk
Rea, Flick (LD - Fortune Green)
flick.rea@camden.gov.uk
Revah, Larraine (LAB - Gospel Oak)
larraine.revah@camden.gov.uk
Risso-Gill, Gillian (LD - West Hampstead)
gillian.risso-gill@camden.gov.uk
Roberts, Kirsty (CON - Hampstead Town)
kirsty.roberts@camden.gov.uk
Robinson, Roger (LAB - St Pancras & Somers Town)
roger.robinson@camden.gov.uk
Sanders, Matthew (LD - Haverstock)
matthew.sanders@camden.gov.uk
Siddig, Tulip (LAB - Regent's Park)
tulip.siddig@camden.gov.uk
Simon, Tom (LD - Belsize)
tom.simon@camden.gov.uk
Spinella, Gio (CON - Frognal & Fitzjohns)
gio.spinella@camden.gov.uk
Trott, Laura (CON - Frognal & Fitzjohns)
laura.trott@camden.gov.uk
Vincent, Sue (LAB - Holborn & Covent Garden)
sue.vincent@camden.gov.uk
Williams, Don (CON - Swiss Cottage)
don.williams@camden.gov.uk

POLITICAL COMPOSITION

LAB: 29, LD: 14, CON: 10, GRN: 1

CABINET

Leader: Mr Adam Harrison

Deputy Leader / Adult Social Care & Health: Ms Patricia Callaghan
Children: Ms Angela Mason
Communities & Culture: Ms Tulip Siddig
Community Safety: Mr Abdul Hai
Finance: Mr Theo Blackwell
Housing: Mr Julian Fulbrook
Regeneration & Growth: Ms Valerie Leach
Sustainability: Mr Phil Jones
Young People: Mr Nasim Ali

COMMITTEE CHAIRS

Audit & Corporate Governance: Mr Peter Brayshaw
Children, Schools & Families Scrutiny (Scrutiny): Ms Jenny Headlam-Wells
Culture & Environment (Scrutiny): Mr Awale Olad
Development Control: Ms Milena Nuti
Health (Scrutiny): Mr John Bryant
Housing & Adult Social Care (Scrutiny): Mr Meric Apak
Licensing: Ms Maryam Eslamdoust
Resources & Corporate Performance (Scrutiny): Mr Don Williams

CANNOCK CHASE D

Cannock Chase District Council, Civic Centre, PO Box 28, Cannock WS11 1BG ☎ 01543 462621 🖷 01543 462317
🖱 customerservices@cannockchasedc.gov.uk
💻 www.cannockchasedc.gov.uk

FACTS & FIGURES

Police Authority: Staffordshire Police Authority
Health Authority: NHS West Midlands
Learning and Skills Council: West Midlands
Parliamentary Constituencies: Cannock Chase
EU Constituencies: West Midlands
Election Frequency: Elections are by thirds
Twinning: Datteln (Germany); Western Springs (USA)

PRINCIPAL OFFICERS

Chief Executive: Mr Stephen Brown, Chief Executive, Civic Centre, Beecroft Road, Cannock WS11 1BG ☎ 01543 462621 🖷 01543 462317 🖱 stephenbrown@cannockchasedc.gov.uk

Senior Management: Mr Tony McGovern, Corporate Director, Civic Centre, Beecroft Road, Cannock WS11 1BG ☎ 01543 462621 🖱 tonymcgovern@cannockchasedc.gov.uk

Architect, Building / Property Services: Mr Robert Phillips, Head of Planning & Regeneration, Civic Centre, Beecroft Road, Cannock WS11 1BG ☎ 01543 462621 🖷 01543 570475 🖱 bobphillips@cannockchasedc.gov.uk

Best Value: Mr Stephen Brown, Chief Executive, Civic Centre, Beecroft Road, Cannock WS11 1BG ☎ 01543 462621 🖷 01543 462317 🖱 stephenbrown@cannockchasedc.gov.uk

Building Control: Mr Paul Beckley, Building Control Manager, Civic Centre, PO Box 28, Beecroft Road, Cannock WS11 1BG ☎ 01543 464408 🖱 paulbeckley@cannockchasedc.gov.uk

Children / Youth Services: Mr Tony McGovern, Corporate Director, Civic Centre, Beecroft Road, Cannock WS11 1BG ☎ 01543 462621 🖱 tonymcgovern@cannockchasedc.gov.uk

Civil Registration: Mr Steve Partridge, Democratic Services Manager, Civic Centre, PO Box 28, Beecroft Road, Cannock WS11 1BG ☎ 01543 462621 🖷 01543 464321 🖱 stevepartridge@cannockchasedc.gov.uk

PR / Communications: Miss Elizabeth Baker, Communications Manager, Civic Centre, PO Box 28, Cannock WS11 1BG ☎ 01543 462621 🖷 01543 464463 🖱 elizabethbaker@cannockchasedc.gov.uk

Community Safety: Mrs Donna Meredith-Wood, Partnerships Manager, Civic Centre, PO Box 28, Cannock WS11 1BG ☎ 01543 462621 🖱 donnameredithwood@cannockchasedc.gov.uk

Computer Management: Mr Tan Ali, ICT Services, Civic Centre, PO Box 28, Cannock WS11 1BG ☎ 01543 464353 🖷 01543 462317 🖱 tanali@cannockchasedc.gov.uk

Contracts: Mrs Judith Aupers, Head of Governance & Operational Development, Civic Centre, PO Box 28, Beecroft Road, Cannock WS11 1BG ☎ 01543 462621 🖱 judithaupers@cannockchasedc.gov.uk

Customer Service: Miss Elizabeth Baker, Communications Manager, Civic Centre, PO Box 28, Cannock WS11 1BG ☎ 01543 462621 🖷 01543 464463 🖱 elizabethbaker@cannockchasedc.gov.uk

Economic Development: Mr Robert Phillips, Head of Planning & Regeneration, Civic Centre, Beecroft Road, Cannock WS11 1BG ☎ 01543 462621 🖷 01543 570475 🖱 bobphillips@cannockchasedc.gov.uk

Electoral Registration: Mr Steve Partridge, Democratic Services Manager, Civic Centre, PO Box 28, Beecroft Road, Cannock WS11 1BG ☎ 01543 462621 🖷 01543 464321 🖱 stevepartridge@cannockchasedc.gov.uk

Emergency Planning: Mrs Judith Aupers, Head of Governance & Operational Development, Civic Centre, PO Box 28, Beecroft Road, Cannock WS11 1BG ☎ 01543 462621 🖱 judithaupers@cannockchasedc.gov.uk

Energy Management: Mr Geoff Winslow, Strategic Asset Manager, Civic Centre, PO Box 28, Beecroft Road, Cannock WS11 1BG ☎ 01543 464524 🖷 01543 570475 🖱 geoffwinslow@cannockchasedc.gov.uk

Environmental / Technical Services: Mr Kevin Lawlor, Head of Environmental Services, Civic Centre, PO Box 28, Beecroft Road, Cannock WS11 1BG ☎ 01543 462621 🖷 01543 573780 🖱 kevinlawlor@cannockchasedc.gov.uk

Environmental Health: Mr Steve Shilvock, Head of Environmental Health & Public Protection, Civic Centre, Beecroft Road, Cannock WS11 1BG ☎ 01543 462621 🖷 01543 464213 🖱 steveshilvock@cannockchasedc.gov.uk

Estates, Property & Valuation: Mr Geoff Winslow, Strategic

Asset Manager, Civic Centre, PO Box 28, Beecroft Road, Cannock WS11 1BG ☎ 01543 464524 🖷 01543 570475 ✉ geoffwinslow@cannockchasedc.gov.uk

European Liaison: Mr Glenn Watson, Economic Development Manager, Civic Centre, PO Box 28, Beecroft Road, Cannock WS11 1BG ☎ 01543 462621 🖷 01543 570475 ✉ glennwatson@cannockchasedc.gov.uk

Facilities: Mr Geoff Winslow, Strategic Asset Manager, Civic Centre, PO Box 28, Beecroft Road, Cannock WS11 1BG ☎ 01543 464524 🖷 01543 570475 ✉ geoffwinslow@cannockchasedc.gov.uk

Finance and Treasurer: Mr Bob Kean, Head of Financial Management, Civic Centre, PO Box 28, Beecroft Road, Cannock WS11 1BG ☎ 01543 462621 🖷 01543 462317 ✉ bobkean@cannockchasedc.gov.uk

Fleet Management: Mr Kevin Lawlor, Head of Environmental Services, Civic Centre, PO Box 28, Beecroft Road, Cannock WS11 1BG ☎ 01543 462621 🖷 01543 573780 ✉ kevinlawlor@cannockchasedc.gov.uk

Grounds Maintenance: Mr Kevin Lawlor, Head of Environmental Services, Civic Centre, PO Box 28, Beecroft Road, Cannock WS11 1BG ☎ 01543 462621 🖷 01543 573780 ✉ kevinlawlor@cannockchasedc.gov.uk

Health and Safety: Mr Carl Morgan, Health & Safety Officer, Civic Centre, PO Box 28, Beecroft Road, Cannock WS11 1BG ☎ 01543 462621 🖷 01543 462317 ✉ carlmorgan@cannockchasedc.gov.uk

Home Energy Conservation: Mr Geoff Winslow, Strategic Asset Manager, Civic Centre, PO Box 28, Beecroft Road, Cannock WS11 1BG ☎ 01543 464524 🖷 01543 570475 ✉ geoffwinslow@cannockchasedc.gov.uk

Housing: Mr Ian Tennant, Head of Housing, Civic Centre, PO Box 28, Beecroft Road, Cannock WS11 1BG ☎ 01543 462621 🖷 01543 462317 ✉ iantennant@cannockchasedc.gov.uk

Housing Maintenance: Mr Ian Tennant, Head of Housing, Civic Centre, PO Box 28, Beecroft Road, Cannock WS11 1BG ☎ 01543 462621 🖷 01543 462317 ✉ iantennant@cannockchasedc.gov.uk

Legal: Mr Alistair Welch, Interim Council Solicitor & Monitoring Officer, Civic Centre, PO Box 28, Cannock WS11 1BG ☎ 01543 462621

Leisure and Cultural Services: Mr Mike Edmonds, Head of Leisure, Culture & Major Projects, Civic Centre, PO Box 28, Beecroft Road, Cannock WS11 1BG ☎ 01543 462621 🖷 01543 562317 ✉ mikeedmonds@cannockchasedc.gov.uk

Licensing: Mr Steve Shilvock, Head of Environmental Health & Public Protection, Civic Centre, Beecroft Road, Cannock WS11 1BG ☎ 01543 462621 🖷 01543 464213 ✉ steveshilvock@cannockchasedc.gov.uk

Member Services: Mr Steve Partridge, Democratic Services Manager, Civic Centre, PO Box 28, Beecroft Road, Cannock WS11 1BG ☎ 01543 462621 🖷 01543 464321 ✉ stevepartridge@cannockchasedc.gov.uk

Parking: Mr Kevin Lawlor, Head of Environmental Services, Civic Centre, PO Box 28, Beecroft Road, Cannock WS11 1BG ☎ 01543 462621 🖷 01543 573780 ✉ kevinlawlor@cannockchasedc.gov.uk

Partnerships: Miss Natasha Swan, Head of Policy, Performance & Partnerships, Civic Centre, PO Box 28, Cannock WS11 1BG ☎ 01543 462621 ✉ natashaswan@cannockchasedc.gov.uk

Personnel / HR: Mrs Anne Bird, Human Resources Manager, Civic Centre, PO Box 28, Cannock WS11 1BG ☎ 01543 462621 🖷 01543 462317 ✉ annebird@cannockchasedc.gov.uk

Planning: Mr Robert Phillips, Head of Planning & Regeneration, Civic Centre, Beecroft Road, Cannock WS11 1BG ☎ 01543 462621 🖷 01543 570475 ✉ bobphillips@cannockchasedc.gov.uk

Procurement: Mrs Judith Aupers, Head of Governance & Operational Development, Civic Centre, PO Box 28, Beecroft Road, Cannock WS11 1BG ☎ 01543 462621 ✉ judithaupers@cannockchasedc.gov.uk

Recycling & Waste Minimisation: Mr Kevin Lawlor, Head of Environmental Services, Civic Centre, PO Box 28, Beecroft Road, Cannock WS11 1BG ☎ 01543 462621 🖷 01543 573780 ✉ kevinlawlor@cannockchasedc.gov.uk

Regeneration: Mr Robert Phillips, Head of Planning & Regeneration, Civic Centre, Beecroft Road, Cannock WS11 1BG ☎ 01543 462621 🖷 01543 570475 ✉ bobphillips@cannockchasedc.gov.uk

Staff Training: Mrs Jan Turner, Training Officer, Civic Centre, PO Box 28, Cannock WS11 1BG ☎ 01543 462621 🖷 01543 462317 ✉ janturner@cannockchasedc.gov.uk

Street Scene: Mr Kevin Lawlor, Head of Environmental Services, Civic Centre, PO Box 28, Beecroft Road, Cannock WS11 1BG ☎ 01543 462621 🖷 01543 573780 ✉ kevinlawlor@cannockchasedc.gov.uk

Sustainable Communities: Miss Natasha Swan, Head of Policy, Performance & Partnerships, Civic Centre, PO Box 28, Cannock WS11 1BG ☎ 01543 462621 ✉ natashaswan@cannockchasedc.gov.uk

Sustainable Development: Mr Robert Phillips, Head of Planning & Regeneration, Civic Centre, Beecroft Road, Cannock WS11 1BG ☎ 01543 462621 🖷 01543 570475 ✉ bobphillips@cannockchasedc.gov.uk

Tourism: Mrs Karen Ward, Economic Development Officer, Tourism & Community, Civic Centre, PO Box 28, Beecroft Road, Cannock WS11 1BG ☎ 01543 462621 🖷 01543 462317 ✉ karenward@cannockchasedc.gov.uk

Town Centre: Mr Glenn Watson, Economic Development Manager, Civic Centre, PO Box 28, Beecroft Road, Cannock WS11 1BG ☎ 01543 462621 🖷 01543 570475

glennwatson@cannockchasedc.gov.uk

Transport: Mr Joss Pressland, Waste & Engineering Services Manager, Civic Centre, PO Box 28, Cannock WS11 1BG ☎ 01543 456807 josspresland@cannockchasedc.gov.uk

Waste Collection and Disposal: Mr Kevin Lawlor, Head of Environmental Services, Civic Centre, PO Box 28, Beecroft Road, Cannock WS11 1BG ☎ 01543 462621 Fax 01543 573780 kevinlawlor@cannockchasedc.gov.uk

Waste Management: Mr Kevin Lawlor, Head of Environmental Services, Civic Centre, PO Box 28, Beecroft Road, Cannock WS11 1BG ☎ 01543 462621 Fax 01543 573780 kevinlawlor@cannockchasedc.gov.uk

Children's Play Areas: Mr Tom Walsh, Parks and Open Spaces Manager, Civic Centre, Beecroft Road, Cannock WS11 1BG ☎ 01543 432621 tomwalsh@cannockchasedc.gov.uk

MEMBERS OF THE COUNCIL (41)

Vice-Chair: **Grice**, Doris (LAB - Hednesford North)
d.grice316@btinternet.com
Deputy Leader of the Council: **Toth**, Janos (LAB - Cannock East)
janostoth@cannockchasedc.gov.uk
Group Leader: **Sutherland**, Mike (CON - Hawks Green)
mikesutherland@cannockchasedc.gov.uk
Adamson, George (LAB - Hednesford Green Heath)
georgeadamson@cannockchasedc.gov.uk
Alcott, Gordon (LAB - Cannock North)
gordonalcott@cannockchasedc.gov.uk
Allen, Frank (LAB - Cannock North)
frankallen@cannockchasedc.gov.uk
Alt, Anne (CON - Western Springs)
annealt@cannockchasedc.gov.uk
Anslow, Chris (CON - Cannock West)
chrisanslow@cannockchasedc.gov.uk
Ball, Gordon (LAB - Hednesford South)
gordonball@cannockchasedc.gov.uk
Bennett, Carl (LAB - Western Springs)
carlbennett@cannockchasedc.gov.uk
Bernard, Ann (CON - Hawks Green)
annbernard@cannockchasedc.gov.uk
Bernard, John (CON - Hawks Green)
Bottomer, Brian (LAB - Hagley)
brianbottomer@cannockchasedc.gov.uk
Cartwright, Sheila (LAB - Hednesford North)
sheilacartwright@cannockchasedc.gov.uk
Davies, Daniel (LD - Etching Hill & the Heath)
danieldavies@cannockchasedc.gov.uk
Davis, Muriel (LAB - Cannock East)
murieldavis@cannockchasedc.gov.uk
Dixon, Dennis (LAB - Cannock North)
dennisdixon@cannockchasedc.gov.uk
Dudson, Alan (LAB - Brereton & Ravenhill)
alandudson@cannockchasedc.gov.uk
Fisher, Paul (LD - Brereton & Ravenhill)
paulfisher@cannockchasedc.gov.uk
Freeman, Maureen (LAB - Cannock South)
maureenfreeman@cannockchasedc.gov.uk
Gamble, Brian (LAB - Hednesford South)
briangamble@cannockchasedc.gov.uk
Gilbert, Peter (CON - Norton Canes)
petergilbert@cannockchasedc.gov.uk
Grocott, Michael (LD - Western Springs)
michaelgrocott@cannockchasedc.gov.uk
Holder, Michael (LAB - Norton Canes)
michaelholder@cannockchasedc.gov.uk
Johnson, Justin (CON - Etching Hill & the Heath)
justinjohnson@cannockchasedc.gov.uk
Jones, Raymond (LD - Etching Hill & the Heath)
raymondjones@cannockchasedc.gov.uk
Jones, Jodie (CON - Rawnsley)
jodiejones@cannockchasedc.gov.uk
Kraujalis, John (LAB - Cannock South)
johnkaye101@yahoo.co.uk
Lovell, Andy (LAB - Hagley)
andylovell@cannockchasedc.gov.uk
Mitchell, Christine (LAB - Cannock East)
christinemitchell@cannockchasedc.gov.uk
Molineux, Gerald (LD - Brereton & Ravenhill)
geraldmolineux@cannockchasedc.gov.uk
Morgan, Clive (LAB - Cannock South)
clivemorgan@cannockchasedc.gov.uk
Pearson, Alan (LAB - Hednesford North)
alanpearson@cannockchasedc.gov.uk
Rowley, John (CON - Heath Hayes East & Wimblebury)
johnrowley@cannockchasedc.gov.uk
Snape, Paul (CON - Cannock West)
paulsnape@cannockchasedc.gov.uk
Spicer, Alison (LAB - Heath Hayes East & Wimblebury)
alisonspicer@cannockchasedc.gov.uk
Stretton, Zaphne (LAB - Norton Canes)
zaphnestretton@cannockchasedc.gov.uk
Sutton, Hyra (CON - Cannock West)
hyrasutton@cannockchasedc.gov.uk
Todd, Diane (LAB - Heath Hayes East & Wimblebury)
dianetodd@cannockchasedc.gov.uk
Todd, Bob (LAB - Hednesford Green Heath)
bobtodd@cannockchasedc.gov.uk
Whitehouse, Linda (CON - Rawnsley)
lindawhitehouse@cannockchasedc.gov.uk

POLITICAL COMPOSITION

LAB: 24, CON: 12, LD: 5

CABINET

Leader: Mr George Adamson
Deputy Leader; Environment: Mr Janos Toth
Corporate Improvement: Mr Dennis Dixon
Culture & Sport: Mrs Christine Mitchell
Economic Development & Planning: Mr Gordon Alcott
Health & Wellbeing: Mrs Muriel Davis
Housing: Mr Frank Allen
Town Centre Regeneration: Ms Diane Todd

COMMITTEE CHAIRS

Culture & Sport Policy Development: Mr Alan Dudson
Economic Development & Planning Policy Development: Ms Linda Whitehouse
Environment Policy Development: Mr Andy Lovell
Health & Wellbeing Policy Development: Ms Maureen Freeman
Licensing & Public Protection: Mr Paul Snape
Scrutiny: Mr John Kraujalis

CANTERBURY CITY D

Canterbury City Council, Council Offices, Military Road, Canterbury CT1 1YW ☎ 01227 862000 🖷 01227 862020 💻 www.canterbury.gov.uk

FACTS & FIGURES

Police Authority: Kent Police Authority
Health Authority: South East Coast Strategic Health Authority
Learning and Skills Council: South East
Parliamentary Constituencies: Canterbury
EU Constituencies: South East
Election Frequency: Elections are of whole council
Twinning: Canterbury: Reims (France); Canterbury Three Towns Association: Canterbury, Vladimir (Russia), Blommington-Normal (USA); Adisham: Campagne-is-Hesdin (France); Herne Bay: Waltrop (Germany); Wimereux (France); Whitstable: Borken (Germany); Albertslund (Denmark); Dainville (France); Sturry and Fordwich: Aire-sur-la-lys (France)

PRINCIPAL OFFICERS

Chief Executive: Mr Colin Carmichael, Chief Executive, Council Offices, Military Road, Canterbury CT1 1YW ☎ 01227 862082 🖷 01227 471646 ✉ colin.carmichael@canterbury.gov.uk

Deputy Chief Executive: Ms Velia Coffey, Deputy Chief Executive, Council Offices, Military Road, Canterbury CT1 1YW ☎ 01227 862149 🖷 01227 862020 ✉ velia.coffey@canterbury.gov.uk

Senior Management: Ms Tricia Marshall, Director of Resources, Council Offices, Military Road, Canterbury CT1 1YW ☎ 01227 862393 🖷 01227 862020 ✉ tricia.marshall@canterbury.gov.uk

Best Value: Mr Mark Bursnell, Head of Policy & Improvement, Council Offices, Military Road, Canterbury CT1 1YW ☎ 01227 862056 🖷 01227 471635 ✉ mark.bursnell@canterbury.gov.uk

Best Value: Mr Dan Hamlin, Improvement Manager, Council Offices, Military Road, Canterbury CT1 1YW ☎ 01227 862059 🖷 01227 471635 ✉ dan.hamlin@canterbury.gov.uk

Building Control: Mr Peter Honey, Building Control Manager, Council Offices, Military Road, Canterbury CT1 1YW ☎ 01227 862500 🖷 01227 471635 ✉ peter.honey@canterbury.gov.uk

PR / Communications: Mrs Celia Glynn-Williams, Head of Communications, Council Offices, Military Road, Canterbury CT1 1YW ☎ 01227 862065 ✉ celia.glynn-williams@canterbury.gov.uk

Community Planning: Mr Ian Brown, Head of Regeneration & Planning, Council Offices, Military Road, Canterbury CT1 1YW ☎ 01227 862193 ✉ ian.brown@canterbury.gov.uk

Community Safety: Ms Larissa Laing, Head of Neighbourhood Services, Council Offices, Military Road, Canterbury CT1 1YW ☎ 01227 862213 🖷 01227 471635 ✉ larissa.laing@canterbury.gov.uk

Computer Management: Mrs Angela Waite, Head of ICT, Council Offices, Military Road, Canterbury CT1 1YW ☎ 01227 862028; 01227 862478; 01227 862478 🖷 01227 862208 ✉ angela.waite@canterbury.gov.uk; angela.waite@ekservices.org; angela.waite@ekservices.org

Contracts: Ms Larissa Laing, Head of Neighbourhood Services, Council Offices, Military Road, Canterbury CT1 1YW ☎ 01227 862213 🖷 01227 471635 ✉ larissa.laing@canterbury.gov.uk

Corporate Services: Mr Mark Burnsell, Head of Policy & Improvement, Council Offices, Military Road, Canterbury CT1 1YW ☎ 01227 862000 ✉ mark.bursnell@canterbury.gov.uk

Corporate Services: Ms Tricia Marshall, Director of Resources, Council Offices, Military Road, Canterbury CT1 1YW ☎ 01227 862393 🖷 01227 862020 ✉ tricia.marshall@canterbury.gov.uk

Customer Service: Ms Carol Gray, Head of Customer Contact Centre, Council Offices, Military Road, Canterbury CT1 1YW ☎ 01227 862000 ✉ carol.gray@ekservices.org

Customer Service: Ms Donna Reed, Shared Services Director, EK Services, Military Road, Canterbury CT1 1YW ☎ 01227 862073; 01227 862073; 01227 862073 ✉ donna.reed@ekservices.org

Economic Development: Mrs Janice McGuinness, Head of Culture & Enterprise, Council Offices, Military Road, Canterbury CT1 1YW ☎ 01227 862492 🖷 01227 470599 ✉ janice.mcguinness@canterbury.gov.uk

E-Government: Mrs Roz Edridge, Business Systems Manager, East Kent Services, Council Offices, Cecil Street, Margate CT9 1XZ ☎ 01843 577033; 01843 577033; 01843 577033 ✉ roz.edridge@thanet.gov.uk

E-Government: Mrs Angela Waite, Head of ICT, Council Offices, Military Road, Canterbury CT1 1YW ☎ 01227 862028; 01227 862478; 01227 862478 🖷 01227 862208 ✉ angela.waite@canterbury.gov.uk; angela.waite@ekservices.org

Electoral Registration: Ms Lyn McDaid, Elections Manager, Council Offices, Military Road, Canterbury CT1 1YW ☎ 01227 862006 🖷 01227 862020 ✉ lyn.mcdaid@canterbury.gov.uk

Energy Management: Mr Philip Kiss, Building Services Engineer (Mechanical) & Energy Officer, Council Offices, Military Road, Canterbury CT1 1YW ☎ 01227 862481 🖷 01227 471635 ✉ philip.kiss@canterbury.gov.uk

Environmental / Technical Services: Ms Larissa Laing, Head of Neighbourhood Services, Council Offices, Military Road, Canterbury CT1 1YW ☎ 01227 862213 🖷 01227 471635 ✉ larissa.laing@canterbury.gov.uk

Environmental Health: Ms Larissa Laing, Head of Neighbourhood Services, Council Offices, Military Road, Canterbury CT1 1YW ☎ 01227 862213 🖷 01227 471635 ✉ larissa.laing@canterbury.gov.uk

Estates, Property & Valuation: Mr Martin Bovingdon, Estates & Valuation Manager, Council Offices, Military Road, Canterbury CT1 1YW ☎ 01227 862088 🖷 01227 764955 ✉ martin.bovingdon@canterbury.gov.uk

Events Manager: Mr John Hawkins, District Events Co-ordinator, Council Offices, Military Road, Canterbury CT1 1YW ☎ 01227 862533 🖱 john.hawkins@canterbury.gov.uk

Facilities: Mrs Alexis Jobson, Central Services Manager, Council Offices, Military Road, Canterbury CT1 1YW ☎ 01227 862255 🖷 01227 862020 🖱 alexis.jobson@canterbury.gov.uk

Finance and Treasurer: Mr Ian Cooke, Head of Finance, Council Offices, Military Road, Canterbury CT1 1YW ☎ 01227 862350 🖷 01227 862350 🖱 ian.cooke@canterbury.gov.uk

Finance and Treasurer: Mr Andrew Stevens, Head of Revenues & Benefits, Council Offices, Military Road, Canterbury CT1 1YW ☎ 01227 862000 🖱 andrew.stevens@canterbury.gov.uk

Grounds Maintenance: Ms Larissa Laing, Head of Neighbourhood Services, Council Offices, Military Road, Canterbury CT1 1YW ☎ 01227 862213 🖷 01227 471635 🖱 larissa.laing@canterbury.gov.uk

Health and Safety: Mr Stephen Turner, Health & Safety Officer, Council Offices, Military Road, Canterbury CT1 1YW ☎ 01227 862079 🖱 stephen.turner@canterbury.gov.uk

Home Energy Conservation: Mr Steve King, Private Sector Housing Manager, Council Offices, Military Road, Canterbury CT1 1YW ☎ 01227 862237 🖱 steve.king@canterbury.gov.uk

Housing: Ms Larissa Laing, Head of Neighbourhood Services, Council Offices, Military Road, Canterbury CT1 1YW ☎ 01227 862213 🖷 01227 471635 🖱 larissa.laing@canterbury.gov.uk

Legal: Mr Mark Ellender, Head of Legal & Democratic Services, Council Offices, Military Road, Canterbury CT1 1YW ☎ 01227 862000 🖷 01227 862020 🖱 mark.ellender@canterbury.gov.uk

Leisure and Cultural Services: Mr David Ford, Assistant Head of Service (Cultural Development), Council Offices, Military Road, Canterbury CT1 1YW ☎ 01227 862526 🖷 01227 470599 🖱 david.ford@canterbury.gov.uk

Leisure and Cultural Services: Mrs Janice McGuinness, Head of Culture & Enterprise, Council Offices, Military Road, Canterbury CT1 1YW ☎ 01227 862492 🖷 01227 470599 🖱 janice.mcguinness@canterbury.gov.uk

Licensing: Mr Roger Vick, Commercial Health Manager, Council Offices, Military Road, Canterbury CT1 1YW ☎ 01227 862214 🖱 roger.vick@canterbury.gov.uk

Lottery Funding, Charity and Voluntary: Ms Suzi Wakeham, Head of Community Development, Council Offices, Military Road, Canterbury CT1 1YW ☎ 01227 862057 🖱 suzi.wakeham@canterbury.gov.uk

Member Services: Mr Mark Ellender, Head of Legal & Democratic Services, Council Offices, Military Road, Canterbury CT1 1YW ☎ 01227 862000 🖷 01227 862020 🖱 mark.ellender@canterbury.gov.uk

Parking: Mr Robert Pollard, Parking Enforcement Manager, Council Offices, Military Road, Canterbury CT1 1YW ☎ 01227 862287 🖱 bob.pollard@canterbury.gov.uk

Personnel / HR: Mrs Charlie Greenway, Head of Personnel Services, Council Offices, Military Road, Canterbury CT1 1YW ☎ 01227 862070

Personnel / HR: Ms Juli Oliver-Smith, Head of EK Human Resources, East Kent HR Partnership, Dover District Council, White Cliffs Business Park, Whitfield, Dover CT16 3PJ ☎ 07917 473616 🖱 hrpartnership@dover.gov.uk; hrpartnership@dover.gov.uk

Planning: Mr Ian Brown, Head of Regeneration & Planning, Council Offices, Military Road, Canterbury CT1 1YW ☎ 01227 862193 🖱 ian.brown@canterbury.gov.uk

Planning: Mr David Reed, Strategic Director, Council Offices, Military Road, Canterbury CT1 1YW ☎ 01227 862468 🖷 01227 862020 🖱 david.reed@canterbury.gov.uk

Procurement: Mrs Alexis Jobson, Central Services Manager, Council Offices, Military Road, Canterbury CT1 1YW ☎ 01227 862255 🖷 01227 862020 🖱 alexis.jobson@canterbury.gov.uk

Recycling & Waste Minimisation: Ms Larissa Laing, Head of Neighbourhood Services, Council Offices, Military Road, Canterbury CT1 1YW ☎ 01227 862213 🖷 01227 471635 🖱 larissa.laing@canterbury.gov.uk

Regeneration: Mr Ian Brown, Head of Regeneration & Planning, Council Offices, Military Road, Canterbury CT1 1YW ☎ 01227 862193 🖱 ian.brown@canterbury.gov.uk

Staff Training: Ms Julia Crawford, Training Manager, Council Offices, Military Road, Canterbury CT1 1YW ☎ 01227 862142 🖱 julia.podd@canterbury.gov.uk

Staff Training: Ms Sonia Godfrey, HR Manager - Business Services, East Kent HR Partnership, Dover District Council, White Cliffs Business Park, Whitfield, Dover CT16 3PJ ☎ 07854 763690 hrpartnership@dover.gov.uk

Sustainable Communities: Ms Suzi Wakeham, Head of Community Development, Council Offices, Military Road, Canterbury CT1 1YW ☎ 01227 862057 🖱 suzi.wakeham@canterbury.gov.uk

Sustainable Development: Ms Dawn Hudd, Deputy Head of Culture & Enterprise, Council Offices, Military Road, Canterbury CT1 1YW ☎ 01227 862054 🖷 01227 471635 🖱 dawn.hudd@canterbury.gov.uk

Tourism: Mrs Caroline Cooper, Tourism Manager, Council Offices, Military Road, Canterbury CT1 1YW ☎ 01227 862571 🖱 caroline.cooper@canterbury.gov.uk

Tourism: Mrs Janice McGuinness, Head of Culture & Enterprise, Council Offices, Military Road, Canterbury CT1 1YW ☎ 01227 862492 🖷 01227 470599 🖱 janice.mcguinness@canterbury.gov.uk

Town Centre: Ms Dawn Hudd, Deputy Head of Culture &

Enterprise, Council Offices, Military Road, Canterbury CT1 1YW
☎ 01227 862054 🖷 01227 471635
dawn.hudd@canterbury.gov.uk

Waste Collection and Disposal: Ms Larissa Laing, Head of Neighbourhood Services, Council Offices, Military Road, Canterbury CT1 1YW ☎ 01227 862213 🖷 01227 471635
larissa.laing@canterbury.gov.uk

MEMBERS OF THE COUNCIL (50)

***Mayor:* Waters**, Robert (CON - St Stephens)
robert.waters@canterbury.gov.uk

***Sheriff:* Taylor**, Heather (CON - Sturry South)
heather.taylor@canterbury.gov.uk

***Leader of the Council:* Gilbey**, John (CON - Blean Forest)
john.gilbey@canterbury.gov.uk

***Deputy Leader of the Council:* Law**, Jean (CON - Seasalter)
jean.law@canterbury.gov.uk

***Group Leader:* Perkins**, Alex (LD - Wincheap)
alex.perkins@canterbury.gov.uk

***Group Leader:* Wratten**, John (LAB - Harbour)
john.wratten@canterbury.gov.uk

Austin, Tony (CON - Sturry North)
tony.austin@canterbury.gov.uk

Baker, Neil (CON - Tankerton)
neil.baker@canterbury.gov.uk

Baldock, Alan (LAB - Northgate)
alan.baldock@canterbury.gov.uk

Bellamy, Jeremy (CON - Barton)
jeremy.bellamy@canterbury.gov.uk

Bissett, Evelyn (CON - Herne & Broomfield)
evelyn.bissett@canterbury.gov.uk

Bright, Robert (CON - Greenhill & Eddington)
robert.bright@canterbury.gov.uk

Byford, Sebastien (CON - West Bay)
sebastien.byford@canterbury.gov.uk

Cartwright, Phil (LAB - Harbour)
phil.cartwright@canterbury.gov.uk

Clark, Ashley (CON - Gorrell)
ashley.clark@canterbury.gov.uk

Cook, Simon (CON - North Nailbourne)
simon.cook@canterbury.gov.uk

Cook, Andrew (CON - Heron)
andrew.cook@canterbury.gov.uk

Cragg, Harry (CON - St Stephens)
harry.cragg@canterbury.gov.uk

Dixey, Michael (LD - Harbledown)
michael.dixey@canterbury.gov.uk

Doyle, Rosemary (CON - Chartham & Stone Street)
rosemary.doyle@canterbury.gov.uk

Eden-Green, Nick (LD - Wincheap)
nick.edengreen@canterbury.gov.uk

Edwards, Jennie (CON - Reculver)
jennie.edwards@canterbury.gov.uk

Ellis, Darren (CON - Northgate)
darren.ellis@canterbury.gov.uk

Flaherty, Ron (LD - Heron)
ron.flaherty@canterbury.gov.uk

Flanagan, James (LD - Westgate)
james.flanagan@canterbury.gov.uk

Glover, Georgina (CON - Marshside)
georgina.glover@canterbury.gov.uk

Harrison, Jeanne (CON - Tankerton)
jeanne.harrison@canterbury.gov.uk

Hirst, David (CON - Greenhill & Eddington)
david.hirst@canterbury.gov.uk

Howes, Joe (CON - Heron)
joe.howes@canterbury.gov.uk

Lee, Peter (CON - West Bay)
peter.lee@canterbury.gov.uk

Linfield, Ida (LD - Westgate)
ida.linfield@canterbury.gov.uk

MacCaul, Charlotte (LD - Wincheap)
charlotte.maccaul@canterbury.gov.uk

McCabe, Hazel (CON - Blean Forest)
hazel.mccabe@canterbury.gov.uk

Oakey, Bill (CON - Barham Downs)
bill.oakey@canterbury.gov.uk

O'Dea, Alison (CON - Gorrell)
alison.o'dea@canterbury.gov.uk

Reuby, Gillian (CON - Reculver)
gillian.reuby@canterbury.gov.uk

Samper, Jennifer (CON - Chestfield & Swalecliffe)
jenny.samper@canterbury.gov.uk

Sharp, Mike (CON - Seasalter)
mike.sharp@canterbury.gov.uk

Sonnex, Sharron (CON - Herne & Broomfield)
sharron.sonnex@canterbury.gov.uk

Staley, Brian (LD - Little Stour)
brian.staley@canterbury.gov.uk

Taylor, Ann (CON - Reculver)
ann.taylor@canterbury.gov.uk

Thomas, Ian (CON - Chestfield & Swalecliffe)
ian.thomas@canterbury.gov.uk

Thomas, Robert (CON - Chartham & Stone Street)
robert.thomas@canterbury.gov.uk

Todd, Pat (CON - Chestfield & Swalecliffe)
pat.todd@canterbury.gov.uk

Vickers, Paula (LD - Barton)
paula.vickers@canterbury.gov.uk

Vickery-Jones, Peter (CON - Herne & Broomfield)
peter.vickeryjones@canterbury.gov.uk

Westgate, Terry (CON - St Stephens)
terry.westgate@canterbury.gov.uk

Williams, Steven (CON - Barton)
steven.williams@canterbury.gov.uk

Windsor, Cyril (CON - Seasalter)
cyril.windsor@canterbury.gov.uk

Wood, Graham
(LD - Westgate)
graham.wood@canterbury.gov.uk

POLITICAL COMPOSITION

CON: 37, LD: 10, LAB: 3

CABINET

Leader; Major Policy, Major Projects & Culture: Mr John Gilbey
Deputy Leader; Communications: Mrs Jean Law
Communications, Culture & Tourism: Mr Neil Baker
Engineering & Transport: Mr Peter Vickery-Jones
Finance, Legal, Personnel & ICT: Mr Peter Lee
Housing: Mr Joe Howes
Licensing & Community Safety: Mr Andrew Cook
Sport & Leisure: Mr Darren Ellis
Waste Collection, Grounds Maintenance & Environment: Ms Rosemary Doyle

COMMITTEE CHAIRS

Development Management: Miss Jennifer Samper
Housing Appeals & Benefits: Ms Sharron Sonnex
Licensing: Ms Jeanne Harrison
Overview: Ms Alison O'Dea
Scrutiny: Mr Alex Perkins

CARDIFF W

Cardiff Council, (Cyngor Caerdydd), County Hall, Atlantic Wharf, Cardiff CF10 4UW ☎ 029 2087 2000 🖷 029 2087 2086 ✉ c2c@cardiff.gov.uk 💻 www.cardiff.gov.uk

FACTS & FIGURES

Police Authority: South Wales Police Authority
Learning and Skills Council: Wales
Parliamentary Constituencies: Cardiff Central, Cardiff North, Cardiff South and Penarth, Cardiff West, Pontypridd
EU Constituencies: Wales
Election Frequency: Elections are of whole council
Twinning: Hordaland County (Norway); Nantes (France); Stuttgart (Germany); Lugansk (Ukraine); Xiamen (China)

PRINCIPAL OFFICERS

Chief Executive: Mr Jonathan House, Chief Executive, County Hall, Atlantic Wharf, Cardiff CF10 4UW ☎ 029 2087 2400 🖷 029 2087 7081 ✉ jon.house@cardiff.gov.uk

Architect, Building / Property Services: Mr David Young, Operational Manager - Design & Construction, Bessemer Close, Leckwith Industrial Estate, Cardiff CF11 8XH ☎ 029 2087 2000 🖷 029 2087 8229 ✉ davy@cardiff.gov.uk

Best Value: Mr Martin Hamilton, Chief Officer - City Management, County Hall, Atlantic Wharf, Cardiff CF10 4UW ☎ 029 2087 2296 🖷 029 2087 2579 ✉ m.hamilton@cardiff.gov.uk

Catering Services: Mr Theo Callendar, Manager - Trading & Quality, County Hall, Atlantic Wharf, Cardiff CF10 4UW ☎ 029 2087 2025 ✉ cntyhallcatering@cardiff.gov.uk

Children / Youth Services: Ms Maria Michael, Chief Children's Services Officer, County Hall, Atlantic Wharf, Cardiff CF10 4UW ☎ 029 2087 3803 🖷 029 2087 3804 ✉ m.michael@cardiff.gov.uk

Computer Management: Mr Steve Durbin, Head of Service, County Hall, Atlantic Wharf, Cardiff CF10 4UW ☎ 029 2087 2100 ✉ s.durbin@cardiff.gov.uk

Consumer Protection and Trading Standards: Mr Dave Holland, Head of Service, Regulatory & Support Service, County Hall, Atlantic Wharf, Cardiff CF10 2TS ☎ 029 2087 2089 🖷 029 2087 2072 ✉ d.holland@cardiff.gov.uk

Contracts: Mr Huw Charles, Purchasing & Contracts Manager, Bessemer Close, Leckwith Industrial Estate, Cardiff CF11 8XH ☎ 029 2087 3744 🖷 029 2037 7030 ✉ h.charles@cardiff.gov.uk

Corporate Services: Mr Gareth Newell, Business Development Manager, County Hall, Atlantic Wharf, Cardiff CF10 4UW ☎ 029 2087 3723 ✉ gnewell@cardiff.gov.uk

Corporate Services: Mr Alan Richards, Superintendent Registrar, Park Place, Cardiff CF10 4UW ☎ 029 2087 1680 🖷 029 2087 1691 ✉ a.richards@cardiff.gov.uk

Education: Mr Chris Jones, Chief Education Officer, County Hall, Atlantic Wharf, Cardiff CF10 4UW ☎ 029 2087 2700 🖷 029 2087 2705 ✉ chjones@cardiff.gov.uk

E-Government: Mr Steve Durbin, Head of Service, County Hall, Atlantic Wharf, Cardiff CF10 4UW ☎ 029 2087 2100 ✉ s.durbin@cardiff.gov.uk

Emergency Planning: Mr Gavin Macho, Principal Emergency Management Officer, Strategic Planning & Environment, Emergency Planning Unit, City Hall, Cardiff CF10 3ND ☎ 029 2087 1831 🖷 029 2087 1836 ✉ gmacho@cardiff.gov.uk

Environmental / Technical Services: Mr Neil Hanratty, City Development Officer, City Hall, Cathays Park, Cardiff CF10 3ND ☎ 029 2087 2052 ✉ nhanratty@cardiff.gov.uk

Environmental Health: Mr Neil Hanratty, City Development Officer, City Hall, Cathays Park, Cardiff CF10 3ND ☎ 029 2087 2052 ✉ nhanratty@cardiff.gov.uk

Estates, Property & Valuation: Mr Charles Coats, Operational Manager - Estates, Strategic Estates, Corporate Services, Cardiff Council, Brindley Road, Cardiff CF10 8TX ☎ 029 2078 5372 ✉ ccoats@cardiff.gov.uk

European Liaison: Mr Gareth Newell, Business Development Manager, County Hall, Atlantic Wharf, Cardiff CF10 4UW ☎ 029 2087 3723 ✉ gnewell@cardiff.gov.uk

Events Manager: Mr Rob Corp, City Centre & Major Events Manager, County Hall, Atlantic Wharf, Cardiff CF10 4UW ☎ 029 2087 3916 🖷 029 2087 3382 ✉ r.corp@cardiff.gov.uk

Finance and Treasurer: Ms Christine Salter, Chief Officer - Corporate Services & Section 151 Officer, County Hall, Atlantic Wharf, Cardiff CF10 4UW ☎ 029 2087 2300 🖷 029 2087 2206 ✉ c.salter@cardiff.gov.uk

Fleet Management: Mr Richard Jones, Tactical Manager - Fleet & Procurement, County Hall, Atlantic Wharf, Cardiff CF10 4UW ☎ 029 2053 7679 ✉ RiJones@cardiff.gov.uk

Grounds Maintenance: Mr Jon Maidment, Operational Manager for Parks & Sport, County Hall, Atlantic Wharf, Cardiff CF10 4UW ☎ ; 029 2068 4020 ✉ j.maidment@cardiff.gov.uk

Health and Safety: Miss Christina Lloyd, Operational Manager - Health & Safety, County Hall, Atlantic Wharf, Cardiff CF10 4UW ☎ 029 2087 2635 🖷 029 2087 2606 ✉ c.c.lloyd@cardiff.gov.uk

Highways: Mr Neil Hanratty, City Development Officer, City Hall, Cathays Park, Cardiff CF10 3ND ☎ 029 2087 2052 ✉ nhanratty@cardiff.gov.uk

Housing: Ms Sarah McGill, Corporate Chief Officer for Housing & Neighbourhood Renewal, Wilcox House, Dunleavy Drive, Celtic Gateway, Cardiff CF11 0BA ☎ 029 2087 2900

s.mcgill@cardiff.gov.uk

Housing Maintenance: Ms Sarah McGill, Corporate Chief Officer for Housing & Neighbourhood Renewal, Wilcox House, Dunleavy Drive, Celtic Gateway, Cardiff CF11 0BA ☎ 029 2087 2900 s.mcgill@cardiff.gov.uk

Legal: Ms Melanie Clay, Chief Officer Legal and Democratic Services, County Hall, Atlantic Wharf, Cardiff CF10 4UW ☎ 029 2087 2421 melanie.clay@cardiff.gov.uk

Licensing: Mr Neil Hanratty, City Development Officer, City Hall, Cathays Park, Cardiff CF10 3ND ☎ 029 2087 2052 nhanratty@cardiff.gov.uk

Lighting: Mr Gary Brown, Operational Manager - Highways Maintenance, County Hall, Atlantic Wharf, Cardiff CF10 4UW ☎ 029 2078 5280 gbrown@cardiff.gov.uk

Member Services: Ms Melanie Clay, Chief Officer Legal and Democratic Services, County Hall, Atlantic Wharf, Cardiff CF10 4UW ☎ 029 2087 2421 melanie.clay@cardiff.gov.uk

Member Services: Mr Mike Davies, Scruitny Performance and Improvement, County Hall, Atlantic Wharf, Cardiff CF10 4UW ☎ 029 2087 2406 🖷 029 2087 2431 m.davies@cardiff.gov.uk

Parking: Mr Paul Carter, Operational Manager - Transportation Strategy & Development, County Hall, Atlantic Wharf, Cardiff CF10 4UW ☎ 029 2087 3243 🖷 029 2087 3108 p.carter@cardiff.gov.uk

Personnel / HR: Mr Laithe Bonni, Specialist Support Manager, County Hall, Atlantic Wharf, Cardiff CF10 4UW ☎ 029 2087 2655 l.bonni@cardiff.gov.uk

Personnel / HR: Mr Philip Lenz, Chief Officer Shared Services, Room 470, County Hall, Atlantic Wharf, Cardiff CF10 4UW ☎ 029 2087 2000 plenz@cardiff.gov.uk

Planning: Mr Neil Hanratty, City Development Officer, City Hall, Cathays Park, Cardiff CF10 3ND ☎ 029 2087 2052 nhanratty@cardiff.gov.uk

Planning: Mr Phil Williams, Operational Manager - Strategic Planning and Development Management, City Hall, Cathays Park, Cardiff CF10 3ND ☎ 029 2087 1379 🖷 029 2087 2665 p.a.williams@cardiff.gov.uk

Procurement: Ms Christine Salter, Chief Officer - Corporate Services & Section 151 Officer, County Hall, Atlantic Wharf, Cardiff CF10 4UW ☎ 029 2087 2300 🖷 029 2087 2206 c.salter@cardiff.gov.uk

Public Libraries: Ms Elspeth Morris, Senior Libraries Officer, County Hall, Atlantic Wharf, Cardiff CF10 4UW ☎ 029 2087 2000

Recycling & Waste Minimisation: Ms Tara King, Chief Officer Waste Management & City Services, Lamby Way, Cardiff CF3 2EQ ☎ 029 2087 5343 🖷 029 2036 3419 t.king@cardiff.gov.uk

Regeneration: Mr Gareth Harcombe, Operational Manager - Regeneration, City Hall, Cathays Park, Cardiff CF10 3ND ☎ 029 2087 3489 gharcombe@cardiff.gov.uk

Road Safety: Mr Mark Foweraker, County Road Safety Officer, County Hall, Atlantic Wharf, Cardiff CF10 4UW ☎ 029 2078 8521 mfoweraker@cardiff.gov.uk

Social Services: Mr Nick Jarman, Corporate Director - Direct Services, County Hall, Atlantic Wharf, Cardiff CF10 4UW ☎ 029 2087 2460 n.jarman@cardiff.gov.uk

Social Services (Adult): Mr Michael Murphy, Chief Adult Services Officer, County Hall, Atlantic Wharf, Cardiff CF10 4UW ☎ 029 2087 3600 🖷 029 2087 3611 michael.murphy@cardiff.gov.uk

Social Services (Children): Ms Maria Michael, Chief Children's Services Officer, County Hall, Atlantic Wharf, Cardiff CF10 4UW ☎ 029 2087 3803 🖷 029 2087 3804 m.michael@cardiff.gov.uk

Staff Training: Mrs Deborah Morley, Operational Manager - Learning & Development, County Hall, Atlantic Wharf, Cardiff CF10 4UW ☎ 029 2087 2000 🖷 029 2087 2633 d.morley@cardiff.gov.uk

Tourism: Ms Sally Edwards Hart, Operational Manager - Venues & Tourism, County Hall, Atlantic Wharf, Cardiff CF10 4UW ☎ 029 2087 3360 🖷 029 2082 7161 sallyhart@cardiff.gov.uk

Tourism: Ms Kathryn Richards, Head of Culture, Tourism & Events, Motorpoint Arena, Executive Suite 1, Mary Ann Street, Cardiff CF10 2EQ ☎ 029 2087 2452 🖷 029 2087 2499 k.richards@cardiff.gov.uk

Town Centre: Mr Rob Corp, City Centre & Major Events Manager, County Hall, Atlantic Wharf, Cardiff CF10 4UW ☎ 029 2066 4723 r.corp@cardiff.gov.uk

Transport: Mr Paul Carter, Operational Manager - Transportation Strategy & Development, County Hall, Atlantic Wharf, Cardiff CF10 4UW ☎ 029 2087 3243 🖷 029 2087 3108 p.carter@cardiff.gov.uk

Transport Planner: Mr Paul Carter, Operational Manager - Transportation Strategy & Development, County Hall, Atlantic Wharf, Cardiff CF10 4UW ☎ 029 2087 3243 🖷 029 2087 3108 p.carter@cardiff.gov.uk

Waste Collection and Disposal: Ms Tara King, Chief Officer Waste Management & City Services, Lamby Way, Cardiff CF3 2EQ ☎ 029 2087 5343 🖷 029 2036 3419 t.king@cardiff.gov.uk

MEMBERS OF THE COUNCIL (75)

***Chair:* Furlong**, Cerys (LAB - Canton)
membersservices@cardiff.gov.uk
***Deputy Chair:* Jones**, Keith (LAB - Llanrumney)
***Leader of the Council:* Joyce**, Heather (LAB - Llanrumney)
membersservices@cardiff.gov.uk
***Deputy Leader of the Council:* Cook**, Ralph (LAB - Trowbridge)
membersservices@cardiff.gov.uk
***Group Leader:* McEvoy**, Neil (PC - Fairwater)
membersservices@cardiff.gov.uk

LOCAL AUTHORITIES

***Group Leader:* Robson**, Adrian (IND - Rhiwbina)
arobson@cardiff.gov.uk
***Group Leader:* Walker**, David (CON - Lisvane)
dwalker@cardiff.gov.uk
***Group Leader:* Woodman**, Judith (LD - Pentwyn)
jwoodman@cardiff.gov.uk
Ahmed, Manzoor (LAB - Adamsdown)
Ahmed, Ali (LAB - Butetown)
Ali, Dilwar (LAB - Llandaff North)
Aubrey, Gareth (LD - Llandaff)
membersservices@cardiff.gov.uk
Bale, Philip (LAB - Llanishen)
Bowden, Fenella (IND - Heath)
Boyle, Joe (LD - Penylan)
Bradbury, Peter (LAB - Caerau)
Bridges, Ed (LD - Gabalfa)
ebridges@cardiff.gov.uk
Burfoot, Patricia (LD - Penylan)
pburfoot@cardiff.gov.uk
Carter, Joseph (LD - Pentwyn)
Chaundy, Paul (LD - Pentwyn)
pchaundy@cardiff.gov.uk
Clark, Elizabeth (LD - Cathays)
membersservices@cardiff.gov.uk
Cook, Richard (LAB - Canton)
ricook@cardiff.gov.uk
Corria, Siobhan (LAB - Llandaff North)
Cowan, Jayne (IND - Rhiwbina)
membersservices@cardiff.gov.uk
Davies, Kirsty (LD - Llandaff)
membersservices@cardiff.gov.uk
Davis, Chris (LAB - Whitchurch & Tongwynlais)
De'Ath, Daniel (LAB - Plasnewydd)
Derbyshire, Bob (LAB - Rumney)
Evans, Jonathan (LAB - Whitchurch & Tongwynlais)
Ford, Lisa (PC - Fairwater)
membersservices@cardiff.gov.uk
Goddard, Susan (LAB - Ely)
sgoddard@cardiff.gov.uk
Goodway, Russell (LAB - Ely)
r.v.goodway@cardiff.gov.uk
Gordon, Iona (LAB - Riverside)
Govier, Ashley (LAB - Grangetown)
Graham, Andrew (CON - Llanishen)
Groves, David (LAB - Whitchurch & Tongwynlais)
Hawkins, Phil (LAB - Riverside)
Hinchey, Graham (LAB - Heath)
Holden, Gareth (LD - Gabalfa)
Holland, Luke (LAB - Splott)
Howells, Nigel (LD - Adamsdown)
n.howells@cardiff.gov.uk
Hudson, Lyn (CON - Heath)
membersservices@cardiff.gov.uk
Hunt, Garry (LAB - Llanishen)
Hyde, Keith (LD - Pentwyn)
khyde@cardiff.gov.uk
Javed, Mohammad (LAB - Plasnewydd)
Jones, Margaret (LD - Cyncoed)
Kelloway, Bill (LD - Penylan)
bkelloway@cardiff.gov.uk
Knight, Sam (LAB - Cathays)
Lent, Sue (LAB - Plasnewydd)
Lloyd, Kathryn (LD - Cyncoed)
Lomax, John (LAB - Grangetown)
Love, Cecelia (LAB - Riverside)
Magill, Julia (LAB - Llanishen)
Marshall, Gretta (LAB - Splott)
McGarry, Mary (LAB - Plasnewydd)
McKerlish, Roderick (CON - Radyr)
membersservices@cardiff.gov.uk
Merry, Sarah (LAB - Cathays)
Michael, Michael (LAB - Trowbridge)
Mitchell, Paul (LAB - Fairwater)
Morgan, Derek (LAB - Llanrumney)
Murphy, Jim (LAB - Ely)
Parry, Jacqueline (LAB - Rumney)
Patel, Ramesh (LAB - Canton)
rapatel@cardiff.gov.uk
Phillips, Georgina (LAB - Pontprennau / Old St. Mellons)
Rees, Diane (CON - Pontprennau / Old St. Mellons)
direes@cardiff.gov.ukw
Rees, David (LD - Cyncoed)
Sanders, Eleanor (IND - Rhiwbina)
Simmons, Elaine (LAB - Caerau)
Thomas, Huw (LAB - Splott)
Thomas, Graham (CON - Creigiau & St Fagans)
Thomas, Benjamin (LAB - Whitchurch & Tongwynlais)
Thorne, Lynda (LAB - Grangetown)
Walsh, Monica (LAB - Trowbridge)
Weaver, Christopher (LAB - Cathays)
Williams, Craig (CON - Pentyrch)

POLITICAL COMPOSITION

LAB: 46, LD: 16, CON: 7, IND: 4, PC: 2

CABINET

Leader: Ms Heather Joyce
Deputy Leader / Strategic Planning, Highways & Transportation: Mr Richard Cook
Education & Lifelong Learning: Ms Julia Magill
Communities, Housing & Social Justice: Ms Lynda Thorne
Environment: Mr Ashley Govier
Environment: Ms Margaret Jones
Finance, Business & Local Economy: Mr Russell Goodway
Social Care, Health & Wellbeing - Children's: Mr Richard Cook
Sport, Leisure & Culture: Mr Huw Thomas

COMMITTEE CHAIRS

Children & Young People (Scrutiny): Mr Bill Kelloway
Community & Adult Services (Scrutiny): Mr Ralph Cook
Constitution: Mr Rodney Berman
Council Appeals: Mr Elgan Morgan
Economic (Scrutiny): Ms Gwenllian Lansdown
Employment Conditions: Mr Rodney Berman
Environmental (Scrutiny): Mr Simon Wakefield
Licensing: Mr Ed Bridges
Planning: Ms Patricia Burfoot
Policy Review & Performance (Scrutiny): Ms Diane Rees
Public Protection: Mr Ed Bridges
Recovery: Mr Roger Burley
Standards & Ethics: Mr Akmal Hanuk (External)

CARLISLE CITY D

Carlisle City Council, Civic Centre, Carlisle CA3 8QG ☎ 01228 817000 🖷 01228 817048 💻 www.carlisle.gov.uk

FACTS & FIGURES

Police Authority: Cumbria Police Authority
Health Authority: North West Strategic Health Authority
Learning and Skills Council: North West
Parliamentary Constituencies: Carlisle, Penrith and The Border
EU Constituencies: North West
Election Frequency: Elections are by thirds
Twinning: Flensburg (Germany); Slupsk (Poland)

PRINCIPAL OFFICERS

Chief Executive: Dr Jason Gooding, Chief Executive, Civic Centre, Carlisle CA3 8QG ☎ 01228 817009 ✉ jasong@carlisle.gov.uk

Senior Management: Mr Darren Crossley, Deputy Chief Executive, Civic Centre, Carlisle CA3 8QG ☎ 01228 817003 ✉ darrenc@carlisle.gov.uk

Access Officer / Social Services (Disability): Mrs Heather Irving, Access Officer, Civic Centre, Carlisle CA3 8QG ☎ 01228 817183 🖷 01228 817513 ✉ heatheri@carlisle.gov.uk

Architect, Building / Property Services: Mr Raymond Simmons, Property Services Manager, Civic Centre, Carlisle CA3 8QG ☎ 01228 817421 ✉ raymonds@carlisle.gov.uk

Best Value: Mr Steven O'Keeffe, Policy & Performance Manager, Civic Centre, Carlisle CA3 8QG ☎ 01228 817258 ✉ steveno@carlisle.gov.uk

Building Control: Mr Mark Bowman, Building Control Manager, Civic Centre, Carlisle CA3 8QG ☎ 01228 817189 ✉ markbo@carlisle.gov.uk

PR / Communications: Mr Steven O'Keefe, Policy & Communications Manager, Civic Centre, Carlisle CA3 8QG ☎ 01228 817258 🖷 01228 817538 ✉ steveno@carlisle.gov.uk

Community Planning: Mr Gavin Capstick, Carlisle Local Strategic Partnership Manager, Civic Centre, Carlisle CA3 8QG ☎ 01228 817030 ✉ gavincap@carlisle.gov.uk

Community Safety: Mr Keith Gerrard, Director - Community Engagement, Civic Centre, Carlisle CA3 8QG ☎ 01228 817350 ✉ keithg@carlisle.gov.uk

Computer Management: Mr Michael Scott, ICT Shared Services Manager, Civic Centre, Carlisle CA3 8QG ☎ 01228 817251 ✉ michael.scott@carlisle.gov.uk

Corporate Services: Dr Jason Gooding, Chief Executive, Civic Centre, Carlisle CA3 8QG ☎ 01228 817009 ✉ jasong@carlisle.gov.uk

Corporate Services: Mr Peter Mason, Director - Resources, Civic Centre, Carlisle CA3 8QG ☎ 01228 817270 ✉ peterm@carlisle.gov.uk

Customer Service: Mrs Jillian Gillespie, Customer Services Manager, Civic Centre, Carlisle CA3 8QG ☎ 01228 817461 ✉ jilliang@carlisle.gov.uk

Economic Development: Ms Jane Meek, Director - Economic Development, Civic Centre, Carlisle CA3 8QG ☎ 01228 817502 ✉ christopherh@carlisle.gov.uk

E-Government: Mr Michael Scott, ICT Shared Services Manager, Civic Centre, Carlisle CA3 8QG ☎ 01228 817251 ✉ michael.scott@carlisle.gov.uk

Electoral Registration: Mr Ian Dixon, Electoral Services Officer, Civic Centre, Carlisle CA3 8QG ☎ 01228 817555 ✉ iand@carlisle.gov.uk

Emergency Planning: Mr Steven O'Keeffe, Emergency Planning Manager, Civic Centre, Carlisle CA3 8QG ☎ 01228 817258 ✉ steveno@carlisle.gov.uk

Environmental / Technical Services: Ms Angela Culleton, Director - Local Environment, Civic Centre, Carlisle CA3 8QG ☎ 01228 817325 ✉ angelacu@carlisle.gov.uk

Environmental Health: Ms Angela Culleton, Director - Local Environment, Civic Centre, Carlisle CA3 8QG ☎ 01228 817325 ✉ angelacu@carlisle.gov.uk

Estates, Property & Valuation: Mr Raymond Simmons, Property Services Manager, Civic Centre, Carlisle CA3 8QG ☎ 01228 817421 ✉ raymonds@carlisle.gov.uk

Events Manager: Mr Margaret Miller, Community, Housing & Health Manager, Civic Centre, Carlisle CA3 8QG ☎ 01228 817330 ✉ margaretmi@carlisle.gov.uk

Facilities: Mr Peter Mason, Director - Resources, Civic Centre, Carlisle CA3 8QG ☎ 01228 817270 ✉ peterm@carlisle.gov.uk

Finance and Treasurer: Mr Peter Mason, Director - Resources, Civic Centre, Carlisle CA3 8QG ☎ 01228 817270 ✉ peterm@carlisle.gov.uk

Grounds Maintenance: Ms Angela Culleton, Director - Local Environment, Civic Centre, Carlisle CA3 8QG ☎ 01228 817325 ✉ angelacu@carlisle.gov.uk

Health and Safety: Mr Arup Majhi, Safety & Health Environmental Manager, Civic Centre, Carlisle CA3 8QG ☎ 01228 817507 ✉ arupm@carlisle.gov.uk

Highways: Ms Angela Culleton, Director - Local Environment, Civic Centre, Carlisle CA3 8QG ☎ 01228 817325 ✉ angelacu@carlisle.gov.uk

Housing: Mr Keith Gerrard, Director - Community Engagement, Civic Centre, Carlisle CA3 8QG ☎ 01228 817350 ✉ keithg@carlisle.gov.uk

Legal: Mr Mark Lambert, Director - Governance, Civic Centre, Carlisle CA3 8QG ☎ 01228 817019 ✉ markl@carlisle.gov.uk

Leisure and Cultural Services: Mr Keith Gerrard, Director - Community Engagement, Civic Centre, Carlisle CA3 8QG ☎ 01228 817350 ✉ keithg@carlisle.gov.uk

Licensing: Mr Mark Lambert, Director - Governance, Civic Centre, Carlisle CA3 8QG ☎ 01228 817019 ✉ markl@carlisle.gov.uk

Lighting: Ms Angela Culleton, Director - Local Environment, Civic Centre, Carlisle CA3 8QG ☎ 01228 817325 ✉ angelacu@carlisle.gov.uk

Member Services: Mr Mark Lambert, Director - Governance, Civic Centre, Carlisle CA3 8QG ☎ 01228 817019 ✉ markl@carlisle.gov.uk

Parking: Ms Angela Culleton, Director - Local Environment, Civic Centre, Carlisle CA3 8QG ☎ 01228 817325 ✉ angelacu@carlisle.gov.uk

Partnerships: Mr Gavin Capstick, Carlisle Local Strategic Partnership Manager, Civic Centre, Carlisle CA3 8QG ☎ 01228 817030 ✉ gavincap@carlisle.gov.uk

Personnel / HR: Ms Jean Cross, Personnel Manager, Civic Centre, Carlisle CA3 8QG ☎ 01228 817081 ✉ jeanc@carlisle.gov.uk

Planning: Mr Christopher Pearson, Economic Development Manager, Civic Centre, Carlisle CA3 8QG ☎ 01228 817015 ✉ christopherp@carlisle.gov.uk

Procurement: Mr Peter Mason, Director - Resources, Civic Centre, Carlisle CA3 8QG ☎ 01228 817270 ✉ peterm@carlisle.gov.uk

Recycling & Waste Minimisation: Ms Angela Culleton, Director - Local Environment, Civic Centre, Carlisle CA3 8QG ☎ 01228 817325 ✉ angelacu@carlisle.gov.uk

Regeneration: Mr Christopher Pearson, Economic Development Manager, Civic Centre, Carlisle CA3 8QG ☎ 01228 817015 ✉ christopherp@carlisle.gov.uk

Staff Training: Ms Linda Mattinson, Learning & Development Co-ordinator, Civic Centre, Carlisle CA3 8QG ☎ 01228 817076 ✉ lindam@carlisle.gov.uk

Street Scene: Ms Angela Culleton, Director - Local Environment, Civic Centre, Carlisle CA3 8QG ☎ 01228 817325 ✉ angelacu@carlisle.gov.uk

Sustainable Communities: Mr Keith Gerrard, Director - Community Engagement, Civic Centre, Carlisle CA3 8QG ☎ 01228 817350 ✉ keithg@carlisle.gov.uk

Tourism: Mr Christopher Pearson, Economic Development Manager, Civic Centre, Carlisle CA3 8QG ☎ 01228 817015 ✉ christopherp@carlisle.gov.uk

Waste Collection and Disposal: Ms Angela Culleton, Director - Local Environment, Civic Centre, Carlisle CA3 8QG ☎ 01228 817325 ✉ angelacu@carlisle.gov.uk

Waste Management: Ms Angela Culleton, Director - Local Environment, Civic Centre, Carlisle CA3 8QG ☎ 01228 817325 ✉ angelacu@carlisle.gov.uk

MEMBERS OF THE COUNCIL (51)

***Mayor:* Wilson**, David (LAB - Upperby)
DavidWi@carlisle.gov.uk
***Deputy Mayor:* Bloxham**, Raynor (CON - Longtown & Rockcliffe)
RayB@carlisle.gov.uk
***Leader of the Council:* Hendry**, Joseph (LAB - Yewdale)
jdhendry@msn.com
***Deputy Leader of the Council:* Glover**, Colin (LAB - Currock)
ColinG@carlisle.gov.uk
***Group Leader:* Allison**, Trevor (LD - Dalston)
TrevorA@carlisle.gov.uk
***Group Leader:* Boaden**, Michael (LAB - Botcherby)
MichaelBo@carlisle.gov.uk
***Group Leader:* Mallinson**, John (CON - Longtown & Rockcliffe)
johnmal@carlisle.gov.uk
Atkinson, Paul (LAB - Denton Holme)
Bainbridge, James (CON - Stanwix Rural)
JamesBa@carlisle.gov.uk
Bell, John (LAB - Morton)
johnbe@carlisle.gov.uk
Betton, Robert (IND - Botcherby)
robertb@carlisle.gov.uk
Bowditch, Steven (LAB - Yewdale)
stevenb@carlisle.gov.uk
Bowman, Cyril (CON - Irthing)
sydb@carlisle.gov.uk
Bowman, Marilyn (CON - Stanwix Rural)
MarilynB@carlisle.gov.uk
Bradley, Heather (LAB - Currock)
HeatherB@carlisle.gov.uk
Cape, Donald (LAB - Upperby)
donaldc@carlisle.gov.uk
Clarke, Nicola (CON - Dalston)
nicolac@carlisle.gov.uk
Collier, John (CON - Burgh)
johnc@carlisle.gov.uk
Craig, Bryan (CON - Dalston)
bryanc@carlisle.gov.uk
Earp, Barry (CON - Wetheral)
BarryE@carlisle.gov.uk
Ellis, Gareth (CON - Belah)
garethe@carlisle.gov.uk
Franklin, Jacqueline (LAB - Belle Vue)
jacquelinef@carlisle.gov.uk
Gallagher, Karen (LAB - Yewdale)
karenga@carlisle.gov.uk
Geddes, Jacquelyne (CON - Stanwix Urban)
JacquelyneG@carlisle.gov.uk
Graham, William (IND - Hayton)
BillG@carlisle.gov.uk
Hamilton Nedved, Paul (CON - Stanwix Urban)
pauln@carlisle.gov.uk
Harid, Abdul (LAB - Currock)
abdulh@carlisle.gov.uk
Layden, Stephen (CON - Brampton)
stephenl@carlisle.gov.uk
Lishman, Neville (CON - Wetheral)

NevilleL@carlisle.gov.uk
Luckley, Olwyn (LD - Castle)
OlwynL@carlisle.gov.uk
Mallinson, Elizabeth (CON - Stanwix Urban)
LizM@carlisle.gov.uk
Martlew, Elsie (LAB - Castle)
elsiem@carlisle.gov.uk
McDevitt, Hugh (LAB - Denton Holme)
HughMcD@carlisle.gov.uk
Mitchelson, Mike (CON - Brampton)
MikeM@carlisle.gov.uk
Morton, David (CON - Belah)
DavidMo@carlisle.gov.uk
Parsons, Doreen (CON - Great Corby & Geltsdale)
DoreenP@carlisle.gov.uk
Patrick, Lucy (LAB - St Aidans)
LucyP@carlisle.gov.uk
Prest, Judith (CON - Lyne)
judyp@carlisle.gov.uk
Quilter, Anne (LAB - St Aidans)
Riddle, Jessica (LAB - Belle Vue)
JessicaR@carlisle.gov.uk
Scarborough, Charles (LAB - Botcherby)
Sherriff, Lee (LAB - Harraby)
leesh@carlisle.gov.uk
Southward, Joan (LAB - Denton Holme)
JoanS@carlisle.gov.uk
Stevenson, Elaine (LAB - Morton)
elaines@carlisle.gov.uk
Stothard, Colin (LAB - Morton)
ColinS@carlisle.gov.uk
Tickner, Les (LAB - Belle Vue)
lesti@carlisle.gov.uk
Vasey, Trish (CON - Belah)
trishv@carlisle.gov.uk
Warwick, Ann (LAB - Upperby)
annw@carlisle.gov.uk
Watson, Reginald (LAB - St Aidans)
RegW@Carlisle.gov.uk
Weber, Cyril (LAB - Harraby)
Whalen, William (LAB - Castle)
williamw@carlisle.gov.uk

POLITICAL COMPOSITION
LAB: 27, CON: 20, IND: 2, LD: 2

CABINET
Leader: Prof Joseph Hendry
Deputy Leader / Economy & Enterprise: Mr Colin Glover
Communities & Housing: Mrs Jessica Riddle
Culture, Health, Leisure & Young People: Ms Anne Quilter
Environment & Transport: Mrs Elsie Martlew
Finance, Governance & Resources: Dr Les Tickner

COMMITTEE CHAIRS
Licensing: Ms Jacqueline Franklin
Regulatory Panel: Mr John Bell

CARMARTHENSHIRE W

Carmarthenshire County Council, (Cyngor Sir Caerfyrddin), County Hall, Carmarthen SA31 1JP ☎ 01267 234567 🖷 01267 224911 ✉ information@carmarthenshire.gov.uk
💻 www.carmarthenshire.gov.uk

FACTS & FIGURES
Police Authority: Dyfed Powys Police Authority
Learning and Skills Council: Wales
Parliamentary Constituencies: Carmarthen East and Dinefwr, Carmarthen West and South Pembrokeshire, Llanelli
EU Constituencies: Wales
Election Frequency: Elections are of whole council

PRINCIPAL OFFICERS
Chief Executive: Mr Mark James, Chief Executive, County Hall, Carmarthen SA31 1JP ☎ 01267 224110 🖷 01267 224652
✉ mjames@carmarthenshire.gov.uk

Deputy Chief Executive: Mr Dave Gilbert, Director - Regeneration & Leisure, County Hall, Carmarthen SA31 1JP
☎ 01267 224141 🖷 01267 224640
✉ dgilbert@carmarthenshire.gov.uk

Assistant Chief Executive: Mr Chris Burns, Assistant Chief Executive - Customer Focus & Policy, County Hall, Carmarthen SA31 1JP ☎ 01267 224112 🖷 01267 224652
✉ cpburns@carmarthenshire.gov.uk

Assistant Chief Executive: Mr Paul Thomas, Assistant Chief Executive - People Management & Performance, Parc Dewi, Carmarthen SA31 3HB ☎ ; 01267 246123
✉ prthomas@carmarthenshire.gov.uk

Senior Management: Mr Roger Jones, Director - Resources, County Hall, Carmarthen SA31 1JP ☎ 01267 224121 🖷 01267 224122 ✉ rjones@carmarthenshire.gov.uk

Senior Management: Mr Bruce McLernon, Director - Social Care, Health & Housing, County Hall, Carmarthen SA31 1JP
☎ 01267 224697 🖷 01267 224681
✉ bmclernon@carmarthenshire.gov.uk

Senior Management: Mr Richard Workman, Director - Technical Services, County Hall, Carmarthen SA31 1JP ☎ 01267 224647
🖷 01267 224620 ✉ rworkman@carmarthenshire.gov.uk

Access Officer / Social Services (Disability): Mr Andrew Russ, Civil Contingency Officer, Parc Myrddin, Wellfield Road, Carmarthen SA13 1DS ☎ ; 01267 228147 🖷 01267 228207
✉ adruss@carmarthenshire.gov.uk

Architect, Building / Property Services: Mr Jonathan Fearn, Head - Corporate Property, Parc Dewi, Carmarthen SA31 3HB
☎ 01267 246244 ✉ jfearn@carmarthenshire.gov.uk

Building Control: Mr Eifion Bowen, Head of Planning Services, 40 Spilman Street, Carmarthen SA31 1LQ ☎ 01267 224850
🖷 01267 237612 ✉ ebowen@carmarthenshire.gov.uk

Catering Services: Mrs Elin Cullen, Head of Business & Specialist Services, Parc Dewi, Carmarthen SA31 3HB
☎ 01267 246480 ✉ ecullen@carmarthenshire.gov.uk

Children / Youth Services: Mr Jake Morgan, Interim Head - Children's Services, Block 2, St David's Park, Jobswewl Road, Carmarthen SA31 3HB ☎ ; 01267 246530 🖷 01267 228908
✉ jakemorgan@carmarthenshire.gov.uk

Civil Registration: Ms Amanda Bebb, Electorial Services Manager, County Hall, Carmarthen SA31 1JP ☎ 01267 228609 ✉ Abebb@carmarthenshire.gov.uk

PR / Communications: Mr Chris Burns, Assistant Chief Executive - Customer Focus & Policy, County Hall, Carmarthen SA31 1JP ☎ 01267 224112 🖷 01267 224652 ✉ cpburns@carmarthenshire.gov.uk

Community Safety: Mrs Kate Thomas, Community Safety Manager, Community Safety, Ammanford Police Station, Foundry Road, Ammanford SA18 2LS ☎ 01554 742182 🖷 01554 742199 ✉ kthomas@carmarthenshire.gov.uk

Computer Management: Mr Steven Havard, Joint Manager - IT, Parc Dewi, Carmarthen SA31 3HB ☎ 01267 234567 ✉ shavard@carmarthenshire.gov.uk

Consumer Protection and Trading Standards: Mr Philip Davies, Head - Public Protection, 3 Spilman Street, Carmarthen SA31 1LE ☎ 01267 228706 🖷 01267 221616 ✉ phdavies@carmarthenshire.gov.uk

Corporate Services: Mrs Linda Reese-Jones, Head - Administration & Law, County Hall, Carmarthen SA31 1JP ☎ 01267 224012 ✉ LRJones@carmarthenshire.gov.uk

Corporate Services: Mr Mike Rogers, Head - Policy & Performance, Parc Myrddin, Richmond Terrace, Carmarthen SA31 1HQ ☎ ; 01267 228171 ✉ mrogers@carmarthenshire.gov.uk

Customer Service: Mr Chris Burns, Assistant Chief Executive - Customer Focus & Policy, County Hall, Carmarthen SA31 1JP ☎ 01267 224112 🖷 01267 224652 ✉ cpburns@carmarthenshire.gov.uk

Direct Labour: Mr Richard Workman, Director - Technical Services, County Hall, Carmarthen SA31 1JP ☎ 01267 224647 🖷 01267 224620 ✉ rworkman@carmarthenshire.gov.uk

Economic Development: Ms Wendy Walters, Head - Economic Development, Nant y Ci, Carmarthen SA33 5DR ☎ 01267 242336 ✉ wswalters@carmarthenshire.gov.uk

E-Government: Mr Steven Havard, Joint Manager - IT, Parc Dewi, Carmarthen SA31 3HB ☎ 01237 234567 ✉ shavard@carmarthenshire.gov.uk

Electoral Registration: Ms Amanda Bebb, Electorial Services Manager, County Hall, Carmarthen SA31 1JP ☎ 01267 228609 ✉ Abebb@carmarthenshire.gov.uk

Emergency Planning: Mr Richard Elms, Civil Contingency Manager, Parc Myrddin, Richmond Terrace, Carmarthen SA31 1HQ ☎ 01267 228195 🖷 01267 228193 ✉ relms@carmarthenshire.gov.uk

Energy Management: Mr Brian Jenkins, Head - Consultancy, County Hall, Carmarthen SA31 1JP ☎ 01267 228133 ✉ BLJenkins@camarthenshire.gov.uk

Environmental / Technical Services: Mr Richard Workman, Director - Technical Services, County Hall, Carmarthen SA31 1JP ☎ 01267 224647 🖷 01267 224620 ✉ rworkman@carmarthenshire.gov.uk

Environmental Health: Mr Philip Davies, Head - Public Protection, 3 Spilman Street, Carmarthen SA31 1LE ☎ 01267 228706 🖷 01267 221616 ✉ phdavies@carmarthenshire.gov.uk

Estates, Property & Valuation: Mr Jonathan Fearn, Head - Corporate Property, Parc Dewi, Carmarthen SA31 3HB ☎ 01267 246244 ✉ jfearn@carmarthenshire.gov.uk

European Liaison: Mr Neville Davies, Head - European Policy & External Funding, Trinity College, Carmarthen SA31 3EP ☎ 01267 224859 🖷 01267 234279 ✉ nevdavies@carmarthenshire.gov.uk

Events Manager: Mr Ian Jones, Head - Leisure, Parc Myrddin, Carmarthen SA13 1DS ☎ 01267 228309 ✉ ijones@carmarthenshire.gov.uk

Facilities: Mrs Elin Cullen, Head of Business & Specialist Services, Parc Dewi, Carmarthen SA31 3HB ☎ 01267 246480 ✉ ecullen@carmarthenshire.gov.uk

Finance and Treasurer: Mr Roger Jones, Director - Resources, County Hall, Carmarthen SA31 1JP ☎ 01267 224121 🖷 01267 224122 ✉ rjones@carmarthenshire.gov.uk

Finance and Treasurer: Mr Christopher Moore, Head - Financial Services, County Hall, Carmarthen SA31 1JP ☎ 01267 224160 ✉ cmoore@carmarthenshire.gov.uk

Fleet Management: Mr Steven Pilliner, Acting Head - Transport & Engineering, Technical Services Department, Street Scene, Pibwrlwyd, Carmarthen SA31 2NH ☎ 01267 228150 ✉ spilliner@carmarthenshire.gov.uk

Grounds Maintenance: Mr David Hughes, Head - Street Scene, Technical Services Department, Street Scene, Pibwrlwyd, Carmarthen SA31 2NH ☎ ; 01267 224502 🖷 01267 221406 ✉ dhughes@carmarthenshire.gov.uk

Health and Safety: Mr Mark Millward, Health & Safety Advisor, Parc Dewi, Carmarthen SA31 3HB ☎ 01267 246131 ✉ mmilward@carmarthenshire.gov.uk

Highways: Mr Steven Pilliner, Acting Head - Transport & Engineering, Technical Services Department, Street Scene, Pibwrlwyd, Carmarthen SA31 2NH ☎ 01267 228150 ✉ spilliner@carmarthenshire.gov.uk

Home Energy Conservation: Mr Brian Jenkins, Head - Consultancy, County Hall, Carmarthen SA31 1JP ☎ 01267 228133 ✉ BLJenkins@camarthenshire.gov.uk

Housing: Mr Robin Staines, Head - Housing, 3 Spilmand Street, Carmarthen SA31 1LE ☎ 01267 228960 ✉ rstaines@carmarthenshire.gov.uk

Housing Maintenance: Mr Robin Staines, Head - Housing, 3 Spilman Street, Carmarthen SA31 1LE ☎ 01267 228960 ✉ rstaines@carmarthenshire.gov.uk

Legal: Mrs Linda Reese-Jones, Head - Administration & Law, County Hall, Carmarthen SA31 1JP ☎ 01267 224012 🖱 LRJones@carmarthenshire.gov.uk

Leisure and Cultural Services: Mr Ian Jones, Head - Leisure, Parc Myrddin, Carmarthen SA13 1DS ☎ 01267 228309 🖱 ijones@carmarthenshire.gov.uk

Licensing: Mr Philip Davies, Head - Public Protection, 3 Spilman Street, Carmarthen SA31 1LE ☎ 01267 228706 🖷 01267 221616 🖱 phdavies@carmarthenshire.gov.uk

Lifelong Learning: Mr Wyn Williams, Head - Improvement & Skills, Parc Dewi, Carmarthen SA31 3HB ☎ 01267 246649 🖷 01267 228312 🖱 wwilliams@carmarthenshire.gov.uk

Lighting: Mr David Hughes, Head - Street Scene, Technical Services Department, Street Scene, Pibwrlwyd, Carmarthen SA31 2NH ☎ ; 01267 224502 🖷 01267 221406 🖱 dhughes@carmarthenshire.gov.uk

Lottery Funding, Charity and Voluntary: Mr Neville Davies, Head - European Policy & External Funding, Trinity College, Carmarthen SA31 3EP ☎ 01267 224859 🖷 01267 234279 🖱 nevdavies@carmarthenshire.gov.uk

Member Services: Mr Ian Llewelyn, Executive Support Manager, County Hall, Carmarthen SA31 1JP ☎ 01267 224051 🖱 ihllewelyn@carmarthenshire.gov.uk

Member Services: Mrs Linda Reese-Jones, Head - Administration & Law, County Hall, Carmarthen SA31 1JP ☎ 01267 224012 🖱 LRJones@carmarthenshire.gov.uk

Parking: Mr Steven Pilliner, Acting Head - Transport & Engineering, Technical Services Department, Street Scene, Pibwrlwyd, Carmarthen SA31 2NH ☎ 01267 228150 🖱 spilliner@carmarthenshire.gov.uk

Partnerships: Mr Chris Burns, Assistant Chief Executive - Customer Focus & Policy, County Hall, Carmarthen SA31 1JP ☎ 01267 224112 🖷 01267 224652 🖱 cpburns@carmarthenshire.gov.uk

Personnel / HR: Mr Paul Thomas, Assistant Chief Executive - People Management & Performance, Parc Dewi, Carmarthen SA31 3HB ☎ ; 01267 246123 🖱 prthomas@carmarthenshire.gov.uk

Planning: Mr Eifion Bowen, Head of Planning Services, 40 Spilman Street, Carmarthen SA31 1LQ ☎ 01267 224850 🖷 01267 237612 🖱 ebowen@carmarthenshire.gov.uk

Procurement: Mr Phil Sexton, Head - Audit, Procurement & ICT, Parc Dewi Sant, Carmarthen SA31 3HB ☎ 01267 246217 🖱 psexton@carmarthenshire.gov.uk

Public Libraries: Mr Wyn Williams, Head - Improvement & Skills, Parc Dewi Sant, Carmarthen SA31 3HB ☎ 01267 246649 🖷 01267 228312 🖱 wwilliams@carmarthenshire.gov.uk

Recycling & Waste Minimisation: Mr David Hughes, Head - Street Scene, Technical Services Department, Street Scene, Pibwrlwyd, Carmarthen SA31 2NH ☎ ; 01267 224502 🖷 01267 221406 🖱 dhughes@carmarthenshire.gov.uk

Regeneration: Mr Dave Gilbert, Director - Regeneration & Leisure, County Hall, Carmarthen SA31 1JP ☎ 01267 224141 🖷 01267 224640 🖱 dgilbert@carmarthenshire.gov.uk

Regeneration: Mr Stuart Walters, Physical Regeneration Manager, Parc Ananwy, Business Resource Centre, Ammanford SA18 3EP ☎ ; 01267 234567 🖱 swalters@carmarthenshire.gov.uk

Road Safety: Mr Steven Pilliner, Acting Head - Transport & Engineering, Technical Services Department, Street Scene, Pibwrlwyd, Carmarthen SA31 2NH ☎ 01267 228150 🖱 spilliner@carmarthenshire.gov.uk

Social Services: Mr Bruce McLernon, Director - Social Care, Health & Housing, County Hall, Carmarthen SA31 1JP ☎ 01267 224697 🖷 01267 224681 🖱 bmclernon@carmarthenshire.gov.uk

Social Services (Adult): Mr Gareth John, Head - Mental Health & Learning Disablities, 3 Spilman Street, Carmarthen SA31 1LE ☎ 01267 228849 🖷 01267 228908 🖱 gjohn@carmarthenshire.gov.uk

Social Services (Adult): Ms Sheila Porter, Head - Primary, Community & Social Care Services, 3 Spilman Street, Carmarthen SA31 1LE ☎ 01267 228900 🖱 Sporter@carmarthenshire.gov.uk

Social Services (Children): Mr Jake Morgan, Interim Head - Children's Services, Block 2, St David's Park, Jobswewl Road, Carmarthen SA31 3HB ☎ ; 01267 246530 🖷 01267 228908 🖱 jakemorgan@carmarthenshire.gov.uk

Street Scene: Mr David Hughes, Head - Street Scene, Technical Services Department, Street Scene, Pibwrlwyd, Carmarthen SA31 2NH ☎ ; 01267 224502 🖷 01267 221406 🖱 dhughes@carmarthenshire.gov.uk

Sustainable Communities: Mr Kendal Davies, Sustainable Development Manager, County Hall, Carmarthen SA31 1JP ☎ 01267 228351 🖷 01267 224652 🖱 jkdavies@carmarthenshire.gov.uk

Sustainable Development: Mr Kendal Davies, Sustainable Development Manager, County Hall, Carmarthen SA31 1JP ☎ 01267 228351 🖷 01267 224652 🖱 jkdavies@carmarthenshire.gov.uk

Tourism: Mr Huw Parsons, Marketing & Tourism Manager, Business Resource Centre, Parc Amanwy, New Road, Ammanford SA18 3EP ☎ ; 01267 234567 🖷 01269 590290 🖱 hlparsons@carmarthenshire.gov.uk

Town Centre: Mr Andrew Shufflebotham, Town Centre Manager, Town Hall, Llanelli SA15 3DD ☎ 01554 742222 🖱 ashufflebotham@carmarthenshire.gov.uk

Traffic Management: Mr Steven Pilliner, Acting Head - Transport & Engineering, Technical Services Department, Street Scene, Pibwrlwyd, Carmarthen SA31 2NH ☎ 01267 228150 🖱 spilliner@carmarthenshire.gov.uk

Transport: Mr Steven Pilliner, Acting Head - Transport & Engineering, Technical Services Department, Street Scene, Pibwrlwyd, Carmarthen SA31 2NH ☎ 01237 228150 ✉ spilliner@carmarthenshire.gov.uk

Transport Planner: Mr Steven Pilliner, Acting Head - Transport & Engineering, Technical Services Department, Street Scene, Pibwrlwyd, Carmarthen SA31 2NH ☎ 01267 228150 ✉ spilliner@carmarthenshire.gov.uk

Waste Collection and Disposal: Mr David Hughes, Head - Street Scene, Technical Services Department, Street Scene, Pibwrlwyd, Carmarthen SA31 2NH ☎ ; 01267 224502 🖷 01267 221406 ✉ dhughes@carmarthenshire.gov.uk

Waste Management: Mr David Hughes, Head - Street Scene, Technical Services Department, Street Scene, Pibwrlwyd, Carmarthen SA31 2NH ☎ ; 01267 224502 🖷 01267 221406 ✉ dhughes@carmarthenshire.gov.uk

MEMBERS OF THE COUNCIL (74)

***Chair:* Jackson**, Ivor (IND - Llandovery)
ijjackson@carmarthenshire.gov.uk
***Leader of the Council:* Gravell**, Meryl (IND - Trimsaran)
mgravell@carmarthenshire.gov.uk
***Deputy Leader of the Council:* Evans**, Wyn (IND - Llanddarog)
wjwevans@carmarthenshire.gov.uk
***Deputy Leader of the Council:* Madge**, Kevin (LAB - Garnant)
kmadge@carmarthenshire.gov.uk
***Group Leader:* Griffiths**, Peter (PC - Carmarthen Town North)
phughes-griffiths@carmarthenshire.gov.uk
Allen, Susan Margaret (IND - Whitland)
smallen@carmarthenshire.gov.uk
Bartlett, John (LAB - Betws)
Bowen, Theresa (LAB - Llwynhendy)
Caiach, Sian (O - Hengoed)
smcaiach@carmarthenshire.gov.uk
Campbell, Cefin (PC - Llanfihangel Aberbythych)
Charles, John (PC - Llanegwad)
mcharles@carmarthenshire.gov.uk
Cooper, Peter (LAB - Saron)
apcooper@carmarthenshire.gov.uk
Cundy, Deryk (LAB - Bynea)
Davies, Joseph (IND - Manordeib & Salem)
Davies, Alun (PC - Saron)
Davies, Terry (LAB - Gorslas)
tedavies@carmarthenshire.gov.uk
Davies, William (LAB - Kidwelly)
wkdavies@carmarthenshire.gov.uk
Davies, Daff (IND - Llansteffan)
dbdavies@carmarthenshire.gov.uk
Davies, Anthony (IND - Llandybie)
antdavies@sirgar.gov.uk
Davies, Ieuan (IND - Llanybydder)
Davies, Sharen (LAB - Llwynhendy)
Davies, Glynog (PC - Quarter Bach)
Defis, Tom (PC - Carmarthen Town West)
Devichand, Tegwen (LAB - Dafen)
tdevichand@carmarthenshire.gov.uk
Dole, Emlyn (PC - Llannon)
edole@carmarthenshire.gov.uk
Edmunds, Jeffrey (LAB - Bigyn)
Edwards, George (LAB - Hengoed)
Evans, David (LAB - Pontamman)
mpbinney@carmarthenshire.gov.uk
Evans, Linda (PC - Llanfihangel-Ar-Arth)
ldaviesevans@carmarthenshire.gov.uk
Evans, Tyssul (PC - Llangyndeyrn)
wtevans@sirgar.gov.uk
Evans, Hazel (PC - Cenarth)
hazelevans@carmarthenshire.gov.uk
Harries, Alun (PC - Ammanford)
Higgins, Calum (LAB - Tycroes)
Hopkins, Gwyn (PC - Llangennech)
wghopkins@carmarthenshire.gov.uk
Howell, John (PC - Llangeler)
Hughes, Philip (IND - St Clears)
pmhughes@carmarthenshire.gov.uk
James, John (LAB - Burry Port)
James, Andrew (IND - Llangadog)
Jenkins, John (INDNA - Elli)
jpjenkins@carmarthenshire.gov.uk
Jenkins, David (PC - Glanamman)
dmjenkins@carmarthenshire.gov.uk
Jones, Gareth (PC - Carmarthen Town North)
gojones@carmarthenshire.gov.uk
Jones, Patricia (LAB - Burry Port)
pemjones@carmarthenshire.gov.uk
Jones, Jim (IND - Glyn)
tjjones@carmarthenshire.gov.uk
Jones, Henry (IND - Cynwyl Elfed)
hijones@sirgar.gov.uk
Jones, Anthony (LAB - Llandybie)
awjones@carmarthenshire.gov.uk
Lemon, Winston (PC - Glanymor)
wjlemon@carmarthenshire.gov.uk
Lenny, Alun (PC - Carmarthen Town South)
Llewellyn, Daniel (PC - Llanboidy)
djrllewellyn@carmarthenshire.gov.uk
Matthews, Shirley (LAB - Pembrey)
Morgan, Giles (IND - Swiss Valley)
agmorgan@carmarthenshire.gov.uk
Morgan, Eryl (LAB - Bigyn)
Owen, Jeff (PC - Tyisha)
Palmer, Pamela (IND - Abergwili)
papalmer@carmarthenshire.gov.uk
Price, Darren (PC - Gorslas)
Richards, Hugh (IND - Felinfoel)
dwhrichards@carmarthenshire.gov.uk
Roberts, Beatrice (LAB - Glanymor)
Shepardson, Hugh Barrie (IND - Pembrey)
hbshepardson@carmarthenshire.gov.uk
Speake, Alan (PC - Carmarthen Town West)
adtspeake@carmarthenshire.gov.uk
Stephens, Mair (IND - St Ishmael)
lmstephens@carmarthenshire.gov.uk
Theophilus, Thomas (IND - Cilycwm)
ttheophilus@carmarthenshire.gov.uk
Thomas, Edward (IND - Llandeilo)
Thomas, Gwyneth (PC - Llangennech)
gwythomas@sirgar.gov.uk
Thomas, William (IND - Trelech)
wdthomas@carmarthenshire.gov.uk
Thomas, Siân (PC - Penygroes)
sethomas@sirgar.gov.uk
Thomas, Margaret (LAB - Llannon)
Thomas, Jeffrey (PC - Carmarthen Town South)

Thomas, Gareth (PC - Hendy)
gbthomas@sirgar.gov.uk
Thomas, Keri (LAB - Tyisha)
kpthomas@carmarthenshire.gov.uk
Thomas, William (LAB - Lliedi)
Tremlett, Jane (IND - Laugharne Township)
jtremlett@carmarthenshire.gov.uk
Williams, Joy Sewell (PC - Pontyberem)
jswilliams@sirgar.gov.uk
Williams, Janice (LAB - Lliedi)
Williams, James Eirwyn (PC - Cynwyl Gaeo)
jewilliams@sirgar.gov.uk
Williams, Dewi (PC - Llangunnor)

POLITICAL COMPOSITION
PC: 28, LAB: 23, IND: 21, INDNA: 1, O: 1

CABINET
Leader / Corporate Leadership & Strategy: Mrs Meryl Gravell
Deputy Leader / Corporate Property, Customer Focus & Community Wellbeing: Mr Kevin Madge
Deputy Leader / Finance & IT: Mr Wyn Evans
Adult Social Care, Corporate Health Co-ordination: Mrs Patricia Jones
Business Management, Public Protection & Youth Services: Mrs Pamela Palmer
Environment & People Management: Mr Philip Hughes

COMMITTEE CHAIRS
Environment Scrutiny: Mr Jim Jones
Health & Social Care: Ms Jane Tremlett
Licensing: Mr Thomas Theophilus
Policy & Resources: Mrs Mair Stephens
Regeneration & Leisure Scrutiny: Mr Anthony Jones

CARRICKFERGUS N

Carrickfergus Borough Council, Museum & Civic Centre, 11 Antrim Street, Carrickfergus BT38 7DG ☎ 028 9335 8000 🖷 028 9336 6676 ✉ info@carrickfergus.org 🖳 www.carrickfergus.org

FACTS & FIGURES
Police Authority: Northern Ireland Policing Board
Health Authority: Health & Social Care Board
Learning and Skills Council: Northern Ireland
Parliamentary Constituencies: Antrim East
EU Constituencies: Northern Ireland
Election Frequency: Elections are of whole council

PRINCIPAL OFFICERS
Chief Executive: Ms Sheila McClelland, Chief Executive, Museum & Civic Centre, 11 Antrim Street, Carrickfergus BT38 7DG ☎ 028 9335 8000

Senior Management: Mr Alan Barkley, Director of Environmental Services, Museum and Civic Centre, 11 Antrim Street, Carrickfergus BT38 7DL ☎ 028 9335 8000 🖷 028 9336 9313 ✉ alan.barkley@carrickfergus.org

Senior Management: Mr Ian Eagleson, Director of Support Services, Museum and Civic Centre, 11 Antrim Street, Carrickfergus BT38 7DL ☎ 028 9335 8000 🖷 028 9336 6676 ✉ ian.eagleson@carrickfergus.org

Senior Management: Mr John McCormick, Director of Development Services, Museum and Civic Centre, 11 Antrim Street, Carrickfergus BT38 8BE ☎ 028 9335 8000 🖷 028 9336 6676 ✉ john.mccormick@carrickfergus.org

Access Officer / Social Services (Disability): Mr Stephen Johnston, Director of Building Services, Museum and Civic Centre, 11 Antrim Street, Carrickfergus BT38 7DG ☎ 028 9335 8000 🖷 028 9335 8088 ✉ stephen.johnston@carrickfergus.org

Architect, Building / Property Services: Mr Stephen Johnston, Director of Building Services, Museum and Civic Centre, 11 Antrim Street, Carrickfergus BT38 7DG ☎ 028 9335 8000 🖷 028 9335 8088 ✉ stephen.johnston@carrickfergus.org

Building Control: Mr Stephen Johnston, Director of Building Services, Museum and Civic Centre, 11 Antrim Street, Carrickfergus BT38 7DG ☎ 028 9335 8000 🖷 028 9335 8088 ✉ stephen.johnston@carrickfergus.org

Civil Registration: Ms Lynn Gordon, Human Resources Manager, Museum and Civic Centre, 11 Antrim Street, Carrickfergus BT38 7DG ☎ 028 9335 8000 🖷 028 9336 6676 ✉ lynn.gordon@carrickfergus.gov.uk

Civil Registration: Mrs E McNeilly, Registrar, Museum and Civic Centre, 11 Antrim Street, Carrickfergus BT38 7DG ☎ 028 9335 8000

PR / Communications: Mr John McCormick, Director of Development Services, Museum and Civic Centre, 11 Antrim Street, Carrickfergus BT38 8BE ☎ 028 9335 8000 🖷 028 9336 6676 ✉ john.mccormick@carrickfergus.org

Community Planning: Mr George Gibson, Development Manager (Community), Museum and Civic Centre, 11 Antrim Street, Carrickfergus BT38 7DG ☎ 028 9335 8000 🖷 028 9335 8088 ✉ george.gibson@carrickfergus.org

Community Safety: Mr John McCormick, Director of Development Services, Museum and Civic Centre, 11 Antrim Street, Carrickfergus BT38 8BE ☎ 028 9335 8000 🖷 028 9336 6676 ✉ john.mccormick@carrickfergus.org

Computer Management: Mr Ian Eagleson, Director of Support Services, Museum and Civic Centre, 11 Antrim Street, Carrickfergus BT38 7DL ☎ 028 9335 8000 🖷 028 9336 6676 ✉ ian.eagleson@carrickfergus.org

Consumer Protection and Trading Standards: Mr Alan Barkley, Director of Environmental Services, Museum and Civic Centre, 11 Antrim Street, Carrickfergus BT38 7DL ☎ 028 9335 8000 🖷 028 9336 9313 ✉ alan.barkley@carrickfergus.org

Contracts: Mr Ian Eagleson, Director of Support Services, Museum and Civic Centre, 11 Antrim Street, Carrickfergus BT38 7DL ☎ 028 9335 8000 🖷 028 9336 6676 ✉ ian.eagleson@carrickfergus.org

Corporate Services: Mr Ian Eagleson, Director of Support

Services, Museum and Civic Centre, 11 Antrim Street, Carrickfergus BT38 7DL ☎ 028 9335 8000 🖷 028 9336 6676 ✉ ian.eagleson@carrickfergus.org

Direct Labour: Mr Ian Eagleson, Director of Support Services, Museum and Civic Centre, 11 Antrim Street, Carrickfergus BT38 7DL ☎ 028 9335 8000 🖷 028 9336 6676 ✉ ian.eagleson@carrickfergus.org

Economic Development: Ms Nicole Mulholland, Development Manager - Economic, Museum and Civic Centre, 11 Antrim Street, Carrickfergus BT38 7DG ☎ 028 9335 8000 🖷 028 9336 6676 ✉ nicole.mulholland@carrickfergus.org

E-Government: Mr Ian Eagleson, Director of Support Services, Museum and Civic Centre, 11 Antrim Street, Carrickfergus BT38 7DL ☎ 028 9335 8000 🖷 028 9336 6676 ✉ ian.eagleson@carrickfergus.org

Electoral Registration: Ms Sheila McClelland, Chief Executive, Museum & Civic Centre, 11 Antrim Street, Carrickfergus BT38 7DG ☎ 028 9335 8000

Emergency Planning: Ms Sheila McClelland, Chief Executive, Museum & Civic Centre, 11 Antrim Street, Carrickfergus BT38 7DG ☎ 028 9335 8000

Energy Management: Mr Stephen Johnston, Director of Building Services, Museum and Civic Centre, 11 Antrim Street, Carrickfergus BT38 7DG ☎ 028 9335 8000 🖷 028 9335 8088 ✉ stephen.johnston@carrickfergus.org

Environmental / Technical Services: Mr Alan Barkley, Director of Environmental Services, Museum and Civic Centre, 11 Antrim Street, Carrickfergus BT38 7DL ☎ 028 9335 8000 🖷 028 9336 9313 ✉ alan.barkley@carrickfergus.org

Environmental Health: Mr Alan Barkley, Director of Environmental Services, Museum and Civic Centre, 11 Antrim Street, Carrickfergus BT38 7DL ☎ 028 9335 8000 🖷 028 9336 9313 ✉ alan.barkley@carrickfergus.org

Estates, Property & Valuation: Mr Stephen Johnston, Director of Building Services, Museum and Civic Centre, 11 Antrim Street, Carrickfergus BT38 7DG ☎ 028 9335 8000 🖷 028 9335 8088 ✉ stephen.johnston@carrickfergus.org

European Liaison: Ms Sheila McClelland, Chief Executive, Museum & Civic Centre, 11 Antrim Street, Carrickfergus BT38 7DG ☎ 028 9335 8000

Events Manager: Ms Lynda Warring, Events Manager, Museum & Civic Centre, 11 Antrim Street, Carrickfergus BT38 7DG ☎ 02893 366 666 ✉ lynda.waring@carrickfergus.org

Finance and Treasurer: Mr Ian Eagleson, Director of Support Services, Museum and Civic Centre, 11 Antrim Street, Carrickfergus BT38 7DL ☎ 028 9335 8000 🖷 028 9336 6676 ✉ ian.eagleson@carrickfergus.org

Fleet Management: Mr Alan Barkley, Director of Environmental Services, Museum and Civic Centre, 11 Antrim Street, Carrickfergus BT38 7DL ☎ 028 9335 8000 🖷 028 9336 9313 ✉ alan.barkley@carrickfergus.org

Grounds Maintenance: Mr John McCormick, Director of Development Services, Museum and Civic Centre, 11 Antrim Street, Carrickfergus BT38 8BE ☎ 028 9335 8000 🖷 028 9336 6676 ✉ john.mccormick@carrickfergus.org

Health and Safety: Mrs Claire Duddy, Health & Safety Adviser, Museum & Civic Centre, 11 Antrim Street, Carrickfergus BT38 7DG ☎ 028 9335 8000 🖷 028 9335 9313 ✉ claire.duddy@carrickfergus.org

Home Energy Conservation: Mr Stephen Johnston, Director of Building Services, Museum and Civic Centre, 11 Antrim Street, Carrickfergus BT38 7DG ☎ 028 9335 8000 🖷 028 9335 8088 ✉ stephen.johnston@carrickfergus.org

Legal: Ms Sheila McClelland, Chief Executive, Museum & Civic Centre, 11 Antrim Street, Carrickfergus BT38 7DG ☎ 028 9335 8000

Leisure and Cultural Services: Mr John McCormick, Director of Development Services, Museum and Civic Centre, 11 Antrim Street, Carrickfergus BT38 8BE ☎ 028 9335 8000 🖷 028 9336 6676 ✉ john.mccormick@carrickfergus.org

Licensing: Mr Alan Barkley, Director of Environmental Services, Museum and Civic Centre, 11 Antrim Street, Carrickfergus BT38 7DL ☎ 028 9335 8000 🖷 028 9336 9313 ✉ alan.barkley@carrickfergus.org

Lottery Funding, Charity and Voluntary: Mr George Gibson, Development Manager (Community), Museum and Civic Centre, 11 Antrim Street, Carrickfergus BT38 7DG ☎ 028 9335 8000 🖷 028 9335 8088 ✉ george.gibson@carrickfergus.org

Member Services: Mr Ian Eagleson, Director of Support Services, Museum and Civic Centre, 11 Antrim Street, Carrickfergus BT38 7DL ☎ 028 9335 8000 🖷 028 9336 6676 ✉ ian.eagleson@carrickfergus.org

Partnerships: Mr George Gibson, Development Manager (Community), Museum and Civic Centre, 11 Antrim Street, Carrickfergus BT38 7DG ☎ 028 9335 8000 🖷 028 9335 8088 ✉ george.gibson@carrickfergus.org

Personnel / HR: Ms Lynn Gordon, Human Resources Manager, Museum and Civic Centre, 11 Antrim Street, Carrickfergus BT38 7DG ☎ 028 9335 8000 🖷 028 9336 6676 ✉ lynn.gordon@carrickfergus.gov.uk

Planning: Ms Sheila McClelland, Chief Executive, Museum & Civic Centre, 11 Antrim Street, Carrickfergus BT38 7DG ☎ 028 9335 8000

Procurement: Mr Ian Eagleson, Director of Support Services, Museum and Civic Centre, 11 Antrim Street, Carrickfergus BT38 7DL ☎ 028 9335 8000 🖷 028 9336 6676 ✉ ian.eagleson@carrickfergus.org

Recycling & Waste Minimisation: Mr Alan Barkley, Director of

Environmental Services, Museum and Civic Centre, 11 Antrim Street, Carrickfergus BT38 7DL ☎ 028 9335 8000 🖷 028 9336 9313 ✉ alan.barkley@carrickfergus.org

Regeneration: Mr John McCormick, Director of Development Services, Museum and Civic Centre, 11 Antrim Street, Carrickfergus BT38 8BE ☎ 028 9335 8000 🖷 028 9336 6676 ✉ john.mccormick@carrickfergus.org

Staff Training: Ms Lynn Gordon, Human Resources Manager, Museum and Civic Centre, 11 Antrim Street, Carrickfergus BT38 7DG ☎ 028 9335 8000 🖷 028 9336 6676 ✉ lynn.gordon@carrickfergus.gov.uk

Street Scene: Mr Alan Barkley, Director of Environmental Services, Museum and Civic Centre, 11 Antrim Street, Carrickfergus BT38 7DL ☎ 028 9335 8000 🖷 028 9336 9313 ✉ alan.barkley@carrickfergus.org

Sustainable Development: Mr Alan Barkley, Director of Environmental Services, Museum and Civic Centre, 11 Antrim Street, Carrickfergus BT38 7DL ☎ 028 9335 8000 🖷 028 9336 9313 ✉ alan.barkley@carrickfergus.org

Tourism: Mr John McCormick, Director of Development Services, Museum and Civic Centre, 11 Antrim Street, Carrickfergus BT38 8BE ☎ 028 9335 8000 🖷 028 9336 6676 ✉ john.mccormick@carrickfergus.org

Town Centre: Ms Nicole Mulholland, Development Manager - Economic, Museum and Civic Centre, 11 Antrim Street, Carrickfergus BT38 7DG ☎ 028 9335 8000 🖷 028 9336 6676 ✉ nicole.mulholland@carrickfergus.org

Transport Planner: Ms Nicole Mulholland, Development Manager - Economic, Museum and Civic Centre, 11 Antrim Street, Carrickfergus BT38 7DG ☎ 028 9335 8000 🖷 028 9336 6676 ✉ nicole.mulholland@carrickfergus.org

Waste Collection and Disposal: Mr Alan Barkley, Director of Environmental Services, Museum and Civic Centre, 11 Antrim Street, Carrickfergus BT38 7DL ☎ 028 9335 8000 🖷 028 9336 9313 ✉ alan.barkley@carrickfergus.org

Waste Management: Mr Alan Barkley, Director of Environmental Services, Museum and Civic Centre, 11 Antrim Street, Carrickfergus BT38 7DL ☎ 028 9335 8000 🖷 028 9336 9313 ✉ alan.barkley@carrickfergus.org

Children's Play Areas: Mr John McCormick, Director of Development Services, Museum and Civic Centre, 11 Antrim Street, Carrickfergus BT38 8BE ☎ 028 9335 8000 🖷 028 9336 6676 ✉ john.mccormick@carrickfergus.org

MEMBERS OF THE COUNCIL (17)

***Mayor:* McClurg**, Jim (DUP - Knockagh Monument)
mcclurgjames@hotmail.com
***Deputy Mayor:* Clements**, Terence (DUP - Kilroot)
***Alderman:* Beattie**, May (DUP - Knockagh Monument)
***Alderman:* Brown**, Jim (IND - Kilroot)
jim.brown@carrickfergus.org
***Alderman:* Neeson**, Sean (ALL - Carrick Castle)
seann@carrickfergus.org
Ashe, Billy (DUP - Kilroot)
billy.ashe@carrickfergus.org
Day, Isobel (ALL - Kilroot)
isobel.day@carrickfergus.org
Dickson, Stewart (ALL - Knockagh Monument)
stewart.dickson@carrickfergus.org
Emerson, Deborah (DUP - Carrick Castle)
deborah.emerson@carrickfergus.org
Ferguson, Eric (UUP - Kilroot)
eric.ferguson@carrickfergus.org
Hamilton, Billy (IND - Carrick Castle)
Hilditch, David (DUP - Carrick Castle)
davidhilditch@btconnect.com
Johnston, Charles (DUP - Knockagh Monument)
charles.johnston@carrickfergus.org
McClurg, Lynn (DUP - Kilroot)
lynn.mcclurg@carrickfergus.org
McKnight, Beryl (UUP - Carrick Castle)
beryl.mcknight@carrickfergus.org
Stewart, John (UUP - Knockagh Monument)
john.stewart@carrickfergus.org
Wilson, Andrew (UUP - Knockagh Monument)
andrew.wilson@carrickfergus.org

POLITICAL COMPOSITION

DUP: 8, UUP: 4, ALL: 3, IND: 2

CASTLE POINT D

Castle Point Borough Council, Council Offices, Kiln Road, Thundersley, Benfleet SS7 1TF ☎ 01268 882200 🖷 01268 882455 ✉ enquiries@castlepoint.gov.uk 🖳 www.castlepoint.gov.uk

FACTS & FIGURES

Police Authority: Essex Police Authority
Health Authority: East of England Strategic Health Authority
Learning and Skills Council: Eastern
Parliamentary Constituencies: Castle Point
EU Constituencies: Eastern
Election Frequency: Elections are by thirds
Twinning: Cologne District 3 (Germany); County Roscommon (Ireland); Romainville (France)

PRINCIPAL OFFICERS

Chief Executive: Mr David Marchant, Chief Executive, Council Offices, Kiln Road, Thundersley, Benfleet SS7 1TF ☎ 01268 882200 🖷 01268 882455 ✉ dmarchant@castlepoint.gov.uk

Deputy Chief Executive: Mrs Devinia Board, Strategic Director - Transformation & Resources, Council Offices, Kiln Road, Thundersley, Benfleet SS7 1TF ☎ 01268 882363 🖷 01268 882455 ✉ dboard@castlepoint.gov.uk

Deputy Chief Executive: Mr Andrew Smith, Strategic Director - Transformation & Resources, Council Offices, Kiln Road, Thundersley, Benfleet SS7 1TF ☎ 01268 882386 🖷 01268 882455 ✉ asmith@castlepoint.gov.uk

Assistant Chief Executive: Mr Craig Watts, Head - Performance & Support Service, Council Offices, Kiln Road, Thundersley, Benfleet SS7 1TF ☎ 01268 882213 🖷 01268 755332 ✉ cwatts@castlepoint.gov.uk

Architect, Building / Property Services: Mr Jarl Jansen,

Facilities & Asset Manager, Council Offices, Kiln Road, Thundersley, Benfleet SS7 1TF ☎ 01268 882408 🖷 01268 882455 ✉ jjansen@castlepoint.gov.uk

Best Value: Mr Craig Watts, Head - Performance & Support Service, Council Offices, Kiln Road, Thundersley, Benfleet SS7 1TF ☎ 01268 882213 🖷 01268 755332 ✉ cwatts@castlepoint.gov.uk

Building Control: Mr Gary Martindill, Principal Building Surveyor, Council Offices, Kiln Road, Thundersley, Benfleet SS7 1TF ☎ 01268 882288 ✉ gmartindill@castlepoint.gov.uk

PR / Communications: Miss Ann Horgan, Head - Governance, Council Offices, Kiln Road, Thundersley, Benfleet SS7 1TF ☎ 01268 882413 ✉ ahorgan@castlepoint.gov.uk

Community Planning: Mr Stephen Rogers, Head - Regeneration & Neighbourhoods, Council Offices, Kiln Road, Thundersley, Benfleet SS7 1TF ☎ 01268 882200 🖷 01268 882382 ✉ srogers@castlepoint.gov.uk

Community Safety: Mrs Mel Harris, Head - Partnerships & Safer Places, Council Offices, Kiln Road, Thundersley, Benfleet SS7 1TF ☎ 01268 882369 ✉ mharris@castlepoint.gov.uk

Computer Management: Mr Barry Delf, ICT Service Manager, Council Offices, Kiln Road, Thundersley, Benfleet SS7 1TF ☎ 01268 882412 🖷 01268 755332 ✉ bdelf@castlepoint.gov.uk

Contracts: Ms Fiona Wilson, Head - Law, Council Offices, Kiln Road, Thundersley, Benfleet SS7 1TF ☎ 01268 882436 🖷 01268 755332 ✉ fwilson@castlepoint.gov.uk

Corporate Services: Mr Andrew Smith, Strategic Director - Transformation & Resources, Council Offices, Kiln Road, Thundersley, Benfleet SS7 1TF ☎ 01268 882386 🖷 01268 882455 ✉ asmith@castlepoint.gov.uk

Customer Service: Ms Wendy Livings, Head - Housing & Communities, Council Offices, Kiln Road, Thundersley, Benfleet SS7 1TF ☎ 01268 882245 ✉ wlivings@castlepoint.gov.uk

Economic Development: Mr Stephen Rogers, Head - Regeneration & Neighbourhoods, Council Offices, Kiln Road, Thundersley, Benfleet SS7 1TF ☎ 01268 882200 🖷 01268 882382 ✉ srogers@castlepoint.gov.uk

Electoral Registration: Mr John Riley, Cabinet & Electoral Services Officer, Council Offices, Kiln Road, Thundersley, Benfleet SS7 1TF ☎ 01268 882417 🖷 01268 755332 ✉ jriley@castlepoint.gov.uk

Emergency Planning: Mr Jarl Jansen, Facilities & Asset Manager, Council Offices, Kiln Road, Thundersley, Benfleet SS7 1TF ☎ 01268 882408 🖷 01268 882455 ✉ jjansen@castlepoint.gov.uk

Energy Management: Mr Rob Lawrence, Property Technical Officer, Council Offices, Kiln Road, Thundersley, Benfleet SS7 1TF ☎ 01268 882200

Environmental / Technical Services: Mrs Trudie Bragg, Head - Environment, Council Offices, Kiln Road, Thundersley, Benfleet SS7 1TF ☎ 01268 882476 ✉ tbragg@castlepoint.gov.uk

Environmental Health: Mrs Debi Waite, Joint Environment Service Manager, Council Offices, Kiln Road, Thundersley, Benfleet SS7 1TF ☎ 01268 882379

Events Manager: Mrs Mel Harris, Head - Partnerships & Safer Places, Council Offices, Kiln Road, Thundersley, Benfleet SS7 1TF ☎ 01268 882369 ✉ mharris@castlepoint.gov.uk

Facilities: Mr Jarl Jansen, Facilities & Asset Manager, Council Offices, Kiln Road, Thundersley, Benfleet SS7 1TF ☎ 01268 882408 🖷 01268 882455 ✉ jjansen@castlepoint.gov.uk

Finance and Treasurer: Ms Chris Mills, Head - Resources, Council Offices, Kiln Road, Thundersley, Benfleet SS7 1TF ☎ 01268 882200 🖷 01268 882211 ✉ cmills@castlepoint.gov.uk

Grounds Maintenance: Mr Ryan Lynch, Operations Services Manager, Council Offices, Kiln Road, Thundersley, Benfleet SS7 1TF ☎ 01268 882377 🖷 01268 793137 ✉ rlynch@castlepoint.gov.uk

Health and Safety: Ms Chris Mills, Head - Resources, Council Offices, Kiln Road, Thundersley, Benfleet SS7 1TF ☎ 01268 882200 🖷 01268 882211 ✉ cmills@castlepoint.gov.uk

Home Energy Conservation: Mr Tim Quinn, Principal Environmental Health Officer, Council Offices, Kiln Road, Thundersley, Benfleet SS7 1TF ☎ 01268 882306 🖷 01268 882306 ✉ tquinn@castlepoint.gov.uk

Housing: Ms Wendy Livings, Head - Housing & Communities, Council Offices, Kiln Road, Thundersley, Benfleet SS7 1TF ☎ 01268 882245 ✉ wlivings@castlepoint.gov.uk

Legal: Ms Fiona Wilson, Head - Law, Council Offices, Kiln Road, Thundersley, Benfleet SS7 1TF ☎ 01268 882436 🖷 01268 755332 ✉ fwilson@castlepoint.gov.uk

Leisure and Cultural Services: Mrs Mel Harris, Head - Partnerships & Safer Places, Council Offices, Kiln Road, Thundersley, Benfleet SS7 1TF ☎ 01268 882369 ✉ mharris@castlepoint.gov.uk

Licensing: Mr Chris Jacob, Licensing Manager, Council Offices, Kiln Road, Thundersley, Benfleet SS7 1TF ☎ 01268 882200 🖷 01268 882455 ✉ cjacob@castlepoint.gov.uk

Member Services: Ms Ann Horgan, Head - Governance, Council Offices, Kiln Road, Thundersley, Benfleet SS7 1TF ☎ 01268 882413 🖷 01268 882455 ✉ ahorgan@castlepoint.gov.uk

Parking: Mr Ryan Lynch, Operational Services Manager, Council Offices, Kiln Road, Thundersley, Benfleet SS7 1TF ☎ 01268 882377 ✉ rlynch@castlepoint.gov.uk

Partnerships: Mrs Mel Harris, Head - Partnerships & Safer Places, Council Offices, Kiln Road, Thundersley, Benfleet SS7 1TF ☎ 01268 882369 ✉ mharris@castlepoint.gov.uk

Personnel / HR: Ms Corinne Birch, Head - Personnel, Council Offices, Kiln Road, Thundersley, Benfleet SS7 1TF ☎ 01268 882200 ✉ cbirch@castlepoint.gov.uk

Personnel / HR: Ms Chris Mills, Head - Resources, Council Offices, Kiln Road, Thundersley, Benfleet SS7 1TF ☎ 01268 882200 🖷 01268 882211 ✉ cmills@castlepoint.gov.uk

Planning: Mr Stephen Rogers, Head - Regeneration & Neighbourhoods, Council Offices, Kiln Road, Thundersley, Benfleet SS7 1TF ☎ 01268 882200 🖷 01268 882382 ✉ srogers@castlepoint.gov.uk

Procurement: Mr Jarl Jansen, Facilities & Asset Manager, Council Offices, Kiln Road, Thundersley, Benfleet SS7 1TF ☎ 01268 882408 🖷 01268 882455 ✉ jjansen@castlepoint.gov.uk

Recycling & Waste Minimisation: Ms Trudie Bragg, Head - Environment & Community, Council Offices, Kiln Road, Thundersley, Benfleet SS7 1TF ☎ 01268 882476 ✉ tbragg@castlepoint.gov.uk

Regeneration: Mr Stephen Rogers, Head - Regeneration & Neighbourhoods, Council Offices, Kiln Road, Thundersley, Benfleet SS7 1TF ☎ 01268 882200 🖷 01268 882382 ✉ srogers@castlepoint.gov.uk

Staff Training: Ms Chris Mills, Head - Resources, Council Offices, Kiln Road, Thundersley, Benfleet SS7 1TF ☎ 01268 882200 🖷 01268 882211 ✉ cmills@castlepoint.gov.uk

Street Scene: Mr Ryan Lynch, Operational Services Manager, Council Offices, Kiln Road, Thundersley, Benfleet SS7 1TF ☎ 01268 882377 ✉ rlynch@castlepoint.gov.uk

Sustainable Communities: Mr Stephen Rogers, Head - Regeneration & Neighbourhoods, Council Offices, Kiln Road, Thundersley, Benfleet SS7 1TF ☎ 01268 882200 🖷 01268 882382 ✉ srogers@castlepoint.gov.uk

Sustainable Development: Mr Rob Lawrence, Property Technical Officer, Council Offices, Kiln Road, Thundersley, Benfleet SS7 1TF ☎ 01268 882200

Traffic Management: Mr Ryan Lynch, Operational Services Manager, Council Offices, Kiln Road, Thundersley, Benfleet SS7 1TF ☎ 01268 882377 ✉ rlynch@castlepoint.gov.uk

Waste Collection and Disposal: Ms Trudie Bragg, Head - Environment & Community, Council Offices, Kiln Road, Thundersley, Benfleet SS7 1TF ☎ 01268 882476 ✉ tbragg@castlepoint.gov.uk

Waste Management: Ms Trudie Bragg, Head - Environment & Community, Council Offices, Kiln Road, Thundersley, Benfleet SS7 1TF ☎ 01268 882476 ✉ tbragg@castlepoint.gov.uk

MEMBERS OF THE COUNCIL (41)

***Mayor:* Burch**, Peter (CON - Cedar Hall)
cllr.pburch@castlepoint.gov.uk
***Deputy Mayor:* Iles**, Maryse (CON - Cedar Hall)
cllr.miles@castlepoint.gov.uk
***Leader of the Council:* Challis**, Pam (CON - St. Peter's)
cllr.pchallis@castlepoint.gov.uk
***Deputy Leader of the Council:* Stanley**, Jeffrey (CON - Boyce)
cllr.jstanley@castlepoint.gov.uk
Anderson, John (IND - Canvey Island Central)
cllr.janderson@castlepoint.gov.uk
Barrett, Lee (IND - Canvey Island East)
cllr.lbarrett@castlepoint.gov.uk
Barton, Gail (IND - Canvey Island East)
Blackwell, Dave (IND - Canvey Island Central)
cllr.dblackwell@castlepoint.gov.uk
Brunt, Cliff (CON - Victoria)
cllr.cbrunt@castlepoint.gov.uk
Campagna, Barry (IND - Canvey Island South)
Cole, Steven (IND - Canvey Island Winter Garden)
Cole, Andy (CON - St. George's)
cllr.acole@castlepoint.gov.uk
Cross, David (CON - St. Mary's)
cllr.dcross@castlepoint.gov.uk
Dick, Bill (CON - St. Peter's)
cllr.wdick@castlepoint.gov.uk
Egan, Beverley (CON - St. Peter's)
cllr.began@castlepoint.gov.uk
Egan, Eoin (CON - Appleton)
cllr.eegan@castlepoint.gov.uk
Freeman, Pam (CON - Appleton)
cllr.pfreeman@castlepoint.gov.uk
Goodwin, Wendy (CON - Boyce)
cllr.wgoodwin@castlepoint.gov.uk
Govier, Jackie (CON - St. George's)
cllr.jgovier@castlepoint.gov.uk
Greig, Peter (IND - Canvey Island Winter Garden)
cllr.pgreig@castlepoint.gov.uk
Hart, Simon (CON - Victoria)
Harvey, Nick (IND - Canvey Island North)
cllr.nharvey@castlepoint.gov.uk
Howard, Ray (CON - Canvey Island West)
cllr.rhoward@castlepoint.gov.uk
Isaacs, Godfrey (CON - St. James')
cllr.gisaacs@castlepoint.gov.uk
King, Jane (IND - Canvey Island West)
cllr.jking@castlepoint.gov.uk
Ladzrie, Norman (CON - St. James')
cllr.nladzrie@castlepoint.gov.uk
Liddiard, Joan (IND - Canvey Island South)
cllr.jliddiard@castlepoint.gov.uk
May, Peter (IND - Canvey Island Central)
cllr.pmay@castlepoint.gov.uk
Partridge, Alf (CON - St. Mary's)
cllr.apartridge@castlepoint.gov.uk
Payne, Janice (IND - Canvey Island South)
cllr.jpayne@castlepoint.gov.uk
Payne, John (IND - Canvey Island East)
cllr.japayne@castlepoint.gov.uk
Riley, Colin (CON - Victoria)
cllr.criley@castlepoint.gov.uk
Sharp, Bill (CON - St. James')
cllr.wsharp@castlepoint.gov.uk
Sheldon, Andrew (CON - St. Mary's)
cllr.asheldon@castlepoint.gov.uk
Skipp, Tom (CON - Appleton)
cllr.tskipp@castlepoint.gov.uk
Smith, Norman (CON - Boyce)
cllr.nsmith@castlepoint.gov.uk

Tucker, Martin (IND - Canvey Island North)
cllr.mtucker@castlepoint.gov.uk
Walter, Clive (CON - St. George's)
cllr.cwalter@castlepoint.gov.uk
Wass, Liz (CON - Cedar Hall)
cllr.lwass@castlepoint.gov.uk
Watson, Grace (IND - Canvey Island North)
cllr.gwatson@castlepoint.gov.uk
Watson, Neville (IND - Canvey Island Winter Garden)
cllr.nwatson@castlepoint.gov.uk

POLITICAL COMPOSITION
CON: 25, IND: 16

CABINET
Leader: Mrs Pam Challis
Deputy Leader / Corporate Policy, Resources & Performance: Mr Jeffrey Stanley
Economic Development & Business Recognition: Mr Norman Smith
Environment & Street Scene: Mr Colin Riley
Leisure & Community Wellbeing: Mrs Wendy Goodwin
Homes & Customer Engagement: Mrs Beverley Egan
Safer Communities: Mr Godfrey Isaacs
Waste, Floods & Water Management: Mr Ray Howard

COMMITTEE CHAIRS
Audit: Mr Clive Walter
Community Policy Development Group (Scrutiny): Mr Eoin Egan
Development Control: Mr Bill Dick
Environment Policy Development Group (Scrutiny): Mr David Cross
Licensing: Mr Cliff Brunt
Overview & Scrutiny: Mr Dave Blackwell
Policy & Performance Policy Development Group (Scrutiny): Mr Cliff Brunt
Standards: Mr Jason Bishop

CASTLEREAGH N

Castlereagh Borough Council, (Stye Braes o Ulidia Burgh Cooncil), Castlereagh Borough Council, Bradford Court, Upper Galwally, Castlereagh BT8 6RB ☏ 028 9049 4500 🖷 028 9049 4515 council@castlereagh.gov.uk www.castlereagh.gov.uk

FACTS & FIGURES
Police Authority: Northern Ireland Policing Board
Health Authority: Eastern Health & Social Services Board
Learning and Skills Council: Northern Ireland
Parliamentary Constituencies: Belfast East, Strangford
EU Constituencies: Northern Ireland
Election Frequency: Elections are of whole council
Twinning: Kent (Washington DC, USA)

PRINCIPAL OFFICERS
Chief Executive: Mr Stephen Reid, Chief Executive, Castlereagh Borough Council, Bradford Court, Upper Galwally, Castlereagh BT8 6RB ☏ 02890 494500 🖷 02890 494507
shernelle@castlereagh.gov.uk

Senior Management: Mr Edwin Campbell, Director of Technical & Environmental Services, Civic & Administrative Offices, Bradford Court, Upper Galwally, Castlereagh, BT8 6RB
☏ 028 9049 4500 🖷 028 9049 4605
edwincampbell@castlereagh.gov.uk

Senior Management: Mrs Joan McCoy, Director of Administration & Community Services, Civic & Administrative Offices, Bradford Court, Upper Galwally, Castlereagh, BT8 6RB
☏ 028 9049 4550 🖷 028 9049 4515
joanmccoy@castlereagh.gov.uk

Senior Management: Mrs Heather Moore, Director of Leisure, Civic & Administrative Offices, Bradford Court, Upper Galwally, Castlereagh, Belfast BT8 6RB ☏ 028 9049 4500 🖷 028 9049 4515 heathermoore@castlereagh.gov.uk

Senior Management: Mr Edward Patterson, Director of Finance, Civic & Administrative Offices, Bradford Court, Upper Galwally, Castlereagh, BT8 6RB ☏ 028 9049 4500 🖷 028 9049 4555
edwardpatterson@castlereagh.gov.uk

Architect, Building / Property Services: Mr Colm Surginor, Capital Projects Officer, Civic & Administrative Offices, Bradford Court, Upper Galwally, Castlereagh, Belfast BT8 6RB ☏ 028 9049 4500 🖷 028 9049 4506 colmsurginor@castlereagh.gov.uk

Best Value: Mr Colin McCabrey, Economic Development Officer, Castlereagh Borough Council, Bradford Court, Upper Galwally, Castlereagh BT8 6RB ☏ 028 9049 4500 🖷 028 9049 4515
colinmccabrey@castlereagh.gov.uk

Building Control: Mr Gordon Bratten, Building Control Manager, Civic & Administrative Offices, Bradford Court, Upper Galwally, Castlereagh, BT8 6RB ☏ 028 9049 4500 🖷 028 9049 4615
gordonbratten@castlereagh.gov.uk

Children / Youth Services: Mr Ryan Black, Community Services Manager, Civil & Administrative Offices, Bradford Court, Upper Galwally, Castlereagh BT8 6RB ☏ 028 9049 4500
ryanblack@castlereagh.gov.uk

Civil Registration: Ms Mary Heaslip, Registrar, Bradford Court, Upper Galwally, Belfast BT8 6RB ☏ 028 9049 4510 🖷 028 9049 4525 maryheaslip@castlereagh.gov.uk

PR / Communications: Mrs Paula Arrell, Public Relations & Marketing, Civic & Administrative Offices, Bradford Court, Upper Galwally, Castlereagh, Belfast BT8 6RB ☏ 028 9049 4500 🖷 028 9049 4515 paulaarrell@castlereagh.gov.uk

Community Planning: Mr Ryan Black, Community Services Manager, Civil & Administrative Offices, Bradford Court, Upper Galwally, Castlereagh BT8 6RB ☏ 028 9049 4500
ryanblack@castlereagh.gov.uk

Community Safety: Mr Roy Lawther, Manager, Castlereagh Borough Council, Bradford Court, Upper Galwally, Castlereagh BT8 6RB ☏ 028 9049 4500 🖷 028 9049 4515
roylawther@castlereagh.gov.uk

Computer Management: Mr Michael Finney, IT Manager, Civic & Administrative Offices, Bradford Court, Upper Galwally,

Castlereagh, Belfast BT8 6RB ☎ 028 9049 4500 🖷 028 9049 4555 ✉ michaelfinney@castlereagh.gov.uk

Corporate Services: Mrs Joan McCoy, Director of Administration & Community Services, Civic & Administrative Offices, Bradford Court, Upper Galwally, Castlereagh, BT8 6RB ☎ 028 9049 4550 🖷 028 9049 4515 ✉ joanmccoy@castlereagh.gov.uk

Direct Labour: Mr Tom Cousins, Operational Services Manager, Civic & Administrative Offices, Bradford Court, Upper Galwally, Castlereagh, Belfast BT8 6RB ☎ 028 9049 4500 🖷 028 9049 4605 ✉ tomcousins@castlereagh.gov.uk

Economic Development: Mr Colin McCabrey, Economic Development Officer, Castlereagh Borough Council, Bradford Court, Upper Galwally, Castlereagh BT8 6RB ☎ 028 9049 4500 🖷 028 9049 4515 ✉ colinmccabrey@castlereagh.gov.uk

E-Government: Mr Edward Patterson, Director of Finance, Civic & Administrative Offices, Bradford Court, Upper Galwally, Castlereagh, BT8 6RB ☎ 028 9049 4500 🖷 028 9049 4555 ✉ edwardpatterson@castlereagh.gov.uk

Electoral Registration: Mr Stephen Reid, Chief Executive, Castlereagh Borough Council, Bradford Court, Upper Galwally, Castlereagh BT8 6RB ☎ 02890 494500 🖷 02890 494507 ✉ shernelle@castlereagh.gov.uk

Emergency Planning: Mr Harry Whan, Emergency Planning Co-ordinator, Civic & Administrative Offices, Bradford Court, Upper Galwally, Castlereagh, Belfast BT8 6RB ☎ 028 9049 4559 🖷 028 9049 4575 ✉ harrywhan@castlereagh.gov.uk

Energy Management: Mr Richard Tracey, M & E Engineer, Civic & Administrative Offices, Bradford Court, Upper Galwally, Castlereagh, Belfast BT8 6RB ☎ 028 9049 4500 🖷 028 9049 4605 ✉ richardtracey@castlereagh.gov.uk

Environmental / Technical Services: Mr Edwin Campbell, Director of Technical & Environmental Services, Civic & Administrative Offices, Bradford Court, Upper Galwally, Castlereagh, BT8 6RB ☎ 028 9049 4500 🖷 028 9049 4605 ✉ edwincampbell@castlereagh.gov.uk

Environmental Health: Mr Richard Harvey, Environmental Health Manager, Civic & Administrative Offices, Bradford Court, Upper Galwally, Castlereagh, Belfast BT8 6RB ☎ 028 9049 4500 🖷 028 9049 4605 ✉ richardharvey@castlereagh.gov.uk

Events Manager: Mrs Edel Patterson, Administrative Manager, Civic & Administrative Offices, Bradford Court, Upper Galwally, Castlereagh, Belfast BT8 6RB ☎ 028 9049 4500 🖷 028 9049 4515 ✉ edelpatterson@castlereagh.gov.uk

Finance and Treasurer: Mr Edward Patterson, Director of Finance, Civic & Administrative Offices, Bradford Court, Upper Galwally, Castlereagh, BT8 6RB ☎ 028 9049 4500 🖷 028 9049 4555 ✉ edwardpatterson@castlereagh.gov.uk

Fleet Management: Mr Tom Cousins, Operational Services Manager, Civic & Administrative Offices, Bradford Court, Upper Galwally, Castlereagh, Belfast BT8 6RB ☎ 028 9049 4500 🖷 028 9049 4605 ✉ tomcousins@castlereagh.gov.uk

Grounds Maintenance: Mr William Torrens, Parks Manager, Civic & Administrative Offices, Bradford Court, Upper Galwally, Castlereagh, Belfast BT8 6RB ☎ 028 9049 4500 🖷 028 9049 4605 ✉ williamtorrens@castlereagh.gov.uk

Health and Safety: Mr Kieran Connelly, Health & Safety Officer, Civic & Administrative Offices, Bradford Court, Upper Galwally, Castlereagh BT8 6RB ☎ 028 9049 4500 🖷 02890 494515 ✉ kieranconnolly@castlereagh.gov.uk

Legal: Mrs Joan McCoy, Director of Administration & Community Services, Castlereagh Borough Council, Bradford Court, Upper Galwally, Castlereagh BT8 6RB ☎ 028 9049 4550 🖷 028 9049 4515 ✉ joanmccoy@castlereagh.gov.uk

Leisure and Cultural Services: Mrs Heather Moore, Director of Leisure, Civic & Administrative Offices, Bradford Court, Upper Galwally, Castlereagh, Belfast BT8 6RB ☎ 028 9049 4500 🖷 028 9049 4515 ✉ heathermoore@castlereagh.gov.uk

Member Services: Mrs Edel Patterson, Administrative Manager, Civic & Administrative Offices, Bradford Court, Upper Galwally, Castlereagh, Belfast BT8 6RB ☎ 028 9049 4500 🖷 028 9049 4515 ✉ edelpatterson@castlereagh.gov.uk

Personnel / HR: Mrs Heather Currie, Human Resources Manager, Castlereagh Borough Council, Bradford Court, Upper Galwally, Castlereagh BT8 6RB ☎ 028 9049 4500 ✉ heathercurrie@castlereagh.gov.uk

Planning: Mrs Catharine McWhirter, Planning Officer, Castlereagh Borough Council, Bradford Court, Upper Galwally, Castlereagh BT8 6RB ☎ 028 9049 4635 ✉ catharinemcwhirter@castlereagh.gov.uk

Procurement: Mr James Sweeney, Procurement Officer, Castlereagh Borough Council, Bradford Court, Upper Galwally, Castlereagh BT8 6RB ☎ 028 9049 4511 🖷 028 9049 4555 ✉ jamessweeney@castlereagh.gov.uk

Recycling & Waste Minimisation: Mr Barry Donaldson, Client Services Manager, Civic & Administrative Offices, Bradford Court, Upper Galwally, Castlereagh, Belfast BT8 6RB ☎ 028 9049 4500 🖷 028 9049 4605 ✉ barrydonaldson@castlereagh.gov.uk

Staff Training: Mrs Heather Currie, Human Resources Manager, Castlereagh Borough Council, Bradford Court, Upper Galwally, Castlereagh BT8 6RB ☎ 028 9049 4500 ✉ heathercurrie@castlereagh.gov.uk

Sustainable Development: Mr Edwin Campbell, Director of Technical & Environmental Services, Civic & Administrative Offices, Bradford Court, Upper Galwally, Castlereagh, BT8 6RB ☎ 028 9049 4500 🖷 028 9049 4605 ✉ edwincampbell@castlereagh.gov.uk

Tourism: Mr Patrick McDonald, ED & Tourism Officer, Civic & Administrative Offices, Bradford Court, Upper Galwally, Castlereagh, Belfast BT8 6RB ☎ 028 9049 4500 🖷 028 9049 4515 ✉ patrickmcdonald@castlereagh.gov.uk

Waste Collection and Disposal: Mr Barry Donaldson, Client Services Manager, Civic & Administrative Offices, Bradford Court, Upper Galwally, Castlereagh, Belfast BT8 6RB ☎ 028 9049 4500 🖷 028 9049 4605 ✉ barrydonaldson@castlereagh.gov.uk

Waste Management: Mr Barry Donaldson, Client Services Manager, Civic & Administrative Offices, Bradford Court, Upper Galwally, Castlereagh, Belfast BT8 6RB ☎ 028 9049 4500 🖷 028 9049 4605 ✉ barrydonaldson@castlereagh.gov.uk

MEMBERS OF THE COUNCIL (22)

***Alderman:* Beattie**, Jack (DUP - Castlereagh South)
beattie.jack@googlemail.com
***Alderman:* Duncan**, Sara (ALL - Castlereagh West)
sara.duncan@allianceparty.org
***Alderman:* Henderson**, Michael (UUP - Castlereagh South)
mjh@utvinternet.com
***Alderman:* Rice**, Geraldine (ALL - Castlereagh South)
***Alderman:* Robinson**, Gareth (DUP - Castlereagh East)
grobinson@dup.org.uk
***Alderman:* White**, Jim (DUP - Castlereagh East)
jimwhite@castlereagh.gov.uk
Beattie, A M (DUP - Castlereagh West)
annbeattie@castlereagh.gov.uk
Chambers, Myreve (DUP - Castlereagh West)
Copeland, Michael (UUP - Castlereagh Central)
michaelcopeland@castlereagh.gov.uk
Drysdale, David (DUP - Castlereagh East)
Gregg, Martin (GRN - Castlereagh East)
martin@bt16plus.co.uk
Hall, Cecil (UUP - Castlereagh West)
cecilhall@castlereagh.gov.uk
Hanvey, Brian (SDLP - Castlereagh South)
brianhanvey@castlereagh.gov.uk
Howard, Carole (ALL - Castlereagh Central)
carole.howard@allianceparty.org
Jeffers, Tommy (DUP - Castlereagh East)
tommyjeffers@castlereagh.gov.uk
Long, Michael (ALL - Castlereagh Central)
long_m_a@hotmail.com
McCoy, Vivienne (DUP - Castlereagh Central)
viviennemccoy@castlereagh.gov.uk
Morrow, T (ALL - Castlereagh East)
O'Reilly, Peter (SDLP - Castlereagh West)
Sandford, T (DUP - Castlereagh Central)
Spratt, Jimmy (DUP - Castlereagh South)
Vitty, D (DUP - Castlereagh Central)

POLITICAL COMPOSITION

DUP: 11, ALL: 5, UUP: 3, SDLP: 2, GRN: 1

CENTRAL BEDFORDSHIRE U

Central Bedfordshire, Priory House, Monks Walk, Chicksands, Shefford SG17 5TQ ☎ 0300 300 8000
✉ customer.services@centralbedfordshire.gov.uk
💻 www.centralbedfordshire.gov.uk

FACTS & FIGURES

Parliamentary Constituencies: Bedfordshire Mid, Bedfordshire North East, Bedfordshire South West, Luton South, South West Bedfordshire

PRINCIPAL OFFICERS

Chief Executive: Mr Richard Carr, Chief Executive, Priory House, Monks Walk, Chicksands, Shefford SG17 5TQ ☎ 0300 300 4004
✉ richard.carr@centralbedfordshire.gov.uk

Deputy Chief Executive: Ms Edwina Grant, Deputy Chief Executive / Director of Children's Services, Priory House, Monks Walk, Chicksands, Shefford SG17 5TQ ☎ 0300 300 4229
✉ edwina.grant@centralbedfordshire.gov.uk

Assistant Chief Executive: Ms Deb Clarke, Interim Assistant Chief Executive, People & Organisation, Priory House, Monks Walk, Chicksands, Shefford SG17 5TQ ☎ 0300 300 6651
✉ deb.clarke@centralbedfordshire.gov.uk

Senior Management: Mr Gary Alderson, Director of Sustainable Communities, Priory House, Monks Walk, Chicksands, Shefford SG17 5TQ ☎ 0300 300 4391
✉ gary.alderson@centralbedfordshire.gov.uk

Senior Management: Mr Alan Fleming, Project Director for Business Services (ICT, Assets and BEaR Project), Priory House, Monks Walk, Chicksands, Shefford SG17 5TQ ☎ 0300 300 6968
✉ alan.fleming@centralbedfordshire.gov.uk

Senior Management: Ms Julie Ogley, Director of Social Care, Health & Housing, Priory House, Monks Walk, Chicksands, Shefford SG17 5TQ ☎ 0300 300 4221
✉ julie.ogley@centralbedfordshire.gov.uk

Building Control: Mr Peter Keates, Head of Building Control & Albion Archaeology, Priory House, Monks Walk, Chicksands SG17 5TQ ☎ 0300 300 4380
✉ peter.keates@centralbedfordshire.gov.uk

Children / Youth Services: Ms Yolanda Corden, Interim Assistant Director, Operations, Watling House, High Street North, Dunstable LU6 1LF ☎ 0300 300 6441
✉ yolanda.corden@centralbedfordshire.gov.uk

Children / Youth Services: Mr Pete Dudley, Assistant Director, Learning, Commissioning & Partnerships, Watling House, High Street North, Dunstable LU6 1LF ☎ 0300 300 4302
✉ pete.dudley@centralbedfordshire.gov.uk

PR / Communications: Ms Georgina Stanton, Chief Communications Manager, Priory House, Monks Walk, Chicksands, Shefford SG17 5TQ ☎ 0300 300 4438
✉ georgina.stanton@centralbedfordshire.gov.uk

Computer Management: Mr Alan Fleming, Project Director for Business Services (ICT, Assets and BEaR Project), Priory House, Monks Walk, Chicksands, Shefford SG17 5TQ ☎ 0300 300 6968
✉ alan.fleming@centralbedfordshire.gov.uk

Computer Management: Mr Matt Scott, ICT Head of Service, Technology House, 239 Ampthill Road, Bedford MK42 9BD
☎ 0300 300 5386 ✉ matt.scott@centralbedfordshire.gov.uk

Computer Management: Mr Brian Vaughan, Stability Programme Manager, Technology House, 239 Ampthill Road, Bedford MK42 9BD ☎ 0300 300 5254

brian.vaughan@centralbedfordshire.gov.uk

Consumer Protection and Trading Standards: Ms Susan Childerhouse, Head of Public Protection, Priory House, Monks Walk, Chicksands, Shefford SG17 5TQ ☎ 0300 300 4394 susan.childerhouse@centralbedfordshire.gov.uk

Customer Service: Mr Bernie McGill, Head of Customer Relations & Services, Priory House, Monks Walk, Chicksands, Shefford SG17 5TQ ☎ 0300 300 5614 bernie.mcgill@centralbedfordshire.gov.uk

Economic Development: Ms Elizabeth Wade, Assistant Director - Economic Growth, Skills & Regeneration, Technology House, 239 Ampthill Road, Bedford MK42 9BD ☎ 0300 300 6288 liz.wade@centralbedfordshire.gov.uk

Education: Mr Pete Dudley, Assistant Director, Learning, Commissioning & Partnerships, Watling House, High Street North, Dunstable LU6 1LF ☎ 0300 300 4302 pete.dudley@centralbedfordshire.gov.uk

Education: Ms Edwina Grant, Deputy Chief Executive / Director of Children's Services, Priory House, Monks Walk, Chicksands, Shefford SG17 5TQ ☎ 0300 300 4229 edwina.grant@centralbedfordshire.gov.uk

Electoral Registration: Mr John Atkinson, Head of Legal & Democratic Services, Priory House, Monks Walk, Chicksands, Shefford SG17 5TQ ☎ 0300 300 6255 john.atkinson@centralbedfordshire.gov.uk

Emergency Planning: Ms Jane Moakes, Assistant Director - Community Safety, Public Protection, Waste & Leisure, Priory House, Monk's Walk, Chicksands, Shefford SG17 5TQ ☎ 0300 300 5441 jane.moakes@centralbedfordshire.gov.uk

Energy Management: Ms Deborah Hoy, Divisional Director, Priory House, Monks Walk, Chicksands, Shefford SG17 5TQ ☎ 0300 300 5974 deborah.hoy@centralbedfordshire.gov.uk

Environmental / Technical Services: Ms Jane Moakes, Assistant Director - Community Safety, Public Protection, Waste & Leisure, Priory House, Monk's Walk, Chicksands, Shefford SG17 5TQ ☎ 0300 300 5441 jane.moakes@centralbedfordshire.gov.uk

Environmental Health: Ms Susan Childerhouse, Head of Public Protection, Priory House, Monks Walk, Chicksands, Shefford SG17 5TQ ☎ 0300 300 4394 susan.childerhouse@centralbedfordshire.gov.uk

Estates, Property & Valuation: Mr Peter Burt, Head of Property Assets, Priory House, Monks Walk, Chicksands, Shefford SG17 5TQ ☎ 0300 300 5281 peter.burt@centralbedfordshire.gov.uk

Estates, Property & Valuation: Mr Alan Fleming, Project Director for Business Services (ICT, Assets and BEaR Project), Priory House, Monks Walk, Chicksands, Shefford SG17 5TQ ☎ 0300 300 6968 alan.fleming@centralbedfordshire.gov.uk

Estates, Property & Valuation: Ms Deborah Hoy, Divisional Director, Priory House, Monks Walk, Chicksands, Shefford SG17 5TQ ☎ 0300 300 5974 deborah.hoy@centralbedfordshire.gov.uk

Facilities: Mr David Cook, Operational Facilities Manager, Watling House, High Street North, Dunstable LU6 1LF ☎ 0300 300 5081 david.cook@centralbedfordshire.gov.uk

Finance and Treasurer: Mr Charles Warboys, Chief Finance Officer, Watling House, High Street North, Dunstable LU6 1LF ☎ 0300 300 6147 charles.warboys@centralbedfordshire.gov.uk

Health and Safety: Ms Elizabeth Dunn, Interim Health & Safety Manager, Technology House, 239 Ampthill Road, Bedford MK42 9BD ☎ 0300 300 6793 elizabeth.dunn@centralbedfordshire.gov.uk

Highways: Mr Basil Jackson, Highways Officer, Priory House, Monk's Walk, Chicksands, Shefford SG17 5TQ ☎ 0300 300 6171 basil.jackson@centralbedfordshire.gov.uk

Housing: Mr Tony Keaveney, Assistant Director, Housing, High Street North, Dunstable LU6 1LF ☎ 0300 300 5210 tony.keaveney@centralbedfordshire.gov.uk

Legal: Mr John Atkinson, Head of Legal & Democratic Services, Priory House, Monks Walk, Chicksands, Shefford SG17 5TQ ☎ 0300 300 6255 john.atkinson@centralbedfordshire.gov.uk

Leisure and Cultural Services: Ms Jane Moakes, Community Safety Officer, Watling House, Dunstable LU6 1LF ☎ 0300 300 5441 jane.moakes@centralbedfordshire.gov.uk

Licensing: Ms Susan Childerhouse, Head of Public Protection, Priory House, Monks Walk, Chicksands, Shefford SG17 5TQ ☎ 0300 300 4394 susan.childerhouse@centralbedfordshire.gov.uk

Member Services: Mr John Atkinson, Head of Legal & Democratic Services, Priory House, Monks Walk, Chicksands, Shefford SG17 5TQ ☎ 0300 300 6255 john.atkinson@centralbedfordshire.gov.uk

Personnel / HR: Ms Deb Clarke, Interim Assistant Chief Executive, People & Organisation, Priory House, Monks Walk, Chicksands, Shefford SG17 5TQ ☎ 0300 300 6651 deb.clarke@centralbedfordshire.gov.uk

Personnel / HR: Ms Catherine Jones, Head of HR & Policy Development, Technology House, 239 Ampthill Road, Bedford MK42 9BD ☎ 0300 300 6048 catherine.jones@centralbedfordshire.gov.uk

Planning: Mr Trevor Saunders, Assistant Director - Planning, Priory House, Monks Walk, Chicksands, Shefford SG17 5TQ ☎ 0300 300 4470 trevor.saunders@centralbedfordshire.gov.uk

Procurement: Mr Robin Edwards, Interim Head of Procurement, Technology House, 239 Ampthill Road, Bedford MK42 9BD robin.edwards@centralbedfordshire.gov.uk

Public Libraries: Ms Elizabeth Wade, Assistant Director - Economic Growth, Skills & Regeneration, Technology House, 239 Ampthill Road, Bedford MK42 9BD ☎ 0300 300 6288

liz.wade@centralbedfordshire.gov.uk

Recycling & Waste Minimisation: Ms Tracey Harris, Head of Waste Management, Technology House, 239 Ampthill Road, Bedford MK42 9BD ☎ 0300 300 4646 tracey.harris@centralbedfordshire.gov.uk

Regeneration: Ms Elizabeth Wade, Assistant Director - Economic Growth, Skills & Regeneration, Technology House, 239 Ampthill Road, Bedford MK42 9BD ☎ 0300 300 6288 liz.wade@centralbedfordshire.gov.uk

Social Services: Mr Stuart Rees, Assistant Director - Adult Social Care, Houghton Lodge, Ampthill, Bedford MK45 2TB ☎ 0300 300 5146 stuart.rees@centralbedfordshire.gov.uk

Social Services (Adult): Mr Stuart Rees, Assistant Director - Adult Social Care, Houghton Lodge, Ampthill, Bedford MK45 2TB ☎ 0300 300 5146 stuart.rees@centralbedfordshire.gov.uk

Social Services (Children): Ms Yolanda Corden, Interim Assistant Director, Operations, Watling House, High Street North, Dunstable LU6 1LF ☎ 0300 300 6441 yolanda.corden@centralbedfordshire.gov.uk

Sustainable Communities: Mr Gary Alderson, Director of Sustainable Communities, Priory House, Monks Walk, Chicksands, Shefford SG17 5TQ ☎ 0300 300 4391 gary.alderson@centralbedfordshire.gov.uk

Tourism: Ms Elizabeth Wade, Assistant Director - Economic Growth, Skills & Regeneration, Technology House, 239 Ampthill Road, Bedford MK42 9BD ☎ 0300 300 6288 liz.wade@centralbedfordshire.gov.uk

Traffic Management: Mr David Bowie, Head of Traffic Management, Technology House, 239 Ampthill Road, Bedford MK42 9BD ☎ 0300 300 6206 david.bowie@centralbedfordshire.gov.uk

Waste Collection and Disposal: Ms Tracey Harris, Head of Waste Management, Technology House, 239 Ampthill Road, Bedford MK42 9BD ☎ 0300 300 4646 tracey.harris@centralbedfordshire.gov.uk

Waste Management: Ms Tracey Harris, Head of Waste Management, Technology House, 239 Ampthill Road, Bedford MK42 9BD ☎ 0300 300 4646 tracey.harris@centralbedfordshire.gov.uk

MEMBERS OF THE COUNCIL (59)

***Chair:* Barker**, Angela (CON - Houghton Conquest & Haynes)
angela.barker@centralbedfordshire.gov.uk
***Vice-Chair:* Maudlin**, Caroline (CON - Sandy)
caroline.maudlin@centralbedfordshire.gov.uk
***Leader of the Council:* Jamieson**, James (CON - Westoning, Flitton & Greenfield)
james.jamieson@centralbedfordshire.gov.uk
***Deputy Leader of the Council:* Jones**, Maurice (CON - Biggleswade North)
maurice.jones@centralbedfordshire.gov.uk
Aldis, Nigel (LD - Sandy)
nigel.aldis@centralbedfordshire.gov.uk
Bastable, Alan (CON - Cranfield & Marston Moretaine)
alan.bastable@centralbedfordshire.gov.uk
Berry, Raymond (CON - Leighton Buzzard South)
raymond.berry@centralbedfordshire.gov.uk
Birt, Lewis (CON - Shefford)
lewis.birt@centralbedfordshire.gov.uk
Blair, Michael (CON - Ampthill)
michael.blair@centralbedfordshire.gov.uk
Bowater, David (CON - Leighton Buzzard South)
david.bowater@centralbedfordshire.gov.uk
Brown, Anthony (CON - Shefford)
anthony.brown@centralbedfordshire.gov.uk
Chapman, Fiona (CON - Flitwick)
fiona.chapman@centralbedfordshire.gov.uk
Clark, Sue (CON - Cranfield & Marston Moretaine)
sue.clark@centralbedfordshire.gov.uk
Clarke, Jon (CON - Stotfold & Langford)
jon.clarke@centralbedfordshire.gov.uk
Costin, Norman (CON - Toddington)
norman.costin@centralbedfordshire.gov.uk
Dalgarno, Ian (CON - Arlesey)
ian.dalgarno@centralbedfordshire.gov.uk
Dodwell, Amanda (CON - Leighton Buzzard South)
amanda.dodwell@centralbedfordshire.gov.uk
Drinkwater, Rita (CON - Arlesey)
rita.drinkwater@centralbedfordshire.gov.uk
Duckett, Paul (CON - Ampthill)
paul.duckett@centralbedfordshire.gov.uk
Egan, Rita (LD - Parkside)
rita.egan@centralbedfordshire.gov.uk
Gammons, Ruth (CON - Caddington)
ruth.gammons@centralbedfordshire.gov.uk
Gomm, Charles (CON - Flitwick)
charles.gomm@centralbedfordshire.gov.uk
Goodchild, Susan (LD - Houghton Hall)
susan.goodchild@centralbedfordshire.gov.uk
Green, Denise (CON - Dunstable Northfields)
denise.green2@centralbedfordshire.gov.uk
Gurney, Doreen (CON - Potton)
doreen.gurney@centralbedfordshire.gov.uk
Hegley, Carole (CON - Dunstable Central)
carole.hegley@centralbedfordshire.gov.uk
Hollick, Peter (CON - Dunstable Watling)
peter.hollick@centralbedfordshire.gov.uk
Hopkin, David (CON - Linslade)
david.hopkin@centralbedfordshire.gov.uk
Janes, Ken (CON - Linslade)
ken.janes@centralbedfordshire.gov.uk
Johnstone, Roy (CON - Leighton Buzzard North)
roy.johnstone@centralbedfordshire.gov.uk
Jones, David (LD - Houghton Hall)
david.jones1@centralbedfordshire.gov.uk
Lawrence, David (CON - Biggleswade South)
david.lawrence@centralbedfordshire.gov.uk
Lawrence, Jane (CON - Biggleswade North)
jane.lawrence@centralbedfordshire.gov.uk
MacKilligan, Iain (CON - Silsoe & Shillington)
iain.mackilligan@centralbedfordshire.gov.uk
Matthews, Ken (CON - Cranfield & Marston Moretaine)
ken.matthews@centralbedfordshire.gov.uk
McVicar, David (CON - Dunstable Icknield)
david.mcvicar@centralbedfordshire.gov.uk
Murray, Julian (IND - Dunstable Northfields)
julian.murray@centralbedfordshire.gov.uk

Mustoe, Marion (CON - Eaton Bray)
marion.mustoe@centralbedfordshire.gov.uk
Nicols, Tom (CON - Toddington)
tom.nicols@centralbedfordshire.gov.uk
Pepworth, Roger (LAB - Dunstable Manshead)
roger.pepworth@centralbeds.gov.uk
Saunders, John (CON - Stotfold & Langford)
Saunders, Brian (CON - Stotfold & Langford)
brian.saunders@centralbedfordshire.gov.uk
Shadbolt, Alan (CON - Leighton Buzzard North)
alan.shadbolt@centralbedfordshire.gov.uk
Sheppard, Naomi (CON - Sandy)
naomi.sheppard@centralbedfordshire.gov.uk
Shingler, Ian (IND - Barton-le-Clay)
ian.shingler@centralbedfordshire.gov.uk
Smith, Mark (IND - Ampthill)
mark.smith@centralbedfordshire.gov.uk
Sparrow, Ann (CON - Dunstable Watling)
ann.sparrow@centralbedfordshire.gov.uk
Spurr, Brian (CON - Leighton Buzzard North)
brian.spurr@centralbedfordshire.gov.uk
Stay, Richard (CON - Caddington)
richard.stay@centralbedfordshire.gov.uk
Turner, Andrew (CON - Flitwick)
andrewturner@flitwickfirst.com
Turner, Patricia (CON - Northill)
tricia.turner@centralbedfordshire.gov.uk
Versallion, Mark (CON - Heath & Reach)
mark.versallion@centralbedfordshire.gov.uk
Vickers, Peter (CON - Biggleswade South)
peter.vickers@centralbedfordshire.gov.uk
Warren, Nigel (CON - Linslade)
nigel.warren@centralbedfordshire.gov.uk
Wells, Budge (CON - Aspley & Woburn)
budge.wells@centralbedfordshire.gov.uk
Wenham, Richard (CON - Arlesey)
richard.wenham@centralbedfordshire.gov.uk
Williams, Peter (LD - Tithe Farm)
peter.williams@centralbedfordshire.gov.uk
Young, Nigel (CON - Dunstable Icknield)
nigel.young@centralbedfordshire.gov.uk
Zerny, Adam (IND - Potton)

POLITICAL COMPOSITION

CON: 49, LD: 5, IND: 4, LAB: 1

CABINET

Leader of the Council & Chairman of the Executive: Mr James Jamieson
Deputy Leader & Executive Member for Corporate Resources: Mr Maurice Jones
Children's Services: Mr Mark Versallion
Economic Partnerships: Mrs Patricia Turner
External Affairs: Mr Richard Stay
Social Care, Health & Housing: Mrs Carole Hegley
Sustainable Communities - Services: Mr Brian Spurr
Sustainable Communities - Strategic Planning & Economic Development: Mr Ken Matthews

COMMITTEE CHAIRS

Audit: Mr David Bowater
Children's Services: Mrs Doreen Gurney
Customer & Central Services (Scrutiny): Mr Paul Duckett
Development Management: Mr Alan Shadbolt
General Purposes: Mrs Jane Lawrence
Licensing: Mr Lewis Birt
Social Care, Health & Housing (Scrutiny): Mrs Rita Drinkwater
Sustainable Communities: Mr David McVicar

CEREDIGION W

Ceredigion County Council, (Cyngor Sir Ceredigion), Neuadd Cyngor Ceredigion, Penmorfa, Aberaeron SA46 0PA ☎ 01545 570881 🖷 01545 572009 ✉ reception@ceredigion.gov.uk
🖳 www.ceredigion.gov.uk

FACTS & FIGURES

Police Authority: Dyfed Powys Police Authority
Learning and Skills Council: Wales
Parliamentary Constituencies: Ceredigion
EU Constituencies: Wales
Election Frequency: Elections are of whole council

PRINCIPAL OFFICERS

Chief Executive: Miss Bronwen Morgan, Chief Executive, Neuadd Cyngor Ceredigion, Penmorfa, Aberaeron SA46 0PA
☎ 01545 572004 🖷 01545 572029
✉ chiefexecutive@ceredigion.ov.uk

Senior Management: Mr Eifon Evans, Director - Education & Community Services, Canolfan Rheidol, Rhodfa Padarn, Llanbadarn Fawr, Aberystwyth SY23 3UE ☎ 01970 633600
🖷 01970 633663 ✉ education@ceredigion.gov.uk

Senior Management: Miss Bronwen Morgan, Chief Executive, Neuadd Cyngor Ceredigion, Penmorfa, Aberaeron SA46 0PA
☎ 01545 572004 🖷 01545 572029
✉ chiefexecutive@ceredigion.ov.uk

Access Officer / Social Services (Disability): Ms Donna Pritchard, Team Manager - Disabilities, Min Areon, Rhiw Goch, Aberaeron SA46 0DY ☎ 01545 570881
✉ donnap@ceredigion.gov.uk

Architect, Building / Property Services: Mr Huw Morgan, Director - Highways, Property & Works, County Hall, Market Street, Aberaeron SA46 0AS ☎ 01545 572400 🖷 01545 571089
✉ huwm@ceredigion.gov.uk

Best Value: Mr Allan Lewis, Assistant Chief Executive - Corporate Strategies & Regeneration, Neuadd Cyngor Ceredigion, Penmorfa, Aberaeron SA46 0PA ☎ 01545 570881
🖷 01545 572029 ✉ allan.lewis@ceredigion.gov.uk

Building Control: Mr Huw Morgan, Director - Highways, Property & Works, County Hall, Market Street, Aberaeron SA46 0AS ☎ 01545 572400 🖷 01545 571089
✉ huwm@ceredigion.gov.uk

Catering Services: Mrs Elonwy James, Catering Services Manager, Canolfan Rheidol, Rhodfa Padarn, Llanbadarn Fawr, Aberystwyth SY23 3UE ☎ 01545 570881
✉ elonwyj@ceredigion.gov.uk

Children / Youth Services: Ms Ann Sweeting, Principal Youth

Officer, Canolfan Rheidol, Rhodfa Padarn, Llanbadarn Fawr, Aberystwyth SY23 3UE ☎ 01970 633712 ✉ anns@ceredigion.gov.uk

Civil Registration: Mr Denfer Morgan, Chief Administration Officer, Neuadd Cyngor Ceredigion, Penmorfa, Aberaeron SA46 0PA ☎ 01545 572036 📠 01545 572029 ✉ denferm@ceredigion.gov.uk

PR / Communications: Ms Anwen Francis, Corporate Communications Officer, Neuadd Cyngor Ceredigion, Penmorfa, Aberaeron SA46 0PA ☎ 01545 572003 ✉ anwenf@ceredigion.gov.uk

Community Planning: Mr Allan Lewis, Assistant Chief Executive - Corporate Strategies & Regeneration, Neuadd Cyngor Ceredigion, Penmorfa, Aberaeron SA46 0PA ☎ 01545 570881 📠 01545 572029 ✉ allan.lewis@ceredigion.gov.uk

Community Safety: Mr Alan Garrod, Manager - Community Safety, Neuadd Cyngor Ceredigion, Penmorfa, Aberaeron SA46 0PA ☎ 01545 570881 📠 01545 572009 ✉ alang@ceredigion.gov.uk

Computer Management: Mr Arwyn Morris, Assistant Director Finance (ICT), Canolfan Rheidol, Rhodfa Padarn, Llanbadarn Fawr, Aberystwyth SY23 3UE ☎ 01970 633200 ✉ arwyn.morris@ceredigion.gov.uk

Consumer Protection and Trading Standards: Mr Bryan Thomas, Director - Environmental Services & Housing, Neuadd Cyngor Ceredigion, Penmorfa, Aberaeron SA46 0PA ☎ 01545 572100 📠 01545 572117 ✉ bryant@ceredigion.gov.uk

Contracts: Mr Huw Morgan, Director - Highways, Property & Works, County Hall, Market Street, Aberaeron SA46 0AS ☎ 01545 572400 📠 01545 571089 ✉ huwm@ceredigion.gov.uk

Customer Service: Mr Iain Marshalsay, Assistant Director - Finance, Revenues & Benefits, Canolfan Rheidol, Rhodfa Padarn, Llanbadarn Fawr, Aberystwyth SY23 3UE ☎ 01970 633160 ✉ iain.marshalsay@ceredigion.gov.uk

Direct Labour: Mr Huw Morgan, Director - Highways, Property & Works, County Hall, Market Street, Aberaeron SA46 0AS ☎ 01545 572400 📠 01545 571089 ✉ huwm@ceredigion.gov.uk

Economic Development: Mr Allan Lewis, Assistant Chief Executive - Corporate Strategies & Regeneration, Neuadd Cyngor Ceredigion, Penmorfa, Aberaeron SA46 0PA ☎ 01545 570881 📠 01545 572029 ✉ allan.lewis@ceredigion.gov.uk

Education: Mr Eifon Evans, Director - Education & Community Services, Canolfan Rheidol, Rhodfa Padarn, Llanbadarn Fawr, Aberystwyth SY23 3UE ☎ 01970 633600 📠 01970 633663 ✉ education@ceredigion.gov.uk

E-Government: Mr Arwyn Morris, Assistant Director Finance (ICT), Canolfan Rheidol, Rhodfa Padarn, Llanbadarn Fawr, Aberystwyth SY23 3UE ☎ 01970 633200 ✉ arwyn.morris@ceredigion.gov.uk

Electoral Registration: Miss Bronwen Morgan, Chief Executive, Neuadd Cyngor Ceredigion, Penmorfa, Aberaeron SA46 0PA ☎ 01545 572004 📠 01545 572029 ✉ chiefexecutive@ceredigion.ov.uk

Emergency Planning: Mr Alan Garrod, Manager - Community Safety, Neuadd Cyngor Ceredigion, Penmorfa, Aberaeron SA46 0PA ☎ 01545 570881 📠 01545 572009 ✉ alang@ceredigion.gov.uk

Energy Management: Mr Huw Morgan, Director - Highways, Property & Works, County Hall, Market Street, Aberaeron SA46 0AS ☎ 01545 572400 📠 01545 571089 ✉ huwm@ceredigion.gov.uk

Environmental / Technical Services: Mr Bryan Thomas, Director - Environmental Services & Housing, Neuadd Cyngor Ceredigion, Penmorfa, Aberaeron SA46 0PA ☎ 01545 572100 📠 01545 572117 ✉ bryant@ceredigion.gov.uk

Environmental Health: Mr Bryan Thomas, Director - Environmental Services & Housing, Neuadd Cyngor Ceredigion, Penmorfa, Aberaeron SA46 0PA ☎ 01545 572100 📠 01545 572117 ✉ bryant@ceredigion.gov.uk

Environmental Health: Mr Huw Williams, Assistant Director - Environmental Health & Trading Standards & Animal Health, Neuadd Cyngor Ceredigion, Penmorfa, Aberaeron SA46 0PA ☎ 01545 572151 📠 01545 572117 ✉ huww@ceredigion.gov.uk

Estates, Property & Valuation: Mr Hywel Raw-Rees, Group Manager - Estates & Valuation, County Hall , Market Street, Aberaeron SA46 0AS ☎ 01545 570881 📠 01545 571089

European Liaison: Mr Mike Shaw, Group Manager- Community Regeneration & Europe, Neuadd Cyngor Ceredigion, Penmorfa, Aberaeron SA46 0PA ☎ 01545 572064 📠 01545 572029 ✉ mikes@ceredigion.gov.uk

Finance and Treasurer: Mr Gwyn Jones, Director - Finance, Town Hall, Aberystwyth SY23 2EB ☎ 01970 633101 📠 01970 633109 ✉ gwynj@ceredigion.gov.uk

Fleet Management: Mr Huw Morgan, Director - Highways, Property & Works, County Hall, Market Street, Aberaeron SA46 0AS ☎ 01545 572400 📠 01545 571089 ✉ huwm@ceredigion.gov.uk

Grounds Maintenance: Mr Huw Morgan, Director - Highways, Property & Works, County Hall, Market Street, Aberaeron SA46 0AS ☎ 01545 572400 📠 01545 571089 ✉ huwm@ceredigion.gov.uk

Health and Safety: Mr Keith Holmes, Corporate Head - Health & Safety, Glanyrafon Depot, Glanyrafon Industrial Estate, Aberystwyth SY23 3JQ ☎ 01970 627543 📠 01970 627301 ✉ keithh@ceredigion.gov.uk

Highways: Mr Huw Morgan, Director - Highways, Property & Works, County Hall, Market Street, Aberaeron SA46 0AS ☎ 01545 572400 📠 01545 571089 ✉ huwm@ceredigion.gov.uk

Home Energy Conservation: Mr Bryan Thomas, Director - Environmental Services & Housing, Neuadd Cyngor Ceredigion, Penmorfa, Aberaeron SA46 0PA ☎ 01545 572100 🖷 01545 572117 🖱 bryant@ceredigion.gov.uk

Housing: Mr Bryan Thomas, Director - Environmental Services & Housing, Neuadd Cyngor Ceredigion, Penmorfa, Aberaeron SA46 0PA ☎ 01545 572100 🖷 01545 572117 🖱 bryant@ceredigion.gov.uk

Housing: Ms Sue Thomas, Manager - Housing Strategy, Neuadd Cyngor Ceredigion, Penmorfa, Aberaeron SA46 0PA ☎ 01545 570881 🖷 01545 572175 🖱 suet@ceredigion.gov.uk

Housing Maintenance: Mr Huw Morgan, Director - Highways, Property & Works, County Hall, Market Street, Aberaeron SA46 0AS ☎ 01545 572400 🖷 01545 571089 🖱 huwm@ceredigion.gov.uk

Legal: Miss Claire Jones, Head - Legal Services, Neuadd Cyngor Ceredigion, Penmorfa, Aberaeron SA46 0PA ☎ 01545 572050 🖷 01545 572029 🖱 clairej@ceredigion.gov.uk

Leisure and Cultural Services: Mr Darryl Evans, Recreation Manager, Canolfan Rheidol, Rhodfa Padarn, Llanbadarn Fawr, Aberystwyth SY23 3UE ☎ 01970 633587 🖷 01970 633663 🖱 darryle@ceredigion.gov.uk

Licensing: Mr Barry Evans, Licensing Officer, Neuadd Cyngor Ceredigion, Penmorfa, Aberaeron SA46 0PA ☎ 01545 570881 🖷 01545 572117 🖱 barrye@ceredigion.gov.uk

Lifelong Learning: Mr Eifon Evans, Director - Education & Community Services, Canolfan Rheidol, Rhodfa Padarn, Llanbadarn Fawr, Aberystwyth SY23 3UE ☎ 01970 633600 🖷 01970 633663 🖱 education@ceredigion.gov.uk

Lighting: Mr Huw Morgan, Director - Highways, Property & Works, County Hall, Market Street, Aberaeron SA46 0AS ☎ 01545 572400 🖷 01545 571089 🖱 huwm@ceredigion.gov.uk

Lottery Funding, Charity and Voluntary: Mr Gareth Rowlands, Manager - Community Regeneration, Neuadd Cyngor Ceredigion, Penmorfa, Aberaeron SA46 0PA ☎ 01545 572066 🖷 01545 572029

Member Services: Mr Denfer Morgan, Chief Administration Officer, Neuadd Cyngor Ceredigion, Penmorfa, Aberaeron SA46 0PA ☎ 01545 572036 🖷 01545 572029 🖱 denferm@ceredigion.gov.uk

Parking: Mr Huw Morgan, Director - Highways, Property & Works, County Hall, Market Street, Aberaeron SA46 0AS ☎ 01545 572400 🖷 01545 571089 🖱 huwm@ceredigion.gov.uk

Personnel / HR: Mr Geraint Gibby, Head - Corporate Human Resources, Neuadd Cyngor Ceredigion, Penmorfa, Aberaeron SA46 0PA ☎ 01545 572014 🖷 01545 572009 🖱 geraintg@ceredigion.gov.uk

Planning: Mr Bryan Thomas, Director - Environmental Services & Housing, Neuadd Cyngor Ceredigion, Penmorfa, Aberaeron SA46 0PA ☎ 01545 572100 🖷 01545 572117 🖱 bryant@ceredigion.gov.uk

Procurement: Mr Gwyn Jones, Director - Finance, Town Hall, Aberystwyth SY23 2EB ☎ 01970 633101 🖷 01970 633109 🖱 gwynj@ceredigion.gov.uk

Public Libraries: Mr Rhodri Llwyd Morgan, Assistant Director - Cultural Services, Canolfan Rheidol, Rhodfa Padarn, Llanbadarn Fawr, Aberystwyth SY23 3UE ☎ 01970 633700 🖷 01970 633663

Recycling & Waste Minimisation: Mr Huw Morgan, Director - Highways, Property & Works, County Hall, Market Street, Aberaeron SA46 0AS ☎ 01545 572400 🖷 01545 571089 🖱 huwm@ceredigion.gov.uk

Regeneration: Mr Allan Lewis, Assistant Chief Executive - Corporate Strategies & Regeneration, Neuadd Cyngor Ceredigion, Penmorfa, Aberaeron SA46 0PA ☎ 01545 570881 🖷 01545 572029 🖱 allan.lewis@ceredigion.gov.uk

Road Safety: Mr Huw Morgan, Director - Highways, Property & Works, County Hall, Market Street, Aberaeron SA46 0AS ☎ 01545 572400 🖷 01545 571089 🖱 huwm@ceredigion.gov.uk

Social Services: Mr Parry Davies, Director - Social Services, Min Aeron, South Road, Aberaeron SA46 0DY ☎ 01545 572601 🖷 01545 572619 🖱 parryd@ceredigion.gov.uk

Social Services (Adult): Ms Sue Darnbrook, Assistant Director - Adult Services, Min Aeron, South Road, Aberaeron SA46 0DY ☎ 01545 572620 🖷 01545 572619 🖱 sue.darnbrook@ceredigion.gov.uk

Social Services (Children): Mr Parry Davies, Director - Social Services, Min Aeron, South Road, Aberaeron SA46 0DY ☎ 01545 572601 🖷 01545 572619 🖱 parryd@ceredigion.gov.uk

Social Services (Children): Mr Buddug Ward, Assistant Director - Children's Services, Min Aeron, Rhiw Goch, Aberaeron SA46 0DY ☎ 01545 572694 🖷 01545 572619 🖱 Buddug.ward@ceredigion.gov.uk

Staff Training: Mrs Rhian Haf Evans, Assistant Personnel Officer - Performance Training, Neuadd Cyngor Ceredigion, Penmorfa, Aberaeron SA46 0PA ☎ 01545 572019 🖷 01545 572009 🖱 rhiane@ceredigion.gov.uk

Street Scene: Mr Bleddyn Jones, Group Manager - Strategy & Procurement, County Hall, Market Street, Aberaeron SA46 0AS ☎ 01545 570881 🖷 01545 571089 🖱 bleddynj@ceredigion.gov.uk

Sustainable Development: Mr Bryan Thomas, Director - Environmental Services & Housing, Neuadd Cyngor Ceredigion, Penmorfa, Aberaeron SA46 0PA ☎ 01545 572100 🖷 01545 572117 🖱 bryant@ceredigion.gov.uk

Tourism: Mr A.E Jones, Manager - Marketing & Tourism Service, Lisburn House, Terrace Road, Aberystwyth SY23 2AG ☎ 01970 633061

Town Centre: Mr Jason Jones, Development Manager, Neuadd

Cyngor Ceredigion, Penmorfa, Aberaeron SA46 0PA ☎ 01545 572070 🖷 01545 572049 ✉ jasonj@ceredigion.gov.uk

Traffic Management: Mr Huw Morgan, Director - Highways, Property & Works, County Hall, Market Street, Aberaeron SA46 0AS ☎ 01545 572400 🖷 01545 571089 ✉ huwm@ceredigion.gov.uk

Transport: Mr Huw Morgan, Director - Highways, Property & Works, County Hall, Market Street, Aberaeron SA46 0AS ☎ 01545 572400 🖷 01545 571089 ✉ huwm@ceredigion.gov.uk

Waste Collection and Disposal: Mr Huw Morgan, Director - Highways, Property & Works, County Hall, Market Street, Aberaeron SA46 0AS ☎ 01545 572400 🖷 01545 571089 ✉ huwm@ceredigion.gov.uk

Waste Management: Mr Huw Morgan, Director - Highways, Property & Works, County Hall, Market Street, Aberaeron SA46 0AS ☎ 01545 572400 🖷 01545 571089 ✉ huwm@ceredigion.gov.uk

MEMBERS OF THE COUNCIL (42)

***Chair:* Cole**, Mark (LD - Cardigan - Rhydyfuwch)
markco@ceredigion.gov.uk
***Vice-Chair:* Adams-Lewis**, John (PC - Cardigan - Mwldan)
john.adams-lewis@ceredigion.gov.uk
***Leader of the Council:* ap Gwynn**, Ellen (PC - Ceulanamaesmawr)
ellen.apgwynn@ceredigion.gov.uk
***Deputy Leader of the Council:* Quant**, Raymond (IND - Borth)
ray.quant@ceredigion.gov.uk
Davies, Peter (IND - Capel Dewi)
peter.davies@ceredigion.gov.uk
Davies, Ceredig (LD - Aberystwyth Central)
ceredigwd@ceredigion.gov.uk
Davies, Steve (PC - Aberystwyth Penparcau)
steve.davies2@ceredigion.gov.uk
Davies, John (PC - Llangybi)
odwyn.davies@ceredigion.gov.uk
Davies, Ifan (IND - Lledrod)
ifan.davies@ceredigion.gov.uk
Davies, Euros (IND - Llanwenog)
euros.davies@ceredigion.gov.uk
Davies, Bryan (PC - Llanarth)
bryan.davies@ceredigion.gov.uk
Davies, Aled (PC - Aberystwyth Rheidol)
aled.davis@ceredigion.gov.uk
Davies, Gareth (PC - Llanbadarn Fawr - Padarn)
gareth.davies@ceredigion.gov.uk
Davies, Rhodri (PC - Melindwr)
rhodri.davies@ceredigion.gov.uk
Edwards, Dafydd (IND - Llansantffraid)
dafydd.edwards@live.co.uk
Evans, David (PC - Llangeitho)
rhodri.evans2@ceredigion.gov.uk
Evans, Peter (PC - Llandysul Town)
peter.evans3@ceredigion.gov.uk
Evans, Benjamin (PC - Llandyfriog)
towyn.evans@ceredigion.gov.uk
Evans, Elizabeth (LD - Aberaeron)
elizabeth.evans@ceredigion.gov.uk
Harris, George (LAB - Lampeter)
hag.harries@ceredigion.gov.uk
Hinge, Paul (LD - Tirymynach)
paul.hinge@ceredigion.gov.uk
Hopley, Sarah (IND - New Quay)
gillhop@ceredigion.gov.uk
Hughes, Catherine (PC - Tregaron)
catherine.hughes@ceredigion.gov.uk
James, Gethin (IND - Aberporth)
gethin.james@ceredigion.gov.uk
James, Gwyn (IND - Penbryn)
gwyn.james@ceredigion.gov.uk
James, Paul (PC - Llanbadarn Fawr - Sulien)
paul.james@ceredigion.gov.uk
Jones, Rowland (LD - Ystwyth)
rowland.jones@ceredigion.gov.uk
Jones-Southgate, Lorrae (PC - Aberystwyth Penparcau)
lorrae.jones-southgate@ceredigion.gov.uk
Lewis, Maldwyn (IND - Troedyraur)
maldwyn.lewis@ceredigion.gov.uk
Lewis, Thomas (IND - Penparc)
thomaslewis34@mypostoffice.co.uk
Lloyd, Gareth (IND - Llandysiliogogo)
garethl@ceredigion.gov.uk
Lloyd, Lyndon (PC - Beulah)
Lloyd Jones, Alun (PC - Llanfarian)
alun.lloydjones@ceredigion.gov.uk
Lumley, John (PC - Ciliau Aeron)
john.lumley@ceredigion.gov.uk
Mason, David (IND - Trefeurig)
dai.mason@ceredigion.gov.uk
Miles, Catrin (PC - Cardigan - Teifi)
catrin.miles@ceredigion.gov.uk
Rees-Evans, David (LD - Llanrhystud)
rowland.rees-evans@ceredigion.gov.uk
Roberts, John (LD - Faenor)
john.roberts@ceredigion.gov.uk
Strong, Mark (PC - Aberystwyth North)
mark.strong@ceredigion.gov.uk
Thomas, Lynford (PC - Llanfihangel Ystrad)
lynford.thomas@ceredigion.gov.uk
Williams, Alun (PC - Aberystwyth Bronglais)
alun.williams@ceredigion.gov.uk
Williams, Ivor (IND - Lampeter)
ivor.williams@ceredigion.gov.uk

POLITICAL COMPOSITION

PC: 21, IND: 13, LD: 7, LAB: 1

CABINET

Leader: Mrs Ellen ap Gwynn
Deputy Leader / Transformation & Performance Management: Mr Raymond Quant
Corporate Resources: Mr Peter Davies
Economic Development, Community Development, Leisure & Culture: Mr Gareth Lloyd
Education & Lifelong Learning: Mr George Harris
Environment, Regulation & Planning: Mr Dafydd Edwards
Social Services & Housing: Mrs Catherine Hughes
Transport, Waste & Carbon Management: Mr Alun Williams

COMMITTEE CHAIRS

Corporate Resources Overview & Scrutiny: Mrs Sarah Hopley
Democratic Services: Mr Ceredig Davies

Healthier Communities Overview & Scrutiny: Mr Alun Lloyd Jones
Learning Communities Overview & Scrutiny: Mr Paul Hinge
Licensing: Mr Paul James

CHARNWOOD D

Charnwood Borough Council, Southfields, Loughborough LE11 2TX ☎ 01509 263151 🖷 01509 263791 ✉ info@charnwood.gov.uk 🖳 www.charnwood.gov.uk

FACTS & FIGURES

Police Authority: Leicestershire Police Authority
Health Authority: East Midlands Strategic Health Authority
Learning and Skills Council: East Midlands
Parliamentary Constituencies: Charnwood, Loughborough
EU Constituencies: East Midlands
Election Frequency: Elections are of whole council
Twinning: Birstall: Rixensart (Belgium); Bradgate Villages: Plateau Est de Rouen (France); East Goscote: Fleury-sur-Andelle (France); Loughborough: Epinal (France); Schwabisch Hall (Germany);Zamosc (Poland); Queniborough: Sceaux-Courtempierre (France); Shepshed: Domont (France); Syston: Deville-les-Rouen (France); Thurmaston: Offranville (France)

PRINCIPAL OFFICERS

Chief Executive: Mr Geoff Parker, Chief Executive & Head of Paid Services, Southfields, Loughborough LE11 2TR ☎ 01509 634800 🖷 01509 263791 ✉ geoff.parker@charnwood.gov.uk

Senior Management: Mr Simon Jackson, Strategic Director of Corporate Services, Southfields, Loughborough LE11 2TX ☎ 01509 634583 🖷 01509 263791 ✉ simon.jackson@charnwood.gov.uk

Senior Management: Ms Eileen Mallon, Strategic Director of Housing, Planning, Regulation and Regulatory Services, Southfields, Loughborough LE11 2TX ☎ 01509 634662 ✉ eileen.mallon@charnwood.gov.uk

Senior Management: Mr David Platts, Head of Revenue, Benefits & Customer Service, Southfields, Loughborough LE11 2TX ☎ 01509 634850 🖷 01509 263791 ✉ david.platts@charnwood.gov.uk

Senior Management: Ms Christine Traill, Strategic Director of Neighbourhood & Community Wellbeing, Southfields, Loughborough LE11 2TX ☎ 01509 634774 ✉ chris.traill@charnwood.gov.uk

Architect, Building / Property Services: Mr Richard Bennett, Head of Planning & Regeneration, Southfields, Loughborough LE11 2TX ☎ 01509 634763 ✉ richard.bennett@charnwood.gov.uk

Architect, Building / Property Services: Mr John Casey, Head Of Finance & Property Services, Southfields, Loughborough LE11 2TX ☎ 01509 634583 ✉ john.casey@charmwood.gov.uk

Architect, Building / Property Services: Mr Dave Wall, Premises Manager, Southfields, Loughborough LE11 2TR ☎ 01509 634686 ✉ dave.wall@charnwood.gov.uk

Best Value: Mr Simon Jackson, Strategic Director of Corporate Services, Southfields, Loughborough LE11 2TX ☎ 01509 634583 🖷 01509 263791 ✉ simon.jackson@charnwood.gov.uk

Best Value: Mr Adrian Ward, Head of Strategic Support, Southfields, Loughborough LE11 2TX ☎ 01509 634612 ✉ adrian.wad@charnwood.gov.uk

Building Control: Mr Richard Bennett, Head of Planning & Regeneration, Southfields, Loughborough LE11 2TX ☎ 01509 634763 ✉ richard.bennett@charnwood.gov.uk

Building Control: Ms Eileen Mallon, Strategic Director of Housing, Planning, Regulation and Regulatory Services, Southfields, Loughborough LE11 2TX ☎ 01509 634662 ✉ eileen.mallon@charnwood.gov.uk

Catering Services: Mr Dave Wall, Premises Manager, Southfields, Loughborough LE11 2TR ☎ ; 01509 634686 ✉ dave.wall@charnwood.gov.uk

Children / Youth Services: Ms Julie Robinson, Head of Leisure Services, Southfields, Loughborough LE11 2TX ☎ 01509 634590 ✉ julie.robinson@charnwood.gov.uk

Children / Youth Services: Ms Christine Traill, Strategic Director of Neighbourhood & Community Wellbeing, Southfields, Loughborough LE11 2TX ☎ 01509 634774 ✉ chris.traill@charnwood.gov.uk

PR / Communications: Mr Michael Underwood, Communications Officer, Southfields, Loughborough LE11 2TX ☎ 01509 634517 ✉ Michael.underwood@charnwood.gov.uk

PR / Communications: Mr Adrian Ward, Head of Strategic Support, Southfields, Loughborough LE11 2TX ☎ 01509 634612 ✉ adrian.wad@charnwood.gov.uk

Community Planning: Ms Julie Robinson, Head of Leisure Services, Southfields, Loughborough LE11 2TX ☎ 01509 634590 ✉ julie.robinson@charnwood.gov.uk

Community Safety: Ms Julie Robinson, Head of Leisure Services, Southfields, Loughborough LE11 2TX ☎ 01509 634590 ✉ julie.robinson@charnwood.gov.uk

Computer Management: Mr Paul Bargewell, Technical Service & Strategy Manager, Southfields, Loughborough LE11 2TX ☎ 01509 634777 ✉ paul.bargewell@charnwood.gov.uk

Computer Management: Mr David Platts, Head of Revenue, Benefits & Customer Service, Southfields, Loughborough LE11 2TX ☎ 01509 634850 🖷 01509 263791 ✉ david.platts@charnwood.gov.uk

Corporate Services: Mr Simon Jackson, Strategic Director of Corporate Services, Southfields, Loughborough LE11 2TX ☎ 01509 634583 🖷 01509 263791 ✉ simon.jackson@charnwood.gov.uk

Customer Service: Mr Adrian Le-Cras, Customer Services Manager, Southfields, Loughborough LE11 2TR ☎ 01509 634860

🖰 adrian.le-cras@charnwood.gov.uk

Customer Service: Mr David Platts, Head of Revenue, Benefits & Customer Service, Southfields, Loughborough LE11 2TX ☎ 01509 634850 🖷 01509 263791 🖰 david.platts@charnwood.gov.uk

Customer Service: Mr Michael Underwood, Communications Officer, Southfields, Loughborough LE11 2TX ☎ 01509 634517 🖰 Michael.underwood@charnwood.gov.uk

Economic Development: Mr Richard Bennett, Head of Planning & Regeneration, Southfields, Loughborough LE11 2TX ☎ 01509 634763 🖰 richard.bennett@charnwood.gov.uk

E-Government: Mr Paul Bargewell, Technical Service & Strategy Manager, Southfields, Loughborough LE11 2TX ☎ 01509 634777 🖰 paul.bargewell@charnwood.gov.uk

E-Government: Mr David Platts, Head of Revenue, Benefits & Customer Service, Southfields, Loughborough LE11 2TX ☎ 01509 634850 🖷 01509 263791 🖰 david.platts@charnwood.gov.uk

Electoral Registration: Mr Adrian Ward, Head of Strategic Support, Southfields, Loughborough LE11 2TX ☎ 01509 634612 🖰 adrian.wad@charnwood.gov.uk

Emergency Planning: Mr Peter Hinton, Community Safety Officer, Southfields, Loughborough LE11 2TR ☎ 01509 634911 🖷 01509 263791 🖰 peter.hinton@charnwood.gov.uk

Emergency Planning: Mr Adrian Ward, Head of Strategic Support, Southfields, Loughborough LE11 2TX ☎ 01509 634612 🖰 adrian.wad@charnwood.gov.uk

Energy Management: Mr Dave Wall, Premises Manager, Southfields, Loughborough LE11 2TR ☎ ; 01509 634686 🖰 dave.wall@charnwood.gov.uk

Environmental / Technical Services: Mr Neil Greenhalgh, Head of Clensing & Open Spaces, Southfields, Loughborough LE11 2TX ☎ 01509 634675 🖰 neil.greenhalgh@charnwood.gov.uk

Environmental / Technical Services: Mr Martin Tincknell, Group Leader Plans, Policys and Place Making, Southfields, Loughborough LE11 2TX ☎ 01509 634767 🖰 martin.tincknell@charnwood.gov.uk

Environmental Health: Ms Eileen Mallon, Strategic Director of Housing, Planning, Regulation and Regulatory Services, Southfields, Loughborough LE11 2TX ☎ 01509 634662 🖰 eileen.mallon@charnwood.gov.uk

Environmental Health: Mr Alan Twells, Head of Regulatory Services, Southfields, Loughborough LE11 2TX ☎ 01509 634650 🖰 alan.twells@charnwood.gov.uk

Estates, Property & Valuation: Mr John Casey, Head of Finance & Property Services, Southfields, Loughborough LE11 2TX ☎ 01509 634583 🖰 john.casey@charmwood.gov.uk

Events Manager: Ms Sylvia Wright, Head of Leisure & Culture, Southfields, Loughborough LE11 2TX ☎ 01509 634658 🖰 sylvia.wright@charnwood.gov.uk

Facilities: Mr Dave Wall, Premises Manager, Southfields, Loughborough LE11 2TR ☎ ; 01509 634686 🖰 dave.wall@charnwood.gov.uk

Finance and Treasurer: Mr John Casey, Head of Finance & Property Services, Southfields, Loughborough LE11 2TX ☎ 01509 634810 🖰 john.casey@charnwood.gov.uk

Finance and Treasurer: Mr Simon Jackson, Strategic Director of Corporate Services, Southfields, Loughborough LE11 2TX ☎ 01509 634583 🖷 01509 263791 🖰 simon.jackson@charnwood.gov.uk

Grounds Maintenance: Mr Colin Bailey, Green Spaces Development Manager, Southfields, Loughborough LE11 2TX ☎ 01509 632530 🖰 colin.bailey@charnwood.gov.uk

Grounds Maintenance: Mr Bernard Sheridan, Green Spaces Operations Manager, Southfields, Loughborough LE11 2TX ☎ 01509 634998 🖰 bernard.sheridan@charnwood.gov.uk

Health and Safety: Mr David Hicks, Health & Safety Officer, Southfields, Loughborough LE11 3DH ☎ 01509 634637 🖷 01509 211703 🖰 david.hicks@charnwood.gov.uk

Health and Safety: Mr Adrian Ward, Head of Strategic Support, Southfields, Loughborough LE11 2TX ☎ 01509 634612 🖰 adrian.wad@charnwood.gov.uk

Housing: Mr David Harris, Head of Housing, Southfields, Loughborough LE11 2TX ☎ 01509 634780 🖰, david.harris@charnwood.gov.uk ()

Housing: Ms Eileen Mallon, Strategic Director of Housing, Planning, Regulation and Regulatory Services, Southfields, Loughborough LE11 2TX ☎ 01509 634662 🖰 eileen.mallon@charnwood.gov.uk

Legal: Mr Adrian Ward, Head of Strategic Support, Southfields, Loughborough LE11 2TX ☎ 01509 634612 🖰 adrian.wad@charnwood.gov.uk

Legal: Mr Adrian Ward, Head of Strategic Support, Southfield Road, Loughborough LE11 2TR ☎ 01509 634612 🖷 01509 634718 🖰 adrian.ward@charnwood.gov.uk

Leisure and Cultural Services: Ms Julie Robinson, Head of Leisure Services, Southfields, Loughborough LE11 2TX ☎ 01509 634590 🖰 julie.robinson@charnwood.gov.uk

Leisure and Cultural Services: Ms Christine Traill, Strategic Director of Neighbourhood & Community Wellbeing, Southfields, Loughborough LE11 2TX ☎ 01509 634774 🖰 chris.traill@charnwood.gov.uk

Leisure and Cultural Services: Ms Sylvia Wright, Head of Leisure & Culture, Southfields, Loughborough LE11 2TX ☎ 01509 634658 🖰 sylvia.wright@charnwood.gov.uk

Licensing: Mr Malcolm Burton, Licensing Officer, Southfields, Loughborough LE11 2TN ☎ 01509 634622 ✉ malcolm.burton@charnwood.gov.uk

Lottery Funding, Charity and Voluntary: Ms Julie Robinson, Head of Leisure Services, Southfields, Loughborough LE11 2TX ☎ 01509 634590 ✉ julie.robinson@charnwood.gov.uk

Member Services: Mr Adrian Ward, Head of Strategic Support, Southfields, Loughborough LE11 2TX ☎ 01509 634612 ✉ adrian.wad@charnwood.gov.uk

Parking: Mr Alan Twells, Head of Regulatory Services, Southfields, Loughborough LE11 2TX ☎ 01509 634650 ✉ alan.twells@charnwood.gov.uk

Partnerships: Ms Julie Robinson, Head of Leisure Services, Southfields, Loughborough LE11 2TX ☎ 01509 634590 ✉ julie.robinson@charnwood.gov.uk

Personnel / HR: Mr Adrian Ward, Head of Strategic Support, Southfields, Loughborough LE11 2TX ☎ 01509 634612 ✉ adrian.wad@charnwood.gov.uk

Planning: Mr Richard Bennett, Head of Planning & Regeneration, Southfields, Loughborough LE11 2TX ☎ 01509 634763 ✉ richard.bennett@charnwood.gov.uk

Planning: Mr Richard Bennett, Head of Planning & Regeneration, Southfields, Loughborough LE11 2TX ☎ 01509 634763 ✉ richard.bennett@charnwood.gov.uk

Planning: Ms Eileen Mallon, Strategic Director of Housing, Planning, Regulation and Regulatory Services, Southfields, Loughborough LE11 2TX ☎ 01509 634662 ✉ eileen.mallon@charnwood.gov.uk

Procurement: Mr David Howkins, Purchasing Manager, Southfields, Loughborough LE11 2TX ☎ 01509 634672 ✉ david.howkins@charnwood.gov.uk

Staff Training: Mr Kevin Brewin, Emergency Planning Co-ordinator, Southfields, Loughborough LE11 2TR ☎ 01509 634904 ✉ kevin.brewin@charnwood.gov.uk

Staff Training: Mr Adrian Ward, Head of Strategic Support, Southfields, Loughborough LE11 2TX ☎ 01509 634612 ✉ adrian.wad@charnwood.gov.uk

Street Scene: Mr Alan Twells, Head of Regulatory Services, Southfields, Loughborough LE11 2TX ☎ 01509 634650 ✉ alan.twells@charnwood.gov.uk

Sustainable Communities: Mr Tom Kiernan, Head of Communities & Partnerships, Southfields, Loughborough LE11 2TX ☎ 01509 634901 ✉ tom.kiernan@charnwood.gov.uk

Sustainable Communities: Ms Julie Robinson, Head of Leisure Services, Southfields, Loughborough LE11 2TX ☎ 01509 634590 ✉ julie.robinson@charnwood.gov.uk

Tourism: Ms Christine Traill, Strategic Director of Neighbourhood & Community Wellbeing, Southfields, Loughborough LE11 2TX ☎ 01509 634774 ✉ chris.traill@charnwood.gov.uk

Town Centre: Mr Michael Bird, Markets & Fairs Manager, Southfields, Loughborough LE11 2TX ☎ 01509 634624 ✉ market.fairs@charnwood.gov.uk

Town Centre: Ms Sylvia Wright, Head of Leisure & Culture, Southfields, Loughborough LE11 2TX ☎ 01509 634658 ✉ sylvia.wright@charnwood.gov.uk

Transport Planner: Mr Richard Bennett, Head of Planning & Regeneration, Southfields, Loughborough LE11 2TX ☎ 01509 634763 ✉ richard.bennett@charnwood.gov.uk

Waste Collection and Disposal: Mr Neil Greenhalgh, Head of Clensing & Open Spaces, Southfields, Loughborough LE11 2TX ☎ 01509 634675 ✉ neil.greenhalgh@charnwood.gov.uk

Waste Management: Mr Neil Greenhalgh, Head of Clensing & Open Spaces, Southfields, Loughborough LE11 2TX ☎ 01509 634675 ✉ neil.greenhalgh@charnwood.gov.uk

MEMBERS OF THE COUNCIL (51)

***Mayor:* Burr**, Bernard (CON - Shepshed West)
cllr.bernard.burr@charnwood.gov.uk
***Leader of the Council:* Slater**, David (CON - Quorn & Mountsorrel Castle)
cllr.david.slater@charnwood.gov.uk
***Deputy Leader of the Council:* Hampson**, Stephen (CON - Syston East)
cllr.stephen.hampson@charnwood.gov.uk
Barkley, Tom (CON - Syston West)
cllr.thomas.barkley@charnwood.gov.uk
Bebbington, Liz (CON - Shepshed East)
cllr.liz.bebbington@charnwood.gov.uk
Bentley, Ian (CON - Birstall Watermead)
cllr.ian.bentley@charnwood.gov.uk
Blain, Matthew (CON - Wreake Villages)
cllr.matthew.blain@charnwood.gov.uk
Bokor, Jenny (CON - The Wolds)
cllr.jenny.bokor@charnwood.gov.uk
Bradshaw, Julie (LAB - Loughborough Ashby)
cllr.julie.bradshaw@charnwood.gov.uk
Campsall, Roy (IND - Loughborough Garendon)
cllr.roy.campsall@charnwood.gov.uk
Capleton, John (CON - Mountsorrel)
cllr.john.capleton@charnwood.gov.uk
Carter, Chris (LAB - Loughborough Ashby)
cllr.christopher.carter@charnwood.gov.uk
Choudhury, Jitu (LAB - Loughborough Hastings)
cllr.jitu.choudhury@charnwood.gov.uk
Day, Paul (CON - Anstey)
cllr.paul.day@charnwood.gov.uk
Duffy, Catherine Ann (BNP - East Goscote)
cllr.catherine.duffy@charnwood.gov.uk
Forrest, Sandie (LAB - Loughborough Storer)
cllr.sandra.forrest@charnwood.gov.uk
Fryer, Hilary (CON - Barrow & Sileby West)
cllr.hilary.fryer@charnwood.gov.uk
Gaskell, David (CON - Birstall Watermead)
cllr.david.gaskell@charnwood.gov.uk
Grimley, David (CON - Queniborough)
cllr.daniel.grimley@charnwood.gov.uk

Harley, Paul (CON - Thurmaston)
cllr.paul.harley@charnwood.gov.uk
Harper-Davies, Leigh (CON - Mountsorrel)
cllr.leigh.harper-davies@charnwood.gov.uk
Harris, Christine (LAB - Loughborough Lemyngton)
cllr.christine.harris@charnwood.gov.uk
Hunt, Jane (CON - Loughborough Nanpantan)
cllr.jane.hunt@charnwood.gov.uk
Hunt, Max (LAB - Loughborough Garendon)
cllr.max.hunt@charnwood.gov.uk
Jones, Stuart (CON - Birstall Wanlip)
cllr.stuart.jones@charnwood.gov.uk
Jukes, Ron (CON - Loughborough Outwoods)
cllr.ron.jukes@charnwood.gov.uk
Lowe, Mark (CON - Thurmaston)
cllr.mark.lowe@charnwood.gov.uk
Miah, Jewel (LAB - Loughborough Lemyngton)
cllr.jewel.miah@charnwood.gov.uk
Morgan, Jonathan (CON - Loughborough Outwoods)
cllr.jonathan.morgan@charnwood.gov.uk
Newton, Betty (LAB - Loughborough Dishley & Hathern)
cllr.betty.newton@charnwood.gov.uk
Osbourne, Peter (CON - Rothley & Thurcaston)
cllr.peter.osborne@charnwood.gov.uk
Pacey, Ken (CON - Syston East)
cllr.ken.pacey@charnwood.gov.uk
Paling, Andy (CON - Sileby)
cllr.andy.paling@charnwood.gov.uk
Poole, Claire (LAB - Shepshed East)
cllr.claire.poole@charnwood.gov.uk
Radford, Christine (CON - Shepshed West)
cllr.christine.radford@charnwood.gov.uk
Ranson, Pauline (CON - Barrow & Sileby West)
cllr.pauline.ranson@charnwood.gov.uk
Seaton, Brenda (CON - Thurmaston)
cllr.brenda.seaton@charnwood.gov.uk
Sharp, Robert (LAB - Loughborough Shelthorpe)
cllr.robert.sharp@charnwood.gov.uk
Shepherd, Richard (CON - Quorn & Mountsorrel Castle)
cllr.richard.shepherd@charnwood.gov.uk
Shergill, Serinda (CON - Birstall Wanlip)
cllr.serinda.shergill@charnwood.gov.uk
Smidowicz, Margaret (CON - Loughborough Nanpantan)
cllr.margaret.smidowicz@charnwood.gov.uk
Smith, Stephen (LAB - Loughborough Dishley & Hathern)
cllr.stephen.smith@charnwood.gov.uk
Smith, Marion (LAB - Loughborough Southfields)
cllr.marion.smith@charnwood.gov.uk
Smith, Graeme (LAB - Loughborough Southfields)
cllr.graeme.smith@charnwood.gov.uk
Snartt, David (CON - Forest Bradgate)
cllr.david.snartt@charnwood.gov.uk
Stork, Nev (LAB - Loughborough Shelthorpe)
cllr.neville.stork@charnwood.gov.uk
Sutherington, John (LD - Anstey)
cllr.john.sutherington@charnwood.gov.uk
Vardy, Eric (CON - Syston West)
cllr.eric.vardy@charnwood.gov.uk
Williams, Anne (LAB - Loughborough Hastings)
cllr.anne.williams@charnwood.gov.uk
Wise, Diane (CON - Rothley & Thurcaston)
cllr.diane.wilson@charnwood.gov.uk
Youell, Patrick (LAB - Loughborough Storer)
cllr.patrick.youell@charnwood.gov.uk

POLITICAL COMPOSITION
CON: 32, LAB: 16, LD: 1, IND: 1, BNP: 1

CABINET
Leader: Mr David Slater
Deputy Leader of the Council & Strategic Support: Mr Stephen Hampson
Cleansing & Open Spaces: Ms Hilary Fryer
Finance & Resources: Mr Tom Barkley
Housing & Regulatory Services: Ms Jane Hunt
Leisure & Culture: Mr Paul Harley
Neighbourhood Services: Mr David Snartt
Planning: Mr Matthew Blain
Revenues & Benefits and Customer Services: Ms Jenny Bokor

COMMITTEE CHAIRS
Appeals & Review: Ms Pauline Ranson
Audit: Mr Paul Blakemore (External)
Licensing: Mr Ken Pacey
Personnel: Mr David Slater
Plans: Mr Paul Day
Policy Scrutiny Management: Mr Roy Brown
Standards: Mr PJ Tomlinson (External)

CHELMSFORD D

Chelmsford Borough Council, Civic Centre, Duke Street, Chelmsford CM1 1JE ☎ 01245 606606 🖷 01245 606310
mailbox@chelmsford.gov.uk 💻 www.chelmsford.gov.uk

FACTS & FIGURES
Police Authority: Essex Police Authority
Health Authority: East of England Strategic Health Authority
Learning and Skills Council: Eastern
Parliamentary Constituencies: Chelmsford
EU Constituencies: Eastern
Election Frequency: Elections are of whole council
Twinning: Chelmsford: Annonay (France); Backnang (Germany); Great Waltham: Cegrat (France); Danbury: Altenglan (Germany)

PRINCIPAL OFFICERS
Chief Executive: Mr Steve Packham, Chief Executive, Civic Centre, Duke Street, Chelmsford CM1 1JE ☎ 01245 606901
steve.packham@chelmsford.gov.uk

Senior Management: Mr Nick Eveleigh, Director of Financial Services, PO Box 457, Civic Centre, Duke Street, Chelmsford CM1 1JE ☎ 01245 606419 🖷 01245 606693
nick.eveleigh@chelmsford.gov.uk

Senior Management: Ms Louise Goodwin, Director of Corporate Services, Civic Centre, Duke Street, Chelmsford CM1 1JE
☎ 01245 606802 🖷 01245 606657
louise.goodwin@chelmsford.gov.uk

Senior Management: Mr David Green, Director of Sustainable Communities, Civic Centre, Duke Street, Chelmsford CM1 1JE
☎ 01245 606503 🖷 01245 606642
david.green@chelmsford.gov.uk

Senior Management: Mr Bernard Mella, Director of Leisure &

Cultural Services, Civic Centre, Duke Street, Chelmsford CM1 1JE ☎ 01245 606471 🖷 01245 606970 ✉ bernard.mella@chelmsford.gov.uk

Senior Management: Mr Keith Nicholson, Director of Public Places, Civic Centre, Duke Street, Chelmsford CM1 1JE ☎ 01245 606606 🖷 01245 606681 ✉ keith.nicholson@chelmsford.gov.uk

Senior Management: Ms Averil Price, Director of Safer Communities, Civic Centre, Duke Street, Chelmsford CM1 1JE ☎ 01245 606473 ✉ averil.price@chelmsford.gov.uk

Access Officer / Social Services (Disability): Mr Paul Houghton, Access Officer, Civic Centre, Duke Street, Chelmsford CM1 1JE ☎ 01245 606328 🖷 01245 606288 ✉ paul.houghton@chelmsford.gov.uk

Architect, Building / Property Services: Mr Neil Smith, Senior Architect, Civic Centre, Duke Street, Chelmsford CM1 1JE ☎ 01245 606606 ✉ neil.smith@chelmsford.gov.uk

Building Control: Mr David Green, Director of Sustainable Communities, Civic Centre, Duke Street, Chelmsford CM1 1JE ☎ 01245 606503 🖷 01245 606642 ✉ david.green@chelmsford.gov.uk

PR / Communications: Mr Ryan De'Ath, Civic Centre, Duke Street, Chelmsford CM1 1JE ☎ 01245 606580 🖷 01245 606657 ✉ ryan.de'ath@chelmsford.gov.uk

Community Planning: Mr David Green, Director of Sustainable Communities, Civic Centre, Duke Street, Chelmsford CM1 1JE ☎ 01245 606503 🖷 01245 606642 ✉ david.green@chelmsford.gov.uk

Community Safety: Mr Spencer Clarke, Community Service & Play Manager, Civic Centre, Duke Street, Chelmsford CM1 1JE ☎ 01245 606477 ✉ spencer.clarke@chelmsford.gov.uk

Computer Management: Mr Tony Preston, Corporate ICT Manager, Civic Centre, Duke Street, Chelmsford CM1 1JE ☎ 01245 606606 ✉ tony.preston@chelmsford.gov.uk

Corporate Services: Ms Louise Goodwin, Director of Corporate Services, Civic Centre, Duke Street, Chelmsford CM1 1JE ☎ 01245 606802 🖷 01245 606657 ✉ louise.goodwin@chelmsford.gov.uk

Customer Service: Mrs Elaine Peck, Customer Services Manager, Civic Centre, Duke Street, Chelmsford CM1 1JE ☎ 01245 606406 🖷 01245 606657 ✉ elaine.peck@chelmsford.gov.uk

Economic Development: Mr Stuart Graham, Inward Investment, Economy & Growth Manager, Civic Centre, Duke Street, Chelmsford CM1 1JE ☎ 01245 606364 ✉ stuart.graham@chelmsford.gov.uk

Electoral Registration: Mr Brian Mayfield, Democratic Services Manager, Democratic Services, Civic Centre, Duke Street, Chelmsford CM1 1JE ☎ 01245 606923 ✉ brian.mayfield@chelmsford.gov.uk

Emergency Planning: Mr Gerry Richardson, Emergency Planning Officer, Civic Centre, Duke Street, Chelmsford CM1 1JE ☎ 01245 606921 ✉ gerry.richardson@chelmsford.gov.uk

Environmental / Technical Services: Mr Paul Brookes, Environmental Services Manager, Civic Centre, Duke Street, Chelmsford CM1 1JE ☎ 01245 606606 ✉ paul.brookes@chelmsford.gov.uk

Environmental / Technical Services: Ms Averil Price, Director of Safer Communities, Civic Centre, Duke Street, Chelmsford CM1 1JE ☎ 01245 606473 ✉ averil.price@chelmsford.gov.uk

Environmental Health: Ms Averil Price, Director of Safer Communities, Civic Centre, Duke Street, Chelmsford CM1 1JE ☎ 01245 606473 ✉ averil.price@chelmsford.gov.uk

Estates, Property & Valuation: Ms Ann Coronel, Legal & Democratic Services Manager, Civic Centre, Duke Street, Chelmsford CM1 1JE ☎ 01245 606560 🖷 01245 606245 ✉ ann.coronel@chelmsford.gov.uk

Events Manager: Mr Jon Gower, Arts & Entertainment Manager, Civic Centre, Duke Street, Chelmsford CM1 1JE ☎ 01245 606495 ✉ jon.gower@chelmsford.gov.uk

Facilities: Mr Richard Pellant, Building Services Manager, Civic Centre, Duke Street, Chelmsford CM1 1JE ☎ 01245 606750 ✉ richard.pellant@chelmsford.gov.uk

Finance and Treasurer: Mr Nick Eveleigh, Director of Financial Services, PO Box 457, Civic Centre, Duke Street, Chelmsford CM1 1JE ☎ 01245 606419 🖷 01245 606693 ✉ nick.eveleigh@chelmsford.gov.uk

Grounds Maintenance: Mr Paul van Damme, Parks & Grounds Operations Manager, Parks Services, Waterhouse Lane, Chelmsford CM1 2RY ☎ 01245 496560 🖷 01245 600803 ✉ paul.vandamme@chelmsford.gov.uk

Home Energy Conservation: Mr Peter McDonagh, Strategic Housing Manager, Civic Centre, Duke Street, Chelmsford CM1 1JE ☎ 01245 606669 🖷 01245 606681 ✉ peter.mcdonagh@chelmsford.gov.uk

Housing: Mr David Green, Director of Sustainable Communities, Civic Centre, Duke Street, Chelmsford CM1 1JE ☎ 01245 606503 🖷 01245 606642 ✉ david.green@chelmsford.gov.uk

Legal: Ms Ann Coronel, Legal & Democratic Services Manager, Civic Centre, Duke Street, Chelmsford CM1 1JE ☎ 01245 606560 🖷 01245 606245 ✉ ann.coronel@chelmsford.gov.uk

Leisure and Cultural Services: Mr Bernard Mella, Director of Leisure & Cultural Services, Civic Centre, Duke Street, Chelmsford CM1 1JE ☎ 01245 606471 🖷 01245 606970 ✉ bernard.mella@chelmsford.gov.uk

Licensing: Mr Ian Weller, Senior Licensing Officer, Civic Centre, Duke Street, Chelmsford CM1 1JE ☎ 01245 606587 🖷 01245 606681 ✉ ian.weller@chelmsford.gov.uk

Member Services: Ms Ann Coronel, Legal & Democratic Services Manager, Civic Centre, Duke Street, Chelmsford CM1 1JE ☎ 01245 606560 🖷 01245 606245 ✉ ann.coronel@chelmsford.gov.uk

Parking: Ms Averil Price, Director of Safer Communities, Civic Centre, Duke Street, Chelmsford CM1 1JE ☎ 01245 606473 ✉ averil.price@chelmsford.gov.uk

Partnerships: Ms Lucy Payne, Chelmsford Partnership Coordinator, Civic Centre, Duke Street, Chelmsford CM1 1JE ☎ 01245 606491 ✉ lucy.payne@chelmsford.gov.uk

Personnel / HR: Ms Louise Goodwin, Director of Corporate Services, Civic Centre, Duke Street, Chelmsford CM1 1JE ☎ 01245 606802 🖷 01245 606657 ✉ louise.goodwin@chelmsford.gov.uk

Planning: Mr David Green, Director of Sustainable Communities, Civic Centre, Duke Street, Chelmsford CM1 1JE ☎ 01245 606503 🖷 01245 606642 ✉ david.green@chelmsford.gov.uk

Procurement: Mr Chris Lay, Procurement Manager, Civic Centre, Duke Street, Chelmsford CM1 1JE ☎ 01245 606485 🖷 01245 606574 ✉ chris.lay@chelmsford.gov.uk

Recycling & Waste Minimisation: Mr Keith Nicholson, Director of Public Places, Civic Centre, Duke Street, Chelmsford CM1 1JE ☎ 01245 606606 🖷 01245 606681 ✉ keith.nicholson@chelmsford.gov.uk

Regeneration: Mr Roger Estop, Planning Design Manager, Town Planning Service, Civic Centre, Duke Street, Chelmsford CM1 1JE ☎ 01245 606281 🖷 01245 606642 ✉ roger.estop@chelmsford.gov.uk

Road Safety: Mrs Gillian Beale, Road Safety Officer for Chelmsford, Essex County Council, Mid Area Office, 2 Beaufort Road, New Dukes Way, Chelmsford CM2 6PS ☎ 01245 240042 🖷 01245 240028 ✉ gillian.beale@essex.gov.uk

Staff Training: Ms Marie Russell, Learning & Organisational Development Officer, Civic Centre, Duke Street, Chelmsford CM1 1JE ☎ 01245 606206 ✉ marie.russell@chelmsford.gov.uk

Street Scene: Ms Averil Price, Director of Safer Communities, Civic Centre, Duke Street, Chelmsford CM1 1JE ☎ 01245 606473 ✉ averil.price@chelmsford.gov.uk

Sustainable Communities: Mr David Green, Director of Sustainable Communities, Civic Centre, Duke Street, Chelmsford CM1 1JE ☎ 01245 606503 🖷 01245 606642 ✉ david.green@chelmsford.gov.uk

Sustainable Development: Mr David Green, Director of Sustainable Communities, Civic Centre, Duke Street, Chelmsford CM1 1JE ☎ 01245 606503 🖷 01245 606642 ✉ david.green@chelmsford.gov.uk

Town Centre: Mr Mike Wray, Town Centre Manager, Civic Centre, Duke Street, Chelmsford CM1 1JE ☎ 01245 606253 🖷 01245 606657

Waste Collection and Disposal: Mr Keith Nicholson, Director of Public Places, Civic Centre, Duke Street, Chelmsford CM1 1JE ☎ 01245 606606 🖷 01245 606681 ✉ keith.nicholson@chelmsford.gov.uk

Waste Management: Mr Paul Brookes, Environmental Services Manager, Civic Centre, Duke Street, Chelmsford CM1 1JE ☎ 01245 606606 ✉ paul.brookes@chelmsford.gov.uk

Children's Play Areas: Mr Spencer Clarke, Community Service & Play Manager, Civic Centre, Duke Street, Chelmsford CM1 1JE ☎ 01245 606477 ✉ spencer.clarke@chelmsford.gov.uk

MEMBERS OF THE COUNCIL (56)

Leader of the Council: **Whitehead**, Roy (CON - South Hanningfield - Stock & Margaretting)
r.whitehead@chelmsford.gov.uk

Deputy Leader of the Council: **Galley**, John (CON - Boreham & the Leighs)
j.gallery@chelmsford.gov.uk

Alcock, Ron (CON - Chelmer Village & Beaulieu Park)
r.alcock@chelmsford.gov.uk

Arnot, Alan (LD - Patching Hall)
a.arnot@chelmsford.gov.uk

Ashford, Delmas (IND - Broomfield & The Walthams)
d.ashford@chelmsford.gov.uk

Burgoyne, Robert (CON - The Lawns)
robert.burgoyne@chelmsford.gov.uk

Chambers, Nicolette (CON - Chelmsford Rural West)
n.chambers@chelmsford.gov.uk

Chambers, Alan (CON - Waterhouse Farm)
alan.chambers@chelmsford.gov.uk

Chandler, Jenny (CON - Great Baddow West)
jenny.chandler@chelmsford.gov.uk

Cousins, Peter (CON - St Andrews)
peter.cousins@chelmsford.gov.uk

Deakin, Jude (LD - Marconi)
jude.deakin@chelmsford.gov.uk

Denston, Bob (CON - South Woodham - Elmwood & Woodville)
r.denston@chelmsford.gov.uk

Fegan, Chris (LAB - Marconi)
chris.fegan@chelmsford.gov.uk

Fuller, Ian (LD - Springfield North)
ian.fuller@chelmsford.gov.uk

Garrett, Christine (CON - The Lawns)
christine.garrett@chelmsford.gov.uk

Grundy, Ian (CON - South Hanningfield - Stock & Margaretting)
i.grundy@chelmsford.gov.uk

Gulliver, Neil (CON - Chelmer Village & Beaulieu Park)
n.gulliver@chelmsford.gov.uk

Harris, Michael (CON - Bicknacre & East & West Hanningfield)
michael.harris@chelmsford.gov.uk

Hindi, Sameh (CON - Moulsham & Central)
s.k.hindi@chelmsford.gov.uk

Hughes, Patricia (CON - South Woodham - Elmwood & Woodville)
p.hughes@chelmsford.gov.uk

Hunnable, John (LD - St Andrews)
j.hunnable@chelmsford.gov.uk

Hutchinson, Paul (CON - Springfield North)
paul.hutchinson@chelmsford.gov.uk

Irwin, Victoria (CON - Moulsham & Central)
victoria.irwin@chelmsford.gov.uk

John, Ashley (CON - South Woodham - Chetwood &

Collingwood)
ashley.john@chelmsford.gov.uk
Jones, David (LD - Moulsham Lodge)
d.jones@chelmsford.gov.uk
Kingsley, Christopher (CON - Little Baddow, Danbury & Sandon)
christopher.kingsley@chelmsford.gov.uk
Lane, Pam (LD - Springfield North)
pamela.lane@chelmsford.gov.uk
Lumley, Duncan (CON - Chelmer Village & Beaulieu Park)
d.lumley@chelmsford.gov.uk
Madden, Dick (CON - Moulsham & Central)
dick.madden@chelmsford.gov.uk
Mascot, Linda (LD - Goat Hall)
linda.mascot@chelmsford.gov.uk
Massey, Bob (CON - South Woodham - Chetwood & Collingwood)
bob.massey@chelmsford.gov.uk
Maybrick, Julie (CON - Trinity)
julie.maybrick@chelmsford.gov.uk
Millane, Lance (CON - Rettendon & Runwell)
lance.millane@chelmsford.gov.uk
Miller, Trevor (LD - Great Baddow East)
t.miller@chelmsford.gov.uk
Moulds, Maureen (CON - South Woodham - Elmwood & Woodville)
maureen.moulds@chelmsford.gov.uk
Mountain, Freda (LD - Goat Hall)
f.mountain@chelmsford.gov.uk
Murray, Jean (CON - Trinity)
jean.murray@chelmsford.gov.uk
Nichols, Gloria (LD - St Andrews)
gloria.nichols@chelmsford.gov.uk
Patient, Brian (CON - Broomfield & The Walthams)
brian.patient@chelmsford.gov.uk
Pontin, Sandra (CON - Broomfield & The Walthams)
sandra.pontin@chelmsford.gov.uk
Potter, Janette (CON - Galleywood)
japotter@chelmsford.gov.uk
Poulter, Richard (CON - Bicknacre & East & West Hanningfield)
r.poulter@chelmsford.gov.uk
Ride, Raymond (CON - Rettendon & Runwell)
r.ride@chelmsford.gov.uk
Robinson, Stephen (LD - Patching Hall)
stephen.robinson@chelmsford.gov.uk
Roper, Tim (CON - Writtle)
t.roper@chelmsford.gov.uk
Rycroft, Chris (LD - Great Baddow East)
c.rycroft@chelmsford.gov.uk
Sach, Tony (CON - Writtle)
tony.sach@chelmsford.gov.uk
Shepherd, Bob (CON - Little Baddow, Danbury & Sandon)
b.shepherd@chelmsford.gov.uk
Sismey, Malcolm (CON - South Woodham - Chetwood & Collingwood)
malcolm.sismey@chelmsford.gov.uk
Sosin, Andrew (LD - Great Baddow East)
a.sosin@chelmsford.gov.uk
Springett, Mark (LD - Moulsham Lodge)
mark.springett@chelmsford.gov.uk
Stevenson, David (CON - Galleywood)
d.stevenson@chelmsford.gov.uk
Villa, Bob (CON - Great Baddow West)
bob.villa@chelmsford.gov.uk
Watson, Malcolm (CON - Waterhouse Farm)
malcolm.watson@chelmsford.gov.uk
Wilson, Philip (CON - Boreham & the Leighs)
p.wilson@chelmsford.gov.uk
Wright, Ian (CON - Little Baddow, Danbury & Sandon)
i.wright@chelmsford.gov.uk

POLITICAL COMPOSITION

CON: 40, LD: 14, IND: 1, LAB: 1

CABINET

Leader: Mr Roy Whitehead
Deputy Leader / Finance: Mr John Galley
Corporate Services: Mr Michael Harris
Leisure & Culture: Mr Raymond Ride
Parks & Heritage: Mrs Nicolette Chambers
Planning & Economic Development: Mr Neil Gulliver
Safer Communities: Mr Ian Grundy
Strategic Housing: Mr Duncan Lumley
Waste Management & Recycling: Mrs Janette Potter

CHELTENHAM D

Cheltenham Borough Council, Municipal Offices, The Promenade, Cheltenham GL50 9SA ☎ 01242 262626 🖷 01242 227131 ✉ enquiries@cheltenham.gov.uk
🖳 www.cheltenham.gov.uk

FACTS & FIGURES

Police Authority: Gloucestershire Police Authority
Health Authority: East of England Strategic Health Authority
Learning and Skills Council: South West
Parliamentary Constituencies: Cheltenham
EU Constituencies: South West
Election Frequency: Elections are biennial
Twinning: Annecy (France); Gottingen (Germany); Kisumu (Kenya); Weihai (China)

PRINCIPAL OFFICERS

Chief Executive: Mr Andrew North, Chief Executive, Municipal Offices, The Promenade, Cheltenham GL50 9SA ☎ 01242 264100 🖷 01242 264360 ✉ andrew.north@cheltenham.gov.uk

Senior Management: Mr Grahame Lewis, Executive Director, Municipal Offices, The Promenade, Cheltenham GL50 9SA ☎ 01242 264312 🖷 01242 264305 ✉ grahame.lewis@cheltenham.gov.uk

Senior Management: Mrs Pat Pratley, Executive Director, Municipal Offices, Promenade, Cheltenham GL50 9SA ☎ 01242 775175 🖷 01242 775127 ✉ pat.pratley@cheltenham.gov.uk

Architect, Building / Property Services: Mr David Roberts, Head of Property & Asset Management, Municipal Offices, The Promenade, Cheltenham GL50 9SA ☎ 01242 264151 🖷 01242 264159 ✉ david.roberts@cheltenham.gov.uk

Building Control: Mr Iain Houston, Building Control Manager, Municipal Offices, The Promenade, Cheltenham GL50 9SA ☎ 01242 264293; 01242 264293 🖷 01242 227323 ✉ iain.houston@cheltenham.gov.uk

Catering Services: Mr Gary Nejrup, Entertainment & Business Manager, Town Hall, Imperial Square, Cheltenham GL50 1QA

☎ 01242 775853 🖷 01242 573902 ✉ gary.nejrup@cheltenham.gov.uk

PR / Communications: Mr Richard Gibson, Policy & Partnerships Manager, Municipal Offices, The Promenade, Cheltenham GL50 9SA ☎ 01242 235354 🖷 01242 264360 ✉ richard.gibson@cheltenham.gov.uk

Community Planning: Mr Mike Redman, Director - Built Environment, Municipal Offices, The Promenade, Cheltenham GL50 9SA ☎ 01242 264160 🖷 01242 227323 ✉ mike.redman@cheltenham.gov.uk

Community Safety: Mrs Barbara Exley, Head of Public Protection, Municipal Offices, Promenade, Cheltenham GL50 9SA ☎ 01242 264220 🖷 01242 264210 ✉ barbara.exley@cheltenham.gov.uk

Community Safety: Mr Trevor Gladding, Community Protection Manager, Municipal Offices, The Promenade, Cheltenham GL50 9SA ☎ 01242 264368 🖷 01242 774941 ✉ trevor.gladding@cheltenham.gov.uk

Computer Management: Mr Paul Woolcock, ICT Infrastructure Manager, Municipal Offices, The Promenade, Cheltenham GL50 9SA ☎ 01242 775102 🖷 01242 227131 ✉ paul.woolcock@cheltenham.gov.uk

Contracts: Mrs Shirin Wotherspoon, Principal Solicitor, Tewkesbury Borough Council, Council Offices, Gloucester Road, Tewkesbury GL20 5TT ☎ 01684 272017; 01684 272017 ✉ shirin.wotherspoon@tewkesbury.gov.uk; shirin.wotherspoon@tewkesbury.gov.uk

Corporate Services: Mr Mark Sheldon, Director - Resources, Municipal Offices, The Promenade, Cheltenham GL50 9SA ☎ 01242 264123 🖷 01242 774989 ✉ mark.sheldon@cheltenham.gov.uk

Customer Service: Mr Mark Sheldon, Director - Resources, Municipal Offices, The Promenade, Cheltenham GL50 9SA ☎ 01242 264123 🖷 01242 774989 ✉ mark.sheldon@cheltenham.gov.uk

Economic Development: Mr Mike Redman, Director - Built Environment, Municipal Offices, The Promenade, Cheltenham GL50 9SA ☎ 01242 264160 🖷 01242 227323 ✉ mike.redman@cheltenham.gov.uk

Electoral Registration: Mrs Kim Smith, Elections & Electoral Registration Manager, Municipal Offices, The Promenade, Cheltenham GL50 9SA ☎ 01242 264948 🖷 01242 264120 ✉ kim.smith@cheltenham.gov.uk

Emergency Planning: Mr Grahame Lewis, Executive Director, Municipal Offices, The Promenade, Cheltenham GL50 9SA ☎ 01242 264312 🖷 01242 264305 ✉ grahame.lewis@cheltenham.gov.uk

Energy Management: Mr Tom Mimnagh, Building Services Manager, Municipal Offices, The Promenade, Cheltenham GL50 9SA ☎ 01242 264164 🖷 01242 264159 ✉ tom.mimnagh@cheltenham.gov.uk

Environmental Health: Mrs Barbara Exley, Head of Public Protection, Municipal Offices, Promenade, Cheltenham GL50 9SA ☎ 01242 264220 🖷 01242 264210 ✉ barbara.exley@cheltenham.gov.uk

Estates, Property & Valuation: Mr David Roberts, Head of Property & Asset Management, Municipal Offices, The Promenade, Cheltenham GL50 9SA ☎ 01242 264151 🖷 01242 264159 ✉ david.roberts@cheltenham.gov.uk

Events Manager: Mr Gary Nejrup, Entertainment & Business Manager, Town Hall, Imperial Square, Cheltenham GL50 1QA ☎ 01242 775853 🖷 01242 573902 ✉ gary.nejrup@cheltenham.gov.uk

Finance and Treasurer: Mr Mark Sheldon, Director - Resources, Municipal Offices, The Promenade, Cheltenham GL50 9SA ☎ 01242 264123 🖷 01242 774989 ✉ mark.sheldon@cheltenham.gov.uk

Fleet Management: Mr Malcolm Carruthers, Fleet Services Manager, Central Depot, Swindon Road, Cheltenham GL51 9JZ ☎ 01242 264361 🖷 01242 264224 ✉ malcolm.carruthers@ubico.co.uk

Grounds Maintenance: Mr Adam Reynolds, Green Space Development Manager, Central Depot, Swindon Road, Cheltenham GL51 9JZ ☎ 01242 774669 ✉ adam.reynolds@cheltenham.gov.uk

Health and Safety: Mrs Barbara Exley, Head of Public Protection, Municipal Offices, Promenade, Cheltenham GL50 9SA ☎ 01242 264220 🖷 01242 264210 ✉ barbara.exley@cheltenham.gov.uk

Home Energy Conservation: Mr Mark Nelson, Public Sector Housing Manager, Municipal Offices, The Promenade, Cheltenham GL50 9SA ☎ 01242 264165 🖷 01242 775119 ✉ mark.nelson@cheltenham.gov.uk

Housing: Mr Martin Stacy, Housing & Communities Manager, Municipal Offices, The Promenade, Cheltenham GL50 9SA ☎ 01242 775213 🖷 01242 264397 ✉ martin.stacy@cheltenham.gov.uk

Housing Maintenance: Mr Paul Stephenson, Acting Chief Executive (Cheltenham Borough Homes), Cheltenham House, Clarence Street, Cheltenham GL50 3RD ☎ 01242 775319 ✉ paul.stephenson@cheltenham.gov.uk

Legal: Ms Sara Freckleton, Borough Solicitor & Monitoring Officer, Council Offices, Gloucester Road, Tewkesbury GL20 5TT ☎ 01684 272010; 01684 272010 ✉ sara.freckleton@tewkesbury.gov.uk

Legal: Mr Peter Lewis, Shared Head of ONE Legal, Council Offices, Gloucester Road, Tewkesbury GL20 5TT ☎ 01684 272012 ✉ peter.lewis@tewkesbury.gov.uk

Leisure and Cultural Services: Mrs Sonia Phillips, Director - Wellbeing & Culture, Municipal Offices, The Promenade, Cheltenham GL50 9SA ☎ 01242 774973 🖷 01242 774989 ✉ sonia.phillips@cheltenham.gov.uk

Licensing: Mrs Barbara Exley, Head of Public Protection, Municipal Offices, Promenade, Cheltenham GL50 9SA ☎ 01242 264220 🖷 01242 264210 ✉ barbara.exley@cheltenham.gov.uk

Lifelong Learning: Mrs Jane Lillystone, Museum, Arts & Tourism Manager, Art Gallery & Museum, Clarence Street, Cheltenham GL50 3JT ☎ 01242 775706 ✉ jane.lillystone@cheltenham.gov.uk

Lottery Funding, Charity and Voluntary: Mr Richard Gibson, Policy & Partnerships Manager, Municipal Offices, The Promenade, Cheltenham GL50 9SA ☎ 01242 235354 🖷 01242 264360 ✉ richard.gibson@cheltenham.gov.uk

Member Services: Mrs Rosalind Reeves, Democratic Services Manager, Municipal Offices, The Promenade, Cheltenham GL50 9SA ☎ 01242 774937 🖷 01242 227131 ✉ rosalind.reeves@cheltenham.gov.uk

Parking: Mr Owen Parry, Head of Integrated Transport & Sustainability, Municipal Offices, The Promenade, Cheltenham GL50 9SA ☎ 01242 774640 ✉ owen.parry@cheltenham.gov.uk

Partnerships: Mr Richard Gibson, Policy & Partnerships Manager, Municipal Offices, The Promenade, Cheltenham GL50 9SA ☎ 01242 235354 🖷 01242 264360 ✉ richard.gibson@cheltenham.gov.uk

Personnel / HR: Mrs Amanda Attfield, Head of Human Resources - GO Shared Services, Cotswold District Council, Trinity Road, Cirencester GL7 1PX ☎ 07920 284313 ✉ amanda.attfield@cheltenham.gov.uk

Planning: Mr Mike Redman, Director - Built Environment, Municipal Offices, The Promenade, Cheltenham GL50 9SA ☎ 01242 264160 🖷 01242 227323 ✉ mike.redman@cheltenham.gov.uk

Procurement: Mrs Angela Cox, Procurement Manager, Municipal Offices, The Promenade, Cheltenham GL50 9SA ☎ 01242 775223 🖷 01242 227131 ✉ angela.cox@cheltenham.gov.uk

Recycling & Waste Minimisation: Ms Beth Boughton, Waste & Recycling Manager, Central Depot, Swindon Road, Cheltenham GL51 9JZ ☎ 01242 774644 🖷 01242 264338 ✉ beth.boughton@ubico.co.uk

Regeneration: Mr Mike Redman, Director - Built Environment, Municipal Offices, The Promenade, Cheltenham GL50 9SA ☎ 01242 264160 🖷 01242 227323 ✉ mike.redman@cheltenham.gov.uk

Staff Training: Mrs Jan Bridges, Learning & Organisational Development Manager, Municipal Offices, Promenade, Cheltenham GL50 9SA ☎ 01242 775189 🖷 01242 264309 ✉ jan.bridges@cheltenham.gov.uk

Street Scene: Mr Owen Parry, Head of Integrated Transport & Sustainability, Municipal Offices, The Promenade, Cheltenham GL50 9SA ☎ 01242 774640 ✉ owen.parry@cheltenham.gov.uk

Sustainable Communities: Mrs Jane Griffiths, Director - Commissioning, Municipal Offices, The Promenade, Cheltenham GL50 9SA ☎ 01242 264126 🖷 01242 264360 ✉ jane.griffiths@cheltenham.gov.uk

Sustainable Development: Ms Gill Morris, Climate Change & Sustainability Officer, Municipal Offices, The Promenade, Cheltenham GL50 9SA ☎ 01242 264229 ✉ gill.morris@cheltenham.gov.uk

Tourism: Mrs Angie Rowlands, Tourist Information Centre Manager, Municipal Offices, The Promenade, Cheltenham GL50 9SA ☎ ; 01242 226033 🖷 01242 264307 ✉ angie.rowlands@cheltenham.gov.uk

Town Centre: Mr Martin Quantock, Cheltenham Business Partnership Manager, Cheltenham Business Partnership, 2 Trafalgar Street, Cheltenham GL50 1UH ☎ 01242 252626 🖷 01242 541255 ✉ manager@cheltenhambp.org.uk

Transport: Mr Owen Parry, Head of Integrated Transport & Sustainability, Municipal Offices, The Promenade, Cheltenham GL50 9SA ☎ 01242 774640 ✉ owen.parry@cheltenham.gov.uk

Waste Collection and Disposal: Mr Rob Bell, Managing Director - UBICO, Central Depot, Swindon Road, Cheltenham GL51 9JZ ☎ 01242 264181 ✉ rob.bell@ubico.co.uk

Waste Management: Mr Scott Williams, Waste & Land Drainage Manager, Cotswold District Council, Trinity Road, Cirencester GL7 1PX ☎ 01285 623123 🖷 01285 623910 ✉ scott.williams@cotswold.gov.uk

MEMBERS OF THE COUNCIL (40)

***Mayor:* Hay**, Colin (LD - Oakley)
cllr.colin.hay@cheltenham.gov.uk

***Leader of the Council:* Jordan**, Stephen (LD - All Saints)
cllr.steve.jordan@cheltenham.gov.uk

***Deputy Leader of the Council:* Rawson**, John (LD - St. Peter's)
cllr.john.rawson@cheltenham.gov.uk

***Group Leader:* Godwin**, Leslie (O - Prestbury)
cllr.les.godwin@cheltenham.gov.uk

***Group Leader:* Smith**, Duncan (CON - Charlton Park)
cllr.duncan.smith@cheltenham.gov.uk

Barnes, Garth (LD - College)
cllr.garth.barnes@cheltenham.gov.uk

Bickerton, Ian (LD - Leckhampton)
cllr.ian.bickerton@cheltenham.gov.uk

Britter, Nigel (LD - Benhall & the Reddings)
cllr.nigel.britter@cheltenham.gov.uk

Chard, Andrew (CON - Leckhampton)

Coleman, Chris (LD - St. Mark's)
cllr.chris.coleman@cheltenham.gov.uk

Driver, Barbara (CON - Lansdown)
cllr.barbara.driver@cheltenham.gov.uk

Fisher, Bernard (LD - Swindon Village)
cllr.bernard.fisher@cheltenham.gov.uk

Fletcher, Jacky (CON - Benhall & the Reddings)
cllr.jacky.fletcher@cheltenham.gov.uk

Flynn, Wendy (LD - Hesters Way)
cllr.wendy.flynn@cheltenham.gov.uk

Garnham, Robert (CON - Park)
rob.garnham@gloucestershire.gov.uk

Hall, Penelope (CON - Charlton Park)
cllr.penelope.hall@cheltenham.gov.uk

Harman, Tim (CON - Park)
Hay, Rowena (LD - Oakley)
cllr.rowena.hay@cheltenham.gov.uk
Hibbert, Diane (O - Pittville)
cllr.diane.hibbert@cheltenham.gov.uk
Holliday, Sandra (LD - St. Mark's)
cllr.sandra.holliday@cheltenham.gov.uk
Jeffries, Peter (LD - Springbank)
cllr.peter.jeffries@cheltenham.gov.uk
Lansley, Andrew (LD - St. Pauls)
Massey, Paul (LD - Swindon Village)
cllr.paul.massey@cheltenham.gov.uk
McCloskey, Helena (LD - Charlton Kings)
cllr.helena.mccloskey@cheltenham.gov.uk
McKinlay, Andrew (LD - Up Hatherley)
cllr.andrew.mckinlay@cheltenham.gov.uk
McLain, Paul (CON - Battledown)
cllr.paul.mclain@cheltenham.gov.uk
Prince, David (O - Pittville)
Regan, Anne (CON - Warden Hill)
cllr.anne.regan@cheltenham.gov.uk
Reid, Rob (LD - Charlton Kings)
Seacome, Diggory (CON - Lansdown)
cllr.diggory.seacome@cheltenham.gov.uk
Stennett, Malcolm (O - Prestbury)
cllr.malcolm.stennett@cheltenham.gov.uk
Stewart, Charles (LD - All Saints)
cllr.charles.stewart@cheltenham.gov.uk
Sudbury, Klara (LD - College)
cllr.klara.sudbury@cheltenham.gov.uk
Teakle, Jo (LD - Warden Hill)
cllr.jo.teakle@cheltenham.gov.uk
Thornton, Pat (LD - St. Peter's)
cllr.pat.thornton@cheltenham.gov.uk
Walklett, Jon (LD - St. Pauls)
cllr.jon.walklett@cheltenham.gov.uk
Wall, Andrew (CON - Battledown)
cllr.andrew.wall@cheltenham.gov.uk
Wheeler, Simon (LD - Hesters Way)
saw50@mac.com
Whyborn, Roger (LD - Up Hatherley)
cllr.roger.whyborn@cheltenham.gov.uk
Williams, Suzanne (LD - Springbank)

POLITICAL COMPOSITION

LD: 25, CON: 11, O: 4

CABINET

Leader: Mr Stephen Jordan
Deputy Leader / Finance: Mr John Rawson
Built Environment: Mr Andrew McKinlay
Corporate Services: Mr Jon Walklett
Housing & Safety: Mr Peter Jeffries
Sport & Culture: Mrs Rowena Hay
Sustainability: Mr Roger Whyborn

COMMITTEE CHAIRS

Appointments: Mrs Rowena Hay
Audit: Mr Paul Massey
Licensing: Mr Garth Barnes
Overview & Scrutiny: Mr Duncan Smith
Planning: Mrs Helena McCloskey

CHERWELL — D

Cherwell District Council, Bodicote House, Bodicote, Banbury OX15 4AA ☎ 01295 252535 🖷 01295 270028
info@cherwell-dc.gov.uk www.cherwell-dc.gov.uk

FACTS & FIGURES

Police Authority: Thames Valley Police Authority
Health Authority: South Central Strategic Health Authority
Learning and Skills Council: South East
Parliamentary Constituencies: Banbury
EU Constituencies: South East
Election Frequency: Elections are by thirds
Twinning: Banbury: Ermont (France), Hennef (Germany); Bicester: Neunkirchen-Seelscheid (Germany); Canton Des Essarts (France)

PRINCIPAL OFFICERS

Chief Executive: Mrs Susan Smith, Chief Executive, Bodicote House, Bodicote, Banbury OX15 4AA ☎ 01295 221573; 01295 221573 sue.smith@cherwellandsouthnorthants.gov.uk

Senior Management: Mr Calvin Bell, Director of Development, Council Offices, Springfields, Towcester NN12 6AE ☎ 0300 003 0103 🖷 01327 322310
calvin.bell@cherwellandsouthnorthants.gov.uk

Senior Management: Mr Martin Henry, Director of Resources, Council Offices, Springfields, Towcester NN12 6AE ☎ 0300 003 0102; 0300 003 0102 🖷 01327 322310
martin.henry@cherwellandsouthnorthants.gov.uk

Senior Management: Ms Viv Hichens, Strategic Procurement, Bodicote House, Bodicote, Banbury OX15 4AA ☎ 01295 221503
viv.hichens@cherwell-dc.gov.uk

Access Officer / Social Services (Disability): Ms Caroline French, Equalities Officer, Bodicote House, Bodicote, Banbury OX15 4AA ☎ 01295 227928
caroline.french@cherwell-dc.gov.uk

Architect, Building / Property Services: Mr Chris Stratford, Head of Regeneration & Housing, Bodicote House, Bodicote, Banbury OX15 4AA ☎ 01295 251871; 0300 003 0111
chris.stratford@cherwellandsouthnorthants.gov.uk

Building Control: Mr Andy Preston, Head of Public Protection & Development Management, Council Offices, Springfields, Towcester NN12 6AE ☎ 01327 322356; 01295 221871 🖷 01327 322074 andy.preston@cherwellandsouthnorthants.gov.uk

PR / Communications: Ms Janet Ferris, Corporate Communications Manager, Bodicote House, Bodicote, Banbury OX15 4AA ☎ 01295 221870; 01295 221870 🖷 01295 270028
janet.ferris@cherwellandsouthnorthants.gov.uk

Community Planning: Ms Claire Taylor, Corporate Performance Manager, Bodicote House, Bodicote, Banbury OX15 4AA
☎ 01295 221563 claire.taylor@cherwellandsouthnorthants.gov.uk

Community Safety: Mr Mike Grant, Safer Communities Manager, Bodicote House, Bodicote, Banbury OX15 4AA ☎ 01295 227989

mike.grant@cherwell-dc.gov.uk

Computer Management: Mr Gareth Jones, Information Services Manager, Council Offices, Springfields, Towcester NN12 6AE 01295 753729 gareth.jones@cherwellandsouthnorthants.gov.uk

Computer Management: Ms Pat Simpson, Programme Manager, Bodicote House, Bodicote, Banbury OX15 4AA 01295 221575; 01295 221575 pat.simpson@cherwellandsouthnorthants.gov.uk

Corporate Services: Mr Chris Rothwell, Head of Community Services, Bodicote House, Bodicote, Banbury OX15 4AA 01295 251774; 0300 003 0104 chris.rothwell@cherwellandsouthnorthants.gov.uk

Customer Service: Ms Jacqui Hurd, Customer Service Manager, Bodicote House, Bodicote, Banbury OX15 4AA 01295 223301 jacqui.hurd@cherwell-dc.gov.uk

Economic Development: Mr Adrian Colwell, Head of Strategic Planning & the Economy, Bodicote House, Bodicote, Banbury OX15 4AA 0300 003 0110; 01295 251871 adrian.colwell@cherwellandsouthnorthants.gov.uk

Economic Development: Mr Steven Newman, Economic Development Officer, Bodicote House, Bodicote, Banbury OX15 4AA 01295 221860 steven.newman@cherwell-dc.gov.uk

Electoral Registration: Mr James Doble, Democratic & Elections Manager, Bodicote House, Bodicote, Banbury OX15 4AA 01295 221587; 01295 221587 james.doble@cherwellandsouthnorthants.gov.uk

Emergency Planning: Mr Jan Southgate, Emergency Co-ordinator, Bodicote House, Bodicote, Banbury OX15 4AA 01295 227906 jan.southgate@cherwell-dc.gov.uk

Energy Management: Ms Gabi Kaiser, Service Development Manager, Bodicote House, Bodicote, Banbury OX15 4AA 01295 221962 01295 277592 gabi.kaiser@cherwell-dc.gov.uk

Environmental / Technical Services: Mr Ian Davies, Director of Environment & Community, Bodicote House, Bodicote, Banbury OX15 4AA 01327 322302; 0300 003 0101 ian.davies@cherwellandsouthnorthants.gov.uk

Environmental / Technical Services: Mr Ed Potter, Head of Envrionmental Services, Thorpe Lane Depot, Banbury OX16 4UT 01295 227023; 0300 003 0105 ed.potter@cherwellandsouthnorthants.gov.uk

Finance and Treasurer: Ms Karen Curtin, Head of Finance & Procurement, Bodicote House, Bodicote, Banbury OX15 4AA 01295 227936 karen.curtin@cherwellandsouthnorthants.gov.uk

Home Energy Conservation: Mr Tim Mills, Private Sector Housing Manager, Bodicote House, Bodicote, Banbury OX15 4AA 01295 221655 tim.mills@cherwell-dc.gov.uk

Housing: Mr Chris Stratford, Head of Regeneration & Housing, Bodicote House, Bodicote, Banbury OX15 4AA 01295 251871; 0300 003 0111 chris.stratford@cherwellandsouthnorthants.gov.uk

Legal: Mr Nigel Bell, Solicitor, Bodicote House, Bodicote, Banbury OX15 4AA 01295 221687 nigel.bell@cherwell-dc.gov.uk

Legal: Mr Kevin Lane, Head of Law & Governance, Council Offices, Springfields, Towcester NN12 6AE 01327 322127; 01327 322127 01327 322114; 01327 322114 kevin.lane@cherwellandsouthnorthants.gov.uk

Leisure and Cultural Services: Mr Ian Davies, Director of Environment & Community, Bodicote House, Bodicote, Banbury OX15 4AA 01327 322302; 0300 003 0101 ian.davies@cherwellandsouthnorthants.gov.uk

Leisure and Cultural Services: Mr Chris Rothwell, Head of Community Services, Bodicote House, Bodicote, Banbury OX15 4AA 01295 251774; 0300 003 0104 chris.rothwell@cherwellandsouthnorthants.gov.uk

Licensing: Ms Natasha Barnes, Licensing & Vehicle Parks Manager, Bodicote House, Bodicote, Banbury OX15 4AA 01295 221599 natasha.barnes@cherwell-dc.gov.uk

Member Services: Ms Natasha Clark, Senior Democratic Services Officer, Bodicote House, Bodicote, Banbury OX15 4AA 01295 221589 natasha.clark@cherwell-dc.gov.uk

Parking: Ms Natasha Barnes, Licensing & Vehicle Parks Manager, Bodicote House, Bodicote, Banbury OX15 4AA 01295 221599 natasha.barnes@cherwell-dc.gov.uk

Personnel / HR: Ms Jo Pitman, Head of Transformation, Bodicote House, Bodicote, Banbury OX15 4AA 01295 221758; 01925 221758 jo.pitman@cherwellandsouthnorthants.gov.uk; jo.pitman@cherwellandsouthnorthants.gov.uk

Planning: Mr Adrian Colwell, Head of Strategic Planning & the Economy, Bodicote House, Bodicote, Banbury OX15 4AA 0300 003 0110; 01295 251871 adrian.colwell@cherwellandsouthnorthants.gov.uk

Planning: Mr Bob Duxbury, Development Control Team Leader, Bodicote House, Bodicote, Banbury OX15 4AA 01295 221821 bob.duxbury@cherwell-dc.gov.uk

Recycling & Waste Minimisation: Ms Gabi Kaiser, Service Development Manager, Bodicote House, Bodicote, Banbury OX15 4AA 01295 221962 01295 277592 gabi.kaiser@cherwell-dc.gov.uk

Staff Training: Mr Chris Harvey, Corporate Training Manager, Bodicote House, Bodicote, Banbury OX15 4AA 01295 221546 chris.harvey@cherwell-dc.gov.uk

Street Scene: Mr Paul Almond, Street & Landscape Services Manager, Bodicote House, Bodicote, Banbury OX15 4AA 01295 221705

Sustainable Communities: Mr Chris Rothwell, Head of Community Services, Bodicote House, Bodicote, Banbury OX15 4AA ☎ 01295 251774; 0300 003 0104 ✉ chris.rothwell@cherwellandsouthnorthants.gov.uk

Sustainable Development: Ms Gabi Kaiser, Service Development Manager, Bodicote House, Bodicote, Banbury OX15 4AA ☎ 01295 221962 🖷 01295 277592 ✉ gabi.kaiser@cherwell-dc.gov.uk

Tourism: Ms Nicola Riley, Arts and Tourism Manager, Bodicote House, Bodicote, Banbury OX15 4AA ☎ 01295 221724 🖷 01295 263155 ✉ nicola.riley@cherwell-dc.gov.uk

Waste Collection and Disposal: Mr Ed Potter, Head of Envrionmental Services, Thorpe Lane Depot, Banbury OX16 4UT ☎ 01295 227023; 0300 003 0105 ✉ ed.potter@cherwellandsouthnorthants.gov.uk

MEMBERS OF THE COUNCIL (50)

***Chair:* Clarke**, Colin (CON - Banbury Calthorpe)
cllr.colin.clarke@cherwell-dc.gov.uk
***Vice-Chair:* Stratford**, Lawrence (CON - Bicester East)
cllr.lawrie.stratford@cherwell-dc.gov.uk
***Leader of the Council:* Wood**, Barry (CON - Fringford)
cllr.barry.wood@cherwell-dc.gov.uk
***Deputy Leader of the Council:* Reynolds**, George (CON - Sibford)
cllr.george.reynolds@cherwell-dc.gov.uk
***Group Leader:* Cartledge**, Patrick (LAB - Banbury Ruscote)
Cllr.Patrick.Cartledge@cherwell-dc.gov.uk
***Group Leader:* Emptage**, Tim (LD - Kidlington South)
cllr.tim.emptage@cherwell-dc.gov.uk
Ahmed, Alyas (CON - Banbury Neithrop)
cllr.alyas.ahmed@cherwell-dc.gov.uk
Atack, Ken (CON - Cropredy)
cllr.ken.atack@cherwell-dc.gov.uk
Beere, Andrew (LAB - Banbury Grimsbury & Castle)
cllr.andrew.beere@cherwell-dc.gov.uk
Billington, Maurice (CON - Kidlington South)
cllr.maurice.billington@cherwell-dc.gov.uk
Blackwell, Fred (CON - Banbury Easington)
cllr.fred.blackwell@cherwell-dc.gov.uk
Bolster, Norman (CON - Bicester West)
cllr.norman.bolster@cherwell-dc.gov.uk
Bonner, Ann (CON - Banbury Grimsbury & Castle)
cllr.ann.bonner@cherwell-dc.gov.uk
Cullip, Margaret (CON - Banbury Grimsbury & Castle)
cllr.margaret.cullip@cherwell-dc.gov.uk
Dhesi, Surinder (LAB - Banbury Neithrop)
surinder.dhesi@cherwell-dc.gov.uk
Donaldson, John (CON - Banbury Hardwick)
cllr.john.donaldson@cherwell-dc.gov.uk
Edwards, Diana (CON - Bicester Town)
cllr.diana.edwards@cherwell-dc.gov.uk
Fulljames, Andrew (CON - Ambrosden & Chesterton)
andrew.fulljames@cherwell-dc.gov.uk
Gibbard, Michael (CON - Yarnton, Gosford & Water Eaton)
cllr.michael.gibbard@cherwell-dc.gov.uk
Hallchurch, Timothy (CON - Otmoor)
cllr.timothy.hallchurch@cherwell-dc.gov.uk
Heath, Chris (CON - Bloxham & Bodicote)
cllr.chris.heath@cherwell-dc.gov.uk
Holland, Simon (CON - Kirtlington)
cllr.simon.holland@cherwell-dc.gov.uk
Hughes, David (CON - Launton)
cllr.david.hughes@cherwell-dc.gov.uk
Hurle, Russell (CON - Bicester West)
cllr.russell.hurle@cherwell-dc.gov.uk
Ilott, Anthony (CON - Banbury Hardwick)
cllr.tony.ilott@cherwell-dc.gov.uk
Irvine, Victoria (CON - Hook Norton)
cllr.victoria.irvine@cherwell-dc.gov.uk
Kerford-Byrnes, Mike (CON - The Astons & Heyfords)
cllr.mike.kerfordbynes@cherwell-dc.gov.uk
MacNamara, James (CON - The Astons & Heyfords)
cllr.james.macnamara@cherwell-dc.gov.uk
Magee, Melanie (CON - Bicester North)
Mallon, Kieron (CON - Banbury Easington)
cllr.kieron.mallon@cherwell-dc.gov.uk
Mawer, Nicholas (CON - Bicester North)
cllr.nicholas.mawer@cherwell-dc.gov.uk
Milne Home, Alastair (CON - Banbury Calthorpe)
cllr.alastair.milnehome@cherwell-dc.gov.uk
Morris, Nigel (CON - Banbury Easington)
O'Neill, Jon (CON - Caversfield)
jon.o'neill@cherwell-dc.gov.uk
O'Sullivan, Paul (CON - Deddington)
cllr.paul.o'sullivan@cherwell-dc.gov.uk
Parish, George (LAB - Banbury Ruscote)
cllr.george.parish@cherwell-dc.gov.uk
Pickford, Debbie (CON - Bicester Town)
cllr.debbie.pickford@cherwell-dc.gov.uk
Pratt, Lynn (CON - Bicester South)
cllr.lynn.pratt@cherwell-dc.gov.uk
Prestidge, Neil (CON - Kidlington South)
cllr.neil.prestidge@cherwell-dc.gov.uk
Randall, Nigel (CON - Adderbury)
nigel.randall@cherwell-dc.gov.uk
Rose, Alaric (LD - Kidlington North)
cllr.alaric.rose@cherwell-dc.gov.uk
Sames, Daniel (CON - Bicester South)
cllr.daniel.sames@cherwell-dc.gov.uk
Sibley, Leslie (LAB - Bicester West)
cllr.leslie.sibley@cherwell-dc.gov.uk
Stevens, Trevor (CON - Yarnton, Gosford & Water Eaton)
cllr.trevor.stevens@cherwell-dc.gov.uk
Stratford, Rose (CON - Bicester East)
cllr.rose.stratford@cherwell-dc.gov.uk
Thirzie Smart, Lynda (CON - Bloxham & Bodicote)
cllr.lynda.thirziesmart@cherwell-dc.gov.uk
Turner, Nicholas (CON - Banbury Hardwick)
cllr.nicholas.turner@cherwell-dc.gov.uk
Webb, Douglas (CON - Wroxton)
cllr.douglas.webb@cherwell-dc.gov.uk
Williamson, Douglas (LD - Kidlington North)
cllr.douglas.williamson@cherwell-dc.gov.uk
Woodcock, Sean (LAB - Banbury Ruscote)
sean.woodcock@cherwell-dc.gov.uk

POLITICAL COMPOSITION

CON: 41, LAB: 6, LD: 3

CABINET

Leader: Mr Barry Wood
Deputy Leader: Mr George Reynolds
Clean & Green: Mr Nigel Morris

Estates & Economy: Mr Norman Bolster
Financial Management: Mr Ken Atack
Performance & Customers: Mr Nicholas Turner
Planning: Mr Michael Gibbard
Public Protection: Mr Anthony Ilott

COMMITTEE CHAIRS

Accounts, Audit & Risk (Scrutiny): Mr Trevor Stevens
Licensing: Mr Fred Blackwell
Overview & Scrutiny: Ms Ann Bonner
Personnel: Ms Lynn Pratt
Planning: Mrs Rose Stratford
Resources & Performance (Scrutiny): Mr Nicholas Mawer

CHESHIRE EAST U

Cheshire East Council, Westfields, Middlewich Road, Sandbach CW11 1HZ ☎ 0300 123 5500 ✉ info@cheshireeast.gov.uk
💻 www.cheshireeast.gov.uk

FACTS & FIGURES

Learning and Skills Council: North West
Parliamentary Constituencies: Congleton, Crewe and Nantwich, Eddisbury, Macclesfield, Tatton
EU Constituencies: North West
Election Frequency: Elections are of whole council

PRINCIPAL OFFICERS

Chief Executive: Ms Erika Wenzel, Chief Executive, Westfields, Middlewich Road, Sandbach CW11 1HZ ☎ 01270 686018 ✉ erika.wenzel@cheshireeast.gov.uk

Senior Management: Mr Paul Bradshaw, Head of HR & Organisational Development, Westfields, Middlewich Road, Sandbach CW11 1HZ ☎ 01270 686027 ✉ paul.bradshaw@cheshireeast.gov.uk

Senior Management: Ms Lorraine Butcher, Director of Children, Families & Adults, Westfields, Middlewich Road, Sandbach CW11 1HZ ☎ 01270 686021 ✉ lorraine.butcher@cheshireeast.gov.uk

Senior Management: Mr John Nicholson, Strategic Director - Places & Organisational Capacity, Westfields, Middlewich Road, Sandbach CW11 1HZ ☎ 01270 686611 ✉ john.nicholson@cheshireeast.gov.uk

Senior Management: Ms Vivienne Quayle, Head of Performance & Customer Capacity, Westfields, Middlewich Road, Sandbach CW11 1HZ ☎ 01270 686623 ✉ vivienne.quayle@cheshireeast.gov.uk

Senior Management: Ms Lisa Quinn, Director of Finance & Business Services, Westfields, Middlewich Road, Sandbach CW11 1HZ ☎ 01270 686628 ✉ lisa.quinn@cheshireeast.gov.uk

Architect, Building / Property Services: Mr Arthur Pritchard, Assets Manager, Floor 1, Emperor Court, Electra Way, Crewe CW1 6ZQ ☎ 01270 686144 ✉ arthur.pritchard@cheshireeast.gov.uk

Best Value: Ms Vivienne Quayle, Head of Performance & Customer Capacity, Westfields, Middlewich Road, Sandbach CW11 1HZ ☎ 01270 686623 ✉ vivienne.quayle@cheshireeast.gov.uk

Best Value: Ms Lisa Quinn, Director of Finance & Business Services, Westfields, Middlewich Road, Sandbach CW11 1HZ ☎ 01270 686628 ✉ lisa.quinn@cheshireeast.gov.uk

Building Control: Mr Steve Irvine, Development Management & Building Control Manager, Macclesfield Town Hall, Market Place, Macclesfield SK10 1EA ☎ 07919 555508

Children / Youth Services: Ms Lorraine Butcher, Director of Children, Families & Adults, Westfields, Middlewich Road, Sandbach CW11 1HZ ☎ 01270 686021 ✉ lorraine.butcher@cheshireeast.gov.uk

Civil Registration: Ms Lindsey Parton, Registration Service & Business Manager, Westfields, Middlewich Road, Sandbach CW11 1HZ ☎ 01270 686477 ✉ lindsey.parton@cheshireeast.gov.uk

PR / Communications: Ms Vivienne Quayle, Head of Performance & Customer Capacity, Westfields, Middlewich Road, Sandbach CW11 1HZ ☎ 01270 686623 ✉ vivienne.quayle@cheshireeast.gov.uk

PR / Communications: Ms Jo Rozsich, Communications & Media Relations Manager, Westfields, Middlewich Road, Sandbach CW11 1HZ ☎ 01270 686577 ✉ jo.rozsich@cheshireeast.gov.uk

Community Planning: Mr Peter Hartwell, Head of Community Services, Westfields, Middlewich Road, Sandbach CW11 1HZ ☎ 01270 686639 ✉ peter.hartwell@cheshireeast.gov.uk

Community Safety: Mr Peter Hartwell, Head of Community Services, Westfields, Middlewich Road, Sandbach CW11 1HZ ☎ 01270 686639 ✉ peter.hartwell@cheshireeast.gov.uk

Computer Management: Mr Gareth Pawlett, ICT Manager, Floor 1, Emperor Court, Electra Way, Crewe CW1 6ZQ ☎ 01270 686166

Consumer Protection and Trading Standards: Ms Kay Roberts, Consumer Protection & Investigations Manager, Westfields, Middlewich Road, Sandbach CW11 1HZ ☎ 01270 686260 ✉ kay.roberts@cheshireeast.gov.uk

Corporate Services: Ms Vivienne Quayle, Head of Performance & Customer Capacity, Westfields, Middlewich Road, Sandbach CW11 1HZ ☎ 01270 686623 ✉ vivienne.quayle@cheshireeast.gov.uk

Customer Service: Mr Paul Bayley, Customer Services & Libraries Manager, Macclesfield Town Hall, Market Place, Macclesfield SK10 1EA ☎ 01606 271567 ✉ paul.bayley@cheshireeast.gov.uk

Customer Service: Ms Vivienne Quayle, Head of Performance & Customer Capacity, Westfields, Middlewich Road, Sandbach CW11 1HZ ☎ 01270 686623 ✉ vivienne.quayle@cheshireeast.gov.uk

Economic Development: Mr Jez Goodman, Economic Development & Regeneration Manager, Westfields, Middlewich Road, Sandbach CW11 1HZ ☎ 07775 220899 ✉ jez.goodman@cheshireeast.gov.uk

Electoral Registration: Ms Lindsey Parton, Registration Service

& Business Manager, Westfields, Middlewich Road, Sandbach CW11 1HZ ☎ 01270 686477 ✉ lindsey.parton@cheshireeast.gov.uk

Electoral Registration: Ms Diane Todd, Electoral Services Team Leader, Westfields, Middlewich Road, Sandbach CW11 1HZ ☎ 01270 686478

Energy Management: Mr Colin Farrelly, Corporate Energy Manager, Emperor Court, Electra Way, Crewe CW1 6ZQ ☎ 01270 686161 ✉ colin.farrelly@cheshireeast.gov.uk

Environmental Health: Ms Tracey Bettaney, Public Protection & Health Manager, Westfields, Middlewich Road, Sandbach CW11 1HZ ☎ 01270 686596 ✉ tracey.bettaney@cheshireeast.gov.uk

Estates, Property & Valuation: Mr Peter Hall, Head of Property Services, Emperor Court, Electra Way, Crewe CW1 6ZQ ☎ 01270 686133 ✉ peter.hall@cheshireeast.gov.uk

Facilities: Mr Richard Jones, Facilities Manager, Emperor Court, Electra Way, Crewe CW1 6ZQ ☎ 01270 686142 ✉ richard.a.jones@cheshireeast.gov.uk

Finance and Treasurer: Ms Christine Mann, Finance Manager, Westfields, Middlewich Road, Sandbach CW11 1HZ ☎ 01244 686229 ✉ christine.mann@cheshireeast.gov.uk

Finance and Treasurer: Ms Lisa Quinn, Director of Finance & Business Services, Westfields, Middlewich Road, Sandbach CW11 1HZ ☎ 01270 686628 ✉ lisa.quinn@cheshireeast.gov.uk

Fleet Management: Mr Murray Halse, Strategic Fleet Manager, Pyms Lane Depot, Pymes Lane, Crewe CW1 3PJ ☎ 07827 954950

Grounds Maintenance: Mr Gareth Edwards, Streetscape & Bereavement Service Manager, Pyms Lane Depot, Pymes Lane, Crewe CW1 3PJ ☎ 01270 537570 ✉ gareth.edwards@cheshireeast.gov.uk

Health and Safety: Ms Bronwen MacArthur-Williams, Corporate Health & Safety Officer, 5th Floor, Delamere House, Delamere Street, Crewe CW1 2JZ ☎ 01270 686331 ✉ bronwen.macarthur-williams@cheshireeast.gov.uk

Housing: Ms Karen Carsberg, Strategic Housing Manager, Westfields, Middlewich Road, Sandbach CW11 1HZ ☎ 01270 686654 ✉ karen.carsberg@cheshireeast.gov.uk

Local Area Agreement: Ms Juliet Blackburn, Partnerships Manager, Westfields, Middlewich Road, Sandbach CW11 1HZ ☎ 01270 686020 ✉ juliet.blackburn@cheshireeast.gov.uk

Legal: Ms Caroline Elwood, Borough Solicitor (Monitoring Officer), Westfields, Middlewich Road, Sandbach CW11 1HZ ☎ 01270 686637 ✉ caroline.elwood@cheshireeast.gov.uk

Leisure and Cultural Services: Mr Guy Kilminster, Head of Health & Wellbeing Services, Westfields, Middlewich Road, Sandbach CW11 1HZ ☎ 01270 686560 ✉ guy.kilminster@cheshireeast.gov.uk

Licensing: Ms Kay Roberts, Consumer Protection & Investigations Manager, Westfields, Middlewich Road, Sandbach CW11 1HZ ☎ 01270 686260 ✉ kay.roberts@cheshireeast.gov.uk

Lifelong Learning: Ms Lesley Richards, Lifelong Learning Projects Coordinator, Emperor Court, Crewe CW1 6ZQ ☎ 01270 686681 ✉ lesley.richards@cheshireeast.gov.uk

Member Services: Mr Brian Reed, Democratic & Registration Services Manager, Westfields, Middlewich Road, Sandbach CW11 1HZ ☎ 01270 686670 ✉ brian.reed@cheshireeast.gov.uk

Parking: Mr Paul Burns, Parking & Markets Manager, Pyms Lane Depot, Pyms Lane, Crewe CW1 3PJ ☎ 01270 537805 ✉ paul.burns@cheshireeast.gov.uk

Partnerships: Ms Juliet Blackburn, Partnerships Manager, Westfields, Middlewich Road, Sandbach CW11 1HZ ☎ 01270 686020 ✉ juliet.blackburn@cheshireeast.gov.uk

Personnel / HR: Mr Paul Bradshaw, Head of HR & Organisational Development, Westfields, Middlewich, Sandbach CW11 1HZ ☎ 01270 686027 ✉ paul.bradshaw@cheshireeast.gov.uk

Personnel / HR: Ms Julie Davies, HR Strategy Manager, Westfields, Middlewich Road, Sandbach CW11 1HZ ☎ 01270 686328 ✉ julie.s.davies@cheshireeast.gov.uk

Planning: Mr Steve Irvine, Development Management & Building Control Manager, Macclesfield Town Hall, Market Place, Macclesfield SK10 1EA ☎ 07919 555508

Planning: Ms Caroline Simpson, Head of Development, Westfields, Middlewich Road, Sandbach CW11 1HZ ☎ 01270 686640 ✉ caroline.simpson@cheshireeast.gov.uk

Public Libraries: Mr Paul Bayley, Customer Services & Libraries Manager, Macclesfield Town Hall, Market Place, Macclesfield SK10 1EA ☎ 01606 271567 ✉ paul.bayley@cheshireeast.gov.uk

Public Libraries: Ms Vivienne Quayle, Head of Performance & Customer Capacity, Westfields, Middlewich Road, Sandbach CW11 1HZ ☎ 01270 686623 ✉ vivienne.quayle@cheshireeast.gov.uk

Recycling & Waste Minimisation: Mr Ray Skipp, Waste & Recycling Manager, Pyms Lane Depot, Pyms Lane, Crewe CW1 3PJ ☎ 01270 537817 ✉ ray.skipp@cheshireeast.gov.uk

Regeneration: Mr Jez Goodman, Economic Development & Regeneration Manager, Westfields, Middlewich Road, Sandbach CW11 1HZ ☎ 07775 220899 ✉ jez.goodman@cheshireeast.gov.uk

Regeneration: Ms Caroline Simpson, Head of Development, Westfields, Middlewich Road, Sandbach CW11 1HZ ☎ 01270 686640 ✉ caroline.simpson@cheshireeast.gov.uk

Road Safety: Ms Andrea Gray, Senior Road Safety Officer, Floor 6, Delamere House, Delamere Road, Crewe CW1 3LL ☎ 01270 686336 ✉ andrea.gray@cheshireeast.gov.uk

Social Services (Adult): Ms Lorraine Butcher, Director of

Children, Families & Adults, Westfields, Middlewich Road, Sandbach CW11 1HZ ☎ 01270 686021 ✉ lorraine.butcher@cheshireeast.gov.uk

Social Services (Children): Ms Lorraine Butcher, Director of Children, Families & Adults, Westfields, Middlewich Road, Sandbach CW11 1HZ ☎ 01270 686021 ✉ lorraine.butcher@cheshireeast.gov.uk

Street Scene: Mr Gareth Edwards, Streetscape & Bereavement Service Manager, Pyms Lane Depot, Pymes Lane, Crewe CW1 3PJ ☎ 01270 537570 ✉ gareth.edwards@cheshireeast.gov.uk

Tourism: Mr Brendan Flanagan, Tatton Park & Visitor Economy Manager, Tatton Park, Tatton, Knutsford WA16 6QN ☎ 01625 374415 ✉ brendan.flanagan@cheshireeast.gov.uk

Town Centre: Mr Jez Goodman, Economic Development & Regeneration Manager, Westfields, Middlewich Road, Sandbach CW11 1HZ ☎ 07775 220899 ✉ jez.goodman@cheshireeast.gov.uk

Waste Collection and Disposal: Mr Ray Skipp, Waste & Recycling Manager, Pyms Lane Depot, Pyms Lane, Crewe CW1 3PJ ☎ 01270 537817 ✉ ray.skipp@cheshireeast.gov.uk

Waste Management: Mr Ray Skipp, Waste & Recycling Manager, Pyms Lane Depot, Pyms Lane, Crewe CW1 3PJ ☎ 01270 537817 ✉ ray.skipp@cheshireeast.gov.uk

MEMBERS OF THE COUNCIL (82)

***Mayor:* Walton**, George (CON - Chelford)
george.walton@cheshireeast.gov.uk
***Deputy Mayor:* Flude**, Dorothy (LAB - Crewe South)
dorothy.flude@cheshireeast.gov.uk
***Leader of the Council:* Jones**, Michael (CON - Bunbury)
michael.e.jones@cheshireeast.gov.uk
***Deputy Leader of the Council:* Brown**, David (CON - Congleton East)
david.brown@cheshireeast.gov.uk
***Group Leader:* Edwards**, Paul (IND - Middlewich)
cllr.paul.edwards@cheshireeast.gov.uk
***Group Leader:* Fletcher**, Rod (LD - Alsager)
rod.fletcher@cheshireeast.gov.uk
***Group Leader:* Newton**, David (LAB - Crewe East)
david.newton@cheshireeast.gov.uk
Andrew, Carolyn (CON - Macclesfield West and Ivy)
carolyn.andrew@cheshireeast.gov.uk
Bailey, Rachel (CON - Audlem)
rachel.bailey@cheshireeast.gov.uk
Bailey, Rhoda (CON - Odd Rode)
rhoda.bailey@cheshireeast.gov.uk
Barratt, Andrew (CON - Odd Rode)
andrew.barratt@cheshireeast.gov.uk
Barton, Gary (CON - Wilmslow West and Chorley)
gary.barton@cheshireeast.gov.uk
Baxendale, Gordon (CON - Congleton West)
gordon.baxendale@cheshireeast.gov.uk
Bebbington, Derek (CON - Leighton)
derek.bebbington@cheshireeast.gov.uk
Boston, Gill (LAB - Macclesfield Hurdsfield)
gill.boston@cheshireeast.gov.uk
Brickhill, David (IND - Shavington)
david.brickhill@cheshireeast.gov.uk
Brown, Louise (CON - Broken Cross and Upton)
louise.brown@cheshireeast.gov.uk
Burkhill, Barry (R - Handforth)
barry.burkhill@cheshireeast.gov.uk
Butterill, Penny (IND - Nantwich North and West)
penny.butterill@cheshireeast.gov.uk
Cartlidge, Roy (LAB - Crewe St Barnabas)
roy.cartlidge@cheshireeast.gov.uk
Clowes, Janet (CON - Wybunbury)
janet.clowes@cheshireeast.gov.uk
Corcoran, Sam (LAB - Sandbach Heath and East)
sam.corcoran@cheshireeast.gov.uk
Davenport, Harold (CON - Disley)
harold.davenport@cheshireeast.gov.uk
Davies, Stan (CON - Wrenbury)
stanley.davies@cheshireeast.gov.uk
Domleo, Roland (CON - Congleton West)
roland.domleo@cheshireeast.gov.uk
Druce, Damien (CON - Macclesfield South)
damien.druce@cheshireeast.gov.uk
Edwards, Ken (LAB - Macclesfield Central)
ken.edwards@cheshireeast.gov.uk
Faseyi, Irene (LAB - Crewe Central)
irene.faseyi@cheshireeast.gov.uk
Findlow, Paul (CON - Prestbury)
paul.findlow@cheshireeast.gov.uk
Fitzgerald, Wesley (CON - Wilmslow West and Chorley)
wesley.fitzgerald@cheshireeast.gov.uk
Gaddum, Hilda (CON - Sutton)
hilda.gaddum@cheshireeast.gov.uk
Gardiner, Stewart (CON - Knutsford)
stewart.gardiner@cheshireeast.gov.uk
Gilbert, Les (CON - Dane Valley)
les.gilbert@cheshireeast.gov.uk
Grant, Mo (LAB - Crewe North)
mo.grant@cheshireeast.gov.uk
Groves, Peter (CON - Nantwich South and Stapeley)
peter.groves@cheshireeast.gov.uk
Hammond, John (CON - Haslington)
john.hammond@cheshireeast.gov.uk
Hardy, Martin (CON - Broken Cross and Upton)
martin.hardy@cheshireeast.gov.uk
Harewood, Alift (LAB - Macclesfield West and Ivy)
alift.harewood@cheshireeast.gov.uk
Hayes, Peter (CON - Bollington)
peter.hayes@cheshireeast.gov.uk
Hogben, Stephen (LAB - Crewe South)
steven.hogben@cheshireeast.gov.uk
Hough, Derek (LD - Alsager)
derek.hough@cheshireeast.gov.uk
Hoyland, Philip (CON - Poynton West and Adlington)
philip.hoyland@cheshireeast.gov.uk
Hunter, Olivia (CON - Knutsford)
olivia.hunter@cheshireeast.gov.uk
Jackson, Janet (LAB - Macclesfield Central)
janet.jackson@cheshireeast.gov.uk
Jeuda, Laura (LAB - Macclesfield South)
laura.jeuda@cheshireeast.gov.uk
Jones, Shirley (LD - Alsager)
shirley.jones@cheshireeast.gov.uk
Keegan, Frank (CON - Alderley Edge)
frank.keegan@cheshireeast.gov.uk
Kolker, Andrew (CON - Dane Valley)
andrew.kolker@cheshireeast.gov.uk
Livesley, Bill (CON - Bollington)

bill.livesley@cheshireeast.gov.uk
Macrea, Jamie (CON - Mobberley)
jamie.macrae@cheshireeast.gov.uk
Mahon, Dennis (R - Handforth)
dennis.mahon@cheshireeast.gov.uk
Marren, David (CON - Haslington)
david.marren@cheshireeast.gov.uk
Martin, Andrew (CON - Nantwich South and Stapeley)
andrew.martin@cheshireeast.gov.uk
Martin, Margaret (LAB - Crewe East)
peggy.martin@cheshireeast.gov.uk
Mason, Peter (CON - Congleton East)
peter.mason@cheshireeast.gov.uk
McGrory, Simon (IND - Middlewich)
simon.mcgrory@cheshireeast.gov.uk
Menlove, Rod (CON - Wilmslow East)
rod.menlove@cheshireeast.gov.uk
Merry, Gill (CON - Sandbach Elworth)
gillian.merry@cheshireeast.gov.uk
Moran, Arthur (IND - Nantwich North and West)
arthur.moran@cheshireeast.gov.uk
Moran, Barry (CON - Sandbach Town)
barry.moran@cheshireeast.gov.uk
Morris, Gail (CON - Sandbach Ettiley Heath and Wheelock)
gail.morris@cheshireeast.gov.uk
Murphy, Brendan (IND - Macclesfield Tytherington)
brendan.murphy@cheshireeast.gov.uk
Murray, Howard (CON - Poynton East and Pott Shrigley)
Neilson, David (LD - Macclesfield East)
david.neilson@cheshireeast.gov.uk
Nurse, Peter (LAB - Crewe West)
peter.nurse@cheshireeast.gov.uk
Parsons, Michael (IND - Middlewich)
michael.parsons@cheshireeast.gov.uk
Raynes, Peter (CON - Knutsford)
peter.raynes@cheshireeast.gov.uk
Roberts, Lloyd (IND - Macclesfield Tytherington)
lloyd.roberts@cheshireeast.gov.uk
Saunders, Jos (CON - Poynton East and Pott Shrigley)
jos.saunders@cheshireeast.gov.uk
Sherratt, Michelle (LAB - Crewe West)
michelle.sherratt@cheshireeast.gov.uk
Silvester, Brian (CON - Willaston and Rope)
brian.silvester@cheshireeast.gov.uk
Simon, Margaret (CON - Wistaston)
margaret.simon@cheshireeast.gov.uk
Smetham, Lesley (CON - Gawsworth)
lesley.smetham@cheshireeast.gov.uk
Stockton, Don (CON - Wilmslow Lacey Green)
don.stockton@cheshireeast.gov.uk
Thorley, Chris (LAB - Crewe East)
chris.thorley@cheshireeast.gov.uk
Thwaite, Andrew (CON - Congleton East)
andrew.thwaite@cheshireeast.gov.uk
Topping, David (CON - Congleton West)
david.topping@cheshireeast.gov.uk
Weatherill, Jaqueline (CON - Wistaston)
jacquie.weatherill@cheshireeast.gov.uk
West, Roger (CON - Poynton West and Adlington)
roger.west@cheshireeast.gov.uk
Whiteley, Paul (CON - Wilmslow Dean Row)
paul.whiteley@cheshireeast.gov.uk
Wilkinson, Steve (CON - High Legh)
steve.wilkinson@cheshireeast.gov.uk
Wray, John (CON - Brereton Rural)
john.wray@cheshireeast.gov.uk

POLITICAL COMPOSITION

CON: 52, LAB: 16, IND: 8, LD: 4, R: 2

CABINET

Leader: Mr Michael Jones
Deputy Leader / Strategic Communities: Mr David Brown
Children & Family Services: Mr Hilda Gaddum
Communities & Regulatory Services: Ms Rachel Bailey
Corporate Policy: Mr Les Gilbert
Environment: Mr Rod Menlove
Finance: Mr Peter Raynes
Health & Adult Social Care: Ms Janet Clowes
Performance: Mr Barry Moran
Prosperity & Economic Regeneration: Mr Jamie Macrea

COMMITTEE CHAIRS

Audit & Governance: Mr John Hammond
Children & Families: Mr Andrew Kolker
Environment & Prosperity (Scrutiny): Mr Bill Livesley
Health & Wellbeing (Scrutiny): Mr Gordon Baxendale
Strategic Planning: Mr Harold Davenport

CHESHIRE WEST & CHESTER U

Cheshire West & Chester, HQ, 58 Nicholas Street, Chester CH1 2NP ☎ 0300 123 8123
enquiries@cheshirewestandchester.gov.uk
www.cheshirewestandchester.gov.uk

FACTS & FIGURES

Parliamentary Constituencies: Chester, City of, Eddisbury, Ellesmere Port and Neston, Tatton, Weaver Vale
E

PRINCIPAL OFFICERS

Chief Executive: Mr Steve Robinson, Chief Executive, HQ, 58 Nicholas Street, Chester CH1 2NP ☎ 01244 977454
steve.robinson@cheshirewestandchester.gov.uk

Children / Youth Services: Mr Paul Boyce, Head of Safeguarding, HQ, 58 Nicholas Street, Chester CH1 2NP ☎ 01244 975924 paul.boyce@cheshirewestandchester.gov.uk

Children / Youth Services: Mr Gerald Meehan, Director of Children's Services, HQ, 58 Nicholas Street, Chester CH1 2NP
gerald.meehan@cheshirewestandchester.gov.uk

Children / Youth Services: Ms Ann Moore, Head of Achievement, HQ, 58 Nicholas Street, Chester CH1 2NP ☎ 01244 975923 ann.moore@cheshirewestandchester.gov.uk

Computer Management: Mr John Callan, Head of ICT Shared Services, Nicholas House, Blackfriars, Chester CH1 4NU ☎ 01244 972001 john.callan@cheshirewestandchester.gov.uk

Computer Management: Mr Dermot Lacey, Head of ICT & Customer Services, HQ, 58 Nicholas Street, Chester CH1 2NP ☎ 01244 977827 dermot.lacey@cheshirewestandchester.gov.uk

Consumer Protection and Trading Standards: Ms Helen Bailey, Head of Regulatory Services, HQ, 58 Nicholas Street, Chester CH1 2NP ☎ 01606 288660

helen.bailey@cheshirewestandchester.gov.uk

Customer Service: Ms Pam Bradley, Head of Marketing & Communications, HQ, 58 Nicholas Street, Chester CH1 2NP ☎ 01244 976996 pam.bradley@cheshirewestandchester.gov.uk

Environmental / Technical Services: Mr John Jeffrey, Head of Waste Management & Streetscene, HQ, 58 Nicholas Street, Chester CH1 2NP ☎ 0300 123 8123 john.jeffrey@cheshirewestandchester.gov.uk

Environmental / Technical Services: Mr Steve Kent, Director of Environment, Area & Community, HQ, 58 Nicholas Street, Chester CH1 2NP ☎ 01244 973575 steve.kent@cheshirewestandchester.gov.uk

Events Manager: Ms Helen Bailey, Head of Regulatory Services, First Floor, Wyvern House, The Drumber, Winsford CW7 1AH ☎ 01606 288660 helen.bailey@cheshirewestandchester.gov.uk

Facilities: Ms Carly Brown, Head of Strategic Support, HQ, 58 Nicholas Street, Chester CH1 2NP ☎ 01244 975916 carly.brown@cheshirewestandchester.gov.uk

Facilities: Ms Julie Gill, Director of Resources, HQ, 58 Nicholas Street, Chester CH1 2NP ☎ 01244 977830 julie.gill@cheshirewestandchester.gov.uk

Facilities: Mr Noel O'Neill, Head of Facilities & Asset Management, HQ, 58 Nicholas Street, Chester CH1 2NP ☎ 01244 977834 noel.oneill@cheshirewestandchester.gov.uk

Finance and Treasurer: Mr Mark Wynn, Head of Finance, HQ, 58 Nicholas Street, Chester CH1 2NP ☎ 01244 972537 mark.wynn@cheshirewestandchester.gov.uk

Housing: Mr David Green, Interim Managing Director of Housing, Ground Floor, Council Offices, Civic Way, Ellesmere Port, CH56 0BE ☎ 0151 356 6514 david.green@cheshirewestandchester.gov.uk

Housing: Mr Alan Slater, Head of Strategic Housing & Spatial Planning, HQ, 58 Nicholas Street, Chester CH1 2NP ☎ 0300 123 8123 alan.slater@cheshirewestandchester.gov.uk

Leisure and Cultural Services: Mr Charlie Seward, Director of Regeneration & Culture, HQ, 58 Nicholas Street, Chester CH1 2NP ☎ 01244 972857 charlie.seward@cheshirewestandchester.gov.uk

Partnerships: Mr Alistair Jeffs, Head of Policy, Performance & Partnerships, HQ, 58 Nicholas Street, Chester CM1 2NP ☎ 01244 972228 alistair.jeffs@cheshirewestandchester.gov.uk

Personnel / HR: Ms Vanessa Coates, Head of HR & Finance Shared Services, Goldsmith House, Hamilton Place, Chester CH1 1SE ☎ 01244 972106 vanessa.coates@cheshirewestandchester.gov.uk

Personnel / HR: Mr Euan Murdoch-Hollies, Head of Human Resources, HQ, 58 Nicholas Street, Chester CH1 2NP ☎ 01244 972860 euan.murdoch-hollies@cheshirewestandchester.gov.uk

Planning: Mr Chris Hindle, Head of Planning & Transport, HQ, 58 Nicholas Street, Chester CH1 2NP ☎ 01244 972859 chris.hindle@cheshirewestandchester.gov.uk

Procurement: Mr Andrew Williams, Head of Procurement, HQ, 58 Nicholas Street, Chester CH1 2NP ☎ 01244 972861 andrew.williams@cheshirewestandchester.gov.uk

Regeneration: Mr Cliff Mallows, Head of Regeneration, HQ, 58 Nicholas Street, Chester CH1 2NP ☎ ; 01244 972684 cliff.mallows@cheshirewestandchester.gov.uk

Regeneration: Mr Charlie Seward, Director of Regeneration & Culture, HQ, 58 Nicholas Street, Chester CH1 2NP ☎ 01244 972857 charlie.seward@cheshirewestandchester.gov.uk

Social Services (Adult): Mr Keith Evans, Head of Strategic Commissioning, HQ, 58 Nicholas Street, Chester CH1 2NP ☎ 01244 972290 🖷 keith.evans@cheshireandwestchester.gov.uk

Social Services (Adult): Mr Mark Palethorpe, Director of Adult Social Care, HQ, 58 Nicholas Street, Chester CH1 2NP mark.palethorpe@cheshirewestandchester.gov.uk

Social Services (Adult): Mr Joe Riley, Head of Service Development & Improvement, HQ, 58 Nicholas Street, Chester CH1 2NP ☎ 01244 972253 joe.riley@cheshirewestandchester.gov.uk

Street Scene: Mr John Jeffrey, Head of Waste Management & Streetscene, HQ, 58 Nicholas Street, Chester CH1 2NP ☎ 0300 123 8123 john.jeffrey@cheshirewestandchester.gov.uk

Waste Management: Mr John Jeffrey, Head of Waste Management & Streetscene, HQ, 58 Nicholas Street, Chester CH1 2NP ☎ 0300 123 8123 john.jeffrey@cheshirewestandchester.gov.uk

MEMBERS OF THE COUNCIL (75)

***Mayor:* Booher**, Pamela (LAB - Winsford Wharton)
pam.booher@cheshirewestandchester.gov.uk

***Deputy Mayor:* Houlbrook**, Jill (CON - Upton)
jill.houlbrook@cheshirewestandchester.gov.uk

***Sheriff:* Crompton**, Bob (CON - Whitby)
bob.crompton@cheshirewestandchester.gov.uk

***Leader of the Council:* Jones**, Mike (CON - Tattenhall)
mike.jones@cheshirewestandchester.gov.uk

***Deputy Leader of the Council:* Ford**, Les (CON - Helsby)
les.ford@cheshirewestandchester.gov.uk

***Group Leader:* Madders**, Justin (LAB - Ellesmere Port Town)
justin.madders@cheshirewestandchester.gov.uk

Anderson, Gareth (CON - Ledsham and Manor)
gareth.anderson@cheshirewestandchester.gov.uk

Armstrong, David (LAB - Winsford Swanlow and Dene)
david.armstrong@cheshirewestandchester.gov.uk

Backett, Don (LAB - Winsford Over and Verdin)
don.beckett@cheshirewestandchester.gov.uk

Black, Alex (LAB - Hoole)
alex.black@cheshirewestandchester.gov.uk

Blackmore, Tom (LAB - Winsford Over and Verdin)
tom.blackmore@cheshirewestandchester.gov.uk

Board, Keith (CON - Great Boughton)
keith.board@cheshirewestandchester.gov.uk

Burns, Stephen (LAB - Winsford Swanlow and Dene)
stephen.burns@cheshirewestandchester.gov.uk
Butcher, Keith (LAB - Ledsham and Manor)
keith.butcher@cheshirewestandchester.gov.uk
Byram, Malcolm (CON - Marbury)
malcolm.byram@cheshirewestandchester.gov.uk
Clare, Lynn (LAB - Ellesmere Port Town)
lynn.clare@cheshirewestandchester.gov.uk
Clarke, Brian (LAB - Winsford Wharton)
brian.clarke@cheshirewestandchester.gov.uk
Claydon, Angela (LAB - St. Paul's)
angela.claydon@cheshirewestandchester.gov.uk
Crowe, Brian (CON - Saughall and Mollington)
brian.crowe@cheshirewestandchester.gov.uk
Daniels, Razia (CON - Handbridge Park)
razia.daniels@cheshirewestandchester.gov.uk
Dawson, Andrew (CON - Frodsham)
andrew.dawson@cheshirewestandchester.gov.uk
Deynem, Hugo (CON - Tarvin and Kelsall)
hugo.deynem@cheshirewestandchester.gov.uk
Dixon, Samantha (LAB - Chester City)
samantha.dixon@cheshirewestandchester.gov.uk
Dolan, Paul (LAB - Winnington and Castle)
paul.dolan@cheshirewestandchester.gov.uk
Donovan, Paul (LAB - Sutton)
paul.donovan@cheshirewestandchester.gov.uk
Dowding, Brenda (CON - Parkgate)
brenda.dowding@cheshirewestandchester.gov.uk
Fifield, Charles (CON - Weaver and Cuddington)
charles.fifield@cheshirewestandchester.gov.uk
Gittins, Louise (LAB - Little Neston and Burton)
louise.gittins@cheshirewestandchester.gov.uk
Graham, Carolyn (LAB - Blacon)
carolyn.graham@cheshirewestandchester.gov.uk
Greenwood, Howard (CON - Farndon)
howard.greenwood@cheshirewestandchester.gov.uk
Grimshaw, John (CON - Weaver and Cuddington)
john.grimshaw@cheshirewestandchester.gov.uk
Hall, Pamela (CON - Great Boughton)
pamela.hall@cheshirewestandchester.gov.uk
Hammond, Don (CON - Marbury)
don.hammond@cheshirewestandchester.gov.uk
Heatley, Graham (CON - Elton)
Graham.Heatley@cheshirewestandchester.gov.uk
Henesy, Mark (LAB - Strawberry)
mark.henesy@cheshirewestandchester.gov.uk
Hogg, Myles (CON - Willaston and Thornton)
myles.hogg@cheshirewestandchester.gov.uk
Johnson, Eleanor (CON - Gowy)
eleanor.johnson@cheshirewestandchester.gov.uk
Jones, Reggie (LAB - Blacon)
reggie.jones@cheshirewestandchester.gov.uk
Jones, Brian (LAB - Whitby)
brian.jones@cheshirewestandchester.gov.uk
Jones, Lynda (CON - Winsford Over and Verdin)
lynda.jones@cheshirewestandchester.gov.uk
Lawrenson, Tony (LAB - Witton and Rudheath)
tony.lawrenson@cheshirewestandchester.gov.uk
Leather, John (CON - Tarvin and Kelsall)
john.leather@cheshirewestandchester.gov.uk
Loch, Kay (CON - Little Neston and Burton)
kay.loch@cheshirewestandchester.gov.uk
Manley, Herbert (CON - Hartford and Greenbank)
herbert.manley@cheshirewestandchester.gov.uk
McKie, Alan (CON - Weaver and Cuddington)
alan.mckie@cheshirewestandchester.gov.uk
McNae, Hilarie (CON - Upton)
hilarie.mcnae@cheshirewestandchester.gov.uk
Meardon, Nicole (LAB - Sutton)
nicole.meardon@cheshirewestandchester.gov.uk
Mercer-Bailey, Amy (LAB - Winnington and Castle)
amy.mercer-bailey@cheshirewestandchester.gov.uk
Merrick, Pat (LAB - Rossmore)
pat.merrick@cheshirewestandchester.gov.uk
Moore, Eveleigh (CON - Tarporley)
eveleigh.mooredutton@cheshirewestandchester.gov.uk
Musgrave, Keith (CON - Hartford and Greenbank)
keith.musgrave@cheshirewestandchester.gov.uk
Nelson, Marie (LAB - Blacon)
marie.nelson@cheshirewestandchester.gov.uk
Oultram, Ralph (CON - Kingsley)
ralph.oultram@cheshirewestandchester.gov.uk
Parker, Margaret (CON - Chester Villages)
margaret.parker@cheshirewestandchester.gov.uk
Parker, Stuart (CON - Chester Villages)
stuart.parker@cheshirewestandchester.gov.uk
Parry, Tom (CON - Newton)
tom.parry@cheshirewestandchester.gov.uk
Powell, Ben (LAB - St. Paul's)
ben.powell@cheshirewestandchester.gov.uk
Riley, Lynn (CON - Frodsham)
lynn.riley@cheshirewestandchester.gov.uk
Roberts, Diane (LAB - Netherpool)
0151 201 6852
Robinson, David (LAB - Boughton)
david.robinson@cheshirewestandchester.gov.uk
Rudd, Bob (LAB - Garden Quarter)
bob.rudd@cheshirewestandchester.gov.uk
Sherlock, Tony (LAB - Grange)
tony.sherlock@cheshirewestandchester.gov.uk
Sinar, Gaynor (CON - Davenham and Moulton)
gaynor.sinar@cheshirewestandchester.gov.uk
Stocks, Mark (CON - Shakerley)
mark.stocks@cheshirewestandchester.gov.uk
Sullivan, Neil (CON - Handbridge Park)
neil.sullivan@cheshirewestandchester.gov.uk
Tate, Alex (LAB - Lache)
alex.tate@cheshirewestandchester.gov.uk
Thompson, Robert (LD - Hoole)
robert.thompson@cheshirewestandchester.gov.uk
Tickridge, Julia (LAB - Witton and Rudheath)
julia.tickridge@cheshirewestandchester.gov.uk
Walmsley, Adrian (CON - Newton)
adrian.walmsley@cheshirewestandchester.gov.uk
Watson, Elton (CON - Davenham and Moulton)
elton.watson@cheshirewestandchester.gov.uk
Weltman, Helen (CON - Davenham and Moulton)
helen.weltman@cheshirewestandchester.gov.uk
Williams, Mark (CON - Dodleston and Huntington)
mark.williams@cheshirewestandchester.gov.uk
Williams, Andy (LAB - Neston)
andy.williams2@cheshirewestandchester.gov.uk
Wright, Ann (CON - Malpas)
ann.wright@cheshirewestandchester.gov.uk
Wright, Norman (CON - Marbury)
norman.wright@cheshirewestandchester.gov.uk

POLITICAL COMPOSITION

CON: 42, LAB: 32, LD: 1

CABINET

Leader: Mr Mike Jones
Deputy Leader / Resources: Mr Leslie Ford
Adult Services: Ms Brenda Dowding
Community & Environment: Ms Lynn Riley
Culture & Recreation: Mr Stuart Parker
Education & Children: Mr Mark Stocks
Prosperity: Mr Herbert Manley

COMMITTEE CHAIRS

Audit & Governance: Mr Keith Musgrave
Children & Education Scrutiny: Ms Nicole Meardon
Community Governance Review: Ms Ann Wright
Corporate Scrutiny: Ms Eveleigh Moore
Health & Wellbeing Scrutiny: Mr Tom Parry
Licensing: Mr Adrian Walmsley
Planning: Ms Helen Weltman
Safeguarding Scrutiny: Ms Margaret Parker

CHESTERFIELD D

Chesterfield Borough Council, Town Hall, Rose Hill, Chesterfield S40 1LP ☎ 01246 345345 🖷 01246 345252 ✉ info@chesterfield.gov.uk 💻 www.chesterfield.gov.uk

FACTS & FIGURES

Police Authority: Derbyshire Police Authority
Health Authority: East Midlands Strategic Health Authority
Learning and Skills Council: East Midlands
Parliamentary Constituencies: Chesterfield
EU Constituencies: East Midlands
Election Frequency: Elections are of whole council
Twinning: Troyes (France); Darmstadt (Germany); Yangquan (China); Tsumeb (Namibia)

PRINCIPAL OFFICERS

Chief Executive: Mr Huw Bowen, Chief Executive, Town Hall, Rose Hill, Chesterfield S40 1LP ☎ 01246 345305 🖷 01246 345252 ✉ huw.bowen@chesterfield.gov.uk

Deputy Chief Executive: Mr Mark Evans, Acting Deputy Chief Executive, Town Hall, Rose Hill, Chesterfield S40 1LP ☎ 01246 345292 🖷 01246 345252 ✉ mark.evans@chesterfield.gov.uk

Architect, Building / Property Services: Mr Roger Farrand, Principal Architect, Town Hall, Rose Hill, Chesterfield S40 1LP ☎ 01246 345401 🖷 01246 345252 ✉ roger.farrand@chesterfield.gov.uk

Best Value: Mr John Moran, Acting Head of Business Transformation, Town Hall, Rose Hill, Chesterfield S40 1LP ☎ 01246 345389 🖷 01246 345252 ✉ john.moran@chesterfield.gov.uk

Building Control: Mr Malcolm Clinton, Business Manager, Unit 2, Dunston Technology Park, Millennium Way, Dunston Road, Chesterfield S41 8ND ☎ 01246 345817 ✉ malcolm.clinton@ne-derbyshire.gov.uk

Building Control: Mr Chris Robinson, Chief Building Control Officer, Town Hall, Rose Hill, Chesterfield S40 1LP ☎ 01246 345818 🖷 01246 345252 ✉ chris.robinson@chesterfield.gov.uk

PR / Communications: Ms Fiona Shepherd, Public Relations Officer, Town Hall, Rose Hill, Chesterfield S40 1LP ☎ 01246 345245 🖷 01246 345252 ✉ fiona.shepherd@chesterfield.gov.uk

Community Safety: Mr Joe Tomlinson, Community Safety Officer, Town Hall, Rose Hill, Chesterfield S40 1LP ☎ 01246 345093 🖷 01246 345252 ✉ joe.tomlinson@chesterfield.gov.uk

Contracts: Mr Bob Trusswell, Head - Procurement, Town Hall, Rose Hill, Chesterfield S40 1LP ☎ 01246 242311; 07800 735086 ✉ bob.trusswell@bolsover.gov.uk

Corporate Services: Mr Martin Illffe, Head of Internal Audit, Town Hall, Rose Hill, Chesterfield S40 1LP ☎ 01246 345345 🖷 01246 345252 ✉ martin.iliffe@chesterfield.gov.uk

Economic Development: Ms Lynda Sharp, Joint Economic Development Manager, Town Hall, Rose Hill, Chesterfield S40 1LP ☎ 01246 345255 🖷 01246 345256 ✉ lynda.sharp@chesterfield.gov.uk

Economic Development: Ms Laurie Thomas, Economic Development Manager, Town Hall, Rose Hill, Chesterfield S40 1LP ☎ 01246 345255 🖷 01246 345256 ✉ laurie.thomas@chesterfield.gov.uk

E-Government: Mr Darren Webber, Information & Communications Technologies Manager, Town Hall, Rose Hill, Chesterfield S40 1LP ☎ 01246 345729 🖷 01246 345252 ✉ darren.webber@chesterfield.gov.uk

Electoral Registration: Mrs Sandra Essex, Democratic Services Manager, Town Hall, Rose Hill, Chesterfield S40 1LP ☎ 01246 345227 🖷 01246 345252 ✉ sandra.essex@chesterfield.gov.uk

Emergency Planning: Ms Sam Sherlock, Emergency Planning Officer, Town Hall, Rose Hill, Chesterfield S40 1LP ☎ 01246 345407 🖷 01246 345252 ✉ sam.sherlock@chesterfield.gov.uk

Energy Management: Mr John Vaughan, Energy Manager, Town Hall, Rose Hill, Chesterfield S40 1LP ☎ 01246 345415 🖷 01246 345252 ✉ john.vaughan@chesterfield.gov.uk

Environmental / Technical Services: Mr Darran West, Head of Environment, Town Hall, Rose Hill, Chesterfield S40 1LP ☎ 01246 345751 🖷 01246 345760 ✉ darran.west@chesterfield.gov.uk

Environmental Health: Mr Darran West, Head of Environment, Town Hall, Rose Hill, Chesterfield S40 1LP ☎ 01246 345751 🖷 01246 345760 ✉ darran.west@chesterfield.gov.uk

Estates, Property & Valuation: Mr Matthew Sorby, Head of Asset Management, Town Hall, Rose Hill, Chesterfield S40 1LP ☎ 01246 345308 🖷 01246 345809 ✉ matthew.sorby@chesterfield.gov.uk

European Liaison: Ms Laurie Thomas, Economic Development Manager, Town Hall, Rose Hill, Chesterfield S40 1LP ☎ 01246 345255 🖷 01246 345256 ✉ laurie.thomas@chesterfield.gov.uk

Finance and Treasurer: Mr Barry Dawson, Head of Finance,

Town Hall, Rose Hill, Chesterfield S40 1LP ☎ 01246 345451 🖷 01246 345252 ✉ barry.dawson@chesterfield.gov.uk

Finance and Treasurer: Ms Fran Rodway, Customer Services & Revenues Manager, Town Hall, Rose Hill, Chesterfield S40 1LP ☎ 01246 345475 🖷 01246 345252 ✉ fran.rodway@chesterfield.gov.uk

Health and Safety: Mr John Moran, Acting Head of Business Transformation, Town Hall, Rose Hill, Chesterfield S40 1LP ☎ 01246 345389 🖷 01246 345252 ✉ john.moran@chesterfield.gov.uk

Home Energy Conservation: Mr Michael Hayden, Head of Regeneration, Town Hall, Rose Hill, Chesterfield S40 1LP ☎ 01246 345789 🖷 01246 345252 ✉ mike.hayden@chesterfield.gov.uk

Housing: Mr Huw Bowen, Chief Executive, Town Hall, Rose Hill, Chesterfield S40 1LP ☎ 01246 345305 🖷 01246 345252 ✉ huw.bowen@chesterfield.gov.uk

Housing: Mr Andy Simpson, Head of Housing, Town Hall, Rose Hill, Chesterfield S40 1LP ☎ 01246 345140 🖷 01246 345252 ✉ andy.simpson@chesterfield.gov.uk

Housing Maintenance: Mr Martyn Bollands, Building Services Manager, Town Hall, Rose Hill, Chesterfield S40 1LP ☎ 01246 345020 🖷 01246 345252 ✉ martyn.bollands@chesterfield.gov.uk

Legal: Ms Sara Goodwin, Head of Governance, Town Hall, Rose Hill, Chesterfield S40 1LP ☎ 01246 345309 🖷 01246 345270 ✉ sara.goodwin@chesterfield.gov.uk

Leisure and Cultural Services: Mr Huw Bowen, Chief Executive, Town Hall, Rose Hill, Chesterfield S40 1LP ☎ 01246 345305 🖷 01246 345252 ✉ huw.bowen@chesterfield.gov.uk

Leisure and Cultural Services: Ms Bernadette Wainwright, Tourism & Town Centre Promotions Manager, Tourist Information Centre, Rykneld Square, Chesterfield S40 1SB ☎ 01246 345305 🖷 01246 345770 ✉ bernadette.wainwright@chesterfield.gov.uk

Licensing: Mr Trevor Durham, Interim Licensing Manager, Town Hall, Rose Hill, Chesterfield S40 1LP ☎ 01246 345230 🖷 01246 345252 ✉ trevor.durham@chesterfield.gov.uk

Member Services: Mrs Sandra Essex, Democratic Services Manager, Town Hall, Rose Hill, Chesterfield S40 1LP ☎ 01246 345227 🖷 01246 345252 ✉ sandra.essex@chesterfield.gov.uk

Member Services: Mr Gerard Rogers, Senior Solicitor & Deputy Monitoring Officer, Town Hall, Rose Hill, Chesterfield S40 1LP ☎ 01246 345310 🖷 01246 345270 ✉ gerard.rogers@chesterfield.gov.uk

Parking: Mr Michael Hayden, Head of Regeneration, Town Hall, Rose Hill, Chesterfield S40 1LP ☎ 01246 345789 🖷 01246 345252 ✉ mike.hayden@chesterfield.gov.uk

Personnel / HR: Ms Jane Dackiewicz, Head of Customer Services, Organisational Development & Business Transformation, Town Hall, Rose Hill, Chesterfield S40 1LP ☎ 01246 345282 🖷 01246 345252 ✉ jane.dackiewicz@chesterfield.gov.uk

Planning: Mr Michael Hayden, Head of Regeneration, Town Hall, Rose Hill, Chesterfield S40 1LP ☎ 01246 345789 🖷 01246 345252 ✉ mike.hayden@chesterfield.gov.uk

Procurement: Mr Richard Somerset, Purchasing Officer, Town Hall, Rose Hill, Chesterfield S40 1LP ☎ 01246 345295 🖷 01246 345252 ✉ richard.somerset@chesterfield.gov.uk

Procurement: Mr Bob Trusswell, Head - Procurement, Sherwood Lodge, Bolsover S44 6NF ☎ 01246 242311; 07800 735086 ✉ bob.trusswell@bolsover.gov.uk

Recycling & Waste Minimisation: Mr David Hibbert, Principal Waste Management Officer, Town Hall, Rose Hill, Chesterfield S40 1LP ☎ 01246 345399 🖷 01246 345760 ✉ david.hibbert@chesterfield.gov.uk

Regeneration: Mr Michael Hayden, Head of Regeneration, Town Hall, Rose Hill, Chesterfield S40 1LP ☎ 01246 345789 🖷 01246 345252 ✉ mike.hayden@chesterfield.gov.uk

Staff Training: Ms Jane Dackiewicz, Head of Customer Services, Organisational Development & Business Transformation, Town Hall, Rose Hill, Chesterfield S40 1LP ☎ 01246 345282 🖷 01246 345252 ✉ jane.dackiewicz@chesterfield.gov.uk

Street Scene: Mr Darran West, Head of Environment, Town Hall, Rose Hill, Chesterfield S40 1LP ☎ 01246 345751 🖷 01246 345760 ✉ darran.west@chesterfield.gov.uk

Sustainable Communities: Mr Peter Corke, Sustainability Officer, Town Hall, Rose Hill, Chesterfield S40 1LP ☎ 01246 345765 🖷 01246 345252 ✉ peter.corke@chesterfield.gov.uk

Sustainable Development: Mr Peter Corke, Sustainability Officer, Town Hall, Rose Hill, Chesterfield S40 1LP ☎ 01246 345765 🖷 01246 345252 ✉ peter.corke@chesterfield.gov.uk

Tourism: Ms Bernadette Wainwright, Tourism & Town Centre Promotions Manager, Tourist Information Centre, Rykneld Square, Chesterfield S40 1SB ☎ 01246 345305 🖷 01246 345770 ✉ bernadette.wainwright@chesterfield.gov.uk

Town Centre: Ms Bernadette Wainwright, Tourism & Town Centre Promotions Manager, Tourist Information Centre, Rykneld Square, Chesterfield S40 1SB ☎ 01246 345305 🖷 01246 345770 ✉ bernadette.wainwright@chesterfield.gov.uk

Waste Collection and Disposal: Mr David Hibbert, Principal Waste Management Officer, Town Hall, Rose Hill, Chesterfield S40 1LP ☎ 01246 345399 🖷 01246 345760 ✉ david.hibbert@chesterfield.gov.uk

Waste Management: Mr David Hibbert, Principal Waste Management Officer, Town Hall, Rose Hill, Chesterfield S40 1LP ☎ 01246 345399 🖷 01246 345760 ✉ david.hibbert@chesterfield.gov.uk

MEMBERS OF THE COUNCIL (48)

***Mayor:* Parsons**, Donald (LAB - Middlecroft & Poolsbrook)
donald.parsons@chesterfield.gov.uk
***Leader of the Council:* Burrows**, John (LAB - Brimington North)
john.burrows@chesterfield.gov.uk
***Deputy Leader of the Council:* Gilby**, Terry (LAB - Brimington North)
terry.gilby@chesterfield.gov.uk
Allen, David (LAB - Hasland)
david.allen@chesterfield.gov.uk
Barr, Peter (LD - Linacre)
peter.barr@chesterfield.gov.uk
Bellamy, Anthony (LAB - Brimington South)
andy.bellamy@chesterfield.gov.uk
Bingham, Barry (LD - Barrow Hill & New Whittington)
barry.bingham@chesterfield.gov.uk
Blank, Sharon (LAB - St Leonards)
sharon.blank@chesterfield.gov.uk
Borrell, Howard (LD - West)
howard.borrell@chesterfield.gov.uk
Bradford, Stewart (LAB - Rother)
stewart.bradbury@chesterfield.gov.uk
Brittain, Stuart (LAB - Rother)
stuart.brittain@chesterfield.gov.uk
Brown, Keith (LAB - Moor)
keith.brown@chesterfield.gov.uk
Callan, Ian (LAB - Brimington South)
ian.callan@chesterfield.gov.uk
Collard, Christopher (LD - Walton)
chris.collard@chesterfield.gov.uk
Davenport, Maureen (LD - Brockwell)
maureen.davenport@chesterfield.gov.uk
Diouf, Alexis (LD - Walton)
alexis.diouf@chesterfield.gov.uk
Dyke, Barry (LAB - Hollingwood & Inkersall)
barry.dyke@chesterfield.gov.uk
Elliott, Helen (LAB - Hollingwood & Inkersall)
helen.elliott@chesterfield.gov.uk
Everitt, Angela (LAB - St Helens)
angela.everitt@chesterfield.gov.uk
Fanshawe, Michael (LAB - Loundsley Green)
michael.fanshawe@chesterfield.gov.uk
Flood, Jenny (LAB - Rother)
jenny.flood@chesterfield.gov.uk
Gibson, Robert (LD - Brockwell)
bob.gibson@chesterfield.gov.uk
Hawksworth, Denise (LD - West)
denise.hawksworth@chesterfield.gov.uk
Higginbottom, Mark (LD - Linacre)
mark.higginbottom@chesterfield.gov.uk
Hill, Anthony (LAB - Hollingwood & Inkersall)
anthony.hill@chesterfield.gov.uk
Hollingworth, Sarah (LAB - Dunston)
sarah.hollingworth@chesterfield.gov.uk
Huckle, Kenneth (LAB - St Leonards)
ken.huckle@chesterfield.gov.uk
Innes, Jean (LAB - Old Whittington)
jean.innes@chesterfield.gov.uk
King, Graham (LAB - Moor)
graham.king@chesterfield.gov.uk
Lang, Vicki (LAB - Lowgates & Woodthorpe)
vicki.lang@chesterfield.gov.uk
Lowe, Julie (LAB - Brimington South)
julie.lowe@chesterfield.gov.uk
Ludlow, Chris (LAB - Middlecroft & Poolsbrook)
chris.ludlow@chesterfield.gov.uk
McManus, Jim (LAB - Lowgates & Woodthorpe)
jim.mcmanus@chesterfield.gov.uk
Miles, Keith (LAB - Holmebrook)
keith.miles@chesterfield.gov.uk
Morgan, Keith (LD - Walton)
keith.morgan@chesterfield.gov.uk
Murphy, Avis (LAB - Loundsley Green)
avis.murphy@chesterfield.gov.uk
Niblock, Shirley (LD - West)
shirley.niblock@chesterfield.gov.uk
Rayner, Neil (LAB - Old Whittington)
neil.rayner@chesterfield.gov.uk
Rayner, Mark (LAB - Dunston)
mark.rayner@chesterfield.gov.uk
Reynolds, Trevor (LAB - St Helens)
trevor.reynolds@chesterfield.gov.uk
Russell, Ray (LD - Brockwell)
ray.russell@chesterfield.gov.uk
Serjeant, Amanda (LAB - Hasland)
amanda.serjeant@chesterfield.gov.uk
Simmons, Gordon (LAB - Dunston)
gordon.simmons@chesterfield.gov.uk
Slack, Andrew (LAB - Hasland)
andy.slack@chesterfield.gov.uk
Stone, David (LD - Barrow Hill & New Whittington)
david.stone@chesterfield.gov.uk
Stone, Paul (LD - Barrow Hill & New Whittington)
paul.stone@chesterfield.gov.uk
Stone, Martin (LAB - Holmebrook)
martin.stone@chesterfield.gov.uk
Stringer, Nicholas (LAB - St Leonards)
nick.stringer@chesterfield.gov.uk

POLITICAL COMPOSITION

LAB: 34, LD: 14

CABINET

Leader / Regeneration: Mr John Burrows
Deputy Leader / Planning: Mr Terry Gilby
Customers & Communities: Ms Sharon Blank
Environment: Mrs Chris Ludlow
Governance & Organisational Development: Mr Graham King
Housing: Mr Jim McManus
Leisure, Culture & Tourism: Mr Nicholas Stringer

COMMITTEE CHAIRS

Appeals, Regulatory & Licensing: Mr Stewart Bradford
Community, Customer & Organisational Development
Scrutiny: Ms Jean Innes
Employment & General: Ms Jenny Flood
Enterprise, Wellbeing & Scrutiny: Mrs Vicki Lang
Planning: Mr Stuart Brittain

CHICHESTER D

Chichester District Council, Council Offices, East Pallant House, East Pallant, Chichester PO19 1TY ☎ 01243 785166 🖷 01243 776766 contact@chichester.gov.uk www.chichester.gov.uk

FACTS & FIGURES

Police Authority: Sussex Police Authority
Health Authority: South East Coast Strategic Health Authority
Learning and Skills Council: South East

Parliamentary Constituencies: Chichester
EU Constituencies: South East
Election Frequency: Elections are of whole council
Twinning: Boxgrove: Lessay (France); Chichester: Chartres (France) and Ravenna (Italy); Midhurst and Petworth: Duren (Germany)

PRINCIPAL OFFICERS

Chief Executive: Mrs Diane Shepherd, Director of Corporate Services, Council Offices, East Pallant House, East Pallant, Chichester PO19 1TY ☎ 01243 534511 🖷 01243 776766 🖱 dshepherd@chichester.gov.uk

Senior Management: Mr Steve Carvell, Director of Environment, Council Offices, East Pallant House, East Pallant, Chichester PO19 1TJ ☎ 01243 534569 🖷 01243 776766 🖱 scarvell@chichester.gov.uk

Senior Management: Mrs Amanda Jobling, Director of Home & Community, Council Offices, East Pallant House, East Pallant, Chichester PO19 1TY ☎ 01243 534599 🖷 01243 776766 🖱 ajobling@chichester.gov.uk

Senior Management: Mr Paul Over, Director of Employment & Prosperity, Council Offices, East Pallant House, East Pallant, Chichester PO19 1TY ☎ 01243 534639 🖷 01243 534673 🖱 pover@chichester.gov.uk

Access Officer / Social Services (Disability): Mr John Bacon, Building & Facility Services Manager, Council Offices, East Pallant House, East Pallant, Chichester PO19 1TY ☎ 01243 534648 🖷 01243 776766 🖱 jbacon@chichester.gov.uk

Architect, Building / Property Services: Mr John Bacon, Building & Facility Services Manager, Council Offices, East Pallant House, East Pallant, Chichester PO19 1TY ☎ 01243 534648 🖷 01243 776766 🖱 jbacon@chichester.gov.uk

Best Value: Mr Stephen Kane, Head of Policy, Council Offices, East Pallant House, East Pallant, Chichester PO1 1TY ☎ 01243 534785 🖷 01243 776766 🖱 skane@chichester.gov.uk

Building Control: Mr Peter Blewden, Environmental Strategy Manager, East Pallant House, East Pallant, Chichester PO19 1TY ☎ 01243 534611

Children / Youth Services: Mr Stephen Hansford, Communities Manager, Council Offices, East Pallant House, East Pallant, Chichester PO19 1TY ☎ 01243 534789 🖷 01243 776766 🖱 shansford@chichester.gov.uk

PR / Communications: Ms Sarah Parker, Public Relations Officer, Council Offices, East Pallant House, East Pallant, Chichester PO19 1TY ☎ 01243 534537 🖱 sparker@chichester.gov.uk

Community Planning: Mr Stephen Kane, Head of Policy, Council Offices, East Pallant House, East Pallant, Chichester PO1 1TY ☎ 01243 534785 🖷 01243 776766 🖱 skane@chichester.gov.uk

Community Safety: Mr Stephen Hansford, Communities Manager, Council Offices, East Pallant House, East Pallant, Chichester PO19 1TY ☎ 01243 534789 🖷 01243 776766 🖱 shansford@chichester.gov.uk

Computer Management: Mrs Jane Dodsworth, Assistant Director - ICT & Customer Services, Council Offices, East Pallant House, East Pallant, Chichester PO19 1TY ☎ 01243 534729 🖷 01243 776766 🖱 jdodsworth@chichester.gov.uk

Contracts: Mr Bob Riley, Contracts Manager, Chichester Contract Services, Stane Street, Westhampnett, Chichester PO18 0NS ☎ 01243 534615 🖷 01243 532695 🖱 briley@chichester.gov.uk

Corporate Services: Mrs Diane Shepherd, Director of Corporate Services, Council Offices, East Pallant House, East Pallant, Chichester PO19 1TY ☎ 01243 534511 🖷 01243 776766 🖱 dshepherd@chichester.gov.uk

Customer Service: Mrs Jane Dodsworth, Assistant Director - ICT & Customer Services, Council Offices, East Pallant House, East Pallant, Chichester PO19 1TY ☎ 01243 534729 🖷 01243 776766 🖱 jdodsworth@chichester.gov.uk

Direct Labour: Mr Rod Darton, Assistant Director - Contract Services, Chichester Contract Services, Stane Street, Westhampnett, Chichester PO18 0NS ☎ 01243 521177 🖷 01243 532695 🖱 rdarton@chichester.gov.uk

Economic Development: Mr Kenrick Garraway, Assistant Director - Economic Development & Tourism, East Pallant House, East Pallant, Chichester PO19 1TY ☎ 01243 534669 🖷 01243 534825 🖱 kgarraway@chichester.gov.uk

E-Government: Mrs Jane Dodsworth, Assistant Director - ICT & Customer Services, Council Offices, East Pallant House, East Pallant, Chichester PO19 1TY ☎ 01243 534729 🖷 01243 776766 🖱 jdodsworth@chichester.gov.uk

Electoral Registration: Ms Jo Timm, Electoral Services Manager, Council Offices, East Pallant House, East Pallant, Chichester PO19 1TY ☎ 01243 534652 🖷 01243 776766 🖱 jtimm@chichester.gov.uk

Emergency Planning: Mr Lloyd Harris, Emergency Planning & Business Continuity Officer, Council Offices, East Pallant House, East Pallant, Chichester PO19 1TY ☎ 01243 534616 🖷 01243 776766 🖱 lharris@chichester.gov.uk

Energy Management: Mr John Bacon, Building & Facility Services Manager, Council Offices, East Pallant House, East Pallant, Chichester PO19 1TY ☎ 01243 534648 🖷 01243 776766 🖱 jbacon@chichester.gov.uk

Environmental / Technical Services: Mr John Bacon, Building & Facility Services Manager, Council Offices, East Pallant House, East Pallant, Chichester PO19 1TY ☎ 01243 534648 🖷 01243 776766 🖱 jbacon@chichester.gov.uk

Environmental Health: Mr Matthew China, Assistant Director - Environmental Health, East Pallant House, East Pallant, Chichester PO19 1TY ☎ 01243 534614 🖷 01243 776766

mchina@chichester.gov.uk

Estates, Property & Valuation: Mr Peter LeGood, Valuation & Estates Manager, East Pallant House, East Pallant, Chichester PO19 1TY ☎ 01243 534668 🖷 01243 776766 plegood@chichester.gov.uk

European Liaison: Mr Kenrick Garraway, Assistant Director - Economic Development & Tourism, East Pallant House, East Pallant, Chichester PO19 1TY ☎ 01243 534669 🖷 01243 534825 kgarraway@chichester.gov.uk

Facilities: Mr John Bacon, Building & Facility Services Manager, Council Offices, East Pallant House, East Pallant, Chichester PO19 1TY ☎ 01243 534648 🖷 01243 776766 jbacon@chichester.gov.uk

Finance and Treasurer: Mr John Ward, Chief Financial Officer, Council Offices, East Pallant House, East Pallant, Chichester PO19 1TY ☎ 01243 776766 jward@chichester.gov.uk

Fleet Management: Mr Rod Darton, Assistant Director - Contract Services, Chichester Contract Services, Stane Street, Westhampnett, Chichester PO18 0NS ☎ 01243 521177 🖷 01243 532695 rdarton@chichester.gov.uk

Grounds Maintenance: Mr Rod Darton, Assistant Director - Contract Services, Chichester Contract Services, Stane Street, Westhampnett, Chichester PO18 0NS ☎ 01243 521177 🖷 01243 532695 rdarton@chichester.gov.uk

Health and Safety: Mr Warren Townsend, Safety Manager, East Pallant House, East Pallant, Chichester PO19 1TY ☎ 01243 534605 🖷 01243 776766 wtownsend@chichester.gov.uk

Home Energy Conservation: Mr Rob Dunmall, Opertions Manager, East Pallant House, East Pallant, Chichester PO19 1TY ☎ 01243 785166

Housing: Mrs Yvonne Thomson, Assistant Director - Strategic Housing Services, East Pallant House, East Pallant, Chichester PO19 1TY ☎ 01243 534591 ythomson@chichester.gov.uk

Legal: Mr David Stewart, Legal Practice Manager, East Pallant House, East Pallant, Chichester PO19 1TY ☎ 01243 534663

Leisure and Cultural Services: Mrs Jane Hotchkiss, Assistant Director - Leisure & Wellbeing, Council Offices, East Pallant House, East Pallant, Chichester PO19 1TY ☎ 01243 534790 🖷 01243 776766 jhotchkiss@chichester.gov.uk

Licensing: Mr Matthew China, Assistant Director - Environmental Health, East Pallant House, East Pallant, Chichester PO19 1TY ☎ 01243 534614 🖷 01243 776766 mchina@chichester.gov.uk

Lifelong Learning: Mr Kenrick Garraway, Assistant Director - Economic Development & Tourism, East Pallant House, East Pallant, Chichester PO19 1TY ☎ 01243 534669 🖷 01243 534825 kgarraway@chichester.gov.uk

Lottery Funding, Charity and Voluntary: Mrs Jane Hotchkiss, Assistant Director - Leisure & Wellbeing, Council Offices, East Pallant House, East Pallant, Chichester PO19 1TY ☎ 01243 534790 🖷 01243 776766 jhotchkiss@chichester.gov.uk

Member Services: Mr Philip Coleman, Member Services Manager, Council Offices, East Pallant House, East Pallant, Chichester PO19 1TY ☎ 01243 534655 pcoleman@chichester.gov.uk

Parking: Mr Robert Clark, Parking Services Manager, East Pallant House, East Pallant, Chichester PO19 1TY ☎ 01243 534701 rclark@chichester.gov.uk

Partnerships: Mr Stephen Hansford, Communities Manager, Council Offices, East Pallant House, East Pallant, Chichester PO19 1TY ☎ 01243 534789 🖷 01243 776766 shansford@chichester.gov.uk

Personnel / HR: Mrs Diane Shepherd, Director of Corporate Services, Council Offices, East Pallant House, East Pallant, Chichester PO19 1TY ☎ 01243 534511 🖷 01243 776766 dshepherd@chichester.gov.uk

Planning: Mr Andrew Frost, Assistant Director - Development Management, East Pallant House, East Pallant, Chichester PO19 1TY ☎ 01243 534892 🖷 01243 776766 afrost@chichester.gov.uk

Procurement: Mr Phil Pickard, Procurement Officer, East Pallant House, East Pallant, Chichester PO19 1TY ☎ 01243 785166

Recycling & Waste Minimisation: Mr Bob Riley, Contracts Manager, Chichester Contract Services, Stane Street, Westhampnett, Chichester PO18 0NS ☎ 01243 534615 🖷 01243 532695 briley@chichester.gov.uk

Regeneration: Mr Kenrick Garraway, Assistant Director - Economic Development & Tourism, East Pallant House, East Pallant, Chichester PO19 1TY ☎ 01243 534669 🖷 01243 534825 kgarraway@chichester.gov.uk

Staff Training: Mr Tim Radcliffe, Senior Personnel Manager, Council Offices, East Pallant House, East Pallant, Chichester PO19 1TY ☎ 01243 534528 🖷 01243 776766 tradcliffe@chichester.gov.uk

Sustainable Communities: Mrs Amanda Jobling, Director of Home & Community, Council Offices, East Pallant House, East Pallant, Chichester PO19 1TY ☎ 01243 785166 🖷 01243 776766 ajobling@chichester.gov.uk

Town Centre: Mrs Kim Long, City Centre Manager, East Pallant House, East Pallant, Chichester PO19 1TY ☎ 01243 534677

Transport: Mr Rod Darton, Assistant Director - Contract Services, Chichester Contract Services, Stane Street, Westhampnett, Chichester PO18 0NS ☎ 01243 521177 🖷 01243 532695 rdarton@chichester.gov.uk

Waste Collection and Disposal: Mr Bob Riley, Contracts Manager, Chichester Contract Services, Stane Street, Westhampnett, Chichester PO18 0NS ☎ 01243 534615 🖷 01243 532695 briley@chichester.gov.uk

Waste Management: Mr Bob Riley, Contracts Manager, Chichester Contract Services, Stane Street, Westhampnett, Chichester PO18 0NS ☎ 01243 534615 🖷 01243 532695 ✉ briley@chichester.gov.uk

Children's Play Areas: Mrs Sarah Peyman, Sport & Leisure Development Manager, East Pallant House, East Pallant, Chichester PO19 1TY ☎ 01243 534791 ✉ speyman@chichester.gov.uk

MEMBERS OF THE COUNCIL (48)

***Chair:* Clementson**, P (CON - East Wittering) p.clementson@btinternet.com
***Leader of the Council:* Caird**, H (CON - Fernhurst) hcaird@chichester.gov.uk
***Deputy Leader of the Council:* Cullen**, M (CON - Bosham) mcullen@chichester.gov.uk
Apel, C (LD - Chichester West) capel@chichester.gov.uk
Barrett, Graeme (CON - East Wittering) graeme.barrett@btinternet.com
Bell, Martyn (CON - Chichester West) mbell@chichester.gov.uk
Budge, Peter (CON - Chichester North) pbudge@chichester.gov.uk
Carr, Simon (LD - Fishbourne) scarr@chichester.gov.uk
Chaplin, A (LD - Chichester South) achaplin@chichester.gov.uk
Cherry, John (CON - Stedham) john@johncherry.plus.com
Connor, J (CON - Selsey North) jconnor@chichester.gov.uk
Cox, Q (LD - Chichester East) qcox@chichester.gov.uk
Dignum, P (CON - Chichester South) pdignum@chichester.gov.uk
Dignum, Tony (CON - Chichester North) pdignum@chichester.gov.uk
Duncton, J (CON - Petworth) janet@duncton.plus.com
Elliott, Maureen (CON - Westbourne) maureen.elliott@btinternet.com
Elliott, John (CON - Bury) john.elliott811929@btopenworld.com
Finch, Bruce (CON - Southbourne) bfinch@chichester.gov.uk
French, T (LD - Chichester East) tfrench@chichester.gov.uk
Graves, N (CON - Fernhurst) ngraves@chichester.gov.uk
Hamilton, E (CON - Easebourne) ehamilton@chichester.gov.uk
Hardwick, P (CON - Plaistow) phardwick@chichester.gov.uk
Hayes, R (CON - Southbourne) rhayes@chichester.gov.uk
Hicks, G (CON - Southbourne) ghicks@chichester.gov.uk
Jarvis, Paul (CON - North Mundham) pjarvis@chichester.gov.uk
Kingston, John (CON - Rogate) jkingston@chichester.gov.uk
Lintill, E (CON - Petworth) elintill@chichester.gov.uk
Lloyd-Williams, Simon (CON - Chichester North) slloyd-williams@chichester.gov.uk
Marshall, Roger (CON - West Wittering) rmarshall@chichester.gov.uk
McAra, Gordon (IND - Midhurst) gmcara@chichester.gov.uk
Montyn, J (CON - West Wittering) pmontyn@chichester.gov.uk
Myers, D (CON - Bosham) dmyers@chichester.gov.uk
Oakley, Simon (CON - Tangmere) soakley@chichester.gov.uk
O'Brien, R (CON - Selsey South) robrien@chichester.gov.uk
Potter, H (CON - Boxgrove) hpotter@chichester.gov.uk
Purnell, Carol (CON - Selsey North) cpurnell@chichester.gov.uk
Ransley, Josef (CON - Wisborough Green) jransley@chichester.gov.uk
Ridd, J (CON - Donnington) jridd@chichester.gov.uk
Robertson, F (CON - Selsey South) frobertson@chichester.gov.uk
Scicluna, Anne (LD - Chichester South) ascicluna@chichester.gov.uk
Shaxson, A (IND - Harting) ashaxson@chichester.gov.uk
Smith, A (LD - Lavant) asmith@chichester.gov.uk
Tassell, J (CON - Funtington) julie.tassell@virgin.net
Thomas, Nick (CON - Plaistow) nthomas@chichester.gov.uk
Tinson, B (CON - Selsey North) btinson@chichester.gov.uk
Tull, T (CON - Sidlesham) ttull@chichester.gov.uk
Weekes, B (IND - Midhurst) bweekes@chichester.gov.uk
Woolley, Michael (LD - Chichester East) mwoolley@chichester.gov.uk

POLITICAL COMPOSITION

CON: 37, LD: 8, IND: 3

CABINET

Leader: Mrs H Caird
Deputy Leader: Mr M Cullen
Corporate Services & Communications: Mr Josef Ransley
Environment: Mr J Connor
Finance: Mrs T Tull
Housing & Planning: Mrs J Duncton
Leisure, Wellbeing & Community Services: Mrs E Lintill

COMMITTEE CHAIRS

Corporate Governance & Audit: Mr J Cherry
Licensing & Enforcement: Mr J Ridd
Overview & Scrutiny (Scrutiny): Mrs C Apel

CHILTERN D

Chiltern District Council, Council Offices, King George V Road, Amersham HP6 5AW ☎ 01494 729000 🖷 01494 586506
💻 www.chiltern.gov.uk

FACTS & FIGURES

Police Authority: Thames Valley Police Authority
Health Authority: South Central Strategic Health Authority
Learning and Skills Council: South East
Parliamentary Constituencies: Aylesbury, Chesham and Amersham
EU Constituencies: South East
Election Frequency: Elections are of whole council
Twinning: Amersham: Bensheim (Germany); Chalfont St. Giles: Graft-De Rijp (Netherlands); Chesham: Friedrichsdorf (Germany), Houilles (France) and Archena (Spain)

PRINCIPAL OFFICERS

Chief Executive: Mr Alan Goodrum, Chief Executive, Council Offices, King George V Road, Amersham HP6 5AW ☎ 01494 732001; 01494 732001 🖷 01494 586506; 01494 586506
🖱 agoodrum@chiltern.gov.uk; agoodrum@chiltern.gov.uk

Senior Management: Mr Alan Goodrum, Chief Executive, Council Offices, King George V Road, Amersham HP6 5AW
☎ 01494 732001; 01494 732001 🖷 01494 586506; 01494 586506
🖱 agoodrum@chiltern.gov.uk; agoodrum@chiltern.gov.uk

Access Officer / Social Services (Disability): Mr Peter Finney, Head of Building Control, Council Offices, King George V Road, Amersham HP6 5AW ☎ 01494 732035 🖷 01494 586508
🖱 pfinney@chiltern.gov.uk

Building Control: Mr Peter Finney, Head of Building Control, Council Offices, King George V Road, Amersham HP6 5AW
☎ 01494 732035 🖷 01494 586508 🖱 pfinney@chiltern.gov.uk

Children / Youth Services: Mr Paul Nanji, Principal Leisure & Community Officer, Council Offices, King George V Road, Amersham HP6 5AW ☎ 01494 732110 🖷 01494 586504
🖱 pnanji@chiltern.gov.uk

PR / Communications: Mrs Rachel Prance, Communications & Public Relations Officer, Council Offices, King George V Road, Amersham HP6 5AW ☎ 01494 732903 🖷 01494 586506
🖱 rprance@chiltern.gov.uk

Community Planning: Mr James Streeter, Policy & Improvement Officer, Council Offices, King George V Road, Amersham HP6 5AW ☎ 01494 732779 🖷 01494 586506
🖱 jstreeter@chiltern.gov.uk

Community Safety: Mrs Katie Galvin, Senior Community Safety Officer, Council Offices, King George V Road, Amersham HP6 5AW ☎ 01494 732265 🖷 01494 586504
🖱 kgalvin@chiltern.gov.uk

Computer Management: Mrs Simonette Dixon, Head of Information Technology, Council Offices, King George V Road, Amersham HP6 5AW ☎ 01494 732087 🖷 01494 586509
🖱 sdixon@chiltern.gov.uk

Contracts: Mr Mike Mitchell, Interim Head of Engineering & Contract Management, Council Offices, King George V Road, Amersham HP6 5AW ☎ 01494 732064
🖱 mmitchell@chiltern.gov.uk

Customer Service: Mrs Sue Trotter, Head of Revenues & Customer Services, Council Offices, King George V Road, Amersham HP6 5AW ☎ 01494 732231 🖱 strotter@chiltern.gov.uk

E-Government: Mrs Simonette Dixon, Head of Information Technology, Council Offices, King George V Road, Amersham HP6 5AW ☎ 01494 732087 🖷 01494 586509
🖱 sdixon@chiltern.gov.uk

Electoral Registration: Mr Richard Harris, Democratic Services Manager, Council Offices, King George V Road, Amersham HP6 5AW ☎ 01494 732010 🖷 01494 586506 🖱 rharris@chiltern.gov.uk

Emergency Planning: Mrs Glynis Chanell, Health & Safety Practitioner, Council Offices, King George V Road, Amersham HP6 5AW ☎ 01494 732062 🖷 01494 586504
🖱 gchanell@chiltern.gov.uk

Environmental Health: Mr Martin Holt, Head of Health & Housing, Council Offices, King George V Road, Amersham HP6 5AW ☎ 01494 732055 🖷 01494 586504 🖱 mholt@chiltern.gov.uk

Estates, Property & Valuation: Miss Frances Read, Estates Officer, Council Offices, King George V Road, Amersham HP6 5AW ☎ 01494 732068 🖱 fread@chiltern.gov.uk

Estates, Property & Valuation: Mrs Joanna Swift, Head of Legal & Estates, Council Offices, The Gateway, Gatehouse Road, Aylesbury HP19 8FF ☎ 01296 585024; 01296 585024 🖷 01296 585585 🖱 jswift@aylesburyvaledc.gov.uk

European Liaison: Mr Alan Goodrum, Chief Executive, Council Offices, King George V Road, Amersham HP6 5AW ☎ 01494 732001; 01494 732001 🖷 01494 586506
🖱 agoodrum@chiltern.gov.uk

Facilities: Mr Simon Rycraft, Administration Manager, Council Offices, King George V Road, Amersham HP6 5AW ☎ 01494 732073 🖱 srycraft@chiltern.gov.uk

Finance and Treasurer: Miss Alison Howes, Head of Financial Services, Council Offices, King George V Road, Amersham HP6 5AW ☎ 01494 732260 🖷 01494 586509
🖱 ahowes@chiltern.gov.uk

Grounds Maintenance: Mr Mike Mitchell, Interim Head of Engineering & Contract Management, Council Offices, King George V Road, Amersham HP6 5AW ☎ 01494 732064
🖱 mmitchell@chiltern.gov.uk

Health and Safety: Mrs Glynis Chanell, Health & Safety Practitioner, Council Offices, King George V Road, Amersham HP6 5AW ☎ 01494 732062 🖷 01494 586504
🖱 gchanell@chiltern.gov.uk

Home Energy Conservation: Mrs Louise Quinn, Senior Private Sector Housing Officer, Council Offices, King George V Road,

Amersham HP6 5AW ☎ 01494 732209 ✉ lquinn@chiltern.gov.uk

Housing: Mr Michael Veryard, Principal Housing Officer, Council Offices, King George V Road, Amersham HP6 5AW ☎ 01494 732200 🖷 01494 586504 ✉ mveryard@chiltern.gov.uk

Legal: Mrs Sue Markham, Legal Services Manager, Council Offices, King George V Road, Amersham HP6 5AW ☎ 01494 732097 🖷 01494 586509 ✉ smarkham@chiltern.gov.uk

Leisure and Cultural Services: Mr Paul Nanji, Principal Leisure & Community Officer, Council Offices, King George V Road, Amersham HP6 5AW ☎ 01494 732110 🖷 01494 586504 ✉ pnanji@chiltern.gov.uk

Licensing: Mr Ian Snudden, Environmental Health Manager, Council Offices, King George V Road, Amersham HP6 5AW ☎ 01494 732057 🖷 01494 586504 ✉ isnudden@chiltern.gov.uk

Lottery Funding, Charity and Voluntary: Mr Paul Nanji, Principal Leisure & Community Officer, Council Offices, King George V Road, Amersham HP6 5AW ☎ 01494 732110 🖷 01494 586504 ✉ pnanji@chiltern.gov.uk

Member Services: Mr Richard Harris, Democratic Services Manager, Council Offices, King George V Road, Amersham HP6 5AW ☎ 01494 732010 🖷 01494 586506 ✉ rharris@chiltern.gov.uk

Parking: Mr Oliver Asbury, Principal Engineer, Council Offices, King George V Road, Amersham HP6 5AW ☎ 01494 732066 ✉ oasbury@chiltern.gov.uk

Personnel / HR: Miss Moraigh Butler, Head of Personnel & Performance, Council Offices, King George V Road, Amersham HP6 5AW ☎ 01494 732015 🖷 01494 586506 ✉ mbutler@chiltern.gov.uk

Planning: Miss Anna Cronin, Interim Head of Planning Services, Council Offices, King George V Road, Amersham HP6 5AW ☎ 01494 732036 🖷 01494 586508 ✉ acronin@chiltern.gov.uk

Procurement: Miss Alison Howes, Head of Financial Services, Council Offices, King George V Road, Amersham HP6 5AW ☎ 01494 732260 🖷 01494 586509 ✉ ahowes@chiltern.gov.uk

Recycling & Waste Minimisation: Mr Mike Mitchell, Interim Head of Engineering & Contract Management, Council Offices, King George V Road, Amersham HP6 5AW ☎ 01494 732064 ✉ mmitchell@chiltern.gov.uk

Regeneration: Mr Martin Holt, Head of Health & Housing, Council Offices, King George V Road, Amersham HP6 5AW ☎ 01494 732055 🖷 01494 586504 ✉ mholt@chiltern.gov.uk

Staff Training: Miss Moraigh Butler, Head of Personnel & Performance, Council Offices, King George V Road, Amersham HP6 5AW ☎ 01494 732015 🖷 01494 586506 ✉ mbutler@chiltern.gov.uk

Sustainable Development: Mr Ben Coakley, Principal Environment Officer, Council Offices, King George V Road, Amersham HP6 5AW ☎ 01494 732060 🖷 01494 586504 ✉ bcoakley@chiltern.gov.uk

Waste Collection and Disposal: Mr Mike Mitchell, Interim Head of Engineering & Contract Management, Council Offices, King George V Road, Amersham HP6 5AW ☎ 01494 732064 ✉ mmitchell@chiltern.gov.uk

Waste Management: Mr Mike Mitchell, Interim Head of Engineering & Contract Management, Council Offices, King George V Road, Amersham HP6 5AW ☎ 01494 732064 ✉ mmitchell@chiltern.gov.uk

MEMBERS OF THE COUNCIL (40)

***Chair:* Warder**, John (CON - Central)
jwarder@chiltern.gov.uk

***Vice-Chair:* Smith**, Linda (CON - Chalfont Common)
lsmith@chiltern.gov.uk

***Leader of the Council:* Rose**, Nicholas (CON - Cholesbury, The Lee & Bellingdon)
nrose@chiltern.gov.uk

***Deputy Leader of the Council:* Smith**, Michael (CON - Chesham Bois & Weedon Hill)
msmith@chiltern.gov.uk

***Group Leader:* Garnett**, Andrew (CON - Prestwood & Heath End)
agarnett@chiltern.gov.uk

***Group Leader:* Jones**, Peter (LD - Ballinger, South Heath & Chartridge)
peter.m.jones@btinternet.com

Appleby, Pam (LD - Amersham Common)
pappleby@chiltern.gov.uk

Bacon, Alan (LD - Asheridge Vale & Lowndes)
abacon@chiltern.gov.uk

Berry, Seb (IND - Great Missenden)
sberry@chiltern.gov.uk

Bhatti, Mohammad (CON - Newtown Chesham)
mbhatti@chiltern.gov.uk

Brown, Noel (CON - Hilltop & Townsend)
nbrown@chiltern.gov.uk

Burns-Green, Robert (CON - Little Missenden)
rburns-green@chiltern.gov.uk

Burton, Julie (CON - Holmer Green)
jburton@chiltern.gov.uk

Cunnane, Mark (CON - Prestwood & Heath End)
mcunnane@chiltern.gov.uk

Darby, Isobel (CON - Gold Hill)
idarby@chiltern.gov.uk

Garth, Andrew (CON - Ashley Green, Latimer & Chenies)
agarth@chiltern.gov.uk

Gladwin, John (CON - Prestwood & Heath End)
jgladwin@chiltern.gov.uk

Groves, Martyn (CON - Central)
mgroves@chiltern.gov.uk

Hardie, Alan (CON - Penn & Coleshill)
ahardie@chiltern.gov.uk

Harker, Mimi (CON - Chesham Bois & Weedon Hill)
mharker@chiltern.gov.uk

Harris, Graham (CON - Penn & Coleshill)
gharris@chiltern.gov.uk

Hudson, Peter (CON - St Mary's & Waterside)
phudson@chiltern.gov.uk

Lacey, Derek (IND - Ridgeway)
dlacey@chiltern.gov.uk

Martin, Peter (CON - Little Chalfont)

pmartin@chiltern.gov.uk
Meacock, David (CON - Chalfont Common)
dmeacock@chiltern.gov.uk
Patel, Siddharth (CON - Seer Green)
spatel@chiltern.gov.uk
Phillips, Don (CON - Little Chalfont)
dphillips@chiltern.gov.uk
Pirouet, Alison (LD - Vale)
apirouet@chiltern.gov.uk
Prince, Michael (CON - Holmer Green)
mprince@chiltern.gov.uk
Ryman, Jeremy (CON - Chalfont St Giles)
chiefexecs@chiltern.gov.uk
Shepherd, Nigel (CON - Amersham on the Hill)
nshepherd@chiltern.gov.uk
Spate, David (CON - Chalfont St Giles)
dspate@chiltern.gov.uk
Spruytenburg, Christopher (LD - Asheridge Vale & Lowndes)
cspruytenburg@chiltern.gov.uk
Stannard, Mike (CON - Chalfont St Giles)
mstannard@chiltern.gov.uk
Stewart, Nik (CON - St Mary's & Waterside)
nstewert@chiltern.gov.uk
Trevette, Howard (CON - Amersham Town)
htrevette@chiltern.gov.uk
Vivis, Mark (CON - Amersham on the Hill)
mvivis@chiltern.gov.uk
Wertheim, John (CON - Austenwood)
jwertheim@chiltern.gov.uk
Williams, Tony (CON - Amersham Town)
shardeloes@msn.com
Wilson, Fred (CON - Hilltop & Townsend)
fwilson@chiltern.gov.uk

POLITICAL COMPOSITION

CON: 33, LD: 5, IND: 2

CABINET

Leader: Mr Nicholas Rose
Deputy Leader: Mr Michael Smith
Community Partnerships: Mr Peter Hudson
Financial & Resource Management: Mr Mike Stannard
Health & Housing: Mrs Isobel Darby
Young People, Leisure, Community & Communications: Mrs Mimi Harker

COMMITTEE CHAIRS

Audit: Mr John Gladwin
Community & Environment (Scrutiny): Mr Alan Bacon
Housing & Planning (Scrutiny): Mrs Julie Burton
Licensing & Regulation: Mr Nigel Shepherd
Performance & Resources (Scrutiny): Mr Andrew Garnett
Personnel: Mr Nicholas Rose
Planning: Mr Don Phillips

CHORLEY D

Chorley Borough Council, Town Hall, Market Street, Chorley PR7 1DP ☎ 01257 515151 🖷 01257 515150
admin.townhall@chorley.gov.uk www.chorley.gov.uk

FACTS & FIGURES

Police Authority: Lancashire Police Authority
Health Authority: North West Strategic Health Authority
Learning and Skills Council: North West
Parliamentary Constituencies: Chorley
EU Constituencies: North West
Election Frequency: Elections are by thirds
Twinning: Sze'kesfehervar' (Hungary)

PRINCIPAL OFFICERS

Chief Executive: Mr Gary Hall, Chief Executive, Town Hall, Market Street, Chorley PR7 1DP ☎ 01257 515151 🖷 01257 515150 chief.exec@chorley.gov.uk

Senior Management: Mr Jamie Carson, Director of People & Places, Town Hall, Market Street, Chorley PR7 1DP ☎ 01257 515151 🖷 01257 515150 jamie.carson@chorley.gov.uk

Senior Management: Mrs Lesley-Ann Fenton, Director of Partnerships, Planning & Policy, Civic Offices, Union Street, Chorley PR7 1AL ☎ 01257 515151 🖷 01257 515150 lesley-ann.fenton@chorley.gov.uk

Best Value: Mrs Lesley-Ann Fenton, Director of Partnerships, Planning & Policy, Civic Offices, Union Street, Chorley PR7 1AL ☎ 01257 515151 🖷 01257 515150 lesley-ann.fenton@chorley.gov.uk

Building Control: Mr John Bethwaite, Principal Building Control Officer, Civic Offices, Union Street, Chorley PR7 1AL ☎ 01257 515151 🖷 01257 515150 john.bethwaite@chorley.gov.uk

PR / Communications: Mr Andrew Daniels, Communications Manager, Town Hall, Market Street, Chorley PR7 1DP ☎ 01257 515151 🖷 01257 515150 andrew.daniels@chorley.gov.uk

Community Planning: Mr Paul Lowe, Chorley & South Ribble Community Safety Manager, Chorley Borough Council, Bengal Street, Chorley PR7 1SA ☎ 01257 515758 🖷 01257 515619 paul.lowe@chorley.gov.uk

Community Safety: Mr Paul Lowe, Chorley & South Ribble Community Safety Manager, Chorley Borough Council, Bengal Street, Chorley PR7 1SA ☎ 01257 515758 🖷 01257 515619 paul.lowe@chorley.gov.uk

Computer Management: Ms Debbie Wilson, ICT Manager, Town Hall, Market Street, Chorley PR7 1DP ☎ 01257 515151 🖷 01251 515150 debbie.wilson@chorley.gov.uk

Customer Service: Mr Asim Khan, Head of Customer & Information Services, Civic Offices, Union Street, Chorley PR7 1AL ☎ 01257 515151 🖷 01257 515150 asim.khan@chorley.gov.uk

Economic Development: Ms Cath Burns, Head of Economic Development, Civic Offices, Union Street, Chorley PR7 1AL ☎ 01257 515151 🖷 01257 515150 cath.burns@chorley.gov.uk

E-Government: Ms Debbie Wilson, ICT Manager, Town Hall, Market Street, Chorley PR7 1DP ☎ 01257 515151 🖷 01251 515150 debbie.wilson@chorley.gov.uk

Electoral Registration: Mr Phil Davies, Principal Corporate Support Officer, Town Hall, Market Street, Chorley PR7 1DP ☎ 01257 515151 🖷 01257 515150 phil.davies@chorley.gov.uk

Emergency Planning: Mr Simon Clark, Head of Environment, Bengal Street Depot, Bengal Street, Chorley PR7 1SA ☎ 01257 515151 🖷 01257 515150 🖰 simon.clark@chorley.gov.uk

Environmental / Technical Services: Mr Jamie Carson, Director of People & Places, Bengal Street Depot, Bengal Street, Chorley PR7 1SA ☎ 01257 515151 🖷 01257 515150 🖰 jamie.carson@chorley.gov.uk

Environmental Health: Mr Simon Clark, Head of Environment, Bengal Street Depot, Bengal Street, Chorley PR7 1SA ☎ 01257 515151 🖷 01257 515150 🖰 simon.clark@chorley.gov.uk

European Liaison: Mrs Lesley-Ann Fenton, Director of Partnerships, Planning & Policy, Civic Offices, Union Street, Chorley PR7 1AL ☎ 01257 515151 🖷 01257 515150 🖰 lesley-ann.fenton@chorley.gov.uk

Events Manager: Mrs Louise Finch, Events & Marketing Manager, Town Hall, Market Street, Chorley PR7 1DP ☎ 01257 515151 🖷 01257 515150 🖰 louise.finch@chorley.gov.uk

Finance and Treasurer: Mr Gary Hall, Chief Executive, Town Hall, Market Street, Chorley PR7 1DP ☎ 01257 515151 🖷 01257 515150 🖰 chief.exec@chorley.gov.uk

Grounds Maintenance: Mr Jamie Dixon, Head of Streetscene & Leisure Contracts, Civic Offices, Union Street, Chorley PR7 1AL ☎ 01257 515151 🖷 01257 515150 🖰 jamie.dixon@chorley.gov.uk

Legal: Mr Chris Moister, Head of Governance, Town Hall, Market Street, Chorley PR7 1DP ☎ 01257 515151 🖷 01257 515150 🖰 chris.moister@chorley.gov.uk

Leisure and Cultural Services: Mr Jamie Carson, Director of People & Places, Bengal Street Depot, Bengal Street, Chorley PR7 1SA ☎ 01257 515151 🖷 01257 515150 🖰 jamie.carson@chorley.gov.uk

Licensing: Mr Jamie Carson, Director of People & Places, Bengal Street Depot, Bengal Street, Chorley PR7 1SA ☎ 01257 515151 🖷 01257 515150 🖰 jamie.carson@chorley.gov.uk

Lottery Funding, Charity and Voluntary: Ms Sarah James, Partnerships Manager, Town Hall, Market Street, Chorley PR7 1DP ☎ 01257 515151 🖷 01257 515150 🖰 sarah.james@chorley.gov.uk

Member Services: Ms Carol Russell, Head of Democratic Services, Town Hall, Market Street, Chorley PR7 1DP ☎ 01257 515151 🖷 01257 515150 🖰 carol.russell@chorley.gov.uk

Parking: Ms Nicola Banks, Business Process Officer (Parking), Town Hall, Market Street, Chorley PR7 1DP ☎ 01257 515151

Partnerships: Mr Chris Sinnott, Head of Policy & Performance, Town Hall, Market Street, Chorley PR7 1DP ☎ 01257 515151 🖷 01257 515150 🖰 chris.sinnott@chorley.gov.uk

Personnel / HR: Ms Camilla Oakes-Scofield, Head of HR & OD, Town Hall, Market Street, Chorley PR7 1DP ☎ 01257 515151 🖷 01257 515150 🖰 camilla.scofield@chorley.gov.uk

Planning: Mrs Lesley-Ann Fenton, Director of Partnerships, Planning & Policy, Civic Offices, Union Street, Chorley PR7 1AL ☎ 01257 515151 🖷 01257 515150 🖰 lesley-ann.fenton@chorley.gov.uk

Procurement: Mrs Janet Hinds, Corporate Procurement Officer & Partnership Manager, Town Hall, Market Street, Chorley PR7 1DP ☎ 01257 515151 🖷 01257 515150 🖰 janet.hinds@chorley.gov.uk

Recycling & Waste Minimisation: Mr Steve Ainscough, Senior Waste Management Officer, Bengal Street Depot, Bengal Street, Chorley PR7 1SA ☎ 01257 515151 🖷 01257 515150 🖰 steve.ainscough@chorley.gov.uk

Regeneration: Mrs Lesley-Ann Fenton, Director of Partnerships, Planning & Policy, Civic Offices, Union Street, Chorley PR7 1AL ☎ 01257 515151 🖷 01257 515150 🖰 lesley-ann.fenton@chorley.gov.uk

Staff Training: Mr Graeme Walmsley, Human Resources & Organisational Development Manager, Town Hall, Market Street, Chorley PR7 1DP ☎ 01257 515151 🖷 01257 515150 🖰 graeme.walmsley@chorley.gov.uk

Street Scene: Mr Jamie Carson, Director of People & Places, Bengal Street Depot, Bengal Street, Chorley PR17 1SA ☎ 01257 515151 🖷 01257 515150 🖰 jamie.carson@chorley.gov.uk

Sustainable Communities: Mrs Lesley-Ann Fenton, Director of Partnerships, Planning & Policy, Civic Offices, Union Street, Chorley PR7 1AL ☎ 01257 515151 🖷 01257 515150 🖰 lesley-ann.fenton@chorley.gov.uk

Sustainable Development: Mrs Lesley-Ann Fenton, Director of Partnerships, Planning & Policy, Civic Offices, Union Street, Chorley PR7 1AL ☎ 01257 515151 🖷 01257 515150 🖰 lesley-ann.fenton@chorley.gov.uk

Tourism: Mr Chris Sinnott, Head of Policy & Performance, Town Hall, Market Street, Chorley PR7 1DP ☎ 01257 515151 🖷 01257 515150 🖰 chris.sinnott@chorley.gov.uk

Town Centre: Mrs Lesley-Ann Fenton, Director of Partnerships, Planning & Policy, Civic Offices, Union Street, Chorley PR7 1AL ☎ 01257 515151 🖷 01257 515150 🖰 lesley-ann.fenton@chorley.gov.uk

Waste Collection and Disposal: Mr Steve Ainscough, Senior Waste Management Officer, Bengal Street Depot, Bengal Street, Chorley PR7 1SA ☎ 01257 515151 🖷 01257 515150 🖰 steve.ainscough@chorley.gov.uk

Waste Management: Mr Steve Ainscough, Senior Waste Management Officer, Bengal Street Depot, Bengal Street, Chorley PR7 1SA ☎ 01257 515151 🖷 01257 515150 🖰 steve.ainscough@chorley.gov.uk

MEMBERS OF THE COUNCIL (47)

***Mayor:* Molyneaux**, June (LAB - Adlington & Anderton) june.molyneaux@chorley.gov.uk

***Deputy Mayor:* Walker**, John (CON - Clayton-le-Woods &

Whittle-le-Woods)
john.walker@chorley.gov.uk
Leader of the Council: **Bradley**, Alistair (LAB - Chorley South East)
alistair.bradley@chorley.gov.uk
Deputy Leader of the Council: **Wilson**, Peter (LAB - Adlington & Anderton)
peter.wilson@chorley.gov.uk
Group Leader: **Goldsworthy**, Peter (CON - Euxton South)
peter.goldsworthy@chorley.gov.uk
Group Leader: **Snape**, Ralph (IND - Chorley North West)
ralph.snape@chorley.gov.uk
Ball, Kenneth (LD - Coppull)
kenneth.ball@chorley.gov.uk
Bell, Eric (CON - Clayton-le-Woods & Whittle-le-Woods)
eric.bell@chorley.gov.uk
Berry, Julia (LAB - Chorley East)
julia.berry@chorley.gov.uk
Brown, Terence (LAB - Chorley East)
terence.brown@chorley.gov.uk
Caunce, Henry (CON - Eccleston & Mawdesley)
henry.caunce@chorley.gov.uk
Cronshaw, Jean (LAB - Clayton-le-Woods North)
Crow, Matthew (LAB - Coppull)
Cullens, Magda (CON - Clayton-le-Woods North)
magda.cullens@chorley.gov.uk
Dalton, John (CON - Lostock)
john.dalton@chorley.gov.uk
Dickinson, Doreen (CON - Lostock)
doreen.dickinson@chorley.gov.uk
Dickinson, David (CON - Brindle & Hoghton)
david.dickinson@chorley.gov.uk
Dunn, Graham (LAB - Adlington & Anderton)
graham.dunn@chorley.gov.uk
Edgerley, Dennis (LAB - Chorley North East)
dennis.edgerley@chorley.gov.uk
Finnamore, Robert (LAB - Coppull)
robert.finnamore@chorley.gov.uk
France, Christopher (LAB - Wheelton & Withnell)
chris.france@chorley.gov.uk
Gee, Anthony (LAB - Chorley South West)
anthony.gee@chorley.gov.uk
Gee, Danny (LAB - Euxton North)
danny.gee@chorley.gov.uk
Gray, Marie (CON - Pennine)
marie.gray@chorley.gov.uk
Hansford, Alison (CON - Wheelton & Withnell)
alison.hansford@chorley.gov.uk
Heaton, Harold (CON - Chisnell)
harold.heaton@chorley.gov.uk
Holgate, Steve (LAB - Chorley South West)
Iddon, Keith (CON - Eccleston & Mawdesley)
keith.iddon@chorley.gov.uk
Joyce, Kevin (CON - Eccleston & Mawdesley)
kevin.joyce@chorley.gov.uk
Khan, Hasina (LAB - Chorley East)
hasina.khan@chorley.gov.uk
Leadbetter, Paul (CON - Chisnell)
paul.leadbetter@chorley.gov.uk
Lees, Roy (LAB - Chorley South West)
roy.lees@chorley.gov.uk
Lowe, Marion (LAB - Chorley North East)
marion.lowe@chorley.gov.uk
Lowe, Adrian (LAB - Chorley North East)
adrian.lowe@chorley.gov.uk
Morgan, Greg (CON - Clayton-le-Woods & Whittle-le-Woods)
greg.morgan@chorley.gov.uk
Muncaster, Michael (CON - Clayton-le-Woods West & Cuerden)
mick.muncaster@chorley.gov.uk
Murfitt, Steve (LAB - Clayton-le-Woods North)
smurfitt01@gmail.com
Murray, Beverley (LAB - Chorley South East)
beverley.murray@chorley.gov.uk
Perks, Mark (CON - Astley & Buckshaw)
mark.perks@chorley.gov.uk
Phipps, Pauline (LAB - Chorley North West)
pauline.phipps@chorley.gov.uk
Platt, Alan (CON - Astley & Buckshaw)
alan.platt@chorley.gov.uk
Rogerson, Dave (LAB - Clayton-le-Woods West & Cuerden)
dave.rogerson@chorley.gov.uk
Russell, Geoffrey (CON - Euxton South)
geoffrey.russell@chorley.gov.uk
Russell, Rosemary (CON - Euxton North)
rosemary.russell@chorley.gov.uk
Snape, Joyce (IND - Chorley North West)
joyce.snape@chorley.gov.uk
Snape, Kim (LAB - Heath Charnock & Rivington)
kim.snape@chorley.gov.uk
Walmsley, Paul (LAB - Chorley South East)
paul.walmsley@chorley.gov.uk

POLITICAL COMPOSITION

LAB: 24, CON: 20, IND: 2, LD: 1

CABINET

Leader / Economic Development & Governance: Mr Alistair Bradley
Deputy Leader / Resources, Policy & Performance: Mr Paul Walmsley
Homes & Businesses: Mr Adrian Lowe
LDF & Planning: Mr Dennis Edgerley
People: Ms Beverley Murray
Places: Mr Terence Brown

COMMITTEE CHAIRS

Community Governance: Mr Peter Goldsworthy
Development Control: Mr Paul Walmsley
General Purposes: Ms Julia Berry
Governance: Mr Paul Leadbetter
Licensing & Public Safety: Mrs Marion Lowe
Overview & Scrutiny: Mr Steve Holgate

CHRISTCHURCH D

Christchurch Borough Council, Civic Offices, Bridge Street, Christchurch BH23 1AZ ☎ 01202 495000 🖷 01202 495234
post@christchurch.gov.uk 💻 www.dorsetforyou.com

FACTS & FIGURES

Police Authority: Dorset Police Authority
Health Authority: NHS South West
Learning and Skills Council: South West
Parliamentary Constituencies: Christchurch County
EU Constituencies: South West
Election Frequency: Elections are of whole council
Twinning: Aalen (Germany); Christchurch (New Zealand); Saint Lo (France); Tatabanya (Hungary)

PRINCIPAL OFFICERS

Chief Executive: Mr David McIntosh, Chief Executive, Civic Offices, Bridge Street, Christchurch BH23 1AZ ☎ 01202 886201 🖷 01202 639030; 01202 495001 ✉ dmcintosh@christchurchandeastdorset.gov.uk

Senior Management: Mr David Barnes, Strategic Director, Civic Offices, Bridge Street, Christchurch BH23 1AZ ☎ 01202 495077 🖷 01202 495107 ✉ dbarnes@christchurchandeastdorset.gov.uk

Senior Management: Mr Neil Farmer, Strategic Director, Civic Offices, Bridge Street, Christchurch BH23 1AZ ☎ 01202 886201; 01202 495979 🖷 01202 639030; 01202 495107 ✉ nfarmer@christchurchandeastdorset.gov.uk

Architect, Building / Property Services: Mr Ashley Harman, Property & Engineering Services Manager, Civic Offices, Bridge Street, Christchurch BH23 1AZ ☎ 01202 495076 🖷 01202 495108 ✉ aharman@christchurchandeastdorset.gov.uk

Best Value: Mr David Barnes, Strategic Director, Civic Offices, Bridge Street, Christchurch BH23 1AZ ☎ 01202 495077 🖷 01202 495107 ✉ dbarnes@christchurchandeastdorset.gov.uk

Building Control: Mr Martin Thompson, Building Control Manager, Civic Offices, Bridge Street, Christchurch BH23 1AZ ☎ 01202 495033 🖷 01202 495105 ✉ mthompson@christchurchandeastdorset.gov.uk

Children / Youth Services: Ms Judith Plumley, Head - Community & Economy, Civic Offices, Bridge Street, Christchurch BH23 1AZ ☎ 01202 886201; 01202 495043 🖷 01202 639030; 01202 495108 ✉ nfarmer@christchurchandeastdorset.gov.uk; jplumpley@christchurchandeastdorset.gov.uk

PR / Communications: Mr Allan Wood, Public Relations Officer, Civic Offices, Bridge Street, Christchurch BH23 1AZ ☎ 01202 495133 🖷 01202 495107 ✉ awood@christchurchandeastdorset.gov.uk

Community Planning: Ms Judith Plumley, Head - Community & Economy, Civic Offices, Bridge Street, Christchurch BH23 1AZ ☎ 01202 886201; 01202 495043 🖷 01202 639030; 01202 495108 ✉ jplumpley@christchurchandeastdorset.gov.uk

Community Planning: Mr Simon Trueick, Community & Planning Policy Manager, Civic Offices, Bridge Street, Christchurch BH23 1AZ ☎ 01202 495038 🖷 01202 495107 ✉ strueick@christchurchandeastdorset.gov.uk

Community Safety: Ms Judith Plumley, Head - Community & Economy, Civic Offices, Bridge Street, Christchurch BH23 1AZ ☎ 01202 886201; 01202 495043 🖷 01202 639030; 01202 495108 ✉ jplumpley@christchurchandeastdorset.gov.uk

Computer Management: Mr Paul Downton, Manager - IT & Information, Civic Offices, Bridge Street, Christchurch BH23 1AZ ☎ 01202 495137 🖷 01202 495107 ✉ pdownton@christchurchandeastdorset.gov.uk

Computer Management: Mr Ian Milner, Head - Finance, Civic Offices, Bridge Street, Christchurch BH23 1AZ ☎ 01202 495176 🖷 01202 482200 ✉ imilner@christchurchandeastdorset.gov.uk

Customer Service: Mr Sean Hawkins, Customer Services Manager, Civic Offices, Bridge Street, Christchurch BH23 1AZ ☎ 01202 495153 🖷 01202 495234 ✉ shawkins@christchurchandeastdorset.gov.uk

Economic Development: Mr Paul Riley, Economic Development Manager, Civic Offices, Bridge Street, Christchurch BH23 1AZ ☎ 01202 495007 🖷 01202 495107 ✉ priley@christchurchandeastdorset.gov.uk

E-Government: Mr David Barnes, Strategic Director, Civic Offices, Bridge Street, Christchurch BH23 1AZ ☎ 01202 495077 🖷 01202 495107 ✉ dbarnes@christchurchandeastdorset.gov.uk

E-Government: Mr Paul Downton, Manager - IT & Information, Civic Offices, Bridge Street, Christchurch BH23 1AZ ☎ 01202 495137 🖷 01202 495107 ✉ pdownton@christchurchandeastdorset.gov.uk

Electoral Registration: Ms Claire Procter, Elections, Licensing & Insurance Manager, Civic Offices, Bridge Street, Christchurch BH23 1AZ ☎ 01202 495119 🖷 01202 495107 ✉ cprocter@christchurchandeastdorset.gov.uk

Emergency Planning: Mr Gary Foyle, Senior Recreation Services Officer, Civic Offices, Bridge Street, Christchurch BH23 1AZ ☎ 01202 495070 🖷 01202 495110 ✉ gfoyle@christchurchandeastdorset.gov.uk

Energy Management: Ms Rachel Sharpe, Sustainability Management Officer, Civic Offices, Bridge Street, Christchurch BH23 1AZ ☎ 01202 495047 🖷 01202 495108 ✉ rsharpe@christchurchandeastdorset.gov.uk

Environmental / Technical Services: Mr Lindsay Cass, Head - Environmental Services, Civic Offices, Bridge Street, Christchurch BH23 1AZ ☎ 01202 886201; 01202 495003 🖷 01202 639030; 01202 495110 ✉ lcass@christchurchandeastdorset.gov.uk; lcass@christchurchandeastdorset.gov.uk

Environmental Health: Mr Steve Duckett, Head - Planning & Health, Civic Offices, Bridge Street, Christchurch BH23 1AZ ☎ 01202 886201; 01202 495987 🖷 01202 639029; 01202 495108 ✉ sduckett@christchurchandeastdorset.gov.uk

Estates, Property & Valuation: Mr Philip Marston, Estates Officer, Civic Offices, Bridge Street, Christchurch BH23 1AZ ☎ 01202 495187 🖷 01202 495108 ✉ pmarston@christchurchandeastdorset.gov.uk

European Liaison: Mr Paul Riley, Economic Development Manager, Civic Offices, Bridge Street, Christchurch BH23 1AZ ☎ 01202 495007 🖷 01202 495107 ✉ priley@christchurchandeastdorset.gov.uk

Events Manager: Mrs Ann Simon, Tourism Manager, Civic Offices, Bridge Street, Christchurch BH23 1AZ ☎ 01202 495127 🖷 01202 495107 ✉ asimon@christchurchandeastdorset.gov.uk

Facilities: Mr Sean Hawkins, Customer Services Manager, Civic Offices, Bridge Street, Christchurch BH23 1AZ ☎ 01202 495153 🖷 01202 495234 ✉ shawkins@christchurchandeastdorset.gov.uk

Finance and Treasurer: Mr Ian Milner, Head - Finance, Civic Offices, Bridge Street, Christchurch BH23 1AZ ☎ 01202 495176 🖷 01202 482200 ✉ imilner@christchurchandeastdorset.gov.uk

Fleet Management: Mr Lindsay Cass, Head - Environmental Services, Civic Offices, Bridge Street, Christchurch BH23 1AZ ☎ 01202 886201; 01202 495003 🖷 01202 639030; 01202 495110 ✉ lcass@christchurchandeastdorset.gov.uk

Grounds Maintenance: Mr Clive Sinden, Countryside & Open Spaces Manager, Civic Offices, Bridge Street, Christchurch BH23 1AZ ☎ 01202 495072 🖷 01202 495110 ✉ csinden@christchurchandeastdorset.gov.uk

Health and Safety: Ms Pauline Miller-McIlravey, Health & Safety Officer, Civic Offices, Bridge Street, Christchurch BH23 1AZ ☎ 01202 495198 ✉ pmiller-mcilraey@christchurchandeastdorset.gov.uk

Home Energy Conservation: Mr Steve Duckett, Head - Planning & Health, Civic Offices, Bridge Street, Christchurch BH23 1AZ ☎ 01202 886201; 01202 495987 🖷 01202 639029; 01202 495108 ✉ sduckett@christchurchandeastdorset.gov.uk

Housing: Ms Kathryn Blatchford, Manager - Stategic Housing Services, Civic Offices, Bridge Street, Christchurch BH23 1AZ ☎ 01202 495155 ✉ kblatchford@christchurchandeastdorset.gov.uk

Legal: Mr Keith Mallett, Head - Legal & Democratic Services, Civic Offices, Bridge Street, Christchurch BH23 1AZ ☎. 01202 886201 🖷 01202 841734 ✉ kmallett@eastdorset.gov.uk; kmallett@christchurchandeastdorset.gov.uk

Leisure and Cultural Services: Mr Matti Raudsepp, Head - Leisure & Open Spaces, Civic Offices, Bridge Street, Christchurch BH23 1AZ ☎ 01202 886201; 01202 495000 🖷 01202 639030 ✉ nfarmer@christchurchandeastdorset.gov.uk; mraudsepp@christchurchandeastdorset.gov.uk

Licensing: Ms Claire Procter, Elections, Licensing & Insurance Manager, Civic Offices, Bridge Street, Christchurch BH23 1AZ ☎ 01202 495119 🖷 01202 495107 ✉ cprocter@christchurchandeastdorset.gov.uk

Lottery Funding, Charity and Voluntary: Mr Paul Riley, Economic Development Manager, Civic Offices, Bridge Street, Christchurch BH23 1AZ ☎ 01202 495007 🖷 01202 495107 ✉ priley@christchurchandeastdorset.gov.uk

Member Services: Mrs Mary Parsa, Democratic Services Manager, Civic Offices, Bridge Street, Christchurch BH23 1AZ ☎ 01202 495050 🖷 01202 495107 ✉ mparsa@christchurchandeastdorset.gov.uk

Parking: Mr Ashley Harman, Property & Engineering Services Manager, Civic Offices, Bridge Street, Christchurch BH23 1AZ ☎ 01202 495076 🖷 01202 495108 ✉ aharman@christchurchandeastdorset.gov.uk

Partnerships: Ms Judith Plumley, Head - Community & Economy, Civic Offices, Bridge Street, Christchurch BH23 1AZ ☎ 01202 886201; 01202 495043 🖷 01202 639030; 01202 495108 ✉ nfarmer@christchurchandeastdorset.gov.uk

Personnel / HR: Mr Mike Harford, Personnel Manager, Civic Offices, Bridge Street, Christchurch BH23 1AZ ☎ 01202 495129 ✉ mharford@christchurchandeastdorset.gov.uk

Planning: Mr Steve Duckett, Head - Planning & Health, Civic Offices, Bridge Street, Christchurch BH23 1AZ ☎ 01202 886201; 01202 495987 🖷 01202 639029; 01202 495108 ✉ sduckett@christchurchandeastdorset.gov.uk

Procurement: Mrs Julia Nobes, Head of Finance, Civic Offices, Bridge Street, Christchurch BH23 1AZ ☎ 01202 495176 🖷 01202 482200 ✉ j.nobes@christchurchandeastdorset.gov.uk

Recycling & Waste Minimisation: Mr Lindsay Cass, Head - Environmental Services, Civic Offices, Bridge Street, Christchurch BH23 1AZ ☎ 01202 886201; 01202 495003 🖷 01202 639030; 01202 495110 ✉ lcass@christchurchandeastdorset.gov.uk

Regeneration: Mr Neil Farmer, Strategic Director, Civic Offices, Bridge Street, Christchurch BH23 1AZ ☎ 01202 886201; 01202 495979 🖷 01202 639030; 01202 495107 ✉ nfarmer@christchurchandeastdorset.gov.uk

Staff Training: Mr Mike Harford, Personnel Manager, Civic Offices, Bridge Street, Christchurch BH23 1AZ ☎ 01202 495129 ✉ mharford@christchurchandeastdorset.gov.uk

Sustainable Communities: Ms Rachel Sharpe, Sustainability Management Officer, Civic Offices, Bridge Street, Christchurch BH23 1AZ ☎ 01202 495047 🖷 01202 495108 ✉ rsharpe@christchurchandeastdorset.gov.uk

Sustainable Development: Ms Judith Plumley, Head - Community & Economy, Civic Offices, Bridge Street, Christchurch BH23 1AZ ☎ 01202 886201; 01202 495043 🖷 01202 639030; 01202 495108 ✉ jplumpley@christchurchandeastdorset.gov.uk

Tourism: Mrs Ann Simon, Tourism Manager, Civic Offices, Bridge Street, Christchurch BH23 1AZ ☎ 01202 495127 🖷 01202 495107 ✉ asimon@christchurchandeastdorset.gov.uk

Town Centre: Mr Paul Riley, Economic Development Manager, Civic Offices, Bridge Street, Christchurch BH23 1AZ ☎ 01202 495007 🖷 01202 495107 ✉ priley@christchurchandeastdorset.gov.uk

Waste Collection and Disposal: Mr Lindsay Cass, Head - Environmental Services, Civic Offices, Bridge Street, Christchurch BH23 1AZ ☎ 01202 886201; 01202 495003 🖷 01202 639030; 01202 495110 ✉ lcass@christchurchandeastdorset.gov.uk

Waste Management: Mr Lindsay Cass, Head - Environmental Services, Civic Offices, Bridge Street, Christchurch BH23 1AZ ☎ 01202 886201; 01202 495003 🖷 01202 639030; 01202 495110 ✉ lcass@christchurchandeastdorset.gov.uk

MEMBERS OF THE COUNCIL (24)

***Deputy Mayor:* Lofts**, John (CON - Highcliffe)
cllr.jlofts@christchurch.gov.uk

***Leader of the Council:* Nottage**, Ray (CON - Purewell & Stanpit)
cllr.rnottage@christchurch.gov.uk

***Deputy Leader of the Council:* Jamieson**, Colin (CON - Burton & Winkton)
cllr.cjamieson@christchurch.gov.uk

Bath, Claire (CON - Mudeford & Friars Cliff)
cllr.cbath@christchurch.gov.uk

Bungey, Colin (IND - Jumpers)
cllr.cbungey@christchurch.gov.uk

Davis, Bernie (CON - Purewell & Stanpit)
cllr.bdavis@christchurch.gov.uk

Dedman, Lesley (CON - West Highcliffe)
cllr.ldedman@christchurch.gov.uk

Derham Wilkes, Sally (CON - North Highcliffe & Walkford)
cllr.sderhamwilkes@christchurch.gov.uk

Duckworth, Michael (CON - Mudeford & Friars Cliff)
cllr.mduckworth@christchurch.gov.uk

Flagg, David (CON - Burton & Winkton)
cllr.dflagg@christchurch.gov.uk

Fox, Travis (CON - St Catherine's and Hurn)
cllr.tfox@christchurch.gov.uk

Geary, Gillian (CON - Town Centre)
Cllr.ggeary@christchurch.gov.uk

Geary, Nick (CON - North Highcliffe & Walkford)
cllr.ngeary@christchurch.gov.uk

Hall, Peter (LD - Town Centre)
cllr.phall@christchurch.gov.uk

Hilliard, Paul (CON - Grange)
cllr.philliard@christchurch.gov.uk

Jamieson, Patricia (CON - West Highcliffe)
cllr.pjamieson@christchurch.gov.uk

Jones, Denise (CON - Grange)
cllr.denisejones@christchurch.gov.uk

Jones, David (CON - West Highcliffe)
cllr.djones@christchurch.gov.uk

Mawbey, Myra (CON - Highcliffe)
cllr.mmawbey@christchurch.gov.uk

Neale, Frederick (IND - Jumpers)
cllr.fneale@christchurch.gov.uk

Phipps, Margaret (CON - Portfield)
cllr.mphipps@christchurch.gov.uk

Smith, Lisle (CON - Portfield)
cllr.lsmith@christchurch.gov.uk

Spittle, Susan (CON - St. Catherine's & Hurn)
cllr.sspittle@christchurch.gov.uk

Watts, Trevor (CON - Mudeford & Friars Cliff)
cllr.trwatts@christchurch.gov.uk

POLITICAL COMPOSITION

CON: 21, IND: 2, LD: 1

CABINET

Leader: Mr Ray Nottage
Deputy Leader: Mr Colin Jamieson
Community: Mr Bernie Davis
Economy: Mr Trevor Watts
Housing: Mrs Susan Spittle
Performance: Mr Michael Duckworth

COMMITTEE CHAIRS

Community Services: Mrs Sally Derham Wilkes
Licensing: Mr David Flagg
Planning: Mr Colin Jamieson
Resources: Mr Ray Nottage

CITY OF LONDON — L

City of London, PO Box 270, Guildhall, London EC2P 2EJ
☎ 020 7332 1400; 020 7606 3030 🖷 020 7796 2621; 020 7332 1119 ✉ pro@cityoflondon.gov.uk 💻 www.cityoflondon.gov.uk

FACTS & FIGURES

Police Authority: City of London Police Authority
Health Authority: NHS London
Learning and Skills Council: London
Parliamentary Constituencies: Cities of London and Westminster
EU Constituencies: London
Election Frequency: Common Councilmen- 4 years, Aldermen- 6 years

PRINCIPAL OFFICERS

Chief Executive: Mr Chris Duffield, Town Clerk & Chief Executive, PO Box 270, Guildhall, London EC2P 2EJ ☎ 020 7332 1400 🖷 020 7796 2621 ✉ townclerk@cityoflondon.gov.uk

Deputy Chief Executive: Ms Susan Attard, Deputy Town Clerk, PO Box 270, Guildhall, London EC2P 2EJ ☎ 020 7332 3724 🖷 020 7796 2621 ✉ susan.attard@cityoflondon.gov.uk

Assistant Chief Executive: Mr Peter Lisley, Assistant Town Clerk, PO Box 270, Guildhall, London EC2P 2EJ ☎ 020 7332 1438 🖷 020 7796 2621 ✉ peter.lisley@cityoflondon.gov.uk

Assistant Chief Executive: Mr Simon Murrells, Assistant Town Clerk, PO Box 270, Guildhall, London EC2P 2EJ ☎ 020 7332 1418 🖷 020 7796 2621 ✉ simon.murrells@cityoflondon.gov.uk

Assistant Chief Executive: Mr Peter Nelson, Assistant Town Clerk, PO Box 270, Guildhall, London EC2P 2EJ ☎ 020 7332 1413 🖷 020 7796 2621 ✉ peter.nelson@cityoflondon.gov.uk

Senior Management: Ms Laura Davison, Research Manager, PO Box 270, Guildhall, London EC2P 2EJ ☎ 020 7332 3610 ✉ laura.davison@cityoflondon.gov.uk

Senior Management: Mr Philip Everett, Director of Environmental Services, Walbrook Wharf, 79-83 Upper Thames Street, London EC4R 4TD ☎ 020 7332 1600 🖷 020 7332 3177 ✉ philip.everett@cityoflondon.gov.uk

Senior Management: Mr Bill Limond, Information Systems Director, 65 Basinghall Street, London EC2V 5DZ ☎ 020 7332 1307 🖷 020 7332 3110 ✉ bill.limond@cityoflondon.gov.uk

Senior Management: Mr Paul Sizeland, Director of Economic Development, PO Box 270, Guildhall, London EC2P 2EJ ☎ 020 7332 3600 🖷 020 7332 3616 ✉ paul.sizeland@cityoflondon.gov.uk

Senior Management: Ms Liz Skelcher, Assistant Director: Performance, Partnerships & Corporate Responibility, PO Box

270, Guildhall, London EC2P 2EJ ☎ 020 7332 3606 ⌂ liz.skelcher@cityoflondon.gov.uk

Access Officer / Social Services (Disability): Mr Rob Oakley, Head of Access Team, PO Box 270, Guildhall, London EC2P 2EJ ☎ 020 7332 3795 ⌂ rob.oakley@cityoflondon.gov.uk

Architect, Building / Property Services: Mr Peter Bennett, City Surveyor, PO Box 270, Guildhall, London EC2P 2EJ ☎ 020 7332 1502 🖷 020 7332 3031 ⌂ peter.bennett@cityoflondon.gov.uk

Best Value: Mr Neil Davies, Head of Corporate Performance & Development, PO Box 270, Guildhall, London EC2P 2EJ ☎ 020 7332 3327 🖷 020 7796 2621 ⌂ neil.davies@cityoflondon.gov.uk

Building Control: Mr David Clements, District Surveyor, PO Box 270, Guildhall, London EC2P 2EJ ☎ 020 7332 1949 ⌂ david.clements@cityoflondon.gov.uk

Catering Services: Ms Helen McCarthy, Home Care Manager, Community and Children's Services Department, PO Box 270, Guildhall, London EC2P 2EJ ☎ 020 7332 1899 ⌂ helen.mccarthy@cityoflondon.gov.uk

Children / Youth Services: Ms Gillian Humble, Family & Young People's Services Director, PO Box 270, Guildhall, London EC2P 2EJ ☎ 020 7332 1465 ⌂ gillian.humble@cityoflondon.gov.uk

Civil Registration: Mr Ian Hussein, Director of Cemetery & Crematorium, PO Box 270, Guildhall, London EC2P 2EJ ☎ 020 8530 9835 ⌂ ian.hussein@cityoflondon.gov.uk

Civil Registration: Ms Andrea Streete, Registrar, St Bartholomew's Hospital, Pathology Block, Room 37, London EC1A 7BE ☎ 020 7600 4977 ⌂ andrea.streete@cityoflondon.gov.uk

PR / Communications: Mr Tony Halmos, Director of Public Relations, PO Box 270, Guildhall, London EC2P 2EJ ☎ 020 7332 1450 ⌂ tony.halmos@cityoflondon.gov.uk

Community Planning: Mr Alan Hughes, Policy & Governance Officer, PO Box 270, Guildhall, London EC2P 2EJ ☎ 020 7332 1411 🖷 020 7796 2621 ⌂ alan.hughes@cityoflondon.gov.uk

Computer Management: Mr Bill Limond, Information Systems Director, 65 Basinghall Street, London EC2V 5DZ ☎ 020 7332 1307 🖷 020 7332 3110 ⌂ bill.limond@cityoflondon.gov.uk

Contracts: Mr Richard Jeffrey, Chief Legal Assistant, PO Box 270, Guildhall, London EC2P 2EJ ☎ 020 7332 1683 ⌂ richard.jeffrey@cityoflondon.gov.uk

Customer Service: Ms Jill Bailey, Access to Services Programme Manager, PO Box 270, Guildhall, London EC2P 2EJ ☎ 020 7332 3422 ⌂ jill.bailey@cityoflondon.gov.uk

Economic Development: Mr Paul Sizeland, Director of Economic Development, PO Box 270, Guildhall, London EC2P 2EJ ☎ 020 7332 3600 🖷 020 7332 3616 ⌂ paul.sizeland@cityoflondon.gov.uk

Energy Management: Mr Paul Kennedy, Corporate Energy Manager, City Surveyor's Department, PO Box 270, Guildhall, London EC2P 2EJ ☎ 020 7332 1130 🖷 020 7332 3031 ⌂ paul.kennedy@cityoflondon.gov.uk

European Liaison: Ms Audrey Nelson, Senior European Officer, PO Box 270, Guildhall, London EC2P 2EJ ☎ 020 7332 1054 🖷 020 7332 3616 ⌂ audrey.nelson@cityoflondon.gov.uk

Events Manager: Ms Fiona Hoban, Assistant Remembrancer (Ceremonial), PO Box 270, Guildhall, London EC2P 2EJ ☎ 020 7332 1261 ⌂ fiona.hoban@cityoflondon.gov.uk

Facilities: Ms Janet Woodvine, Guildhall Facilities Manager, PO Box 270, Guildhall, London EC2P 2EJ ☎ 020 7606 1157

Finance and Treasurer: Mr Chris Bilsland, Chamberlain, PO Box 270, Guildhall, London EC2P 2EJ ☎ 020 7332 1300 🖷 020 7332 1535 ⌂ chamberlain@cityoflondon.gov.uk

Finance and Treasurer: Mrs Carla-Maria Heath, Head of Revenues, PO Box 270, Guildhall, London EC2P 2EJ ☎ 020 7332 1387 ⌂ carla-maria.heath@cityoflondon.gov.uk

Fleet Management: Mr Douglas Wilkinson, Cleansing Services Assistant Director, Walbrook Wharf, Upper Thames Street, London EC4R 3TD ☎ 020 7332 4998 🖷 020 7236 6560 ⌂ douglas.wilkinson@cityoflondon.gov.uk

Grounds Maintenance: Mr Ian Hussein, Director of Cemetery & Crematorium, PO Box 270, Guildhall, London EC2P 2EJ ☎ 020 8530 9835 ⌂ ian.hussein@cityoflondon.gov.uk

Grounds Maintenance: Mr Martin Rodman, Superintendant of West Ham Park & City Gardens, PO Box 270, Guildhall, London EC2P 2EJ ☎ 020 7374 4152 🖷 020 7374 4116 ⌂ martin.rodman@cityoflondon.gov.uk

Health and Safety: Mr Shahnaz Keane, Corporate Health & Safety Officer, PO Box 270, Guildhall, London EC2P 2EJ ☎ 020 7332 1347 🖷 020 7332 3031 ⌂ shahnaz.keane@cityoflondon.gov.uk

Highways: Mr Paul Levett, Senior Engineer, PO Box 270, Guildhall, London EC2P 2EJ ☎ 020 7332 1544 🖷 020 7332 3531 ⌂ paul.levett@cityoflondon.gov.uk

Highways: Mr Steve Presland, Transportation & Public Realm Director, PO Box 270, Guildhall, London EC2P 2EJ ☎ 020 7332 4999 ⌂ steve.presland@cityoflondon.gov.uk

Housing: Mr Stewart Crook, Area Housing Manager, PO Box 270, Guildhall, London EC2P 2EJ ☎ 020 7332 3005 🖷 020 7332 1642 ⌂ stewart.crook@cityoflondon.gov.uk

Housing: Mr Peter Snowdon, Projects Director, PO Box 270, Guildhall, London EC2P 2EJ ☎ 020 7332 1802 ⌂ peter.snowdon@cityoflondon.gov.uk

Housing Maintenance: Mr Edwin Stevens, Housing & Technical Services Director, 3 Lauderdale Place, Barbican, London EC2Y 8EN ☎ 020 7332 3015 ⌂ edwin.stevens@cityoflondon.gov.uk

LOCAL AUTHORITIES

Local Area Agreement: Mr Alan Hughes, Policy & Governance Officer, PO Box 270, Guildhall, London EC2P 2EJ ☎ 020 7332 1411 🖷 020 7796 2621 ✉ alan.hughes@cityoflondon.gov.uk

Legal: Mr Michael Cogher, Comptroller & City Solicitor, PO Box 270, Guildhall, London EC2P 2EJ ☎ 020 7332 3699 🖷 020 7332 1992 ✉ michael.cogher@cityoflondon.gov.uk

Leisure and Cultural Services: Mrs Sue Ireland, Director of Open Spaces, City of London Open Space Department, 1 Guildhall Yard, London EC2V 5AE ☎ 020 7332 3033 🖷 020 7332 3522 ✉ sue.ireland@cityoflondon.gov.uk

Leisure and Cultural Services: Sir Nicholas Kenyon, Managing Director of the Barbican Centre, Barbican Centre, Silk Street, London EC2Y 8DS ☎ 020 7382 7001 🖷 020 7382 7245 ✉ nkenyon@barbican.org.uk

Leisure and Cultural Services: Mr David Pearson, Director of Culture, Heritage & Libraries, PO Box 270, Guildhall, London EC2P 2EJ ☎ 020 7606 1850 ✉ david.pearson@cityoflondon.gov.uk

Licensing: Mr Bryn Aldridge, Port Health & Veterinary Services Director, Walbrook Wharf, Upper Thames Street, London EC4R 3TD ☎ 020 7332 3405 ✉ bryn.aldridge@cityoflondon.gov.uk

Lifelong Learning: Ms Susan Lacey, Learning & Development Manager, PO Box 270, Guildhall, London EC2P 2EJ ☎ 020 7606 3289 ✉ susan.lacey@cityoflondon.gov.uk

Lighting: Mr John Burke, Mechanical & Electrical Services Manager, PO Box 270, Guildhall, London EC2P 2EJ ☎ 020 7332 1102 ✉ john.burke@cityoflondon.gov.uk

Lottery Funding, Charity and Voluntary: Ms Clare Thomas, Chief Grants Officer, The City Bridge Trust Fund, PO Box 270, Guildhall, London EC2P 2EJ ☎ 020 7332 3713 🖷 020 7332 2621 ✉ clare.thomas@cityoflondon.gov.uk

Parking: Mr Ian Hughes, Assistant Highways Director, PO Box 270, Guildhall, London EC2P 2EJ ☎ 020 7332 1977 ✉ ian.hughes@cityoflondon.gov.uk

Personnel / HR: Ms Chrissie Morgan, Director of Human Resources, PO Box 270, Guildhall, London EC2P 2EJ ☎ 020 7332 1424 ✉ chrissie.morgan@cityoflondon.gov.uk

Planning: Mr Peter Rees, City Planning Officer, PO Box 270, Guildhall, London EC2P 2EJ ☎ 020 7332 1700 🖷 020 7332 1806 ✉ peterwynne.rees@cityoflondon.gov.uk

Procurement: Mr Gary Dowding, Head of Strategic Procurement, PO Box 270, Guildhall, London EC2P 2EJ ☎ 020 7332 1180 🖷 020 7332 1535 ✉ gary.dowding@cityoflondon.gov.uk

Public Libraries: Mr David Pearson, Director of Culture, Heritage & Libraries, PO Box 270, Guildhall, London EC2P 2EJ ☎ 020 7606 1850 ✉ david.pearson@cityoflondon.gov.uk

Road Safety: Mr Matthew Collins, Road Safety Team Leader, PO Box 270, Guildhall, London EC2P 2EJ ☎ 020 7332 1546 🖷 020 7332 1806 ✉ matthew.collins@cityoflondon.gov.uk

Social Services (Adult): Mr Dave Mason, Interim Head of Adult Social Care, North Wing 2nd Floor, PO Box 270, Guildhall, London EC2P 2EJ ☎ 020 7332 1636 ✉ dave.mason@cityoflondon.gov.uk

Social Services (Children): Ms Joy Hollister, Director of Community & Children's Services, PO Box 270, Guildhall, London EC2P 2EJ ☎ 020 7332 1650 ✉ joy.hollister@cityoflondon.gov.uk

Street Scene: Mr Victor Callister, Assistant Director (Department of the Built Environment), PO Box 270, Guildhall, London EC2P 2EJ ☎ 020 7332 3468 ✉ victor.callister@cityoflondon.gov.uk

Street Scene: Mr Steve Presland, Transportation & Public Realm Director, PO Box 270, Guildhall, London EC2P 2EJ ☎ 020 7332 4999 ✉ steve.presland@cityoflondon.gov.uk

Sustainable Communities: Mr Neal Hounsell, Strategy & Performance Director, Department of Community and Children's Services, PO Box 270, Guildhall, London EC2P 2EJ ☎ 020 7332 1638 ✉ neal.hounsell@cityoflondon.gov.uk

Traffic Management: Mr Iain Simmons, Assitant Director (Local Transportation), PO Box 270, Guildhall, London EC2P 2EJ ☎ 020 7332 1151 🖷 020 7332 1806 ✉ iain.simmons@cityoflondon.gov.uk

Waste Collection and Disposal: Mr Jim Graham, Assistant Director of Operations/Cleansing, Walbrook Wharf, Upper Thames Street, London EC4R 3TD ☎ 020 7332 4972 🖷 020 7236 6560 ✉ jim.graham@cityoflondon.gov.uk

Waste Collection and Disposal: Mr Steve Presland, Transportation & Public Realm Director, PO Box 270, Guildhall, London EC2P 2EJ ☎ 020 7332 4999 ✉ steve.presland@cityoflondon.gov.uk

Waste Management: Mr Lee Turner, Senior Waste Disposal Officer, Walbrook Wharf, Upper Thames Street, London EC4R 3TD ☎ 020 7332 4976 🖷 020 7236 6560 ✉ lee.turner@cityoflondon.gov.uk

MEMBERS OF THE COUNCIL (124)

***The Lord Mayor:* Wootton**, David (NP - Langbourn)
david.wootton@cityoflondon.gov.uk

***Alderman:* Anstee**, Nick (NP - Aldersgate)
nicholas.anstee@cityoflondon.gov.uk

***Alderman:* Bear**, Michael (NP - Portsoken)
michael.bear@cityoflondon.gov.uk

***Alderman:* Evans**, Jeffrey (NP - Cheap)
jeffrey.evans@cityoflondon.gov.uk

***Alderman:* Finch**, Robert (NP - Coleman Street)
robert@thefinches.org

***Alderman:* Garbutt**, John (NP - Walbrook)
john.garbutt@halbis.com

***Alderman:* Gifford**, Roger (NP - Cordwainer)
roger.gifford@seb.co.uk

***Alderman:* Gowman**, Alison (NP - Dowgate)
alison.gowman@dlapiper.com

***Alderman:* Graves**, David (NP - Cripplegate)
david.graves@cityoflondon.gov.uk

***Alderman:* Haines**, Gordon (NP - Queenhithe)

gordon.haines@cityoflondon.gov.uk
***Alderman:* Hall**, Benjamin (NP - Farringdon Within)
bob_rh_hall@hotmail.com
***Alderman:* Hewitt**, Peter (NP - Aldgate)
peter.hewitt@cityoflondon.gov.uk
***Alderman:* Howard**, David (NP - Cornhill)
david.howard@charles-stanley.co.uk
***Alderman:* Judge**, Paul (NP - Tower)
paul@paulrjudge.com
***Alderman:* Lewis**, David (NP - Broad Street)
david.lewis@cityoflondon.gov.uk
***Alderman:* Luder**, Ian (NP - Castle Baynard)
ian.luder@cityoflondon.gov.uk
***Alderman:* Parmley**, Andrew (NP - Vintry)
andrew.parmley@cityoflondon.gov.uk
***Alderman:* Redcliffe**, Neil (NP - Bishopsgate Within)
neil@redcliffe.me.uk
***Alderman:* Remnant**, Philip (NP - Bassishaw)
philip.remnant@credit-suisse.com
***Alderman:* Savory**, Michael (NP - Bread Street)
michael.savory@cityoflondon.gov.uk
***Alderman:* Stuttard**, John (NP - Lime Street)
john.stuttard@uk.pwc.com
***Alderman:* Walsh**, Simon (NP - Farringdon Without North Side)
aldermanfarringdonwithout@gmail.com
***Alderman:* White**, John (NP - Billingsgate)
john.white@cottamrhodes.com
***Alderman:* Woolf**, Fiona (NP - Candlewick)
fiona.woolf@cms-cmck.com
***Alderman:* Yarrow**, Alan (NP - Bridge & Bridge Without)
alan.yarrow@dkib.com
***Common Councilman:* Abrahams**, George (NP - Farringdon Without North Side)
georgea@georgeabrahams.co.uk
***Common Councilman:* Absalom**, John (NP - Farringdon Without North Side)
john.absalom@cityoflondon.gov.uk
***Common Councilman:* Ayers**, Ken (NP - Bassishaw)
kenneth.ayers@cityoflondon.gov.uk
***Common Councilman:* Bain-Stewart**, Alex (NP - Farringdon Within North Side)
alex.bain-stewart@cityoflondon.gov.uk
***Common Councilman:* Barker**, John (NP - Cripplegate Within)
john.barker@cityoflondon.gov.uk
***Common Councilman:* Barrow**, Douglas (NP - Aldgate)
***Common Councilman:* Bennett**, John (NP - Broad Street)
john.bennett@cityoflondon.gov.uk
***Common Councilman:* Bird**, John (NP - Tower)
col-eb-tc@cityoflondon.gov.uk
***Common Councilman:* Boleat**, Mark (NP - Cordwainer)
mark.boleat@cityoflondon.gov.uk
***Common Councilman:* Bradshaw**, David (NP - Cripplegate Within)
david.bradshaw@cityoflondon.gov.uk
***Common Councilman:* Brewster**, John (NP - Bishopsgate Within)
***Common Councilman:* Cassidy**, Michael (NP - Coleman Street)
michael.cassidy@dlapiper.com
***Common Councilman:* Catt**, Ray (NP - Castle Baynard)
ray.catt@nab.co.uk
***Common Councilman:* Chadwick**, Roger (NP - Tower)
roger.chadwick@cityoflondon.gov.uk
***Common Councilman:* Challis**, Nigel (NP - Castle Baynard)
nigel.challis@cityoflondon.gov.uk
***Common Councilman:* Chapman**, John (NP - Langbourn)
johnc@jdconsultants.com
***Common Councilman:* Cotgrove**, Dennis (NP - Lime Street)
dennis.cotgrove@cityoflondon.gov.uk
***Common Councilman:* Cressey**, Nicolas (NP - Portsoken)
nicolas.cressey@cityoflondon.gov.uk
***Common Councilman:* Currie**, Stephanie (NP - Cripplegate Without)
stella.currie@cityoflondon.gov.uk
***Common Councilman:* Davies**, Pollyanna (NP - Broad Street)
pollyanna.davies@cityoflondon.gov.uk
***Common Councilman:* Day**, Martin (NP - Bishopsgate Without)
martin.j.day@hotmail.co.uk
***Common Councilman:* Deane**, Alexander (NP - Farringdon Without North Side)
alexanderdeane@ymail.com
***Common Councilman:* D'Olier Duckworth**, Simon (NP - Bishopsgate Within)
***Common Councilman:* Dove**, William (NP - Bishopsgate Without)
***Common Councilman:* Dudley**, Martin (NP - Aldersgate)
martin.dudley@cityoflondon.gov.uk
***Common Councilman:* Duffield**, Robert (NP - Farringdon Within)
rwd@yltd.co.uk
***Common Councilman:* Dunphy**, Peter (NP - Cornhill)
p.dunphy@darwinrhodes.com
***Common Councilman:* Eskenzi**, Anthony (NP - Farringdon Within South Side)
anthony.eskenzi@cityoflondon.gov.uk
***Common Councilman:* Eve**, Robin (NP - Cheap)
robin.eve@btopenworld.com
***Common Councilman:* Everett**, Kevin (NP - Candlewick)
kevin.everett@cityoflondon.gov.uk
***Common Councilman:* Farr**, Martin (NP - Walbrook)
martin.farr@gvagrimley.co.uk
***Common Councilman:* Fernandes**, Sophie (NP - Coleman Street)
sophieannefernandes@gmail.com
***Common Councilman:* Fraser**, Bill (NP - Vintry)
william.fraser@cityoflondon.gov.uk
***Common Councilman:* Fraser**, Stuart (NP - Coleman Street)
stuart.fraser@cityoflondon.gov.uk
***Common Councilman:* Fredericks**, Marianne (NP - Tower)
marianne_fredericks@hotmail.com
***Common Councilman:* Galloway**, Archibald (NP - Bishopsgate Without)
archie.galloway@cityoflondon.gov.uk
***Common Councilman:* Gillon**, George (NP - Cordwainer)
george.gillon@cityoflondon.gov.uk
***Common Councilman:* Ginsbury**, Stanley (NP - Bishopsgate Within)
stanley.ginsburg@cityoflondon.gov.uk
***Common Councilman:* Graves**, Anthony (NP - Bishopsgate Within)
colin.graves@cityoflondon.gov.uk
***Common Councilman:* Haines**, Stephen (NP - Cornhill)
stephen.haines@cityoflondon.gov.uk
***Common Councilman:* Halliday**, Pauline (NP - Walbrook)
halliday.p@tiscali.co.uk
***Common Councilman:* Hardwick**, Peter (NP - Aldgate)
peter.hardwick@cityoflondon.gov.uk
***Common Councilman:* Harris**, Brian (NP - Bridge & Bridge Without)

brian.harris@cityoflondon.gov.uk
***Common Councilman:* Henderson-Begg**, Michael (NP - Coleman Street)
clerk@tinplateworkers.co.uk
***Common Councilman:* Hoffman**, Tom (NP - Vintry)
tom.hoffman@cityoflondon.gov.uk
***Common Councilman:* Howard**, Robert (NP - Lime Street)
COL-EB-TC@cityoflondon.gov.uk
***Common Councilman:* Hudson**, Michael (NP - Castle Baynard)
city@mhlaw.co.uk
***Common Councilman:* Hunt**, William (NP - Castle Baynard)
william.hunt@cityoflondon.gov.uk
***Common Councilman:* Hyde**, Wendy (NP - Bishopsgate Without)
wendy.hyde@cityoflondon.gov.uk
***Common Councilman:* James**, Clare (NP - Farringdon Within South Side)
clare.james@puntersouthall.com
***Common Councilman:* Jones**, Henry (NP - Portsoken)
henry.jones@cityoflondon.gov.uk
***Common Councilman:* King**, Alastair (NP - Queenhithe)
alastair.king@cityoflondon.gov.uk
***Common Councilman:* Knowles**, Keith (NP - Candlewick)
keith.knowles@cityoflondon.gov.uk
***Common Councilman:* Lawrence**, Greg (NP - Farringdon Without North Side)
col-eb-tc@cityoflondon.gov.uk
***Common Councilman:* Leck**, Peter (NP - Aldersgate)
peter.leck@hotmail.co.uk
***Common Councilman:* Littlechild**, Vivienne (NP - Cripplegate Within)
vivienne.littlechild@cityoflondon.gov.uk
***Common Councilman:* Llewelyn-Davies**, Anthony (NP - Billingsgate)
anthony.llewelyn-davies@cityoflondon.gov.uk
***Common Councilman:* Lodge**, Oliver (NP - Bread Street)
oliver.lodge@cityoflondon.gov.uk
***Common Councilman:* Lord**, Charles Edward (NP - Farringdon Without South Side)
edward.lord@cityoflondon.gov.uk
***Common Councilman:* Malins**, Julian (NP - Farringdon Without South Side)
malins@btinternet.com
***Common Councilman:* Martinelli**, Peter (NP - Farringdon Without South Side)
peter.martinelli@cityoflondon.gov.uk
***Common Councilman:* Mayhew**, Jeremy (NP - Aldersgate)
jeremymayhew@btinternet.com
***Common Councilman:* McGuinness**, Catherine (NP - Castle Baynard)
catherine.mcguinness@cityoflondon.gov.uk
***Common Councilman:* Mead**, Wendy (NP - Farringdon Without South Side)
wendy.mead@cityoflondon.gov.uk
***Common Councilman:* Merrett**, Robert (NP - Bassishaw)
robert.merrett@jpmorgan.com
***Common Councilman:* Mooney**, Brian (NP - Queenhithe)
brian.mooney@btinternet.com
***Common Councilman:* Moore**, Gareth (NP - Cripplegate Within)
gareth.moore@cityoflondon.gov.uk
***Common Councilman:* Morris**, Hugh (NP - Aldgate)
***Common Councilman:* Moys**, Sylvia (NP - Aldgate)
sylvia.moys@cityoflondon.gov.uk
***Common Councilman:* Nash**, Joyce (NP - Aldersgate)
joyce.nash@cityoflondon.gov.uk
***Common Councilman:* Newman**, Barbara (NP - Aldersgate)
barbara.newman@cityoflondon.gov.uk
***Common Councilman:* Owen**, Janet (NP - Langbourn)
janet.owen@cityoflondon.gov.uk
***Common Councilman:* Owen-Ward**, John (NP - Bridge & Bridge Without)
john.owen-ward@cityoflondon.gov.uk
***Common Councilman:* Page**, Michael (NP - Farringdon Within South Side)
bindonbear@live.co.uk
***Common Councilman:* Pembroke**, Anne (NP - Cheap)
ann.pembroke@cityoflondon.gov.uk
***Common Councilman:* Pollard**, Henry (NP - Dowgate)
henry_pollard@invescoperpetual.co.uk
***Common Councilman:* Priest**, Henrika (NP - Castle Baynard)
henrika.priest@cityoflondon.gov.uk
***Common Councilman:* Pulman**, Gerald (NP - Tower)
geraldpulman@hotmail.com
***Common Councilman:* Punter**, Christopher (NP - Cripplegate Within)
chris.punter@cityoflondon.gov.uk
***Common Councilman:* Quilter**, Stephen (NP - Cripplegate Without)
vision@totalise.co.uk
***Common Councilman:* Regan**, Richard (NP - Farringdon Within North Side)
richard.regan@cityoflondon.gov.uk
***Common Councilman:* Regis**, Delis (NP - Portsoken)
delis.regis@cityoflondon.gov.uk
***Common Councilman:* Richardson**, Matthew (NP - Coleman Street)
matthew.richardson@cityoflondon.gov.uk
***Common Councilman:* Rogula**, Elizabeth (NP - Lime Street)
er@btinternet.com
***Common Councilman:* Rounding**, Virginia (NP - Farringdon Within North Side)
virginia.rounding@cityoflondon.gov.uk
***Common Councilman:* Scott**, John (NP - Broad Street)
john.scott@cityoflondon.gov.uk
***Common Councilman:* Seaton**, Ian (NP - Bassishaw)
***Common Councilman:* Sherlock**, Robin (NP - Dowgate)
robin.sherlock@cityoflondon.gov.uk
***Common Councilman:* Shilson**, Giles (NP - Bread Street)
giles.shilson@cityoflondon.gov.uk
***Common Councilman:* Simons**, Jeremy (NP - Castle Baynard)
jeremy.simons@cityoflondon.gov.uk
***Common Councilman:* Snyder**, Michael (NP - Cordwainer)
michael.snyder@cityoflondon.gov.uk
***Common Councilman:* Spanner**, John (NP - Farringdon Without South Side)
john.spanner@cityoflondon.gov.uk
***Common Councilman:* Starling**, Angela (NP - Cripplegate Without)
angela.starling@cityoflondon.gov.uk
***Common Councilman:* Thompson**, David (NP - Aldgate)
***Common Councilman:* Tomlinson**, John (NP - Cripplegate Without)
john@johnandpaula.com
***Common Councilman:* Tumbridge**, James (NP - Tower)
james.tumbridge@cityoflondon.gov.uk
***Common Councilman:* Twogood**, Mark (NP - Farringdon Without North Side)
mark_twogood@yahoo.co.uk

Common Councilman: **Welbank**, Michael (NP - Billingsgate)
michael.welbank@cityoflondon.gov.uk
Fletcher, John William (NP - Portsoken)

COMMITTEE CHAIRS

Community & Children's Services (Scrutiny): Rev Dr Martin Dudley
Culture, Heritage & Libraries (Scrutiny): Mr John Scott
Establishment: Mr John Barker
Finance: Mr Roger Chadwick
Policy & Resources: Mr Mark Boleat
Port Health & Environmental Services: Mr John Tomlinson
Standards: Dr Colin Kolbert (External)

CLACKMANNANSHIRE S

Clackmannanshire Council, Greenfield House, Alloa FK10 2AD
☎ 01259 450000 🖷 01259 452010
contactcentre@clacks.gov.uk 💻 www.clacksweb.org.uk

FACTS & FIGURES

Police Authority: Central Scotland Police Authority
Health Authority: NHS Forth Valley
Learning and Skills Council: Scotland
EU Constituencies: Scotland
Election Frequency: Elections are of whole council

PRINCIPAL OFFICERS

Chief Executive: Ms Elaine McPherson, Chief Executive, Greenfield House, Alloa FK10 1EX ☎ 01259 452013 emcpherson@clacks.gov.uk

Senior Management: Mrs Nikki Bridle, Director - Finance & Corporate Services, Greenfield, Alloa FK10 2AD ☎ 01259 452030 nbridle@clacks.gov.uk

Senior Management: Mr Garry Dallas, Director - Services to Communities, Lime Tree House, Castle Street, Alloa FK10 1EX ☎ 01259 450000 🖷 01259 452530 gdallas@clacks.gov.uk

Senior Management: Ms Elaine McPherson, Chief Executive, Greenfield House, Alloa FK10 1EX ☎ 01259 452013 emcpherson@clacks.gov.uk

Architect, Building / Property Services: Mr Stephen Crawford, Head - Facilities Management, Kilncraigs House, Greenside Street, Alloa FK10 1EB ☎ 01259 452533 🖷 01259 452660 scrawford@clacks.gov.uk

Building Control: Mr Alistair Mackenzie, Team Leader - Building, Standards & Llicensing, Kilncraigs House, Greenside Street, Alloa FK10 1EB ☎ 01259 452554 🖷 01259 452547 amackenzie@clacks.gov.uk

Catering Services: Ms Diane MacKenzie, Services Officer, Greenfield House, Alloa FK10 2AD ☎ 01259 452190

Children / Youth Services: Ms Deirdre Cilliers, Head of Joint Services / Chief Social Work Officer, Limetree House, Castle Street, Alloa FK10 1EX ☎ 01259 450000; 01786 442935 🖷 01259 452440; 01786 442782 dcilliers@clacks.gov.uk

Civil Registration: Mr Andrew Hunter, Senior Governance Officer, Greenfield, Alloa FK10 2AD ☎ 01259 452111 🖷 01259 452245 ahunter@clacks.gov.uk

PR / Communications: Mrs Karen Payton, Acting Head - Communications, Greenfield House, Alloa FK10 2AD ☎ 01259 452027 kpayton@clackmannanshire.gov.uk

PR / Communications: Ms Karen Payton, Communications & Marketing Team Leader, Greenfield House, Alloa FK10 2AD ☎ 01259 452027 kpayton@clacks.gov.uk

Computer Management: Mr John Munro, ICT Service Manager, Greenfield, Alloa FK10 2AD ☎ 01259 452510 jmunro@clacks.gov.uk

Computer Management: Mr John Munro, IT Manager, Greenfield, Alloa FK10 2AD ☎ 01259 452055 jmunro@clackmannanshire.gov.uk

Consumer Protection and Trading Standards: Mr Ian Doctor, Service Manager - Environmental Health & Consumer Protection, Kilncraigs, Greenside Place, Alloa FK10 1EB ☎ 01259 452572 🖷 01259 452535 idoctor@clacks.gov.uk

Contracts: Mr Garry Dallas, Director - Services to Communities, Lime Tree House, Castle Street, Alloa FK10 1EX ☎ 01259 450000 🖷 01259 452530 gdallas@clacks.gov.uk

Corporate Services: Mrs Nikki Bridle, Director - Finance & Corporate Services, Greenfield, Alloa FK10 2AD ☎ 01259 452030 nbridle@clacks.gov.uk

Customer Service: Mr Brian Forbes, Customer Services Manager, Greenfield House, Alloa FK10 2AD ☎ 01259 452187 🖷 01259 452170 bforbes@clacks.gov.uk

Customer Service: Ms Elaine McPherson, Chief Executive, Greenfield House, Alloa FK10 1EX ☎ 01259 452013 emcpherson@clacks.gov.uk

Economic Development: Ms Helen Blenkharn, Development Officer - Sustainability, Greenfield House, Alloa FK10 2AD ☎ 01259 450000

Education: Mr Kevin Kelman, Assistant Head of Education, Viewforth, Stirling FK8 2ET ☎ 01786 442680; 01786 442680 kelmank@stirling.gov.uk; kelmank@stirling.gov.uk

Education: Mr Alan Millikin, Assistant Head of Education, Viewforth, Stirling FK8 2ET ☎ 01786 442945; 01786 442945 millikina@stirling.gov.uk; millikina@stirling.gov.uk

Electoral Registration: Mr Andrew Hunter, Senior Governance Officer, Greenfield, Alloa FK10 2AD ☎ 01259 452111 🖷 01259 452245 ahunter@clacks.gov.uk

Electoral Registration: Mr Andrew Hunter, Senior Governance Officer, Greenfield House, Alloa FK10 2AD ☎ 01259 452103 ahunter2@clackmannanshire.gov.uk

Emergency Planning: Mr David Johnstone, Emergency Planning

Officer, Lime Tree House, Castle Street, Alloa FK10 1EX ☎ 01259 452537 🖷 01259 452350 ✉ djohnstone@clacks.gov.uk

Emergency Planning: Mr David Johnstone, Emergency Planning Officer, Lime Tree House, Castle Street, Alloa FK10 1EX ☎ 01259 452537 🖷 01259 452350 ✉ djohnstone@clacks.gov.uk

Energy Management: Mr Richard Scobie, Energy Officer, Kilncraigs House, Greenside Street, Alloa FK10 1EB ☎ 01259 450000 ✉ rscobbie@clacks.gov.uk

Environmental / Technical Services: Mr Garry Dallas, Director - Services to Communities, Lime Tree House, Castle Street, Alloa FK10 1EX ☎ 01259 450000 🖷 01259 452530 ✉ gdallas@clacks.gov.uk

Environmental Health: Mr Graeme Cunningham, Integrated Waste Manager, Kilncraigs House, Greenside Street, Alloa FK10 1EB ☎ 01259 452548 🖷 01259 452547 ✉ gcunningham@clacks.gov.uk

Estates, Property & Valuation: Mr George Adamson, Team Leader - Estates, Kilncraigs House, Greenside Street, Alloa FK10 1EB ☎ 01259 450000

European Liaison: Ms Elaine McPherson, Chief Executive, Greenfield House, Alloa FK10 1EX ☎ 01259 452013 ✉ emcpherson@clacks.gov.uk

Events Manager: Mrs Karen Kirkwood, Soft Facilities Management Services Officer, Kilncraigs , Greenside Place, Alloa, Alloa FK10 3JY ☎ 01259 450000 ✉ kkirkwood@clacks.gov.uk

Facilities: Mr Stephen Crawford, Head - Facilities Management, Kilncraigs House, Greenside Street, Alloa FK10 1EB ☎ 01259 452533 🖷 01259 452660 ✉ scrawford@clacks.gov.uk

Finance and Treasurer: Mrs Nikki Bridle, Director - Finance & Corporate Services, Greenfield, Alloa FK10 2AD ☎ 01259 452030 ✉ nbridle@clacks.gov.uk

Finance and Treasurer: Mr Martin Dunsmore, Head of Accounting & Budgeting, Greenfield House, Alloa FK10 2AD ☎ 01259 452041 ✉ mdunsmore@clacks.gov.uk

Grounds Maintenance: Mr Graeme Cunningham, Integrated Waste Manager, Kilncraigs House, Greenside Street, Alloa FK10 1EB ☎ 01259 452548 🖷 01259 452547 ✉ gcunningham@clacks.gov.uk

Health and Safety: Mrs Sarah Robertson, Health & Safety Adviser, Greenfield House, Alloa FK10 1EX ☎ 01259 452174

Highways: Mr Stephen Crawford, Head - Facilities Management, Kilncraigs House, Greenside Street, Alloa FK10 1EB ☎ 01259 452533 🖷 01259 452660 ✉ scrawford@clacks.gov.uk

Housing: Mr John Gillespie, Head - Community & Regulatory, Lime Tree House, Castle Street, Alloa FK10 1EX ☎ 01259 452360 🖷 01259 452400 ✉ jgillespie@clacks.gov.uk

Housing Maintenance: Ms Jennifer Queripel, Service Manager Housing Operations, Lime Tree House, North Castle Street, Alloa FK10 1EX ☎ 01259 45 2475

Legal: Mr David Thomson, Legal Services Manager, Greenfield House, Alloa FK10 2AD ☎ 01259 450000 ✉ dthomson@clacks.gov.uk

Licensing: Ms June Andison, Administrator/ Licensing, Kilncraigs House, Alloa FK10 1AB ☎ 01259 450000 🖷 01259 452230 ✉ jandison@clacks.gov.uk

Lighting: Mr Malcolm West, Manager - Roads & Transportation, Kilncraigs House, Greenside Street, Alloa FK10 1EX ☎ 01259 452624 🖷 01259 452535 ✉ mwest@clacks.gov.uk

Member Services: Mrs Aileen Littlejohn, Business Support Manager, Greenfield, Alloa FK10 2AD ☎ 01259 452003 🖷 01259 452230 ✉ alittlejohn@clacks.gov.uk

Planning: Mr Grant Baxter, Principal Planner, Kilncraigs House, Alloa FK10 1AB ☎ 01259 450000 ✉ gbaxter@clacks.gov.uk

Procurement: Mr Derek Barr, Procurement Manager, Greenfield, Alloa FK10 1EX ☎ 01259 452017 ✉ dbarr@clacks.gov.uk

Public Libraries: Mr Derek Barr, Procurement Manager, Greenfield, Alloa FK10 1EX ☎ 01259 452017 ✉ dbarr@clacks.gov.uk

Recycling & Waste Minimisation: Mr Graeme Cunningham, Manager - Environment, Lime Tree House, Castle Street, Alloa FK10 1EX ☎ 01259 452548 🖷 01259 452535 ✉ wasteservices@clacks.gov.uk

Regeneration: Ms Cherie Jarvie, Team Leader - Research & Information, Greenfield House, Alloa FK10 2AD ☎ 01259 211438 ✉ cjarvie@clacks.gov.uk

Road Safety: Mr Malcolm West, Manager - Roads & Transportation, Kilncraigs House, Greenside Street, Alloa FK10 1EX ☎ 01259 452624 🖷 01259 452535 ✉ mwest@clacks.gov.uk

Social Services: Mr Grahame Blair, Director - Services to People, Lime Tree House, Castle Street, Alloa FK10 1EX ☎ 01259 452374 ✉ gblair@clacks.gov.uk

Social Services (Adult): Ms Deirdre Cilliers, Head of Joint Services / Chief Social Work Officer, Limetree House, Castle Street, Alloa FK10 1EX ☎ 01259 450000; 01786 442935 🖷 01259 452440; 01786 442782 ✉ dcilliers@clacks.gov.uk

Social Services (Children): Ms Joan Lyle, Service Manager - Child Care, Greenfield House, Alloa FK10 2AD ☎ 01259 450000

Staff Training: Ms Lorna Young, Learning & Development Advisor, Greenfield House, Alloa FK10 2AD ☎ 01259 450000 ✉ lorna.young@clacksweb.org.uk

Street Scene: Mr Charlie Norman, Team Leader of Road Services, Kilncraigs House, Greenside Street, Alloa FK10 1EB ☎ 01259 452590 ✉ cnorman@clacks.gov.uk

Tourism: Ms Carolyn McGill, Business Development & Liaison Advisor, Greenfield House, Alloa FK10 2AD ☎ 01259 450000 ✉ carolynmcgill@clacks.gov.uk

Town Centre: Mr Andy Mitchell, BID Project Leader, Greenfield House, Alloa FK10 2AD ☎ 01259 727313 ✉ andrew@atcbid.com

Traffic Management: Mr Malcolm West, Manager - Roads & Transportation, Kilncraigs House, Greenside Street, Alloa FK10 1EX ☎ 01259 452624 🖷 01259 452535 ✉ mwest@clacks.gov.uk

Transport: Mr Malcolm West, Manager - Roads & Transportation, Kilncraigs House, Greenside Street, Alloa FK10 1EX ☎ 01259 452624 🖷 01259 452535 ✉ mwest@clacks.gov.uk

Transport Planner: Mr Malcolm West, Manager - Roads & Transportation, Kilncraigs House, Greenside Street, Alloa FK10 1EX ☎ 01259 452624 🖷 01259 452535 ✉ mwest@clacks.gov.uk

Waste Collection and Disposal: Mr Graeme Cunningham, Integrated Waste Manager, Kilncraigs House, Greenside Street, Alloa FK10 1EB ☎ 01259 452548 🖷 01259 452547 ✉ gcunningham@clacks.gov.uk

Waste Management: Mr Graeme Cunningham, Integrated Waste Manager, Kilncraigs House, Greenside Street, Alloa FK10 1EB ☎ 01259 452548 🖷 01259 452547 ✉ gcunningham@clacks.gov.uk

MEMBERS OF THE COUNCIL (18)

***Deputy Provost:* Balsillie**, Donald (SNP - Clackmannanshire North)
dbalsillie@clacks.gov.uk
***Deputy Provost:* Hamilton**, Irene (SNP - Clackmannanshire East)
ihamilton@clacks.gov.uk
***Leader of the Council:* Womersley**, Gary (SNP - Clackmannanshire Central)
gwomersley@clacks.gov.uk
Cadenhead, Janet (LAB - Clackmannanshire South)
jcadenhead@clacks.gov.uk
Campbell, Alastair (CON - Clackmannanshire East)
acampbell@clacks.gov.uk
Drummond, Archie (IND - Clackmannanshire North)
adrummond@clacks.gov.uk
Earle, Kenneth (LAB - Clackmannanshire South)
kearle@clacks.gov.uk
Forson, Ellen (SNP - Clackmannanshire South)
eforson@clacks.gov.uk
Holden, Craig (IND - Clackmannanshire South)
cholden@clacks.gov.uk
Martin, Kathleen (LAB - Clackmannanshire East)
kmartin@clacks.gov.uk
Matchett, George (LAB - Clackmannanshire West)
gmatchett@clacks.gov.uk
McAdam, Walter (SNP - Clackmannanshire North)
wmcadam@clacks.gov.uk
McGill, Robert (LAB - Clackmannanshire North)
rmcgill@clacks.gov.uk
Murphy, Tina (SNP - Clackmannanshire West)
tmurphy@clacks.gov.uk
Sharp, Les (SNP - Clackmannanshire West)
lsharp@clacks.gov.uk
Stalker, Jim (LAB - Clackmannanshire West)
jstalker@clacks.gov.uk
Stewart, Derek (LAB - Clackmannanshire Central)
dstewart@clacks.gov.uk
Watt, Graham (LAB - Clackmannanshire Central)
grahamwatt@clacks.gov.uk

POLITICAL COMPOSITION

LAB: 8, SNP: 7, IND: 2, CON: 1

COMMITTEE CHAIRS

Planning: Mr Alastair Campbell
Scrutiny: Mr Donald Balsillie
Workforce: Mr Derek Stewart

COLCHESTER D

Colchester Borough Council, Rowan House, 33 Sheepen Road, Colchester CO3 3WG ☎ 01206 282222 🖷 01206 282288
✉ customerservicecentre@colchester.gov.uk
🖳 www.colchester.gov.uk

FACTS & FIGURES

Police Authority: Essex Police Authority
Health Authority: East of England Strategic Health Authority
Learning and Skills Council: Eastern
Parliamentary Constituencies: Colchester, Harwich and Essex North
EU Constituencies: Eastern
Election Frequency: Elections are by thirds
Twinning: Avignon (France); Wetzlar (Germany); Imola (Italy)

PRINCIPAL OFFICERS

Chief Executive: Mr Adrian Pritchard, Chief Executive, Rowan House, 33 Sheepen Road, Colchester CO3 3WG ☎ 01206 282211 🖷 01206 282358 ✉ adrian.pritchard@colchester.gov.uk

Senior Management: Mrs Pam Donnelly, Executive Director - Customer Excellence, Rowan House, 33 Sheepen Road, Colchester CO3 3WG ☎ 01206 282212 🖷 01206 282358 ✉ pamela.donnelly@colchester.gov.uk

Senior Management: Mrs Ann Hedges, Executive Director - People & Performance, Rowan House, 33 Sheepen Road, Colchester CO3 3WG ☎ 01206 282212 🖷 01206 282358 ✉ ann.hedges@colchester.gov.uk

Senior Management: Mr Ian Vipond, Executive Director - Leadership of Place, Rowan House, 33 Sheepen Road, Colchester CO3 3WG ☎ 01206 282717 🖷 01206 282358 ✉ ian.vipond@colchester.gov.uk

Access Officer / Social Services (Disability): Mr Malcolm Pleiksnis, Specialist Support Officer, Rowan House, 33 Sheepen Road, Colchester CO3 3WG ☎ 01206 282598 🖷 01206 500179 ✉ malcolm.pleiksnis@colchester.gov.uk

Best Value: Ms Chris Reed, Policy & Projects Officer, Rowan House, 33 Sheepen Road, Colchester CO3 3WG ☎ 01206 282240 🖷 01206 282533 ✉ chris.reed@colchester.gov.uk

Building Control: Mr Vincent Pearce, Development Service Manager, Rowan House, 33 Sheepen Road, Colchester CO3 3WG

☎ 01206 282452 🖷 01206 282598
✉ vincent.pearce@colchester.gov.uk

Catering Services: Ms Jessica Douglas, Senior Manager - Corporate Management, Rowan House, 33 Sheepen Road, Colchester CO3 3WG ☎ 01206 282239 🖷 01206 282533 ✉ jessica.douglas@colchester.gov.uk

Catering Services: Mr Lee Spalding, Building Services & Facilities Manager, Rowan House, 33 Sheepen Road, Colchester CO3 3WG ☎ 01206 506905 ✉ lee.spalding@colchester.gov.uk

Children / Youth Services: Mrs Lucie Breadman, Head of Life Opportunities, Rowan House, 33 Sheepen Road, Colchester CO3 3WG ☎ 01206 506517 ✉ lucie.breadman@colchester.gov.uk

PR / Communications: Ms Jessica Douglas, Senior Manager - Corporate Management, Rowan House, 33 Sheepen Road, Colchester CO3 3WG ☎ 01206 282239 🖷 01206 282533 ✉ jessica.douglas@colchester.gov.uk

PR / Communications: Ms Joanne Partlett, Communications & Marketing Manager, Rowan House, 33 Sheepen Road, Colchester CO3 3WG ☎ 01206 282262 🖷 01206 282533 ✉ joanne.partlett@colchester.gov.uk

Community Planning: Mr Gareth Mitchell, Head of Strategic Policy & Regeneration, Rowan House, 33 Sheepen Road, Colchester CO3 3WG ☎ 01206 506972 🖷 01206 507814 ✉ gareth.mitchell@colchester.gov.uk

Community Safety: Mr Matthew Sterling, Senior Manager, PO Box 52215, Town Hall, Colchester CO1 1GG ☎ 01206 282577 🖷 01206 507814 ✉ matthew.sterling@colchester.gov.uk

Computer Management: Mr Lee French, ICT Manager, Rowan House, 33 Sheepen Road, Colchester CO3 3WG ☎ 01206 282350 🖷 01206 282533 ✉ lee.french@colchester.gov.uk

Contracts: Mr Julian Wilkins, Principal Lawyer, Rowan House, 33 Sheepen Road, Colchester CO3 3WG ☎ 01206 282257 🖷 01206 282533 ✉ julian.wilkins@colchester.gov.uk

Corporate Services: Ms Jessica Douglas, Senior Manager - Corporate Management, Rowan House, 33 Sheepen Road, Colchester CO3 3WG ☎ 01206 282239 🖷 01206 282533 ✉ jessica.douglas@colchester.gov.uk

Customer Service: Ms Pamela Donnelly, Executive Director, Rowan House, 33 Sheepen Road, Colchester CO3 3WG ☎ 01206 282901 🖷 01206 282261 ✉ pamela.donnelly@colchester.gov.uk

Customer Service: Ms Leonie Rathbone, Customer Services Manager, Rowan House, 33 Sheepen Road, Colchester CO3 3WG ☎ 01206 507887 🖷 01206 282288 ✉ leonie.rathbone@colchester.gov.uk

Economic Development: Mr Nigel Myers, Enterprise & Tourism Manager, Rowan House, 33 Sheepen Road, Colchester CO3 3WG ☎ 01206 282878 🖷 01206 507814 ✉ nigel.myers@colchester.gov.uk

E-Government: Mr Lee French, Corporate ICT Manager, Rowan House, 33 Sheepen Road, Colchester CO3 3WG ☎ 01206 282350 🖷 01206 282533 ✉ lee.french@colchester.gov.uk

Electoral Registration: Mrs Sarah Cheek, Electoral Services Manager, Rowan House, 33 Sheepen Road, Colchester CO3 3WG ☎ 01206 282271 🖷 01206 282533 ✉ sarah.cheek@colchester.gov.uk

Electoral Registration: Ms Amanda Chidgey, Democratic Services Manager, Rowan House, 33 Sheepen Road, Colchester CO3 3WG ☎ 01206 282227 🖷 01206 282533 ✉ amanda.chidgey@colchester.gov.uk

Emergency Planning: Mr Paul Walker, Protective Services Manager, Rowan House, 33 Sheepen Road, Colchester CO3 3WG ☎ 01206 507157; 01206 507157 ✉ paul.walker@colchester.gov.uk; paul.walker@colchester.gov.uk

Energy Management: Ms Samantha Preston, Strategy Performance Officer, Rowan House, 33 Sheepen Road, Colchester CO3 3WG ☎ 01206 282707 ✉ samantha.preston@colchester.gov.uk

Environmental Health: Mrs Beverley Jones, Head of Environmental & Protective Services, Rowan House, 33 Sheepen Road, Colchester CO3 3WG ☎ 01206 282593 🖷 01206 282598 ✉ beverley.jones@colchester.gov.uk

Environmental Health: Ms Karen Newman, Public Health & Enforcement Service Manager, Rowan House, 33 Sheepen Road, Colchester CO3 3WG ☎ 01206 507855 ✉ karen.newman@colchester.gov.uk

Estates, Property & Valuation: Mr Michael Shorten, Estates Services Manager, Rowan House, 33 Sheepen Road, Colchester CO3 3WG ☎ 01206 282252 🖷 01206 282236 ✉ michael.shorten@colchester.gov.uk

Events Manager: Mr Frank Turmel, Events Manager, Charter Hall, Cowdray Avenue, Colchester CO1 1YH ☎ 01206 282946 ✉ frank.turmel@colchester.gov.uk

Facilities: Mr Lee Spalding, Building Services & Facilities Manager, Rowan House, 33 Sheepen Road, Colchester CO3 3WG ☎ 01206 506905 ✉ lee.spalding@colchester.gov.uk

Finance and Treasurer: Mr Ian Blofield, Head of Resource Management (Interim), Rowan House, 33 Sheepen Road, Colchester CO3 3WG ☎ 01473 433710; 01206 282350 🖷 01206 282358 ✉ ian.blofield@ipswich.gov.uk; ian.blofield@colchester.gov.uk

Fleet Management: Mr Paul English, Group Manager - Recycling & Fleet, 221 Shrub End Road, Colchester CO3 4RN ☎ 01206 282620 ✉ paul.english@colchester.gov.uk

Grounds Maintenance: Mr Bob Penny, Parks & Recreation Manager, Rowan House, 33 Sheepen Road, Colchester CO3 3WG ☎ 01206 282903 🖷 01206 507814 ✉ bob.penny@colchester.gov.uk

Health and Safety: Ms Pamela Donnelly, Executive Director, Rowan House, 33 Sheepen Road, Colchester CO3 3WG ☎ 01206 282901 🖷 01206 282261 ✉ pamela.donnelly@colchester.gov.uk

Health and Safety: Ms Karen Newman, Public Health & Enforcement Service Manager, Rowan House, 33 Sheepen Road, Colchester CO3 3WG ☎ 01206 507855 ✉ karen.newman@colchester.gov.uk

Health and Safety: Mr Tudor Smith, Health & Safety Advisor, Rowan House, 33 Sheepen Road, Colchester CO3 3WG ☎ 01206 506579 🖷 01206 282533 ✉ tudor.smith@colchester.gov.uk

Housing: Mr Matthew Sterling, Senior Manager, PO Box 52215, Town Hall, Colchester CO1 1GG ☎ 01206 282577 🖷 01206 507814 ✉ matthew.sterling@colchester.gov.uk

Housing Maintenance: Mr Chris Morris, Operations Manager (Colchester Borough Homes), Rowan House, 33 Sheepen Road, Colchester CO3 3WG ☎ 01206 282608

Legal: Ms Jessica Douglas, Senior Manager - Corporate Management, Rowan House, 33 Sheepen Road, Colchester CO3 3WG ☎ 01206 282239 🖷 01206 282533 ✉ jessica.douglas@colchester.gov.uk

Legal: Mr Andrew Weavers, Legal Services Manager & Monitoring Officer, Rowan House, 33 Sheepen Road, Colchester CO3 3WG ☎ 01206 282213 🖷 01206 573911 ✉ andrew.weavers@colchester.gov.uk

Leisure and Cultural Services: Mr Simon Grady, Sport & Leisure Manager, Rowan House, 33 Sheepen Road, Colchester CO3 3WG ☎ 01206 282908 🖷 01206 507814 ✉ simon.grady@colchester.gov.uk

Licensing: Mrs Beverley Jones, Head of Environmental & Protective Services, Rowan House, 33 Sheepen Road, Colchester CO3 3WG ☎ 01206 282593 🖷 01206 282598 ✉ beverley.jones@colchester.gov.uk

Licensing: Ms Karen Newman, Public Health & Enforcement Service Manager, Rowan House, 33 Sheepen Road, Colchester CO3 3WG ☎ 01206 507855 ✉ karen.newman@colchester.gov.uk

Member Services: Ms Amanda Chidgey, Democratic Services Manager, Rowan House, 33 Sheepen Road, Colchester CO3 3WG ☎ 01206 282227 🖷 01206 282533 ✉ amanda.chidgey@colchester.gov.uk

Member Services: Ms Jessica Douglas, Senior Manager - Corporate Management, Rowan House, 33 Sheepen Road, Colchester CO3 3WG ☎ 01206 282239 🖷 01206 282533 ✉ jessica.douglas@colchester.gov.uk

Parking: Mr Richard Walker, Parking Partnership Group Manager, Rowan House, 33 Sheepen Road, Colchester CO3 3WG ☎ 01206 282708 🖷 01206 282716 ✉ richard.walker@colchester.gov.uk

Personnel / HR: Mr Mike Thurston, Human Resources Service Centre Manager, Rowan House, 33 Sheepen Road, Colchester CO3 3WG ☎ 01206 282396 🖷 01206 764023 ✉ mike.thurston@colchester.gov.uk

Planning: Mrs Beverley Jones, Head of Environmental & Protective Services, Rowan House, 33 Sheepen Road, Colchester CO3 3WG ☎ 01206 282593 🖷 01206 282598 ✉ beverley.jones@colchester.gov.uk

Planning: Mr Vincent Pearce, Development Service Manager, Rowan House, 33 Sheepen Road, Colchester CO3 3WG ☎ 01206 282452 🖷 01206 282598 ✉ vincent.pearce@colchester.gov.uk

Procurement: Mrs Elfreda Walker, Finance Manager, Rowan House, 33 Sheepen Road, Colchester CO3 3WG ☎ 01206 282461 🖷 01206 282358 ✉ elfreda.walker@colchester.gov.uk

Recycling & Waste Minimisation: Mr Paul English, Group Manager - Recycling & Fleet, 221 Shrub End Road, Colchester CO3 4RN ☎ 01206 282620 ✉ paul.english@colchester.gov.uk

Regeneration: Mr Gareth Mitchell, Head of Strategic Policy & Regeneration, Rowan House, 33 Sheepen Road, Colchester CO3 3WG ☎ 01206 506972 🖷 01206 507814 ✉ gareth.mitchell@colchester.gov.uk

Street Scene: Mr Matthew Young, Head of Street Services, Rowan House, 33 Sheepen Road, Colchester CO3 3WG ☎ 01206 282902 🖷 01206 282711 ✉ matthew.young@colchester.gov.uk

Sustainable Communities: Mrs Lucie Breadman, Head of Life Opportunities, Rowan House, 33 Sheepen Road, Colchester CO3 3WG ☎ 01206 506517 ✉ lucie.breadman@colchester.gov.uk

Sustainable Development: Mr Gareth Mitchell, Head of Strategic Policy & Regeneration, Rowan House, 33 Sheepen Road, Colchester CO3 3WG ☎ 01206 506972 🖷 01206 507814 ✉ gareth.mitchell@colchester.gov.uk

Tourism: Mr Gareth Mitchell, Head of Strategic Policy & Regeneration, Rowan House, 33 Sheepen Road, Colchester CO3 3WG ☎ 01206 506972 🖷 01206 507814 ✉ gareth.mitchell@colchester.gov.uk

Tourism: Ms Karen Turnbull, Tourism & Visitor Development Officer, Rowan House, 33 Sheepen Road, Colchester CO3 3WG ☎ 01206 282915 🖷 01206 282916 ✉ karen.turnbull@colchester.gov.uk

Town Centre: Mr Howard Davies, Town Centre Project Manager, Rowan House, 33 Sheepen Road, Colchester CO3 3WG ☎ 01206 507885 🖷 01206 282711 ✉ howard.davies@colchester.gov.uk

Transport Planner: Mr Gareth Mitchell, Head of Strategic Policy & Regeneration, Rowan House, 33 Sheepen Road, Colchester CO3 3WG ☎ 01206 506972 🖷 01206 507814 ✉ gareth.mitchell@colchester.gov.uk

Waste Collection and Disposal: Mr Paul English, Group Manager - Recycling & Fleet, 221 Shrub End Road, Colchester CO3 4RN ☎ 01206 282620 ✉ paul.english@colchester.gov.uk

Waste Management: Mr Paul English, Group Manager -

Recycling & Fleet, 221 Shrub End Road, Colchester CO3 4RN
☏ 01206 282620 ✉ paul.english@colchester.gov.uk

Children's Play Areas: Mr Bob Penny, Parks & Recreation Manager, Rowan House, 33 Sheepen Road, Colchester CO3 3WG
☏ 01206 282903 🖷 01206 507814
✉ bob.penny@colchester.gov.uk

MEMBERS OF THE COUNCIL (60)

***Mayor:* Arnold**, Christopher (CON - Fordham & Stour)
cllr.christopher.arnold@colchester.gov.uk
***Deputy Mayor:* Sykes**, Colin (LD - Stanway)
cllr.colin.sykes@colchester.gov.uk
***Leader of the Council:* Turrell**, Anne (LD - Mile End)
cllr.anne.turrell@colchester.gov.uk
***Deputy Leader of the Council:* Hunt**, Martin (LD - Christ Church)
cllr.martin.hunt@colchester.gov.uk
Barlow, Nick (LD - Castle)
cllr.nick.barlow@colchester.gov.uk
Barton, Lynn (LD - Shrub End)
cllr.lyn.barton@colchester.gov.uk
Bentley, Kevin (CON - Birch & Winstree)
cllr.kevin.bentley@colchester.gov.uk
Blandon, Mary (LD - Harbour)
cllr.mary.blandon@colchester.gov.uk
Blundell, Elizabeth (CON - Marks Tey)
cllr.elizabeth.blundell@colchester.gov.uk
Cable, Mark (CON - Dedham & Langham)
Chapman, Nigel (CON - Fordham & Stour)
cllr.nigel.chapman@colchester.gov.uk
Chillingworth, Peter (CON - Great Tey)
cllr.peter.chillingworth@colchester.gov.uk
Chuah, Helen (LD - St Anne's)
cllr.helen.chuah@colchester.gov.uk
Cook, Barrie (LD - St Anne's)
cllr.barrie.cook@colchester.gov.uk
Cope, Nick (LD - Christ Church)
cllr.nick.cope@colchester.gov.uk
Cory, Mark (LD - Wivenhoe Cross)
cllr.mark.cory@colchester.gov.uk
Davies, Beverly (CON - Prettygate)
cllr.beverly.davies@colchester.gov.uk
Dopson, Tina (LAB - St Andrew's)
cllr.tina.dobson@colchester.gov.uk
Elliott, John (CON - Tiptree)
cllr.john.elliott@colchester.gov.uk
Ellis, Andrew (CON - Birch & Winstree)
andrew.ellis@colchester.gov.uk
Fairley-Crowe, Margaret (CON - Tiptree)
cllr.margaret.fairley-crowe@colchester.gov.uk
Feltham, Annie (LD - New Town)
cllr.Annie.Feltham@colchester.gov.uk
Ford, Stephen (LAB - Wivenhoe Quay)
cllr.stephen.ford@colchester.gov.uk
Frame, Bill (LD - Castle)
cllr.bill.frame@colchester.gov.uk
Gamble, Ray (LD - St John's)
cllr.ray.gamble@colchester.gov.uk
Goss, Martin (LD - Mile End)
cllr.martin.goss@colchester.gov.uk
Granger, Glenn (CON - West Mersea)
Greenhill, Scott (LD - Mile End)
cllr.scott.greenhill@colchester.gov.uk
Harrington, Marcus (CON - West Bergholt & Eight Ash Green)
cllr.Marcus.Harrington@colchester.gov.uk
Harris, David (LAB - Berechurch)
cllr.david.harris@colchester.gov.uk
Havis, Julia (LD - Harbour)
Hayes, Jo (LD - Castle)
Hazell, Pauline (CON - Shrub End)
cllr.pauline.hazell@colchester.gov.uk
Higgins, Peter (LD - New Town)
cllr.peter.higgins@colchester.gov.uk
Higgins, Theresa (LD - New Town)
cllr.theresa.higgins@colchester.gov.uk
Hogg, Mike (LD - St Anne's)
cllr.mike.hogg@colchester.gov.uk
Jarvis, Brian (CON - Lexden)
Jowers, John (CON - West Mersea)
cllr.john.jowers@colchester.gov.uk
Kimberley, Margaret (CON - West Mersea)
cllr.margaret.kimberley@colchester.gov.uk
Lewis, Sonia (CON - Lexden)
cllr.sonia.lewis@colchester.gov.uk
Liddy, Cyril (LAB - Wivenhoe Quay)
Lilley, Michael (LAB - East Donyland)
cllr.mike.lilley@colchester.gov.uk
Lissimore, Sue (CON - Prettygate)
cllr.sue.lissimore@colchester.gov.uk
Maclean, Jackie (CON - Copford & West Stanway)
cllr.jackie.maclean@colchester.gov.uk
Manning, Jon (LD - Wivenhoe Cross)
cllr.jon.manning@colchester.gov.uk
Martin, Richard (CON - Tiptree)
cllr.richard.martin@colchester.gov.uk
Mudie, Colin (LD - Berechurch)
cllr.colin.mudie@colchester.gov.uk
Naish, Kim (LAB - Berechurch)
cllr.kim.naish@colchester.gov.uk
Offen, Nigel (LD - Shrub End)
cllr.nigel.offen@colchester.gov.uk
Oxford, Beverley (R - Highwoods)
cllr.beverley.oxford@colchester.gov.uk
Oxford, Gerard (R - Highwoods)
cllr.gerard.oxford@colchester.gov.uk
Oxford, Philip (R - Highwoods)
cllr.philip.oxford@colchester.gov.uk
Quince, Will (CON - Prettygate)
cllr.Will.Quince@colchester.gov.uk
Scott-Boutell, Lesley (LD - Stanway)
cllr.leslie.scott-boutell@colchester.gov.uk
Smith, Paul (LD - St John's)
cllr.paul.smith@colchester.gov.uk
Sutton, Terry (CON - Pyefleet)
cllr.terry.sutton@colchester.gov.uk
Sykes, Laura (LD - Stanway)
cllr.laura.sykes@colchester.gov.uk
Willetts, Dennis (CON - West Bergholt & Eight Ash Green)
cllr.dennis.willetts@colchester.gov.uk
Young, Tim (LAB - St Andrew's)
cllr.tim.young@colchester.gov.uk
Young, Julie (LAB - St Andrew's)
cllr.julie.young@colchester.gov.uk

POLITICAL COMPOSITION

LD: 26, CON: 23, LAB: 8, R: 3

CABINET
Leader / Strategy: Mrs Anne Turrell
Deputy Leader / Street & Waste Services: Mr Martin Hunt
Business & Resources: Mr Paul Smith
Communites & Leisure Services: Ms Annie Feltham
Customers: Ms Beverley Oxford
Housing: Mrs Tina Dopson
Planning, Community Safety & Culture: Mr Tim Young
Renaissance: Ms Lynn Barton

COMMITTEE CHAIRS
Accounts & Regulatory: Mr Dennis Willetts
Finance & Audit (Scrutiny): Mr Dennis Willetts
Licensing: Mr Nick Cope
Planning: Mrs Theresa Higgins
Policy Review & Development (Scrutiny): Mrs Julie Young

COLERAINE N

Coleraine Borough Council, Cloonavin, 66 Portstewart Road, Coleraine BT52 1EY ☎ 028 7034 7034 🖷 028 7034 7026 🖰 info@colerainebc.gov.uk 💻 www.colerainebc.gov.uk

FACTS & FIGURES
Police Authority: Northern Ireland Policing Board
Health Authority: Health & Social Care Board
Learning and Skills Council: Northern Ireland
Parliamentary Constituencies: Londonderry East
EU Constituencies: Northern Ireland
Election Frequency: Elections are of whole council
Twinning: La Roche-sur-Yon, Vendee (France)

PRINCIPAL OFFICERS
Chief Executive: Mr Roger Wilson, Town Clerk & Chief Executive, Cloonavin, 66 Portstewart Road, Coleraine BT52 1EY ☎ 028 7034 7034 🖷 028 7034 7026 🖰 townclerk@colerainebc.gov.uk

Deputy Chief Executive: Mr Keiran Doherty, Director of Environmental Services, Cloonavin, 66 Portstewart Road, Coleraine BT52 1EY ☎ 028 7034 7171 🖷 028 7034 7195 🖰 eh@colerainebc.gov.uk

Architect, Building / Property Services: Mr John Richardson, Head of Estates & Facilites Manager, Cloonavin, 66 Portstewart Road, Coleraine BT52 1EY ☎ 028 7034 7272 🖷 028 7034 7256 🖰 john.richardson@coleraine.gov.uk

Building Control: Mr David Robinson, Principal Building Control Officer, Cloonavin, 66 Portstewart Road, Coleraine BT52 1EY ☎ 028 7034 7272 🖷 028 7034 7256 🖰 david.robinson@colerainebc.gov.uk

Civil Registration: Miss Gwyneth Kerr, Registrar, Cloonavin, 66 Portstewart Road, Coleraine BT52 1EY ☎ 028 7034 7020 🖷 028 7034 7022 🖰 gwyneth.kerr@colerainebc.gov.uk

PR / Communications: Ms Tara Cunningham, PR Manager, Cloonavin, 66 Portstewart Road, Coleraine BT52 1EY ☎ 028 7034 7034 🖷 028 7034 7026 🖰 pr@colerainebc.gov.uk

Computer Management: Mr Patrick McColgan, Information Technology Manager, Cloonavin, 66 Portstewart Road, Coleraine BT52 1EY ☎ 028 7034 7134 🖷 028 7034 7143 🖰 patrick.mccolgan@colerainebc.gov.uk

Consumer Protection and Trading Standards: Mr Keiran Doherty, Director of Environmental Services, Cloonavin, 66 Portstewart Road, Coleraine BT52 1EY ☎ 028 7034 7171 🖷 028 7034 7195 🖰 eh@colerainebc.gov.uk

Customer Service: Miss Moira Mann, Head of Development Services, Cloonavin, 66 Portstewart Road, Coleraine BT52 1EY ☎ 028 7034 7044 🖷 028 7034 7026 🖰 moira.mann@colerainebc.gov.uk

Economic Development: Mrs Linda Williams, Economic Development Manager, Cloonavin, 66 Portstewart Road, Coleraine BT52 1EY ☎ 028 7034 7045 🖷 028 7034 7026 🖰 linda.williams@colerainebc.gov.uk

Emergency Planning: Mr Keiran Doherty, Director of Environmental Services, Cloonavin, 66 Portstewart Road, Coleraine BT52 1EY ☎ 028 7034 7171 🖷 028 7034 7195 🖰 eh@colerainebc.gov.uk

Energy Management: Mr John Richardson, Head of Estates & Facilites Manager, Cloonavin, 66 Portstewart Road, Coleraine BT52 1EY ☎ 028 7034 7272 🖷 028 7034 7256 🖰 john.richardson@coleraine.gov.uk

Environmental Health: Mr Keiran Doherty, Director of Environmental Services, Cloonavin, 66 Portstewart Road, Coleraine BT52 1EY ☎ 028 7034 7171 🖷 028 7034 7195 🖰 eh@colerainebc.gov.uk

Estates, Property & Valuation: Ms Bernadette McGuinness, Principal Administrative Officer, Cloonavin, 66 Portstewart Road, Coleraine BT52 1EY ☎ 028 7034 7015 🖷 028 7034 7026 🖰 bernadette.mcguinness@colerainebc.gov.uk

European Liaison: Mr Martin Clark, Economic Development Assistant, Cloonavin, 66 Portstewart Road, Coleraine BT52 1EY ☎ 028 7034 7034 🖷 028 7034 7026 🖰 martin.clark@colerainebc.gov.uk

Events Manager: Ms Christine McKee, Events Manager, Cloonavin, 66 Portstewart Road, Coleraine BT52 1EY ☎ 028 7034 7208 🖰 christine.mckee@colerainebc.gov.uk

Facilities: Mr John Richardson, Head of Estates & Facilites Manager, Cloonavin, 66 Portstewart Road, Coleraine BT52 1EY ☎ 028 7034 7272 🖷 028 7034 7256 🖰 john.richardson@coleraine.gov.uk

Finance and Treasurer: Mr Richard Cox, Acting Head of Finance, Cloonavin, 66 Portstewart Road, Coleraine BT52 1EY ☎ 028 7034 7134 🖷 028 7034 7143 🖰 corporate@colerainebc.gov.uk

Grounds Maintenance: Mr Paul Jess, Acting General Manager, Parks Nursery, Newmills Road, Coleraine BT52 2JB ☎ 028 7035 1718 🖷 028 7032 7884 🖰 paul.jess@colerainebc.gov.uk

Health and Safety: Mr Rory Donnelly, Health & Safety Officer, Cloonavin, 66 Portstewart Road, Coleraine BT52 1EY ☎ 028 7034 7171 🖷 028 7034 7195 ✉ rory.donnelly@colerainebc.gov.uk

Home Energy Conservation: Ms Nicola Neill, Energy Efficiency Officer, Cloonavin, 66 Portstewart Road, Coleraine BT52 1EY ☎ 028 7034 7225 🖷 028 7034 7195

Leisure and Cultural Services: Mr Richard Baker, Corporate Director of Leisure and Development, Cloonavin, 66 Portstewart Road, Coleraine BT52 1EY ☎ 028 7034 7234 🖷 028 7034 7239 ✉ leisure@colerainebc.gov.uk

Licensing: Mrs Mary McKinney, Licensing Officer, Cloonavin, 66 Portstewart Road, Coleraine BT52 1EY ☎ 028 7034 7272 🖷 028 7034 7026 ✉ mary.mckinney@colerainebc.gov.uk

Lottery Funding, Charity and Voluntary: Ms Julie Welsh, Community Development Manager, Cloonavin, 66 Portstewart Road, Coleraine BT52 1EY ☎ 028 7034 7034 🖷 028 7034 7026 ✉ julie.welsh@colerainebc.gov.uk

Member Services: Ms Bernadette McGuinness, Principal Administrative Officer, Cloonavin, 66 Portstewart Road, Coleraine BT52 1EY ☎ 028 7034 7015 🖷 028 7034 7026 ✉ bernadette.mcguinness@colerainebc.gov.uk

Personnel / HR: Mrs Anne Lennon, Human Resources Manager, Cloonavin, 66 Portstewart Road, Coleraine BT52 1EY ☎ 028 7034 7133 🖷 028 7034 7026 ✉ anne.lennon@colerainebc.gov.uk

Recycling & Waste Minimisation: Mr Jonathan Wilson, Technical & Waste Management Officer, Cloonavin, 66 Portstewart Road, Coleraine BT52 1EY ☎ 028 7034 7272 🖷 028 7034 7256 ✉ jonathan.wilson@colerainebc.gov.uk

Staff Training: Mrs Lucille McElholm, Training Officer, Cloonavin, 66 Portstewart Road, Coleraine BT52 1EY ☎ 028 7034 7131 ✉ lucille.mcelholm@colerainebc.gov.uk

Sustainable Development: Ms Rachel Bain, Bio Diversity Officer, Cloonavin, 66 Portstewart Road, Coleraine BT52 1EY ☎ 028 7034 7272 🖷 028 7034 7256 ✉ rachel.bain@colerainebc.gov.uk

Tourism: Mr Peter Thompson, Tourism Manager, Cloonavin, 66 Portstewart Road, Coleraine BT52 1EY ☎ 028 7034 7044 🖷 028 7034 7026 ✉ peter.thompson@colerainebc.gov.uk

Town Centre: Mrs Julienne Elliott, Town Centre Manager, 2 Abbey Street, Coleraine BT52 1DS ☎ 028 7034 4067 🖷 028 7032 1416 ✉ tcm@colerainebc.gov.uk

Waste Collection and Disposal: Mr Jonathan Wilson, Technical & Waste Management Officer, Cloonavin, 66 Portstewart Road, Coleraine BT52 1EY ☎ 028 7034 7272 🖷 028 7034 7256 ✉ jonathan.wilson@colerainebc.gov.uk

Waste Management: Mr Jonathan Wilson, Technical & Waste Management Officer, Cloonavin, 66 Portstewart Road, Coleraine BT52 1EY ☎ 028 7034 7272 🖷 028 7034 7256 ✉ jonathan.wilson@colerainebc.gov.uk

MEMBERS OF THE COUNCIL (22)

***Mayor:* Cole**, Samuel (DUP - Bann)
samuel.cole@hotmail.com

***Deputy Mayor:* Hickey**, Maura (SDLP - The Skerries)
maurahickey@tiscali.co.uk

***Alderman:* Creelman**, William (DUP - Coleraine East)
william.creelman@colerainebc.gov.uk

***Alderman:* Harding**, David (UUP - Coleraine East)
dhmrcvs@hotmail.com

***Alderman:* Hillis**, Norman (UUP - The Skerries)
norman.hills@colerainebc.gov.uk

***Alderman:* McClure**, James (DUP - Coleraine Central)
james.mcclure@colerainebc.gov.uk

Alexander, Christine (IND - The Skerries)
christine.alexander@colerainebc.gov.uk

Archibald, Ciaran (SF - Bann)
ciaran.archibald@gmail.com

Barbour, David (UUP - Coleraine Central)
david.babour@colerainebc.gov.uk

Boyle, Yvonne (ALL - Coleraine East)
yvonne.boyle@allianceparty.org

Bradley, Maurice (DUP - Coleraine East)
maurice.bradley@colerainebc.gov.uk

Duddy, G (DUP - Coleraine Central)
william.duddy7@btinternet.com

Fielding, Phyllis (DUP - Coleraine East)
phyllis.fielding@colerainebc.gov.uk

Fielding, Mark (DUP - The Skerries)
mark.fielding@colerainebc.gov.uk

Fitzpatrick, Barney (ALL - The Skerries)
bernard.fitzpatrick@colerainebc.gov.uk

Holmes, Richard (UUP - Bann)
richard.holmes@colerainebc.gov.uk

King, William (UUP - Bann)
william.king@colerainebc.gov.uk

Loftus, Roisin (SDLP - Bann)
roisin.loftus@colerainebc.gov.uk

McCandless, William (DUP - Coleraine Central)
william.mccandless@colerainebc.gov.uk

McClarty, David (UUP - Coleraine Central)
david.mcclarty@colerainebc.gov.uk

McLaughlin, Gerry (SDLP - Coleraine Central)
gerry.mclaughlin@colerainebc.gov.uk

McQuillan, Adrian (DUP - Bann)
adrian.mcquillan@colerainebc.gov.uk

POLITICAL COMPOSITION

DUP: 9, UUP: 6, SDLP: 3, ALL: 2, IND: 1, SF: 1

CONWY — W

Conwy County Borough Council, (Cyngor Bwrdeistref Sirol Conwy), Bodlondeb, Bangor Road, Conwy LL32 8DU
☎ 01492 574000 🖷 01492 592114
✉ information@conwy.gov.uk
🖳 www.conwy.gov.uk

FACTS & FIGURES

Police Authority: North Wales Police Authority
Learning and Skills Council: Wales
Parliamentary Constituencies: Aberconwy, Clwyd West
EU Constituencies: Wales
Election Frequency: Elections are of whole council

PRINCIPAL OFFICERS

Chief Executive: Mr Iwan Davies, Chief Executive, Bodlondeb, Bangor Road, Conwy LL32 8DU ☎ 01492 576015 🖷 01492 576135 🖱 iwan.davies@conwy.gov.uk

Senior Management: Mr Ken Finch, Strategic Director, Bodlondeb, Bangor Road, Conwy LL32 8DU ☎ 01492 576200 🖷 01492 576203 🖱 ken.finch@conwy.gov.uk

Senior Management: Mr Andrew Kirkham, Strategic Director, Bodlondeb, Bangor Road, Conwy LL32 8DU ☎ 01492 576170 🖱 andrew.kirkham@conwy.gov.uk

Architect, Building / Property Services: Mr Derwyn Owen, Head of Engineering & Design Service, Government Buildings, Dinerth Road, Rhos on Sea, Colwyn Bay LL28 4UL ☎ 01492 574286 🖷 01492 574040 🖱 property.services@conwy.gov.uk

Building Control: Mr Phil Hardwick, Development & Building Control Manager, Civic Offices, Colwyn Bay LL29 8AR ☎ 01492 575274 🖱 phil.hardwick@conwy.gov.uk

Children / Youth Services: Mr Geraint James, Statutory Head of Education Services, Government Buildings, Dinerth Road, Rhos-on-Sea, LL28 4UL ☎ 01492 575001 🖱 geraint.james@conwy.gov.uk

Children / Youth Services: Ms Jenny Williams, Interim Director of Social Services, Civic Offices, Colwyn Bay LL29 8AR ☎ 01492 575687 🖷 01492 575687 🖱 jenny.williams@conwy.gov.uk

PR / Communications: Mrs Rachael Gill, Marketing & Communications Manager, Bodlondeb, Bangor Road, Conwy LL32 8DU ☎ 01492 575941 🖱 rachael.gill@conwy.gov.uk

Community Planning: Ms Marianne Jackson, Head of Community Development Services, Library Building, Mostyn Street, Llandudno LL30 2NG ☎ 01492 576314 🖱 marianne.jackson@conwy.gov.uk

Community Safety: Ms Sian Taylor, Community Safety Manager, Civic Offices, Colwyn Bay LL29 8AR ☎ 01492 575190 🖱 sian.taylor@conwy.gov.uk

Computer Management: Mr Steve Jones, Head of Information Technology, Bodlondeb, Conwy LL32 8DU ☎ 01492 576020 🖷 01492 592114 🖱 steve.jones@conwy.gov.uk

Consumer Protection and Trading Standards: Mr John Donnelly, Principal Licensing & Registration Officer, Civic Offices, Colwyn Bay LL29 8AR ☎ 01492 575197 🖱 john.donnelly@conwy.gov.uk

Economic Development: Mr Rob Dix, Section Head: Business & Enterprise, 28 Wynnstay Road, Colwyn Bay LL29 8NB ☎ 01492 574506 🖱 rob.dix@conwy.gov.uk

Education: Mr Geraint James, Statutory Head of Education Services, Government Buildings, Dinerth Road, Rhos-on-Sea, LL28 4UL ☎ 01492 575001 🖱 geraint.james@conwy.gov.uk

Education: Mr John Roberts, Head of Resources & Performance (Education), Government Buildings, Dinerth Road, Rhos on Sea, Colwyn Bay LL28 4UL ☎ 01492 575050 🖱 john.roberts@conwy.gov.uk

E-Government: Mrs Sarah Davies, E-Government Manager, 26 Castle Street, Conwy LL32 8AY ☎ 01492 576290 🖱 sarah.davies@conwy.gov.uk

Electoral Registration: Mrs Sian Williams, Democratic Services Manager, Bodlondeb, Bangor Road, Conwy LL32 8DU ☎ 01492 576062 🖱 sian.williams@conwy.gov.uk

Emergency Planning: Mr Jonathan Williams, Civil Contigencies Manager, Bodlondeb, Conwy LL32 8DU ☎ 01492 576099 🖱 jonathan.williams@conwy.gov.uk

Energy Management: Mr Derwyn Owen, Head of Engineering & Design Service, Government Buildings, Dinerth Road, Rhos on Sea, Colwyn Bay LL28 4UL ☎ 01492 574286 🖷 01492 574040 🖱 property.services@conwy.gov.uk

Environmental / Technical Services: Mr Geraint Edwards, Head of Environmental Services, Mochdre Offices, Conway Road, Mochdre, LL28 5AB ☎ 01492 575207 🖷 01492 575199 🖱 geraint.edwards@conwy.gov.uk

Environmental Health: Mr Nick Jones, Environmental Enforcement Manager, Civic Offices, Colwyn Bay LL29 8AR ☎ 01492 574281 🖱 nick.jones@conwy.gov.uk

Estates, Property & Valuation: Mr Bleddyn Evans, County Valuer, Government Buildings, Dinerth Road, Rhos on Sea, Colwyn Bay LL28 4UL ☎ 01492 574283 🖷 01492 574040 🖱 bleddyn.evans@conwy.gov.uk

Estates, Property & Valuation: Mr Derwyn Owen, Head of Engineering & Design Service, Government Buildings, Dinerth Road, Rhos on Sea, Colwyn Bay LL28 4UL ☎ 01492 574286 🖷 01492 574040 🖱 property.services@conwy.gov.uk

European Liaison: Mr Rob Dix, Section Head: Business & Enterprise, 28 Wynnstay Road, Colwyn Bay LL29 8NB ☎ 01492 574506 🖱 rob.dix@conwy.gov.uk

Events Manager: Mrs Rachael Gill, Marketing & Communications Manager, Bodlondeb, Bangor Road, Conwy LL32 8DU ☎ 01492 575941 🖱 rachael.gill@conwy.gov.uk

Facilities: Mr Adrian Ives, Property Maintenance & Facilities Manager, Government Buildings, Dinerth Road, Rhos on Sea, Colwyn Bay LL28 4UL ☎ 01492 574286 🖷 ; 01492 574040 🖱 adrian.ives@conwy.gov.uk

Finance and Treasurer: Mr Andrew Kirkham, Strategic Director, Bodlondeb, Conwy LL32 8DU ☎ 01492 576170 🖱 andrew.kirkham@conwy.gov.uk

Fleet Management: Mr Peter Barton-Price, Parks & Fleet Management, Mochdre Offices, Conway Road, Mochdre, Colwyn Bay LL28 5AB ☎ 01492 575395 🖱 peter.barton-price@conwy.gov.uk

Grounds Maintenance: Mr Lyn Davies, Street Scene Manager, Mochdre Offices, Conway Road, Mochdre, Colwyn Bay LL28 5AB ☎ 01492 575299 🖷 01492 575199 ✉ lyn.davies@conwy.gov.uk

Health and Safety: Mr Ken Ellis, Corporate Safety Officer, Bodlondeb, Bangor Road, Conwy LL32 8DU ☎ 01492 576092 🖷 01492 576003 ✉ ken.ellis@conwy.gov.uk

Highways: Mr Stuart Davies, Head of Highways & Infrastructure, The Heath, Penmaenmawr Road, Llanfairfechan, LL33 0PF ☎ 01492 575401 ✉ highways@conwy.gov.uk

Highways: Mr Gwyn Hughes, Head of Operations, The Heath, Penmaenmawr Road, Llanfairfechan, LL33 0PF ☎ 01492 575401 ✉ gwyn.hughes@conwy.gov.uk

Home Energy Conservation: Mrs Sam Parry, Acting Head of Housing Strategy, Civic Offices, Colwyn Bay LL29 8AR ☎ 01492 574224 ✉ sam.parry@conwy.gov.uk

Housing: Mrs Sam Parry, Acting Head of Housing Strategy, Civic Offices, Colwyn Bay LL29 8AR ☎ 01492 574224 ✉ sam.parry@conwy.gov.uk

Legal: Mrs Delyth Jones, Head of Law & Governance, Bodlondeb, Bangor Road, Conwy LL32 8DU ☎ 01492 576075 ✉ delyth.e.jones@conwy.gov.uk

Leisure and Cultural Services: Ms Marianne Jackson, Head of Community Development Services, Library Building, Mostyn Street, Llandudno LL30 2NG ☎ 01492 576314 ✉ marianne.jackson@conwy.gov.uk

Licensing: Mr John Donnelly, Principal Licensing & Registration Officer, Civic Offices, Colwyn Bay LL29 8AR ☎ 01492 575197 ✉ john.donnelly@conwy.gov.uk

Lifelong Learning: Mr Geraint James, Statutory Head of Education Services, Government Buildings, Dinerth Road, Rhos-on-Sea, LL28 4UL ☎ 01492 575001 ✉ geraint.james@conwy.gov.uk

Lighting: Mr Andy Clark, Street Lighting Manager, The Heath, Penmaenmawr Road, Llanfairfechan, LL33 0PF ☎ 01492 575489 ✉ andy.clark@conwy.gov.uk

Member Services: Ms Gill Hayes, Democratic Services Manager, Bodlondeb, Bangor Road, Conwy LL32 8DU ☎ 01492 576122 ✉ gill.hayes@conwy.gov.uk

Member Services: Mrs Sian Williams, Democratic Services Manager, Bodlondeb, Bangor Road, Conwy LL32 8DU ☎ 01492 576062 ✉ sian.williams@conwy.gov.uk

Parking: Mr Paul Evans, Traffic Engineer, The Heath, Penmaenmawr Road, Llanfairfechan, LL33 0PF ☎ 01492 575422 🖷 01248 681881 ✉ paul.evans@conwy.gov.uk

Partnerships: Ms Andrea Williams, Partnership Co-ordination Manager, Bodlondeb, Bangor Road, Conwy LL32 8DU ☎ 01492 576239 ✉ andrea.williams2@conwy.gov.uk

Personnel / HR: Mr Phillip Davies, Head of Corporate Personnel Services, Bodlondeb, Bangor Road, Conwy LL32 8DU ☎ 01492 576124 🖷 01492 576135 ✉ phillip.davies@conwy.gov.uk

Planning: Mr Phil Hardwick, Development & Building Control Manager, Civic Offices, Colwyn Bay LL29 8AR ☎ 01492 575274 ✉ phil.hardwick@conwy.gov.uk

Procurement: Mr Mike Halstead, Head of Audit & Procurement, Bodlondeb, Bangor Road, Conwy LL32 8DU ☎ 01492 574000 🖷 01492 592114 ✉ mike.halstead@conwy.gov.uk

Public Libraries: Ms Rhian Williams, Section Head: Culture & Information, Library Building, Mostyn Street, Llandudno LL30 2NG ☎ 01492 576139 ✉ rhian.williams@conwy.gov.uk

Recycling & Waste Minimisation: Mr Andrew Wilkinson, Waste Manager, Mochdre Offices, Conway Road, Mochdre, Colwyn Bay LL28 5AB ☎ 01492 575127 ✉ andrew.j.wilkinson@conwy.gov.uk

Regeneration: Mr Rob Dix, Section Head: Business & Enterprise, 28 Wynnstay Road, Colwyn Bay LL29 8NB ☎ 01492 574506 ✉ rob.dix@conwy.gov.uk

Regeneration: Ms Marianne Jackson, Head of Community Development Services, Library Building, Mostyn Street, Llandudno LL30 2NG ☎ 01492 576314 ✉ marianne.jackson@conwy.gov.uk

Road Safety: Mr Paul Evans, Traffic Engineer, The Heath, Penmaenmawr Road, Llanfairfechan, LL33 0PF ☎ 01492 575422 🖷 01248 681881 ✉ paul.evans@conwy.gov.uk

Social Services: Ms Jenny Williams, Interim Director of Social Services, Civic Offices, Colwyn Bay LL29 8AR ☎ 01492 575687 🖷 01492 575687 ✉ jenny.williams@conwy.gov.uk

Social Services (Adult): Ms Jenny Williams, Interim Director of Social Services, Civic Offices, Colwyn Bay LL29 8AR ☎ 01492 575687 🖷 01492 575687 ✉ jenny.williams@conwy.gov.uk

Social Services (Children): Ms Jenny Williams, Interim Director of Social Services, Civic Offices, Colwyn Bay LL29 8AR ☎ 01492 575687 🖷 01492 575687 ✉ jenny.williams@conwy.gov.uk

Staff Training: Mr Phillip Davies, Head of Corporate Personnel Services, Bodlondeb, Bangor Road, Conwy LL32 8DU ☎ 01492 576124 🖷 01492 576135 ✉ phillip.davies@conwy.gov.uk

Street Scene: Mr Lyn Davies, Street Scene Manager, Mochdre Offices, Conway Road, Mochdre, Colwyn Bay LL28 5AB ☎ 01492 575299 🖷 01492 575199 ✉ lyn.davies@conwy.gov.uk

Sustainable Communities: Ms Marianne Jackson, Head of Community Development Services, Library Building, Mostyn Street, Llandudno LL30 2NG ☎ 01492 576314 ✉ marianne.jackson@conwy.gov.uk

Sustainable Development: Ms Marianne Jackson, Head of Community Development Services, Library Building, Mostyn Street, Llandudno LL30 2NG ☎ 01492 576314 ✉ marianne.jackson@conwy.gov.uk

Tourism: Ms Marianne Jackson, Head of Community Development Services, Library Building, Mostyn Street, Llandudno LL30 2NG ☎ 01492 576314 ⌘ marianne.jackson@conwy.gov.uk

Town Centre: Ms Marianne Jackson, Head of Community Development Services, Library Building, Mostyn Street, Llandudno LL30 2NG ☎ 01492 576314 ⌘ marianne.jackson@conwy.gov.uk

Traffic Management: Mr Paul Evans, Traffic Engineer, The Heath, Penmaenmawr Road, Llanfairfechan, LL33 0PF ☎ 01492 575422 🖷 01248 681881 ⌘ paul.evans@conwy.gov.uk

Transport: Mr Gwyn Hughes, Head of Operations, The Heath, Penmaenmawr Road, Llanfairfechan, LL33 0PF ☎ 01492 575401 ⌘ gwyn.hughes@conwy.gov.uk

Transport: Mr Bob Saxby, Section Head: Integrated Transport (Policy), Library Building, Mostyn Street, Llandudno LL30 2NG ☎ 01492 575469 🖷 01248 681881 ⌘ bob.saxby@conwy.gov.uk

Transport Planner: Mr Bob Saxby, Section Head: Integrated Transport (Policy), Library Building, Mostyn Street, Llandudno LL30 2NG ☎ 01492 575469 🖷 01248 681881 ⌘ bob.saxby@conwy.gov.uk

Waste Collection and Disposal: Mr Andrew Wilkinson, Waste Manager, Mochdre Offices, Conway Road, Mochdre, Colwyn Bay LL28 5AB ☎ 01492 575127 ⌘ andrew.j.wilkinson@conwy.gov.uk

Waste Management: Mr Andrew Wilkinson, Waste Manager, Mochdre Offices, Conway Road, Mochdre, Colwyn Bay LL28 5AB ☎ 01492 575127 ⌘ andrew.j.wilkinson@conwy.gov.uk

Children's Play Areas: Mr Peter Barton-Price, Parks & Fleet Management, Mochdre Offices, Conway Road, Mochdre, Colwyn Bay LL28 5AB ☎ 01492 575395 ⌘ peter.barton-price@conwy.gov.uk

MEMBERS OF THE COUNCIL (59)

***Chair:* Anderson**, Stuart (IND - Bae Cinmel / Kinmel Bay)
cllr.dr.stuart.anderson@conwy.gov.uk
***Vice-Chair:* Roberts**, Liz (PC - Betws Y Coed)
cllr.liz.roberts@conwy.gov.uk
***Leader of the Council:* Roberts**, Dilwyn (PC - Llangernyw)
cllr.dilwyn.roberts@conwy.gov.uk
Allardice, Sarah Louise (LAB - Conwy)
cllr.sara.allardice@conwy.gov.uk
Bradfield, Frank (CON - Craig Y Don)
Carlisle, Cheryl (CON - Colwyn)
cllr.cheryl.carlisle@conwy.gov.uk
Cater, Christopher (IND - Penrhyn)
cllr.christopher.cater@conwy.gov.uk
Cossey, Brian (LD - Colwyn)
cllr.brian.cossey@conwy.gov.uk
Cotton, Samantha (CON - Deganwy)
cllr.samantha.cotton@conwy.gov.uk
Cowans, Dave (IND - Eirias)
cllr.dave.cowans@conwy.gov.uk
Darwin, William (IND - Bae Cinmel / Kinmel Bay)
cllr.bill.darwin@conwy.gov.uk
Doyle, Mary (CON - Rhiw)
cllr.mary.doyle@conwy.gov.uk
Edwards, Philip (PC - Llandrillo-yn-Rhos)
cllr.phil.edwards@conwy.gov.uk
Eeles, Keith (IND - Llanddulas)
cllr.keith.eeles@conwy.gov.uk
Evans, Philip (IND - Tudno)
cllr.philip.evans@conwy.gov.uk
Groom, Linda (IND - Penrhyn)
cllr.linda.groom@conwy.gov.uk
Haworth, Janet (CON - Gogarth)
cllr.janet.haworth@conwy.gov.uk
Hinchliff, Andrew (LAB - Bryn)
cllr.andrew.hinchliff@conwy.gov.uk
Hold, Jobi (LAB - Mostyn)
cllr.jobi.hold@conwy.gov.uk
Hughes, Ronnie (LAB - Tudno)
cllr.ronnie.hughes@conwy.gov.uk
Hughes, Meirion (PC - Pensarn)
cllr.meirion.hughes@conwy.gov.uk
Hughes, Chris (LAB - Glyn)
cllr.chris.hughes@conwy.gov.uk
Jamil, Ahmed (IND - Betws-Yn-Rhos)
cllr.dr.ahmed.jamil@conwy.gov.uk
Jenkins, Ian (PC - Gower)
cllr.ian.jenkins@conwy.gov.uk
Jones, Wyn (PC - Uwch Conwy)
cyng.wyn.ellis.jones@conwy.gov.uk
Jones, Ray (LAB - Pandy)
cllr.ray.jones@conwy.gov.uk
Jones, Gareth (PC - Craig Y Don)
cllr.gareth.jones@conwy.gov.uk
Khan, Abdul (PC - Glyn)
cllr.abdul.khan@conwy.gov.uk
Knightly, William (CON - Tywyn)
cllr.william.knightly@conwy.gov.uk
Lewis, Peter (IND - Uwchaled)
Lloyd-Williams, Sue (IND - Llansannan)
cllr.sue.lloyd-williams@conwy.gov.uk
Lyon, Margaret (CON - Gogarth)
cllr.margaret.lyon@conwy.gov.uk
MacLennan, John (CON - Pentre Mawr)
cllr.john.maclennan@conwy.gov.uk
MacRae, Delyth (PC - Gele)
cllr.delyth.macrae@conwy.gov.uk
McCaffrey, Anne (IND - Capelulo)
cllr.anne.mccaffrey@conwy.gov.uk
Miles, Dewi (IND - Mostyn)
cllr.dewi.miles@conwy.gov.uk
Milne, Donald (CON - Llandrillo-yn-Rhos)
cllr.donald.milne@conwy.gov.uk
Parry, Edgar (IND - Crwst)
cllr.edgar.parry@conwy.gov.uk
Parry, Roger (CON - Llandrillo-yn-Rhos)
cllr.roger.parry@conwy.gov.uk
Priestley, Michael (LD - Marl)
cllr.michael.priestley@conwy.gov.uk
Rayner, Mike (PC - Eglwysbach)
cllr.mike.rayner@conwy.gov.uk
Rees, Graham (IND - Llansanffraid)
cllr.graham.rees@conwy.gov.uk
Roberts, Dave (CON - Llandrillo-yn-Rhos)
cllr.david.m.roberts@conwy.gov.uk
Roberts, Paul (CON - Caerhun)
cllr.paul.roberts@conwy.gov.uk
Roberts, John (LD - Rhiw)
cllr.john.roberts@conwy.gov.uk
Rogers-Jones, Hilary (PC - Trefriw)

cllr.hilary.rogers-jones@conwy.gov.uk
Rowlands, Tim (CON - Gele)
cllr.tim.rowlands@conwy.gov.uk
Rowlands, Sam (CON - Pentre Mawr)
cllr.sam.rowlands@conwy.gov.uk
Shotter, Susan (LD - Marl)
Smith, Deion (LAB - Llysfaen)
cllr.deion.smith@conwy.gov.uk
Smith, Nigel (IND - Bae Cinmel / Kinmel Bay)
cllr.nigel.smith@conwy.gov.uk
Squire, Bob (IND - Eirias)
cllr.bob.squire@conwy.gov.uk
Stevens, Ken (LAB - Pant Yr Afon / Penmaenan)
cllr.ken.stevens@conwy.gov.uk
Stott, Trevor (LD - Rhiw)
cllr.trevor.stott@conwy.gov.uk
Stubbs, Jean (LAB - Abergele Pensarn)
cllr.jean.stubbs@conwy.gov.uk
Tansley, Adrian (LAB - Mochdre)
cllr.adrian.tansley@conwy.gov.uk
Vaughan, Joan (IND - Conwy)
cllr.joan.vaughan@conwy.gov.uk
Weyman, Jason (IND - Deganwy)
cllr.jason.weyman@conwy.gov.uk
Wood, Andrew (IND - Gele)
cllr.andrew.wood@conwy.gov.uk

POLITICAL COMPOSITION
IND: 19, CON: 14, PC: 11, LAB: 10, LD: 5

CABINET
Leader: Mr Dilwyn Roberts
Deputy Leader: Mr Ronnie Hughes
Communication, Marketing & Leisure: Mr Graham Rees
Communities: Mr Philip Edwards
Environment & Sustainability: Mr Dave Cowans
Finance & Resources: Mr Jason Weyman
Governance & Regulation: Mr Philip Evans
Highways & Property: Mr Michael Priestley
Skills & Lifelong Learning: Mr Wyn Jones
Social Care & Health: Mr Chris Hughes

COMMITTEE CHAIRS
Communities Overview & Scrutiny: Mrs Linda Groom
Democratic Services: Mrs Cheryl Carlisle
Licensing & Regulation: Mr Ken Stevens
Partnerships Overview & Scrutiny: Mrs Sue Lloyd-Williams
Principal Overview & Scrutiny: Mr William Knightly

COOKSTOWN N

Cookstown District Council, Council Offices, Burn Road, Cookstown BT80 8DT ☎ 028 8676 2205
✉ info@cookstown.gov.uk
🖳 www.cookstown.gov.uk

FACTS & FIGURES
Police Authority: Northern Ireland Policing Board
Health Authority: Health & Social Care Board
Learning and Skills Council: Northern Ireland
EU Constituencies: Northern Ireland
Election Frequency: Elections are of whole council

PRINCIPAL OFFICERS
Chief Executive: Mr Adrian McCreesh, Acting Clerk & Chief Executive, Council Offices, Burn Road, Cookstown BT80 8DT
☎ 028 8676 2205 🖷 028 8676 4360
✉ adrian.mccreesh@cookstown.gov.uk

Senior Management: Mr Derek Duncan, Director of Operational Services, Council Offices, Burn Road, Cookstown BT80 8DT
☎ 028 8676 2205 🖷 028 8676 4360
✉ derek.duncan@cookstown.gov.uk

Senior Management: Mr Mark Kelso, Director of Environmental Health, Council Offices, Burn Road, Cookstown BT80 8DT ☎ 028 8676 2205 🖷 028 8676 4360 ✉ mark.kelso@cookstown.gov.uk

Senior Management: Mr Trevor McAdoo, Director of Building Control, Council Offices, Burn Road, Cookstown BT80 8DT
☎ 028 8676 2205 🖷 028 8676 4360
✉ trevor.mcadoo@cookstown.gov.uk

Senior Management: Mr Adrian McCreesh, Acting Clerk & Chief Executive, Council Offices, Burn Road, Cookstown BT80 8DT
☎ 028 8676 2205 🖷 028 8676 4360
✉ adrian.mccreesh@cookstown.gov.uk

Senior Management: Mr Ivor Paisley, Director of Corporate Services, Council Offices, Burn Road, Cookstown BT80 8DT
☎ 028 8676 2205 🖷 028 8676 4360
✉ ivor.paisley@cookstown.gov.uk

Best Value: Mr Ivor Paisley, Director of Corporate Services, Council Offices, Burn Road, Cookstown BT80 8DT ☎ 028 8676 2205 🖷 028 8676 4360 ✉ ivor.paisley@cookstown.gov.uk

Building Control: Mr Trevor McAdoo, Director of Building Control, Council Offices, Burn Road, Cookstown BT80 8DT
☎ 028 8676 2205 🖷 028 8676 4360
✉ trevor.mcadoo@cookstown.gov.uk

Community Safety: Mrs Shauna McCloskey, Community Safety, Council Offices, Burn Road, Cookstown BT80 8DT ☎ 028 8676 2205 ✉ shauna.mccloskey@cookstown.gov.uk

Computer Management: Mr Barry O'Hagan, IT Officer, Council Offices, Burn Road, Cookstown BT80 8DT ☎ 028 8676 2205
✉ barry.ohagan@cookstown.gov.uk

Corporate Services: Mr Ivor Paisley, Director of Corporate Services, Council Offices, Burn Road, Cookstown BT80 8DT
☎ 028 8676 2205 🖷 028 8676 4360
✉ ivor.paisley@cookstown.gov.uk

Economic Development: Mr Adrian McCreesh, Acting Clerk & Chief Executive, Council Offices, Burn Road, Cookstown BT80 8DT ☎ 028 8676 2205 🖷 028 8676 4360
✉ adrian.mccreesh@cookstown.gov.uk

E-Government: Mr Barry O'Hagan, IT Officer, Council Offices, Burn Road, Cookstown BT80 8DT ☎ 028 8676 2205
✉ barry.ohagan@cookstown.gov.uk

Emergency Planning: Mr Mark Kelso, Director of Environmental

Health, Council Offices, Burn Road, Cookstown BT80 8DT ☎ 028 8676 2205 🖷 028 8676 4360 ✉ mark.kelso@cookstown.gov.uk

Environmental Health: Mr Mark Kelso, Director of Environmental Health, Council Offices, Burn Road, Cookstown BT80 8DT ☎ 028 8676 2205 🖷 028 8676 4360 ✉ mark.kelso@cookstown.gov.uk

Finance and Treasurer: Mr Ivor Paisley, Director of Corporate Services, Council Offices, Burn Road, Cookstown BT80 8DT ☎ 028 8676 2205 🖷 028 8676 4360 ✉ ivor.paisley@cookstown.gov.uk

Health and Safety: Mr Ray Hall, Health & Safety Officer, Council Offices, Burn Road, Cookstown BT80 8DT ☎ 028 8676 2205 🖷 028 8676 4360 ✉ ray.hall@cookstown.gov.uk

Leisure and Cultural Services: Mr Derek Duncan, Director of Operational Services, Council Offices, Burn Road, Cookstown BT80 8DT ☎ 028 8676 2205 🖷 028 8676 4360 ✉ derek.duncan@cookstown.gov.uk

Licensing: Mr Trevor McAdoo, Director of Building Control, Council Offices, Burn Road, Cookstown BT80 8DT ☎ 028 8676 2205 🖷 028 8676 4360 ✉ trevor.mcadoo@cookstown.gov.uk

Member Services: Ms Carmel McCann, Personal Assistant, Council Offices, Burn Road, Cookstown BT80 8DT ☎ 028 8676 2205 🖷 028 8676 9165 ✉ carmel.mccann@cookstown.gov.uk

Personnel / HR: Miss Sandra Matchett, Personnel Officer, Council Offices, Burn Road, Cookstown BT80 8DT ☎ 028 8676 2205 🖷 028 8676 4360 ✉ sandra.matchett@cookstown.gov.uk

Planning: Mr Trevor McAdoo, Director of Building Control, Council Offices, Burn Road, Cookstown BT80 8DT ☎ 028 8676 2205 🖷 028 8676 4360 ✉ trevor.mcadoo@cookstown.gov.uk

Recycling & Waste Minimisation: Mr Derek Duncan, Director of Operational Services, Council Offices, Burn Road, Cookstown BT80 8DT ☎ 028 8676 2205 🖷 028 8676 4360 ✉ derek.duncan@cookstown.gov.uk

Recycling & Waste Minimisation: Mr Mark McAdoo, Operations Officer, Council Offices, Burn Road, Cookstown BT80 8DT ☎ 028 8676 2205 🖷 028 8676 4360 ✉ mark.mcadoo@cookstown.gov.uk

Sustainable Communities: Mr Mark Kelso, Director of Environmental Health, Council Offices, Burn Road, Cookstown BT80 8DT ☎ 028 8676 2205 🖷 028 8676 4360 ✉ mark.kelso@cookstown.gov.uk

Tourism: Ms Denise Campbell, Tourism Officer, Burnavon Centre, Burn Road, Cookstown BT80 8DT ☎ 028 8676 9949 🖷 928 8676 5853 ✉ denise.campbell@cookstown.gov.uk

Town Centre: Mr Terry Scullion, Town Strategy Manager, Council Offices, Burn Road, Cookstown BT80 8DT ☎ 028 8676 2205 🖷 028 8676 4360 ✉ terry.scullion@cookstown.gov.uk

Waste Collection and Disposal: Mr Derek Duncan, Director of Operational Services, Council Offices, Burn Road, Cookstown BT80 8DT ☎ 028 8676 2205 🖷 028 8676 4360 ✉ derek.duncan@cookstown.gov.uk

Waste Management: Mr Derek Duncan, Director of Operational Services, Council Offices, Burn Road, Cookstown BT80 8DT ☎ 028 8676 2205 🖷 028 8676 4360 ✉ derek.duncan@cookstown.gov.uk

MEMBERS OF THE COUNCIL (16)

***Chair:* Clarke**, Sean (SF - Drum Manor)
clerke@hotmail.com
Glasgow, Samuel (UUP - Drum Manor)
Kelly, Robert (UUP - Ballinderry)
robertkelly538@btinternet.com
Lees, Maureen (DUP - Drum Manor)
maureen.lees@cookstown.gov.uk
Mallaghan, Cáthal (SF - Drum Manor)
cathalmallaghan@hotmail.com
Mayo, Deidre (SDLP - Ballinderry)
deirdre.mayo@cookstown.gov.uk
McAleer, Patrick (SF - Ballinderry)
pearse@pearse6.wanado.co.uk
McCartney, Samuel (DUP - Ballinderry)
McCrea, Ian (DUP - Cookstown Central)
ian@ianmccrea.com
McElhone, Ciarán (SF - Cookstown Central)
ciaran.mcelhone@yahoo.ie
McFlynn, Christine (SDLP - Ballinderry)
cllrcmcflynn@hotmail.com
McGarvey, James (SDLP - Drum Manor)
jamessmcgarvey@aol.com
McIvor, Michael (SF - Ballinderry)
McNamee, John (SF - Cookstown Central)
john.mcnamee@cookstown.gov.uk
Quinn, Tony (SDLP - Cookstown Central)
tony.quinn@cookstown.gov.uk
Wilson, Trevor (UUP - Cookstown Central)
trevor.wilson@cookstown.gov.uk

POLITICAL COMPOSITION

SF: 6, SDLP: 4, UUP: 3, DUP: 3

COMMITTEE CHAIRS

Audit & Risk: Mr Trevor Wilson
Development: Mr Patrick McAleer
Policy & Resources: Mr Ciarán McElhone
Sports & Leisure: Mr Trevor Wilson

COPELAND D

Copeland Borough Council, The Copeland Centre, Catherine Street, Whitehaven CA28 7SJ ☎ 0845 054 8600 ✉ info@copelandbc.gov.uk 🖳 www.copelandbc.gov.uk

FACTS & FIGURES

Police Authority: Cumbria Police Authority
Health Authority: North West Strategic Health Authority
Learning and Skills Council: North West
Parliamentary Constituencies: Copeland
EU Constituencies: North West
Election Frequency: Elections are of whole council

LOCAL AUTHORITIES

PRINCIPAL OFFICERS

Chief Executive: Mr Paul Walker, Chief Executive, The Copeland Centre, Catherine Street, Whitehaven CA28 7SJ ☎ 01946 598324

Senior Management: Ms Cath Coombs, Acting Head of Leisure & Environmental Services, Whitehaven Commercial Park, Moresby Parks, Whitehaven CA28 8YD ☎ 01946 852960 🖷 01946 852965 ✉ ccoombs@copelandbc.gov.uk

Senior Management: Mrs Pat Graham, Corporate Director (People & Places), The Copeland Centre, Catherine Street, Whitehaven CA28 7SJ ☎ 01946 598415 🖷 01946 598440 ✉ pgraham@copelandbc.gov.uk

Senior Management: Mr Steve Smith, Interim Head of Regeneration, The Copeland Centre, Catherine Street, Whitehaven CA28 7SJ ☎ 01946 598415 🖷 01946 598307 ✉ ssmith@copelandbc.gov.uk

Senior Management: Ms Joanne Wagstaffe, Corporate Director (Resources & Transformation), The Copeland Centre, Catherine Street, Whitehaven CA28 7SJ ☎ 01946 598322 ✉ jwagstaffe@copelandbc.gov.uk

Access Officer / Social Services (Disability): Ms Heather Morrison, Planning Officer, The Copeland Centre, Catherine Street, Whitehaven CA28 7SJ ☎ 01946 598420 🖷 01946 598306 ✉ hmorrison@copelandbc.gov.uk

Building Control: Mrs Pat Graham, Corporate Director (People & Places), The Copeland Centre, Catherine Street, Whitehaven CA28 7SJ ☎ 01946 598440 🖷 01946 598440 ✉ pgraham@copelandbc.gov.uk

Building Control: Mr Mark Key, Principal Building Control Surveyor, The Copeland Centre, Catherine Street, Whitehaven CA28 7SJ ☎ 01946 598407 ✉ mkey@copelandbc.gov.uk

Building Control: Mr Keith Parker, Head of Neighbourhoods, Whitehaven Commercial Park, Moresby Parks, Whitehaven CA28 8YD ☎ 01946 593021 🖷 01946 852965 ✉ kparker@copelandbc.gov.uk

Building Control: Mr Keith Parker, Head of Neighbourhoods, Whitehaven Commercial Park, Moresby Parks, Whitehaven CA28 8YD ☎ 01946 593021 ✉ keith.parker@copelandbc.gov.uk

Children / Youth Services: Ms Cath Coombs, Acting Head of Leisure & Environmental Services, Whitehaven Commercial Park, Moresby Parks, Whitehaven CA28 8YD ☎ 01946 852960 🖷 01946 852965 ✉ ccoombs@copelandbc.gov.uk

PR / Communications: Mr Ian Curwen, Communications Officer, The Copeland Centre, Catherine Street, Whitehaven CA28 7SJ ☎ 01946 598504 ✉ icurwen@copelandbc.gov.uk

Computer Management: Mr Martin Stroud, ICT Manager, The Copeland Centre, Catherine Street, Whitehaven CA28 7SJ ☎ 01946 598481 ✉ mstroud@copelandbc.gov.uk

Consumer Protection and Trading Standards: Ms Jackie O'Reilly, Environmental Health Manager, The Copeland Centre, Catherine Street, Whitehaven CA28 7SJ ☎ 01946 598335 🖷 01946 598304 ✉ joreilly@copelandbc.gov.uk

Contracts: Ms Cath Coombs, Acting Head of Leisure & Environmental Services, Whitehaven Commercial Park, Moresby Parks, Whitehaven CA28 8YD ☎ 01946 852960 🖷 01946 852965 ✉ ccoombs@copelandbc.gov.uk

Contracts: Mrs Darienne Law, Head of Corporate Resources, The Copeland Centre, Catherine Street, Whitehaven CA28 7SJ ☎ 01946 598457 ✉ darienne.law@copeland.gov.uk

Corporate Services: Mr Keith Parker, Acting Corporate Director (Quality of Life), The Copeland Centre, Catherine Street, Whitehaven CA28 7SJ ☎ 01946 598322 🖷 01946 598303 ✉ kparker@copelandbc.gov.uk

Customer Service: Mrs Pat Graham, Corporate Director (People & Places), The Copeland Centre, Catherine Street, Whitehaven CA28 7SJ ☎ 01946 598415 🖷 01946 598440 ✉ pgraham@copelandbc.gov.uk

Customer Service: Dr Penny Mell, Head of Policy & Transformation, The Copeland Centre, Catherine Street, Whitehaven CA28 7SJ ☎ 01946 598450 🖷 01946 852585 ✉ penny.mell@copeland.gov.uk

Economic Development: Mrs Julie Betteridge, Head of Development Strategy, The Copeland Centre, Catherine Street, Whitehaven CA28 7SJ ☎ 01946 598415 🖷 01946 598307 ✉ jbetteridge@copelandbc.gov.uk

Economic Development: Mr Steve Smith, Interim Head of Regeneration, The Copeland Centre, Catherine Street, Whitehaven CA28 7SJ ☎ 01946 598415 🖷 01946 598307 ✉ ssmith@copelandbc.gov.uk

Electoral Registration: Miss Stephanie Shaw, Elections Manager, The Copeland Centre, Catherine Street, Whitehaven CA28 7SJ ☎ 01946 598533 🖷 01946 598311 ✉ sshaw@copelandbc.gov.uk

Emergency Planning: Miss Stephanie Shaw, Elections Manager, The Copeland Centre, Catherine Street, Whitehaven CA28 7SJ ☎ 01946 598533 🖷 01946 598311 ✉ sshaw@copelandbc.gov.uk

Environmental Health: Mrs Pat Graham, Corporate Director (People & Places), The Copeland Centre, Catherine Street, Whitehaven CA28 7SJ ☎ 01946 598440 🖷 01946 598440 ✉ pgraham@copelandbc.gov.uk

Environmental Health: Ms Jackie O'Reilly, Environmental Health Manager, The Copeland Centre, Catherine Street, Whitehaven CA28 7SJ ☎ 01946 598335 🖷 01946 598304 ✉ joreilly@copelandbc.gov.uk

Environmental Health: Mr Keith Parker, Head of Neighbourhoods, Whitehaven Commercial Park, Moresby Parks, Whitehaven CA28 8YD ☎ 01946 593021 ✉ keith.parker@copelandbc.gov.uk

Environmental Health: Mr Keith Parker, Head of

Neighbourhoods, Whitehaven Commercial Park, Moresby Parks, Whitehaven CA28 8YD ☎ 01946 593021 🖷 01946 852965 ✉ kparker@copelandbc.gov.uk

Estates, Property & Valuation: Mrs Pat Graham, Corporate Director (People & Places), The Copeland Centre, Catherine Street, Whitehaven CA28 7SJ ☎ 01946 598440 🖷 01946 598440 ✉ pgraham@copelandbc.gov.uk

European Liaison: Mr Steve Smith, Interim Head of Regeneration, The Copeland Centre, Catherine Street, Whitehaven CA28 7SJ ☎ 01946 598415 🖷 01946 598307 ✉ ssmith@copelandbc.gov.uk

Finance and Treasurer: Ms Angela Brown, Head of Finance, The Copeland Centre, Catherine Street, Whitehaven CA28 7SJ ☎ 0845 054 8600

Finance and Treasurer: Mrs Darienne Law, Head of Corporate Resources, The Copeland Centre, Catherine Street, Whitehaven CA28 7SJ ☎ 01946 598457 ✉ darienne.law@copeland.gov.uk

Finance and Treasurer: Ms Joanne Wagstaffe, Corporate Director (Resources & Transformation), The Copeland Centre, Catherine Street, Whitehaven CA28 7SJ ☎ 01946 598322 ✉ jwagstaffe@copelandbc.gov.uk

Fleet Management: Ms Cath Coombs, Acting Head of Leisure & Environmental Services, Whitehaven Commercial Park, Moresby Parks, Whitehaven CA28 8YD ☎ 01946 852960 🖷 01946 852965 ✉ ccoombs@copelandbc.gov.uk

Grounds Maintenance: Mr Keith Parker, Head of Neighbourhoods, Whitehaven Commercial Park, Moresby Parks, Whitehaven CA28 8YD ☎ 01946 593021 ✉ keith.parker@copelandbc.gov.uk

Highways: Mr John Hughes, Principal Strategic Planning & Development Officer, The Copeland Centre, Catherine Street, Whitehaven CA28 7SJ ☎ 01946 598435 🖷 01946 598307 ✉ jhughes@copelandbc.gov.uk

Housing: Mrs Julie Betteridge, Head of Development Strategy, The Copeland Centre, Catherine Street, Whitehaven CA28 7SJ ☎ 01946 598415 🖷 01946 598307 ✉ jbetteridge@copelandbc.gov.uk

Housing: Mrs Pat Graham, Corporate Director (People & Places), The Copeland Centre, Catherine Street, Whitehaven CA28 7SJ ☎ 01946 598440 🖷 01946 598440 ✉ pgraham@copelandbc.gov.uk

Local Area Agreement: Mrs Julie Betteridge, Head of Development Strategy, The Copeland Centre, Catherine Street, Whitehaven CA28 7SJ ☎ 01946 598415 🖷 01946 598307 ✉ jbetteridge@copelandbc.gov.uk

Leisure and Cultural Services: Mrs Pat Graham, Corporate Director (People & Places), The Copeland Centre, Catherine Street, Whitehaven CA28 7SJ ☎ 01946 598440 🖷 01946 598440 ✉ pgraham@copelandbc.gov.uk

Leisure and Cultural Services: Mr Keith Parker, Head of Neighbourhoods, Whitehaven Commercial Park, Moresby Parks, Whitehaven CA28 8YD ☎ 01946 593021 🖷 01946 852965 ✉ kparker@copelandbc.gov.uk

Lighting: Ms Cath Coombs, Acting Head of Leisure & Environmental Services, Whitehaven Commercial Park, Moresby Parks, Whitehaven CA28 8YD ☎ 01946 852960 🖷 01946 852965 ✉ ccoombs@copelandbc.gov.uk

Lottery Funding, Charity and Voluntary: Mr Steve Smith, Interim Head of Regeneration, The Copeland Centre, Catherine Street, Whitehaven CA28 7SJ ☎ 01946 598415 🖷 01946 598307 ✉ ssmith@copelandbc.gov.uk

Member Services: Mr Tim Capper, Democratic Services Manager, The Copeland Centre, Catherine Street, Whitehaven CA28 7SJ ☎ 01946 598526 🖷 01946 598303 ✉ tcapper@copelandbc.gov.uk

Member Services: Mrs Darienne Law, Head of Corporate Resources, The Copeland Centre, Catherine Street, Whitehaven CA28 7SJ ☎ 01946 598457 ✉ darienne.law@copeland.gov.uk

Parking: Ms Cath Coombs, Acting Head of Leisure & Environmental Services, Whitehaven Commercial Park, Moresby Parks, Whitehaven CA28 8YD ☎ 01946 852960 🖷 01946 852965 ✉ ccoombs@copelandbc.gov.uk

Partnerships: Mrs Julie Betteridge, Head of Development Strategy, The Copeland Centre, Catherine Street, Whitehaven CA28 7SJ ☎ 01946 598415 🖷 01946 598307 ✉ jbetteridge@copelandbc.gov.uk

Partnerships: Mr Keith Parker, Acting Corporate Director (Quality of Life), The Copeland Centre, Catherine Street, Whitehaven CA28 7SJ ☎ 01946 598322 🖷 01946 598303 ✉ kparker@copelandbc.gov.uk

Personnel / HR: Mr Len Gleed, Human Resources Manager, The Copeland Centre, Catherine Street, Whitehaven CA28 7SJ ☎ 01946 598505 🖷 01946 598303 ✉ lgleed@copelandbc.gov.uk

Personnel / HR: Mrs Darienne Law, Head of Corporate Resources, The Copeland Centre, Catherine Street, Whitehaven CA28 7SJ ☎ 01946 598457 ✉ darienne.law@copeland.gov.uk

Planning: Mrs Pat Graham, Corporate Director (People & Places), The Copeland Centre, Catherine Street, Whitehaven CA28 7SJ ☎ 01946 598440 🖷 01946 598440 ✉ pgraham@copelandbc.gov.uk

Planning: Mr Tony Pomfret, Development Services Manager, The Copeland Centre, Catherine Street, Whitehaven CA28 7SJ ☎ 01946 598416 🖷 01946 598307 ✉ tpomfret@copelandbc.gov.uk

Recycling & Waste Minimisation: Ms Janice Carrol, Waste Services Manager, Whitehaven Commercial Park, Moresby Parks, Whitehaven CA28 8YD ☎ 01946 852915 🖷 01946 852965 ✉ jcarrol@copelandbc.gov.uk

Recycling & Waste Minimisation: Mr Keith Parker, Head of Neighbourhoods, Whitehaven Commercial Park, Moresby Parks, Whitehaven CA28 8YD ☎ 01946 593021 🖷 01946 852965 ✉ kparker@copelandbc.gov.uk

Regeneration: Mrs Julie Betteridge, Head of Development Strategy, The Copeland Centre, Catherine Street, Whitehaven CA28 7SJ ☎ 01946 598415 🖷 01946 598307 ✉ jbetteridge@copelandbc.gov.uk

Regeneration: Mrs Pat Graham, Corporate Director (People & Places), The Copeland Centre, Catherine Street, Whitehaven CA28 7SJ ☎ 01946 598440 🖷 01946 598440 ✉ pgraham@copelandbc.gov.uk

Road Safety: Mr John Hughes, Principal Strategic Planning & Development Officer, The Copeland Centre, Catherine Street, Whitehaven CA28 7SJ ☎ 01946 598435 🖷 01946 598307 ✉ jhughes@copelandbc.gov.uk

Staff Training: Mrs Darienne Law, Head of Corporate Resources, The Copeland Centre, Catherine Street, Whitehaven CA28 7SJ ☎ 01946 598457 ✉ darienne.law@copeland.gov.uk

Street Scene: Ms Cath Coombs, Acting Head of Leisure & Environmental Services, Whitehaven Commercial Park, Moresby Parks, Whitehaven CA28 8YD ☎ 01946 852960 🖷 01946 852965 ✉ ccoombs@copelandbc.gov.uk

Sustainable Communities: Mrs Julie Betteridge, Head of Development Strategy, The Copeland Centre, Catherine Street, Whitehaven CA28 7SJ ☎ 01946 598415 🖷 01946 598307 ✉ jbetteridge@copelandbc.gov.uk

Sustainable Communities: Mr Steve Smith, Interim Head of Regeneration, The Copeland Centre, Catherine Street, Whitehaven CA28 7SJ ☎ 01946 598415 🖷 01946 598307 ✉ ssmith@copelandbc.gov.uk

Sustainable Development: Mrs Julie Betteridge, Head of Development Strategy, The Copeland Centre, Catherine Street, Whitehaven CA28 7SJ ☎ 01946 598415 🖷 01946 598307 ✉ jbetteridge@copelandbc.gov.uk

Sustainable Development: Ms Rachel Osbourne, Sustainability Officer, The Copeland Centre, Catherine Street, Whitehaven CA28 7SJ ☎ 0845 054 8600

Traffic Management: Mr John Hughes, Principal Strategic Planning & Development Officer, The Copeland Centre, Catherine Street, Whitehaven CA28 7SJ ☎ 01946 598435 🖷 01946 598307 ✉ jhughes@copelandbc.gov.uk

Transport: Mrs Julie Betteridge, Head of Development Strategy, The Copeland Centre, Catherine Street, Whitehaven CA28 7SJ ☎ 01946 598415 🖷 01946 598307 ✉ jbetteridge@copelandbc.gov.uk

Transport: Ms Cath Coombs, Acting Head of Leisure & Environmental Services, Whitehaven Commercial Park, Moresby Parks, Whitehaven CA28 8YD ☎ 01946 852960 🖷 01946 852965 ✉ ccoombs@copelandbc.gov.uk

Waste Collection and Disposal: Ms Janice Carrol, Waste Services Manager, Whitehaven Commercial Park, Moresby Parks, Whitehaven CA28 8YD ☎ 01946 852915 🖷 01946 852965 ✉ jcarrol@copelandbc.gov.uk

Waste Collection and Disposal: Mr Keith Parker, Head of Neighbourhoods, Whitehaven Commercial Park, Moresby Parks, Whitehaven CA28 8YD ☎ 01946 593021 ✉ keith.parker@copelandbc.gov.uk

Waste Management: Mrs Pat Graham, Corporate Director (People & Places), The Copeland Centre, Catherine Street, Whitehaven CA28 7SJ ☎ 01946 598440 🖷 01946 598440 ✉ pgraham@copelandbc.gov.uk

Waste Management: Mr Keith Parker, Head of Neighbourhoods, Whitehaven Commercial Park, Moresby Parks, Whitehaven CA28 8YD ☎ 01946 593021 🖷 01946 852965 ✉ kparker@copelandbc.gov.uk

Waste Management: Mr Keith Parker, Head of Neighbourhoods, Whitehaven Commercial Park, Moresby Parks, Whitehaven CA28 8YD ☎ 01946 593021 ✉ keith.parker@copelandbc.gov.uk

MEMBERS OF THE COUNCIL (51)

***Mayor:* Jackson**, John (CON - Beckermet)
john.jackson@copeland.gov.uk

***Deputy Mayor:* Tyson**, Peter (LAB - Sandwith)
peter.tyson@copeland.gov.uk

***Leader of the Council:* Woodburn**, Elaine (LAB - Egremont North)
elaine.woodburn@copeland.gov.uk

Banks, David (LAB - Cleator Moor South)
david.banks@copeland.gov.uk

Blackwell, Geoffrey (LAB - Moresby)
geoffrey.blackwell@copeland.gov.uk

Bowman, John (LAB - Distington)
john.bowman@copeland.gov.uk

Bowman, Jackie (LAB - Distington)
jackie.bowman@copeland.gov.uk

Branney, Hugh (LAB - Cleator Moor North)
hugh.branney@copeland.gov.uk

Clarkson, Yvonne (CON - Beckermet)
yvonne.clarkson@copeland.gov.uk

Clements, George (LAB - Kells)
george.clements@copeland.gov.uk

Conner, Karl (LAB - Egremont North)
karl.connor@copeland.gov.uk

Connolly, Peter (LAB - Frizington)
peter.connnolly@copeland.gov.uk

Dixon, Brian (O - Distington)
bdixon@copeland.gov.uk

Docherty, Margarita (LAB - Hensingham)
margarita.docherty@copeland.gov.uk

Downie, Jon (LAB - Frizington)
jon.downie@copeland.gov.uk

Eastwood, Eileen (CON - Seascale)
eileen.eastwood@copeland.gov.uk

Faichney, Dorothy Anne (LAB - Mirehouse)
membersservices@copeland.gov.uk

Fallows, John (LAB - Newtown)
john.fallows@copeland.gov.uk

Garrity, Geoffrey (LAB - Hensingham)

geoffrey.garrity@copeland.gov.uk
Gleaves, Frederick (CON - Holborn Hill)
fred.gleaves@copeland.gov.uk
Greatorex, Phil (LAB - Bransty)
philip.greatorex@copeland.gov.uk
Haraldsen, Stephen (CON - Hillcrest)
stephen.haraldsen@copeland.gov.uk
Heathcote, Francis (CON - Newtown)
francis.heathcote@copeland.gov.uk
Hill, Ian (CON - St Bees)
ian.hill@copeland.gov.uk
Hitchen, Keith (CON - Bootle)
keith.hitchen@copeland.gov.uk
Hogg, Lena (LAB - Egremont South)
lena.hogg@copeland.gov.uk
Holliday, Allan (LAB - Kells)
allan.holliday@copeland.gov.uk
Hully, Joan (LAB - Cleator Moor North)
membersservices@copeland.gov.uk
Jacob, Alan (CON - Gosforth)
alan.jacob@copeland.gov.uk
Kane, Peter (LAB - Mirehouse)
peter.kane@copeland.gov.uk
Kane, John (LAB - Harbour)
john.kane@copeland.gov.uk
McVeigh, Michael (LAB - Egremont South)
micheal.mcveigh@copeland.gov.uk
Moore, David (CON - Seascale)
david.moore@copeland.gov.uk
Norwood, Alistair (CON - Hillcrest)
alistair.norwood@copeland.gov.uk
Park, John (LAB - Holborn Hill)
john.park@copeland.gov.uk
Pollen, Sam (LAB - Egremont North)
sam.pollen@copeland.gov.uk
Riley, David (LAB - Cleator Moor South)
david.riley@copeland.gov.uk
Salkeld, Robert (CON - Ennerdale)
robert.salkfied@copeland.gov.uk
Scurrah, Gilbert (CON - Millom Without)
membersservices@copeland.gov.uk
Smith, Dave (LAB - Bransty)
dave.smith@copeland.gov.uk
Southward, William (LAB - Cleator Moor North)
membersservices@copeland.gov.uk
Stephenson, Peter (LAB - Sandwith)
peter.stephenson@copeland.gov.uk
Sunderland, Joseph (IND - Arlecdon)
membersservices@copeland.gov.uk
Troughton, Gillian (LAB - Bransty)
gillian.troughton@copeland.gov.uk
Whalley, Paul (LAB - Mirehouse)
paul.whalley@copeland.gov.uk
Williams, Jeanette (LAB - Harbour)
jeanette.williams@copeland.gov.uk
Williams, Norman (LAB - Hensingham)
norman.williams@copeland.gov.uk
Wilson, Douglas (CON - Haverigg)
douglas.wilson@copeland.gov.uk
Wilson, Fee (CON - Newtown)
felicity.wilson@copeland.gov.uk
Woodman, Carole (LAB - Egremont South)
carole.woodman@copeland.gov
Wormstrup, Henry (LAB - Harbour)
henry.wormstrup@copeland.gov.uk

POLITICAL COMPOSITION
LAB: 34, CON: 15, IND: 1, O: 1

CABINET
Leader: Miss Elaine Woodburn
Environment & Sustainability: Mr Allan Holliday
Finance & Resources: Ms Gillian Troughton
Housing & Planning: Mr George Clements
Leisure, Culture & Youth: Mr Hugh Branney
Partnerships & Policy: Mr Karl Conner
Performance & Transformation: Mr John Bowman
Regeneration: Mr Phil Greatorex

CORBY D

Corby Borough Council, Grosvenor House, George Street, Corby NN17 1QB ☎ 01536 464000 🖷 01536 400200
💻 www.corby.gov.uk

FACTS & FIGURES
Police Authority: Northamptonshire Police Authority
Health Authority: East Midlands Strategic Health Authority
Learning and Skills Council: East Midlands
Parliamentary Constituencies: Corby
EU Constituencies: East Midlands
Election Frequency: Every 4 years
Twinning: Chatellerault (France); Velbert (Germany)

PRINCIPAL OFFICERS
Chief Executive: Mr Norman Stronach, Acting Chief Executive, The Cube, Parkland Gateway, Corby NN17 1QG ☎ 01536 464001 ✉ norman.stronach@corby.gov.uk

Assistant Chief Executive: Mrs Angela Warburton, Assistant Chief Executive, Deene House, New Post Office Square, Corby NN17 1GD ☎ 01536 464000 ✉ angela.warburton@corby.gov.uk

Senior Management: Mr Norman Stronach, Acting Chief Executive, The Cube, Parklands Gateway, Corby NN17 1QG ☎ 01536 464001 ✉ norman.stronach@corby.gov.uk

Access Officer / Social Services (Disability): Mr Colin Cox, Principal Building Control Officer, Deene House, New Post Office Square, Corby NN17 1GD ☎ 01536 464172 ✉ colin.cox@corby.gov.uk

Architect, Building / Property Services: Mr Steven Redfern, Head of CB Property Services, The Cube, Parklands Gateway, Corby NN17 1QG ☎ 01536 464686 ✉ steven.redfern@corby.gov.uk

Building Control: Mr Colin Cox, Principal Building Control Officer, Deene House, New Post Office Square, Corby NN17 1GD ☎ 01536 464172 ✉ colin.cox@corby.gov.uk

PR / Communications: Ms Kimberley Buzzard, Communications Officer, The Cube, Parklands Gateway, Corby NN17 1QG ☎ 01536 464020 ✉ kimberley.buzzard@corby.gov.uk

Community Safety: Mrs Vicki Rockall, Principal Community Safety Officer, Deene House, New Post Office Square, Corby NN17 1GD ☎ 01536 464647 ✉ vicki.rockall@corby.gov.uk

Community Safety: Mr Tom Todkill, Head of CCTV Control Room, Grosvenor House, George Street, Corby NN17 1QB ☎ 01536 464000 ✉ t.todkill@corby.gov.uk

Computer Management: Mr Will McAlindon, ICT Manager, Deene House, New Post Office Square, Corby NN17 1GD ☎ 01536 464089 ✉ will.mcalindon@corby.gov.uk

Contracts: Ms Cheri Faulkner, Procurement Officer, Deene House, New Post Office Square, Corby NN17 1GD ☎ 01536 464680 ✉ cheri.falkner@corby.gov.uk

Corporate Services: Mr Adrian Sibley, Director of Corporate Services, Deene House, New Post Office Square, Corby NN17 1GD ☎ 01536 464031 ✉ adrian.sibley@corby.gov.uk

Corporate Services: Mr Norman Stronach, Acting Chief Executive, The Cube, Parklands Gateway, Corby NN17 1QG ☎ 01536 464001 ✉ norman.stronach@corby.gov.uk

Customer Service: Mr Adrian Sibley, Director of Corporate Services, Deene House, New Post Office Square, Corby NN17 1GD ☎ 01536 464031 ✉ adrian.sibley@corby.gov.uk

Direct Labour: Mr Iain Smith, Head of Service - Environmental Quality, Deene House, New Post Office Square, Corby NN17 1GD ☎ 01536 464061 ✉ iain.smith@corby.gov.uk

Electoral Registration: Mrs Beverley Wilson, Electoral Services Officer, Grosvenor House, George Street, Corby NN17 1QB ☎ 01536 464012 🖷 01536 464657 ✉ beverley.wilson@corby.gov.uk

Environmental / Technical Services: Mr Iain Smith, Head of Service - Environmental Quality, Deene House, New Post Office Square, Corby NN17 1GD ☎ 01536 464061 ✉ iain.smith@corby.gov.uk

Environmental Health: Mr Iain Smith, Head of Service - Environmental Quality, Deene House, New Post Office Square, Corby NN17 1GD ☎ 01536 464061 ✉ iain.smith@corby.gov.uk

Estates, Property & Valuation: Mr Steven Redfern, Head of CB Property Services, Deene House, New Post Office Square, Corby NN17 1GD ☎ 01536 464650 ✉ steven.redfern@corby.gov.uk

Facilities: Mr Steven Redfern, Head of CB Property Services, Deene House, New Post Office Square, Corby NN17 1GD ☎ 01536 464650 ✉ steven.redfern@corby.gov.uk

Health and Safety: Ms Anne-Marie Smith, Environmental Health Officer, Deene House, New Post Office Square, Corby NN17 1GD ☎ 01536 464000

Housing: Mrs Angela Warburton, Assistant Chief Executive, Deene House, New Post Office Square, Corby NN17 1GD ☎ 01536 464000 ✉ angela.warburton@corby.gov.uk

Housing Maintenance: Mr Iain Smith, Head of Service - Environmental Quality, Deene House, New Post Office Square, Corby NN17 1GD ☎ 01536 464061 ✉ iain.smith@corby.gov.uk

Legal: Mr Nigel Channer, Manager, Deene House, New Post Office Square, Corby NN17 1GD ☎ 01536 464000 ✉ nigel.channer@corby.gov.uk

Legal: Mrs Emma Granger, Manager, Deene House, New Post Office Square, Corby NN17 1GD ☎ 01536 464000 ✉ emma.granger@corby.gov.uk

Leisure and Cultural Services: Mr Chris Stephenson, Head of Service - Culture & Leisure, Deene House, New Post Office Square, Corby NN17 1GD ☎ 01536 464041 ✉ chris.stephenson@corby.gov.uk

Licensing: Mr Iain Smith, Head of Service - Environmental Quality, Deene House, New Post Office Square, Corby NN17 1GD ☎ 01536 464061 ✉ iain.smith@corby.gov.uk

Lottery Funding, Charity and Voluntary: Mr Chris Stephenson, Head of Service - Culture & Leisure, Deene House, New Post Office Square, Corby NN17 1GD ☎ 01536 464041 ✉ chris.stephenson@corby.gov.uk

Member Services: Mr Paul Goult, Democratic Services Manager, Grosvenor House, George Street, Corby NN17 1QB ☎ 01536 464013 🖷 01536 464635 ✉ paul.goult@corby.gov.uk

Personnel / HR: Mrs Stella Jinks, Human Resources Manager, Deene House, New Post Office Square, Corby NN17 1GD ☎ 01536 464032 ✉ stella.jinks@corby.gov.uk

Planning: Mr Rob Temperley, Principal Planning Officer, Deene House, New Post Office Square, Corby NN17 1GD ☎ 01536 464161 ✉ rob.temperley@corby.gov.uk

Procurement: Ms Cheri Faulkner, Procurement Officer, Deene House, New Post Office Square, Corby NN17 1GD ☎ 01536 464680 ✉ cheri.falkner@corby.gov.uk

Regeneration: Mr Norman Stronach, Acting Chief Executive, The Cube, Parklands Gateway, Corby NN17 1QB ☎ 01536 464001 ✉ norman.stronach@corby.gov.uk

Staff Training: Mrs Stella Jinks, Human Resources Manager, Deene House, New Post Office Square, Corby NN17 1GD ☎ 01536 464032 ✉ stella.jinks@corby.gov.uk

Street Scene: Mr Iain Smith, Head of Service - Environmental Quality, Deene House, New Post Office Square, Corby NN17 1GD ☎ 01536 464061 ✉ iain.smith@corby.gov.uk

Sustainable Communities: Mr Norman Stronach, Acting Chief Executive, The Cube, Parklands Gateway, Corby NN17 1GD ☎ 01536 464001 ✉ norman.stronach@corby.gov.uk

Sustainable Development: Mr Simon Winch, Sustainability Officer, Deene House, New Post Office Square, Corby NN17 1GD ☎ 01536 464685 ✉ simon.winch@corby.gov.uk

Waste Collection and Disposal: Mr Iain Smith, Head of Service - Environmental Quality, Deene House, New Post Office Square, Corby NN17 1GD ☎ 01536 464061 ✉ iain.smith@corby.gov.uk

Waste Management: Mr Iain Smith, Head of Service - Environmental Quality, Deene House, New Post Office Square, Corby NN17 1GD ☎ 01536 464061 ✉ iain.smith@corby.gov.uk

Children's Play Areas: Mr Lloyd Baines-Davies, Culture & Leisure Manager, Deene House, New Post Office Square, Corby NN17 1GD ☎ 01536 464674 ✉ lloyd.bainesdavies@corby.gov.uk

MEMBERS OF THE COUNCIL (28)

***Mayor:* McDade**, Gail (LAB - Lodge Park)
gail.mcdade@corby.gov.uk
***Deputy Mayor:* Rahman**, Mohammed (LAB - Oakley Vale)
Mohammed.rahman@corby.gov.uk
***Leader of the Council:* Beattie**, Tom (LAB - Shire Lodge)
tommy.beattie@corby.gov.uk
***Deputy Leader of the Council:* Pengelly**, Mark (LAB - East)
mark.pengelly@corby.gov.uk
***Group Leader:* Sims**, David (CON - Oakley Vale)
david@oakleyvaleconservatives.co.uk
***Group Leader:* Stanbra**, Chris (LD - Danesholme)
christopher.stanbra@corby.gov.uk
Addison, Jean (LAB - Rowlett)
jean.addison@corby.gov.uk
Beattie, Paul (LAB - Kingswood)
paul.beattie@corby.gov.uk
Beeby, Ray (LAB - Shire Lodge)
ray.beeby@corby.gov.uk
Bromhall, Philip (LD - Weldon & Gretton)
philip.bromhall@corby.gov.uk
Brown, Ann (LAB - Beanfield)
ann.brown@corby.gov.uk
Butcher, Mary (LAB - Beanfield)
mary.butcher@corby.gov.uk
Caine, Judy (LAB - Oakley Vale)
judy.caine@corby.gov.uk
Chaudhury, Eyusuf (LAB - Great Oakley)
Eyusuf.chaudhury@corby.gov.uk
Dady, Anthony (LAB - Tower Hill)
anthony.dady@corby.gov.uk
Eyles, Bob (LAB - Lodge Park)
bob.eyles@corby.gov.uk
Ferguson, Lawrence (LAB - Exeter)
lawrence.ferguson@corby.gov.uk
Forshaw, Maureen (LAB - Kingswood)
Goult, Lucy (LAB - East)
Lucy.goult@corby.gov.uk
Heggs, Stan (CON - Stanion & Corby Village)
stan.heggs@corby.gov.uk
Latta, William (LAB - Rowlett)
william.latta@corby.gov.uk
Lilley, Ray (CON - Stanion & Corby Village)
ray.lilley@corby.gov.uk
McEwan, Peter (LAB - Tower Hill)
peter.mcewan@corby.gov.uk
McGhee, John (LAB - Kingswood)
jmcghee@northamptonshire.gov.uk
McKellar, Robert (CON - Weldon & Gretton)
robert.mckellar@corby.gov.uk
Noble, Jimmy (LAB - Central)
jimmy.noble@corby.gov.uk
Petch, Peter (LAB - Danesholme)
peter.petch@corby.gov.uk
Riley, Bob (LD - Rural West)
bob.riley@corby.gov.uk

POLITICAL COMPOSITION

LAB: 21, CON: 4, LD: 3

CABINET

Leader: Mr Tom Beattie
Deputy Leader: Mr Mark Pengelly
Community: Mr John McGhee
Environment: Mr Peter McEwan
Housing: Mr Bob Eyles
Regeneration: Mr Jimmy Noble

COMMITTEE CHAIRS

Audit & Governance: Mrs Jean Addison
Development Control: Mr William Latta

CORNWALL U

Cornwall, County Hall, Treyew Road, Truro TR1 3AY
☎ 0300 1234 100 ✉ customerservices@cornwall.gov.uk
🖳 www.cornwall.gov.uk

FACTS & FIGURES

Parliamentary Constituencies: Camborne and Redruth, St. Austell and Newquay, St. Ives, Truro and Falmouth
E

PRINCIPAL OFFICERS

Chief Executive: Mr Kevin Lavery, Chief Executive, County Hall, Treyew Road, Truro TR1 3AY ☎ 01872 322100 🖷 01872 322580 ✉ klavery@cornwall.gov.uk

Assistant Chief Executive: Mr Paul Masters, Assistant Chief Executive, New County Hall, Truro TR1 3AY ☎ 01872 322121 🖷 01872 322580 ✉ pmasters@cornwall.gov.uk

Senior Management: Ms Kim Carey, Corporate Director - Adult Care & Support, Old County Hall, Truro TR1 3AY ☎ 01872 323612 ✉ kcarey@cornwall.gov.uk

Senior Management: Mr Michael Crich, Corporate Director, County Hall, Treyew Road, Truro TR1 3AY ☎ 01872 323262 🖷 01872 322580 ✉ mcrich@cornwall.gov.uk

Senior Management: Mr Trevor Doughty, Corporate Director - Children, Schools & Families, County Hall, Treyew Road, Truro TR1 3AY ☎ 01872 322403 ✉ tdoughty@cornwall.gov.uk

Senior Management: Ms Gill Steward, Corporate Director - Communities, New County Hall, Truro TR1 3AY ☎ 01872 322582 ✉ gsteward@cornwall.gov.uk

Architect, Building / Property Services: Mr Peter Marsh, Head of Property, Ocean House, Truro Business Park, Threemilestone, Truro TR4 9LD ☎ 01872 326949 🖷 01872 326948 ✉ pmarsh@cornwall.gov.uk

Building Control: Mr Phil Mason, Head of Planning & Regeneration, Room 209, Restormel Offices, 39 Penwinnick Road, St. Austell PL25 5DR ☎ 01726 223452 ✉ phil.mason@cornwall.gov.uk

Children / Youth Services: Mr Trevor Doughty, Corporate Director - Children, Schools & Families, County Hall, Treyew

Road, Truro TR1 3AY ☎ 01872 322403
✉ tdoughty@cornwall.gov.uk

Civil Registration: Ms Anne McSeveney, Registration Manager, Dalvenie House, Country Hall, Treyew Road, Truro TR1 3AY ☎ 01872 224250 ✉ amcseveney@cornwall.gov.uk

PR / Communications: Ms Carole Theobald, Head of Strategy, Localism & Communications, The Exchange, New County Hall, Treyew Road, Truro TR1 3AY ☎ 01872 322572
✉ ctheobald@cornwall.gov.uk

Community Safety: Mr Des Tidbury, Chief Fire Officer & Head of Community Safety, Old County Hall, Treyew Road, Truro TR1 3AY ☎ 01872 323739 ✉ dtidbury@fire.cornwall.gov.uk

Computer Management: Mr David Picknett, Head of Information Technology, County Hall, Truro TR1 3AY
✉ dpicknett@cornwall.gov.uk

Consumer Protection and Trading Standards: Mr Allan Hampshire, Head of Public Health & Protection, County Hall, Treyew Road, Truro TR1 3AY ☎ 01872 224409
✉ allan.hampshire@cornwall.gov.uk

Contracts: Ms Liz Calcutt, Head of Procurement & Commissioning, Room 5, First Floor, Dalvenie House, County Hall, Treyew Road, Truro TR1 3AY ☎ 01872 322195
✉ lcalcutt@cornwall.gov.uk

Corporate Services: Mr Michael Crich, Corporate Director, County Hall, Treyew Road, Truro TR1 3AY ☎ 01872 323262
🖷 01872 322580 ✉ mcrich@cornwall.gov.uk

Customer Service: Mr Mark Read, Head of Shared Services, Room 204, Central 2 Office, 39 Penwinnick Road, St. Austell PL25 5DR ☎ 01726 223316 ✉ mark.read@cornwall.gov.uk

Economic Development: Ms Sandra Rothwell, Head of Economic Development, Room 236, New County Hall, Treyew Road, Truro TR1 3AY ☎ 01872 322160
✉ srothwell@cornwall.gov.uk

Education: Mr David Wood, Head of Schools & Achievement, Room 412, Council Offices, Dolcoath Avenue, Camborne TR14 8SX ☎ 01209 615089 🖷 01209 614494 ✉ dwood@cornwall.gov.uk

Electoral Registration: Mr Richard Williams, Head of Legal & Democratic Services, Room 470, New County Hall, Treyew Road, Truro TR1 3AY ☎ 01872 322120 🖷 01872 323833
✉ rawilliams@cornwall.gov.uk

Emergency Planning: Mr Richard Fedorowicz, Head of Emergency Management, Room 709, Old County Hall, Station Road, Truro TR1 3AY ☎ 01872 323121
✉ rfedorowicz@cornwall.gov.uk

Energy Management: Mr Peter Marsh, Head of Property, Ocean House, Truro Business Park, Threemilestone, Truro TR4 9LD
☎ 01872 326949 🖷 01872 326948 ✉ pmarsh@cornwall.gov.uk

Environmental / Technical Services: Mr Nigel Blackler, Head of Transport, Waste & Environment, ☎ 01872 324124
✉ nblackler@cornwall.gov.uk

Environmental Health: Mr Allan Hampshire, Head of Public Health & Protection, County Hall, Treyew Road, Truro TR1 3AY
☎ 01872 224409 ✉ allan.hampshire@cornwall.gov.uk

Estates, Property & Valuation: Mr Peter Marsh, Head of Property, Ocean House, Truro Business Park, Threemilestone, Truro TR4 9LD ☎ 01872 326949 🖷 01872 326948
✉ pmarsh@cornwall.gov.uk

European Liaison: Ms Sandra Rothwell, Head of Economic Development, Room 236, New County Hall, Treyew Road, Truro TR1 3AY ☎ 01872 322160 ✉ srothwell@cornwall.gov.uk

Facilities: Mr Peter Marsh, Head of Property, Ocean House, Truro Business Park, Threemilestone, Truro TR4 9LD ☎ 01872 326949 🖷 01872 326948 ✉ pmarsh@cornwall.gov.uk

Finance and Treasurer: Ms Cath Robinson, Head of Finance, County Hall, Treyew Road, Truro TR1 3AY ☎ 01872 324449
✉ crobinson@cornwall.gov.uk

Fleet Management: Mr Arthur Hooper, Head of Highways, North Building, Central GP Centre, Castle Canyke Road, Bodmin PL31 1DZ ☎ 01872 327838 ✉ ahooper@cornwall.gov.uk

Health and Safety: Mr Allan Hampshire, Head of Public Health & Protection, Room C3.11, Carrick House, Pydar Street, Truro TR1 1EB ☎ 01872 224409 ✉ allan.hampshire@cornwall.gov.uk

Highways: Mr Arthur Hooper, Head of Highways, County Hall, Treyew Road, Truro TR1 3AY ☎ 01872 327838
✉ ahooper@cornwall.gov.uk

Housing: Ms Jane Barlow, Head of Housing, County Hall, Treyew Road, Truro TR1 3AY ☎ 01209 614322
✉ jane.barlow@cornwall.gov.uk

Local Area Agreement: Ms Carole Theobald, Head of Strategy, Localism & Communications, The Exchange, New County Hall, Treyew Road, Truro TR1 3AY ☎ 01872 322572
✉ ctheobald@cornwall.gov.uk

Legal: Mr Richard Williams, Head of Legal & Democratic Services, Room 470, New County Hall, Treyew Road, Truro TR1 3AY ☎ 01872 322120 🖷 01872 323833
✉ rawilliams@cornwall.gov.uk

Leisure and Cultural Services: Ms Gill Steward, Corporate Director - Communities, New County Hall, Truro TR1 3AY
☎ 01872 322582 ✉ gsteward@cornwall.gov.uk

Licensing: Mr Allan Hampshire, Head of Public Health & Protection, Room C3.11, Carrick House, Pydar Street, Truro TR1 1EB ☎ 01872 224409 ✉ allan.hampshire@cornwall.gov.uk

Member Services: Mr Richard Williams, Head of Democratic & Legal Services, New County Hall, Truro TR1 3AY ☎ 01872 322120
✉ rawilliams@cornwall.gov.uk

Parking: Mr Peter Moore, Community Transport Manager, Room A3.12, Carrick House, Pydar Street, Truro TR1 1EB ☎ 01872 224459 ✉ pmoore@cornwall.gov.uk

Partnerships: Ms Carole Theobald, Head of Strategy, Localism & Communications, The Exchange, New County Hall, Treyew Road, Truro TR1 3AY ☎ 01872 322572 ✉ ctheobald@cornwall.gov.uk

Personnel / HR: Ms Dawn Aunger, Head of Human Resources & Organisation Development, County Hall, Treyew Road, Truro TR1 3AY ☎ 01872 323119 ✉ daunger@cornwall.gov.uk

Planning: Mr Phil Mason, Head of Planning & Regeneration, County Hall, Treyew Road, Truro TR1 3AY ☎ 01726 223452 ✉ phil.mason@cornwall.gov.uk

Procurement: Ms Liz Calcutt, Head of Procurement & Commissioning, Room 5, First Floor, Dalvenie House, County Hall, Treyew Road, Truro TR1 3AY ☎ 01872 322195 ✉ lcalcutt@cornwall.gov.uk

Public Libraries: Mr Mark Read, Head of Shared Services, Room 204, Central 2 Office, 39 Penwinnick Road, St. Austell PL25 5DR ☎ 01726 223316 ✉ mark.read@cornwall.gov.uk

Recycling & Waste Minimisation: Mr Nigel Blackler, Head of Transport, Waste & Environment, County Hall, Treyew Road, Truro TR1 3AY ☎ ; 01872 324124 ✉ nblackler@cornwall.gov.uk

Regeneration: Mr Phil Mason, Head of Planning & Regeneration, County Hall, Treyew Road, Truro TR1 3AY ☎ 01726 223452 ✉ phil.mason@cornwall.gov.uk

Road Safety: Mr Peter Moore, Community Transport Manager, Room A3.12, Carrick House, Pydar Street, Truro TR1 1EB ☎ 01872 224459 ✉ pmoore@cornwall.gov.uk

Social Services (Adult): Ms Kim Carey, Corporate Director - Adult Care & Support, The Exchange, New County Hall, Treyew Road, Truro TR1 1EB ☎ 01872 323612 ✉ kcarey@cornwall.gov.uk

Social Services (Children): Mr Jack Cordery, Head of Service (Social Work), Room 424, New County Hall, Treyew Road, Truro TR1 3AY ☎ 01872 323637 ✉ jcordery@cornwall.gov.uk

Staff Training: Ms Dawn Aunger, Head of Human Resources & Organisation Development, County Hall, Treyew Road, Truro TR1 3AY ☎ 01872 323119 ✉ daunger@cornwall.gov.uk

Tourism: Mr Malcom Bell, Head of Tourism, Pydar House, Pydar Street, Truro TR1 1EA ☎ 01872 322820 ✉ malcolm.bell@cornwallenterprise.co.uk

Town Centre: Mr Rob Andrew, Local Area Manager, Room B2.07, Carrick House, Pydar House, Truro TR1 1EB ☎ 01872 224239 ✉ randrew@cornwall.gov.uk

Traffic Management: Mr Arthur Hooper, Head of Highways, North Building, Central GP Centre, Castle Canyke Road, Bodmin PL31 1DZ ☎ 01872 327838 ✉ ahooper@cornwall.gov.uk

Transport: Mr Nigel Blackler, Head of Transport, Waste & Environment, County Hall, Treyew Road, Truro TR1 3AY ☎ 01872 324124 ✉ nblackler@cornwall.gov.uk

Transport Planner: Mr Nigel Blackler, Head of Transport, Waste & Environment, County Hall, Treyew Road, Truro TR1 3AY ☎ 01872 324124 ✉ nblackler@cornwall.gov.uk

Waste Collection and Disposal: Mr Nigel Blackler, Head of Transport, Waste & Environment, County Hall, Treyew Road, Truro TR1 3AY ☎ 01872 324124 ✉ nblackler@cornwall.gov.uk

Waste Management: Mr Nigel Blackler, Head of Transport, Waste & Environment, County Hall, Treyew Road, Truro TR1 3AY ☎ 01872 324124 ✉ nblackler@cornwall.gov.uk

MEMBERS OF THE COUNCIL (123)

***Chair:* Harvey**, Pat (IND - St Columb)
pharvey@cornwall.gov.uk
***Vice-Chair:* Dyer**, John (CON - Chacewater & Kenwyn)
fjdyer@cornwall.gov.uk
***Leader of the Council:* Robertson**, Alec (CON - Helston North)
leader@cornwall.gov.uk
***Group Leader:* Cole**, Dick (O - St Enoder)
ricole@cornwall.gov.uk
***Group Leader:* Rowe**, Jeremy (LD - St Issey)
jeremy.rowe27@gmail.com
Ansari, Doris (LD - Truro Tregolls)
dansari@cornwall.gov.uk
Austin, Bob (LD - Saltash Essa)
baustin@cornwall.gov.uk
Bailey, Irene (IND - Ludgvan)
Bain, Sally (CON - Fowey)
sbain@cornwall.gov.uk
Bartlett, Russell (CON - Gunnislake)
rbartlett@cornwall.gov.uk
Biggs, David (CON - Camborne West)
dbiggs@cornwall.gov.uk
Biscoe, B M M (IND - Truro Moresk)
bertbiscoe@btinternet.com
Brewer, Colin (IND - Wadebridge East)
cbrewer@cornwall.gov.uk
Brown, Geoff (LD - Newquay Central)
geoff-brown@talktalk.net
Brown, Glenton (LD - Tintagel)
gbrown@cornwall.gov.uk
Bull, Jackie (LD - Bugle)
jbull@cornwall.gov.uk
Burden, Neil (IND - Stokeclimsland)
nburden@cornwall.gov.uk
Callan, Michael (IND - Perranporth)
mcallan@cornwall.gov.uk
Chappel, Grenville (IND - Falmouth Penwerris)
gchappel@cornwall.gov.uk
Clark, Jinny (CON - Newlyn & Goonhavern)
jclark@cornwall.gov.uk
Coombe, John (IND - Hayle South)
jcoombe@cornwall.gov.uk
Cullimore, Stuart (O - Camborne South)
scullimore@cornwall.gov.uk
Curnow, Des (IND - St Stephen)
descurnow@cornwall.gov.uk
Currie, Jim (CON - Feock & Kea)
jcurrie@cornwall.gov.uk
Dolley, Lisa (IND - Redruth North)

ldolley@cornwall.gov.uk
Dolphin, Paula (LD - Flexbury & Poughill)
pdolphin@cornwall.gov.uk
Donnithorne, Les (LD - St Agnes)
ldonnithorne@cornwall.gov.uk
Double, Steve (CON - St Austell Poltair)
sdouble@cornwall.gov.uk
Duffin, Joyce (LD - Mount Hawke & Portreath)
jmduffin@cornwall.gov.uk
Eathorne-Gibbons, Mike (CON - Ladock, St Clement & St Erme)
meathornegibbons@cornwall.gov.uk
Eddowes, Mike (CON - Redruth Central)
meddowes@cornwall.gov.uk
Edwards, George (LD - Newquay Treloggan)
Egerton, Bob (IND - Probus)
begerton@cornwall.gov.uk
Eggleston, Olive (CON - St Germans)
oeggleston@cornwall.gov.uk
Ellis, Bernie (CON - Menheniot)
bellis2@cornwall.gov.uk
Eva, Steve (IND - Falmouth Arwenack)
seva@cornwall.gov.uk
Evans, Geoffrey (CON - Falmouth Gyllyngvase)
Ferguson, Fiona (CON - Truro Trehaverne)
fiferguson@cornwall.gov.uk
Fitter, John (CON - Colan & Mawgan)
jfitter@cornwall.gov.uk
Flashman, Jim (CON - Kelly Bray)
jflashman@cornwall.gov.uk
Folkes, Alex (LD - Launceston Central)
alexfolkes@gmail.com
Fonk, Mario (LD - Gulval & Heamoor)
mfonk@cornwall.gov.uk
George, Mike (LD - Liskeard South & Dobwalls)
German, Julian (IND - Roseland)
jgerman@cornwall.gov.uk
Gillard-Loft, Sasha (LD - Launceston South)
sgillardloft@cornwall.gov.uk
Gisbourne, Brian (CON - St Endellion)
bgisbourne@cornwall.gov.uk
Goninan, Chris (IND - St Just in Penwith)
cgoninan@cornwall.gov.uk
Goodenough, Keith (CON - Camelford)
kgoodenough@cornwall.gov.uk
Greenslade, Fred (IND - St Dennis)
fred.greenslade@cornwall.gov.uk
Hannaford, Edwina (LD - Looe West & Lansallos)
ehannaford@cornwall.gov.uk
Harding, Roger (CON - Newlyn & Mousehole)
sales@rchardingandson.co.uk
Hatton, Neil (CON - Constantine)
neilhatton@constantinecornwall.co.uk
Haycock, Judith (IND - Helston Central)
jhaycock@cornwall.gov.uk
Heywood, Harry (IND - Newquay Treviglas)
hheywood@cornwall.gov.uk
Hicks, Graeme (IND - Redruth South)
ghicks@cornwall.gov.uk
Hobbs, Brian (LD - Torpoint East)
bhobbs@cornwall.gov.uk
Holley, Derek (IND - Saltash Pill)
dholley@cornwall.gov.uk
Hughes, David (LD - Tywardreath)
dhughes@cornwall.gov.uk
Jenkin, Loveday (O - Wendron)
letjenkin@cornwall.gov.uk
Kaczmarek, Mark (IND - St Day & Lanner)
mkaczmarek@cornwall.gov.uk
Keeling, John (IND - Breage)
jkeeling@cornwall.gov.uk
Kennedy, Lance (CON - Bodmin East)
lkennedy@cornwall.gov.uk
Kenny, Joanna (LD - Newquay Pentire)
jkenny@cornwall.gov.uk
Kerridge, Ann (LD - Bodmin West)
akerridge@cornwall.gov.uk
Lambshead, Patrick (CON - Newquay Tretherras)
plambshead@cornwall.gov.uk
Lewarne, Ruth (LD - Penzance East)
rlewarne@cornwall.gov.uk
Long, Andrew (O - Callington)
ajlong@cornwall.gov.uk
Lugg, John (IND - St Teath)
jlugg@cornwall.gov.uk
Lyne, Pam (IND - St Keverne & Meneage)
plyne@cornwall.gov.uk
Maddern, Bill (CON - St Buryan)
william.maddern@cornwall.gov.uk
Mann, Scott (CON - Wadebridge West)
smann@cornwall.gov.uk
Martin, Mick (CON - Lanivet)
mmartin@cornwall.gov.uk
Martin, Tony (CON - Penryn East & Mylor)
tomartin@cornwall.gov.uk
May, Mary (IND - Penryn West)
mamay@cornwall.gov.uk
Mutton, Denise (CON - Mevagissey)
dmutton2@cornwall.gov.uk
Nicholas, Sue (CON - Marazion)
sunicholas@cornwall.gov.uk
Nolan, Rob (LD - Truro Boscawen)
rnolan@cornwall.gov.uk
Oxenham, John (LD - St Austell Bay)
joxenham@cornwall.gov.uk
Parsons, Philip (CON - Altarnun)
pparsons@cornwall.gov.uk
Parsons, David (LD - Bude North & Stratton)
davidparsons 56@gmail.com
Pascoe, Chris (LD - Threemilestone & Gloweth)
chpascoe@cornwall.gov.uk
Pass, Sue (IND - Penzance Promenade)
spass@cornwall.gov.uk
Paynter, Adam (LD - Launceston North)
apaynter@cornwall.gov.uk
Pearce, Nigel (LD - Bude South)
nigelpearce33@hotmail.com
Pearn, Mike (CON - Torpoint West)
mpearn@cornwall.gov.uk
Penhaligon, Liz (CON - Lelant & Carbis Bay)
epenhaligon@cornwall.gov.uk
Plummer, Neil (O - Stithians)
nplummer@cornwall.gov.uk
Pollard, John (IND - Hayle North)
jpollard1@cornwall.gov.uk
Polmounter, Shirley (LD - Mount Charles)
spolmounter@cornwall.gov.uk
Powell, Jan (CON - Liskeard North)
jpowell1@cornwall.gov.uk
Preston, Bryan (LD - Saltash Burraton)

bpreston@cornwall.gov.uk
Pugh, Richard (CON - Pelynt)
rpugh2@cornwall.gov.uk
Riches, Colin (LD - Saltash St Stephens)
criches@cornwall.gov.uk
Ridgers, Chris (CON - Mabe)
chridgers@cornwall.gov.uk
Robinson, Jude (LAB - Camborne North)
jrobinson1@cornwall.gov.uk
Rogerson, Pat (LD - Bodmin Central)
progerson@cornwall.gov.uk
Rowe, Christopher (LD - Penwithick)
chrisrowe@sanfernando.fsnet.uk
Rule, Carolyn (CON - Mullion)
carorule@cornwall.gov.uk
Rushworth, Stephen (CON - Padstow)
srushworth@cornwall.gov.uk
Saunby, David (IND - Falmouth Trescobeas)
Schofield, Jay (LD - Liskeard Central)
jayschofield.uk@gmail.com
Shakerley, Gavin (CON - Lostwithiel)
gshakerley@cornwall.gov.uk
Sheppard, Peter (CON - Carn Brea North)
psheppard@cornwall.gov.uk
Stoneman, Jon (CON - Camborne Central)
jstoneman@cornwall.gov.uk
Stuart, Jenny (CON - St Austell Gover)
jestewart@cornwall.gov.uk
Symons, Joan (CON - St Ives South)
jhsymons@cornwall.gov.uk
Tanner, Joan (CON - St Ives North)
jtanner@cornwall.gov.uk
Taylor, Roy (LD - St Blaise)
roytaylor@cornwall.gov.uk
Teverson, Robin (LD - St Mewan)
robinteverson@googlemail.com
Toms, Armand (CON - Looe East)
atoms@cornwall.gov.uk
Tovey, Ray (CON - Gwinear-Gwithian & St Erth)
rtovey@cornwall.gov.uk
Trubody, George (CON - Rame)
gtrubody@cornwall.gov.uk
Tucker, Phil (CON - Poundstock)
ptucker@cornwall.gov.uk
Turner, John (LD - St Ives)
johnturner@cornwall.gov.uk
Varney, Mike (IND - Falmouth Boslowick)
mvarney@cornwall.gov.uk
Walker, Graham (LD - St Austell Bethel)
gwalkera1@gmail.com
Wallis, Andrew (IND - Porthleven & Helston South)
awallis@cornwall.gov.uk
Watson, Derris (LD - St Cleer)
dwatson@cornwall.gov.uk
Wilkins, Terry (CON - Illogan)
tewilkins@cornwall.gov.uk
Williams, Morwenna (CON - Troon & Beacon)
mowilliams@cornwall.gov.uk
Williams, Tamsin (LD - Penzance Central)
cllrtwilliams@gmail.com
Willoughby, Kym (LD - Carn Brea South)
kwilloughby@cornwall.gov.uk
Wood, John (IND - Roche)

POLITICAL COMPOSITION
CON: 48, LD: 39, IND: 30, O: 5, LAB: 1

CABINET
Leader: Mr Alec Robertson
Adult Care & Support: Mr Armand Toms
Children's Services: Mr Neil Burden
Community Safety & Public Protection: Mr Lance Kennedy
Corporate Resources: Mr Jim Currie
Economy & Regeneration: Mr Chris Ridgers
Environment, Waste Management Policy & Shared Services: Mr Steve Double
Health & Wellbeing / Human Resources: Ms Carolyn Rule
Housing & Planning: Mr Mark Kaczmarek
Localism, Sustainability & Devolution: Mr Julian German
Tourism, Culture & Leisure: Ms Joan Symons
Transportation, Highways & Environment Operations: Mr Graeme Hicks

COMMITTEE CHAIRS
Audit: Mr Mike Eathorne-Gibbons
Children, Education & Families (Scrutiny): Mr John Pollard
Community (Scrutiny): Ms Judith Haycock
Corporate Resources (Scrutiny): Mr John Keeling
Environment & Economy (Scrutiny): Mr Fred Greenslade
Health & Adults (Scrutiny): Ms Sue Nicholas
Human Resources: Mr John Wood
Licensing: Mr Jon Stoneman
Pensions: Ms Morwenna Williams
Strategic Planning: Mr Mike Varney

COTSWOLD D

Cotswold District Council, Council Offices, Trinity Road, Cirencester GL7 1PX ☎ 01285 623000 🖷 01285 623900 ✉ cdc@cotswold.gov.uk 💻 www.cotswold.gov.uk

FACTS & FIGURES
Police Authority: Gloucestershire Police Authority
Health Authority: NHS South West
Learning and Skills Council: South West
Parliamentary Constituencies: Cotswold
EU Constituencies: South West
Election Frequency: Elections are of whole council
Twinning: Chipping Campden: Port d'Ouilly (France); Cirencester: Itzehoe (Germany); Tetbury: Zwingenburg (Germany)

PRINCIPAL OFFICERS
Chief Executive: Mr David Neudegg, Chief Executive, Council Offices, Trinity Road, Cirencester GL7 1PX ☎ 01285 623100 🖷 01285 623906 ✉ david.neudegg@cotswold.gov.uk

Senior Management: Mr Andrew Fotherby, Strategic Director, Council Offices, Trinity Road, Cirencester GL7 1PX ☎ 01285 623500 🖷 01285 623906 ✉ andrew.fotherby@cotswold.gov.uk

Senior Management: Mr Frank Wilson, Strategic Director, Council Offices, Trinity Road, Cirencester GL7 1PX ☎ 01285 623402 🖷 01285 623906 ✉ frank.wilson@cotswold.gov.uk

Senior Management: Mr Ralph Young, Strategic Director,

Council Offices, Trinity Road, Cirencester GL7 1PX ☎ 01285 623600 🖷 01285 623906 ✉ ralph.young@cotswold.gov.uk

Architect, Building / Property Services: Mrs Bhavna Patel, Head of Legal & Property Services, Council Offices, Trinity Road, Cirencester GL7 1PX ☎ 01285 623219 🖷 01285 623900 ✉ bhavna.patel@cotswold.gov.uk

Best Value: Ms Kath Hoare, Business Improvement Manager, Council Offices, Trinity Road, Cirencester GL7 1PX ☎ 01285 623573 🖷 01285 623900 ✉ kath.hoare@cotswold.gov.uk

Building Control: Mr John Hill, Building Control Manager, Council Offices, Trinity Road, Cirencester GL7 1PX ☎ 01285 623633 🖷 01285 623905 ✉ john.hill@cotswold.gov.uk

PR / Communications: Mr Bob McNally, Press & Media Liaison Officer, Council Offices, Trinity Road, Cirencester GL7 1PX ☎ 01285 623120 🖷 01285 623900 ✉ bob.mcnally@cotswold.gov.uk

Community Planning: Mr Mike Clark, Corporate Planning Manager, Council Offices, Trinity Road, Cirencester GL7 1PX ☎ 01285 623565 🖷 01285 623900 ✉ mike.clark@cotswold.gov.uk

Community Safety: Mrs Rosemary Lynn, Head of Sustainable Communities & Housing, Council Offices, Trinity Road, Cirencester GL7 1PX ☎ 01285 623560 🖷 01285 623923 ✉ rosemary.lynn@cotswold.gov.uk

Computer Management: Mr Mike Brown, ICT Services Manager, Council Offices, Trinity Road, Cirencester GL7 1PX ☎ 01285 623000 🖷 01285 623900 ✉ mike.brown@cotswold.gov.uk

Customer Service: Ms Monica Stephens, Joint Head of Customer Services, Council Offices, Trinity Road, Cirencester GL7 1PX ☎ 01285 621400 🖷 01285 623900 ✉ monica.stephens@cotswold.gov.uk

E-Government: Mr Dave Pennington, Web Developer, Council Offices, Trinity Road, Cirencester GL7 1PX ☎ 01285 623000 🖷 01285 623900 ✉ dave.pennington@cotswold.gov.uk

Electoral Registration: Mr Nigel Adams, Head of Democratic Services, Council Offices, Trinity Road, Cirencester GL7 1PX ☎ 01285 623202 🖷 01285 623900 ✉ nigel.adams@cotswold.gov.uk

Emergency Planning: Mrs Claire Locke, Head of Environmental Services, Council Offices, Trinity Road, Cirencester GL7 1PX ☎ 01285 623427 🖷 01285 623000 ✉ claire.locke@cotswold.gov.uk

Energy Management: Mr Gary Packer, Sustainable Energy Officer, Council Offices, Trinity Road, Cirencester GL7 1PX ☎ 01285 623428 🖷 01285 623900 ✉ gary.packer@cotswold.gov.uk

Environmental / Technical Services: Mrs Claire Locke, Head of Environmental Services, Council Offices, Trinity Road, Cirencester GL7 1PX ☎ 01285 623427 🖷 01285 623000 ✉ claire.locke@cotswold.gov.uk

Environmental Health: Ms Kate Bishop, Head of Public Protection, Council Offices, Trinity Road, Cirencester GL7 1PX ☎ 01285 623442 🖷 01285 623900 ✉ kate.bishop@cotswold.gov.uk

Estates, Property & Valuation: Mrs Bhavna Patel, Head of Legal & Property Services, Council Offices, Trinity Road, Cirencester GL7 1PX ☎ 01285 623219 🖷 01285 623900 ✉ bhavna.patel@cotswold.gov.uk

Finance and Treasurer: Ms Jenny Poole, Head of Financial Services & Audit, Council Offices, Trinity Road, Cirencester GL7 1PX ☎ 01285 623313 🖷 01285 623900 ✉ jenny.poole@cotswold.gov.uk

Health and Safety: Ms Pauline Smith, Health & Safety Officer, Council Offices, Trinity Road, Cirencester GL7 1PX ☎ 01285 623111 🖷 01285 623900 ✉ ruth.woolridge@cotswold.gov.uk

Home Energy Conservation: Mr Gary Packer, Sustainable Energy Officer, Council Offices, Trinity Road, Cirencester GL7 1PX ☎ 01285 623428 🖷 01285 623900 ✉ gary.packer@cotswold.gov.uk

Housing: Mrs Rosemary Lynn, Head of Sustainable Communities & Housing, Council Offices, Trinity Road, Cirencester GL7 1PX ☎ 01285 623560 🖷 01285 623923 ✉ rosemary.lynn@cotswold.gov.uk

Legal: Mrs Bhavna Patel, Head of Legal & Property Services, Council Offices, Trinity Road, Cirencester GL7 1PX ☎ 01285 623219 🖷 01285 623900 ✉ bhavna.patel@cotswold.gov.uk

Leisure and Cultural Services: Mr Jamie Nesbit, Head of Leisure & Cultural Services, Council Offices, Trinity Road, Cirencester GL7 1PX ☎ 01285 623144 🖷 01285 623900 ✉ jamie.nesbit@cotswold.gov.uk

Licensing: Ms Kate Bishop, Head of Public Protection, Council Offices, Trinity Road, Cirencester GL7 1PX ☎ 01285 623442 🖷 01285 623900 ✉ kate.bishop@cotswold.gov.uk

Member Services: Mr Nigel Adams, Head of Democratic Services, Council Offices, Trinity Road, Cirencester GL7 1PX ☎ 01285 623202 🖷 01285 623900 ✉ nigel.adams@cotswold.gov.uk

Parking: Ms Maria Wheatley, Car Parks Manager, Council Offices, Trinity Road, Cirencester GL7 1PX ☎ 01285 623228 🖷 01285 623900 ✉ maria.wheatley@cotswold.gov.uk

Personnel / HR: Ms Sara Mullen, HR Service Manager, Council Offices, Trinity Road, Cirencester GL7 1PX ☎ 01285 623112 🖷 01285 623900 ✉ sara.mullen@cotswold.gov.uk

Planning: Ms Philippa Lowe, Head of Development Services, Council Offices, Trinity Road, Cirencester GL7 1PX ☎ 01285 623515 🖷 01285 623900 ✉ philippa.field@cotswold.gov.uk

Procurement: Ms Kath Hoare, Business Improvement Manager, Council Offices, Trinity Road, Cirencester GL7 1PX ☎ 01285 623573 🖷 01285 623900 ✉ kath.hoare@cotswold.gov.uk

Recycling & Waste Minimisation: Mr Scott Williams, Waste Manager, Council Offices, Trinity Road, Cirencester GL7 1PX ☎ 01285 623096 🖷 01285 623900 ✉ scott.williams@cotswold.gov.uk

Staff Training: Ms Sara Mullen, HR Service Manager, Council Offices, Trinity Road, Cirencester GL7 1PX ☎ 01285 623112 🖷 01285 623900 ✉ sara.mullen@cotswold.gov.uk

Tourism: Ms Sally Graff, Tourism Manager, Council Offices, Trinity Road, Cirencester GL7 1PX ☎ 01608 650881 🖷 01285 623900 ✉ sally.graff@cotswold.gov.uk

Waste Collection and Disposal: Mr Scott Williams, Waste Manager, Council Offices, Trinity Road, Cirencester GL7 1PX ☎ 01285 623096 🖷 01285 623900 ✉ scott.williams@cotswold.gov.uk

Waste Management: Mr Scott Williams, Waste Manager, Council Offices, Trinity Road, Cirencester GL7 1PX ☎ 01285 623096 🖷 01285 623900 ✉ scott.williams@cotswold.gov.uk

MEMBERS OF THE COUNCIL (43)

***Vice-Chair:* Bennett**, Clive (CON - Water Park)
clive.bennett@cotswold.gov.uk
***Leader of the Council:* Stowe**, Lynden (CON - Campden - Vale)
lynden.stowe@cotswold.gov.uk
***Group Leader:* Hodgkinson**, Paul (LD - Churn Valley)
paul.hodgkinson@cotswold.gov.uk
Annett, Mark (CON - Campden - Vale)
mark.annett@cotswold.gov.uk
Birch, John (CON - Thames-Head)
john.birch@cotswold.gov.uk
Broad, David (CON - Chedworth)
david.broad@cotswold.gov.uk
Burgess, John (CON - Cirencester - Beeches)
john.burgess@cotswold.gov.uk
Carter, Sandra (CON - Kempsford-Lechlade)
sandra.carter@cotswold.gov.uk
Coakley, Susan (IND - Kempsford-Lechlade)
susan.coakley@cotswold.gov.uk
Coleman, Patrick (LD - Cirencester - Stratton - Whiteway)
patrick.coleman@cotswold.gov.uk
Collier, Dominic (CON - Three Rivers)
dominic.collier@cotswold.gov.uk
Crosbie-Dawson, Venetia (CON - Rissingtons)
venetia.crosbiedawson@cotswold.gov.uk
Dare, Barry (CON - Blockley)
barry.dare@cotswold.gov.uk
Dutton, Robert (CON - Moreton-in-Marsh)
robert.dutton@cotswold.gov.uk
Fowles, David (CON - Hampton)
david.fowles@cotswold.gov.uk
Gibbs, Barry (CON - Tetbury)
barry.gibbs@cotswold.gov.uk
Hancock, Christopher (IND - Northleach)
christopher.hancock@cotswold.gov.uk
Harris, Joseph (LD - Cirencester - Park)
joe.harris@cotswold.gov.uk
Hicks, Diana (CON - Tetbury)
diana.hicks@cotswold.gov.uk
Hincks, Jenny (LD - Cirencester - Watermoor)
jenny.hincks@cotswold.gov.uk
Hirst, Stephen (IND - Tetbury)
stephen.hirst@cotswold.gov.uk
Hooper, Rodney (IND - Moreton-in-Marsh)
rod.hooper@cotswold.gov.uk
Horsfall, Edward (CON - Ampney - Coln)
edward.horsfall@cotswold.gov.uk
Hughes, Johnathan (LD - Cirencester - Beeches)
johnathan.hughes@cotswold.gov.uk
Hughes, Robin (CON - Sandywell)
robin.hughes@cotswold.gov.uk
Jeffery, Sheila (CON - Bourton-on-the-Water)
sheila.jeffery@cotswold.gov.uk
Jenkins, Esmond (LD - Water Park)
esmond.jenkins@cotswold.gov.uk
Jepson, Susan (CON - Campden - Vale)
sue.jepson@cotswold.gov.uk
Layton, Juliet (LD - Water Park)
juliet.layton@cotswold.gov.uk
Lichnowsk, Andrew (LD - Cirencester - Stratton - Whiteway)
andrew.lichnowski@cotswold.gov.uk
Nash, Deryck (LD - Cirencester - Chesterton)
deryck.nash@cotswold.gov.uk
Nicolle, Carolyn (CON - Grumbolds Ash)
carolyn.nicolle@cotswold.gov.uk
Parsons, Jim (CON - Avening)
jim.parsons@cotswold.gov.uk
Parsons, Nicholas (CON - Ermin)
nicholas.parsons@cotswold.gov.uk
Penman, David (CON - Beacon-Stow)
david.penman@cotswold.gov.uk
Phillips, Merryl (CON - Beacon-Stow)
merryl.phillips@cotswold.gov.uk
Rickman, Margaret (LD - Cirencester - Chesterton)
margaret.rickman@cotswold.gov.uk
Searles, Lee (LD - Cirencester - Park)
lee.searles@cotswold.gov.uk
Selwyn, Gary (LD - Cirencester - Watermoor)
gary.selwyn@cotswold.gov.uk
Theodoulou, Raymond (CON - Fairford)
raymond.theodoulou@cotswold.gov.uk
Topple, Carole (CON - Riversmeet)
carole.topple@cotswold.gov.uk
Wardle, Mark (IND - Fairford)
mark.wardle@cotswold.gov.uk
Wilkins, Len (CON - Bourton-on-the-Water)
len.wilkins@cotswold.gov.uk

POLITICAL COMPOSITION

CON: 26, LD: 12, IND: 5

CABINET

Leader: Mr Lynden Stowe
Corporate Resources: Mr Barry Dare
Customer Services: Mr Barry Gibbs
Environment: Mr David Fowles
Forward Planning: Mr Nicholas Parsons
Housing & Communities: Mrs Carole Topple
Planning: Mrs Susan Jepson
Support Services: Mr John Burgess

COMMITTEE CHAIRS

Audit: Mr Raymond Theodoulou
Licensing: Mr Clive Bennett
Overview & Scrutiny: Mrs Sandra Carter

Planning (Regulatory): Mrs Venetia Crosbie-Dawson

COVENTRY CITY M

Coventry City Council, The Council House, Earl Street, Coventry CV1 5RR ☎ 024 7683 3333 🖷 024 7683 3680 ✉ coventrydirect@coventry.gov.uk 💻 www.coventry.gov.uk

FACTS & FIGURES

Police Authority: West Midlands Police Authority
Health Authority: NHS West Midlands
Learning and Skills Council: West Midlands
Parliamentary Constituencies: Coventry North East, Coventry North West, Coventry South
EU Constituencies: West Midlands
Election Frequency: Elections are by thirds
Twinning: Arnhem (Netherlands); Belgrade (Serbia); Bologna (Italy); Caen (France); Cork (Republic of Ireland); Cornwall, Ontario (Canada); Coventry (CT, USA); Coventry, New York State (USA); Coventry (RI, USA); Dresden (Germany); Dunaujvaros and Kecskemet (Hungary); Galati (Romania); Granby (Canada); Graz (Austria) Kiel (Germany); Ostrava and Lidice (Czech Rep); Parkes (Australia); Sarajevo (Bosnia and Herzegovina); St. Etienne (France); Windsor (Canada); Kingston (Jamaica); Volgograd (Russia); Warsaw (Poland)

PRINCIPAL OFFICERS

Chief Executive: Mr Martin Reeves, Chief Executive, The Council House, Earl Street, Coventry CV1 5RR ☎ 024 7683 1100 🖷 024 7683 3680 ✉ martin.reeves@coventry.gov.uk

Assistant Chief Executive: Dr Jocelyn Parry, Assistant Chief Executive, Council House, Earl Street, Coventry CV1 5RR ☎ 024 7683 1077 🖷 0247683 1106 ✉ jos.parry@coventry.gov.uk

Senior Management: Ms Tracy Darke, Head of Development Services, PO Box 2178, Riverside House, Milverton Hill, Leamington Spa CV32 5QH ☎ 01926 456016 🖷 01926 456542 ✉ tracy.darke@warwickdc.gov.uk

Senior Management: Mr Colin Green, Director of Children, Learning & Young People, Council House, Earl Street, Coventry CV1 5RS ☎ 024 7683 1500 🖷 024 7683 1505 ✉ colin.green@coventry.gov.uk

Best Value: Dr Jocelyn Parry, Assistant Chief Executive, Council House, Earl Street, Coventry CV1 5RR ☎ 024 7683 1077 🖷 0247683 1106 ✉ jos.parry@coventry.gov.uk

Children / Youth Services: Ms A Parks, Head of Service (Youth Offending), Ground Floor Christchurch House, Greyfriars Lane, Coventry CV1 2GY ☎ 024 7683 4297 ✉ a.parks@coventry-yos.org.uk

Civil Registration: Ms Susan Hammond, Superintendent Registrar/Business Manager, The Register Office, Chelesmore Manor House, Manor House Drive, Coventry CV1 2ND ☎ 024 7683 3136 🖷 024 7683 3110 ✉ susan.hammond@coventry.gov.uk

PR / Communications: Ms Fran Collingham, Media & Communications Manager, Council House, Earl Street, Coventry CV1 5RS ☎ 024 7683 1088 🖷 024 7683 1132 ✉ fran.collingham@coventry.gov.uk

Community Planning: Ms Janice Nichols, Head of Neighbourhood Management, Council House, Earl Street, Coventry CV1 5RS ☎ 024 7683 1074 🖷 024 7683 1080 ✉ janice.nichols@coventry.gov.uk

Community Safety: Ms Mandie Watson, Community Safety Manager, Broadgate House, Broadgate, Coventry CV1 1NH ☎ 024 7683 2580 🖷 024 7683 2978 ✉ mandie.watson@coventry.gov.uk

Computer Management: Ms Bev Messinger, Director of Customer & Workforce Services, Council House, Earl Street, Coventry CV1 5RS ☎ 024 7683 3206 🖷 024 7683 3266 ✉ bev.messinger@coventry.gov.uk

Consumer Protection and Trading Standards: Mr Hamish Simmonds, Head of Trading Standards, City Services, 5th Floor Broadgate House, Broadgate, Coventry CV1 5RS ☎ 024 7683 1871 🖷 024 7683 2128 ✉ hamish.simmonds@coventry.gov.uk

Contracts: Mr Mick Burn, Procurement Manager, City Procurement, Tower Block, Much Park Street, Coventry CV3 4AR ☎ 024 7683 3767 🖷 024 7683 3780 ✉ mick.burn@coventry.gov.uk

Corporate Services: Ms Helen Abraham, Head of Democratic Services, Council House, Earl Street, Coventry CV1 5RS ☎ 024 7683 2199 🖷 024 7683 3070 ✉ helen.abraham@coventry.gov.uk

Customer Service: Mr Martin Yardley, Director of City Services & Development, Tower Block, Much Park Street, Coventry CV1 2PY ☎ 024 7683 1200 ✉ martin.yardley@coventry.gov.uk

Education: Ms Sue Heawood, Head of School Admissions, The Council House, Earl Street, Coventry CV1 5RR ☎ 024 7683 1500 ✉ sue.heawood@coventry.gov.uk

E-Government: Ms Bev Messinger, Director of Customer & Workforce Services, Council House, Earl Street, Coventry CV1 5RS ☎ 024 7683 3206 🖷 024 7683 3266 ✉ bev.messinger@coventry.gov.uk

Electoral Registration: Ms Helen Abraham, Head of Democratic Services, Council House, Earl Street, Coventry CV1 5RS ☎ 024 7683 2199 🖷 024 7683 3070 ✉ helen.abraham@coventry.gov.uk

Emergency Planning: Mr Peter Streets, Emergency Planning Officer, The Council House, Earl Street, Coventry CV1 5RR ☎ 024 7683 1837 🖷 024 7683 2128 ✉ peter.streets@coventry.gov.uk

Energy Management: Mr Kevin Palmer, Senior Energy Conservation Engineer, City Development, Tower Block, Much Park Street, Coventry CV1 2QE ☎ 024 7683 2711 🖷 024 7683 3670 ✉ kevin.palmer@coventry.gov.uk

Estates, Property & Valuation: Mr Nigel Clews, Head of Property & Projects, Tower Block, Much Park Street, Coventry CV1 2PY ☎ 024 7683 2620 🖷 024 7683 1203

nigel.clews@coventry.gov.uk

Events Manager: Ms Lee House, Events Manager, Floor 2, West Orchard House, Corporation Street, Coventry CV1 1GF ☎ 024 7683 2351 lee.house@coventry.gov.uk

Finance and Treasurer: Mr Chris West, Director of Finance & Legal Services, Council House, Earl Street, Coventry CV1 5RS ☎ 028 7683 3710 chris.west@coventry.gov.uk

Fleet Management: Ms Mary Morrissey, Assistant Director - Street Pride & Fleet Management, Tower Block, Much Park Street, Coventry CV1 2PY ☎ 024 7683 2632 mary.morrissey@coventry.gov.uk

Grounds Maintenance: Mr Martin Yardley, Director of City Services & Development, Tower Block, Much Park Street, Coventry CV1 2PY ☎ 024 7683 1200 martin.yardley@coventry.gov.uk

Health and Safety: Ms Jane Don, Health & Safety Manager, Broadgate House, Broadgate, Coventry CV1 1NH ☎ 024 7683 3293 jane.don@coventry.gov.uk

Highways: Mr Colin Knight, Assistant Director - Planning, Transport & Highways, Tower Block, Much Park Street, Coventry CV1 2PY ☎ 024 7683 2322 colin.knight@coventry.gov.uk

Home Energy Conservation: Mr Kevin Palmer, Senior Energy Conservation Engineer, City Development, Tower Block, Much Park Street, Coventry CV1 2QE ☎ 024 7683 2711 🖷 024 7683 3670 kevin.palmer@coventry.gov.uk

Housing: Mrs Sara Roach, Head of Housing, Broadgate House, Broadgate, Coventry CV1 1NH ☎ 024 7683 2123 sara.rudge@coventry.gov.uk

Local Area Agreement: Ms Jenni Venn, Corporate Policy & Research Manager, The Council House, Earl Street, Coventry CV1 5RR ☎ 024 7683 1077 jenni.venn@coventry.gov.uk

Legal: Mr Chris West, Director of Finance & Legal Services, Council House, Earl Street, Coventry CV1 5RS ☎ 028 7683 3710 chris.west@coventry.gov.uk

Licensing: Ms Davina Blackburn, Principal Licensing Officer, The Council House, Earl Street, Coventry CV1 5RR ☎ 024 7683 1874 davina.blackburn@coventry.gov.uk

Lottery Funding, Charity and Voluntary: Mr Stephen Weir, Advice Service, 1st Floor, West Orchard House, 28-34 Corporation Street, Coventry CV1 1GF ☎ 024 7683 1394

Member Services: Ms Helen Abraham, Head of Democratic Services, Council House, Earl Street, Coventry CV1 5RS ☎ 024 7683 2199 🖷 024 7683 3070 helen.abraham@coventry.gov.uk

Parking: Ms Annette Ward, Parking Supervisor, The Council House, Earl Street, Coventry CV1 5RR ☎ 024 7660 7081

Personnel / HR: Ms Sue Iannantuoni, Head of Human Resources, The Council House, Earl Street, Coventry CV1 5RR ☎ 024 7683 3543 sue.iannantuoni@coventry.gov.uk

Personnel / HR: Ms Bev Messinger, Director of Customer & Workforce Services, Council House, Earl Street, Coventry CV1 5RS ☎ 024 7683 3206 🖷 024 7683 3266 bev.messinger@coventry.gov.uk

Planning: Ms Carol Pullen, Head of Strategic Planning, The Council House, Earl Street, Coventry CV1 5RR ☎ 024 7683 1530 carol.pullen@coventry.gov.uk

Procurement: Mr Mick Burn, Procurement Manager, City Procurement, Tower Block, Much Park Street, Coventry CV3 4AR ☎ 024 7683 3767 🖷 024 7683 3780 mick.burn@coventry.gov.uk

Public Libraries: Ms Carmel Reed, Head of Library Services, West Orchard House, 28-34 Corporation Street, New Union Street, Coventry CV1 1GF ☎ 024 7683 1579 carmel.reed@coventry.gov.uk

Recycling & Waste Minimisation: Ms Julie Bird, Recycling Officer, Broadgate House, Broadgate, Coventry CV1 1NH ☎ 024 7683 3945 🖷 024 7683 1831 julie.bird@coventry.gov.uk

Regeneration: Mr Martin Yardley, Director of City Services & Development, Tower Block, Much Park Street, Coventry CV1 2PY ☎ 024 7683 1200 martin.yardley@coventry.gov.uk

Road Safety: Ms Melanie Statham, Senior Road Safety Officer, The Council House, Earl Street, Coventry CV1 5RR ☎ 024 7683 2007 🖷 024 7683 2150 melanie.statham@coventry.gov.uk

Social Services (Adult): Mr Mark Godfrey, Assistant Director - Adult Services, The Council House, Earl Street, Coventry CV1 5RR ☎ 024 7683 3402 mark.godfrey@coventry.gov.uk

Staff Training: Mr Shokat Lal, Human Resources Manager (Workforce Development), Council House, Earl Street, Coventry CV1 5RS ☎ 024 7683 3243 🖷 024 7683 3266 shokat.lal@coventry.gov.uk

Street Scene: Ms Mary Morrissey, Assistant Director - Street Pride & Fleet Management, Tower Block, Much Park Street, Coventry CV1 2PY ☎ 024 7683 2632 mary.morrissey@coventry.gov.uk

Sustainable Communities: Mr Andy Littlewood, Sustainable Communities Officer, Broadgate House, Broadgate, Coventry CV1 1NH ☎ 024 7683 2330 andy.littlewood@coventry.gov.uk

Sustainable Communities: Ms Mary Morrissey, Assistant Director - Street Pride & Fleet Management, Tower Block, Much Park Street, Coventry CV1 2PY ☎ 024 7683 2632 mary.morrissey@coventry.gov.uk

Sustainable Development: Mr Michael Checkley, Sustainability & Climate Change Manager, The Council House, Earl Street, Coventry CV1 5RR ☎ 024 7683 2155 michael.checkley@coventry.gov.uk

Tourism: Mr David Cockcroft, Assistant Director - City Centre

and Development Services, Tower Block, Much Park Street, Coventry CV1 2PY ☎ 024 7660 3964
david.cockcroft@discover.co.uk

Traffic Management: Mr Colin Knight, Assistant Director - Planning, Transport & Highways, Tower Block, Much Park Street, Coventry CV1 2PY ☎ 024 7683 2322
colin.knight@coventry.gov.uk

Transport: Mr Colin Knight, Assistant Director - Planning, Transport & Highways, Tower Block, Much Park Street, Coventry CV1 2PY ☎ 024 7683 2322 colin.knight@coventry.gov.uk

MEMBERS OF THE COUNCIL (54)

The Lord Mayor: **Sawdon**, Tim (CON - Wainbody)
tim.sawdon@coventry.gov.uk
Chair: **Mullhall**, Keiran (LAB - Radford)
keiran.mulhall@coventry.gov.uk
Deputy Mayor: **Crookes**, Gary (CON - Wainbody)
gary.crookes@coventry.gov.uk
Abbott, Faye (LAB - Wyken)
faye.abbott@coventry.gov.uk
Akhtar, Naeem (LAB - St Michaels)
naeem.akhtar@coventry.gov.uk
Ali, Maya (LAB - Westwood)
maya.ali@coventry.gov.uk
Andrews, Allan (CON - Earlsdon)
allan.andrews@coventry.gov.uk
Auluck, Malkiat (LAB - Foleshill)
malkiat.auluck@coventry.gov.uk
Bains, Sucha (LAB - Upper Stoke)
sucha.bains@coventry.gov.uk
Bigham, Linda (LAB - Longford)
linda.bigham@coventry.gov.uk
Blundell, John (CON - Wainbody)
john.blundell@coventry.gov.uk
Caan, Kamram (LAB - Upper Stoke)
kamran.caan@coventry.gov.uk
Chater, Dave (LAB - Binley & Willenhall)
dave.chater@coventry.gov.uk
Clifford, Joe (LAB - Holbrook)
joseph.clifford@coventry.gov.uk
Duggins, George (LAB - Longford)
george.duggins@coventry.gov.uk
Fletcher, Colleen (LAB - Upper Stoke)
colleen.fletcher@coventry.gov.uk
Foster, Kevin (CON - Cheylesmore)
kevin.foster@coventry.gov.uk
Galliers, David (LAB - Bablake)
david.galliers@coventry.gov.uk
Gannon, Damian (LAB - Sherbourne)
damian.gannon@coventry.gov.uk
Gingell, Alison (LAB - Sherbourne)
alison.gingell@coventry.gov.uk
Hammon, Michael (CON - Earlsdon)
michael.hammon@coventry.gov.uk
Harvard, Lindsley (LAB - Longford)
lindsley@harvard.freeserve.co.uk
Hetherton, Patricia (LAB - Woodlands)
patricia.hetherton@coventry.gov.uk
Howells, Dan (LAB - Whoberley)
dan.howells@coventry.gov.uk
Innes, Jayne (LAB - Whoberley)
jayne.innes@coventry.gov.uk
Kelly, Lynette (LAB - Henley)
lynnette.kelly@coventry.gov.uk
Kershaw, David (LAB - Bablake)
david.kershaw@coventry.gov.uk
Khan, Tariq (LAB - Foleshill)
tariq.khan@coventry.gov.uk
Khan, Abdul (LAB - Foleshill)
abdul.khan@coventry.gov.uk
Lakha, Ram (LAB - Binley & Willenhall)
ram.lakha@coventry.gov.uk
Lancaster, Rachel (LAB - Holbrook)
rachel.lancaster@coventry.gov.uk
Lepoidevin, Julia (CON - Woodlands)
julia.lepoidevin@coventry.gov.uk
Lucas, Ann (LAB - Holbrook)
ann.lucas@coventry.gov.uk
Maton, Kevin (LAB - Henley)
kevin.maton@coventry.gov.uk
McNicholas, John (LAB - Lower Stoke)
john.mcnicholas@coventry.gov.uk
Miks, Catherine (LAB - Lower Stoke)
catherine.miks@coventry.gov.uk
Mutton, John (LAB - Binley & Willenhall)
john.mutton@coventry.gov.uk
Mutton, Mal (LAB - Radford)
mal.mutton@coventry.gov.uk
Noonan, Hazel (CON - Cheylesmore)
hazel.noonan@coventry.gov.uk
O'Boyle, Jim (LAB - St Michaels)
jim.o'boyle@coventry.gov.uk
Ruane, Ed (LAB - Henley)
ed.ruane@coventry.gov.uk
Sandy, Richard (LAB - Westwood)
richard.sandy@coventry.gov.uk
Singh, Bally (LAB - Whoberley)
bally.singh@coventry.gov.uk
Singh Sehmi, Harjinder (LAB - Cheylesmore)
harjinder.singhsehmi@coventry.gov.uk
Skinner, David (CON - Westwood)
david.skinner@coventry.gov.uk
Skipper, Tony (LAB - Radford)
tony.skipper@coventry.gov.uk
Sweet, Hazel (LAB - Wyken)
hazel.sweet@coventry.gov.uk
Taylor, Ken (CON - Earlsdon)
ken.taylor@coventry.gov.uk
Thay, Robert (LAB - Wyken)
robert.thay@coventry.gov.uk
Thomas, Steven (LAB - Woodlands)
steven.thomas@coventry.gov.uk
Townshend, Phil (LAB - Lower Stoke)
phil.townshend@coventry.gov.uk
Walsh, Seamus (LAB - Sherbourne)
seamus.walsh@coventry.gov.uk
Welsh, David (LAB - St. Michaels)
david.welsh@coventry.gov.uk
Williams, Andrew (CON - Bablake)
andrew.williams@coventry.gov.uk

POLITICAL COMPOSITION

LAB: 43, CON: 11

CABINET

Leader: Mr John Mutton

Children & Young People: Mr Jim O'Boyle
City Development: Dr Lynette Kelly
City Services: Mr Lindsley Harvard
Community Safety & Equalities: Mr Phil Townshend
Education: Mr David Kershaw
Health & Community Services: Mrs Ann Lucas
Neighbourhood Action, Housing, Leisure & Culture: Mr Ed Ruane
Strategic Finance & Resources: Mr George Duggins
Sustainability & Local Infrastructure: Mr Abdul Khan

COMMITTEE CHAIRS

Audit & Governance: Mr Dave Chater
Ethics: Ms Patricia Hetherton
Licensing & Regulatory: Ms Rachel Lancaster
Planning: Mr Kevin Maton
Scrutiny Co-ordination: Ms Linda Bigham

CRAIGAVON N

Craigavon Borough Council, Civic Centre, Lakeview Road, Craigavon BT64 1AL ☎ 028 3831 2400 🖷 028 3831 2444 ✉ info@craigavon.gov.uk 💻 www.craigavon.gov.uk

FACTS & FIGURES

Police Authority: Northern Ireland Policing Board
Health Authority: Southern Health & Social Care Board
Learning and Skills Council: Northern Ireland
Parliamentary Constituencies: Upper Bann
EU Constituencies: Northern Ireland
Election Frequency: Elections are of whole council
Twinning: LaGrange, Georgia (USA)

PRINCIPAL OFFICERS

Chief Executive: Dr Theresa Donaldson, Chief Executive, Civic Centre, Lakeview Road, Craigavon BT64 1AL ☎ 028 3831 2402 ✉ theresa.donaldson@craigavon.gov.uk

Architect, Building / Property Services: Mr Stewart Kerr, Head of Technical Services, Civic Centre, Lakeview Road, Craigavon BT64 1AL 🖷 stewart.kerr@craigavon.gov.uk

Best Value: Miss Stephanie Harte, Policy Development Officer, Civic Centre, Lakeview Road, Craigavon BT64 1AL ☎ 028 3831 2501 🖷 028 3831 2444 ✉ stephanie.harte@craigavon.gov.uk

Building Control: Mr Robert Colvin, Director of Building Control Services, Civic Centre, Lakeview Road, Craigavon BT64 1AL ☎ 028 3831 2591 🖷 028 2831 2444 ✉ robert.colvin@craigavon.gov.uk

Building Control: Mr Richard Dale, Principal Building Control Surveyor, Civic Centre, Lakeview Road, Craigavon BT64 1AL ☎ 028 3831 2400 ✉ richard.dale@craigavon.gov.uk

Catering Services: Mrs Margaret Parks, Catering Manager, Civic Centre, Lakeview Road, Craigavon BT64 1AL ☎ 028 3831 2557 ✉ margaret.parks@craigavon.gov.uk

Civil Registration: Mrs Linda Steenson, Registrar, Civic Centre, Lakeview Road, Craigavon BT64 1AL ☎ 028 3831 2400 🖷 028 3831 2444 ✉ registrar@craigavon.gov.uk

PR / Communications: Mrs Pauline Nixon-Black, Public Relations Officer, Civic Centre, Lakeview Road, Craigavon BT64 1AL ☎ 028 3831 2429 🖷 028 3831 2444 ✉ pauline.nixon.black@craigavon.gov.uk

Community Planning: Ms Diane Clarke, Principal Community Services Manager, Civic Centre, Lakeview Road, Craigavon BT64 1AL ☎ 028 3831 2400 ✉ diane.clarke@craigavon.gov.uk

Community Planning: Miss Nicola Lane, Head of Community Development, Civic Centre, Lakeview Road, Craigavon BT64 1AL ☎ 028 3831 2457 🖷 028 3831 2488 ✉ nicola.lane@craigavon.gov.uk

Community Safety: Miss Sarah Wilson, Community Safety Officer, Civic Centre, Lakeview Road, Craigavon BT64 1AL ☎ 028 3831 2484 🖷 028 3831 2444 ✉ sarah.wilson@craigavon.gov.uk

Computer Management: Mr Barry McQueen, IT Officer, Civic Centre, Lakeview Road, Craigavon BT64 1AL ☎ 028 3831 2465 🖷 028 3831 2444 ✉ barry.mcqueen@craigavon.gov.uk

Consumer Protection and Trading Standards: Ms Audrey McClune, Head of Environmental Health, Civic Centre, Lakeview Road, Craigavon BT64 1AL ☎ 028 3831 2521 🖷 028 3831 2444 ✉ audrey.mcclune@craigavon.gov.uk

Contracts: Mr Stewart Kerr, Head of Technical Services, Civic Centre, Lakeview Road, Craigavon BT64 1AL 🖷 stewart.kerr@craigavon.gov.uk

Corporate Services: Ms Brona Slevin, Director of Corporate Services, Civic Centre, Lakeview Road, Craigavon BT64 1AL ☎ 028 3831 2460 🖷 028 3831 2444 ✉ brona.slevin@craigavon.gov.uk

Corporate Services: Mr Michael Watson, Audit, Governance & Risk, Civic Centre, Lakeview Road, Craigavon BT64 1AL ☎ 028 3831 2400 ✉ michael.watson@craigavon.gov.uk

Customer Service: Mrs Joanne Grattan, Customer Services Officer, Civic Centre, Lakeview Road, Craigavon BT64 1AL ☎ 028 3831 2554 ✉ joanne.grattan@craigavon.gov.uk

Direct Labour: Mr Stewart Kerr, Head of Technical Services, Civic Centre, Lakeview Road, Craigavon BT64 1AL 🖷 stewart.kerr@craigavon.gov.uk

Economic Development: Mrs Nicola Wilson, Head of Economic Development, Civic Centre, Lakeview Road, Craigavon BT64 1AL ☎ 028 3831 2571 🖷 028 3831 2444 ✉ nicola.wilson@craigavon.gov.uk

E-Government: Mr Liam McStravick, Head of Finance, Civic Centre, Lakeview Road, Craigavon BT64 1AL ☎ 028 3831 2481 ✉ liam.mcstravick@craigavon.gov.uk

Emergency Planning: Mr Lewis Porter, Principal Administration Officer, Civic Centre, Lakeview Road, Craigavon BT64 1AL ☎ 028 3831 2442 🖷 028 3831 2444 ✉ lewis.porter@craigavon.gov.uk

Environmental / Technical Services: Mrs Lorraine Crawford,

Director of Environmental Services, Civic Centre, Lakeview Road, Craigavon BT64 1AL ☎ 028 3831 2531 🖷 028 3831 2444 lorraine.crawford@craigavon.gov.uk

Environmental / Technical Services: Ms Audrey McClune, Head of Environmental Health, Civic Centre, Lakeview Road, Craigavon BT64 1AL ☎ 028 3831 2521 🖷 028 3831 2444 audrey.mcclune@craigavon.gov.uk

Environmental Health: Ms Audrey McClune, Head of Environmental Health, Civic Centre, Lakeview Road, Craigavon BT64 1AL ☎ 028 3831 2521 🖷 028 3831 2444 audrey.mcclune@craigavon.gov.uk

Estates, Property & Valuation: Mr Lewis Porter, Principal Administration Officer, Civic Centre, Lakeview Road, Craigavon BT64 1AL ☎ 028 3831 2442 🖷 028 3831 2444 lewis.porter@craigavon.gov.uk

European Liaison: Mrs Nicola Wilson, Head of Economic Development, Civic Centre, Lakeview Road, Craigavon BT64 1AL ☎ 028 3831 2571 🖷 028 3831 2444 nicola.wilson@craigavon.gov.uk

Facilities: Mrs Denise McCluskey, Facilities Manager, Civic Centre, Lakeview Road, Craigavon BT64 1AL ☎ 028 38312422 denise.mccluskey@craigavon.gov.uk

Finance and Treasurer: Mr Liam McStravick, Head of Finance, Civic Centre, Lakeview Road, Craigavon BT64 1AL ☎ 028 3831 2481 liam.mcstravick@craigavon.gov.uk

Fleet Management: Mr Andrew Shields, Depot Fleet Manager, Carn Depot, Craigavon BT63 5WG ☎ 028 3833 9031 🖷 028 3839 6060 andrew.shields@craigavon.gov.uk

Grounds Maintenance: Mr Kieran Cahoon, Parks Manager, Civic Centre, Lakeview Road, Craigavon BT64 1AL ☎ 028 3832 2870 kieran.cahoon@craigavon.gov.uk

Health and Safety: Mr Danny Dugdale, Health & Safety Adviser, Civic Centre, Lakeview Road, Craigavon BT64 1AL ☎ 028 3831 2526 🖷 028 3831 2636 danny.dugdale@craigavon.gov.uk

Leisure and Cultural Services: Mr Stephen Fraser, Director of Leisure Services, Civic Centre, Lakeview Road, Craigavon BT64 1AL ☎ 028 3831 2400 stephen.fraser@craigavon.gov.uk

Leisure and Cultural Services: Ms Rosemary Mulholland, Head of Conservation & Heritage, Civic Centre, Lakeview Road, Craigavon BT64 1AL ☎ 028 3831 2400 rosemary.mulholland@craigavon.gov.uk

Licensing: Mrs Maureen Briggs, Licensing Officer, Civic Centre, Lakeview Road, Craigavon BT64 1AL ☎ 028 3831 2524 🖷 028 3831 2444 maureen.briggs@craigavon.gov.uk

Lottery Funding, Charity and Voluntary: Ms Olga Murtagh, Director of Development, Civic Centre, Lakeview Road, Craigavon BT64 1AL ☎ 028 3831 2570 olga.murtagh@craigavon.gov.uk

Member Services: Ms Wendy Geary, Senior Member Services Officer, Civic Centre, Lakeview Road, Craigavon BT64 1AL ☎ 028 3831 2412 🖷 028 3831 2597 wendy.geary@craigavon.gov.uk

Personnel / HR: Mr Raymond Donnelly, Head of Human Resources, Civic Centre, Lakeview Road, Craigavon BT64 1AL ☎ 028 3831 2409 raymond.donnelly@craigavon.gov.uk

Procurement: Mr Stewart Kerr, Head of Technical Services, Civic Centre, Lakeview Road, Craigavon BT64 1AL 🖷 stewart.kerr@craigavon.gov.uk

Recycling & Waste Minimisation: Ms J Wilson, Recycling Officer, Civic Centre, Lakeview Road, Craigavon BT64 1AL ☎ 028 3831 2400 jennifer.wilson@craigavon.gov.uk

Staff Training: Ms Niamh Shannon, Learning & Development Manager, Civic Centre, Lakeview Road, Craigavon BT64 1AL ☎ 028 3831 2409 🖷 028 3831 2444 niamh.shannon@craigavon.gov.uk

Street Scene: Ms Olga Murtagh, Director of Development, Civic Centre, Lakeview Road, Craigavon BT64 1AL ☎ 028 3831 2570 olga.murtagh@craigavon.gov.uk

Sustainable Development: Mrs Lorraine Crawford, Director of Environmental Services, Civic Centre, Lakeview Road, Craigavon BT64 1AL ☎ 028 3831 2531 🖷 028 3831 2444 lorraine.crawford@craigavon.gov.uk

Tourism: Ms Sandra Durand, Assistant Economic Development Officer, Civic Centre, Lakeview Road, Craigavon BT64 1AL ☎ 028 3831 2575 🖷 028 3831 2488 sandra.durand@crigavon.gov.uk

Town Centre: Ms Lyn McNeil, Town Centre Manager, Civic Centre, Lakeview Road, Craigavon BT64 1AL ☎ 02838 312400

Transport: Mr Stewart Kerr, Head of Technical Services, Civic Centre, Lakeview Road, Craigavon BT64 1AL 🖷 stewart.kerr@craigavon.gov.uk

Waste Collection and Disposal: Mr Paul Topley, Waste Management Officer, Carn Depot, Craigavon BT63 5WG ☎ 028 3839 6062 🖷 028 3839 6060 paul.topley@craigavon.gov.uk

Waste Management: Mr Paul Topley, Waste Management Officer, Carn Depot, Craigavon BT63 5WG ☎ 028 3839 6062 🖷 028 3839 6060 paul.topley@craigavon.gov.uk

MEMBERS OF THE COUNCIL (25)

***Mayor:* Lockhart**, Carla (DUP - Lurgan)
carla.lockhart@craigavon.gov.uk
***Deputy Mayor:* Hatch**, Arnold (UUP - Portadown)
arnold.hatch@craigavon.gov.uk
***Alderman:* Anderson**, Sydney (DUP - Portadown)
sidney.anderson@craigavon.gov.uk
***Alderman:* Crozier**, Meta (UUP - Lurgan)
meta.crozier@craigavon.gov.uk
***Alderman:* McCullough**, Gladys (DUP - Portadown)
gladys.mccullough@craigavon.gov.uk

***Alderman:* Moutray**, Stephen (DUP - Lurgan)
stephen.moutray@craigavon.gov.uk
***Alderman:* Smith**, Woolsey (DUP - Central)
woolsey.smith@craigavon.gov.uk
Baxter, Mark (DUP - Lurgan)
mark.baxter@craigavon.gov.uk
Carson, Alan (DUP - Portadown)
alan.carson@craigavon.gov.uk
Causby, Darryn (DUP - Portadown)
darryn.causby@craigavon.gov.uk
Dixon, Conrad (ALL - Central)
Duffy, Paul (SF - Portadown)
paul.duffy@craigavon.gov.uk
Harkness, Ronnie (UUP - Central)
ronnieharkness@hotmail.com
Mackle, Liam (SF - Lurgan)
liam.mackle@craigavon.gov.uk
McAlinden, Declan (SDLP - Loughside)
declan.mcalinden@craigavon.gov.uk
McGeown, Noel (SF - Loughside)
noel.mcgeown@craigavon.gov.uk
McGibbon, Jonathan (SF - Loughside)
jonathan.mcgibbon@craigavon.gov.uk
McKenna, Gemma (SF - Portadown)
gemma.mckenna@craigavon.gov.uk
Nelson, Jospeh (SDLP - Loughside)
joe.nelson@craigavon.gov.uk
O'Connor, Thomas (SF - Central)
tommy.oconnor@craigavon.gov.uk
O'Dowd, Mairead (SF - Loughside)
mairead.odowd@craigavon.gov.uk
O'Dowd, Mark (SF - Central)
mark.odowd@craigavon.gov.uk
Savage, George (UUP - Lurgan)
george.savage@craigavon.gov.uk
Smith, Robert (DUP - Central)
robert.smith@craigavon.gov.uk
Twyble, Kenneth (UUP - Central)
kenneth.twyble@craigavon.gov.uk

POLITICAL COMPOSITION

DUP: 9, SF: 8, UUP: 5, SDLP: 2, ALL: 1

COMMITTEE CHAIRS

Audit: Mr Stephen Moutray
Environmental Services: Ms Gemma McKenna
Leisure Services: Mr Ronnie Harkness
Policy & Resources: Mr Mark Baxter

CRAVEN D

Craven District Council, 1 Belle Vue Square, Broughton Road, Skipton BD23 1FJ ☎ 01756 700600
🖷 01756 700658
💻 www.cravendc.gov.uk

FACTS & FIGURES

Police Authority: North Yorkshire Police Authority
Health Authority: NHS Yorkshire & the Humber
Learning and Skills Council: Yorkshire and the Humber
Parliamentary Constituencies: Skipton and Ripon
EU Constituencies: Yorkshire and the Humber
Election Frequency: Elections are by thirds

PRINCIPAL OFFICERS

Chief Executive: Mr Paul Shevlin, Chief Executive, 1 Belle Vue Square, Broughton Road, Skipton BD23 1FJ ☎ 01756 706201 🖷 01756 706219 ✉ pshevlin@cravendc.gov.uk

Deputy Chief Executive: Mr Paul Ellis, Deputy Chief Executive, 1 Belle Vue Square, Broughton Road, Skipton BD23 1FJ ☎ 01756 700600 🖷 01756 706413 ✉ pellis@cravendc.gov.uk

Senior Management: Ms Joanna Miller, Corporate Head (Financial Management), 1 Belle Vue Square, Broughton Road, Skipton BD23 1FJ ☎ 01756 706302 🖷 01756 700658 ✉ jmiller@cravendc.gov.uk

Best Value: Mrs Claire Hudson, Corporate Performance & Improvement Manager, 1 Belle Vue Square, Broughton Road, Skipton BD23 1FJ ☎ 01756 706493 ✉ chudson@cravendc.gov.uk

Building Control: Mr Ian Swain, Planning & Development Control Building Control Manager, 1 Belle Vue Square, Broughton Road, Skipton BD23 1FJ ☎ 01756 706465 🖷 01756 706658 ✉ wgudger@cravendc.gov.uk

PR / Communications: Mrs Sharon Hudson, Communications Manager, 1 Belle Vue Square, Broughton Road, Skipton BD23 1FJ ☎ 01756 706246 🖷 01756 700658 ✉ shudson@cravendc.gov.uk

Community Safety: Ms Stacey Mitchell, Craven Safety Community Partnership Co-ordinator, 1 Belle Vue Square, Broughton Road, Skipton BD23 1FJ ☎ 01756 700600 ✉ smitchell@cravendc.gov.uk

Computer Management: Mr Graham Thistlewhaite, Head - IS, 1 Belle Vue Square, Broughton Road, Skipton BD23 1FJ ☎ 01757 705101; 01756 706313 🖷 01756 700657; 01757 292229 ✉ gthistlewhaite@cravendc.gov.uk

Corporate Services: Ms Samia Hussain, Corporate Manager - Business Support, 1 Belle Vue Square, Broughton Road, Skipton BD23 1FJ ☎ 01756 706207 🖷 01756 706218 ✉ shussain@cravendc.gov.uk

Customer Service: Ms Deborah Davies, Customer & Benefit Services Manager, Town Hall, High Street, Skipton BD23 1AH ☎ 01756 700600 🖷 01756 700657 ✉ ddavies@cravendc.gov.uk

Economic Development: Mr David Smurthwaite, Strategic Manager - Planning, 1 Belle Vue Square, Broughton Road, Skipton BD23 1FJ ☎ 01756 706409 🖷 01756 700658 ✉ dsmurthwaite@cravendc.gov.uk

E-Government: Mr Graham Thistlewhaite, Head - IS, 1 Belle Vue Square, Broughton Road, Skipton BD23 1FJ ☎ 01757 705101; 01756 706313 🖷 01756 700657; 01757 292229 ✉ gthistlewhaite@cravendc.gov.uk

Electoral Registration: Mr Colin Iveson, Democratic Services Manager, 1 Belle Vue Square, Broughton Road, Skipton BD23 1FJ ☎ 01756 706231 🖷 01756 706257 ✉ civeson@cravendc.gov.uk

Emergency Planning: Mr Paul Shevlin, Chief Executive, 1 Belle Vue Square, Broughton Road, Skipton BD23 1FJ ☎ 01756 706201

🖷 01756 706219 ✉ pshevlin@cravendc.gov.uk

Environmental / Technical Services: Mr Phil Greenup, Environment and Housing Manager, South Lakeland House, Lowther Street, Kendal LA9 4UQ ☎ 0845 050 4434; 0845 050 4434 🖷 01539 740300 ✉ p.greenup@southlakeland.gov.uk

Environmental Health: Mr Mark Richardson, Environmental Health Manager, 1 Belle Vue Square, Broughton Road, Skipton BD23 1FJ ☎ 01756 706356 ✉ mrichardson@cravendc.gov.uk

Finance and Treasurer: Ms Joanna Miller, Corporate Head (Financial Management), 1 Belle Vue Square, Broughton Road, Skipton BD23 1FJ ☎ 01756 706302 🖷 01756 700658 ✉ jmiller@cravendc.gov.uk

Grounds Maintenance: Ms Hazel Smith, Projects Manager, 1 Belle Vue Square, Broughton Road, Skipton BD23 1FJ ☎ 01756 706310 🖷 01756 706219 ✉ hsmith@cravendc.gov.uk

Health and Safety: Ms Samia Hussain, Corporate Manager - Business Support, 1 Belle Vue Square, Broughton Road, Skipton BD23 1FJ ☎ 01756 706207 🖷 01756 706218 ✉ shussain@cravendc.gov.uk

Home Energy Conservation: Mr Wyn Ashton, Head - Strategic Housing, 1 Belle Vue Square, Broughton Road, Skipton BD23 1FJ ☎ 01756 706338 🖷 01756 700658 ✉ washton@cravendc.gov.uk

Housing: Mr Wyn Ashton, Head - Strategic Housing, 1 Belle Vue Square, Broughton Road, Skipton BD23 1FJ ☎ 01756 706338 🖷 01756 700658 ✉ washton@cravendc.gov.uk

Legal: Mrs Gill Cooper, Strategic Manager - Legal & Democratic Services, 1 Belle Vue Square, Broughton Road, Skipton BD23 1FJ ☎ 01756 706249 🖷 01756 706257 ✉ gcooper@cravendc.gov.uk

Leisure and Cultural Services: Mr David Smurthwaite, Strategic Manager - Planning, 1 Belle Vue Square, Broughton Road, Skipton BD23 1FJ ☎ 01756 706409 🖷 01756 700658 ✉ dsmurthwaite@cravendc.gov.uk

Licensing: Mr Tim Bassett, Temporary Environmental Health Manager, 1 Belle Vue Square, Broughton Road, Skipton BD23 1FJ ☎ 01756 706334 🖷 01756 700658 ✉ tbassett@cravendc.gov.uk

Lottery Funding, Charity and Voluntary: Ms Kate Senior, Partnerships Manager, 1 Belle Vue Square, Broughton Road, Skipton BD23 1FJ ☎ 01756 706414 🖷 01756 700658 ✉ ksenior@cravendc.gov.uk

Member Services: Mr Colin Iveson, Democratic Services Manager, 1 Belle Vue Square, Broughton Road, Skipton BD23 1FJ ☎ 01756 706231 🖷 01756 706257 ✉ civeson@cravendc.gov.uk

Parking: Mr Shane Reffin, Parking & Markets Manager, 1 Belle Vue Square, Broughton Road, Skipton BD23 1FJ ☎ 01756 706421 ✉ sreffin@cravendc.gov.uk

Partnerships: Ms Kate Senior, Partnerships Manager, 1 Belle Vue Square, Broughton Road, Skipton BD23 1FJ ☎ 01756 706414 🖷 01756 700658 ✉ ksenior@cravendc.gov.uk

Personnel / HR: Ms Samia Hussain, Corporate Manager - Business Support, 1 Belle Vue Square, Broughton Road, Skipton BD23 1FJ ☎ 01756 706207 🖷 01756 706218 ✉ shussain@cravendc.gov.uk

Planning: Mr David Smurthwaite, Strategic Manager - Planning, 1 Belle Vue Square, Broughton Road, Skipton BD23 1FJ ☎ 01756 706409 🖷 01756 700658 ✉ dsmurthwaite@cravendc.gov.uk

Recycling & Waste Minimisation: Mr Paul Florentine, Waste & Recycling Manager, 1 Belle Vue Square, Broughton Road, Skipton BD23 1FJ ☎ 01756 706320 🖷 01756 700658 ✉ pflorentine@cravendc.gov.uk

Regeneration: Mr David Smurthwaite, Strategic Manager - Planning, 1 Belle Vue Square, Broughton Road, Skipton BD23 1FJ ☎ 01756 706409 🖷 01756 700658 ✉ dsmurthwaite@cravendc.gov.uk

Sustainable Communities: Ms Kate Senior, Partnerships Manager, 1 Belle Vue Square, Broughton Road, Skipton BD23 1FJ ☎ 01756 706414 🖷 01756 700658 ✉ ksenior@cravendc.gov.uk

Sustainable Development: Mr David Smurthwaite, Strategic Manager - Planning, 1 Belle Vue Square, Broughton Road, Skipton BD23 1FJ ☎ 01756 706409 🖷 01756 700658 ✉ dsmurthwaite@cravendc.gov.uk

Tourism: Mr David Smurthwaite, Strategic Manager - Planning, 1 Belle Vue Square, Broughton Road, Skipton BD23 1FJ ☎ 01756 706409 🖷 01756 700658 ✉ dsmurthwaite@cravendc.gov.uk

Town Centre: Mr Dave Parker, Chief Officer - Skipton, Skipton Town Council Office, 2nd Floor, Barclays Bank Chambers, Skipton BD23 1DT ☎ 01756 794357

Transport Planner: Mr Dave Parker, Chief Officer - Skipton, Skipton Town Council Office, 2nd Floor, Barclays Bank Chambers, Skipton BD23 1DT ☎ 01756 794357

Waste Collection and Disposal: Mr Paul Florentine, Waste & Recycling Manager, 1 Belle Vue Square, Broughton Road, Skipton BD23 1FJ ☎ 01756 706320 🖷 01756 700658 ✉ pflorentine@cravendc.gov.uk

Waste Management: Mr Paul Florentine, Waste & Recycling Manager, 1 Belle Vue Square, Broughton Road, Skipton BD23 1FJ ☎ 01756 706320 🖷 01756 700658 ✉ pflorentine@cravendc.gov.uk

MEMBERS OF THE COUNCIL (30)

***Chair:* Harbron**, Christopher (CON - Skipton East)
Vote4harbron@tiscali.co.uk
***Vice-Chair:* Whaites**, Donald (CON - Settle & Ribblebanks)
donnywhaites@hotmail.com
***Leader of the Council:* Knowles-Fitton**, Christopher (CON - Barden Fell)
chris@knowleslodge.com
***Deputy Leader of the Council:* Foster**, Richard (CON - Grassington)
confoster@fsmail.net
***Group Leader:* Barrett**, Philip (IND - Glusburn)
cllr.philip.barrett@northyorks.gov.uk

Barrington, Lin (IND - Bentham)
linbarrington@live.co.uk
Beck, Graham (IND - Glusburn)
GRHB4@aol.com
Brockbank, Linda (CON - Bentham)
ccprod@uwclub.net
English, Polly (LD - Skipton West)
pollyenglish@hotmail.co.uk
English, Paul (LD - Skipton West)
englishpa@hotmail.com
Fairbank, Patricia (CON - Aire Valley with Lothersdale)
Green, Adrian (CON - Cowling)
adygreen@msn.com
Hart, Kenneth (IND - Sutton-in-Craven)
kenhart2001@yahoo.co.uk
Heseltine, Robert (IND - Skipton South)
cllr.robert.heseltine@northyorks.gov.uk
Ireton, David (IND - Ingleton & Clapham)
cllr.david.ireton@northyorks.gov.uk
Jaquin, Eric (LD - Skipton East)
eric.jaquin@freeserve.co.uk
Kerwin-Davey, John (IND - Skipton North)
j.kerwindavey@btinternet.com
Lis, Carl (CON - Ingleton & Clapham)
chlis@btinternet.com
Mason, Robert (IND - West Craven)
Moorby, Robert (IND - Hellifield and Long Preston)
r.moorby470@btinternet.com
Myers, Simon (CON - Gargrave & Malhamdale)
SimonMyersCDC@aol.com
Place, Stephen (IND - Sutton-in-Craven)
ssplace@hotmail.com
Quinn, John (CON - Embsay-with-Eastby)
andygill.quinn@virgin.net
Roberts, John (CON - Upper Wharfdale)
j-roberts@supanet.com
Solloway, Andrew (IND - Skipton South)
andy.solloway@virgin.net
Staveley, David (CON - Settle & Ribblebanks)
dstav@hotmail.co.uk
Sutcliffe, Alan (CON - Gargrave & Malhamdale)
alansutcliffe952@btinternet.com
Turner, Marcia (CON - Skipton North)
MARCIA@turner3.fsbusiness.co.uk
Welch, Richard (CON - Penyghent)
rcw.gigg@googlemail.com
Wheeler, Mark (LD - Aire Valley with Lothersdale)
markandnicolawheeler@supanet.com

POLITICAL COMPOSITION

CON: 15, IND: 11, LD: 4

CABINET

Leader: Mr Christopher Knowles-Fitton
Deputy Leader: Mr Richard Foster
Children & Young People: Mr Christopher Harbron

COMMITTEE CHAIRS

Audit & Governance: Mr Stephen Place
Licensing: Mr John Quinn
Overview & Scrutiny: Mr John Roberts
Planning: Mr Richard Welch
Policy: Mr Christopher Knowles-Fitton

CRAWLEY — D

Crawley Borough Council, Town Hall, The Boulevard, Crawley RH10 1UZ ☎ 01293 438000 🖷 01293 511803
✉ crawleybc@crawley.gov.uk 🖳 www.crawley.gov.uk

FACTS & FIGURES

Police Authority: Sussex Police Authority
Health Authority: South East Coast Strategic Health Authority
Learning and Skills Council: South East
Parliamentary Constituencies: Crawley
EU Constituencies: South East
Election Frequency: Elections are by thirds
Twinning: Dorsten (Germany)

PRINCIPAL OFFICERS

Chief Executive: Mr Lee Harris, Chief Executive, Town Hall, The Boulevard, Crawley RH10 1UZ ☎ 01293 438626 🖷 01293 438723 ✉ lee.harris@crawley.gov.uk

Senior Management: Mr Peter Browning, Director of Environment & Housing, Town Hall, The Boulevard, Crawley RH10 1UZ ☎ 01293 438754 🖷 01293 438606 ✉ peter.browning@crawley.gov.uk

Senior Management: Mr David Covill, Director of Resources, Town Hall, The Boulevard, Crawley RH10 1UZ ☎ 01293 438335 🖷 01293 511803 ✉ david.covill@crawley.gov.uk

Senior Management: Mr Phil Rogers, Director of Community Services, Town Hall, The Boulevard, Crawley RH10 1UZ ☎ 01293 438462 🖷 01293 438443 ✉ phil.rogers@crawley.gov.uk

Access Officer / Social Services (Disability): Mr Damian Brewer, Access Officer (Horsham District Council), Town Hall, The Boulevard, Crawley RH10 1UZ ☎ 01403 215648 🖷 01403 215599 ✉ damian.brewer@crawley.gov.uk

Architect, Building / Property Services: Mr Peter Allen, Head of Property, Town Hall, The Boulevard, Crawley RH10 1UZ ☎ 01293 438344 ✉ peter.allen@crawley.gov.uk

Building Control: Ms Jo Newton-Smith, Procurement Manager, Town Hall, The Boulevard, Crawley RH10 1UZ ☎ 01403 215299 ✉ jo.newton-smith@crawley.gov.uk

PR / Communications: Mr Allan Hambly, Communications Manager, Town Hall, The Boulevard, Crawley RH10 1UZ ☎ 01293 438781 🖷 01293 438602 ✉ allan.hambly@crawley.gov.uk

Community Planning: Ms Carrie Burton, Corporate Policy Manager, Town Hall, The Boulevard, Crawley RH10 1UZ ☎ 01293 438473 🖷 01293 438718 ✉ carrie.burton@crawley.gov.uk

Community Safety: Mr Don Edwardson, Community Safety Officer, Town Hall, The Boulevard, Crawley RH10 1UZ ☎ 01293 438681 🖷 01293 438606 ✉ don.edwardson@crawley.gov.uk

Computer Management: Mrs Lucasta Grayson, Head of People & Technology, Town Hall, The Boulevard, Crawley RH10 1UZ ☎ 01293 438213 ✉ lucasta.grayson@crawley.gov.uk

Contracts: Ms Jo Newton-Smith, Procurement Manager, Town Hall, The Boulevard, Crawley RH10 1UZ ☎ 01403 215299 ✉ jo.newton-smith@crawley.gov.uk

Customer Service: Mrs Lucasta Grayson, Head of People & Technology, Town Hall, The Boulevard, Crawley RH10 1UZ ☎ 01293 438213 ✉ lucasta.grayson@crawley.gov.uk

Direct Labour: Mr Peter Browning, Director of Environment & Housing, Town Hall, The Boulevard, Crawley RH10 1UZ ☎ 01293 438754 🖷 01293 438606 ✉ peter.browning@crawley.gov.uk

Economic Development: Mr Steve Sawyer, Economic Development Officer, Town Hall, The Boulevard, Crawley RH10 1UZ ☎ 01293 438704 ✉ steve.sawyer@crawley.gov.uk

E-Government: Mrs Lucasta Grayson, Head of People & Technology, Town Hall, The Boulevard, Crawley RH10 1UZ ☎ 01293 438213 ✉ lucasta.grayson@crawley.gov.uk

Electoral Registration: Ms Ann-Maria Brown, Head of Legal & Democratic Services, Town Hall, The Boulevard, Crawley RH10 1UZ ☎ 01293 438292 🖷 01293 511803 ✉ ann-maria.brown@crawley.gov.uk

Electoral Registration: Mr Andrew Oakley, Electoral Services Manager, Town Hall, The Boulevard, Crawley RH10 1UZ ☎ 01293 438346 🖷 01293 511803 ✉ andrew.oakley@crawley.gov.uk

Emergency Planning: Mr Andrew Gaffney, Emergency Planning Officer, Town Hall, The Boulevard, Crawley RH10 1UZ ☎ 01293 468454 ✉ andy.gaffney@crawley.gov.uk

Energy Management: Mr Brett Hagen, Environment Manager, Town Hall, The Boulevard, Crawley RH10 1UZ ☎ 01293 438543 🖷 01293 438604 ✉ brett.hagen@crawley.gov.uk

Environmental / Technical Services: Mr Peter Browning, Director of Environment & Housing, Town Hall, The Boulevard, Crawley RH10 1UZ ☎ 01293 438754 🖷 01293 438606 ✉ peter.browning@crawley.gov.uk

Environmental / Technical Services: Mrs Angela Tanner, Head of Environmental Services, Town Hall, The Boulevard, Crawley RH10 1UZ ☎ 01293 438220 🖷 01293 438488 ✉ angela.tanner@crawley.gov.uk

Environmental Health: Mrs Angela Tanner, Head of Environmental Services, Town Hall, The Boulevard, Crawley RH10 1UZ ☎ 01293 438220 🖷 01293 438488 ✉ angela.tanner@crawley.gov.uk

Estates, Property & Valuation: Mr Peter Allen, Head of Property, Town Hall, The Boulevard, Crawley RH10 1UZ ☎ 01293 438344 ✉ peter.allen@crawley.gov.uk

European Liaison: Mr Lee Harris, Chief Executive, Town Hall, The Boulevard, Crawley RH10 1UZ ☎ 01293 438626 🖷 01293 438723 ✉ lee.harris@crawley.gov.uk

Facilities: Mr Mike Pidgeon, Facilities Manager, Town Hall, The Boulevard, Crawley RH10 1UZ ☎ 01293 438291 🖷 01293 438602 ✉ mike.pidgeon@crawley.gov.uk

Finance and Treasurer: Mr David Covill, Director of Resources, Town Hall, The Boulevard, Crawley RH10 1UZ ☎ 01293 438335 🖷 01293 511803 ✉ david.covill@crawley.gov.uk

Grounds Maintenance: Mrs Karen Rham, Parks and Green Spaces Officer, Town Hall, The Boulevard, Crawley RH10 1UZ ☎ 01293 535624 ✉ karen.rham@crawley.gov.uk

Health and Safety: Mr Andrew Gaffney, Emergency Planning Officer, Town Hall, The Boulevard, Crawley RH10 1UZ ☎ 01293 468454 ✉ andy.gaffney@crawley.gov.uk

Home Energy Conservation: Mr Brett Hagen, Environment Manager, Town Hall, The Boulevard, Crawley RH10 1UZ ☎ 01293 438543 🖷 01293 438604 ✉ brett.hagen@crawley.gov.uk

Housing: Mr Peter Browning, Director of Environment & Housing, Town Hall, The Boulevard, Crawley RH10 1UZ ☎ 01293 438754 🖷 01293 438606 ✉ peter.browning@crawley.gov.uk

Housing: Ms Diana Maughan, Head of Housing Strategic Services, Town Hall, The Boulevard, Crawley RH10 1UZ ☎ 01293 438234 ✉ diana.maughan@crawley.gov.uk

Housing Maintenance: Mr Tim Honess, Maintenance Operations Manager, Town Hall, The Boulevard, Crawley RH10 1UZ ☎ 01293 438253 ✉ tim.honess@crawley.gov.uk

Legal: Ms Ann-Maria Brown, Head of Legal & Democratic Services, Town Hall, The Boulevard, Crawley RH10 1UZ ☎ 01293 438292 🖷 01293 511803 ✉ ann-maria.brown@crawley.gov.uk

Leisure and Cultural Services: Mr Phil Rogers, Director of Community Services, Town Hall, The Boulevard, Crawley RH10 1UZ ☎ 01293 438462 🖷 01293 438443 ✉ phil.rogers@crawley.gov.uk

Licensing: Mrs Angela Tanner, Head of Environmental Services, Town Hall, The Boulevard, Crawley RH10 1UZ ☎ 01293 438220 🖷 01293 438488 ✉ angela.tanner@crawley.gov.uk

Lottery Funding, Charity and Voluntary: Mr Phil Rogers, Director of Community Services, Town Hall, The Boulevard, Crawley RH10 1UZ ☎ 01293 438462 🖷 01293 438443 ✉ phil.rogers@crawley.gov.uk

Member Services: Ms Ann-Maria Brown, Head of Legal & Democratic Services, Town Hall, The Boulevard, Crawley RH10 1UZ ☎ 01293 438292 🖷 01293 511803 ✉ ann-maria.brown@crawley.gov.uk

Parking: Mr Graham Marriott, Technical Officer, Town Hall, The Boulevard, Crawley RH10 1UZ ☎ 01293 438520 ✉ graham.marriott@crawley.gov.uk

Personnel / HR: Mrs Lucasta Grayson, Head of People & Technology, Town Hall, The Boulevard, Crawley RH10 1UZ ☎ 01293 438213 ✉ lucasta.grayson@crawley.gov.uk

Planning: Mrs Jean McPherson, Development Control Manager, Town Hall, The Boulevard, Crawley RH10 1UZ ☎ 01293 438577 🖷 01293 438495 ✉ jean.mcpherson@crawley.gov.uk

Procurement: Ms Jo Newton-Smith, Procurement Manager, Town Hall, The Boulevard, Crawley RH10 1UZ ☎ 01293 438363 ✉ jo.newton-smith@crawley.gov.uk

Recycling & Waste Minimisation: Mr Christian Harris, Head of Amenity Services, Town Hall, The Boulevard, Crawley RH10 1UZ ☎ 01293 438420 ✉ christian.harris@crawley.gov.uk

Staff Training: Mr Andrew Davies, Training & Development Manager, Town Hall, The Boulevard, Crawley RH10 1UZ ☎ 01293 438948 🖷 01293 438600 ✉ andrew.davies@crawley.gov.uk

Street Scene: Mr Graham Rowe, Street Scene Services & Cleansing Manager, Town Hall, The Boulevard, Crawley RH10 1UZ ☎ 01293 438460 🖷 01293 438606 ✉ graham.rowe@crawley.gov.uk

Sustainable Communities: Mr Peter Browning, Director of Environment & Housing, Town Hall, The Boulevard, Crawley RH10 1UZ ☎ 01293 438754 🖷 01293 438606 ✉ peter.browning@crawley.gov.uk

Sustainable Development: Mr Brett Hagen, Environment Manager, Town Hall, The Boulevard, Crawley RH10 1UZ ☎ 01293 438543 🖷 01293 438604 ✉ brett.hagen@crawley.gov.uk

Town Centre: Mr Alfredo Mendes, Town Centre Co-ordinator, Town Hall, The Boulevard, Crawley RH10 1UZ ☎ 01293 438237 ✉ alfredo.mendes@crawley.gov.uk

Transport: Mr Graham Rowe, Street Scene Services & Cleansing Manager, Town Hall, The Boulevard, Crawley RH10 1UZ ☎ 01293 438460 🖷 01293 438606 ✉ graham.rowe@crawley.gov.uk

Waste Collection and Disposal: Mr Peter Browning, Director of Environment & Housing, Town Hall, The Boulevard, Crawley RH10 1UZ ☎ 01293 438754 🖷 01293 438606 ✉ peter.browning@crawley.gov.uk

Waste Collection and Disposal: Mr Christian Harris, Head of Amenity Services, Town Hall, The Boulevard, Crawley RH10 1UZ ☎ 01293 438420 ✉ christian.harris@crawley.gov.uk

Waste Management: Mr Peter Browning, Director of Environment & Housing, Town Hall, The Boulevard, Crawley RH10 1UZ ☎ 01293 438754 🖷 01293 438606 ✉ peter.browning@crawley.gov.uk

Waste Management: Mr Christian Harris, Head of Amenity Services, Town Hall, The Boulevard, Crawley RH10 1UZ ☎ 01293 438420 ✉ christian.harris@crawley.gov.uk

MEMBERS OF THE COUNCIL (37)

***Mayor:* Blake**, Keith (CON - Gossops Green)
keith.blake@crawley.gov.uk
***Deputy Mayor:* Burgess**, Bob (CON - Three Bridges)
bob.burgess@crawley.gov.uk
***Leader of the Council:* Lanzer**, Bob (CON - Pound Hill South & Worth)
bob.lanzer@crawley.gov.uk
***Deputy Leader of the Council:* Denman**, Claire (CON - Pound Hill South & Worth)
claire.denman@crawley.gov.uk
Ayling, Marion (LAB - Bewbush)
marion.ayling@crawley.gov.uk
Blake, Sally (CON - Pound Hill North)
sally.blake@crawley.gov.uk
Bloom, Howard (CON - Southgate)
howard.bloom@crawley.gov.uk
Boxall, Nigel (CON - Tilgate)
nigel.boxall@crawley.gov.uk
Brockwell, Keith (CON - Pound Hill North)
keith.brockwell@crawley.gov.uk
Burgess, Brenda (CON - Three Bridges)
brenda.burgess@crawley.gov.uk
Burke, Lee (CON - Pound Hill South & Worth)
lee.burke@crawley.gov.uk
Burrett, Richard (CON - Pound Hill North)
richard.burrett@crawley.gov.uk
Cheshire, Chris (LAB - Bewbush)
chris.cheshire@crawley.gov.uk
Crow, Duncan (CON - Furnace Green)
duncan.crow@crawley.gov.uk
Cumper, Vanessa (CON - West Green)
vanessa.cumper@crawley.gov.uk
Denman, John (CON - Ifield)
john.denman@crawley.gov.uk
Eade, Carol (CON - Furnace Green)
carol.eade@crawley.gov.uk
Irvine, Ian (LAB - Broadfield North)
ian.irvine@crawley.gov.uk
Jones, Michael (LAB - Bewbush)
michael.jones@crawley.gov.uk
Joyce, Stephen (LAB - Langley Green)
stephen.joyce@crawley.gov.uk
Lamb, Peter (LAB - Northgate)
peter.lamb@crawley.gov.uk
Lloyd, Colin (LAB - Tilgate)
colin.lloyd@crawley.gov.uk
Marshall-Ascough, Liam (CON - Southgate)
liam.marshall-ascough@crawley.gov.uk
Moffatt, Colin (LAB - Broadfield South)
colin.moffatt@crawley.gov.uk
Mullins, Chris (LAB - Gossops Green)
chris.mullins@crawley.gov.uk
Oxlade, Chris (LAB - Ifield)
chris.oxlade@crawley.gov.uk
Peck, Duncan (CON - Maidenbower)
duncan.peck@crawley.gov.uk
Quinn, Brian (LAB - Broadfield North)
brian.quinn@crawley.gov.uk
Quirk, Alan (CON - Broadfield South)
alan.quirk@crawley.gov.uk
Shreeves, David (LAB - Langley Green)
david.shreeves@crawley.gov.uk
Smith, Brenda (LAB - Langley Green)
brenda.smith@crawley.gov.uk
Smith, Peter (LAB - Ifield)
peter.smith@crawley.gov.uk
Thomas, Geraint (LAB - Northgate)
geraint.thomas@crawley.gov.uk
Trussell, Ken (CON - Maidenbower)
ken.trussell@crawley.gov.uk

Walker, Lenny (CON - Maidenbower)
lenny.walker@crawley.gov.uk
Ward, Bill (LAB - West Green)
bill.ward@crawley.gov.uk
Williamson, Karl (CON - Southgate)
karl.williamson@crawley.gov.uk

POLITICAL COMPOSITION
CON: 21, LAB: 16

CABINET
Leader: Mr Bob Lanzer
Deputy Leader / Planning & Economic Development: Mrs Claire Denman
Community Engagement: Mr Nigel Boxall
Environment Services: Mr Ken Trussell
Housing: Mr Richard Burrett
Leisure & Cultural Services: Mr Lenny Walker

COMMITTEE CHAIRS
Audit & Governance: Mr Alan Quirk
Development Control: Mr John Denman
General Purposes: Mr Richard Burrett
Licensing: Mrs Beryl MeCrow

CROYDON L

Croydon London Borough Council, The Town Hall, Katharine Street, Croydon CR0 1NX ☎ 020 8726 6000 🖷 020 8760 5657 💻 www.croydon.gov.uk

FACTS & FIGURES
Police Authority: Metropolitan Police Authority
Health Authority: NHS London
Learning and Skills Council: London
Parliamentary Constituencies: Croydon Central, Croydon North, Croydon South
EU Constituencies: London
Election Frequency: Elections are of whole council
Twinning: Arnhem (Netherlands)

PRINCIPAL OFFICERS
Chief Executive: Mr Jon Rouse, Chief Executive, Taberner House, Park Lane, Croydon CR9 3JS ☎ 020 8726 6000 🖷 020 8760 5674 ✉ jon.rouse@croydon.gov.uk

Deputy Chief Executive: Mr Nathan Elvery, Executive Director, Taberner House, Park Lane, Croydon CR9 3JS ☎ 020 8726 6000 Extn 62822 🖷 020 8686 7405 ✉ nathan.elvery@croydon.gov.uk

Deputy Chief Executive: Ms Hannah Miller, Executive Director, Taberner House, Park Lane, Croydon CR9 1JT ☎ 020 8726 6000 Extn 64590 ✉ hannah.miller@croydon.gov.uk

Senior Management: Mrs Julie Belvir, Council Solicitor & Director of Democratic & Legal Services, Taberner House, Park Lane , Croydon CR9 3JS ☎ 020 8726 6000 Extn 64985 ✉ julie.belvir@croydon.gov.uk

Senior Management: Mr Nathan Elvery, Executive Director, Taberner House, Park Lane, Croydon CR9 3JS ☎ 020 8726 6000 Extn 62822 🖷 020 8686 7405 ✉ nathan.elvery@croydon.gov.uk

Senior Management: Mr Paul Greenhalgh, Executive Director - Children, Young People & Learners, 7th Floor, Taberner House, Park Lane, Croydon CR9 3JS ☎ 020 8726 6000 Ext 65787 ✉ paul.greenhalgh@croydon.gov.uk

Senior Management: Ms Hannah Miller, Executive Director, Taberner House, Park Lane, Croydon CR9 2BA ☎ 020 8726 6000 Extn 64590 ✉ hannah.miller@croydon.gov.uk

Architect, Building / Property Services: Mr Stephen Wingrave, Strategic Estates Manager, Taberner House, Park Lane, Croydon CR9 1JR ☎ 020 8726 6000 extn 61512 🖷 020 8760 5728 ✉ stephen.wingrave@croydon.gov.uk

Building Control: Mr Mike Kiely, Director of Planning & Building Control, Taberner House, Park Lane, Croydon CR9 1JT ☎ 020 8760 5599 ✉ mike.kiely@croydon.gov.uk

Catering Services: Ms Allyson Lloyd, Corporate Catering Manager, Taberner House, Park Lane, Croydon CR9 3JS ☎ 020 8760 5467 ✉ allyson.lloyd@croydon.gov.uk

Community Safety: Mr Andy Opie, Head of Community Safety, Taberner House, Park Lane, Croydon CR9 3JS ☎ 020 8726 6000 Extn 65686 ✉ andy.opie@croydon.gov.uk

Computer Management: Mr Nathan Elvery, Executive Director, Taberner House, Park Lane, Croydon CR9 3JS ☎ 020 8726 6000 Extn 62822 🖷 020 8686 7405 ✉ nathan.elvery@croydon.gov.uk

Consumer Protection and Trading Standards: Mr Paul Foster, Head of Regulatory Services, Taberner House, Park Lane, Croydon CR9 3JS ☎ 020 8726 6000 Extn 65475 🖷 020 8760 5786 ✉ paul.foster@croydon.gov.uk

Contracts: Ms Sarah Ireland, Director of Strategy Commissioning Procurement & Performance, Taberner House, Park Lane, Croydon CR9 3JS ☎ 020 8726 6000 Extn 62070 ✉ sarah.ireland@croydon.gov.uk

Customer Service: Mr Graham Cadle, Director of Customer Services, Taberner House, Park Lane, Croydon CR9 1JT ☎ 020 8726 6000 Extn 63295 ✉ graham.cadle@croydon.gov.uk

Economic Development: Ms Lisa McCance, Head of Economic Development Development, Taberner House, Park Lane, Croydon CR9 3RN ☎ 020 8760 5655 ✉ lisa.mccance@croydon.gov.uk

E-Government: Mr Nathan Elvery, Executive Director, Taberner House, Park Lane, Croydon CR9 3JS ☎ 020 8726 6000 Extn 62822 🖷 020 8686 7405 ✉ nathan.elvery@croydon.gov.uk

Electoral Registration: Mr Lea Goddard, Head of Registration Services & Electoral, Town Hall, Katherine Street, Croydon CR9 1DE ☎ 020 8726 6000 Extn 65730 🖷 020 8407 1308 ✉ lea.goddard@croydon.gov.uk

Emergency Planning: Mr Maurice Egan, Corporate Security Manager, Taberner House, Park Lane, Croydon CR9 3JS ☎ 020 8760 5678 🖷 020 8760 5630 ✉ mo.egan@croydon.gov.uk

Estates, Property & Valuation: Mr Stephen Wingrave, Strategic

Estates Manager, Taberner House, Park Lane, Croydon CR9 1JR ☎ 020 8726 6000 extn 61512 🖷 020 8760 5728 🖰 stephen.wingrave@croydon.gov.uk

Finance and Treasurer: Mr Nigel Cook, Head of Pensions & Treasury, Taberner House, Park Lane, Croydon CR9 3RN ☎ 020 8726 6000 🖰 nigel.cook@croydon.gov.uk

Finance and Treasurer: Mr Nathan Elvery, Executive Director, Taberner House, Park Lane, Croydon CR9 3JS ☎ 020 8726 6000 Extn 62822 🖷 020 8686 7405 🖰 nathan.elvery@croydon.gov.uk

Health and Safety: Ms Liz Johnston, Health & Safety Senior Consultant, Taberner House, Park Lane, Croydon CR9 3JS ☎ 020 8726 6000 Extn 62001 🖷 020 8760 5749 🖰 elizabeth.johnston@croydon.gov.uk

Highways: Mr Anthony Brooks, Director - Public Safety & Public Realm, Taberner House, Park Lane, Croydon CR9 3RN ☎ 020 8726 6000 🖰 anthony.brooks@croydon.gov.uk

Home Energy Conservation: Mr George Simms, Planning & Sustainability Officer, Taberner House, Park Lane, Croydon CR9 1JT ☎ 020 8726 6000 Extn 62314 🖰 george.simms@croydon.gov.uk

Housing: Mr Peter Brown, Director of Housing Needs & Renewal, Taberner House, Park Lane, Croydon CR9 1JT ☎ 020 8726 6100 🖰 peter.brown@croydon.gov.uk

Housing: Ms Hannah Miller, Executive Director, Taberner House, Park Lane, Croydon CR9 1JT ☎ 020 8726 6000 Extn 64590 🖰 hannah.miller@croydon.gov.uk

Housing Maintenance: Mr Dave Sutherland, Divisional Director (Housing Management Services), Taberner House, Park Lane, Croydon CR9 1DH ☎ 020 8726 6000 Extn 4957 🖷 020 8760 5745 🖰 dave.sutherland@croydon.gov.uk

Legal: Mrs Julie Belvir, Council Solicitor & Director of Democratic & Legal Services, Taberner House, Park Lane , Croydon CR9 3JS ☎ 020 8726 6000 Extn 64985 🖰 julie.belvir@croydon.gov.uk

Leisure and Cultural Services: Mr Anthony Brooks, Director - Public Safety & Public Realm, Taberner House, Park Lane, Croydon CR9 3RN ☎ 020 8726 6000 🖰 anthony.brooks@croydon.gov.uk

Licensing: Mr Michael Goddard, Licensing Team Leader, Taberner House, Park Lane, Croydon CR9 3JS ☎ 020 8726 6000 🖰 michael.goddard@croydon.gov.uk

Lifelong Learning: Ms Alison Critchley, Director of Commissioning, Performance & Partnerships, Taberner House, Park Lane, Croydon CR9 1JT ☎ 020 8726 6000 🖰 alison.critchley@croydon.gov.uk

Lottery Funding, Charity and Voluntary: Mr David Freeman, Policy Manager, Taberner House, Park Lane, Croydon CR9 3JS ☎ 020 8726 6000 🖷 020 8760 5463 🖰 david.freeman@croydon.gov.uk

Member Services: Mr Solomon Agutu, Head of Democratic Services & Scrutiny, Taberner House, Park Lane, Croydon CR9 3JS ☎ 020 8726 6000 extn 62920 🖰 soloman.agutu@croydon.gov.uk

Parking: Mr Anthony Brooks, Director - Public Safety & Public Realm, Taberner House, Park Lane, Croydon CR9 3RN ☎ 020 8726 6000 🖰 anthony.brooks@croydon.gov.uk

Partnerships: Ms Sharon Godman, Head of Corporate Equalities & Cohesion Unit, Taberner House, Park Lane, Croydon CR9 3RN ☎ 020 8726 6000 🖰 sharon.godman@croydon.gov.uk

Personnel / HR: Mrs Pam Parkes, Director of Workforce & Community Relations, Taberner House, Park Lane, Croydon CR9 3JS ☎ 020 8760 5651 🖷 020 8760 5611 🖰 pam.parkes@croydon.gov.uk

Planning: Mr Mike Kiely, Director of Planning & Building Control, Taberner House, Park Lane, Croydon CR9 1JT ☎ 020 8760 5599 🖰 mike.kiely@croydon.gov.uk

Planning: Mr Rory Macleod, Head of Planning Control, Taberner House, Park Lane, Croydon CR9 3RN ☎ 020 8726 6000 🖰 rory.macleod@croydon.gov.uk

Procurement: Ms Sarah Ireland, Director of Strategy Commissioning Procurement & Performance, Taberner House, Park Lane, Croydon CR9 3JS ☎ 020 8726 6000 Extn 62070 🖰 sarah.ireland@croydon.gov.uk

Public Libraries: Ms Aileen Cahill, Head of Libraries, Central Library, Katharine Street, Croydon CR9 1ET ☎ 020 8726 6000 Extn 1123 🖰 aileen.cahill@croydon.gov.uk

Recycling & Waste Minimisation: Mr Malcolm Kendall, Head of Environment & Leisure, Stubbs Mead Depot, Factory Lane, Croydon CR0 3RL 🖰 malcolm.kendall@croydon.gov.uk

Regeneration: Mr Tony Antoniou, Director of Regeneration & Planning, Taberner House, Park Lane, Croydon CR9 3JS ☎ 020 8726 6000 Extn 65407 🖰 tony.antoniou@croydon.gov.uk

Road Safety: Mr Mike Barton, Strategic Technical Manager, Taberner House, Park Lane, Croydon CR9 1JR ☎ 020 8760 6197 🖰 mike.barton@croydon.gov.uk

Social Services: Mrs Hannah Miller, Executive Director of Housing & Social Services, Taberner House, Park Lane, Croydon CR9 2BA ☎ 020 8760 5490 🖷 020 8686 1251 🖰 hannah.miller@croydon.gov.uk

Social Services (Adult): Ms Pauline French, Director of Personal Support, Taberner House, Park Lane, Croydon CR9 3JS ☎ 020 8760 5416 🖷 020 8686 2978 🖰 pauline.french@croydon.gov.uk

Social Services (Adult): Ms Brenda Scanlon, Director of Adult Care Commissioning, Taberner House, Park Lane, Croydon CR9 2BA ☎ 020 8760 5727 🖰 brenda.scanlon@croydon.gov.uk

Street Scene: Mr Andy Opie, Head of Community Safety,

Taberner House, Park Lane, Croydon CR9 3JS ☎ 020 8726 6000 Extn 65686 ✉ andy.opie@croydon.gov.uk

Traffic Management: Mr Dave Tomlinson, Traffic Manager, The Town Hall, Katharine Street, Croydon CR0 1NX ☎ 020 8760 5425 ✉ dave.tomlinson@croydon.gov.uk

Transport: Mr Ian Plowright, Head of Strategic Transport, Taberner House, Park Lane, Croydon CR9 3JS ☎ 020 8726 6000 Extn 62927 ✉ ian.plowright@croydon.gov.uk

Waste Collection and Disposal: Mr Malcolm Kendall, Head of Environment & Leisure, Stubbs Mead Depot, Factory Lane, Croydon CR0 3RL ✉ malcolm.kendall@croydon.gov.uk

Waste Management: Mr Malcolm Kendall, Head of Environment & Leisure, Stubbs Mead Depot, Factory Lane, Croydon CR0 3RL ✉ malcolm.kendall@croydon.gov.uk

MEMBERS OF THE COUNCIL (70)

***Mayor:* Arram**, Eddy (CON - Ashburton)
eddy.arram@croydon.gov.uk
***Deputy Mayor:* Harris**, Tony (CON - Waddon)
tony.harris@croydon.gov.uk
***Leader of the Council:* Fisher**, Mike (CON - Shirley)
mike.fisher@croydon.gov.uk
***Deputy Leader of the Council:* Pollard**, Timothy (CON - Sanderstead)
councillor@timpollard.co.uk
***Group Leader:* Scott**, Paul (LAB - Woodside)
paul.scott@croydon.gov.uk
Avis, Jane (LAB - South Norwood)
jane.avis@croydon.gov.uk
Ayres, George (LAB - New Addington)
george.ayres@croydon.gov.uk
Bains, Jeet (CON - Coulsdon West)
jeet.bains@croydon.gov.uk
Bashford, Sara (CON - Selsdon & Ballards)
sara.bashford@croydon.gov.uk
Bass, Graham (CON - Purley)
graham.bass@croydon.gov.uk
Bee, Kathy (LAB - South Norwood)
kathy.bee@croydon.gov.uk
Bonner, Carole (LAB - Fieldway)
carole.bonner@croydon.gov.uk
Butler, Alison (LAB - Bensham Manor)
alison.butler@croydon.gov.uk
Buttinger, Janice (CON - Kenley)
janice.buttinger@croydon.gov.uk
Chatterjee, Richard (CON - Shirley)
richard.chatterjee@croydon.gov.uk
Chowdhury, Sherwan (LAB - Norbury)
sherwan.chowdhury@croydon.gov.uk
Clouder, Pat (LAB - Thornton Heath)
pat.clouder@croydon.gov.uk
Collins, Stuart (LAB - Broad Green)
stuart.collins@croydon.gov.uk
Cromie, Justin (CON - Coulsdon East)
justin.cromie@croydon.gov.uk
Cummings, Jason (CON - Heathfield)
jason.cummings@croydon.gov.uk
Fitze, David (CON - Fairfield)
david.fitze@croydon.gov.uk
Fitzsimons, Sean (LAB - Addiscombe)
sean.fitzsimons@croydon.gov.uk
Flemming, Alisa (LAB - Upper Norwood)
alisa.flemming@croydon.gov.uk
Gatland, Maria (CON - Croham)
maria.gatland@croydon.gov.uk
George-Hilley, Clare (CON - Waddon)
clare.hilley@croydon.gov.uk
Godfrey, Timothy (LAB - Selhurst)
timothy.godfrey@croydon.gov.uk
Gray, Donna (LAB - Bensham Manor)
donna.gray@croydon.gov.uk
Hale, Lynne (CON - Sanderstead)
lynne.hale@croydon.gov.uk
Hall, Simon (LAB - Fieldway)
simon.hall@croydon.gov.uk
Hay-Justice, Patricia (LAB - Addiscombe)
patricia.hay-justice@croydon.gov.uk
Hoar, Simon (CON - Waddon)
simon.hoar@croydon.gov.uk
Hollands, Steve (CON - Kenley)
steve.hollands@croydon.gov.uk
Hopley, Yvette (CON - Sanderstead)
yvette.hopley@croydon.gov.uk
Jewitt, Karen (LAB - Woodside)
karen.jewitt@croydon.gov.uk
Kabir, Humayun (LAB - West Thornton)
humayun.kabir@croydon.gov.uk
Kellett, Adam (CON - Ashburton)
adam.kellett@croydon.gov.uk
Khan, Shafi (LAB - Norbury)
bernadette.khan@croydon.gov.uk
Khan, Bernadette (LAB - West Thornton)
shafi.khan@croydon.gov.uk
Kyeremeh, Matthew (LAB - Thornton Heath)
matthew.kyeremeh@croydon.gov.uk
Lawlor, Wayne (LAB - South Norwood)
wayne.lawlor@croydon.gov.uk
Lenton, Terry (CON - Coulsdon East)
terry.lenton@croydon.gov.uk
Letts, Toni (LAB - Selhurst)
toni.letts@croydon.gov.uk
Mansell, Maggie (LAB - Norbury)
maggie.mansell@croydon.gov.uk
Marshall, Janet (CON - Shirley)
janet.marshall@croydon.gov.uk
Mead, Dudley (CON - Selsdon & Ballards)
dudley.mead@croydon.gov.uk
Mead, Margaret (CON - Heathfield)
margaret.mead@croydon.gov.uk
Mohan, Vidhyacharan (CON - Fairfield)
vidhi.mohan@croydon.gov.uk
Neal, Michael (CON - Croham)
michael.neal@croydon.gov.uk
Newman, Tony (LAB - Woodside)
tony.newman@croydon.gov.uk
O'Connell, Steve (CON - Kenley)
steve.o'connell@croydon.gov.uk
Osland, David (CON - Coulsdon West)
david.osland@croydon.gov.uk
Parker, Ian (CON - Coulsdon West)
ian.parker@croydon.gov.uk
Pearson, Tony (CON - New Addington)
tony.pearson@croydon.gov.uk
Perry, Jason (CON - Croham)
jason.perry@croydon.gov.uk

Pollard, Helen (CON - Heathfield)
councillor@helenpollard.co.uk
Quadir, Badsha (CON - Purley)
badsha.quadia@croydon.gov.uk
Rajendran, Raj (LAB - Bensham Manor)
raj.rajendran@croydon.gov.uk
Ryan, Pat (LAB - Upper Norwood)
pat.ryan@croydon.gov.uk
Ryan, Gerry (LAB - Selhurst)
gerry.ryan@croydon.gov.uk
Selva, Mike (LAB - Broad Green)
mike.selva@croydon.gov.uk
Shahul-Hameed, Manju (LAB - Broad Green)
manju.shahul-hameed@croydon.gov.uk
Slipper, Avril (CON - Ashburton)
the.mayor@croydon.gov.uk
Smith, Paul (LAB - West Thornton)
paul.j.smith@croydon.gov.uk
Speakman, Donald (CON - Purley)
donald.speakman@croydon.gov.uk
Thomas, Phil (CON - Selsdon & Ballards)
phil.thomas@croydon.gov.uk
Watson, Mark (LAB - Addiscombe)
mark.watson@croydon.gov.uk
Wentworth, John (LAB - Upper Norwood)
john.wentworth@croydon.gov.uk
Winborn, Susan (CON - Fairfield)
susan.winborn@croydon.gov.uk
Woodley, Louisa (LAB - Thornton Heath)
louisa.woodley@croydon.gov.uk
Wright, Christopher (CON - Coulsdon East)
christopher.wright@croydon.gov.uk

POLITICAL COMPOSITION

CON: 37, LAB: 33

CABINET

Leader: Mr Mike Fisher
Deputy Leader, Children, Young People & Learners (Communication): Mr Timothy Pollard
Adult Services & Health: Ms Margaret Mead
Communities & Economic Development: Mr Vidhyacharan Mohan
Community Safety & Public Protection: Mr Simon Hoar
Corporate & Voluntary Services: Ms Sara Bashford
Finance & Performance Management: Mr Steve O'Connell
Highways & Environmental Services: Mr Phil Thomas
Housing: Mr Dudley Mead
Planning, Regeneration & Transport: Mr Jason Perry

COMMITTEE CHAIRS

Audit: Ms Yvette Hopley
Licensing: Ms Maria Gatland
Pensions: Mr Dudley Mead
Planning: Mr David Osland
Scrutiny & Strategic Overview: Mr Steve Hollands

CUMBRIA — C

Cumbria County Council, The Courts, English Street, Carlisle CA3 8NA ☎ 01228 606060 🖷 01228 606327 ✉ information@cumbriacc.gov.uk 🖳 www.cumbria.gov.uk

FACTS & FIGURES

Police Authority: Cumbria Police Authority
Health Authority: North West Strategic Health Authority
Learning and Skills Council: North West
EU Constituencies: North West
Election Frequency: Elections are of whole council
Twinning: Rheinisch-Bergischer Kreis (Germany)

PRINCIPAL OFFICERS

Chief Executive: Ms Jill Stannard, Chief Executive, The Courts, English Street, Carlisle CA3 8NA ☎ 01228 226301 ✉ jill.stannard@cumbria.gov.uk

Assistant Chief Executive: Ms Dawn Roberts, Assistant Chief Executive, The Courts, English Street, Carlisle CA3 8NA ☎ 01228 226310 ✉ dawn.roberts@cumbria.gov.uk

Senior Management: Mr Dominic Harrison, Corporate Director - Safer & Stronger Communities, Fire Service HQ, Station Road, Cockermouth CA13 9PR ☎ 01900 820211 🖷 01900 820219 ✉ dominic.harrison@cumbria.gov.uk

Senior Management: Mrs Julia Morrison, Corporate Director - Children's Services, 5 Portland Square, Carlisle CA1 1PU ☎ 01228 226857 ✉ julia.morrison@cumbria.gov.uk

Senior Management: Mr Richard Parry, Corporate Director - Adult & Local Services, 15 Portland Square, Carlisle CA1 1PU ☎ 01228 227116 ✉ richard.parry@cumbria.gov.uk

Senior Management: Mr Jim Savage, Corporate Director - Organisational Development, The Courts, English Street, Carlisle CA3 8NA ☎ 01228 226342 ✉ jim.savage@cumbria.gov.uk

Senior Management: Mrs Diane Wood, Corporate Director - Resources, The Courts, English Street, Carlisle CA3 8NA ☎ 01228 226263 ✉ diane.wood@cumbria.gov.uk

Access Officer / Social Services (Disability): Mr Richard Parry, Corporate Director - Adult & Local Services, 15 Portland Square, Carlisle CA1 1QQ ☎ 01228 227116 ✉ richard.parry@cumbria.gov.uk

Architect, Building / Property Services: Mr Mike Smith, Land & Property Manager, 18 Portland Square, Carlisle CA1 1PE ☎ 01228 226030 🖷 01228 226016 ✉ mike.smith@cumbria.gov.uk

Best Value: Mr Duncan McQueen, Performance & Intelligence Manager, The Courts, Carlisle CA3 8NA ☎ 01228 226293 🖷 01228 226331 ✉ duncan.mcqueen@cumbria.gov.uk

Building Control: Mr Sean Reed, Facilities Management Manager, 18 Portland Square, Carlisle CA1 1PE ☎ 01228 226030 ✉ sean.reed@cumbria.gov.uk

Children / Youth Services: Mrs Julia Morrison, Corporate Director - Children's Services, 5 Portland Square, Carlisle CA1 1PU ☎ 01228 226857 ✉ julia.morrison@cumbria.gov.uk

Children / Youth Services: Ms Catherine Witt, Locality Director, 5 Portland Square, Carlisle CA1 1PU ☎ 01228 226865 ✉ catherine.witt@cumbria.gov.uk

Civil Registration: Mrs Diane Wood, Corporate Director - Resources, The Courts, English Street, Carlisle CA3 8NA ☎ 01228 226263 ✉ diane.wood@cumbria.gov.uk

Community Safety: Ms Cate Bowman, Head of Service Community Care, 15 Portland Square, Carlisle CA1 1QQ ☎ 01228 227118 ✉ cate.bowman@cumbria.gov.uk

Community Safety: Mr Dominic Harrison, Corporate Director - Safer & Stronger Communities, Fire Service HQ, Station Road, Cockermouth CA13 9PR ☎ 01900 820211 🖷 01900 820219 ✉ dominic.harrison@cumbria.gov.uk

Computer Management: Ms Angie Reid, Senior Manager - Corporate Information, The Courts, English Street, Carlisle CA3 8NA ☎ 01228 221002 🖷 01228 601017 ✉ angie.reid@cumbria.gov.uk

Consumer Protection and Trading Standards: Ms Angela Jones, Senior Manager - Trading Standards, County Offices, Kendal LA4 4RQ ☎ 01539 773586 🖷 01539 773580 ✉ angela.jones@cumbria.gov.uk

Contracts: Mr Conway Stewart, Senior Manager - Strategic Procurement, Barras Lane, Dalston, Carlisle CA5 7NY ☎ 01228 226762 🖷 01228 607605 ✉ conway.stewart@cumbria.gov.uk

Corporate Services: Mr Simon Smith, Head of Management Audit, The Courts, English Street, Carlisle CA3 8NA ☎ 01228 226280 ✉ simon.smith@cumbria.gov.uk

Customer Service: Mr Jim Grisenthwaite, Assistant Director - Local Services, Arroyo Block, The Castle, Carlisle CA3 8UR ☎ 01228 227282 ✉ jim.grisenthwaite@cumbria.gov.uk

Economic Development: Mr Allan Haile, Assistant Director - Economic Development, The Courts, English Street, Carlisle CA3 8NA ☎ 01228 226682 🖷 01228 606689 ✉ allan.haile@cumbria.gov.uk

Education: Mrs Julia Morrison, Corporate Director - Children's Services, 5 Portland Square, Carlisle CA2 6PU ☎ 01228 226857 ✉ julia.morrison@cumbria.gov.uk

Education: Ms Caroline Sutton, Assistant Director - Schools & Learning, 5 Portland Square, Carlisle CA1 1PU ☎ 01228 226877 ✉ caroline.sutton@cumbria.gov.uk

Education: Ms Brenda Wile, Senior Manager - Learning Support Services, 5 Portland Square, Carlisle CA1 1PU ☎ 01228 226877 ✉ brenda.wile@cumbria.gov.uk

E-Government: Mr Alan Cook, Senior Project Manager, The Courts, English Street, Carlisle CA3 8NA ☎ 01228 221002 🖷 01228 606608 ✉ alan.cook@cumbria.gov.uk

Electoral Registration: Ms Diane Wood, Corporate Director - Resources, The Courts, English Street, Carlisle CA3 8NA ☎ 01228 226263 🖷 01228 606264 ✉ diane.wood@cumbria.gov.uk

Emergency Planning: Mr Mike Smyth, Assistant Director - Community Protection, Arroyo Block, The Castle, Carlisle CA3 8UR ☎ 01228 815703 🖷 01228 815701 ✉ mike.smyth@cumbria.gov.uk

Energy Management: Ms Katherine Tyer, Environment Performance Officer, The Courts, English Street, Carlisle CA3 8NA ☎ 01228 226313 🖷 01228 606322 ✉ katherine.tyer@cumbria.gov.uk

Estates, Property & Valuation: Mr Mike Smith, Land & Property Manager, 18 Portland Square, Carlisle CA1 1PE ☎ 01228 226030 🖷 01228 226016 ✉ mike.smith@cumbria.gov.uk

Facilities: Mr Sean Reed, Facilities Management Manager, 18 Portland Square, Carlisle CA1 1PE ☎ 01228 226030 ✉ sean.reed@cumbria.gov.uk

Finance and Treasurer: Ms Julie Crellin, Head of Accountancy Services & Deputy Chief Finance Officer, The Courts, English Street, Carlisle CA3 8NA ☎ 01228 227291 ✉ julie.crellin@cumbria.gov.uk

Finance and Treasurer: Ms Diane Wood, Corporate Director - Resources, The Courts, English Street, Carlisle CA3 8NA ☎ 01228 226263 🖷 01228 606264 ✉ diane.wood@cumbria.gov.uk

Grounds Maintenance: Mr Mike Smith, Land & Property Manager, 18 Portland Square, Carlisle CA1 1PE ☎ 01228 226030 🖷 01228 226016 ✉ mike.smith@cumbria.gov.uk

Health and Safety: Mr Julian Stainton, Health & Safety Manager, The Courts, English Street, Carlisle CA3 8NA ☎ 01228 226340 ✉ julian.stainton@cumbria.gov.uk

Highways: Mr Andrew Moss, Assistant Director - Environment, Barras Lane, Dalston, Carlisle CA5 7NY ☎ 01228 227732 🖷 01228 607605 ✉ andrew.moss@cumbria.gov.uk

Local Area Agreement: Ms Clare Killeen, Senior Policy Officer, The Courts, English Street, Carlisle CA3 8NA ☎ 01228 226514 ✉ clare.killeen@cumbria.gov.uk

Legal: Ms Angela Harwood, Head of Legal Services, The Courts, English Street, Carlisle CA3 8NA ☎ 01228 227352 🖷 01228 607376 ✉ angela.harwood@cumbria.gov.uk

Leisure and Cultural Services: Mr Bruce Bennison, Head of Cultural Policy, Arroyo Block, The Castle, Carlisle CA3 8XF ☎ 01228 227305 ✉ bruce.bennison@cumbria.gov.uk

Leisure and Cultural Services: Mr Jim Grisenthwaite, Assistant Director - Local Services, Arroyo Block, The Castle, Carlisle CA3 8UR ☎ 01228 227282 ✉ jim.grisenthwaite@cumbria.gov.uk

Lighting: Mr Andrew Moss, Assistant Director - Environment, The Courts, English Street, Carlisle CA3 8NA ☎ 01228 227732 🖷 01228 607605 ✉ andrew.moss@cumbria.gov.uk

Member Services: Mrs Diane Wood, Corporate Director - Resources, The Courts, English Street, Carlisle CA3 8NA ☎ 01228 226263 ✉ diane.wood@cumbria.gov.uk

Personnel / HR: Mr Jim Savege, Corporate Director -

Organisational Development, The Courts, English Street, Carlisle CA3 8NA ☎ 01228 226340 ✉ jim.savege@cumbria.gov.uk

Procurement: Mr Conway Stewart, Senior Manager - Strategic Procurement, Barras Lane, Dalston, Carlisle CA5 7NY ☎ 01228 226762 🖷 01228 607605 ✉ conway.stewart@cumbria.gov.uk

Public Libraries: Mr Jim Grisenthwaite, Assistant Director - Local Services, Arroyo Block, The Castle, Carlisle CA3 8UR ☎ 01228 227282 ✉ jim.grisenthwaite@cumbria.gov.uk

Recycling & Waste Minimisation: Mr Paul Feehily, Senior Manager - Waste Management, Barras Lane, Dalston, Carlisle CA5 7NY ☎ 01228 227724 🖷 01228 607605 ✉ paul.feehily@cumbria.gov.uk

Regeneration: Mr Allan Haile, Assistant Director - Economic Development, The Courts, English Street, Carlisle CA3 8NA ☎ 01228 226682 🖷 01228 606689 ✉ allan.haile@cumbria.gov.uk

Road Safety: Mr Chris Broadbent, Road Safety Co-ordinator, The Courts, English Street, Carlisle CA3 8NA ☎ 01228 221751 🖷 01228 226728 ✉ chris.broadbent@cumbria.gov.uk

Social Services: Mr Richard Parry, Corporate Director - Adult & Local Services, 15 Portland Square, Carlisle CA1 1QQ ☎ 01228 227116 ✉ richard.parry@cumbria.gov.uk

Social Services (Adult): Ms Amanda Evans, Assistant Director - Social Care - Adult & Local Services, The Courts, English Street, Carlisle CA3 8NA ✉ amanda.evans@cumbria.gov.uk

Social Services (Adult): Mr Richard Parry, Corporate Director - Adult & Local Services, 15 Portland Square, Carlisle CA1 1QQ ☎ 01228 227116 ✉ richard.parry@cumbria.gov.uk

Social Services (Children): Mrs Julia Morrison, Corporate Director - Children's Services, 5 Portland Square, Carlisle CA2 6PU ☎ 01228 226857 ✉ julia.morrison@cumbria.gov.uk

Staff Training: Mr Jim Savege, Corporate Director - Organisational Development, The Courts, English Street, Carlisle CA3 8NA ☎ 01228 226340 ✉ jim.savege@cumbria.gov.uk

Sustainable Communities: Mrs Helen Blake, Service Manager - Policy Planning, The Courts, English Street, Carlisle CA3 8NA ☎ 01228 226687 ✉ helen.blake@cumbria.gov.uk

Sustainable Communities: Mr Jim Grisenthwaite, Assistant Director - Local Services, Arroyo Block, The Castle, Carlisle CA3 8UR ☎ 01228 227282 ✉ jim.grisenthwaite@cumbria.gov.uk

Sustainable Communities: Mr Dominic Harrison, Corporate Director - Safer & Stronger Communities, Fire Service HQ, Station Road, Cockermouth CA13 9PR ☎ 01900 820211 🖷 01900 820219 ✉ dominic.harrison@cumbria.gov.uk

Sustainable Communities: Mr John Macilwraith, Assistant Director - Strategy & Commissioning, 5 Portland Square, Carlisle CA1 1PU ☎ 01228 226833 ✉ john.macilwraith@cumbria.gov.uk

Traffic Management: Mr Andrew Moss, Assistant Director - Environment, Barras Lane, Dalston, Carlisle CA5 7NY ☎ 01228 227732 🖷 01228 607605 ✉ andrew.moss@cumbria.gov.uk

Transport: Mr Rob Terwey, Senior Management - Transport, The Courts, English Street, Carlisle CA3 8NA ☎ 01228 226717 🖷 01228 606728 ✉ rob.terwey@cumbria.gov.uk

Transport Planner: Mr Rob Terwey, Senior Management - Transport, The Courts, English Street, Carlisle CA3 8NA ☎ 01228 226717 🖷 01228 606728 ✉ rob.terwey@cumbria.gov.uk

Waste Collection and Disposal: Mr Paul Feehily, Senior Manager - Waste Management, Barras Lane, Dalston, Carlisle CA5 7NY ☎ 01228 227724 🖷 01228 607605 ✉ paul.feehily@cumbria.gov.uk

Waste Management: Mr Paul Feehily, Senior Manager - Waste Management, Barras Lane, Dalston, Carlisle CA5 7NY ☎ 01228 227724 🖷 01228 607605 ✉ paul.feehily@cumbria.gov.uk

MEMBERS OF THE COUNCIL (84)

***Chair:* Woolley**, John (LAB - Mirehouse)
john.woolley@cumbriacc.gov.uk
***Vice-Chair:* Clarkson**, Norman (CON - Gosforth & Ennerdale)
norman.clarkson@cumbriacc.gov.uk
***Leader of the Council:* Martin**, Eddie (CON - Dearham & Broughton)
eddie.martin@cumbria.gov.uk
***Deputy Leader of the Council:* Young**, Stewart (LAB - Upperby)
stewart.young@cumbria.gov.uk
***Group Leader:* Fee**, Trevor (IND - Seaton)
trevor.fee@cumbria.gov.uk
Airey, James (CON - Ulverston West)
james.airey@cumbria.gov.uk
Allison, Trevor (LD - Dalston & Cummersdale)
trevor.allison@cumbria.gov.uk
Barry, Alan (LAB - St Michaels)
alan.barry@cumbria.gov.uk
Bell, John (LAB - Morton)
john.bell@cumbria.gov.uk
Bell, Patricia (LD - Penrith East)
patricia.bell@cumbriacc.gov.uk
Betton, Robert (IND - Botcherby)
robert.betton@cumbriacc.gov.uk
Bingham, Roger (CON - Lower Kentdale)
roger.bingham@cumbria.gov.uk
Bland, James (CON - Lyth Valley)
james.bland@cumbria.gov.uk
Bleasdale, William (CON - Dalton South)
bill.bleasdale@cumbria.gov.uk
Bradley, Heather (LAB - Currock)
heather.bradley@cumbria.gov.uk
Brown, Susan (CON - Seascale & Whicham)
susan.brown@cumbria.gov.uk
Burns, Anne (LAB - Hindpool)
anne.burns@cumbriacc.gov.uk
Cameron, Bill (LAB - Maryport West)
bill.cameron@cumbria.gov.uk
Cannon, Barbara (LAB - Moss Bay)
barbara.cannon@cumbria.gov.uk
Carrick, Hilary (CON - Penrith North)
hilary.carrick@cumbria.gov.uk
Clare, Thomas (LD - Kendal Castle)

thomas.clare@cumbria.gov.uk
Cole, Raymond (CON - Millom)
raymond.cole@cumbria.gov.uk
Collins, Stan (LD - Upper Kent)
stan.collins@cumbriacc.gov.uk
Cook, Geoffrey (LD - Kendal Highgate)
geoffrey.cook@cumbriacc.gov.uk
Cowell, Joseph (CON - Wigton)
joe.cowell@cumbria.gov.uk
Earnshaw, David (LD - Lakes)
david.earnshaw@cumbria.gov.uk
Fairbairn, Duncan (CON - Bowness, Thursby & Caldbeck)
duncan.s.fairbairn@cumbriacc.gov.uk
Fearon, Helen (CON - Penrith West)
helen.fearon@cumbria.gov.uk
Feeney-Johnson, Clare (LD - Kendal Nether)
clare.feeney-johnson@cumbriacc.gov.uk
Fisher, Lawrence (CON - Brampton Gilsland)
lawrence.fisher@cumbriacc.gov.uk
Gray, Brenda (LD - Kendal South)
brenda.gray@cumbria.gov.uk
Guselli, Ramon (CON - Roosecote)
ray.guselli@cumbria.gov.uk
Hamezeian, Jim (IND - Ormsgill)
jim.hamezeian@cumbria.gov.uk
Hamilton, Kevin (LAB - Risedale)
kevin.hamilton@cumbria.gov.uk
Hammond, Lisa (IND - Parkside)
lisa.hammond@cumbria.gov.uk
Hawkins, Michael (LAB - Hensingham & Arlecdon)
mike.hawkins@cumbria.gov.uk
Heath, Jillian (CON - Dalton North)
jill.heath@cumbria.gov.uk
Holliday, Joseph (LAB - St John's)
joe.holliday@cumbria.gov.uk
Hornby, Peter (CON - Ulverston East)
peter.hornby@cumbria.gov.uk
Humes, Gerald (LAB - Moorclose)
gerald.humes@cumbria.gov.uk
Kennon, Alan (CON - Cockermouth West)
alan.kennon@cumbria.gov.uk
Knowles, Timothy (LAB - Cleator Moor North & Frizington)
timothy.knowles@cumbriacc.gov.uk
Lancaster, Kevin (CON - Sedbergh & Kirkby Lonsdale)
kevin.lancaster@cumbria.gov.uk
Lister, Jim (CON - Aspatria & Wharrells)
Little, Keith (LAB - Maryport East)
keith.little@cumbria.gov.uk
Lowther, Thomas (CON - Eden Lakes)
thomas.lowther@cumbria.gov.uk
Macur, Tina (CON - Newbarns)
tina.macur@cumbria.gov.uk
Mallinson, John (CON - Stanwix & Irthington)
john.mallinson@cumbria.gov.uk
Mallinson, Elizabeth (CON - Stanwix Urban)
elizabeth.mallinson@cumbria.gov.uk
Marcus, David (CON - Walney South)
david.marcus@cumbria.gov.uk
Markley, Anthony (CON - Solway Coast)
anthony.markley@cumbria.gov.uk
Marriner, Nicholas (CON - Wetheral)
nick.marriner@cumbria.gov.uk
McCreesh, John (LD - Kendal Strickland & Fell)
john.mccreesh@cumbria.gov.uk
McDevitt, Hugh (LAB - Denton Holme)
hugh.mcdevitt@cumbria.gov.uk
Morgan, Frank (LAB - Cleator Moor South & Egremont)
frank.morgan@cumbriacc.gov.uk
Munby, Robery (CON - Keswick & Derwent)
ronald.munby@cumbria.gov.uk
Nicholson, Eric (CON - Cockermouth East)
eric.nicholson@cumbriacc.gov.uk
Pearson, Oliver (IND - Old Barrow)
oliver.pearson@cumbria.gov.uk
Rae, Marjorie (LAB - Harrington, Clifton & Stainburn)
marjorie.rae@cumbria.gov.uk
Richardson, Albert (CON - Greystoke & Hesket)
albert.p.richardson@cumbria.gov.uk
Roberts, Graham (CON - Bransty)
graham.roberts@cumbria.gov.uk
Roberts, David (CON - Hawcoat)
david.roberts@cumbria.gov.uk
Robinson, Mary (IND - Alston & East Fellside)
mary.robinson@cumbriacc.gov.uk
Robson, Fiona (CON - Yewdale)
fiona.j.robson@cumbriacc.gov.uk
Ross, Archibald (LAB - Distington & Moresby)
archibald.ross@cumbria.gov.uk
Salisbury, Claire (CON - High Furness)
claire.salisbury@cumbria.gov.uk
Skillicorn, Wendy (LAB - Kells & Sandwith)
wendy.skillicorn@cumbria.gov.uk
Southward, David (LAB - St Bees & Egremont)
david.southward@cumbria.gov.uk
Stephenson, Martin (CON - Appleby)
martin.stephenson@cumbriacc.gov.uk
Stephenson, Jonathan (LD - Windermere)
jo.stephenson@cumbria.gov.uk
Stewart, Ian (LD - Kent Estuary)
ian.stewart@cumbria.gov.uk
Stockdale, Ian (LAB - Belle Vue)
ian.stockdale@cumbriacc.gov.uk
Strong, Gary (CON - Penrith Rural)
gary.b.strong@cumbria.gov.uk
Tarbitt, Val (CON - Longtown & Bewcastle)
val.tarbitt@cumbria.gov.uk
Thornton, Peter (LD - Kirkby Stephen)
peter.thornton@cumbria.gov.uk
Toole, Alan (CON - Belah)
alan.toole@cumbriacc.gov.uk
Watson, Reg (LAB - St Aidan's)
reg.watson@cumbria.gov.uk
Wearing, Bill (CON - Grange)
bill.wearing@cumbria.gov.uk
Weber, Cyril (LAB - Harraby)
Whalen, William (LAB - Castle)
Willis, Janet (LD - Low Furness)
janet.willis@cumbria.gov.uk
Wilson, Roderick (LD - Cartmel)
rod.wilson@cumbriacc.gov.uk
Wonnacott, Andrew (CON - Hillcrest)
andrew.wonnacott@cumbria.gov.uk
Worth, Melvyn
(LAB - Walney North)
melvyn.worth@cumbria.gov.uk

POLITICAL COMPOSITION

CON: 39, LAB: 25, LD: 14, IND: 6

CABINET
Leader: Mr Eddie Martin
Deputy Leader: Mr Stewart Young
Adult Social Care: Mr James Airey
Children's Social Care: Mrs Anne Burns
Communities: Mr Oliver Pearson
Economy & Highways: Mr Anthony Markley
Organisational Development: Mrs Elizabeth Mallinson
Safer & Stronger Communities: Mr Gary Strong
Schools & Learning: Mr Duncan Fairbairn
Transport & Environment: Mr Timothy Knowles

COMMITTEE CHAIRS
Audit & Assurance: Ms Hilary Carrick
Development Control & Regulation: Mr Lawrence Fisher
Economy & Environment: Mr David Roberts
Health Scrutiny: Mr Bill Wearing
Pensions: Mr Melvyn Worth
Safe, Stronger & Inclusive Communities: Mr Jonathan Stephenson
Scrutiny Advisory: Mrs Barbara Cannon

DACORUM D

Dacorum Borough Council, Civic Centre, Marlowes, Hemel Hempstead HP1 1HH ☎ 01442 228000 🖷 01442 228995 communications@dacorum.gov.uk www.dacorum.gov.uk

FACTS & FIGURES
Police Authority: Hertfordshire Police Authority
Health Authority: East of England Strategic Health Authority
Learning and Skills Council: Eastern
Parliamentary Constituencies: Hemel Hempstead
EU Constituencies: Eastern
Election Frequency: Elections are of whole council
Twinning: Berkhamstead: Baune (France); Hemel Hempstead: Neu-Isenburg (Germany); Tring: Mosbach (Germany)

PRINCIPAL OFFICERS
Chief Executive: Mr Daniel Zammit, Chief Executive, Civic Centre, Marlowes, Hemel Hempstead HP1 1HH ☎ 01442 228213 🖷 01442 228995 daniel.zammit@dacorum.gov.uk

Senior Management: Mrs Sally Marshall, Corporate Director - Finance & Governance, Civic Centre, Marlowes, Hemel Hempstead HP1 1HH ☎ 01442 228313 sally.marshall@dacorum.gov.uk

Access Officer / Social Services (Disability): Mr John Gavin, Building Control Manager, Civic Centre, Marlowes, Hemel Hempstead HP1 1HH ☎ 01442 228578 🖷 01442 228581 john.gavin@dacorum.gov.uk

Best Value: Ms Janice Milsom, Assistant Director - Strategy & Transformation, Community & Organisation, Civic Centre, Marlowes, Hemel Hempstead HP1 1HH ☎ 01442 228009 🖷 01442 228995 janice.milsom@dacorum.gov.uk

Building Control: Mr John Gavin, Building Control Manager, Civic Centre, Marlowes, Hemel Hempstead HP1 1HH ☎ 01442 228578 🖷 01442 228581 john.gavin@dacorum.gov.uk

Community Planning: Mr David Gill, Group Leader - Partnerships, Policy & Communications, Civic Centre, Marlowes, Hemel Hempstead HP1 1HH ☎ 01442 228511 david.gill@dacorum.gov.uk

Community Safety: Mr Clive Townsley, Community Safety Co-ordinator, Civic Centre, Marlowes, Hemel Hempstead HP1 1HH ☎ 01442 228641 🖷 01442 228995 clive.townsley@dacorum.gov.uk

Corporate Services: Ms Lesley Crisp, Maylands Business Manager, Civic Centre, Marlowes, Hemel Hempstead HP1 1HH ☎ 01756 700600 lesley.crisp@dacorum.gov.uk

Corporate Services: Mr Jim Doyle, Group Manager - Democratic Services, Civic Centre, Marlowes, Hemel Hempstead HP1 1HH ☎ 01442 228222 🖷 01442 228264 jim.doyle@dacorum.gov.uk

Customer Service: Mrs Karen Tarbox, Head of Housing, Customer & Community Services, Civic Centre, Marlowes, Hemel Hempstead HP1 1HH ☎ 01442 228776 🖷 01442 228995 karen.tarbox@dacorum.gov.uk

Economic Development: Ms Lesley Crisp, Maylands Business Manager, Civic Centre, Marlowes, Hemel Hempstead HP1 1HH ☎ 01756 700600 lesley.crisp@dacorum.gov.uk

Economic Development: Mrs Chris Taylor, Group Manager - Strategic Planning & Regeneration, Civic Centre, Marlowes, Hemel Hempstead HP1 1HH ☎ 01442 867805 🖷 01442 266056 chris.taylor@dacorum.gov.uk

E-Government: Mr Nick Yarham, Service Provision Manager, Civic Centre, Marlowes, Hemel Hempstead HP1 1HH ☎ 01442 228115 🖷 01442 228178 nick.yarham@dacorum.gov.uk

Electoral Registration: Mr Jim Doyle, Group Manager - Democratic Services, Civic Centre, Marlowes, Hemel Hempstead HP1 1HH ☎ 01442 228222 🖷 01442 228264 jim.doyle@dacorum.gov.uk

Emergency Planning: Mr John Clarke, Head - Public Protection, Civic Centre, Marlowes, Hemel Hempstead HP1 1HH ☎ 01442 228480 🖷 01442 228477 john.clarke@dacorum.gov.uk

Environmental / Technical Services: Mr Brian Scott, Head of Street Care, Civic Centre, Marlowes, Hemel Hempstead HP1 1HH ☎ 01442 228355 🖷 01442 228340 brian.scott@dacorum.gov.uk

Environmental Health: Mr John Clarke, Head - Public Protection, Civic Centre, Marlowes, Hemel Hempstead HP1 1HH ☎ 01442 228480 🖷 01442 228477 john.clarke@dacorum.gov.uk

Estates, Property & Valuation: Ms Adriana Livingstone, Team Leader - Estates & Valuation, Civic Centre, Marlowes, Hemel Hempstead HP1 1HH ☎ 01442 228776 adriana.livingstone@dacroum.gov.uk

Facilities: Mr Alan Beare, Facilities Manager, Civic Centre, Marlowes, Hemel Hempstead HP1 1HH ☎ 01442 228000 🖷 01442 228340 alan.beare@dacorum.gov.uk

Finance and Treasurer: Mrs Sally Marshall, Corporate Director - Finance & Governance, Civic Centre, Marlowes, Hemel Hempstead HP1 1HH ☎ 01442 228313 ✉ sally.marshall@dacorum.gov.uk

Grounds Maintenance: Mr Simon Coultas, Assistant Operations Manager, Civic Centre, Marlowes, Hemel Hempstead HP1 1HH ☎ 01442 228032 🖷 01442 228884 ✉ simon.coultas@dacorum.gov.uk

Health and Safety: Mrs Helen Price, Corporate Health, Safety & Wellbeing Officer, Civic Centre, Marlowes, Hemel Hempstead HP1 1HH ☎ 01442 228518 🖷 01442 228629 ✉ helen.price@dacorum.gov.uk

Housing: Mrs Karen Tarbox, Head of Housing, Customer & Community Services, Civic Centre, Marlowes, Hemel Hempstead HP1 1HH ☎ 01442 228776 🖷 01442 228995 ✉ karen.tarbox@dacorum.gov.uk

Housing Maintenance: Mr Neil Brown, Programme & Procurement Team Leader, Civic Centre, Marlowes, Hemel Hempstead HP1 1HH ☎ 01442 228639

Legal: Mr Steven Baker, Head - Legal & Democratic Services, Civic Centre, Marlowes, Hemel Hempstead HP1 1HH ☎ 01442 228000 ✉ steve.baker@dacorum.gov.uk

Lifelong Learning: Ms Hilary Fyson, Learning Partnerships Manager, Civic Centre, Marlowes, Hemel Hempstead HP1 1HH ☎ 01442 867432 ✉ hilary.fyson@dacorum.gov.uk

Lottery Funding, Charity and Voluntary: Mr David Gill, Group Leader - Partnerships, Policy & Communications, Civic Centre, Marlowes, Hemel Hempstead HP1 1HH ☎ 01442 228511 ✉ david.gill@dacorum.gov.uk

Member Services: Mr Jim Doyle, Group Manager - Democratic Services, Civic Centre, Marlowes, Hemel Hempstead HP1 1HH ☎ 01442 228222 🖷 01442 228264 ✉ jim.doyle@dacorum.gov.uk

Parking: Mr Steve Barnes, Parking Policy Officer, Civic Centre, Marlowes, Hemel Hempstead HP1 1HH ☎ 01442 249484 ✉ steve.barnes@dacorum.gov.uk

Personnel / HR: Ms Karen Winser, Senior HR Manager, Civic Centre, Marlowes, Hemel Hempstead HP1 1HH ☎ 01442 228517 🖷 01442 228995 ✉ karen.winser@dacorum.gov.uk

Planning: Mr James Doe, Assistant Director - Planning, Development & Regeneration, Civic Centre, Marlowes, Hemel Hempstead HP1 1HH ☎ 01442 228353 🖷 01442 228340 ✉ james.doe@dacorum.gov.uk

Procurement: Mr Ben Hosier, Group Manager - Commissioning, Procurement & Compliance, Civic Centre, Marlowes, Hemel Hempstead HP1 1HH ☎ 01442 228215 🖷 01442 228995 ✉ ben.hosier@dacorum.gov.uk

Recycling & Waste Minimisation: Mr Craig Thorpe, Group Manager - Enviromental Services, Civic Centre, Marlowes, Hemel Hempstead HP1 1HH ☎ 01442 228030 ✉ craig.thorpe@dacorum.gov.uk

Regeneration: Mr James Doe, Assistant Director - Planning, Development & Regeneration, Civic Centre, Marlowes, Hemel Hempstead HP1 1HH ☎ 01442 228352 🖷 01442 228929 ✉ james.doe@dacorum.gov.uk

Staff Training: Ms Lana Linden, Corporate Training Co-ordinator, Civic Centre, Marlowes, Hemel Hempstead HP1 1HH ☎ 01442 228515 🖷 01442 228629 ✉ lana.linden@dacorum.gov.uk

Street Scene: Mr David Austin, Assistant Director - Neighbourhood Delivery, Civic Centre, Marlowes, Hemel Hempstead HP1 1HH ☎ 01442 228355 ✉ david.austin@dacorum.gov.uk

Town Centre: Mr James Doe, Assistant Director - Planning, Development & Regeneration, Civic Centre, Marlowes, Hemel Hempstead HP1 1HH ☎ 01442 228353 🖷 01442 228340 ✉ james.doe@dacorum.gov.uk

Transport Planner: Mr James Doe, Assistant Director - Planning, Development & Regeneration, Civic Centre, Marlowes, Hemel Hempstead HP1 1HH ☎ 01442 228353 🖷 01442 228340 ✉ james.doe@dacorum.gov.uk

Waste Collection and Disposal: Mr Craig Thorpe, Group Manager - Enviromental Services, Civic Centre, Marlowes, Hemel Hempstead HP1 1HH ☎ 01442 228030 ✉ craig.thorpe@dacorum.gov.uk

Waste Management: Mr Craig Thorpe, Group Manager - Enviromental Services, Civic Centre, Marlowes, Hemel Hempstead HP1 1HH ☎ 01442 228030 ✉ craig.thorpe@dacorum.gov.uk

MEMBERS OF THE COUNCIL (50)

Adeleke, Gbola (CON - Bovingdon, Flaunden & Chipperfield)
gbola.adeleke@dacorum.gov.uk
Adshead, Graham (CON - Hemel Hempstead Town)
graham.adshead@dacorum.gov.uk
Anderson, Alan (CON - Kings Langley)
alan.anderson@dacorum.gov.uk
Ayling, Brian (CON - Apsley & Corner Hall)
brian.ayling@dacorum.gov.uk
Bassadone, Hazel (CON - Leverstock Green)
hazel.bassadone@dacorum.gov.uk
Bateman, Stephen (CON - Berkhamstead East)
stephen.bateman@dacorum.gov.uk
Bhinder, Alexander (CON - Grovehill)
alexander.bhinder@dacorum.gov.uk
Chapman, Gill (CON - Bovingdon, Flaunden & Chipperfield)
gill.chapman@dacorum.gov.uk
Chapman, Bert (CON - Watling)
herbert.chapman@dacorum.gov.uk
Clark, Michael (CON - Apsley & Corner Hall)
michael.clark@dacorum.gov.uk
Collins, David (CON - Berkhamstead Castle)
david.collins@dacorum.gov.uk
Conwy, Olive (CON - Tring West & Rural)
olive.conway@dacorum.gov.uk
Doole, Geoffrey (CON - Nash Mills)
geoff.doole@dacorum.gov.uk
Douris, Terry (CON - Grovehill)

terry.douris@dacorum.gov.uk
Elliot, Graeme (CON - Chaulden & Warners End)
graeme.elliott@dacorum.gov.uk
Fantham, Alan (CON - Northchurch)
alan.fantham@dacorum.gov.uk
Flint, Maureen (LAB - Gadebridge)
maureen.flint@dacorum.gov.uk
Green, Carol (CON - Berkhamsted West)
carol.green@dacorum.gov.uk
Griffiths, Margaret (CON - Leverstock Green)
margaret.griffiths@dacorum.gov.uk
Guest, Fiona (CON - Chaulden & Warners End)
fiona@dandfguest.freeserve.co.uk
Harden, Neil (CON - Boxmoor)
neil.harden@dacorum.gov.uk
Harris, Lloyd (LD - Highfield)
lloyd.harris@dacorum.gov.uk
Hearn, Penny (CON - Tring East)
penny.hearn@dacorum.gov.uk
Hollinghurst, Rosemarie (LD - Aldbury & Wiggington)
rosemarie.hollinghurst@dacorum.gov.uk
Hollinghurst, Nicholas (LD - Tring Central)
nicholas.hollinghurst@dacorum.gov.uk
Laws, Julie (CON - Berkhamstead East)
julie.laws@dacorum.gov.uk
Lawson, Allan (CON - Adeyfield East)
allan.lawson@dacorum.gov.uk
Link, Brenda (LD - Highfield)
brenda.link@dacorum.gov.uk
Lloyd, David (CON - Watling)
david.lloyd@dacorum.gov.uk
MacDonald, Fiona (CON - Berkhamstead Castle)
fiona.macdonald@dacorum.gov.uk
Mahmood, Suqlain (CON - Bennetts End)
suqlain.mahmood@dacorum.gov.uk
Marshall, Janice (CON - Boxmoor)
janice.marshall@dacorum.gov.uk
McKay, Anthony (CON - Hemel Hempstead Town)
anthony.mckay@dacorum.gov.uk
McLean, Bob (CON - Kings Langley)
bob.mclean@dacorum.gov.uk
Organ, Jack (CON - Bovingdon, Flaunden & Chipperfield)
jack.organ@dacorum.gov.uk
Peter, Colin (CON - Apsley & Corner Hall)
colin.peter@dacorum.gov.uk
Rance, Denise (LD - Tring Central)
denise.rance@dacorum.gov.uk
Reay, Ian (CON - Berkhamsted West)
ian.reay@dacorum.gov.uk
Ryan, Ann (CON - Grovehill)
ann.ryan@dacorum.gov.uk
Sutton, Graham (CON - Leverstock Green)
graham.sutton@dacorum.gov.uk
Taylor, Roger (CON - Gadebridge)
roger.taylor@dacorum.gov.uk
Tiley, Nicholas (CON - Ashridge)
nicholas.tiley@dacorum.gov.uk
Townsend, Christopher (LD - Tring West & Rural)
christopher.townsend@dacorum.gov.uk
White, Keith (LAB - Adeyfield West)
keith.white@dacorum.gov.uk
Whitman, John (CON - Chaulden & Warners End)
john.whitman@dacorum.gov.uk
Williams, Andrew (CON - Boxmoor)
andrew.williams@dacorum.gov.uk
Wixted, Joann (CON - Bennetts End)
joann.wixted@dacorum.gov.uk
Wood, Dan (CON - Adeyfield West)
dan.wood@dacorum.gov.uk
Wyatt-Lowe, Colette (CON - Woodhall Farm)
colette.wyatt-lowe@dacorum.gov.uk
Wyatt-Lowe, William (CON - Adeyfield East)
william.wyatt-lowe@dacorum.gov.uk

POLITICAL COMPOSITION
CON: 42, LD: 6, LAB: 2

CABINET
Leader: Mr Andrew Williams
Deputy Leader: Ms Margaret Griffiths
Community Leadership: Mr Andrew Williams
Environmental Services & Sustainability: Ms Julie Laws
Finance & Resources: Mr Nicholas Tiley
Housing: Ms Margaret Griffiths
Planning & Regeneration: Mr Terry Douris
Resident & Regulatory Services: Mr Neil Harden

COMMITTEE CHAIRS
Appeals: Ms Hazel Bassadone
Audit: Mr Roger Taylor
Development Control: Mr David Lloyd
Electoral Review: Mr Andrew Williams
Finance & Resources Overview & Scrutiny: Mr Graham Sutton
Housing & Community Overview & Scrutiny: Ms Janice Marshall
Licensing & Health & Safety Enforcement: Mr Allan Lawson
Strategic Planning & Environment Overview & Scrutiny: Mr Alan Anderson

DARLINGTON U

Darlington Borough Council, Town Hall, Feethams, Darlington DL1 5QT ☎ 01325 380651 🖷 01325 382032 ✉ enquiries@darlington.gov.uk 💻 www.darlington.gov.uk

FACTS & FIGURES
Police Authority: Durham Police Authority
Health Authority: North East Strategic Health Authority
Learning and Skills Council: North East
Parliamentary Constituencies: Darlington
EU Constituencies: North East
Election Frequency: Elections are of whole council
Twinning: Amiens (France); Mulhheim an der Ruhr (Germany)

PRINCIPAL OFFICERS
Chief Executive: Ms Ada Burns, Chief Executive, Town Hall, Feethams, Darlington DL1 5QT ☎ 01325 388011 🖷 01325 388018 ✉ ada.burns@darlington.gov.uk

Senior Management: Mr Richard Alty, Director - Place, Town Hall, Feethams, Darlington DL1 5QT ☎ 01325 347401; 01325 388946 🖷 01325 382032 ✉ richard.alty@darlington.gov.uk

Senior Management: Mr Murray Rose, Director - People, Town Hall, Feethams, Darlington DL1 5QT ☎ 01325 388099 🖷 01325 382032 ✉ murray.rose@darlington.gov.uk

Senior Management: Mr Paul Wildsmith, Director - Resources, Town Hall, Feethams, Darlington DL1 5QT ☎ 01325 388001 🖷 01325 382032 ✉ paul.wildsmith@darlington.gov.uk

Architect, Building / Property Services: Mr Brian Dobinson, Head of Building Design Services & Acting Assistant Director - Place, Vicarage Road Depot, Darlington DL1 1JW ☎ 01325 347446 🖷 01325 486987 ✉ brian.dobinson@darlington.gov.uk

Building Control: Mr Richard Collinson, Building Control Manager, Town Hall, Feethams, Darlington DL1 5QT ☎ 01325 388428 🖷 01325 382032 ✉ richard.collinson@darlington.gov.uk

Catering Services: Mr Graham Carey, Catering Manager, Dolphin Centre, Horsemarket, Darlington DL1 5RP ☎ 01325 388415 🖷 01325 369400 ✉ graham.carey@darlington.gov.uk

Children / Youth Services: Ms Yvonne Coates, Head of Family Support, Town Hall, Feethams, Darlington DL1 5QT ☎ 01325 388884 🖷 01325 382032 ✉ yvonne.coates@darlington.gov.uk

Children / Youth Services: Mr David Mason, Head of Social Care & YOS, Town Hall, Feethams, Darlington DL1 5QT ☎ 01325 406022 ✉ david.mason@darlington.gov.uk

Civil Registration: Mr Anthony Hall, Superintendant Registrar, The Registrar Office, Backhouse Hall, Bull Wynd, Darlington DL1 5RG ☎ 01325 346604 🖷 01325 346898 ✉ anthony.hall@darlington.gov.uk

PR / Communications: Ms Cassandra Ferguson, Head of Communications, Town Hall, Feethams, Darlington DL1 5QT ☎ 01325 388020 🖷 01325 388018 ✉ cassandra.ferguson@darlington.gov.uk

Community Planning: Mr David Plews, Head of Communities, Town Hall, Feethams, Darlington DL1 5QT ☎ 01325 388023 🖷 01325 382032 ✉ david.plews@darlington.gov.uk

Community Safety: Mr David Plews, Head of Communities, Town Hall, Feethams, Darlington DL1 5QT ☎ 01325 388023 🖷 01325 382032 ✉ david.plews@darlington.gov.uk

Computer Management: Ms Margaret Elsworth, Assistant Head of ICT (Business Services), The Studios, Lingfield Point, Darlington DL1 1RT ☎ 01642 526334 🖷 01642 524981 ✉ margaret.elsworth@xentrall.org.uk

Computer Management: Mr Oliver Plumpton, Assistant Head of ICT Services (Transaction & Operations), The Studios, Lingfield Point, Darlington DL1 1RT ☎ 01642 526339 🖷 01642 524981 ✉ oliver.plumpton@xentrall.gov.uk

Consumer Protection and Trading Standards: Mr Nigel Green, Principal Trading Standards Officer, Town Hall, Feethams, Darlington DL1 5QT ☎ 01325 388989 🖷 01325 382032 ✉ nigel.green@darlington.gov.uk

Contracts: Ms Susan White, Head of Strategic Procurement & Contract Management, Town Hall, Feethams, Darlington DL1 5QT ☎ 01325 388019 🖷 01325 382032 ✉ susan.white@darlington.gov.uk

Customer Service: Ms Linda Todd, Head of Democratic & Customer Services, Town Hall, Feethams, Darlington DL1 5QT ☎ 01325 388354 🖷 01325 382032 ✉ linda.todd@darlington.gov.uk

Economic Development: Mr Nik Grewer, Head of Economic Regeneration, Town Hall, Feethams, Darlington DL1 5QT ☎ 01325 388687 🖷 01325 382032 ✉ nik.grewer@darlington.gov.uk

Education: Ms Jenni Cooke, Assistant Director - Children, Families & Learning, Town Hall, Feethams, Darlington DL1 5QT ☎ 01325 388861 🖷 01325 382032 ✉ jenni.cooke@darlington.gov.uk

E-Government: Ms Margaret Elsworth, Assistant Head of ICT (Business Services), The Studios, Lingfield Point, Darlington DL1 1RT ☎ 01642 526334 🖷 01642 524981 ✉ margaret.elsworth@xentrall.org.uk

Electoral Registration: Ms Lynne Wood, Elections Manager, Town Hall, Feethams, Darlington DL1 5QT ☎ 01325 388287 🖷 01325 382032 ✉ lynne.wood@darlington.gov.uk

Emergency Planning: Mr Bill Westland, Head of Regulatory Services, Town Hall, Feethams, Darlington DL1 5QT ☎ 01325 388552 🖷 01325 382032 ✉ bill.westland@darlington.gov.uk

Energy Management: Mr Guy Metcalfe, Estates & Property Manager, Town Hall, Feethams, Darlington DL1 5QT ☎ 01325 388735 🖷 01325 382032 ✉ guy.metcalf@darlington.gov.uk

Environmental / Technical Services: Mr Brian Graham, Head of Environmental Services, Vicarage Road Depot, Darlington DL1 4RF ☎ 01325 347541 🖷 01325 486987 ✉ brian.graham@darlington.gov.uk

Environmental Health: Mr Barry Pearson, Environmental Health Manager, Town Hall, Feethams, Darlington DL1 5QT ☎ 01325 388560 🖷 01325 388032 ✉ barry.pearson@darlington.gov.uk

Estates, Property & Valuation: Mr Guy Metcalfe, Estates & Property Manager, Town Hall, Feethams, Darlington DL1 5QT ☎ 01325 388735 🖷 01325 382032 ✉ guy.metcalf@darlington.gov.uk

Events Manager: Mr Jeff Dawson, Events Manager, Dolphin Centre, Horsemarket, Darlington DL1 5RP ☎ 01325 388427 🖷 01325 369400 ✉ jeff.dawson@darlington.gov.uk

Facilities: Mr Sean Thomas, Facilities Support Manager, Dolphin Centre, Horsemarket, Darlington DL1 5RP ☎ 01325 388929 🖷 01325 369400 ✉ sean.thomas@darlington.gov.uk

Finance and Treasurer: Mr Paul Wildsmith, Director - Resources, Town Hall, Feethams, Darlington DL1 5QT ☎ 01325 388001 🖷 01325 382032 ✉ paul.wildsmith@darlington.gov.uk

Finance and Treasurer: Mr Paul Wildsmith, Director - Resources, Town Hall, Feethams, Darlington DL1 5QT ☎ 01325

388001 🖷 01325 382032 ✉ paul.wildsmith@darlington.gov.uk

Fleet Management: Mr Roger Scott, Transport Services Manager, Vicarage Road Depot, Darlington DL1 1JW ☎ 01325 347475 🖷 01325 486987 ✉ roger.scott@darlington.gov.uk

Grounds Maintenance: Mr Brian Graham, Head of Environmental Services, Vicarage Road Depot, Darlington DL1 4RF ☎ 01325 347541 🖷 01325 486987 ✉ brian.graham@darlington.gov.uk

Health and Safety: Ms Joanne Skelton, Acting Health & Safety Manager, Arts Centre, Vane Terrace, Darlington DL3 7AX ☎ 01325 388113 🖷 01325 365794 ✉ joanne.skelton@darlington.gov.uk

Highways: Mr Steve Brannan, Head of Highway Asset Management, The Beehive, Lingfield Point, Darlington DL1 1YN ☎ 01325 388755 🖷 01325 388724 ✉ steve.brannan@darlington.gov.uk

Highways: Mr Dave Winstanley, Assistant Director - Highways, Design & Projects, The Beehive, Lingfield Point, Darlington DL1 1YN ☎ 01325 388752 🖷 01325 388724 ✉ david.winstanley@darlington.gov.uk

Home Energy Conservation: Mr Alan Glew, Head of Programmes & Projects, Town Hall, Feethams, Darlington DL1 5QT ☎ 01235 388202 🖷 01325 382032 ✉ alan.glew@darlington.gov.uk

Housing: Mrs Pauline Mitchell, Assistant Director - Adult Social Care & Housing, Town Hall, Feethams, Darlington DL1 5QT ☎ 01325 388505 🖷 01325 382032 ✉ pauline.mitchell@darlington.gov.uk

Housing Maintenance: Ms Hazel Neasham, Head of Housing Services, Town Hall, Feethams, Darlington DL1 5QT ☎ 01325 388535 🖷 01325 382032 ✉ hazel.neasham@darlington.gov.uk

Legal: Mr Luke Swinhoe, Head of Legal Services, Town Hall, Feethams, Darlington DL1 5QT ☎ 01325 388055 🖷 01325 382032 ✉ luke.swinhoe@darlington.gov.uk

Leisure and Cultural Services: Mr Mike Crawshaw, Head of Culture, Dolphin Centre, Horsemarket, Darlington DL1 5RP ☎ 01325 388431 🖷 01325 369400 ✉ mike.crawshaw@darlington.gov.uk

Licensing: Ms Pam Ross, Licensing, Parking & Trading Standards Manager, Town Hall, Feethams, Darlington DL1 5QT ☎ 01325 388647 🖷 01325 382032 ✉ pam.ross@darlington.gov.uk

Lifelong Learning: Mr Mike Crawshaw, Head of Culture, Dolphin Centre, Horsemarket, Darlington DL1 5RP ☎ 01325 388431 🖷 01325 369400 ✉ mike.crawshaw@darlington.gov.uk

Lighting: Mr Paul Brownbridge, Street Lighting Engineer, The Beehive, Lingfield Point, Darlington DL1 1YN ☎ 01325 388765 🖷 01325 388724 ✉ paul.brownbridge@darlington.gov.uk

Lighting: Mr Tom Russell, Street Lighting Engineer, The Beehive, Lingfield Point, Darlington DL1 1YN ☎ 01325 388754 🖷 01325 388724 ✉ tom.russell@darlington.gov.uk

Lottery Funding, Charity and Voluntary: Ms Pearl Berry, Economic Regeneration Officer, Town Hall, Feethams, Darlington DL1 5QT ☎ 01325 388642 🖷 01325 382032 ✉ pearl.berry@darlington.gov.uk

Member Services: Ms Linda Todd, Head of Democratic & Customer Services, Town Hall, Feethams, Darlington DL1 5QT ☎ 01325 388354 🖷 01325 382032 ✉ linda.todd@darlington.gov.uk

Parking: Ms Pam Ross, Licensing, Parking & Trading Standards Manager, Town Hall, Feethams, Darlington DL1 5QT ☎ 01325 388647 🖷 01325 382032 ✉ pam.ross@darlington.gov.uk

Partnerships: Mr Seth Pearson, Director, Town Hall, Feethams, Darlington DL1 5QT ☎ 01325 388462 🖷 01325 388018 ✉ seth.pearson@darlington.gov.uk

Personnel / HR: Ms Joanne Machers, Assistant Director - Human Resources Management, Town Hall, Feethams, Darlington DL1 5QT ☎ 01325 388210 🖷 01325 382032 ✉ joanne.machers@darlington.gov.uk

Planning: Mr John Anderson, Assistant Director - Policy & Regeneration, Town Hall, Feethams, Darlington DL1 5QT ☎ 01325 388501 🖷 01325 382032 ✉ john.anderson@darlington.gov.uk

Planning: Mr Roy Merrett, Development Manager, Town Hall, Feethams, Darlington DL1 5QT ☎ 01325 388037 🖷 01325 382032 ✉ roy.merrett@darlington.gov.uk

Procurement: Ms Susan White, Head of Strategic Procurement & Contract Management, Town Hall, Feethams, Darlington DL1 5QT ☎ 01325 388019 🖷 01325 382032 ✉ susan.white@darlington.gov.uk

Public Libraries: Mr Mike Crawshaw, Head of Culture, Dolphin Centre, Horsemarket, Darlington DL1 5RP ☎ 01325 388431 🖷 01325 369400 ✉ mike.crawshaw@darlington.gov.uk

Recycling & Waste Minimisation: Ms Phillippa Scrafton, Waste Minimisation & Recycling Officer, Vicarage Road Depot, Darlington DL1 1JW ☎ 01325 347434 🖷 01325 486987 ✉ phillippa.scrafton@darlington.gov.uk

Regeneration: Mr John Anderson, Assistant Director - Policy & Regeneration, Town Hall, Feethams, Darlington DL1 5QT ☎ 01325 388501 🖷 01325 382032 ✉ john.anderson@darlington.gov.uk

Road Safety: Mr Andrew Casey, Head of Highway Network Management, The Beehive, Lingfield Point, Darlington DL1 1YN ☎ 01325 388746 🖷 01325 388724 ✉ andrew.casey@darlington.gov.uk

Social Services: Mr Murray Rose, Director - People, Town Hall, Feethams, Darlington DL1 5QT ☎ 01325 388099

🖷 01325 382032 ✉ murray.rose@darlington.gov.uk

Social Services (Adult): Mrs Pauline Mitchell, Assistant Director - Adult Social Care & Housing, Town Hall, Feethams, Darlington DL1 5QT ☎ 01325 388505 🖷 01325 382032 ✉ pauline.mitchell@darlington.gov.uk

Social Services (Children): Ms Jenni Cooke, Assistant Director - Children, Families & Learning, Town Hall, Feethams, Darlington DL1 5QT ☎ 01325 388861 🖷 01325 382032 ✉ jenni.cooke@darlington.gov.uk

Staff Training: Ms Carol Hambleton, HR Manager (Organisational & Workforce Development), Town Hall, Feethams, Darlington DL1 5QT ☎ 01325 388239 🖷 01325 382032 ✉ carol.hambleton@darlington.gov.uk

Street Scene: Mr Brian Graham, Head of Environmental Services, Vicarage Road Depot, Darlington DL1 4RF ☎ 01325 347541 🖷 01325 486987 ✉ brian.graham@darlington.gov.uk

Sustainable Communities: Mr Steve Petch, Head of Strategy & Commissioning, Town Hall, Feethams, Darlington DL1 5QT ☎ 01325 388627 🖷 01325 382032 ✉ steve.petch@darlington.gov.uk

Sustainable Development: Ms Paula Jamieson, Sustainable Development Officer, Town Hall, Feethams, Darlington DL1 5QT ☎ 01325 388920 🖷 01325 382032 ✉ paula.jamieson@darlington.gov.uk

Town Centre: Mr Nik Grewer, Head of Economic Regeneration, Town Hall, Feethams, Darlington DL1 5QT ☎ 01325 388687 🖷 01325 382032 ✉ nik.grewer@darlington.gov.uk

Traffic Management: Mr Andrew Casey, Head of Highway Network Management, The Beehive, Lingfield Point, Darlington DL1 1YN ☎ 01325 388746 🖷 01325 388724 ✉ andrew.casey@darlington.gov.uk

Transport: Mr Roger Scott, Transport Services Manager, Vicarage Road Depot, Darlington DL1 1JW ☎ 01325 347475 🖷 01325 486987 ✉ roger.scott@darlington.gov.uk

Transport Planner: Mr Owen Wilson, Transformation Programme/Transport Policy, The Beehive, Lingfield Point, Darlington DL1 1YN ☎ 01325 388464 🖷 01325 388018 ✉ owen.wilson@darlington.gov.uk

Waste Collection and Disposal: Mr Ian Thompson, Assistant Director - Community Services, Vicarage Road Depot, Darlington DL1 1JW ☎ 01325 347447 🖷 01325 486987 ✉ ian.thompson@darlington.gov.uk

Waste Management: Ms Phillippa Scrafton, Waste Minimisation & Recycling Officer, Vicarage Road Depot, Darlington DL1 1JW ☎ 01325 347434 🖷 01325 486987 ✉ phillippa.scrafton@darlington.gov.uk

MEMBERS OF THE COUNCIL (53)

***Mayor:* Baldwin**, Paul (LAB - Cockerton East)
paul.baldwin@darlington.gov.uk

***Deputy Mayor:* Coultas**, Alan (CON - Hummersknott)
alan.coultas@darlington.gov.uk

***Leader of the Council:* Dixon**, Bill (LAB - Eastbourne)
bill.dixon@darlington.gov.uk

***Group Leader:* Curry**, Anne-Marie (LD - North Road)
annemarie.curry@darlington.gov.uk

***Group Leader:* Scott**, Heather (CON - Park West)
heather.scott@darlington.gov.uk

Carson, Bob (LAB - Pierremont)
bob.carson@darlington.gov.uk

Cartwright, Gill (CON - Harrowgate Hill)
gill.cartwright@darlington.gov.uk

Copeland, Veronica (LAB - Banktop)
veronica.copeland@darlington.gov.uk

Cossins, Jan (LAB - Cockerton West)
jan.cossins@darlingon.gov.uk

Crudass, Paul (CON - Heighington & Coniscliffe)
paul.crudass@darlington.gov.uk

Donoghue, Bob (CON - Park West)
bob.donoghue@darlington.gov.uk

Francis, Roderick (LAB - Eastbourne)
roderick.francis@darlington.gov.uk

Galletley, Ian (CON - College)
ian.galletley@darlington.gov.uk

Grundy, Richard (CON - Faverdale)
richard.grundy@darlington.gov.uk

Harker, Stephen (LAB - Pierremont)
stephen.harker@darlington.gov.uk

Harman, Paul (LAB - Park East)
paul.harman@darlington.gov.uk

Haszeldine, Lynne (LAB - Lingfield)
lynne.haszeldine@darlington.gov.uk

Haszeldine, Ian (LAB - Lingfield)
ian.haszeldine@darlington.gov.uk

Hughes, Cyndi (LAB - Park East)
cyndi.hughes@darlington.gov.uk

Hughes, Linda (LAB - Pierremont)
linda.hughes@darlington.gov.uk

Hutchinson, Beverley (LAB - Haughton North)
bev.hutchinson@darlington.gov.uk

Johnson, Charles (CON - Hummersknott)
charles.johnson@darlington.gov.uk

Jones, Doris (CON - Middleton St George)
doris.jones@darlington.gov.uk

Jones, Brian (CON - Sadberge & Whessoe)
brian.jones@darlington.gov.uk

Kelly, Joe (LD - Hurworth)
joe.kelley@darlington.gov.uk

Knowles, Marjory (LAB - Harrowgate Hill)
marjory.knowles@darlington.gov.uk

Landers, Martin (LAB - Haughton East)
martin.landers@darlington.gov.uk

Lawton, Fred (LD - North Road)
fred.lawton@darlington.gov.uk

Lee, Gerald (CON - Heighington & Coniscliffe)
gerald.lee@darlington.gov.uk

Lewis, Ron (CON - Mowden)
ronald.lewis@darlington.gov.uk

Lister, Eleanor (LAB - Northgate)
eleanor.lister@darlington.gov.uk

Long, Dorothy (LAB - Northgate)
dorothy.long@darlington.gov.uk

Lyonette, David (LAB - Haughton West)
david.lyonette@darlington.gov.uk

Lyonette, Joe (LAB - Park East)

joe.lyonette@darlington.gov.uk
Macnab, Alan (LD - North Road)
alan.macnab@darlington.gov.uk
Maddison, Jackie (LAB - Lascelles)
jackie.maddison@darlington.gov.uk
McEwan, Chris (LAB - Haughton East)
chris.mcewan@darlington.gov.uk
Newall, Wendy (LAB - Lascelles)
wendy.newall@darlington.gov.uk
Nutt, Thomas (LAB - Haughton North)
thomas.nutt@darlington.gov.uk
Regan, David (LAB - Cockerton West)
david.regan@darlington.gov.uk
Richmond, Tony (CON - College)
tony.richmond@darlington.gov.uk
Richmond, Sue (LAB - Cockerton East)
sue.richmond@darlington.gov.uk
Scott, Andrew (LAB - Haughton West)
andrew.scott@darlington.gov.uk
Stenson, Bill (CON - Mowden)
bill.stenson@darlington.gov.uk
Swainston, Martin (LD - Hurworth)
martin.swainston@darlington.gov.uk
Taylor, Chris (LAB - Banktop)
chris.taylor@darlington.gov.uk
Taylor, Jan (LAB - Central)
jan.taylor@darlington.gov.uk
Thistlethwaite, Bryan (LAB - Cockerton East)
bryan.thistlethwaite@darlington.gov.uk
Vasey, John (LAB - Harrowgate Hill)
john.vasey@darlington.gov.uk
Vasey, Lee (LAB - Eastbourne)
lee.vasey@darlington.gov.uk
Wallis, Nick (LAB - Haughton West)
nick.wallis@darlington.gov.uk
Wright, Malcolm (LAB - Central)
malcolm.wright@darlington.gov.uk
York, Steve (CON - Middleton St George) steve.york@darlington.gov.uk

POLITICAL COMPOSITION

LAB: 33, CON: 15, LD: 5

CABINET

Leader: Mr Bill Dixon
Deputy Leader: Mr Stephen Harker
Adult Social Care & Housing: Ms Veronica Copeland
Children & Young Peopple: Ms Cyndi Hughes
Economy & Regeneration: Mr Chris McEwan
Efficiency & Resources: Mr Stephen Harker
Health & Partnerships: Mr Andrew Scott
Leisure & Local Environment: Mr Nick Wallis
Transport: Mr David Lyonette

COMMITTEE CHAIRS

Adults & Housing Scrutiny: Mr Bryan Thistlethwaite
Audit: Mr Paul Baldwin
Children & Young People Scrutiny: Ms Eleanor Lister
Efficiency & Resources Scrutiny: Mr Ian Haszeldine
General Licensing: Mr Thomas Nutt
Health & Partnerships Scrutiny: Ms Wendy Newall
Place Scrutiny: Ms Dorothy Long
Planning Applications: Mr Paul Baldwin

DARTFORD — D

Dartford Borough Council, Civic Centre, Home Gardens, Dartford DA1 1DR ☎ 01322 343434 🖷 01322 343422
💻 www.dartford.gov.uk

FACTS & FIGURES

Police Authority: Kent Police Authority
Health Authority: South East Coast Strategic Health Authority
Learning and Skills Council: South East
Parliamentary Constituencies: Dartford
EU Constituencies: South East
Election Frequency: Elections are of whole council
Twinning: Gravelines (France); Hanau (Germany); Economic accords: Cappelle (Holland), Dunkerque (France), Tallinn (Estonia); Treaty of Friendship: Nam Yang Ju City (South Korea)

PRINCIPAL OFFICERS

Chief Executive: Mr Graham Harris, Managing Director, Civic Centre, Home Gardens, Dartford DA1 1DR ☎ 01322 343434 🖷 01322 343422 ✉ graham.harris@dartford.gov.uk

Senior Management: Chris Oliver, Executive Director, Civic Centre, Home Gardens, Dartford DA1 1DR ☎ 01322 343434 🖷 01322 343045 ✉ chris.oliver@dartford.gov.uk

Architect, Building / Property Services: Mr David Fletcher, Project Director, Civic Centre, Home Gardens, Dartford DA1 1DR ☎ 01322 343434 🖷 01322 343422 ✉ david.fletcher@dartford.gov.uk

Building Control: Mr Andrew Nichols, Building & Control Manager, Civic Centre, Home Gardens, Dartford DA1 1DR ☎ 01322 343434 🖷 01322 343422 ✉ andrew.nichols@dartford.gov.uk

PR / Communications: Ms Helen Clark, Press & Design Officer, Civic Centre, Home Gardens, Dartford DA1 1DR ☎ 01322 343069 ✉ helen.clark@dartford.gov.uk

Community Planning: Ms Teresa Ryszkowska, Planning Policy Manager, Civic Centre, Home Gardens, Dartford DA1 1DR ☎ 01322 343631 🖷 01322 343422 ✉ teresa.ryszkowska@dartford.gov.uk

Community Safety: Mrs Sheri Green, Strategic Director, Civic Centre, Home Gardens, Dartford DA1 1DR ☎ 01322 343434 🖷 01322 343422 ✉ sheri.green@dartford.gov.uk

Computer Management: Mrs Sheri Green, Strategic Director, Civic Centre, Home Gardens, Dartford DA1 1DR ☎ 01322 343434 🖷 01322 343422 ✉ sheri.green@dartford.gov.uk

Corporate Services: Mr Steve Brooks, Head of Financial & Human Resources, Civic Centre, Home Gardens, Dartford DA1 1DR ☎ 01322 343434 🖷 01322 343422 ✉ steve.brooks@dartford.gov.uk

Corporate Services: Mr Andrew Hall, Assistant Building Surveyor, Civic Centre, Home Gardens, Dartford DA1 1DR ☎ 01322 343489 🖷 01322 343422 ✉ andrew.hall@dartford.gov.uk

E-Government: Mrs Sheri Green, Strategic Director, Civic Centre, Home Gardens, Dartford DA1 1DR ☎ 01322 343434 🖷 01322 343422 ✉ sheri.green@dartford.gov.uk

Electoral Registration: Mr Graham Harris, Managing Director, Civic Centre, Home Gardens, Dartford DA1 1DR ☎ 01322 343434 🖷 01322 343422 ✉ graham.harris@dartford.gov.uk

Emergency Planning: Mr Ken Follett, Drainage & Engineering Manager, Civic Centre, Home Gardens, Dartford DA1 1DR ☎ 01322 343434 🖷 01322 343422 ✉ ken.follett@dartford.gov.uk

Environmental Health: Mrs Annie Sargent, Environmental Health Manager, Dartford Borough Council, Civic Centre, Home Gardens, Dartford DA1 1DR ✉ annie.sargent@dartford.gov.uk

Estates, Property & Valuation: Mr Andrew Hall, Assistant Building Surveyor, Civic Centre, Home Gardens, Dartford DA1 1DR ☎ 01322 343489 🖷 01322 343422 ✉ andrew.hall@dartford.gov.uk

Finance and Treasurer: Mr Steve Brooks, Head of Financial & Human Resources, Civic Centre, Home Gardens, Dartford DA1 1DR ☎ 01322 343434 🖷 01322 343422 ✉ steve.brooks@dartford.gov.uk

Fleet Management: Ms Lynn Stewart, Senior Finance Assistant, Civic Centre, Home Gardens, Dartford DA1 1DR ☎ 01322 343434 🖷 01322 343422 ✉ lynn.stewart@dartford.gov.uk

Grounds Maintenance: Mr Dave Thomas, Waste & Recycling Manager, Civic Centre, Home Gardens, Dartford DA1 1DR ☎ 01322 343434 🖷 01322 343422 ✉ dave.thomas@dartford.gov.uk

Health and Safety: Mrs Annie Sargent, Environmental Health Manager, Dartford Borough Council, Civic Centre, Home Gardens, Dartford DA1 1DR ✉ annie.sargent@dartford.gov.uk

Home Energy Conservation: Ms Sandra Woodfall, Environmental Promotions Officer, Civic Centre, Home Gardens, Dartford DA1 1DR ☎ 01322 343434 🖷 01322 343422 ✉ sandra.woodfall@dartford.gov.uk

Housing: Mr Peter Dosad, Head of Housing, Civic Centre, Home Gardens, Dartford DA1 1DR ☎ 01322 343434 🖷 01322 343422 ✉ peter.dosad@dartford.gov.uk

Legal: Ms Marie Kelly-Stone, Head of Legal Services, Civic Centre, Home Gardens, Dartford DA1 1DR ☎ 01322 343434 🖷 01322 343422 ✉ marie.kelly-stone@dartford.gov.uk

Leisure and Cultural Services: Mr Stephen Jefferson, Policy & Corporate Support Manager, Civic Centre, Home Gardens, Dartford DA1 1DR ☎ 01322 343434 ✉ stephen.jefferson@dartford.gov.uk

Licensing: Mr David Court, Senior Licensing Officer, Civic Centre, Home Gardens, Dartford DA1 1DR ☎ 01322 343434 🖷 01322 343422 ✉ david.court@dartford.gov.uk

Member Services: Ms Marie Kelly-Stone, Head of Legal Services, Civic Centre, Home Gardens, Dartford DA1 1DR ☎ 01322 343434 🖷 01322 343422 ✉ marie.kelly-stone@dartford.gov.uk

Parking: Mr Lewis Boudville, Parking Services Manager, Civic Centre, Home Gardens, Dartford DA1 1DR ☎ 01322 434434 🖷 01322 343422 ✉ lewis.boudville@dartford.gov.uk

Planning: Mr Rob Scott, Regeneration Director, Civic Centre, Home Gardens, Dartford DA1 1DR ☎ 01322 343434 🖷 01322 343422 ✉ rob.scott@dartford.gov.uk

Procurement: Mr Bami Cole, Audit, Risk & Anti-Fraud Manager, Dartford Borough Council, Civic Centre, Home Gardens, Dartford DA1 1DR ☎ ; 01322 343023 ✉ bami.cole@dartford.gov.uk

Recycling & Waste Minimisation: Mr Dave Thomas, Waste and Parks Manager, Civic Centre, Home Gardens, Dartford DA1 1DR ☎ 01322 343334 🖷 01322 343422 ✉ dave.thomas@dartford.gov.uk

Regeneration: Mr Rob Scott, Regeneration Director, Civic Centre, Home Gardens, Dartford DA1 1DR ☎ 01322 343434 🖷 01322 343422 ✉ rob.scott@dartford.gov.uk

Street Scene: Mr Rob Scott, Regeneration Director, Civic Centre, Home Gardens, Dartford DA1 1DR ☎ 01322 343434 🖷 01322 343422 ✉ rob.scott@dartford.gov.uk

Sustainable Development: Ms Sandra Woodfall, Environmental Promotions Officer, Civic Centre, Home Gardens, Dartford DA1 1DR ☎ 01322 343434 🖷 01322 343422 ✉ sandra.woodfall@dartford.gov.uk

Town Centre: Mr Lewis Kirnon, Town Centre Liaison Officer, Civic Centre, Home Gardens, Dartford DA1 1DR ☎ 01322 343434 🖷 01322 343422 ✉ lewis.kirnon@dartford.gov.uk

Waste Collection and Disposal: Mr Dave Thomas, Waste & Recycling Manager, Civic Centre, Home Gardens, Dartford DA1 1DR ☎ 01322 343434 🖷 01322 343422 ✉ dave.thomas@dartford.gov.uk

Waste Management: Mr Dave Thomas, Waste & Recycling Manager, Civic Centre, Home Gardens, Dartford DA1 1DR ☎ 01322 343434 🖷 01322 343422 ✉ dave.thomas@dartford.gov.uk

MEMBERS OF THE COUNCIL (44)

***Mayor:* Allen**, Ann (CON - Joydens Wood)
ann.allen@dartford.gov.uk

***Deputy Mayor:* Thurlow**, Patsy (CON - Heath)
patsy.thurlow@dartford.gov.uk

***Group Leader:* Bardoe**, Arron (CON - West Hill)
arron.bardoe@dartford.gov.uk

***Group Leader:* Brown**, Steve (CON - Longfield, New Barn & Southfleet)
steve.brown@dartford.gov.uk

***Group Leader:* Hunnisett**, Derek (CON - Wilmington)
derek.hunnisett@btintenet.com

***Group Leader:* Read**, Bryan (R - Swanscombe)
bryan.read@dartford.gov.uk

Castle: Vacant

Adams, John (LAB - Stone)
john.adams@dartford.gov.uk
Armitt, Ian (CON - Bean & Darenth)
ian.armitt@dartford.gov.uk
Bobby, Leslie (R - Swanscombe)
leslie.bobby@dartford.gov.uk
Bryant, Rosie (LAB - Princes)
rosie.bryant@dartford.gov.uk
Bryant, Matthew (LAB - Joyce Green)
matthew.bryant@dartford.gov.uk
Burrell, John (CON - Stone)
john.burrell@dartford.gov.uk
Butterfill, Susan (R - Greenhithe)
susan.butterfill@dartford.gov.uk
Cannon, Peter (CON - Brent)
peter.cannon@dartford.gov.uk
Coleman, Pat (CON - Sutton-at-Hone & Hawley)
pat.coleman@dartford.gov.uk
Davis, Matthew (CON - Town)
matthew.davis@dartford.gov.uk
Hammock, David (CON - Bean & Darenth)
david.hammock@dartford.gov.uk
Hawkes, Jonathon (LAB - Stone)
jonathon.hawkes@dartford.gov.uk
Hayes, John (R - Swanscombe)
john.hayes@dartford.gov.uk
Kelly, Patrick (LAB - Princes)
patrick.kelly@dartford.gov.uk
Kelly, Keith (CON - Greenhithe)
keith.kelly@dartford.gov.uk
Kite, Jeremy (CON - Longfield, New Barn & Southfleet)
jeremy.kite@dartford.gov.uk
Lampkin, Eddy (CON - Wilmington)
eddy.lampkin@dartford.gov.uk
Lloyd, Andy (CON - Heath)
andy.lloyd@dartford.gov.uk
Madison, Tom (LAB - Littlebrook)
tom.maddison@dartford.gov.uk
Martin, Tony (CON - Sutton-at-Hone & Hawley)
tony.martin@dartford.gov.uk
Mote, David (CON - Greenhithe)
david.mote@dartford.gov.uk
Muckle, Ann (LAB - Joyce Green)
ann.muckle@ntlworld.com
Muckle, John (LAB - Littlebrook)
john.muckle@dartford.gov.uk
Ozog, Jan (CON - West Hill)
jan.ozog@dartford.gov.uk
Perfitt, Roger (CON - Longfield, New Barn & Southfleet)
Peters, Marilyn (CON - Joydens Wood)
marilyn.peters@kcl.ac.uk
Prout, Geoffrey (LAB - Princes)
geoff.prout@dartford.gov.uk
Reynolds, Gary (CON - Newtown)
gary.reynolds@dartford.gov.uk
Rickwood, Jennifer (CON - Joydens Wood)
Sandhu, Avtar (CON - Newtown)
avtar.sandhu@dartford.gov.uk
Shanks, Rebecca (CON - Bean & Darenth)
rebecca.shanks@dartford.gov.uk
Shippham, Chris (CON - Town)
chris.shippam@dartford.gov.uk
Street, Michael (CON - Newtown)
michael.street@dartford.gov.uk
Swinerd, Drew (CON - Brent)
drew.swinerd@dartford.gov.uk
Wells, Anthony (CON - West Hill)
anthony.wells@dartford.gov.uk
Wells, Richard (CON - Heath)
richard.wells@dartford.gov.uk
Wightman, Nancy (CON - Brent)
nancy.wightman@dartford.gov.uk

POLITICAL COMPOSITION
CON: 30, LAB: 9, R: 4, Vacant: 1

CABINET
Leader: Mr Jeremy Kite
Deputy Leader/ Strategic Council Finance Services: Mr Tony Martin
Business & Enterprise, Procurement, Trading & Income: Mr Arron Bardoe
Customer Experience & Services Profiles: Mr Eddy Lampkin
Environment, Leisure & Events: Mr Andy Lloyd
Front Line Services, Customer Champion & Housing: Mr Pat Coleman
Licensing, Obligations & Enforcement: Mr David Hammock
Policy Development: Mr Steve Brown
Town Centre: Mr Chris Shippham
Urban Regeneration: Mr Bryan Read

COMMITTEE CHAIRS
Appeals: Ms Patsy Thurlow
Appointments: Mr Jeremy Kite
Audit: Mr David Hammock
Crime & Disorder Overview & Scrutiny: Mr Richard Wells
Development Control Board: Mr Derek Hunnisett
Licensing: Mr Ian Armitt
Policy Overview: Mr Eddy Lampkin
Scrutiny: Mr Geoffrey Prout

DAVENTRY D

Daventry District Council, Lodge Road, Daventry NN11 4FP
☎ 01327 871100 🖷 01327 300011 ✉ comments@daventrydc.gov.uk
💻 www.daventrydc.gov.uk

FACTS & FIGURES
Police Authority: Northamptonshire Police Authority
Health Authority: East Midlands Strategic Health Authority
Learning and Skills Council: East Midlands
Parliamentary Constituencies: Daventry, Kettering
EU Constituencies: East Midlands
Election Frequency: Elections are by thirds
Twinning: Daventry Town: Westerburg (Germany)

PRINCIPAL OFFICERS
Chief Executive: Mr Ian Vincent, Managing Director & Returning Officer, Council Offices, Lodge Road, Daventry NN11 5AF
☎ 01327 871100 ✉ ivincent@daventrydc.gov.uk

Senior Management: Mr Simon Bovey, Executive Director & Monitoring Officer, Council Offices, Lodge Road, Daventry NN11 5AF ☎ 01327 302595 🖷 01327 300011
✉ sbovey@daventrydc.gov.uk

Architect, Building / Property Services: Mr Simon Bowers,

Corporate Manager - Development & Property, Council Offices, Lodge Road, Daventry NN11 4FP ☎ 01327 302432 ✉ sbowers@daventrydc.gov.uk

Best Value: Ms Katie Jones, Performance Manager, Lodge Road, Daventry NN11 4FP ☎ 01327 302417 ✉ kjones@daventrydc.gov.uk

Building Control: Mr Tony Gillet, Corporate Manager - Environment Protection, Council Offices, Lodge Road, Daventry NN11 4FP ☎ 01327 302276 🖷 01327 300011 ✉ tgillet@daventrydc.gov.uk

PR / Communications: Ms Becky Hutson, PR Officer, Lodge Road, Daventry NN11 4FP ☎ 01327 302404 ✉ bhutson@daventrydc.gov.uk

Community Safety: Mr Kevin Fagan, Community Partnership Team Manager, Lodge Road, Daventry NN11 4FP ☎ 01327 302424 ✉ kfagan@daventrydc.gov.uk

Computer Management: Miss Paula Green, Corporate Manager - Customer Access, Council Offices, Lodge Road, Daventry NN11 4FP ☎ 01327 302326 🖷 01327 300011 ✉ pgreen@daventrydc.gov.uk

Customer Service: Miss Paula Green, Corporate Manager - Customer Access, Council Offices, Lodge Road, Daventry NN11 4FP ☎ 01327 302326 🖷 01327 300011 ✉ pgreen@daventrydc.gov.uk

Economic Development: Mr Simon Bowers, Corporate Manager - Development & Property, Council Offices, Lodge Road, Daventry NN11 4FP ☎ 01327 302432 ✉ sbowers@daventrydc.gov.uk

Emergency Planning: Mr Simon Bowers, Corporate Manager (Development & Property), Council Offices, Lodge Road, Daventry NN11 5AF ☎ 01327 302432 🖷 01327 302446 ✉ sbowers@daventrydc.gov.uk

Energy Management: Mr Tony Gillet, Corporate Manager - Environment Protection, Council Offices, Lodge Road, Daventry NN11 4FP ☎ 01327 302276 🖷 01327 300011 ✉ tgillet@daventrydc.gov.uk

Environmental / Technical Services: Mr Tony Gillet, Corporate Manager - Environment Protection, Council Offices, Lodge Road, Daventry NN11 4FP ☎ 01327 302276 🖷 01327 300011 ✉ tgillet@daventrydc.gov.uk

Environmental Health: Mr Tony Gillet, Corporate Manager - Environment Protection, Council Offices, Lodge Road, Daventry NN11 4FP ☎ 01327 302276 🖷 01327 300011 ✉ tgillet@daventrydc.gov.uk

Estates, Property & Valuation: Mr Simon Bowers, Corporate Manager - Development & Property, Council Offices, Lodge Road, Daventry NN11 4FP ☎ 01327 302432 ✉ sbowers@daventrydc.gov.uk

Facilities: Mr Simon Bowers, Corporate Manager (Development & Property), Council Offices, Lodge Road, Daventry NN11 5AF ☎ 01327 302432 🖷 01327 302446 ✉ sbowers@daventrydc.gov.uk

Health and Safety: Mr Tony Gillet, Corporate Manager - Environment Protection, Council Offices, Lodge Road, Daventry NN11 4FP ☎ 01327 302276 🖷 01327 300011 ✉ tgillet@daventrydc.gov.uk

Home Energy Conservation: Mr Tony Gillet, Corporate Manager - Environment Protection, Council Offices, Lodge Road, Daventry NN11 4FP ☎ 01327 302276 🖷 01327 300011 ✉ tgillet@daventrydc.gov.uk

Home Energy Conservation: Mrs Maria Taylor, Corporate Manager - Community, Council Offices, Lodge Road, Daventry NN11 4FP ☎ 01327 302229 ✉ mtaylor@daventrydc.gov.uk

Housing: Mrs Maria Taylor, Corporate Manager - Community, Council Offices, Lodge Road, Daventry NN11 4FP ☎ 01327 302229 ✉ mtaylor@daventrydc.gov.uk

Housing Maintenance: Mrs Maria Taylor, Corporate Manager - Community, Council Offices, Lodge Road, Daventry NN11 4FP ☎ 01327 302229 ✉ mtaylor@daventrydc.gov.uk

Legal: Mr Gideon Mclean, Programme & Performance Officer, Lodge Road, Daventry NN11 4FP ☎ 01327 871100

Licensing: Mr Tony Gillet, Corporate Manager - Environment Protection, Council Offices, Lodge Road, Daventry NN11 4FP ☎ 01327 302276 🖷 01327 300011 ✉ tgillet@daventrydc.gov.uk

Member Services: Mrs Sue Thomas, Member Services Officer, Council Offices, Lodge Road, Daventry NN11 5AF ☎ 01327 302595 🖷 01327 876543 ✉ sthomas1@daventrydc.gov.uk

Partnerships: Mrs Maria Taylor, Corporate Manager - Community, Council Offices, Lodge Road, Daventry NN11 4FP ☎ 01327 302229 ✉ mtaylor@daventrydc.gov.uk

Personnel / HR: Mrs Maria Taylor, Corporate Manager - Community, Council Offices, Lodge Road, Daventry NN11 4FP ☎ 01327 302229 ✉ mtaylor@daventrydc.gov.uk

Planning: Mr Tony Gillet, Corporate Manager - Environment Protection, Council Offices, Lodge Road, Daventry NN11 4FP ☎ 01327 302276 🖷 01327 300011 ✉ tgillet@daventrydc.gov.uk

Procurement: Mr Simon Bowers, Corporate Manager - Development & Property, Council Offices, Lodge Road, Daventry NN11 4FP ☎ 01327 302432 ✉ sbowers@daventrydc.gov.uk

Staff Training: Ms Rosemary Daniels, Governance and HR, Lodge Road, Daventry NN11 4FP ☎ 01327 871100

Sustainable Communities: Mr Simon Bovey, Executive Director & Monitoring Officer, Council Offices, Lodge Road, Daventry NN11 5AF ☎ 01327 302595 🖷 01327 300011 ✉ sbovey@daventrydc.gov.uk

Sustainable Communities: Mrs Maria Taylor, Corporate Manager - Community, Council Offices, Lodge Road, Daventry NN11 4FP ☎ 01327 302229 ✉ mtaylor@daventrydc.gov.uk

Town Centre: Mr Simon Bowers, Corporate Manager - Development & Property, Council Offices, Lodge Road, Daventry NN11 4FP ☎ 01327 302432 ✉ sbowers@daventrydc.gov.uk

MEMBERS OF THE COUNCIL (36)

***Chair:* Osborne**, Diana (CON - Long Buckby)
dosborne@daventrydc.gov.uk
***Vice-Chair:* Long**, Chris (CON - Abbey North)
clong@daventrydc.gov.uk
Atterbury, Richard (CON - Barby & Kilsby)
ratterbury@daventrydc.gov.uk
Bunting, Nick (CON - Brixworth)
nbunting@daventrydc.gov.uk
Campbell, Abigail (LAB - Braunston & Welton)
acampbell@daventrydc.gov.uk
Carter, Ann (CON - Walgrave)
acarter@daventrydc.gov.uk
Chantler, Alan (CON - Yelvertoft)
aechantler@daventrydc.gov.uk
Cribbin, Daniel (CON - Moulton)
dcribbin@daventrydc.gov.uk
Driver, Kay (CON - Welford)
kdriver@daventrydc.gov.uk
Duly, Ian (CON - Weedon)
iduly@daventrydc.gov.uk
Eddon, Deanna (CON - Abbey South)
deddon@daventrydc.gov.uk
Frenchman, Barry (CON - Spratton)
bfrenchman@daventrydc.gov.uk
Gilford, Jo (CON - Woodford)
jmgilford@daventrydc.gov.uk
Griffin, Elizabeth (CON - Woodford)
egriffin@daventrydc.gov.uk
Harris, Andrew (CON - Hill)
aharris@daventrydc.gov.uk
Hills, Alan (CON - Hill)
ahills@daventrydc.gov.uk
Howard, Wayne (CON - Hill)
whoward@daventrydc.gov.uk
Irving-Swift, Cecile (CON - Welford)
cirving-swift@daventrydc.gov.uk
James, David (LAB - Abbey North)
djames@daventrydc.gov.uk
Lee, Chris (LAB - Drayton)
clee@daventrydc.gov.uk
Lomax, Catherine (LD - Barby & Kilsby)
clomax@daventrydc.gov.uk
Loud, Olwen (LAB - Drayton)
oloud@daventrydc.gov.uk
Luke, Maureen (LAB - Abbey North)
mluke@daventrydc.gov.uk
Melling, Ken (CON - Ravensthorpe)
kmelling@daventrydc.gov.uk
Millar, Chris (CON - West Haddon & Guilsborough)
cmillar@daventrydc.gov.uk
Morgan, Colin (CON - Abbey South)
cmorgan@daventrydc.gov.uk
Osborne, Steve (CON - Long Buckby)
sosborne@daventrydc.gov.uk
Over, Chris (CON - Abbey South)
cover@daventrydc.gov.uk
Patchett, Bob (CON - Woodford)
bpatchett@daventrydc.gov.uk
Perry, Kevin (CON - Weedon)
kperry@daventrydc.gov.uk
Randall, Wendy (LAB - Abbey North)
wrandall@daventrydc.gov.uk
Reeves, Eddie (CON - Weedon)
ereeves@daventrydc.gov.uk
Shephard, John (CON - Spratton)
jshephard@daventrydc.gov.uk
Warren, Mike (CON - Moulton)
mwarren@daventrydc.gov.uk
Wiig, Elizabeth (CON - Brixworth)
ewiig@daventrydc.gov.uk
Wiig, Frank (CON - Brixworth)
fwiig@daventrydc.gov.uk

POLITICAL COMPOSITION

CON: 29, LAB: 6, LD: 1

CABINET

Leader: Mr Chris Millar

COMMITTEE CHAIRS

Appeals: Mr Andrew Harris
Corporate Governance: Mr John Shephard
Licensing: Mrs Ann Carter
Planning: Mr Steve Osborne
Scrutiny & Improvement: Mr Alan Chantler

DENBIGHSHIRE — W

Denbighshire County Council, (Cyngor Sir Ddinbych), County Hall, Wynnstay Road, Ruthin LL15 1YN ☎ 01824 706000 🖷 01824 707446 ✉ customerservicecentre@denbighshire.gov.uk or canolfangwasanaethcwsmer@sirddinbych.gov.uk 💻 www.denbighshire.gov.uk or www.sirddinbych.gov.uk

FACTS & FIGURES

Police Authority: North Wales Police Authority
Learning and Skills Council: Wales
Parliamentary Constituencies: Clwyd South, Clwyd West, Vale of Clwyd
EU Constituencies: Wales
Election Frequency: Elections are of whole council

PRINCIPAL OFFICERS

Chief Executive: Dr Mohammed Mehmet, Chief Executive, County Hall, Wynnstay Road, Ruthin LL15 1YN ☎ 01824 706128 🖷 01824 706045 ✉ mohammed.mehmet@denbighshire.gov.uk

Senior Management: Ms Sally Ellis, Corporate Director - Demographic Change & Well-being, County Hall, Wynnstay Road, Ruthin LL15 1AT ☎ 01824 706149 🖷 01824 706646 ✉ sally.ellis@denbighshire.gov.uk

Senior Management: Mrs Bethan Jones, Corporate Director - Business Transformation & Regeneration, County Hall, Wynnstay Road, Ruthin LL15 1AT ☎ 01824 706060 🖷 01824 706045 ✉ bethan.jones@denbighshire.gov.uk

Senior Management: Mr Hywyn Williams, Corporate Director - Learning & Communities, County Hall, Wynnstay Road, Ruthin LL15 1YN ☎ 01824 708224 ✉ hywyn.williams@denbighshire.gov.uk

Access Officer / Social Services (Disability): Ms Karen

Beattie, Corporate Equalities Officer, County Hall, Wynnstay Road, Ruthin LL15 1YN ☎ 01745 888746 🖷 01824 708088 karen.beattie@denbighshire.gov.uk

Architect, Building / Property Services: Mr David Mathews, Valutation & Estates Team Manager, Caledfryn, Smithfield Road, Denbigh L16 3RJ ☎ 01824 706798 🖷 01824 708088 david.mathews@denbighshire.gov.uk

Building Control: Mr Robin Johnston, Building Control Officer, Caledfryn, Smithfield Road, Denbigh LL16 3RJ ☎ 01824 706714 🖷 01824 706953 robin.johnston@denbighshire.gov.uk

Catering Services: Ms Hayley Jones, Catering Manager, Kinmel Park Depot, Bodelwyddan, LL18 5UX ☎ 01824 712131 hayley.jones@denbighshire.gov.uk

Catering Services: Mr Ian Kemp, Catering Services Manager, Kinmel Park Depot, Bodelwyddan, LL18 5UX ☎ 01824 712125 🖷 01824 712131 ian.kemp@denbighshire.gov.uk

Children / Youth Services: Mr Jamie Groves, Head of Leisure, Libraries & Community Development, County Hall, Wynnstay Road, Ruthin LL15 1YN ☎ 01824 712723 jamie.groves@denbighshire.gov.uk

Civil Registration: Mr Gary Williams, County Clerk, County Hall, Wynnstay Road, Ruthin LL15 1YN ☎ 01824 712562 🖷 01824 706293 gary.williams@denbighshire.gov.uk

PR / Communications: Mr Gareth Watson, Corporate Communications Manager, County Hall, Wynnstay Road, Ruthin LL15 1YN ☎ 01824 706222 🖷 01824 707446 gareth.watson@denbigshire.gov.uk

Community Safety: Mr Roly Schwarz, Community Safety Manager, Divisional Police Headquarters, St Asaph Business Park, St Asaph, Denbigh LL17 0JG ☎ 01824 708036 🖷 01824 708039 roly.schwarz@denbighshire.gov.uk

Computer Management: Ms Cara Williams, Head of ICT, County Hall, Wynnstay Road, Ruthin LL15 1YN ☎ 01824 706211 cara.williams@denbighshire.gov.uk

Consumer Protection and Trading Standards: Mr Graham Boase, Head of Regeneration & Regulatory Services, County Hall, Wynnstay Road, Ruthin LL15 1YN ☎ 01824 706925 graham.boase@denbighshire.gov.uk

Contracts: Mr Steve Parker, Head of Environmental Services, Kinmel Park Depot, Kinmel Park, Abergele Road, Bodelwyddan, Rhyl LL18 5UX ☎ 01824 712123 🖷 01824 712123 steve.parker@denbighshire.gov.uk

Customer Service: Ms Cara Williams, Head of ICT, County Hall, Wynnstay Road, Ruthin LL15 1YN ☎ 01824 706211 cara.williams@denbighshire.gov.uk

Direct Labour: Mr Steve Parker, Head of Environmental Services, Kinmel Park Depot, Kinmel Park, Abergele Road, Bodelwyddan, Rhyl LL18 5UX ☎ 01824 712123 🖷 01824 712123 steve.parker@denbighshire.gov.uk

Economic Development: Mr Mark Dixon, Regeneration & Strategic Manager, Trem Clwyd, Canol y Dre, Ruthin LL15 1QA ☎ 01824 706860 🖷 01824 708088 mark.dixon@denbighshire.gov.uk

Education: Ms Karen Evans, Head of School Improvement & Inclusion, Trem Clwyd, Canol y Dre, Ruthin LL15 1QA ☎ 01824 708009 karen.evans@denbighshire.gov.uk

Education: Mr Hywyn Williams, Corporate Director - Learning & Communities, County Hall, Wynnstay Road, Ruthin LL15 1YN ☎ 01824 708224 hywyn.williams@denbighshire.gov.uk

E-Government: Ms Cara Williams, Head of ICT, County Hall, Wynnstay Road, Ruthin LL15 1YN ☎ 01824 706211 cara.williams@denbighshire.gov.uk

Electoral Registration: Mr Gareth Evans, County Electoral Services Administrator, County Hall, Wynnstay Road, Ruthin LL15 1YN ☎ 01824 706114 g.evans@denbighshire.gov.uk

Emergency Planning: Mr Don Norris, Emergency Planning Co-ordinator, County Hall, Mold CH7 6NJ ☎ 01352 752121 don.norris@flintshire.gov.uk

Environmental Health: Mr Graham Boase, Head of Planning & Public Protection, Caledfryn, Smithfield Road, Denbigh LL16 3RJ ☎ 01824 706925 graham.boase@denbighshire.gov.uk

Estates, Property & Valuation: Mr David Mathews, Valutation & Estates Team Manager, Caledfryn, Smithfield Road, Denbigh LL16 3RJ ☎ 01824 706798 🖷 01824 708088 david.mathews@denbighshire.gov.uk

Events Manager: Ms Sian Davies, Events Manager, Rhyl Pavillion Theatre, The Promenade, Rhyl LL18 3AQ ☎ 01745 332414

Finance and Treasurer: Mrs Bethan Jones, Corporate Director - Business Transformation & Regeneration, County Hall, Wynnstay Road, Ruthin LL15 1AT ☎ 01824 706060 🖷 01824 706045 bethan.jones@denbighshire.gov.uk

Finance and Treasurer: Mr Paul McGrady, Financial Controller, County Hall, Wynnstay Road, Ruthin LL15 1YN ☎ 01824 706132 paul.mcrady@denbighshire.gov.uk

Fleet Management: Mr Graham Taylor, Transport Manager, Fleet Depot, Expressway Business Park, Bodelwyddan, LL18 5SQ ☎ 01745 832231 🖷 01745 839242 graham.taylor@denbighshire.gov.uk

Grounds Maintenance: Mr Steve Parker, Head of Environmental Services, Kinmel Park Depot, Kinmel Park, Abergele Road, Bodelwyddan, Rhyl LL18 5UX ☎ 01824 712123 🖷 01824 712123 steve.parker@denbighshire.gov.uk

Health and Safety: Ms Helen Tapley, Corporate Health & Safety Manager, County Hall, Wynnstay Road, Ruthin LL15 1YN ☎ 01824 712582 helen.tapley@denbighshire.gov.uk

Highways: Mr Stuart Davies, Head of Transport & Infrastructure, Caledfryn, Smithfield Road, Denbigh LL16 3RJ ☎ 01824 706801

🖷 01824 706970 ✉ stuart.davies@denbighshire.gov.uk

Home Energy Conservation: Mr Gareth Roberts, Housing & Renewal Officer, Ty Nant, 6/8 Nant Hall Road, Prestatyn LL19 9LL ☎ 01824 706679 🖷 01824 706575 ✉ gareth.roberts@denbighshire.gov.uk

Housing: Mr Peter McHugh, Head of Housing Services, Russell House, Churton Road, Rhyl LL18 3DP ☎ 01824 708461 🖷 01824 708453 ✉ peter.mchugh@denbighshire.gov.uk

Housing Maintenance: Mr Alan Jones, Principal Housing Maintenance Officer, Kinmel Park Depot, Abergele Road, Bodelwyddan, Rhyl LL18 5UX ☎ 01824 712137 ✉ alan.jones@denbighshire.gov.uk

Legal: Mr Gary Williams, County Clerk, County Hall, Wynnstay Road, Ruthin LL15 1YN ☎ 01824 712562 🖷 01824 706293 ✉ gary.williams@denbighshire.gov.uk

Leisure and Cultural Services: Mr Jamie Groves, Head of Leisure, Libraries & Community Development, County Hall, Wynnstay Road, Ruthin LL15 1YN ☎ 01824 706476 🖷 01745 344516 ✉ jamie.groves@denbighshire.gov.uk

Leisure and Cultural Services: Mr Huw Rees, Acting Head of Countryside Services, Yr Hen Garchar, Ruthin LL15 1QA ☎ 01824 708228 ✉ huw.rees@denbighshire.gov.uk

Lifelong Learning: Mr Hywyn Williams, Corporate Director - Learning & Communities, County Hall, Wynnstay Road, Ruthin LL15 1YN ☎ 01824 708224 ✉ hywyn.williams@denbighshire.gov.uk

Lighting: Mr Andy Clark, Street Lighting Engineer, Kinmel Park Depot, Abergele Road, Bodelwyddan, LL18 5UX ☎ 01824 712140 ✉ andy.clark@denbighshire.gov.uk

Member Services: Mr Eleri Woodford, Member Support & Development Manager, County Hall, Wynnstay Road, Ruthin LL15 1YN ☎ 01824 706196 🖷 01824 706293 ✉ eleri.woodford@denbighshire.gov.uk

Parking: Mr Stuart Davies, Head of Transport & Infrastructure, Caledfryn, Smithfield Road, Denbigh LL16 3RJ ☎ 01824 706801 🖷 01824 706970 ✉ stuart.davies@denbighshire.gov.uk

Partnerships: Mr Alan Smith, Head of Business Planning & Performance, County Hall, Wynnstay Road, Ruthin LL15 1AT ☎ 01824 706246 🖷 01824 706045 ✉ alan.smith@denbighshire.gov.uk

Personnel / HR: Ms Linda Atkin, Head of Personnel, County Hall, Wynnstay Road, Ruthin LL15 1YN ☎ 01824 706565 🖷 01824 706575 ✉ linda.atkin@denbighshire.gov.uk

Planning: Mr Graham Boase, Head of Planning & Public Protection, Caledfryn, Smithfield Road, Denbigh LL16 3RJ ☎ 01824 706925 ✉ graham.boase@denbighshire.gov.uk

Procurement: Mr Arwel Staples, Strategic Procurement Officer, County Hall, Wynnstay Road, Ruthin LL15 1YN ☎ 01824 706042 🖷 01824 706045 ✉ arwel.staples@denbighshire.gov.uk

Public Libraries: Mr Robert Arwyn Jones, Principal Librarian, Yr Hen Garchar, 46 Clwyd Street, Ruthin LL15 1HP ☎ 01824 708203 🖷 01824 708202 ✉ arwyn.jones@denbighshire.gov.uk

Recycling & Waste Minimisation: Mr Alan Roberts, Senior Waste Officer, Kinmel Park Depot, Engine Hill, LL18 5UX ☎ 01824 712408 🖷 01824 712125 ✉ alan.l.roberts@denbighshire.gov.uk

Regeneration: Mr Mark Dixon, Regeneration & Strategic Manager, Trem Clwyd, Canol y Dre, Ruthin LL15 1QA ☎ 01824 706860 🖷 01824 708088 ✉ mark.dixon@denbighshire.gov.uk

Road Safety: Mr Alan Hinchcliffe, Road Safety Officer, Caledfryn, Smithfield Road, Denbigh LL16 3RJ ☎ 01824 706970 🖷 01824 706865 ✉ alan.hinchcliffe@denbighshire.gov.uk

Social Services: Mr Neil Ayling, Head of Adult Services (Community & Intermediate Care), Ty Nant, Nant Hall Road, Prestatyn LL19 9LG ☎ 01824 706654 🖷 01824 706646 ✉ neil.ayling@denbighshire.gov.uk

Social Services: Ms Sally Ellis, Corporate Director - Demographic Change & Well-being, County Hall, Wynnstay Road, Ruthin LL15 1AT ☎ 01824 706149 🖷 01824 706646 ✉ sally.ellis@denbighshire.gov.uk

Social Services (Children): Mr Leighton Rees, Head of Children & Family Services, Ty Nant, Nant Hall Road, Prestatyn LL19 9LL ☎ 01824 706655 ✉ leighton.rees@denbighshire.gov.uk

Staff Training: Mr John Rees, Principal Personnel Officer, Employee & Member Development, County Hall, Wynnstay Road, Ruthin LL15 1YN ☎ 01824 712537 🖷 01824 712526 ✉ john.rees@denbighshire.gov.uk

Tourism: Dr Carolyn Brindle, Marketing & Tourism Manager, Trem Clwyd, Canol y Dre, Ruthin LL15 1QA ☎ 01824 708089 🖷 01824 708088 ✉ carolyn.brindle@denbighshire.gov.uk

Traffic Management: Mr Stuart Davies, Head of Transport & Infrastructure, Caledfryn, Smithfield Road, Denbigh LL16 3RJ ☎ 01824 706801 🖷 01824 706970 ✉ stuart.davies@denbighshire.gov.uk

Transport: Mr Stuart Davies, Head of Transport & Infrastructure, Caledfryn, Smithfield Road, Denbigh LL16 3RJ ☎ 01824 706801 🖷 01824 706970 ✉ stuart.davies@denbighshire.gov.uk

Transport Planner: Mr Stuart Davies, Head of Transport & Infrastructure, Caledfryn, Smithfield Road, Denbigh LL16 3RJ ☎ 01824 706801 🖷 01824 706970 ✉ stuart.davies@denbighshire.gov.uk

Waste Collection and Disposal: Mr Alan Roberts, Senior Waste Officer, Kinmel Park Depot, Engine Hill, LL18 5UX ☎ 01824 712408 🖷 01824 712125 ✉ alan.l.roberts@denbighshire.gov.uk

Waste Management: Mr Alan Roberts, Senior Waste Officer, Kinmel Park Depot, Engine Hill, LL18 5UX ☎ 01824 712408

🖷 01824 712125 ✉ alan.l.roberts@denbighshire.gov.uk

MEMBERS OF THE COUNCIL (47)

***Chair:* Chamberlain Jones**, Jeanette (LAB - Rhyl South)
jeanette.c.jones@denbighshire.gov.uk
***Vice-Chair:* Bartley**, R (IND - Denbigh Lower)
ray.bartley@denbighshire.gov.uk
***Group Leader:* Butterfield**, Joan (LAB - Rhyl West)
joan.butterfield@denbighshire.gov.uk
***Group Leader:* Kensler**, Gwyneth (PC - Denbigh Central)
gwyneth.kensler@denbighshire.gov.uk
***Group Leader:* Smith**, David (IND - Ruthin)
david.smith@denbighshire.gov.uk
***Group Leader:* Thompson-Hill**, Julian (CON - Prestatyn East)
julian.thompson-hill@denbighshire.gov.uk
Armstrong, Ian (LAB - Rhyl West)
ian.armstrong@denbighshire.gov.uk
Blakeley, Brian (LAB - Rhyl South East)
brian.blakeley@denbighshire.gov.uk
Cowie, Bill (IND - St Asaph West)
bill.cowie@denbighshire.gov.uk
Davies, Anne (CON - Rhuddlan)
j.ann.davies@denbighshire.gov.uk
Davies, James (CON - Prestatyn East)
james.davies@denbighshire.gov.uk
Davies, Richard (IND - Denbigh Lower)
richard.lulu.davies@denbighshire.gov.uk
Davies, Meirick Lloyd (PC - Trefnant)
meirick.davies@denbighshire.gov.uk
Davies, Stuart (IND - Llangollen)
stuart.a.davies@denbighshire.gov.uk
Duffy, Peter (LAB - Prestatyn Central)
peter.duffy@denbighshire.gov.uk
Evans, Hugh (IND - Llanfair Dyffryn Clwyd / Gwyddelwern)
hugh.evans@denbighshire.gov.uk
Evans, Peter (IND - Meliden)
peter.evans@denbighshire.gov.uk
Feeley, Bobby (IND - Ruthin)
bobby.feeley@denbighshire.gov.uk
Guy-Davies, Carys (LAB - Prestatyn North)
carys.guy-davies@denbighshire.gov.uk
Hilditch-Roberts, Huw (IND - Ruthin)
huw.hilditch-roberts@denbighshire.gov.uk
Holland, Martyn (CON - Llanarmon-yn-Iâl/ Llandegla)
martyn.holland@denbighshire.gov.uk
Hughes, Colin (LAB - Denbigh Upper & Henllan)
colin.hughes@denbighshire.gov.uk
Hughes, Rhys (PC - Llangollen)
rhys.hughes@denbighshire.gov.uk
Irving, Hugh (CON - Prestatyn Central)
hugh.irving@denbighshire.gov.uk
Jones, Pat (LAB - Rhyl South West)
pat.jones@denbighshire.gov.uk
Jones, Huw (PC - Corwen)
huw.jones@denbighshire.gov.uk
Jones, Alice (IND - Bodelwyddan)
alice.jones@denbighshire.gov.uk
Lloyd-Williams, Geraint (LAB - Denbigh Upper & Henllan)
geraint.lloyd-williams@denbighshire.gov.uk
McCarroll, Margaret (LAB - Rhyl South West)
margaret.mccarroll@denbighshire.gov.uk
McLellan, Jason (LAB - Prestatyn North)
jason.mcclellan@denbighshire.gov.uk
Mellor, Barry (LAB - Rhyl East)
barry.mellor@denbighshire.gov.uk
Mullen-James, Win (LAB - Rhyl South East)
win.mullen-james@denbighshire.gov.uk
Murray, Bob (LAB - Prestatyn South West)
bob.murray@denbighshire.gov.uk
Owen, Peter (CON - Dyserth)
peter.owen@denbighshire.gov.uk
Owens, Dewi (CON - St Asaph East)
dewi.owens@denbighshire.gov.uk
Parry, Merfyn (IND - Llandyrnog)
merfyn.parry@denbighshire.gov.uk
Pennington, Allan (CON - Prestatyn North)
allan.pennington@denbighshire.gov.uk
Roberts, Arwel (PC - Rhuddlan)
arwel.roberts@denbighshire.gov.uk
Sandilands, Gareth (LAB - Prestatyn South West)
gareth.sandilands@denbighshire.gov.uk
Simmons, David (LAB - Rhyl East)
david.simmons@denbighshire.gov.uk
Smith, Barbara (IND - Tremeirchion)
barbara.smith@denbighshire.gov.uk
Tasker, Bill (LAB - Rhyl South East)
bill.tasker@denbighshire.gov.uk
Welch, Joe (IND - Llanrhaeadr-yng-Nghinmeirch)
joseph.welch@denbighshire.gov.uk
Williams, Huw (CON - Llanbedr Dyffryn Clwyd/ Llangynhafal)
huw.o.williams@denbighshire.gov.uk
Williams, Eryl (PC - Efenechtyd)
eryl.williams@denbighshire.gov.uk
Williams, Cefyn (PC - Llandrillo)
cefyn.williams@denbighshire.gov.uk
Williams, Cheryl (LAB - Rhyl South)
cheryl.williams@denbighshire.gov.uk

POLITICAL COMPOSITION

LAB: 18, IND: 13, CON: 9, PC: 7

CABINET

Leader: Mr Hugh Evans
Deputy Leader: Mr Eryl Williams
Customers & Communications: Mr Hugh Irving
Economic Development: Mr Hugh Evans
Education: Mr Eryl Williams
Finance & Assets: Mr Julian Thompson-Hill
Modernising & Performance: Ms Barbara Smith
Public Realm: Mr David Smith
Social Care & Children's Services: Ms Bobby Feeley
Tourism, Youth & Leisure: Mr Huw Jones

COMMITTEE CHAIRS

Communities Scrutiny: Mr Huw Hilditch-Roberts
Corporate Governance: Mr Jason McLellan
Partnerships Scrutiny: Mr Brian Blakeley
Performance Scrutiny: Mr Colin Hughes
Planning: Mr Dewi Owens

DERBY CITY U

Derby City Council, The Council House, Corporation Street, Derby DE1 2FS ☎ 01332 293111 🖷 01332 255500 💻 www.derby.gov.uk

FACTS & FIGURES

Police Authority: Derbyshire Police Authority
Health Authority: East Midlands Strategic Health Authority
Learning and Skills Council: East Midlands
Parliamentary Constituencies: Derby North, Derby South, Derbyshire Mid
EU Constituencies: East Midlands
Election Frequency: Elections are by thirds
Twinning: Osnabrück (Germany), Toyota City (Japan)

PRINCIPAL OFFICERS

Chief Executive: Mr Adam Wilkinson, Chief Executive, 4th Floor Saxon House, Heritage Gate, Friary Street, Derby DE1 1AN ☎ 01332 643547 ✉ adam.wilkinson@derby.gov.uk

Senior Management: Mr Andrew Bunyan, Strategic Director - Children & Young People, 5th Floor, Saxon House, Heritage Gate, Friary Street, Derby DE1 1AN ☎ 01332 643557 ✉ andrew.bunyan@derby.gov.uk

Senior Management: Ms Cath Roff, Strategic Director - Adults Health & Housing, 5th Floor, Saxon House, Heritage Gate, Friary Street, Derby DE1 1AN ☎ 01332 643550 ✉ cath.roff@derby.gov.uk

Access Officer / Social Services (Disability): Ms Angela Cole, Head of Intervention & Inclusion, Middleton House, 27 St Mary's Gate, Derby DE1 3NS ☎ 01332 256753 ✉ angela.cole@derby.gov.uk

Access Officer / Social Services (Disability): Ms Libby Johnston, Head of Integrated Disabled Childrens Services, The Lighthouse, St Marks Road, Derby DE21 6AL ☎ 01332 256950 ✉ elizabeth.johnston@derby.gov.uk

Access Officer / Social Services (Disability): Ms Cath Roff, Strategic Director - Adults Health & Housing, 5th Floor, Saxon House, Heritage Gate, Friary Street, Derby DE1 1AN ☎ 01332 643550 ✉ cath.roff@derby.gov.uk

Architect, Building / Property Services: Mr Paul Glowacki, Head of Design, Corporate and Adult Services, Roman House, Friars Gate, Derby DE1 1XB ☎ 01332 255032 ✉ paul.glowacki@derby.gov.uk

Best Value: Mr Gordon Stirling, Acting Assistant Director - Policy, Performance & Communication, 5th Floor, Saxon House, Heritage Gate, Friary Street, Derby DE1 1AN ☎ 01332 643430 ✉ gordon.stirling@derby.gov.uk

Building Control: Mr Paul Clarke, Head of Development Management, Roman House, Friar Gate, Derby DE1 1XB ☎ 01332 255942 ✉ paul.clarke@derby.gov.uk

Building Control: Mr Mick Henman, Head of Building Consultancy, Roman House, Friar Gate, Derby DE1 1XB ☎ 01332 255006 ✉ mick.henman@derby.gov.uk

Catering Services: Mrs Sandra Cole, Head of Facilities Management, 839 London Road, Alvaston, Derby DE24 8UZ ☎ 01332 642142 ✉ sandra.cole@derby.gov.uk

Children / Youth Services: Mr Steve Baguley, Head of Service Connexions Locality 1&5 Youth Support, Beaufort Street, Chaddesden, Derby DE21 6AX ☎ 01332 641340 ✉ steve.baguley@derby.gov.uk

Children / Youth Services: Mrs Jacqui Jensen, Director of Early Intervention & Integrated Services, Middleton House, 27 St. Mary's Gate, Derby DE1 3NN ☎ 01332 642668 🖷 01332 716870 ✉ jacqui.jensen@derby.gov.uk

Children / Youth Services: Ms Sally Penrose, Interim Head of Service - Fostering & Adoption, Fostering and Adoption Centre, Perth Street, Derby DE21 6XX ☎ 01332 643817 ✉ sally.penrose@derby.gov.uk

Civil Registration: Mr James Clark, Registration Services Manager, Royal Oak House, Market Place, Derby DE1 3AR ☎ 01332 256527 ✉ james.clark@derby.gov.uk

PR / Communications: Ms Yvonne Wilkinson, Head of Communications, Norman House, Heritage Gate, Friary Street, Derby DE1 1AN ☎ 01332 643501 ✉ yvonne.wilkinson@derby.gov.uk

Community Safety: Mr Tim Clegg, Director for Streetpride and City & Neighbourhood Partnerships, 15 Stores Road, Derby DE21 4BD ☎ 01332 641516 ✉ tim.clegg@derby.gov.uk

Computer Management: Mr Nick O'Reilly, Director of ICT, The Council House, Corporation Street, Derby DE1 2FS ☎ 01332 643254 ✉ nick.oreilly@derby.gov.uk

Consumer Protection and Trading Standards: Mr John Tomlinson, Director of Environmental & Regulatory Services, Environmental Services, Celtic House, Heritage Gate, Friary Street, Derby DE1 1QX ☎ 01332 251507 🖷 01332 716330 ✉ john.tomlinson@derby.gov.uk

Corporate Services: Mr Richard Boneham, Head of Audit & Risk Management, The Council House, Corporation Street, Derby DE1 2FS ☎ 01332 643280 ✉ richard.boneham@derby.gov.uk

Corporate Services: Ms Lynda Innocent, Head of Business Systems, The Council House, Corporation Street, Derby DE1 2FS ☎ 01332 643235 ✉ lynda.innocent@derby.gov.uk

Corporate Services: Mr Rob Salmon, Head of Spatial Planning & Climate Change, Roman House, Friar Gate, Derby DE1 1XB ☎ 01332 255020 ✉ rob.salmon@derby.gov.uk

Customer Service: Mr Bernard Fenton, Head of Customer Services, The Council House, Corporation Street, Derby DE1 2FS ☎ 01332 643758 ✉ bernard.fenton@derby.gov.uk

Customer Service: Mrs Pat Gallimore, Head of Access & Direct Services, Middleton House, 29 St Mary's Gate, Derby DE1 3NS ☎ 01332 717280 ✉ pat.gallimore@derby.gov.uk

Economic Development: Mr Richard Williams, Director of Regeneration, Roman House, Friar Gate, Derby DE1 1XB ☎ 01332 255974 ✉ richard.williams@derby.gov.uk

Education: Mr Andrew Bunyan, Strategic Director - Children &

Young People, 5th Floor, Saxon House, Heritage Gate, Friary Street, Derby DE1 1AN ☎ 01332 643557 ✉ andrew.bunyan@derby.gov.uk

Education: Ms Angela Cole, Head of Intervention & Inclusion, Middleton House, 27 St Mary's Gate, Derby DE1 3NS ☎ 01332 256753 ✉ angela.cole@derby.gov.uk

Education: Mr Gurmail Nizzer, Head of School Place Planning & Organisation, Middleton House, 27 St Mary's Gate, Derby DE1 3NN ☎ 01332 642720 ✉ gurmail.nizzer@derby.gov.uk

Education: Ms Lynda Poole, Service Director - Learning & Inclusion, Middleton House, 27 St Mary's Gate, Derby DE1 3NN ☎ 01332 642665 ✉ lynda.poole@derby.gov.uk

Electoral Registration: Mr Mike Styne, Electoral Service & Land Charges Manager, Roman House, Friar Gate, Derby DE1 1AN ☎ 01332 287280 ✉ mick.styne@derby.gov.uk

Emergency Planning: Mr Rob Ashton, Chief Emergency Planning Officer, Roman House, Friar Gate, Derby DE1 1XB ☎ 01332 641984 ✉ rob.ashton@derby.gov.uk

Energy Management: Mr Richard Murrell, Principal Home Energy Advisor, Roman House, Friar Gate, Derby DE1 1XB ☎ 01332 255971 ✉ richard.murrell@derby.gov.uk

Environmental Health: Mr Michael Kay, Head of Environmental Health & Licensing, Celtic House, Heritage Gate, Friary Street, Derby DE1 1QX ☎ 01332 641940 ✉ michael.kay@derby.gov.uk

Estates, Property & Valuation: Mr Steve Meynell, Head of Estates, 3rd Floor, Norman House, Friar Gate, Derby DE1 1NU ☎ 01332 643337 ✉ steve.meynell@derby.gov.uk

Facilities: Ms Sandra Cole, Head of Facilities Management, 839 London Road, Derby DE24 8UZ ☎ 01332 716440 ✉ sandra.cole@derby.gov.uk

Facilities: Mr Ian Shepherd, Corporate Facilities Manager, Saxon House, Heritage Gate, Friary Street, Derby DE1 1AN ☎ 01332 643338 ✉ ian.shepherd@derby.gov.uk

Finance and Treasurer: Mr Roger Kershaw, Strategic Director of Resources, 4th Floor, Saxon House, Heritage Gate, Friary Street, Derby DE1 2FS ☎ 01332 643552 ✉ roger.kershaw@derby.gov.uk

Finance and Treasurer: Mr Martyn Marples, Director of Finance & Procurement, 3rd Floor, Norman House, Heritage Gate, Friary Street, Derby DE1 3NS ☎ 01332 643377 ✉ martyn.marples@derby.gov.uk

Fleet Management: Mr Richard Kniveton, Fleet & Depot Manager, 15 Stores Road, Derby DE21 4BD ☎ 01332 641514 🖷 01332 716469 ✉ richard.kniveton@derby.gov.uk

Grounds Maintenance: Mr Ian Wheatley, Head of Grounds Maintenance & Cleansing, 15 Stores Road, Derby DE21 4BD ☎ 01332 641530 🖷 01332 641510 ✉ ian.wheatley@derby.gov.uk

Health and Safety: Mr Nigel Parkes-Rolfe, Head of Corporate Health & Safety, Celtic House, Heritage Gate, Friary Street, Derby DE1 1QX ☎ 01332 641935 ✉ nigel.parkes-rolfe@derby.gov.uk

Highways: Mr Dave Bartram, Head of Highways & Engineering, 15 Stores Road, Derby DE21 4BD ☎ 01332 641516 ✉ dave.bartram@derby.gov.uk

Highways: Ms Christine Durrant, Director of Planning & Facilities Management, Roman House, Friar Gate, Derby DE1 1XB ☎ 01332 256004 ✉ christine.durrant@derby.gov.uk

Home Energy Conservation: Mr Richard Murrell, Principal Home Energy Advisor, Roman House, Friar Gate, Derby DE1 1XB ☎ 01332 255971 ✉ richard.murrell@derby.gov.uk

Housing: Mr Phil Davies, Chief Executive of Derby Homes, Floor 2, Southpoint, Cardinal Square, 10 Nottingham Road, Derby DE1 3QT ☎ 01332 711010 🖷 01332 711003 ✉ phil.davies@derby.gov.uk

Legal: Mr Stuart Leslie, Director of Legal & Democratic Services, The Council House, Corporation Street, Derby DE1 2FS ☎ 01332 643616 🖷 01332 255834 ✉ stuart.leslie@derby.gov.uk

Leisure and Cultural Services: Mr Andrew Beddow, Head of Service Facilities, Celtic House, Friar Gate, Derby DE1 1QX ☎ 01332 641230 ✉ andrew.beddow@derby.gov.uk

Leisure and Cultural Services: Dr Peter Meakin, Artistic Producer, Assembly Rooms, Market Place, Derby DE1 3AH ☎ 01332 255806 ✉ peter.meakin@derby.gov.uk

Leisure and Cultural Services: Mr David Potton, Head of Libraries & Museums, Celtic House, Friar Gate, Derby DE1 1QX ☎ 01332 641719 ✉ david.potton@derby.gov.uk

Licensing: Mr John Tomlinson, Director of Environmental & Regulatory Services, Environmental Services, Celtic House, Heritage Gate, Friary Street, Derby DE1 1QX ☎ 01332 251507 🖷 01332 716330 ✉ john.tomlinson@derby.gov.uk

Lifelong Learning: Ms Cath Harcula, Head of Adult Learning, Allen Park Centre, Derby DE24 9DE ☎ 01332 42304 🖷 01332 256717 ✉ cath.harcula@derby.gov.uk

Member Services: Mr Phil O'Brien, Head of Democratic Services, 5th Floor, Saxon House, Heritage Gate, Friary Street, Derby DE1 1AN ☎ 01332 643644 🖷 01332 255500 ✉ phil.o'brien@derby.gov.uk

Parking: Mr Tim Clegg, Director for Streetpride and City & Neighbourhood Partnerships, 15 Stores Road, Derby DE21 4BD ☎ 01332 641516 ✉ tim.clegg@derby.gov.uk

Partnerships: Mr Tim Clegg, Director for Streetpride and City & Neighbourhood Partnerships, 15 Stores Road, Derby DE21 4BD ☎ 01332 641516 ✉ tim.clegg@derby.gov.uk

Personnel / HR: Ms Karen Jewell, Director of HR & Business Support, 3rd Floor, Norman House, Friar Gate, Derby DE1 1NU ☎ 01332 643724 ✉ karen.jewell@derby.gov.uk

Planning: Mr Paul Clarke, Head of Development Management, Roman House, Friar Gate, Derby DE1 1XB ☎ 01332 255942 ✉ paul.clarke@derby.gov.uk

Procurement: Mr Martyn Marples, Director of Finance & Procurement, 3rd Floor, Norman House, Heritage Gate, Friary Street, Derby DE1 3NS ☎ 01332 643377 ✉ martyn.marples@derby.gov.uk

Procurement: Mr Ray Poxon, Head of Procurement, Norman House, Heritage Gate, Friary Street, Derby DE1 1AN ☎ 01332 643271 ✉ ray.poxon@derby.gov.uk

Public Libraries: Mr David Potton, Head of Libraries & Museums, Celtic House, Friar Gate, Derby DE1 1QX ☎ 01332 641719 ✉ david.potton@derby.gov.uk

Public Libraries: Ms Jennie Preedy, Libraries Support Manager, Celtic House, Friar Gate, Derby DE1 1QX ☎ 01332 641723 ✉ jennie.preedy@derby.gov.uk

Recycling & Waste Minimisation: Mr Mick McLachlan, Head of Waste Management, 15 Stores Road, Derby DE21 4BE ☎ 01332 641503 ✉ mick.mclachlan@derby.gov.uk

Regeneration: Mr Richard Williams, Director of Regeneration, Roman House, Friar Gate, Derby DE1 1XB ☎ 01332 255974 ✉ richard.williams@derby.gov.uk

Social Services: Ms Sally Curtis, Acting Assistant Director (Operations), Middleton House, 27 St Mary's Gate, Derby DE1 3NS ☎ 01332 642798 ✉ sally.curtis@derby.gov.uk

Social Services: Ms Cath Roff, Strategic Director - Adults Health & Housing, 5th Floor, Saxon House, Heritage Gate, Friary Street, Derby DE1 1AN ☎ 01332 643550 ✉ cath.roff@derby.gov.uk

Social Services (Adult): Ms Cath Roff, Strategic Director - Adults Health & Housing, 5th Floor, Saxon House, Heritage Gate, Friary Street, Derby DE1 1AN ☎ 01332 643550 ✉ cath.roff@derby.gov.uk

Social Services (Children): Mr Mark Barratt, Service Director - Specialist Services, Fostering and Adoption Centre, Perth Street, Derby DE21 6XX ☎ 01332 642669 ✉ mark.barratt@derby.gov.uk

Social Services (Children): Mr Andrew Bunyan, Strategic Director - Children & Young People, 5th Floor, Saxon House, Heritage Gate, Friary Street, Derby DE1 1AN ☎ 01332 643557 ✉ andrew.bunyan@derby.gov.uk

Social Services (Children): Mrs Jacqui Jensen, Director of Early Intervention & Integrated Services, Middleton House, 27 St. Mary's Gate, Derby DE1 3NN ☎ 01332 642668 🖷 01332 716870 ✉ jacqui.jensen@derby.gov.uk

Tourism: Mr Alan Smith, Head of Economic Regeneration, Roman House, Friar Gate, Derby DE1 1XB ☎ 01332 641624 ✉ alan.smith@derby.gov.uk

Tourism: Mr Richard Williams, Director of Regeneration, Roman House, Friar Gate, Derby DE1 1XB ☎ 01332 255974 ✉ richard.williams@derby.gov.uk

Traffic Management: Mr Tim Clegg, Director for Streetpride and City & Neighbourhood Partnerships, 15 Stores Road, Derby DE21 4BD ☎ 01332 641516 ✉ tim.clegg@derby.gov.uk

Traffic Management: Mr David Gartside, Head of Traffic & Transportation, Roman House, Friar Gate, Derby DE1 1XB ☎ 01332 641821 ✉ david.gartside@derby.gov.uk

Transport: Mr Tony Gascoigne, Sustainable Transport Group Manager, Roman House, Friar Gate, Derby DE1 1XB ☎ 01332 641779 ✉ tony.gascoigne@derby.gov.uk

Waste Management: Mr Mick McLachlan, Head of Waste Management, 15 Stores Road, Derby DE21 4BE ☎ 01332 641503 ✉ mick.mclachlan@derby.gov.uk

MEMBERS OF THE COUNCIL (51)

***Chair:* Hickson**, Philip (CON - Allestree)
philip.hickson@derby.gov.uk

***Mayor:* Allen**, Les (LD - Littleover)
les.allen@derby.gov.uk

***Leader of the Council:* Bayliss**, Paul (LAB - Alvaston)
paul.bayliss@derby.gov.uk

Afzal, Asaf (LAB - Abbey)
asaf.afzal@derby.gov.uk

Ashburner, Eric (LD - Littleover)
eric.ashburner@derby.gov.uk

Atwal, Ajit (LD - Abbey)
ajit.atwal@derby.gov.uk

Bailey, Phil (CON - Chellaston)
phil.bailey@derby.gov.uk

Banwait, Ranjit (LAB - Boulton)
ranjit.banwait@derby.gov.uk

Barker, Mick (CON - Oakwood)
mick.barker@derby.gov.uk

Bolton, Sara (LAB - Chaddesden)
sara.bolton@derby.gov.uk

Campbell, Paul (LAB - Chaddesden)
paul.campbell@derby.gov.uk

Carr, Michael (LD - Littleover)
michael.carr@derby.gov.uk

Davis, Saadia (CON - Allestree)
saadia.davis@derby.gov.uk

Dhindsa, Hardyal (LAB - Normanton)
hardyal.dhindsa@derby.gov.uk

Harwood, Frank (CON - Oakwood)
frank.harwood@derby.gov.uk

Higginbottom, Lisa (LAB - Mackworth)
lisa.higginbottom@derby.gov.uk

Hillier, Karen (LAB - Sinfin)
karen.hillier@derby.gov.uk

Holmes, Matthew (CON - Chellaston)
matthew.holmes@derby.gov.uk

Hussain, Fareed (LAB - Arboretum)
fareed.hussain@derby.gov.uk

Ingall, Philip John (CON - Chellaston)
philip.ingall@derby.gov.uk

Jackson, Barbara (LAB - Boulton)
barbara.jackson@derby.gov.uk

Jennings, Harvey (CON - Spondon)
harvey.jennings@derby.gov.uk

Jones, Hilary (LD - Mickleover)
hilary.jones@derby.gov.uk
Keith, John (CON - Mickleover)
john.keith@derby.gov.uk
Khan, Jangir (LAB - Normanton)
jangir.khan@derby.gov.uk
Khan, Shiraz (LD - Arboretum)
shiraz.khan@derby.gov.uk
MacDonald, Anne (LAB - Chaddesden)
anne.macdonald@derby.gov.uk
Martin, Alison (LAB - Boulton)
alison.martin@derby.gov.uk
Naitta, Joe (LD - Blagreaves)
joe.naitta@derby.gov.uk
Nawaz, Gulfraz (LAB - Arboretum)
gulfraz.nawaz@derby.gov.uk
Pegg, Paul (LAB - Mackworth)
paul.pegg@derby.gov.uk
Poulter, Christopher Paul (CON - Spondon)
christopher.poulter@derby.gov.uk
Radford, Lorraine (CON - Darley)
lorraine.radford@derby.gov.uk
Rawson, Martin (LAB - Derwent)
martin.rawson@derby.gov.uk
Redfern, Margaret (LAB - Derwent)
margaret.redfern@derby.gov.uk
Repton, Martin (LAB - Darley)
martin.repton@derby.gov.uk
Roberts, David (LAB - Derwent)
dave.roberts@derby.gov.uk
Russell, Sarah (LAB - Abbey)
sarah.russell@derby.gov.uk
Sandhu, Balbir (LAB - Normanton)
balbir.sandhu@derby.gov.uk
Shanker, Baggy (LAB - Sinfin)
baggy.shankar@derby.gov.uk
Skelton, Ruth (LD - Blagreaves)
ruth.skelton@derby.gov.uk
Stanton, Jack (LAB - Darley)
jack.stanton@derby.gov.uk
Tittley, Mark (LAB - Alvaston)
mark.titley@derby.gov.uk
Troup, Robert (LD - Blagreaves)
robert.troup@derby.gov.uk
Turner, Robin (LAB - Sinfin)
robin.turner@derby.gov.uk
Webb, Roy (CON - Allestree)
roy.webb@derby.gov.uk
Whitby, John (LAB - Mackworth)
john.whitby@derby.gov.uk
Williams, Evonne (CON - Spondon)
evonne.williams@derby.gov.uk
Winter, Fay (LD - Mickleover)
fay.winter@derby.gov.uk
Winter, Linda (LAB - Alvaston)
linda.winter@derby.gov.uk
Wood, Robin (CON - Oakwood)
robin.wood@derby.gov.uk

POLITICAL COMPOSITION

LAB: 27, CON: 14, LD: 10

CABINET

Leader: Mr Paul Bayliss
Adults & Health: Mr Fareed Hussain
Business, Finance & Democracy: Ms Sarah Russell
Children & Young People: Mr Martin Repton
Housing & Advice: Mr Baggy Shanker
Leisure & Culture: Mr Martin Rawson
Neighbourhoods & Streetpride: Mr Ranjit Banwait
Planning, Environment & Public Protection: Mr Hardyal Dhindsa

COMMITTEE CHAIRS

Adults & Public Health Overview & Scrutiny: Ms Karen Hillier
Audit & Accounts: Mr David Roberts
Children & Young People: Mr John Whitby
Corporate Scrutiny & Climate Change Overview & Scrutiny: Mr Mark Tittley
Governance: Mr Philip Hickson
Neighbourhood Overview & Scrutiny: Mr Asaf Afzal
Planning Control: Ms Sara Bolton
Planning, Housing & Leisure Overview & Scrutiny: Ms Margaret Redfern
Resources & Governance Overview & Scrutiny: Ms Linda Winter

DERBYSHIRE — C

Derbyshire County Council, County Hall, Matlock DE4 3AG
☎ 01629 580000 🖷 01629 585280 💻 www.derbyshire.gov.uk

FACTS & FIGURES

Police Authority: Derbyshire Police Authority
Health Authority: East Midlands Strategic Health Authority
Learning and Skills Council: East Midlands
EU Constituencies: East Midlands
Election Frequency: Elections are of whole council
Twinning: China- links with Yangpu district in Shanghai; South Africa- links with Mamelodi in the Tshwane Province

PRINCIPAL OFFICERS

Chief Executive: Mr Nick Hodgson, Chief Executive, County Hall, Matlock DE4 3AG ☎ 01629 538300 🖷 01629 538398 ✉ nick.hodgson@derbyshire.gov.uk

Senior Management: Mr Ian Stephenson, Strategic Director - Environmental Services, County Hall, Matlock DE4 3AG ☎ 01629 538100 🖷 01629 538698 ✉ ian.stephenson@derbyshire.gov.uk

Architect, Building / Property Services: Mr David Beard, Design Manager, Chatsworth Hall, Chesterfield Road, Matlock DE4 3FW ☎ 01629 536337 🖷 01629 536266 ✉ david.beard@derbyshire.gov.uk

Architect, Building / Property Services: Mrs Sarah Morris, Assistant Director - Property (Design), Corporate Resources Department, Chatsworth Hall, Chesterfield Road, Matlock DE4 3FW ☎ 01629 536260 🖷 01629 536266 ✉ sarah.morris@derbyshire.gov.uk

Best Value: Mr Richard Corker, Head of Service - Quality Assurance, County Hall, Matlock DE4 3AG ☎ 01629 532022 ✉ richard.corker@derbyshire.gov.uk

Best Value: Mrs Jane Cox, Policy Manager - Performance,

County Hall, Matlock DE4 3AG ☎ 01629 538267 ✉ jane.cox@derbyshire.gov.uk

Best Value: Mrs Ester Croll, Policy Manager - Performance, County Hall, Matlock DE4 3AG ☎ 01629 538267 ✉ ester.croll@derbyshire.gov.uk

Building Control: Mr David Humphrey, Head of Development, Chatsworth Hall, Chesterfield Road, Matlock DE4 3FW ☎ 01629 535766 🖷 01629 536435 ✉ david.humphrey@derbyshire.gov.uk

Catering Services: Ms Sheila Murdoch, Catering & Domestic Services Manager, County Hall, Matlock DE4 3AG ☎ 01629 532183 ✉ sheila.murdoch@derbyshire.gov.uk

Children / Youth Services: Mr Jim Hickman, Assistant Director - Schools & Learning, County Hall, Matlock DE4 3AG ☎ 01629 532750 🖷 01629 580350 ✉ jim.hickman@derbyshire.gov.uk

Children / Youth Services: Mr Ian Johnson, Deputy Strategic Director - Children & Younger Adults, County Hall, Matlock DE4 3AG ☎ 01629 532005 🖷 01629 580350 ✉ ian.johnson@derbyshire.gov.uk

Children / Youth Services: Ms Melanie Meggs, Assistant Director - Universal & Targeted Services, County Hall, Matlock DE4 3AG ☎ 01629 532016 🖷 01629 580350 ✉ melanie.meggs@derbyshire.gov.uk

Children / Youth Services: Ms Sally Savage, Assistant Director - Commissioning & Performance Management, County Hall, Matlock DE4 3AG ☎ 01629 532211 🖷 01629 580350 ✉ sally.savage@derbyshire.gov.uk

Children / Youth Services: Mr Ian Thomas, Strategic Director - Children & Younger Adults, County Hall, Matlock DE4 3AG ☎ 01629 532062 🖷 01629 580350 ✉ ian.thomas@derbyshire.gov.uk

PR / Communications: Mr Rod Cook, Director - Communication & Access to Services, County Hall, Matlock DE4 3AG ☎ 01629 538200 🖷 01629 538209 ✉ rod.cook@derbyshire.gov.uk

PR / Communications: Mrs Jenny Tozer, Assistant Director - Communications, County Hall, Matlock DE4 3AG ☎ 01629 538203 🖷 01629 538209 ✉ jenny.tozer@derbyshire.gov.uk

Community Planning: Mrs Jude Wildgoose, Policy Manager, County Hall, Matlock DE4 3AG ☎ 01629 538439 ✉ jude.wildgoose@derbyshire.gov.uk

Community Safety: Mr David Lowe, Strategic Director - Policy & Community Safety, County Hall, Matlock DE4 3AG ☎ 01629 538340 ✉ david.lowe@derbyshire.gov.uk

Computer Management: Mr Bob Busby, Core Systems Programme Manager, County Hall, Matlock DE4 3AG ☎ 01629 536806 ✉ bob.busby@derbyshire.gov.uk

Consumer Protection and Trading Standards: Mr Rob Taylour, Assistant Director - Cultural & Community Services & Head of Trading Standards, County Hall, Matlock DE4 3AG ☎ 01629 539830 🖷 01629 536522 ✉ rob.taylour@derbyshire.gov.uk

Contracts: Mr Steve Gerrard, Deputy Director - Property, Corporate Resources Department, Chatsworth Hall, Chesterfield Road, Matlock DE4 3FW ☎ 01629 536204 🖷 01629 536266 ✉ steve.gerrard@derbyshire.gov.uk

Corporate Services: Mr Peter Handford, Director - Finance, County Hall, Matlock DE4 3AG ☎ 01629 538700 ✉ peter.handford@derbyshire.gov.uk

Direct Labour: Mr Steve Gerrard, Deputy Director - Property, Chatsworth Hall, Chesterfield Road, Matlock DE4 3FW ☎ 01629 536204 🖷 01629 536266 ✉ steve.gerrard@derbyshire.gov.uk

Economic Development: Mr Frank Horsley, Head of Economic Regeneration, County Hall, Matlock DE4 3AG ☎ 01629 538348 🖷 01629 538368 ✉ frank.horsley@derbyshire.gov.uk

E-Government: Mr David Hickman, Director - Transformation, County Hall, Matlock DE4 3AG ☎ 01629 535801 🖷 01629 772009 ✉ david.hickman@derbyshire.gov.uk

Emergency Planning: Mr Ian Shuttleworth, Chief Emergency Planning Officer, County Hall, Matlock DE4 3AG ☎ 01629 538360 🖷 01629 585358 ✉ ian.shuttleworth@derbyshire.gov.uk

Energy Management: Mr Alan Dawson, Group Manager M & E Operations, Corporate Resources Department, Chatsworth Hall, Chesterfield Road, Matlock DE4 3FW ☎ 01629 539985 🖷 01629 536266 ✉ alan.dawson@derbyshire.gov.uk

Environmental / Technical Services: Mr Ian Stephenson, Strategic Director - Environmental Services, County Hall, Matlock DE4 3AG ☎ 01629 538100 🖷 01629 538698 ✉ ian.stephenson@derbyshire.gov.uk

Estates, Property & Valuation: Mr Steve Dolby, Group Manager - Estates, Chatsworth Hall, Chesterfield Road, Matlock DE4 3FW ☎ 01629 536333 🖷 01629 536266 ✉ steve.dolby@derbyshire.gov.uk

Estates, Property & Valuation: Mr Peter Hirst, Group Manager - Estates, Chatsworth Hall, Chesterfield Road, Matlock DE4 3FW ☎ 01629 536322 🖷 01629 536266 ✉ peter.hirst@derbyshire.gov.uk

European Liaison: Mr Frank Horsley, Head of Economic Regeneration, County Hall, Matlock DE4 3AG ☎ 01629 538348 🖷 01629 538368 ✉ frank.horsley@derbyshire.gov.uk

Events Manager: Miss Stephanie Walsh, Economic Development Officer, County Hall, Matlock DE4 3AG ☎ 01629 538464 🖷 01629 538368 ✉ stephanie.walsh@derbyshire.gov.uk

Facilities: Mr Stewart Ibbotson, Assistant Director - Consultancy & Contracting, Station Road, Darley Dale, Matlock DE4 2EQ ☎ 01629 535400 🖷 01629 535469 ✉ stewart.ibbotson@derbyshire.gov.uk

Finance and Treasurer: Mr Peter Handford, Director - Finance, County Hall, Matlock DE4 3AG ☎ 01629 538700

peter.handford@derbyshire.gov.uk

Fleet Management: Mr Brian Hattersley, Principal Engineer, County Transport, Fleet Management, Ripley Road, Ambergate, Derby DE4 2ER ☎ 01629 532110 🖷 01773 856535 brian.hattersley@derbyshire.gov.uk

Grounds Maintenance: Mr Steve Gerrard, Deputy Director - Property, Corporate Resources Department, Chatsworth Hall, Chesterfield Road, Matlock DE4 3FW ☎ 01629 536204 🖷 01629 536266 steve.gerrard@derbyshire.gov.uk

Health and Safety: Mr John Davis, Corporate Health & Safety Advisor, County Hall, Matlock DE4 3AG ☎ 01629 536950 john.davis@derbyshire.gov.uk

Highways: Mr Mike Ashworth, Deputy Director - Environmental Services, County Hall, Matlock DE4 3AG ☎ 01629 538544 🖷 01629 538698 mike.ashworth@derbyshire.gov.uk

Legal: Mr John McEivaney, Director - Legal Services, County Hall, Matlock DE4 3AG ☎ 01629 580000 john.mcelvaney@derbyshire.gov.uk

Leisure and Cultural Services: Mr Martin Molloy, Strategic Director - Cultural & Community Services, County Hall, Matlock DE4 3AG ☎ 01629 536500 🖷 ; 01629 536522 martin.malloy@derbyshire.gov.uk

Licensing: Mr Rob Taylour, Assistant Director - Cultural & Community Services & Head of Trading Standards, County Hall, Matlock DE4 3AG ☎ 01629 539830 🖷 01629 536522 rob.taylour@derbyshire.gov.uk

Lighting: Mr Stewart Ibbotson, Assistant Director - Consultancy & Contracting, Station Road, Darley Dale, Matlock DE4 2EQ ☎ 01629 535400 🖷 01629 535469 stewart.ibbotson@derbyshire.gov.uk

Lottery Funding, Charity and Voluntary: Ms Sarah Eaton, Head of Policy & Research, County Hall, Matlock DE4 3AG ☎ 01629 538268 sarah.eaton@derbyshire.gov.uk

Partnerships: Mr Nick Hodgson, Chief Executive, County Hall, Matlock DE4 3AG ☎ 01629 538300 🖷 01629 538398 nick.hodgson@derbyshire.gov.uk

Personnel / HR: Mr Toni Compai, Director of HR, County Hall, Matlock DE4 3AG ☎ 01629 536927 🖷 01629 536937 toni.compai@derbyshire.gov.uk

Planning: Mrs Allison Thomas, Assistant Director - Planning & Environment (Including Waste), Stand House, Dale Road South, Matlock DE4 3RY ☎ 01629 533300 🖷 01629 533308 allison.thomas@derbyshire.gov.uk

Procurement: Mr Andrew Ayling, County Procurement Officer, Chatsworth Hall, Chesterfield Road, Matlock DE4 3FW ☎ 01629 536804 🖷 ; 01629 536866 andrew.ayling@derbyshire.gov.uk

Public Libraries: Mr Don Gibbs, Assistant Director - Libraries & Heritage, County Hall, Matlock DE4 3AG ☎ 01629 536572 🖷 01629 536522 don.gibbs@derbyshire.gov.uk

Recycling & Waste Minimisation: Ms Claire Brailsford, Head of Waste Management, County Hall, Matlock DE4 3AG ☎ 01629 539775 🖷 01629 533308 claire.brailsford@derbyshire.gov.uk

Regeneration: Mr Frank Horsley, Head of Economic Regeneration, County Hall, Matlock DE4 3AG ☎ 01629 538348 🖷 01629 538368 frank.horsley@derbyshire.gov.uk

Road Safety: Mr Mike Ashworth, Deputy Director - Environmental Services, County Hall, Matlock DE4 3AG ☎ 01629 538544 🖷 01629 538698 mike.ashworth@derbyshire.gov.uk

Social Services (Adult): Mr Kieran Hickey, Assistant Director - Direct Care Services, County Hall, Matlock DE4 3AG ☎ 01629 532001 🖷 01629 581922 kieran.hickey@derbyshire.gov.uk

Social Services (Adult): Mr James Matthews, Assistant Director - Strategy & Commissioning, County Hall, Matlock DE4 3AG ☎ 01629 532004 🖷 01629 581922 james.matthews@derbyshire.gov.uk

Social Services (Adult): Ms Mary McElvaney, Assistant Director - Field Work Services - Sth, County Hall, Matlock DE4 3AG ☎ 01629 532002 🖷 01629 581922 mary.mcelvaney@derbyshire.gov.uk

Social Services (Adult): Mr Andrew Milroy, Assistant Director - Field Work Services - Nth, County Hall, Matlock DE4 3AG ☎ 01629 532177 🖷 01629 581922 andrew.milroy@derbyshire.gov.uk

Social Services (Adult): Mr Bill Robertston, Strategic Director - Adult Care, County Hall, Matlock DE4 3AG ☎ 01629 532432 🖷 01629 581922 bill.robertson@derbyshire.gov.uk

Staff Training: Mr Toni Compai, Director of HR, County Hall, Matlock DE4 3AG ☎ 01629 536927 🖷 01629 536937 toni.compai@derbyshire.gov.uk

Sustainable Communities: Mr Ian Stephenson, Strategic Director - Environmental Services, County Hall, Matlock DE4 3AG ☎ 01629 538100 🖷 01629 538698 ian.stephenson@derbyshire.gov.uk

Tourism: Miss Stephanie Walsh, Economic Development Officer, County Hall, Matlock DE4 3AG ☎ 01629 538464 🖷 01629 538368 stephanie.walsh@derbyshire.gov.uk

Traffic Management: Mr Mike Ashworth, Deputy Director - Environmental Services, County Hall, Matlock DE4 3AG ☎ 01629 538544 🖷 01629 538698 mike.ashworth@derbyshire.gov.uk

Transport: Mr Brian Hattersley, Principal Engineer, County Transport, Fleet Management, Ripley Road, Ambergate, Derby DE4 2ER ☎ 01629 532110 🖷 01773 856535 brian.hattersley@derbyshire.gov.uk

Waste Collection and Disposal: Ms Claire Brailsford, Head of Waste Management, County Hall, Matlock DE4 3AG ☎ 01629 539775 🖷 01629 533308 claire.brailsford@derbyshire.gov.uk

Waste Management: Ms Claire Brailsford, Head of Waste Management, County Hall, Matlock DE4 3AG ☎ 01629 539775 🖷 01629 533308 ✉ claire.brailsford@derbyshire.gov.uk

MEMBERS OF THE COUNCIL (64)

***Chair:* Wharmby**, George (CON - Glossop North & Rural)
george.wharmby@derbyshire.gov.uk

***Leader of the Council:* Lewer**, Andrew (CON - Ashbourne)
andrew.lewer@derbyshire.gov.uk

***Group Leader:* Western**, Anne (LAB - Barlborough & Clowne)
anne.western@derbyshire.gov.uk

Allen, David (LAB - Birdholme)
dave.allen@derbyshire.gov.uk

Allsop, John (CON - Dronfield North)
john.allsop@derbyshire.gov.uk

Allsop, Susan (CON - Dronfield South)
susan.allsop@derbyshire.gov.uk

Atkins, Elizabeth (LD - New Mills)
beth.atkins@derbyshire.gov.uk

Baldry, Robin (IND - Buxton West)
robin.baldry@derbyshire.gov.uk

Birkin, Glennice (LAB - Ilkeston)
glennice.birkin@derbyshire.gov.uk

Blank, Sharon (LAB - Spire)
sharon.blank@derbyshire.gov.uk

Booth, Michelle (LAB - Kirk Hallam)
michelle.booth@derbyshire.gov.uk

Bowley, David (CON - Ripley)
david.bowley@derbyshire.gov.uk

Bradford, Stuart (CON - Duffield & Belper South)
stuart.bradford@derbyshire.gov.uk

Burrows, Walter (LAB - Brimington)
walter.burrows@derbyshire.gov.uk

Chapman, David (LAB - Sutton)
david.chapman@derbyshire.gov.uk

Charles, Alan (LAB - Killamarsh)
alan.charles@derbyshire.gov.uk

Cox, Celia (LAB - Heanor Central)
celia.cox@derbyshire.gov.uk

Coyle, Jim (LAB - Pinxton & South Normanton West)
jim.coyle@derbyshire.gov.uk

Critchlow, Tracy (CON - Chapel & Hope Valley)
tracy.critchlow@derbyshire.gov.uk

Dixon, Joan (LAB - Bolsover South West & Scarcliffe)
joan.dixon@derbyshire.gov.uk

Ellis, Stuart (CON - Holymoorside & Wingerworth)
stuart.ellis@derbyshire.gov.uk

Farrington, Gillian (CON - Swadlincote Central & Woodville)
gill.farrington@derbyshire.gov.uk

Flitter, Steve (LD - Matlock)
steve.flitter@derbyshire.gov.uk

Ford, Martyn (CON - Repton & Willington)
martyn.ford@derbyshire.gov.uk

Gillott, Kevin (LAB - North Wingfield & Tupton)
kevin.gillott@derbyshire.gov.uk

Harrison, John (CON - Aston & Melbourne)
john.harrison@derbyshire.gov.uk

Hart, Carol (CON - Breadsall & West Hallam)
carol.hart@derbyshire.gov.uk

Hickton, Garry (CON - Petersham)
garry.hickton@derbyshire.gov.uk

Higginbottom, Mark (LD - St Marys)
mark.higginbottom@derbyshire.gov.uk

Hosker, Roland (LAB - Long Eaton)
roland.hosker@derbyshire.gov.uk

Jackson, Christopher (CON - Alport & Derwent)
chris.jackson@derbyshire.gov.uk

Jones, Charles (CON - Linton & Church Gresley)
charles.jones@derbyshire.gov.uk

Lacey, Mike (CON - Newhall & Seales)
mike.lacey@derbyshire.gov.uk

Lewis, Barry (CON - Stonebroom & Pilsey)
barry.lewis@derbyshire.gov.uk

Longden, Mike (CON - Derwent Valley)
michael.longden@derbyshire.gov.uk

Lucas, Brian (LAB - Cotmanhay)
brian.lucas@derbyshire.gov.uk

MacDonald, Gregory (CON - Horsley)
greg.macdonald@derbyshire.gov.uk

Major, Wayne (CON - Sandiacre)
wayne.major@derbyshire.gov.uk

Makin, Peter (CON - Belper)
peter.makin@derbyshire.gov.uk

Moesby, Clive (LAB - South Normanton East & Tibshelf)
clive.moesby@derbyshire.gov.uk

Morgan, Keith (LD - Hipper)
keith.morgan@derbyshire.gov.uk

Murray, Pat (CON - Midway & Hartshorn)
pat.murray@derbyshire.gov.uk

Parkinson, Kevin (CON - Greater Heanor)
kevin.parkinson@derbyshire.gov.uk

Parkinson, Robert (CON - Breaston)
robert.parkinson@derbyshire.gov.uk

Patten, Julie (CON - Hatton & Hilton)
julie.patten@derbyshire.gov.uk

Pidgeon, Cheryl (LAB - Sawley)
cheryl.pidgeon@derbyshire.gov.uk

Purdy, Garry (CON - Wirksworth)
garry.purdy@derbyshire.gov.uk

Reddy, Pam (CON - Buxton North & East)
pam.reddy@derbyshire.gov.uk

Ridgway, Brian (LAB - Eckington)
brian.ridgway@derbyshire.gov.uk

Riggott, Peter (LAB - Clay Cross)
peter.riggott@derbyshire.gov.uk

Rogers, Tony (LD - Newbold)
tony.rogers@derbyshire.gov.uk

Russell, Ray (LD - Ashgate)
ray.russell@derbyshire.gov.uk

Smith, Paul (LAB - Somercotes)
paul.smith@derbyshire.gov.uk

Spencer, Simon (CON - Dovedale)
simon.spencer@derbyshire.gov.uk

Stevens, Juliette (CON - Heage)
juliette.stevens@derbyshire.gov.uk

Stevenson, Kenneth (LAB - Bolsover North West, Elmton & Whitwell)
ken.stevenson@derbyshire.gov.uk

Stockdale, Marion (LAB - Shirebrook & Pleasley)
marian.stockdale@derbyshire.gov.uk

Stone, David (IND - Staveley North & Whittington)
david.stone@derbyshire.gov.uk

Taylor, Barrie (LD - Whaley Bridge & Blackbrook)
barrie.taylor@derbyshire.gov.uk

Twigg, Judith (CON - Bakewell)
judith.twigg@derbyshire.gov.uk

Wharmby, Jean (CON - Glossop South)
jean.wharmby@derbyshire.gov.uk

Wilcox, Dave (LAB - Etherow)
dave.wilcox@derbyshire.gov.uk

Williams, John (LAB - Staveley South)
john.williams@derbyshire.gov.uk
Wilson, David (CON - Alfreton)
david.wilson@derbyshire.gov.uk

POLITICAL COMPOSITION
CON: 32, LAB: 23, LD: 7, IND: 2

CABINET
Leader/ Culture: Mr Andrew Lewer
Adult Care: Mr Charles Jones
Education: Mr Mike Longden
Finance & Management: Mr John Harrison
Highways & Transport: Mr Simon Spencer
Public Health: Ms Carol Hart
Recycling & Technology: Mr John Allsop
Regeneration: Mr Kevin Parkinson
Young People: Mr Barry Lewis

COMMITTEE CHAIRS
Audit: Mr Stuart Bradford
Pensions: Mr Peter Makin
Places Improvement & Scrutiny: Mrs Judith Twigg
Regulatory Planning: Mr Martyn Ford
Regulatory, Licensing & Appeals: Mr Robert Parkinson
Resources Improvement & Scrutiny: Ms Pat Murray

DERBYSHIRE DALES D

Derbyshire Dales District Council, Town Hall, Matlock DE4 3NN ☎ 01629 761100 🖷 01629 761148 💻 www.derbyshiredales.gov.uk

FACTS & FIGURES
Police Authority: Derbyshire Police Authority
Health Authority: East Midlands Strategic Health Authority
Learning and Skills Council: East Midlands
Parliamentary Constituencies: Derbyshire Dales, High Peak
EU Constituencies: East Midlands
Election Frequency: Elections are of whole council
Twinning: Vogelsbergkreis (Germany)

PRINCIPAL OFFICERS
Chief Executive: Mrs Dorcas Bunton, Chief Executive, Town Hall, Matlock DE4 3NN ☎ 01629 761126 🖷 01629 761149 ✉ dorcas.bunton@derbyshiredales.gov.uk

Senior Management: Mr Peter Foley, Director of Community Services, Town Hall, Matlock DE4 3NN ☎ 01629 761370 🖷 01629 761165 ✉ peter.foley@derbyshiredales.gov.uk

Senior Management: Mr Paul Wilson, Director of Planning & Housing Services, Town Hall, Matlock DE4 3NN ☎ 01629 761325 🖷 01629 761163 ✉ paul.wilson@derbyshiredales.gov.uk

Architect, Building / Property Services: Mr Paul Wilson, Director of Planning & Housing Services, Town Hall, Matlock DE4 3NN ☎ 01629 761325 🖷 01629 761163 ✉ paul.wilson@derbyshiredales.gov.uk

Best Value: Dr Steve Capes, Head of Regeneration & Organisational Development, Town Hall, Matlock DE4 3NN ☎ 01629 761371 🖷 01629 761165 ✉ steve.capes@derbyshiredales.gov.uk

Building Control: Mr David Harris, Building Control Manager, Town Hall, Matlock DE4 3NN ☎ 01629 761320 🖷 01629761163 ✉ david.harris@derbyshiredales.gov.uk

PR / Communications: Mr Jim Fearn, Communications & Marketing Manager, Town Hall, Matlock DE4 3NN ☎ 01629 761195 🖷 01629 761165 ✉ jim.fearn@derbyshiredales.gov.uk

Community Planning: Mr Giles Dann, Policy & Economic Development Manager, Town Hall, Matlock DE4 3NN ☎ 01629 761211 🖷 01629 761165 ✉ giles.dann@derbyshiredales.gov.uk

Community Safety: Dr Steve Capes, Head of Regeneration & Organisational Development, Town Hall, Matlock DE4 3NN ☎ 01629 761371 🖷 01629 761165 ✉ steve.capes@derbyshiredales.gov.uk

Computer Management: Mr Nick Blaney, Joint IT Services Manager, Town Hall, Matlock DE4 3NN ☎ 01246 217103; 01246 717097 🖷 01246 242423 ✉ nick.blaney@ne-derbyshire.gov.uk

Contracts: Mr Peter Foley, Director of Community Services, Town Hall, Matlock DE4 3NN ☎ 01629 761370 🖷 01629 761165 ✉ peter.foley@derbyshiredales.gov.uk

Customer Service: Ms Sandra Lamb, Head of Democratic Services, Town Hall, Matlock DE4 3NN ☎ 01629 761281 🖷 01629 761307 ✉ sandra.lamb@derbyshiredales.gov.uk

Economic Development: Mr Giles Dann, Policy & Economic Development Manager, Town Hall, Matlock DE4 3NN ☎ 01629 761211 🖷 01629 761165 ✉ giles.dann@derbyshiredales.gov.uk

E-Government: Mr Nick Blaney, Joint IT Services Manager, Town Hall, Matlock DE4 3NN ☎ 01246 717097 ✉ nick.blaney@ne-derbyshire.gov.uk

Electoral Registration: Mrs Dorcas Bunton, Chief Executive, Town Hall, Matlock DE4 3NN ☎ 01629 761126 🖷 01629 761149 ✉ dorcas.bunton@derbyshiredales.gov.uk

Emergency Planning: Mrs Dorcas Bunton, Chief Executive, Town Hall, Matlock DE4 3NN ☎ 01629 761126 🖷 01629 761149 ✉ dorcas.bunton@derbyshiredales.gov.uk

Energy Management: Mr Mike Galsworthy, Estates Manager, Town Hall, Matlock DE4 3NN ☎ 01629 761362 🖷 01629 761146 ✉ mike.galsworthy@derbyshiredales.gov.uk

Environmental / Technical Services: Mr Peter Foley, Director of Community Services, Town Hall, Matlock DE4 3NN ☎ 01629 761370 🖷 01629 761165 ✉ peter.foley@derbyshiredales.gov.uk

Environmental / Technical Services: Mrs Heidi McDougall, Head of Environmental Services, Town Hall, Matlock DE4 3NN ☎ 01629 761372 ✉ heidi.mcdougall@derbyshiredales.gov.uk

Environmental Health: Mr Peter Foley, Director of Community Services, Town Hall, Matlock DE4 3NN ☎ 01629 761370 🖷 01629 761165 ✉ peter.foley@derbyshiredales.gov.uk

Estates, Property & Valuation: Mr Mike Galsworthy, Estates Manager, Town Hall, Matlock DE4 3NN ☎ 01629 761362 🖷 01629 761146 ✉ mike.galsworthy@derbyshiredales.gov.uk

Events Manager: Ms Nicola Wildgoose, Events Manager, Town Hall, Matlock DE4 3NN ☎ 01629 761390 ✉ nicola.wildgoose@derbyshiredales.gov.uk

Finance and Treasurer: Mr Philip Colledge, Head of Finance, Town Hall, Matlock DE4 3NN ☎ 01629 761203 🖷 01629 761148 ✉ philip.colledge@derbyshiredales.gov.uk

Fleet Management: Mr Mark Kiddier, Street Scene & Works Transport Manager, Town Hall, Matlock DE4 3NN ☎ 01629 735497 🖷 01629 761165 ✉ mark.kiddier@derbyshiredales.gov.uk

Grounds Maintenance: Mr Peter Foley, Director of Community Services, Town Hall, Matlock DE4 3NN ☎ 01629 761370 🖷 01629 761165 ✉ peter.foley@derbyshiredales.gov.uk

Health and Safety: Mr Peter Foley, Director of Community Services, Town Hall, Matlock DE4 3NN ☎ 01629 761370 🖷 01629 761165 ✉ peter.foley@derbyshiredales.gov.uk

Health and Safety: Mr Robin Walsh, Health & Safety Officer, Town Hall, Matlock DE4 3NN ☎ 01629 761151 ✉ robin.walsh@derbyshiredales.gov.uk

Home Energy Conservation: Mr Peter Foley, Director of Community Services, Town Hall, Matlock DE4 3NN ☎ 01629 761370 🖷 01629 761165 ✉ peter.foley@derbyshiredales.gov.uk

Housing: Mr Paul Wilson, Director of Planning & Housing Services, Town Hall, Matlock DE4 3NN ☎ 01629 761325 🖷 01629 761163 ✉ paul.wilson@derbyshiredales.gov.uk

Legal: Mr Philip Horsfield, Solicitor, Town Hall, Matlock DE4 3NN ☎ 01629 761319 🖷 01629 761307 ✉ philip.horsfield@derbyshiredales.gov.uk

Leisure and Cultural Services: Mr Peter Foley, Director of Community Services, Town Hall, Matlock DE4 3NN ☎ 01629 761370 🖷 01629 761165 ✉ peter.foley@derbyshiredales.gov.uk

Leisure and Cultural Services: Mr Les Warren, Leisure Officer, Town Hall, Matlock DE4 3NN ☎ 01629 761382 🖷 01629 761165 ✉ les.warren@derbyshiredales.gov.uk

Licensing: Mr Peter Foley, Director of Community Services, Town Hall, Matlock DE4 3NN ☎ 01629 761370 🖷 01629 761165 ✉ peter.foley@derbyshiredales.gov.uk

Lottery Funding, Charity and Voluntary: Ms Sandra Lamb, Head of Democratic Services, Town Hall, Matlock DE4 3NN ☎ 01629 761281 🖷 01629 761307 ✉ sandra.lamb@derbyshiredales.gov.uk

Member Services: Ms Sandra Lamb, Head of Democratic Services, Town Hall, Matlock DE4 3NN ☎ 01629 761281 🖷 01629 761307 ✉ sandra.lamb@derbyshiredales.gov.uk

Parking: Mr Peter Foley, Director of Community Services, Town Hall, Matlock DE4 3NN ☎ 01629 761370 🖷 01629 761165 ✉ peter.foley@derbyshiredales.gov.uk

Partnerships: Dr Steve Capes, Head of Regeneration & Organisational Development, Town Hall, Matlock DE4 3NN ☎ 01629 761371 🖷 01629 761165 ✉ steve.capes@derbyshiredales.gov.uk

Personnel / HR: Ms Liz Aris, Personnel Assistant, Town Hall, Matlock DE4 3NN ☎ 01629 761155 🖷 01629 761167 ✉ liz.aris@derbyshiredales.gov.uk

Personnel / HR: Mr John Hopkinson, Personnel & Management Services Officer, Town Hall, Matlock DE4 3NN ☎ 01629 761364 🖷 01629 761165 ✉ john.hopkinson@derbyshiredales.gov.uk

Planning: Mr Paul Wilson, Director of Planning & Housing Services, Town Hall, Matlock DE4 3NN ☎ 01629 761325 🖷 01629 761163 ✉ paul.wilson@derbyshiredales.gov.uk

Recycling & Waste Minimisation: Mr Peter Foley, Director of Community Services, Town Hall, Matlock DE4 3NN ☎ 01629 761370 🖷 01629 761165 ✉ peter.foley@derbyshiredales.gov.uk

Recycling & Waste Minimisation: Mr Keith Hollinshead, Waste Management & Recycling Officer, Town Hall, Matlock DE4 3NN ☎ 01629 761112 🖷 01629 761165 ✉ keith.hollinshead@derbyshiredales.gov.uk

Regeneration: Dr Steve Capes, Head of Regeneration & Organisational Development, Town Hall, Matlock DE4 3NN ☎ 01629 761371 🖷 01629 761165 ✉ steve.capes@derbyshiredales.gov.uk

Staff Training: Mr John Hopkinson, Personnel & Management Services Officer, Town Hall, Matlock DE4 3NN ☎ 01629 761364 🖷 01629 761165 ✉ john.hopkinson@derbyshiredales.gov.uk

Street Scene: Mr Peter Foley, Director of Community Services, Town Hall, Matlock DE4 3NN ☎ 01629 761370 🖷 01629 761165 ✉ peter.foley@derbyshiredales.gov.uk

Street Scene: Mrs Heidi McDougall, Head of Environmental Services, Town Hall, Matlock DE4 3NN ☎ 01629 761372 ✉ heidi.mcdougall@derbyshiredales.gov.uk

Street Scene: Mr Paul Wilson, Director of Planning & Housing Services, Town Hall, Matlock DE4 3NN ☎ 01629 761325 🖷 01629 761163 ✉ paul.wilson@derbyshiredales.gov.uk

Sustainable Communities: Mr Paul Wilson, Director of Planning & Housing Services, Town Hall, Matlock DE4 3NN ☎ 01629 761325 🖷 01629 761163 ✉ paul.wilson@derbyshiredales.gov.uk

Sustainable Development: Mrs Dorcas Bunton, Chief Executive, Town Hall, Matlock DE4 3NN ☎ 01629 761126 🖷 01629 761149 ✉ dorcas.bunton@derbyshiredales.gov.uk

Tourism: Ms Gill Chapman, Tourism Officer, Town Hall, Matlock DE4 3NN ☎ 01629 761145 ✉ gill.chapman@derbyshiredales.gov.uk

Transport: Mr Peter Foley, Director of Community Services, Town Hall, Matlock DE4 3NN ☎ 01629 761370 🖷 01629 761165 ✉ peter.foley@derbyshiredales.gov.uk

Transport: Mr Mark Kiddier, Street Scene & Works Transport Manager, Town Hall, Matlock DE4 3NN ☎ 01629 735497 🖷 01629 761165 ✉ mark.kiddier@derbyshiredales.gov.uk

Waste Collection and Disposal: Mr Peter Foley, Director of Community Services, Town Hall, Matlock DE4 3NN ☎ 01629 761370 🖷 01629 761165 ✉ peter.foley@derbyshiredales.gov.uk

Waste Management: Mr Peter Foley, Director of Community Services, Town Hall, Matlock DE4 3NN ☎ 01629 761370 🖷 01629 761165 ✉ peter.foley@derbyshiredales.gov.uk

Children's Play Areas: Mr Les Warren, Leisure Officer, Town Hall, Matlock DE4 3NN ☎ 01629 761382 🖷 01629 761165 ✉ les.warren@derbyshiredales.gov.uk

MEMBERS OF THE COUNCIL (39)

Bevan, Jacqueline (CON - Hathersage & Eyam)
jacque.bevan@derbyshiredales.gov.uk
Bower, Jennifer (CON - Tideswell)
jennifer.bower@derbyshiredales.gov.uk
Bright, Richard (CON - Hulland)
richard.bright@derbyshiredales.gov.uk
Bull, Kenneth (CON - Norbury)
ken.bull@derbyshiredales.gov.uk
Bull, Stephen (CON - Ashbourne North)
stephen.bull@derbyshiredales.gov.uk
Burfoot, Susan (LD - Matlock All Saints)
sue.burfoot@derbyshiredales.gov.uk
Burton, David (LD - Darley Dale)
david.burton@derbyshiredales.gov.uk
Cartwright, Bob (LAB - Masson)
bob.cartwright@derbyshiredales.gov.uk
Catt, Albert (CON - Doveridge & Sudbury)
albert.catt@derbyshiredales.gov.uk
Chapman, David (CON - Hartington & Taddington)
david.chapman@derbyshiredales.gov.uk
Donnelly, Thomas (CON - Ashbourne South)
thomas.donnelly@derbyshiredales.gov.uk
Elliott, Ann (CON - Matlock All Saints)
ann.elliott@derbyshiredales.gov.uk
Fearn, David (LD - Darley Dale)
david.fearn@derbyshiredales.gov.uk
Fitzherbert, Richard (CON - Dovedale & Parwich)
richard.fitzherbert@derbyshiredales.gov.uk
Flitter, Stephen (LD - Matlock St. Giles)
steve.flitter@derbyshiredales.gov.uk
Frederickson, David (IND - Lathkill & Bradford)
david.frederickson@derbyshiredales.gov.uk
Goodison, Janet (CON - Bradwell)
janet.goodison@derbyshiredales.gov.uk
Hunt, Catherine (CON - Calver)
cate.hunt@derbyshiredales.gov.uk
Jenkins, Angus (CON - Brailsford)
angus.jenkins@derbyshiredales.gov.uk
Lewer, Andrew (CON - Ashbourne South)
andrew.lewer@derbyshiredales.gov.uk
Longden, Michael (CON - Chatsworth)
mike.longden@derbyshiredales.gov.uk
Longstone, Neil (CON - Litton & Longstone)
neil.horton@derbyshiredales.gov.uk
Millward, Anthony (CON - Ashbourne North)
tony.millward@derbyshiredales.gov.uk
Monks, Jean (CON - Hathersage & Eyam)
jean.monks@derbyshiredales.gov.uk
Purdy, Garry (CON - Masson)
garry.purdy@derbyshiredales.gov.uk
Ratcliffe, Mike (LAB - Wirksworth)
mike.ratclife@derbyshiredales.gov.uk
Ratcliffe, Irene (LAB - Wirksworth)
irene.ratcliffe@derbyshiredales.gov.uk
Rose, Lewis (CON - Carsington Water)
lewis.rose@derbyshiredales.gov.uk
Shirley, Andrew (CON - Clifton & Bradley)
andrew.shirley@derbyshiredales.gov.uk
Slack, Peter (LAB - Wirksworth)
peter.slack@derbyshiredales.gov.uk
Statham, Andrew (CON - Darley Dale)
andrew.statham@derbyshiredales.gov.uk
Stevens, Geoffrey (CON - Matlock All Saints)
geoff.stevens@derbyshiredales.gov.uk
Stevens, Jacquie (CON - Matlock St. Giles)
jacquie.stevens@derbyshiredales.gov.uk
Swindell, Colin (LAB - Winster & South Darley)
colin.swindell@derbyshiredales.gov.uk
Tilbrook, Philippa (CON - Bakewell)
philippa.tilbrook@derbyshiredales.gov.uk
Tipping, Barrie (CON - Matlock St. Giles)
barrie.tipping@derbyshiredales.gov.uk
Twigg, Judith (CON - Bakewell)
judith.twigg@derbyshiredales.gov.uk
Walker, Carol (CON - Bakewell)
carol.walker@derbyshiredales.gov.uk
Wild, Joanne (CON - Stanton)
joanna.wild@derbyshiredales.gov.uk

POLITICAL COMPOSITION

CON: 29, LAB: 5, LD: 4, IND: 1

CABINET

Leader: Mr Lewis Rose
Culture: Mr Andrew Lewer

COMMITTEE CHAIRS

Community & Environment: Mr Stephen Bull
Licensing & Appeals: Mrs Jacqueline Bevan

DERRY CITY — N

Derry City Council, 98 Strand Road, Derry BT48 7NN
☎ 028 7136 5151 🖷 028 7136 8536 🖳 www.derrycity.gov.uk

FACTS & FIGURES

Police Authority: Northern Ireland Policing Board
Health Authority: Western Local Commissioning Group
Learning and Skills Council: Northern Ireland
Parliamentary Constituencies: Foyle
EU Constituencies: Northern Ireland
Election Frequency: Elections are of whole council

PRINCIPAL OFFICERS

Chief Executive: Ms Sharon O'Connor, Chief Executive & Town Clerk, 98 Strand Road, Derry BT48 7NN ☎ 028 7136 5151

Architect, Building / Property Services: Mr John Kelpie, Strategic Director, Council Offices, 98 Strand Road, Derry BT48 7NN ☎ 028 7136 5151 🖷 028 7136 8536 ✉ john.kelpie@derrycity.gov.uk

Building Control: Mr Anthony Tohill, Strategic Director, 98 Strand Road, Derry BT48 7NN ☎ 028 7137 6521 🖷 028 7126 0749 ✉ anthony.tohill@derrycity.gov.uk

PR / Communications: Ms Claire Lundy, Marketing & Communications Officer, Council Offices, 98 Strand Road, Derry BT48 7NN ☎ 028 7137 6504 🖷 028 7126 4858 ✉ claire.lundy@derrycity.gov.uk

Computer Management: Mr Joseph Campbell, City Treasurer, Council Offices, 98 Strand Road, Derry BT48 7NN ☎ 028 7137 6526 🖷 028 7126 0359 ✉ joe.campbell@derrycity.gov.uk

Computer Management: Mr Samuel Harvey, Head - Information Technology Officer, Council Offices, 98 Strand Road, Derry BT48 7NN ☎ 028 7136 5151 🖷 028 7126 0359 ✉ samuel.harvey@derrycity.gov.uk

Consumer Protection and Trading Standards: Mr Paul McSwiggan, Senior Environmental Health Officer, Council Offices, 98 Strand Road, Derry BT48 7NN ☎ 028 7136 5151 🖷 028 7126 6009 ✉ paul.mcswiggan@derrycity.gov.uk

Economic Development: Mr Tony Monaghan, Acting Senior Economic Development Officer, 98 Strand Road, Derry BT48 7NN ☎ 028 7136 5151 🖷 028 7126 4858 ✉ tony.monaghan@derrycity.gov.uk

Emergency Planning: Mr Philip O'Doherty, Chief Environmental Health Officer, Council Offices, 98 Strand Road, Derry BT48 7NN ☎ 028 7136 5151 🖷 028 7126 6009 ✉ philip.odoherty@derrycity.gov.uk

Environmental / Technical Services: Mr John Kelpie, Strategic Director, Council Offices, 98 Strand Road, Derry BT48 7NN ☎ 028 7136 5151 🖷 028 7136 8536 ✉ john.kelpie@derrycity.gov.uk

Environmental Health: Mr Philip O'Doherty, Chief Environmental Health Officer, Council Offices, 98 Strand Road, Derry BT48 7NN ☎ 028 7136 5151 🖷 028 7126 6009 ✉ philip.odoherty@derrycity.gov.uk

European Liaison: Mr Tony Monaghan, Acting Senior Economic Development Officer, 98 Strand Road, Derry BT48 7NN ☎ 028 7136 5151 🖷 028 7126 4858 ✉ tony.monaghan@derrycity.gov.uk

Events Manager: Mr Gerry McColgan, Community Services Programme Organiser, 98 Strand Road, Derry BT48 7NN ☎ 028 7136 5151 ✉ gerald.mccolgan@derrycity.gov.uk

Finance and Treasurer: Mr Joseph Campbell, City Treasurer, Council Offices, 98 Strand Road, Derry BT48 7NN ☎ 028 7137 6526 🖷 028 7126 0359 ✉ joe.campbell@derrycity.gov.uk

Fleet Management: Mr John Kelpie, Strategic Director, Council Offices, 98 Strand Road, Derry BT48 7NN ☎ 028 7136 5151 🖷 028 7136 8536 ✉ john.kelpie@derrycity.gov.uk

Grounds Maintenance: Mr Danny McCartney, Grounds Maintenance Manager, Council Offices, 98 Strand Road, Derry BT48 7NN ☎ 028 7136 5151 ✉ danny.mccartney@derrycity.gov.uk

Health and Safety: Mr Barry Doherty, Senior Environmental Health Officer, 98 Strand Road, Derry BT48 7NN ☎ 028 7136 5151 🖷 028 7126 6009 ✉ barry.doherty@derrycity.gov.uk

Leisure and Cultural Services: Ms Roisin Doherty, Temporary Head of Heritage & Museums Service, Harbour Museum, Harbour Square, Londonderry BT48 6AF ☎ 028 7137 7331 ✉ roisin.doherty@derrycity.gov.uk

Leisure and Cultural Services: Ms Oonagh McGillion, Director - Development, 98 Strand Road, Derry BT48 7NN ☎ 028 7136 5151 🖷 028 7126 6009 ✉ oonagh.mcgillion@derrycity.gov.uk

Member Services: Ms Karen Henderson, Member Services Officer, 9 Strand Road, Derry BT48 7NN ☎ 028 7136 5151 ✉ karen.henderson@derrycity.gov.uk

Personnel / HR: Mrs Sinead McNicholl, Head - Human Resources, 98 Strand Road, Derry BT48 7NN ☎ 028 7136 5151 ✉ sinead.mcnicholl@derrycity.gov.uk

Procurement: Mr Colin Killeen, Central Purchasing Officer, Council Offices, 98 Strand Road, Derry BT48 7NN ☎ 028 7137 6526 🖷 028 7126 0359 ✉ colin.killeen@derrycity.gov.uk

Recycling & Waste Minimisation: Mr Conor Canning, Waste Services Manager, Council Offices, 98 Strand Road, Derry BT48 7NN ☎ 028 7136 5151 🖷 028 7136 3569 ✉ conor.canning@derrycity.gov.uk

Regeneration: Mr Tony Monaghan, Acting Senior Economic Development Officer, 98 Strand Road, Derry BT48 7NN ☎ 028 7136 5151 🖷 028 7126 4858 ✉ tony.monaghan@derrycity.gov.uk

Staff Training: Mrs Sinead McNicholl, Head - Human Resources, 98 Strand Road, Derry BT48 7NN ☎ 028 7136 5151 ✉ sinead.mcnicholl@derrycity.gov.uk

Sustainable Development: Mr Philip O'Doherty, Chief Environmental Health Officer, Council Offices, 98 Strand Road, Derry BT48 7NN ☎ 028 7136 5151 🖷 028 7126 6009 ✉ philip.odoherty@derrycity.gov.uk

Tourism: Ms Oonagh McGillion, Director - Development, 98 Strand Road, Derry BT48 7NN ☎ 028 7136 5151 🖷 028 7126 6009 ✉ oonagh.mcgillion@derrycity.gov.uk

Waste Collection and Disposal: Mr Conor Canning, Waste Services Manager, Council Offices, 98 Strand Road, Derry BT48 7NN ☎ 028 7136 5151 🖷 028 7136 3569 ✉ conor.canning@derrycity.gov.uk

MEMBERS OF THE COUNCIL (30)

***Mayor:* Cambell**, Kevin (SF - Cityside)
kevin.campbell@derry-city.org
***Deputy Mayor:* Hamilton**, Mary (UUP - Waterside)

mary.hamilton@derrycity.gov.uk
***Alderman:* Devenney**, Maurice (DUP - Rural)
maurice.devenney@derrycity.gov.uk
***Alderman:* Garfield-Kidd**, April (DUP - Waterside)
april.garfield-kidd@derrycity.gov.uk
***Alderman:* Miller**, Joe (DUP - Waterside)
joe.miller@derrycity.gov.uk
Boyle, John (SDLP - Northland)
john.boyle@derrycity.gov.uk
Carr, Jimmy (SDLP - Shantallow)
jimmy.carr@derrycity.gov.uk
Carr, Sean (SDLP - Northland)
sean.carr@derrycity.gov.uk
Clifford, Jim (SDLP - Cityside)
jim.clifford@derrycity.gov.uk
Conway, Thomas (SDLP - Rural)
thomas.conway@derrycity.gov.uk
Cooper, Michael (SF - Northland)
michael.cooper@derry-city.org
Diver, Gerard (SDLP - Waterside)
gerard.diver@derrycity.gov.uk
Dobbins, Angela (SDLP - Shantallow)
angela.dobbins@derrycity.gov.uk
Donnelly, Ann (SDLP - Cityside)
ann.donnelly@derrycity.gov.uk
Fleming, Paul (SF - Rural)
paul.fleming@derry-city.org
Fleming, Lynn (SF - Waterside)
lynn.fleming@derry-city.org
Gallagher, Shaun (SDLP - Shantallow)
shaun.gallagher@derrycity.gov.uk
Hassan, Tony (SF - Shantallow)
tony.hassan@derry-city.org
Hastings, Gus (SDLP - Rural)
gus.hastings@derrycity.gov.uk
Kelly, Colly (SF - Cityside)
colly.kelly@derry-city.org
Logue, Patricia (SF - Cityside)
patricia.logue@derry-city.org
McAuley, Eamon (SDLP - Northland)
eamon.mcauley@derrycity.gov.uk
McCallion, Elisha (SF - Shantallow)
elishamclaughlin@hotmail.com
McGinley, Eric (SF - Northland)
eric.mcginley@derrcyity.gov.uk
McLaughlin, Maeve (SF - Northland)
maeve.mc@btopenworld.com
Middleton, Gary (DUP - Rural)
gary.middleton@derrycity.gov.uk
Reilly, Martin (SDLP - Waterside)
martin.reilly@derrycity.gov.uk
Stevenson, Brenda (SDLP - Rural)
brenda.stevenson@derrycity.gov.uk
Thompson, Drew (DUP - Waterside)
drew.thompson@derrycity.gov.uk
Tierney, John (SDLP - Northland)
john.tierney@derrycity.gov.uk

POLITICAL COMPOSITION
SDLP: 14, SF: 10, DUP: 5, UUP: 1

COMMITTEE CHAIRS
Development: Ms Lynn Fleming
Environmental Services: Mr Jimmy Carr
Planning: Ms Brenda Stevenson
Policy & Resources: Mr Paul Fleming
Regional Services: Ms Maeve McLaughlin
Staff: Ms Patricia Logue

DEVON — C

Devon County Council, County Hall, Topsham Road, Exeter EX2 4QD ☎ 0845 155 1015 🖷 01392 382324 💻 www.devon.gov.uk

FACTS & FIGURES
Police Authority: Devon & Cornwall Police Authority
Health Authority: NHS South West
Learning and Skills Council: South West
Parliamentary Constituencies: Devon Central, Devon East, Devon North, Devon South West, Devon West and Torridge, Exeter, Newton Abbot, Plymouth Moor View, Plymouth Sutton and Devonport, Tiverton and Honiton, Totnes
EU Constituencies: South West
Election Frequency: Elections are of whole council
Twinning: Calvados, Normandy

PRINCIPAL OFFICERS
Chief Executive: Dr Phil Norrey, Chief Executive, County Hall, Topsham Road, Exeter EX2 4QD ☎ 01392 383201 🖷 01392 382286 🖱 phil.norrey@devon.gov.uk

Senior Management: Mr Mary Davis, County Treasurer, County Hall, Topsham Road, Exeter EX2 4QD ☎ 01392 383310 🖷 01392 382959 🖱 mary.davis@devon.gov.uk

Senior Management: Mr John Smith, Head of Services for Communities, County Hall, Topsham Road, Exeter EX2 4QW ☎ 01392 383075 🖷 01392 382286 🖱 john.smith@devon.gov.uk

Senior Management: Mrs Jennie Stephens, Strategic Director - People, County Hall, Topsham Road, Exeter EX2 4QR ☎ 01392 383299 🖷 01392 382684 🖱 jennie.stephens@devon.gov.uk

Access Officer / Social Services (Disability): Ms Carolyn Elliott, Assistant Director/Learning Disability, Estuary House, Collet Way, Brunel Industrial Estate, Newton Abbot TQ12 4PH ☎ 01392 384747 🖱 carolyn.elliott@devon.gov.uk

Architect, Building / Property Services: Ms Karen Dyson, Corporate Property Manager, County Hall, Topsham Road, Exeter EX2 4QD ☎ 01392 382194 🖱 karen.dyson@devon.gov.uk

Best Value: Ms Annette-Marie Ball, Head of Procurement & Estates, County Hall, Topsham Road, Exeter EX2 4QD ☎ 01392 384635 🖱 annette-marie.ball@devon.gov.uk

Building Control: Mr Stewart Redding, County Development Manager, Lucombe House, County Hall, Topsham Road, Exeter EX2 4QW ☎ 01392 383368 🖱 stewart.redding@devon.gov.uk

Catering Services: Ms Fran Perry, Function & Food Procurement Manager, Falcon Road Offices, Exeter EX2 7PL ☎ 01392 384363 🖱 fran.perry@devon.gov.uk

Children / Youth Services: Mr Dillon Hughes, Strategic Lead - Youth Services, County Hall, Topsham Road, Exeter EX2 4QD

☎ 01392 383517 ✉ dillon.hughes@devon.gov.uk

Civil Registration: Ms Trish Harrogate, Registration Service Manager, Devon Register Office, Castle Street, Exeter EX4 3PQ ☎ 01392 385618 🖷 01392 384232 ✉ trish.harrogate@devon.gov.uk

PR / Communications: Mr Peter Doyle, Head of External Communications, County Hall, Topsham Road, Exeter EX2 4QW ☎ 01392 383264 ✉ peter.doyle@devon.gov.uk

PR / Communications: Mr Tony Parker, Head of Communications & Media, County Hall, Topsham Road, Exeter EX2 4QW ☎ 01392 384770 🖷 01392 382286 ✉ tony.parker@devon.gov.uk

Community Safety: Mr John Smith, Head of Services for Communities, County Hall, Topsham Road, Exeter EX2 4QD ☎ 01392 383075 🖷 01392 382286 ✉ john.smith@devon.gov.uk

Computer Management: Mr Rob Parkhouse, Head of Business Strategy & Support, County Hall, Topsham Road, Exeter EX2 4QJ ☎ 01392 382458 ✉ rob.parkhouse@devon.gov.uk

Consumer Protection and Trading Standards: Mr Paul Thomas, Head of Trading Standards, County Hall, Topsham Road, Exeter EX2 4QD ☎ 01392 382728 ✉ paul.thomas@devon.gov.uk

Contracts: Mr Jan Shadbolt, County Solicitor, County Hall, Topsham Road, Exeter EX2 4QD ☎ 01392 382285 🖷 01392 382286 ✉ jan.shadbolt@devon.gov.uk

Customer Service: Mr Roger Jenkins, Customer Service Centre Manager, Customer Service Centre, 7 Millennium Place, Lowman Way, Tiverton EX16 6SB ☎ 01392 386888 ✉ roger.jenkins@devon.gov.uk

Economic Development: Ms Kerry Denton, Head of Economy & Enterprise, County Hall, Topsham Road, Exeter EX2 4QD ☎ 01392 382150 ✉ kerry.denton@devon.gov.uk

Education: Ms Sue Clarke, Head of Education & Learning, County Hall, Topsham Road, Exeter EX2 4QD ☎ 01392 383212 ✉ sue.clarke@devon.gov.uk

Emergency Planning: Mr Simon Kitchen, Acting Head of Organisation Development, County Hall, Topsham Road, Exeter EX2 4QD ☎ 01392 382699 ✉ simon.kitchen@devon.gov.uk

European Liaison: Ms Kerry Denton, Head of Economy & Enterprise, County Hall, Topsham Road, Exeter EX2 4QD ☎ 01392 382150 ✉ kerry.denton@devon.gov.uk

Events Manager: Ms Samantha Hill, Marketing Manager, County Hall, Topsham Road, Exeter EX2 4QD ☎ 01392 382954 ✉ sam.hill@devon.gov.uk

Facilities: Mr Charlie Bottrell, County Hall Facilities Manager, County Hall, Topsham Road, Exeter EX2 4QW ☎ 01392 383279 🖷 01392 382830 ✉ charlie.bottrell@devon.gov.uk

Finance and Treasurer: Mr Mary Davis, County Treasurer, County Hall, Topsham Road, Exeter EX2 4QD ☎ 01392 383310 🖷 01392 382959 ✉ mary.davis@devon.gov.uk

Grounds Maintenance: Mr Charlie Bottrell, County Hall Facilities Manager, County Hall, Topsham Road, Exeter EX2 4QD ☎ 01392 383279 🖷 01392 382830 ✉ charlie.bottrell@devon.gov.uk

Health and Safety: Ms Margaret Bullock, County Health & Safety Manager, Arlington House, Ground Floor, Park 5, Harrier Way, Exeter EX2 7HU ☎ 01392 382788 🖷 01392 382542 ✉ margaret.bullock@devon.gov.uk

Highways: Mr Lester Willmington, Head of Highway & Traffic Management, Lucombe House, County Hall, Topsham Road, Exeter EX2 4QW ☎ 01392 383379 🖷 01392 382135 ✉ lester.willmington@devon.gov.uk

Local Area Agreement: Mr Roger Grainger, Team Manager, County Hall, Topsham Road, Exeter EX2 4QD ☎ 01932 382153; 01392 382865 ✉ roger.grainger@devon.gov.uk

Legal: Mr Jan Shadbolt, County Solicitor, County Hall, Topsham Road, Exeter EX2 4QD ☎ 01392 382285 🖷 01392 382286 ✉ jan.shadbolt@devon.gov.uk

Leisure and Cultural Services: Dr Ian Harrison, Deputy Executive Director of Environment, Economy & Culture, County Hall, Topsham Road, Exeter EX2 4QW ☎ 01392 382150 ✉ ian.harrison@devon.gov.uk

Lifelong Learning: Ms Margaret Davidson, Principal Adult & Community Learning Officer, Buckland House, Park Five, Sowton, Exeter EX2 7ND ☎ 01392 385722 ✉ margaret.davidson@devon.gov.uk

Lighting: Mr Andy Ware, Team Leader - Street Lighting, County Hall, Topsham Road, Exeter EX2 4QD ☎ 01392 383384 🖷 01392 382342 ✉ andy.ware@devon.gov.uk

Member Services: Mr Rob Hooper, Democratic Services & Scrutiny Manager, County Hall, Topsham Road, Exeter EX2 4QD ☎ 01392 382300 🖷 01392 382286 ✉ rob.hooper@devon.gov.uk

Member Services: Mrs Alison Howell, Member Services Officer, County Hall, Topsham Road, Exeter EX2 4QD ☎ 01392 382888 🖷 01392 382324 ✉ alison.howell@devon.gov.uk

Member Services: Ms Karen Strahan, Deputy Committee & Scrutiny Manager, County Hall, Topsham Road, Exeter EX2 4QD ☎ 01392 382264 🖷 01392 382324 ✉ karen.strahan@devon.gov.uk

Parking: Mr Gary Powell, Traffic Management Team Manager, Lucombe House, County Hall, Topsham Road, Exeter EX2 4QW ☎ 01392 382244 🖷 01392 382135 ✉ gary.powell@devon.gov.uk

Personnel / HR: Mr Paul Jones, Head of Human Resources, County Hall, Topsham Road, Exeter EX2 4QD ☎ 01392 383309 ✉ paul.jones@devon.gov.uk

Planning: Mr Stewart Redding, County Development Manager,

LOCAL AUTHORITIES

Lucombe House, County Hall, Topsham Road, Exeter EX2 4QW ☎ 01392 383368 ✉ stewart.redding@devon.gov.uk

Procurement: Mrs Annette-Marie Ball, Head of Procurement & Estates, County Hall, Topsham Road, Exeter EX2 4QD ☎ 01392 384635 📠 01392 384636 ✉ annette-marie.ball@devon.gov.uk

Public Libraries: Ms Ciara Eastell, Head of Libraries, Great Moor House, Bittern Road, Sowton, Exeter EX2 7NL ☎ 01392 384315 ✉ ciara.eastell@devon.gov.uk

Recycling & Waste Minimisation: Mr David Whitton, Head of Capital Development & Waste Management, County Hall, Topsham Road, Exeter EX2 4QD ☎ 01392 382701 ✉ david.whitton@devon.gov.uk

Regeneration: Mr Andrew Lightfoot, Head of Regeneration, Lucombe House, Topsham Road, Exeter EX2 4QD ☎ 01392 382889 ✉ andrew.lightfoot@devon.gov.uk

Road Safety: Mr Jeremy Phillips, Sustainable & Safer Travel Team Manager, County Hall, Topsham Road, Exeter EX2 4QD ☎ 01392 383289 ✉ peter.gimber@devon.gov.uk

Social Services: Mrs Jennie Stephens, Strategic Director - People, County Hall, Topsham Road, Exeter EX2 4QR ☎ 01392 383299 📠 01392 382684 ✉ jennie.stephens@devon.gov.uk

Social Services (Adult): Mrs Jennie Stephens, Strategic Director - People, County Hall, Topsham Road, Exeter EX2 4QR ☎ 01392 383299 📠 01392 382684 ✉ jennie.stephens@devon.gov.uk

Social Services (Children): Ms Sally Slade, Head of Integrated Children's Services & Adult Care Management, Room 137, County Hall, Topsham Road, Exeter EX2 4QD ☎ 01392 356908 ✉ sally.slade@devon.gov.uk

Staff Training: Mr Bill Heasman, Manager - Leadership & Management Development, Room 220, County Hall, Topsham Road, Exeter EX2 4QD ☎ 01392 382344 ✉ bill.heasman@devon.gov.uk

Tourism: Ms Kerry Denton, Head of Economy & Enterprise, Lucombe House, County Hall, Topsham Road, Exeter EX2 4QD ☎ 01392 382150 ✉ kerry.denton@devon.gov.uk

Traffic Management: Mr Lester Willmington, Head of Highway & Traffic Management, Lucombe House, County Hall, Topsham Road, Exeter EX2 4QW ☎ 01392 383379 📠 01392 382135 ✉ lester.willmington@devon.gov.uk

Transport: Mr Bruce Thompson, Transport Co-ordination Service Manager, County Hall, Topsham Road, Exeter EX2 4QD ☎ 01392 383244 ✉ bruce.thompson@devon.gov.uk

Waste Collection and Disposal: Mr David Whitton, Head of Capital Development & Waste Management, Matford Lane Offices, County Hall, Exeter EX2 4QW ☎ 01392 382701 ✉ david.whitton@devon.gov.uk

MEMBERS OF THE COUNCIL (62)

Leader of the Council: **Hart**, John (CON - Bickleigh & Wembury)
john.hart@devon.gov.uk

Barker, Stuart (CON - Ashburton & Buckfastleigh)
stuart.barker@devon.gov.uk

Berry, John (CON - Cullompton Rural)
john.berry@devon.gov.uk

Black, Paula (LAB - Totnes Rural)
paula.black@devon.gov.uk

Bowden, Peter (CON - Broadclyst & Whimple)
peter.bowden@devon.gov.uk

Boyd, Andy (CON - Torrington Rural)
andy.boyd@devon.gov.uk

Boyle, Alison (CON - Bideford South & Hartland)
alison.boyle@devon.gov.uk

Brazil, Julian (LD - Kingsbridge & Stokenham)
julian.brazil@devon.gov.uk

Brock, Philip (LD - St David's & St James)
philip.brock@devon.gov.uk

Brook, Jerry (CON - Chudleigh Rural)
jerry.brook@devon.gov.uk

Cann, Rodney (IND - Fremington Rural)
rodney.s.cann@devon.gov.uk

Channon, Christine (CON - Budleigh)
christine.channon@devon.gov.uk

Chugg, Caroline (CON - Braunton Rural)
caroline.chugg@devon.gov.uk

Clarence, Chris (CON - Teign Estuary)
chris.clarence@devon.gov.uk

Clatworthy, John (CON - Dawlish)
john.clatworthy@devon.gov.uk

Colthorpe, Polly (CON - Tiverton West)
polly.colthorpe@devon.gov.uk

Connett, Alan (LD - Exminster & Kenton)
alan.connett@devon.gov.uk

Croad, Roger (CON - Ivybridge)
roger.croad@devon.gov.uk

Davis, Andrea (CON - Combe Martin Rural)
andrea.davis@devon.gov.uk

Day, Simon (CON - Thurlestone, Salcombe & Allington)
simon.day@devon.gov.uk

Diviani, Paul (CON - Honiton St Paul's)
paul.diviani@devon.gov.uk

Eastman, Andrew (CON - Northam)
andrew.eastman@devon.gov.uk

Edgell, Richard (CON - Chulmleigh & Swimbridge)
richard.edgell@devon.gov.uk

Foggin, Olwen (LAB - Heavitree & Whipton Barton)
olwen.foggin@devon.gov.uk

Fowler, Geoffrey (LD - Ilfracombe)
geoff.fowler@devon.gov.uk

Fry, Anne (LD - Newton Abbot North)
anne.fry@devon.gov.uk

Giles, Roger (IND - Ottery St Mary Rural)
roger.giles@devon.gov.uk

Greenslade, Brian (LD - Barnstaple North)
brian.greenslade@devon.gov.uk

Gribble, George (CON - Bovey Tracey Rural)
george.gribble@devon.gov.uk

Hannaford, Rob (LAB - Exwick & St Thomas)
rob.hannaford@devon.gov.uk

Hannon, Des (LD - Tiverton East)
des.hannon@devon.gov.uk

Hawkins, Jonathan (CON - Dartmouth & Kingswear)
jonathan.hawkins@devon.gov.uk

Haywood, Chris (LD - Barnstaple South)
chris.haywood@devon.gov.uk

Hook, Gordon (LD - Newton Abbot South)

gordon.hook@devon.gov.uk
Hughes, Bernard (CON - Exmouth Halsdon & Woodbury)
bernard.hughes@devon.gov.uk
Hughes, Stuart (CON - Sidmouth Sidford)
stuart.hughes@devon.gov.uk
Knight, Jim (CON - Seaton Coastal)
jim.knight@devon.gov.uk
Leadbetter, Andrew (CON - St Loyes & Topsham)
andrew.leadbetter@devon.gov.uk
Lee, Michael (CON - Newton St Cyres & Sandford)
michael.lee@devon.gov.uk
Marsh, Christine (CON - Okehampton Rural)
christine.marsh@devon.gov.uk
McInnes, James (CON - Hatherleigh & Chagford)
james.mcinnes@devon.gov.uk
McMurray, James (CON - Teignmouth)
james.mcmurray@devon.gov.uk
Moulding, Andrew (CON - Axminster)
andrew.moulding@devon.gov.uk
Mumford, William (CON - Yealmpton)
william.mumford@devon.gov.uk
Newcombe, Vanessa (LD - Alphington & Cowick)
vanessa.newcombe@devon.gov.uk
Owen, Jill (LAB - Priory & St Leonard's)
jill.owen@devon.gov.uk
Parsons, Barry (CON - Holsworthy Rural)
barry.parsons@devon.gov.uk
Pennington, Trevor (CON - South Brent & Dartington)
trevor.pennington@devon.gov.uk
Prowse, Percy (CON - Duryard & Pennsylvania)
percy.prowse@devon.gov.uk
Radford, Ray (CON - Willand & Uffculme)
ray.radford@devon.gov.uk
Randall-Johnson, Sara (CON - Honiton St Michael's)
sara.randalljohnson@devon.gov.uk
Robinson, Sam (CON - Bideford East)
sam.robinson@devon.gov.uk
Sanders, Philip (CON - Yelverton Rural)
philip.sanders@devon.gov.uk
Sellis, Debo (CON - Tavistock)
debo.sellis@devon.gov.uk
Smith, Dennis (CON - Teignbridge South)
dennis.smith@devon.gov.uk
Spence, Saxon (LAB - Pinhoe & Mincinglake)
saxon.spence@devon.gov.uk
Taylor, Brenda (LD - Exmouth Brixington & Withycombe)
brenda.taylor@devon.gov.uk
Walters, Mike (CON - Kingsteignton)
mike.walters@devon.gov.uk
Way, Nick (LD - Crediton Rural)
nick.way@devon.gov.uk
Westlake, Richard (LAB - Newtown & Polsloe)
richard.westlake@devon.gov.uk
Wragg, Eileen (LD - Exmouth Littleham & Town)
eileen.wragg@devon.gov.uk
Yabsley, Jeremy (CON - South Molton Rural)
jeremy.yabsley@devon.gov.uk

POLITICAL COMPOSITION
CON: 41, LD: 13, LAB: 6, IND: 2

CABINET
Leader/ Policy & Corporate: Mr John Hart
Adult Social Care, Families & Post 16: Mr Stuart Barker
Business Services: Mr Andrew Leadbetter
Children, Health & Wellbeing: Miss Andrea Davis
Economy, Enterprise & Employment: Mr William Mumford
Environment & Community: Mr Roger Croad
Highways & Transportation: Mr Stuart Hughes
Resources: Mr John Clatworthy

COMMITTEE CHAIRS
Appeals: Mr Jim Knight
Corporate Services Scrutiny: Mr Brian Greenslade
Development Management: Mr James McInnes
Health & Wellbeing Scrutiny: Mr Richard Westlake
Investment & Pension Fund: Mr Barry Parsons
Peoples Scrutiny: Mrs Vanessa Newcombe
Personnel Partnership: Mr John Hart
Places Scrutiny: Mr Gordon Hook

DONCASTER M

Doncaster Metropolitan Borough Council, Floor 8, Council House, College Road, Doncaster DN1 3AJ ☎ 01302 734444 askus@doncaster.gov.uk www.doncaster.gov.uk

FACTS & FIGURES
Police Authority: South Yorkshire Police Authority
Health Authority: NHS Yorkshire & the Humber
Learning and Skills Council: Yorkshire and the Humber
Parliamentary Constituencies: Don Valley, Doncaster Central, Doncaster North
EU Constituencies: Yorkshire and the Humber
Election Frequency: Elections are by thirds
Twinning: Avion (France); Dandong (China); Gliwice (Poland); Herten (Germany); Wilmington (USA)

PRINCIPAL OFFICERS
Chief Executive: Ms Jo Miller, Chief Executive, Floor 8, Council House, College Road, Doncaster DN1 3AJ ☎ 01302 862230 jo.miller@doncaster.gov.uk

Senior Management: Mrs Joan Beck, Director of Adults & Communities, Floor 2, Council House, College Road, Doncaster DN1 3AJ ☎ 01302 737808 joan.beck@doncaster.gov.uk

Senior Management: Mr Peter Dale, Director of Regeneration & Environment, Floor 2, Council House, College Road, Doncaster DN1 3AJ ☎ 01302 862505 🖷 01302 737685 peter.dale@doncaster.gov.uk

Senior Management: Mr Chris Pratt, Director of Children & Young People's Services, Floor 4, Council House, College Road, Doncaster DN1 3AJ ☎ 01302 737800 chris.pratt@doncaster.gov.uk

Senior Management: Mr Simon Wiles, Director of Finance & Corporate Services, Floor 2, Council House, College Road, Doncaster DN1 3AJ ☎ ; 01302 736907 🖷 01302 737384 simon.wiles@doncater.gov.uk

Access Officer / Social Services (Disability): Mr Pat Higgs, Assistant Director of Adult Social Care, Floor 7, Council House, College Road, Doncaster DN1 3AJ ☎ 01302 737620 pat.higgs@doncaster.gov.uk

Architect, Building / Property Services: Mr Chris Fairbrother, Property Manager, Floor 1, Council House, College Road, Doncaster DN1 3AJ ☎ 01302 737363 🖷 01302 862329 ✉ chris.fairbrother@doncaster.gov.uk

Building Control: Mr Richard Purcell, Head of Development Management, 2nd Floor, Danum House, St Sepulchre Gate, Doncaster DN1 1UB ☎ 01302 734862 🖷 01302 734949 ✉ richard.purcell@doncaster.gov.uk

Catering Services: Ms Andrea Swaby, Catering Manager, Ground Floor, Council House, College Road, Doncaster DN1 3AJ ☎ 01302 737600 ✉ andrea.swaby@doncaster.gov.uk

Children / Youth Services: Ms Vicki Lawson, Assistant Director of Children & Families, Floor 4, Council House, College Road, Doncaster DN1 3AJ ☎ 01302 737197 ✉ vicki.lawson@doncaster.gov.uk

Children / Youth Services: Mr Chris Pratt, Director of Children & Young People's Services, Floor 4, Council House, College Road, Doncaster DN1 3AJ ☎ 01302 737800 ✉ chris.pratt@doncaster.gov.uk

Civil Registration: Mr William Templeton, Superintendent Registrar, Elmfield House, South Parade, Doncaster DN1 2EH ☎ 01302 364922 ✉ william.templeton@doncaster.gov.uk

PR / Communications: Ms Lorna Thornley, Head of Communications, Floor 1, Council House, College Road, Doncaster DN1 3AJ ☎ 01302 737988 ✉ lorna.thornley@doncaster.gov.uk

Community Planning: Mr Scott Cardwell, Assistant Director of Development, Floor 11, Council House, College Road, Doncaster DN1 3AJ ☎ 01302 737655 ✉ scott.cardwell@doncaster.gov.uk

Community Safety: Ms Karen Johnson, Assistant Director of Communities, Floor 7, Council House, College Road, Doncaster DN1 3AJ ☎ 01302 862507 🖷 01302 862338 ✉ karen.johnson@doncaster.gov.uk

Computer Management: Ms Julie Grant, Assistant Director of Customer Services & ICT, Floor 2, Council House, College Road, Doncaster DN1 3AJ ☎ 01302 862496 ✉ julie.grant@doncaster.gov.uk

Consumer Protection and Trading Standards: Ms Gill Gillies, Assistant Director of Environment, Floor 2, Council House, College Road, Doncaster DN1 3AJ ☎ 01302 736018 ✉ gill.gillies@doncaster.gov.uk

Consumer Protection and Trading Standards: Mr Dave McMurdo, Trading Standards Manager, Floor 3, Council House, College Road, Doncaster DN1 3AJ ☎ 01302 737522 🖷 01302 737950 ✉ dave.mcmurdo@doncaster.gov.uk

Contracts: Mr Tony Coffey, Head of Corporate Procurement, Floor 10, Council House, College Road, Doncaster DN1 3AJ ☎ 01302 862222 🖷 01302 736681 ✉ tony.coffey@doncaster.gov.uk

Corporate Services: Mr Simon Wiles, Director of Finance & Corporate Services, Floor 11, Council House, College Road, Doncaster DN1 3AJ ☎ ; 01302 736907 🖷 01302 737384 ✉ simon.wiles@doncater.gov.uk

Customer Service: Ms Julie Grant, Assistant Director of Customer Services & ICT, Floor 2, Council House, College Road, Doncaster DN1 3AJ ☎ 01302 862496 ✉ julie.grant@doncaster.gov.uk

Economic Development: Mr Scott Cardwell, Assistant Director of Development, Floor 11, Council House, College Road, Doncaster DN1 3AJ ☎ 01302 737655 ✉ scott.cardwell@doncaster.gov.uk

Economic Development: Mr Lee Tillman, Head of Strategy & Programmes, Danum House, St Sepulchre Gate, Doncaster DN1 1UB ☎ 01302 734552 ✉ lee.tillman@doncaster.gov.uk

Education: Ms Jo Moxon, Assistant Director for Education, Floor 4, Council House, College Road, Doncaster DN1 3AJ ☎ 01302 737201 ✉ jo.moxon@doncaster.gov.uk

E-Government: Ms Julie Grant, Assistant Director of Customer Services & ICT, Floor 2, Council House, College Road, Doncaster DN1 3AJ ☎ 01302 862496 ✉ julie.grant@doncaster.gov.uk

Electoral Registration: Mr Roger Harvey, Assistant Director of Legal & Democratic Services, Copley House, Waterdale, Doncaster DN1 3EQ ☎ 01302 734646 🖷 ; 01302 736273 ✉ roger.harvey@doncaster.gov.uk

Electoral Registration: Mr Brendan Martin, Head of Democratic Services, Copley House, Waterdale, Doncaster DN1 3EQ ☎ 01302 736707 ✉ brendan.martin@doncaster.gov.uk

Emergency Planning: Ms Gill Gillies, Assistant Director of Environment, Floor 7, Council House, College Road, Doncaster DN1 3AJ ☎ 01302 736018 ✉ gill.gillies@doncaster.gov.uk

Energy Management: Mr Dave Wilkinson, Assistant Director of Trading & Support Services, PO Box 117, Floor 11, Council House, College Road, Doncaster DN1 3AJ ☎ 01302 737501 🖷 01302 737644 ✉ dave.wilkinson@doncaster.gov.uk

Environmental / Technical Services: Mr Dave Wilkinson, Assistant Director of Trading & Support Services, PO Box 117, Floor 11, Council House, College Road, Doncaster DN1 3AJ ☎ 01302 737501 🖷 01302 737644 ✉ dave.wilkinson@doncaster.gov.uk

Environmental Health: Ms Gill Gillies, Assistant Director of Environment, Floor 2, Council House, College Road, Doncaster DN1 3AJ ☎ 01302 736018 ✉ gill.gillies@doncaster.gov.uk

Estates, Property & Valuation: Mr Scott Cardwell, Assistant Director of Development, Floor 11, Council House, College Road, Doncaster DN1 3AJ ☎ 01302 737655 ✉ scott.cardwell@doncaster.gov.uk

European Liaison: Mr Christian Foster, Programmes Manager, Floor 10, Council House, College Road, Doncaster DN1 3AJ

☎ 01302 736614 ✉ christian.foster@doncaster.gov.uk

Events Manager: Ms Valerie Constantine, Events Manager, The Blue Building, 38 - 40 Blue Building, Doncaster DN1 1DA ☎ 01302 736033 🖷 01302 762341 ✉ valerie.constantine@doncaster.gov.uk

Facilities: Mr Drew Oxley, Head of Facilities Management, North Bridge Depot, North Bridge Road, Doncaster DN5 9AN ☎ 01302 736857 🖷 01302 736897 ✉ drew.oxley@doncaster.gov.uk

Finance and Treasurer: Mr Steve Mawson, Assistant Director of Resources - Finance & Performance, Floor 9, Council House, College Road, Doncaster DN1 3AJ ☎ 01302 737650 🖷 01302 737923 ✉ steve.mawson@doncaster.gov.uk

Finance and Treasurer: Mr Simon Wiles, Director of Finance & Corporate Services, Floor 11, Council House, College Road, Doncaster DN1 3AJ ☎ ; 01302 736907 🖷 01302 737384 ✉ simon.wiles@doncater.gov.uk

Fleet Management: Mr Mick Hepple, Head of Transport Services, North Bridge Depot, North Bridge Road, Doncaster DN5 9AN ☎ 01302 736810 🖷 01302 736819 ✉ mick.hepple@doncaster.gov.uk

Grounds Maintenance: Ms Gill Gillies, Assistant Director of Environment, Floor 7, Council House, College Road, Doncaster DN1 3AJ ☎ 01302 736018 ✉ gill.gillies@doncaster.gov.uk

Health and Safety: Ms Gill Gillies, Assistant Director of Environment, Floor 7, Council House, College Road, Doncaster DN1 3AJ ☎ 01302 736018 ✉ gill.gillies@doncaster.gov.uk

Highways: Mr Peter Dale, Director of Regeneration & Environment, Floor 2, Council House, College Road, Doncaster DN1 3AJ ☎ 01302 862505 🖷 01302 737685 ✉ peter.dale@doncaster.gov.uk

Highways: Ms Gill Gillies, Assistant Director of Environment, Floor 7, Council House, College Road, Doncaster DN1 3AJ ☎ 01302 736018 ✉ gill.gillies@doncaster.gov.uk

Home Energy Conservation: Ms Kim Goldberg, Home Energy Officer, Floor 3, Council House, College Road, Doncaster DN1 3AJ ☎ 01302 737056 🖷 01302 737950 ✉ kim.goldberg@doncaster.gov.uk

Housing: Mr Gary Wells, Assistant Director of Strategic Housing, Floor 2, Council House, College Road, Doncaster DN1 3AJ ☎ 01302 862485 🖷 01302 736260 ✉ gary.wells@doncaster.gov.uk

Housing Maintenance: Ms Susan Jordan, Chief Executive St Leger Homes of Doncaster, St Leger Court, White Road Way, Doncaster DN4 5ND ☎ 01302 862700 🖷 01302 862715 ✉ susan.jordan@stlegerhomes.co.uk ;

Local Area Agreement: Mr Howard Monk, Head of Corporate Policy & Performance, Floor 8, Council House, College Road, Doncaster DN1 3PY ☎ 01302 736911 🖷 01302 737769 ✉ howard.monk@doncaster.gov.uk

Legal: Mr Roger Harvey, Assistant Director of Legal & Democratic Services, Copley House, Waterdale, Doncaster DN1 3EQ ☎ 01302 734646 🖷 01302 736273 ✉ roger.harvey@doncaster.gov.uk

Leisure and Cultural Services: Mr John Sherburn, Leisure Services Manager, Floor 7, Council House, College Road, Doncaster DN1 3AJ ☎ 01302 737108 ✉ john.sherburn@doncaster.gov.uk

Licensing: Mr Harold Hudson, Licensing Manager, Ground Floor, Council House, College Road, Doncaster DN1 3AJ ☎ 01302 736257 🖷 ; 01302 737323 ✉ harold.hudson@doncaster.gov.uk

Lifelong Learning: Ms Ruth Brook, Head of Family & Community Learning Service, Richmond Hill, Melton Road, Sprotbrough, Doncaster DN5 7SB ☎ 01302 862688 ✉ ruth.brook@doncaster.gov.uk

Lighting: Ms Gill Gillies, Assistant Director of Environment, Floor 7, Council House, College Road, Doncaster DN1 3AJ ☎ 01302 736018 ✉ gill.gillies@doncaster.gov.uk

Lottery Funding, Charity and Voluntary: Mr Christian Foster, Programmes Manager, Floor 10, Council House, College Road, Doncaster DN1 3AJ ☎ 01302 736614 ✉ christian.foster@doncaster.gov.uk

Member Services: Mr Andrew Sercombe, Scrutiny & Member Support Manager, 2 Priory Place, Doncaster DN1 1BN ☎ 01302 734354 ✉ andrew.sercombe@doncaster.gov.uk

Parking: Mr Tony Bidmead, Parking & Enforcement Manager, North Bridge Depot, North Bridge Road, Doncaster DN5 9AN ☎ 01302 736861 ✉ tony.bidmead@doncaster.gov.uk

Partnerships: Mr Howard Monk, Head of Corporate Policy & Performance, Floor 8, Council House, College Road, Doncaster DN1 3PY ☎ 01302 736911 🖷 01302 737769 ✉ howard.monk@doncaster.gov.uk

Personnel / HR: Ms Jill Higgs, Assistant Director of Human Resources & Communications, Floor 8, Council House, College Road, Doncaster DN1 3AJ ☎ 01302 737004 ✉ jill.higgs@doncaster.gov.uk

Planning: Mr Scott Cardwell, Assistant Director of Development, Floor 11, Council House, College Road, Doncaster DN1 3AJ ☎ 01302 737655 ✉ scott.cardwell@doncaster.gov.uk

Procurement: Mr Tony Coffey, Head of Corporate Procurement, Floor 10, Council House, College Road, Doncaster DN1 3AJ ☎ 01302 862222 🖷 01302 736681 ✉ tony.coffey@doncaster.gov.uk

Public Libraries: Ms Julie Grant, Assistant Director of Customer Services & ICT, Floor 2, Council House, College Road, Doncaster DN1 3AJ ☎ 01302 862496 ✉ julie.grant@doncaster.gov.uk

Recycling & Waste Minimisation: Ms Gill Gillies, Assistant Director of Environment, Floor 2, Council House, College Road, Doncaster DN1 3AJ ☎ 01302 736018

gill.gillies@doncaster.gov.uk

Regeneration: Mr Scott Cardwell, Assistant Director of Development, Floor 11, Council House, College Road, Doncaster DN1 3AJ 01302 737655 scott.cardwell@doncaster.gov.uk

Road Safety: Ms Gill Gillies, Assistant Director of Environment, Floor 2, Council House, College Road, Doncaster DN1 3AJ 01302 736018 gill.gillies@doncaster.gov.uk

Social Services (Adult): Mrs Joan Beck, Director of Adults & Communities, Floor 2, Council House, College Road, Doncaster DN1 3AJ 01302 737808 joan.beck@doncaster.gov.uk

Social Services (Children): Ms Vicki Lawson, Assistant Director of Children & Families, Floor 4, Council House, College Road, Doncaster DN1 3AJ 01302 737197 vicki.lawson@doncaster.gov.uk

Social Services (Children): Mr Chris Pratt, Director of Children & Young People's Services, Floor 4, Council House, College Road, Doncaster DN1 3AJ 01302 737800 chris.pratt@doncaster.gov.uk

Staff Training: Ms Jill Higgs, Assistant Director of Human Resources & Communications, Floor 8, Council House, College Road, Doncaster DN1 3AJ 01302 737004 jill.higgs@doncaster.gov.uk

Street Scene: Ms Gill Gillies, Assistant Director of Environment, Floor 7, Council House, College Road, Doncaster DN1 3AJ 01302 736018 gill.gillies@doncaster.gov.uk

Sustainable Communities: Ms Gill Gillies, Assistant Director of Environment, Floor 7, Council House, College Road, Doncaster DN1 3AJ 01302 736018 gill.gillies@doncaster.gov.uk

Tourism: Mr Colin Joy, Tourism & Visitor Economy Manager, The Blue Building, 38-40 High Street, Doncaster DN1 1DE 01302 737967 01302 736362 colin.joy@doncaster.gov.uk

Town Centre: Mr Roy Dean, Town Centre Manager, The Blue Building, 38 - 40 High Street, Doncaster DN1 1DE 01302 862349 01302 862341 roy.dean@doncaster.gov.uk

Town Centre: Mr Richard Young, Tourism & Visitor Economy Manager, The Blue Building, 38 - 40 High Street, Doncaster DN1 1DE 01302 734920 r.young@doncaster.gov.uk

Traffic Management: Ms Gill Gillies, Assistant Director of Environment, Floor 7, Council House, College Road, Doncaster DN1 3AJ 01302 736018 gill.gillies@doncaster.gov.uk

Transport: Mr Neil Firth, Head of Transport & Accessibility, Scarborough House, Chequer Road, Doncaster DN1 2DB 01302 735002 neil.firth@doncaster.gov.uk

Transport Planner: Mr Stephen King, Principal Transport Planner, Scarborough House, Chequer Road, Doncaster DN1 2DB 01302 735122 01302 735028 stephen.king@doncaster.gov.uk

Waste Collection and Disposal: Ms Gill Gillies, Assistant Director of Environment, Floor 7, Council House, College Road, Doncaster DN1 3AJ 01302 736018 gill.gillies@doncaster.gov.uk

Waste Management: Ms Gill Gillies, Assistant Director of Environment, Floor 7, Council House, College Road, Doncaster DN1 3AJ 01302 736018 gill.gillies@doncaster.gov.uk

Children's Play Areas: Ms Gill Gillies, Assistant Director of Environment, Floor 7, Council House, College Road, Doncaster DN1 3AJ 01302 736018 gill.gillies@doncaster.gov.uk

MEMBERS OF THE COUNCIL (64)

***Chair:* Mills**, Chris (LAB - Conisbrough & Denaby)
christine.mills@doncaster.gov.uk

***Mayor:* Davies**, Peter (O -)
peter.davies@doncaster.gov.uk

***Deputy Mayor:* Schofield**, Patricia (CON - Finningley)
patricia.schofield@doncaster.gov.uk

***Group Leader:* Coddington**, Paul (LD - Bessacarr & Cantley)
paul.coddington@doncaster.gov.uk

***Group Leader:* Jones**, Glyn (LAB - Central)
glyn.jones@doncaster.gov.uk

***Group Leader:* Woodcock**, Yvonne (CON - Finningley)
yvonne.woodcock@doncaster.gov.uk

Bartlett, Patricia (CON - Torne Valley)
patricia.bartlett@doncaster.gov.uk

Blackham, Joe (LAB - Stainforth & Moorends)
joe.blackham@doncaster.gov.uk

Bolton, Susan (LAB - Adwick)
susan.bolton@doncaster.gov.uk

Bosmans, Andrew (LAB - Balby)
andrew.bosmans@doncaster.gov.uk

Butler, Elsie (LAB - Edlington & Warmsworth)
elsie.butler@doncaster.gov.uk

Cole, Phil (LAB - Edlington & Warmsworth)
phil.cole@doncaster.gov.uk

Cooper-Holmes, Richard (LAB - Rossington)
richard.cooper-holmes@doncaster.gov.uk

Corden, Tony (LAB - Armthorpe)
Tony.Corden@doncaster.gov.uk

Curran, Linda (LAB - Hatfield)
linda.curran@doncaster.gov.uk

Cuthbert, Monty (LD - Bessacarr & Cantley)
monty.cuthbert@doncaster.gov.uk

Dobbs, Edward (LAB - Thorne)
edward.dobbs@doncaster.gov.uk

Fennelly, Nuala (LAB - Balby)
nuala.fennelly@doncaster.gov.uk

Ford, Bob (CON - Torne Valley)
bob.ford@doncaster.gov.uk

Haith, Pat (LAB - Hatfield)
pat.haith@doncaster.gov.uk

Hall, Pat (LAB - Edenthorpe Kirk Sandall & Barnby Dun)
pat.hall@doncaster.gov.uk

Hardy, Stuart (LAB - Bentley)
stuart.hardy@doncaster.gov.uk

Hedley, Barbara (LAB - Stainforth & Moorends)
barbara.hedley@doncaster.gov.uk

Hodson, Rachel (LAB - Thorne)
Rachel.Hodson@doncaster.gov.uk

Hogarth, Charlie (LAB - Bentley)
Charlie.Hogarth@doncaster.gov.uk

Holland, David (LAB - Mexborough)
david.holland@doncaster.gov.uk
Holland, Sandra (LAB - Conisbrough & Denaby)
sandra.holland@doncaster.gov.uk
Hood, Moira (LAB - Wheatley)
moira.hood@doncaster.gov.uk
Hoyle, Barbara (CON - Torne Valley)
barbara.hoyle@doncaster.gov.uk
Hughes, Eva (LAB - Wheatley)
eva.hughes@doncaster.gov.uk
Hutchinson, Deborah (IND - Great North Road)
deborah.hutchinson@doncaster.gov.uk
Jameson, Mick (LAB - Balby)
george.jameson@doncaster.gov.uk
Johnson, Barry (LAB - Rossington)
barry.johnson@doncaster.gov.uk
Johnson, Bob (LAB - Edlington & Warmsworth)
Bob.Johnson@doncaster.gov.uk
Jones, Roselyn (LAB - Askern Spa)
ros.jones@doncaster.gov.uk
Jones, R. Allan (CON - Finningley)
richard.jones@doncaster.gov.uk
Jones, Alan (LAB - Askern Spa)
a.jones@doncaster.gov.uk
Keegan, Ken (LAB - Stainforth & Moorends)
kenneth.keegan@doncaster.gov.uk
Kidd, Jane (LAB - Town Moor)
jane.kidd@doncaster.gov.uk
Kitchen, Ted (LAB - Adwick)
edwin.kitchen@doncaster.gov.uk
Knight, Pat (LAB - Hatfield)
Pat.Knight@doncaster.gov.uk
Knowles, Sue (LAB - Town Moor)
S.Knowles@doncaster.gov.uk
Leyland-Jepson, Tracey (LAB - Mexborough)
tracey.leyland-jepson@doncaster.gov.uk
McGuinness, Sue (LAB - Armthorpe)
sue.mcguinness@doncaster.gov.uk
McGuinness, Chris (LAB - Armthorpe)
chris.mcguinness@doncaster.gov.uk
McHale, John (LAB - Central)
john.mchale@doncaster.gov.uk
McNamee, Hilary (LAB - Rossington)
Hilary.McNamee@doncaster.gov.uk
Mordue, Bill (LAB - Great North Road)
bill.mordue@doncaster.gov.uk
Mounsey, John (LAB - Adwick)
j.mounsey@doncaster.gov.uk
Nevett, David (LAB - Edenthorpe Kirk Sandall & Barnby Dun)
david.nevett@doncaster.gov.uk
Nightingale, Jane (LAB - Bentley)
Jane.nightingale@doncaster.gov.uk
Phillips, Susan (LD - Mexborough)
sue.phillips@doncaster.gov.uk
Ransome, Cynthia (CON - Sprotbrough)
cynthia.ransome@doncaster.gov.uk
Revill, Tony (LAB - Edenthorpe Kirk Sandall & Barnby Dun)
Tony.Revill@doncaster.gov.uk
Rodgers, Kevin (LAB - Great North Road)
kevin.rodgers@doncaster.gov.uk
Sahman, Craig (LAB - Conisbrough & Denaby)
craig.sahman@doncaster.gov.uk
Sheppard, John (LAB - Wheatley)
John.Sheppard@doncaster.gov.uk
Tatton-Kelly, Eric (LD - Bessacarr & Cantley)
eric.tatton-kelly@doncaster.gov.uk
White, Austen (LAB - Askern Spa)
austen.white@doncaster.gov.uk
Wilkinson, Sue (LAB - Central)
Sue.Wilkinson@doncaster.gov.uk
Williams, Martin (IND - Thorne)
martin.williams@doncaster.gov.uk
Wood, Jonathan (CON - Sprotbrough)
jonathan.wood@doncaster.gov.uk
Woodhouse, Doreen (CON - Sprotbrough)
doreen.woodhouse@doncaster.gov.uk
Wray, Paul (LAB - Town Moor)
paul.wray@doncaster.gov.uk

POLITICAL COMPOSITION
LAB: 48, CON: 9, LD: 4, IND: 2, O: 1

CABINET
Leader: Mr Peter Davies
Adult Social Care & Health: Mrs Patricia Schofield
Children & Young People: Mr Eric Tatton-Kelly
Communities & Environmental Protection: Mrs Cynthia Ransome
Development, Transport, Equalities & Cohesion: Mr Peter Davies
Finance & Corporate Services: Mr Paul Coddington
Housing: Mrs Barbara Hoyle

COMMITTEE CHAIRS
Adults & Communities Overview & Scrutiny: Ms Pat Knight
Audit: Mrs Roselyn Jones
Chief Officer Appointments: Mr Bob Johnson
Licensing: Mr David Nevett
Planning: Mrs Eva Hughes
Regeneration & Environment Overview & Scrutiny: Mr Kevin Rodgers
Schools, Children & Young People Overview & Scrutiny: Ms Hilary McNamee
Standards: Mrs Moira Hood

DORSET — C

Dorset County Council, County Hall, Colliton Park, Dorchester DT1 1XJ ☎ 01305 221000 🖷 01305 224839
dorsetdirect@dorsetcc.gov.uk 💻 www.dorsetforyou.com

FACTS & FIGURES
Police Authority: Dorset Police Authority
Health Authority: NHS South West
Learning and Skills Council: South West
EU Constituencies: South West
Election Frequency: Elections are of whole council

PRINCIPAL OFFICERS
Chief Executive: Ms Debbie Ward, Chief Executive, County Hall, Colliton Park, Dorchester DT1 1XJ ☎ 01305 224317
d.ward@dorsetcc.gov.uk

Deputy Chief Executive: Mrs Elaine Taylor, Director for Corporate Resources, County Hall, Colliton Park, Dorchester DT1 1XJ ☎ 01305 224177 🖷 01305 224114
e.m.taylor@dorsetcc.gov.uk

Senior Management: Mr Miles Butler, Director for Environment, County Hall, Colliton Park, Dorchester DT1 1XJ ☎ 01305 224216 🖷 01305 224914 🖰 m.butler@dorsetcc.gov.uk

Senior Management: Mr John Nash, Director for Children's Services, County Hall, Colliton Park, Dorchester DT1 1XJ ☎ 01305 224166 🖷 01305 224499 🖰 j.g.nash@dorsetcc.gov.uk

Senior Management: Mrs Elaine Taylor, Director for Corporate Resources, County Hall, Colliton Park, Dorchester DT1 1XJ ☎ 01305 224177 🖷 01305 224114 🖰 e.m.taylor@dorsetcc.gov.uk

Architect, Building / Property Services: Mr Mike Harries, Head of Dorset Property, Princes House, Princes Street, Dorchester DT1 1TP ☎ 01305 225227 🖷 01305 225254 🖰 m.j.harries@dorsetcc.gov.uk

Best Value: Mr Andy Ray, Head of Business Change & Efficiency, County Hall, Colliton Park, Dorchester DT1 1XJ ☎ 01305 224113 🖷 01305 228567 🖰 a.r.ray@dorsetcc.gov.uk

Building Control: Mr Mike Harries, Head of Dorset Property, Princes House, Princes Street, Dorchester DT1 1TP ☎ 01305 225227 🖷 01305 225254 🖰 m.j.harries@dorsetcc.gov.uk

Catering Services: Ms Jackie Garland, Category Manager, County Hall, Colliton Park, Dorchester DT1 1XJ ☎ 01305 221267 🖷 01305 228567 🖰 j.a.garland@dorsetcc.gov.uk

Catering Services: Mrs Sue Hawkins, Care Catering Services Manager, Vespasian House Catering 2nd Floor, West Wing, Bridport Road, Dorchester DT1 1PX ☎ 01305 225930 🖰 s.hawkins@dorsetcc.gov.uk

Children / Youth Services: Mr Les Gardner, Head of Early Intervention Services, County Hall, Colliton Park, Dorchester DT1 1XJ ☎ 01305 224164 🖷 01305 224499 🖰 l.gardner@dorsetcc.gov.uk

Children / Youth Services: Mr Mike Hogan, Youth & Community Services Manager, Youth Headquarters, Princes House, Prices Street, Dorchester DT1 1TP ☎ 01305 221975 🖰 m.hogan@dorsetcc.gov.uk

Civil Registration: Mrs Sam Porter, Regulatory Services Support Manager, Colliton Annexe, Colliton Park, Dorchester DT1 1XJ ☎ 01305 224927 🖷 01305 224951 🖰 s.l.porter@dorsetcc.gov.uk

Community Safety: Mr Andrew Archibald, Head of Adult Services, County Hall, Colliton Park, Dorchester DT1 1XJ ☎ 01305 216665 🖰 a.archibald@dorsetcc.gov.uk

Community Safety: Mr Andy Frost, Strategic Manager Dat and Community Safety, County Hall, Colliton Park, Dorchester DT1 1XJ ☎ 01305 224331 🖷 01305 224325 🖰 a.frost@dorsetcc.gov.uk

Computer Management: Mr Richard Pascoe, Head of ICT Strategy & Systems, County Hall, Colliton Park, Dorchester DT1 1XJ ☎ 01305 224117 🖷 01305 224391 🖰 r.j.pascoe@dorsetcc.gov.uk

Consumer Protection and Trading Standards: Mrs Sam Porter, Regulatory Services Support Manager, Colliton Annexe, Colliton Park, Dorchester DT1 1XJ ☎ 01305 224927 🖷 01305 224951 🖰 s.l.porter@dorsetcc.gov.uk

Contracts: Mr Andy Ray, Head of Business Change & Efficiency, County Hall, Colliton Park, Dorchester DT1 1XJ ☎ 01305 224113 🖷 01305 228567 🖰 a.r.ray@dorsetcc.gov.uk

Corporate Services: Mr David Ayre, Head of Countryside & Business Development, County Hall, Colliton Park, Dorchester DT1 1XJ ☎ 01305 224257 🖰 d.n.ayre@dorsetcc.gov.uk

Corporate Services: Mr Mark Taylor, Head of Internal Audit, Insurance & Risk Management, County Hall, Colliton Park, Dorchester DT1 1XJ ☎ ; 01305 224982 🖰 m.taylor@dorsetcc.gov.uk

Corporate Services: Mrs Elaine Taylor, Director for Corporate Resources, County Hall, Colliton Park, Dorchester DT1 1XJ ☎ 01305 224177 🖷 01305 224114 🖰 e.m.taylor@dorsetcc.gov.uk

Direct Labour: Mr Andrew Martin, Head of Highways Operations, Charminster Depot, Wanchard Lane, Charminster, Dorchester DT2 9RP ☎ 01305 228100 🖷 01305 228101 🖰 a.j.martin@dorsetcc.gov.uk

Economic Development: Ms Helen Heanes, Senior Economic Development Officer, County Hall, Colliton Park, Dorchester DT1 1XJ ☎ 01305 224677 🖷 01305 225049 🖰 h.e.heanes@dorsetcc.gov.uk

Education: Mr John Nash, Director for Children's Services, County Hall, Colliton Park, Dorchester DT1 1XJ ☎ 01305 224166 🖷 01305 224499 🖰 j.g.nash@dorsetcc.gov.uk

E-Government: Mr Richard Pascoe, Head of ICT Strategy & Systems, County Hall, Colliton Park, Dorchester DT1 1XJ ☎ 01305 224117 🖷 01305 224391 🖰 r.j.pascoe@dorsetcc.gov.uk

Electoral Registration: Miss Kirsty Riglar, Democratic Services Manager, County Hall, Colliton Park, Dorchester DT1 1XJ ☎ 01305 225184 🖷 01305 224395 🖰 k.riglar@dorsetcc.gov.uk

Emergency Planning: Mr Simon Parker, County Emergency Planning Officer, County Hall, Colliton Park, Dorchester DT1 1XJ ☎ 01305 224510 🖷 01305 224108 🖰 s.parker@dorsetcc.gov.uk

Energy Management: Mr Mike Petitdemange, Senior Energy Engineer, Princes House, Princes Street, Dorchester DT1 1TP ☎ 01305 225279 🖷 01305 225222 🖰 m.j.petitdemange@dorsetcc.gov.uk

Environmental / Technical Services: Mr Miles Butler, Director for Environment, County Hall, Colliton Park, Dorchester DT1 1XJ ☎ 01305 224216 🖷 01305 224914 🖰 m.butler@dorsetcc.gov.uk

Estates, Property & Valuation: Mr Peter Scarlett, Valuation & Estates Manager, County Hall, Colliton Park, Dorchester DT1 1XJ ☎ 01305 221941 🖰 p.scarlett@dorsetcc.gov.uk

European Liaison: Mrs Ann Minto, Principal Europe & External Policy Officer, County Hall, Colliton Park, Dorchester DT1 1XJ

☎ 01305 224602 🖷 01305 225158 ✉ a.minto@dorsetcc.gov.uk

Events Manager: Mr Jonathan Slater, Senior Public Relations Officer, County Hall, Colliton Park, Dorchester DT1 1XJ ☎ 01305 228538 ✉ j.slater@dorsetcc.gov.uk

Facilities: Mr Steve Cheeseman, Business & Facilities Manager, County Hall, Colliton Park, Dorchester DT1 1XJ ☎ 01305 224204 🖷 01305 224399 ✉ s.w.cheeseman@dorsetcc.gov.uk

Finance and Treasurer: Mr Richard Bates, Head of Accountancy Support, County Hall, Colliton Park, Dorchester DT1 1XJ ☎ 01305 228548 ✉ r.bates@dorsetcc.gov.uk

Finance and Treasurer: Mr Peter Illsley, Head of Corporate Finance, County Hall, Colliton Park, Dorchester DT1 1XJ ☎ 01305 224940 ✉ p.illsley@dorsetcc.gov.uk

Finance and Treasurer: Mr Paul Kent, Chief Financial Officer/Deputy Director for Chief Financial Officer/Deputy Director for Corporate Resources, County Hall, Colliton Park, Dorchester DT1 1XJ ☎ 01305 224115 🖷 01305 224114 ✉ p.j.kent@dorsetcc.gov.uk

Fleet Management: Mr Sean Adams, Senior Category Manager, County Hall, Colliton Park, Dorchester DT1 1XJ ☎ 01305 221263 🖷 01305 228567 ✉ s.w.adams@dorsetcc.gov.uk

Fleet Management: Mr Michael Winter, Head of Dorset Highways Management, Pullman Court, Dorchester DT1 1GA ☎ 01305 225302 ✉ m.w.winter@dorsetcc.gov.uk

Grounds Maintenance: Mr Steve Harris, Grounds Maintenance Manager, Dorset Works Organisation, Charminster Depot, Wanchard Lane, Charminster, Dorchester DT2 9RP ☎ 01305 228192 🖷 01305 228101 ✉ s.jb.harris@dorsetcc.gov.uk

Health and Safety: Miss Karen Butters, Employee Wellbeing Manager, County Hall, Colliton Park, Dorchester DT1 1XJ ☎ 01305 224095 🖷 01305 224620 ✉ k.butters@dorsetcc.gov.uk

Highways: Mr Andrew Martin, Head of Highways Operations, Charminster Depot, Wanchard Lane, Charminster, Dorchester DT2 9RP ☎ 01305 228100 🖷 01305 228101 ✉ a.j.martin@dorsetcc.gov.uk

Highways: Mr Michael Winter, Head of Dorset Highways Management, County Hall, Colliton Park, Dorchester DT1 1XJ ☎ 01305 225302 ✉ m.w.winter@dorsetcc.gov.uk

Legal: Mr Jonathan Mair, Head of Legal & Democratic Services, County Hall, Colliton Park, Dorchester DT1 1XJ ☎ 01305 224181 🖷 01305 224399 ✉ j.e.mair@dorsetcc.gov.uk

Leisure and Cultural Services: Mr Paul Leivers, Head of Cultural Services, Library Headquarters, Colliton Park, Dorchester DT1 1XJ ☎ 01305 224455 🖷 01305 224456 ✉ p.leivers@dorsetcc.gov.uk

Lifelong Learning: Mr Les Gardner, Head of Early Intervention Services, County Hall, Colliton Park, Dorchester DT1 1XJ ☎ 01305 224164 🖷 01305 224299 ✉ l.gardner@dorsetcc.gov.uk

Lighting: Mr Rod Mainstone, Principal Engineer - Streetlighting, Dorset Engineering Consultancy, Pullman Court, Station Approach, Dorchester DT1 1GA ☎ 01305 225355 🖷 01305 225301 ✉ r.l.mainstone@dorsetcc.gov.uk

Lottery Funding, Charity and Voluntary: Mr Chris Scally, External Funding & Development Manager, County Hall, Colliton Park, Dorchester DT1 1XJ ☎ 01305 228624 🖷 01305 224886 ✉ c.scally@dorsetcc.gov.uk

Member Services: Miss Kirsty Riglar, Democratic Services Manager, County Hall, Colliton Park, Dorchester DT1 1XJ ☎ 01305 225184 🖷 01305 224395 ✉ k.riglar@dorsetcc.gov.uk

Personnel / HR: Miss Sheralyn Huntingford, Head of Human Resources & Exchequer Services, County Hall, Colliton Park, Dorchester DT1 1XJ ☎ 01305 224090 🖷 01305 224620 ✉ s.huntingford@dorsetcc.gov.uk

Planning: Mr Don Gobbett, Head of Planning Division, County Hall, Colliton Park, Dorchester DT1 1XJ ☎ 01305 224490 🖷 01305 224914 ✉ d.m.gobbett@dorsetcc.gov.uk

Procurement: Mr Andy Ray, Head of Business Change & Efficiency, County Hall, Colliton Park, Dorchester DT1 1XJ ☎ 01305 224113 🖷 01305 228567 ✉ a.r.ray@dorsetcc.gov.uk

Public Libraries: Mr Paul Leivers, Head of Cultural Services, Library Headquarters, Colliton Park, Dorchester DT1 1XJ ☎ 01305 224455 🖷 01305 224456 ✉ p.leivers@dorsetcc.gov.uk

Recycling & Waste Minimisation: Mr Steve Burdis, Director - Dorset Waste Partnership, Wadham House, 50 High West Street, Dorchester DT1 1UT ☎ 01305 224691 🖷 01305 225002 ✉ steve.burdis@dorsetcc.gov.uk

Regeneration: Mr Dave Walsh, Group Leader - Community, Economic Policies & Programmes, County Hall, Colliton Park, Dorchester DT1 1XJ ☎ 01305 224254 🖷 01305 224602 ✉ d.walsh@dorsetcc.gov.uk

Road Safety: Mr Robert Smith, Road Safety Officer, County Hall, Colliton Park, Dorchester DT1 1XJ ☎ 01305 224680 🖷 01305 224835 ✉ r.smith@dorsetcc.gov.uk

Social Services (Adult): Mr Andrew Archibald, Head of Adult Services, Dorchester Local Office, Acland Road, Dorchester DT1 1SH ☎ 01305 216665 ✉ a.archibald@dorsetcc.gov.uk

Social Services (Children): Mrs Jackie Last, Head of Children & Family Services, County Hall, Colliton Park, Dorchester DT1 1XJ ☎ 01305 225089 🖷 01305 224499 ✉ j.last@dorsetcc.gov.uk

Staff Training: Mrs Helen Sotheran, Learning & Development Manager, County Hall, Colliton Park, Dorchester DT1 1XJ ☎ 01305 224088 🖷 01305 224620 ✉ h.l.sotheran@dorsetcc.gov.uk

Sustainable Communities: Mr Don Gobbett, Head of Planning Division, County Hall, Colliton Park, Dorchester DT1 1XJ ☎ 01305 224490 🖷 01305 224914 ✉ d.m.gobbett@dorsetcc.gov.uk

Sustainable Development: Ms Kate Hall, Sustainability Manager, County Hall, Colliton Park, Dorchester DT1 1XJ ☎ 01305 224774 🖷 01305 224602 🖱 k.m.hall@dorsetcc.gov.uk

Tourism: Mr Dave Walsh, Group Leader - Community, Economic Policies & Programmes, County Hall, Colliton Park, Dorchester DT1 1XJ ☎ 01305 224254 🖷 01305 224602 🖱 d.walsh@dorsetcc.gov.uk

Traffic Management: Mr Andy Ackerman, Group Manager - Traffic Management, County Hall, Colliton Park, Dorchester DT1 1XJ ☎ 01305 225302 🖷 01305 225186 🖱 a.ackerman@dorsetcc.gov.uk

Transport: Mr David Coates, Public Transport Manager, County Hall, Colliton Park, Dorchester DT1 1XJ ☎ 01305 221587 🖱 d.coates@dorsetcc.gov.uk

Waste Collection and Disposal: Mr Steve Burdis, Director - Dorset Waste Partnership, Wadham House, 50 High West Street, Dorchester DT1 1UT ☎ 01305 224691 🖷 01305 225002 🖱 steve.burdis@dorsetcc.gov.uk

Waste Management: Mr Steve Burdis, Director - Dorset Waste Partnership, Wadham House, 50 High West Street, Dorchester DT1 1UT ☎ 01305 224691 🖷 01305 225002 🖱 steve.burdis@dorsetcc.gov.uk

MEMBERS OF THE COUNCIL (45)

***Chair:* Wilson**, John (CON - Ferndown)
j.l.wilson@dorsetcc.gov.uk
***Leader of the Council:* Campbell**, Angus (CON - Hambledon)
i.a.campbell@dorsetcc.gov.uk
***Group Leader:* Dover**, Janet (LD - Colehill & Stapehill)
j.dover@dorsetcc.gov.uk
Ames, Les (IND - Portland Tophill)
l.h.ames@dorsetcc.gov.uk
Bevan, Michael (CON - Sherborne Rural)
m.bevan@dorsetcc.gov.uk
Biggs, Richard (LD - Dorchester)
r.m.biggs@dorsetcc.gov.uk
Brenton, Alex (LD - Egdon Heath)
a.brenton@dorsetcc.gov.uk
Brierley, Geoffrey (CON - Marshwood Vale)
g.j.brierley@dorsetcc.gov.uk
Budd, David (LD - Wareham)
d.a.budd@dorsetcc.gov.uk
Burt, Derek (CON - Ferndown)
d.b.burt@dorsetcc.gov.uk
Cattaway, Andrew (CON - Stour Vale)
a.r.cattaway@dorsetcc.gov.uk
Coatsworth, Ronald (CON - Bride Valley)
r.w.coatsworth@dorsetcc.gov.uk
Cook, Robin (CON - Minister)
r.cook@dorsetcc.gov.uk
Cooke, Andy (CON - Broadwey)
a.cooke@dorsetcc.gov.uk
Coombs, Toni (CON - Verwood & Three Legged Cross)
t.b.coombs@dorsetcc.gov.uk
Cooper, Barrie (LD - Blandford)
b.g.cooper@dorsetcc.gov.uk
Cox, Hilary (CON - Winterborne)
h.a.cox@dorsetcc.gov.uk
Crowhurst, David (CON - Linden Lea)
d.crowhurst@dorsetcc.gov.uk
Drane, Fred (LD - Lytchett)
f.h.drane@dorsetcc.gov.uk
Ellis, Brian (LD - Lodmoor)
b.e.ellis@dorsetcc.gov.uk
Finney, Peter (CON - West Moors & Holt)
p.finney@dorsetcc.gov.uk
Flower, Spencer (CON - Verwood & Three Legged Cross)
s.g.flower@dorsetcc.gov.uk
Fox, David J (CON - Commons)
d.j.fox@dorsetcc.gov.uk
Fox, David C (LD - Blackmore Vale)
d.c.fox@dorsetcc.gov.uk
Gardner, Ian (CON - Chickerell & Chesil Bank)
i.gardner@dorsetcc.gov.uk
Gould, Robert (CON - Sherborne)
r.gould@dorsetcc.gov.uk
Griffiths, Alan (CON - Mudeford & Highcliffe)
a.griffiths@dorsetcc.gov.uk
Hall, Peter (CON - Christchurch Central)
p.r.hall@dorsetcc.gov.uk
Harris, David (LD - Westham)
david.harris@dorsetcc.gov.uk
Haynes, Jill (CON - Three Valleys)
jill.haynes@dorsetcc.gov.uk
Jamieson, Colin (CON - Highcliffe & Walkford)
c.jamieson@dorsetcc.gov.uk
Jefferies, Susan (LD - Corfe Mullen)
s.jefferies@dorsetcc.gov.uk
Jeffery, Mervyn (LD - Shaftesbury)
m.jeffrey@dorsetcc.gov.uk
Jones, David (CON - Burton Grange)
david.jones@dorsetcc.gov.uk
Jones, Trevor (LD - Dorchester)
d.t.jones@dorsetcc.gov.uk
Knox, Rebecca (CON - Beaminster)
r.knox@dorsetcc.gov.uk
Legg, Howard (LD - Weymouth Town)
h.legg@dorsetcc.gov.uk
Lovell, Mike (CON - Purbeck Hills)
m.v.lovell@dorsetcc.gov.uk
Milsted, David (LD - Gillingham)
d.milsted@dorsetcc.gov.uk
Munro, Tim (CON - Portland Harbour)
tim.munro@dorsetcc.gov.uk
Palmer, Timothy (CON - Cranborne Chase)
t.j.palmer@dorsetcc.gov.uk
Reed, Nigel (CON - Rodwell)
n.reed@dorsetcc.gov.uk
Richardson, Peter (CON - St Leonards & St Ives)
p.richardson@dorsetcc.gov.uk
Trite, William (CON - Swanage)
w.trite@dorsetcc.gov.uk
Wallace, Karl (LAB - Bridport)
k.wallace@dorsetcc.gov.uk

POLITICAL COMPOSITION

CON: 29, LD: 14, IND: 1, LAB: 1

CABINET

Leader: Mr Angus Campbell
Adult Social Care: Mr Andrew Cattaway
Children's Services: Mrs Toni Coombs

Community Services: Mrs Hilary Cox
Corporate Resources: Mr Spencer Flower
Environment: Mr Robert Gould
Highways & Transportation: Mr Peter Finney

COMMITTEE CHAIRS

Adult & Community Services Overview & Scrutiny: Mrs Jill Haynes
Audit & Scrutiny: Mr Trevor Jones
Children's Services: Mr Michael Bevan
Dorset Health Scrutiny: Mr Ronald Coatsworth
Environment Overview: Mr Robin Cook
Planning: Mr Derek Burt
Staffing: Mr Angus Campbell

DOVER D

Dover District Council, Council Offices, White Cliffs Business Park, Dover CT16 3PJ ☎ 01304 821199 🖷 01304 872300 ✉ customerservices@dover.gov.uk 💻 www.dover.gov.uk

FACTS & FIGURES

Police Authority: Kent Police Authority
Health Authority: South East Coast Strategic Health Authority
Learning and Skills Council: South East
Parliamentary Constituencies: Dover
EU Constituencies: South East
Election Frequency: Elections are of whole council
Twinning: Dover: Calais (France); Split (Yugoslavia); Deal: St. Omer (France); Vlissingen (Netherlands); Aylesham: Courrieres (France); Eastry: Longpre-les-Corps-Saints (France); Ringwould with Kingsdown: Wissant (France); Sandwich: Honfleur (France); Renoix (Belgium)

PRINCIPAL OFFICERS

Chief Executive: Mr Nadeem Aziz, Chief Executive, Council Offices, White Cliffs Business Park, Dover CT16 3PJ ☎ 01304 872400 🖷 01304 872004 ✉ nadeemaziz@dover.gov.uk

Senior Management: Mr Mike Davis, Director of Finance, Housing & Community, Council Offices, White Cliffs Business Park, Dover CT16 3PJ ☎ 01304 872107 🖷 01304 872104 ✉ mikedavis@dover.gov.uk

Senior Management: Mr Michael Dawson, Director of Regeneration & Development, Council Offices, White Cliffs Business Park, Dover CT16 3PJ ☎ 01304 872460 🖷 01304 872416 ✉ michaeldawson@dover.gov.uk

Senior Management: Mr David Randall, Director of Governance, Council Offices, White Cliffs Business Park, Dover CT16 3PJ ☎ 01304 872141 🖷 01304 872300 ✉ davidrandall@dover.gov.uk

Senior Management: Mr Roger Walton, Director of Environment & Corporate Assets, Council Offices, White Cliffs Business Park, Dover CT16 3PJ ☎ 01304 872240 🖷 01304 872416 ✉ rogerwalton@dover.gov.uk

Architect, Building / Property Services: Mr Roger Walton, Director of Environment & Corporate Assets, Council Offices, White Cliffs Business Park, Dover CT16 3PJ ☎ 01304 872240 🖷 01304 872416 ✉ rogerwalton@dover.gov.uk

Best Value: Mr David Randall, Director of Governance, Council Offices, White Cliffs Business Park, Dover CT16 3PJ ☎ 01304 872141 🖷 01304 872300 ✉ davidrandall@dover.gov.uk

Building Control: Mr Michael Dawson, Director of Regeneration & Development, Council Offices, White Cliffs Business Park, Dover CT16 3PJ ☎ 01304 872460 🖷 01304 872416 ✉ michaeldawson@dover.gov.uk

PR / Communications: Mr Nadeem Aziz, Chief Executive, Council Offices, White Cliffs Business Park, Dover CT16 3PJ ☎ 01304 872400 🖷 01304 872004 ✉ nadeemaziz@dover.gov.uk

Community Planning: Mr Michael Dawson, Director of Regeneration & Development, Council Offices, White Cliffs Business Park, Dover CT16 3PJ ☎ 01304 872460 🖷 01304 872416 ✉ michaeldawson@dover.gov.uk

Community Safety: Mr Roger Walton, Director of Environment & Corporate Assets, Council Offices, White Cliffs Business Park, Dover CT16 3PJ ☎ 01304 872240 🖷 01304 872416 ✉ rogerwalton@dover.gov.uk

Computer Management: Mrs Angela Waite, Head of ICT, EK Services, Military Road, Canterbury CT1 1YW ☎ 01227 862028; 01227 862478; 01227 862478 🖷 01227 862208 ✉ angela.waite@canterbury.gov.uk; angela.waite@ekservices.org; angela.waite@ekservices.org

Contracts: Mr Mike Davis, Director of Finance, Housing & Community, Council Offices, White Cliffs Business Park, Dover CT16 3PJ ☎ 01304 872107 🖷 01304 872104 ✉ mikedavis@dover.gov.uk

Corporate Services: Mr David Randall, Director of Governance, Council Offices, White Cliffs Business Park, Dover CT16 3PJ ☎ 01304 872141 🖷 01304 872300 ✉ davidrandall@dover.gov.uk

Customer Service: Mr Nadeem Aziz, Chief Executive, Council Offices, White Cliffs Business Park, Dover CT16 3PJ ☎ 01304 872400 🖷 01304 872004 ✉ nadeemaziz@dover.gov.uk

Customer Service: Ms Donna Reed, Shared Services Director, EK Services, Military Road, Canterbury CT1 1YW ☎ 01227 862073 ✉ donna.reed@ekservices.org

Economic Development: Mr Michael Dawson, Director of Regeneration & Development, Council Offices, White Cliffs Business Park, Dover CT16 3PJ ☎ 01304 872460 🖷 01304 872416 ✉ michaeldawson@dover.gov.uk

E-Government: Mr Mike Davis, Director of Finance, Housing & Community, Council Offices, White Cliffs Business Park, Dover CT16 3PJ ☎ 01304 872107 🖷 01304 872104 ✉ mikedavis@dover.gov.uk

E-Government: Mrs Roz Edridge, Business Systems Manager, East Kent Services, Council Offices, Cecil Street, Margate CT9 1XZ ☎ 01843 577033 ✉ roz.edridge@thanet.gov.uk

Electoral Registration: Mr David Randall, Director of Governance, Council Offices, White Cliffs Business Park, Dover

CT16 3PJ ☎ 01304 872141 🖷 01304 872300 ✉ davidrandall@dover.gov.uk

Emergency Planning: Mr David Randall, Director of Governance, Council Offices, White Cliffs Business Park, Dover CT16 3PJ ☎ 01304 872141 🖷 01304 872300 ✉ davidrandall@dover.gov.uk

Environmental / Technical Services: Mr Roger Walton, Director of Environment & Corporate Assets, Council Offices, White Cliffs Business Park, Dover CT16 3PJ ☎ 01304 872240 🖷 01304 872416 ✉ rogerwalton@dover.gov.uk

Environmental Health: Mr Michael Dawson, Director of Regeneration & Development, Council Offices, White Cliffs Business Park, Dover CT16 3PJ ☎ 01304 872460 🖷 01304 872416 ✉ michaeldawson@dover.gov.uk

Estates, Property & Valuation: Mr Roger Walton, Director of Environment & Corporate Assets, Council Offices, White Cliffs Business Park, Dover CT16 3PJ ☎ 01304 872240 🖷 01304 872416 ✉ rogerwalton@dover.gov.uk

Finance and Treasurer: Mr Mike Davis, Director of Finance, Housing & Community, Council Offices, White Cliffs Business Park, Dover CT16 3PJ ☎ 01304 872107 🖷 01304 872104 ✉ mikedavis@dover.gov.uk

Fleet Management: Mr Mike Davis, Director of Finance, Housing & Community, Council Offices, White Cliffs Business Park, Dover CT16 3PJ ☎ 01304 872107 🖷 01304 872104 ✉ mikedavis@dover.gov.uk

Grounds Maintenance: Mr Roger Walton, Director of Environment & Corporate Assets, Council Offices, White Cliffs Business Park, Dover CT16 3PJ ☎ 01304 872240 🖷 01304 872416 ✉ rogerwalton@dover.gov.uk

Health and Safety: Mr David Randall, Director of Governance, Council Offices, White Cliffs Business Park, Dover CT16 3PJ ☎ 01304 872141 🖷 01304 872300 ✉ davidrandall@dover.gov.uk

Home Energy Conservation: Mr Roger Walton, Director of Environment & Corporate Assets, Council Offices, White Cliffs Business Park, Dover CT16 3PJ ☎ 01304 872240 🖷 01304 872416 ✉ rogerwalton@dover.gov.uk

Housing: Mr Mike Davis, Director of Finance, Housing & Community, Council Offices, White Cliffs Business Park, Dover CT16 3PJ ☎ 01304 872107 🖷 01304 872104 ✉ mikedavis@dover.gov.uk

Housing Maintenance: Mr Elliot Austin, Housing Maintenance Manager, East Kent Housing Ltd, c/o Council Offices, Cecil Street, Margate CT9 1XZ ☎ 01843 577085; 01843 577085 🖷 01843 290906; 01843 290906 ✉ elliot.austin@thanet.gov.uk; elliot.austin@thanet.gov.uk

Housing Maintenance: Mr Mike Davis, Director of Finance, Housing & Community, Council Offices, White Cliffs Business Park, Dover CT16 3PJ ☎ 01304 872107 🖷 01304 872104 ✉ mikedavis@dover.gov.uk

Legal: Mr Harvey Rudd, Solicitor to the Council, Council Offices, White Cliffs Business Park, Dover CT16 3PJ ☎ 01304 872321 🖷 01304 872300 ✉ harveyrudd@dover.gov.uk

Leisure and Cultural Services: Mr Mike Davis, Director of Finance, Housing & Community, Council Offices, White Cliffs Business Park, Dover CT16 3PJ ☎ 01304 872107 🖷 01304 872104 ✉ mikedavis@dover.gov.uk

Licensing: Mr Roger Walton, Director of Environment & Corporate Assets, Council Offices, White Cliffs Business Park, Dover CT16 3PJ ☎ 01304 872240 🖷 01304 872416 ✉ rogerwalton@dover.gov.uk

Lighting: Mr Roger Walton, Director of Environment & Corporate Assets, Council Offices, White Cliffs Business Park, Dover CT16 3PJ ☎ 01304 872240 🖷 01304 872416 ✉ rogerwalton@dover.gov.uk

Member Services: Mr David Randall, Director of Governance, Council Offices, White Cliffs Business Park, Dover CT16 3PJ ☎ 01304 872141 🖷 01304 872300 ✉ davidrandall@dover.gov.uk

Parking: Mr Roger Walton, Director of Environment & Corporate Assets, Council Offices, White Cliffs Business Park, Dover CT16 3PJ ☎ 01304 872240 🖷 01304 872416 ✉ rogerwalton@dover.gov.uk

Personnel / HR: Ms Juli Oliver-Smith, Head of EK Human Resources, East Kent HR Partnership, Dover District Council, White Cliffs Business Park, Whitfield, Dover CT16 3PJ ☎ 07917 473616 ✉ hrpartnership@dover.gov.uk

Personnel / HR: Mr David Randall, Director of Governance, Council Offices, White Cliffs Business Park, Dover CT16 3PJ ☎ 01304 872141 🖷 01304 872300 ✉ davidrandall@dover.gov.uk

Planning: Mr Michael Dawson, Director of Regeneration & Development, Council Offices, White Cliffs Business Park, Dover CT16 3PJ ☎ 01304 872460 🖷 01304 872416 ✉ michaeldawson@dover.gov.uk

Procurement: Mr Mike Davis, Director of Finance, Housing & Community, Council Offices, White Cliffs Business Park, Dover CT16 3PJ ☎ 01304 872107 🖷 01304 872104 ✉ mikedavis@dover.gov.uk

Recycling & Waste Minimisation: Mr Roger Walton, Director of Environment & Corporate Assets, Council Offices, White Cliffs Business Park, Dover CT16 3PJ ☎ 01304 872240 🖷 01304 872416 ✉ rogerwalton@dover.gov.uk

Regeneration: Mr Tim Ingleton, Head of Inward Investment, Council Offices, White Cliffs Business Park, Dover CT16 3PJ ☎ 01304 872423 🖷 01304 872445 ✉ timingleton@dover.gov.uk

Staff Training: Ms Sonia Godfrey, HR Manager - Business Services, East Kent HR Partnership, Dover District Council, White Cliffs Business Park, Whitfield, Dover CT16 3PJ ☎ 07854 763690 ✉ hrpartnership@dover.gov.uk

Staff Training: Mr David Randall, Director of Governance,

Council Offices, White Cliffs Business Park, Dover CT16 3PJ
☎ 01304 872141 🖷 01304 872300 ✉ davidrandall@dover.gov.uk

Street Scene: Mr Roger Walton, Director of Environment & Corporate Assets, Council Offices, White Cliffs Business Park, Dover CT16 3PJ ☎ 01304 872240 🖷 01304 872416 ✉ rogerwalton@dover.gov.uk

Sustainable Communities: Mr Mike Davis, Director of Finance, Housing & Community, Council Offices, White Cliffs Business Park, Dover CT16 3PJ ☎ 01304 872107 🖷 01304 872104 ✉ mikedavis@dover.gov.uk

Tourism: Mr Mike Davis, Director of Finance, Housing & Community, Council Offices, White Cliffs Business Park, Dover CT16 3PJ ☎ 01304 872107 🖷 01304 872104 ✉ mikedavis@dover.gov.uk

Traffic Management: Mr Roger Walton, Director of Environment & Corporate Assets, Council Offices, White Cliffs Business Park, Dover CT16 3PJ ☎ 01304 872240 🖷 01304 872416 ✉ rogerwalton@dover.gov.uk

Waste Collection and Disposal: Mr Roger Walton, Director of Environment & Corporate Assets, Council Offices, White Cliffs Business Park, Dover CT16 3PJ ☎ 01304 872240 🖷 01304 872416 ✉ rogerwalton@dover.gov.uk

Waste Management: Mr Roger Walton, Director of Environment & Corporate Assets, Council Offices, White Cliffs Business Park, Dover CT16 3PJ ☎ 01304 872240 🖷 01304 872416 ✉ rogerwalton@dover.gov.uk

MEMBERS OF THE COUNCIL (45)

***Chair:* Nicholas**, Sue (CON - River)
cllrsuenicholas@dover.gov.uk
***Vice-Chair:* Le Chevalier**, Paul (CON - Walmer)
cllrpaullechevalier@dover.gov.uk
Back, Jim (CON - Whitfield)
cllrjames.back@dover.gov.uk
Bano, Ben (LAB - Mill Hill)
cllrbenbano@dover.gov.uk
Bartlett, Trevor (CON - Little Stour & Ashstone)
cllrtrevorbartlett@dover.gov.uk
Beresford, Pauline (CON - River)
cllrpauline.beresford@dover.gov.uk
Bond, Trevor (CON - Middle Deal & Sholden)
cllrtrevorbond@dover.gov.uk
Brivio, Pamela (LAB - Tower Hamlets)
cllrpamela.brivio@dover.gov.uk
Butcher, Bernard (CON - Sandwich)
cllrbernardbutcher@dover.gov.uk
Carter, Paul (CON - Sandwich)
cllrpaul.carter@dover.gov.uk
Chandler, Susan (CON - Little Stour & Ashstone)
cllrsusanchandler@dover.gov.uk
Collor, Nigel (CON - Castle)
cllrnigelcollor@dover.gov.uk
Connolly, Michael (CON - Little Stour & Ashstone)
cllrmichaelconolly@dover.gov.uk
Cowan, Gordon (LAB - St Radigunds)
cllrgordoncowan@dover.gov.uk
Cronk, James (LAB - Middle Deal & Sholden)
cllrjimcronk@dover.gov.uk
Eddy, Mike (LAB - Mill Hill)
cllrmichaeleddy@dover.gov.uk
Frost, Bob (CON - North Deal)
cllrbob.frost@dover.gov.uk
Gardner, Bill (LAB - North Deal)
billkimi@hotmail.co.uk
Goodwin, John (LAB - Tower Hamlets)
cllrjohngoodwin@dover.gov.uk
Hannent, David (CON - Whitfield)
cllrdavid.hannent@dover.gov.uk
Hawkins, Pam (LAB - Middle Deal & Sholden)
cllrpamela.hawkins@dover.gov.uk
Heath, Patrick (CON - Walmer)
cllrpatrickheath@dover.gov.uk
Hood, Jim (LAB - Town & Pier)
cllrgeorgehood@dover.gov.uk
Jones, Sue (LAB - Maxton, Elms Vale & Priory)
cllrsuejones@dover.gov.uk
Keen, Linda (LAB - Aylesham)
linda.keen@clara.co.uk
Kenton, Nicholas (CON - Eastry)
cllrnicholaskenton@dover.gov.uk
Le Chevalier, Sue (CON - Ringwould)
cllrsuzannelechevalier@dover.gov.uk
Lymer, Geoffrey (CON - Lydden & Temple Ewell)
cllrgeoffreylymer@dover.gov.uk
Manion, Stephen (CON - Eastry)
cllrstephenmanion@dover.gov.uk
Mills, Kevin (LAB - St Radigunds)
cllrkevinmills@dover.gov.uk
Morris, Keith (CON - St Margaret's-at-Cliffe)
cllrkeith.morris@dover.gov.uk
Ovenden, Marjorie (Mog) (CON - Eythorne & Shepherdswell)
cllrmog.ovenden@dover.gov.uk
Pollitt, Sid (LAB - Mill Hill)
cllrsid.pollitt@dover.gov.uk
Rook, Julie (CON - North Deal)
cllrjulierook@dover.gov.uk
Russell, Pip (CON - Sandwich)
cllrpip.russell@dover.gov.uk
Scales, Frederick (CON - Capel-le-Ferne)
cllrfrederickscales@dover.gov.uk
Smallwood, Diane (LAB - Maxton, Elms Vale & Priory)
cllrdianesmallwood@dover.gov.uk
Smith, Anne (LAB - Buckland)
cllrannesmith@dover.gov.uk
Smith, Christopher (Kit) (CON - Walmer)
cllrkitsmith@dover.gov.uk
Smith, Mick (LAB - Buckland)
cllrjohnsmith@dover.gov.uk
Thomson, Robert (LAB - Aylesham)
cllrrobertthompson@dover.gov.uk
Tranter, Janet (LAB - Buckland)
cllrjanettranter@dover.gov.uk
Walkden, Roger (CON - Maxton, Elms Vale & Priory)
cllrrogerwalkden@dover.gov.uk
Walker, Peter (LAB - Eythorne & Shepherdswell)
cllrpeter.walker@dover.gov.uk
Watkins, Paul (CON - St Margaret's-at-Cliffe)
cllrpaulwatkins@dover.gov.uk

POLITICAL COMPOSITION

CON: 26, LAB: 19

CABINET

Leader: Mr Paul Watkins
Deputy Leader: Mrs Susan Chandler
Access & Property Management: Mr Nigel Collor
Corporate Resources & Performance: Mr Michael Connolly
Environment, Waste & Planning: Mr Nicholas Kenton
Health, Wellbeing & Public Protection: Mr Patrick Heath
Skills, Training & External Relations: Mr Christopher (Kit) Smith

COMMITTEE CHAIRS

Community Regeneration Scrutiny: Mr Jim Hood
Licensing: Mr Bernard Butcher
Planning: Mr Frederick Scales
Policy & Reform Scrutiny: Mr Kevin Mills
Regulatory: Mr Bernard Butcher

DOWN N

Down District Council, Council Offices, 24 Strangford Road, Downpatrick BT30 6SR ☎ 028 4461 0800 🖷 028 4461 0801 ✉ council@downdc.gov.uk 💻 www.downdc.gov.uk

FACTS & FIGURES

Police Authority: Northern Ireland Policing Board
Health Authority: Eastern Health & Social Services Board
Learning and Skills Council: Northern Ireland
Parliamentary Constituencies: Down South, Strangford
EU Constituencies: Northern Ireland
Election Frequency: Elections are of whole council
Twinning: Downpatrick: Listowel (Ireland), Bezons (France), Glenview (USA); Newcastle: New Ross (Ireland); Ballynahinch: Lamourlaye (France)

PRINCIPAL OFFICERS

Chief Executive: Mr John Dumigan, Clerk & Chief Executive, Council Offices, 24 Strangford Road, Downpatrick BT30 6SR ☎ 028 4461 0800 🖷 028 4461 0801 ✉ john.dumigan@downdc.gov.uk

Architect, Building / Property Services: Mrs Marie Ward, Group Chief Building Control Officer, Council Offices, 24 Strangford Road, Downpatrick BT30 6SR ☎ 028 4461 0829 🖷 028 4461 0801 ✉ marie.ward@downdc.gov.uk

Building Control: Mrs Marie Ward, Group Chief Building Control Officer, Council Offices, 24 Strangford Road, Downpatrick BT30 6SR ☎ 028 4461 0829 🖷 028 4461 0801 ✉ marie.ward@downdc.gov.uk

Civil Registration: Ms Helen Matthews, Registrar, Council Offices, 24 Strangford Road, Downpatrick BT30 6SR ☎ 028 4461 0800 🖷 028 4461 0801 ✉ helen.matthews@downdc.gov.uk

PR / Communications: Ms Veronica Keegan, Marketing Manager, Council Offices, 24 Strangford Road, Downpatrick BT30 6SR ☎ 028 4461 0800 🖷 028 4461 0801 ✉ veronica.keegan@downdc.gov.uk

Community Safety: Mr Mark Kent, Community Safety Officer, Council Offices, 24 Strangford Road, Downpatrick BT30 6SR ☎ 028 4461 0800 🖷 028 4461 0801 ✉ mark.kent@downdc.gov.uk

Computer Management: Mr Gavin Ringland, IT Advisor, Council Offices, 24 Strangford Road, Downpatrick BT30 6SR ☎ 028 4461 0800 🖷 028 4461 0801 ✉ gavin.ringland@downdc.gov.uk

Contracts: Ms Alison White, Principal Administrative Officer, Council Offices, 24 Strangford Road, Downpatrick BT30 6SR ☎ 028 4461 0804 🖷 028 4461 0801 ✉ alison.white@downdc.gov.uk

Customer Service: Mr Gerry McBride, Customer Relations Manager, 24 Stangford Road, Downpatrick BT30 6SR

Economic Development: Mr David Patterson, Economic Development Manager, Council Offices, 24 Strangford Road, Downpatrick BT30 6SR ☎ 028 4461 9870 🖷 028 4461 9879 ✉ david.patterson@downdc.gov.uk

Emergency Planning: Ms Loreto McManus, Insurance & Risk Officer, Council Offices, 24 Strangford Road, Downpatrick BT30 6SR ☎ 028 4461 0800 🖷 028 4461 0801 ✉ loreto.mcmanus@downdc.gov.uk

Energy Management: Mrs Marie Ward, Group Chief Building Control Officer, Council Offices, 24 Strangford Road, Downpatrick BT30 6SR ☎ 028 4461 0829 🖷 028 4461 0801 ✉ marie.ward@downdc.gov.uk

Environmental / Technical Services: Ms Canice O'Rourke, Director of Environmental Services, Council Offices, 24 Strangford Road, Downpatrick BT30 6SR ☎ 028 4461 0827 🖷 028 4461 0801 ✉ canice.o'rourke@downdc.gov.uk

Environmental Health: Mr T McCrory, Principal Environmental Health Officer, Council Offices, 24 Strangford Road, Downpatrick BT30 6SR ☎ 028 4461 0824 🖷 028 4461 0801 ✉ tmccrory@downdc.gov.uk

Estates, Property & Valuation: Mrs Marie Ward, Group Chief Building Control Officer, Council Offices, 24 Strangford Road, Downpatrick BT30 6SR ☎ 028 4461 0829 🖷 028 4461 0801 ✉ marie.ward@downdc.gov.uk

European Liaison: Mrs Margaret Quinn, Project Development Manager, Council Offices, 24 Strangford Road, Downpatrick BT30 6SR ☎ 028 4461 9870 ✉ margaret.quinn@downdc.gov.uk

Events Manager: Ms Ann Moreland, Events Manager, Offices 9 & 10, Innovation House, 46 Belfast Road, Downpatrick BT30 9UP ☎ 028 4461 9870 🖷 028 4461 9879 ✉ ann.moreland@downdc.gov.uk

Finance and Treasurer: Mr Ken Montgomery, Principal Accounting Officer, Council Offices, 24 Strangford Road, Downpatrick BT30 6SR ☎ 028 4461 0800 🖷 ; 028 4461 0801

Fleet Management: Ms Canice O'Rourke, Director of Environmental Services, Council Offices, 24 Strangford Road, Downpatrick BT30 6SR ☎ 028 4461 0827 🖷 028 4461 0801 ✉ canice.o'rourke@downdc.gov.uk

Grounds Maintenance: Mr Damien Morgan, Parks Officer, Council Offices, 24 Strangford Road, Downpatrick BT30 6SR ☎ 028 4461 0800 🖷 028 4461 0801 🖰 damien.morgan@downdc.gov.uk

Health and Safety: Miss Kelly Rusk, Health & Safety Advisor, Council Offices, 24 Strangford Road, Downpatrick BT30 6SR 🖰 kelly.rusk@downdc.gov.uk

Legal: Ms Alison White, Principal Administrative Officer, Council Offices, 24 Strangford Road, Downpatrick BT30 6SR ☎ 028 4461 0804 🖷 028 4461 0801 🖰 alison.white@downdc.gov.uk

Leisure and Cultural Services: Mr Patrick McCluskey, Sports & Community Services Manager, Council Offices, 24 Strangford Road, Downpatrick BT30 6SR ☎ 028 4461 0815 🖷 028 4461 0801 🖰 patrick.mccluskey@downdc.gov.uk

Licensing: Ms Alison White, Principal Administrative Officer, Council Offices, 24 Strangford Road, Downpatrick BT30 6SR ☎ 028 4461 0804 🖷 028 4461 0801 🖰 alison.white@downdc.gov.uk

Member Services: Ms Alison White, Principal Administrative Officer, Council Offices, 24 Strangford Road, Downpatrick BT30 6SR ☎ 028 4461 0804 🖷 028 4461 0801 🖰 alison.white@downdc.gov.uk

Personnel / HR: Mrs Catrina Miskelly, Human Resources Manager, Council Offices, 24 Strangford Road, Downpatrick BT30 6SR ☎ 028 4461 0805 🖷 028 4461 0801 🖰 catrina.miskelly@downdc.gov.uk

Planning: Mrs Marie Ward, Group Chief Building Control Officer, Council Offices, 24 Strangford Road, Downpatrick BT30 6SR ☎ 028 4461 0829 🖷 028 4461 0801 🖰 marie.ward@downdc.gov.uk

Procurement: Ms Alison White, Principal Administrative Officer, Council Offices, 24 Strangford Road, Downpatrick BT30 6SR ☎ 028 4461 0804 🖷 028 4461 0801 🖰 alison.white@downdc.gov.uk

Recycling & Waste Minimisation: Ms Canice O'Rourke, Director of Environmental Services, Council Offices, 24 Strangford Road, Downpatrick BT30 6SR ☎ 028 4461 0827 🖷 028 4461 0801 🖰 canice.o'rourke@downdc.gov.uk

Staff Training: Mrs Catrina Miskelly, Human Resources Manager, Council Offices, 24 Strangford Road, Downpatrick BT30 6SR ☎ 028 4461 0805 🖷 028 4461 0801 🖰 catrina.miskelly@downdc.gov.uk

Street Scene: Mr Tom McClean, Building & Estates Manager, Council Offices, 24 Strangford Road, Downpatrick BT30 6SR ☎ 028 4461 0800 🖷 028 4461 0801 🖰 tom.mcclean@downdc.gov.uk

Tourism: Ms Angela Gilchrist, Tourism Manager, The St. Patrick Centre, 53a Market Street, Downpatrick BT30 6LZ ☎ 028 4461 6625 🖰 angela.gilchrist@downdc.gov.uk

Waste Collection and Disposal: Ms Canice O'Rourke, Director of Environmental Services, Council Offices, 24 Strangford Road, Downpatrick BT30 6SR ☎ 028 4461 0827 🖷 028 4461 0801 🖰 canice.o'rourke@downdc.gov.uk

Waste Management: Ms Canice O'Rourke, Director of Environmental Services, Council Offices, 24 Strangford Road, Downpatrick BT30 6SR ☎ 028 4461 0827 🖷 028 4461 0801 🖰 canice.o'rourke@downdc.gov.uk

Children's Play Areas: Mr Patrick McCluskey, Sports & Community Services Manager, Council Offices, 24 Strangford Road, Downpatrick BT30 6SR ☎ 028 4461 0815 🖷 028 4461 0801 🖰 patrick.mccluskey@downdc.gov.uk

MEMBERS OF THE COUNCIL (23)

***Vice-Chair:* McCarthy**, Maria (SDLP - Rowallane)
maria.mccarthy@downdc.gov.uk
Andrews, Terry (IND - Rowallane)
terry.andrews@downdc.gov.uk
Burgess, Robert (UUP - Rowallane)
robert.burgess@downdc.gov.uk
Burns, Stephen (SF - Newcastle)
stephen.burns@downdc.gov.uk
Clarke, Patrick (ALL - Newcastle)
patrick.clarke@downdc.gov.uk
Clarke, William (SF - Newcastle)
william.clarke@downdc.gov.uk
Coogan, Michael (SF - Ballynahinch)
michael.coogan@downdc.gov.uk
Craig, Garth (DUP - Ballynahinch)
garth.craig@downdc.gov.uk
Curran, Dermot (SDLP - Downpatrick)
dermot.curran@downdc.gov.uk
Dick, William (DUP - Rowallane)
william.dick@downdc.gov.uk
Doris, John (SDLP - Downpatrick)
john.doris@downdc.gov.uk
Enright, Cadogan (GRN - Downpatrick)
cadogan.enright@downdc.gov.uk
Johnston, Liam (SF - Downpatrick)
liam.johnston@downdc.gov.uk
Lyons, Walter (UUP - Ballynahinch)
walter.lyons@downdc.gov.uk
Mac Con Midhe, Eamonn (SF - Downpatrick)
eamonn.macconmidhe@downdc.gov.uk
McAleenan, Anne (SDLP - Ballynahinch)
anne.mcaleenan@downdc.gov.uk
McGrath, Colin (SDLP - Downpatrick)
colin.mcgrath@downdc.gov.uk
O'Boyle, Carmel (SDLP - Newcastle)
carmel.o'boyle@downdc.gov.uk
O'Neill, Eamonn (SDLP - Newcastle)
eamonn.o'neill@downdc.gov.uk
Patterson, Desmond (UUP - Newcastle)
desmond.patterson@downdc.gov.uk
Sharvin, Gareth (SDLP - Downpatrick)
gareth.sharvin@downdc.gov.uk
Toman, Patrick (SDLP - Ballynahinch)
patrick.toman@downdc.gov.uk
Walker, William (DUP - Rowallane)
william.walker@downdc.gov.uk

POLITICAL COMPOSITION
SDLP: 9, SF: 5, DUP: 3, UUP: 3, GRN: 1, IND: 1, ALL: 1

COMMITTEE CHAIRS
Audit: Mr Eamonn Mac Con Midhe
Corporate Services: Mr Colin McGrath
Cultural & Economic Development: Mr McAleenan (External)
Environmental Services: Mr Eamonn O'Neill
Recreation & Community Services: Mr Stephen Burns
Strategic Policy & Resources: Mr Walter Lyons

DUDLEY M
Dudley Metropolitan Borough Council, The Council House, Priory Road , Dudley DY1 1HF ☎ 0300 555 2345 🖷 01384 815275 ✉ dudleycouncilplus@dudley.gov.uk 💻 www.dudley.gov.uk

FACTS & FIGURES
Police Authority: West Midlands Police Authority
Health Authority: NHS West Midlands
Learning and Skills Council: West Midlands
Parliamentary Constituencies: Dudley North, Dudley South, Halesowen and Rowley Regis, Stourbridge
EU Constituencies: West Midlands
Election Frequency: Elections are by thirds

PRINCIPAL OFFICERS
Chief Executive: Mr John Polychronakis, Chief Executive, Council House, Priory Road, Dudley DY1 1HF ☎ 01384 815201 🖷 01384 815275 ✉ john.polychronakis@dudley.gov.uk

Senior Management: Mr John Millar, Director of the Urban Environment, 3-5 St. James's Road, Dudley DY1 1HZ ☎ 01384 814150 🖷 01384 814109 ✉ john.millar@dudley.gov.uk

Senior Management: Mrs Andrea Pope-Smith, Director of Adult, Community & Housing Services, Ednam House, St James's Road, Dudley DY1 3JJ ☎ 01384 815800 🖷 01384 811995 ✉ andrea.pope-smith@dudley.gov.uk

Senior Management: Ms Jane Porter, Acting Director of Children's Services & e-Champion, Westox House, 1 Trinity Road, Dudley DY1 1JQ ☎ 01384 814250 🖷 01384 814202 ✉ jane.porter@dudley.gov.uk

Senior Management: Mr Philip Tart, Director of Law, Property & Human Resources, The Council House, Priory Road , Dudley DY1 1HF ☎ 01384 815300 🖷 01384 815379 ✉ philip.tart@dudley.gov.uk

Access Officer / Social Services (Disability): Mrs Ann Askew, Head Service Physical & Sensory Disabilities, Brierley Hill Health & Social Care Centre, 2nd Floor, Venture Way, Brierley Hill DY5 1RU ☎ 01384 813090 ✉ ann.askew@dudley.gov.uk

Best Value: Mr Pete Sanford, Review Manager, Corporate Policy & Research, 3 St. James's Road, Dudley DY1 1H2 ☎ 01384 814717 ✉ pete.sanford@dudley.gov.uk

Building Control: Mrs Sue Holmyard, Assistant Director - Planning & Environmental Health, 3 St James's Road, Dudley DY1 1HZ ☎ 01384 814030 🖷 01384 814186 ✉ sue.holmyard@dudley.gov.uk

Catering Services: Ms Jill Seymour, Catering Manager, The Council House, Priory Road , Dudley DY1 1HF ☎ 01384 815261 ✉ jill.seymour@dudley.gov.uk

Civil Registration: Mrs Teresa Reilly, Assistant Director - HR & Organisational Development, 4 Ednam Road, Dudley DY1 1HW ☎ 01384 815330 🖷 01384 813391 ✉ teresa.reilly@dudley.gov.uk

PR / Communications: Mrs Jan Jennings, Head of Communication & Public Affairs, The Council House, Priory Road , Dudley DY1 1HF ☎ 01384 815224 🖷 01384 815231 ✉ jan.jennings@dudley.gov.uk

Community Planning: Mr Geoff Thomas, Assistant Director - Policy & Improvement, Falcon House, The Minnories, Dudley DY1 1HF ☎ 01384 815270 🖷 01384 815257 ✉ geoff.thomas@dudley.gov.uk

Community Safety: Ms Sue Haywood, Acting Head of Community Safety, Brierley Hill Police Station, Bank Street, Brierley Hill DY5 3DH ☎ 01384 815215 🖷 01384 818218 ✉ sue.haywood@dudley.gov.uk

Computer Management: Mr Lance Cartwright, Head of ICT Services, Blowers Green Road, Dudley DY2 8UZ ☎ 01384 815600 🖷 01384 815660 ✉ lance.cartwright@dudley.gov.uk

Computer Management: Mr John O'Neil, Team Manager, Ednam House, St James's Road, Dudley DY1 3JJ ☎ 01384 813173 ✉ john.oneil@dudley.gov.uk

Computer Management: Mrs Christine Ward, Team Manager, Ednam House, St. James's Road, Dudley DY1 3JJ ☎ 01384 813173 ✉ chris.ward@dudley.gov.uk

Consumer Protection and Trading Standards: Mrs Sue Holmyard, Assistant Director - Planning & Environmental Health, 3 St James's Road, Dudley DY1 1HZ ☎ 01384 814030 🖷 01384 814186 ✉ sue.holmyard@dudley.gov.uk

Contracts: Mr Ian Clarke, Head of Procurement, The Council House, Priory Road, Dudley DY1 1HF ☎ 01384 814884 🖷 01384 814831 ✉ ian.clarke@dudley.gov.uk

Corporate Services: Ms Christine Ballinger, Divisional Manager Assessment, 23 - 25 St. James's Road, Dudley DY1 3JD ☎ 01384 813200 ✉ christine.ballinger@dudley.gov.uk

Customer Service: Mr Sean Beckett, Customer Services Manager, Dudley Council Plus, Castle Street, Dudley DY1 1JQ ☎ 01384 815281 ✉ sean.beckett@dudley.gov.uk

Economic Development: Mr Phil Coyne, Assistant Director - Economic Regeneration & Transportation, Mary Stevens Park, Stourbridge DY8 2AA ☎ 01384 814004 🖷 01384 814455 ✉ phil.coyne@dudley.gov.uk

Education: Ms Nikki Hubbard, Head of School Admissions, Westox House, 1 Trinity Road, Dudley DY1 1JQ ☎ 01384 814264 ✉ nikki.hubbard@dudley.gov.uk

Education: Mr Dave Perrett, Assistant Director - Education, Play

& Learning, Westox House, 1 Trinity Road, Dudley DY1 1JQ ☎ 01384 814250 🖷 01384 814202 ✉ dave.perrett@dudley.gov.uk

Electoral Registration: Ms Alison Malkin, Head of Electoral Services, Old Crown Court, Priory Street, Dudley DY1 1EY ☎ 01384 815274 🖷 01384 815299 ✉ alison.malkin@dudley.gov.uk

Emergency Planning: Mr John Hodt, Head of Contingency & Disaster Management, The Council House, Room 18, Priory Road, Dudley DY1 1HF ☎ 01384 818066 ✉ john.hodt@dudley.gov.uk

Environmental / Technical Services: Mr Matt Williams, Assistant Director - Environment Management, Lister Road Depot, Lister Road, Netherton, Dudley DY2 8JW ☎ 01384 814510 🖷 01384 814592 ✉ matt.williams@dudley.gov.uk

Environmental Health: Mrs Sue Holmyard, Assistant Director - Planning & Environmental Health, 3 St James's Road, Dudley DY1 1HZ ☎ 01384 814030 🖷 01384 814186 ✉ sue.holmyard@dudley.gov.uk

Events Manager: Ms Sally Newell, Director of the Urban Environment, The Council House, Priory Road , Dudley DY1 1HF ☎ 01384 815500 🖷 01384 814181 ✉ sally.newell@dudley.gov.uk

Finance and Treasurer: Mr Iain Newman, Treasurer, The Council House, Priory Road , Dudley DY1 1HF ☎ ; 01384 814802 🖷 01384 815379 ✉ iain.newman@dudley.gov.uk

Fleet Management: Mr Matt Williams, Assistant Director - Environment Management, Lister Road Depot, Lister Road, Netherton, Dudley DY2 8JT ☎ 01384 814510 🖷 01384 814592 ✉ matt.williams@dudley.gov.uk

Grounds Maintenance: Mr Matt Williams, Assistant Director - Environment Management, Lister Road Depot, Lister Road, Netherton, Dudley DY2 8JT ☎ 01384 814510 🖷 01384 814592 ✉ matt.williams@dudley.gov.uk

Health and Safety: Mr Ray Faulkner, Corporate Health & Safety Manager, 3 - 5 St. James's Road, Dudley DY1 1HZ ☎ 01384 814722 🖷 01384 815979 ✉ ray.faulkner@dudley.gov.uk

Highways: Mr Matt Williams, Assistant Director - Environment Management, Lister Road Depot, Lister Road, Netherton, Dudley DY2 8JT ☎ 01384 814510 🖷 01384 814592 ✉ matt.williams@dudley.gov.uk

Home Energy Conservation: Ms Helen Barlow, Head of Service Private Sector Housing, 15 St James' Road, Dudley DY1 1HT ☎ 01384 812633 ✉ helen.barlow@dudley.gov.uk

Housing: Ms Diane Channings, Assistant Director of Adult, Community & Housing Services, Capstan House, Waterfront East, Brierley Hill DY5 1XL ☎ 01384 815076 🖷 01384 815167 ✉ diane.channings@dudley.gov.uk

Local Area Agreement: Mr Dennis Hodson, Director, Dudley Community Partnership, Unit 47, Waterfront East, Brierley Hill DY5 1XJ ☎ 01384 814756 ✉ dennis.hodson@dudley.gov.uk

Legal: Mr Mohammed Farooq, Interim Assistant Director, 5 Ednam Road, Dudley DY1 1HL ☎ 01384 815301 🖷 01384 815325 ✉ mohammed.farooq@dudley.gov.uk

Leisure and Cultural Services: Mr Duncan Lowndes, Assistant Director - Culture & Leisure, Claughton House, Blowers Green Road, Dudley DY2 8UZ ☎ 01384 815500 🖷 01384 814181 ✉ duncan.lowndes@dudley.gov.uk

Licensing: Mrs Janet Elliott, Licensing & Service Improvement Officer, 5 Ednam Road, Dudley DY1 1HL ☎ 01384 815763 🖷 01384 815325 ✉ janet.elliott@dudley.gov.uk

Lifelong Learning: Ms Kate Millin, Assistant Director of Adult Community & Housing Services - Libraries, Archives & Adult Learning, Ednam House, 1 St James' Road, Dudley DY1 3JJ ☎ 01384 812295 🖷 01384 811995 ✉ kate.millin@dudley.gov.uk

Lighting: Mr Matt Williams, Assistant Director - Environment Management, Lister Road Depot, Lister Road, Netherton, Dudley DY2 8JT ☎ 01384 814510 🖷 01384 814592 ✉ matt.williams@dudley.gov.uk

Member Services: Mr Steve Griffiths, Democratic Services Manager, The Council House, Priory Road , Dudley DY1 1HF ☎ 01384 815235 🖷 01384 815202 ✉ steve.griffiths@dudley.gov.uk

Parking: Mr Garry Dean, Head of Street & Green Care, Lister Road Depot, Lister Road, Netherton, Dudley DY2 8JW ☎ 01384 814506 🖷 01384 818393 ✉ garry.dean@dudley.gov.uk

Partnerships: Mr Mike Marshall, Head of Commissioning/Partnership, 6 St James Road, Dudley DY1 3JL ☎ 01384 818181 ✉ mike.marshall@dudley.gov.uk

Partnerships: Mr Ian McGuff, Assistant Director, Quality & Partnership, Westox House, 1 Trinity Road, Dudley DY1 1JQ ☎ 01384 814387 🖷 01384 814202 ✉ ian.mcguff@dudley.gov.uk

Personnel / HR: Mrs Teresa Reilly, Assistant Director - HR & Organisational Development, 4 Ednam Road, Dudley DY1 1HW ☎ 01384 815330 🖷 01384 813391 ✉ teresa.reilly@dudley.gov.uk

Personnel / HR: Ms Jill Snow, Payroll Manager, The Council House, Priory Road , Dudley DY1 1HF ☎ 01384 814898 ✉ jill.snow@dudley.gov.uk

Planning: Mrs Helen Martin, Head of Planning, 3 St. James's Road, Dudley DY1 1HZ ☎ 01384 814186 🖷 01384 814186 ✉ helen.martin@dudley.gov.uk

Procurement: Mr Ian Clarke, Head of Procurement, The Council House, Priory Road, Dudley DY1 1HF ☎ 01384 814884 🖷 01384 814831 ✉ ian.clarke@dudley.gov.uk

Public Libraries: Ms Kate Millin, Assistant Director of Adult Community & Housing Services - Libraries, Archives & Adult Learning, Ednam House, 1 St James' Road, Dudley DY1 3JJ ☎ 01384 812295 🖷 01384 811995 ✉ kate.millin@dudley.gov.uk

Recycling & Waste Minimisation: Mr Matt Williams, Assistant Director - Environment Management, Lister Road Depot, Lister Road, Netherton, Dudley DY2 8JT ☎ 01384 814510 🖷 01384

814592 ✉ matt.williams@dudley.gov.uk

Regeneration: Mr Phil Coyne, Assistant Director - Economic Regeneration & Transportation, Mary Stevens Park, Stourbridge DY8 2AA ☎ 01384 814004 📠 01384 814455 ✉ phil.coyne@dudley.gov.uk

Road Safety: Mr Phil Coyne, Assistant Director - Economic Regeneration & Transportation, Mary Stevens Park, Stourbridge DY8 2AA ☎ 01384 814004 📠 01384 814455 ✉ phil.coyne@dudley.gov.uk

Social Services: Mr Richard Carter, Assistant Director - Learning Disabilities and Mental Health, Ednam House, 6 St. James's Road, Dudley DY1 3JJ ☎ 01384 815804 ✉ richard.carter@dudley.gov.uk

Social Services: Mr Brendan Clifford, Assistant Director - Adult Community & Housing Services - Policy Performance and Resources, Ednam House, St. James' Road, Dudley DY1 3JJ ☎ 01384 815805 📠 01384 811995 ✉ brendan.clifford@dudley.gov.uk

Social Services (Adult): Ms Maggie Venables, Assistant Director - Older People & Physical Disabilities, Ednam House, St James's Road, Dudley DY1 3JJ ☎ 01384 815802 📠 01384 811995 ✉ Maggie.venables@dudley.gov.uk

Social Services (Children): Ms Pauline Sharratt, Assistant Director - Children & Families, Westox House, 1 Trinity Road, Dudley DY1 1JQ ☎ 01384 815803 📠 01384 815865 ✉ pauline.sharratt@dudley.gov.uk

Staff Training: Mrs Sarah Treneer, Head of Learning & Organisational Development, 4 Ednam Road, Dudley DY1 1HW ☎ 01384 814727 📠 01384 815204 ✉ sarah.treneer@dudley.gov.uk

Street Scene: Mr Matt Williams, Assistant Director - Environment Management, Lister Road Depot, Lister Road, Netherton, Dudley DY2 8JT ☎ 01384 814510 📠 01384 814592 ✉ matt.williams@dudley.gov.uk

Sustainable Communities: Mr Geoff Thomas, Assistant Director - Policy & Improvement, Falcon House, The Minnories, Dudley DY1 1HF ☎ 01384 815270 📠 01384 815257 ✉ geoff.thomas@dudley.gov.uk

Sustainable Development: Mrs Sue Holmyard, Assistant Director - Planning & Environmental Health, 3 St James's Road, Dudley DY1 1HZ ☎ 01384 814030 📠 01384 814186 ✉ sue.holmyard@dudley.gov.uk

Tourism: Mr Duncan Lowndes, Assistant Director - Culture & Leisure, Claughton House, Blowers Green Road, Dudley DY2 8UZ ☎ 01384 815500 📠 01384 814181 ✉ duncan.lowndes@dudley.gov.uk

Town Centre: Mr Phil Coyne, Assistant Director - Economic Regeneration & Transportation, Mary Stevens Park, Stourbridge DY8 2AA ☎ 01384 814004 📠 01384 814455 ✉ phil.coyne@dudley.gov.uk

Traffic Management: Mr Phil Coyne, Assistant Director - Economic Regeneration & Transportation, Mary Stevens Park, Stourbridge DY8 2AA ☎ 01384 814004 📠 01384 814455 ✉ phil.coyne@dudley.gov.uk

Transport: Mr Matt Williams, Assistant Director - Environment Management, Lister Road Depot, Lister Road, Netherton, Dudley DY2 8JT ☎ 01384 814510 📠 01384 814592 ✉ matt.williams@dudley.gov.uk

Waste Collection and Disposal: Mr Matt Williams, Assistant Director - Environment Management, Lister Road Depot, Lister Road, Netherton, Dudley DY2 8JT ☎ 01384 814510 📠 01384 814592 ✉ matt.williams@dudley.gov.uk

Waste Management: Mr Matt Williams, Assistant Director - Environment Management, Lister Road Depot, Lister Road, Netherton, Dudley DY2 8JT ☎ 01384 814510 📠 01384 814592 ✉ matt.williams@dudley.gov.uk

MEMBERS OF THE COUNCIL (72)

***Mayor:* Mottram**, Melvyn (LAB - Coseley East)
cllr.melvyn.mottram@dudley.gov.uk

***Deputy Mayor:* Finch**, Alan (LAB - Castle & Priory)
cllr.alan.finch@dudley.gov.uk

***Group Leader:* Jones**, Les (CON - Pedmore & Stourbridge East)
cllr.les.jones@dudley.gov.uk

Ahmed, Khurshid (LAB - St James's)
cllr.khurshid.ahmed@dudley.gov.uk

Ahmed, Asif (LAB - St James's)
cllr.asif.ahmed@dudley.gov.uk

Ali, Shaukat (LAB - St Thomas's)
cllr.shaukat.ali@dudley.gov.uk

Ameson, Doreen (CON - Upper Gornal & Woodsetton)
cllr.doreen.ameson@dudley.gov.uk

Arshad, Safeena (LAB - St Thomas's)
cllr.safeena.arshad@dudley.gov.uk

Aston, Margaret (LAB - Castle & Priory)

Aston, Adam (LAB - Upper Gornal & Woodsetton)
cllr.adam.aston@dudley.gov.uk

Attwood, Mike (CON - Norton)
cllr.mike.attwood@dudley.gov.uk

Billingham, Cheryl (CON - Kingswinford North & Wall Heath)
cllr.cheryl.billingham@dudley.gov.uk

Bills, Hilary (LAB - Halesowen North)
cllr.hilary.bills@dudley.gov.uk

Blood, David (CON - Kingswinford South)
cllr.david.blood@dudley.gov.uk

Body, Richard (LAB - Cradley & Wollescote)
cllr.richard.body@dudley.gov.uk

Boleyn, Lynn (LAB - Kingswinford North & Wall Heath)
cllr.lynn.boleyn@dudley.gov.uk

Branwood, Dave (LAB - Gornal)
cllr.dave.branwood@dudley.gov.uk

Burston, Ray (CON - Hayley Green & Cradley South)
cllr.ray.burston@dudley.gov.uk

Casey, Keiran (LAB - Upper Gornal & Woodsetton)
cllr.keiran.casey@dudley.gov.uk

Caunt, David (CON - Sedgley)
cllr.david.caunt@dudley.gov.uk

Cotterill, Bryan (LAB - Quarry Bank & Dudley Wood)
cllr.bryan.cotterill@dudley.gov.uk

Cowell, Jackie (LAB - Quarry Bank & Dudley Wood)

cllr.jackie.cowell@dudley.gov.uk
Crumpton, Timothy (LAB - Cradley & Wollescote)
cllr.timothy.crumpton@dudley.gov.uk
Davies, George (LAB - Coseley East)
cllr.george.davies@dudley.gov.uk
Duckworth, Will (GRN - Netherton, Woodside & St Andrews)
cllr.will.duckworth@dudley.gov.uk
Elcock, Colin (CON - Norton)
Evans, Michael (CON - Sedgley)
cllr.michael.evans@dudley.gov.uk
Finch, Ken (LAB - Castle & Priory)
cllr.ken.finch@dudley.gov.uk
Foster, Judy (LAB - Brookmoor & Pensnett)
cllr.judy.foster@dudley.gov.uk
Hale, Chris (LAB - Wollaston & Stourbridge Town)
cllr.chris.hale@dudley.gov.uk
Hanif, Mohammed (LAB - Lye & Stourbridge North)
cllr.mohammed.hanif@dudley.gov.uk
Harley, Patrick (CON - Kingswinford South)
cllr.patrick.harley@dudley.gov.uk
Harris, Rachel (LAB - Brierley Hill)
cllr.rachel.harris@dudley.gov.uk
Hemingsley, Derrick (LAB - Wordsley)
cllr.derrick.hemingsley@dudley.gov.uk
Herbert, Tremaine (LAB - Lye & Stourbridge North)
cllr.tremaine.herbert@dudley.gov.uk
Hill, Jeffrey (CON - Halesowen North)
cllr.jeff.hill@dudley.gov.uk
Islam, Zafar (LAB - Brierley Hill)
cllr.zafar.islam@dudley.gov.uk
James, Bob (CON - Belle Vale)
cllr.robert.james@dudley.gov.uk
Jones, John (CON - Wordsley)
cllr.john.jones@dudley.gov.uk
Jordan, Karen (LAB - Brookmoor & Pensnett)
cllr.karen.jordan@dudley.gov.uk
Kettle, Ian (CON - Pedmore & Stourbridge East)
cllr.ian.kettle@dudley.gov.uk
Knowles, Malcolm (CON - Wollaston & Stourbridge Town)
cllr.malcolm.knowles@dudley.gov.uk
Lowe, Peter (LAB - Lye & Stourbridge North)
cllr.peter.lowe@dudley.gov.uk
Marrey, Ian (LAB - Wollaston & Stourbridge West)
cllr.ian.marrey@dudley.gov.uk
Martin, John (LAB - Brockmoor & Pensnett)
cllr.john.martin@dudley.gov.uk
Martin, Patricia (CON - Amblecombe)
cllr.pat.martin@dudley.gov.uk
Miller, Peter (CON - Kingswinford South)
cllr.peter.miller@dudley.gov.uk
Nicholls, Jill (CON - Belle Vale)
cllr.jill.nicholls@dudley.gov.uk
Partridge, Gaye (LAB - Cradley & Wollescote)
cllr.gaye.partridge@dudley.gov.uk
Perks, Christine (LAB - Amblecote)
cllr.christine.perks@dudley.gov.uk
Ridney, Susan (LAB - Coseley East)
cllr.susan.ridney@dudley.gov.uk
Roberts, Mary (LAB - St James's)
cllr.mary.roberts@dudley.gov.uk
Rogers, Heather (CON - Norton)
cllr.heather.rogers@dudley.gov.uk
Russell, Donella (LAB - Belle Vale)
cllr.donella.russell@dudley.gov.uk
Shakespeare, Karen (CON - Halesowen North)
cllr.karen.shakespeare@dudley.gov.uk
Simms, Glenis (CON - Wordsley)
cllr.glenis.simms@dudley.gov.uk
Sparks, David (LAB - Quarry Bank & Dudley Wood)
cllr.david.sparks@dudley.gov.uk
Taylor, Alan (CON - Halesowen South)
cllr.alan.taylor@dudley.gov.uk
Turner, Kenneth (CON - Hayley Green & Cradley South)
cllr.kenneth.turner@dudley.gov.uk
Turner, Stuart (LAB - Gornal)
cllr.stuart.turner@dudley.gov.uk
Turners, Hazel (CON - Hayley Green & Cradley South)
cllr.hazel.turner@dudley.gov.uk
Tyler, Dave (LAB - Kingswinford North & Wall Heath)
cllr.dave.tyler@dudley.gov.uk
Vickers, David (CON - Halesowen South)
cllr.david.vickers@dudley.gov.uk
Walker, Elizabeth (CON - Amblecote)
cllr.elizabeth.walker@dudley.gov.uk
Waltho, Steve (LAB - St Thomas's)
cllr.steve.waltho@dudley.gov.uk
Westwood, Tina (CON - Sedgley)
cllr.tina.westwood@dudley.gov.uk
Wilson, Colin (CON - Pedmore & Stourbridge East)
cllr.colin.wilson@dudley.gov.uk
Wilson, Margaret (LAB - Brierley Hill)
cllr.margaret.wilson@dudley.gov.uk
Wood, Tracy (LAB - Netherton, Woodside & St Andrews)
cllr.tracy.wood@dudley.gov.uk
Woodall, John (CON - Halesowen South)
cllr.john.p.woodall@dudley.gov.uk
Wright, Timothy (CON - Gornal)
cllr.timothy.wright@dudley.gov.uk
Zada, Qadar (LAB - Netherton, Woodside & St Andrews)
cllr.qadar.zada@dudley.gov.uk

POLITICAL COMPOSITION

LAB: 41, CON: 30, GRN: 1

CABINET

Leader/ Policy: Mr David Sparks
Deputy Leader: Mr Shaukat Ali
Adult & Community Services: Mr Steve Waltho
Environment & Culture: Ms Tracy Wood
Finance: Mr Peter Lowe
Health & Wellbeing: Mr Zafar Islam
Housing, Libraries & Adult Learning: Mr Khurshid Ahmed
Integrated Children's Services: Mr Timothy Crumpton

COMMITTEE CHAIRS

Audit & Standards: Mr Qadar Zada
Children Service's Scrutiny: Mr Stuart Turner
Community Safety & Services Scrutiny: Mr Ian Kettle
Development Control: Ms Rachel Harris
Environment Scrutiny: Mr Mohammed Hanif
Health & Adult Social Care Scrutiny: Mrs Susan Ridney
Licensing & Safety: Ms Hilary Bills
Regeneration Culture & Adult Education: Mr Dave Tyler

DUMFRIES & GALLOWAY S

Dumfries & Galloway Council, Council Offices, English Street, Dumfries DG1 2DD ☎ 01387 260000 🖷 01387 260034
cis@dumgal.gov.uk www.dumgal.gov.uk

LOCAL AUTHORITIES

FACTS & FIGURES

Police Authority: Dumfries & Galloway Police & Fire & Rescue Authority
Health Authority: NHS Dumfries & Galloway
Learning and Skills Council: Scotland
Parliamentary Constituencies: Dumfries and Galloway, Dumfriesshire, Clydesdale and Tweedale
EU Constituencies: Scotland
Election Frequency: Elections are of whole council

PRINCIPAL OFFICERS

Chief Executive: Mr Gavin Stevenson, Chief Executive, Council Offices, English Street, Dumfries DG1 2DD ☎ 01387 260001 🖷 01387 260034 ✉ chief.executive@dumgal.gov.uk

Assistant Chief Executive: Ms Lorna Meahan, Assistant Chief Executive, Council Offices, English Street, Dumfries DG1 2DD ☎ 01387 260003 ✉ lorna.meahan@dumgal.gov.uk

Catering Services: Ms Anne Vance, Catering Officer, School Services, Woodbank, 30 Edinburgh Road, Dumfries DG1 1NW ☎ 01387 260432 ✉ annev@dumgal.gov.uk

Children / Youth Services: Mr John Alexander, Director - Social Work Services, Woodbank, 30 Edinburgh Road, Dumfries DG1 1NW ☎ 01387 260451

Children / Youth Services: Mr John McVie, Head of Service Pupil Support & Integration, Council Offices, English Street, Dumfries DG1 2DD

Civil Registration: Mrs Alison Quigley, Chief Registrar, 15 Ednam Street, Annan DG12 5EF ☎ 01461 204914 🖷 01461 206896 ✉ alisonq@dumgal.gov.uk

PR / Communications: Ms Claire Aitken, Team Leader - Internal Communication & Marketing, Council Offices, English Street, Dumfries DG1 2DD ☎ 01387 260058 🖷 01387 260334 ✉ clarie.aitkens@dumgal.gov.uk

Community Planning: Ms Liz Manson, Operations Manager - Corporate & Community Planning, Council Offices, English Street, Dumfries DG1 2DD ☎ 01387 260074 ✉ liz.manson@dumgal.gov.uk

Community Safety: Mr David Gurney, Acting Emergency Planning & Community Safety Manager, Emergency Planning Unit, Carruthers House, English Street, Dumfries DG1 2HP ☎ 01387 260046 🖷 01387 265467

Computer Management: Mr Derek Shaw, Operations Manager - Technology Solutions, Council Offices, English Street, Dumfries DG1 2DD ☎ 01387 260 300 ✉ dereks@dumgal.gov.uk

Consumer Protection and Trading Standards: Mr Alan Gass, Chief Trading Standards Officer, 1 Newall Terrace, Dumfries DG1 1LN ☎ 01387 260080 🖷 01387 260094

Contracts: Mr Alistair Speedie, Director - Sustainable Development, Militia House, English Street, Dumfries DG1 2HR ☎ 01387 260376 ✉ alistair.speedie@dumgal.gov.uk

Corporate Services: Ms Liz Manson, Operations Manager - Corporate & Community Planning, Council Offices, English Street, Dumfries DG1 2DD ☎ 01387 260074 ✉ liz.manson@dumgal.gov.uk

Corporate Services: Mr Martin Ogilvie, Operations Manager - Civil Protection, Resilience & Corporate Risk, Council Offices, English Street, Dumfries DG1 2DD ✉ martin.ogilvie@dumgal.gov.uk

Customer Service: Mr Justin Tracy, Director - Community & Customer Services, Council Offices, English Street, Dumfries DG1 2DD ☎ 01387 273874 ✉ justin.tracy@dumgal.gov.uk

Economic Development: Mr Ewan Green, Operations Manager Economic Development, Council Offices, English Street, Dumfries DG1 2DD

Education: Ms Rachel Doherty, Head of Service - Strategic Planning & Support, Council Offices, English Street, Dumfries DG1 2DD

Education: Mr Colin Grant, Director - Education Services, Council Offices, English Street, Dumfries DG1 2DD

E-Government: Mr Keith Percival, Service Manager - Customer Services, Council Offices, English Street, Dumfries DG1 2DD ☎ 01387 260384 🖷 01387 260034 ✉ keithp@dumgal.gov.uk

Electoral Registration: Mr Keith Mossop, Assessor & Electoral Registration Officer, Council Offices, English Street, Dumfries DG1 2DD ☎ 01387 260627 🖷 01387 260632 ✉ ero@dumgal.gov.uk

Emergency Planning: Mr David Gurney, Acting Emergency Planning & Community Safety Manager, Emergency Planning Unit, Carruthers House, English Street, Dumfries DG1 2HP ☎ 01387 260046 🖷 01387 265467

Energy Management: Mr John Currie, Service Leader Energy, County House, 2 Great King Street, Dumfries DG1 1AE ☎ 01387 260718 🖷 01387 261661 ✉ johncu@dumgal.gov.uk

Estates, Property & Valuation: Ms Rhona Wells, Operations Manager for Strategic Property Services, Council Offices, English Street, Dumfries DG1 2DD ☎ 01387 260432 ✉ rhona.wells@dumgal.gov.uk

Finance and Treasurer: Mr Paul Garrett, Operations Manager, Council Offices, English Street, Dumfries DG1 2DD

Fleet Management: Mr Ian Anderson, Fleet Management Supervisor, Garroch Business Park, Garroch Loaning, Dumfries DG2 8PY ☎ 01387 274184 🖷 01387 243186 ✉ ian.anderson@dumgal.gov.uk

Health and Safety: Mr George Brown, Health & Safety Manager, Council Offices, English Street, Dumfries DG1 2DD ☎ 01387 260000 🖷 01387 260061 ✉ george.brown2@dumgal.gov.uk

Highways: Mr Alistair Speedie, Director - Sustainable Development, Militia House, English Street, Dumfries DG1 2HR

☎ 01387 260376 ✉ alistair.speedie@dumgal.gov.uk

Housing: Mr John Lynch, Operations Manager - Strategic Housing & Commissioning, Carmont House, Bankend Road, Dumfries DG1 4ZJ ☎ 01387 245123 🖷 01387 245133 ✉ johnl@dumgal.gov.uk

Legal: Mr Brendan Kearney, Operational Manager - Legal Services, Council Offices, Buccleuch Street, Dumfries DG1 2AD ☎ 01387 245924 🖷 01387 247803 ✉ brendan.kearney@dumgal.gov.uk

Legal: Mr Willie Taylor, Service Manager - Courts & Licensing, Council Offices, English Street, Dumfries DG1 2DD ☎ 01387 245913 🖷 01387 252978 ✉ willie.taylor@dumgal.gov.uk

Leisure and Cultural Services: Mr Richard Grieveson, Head of Resource Planning & Community Services, Marchmount House, Dumfries DG1 1PY ☎ 01387 273875 ✉ richard.grieveson@dumgal.gov.uk

Licensing: Mr Alex Haswell, Director - Chief Executive Service, Council Offices, English Street, Dumfries DG1 2DD ☎ 01387 260000 🖷 01387 260034 ✉ alex.haswell@dumgal.gov.uk

Licensing: Mr Willie Taylor, Service Manager - Courts & Licensing, Council Offices, English Street, Dumfries DG1 2DD ☎ 01387 245913 🖷 01387 252978 ✉ willie.taylor@dumgal.gov.uk

Lighting: Mr Alistair Speedie, Director - Sustainable Development, Militia House, English Street, Dumfries DG1 2HR ☎ 01387 260376 ✉ alistair.speedie@dumgal.gov.uk

Lottery Funding, Charity and Voluntary: Ms Emma Berger, Voluntary Sector Manager, Marchmount House, Dumfries DG1 1PY ☎ 01387 260000 ✉ emma.berger@dumgal.gov.uk

Member Services: Ms Carol Henshall, Service Manager - Committee & Member Services, Council Offices, English Street, Dumfries DG1 2DD ☎ 01387 260000 🖷 01387 260034 ✉ carol.henshall@dumgal.gov.uk

Parking: Mr Alistair Speedie, Director - Sustainable Development, Militia House, English Street, Dumfries DG1 2HR ☎ 01387 260376 ✉ alistair.speedie@dumgal.gov.uk

Personnel / HR: Mr Paul Clarkin, Operations Manager - Human Resources, Council Offices, English Street, Dumfries DG1 2DD ☎ 01387 273842 ✉ paul.clarkin@dumgal.gov.uk

Planning: Mr Alistair Speedie, Director - Sustainable Development, Militia House, English Street, Dumfries DG1 2HR ☎ 01387 260376 ✉ alistair.speedie@dumgal.gov.uk

Procurement: Ms Rhona MacPherson, Corporate Procurement Manager, Council Offices, English Street, Dumfries DG1 2DD

Public Libraries: Ms Janice Goldie, Principal Policy Officer: Libraries, Information & Archives, Marchmount House, Dumfries DG1 1PY ☎ 01387 273887 ✉ janice.goldie@dumgal.gov.uk

Recycling & Waste Minimisation: Mr Alistair Speedie, Director - Sustainable Development, Militia House, English Street, Dumfries DG1 2HR ☎ 01387 260376 ✉ alistair.speedie@dumgal.gov.uk

Social Services: Mr John Alexander, Director - Social Work Services, Woodbank, 30 Edinburgh Road, Dumfries DG1 1NW ☎ 01387 260451

Social Services: Mr Peter David, Senior Social Work Manager, Council Offices, English Street, Dumfries DG1 2DD

Social Services: Mr Geoff Dean, Senior Social Work Manager, Longacres Road, Kirkcudbright DG6 4AT ☎ 01557 339260

Social Services: Mr Sean McGleenan, Senior Social Work Manager, 122 Irish Street, Dumfries DG1 2AW ☎ 01387 273686

Social Services: Mr Allan Monteforte, Senior Social Work Manager, 39 Lewis Street, Stranraer DG9 7AD ☎ 01776 706884

Social Services (Adult): Mr John Alexander, Director - Social Work Services, Woodbank, 30 Edinburgh Road, Dumfries DG1 1NW ☎ 01387 260451

Social Services (Children): Mr John Alexander, Director - Social Work Services, Woodbank, 30 Edinburgh Road, Dumfries DG1 1NW ☎ 01387 260451

Staff Training: Mr Paul Clarkin, Operations Manager - Human Resources, Marchmount House, Dumfries DG1 1PY ☎ 01387 273842 ✉ paul.clarkin@dumgal.gov.uk

Sustainable Communities: Mr Bill Barker, Operations Manager - Infrastructure & Commissioning, Cargen Towers, Garroch Business Park, Garroch Loaning, Dumfries DG2 8PN

Sustainable Communities: Mr Justin Tracy, Director - Community & Customer Services, Marchmount House, Dumfries DG1 1PY ☎ 01387 273874 ✉ justin.tracy@dumgal.gov.uk

Traffic Management: Mr Alistair Speedie, Director - Sustainable Development, Militia House, English Street, Dumfries DG1 2HR ☎ 01387 260376 ✉ alistair.speedie@dumgal.gov.uk

Transport: Mr Ian Anderson, Fleet Management Supervisor, Garroch Business Park, Garroch Loaning, Dumfries DG2 8PY ☎ 01387 274184 🖷 01387 243186 ✉ ian.anderson@dumgal.gov.uk

Transport Planner: Mr Ian Anderson, Fleet Management Supervisor, Garroch Business Park, Garroch Loaning, Dumfries DG2 8PY ☎ 01387 274184 🖷 01387 243186 ✉ ian.anderson@dumgal.gov.uk

Waste Management: Mr Alistair Speedie, Director - Sustainable Development, Militia House, English Street, Dumfries DG1 2HR ☎ 01387 260376 ✉ alistair.speedie@dumgal.gov.uk

MEMBERS OF THE COUNCIL (48)

Bell, Graham (CON - North West Dumfries)
john.bell2@dumgal.gov.uk
Blake, Ian (CON - Abbey)
ian.blake@dumgal.gov.uk
Brodie, Richard (LD - Annandale South)
richard.brodie@dumgal.gov.uk

Brown, Ted (LAB - Annandale North)
ted.brown@dumgal.gov.uk
Carruthers, Ian (CON - Annandale South)
ian.carruthers@dumgal.gov.uk
Carruthers, Karen (CON - Annandale East & Eskdale)
karen.carruthers3@dumgal.gov.uk
Carson, Finlay (CON - Castle Douglas & Glenkens)
finlay.carson@dumgal@gov.uk
Collins, Brian (SNP - Castle Douglas & Glenkens)
brian.collins@dumgal.gov.uk
Davidson, Rob (SNP - Abbey)
rob.davidson@dumgal.gov.uk
Dempster, James (LAB - Mid & Upper Nithsdale)
james.dempster@dumgal.gov.uk
Dick, Iain (SNP - Stranraer & North Rhins)
iain.dick@dumgal.gov.uk
Diggle, Peter (CON - Annandale North)
peter.diggle@dumgal.gov.uk
Dryburgh, Archie (LAB - Annandale East & Eskdale)
archie.dryburgh@dumgal.gov.uk
Dykes, Gillian (CON - Mid & Upper Nithsdale)
gill.dykes@dumgal.gov.uk
Ferguson, Andy (SNP - North West Dumfries)
andy.ferguson@dumgal.gov.uk
Forster, Grahame (NP - Wigtown West)
grahame.forster@dumgal.gov.uk
Geddes, Alistair (SNP - Mid Galloway)
alistair.geddes@dumgal.gov.uk
Gilroy, Patsy (CON - Dee)
patsy.gilroy@dumgal.gov.uk
Groom, Jack (CON - Nith)
jack.groom@dumgal.gov.uk
Higgins, Robert (SNP - Wigtown West)
robert.higgins@dumgal.gov.uk
Hongmei Jin, Yen (SNP - Lochar)
yen.hongmeijin@dumgal.gov.uk
Hyslop, Ivor (CON - Lochar)
ivor.hyslop@dumgal.gov.uk
Leaver, Jeff (LAB - Lochar)
jeff.leaver@dumgal.gov.uk
MacGregor, Gail (CON - Annandale North)
gail.macgregor@dumgal.gov.uk
Maitland, Jane (IND - Dee)
jane.maitland@dumgal.gov.uk
Male, Denis (CON - Annandale East & Eskdale)
denis.male@dumgal.gov.uk
Marshall, Sean (LAB - Annandale South)
sean.marshall@dumgal.gov.uk
Martin, John (LAB - Nith)
john.martin@dumgal.gov.uk
McAughtrie, Tom (LAB - Abbey)
tom.mcaughtrie@dumgal.gov.uk
McClung, Jim (SNP - Wigtown West)
jim.mcclung@dumgal.gov.uk
McColm, Jim (IND - Mid Galloway)
jim.mccolm@dumgal.gov.uk
McCutcheon, Marion (LAB - Stranraer & North Rhins)
marion.mccutcheon@dumgal.gov.uk
McKie, David (LAB - North West Dumfries)
david.mckie@dumgal.gov.uk
Nicholson, Ronnie (LAB - North West Dumfries)
ronnie.nicholson@dumgal.gov.uk
Nicol, Graham (CON - Mid Galloway)
graham.nicol@dumgal.gov.uk
Oglivie, Ronald (LAB - Annandale South)
ronal.ogilvie@dumgal.gov.uk
Peacock, Craig (IND - Annandale East & Eskdale)
craig.peacock@dumgal.gov.uk
Prentice, George (IND - Castle Douglas & Glenkens)
george.prentice@dumgal.gov.uk
Scobie, William (NP - Stranraer & North Rhins)
william.scobie@dumgal.gov.uk
Smyth, Colin (LAB - Nith)
colin.smyth@dumgal.gov.uk
Stitt, David (LAB - Abbey)
davie.stitt@dumgal.gov.uk
Syme, John (LAB - Mid & Upper Nithsdale)
john.syme@dumgal.gov.uk
Thompson, Stephen (SNP - Annandale North)
stephen.thompson@dumgal.gov.uk
Thompson, Ted (LAB - lochar)
ted.thompson@dumgal.gov.uk
Tuckfield, Roberta (CON - Wigtown West)
roberta.tuckfield@dumgal.gov.uk
Witts, Alistair (SNP - Nith)
alistair.witts@dumgal.gov.uk
Wood, Andrew (SNP - Mid & Upper Nithsdale)
andrew.wood@dumgal.gov.uk
Wyper, Colin (IND - Dee)
colin.wyper@dumgal.gov.uk

POLITICAL COMPOSITION

LAB: 15, CON: 14, SNP: 11, IND: 5, NP: 2, LD: 1

COMMITTEE CHAIRS

Education: Ms Gail MacGregor
Planning, Housing & Environmental Services: Mr Ian Carruthers
Policy & Resources: Mr Ivor Hyslop
Scrutiny & Performance: Mr Alistair Geddes
Social Work Services: Mr Andy Ferguson

DUNDEE CITY — S

Dundee City Council, 21 City Square, Dundee DD1 3BY ☎ 01382 434000 🖷 01382 434666 💻 www.dundeecity.gov.uk

FACTS & FIGURES

Police Authority: Tayside Joint Police Board
Health Authority: NHS Tayside
Learning and Skills Council: Scotland
Parliamentary Constituencies: Dundee East, Dundee West
EU Constituencies: Scotland
Election Frequency: Elections are of whole council

PRINCIPAL OFFICERS

Chief Executive: Mr David Dorward, Chief Executive, 21 City Square, Dundee DD1 3BY ☎ 01382 434201 🖷 01382 434996 david.dorward@dundeecity.gov.uk

Access Officer / Social Services (Disability): Ms Dorothy Wilson, Access Officer, Dundee House, 50 North Lindsay Street, Dundee DD1 1LS ☎ 01382 433865 🖷 01382 433034 dorothy.wilson@dundeecity.gov.uk

Architect, Building / Property Services: Mr Rob Pedersen, City Architectural Services Officer, Dundee House, 50 North Linday Street, Dundee DD1 1LS ☎ 01382 433640 🖷 01382 433034

rob.pedersen@dundeecity.gov.uk

Best Value: Mr Paul Carroll, Performance & Improvement Manager, 21 City Square, Dundee DD1 3BY ☎ 01382 434452 🖷 01382 434996 paul.carroll@dundeecity.gov.uk

Building Control: Mr Kenneth Findlay, Team Leader, Building Control, Dundee House, 50 North Lindsay Street, Dundee DD1 1LS ☎ 01382 433001 🖷 01382 433013 ken.findlay@dundeecity.gov.uk

Children / Youth Services: Ms Jane Martin, Manager, Children's Services & Criminal Justice, Friarfield House, Barrack Street, Dundee DD1 1PQ ☎ 01382 435017 jane.martin@dundeecity.gov.uk

Civil Registration: Mr Grant Law, Registrar, 21 City Square, Dundee DD1 3BY ☎ 01382 435223 grant.law@dundeecity.gov.uk

PR / Communications: Mr Les Roy, Head of Public Relations, 21 City Square, Dundee DD1 3BY ☎ 01382 434501 🖷 01382 434834 les.roy@dundeecity.gov.uk

Community Planning: Mr Peter Allan, Community Planning Manager, 21 City Square, Dundee DD1 3BY ☎ 01382 434465 🖷 01382 434996 peter.allan@dundeecity.gov.uk

Community Safety: Mr Neil Gunn, Head of Community Learning & Development, Central Library, Dundee DD1 3RZ ☎ 01382 307464 🖷 01382 307487 neil.gunn@dundeecity.gov.uk

Computer Management: Mr Ged Bell, Head of Information Technology, Downfield House, East School Road, Dundee DD3 8NX ☎ 01382 438060 🖷 01382 438002 ged.bell@dundeecity.gov.uk

Consumer Protection and Trading Standards: Mr Ken Daly, Trading Standards Manager, Claverhouse West Industrial Park, Jack Martin Way, Dundee DD1 ☎ 01382 436263 ken.daly@dundeecity.gov.uk

Contracts: Mr Kenneth Laing, Director of Environment, 353 Clepington Road, Dundee DD3 8PL ☎ 01382 434729 🖷 01382 434777 ken.laing@dundeecity.gov.uk

Corporate Services: Ms Marjory Stewart, Director of Corporate Services, Dundee House, 50 North Linday Street, Dundee DD1 1LS ☎ 01382 433555 🖷 01382 433045 marjory.stewart@dundeecity.gov.uk

Direct Labour: Mr Kenneth Laing, Director of Environment, 353 Clepington Road, Dundee DD3 8PL ☎ 01382 434729 🖷 01382 434777 ken.laing@dundeecity.gov.uk

Economic Development: Mr Mike Galloway, Director of City Development, Dundee House, 50 North Linday Street, Dundee DD1 1LS ☎ 01382 433610 🖷 01382 433013 mike.galloway@dundeecity.gov.uk

Education: Mr Michael Wood, Director of Education, Dundee House, 50 North Lindsay Street, Dundee DD1 1LS ☎ 01382 433088 🖷 01382 433080 michael.wood@dundeecity.gov.uk

E-Government: Mr Paul Carroll, Performance & Improvement Manager, 21 City Square, Dundee DD1 3BY ☎ 01382 434452 🖷 01382 434996 paul.carroll@dundeecity.gov.uk

Electoral Registration: Mr Roger Mennie, Head of Legal & Democratic Services, 21 City Square, Dundee DD1 3BY ☎ 01382 434577 roger.mennie@dundeecity.gov.uk

Emergency Planning: Mr John Handling, Emergency Planning Officer, 21 City Square, Dundee DD1 3BY ☎ 01382 434264 🖷 01382 434666 john.handling@dundeecity.gov.uk

Energy Management: Mr Alex Gibson, Team Leader (Property Services), 3 City Square, Dundee DD1 3BA ☎ 01382 434814 🖷 01382 434650 alex.gibson@dundeecity.gov.uk

Environmental Health: Mr Kenny Kerr, Head of Environmental Protection, 34 Harefield Road, Dundee DD2 3JW ☎ 01382 436201 🖷 01382 436226 kenny.kerr@dundeecity.gov.uk

Estates, Property & Valuation: Mr Mike Galloway, Director of City Development, Dundee House, 50 North Lindsay Street, Dundee DD1 1LS ☎ 01382 433610 🖷 01382 433013 mike.galloway@dundeecity.gov.uk

European Liaison: Mr Stan Ure, Head of Economic Development, City Development, 3 City Square, Dundee DD1 3BA ☎ 01382 434908 🖷 01382 434650 stan.ure@dundeecity.gov.uk

Finance and Treasurer: Ms Marjory Stewart, Director of Corporate Services, Dundee House, 50 North Lindsay Street, Dundee DD1 1NZ ☎ 01382 433555 🖷 01382 433045 marjory.stewart@dundeecity.gov.uk

Grounds Maintenance: Mr Rod Houston, Land Services Manager, 353 Clepington Road, Dundee DD3 8PL ☎ 01382 434747 🖷 01382 434777 rod.houston@dundeecity.gov.uk

Health and Safety: Mr Neil Doherty, Council Health & Safety Co-ordinator, 8 City Square, Dundee DD1 3BG ☎ 01382 434878 🖷 01382 434614 neil.doherty@dundeecity.gov.uk

Highways: Mr Fergus Wison, City Engineer, Dundee House, 50 North Linday Street, Dundee DD1 1LS ☎ 01382 433711 🖷 01382 433313 fergus.wilson@dundeecity.gov.uk

Home Energy Conservation: Ms Heather Mcquillan, HECA Officer, Housing Investment Unit, Dundee House, 50 North Lindsay Street, Dundee DD1 1NB ☎ 01382 434872 🖷 01382 434597 heather.mcquillan@dundeecity.gov.uk

Housing: Mrs Elaine Zwirlein, Director of Housing, 50 North Lindsay Street, Dundee DD1 1LS ☎ 01382 434538 🖷 01382 434942 elaine.zwirlein@dundeecity.gov.uk

Housing Maintenance: Mrs Elaine Zwirlein, Director of Housing, 50 North Lindsay Street, Dundee DD1 1LS ☎ 01382 434538 🖷 01382 434942 elaine.zwirlein@dundeecity.gov.uk

Legal: Mr Roger Mennie, Head of Legal & Democratic Services,

21 City Square, Dundee DD1 3BY ☎ 01382 434577
✉ roger.mennie@dundeecity.gov.uk

Leisure and Cultural Services: Mr Stewart Murdoch, Director of Leisure & Communities, Central Library, Dundee DD1 2DB
☎ 01382 437460 🖷 01382 437487
✉ stewart.murdoch@dundeecity.gov.uk

Licensing: Mr Roger Mennie, Head of Legal & Democratic Services, 21 City Square, Dundee DD1 3BY ☎ 01382 434577
✉ roger.mennie@dundeecity.gov.uk

Lifelong Learning: Mr Stewart Murdoch, Director of Leisure & Communities, Central Library, Dundee DD1 2DB ☎ 01382 437460
🖷 01382 437487 ✉ stewart.murdoch@dundeecity.gov.uk

Lighting: Mr Lindsay McGregor, Team Leader (Street Lighting), Dundee House, 50 North Lindsay Street, Dundee DD1 1LS
☎ 01382 834132 🖷 01382 433013
✉ lindsay.mcgregor@dundeecity.gov.uk

Lottery Funding, Charity and Voluntary: Ms Diane Milne, Senior Policy Officer, 3 City Square, Dundee DD1 3BY ☎ 01382 434653 🖷 01382 434650 ✉ diane.milne@dundeecity.gov.uk

Member Services: Mr Paul Carroll, Performance & Improvement Manager, 21 City Square, Dundee DD1 3BY ☎ 01382 434452
🖷 01382 434996 ✉ paul.carroll@dundeecity.gov.uk

Parking: Mr Mike Galloway, Director of City Development, Dundee House, 50 North Lindsay Street, Dundee DD1 1LS
☎ 01382 433610 🖷 01382 433013
✉ mike.galloway@dundeecity.gov.uk

Personnel / HR: Mr Iain Martin, Head of Personnel, 8 City Square, Dundee DD1 3BG ☎ 01382 434438 🖷 01382 434614
✉ iain.martin@dundeecity.gov.uk

Planning: Mr Mike Galloway, Director of City Development, Dundee House, 50 North Lindsay Street, Dundee DD1 1LS
☎ 01382 433610 🖷 01382 433013
✉ mike.galloway@dundeecity.gov.uk

Public Libraries: Mr Stewart Murdoch, Director of Leisure & Communities, Central Library, Dundee DD1 2DB ☎ 01382 437460
🖷 01382 437487 ✉ stewart.murdoch@dundeecity.gov.uk

Recycling & Waste Minimisation: Mr Kenny Kerr, Head of Environmental Protection, 34 Harefield Road, Dundee DD2 3JW
☎ 01382 436201 🖷 01382 436226
✉ kenny.kerr@dundeecity.gov.uk

Road Safety: Mr Neil Gellatly, Head of Transportation, Dundee House, 50 North Lindsay Street, Dundee DD1 1LS ☎ 01382 433116 🖷 01382 433313 ✉ neil.gellatly@dundeecity.gov.uk

Social Services: Mr Alan Baird, Director of Social Work, Dundee House, 50 North Lindsay Street, Dundee DD1 1LS ☎ 01382 433205 🖷 01382 433012 ✉ alan.baird@dundeecity.gov.uk

Social Services (Adult): Ms Laura Bannerman, Community Care Manager, Claverhouse East Industrial Park, Jack Martin Way, Dundee DD1 ☎ 01382 438302 🖷 01382 438360
✉ laura.bannerman@dundeecity.gov.uk

Social Services (Children): Ms Jane Martin, Manager, Children's Services & Criminal Justice, Friarfield House, Barrack Street, Dundee DD1 1PQ ☎ 01382 435017
✉ jane.martin@dundeecity.gov.uk

Staff Training: Mr Iain Martin, Head of Personnel, 8 City Square, Dundee DD1 3BG ☎ 01382 434224 🖷 01382 434614
✉ iain.martin@dundeecity.gov.uk

Town Centre: Mrs Lorna McKenzie, City Centre Manager, 3 City Square, Dundee DD1 3BA ☎ 01382 434548 🖷 01382 434650
✉ lorna.mckenzie@dundeecity.gov.uk

Traffic Management: Mr Neil Gellatly, Head of Transportation, Dundee House, 50 North Lindsay Street, Dundee DD1 1LS
☎ 01382 433116 🖷 01382 433313
✉ neil.gellatly@dundeecity.gov.uk

Transport: Mr Mike Galloway, Director of City Development, Dundee House, 50 North Lindsay Street, Dundee DD1 1LS
☎ 01382 433610 🖷 01382 433013
✉ mike.galloway@dundeecity.gov.uk

Transport Planner: Mr Mike Galloway, Director of City Development, Dundee House, 50 North Lindsay Street, Dundee DD1 1LS ☎ 01382 433610 🖷 01382 433013
✉ mike.galloway@dundeecity.gov.uk

Waste Collection and Disposal: Mr Kenny Kerr, Head of Environmental Protection, 34 Harefield Road, Dundee DD2 3JW
☎ 01382 436201 🖷 01382 436226
✉ kenny.kerr@dundeecity.gov.uk

Waste Management: Mr Kenny Kerr, Head of Environmental Protection, 34 Harefield Road, Dundee DD2 3JW ☎ 01382 436201 🖷 01382 436226 ✉ kenny.kerr@dundeecity.gov.uk

Children's Play Areas: Mr Gary Robertson, Head of Environmental Management, 353 Clepington Road, Dundee DD3 8PL ☎ 01382 436894 ✉ gary.robertson@dundeecity.gov.uk

MEMBERS OF THE COUNCIL (29)

Alexander, John (SNP - Strathmartine)
john.alexander@dundeecity.gov.uk
Asif, Mohammed (LAB - Coldside)
mohammed.asif@dundeecity.gov.uk
Bidwell, Laurie (LAB - The Ferry)
laurie.bidwell@dundeecity.gov.uk
Black, Jimmy (SNP - Coldside)
jimmy.black@dundeecity.gov.uk
Borthwick, Ian (IND - Strathmartine)
ian.borthwick@dundeecity.gov.uk
Bowes, Dave (SNP - Coldside)
david.bowes@dundeecity.gov.uk
Brennan, Lesley (LAB - East End)
lesley.brennan@dundeecity.gov.uk
Campbell, Bill (SNP - West End)
bill.campbell@dundeecity.gov.uk
Cordell, Kevin (SNP - The Ferry)
kevin.cordell@dundeecity.gov.uk

Cruikshank, Georgia (LAB - Maryfield)
georgia.cruikshank@dundeecity.gov.uk
Dawson, Will (SNP - East End)
will.dawson@dundeecity.gov.uk
Duncan, Bob (SNP - Lochee)
bob.duncan@dundeecity.gov.uk
Ferguson, Tom (LAB - Lochee)
tom.ferguson@dundeecity.gov.uk
Gordon, Brian (LAB - North East)
brian.gordon@dundeecity.gov.uk
Guild, Kenneth (SNP - The Ferry)
ken.guild@dundeecity.gov.uk
Hunter, Stewart (SNP - Strathmartine)
stewart.hunter@dundeecity.gov.uk
Keenan, Kevin (LAB - Strathmartine)
kevin.keenan@dundeecity.gov.uk
Lynn, Ken (SNP - Maryfield)
ken.lynn@dundeecity.gov.uk
MacPherson, Fraser (LD - West End)
fraser.macpherson@dundeecity.gov.uk
McCready, Richard (LAB - West End)
richard.mccready@dundeecity.gov.uk
McDonald, Vari (SNP - West End)
vari.mcdonald@dundeecity.gov.uk
McGovern, Norma (LAB - Lochee)
Norma.mcgovern@dundeecity.gov.uk
Melville, Craig (SNP - Maryfield)
craig.melville@dundeecity.gov.uk
Murray, Gregor (SNP - North East)
gregor.murray@dundeecity.gov.uk
Roberts, Christina (SNP - East End)
christina.roberts@dundeecity.gov.uk
Ross, Alan (SNP - Lochee)
alan.ross@dundeecity.gov.uk
Sawers, Willie (SNP - North East)
willie.sawers@dundeecity.gov.uk
Scott, Derek (CON - The Ferry)
derek.scott@dundeecity.gov.uk
Wright, Helen (LAB - Coldside)
helen.wright@dundeecity.gov.uk

POLITICAL COMPOSITION

SNP: 16, LAB: 10, LD: 1, CON: 1, IND: 1

DUNGANNON & SOUTH TYRONE N

Dungannon and South Tyrone Borough Council, Council Offices, Circular Road, Dungannon BT71 6DT ☎ 028 8772 0300 🖷 028 8772 0368 💻 www.dungannon.gov.uk

FACTS & FIGURES

Police Authority: Northern Ireland Policing Board
Health Authority: Southern Health & Social Care Board
Learning and Skills Council: Northern Ireland
Parliamentary Constituencies: Fermanagh and South Tyrone, Ulster Mid
EU Constituencies: Northern Ireland
Election Frequency: Elections are of whole council

PRINCIPAL OFFICERS

Chief Executive: Mr Alan Burke, Joint Chief Executive (Acting) & Director of Environmental Services, Council Offices, Circular Road, Dungannon BT71 6DT ☎ 028 8772 0343 🖷 028 8772 0333 ✉ alan.burke@dungannon.gov.uk

Chief Executive: Mr Iain Frazer, Joint Chief Executive (Acting) & Director of Development, Council Offices, Circular Road, Dungannon BT71 6DT ☎ 028 8772 0343 🖷 028 8772 0333 ✉ iain.frazer@dungannon.gov.uk

Senior Management: Mr Brendan Currie, Head of Human Resources, Council Offices, 24 Northland Row, Dungannon BT71 6AP ☎ 028 8772 8130 🖷 028 8772 8121 ✉ brendan.currie@dungannon.gov.uk

Senior Management: Mrs Paula Kerr, Director of Finance, Council Offices, Circular Road, Dungannon BT71 6DT ☎ 028 8772 0300 🖷 028 8772 0368 ✉ paula.kerr@dungannon.gov.uk

Senior Management: Mr Jim McClelland, Director of Building Services, Council Offices, Circular Road, Dungannon BT71 6DT ☎ 028 8772 0346 🖷 028 8772 0356 ✉ jim.mcclelland@dungannon.gov.uk

Architect, Building / Property Services: Mr Jim McClelland, Director of Building Services, Council Offices, Circular Road, Dungannon BT71 6DT ☎ 028 8772 0346 🖷 028 8772 0356 ✉ jim.mcclelland@dungannon.gov.uk

Best Value: Mrs Paula Kerr, Director of Finance, Council Offices, Circular Road, Dungannon BT71 6DT ☎ 028 8772 0300 🖷 028 8772 0368 ✉ paula.kerr@dungannon.gov.uk

Building Control: Mr Jim McClelland, Director of Building Services, Council Offices, Circular Road, Dungannon BT71 6DT ☎ 028 8772 0346 🖷 028 8772 0356 ✉ jim.mcclelland@dungannon.gov.uk

Civil Registration: Ms Anne McCourt, Registrar, Council Offices, Circular Road, Dungannon BT71 6DT ☎ 028 8772 0329 🖷 028 8772 0368 ✉ registrar@dungannon.gov.uk

PR / Communications: Mr Alan Burke, Joint Chief Executive (Acting) & Director of Environmental Services, Council Offices, Circular Road, Dungannon BT71 6DT ☎ 028 8772 0343 🖷 028 8772 0333 ✉ alan.burke@dungannon.gov.uk

PR / Communications: Mr Iain Frazer, Joint Chief Executive (Acting) & Director of Development, Council Offices, Circular Road, Dungannon BT71 6DT ☎ 028 8772 0343 🖷 028 8772 0333 ✉ iain.frazer@dungannon.gov.uk

Community Safety: Mr Philip Clarke, Community Services Manager, Council Offices, Circular Road, Dungannon BT71 6DT ☎ 028 8772 8616 🖷 028 8772 0368 ✉ philip.clarke@dungannon.gov.uk

Computer Management: Mr Ciaran McKeown, Acting ICT Manager, Council Offices, Circular Road, Dungannon BT71 6DT ☎ 028 8772 0323 ✉ ciaran.mckeown@dungannon.gov.uk

Consumer Protection and Trading Standards: Mr Alan Burke, Joint Chief Executive (Acting) & Director of Environmental Services, Council Offices, Circular Road, Dungannon BT71 6DT ☎ 028 8772 0343 🖷 028 8772 0333 ✉ alan.burke@dungannon.gov.uk

Contracts: Mr Jim McClelland, Director of Building Services, Council Offices, Circular Road, Dungannon BT71 6DT ☎ 028 8772 0346 🖷 028 8772 0356 ✉ jim.mcclelland@dungannon.gov.uk

Economic Development: Mr Vincent Beggs, Enterprise, Investment & Grants Manager, Council Offices, Circular Road, Dungannon BT71 6DT ☎ 028 8772 0347 🖷 028 8772 0333 ✉ vinny.beggs@dungannon.gov.uk

Emergency Planning: Mr Alan Burke, Joint Chief Executive (Acting) & Director of Environmental Services, Council Offices, Circular Road, Dungannon BT71 6DT ☎ 028 8772 0343 🖷 028 8772 0333 ✉ alan.burke@dungannon.gov.uk

Energy Management: Mr Jim McClelland, Director of Building Services, Council Offices, Circular Road, Dungannon BT71 6DT ☎ 028 8772 0346 🖷 028 8772 0356 ✉ jim.mcclelland@dungannon.gov.uk

Environmental / Technical Services: Mr Alan Burke, Joint Chief Executive (Acting) & Director of Environmental Services, Council Offices, Circular Road, Dungannon BT71 6DT ☎ 028 8772 0343 🖷 028 8772 0333 ✉ alan.burke@dungannon.gov.uk

Environmental Health: Mr Alan Burke, Joint Chief Executive (Acting) & Director of Environmental Services, Council Offices, Circular Road, Dungannon BT71 6DT ☎ 028 8772 0343 🖷 028 8772 0333 ✉ alan.burke@dungannon.gov.uk

Estates, Property & Valuation: Mrs Paula Kerr, Director of Finance, Council Offices, Circular Road, Dungannon BT71 6DT ☎ 028 8772 0300 🖷 028 8772 0368 ✉ paula.kerr@dungannon.gov.uk

European Liaison: Mr Vincent Beggs, Enterprise, Investment & Grants Manager, Council Offices, Circular Road, Dungannon BT71 6DT ☎ 028 8772 0347 🖷 028 8772 0333 ✉ vinny.beggs@dungannon.gov.uk

Finance and Treasurer: Mrs Paula Kerr, Director of Finance, Council Offices, Circular Road, Dungannon BT71 6DT ☎ 028 8772 0300 🖷 028 8772 0368 ✉ paula.kerr@dungannon.gov.uk

Fleet Management: Mr Alan Burke, Joint Chief Executive (Acting) & Director of Environmental Services, Council Offices, Circular Road, Dungannon BT71 6DT ☎ 028 8772 0343 🖷 028 8772 0333 ✉ alan.burke@dungannon.gov.uk

Grounds Maintenance: Mr Iain Frazer, Joint Chief Executive (Acting) & Director of Development, Council Offices, Circular Road, Dungannon BT71 6DT ☎ 028 8772 0343 🖷 028 8772 0333 ✉ iain.frazer@dungannon.gov.uk

Health and Safety: Ms Elaine Girvan, Health & Safety Officer, Council Offices, Circular Road, Dungannon BT71 6DT ☎ 028 8772 8120 🖷 028 8772 0368 ✉ elaine.girvan@dungannon.gov.uk

Leisure and Cultural Services: Mr Ken Barrett, Recreation Manager, Dungannon Leisure Centre, Circular Road, Dungannon BT71 6DT ☎ 028 8772 0372 🖷 028 8772 0380 ✉ ken.barrett@dungannon.gov.uk

Licensing: Mr Rodney Gillis, Senior Licensing Officer, Council Offices, Circular Road, Dungannon BT71 6DT ☎ 028 8772 0349 🖷 028 8772 0368 ✉ rodney.gillis@dungannon.gov.uk

Lifelong Learning: Ms Sinead Mullan, Skills, Learning & Development Officer, Council Offices, Circular Road, Dungannon BT71 6AP ☎ 028 8772 8123 🖷 028 8772 8121 ✉ sinead.mullan@dungannon.gov.uk

Lottery Funding, Charity and Voluntary: Mr Philip Clarke, Community Services Manager, Council Offices, Circular Road, Dungannon BT71 6DT ☎ 028 8772 8616 🖷 028 8772 0368 ✉ philip.clarke@dungannon.gov.uk

Member Services: Mrs Eileen Forde, Member Support Officer, Council Offices, Circular Road, Dungannon BT71 6DT ☎ 028 8772 0309 🖷 028 8772 0333 ✉ eileen.forde@dungannon.gov.uk

Partnerships: Mr Philip Clarke, Community Services Manager, Council Offices, Circular Road, Dungannon BT71 6DT ☎ 028 8772 8616 🖷 028 8772 0368 ✉ philip.clarke@dungannon.gov.uk

Personnel / HR: Mr Brendan Currie, Head of Human Resources, Council Offices, 24 Northland Row, Dungannon BT71 6AP ☎ 028 8772 8130 🖷 028 8772 8121 ✉ brendan.currie@dungannon.gov.uk

Procurement: Mrs Linda Ferguson, Procurement Officer, Council Offices, Circular Road, Dungannon BT71 6DT ☎ 028 8772 0321 ✉ linda.ferguson@dungannon.gov.uk

Recycling & Waste Minimisation: Mr Alan Burke, Joint Chief Executive (Acting) & Director of Environmental Services, Council Offices, Circular Road, Dungannon BT71 6DT ☎ 028 8772 0343 🖷 028 8772 0333 ✉ alan.burke@dungannon.gov.uk

Regeneration: Mr Iain Frazer, Joint Chief Executive (Acting) & Director of Development, Council Offices, Circular Road, Dungannon BT71 6DT ☎ 028 8772 0343 🖷 028 8772 0333 ✉ iain.frazer@dungannon.gov.uk

Staff Training: Ms Sinead Mullan, Skills, Learning & Development Officer, Council Offices, Circular Road, Dungannon BT71 6AP ☎ 028 8772 8123 🖷 028 8772 8121 ✉ sinead.mullan@dungannon.gov.uk

Sustainable Development: Ms Yvonne Zellmann, Local Agenda 21 Co-ordinator, Council Offices, Circular Road, Dungannon BT71 6DT ☎ 028 8772 0338 🖷 028 8772 0368 ✉ yvonne.zellmann@dungannon.gov.uk

Tourism: Mr Nigel Hill, Parks & Tourism Manager, Dungannon Park, Park Lake, Moy Road, Dungannon BT71 6DY ☎ 028 8776 7259 ✉ nigel.hill@dungannon.gov.uk

Town Centre: Mr Paul McCreedy, Town Centre Manager, Council Offices, Circular Road, Dungannon BT71 6DT ☎ 028 8772 8615 🖷 028 8772 0368 ✉ paul.mccreedy@dungannon.gov.uk

Waste Collection and Disposal: Mr Alan Burke, Joint Chief Executive (Acting) & Director of Environmental Services, Council Offices, Circular Road, Dungannon BT71 6DT ☎ 028 8772 0343 🖷 028 8772 0333 ✉ alan.burke@dungannon.gov.uk

Waste Management: Mr Alan Burke, Joint Chief Executive (Acting) & Director of Environmental Services, Council Offices, Circular Road, Dungannon BT71 6DT ☎ 028 8772 0343 🖷 028 8772 0333 ✉ alan.burke@dungannon.gov.uk

Children's Play Areas: Mr Nigel Hill, Parks & Tourism Manager, Dungannon Park, Park Lake, Moy Road, Dungannon BT71 6DY ☎ 028 8776 7259 ✉ nigel.hill@dungannon.gov.uk

MEMBERS OF THE COUNCIL (23)

***Mayor:* Gildernew**, Phelim (SF - Blackwater)
phelim.gildernew@dstbc.org
Ashton, Kim (DUP - Dungannon Town)
kim.aston@dstbc.org
Brush, Samuel (DUP - Blackwater)
samuel.brush@dstbc.org
Burton, Roger (DUP - Blackwater)
roger.burton@dstbc.org
Burton, Frances (DUP - Clogher Valley)
frances.burton@dstbc.org
Cavanagh, Jim (SDLP - Torrent)
jim.cavnagh@dstbc.org
Cuddy, Walter (UUP - Dungannon Town)
walter.cuddy@dstbc.org
Daly, Pat (SDLP - Blackwater)
pat.daly@dstbc.org
Donnelly, Desmond (SF - Torrent)
desmond.donnelly@dstbc.org
Gildernew, Phelim (SF - Blackwater)
Gillespie, Michael (SF - Torrent)
michael.gillespie@dstbc.org
Hamilton, Jim (UUP - Blackwater)
jim.hamilton@dstbc.org
McGaghan, Bronwyn (SF - Dungannon Town)
bronwyn.mcgahan@dstbc.org
McGonnell, Anthony (SDLP - Clogher Valley)
mcgonnella@aol.com
McGuigan, Sean (SF - Clogher Valley)
sean.mcguigan@dstbc.org
McLarnon, Larry (SF - Dungannon Town)
larry.mclarnon@dstbc.org
Monteith, Barry (IND - Dungannon Town)
barry.monteith@dstbc.org
Morrow, Maurice (DUP - Dungannon Town)
mauricemorrow@hotmail.com
Mulligan, Robert (UUP - Clogher Valley)
robert.mulligan@dstbc.org
O'Neill, Joe (SF - Torrent)
joe.oneill@dstbc.org
Quinn, Padraig (SF - Torrent)
padraig.quinn@dstbc.org
Reid, Kenneth (UUP - Torrent)
kenneth.reid@dstbc.org
Robinson, Wills (DUP - Clogher Valley)
wills.robinson@dstbc.org

POLITICAL COMPOSITION

SF: 9, DUP: 6, UUP: 4, SDLP: 3, IND: 1

DURHAM U

Durham, Durham County Council, County Hall, Durham DH1 5QF
☎ 0300 123 7070 🖷 0191 383 4500
💻 www.durham.gov.uk

FACTS & FIGURES

Parliamentary Constituencies: Bishop Auckland, Durham North, Durham North West, Durham, City of , Easington, Sedgefield
E

PRINCIPAL OFFICERS

Chief Executive: Mr George Garlick, Chief Executive, Durham County Council, County Hall, Durham DH1 5UF ☎ 0191 372 7600 ✉ george.garlick@durham.gov.uk

Assistant Chief Executive: Ms Lorraine O'Donnell, Assistant Chief Executive, Durham County Council, County Hall, Durham DH1 5UF ☎ 0191 372 7603 ✉ lorraine.odonnell@durham.gov.uk

Senior Management: Mr Terry Collins, Corporate Director - Neighbourhood Services, Durham County Council, County Hall, Durham DH1 5UQ ☎ 0191 383 4447 ✉ terry.collins@durham.gov.uk

Senior Management: Mr Don McLure, Corporate Director - Resources, Durham County Council, County Hall, Durham DH1 5QF ☎ 0191 383 3550 ✉ don.mclure@durham.gov.uk

Senior Management: Ms Rachael Shimmin, Corporate Director - Adults, Wellbeing & Health, Durham County Council, County Hall, Durham DH1 5UG ☎ 0191 383 3296 ✉ rachael.shimmin@durham.gov.uk

Senior Management: Mr Ian Thompson, Corporate Director - Regeneration & Economic Development, Durham County Council, County Hall, Durham DH1 5QF ☎ 0191 383 6590 ✉ ian_thompson@durham.gov.uk

Senior Management: Mr David Williams, Corporate Director - Children & Young People's Service, Durham County Council, County Hall, Durham DH1 5QF ☎ 0191 383 3319 ✉ d.c.williams@durham.gov.uk

Access Officer / Social Services (Disability): Ms Maureen Clare, Head of Access - County Wide Services, Durham County Council, County Hall, Durham DH1 5UJ ☎ 0191 383 3535 ✉ maureen.clare@durham.gov.uk

Access Officer / Social Services (Disability): Ms Jeanette Stephenson, Strategic Manager - Inclusion, Durham County Council, County Hall, Durham DH1 5QF ☎ 0191 383 3738 ✉ jeanette.stephenson@durham.gov.uk

Access Officer / Social Services (Disability): Ms Geraldine Waugh, Operations Manager, Durham County Council, County Hall, Durham DH1 5QF ☎ 0191 383 5149 ✉ geraldine.waugh@durham.gov.uk

Access Officer / Social Services (Disability): Mr Frank Whitelock, Strategic Manager for Integrated Services, Durham County Council, County Hall, Durham DH1 5QF ☎ 0191 383 3744 ✉ frank.whitelock@durham.gov.uk

Architect, Building / Property Services: Mr David Taylor, Property, Planning & Projects Manager, Durham County Council, County Hall, Durham DH1 5QF ☎ 0191 383 3509 ✉ david.taylor3@durham.gov.uk

Best Value: Mr Roger Goodes, Head of Policy & Communications, Durham County Council, County Hall, Durham DH1 5UL ☎ 0191 383 5714 roger.goodes@durham.gov.uk

Building Control: Mr Paul Burr, Building & Facilities Maintenance Manager, Durham County Council, County Hall, Durham DH1 5QF ☎ 0191 372 5030 paul.burr@durham.gov.uk

Children / Youth Services: Ms Gill Eshelby, Head of County Durham Youth Offending Services, Durham County Council, County Hall, Durham DH1 5QF ☎ 0191 383 4752 gill.eshelby@durham.gov.uk

Children / Youth Services: Mr Paul Hebron, Positive Activities for Young People Manager, Durham County Council, County Hall, Durham DH1 5QF ☎ 03000 260513 paul.hebron@durham.gov.uk

Children / Youth Services: Ms Carol Payne, Head of Early Intervention & Partnerships, Durham County Council, County Hall, Durham DH1 5QF ☎ 0191 383 3320 carole.payne@durham.gov.uk

Children / Youth Services: Mr David Williams, Director - Children & Young People, Durham County Council, County Hall, Durham DH1 5UJ ☎ 0191 383 3319 d.c.williams@durham.gov.uk

PR / Communications: Mr Roger Goodes, Head of Policy & Communications, Durham County Council, County Hall, Durham DH1 5QF ☎ 0191 383 5714 roger.goodes@durham.gov.uk

Community Planning: Ms Melanie Campbell, Strategic Manager - Healthier Communities, Durham County Council, County Hall, Durham DH1 5QF ☎ 0191 383 5696 melanie.campbell@durham.gov.uk

Community Planning: Ms Jenny Haworth, Head of Planning & Performance, Durham County Council, County Hall, Durham DH1 5QF ☎ 0191 383 6598 jenny.haworth@durham.gov.uk

Community Safety: Mr Steven Arkley, Strategic Manager - Safer Communities, Durham County Council, County Hall, Durham DH1 5QF ☎ 0191 383 3195 steven.arkley@durham.gov.uk

Computer Management: Mr Keith Forster, Strategic Manager - Performance & Systems, Durham County Council, County Hall, Durham DH1 5QF ☎ 0191 383 3051 keith.forster@durham.gov.uk

Computer Management: Mr Phil Jackman, Head of ICT Services, Durham County Council, County Hall, Durham DH1 5QF ☎ 07775 025096 phil.jackman@durham.gov.uk

Consumer Protection and Trading Standards: Mr Owen Cleugh, Consumer Protection Manager, Durham County Council, County Hall, Durham DH1 5QF ☎ 03000 260925 owen.cleugh@durham.gov.uk

Consumer Protection and Trading Standards: Ms Joanne Waller, Head of Environment, Health & Consumer Protection, Durham County Council, County Hall, Durham DH1 5UQ ☎ 03000 260924 joanne.waller@durham.gov.uk

Contracts: Ms Denise Elliot, Strategic Commissioning Manager, Durham County Council, County Hall, Durham DH1 5QF ☎ 0191 383 4980 denise.elliot@durham.gov.uk

Contracts: Mr Dave Shipman, Strategic Commissioning Manager, Durham County Council, County Hall, Durham DH1 5QF ☎ 0191 383 4412 dave.shipman@durham.gov.uk

Corporate Services: Mr Kevin Edworthy, Corporate Policy & Planning Team Leader, Durham County Council, County Hall, Durham DH1 5QF ☎ 0191 383 6514 kevin.edworthy@durham.gov.uk

Corporate Services: Mr Tom Gorman, Corporate Improvement Manager, Durham County Council, County Hall, Durham DH1 5QF ☎ 0191 383 6518 tom.gorman@durham.gov.uk

Corporate Services: Ms Jan Hillary, Corporate Communications Manager, Durham County Council, County Hall, Durham DH1 5QF ☎ 0191 372 7677 jan.hillary@durham.gov.uk

Corporate Services: Ms Su Jordan, Corporate Programme Team Leader, Durham County Council, County Hall, Durham DH1 5QF ☎ 0191 383 6515 su.jordan@durham.gov.uk

Customer Service: Mr Craig Etherington, Customer Service Manager, Durham County Council, County Hall, Durham DH1 5QF ☎ 0191 372 7669 craig.etherington@durham.gov.uk

Customer Service: Mr Lawrence Serewicz, Principal Information Manager, Durham County Council, County Hall, Durham DH1 5QF ☎ 0191 372 8371 lawrence.serewicz@durham.gov.uk

Customer Service: Mr Oliver Sherratt, Head of Direct Services, Durham County Council, County Hall, Durham DH1 5QF ☎ 0191 372 5205 oliver.sherratt@durham.gov.uk

Economic Development: Ms Sarah Robson, Head of Economic Development & Housing, Durham County Council, County Hall, Durham DH1 5QF ☎ 0191 383 3444 sarah_robson@durham.gov.uk

Economic Development: Mr Graham Wood, Economic Development Manager, Durham County Council, County Hall, Durham DH1 5QF ☎ 03000 262002 graham.wood@durham.gov.uk

Education: Ms Jane le Sage, Educational Support Services Manager, Durham County Council, County Hall, Durham DH1 5QF ☎ 01740 656998 jane.le.sage@durham.gov.uk

Education: Ms Caroline O'Neill, Head of Achievement Services & Head of Education Development Service, Durham County Council, County Hall, Durham DH1 5QF ☎ 0191383 3331 caroline.oneill@durham.gov.uk

Electoral Registration: Ms Colette Longbottom, Legal & Democratic Services, Durham County Council, County Hall, Durham DH1 5QF ☎ 0191 383 5643 colette.longbottom@durham.gov.uk

Emergency Planning: Mr Anthony McDermott, Chief Civil

Contingency Officer, Durham County Council, County Hall, Durham DH1 5QF ☎ 01388 824020 ✉ anthony.mcdermott@durhamdarlingtonccu.gov.uk

Environmental / Technical Services: Mr John Reed, Head of Technical Services, Durham County Council, County Hall, Durham DH1 5QF ☎ 0191 383 3465 ✉ john.reed@durham.gov.uk

Environmental Health: Mr Gary Hutchinson, Environment Protection Manager, Durham County Council, County Hall, Durham DH1 5QF ☎ 03000 261007 ✉ gary.hutchinson@durham.gov.uk

Environmental Health: Ms Joanne Waller, Head of Environment, Health & Consumer Protection, Durham County Council, County Hall, Durham DH1 5UQ ☎ 03000 260924 ✉ joanne.waller@durham.gov.uk

Environmental Health: Mr Michael Yeadon, Health Protection Manager, Durham County Council, County Hall, Durham DH1 5QF ☎ 01388 816166 Ext 4454 ✉ michael.yeadon@durham.gov.uk

Estates, Property & Valuation: Mr Chris Rolle, Asset Manager, Durham County Council, County Hall, Durham DH1 5QF ☎ 0191 383 3223 ✉ chris.rolle@durham.gov.uk

Finance and Treasurer: Mr Graham Bainbridge, Head of Finance, Durham County Council, County Hall, Durham DH1 5QF ☎ 0191 383 3388 ✉ graham.bainbridge@durham.gov.uk

Finance and Treasurer: Mr Paul Darby, Head of Financial Services, Durham County Council, County Hall, Durham DH1 5QF ☎ 03000 261930 ✉ paul.darby@durham.gov.uk

Finance and Treasurer: Ms Susan Elliott, Financial Services Manager, Durham County Council, County Hall, Durham DH1 5QF ☎ 0191 383 5245 ✉ susan.elliott@durham.gov.uk

Finance and Treasurer: Mr Jeff Garfoot, Head of Corporate Finance, Durham County Council, County Hall, Durham DH1 5QF ☎ 0191 383 3551 ✉ jeff.garfoot@durham.gov.uk

Finance and Treasurer: Mr Andrew Gilmore, Strategic Financial Services Manager, Durham County Council, County Hall, Durham DH1 5QF ☎ 0191 383 3098 ✉ andrew.gilmore@durham.gov.uk

Finance and Treasurer: Mr Nick Orton, Payroll & Pensions Manager, Durham County Council, County Hall, Durham DH1 5QF ☎ 0191 383 4429 ✉ nick.orton@durham.gov.uk

Fleet Management: Mr Norman Ramsey, County Fleet Manager, Durham County Council, County Hall, Durham DH1 5QF ☎ 0191 372 5159 ✉ norman.ramsey@durham.gov.uk

Health and Safety: Ms Kim Jobson, Human Resources & Organisational Development Manager, Durham County Council, County Hall, Durham DH1 5QF ☎ 0191 383 3240 ✉ kim.jobson@durham.gov.uk

Highways: Mr Mark Readman, Highways Operations Manager, Durham County Council, County Hall, Durham DH1 5QF ☎ 0191 372 5081 ✉ mark.readman@durham.gov.uk

Highways: Mr David Wilcox, Strategic Highways Manager, Durham County Council, County Hall, Durham DH1 5QF ☎ 0191 383 3468 ✉ dave.wilcox@durham.gov.uk

Housing: Ms Sarah Robson, Head of Economic Development & Housing, Durham County Council, County Hall, Durham DH1 5QF ☎ 0191 383 3444 ✉ sarah_robson@durham.gov.uk

Housing Maintenance: Ms Kath Heathcote, Housing Regeneration Manager, Durham County Council, County Hall, Durham DH1 5QF ☎ 01207 218930 ✉ kath.heathcote@durham.gov.uk

Legal: Ms Colette Longbottom, Legal & Democratic Services, Durham County Council, County Hall, Durham DH1 5QF ☎ 0191 383 5643 ✉ colette.longbottom@durham.gov.uk

Legal: Ms Elizabeth Wilson, Business Manager - Legal Services, Durham County Council, County Hall, Durham DH1 5QF ☎ 0191 383 3513 ✉ elizabeth.wilson@durham.gov.uk

Leisure and Cultural Services: Mr Neil Hillier, Strategic Manager - Heritage & Culture, Durham County Council, County Hall, Durham DH1 5QF ☎ 0191 383 3208 ✉ neil.hillier@durham.gov.uk

Leisure and Cultural Services: Mr Stephen Howell, Head of Sport & Leisure Services, Durham County Council, County Hall, Durham DH1 5UQ ☎ 0191 383 5728 ✉ stephen.howell@durham.gov.uk

Lifelong Learning: Ms Rosemary Laxton, Head of Libraries, Learning & Culture, Durham County Council, County Hall, Durham DH1 5QF ☎ 0191 383 6543 ✉ rosemary.laxton@durham.gov.uk

Member Services: Ms Sharon Spence, Democratic Services Manager, Durham County Council, County Hall, Durham DH1 5QF ☎ 0191 383 3507 ✉ sharon.spence@durham.gov.uk

Partnerships: Mr Gordon Elliott, Head of Partnership & Community Engagement, Durham County Council, County Hall, Durham DH1 5UF ☎ 0191 372 5323 ✉ gordon.elliott@durham.gov.uk

Personnel / HR: Ms Lorraine Anderson, Human Resources Manager - Operations & Projects, Durham County Council, County Hall, Durham DH1 5QF ☎ 0191 372 7620 ✉ lorraine.anderson@durham.gov.uk

Personnel / HR: Ms Kim Jobson, Head of Human Resources & Organisational Development, Durham County Council, County Hall, Durham DH1 5UL ☎ 0191 383 3240 ✉ kim.jobson@durham.gov.uk

Personnel / HR: Ms Joanne Kemp, Human Resources Manager - Policy & Organisational Development, Durham County Council, County Hall, Durham DH1 5QF ☎ 0191 372 7621 ✉ joanne.kemp@durham.gov.uk

Planning: Ms Jenny Haworth, Head of Planning & Performance, Durham County Council, County Hall, Durham DH1 5QF ☎ 0191 383 6598 ✉ jenny.haworth@durham.gov.uk

Planning: Ms Andrea Petty, Policy & Planning Manager, Durham County Council, County Hall, Durham DH1 5QF ☎ 0191 383 3328 ✉ andrea.petty@durham.gov.uk

Planning: Ms Beverley Stobbart, Policy Performance & Planning Manager, Durham County Council, County Hall, Durham DH1 5QF ☎ 0191 383 3602 ✉ bev.stobbart@durham.gov.uk

Planning: Mr Stuart Timmiss, Head of Planning, Durham County Council, County Hall, Durham DH1 5QF ☎ 0191 372 7619 ✉ stuart.timmiss@durham.gov.uk

Procurement: Mr Darren Knowd, Corporate Procurement Manager, Durham County Council, County Hall, Durham DH1 5QF ☎ 0191 383 4187 ✉ darren.knowd@durham.gov.uk

Procurement: Ms Louise Lyons, Commissioning Services Manager, Durham County Council, County Hall, Durham DH1 5QF ☎ 0191 383 3330 ✉ louise.lyons@durham.gov.uk

Public Libraries: Ms Anne Davison, Strategic Manager - Libraries, Durham County Council, County Hall, Durham DH1 5QF ☎ 0191 383 3742 ✉ anne.davison@durham.gov.uk

Regeneration: Mr Peter Coe, Regeneration & Development Manager, Durham County Council, County Hall, Durham DH1 5QF ☎ 03000 262042 ✉ peter.coe@durham.gov.uk

Social Services (Adult): Mr Philip Emberson, Operations Manager - County Durham Care & Support, Durham County Council, County Hall, Durham DH1 5QF ☎ 0191 383 5102 ✉ philip.emberson@durham.gov.uk

Social Services (Adult): Mrs Lesley Jeavons, Head of Adult Care, Durham County Council, County Hall, Durham DH1 5UG ☎ 0191 383 3293 ✉ lesley.tickell@durham.gov.uk

Social Services (Adult): Ms Tracy Joisce, Operations Manager, Durham County Council, County Hall, Durham DH1 5QF ☎ 0191 383 5106 ✉ tracy.joisce@durham.gov.uk

Social Services (Adult): Mr Gerald Tompkins, Head of Social Inclusion, Durham County Council, County Hall, Durham DH1 5QF ☎ 0191 383 3176 ✉ gerald.tompkins@durham.gov.uk

Social Services (Adult): Mr Nick Whitton, Head of Commissioning, Durham County Council, County Hall, Durham DH1 5QF ☎ 0191 383 4188 ✉ nick.whitton@durham.gov.uk

Social Services (Children): Mr Mark Gurney, Safeguarding Children's Services Strategic Manager, Durham County Council, County Hall, Durham DH1 5QF ☎ 0191 383 4541 ✉ mark.gurney@durham.gov.uk

Social Services (Children): Ms Gail Hopper, Head of Safeguarding & Specialist Services, Durham County Council, County Hall, Durham DH1 5UG ☎ 0191 383 3322 ✉ gail.h.hopper@durham.gov.uk

Social Services (Children): Ms Karen Robb, Looked-After Children & Young People's Services Strategic Manager, Durham County Council, County Hall, Durham DH1 5QF ☎ 0191 383 4542 ✉ karen.robb@durham.gov.uk

Staff Training: Ms Kim Jobson, Human Resources & Organisational Development Manager, Durham County Council, County Hall, Durham DH1 5QF ☎ 0191 383 3240 ✉ kim.jobson@durham.gov.uk

Street Scene: Mr Jimmy Bennett, Streetscene Area Manager South, Durham County Council, County Hall, Durham DH1 5QF ☎ 01388 728880 ✉ james.bennett@durham.gov.uk

Street Scene: Mr Ian Hoult, Streetscene Are Manager North, Durham County Council, County Hall, Durham DH1 5QF ☎ 01207 218733 ✉ ian.hoult@durham.gov.uk

Street Scene: Mr Keith Parkinson, Streetscene Area Manager East, Durham County Council, County Hall, Durham DH1 5QF ☎ 0191 527 4401 ✉ keith.parkinson@durham.gov.uk

Sustainable Communities: Mr Peter Appleton, Head of Policy, Planning & Performance, Durham County Council, County Hall, Durham DH1 5QF ☎ 0191 383 3628 ✉ peter.appleton@durham.gov.uk

Transport: Mr Adrian White, Head of Transport & Transport Services, Durham County Council, County Hall, Durham DH1 5UQ ☎ 0191 383 3435 ✉ adrian.white@durham.gov.uk

Transport Planner: Mr Adrian White, Head of Transport, Durham County Council, County Hall, Durham DH1 5QF ☎ 0191 383 3435 ✉ adrian.white@durham.gov.uk

Total Place: Ms Jenny Haworth, Head of Planning & Performance, Durham County Council, County Hall, Durham DH1 5QF ☎ 0191 383 6598 ✉ jenny.haworth@durham.gov.uk

Waste Management: Mr John Shannon, Strategic Waste Manager, Durham County Council, County Hall, Durham DH1 5QF ☎ 0191 383 3093 ✉ john.shannon@durham.gov.uk

MEMBERS OF THE COUNCIL (126)

***Chair:* Marshall**, Linda (LAB - Chester-le-Street West Central)
linda.marshall@durham.gov.uk

***Leader of the Council:* Henig**, Simon (LAB - Chester-le-Street West Central)
simon.henig@durham.gov.uk

Alderson, Bob (IND - Burnopfield & Dipton)
bob.alderson@durham.gov.uk

Alvey, Jimmy (LAB - Peterlee West)
jimmy.alvey@durham.gov.uk

Armstrong, Joseph (LAB - Esh)
joseph.armstrong@durham.gov.uk

Arthur, Bob (IND - Dawdon)
bob.arthur@durham.gov.uk

Avery, Brian (LAB - Chilton)
brian.avery@durham.gov.uk

Bailey, John (IND - Crook North & Tow Law)
john.bailey@durham.gov.uk

Bainbridge, Beaty (CON - Chester-le-Street North & East)
beaty.bainbridge@durham.gov.uk

Bainbridge, Allan (CON - Chester-le-Street South)
a.bainbridge@durham.gov.uk

Barker, Alan (LAB - Easington)

alan.barker@durham.gov.uk
Barnett, Duncan (IND - Benfieldside)
duncan.barnett@durham.gov.uk
Bell, Alan (IND - Lumley)
alan.bell@durham.gov.uk
Bell, Edward (LAB - Deneside)
edward.bell@durham.gov.uk
Bell, Jennifer (LAB - Deneside)
jennifer.bell@durham.gov.uk
Bell, Richard (CON - Barnard Castle West)
richard.bell@durham.gov.uk
Blakey, Jan (LAB - Durham South)
jan.blakey@durham.gov.uk
Bleasdale, Gerry (LAB - Seaham)
gerry.bleasdale@durham.gov.uk
Bowman, Dorothy (LAB - Shildon East)
dorothy.bowman@durham.gov.uk
Boyes, David (LAB - Easington)
david.boyes@durham.gov.uk
Brookes, Peter (LAB - Trimdon)
peter.brookes@durham.gov.uk
Brown, Jane (LAB - Delves Lane & Consett South)
jane.brown@durham.gov.uk
Brown, David (CON - Sedgefield)
d.brown@durham.gov.uk
Brunskill, Becky (CON - Willington)
becky.brunskill@durham.gov.uk
Burn, Dorothy (LD - Coundon)
dororthy.burn@durham.gov.uk
Campbell, Malcolm (IND - Esh)
malcolm.campbell@durham.gov.uk
Carr, Colin (LAB - Ouston & Urpeth)
colin.carr@durham.gov.uk
Chaplow, Jean (LAB - Deerness Valley)
jean.chaplow@durham.gov.uk
Charlton, Pauline (LAB - Evenwood)
paulinecharlton@durham.gov.uk
Cordon, James (LAB - Pelton)
james.cordon@durham.gov.uk
Cox, Alan (LAB - Blackhalls)
alan.cox@durham.gov.uk
Crooks, Rev (LD - Framwellgate Moor)
rev.crooks@durham.gov.uk
Crute, Robert (LAB - Blackhalls)
rob.crute@durham.gov.uk
Davidson, Keith (LAB - Chester-le-Street South)
keith.davidson@durham.gov.uk
Dixon, Mike (LAB - Aycliffe West)
mike.dixon@durham.gov.uk
Docherty, Janice (LAB - Craghead & South Moor)
janice.docherty@durham.gov.uk
Farry, David (IND - Ferryhill)
david.farry@durham.gov.uk
Foster, Neil (LAB - Tudhoe)
neil.foster@durham.gov.uk
Freeman, David (LD - Elvet)
david.freeman@durham.gov.uk
Gittins, Paul (IND - Aycliffe North)
paul.gittins@durham.gov.uk
Graham, Barbara (LAB - Tudhoe)
barbara.graham@durham.gov.uk
Gray, Joan (LAB - Aycliffe North)
joan.gray@durham.gov.uk
Hancock, David (IND - Shildon West)
david.hancock@durham.gov.uk
Harrison, Neil (LD - Bishop Auckland Town)
n.harrison@durham.gov.uk
Harrison, Barbara (CON - Barnard Castle West)
barbara.harrison@durham.gov.uk
Hodgson, Michele (LAB - Annfield Plain)
michele.hodgson@durham.gov.uk
Holland, Grenville (LD - Nevilles Cross)
grenville.holland@durham.gov.uk
Holroyd, Kenneth (LD - Belmont)
ken.holroyd@durham.gov.uk
Hopgood, Amanda (LD - Newton Hall)
amanda.hopgood@durham.gov.uk
Hovvells, Lucy (LAB - Trimdon)
lucy.hovvels@durham.gov.uk
Hugill, Stephen (CON - Evenwood)
stephen.hugill@durham.gov.uk
Hunter, John (IND - Tanfield)
john.hunter@durham.gov.uk
Huntington, Garry (LD - Shildon West)
garry.huntington@durham.gov.uk
Huntington, Eunice (LAB - Shotton)
eunice.huntington@durham.gov.uk
Iveson, Sarah (LAB - Aycliffe East)
sarah.iveson@durham.gov.uk
Johnson, Ossie (LAB - Lanchester)
ossie.johnson@durham.gov.uk
Jopling, Patricia (IND - Crook North & Tow Law)
patricia.jopling@durham.gov.uk
Laing, Audrey (LAB - Peterlee East)
audrey.laing@durham.gov.uk
Lee, June (LAB - Woodhouse Close)
june.lee@durham.gov.uk
Lethbridge, John (LAB - Woodhouse Close)
john.lethbridge@durham.gov.uk
Liddle, Ralph (LD - Peterlee West)
ralph.liddle@durham.gov.uk
Maddison, Dennis (LAB - Horden)
dennis.maddison@durham.gov.uk
Magee, Charles (LAB - Ferryhill)
charles.magee@durham.gov.uk
Marshall, Carl (LAB - Stanley)
carl.marshall@durham.gov.uk
Marshall, David (LAB - Craghead & South Moor)
da.marshall@durham.gov.uk
Martin, Nigel (LD - Nevilles Cross)
nigel.martin@durham.gov.uk
Maslin, Joan (IND - Wingate)
joan.maslin@durham.gov.uk
Mavin, Eric (LD - Belmont)
eric.mavin@durham.gov.uk
May, Peter (CON - Pelton)
peter.may@durham.gov.uk
Moran, John (LAB - Aycliffe East)
john.moran@durham.gov.uk
Morgan, Dennis (LAB - Coxhoe)
dennis.morgan@durham.gov.uk
Murphy, Eddie (IND - Crook South)
eddie.murphy@durham.gov.uk
Myers, Dan (LAB - Seaham)
dan.myers@durham.gov.uk
Myers, Brian (LAB - Willington)
blmyers@durham.gov.uk
Napier, Alan (LAB - Murton)
alan.napier@durham.gov.uk
Naylor, Alice (LAB - Murton)

alice.naylor@durham.gov.uk
Nicholls, Morris (LAB - Thornley)
morris.nicholls@durham.gov.uk
Nicholson, Joan (IND - Annfield Plain)
joan.nicholson@durham.gov.uk
O'Donnell, Len (LAB - Wingate)
leonard.odonnell@durham.gov.uk
Ord, Reginald (IND - Burnopfield & Dipton)
reg.ord@durham.gov.uk
Ord, Ben (LD - Spennymoor & Middlestone)
ben.ord@durham.gov.uk
Paylor, Enid (LAB - Aycliffe West)
enid.paylor@durham.gov.uk
Plews, Maria (LAB - Coxhoe)
maria.plews@durham.gov.uk
Potts, Christine (LAB - Chilton)
christine.potts@durham.gov.uk
Potts, Maureen (LAB - Ouston & Urpeth)
maureen.potts@durham.gov.uk
Richardson, George (CON - Barnard Castle East)
george.richardson@durham.gov.uk
Robinson, John (LAB - Sedgefield)
john.robinson@durham.gov.uk
Robinson, Stephen (IND - Benfieldside)
s.robinson@durham.gov.uk
Robson, Clive (LAB - Consett North)
clive.robson@durham.gov.uk
Rowlandson, James (CON - Barnard Castle East)
james.rowlandson@durham.gov.uk
Savory, Anita (IND - Weardale)
anita.savory@durham.gov.uk
Shield, Alan (IND - Leadgate & Medomsley)
alan.shield@durham.gov.uk
Shiell, John (LAB - Chester-le-Street North & East)
john.shiell@durham.gov.uk
Shuttleworth, John (IND - Weardale)
jshuttleworth@durham.gov.uk
Simmons, Mamie (LD - Newton Hall)
mamie.simmons@durham.gov.uk
Southwell, Dennis (LD - Gilesgate)
dennis.southwell@durham.gov.uk
Stelling, Watts (IND - Leadgate & Medomsley)
watts.stelling@durham.gov.uk
Stephens, Brian (LAB - Shildon East)
brian.stephens@durham.gov.uk
Stoker, David (LD - Elvet)
david.stoker@durham.gov.uk
Stradling, Paul (LAB - Horden)
paul.stradling@durham.gov.uk
Taylor, Paul (LAB - Brandon)
paul.taylor@durham.gov.uk
Taylor, Thomas (LD - Coundon)
tommy.taylor@durham.gov.uk
Temple, Owen (LD - Consett North)
owen.temple@durham.gov.uk
Tennant, Gordon (LAB - Peterlee East)
gordon.tennant@durham.gov.uk
Thompson, Kevin (LD - Spennymoor & Middlestone)
kevin.thompson@durham.gov.uk
Thomson, Les (LD - Gilesgate)
les.thomson@durham.gov.uk
Todd, Robin (LAB - Shotton)
robin.todd@durham.gov.uk
Tomlinson, Eddie (LAB - Crook South)
eddie.tomlinson@durham.gov.uk
Turnbull, John (LAB - Brandon)
john.turnbull@durham.gov.uk
Turner, Allen (LAB - Sacriston)
allen.turner@durham.gov.uk
Turner, Andrew (LAB - West Auckland)
andy.turner@durham.gov.uk
Vasey, Claire (LAB - Stanley)
claire.l.vasey@durham.gov.uk
Walker, Charlie (LAB - Dawdon)
charlie.walker@durham.gov.uk
Wilkes, Mark (LD - Framwellgate Moor)
mark.wilkes@durham.gov.uk
Wilkinson, John (LD - Deerness Valley)
john.wilkinson@durham.gov.uk
Williams, Mac (LAB - Durham South)
mac.williams@durham.gov.uk
Willis, Audrey (IND - Lumley)
audrey.willis@durham.gov.uk
Wilson, Brian (IND - Thornley)
brian.wilson@durham.gov.uk
Wilson, Joe (LAB - Tanfield)
joe.wilson@durham.gov.uk
Wood, Maureen (LD - Sherburn)
maureen.wood@durham.gov.uk
Woods, Carol (LD - Sherburn)
carol.woods@durham.gov.uk
Wright, Anne (LAB - Sacriston)
anne.wright@durham.gov.uk
Yorke, Robert (LAB - West Auckland)
robert.yorke@durham.gov.uk
Young, Robert (LAB - Delves Lane & Consett South)
bob.young@durham.gov.uk
Young, Richard (IND - Lanchester)
richie.young@durham.gov.uk
Zair, Samuel (IND - Bishop Auckland Town)
sam.zair@durham.gov.uk

POLITICAL COMPOSITION

LAB: 69, IND: 24, LD: 23, CON: 10

CABINET

Leader: Mr Simon Henig
Deputy Leader/ Resources: Mr Alan Napier
Adult Services: Mr Morris Nicholls
Children & Young People's Services: Ms Claire Vasey
Economic Regeneration: Mr Neil Foster
Housing: Mr Clive Robson
Leisure, Libraries & Lifelong Learning: Ms Maria Plews
Neighbourhoods & Local Partnerships: Mr Brian Stephens
Safer & Healthier Communities: Ms Lucy Hovvells
Strategic Environment & Leisure: Mr Robert Young

COMMITTEE CHAIRS

Adults, Wellbeing & Health Overview & Scrutiny: Mr Dan Myers
Audit: Mr Edward Bell
Chief Officer's Appointment: Mr Simon Henig
Children & Young People's Overview & Scrutiny: Ms Jan Blakey
Corporate Issues: Mr Brian Avery
County Planning: Mr Keith Davidson
Economy & Enterprise Overview & Scrutiny: Mr John Moran
Environment & Sustainable Communities Overview &

Scrutiny: Mr Dan Myers
General Licensing & Registration: Mr Colin Carr
Human Resources: Mr Mac Williams
Overview & Scrutiny Management Board: Mr Joseph Armstrong
Pension Fund: Mr Andrew Turner
Safer & Stronger Communities Overview & Scrutiny: Mr David Boyes
Standards: Ms Pauline Charlton
Statutory Licensing: Mr Colin Carr

EALING L

Ealing London Borough Council, Perceval House, 14-16 Uxbridge Road, Ealing, London W5 2HL ☎ 020 8825 5000 🖷 020 8579 5224 ✉ webmaster@ealing.gov.uk 💻 www.ealing.gov.uk

FACTS & FIGURES

Police Authority: Metropolitan Police Authority
Health Authority: NHS London
Learning and Skills Council: London
Parliamentary Constituencies: Ealing Central and Acton, Ealing North, Ealing, Southall
EU Constituencies: London
Election Frequency: Elections are of whole council
Twinning: Bielany (Poland); Kreis Steinfurt (Germany); Marcq-en-Baroeul (France)

PRINCIPAL OFFICERS

Chief Executive: Mr Martin Smith, Chief Executive, Perceval House, 14-16 Uxbridge Road, Ealing W5 2HL ☎ 020 8825 7089 ✉ chiefexecutive@ealing.gov.uk

Senior Management: Mr David Archibald, Executive Director - Children & Adults, Perceval House, 14-16 Uxbridge Road, Ealing, London W5 2HL ☎ 020 8825 8107 🖷 020 8840 5500 ✉ darchibald@ealing.gov.uk

Senior Management: Mr Pat Hayes, Executive Director - Regeneration & Housing, Perceval House, 14-16 Uxbridge Road, Ealing W5 2HL ☎ 020 8825 9120 🖷 020 8825 5500 ✉ pat.hayes@ealing.gov.uk

Senior Management: Mr Ian O'Donnell, Executive Director - Corporate Resources, Perceval House, 14-16 Uxbridge Road, Ealing W5 2HL ☎ 020 8828 5269 🖷 020 8825 5500 ✉ odonnelli@ealing.gov.uk

Senior Management: Mr Keith Townsend, Executive Director - Environment & Customer Services, Perceval House, 14-16 Uxbridge Road, Ealing, London W5 2NL ☎ 020 8825 9551 🖷 020 8840 5500 ✉ townsendk@ealing.gov.uk

Architect, Building / Property Services: Mr Mark Newton, Director of Business Services, Perceval House, 14-16 Uxbridge Road, Ealing W5 2HL ☎ 020 8825 7509 🖷 020 8825 7476 ✉ mark.newton@ealing.gov.uk

Best Value: Mr Matthew Booth, Director of Policy & Performance, Perceval House, 14-16 Uxbridge Road, Ealing, London W5 2HL ☎ 020 8825 8556 ✉ boothm@ealing.gov.uk

Building Control: Ms Aileen Jones, Head of Planning Services, Perceval House, 14-16 Uxbridge Road, Ealing, London W5 2HL ☎ 020 8825 8371 🖷 020 8825 6610 ✉ jonesa@ealing.gov.uk

Building Control: Mr Noel Rutherford, Director of Built Environment, Perceval House, 14-16 Uxbridge Road, Ealing, London W5 2HL ☎ 020 8825 6639 🖷 020 8825 6610 ✉ rutherfn@ealing.gov.uk

Children / Youth Services: Ms Elaine Cunningham, Head of Youth & Connexions Service, Perceval House, 14-16 Uxbridge Road, Ealing, London W5 2HL ☎ 020 8825 6593 🖷 020 8825 5775 ✉ ecunningham@ealing.gov.uk

Children / Youth Services: Ms Judith Finlay, Director of Children's Services, Perceval House, 14-16 Uxbridge Road, Ealing, London W5 2HL ☎ 020 8825 7106 🖷 020 8825 6934 ✉ finlayj@ealing.gov.uk

Civil Registration: Ms Franchene Allen, Registration Services Manager, Perceval House, 14-16 Uxbridge Road, Ealing, London W5 2HL ☎ 020 8825 9277 🖷 020 8825 8560 ✉ fran.allen@ealing.gov.uk

PR / Communications: Mr Peter Morris, Director of Marketing & Communications, Perceval House, 14-16 Uxbridge Road, Ealing, London W5 2HL ☎ 020 8825 5374 🖷 020 8579 9909 ✉ morrisp@ealing.gov.uk

Community Safety: Ms Susan Parsonage, Director of Community Safety, Perceval House, 14-16 Uxbridge Road, Ealing, London W5 2HL ☎ 020 8825 7398 🖷 020 8825 6661 ✉ parsonas@ealing.gov.uk

Computer Management: Mr Mark Newton, Director of Business Services, Perceval House, 14-16 Uxbridge Road, Ealing W5 2HL ☎ 020 8825 7509 🖷 020 8825 7476 ✉ mark.newton@ealing.gov.uk

Consumer Protection and Trading Standards: Mr Mark Wiltshire, Head of Regulatory Services, Perceval House, 14-16 Uxbridge Road, Ealing, London W5 2HL ☎ 020 8825 8197 ✉ wiltshirema@ealing.gov.uk

Contracts: Mrs Kate Graefe, Head of Strategic Procurement, Perceval House, 14-16 Uxbridge Road, Ealing, London W5 2HL ☎ 020 8825 9843 ✉ graefek@ealing.gov.uk

Corporate Services: Mr Simon George, Director of Corporate Finance & Audit, Perceval House, 14-16 Uxbridge Road, Ealing, London W5 2HL ☎ 020 8825 6193 🖷 020 8825 6590 ✉ sigeorge@ealing.gov.uk

Corporate Services: Mr Mark Wiltshire, Head of Regulatory Services, Perceval House, 14-16 Uxbridge Road, Ealing, London W5 2HL ☎ 020 8825 8197 ✉ wiltshirema@ealing.gov.uk

Customer Service: Ms Alison Reynolds, Director of Customer Services, Perceval House, 14-16 Uxbridge Road, Ealing, London W5 2HL ☎ 020 8825 5329 ✉ reynolda@ealing.gov.uk

Economic Development: Mr Brendon Walsh, Director of

Property & Regeneration, Perceval House, Ealing Council, 14-16 Oxbridge Road, Ealing, London W5 2HL ☎ 020 8825 6539 ✉ walshb@ealing.gov.uk

Education: Ms Eileen Lustig, Head of Admissions, Perceval House, 14-16 Uxbridge Road, Ealing, London W5 2HL ☎ 020 8825 5059 ✉ elustig@ealing.gov.uk

Electoral Registration: Mr Ross Jackson, Head of Elections & Members' Services, Perceval House, 14-16 Uxbridge Road, Ealing, London W5 2HL ☎ 020 8825 6854 ✉ jacksonr@ealing.gov.uk

Emergency Planning: Ms Chris Begley, Interim Head of Civil Protection, Perceval House, 14-16 Uxbridge Road, Ealing, London W5 2HL ☎ 020 8825 7806 🖷 020 8825 6909 ✉ begleyc@ealing.gov.uk

Environmental / Technical Services: Mr Noel Rutherford, Director of Built Environment, Perceval House, 14-16 Uxbridge Road, Ealing, London W5 2HL ☎ 020 8825 6639 🖷 020 8825 6610 ✉ rutherfn@ealing.gov.uk

Estates, Property & Valuation: Mr Brendon Walsh, Director of Property & Regeneration, Perceval House, 14-16 Uxbridge Road, Ealing, London W5 2HL ☎ 020 8825 6539 ✉ walshb@ealing.gov.uk

European Liaison: Mr Calum Murdoch, External Funding Officer, Perceval House, 14-16 Uxbridge Road, Ealing, London W5 2HL ☎ 020 8825 7443 ✉ murdochc@ealing.gov.uk

Events Manager: Miss Fiona Elliot, Head of Hospitality & Events, Perceval House, 14-16 Uxbridge Road, Ealing, London W5 2HL ☎ 020 8825 6061 ✉ elliotf@ealing.gov.uk

Facilities: Mr Mark Newton, Director of Business Services, Perceval House, 14-16 Uxbridge Road, Ealing W5 2HL ☎ 020 8825 7509 🖷 020 8825 7476 ✉ mark.newton@ealing.gov.uk

Finance and Treasurer: Mr David Ewart, Director of Finance Regeneration & Housing, Perceval House, 14-16 Uxbridge Road, Ealing, London W5 2HL ☎ 020 8825 7884 ✉ ewartd@ealing.gov.uk

Finance and Treasurer: Mr Simon George, Director of Corporate Finance & Audit, Perceval House, 14-16 Uxbridge Road, Ealing, London W5 2HL ☎ 020 8825 6193 🖷 020 8825 6590 ✉ sigeorge@ealing.gov.uk

Finance and Treasurer: Mr Ian O'Donnell, Executive Director - Corporate Resources, Perceval House, 14-16 Uxbridge Road, Ealing, London W5 2HL ☎ 020 8828 5269 🖷 020 8825 5500 ✉ odonnelli@ealing.gov.uk

Finance and Treasurer: Ms Adele Taylor, Director of Financial Services, Perceval House, 14-16 Uxbridge Road, Ealing, London W5 2HL ☎ 020 8825 7548 ✉ taylora@ealing.gov.uk

Grounds Maintenance: Mr Roger Jones, Director of Environment & Leisure, Perceval House, 14-16 Uxbridge Road, Ealing, London W5 2HL ☎ 020 8825 8576

Highways: Mr Shahid Iqbal, Assistant Director of Highways, 4th Floor Perceval House, 14-16 Uxbridge Road, Ealing, London W5 2HL ☎ 020 8825 7802 🖷 020 8825 5858 ✉ iqbalsp@ealing.gov.uk

Local Area Agreement: Mr Jarvis Garrett, Improvement Manager, Town Hall, London W5 2BY ☎ 020 8825 7893 ✉ garrettj@ealing.gov.uk

Legal: Ms Helen Harris, Head of Legal & Democratic Services, Perceval House, 14-16 Uxbridge Road, Ealing, London W5 2HL ☎ 020 8825 8615 ✉ harrish@ealing.gov.uk

Licensing: Ms Loraine Abbott, Regulatory Services Officer, Perceval House, 14-16 Uxbridge Road, Ealing, London W5 2HL ☎ 020 8825 6298 ✉ abbottl@ealing.gov.uk

Lottery Funding, Charity and Voluntary: Mr Nigel Fogg, Grants Unit Manager, Perceval House, 14-16 Uxbridge Road, Ealing, London W5 2HL ☎ 020 8825 7589 ✉ foggn@ealing.gov.uk

Member Services: Mr Ross Jackson, Head of Elections & Members' Services, Perceval House, 14-16 Uxbridge Road, Ealing, London W5 2HL ☎ 020 8825 6854 ✉ jacksonr@ealing.gov.uk

Parking: Mr Keiron Clarke, Parking Operations Manager, Perceval House, 14-16 Uxbridge Road, Ealing, London W5 2HL ☎ 020 8825 7584 ✉ clarkek@ealing.gov.uk

Partnerships: Mr Matthew Booth, Director of Policy & Performance, Perceval House, 14-16 Uxbridge Road, Ealing, London W5 2HL ☎ 020 8825 8556 ✉ boothm@ealing.gov.uk

Personnel / HR: Mr David Veale, Assistant Director of HR & Organisational Development, Perceval House, 14-16 Uxbridge Road, Ealing, London W5 2HL ☎ 020 8825 7359 ✉ vealed@ealing.gov.uk

Planning: Ms Aileen Jones, Head of Planning Services, Perceval House, 14-16 Uxbridge Road, Ealing, London W5 2HL ☎ 020 8825 8371 🖷 020 8825 6610 ✉ jonesa@ealing.gov.uk

Procurement: Mrs Kate Graefe, Head of Strategic Procurement, Perceval House, 14-16 Uxbridge Road, Ealing, London W5 2HL ☎ 020 8825 9843 ✉ graefek@ealing.gov.uk

Public Libraries: Ms Carole Stewart, Assistant Director of Arts, Heritage & Libraries, Perceval House, 14-16 Uxbridge Road, Ealing, London W5 2HL ☎ 020 8825 7216 ✉ stewartc@ealing.gov.uk

Recycling & Waste Minimisation: Mr Earl McKenzie, Assistant Director of Street Services, Perceval House, 14-16 Uxbridge Road, Ealing, London W5 2LX ☎ 020 8825 5194 ✉ mckenzie@ealing.gov.uk

Regeneration: Mr Brendon Walsh, Director of Property & Regeneration, Perceval House, 14-16 Uxbridge Road, Ealing, London W5 2HL ☎ 020 8825 6539 ✉ walshb@ealing.gov.uk

Road Safety: Mr Shahid Iqbal, Assistant Director of Highways, 4th Floor Perceval House, 14-16 Uxbridge Road, Ealing, London

W5 2HL ☎ 020 8825 7802 🖷 020 8825 5858
✉ iqbalsp@ealing.gov.uk

Social Services (Adult): Mr Steven Day, Director of Adult Services, Perceval House, 14-16 Uxbridge Road, Ealing, London W5 2HL ☎ 020 8825 6286 ✉ days@ealing.gov.uk

Social Services (Children): Ms Judith Finlay, Director of Children's Services, Perceval House, 14-16 Uxbridge Road, Ealing, London W5 2HL ☎ 020 8825 7106 🖷 020 8825 6934 ✉ finlayj@ealing.gov.uk

Sustainable Communities: Ms Joanne Mortensen, Sustainability Co-ordinator, Perceval House, 14-16 Uxbridge Road, Ealing, London W5 2HL ☎ 020 8825 9183 ✉ Mortensenj@ealing.gov.uk

Sustainable Development: Ms Joanne Mortensen, Sustainability Co-ordinator, Perceval House, 14-16 Uxbridge Road, Ealing, London W5 2HL ☎ 020 8825 9183 ✉ Mortensenj@ealing.gov.uk

Town Centre: Ms Lucy Taylor, Assistant Director of Regeneration & Planning Policy, Perceval House, 14-16 Uxbridge Road, Ealing, London W5 2HL ☎ 020 8825 9036 ✉ taylorl@ealing.gov.uk

Traffic Management: Mr Shahid Iqbal, Assistant Director of Highways, 4th Floor Perceval House, 14-16 Uxbridge Road, Ealing, London W5 2HL ☎ 020 8825 7802 🖷 020 8825 5858 ✉ iqbalsp@ealing.gov.uk

Transport: Mr Francis Torto, Transport Development Manager, Perceval House, 14-16 Uxbridge Road, Ealing, London W5 2HL ☎ 020 8825 7382 ✉ tortof@ealing.gov.uk

Total Place: Mr Brendon Walsh, Director of Property & Regeneration, Perceval House, 14-16 Uxbridge Road, Ealing, London W5 2HL ☎ 020 8825 6539 ✉ walshb@ealing.gov.uk

Waste Management: Mr Earl McKenzie, Assistant Director of Street Services, Perceval House, 14-16 Uxbridge Road, Ealing, London W5 2LX ☎ 020 8825 5194 ✉ mckenzie@ealing.gov.uk

Waste Management: Mr Earl McKenzie, Assistant Director of Street Services, Perceval House, 14-16 Uxbridge Road, Ealing, London W5 2LX ☎ 020 8825 5194 ✉ mckenzie@ealing.gov.uk

MEMBERS OF THE COUNCIL (69)

***Deputy Mayor:* Ahmed**, Shahbaz (LAB - North Greenford)
shahbaz.ahmed@ealing.gov.uk
***Leader of the Council:* Bell**, Julian (LAB - Greenford Broadway)
julian.bell@ealing.gov.uk
***Deputy Leader of the Council:* Dheer**, Ranjit (LAB - Dormers Wells)
ranjit.dheer@ealing.gov.uk
***Group Leader:* Millican**, David (CON - Northfield)
david.millican@ealing.gov.uk
Anand, Jasbir (LAB - Southall Green)
jasbir.anand@ealing.gov.uk
Anderson, Justin (CON - Perivale)
justin.anderson@ealing.gov.uk
Anjum, Sitarah (LAB - Perivale)
sitarah.anjum@ealing.gov.uk
Aslam, Mohammad (LAB - Norwood Green)
mohammad.aslam@ealing.gov.uk
Bagha, Tej Ram (LAB - Dormers Wells)
tej.bagha@ealing.gov.uk
Bakhai, Nigel (LD - Elthorne)
nigel.bakhai@ealing.gov.uk
Ball, Jon (LD - Ealing Common)
jon.ball@ealing.gov.uk
Brooks, Will (CON - Greenford Green)
william.brooks@ealing.gov.uk
Byrne, Theresa (LAB - North Greenford)
theresa.byrne@ealing.gov.uk
Chapman, Ann (CON - Walpole)
ann.chapman@ealing.gov.uk
Costello, Colm (CON - Hobbayne)
colm.costello@ealing.gov.uk
Cowing, John (CON - Walpole)
john.cowing@ealing.gov.uk
Crawford, Daniel (LAB - Acton Central)
daniel.crawford@ealing.gov.uk
Crawford, Kate (LAB - East Acton)
katherine.crawford@ealing.gov.uk
Dabrowska, Joanna (CON - Ealing Common)
joanna.dabrowska@ealing.gov.uk
Dennehy, Benjamin (CON - Hanger Hill)
benjamin.dennehy@ealing.gov.uk
Dhami, Tejinder Singh (LAB - Dormers Wells)
tejinder.dhami@ealing.gov.uk
Dhindsa, Kamaljit (LAB - Southall Green)
kamaljit.dhindsa@ealing.gov.uk
Emment, Susan (CON - Greenford Green)
susan.emment@ealing.gov.uk
Gallagher, John (LAB - South Acton)
john.gallagher@ealing.gov.uk
Gordon, Yoel (LAB - Elthorne)
yoel.gordon@ealing.gov.uk
Grant, Isobel (CON - Cleveland)
isobel.grant@ealing.gov.uk
Gulaid, Abdullah (LAB - Acton Central)
abdullah.gulaid@ealing.gov.uk
Harris, Eileen (CON - Northolt Mandeville)
eileen.harris@ealing.gov.uk
Iskanderian, Ara (LAB - Northolt Mandeville)
ara.iskanderian@ealing.gov.uk
Johnson, Yvonne (LAB - South Acton)
yvonne.johnson@ealing.gov.uk
Kang, Swarn Singh (LAB - Southall Green)
swarn.kang@ealing.gov.uk
Kapoor, Anita (CON - Elthorne)
anita.kapoor@ealing.gov.uk
Kapoor, Ashok (CON - Walpole)
ashok.kapoor@ealing.gov.uk
Kaur, Harbhajan (LAB - Greenford Broadway)
harbhajan.kaur@ealing.gov.uk
Kausar, Mohammed (LAB - Southall Broadway)
mohammed.kausar@ealing.gov.uk
Langan, Wendy (LAB - Hobbayne)
wendy.langan@ealing.gov.uk
Mahfouz, Bassam (LAB - Northolt West End)
bassam.mahfouz@ealing.gov.uk
Malcolm, Gary (LD - Southfield)
gary.malcolm@ealing.gov.uk
Mann, Gurmit Kaur (LAB - Norwood Green)
gurmit.mann@ealing.gov.uk
Mann, Rajinder Singh (LAB - Norwood Green)
rajinder.mann@ealing.gov.uk

Manro, Shital (LAB - North Greenford)
shital.manro@ealing.gov.uk
Midha, Mohinder Kaur (LAB - Lady Margaret)
mohinder.midha@ealing.gov.uk
Mohan, Karam (LAB - Lady Margaret)
karam.mohan@ealing.gov.uk
Murtagh, Tim (LAB - Greenford Broadway)
tim.murtagh@ealing.gov.uk
Noori, Zahida (LAB - Southall Broadway)
Zahida.Abbas.Noori@ealing.gov.uk
Padda, Swaran (LAB - Lady Margaret)
swaran.padda@ealing.gov.uk
Pagan, Diana (CON - Hanger Hill)
diana.pagan@ealing.gov.uk
Popham, John (CON - Cleveland)
john.popham@ealing.gov.uk
Potts, Ian (CON - Ealing Broadway)
ian.potts@ealing.gov.uk
Reece, Rosamund (CON - Ealing Common)
roz.reece@ealing.gov.uk
Reen, Mark (CON - Northfield)
mark.reen@ealing.gov.uk
Reeves, Brian (LAB - Northolt West End)
brian.reeves@ealing.gov.uk
Rennie, Edward (LAB - Perivale)
edward.rennie@ealing.gov.uk
Rose, Harvey (LD - Southfield)
harvey.rose@ealing.gov.uk
Sabiers, Mik (LAB - South Acton)
mik.sabiers@ealing.gov.uk
Said, Atallah (LAB - East Acton)
atallah.said@ealing.gov.uk
Scott, David (CON - Ealing Broadway)
david.scott@ealing.gov.uk
Stacey, Jason (CON - Greenford Green)
jason.stacey@ealing.gov.uk
Stafford, Gregory (CON - Cleveland)
gregory.stafford@ealing.gov.uk
Steed, Andrew (LD - Southfield)
andrew.steed@ealing.gov.uk
Summers, Chris (LAB - Northolt Mandeville)
chris.summers@ealing.gov.uk
Sumner, Nigel (CON - Hanger Hill)
nigel.sumner@ealing.gov.uk
Tailor, Hitesh (LAB - East Acton)
hitesh.tailor@ealing.gov.uk
Taylor, Philip (CON - Northfield)
philip.taylor@ealing.gov.uk
Varma, Surinder (LAB - Southall Broadway)
surinder.varma@ealing.gov.uk
Walker, Patricia (LAB - Acton Central)
patricia.walker@ealing.gov.uk
Wall, Lauren (LAB - Northolt West End)
lauren.wall@ealing.gov.uk
Wall, Ray (LAB - Hobbayne)
ray.wall@ealing.gov.uk
Young, Anthony (CON - Ealing Broadway)
anthony.young@ealing.gov.uk

POLITICAL COMPOSITION
LAB: 40, CON: 24, LD: 5

CABINET
Leader of the Council / Policy: Mr Julian Bell
Deputy Leader / Community Services & Safety: Mr Ranjit Dheer
Children & Young People: Ms Patricia Walker
Health & Adult Services: Ms Jasbir Anand
Housing: Mr Hitesh Tailor
Finance & Performance: Ms Yvonne Johnson
Transport & Environment: Ms Bassam Mahfouz

COMMITTEE CHAIRS
Development Advisory: Mr Julian Bell
Education: Ms Patricia Walker
Emergency: Mr Julian Bell
Health & Adult Social Services: Mr Abdullah Gulaid
Licensing: Ms Kate Crawford
Overview & Scrutiny: Mr Shital Manro
Pensions: Ms Yvonne Johnson
Planning: Mr Ray Wall
Regulatory: Ms Kate Crawford

EAST AYRSHIRE — S

East Ayrshire Council, Council Headquarters, London Road, Kilmarnock KA3 7BU ☎ 01563 576000 🖷 01563 576500
the.council@east-ayrshire.gov.uk 💻 www.east-ayrshire.gov.uk

FACTS & FIGURES
Police Authority: Strathclyde Police Authority
Health Authority: NHS Ayrshire & Arran
Learning and Skills Council: Scotland
Parliamentary Constituencies: Ayr, Carrick and Cumnock, Kilmarnock and Loudoun
EU Constituencies: Scotland
Election Frequency: Elections are of whole council
Twinning: Ales (France); Herstal (Belgium); Joue-les-tours (France); Kulmbach (Germany); Santa Coloma de Gramenet (Spain)

PRINCIPAL OFFICERS
Chief Executive: Ms Fiona Lees, Chief Executive, Council Headquarters, London Road, Kilmarnock KA3 7BU ☎ 01563 576019 🖷 01563 576200 fiona.lees@east-ayrshire.gov.uk

Deputy Chief Executive: Mrs Elizabeth Morton, Depute Chief Executive / Executive Director of Neighbourhood Services, Council Headquarters, London Road, Kilmarnock KA3 7BU ☎ 01563 576001 elizabeth.morton@east-ayrshire.gov.uk

Senior Management: Mr Alex McPhee, Executive Director of Finance & Corporate Support, Council Headquarters, London Road, Kilmarnock KA3 7BU ☎ 01563 576279 alex.mcphee@east-ayrshire.gov.uk

Senior Management: Mr Graham Short, Executive Director of Educational & Social Services, Council Headquarters, London Road, Kilmarnock KA3 7BU ☎ 01563 576003 graham.short@east-ayrshire.gov.uk

Architect, Building / Property Services: Mr Donald Meldrum, Asset Manager, 17-19 Hill Street, Kilmarnock KA3 1HB ☎ 01563 503460 donald.meldrum@east-ayrshire.gov.uk

Best Value: Ms Gwen Barker, Policy, Planning & Performance

Manager, Council Headquarters, London Road, Kilmarnock KA3 7BU ☎ 01563 554602 ✉ gwen.barker@east-ayrshire.gov.uk

Building Control: Mr David McDowall, Building Standards & Development Manager, The Johnnie Walker Bond, 15 Strand Street, Kilmarnock KA1 1HU ☎ 01563 576749 ✉ david.mcdowall@east-ayrshire.gov.uk

Catering Services: Mr Andrew Kennedy, Acting Head of Facilities Management, Council Headquarters, London Road, Kilmarnock KA3 7BU ☎ 01563 576089 ✉ andrew.kennedy@east-ayrshire.gov.uk

Civil Registration: Ms Catherine Dunlop, Senior Registrar, Burns Monument Centre, Kay Park, Kilmarnock KA3 7RU ☎ 01563 576692 ✉ catherine.dunlop@east-ayrshire.gov.uk

PR / Communications: Ms Lynne Buchanan, Communications & Customer First Manager, Council Headquarters, London Road, Kilmarnock KA3 7BU ☎ 01563 576520 ✉ lynne.buchanan@east-ayrshire.gov.uk

Community Planning: Ms Gwen Barker, Policy, Planning & Performance Manager, Council Headquarters, London Road, Kilmarnock KA3 7BU ☎ 01563 554602 ✉ gwen.barker@east-ayrshire.gov.uk

Community Safety: Mr Chris McAleavey, Head of Housing & Environment Services, Council Headquarters, London Road, Kilmarnock KA3 7BU ☎ 01563 576598 ✉ chris.mcaleavey@east-ayrshire.gov.uk

Computer Management: Mr Malcolm Roulston, Head of Corporate Infrastructure, Civic Centre South, John Dickie Street, Kilmarnock KA1 1HW ☎ 01563 576809 ✉ malcolm.roulston@east-ayrshire.gov.uk

Consumer Protection and Trading Standards: Mr Les Aitchison, Assistant Principal Officer, Civic Centre South, John Dickie Street, Kilmarnock KA1 1HW ☎ 01563 554381 ✉ les.aitchison@east-ayrshire.gov.uk

Contracts: Mr Stuart McCall, Legal & Procurement Services Manager, Council Headquarters, London Road, Kilmarnock KA3 7BU ☎ 01563 576085 ✉ stuart.mccall@east-ayrshire.gov.uk

Corporate Services: Mr Bill Walkinshaw, Head of Democratic Services, Council Headquarters, London Road, Kilmarnock KA3 7BU ☎ 01563 576135 ✉ bill.walkinshaw@east-ayrshire.gov.uk

Direct Labour: Mr Derek Spence, Housing Asset Services Manager, Burnside Street, Kilmarnock, KA1 4EX ☎ 01563 555501 ✉ derek.spence@east-ayrshire.gov.uk

Economic Development: Mr Alan Neish, Head of Planning & Economic Development, The Johnnie Walker Bond, 15 Strand Street, Kilmarnock KA1 1HU ☎ 01563 576767 ✉ alan.neish@east-ayrshire.gov.uk

Education: Mr Graham Short, Executive Director of Educational & Social Services, Council Headquarters, London Road, Kilmarnock KA3 7BU ☎ 01563 576003 ✉ graham.short@east-ayrshire.gov.uk

Education: Mr Alan Ward, Acting Head of Service, Council Headquarters, London Road, Kilmarnock KA3 7BU ☎ 01563 576126 ✉ alan.ward@east-ayrshire.gov.uk

E-Government: Mr Alex McPhee, Executive Director of Finance & Corporate Support, Council Headquarters, London Road, Kilmarnock KA3 7BU ☎ 01563 576279 ✉ alex.mcphee@east-ayrshire.gov.uk

E-Government: Mr Malcolm Roulston, Head of Corporate Infrastructure, Civic Centre South, John Dickie Street, Kilmarnock KA1 1HW ☎ 01563 576809 ✉ malcolm.roulston@east-ayrshire.gov.uk

Emergency Planning: Mrs Monica Orr, Civil Contingencies Officer, Building 372, Alpha Freight Area, Robertson Road, Glasgow Prestwick International Airport, Prestwick KA9 2PL ☎ 01292 692185 ✉ monica.orr@east-ayrshire.gov.uk

Energy Management: Mrs Sarah Farrell, Energy Adviser, 2 The Cross, Kilmarnock KA1 1LR ☎ 01563 555224 ✉ sarah.farrell@east-ayrshire.gov.uk

Environmental / Technical Services: Mr Chris McAleavey, Head of Housing & Environment Services, Council Headquarters, London Road, Kilmarnock KA3 7BU ☎ 01563 576598 ✉ chris.mcaleavey@east-ayrshire.gov.uk

Environmental Health: Mr David Mitchell, Head Legal, Procurement & Regulatory Services, Council Headquarters, London Road, Kilmarnock KA3 7BU ☎ 01563 576061 🖷 01563 576179 ✉ david.mitchell@east-ayrshire.gov.uk

Estates, Property & Valuation: Mr Donald Meldrum, Asset Manager, 17-19 Hill Street, Kilmarnock KA3 1HB ☎ 01563 503460 ✉ donald.meldrum@east-ayrshire.gov.uk

Finance and Treasurer: Mr Alex McPhee, Executive Director of Finance & Corporate Support, Council Headquarters, London Road, Kilmarnock KA3 7BU ☎ 01563 576279 ✉ alex.mcphee@east-ayrshire.gov.uk

Fleet Management: Mr Robert Stevenson, Transport Services Manager, Transport Unit, 34 Main Road, Crookedholm, Kilmarnock KA3 6JS ☎ 01563 503250 ✉ robert.stevenson@east-ayrshire.gov.uk

Grounds Maintenance: Mr Robert McCulloch, Outdoor Amenities Manager, Outdoor Amenities, Western Road Depot, Kilmarnock KA3 1LL ☎ 01563 554066 ✉ robert.mcculloch@east-ayrshire.gov.uk

Health and Safety: Mr Ian McArthur, Health & Safety Manager, Civic Centre South, John Dickie Street, Kilmarnock KA1 1HW ☎ 01563 576901 ✉ ian.mcarthur@east-ayrshire.gov.uk

Highways: Mr John Bryson, Head of Roads & Transportation, The Johnnie Walker Bond, 15 Strand Street, Kilmarnock KA1 1HU ☎ 01563 503164 ✉ john.bryson@east-ayrshire.gov.uk

Housing: Mr Chris McAleavey, Head of Housing & Environment Services, Council Headquarters, London Road, Kilmarnock KA3 7BU ☎ 01563 576598 ✉ chris.mcaleavey@east-ayrshire.gov.uk

Housing: Mrs Elizabeth Morton, Depute Chief Executive / Executive Director of Neighbourhood Services, Council Headquarters, London Road, Kilmarnock KA3 7BU ☎ 01563 576001 ✉ elizabeth.morton@east-ayrshire.gov.uk

Housing Maintenance: Mr Chris McAleavey, Head of Housing & Environment Services, Council Headquarters, London Road, Kilmarnock KA3 7BU ☎ 01563 576598 ✉ chris.mcaleavey@east-ayrshire.gov.uk

Legal: Mr Alex McPhee, Executive Director of Finance & Corporate Support, Council Headquarters, London Road, Kilmarnock KA3 7BU ☎ 01563 576279 ✉ alex.mcphee@east-ayrshire.gov.uk

Legal: Mr David Mitchell, Head Legal, Procurement & Regulatory Services, Council Headquarters, London Road, Kilmarnock KA3 7BU ☎ 01563 576061 🖷 01563 576179 ✉ david.mitchell@east-ayrshire.gov.uk

Leisure and Cultural Services: Mr John Griffiths, Head of Leisure Services, Council Headquarters, London Road, Kilmarnock KA3 7BU ☎ 01563 576264 🖷 01563 576130 ✉ john.griffiths@east-ayrshire.gov.uk

Leisure and Cultural Services: Mrs Elizabeth Morton, Depute Chief Executive / Executive Director of Neighbourhood Services, Council Headquarters, London Road, Kilmarnock KA3 7BU ☎ 01563 576001 ✉ elizabeth.morton@east-ayrshire.gov.uk

Licensing: Mr David Mitchell, Head Legal, Procurement & Regulatory Services, Council Headquarters, London Road, Kilmarnock KA3 7BU ☎ 01563 576061 🖷 01563 576179 ✉ david.mitchell@east-ayrshire.gov.uk

Lighting: Mr John Bryson, Head of Roads & Transportation, The Johnnie Walker Bond, 15 Strand Street, Kilmarnock KA1 1HU ☎ 01563 503164 ✉ john.bryson@east-ayrshire.gov.uk

Member Services: Mr Bill Walkinshaw, Head of Democratic Services, Council Headquarters, London Road, Kilmarnock KA3 7BU ☎ 01563 576135 🖷 01563 576245 ✉ bill.walkinshaw@east-ayrshire.gov.uk

Parking: Mr John Bryson, Head of Roads & Transportation, The Johnnie Walker Bond, 15 Strand Street, Kilmarnock KA1 1HU ☎ 01563 503164 ✉ john.bryson@east-ayrshire.gov.uk

Personnel / HR: Mr Alex McPhee, Executive Director of Finance & Corporate Support, Council Headquarters, London Road, Kilmarnock KA3 7BU ☎ 01563 576279 ✉ alex.mcphee@east-ayrshire.gov.uk

Personnel / HR: Mr Martin Rose, Head of Human Resources, Council Headquarters, London Road, Kilmarnock KA3 7BU ☎ 01563 576092 ✉ martin.rose@east-ayrshire.gov.uk

Planning: Mrs Elizabeth Morton, Depute Chief Executive / Executive Director of Neighbourhood Services, Council Headquarters, London Road, Kilmarnock KA3 7BU ☎ 01563 576001 ✉ elizabeth.morton@east-ayrshire.gov.uk

Planning: Mr Alan Neish, Head of Planning & Economic Development, The Johnnie Walker Bond, 15 Strand Street, Kilmarnock KA1 1HU ☎ 01563 576767 ✉ alan.neish@east-ayrshire.gov.uk

Procurement: Mr Alex Reid, Procurement Team Leader, Council Headquarters, London Road, Kilmarnock KA3 7BU ☎ 01563 576186 ✉ alex.reid@east-ayrshire.gov.uk

Public Libraries: Mr Gerard Cairns, Library, Registration & Information Services Manager, The Burns Monument Centre, Kay Park, Kilmarnock KA3 7RU ☎ 01563 554330 ✉ gerard.cairns@east-ayrshire.gov.uk

Recycling & Waste Minimisation: Mr Chris McAleavey, Head of Housing & Environment Services, Council Headquarters, London Road, Kilmarnock KA3 7BU ☎ 01563 576598 ✉ chris.mcaleavey@east-ayrshire.gov.uk

Regeneration: Mr Alan Neish, Head of Planning & Economic Development, The Johnnie Walker Bond, 15 Strand Street, Kilmarnock KA1 1HU ☎ 01563 576767 ✉ alan.neish@east-ayrshire.gov.uk

Road Safety: Mr Jim Melville, Road Safety Officer, The Johnnie Walker Bond, 15 Strand Street, Kilmarnock KA3 1HU ☎ 01563 503132 ✉ jim.melville@east-ayrshire.gov.uk

Social Services: Mr Graham Short, Executive Director of Educational & Social Services, Council Headquarters, London Road, Kilmarnock KA3 7BU ☎ 01563 576003 ✉ graham.short@east-ayrshire.gov.uk

Social Services (Adult): Mr Eddie Fraser, Head of Community Support, Council Headquarters, London Road, Kilmarnock KA3 7BU ☎ 01563 576546 ✉ eddie.fraser@east-ayrshire.gov.uk

Social Services (Children): Ms Susan Taylor, Head of Children & Families & Criminal Justice, Council Headquarters, London Road, Kilmarnock KA3 7BU ☎ 01563 576920 ✉ susan.taylor@east-ayrshire.gov.uk

Staff Training: Ms Ailie Macpherson, Organisational Development Manager, 17 - 19 Hill Street, Kilmarnock KA3 1HA ☎ 01563 503441 ✉ allie.macpherson@east-ayrshire.gov.uk

Street Scene: Mr John Bryson, Head of Roads & Transportation, The Johnnie Walker Bond, 15 Strand Street, Kilmarnock KA1 1HU ☎ 01563 503164 ✉ john.bryson@east-ayrshire.gov.uk

Sustainable Development: Mr Alan Neish, Head of Planning & Economic Development, The Johnnie Walker Bond, 15 Strand Street, Kilmarnock KA1 1HU ☎ 01563 576767 ✉ alan.neish@east-ayrshire.gov.uk

Tourism: Mr Alan Neish, Head of Planning & Economic Development, The Johnnie Walker Bond, 15 Strand Street, Kilmarnock KA1 1HU ☎ 01563 576767

alan.neish@east-ayrshire.gov.uk

Town Centre: Ms Kathryn Howell, Town Centre Manager - Cumnock, Unit 14, 14 Townhead Street, Cumnock KA18 1LE ☎ 01290 429350 kathryn.howell@east-ayrshire.gov.uk

Town Centre: Ms Fiona Nicolson, Town Centre Manager - Kilmarnock, CARS Office, 34 John Finnie Street, Kilmarnock KA1 1DD ☎ 01563 503014 fiona.nicolson@east-ayrshire.gov.uk

Traffic Management: Mr John Bryson, Head of Roads & Transportation, The Johnnie Walker Bond, 15 Strand Street, Kilmarnock KA1 1HU ☎ 01563 503164 john.bryson@east-ayrshire.gov.uk

Transport: Mr Robert Stevenson, Transport Services Manager, Transport Unit, 34 Main Road, Crookedholm, Kilmarnock KA3 6JS ☎ 01563 503250 robert.stevenson@east-ayrshire.gov.uk

Transport Planner: Mr John Bryson, Head of Roads & Transportation, The Johnnie Walker Bond, 15 Strand Street, Kilmarnock KA1 1HU ☎ 01563 503164 john.bryson@east-ayrshire.gov.uk

Waste Collection and Disposal: Mr Chris McAleavey, Head of Housing & Environment Services, Council Headquarters, London Road, Kilmarnock KA3 7BU ☎ 01563 576598 chris.mcaleavey@east-ayrshire.gov.uk

Waste Management: Mr Chris McAleavey, Head of Housing & Environment Services, Council Headquarters, London Road, Kilmarnock KA3 7BU ☎ 01563 576598 chris.mcaleavey@east-ayrshire.gov.uk

MEMBERS OF THE COUNCIL (32)

***Provost:* McFadzean**, John (CON - Irvine Valley)
john.mcfadzean@east-ayrshire.gov.uk
***Deputy Provost:* Campbell**, John (SNP - Kilmarnock East & Hurlford)
john.campbell@east-ayrshire.gov.uk
***Leader of the Council:* Reid**, Douglas (SNP - Kilmarnock West & Crosshouse)
douglas.reid@east-ayrshire.gov.uk
***Deputy Leader of the Council:* Linton**, Iain (SNP - Kilmarnock West & Crosshouse)
iain.linton@east-ayrshire.gov.uk
Bell, John (SNP - Doon Valley)
john.bell@east-ayrshire.gov.uk
Brown, Alan (SNP - Irvine Valley)
alan.brown@east-ayrshire.gov.uk
Buchanan, Jim (SNP - Kilmarnock East & Hurlford)
jim.buchanan@east-ayrshire.gov.uk
Coffey, Helen (SNP - Kilmarnock North)
willie.coffey@east-ayrshire.gov.uk
Cook, Tom (CON - Kilmarnock West & Crosshouse)
tom.cook@east-ayrshire.gov.uk
Crawford, William (LAB - Cumnock & New Cumnock)
william.crawford@east-ayrshire.gov.uk
Cree, Gordon (LAB - Kilmarnock East & Hurlford)
gordon.cree@east-ayrshire.gov.uk
Dinwoodie, Elaine (LAB - Doon Valley)
elaine.dinwoodie@east-ayrshire.gov.uk
Freel, Ellen (IND - Annick)
ellen.freel2@east-ayrshire.gov.uk
Hershaw, Andrew (SNP - Kilmarnock North)
andrew.hershaw@east-ayrshire.gov.uk
Jones, Lillian (LAB - Kilmarnock West & Crosshouse)
lillian.jones@east-ayrshire.gov.uk
Knapp, John (LAB - Kilmarnock South)
john.knapp@east-ayrshire.gov.uk
MacColl, Eoghann (SNP - Annick)
eoghann.maccoll@east-ayrshire.gov.uk
Mair, George (LAB - Irvine Valley)
george.mair@east-ayrshire.gov.uk
McDill, Robert (SNP - Irvine Valley)
robert.mcdill@east-ayrshire.gov.uk
McGhee, John (LAB - Annick)
john.mcghee@east-ayrshire.gov.uk
McGhee, Neil (LAB - Ballochmyle)
neil.mcghee@east-ayrshire.gov.uk
McIntyre, Drew (LAB - Kilmarnock East & Hurlford)
andrew.mcintyre@east-ayrshire.gov.uk
McKay, Maureen (LAB - Kilmarnock North)
maureen.mckay@east-ayrshire.gov.uk
Menzies, William (LAB - Cumnock & New Cumnock)
william.menzies@east-ayrshire.gov.uk
Morrice, Kathy (SNP - Cumnock & New Cumnock)
kathy.morrice@east-ayrshire.gov.uk
Pirie, Moira (LAB - Doon Valley)
moira.pirie@east-ayrshire.gov.uk
Primrose, Stephanie (SNP - Ballochmyle)
stephanie.primrose@east-ayrshire.gov.uk
Roberts, Jim (SNP - Ballochmyle)
jim.roberts@east-ayrshire.gov.uk
Ross, Eric (LAB - Cumnock & New Cumnock)
eric.ross@east-ayrshire.gov.uk
Ross, Hugh (SNP - Kilmarnock South)
hugh.ross@east-ayrshire.gov.uk
Shaw, David (LAB - Ballochmyle)
david.shaw@east-ayrshire.gov.uk
Todd, Jim (SNP - Kilmarnock South)
jim.todd@east-ayrshire.gov.uk

POLITICAL COMPOSITION

SNP: 15, LAB: 14, CON: 2, IND: 1

CABINET

Leader: Mr Douglas Reid
Deputy Leader: Mr Iain Linton
Delivering Community Regeneration: Mr Jim Buchanan
Delivering Community Regeneration: Mr Robert McDill
Improving Community Health & Wellbeing: Mr Eoghann MacColl
Improving Community Safety: Mr Tom Cook
Promoting Lifelong Learning: Ms Stephanie Primrose
Strategic Planning, Management & Resources and Equalities: Mr Alan Brown
Strategic Planning, Management & Resources and Equalities: Mr Douglas Reid

EAST CAMBRIDGESHIRE D

East Cambridgeshire District Council, The Grange, Nutholt Lane, Ely CB7 4EE ☎ 01353 665555 🖷 01353 665240
info@eastcambs.gov.uk
www.eastcambs.gov.uk

FACTS & FIGURES

Police Authority: Cambridgeshire Police Authority
Health Authority: East of England Strategic Health Authority
Learning and Skills Council: Eastern
Parliamentary Constituencies: Cambridgeshire South East
EU Constituencies: Eastern
Election Frequency: Elections are of whole council
Twinning: District: Orsay (France); Kempen (Germany); Ely: Ribe (Denmark)

PRINCIPAL OFFICERS

Chief Executive: Mr John Hill, Chief Executive, The Grange, Nutholt Lane, Ely CB7 4EE ☎ 01353 616274 🖷 01353 616326 ✉ john.hill@eastcambs.gov.uk

Deputy Chief Executive: Mr Andrew Killington, Deputy Chief Executive, The Grange, Nutholt Lane, Ely CB7 4EE ☎ 01353 616303 🖷 01353 665240 ✉ andrew.killington@eastcambs.gov.uk

Access Officer / Social Services (Disability): Mr Rob Fysh, Team Leader, Building Control, The Grange, Nutholt Lane, Ely CB7 4EE ✉ rob.fysh@eastcambs.gov.uk

Best Value: Mr John Hill, Chief Executive, The Grange, Nutholt Lane, Ely CB7 4EE ☎ 01353 616274 🖷 01353 616326 ✉ john.hill@eastcambs.gov.uk

Building Control: Mr Rob Fysh, Team Leader, Building Control, The Grange, Nutholt Lane, Ely CB7 4EE ✉ rob.fysh@eastcambs.gov.uk

PR / Communications: Mr Tony Taylorson, Communications & Media Manager, The Grange, Nutholt Lane, Ely CB7 4EE ☎ 01353 665555 🖷 01353 665240 ✉ tony.taylorson@eastcambs.gov.uk

Community Planning: Mr Darren Dixon, Head of Community Services, The Grange, Nutholt Lane, Ely CB7 4EE ☎ 01353 616454 🖷 01353 668819 ✉ darren.dixon@eastcambs.gov.uk

Community Safety: Mr Nick Ball, Community Safety Officer, The Grange, Nutholt Lane, Ely CB7 4EE ☎ 01353 616455 🖷 01353 665240 ✉ nick.ball@eastcambs.gov.uk

Computer Management: Mr Andrew Killington, Deputy Chief Executive, The Grange, Nutholt Lane, Ely CB7 4EE ☎ 01353 616303 🖷 01353 665240 ✉ andrew.killington@eastcambs.gov.uk

Customer Service: Mr Andrew Killington, Deputy Chief Executive, The Grange, Nutholt Lane, Ely CB7 4EE ☎ 01353 616303 🖷 01353 665240 ✉ andrew.killington@eastcambs.gov.uk

Direct Labour: Mr Keith Stronach, Principal Facilities & Asset Management Officer, The Grange, Nutholt Lane, Ely CB7 4EE ☎ 01353 616300 ✉ keith.stronach@eastcambs.gov.uk

Economic Development: Ms Shirley Blake, Principal Sustainable Development Officer, The Grange, Nutholt Lane, Ely CB7 4EE ☎ 01353 616385 🖷 01353 665240 ✉ shirley.blake@eastcambs.gov.uk

Economic Development: Mr Giles Hughes, Head of Planning & Sustainable Development Services, The Grange, Nutholt Lane, Ely CB7 4EE ☎ 01353 665555 🖷 01353 665240 ✉ giles.hughes@eastcambs.gov.uk

E-Government: Mr Andrew Killington, Deputy Chief Executive, The Grange, Nutholt Lane, Ely CB7 4EE ☎ 01353 616303 🖷 01353 665240 ✉ andrew.killington@eastcambs.gov.uk

Electoral Registration: Mrs Joan Cox, Electoral Services Officer, The Grange, Nutholt Lane, Ely CB7 4EE ☎ 01353 616460 🖷 01353 665240 ✉ joan.cox@eastcambs.gov.uk

Emergency Planning: Mr John Hill, Chief Executive, The Grange, Nutholt Lane, Ely CB7 4EE ☎ 01353 616274 🖷 01353 616326 ✉ john.hill@eastcambs.gov.uk

Energy Management: Mrs Liz Knox, Head of Environmental Services, The Grange, Nutholt Lane, Ely CB7 4EE ☎ 01353 616313 ✉ liz.knox@eastcambs.gov.uk

Environmental Health: Mrs Liz Knox, Head of Environmental Services, The Grange, Nutholt Lane, Ely CB7 4EE ☎ 01353 616313 ✉ liz.knox@eastcambs.gov.uk

Estates, Property & Valuation: Mr Keith Stronach, Principal Facilities & Asset Management Officer, The Grange, Nutholt Lane, Ely CB7 4EE ☎ 01353 616300 ✉ keith.stronach@eastcambs.gov.uk

European Liaison: Ms Shirley Blake, Principal Sustainable Development Officer, The Grange, Nutholt Lane, Ely CB7 4EE ☎ 01353 616385 🖷 01353 665240 ✉ shirley.blake@eastcambs.gov.uk

Facilities: Mr Keith Stronach, Principal Facilities & Asset Management Officer, The Grange, Nutholt Lane, Ely CB7 4EE ☎ 01353 616300 ✉ keith.stronach@eastcambs.gov.uk

Finance and Treasurer: Mrs Linda Grinnell, Head of Finance, The Grange, Nutholt Lane, Ely CB7 4EE ☎ 01353 665555 ✉ linda.grinnell@eastcambs.gov.uk

Health and Safety: Mr Keith Stronach, Principal Facilities & Asset Management Officer, The Grange, Nutholt Lane, Ely CB7 4EE ☎ 01353 616300 ✉ keith.stronach@eastcambs.gov.uk

Home Energy Conservation: Mrs Liz Knox, Head of Environmental Services, The Grange, Nutholt Lane, Ely CB7 4EE ☎ 01353 616313 ✉ liz.knox@eastcambs.gov.uk

Housing: Ms Jane Hollingworth, Head of Housing, The Grange, Nutholt Lane, Ely CB7 4EE ☎ 01353 616236 🖷 01353 665240 ✉ jane.hollingworth@eastcambs.gov.uk

Legal: Mrs Jeanette Thompson, Head of Legal & Democratic Services, The Grange, Nutholt Lane, Ely CB7 4EE ☎ 01353 616372 🖷 01353 668803 ✉ jeanette.thompson@eastcambs.gov.uk

Leisure and Cultural Services: Mr Darren Dixon, Head of Community Services, The Grange, Nutholt Lane, Ely CB7 4EE ☎ 01353 616454 🖷 01353 668819

🖱 darren.dixon@eastcambs.gov.uk

Licensing: Mrs Liz Knox, Head of Environmental Services, The Grange, Nutholt Lane, Ely CB7 4EE ☎ 01353 616313 🖱 liz.knox@eastcambs.gov.uk

Parking: Mrs Tracey Harding, Team Leader, Tourism and Town Centre Services, The Grange, Nutholt Lane, Ely CB7 4EE ☎ 01363 665555 🖷 01353 665240 🖱 tracey.harding@eastcambs.gov.uk

Personnel / HR: Mrs Kathy Batey, Head of HR & Facilities Management, The Grange, Nutholt Lane, Ely CB7 4EE ☎ 01353 665555 🖷 01353 665240 🖱 kathy.batey@eastcambs.gov.uk

Personnel / HR: Mr Andrew Killington, Deputy Chief Executive, The Grange, Nutholt Lane, Ely CB7 4EE ☎ 01353 616303 🖷 01353 665240 🖱 andrew.killington@eastcambs.gov.uk

Planning: Mr Giles Hughes, Head of Planning & Sustainable Development Services, The Grange, Nutholt Lane, Ely CB7 4EE ☎ 01353 665555 🖷 01353 665240 🖱 giles.hughes@eastcambs.gov.uk

Procurement: Mr Keith Stronach, Principal Facilities & Asset Management Officer, The Grange, Nutholt Lane, Ely CB7 4EE ☎ 01353 616300 🖱 keith.stronach@eastcambs.gov.uk

Recycling & Waste Minimisation: Mrs Liz Knox, Head of Environmental Services, The Grange, Nutholt Lane, Ely CB7 4EE ☎ 01353 616313 🖱 liz.knox@eastcambs.gov.uk

Staff Training: Mrs Kathy Batey, Head of HR & Facilities Management, The Grange, Nutholt Lane, Ely CB7 4EE ☎ 01353 665555 🖷 01353 665240 🖱 kathy.batey@eastcambs.gov.uk

Sustainable Communities: Ms Suzanne Goff, Sustainability Officer, The Grange, Nutholt Lane, Ely CB7 4EE ☎ 01353 616379 🖷 01353 665240 🖱 suzanne.goff@eastcambs.gov.uk

Tourism: Mrs Tracey Harding, Team Leader, Tourism and Town Centre Services, The Grange, Nutholt Lane, Ely CB7 4EE ☎ 01363 665555 🖷 01353 665240 🖱 tracey.harding@eastcambs.gov.uk

Town Centre: Mrs Tracey Harding, Team Leader, Tourism and Town Centre Services, The Grange, Nutholt Lane, Ely CB7 4EE ☎ 01363 665555 🖷 01353 665240 🖱 tracey.harding@eastcambs.gov.uk

Waste Collection and Disposal: Mrs Liz Knox, Head of Environmental Services, The Grange, Nutholt Lane, Ely CB7 4EE ☎ 01353 616313 🖱 liz.knox@eastcambs.gov.uk

Waste Management: Mrs Liz Knox, Head of Environmental Services, The Grange, Nutholt Lane, Ely CB7 4EE ☎ 01353 616313 🖱 liz.knox@eastcambs.gov.uk

MEMBERS OF THE COUNCIL (39)

***Chair:* Parramint**, Tony (CON - Soham South)
tony.parramint@eastcambs.gov.uk
***Vice-Chair:* Cornell**, Tony (CON - Soham North)
tony.cornell@eastcambs.gov.uk
***Leader of the Council:* Moakes**, Peter (CON - Sutton)
peter.moakes@eastcambs.gov.uk
***Deputy Leader of the Council:* Palmer**, James (CON - Soham North)
james.palmer@eastcambs.gov.uk
***Group Leader:* Allen**, Ian (LD - Haddenham)
ian.allen@eastcambs.gov.uk
***Group Leader:* Wilson**, Gareth (LD - Haddenham)
gareth.wilson@eastcambs.gov.uk
***Group Leader:* Wright**, Andrew (IND - Littleport East)
andrew.wright@eastcambs.gov.uk
Alderson, Allen (CON - Swaffhams)
allen.alderson@eastcambs.gov.uk
Allan, Michael (LD - Fordham Villages)
michael.allan@eastcambs.gov.uk
Ambrose-Smith, Christine (CON - Littleport West)
christine.ambrose-smith@eastcambs.gov.uk
Austen, Sue (LD - Ely West)
sue.austen@eastcambs.gov.uk
Bailey, Anna (CON - Downham Villages)
anna.bailey@eastcambs.gov.uk
Beckett, Derrick (IND - Isleham)
derrick.beckett@eastcambs.gov.uk
Brown, David (CON - Burwell)
david.brown@eastcambs.gov.uk
Burton, Will (CON - Ely East)
will.burton@eastcambs.gov.uk
Edwards, Lavinia (CON - Burwell)
lavinia.edwards@eastcambs.gov.uk
Ellis, Kevin (CON - Bottisham)
kevin.ellis@eastcambs.gov.uk
Fordham, Colin (IND - Soham South)
colin.fordham@eastcambs.gov.uk
Friend-Smith, Sheila (LD - Ely West)
sheila.friend-smith@eastcambs.gov.uk
Friend-Smith, Jeremy (LD - Ely South)
jeremy.friend-smith@eastcambs.gov.uk
Goodge, Tony (CON - Downham Villages)
tony.goodge@eastcambs.gov.uk
Griffin-Singh, Elaine (CON - Ely North)
elaine.griffin-singh@eastcambs.gov.uk
Harris, Lindsey (LD - Ely North)
lindsey.harris@eastcambs.gov.uk
Hobbs, Richard (CON - Ely East)
richard.hobbs@eastcambs.gov.uk
Hunt, Bill (CON - Stretham)
bill.hunt@eastcambs.gov.uk
Hunt, Tom (CON - Ely South)
tom.hunt@eastcambs.gov.uk
Kerby, Tom (CON - Cheveley)
tom.kerby@eastcambs.gov.uk
Morris, Chris (CON - Dullingham Villages)
chris.morris@eastcambs.gov.uk
Morrison, Neil (LD - Littleport West)
neil.morrison@eastcambs.gov.uk
Palmer, John (IND - Soham South)
john.palmer@eastcambs.gov.uk
Read, Philip (CON - Sutton)
philip.read@eastcambs.gov.uk
Roberts, Charles (CON - Stretham)
charles.roberts@eastcambs.gov.uk
Rouse, Mike (CON - Ely North)
mike.rouse@eastcambs.gov.uk
Schumann, Joshua (CON - Fordham Villages)

joshua.schumann@eastcambs.gov.uk
Smith, David (CON - Littleport East)
david.ambrose-smith@eastcambs.gov.uk
Stevens, Robert (LD - Bottisham)
robert.stevens@eastcambs.gov.uk
Williams, Hazel (LD - Burwell)
hazel.williams@eastcambs.gov.uk
Willows, Sue (CON - Cheveley)
sue.willows@eastcambs.gov.uk
Wilson, Pauline (LD - Haddenham)
pauline.wilson@eastcambs.gov.uk

POLITICAL COMPOSITION
CON: 24, LD: 11, IND: 4

COMMITTEE CHAIRS
Community & Environment: Mr Richard Hobbs
Development & Transport: Mr Peter Moakes
Licensing: Mr Tony Goodge
Personnel & Corporate Services: Mr John Palmer
Planning: Mr Philip Read
Scrutiny: Mr Michael Allan

EAST DEVON D

East Devon District Council, Council Offices, Knowle, Sidmouth EX10 8HL ☎ 01395 516551 🖷 01395 517507
info@eastdevon.gov.uk www.eastdevon.gov.uk

FACTS & FIGURES
Police Authority: Devon & Cornwall Police Authority
Health Authority: NHS South West
Learning and Skills Council: South West
EU Constituencies: South West
Election Frequency: Elections are of whole council
Twinning: Clyst St. Mary: Merville-Franciville-Plage (France); Exmouth: Dinan (France); Farringdon: Sequeville-en-Bassin (France); Feniton: Louvigny (France); Honiton: Mezidon-Canon (France); Lympstone: Beuville-Bieville (France); Newton Poppleford: Crevecoeur-en-Auge (France); Otterton: Vieux (France); Ottery St. Mary: Pont l'Eveque (France); Seaton: Thury Harcourt (France); Stoke Canon: Bavent (France); Woodbury: Bretteville-sur-Odon (France)

PRINCIPAL OFFICERS
Chief Executive: Mr Mark Williams, Chief Executive, Council Offices, Knowle, Sidmouth EX10 8HL ☎ 01395 517408 🖷 01395 517507 mwilliams@eastdevon.gov.uk

Deputy Chief Executive: Mr Richard Cohen, Deputy Chief Executive - Development, Regeneration & Partnerships, Council Offices, Knowle, Sidmouth EX10 8HL
rcohen@eastdevon.gov.uk

Deputy Chief Executive: Mrs Denise Lyon, Deputy Chief Executive - Transformation & Systems Thinking, Council Offices, Knowle, Sidmouth EX10 8HL ☎ 01395 517480 🖷 01395 517507
dlyon@eastdevon.gov.uk

Architect, Building / Property Services: Mr Paul Seager, Principal Building Control Surveyor, Council Offices, Knowle, Sidmouth EX10 8HL ☎ 01395 517482
buildingcontrol@eastdevon.gov.uk

Building Control: Mr Paul Seager, Principal Building Control Surveyor, Council Offices, Knowle, Sidmouth EX10 8HL ☎ 01395 517482 buildingcontrol@eastdevon.gov.uk

PR / Communications: Mr Nick Stephens, Communications Officer, Council Offices, Knowle, Sidmouth EX10 8HL ☎ 01395 517559 🖷 01395 517507 nstephens@eastdevon.gov.uk

Community Planning: Mrs Kate Little, Head of Economy, Council Offices, Knowle, Sidmouth EX10 8HL ☎ 01395 519981 🖷 01395 517509 klittle@eastdevon.gov.uk

Community Safety: Mr G Moore, Community Safety Officer, Exmouth Police Station, North Street, Sidmouth EX8 1JZ ☎ 01395 273802 gmoore@eastdevon.gov.uk

Computer Management: Mr Chris Powell, Corporate ICT Manager, Council Offices, Knowle, Sidmouth EX10 8HL ☎ 01395 517433 🖷 01395 517501 cpowell@eastdevon.gov.uk

Customer Service: Ms Cherise Foster, Customer Service Manager, Council Offices, Knowle, Sidmouth EX10 8HL ☎ 01395 517535 🖷 01395 517504 cfoster@eastdevon.gov.uk

Economic Development: Mr Nigel Harrison, Economic Development Manager, Council Offices, Knowle, Sidmouth EX10 8HL ☎ 01395 517406 🖷 01395 517501
nharrison@eastdevon.gov.uk

E-Government: Mr Chris Powell, Corporate ICT Manager, Council Offices, Knowle, Sidmouth EX10 8HL ☎ 01395 517433 🖷 01395 517501 cpowell@eastdevon.gov.uk

Electoral Registration: Mr Philip Seccombe, Electoral Services Officer, Council Offices, Knowle, Sidmouth EX10 8HL ☎ 01395 517402 🖷 01395 517507 pseccombe@eastdevon.gov.uk

Facilities: Mr Brian Kohl, Property Services Manager, Council Offices, Knowle, Sidmouth EX10 8HL ☎ 01395 516551 🖷 01395 517509 bkohl@eastdevon.gov.uk

Finance and Treasurer: Mr S Davey, Head of Finance, Council Offices, Knowle, Sidmouth EX10 8HL ☎ 01395 517490
sdavey@eastdevon.gov.uk

Health and Safety: Mr S Cross, Safety Advisor, Council Offices, Knowle, Sidmouth EX10 8HL ☎ 01395 516551 🖷 01395 517508
scross@eastdevon.gov.uk

Housing: Mr John Golding, Head of Housing, Council Offices, Knowle, Sidmouth EX10 8HL ☎ 01395 517567 🖷 01395 517508
jgolding@eastdevon.gov.uk

Legal: Mrs Rachel Pocock, Corporate Legal & Democratic Services Manager, Council Offices, Knowle, Sidmouth EX10 8HL ☎ 01395 517401 🖷 01395 517507 rpocock@eastdevon.gov.uk

Licensing: Mr J Tippin, Licensing Manager, Council Offices, Knowle, Sidmouth EX10 8HL ☎ 01395 516551 🖷 01395 517507
jtippin@eastdevon.gov.uk

Lifelong Learning: Mrs Rachel Pocock, Corporate Legal & Democratic Services Manager, Council Offices, Knowle, Sidmouth EX10 8HL ☎ 01395 517401 🖷 01395 517507 ✉ rpocock@eastdevon.gov.uk

Lottery Funding, Charity and Voluntary: Miss Jamie Buckley, Funding Officer, Council Offices, Knowle, Sidmouth EX10 8HL ☎ 01395 517569 🖷 01395 517507 ✉ jbuckley@eastdevon.gov.uk

Member Services: Mrs Rachel Pocock, Corporate Legal & Democratic Services Manager, Council Offices, Knowle, Sidmouth EX10 8HL ☎ 01395 517401 🖷 01395 517507 ✉ rpocock@eastdevon.gov.uk

Personnel / HR: Ms Karen Jenkins, Corporate Organisational Development Manager, Council Offices, Knowle, Sidmouth EX10 8HL ☎ 01395 516551 🖷 01395 5175057 ✉ kjenkin@eastdevon.gov.uk

Planning: Mrs Kate Little, Head of Economy, Council Offices, Knowle, Sidmouth EX10 8HL ☎ 01395 519981 🖷 01395 517509 ✉ klittle@eastdevon.gov.uk

Procurement: Mr Colin Slater, Procurement Officer, Council Offices, Knowle, Sidmouth EX10 8HL ☎ 01395 516551 🖷 01395 517509 ✉ procurement@eastdevon.gov.uk

Recycling & Waste Minimisation: Mr Paul Deakin, Waste & Recycling Interim Manager, Council Offices, Knowle, Sidmouth EX10 8HL ☎ 01395 517615 🖷 01395 517504 ✉ pdeakin@eastdevon.gov.uk

Waste Collection and Disposal: Mr Paul Deakin, Waste & Recycling Interim Manager, Council Offices, Knowle, Sidmouth EX10 8HL ☎ 01395 517615 🖷 01395 517504 ✉ pdeakin@eastdevon.gov.uk

Waste Management: Mr Paul Deakin, Waste & Recycling Interim Manager, Council Offices, Knowle, Sidmouth EX10 8HL ☎ 01395 517615 🖷 01395 517504 ✉ pdeakin@eastdevon.gov.uk

MEMBERS OF THE COUNCIL (59)

***Chair:* Halse**, Peter (CON - Honiton St Michaels)
phalse@eastdevon.gov.uk
***Vice-Chair:* Newth**, Fraces (CON - Sidmouth Town)
fnewth@eastdevon.gov.uk
***Leader of the Council:* Diviani**, Paul (CON - Yarty)
pdiviani@eastdevon.gov.uk
***Deputy Leader of the Council:* Moulding**, Andrew (CON - Axminster Town)
amoulding@eastdevon.gov.uk
Allen, Mike (CON - Honiton St Michaels)
mallen@eastdevon.gov.uk
Atkins, David (CON - Woodbury & Lympstone)
datkins@eastdevon.gov.uk
Bloxham, Raymond (CON - Raleigh)
rbloxham@eastdevon.gov.uk
Boote, Roger (CON - Honiton St Pauls)
rboote@eastdevon.gov.uk
Bowden, Peter (CON - Broadclyst)
pbowden@eastdevon.gov.uk
Brown, Graham (CON - Feniton and Buckerell)
gbrown@eastdevon.gov.uk
Burrows, Peter (LD - Seaton)
dbutton@eastdevon.gov.uk
Button, Derek (LD - Broadclyst)
dbutton@eastdevon.gov.uk
Buxton, Bob (CON - Dunkeswell)
bbuxton@eastdevon.gov.uk
Chamberlain, Geoffrey (LD - Exmouth Withycombe Raleigh)
gchamberlain@eastdevon.gov.uk
Chapman, Maddy (CON - Exmouth Brixington)
mchapman@eastdevonn.gov.uk
Chapman, David (CON - Exmouth Brixington)
dchapman@eastdevon.gov.uk
Chubb, Iain (CON - Newbridges)
ichubb@eastdevon.gov.uk
Cope, Trevor (IND - Exmouth Brixington)
tcope@eastdevon.gov.uk
Cox, David (CON - Ottery St Mary Town)
dcox@eastdevon.gov.uk
Custance-Baker, Deborah (CON - Exe Valley)
dcustancebaker@eastdevon.gov.uk
Dent, Alan (CON - Budleigh)
adent@eastdevon.gov.uk
Drew, Christine (CON - Sidmouth Sidford)
cdrew@eastdevon.gov.uk
Duval-Steer, Vivien (CON - Exmouth Halsdon)
vduval-steer@eastdevon.gov.uk
Elson, Jill (CON - Exmouth Halsdon)
jelson@eastdevon.gov.uk
Gammell, Martin (LD - Whimple)
mgammell@eastdevon.gov.uk
Gazzard, Steve (LD - Exmouth Town)
Giles, Roger (IND - Ottery St Mary Town)
rgiles@eastdevon.gov.uk
Godbeer, Graham (CON - Coly Valley)
ggodbeer@eastdevon.gov.uk
Graham, Pat (LD - Exmouth Town)
pgraham@eastdevon.gov.uk
Hall, Steve (CON - Budleigh)
shall@eastdevon.gov.uk
Howard, Tony (CON - Ottery St Mary Rural)
thoward@eastdevon.gov.uk
Howe, Michael (CON - Clyst Valley)
mhowe@eastdevon.gov.uk
Hughes, Stuart (CON - Sidmouth Sidford)
shughes@eastdevon.gov.uk
Hull, Douglas (LD - Axminster Town)
dhull@eastdevon.gov.uk
Humphreys, John (CON - Exmouth Littleham)
jhumphreys@eastdevon.gov.uk
Ingham, Ben (IND - Woodbury & Lympstone)
bingham@eastdevon.gov.uk
Jeffery, John (IND - Axminster Rural)
jjeffery@eastdevon.gov.uk
Jones, Stephanie (CON - Seaton)
sjones@eastdevon.gov.uk
Kerridge, Sheila (CON - Sidmouth Town)
skerridge@eastdevon.gov.uk
Key, D (CON - Otterhead)
dkey@eastdevon.gov.uk
Knight, Jim (CON - Seaton)
jknight@eastdevon.gov.uk
O'Leary, John (CON - Honiton St Pauls)
Parr, Helen (CON - Coly Valley)
hparr@eastdevon.gov.uk
Pook, Geoff (IND - Beer & Branscome)

gpook@eastdevon.gov.uk
Potter, Ken (CON - Newton Pop. & Harpford)
kpotter@eastdevon.gov.uk
Skinner, Philip (CON - Tale Vale)
pskinner@eastdevon.gov.uk
Stott, Pauline (CON - Exmouth Halsdon)
pstott@eastdevon.gov.uk
Sullivan, Peter (CON - Sidmouth Town)
psullivan@eastdevon.gov.uk
Taylor, Brenda (LD - Exmouth Withycombe Raleigh)
btaylor@eastdevon.gov.uk
Thomas, Ian (CON - Trinity)
ithomas@eastdevon.gov.uk
Troman, Graham (CON - Sidmouth Sidford)
gtroman@eastdevon.gov.uk
Twiss, Phil (CON - Honiton St Michaels)
ptwiss@eastdevon.gov.uk
Wale, Chris (CON - Sidmouth Rural)
cwale@eastdevon.gov.uk
Williamson, Mark (CON - Exmouth Littleham)
mwilliamson@eastdevon.gov.uk
Wood, Tim (CON - Exmouth Littleham)
twood@eastdevon.gov.uk
Wragg, Eileen (LD - Exmouth Town)
ewragg@eastdevon.gov.uk
Wragg, Stephen (LD - Exmouth Withycombe Raleigh)
swragg@eastdevon.gov.uk
Wright, Claire (IND - Ottery St Mary Rural)
cwright@eastdevon.gov.uk
Wright, Thomas (CON - Budleigh)
twright@eastdevon.gov.uk

POLITICAL COMPOSITION

CON: 43, LD: 10, IND: 6

CABINET

Leader of the Council: Mr Paul Diviani
Deputy Leader / Strategic Development & Partnerships: Mr Andrew Moulding
Corporate Business: Mr Raymond Bloxham
Corporate Services: Mr Ian Thomas
Environment: Mr Iain Chubb
Finance: Mr David Cox
Sustainable Homes & Communities: Ms Jill Elson

COMMITTEE CHAIRS

Audit & Corporate Governance: Mr Ken Potter
Development Management: Mr Mark Williamson
Housing Review Board: Mrs Pauline Stott
Licensing & Enforcement: Mr Steve Hall
Overview & Scrutiny: Mr Stuart Hughes
Planning Inspections: Mr Mark Williamson

EAST DORSET D

East Dorset District Council, Council Offices, Furzehill, Wimborne BH21 4HN ☎ 01202 886201 🖷 01202 841390
💻 www.dorsetforyou.com

FACTS & FIGURES

Police Authority: Dorset Police Authority
Health Authority: NHS South West
Learning and Skills Council: South West
Parliamentary Constituencies: Christchurch County, Dorset Mid and Poole North
EU Constituencies: South West
Election Frequency: Elections are of whole council

PRINCIPAL OFFICERS

Chief Executive: Mr David McIntosh, Chief Executive, Council Offices, Furzehill, Wimborne BH21 4HN ☎ 01202 886201 🖷 01202 639030; 01202 495001
✉ dmcintosh@christchurchandeastdorset.gov.uk

Senior Management: Mr David Barnes, Strategic Director, Civic Offices, Bridge Street, Christchurch BH23 1AZ ☎ 01202 495077 🖷 01202 495107; 01202 495107
✉ dbarnes@christchurchandeastdorset.gov.uk

Access Officer / Social Services (Disability): Mr David Gale, Manager - Building Control, Council Offices, Furzehill, Wimborne BH21 4HN ☎ 01202 886201 🖷 01202 849182
✉ dgale@eastdorset.gov.uk

Architect, Building / Property Services: Mr Jonathan Ross, Property Services Manager, Council Offices, Furzehill, Wimborne BH21 4HN ☎ 01202 886201 🖷 01202 639030
✉ jross@eastdorset.gov.uk

Children / Youth Services: Ms Judith Plumley, Head - Community & Economy, Council Offices, Furzehill, Wimborne BH21 4HN ☎ 01202 886201; 01202 495043 🖷 01202 639030; 01202 495108 ✉ nfarmer@christchurchandeastdorset.gov.uk

PR / Communications: Mr Steve Welsby, Communications Officer, Council Offices, Furzehill, Wimborne BH21 4HN ☎ 01202 886201 🖷 01202 841390 ✉ swelsby@eastdorset.gov.uk

Community Planning: Mr Neil Farmer, Strategic Director, Council Offices, Furzehill, Wimborne BH21 4HN ☎ 01202 886201; 01202 495979 🖷 01202 639030; 01202 495107 ✉ nfarmer@christchurchandeastdorset.gov.uk

Community Safety: Mrs Martha Perry, Community Safety Officer, Council Offices, Furzehill, Wimborne BH21 4HN ☎ 01202 886201 🖷 01202 639030 ✉ mperry@eastdorset.gov.uk

Computer Management: Mr Paul Downton, Manager - IT & Information, Civic Offices, Bridge Street, Christchurch BH23 1AZ ☎ 01202 495137 🖷 01202 495107
✉ pdownton@christchurchandeastdorset.gov.uk

Computer Management: Mr Ian Milner, Head - Finance, Civic Offices, Bridge Street, Christchurch BH23 1AZ ☎ 01202 495176; 🖷 01202 482200
✉ imilner@christchurchandeastdorset.gov.uk

Economic Development: Mr Kevin Poulton, Manager - Economic Regeneration, Council Offices, Furzehill, Wimborne BH21 4HN ☎ 01202 886201 🖷 01202 849182
✉ kpoulton@eastdorset.gov.uk

Emergency Planning: Mr Jonathan Ross, Property Services Manager, Council Offices, Furzehill, Wimborne BH21 4HN ☎ 01202 886201 🖷 01202 639030 ✉ jross@eastdorset.gov.uk

Energy Management: Mr Steve Duckett, Head - Planning & Health, Council Offices, Furzehill, Wimborne BH21 4HN ☎ 01202 886201; 01202 495987 🖷 01202 639029; 01202 495108 ✉ sduckett@christchurchandeastdorset.gov.uk; sduckett@christchurchandeastdorset.gov.uk

Environmental / Technical Services: Mr Lindsay Cass, Head - Environmental Services, Council Offices, Furzehill, Wimborne BH21 4HN ☎ 01202 886201; 01202 495003 🖷 01202 639030; 01202 495110 ✉ lcass@christchurchandeastdorset.gov.uk; lcass@christchurchandeastdorset.gov.uk

Environmental Health: Mr Steve Duckett, Head - Planning & Health, Council Offices, Furzehill, Wimborne BH21 4HN ☎ 01202 886201; 01202 495987 🖷 01202 639029; 01202 495108 ✉ sduckett@christchurchandeastdorset.gov.uk; sduckett@christchurchandeastdorset.gov.uk

European Liaison: Mr Kevin Poulton, Manager - Economic Regeneration, Council Offices, Furzehill, Wimborne BH21 4HN ☎ 01202 886201 🖷 01202 849182 ✉ kpoulton@eastdorset.gov.uk

Facilities: Mr Jonathan Ross, Property Services Manager, Council Offices, Furzehill, Wimborne BH21 4HN ☎ 01202 886201 🖷 01202 639030 ✉ jross@eastdorset.gov.uk

Finance and Treasurer: Mr Paul Bliss, Revenues Manager, Council Offices, Furzehill, Wimborne BH21 4HN ☎ 01202 886201

Finance and Treasurer: Mr Ian Milner, Head - Finance, Civic Offices, Bridge Street, Christchurch BH23 1AZ ☎ 01202 495176 🖷 01202 482200 ✉ imilner@christchurchandeastdorset.gov.uk

Health and Safety: Mr Steve Duckett, Head - Planning & Health, Council Offices, Furzehill, Wimborne BH21 4HN ☎ 01202 886201; 01202 495987 🖷 01202 639029; 01202 495108 ✉ sduckett@christchurchandeastdorset.gov.uk

Housing: Ms Kathryn Blatchford, Manager - Stategic Housing Services, Civic Offices, Bridge Street, Christchurch BH23 1AZ ☎ 01202 495155 ✉ kblatchford@christchurchandeastdorset.gov.uk

Housing: Mr Graeme Stanley, Chief Executive - East Dorset Housing Association, Council Offices, Furzehill, Wimborne BH21 4HN ☎ 01202 308600 ✉ gstanley@christchurchandeastdorset.gov.uk

Housing Maintenance: Mr Graeme Stanley, Chief Executive - East Dorset Housing Association, Council Offices, Furzehill, Wimborne BH21 4HN ☎ 01202 308600 ✉ gstanley@christchurchandeastdorset.gov.uk

Legal: Mr Keith Mallett, Head - Legal & Democratic Services, Council Offices, Furzehill, Wimborne BH21 4HN ☎ 01202 886201; 01202 495989 🖷 01202 841734; 01202 495107 ✉ kmallett@eastdorset.gov.uk; kmallett@christchurchandeastdorset.gov.uk

Leisure and Cultural Services: Mr Matti Raudsepp, Head - Leisure & Open Spaces, Council Offices, Furzehill, Wimborne BH21 4HN ☎ 01202 886201; 01202 495000 🖷 01202 639030 ✉ mraudsepp@christchurchandeastdorset.gov.uk

Licensing: Mr Steve Ricketts, Manager - Licensing & Administration, Council Offices, Furzehill, Wimborne BH21 4HN ☎ 01202 886201 🖷 01202 841390

Lottery Funding, Charity and Voluntary: Mr Matti Raudsepp, Head - Leisure & Open Spaces, Council Offices, Furzehill, Wimborne BH21 4HN ☎ 01202 886201; 01202 495000 🖷 01202 639030 ✉ nfarmer@christchurchandeastdorset.gov.uk

Parking: Mr Trevor Thomas, Engineering Services Manager, Council Offices, Furzehill, Wimborne BH21 4HN ☎ 01202 886201 🖷 01202 639030 ✉ tthomas@eastdorset.gov.uk

Personnel / HR: Mrs Sue Weal, Personnel Manager, Council Offices, Furzehill, Wimborne BH21 4HN ☎ 01202 886201 🖷 01202 841390 ✉ sweal@eastdorset.gov.uk

Planning: Mr Steve Duckett, Head - Planning & Health, Council Offices, Furzehill, Wimborne BH21 4HN ☎ 01202 886201; 01202 495987 🖷 01202 639029; 01202 495108 ✉ sduckett@christchurchandeastdorset.gov.uk

Recycling & Waste Minimisation: Miss Gemma Coles, Enforcement Officer, Council Offices, Furzehill, Wimborne BH21 4HN ☎ 01202 886201 🖷 01202 639030 ✉ gcoles@eastdorset.gov.uk

Staff Training: Mrs Sue Weal, Personnel Manager, Council Offices, Furzehill, Wimborne BH21 4HN ☎ 01202 886201 🖷 01202 841390 ✉ sweal@eastdorset.gov.uk

Tourism: Mrs Rachel Limb, Manager - Tourism, Council Offices, Furzehill, Wimborne BH21 4HN ☎ 01202 886201 🖷 01202 639030 ✉ rlimb@eastdorset.gov.uk

Waste Management: Miss Gemma Coles, Enforcement Officer, Council Offices, Furzehill, Wimborne BH21 4HN ☎ 01202 886201 🖷 01202 639030 ✉ gcoles@eastdorset.gov.uk

MEMBERS OF THE COUNCIL (36)

***Chair:* Clark**, Lucy (CON - Verwood Stephen's Castle)
lucyclark@talktalk.net

***Vice-Chair:* Birr**, Malcolm (CON - Ferndown Links)
cllr.mbirr@eastdorset.gov.uk

***Leader of the Council:* Flower**, Spencer (CON - Holt)
spencerflower@btinternet.com

***Group Leader:* Holland**, Anne (LD - Corfe Mullen North)
aholland@corfemullenlibdems.org.uk

Bennett, Paul (CON - Stour)
paul.bennett@insleyandpartners.com

Burns, Sarah (CON - Corfe Mullen Central)
cllr.sburns@eastdorsetdc.gov.uk

Burt, Derek (CON - Ferndown Central)
derekburt@dsl.pipex.com

Butler, Stephen (CON - Crane)
cllr.sbutler@eastdorsetdc.gov.uk

Clarke, Alex (CON - West Moors)
cllr.aclarke@eastdorset.gov.uk

Cook, Robin (CON - Winborne Minster)

cllr.rcook@eastdorsetdc.gov.uk
Coombs, Toni (CON - Verwood Dewlands)
T.B.Coombs@dorsetcc.gov.uk
Dover, Janet (LD - Colehill East)
cllr.jdover@eastdorset.gov.uk
Dudman, Ray (CON - St Leonards & St Ives West)
raymonddudman790@btinternet.com
Dyer, Mike (CON - St Leonards & St Ives East)
cllr.mdyer@eastdorset.gov.uk
Edwards, Patrick (CON - Corfe Mullen South)
cllr.pedwards@eastdorsetdc.gov.uk
Elliot, Sally (CON - Longham)
sally_elliot@talk21.com
Gibson, Simon (CON - Verwood Stephen's Castle)
cllr.sgibson@eastdorsetdc.gov.uk
Hazel, Jean (CON - Verwood Dewlands)
cllr.jhazel@eastdorset.gov.uk
Holland, Paul (LD - Corfe Mullen Central)
pholland@corfemullenlibdems.org.uk
Hymers, Pat (LD - Wimborne Minster)
pat.hymers2@tiscali.co.uk
Little, John (CON - Ferndown Links)
cllr.jlittle@eastdorset.gov.uk
Lugg, Steven (CON - Ferndown Central)
cllr.slugg@eastdorsetdc.gov.uk
Manuel, Barbara (CON - Parley)
cllr.bmanuel@eastdorset.gov.uk
Monks, Ian (CON - Alderholt)
ijmonks@aol.com
Morgan, David (LD - Wimborne Minster)
cllr.dmorgan@eastdorset.gov.uk
Mortimer, Boyd (CON - Verwood Newtown)
boyden69@aol.com
Packer, David (CON - Colehill West)
david.packer@btinternet.com
Reynolds, Pauline (CON - Ameysford)
cllr.preynolds@eastdorset.gov.uk
Richardson, Peter (CON - Three Cross & Potterne)
Russell, George (CON - Stapehill)
cllr.grussell@eastdorset.gov.uk
Shortell, David (CON - West Moors)
cllr.dshortell@eastdorsetdc.gov.uk
Skeats, Andy (CON - West Moors)
cllr.askeats@eastdorsetdc.gov.uk
Tong, Simon (CON - Handley Vale)
cllr.stong@eastdorset.gov.uk
Wallace, Don (LD - Colehill East)
cllr.dwallace@eastdorset.gov.uk
Warman, Ann (CON - St Leonards & St Ives East)
ann_warman@hotmail.co.uk
Wilson, John
(CON - Parley)
cllr.jwilson@eastdorsetdc.gov.uk

POLITICAL COMPOSITION

CON: 30, LD: 6

COMMITTEE CHAIRS

Audit & Scrutiny: Mr Paul Bennett
Efficiency & Improvement: Mr John Little
Licensing: Mr David Packer
Planning: Mr Simon Tong
Policy & Resources: Mr Spencer Flower

EAST DUNBARTONSHIRE — S

East Dunbartonshire Council, Tom Johnston House, Civic Way, Kirkintilloch, Glasgow G66 4TJ ☎ 0141 578 8000 🖷 0141 777 5576 ✉ general@eastdunbarton.gov.uk 💻 www.eastdunbarton.gov.uk

FACTS & FIGURES

Police Authority: Strathclyde Police Authority
Health Authority: NHS Greater Glasgow & Clyde Health Board
Learning and Skills Council: Scotland
Parliamentary Constituencies: Cumbernauld, Kilsyth and Kirkintilloch East
EU Constituencies: Scotland
Election Frequency: Elections are of whole council
Twinning: Corbeil - Essonnes (France) Yoichi (Japan)

PRINCIPAL OFFICERS

Chief Executive: Mr Gerry Cornes, Chief Executive, Tom Johnston House, Civic Way, Kirkintilloch, Glasgow G66 4TJ ☎ 0141 578 8080; 0141 578 8082 🖷 0141 578 8330 ✉ gerry.cornes@eastdunbarton.gov.uk

Senior Management: Ms Diane Campbell, Director - Corporate & Customer Services, Tom Johnston House, Civic Way, Kirkintilloch, Glasgow G66 4TJ ☎ 0141 578 8039 🖷 0141 578 8470 ✉ diane.campbell@eastdunbarton.gov.uk

Senior Management: Mr Derek Cunningham, Director - Development & Infrastructure, Tom Johnston House, Civic Way, Kirkintilloch, Glasgow G66 4TJ ☎ 0141 578 8420 🖷 0141 578 8333 ✉ derek.cunningham@eastdunbarton.gov.uk

Senior Management: Ms Grace Irvine, Head - Assets & Property Services, Broomhill Industrial Estate, Kilsyth Road, Kirkintilloch, Glasgow G66 1TF ☎ 0141 574 5504 🖷 0141 574 5529 ✉ grace.irvine@eastdunbarton.gov.uk

Senior Management: Mr Tony Keogh, Head - Social Work, The Triangle, Kirkintilloch Road, Bishopbriggs, Glasgow G64 2TR ☎ 0141 777 3000 ✉ tony.keogh@eastdunbarton.gov.uk

Senior Management: Mr John Simmons, Director - Community Services, Tom Johnston House, Civic Way, Kirkintilloch, Glasgow G66 4TJ ☎ 0141 578 8460 🖷 0141 578 8470 ✉ john.simmons@eastdunbarton.gov.uk

Computer Management: Mr Ian Black, Head - Finance & ICT, Tom Johnston House, Civic Way, Kirkintilloch, Glasgow G66 4TJ ☎ 0141 578 8212 🖷 0141 578 8181 ✉ ian.black@eastdunbarton.gov.uk

Corporate Services: Mr Alistair Crighton, Head - Legal & Democratic Services, Tom Johnston House, Civic Way, Kirkintilloch, Glasgow G66 4TJ ☎ 0141 578 8310 🖷 0141 578 8468 ✉ alistair.crighton@eastdunbarton.gov.uk

Customer Service: Ms Ann Davie, Head - Customer Relations & Organisational Development, Tom Johnston House, Civic Way, Kirkintilloch, Glasgow G66 4TJ ☎ 0141 578 8070 🖷 0141 578 8283 ✉ ann.davie@eastdunbarton.gov.uk

Economic Development: Mr Thomas Glen, Head - Development & Enterprise, The Triangle, Kirkintilloch Road, Bishopbriggs, Glasgow G64 2TR ☎ 0141 578 8525 🖷 0141 578 8580 ✉ thomas.glen@eastdunbarton.gov.uk

Education: Mr Gordon Currie, Head - Education, Boclair House, 100 Milngavie Road, Bearsden, Glasgow G61 2TQ ☎ 0141 578 8720 🖷 0141 578 8653 ✉ gordon.currie@eastdunbarton.gov.uk

Electoral Registration: Mrs Lynn Kane, Legal & Democratic Services Officer, Tom Johnston House, Civic Way, Kirkintilloch, Glasgow G66 4TJ ☎ 0141 578 8098 🖷 0141 578 8096 ✉ lynn.kane@eastdunbarton.gov.uk

Emergency Planning: Mr Martin Cunningham, Manager - Democratic Services, Tom Johnston House, Civic Way, Kirkintilloch, Glasgow G66 4TJ ☎ 0141 578 8251 🖷 0141 777 8576 ✉ martin.cunningham@eastdunbarton.gov.uk

Energy Management: Mr Gerry Murphy, Environmental Engineer, Grange 1, Milngavie, Glasgow G62 8AQ ☎ 0141 5788000 🖷 0141 578 8779 ✉ gerry.murphy@eastdunbarton.gov.uk

Estates, Property & Valuation: Mr Alan Sim, Head - Planning, Development & Property Assets, The Triangle, Kirkintilloch Road, Bishopbriggs, Glasgow G64 2TR ☎ 0141 578 8545 🖷 0141 761 9006 ✉ alan.sim@eastdunbarton.gov.uk

European Liaison: Ms Mary Coulshed, Economic Development Team Leader, The Triangle, Kirkintilloch Road, Bishopbriggs, Glasgow G64 2TR ☎ 0141 578 8511 🖷 0141 578 8575 ✉ mary.coulshed@eastdunbarton.gov.uk

Facilities: Ms Grace Irvine, Head - Assets & Property Services, Broomhill Industrial Estate, Kilsyth Road, Kirkintilloch, Glasgow G66 1TF ☎ 0141 574 5504 🖷 0141 574 5529 ✉ grace.irvine@eastdunbarton.gov.uk

Finance and Treasurer: Mr Ian Black, Head - Finance & ICT, Tom Johnston House, Civic Way, Kirkintilloch, Glasgow G66 4TJ ☎ 0141 578 8212 🖷 0141 578 8181 ✉ ian.black@eastdunbarton.gov.uk

Fleet Management: Mr David Devine, Head - Roads & Neighbourhood Services, Broomhill Industrial Estate, Kilsyth Road, Kirkintilloch, Glasgow G66 1TF ☎ 0141 574 5503 🖷 0141 574 5529 ✉ david.devine@eastdunbarton.gov.uk

Health and Safety: Ms Debbie Gray, Health & Safety Officer, Tom Johnston House, Civic Way, Kirkintilloch, Glasgow G66 4TJ ☎ 0141 5788000 ✉ debbue.gray@eastdunbartonshire.gov.uk

Health and Safety: Mr Tommy Sullivan, Health & Safety Advisor, Tom Johnston House, Civic Way, Kirkintilloch, Glasgow G66 4TJ ☎ 0141 5788000 ✉ tommy.sullivan@eastdunbartonshire.gov.uk

Highways: Mr David Devine, Head - Roads & Neighbourhood Services, Broomhill Industrial Estate, Kilsyth Road, Kirkintilloch, Glasgow G66 1TF ☎ 0141 574 5503 🖷 0141 574 5529 ✉ david.devine@eastdunbarton.gov.uk

Home Energy Conservation: Mr Gerry Murphy, Environmental Engineer, Grange 1, Milngavie, Glasgow G62 8AQ ☎ 0141 5788000 🖷 0141 578 8779 ✉ gerry.murphy@eastdunbarton.gov.uk

Housing: Mr Kenny Simpson, Head - Housing & Community Services, Tom Johnston House, Civic Way, Kirkintilloch, Glasgow G66 4TJ ☎ 0141 578 8409 🖷 0141 578 8013 ✉ kenny.simpson@eastdunbarton.gov.uk

Housing Maintenance: Mr Kenny Simpson, Head - Housing & Community Services, Tom Johnston House, Civic Way, Kirkintilloch, Glasgow G66 4TJ ☎ 0141 578 8409 🖷 0141 578 8013 ✉ kenny.simpson@eastdunbarton.gov.uk

Legal: Mr Alistair Crighton, Head - Legal & Democratic Services, Tom Johnston House, Civic Way, Kirkintilloch, Glasgow G66 4TJ ☎ 0141 578 8310 🖷 0141 578 8468 ✉ alistair.crighton@eastdunbarton.gov.uk

Leisure and Cultural Services: Mr Mark Grant, Leisure & Cultural Services Manager, Tom Johnston House, Civic Way, Kirkintilloch, Glasgow G66 4TJ ☎ 0141 578 8142 ✉ mark.grant@eastdunbarton.gov.uk

Licensing: Mr Peter Kelly, Head - Licensing regulatroy & sevices manager, Tom Johnston House, Civic Way, Kirkintilloch, Glasgow G66 4TJ ☎ 0141 578 8000 ✉ peter.kelly@eastdunbarton.gov.uk

Lifelong Learning: Ms Elizabeth Brown, Information & Lifelong Learning Manager, William Patrick Library, 2 West High Street, Kirkintilloch, Glasgow G66 1AD ☎ 0141 775 5666 🖷 0141 776 0408 ✉ elizabeth.brown@eastdunbarton.gov.uk

Lighting: Mr David Devine, Head - Roads & Neighbourhood Services, Broomhill Industrial Estate, Kilsyth Road, Kirkintilloch, Glasgow G66 1TF ☎ 0141 574 5503 🖷 0141 574 5529 ✉ david.devine@eastdunbarton.gov.uk

Member Services: Mr Martin Cunningham, Manager - Democratic Services, Tom Johnston House, Civic Way, Kirkintilloch, Glasgow G66 4TJ ☎ 0141 578 8251 🖷 0141 777 8576 ✉ martin.cunningham@eastdunbarton.gov.uk

Partnerships: Mr Thomas Glen, Head - Development & Enterprise, The Triangle, Kirkintilloch Road, Bishopbriggs, Glasgow G64 2TR ☎ 0141 578 8525 🖷 0141 578 8580 ✉ thomas.glen@eastdunbarton.gov.uk

Personnel / HR: Ms Ann Davie, Head - Customer Relations & Organisational Development, Tom Johnston House, Civic Way, Kirkintilloch, Glasgow G66 4TJ ☎ 0141 578 8070 🖷 0141 578 8283 ✉ ann.davie@eastdunbarton.gov.uk

Planning: Mr Sandy McGarvey, Head - Integrated Support - Community Services, Boclair House, 100 Milngavie Road, Bearsden, Glasgow G61 2TQ ☎ 0141 578 8717 🖷 0141 578 8653 ✉ sandy.mcgarvey@eastdunbarton.gov.uk

Planning: Mr Alan Sim, Head - Planning, Development & Property Assets, The Triangle, Kirkintilloch Road, Bishopbriggs, Glasgow G64 2TR ☎ 0141 578 8545 🖷 0141 761 9006 ✉ alan.sim@eastdunbarton.gov.uk

Procurement: Mr Ken Middlemarsh, Procurement Manager, Tom Johnston House, Civic Way, Kirkintilloch, Glasgow G66 4TJ ☎ 0141 5788000 ✉ ken.middlemarsh@eastdunbartonshire.gov.uk

Public Libraries: Ms Elizabeth Brown, Information & Lifelong Learning Manager, William Patrick Library, 2 West High Street, Kirkintilloch, Glasgow G66 1AD ☎ 0141 775 5666 🖷 0141 776 0408 ✉ elizabeth.brown@eastdunbarton.gov.uk

Regeneration: Mr Crawford McGhie, Enterprise manager, The Triangle, Kirkintilloch Road, Bishopbriggs, Glasgow G64 1TR ☎ 0141 578 8000 ✉ crawford.mcghie@eastdunbarton.gov.uk

Road Safety: Mr David Devine, Head - Roads & Neighbourhood Services, Broomhill Industrial Estate, Kilsyth Road, Kirkintilloch, Glasgow G66 1TF ☎ 0141 574 5503 🖷 0141 574 5529 ✉ david.devine@eastdunbarton.gov.uk

Social Services: Mr Tony Keogh, Head - Social Work, William Patrick Library, 2 West High Street, Kirkintilloch, Glasgow G66 1AD ☎ 0141 777 3000 ✉ tony.keogh@eastdunbarton.gov.uk

Staff Training: Ms Ann Davie, Head - Customer Relations & Organisational Development, Tom Johnston House, Civic Way, Kirkintilloch, Glasgow G66 4TJ ☎ 0141 578 8070 🖷 0141 578 8283 ✉ ann.davie@eastdunbarton.gov.uk

Sustainable Communities: Ms Sylvia Gray, Sustainable Development Officer, Omnia Building, Westerhill Road, Bishopbriggs, G64 2TQ ☎ 0141 761 4860 🖷 0141 761 4888 ✉ sylvia.gray@eastdunbarton.gov.uk

Sustainable Development: Mr John King, Environmental Health Manager, 2 Grange Avenue, Milngavie, Glasgow G62 8AQ ☎ 0141 578 8837 🖷 0141 578 8787 ✉ john.king@eastdunbarton.gov.uk

Tourism: Ms Mary Coulshed, Economic Development Team Leader, The Triangle, Kirkintilloch Road, Bishopbriggs, Glasgow G64 2TR ☎ 0141 578 8511 🖷 0141 578 8575 ✉ mary.coulshed@eastdunbarton.gov.uk

Traffic Management: Mr David Devine, Head - Roads & Neighbourhood Services, Broomhill Industrial Estate, Kilsyth Road, Kirkintilloch, Glasgow G66 1TF ☎ 0141 574 5503 🖷 0141 574 5529 ✉ david.devine@eastdunbarton.gov.uk

Transport Planner: Mr Crawford McGhie, Enterprise manager, The Triangle, Kirkintilloch Road, Bishopbriggs, Glasgow G64 1TR ☎ 0141 578 8000 ✉ crawford.mcghie@eastdunbarton.gov.uk

MEMBERS OF THE COUNCIL (24)

***Provost:* Walker**, Una (LAB - Bishopbriggs North & Torrance)
una.walker@eastdunbarton.gov.uk
***Deputy Provost:* Jarvis**, Anne (CON - Lenzie & Kirkintilloch South)
anna.jarvis@eastdunbarton.gov.uk
***Leader of the Council:* Geekie**, Rhondda (LAB - Lenzie & Kirkintilloch South)
rhondda.geekie@eastdunbarton.gov.uk
***Deputy Leader of the Council:* Ghai**, Ashay (LD - Bearsden North)
ashay.ghai@eastdunbarton.gov.uk
Cumming, Duncan (LD - Bearsden North)
duncan.cumming@eastdunbarton.gov.uk
Dempsey, John (LAB - Campsie & Kirkintilloch North)
john.dempsey@eastdunbarton.gov.uk
Gibbons, Jim (SNP - Milngavie)
jim.gibbons@eastdunbarton.gov.uk
Gotts, Eric (LD - Milngavie)
eric.gotts@eastdunbarton.gov.uk
Hendry, Bill (CON - Bishopbriggs North & Torrance)
billy.hendry@eastdunbarton.gov.uk
Henry, Maureen (LAB - Milngavie)
mauree.henry@eastdunbarton.gov.uk
Jamieson, John (SNP - Kirkintilloch East & Twechar)
john.jamieson@eastdunbarton.gov.uk
Kennedy, Charles (IND - Campsie & Kirkintilloch North)
charles.kennedy@eastdunbarton.gov.uk
Low, Gordon (SNP - Bishopbriggs South)
gordan.low@eastdunbarton.gov.uk
Macdonald, Stewart (LAB - Kirkintilloch East & Twechar)
stewart.macdonald@eastdunbarton.gov.uk
Mackay, Ian (SNP - Bearsden North)
ian.mackay@eastdunbarton.gov.uk
McNair, Anne (SNP - Bishopbriggs North & Torrance)
anne.mcnair@eastdunbarton.gov.uk
Moir, Alan (LAB - Bishopbriggs South)
alan.moir@eastdunbarton.gov.uk
Moody, Vaughan (LD - Bearsden South)
vaughan.moody@eastdunbarton.gov.uk
O'Donnell, Michael (LAB - Bishopbriggs South)
michael.o'donnell@eastdunbarton.gov.uk
Renwick, Gillian (SNP - Lenzie & Kirkintilloch South)
gillian.renwick@eastdunbarton.gov.uk
Ritchie, David (SNP - Campsie & Kirkintilloch North)
david.ritchie@eastdunbarton.gov.uk
Shergill, Manjinder (LAB - Bearsden South)
manjinder.shergill@eastdunbarton.gov.uk
Small, Keith (SNP - Bearsden South)
keith.small@eastdunbarton.gov.uk
Young, Jack (IND - Kirkintilloch East & Twechar)
jack.young@eastdunbarton.gov.uk

POLITICAL COMPOSITION

LAB: 8, SNP: 8, LD: 4, CON: 2, IND: 2

COMMITTEE CHAIRS

Education: Mr Eric Gotts
Housing & Community Services: Mr Ashay Ghai
Policy & Resources: Ms Rhondda Geekie

EAST HAMPSHIRE D

East Hampshire District Council, Penns Place, Petersfield GU31 4EX ☎ 01730 266551 💻 www.easthants.gov.uk

FACTS & FIGURES

Police Authority: Hampshire Police Authority
Health Authority: South Central Strategic Health Authority
Learning and Skills Council: South East
Parliamentary Constituencies: Hampshire East
EU Constituencies: South East
Election Frequency: Elections are of whole council
Twinning: Clanfield: Val d'Olson (France); Petersfield: Barentin (France); Whitehill: Conde-sur-Vire (France)

PRINCIPAL OFFICERS

Chief Executive: Ms Sandy Hopkins, Joint Chief Executive, Penns Place, Petersfield GU31 4EX ☎ 023 9244 6150 🖷 023 9248 0263 ✉ sandy.hopkins@havant.gov.uk

Deputy Chief Executive: Miss Daphne Gardner, Eco-Town Project Co-ordinator, Penns Place, Petersfield GU31 4EX ☎ 01730 234005 🖷 01730 267760 ✉ daphne_gardner@easthants.gov.uk

Senior Management: Mr Tom Horwood, Executive Director, Penns Place, Petersfield GU31 4EX ☎ 01730 234025; 023 9244 6151 🖷 01730 267760; 023 9248 0263 ✉ tom.horwood@easthants.gov.uk

Senior Management: Ms Gill Kneller, Executive Director, Penns Place, Petersfield GU31 4EX ☎ 01730 234004; 023 9244 6151 🖷 01730 234012; 023 9248 0263 ✉ gill.kneller@easthants.gov.uk; gill.kneller@easthants.gov.uk

Architect, Building / Property Services: Mr Chris Fairhead, Land & Property Manager, Penns Place, Petersfield GU31 4EX ☎ 01730 234040 🖷 01730 234039 ✉ chris_fairhead@easthants.gov.uk

Best Value: Mr Robert Chambers, Service Manager Finance, Penns Place, Petersfield GU31 4EX ☎ 01730 234104 🖷 01730 267760 ✉ robert_chambers@easthants.gov.uk

Building Control: Mrs Julia Potter, Executive Head - Planning & Built Environment, Penns Place, Petersfield GU31 4EX ☎ 01730 234376; 023 9244 6520 🖷 01730 234385; 023 9244 6588 ✉ julia.potter@easthants.gov.uk

Children / Youth Services: Mr Michael O'Mahony, Interim Head of Community Services, Penns Place, Petersfield GU31 4EX ☎ 01730234383 ✉ michael_omahony@easthants.gov.uk

Children / Youth Services: Mr Tim Slater, Executive Head - Economy & Communities, Penns Place, Petersfield GU31 4EX ☎ 01730 234613

PR / Communications: Mr Tom Horwood, Executive Director, Penns Place, Petersfield GU31 4EX ☎ 01730 234025; 023 9244 6151 🖷 01730 267760; 023 9248 0263 ✉ tom.horwood@easthants.gov.uk

Community Planning: Miss Daphne Gardner, Eco-Town Project Co-ordinator, Penns Place, Petersfield GU31 4EX ☎ 01730 234005 🖷 01730 267760 ✉ daphne_gardner@easthants.gov.uk

Community Safety: Mrs Jackie Batchelor, Executive Head - Environment & Neighbourhood Quality, Penns Place, Petersfield GU31 4EX ☎ 01730 234271

Community Safety: Ms Karen Dawes, Community Safety Manager, Penns Place, Petersfield GU31 4EX ☎ 01730 234167 ✉ karen_dawes@easthants.gov.uk

Computer Management: Mrs Debbie Fox, Executive Head of Marketing & Development, Penns Place, Petersfield GU31 4EX ☎ 01730 234035 ✉ debbie.fox@havant.gov.uk

Computer Management: Mr Howard Puddy, IT Services Manager, Penns Place, Petersfield GU31 4EX ☎ 01730 266551 ✉ howard_puddy@easthants.gov.uk

Contracts: Mrs Joanna Davis, Project Manager - Business Transformation, Penns Place, Petersfield GU31 4EX ☎ 01730 234305 🖷 01730 234291 ✉ joanna.davis@easthants.gov.uk

Contracts: Mr Brian Turner, Environmental Services Manager - Contracts, Penns Place, Petersfield GU31 4EX ☎ 01730 234283; 01730 234383 ✉ brian.turner@easthants.gov.uk

Corporate Services: Miss Daphne Gardner, Eco-Town Project Co-ordinator, Penns Place, Petersfield GU31 4EX ☎ 01730 234005 🖷 01730 267760 ✉ daphne_gardner@easthants.gov.uk

Corporate Services: Mr Tom Horwood, Executive Director, Penns Place, Petersfield GU31 4EX ☎ 01730 234025; 023 9244 6151 🖷 01730 267760; 023 9248 0263 ✉ tom.horwood@easthants.gov.uk

Corporate Services: Ms Gill Kneller, Executive Director, Penns Place, Petersfield GU31 4EX ☎ 01730 234004; 023 9244 6151 🖷 01730 234012; 023 9248 0263 ✉ gill.kneller@easthants.gov.uk

Customer Service: Mr Tom Horwood, Executive Director, Penns Place, Petersfield GU31 4EX ☎ 01730 234025; 023 9244 6151 🖷 01730 267760 ✉ tom.horwood@easthants.gov.uk

Economic Development: Mr Tim Slater, Executive Head - Economy & Communities, Penns Place, Petersfield GU31 4EX ☎ 01730 234613

Electoral Registration: Ms Lianne Hall, Elections Manager, Penns Place, Petersfield GU31 4EX ☎ 01730 234370 ✉ eservices@easthants.gov.uk

Energy Management: Mrs Jackie Batchelor, Executive Head - Environment & Neighbourhood Quality, Penns Place, Petersfield GU31 4EX ☎ 01730 234271

Energy Management: Mr Jon Sanders, Service Manager - Property, Penns Place, Petersfield GU31 4EX ☎ 01730 234091 🖷 023 9248 0263 ✉ jon_sanders@easthants.gov.uk

Environmental / Technical Services: Mrs Jackie Batchelor, Executive Head - Environment & Neighbourhood Quality, Penns Place, Petersfield GU31 4EX ☎ 01730 234271

Environmental / Technical Services: Ms Gill Kneller, Executive Director, Penns Place, Petersfield GU31 4EX ☎ 01730 234004; 023 9244 6151 🖷 01730 234012; 023 9248 0263 ✉ gill.kneller@easthants.gov.uk

Environmental Health: Mrs Jackie Batchelor, Executive Head - Environment & Neighbourhood Quality, Penns Place, Petersfield GU31 4EX ☎ 01730 234271

Environmental Health: Ms Gill Kneller, Executive Director, Penns Place, Petersfield GU31 4EX ☎ 01730 234004; 023 9244 6151 🖷 01730 234012; 023 9248 0263 ✉ gill.kneller@easthants.gov.uk

Environmental Health: Mr Stuart Wedgebury, Service Manager - Environmental Health, Public Service Plaza, Civic Centre Road, Havant PO9 2AX ☎ 023 9244 6651 🖷 023 9244 6659 🖰 stuart.wedgebury@easthants.gov.uk

Estates, Property & Valuation: Mr Chris Fairhead, Land & Property Manager, Penns Place, Petersfield GU31 4EX ☎ 01730 234040 🖷 01730 234039 🖰 chris_fairhead@easthants.gov.uk

Estates, Property & Valuation: Miss Daphne Gardner, Eco-Town Project Co-ordinator, Penns Place, Petersfield GU31 4EX ☎ 01730 234005 🖷 01730 267760 🖰 daphne_gardner@easthants.gov.uk

Facilities: Mr Jon Sanders, Service Manager - Property, Penns Place, Petersfield GU31 4EX ☎ 01730 234091; 023 9244 6241 🖷 023 9248 0263 🖰 jon_sanders@easthants.gov.uk; jon.sanders@easthants.gov.uk

Finance and Treasurer: Mr Mike Ball, Revenues & Benefits Service Manager, Penns Place, Petersfield GU31 4EX ☎ 01730 234171 🖷 01730 260645 🖰 mike.ball@easthants.gov.uk

Finance and Treasurer: Mr Robert Chambers, Service Manager Finance, Penns Place, Petersfield GU31 4EX ☎ 01730 234104 🖷 01730 267760 🖰 robert_chambers@easthants.gov.uk

Finance and Treasurer: Mrs Jane Eaton, Executive Head - Governance & Logistics, Penns Place, Petersfield GU31 4EX ☎ 01730 234035

Finance and Treasurer: Mrs Tracey Hughes, Benefits Manager, Penns Place, Petersfield GU31 4EX ☎ 01730 234173 🖷 01730 260645 🖰 tracey_hughes@easthants.gov.uk

Finance and Treasurer: Mr Nigel Street, Executive Head - Governance & Logistics, Penns Place, Petersfield GU31 4EX ☎ 01730 234111 🖰 nigel.street@easthants.gov.uk

Finance and Treasurer: Mr Brian Wood, Revenues Manager, Penns Place, Petersfield GU31 4EX ☎ 01730 234150 🖷 01730 260645 🖰 brian_wood@easthants.gov.uk

Health and Safety: Mrs Jackie Batchelor, Executive Head - Environment & Neighbourhood Quality, Penns Place, Petersfield GU31 4EX ☎ 01730 234271

Health and Safety: Mrs Jackie Batchelor, Executive Head - Environment & Neighbourhood Quality, Penns Place, Petersfield GU31 4EX ☎ 01730 234271

Health and Safety: Mr Nigel Street, Executive Head - Governance & Logistics, Penns Place, Petersfield GU31 4EX ☎ 01730 234111 🖰 nigel.street@easthants.gov.uk

Home Energy Conservation: Mrs Julia Potter, Executive Head - Planning & Built Environment, Penns Place, Petersfield GU31 4EX ☎ 01730 234376; 023 9244 6520 🖷 01730 234385; 023 9244 6588 🖰 julia.potter@easthants.gov.uk

Housing: Ms Tracey Howard, Service Manager - Housing, Public Service Plaza, Civic Centre Road, Havant PO9 2AX ☎ 023 9244 6626 🖷 023 9248 0263 🖰 tracey.howard@easthants.gov.uk

Housing: Mrs Julia Potter, Executive Head - Planning & Built Environment, Penns Place, Petersfield GU31 4EX ☎ 01730 234376; 023 9244 6520 🖷 01730 234385; 023 9244 6588 🖰 julia.potter@easthants.gov.uk

Housing: Mr Tim Slater, Executive Head - Economy & Communities, Penns Place, Petersfield GU31 4EX ☎ 01730 234613

Legal: Mrs Jo Barden-Hernandez, Solicitor to the Council, Penns Place, Petersfield GU31 4EX ☎ 01730 234068; 023 9244 6212 🖷 023 9248 0263 🖰 jo_gabell@easthants.gov.uk

Legal: Mrs Jane Eaton, Executive Head - Governance & Logistics, Penns Place, Petersfield GU31 4EX ☎ 01730 234035; 023 9244 6151 🖷 023 9248 0263 🖰 jane.eaton@havant.gov.uk

Legal: Mr Nigel Street, Executive Head - Governance & Logistics, Penns Place, Petersfield GU31 4EX ☎ 01730 234111 🖰 nigel.street@easthants.gov.uk

Leisure and Cultural Services: Mr Tim Slater, Executive Head - Economy & Community, Penns Place, Petersfield GU31 4EX ☎ 01730 234613; 023 9244 6401 🖷 023 9248 0263 🖰 tim.slater@havant.gov.uk

Member Services: Ms Jackie Kelsey, Democratic Services Officer, Penns Place, Petersfield GU31 4EX ☎ 01730 234097 🖰 jackie.kelsey@easthants.gov.uk

Parking: Mr Jon Sanders, Service Manager - Property, Penns Place, Petersfield GU31 4EX ☎ 01730 234091; 023 9244 6241 🖷 023 9248 0263 🖰 jon_sanders@easthants.gov.uk

Personnel / HR: Mrs Debbie Fox, Executive Head - Marketing & Development, Penns Place, Petersfield GU31 4EX ☎ 01730 234035 🖰 debbie.fox@havant.gov.uk

Planning: Mr Chris Murray, Service Manager - Planning, Penns Place, Petersfield GU31 4EX ☎ 01730 234331; 023 9244 6512 🖰 chris.murray@easthants.gov.uk

Planning: Mrs Julia Potter, Executive Head - Planning & Built Environment, Penns Place, Petersfield GU31 4EX ☎ 01730 234376; 023 9244 6520 🖷 01730 234385; 023 9244 6588 🖰 julia.potter@easthants.gov.uk

Recycling & Waste Minimisation: Mrs Jackie Batchelor, Executive Head - Environment & Neighbourhood Quality, Penns Place, Petersfield GU31 4EX ☎ 01730 234271

Town Centre: Mr Chris Fairhead, Land & Property Manager, Penns Place, Petersfield GU31 4EX ☎ 01730 234040 🖷 01730 234039 🖰 chris_fairhead@easthants.gov.uk

Transport: Mrs Julia Potter, Executive Head - Planning & Built Environment, Penns Place, Petersfield GU31 4EX ☎ 01730 234376; 023 9244 6520 🖷 01730 234385; 023 9244 6588 🖰 julia.potter@easthants.gov.uk

Waste Collection and Disposal: Mrs Jackie Batchelor, Executive Head - Environment & Neighbourhood Quality, Penns Place, Petersfield GU31 4EX ☎ 01730 234271

Waste Collection and Disposal: Mrs Jackie Batchelor, Executive Head - Environment & Neighbourhood Quality, Penns Place, Petersfield GU31 4EX ☎ 01730 234271

Waste Collection and Disposal: Mrs Joanna Davis, Project Manager - Business Transformation, Penns Place, Petersfield GU31 4EX ☎ 01730 234305 🖷 01730 234291 🖱 joanna.davis@easthants.gov.uk

Waste Management: Mrs Jackie Batchelor, Executive Head - Environment & Neighbourhood Quality, Penns Place, Petersfield GU31 4EX ☎ 01730 234271

Waste Management: Mrs Jackie Batchelor, Executive Head - Environment & Neighbourhood Quality, Penns Place, Petersfield GU31 4EX ☎ 01730 234271

MEMBERS OF THE COUNCIL (44)

***Chair:* Seward**, Pat (CON - Four Marks and Medstead)
pat.steward@easthants.gov.uk
***Vice-Chair:* Graham**, Christopher (LD - Ropley and Tisted)
christopher.graham@easthants.gov.uk
***Leader of the Council:* Moon**, Ken (CON - Clanfield and Finchdean)
ken.moon@easthants.gov.uk
***Deputy Leader of the Council:* Watts**, Glynis (CON - Holybourne and Froyle)
glynis.watts@easthants.gov.uk
Horndean (Downs): Vacant
Aiston, Philip (CON - Petersfield (Causeway))
philip.aiston@easthants.gov.uk
Ashcroft, David (CON - Selborne)
david.ashcroft@easthants.gov.uk
Ashton, Lynn (CON - Bramshott and Liphook)
Ayer, Hilary (CON - Petersfield (St. Peters))
hilary.ayer@easthants.gov.uk
Ayer, Robert (CON - Petersfield (Rother))
bob.ayer@easthants.gov.uk
Branch, Nicholas (CON - Alton (Westbrooke))
nicholas.branch@easthants.gov.uk
Burridge, Patrick (CON - Downland)
patrick.burridge@easthants.gov.uk
Butler, Julie (CON - Petersfield (Heath))
julie.butler@easthants.gov.uk
Carew, Adam (LD - Whitehill (Walldown))
adam.carew@easthants.gov.uk
Carter, Ken (CON - Binsted and Bentley)
ken.carter@easthants.gov.uk
Cowper, Ferris (CON - Grayshott)
fcowper@aol.com
Denston, Dorothy (CON - Horndean (Hazelton and Blendworth))
dorothy.denston@easthants.gov.uk
Drew, Nick (CON - Froxfield and Steep)
nick.drew@easthants.gov.uk
Drury, Philip (LD - Whitehill (Hogmoor))
philip.drury@easthants.gov.uk
Evans, Lynn (CON - Horndean (Murray))
lynn.evans@easthants.gov.uk
Evans, David (CON - Horndean (Kings))
david.evans@easthants.gov.uk
Faddy, Zoya (LD - Whitehill (Chase))
zoya.faddy@easthants.gov.uk
Glass, Angela (CON - Bramshott and Liphook)
angela.glass@easthants.gov.uk
Gray, Jennifer (CON - Liss) steeples@easynet.co.uk
Harvey, Marjorie (LD - Rowlands Castle)
margieanddave@aol.com
Johnson, Maurice (CON - Four Marks and Medstead)
maurice.johnson@easthants.gov.uk
Joy, Andrew (CON - Alton (Ashdell))
andrew.joy@easthants.gov.uk
Logan, Gina (CON - Liss)
gina.logan@easthants.gov.uk
Maynard, Melissa (CON - Alton (Whitedown))
melissa.maynard@easthants.gov.uk
Millard, Richard (CON - Headley)
richard.millard@easthants.gov.uk
Mouland, William (CON - Bramshott and Liphook)
bill.mouland@easthants.gov.uk
Muldoon, Anthony (LD - Whitehill (Deadwater))
am48@btinternet.com
Newberry, David (CON - Clanfield and Finchdean)
david.newberry@easthants.gov.uk
Onslow, Judith (CON - The Hangers and Forest)
judyonslow@btinternet.com
Orme, David (CON - Alton (Wooteys))
david.orme@easthants.gov.uk
Parker-Smith, Yvonne (CON - Lindford)
yvonne.parker-smith@easthants.gov.uk
Parkinson, David (CON - East Meon)
david.parkinson@easthants.gov.uk
Phillips, Dean (CON - Alton (Eastbrooke))
dean.phillips@easthants.gov.uk
Saunders, Robert (CON - Alton (Amery))
robert.saunders@easthants.gov.uk
Schillemore, Sara (CON - Horndean (Catherington and Lovedean))
sara.schillemore@easthants.gov.uk
Stacpoole, Guy (CON - Petersfield (St. Mary's))
guy.stacpoole@easthants.gov.uk
West, John (CON - Petersfield (Bell Hill))
john.west@easthants.gov.uk
Wherrell, Chris (LD - Whitehill (Pinewood))
chris.wherrell@easthants.gov.uk
Williams, Anthony (CON - Headley)
anthony.williams@easthants.gov.uk

POLITICAL COMPOSITION

CON: 36, LD: 7, Vacant: 1

CABINET

Leader / Planning & Development: Mr Ken Moon
Deputy Leader / Regeneration & Community: Mrs Glynis Watts
Assets & Contracts: Mr Richard Millard
Corporate Affairs: Mr David Parkinson
Environment: Mrs Hilary Ayer
Finance: Mrs Julie Butler
Housing & South Downs National Park: Ms Jennifer Gray

COMMITTEE CHAIRS

Development Policy: Mr Ken Moon
Licensing: Mrs Judith Onslow
Planning Committee: Mr Ken Moon

EAST HERTFORDSHIRE D

East Herts Council, The Causeway, Bishop's Stortford CM23 2EN ☎ 01279 655261 ✉ info@eastherts.gov.uk
💻 www.eastherts.gov.uk

FACTS & FIGURES

Police Authority: Hertfordshire Police Authority
Health Authority: East of England Strategic Health Authority
Learning and Skills Council: Eastern
Parliamentary Constituencies: Hertford and Stortford, Hertfordshire North East
EU Constituencies: Eastern
Election Frequency: Elections are of whole council
Twinning: Bishop's Stortford: Villiers-sur-Marne (France), Friedberg (Germany); Buntingford: Luynes (France); Hertford: Evron (France), Wildeshausen (Germany); Sawbridgeworth: Bry-sur-Marne (France); The Hadhams: Haddam (USA); Ware: Wulfrath (Germany)

PRINCIPAL OFFICERS

Chief Executive: Mr George A Robertson, Chief Executive & Director of Customer & Community Services, Wallfields, Pegs Lane, Hertford SG13 8EQ ☎ 01992 531410 ✉ george.a.robertson@eastherts.gov.uk

Senior Management: Mr Simon Chancellor, Head of Financial Services & Performance, Wallfields, Pegs Lane, Hertford SG13 8EG ☎ 01279 502050 ✉ simon.chancellor@eastherts.gov.uk

Senior Management: Mr Simon Drinkwater, Director of Neighbourhood Services, Wallfields, Pegs Lane, Hertford SG13 8EQ ☎ 01279 501405 🖷 01279 757582 ✉ simon.drinkwater@eastherts.gov.uk

Senior Management: Mr Alan Madin, Director of Internal Services, Wallfields, Pegs Lane, Hertford SG13 8EQ ☎ 01279 655261 ✉ alan.madin@eastherts.gov.uk

Senior Management: Mr George A Robertson, Director of Customer & Community Services, Wallfields, Pegs Lane, Hertford SG13 8EQ ☎ 01992 531410 ✉ george.a.robertson@eastherts.gov.uk

Senior Management: Mrs Su Tarran, Head of Revenues & Benefits, Wallfields, Pegs Lane, Hertford SG13 8EQ ☎ 01279 502075 ✉ su.tarran@eastherts.gov.uk

Architect, Building / Property Services: Mr Roy Crow, Facilities & Property Manager, Wallfields, Pegs Lane, Hertford SG13 8EQ ☎ 01992 531695 ✉ roy.crow@eastherts.gov.uk

Best Value: Ms Ceri Pettit, Corporate Planning & Performance Manager, Council Offices, The Causeway, Bishop's Stortford CM23 2EN ☎ 01279 502240 🖷 01279 502015 ✉ ceri.pettit@eastherts.gov.uk

Building Control: Mr Kevin Steptoe, Head of Planning & Building Control, East Herts Council, Wallfields, Pegs Lane, Hertford SG13 8EQ ☎ 01992 531407 ✉ kevin.steptoe@eastherts.gov.uk

PR / Communications: Ms Lorna Georgiou, Communications Team Leader, Wallfields, Pegs Lane, Hertford SG13 8EQ ☎ 01992 532244 ✉ lorna.georgiou@eastherts.gov.uk

Community Safety: Mr Brian Simmonds, Head of Community Safety & Health Services, Wallfields, Pegs Lane, Hertford SG13 8EQ ☎ 01992 531498 ✉ brian.simmonds@eastherts.gov.uk

Computer Management: Mr David Frewin, Network & Systems Support Manager, Wallfields, Pegs Lane, Hertford SG13 8EQ ☎ 01279 502158 ✉ david.frewin@eastherts.gov.uk

Contracts: Mr Cliff Cardoza, Head of Environmental Services, Wallfields, Pegs Lane, Hertford SG13 8EQ ☎ 01992 531698 ✉ cliff.cardoza@eastherts.gov.uk

Customer Service: Mr Neil Sloper, Head of Customer Services & Parking, Wallfields, Pegs Lane, Hertford SG13 8EQ ☎ 01992 531611 ✉ neil.sloper@eastherts.gov.uk

Economic Development: Mr Paul Pullin, Economic Development Manager, Wallfields, Pegs Lane, Hertford SG13 8EQ ☎ 01992 531606 ✉ paul.pullin@eastherts.gov.uk

Electoral Registration: Mr Jeff Hughes, Head of Democratic & Legal Services, Wallfields, Pegs Lane, Hertford SG13 8EQ ☎ 01279 502170 ✉ jeff.hughes@eastherts.gov.uk

Emergency Planning: Mr Brian Simmonds, Head of Community Safety & Health Services, Wallfields, Pegs Lane, Hertford SG13 8EQ ☎ 01992 531498 ✉ brian.simmonds@eastherts.gov.uk

Environmental / Technical Services: Mr Cliff Cardoza, Head of Environmental Services, Wallfields, Pegs Lane, Hertford SG13 8EQ ☎ 01992 531698 ✉ cliff.cardoza@eastherts.gov.uk

Environmental Health: Mr Brian Simmonds, Head of Community Safety & Health Services, Wallfields, Pegs Lane, Hertford SG13 8EQ ☎ 01992 531498 ✉ brian.simmonds@eastherts.gov.uk

Estates, Property & Valuation: Mr Martin Shrosbree, Assets & Estates Manager, Wallfields, Pegs Lane, Hertford SG13 8EQ ☎ 01992 531655 ✉ martin.shrosbree@eastherts.gov.uk

European Liaison: Mr Paul Pullin, Economic Development Manager, Wallfields, Pegs Lane, Hertford SG13 8EQ ☎ 01992 531606 ✉ paul.pullin@eastherts.gov.uk

Facilities: Mr Roy Crow, Facilities & Property Manager, Wallfields, Pegs Lane, Hertford SG13 8EQ ☎ 01992 531695 ✉ roy.crow@eastherts.gov.uk

Finance and Treasurer: Mr Simon Chancellor, Head of Financial Services & Performance, Wallfields, Pegs Lane, Hertford SG13 8EG ☎ 01279 502050 ✉ simon.chancellor@eastherts.gov.uk

Finance and Treasurer: Mr Alan Madin, Director of Internal Services, Wallfields, Pegs Lane, Hertford SG13 8EQ ☎ 01279 655261 ✉ alan.madin@eastherts.gov.uk

Grounds Maintenance: Mr Ian Sharratt, Environmental Manager - Open Spaces, Wallfields, Pegs Lane, Hertford SG13 8EQ

☎ 01992 531525 ✉ ian.sharratt@eastherts.gov.uk

Health and Safety: Mr Peter Dickinson, Health & Safety Officer, Wallfields, Pegs Lane, Hertford SG13 8EQ ☎ 01992 531636 ✉ peter.dickinson@eastherts.gov.uk

Home Energy Conservation: Mr David Thorogood, Environmental Co-ordinator, Wallfields, Pegs Lane, Hertford SG13 8EQ ☎ 01992 531621 ✉ david.thorogood@eastherts.gov.uk

Housing: Ms Claire Bennett, Manager of Housing Services, Wallfields, Pegs Lane, Hertford SG13 8EQ ☎ 01992 531603 ✉ claire.bennet@eastherts.gov.uk

Legal: Mr George Robertson, Legal Services Manager, Wallfields, Pegs Lane, Hertford SG13 8EQ ☎ 01279 502193 ✉ george.robertson@eastherts.gov.uk

Leisure and Cultural Services: Mr Mark Kingsland, Leisure Services Manager, Wallfields, Pegs Lane, Hertford SG13 8EQ ☎ 01279 655880 ✉ mark.kingsland@eastherts.gov.uk

Licensing: Mr Paul Newman, Licensing Process Manager, Wallfields, Pegs Lane, Hertford SG13 8EQ ☎ 01992 531521 ✉ paul.newman@eastherts.gov.uk

Lottery Funding, Charity and Voluntary: Ms Claire Pullen, Engagement & Partnerships Officer (Grants), Wallfields, Pegs Lane, Hertford SG13 8EQ ☎ 01992 531593 ✉ claire.pullen@eastherts.gov.uk

Member Services: Mr Jeff Hughes, Head of Democratic & Legal Services, Wallfields, Pegs Lane, Hertford SG13 8EQ ☎ 01279 502170 ✉ jeff.hughes@eastherts.gov.uk

Parking: Mr Andrew Pulham, Parking Services Manager, Wallfields, Pegs Lane, Hertford SG13 8EG ☎ 01279 502030 ✉ andrew.pulham@eastherts.gov.uk

Partnerships: Mrs Mekhola Ray, Engagement & Partnerships Team Leader, Wallfields, Pegs Lane, Hertford SG13 8EQ ☎ 01992 531613 ✉ mekhola.ray@eastherts.gov.uk

Personnel / HR: Ms Emma Freeman, Head of People, ICT & Property Services, Wallfields, Pegs Lane, Hertford SG13 8EQ ☎ 01992 531635 ✉ emma.freeman@eastherts.gov.uk

Planning: Mr Kevin Steptoe, Head of Planning & Building Control, Wallfields, Pegs Lane, Hertford SG13 8EQ ☎ 01992 531407 ✉ kevin.steptoe@eastherts.gov.uk

Procurement: Ms Tracey Sargent, Procurement Officer, Wallfields, Pegs Lane, Hertford SG13 8EQ ☎ 01992 532122 ✉ tracey.sargent@eastherts.gov.uk

Recycling & Waste Minimisation: Mr Trevor Watkins, Waste Services Manager, Wallfields, Pegs Lane, Hertford SG13 8EQ ☎ 01992 531549 ✉ trevor.watkins@eastherts.gov.uk

Sustainable Communities: Mr George A Robertson, Chief Executive & Director of Customer & Community Services, Wallfields, Pegs Lane, Hertford SG13 8EQ ☎ 01992 531410 ✉ george.a.robertson@eastherts.gov.uk

Sustainable Development: Mr David Thorogood, Environmental Co-ordinator, Wallfields, Pegs Lane, Hertford SG13 8EQ ☎ 01992 531621 ✉ david.thorogood@eastherts.gov.uk

Tourism: Ms Tilly Andrews, Economic & Tourism Development Officer, Wallfields, Pegs Lane, Hertford SG13 8EQ ☎ 01992 531506 ✉ tilly.andrews@eastherts.gov.uk

Town Centre: Mr Paul Pullin, Economic Development Manager, Wallfields, Pegs Lane, Hertford SG13 8EQ ☎ 01992 531606 ✉ paul.pullin@eastherts.gov.uk

Traffic Management: Mr Andrew Pulham, Parking Services Manager, Wallfields, Pegs Lane, Hertford SG13 8EQ ☎ 01279 502030 ✉ andrew.pulham@eastherts.gov.uk

Waste Collection and Disposal: Mr Cliff Cardoza, Head of Environmental Services, Wallfields, Pegs Lane, Hertford SG13 8EQ ☎ 01992 531698 ✉ cliff.cardoza@eastherts.gov.uk

Waste Management: Mr Cliff Cardoza, Head of Environmental Services, Wallfields, Pegs Lane, Hertford SG13 8EQ ☎ 01992 531698 ✉ cliff.cardoza@eastherts.gov.uk

MEMBERS OF THE COUNCIL (50)

***Chair:* Rutland-Barsby**, Suzanne (CON - Hertford (Castle))
suzanne.rutland-barsby@eastherts.gov.uk

***Chair:* Taylor**, Jeanette (CON - Ware (St Mary's))
jeanette.taylor@eastherts.gov.uk

***Vice-Chair:* McAndrew**, Graham (CON - Bishop's Stortford (Silverleys))
graham.mcandrew@eastherts.gov.uk

***Leader of the Council:* Jackson**, Tony (CON - Datchworth and Aston)
anthony.jackson@eastherts.gov.uk

***Deputy Leader of the Council:* Alexander**, Malcolm (CON - Ware (Trinity))
malcolm.alexander@eastherts.gov.uk

Abbott, Daniel (CON - Bishop's Stortford (All Saints))
daniel.abbot@eastherts.gov.uk

Andrews, David (CON - Thundridge and Standon)
david.andrews@eastherts.gov.uk

Ashley, William (CON - Hertford Heath)
william.ashley@eastherts.gov.uk

Ballam, Phyllis (CON - Ware (Christchurch))
phyllis.ballam@eastherts.gov.uk

Basra, Surjit (CON - Buntingford)
surjit.basra@eastherts.gov.uk

Bedford, Edward (CON - Ware (Christchurch))
edward.bedford@eastherts.gov.uk

Beeching, Roger (CON - Sawbridgeworth)
roger.beeching@eastherts.gov.uk

Buckmaster, Eric (IND - Sawbridgeworth)

Bull, Stan (CON - Buntingford)
stan.bull@eastherts.gov.uk

Burlton, Allen (CON - Bishop's Stortford (South))
allen.burlton@eastherts.gov.uk

Carver, Mike (CON - Much Hadham)
mike.carver@eastherts.gov.uk

Cheswright, Rose (CON - Braughing)
rosemary.cheswright@eastherts.gov.uk

Crofton, Ken (CON - Walkern)
henry.crofton@eastherts.gov.uk
Dearman, Andrew (CON - Puckeridge)
andrew.dearman@eastherts.gov.uk
Demonti, Jill (CON - Bishop's Stortford (Meads))
jill.demonti@eastherts.gov.uk
Gray, Peter (CON - Bishop's Stortford (Central))
peter.gray@eastherts.gov.uk
Haysey, Linda (CON - Hertford Rural South)
linda.haysey@eastherts.gov.uk
Herbert, Tim (CON - Bishop's Stortford (Meads))
tim.herbert@eastherts.gov.uk
Hollebon, Diane (CON - Bishop's Stortford (South))
diane.hollebon@eastherts.gov.uk
Hone, Dorothy (CON - Hertford (Castle))
dorothy.hone@eastherts.gov.uk
Jones, Gary (CON - Bishop's Stortford (Silverleys))
gary.jones@eastherts.gov.uk
Lawrence, Graham (CON - Hertford (Bengeo))
graham.lawrence@eastherts.gov.uk
Mayes, Janet (CON - Great Amwell)
janet.mayes@eastherts.gov.uk
McMullen, Michael (CON - Hertford Rural North)
michael.mcmullen@eastherts.gov.uk
Moore, Patricia (CON - Hertford (Sele))
patricia.moore@eastherts.gov.uk
Mortimer, William (CON - Sawbridgeworth)
william.mortimer@eastherts.gov.uk
Newman, Michael (IND - Hunsdon)
michael.newman@eastherts.gov.uk
Page, Tim (CON - Bishop's Stortford (Central))
tim.page@eastherts.gov.uk
Phillips, Paul (CON - Hertford (Bengeo))
paul.phillips@eastherts.gov.uk
Pope, Mark (CON - Ware (Chadwell))
mark.pope@eastherts.gov.uk
Poulton, Nigel (CON - Watton-at-Stone)
nigel.poulton@eastherts.gov.uk
Radford, Russell (CON - Hertford (Castle))
russell.radford@eastherts.gov.uk
Ranger, Jim (CON - The Mundens and Cottered)
jim.ranger@eastherts.gov.uk
Rowley, Charles (CON - Hertford (Sele))
charles.rowley@eastherts.gov.uk
Ruffles, Peter (CON - Hertford (Bengeo))
peter.ruffles@eastherts.gov.uk
Symonds, Norma (CON - Bishop's Stortford (Central))
norma.symonds@eastherts.gov.uk
Tindale, Michael (CON - Little Hadham)
michael.tindale@eastherts.gov.uk
Warman, Alan (CON - Ware (St Mary's))
alan.warman@eastherts.gov.uk
Williamson, Geoffrey (CON - Stanstead Abbotts)
geoffrey.williamson@eastherts.gov.uk
Wilson, Nicholas (CON - Hertford (Kingsmead))
nicholas.wilson@eastherts.gov.uk
Wing, John (LD - Ware (Trinity))
john.wing@easthearts.gov.uk
Wood, Mike (LD - Bishop's Stortford (All Saints))
mike.wood@eastherts.gov.uk
Woodward, Colin (CON - Bishop's Stortford (All Saints))
colin.woodward@eastherts.gov.uk
Wrangles, Beryl (CON - Hertford (Kingsmead))
beryl.wrangles@eastherts.gov.uk
Wyllie, John (CON - Bishop's Stortford (South))
john.wyllie@eastherts.gov.uk

POLITICAL COMPOSITION

CON: 46, IND: 2, LD: 2

CABINET

Leader: Mr Anthony Jackson
Deputy Leader / Community Saftey & Environment: Mr Malcolm Alexander
Economic Development: Mr Paul Phillips
Finance: Mr Michael Tindale
Health, Housing & Community Support: Mrs Linda Haysey
Strategic Planning & Transport: Mr Mike Carver

COMMITTEE CHAIRS

Audit (Scrutiny): Mr Jim Ranger
Community Scrutiny: Mr Graham McAndrew
Corporate Business Scrutiny (Scrutiny): Mr David Andrews
Development Control: Ms Suzanne Rutland-Barsby
Environment Scrutiny (Scrutiny): Mr Daniel Abbott
Health Engagement Panel: Ms Norma Symonds
Highways: Mr Nigel Poulton
Human Resources: Mr Colin Woodward
Licensing: Mrs Rose Cheswright

EAST LINDSEY D

East Lindsey District Council, Tedder Hall, Manby Park, Louth LN11 8UP ☎ 01507 601111 🖷 01507 600206
customerservices@e-lindsey.gov.uk 💻 www.e-lindsey.gov.uk

FACTS & FIGURES

Police Authority: Lincolnshire Police Authority
Health Authority: East Midlands Strategic Health Authority
Learning and Skills Council: East Midlands
Parliamentary Constituencies: Boston and Skegness, Louth and Horncastle
EU Constituencies: East Midlands
Election Frequency: Elections are of whole council
Twinning: Louth: La Ferte Bernard (France); Old Bolingbroke: Bolingbrook (USA); Skegness: Bad Gandersheim (Germany)

PRINCIPAL OFFICERS

Chief Executive: Mr Nigel Howells, Chief Executive, Tedder Hall, Manby Park, Louth LN11 8UP ☎ 01507 61340 🖷 01507 329486 nigel.howells@e-lindsey.gov.uk

Deputy Chief Executive: Mr Robert Barlow, Deputy Chief Executive/Section 151 Officer, Tedder Hall, Manby Park, Louth LN11 8UP ☎ 01205 314200 🖷 01205 364604 robert.barlow@boston.gov.uk

Deputy Chief Executive: Mr Stuart Davy, Deputy Chief Executive, Tedder Hall, Manby Park, Louth LN11 8UP ☎ 01507 613411 🖷 01507 329486 stuart.davy@e-lindsey.gov.uk

Senior Management: Ms Alison Penn, Strategic Development Officer, Tedder Hall, Manby Park, Louth LN11 8UP ☎ 01507 329413 alison.penn@e-lindsey.gov.uk

Senior Management: Mr Paul Wilson, Head of Customer Services, Tedder Hall, Manby Park, Louth LN11 8UP ☎ 01507

613271 ✉ paul.wilson@cpbs.com

Architect, Building / Property Services: Mr Gary Sargeant, Property & Technical Services Manager, Tedder Hall, Manby Park, Louth LN11 8UP ☎ 01507 613020 ✉ gary.sargeant@e-lindsey.gov.uk

Building Control: Mr Garry Winterton, Building Control Team Leader, Tedder Hall, Manby Park, Louth LN11 8UP ☎ 01507 613189 🖷 01507 327069 ✉ garry.winterton@e-lindsey.gov.uk

Children / Youth Services: Ms Semantha Neal, Strategic Development Manager, Tedder Hall, Manby Park, Louth LN11 8UP ☎ 01507 613440 ✉ semantha.neal@e-lindsey.gov.uk

PR / Communications: Mr James Gilbert, Communications & Consultation Team Leader, Tedder Hall, Manby Park, Louth LN11 8UP ☎ 01507 613415 🖷 01507 329190 ✉ james.gilbert@e-lindsey.gov.uk

Community Safety: Mr Jonathan Challen, Private Sector Housing Team Leader, Tedder Hall, Manby Park, Louth LN11 8UP ☎ 01507 613051 ✉ jonathan.challen@e-lindsey.gov.uk

Computer Management: Mr Marcus Coleman, Operations Director, Tedder Hall, Manby Park, Louth LN11 8UP ☎ 01507 613307; 01507 613307 🖷 01507 329599; 01507 329599 ✉ marcus.coleman@cpbs.com

Customer Service: Mr Paul Wilson, Head of Customer Services, Tedder Hall, Manby Park, Louth LN11 8UP ☎ 01507 613271 ✉ paul.wilson@cpbs.com

Economic Development: Mr Jonathan Burgess, Economic & Tourism Team Leader, Tedder Hall, Manby Park, Louth LN11 8UP ☎ 01507 613117 ✉ jonathan.burgess@e-lindsey.gov.uk

Electoral Registration: Mrs Sue Brewitt, Elections Officer, Tedder Hall, Manby Park, Louth LN11 8UP ☎ 01507 613430 ✉ sue.brewitt@e-lindsey.gov.uk

Emergency Planning: Mr Mike Harrison, Commercial Team Leader, Tedder Hall, Manby Park, Louth LN11 8UP ☎ 01507 613470 🖷 01507 600206 ✉ mike.harrison@e-lindsey.gov.uk

Energy Management: Mr Robert Frost, Technical Services Officer, Tedder Hall, Manby Park, Louth LN11 8UP ☎ 01507 613038 ✉ robert.frost@e-lindsey.gov.uk

Environmental / Technical Services: Mrs Anneliese Johnson, Environment Team Leader, Tedder Hall, Manby Park, Louth LN11 8UP ☎ 01507 613497 🖷 01507 600206 ✉ anneliese.johnson@e-lindsey.gov.uk

Environmental Health: Mr Mike Harrison, Commercial Team Leader, Tedder Hall, Manby Park, Louth LN11 8UP ☎ 01507 613470 🖷 01507 600206 ✉ mike.harrison@e-lindsey.gov.uk

Estates, Property & Valuation: Mr Richard Sands, Property Services Officer, Tedder Hall, Manby Park, Louth LN11 8UP ☎ 01507 613021 ✉ richard.sands@e-lindsey.gov.uk

Estates, Property & Valuation: Mr Gary Sargeant, Property & Technical Services Manager, Tedder Hall, Manby Park, Louth LN11 8UP ☎ 01507 613020 ✉ gary.sargeant@e-lindsey.gov.uk

Events Manager: Mr James Brindle, Culture Team Leader, Tedder Hall, Manby Park, Louth LN11 8UP ☎ 01507 613450 ✉ james.brindle@e-lindsey.gov.uk

Facilities: Mr Mark Humphreys, Strategic Development Manager, Tedder Hall, Manby Park, Louth LN11 8UP ☎ 01507 613441 ✉ mark.humphreys@e-lindsey.gov.uk

Finance and Treasurer: Mr Robert Barlow, Deputy Chief Executive/Section 151 Officer, Tedder Hall, Manby Park, Louth LN11 8UP ☎ 01205 314200; 01507 613413 🖷 01205 364604; 01507 329486 ✉ robert.barlow@boston.gov.uk; robert.barlow@boston.gov.uk

Fleet Management: Mr Nick Davis, Team Leader - Waste Services, Tedder Hall, Manby Park, Louth LN11 8UP ☎ 01507 613540 ✉ nick.davis@e-lindsey.gov.uk

Grounds Maintenance: Ms Victoria Burgess, Service Development Team Leader, Tedder Hall, Manby Park, Louth LN11 8UP ☎ 01507 613536 ✉ V.B@e-lindsey.gov.uk

Grounds Maintenance: Mr Danny Wilson, Area Manager - North, Tedder Hall, Manby Park, Louth LN11 8UP ☎ 01507 613541 ✉ danny.wilson@e-lindsey.gov.uk

Health and Safety: Mr Tony Lascelles, Head of HR, Tedder Hall, Manby Park, Louth LN11 8UP ☎ 01507 613230; 01507 613230 🖷 01507 600206; 01507 600206 ✉ tony.lascelles@cpbs.com; tony.lascelles@cpbs.com

Home Energy Conservation: Mr Jonathan Challen, Private Sector Housing Team Leader, Tedder Hall, Manby Park, Louth LN11 8UP ☎ 01507 613051 ✉ jonathan.challen@e-lindsey.gov.uk

Housing: Mr Jason Oxby, Housing Advice & Homelessness Team Leader, Tedder Hall, Manby Park, Louth LN11 8UP ☎ 01507 613120 ✉ jason.oxby@e-lindsey.gov.uk

Licensing: Mr Adrian Twiddy, Licensing Officer, Tedder Hall, Manby Park, Louth LN11 8UP ☎ 01507 613011 🖷 01507 600206 ✉ adrian.twiddy@e-lindsey.gov.uk

Lottery Funding, Charity and Voluntary: Mr James Ward, Community Development Officer, Tedder Hall, Manby Park, Louth LN11 8UP ☎ 01507 613073 🖷 01507 600206 ✉ james.ward@e-lindsey .gov.uk

Member Services: Mrs Ann Good, Senior Member Services Officer, Tedder Hall, Manby Park, Louth LN11 8UP ☎ 01507 613420 ✉ ann.good@e-lindsey@gov.uk

Parking: Mr Duncan Hollingworth, Team Leader - Enforcement, Tedder Hall, Manby Park, Louth LN11 8UP ☎ 01507 613558 ✉ duncan.hollingworth@e-lindsey.gov.uk

Partnerships: Mr John Medler, Team Leader - Performance, Commissioning & Governance, Tedder Hall, Manby Park, Louth

LN11 8UP ☎ 01507 613072 ✉ john.medler@e-lindsey.gov.uk

Personnel / HR: Mr Tony Lascelles, Head of HR, Tedder Hall, Manby Park, Louth LN11 8UP ☎ 01507 613230 🖷 01507 600206 ✉ tony.lascelles@cpbs.com

Planning: Mr Chris Panton, Planning Team Leader, Tedder Hall, Manby Park, Louth LN11 8UP ☎ 01507 613158 ✉ chris.panton@e-lindsey.gov.uk

Recycling & Waste Minimisation: Mr Nick Davis, Team Leader - Waste Services, Tedder Hall, Manby Park, Louth LN11 8UP ☎ 01507 613540 ✉ nick.davis@e-lindsey.gov.uk

Regeneration: Mr Jonathan Burgess, Economic & Tourism Team Leader, Tedder Hall, Manby Park, Louth LN11 8UP ☎ 01507 613117 ✉ jonathan.burgess@e-lindsey.gov.uk

Staff Training: Mr Tony Lascelles, Head of HR, Tedder Hall, Manby Park, Louth LN11 8UP ☎ 01507 613230 🖷 01507 600206 ✉ tony.lascelles@cpbs.com

Street Scene: Ms Victoria Burgess, Service Development Team Leader, Tedder Hall, Manby Park, Louth LN11 8UP ☎ 01507 613536 ✉ V.B@e-lindsey.gov.uk

Sustainable Communities: Ms Debbie Prince, Neighbourhood Projects Officer, Tedder Hall, Manby Park, Louth LN11 8UP ☎ 01507 613652 ✉ debbie.prince@e-lindsey.gov.uk

Sustainable Development: Ms Sarah Cocker, Community Safety Partnership Officer, Tedder Hall, Manby Park, Louth LN11 8UP ☎ 01507 613050 ✉ sarah.cocker@e-lindsey.gov.uk

Tourism: Mr Jonathan Burgess, Economic & Tourism Team Leader, Tedder Hall, Manby Park, Louth LN11 8UP ☎ 01507 613117 ✉ jonathan.burgess@e-lindsey.gov.uk

Town Centre: Mr Jonathan Burgess, Economic & Tourism Team Leader, Tedder Hall, Manby Park, Louth LN11 8UP ☎ 01507 613117 ✉ jonathan.burgess@e-lindsey.gov.uk

Town Centre: Ms Stefan Krause, Skegness Town Centre Manager, Tedder Hall, Manby Park, Louth LN11 8UP ☎ 01754 896977 ✉ stefan.krause@e-lindsey.gov.uk

Waste Collection and Disposal: Mr Nick Davis, Team Leader - Waste Services, Tedder Hall, Manby Park, Louth LN11 8UP ☎ 01507 613540 ✉ nick.davis@e-lindsey.gov.uk

Waste Management: Mr Nick Davis, Team Leader - Waste Services, Tedder Hall, Manby Park, Louth LN11 8UP ☎ 01507 613540 ✉ nick.davis@e-lindsey.gov.uk

MEMBERS OF THE COUNCIL (60)

***Chair:* Avison**, Stanley (CON - Coningsby / Tattershall)
stanley.avison@e-lindsey.gov.uk

***Leader of the Council:* Stephenson**, Doreen (CON - North Thoresby)
doreen.stephenson@e-lindsey.gov.uk

Aldridge, Terrence (CON - Holton le Clay)
terry.aldridge@e-lindsey.gov.uk

Anderson, Mark (LAB - Skegness St. Clements)
mark.anderson@e-lindsey.gov.uk

Archer, Graham (LAB - Ingoldmells)
graham.archer@e-lindsey.gov.uk

Ayling, Victoria (CON - Stickney)
victoria.ayling@e-lindsey.gov.uk

Blacklock, Clive (CON - Holton le Clay)
clive.blacklock@e-lindsey.gov.uk

Bradley, Jean (IND - Alford)
jean.bradley@e-lindsey.gov.uk

Bridges, Anthony (CON - Tetney)
tony.bridges@e-lindsey.gov.uk

Burnett, Brian (IND - Binbrook)
brian.burnett@e-lindsey.gov.uk

Byford, John (CON - Skegness Seacroft)
john.byford@e-lindsey.gov.uk

Campbell-Wardman, Sandra (LD - Horncastle)
sandra.campbell-wardman@e-lindsey.gov.uk

Cooper, Neil (CON - Burgh le Marsh)
neil.cooper@e-lindsey.gov.uk

Cooper, Pauline (CON - Croft)
pauline.cooper@e-lindsey.gov.uk

Cullen, Graham (LAB - Mablethorpe Central)
graham.cullen@e-lindsey.gov.uk

Curtis, Raymond (LD - Coningsby / Tattershall)
raymond.curtis@e-lindsey.gov.uk

Dennis, Sidney (CON - Skegness St. Clements)
sidney.dennis@e-lindsey.gov.uk

Dodds, Sarah (LAB - Louth Priory)
sarah.dodds@e-lindsey.gov.uk

Doughty, Stephen (IND - Frithville)
steve.doughty@e-lindsey.gov.uk

Edginton, Dick (CON - Skegness Seacroft)
david.edginton@e-lindsey.gov.uk

Ferryman, Andrew (IND - Sutton on Sea North)
andrew.ferryman@e-lindsey.gov.uk

Gray, William (CON - Roughton)
william.gray@e-lindsey.gov.uk

Grist, Adam (CON - Legbourne)
adam.grist@e-lindsey.gov.uk

Harness, Philip (CON - Woodhall Spa)
philip.harness@e-lindsey.gov.uk

Harrison, Sandra (CON - Skidbrooke with Saltfleet Haven)
sandra.harrison@e-lindsey.gov.uk

Harrison, Janet (IND - Mareham le Fen)
janet.harrison@e-lindsey.gov.uk

Harvery, Rick (IND - Sibsey)
rick.harvey@e-lindsey.gov.uk

Hopkins, James (CON - Hunleby)
james.hopkins@e-lindsey.gov.uk

Horton, George (LD - Louth St. Michaels)
george.horton@e-lindsey.gov.uk

Howard, Tony (LAB - Mablethorpe East)
tony.howard@e-lindsey.gov.uk

Kemp, Phillip (LAB - Skegness Scarbrough)
phillip.kemp@e-lindsey.gov.uk

Knowles, Terence (IND - Grimoldby)
terence.knowles@e-lindsey.gov.uk

Leivers, Phil (IND - Chapel St. Leonards)
phil.leivers@e-lindsey.gov.uk

Leyland, Craig (CON - Woodhall Spa)
craig.leyland@e-lindsey.gov.uk

Macey, Carl (CON - Skegness Winthorpe)
carl.macey@e-lindsey.gov.uk

Makinson-Sanders, Jill (IND - Louth St. Mary's)

jill.makinson-sanders@e-lindsey.gov.uk
Marfleet, Hugo (CON - Withern with Stain)
hugo.marfleet@e-lindsey.gov.uk
Marfleet, L-J (CON - Tetford)
l-j.marfleet@e-lindsey.gov.uk
Martin, Fiona (LD - Horncastle)
fiona.martin@e-lindsey.gov.uk
Milner, Kenneth (CON - Skegness Scarbrough)
kenneth.milner@e-lindsey.gov.uk
Mossop, Edward (IND - Marshchapel)
edward.mossop@e-lindsey.gov.uk
Newcombe, Hazel (IND - Chapel St. Leonards)
hazel.newcombe@e-lindsey.gov.uk
Newton, Stephen (CON - Horncastle)
stephen.newton@e-lindsey.gov.uk
O'Dare, Steve (CON - Skegness Winthorpe)
steve.odare@e-lindsey.gov.uk
Palmer, Robert (CON - North Somercotes)
robert.palmer@e-lindsey.gov.uk
Phillipson, Peter (IND - Wragby)
Preen, Michael (LAB - Louth Trinity)
michael.preen@e-lindsey.gov.uk
Prince, Paddy (LAB - Mablethorpe North)
paddy.prince@e-lindsey.gov.uk
Simpson, Daniel (IND - Ludford)
daniel.simpson@e-lindsey.gov.uk
Smith, Kevin (CON - Wainfleet/Friskney)
kevin.smith@e-lindsey.gov.uk
Smith, Angie (CON - Willoughby/Sloothby)
angie.smith@e-lindsey.gov.uk
Stephenson, Laura (LAB - Louth St. Margarets)
laura.stephenson@e-lindsey.gov.uk
Sturman, Philip (LAB - Louth North Holme)
philip.sturman@e-lindsey.gov.uk
Swanson, Jim (IND - Halton Holegate)
jim.swanson@e-lindsey.gov.uk
Upsall, John (CON - Wainfleet/Friskney)
john.upsall@e-lindsey.gov.uk
Veasey, Anne (IND - Sutton on Sea South)
anne.veasey@e-lindsey.gov.uk
Watson, Stuart (CON - Thusthorpe / Mablethorpe South)
stuart.watson@e-lindsey.gov.uk
Watson, Pauline (CON - Louth St James)
pauline.watson@e-lindsey.gov.uk
Webb, Jeremy (IND - Alford)
jeremy.webb@e-lindsey.gov.uk
Williams, Roderick (CON - Spilsby)
roderick.williams@e-lindsey.gov.uk

POLITICAL COMPOSITION

CON: 30, IND: 16, LAB: 10, LD: 4

CABINET

Leader: Mrs Doreen Stephenson
Communities: Mrs Sandra Harrison
Corporate Affairs: Ms Victoria Ayling
Culture, Leisure & Tourism: Mr Adam Grist
Economic Regeneration: Mr Craig Leyland
Environment: Mr Stephen Newton
Finance: Mr John Upsall
Housing: Mr William Gray

COMMITTEE CHAIRS

Audit: Mr Anthony Bridges
General Licensing: Mr George Horton
Overview: Mrs Fiona Martin
Planning: Mr Neil Cooper

EAST LOTHIAN S

East Lothian Council, John Muir House, Brewery Park, Haddington EH41 3HA ☎ 01620 827827
🖱 feedback@eastlothian.gov.uk 💻 www.eastlothian.gov.uk

FACTS & FIGURES

Police Authority: Lothian & Borders Police Board
Health Authority: NHS Lothian
Learning and Skills Council: Scotland
Parliamentary Constituencies: East Lothian
EU Constituencies: Scotland
Election Frequency: Elections are of whole council
Twinning: Dunbar: Lignieres (France) and Martinez (USA); East Lothian: Kreis Spree-Neisse (Germany); Haddington: Aubigny (France); Musselburgh: Champigny (France) and Rosignano Marittimo (Italy); North Berwick: Kerteminde (Denmark)

PRINCIPAL OFFICERS

Chief Executive: Ms Angela Leitch, Chief Executive, John Muir House, Brewery Park, Haddington EH41 3HA ☎ 01620 827588 🖷 01620 827410 🖱 aleitch@eastlothian.gov.uk

Senior Management: Mr Peter Collins, Executive Director of Environment, John Muir House, Haddington EH41 3HA ☎ 01620 827247 🖷 01620 827457 🖱 pcollins@eastlothian.gov.uk

Senior Management: Mr Alex McCrorie, Executive Director of Corporate Resources, John Muir House, Haddington EH41 3HA ☎ 01620 827204 🖷 01620 827446 🖱 amccrorie@eastlothian.gov.uk

Architect, Building / Property Services: Ms Liz McLean, Principal Architect, Penston House, Macmerry Industrial Estate, Macmerry, EH33 1EX ☎ 01620 827353 🖷 01620 827454 🖱 lmclean@eastlothian.gov.uk

Best Value: Mr Jim Lamond, Head of Council Resources, John Muir House, Haddington EH41 3HA ☎ 01620 827278 🖱 jlamond@eastlothian.gov.uk

Building Control: Mr John Murdoch, Building Control Manager, John Muir House, Haddington EH41 3HA ☎ 01620 827266 🖷 01620 827723 🖱 jmurdoch@eastlothian.gov.uk

Catering Services: Ms Joyce Marlow, Catering Manager, Block B, Brewery Park, Haddington EH41 3HA ☎ 01620 827481 🖱 jmarlow@eastlothian.gov.uk

Children / Youth Services: Mr Alan Ross, Head of Children's Services, John Muir House, Haddington EH41 3HA ☎ 01620 827881 🖷 01620 824295 🖱 aross@eastlothian.gov.uk

Civil Registration: Ms Sandra Ross, Senior Registrar, John Muir House, Haddington EH41 3HA ☎ 01620 827308 🖷 01620 827529 🖱 sross@eastlothian.gov.uk

PR / Communications: Mr David Russell, Democratic Services

Manager, John Muir House, Haddington EH41 3HA ☎ 01620 827655 🖷 01620 827442 ✉ drussell@eastlothian.gov.uk

Community Planning: Mr Paulo Vestri, Corporate Policy Manager, John Muir House, Haddington EH41 3HA ☎ 01620 827320 🖷 01620 827442 ✉ pvestri@eastlothian.gov.uk

Community Safety: Ms Claire Goodwin, Policy Officer, John Muir House, Haddington EH41 3HA ☎ 01620 827270 🖷 01620 827442 ✉ cgoodwin@eastlothian.gov.uk

Consumer Protection and Trading Standards: Mr David Evans, Chief Environmental & Consumer Protection Officer, John Muir House, Haddington EH41 3HA ☎ 01620 827286 🖷 01620 827918 ✉ devans@eastlothian.gov.uk

Corporate Services: Mr Jim Lamond, Head of Council Resources, John Muir House, Brewery Park, Haddington EH41 3HA ☎ 01620 827278 ✉ jlamond@eastlothian.gov.uk

Customer Service: Ms Eileen Morrison, Customer Services Manager, Penston House, Macmerry Industrial Estate, Tranent EH33 1EX ☎ 01620 827211 🖷 01620 827253 ✉ emorrison@eastlothian.gov.uk

Customer Service: Mr Tom Shearer, Head of Policy & Partnerships, John Muir House, Brewery Park, Haddington EH41 3HA ☎ 01620 827560 🖷 01620 827291 ✉ tshearer@eastlothian.gov.uk

Economic Development: Mr Tom Shearer, Head of Policy & Partnerships, John Muir House, Brewery Park, Haddington EH41 3HA ☎ 01620 827560 🖷 01620 827291 ✉ tshearer@eastlothian.gov.uk

Economic Development: Ms Susan Smith, Economic Development Manager, Carlyle House, Lodge Street, Haddington EH41 3DX ☎ 01620 827282 🖷 01620 827482 ✉ ssmith@eastlothian.gov.uk

Education: Ms Maureen Jobson, Acting Head of Education, John Muir House, Haddington EH41 3HA ☎ 01620 827596 ✉ mjobson@eastlothian.gov.uk

Education: Mr Don Ledingham, Joint Director of Education & Children's Services, John Muir House, Brewery Park, Haddington EH41 3HA ☎ 01620 827596; 0131 270 7500 🖷 0131 271 3751 ✉ dledingham@eastlothian.gov.uk

Electoral Registration: Mr Jim Lamond, Head of Council Resources, John Muir House, Haddington EH41 3HA ☎ 01620 827278 ✉ jlamond@eastlothian.gov.uk

Emergency Planning: Ms Elizabeth Dobson, Emergency Planning Officer, John Muir House, Brewery Park, Haddington EH41 3HA ☎ 01620 827779 🖷 01620 827438 ✉ edobson@eastlothian.gov.uk

Energy Management: Mr Mark McArthur, Home Energy Officer, John Muir House, Haddington EH41 3HA ☎ 01620 827862 🖷 01620 826202 ✉ mmcarthur@eastlothian.gov.uk

Environmental / Technical Services: Mr Peter Collins, Executive Director of Environment, John Muir House, Haddington EH41 3HA ☎ 01620 827247 🖷 01620 827457 ✉ pcollins@eastlothian.gov.uk

Environmental / Technical Services: Mr Richard Jennings, Head of Housing and Environment, John Muir House, Brewery Park, Haddington EH41 3HA ☎ 01620 827572 ✉ rjennings@eastlothian.gov.uk

Environmental Health: Mr David Evans, Chief Environmental & Consumer Protection Officer, John Muir House, Haddington EH41 3HA ☎ 01620 827286 🖷 01620 827918 ✉ devans@eastlothian.gov.uk

Environmental Health: Mr Richard Jennings, Head of Housing and Environment, John Muir House, Brewery Park, Haddington EH41 3HA ☎ 01620 827572 ✉ rjennings@eastlothian.gov.uk

Estates, Property & Valuation: Mr Richard Jennings, Head of Housing and Environment, John Muir House, Brewery Park, Haddington EH41 3HA ☎ 01620 827572 ✉ rjennings@eastlothian.gov.uk

European Liaison: Ms Susan Smith, Economic Development Manager, Carlyle House, Lodge Street, Haddington EH41 3DX ☎ 01620 827282 🖷 01620 827482 ✉ ssmith@eastlothian.gov.uk

Facilities: Ms Angela Hegarty, Acting Manager, Facility Management, John Muir House, Haddington EH41 3HA ☎ 01620 827298 ✉ ahegarty@eastlothian.gov.uk

Finance and Treasurer: Mr Jim Lamond, Head of Council Resources, John Muir House, Brewery Park, Haddington EH41 3HA ☎ 01620 827278 ✉ jlamond@eastlothian.gov.uk

Finance and Treasurer: Mr Alex McCrorie, Executive Director of Corporate Resources, John Muir House, Haddington EH41 3HA ☎ 01620 827204 🖷 01620 827446 ✉ amccrorie@eastlothian.gov.uk

Fleet Management: Mr Ray Montgomery, Head of Infrastructure, John Muir House, Haddington EH41 3HA ☎ 01620 827658 🖷 01620 827923 ✉ rmontgomery@eastlothian.gov.uk

Grounds Maintenance: Ms Maree Johnston, Landscape & Countryside Manager, John Muir House, Haddington EH41 3HA ☎ 01620 827427 🖷 01620 827456 ✉ mjohnston@eastlothian.gov.uk

Health and Safety: Mr Keith Flockhart, Health & Safety Advisor, John Muir House, Brewery Park, Haddington EH41 3HA ☎ 01620 827337 🖷 01620 827612 ✉ clawson@eastlothian.gov.uk

Highways: Mr Ray Montgomery, Head of Infrastructure, John Muir House, Haddington EH41 3HA ☎ 01620 827658 🖷 01620 827923 ✉ rmontgomery@eastlothian.gov.uk

Housing: Mr Richard Jennings, Head of Housing & Environment, John Muir House, Brewery Park, Haddington EH41 3HA ☎ 01620 827572 ✉ rjennings@eastlothian.gov.uk

Housing Maintenance: Mr Richard Jennings, Head of Housing & Environment, John Muir House, Brewery Park, Haddington EH41 3HA ☎ 01620 827572 ✉ rjennings@eastlothian.gov.uk

Legal: Mr Jim Lamond, Head of Council Resources, John Muir House, Brewery Park, Haddington EH41 3HA ☎ 01620 827278 ✉ jlamond@eastlothian.gov.uk

Leisure and Cultural Services: Mr Tom Shearer, Head of Policy & Partnerships, John Muir House, Haddington EH41 3HA ☎ 01620 827560 🖷 01620 827291 ✉ tshearer@eastlothian.gov.uk

Lifelong Learning: Ms Myra Galloway, Principal Community Development Officer, John Muir House, Haddington EH41 3HA ☎ 01620 827568 🖷 01620 827291 ✉ mgalloway@eastlothian.gov.uk

Lighting: Mr Nicholas Flynn, Street Lighting Officer, John Muir House, Brewery Park, Haddington EH41 3HA ☎ 01620 827622 🖷 01620 827710 ✉ nflynn@eastlothian.gov.uk

Lottery Funding, Charity and Voluntary: Ms Susan Smith, Economic Development Manager, Carlyle House, Lodge Street, Haddington EH41 3DX ☎ 01620 827282 🖷 01620 827482 ✉ ssmith@eastlothian.gov.uk

Member Services: Ms Lel Gillingwater, Democratic Support Services Manager, John Muir House, Haddington EH41 3HA ☎ 01620 827225 ✉ lgillingwater@eastlothian.gov.uk

Member Services: Mr Jim Lamond, Head of Council Resources, John Muir House, Brewery Park, Haddington EH41 3HA ☎ 01620 827278 ✉ jlamond@eastlothian.gov.uk

Member Services: Ms Jill Totney, Democratic Services Manager, John Muir House, Brewery Park, Haddington EH41 3HA ☎ 01620 827225 ✉ jtotney@eastlothian.gov.uk

Partnerships: Mr Tom Shearer, Head of Policy & Partnerships, John Muir House, Brewery Park, Haddington EH41 3HA ☎ 01620 827560 🖷 01620 827291 ✉ tshearer@eastlothian.gov.uk

Personnel / HR: Mr Jim Lamond, Head of Council Resources, John Muir House, Brewery Park, Haddington EH41 3HA ☎ 01620 827278 ✉ jlamond@eastlothian.gov.uk

Personnel / HR: Ms Sharon Saunders, Head of Children's Wellbeing, John Muir House, Haddington EH41 3HA ☎ 01620 827259 🖷 01620 827612 ✉ ssaunders@eastlothian.gov.uk

Planning: Mr Peter Collins, Executive Director of Environment, John Muir House, Haddington EH41 3HA ☎ 01620 827247 🖷 01620 827457 ✉ pcollins@eastlothian.gov.uk

Procurement: Ms Julie Caughey, Finance Manager, John Muir House, Haddington EH41 3HA ☎ 01620 827998 ✉ jcaughey@eastlothian.gov.uk

Public Libraries: Ms Alison Hunter, Libraries Officer, Library Headquarters, Dunbar Road, Haddington EH41 3PJ ☎ 01620 828202 🖷 01620 828201 ✉ ahunter@eastlothian.gov.uk

Public Libraries: Mr Tom Shearer, Head of Policy & Partnerships, John Muir House, Brewery Park, Haddington EH41 3HA ☎ 01620 827560 🖷 01620 827291 ✉ tshearer@eastlothian.gov.uk

Recycling & Waste Minimisation: Mr Colin Clark, Waste Services Manager, John Muir House, Haddington EH41 3HA ☎ 01620 827830 🖷 01620 827899 ✉ cclark@eastlothian.gov.uk

Road Safety: Mr Colin Bathgate, Senior Traffic & Safety Officer, John Muir House, Haddington EH41 3HA ☎ 01620 827675 🖷 01620 827710 ✉ cbathgate@eastlothian.gov.uk

Social Services (Adult): Mr Gordon Miller, Acting Head of Adult Social Care, 6-8 Lodge Road, Haddington EH41 3DX ☎ 01620 827577 ✉ gmiller@eastlothian.gov.uk

Social Services (Children): Mr Alan Ross, Head of Children's Services, John Muir House, Haddington EH41 3HA ☎ 01620 827881 🖷 01620 824295 ✉ aross@eastlothian.gov.uk

Social Services (Children): Ms Sharon Saunders, Head of Children's Wellbeing, John Muir House, Brewery Park, Haddington EH41 3HA ☎ 01620 827259 🖷 01620 827612 ✉ ssaunders@eastlothian.gov.uk

Staff Training: Mr Gavin Macgregor, OD Manager, John Muir House, Haddington EH41 3HA ☎ 01620 827827 ✉ gmacgregor1@eastlothian.gov.uk

Sustainable Communities: Mr Paulo Vestri, Corporate Policy Manager, John Muir House, Haddington EH41 3HA ☎ 01620 827320 🖷 01620 827442 ✉ pvestri@eastlothian.gov.uk

Sustainable Development: Mr David Evans, Chief Environmental & Consumer Protection Officer, John Muir House, Haddington EH41 3HA ☎ 01620 827286 🖷 01620 827918 ✉ devans@eastlothian.gov.uk

Tourism: Ms Claire Dutton, Tourism Officer, Carlyle House, Lodge Street, Haddington EH41 3DX ☎ 01620 827482 🖷 01620 827482 ✉ cdutton@eastlothian.gov.uk

Tourism: Mr Tom Shearer, Head of Policy & Partnerships, John Muir House, Brewery Park, Haddington EH41 3HA ☎ 01620 827560 🖷 01620 827291 ✉ tshearer@eastlothian.gov.uk

Town Centre: Mr Peter Collins, Executive Director of Environment, John Muir House, Haddington EH41 3HA ☎ 01620 827247 🖷 01620 827457 ✉ pcollins@eastlothian.gov.uk

Traffic Management: Mr Ray Montgomery, Head of Infrastructure, John Muir House, Haddington EH41 3HA ☎ 01620 827658 🖷 01620 827923 ✉ rmontgomery@eastlothian.gov.uk

Waste Collection and Disposal: Mr Colin Clark, Waste Services Manager, John Muir House, Haddington EH41 3HA ☎ 01620 827830 🖷 01620 827899 ✉ cclark@eastlothian.gov.uk

Waste Management: Mr Colin Clark, Waste Services Manager, John Muir House, Haddington EH41 3HA ☎ 01620 827830 🖷 01620 827899 ✉ cclark@eastlothian.gov.uk

MEMBERS OF THE COUNCIL (23)

***Provost:* Broun-Lindsay**, Ludovic (CON - Haddington and Lammermuir)
lbroun-linday@eastlothian.gov.uk
***Deputy Provost:* Gillies**, Jim (LAB - Fa'side)
jgillies@eastlothian.gov.uk
***Leader of the Council:* Innes**, William (LAB - Preston/Seton/Gosford)
winnes@eastlothian.gov.uk
***Deputy Leader of the Council:* Veitch**, Michael (CON - Dunbar and East Linton)
mleitch@eastlothian.gov.uk
***Deputy Leader of the Council:* Veitch**, Michael (CON - Dunbar and East Linton)
mveitch1@eastlothian.gov.uk
***Group Leader:* McLennan**, Paul (SNP - Dunbar and East Linton)
pmclennan@eastlothian.gov.uk
Akhtar, Shamin (LAB - Fa'side)
sakhtar@eastlothian.gov.uk
Berry, David (SNP - North Berwick Coastal)
dberry@eastlothian.gov.uk
Brown, Steven (SNP - Preston/Seton/Gosford)
sbrown@eastlothian.gov.uk
Brown, Steven (SNP - Preston/Seton/Gosford)
sbrown1@eastlothian.gov.uk
Caldwell, John (IND - Musselburgh East and Carberry)
jcaldwell1@eastlothian.gov.uk
Currie, Stuart (SNP - Musselburgh East and Carberry)
scurrie@eastlothian.gov.uk
Day, Tim (CON - North Berwick Coastal)
tday@eastlothian.gov.uk
Forrest, Andrew (LAB - Musselburgh East and Carberry)
aforrest2@eastlothian.gov.uk
Goodfellow, Jim (LAB - North Berwick Coastal)
jgoodfellow@eastlothian.gov.uk
Grant, Donald (LAB - Fa'side)
dgrant@eastlothian.gov.uk
Hampshire, Norman (LAB - Dunbar and East Linton)
nhampshire@eastlothian.gov.uk
Libberton, Margaret (LAB - Preston/Seton/Gosford)
mlibberton1@eastlothian.gov.uk
MacKenzie, Peter (SNP - Preston/Seton/Gosford)
pmackenzie@eastlothian.gov.uk
McAllister, Fraser (SNP - Musselburgh West)
fmcallister@eastlothian.gov.uk
McLeod, Kenny (SNP - Fa'side)
kmcleod1@eastlothian.gov.uk
McMillan, John (LAB - Haddington and Lammermuir)
jmcmillan@eastlothian.gov.uk
McNeil, John (LAB - Musselburgh West)
jmcneil@eastlothian.gov.uk
Trotter, Tom (SNP - Haddington and Lammermuir)
ttrotter@eastlothian.gov.uk
Williamson, John (SNP - Musselburgh West)
jwilliamson@eastlothian.gov.uk

POLITICAL COMPOSITION

LAB: 10, SNP: 9, CON: 3, IND: 1

CABINET

Community Wellbeing: Mrs Ruth Currie
Depute Provost: Mr Roger Knox
Deputy Leader: Mr Stuart Mackinnon
Education & Children's Services: Mr Peter MacKenzie
Environment: Mr Barry Turner
Housing & Community Safety: Mr Stuart Currie
Leader/Health and Social Care: Mr Paul McLennan
Provost: Mrs Sheena Richardson

EAST NORTHAMPTONSHIRE D

East Northamptonshire District Council, (East Northamptonshire Council), East Northamptonshire House, Cedar Drive, Thrapston NN14 4LZ ☎ 01832 742000 🖷 01832 734839 ✉ info@east-northamptonshire.gov.uk 💻 www.east-northamptonshire.gov.uk

FACTS & FIGURES

Police Authority: Northamptonshire Police Authority
Health Authority: East Midlands Strategic Health Authority
Learning and Skills Council: East Midlands
Parliamentary Constituencies: Corby, Wellingborough
EU Constituencies: East Midlands
Election Frequency: Elections are of whole council
Twinning: Loreley (Germany)

PRINCIPAL OFFICERS

Chief Executive: Mr David Oliver, Chief Executive, East Northamptonshire House, Cedar Drive, Thrapston NN14 4LZ ☎ 01832 742000 ✉ doliver@east-northamptonshire.gov.uk

Senior Management: Ms Sharn Matthews, Director & Monitoring Officer, East Northamptonshire House, Cedar Drive, Thrapston NN14 4LZ ☎ 01832 742108
✉ smatthews@east-northamptonshire.gov.uk

Best Value: Mrs Lisa Hyde, Head of Policy & Community Development, East Northamptonshire House, Cedar Drive, Thrapston NN14 4LZ ☎ 01832 742162 🖷 01832 734839
✉ lhyde@east-northamptonshire.gov.uk

Building Control: Mr Malcolm Shepherd, Building Control Manager, Community Services Directorate, East Northamptonshire House, Cedar Drive, Thrapston NN14 4LZ ☎ 01832 742122 🖷 01832 734839
✉ building.control@east-northamptonshire.gov.uk

Children / Youth Services: Mr Mike Greenway, Community Development Manager, East Northamptonshire House, Cedar Drive, Thrapston NN14 4LZ ☎ 01832 742059 🖷 01832 734839
✉ mgreenway@east-northamptonshire.gov.uk

PR / Communications: Mrs Janet Walls, Communications Manager, East Northamptonshire House, Cedar Drive, Thrapston NN14 4LZ ☎ 01832 742169 🖷 01832 742160
✉ jwalls@east-northamptonshire.gov.uk

Community Planning: Mr Mike Greenway, Community Development Manager, East Northamptonshire Council, Cedar Drive, Thrapston NN10 4LZ ☎ 01832 742000
✉ mgreenway@east-northamptonshire.gov.uk

Community Safety: Mr Mike Greenway, Community Development Manager, East Northamptonshire House, Cedar Drive, Thrapston NN14 4LZ ☎ 01832 742059 🖷 01832 734839
✉ mgreenway@east-northamptonshire.gov.uk

Computer Management: Mr Gareth Jones, Head of ICT, East Northamptonshire House, Cedar Drive, Thrapston NN14 4LZ ☎ 01832 742076 🖷 01832 734839 ✉ gjones@east-northamptonshire.gov.uk

Corporate Services: Mrs Katy Everitt, Head of Organisational Development, East Northamptonshire House, Cedar House, Thrapston NN14 4LZ ☎ 01832 742113 🖷 01832 742234 ✉ personnel@east-northamptonshire.gov.uk

Customer Service: Ms Alison Cressey, Head of Customer Services, East Northamptonshire House, Cedar Drive, Thrapston NN14 4LZ ☎ 01832 742250 🖷 01832 734839 ✉ acressey@east-northamptonshire.gov.uk

Economic Development: Mr Tom Grozdoski, Economic Development Officer, East Northamptonshire House, Cedar Drive, Thrapston NN14 4LZ ☎ 01832 742195 ✉ tgrozdoski@east-northamptonshire.gov.uk

E-Government: Mrs Pat Bird, E-Government & Information Manager, East Northamptonshire House, Cedar Drive, Thrapston NN14 4LZ ☎ 01832 742229 🖷 01832 734839 ✉ pbird@east-northamptonshire.gov.uk

Electoral Registration: Mrs Judi Miles, Electoral Services Manager, East Northamptonshire House, Cedar Drive, Thrapston NN14 4LZ ☎ 01832 742119 🖷 01832 734839 ✉ jmiles@east-northamptonshire.gov.uk

Environmental Health: Mr Mike Deacon, Head of Environmental Services, East Northamptonshire House, Cedar Drive, Thrapston NN14 4LZ ☎ 01832 742060 🖷 01832 734839 ✉ environmentalservices@east-northamptonshire.gov.uk

Facilities: Mr Richard Hankins, Amenities Manager, East Northamptonshire House, Cedar Drive, Thrapston NN14 4LZ ☎ 01832 742031 ✉ rhankins@east-northamptonshire.gov.uk

Legal: Mr Neil Pritchard, Solicitor to the Council, East Northamptonshire House, Cedar Drive, Thrapston NN14 4LZ ☎ 01832 742151 🖷 01832 734839 ✉ npritchard@east-northamptonshire.gov.uk

Licensing: Mr Mike Deacon, Head of Environmental Services, East Northamptonshire House, Cedar Drive, Thrapston NN14 4LZ ☎ 01832 742060 🖷 01832 734839 ✉ environmentalservices@east-northamptonshire.gov.uk

Member Services: Mr James McLaughlin, Democratic & Electoral Services Manager, Cedar Drive, Thrapston NN14 4LZ ☎ 01832 742113

Member Services: Mr David Pope, Member Services Officer, East Northamptonshire House, Cedar Drive, Thrapston NN14 4LZ ☎ 01832 742198 🖷 01832 734839 ✉ memberservices@east-northamptonshire.gov.uk

Partnerships: Mr Mike Greenway, Community Development Manager, East Northamptonshire Council, Cedar Drive, Thrapston NN10 4LZ ☎ 01832 742000 ✉ mgreenway@east-northamptonshire.gov.uk

Personnel / HR: Mrs Katy Everitt, Head of Organisational Development, East Northamptonshire House, Cedar House, Thrapston NN14 4LZ ☎ 01832 742113 🖷 01832 742234 ✉ personnel@east-northamptonshire.gov.uk

Planning: Mr James Wilson, Interim Head of Planning Services, East Northamptonshire House, Cedar Drive, Thrapston NN14 4LZ ☎ 01832 742218 ✉ jwilson@east-northamptonshire.gov.uk

Recycling & Waste Minimisation: Mr Michael Bailey, Waste Management Officer (Recycling), East Northamptonshire House, Cedar Drive, Thrapston NN14 4LZ ☎ 01832 742043 🖷 01832 734839 ✉ mbailey@east-northamptonshire.gov.uk

Regeneration: Mr Mike Greenway, Community Development Manager, East Northamptonshire Council, Cedar Drive, Thrapston NN10 4LZ ☎ 01832 742000 ✉ mgreenway@east-northamptonshire.gov.uk

Staff Training: Mrs Katy Everitt, Head of Organisational Development, East Northamptonshire House, Cedar House, Thrapston NN14 4LZ ☎ 01832 742113 🖷 01832 742234 ✉ personnel@east-northamptonshire.gov.uk

Sustainable Communities: Mr Mike Greenway, Community Development Manager, East Northamptonshire Council, Cedar Drive, Thrapston NN10 4LZ ☎ 01832 742000 ✉ mgreenway@east-northamptonshire.gov.uk

Sustainable Development: Ms Hayley Blundell, Urban Design Officer, East Northamptonshire House, Cedar Drive, Thrapston NN14 4LZ ☎ 01832 742351 ✉ hblundell@east-northamptonshire.gov.uk

Sustainable Development: Mr Mike Greenway, Community Development Manager, East Northamptonshire Council, Cedar Drive, Thrapston NN10 4LZ ☎ 01832 742000 ✉ mgreenway@east-northamptonshire.gov.uk

Tourism: Miss Karen Williams, Tourism Development Officer, East Northamptonshire House, Cedar Drive, Thrapston NN14 4LZ ☎ 01832 742064 🖷 01832 734839 ✉ kwilliams@east-northamptonshire.gov.uk

Waste Collection and Disposal: Ms Charlotte Tompkins, Waste Manager, East Northamptonshire House, Cedar Drive, Thrapston NN14 4LZ ☎ 01832 742034 🖷 01832 734839 ✉ waste@east-northamptonshire.gov.uk

Waste Management: Ms Charlotte Tompkins, Waste Manager, East Northamptonshire House, Cedar Drive, Thrapston NN14 4LZ ☎ 01832 742034 🖷 01832 734839 ✉ waste@east-northamptonshire.gov.uk

MEMBERS OF THE COUNCIL (40)

***Chair:* Homer**, Sue (CON - Rushden Bates)
shomer@east-northamptonshire.gov.uk

***Chair:* Wood**, Clive (CON - Rushden Spencer)
cwood@east-northamptonshire.gov.uk

***Vice-Chair:* Hughes**, Sylvia (CON - Lyveden)
shughes@east-northamptonshire.gov.uk

***Vice-Chair:* Whiting**, Pam (CON - Higham Ferrers Lancaster)

pwhiting@east-northamptonshire.gov.uk
***Leader of the Council:* North**, Steven (CON - Rushden Sartoris)
snorth@east-northamptonshire.gov.uk
***Deputy Leader of the Council:* Harwood**, Glenn (CON - Higham Ferrers Lancaster)
gharwood@east-northamptonshire.gov.uk
***Group Leader:* Gell**, Richard (IND - Higham Ferrers Chichele)
rgell@east-northamptonshire.gov.uk
***Group Leader:* Nightingale**, Bob (LAB - Irthlingborough Waterloo)
bnightingale@east-northamptonshire.gov.uk
Barnwell: Vacant
Baden, Peter (IND - Thrapston Market)
pbaden@east-northamptonshire.gov.uk
Bateman, David (CON - Oundle)
dbateman@east-northamptonshire.gov.uk
Boto, Tony (CON - Raunds Saxon)
tboto@east-northamptonshire.gov.uk
Brackenbury, Wendy (CON - Thrapston Lakes)
wbrackenbury@east-northamptonshire.gov.uk
Brackenbury, David (CON - Lower Nene)
dbrackenbury@east-northamptonshire.gov.uk
Bradberry, Pauline (CON - Fineshade)
pbradberry@east-northamptonshire.gov.uk
Farrar, John (LAB - Irthlingborough John Pyel)
jfarrar@east-northamptonshire.gov.uk
Finch, Michael (CON - Thrapston Market)
mfinch@east-northamptonshire.gov.uk
Glithero, Roger (CON - Kings Forest)
rglithero@east-northamptonshire.gov.uk
Greenwood-Smith, Glenvil (CON - Raunds Windmill)
glenvil@east-northamptonshire.gov.uk
Hillson, Marika (CON - Irthlingborough Waterloo)
mhillson@east-northamptonshire.gov.uk
Hobbs, Sylvia (CON - Irthlingborough John Pyel)
shobbs@east-northamptonshire.gov.uk
Hollomon, Marian (CON - Rushden Hayden)
mhollomon@east-northamptonshire.gov.uk
Hughes, Dudley (CON - Woodford)
dhughes@east-northamptonshire.gov.uk
Jenney, Barbara (CON - Rushden Hayden)
bjenney@east-northamptonshire.gov.uk
Jenney, David (CON - Rushden Pemberton)
memberservices@east-northamptonshire.gov.uk
Lewis, Richard (CON - Rushden Hayden)
rlewis@east-northamptonshire.gov.uk
Lucille, Eloise (CON - Stanwick)
elucille@east-northamptonshire.gov.uk
Mercer, Andy (CON - Rushden Spencer)
amercer@east-northamptonshire.gov.uk
Mercer, Gill (CON - Rushden Pemberton)
gmercer@east-northamptonshire.gov.uk
Northall, Brian (CON - Raunds Saxon)
bnorthall@east-northamptonshire.gov.uk
Peacock, Sarah (CON - Rushden Spencer)
speacock@east-northamptonshire.gov.uk
Pinnock, Ron (CON - Rushden Sartoris)
rpinnock@east-northamptonshire.gov.uk
Read, David (IND - Thrapston Lakes)
dread@east-northamptonshire.gov.uk
Reichhold, Rupert (CON - Oundle)
Saunston, Anna (CON - Higham Ferrers Chichele)
asaunton@east-northamptonshire.gov.uk
Stearn, Phillip (CON - Oundle)
pstearn@east-northamptonshire.gov.uk
Taylor, Jeremy (CON - Prebendal)
memberservices@east-northamptonshire.gov.uk
Underwood, Robin (CON - Rushden Bates)
runderwood@east-northamptonshire.gov.uk
Wathen, Peter (CON - Raunds Windmill)
pwathen@east-northamptonshire.gov.uk
Wright, Colin (CON - Rushden Pemberton)
cwright@east-northamptonshire.gov.uk

POLITICAL COMPOSITION

CON: 34, IND: 3, LAB: 2, Vacant: 1

COMMITTEE CHAIRS

Development Control: Miss Pauline Bradberry
Licensing: Mr Glenn Harwood
Planning Policy: Mr David Brackenbury
Policy & Resources: Mr Richard Lewis
Scrutiny: Mr Phillip Stearn

EAST RENFREWSHIRE S

East Renfrewshire Council, Council Headquarters, Eastwood Park, Rouken Glen Road, Giffnock G46 6UG ☎ 0141 577 3000 🖷 0141 620 0884 ✉ customerservices@eastrenfrewshire.gov.uk 💻 www.eastrenfrewshire.gov.uk

FACTS & FIGURES

Police Authority: Strathclyde Police Authority
Health Authority: NHS Greater Glasgow & Clyde Health Board
Learning and Skills Council: Scotland
Parliamentary Constituencies: Renfrewshire East
EU Constituencies: Scotland
Election Frequency: Elections are of whole council
Twinning: Albertslund

PRINCIPAL OFFICERS

Chief Executive: Mrs Lorraine McMillan, Chief Executive, Council Headquarters, Eastwood Park, Rouken Glen Road, Giffnock G46 6UG ☎ 0141 577 3009 🖷 0141 577 3017
✉ lorraine.mcmillan@eastrenfrewshire.gov.uk

Deputy Chief Executive: Mrs Caroline Innes, Deputy Chief Executive, Council Headquarters, Eastwood Park, Rouken Glen Road, Giffnock G46 6UG ☎ 0141 577 3161 🖷 0141 577 3155
✉ caroline.innes@eastrenfrewshire.gov.uk

Senior Management: Mr Andrew Cahill, Director of Environment, 2 Spiersbridge Way, Spiersbridge Business Park, Thornliebank G46 8NG ☎ 0141 577 3036 🖷 0141 577 3078
✉ andrew.cahill@eastrenfrewshire.gov.uk

Senior Management: Mrs Julie Murray, CHCP Director, Council Headquarters, Eastwood Park, Rouken Glen Road, Giffnock G46 6UG ☎ 0141 577 3840 🖷 0141 577 3846
✉ julie.murray@eastrenfrewshire.gov.uk

Senior Management: Mr Norie Williamson, Director of Finance, Council Headquarters, Eastwood Park, Rouken Glen Road, Giffnock G46 6UG ☎ 0141 577 3000
✉ norie.williamson@eastrenfrewshire.gov.uk

Senior Management: Mr John Wilson, Director of Education & Community Services, Barrhead Council Offices, 211 Main Street, Barrhead G78 1SY ☎ 0141 577 3404 ✉ john.wilson@eastrenfrewshire.gov.uk

Children / Youth Services: Ms Safaa Baxter, Head of Children's Services, 1 Burnfield Avenue, Giffnock G46 7TT ☎ 0141 577 3841 ✉ safaa.baxter@eastrenfrewshire.gov.uk

Children / Youth Services: Mrs Julie Murray, CHCP Director, Council Headquarters, Eastwood Park, Rouken Glen Road, Giffnock G46 6UG ☎ 0141 577 3840 🖷 0141 577 3846 ✉ julie.murray@eastrenfrewshire.gov.uk

Civil Registration: Mr Jim Clarke, Registrar, Council Headquarters, Eastwood Park, Rouken Glen Road, Giffnock G46 6UG ☎ ; 0141 577 3452 ✉ jim.clarke@eastrenfrewshire.gov.uk

PR / Communications: Ms Louisa Mahon, Communications Manager, Council Headquarters, Eastwood Park, Rouken Glen Road, Giffnock G46 6UG ☎ 0141 577 3851 🖷 0141 577 3852 ✉ louisa.mahon@eastrenfrewshire.gov.uk

Community Planning: Mr Jamie Reid, Community Resources Officer, Council Headquarters, Eastwood Park, Rouken Glen Road, Giffnock G46 6UG ☎ 0141 577 8557 ✉ jamie.reid@eastrenfrewshire.gov.uk

Community Safety: Mr Jim Sneddon, Head of Community Resources, Council Headquarters, Eastwood Park, Rouken Glen Road, Giffnock G46 6UG ☎ 0141 577 3744 ✉ jim.sneddon@eastrenfrewshire.gov.uk

Consumer Protection and Trading Standards: Mr Andrew Corry, Head of Enviromental Services, Council Headquarters, Eastwood Park, Rouken Glen Road, Giffnock G46 6UG ☎ 0141 577 3756 🖷 0141 577 3181 ✉ andrew.corry@eastrenfrewshire.gov.uk

Contracts: Mr Jim Livingstone, Purchasing & Procurement Manager, Capelrig House, Capelrig Road, Newton Mearns G77 6NH ☎ 0141 577 8555 ✉ jim.livingstone@eastrenfrewshire.gov.uk

Customer Service: Mrs Louise Pringle, Head of Customer & Business Change Services, Council Headquarters, Eastwood Park, Rouken Glen Road, Giffnock G46 6UG ☎ 0141 577 3000 ✉ louise.smith@eastrenfrewshire.gov.uk

Education: Ms Susan Gow, Head Education Services (Children & Young People), Barrhead Council Offices, 211 Main Street, Barrhead G78 1SY ☎ 0141 577 3204 ✉ susan.gow@eastrenfrewshire.gov.uk

Education: Ms Fiona Morrison, Head Education Services (School Performance & Provision), Barrhead Council Offices, 211 Main Street, Barrhead G78 1SY ☎ 0141 577 3229 ✉ fiona.morrison@eastrenfrewshire.gov.uk

Education: Ms Mhairi Shaw, Head Education Services (Inclusion Skills & Quality Improvement), Barrhead Council Offices, 211 Main Street, Barrhead G78 1SY ☎ 0141 577 3481 ✉ mhairi.shaw@eastrenfrewshire.gov.uk

Education: Mr John Wilson, Director of Education & Community Services, Barrhead Council Offices, 211 Main Street, Barrhead G78 1SY ☎ 0141 577 3404 ✉ john.wilson@eastrenfrewshire.gov.uk

E-Government: Mr Patrick Murray, IT Manager - Systems, Barrhead Council Offices, 211 Main Street, Barrhead G78 1YS ☎ 0141 577 3400 ✉ patrick.murray@eastrenfrewshire.gov.uk

Environmental / Technical Services: Mr Andrew Cahill, Director of Environment, 2 Spiersbridge Way, Spiersbridge Business Park, Thornliebank G46 8NG ☎ 0141 577 3036 🖷 0141 577 3078 ✉ andrew.cahill@eastrenfrewshire.gov.uk

Environmental Health: Mr Andrew Corry, Head of Enviromental Services, Council Headquarters, Eastwood Park, Rouken Glen Road, Giffnock G46 6UG ☎ 0141 577 3756 🖷 0141 577 3181 ✉ andrew.corry@eastrenfrewshire.gov.uk

Events Manager: Mr Malcolm Wright, Events Co-ordinator, Council Headquarters, Eastwood Park, Rouken Glen Road, Giffnock G46 6UG ☎ 0141 577 4854 ✉ malcolm.wright@eastrenfrewshire.gov.uk

Finance and Treasurer: Ms Margaret McCrossan, Head of Accountancy Services, Council Headquarters, Eastwood Park, Rouken Glen Road, Giffnock G46 6UG ☎ 0141 577 3035 ✉ margaret.mccrossan@eastrenfrewshire.gov.uk

Finance and Treasurer: Mr David Miller, Head of Revenue Services, Barrhead Council Offices, 211 Main Street, Barrhead G78 1SY ☎ 0141 577 3203 ✉ david.miller@eastrenfrewshire.gov.uk

Finance and Treasurer: Mr Norie Williamson, Director of Finance, Council Headquarters, Eastwood Park, Rouken Glen Road, Giffnock G46 6UG ☎ 0141 577 3000 ✉ norie.williamson@eastrenfrewshire.gov.uk

Legal: Mr Gerry Mahon, Chief Solicitor to the Council, Council Headquarters, Eastwood Park, Rouken Glen Road, Giffnock G46 6UG ☎ 0141 577 3024 ✉ gerry.mahon@eastrenfrewshire.gov.uk

Member Services: Ms Margaret Pettigrew, Member Services Officer, Council Headquarters, Eastwood Park, Rouken Glen Road, Giffnock G46 6UG ☎ 0141 577 3107 🖷 0141 577 3119 ✉ margaret.pettigrew@eastrenfrewshire.gov.uk

Partnerships: Mrs Julie Murray, CHCP Director, Council Headquarters, Eastwood Park, Rouken Glen Road, Giffnock G46 6UG ☎ 0141 577 3840 🖷 0141 577 3846 ✉ julie.murray@eastrenfrewshire.gov.uk

Personnel / HR: Mrs Caroline Innes, Deputy Chief Executive, Council Headquarters, Eastwood Park, Rouken Glen Road, Giffnock G46 6UG ☎ 0141 577 3161 🖷 0141 577 3155 ✉ caroline.innes@eastrenfrewshire.gov.uk

Procurement: Mr Jim Livingstone, Purchasing & Procurement Manager, Capelrig House, Capelrig Road, Newton Mearns G77 6NH ☎ 0141 577 8555 ✉ jim.livingstone@eastrenfrewshire.gov.uk

Public Libraries: Mr Ken McKinlay, Head of Education Services (Culture, Sport & Continuing Education), Council Headquarters,

Eastwood Park, Rouken Glen Road, Giffnock G46 6UG
☎ 0141 577 3103 🖷 0141 577 3100
ken.mckinlay@eastrenfrewshire.gov.uk

Recycling & Waste Minimisation: Mr Andrew Corry, Head of Enviromental Services, Council Headquarters, Eastwood Park, Rouken Glen Road, Giffnock G46 6UG ☎ 0141 577 3756 🖷 0141 577 3181 andrew.corry@eastrenfrewshire.gov.uk

Social Services: Mrs Julie Murray, CHCP Director, Council Headquarters, Eastwood Park, Rouken Glen Road, Giffnock G46 6UG ☎ 0141 577 3840 🖷 0141 577 3846
julie.murray@eastrenfrewshire.gov.uk

Social Services (Adult): Mrs Julie Murray, CHCP Director, Council Headquarters, Eastwood Park, Rouken Glen Road, Giffnock G46 6UG ☎ 0141 577 3840 🖷 0141 577 3846
julie.murray@eastrenfrewshire.gov.uk

Social Services (Children): Mrs Julie Murray, CHCP Director, Council Headquarters, Eastwood Park, Rouken Glen Road, Giffnock G46 6UG ☎ 0141 577 3840 🖷 0141 577 3846
julie.murray@eastrenfrewshire.gov.uk

Sustainable Development: Mr Andrew Cahill, Director of Environment, 2 Spiersbridge Way, Spiersbridge Business Park, Thornliebank G46 8NG ☎ 0141 577 3036 🖷 0141 577 3078
andrew.cahill@eastrenfrewshire.gov.uk

Waste Management: Mr Andrew Corry, Head of Enviromental Services, Council Headquarters, Eastwood Park, Rouken Glen Road, Giffnock G46 6UG ☎ 0141 577 3756 🖷 0141 577 3181
andrew.corry@eastrenfrewshire.gov.uk

MEMBERS OF THE COUNCIL (20)

***Provost:* Carmichael**, Alistair (SNP - Busby, Clarkston and Eaglesham)
alistair.carmichael@eastrenfrewshire.gov.uk
***Leader of the Council:* Fletcher**, James (LAB - Giffnock and Thornliebank)
jim.fletcher@eastrenfrewshire.gov.uk
Buchanan, Tony (SNP - Neilston, Uplawmoor and Newton Mearns North)
tony.buchanan@eastrenfrewshire.gov.uk
Cunningham, Betty (LAB - Barrhead)
betty.cunningham@eastrenfrewshire.gov.uk
Devlin, Danny (IND - Barrhead)
danny.devlin@eastrenfrewshire.gov.uk
Gilbert, Charlie (CON - Neilston, Uplawmoor and Newton Mearns North)
charlie.gilbert@eastrenfrewshire.gov.uk
Grant, Barbara (CON - Newton Mearns South)
barbara.grant@eastrenfrewshire.gov.uk
Green, Elaine (LAB - Neilston, Uplawmoor and Newton Mearns North)
elaine.green@eastrenfrewshire.gov.uk
Hay, Kenny (LAB - Barrhead)
kenny.hay@eastrenfrewshire.gov.uk
Lafferty, Alan (LAB - Busby, Clarkston and Eaglesham)
alan.lafferty@eastrenfrewshire.gov.uk
McAlpine, Ian (LAB - Newton Mearns South)
ian.mcalpine@eastrenfrewshire.gov.uk
McCaskill, Gordon (CON - Netherlee, Stamplerland and Williamwood)
gordon.mccaskil@eastrenfrewshire.gov.uk
Miller, Stewart (CON - Busy, Clarkston and Eaglesham)
stewart.miller@eastrenfrewshire.gov.uk
Montague, Mary (LAB - Netherlee, Stamplerland and Williamwood)
mary.montague@eastrenfrewshire.gov.uk
O'Kane, Paul (LAB - Neilston, Uplawmoor and Newton Mearns North)
paul.o'kane@eastrenfrewshire.gov.uk
Reilly, Tommy (SNP - Barrhead)
tommy.reilly@eastrenfrewshire.gov.uk
Robertson, Ralph (IND - Netherlee, Stamplerland and Williamwood)
ralph.robertson@eastrenfrewshire.gov.uk
Swift, Jim (CON - Newton Mearns South)
jim.swift@eastrenfrewshire.gov.uk
Wallace, Gordon (CON - Giffnock and Thornliebank)
gordon.wallace@eastrenfrewshire.gov.uk
Waters, Vincent (SNP - Giffnock and Thornliebank)
vincent.waters@eastrenfrewshire.gov.uk

POLITICAL COMPOSITION

LAB: 8, CON: 6, SNP: 4, IND: 2

EAST RIDING OF YORKSHIRE U

East Riding of Yorkshire Council, County Hall, Beverley HU17 9BA ☎ 01482 887700 🖷 01482 884150 www.eastriding.gov.uk

FACTS & FIGURES

Police Authority: Humberside Police Authority
Health Authority: NHS Yorkshire & the Humber
Learning and Skills Council: Yorkshire and the Humber
Parliamentary Constituencies: Beverley & Holderness, Haltemprice and Howden, Yorkshire East
EU Constituencies: Yorkshire and the Humber
Election Frequency: Elections are of whole council

PRINCIPAL OFFICERS

Chief Executive: Mr Nigel Pearson, Chief Executive, County Hall, Beverley HU17 9BA ☎ 01482 391000 🖷 01482 391002
nigel.pearson@eastriding.gov.uk

Senior Management: Mr Tim Allison, Director of Public Health, County Hall, Beverley HU17 9BA ☎ 01482 391551; 01482 672068 🖷 01482 393009 tim.allison@eastriding.gov.uk; tim.allison@nhs.net

Senior Management: Mr Steve Button, Director of Policy, Partnerships & Improvement, County Hall, Beverley HU17 9BA ☎ 01482 396000 🖷 01482 393009
steve.button@eastriding.gov.uk

Senior Management: Mr Nigel Leighton, Director of Environment & Neighbourhood Services, County Hall, Beverley HU17 9BA ☎ 01482 395000 🖷 01482 393009
nigel.leighton@eastriding.gov.uk

Senior Management: Mr Alan Menzies, Director of Planning & Economic Regeneration, County Hall, Beverley HU17 9BA ☎ 01482 391600 🖷 01482 393009

alan.menzies@eastriding.gov.uk

Senior Management: Mrs Alison Michalska, Director of Children, Family & Adult Services, County Hall, Beverley HU17 9BA ☎ 01482 392000 🖷 01482 392102 alison.michalska@eastriding.gov.uk

Senior Management: Mr Malcolm Sims, Director of Corporate Resources, County Hall, Beverley HU17 9BA ☎ 01482 393000 🖷 01482 393009 malcolm.sims@eastriding.gov.uk

Access Officer / Social Services (Disability): Mr Derek Newton, Performance Manager - Adult Care Management, County Hall, Beverley HU17 9BA ☎ 01482 396442 derek.newton@eastriding.gov.uk

Architect, Building / Property Services: Mr Dave Waudby, Head of Infrastructure & Facilities, County Hall, Beverley HU17 9BA ☎ 01482 395800 🖷 01482 395063 dave.waudby@eastriding.gov.uk

Best Value: Mr Simon Laurie, VFM & Commissioning Manager, County Hall, Beverley HU17 9BA ☎ 01482 391480 🖷 01482 391405 simon.laurie@eastriding.gov.uk

Building Control: Mr Chris Ducker, Buidling Control & Sustainable Construction Manager, County Hall, Beverley HU17 9BA ☎ 01482 393810 🖷 01482 393779 chris.ducker@eastriding.gov.uk

Catering Services: Mr Alan Woods, Catering Service Manager, County Hall, Beverley HU17 9BA ☎ 01482 395121 alan.woods@eastriding.gov.uk

Children / Youth Services: Mrs Alison Michalska, Director of Children, Family & Adult Services, County Hall, Beverley HU17 9BA ☎ 01482 392000 🖷 01482 392102 alison.michalska@eastriding.gov.uk

Children / Youth Services: Mr John Wilson, Assistant Director of Children & Young People Services, County Hall, Beverley HU17 9BA ☎ 01482 392050 🖷 01482 392102 johnf.wilson@eastriding.gov.uk

Civil Registration: Ms Patricia Mann, Superintendent Registrar, Walkergate House, Beverley HU17 9BP ☎ 01482 393601 🖷 01482 873414 patricia.mann@eastriding.gov.uk

PR / Communications: Ms Lisa Mansell, Press Manager & Editor, County Hall, Beverley HU17 9BA ☎ 01482 391440 lisa.mansell@eastriding.gov.uk

Community Planning: Mr Carl Duck, Local Strategic Partnership Manager, County Hall, Beverley HU17 9BA ☎ 01482 391424 🖷 01482 391409 carl.duck@eastriding.gov.uk

Community Safety: Mr Max Hough, Crime & Disorder Reduction Manager, County Hall, Beverley HU17 9BA ☎ 01482 391016 max.hough@eastriding.gov.uk

Computer Management: Mr Michael Jackson, Corporate ICT Manager, County Hall, Beverley HU17 9BA ☎ 01482 394560 michael.jackson@eastriding.gov.uk

Consumer Protection and Trading Standards: Mr Colin Briggs, Trading Standards Services Manager, County Hall, Beverley HU17 9BA ☎ 01482 396238 colin.briggs@eastriding.gov.uk

Contracts: Mr Dave Morley, Head of Support & Procurement Services Manager, County Hall, Beverley HU17 9BA ☎ 01482 395101 dave.morley@eastriding.gov.uk

Corporate Services: Mr Malcolm Sims, Director of Corporate Resources, County Hall, Beverley HU17 9BA ☎ 01482 393000 🖷 01482 393009 malcolm.sims@eastriding.gov.uk

Customer Service: Ms Amanda Wilde, Customer Service Strategy & Liaison Manager, County Hall, Beverley HU17 9BA ☎ 01482 393360 amanda.wilde@eastriding.gov.uk

Economic Development: Mr Paul Bell, Head of Economic Development, County Hall, Beverley HU17 9BA ☎ 01482 391610 paul.bell@eastriding.gov.uk

Education: Mr Mike Furbank, Head of Achievement & Learning, County Hall, Beverley HU17 9BA ☎ 01482 392402 mike.furbank@eastriding.gov.uk

E-Government: Mr Michael Jackson, Corporate ICT Manager, County Hall, Beverley HU17 9BA ☎ 01482 394560 michael.jackson@eastriding.gov.uk

Electoral Registration: Ms Helena Coates, Democratic Services Manager, County Hall, Beverley HU17 9BA ☎ 01482 393210 🖷 01482 393319 helena.coates@eastriding.gov.uk

Emergency Planning: Mr Alan Bravey, Emergency Planning Manager, County Hall, Beverley HU17 9BA ☎ 01482 393050 🖷 01482 393059 alan.bravey@eastriding.gov.uk

Energy Management: Ms Karen Williamson, Strategic Investment & Development Manager, County Hall, Beverley HU17 9BA ☎ 01482 393907 🖷 01482 393990 karen.williamson@eastriding.gov.uk

Environmental / Technical Services: Mr John Skidmore, Head of Streetscene Services, County Hall, Beverley HU17 9BA ☎ 01482 395505 🖷 01482 391002 john.skidmore@eastriding.gov.uk

Estates, Property & Valuation: Mr John Read, Valuation & Estates Manager, County Hall, Beverley HU17 9BA ☎ 01482 393930 🖷 01482 391726 john.read@eastriding.gov.uk

European Liaison: Miss Claire Watts, External Funding & Policy Manager, County Hall, Beverley HU17 9BA ☎ 01482 391618 🖷 01482 391666 claire.watts@eastriding.gov.uk

Events Manager: Mr Paul Roggeman, Conference & Events Manager, County Hall, Beverley HU17 9BA ☎ 01482 391668 paul.roggeman@eastriding.gov.uk

Facilities: Mr Darren Stevens, Head of Culture & Information, County Hall, Beverley HU17 9BA ☎ 01482 392500 🖷 01482

395052 ✉ darren.stevens@eastriding.gov.uk

Finance and Treasurer: Mrs Caroline Lacey, Head of Finance, County Hall, Beverley HU17 9BA ☎ 01482 394100 ✉ caroline.lacey@eastriding.gov.uk

Fleet Management: Mr Nigel Rowe, Transportation Services Manager, Fleet Management Unit, Grovehill Road, Beverley HU17 0JP ☎ 01482 395501 🖷 01482 395054 ✉ nigel.rowe@eastriding.gov.uk

Grounds Maintenance: Mr Malcolm Sleight, Grounds Service Manager, County Hall, Beverley HU17 9BA ☎ 01482 395860 🖷 01482 395883 ✉ malcolm.sleight@eastriding.gov.uk

Health and Safety: Mr Garry Smith, Safety Services Manager, County Hall, Beverley HU17 9BA ☎ 01482 391110 ✉ garry.smith@eastriding.gov.uk

Highways: Mr Mike White, Group Manager Technical Services, County Hall, Beverley HU17 9BA ☎ 01482 395684 ✉ mike.white@eastriding.gov.uk

Home Energy Conservation: Mrs Jane Mears, Senior Environmental Health Officer, Town Hall, Quay Road, Bridlington YO16 4LT ☎ 01482 396278 🖷 01482 396103 ✉ jane.mears@eastriding.gov.uk

Housing: Mr Richard Ikin, Housing Services Group Manager, County Hall, Beverley HU17 9BA ☎ 01482 396120 🖷 01482 396102 ✉ dick.ikin@eastriding.gov.uk

Housing Maintenance: Mr Sid Coates, Housing Maintenance Unit Manager, 1st Floor, Beverley Depot, Annie Reed Road, Beverley HU17 0LE ☎ 01482 395817 ✉ sid.coates@eastriding.gov.uk

Legal: Mr Mathew Buckley, Head of Legal & Democratic Services, County Hall, Beverley HU17 9BA ☎ 01482 393100 🖷 01482 393103 ✉ mathew.buckley@eastriding.gov.uk

Legal: Mr Tom Spencer, Litigation & Regulatory Services Manager, County Hall, Beverley HU17 9BA ☎ 01482 393135 ✉ thomas.spencer@eastriding.gov.uk

Leisure and Cultural Services: Mr Darren Stevens, Head of Culture & Information, County Hall, Beverley HU17 9BA ☎ 01482 392500 🖷 01482 395052 ✉ darren.stevens@eastriding.gov.uk

Licensing: Ms Tina Holtby, Licensing Manager, County Hall, Beverley HU17 9BA ☎ 01482 396291 ✉ tina.holtby@eastriding.gov.uk

Lifelong Learning: Mr Mike Furbank, Head of Achievement & Learning, County Hall, Beverley HU17 9BA ☎ 01482 392402 ✉ mike.furbank@eastriding.gov.uk

Lighting: Mr Iain Ferguson, Lighting Engineer, County Hall, Beverley HU17 9BA ☎ 01482 395645 🖷 01482 395060 ✉ iain.ferguson@eastriding.gov.uk

Lottery Funding, Charity and Voluntary: Mr Simon Lowe, Policy & Partnerships Manager, County Hall, Beverley HU17 9BA ☎ 01482 391422 🖷 01482 391409 ✉ simon.lowe@eastriding.gov.uk

Member Services: Ms Helena Coates, Democratic Services Manager, County Hall, Beverley HU17 9BA ☎ 01482 393210 🖷 01482 393319 ✉ helena.coates@eastriding.gov.uk

Parking: Mrs Paula Danby, Service Manager, Beverley Depot, Annie Reed Road, Beverley HU17 0LF ☎ 01482 395570 ✉ paula.danby@eastriding.gov.uk

Partnerships: Mrs Ann Woodward, Head of Performance & Strategic Partnerships, County Hall, Beverley HU17 9BA ☎ 01482 391420 🖷 01482 391409 ✉ ann.woodward@eastriding.gov.uk

Personnel / HR: Mr David Smith, Head of Human Resources, County Hall, Beverley HU17 9BA ☎ 01482 391100 🖷 01482 393009 ✉ david.smith@eastriding.gov.uk

Planning: Mr Pete Ashcroft, Head of Planning & Development Management, County Hall, Beverley HU17 9BA ☎ 01482 393700 🖷 01482 393779 ✉ pete.ashcroft@eastriding.gov.uk

Procurement: Mr Chris Allison, Procurement Manager, County Hall, Beverley HU17 9BA ☎ 01482 395104 🖷 01482 395096 ✉ chris.allison@eastriding.gov.uk

Procurement: Mr Dave Morley, Head of Support & Procurement Services Manager, County Hall, Beverley HU17 9BA ☎ 01482 395101 ✉ dave.morley@eastriding.gov.uk

Public Libraries: Ms Libby Herbert, Libraries, Archives & Museums Service Manager, Council Offices, Main Road, Skirlaugh, Hull HU11 5HN ☎ 01482 392701 ✉ libby.herbert@eastriding.gov.uk

Recycling & Waste Minimisation: Mr John Skidmore, Head of Streetscene Services, County Hall, Beverley HU17 9BA ☎ 01482 395505 🖷 01482 391002 ✉ john.skidmore@eastriding.gov.uk

Regeneration: Ms Sue Lang, Regeneration & Funding Group Manager, County Hall, Beverley HU17 9BA ☎ 01482 391617 🖷 01482 391666 ✉ sue.lang@eastriding.gov.uk

Road Safety: Mr Dave Waudby, Head of Infrastructure & Facilities, County Hall, Beverley HU17 9BA ☎ 01482 395800 🖷 01482 395063 ✉ dave.waudby@eastriding.gov.uk

Social Services: Mrs Alison Michalska, Director of Children, Family & Adult Services, County Hall, Beverley HU17 9BA ☎ 01482 392000 🖷 01482 392102 ✉ alison.michalska@eastriding.gov.uk

Social Services (Adult): Ms Rosy Pope, Head of Adult Services, County Hall, Beverley HU17 9BA ☎ 01482 396400 🖷 01482 396003 ✉ rosy.pope@eastriding.gov.uk

Social Services (Children): Ms Pam Allen, Head of Children & Young People's Support & Safeguarding Services, County Hall, Room AF37, Beverley HU17 9BA ☎ 01482 396404 🖷 01482

396003 pam.allen@eastriding.gov.uk

Staff Training: Mrs Tina Tate, Training & Development Manager, Council Offices, Main Road, Skirlaugh, Beverley HU11 5HN ☎ 01482 391170 🖷 01482 391299 tina.tate@eastriding.gov.uk

Street Scene: Mr John Skidmore, Head of Streetscene Services, County Hall, Beverley HU17 9BA ☎ 01482 395505 🖷 01482 391002 john.skidmore@eastriding.gov.uk

Sustainable Communities: Mr David Renwick, Principal Sustainable Communities and Coast Officer, County Hall, Beverley HU17 9BA ☎ 01482 391720 🖷 01482 391726 david.renwick@eastriding.gov.uk

Sustainable Development: Mr David Renwick, Principal Sustainable Communities and Coast Officer, County Hall, Beverley HU17 9BA ☎ 01482 391720 🖷 01482 391726 david.renwick@eastriding.gov.uk

Tourism: Mr Andy Gray, Tourism Manager, Wykeland House, 47 Queen Street, Hull HU1 1UU ☎ 01482 486604 🖷 01482 391666 andy.gray@eastriding.gov.uk

Town Centre: Ms Sue Lang, Regeneration & Funding Group Manager, County Hall, Beverley HU17 9BA ☎ 01482 391617 🖷 01482 391666 sue.lang@eastriding.gov.uk

Traffic Management: Mr Mike White, Group Manager - Technical Services, Grove Hill Depot, 2nd Floor, Beverley HU17 0JP ☎ 01482 395684 mike.white@eastriding.gov.uk

Transport: Ms Paula Danby, Parking Manager, Annie Reed Road Depot Top Floor, Beverley HU17 0LF ☎ 01482 395570 paula.danby@eastriding.gov.uk

Transport: Mr Nigel Rowe, Transportation Services Manager, Annie Reed Road, 1st Floor, Beverley HU17 0JP ☎ 01482 395501 🖷 01482 395054 nigel.rowe@eastriding.gov.uk

Transport Planner: Mr Ian Burnett, Strategic Transport Planning Manager, County Hall, Room AS67, Beverley HU17 9BA ☎ 01482 391744 🖷 01482 393990 ian.burnett@eastriding.gov.uk

Waste Management: Mr John Skidmore, Head of Streetscene Services, County Hall, Beverley HU17 9BA ☎ 01482 395505 🖷 01482 391002 john.skidmore@eastriding.gov.uk

Children's Play Areas: Ms Louise Adams, Sport, Play & Arts Service Manager, County Hall, Beverley HU17 9BA ☎ 01482 392520 louise.adams@eastriding.gov.uk

MEMBERS OF THE COUNCIL (67)

Leader of the Council: **Parnaby**, Stephen (CON - Beverley Rural)
councillor.parnaby@eastriding.gov.uk

Abraham, Julie (CON - South Hunsley)
julie@mjabraham.karoo.co.uk

Aird, Elaine (CON - St Marys)
councillor.aird@eastriding.gov.uk

Allerston, Raymond (SD - Bridlington Old Town)

Barrett, John (CON - Snaith Airmyn and Rawcliffe and Marshlands)
councillor.barrett@eastriding.gov.uk

Bayram, Charlie (CON - Howden)
cbayram@cbayram.karoo.co.uk

Birmingham, Bradley (CON - Beverley Rural)
councillor.birmingham@eastriding.gov.uk

Boatman, Mally (LAB - Goole South)
councillor.boatman@eastriding.gov.uk

Bryan, Mike (CON - South West Holderness)
councillor.bryan@eastriding.gov.uk

Burton, Andy (CON - Wolds Weighton)
cllr.burton@googlemail.com

Burton, Richard (CON - Bridlington Central and Old Town)
richardrockville@aol.com

Chadwick, Chad (CON - Bridlington South)
chad61@tesco.net

Chadwick, Margaret (CON - Bridlington South)
chad61@tesco.net

Chapman, Margaret (CON - East Wolds and Coastal)
margaret173@btinternet.com

Charis, Irene (CON - St Marys)
councillor.charis@eastriding.gov.uk

Cracknell, Jackie (CON - South East Holderness)
councillor.cracknell@eastriding.gov.uk

Davison, Philip (LD - Hessle)
philnliz@philnliz.karoo.co.uk

Dennis, John (CON - South West Holderness)
councillor.dennis@eastriding.gov.uk

Elvidge, David (CON - Minster and Woodmansey)
councillor.elvidge@eastriding.gov.uk

Engall, Doreen (CON - Howdenshire)
councillor.engall@eastriding.gov.uk

Evans, Nicholas (CON - Howdenshire)
councillor.evans@eastriding.gov.uk

Evison, Jane (CON - East Wolds and Coastal)
janeevison@btinternet.com

Finlay, Shelagh (LAB - Bridlington South)
councillor.finaly@eastriding.gov.uk

Fox, Caroline (CON - Snaith Airmyn and Rawcliffe and Marshlands)
carolineF071@aol.com

Fraser, Symon (CON - Driffield and Rural)
symon.fraser@farmline.com

Galbraith, Tony (CON - Dale)
tony@galbraith1.karoo.co.uk

Gilmour, Helen (CON - South Hunsley)
helen@gilmourco.karoo.co.uk

Green, Helen (CON - Cottingham South)
councillor.green@eastriding.gov.uk

Grove, Matthew (CON - Mid Holderness)
m.grove@cssyorkshire.com

Hall, Barbara (CON - Driffield and Rural)
cllr.bhall@yahoo.co.uk

Hardy, Mary-Rose (LD - Tranby)
maryrosehardy@hotmail.co.uk

Harold, Kerri (CON - Minster and Woodmansey)
kerri@westholmecars.karoo.co.uk

Harrap, Richard (CON - Bridlington North)
councillor.harrap@eastriding.gov.uk

Head, Josie (IND - Goole North)
josiejoise10@sky.com

Hodgson, Arthur
(CON - South East Holderness)
councillor.hodgson@eastriding.gov.uk

Hogan, Paul (LAB - Hessle)
paul@mpdhogan.karoo.co.uk
Horton, Shaun (CON - Willerby and Kirk Ella)
cllr.shaunhorton@yahoo.co.uk
Hough, Kevan (CON - South East Holderness)
councillor.hough@eastriding.gov.uk
Hudson, Rita (CON - Dale)
councillor.hudson@eastriding.gov.uk
Ibson, Angela (CON - Willerby and Kirk Ella)
ibson.ibson@karoo.co.uk
Jefferies, Brian (LD - Hessle)
jefferies@jefferies.karoo.co.uk
Jefferson, Barbara (IND - North Holderness)
BYJefferson@aol.com
Jump, Ros (CON - Cottingham North)
councillor.jump@eastriding.gov.uk
Lane, Stephen (CON - Pocklington Provincial)
stephen.a.lane@btinternet.com
Mathieson, Geraldine (CON - Cottingham North)
cllr@mathieson1.karoo.co.uk
Matthews, Chris (CON - Bridlington North)
chris.matthews35@btinternet.com
Mole, Claude (CON - Pocklington Provincial)
allthemoles@aol.com
Moore, Keith (LAB - Goole North)
mookei440@aol.com
Newlove, Josh (LAB - Tranby)
councillor.newlove@tranbylabour.com
O'Neil, Pat (LAB - Goole South)
patricia.oneil1@btinternet.com
Owen, Jonathan (CON - East Wolds and Coastal)
jvg.owen@btopenworld.com
Peacock, Dominic (CON - Minster and Woodmansey)
councillor.peacock@eastriding.gov.uk
Pearson, Bryan (CON - St Marys)
councillor.pearson@eastriding.gov.uk
Pollard, Phyllis (CON - Beverley Rural)
phyllispollard1@gmail.com
Robinson, Paul (CON - Howdenshire)
cllrpaulrobinson@aol.com
Rudd, David (CON - Wolds Weighton)
davidrudd@btopenworld.com
Sharpe, Dee (CON - Wolds Weighton)
councillor.sharpe@eastriding.gov.uk
Skow, Brian (CON - Mid Holderness)
brian@skow.orangehome.co.uk
Slater, Lena (CON - Cottingham South)
councillor.slater@eastriding.gov.uk
Smith, Pat (CON - Dale)
smith36@smith36.karoo.co.uk
Suggit, Ann (IND - South West Holderness)
nicholasgate70@nicholasgate70.karoo.co.uk
Temple, Felicity (CON - Driffield and Rural)
felicity.temple@yahoo.com
Turner, Peter (CON - Mid Holderness)
peter@peterturner.karoo.co.uk
West, Kay (CON - Pocklington Provincial)
kaywestbb@hotmail.com
Whitehead, Michael (CON - Willerby and Kirk Ella)
councillor.whitehead@eastriding.gov.uk
Whittle, John (IND - North Holderness)
jwhittle@tiscali.co.uk
Wilkinson, John (CON - Bridlington North)
jaycee.wilkinson@btinternet.com

POLITICAL COMPOSITION
CON: 53, LAB: 6, IND: 4, LD: 3, SD: 1

CABINET
Leader / Key Strategic Issues: Mr S Parnaby
Deputy Leader / Performance Improvement & Partnerships: Mr J Owen
Adult & Carer Services: Mr Richard Harrap
Children, Young People & Local Authority Schools: Ms Julie Abraham
Civic Wellbeing & Culture: Mr Richard Burton
Community Partnerships: Ms Jackie Cracknell
Council Support Services: Mrs Margaret Chadwick
Economic Development, Tourism & Rural Issues: Ms Jane Evison
Environment, Housing & Planning: Mr Symon Fraser
Infrastructure, Highways & Emergency Planning: Mr Chris Matthews

COMMITTEE CHAIRS
Audit: Ms Barbara Jefferson
Licensing: Ms Angela Ibson
Pensions: Mr Chad Chadwick
Planning: Ms Phyllis Pollard
Standards: Ms Catherine Shannon (External)

EAST STAFFORDSHIRE D

East Staffordshire Borough Council, Town Hall, Burton-on-Trent DE14 2EB ☎ 01283 508000 🖷 01283 535412
firstname.lastname@eaststaffsbc.gov.uk
www.eaststaffsbc.gov.uk

FACTS & FIGURES
Police Authority: Staffordshire Police Authority
Health Authority: NHS West Midlands
Learning and Skills Council: West Midlands
Parliamentary Constituencies: Burton
EU Constituencies: West Midlands
Election Frequency: Elections are of whole council
Twinning: East Staffordshire: Kurdjali (Bulgaria); Lingen (Germany); Blantyre (Malawi); Elkhart (USA); Marchington: Neudrossenfeld (Bavaria); Uttoxeter: Raisdorf (Germany)

PRINCIPAL OFFICERS
Chief Executive: Mr Andy O'Brien, Chief Executive, The Maltsters, Wetmore Road, Burton-on-Trent DE14 1LS ☎ 01283 508300 🖷 01283 508388 andy.o'brien@eaststaffsbc.gov.uk

Senior Management: Mr Paul Costiff, Head of Built Environment, The Maltsters, Wetmore Road, Burton-on-Trent DE14 1LS ☎ 01283 505407 🖷 01283 508388
paul.costiff@eaststaffsbc.gov.uk

Senior Management: Mr David Duckitt, Head of Legal & Democratic Services, The Maltsters, Wetmore Road, Burton-on-Trent DE14 1LS ☎ 01283 508512 🖷 01283 508388
david.duckitt@eaststaffsbc.gov.uk

Senior Management: Mr Stephen Hinds, Head of Finance, The Maltsters, Wetmore Road, Burton-on-Trent DE14 1LS ☎ 01283

508305 🖷 01283 508388 ✉ stephen.hinds@eaststaffsbc.gov.uk

Senior Management: Mr Sal Khan, Head of Service Commissioning, The Maltsters, Wetmore Road, Burton-on-Trent DE14 1LS ☎ 01283 508674 🖷 01283 508388 ✉ sal.khan@eaststaffsbc.gov.uk

Senior Management: Mr Philip Somerfield, Head of Regulatory Services, The Maltsters, Wetmore Road, Burton-on-Trent DE14 1LS ☎ 01283 508622 🖷 01283 508388 ✉ philip.somerfield@eaststaffsbc.gov.uk

Building Control: Mr Geoff Sherratt, Building Control Manager, The Maltsters, Wetmore Road, Burton-on-Trent DE14 1LS ☎ 01283 508614 🖷 01283 508388 ✉ geoff.sherratt@eaststaffsbc.gov.uk

PR / Communications: Mr Chris Ebberley, Programmes & Information Manager, The Maltsters, Wetmore Road, Burton-on-Trent DE14 1LS ☎ 01283 508772 🖷 01283 508388 ✉ chris.ebberley@eaststaffsbc.gov.uk

Computer Management: Mr Guy Thornhill, Head of ICT, The Maltsters, Wetmore Road, Burton-on-Trent DE14 1LS ☎ 01283 504351 🖷 01283 508388 ✉ guy.thornhill@eaststaffsbc.gov.uk

Corporate Services: Mr Sal Khan, Head of Service Commissioning, The Maltsters, Wetmore Road, Burton-on-Trent DE14 1LS ☎ 01283 508674 🖷 01283 508388 ✉ sal.khan@eaststaffsbc.gov.uk

Customer Service: Mr Sal Khan, Head of Service Commissioning, The Maltsters, Wetmore Road, Burton-on-Trent DE14 1LS ☎ 01283 508674 🖷 01283 508388 ✉ sal.khan@eaststaffsbc.gov.uk

Economic Development: Mr Paul Costiff, Head of Built Environment, The Maltsters, Wetmore Road, Burton-on-Trent DE14 1LS ☎ 01283 505407 🖷 01283 508388 ✉ paul.costiff@eaststaffsbc.gov.uk

E-Government: Mr Sal Khan, Head of Service Commissioning, The Maltsters, Wetmore Road, Burton-on-Trent DE14 1LS ☎ 01283 508674 🖷 01283 508388 ✉ sal.khan@eaststaffsbc.gov.uk

Electoral Registration: Mr Peter Davies, Democratic Services & Resilience Manager, Town Hall, Burton-on-Trent DE14 2EB ☎ 01283 508309 🖷 01283 508388 ✉ peter.davies@eaststaffsbc.gov.uk

Emergency Planning: Mr Peter Davies, Democratic Services & Resilience Manager, Town Hall, Burton-on-Trent DE14 2EB ☎ 01283 508309 🖷 01283 508388 ✉ peter.davies@eaststaffsbc.gov.uk

Environmental / Technical Services: Mr Philip Somerfield, Head of Regulatory Services, The Maltsters, Wetmore Road, Burton-on-Trent DE14 1LS ☎ 01283 508622 🖷 01283 508388 ✉ philip.somerfield@eaststaffsbc.gov.uk

Environmental Health: Mr Philip Somerfield, Head of Regulatory Services, The Maltsters, Wetmore Road, Burton-on-Trent DE14 1LS ☎ 01283 508622 🖷 01283 508388 ✉ philip.somerfield@eaststaffbc.gov.uk

Facilities: Mr Ian Boam, Shared Services Centre Manager (H&S Facilities & Functions), Town Hall, Burton-on-Trent DE14 2EB ☎ 01283 508653 🖷 01283 508388 ✉ ian.boam@eaststaffsbc.gov.uk

Finance and Treasurer: Mr Stephen Hinds, Head of Finance, The Maltsters, Wetmore Road, Burton-on-Trent DE14 1LS ☎ 01283 508305 🖷 01283 508388 ✉ stephen.hinds@eaststaffsbc.gov.uk

Health and Safety: Mr Ian Boam, Shared Services Centre Manager (H&S Facilities & Functions), Town Hall, Burton-on-Trent DE14 2EB ☎ 01283 508653 🖷 01283 508388 ✉ ian.boam@eaststaffsbc.gov.uk

Housing: Mr Paul Costiff, Head of Built Environment, The Maltsters, Wetmore Road, Burton-on-Trent DE14 1LS ☎ 01283 505407 🖷 01283 508388 ✉ paul.costiff@eaststaffsbc.gov.uk

Legal: Ms Diane Passam, Legal Team Leader (Solicitor), The Maltsters, Wetmore Road, Burton-on-Trent DE14 1LS ☎ 01283 508386 🖷 01283 535412 ✉ diane.passam@eaststaffsbc.gov.uk

Leisure and Cultural Services: Mr Sal Khan, Head of Service Commissioning, The Maltsters, Wetmore Road, Burton-on-Trent DE14 1LS ☎ 01283 508674 🖷 01283 508388 ✉ sal.khan@eaststaffsbc.gov.uk

Licensing: Mr Philip Somerfield, Head of Regulatory Services, The Maltsters, Wetmore Road, Burton-on-Trent DE14 1LS ☎ 01283 508622 🖷 01283 508388 ✉ philip.somerfield@eaststaffsbc.gov.uk

Member Services: Mr Peter Davies, Democratic Services & Resilience Manager, Town Hall, Burton-on-Trent DE14 2EB ☎ 01283 508309 🖷 01283 508388 ✉ peter.davies@eaststaffsbc.gov.uk

Parking: Mr Philip Somerfield, Head of Regulatory Services, The Maltsters, Wetmore Road, Burton-on-Trent DE14 1LS ☎ 01283 508622 🖷 01283 508388 ✉ philip.somerfield@eaststaffbc.gov.uk

Partnerships: Mr Dean Piper, Enterprise & Partnerships Manager, The Maltsters, Wetmore Road, Burton-on-Trent DE14 1LS ☎ 01283 508893 🖷 01283 508388 ✉ dean.piper@eaststaffsbc.gov.uk

Personnel / HR: Mr Sal Khan, Head of Service Commissioning, The Maltsters, Wetmore Road, Burton-on-Trent DE14 1LS ☎ 01283 508674 🖷 01283 508388 ✉ sal.khan@eaststaffsbc.gov.uk

Planning: Mr Philip Somerfield, Head of Regulatory Services, The Maltsters, Wetmore Road, Burton-on-Trent DE14 1LS ☎ 01283 508622 🖷 01283 508388 ✉ philip.somerfield@eaststaffbc.gov.uk

Procurement: Mr Chris Ebberley, Programmes & Information

Manager, The Maltsters, Wetmore Road, Burton-on-Trent DE14 1LS ☎ 01283 508772 🖷 01283 508388 ✉ chris.ebberley@eaststaffsbc.gov.uk

Recycling & Waste Minimisation: Ms Amy Cunnington, Recycling Officer, The Maltsters, Wetmore Road, Burton-on-Trent DE14 1LS ☎ 01283 508666 🖷 01283 508388 ✉ amy.cunnington@eaststaffsbc.gov.uk

Regeneration: Mr Paul Costiff, Head of Built Environment, The Maltsters, Wetmore Road, Burton-on-Trent DE14 1LS ☎ 01283 505407 🖷 01283 508388 ✉ paul.costiff@eaststaffsbc.gov.uk

Staff Training: Mr Sal Khan, Head of Service Commissioning, The Maltsters, Wetmore Road, Burton-on-Trent DE14 1LS ☎ 01283 508674 🖷 01283 508388 ✉ sal.khan@eaststaffsbc.gov.uk

Street Scene: Mr Paul Farrer, Environment Manager, Town Hall, Burton-on-Trent DE14 2EB ☎ 01283 505899 🖷 01283 508388 ✉ paul.farrer@eaststaffsbc.gov.uk

Sustainable Communities: Mr Peter Robinson, Climate Change & Adaptation Officer, The Maltsters, Wetmore Road, Burton-on-Trent DE14 1LS ☎ 01283 508483 🖷 01283 508388 ✉ peter.robinson@eaststaffsbc.gov.uk

Tourism: Mr Paul Costiff, Head of Built Environment, The Maltsters, Wetmore Road, Burton-on-Trent DE14 1LS ☎ 01283 505407 🖷 01283 508388 ✉ paul.costiff@eaststaffsbc.gov.uk

Waste Collection and Disposal: Mr Paul Farrer, Environment Manager, Town Hall, Burton-on-Trent DE14 2EB ☎ 01283 505899 🖷 01283 508388 ✉ paul.farrer@eaststaffsbc.gov.uk

Waste Management: Mr Paul Farrer, Environment Manager, Town Hall, Burton-on-Trent DE14 2EB ☎ 01283 505899 🖷 01283 508388 ✉ paul.farrer@eaststaffsbc.gov.uk

MEMBERS OF THE COUNCIL (39)

***Leader of the Council:* Grosvenor**, Richard (CON - Branston)
richard.grosvenor@eaststaffsbc.gov.uk
***Deputy Leader of the Council:* Peters**, Bernard (CON - Brizlincote)
bernard.peters@eaststaffsbc.gov.uk
Ackroyd, Patricia (CON - Branston)
patricia.ackroyd@eaststaffsbc.gov.uk
Andjelkovic, Sonia (LAB - Eton Park)
sonia.andjelkovic@eaststaffsbc.gov.uk
Bahague, Beryl (CON - Yoxall)
beryl.behague@eaststaffsbc.gov.uk
Ball, Peter (CON - Town)
peter.ball@eaststaffsbc.gov.uk
Barrett, Malcolm (CON - Town)
malcolm.barrett@eaststaffsbc.gov.uk
Birnie, Nathan (CON - Weaver)
nathan.birnie@eaststaffsbc.gov.uk
Blencowe, Martin (LAB - Heath)
martin.blencowe@eaststaffsbc.gov.uk
Bowering, Michael (CON - Branston)
michael.bowering@eaststaffsbc.gov.uk
Builth, Ken (LAB - Horninglow)
ken.builth@eaststaffsbc.gov.uk
Carlton, Rebecca (CON - Stretton)
rebecca.carlton@eaststaffsbc.gov.uk
Carruthers, Michael (LAB - Anglesey)
mick.carruthers@eaststaffsbc.gov.uk
Chaudhry, Ali (LAB - Anglesey)
ali.chaudhry@eaststaffsbc.gov.uk
Clarke, Ron (LAB - Eton Park)
ron.clarke@eaststaffsbc.gov.uk
Fellows, Jake (CON - Brizlincote)
jake.fellows@eaststaffsbc.gov.uk
Fitzpatrick, Michael (LAB - Stapenhill)
michael.fitzpatrick@eaststaffsbc.gov.uk
Fletcher, Dennis (LAB - Winshill)
dennis.fletcher@eaststaffsbc.gov.uk
Fowkes, Maggie (CON - Stretton)
maggie.fowkes@eaststaffsbc.gov.uk
Ganley, Bev (LAB - Shobnall)
beverley.ganley@eaststaffsbc.gov.uk
Ganley, William (LAB - Shobnall)
william.ganley@eaststaffsbc.gov.uk
Grier, Susan (LAB - Stapenhill)
susan.grier@eaststaffsbc.gov.uk
Hall, Greg (CON - Bagots)
greg.hall@eaststaffsbc.gov.uk
Hardwick, Robert (CON - Crown)
robert.hardwick@eaststaffsbc.gov.uk
Jessel, Julia (CON - Needwood)
julia.jessel@eaststaffsbc.gov.uk
Johnston, Bob (LAB - Horninglow)
robert.johnston@eaststaffsbc.gov.uk
Jones, Jacqui (CON - Needwood)
jacqui.jones@eaststaffsbc.gov.uk
Leese, David (CON - Winshill)
david.leese@eaststaffsbc.gov.uk
Legg, Alison (LAB - Stapenhill)
alison.legg@eaststaffsbc.gov.uk
Milner, Len (CON - Stretton)
len.milner@eaststaffsbc.gov.uk
Mott, Julian (LAB - Horninglow)
julian.mott@eaststaffsbc.gov.uk
North, Ian (LAB - Winshill)
ian.north@eaststaffsbc.gov.uk
Riley, Andrew (LAB - Heath)
andrew.riley@eaststaffsbc.gov.uk
Rodgers, Michael (LD - Burton)
michael.rodgers@eaststaffsbc.gov.uk
Smith, Chris (CON - Churnett)
chris.smith@eaststaffsbc.gov.uk
Smith, Stephen (CON - Tutbury and Outwoods)
stephen.smith@eaststaffsbc.gov.uk
Staples, Elizabeth (CON - Tutbury and Outwoods)
elizabeth.staples@eaststaffsbc.gov.uk
Toon, Beryl (CON - Rolleston on Dove)
beryl.toon@eaststaffsbc.gov.uk
Whittaker, Colin (CON - Abbey)
colin.whittaker@eaststaffsbc.gov.uk

POLITICAL COMPOSITION

CON: 22, LAB: 16, LD: 1

CABINET

Leader: Mr Richard Grosvenor
Deputy Leader / Built Environment: Mrs Julia Jessel
Corporate Services: Mr David Leese

Regulatory Services: Mr Robert Hardwick
Service Commissioning: Mr Bernard Peters

COMMITTEE CHAIRS

Audit: Mr Stephen Smith
Licensing: Mrs Patricia Ackroyd
Planning Applications: Mr David Brookes
Scrutiny Programme Board: Mr Colin Whittaker

EAST SUSSEX C

East Sussex County Council, County Hall, St Anne's Crescent, Lewes BN7 1UE ☎ 0345 6080190
💻 www.eastsussex.gov.uk

FACTS & FIGURES

Police Authority: Sussex Police Authority
Health Authority: South East Coast Strategic Health Authority
Learning and Skills Council: South East
Parliamentary Constituencies: Bexhill and Battle, Eastbourne, Hastings and Rye, Lewes, Wealden
EU Constituencies: South East
Election Frequency: Elections are of whole council
Twinning: Battle: St Valery sur Somme (France); Bexhill: Merris (France); Crowborough: Montargis (France), Horwich, Lancashire (UK); East Hoathly and Halland: Juziers (France); East Sussex: Essonne (France); Kreis Pinneberg (Germany); Forest Row: Milly-la-Foret (France); Hailsham: Gournay-En-Bray (France); Hastings: Béthune (France), Oudenaarde (Belgium), Dordrecht (Netherlands), Schwerte (Germany); Heathfield and Waldron: Forges-Les-Eaux (France); Hurst Green: Ellerhoop (Germany); Lewes: Blois (France),

PRINCIPAL OFFICERS

Chief Executive: Ms Becky Shaw, Chief Executive, County Hall, St Anne's Crescent, Lewes BN7 1SW ☎ 01273 481950 🖷 01273 483317 ✉ becky.shaw@eastsussex.gov.uk

Assistant Chief Executive: Mr Simon Hughes, Assistant Chief Executive, County Hall, St Anne's Crescent, Lewes BN7 1UE ☎ 01273 481193 ✉ simon.hughes@eastsussex.gov.uk

Senior Management: Mr Rupert Clubb, Director of Economy, Transport & Environment, County Hall, St Anne's Crescent , Lewes BN7 1SW ☎ 01273 482200 🖷 01273 479536 ✉ rupert.clubb@eastsussex.gov.uk

Senior Management: Mr Matt Dunkley, Director of Children's Services, PO Box 4, County Hall, St Anne's Crescent, Lewes BN7 1SW ☎ 01273 481316 ✉ matt.dunkley@eastsussex.gov.uk

Senior Management: Mr Keith Hinkley, Director of Adult Social Care, PO Box 5, County Hall, St Anne's Crescent, Lewes BN7 1SW ☎ 01273 481288 🖷 01273 481331 ✉ keith.hinkley@eastsussex.gov.uk

Access Officer / Social Services (Disability): Mr Keith Hinkley, Director of Adult Social Care, PO Box 5, County Hall, St Anne's Crescent, Lewes BN7 1SW ☎ 01273 481288 🖷 01273 481331 ✉ keith.hinkley@eastsussex.gov.uk

Architect, Building / Property Services: Mr John Morris, Assistant Director - Corporate Resources - Property, PO Box 3, County Hall, St Anne's Crescent , Lewes BN7 1SF ☎ 01273 482404 🖷 01273 481687 ✉ john.morris@eastsussex.gov.uk

Best Value: Mr Duncan Savage, Assistant Director - Audit & Performance, PO Box 3, County Hall, St Anne's Crescent, Lewes BN7 1SF ☎ 01273 482330 🖷 01273 482848 ✉ duncan.savage@eastsussex.gov.uk

Catering Services: Ms Jane Carter, Contracts Manager (Catering), PO Box 4, County Hall, St Anne's Crescent, Lewes BN7 1SG ☎ 01273 482513 🖷 01273 481261 ✉ j.carter@eastsussexcc.gov.uk

Children / Youth Services: Mr Matt Dunkley, Director of Children's Services, County Hall, St Anne's Crescent , Lewes BN7 1SW ☎ 01273 481316 ✉ matt.dunkley@eastsussex.gov.uk

PR / Communications: Mrs Lynn Evans, Head of Communications, County Hall, St Anne's Crescent, Lewes BN7 1SW ☎ 01273 481522 🖷 01273 474434 ✉ lynn.evans@eastsussex.gov.uk

Community Planning: Ms Sarah Dyde, Policy Manager (Equalities), County Hall, St Anne's Crescent, Lewes BN7 1UE ☎ 01273 481000 ✉ sarah.dyde@eastsussex.gov.uk

Computer Management: Ms Shirley Hamilton, Assistant Director ICT, PO Box 3, County Hall, St Anne's Crescent, Lewes BN7 1SF ☎ 01273 481197 🖷 01273 481485 ✉ shirley.hamilton@eastsussex.gov.uk

Consumer Protection and Trading Standards: Mr Brian Johnson, Head of Trading Standards, St Mary's House, 52 St Leonard's Road, Eastbourne BN7 1AKL ☎ 01323 463421 🖷 01323 418227 ✉ brian.johnson@eastsussex.gov.uk

Contracts: Ms Jane Carter, Contracts Manager (Catering), PO Box 4, County Hall, St Anne's Crescent, Lewes BN7 1SG ☎ 01273 482513 🖷 01273 481261 ✉ j.carter@eastsussexcc.gov.uk

Contracts: Ms Debbie Endersby, Head of Strategic Commissioning, County Hall, St Anne's Crescent, Lewes BN7 1UE ☎ 01273 481125 ✉ debbie.endersby@eastsussex.gov.uk

Corporate Services: Mr Sean Nolan, Director of Corporate Resources, County Hall, St Anne's Crescent, Lewes BN7 1SF ☎ 01273 481412 🖷 01273 482848 ✉ sean.nolan@eastsussex.gov.uk

Economic Development: Mr Kieran McNamara, Assistant Director - Economy & Community Services, PO Box 5, County Hall, St Anne's Crescent , Lewes BN7 1SW ☎ 01273 481268 🖷 01273 482023 ✉ kieran.mcnamara@eastsussex.gov.uk

Education: Mr Matt Dunkley, Director of Children's Services, County Hall, St Anne's Crescent , Lewes BN7 1SW ☎ 01273 481316 ✉ matt.dunkley@eastsussex.gov.uk

E-Government: Mr Sean Nolan, Director of Corporate Resources, County Hall, St Anne's Crescent, Lewes BN7 1SF ☎ 01273 481412 🖷 01273 482848 ✉ sean.nolan@eastsussex.gov.uk

LOCAL AUTHORITIES

Emergency Planning: Mr David Broadley, Interim Head of Emergency Planning, St Mary's House, 52 St Leonard's Road, Eastbourne BN21 3UU ☎ 01273 481458 🖷 01273 482582 ✉ david.broadley@eastsussex.gov.uk

Energy Management: Mr John Morris, Assistant Director - Corporate Resources - Property, PO Box 3, County Hall, St Anne's Crescent , Lewes BN7 1SF ☎ 01273 482404 🖷 01273 481687 ✉ john.morris@eastsussex.gov.uk

Environmental / Technical Services: Mr Nick Skelton, Head of Environmental Operations, County Hall, St Anne's Crescent, Lewes BN7 1UE ☎ 01273 481804 ✉ nick.skelton@eastsussex.gov.uk

Environmental / Technical Services: Mr Carl Valentine, Head of Environment, County Hall, St Anne's Crescent, Lewes BN7 1UE ☎ 01273 336199 🖷 01273 486934 ✉ carl.valentine@eastsussexcc.gov.uk

Estates, Property & Valuation: Mr John Morris, Assistant Director - Corporate Resources - Property, PO Box 3, County Hall, St Anne's Crescent , Lewes BN7 1SF ☎ 01273 482404 🖷 01273 481687 ✉ john.morris@eastsussex.gov.uk

European Liaison: Mr Kieran McNamara, Assistant Director - Economy & Community Services, PO Box 5, County Hall, St Anne's Crescent , Lewes BN7 1SW ☎ 01273 481268 🖷 01273 482023 ✉ kieran.mcnamara@eastsussex.gov.uk

Facilities: Mr Paul Barnard, Facilities Manager, PO Box 3, County Hall, St Anne's Crescent , Lewes BN7 1SF ☎ 01273 482120 ✉ paul.barnard@eastsussex.gov.uk

Finance and Treasurer: Mr Sean Nolan, Director of Corporate Resources, County Hall, St Anne's Crescent, Lewes BN7 1SF ☎ 01273 481412 🖷 01273 482848 ✉ sean.nolan@eastsussex.gov.uk

Fleet Management: Mr Richard Merrill, Fleet Management Officer, Ringmer Depot, The Broyle, Ringmer, BN8 5NP ☎ 01273 482933 ✉ richard.merrill@eastsussex.gov.uk

Health and Safety: Ms Judy Benoy, Senior Health & Safety Adviser, County Hall, St Anne's Crescent, Lewes BN7 1UE ☎ 01273 481227 ✉ judy.benoy@eastsussex.gov.uk

Highways: Mr Rupert Clubb, Director of Economy, Transport & Environment, County Hall, St Anne's Crescent , Lewes BN7 1SW ☎ 01273 482200 🖷 01273 479536 ✉ rupert.clubb@eastsussex.gov.uk

Local Area Agreement: Ms Becky Shaw, Chief Executive, County Hall, St Anne's Crescent, Lewes BN7 1SW ☎ 01273 481950 🖷 01273 483317 ✉ becky.shaw@eastsussex.gov.uk

Legal: Mr Philip Baker, Assistant Director - Legal & Democratic Services, County Hall, St Annes Crescent, Lewes BN7 1UN ☎ 01273 481564 ✉ philip.baker@eastsussex.gov.uk

Leisure and Cultural Services: Ms Sally Staples, Cultural Strategy Manager, County Hall, St Anne's Crescent, Lewes BN7 1UE ☎ 01273 481871 ✉ arts@eastsussex.gov.uk

Lighting: Mr Tony Pike, Finance & Policy Manager, County Hall, St Anne's Crescent, Lewes BN7 1UE ☎ 01273 482130 🖷 01273 479536 ✉ tony.pike@eastsussex.gov.uk

Member Services: Mr Andy Cottell, Democratic Services Manager, Room C3F County Hall, St Anne's Crescent, Lewes BN7 1SW ☎ 01273 481955 🖷 01273 481208 ✉ andy.cottell@eastsussex.gov.uk

Parking: Mr Brian Deval, Transport Strategy Promotions Officer, County Hall, St Anne's Crescent , Lewes BN7 1SW ☎ 01273 482134 ✉ brian.deval@eastsussex.gov.uk

Personnel / HR: Mr Leatham Green, Assistant Director of Personnel & Training, County Hall, St Anne's Crescent, Lewes BN7 1UE ☎ 01273 481415 ✉ leatham.green@eastsussex.gov.uk

Planning: Mr Rupert Clubb, Director of Economy, Transport & Environment, County Hall, St Anne's Crescent , Lewes BN7 1SW ☎ 01273 482200 🖷 01273 479536 ✉ rupert.clubb@eastsussex.gov.uk

Planning: Mr Tony Cook, Head of Planning, C Floor, West Block, County Hall, Lewes BN7 1UE ☎ 01273 481653 ✉ tony.cook@eastsussex.gov.uk

Procurement: Mr Chris Andrews, Acting Corporate Procurement Team Manager, PO Box 3, County Hall, St Anne's Crescent, Lewes BN7 1SF ☎ 01273 481737 🖷 01273 481485 ✉ chris.andrews@eastsussex.gov.uk

Public Libraries: Dr Irene Campbell, Assistant Director - Libraries, Culture & Community Learning, County Hall, St Anne's Crescent , Lewes BN7 1SW ☎ 01273 481347 🖷 01273 481716 ✉ irene.campbell@eastsussex.gov.uk

Recycling & Waste Minimisation: Ms Michelle Erskine, Maternity Cover - Recycling Officer, County Hall, St Anne's Crescent, Lewes BN7 1UE ☎ 01273 482144 ✉ michelle.erskine@eastsussex.gov.uk

Regeneration: Mr Kieran McNamara, Assistant Director - Economy & Community Services, PO Box 5, County Hall, St Anne's Crescent , Lewes BN7 1SW ☎ 01273 481268 🖷 01273 482023 ✉ kieran.mcnamara@eastsussex.gov.uk

Road Safety: Mr Andy Cook, Team Leader - Transport Strategy, County Hall, St Anne's Crescent, Lewes BN7 1UE ☎ 01273 482263 🖷 01273 479536 ✉ andy.cook@eastsussex.gov.uk

Social Services: Mr Keith Hinkley, Director of Adult Social Care, PO Box 5, County Hall, St Anne's Crescent, Lewes BN7 1SW ☎ 01273 481288 🖷 01273 481331 ✉ keith.hinkley@eastsussex.gov.uk

Social Services (Adult): Mr Mark Stainton, Assistant Director - Adult Social Care - Operations, PO Box 5, County Hall, St Anne's Crescent , Lewes BN7 1SW ☎ 01273 481238 🖷 01273 481331 ✉ mark.stainton@eastsussex.gov.uk

Social Services (Children): Ms Liz Rugg, Assistant Director - Children & Families Services, PO Box 4, County Hall, St Anne's

Crescent, Lewes BN7 1SG ☎ 01273 481274 🖷 01273 481331 ✉ liz.rugg@eastsussex.gov.uk

Social Services (Children): Mr Douglas Sinclair, Head of Children's Safeguards & Quality Assurance, County Hall, St Anne's Crescent, Lewes BN7 1UE ☎ 01273 481289 ✉ douglas.sinclair@eastsussex.gov.uk

Staff Training: Ms Niki Sharp, Lead ICT Training Consultant, County Hall, St Anne's Crescent, Lewes BN7 1UE ☎ 01273 481836 ✉ niki.sharp@eastsussex.gov.uk

Sustainable Communities: Ms Becky Shaw, Chief Executive, County Hall, St Anne's Crescent, Lewes BN7 1SW ☎ 01273 481950 🖷 01273 483317 ✉ becky.shaw@eastsussex.gov.uk

Sustainable Development: Mr Rupert Clubb, Director of Transport & Environment, County Hall, St Anne's Crescent, Lewes BN7 1UE ☎ 01273 4822000 🖷 01273 479536 ✉ rupert.clubb@eastsussex.gov.uk

Sustainable Development: Mr Carl Valentine, Head of Environment, County Hall, St Anne's Crescent, Lewes BN7 1UE ☎ 01273 336199 🖷 01273 486934 ✉ carl.valentine@eastsussexcc.gov.uk

Traffic Management: Mr Rupert Clubb, Director of Economy, Transport & Environment, County Hall, St Anne's Crescent , Lewes BN7 1SW ☎ 01273 482200 🖷 01273 479536 ✉ rupert.clubb@eastsussex.gov.uk

Transport: Mr Rupert Clubb, Director of Economy, Transport & Environment, County Hall, St Anne's Crescent , Lewes BN7 1SW ☎ 01273 482200 🖷 01273 479536 ✉ rupert.clubb@eastsussex.gov.uk

Transport: Mr Brian Deval, Transport Strategy Promotions Officer, County Hall, St Anne's Crescent, Lewes BN7 1UE ☎ 01273 482134 ✉ brian.deval@eastsussex.gov.uk

Transport: Mr Roger Williams, Head of Highways, County Hall, St Anne's Crescent, Lewes BN7 1UE ☎ 01273 481000 ✉ roger.williams@eastsussex.gov.uk

Waste Collection and Disposal: Mr Rupert Clubb, Director of Economy, Transport & Environment, County Hall, St Anne's Crescent , Lewes BN7 1SW ☎ 01273 482200 🖷 01273 479536 ✉ rupert.clubb@eastsussex.gov.uk

Waste Management: Mr Rupert Clubb, Director of Economy, Transport & Environment, County Hall, St Anne's Crescent , Lewes BN7 1SW ☎ 01273 482200 🖷 01273 479536 ✉ rupert.clubb@eastsussex.gov.uk

MEMBERS OF THE COUNCIL (49)

***Chair:* Dowling**, Chris (CON - Framfield and Horam)
cllr.chris.dowling@eastsussex.gov.uk

***Vice-Chair:* Lock**, Matthew (CON - Hastings - St Helen's and Silverhill)
cllr.matthew.lock@eastsussex.gov.uk

***Leader of the Council:* Jones**, Peter (CON - Northern Rother)
cllr.peter.jones@eastsussexcc.gov.uk

***Deputy Leader of the Council:* Glazier**, Keith (CON - Rye and Eastern Rother)
cllr.keith.glazier@eastsussex.gov.uk

***Group Leader:* Shing**, Stephen (IND - Polegate, Willingdon & East Dean)
cllr.stephen.shing@eastsussex.gov.uk

***Group Leader:* Tutt**, David (LD - Eastbourne - St Anthony's)
cllr.david.tutt@eastsussex.gov.uk

***Group Leader:* Webb**, Trevor (LAB - Hastings - Central St Leonards & Gensing)
cllr.trevor.webb@eastsussex.gov.uk

Barnes, John (CON - Rother North West)
Cll.john.barnes@eastsussex.gov.uk

Belsey, Colin (CON - Eastbourne - Ratton)
Cllr.Colin.Belsey@eastsussex.gov.uk

Bennett, Nick (CON - Alfriston, East Hoathly & Hellingly)
Cllr.Nick.Bennett@eastsussex.gov.uk

Bentley, Bill (CON - Hailsham and Herstmonceux)
cllr.bill.bentley@eastsussexcc.gov.uk

Birch, Jeremy (LAB - Hastings - Old Hastings & Tressell)
cllr.jeremy.birch@eastsussex.gov.uk

Daniel, Godfrey (LAB - Hastings - Braybrooke & Castle)
cllr.godfrey.daniel@eastsussex.gov.uk

Elkin, David (CON - Eastbourne - Sovereign)
cllr.david.elkin@eastsussex.gov.uk

Ensor, Michael (CON - Bexhill King Offa)
Cllr.michael.ensor@eastsussex.gov.uk

Fawthrop, Terry (CON - Hastings - Baird & Ore)
Cllr.Terry.Fawthrop@eastsussex.gov.uk

Field, Kathryn (LD - Battle and Crowhurst)
cllr.kathryn.field@eastsussex.gov.uk

Freebody, Tony (CON - Pevensey & Westham)
Cllr.Tony.Freebody@eastsussex.gov.uk

Freeman, Jon (LD - Seaford Blatchington)
cllr.jon.freeman@eastsussex.gov.uk

Gadd, Brian (CON - Bexhill West)
cllr.brian.gadd@eastsussex.gov.uk

Harris, Jon (LD - Eastbourne - Langney)
cllr.jon.harris@eastsussex.gov.uk

Healy, Beryl (LD - Eastbourne - Devonshire)
cllr.beryl.healy@eastsussex.gov.uk

Heaps, Carolyn (LD - Eastbourne - Old Town)
Cllr.Carolyn.Heaps@eastsussex.gov.uk

Howson, Phil (CON - Peacehaven and Telscombe Towns)
cllr.phillip.howson@eastsussexcc.gov.uk

Hughes, Joy (CON - Bexhill King Offa)
Cllr.Joy.Hughes@eastsussex.gov.uk

Kenward, Martin (CON - Bexhill East)
Cllr.Martin.Kenward@eastsussex.gov.uk

Lambert, Carolyn (LD - Seaford Sutton)
Cllr.Carolyn.Lambert@eastsussex.gov.uk

Livings, John (CON - Peacehaven and Telscombe Towns)
cllr.john.livings@eastsussex.gov.uk

Maynard, Carl (CON - Brede Valley and Marsham)
cllr.carl.maynard@eastsussexcc.gov.uk

O'Keeffe, Ruth (IND - Lewes)
cllr.ruth.o'keefe@eastsussexcc.gov.uk

Ost, Pat (LD - Ouse Valley East)
cllr.thomas.ost@eastsussexcc.gov.uk

Pragnell, Peter (CON - Hastings - Ashdown & Conquest)
Cllr.Peter.Pragnell@eastsussex.gov.uk

Reid, Tony (CON - Buxted Maresfield)
cllr.anthony.reid@eastsussex.gov.uk

Rodohan, Pat (LD - Eastbourne - Upperton)
Cllr.Pat.Rodohan@eastsussex.gov.uk

Rogers, David (LD - Newhaven and Ouse Valley West)
cllr.david.rogers@eastsussex.gov.uk
Scott, Philip (LAB - Hastings - Hollington & Wishing Tree)
cllr.phil.scott@eastsussex.gov.uk
Shing, Daniel (IND - Polegate, Willingdon & East Dean)
Cllr.Daniel.Shing@eastsussex.gov.uk
Simmons, Rupert (CON - Heathfield)
cllr.rupert.simmons@eastsussex.gov.uk
Sparks, Paul (LD - Uckfield)
cllr.paul.sparks@eastsussexcc.gov.uk
St Pierre, Rosalyn (LD - Ringmer and Lewes Bridge)
cllr.rosalyn.stpierre@eastsussexcc.gov.uk
Stogdon, Richard (CON - Crowborough)
cllr.richard.stogdon@eastsussexcc.gov.uk
Stroude, Meg (CON - Chailey)
cllr.meg.stroude@eastsussex.gov.uk
Taylor, Barry (CON - Eastbourne - Meads)
cllr.barry.taylor@eastsussex.gov.uk
Thomas, Roger (CON - Hailsham and Hertsmonceux)
cllr.roger.thomas@eastsussexcc.gov.uk
Thompson, Mike (LD - Eastbourne - Hampden Park)
Cllr.Mike.Thompson@eastsussex.gov.uk
Tidy, Sylvia (CON - Crowborough)
cllr.sylvia.tidy@eastsussexcc.gov.uk
Tidy, Robert (CON - Wadhurst)
cllr.bob.tidy@eastsussex.gov.uk
Waite, Joy (CON - Hastings - Maze Hill and West St Leonards)
cllr.joy.waite@eastsussex.gov.uk
Whetstone, Francis (CON - Forest Row)
cllr.francis.whetstone@eastsussex.gov.uk

POLITICAL COMPOSITION

CON: 29, LD: 13, LAB: 4, IND: 3

CABINET

Leader / Strategic Management & Economic Development: Mr Peter Jones
Deputy Leader / Community & Resources: Mr Keith Glazier
Adult Social Care: Mr Bill Bentley
Children's & Adults' Services: Mr David Elkin
Children & Families: Mr Colin Belsey
Economy, Transport & Environment: Mr Carl Maynard
Learning & School Effectiveness: Mr Nick Bennett

COMMITTEE CHAIRS

Adult Social Care & Community Safety (Scrutiny): Mr Peter Pragnell
Audit, Best Value & Community Services (Scrutiny): Mr Paul Sparks
Children's Services (Scrutiny): Mr Michael Ensor
Economy, Transport & Environment (Scrutiny): Mr Richard Stogdon
Governance: Mr Peter Jones
Pension Fund Investment Panel: Mr Tony Reid
Planning: Mr Godfrey Daniel
Regulatory: Mr Terry Fawthrop

EASTBOURNE D

Eastbourne Borough Council, 1 Grove Road, Eastbourne BN21 4TW ☎ 01323 415000 🖷 01323 415130
enquiries@eastbourne.gov.uk www.eastbourne.gov.uk

FACTS & FIGURES

Police Authority: Sussex Police Authority
Health Authority: South East Coast Strategic Health Authority
Learning and Skills Council: South East
Parliamentary Constituencies: Eastbourne
EU Constituencies: South East
Election Frequency: Elections are of whole council

PRINCIPAL OFFICERS

Chief Executive: Mr Robert Cottrill, Chief Executive, 1 Grove Road, Eastbourne BN21 4TW ☎ 01323 415046 🖷 01323 430745 robert.cottrill@eastbourne.gov.uk

Assistant Chief Executive: Mr Julian Osgathorpe, Deputy Chief Executive, 1 Grove Road, Eastbourne BN21 4TW ☎ 01323 415008 julian.osgathorpe@eastbourne.gov.uk

Architect, Building / Property Services: Mr Henry Branson, Head of Infrastructure, 1 Grove Road, Eastbourne BN21 4TW ☎ 01323 41555 henry.branson@eastbourne.gov.uk

Best Value: Mr William Tompsett, Policy & Performance Officer, 1 Grove Road, Eastbourne BN21 4TW ☎ 01323 415418 william.tompsett@eastbourne.gov.uk

Building Control: Mr Jefferson Collard, Senior Head of Development & Environment, 68 Grove Road, Eastbourne BN21 4UH ☎ 01323 415252 🖷 01323 641842 jeff.collard@eastbourne.gov.uk

PR / Communications: Mrs Annie Wills, Tourism Manager, 1 Grove Road, Eastbourne BN21 4TW ☎ 01323 415410 annie.wills@eastbourne.gov.uk

Community Planning: Mr Ian Fitzpatrick, Senior Head of Community, 1 Grove Road, Eastbourne BN21 4TW ☎ 01323 415935 ian.fitzpatrick@eastbourne.gov.uk

Community Safety: Mr Ian Fitzpatrick, Senior Head of Community, 1 Grove Road, Eastbourne BN21 4TW ☎ 01323 415935 ian.fitzpatrick@eastbourne.gov.uk

Computer Management: Mr Henry Branson, Head of Infrastructure, 1 Grove Road, Eastbourne BN21 4TW ☎ 01323 41555 henry.branson@eastbourne.gov.uk

Contracts: Miss Diane Linsdell, Strategic Projects Co-ordinator, 1 Grove Road, Eastbourne BN21 4TW ☎ 01323 415143 🖷 01323 439558 diane.linsdell@eastbourne.gov.uk

Customer Service: Mr Ian Fitzpatrick, Senior Head of Community, 1 Grove Road, Eastbourne BN21 4TW ☎ 01323 415935 ian.fitzpatrick@eastbourne.gov.uk

Economic Development: Ms Kerry Band, Economic Development Officer, 1 Grove Road, Eastbourne BN21 4TW ☎ 01323 415054 kerry.band@eastbourne.gov.uk

Economic Development: Mr Jefferson Collard, Senior Head of Development & Environment, 1 Grove Road, Eastbourne BN21 4TW ☎ 01323 415252 🖷 01323 641842 jeff.collard@eastbourne.gov.uk

Economic Development: Mrs Penny Shearer, Economic Development Manager, 1 Grove Road, Eastbourne BN21 4TW ☎ 01323 415030 🖷 01323 439407 🖰 penny.shearer@eastbourne.gov.uk

E-Government: Mr Henry Branson, Head of Infrastructure, 1 Grove Road, Eastbourne BN21 4TW ☎ 01323 41555 🖰 henry.branson@eastbourne.gov.uk

Electoral Registration: Mr Peter Finnis, Head of Strategy & Democracy, 1 Grove Road, Eastbourne BN21 4TW ☎ 01323 415003 🖷 01323 410322 🖰 peter.finnis@eastbourne.gov.uk

Electoral Registration: Mrs Tracey Pannett, Electoral Services Manager, Town Hall, Grove Road, Eastbourne BN21 4UG ☎ 01323 415074 🖰 tracey.pannett@eastbourne.gov.uk

Emergency Planning: Mr Peter Finnis, Head of Strategy & Democracy, Town Hall, Grove Road, Eastbourne BN21 4UG ☎ 01323 415003 🖷 01323 410322 🖰 peter.finnis@eastbourne.gov.uk

Environmental Health: Mr Jefferson Collard, Senior Head of Development & Environment, 1 Grove Road, Eastbourne BN21 4TW ☎ 01323 415252 🖷 01323 641842 🖰 jeff.collard@eastbourne.gov.uk

Environmental Health: Mrs Sue Oliver, Environmental Health and Amenities Manager, 1 Grove Road, Eastbourne BN21 4TW ☎ 01323 415360 🖷 01323 415997 🖰 sue.oliver@eastbourne.gov.uk

Estates, Property & Valuation: Mr Henry Branson, Head of Infrastructure, 1 Grove Road, Eastbourne BN21 4TW ☎ 01323 41555 🖰 henry.branson@eastbourne.gov.uk

European Liaison: Mr Jefferson Collard, Senior Head of Development & Environment, 1 Grove Road, Eastbourne BN21 4TW ☎ 01323 415252 🖷 01323 641842 🖰 jeff.collard@eastbourne.gov.uk

European Liaison: Mrs Penny Shearer, Economic Development Manager, 1 Grove Road, Eastbourne BN21 4TW ☎ 01323 415030 🖷 01323 439407 🖰 penny.shearer@eastbourne.gov.uk

Events Manager: Mr Mike Marchant, Events Development Manager, 1 Grove Road, Eastbourne BN21 4TW ☎ 01323 415407 🖰 mike.marchant@eastbourne.gov.uk

Facilities: Mr Jefferson Collard, Senior Head of Development & Environment, 68 Grove Road, Eastbourne BN21 4UH ☎ 01323 415252 🖷 01323 641842 🖰 jeff.collard@eastbourne.gov.uk

Finance and Treasurer: Mr Alan Osborne, Chief Finance Officer, 1 Grove Road, Eastbourne BN21 4TW ☎ 01323 415149 🖰 alan.osborne@eastbourne.gov.uk

Grounds Maintenance: Mr Mike Smith, Downland, Trees & Woodland Manager, 1 Grove Road, Eastbourne BN21 4TW ☎ 01323 415273 🖷 01323 641842 🖰 mike.smith@eastbourne.gov.uk

Grounds Maintenance: Mr Gareth Williams, Parks & Gardens Manager, 1 Grove Road, Eastbourne BN21 4TW ☎ 01323 415281 🖷 01323 641842 🖰 gareth.williams@eastbourne.gov.uk

Health and Safety: Mr Jefferson Collard, Senior Head of Development & Environment, 68 Grove Road, Eastbourne BN21 4UH ☎ 01323 415252 🖷 01323 641842 🖰 jeff.collard@eastbourne.gov.uk

Health and Safety: Mrs Sue Oliver, Environmental Health and Amenities Manager, 1 Grove Road, Eastbourne BN21 4TW ☎ 01323 415360 🖷 01323 415997 🖰 sue.oliver@eastbourne.gov.uk

Home Energy Conservation: Mr Nick Adlam, Energy Efficiency Officer, 1 Grove Road, Eastbourne BN21 4TW ☎ 01323 415963 🖰 nick.adlam@eastbourne.gov.uk

Housing: Mr Ian Fitzpatrick, Senior Head of Community, 1 Grove Road, Eastbourne BN21 4TW ☎ 01323 415935 🖰 ian.fitzpatrick@eastbourne.gov.uk

Local Area Agreement: Mr Jefferson Collard, Senior Head of Development & Environment, 1 Grove Road, Eastbourne BN21 4TW ☎ 01323 415252 🖷 01323 641842 🖰 jeff.collard@eastbourne.gov.uk

Legal: Mr Peter Finnis, Head of Strategy & Democracy, 1 Grove Road, Eastbourne BN21 4TW ☎ 01323 415003 🖷 01323 410322 🖰 peter.finnis@eastbourne.gov.uk

Legal: Alice Rowland, Lawyer to the Council (Jobshare), 1 Grove Road, Eastbourne BN21 4TW ☎ 01323 410000 🖰 alice.rowland@eastbourne.gov.uk

Legal: Ms Victoria Simpson, Lawyer to the Council (Jobshare), 1 Grove Road, Eastbourne BN21 4TW ☎ 01323 410000 🖰 victoria.simpson@eastbourne.gov.uk

Leisure and Cultural Services: Mrs Tracey McNulty, Senior Head of Tourism & Leisure, 1 Grove Road, Eastbourne BN21 4TW ☎ 01323 415432 🖰 tracey.mcnulty@eastbourne.gov.uk

Licensing: Mr Jefferson Collard, Senior Head of Development & Environment, 1 Grove Road, Eastbourne BN21 4TW ☎ 01323 415252 🖷 01323 641842 🖰 jeff.collard@eastbourne.gov.uk

Licensing: Ms Kareen Plympton, Licensing Manager, 1 Grove Road, Eastbourne BN21 4TW ☎ 01323 415937 🖷 01323 415997 🖰 kareen.plympton@eastbourne.gov.uk

Member Services: Mr David Robinson, Member Services Manager, 1 Grove Road, Eastbourne BN21 4TW ☎ 01323 415022 🖷 01323 410322 🖰 david.robinson@eastbourne.gov.uk

Parking: Mr Jefferson Collard, Senior Head of Development & Environment, 1 Grove Road, Eastbourne BN21 4TW ☎ 01323 415252 🖷 01323 641842 🖰 jeff.collard@eastbourne.gov.uk

Partnerships: Mr Ian Fitzpatrick, Senior Head of Community, 1 Grove Road, Eastbourne BN21 4TW ☎ 01323 415935 🖰 ian.fitzpatrick@eastbourne.gov.uk

Planning: Mr Jefferson Collard, Senior Head of Development & Environment, 1 Grove Road, Eastbourne BN21 4TW ☎ 01323 415252 🖷 01323 641842 ✉ jeff.collard@eastbourne.gov.uk

Procurement: Mr Peter MacCabe, Purchasing Officer, 1 Grove Road, Eastbourne BN21 4TW ☎ 01323 415463 ✉ purchasing@eastbourne.gov.uk

Recycling & Waste Minimisation: Mr Jefferson Collard, Senior Head of Development & Environment, 1 Grove Road, Eastbourne BN21 4TW ☎ 01323 415252 🖷 01323 641842 ✉ jeff.collard@eastbourne.gov.uk

Recycling & Waste Minimisation: Mr Paul Marsden, Cleansing Manager, 1 Grove Road, Eastbourne BN21 4TW ☎ 01323 415278 🖷 01323 641842 ✉ paul.marsden@eastbourne.gov.uk

Regeneration: Mr Jefferson Collard, Senior Head of Development & Environment, 1 Grove Road, Eastbourne BN21 4TW ☎ 01323 415252 🖷 01323 641842 ✉ jeff.collard@eastbourne.gov.uk

Regeneration: Mrs Penny Shearer, Economic Development Manager, 1 Grove Road, Eastbourne BN21 4TW ☎ 01323 415030 🖷 01323 439407 ✉ penny.shearer@eastbourne.gov.uk

Staff Training: Ms Elaine Wyatt, Resourcing & Development Manager, Town Hall, Grove Road, Eastbourne BN21 4UG ☎ 01323 415005 🖷 01323 410322 ✉ elaine.wyatt@eastbourne.gov.uk

Street Scene: Mr Jefferson Collard, Senior Head of Development & Environment, 1 Grove Road, Eastbourne BN21 4TW ☎ 01323 415252 🖷 01323 641842 ✉ jeff.collard@eastbourne.gov.uk

Sustainable Communities: Mr Ian Fitzpatrick, Senior Head of Community, 1 Grove Road, Eastbourne BN21 4TW ☎ 01323 415935 ✉ ian.fitzpatrick@eastbourne.gov.uk

Sustainable Development: Ms Kerry Band, Economic Development Officer, 1 Grove Road, Eastbourne BN21 4TW ☎ 01323 415054 ✉ kerry.band@eastbourne.gov.uk

Tourism: Mrs Tracey McNulty, Senior Head of Tourism & Leisure, 68 Grove Road, Eastbourne BN21 4UG ☎ 01323 415432 ✉ tracey.mcnulty@eastbourne.gov.uk

Tourism: Mrs Annie Wills, Tourism Manager, 1 Grove Road, Eastbourne BN21 4TW ☎ 01323 415410 ✉ annie.wills@eastbourne.gov.uk

Town Centre: Mr Chris Richards, Town Centre Manager, 1 Grove Road, Eastbourne BN21 4TW ☎ 01323 415413 🖷 01323 439407 ✉ chris.richards@eastbourne.gov.uk

Waste Collection and Disposal: Mr Paul Marsden, Cleansing Manager, 1 Grove Road, Eastbourne BN21 4TW ☎ 01323 415278 🖷 01323 641842 ✉ paul.marsden@eastbourne.gov.uk

Waste Management: Mr Paul Marsden, Cleansing Manager, 1 Grove Road, Eastbourne BN21 4TW ☎ 01323 415278 🖷 01323 641842 ✉ paul.marsden@eastbourne.gov.uk

MEMBERS OF THE COUNCIL (28)

***Mayor:* Heaps**, Carolyn (LD - Old Town)
***Deputy Mayor:* Thompson**, Mike (LD - Hampden Park)
***Leader of the Council:* Tutt**, David (LD - St Anthony's)
***Deputy Leader of the Council:* Mattock**, Gill (LD - St Anthony's)
***Group Leader:* Elkin**, David (CON - Meads)
Meads: Vacant
Bannister, Margaret (LD - Devonshire)
Belsey, Colin (CON - Ratton)
Coles, Janet (LD - Old Town)
councillor.coles@eastbourne.gov.uk
Cooke, Alun (CON - Upperton)
councillor.cooke@eastbourne.gov.uk
Ede, Philip (CON - Sovereign)
councillor.ede@eastbourne.gov.uk
Harris, Jon (LD - St Anthony's)
Hearn, Pat (LD - Hampden Park)
councillor.hearn@eastbourne.gov.uk
Howlett, Sandie (CON - Ratton)
Jenkins, Gordon (CON - Sovereign)
councillor.jenkins@eastbourne.gov.uk
Liddiard, Tom (CON - Upperton)
councillor.liddiard@eastbourne.gov.uk
Miah, Harun (LD - Langney)
Murdoch, Colin (CON - Ratton)
Murdoch, Colin (CON - Ratton)
councillor.murdoch@eastbourne.gov.uk
Murray, Jim (LD - Hampden Park)
councillor.murray@eastbourne.gov.uk
Shuttleworth, Alan (LD - Langney)
councillor.shuttleworth@eastbourne.gov.uk
Stanley, Neil (LD - Devonshire)
Taylor, Barry (CON - Meads)
Tester, Troy (LD - Langney)
Ungar, John (LD - Old Town)
councillor.ungar@eastbourne.gov.uk
Wallis, Steven (LD - Devonshire)
Warner, Patrick (CON - Sovereign)
councillor.warner@eastbourne.gov.uk
West, Annabelle (CON - Upperton)
councillor.west@eastbourne.gov.uk

POLITICAL COMPOSITION

LD: 15, CON: 12, Vacant: 1

CABINET

Leader / Community Strategy & Local Strategic Partnership: Mr David Tutt
Deputy Leader / Financial Services: Ms Gill Mattock
Commercial & Recreational Services: Mr Neil Stanley
Core Support & Strategic Services: Mr Troy Tester
Direct Assistance Services: Cllr Margaret Bannister
Place Services: Mr Steven Wallis

COMMITTEE CHAIRS

Audit: Cllr John Ungar
Licensing: Mr Mike Thompson
Planning: Cllr John Ungar

EASTLEIGH D

Eastleigh Borough Council, Civic Offices, Leigh Road, Eastleigh SO50 9YN ☎ 023 8068 8000 🖷 023 8064 3952 ✉ boroughcouncil@eastleigh.gov.uk 💻 www.eastleigh.gov.uk

FACTS & FIGURES

Police Authority: Hampshire Police Authority
Health Authority: South Central Strategic Health Authority
Learning and Skills Council: South East
Parliamentary Constituencies: Eastleigh
EU Constituencies: South East
Election Frequency: Elections are by thirds
Twinning: Kornwestheim (Germany); Villeneuve-St; Georges (France)

PRINCIPAL OFFICERS

Chief Executive: Ms Bernie Topham, Chief Executive, Civic Offices, Leigh Road, Eastleigh SO50 9YN ☎ 023 8068 8101 🖷 023 8061 1528 ✉ bernie.topham@eastleigh.gov.uk

Senior Management: Mr Alex Parmley, Corporate Director, Civic Offices, Leigh Road, Eastleigh SO50 9YN ☎ 023 8068 8305 🖷 023 8061 1528 ✉ alex.parmley@eastleigh.gov.uk

Senior Management: Mr Nick Tustian, Corporate Director/ Chief Financial Officer, Civic Offices, Leigh Road, Eastleigh SO50 9YN ☎ 023 8068 8003 🖷 023 8064 3952 ✉ nick.tustian@eastleigh.gov.uk

Architect, Building / Property Services: Mr Paul Ramshaw, Head - Regeneration & Planning Policy, Civic Offices, Leigh Road, Eastleigh SO50 9YN ☎ 023 8068 8132 ✉ paul.ramshaw@eastleigh.gov.uk

Best Value: Mr Vince Johnston, Performance & Development Manager, Civic Offices, Leigh Road, Eastleigh SO50 9YN ☎ 023 8068 8000 🖷 023 8064 3952 ✉ vince.johnston@eastleigh.gov.uk

Building Control: Mr Neil Ferris, Head - Building Control, Civic Offices, Leigh Road, Eastleigh SO50 9YN ☎ 023 8068 8272 🖷 023 8064 3952 ✉ neil.ferris@eastleigh.gov.uk

PR / Communications: Mr Steve Collins, Communications Officer, Civic Offices, Leigh Road, Eastleigh SO50 9YN ☎ 023 8068 8135 🖷 023 8061 1528 ✉ steve.collins@eastleigh.gov.uk

Community Planning: Ms Helen Coleman, Health & Community Team Manager, Civic Offices, Leigh Road, Eastleigh SO50 9YN ☎ 023 8068 8017 🖷 023 8068 8257 ✉ helen.coleman@eastleigh.gov.uk

Community Safety: Mr Peter Baldry, Head - Community Safety, Civic Offices, Leigh Road, Eastleigh SO50 9YN ☎ 023 8068 8000 ✉ peter.baldry@eastleigh.gov.uk

Computer Management: Ms Jasvir Chohan, Head - Customer Services & ICT, Civic Offices, Leigh Road, Eastleigh SO50 9YN ☎ 023 8068 8070 🖷 023 8064 3952 ✉ jasvir.chohan@eastleigh.gov.uk

Customer Service: Ms Jessica Mendez, Customer Services Manager, Civic Offices, Leigh Road, Eastleigh SO50 9YN ☎ 023 8068 8000 ✉ jessica.mendez@eastleigh.gov.uk

Direct Labour: Mrs Gail Grant, Head - Direct Services, Contract Services, Botley Road, Hedge End, Eastleigh SO30 2RA ☎ 023 8068 8370 🖷 01489 789146 ✉ gail.grant@eastleigh.gov.uk

Economic Development: Mrs Teresa Smith, Economic Development Officer, Civic Offices, Leigh Road, Eastleigh SO50 9YN ☎ 023 8068 8405 🖷 023 8064 3952 ✉ teresa.smith@eastleigh.gov.uk

Electoral Registration: Mrs Samantha Jones, Elections Officer, Civic Offices, Leigh Road, Eastleigh SO50 9YN ☎ 023 8068 8201 🖷 023 8064 3952 ✉ sam.jones@eastleigh.gov.uk

Emergency Planning: Mr David Pollard, Emergency Planning Officer, Civic Offices, Leigh Road, Eastleigh SO50 9YN ☎ 023 8068 8234 🖷 023 8064 3952 ✉ david.pollard@eastleigh.gov.uk

Energy Management: Ms Judith Beard, Sustainability & Policy Co-ordinator, Civic Offices, Leigh Road, Eastleigh SO50 9YN ☎ 023 8068 8085 ✉ judith.beard@eastleigh.gov.uk

Estates, Property & Valuation: Mr Paul Phillips, Regeneration & Planning Policy Officer, Civic Offices, Leigh Road, Eastleigh SO50 9YN ☎ 023 8068 8000 ✉ paul.phillips@eastleigh.gov.uk

European Liaison: Mrs Teresa Smith, Economic Development Officer, Civic Offices, Leigh Road, Eastleigh SO50 9YN ☎ 023 8068 8405 🖷 023 8064 3952 ✉ teresa.smith@eastleigh.gov.uk

Facilities: Mrs Jennifer Filer, Facilities Manager, Civic Offices, Leigh Road, Eastleigh SO50 9YN ☎ 023 8068 8000 🖷 023 8064 3952 ✉ jennifer.filer@eastleigh.gov.uk

Finance and Treasurer: Mrs Loraine Radford, Head - Revenue & Benefits, Civic Offices, Leigh Road, Eastleigh SO50 9YN ☎ 023 8068 8000 ✉ loraine.radford@eastleigh.gov.uk

Finance and Treasurer: Mr Nick Tustian, Corporate Director/ Chief Financial Officer, Civic Offices, Leigh Road, Eastleigh SO50 9YN ☎ 023 8068 8003 🖷 023 8064 3952 ✉ nick.tustian@eastleigh.gov.uk

Fleet Management: Mrs Gail Grant, Head - Direct Services, Contract Services, Botley Road, Hedge End, Eastleigh SO30 2RA ☎ 023 8068 8370 🖷 01489 789146 ✉ gail.grant@eastleigh.gov.uk

Grounds Maintenance: Mr Paul Naylor, Streetscene Manager, Civic Offices, Leigh Road, Eastleigh SO50 9YN ☎ 023 8065 0970 ✉ paul.naylor@eastleigh.gov.uk

Health and Safety: Ms Phillippa Banner, Corporate Health & Safety Officer, Civic Offices, Leigh Road, Eastleigh SO50 9YN ☎ 023 8068 8358 🖷 023 8064 3952 ✉ philippa.banner@eastleigh.gov.uk

Home Energy Conservation: Ms Judith Beard, Sustainability & Policy Co-ordinator, Civic Offices, Leigh Road, Eastleigh SO50 9YN ☎ 023 8068 8085 ✉ judith.beard@eastleigh.gov.uk

Housing: Mr Nick James, Senior Housing Advisor, Civic Offices, Leigh Road, Eastleigh SO50 9YN ☎ 023 8068 8326 ✉ nick.james@oxford.gov.uk ()

Legal: Mr Richard Ward, Head - Legal & Democratic Services, Civic Offices, Leigh Road, Eastleigh SO50 9YN ☎ 023 8068 8103 🖷 023 8064 3952 ✉ richard.ward@eastleigh.gov.uk

Leisure and Cultural Services: Mrs Julia Birt, Sport & Active Lifestyles Manager, Civic Offices, Leigh Road, Eastleigh SO50 9YN ☎ 023 8068 8000 ✉ julia.birt@eastleigh.gov.uk

Licensing: Mr Richard Ward, Head - Legal & Democratic Services, Civic Offices, Leigh Road, Eastleigh SO50 9YN ☎ 023 8068 8103 🖷 023 8064 3952 ✉ richard.ward@eastleigh.gov.uk

Lottery Funding, Charity and Voluntary: Mrs Cheryl Butler, Head - Culture, Civic Offices, Leigh Road, Eastleigh SO50 9YN ☎ 023 8068 8187 🖷 023 8064 3952 ✉ cheryl.butler@eastleigh.gov.uk

Member Services: Mr Jon Brown, Head - Democratic Services, Civic Offices, Leigh Road, Eastleigh SO50 9YN ☎ 023 8068 8000 🖷 023 8064 3952 ✉ jon.brown@eastleigh.gov.uk

Parking: Mr Wayne Bailey, Parking Services Manager, Civic Offices, Leigh Road, Eastleigh SO50 9YN ☎ 023 8068 8000 ✉ wayne.bailey@eastleigh.gov.uk

Personnel / HR: Mrs Melanie Swain, Head - Human Resources, Civic Offices, Leigh Road, Eastleigh SO50 9YN ☎ 023 8068 8141 ✉ melanie.swain@eastleigh.gov.uk

Planning: Ms Caroline Thomas, Head - Development Control, Civic Offices, Leigh Road, Eastleigh SO50 9YN ☎ 023 8068 8248 🖷 023 8064 3952 ✉ caroline.thomas@eastleigh.gov.uk

Procurement: Mrs Jennifer Filer, Facilities Manager, Civic Offices, Leigh Road, Eastleigh SO50 9YN ☎ 023 8068 8000 🖷 023 8064 3952 ✉ jennifer.filer@eastleigh.gov.uk

Recycling & Waste Minimisation: Mrs Angela Taylor, Waste & Recyling Team Leader, Contract Services, Botley Road, Hegde End, Eastleigh SO30 2RA ☎ 023 8068 8000 🖷 01489 789146 ✉ angela.taylor@eastleigh.gov.uk

Regeneration: Mr Paul Ramshaw, Head - Regeneration & Planning Policy, Civic Offices, Leigh Road, Eastleigh SO50 9YN ☎ 023 8068 8132 ✉ paul.ramshaw@eastleigh.gov.uk

Staff Training: Mrs Melanie Swain, Head - Human Resources, Civic Offices, Leigh Road, Eastleigh SO50 9YN ☎ 023 8068 8141 ✉ melanie.swain@eastleigh.gov.uk

Street Scene: Mr Paul Naylor, Streetscene Manager, Civic Offices, Leigh Road, Eastleigh SO50 9YN ☎ 023 8065 0970 ✉ paul.naylor@eastleigh.gov.uk

Sustainable Development: Ms Judith Beard, Sustainability & Policy Co-ordinator, Civic Offices, Leigh Road, Eastleigh SO50 9YN ☎ 023 8068 8085 ✉ judith.beard@eastleigh.gov.uk

Traffic Management: Mr Stuart Robinson-Woledge, Traffic &Transport Sevices Manager, Civic Offices, Leigh Road, Eastleigh SO50 9YN ☎ 023 8068 8229 🖷 023 8068 3952 ✉ stuart.robinson-woledge@eastleigh.gov.uk

Transport: Mr Ed Vokes, Head - Transportation & Engineering, Civic Offices, Leigh Road, Eastleigh SO50 9YN ☎ 023 8068 8234 🖷 023 8064 3952 ✉ ed.vokes@eastleigh.gov.uk

Waste Collection and Disposal: Mr Colin Ellis, Senior Inspector/ Refuse Collection, Contract Services, Botley Road, Hedge End, Eastleigh SO30 2RA ☎ 023 8068 8000 🖷 01489 789146 ✉ colin.ellis@eastleigh.gov.uk

Waste Management: Mr Colin Ellis, Senior Inspector/ Refuse Collection, Contract Services, Botley Road, Hedge End, Eastleigh SO30 2RA ☎ 023 8068 8000 🖷 01489 789146 ✉ colin.ellis@eastleigh.gov.uk

MEMBERS OF THE COUNCIL (44)

***Mayor:* Kyrle**, Rupert (LD - Botley)
rupert.kyrle@eastleigh.gov.uk

***Deputy Mayor:* Cross**, Malcolm (LD - Hamble-le-Rice and Butlocks Heath)
malcolm.cross@eastleigh.gov.uk

***Leader of the Council:* House**, Keith (LD - Hedge End Wildern)
keith.house@eastleigh.gov.uk

***Deputy Leader of the Council:* Winstanley**, Anne (LD - Bishopstoke West)
anne.winstanley@eastleigh.gov.uk

***Group Leader:* Olson**, Godfrey (CON - Hiltingbury East)
godfrey.olson@eastleigh.gov.uk

Airey, David (LD - Netley Abbey)
david.airey@eastleigh.gov.uk

Bancroft, Simon (LD - Eastleigh Central)
simon.bancroft@eastleigh.gov.uk

Bicknell, Paul (LD - Eastleigh South)
paul.bicknell@eastleigh.gov.uk

Bloom, Louise (LD - Hedge End and Grange Park)
louise.bloom@eastleigh.gov.uk

Broadhurst, Alan (LD - Chandlers Ford West)
alan.broadhurst@eastleigh.gov.uk

Broadhurst, Haulwen (LD - Chandlers Ford East)
haulwen.broadhurst@eastleigh.gov.uk

Caldwell, John (CON - Hiltingbury East)
john.caldwell@eastleigh.gov.uk

Clarke, Daniel (LD - West End South)
daniel.clarke@eastleigh.gov.uk

Cossey, Andrew (LD - Fair Oak and Horton Heath)
andrew.cossey@eastleigh.gov.uk

Craig, Tonia (LD - Burlesden and Old Netley)
tonia.craig@eastleigh.gov.uk

Fraser, Cathie (LD - Botley)
cathie.fraser@eastleigh.gov.uk

Goodall, David (LD - West End South)
david.goodall@eastleigh.gov.uk

Grajewski, Judith (CON - Hiltingbury West)
judith.grajewski@eastleigh.gov.uk

Hamel, Suzy (LD - Hamble-le-Rice and Butlocks Heath)
suzy.hamel@eastleigh.gov.uk

Holden-Brown, Pamela (LD - Chandlers Ford East)
pamela.holden-brown@eastleigh.gov.uk

Holes, Steve (LD - Burlesdon and Old Netley)

steve.holes@eastleigh.gov.uk
Hughes, Michael (CON - Hiltingbury West)
michael.hughes@eastleigh.gov.uk
Hughes, Jenny (LD - Hedge End Wildern)
jenny.hughes@eastleigh.gov.uk
Hughes, Peter (LD - Hedge End St Johns)
peter.hughes@eastleigh.gov.uk
Irish, Wayne (LD - Eastleigh Central)
Mann, Darshan (LD - Eastleigh South)
darshan.mann@eastleigh.gov.uk
McNulty, Luke (LD - Netley Abbey)
luke.mcnulty@eastleigh.gov.uk
Mignot, Trevor (LD - Bishopstoke East)
trevor.mignot@eastleigh.gov.uk
Noyce, Tony (LD - West End North)
tony.noyce@eastleigh.gov.uk
O'Sullivan, Jane (LD - Bursledon and Old Netley)
jane.o'sullivan@eastleigh.gov.uk
Pragnell, David (LD - Chandlers Ford West)
david.pragnell@eastleigh.gov.uk
Pretty, Derek (LD - Hedge End and Grange Park)
derek.pretty@eastleigh.gov.uk
Roling, Angela (LD - Bishopstoke East)
angela.roling@eastleigh.gov.uk
Scott, Desmond (LD - Fair Oak and Horton Heath)
des.scott@eastleigh.gov.uk
Smith, Roger (LD - Fair Oak and Horton Heath)
roger.smith@eastleigh.gov.uk
Sollitt, Maureen (LD - Eastleigh North)
maureen.sollitt@eastleigh.gov.uk
Sollitt, Steve (LD - Eastleigh South)
steve.sollitt@eastleigh.gov.uk
Tennent, Bruce (LD - West End North)
bruce.tennent@eastleigh.gov.uk
Thomas, Chris (LD - Eastleigh North)
chris.thomas@eastleigh.gov.uk
Thornton, Michael (LD - Bishopstoke West)
michael.thornton@eastleigh.gov.uk
Trenchard, Keith (LD - Eastleigh Central)
keith.trenchard@eastleigh.gov.uk
Wall, Peter (LD - Eastleigh North)
peter.wall@eastleigh.gov.uk
Welsh, Jane (LD - Hedge End St Johns)
jane.welsh@eastleigh.gov.uk
Wheatley, Mick (LD - Hedge End St Johns)
mick.wheatley@eastleigh.gov.uk

POLITICAL COMPOSITION

LD: 40, CON: 4

CABINET

Leader / Regeneration & Resources: Mr Keith House
Deputy Leader / Housing & Customer Service: Ms Anne Winstanley
Business & Skills: Mr Peter Wall
Communities: Mr Roger Smith
Environment: Ms Louise Bloom
Health: Mrs Cathie Fraser
Leisure: Mr Alan Broadhurst
Transport & Streetscene: Mr David Airey

COMMITTEE CHAIRS

Audit & Resources: Mr Steve Holes
Licensing: Mr Peter Wall
Policy & Performance Scrutiny: Mrs Tonia Craig

EDEN — D

Eden District Council, Town Hall, Penrith CA11 7QF ☎ 01768 817817 🖷 01768 890470 ✉ customer.services@eden.gov.uk
🖳 www.eden.gov.uk

FACTS & FIGURES

Police Authority: Cumbria Police Authority
Health Authority: North West Strategic Health Authority
Learning and Skills Council: North West
Parliamentary Constituencies: Penrith and The Border, Westmorland and Lonsdale
EU Constituencies: North West
Election Frequency: Elections are of whole council
Twinning: Sister City- Penrith (NSW, Australia)

PRINCIPAL OFFICERS

Chief Executive: Mr Robin Hooper, Chief Executive, Town Hall, Penrith CA11 7QF ☎ 01768 212200 ✉ chief.exec@eden.gov.uk

Deputy Chief Executive: Mr Paul Foote, Director of Corporate & Legal Services, Town Hall, Penrith CA11 7QF ☎ 01768 212205 🖷 01768 890470 ✉ paul.foote@eden.gov.uk

Architect, Building / Property Services: Mr Adrian Cozens, Engineering Manager, Mansion House, Penrith CA11 7YG ☎ 01768 212448 ✉ adrian.cozens@eden.gov.uk

Architect, Building / Property Services: Mr Paul Foote, Director of Corporate & Legal Services, Town Hall, Penrith CA11 7QF ☎ 01768 212205 🖷 01768 890470 ✉ paul.foote@eden.gov.uk

Best Value: Mrs Ruth Atkinson, Communities Director, Mansion House, Penrith CA11 7YG ☎ 01768 212202 🖷 01768 890470 ✉ ruth.atkinson@eden.gov.uk

Building Control: Mrs Ruth Atkinson, Communities Director, Mansion House, Penrith CA11 7YG ☎ 01768 212202 🖷 01768 890470 ✉ ruth.atkinson@eden.gov.uk

Building Control: Mr Gwyn Clark, Head of Planning Services, Mansion House, Penrith CA11 7YG ☎ 01768 212388 🖷 01768 890732 ✉ gwyn.clark@eden.gov.uk

PR / Communications: Mr Barry Cooper, Communications Officer, Town Hall, Penrith CA11 7QF ☎ 01768 212137 🖷 01768 890470 ✉ barry.cooper@eden.gov.uk

PR / Communications: Mr Oliver Shimell, Communities Manager, Town Hall, Penrith CA11 7QF ☎ 01768 212143 ✉ oliver.shimell@eden.gov.uk

Community Planning: Mrs Ruth Atkinson, Communities Director, Mansion House, Penrith CA11 7YG ☎ 01768 212202 🖷 01768 890470 ✉ ruth.atkinson@eden.gov.uk

Community Planning: Ms Deborah Garnett, Senior Communities Officer, Mansion House, Penrith CA11 7YG ☎ 01768 212268 🖷 01768 890470 ✉ deborah.garnett@eden.gov.uk

Community Planning: Mr Oliver Shimell, Communities Manager, Town Hall, Penrith CA11 7QF ☎ 01768 212143 ✉ oliver.shimell@eden.gov.uk

Computer Management: Mr Ben Wright, IT Manager, Town Hall, Penrith CA11 7QF ☎ 01768 212206; 0845 050 4434 🖷 01768 890470; 01539 740300 ✉ ben.wright@eden.gov.uk; b.wright@southlakeland.gov.uk

Contracts: Mr Adrian Cozens, Engineering Manager, Mansion House, Penrith CA11 7YG ☎ 01768 212448 ✉ adrian.cozens@eden.gov.uk

Corporate Services: Mrs Linda Methven, Customer Services Manager, Town Hall, Penrith CA11 7QF ☎ 01768 212130 🖷 01768 890470 ✉ linda.methven@eden.gov.uk

Customer Service: Mrs Linda Methven, Customer Services Manager, Town Hall, Penrith CA11 7QF ☎ 01768 212130 🖷 01768 890470 ✉ linda.methven@eden.gov.uk

Economic Development: Mrs Ruth Atkinson, Communities Director, Mansion House, Penrith CA11 7YG ☎ 01768 212202 🖷 01768 890470 ✉ ruth.atkinson@eden.gov.uk

Economic Development: Mr Oliver Shimell, Communities Manager, Town Hall, Penrith CA11 7QF ☎ 01768 212143 ✉ oliver.shimell@eden.gov.uk

E-Government: Mr Ben Wright, IT Manager, Town Hall, Penrith CA11 7QF ☎ 01768 212206; 0845 050 4434 🖷 01768 890470; 01539 740300 ✉ ben.wright@eden.gov.uk; b.wright@southlakeland.gov.uk

Electoral Registration: Mr Paul Foote, Director of Corporate & Legal Services, Town Hall, Penrith CA11 7QF ☎ 01768 212205 🖷 01768 890470 ✉ paul.foote@eden.gov.uk

Electoral Registration: Mr Robin Hooper, Chief Executive, Town Hall, Penrith CA11 7QF ☎ 01768 212200 ✉ chief.exec@eden.gov.uk

Environmental Health: Mrs Ruth Atkinson, Communities Director, Mansion House, Penrith CA11 7YG ☎ 01768 212202 🖷 01768 890470 ✉ ruth.atkinson@eden.gov.uk

Environmental Health: Miss Julie Monk, Head of Environmental Services, Mansion House, Penrith CA11 7YG ☎ 01768 212328 ✉ julie.monk@eden.gov.uk

Estates, Property & Valuation: Mr Adrian Cozens, Engineering Manager, Mansion House, Penrith CA11 7YG ☎ 01768 212448 ✉ adrian.cozens@eden.gov.uk

Estates, Property & Valuation: Mr Paul Foote, Director of Corporate & Legal Services, Town Hall, Penrith CA11 7QF ☎ 01768 212205 🖷 01768 890470 ✉ paul.foote@eden.gov.uk

Events Manager: Mr Barry Cooper, Communications Officer, Town Hall, Penrith CA11 7QF ☎ 01768 212137 🖷 01768 890470 ✉ barry.cooper@eden.gov.uk

Events Manager: Mr Oliver Shimell, Communities Manager, Town Hall, Penrith CA11 7QF ☎ 01768 212143 ✉ oliver.shimell@eden.gov.uk

Facilities: Mr Adrian Cozens, Engineering Manager, Mansion House, Penrith CA11 7YG ☎ 01768 212448 ✉ adrian.cozens@eden.gov.uk

Facilities: Mr Paul Foote, Director of Corporate & Legal Services, Town Hall, Penrith CA11 7QF ☎ 01768 212205 🖷 01768 890470 ✉ paul.foote@eden.gov.uk

Finance and Treasurer: Mr David Rawsthorn, Director of Finance, Town Hall, Penrith CA11 7QF ☎ 01768 212211 🖷 01768 890470 ✉ david.rawsthorn@eden.gov.uk

Grounds Maintenance: Mr Adrian Cozens, Engineering Manager, Mansion House, Penrith CA11 7YG ☎ 01768 212448 ✉ adrian.cozens@eden.gov.uk

Grounds Maintenance: Mr Paul Foote, Director of Corporate & Legal Services, Town Hall, Penrith CA11 7QF ☎ 01768 212205 🖷 01768 890470 ✉ paul.foote@eden.gov.uk

Health and Safety: Mrs Ruth Atkinson, Communities Director, Mansion House, Penrith CA11 7YG ☎ 01768 212202 🖷 01768 890470 ✉ ruth.atkinson@eden.gov.uk

Health and Safety: Mrs Bibian McRoy, Human Resources Manager (Job Share), Town Hall, Penrith CA11 7QF ☎ 01768 212243 ✉ bibian.mcroy@eden.gov.uk

Health and Safety: Ms Claire Robinson, Environmental Health Officer (Food, Health & Safety), Mansion House, Penrith CA11 7YG ☎ 01768 212352 🖷 01768 890732 ✉ claire.robinson@eden.gov.uk

Highways: Mr Adrian Cozens, Engineering Manager, Mansion House, Penrith CA11 7YG ☎ 01768 212448 ✉ adrian.cozens@eden.gov.uk

Housing: Mrs Ruth Atkinson, Communities Director, Mansion House, Penrith CA11 7YG ☎ 01768 212202 🖷 01768 890470 ✉ ruth.atkinson@eden.gov.uk

Housing: Miss Julie Monk, Head of Environmental Services, Mansion House, Penrith CA11 7YG ☎ 01768 212328 ✉ julie.monk@eden.gov.uk

Legal: Mr Paul Foote, Director of Corporate & Legal Services, Town Hall, Penrith CA11 7QF ☎ 01768 212205 🖷 01768 890470 ✉ paul.foote@eden.gov.uk

Legal: Mr Christopher Potter, Legal Services Manager, Town Hall, Penrith CA11 7QF ☎ 01768 212249 🖷 01768 890470 ✉ christopher.potter@eden.gov.uk

Leisure and Cultural Services: Mrs Ruth Atkinson, Communities Director, Mansion House, Penrith CA11 7YG ☎ 01768 212202 🖷 01768 890470 ✉ ruth.atkinson@eden.gov.uk

Leisure and Cultural Services: Mr Oliver Shimell, Communities

Manager, Town Hall, Penrith CA11 7QF ☎ 01768 212143 ✉ oliver.shimell@eden.gov.uk

Licensing: Mr Paul Foote, Director of Corporate & Legal Services, Town Hall, Penrith CA11 7QF ☎ 01768 212205 🖷 01768 890470 ✉ paul.foote@eden.gov.uk

Licensing: Mr Christopher Potter, Legal Services Manager, Town Hall, Penrith CA11 7QF ☎ 01768 212249 🖷 01768 890470 ✉ christopher.potter@eden.gov.uk

Member Services: Mr Paul Foote, Director of Corporate & Legal Services, Town Hall, Penrith CA11 7QF ☎ 01768 212205 🖷 01768 890470 ✉ paul.foote@eden.gov.uk

Member Services: Mr Paul Foote, Director of Corporate & Legal Services, Town Hall, Penrith CA11 7QF ☎ 01768 212205 🖷 01768 890470 ✉ paul.foote@eden.gov.uk

Member Services: Mr Christopher Potter, Legal Services Manager, Town Hall, Penrith CA11 7QF ☎ 01768 212249 🖷 01768 890470 ✉ christopher.potter@eden.gov.uk

Parking: Mr Adrian Cozens, Engineering Manager, Mansion House, Penrith CA11 7YG ☎ 01768 212448 ✉ adrian.cozens@eden.gov.uk

Parking: Mr Paul Foote, Director of Corporate & Legal Services, Town Hall, Penrith CA11 7QF ☎ 01768 212205 🖷 01768 890470 ✉ paul.foote@eden.gov.uk

Partnerships: Mrs Ruth Atkinson, Communities Director, Mansion House, Penrith CA11 7YG ☎ 01768 212202 🖷 01768 890470 ✉ ruth.atkinson@eden.gov.uk

Partnerships: Mr Oliver Shimell, Communities Manager, Town Hall, Penrith CA11 7QF ☎ 01768 212143 ✉ oliver.shimell@eden.gov.uk

Personnel / HR: Mr Paul Foote, Director of Corporate & Legal Services, Town Hall, Penrith CA11 7QF ☎ 01768 212205 🖷 01768 890470 ✉ paul.foote@eden.gov.uk

Personnel / HR: Mrs Bibian McRoy, Human Resources Manager (Job Share), Town Hall, Penrith CA11 7QF ☎ 01768 212243 ✉ bibian.mcroy@eden.gov.uk

Planning: Mrs Ruth Atkinson, Communities Director, Mansion House, Penrith CA11 7YG ☎ 01768 212202 🖷 01768 890470 ✉ ruth.atkinson@eden.gov.uk

Planning: Mr Gwyn Clark, Head of Planning Services, Mansion House, Penrith CA11 7YG ☎ 01768 212388 🖷 01768 890732 ✉ gwyn.clark@eden.gov.uk

Procurement: Mr Clive Howey, Financial Services Manager, Town Hall, Penrith CA11 7QF ☎ 01768 212213 ✉ clive.howey@eden.gov.uk

Recycling & Waste Minimisation: Mr Paul Foote, Director of Corporate & Legal Services, Town Hall, Penrith CA11 7QF ☎ 01768 212205 🖷 01768 890470 ✉ paul.foote@eden.gov.uk

Recycling & Waste Minimisation: Ms Deborah Garnett, Senior Communities Officer, Mansion House, Penrith CA11 7YG ☎ 01768 212268 🖷 01768 890470 ✉ deborah.garnett@eden.gov.uk

Regeneration: Mrs Ruth Atkinson, Communities Director, Mansion House, Penrith CA11 7YG ☎ 01768 212202 🖷 01768 890470 ✉ ruth.atkinson@eden.gov.uk

Street Scene: Mrs Ruth Atkinson, Communities Director, Mansion House, Penrith CA11 7YG ☎ 01768 212202 🖷 01768 890470 ✉ ruth.atkinson@eden.gov.uk

Street Scene: Mr Oliver Shimell, Communities Manager, Town Hall, Penrith CA11 7QF ☎ 01768 212143 ✉ oliver.shimell@eden.gov.uk

Sustainable Communities: Mrs Ruth Atkinson, Communities Director, Mansion House, Penrith CA11 7YG ☎ 01768 212202 🖷 01768 890470 ✉ ruth.atkinson@eden.gov.uk

Sustainable Communities: Mr Oliver Shimell, Communities Manager, Town Hall, Penrith CA11 7QF ☎ 01768 212143 ✉ oliver.shimell@eden.gov.uk

Sustainable Development: Mrs Ruth Atkinson, Communities Director, Mansion House, Penrith CA11 7YG ☎ 01768 212202 🖷 01768 890470 ✉ ruth.atkinson@eden.gov.uk

Tourism: Mrs Ruth Atkinson, Communities Director, Mansion House, Penrith CA11 7YG ☎ 01768 212202 🖷 01768 890470 ✉ ruth.atkinson@eden.gov.uk

Tourism: Mr Oliver Shimell, Communities Manager, Town Hall, Penrith CA11 7QF ☎ 01768 212143 ✉ oliver.shimell@eden.gov.uk

Town Centre: Mrs Ruth Atkinson, Communities Director, Mansion House, Penrith CA11 7YG ☎ 01768 212202 🖷 01768 890470 ✉ ruth.atkinson@eden.gov.uk

Town Centre: Mr Oliver Shimell, Communities Manager, Town Hall, Penrith CA11 7QF ☎ 01768 212143 ✉ oliver.shimell@eden.gov.uk

Waste Collection and Disposal: Miss Julie Monk, Assistant Director (Environmental Services), Mansion House, Penrith CA11 7YG ☎ 01768 817817 ✉ julie.monk@eden.gov.uk

Waste Management: Miss Julie Monk, Assistant Director (Environmental Services), Mansion House, Penrith CA11 7YG ☎ 01768 817817 ✉ julie.monk@eden.gov.uk

Children's Play Areas: Mrs Ruth Atkinson, Communities Director, Mansion House, Penrith CA11 7YG ☎ 01768 212202 🖷 01768 890470 ✉ ruth.atkinson@eden.gov.uk

Children's Play Areas: Mr Oliver Shimell, Communities Manager, Town Hall, Penrith CA11 7QF ☎ 01768 212143 ✉ oliver.shimell@eden.gov.uk

MEMBERS OF THE COUNCIL (38)

***Chair:* Morgan**, Keith (IND - Appleby (Appleby))
keith.morgan@eden.gov.uk

Vice-Chair: **Thompson**, John (CON - Penrith West)
john.thompson@eden.gov.uk
Leader of the Council: **Nicolson**, Gordon (CON - Lazonby)
gordon.nicolson@eden.gov.uk
Deputy Leader of the Council: **Robinson**, Mary (IND - Kirkoswald)
mary.robinson@eden.gov.uk
Beaty, Kevin (CON - Skelton)
kevin.beaty@eden.gov.uk
Bowen, Gratten (LD - Penrith Carleton)
grattan.bowen@eden.gov.uk
Clark, Margaret (IND - Penrith South)
margaret.clark@eden.gov.uk
Connell, Andrew (LD - Appleby (Bongate))
andrew.connell@eden.gov.uk
Derbyshire, Judith (LD - Penrith North)
judith.derbyshire@eden.gov.uk
Eyles, Michael (LD - Penrith East)
michael.eyles@eden.gov.uk
Godwin, Pat (IND - Alston Moor)
patricia.godwin@eden.gov.uk
Grisedale, Lesley (CON - Hesket)
lesley.grisedale@eden.gov.uk
Harding, David (CON - Penrith Pategill)
david.harding@eden.gov.uk
Harrison, Chris (CON - Alston Moor)
christopher.harrison@eden.gov.uk
Harrison, Hugh (IND - Dacre)
hugh.harrison@eden.gov.uk
Holliday, Michael (IND - Langwathby)
michael.holliday@eden.gov.uk
Howse, Robin (LD - Penrith North)
robin.howse@eden.gov.uk
Hughes, Neil (LD - Shap)
neil.hughes@eden.gov.uk
Huxley, David (CON - Greystoke)
david.huxley@eden.gov.uk
Ladhams, Trevor (IND - Kirkby Stephen)
trevor.ladhams@eden.gov.uk
Lynch, John (CON - Penrith East)
john.lynch@eden.gov.uk
Orchard, Sheila (CON - Hartside)
sheila.orchard@eden.gov.uk
Patterson, William (IND - Warcop)
william.patterson@eden.gov.uk
Raine, Joan (CON - Crosby Ravensworth)
joan.raine@eden.gov.uk
Richardson, Paul (IND - Kirkby Stephen)
paul.richardson@eden.gov.uk
Sawrey-Cookson, Henry (IND - Kirkby Thore)
henry.sawrey-cookson@eden.gov.uk
Simpson, Sydney (CON - Ullswater)
sydney.simpson@eden.gov.uk
Slee, Michael (CON - Askham)
michael.slee@eden.gov.uk
Smith, Malcolm (IND - Brough)
malcolm.smith@eden.gov.uk
Spence, Dorothy (LD - Long Marton)
dorothy.spence@eden.gov.uk
Stobbart, Dawn (LD - Penrith West)
dawn.stobbart@eden.gov.uk
Temple, Malcolm (CON - Penrith South)
malcolm.temple@eden.gov.uk
Threlkeld, Harold (IND - Eamont)
harold.threlkeld@eden.gov.uk
Todd, Adrian (CON - Orton with Tebay)
adrian.todd@eden.gov.uk
Tonkin, Michael (IND - Morland)
michael.tonkin@eden.gov.uk
Torkington, Ian (LD - Ravenstonedale)
ian.torkington@eden.gov.uk
Whipp, David (CON - Penrith North)
david.whipp@eden.gov.uk
Wicks, Debra (CON - Hesket)
debra.wicks@eden.gov.uk

POLITICAL COMPOSITION

CON: 16, IND: 13, LD: 9

CABINET

Leader / Strategic & Community Leadership: Mr Gordon Nicolson
Deputy Leader / Communities: Mrs Mary Robinson
Economy & Planning: Mr Malcolm Smith
Environment: Mr Michael Tonkin
Housing: Mrs Lesley Grisedale
Resources: Mr John Lynch

COMMITTEE CHAIRS

Accounts & Governance: Mr David Huxley
Environment & Economy: Mr Michael Holliday
Housing & Community: Major Henry Sawrey-Cookson
Human Resources & Appeals: Mr Sydney Simpson
Licensing: Mr Malcolm Temple
Planning: Mr John Thompson
Scrutiny Co-ordinating Board (Scrutiny): Mr Michael Holliday
Standards: Mr David Tweddle (External)

EDINBURGH, CITY OF S

City of Edinburgh Council, Waverley Court, 4 East Market Street, Edinburgh EH8 8BG ☎ 0131 200 2000
council.info@edinburgh.gov.uk www.edinburgh.gov.uk

FACTS & FIGURES

Police Authority: Lothian & Borders Police Board
Health Authority: NHS Lothian
Learning and Skills Council: Scotland
Parliamentary Constituencies: Edinburgh East, Edinburgh North and Leith, Edinburgh South, Edinburgh South West, Edinburgh West
EU Constituencies: Scotland
Election Frequency: Elections are of whole council

PRINCIPAL OFFICERS

Chief Executive: Mrs Sue Bruce, Chief Executive, Waverley Court, 4 East Market Street, Edinburgh EH8 8BG ☎ 0131 200 2000 sue.bruce@edinburgh.gov.uk

Senior Management: Mr Dave Anderson, Director of City Development, Council Headquarters, Waverley Court, 4 East Market Street, Edinburgh EH8 8BG ☎ 0131 529 3595
dave.anderson@edinburgh.gov.uk

Senior Management: Mr Peter Gabbitas, Director of Health & Social Care, Level 1/8, Waverley Court, 4 East Market Street,

Edinburgh EH8 8BG ☎ 0131 553 8201 🖷 0131 554 0838
🖰 peter.gabbitas@edinburgh.gov.uk

Senior Management: Ms Gillian Tee, Director of Children & Families, Council Headquarters, Waverley Court, 4 East Market Street, Edinburgh EH8 8BG ☎ 0131 469 3000
🖰 gillian.tee@edinburgh.gov.uk

Senior Management: Mr Mark Turley, Director of Services for Communities, Courtyard Level, Waverley Court, 4 East Market Street, Edinburgh EH8 8BG ☎ 0131 200 2000
🖰 mark.turley@edinburgh.gov.uk

Architect, Building / Property Services: Mr Peter Long, Interim Head of Property Management, Waverley Court, 4 East Market Street, Edinburgh EH8 8BG ☎ 0131 200 2000
🖰 peter.long@edinburgh.gov.uk

Building Control: Mr Peter Long, Interim Head of Property Management, Waverley Court, 4 East Market Street, Edinburgh EH8 8BG ☎ 0131 200 2000 🖰 peter.long@edinburgh.gov.uk

Catering Services: Ms Carol McGhie, General Manager, Council Headquarters, Waverley Court, 4 East Market Street, Edinburgh EH8 8BG ☎ 0131 669 5767

Children / Youth Services: Ms Gillian Tee, Director of Children & Families, Council Headquarters, Waverley Court, 4 East Market Street, Edinburgh EH8 8BG ☎ 0131 469 3000
🖰 gillian.tee@edinburgh.gov.uk

Community Planning: Mr David Lyon, Head of Service - Environmental, Waverley Court, 4 East Market Street, Edinburgh EH8 8BG ☎ 0131 200 2000 🖰 david.lyon@edinburgh.gov.uk

Community Safety: Ms Susan Mooney, Acting Head of Service, Community Safety, Waverley Court, 4 East Market Street, Edinburgh EH8 8BG ☎ 0131 200 2000
🖰 susan.mooney@edinburgh.gov.uk

Consumer Protection and Trading Standards: Mr Mark Turley, Director of Services for Communities, Courtyard Level, Waverley Court, 4 East Market Street, Edinburgh EH8 8BG
☎ 0131 200 2000 🖰 mark.turley@edinburgh.gov.uk

Corporate Services: Mr Billy MacIntyre, Head of Resources, Waverley Court, 4 East Market Street, Edinburgh EH8 8BG
☎ 0131 469 3344 🖰 billy.macintyre@edinburgh.gov.uk

Economic Development: Mr Dave Anderson, Director of City Development, Council Headquarters, Waverley Court, 4 East Market Street, Edinburgh EH8 8BG ☎ 0131 529 3595
🖰 dave.anderson@edinburgh.gov.uk

Economic Development: Mr Marshall Poulton, Head of Transport, Level 2/1, Waverley Court, 4 East Market Street, Edinburgh EH8 8BG ☎ 0131 200 2000
🖰 marshall.poulton@edinburgh.gov.uk

Economic Development: Mr Greg Ward, Head of Economic Development, Waverley Court, 4 East Market Street, Edinburgh EH8 8BG ☎ 0131 529 4298 🖰 greg.ward@edinburgh.gov.uk

Education: Mr Mike Rosendale, Head of School & Communities Services, Waverley Court, 4 East Market Street, Edinburgh EH8 8BG ☎ 0131 529 2218 🖰 mike.rosendale@edinburgh.gov.uk

Education: Ms Gillian Tee, Director of Children & Families, Council Headquarters, Waverley Court, 4 East Market Street, Edinburgh EH8 8BG ☎ 0131 469 3000
🖰 gillian.tee@edinburgh.gov.uk

Emergency Planning: Mr Paul Young, Council Emergency Planning Officer, Level G/4, Waverley Court, 4 East Market Street, Edinburgh EH8 8BG ☎ 0131 529 4687
🖰 paul.young@edinburgh.gov.uk

Environmental / Technical Services: Mr Mark Turley, Director of Services for Communities, Courtyard Level, Waverley Court, 4 East Market Street, Edinburgh EH8 8BG ☎ 0131 200 2000
🖰 mark.turley@edinburgh.gov.uk

Environmental Health: Mr David Lyon, Head of Service - Environmental, Waverley Court, 4 East Market Street, Edinburgh EH8 8BG ☎ 0131 200 2000 🖰 david.lyon@edinburgh.gov.uk

Estates, Property & Valuation: Mr Peter Long, Interim Head of Property Management, Waverley Court, 4 East Market Street, Edinburgh EH8 8BG ☎ 0131 200 2000
🖰 peter.long@edinburgh.gov.uk

European Liaison: Mr Marshall Poulton, Head of Transport, Level 2/1, Waverley Court, 4 East Market Street, Edinburgh EH8 8BG ☎ 0131 200 2000 🖰 marshall.poulton@edinburgh.gov.uk

Facilities: Mr Peter Long, Interim Head of Property Management, Waverley Court, 4 East Market Street, Edinburgh EH8 8BG
☎ 0131 200 2000 🖰 peter.long@edinburgh.gov.uk

Finance and Treasurer: Mr Danny Gallacher, Head of Revenues & Benefits, Chesser House, 500 Gorgie Road, Edinburgh EH11 3YJ ☎ 0131 469 5006 🖰 danny.gallacher@edinburgh.gov.uk

Finance and Treasurer: Ms Karen Kelly, Head of Financial Services, Council Headquarters, Waverley Court, 4 East Market Street, Edinburgh EH8 8BG ☎ 0131 469 3184

Finance and Treasurer: Ms Clare Scott, Investments & Pensions Service Manager, Waverley Court, 4 East Market Street, Edinburgh EH8 8BG ☎ 0131 469 3830
🖰 clare.scott@edinburgh.gov.uk

Housing: Ms Cathy King, Head of Housing & Regeneration, Waverley Court, 4 East Market Street, Edinburgh EH8 8BG
☎ 0131 529 7383 🖰 cathy.king@edinburgh.gov.uk

Housing: Mr Mark Turley, Director of Services for Communities, Courtyard Level, Waverley Court, 4 East Market Street, Edinburgh EH8 8BG ☎ 0131 200 2000 🖰 mark.turley@edinburgh.gov.uk

Housing Maintenance: Mr Alex Burns, Head of Edinburgh Building Services, 33 Murrayburn Road, Edinburgh EH8 8BG
☎ 0131 200 2000 🖰 alexander.burns@edinburgh.gov.uk

Legal: Mr Alistair Maclean, Council Solicitor, Level 3/1, Waverley

Court, 4 East Market Street, Edinburgh EH8 8BG ☎ 0131 529 4136 ✉ alastair.maclean@edinburgh.gov.uk

Leisure and Cultural Services: Ms Lynne Halfpenny, Head of Culture & Sport, Waverley Court, 4 East Market Street, Edinburgh EH8 8BG ☎ 0131 529 3567 ✉ lynne.halfpenny@edinburgh.gov.uk

Licensing: Mr Alistair Maclean, Council Solicitor, Level 3/1, Waverley Court, 4 East Market Street, Edinburgh EH8 8BG ☎ 0131 529 4136 ✉ alastair.maclean@edinburgh.gov.uk

Lifelong Learning: Ms Gillian Hunt, Head of Professional Development & Lifelong Learning, Council Headquarters, Waverley Court, 4 East Market Street, Edinburgh EH8 8BG ☎ 0131 469 3072 ✉ gillian.hunt@edinburgh.gov.uk

Lighting: Mr Mark Turley, Director of Services for Communities, Courtyard Level, Waverley Court, 4 East Market Street, Edinburgh EH8 8BG ☎ 0131 200 2000 ✉ mark.turley@edinburgh.gov.uk

Member Services: Mr Tom Little, Head of Performance, Strategy & Policy, Waverley Court, 4 East Market Street, Edinburgh EH8 8BG ☎ 0131 469 3846 ✉ tom.little@edinburgh.gov.uk

Member Services: Ms Beverley Wilson, Civic & Members' Services Manager, Waverley Court, 4 East Market Street, Edinburgh EH8 8BG ☎ 0131 200 2000 ✉ beverley.wilson@edinburgh.gov.uk

Parking: Mr Gavin Brown, Interim Transport Services Manager, Council Headquarters, Waverley Court, 4 East Market Street, Edinburgh EH8 8BG ☎ 0131 469 3775 🖷 0131 469 3730 ✉ gavin.brown@edinburgh.gov.uk

Personnel / HR: Mr Philip Barr, Head of Human Resources, Level 2/3, Waverley Court, 4 East Market Street, Edinburgh EH8 8BG ☎ 0131 200 2000 ✉ philip.barr@edinburgh.gov.uk

Planning: Mr Dave Anderson, Director of City Development, Council Headquarters, Waverley Court, 4 East Market Street, Edinburgh EH8 8BG ☎ 0131 529 3595 ✉ dave.anderson@edinburgh.gov.uk

Planning: Mr John Bury, Head of Planning & Strategy, Waverley Court, 4 East Market Street, Edinburgh EH8 8BG ☎ 0131 529 3494 ✉ john.bury@edinburgh.gov.uk

Procurement: Mr Graeme Hastie, Procurement Manager, Level 3, Waverley Court, 4 East Market Street, Edinburgh EH8 8BG ☎ 0131 469 3851 ✉ graeme.hastie@edinburgh.gov.uk

Public Libraries: Ms Liz McGelligan, Head of Libraries & Information Services, Level C5, Waverley Court, 4 East Market Street, Edinburgh EH8 8BG ☎ 0131 529 7894 ✉ liz.mcgettigan@edinburgh.gov.uk

Recycling & Waste Minimisation: Mr Mark Turley, Director of Services for Communities, Courtyard Level, Waverley Court, 4 East Market Street, Edinburgh EH8 8BG ☎ 0131 200 2000 ✉ mark.turley@edinburgh.gov.uk

Social Services: Ms Monica Boyle, Head of Social Care Performance, Waverley Court, 4 East Market Street, Edinburgh EH8 8BG ☎ 0131 553 8319 ✉ monica.boyle@edinburgh.gov.uk

Social Services: Mr Peter Gabbitas, Director of Health & Social Care, Level 1/8, Waverley Court, 4 East Market Street, Edinburgh EH8 8BG ☎ 0131 553 8201 🖷 0131 554 0838 ✉ peter.gabbitas@edinburgh.gov.uk

Social Services: Ms Michelle Miller, Head of Quality & Standards & Chief Social Work Officer, Waverley Court, 4 East Market Street, Edinburgh EH8 8BG ☎ 0131 553 8520 ✉ michelle.miller@edinburgh.gov.uk

Social Services (Adult): Mr Peter Gabbitas, Director of Health & Social Care, Level 1/8, Waverley Court, 4 East Market Street, Edinburgh EH8 8BG ☎ 0131 553 8201 🖷 0131 554 0838 ✉ peter.gabbitas@edinburgh.gov.uk

Social Services (Children): Ms Gillian Tee, Director of Children & Families, Council Headquarters, Waverley Court, 4 East Market Street, Edinburgh EH8 8BG ☎ 0131 469 3000 ✉ gillian.tee@edinburgh.gov.uk

Staff Training: Mr Philip Barr, Head of Human Resources, Level 2/3, Waverley Court, 4 East Market Street, Edinburgh EH8 8BG ☎ 0131 200 2000 ✉ philip.barr@edinburgh.gov.uk

Sustainable Development: Ms Janice Pauwels, Senior Policy Officer, Environment, Level 2/1, Waverley Court, 4 East Market Street, Edinburgh EH8 8BG ☎ 0131 200 2000 ✉ janice.pauwels@edinburgh.gov.uk

Traffic Management: Mr Dave Anderson, Director of City Development, Council Headquarters, Waverley Court, 4 East Market Street, Edinburgh EH8 8BG ☎ 0131 529 3595 ✉ dave.anderson@edinburgh.gov.uk

Transport: Mr Gavin Brown, Interim Transport Services Manager, Council Headquarters, Waverley Court, 4 East Market Street, Edinburgh EH8 8BG ☎ 0131 469 3775 🖷 0131 469 3730 ✉ gavin.brown@edinburgh.gov.uk

Transport: Mr Marshall Poulton, Head of Transport, Level 2/1, Waverley Court, 4 East Market Street, Edinburgh EH8 8BG ☎ 0131 200 2000 ✉ marshall.poulton@edinburgh.gov.uk

Transport Planner: Mr Dave Anderson, Director of City Development, Council Headquarters, Waverley Court, 4 East Market Street, Edinburgh EH8 8BG ☎ 0131 529 3595 ✉ dave.anderson@edinburgh.gov.uk

Waste Management: Mr Mark Turley, Director of Services for Communities, Courtyard Level, Waverley Court, 4 East Market Street, Edinburgh EH8 8BG ☎ 0131 200 2000 ✉ mark.turley@edinburgh.gov.uk

MEMBERS OF THE COUNCIL (58)

***Provost:* Wilson**, Donald (LAB - Sighthill and Gorgie)
donald.wilson@edinburgh.gov.uk
***Deputy Provost:* Brock**, Deirdre (SNP - Leith Walk)
deirdre.brock@edinburgh.gov.uk
***Leader of the Council:* Burns**, Andrew (LAB - Fountainbridge

and Craiglockhart)
andrew.burns@edinburgh.gov.uk
Aitken, Elaine (CON - Colinton and Fairmilehead)
elaine.aitken@edinburgh.gov.uk
Aldridge, Robert (LD - Drum Brae and Gyle)
robert.aldridge@edinburgh.gov.uk
Bagshaw, Nigel (SGP - Inverleith)
nigel.bagshaw@edinburgh.gov.uk
Balfour, Jeremy (CON - Corstorphine and Murrayfield)
jeremy.balfour@edinburgh.gov.uk
Barrie, Gavin (SNP - Inverleith)
gavin.barrie@edinburgh.gov.uk
Blacklock, Angela (LAB - Leith Walk)
angela.blacklock@edinburgh.gov.uk
Booth, Chas (SGP - Leith)
chas.booth@edinburgh.gov.uk
Bridgman, Michael (SNP - Portobello and Craigmillar)
michael.bridgman@edinburgh.gov.uk
Buchanan, Tom (SNP - Liberton and Gilberton)
tom.buchanan@edinburgh.gov.uk
Burgess, Steve (GRN - Southside and Newington)
steve.burgess@edinburgh.gov.uk
Cairns, Ronald (SNP - Drum Brae and Gyle)
ronald.cairns@edinburgh.gov.uk
Cardownie, Stephen (SNP - Forth)
steve.cardownie@edinburgh.gov.uk
Chapman, Maggie (GRN - Leith Walk)
maggie.chapman@edinburgh.gov.uk
Child, Maureen (LAB - Portobello and Craigmillar)
maureen.child@edinburgh.gov.uk
Cook, Bill (LAB - Liberton and Gilmerton)
bill.cook@edinburgh.gov.uk
Cook, Nick (CON - Liberton and Gilmerton)
nick.cook@edinburgh.gov.uk
Corbett, Gavin (SGP - Fountainbridge and Craiglockhart)
gavin.corbett@edinburgh.gov.uk
Day, Cammy (LAB - Forth)
cammy.day@edinburgh.gov.uk
Dixon, Denis (SNP - Sighthill and Gorgie)
denis.dixon@edinburgh.gov.uk
Doran, Karen (LAB - City Centre)
karen.doran@edinburgh.gov.uk
Edie, Paul (LD - Corstorphine and Murrayfield)
paul.edie@edinburgh.gov.uk
Fullerton, Catherine (SNP - Sighthill and Gorgie)
cathy.fullerton@edinburgh.gov.uk
Gardner, Nick (LAB - Leith Walk)
nick.gardner@edinburgh.gov.uk
Godzik, Paul (LAB - Meadows and Morningside)
paul.godzik@edinburgh.gov.uk
Griffiths, Joan (LAB - Craigentinny and Duddingston)
joan.griffiths@edinburgh.gov.uk
Hart, Norma (LAB - Liberton and Gilmerton)
norma.hart@edinbirgh.gov.uk
Henderson, Ricky (LAB - Pentland Hills)
ricky.henderson@edinburgh.gov.uk
Henderson, Bill (SNP - Pentland Hills)
bill.rhenderson@edinburgh.gov.uk
Heslop, Dominic (CON - Pentland Hills)
dominic.heslop@edinburgh.gov.uk
Hinds, Lesley (LAB - Inverleith)
lesley.hinds@edinburgh.gov.uk
Howat, Sandy (SNP - Meadows and Morningside)
sandy.howat@edinburgh.gov.uk
Jackson, Allan (CON - Forth)
allan.jackson@edinburgh.gov.uk
Keil, Karen (LAB - Drum Brae and Gyle)
karen.keil@edinburgh.gov.uk
Key, David (SNP - Fountainbridge and Craiglockhart)
david.key@edinburgh.gov.uk
Lewis, Richard (SNP - Colinton and Fairmilehead)
richard.lewis@edinburgh.gov.uk
Lunn, Alex (LAB - Craigentinny and Duddingston)
alex.lunn@edinburgh.gov.uk
Main, Melanie (SGP - Meadows and Morningside)
melanie.main@edinburgh.gov.uk
McInnes, Mark (CON - Meadows and Morningside)
mark.mcinnes@edinburgh.gov.uk
McVey, Adam (SNP - Leith)
adam.mcvey@edinburgh.gov.uk
Milligan, Eric (LAB - Sighthill and Gorgie)
eric.milligan@edinburgh.gov.uk
Mowat, Joanna (CON - City Centre)
joanna.mowat@edinburgh
Munro, Gordon (LAB - Leith)
gordon.munro@edinburgh.gov.uk
Orr, Jim (SNP - Southside and Newington)
jim.orr@edinburgh.gov.uk
Paterson, Lindsay (CON - Almond)
linday.paterson@edinburgh.gov.uk
Perry, Ian (LAB - Southside and Newington)
ian.perry@edinburgh.gov.uk
Rankin, Alasdair (SNP - City Centre)
alasdair.rankin@edinburgh.gov.uk
Redpath, Vicki (LAB - Forth)
vicki.redpath@edinburgh.gov.uk
Rose, Cameron (CON - Southside and Newington)
cameron.rose@edinburgh.gov.uk
Ross, Frank (SNP - Corstorphine and Murrayfield)
frank.ross@edinburgh.gov.uk
Rust, Jason (CON - Colinton and Fairmilehead)
jason.rust@edinburgh.gov.uk
Shields, Alastair (LD - Almond)
alastair.shields@edinburgh.gov.uk
Tymkewwycz, Stefan (SNP - Craigentinny and Duddingston)
stefan.tymkewycz@edinburgh.gov.uk
Walker, David (LAB - Portobello and Craigmillar)
david.walker1@edinburgh.gov.uk
Whyte, Iain (CON - Inverleith)
iain.whyte@edinburgh.gov.uk
Work, Norman (SNP - Almond)
norman.work@edinburgh.gov.uk

POLITICAL COMPOSITION

LAB: 20, SNP: 18, CON: 11, SGP: 4, LD: 3, GRN: 2

ELMBRIDGE D

Elmbridge Borough Council, Civic Centre, High Street, Esher KT10 9SD ☎ 01372 474474 🖷 01372 474972
✉ civiccentre@elmbridge.gov.uk 💻 www.elmbridge.gov.uk

FACTS & FIGURES

Police Authority: Surrey Police Authority
Health Authority: South East Coast Strategic Health Authority
Learning and Skills Council: South East
Parliamentary Constituencies: Esher and Walton
EU Constituencies: South East
Election Frequency: Elections are by thirds
Twinning: Rueil-Malmaison (France)

PRINCIPAL OFFICERS

Chief Executive: Mr Robert Moran, Chief Executive, Civic Centre, High Street, Esher KT10 9SD ☎ 01372 474380 🖷 01372 474933 🖱 chiefexec@elmbridge.gov.uk

Senior Management: Mr Ray Lee, Strategic Director, Civic Centre, High Street, Esher KT10 9SD ☎ 01372 474700 🖷 01372 474910 🖱 sds@elmbridge.gov.uk

Senior Management: Mrs Sarah Selvanathan, Strategic Director, Civic Centre, High Street, Esher KT10 9SD ☎ 01372 474100 🖷 01372 474971 🖱 sdr@elmbridge.gov.uk

Architect, Building / Property Services: Mrs Alexandra Williams, Head of Asset Management & Property Services, Civic Centre, High Street, Esher KT10 9SD ☎ 01372 474218 🖷 01372 474927 🖱 awilliams@elmbridge.gov.uk

Best Value: Mrs Natalie Anderson, Head of Corporate Policy & Partnerships, Civic Centre, High Street, Esher KT10 9SD ☎ 01372 474111 🖷 01372 474932 🖱 corporatepolicy@elmbridge.gov.uk

Building Control: Mr Mark Webb, Building Control Manager, Civic Centre, High Street, Esher KT10 9SD ☎ 01372 474801 🖷 01372 474912 🖱 bcon@elmbridge.gov.uk

PR / Communications: Ms Jane Connolly, Communications & New Media Manager, Civic Centre, High Street, Esher KT10 9SD ☎ 01372 474392 🖷 01372 474932 🖱 communications@elmbridge.gov.uk

Community Safety: Ms Annabel Crouch, Community Safety Co-ordinator, Civic Centre, High Street, Esher KT10 9SD ☎ 01372 474398 🖷 01372 474932 🖱 communitysafety@elmbridge.gov.uk

Community Safety: Mr Peter Kipps, Community Safety Partnership Manager, Civic Centre, High Street, Esher KT10 9SD ☎ 01372 474399 🖷 01372 474932 🖱 communitysafety@elmbridge.gov.uk

Computer Management: Mr Mark Lumley, Head of Information Systems, Civic Centre, High Street, Esher KT10 9SD 🖷 01372 474158 🖱 isd@elmbridge.gov.uk

Contracts: Mr Alan Harrison, Head of Legal Services, Civic Centre, High Street, Esher KT10 9SD ☎ 01372 474192 🖷 01372 474973 🖱 legalservices@elmbridge.gov.uk

Corporate Services: Mrs Deanna Harris, Head of Internal Audit Partnership, Civic Centre, High Street, Esher KT10 9SD ☎ 01372 474108 🖷 01372 474971 🖱 internalaudit@elmbridge.gov.uk

Corporate Services: Mrs Sarah Selvanathan, Strategic Director, Civic Centre, High Street, Esher KT10 9SD ☎ 01372 474100 🖷 01372 474971 🖱 sdr@elmbridge.gov.uk

Customer Service: Ms Teresa Smith, Policy Manager - Business Improvement, Civic Centre, High Street, Esher KT10 9SD ☎ 01372 474385 🖷 01372 474932 🖱 corporatepolicy@elmbridge.gov.uk

Economic Development: Mr Ray Lee, Strategic Director, Civic Centre, High Street, Esher KT10 9SD ☎ 01372 474700 🖷 01372 474910 🖱 sds@elmbridge.gov.uk

Electoral Registration: Miss Alex Mammous, Electoral Services Manager, Civic Centre, High Street, Esher KT10 9SD ☎ 01372 474182 🖷 01372 474981 🖱 electoral@elmbridge.gov.uk

Emergency Planning: Mrs Gill Marchbank, Emergency Planning & Business Continuity Officer, Civic Centre, High Street, Esher KT10 9SD ☎ 01372 474208 🖷 01372 474208 🖱 gmarchbank@elmbridge.gov.uk

Energy Management: Miss Cristina Royo, Sustainable Energy Officer, Civic Centre, High Street, Esher KT10 9SD ☎ 01372 474211 🖷 01372 474935 🖱 croyo@elmbridge.gov.uk

Environmental / Technical Services: Mr Anthony Jeziorski, Head of Environmental Care, Civic Centre, High Street, Esher KT10 9SD ☎ 01372 474762 🖷 01372 474929 🖱 envcare@elmbridge.gov.uk

Estates, Property & Valuation: Mrs Alexandra Williams, Head of Asset Management & Property Services, Civic Centre, High Street, Esher KT10 9SD ☎ 01372 474218 🖷 01372 474927 🖱 awilliams@elmbridge.gov.uk

Facilities: Mrs Alexandra Williams, Head of Asset Management & Property Services, Civic Centre, High Street, Esher KT10 9SD ☎ 01372 474218 🖷 01372 474927 🖱 awilliams@elmbridge.gov.uk

Finance and Treasurer: Mrs Sarah Selvanathan, Strategic Director, Civic Centre, High Street, Esher KT10 9SD ☎ 01372 474100 🖷 01372 474971 🖱 sdr@elmbridge.gov.uk

Grounds Maintenance: Mr Ian Burrows, Head of Leisure & Cultural Services, Civic Centre, High Street, Esher KT10 9SD ☎ 01372 474572 🖷 01372 474939 🖱 leisure@elmbridge.gov.uk

Health and Safety: Mr Richard Simms, Health & Safety Advisor, Civic Centre, High Street, Esher KT10 9SD ☎ 01372 474215 🖷 01372 474979 🖱 rsimms@elmbridge.gov.uk

Housing: Ms Julie Cook, Head of Housing Services, Civic Centre, High Street, Esher KT10 9SD ☎ 01372 474640 🖷 01372 474934 🖱 jcook@elmbridge.gov.uk

Legal: Mr Alan Harrison, Head of Legal Services, Civic Centre, High Street, Esher KT10 9SD ☎ 01372 474192 🖷 01372 474973 🖱 legalservices@elmbridge.gov.uk

Leisure and Cultural Services: Mr Ian Burrows, Head of Leisure & Cultural Services, Civic Centre, High Street, Esher KT10 9SD ☎ 01372 474572 🖷 01372 474939 🖱 leisure@elmbridge.gov.uk

Lottery Funding, Charity and Voluntary: Mrs Gail McKenzie, Voluntary Sector Support Officer, Civic Centre, High Street, Esher KT10 9SD ☎ 01372 474549 🖷 01372 474937 🖱 commservices@elmbridge.gov.uk

Member Services: Ms Beverley Greenstein, Head of Executive & Member Services, Civic Centre, High Street, Esher KT10 9SD ☎ 01372 474173 🖷 01372 474933

✉ committee@elmbridge.gov.uk

Parking: Mr Anthony Jeziorski, Head of Environmental Care, Civic Centre, High Street, Esher KT10 9SD ☎ 01372 474762 🖷 01372 474929 ✉ envcare@elmbridge.gov.uk

Partnerships: Mrs Natalie Anderson, Head of Corporate Policy & Partnerships, Civic Centre, High Street, Esher KT10 9SD ☎ 01372 474111 🖷 01372 474932 ✉ corporatepolicy@elmbridge.gov.uk

Personnel / HR: Mrs Caroline Hall, Head of Personnel, Civic Centre, High Street, Esher KT10 9SD ☎ 01372 474214 🖷 01372 474979 ✉ personnel@elmbridge.gov.uk

Procurement: Mr Alan Harrison, Head of Legal Services, Civic Centre, High Street, Esher KT10 9SD ☎ 01372 474192 🖷 01372 474973 ✉ legalservices@elmbridge.gov.uk

Recycling & Waste Minimisation: Mr Anthony Jeziorski, Head of Environmental Care, Civic Centre, High Street, Esher KT10 9SD ☎ 01372 474762 🖷 01372 474929 ✉ envcare@elmbridge.gov.uk

Regeneration: Mr Ray Lee, Strategic Director, Civic Centre, High Street, Esher KT10 9SD ☎ 01372 474700 🖷 01372 474910 ✉ sds@elmbridge.gov.uk

Staff Training: Ms Caroline Swift, Personnel & Training Manager, Civic Centre, High Street, Esher KT10 9SD ☎ 01372 474213 🖷 01372 474979 ✉ personnel@elmbridge.gov.uk

Street Scene: Mr Anthony Jeziorski, Head of Environmental Care, Civic Centre, High Street, Esher KT10 9SD ☎ 01372 474762 🖷 01372 474929 ✉ envcare@elmbridge.gov.uk

Sustainable Development: Mrs Lesley Underwood, LDF & Policy Manager, Civic Centre, High Street, Esher KT10 9SD ☎ 01372 474799 ✉ tplan@elmbridge.gov.uk

Waste Collection and Disposal: Mr Anthony Jeziorski, Head of Environmental Care, Civic Centre, High Street, Esher KT10 9SD ☎ 01372 474762 🖷 01372 474929 ✉ envcare@elmbridge.gov.uk

Waste Management: Mr Anthony Jeziorski, Head of Environmental Care, Civic Centre, High Street, Esher KT10 9SD ☎ 01372 474762 🖷 01372 474929 ✉ envcare@elmbridge.gov.uk

MEMBERS OF THE COUNCIL (59)

***Mayor:* Turner**, Janet (R - Hinchley Wood)
jturner@elmbridge.gov.uk

***Deputy Mayor:* Bennison**, Mike (CON - Cobham and Downside)
mbennison@elmbridge.gov.uk

***Leader of the Council:* O'Reilly**, John (CON - Hersham South)
joreilly@elmbridge.gov.uk

***Deputy Leader of the Council:* Dodsworth**, Simon (CON - Weybridge South)
sdodsworth@elmbridge.gov.uk

***Group Leader:* Fairbank**, Barry (LD - Long Ditton)
bfairbank@elmbridge.gov.uk

***Group Leader:* Selleck**, Stuart (R - Molesey North)
sselleck@elmbridge.gov.uk

Archer, David (CON - Esher)
darcher@elmbridge.gov.uk

Axton, Mike (R - Molesey South)
maxton@elmbridge.gov.uk

Browne, James (CON - Cobham Fairmile)
jbrowne@elmbridge.gov.uk

Bruce, Ruth (R - Weston Green)
rbruce@elmbridge.gov.uk

Butcher, John (CON - Cobham and Downside)
jbutcher@elmbridge.gov.uk

Cartwright, Jimmy (LD - Claygate)
jcartwright@elmbridge.gov.uk

Cheyne, Barry (CON - Oatlands Park)
bcheyne@elmbridge.gov.uk

Coomes, Alex (LD - Claygate)
acoomes@elmbridge.gov.uk

Cooper, Elizabeth (R - Molesey East)
ecooper@elmbridge.gov.uk

Cooper, Nigel (R - Molesey East)
ncooper@elmbridge.gov.uk

Cowin, Barbara (CON - Walton North)
bcowin@elmbridge.gov.uk

Cross, Christine (CON - Walton North)
ccross@elmbridge.gov.uk

Dabell, Frank (R - Hinchley Wood)
fdabell@elmbridge.gov.uk

Davis, Andrew (LD - Weybridge North)
adavis@elmbridge.gov.uk

Dearlove, Glenn (CON - Weybridge South)
gdearlove@elmbridge.gov.uk

Dennis, Sandra (R - Thames Ditton)
sdennis@elmbridge.gov.uk

Donaldson, Ian (CON - Hersham North)
iandonaldson@elmsbridge.gov.uk

Donaldson, Ian Travis (R - Molesey South)
idonaldson@elmbridge.gov.uk

Egan, Keith (CON - St George's Hill)
kegan@elmbridge.gov.uk

Eldridge, Victor (R - Molesey South)
veldridge@elmbridge.gov.uk

Elmer, Christine (CON - Walton South)
celmer@elmbridge.gov.uk

Elmer, Chris (CON - Walton South)
chriselmer@elmbridge.gov.uk

Fairclough, Brian (R - St. George's Hill)
bfairclough@elmbridge.gov.uk

Fuller, Jan (CON - Oxshott and Stoke D'Abernon)
jfuller@elmbridge.gov.uk

Gray, Ramon (CON - Weybridge North)
rgray@elmbridge.gov.uk

Green, Roy (O - Hersham North)
rgreen@elmbridge.gov.uk

Harman, Peter (R - St George's Hill)
pharman@elmbridge.gov.uk

Hawkins, Stuart (CON - Walton South)
shawkins@embridge.gov.uk

Herbert, Geoffrey (CON - Claygate)
gherbert@elmbridge.gov.uk

Hopkins, Alan (R - Molesey North)
ahopkins@elmbridge.gov.uk

Hughes, Kay (CON - Oatlands Park)
khughes@elmbridge.gov.uk

Izard, Toni (LD - Long Ditton)
tizard@elmbridge.gov.uk

Kapadia, Shetwa (LD - Long Ditton)
skapadia@elmbridge.gov.uk

Kelly, Andrew (CON - Walton Ambleside)

akelly@elmbridge.gov.uk
Kopitko, Alan (CON - Walton Ambleside)
akopitko@elmbridge.gov.uk
Lake, Rachael (CON - Walton North)
rlake@elmbridge.gov.uk
Luxton, Neil (O - Walton Central)
nluxton@elmbridge.gov.uk
Lyon, Ruth (R - Thames Ditton)
rlyon@elmbridge.gov.uk
Mills, Melvyn (R - Walton Central)
mmills@elmbridge.gov.uk
Mitchell, Dorothy (CON - Cobham and Downside)
dmitchell@elmbridge.gov.uk
Mitchell, Ruth (CON - Hersham South)
rmitchell@elmbridge.gov.uk
Odone, Maria (CON - Cobham Fairmile)
modone@elmbridge.gov.uk
Popham, Tony (R - Molesey East)
tpopham@elmbridge.gov.uk
Randolph, Karen (R - Thames Ditton)
krandolph@elmbridge.gov.uk
Robertson, Liz (R - Molesey North)
lrobertson@elmbridge.gov.uk
Sadler, Chris (R - Walton Central)
csadler@elmbridge.gov.uk
Samuels, Lorraine (CON - Oatlands Park)
lsamuels@elmbridge.gov.uk
Saunders, Elise (CON - Oxshott and Stoke D'Abernon)
esaunders@elmbridge.gov.uk
Sheldon, John (CON - Hersham South)
jsheldon@elmbridge.gov.uk
Sheldon, Mary (CON - Hersham North)
msheldon@elmbridge.gov.uk
Shipley, Tannia (R - Weston Green)
tshipley@elmbridge.gov.uk
Vickers, James (CON - Oxshott and Stoke D'Abernon)
jvickers@elmbridge.gov.uk
Waugh, Simon (CON - Esher) swaugh@elmbridge.gov.uk

POLITICAL COMPOSITION

CON: 31, R: 20, LD: 6, O: 2

CABINET

Leader: Mr John O'Reilly
Deputy Leader / Regulatory Affairs: Mr Simon Dodsworth
Community Development: Mrs Christine Cross
Corporate Development: Ms Barbara Cowin
Environment: Mr Glenn Dearlove
Highways & Transport: Ms Dorothy Mitchell
Housing: Mr James Browne
Leisure & Culture: Ms Jan Fuller
Social Affairs: Mrs Christine Elmer

COMMITTEE CHAIRS

Licensing: Mr Ian Donaldson
Overview & Scrutiny: Mr Alan Hopkins
Planning: Mr Chris Elmer

ENFIELD L

Enfield London Borough Council, Civic Centre, Silver Street, Enfield EN1 3XA ☎ 020 8379 1000 🖷 020 8379 4453
💻 www.enfield.gov.uk

FACTS & FIGURES

Police Authority: Metropolitan Police Authority
Health Authority: NHS London
Learning and Skills Council: London
Parliamentary Constituencies: Edmonton, Enfield North, Enfield, Southgate
EU Constituencies: London
Election Frequency: Elections are of whole council
Twinning: Gladbeck (Germany); Courbevoie (France)

PRINCIPAL OFFICERS

Chief Executive: Mr Rob Leak, Chief Executive, PO Box 61, Civic Centre, Silver Street, Enfield EN1 3XY ☎ 020 8379 3901 ✉ chief.executive@enfield.gov.uk

Senior Management: Mr Ian Davis, Director of Environment, PO Box 52, Civic Centre, Silver Street, Enfield EN1 3XD ☎ 020 8379 3500 🖷 020 8379 3475 ✉ ian.davis@enfield.gov.uk

Senior Management: Mr Andrew Fraser, Director of Schools & Children's Services, PO Box 56, Civic Centre, Silver Street, Enfield EN1 3XQ ☎ 020 8379 3200 🖷 020 8379 3351 ✉ andrew.fraser@enfield.gov.uk

Senior Management: Mr Ray James, Director of Health, Housing & Adult Social Care, PO Box 59, Civic Centre, Silver Street, Enfield EN1 3XL ☎ 020 8379 4160 🖷 020 8379 4274 ✉ ray.james@enfield.gov.uk

Senior Management: Mr James Rolfe, Director of Finance, Resources & Customer Services, PO Box 54, Civic Centre, Silver Street, Enfield EN1 3XF ☎ 020 8379 4600 🖷 020 8379 5193 ✉ james.rolfe@enfield.gov.uk

Senior Management: Mr Neil Rousell, Director of Regeneration, Leisure & Culture, PO Box 56, Civic Centre, Silver Street, Enfield EN1 3XQ ☎ 020 8379 4968 🖷 020 8379 4293 ✉ neil.rousell@enfield.gov.uk

Architect, Building / Property Services: Mr Brian Smart, Interim Assistant Director, Property Services, PO Box 51, Civic Centre, Silver Street, Enfield EN1 3XB ☎ ; 020 8379 4605 🖷 020 8379 5193 ✉ brian.smart@enfield.gov.uk

Best Value: Mr Simon Tendeter, Assistant Director, Communities, Communications, Policy & Performance, PO Box 61, Civic Centre, Silver Street, Enfield EN1 3XY ☎ 020 8379 3880 🖷 020 8379 4293 ✉ simon.tendeter@enfield.gov.uk

Building Control: Mr Bob Griffiths, Assistant Director, Planning & Environmental Protection, PO Box 52, Civic Centre, Silver Street, Enfield EN1 3XD ☎ 020 8379 3676 🖷 020 8379 5120 ✉ bob.griffiths@enfield.gov.uk

Catering Services: Ms Jennifer Hill, Assistant Director, Commissioning, PO Box 56, Civic Centre, Silver Street, Enfield EN1 3XQ ☎ 020 8379 4910 🖷 020 8379 3243 ✉ jennifer.hill@enfield.gov.uk

Children / Youth Services: Mr Andrew Fraser, Director of Schools & Children's Services, PO Box 56, Civic Centre, Silver

Street, Enfield EN1 3XQ ☎ 020 8379 3200 🖷 020 8379 3351 ✉ andrew.fraser@enfield.gov.uk

Civil Registration: Ms Valerie Parsons, Superintendant Registrar, Civic Centre, Silver Street, Enfield EN1 3XA ☎ 020 8379 8501 🖷 020 8379 8588 ✉ valerie.parsons@enfield.gov.uk

PR / Communications: Ms Kate Robertson, Assistant Director of Customer Services, Information & Transformation, PO Box 61, Civic Centre, Silver Street, Enfield EN1 3XY ☎ 020 8379 5165 🖷 020 8379 4031 ✉ kate.robertson@enfield.gov.uk

Community Planning: Mr Simon Tendeter, Assistant Director, Communities, Communications, Policy & Performance, PO Box 61, Civic Centre, Silver Street, Enfield EN1 3XY ☎ 020 8379 3880 🖷 020 8379 4293 ✉ simon.tendeter@enfield.gov.uk

Community Safety: Ms Andrea Clemons, Head of Community Safety, PO Box 52, Civic Centre, Silver Street, Enfield EN1 3XD ☎ 020 8379 4085 🖷 020 8379 4005 ✉ andrea.clemons@enfield.gov.uk

Computer Management: Ms Kate Robertson, Assistant Director of Customer Services, Information & Transformation, PO Box 61, Civic Centre, Silver Street, Enfield EN1 3XY ☎ 020 8379 5165 🖷 020 8379 4031 ✉ kate.robertson@enfield.gov.uk

Consumer Protection and Trading Standards: Ms Sue McDaid, Head of Trading Standards & Licensing, Civic Centre, Silver Street, Enfield EN1 3XA ☎ 020 8379 3680 🖷 020 8379 8506 ✉ sue.mcdaid@enfield.gov.uk

Contracts: Mr Gary Barnes, Assistant Director, Highways & Transportation, PO Box 52, Civic Centre, Silver Street, Enfield EN1 3XD ☎ 020 8379 3600 🖷 020 8379 3475 ✉ gary.barnes@enfield.gov.uk

Corporate Services: Mr James Rolfe, Director of Finance, Resources & Customer Services, PO Box 54, Civic Centre, Silver Street, Enfield EN1 3XF ☎ 020 8379 4600 🖷 020 8379 5193 ✉ james.rolfe@enfield.gov.uk

Customer Service: Ms Tracey Chamberlain, Head of Customer Access, Civic Centre, Silver Street, Enfield EN1 3XY ☎ 020 8379 6525 🖷 020 8379 6458 ✉ tracey.chamberlain@enfield.gov.uk

Direct Labour: Mr Gary Barnes, Assistant Director, Highways & Transportation, PO Box 52, Civic Centre, Silver Street, Enfield EN1 3XD ☎ 020 8379 3600 🖷 020 8379 3475 ✉ gary.barnes@enfield.gov.uk

Economic Development: Mr John Haslem, Head of Economic Development, PO Box 52, Civic Centre, Silver Street, Enfield EN1 3XD ☎ 020 8379 3779 🖷 020 8379 3000 ✉ john.haslem@enfield.gov.uk

Education: Mr Andrew Fraser, Director of Schools & Children's Services, PO Box 56, Civic Centre, Silver Street, Enfield EN1 3XQ ☎ 020 8379 3200 🖷 020 8379 3351 ✉ andrew.fraser@enfield.gov.uk

Electoral Registration: Mr Peter Stanyon, Head of Electoral & Democratic Services, Civic Centre, Silver Street, Enfield EN1 3XA ☎ 020 8379 8580 🖷 020 8379 8588 ✉ peter.stanyon@enfield.gov.uk

Emergency Planning: Ms Andrea Clemons, Head of Community Safety, PO Box 52, Civic Centre, Silver Street, Enfield EN1 3XD ☎ 020 8379 4085 🖷 020 8379 4005 ✉ andrea.clemons@enfield.gov.uk

Energy Management: Mr Bob Griffiths, Assistant Director, Planning & Environmental Protection, PO Box 52, Civic Centre, Silver Street, Enfield EN1 3XD ☎ 020 8379 3676 🖷 020 8379 5120 ✉ bob.griffiths@enfield.gov.uk

Environmental / Technical Services: Mr Ian Davis, Director of Environment, PO Box 52, Civic Centre, Silver Street, Enfield EN1 3XD ☎ 020 8379 3500 🖷 020 8379 3475 ✉ ian.davis@enfield.gov.uk

Environmental Health: Mr Ian Davis, Director of Environment, PO Box 52, Civic Centre, Silver Street, Enfield EN1 3XD ☎ 020 8379 3500 🖷 020 8379 3475 ✉ ian.davis@enfield.gov.uk

Environmental Health: Mr Bob Griffiths, Assistant Director, Planning & Environmental Protection, PO Box 52, Civic Centre, Silver Street, Enfield EN1 3XD ☎ 020 8379 3676 🖷 020 8379 5120 ✉ bob.griffiths@enfield.gov.uk

Estates, Property & Valuation: Mr Brian Smart, Interim Assistant Director, Property Services, PO Box 51, Civic Centre, Silver Street, Enfield EN1 3XB ☎ 020 8379 4605 🖷 020 8379 5193 ✉ brian.smart@enfield.gov.uk

European Liaison: Ms Lorraine Cox, Cultural Services Manager, PO Box 56, Civic Centre, Silver Street, Enfield EN1 3XQ ☎ 020 8379 3659 🖷 020 8379 3777 ✉ lorraine.cox@enfield.gov.uk

Facilities: Mr Stuart Simper, Acting Head of Facilities, PO Box 54, Civic Centre, Silver Street, Enfield EN1 3XF ☎ 020 8379 3032 🖷 020 8379 4455 ✉ stuart.simper@enfield.gov.uk

Finance and Treasurer: Mr Richard Tyler, Assistant Director, Finance, PO Box 54, Civic Centre, Silver Street, Enfield EN1 3XF ☎ 020 8379 4732 🖷 020 8379 5193 ✉ richard.tyler@enfield.gov.uk

Fleet Management: Mr Gary Barnes, Assistant Director, Highways & Transportation, PO Box 52, Civic Centre, Silver Street, Enfield EN1 3XD ☎ 020 8379 3600 🖷 020 8379 3475 ✉ gary.barnes@enfield.gov.uk

Grounds Maintenance: Mr Neil Issac, Assistant Director, Waste Management, Street Scene & Parks, PO Box 52, Civic Centre, Silver Street, Enfield EN1 3XD ☎ ; 020 8379 3760 🖷 020 8379 3475 ✉ neil.issac@enfield.gov.uk

Health and Safety: Mr John Griffiths, Corporate Safety Manager, PO Box 61, Civic Centre, Silver Street, Enfield EN1 3XY ☎ 020 8379 3696 🖷 020 8379 3922 ✉ john.griffiths@enfield.gov.uk

Highways: Mr Gary Barnes, Assistant Director, Highways & Transportation, PO Box 52, Civic Centre, Silver Street, Enfield

EN1 3XD ☎ 020 8379 3600 🖷 020 8379 3475
gary.barnes@enfield.gov.uk

Home Energy Conservation: Mr Stephen Tapper, Assistant Director, Place Shaping, Civic Centre, Silver Street, Enfield EN1 3XA ☎ 020 8379 3800 🖷 020 8379 4293
stephen.tapper@enfield.gov.uk

Housing: Ms Sally McTernan, Assistant Director of Community Housing Services, Civic Centre, Silver Street, Enfield EN1 3XA ☎ 020 8379 4465 🖷 020 8379 4274
sally.mcternan@enfield.gov.uk

Housing Maintenance: Ms Sally McTernan, Assistant Director of Community Housing Services, Civic Centre, Silver Street, Enfield EN1 3XA ☎ 020 8379 4465 🖷 020 8379 4274
sally.mcternan@enfield.gov.uk

Local Area Agreement: Ms Alison Trew, Head of Corporate Policy & Performance, Civic Centre, Silver Street, Enfield EN1 3XA ☎ 020 8379 3186 alison.trew@enfield.gov.uk

Legal: Ms Asmat Hussain, Assistant Director of Legal Services, PO Box 54, Civic Centre, Silver Street, Enfield EN1 3XF ☎ 020 8379 6438 🖷 020 8379 5138 asmat.hussain@enfield.gov.uk

Leisure and Cultural Services: Mr Neil Rousell, Director of Regeneration, Leisure & Culture, PO Box 56, Civic Centre, Silver Street, Enfield EN1 3XQ ☎ 020 8379 4968 🖷 020 8379 4293
neil.rousell@enfield.gov.uk

Licensing: Ms Sue McDaid, Head of Trading Standards & Licensing, Civic Centre, Silver Street, Enfield EN1 3XA ☎ 020 8379 3680 🖷 020 8379 8506 sue.mcdaid@enfield.gov.uk

Lifelong Learning: Mr Andrew Fraser, Director of Schools & Children's Services, PO Box 56, Civic Centre, Silver Street, Enfield EN1 3XQ ☎ 020 8379 3200 🖷 020 8379 3351
andrew.fraser@enfield.gov.uk

Lighting: Mr Gary Barnes, Assistant Director, Highways & Transportation, PO Box 52, Civic Centre, Silver Street, Enfield EN1 3XD ☎ 020 8379 3600 🖷 020 8379 3475
gary.barnes@enfield.gov.uk

Lottery Funding, Charity and Voluntary: Mr Shaun Rogan, Head of Communities, Partnerships & External Relations, Civic Centre, Silver Street, Enfield EN1 3XY ☎ 020 8379 3836 🖷 020 8379 4293 shaun.rogan@enfield.gov.uk

Member Services: Mr John Austin, Assistant Director, Corporate Governance, PO Box 54, Civic Centre, Silver Street, Enfield EN1 3XF ☎ 020 8379 4094 🖷 020 8379 5157
john.austin@enfield.gov.uk

Parking: Ms Elena Dellafiora, Head of Parking, Civic Centre, Silver Street, Enfield EN1 3XD ☎ 020 8379 6402
elena.dellafiora@enfield.gov.uk

Partnerships: Mr Shaun Rogan, Head of Communities, Partnerships & External Relations, Civic Centre, Silver Street, Enfield EN1 3XY ☎ 020 8379 3836 🖷 020 8379 4293
shaun.rogan@enfield.gov.uk

Personnel / HR: Mr Timothy Strong, Assistant Director, Human Resources, PO Box 61, Civic Centre, Silver Street, Enfield EN1 3XA ☎ 020 8379 4141 🖷 020 8379 3567
timothy.strong@enfield.gov.uk

Planning: Mr Bob Griffiths, Assistant Director, Planning & Environmental Protection, PO Box 52, Civic Centre, Silver Street, Enfield EN1 3XD ☎ 020 8379 3676 🖷 020 8379 5120
bob.griffiths@enfield.gov.uk

Procurement: Mr James Rolfe, Director of Finance, Resources & Customer Services, PO Box 54, Civic Centre, Silver Street, Enfield EN1 3XF ☎ 020 8379 4600 🖷 020 8379 5193
james.rolfe@enfield.gov.uk

Public Libraries: Ms Julie Gibson, Head of Libraries & Museums, Civic Centre, Silver Street, Enfield EN1 3XA ☎ 020 8379 3749
julie.gibson@enfield.gov.uk

Recycling & Waste Minimisation: Mr Neil Issac, Assistant Director, Waste Management, Street Scene & Parks, PO Box 52, Civic Centre, Silver Street, Enfield EN1 3XD ☎ 020 8379 3760 🖷 020 8379 3475 neil.issac@enfield.gov.uk

Regeneration: Ms Judy Flight, Head of Sustainable Communities, Civic Centre, Silver Street, Enfield EN1 3XA ☎ 020 8379 3175 🖷 020 8379 3000 judy.flight@enfield.gov.uk

Road Safety: Mr Roger Miles, Section Manager - Road Safety, PO Box 52, Civic Centre, Silver Street, Enfield EN1 3XD
☎ 020 8379 8545 roger.miles@enfield.gov.uk

Social Services: Mr Ray James, Director of Health, Housing & Adult Social Care, PO Box 59, Civic Centre, Silver Street, Enfield EN1 3XL ☎ 020 8379 4160 🖷 020 8379 4274
ray.james@enfield.gov.uk

Social Services (Adult): Mr Ray James, Director of Health, Housing & Adult Social Care, PO Box 59, Civic Centre, Silver Street, Enfield EN1 3XL ☎ 020 8379 4160 🖷 020 8379 4274
ray.james@enfield.gov.uk

Social Services (Children): Mr Andrew Fraser, Director of Schools & Children's Services, PO Box 56, Civic Centre, Silver Street, Enfield EN1 3XQ ☎ 020 8379 3200 🖷 020 8379 3351
andrew.fraser@enfield.gov.uk

Staff Training: Mr Timothy Strong, Assistant Director, Human Resources, PO Box 61, Civic Centre, Silver Street, Enfield EN1 3XA ☎ 020 8379 4141 🖷 020 8379 3567
timothy.strong@enfield.gov.uk

Street Scene: Mr Ian Davis, Director of Environment, PO Box 52, Civic Centre, Silver Street, Enfield EN1 3XD ☎ 020 8379 3500 🖷 020 8379 3475 ian.davis@enfield.gov.uk

Sustainable Communities: Ms Judy Flight, Head of Sustainable Communities, Civic Centre, Silver Street, Enfield EN1 3XA ☎ 020 8379 3175 🖷 020 8379 3000 judy.flight@enfield.gov.uk

Sustainable Development: Mr Stephen Tapper, Assistant Director, Place Shaping, Civic Centre, Silver Street, Enfield EN1 3XA ☎ 020 8379 3800 🖷 020 8379 4293 ✉ stephen.tapper@enfield.gov.uk

Tourism: Mr Neil Rousell, Director of Regeneration, Leisure & Culture, PO Box 56, Civic Centre, Silver Street, Enfield EN1 3XQ ☎ 020 8379 4968 🖷 020 8379 4293 ✉ neil.rousell@enfield.gov.uk

Town Centre: Mr Gary Barnes, Assistant Director, Highways & Transportation, PO Box 52, Civic Centre, Silver Street, Enfield EN1 3XD ☎ 020 8379 3600 🖷 020 8379 3475 ✉ gary.barnes@enfield.gov.uk

Traffic Management: Mr Gary Barnes, Assistant Director, Highways & Transportation, PO Box 52, Civic Centre, Silver Street, Enfield EN1 3XD ☎ 020 8379 3600 🖷 020 8379 3475 ✉ gary.barnes@enfield.gov.uk

Transport: Mr Gary Barnes, Assistant Director, Highways & Transportation, PO Box 52, Civic Centre, Silver Street, Enfield EN1 3XD ☎ 020 8379 3600 🖷 020 8379 3475 ✉ gary.barnes@enfield.gov.uk

Transport Planner: Mr Bob Griffiths, Assistant Director, Planning & Environmental Protection, PO Box 52, Civic Centre, Silver Street, Enfield EN1 3XD ☎ 020 8379 3676 🖷 020 8379 5120 ✉ bob.griffiths@enfield.gov.uk

Waste Collection and Disposal: Mr Neil Issac, Assistant Director, Waste Management, Street Scene & Parks, PO Box 52, Civic Centre, Silver Street, Enfield EN1 3XD ☎ 020 8379 3760 🖷 020 8379 3475 ✉ neil.issac@enfield.gov.uk

Waste Management: Mr Neil Issac, Assistant Director, Waste Management, Street Scene & Parks, PO Box 52, Civic Centre, Silver Street, Enfield EN1 3XD ☎ ; 020 8379 3760 🖷 020 8379 3475 ✉ neil.issac@enfield.gov.uk

MEMBERS OF THE COUNCIL (63)

***Mayor:* Anolue**, Kate (LAB - Upper Edmonton)
kate.anolue@enfield.gov.uk

***Deputy Mayor:* Anwar**, Chaudrey (LAB - Ponders End)
chaudrey.anwar@enfield.gov.uk

***Leader of the Council:* Taylor**, Doug (LAB - Ponders End)
doug.taylor@enfield.gov.uk

***Deputy Leader of the Council:* Georgiou**, Achilleas (LAB - Bowes)
cllr.achilleas.georgiou@enfield.gov.uk

Bakir, Ali (LAB - Haselbury)
ali.bakir@enfield.gov.uk

Barker, Alan (CON - Southgate Green)
alan.barker@enfield.gov.uk

Bearryman, Caitriona (LAB - Southbury)
caitriona.bearryman@enfield.gov.uk

Bond, Chris (LAB - Southbury)
chris.bond@enfield.gov.uk

Brett, Yasemin (LAB - Bowes)
yasemin.brett@enfield.gov.uk

Buckland, Jayne (LAB - Edmonton Green)
jayne.buckland@enfield.gov.uk

Cazimoglu, Alev (LAB - Enfield Highway)
alev.cazimoglu@enfield.gov.uk

Chamberlain, Lee (CON - Bush Hill Park)
cllr.lee.chamberlain@enfield.gov.uk

Charalambous, Bambos (LAB - Palmers Green)
bambos.charalambous@enfield.gov.uk

Cicek, Yusuf (LAB - Turkey Street)
yusuf.cicek@enfield.gov.uk

Cole, Christopher (LAB - Palmers Green)
christopher.cole@enfield.gov.uk

Constantinides, Andreas (LAB - Upper Edmonton)
andreas.constantinides@enfield.gov.uk

Cranfield, Ingrid (LAB - Lower Edmonton)
ingrid.cranfield@enfield.gov.uk

Deacon, Christopher (LAB - Jubilee)
christopher.deacon@enfield.gov.uk

Delman, Don (CON - Highlands)
don.delman@enfield.gov.uk

During, Christiana (LAB - Upper Edmonton)
christiana.during@enfield.gov.uk

East, Marcus (CON - Chase)
marcus.east@enfield.gov.uk

Ekechi, Patricia (LAB - Haselbury)
patricia.ekechi@enfield.gov.uk

Goddard, Del (LAB - Palmers Green)
del.goddard@enfield.gov.uk

Hall, Jonas (CON - Bush Hill Park)
jonas.hall@enfield.gov.uk

Hamilton, Christine (LAB - Enfield Lock)
christine.hamilton@enfield.gov.uk

Hasan, Ahmet (LAB - Jubilee)
ahmet.hasan@enfield.gov.uk

Hayward, Robert (CON - Southgate)
robert.hayward@enfield.gov.uk

Hayward, Elaine (CON - Winchmore Hill)
elaine.hayward@enfield.gov.uk

Headley, Denise (CON - Bush Hill Park)
denise.headley@enfield.gov.uk

Hurer, Ertan (CON - Winchmore Hill)
ertan.hurer@enfield.gov.uk

Ibrahim, Tahsin (LAB - Turkey Street)
tahsin.ibrahim@enfield.gov.uk

Joannides, Chris (CON - Grange)
chris.joannides@enfield.gov.uk

Jukes, Eric (CON - Town)
eric.jukes@enfield.gov.uk

Kaye, John (CON - Highlands)
jon.kaye@enfield.gov.uk

Keazor, Nneka (LAB - Enfield Lock)
nneka.keazor@enfield.gov.uk

Laban, Joanne (CON - Town)
joanne.laban@enfield.gov.uk

Lamprecht, Henry (CON - Southgate Green)
henry.lamprecht@enfield.gov.uk

Lavender, Michael (CON - Cockfosters)
michael.lavender@enfield.gov.uk

Lemonides, Dino (LAB - Enfield Highway)
dino.lemonides@enfield.gov.uk

Levy, Derek (LAB - Southbury)
derek.levy@enfield.gov.uk

Maynard, Simon (LAB - Chase)
simon.maynard@enfield.gov.uk

McCannah, Paul (CON - Cockfosters)
paul.mccannah@enfield.gov.uk

McGowan, Donald (LAB - Turkey Street)
donald.mcgowan@enfield.gov.uk

Murphy, Chris (LAB - Edmonton Green)
chris.murphy@enfield.gov.uk
Neville, Terence (CON - Grange)
terence.neville@enfield.gov.uk
Orhan, Ayfer (LAB - Ponders End)
ayfer.orhan@enfield.gov.uk
Oykener, Ahmet (LAB - Lower Edmonton)
ahmet.oykener@enfield.gov.uk
Peace, Anne-Marie (CON - Highlands)
annemarie.peace@enfield.gov.uk
Pearce, Daniel (CON - Southgate)
daniel.pearce@enfield.gov.uk
Prescott, Martin (CON - Winchmore Hill)
martin.prescott@enfield.gov.uk
Robinson, Geoffrey (LAB - Lower Edmonton)
geoffrey.robinson@enfield.gov.uk
Rye, Michael (CON - Town)
michael.rye@enfield.gov.uk
Savva, George (LAB - Haselbury)
george.savva@enfield.gov.uk
Simbodyal, Rohini (LAB - Jubilee)
rohini.simbodyal@enfield.gov.uk
Simon, Toby (LAB - Enfield Highway)
toby.simon@enfield.gov.uk
Sitkin, Alan (LAB - Bowes)
alan.sitkin@enfield.gov.uk
Smith, Edward (CON - Southgate)
edward.smith@enfield.gov.uk
Stafford, Andrew (LAB - Edmonton Green)
andrew.stafford@enfield.gov.uk
Uzoanya, Ozzie (LAB - Enfield Lock)
Cllr.Ozzie.Uzoanya@enfield.gov.uk
Vince, Glynis (CON - Grange)
glynis.vince@enfield.gov.uk
Waterhouse, Tom (CON - Chase)
tom.waterhouse@enfield.gov.uk
Zetter, Lionel (CON - Cockfosters)
lional.zetter@enfield.gov.uk
Zinkin, Ann (CON - Southgate Green)
ann.zinkin@enfield.gov.uk

POLITICAL COMPOSITION
LAB: 37, CON: 26

CABINET
Leader: Mr Doug Taylor
Deputy Leader: Mr Achilleas Georgiou
Adult Services, Care & Health: Mr Donald McGowan
Business & Regeneration: Mr Del Goddard
Children & Young People: Ms Ayfer Orhan
Community Wellbeing & Public Health: Ms Christine Hamilton
Culture, Leisure, Youth & Localism: Mr Bambos Charalambous
Environment: Mr Chris Bond
Finance & Property: Mr Andrew Stafford
Housing: Mr Ahmet Oykener

COMMITTEE CHAIRS
Audit: Mr Dino Lemonides
Children & Young People Scrutiny Panel: Ms Rohini Simbodyal
Crime & Safety & Strong Communities Scrutiny Panel: Mr Michael Rye
Health & Wellbeing Scrutiny Panel: Ms Alev Cazimoglu
Housing, Growth & Regeneration Scrutiny Panel: Mr Edward Smith
Licensing: Mr Derek Levy
Member & Democratic Services Group: Mr Toby Simon
Older People & Vulnerable Adults Scrutiny Panel: Mr George Savva
Overview & Scrutiny Committee: Mr Toby Simon
Pensions Fund: Mr Tahsin Ibrahim
Planning: Mr Andreas Constantinides

EPPING FOREST D

Epping Forest District Council, Civic Offices, High Street, Epping CM16 4BZ ☎ 01992 564000 🖷 01992 578018
information@eppingforestdc.gov.uk
www.eppingforestdc.gov.uk

FACTS & FIGURES
Police Authority: Essex Police Authority
Health Authority: East of England Strategic Health Authority
Learning and Skills Council: Eastern
Parliamentary Constituencies: Epping Forest
EU Constituencies: Eastern
Election Frequency: Elections are by thirds

PRINCIPAL OFFICERS
Chief Executive: Mr Derek Macnab, Acting Chief Executive, Civic Offices, High Street, Epping CM16 4BZ
shawkins@eppingforestdc.gov.uk

Deputy Chief Executive: Mr Derek Macnab, Deputy Chief Executive, Civic Offices, High Street, Epping CM16 4BZ ☎ 01992 564050 🖷 01992 564445 dmacnab@eppingforestdc.gov.uk

Assistant Chief Executive: Mr Ian Willett, Assistant Chief Executive, Civic Offices, High Street, Epping CM16 4BZ ☎ 01992 564243 🖷 01992 564445 iwillett@eppingforestdc.gov.uk

Architect, Building / Property Services: Mr Qasim Durrani, Assistant Director (Technical) Environment & Street Scene, Civic Offices, High Street, Epping CM16 4BZ ☎ 01992 564055 🖷 01992 561016 qdurrani@eppingforestdc.gov.uk

Best Value: Mr Steve Tautz, Performance Improvements Manager, Civic Offices, High Street, Epping CM16 4BZ ☎ 01992 564180 stautz@eppingforestdc.gov.uk

Building Control: Mr John Kershaw, Assistant Director (Building Control), Civic Offices, High Street, Epping CM16 4BZ ☎ 01992 564142 🖷 01992 564229 jkershaw@eppingforestdc.gov.uk

Children / Youth Services: Ms Julie Chandler, Assistant Director (Community Services & Customer Relations), Hemnall Street, Epping CM16 4LU ☎ 01992 564214
jchandler@eppingforestdc.gov.uk

PR / Communications: Mr Tom Carne, Public Relations & Marketing Officer, Civic Offices, High Street, Epping CM16 4BZ ☎ 01992 564039 🖷 01992 564488
tcarne@eppingforestdc.gov.uk

Community Planning: Ms Gill Wallis, Community Development Officer, Civic Offices, High Street, Epping CM16 4BZ ☎ 01992

564557 gwallis@eppingforest.gov.uk

Community Safety: Mrs Caroline Wiggins, Safer Communities Manager, Civic Offices, High Street, Epping CM16 4BZ ☎ 01992 564122 cwiggins@eppingforestdc.gov.uk

Computer Management: Mr David Newton, Assistant Director (ICT), Civic Offices, High Street, Epping CM16 4BZ ☎ 01992 564580 dnewton@eppingforest.gov.uk

Computer Management: Mr Bob Palmer, Director of Finance & ICT, Civic Offices, High Street, Epping CM16 4BZ ☎ 01992 564279 🖷 01992 564510 bpalmer@eppingforestdc.gov.uk

Contracts: Mr Derek Macnab, Deputy Chief Executive, Civic Offices, High Street, Epping CM16 4BZ ☎ 01992 564050 🖷 01992 564445 dmacnab@eppingforestdc.gov.uk

Customer Service: Ms Jenny Filby, Complaints Officer, Civic Offices, High Street, Epping CM16 4BZ ☎ 01992 564512 jfilby@eppingforest.gov.uk

Customer Service: Mr Derek Macnab, Deputy Chief Executive, Civic Offices, High Street, Epping CM16 4BZ ☎ 01992 564050 🖷 01992 564445 dmacnab@eppingforestdc.gov.uk

Economic Development: Mr John de Wilton Preston, Director of Planning & Economic Development, Civic Offices, High Street, Epping CM16 4BZ ☎ 01992 564111 jdewiltonpreston@eppingforest.gov.uk

E-Government: Mr Bob Palmer, Director of Finance & ICT, Civic Offices, High Street, Epping CM16 4BZ ☎ 01992 564279 🖷 01992 564510 bpalmer@eppingforestdc.gov.uk

Electoral Registration: Ms Wendy Macleod, Senior Electoral Services Officer, Civic Offices, High Street, Epping CM16 4BZ ☎ 01992 564023 🖷 01992 578018 wmacleod@eppingforestdc.gov.uk

Emergency Planning: Mr Mike Tipping, Assistant Director (Facilities Management & Emergency Planning), Civic Offices, High Street, Epping CM16 4BZ ☎ 01992 564280 🖷 01992 564116 mtipping@eppingforestdc.gov.uk

Energy Management: Mr Qasim Durrani, Assistant Director (Technical) Environment & Street Scene, Civic Offices, High Street, Epping CM16 4BZ ☎ 01992 564055 🖷 01992 561016 qdurrani@eppingforestdc.gov.uk

Environmental / Technical Services: Mr John Gilbert, Director of Environment & Street Scene, Civic Offices, High Street, Epping CM16 4BZ ☎ 01992 564062 🖷 01992 561016 jgilbert@eppingforestdc.gov.uk

Environmental Health: Mr James Nolan, Assistant Director (Environments & Neighbourhoods), Civic Offices, High Street, Epping CM16 4BZ ☎ 01992 564083 🖷 01992 561016 jnolan@eppingforestdc.gov.uk

Facilities: Mr Mike Tipping, Assistant Director (Facilities Management & Emergency Planning), Civic Offices, High Street, Epping CM16 4BZ ☎ 01992 564280 🖷 01992 564116 mtipping@eppingforestdc.gov.uk

Finance and Treasurer: Mr Peter Maddock, Assistant Director (Accountancy), Civic Offices, High Street, Epping CM16 4BZ ☎ 01992 564602 pmaddock@eppingforest.gov.uk

Finance and Treasurer: Mr Bob Palmer, Director of Finance & ICT, Civic Offices, High Street, Epping CM16 4BZ ☎ 01992 564279 🖷 01992 564510 bpalmer@eppingforestdc.gov.uk

Finance and Treasurer: Mr Robert Pavey, Assistant Director (Revenues), Civic Offices, High Street, Epping CM16 4BZ ☎ 01992 564211 rpavey@eppingforest.gov.uk

Finance and Treasurer: Ms Janet Twinn, Assistant Director (Benefits), Civic Offices, High Street, Epping CM16 4BZ ☎ 01992 564215 jtwinn@eppingforest.gov.uk

Grounds Maintenance: Ms Laura MacNeill, Assistant Director (Performance & Operations), 25 Hemnall Street, Epping CM16 4LX ☎ 01992 564223 🖷 01992 564250 lmacneill@eppingforestdc.gov.uk

Home Energy Conservation: Mr James Nolan, Assistant Director (Environments & Neighbourhoods), Civic Offices, High Street, Epping CM16 4BZ ☎ 01992 564083 🖷 01992 561016 jnolan@eppingforestdc.gov.uk

Housing: Mr Alan Hall, Director of Housing, Civic Offices, High Street, Epping CM16 4BZ ☎ 01992 564004 🖷 01992 564230 ahall@eppingforestdc.gov.uk

Housing: Ms Lyndsay Swan, Assistant Director (Private Sector & Resources), Civic Offices, High Street, Epping CM16 4BZ ☎ 01992 564146 lswan@eppingforest.gov.uk

Housing Maintenance: Mr Paul Pledger, Assistant Director (Property), Civic Offices, High Street, Epping CM16 4BZ ☎ 01992 564248 🖷 01992 564230 ppledger@eppingforestdc.gov.uk

Housing Maintenance: Mr Roger Wilson, Assistant Director (Operations), Civic Offices, High Street, Epping CM16 4BZ ☎ 01992 564419 rwilson@eppingforest.gov.uk

Legal: Ms Alison Mitchell, Assistant Director (Legal), Civic Offices, High Street, Epping CM16 4BZ ☎ 01992 564017 amitchell@eppingforest.gov.uk

Legal: Ms Colleen O'Boyle, Director of Corporate Support Services/Solicior to the Council, Civic Offices, High Street, Epping CM16 4BZ ☎ 01992 564475 🖷 01992 578018 coboyle@eppingforestdc.gov.uk

Leisure and Cultural Services: Ms Felicity Hall, Arts Officer, Civic Offices, High Street, Epping CM16 4BZ ☎ 01992 564553 fhall@eppingforest.gov.uk

Leisure and Cultural Services: Mr Derek Macnab, Deputy Chief Executive, Civic Offices, High Street, Epping CM16 4BZ ☎ 01992 564050 🖷 01992 564445 dmacnab@eppingforestdc.gov.uk

Leisure and Cultural Services: Mr Tony O'Connor, Museum Offier, Civic Offices, High Street, Epping CM16 4BZ ☎ 01992 716882 ✉ toconnor@eppingforest.gov.uk

Leisure and Cultural Services: Mr James Warwick, Sports Development Manager, Civic Offices, High Street, Epping CM16 4BZ ☎ 01992 564350 ✉ jwarwick@eppingforest.gov.uk

Lottery Funding, Charity and Voluntary: Mr Chris Overend, Policy & Research Officer, Civic Offices, High Street, Epping CM16 4BZ ☎ 01992 564247 🖷 01992 564445 ✉ coverend@eppingforestdc.gov.uk

Member Services: Mr Simon Hill, Senior Democratic Services Manager, Civic Offices, High Street, Epping CM16 4BZ ☎ 01992 564240 ✉ shill@eppingforest.gov.uk

Member Services: Mr Graham Lunnun, Assistant Director (Democratic Services), Civic Offices, High Street, Epping CM16 4BZ ☎ 01992 564244 🖷 01992 564445 ✉ glunnun@eppingforestdc.gov.uk

Parking: Mr John Gilbert, Director of Environment & Street Scene, Civic Offices, High Street, Epping CM16 4BZ ☎ 01992 564062 🖷 01992 561016 ✉ jgilbert@eppingforestdc.gov.uk

Personnel / HR: Mrs Paula Maginnis, Assistant Director (Human Resources), Civic Offices, High Street, Epping CM16 4BZ ☎ 01992 564536 🖷 01992 564075 ✉ pmaginnis@eppingforestdc.gov.uk

Planning: Mr John de Wilton Preston, Director of Planning & Economic Development, Civic Offices, High Street, Epping CM16 4BZ ☎ 01992 564111 ✉ jdewiltonpreston@eppingforest.gov.uk

Planning: Ms Kassandra Polyzoidea, Assistant Director of Policy & Conservation (Planning), Civic Offices, High Street, Epping CM16 4BZ ☎ 01992 564119 ✉ kpolyzoidea@eppingforest.gov.uk

Planning: Mr Nigel Richardson, Assistant Director (Development Control), Civic Offices, High Street, Epping CM16 4BZ ☎ 01992 564110 ✉ nrichardson@eppingforest.gov.uk

Procurement: Mr Mike Tipping, Assistant Director (Facilities Management & Emergency Planning), Civic Offices, High Street, Epping CM16 4BZ ☎ 01992 564280 🖷 01992 564116 ✉ mtipping@eppingforestdc.gov.uk

Staff Training: Mrs Paula Maginnis, Assistant Director (Human Resources), Civic Offices, High Street, Epping CM16 4BZ ☎ 01992 564536 🖷 01992 564075 ✉ pmaginnis@eppingforestdc.gov.uk

Street Scene: Mr John Gilbert, Director of Environment & Street Scene, Civic Offices, High Street, Epping CM16 4BZ ☎ 01992 564062 🖷 01992 561016 ✉ jgilbert@eppingforestdc.gov.uk

Waste Management: Mr John Gilbert, Director of Environment & Street Scene, Civic Offices, High Street, Epping CM16 4BZ ☎ 01992 564062 🖷 01992 561016 ✉ jgilbert@eppingforestdc.gov.uk

MEMBERS OF THE COUNCIL (58)

***Chair:* Rolfe**, Brian (CON - Lambourne)
cllrbrianrolfe@hotmail.co.uk

***Vice-Chair:* Sartin**, Mary (CON - Roydon)
marysartin@yahoo.com

***Leader of the Council:* Whitbread**, Chris (CON - Epping Lindsey and Thornwood Common)
chris.whitbread@btinternet.com

***Deputy Leader of the Council:* Stavrou**, Syd (CON - Waltham Abbey High Beach)
sydstavrou@yahoo.com

Angold-Stephens, Kenneth (R - Loughton Roding)
ken@angold-stephens.co.uk

Avery, Kenneth (CON - Epping Hemnall)
kfcavey@btinternet.com

Bassett, Richard (CON - Lower Nazeing)
richard.d.bassett@ntlworld.com

Boyce, Tony (CON - Moreton and Fyfield)
tonyboyce@aol.com

Brady, Heather (CON - Passingford)
heatherbrady@hotmail.co.uk

Breare-Hall, Will (CON - Epping Lindsey and Thornwood Common)
wsbh@hotmail.co.uk

Chambers, Gavin (CON - Buckhurst Hill West)
cllr.g.chambers@gmail.com

Chana, Kewel (CON - Grange Hill)
kewalchana@yahoo.co.uk

Church, Tony (CON - Epping Lindsey and Thornwood Common)
tony@churchspires.com

Cochrane, Tessa (R - Loughton Fairmead)
tessa.cochrane@ntlworld.com

Cohen, Richard (R - Loughton St Mary's)
rcohenfdc@hotmail.com

Finn, Colin (R - Loughton Forest)
finnsathome@msn.com

Gadsby, Ricki (CON - Waltham Abbey South West)

Girling, Leon (R - Loughton Broadway)
leongirling@gmail.com

Gode, Peter (LAB - Shelley)

Grigg, Anne (CON - North Weald Bassett)
annegrigg@live.co.uk

Hart, James (CON - Loughton Forest)
hartjmh@bloomberg.net

Hart, Jennie (R - Loughton Broadway)
jennie.hart@loughtonresidents.co.uk

Jacobs, Derek (LD - Chipping Ongar, Greensted and Marden Ash)
derek-elaine@d-e-jacobs.fsnet.co.uk

Johnson, David (CON - Waltham Abbey Honey Lane)
david.john5on@virgin.net

Jones, Sue (CON - Theydon Bois)
sue.jones193@ntlworld.com

Kane, Helen (CON - Waltham Abbey South West)
helen@samkane.co.uk

Keska, Paul (CON - Chipping Ongar, Greensted and Marden Ash)
cllr.ps.keska@hotmail.co.uk

Knapman, John (CON - Chigwell Village)
jknapman@msn.com

Knight, Yolanda (CON - Lower Nazeing)
yogard@hotmail.co.uk

Lea, Jeanne (CON - Waltham Abbey North East)

Leonard, Lance (R - Loughton Alderton)

ltleonard@aol.com
Lion, Alan (CON - Grange Hill)
al.lion@btinternet.com
Mann, Harvey (R - Loughton St Mary's)
Markham, John (R - Loughton St Johns)
McEwen, Maggie (CON - High Ongar, Willingale and The Rodings)
heath.lands@btinternet.com
Mitchell, Ann (CON - Waltham Abbey North East)
lillianmitchell@sky.com
Mohindra, Gagan (CON - Grange Hill)
gagan.mohindra@chromexgroup.com
Morgan, Richard (IND - Hastingwood, Matching and Sheering Village)
richard@littlefaggoters.wanadoo.co.uk
Murray, Stephen (IND - Loughton Roding)
Philip, John (CON - Theydon Bois)
john.philip1@ntlworld.com
Pond, Caroline (R - Loughton St Johns)
caroline_pond@hotmail.com
Sandler, Brian (CON - Chigwell Row)
bpsandler@aol.com
Shiell, Glynis (CON - Waltham Abbey Honey Lane)
Smith, Penny (CON - Broadley Common, Epping Green and Nazeing)
pennysmith@btinternet.com
Spencer, Peter (LD - Buckhurst Hill East)
Stallan, David (CON - North Weald Bassett)
dave.stallan@tesco.net
Thomas, Tracey (R - Loughton Alderton)
traceythomas210@msn.com
Ulkun, Haluk (CON - Buckhurst Hill West)
Wagland, Lesley (CON - Chigwell Village)
lwebber@live.co.uk
Waller, Gary (CON - Lower Sheering)
gary.waller@which.net
Watson, Sylvia (CON - Buckhurst Hill West)
sylvia_watson@btconnect.com
Watts, Antony (CON - Waltham Abbey Honey Lane)
Webster, Elizabeth (CON - Waltham Abbey Paternoster)
cllr.elizabeth.webster@essexcc.gov.uk
Whitehouse, Janet (LD - Epping Hemnall)
janet.whitehouse@eflibdems.org.uk
Whitehouse, Jon (LD - Epping Hemnall)
jon@jonwhitehouse.org.uk
Wixley, David (R - Loughton Fairmead)
david.wixley@talktalk.net
Wright, Neville (CON - Buckhurst Hill East)
nevillewright64@hotmail.com
Wyatt, John (CON - Waltham Abbey Paternoster)
wyatt_john1@sky.com

POLITICAL COMPOSITION
CON: 39, R: 12, LD: 4, IND: 2, LAB: 1

CABINET
Leader: Mr Chris Whitbread
Deputy Leader / Finance & Technology: Ms Syd Stavrou
Economic Development: Ms Anne Grigg
Environment: Mr Will Breare-Hall
Housing: Mr David Stallan
Leisure & Wellbeing: Ms Elizabeth Webster
Planning: Mr Richard Bassett
Safer, Greener & Highways: Mr Gary Waller
Support Services: Mr Haluk Ulkun

COMMITTEE CHAIRS
Audit & Governance: Mr Antony Watts
Electoral & Community Governance Review: Mr John Philip
Finance & Performance Management: Mr Alan Lion
Housing Appeals: Mr Ann Mitchell
Housing Scrutiny: Mr Stephen Murray
Licensing: Mr Kenneth Angold-Stephens
Overview & Scrutiny: Mr Richard Morgan
Planning Services: Mr John Wyatt
Safer, Cleaner, Greener Scrutiny Standing (Scrutiny): Ms Jeanne Lea

EPSOM & EWELL D
Epsom & Ewell Borough Council, Town Hall, The Parade, Epsom KT18 5BY ☎ 01372 732000 🖷 01372 732020
contactus@epsom-ewell.gov.uk
www.epsom-ewell.gov.uk

FACTS & FIGURES
Police Authority: Surrey Police Authority
Health Authority: South East Coast Strategic Health Authority
Learning and Skills Council: South East
Parliamentary Constituencies: Epsom and Ewell
EU Constituencies: South East
Election Frequency: Elections are of whole council
Twinning: Chantilly (France)

PRINCIPAL OFFICERS
Chief Executive: Mrs Frances Rutter, Chief Executive, Town Hall, The Parade, Epsom KT18 5BY ☎ 01372 732104 🖷 01372 732111 frutter@epsom-ewell.gov.uk

Senior Management: Mrs Irene Clarke, Director of HR & Communications, Town Hall, The Parade, Epsom KT18 5BY ☎ 01372 732104 iclarke@epsom-ewell.gov.uk

Senior Management: Mr Steve Davies, Director of Operations, Town Hall, The Parade, Epsom KT18 5BY ☎ 01372 732102 🖷 01372 732111 sdavies@epsom-ewell.gov.uk

Senior Management: Mr John Turnbull, Director of Finance, Town Hall, The Parade, Epsom KT18 5BY ☎ 01372 732102 🖷 01372 732288 jturnbull@epsom-ewell.gov.uk

Building Control: Mr Mark Berry, Head of Planning & Building Control, Town Hall, The Parade, Epsom KT18 5BY ☎ 01372 732391 🖷 01372 732365 mberry@epsom-ewell.gov.uk

PR / Communications: Mr Mark Rouson, Communications Officer, Town Hall, The Parade, Epsom KT18 5BY ☎ 01372 732080 mrouson@epson-ewell.gov.uk

Community Planning: Mr Andrew Eperson, Head of Policy & Partnerships, Town Hall, The Parade, Epsom KT18 5BY ☎ 01372 732402 🖷 01372 732452 aeperson@epsom-ewell.gov.uk

Community Safety: Ms Katrina Best, Community Safety Officer, Town Hall, The Parade, Epsom KT18 5BY ☎ 01372 732133

kbest@epsom-ewell.gov.uk

Computer Management: Mr Mark Lumley, Head of ICT, Town Hall, The Parade, Epsom KT18 5BY ☎ 01372 732174 mlumley@epsom-ewell.gov.uk

Customer Service: Mrs Joy Stevens, Head of Customer Services, Town Hall, The Parade, Epsom KT18 5BY ☎ 01372 732701 jstevens@epsom-ewell.gov.uk

Direct Labour: Mr Ian Dyer, Head of Operational Services, Longmead Depot, Blenheim Road, Epsom KT19 9AP ☎ 01372 732520 idyer@epsom-ewell.gov.uk

E-Government: Mr Steve Davies, Director of Operations, Town Hall, The Parade, Epsom KT18 5BY ☎ 01372 732102 🖷 01372 732111 sdavies@epsom-ewell.gov.uk

Electoral Registration: Ms Kerry Blundell, Electoral Registration Officer, Town Hall, The Parade, Epsom KT18 5BY ☎ 01372 732152 kblundell@epsom-ewell.gov.uk

Emergency Planning: Mr Doug Earle, Head of Corporate Risk & Facilities, Town Hall, The Parade, Epsom KT18 5BY ☎ 01372 732211 dearle@epsom-ewell.gov.uk

Environmental Health: Mr David Rowley, Head of Housing and Environment, Town Hall, The Parade, Epsom KT18 5BY ☎ 01372 732000 drowley@epsom-ewell.gov.uk

Estates, Property & Valuation: Mr Brendan Smith, Estates Manager, Town Hall, The Parade, Epsom KT18 5BY ☎ 01372 732143 bsmith@epsom-ewell.gov.uk

Facilities: Mr Doug Earle, Head of Corporate Risk & Facilities, Town Hall, The Parade, Epsom KT18 5BY ☎ 01372 732211 dearle@epsom-ewell.gov.uk

Finance and Treasurer: Ms J Doney, Head of Revenues & Benefits, Town Hall, The Parade, Epsom KT18 5BY ☎ 01372 732000 jdoney@epsom-ewell.gov.uk

Finance and Treasurer: Mr Lee Duffy, Head of Financial Services, Town Hall, The Parade, Epsom KT18 5BY ☎ 01372 732210 lduffy@epsom-ewell.gov.uk

Finance and Treasurer: Mr Doug Earle, Head of Corporate Risk & Facilities, Town Hall, The Parade, Epsom KT18 5BY ☎ 01372 732211 dearle@epsom-ewell.gov.uk

Health and Safety: Ms Pauline Baxter, Corporate Health & Safety Officer, Town Hall, The Parade, Epsom KT18 5BY ☎ 01372 732410 🖷 01372 732452 pbaxter@epsom-ewell.gov.uk

Housing: Ms Annette Snell, Housing Manager, Town Hall, The Parade, Epsom KT18 5BY ☎ 01372 732436 🖷 01372 732440 asnell@epsom-ewell.gov.uk

Legal: Mr Simon Young, Head of Legal & Democratic Services, Town Hall, The Parade, Epsom KT18 5BY ☎ 01372 732148 syoung@epsom-ewell.gov.uk

Leisure and Cultural Services: Mr Andrew Eperson, Head of Policy & Partnerships, Town Hall, The Parade, Epsom KT18 5BY ☎ 01372 732402 🖷 01372 732452 aeperson@epsom-ewell.gov.uk

Licensing: Mrs Rachel Jackson, Licensing Officer, Town Hall, The Parade, Epsom KT18 5BY ☎ 01372 732449 🖷 01372 732365 rjackson@epsom-ewell.gov.uk

Member Services: Miss Fiona Cotter, Democratic Services Manager, Town Hall, The Parade, Epsom KT18 5BY ☎ 01372 732124 🖷 01372 732111 fcotter@epsom-ewell.gov.uk

Parking: Mr Robin Muir, Parking Manager, Town Hall, The Parade, Epsom KT18 5BY ☎ 01372 732000 (option 3)

Personnel / HR: Mrs Jenny Lester, HR Manager, Town Hall, The Parade, Epsom KT18 5BY ☎ 01372 732127 jlester@epsom-ewell.gov.uk

Planning: Mr Mark Berry, Head of Planning & Building Control, Town Hall, The Parade, Epsom KT18 5BY ☎ 01372 732391 🖷 01372 732365 mberry@epsom-ewell.gov.uk

Procurement: Mr Derek Smith, Procurement Officer, Town Hall, The Parade, Epsom KT18 5BY ☎ 01372 732000 dsmith@epsom-ewell.gov.uk

Recycling & Waste Minimisation: Mr Ian Dyer, Head of Operational Services, Longmead Depot, Blenheim Road, Epsom KT19 9AP ☎ 01372 732520 idyer@epsom-ewell.gov.uk

Regeneration: Mr Andrew Eperson, Head of Policy & Partnerships, Town Hall, The Parade, Epsom KT18 5BY ☎ 01372 732402 🖷 01372 732452 aeperson@epsom-ewell.gov.uk

Sustainable Communities: Mr Andrew Eperson, Head of Policy & Partnerships, Town Hall, The Parade, Epsom KT18 5BY ☎ 01372 732402 🖷 01372 732452 aeperson@epsom-ewell.gov.uk

Waste Collection and Disposal: Mr Ian Dyer, Head of Operational Services, Longmead Depot, Blenheim Road, Epsom KT19 9AP ☎ 01372 732520 idyer@epsom-ewell.gov.uk

Waste Management: Mr Ian Dyer, Head of Operational Services, Longmead Depot, Blenheim Road, Epsom KT19 9AP ☎ 01372 732520 idyer@epsom-ewell.gov.uk

MEMBERS OF THE COUNCIL (38)

Ardern-Jones, Paul (R - Stamford)
parden-jones@epsom-ewell.gov.uk

Arthur, Michael (R - Ewell)
marthur@epsom-ewell.gov.uk

Beckett, John (R - Auriol)
jbeckett@epsom-ewell.gov.uk

Booker, Ian (R - Town)
ibooker@epsom-ewell.gov.uk

Bradley, Pamela (R - Stoneleigh)
pbradley@epsom-ewell.gov.uk

Cahill-Sawford, Ben (R - Woodcote)
bchaill-sawford@epsom-ewell.gov.uk

Carlson, Sheila (LAB - Court)
scarlson@epsom-ewell.gov.uk
Clarke, James (CON - Ruxley)
jamesclarke@epsom-ewell.gov.uk
Crawford, George (R - Cuddington)
gcrawford@epsom-ewell.gov.uk
Dale, Darren (CON - Stoneleigh)
ddale@epsom-ewell.gov.uk
Dallen, Lucie (R - West Ewell)
ldallen@epsom-ewell.gov.uk
Dallen, Paul (R - Woodcote)
pdallen@epsom-ewell.gov.uk
Dallen, Neil (R - Town)
ndallen@epsom-ewell.gov.uk
Dudley, Graham (R - Nonsuch)
gdudley@epsom-ewell.gov.uk
Foote, Robert (R - Cuddington)
rfoote@epsom-ewell.gov.uk
Frost, Chris (R - Nonsuch)
cfrost@epsom-ewell.gov.uk
Frost, Liz (R - Woodcote)
lfrost@epsom-ewell.gov.uk
Geleit, Rob (LAB - Court)
rgeleit@epsom-ewell.gov.uk
Glover, Judith (R - Cuddington)
jglover@epsom-ewell.gov.uk
Jones, Anna (LD - College)
ajones@epsom-ewell.gov.uk
Keen, William (CON - Ruxley)
wkeen@epsom-ewell.gov.uk
Kelly, Alison (LD - Town)
akelly@epsom-ewell.gov.uk
Key, Christine (LD - College)
ckey@epsom-ewell.gov.uk
Kington, Eber (R - Ewell Court)
ekington@merton.atl.org.uk
Long, Christine (R - Auriol)
clong@epsom-ewell.gov.uk
Mason, Janet (R - Ruxley)
jmason@epsom-ewell.gov.uk
Mayall, Dave (R - Ewell Court)
dmayall@epsom-ewell.gov.uk
Morris, Julie (LD - College)
jmorris@epsom-ewell.gov.uk
Pavey, Nigel (LD - Stamford)
npavey@epsom-ewell.gov.uk
Reynolds, Humphrey (R - Ewell)
hreynolds@epsom-ewell.gov.uk
Smith, Jean (R - Ewell Court)
jsmith@epsom-ewell.gov.uk
Smitherham, Clive (R - West Ewell)
csmitherham@epsom-ewell.gov.uk
Steer, Jean (R - West Ewell)
jsteer@epsom-ewell.gov.uk
Stevens, Dan (LAB - Court)
dstevens@epsom-ewell.gov.uk
Taylor, Colin (LD - Stamford)
colintaylor@epsom-ewell.gov.uk
Teasdale, Michael (R - Stoneleigh)
mteasdale@epsom-ewell.gov.uk
Wood, David (R - Nonsuch)
dwood@epsom-ewell.gov.uk
Woodbridge, Clive (R - Ewell)
cwoodbridge@epsom-ewell.gov.uk

POLITICAL COMPOSITION

R: 26, LD: 6, CON: 3, LAB: 3

EREWASH D

Erewash Borough Council, Sandiacre Friesland Sports Centre, Nursery Avenue, Sandiacre NG10 5HG ☎ 0845 907 2244 🖷 0115 907 1121 💻 www.erewash.gov.uk

FACTS & FIGURES

Police Authority: Derbyshire Police Authority
Health Authority: East Midlands Strategic Health Authority
Learning and Skills Council: Eastern
Parliamentary Constituencies: Erewash
EU Constituencies: Eastern
Election Frequency: Elections are of whole council
Twinning: Ilkeston: Chalons-sur-Marne (France); Long Eaton: Romorantin (France); Langen (Germany)

PRINCIPAL OFFICERS

Chief Executive: Mr Jeremy Jaroszek, Chief Executive, Town Hall, Ilkeston DE7 5RP ☎ 0845 907 2244 🖷 0115 944 3269 ✉ jeremy.jaroszek@erewash.gov.uk

Deputy Chief Executive: Mr Ian Sankey, Director for Resources / Deputy Chief Executive, Town Hall, Ilkeston DE7 5RP ☎ 0845 907 2244 🖷 0115 944 3269 ✉ ian.sankey@erewash.gov.uk

Assistant Chief Executive: Ms Lorraine Poyser, Assistant Chief Executive, Town Hall, Ilkeston DE7 5RP ☎ 0845 907 2244 🖷 0115 907 1121 ✉ lorraine.poyser@erewash.gov.uk

Senior Management: Mr Phillip Wright, Director for Operational Services, Merlin House, Merlin Way, Ilkeston DE7 4RA ☎ 0845 907 2244 🖷 0115 931 6079 ✉ phillip.wright@erewash.gov.uk

Best Value: Mrs Rachel Fernandez, Corporate Planning Manager, Town Hall, Ilkeston DE7 5RP ☎ 0845 907 2244 🖷 0115 907 1211 ✉ rachel.fernandez@erewash.gov.uk

Building Control: Mr Peter Baker, Building Control Manager, Town Hall, Long Eaton NG10 1HU ☎ 0845 907 2244 🖷 0115 907 2343 ✉ peter.baker@erewash.gov.uk

PR / Communications: Mr Stewart Millar, Communications & Consultation Manager, Town Hall, Ilkeston DE7 5RP ☎ 0845 907 2244 🖷 0115 907 1121 ✉ stewart.millar@erewash.gov.uk

Community Safety: Mr Nick Thurstan, Head of Environment & Community Safety, Merlin House, Merlin Way, Ilkeston DE7 4RA ☎ 0845 907 2244 🖷 0115 931 6079 ✉ nick.thurstan@erewash.gov.uk

Computer Management: Mr Neil Webster, ICT Manager, Town Hall, Long Eaton NG10 1HU ☎ 0845 907 2244 🖷 0115 931 6001 ✉ neil.webster@erewash.gov.uk

Corporate Services: Mr Ian Sankey, Director for Resources / Deputy Chief Executive, Town Hall, Ilkeston DE7 5RP ☎ 0845 907 2244 🖷 0115 944 3269 ✉ ian.sankey@erewash.gov.uk

Customer Service: Mr Stuart Lloyd, Head of Customer &

Support Services, Town Hall, Long Eaton NG10 1HU ☎ 0845 907 2244 🖷 0115 931 6001 🖱 stuart.lloyd@erewash.gov.uk

Electoral Registration: Mrs Hayley Brailsford, Electoral Services Manager, Town Hall, Ilkeston DE7 5RP ☎ 0845 907 2244 🖷 0115 907 1121 🖱 hayley.brailsford@erewash.gov.uk

Emergency Planning: Mr David Bramwell, Head of Green Space & Street Scene, West Park Nursery, Wilsthorpe Road, Long Easton NG10 4AA ☎ 0845 907 2244 🖷 0115 931 6079 🖱 dave.bramwell@erewash.gov.uk

Environmental / Technical Services: Mr Phillip Wright, Director for Operational Services, Merlin House, Merlin Way, Ilkeston DE7 4RA ☎ 0845 907 2244 🖷 0115 931 6079 🖱 phillip.wright@erewash.gov.uk

Environmental Health: Mr Nick Thurstan, Head of Environment & Community Safety, Merlin House, Merlin Way, Ilkeston DE7 4RA ☎ 0845 907 2244 🖷 0115 931 6079 🖱 nick.thurstan@erewash.gov.uk

Estates, Property & Valuation: Mr Stuart Lloyd, Head of Customer & Support Services, Town Hall, Long Eaton NG10 1HU ☎ 0845 907 2244 🖷 0115 931 6001 🖱 stuart.lloyd@erewash.gov.uk

Events Manager: Mrs Jan Oldham, Marketing & Research Manager, Sandiacre Friesland Sports Centre, Nursery Avenue, Sandiacre NG10 5AE ☎ 0845 907 2244 🖷 0115 949 7062 🖱 jan.oldham@erewash.gov.uk

Finance and Treasurer: Mr Ian Sankey, Director for Resources / Deputy Chief Executive, Town Hall, Ilkeston DE7 5RP ☎ 0845 907 2244 🖷 0115 944 3269 🖱 ian.sankey@erewash.gov.uk

Finance and Treasurer: Mr David Watson, Head of Finance, Town Hall, Ilkeston DE7 5RP ☎ 0845 907 2244 🖷 0115 907 1018 🖱 david.watson@erewash.gov.uk

Fleet Management: Mr Trevor Patchitt, Transport Manager, Merlin House, Merlin Way, Ilkeston DE7 4RA ☎ 0845 907 2244 🖷 0115 931 6079 🖱 trevor.patchitt@erewash.gov.uk

Grounds Maintenance: Mr David Bramwell, Head of Green Space & Street Scene, West Park Nursery, Wilsthorpe Road, Long Easton NG10 4AA ☎ 0845 907 2244 🖷 0115 931 6079 🖱 dave.bramwell@erewash.gov.uk

Health and Safety: Ms Liz Street, Environmental Health Manager (Commercial), Merlin House, Merlin Way, Ilkeston DE7 4RA ☎ 0845 907 2244 🖷 0115 931 6079 🖱 elizabeth.street@erewash.gov.uk

Housing: Ms Sara Dinsdale, Housing Options Manager, Town Hall, Ilkeston DE7 5RP ☎ 0845 907 2244 🖷 0115 931 6013 🖱 sara.dinsdale@erewash.gov.uk

Legal: Mr Brendan Morris, Borough Solicitor, Town Hall, Ilkeston DE7 5RP ☎ 0845 907 2244 🖷 0115 907 1121 🖱 brendan.morris@erewash.gov.uk

Leisure and Cultural Services: Mr Tim Spencer, Head of Culture & Leisure, Sandiacre Friesland Sports Centre, Nursery Avenue, Sandiacre NG10 5HG ☎ 0845 907 2244 🖷 0115 949 7062 🖱 tim.spencer@erewash.gov.uk

Licensing: Mr Phillip Wright, Director for Operational Services, Merlin House, Merlin Way, Ilkeston DE7 4RA ☎ 0845 907 2244 🖷 0115 931 6079 🖱 phillip.wright@erewash.gov.uk

Member Services: Mr Andrew Sharpe, Head of Democratic Services, Town Hall, Ilkeston DE7 5RP ☎ 0845 907 2244 🖷 0115 907 1121 🖱 andrew.sharpe@erewash.gov.uk

Parking: Mr David Bramwell, Head of Green Space & Street Scene, West Park Nursery, Wilsthorpe Road, Long Easton NG10 4AA ☎ 0845 907 2244 🖷 0115 931 6079 🖱 dave.bramwell@erewash.gov.uk

Partnerships: Ms Lorraine Poyser, Assistant Chief Executive, Town Hall, Ilkeston DE7 5RP ☎ 0845 907 2244 🖷 0115 907 1121 🖱 lorraine.poyser@erewash.gov.uk

Personnel / HR: Ms Jennifer Browne, Head of Personnel, Town Hall, Long Eaton NG10 1HU ☎ 0845 907 2244 🖷 0115 907 2266 🖱 jennifer.browne@erewash.gov.uk

Planning: Mr Steve Birkinshaw, Head of Planning & Regeneration, Town Hall, Long Easton NG10 1HU ☎ 0845 907 2244 🖷 0115 907 2237 🖱 steve.birkinshaw@erewash.gov.uk

Procurement: Mr Howard Lane, Procurement Officer, Town Hall, Ilkeston DE7 5RP ☎ 0845 907 2244 🖷 0115 907 1018 🖱 howard.lane@erewash.gov.uk

Recycling & Waste Minimisation: Ms Julie Harvey, Head of Waste & Fleet Operations, Merlin House, Merlin Way, Ilkeston DE7 4RA ☎ 0845 907 2244 🖷 0115 931 6079 🖱 julie.harvey@erewash.gov.uk

Regeneration: Mr Ian Sankey, Director for Resources / Deputy Chief Executive, Town Hall, Ilkeston DE7 5RP ☎ 0845 907 2244 🖷 0115 944 3269 🖱 ian.sankey@erewash.gov.uk

Staff Training: Ms Joanna Till, Personnel Manager, Town Hall, Long Eaton NG10 1HU ☎ 0845 907 2244 🖷 0115 907 2266 🖱 joanna.till@erewash.gov.uk

Street Scene: Mr David Bramwell, Head of Green Space & Street Scene, West Park Nursery, Wilsthorpe Road, Long Easton NG10 4AA ☎ 0845 907 2244 🖷 0115 931 6079 🖱 dave.bramwell@erewash.gov.uk

Sustainable Development: Mr Ian Sankey, Director for Resources / Deputy Chief Executive, Town Hall, Ilkeston DE7 5RP ☎ 0845 907 2244 🖷 0115 944 3269 🖱 ian.sankey@erewash.gov.uk

Tourism: Mr Tim Spencer, Head of Culture & Leisure, Sandiacre Friesland Sports Centre, Nursery Avenue, Sandiacre NG10 5HG ☎ 0845 907 2244 🖷 0115 949 7062 🖱 tim.spencer@erewash.gov.uk

Waste Collection and Disposal: Ms Julie Harvey, Head of Waste & Fleet Operations, Merlin House, Merlin Way, Ilkeston DE7 4RA ☎ 0845 907 2244 🖷 0115 931 6079 ✉ julie.harvey@erewash.gov.uk

Waste Management: Ms Julie Harvey, Head of Waste & Fleet Operations, Merlin House, Merlin Way, Ilkeston DE7 4RA ☎ 0845 907 2244 🖷 0115 931 6079 ✉ julie.harvey@erewash.gov.uk

Children's Play Areas: Mr Richard Ashley, Green Space & Street Scene Manager, Merlin House, Merlin Way, Ilkeston DE7 4RA ☎ 0845 907 2244 🖷 0115 931 6079 ✉ richard.ashley@erewash.gov.uk

MEMBERS OF THE COUNCIL (51)

***Mayor:* Hulls**, Jennifer (CON - Sandiacre South)
councillor.jennifer.hulls@erewash.gov.uk
***Deputy Mayor:* Clare**, Valerie (CON - Draycott and Stanton By Dale)
councillor.val.clare@erewash.gov.uk
***Leader of the Council:* Corbett**, Christopher (CON - Wilsthorpe)
councillor.chris.corbett@erewash.gov.uk
***Deputy Leader of the Council:* Hart**, Carol (CON - West Hallam and Dale Abbey)
councillor.carol.hart@erewash.gov.uk
***Group Leader:* Griffiths**, Howard (LAB - Derby Road East)
councillor.howard.griffiths@erewash.gov.uk
***Group Leader:* Phillips**, Alex (LAB - Hallam Fields)
councillor.alex.phillips@erewash.gov.uk
Athwal, Kewal (CON - Wilsthorpe)
councillor.kewal.athwal@erewash.gov.uk
Bevan, Ernest (LAB - Ilkeston North)
councillor.ernest.bevan@erewash.gov.uk
Bilbie, Steve (CON - Sandiacre North)
councillor.steve.bilbie@erewash.gov.uk
Birkin, Glennice (LAB - Ilkeston Central)
councillor.glennice.birkin@erewash.gov.uk
Bishop, Edward (LAB - Hallam Fields)
councillor.ted.bishop@erewash.gov.uk
Bonam, Joanne (CON - Sawley)
councillor.jo.bonam@erewash.gov.uk
Booth, John (LAB - Cotmanhay)
councillor.john.booth@erewash.gov.uk
Booth, Louis (LAB - Kirk Hallam)
councillor.louis.booth@erewash.gov.uk
Booth, Michelle (LAB - Sandiacre North)
councillor.michelle.booth@erewash.gov.uk
Briggs, Donna (CON - Long Eaton Central)
councillor.donna.briggs@erewash.gov.uk
Broughton, Bruce (CON - West Hallam and Dale Abbey)
councillor.bruce.broughton@erewash.gov.uk
Custance, Valerie (CON - Abbotsford)
councillor.val.custance@erewash.gov.uk
Dawson, James (LAB - Abbotsford)
councillor.james.dawson@erewash.gov.uk
Dinsdale, Gary (CON - Sandiacre South)
councillor.gary.dinsdale@erewash.gov.uk
Frudd, John (LAB - Kirk Hallam)
councillor.john.frudd@erewash.gov.uk
Green, Stephen (LAB - Kirk Hallam)
councillor.stephen.green@erewash.gov.uk
Griffiths, Margaret (LAB - Derby Road East)
councillor.margaret.griffiths@erewash.gov.uk
Harrison, Barbara (CON - West Hallam and Dale Abbey)
councillor.barbara.harrison@erewash.gov.uk
Hickton, Garry (CON - Derby Road West)
councillor.garry.hickton@erewash.gov.uk
Holbrook, Terence (CON - Ockbrook and Borrowash)
councillor.terry.holbrook@erewash.gov.uk
Hopkinson, Mary (CON - Little Hallam)
councillor.mary.hopkinson@erewash.gov.uk
Hosker, Roland (LAB - Nottingham Road)
councillor.roland.hosker@erewash.gov.uk
Keen, Keri (LAB - Derby Road West)
councillor.keri.keen@erewash.gov.uk
McGraw, Linda (LAB - Stanley)
councillor.linda.mcgraw@erewash.gov.uk
Mellors, Denise (LAB - Nottingham Road)
councillor.denise.mellors@erewash.gov.uk
Miller, Kevin (CON - Derby Road West)
councillor.kevin.miller@erewash.gov.uk
Moloney, Patrick (LAB - Old Park)
councillor.tim.moloney@erewash.gov.uk
Morgan, David (LAB - Cotmanhay)
councillor.david.morgan@erewash.gov.uk
Neill, Clare (LAB - Long Eaton Central)
councillor.clare.neill@erewash.gov.uk
Orchard, Derek (CON - Draycott and Stanton By Dale)
councillor.derek.orchard@erewash.gov.uk
Orchard, Margaret (CON - Breaston)
councillor.margaret.orchard@erewash.gov.uk
Parkinson, Robert (CON - Breaston)
councillor.robert.parkinson@erewash.gov.uk
Phillips, Frank (LAB - Ilkeston Central)
councillor.frank.phillips@erewash.gov.uk
Phillips, Pamela (LAB - Old Park)
councillor.pam.phillips@erewash.gov.uk
Pidgeon, Cheryl (LAB - Nottingham Road)
councillor.cheryl.pidgeon@erewash.gov.uk
Smith, Geoffrey (CON - Wilsthorpe)
councillor.geoffrey.smith@erewash.gov.uk
Stephenson, David (CON - Little Hallam)
councillor.david.stephenson@erewash.gov.uk
Stevenson, Abey (CON - Little Eaton and Breadsall)
councillor.abey.stevenson@erewash.gov.uk
Stevenson, Ann (LAB - Long Eaton Central)
councillor.ann.stevenson@erewash.gov.uk
Summerfield, Alan (CON - Little Eaton and Breadsall)
councillor.alan.summerfield@erewash.gov.uk
Tumanow, Vera (CON - Ockbrook and Borrowash)
councillor.vera.tumanow@erewash.gov.uk
Wallis, Michael (CON - Ockbrook and Borrowash)
councillor.michael.wallis@erewash.gov.uk
Walton, Daniel (CON - Sawley)
councillor.daniel.walton@erewash.gov.uk
Wilson, Jane (LAB - Ilkeston North)
councillor.jane.wilson@erewash.gov.uk
Woollford, Russell (LAB - Sawley)
councillor.russell.woollford@erewash.gov.uk

POLITICAL COMPOSITION

CON: 26, LAB: 25

CABINET

Leader / Strategic Policy: Mr Christopher Corbett
Deputy Leader / Community Engagement: Mrs Carol Hart
Culture & Leisure: Mr Michael Wallis
Environment: Mrs Barbara Harrison

Personnel & Legal Services: Mrs Jennifer Hulls
Resources: Mr David Stephenson
Regeneration & Planning: Mr Geoffrey Smith

COMMITTEE CHAIRS

Audit: Mr Garry Hickton
General Purposes: Mr Kevin Miller
Licensing & Public Protection: Mrs Vera Tumanow
Planning: Mr Robert Parkinson
Scrutiny (Scrutiny): Mr Alan Summerfield

ESSEX C

Essex County Council, County Hall, Market Road, Chelmsford CM1 1LX ☎ 03456 080190 💻 www.essexcc.gov.uk

FACTS & FIGURES

Police Authority: Essex Police Authority
Health Authority: East of England Strategic Health Authority
Learning and Skills Council: Eastern
Parliamentary Constituencies: Maldon
EU Constituencies: Eastern
Election Frequency: Elections are of whole council

PRINCIPAL OFFICERS

Chief Executive: Ms Joanna Killian, Chief Executive, County Hall, Market Road, Chelmsford CM1 1QH ☎ 01245 430047 🖷 01245 430741 ✉ joanna.killian@essex.gov.uk

Deputy Chief Executive: Mr Robert Overall, Deputy Chief Executive & Executive Director for Environment Sustainability & Highways, County Hall, Market Road, Chelmsford CM1 1LX ☎ 01245 434409 🖷 01245 437697 ✉ robert.overall@essex.gov.uk

Senior Management: Mr Dave Hill, Executive Director - Schools, Children & Family, County Hall, Market Road, Chelmsford CM1 1LX ☎ 01245 431891 ✉ dave.hill@essex.gov.uk

Senior Management: Ms Margaret Lee, Executive Director - Finance, County Hall, Market Road, Chelmsford CM1 1LX ☎ 01245 431010 🖷 01245 431960 ✉ margaret.lee@essex.gov.uk

Senior Management: Mr Keir Lynch, Executive Director - Transformation, County Hall, Market Road, Chelmsford CM1 1LX ☎ 01245 431117 ✉ keir.lynch@essex.gov.uk

Senior Management: Mr Robert Overall, Deputy Chief Executive & Executive Director for Environment Sustainability & Highways, County Hall, Market Road, Chelmsford CM1 1LX ☎ 01245 434409 🖷 01245 437697 ✉ robert.overall@essex.gov.uk

Senior Management: Mr David Wilde, Chief Information Officer, County Hall, Market Road, Chelmsford CM1 1LX ☎ 01245 433172 ✉ david.wilde@essex.gov.uk

Access Officer / Social Services (Disability): Ms Liz Chidgey, Executive Director - Adult Social Care, County Hall, Market Road, Chelmsford CM1 1LX ☎ 01245 434123 ✉ liz.chidgey@essex.gov.uk

Building Control: Mr Roy Leavitt, Head of Development Control, County Hall, Market Road, Chelmsford CM1 1LX ☎ 01245 437522 ✉ roy.leavitt@essex.gov.uk

Building Control: Mr Roger Moore, Head of Property Commissioning, County Hall, Market Road, Chelmsford CM1 1LX ☎ 01245 435310 ✉ roger.moore@essex.gov.uk

Children / Youth Services: Ms Stephanie Bishop, Head of Fostering & Adoption, County Hall, Market Road, Chelmsford CM1 1LX ☎ 01245 434839 ✉ stephanie.bishop@essex.gov.uk

Children / Youth Services: Mr Tim Coulson, Director - Education & Learning, County Hall, Market Road, Chelmsford CM1 1LX ☎ 01245 436031 ✉ tim.coulson@essex.gov.uk

Children / Youth Services: Ms Helen Lincoln, Director - Children's Social Care, County Hall, Market Road, Chelmsford CM1 1LX ☎ 01245 430494 ✉ helen.lincoln@essex.gov.uk

Civil Registration: Mr Philip Thomson, County Solicitor, New Bridge House, 60-68 New London Road, Chelmsford CM2 0PD ☎ 01245 506760 🖷 01245 357335 ✉ philip.thomson@essex.gov.uk

Computer Management: Ms Helen Burley, IS Business Development Officer & Partnerships, County Hall, Market Road, Chelmsford CM1 1LX ☎ 01245 435297 ✉ helen.burley@essex.gov.uk

Computer Management: Mr David Wilde, Chief Information Officer, County Hall, Market Road, Chelmsford CM1 1LX ☎ 01245 433172 ✉ david.wilde@essex.gov.uk

Contracts: Mr Anthony Doyle, Chief Procurement Officer, County Hall, Market Road, Chelmsford CM1 1LX ☎ 01245 431880 ✉ anthony.doyle@essex.gov.uk

Contracts: Mr Mark Paget, Contract Manager, County Hall, Market Road, Chelmsford CM1 1LX ☎ 01245 431846 ✉ mark.paget@essex.gov.uk

Corporate Services: Ms Katie Hadgraft, Head of Employee Communications & Engagement, County Hall, Market Road, Chelmsford CM1 1LX ☎ 01245 434010 ✉ katie.hadgraft@essex.gov.uk

Corporate Services: Mr Mark Hobson, Assistant Director - Shared Services, County Hall, Market Road, Chelmsford CM1 1LX ☎ 01245 431026 ✉ mark.hobson@essex.gov.uk

Corporate Services: Ms Denise Murray, Directorate Head of Finance & Resources, Schools, Children & Families, County Hall, Market Road, Chelmsford CM1 1LX ☎ 01245 436721 ✉ denise.murray@essex.gov.uk

Education: Mr Tim Coulson, Director - Education & Learning, County Hall, Market Road, Chelmsford CM1 1LX ☎ 01245 436031 ✉ tim.coulson@essex.gov.uk

Education: Mr Graham Ranby, Lead Strategic Comissioner - Planning & Provision, County Hall, Market Road, Chelmsford CM1 1LX ☎ 01245 436704 ✉ graham.ranby@essex.gov.uk

Emergency Planning: Mr David Johnson, Chief Fire Officer & Head of Emergency Planning, County Hall, Market Road, Chelmsford CM1 1LX ☎ 01245 430366 ✉ david.johnson@essex.gov.uk

European Liaison: Ms Lorraine George, Head of EU & External Funding, County Hall, Market Road, Chelmsford CM1 1QH ☎ 01245 430472 ✉ lorraine.george@essex.gov.uk

Events Manager: Ms Sharon Collier, Events Management & Community Budgets, County Hall, Market Road, Chelmsford CM1 1QH ☎ 01245 436569 🖷 01245 430734 ✉ sharon.collier@essex.gov.uk

Finance and Treasurer: Ms Margaret Lee, Executive Director - Finance, County Hall, Market Road, Chelmsford CM1 1LX ☎ 01245 431010 🖷 01245 431960 ✉ margaret.lee@essex.gov.uk

Finance and Treasurer: Mr Martin Quinn, Head of Investments, County Hall, Market Road, Chelmsford CM1 1LX ☎ 01245 431412 ✉ martin.quinn@essex.gov.uk

Finance and Treasurer: Mr Peter Tanton, Head of Internal Audit, County Hall, Market Road, Chelmsford CM1 1LX ☎ 01245 43110 ✉ peter.tanton@essex.gov.uk

Fleet Management: Mr John Pope, Head of Passenger Transport, County Hall, Market Road, Chelmsford CM1 1QH ☎ 01245 437506 🖷 01245 496764 ✉ john.pope@essex.gov.uk

Grounds Maintenance: Mr Tim Dixon, Head of Country Parks, County Hall, Market Road, Chelmsford CM1 1LX ☎ 01245 437706 ✉ tim.dixon@essex.gov.uk

Health and Safety: Ms Janet Ross, Health, Safety & Risk Manager, County Hall, Market Road, Chelmsford CM1 1QH ☎ 01245 430289 🖷 01245 352710 ✉ janet.ross@essex.gov.uk

Highways: Mr Paul Bird, Director for Highways & Transportation, County Hall, Market Road, Chelmsford CM1 1QH ☎ 01245 437003 🖷 01245 251601 ✉ paul.bird@essex.gov.uk

Legal: Mr Philip Thomson, County Solicitor, New Bridge House, 60-68 New London Road, Chelmsford CM2 0PD ☎ 01245 506760 🖷 01245 357335 ✉ philip.thomson@essex.gov.uk

Lifelong Learning: Mrs Susan Carragher, Director of Libraries & Culture, County Hall, Market Road, Chelmsford CM1 1LX ☎ 01245 434105 🖷 01245 434016 ✉ susan.carragher@essex.gov.uk

Partnerships: Mr Dan Gascoyne, Partnership, Delivery & Quality of Life Team Leader, County Hall, Market Road, Chelmsford CM1 1LX ☎ 01245 437302 ✉ dan.gascoyne@essex.gov.uk

Personnel / HR: Mr Keir Lynch, Executive Director - Transformation, County Hall, Market Road, Chelmsford CM1 1LX ☎ 01245 431117 ✉ keir.lynch@essex.gov.uk

Planning: Mr Paul Bird, Director for Highways & Transportation, County Hall, Market Road, Chelmsford CM1 1QH ☎ 01245 437003 🖷 01245 251601 ✉ paul.bird@essex.gov.uk

Procurement: Mr Anthony Doyle, Chief Procurement Officer, County Hall, Market Road, Chelmsford CM1 1LX ☎ 01245 431880 ✉ anthony.doyle@essex.gov.uk

Public Libraries: Mrs Susan Carragher, Director of Libraries & Culture, County Hall, Market Road, Chelmsford CM1 1LX ☎ 01245 434105 🖷 01245 434016 ✉ susan.carragher@essex.gov.uk

Recycling & Waste Minimisation: Mr Jason Searles, Head of Waste & Recycling, County Hall, Market Road, Chelmsford CM1 1QH ☎ 01245 437283 🖷 01245 437691 ✉ jason.searles@essex.gov.uk

Road Safety: Ms Katie Brimley, Road Safety ETP Team Leader, County Hall, Market Road, Chelmsford CM1 1LX ☎ 01245 437781 🖷 01245 490705 ✉ katie.brimley@essex.gov.uk

Social Services (Children): Ms Helen Lincoln, Director - Children's Social Care, County Hall, Market Road, Chelmsford CM1 1LX ☎ 01245 430494 ✉ helen.lincoln@essex.gov.uk

Social Services (Children): Ms Helen Lincoln, Director - Children's Social Care, County Hall, Market Road, Chelmsford CM1 1LX ☎ 01245 430494 ✉ helen.lincoln@essex.gov.uk

Staff Training: Mr Jeff Wren, Head of Leadership & Development, County Hall, Market Road, Chelmsford CM1 1LX ☎ 01245 437806 ✉ jeff.wren@essex.gov.uk

Tourism: Ms Lisa Bone, Strategic Tourism Manager, County Hall, Market Road, Chelmsford CM1 1LX ☎ 01245 437305 ✉ lisa.bone@essex.gov.uk

Traffic Management: Ms Nicola Foster, Group Manager - Road Safety, County Hall, Market Road, Chelmsford CM1 1LX ☎ 01245 437004 ✉ nicola.foster@essex.gov.uk

Traffic Management: Mr John Pope, Head of Passenger Transport, County Hall, Market Road, Chelmsford CM1 1QH ☎ 01245 437506 🖷 01245 496764 ✉ john.pope@essex.gov.uk

Transport: Mr John Pope, Head of Passenger Transport, County Hall, Market Road, Chelmsford CM1 1QH ☎ 01245 437506 🖷 01245 496764 ✉ john.pope@essex.gov.uk

Transport Planner: Mr Christopher Stevenson, Head of Transport, Strategy & Engagement, County Hall, Market Road, Chelmsford CM1 1LX ☎ 01245 437287 ✉ chris.stevenson@essex.gov.uk

Children's Play Areas: Mr Tim Dixon, Head of Country Parks, County Hall, Market Road, Chelmsford CM1 1LX ☎ 01245 437706 ✉ tim.dixon@essex.gov.uk

MEMBERS OF THE COUNCIL (74)

***Chair:* Twitchen**, Kay (CON - Billericay and Burstead)
cllr.kay.twitchen@essexcc.gov.uk

***Vice-Chair:* Hume**, Norman (CON - South Woodham Ferrers)
cllr.norman.hume@essex.gov.uk

***Leader of the Council:* Martin**, Peter (CON - Chelmer)
cllr.peter.martin@essexcc.gov.uk

***Deputy Leader of the Council:* Finch**, David (CON - Hedingham)
cllr.david.finch@essexcc.gov.uk
***Group Leader:* Mackrory**, Michael (LD - Springfield)
cllr.mike.mackrory@essexcc.gov.uk
Abrahall, David (CON - Pitsea)
cllr.david.abrahall@essex.gov.uk
Aldridge, John (CON - Broomfield and Writtle)
cllr.john.aldridge@essexcc.gov.uk
Aspinell, Barry (LD - Brentwood North)
cllr.barry.aspinell@essex.gov.uk
Barker, Susan (CON - Dunmow)
cllr.susan.barker@essexcc.gov.uk
Barton, Lyn (LD - Maypole)
cllr.linda.barton@essex.gov.uk
Bass, Rodney (CON - Heybridge and Tollesbury)
cllr.rodney.bass@essexcc.gov.uk
Baugh, John (CON - Bocking)
cllr.john.baugh@essex.gov.uk
Bentley, Kevin (CON - Stanway and Pyefleet)
cllr.kevin.bentley@essex.gov.u
Boyce, Bob (CON - Southminster)
cllr.bob.boyce@essexcc.gov.uk
Brown, Anne (CON - Constable)
cllr.anne.brown@essex.gov.uk
Butland, Graham (CON - Braintree Town)
cllr.graham.butland@essex.gov.uk
Callender, Ricky (CON - Harwich)
cllr.ricky.calleneder@essex.gov.uk
Candy, Sarah (CON - Tendring Rural West)
cllr.sarah.candy@essex.gov.uk
Castle, Stephen (CON - Rayleigh North)
cllr.stephen.castle@essex.gov.uk
Chambers, Robert (CON - Saffron Walden)
cllr.robert.chambers@essex.gov.uk
Channer, Penny (CON - Maldon)
cllr.penny.channer@essex.gov.uk
Chapman, Tracey (CON - Rochford North)
cllr.tracey.chapman@essexcc.gov.uk
Deakin, Judith (LD - Chelmsford West)
cllr.jude.deakin@essex.gov.uk
Dick, William (CON - Thundersley)
cllr.bill.dick@essex.gov.uk
Dornan, John (CON - Laindon Park and Fryerns)
cllr.john.dornan@essex.gov.uk
Durcan, Anthony (LAB - Harlow West)
cllr.tony.durcan@essex.gov.uk
Edey, Nigel (CON - Braintree Eastern)
cllr.nigel.edey@essexcc.gov.uk
Fisher, Magaret (LD - Abbey)
cllr.margaret.fissher@essex.gov.uk
Garnett, Michael (CON - Harlow North)
cllr.mike.garnett@essex.gov.uk
Gooding, Raymond (CON - Stanstead)
cllr.ray.gooding@essex.gov.uk
Griffiths, Chris (CON - Clacton West)
cllr.chris.griffiths@essex.gov.uk
Grundy, Ian (CON - Stock)
cllr.ian.grundy@essex.gov.uk
Hart, Elizabeth (CON - Rochford West)
cllr.elizabeth.hart@essexcc.gov.uk
Hedley, Anthony (CON - Billericay and Burstead)
cllr.anthony.hedley@essexcc.gov.uk
Higgins, Theresa (LD - Parsons Heath and East Gates)
cllr.theresa.higgins@essex.gov.uk
Hillier, Sandra (CON - Pitsea)
cllr.sandra.hillier@essex.gov.uk
Howard, Raymond (CON - Canvey Island West)
cllr.ray.howard@essexcc.gov.uk
Jackson, Anthony (CON - North Weald and Nazeing)
cllr.anthony.jackson@essex.gov.uk
Johnson, Edward (CON - Harlow South East)
cllr.edward.johnson@essexcc.gov.uk
Jowers, John (CON - Mersea and Tiptree)
cllr.john.jowers@essex.gov.uk
Kendall, David (LD - Brentwood South)
cllr.david.kendall@essex.gov.uk
Knapman, John (CON - Chigwell and Loughton Broadway)
cllr.john.knapman@essex.gov.uk
Lager, Michael (CON - Witham Northern)
cllr.Michael.Lager@essex.gov.uk
Louis, Derrick (CON - Witham Southern)
cllr.derrek.louis@essex.gov.uk
Lucas, Jeremy (CON - Drury)
cllr.jeremy.lucas@essexcc.gov.uk
Madden, Dick (IND - Chelmsford Central)
cllr.dick.madden@essex.gov.uk
Mayzes, Stephen (CON - Clacton North)
cllr.stephen.mayzes@essex.gov.uk
McEwen, Gerald (CON - Ongar and Rural)
cllr.gerard.mcewan@essex.gov.uk
Mead, Linda (CON - Clacton East)
cllr.linda.mead@essex.gov.uk
Metcalfe, Valerie (CON - Buckhurst Hill and Loughton South)
Cllr.valerie.metcalfe@essex.gov.uk
Miller, Maureen (LD - Great Baddow)
cllr.maureen.miller@essexcc.gov.uk
Mitchinson, Guy (CON - Harlow West)
cllr.guy.mitchinson@essex.gov.uk
Morris, Donald (CON - Wickford Crouch)
cllr.don.morris@essex.gov.uk
Naylor, Ann (CON - Brentwood Rural)
cllr.ann.naylor@essexcc.gov.uk
Page, Michael (CON - Frinton and Walton)
cllr.mick.page@essex.gov.uk
Pearson, Roy (CON - Rochford South)
roy.pearson@essex.gov.uk
Pike, Joe (CON - Halstead)
cllr.joe.pike@essex.gov.uk
Pond, Chris (R - Loughton Central)
cllr.chris.pond@essexcc.gov.uk
Pummell, Iris (CON - Wickford Crouch)
cllr.iris.pummell@essex.gov.uk
Reeves, Jillian (CON - Hadleigh)
cllr.jillian.reeves@essexcc.gov.uk
Riley, Colin (CON - South Benfleet)
cllr.colin.riley@essexcc.gov.uk
Roberts, John (CON - Brentwood Hutton)
cllr.john.roberts@essexcc.gov.uk
Robinson, Derek (CON - Brightlingsea)
cllr.derek.robinson@essexcc.gov.uk
Sargent, Terri (CON - Laindon Park and Fryerns)
cllr.terri.sargent@essex.gov.uk
Schofield, John (CON - Basildon Westley Heights)
cllr.john.schofield@essexcc.gov.uk
Skeels, John (CON - Tendring Rural East)
cllr.michael.skeels@essex.gov.uk
Turrell, Anne (LD - Mile End and Highwoods)
cllr.anne.turrell@essexcc.gov.uk

Walsh, Simon (CON - Thaxted)
cllr.simon.walsh@essex.gov.uk
Walters, Roger (CON - Three Fields with Great Notley)
cllr.roger.walters@essex.gov.uk
Webster, Elizabeth (CON - Waltham Abbey)
cllr.elizabeth.webster@essexcc.gov.uk
Webster, Mavis (CON - Rayleigh South)
Cllr.Mavis.Webster@essex.gov.uk
Whitehouse, Janet (LD - Epping and Theydon Bois)
cllr.janet.whitehouse@essex.gov.uk
Wood, Brian (IND - Canvey Island East)
cllr.brian.wood@essex.gov.uk
Young, Julie (LAB - Wivenhoe St Andrew)
cllr.julie.young@essex.gov.uk

POLITICAL COMPOSITION
CON: 58, LD: 10, IND: 2, LAB: 2, R: 1

CABINET
Leader: Mr Peter Martin
Deputy Leader / Finance & Transformation Programme: Mr David Finch
Adult Social Care: Mr John Aldridge
Children's Services: Mr Raymond Gooding
Economic Growth, Waste & Recycling: Mr Kevin Bentley
Education, Lifelong Learning & 2012 Games: Mr Stephen Castle
Environment & Culture: Mr Jeremy Lucas
Health & Wellbeing: Ms Ann Naylor
Highways & Transportation: Mr Derrick Louis

COMMITTEE CHAIRS
Audit: Mr Michael Lager
Children & Young People: Mrs Tracey Chapman
Community & Older People (Scrutiny): Mr William Dick
Development & Regulation: Mr Nigel Edey
Economic Development, Environment & Highways (Scrutiny): Mrs Susan Barker
Health: Mr Graham Butland
Safer & Stronger Communities: Mr Simon Walsh
Scrutiny: Mr Simon Walsh

EXETER CITY D

Exeter City Council, Civic Centre, Paris Street, Exeter EX1 1JN
☎ 01392 277888 🖷 01392 265265 ✉ exeter@exeter.gov.uk
💻 www.exeter.gov.uk

FACTS & FIGURES
Police Authority: Devon & Cornwall Police Authority
Health Authority: NHS South West
Learning and Skills Council: South West
Parliamentary Constituencies: Exeter
EU Constituencies: South West
Election Frequency: Elections are by thirds
Twinning: Bad Homburg (Germany); Rennes (France); Terracina (Italy); Yaroslavl (Russia)

PRINCIPAL OFFICERS
Chief Executive: Mr Philip Bostock, Chief Executive, Civic Centre, Paris Street, Exeter EX1 1JN ☎ 01392 265188 🖷 01392 265268 ✉ philip.bostock@exeter.gov.uk

Assistant Chief Executive: Ms Bindu Arjoon, Assistant Director - Business Transformation, Civic Centre, Paris Street, Exeter EX1 1JN ☎ 01392 265199 🖷 01392 265268 ✉ bindu.arjoon@exeter.gov.uk

Senior Management: Mr Karime Hassan, Strategic Director, Civic Centre, Paris Street, Exeter EX1 1JN ☎ 01392 265192 🖷 01392 265179 ✉ karime.hassan@exeter.gov.uk

Best Value: Mr Bruce Luxton, Corporate Manager Policy - Communications & Community Engagement, Civic Centre, Paris Street, Exeter EX1 1JN ☎ 01392 265166 🖷 01392 265268 ✉ bruce.luxton@exeter.gov.uk

Building Control: Mr Alan Stokes, Building Control Manager & Access Officer, Civic Centre, Paris Street, Exeter EX1 1JN ☎ 01392 265218 🖷 01392 265628 ✉ alan.stokes@exeter.gov.uk

PR / Communications: Mr Bruce Luxton, Corporate Manager Policy - Communications & Community Engagement, Civic Centre, Paris Street, Exeter EX1 1JN ☎ 01392 265166 🖷 01392 265268 ✉ bruce.luxton@exeter.gov.uk

Community Safety: Mr Bruce Luxton, Corporate Manager Policy - Communications & Community Engagement, Civic Centre, Paris Street, Exeter EX1 1JN ☎ 01392 265166 🖷 01392 265268 ✉ bruce.luxton@exeter.gov.uk

Computer Management: Ms Bindu Arjoon, Assistant Director - Business Transformation, Civic Centre, Paris Street, Exeter EX1 1JN ☎ 01392 265199 🖷 01392 265268 ✉ bindu.arjoon@exeter.gov.uk

Corporate Services: Mr John Street, Corporate Manager - Democratic & Civic Support, Civic Centre, Paris Street, Exeter EX1 1JN ☎ 01392 265106 🖷 01392 265265 ✉ john.street@exeter.gov.uk

Customer Service: Ms Bindu Arjoon, Assistant Director - Business Transformation, Civic Centre, Paris Street, Exeter EX1 1JN ☎ 01392 265199 🖷 01392 265268 ✉ bindu.arjoon@exeter.gov.uk

Customer Service: Mr John Street, Corporate Manager - Democratic & Civic Support, Civic Centre, Paris Street, Exeter EX1 1JN ☎ 01392 265106 🖷 01392 265265 ✉ john.street@exeter.gov.uk

Economic Development: Mr Richard Ball, Assistant Director - Economy, Civic Centre, Paris Street, Exeter EX1 1JN ☎ 01392 265140 🖷 01392 265625 ✉ richard.ball@exeter.gov.uk

Economic Development: Mr Karime Hassan, Strategic Director, Civic Centre, Paris Street, Exeter EX1 1JN ☎ 01392 265192 🖷 01392 265179 ✉ karime.hassan@exeter.gov.uk

E-Government: Mrs Christine Sheldon, Web & IT Programme Manager, Civic Centre, Paris Street, Exeter EX1 1JN ☎ 01392 265719 🖷 01392 265217 ✉ christine.sheldon@exeter.gov.uk

Electoral Registration: Mr Jeff Chalk, Electoral Services Manager, Civic Centre, Paris Street, Exeter EX1 1JN ☎ 01392

265640 🖷 01392 265752 ✉ jeff.chalk@exeter.gov.uk

Electoral Registration: Mr John Street, Corporate Manager - Democratic & Civic Support, Civic Centre, Paris Street, Exeter EX1 1JN ☎ 01392 265106 🖷 01392 265265 ✉ john.street@exeter.gov.uk

Emergency Planning: Ms Bindu Arjoon, Assistant Director - Business Transformation, Civic Centre, Paris Street, Exeter EX1 1JN ☎ 01392 265199 🖷 01392 265268 ✉ bindu.arjoon@exeter.gov.uk

Environmental / Technical Services: Mr Robert Norley, Assistant Director - Environment, Civic Centre, Paris Street, Exeter EX1 1RQ ☎ 01392 265170 🖷 01392 265852 ✉ robert.norley@exeter.gov.uk

Environmental Health: Mr Robert Norley, Assistant Director - Environment, Civic Centre, Paris Street, Exeter EX1 1RQ ☎ 01392 265170 🖷 01392 265852 ✉ robert.norley@exeter.gov.uk

Estates, Property & Valuation: Mr Michael Carson, Acting Head of Estates Service, Civic Centre, Paris Street, Exeter EX1 1JN ☎ 01392 265169 ✉ michael.carson@exeter.gov.uk

European Liaison: Mr Bruce Luxton, Corporate Manager Policy - Communications & Community Engagement, Civic Centre, Paris Street, Exeter EX1 1JN ☎ 01392 265166 🖷 01392 265268 ✉ bruce.luxton@exeter.gov.uk

Events Manager: Ms Valerie Wilson, Festivals & Events Manager, Civic Centre, Paris Street, Exeter EX1 1JN ☎ 01392 265205 🖷 01392 265268 ✉ val.wilson@exeter.gov.uk

Facilities: Mr John Street, Corporate Manager - Democratic & Civic Support, Civic Centre, Paris Street, Exeter EX1 1JN ☎ 01392 265106 🖷 01392 265265 ✉ john.street@exeter.gov.uk

Finance and Treasurer: Mr Andrew Stark, Assistant Director Finance, Civic Centre, Paris Street, Exeter EX1 1JN ☎ 01392 265153 🖷 01392 265217 ✉ andy.stark@exeter.gov.uk

Fleet Management: Mr Haydn Davies, Fleet Manager, Exton Road, Marsh Barton, Exeter EX2 8EQ ☎ 01392 665037 🖷 01392 665039 ✉ haydn.davies@exeter.gov.uk

Grounds Maintenance: Mr Paul Faulkner, Parks & Open Spaces Manager, Belle Isle Nursery, Belle Isle Drive, Exeter EX2 4RY ☎ 01392 262638 🖷 01392 262631 ✉ paul.faulkner@exeter.gov.uk

Health and Safety: Mr Robert Norley, Assistant Director - Environment, Civic Centre, Paris Street, Exeter EX1 1RQ ☎ 01392 265170 🖷 01392 265852 ✉ robert.norley@exeter.gov.uk

Home Energy Conservation: Mr Keith Williams, Environmental Health Manager (Private Sector Housing), Civic Centre, Paris Street, Exeter EX1 1RQ ☎ 01392 265777 🖷 01392 265852 ✉ keith.williams@exeter.gov.uk

Housing: Mr Lawrence Blake, Acting Head of Housing Services, Civic Centre, Paris Street, Exeter EX1 1JN ☎ 01392 265691 🖷 01392 265533 ✉ lawrence.blake@exeter.gov.uk

Legal: Miss Baan Al-Khafaji, Corporate Manager Legal, Civic Centre, Paris Street, Exeter EX1 1JN ☎ 01392 265874 🖷 01392 265265 ✉ bkhafaji@exeter.gov.uk

Licensing: Mr Robert Norley, Assistant Director - Environment, Civic Centre, Paris Street, Exeter EX1 1RQ ☎ 01392 265170 🖷 01392 265852 ✉ robert.norley@exeter.gov.uk

Member Services: Mr John Street, Corporate Manager - Democratic & Civic Support, Civic Centre, Paris Street, Exeter EX1 1JN ☎ 01392 265106 🖷 01392 265265 ✉ john.street@exeter.gov.uk

Member Services: Ms Rowena Whiter, Member Services Manager, Civic Centre, Paris Street, Exeter EX1 1JN ☎ 01392 265110 🖷 01392 265268 ✉ rowena.whiter@exeter.gov.uk

Parking: Mr Roger Coombes, Assistant Director Public Realm, Civic Centre, Paris Street, Exeter EX1 1JN ☎ 01392 265468 🖷 01392 265179 ✉ roger.coombes@exeter.gov.uk

Personnel / HR: Ms Bindu Arjoon, Assistant Director - Business Transformation, Civic Centre, Paris Street, Exeter EX1 1JN ☎ 01392 265199 🖷 01392 265268 ✉ bindu.arjoon@exeter.gov.uk

Personnel / HR: Ms Debbie Hartman, Head of Human Resources, Civic Centre, Paris Street, Exeter EX1 1JN ☎ 01392 265125 ✉ debbie.hartman@exeter.gov.uk

Planning: Mr Richard Short, Assistant Director - City Development, Civic Centre, Paris Street, Exeter EX1 1JN ☎ 01392 265219 🖷 01392 265431 ✉ richard.short@exeter.gov.uk

Recycling & Waste Minimisation: Mr Robert Norley, Assistant Director - Environment, Civic Centre, Paris Street, Exeter EX1 1RQ ☎ 01392 265170 🖷 01392 265852 ✉ robert.norley@exeter.gov.uk

Staff Training: Mr Ian Walker, Learning & Development Manager, Civic Centre, Paris Street, Exeter EX1 1JN ☎ 01392 265680 🖷 01392 265667 ✉ ian.walker@exeter.gov.uk

Street Scene: Mr Robert Norley, Assistant Director - Environment, Civic Centre, Paris Street, Exeter EX1 1RQ ☎ 01392 265170 🖷 01392 265852 ✉ robert.norley@exeter.gov.uk

Sustainable Communities: Mr Karime Hassan, Strategic Director, Civic Centre, Paris Street, Exeter EX1 1JN ☎ 01392 265192 🖷 01392 265179 ✉ karime.hassan@exeter.gov.uk

Tourism: Mr Richard Ball, Assistant Director - Economy, Civic Centre, Paris Street, Exeter EX1 1JN ☎ 01392 265140 🖷 01392 265625 ✉ richard.ball@exeter.gov.uk

Tourism: Ms Victoria Hatfield, Tourism Development Manager, Civic Centre, Paris Street, Exeter EX1 1JJ ☎ 01392 265104 🖷 01392 265695 ✉ victoria.hatfield@exeter.gov.uk

Town Centre: Mr John Harvey, City Centre Manager, Civic Centre, Paris Street, Exeter EX1 1JN ☎ 01392 265210 ✉ john.harvey@exeter.gov.uk

Waste Management: Mr Robert Norley, Assistant Director -

Environment, Civic Centre, Paris Street, Exeter EX1 1RQ ☎ 01392 265170 🖷 01392 265852 ✉ robert.norley@exeter.gov.uk

MEMBERS OF THE COUNCIL (40)

***The Lord Mayor:* Newby**, Rob (CON - Topsham)
cllr.rob.newby@exeter.gov.uk

***Deputy Mayor:* Prowse**, Percy (CON - Duryard)
cllr.percy.prowse@exeter.gov.uk

***Leader of the Council:* Edwards**, Peter (LAB - Whipton Barton)
cllr.peter.edwards@exeter.gov.uk

***Group Leader:* Fullham**, Adrian (LD - St Thomas)
cllr.adrian.fullam@exeter.gov.uk

***Group Leader:* Henson**, Yolanda (CON - Polsloe)
cllr.yolonda.henson@exeter.gov.uk

Baldwin, Margaret (CON - Topsham)
cllr.margaret.baldwin@exeter.gov.uk

Bialyk, Philip (LAB - Exwick)
cllr.philip.bialyk@exeter.gov.uk

Bowkett, Simon (LAB - Pinhoe)
cllr.simon.bowkett@exeter.gov.uk

Branston, Richard (LAB - Newtown)
cllr.richard.branston@exeter.gov.uk

Brock, Stella (LD - St David's)
cllr.stella.brock@exeter.gov.uk

Bull, Paul (LAB - Cowick)
cllr.paul.bull@exter.gov.uk

Choules, Marcel (LAB - Priory)
cllr.marcel.choules@exeter.gov.uk

Clark, Margaret (LAB - Alphington)
cllr.margaret.clark@exeter.gov.uk

Crew, Rob (LAB - Alphington)
cllr.rob.crew@exeter.gov.uk

Crow, Tyna (CON - Heavitree)
cllr.tyna.crow@exeter.gov.uk

Dawson, Catherine (LAB - Mincinglake)
cllr.catherine.dawson@exeter.gov.uk

Denham, Rosie (LAB - Whipton Barton)
cllr.rosie.denham@exeter.gov.uk

Donovan, Jake (CON - Pennsylvania)

Hannaford, Rob (LD - St Thomas)
cllr.rob.hannaford@exeter.co.uk

Henson, David (CON - St Loyes)
cllr.david.henson@exeter.gov.uk

Laws, Sarah (LAB - St David's)
cllr.sarah.laws@exter.gov.uk

Leadbetter, Andrew (CON - St Loyes)
cllr.andrew.leadbetter@exter.gov.uk

Lyons, Rachel (LAB - Polsloe)
cllr.rachel.lyons@exeter.gov.uk

Martin, Ian (LAB - Mincinglake)
cllr.ian.martin@exeter.gov.uk

McDonald, Moira (LAB - Pinhoe)
cllr.moira.macdonald@exeter.gov.uk

Mitchell, Kevin (LD - St James)
cllr.kevin.mitchell@exeter.gov.uk

Morris, Heather (LAB - Cowick)
cllr.heather.morris@exeter.gov.uk

Mottram, Lee (CON - Duryard)
cllr.lee.mottram@exeter.gov.uk

Owen, Keith (LAB - St James)
cllr.keith.owen@exeter.gov.uk

Payne, Tim (LD - Pennyslvania)
cllr.tim.payne@exeter.gov.uk

Pearson, Ollie (LAB - Exwick)
cllr.ollie.pearson@exeter.gov.uk

Robson, Lesley (LAB - Priory)
cllr.lesley.robson@exeter.gov.uk

Ruffle, Rod (LD - Alphington)
cllr.rod.ruffle@exeter.gov.uk

Sheldon, Greg (LAB - Heavitree)
cllr.greg.sheldon@exeter.gov.uk

Shiel, Norman (CON - St Leonard's)
cllr.norman.shiel@exeter.gov.uk

Spackman, Roger (LAB - Newtown)
cllr.roger.spackman@exeter.gov.uk

Sutton, Rachel (LAB - Exwick)
cllr.rachel.sutton@exeter.gov.uk

Tippins, Gill (LAB - Priory)
cllr.gill.tippins@exeter.gov.uk

Wardle, Tony (LAB - Whipton Barton)
cllr.tony.wardle@exeter.gov.uk

Winterbottom, John (CON - St Leonard's)
cllr.john.winterbottom@exeter.gov.uk

POLITICAL COMPOSITION

LAB: 23, CON: 11, LD: 6

CABINET

Leader / Budget & Strategic Vision: Mr Peter Edwards
Business Transformation & Human Resources: Mr Ian Martin
Economy & Tourism: Ms Rosie Denham
Environment & Leisure: Mr Greg Sheldon
Housing & Community Involvement: Mr Rob Hannaford
Sustainable Development & Transport: Ms Rachel Sutton

COMMITTEE CHAIRS

Final Accounts: Mr Peter Edwards
Licensing: Ms Moira McDonald
Planning: Mr Philip Bialyk
Scrutiny Committee - Community: Mr Norman Shiel
Scrutiny Committee - Economy: Ms Tyna Crow
Scrutiny Committee - Resources: Ms Margaret Baldwin

FALKIRK S

Falkirk Council, Municipal Buildings, Falkirk FK1 5RS ☎ 01324 506070 🖷 01324 506071 ✉ info@falkirk.gov.uk
🖳 www.falkirk.gov.uk

FACTS & FIGURES

Police Authority: Central Scotland Police Authority
Health Authority: NHS Forth Valley
Learning and Skills Council: Scotland
Parliamentary Constituencies: Falkirk, Linlithgow and Falkirk East
EU Constituencies: Scotland
Election Frequency: Elections are of whole council

PRINCIPAL OFFICERS

Chief Executive: Mrs Mary Pitcaithly, Chief Executive, Municipal Buildings, Falkirk FK1 5RS ☎ 01324 506002 🖷 01324 506001 ✉ mary.pitcaithly@falkirk.gov.uk

Senior Management: Mr Andrew Sutherland, Director of Education Services, Sealock House, 2 Inchyra Road, Grangemouth FK3 9XB ☎ 01324 506680 🖷 01324 506664 ✉ andrew.sutherland@falkirk.gov.uk

Senior Management: Mrs Julia Swan, Director of Education Services, Sealock House, 2 Inchyra Road, Grangemouth FK3 9XB ☎ 01324 506680 🖷 01324 506664 ✉ julia.swan@falkirk.gov.uk

Access Officer / Social Services (Disability): Ms Karen Algie, Head of Human Resources & Customer First, Municipal Buildings, Falkirk FK1 5RS ☎ 01324 506223 🖷 01324 506220 ✉ karen.algie@falkirk.gov.uk

Architect, Building / Property Services: Mr Robert McMaster, Head of Roads & Design Services, Abbotsford House, David's Loan, Falkirk FK2 7YZ ☎ 01324 504953 🖷 01324 504888 ✉ robert.mcmaster@falkirk.gov.uk

Best Value: Mr Stuart Ritchie, Director of Corporate & Neighbourhood Services, Municipal Buildings, Falkirk FK1 5RS ☎ 01324 506005 🖷 01324 506001 ✉ stuart.ritchie@falkirk.gov.uk

Building Control: Mr Russell Cartwright, Building Standards Manager, Falkirk Development Services, Abbotsford House, David's Loan, Falkirk FK2 7YZ ☎ 01324 504801 🖷 01324 504848 ✉ russell.cartwright@falkirk.gov.uk

Catering Services: Ms Judith Borg, Catering Co-ordinator, Municipal Buildings, Falkirk FK1 5RS ☎ 01324 590461 ✉ judith.borg@falkirk.gov.uk

Civil Registration: Ms Gillian McIntyre, Customer & Development Manager, Municipal Buildings, Falkirk FK1 5RS ☎ 01324 506104 ✉ gillian.mcintyre@falkirk.gov.uk

PR / Communications: Ms Caroline Binnie, Communications Manager, Municipal Buildings, Falkirk FK1 5RS ☎ 01324 506051 🖷 01324 506061 ✉ caroline.binnie@falkirk.gov.uk

Community Planning: Ms Fiona Campbell, Head of Policy, Technology & Improvement, Municipal Buildings, Falkirk FK1 5RS ☎ 01324 506004 🖷 01324 506061 ✉ fiona.campbell@falkirk.gov.uk

Community Safety: Ms Fiona Campbell, Head of Policy, Technology & Improvement, Municipal Buildings, Falkirk FK1 5RS ☎ 01324 506004 🖷 01324 506061 ✉ fiona.campbell@falkirk.gov.uk

Computer Management: Mr Donald Maclennan, ICT Officer, Municipal Buildings, Falkirk FK1 5RS ☎ 01324 501550 ✉ donnie.maclennan@falkirk.gov.uk

Consumer Protection and Trading Standards: Mr Douglas Duff, Head of Economic Development & Envrionmental Services, Falkirk Council Development Services, Abbotsford House, David's Loan, Falkirk FK2 7YZ ☎ 01324 590905 🖷 01324 504848 ✉ douglas.duff@falkirk.gov.uk

Contracts: Mr Stuart Ritchie, Director of Corporate & Neighbourhood Services, Municipal Buildings, Falkirk FK1 5RS ☎ 01324 506005 🖷 01324 506001 ✉ stuart.ritchie@falkirk.gov.uk

Corporate Services: Mr Stuart Ritchie, Director of Corporate & Neighbourhood Services, Municipal Buildings, Falkirk FK1 5RS ☎ 01324 506005 🖷 01324 506001 ✉ stuart.ritchie@falkirk.gov.uk

Customer Service: Ms Karen Algie, Head of Human Resources & Customer First, Municipal Buildings, Falkirk FK1 5RS ☎ 01324 506223 🖷 01324 506220 ✉ karen.algie@falkirk.gov.uk

Direct Labour: Mr Stuart Ritchie, Director of Corporate & Neighbourhood Services, Municipal Buildings, Falkirk FK1 5RS ☎ 01324 506005 🖷 01324 506001 ✉ stuart.ritchie@falkirk.gov.uk

Economic Development: Mr Douglas Duff, Head of Economic Development & Envrionmental Services, Falkirk Council Development Services, Abbotsford House, David's Loan, Falkirk FK2 7YZ ☎ 01324 590905 🖷 01324 504848 ✉ douglas.duff@falkirk.gov.uk

Education: Mr Nigel Fletcher, Head of Educational Support & Improvement, Sealock House, 2 Inchyra Road, Grangemouth FK3 9XB ☎ 01324 506686 🖷 01324 506664 ✉ nigel.fletcher@falkirk.gov.uk

Education: Mr Gary Greenhorn, Head of Educational Planning & Resources, Sealock House, 2 Inchyra House, Grangemouth FK3 9XB ☎ 01324 506683 🖷 01324 506664 ✉ gary.greenhorn@falkirk.gov.uk

Education: Mr Andrew Sutherland, Director of Education Services, Sealock House, 2 Inchyra Road, Grangemouth FK3 9XB ☎ 01324 506680 🖷 01324 506664 ✉ andrew.sutherland@falkirk.gov.uk

E-Government: Ms Fiona Campbell, Head of Policy, Technology & Improvement, Municipal Buildings, Falkirk FK1 5RS ☎ 01324 506004 🖷 01324 506061 ✉ fiona.campbell@falkirk.gov.uk

Emergency Planning: Mr Malcolm Wilson, Civil Contingencies Co-Ordinator, Development Services, Abbotsford House, David's Loan, Falkirk FK2 7YZ ☎ 01324 501000 🖷 01324 501001 ✉ m.wilson@falkirk.gov.uk

Environmental / Technical Services: Ms Rhona Geisler, Director of Development Services, Abbotsford House, David's Loan, Falkirk FK2 7YZ ☎ 01324 504949 🖷 01324 504848 ✉ rhona.geisler@falkirk.gov.uk

Environmental Health: Mr Graeme Webster, Environmental Health Co-ordinator, Abbotsford House, David's Loan, Falkirk FK2 7YZ ☎ 01324 504762

Estates, Property & Valuation: Mr Colin Cunningham, Estates Manager, Earls Road Depot, Grangemouth FK3 8XB ☎ 01324 501137 🖷 01324 504613 ✉ colin.cunningham@falkirk.gov.uk

European Liaison: Ms Fiona Campbell, Head of Policy, Technology & Improvement, Municipal Buildings, Falkirk FK1 5RS ☎ 01324 506004 🖷 01324 506061 ✉ fiona.campbell@falkirk.gov.uk

Facilities: Ms Jennifer Litts, Head of Facilities Management, Suite 4, The Forum, Callendar Business Park, Falkirk FK1 1XR ☎ 01324 590789 🖷 01324 590781 ✉ jennifer.litts@falkirk.gov.uk

Finance and Treasurer: Mr John Flannigan, Depute Chief Finance Officer, Municipal Buildings, Falkirk FK1 5RS ☎ 01324

506371 ✉ john.flannigan@falkirk.gov.uk

Finance and Treasurer: Mrs Susan Mathers, Depute Chief Finance Officer, Callendar Square, Falkirk FK1 1UJ ☎ 01324 506371 ✉ susan.mathers@falkirk.gov.uk

Finance and Treasurer: Mr Bryan Smail, Chief Finance Officer, Municipal Buildings, Falkirk FK1 5RS ☎ 01324 506300 ✉ bryan.smail@falkirk.gov.uk

Fleet Management: Mr John Paterson, Head of Operations, Dalgrain, Earls Road, Grangemouth FK3 9XB ☎ 01324 594626 ✉ john.paterson@falkirk.gov.uk

Grounds Maintenance: Mr Colin Cunningham, Estates Manager, Earls Road Depot, Grangemouth FK3 8XB ☎ 01324 501137 📠 01324 504613 ✉ colin.cunningham@falkirk.gov.uk

Health and Safety: Ms Karen Algie, Head of Human Resources & Customer First, Municipal Buildings, Falkirk FK1 5RS ☎ 01324 506223 📠 01324 506220 ✉ karen.algie@falkirk.gov.uk

Highways: Mr Robert McMaster, Head of Roads & Design Services, Abbotsford House, David's Loan, Falkirk FK2 7YZ ☎ 01324 504953 📠 01324 504888 ✉ robert.mcmaster@falkirk.gov.uk

Home Energy Conservation: Mr Robin Millard, Building Design Manager, Falkirk Council Development Services, Abbotsford House, David's Loan, Falkirk FK2 7YZ ☎ 01324 504868 📠 01324 504888 ✉ robin.millard@falkirk.gov.uk

Housing: Mr Stuart Ritchie, Director of Corporate & Neighbourhood Services, Municipal Buildings, Falkirk FK1 5RS ☎ 01324 506005 📠 01324 506001 ✉ stuart.ritchie@falkirk.gov.uk

Housing Maintenance: Ms Jennifer Litts, Head of Facilities Management, Suite 4, The Forum, Callendar Business Park, Falkirk FK1 1XR ☎ 01324 590789 📠 01324 590781 ✉ jennifer.litts@falkirk.gov.uk

Legal: Ms Rose Mary Glackin, Chief Governance Officer, Municipal Buildings, Falkirk FK1 5RS ☎ 01324 506076 📠 01324 506288 ✉ rosemary.glackin@falkirk.gov.uk

Licensing: Ms Alison Barr, Consumer Protection Manager, Municipal Buildings, Falkirk FK1 5RS ☎ 01324 501265 📠 01324 501588 ✉ alison.barr@falkirk.gov.uk

Lighting: Mr Graham Speirs, Area Lighting Engineer, Falkirk Council Development Services, Abbotsford House, David's Loan, Falkirk FK2 7YZ ☎ 01324 504823 📠 01324 504843 ✉ graham.speirs@falkirk.gov.uk

Lottery Funding, Charity and Voluntary: Ms Fiona Campbell, Head of Policy, Technology & Improvement, Municipal Buildings, Falkirk FK1 5RS ☎ 01324 506004 📠 01324 506061 ✉ fiona.campbell@falkirk.gov.uk

Member Services: Mr Harry Forster, Member Services Administrator, Municipal Buildings, Falkirk FK1 5RS ☎ 01324 506152 📠 01324 506151 ✉ harry.forster@falkirk.gov.uk

Parking: Mr Russell Steedman, Network Co-ordinator, Abbotsford House, David's Loan, Falkirk FK1 5RS ☎ 01324 504830 📠 01324 504843 ✉ russell.steedman@falkirk.gov.uk

Personnel / HR: Ms Karen Algie, Head of Human Resources & Customer First, Municipal Buildings, Falkirk FK1 5RS ☎ 01324 506223 📠 01324 506220 ✉ karen.algie@falkirk.gov.uk

Personnel / HR: Mr Stuart Ritchie, Director of Corporate & Neighbourhood Services, Municipal Buildings, Falkirk FK1 5RS ☎ 01324 506005 📠 01324 506001 ✉ stuart.ritchie@falkirk.gov.uk

Planning: Mr Ian Dryden, Development Control Manager, Falkirk Council Development Services, Abbotsford House, David's Loan, Falkirk FK2 7HZ ☎ 01324 504756 📠 01324 504747 ✉ ian.dryden@falkirk.gov.uk

Procurement: Mr Allan Currie, Purchasing Adviser, Corporate and Neighbourhood Services, Callendar Business Park, Falkirk FK1 1XR ☎ 01324 590818 📠 01324 503081 ✉ allan.currie@falkirk.gov.uk

Recycling & Waste Minimisation: Mr Robin Baird, Waste Strategy Co-ordinator, Abbotsford House, David's Loan, Falkirk FK2 7YZ ☎ 01324 590437 📠 01324 590421 ✉ robin.baird@falkirk.gov.uk

Regeneration: Ms Fiona Campbell, Head of Policy, Technology & Improvement, Municipal Buildings, Falkirk FK1 5RS ☎ 01324 506004 📠 01324 506061 ✉ fiona.campbell@falkirk.gov.uk

Road Safety: Mr John Angell, Head of Planning & Transportation, Falkirk Council Development Services, Abbotsford House, David's Loan, Falkirk FK2 7YZ ☎ 01324 504951 📠 01324 504848 ✉ john.angell@falkirk.gov.uk

Social Services: Ms Margaret Anderson, Director: Social Work Services, Social Work Headquarters, Denny Town House, 23 Glasgow Road, Denny FK6 5DL ☎ 01324 506400 📠 01324 065401 ✉ margaret.anderson@falkirk.gov.uk

Social Services (Adult): Ms Marion Reddie, Head of Community Care, Denny Town House, Glasgow Road, Denny FK6 5DL ☎ 01324 506400 📠 01324 506401 ✉ marion.reddie@falkirk.gov.uk

Social Services (Children): Ms Kathy McCarroll, Head of Children & Families & Criminal Justice, Social Work Headquarters, Denny Town House, 23 Glasgow Road, Denny FK6 5DL ☎ 01324 506400 📠 01324 506401 ✉ kathy.mccarroll@falkirk.gov.uk

Staff Training: Ms Karen Algie, Head of Human Resources & Customer First, Municipal Buildings, Falkirk FK1 5RS ☎ 01324 506223 📠 01324 506220 ✉ karen.algie@falkirk.gov.uk

Street Scene: Mr Raymond Smith, Street Scene, Development Services, Roads Unit, Earls Road, Grangemouth FK3 8XD ☎ 01324 506070

Sustainable Communities: Mr Alan Rodger, Planning & Environment Manager, Falkirk Council Development Services, Abbotsford House, David's Loan, Falkirk FK2 7YZ ☎ 01324

504710 🖷 01324 504709 ✉ alan.rodger@falkirk.gov.uk

Sustainable Development: Mr Alan Rodger, Planning & Environment Manager, Falkirk Council Development Services, Abbotsford House, David's Loan, Falkirk FK2 7YZ ☎ 01324 504710 🖷 01324 504709 ✉ alan.rodger@falkirk.gov.uk

Town Centre: Mr Alastair Mitchell, Town Centre Manager, Old Burgh Buildings, 12-14 Newmarket Street, Falkirk FK1 1JE ☎ 01324 611293 🖷 01324 632644 ✉ alastair.mitchell@btconnect.com

Traffic Management: Mr Russell Steedman, Network Co-ordinator, Abbotsford House, David's Loan, Falkirk FK1 5RS ☎ 01324 504830 🖷 01324 504843 ✉ russell.steedman@falkirk.gov.uk

Transport: Mr John Paterson, Head of Operations, Dalgrain, Earls Road, Grangemouth FK3 9XB ☎ 01324 594626 ✉ john.paterson@falkirk.gov.uk

Transport Planner: Mrs Julie Cole, Acting Transport Planning Manager, Development Services, Abbotsford House, David's Loan, Falkirk FK2 7YZ ☎ 01324 404820 🖷 01324 504914 ✉ julie.cole@falkirk.gov.uk

Waste Collection and Disposal: Mr Robin Baird, Waste Strategy Co-ordinator, Abbotsford House, David's Loan, Falkirk FK2 7YZ ☎ 01324 590437 🖷 01324 590421 ✉ robin.baird@falkirk.gov.uk

Waste Collection and Disposal: Mr John Paterson, Head of Operations, Dalgrain, Earls Road, Grangemouth FK3 9XB ☎ 01324 594626 ✉ john.paterson@falkirk.gov.uk

Waste Management: Mr John Paterson, Head of Operations, Dalgrain, Earls Road, Grangemouth FK3 9XB ☎ 01324 594626 ✉ john.paterson@falkirk.gov.uk

MEMBERS OF THE COUNCIL (32)

***Provost:* Reid**, Pat (LAB - Falkirk North)
pat.reid@falkirk.gov.uk
***Deputy Provost:* Patrick**, John (CON - Falkirk South)
john.patrick@falkirk.gov.uk
Alexander, David (SNP - Falkirk North)
david.alexander@falkirk.gov.uk
Balfour, David (SNP - Grangemouth)
david.balfour@falkirk.gov.uk
Bird, Stephen (SNP - Carse Kinnaird and Tryst)
stephen.bird@falkirk.gov.uk
Black, Allyson (LAB - Grangemouth)
allyson.black@falkirk.gov.uk
Blackwood, Jim (LAB - Denny and Banknock)
jim.blackwood@falkirk.gov.uk
Buchanan, Billy (IND - Bonnybridge and Larbert)
william.buchanan@falkirk.gov.uk
Carleschi, Steven (SNP - Carse Kinnaird and Tryst)
steven.carleschi@falkirk.gov.uk
Chalmers, Colin (SNP - Falkirk South)
colin.chalmers@falkirk.gov.uk
Coleman, Tom (SNP - Bonnybridge and Larbert)
thomas.coleman@falkirk.gov.uk
Goldie, Gerald (LAB - Falkirk South)
gerry.goldie@falkirk.gov.uk
Goldie, Dennis (LAB - Falkirk South)
dennis.goldie@falkirk.gov.uk
Gow, Linda (O - Bonnybridge and Larbert)
linda.gow@falkirk.gov.uk
Hughes, Gordon (SNP - Upper Braes)
gordon.hughes@falkirk.gov.uk
Jackson, Steven (SNP - Lower Braes)
steven.jackson@falkirk.gov.uk
MacDonald, Charles (LAB - Carse Kinnaird and Tryst)
charles.macdonald@falkirk.gov.uk
Mahoney, Adrian (LAB - Bo'ness and Blackness)
adrian.mahoney@falkirk.gov.uk
Martin, Craig (LAB - Falkirk North)
craigr.martin@falkirk.gov.uk
Martin, Craig (LAB - Carse Kinnaird and Tryst)
craig.martin@falkirk.gov.uk
McCabe, Brian (IND - Denny and Banknock)
brian.mccabe@falkirk.gov.uk
McLuckie, John (LAB - Upper Braes)
john.mcluckie@falkirk.gov.uk
McNally, John (SNP - Denny and Banknock)
john.mcnally@falkirk.gov.uk
Meiklejohn, Cecil (SNP - Falkirk North)
cecil.meiklejohn@falkirk.gov.uk
Murray, Roise (LAB - Upper Braes)
rosie.murray@falkirk.gov.uk
Nicol, Malcolm (CON - Lower Braes)
malcolm.nicol@falkirk.gov.uk
Nimmo, Alan (LAB - Lower Braes)
alan.nimmo@falkirk.gov.uk
Oliver, Martin (SNP - Denny and Banknock)
martin.oliver@falkirk.gov.uk
Paterson, Joan (LAB - Grangemouth)
joan.paterson@falkirk.gov.uk
Ritchie, Ann (SNP - Bo'ness and Blackness)
ann.ritchie@falkirk.gov.uk
Spears, Robert (IND - Grangemouth)
robert.spears@falkirk.gov.uk
Turner, Sandy (SNP - Bo'ness and Blackness)
sandy.turner@falkirk.gov.uk

POLITICAL COMPOSITION

LAB: 13, SNP: 13, IND: 3, CON: 2, O: 1

COMMITTEE CHAIRS

Economic Strategy & Development: Mr Dennis Goldie
Education: Mr Alan Nimmo
Environment & Coummunity Safety: Dr Craig Martin
Housing & Social Care: Mr Gerald Goldie
Leisure, Tourism & Community: Mr Adrian Mahoney
Licensing: Mr Malcolm Nicol
Pensions: Mr John Patrick
Planning: Mr William Buchanan
Policy & Resources: Dr Craig Martin

FAREHAM D

Fareham Borough Council, Civic Offices, Civic Way, Fareham PO16 7AZ ☎ 01329 236100 🖷 01329 822732 ✉ cx@fareham.gov.uk 💻 www.fareham.gov.uk

FACTS & FIGURES

Police Authority: Hampshire Police Authority

Health Authority: South Central Strategic Health Authority
Learning and Skills Council: South East
Parliamentary Constituencies: Fareham
EU Constituencies: South East
Election Frequency: Elections are biennial
Twinning: Vannes (France); Pulheim (Germany)

PRINCIPAL OFFICERS

Chief Executive: Mr Peter Grimwood, Chief Executive, Civic Offices, Civic Way, Fareham PO16 7AZ ☎ 01329 824300 ✉ pgrimwood@fareham.gov.uk

Senior Management: Mrs Lindsey Ansell, Head of Corporate Services, Civic Offices, Civic Way, Fareham PO16 7AZ ☎ 01329 824567 🖷 01329 822732 ✉ lansell@fareham.gov.uk

Access Officer / Social Services (Disability): Mr Richard Sturgess, Access Officer, Civic Offices, Civic Way, Fareham PO16 7AZ ☎ 023 9254 5535 ✉ rsturgess@fareham.gov.uk

Architect, Building / Property Services: Mr Graham Lloyd, Head of Estates, Civic Offices, Civic Way, Fareham PO16 7AZ ☎ 01329 824320 ✉ glloyd@fareham.gov.uk

Architect, Building / Property Services: Mr Chris Newman, Head of Building Services, Civic Offices, Civic Way, Fareham PO16 7AZ ☎ 01329 236100 ✉ cnewman@fareham.gov.uk

Building Control: Mr John Shaw, Building Control Manager, Civic Offices, Civic Way, Fareham PO16 7AZ ☎ 01329 236100 🖷 01329 821461 ✉ jshaw@fareham.gov.uk

Building Control: Mr Lee Smith, Head of Development Control, Civic Offices, Civic Way, Fareham PO16 7AZ ☎ 01329 236100 ✉ lsmith@fareham.gov.uk

Children / Youth Services: Mr Martyn George, Director of Community & Streetscene, Civic Offices, Civic Way, Fareham PO16 7AZ ☎ 01329 824400 ✉ mgeorge@fareham.gov.uk

PR / Communications: Mrs Sue Mills, PR & Marketing Manager, Civic Offices, Civic Way, Fareham PO16 7AZ ☎ 01329 236100 🖷 01329 822732 ✉ smills@fareham.gov.uk

Community Planning: Mr Richard Jolley, Director of Planning & Environment, Civic Offices, Civic Way, Fareham PO16 7AZ ☎ 01329 824388 ✉ rjolley@fareham.gov.uk

Community Safety: Ms Naerinder Bains, Community Safety Officer, Civic Offices, Civic Way, Fareham PO16 7AZ ☎ 01329 824496 ✉ nbains@fareham.gov.uk

Computer Management: Mr Peter Harper, Head of ICT, Civic Offices, Civic Way, Fareham PO16 7AZ ☎ 01329 824537 ✉ pharper@fareham.gov.uk

Corporate Services: Mrs Lindsey Ansell, Head of Corporate Services, Civic Offices, Civic Way, Fareham PO16 7AZ ☎ 01329 824567 🖷 01329 822732 ✉ lansell@fareham.gov.uk

Corporate Services: Ms Elaine Hammell, Head of Audit & Assurance, Civic Offices, Civic Way, Fareham PO16 7AZ ☎ 01329 236100 ✉ ehammell@fareham.gov.uk

Customer Service: Ms Leigh Usher, Head of Customer & Democratic Services, Civic Offices, Civic Way, Fareham PO16 7AZ ☎ 01329 236100 ✉ lusher@fareham.gov.uk

Economic Development: Mr Tony Mundy, Economic Development Manager, Civic Offices, Civic Way, Fareham PO16 7AZ ☎ 01329 824686 ✉ tmundy@fareham.gov.uk

E-Government: Mr Peter Grimwood, Chief Executive, Civic Offices, Civic Way, Fareham PO16 7AZ ☎ 01329 824300 ✉ pgrimwood@fareham.gov.uk

Electoral Registration: Mrs Elaine Wildig, Electoral Services Manager, Civic Offices, Civic Way, Fareham PO16 7AZ ☎ 01329 824587 🖷 01329 822732 ✉ electionservices@fareham.gov.uk

Emergency Planning: Mr Garry White, Director of Regulatory & Democratic Services, Civic Offices, Civic Way, Fareham PO16 7AZ ☎ 01329 236100 🖷 01329 821511 ✉ gwhite@fareham.gov.uk

Energy Management: Mr Robert Dunn, Facilities Services Officer, Civic Offices, Civic Way, Fareham PO16 7AZ ☎ 01329 824559 🖷 01329 821411 ✉ rdunn@fareham.gov.uk

Environmental / Technical Services: Mr Martyn George, Director of Community & Streetscene, Civic Offices, Civic Way, Fareham PO16 7AZ ☎ 01329 824400 ✉ mgeorge@fareham.gov.uk

Environmental Health: Mr Garry White, Director of Regulatory & Democratic Services, Civic Offices, Civic Way, Fareham PO16 7AZ ☎ 01329 236100 🖷 01329 821511 ✉ gwhite@fareham.gov.uk

Estates, Property & Valuation: Mr Graham Lloyd, Head of Estates, Civic Offices, Civic Way, Fareham PO16 7AZ ☎ 01329 824320 ✉ glloyd@fareham.gov.uk

European Liaison: Mr Tony Mundy, Economic Development Manager, Civic Offices, Civic Way, Fareham PO16 7AZ ☎ 01329 824686 ✉ tmundy@fareham.gov.uk

Finance and Treasurer: Mrs Caroline Quirk, Head of Benefits, Civic Offices, Civic Way, Fareham PO16 7AZ ☎ 01329 236100 ✉ cquirk@fareham.gov.uk

Finance and Treasurer: Mr Andy Wannell, Director of Finance & Resources, Civic Offices, Civic Way, Fareham PO16 7AZ ☎ 01329 824620 🖷 01329 821541 ✉ awannell@fareham.gov.uk

Fleet Management: Mr Trevor Beard, Transport Manager, Civic Offices, Civic Way, Fareham PO16 7AZ ☎ 01329 824836 ✉ tbeard@fareham.gov.uk

Grounds Maintenance: Mr Martyn George, Director of Community & Streetscene, Civic Offices, Civic Way, Fareham PO16 7AZ ☎ 01329 824400 ✉ mgeorge@fareham.gov.uk

Health and Safety: Mr Tom Rodgers, Health & Safety Officer, Civic Offices, Civic Way, Fareham PO16 7AZ ☎ 01329 236100 🖷 01329 821411 ✉ trodgers@fareham.gov.uk

Housing: Mr Andrew Fiske, Head of Strategic Housing, Civic Offices, Civic Way, Fareham PO16 7AZ ☎ 01329 236100 ✉ afiske@fareham.gov.uk

Housing: Mr Martyn George, Director of Community & Streetscene, Civic Offices, Civic Way, Fareham PO16 7AZ ☎ 01329 824400 ✉ mgeorge@fareham.gov.uk

Legal: Mr Richard Ivory, Acting Head of Legal & Democratic Services, Civic Offices, Civic Way, Fareham PO16 7AZ ☎ 02380 832794 ✉ richard.ivory@southampton.gov.uk

Leisure and Cultural Services: Mr Mark Bowler, Head of Leisure & Community, Civic Offices, Civic Way, Fareham PO16 7AZ ☎ 01329 824420 ✉ mbowler@fareham.gov.uk

Licensing: Mrs Mandy Hovey, Licensing Officer, Civic Offices, Civic Way, Fareham PO16 7AZ ☎ 01329 824428 🖷 01329 822732 ✉ mhovey@fareham.gov.uk

Lottery Funding, Charity and Voluntary: Mr Mark Bowler, Head of Leisure & Community, Civic Offices, Civic Way, Fareham PO16 7AZ ☎ 01329 824420 ✉ mbowler@fareham.gov.uk

Member Services: Ms Leigh Usher, Head of Customer & Democratic Services, Civic Offices, Civic Way, Fareham PO16 7AZ ☎ 01329 236100 ✉ lusher@fareham.gov.uk

Parking: Mr K Wright, Head of Community Safety & Enforcement, Civic Offices, Civic Way, Fareham PO16 7AZ ☎ 01329 236100 🖷 01329 824377 ✉ kwright@fareham.gov.uk

Personnel / HR: Ms Sarah Robinson, Head of Personnel & Development, Civic Offices, Civic Way, Fareham PO16 7AZ ☎ 01329 824564 ✉ srobinson@fareham.gov.uk

Planning: Ms Linda Jewell, Head of Strategic Planning & Design, Civic Offices, Civic Way, Fareham PO16 7AZ ☎ 01329 236100 ✉ ljewell@fareham.gov.uk

Planning: Mr Richard Jolley, Director of Planning & Environment, Civic Offices, Civic Way, Fareham PO16 7AZ ☎ 01329 824388 ✉ rjolley@fareham.gov.uk

Procurement: Mr Gary Jarvis, Procurement Officer, Civic Offices, Civic Way, Fareham PO16 7AZ ☎ 01329 824508 ✉ gjarvis@fareham.gov.uk

Recycling & Waste Minimisation: Mr Martyn George, Director of Community & Streetscene, Civic Offices, Civic Way, Fareham PO16 7AZ ☎ 01329 824400 ✉ mgeorge@fareham.gov.uk

Street Scene: Mr Paul Doran, Head of Street Scene Services, Civic Offices, Civic Way, Fareham PO16 7AZ ☎ 01329 236100 ✉ pdoran@fareham.gov.uk

Sustainable Communities: Mr Peter Grimwood, Chief Executive, Civic Offices, Civic Way, Fareham PO16 7AZ ☎ 01329 824300 ✉ pgrimwood@fareham.gov.uk

Sustainable Development: Mr Garry White, Director of Regulatory & Democratic Services, Civic Offices, Civic Way, Fareham PO16 7AZ ☎ 01329 236100 🖷 01329 821511 ✉ gwhite@fareham.gov.uk

Town Centre: Mrs Patricia Gray, Fareham Town Centre Manager, Civic Offices, Civic Way, Fareham PO16 7PU ☎ 01329 236100 ✉ pgray@fareham.gov.uk

Traffic Management: Mr C Oldham, Traffic & Design Manager, Civic Offices, Civic Way, Fareham PO16 7AZ ☎ 01329 236100 ✉ coldham@fareham.gov.uk

Transport: Mr Trevor Beard, Transport Manager, Civic Offices, Civic Way, Fareham PO16 7AZ ☎ 01329 824836 ✉ tbeard@fareham.gov.uk

Transport Planner: Ms Rosemary Fletcher, Principal Transport Planner, Civic Offices, Civic Way, Fareham PO16 7AZ ✉ rfletcher@fareham.gov.uk

Waste Collection and Disposal: Mr Nye Onosey, Refuse & Recycling Manager, Civic Offices, Civic Way, Fareham PO16 7AZ ☎ 01329 236100 ✉ nonosey@fareham.gov.uk

Waste Management: Mr Martyn George, Director of Community & Streetscene, Civic Offices, Civic Way, Fareham PO16 7PU ☎ 01329 824400 ✉ mgeorge@fareham.gov.uk

MEMBERS OF THE COUNCIL (31)

Mayor: **Steadman**, Dennis (CON - Fareham South)
dsteadman@fareham.gov.uk
Deputy Mayor: **Bayford**, Susan (CON - Locks Heath)
sbayford@fareham.gov.uk
Leader of the Council: **Woodward**, Sean (CON - Sarisbury)
swoodward@fareham.gov.uk
Deputy Leader of the Council: **Price**, Roger (LD - Portchester East)
rprice@fareham.gov.uk
Bayford, Brian (CON - Park Gate)
bbayford@fareham.gov.uk
Bell, Susan (CON - Portchester West)
sbell@fareham.gov.uk
Bryant, John (CON - Fareham North)
cllrbryant@fareham.gov.uk
Bryant, Pamela (CON - Fareham North)
cllrbryant@fareham.gov.uk
Cartwright, Trevor (CON - Warsash)
tcartwright@fareham.gov.uk
Davies, Peter Fareham North West: Vacant
pdavies@fareham.gov.uk
Ellerton, Marian (CON - Park Gate)
mellerton@fareham.gov.uk
Englefield, Jack (LD - Titchfield Common)
jenglefield@fareham.gov.uk
Evans, Keith (CON - Locks Heath)
kevans@fareham.gov.uk
Fazackarley, Geoff (LD - Portchester East)
Ford, Michael (CON - Warsash)
Forrest, James (LD - Stubbington)
jforrest@fareham.gov.uk
Gregory, Nick (CON - Fareham West)
ngregory@fareham.gov.uk
Harper, Tifanny (CON - Titchfield)
tharper@fareham.gov.uk

Hockley, Connie (CON - Titchfield)
chockley@fareham.gov.uk
Howard, Trevor (CON - Fareham South)
thoward@fareham.gov.uk
Keeble, Leslie (CON - Fareham West)
lkeeble@fareham.gov.uk
Knight, Tim (CON - Hill Head)
tknight@fareham.gov.uk
Mandry, Arthur (CON - Hill Head)
amandry@fareham.gov.uk
Mandry, Kay (CON - Stubbington)
kmandry@fareham.gov.uk
Norris, David (LD - Portchester East)
dnorris@fareham.gov.uk
Pankhurst, Sarah (CON - Titchfield Common)
Swanbrow, David (CON - Sarisbury)
dswanbrow@fareham.gov.uk
Trott, Katrina (LD - Fareham East)
ktrott@fareham.gov.uk
Walker, Nick (CON - Portchester West)
nwalker@fareham.gov.uk
Whittingham, David (CON - Fareham North West)
dwhittingham@fareham.gov.uk
Whittle, Paul (LD - Fareham East)
pwhittle@fareham.gov.uk

POLITICAL COMPOSITION
CON: 23, LD: 7, UKWN: 1

COMMITTEE CHAIRS
Audit & Governance: Mr Tim Knight
Housing: Mrs Marian Ellerton
Leisure & Community: Cllr Susan Bell
Licensing & Regulatory Affairs: Mrs Pamela Bryant
Planning & Development Control: Mr Nick Walker
Public Protection: Mrs Kay Mandry
Scrutiny: Mr David Swanbrow
Strategic Planning & Environment: Cllr John Bryant

FENLAND D

Fenland District Council, Fenland Hall, County Road, March PE15 8NQ ☎ 01354 654321 🖷 01354 622259 ✉ info@fenland.gov.uk 💻 www.fenland.gov.uk

FACTS & FIGURES
Police Authority: Cambridgeshire Police Authority
Health Authority: East of England Strategic Health Authority
Learning and Skills Council: Eastern
Parliamentary Constituencies: Cambridgeshire North East
EU Constituencies: Eastern
Election Frequency: Elections are of whole council
Twinning: Stadt Nettetal (Germany); Maroochyshire (Australia)

PRINCIPAL OFFICERS
Chief Executive: Mr Paul Medd, Chief Executive, Fenland Hall, County Road, March PE15 8NQ ☎ 01354 622303 ✉ paulmedd@fenland.gov.uk

Architect, Building / Property Services: Mr Gary Garford, Corporate Director, Fenland Hall, County Road, March PE15 8NQ ☎ 01354 622373 ✉ garygarford@fenland.gov.uk

Best Value: Ms Carol Pilson, Corporate Director, Fenland Hall, County Road, March PE15 8NQ ☎ 01354 622360 ✉ cpilson@fenland.gov.uk

Building Control: Mr Alan Pain, Corporate Director, Fenland Hall, County Road, March PE15 8NQ ☎ 01354 622302 ✉ alanpain@fenland.gov.uk

PR / Communications: Ms Carol Pilson, Corporate Director, Fenland Hall, County Road, March PE15 8NQ ☎ 01354 622360 ✉ cpilson@fenland.gov.uk

Community Planning: Mr Gary Garford, Corporate Director, Fenland Hall, County Road, March PE15 8NQ ☎ 01354 622373 ✉ garygarford@fenland.gov.uk

Community Safety: Mr Richard Cassidy, Corporate Director, Fenland Hall, County Road, March PE15 8NQ ☎ 01354 622300 ✉ richardcassidy@fenland.gov.uk

Computer Management: Mr Rob Bridge, Corporate Director & Chief Finance Officer, Fenland Hall, County Road, March PE15 8NQ ☎ 01354 622201 ✉ robbridge@fenland.gov.uk

Computer Management: Mr Geoff Kent, Head of Income & ICT, Fenland Hall, County Road, March PE15 8NQ ☎ 01354 654321 ✉ gkent@fenland.gov.uk

Customer Service: Mr Rob Bridge, Corporate Director & Chief Finance Officer, Fenland Hall, County Road, March PE15 8NQ ☎ 01354 622201 ✉ robbridge@fenland.gov.uk

Economic Development: Mr Alan Pain, Corporate Director, Fenland Hall, County Road, March PE15 8NQ ☎ 01354 622302 ✉ alanpain@fenland.gov.uk

E-Government: Mr Rob Bridge, Corporate Director & Chief Finance Officer, Fenland Hall, County Road, March PE15 8NQ ☎ 01354 622201 ✉ robbridge@fenland.gov.uk

Electoral Registration: Mr Paul Medd, Chief Executive, Fenland Hall, County Road, March PE15 8NQ ☎ 01354 622303 ✉ paulmedd@fenland.gov.uk

Emergency Planning: Mr David Vincent, Health, Safety and Emergency Planning Manager, Fenland Hall, County Road, March PE15 8NQ ☎ 01354 622353 ✉ dvincent@fenland.gov.uk

Energy Management: Mr Richard Cassidy, Corporate Director, Fenland Hall, County Road, March PE15 8NQ ☎ 01354 622300 ✉ richardcassidy@fenland.gov.uk

Environmental / Technical Services: Mr Richard Cassidy, Corporate Director, Fenland Hall, County Road, March PE15 8NQ ☎ 01354 622300 ✉ richardcassidy@fenland.gov.uk

Environmental Health: Mr Richard Cassidy, Corporate Director, Fenland Hall, County Road, March PE15 8NQ ☎ 01354 622300 ✉ richardcassidy@fenland.gov.uk

Estates, Property & Valuation: Mr Gary Garford, Corporate Director, Fenland Hall, County Road, March PE15 8NQ ☎ 01354

622373 ✉ garygarford@fenland.gov.uk

Facilities: Mr Gary Garford, Corporate Director, Fenland Hall, County Road, March PE15 8NQ ☎ 01354 622373 ✉ garygarford@fenland.gov.uk

Finance and Treasurer: Mr Rob Bridge, Corporate Director & Chief Finance Officer, Fenland Hall, County Road, March PE15 8NQ ☎ 01354 622201 ✉ robbridge@fenland.gov.uk

Fleet Management: Mr Richard Cassidy, Corporate Director, Fenland Hall, County Road, March PE15 8NQ ☎ 01354 622300 ✉ richardcassidy@fenland.gov.uk

Grounds Maintenance: Mr Richard Cassidy, Corporate Director, Fenland Hall, County Road, March PE15 8NQ ☎ 01354 622300 ✉ richardcassidy@fenland.gov.uk

Health and Safety: Mr Richard Cassidy, Corporate Director, Fenland Hall, County Road, March PE15 8NQ ☎ 01354 622300 ✉ richardcassidy@fenland.gov.uk

Home Energy Conservation: Mr Alan Pain, Corporate Director, Fenland Hall, County Road, March PE15 8NQ ☎ 01354 622302 ✉ alanpain@fenland.gov.uk

Housing: Mr Alan Pain, Corporate Director, Fenland Hall, County Road, March PE15 8NQ ☎ 01354 622302 ✉ alanpain@fenland.gov.uk

Local Area Agreement: Ms Carol Pilson, Corporate Director, Fenland Hall, County Road, March PE15 8NQ ☎ 01354 622360 ✉ cpilson@fenland.gov.uk

Legal: Mr Ian Hunt, Chief Solicitor, Fenland Hall, County Road, March PE15 8NQ ☎ 01354 622214 🖷 01354 606904 ✉ ihunt@fenland.gov.uk

Leisure and Cultural Services: Mr Richard Cassidy, Corporate Director, Fenland Hall, County Road, March PE15 8NQ ☎ 01354 622300 ✉ richardcassidy@fenland.gov.uk

Licensing: Mr Alan Pain, Corporate Director, Fenland Hall, County Road, March PE15 8NQ ☎ 01354 622302 ✉ alanpain@fenland.gov.uk

Lottery Funding, Charity and Voluntary: Mr Alan Pain, Corporate Director, Fenland Hall, County Road, March PE15 8NQ ☎ 01354 622302 ✉ alanpain@fenland.gov.uk

Member Services: Mr Paul Medd, Chief Executive, Fenland Hall, County Road, March PE15 8NQ ☎ 01354 622303 ✉ paulmedd@fenland.gov.uk

Parking: Mr Gary Garford, Corporate Director, Fenland Hall, County Road, March PE15 8NQ ☎ 01354 622373 ✉ garygarford@fenland.gov.uk

Partnerships: Mr Richard Cassidy, Corporate Director, Fenland Hall, County Road, March PE15 8NQ ☎ 01354 622300 ✉ richardcassidy@fenland.gov.uk

Personnel / HR: Mrs Sam Anthony, Head of HR & OD, Fenland Hall, County Road, March PE15 8NQ ☎ 01354 654321 ✉ santhony@fenland.gov.uk

Planning: Mr Alan Pain, Corporate Director, Fenland Hall, County Road, March PE15 8NQ ☎ 01354 622302 ✉ alanpain@fenland.gov.uk

Procurement: Mr Rob Bridge, Corporate Director & Chief Finance Officer, Fenland Hall, County Road, March PE15 8NQ ☎ 01354 622201 ✉ robbridge@fenland.gov.uk

Recycling & Waste Minimisation: Mr Richard Cassidy, Corporate Director, Fenland Hall, County Road, March PE15 8NQ ☎ 01354 622300 ✉ richardcassidy@fenland.gov.uk

Regeneration: Mr Alan Pain, Corporate Director, Fenland Hall, County Road, March PE15 8NQ ☎ 01354 622302 ✉ alanpain@fenland.gov.uk

Staff Training: Mrs Sam Anthony, Head of HR & OD, Fenland Hall, County Road, March PE15 8NQ ☎ 01354 654321 ✉ santhony@fenland.gov.uk

Street Scene: Mr Richard Cassidy, Corporate Director, Fenland Hall, County Road, March PE15 8NQ ☎ 01354 622300 ✉ richardcassidy@fenland.gov.uk

Sustainable Communities: Mr Alan Pain, Corporate Director, Fenland Hall, County Road, March PE15 8NQ ☎ 01354 622302 ✉ alanpain@fenland.gov.uk

Tourism: Mr Alan Pain, Corporate Director, Fenland Hall, County Road, March PE15 8NQ ☎ 01354 622302 ✉ alanpain@fenland.gov.uk

Town Centre: Mr Gary Garford, Corporate Director, Fenland Hall, County Road, March PE15 8NQ ☎ 01354 622373 ✉ garygarford@fenland.gov.uk

Transport Planner: Mr Gary Garford, Corporate Director, Fenland Hall, County Road, March PE15 8NQ ☎ 01354 622373 ✉ garygarford@fenland.gov.uk

Waste Collection and Disposal: Mr Richard Cassidy, Corporate Director, Fenland Hall, County Road, March PE15 8NQ ☎ 01354 622300 ✉ richardcassidy@fenland.gov.uk

Waste Management: Mr Richard Cassidy, Corporate Director, Fenland Hall, County Road, March PE15 8NQ ☎ 01354 622300 ✉ richardcassidy@fenland.gov.uk

MEMBERS OF THE COUNCIL (40)

***Chair:* Humphrey**, Michael (CON - Roman Bank - Wisbech)
mhumphrey@fenland.gov.uk

***Vice-Chair:* Mayor**, Ken (CON - Bassenhally - Whittlesey)
kenmayor@fenlands.gov.uk

***Leader of the Council:* Melton**, Alan (CON - Birch - Chatteris)
meltonalan@aol.com

***Deputy Leader of the Council:* Seaton**, Chris (CON - Roman Bank - Wisbech)
cseaton@fenland.gov.uk

Archer, Mark (IND - Manea)
marcher@fenland.gov.uk
Booth, Gavin (LD - Parson Drove and Wisbech St Mary)
gbooth@fenland.gov.uk
Bucknor, Michael (IND - Waterlees - Wisbech)
mbucknor@fenland.gov.uk
Bucknor, Virginia (IND - Waterlees - Wisbech)
vbucknor@fenland.gov.uk
Butcher, Ralph (CON - Benwick, Coates and Estrea)
rbutcher@fenland.gov.uk
Chambers, John (CON - The Mills - Chatteris)
jchambers@fenland.gov.uk
Clark, John (CON - March East)
jclark@fenland.gov.uk
Connor, David (CON - Doddington)
dconnor@fenland.gov.uk
Cornwell, Mike (CON - March North)
mcornwell@fenland.gov.uk
Cotterell MBE, Mac (CON - Elm and Christchurch)
mcotterell@fenland.gov.uk
Cox, Carol (CON - Clarkson - Wisbech)
ccox@fenland.gov.uk
Curtis, Martin (CON - Kingsmoor - Whittlesey)
mcurtis@fenland.gov.uk
Farmer, Jonathan (CON - Medworth - Wisbech)
jfarmer@fenland.gov.uk
French, Jan (CON - March West)
jfrench@fenland.gov.uk
Garratt, Steve (CON - Lattersey - Whittlesey)
sgarratt@fenland.gov.uk
Hatton, Philip (CON - Roman Bank - Wisbech)
phatton@fenland.gov.uk
Hodgson, David (CON - Staithe - Wisbech)
dhodgson@fenland.gov.uk
Jolley, Paul (CON - Wimblington)
pjolley@fenland.gov.uk
Keane, Bernard (CON - March East)
bkeane@fenland.gov.uk
King, Simon (CON - Hill - Wisbech)
sking@fenland.gov.uk
Mayor, Kay (CON - Delph - Whittlesey)
kaymayor@fenland.gov.uk
Miscandlon, Alex (CON - Benwick, Coates and Eastrea)
amiscandlon@fenland.gov.uk
Murphy, Peter (CON - Wenneye - Chatteris)
pmurphy@fenland.gov.uk
Newell, Florence (CON - Slade Lode - Chatteris)
fnewell@fenland.gov.uk
Oliver, David (CON - Peckover - Wisbech)
doliver@fenland.gov.uk
Owen, Kit (CON - March West)
kowen@fenland.gov.uk
Patrick, David (LD - Kirkgate - Wisbech)
dpatrick@fenland.gov.uk
Peachey, Ken (CON - St Marys - Whittlesey)
kpeachey@fenland.gov.uk
Quince, Trevor (CON - March North)
tquince@fenland.gov.uk
Scrimshaw, Robert (CON - Parson Drove / Wisbech St. Mary)
rscrimshaw@fenland.gov.uk
Skoulding, Robert (IND - March West)
rskoulding@fenland.gov.uk
Stebbing, Derek (CON - St Andrews - Whittlesey)
dstebbing@fenland.gov.uk
Sutton, Will (CON - Elm and Christchurch)
wsutton@fenland.gov.uk
Tunley, Peter (CON - March North)
ptunley@fenland.gov.uk
Wegg, Bruce (CON - Hill - Wisbech)
bwegg@fenland.gov.uk
Yeulett, Fred (CON - March East)
fyeulett@fenland.gov.uk

POLITICAL COMPOSITION

CON: 34, IND: 4, LD: 2

CABINET

Leader / Policy & Resources: Mr Alan Melton
Deputy Leader / Economy, Inward Investment, Business & Skills Development: Mr Chris Seaton
Environment & Street Scene: Mr Peter Murphy
Growth & Transport: Mr Kit Owen
Leisure: Mr Steve Garratt
Planning Improvements: Mrs Jan French
Quality Organisation, Finance & Performance Management: Mr John Clark
Rural Affairs & Health and Well Being: Mr Ralph Butcher
Special Projects: Mr Mac Cotterell MBE
Wisbech Affairs: Mr David Oliver

COMMITTEE CHAIRS

Corporate Governance: Mrs Florence Newell
Licensing: Mrs Kay Mayor
Overview & Scrutiny: Mr Paul Jolley
Planning: Mr Roger Green

FERMANAGH N

Fermanagh District Council, Town Hall, Enniskillen BT74 7BA
☎ 028 6632 5050 🖷 028 6632 2024 ✉ fdc@fermanagh.gov.uk
💻 www.fermanagh.gov.uk

FACTS & FIGURES

Police Authority: Northern Ireland Policing Board
Health Authority: Western Local Commissioning Group
Learning and Skills Council: Northern Ireland
Parliamentary Constituencies: Fermanagh and South Tyrone
EU Constituencies: Northern Ireland
Election Frequency: Elections are of whole council
Twinning: Fermanagh: Bielefeld, Brackwede (Germany)

PRINCIPAL OFFICERS

Chief Executive: Mr Brendan Hegarty, Chief Executive, Town Hall, Enniskillen BT74 7BA ☎ 028 6632 5050 🖷 028 6632 2024 ✉ brendan.hegarty@fermanagh.gov.uk

Deputy Chief Executive: Mr Brendan Hegarty, Chief Executive, Town Hall, Enniskillen BT74 7BA ☎ 028 6632 5050 🖷 028 6632 2024 ✉ brendan.hegarty@fermanagh.gov.uk

Senior Management: Mr Robert Forde, Director of Environmental Health, Town Hall, Enniskillen BT74 7BA ☎ 028 6632 5050 🖷 028 6632 2024 ✉ robert.forde@fermanagh.gov.uk

Senior Management: Mr Robert Gibson, Director of Leisure, Tourism & Arts, Town Hall, Enniskillen BT74 7BA ☎ 028 6632 5050 🖷 028 6632 2024 ✉ robert.gibson@fermanagh.gov.uk

Senior Management: Mr Gerald Knox, Director of Technical Services, Killyvilly Depot, Enniskillen BT74 6HR ☎ 028 6632 3533 🖷 028 6632 6360 ✉ gerry.knox@fermanagh.gov.uk

Senior Management: Mr Desmond Reid, Director of Building Control, Administrative Office, Town Hall, Enniskillen BT74 7BA ☎ 028 6632 5050 🖷 028 6632 9112 ✉ desmond.reid@fermanagh.gov.uk

Best Value: Mr Tom McCabe, Personnel Manager, Town Hall, Enniskillen BT74 7BA ☎ 028 6632 5050 🖷 028 6632 2024 ✉ tom.mccabe@fermanagh.gov.uk

Building Control: Mr Desmond Reid, Director of Building Control, Administrative Office, Town Hall, Enniskillen BT74 7BA ☎ 028 6632 5050 🖷 028 6632 9112 ✉ desmond.reid@fermanagh.gov.uk

Community Safety: Mr Neville Armstrong, Community Safety Co-ordinator, Town Hall, Enniskillen BT74 7BA ☎ 028 6632 5050 🖷 028 6632 2024 ✉ neville.armstrong@fermanagh.gov.uk

Computer Management: Mr Brendan Hegarty, Chief Executive, Town Hall, Enniskillen BT74 7BA ☎ 028 6632 5050 🖷 028 6632 2024 ✉ brendan.hegarty@fermanagh.gov.uk

Consumer Protection and Trading Standards: Mr Robert Forde, Director of Environmental Health, Town Hall, Enniskillen BT74 7BA ☎ 028 6632 5050 🖷 028 6632 2024 ✉ robert.forde@fermanagh.gov.uk

Direct Labour: Mr Gerald Knox, Director of Technical Services, Killyvilly Depot, Enniskillen BT74 6HR ☎ 028 6632 3533 🖷 028 6632 6360 ✉ gerry.knox@fermanagh.gov.uk

Economic Development: Mr Brendan Hegarty, Chief Executive, Town Hall, Enniskillen BT74 7BA ☎ 028 6632 5050 🖷 028 6632 2024 ✉ brendan.hegarty@fermanagh.gov.uk

E-Government: Mr Brendan Hegarty, Chief Executive, Town Hall, Enniskillen BT74 7BA ☎ 028 6632 5050 🖷 028 6632 2024 ✉ brendan.hegarty@fermanagh.gov.uk

Emergency Planning: Mr David Phair, Head of Administration, Town Hall, Enniskillen BT74 7BA ☎ 028 6632 5050 🖷 028 6632 2024 ✉ david.phair@fermanagh.gov.uk

Environmental / Technical Services: Mr Robert Gibson, Director of Leisure, Tourism & Arts, Town Hall, Enniskillen BT74 7BA ☎ 028 6632 5050 🖷 028 6632 2024 ✉ robert.gibson@fermanagh.gov.uk

Environmental Health: Mr Robert Forde, Director of Environmental Health, Town Hall, Enniskillen BT74 7BA ☎ 028 6632 5050 🖷 028 6632 2024 ✉ robert.forde@fermanagh.gov.uk

Events Manager: Mr Robert Gibson, Director of Leisure, Tourism & Arts, Town Hall, Enniskillen BT74 7BA ☎ 028 6632 5050 🖷 028 6632 2024 ✉ robert.gibson@fermanagh.gov.uk

Finance and Treasurer: Mr Brendan Hegarty, Chief Executive, Town Hall, Enniskillen BT74 7BA ☎ 028 6632 5050 🖷 028 6632 2024 ✉ brendan.hegarty@fermanagh.gov.uk

Fleet Management: Mr Gerald Knox, Director of Technical Services, Killyvilly Depot, Enniskillen BT74 6HR ☎ 028 6632 3533 🖷 028 6632 6360 ✉ gerry.knox@fermanagh.gov.uk

Grounds Maintenance: Mr Gerald Knox, Director of Technical Services, Killyvilly Depot, Enniskillen BT74 6HR ☎ 028 6632 3533 🖷 028 6632 6360 ✉ gerry.knox@fermanagh.gov.uk

Health and Safety: Mr Robert Forde, Director of Environmental Health, Town Hall, Enniskillen BT74 7BA ☎ 028 6632 5050 🖷 028 6632 2024 ✉ robert.forde@fermanagh.gov.uk

Leisure and Cultural Services: Mr Robert Gibson, Director of Leisure, Tourism & Arts, Town Hall, Enniskillen BT74 7BA ☎ 028 6632 5050 🖷 028 6632 2024 ✉ robert.gibson@fermanagh.gov.uk

Licensing: Mr Francis Gilleece, Licensing Officer, Town Hall, Enniskillen BT74 7BA ☎ 028 6632 5050 🖷 028 6632 2024 ✉ francis.gilleece@fermanagh.gov.uk

Member Services: Mr David Phair, Head of Administration, Town Hall, Enniskillen BT74 7BA ☎ 028 6632 5050 🖷 028 6632 2024 ✉ david.phair@fermanagh.gov.uk

Partnerships: Mr Neville Armstrong, Community Safety Co-ordinator, Town Hall, Enniskillen BT74 7BA ☎ 028 6632 5050 🖷 028 6632 2024 ✉ neville.armstrong@fermanagh.gov.uk

Personnel / HR: Mr Tom McCabe, Personnel Manager, Town Hall, Enniskillen BT74 7BA ☎ 028 6632 5050 🖷 028 6632 2024 ✉ tom.mccabe@fermanagh.gov.uk

Procurement: Mr David Phair, Head of Administration, Town Hall, Enniskillen BT74 7BA ☎ 028 6632 5050 🖷 028 6632 2024 ✉ david.phair@fermanagh.gov.uk

Recycling & Waste Minimisation: Mr Paul Slowey, Technical Officer, Killyvilly Depot, Enniskillen BT74 6HR ☎ 028 6632 3533 🖷 028 6632 3630 ✉ paul.slowey@fermanagh.gov.uk

Staff Training: Mr Tom McCabe, Personnel Manager, Town Hall, Enniskillen BT74 7BA ☎ 028 6632 5050 🖷 028 6632 2024 ✉ tom.mccabe@fermanagh.gov.uk

Sustainable Communities: Mr Robert Gibson, Director of Leisure, Tourism & Arts, Town Hall, Enniskillen BT74 7BA ☎ 028 6632 5050 🖷 028 6632 2024 ✉ robert.gibson@fermanagh.gov.uk

Sustainable Development: Mr Robert Gibson, Director of Leisure, Tourism & Arts, Town Hall, Enniskillen BT74 7BA ☎ 028 6632 5050 🖷 028 6632 2024 ✉ robert.gibson@fermanagh.gov.uk

Tourism: Mr Robert Gibson, Director of Leisure, Tourism & Arts, Town Hall, Enniskillen BT74 7BA ☎ 028 6632 5050 🖷 028 6632 2024 ✉ robert.gibson@fermanagh.gov.uk

Town Centre: Mr Robert Gibson, Director of Leisure, Tourism & Arts, Town Hall, Enniskillen BT74 7BA ☎ 028 6632 5050

🖷 028 6632 2024 ✉ robert.gibson@fermanagh.gov.uk

Transport Planner: Mr Gerald Knox, Director of Technical Services, Killyvilly Depot, Enniskillen BT74 6HR ☎ 028 6632 3533 🖷 028 6632 6360 ✉ gerry.knox@fermanagh.gov.uk

Waste Collection and Disposal: Mr Robert Gibson, Director of Leisure, Tourism & Arts, Town Hall, Enniskillen BT74 7BA ☎ 028 6632 5050 🖷 028 6632 2024 ✉ robert.gibson@fermanagh.gov.uk

Waste Collection and Disposal: Mr Gerald Knox, Director of Technical Services, Killyvilly Depot, Enniskillen BT74 6HR ☎ 028 6632 3533 🖷 028 6632 6360 ✉ gerry.knox@fermanagh.gov.uk

Waste Management: Mr Robert Gibson, Director of Leisure, Tourism & Arts, Town Hall, Enniskillen BT74 7BA ☎ 028 6632 5050 🖷 028 6632 2024 ✉ robert.gibson@fermanagh.gov.uk

MEMBERS OF THE COUNCIL (23)

Andrews, Harold (UUP - Erne East)
harold.andrews@fermanagh.gov.uk
Baird, Alex (UUP - Erne West)
alex.baird@fermanagh.gov.uk
Barton, Rosemary (UUP - Erne North)
rosemary.barton@fermanagh.gov.uk
Brimstone, Alison (DUP - Enniskillen)
alison.brimstone@fermanagh.gov.uk
Britton, Frank (SDLP - Enniskillen)
frank.britton@fermanagh.gov.uk
Brownlee, Cyril (DUP - Enniskillen)
cyril.brownlee@fermanagh.gov.uk
Coyle, Debbie (SF - Enniskillen)
debbie.coyle@fermanagh.gov.uk
Doherty, Barry (SF - Erne West)
barry.doherty@fermanagh.gov.uk
Farrell, Raymond (UUP - Erne North)
raymond.farrell@fermanagh.gov.uk
Gallagher, Brendan (SDLP - Erne West)
gallagherb@fermanagh.gov.uk
Greene, Sheamus (SF - Erne East)
sheamus.greene@fermanagh.gov.uk
Hugget, Stephen (SF - Erne North)
stephen.hugget@fermanagh.gov.uk
Irvine, Robert (UUP - Enniskillen)
robert.irvine@fermanagh.gov.uk
Johnston, Bert (DUP - Erne North)
bert.johnstone@fermanagh.gov.uk
Johnston, Basil (UUP - Enniskillen)
basil.johnston@fermanagh.gov.uk
Lynch, Ruth (SF - Erne East)
ruth.lynch@fermanagh.gov.uk
Maguire, Thomas (SF - Enniskillen)
thomas.maguire@fermanagh.gov.uk
McCaffrey, Brian (SF - Erne East)
brian.mccaffrey@fermanagh.gov.uk
O'Kane, John (SDLP - Erne North)
john.okane@fermanagh.gov.uk
O'Reilly, Thomas (SF - Erne East)
thomas.oreilly@fermanagh.gov.uk
Rice, Frankie (SF - Erne West)
frank.rice@fermanagh.gov.uk
Robinson, Paul (DUP - Erne East)
paul.robinson@fermanagh.gov.uk
Swift, Bernice (IND - Erne West)
bernice.swift@fermanagh.gov.uk

POLITICAL COMPOSITION

SF: 9, UUP: 6, DUP: 4, SDLP: 3, IND: 1

COMMITTEE CHAIRS

Audit: Mr Brian McCaffrey
Development: Ms Debbie Coyle
Environmental Health: Mr Paul Robinson
Environmental Services: Mr Alex Baird
Planning: Mr Sheamus Greene

FIFE S

Fife Council, Fife House, North Street, Glenrothes KY7 5LT
☎ 0845 155 0000 ✉ fife.council@fife.gov.uk
💻 www.fifedirect.org.uk

FACTS & FIGURES

Police Authority: Fife Police Authority
Health Authority: NHS Fife
Learning and Skills Council: Scotland
Parliamentary Constituencies: Dunfermline and West Fife, Fife North East, Glenrothes, Kirkcaldy and Cowdenbeath
EU Constituencies: Scotland
Election Frequency: Elections are of whole council

PRINCIPAL OFFICERS

Chief Executive: Mr Ronnie Hinds, Chief Executive, Fife House, North Street, Glenrothes KY7 5LT ☎ 08451 555555 Ext 442332 ✉ ronnie.hinds@fife.gov.uk

Access Officer / Social Services (Disability): Ms Roseanne Fearon, Head of Service, Adult Services, 5th Floor, Rothesay House, Rothesay Place, Glenrothes KY7 5PQ ☎ 08451 555555 Ext 441180 ✉ roseanne.fearon@fife.gov.uk

Best Value: Mr Michael Enston, Executive Director, Fife House, North Street, Glenrothes KY7 5LT ☎ 08451 555555 Ext 441198 ✉ michael.enston@fife.gov.uk

Building Control: Mr Keith Winter, Head of Development Services, Fife House, North Street, Glenrothes KY7 5LT ☎ 08451 555555 Ext 442284 ✉ keith.winter@fife.gov.uk

Catering Services: Mr Ken Gourlay, Head of Asset & Facilities Management Services, Kingdom House, North Street, Glenrothes KY7 5LT ☎ 08451 555555

Children / Youth Services: Mr Stephen Moore, Executive Director (Social Work) and Lead for Health, Rothesay House, North Street, Glenrothes KY7 5PQ ☎ 08451 555555 Ext 444112 ✉ stephen.moore@fife.gov.uk

Community Planning: Mr Michael Enston, Executive Director, Fife House, North Street, Glenrothes KY7 5LT ☎ 08451 555555 Ext 441198 ✉ michael.enston@fife.gov.uk

Community Safety: Mr Michael Enston, Executive Director, Fife House, North Street, Glenrothes KY7 5LT ☎ 08451 555555 Ext 441198 ✉ michael.enston@fife.gov.uk

Computer Management: Mr Charlie Anderson, Interim Head of I.T. Services, Carleton House, Balgonie Road, Markinch, KY7 6AQ ☎ 08451 555555 ✉ charlie.anderson@fife.gov.uk

Consumer Protection and Trading Standards: Mr Fraser Thomson, Programme Director, 1st Floor, Bankhead Central, Bankhead Park, Glenrothes KY7 6GH ☎ 08451 555555 Ext 440470 ✉ fraser.thomson@fife.gov.uk

Contracts: Mr John Cosgrove, Procurement and Supplies Manager, Fife House, North Street, Glenrothes KY7 5LT ☎ 08451 555555 ✉ John.Cosgrove@fife.gov.uk

Corporate Services: Mr Michael Enston, Executive Director, Fife House, North Street, Glenrothes KY7 5LT ☎ 08451 555555 Ext 441198 ✉ michael.enston@fife.gov.uk

Corporate Services: Mr Sandy Gallanders, Projects Director, Fife House, North Street, Glenrothes KY7 5LT ☎ 08451 555555 Etx 444264 ✉ sandy.gallanders@fife.gov.uk

Direct Labour: Mr Bob McLellan, Head of Transportation Services, First Floor, Bankhead Central, Bankhead Park, Glenrothes KY7 6GH ☎ 08451 555555 Ext 444424 ✉ bob.mclellan@fife.gov.uk

Economic Development: Mr Keith Winter, Head of Development Services, Fife House, North Street, Glenrothes KY7 5LT ☎ 08451 555555 Ext 442284 ✉ keith.winter@fife.gov.uk

Education: Mr Kenneth Greer, Executive Director, Children's Services, Rothesay House, North Street, Glenrothes KY7 5PQ ☎ 08451 555555 Ext 444219 ✉ kenneth.greer@fife.gov.uk

E-Government: Mr Charlie Anderson, Interim Head of I.T. Services, Carleton House, Balgonie Road, Markinch, KY7 6AQ ☎ 08451 555555 ✉ charlie.anderson@fife.gov.uk

Electoral Registration: Mr Lawrence Cooper, Depute Electoral Registration Officer & Service Manager, Fife House, North Street, Glenrothes KY7 5TL ☎ Lawrence.Cooper@fife.gov.uk

Emergency Planning: Mr Dougie Potter, Emergency Planning Officer, Fife Fire & Rescue Headquarters, Strathore Road, Thornton, Kirkcaldy KY1 4DF ☎ 01592 778376 ✉ dougie.potter@fife.gov.uk

Energy Management: Mr Ken Gourlay, Head of Asset & Facilities Management Services, Ground Floor, Bankhead Central, Bankhead Park, Glenrothes KY7 6GH ☎ 08451 555555

Environmental / Technical Services: Mr Fraser Thomson, Programme Director, 1st Floor, Bankhead Central, Bankhead Park, Glenrothes KY7 6GH ☎ 08451 555555 Ext 440470 ✉ fraser.thomson@fife.gov.uk

Environmental Health: Mr Fraser Thomson, Programme Director, 1st Floor, Bankhead Central, Bankhead Park, Glenrothes KY7 6GH ☎ 08451 555555 Ext 440470 ✉ fraser.thomson@fife.gov.uk

Estates, Property & Valuation: Mr Alan Paul, Senior Manager (Property Services), Bankhead Central, Bankhead Park, Glenrothes KY7 6GH ☎ 08451 555555 ✉ alan.paul@fife.gov.uk

European Liaison: Mr Michael Enston, Executive Director, Fife House, North Street, Glenrothes KY7 5LT ☎ 08451 555555 Ext 441198 ✉ michael.enston@fife.gov.uk

Facilities: Mr Ken Gourlay, Head of Asset & Facilities Management Services, Kingdom House, North Street, Glenrothes KY7 5LT ☎ 08451 555555

Finance and Treasurer: Mr Brian Livingston, Executive Director Finance and Resources, Fife House, North Street, Glenrothes KY7 5LT ☎ 08451 55 55 55 Ext 44 09 72 ✉ Brian.Livingston@fife.gov.uk

Fleet Management: Mr Ken Gourlay, Head of Asset & Facilities Management Services, Kingdom House, North Street, Glenrothes KY7 5LT ☎ 08451 555555

Grounds Maintenance: Mr Steve Grimmond, Executive Director, Fife House, North Street, Glenrothes KY7 5LT ☎ 08451 555555 Ext 444143 ✉ steven.grimmond@fife.gov.uk

Health and Safety: Mr Michael Enston, Executive Director, Fife House, North Street, Glenrothes KY7 5LT ☎ 08451 555555 Ext 441198 ✉ michael.enston@fife.gov.uk

Highways: Mr Bob McLellan, Head of Transportation Services, First Floor, Bankhead Central, Bankhead Park, Glenrothes KY7 6GH ☎ 08451 555555 Ext 444424 ✉ bob.mclellan@fife.gov.uk

Home Energy Conservation: Mr Derek Muir, Head of Housing, 3rd Floor, Rothesay House, North Street, Glenrothes KY5 5LT ☎ 08451 555555 Ext 444513 ✉ derek.muir@fife.gov.uk

Housing: Mr Derek Muir, Head of Housing, 3rd Floor, Rothesay House, North Street, Glenrothes KY5 5LT ☎ 08451 555555 Ext 444513 ✉ derek.muir@fife.gov.uk

Housing Maintenance: Mr Derek Muir, Head of Housing, 3rd Floor, Rothesay House, North Street, Glenrothes KY5 5LT ☎ 08451 555555 Ext 444513 ✉ derek.muir@fife.gov.uk

Leisure and Cultural Services: Mr Steve Grimmond, Executive Director, Fife House, North Street, Glenrothes KY7 5LT ☎ 08451 555555 Ext 444143 ✉ steven.grimmond@fife.gov.uk

Lifelong Learning: Mr Stephen Moore, Executive Director (Social Work) and Lead for Health, Rothesay House, North Street, Glenrothes KY7 5PQ ☎ 08451 555555 Ext 444112 ✉ stephen.moore@fife.gov.uk

Lighting: Mr Bob McLellan, Head of Transportation Services, First Floor, Bankhead Central, Bankhead Park, Glenrothes KY7 6GH ☎ 08451 555555 Ext 444424 ✉ bob.mclellan@fife.gov.uk

Lottery Funding, Charity and Voluntary: Mr Michael Enston, Executive Director, Fife House, North Street, Glenrothes KY7 5LT ☎ 08451 555555 Ext 441198 ✉ michael.enston@fife.gov.uk

Lottery Funding, Charity and Voluntary: Mr Steve Grimmond,

Executive Director, Fife House, North Street, Glenrothes KY7 5LT ☎ 08451 555555 Ext 444143 ✉ steven.grimmond@fife.gov.uk

Member Services: Mr Michael Enston, Executive Director, Fife House, North Street, Glenrothes KY7 5LT ☎ 08451 555555 Ext 441198 ✉ michael.enston@fife.gov.uk

Parking: Mr Bob McLellan, Head of Transportation Services, First Floor, Bankhead Central, Bankhead Park, Glenrothes KY7 6GH ☎ 08451 555555 Ext 444424 ✉ bob.mclellan@fife.gov.uk

Partnerships: Mr Michael Enston, Executive Director, Fife House, North Street, Glenrothes KY7 5LT ☎ 08451 555555 Ext 441198 ✉ michael.enston@fife.gov.uk

Partnerships: Mr Steve Grimmond, Executive Director, Fife House, North Street, Glenrothes KY7 5LT ☎ 08451 555555 Ext 444143 ✉ steven.grimmond@fife.gov.uk

Personnel / HR: Mr Sandy Gallanders, Projects Director, Fife House, North Street, Glenrothes KY7 5LT ☎ 08451 555555 Etx 444264 ✉ sandy.gallanders@fife.gov.uk

Procurement: Mr John Cosgrove, Procurement and Supplies Manager, Fife House, North Street, Glenrothes KY7 5LT ☎ 08451 555555 ✉ John.Cosgrove@fife.gov.uk

Public Libraries: Mr Steve Grimmond, Executive Director, Fife House, North Street, Glenrothes KY7 5LT ☎ 08451 555555 Ext 444143 ✉ steven.grimmond@fife.gov.uk

Recycling & Waste Minimisation: Mr Fraser Thomson, Programme Director, 1st Floor, Bankhead Central, Bankhead Park, Glenrothes KY7 6GH ☎ 08451 555555 Ext 440470 ✉ fraser.thomson@fife.gov.uk

Road Safety: Mr Bob McLellan, Head of Transportation Services, First Floor, Bankhead Central, Bankhead Park, Glenrothes KY7 6GH ☎ 08451 555555 Ext 444424 ✉ bob.mclellan@fife.gov.uk

Social Services: Mr Stephen Moore, Executive Director (Social Work) and Lead for Health, Rothesay House, North Street, Glenrothes KY7 5PQ ☎ 08451 555555 Ext 444112 ✉ stephen.moore@fife.gov.uk

Social Services (Adult): Mr Stephen Moore, Executive Director (Social Work) and Lead for Health, Rothesay House, North Street, Glenrothes KY7 5PQ ☎ 08451 555555 Ext 444112 ✉ stephen.moore@fife.gov.uk

Social Services (Children): Mr Stephen Moore, Executive Director (Social Work) and Lead for Health, Rothesay House, North Street, Glenrothes KY7 5PQ ☎ 08451 555555 Ext 444112 ✉ stephen.moore@fife.gov.uk

Staff Training: Mr Michael Enston, Executive Director, Fife House, North Street, Glenrothes KY7 5LT ☎ 08451 555555 Ext 441198 ✉ michael.enston@fife.gov.uk

Sustainable Development: Mr Neil Gateley, Team Leader, Environmental Partnerships & Projects Team, Kingdom House, North Street, Glenrothes KY7 5LT ☎ 08451 555555 Ext 440457 ✉ neil.gateley@fife.gov.uk

Traffic Management: Mr Bob McLellan, Head of Transportation Services, First Floor, Bankhead Central, Bankhead Park, Glenrothes KY7 6GH ☎ 08451 555555 Ext 444424 ✉ bob.mclellan@fife.gov.uk

Transport: Mr Bob McLellan, Head of Transportation Services, First Floor, Bankhead Central, Bankhead Park, Glenrothes KY7 6GH ☎ 08451 555555 Ext 444424 ✉ bob.mclellan@fife.gov.uk

Transport Planner: Mr Bob McLellan, Head of Transportation Services, First Floor, Bankhead Central, Bankhead Park, Glenrothes KY7 6GH ☎ 08451 555555 Ext 444424 ✉ bob.mclellan@fife.gov.uk

Waste Collection and Disposal: Mr Fraser Thomson, Programme Director, 1st Floor, Bankhead Central, Bankhead Park, Glenrothes KY7 6GH ☎ 08451 555555 Ext 440470 ✉ fraser.thomson@fife.gov.uk

Waste Management: Mr Fraser Thomson, Programme Director, 1st Floor, Bankhead Central, Bankhead Park, Glenrothes KY7 6GH ☎ 08451 555555 Ext 440470 ✉ fraser.thomson@fife.gov.uk

MEMBERS OF THE COUNCIL (78)

***Provost:* Leishman**, Jim (LAB - Dunfermline Central)
***Provost:* Melville**, Frances (LD - St Andrews)
***Leader of the Council:* Rowley**, Alex (LAB - The Lochs)
Adam, Tom (LAB - Leven, Kennoway and Largo)
Alexander, David (SNP - Leven, Kennoway and Largo)
Bain, Ann (SNP - The Lochs)
Bain, Alistair (SNP - Cowdenbeath)
Baxter, Jayne (LAB - Cowdenbeath)
Beare, John (SNP - Glenrothes North, Leslie and Markinch)
Brett, Tim (LD - Tay Bridgehead)
Brown, Bill (SNP - Glenrothes West and Kinglassie)
Brown, Lawrence (LAB - Kirkcaldy East)
Callaghan, Alice (LAB - West Fife and Coastal Villages)
Callaghan, Pat (LAB - Rosyth)
Campbell, William (LAB - Dunfermline North)
Campbell, Betty (LAB - Glenrothes West and Kinglassie)
Carrington, Kay (LAB - Kirkcaldy East)
Chapman, Douglas (SNP - Rosyth)
Chisholm, Ian (SNP - Lochgelly and Cardenden)
Clarke, William (IND - The Lochs)
Clelland, Bob (LAB - West Fife and Coastal Villages)
Connor, Bill (SNP - Tay Bridgehead)
Craik, Altany (LAB - Glenrothes West and Kinglassie)
Crichton, Ian (LAB - Glenrothes Central and Thornton)
Crooks, Neil (LAB - Kirkcaldy North)
Dempsey, Dave (CON - Inverkeithing and Dalgety Bay)
Docherty, John (SNP - East Neuk and Landward)
Erskine, Linda (LAB - Lochgelly and Cardenden)
Ferguson, William (IND - West Fife and Coastal Villages)
George, Peter (LAB - Burntisland, Kinghorn and Western Kirkcaldy)
Goodall, Brian (SNP - Dunfermline South)
Graham, David (LAB - Buckhaven, Methil and Wemyss)
Grant, Peter (SNP - Glenrothes West and Kinglassie)
Grant, Fiona (SNP - Glenrothes North, Leslie and Markinch)

Haffey, Charles (LAB - Leven, Kennoway and Largo)
Hamilton, Judy (LAB - Kirkcaldy Central)
Hanvey, Neale (SNP - Dunfermline Central)
Heer, Andy (CON - Howe of Fife and Tay Coast)
Hilton, Cara (LAB - Dunfermline South)
Hood, Mark (LAB - Lochgelly and Cardenden)
Hunter, Alistair (SNP - Leven, Kennoway and Largo)
Kay, George (SNP - Burntisland, Kinghorn and Western Kirkcaldy)
Kay, William (LAB - Glenrothes North, Leslie and Markinch)
Kennedy, Margaret (LD - Cupar)
Laird, Lesley (LAB - Inverkeithing and Dalgety Bay)
Law, Helen (LAB - Dunfermline North)
Leslie, Susan (LD - Burntisland, Kinghorn and Western Kirkcaldy)
Lindsay, Carol (SNP - Kirkcaldy North)
Lockheart, Peter (LAB - Cowdenbeath)
Lothian, Donald (LD - Howe of Fife and Tay Coast)
MacDiarmid, David (SNP - Howe of Fife and Tay Coast)
MacGregor, Donald (LD - East Neuk and Landward)
MacPhail, Stuart (SNP - Kirkcaldy Central)
Marjoram, Karen (SNP - Cupar)
Martin, Anthony (LD - Dunfermline South)
McCartney, Keith (SNP - St Andrews)
McGarry, Alice (SNP - Inverkeithing and Dalgety Bay)
Mogg, David (SNP - Dunfermline North)
Morrison, Dorothea (CON - St Andrews)
Morrison, Arthur (SNP - Kirkcaldy East)
Morrison, Kay (LAB - Glenrothes North, Leslie and Markinch)
O'Brien, John (SNP - Buckhaven, Methil and Wemyss)
Poole, Bryan (IND - Cupar)
Riches, Elizabeth (LD - East Neuk and Landward)
Rodger, Andrew (IND - Buckhaven, Methil and Wemyss)
Rosiejak, Joe (LD - Dunfermline Central)
Ross, David (LAB - Kirkcaldy North)
Rumney, Mike (LAB - Dunfermline South)
Selbie, Kenny (LAB - Kirkcaldy Central)
Shirkie, Mike (LAB - Rosyth)
Sloan, Ian (LAB - Glenrothes Central and Thornton)
Stewart, Kate (SNP - West Fife and Coastal Villages)
Taylor, Margaret (LD - Tay Bridgehead)
Thomson, Brian (LAB - St Andrews)
Vettraino, Ross (SNP - Glenrothes Central and Thornton)
Yates, Gavin (LAB - Inverkeithing and Dalgety Bay)
Young, Bob (LAB - Dunfermline Central)
Young, Jim (LAB - Buckhaven, Methil and Wemyss)

POLITICAL COMPOSITION
LAB: 35, SNP: 26, LD: 10, IND: 4, CON: 3

FLINTSHIRE W

Flintshire County Council, (Cyngor Sir y Fflint), County Hall, Mold CH7 6NF ☎ 01352 752121 🖷 01352 758240
✉ info@flintshire.gov.uk 💻 www.flintshire.gov.uk

FACTS & FIGURES
Police Authority: North Wales Police Authority
Learning and Skills Council: Wales
Parliamentary Constituencies: Alyn and Deeside, Delyn
EU Constituencies: Wales
Election Frequency: Elections are by thirds

PRINCIPAL OFFICERS
Chief Executive: Mr Colin Everett, Chief Executive, County Hall, Mold CH7 6NB ☎ 01352 702100
✉ chief.executive@flintshire.gov.uk

Senior Management: Mr Ian Budd, Director of Lifelong Learning, County Hall, Mold CH7 6NF ☎ 01352 704010 🖷 01352 704040 ✉ ian.budd@flintshire.gov.uk

Senior Management: Mr Carl Longland, Director of Environment, County Hall, Mold CH7 6NF ☎ 01352 704500 🖷 01352 704550 ✉ carl.longland@flintshire.gov.uk

Access Officer / Social Services (Disability): Ms Jo Taylor, Service Manager, County Hall, Mold CH7 6NF ☎ 01352 701350 🖷 01352 702635 ✉ jo.taylor@flintshire.gov.uk

Architect, Building / Property Services: Mr Andy Smith, Corporate Property Maintenance Manager, County Offices, Chapel Street, Flint CH6 5BD ☎ 01352 703127 🖷 01352 762915 ✉ andy.smith@flintshire.gov.uk

Best Value: Mrs Karen Armstrong, Policy, Performance & Partnership Manager, County Hall, Mold CH7 6NT ☎ 01352 702740 🖷 01352 702807 ✉ karen.armstrong@flintshire.gov.uk

Building Control: Mr Scott Rowley, Team Manager, County Hall, Mold CH7 6NF ☎ 01352 703272 🖷 01352 703615
✉ scott.rowley@flintshire.gov.uk

Catering Services: Ms Vicky Bell, Catering Manager, County Hall, Mold CH7 6ND ☎ 01352 704045 🖷 01352 754202
✉ vicky.bell@flintshire.gov.uk

Children / Youth Services: Mr Rob Edwards, County Youth & Community Officer, County Hall, Mold CH7 6ND ☎ 01352 704031 🖷 01352 704055 ✉ rob.edwards@flintshire.gov.uk

Civil Registration: Mrs Denise Naylor, Customer Services Manager, County Hall, Mold CH7 6NT ☎ 01352 702421 🖷 01352 702807 ✉ denise.naylor@flintshire.gov.uk

PR / Communications: Ms Barbara Milne, Corporate Communications Manager, County Hall, Mold CH7 6NB ☎ 01352 702111 🖷 01352 704949 ✉ barbara.milne@flintshire.gov.uk

Community Planning: Mrs Karen Armstrong, Policy, Performance & Partnership Manager, County Hall, Mold CH7 6NT ☎ 01352 702740 🖷 01352 702807
✉ karen.armstrong@flintshire.gov.uk

Community Safety: Mrs Sian Jones, Team Leader, County Hall, Mold CH7 6NT ☎ 01352 702132 🖷 01352 700152
✉ sian.l.jones@flintshire.gov.uk

Computer Management: Mr Chris Guest, Head of ICT & Customer Services, County Hall, Mold CH7 6NT ☎ 01352 702800 🖷 01352 700149 ✉ chris.guest@flintshire.gov.uk

Consumer Protection and Trading Standards: Mr Michael

Lovatt, Community Protection Manager, County Hall, Mold CH7 6NF ☎ 01352 703393 🖷 01352 703441 ✉ michael.lovatt@flintshire.gov.uk

Consumer Protection and Trading Standards: Mrs Sylvia Portbury, Health Protection Manager, County Hall, Mold CH7 6NF ☎ 01352 703378 🖷 01352 703441 ✉ sylvia.portbury@flintshire.gov.uk

Corporate Services: Mrs Kerry Feather, Head of Finance, County Hall, Mold CH7 6NA ☎ 01352 702200 🖷 01352 700149 ✉ kerry.feather@flintshire.gov.uk

Corporate Services: Mr Chris Guest, Head of ICT & Customer Services, County Hall, Mold CH7 6NT ☎ 01352 702800 🖷 01352 700149 ✉ chris.guest@flintshire.gov.uk

Corporate Services: Mr Gareth Owens, Head of Legal & Democratic Services, County Hall, Mold CH7 6NF ☎ 01352 702344 🖷 01352 702494 ✉ gareth.owens@flintshire.gov.uk

Corporate Services: Mrs Helen Stappleton, Head of HR & Organisational Development, County Hall, Mold CH7 6NG ☎ 01352 702720 🖷 01352 700152 ✉ helen.stappleton@flintshire.gov.uk

Customer Service: Mrs Denise Naylor, Customer Services Manager, County Hall, Mold CH7 6NT ☎ 01352 702421 🖷 01352 702807 ✉ denise.naylor@flintshire.gov.uk

Direct Labour: Mr Harvey Mitchell, Streetscene Manager, Alltami Depot, Alltami, Mold CH7 6LG ☎ 01352 701200 🖷 01352 701270 ✉ harvey.mitchell@flintshire.gov.uk

Economic Development: Mr Dave Heggarty, Head of Regeneration, County Hall, Mold CH7 6NF ☎ 01352 703203 🖷 01352 704550 ✉ dave.heggarty@flintshire.gov.uk

E-Government: Mr Chris Guest, Head of ICT & Customer Services, County Hall, Mold CH7 6NT ☎ 01352 702800 🖷 01352 700149 ✉ chris.guest@flintshire.gov.uk

Electoral Registration: Mrs Lyn Phillips, Electoral Services Manager, County Hall, Mold CH7 6NF ☎ 01352 702329 🖷 01352 702494 ✉ lyn.phillips@flintshire.gov.uk

Emergency Planning: Mr Don Norris, Civil Contingencies Manager, County Hall, Mold CH7 6NG ☎ 01352 702120 🖷 01352 754005 ✉ don.norris@flintshire.gov.uk

Energy Management: Mr Will Pierce, Energy Manager, County Offices, Chapel Street, Flint CH6 5BD ☎ 01352 703137 🖷 01352 703786 ✉ will.pierce@flintshire.gov.uk

Environmental / Technical Services: Mr Neal Cockerton, Head of Assets & Transportation, County Hall, Mold CH7 6NF ☎ 01352 703169 🖷 01352 704550 ✉ neal.cockerton@flintshire.gov.uk

Environmental / Technical Services: Mr Kevin Gardiner, Waste Services Manager, County Depot, Chester Road East, Queensferry, Deeside CH5 1TD ☎ 01352 701234 🖷 01352 701727 ✉ kevin.gardiner@flintshire.gov.uk

Environmental Health: Mr Ian Vaughan-Evans, Interim Head of Public Protection, County Hall, Mold CH7 6NF ☎ 01352 703413 🖷 01352 703441 ✉ ian.vaughan-evans@flintshire.gov.uk

Estates, Property & Valuation: Mr Anthony Bamford, Corporate Valuer, County Offices, Chapel Street, Flint CH6 5BD ☎ 01352 703102 🖷 01352 703111 ✉ tony.bamford@flintshire.gov.uk

European Liaison: Mr Dave Heggarty, Head of Regeneration, County Hall, Mold CH7 6NF ☎ 01352 703203 🖷 01352 704550 ✉ dave.heggarty@flintshire.gov.uk

Facilities: Mr Rudy Imhoof, Interim Facilities Service Manager, County Hall, Mold CH7 6NF ☎ 01352 704039 🖷 01352 754207 ✉ rudy.imhoof@flintshire.gov.uk

Finance and Treasurer: Mrs Kerry Feather, Head of Finance, County Hall, Mold CH7 6NA ☎ 01352 702200 🖷 01352 700149 ✉ kerry.feather@flintshire.gov.uk

Finance and Treasurer: Mr Gary Ferguson, Corporate Finance Manager, County Hall, Mold CH7 6NF ☎ 01352 702271 ✉ gary.ferguson@flintshire.gov.uk

Fleet Management: Mr Barry Wilkinson, Fleet Services Operations Manager, Alltami Depot, Alltami, Mold CH7 6LG ☎ 01244 704656 🖷 01244 704660 ✉ barry.wilkinson@flintshire.gov.uk

Grounds Maintenance: Mr Harvey Mitchell, Streetscene Manager, County Hall, Mold CH7 6NB ☎ 01352 701200 🖷 01352 701270 ✉ harvey.mitchell@flintshire.gov.uk

Health and Safety: Ms Vanessa Johnson, Corporate Health & Safety Manager, County Hall, Mold CH7 6NB ☎ 01352 702962 🖷 01352 703441 ✉ vanessa.johnson@flintshire.gov.uk

Highways: Mr Steve Jones, Head of Streetscene, County Hall, Mold CH7 6NF ☎ 01352 704700 ✉ stephen.o.jones@flintshire.gov.uk

Highways: Mr Harvey Mitchell, Streetscene Manager, County Hall, Mold CH7 6NB ☎ 01352 701200 🖷 01352 701270 ✉ harvey.mitchell@flintshire.gov.uk

Home Energy Conservation: Mr Will Pierce, Energy Manager, County Offices, Chapel Street, Flint CH6 5BD ☎ 01352 703137 🖷 01352 703786 ✉ will.pierce@flintshire.gov.uk

Housing: Ms Clare Budden, Head of Housing, County Hall, Mold CH7 6NF ☎ 01352 703800 🖷 01352 762915 ✉ clare.budden@flintshire.gov.uk

Housing Maintenance: Mr Mike Barnard, Housing & Property Maintenance Manager, Flint Offices, Flint CH6 5BE ☎ 01352 701658 ✉ mike.barnard@flintshire.gov.uk

Legal: Mr Gareth Owens, Head of Legal & Democratic Services, County Hall, Mold CH7 6NF ☎ 01352 702344 🖷 01352 702494 ✉ gareth.owens@flintshire.gov.uk

Leisure and Cultural Services: Mr Lawrence Rawsthorne, Head of Culture & Leisure, Library Headquarters, County Hall, Mold CH7 6NW ☎ 01352 704400 🖷 01352 753662 ✉ lawrence.rawsthorne@flintshire.gov.uk

Licensing: Mr Michael Lovatt, Community Protection Manager, County Hall, Mold CH7 6NF ☎ 01352 703393 🖷 01352 703441 ✉ michael.lovatt@flintshire.gov.uk

Lifelong Learning: Mr Ian Budd, Director of Lifelong Learning, County Hall, Mold CH7 6NF ☎ 01352 704010 🖷 01352 704040 ✉ ian.budd@flintshire.gov.uk

Lighting: Mr Darell Jones, Streetlighting Manager, Halkyn Depot, Fulbrook Buildings, Halkyn, Mold CH8 8BY ☎ 01352 701290 🖷 01352 701270 ✉ darell.jones@flintshire.gov.uk

Member Services: Mrs Karen Jones, Chairman's & Members' Assistant, County Hall, Mold CH7 6NR ☎ 01352 702151 🖷 01352 702150 ✉ karen.jones@flintshire.gov.uk

Member Services: Mrs Lesley Wood, Chairman's & Members' Assistant, County Hall, Mold CH7 6NR ☎ 01352 702151 🖷 01352 702150 ✉ lesley.wood@flintshire.gov.uk

Parking: Mr Neal Cockerton, Head of Assets & Transportation, County Hall, Mold CH7 6NF ☎ 01352 703169 🖷 01352 704550 ✉ neal.cockerton@flintshire.gov.uk

Partnerships: Mrs Karen Armstrong, Policy, Performance & Partnership Manager, County Hall, Mold CH7 6NT ☎ 01352 702740 🖷 01352 702807 ✉ karen.armstrong@flintshire.gov.uk

Personnel / HR: Mrs Helen Stappleton, Head of HR & Organisational Development, County Hall, Mold CH7 6NG ☎ 01352 702720 🖷 01352 700152 ✉ helen.stappleton@flintshire.gov.uk

Planning: Mr A Farrow, Head of Planning, County Hall, Mold CH7 6NB ☎ 01352 703201 🖷 01352 756444 ✉ andy.farrow@flintshire.gov.uk

Procurement: Mr Chris Guest, Head of ICT & Customer Services, County Hall, Mold CH7 6NT ☎ 01352 702800 🖷 01352 700149 ✉ chris.guest@flintshire.gov.uk

Public Libraries: Mr Lawrence Rawsthorne, Head of Culture & Leisure, Library Headquarters, County Hall, Mold CH7 6NW ☎ 01352 704400 🖷 01352 753662 ✉ lawrence.rawsthorne@flintshire.gov.uk

Recycling & Waste Minimisation: Mr Kevin Gardiner, Waste Services Manager, County Depot, Chester Road East, Queensferry, Deeside CH5 1TD ☎ 01352 701234 🖷 01352 701727 ✉ kevin.gardiner@flintshire.gov.uk

Regeneration: Mr Dave Heggarty, Head of Regeneration, County Hall, Mold CH7 6NF ☎ 01352 703203 🖷 01352 704550 ✉ dave.heggarty@flintshire.gov.uk

Road Safety: Mr Geraint Jones, Senior Engineer (Road Safety Officer), County Hall, Mold CH7 6NF ☎ 01352 704527 🖷 01352 756444 ✉ geraint.jones@flintshire.gov.uk

Social Services: Mr Neil Ayling, Director of Community Services, County Hall, Mold CH7 6NF ☎ 01352 702500 🖷 01352 70255 ✉ neil.j.ayling@flintshire.gov.uk

Social Services (Adult): Mr Alan Butterworth, Head of Development & Resources, County Hall, Mold CH7 6NN ☎ 01352 702510 🖷 01352 702555 ✉ alan.butterworth@flintshire.gov.uk

Social Services (Adult): Ms Maureen Mullaney, Head of Social Services for Adults, County Hall, Mold CH7 6NF ☎ 01352 702512 🖷 01352 702555 ✉ maureen.mullaney@flintshire.gov.uk

Social Services (Children): Ms Carol Salmon, Head of Social Services for Children, County Hall, Mold CH7 6NN ☎ 01352 702504 🖷 01352 702555 ✉ carol.salmon@flintshire.gov.uk

Staff Training: Mr Stephen Hughes, Corporate Training Manager, Northop Campus, Deeside College, Northop, Mold CH7 6AA ☎ 01352 841059 ✉ stephen.r.hughes@flintshire.gov.uk

Street Scene: Mr Harvey Mitchell, Streetscene Manager, County Hall, Mold CH7 6NB ☎ 01352 701200 🖷 01352 701270 ✉ harvey.mitchell@flintshire.gov.uk

Sustainable Communities: Ms Erica Mackie, Sustainable Development Officer, County Hall, Mold CH7 6NT ☎ 01352 703217 🖷 01352 700152 ✉ erica.mackie@flintshire.gov.uk

Sustainable Development: Ms Erica Mackie, Sustainable Development Officer, County Hall, Mold CH7 6NT ☎ 01352 703217 🖷 01352 700152 ✉ erica.mackie@flintshire.gov.uk

Tourism: Mr David Evans, Tourism Manager, County Hall, Mold CH7 6NB ☎ 01352 702468 🖷 01352 702050 ✉ david.p.evans@flintshire.gov.uk

Town Centre: Mr Dave Heggarty, Head of Regeneration, County Hall, Mold CH7 6NF ☎ 01352 703203 🖷 01352 704550 ✉ dave.heggarty@flintshire.gov.uk

Traffic Management: Mr Ian Wellwood, Interim Head of Engineering Services, County Hall, Mold CH7 6NF ☎ 01352 704701 🖷 01352 756444 ✉ ian.wellwood@flintshire.gov.uk

Transport: Mr Neal Cockerton, Head of Assets & Transportation, County Hall, Mold CH7 6NF ☎ 01352 703169 🖷 01352 704550 ✉ neal.cockerton@flintshire.gov.uk

Transport: Mr Kevin Sutton, Highways Strategy Manager, County Hall, Mold CH7 6NF ☎ 01352 704605 🖷 01352 704540 ✉ kevin.sutton@flintshire.gov.uk

Waste Collection and Disposal: Mr Kevin Gardiner, Waste Services Manager, County Depot, Chester Road East, Queensferry, Deeside CH5 1TD ☎ 01352 701234 🖷 01352 701727 ✉ kevin.gardiner@flintshire.gov.uk

Waste Management: Mr Kevin Gardiner, Waste Services Manager, County Depot, Chester Road East, Queensferry, Deeside CH5 1TD ☎ 01352 701234 🖷 01352 701727 ✉ kevin.gardiner@flintshire.gov.uk

MEMBERS OF THE COUNCIL (70)

***Chair:* Minshull**, Ann (LAB - Shotton West)
ann.minshull@flintshire.gov.uk
***Vice-Chair:* Thomas**, Carolyn (IND - Treuddyn)
carolyn.thomas@flintshire.gov.uk
***Leader of the Council:* Shotton**, Aaron (LAB - Connah's Quay Central)
aaron.shotton@flintshire.gov.uk
***Deputy Leader of the Council:* Attridge**, Bernie (LAB - Connah's Quay Central)
bernie.attridge@flintshire.gov.uk
***Group Leader:* Carver**, Clive (CON - Hawarden)
clive.carver@flintshire.gov.uk
***Group Leader:* Guest**, Robin (LD - Mold South)
robin.guest@flintshire.gov.uk
***Group Leader:* Heesom**, Patrick (IND - Mostyn)
patrick.heesom@flintshire.gov.uk
Aldridge, Alex (LAB - Flint Coleshill)
alex.aldridge@flintshire.gov.uk
Banks, Glyn (LAB - Ffynnongroyw)
glyn.banks@flintshire.gov.uk
Bateman, Haydn (IND - Mold Broncoed)
haydn.bateman@flintshire.gov.uk
Bateman, Marion (IND - Northop)
marion.bateman@flintshire.gov.uk
Bithell, Chris (LAB - Mold East)
christopher.bithell@flintshire.gov.uk
Bragg, Amanda (LD - New Brighton)
amanda.bragg@flintshire.gov.uk
Brown, Helen (IND - Aston)
helenyale@flintshire.gov.uk
Butler, Derek (LAB - Broughton South)
derek.butler@flintshire.gov.uk
Cox, David (LAB - Flint Coleshill)
david.cox@flintshire.gov.uk
Curtis, Peter (LAB - Holywell Central)
peter.curtis@flintshire.gov.uk
Davies, Ron (LAB - Shotton Higher)
ronald.davies@flintshire.gov.uk
Davies-Cooke, Adele (CON - Gwernaffield)
adele.daviescooke@flintshire.gov.uk
Diskin, Glenys (LAB - Mancot)
glenys.diskin@flintshire.gov.uk
Diskin, Alan (LAB - Mancot)
alan.diskin@flintshire.gov.uk
Dolphin, Rosetta (LD - Greenfield)
rosetta.dolphin@flintshire.gov.uk
Dolphin, Chris (LD - Whitford)
chris_dolphin@hotmail.co.uk
Dunbar, Ian (LAB - Connah's Quay South)
ian.dunbar@flintshire.gov.uk
Dunn, Brian (IND - Connah's Quay Wepre)
brian.dunn@flintshire.gov.uk
Ellis, Carol (IND - Buckley Mountain)
carol.ellis@flintshire.gov.uk
Evans, Ted (LAB - Flint Trelawny)
ted.evans@flintshire.gov.uk
Evans, David (LAB - Shotton East)
david.evans@flintshire.gov.uk
Falshaw, Jim (CON - Caerwys)
jim.falshaw@flintshire.gov.uk
Gay, Veronica (IND - Saltney Stonebridge)
veronica.gay@flintshire.gov.uk
Halford, Alison (CON - Ewloe)
alison.halford@flintshire.gov.uk
Hampson, Ron (LAB - Buckley Bistre West)
ronald.hampson@flintshire.gov.uk
Hardcastle, George (IND - Aston)
george.hardcastle@flintshire.gov.uk
Hinds, Cindy (LAB - Pen-y-Ffordd)
cindy.hinds@flintshire.gov.uk
Howorth, Trefor (LAB - Flint Trelawny)
margaret@howorth2.wanadoo.co.uk
Hughes, Raymond (IND - Leeswood)
raymond.hughes@flintshire.gov.uk
Hutchinson, Dennis (IND - Buckley Pentrobin)
dennis.hutchinson@flintshire.gov.uk
Isherwood, Hilary (CON - Llanfynydd)
hilaryisherwood@googlemail.com
Johnson, Joe (LAB - Holywell East)
joe.johnson@flintshire.gov.uk
Johnson, Rita (IND - Flint Oakenholt)
rita.johnson@flintshire.gov.uk
Jones, Christine (LAB - Sealand)
christine.m.jones@flintshire.gov.uk
Jones, Kevin (LAB - Bagillt East)
kevin.jones@flintshire.gov.uk
Jones, Richard (LD - Buckley Bistre East)
richard.jones@flintshire.gov.uk
Jones, Stella (LAB - Caergwrle)
stella.jones@flintshire.gov.uk
Legg, Colin (IND - Halkyn)
colin.legg@flintshire.gov.uk
Lightfoot, Phil (IND - Higher Kinnerton)
phil.lightfoot@flintshire.gov.uk
Lloyd, Brian (IND - Mold West)
brian.lloyd@flintshire.gov.uk
Lloyd, Richard (IND - Saltney Mold Junction)
richard.lloyd@flintshire.gov.uk
Lowe, Mike (LAB - Broughton South)
mike.lowe@flintshire.gov.uk
Macfarlane, Peter (LAB - Connah's Quay Golftyn)
peter.macfarlane@flintshire.gov.uk
Mackie, Dave (IND - Ewloe)
david.mackie@flintshire.gov.uk
Matthews, Nancy (LD - Gwernymynydd)
nancy.matthews@flintshire.gov.uk
McGuill, Hilary (LD - Argoed)
hilary.mcguill@flintshire.gov.uk
Mullin, Billy (LAB - Broughton North East)
billy.mullin@flintshire.gov.uk
Newhouse, Tim (IND - Hope)
tim.newhouse@flintshire.gov.uk
Peers, Mike (IND - Buckley Pentrobin)
mike.peers@flintshire.gov.uk
Phillips, Neville (LD - Buckley Bistre West)
neville.phillips@flintshire.gov.uk
Reece, Mike (LAB - Bagillt West)
mikereece@talktalk.net
Roberts, Ian (LAB - Flint Castle)
ian.roberts@flintshire.gov.uk
Roberts, Gareth (PC - Holywell West)
h.gareth.roberts@flintshire.gov.uk
Sharps, Tony (IND - Northop Hall)
tony.sharps@flintshire.gov.uk
Shotton, Paul (LAB - Connah's Quay Golftyn)
paul.shotton@flintshire.gov.uk
Smith, Ian (LAB - Connah's Quay South)
ian.smith@flintshire.gov.uk
Steele-Mortimer, Nigel (CON - Trelawnyd and Gwaenysgor)

nigel.ann.mortimer@lineone.net
Thomas, Owen (CON - Cilcain)
owen.thomas@flintshire.gov.uk
Williams, Sharon (LAB - Gronant)
sharon.williams@flintshire.gov.uk
Williams, David (IND - Pen-y-Ffordd)
david.m.williams@flintshire.gov.uk
Wisinger, David (LAB - Queensferry)
david.wisinger@flintshire.gov.uk
Woolley, Arnold (IND - Buckley Bistre East)
arnold.woolley@flintshire.gov.uk
Wright, Matt (CON - Brynford)
matt@valeofclwyd.orangehome.co.uk

POLITICAL COMPOSITION
LAB: 31, IND: 22, CON: 8, LD: 8, PC: 1

CABINET
Leader / Finance: Mr Aaron Shotton
Deputy Leader / Environment: Mr Bernie Attridge
Corporate Management: Mr Billy Mullin
Education: Mr Chris Bithell
Housing: Ms Helen Brown
Public Protection, Waste & Recycling: Mr Kevin Jones
Regeneration, Enterprise & Leisure: Mr Peter Macfarlane
Social Services: Ms Christine Jones

COMMITTEE CHAIRS
Audit: Ms Alison Halford
Corporate Resources (Scrutiny): Mr Richard Jones
Environment and Regeneration (Scrutiny): Mr Matt Wright
Housing: Mr Ron Hampson
Licensing: Mr Tony Sharps
Lifelong Learning: Mr Ian Roberts
Planning & Development Control: Mr David Wisinger
Social & Health Care: Mrs Carol Ellis

FOREST HEATH D
Forest Heath District Council, District Offices, College Heath Road, Mildenhall IP28 7EY ☎ 01638 719000 🖷 01638 716493 ✉ info@forest-heath.gov.uk 💻 www.forest-heath.gov.uk

FACTS & FIGURES
Police Authority: Suffolk Police Authority
Health Authority: East of England Strategic Health Authority
Learning and Skills Council: Eastern
EU Constituencies: Eastern
Election Frequency: Elections are of whole council
Twinning: Maisons-Laffitte (France); Le Mesnil-le-Roi (France)

PRINCIPAL OFFICERS
Chief Executive: Mr Ian Gallin, Joint Chief Executive, District Offices, College Heath Road, Mildenhall IP28 7EY ☎ 01638 719324 🖷 01638 719310
✉ ian.gallin@forest-heath.gov.uk

Senior Management: Mr Andrew Claydon, Strategic Director (Resources), District Offices, College Heath Road, Mildenhall IP28 7EY ☎ 01638 719701 🖷 01638 719310
✉ andrew.claydon@forest-heath.gov.uk

Senior Management: Mr Nigel McCurdy, Strategic Director (Resources), District Offices, College Heath Road, Mildenhall IP28 7EY ☎ 01638 719000 🖷 01638 719310
✉ nigel.mccurdy@forest-heath.gov.uk

Architect, Building / Property Services: Mr Nigel McCurdy, Strategic Director (Resources), District Offices, College Heath Road, Mildenhall IP28 7EY ☎ 01638 719000 🖷 01638 719310
✉ nigel.mccurdy@forest-heath.gov.uk

Best Value: Ms Janice Rees, Head of Corporate Development, District Offices, College Heath Road, Mildenhall IP28 7EY
☎ 01638 719231 🖷 01638 716493
✉ janice.rees@forest-heath.gov.uk

Building Control: Mr Adrian Leeds, Building Control Manager, District Offices, College Heath Road, Mildenhall IP28 7EY
☎ 01638 719230 🖷 01638 719230
✉ adrian.leeds@forest-heath.gov.uk

Children / Youth Services: Mr Simon Phelan, Head of Community Development, District Offices, College Heath Road, Mildenhall IP28 7EY ☎ 01638 719440 🖷 01638 716493
✉ simon.phelan@forest-heath.gov.uk

PR / Communications: Ms Marianne Hulland, Communications Manager, District Offices, College Heath Road, Mildenhall IP28 7EY ☎ 01284 757034; 01638 719361 🖷 01284 757032; 01638 716493 ✉ marianne.hulland@stedsbc.gov.uk; marianne.hulland@forest-heath.gov.uk

Community Planning: Mr Simon Phelan, Head of Community Development, District Offices, College Heath Road, Mildenhall IP28 7EY ☎ 01638 719440 🖷 01638 716493
✉ simon.phelan@forest-heath.gov.uk

Community Safety: Mr Simon Phelan, Head of Community Development, District Offices, College Heath Road, Mildenhall IP28 7EY ☎ 01638 719440 🖷 01638 716493
✉ simon.phelan@forest-heath.gov.uk

Computer Management: Mr Steve Newey, ICT Manager, PO Box 1, College Heath Road, Mildenhall IP28 7UZ ☎ 01638 719762 🖷 01638 716493
✉ steve.newey@forest-heath.gov.uk

Corporate Services: Mrs Ruth Littlechild, Head of Human Resources & Corporate Support Services, District Offices, College Heath Road, Mildenhall IP28 7EY ☎ 01638 719326 🖷 01638 716493 ✉ ruth.littlechild@forest-heath.gov.uk

Economic Development: Mr Simon Phelan, Head of Community Development, District Offices, College Heath Road, Mildenhall IP28 7EY ☎ 01638 719440 🖷 01638 716493
✉ simon.phelan@forest-heath.gov.uk

E-Government: Mr Steve Newey, ICT Manager, PO Box 1, College Heath Road, Mildenhall IP28 7UZ ☎ 01638 719762 🖷 01638 716493 ✉ steve.newey@forest-heath.gov.uk

Electoral Registration: Mr Ken Crow, Electoral Services Manager, District Offices, College Heath Road, Mildenhall IP28

7EY ☎ 01638 719364 🖷 01638 716493
✉ ken.crow@forest-heath.gov.uk

Emergency Planning: Mr Stephen Henthorn, Emergency Planning Officer, District Offices, College Heath Road, Mildenhall IP28 7EY ☎ 01638 719321 🖷 01638 716493
✉ stephen.henthorn@forest-heath.gov.uk

Energy Management: Mr Mark Christie, Environmental Services Manager, District Offices, College Heath Road, Mildenhall IP28 7EY ☎ 01638 719220 🖷 01638 716493
✉ mark.christie@forest-heath.gov.uk

Environmental / Technical Services: Mr Mark Christie, Environmental Services Manager, District Offices, College Heath Road, Mildenhall IP28 7EY ☎ 01638 719220 🖷 01638 716493
✉ mark.christie@forest-heath.gov.uk

Environmental Health: Mr Andrew Newman, Service Manager, Environmental Health, District Offices, College Heath Road, Mildenhall IP28 7EY ☎ 01638 719276 🖷 01638 716493
✉ andrew.newman@forest-heath.gov.uk

Estates, Property & Valuation: Mr Andrew Claydon, Strategic Director (Resources), District Offices, College Heath Road, Mildenhall IP28 7EY ☎ 01638 719701 🖷 01638 719310
✉ andrew.claydon@forest-heath.gov.uk

European Liaison: Mr Ian Gallin, Joint Chief Executive, District Offices, College Heath Road, Mildenhall IP28 7EY ☎ 01638 719324 🖷 01638 719310 ✉ ian.gallin@forest-heath.gov.uk

Finance and Treasurer: Ms Lynda Pope, Head of Finance, District Offices, College Heath Road, Mildenhall IP28 7EY ☎ 01638 719233 ✉ lynda.pope@forest-heath.gov.uk

Fleet Management: Mr Keith Marley, Head of Environmental Services, District Offices, College Heath Road, Mildenhall IP28 7EY ☎ 01638 719233 ✉ keith.marley@forest-heath.gov.uk

Home Energy Conservation: Mr Mark Christie, Environmental Services Manager, District Offices, College Heath Road, Mildenhall IP28 7EY ☎ 01638 719220 🖷 01638 716493
✉ mark.christie@forest-heath.gov.uk

Housing: Mr Simon Phelan, Head of Community Development, District Offices, College Heath Road, Mildenhall IP28 7EY ☎ 01638 719440 🖷 01638 716493
✉ simon.phelan@forest-heath.gov.uk

Legal: Mr Peter Heard, Solicitor, District Offices, College Heath Road, Mildenhall IP28 7EY ☎ 01638 719309 🖷 01638 716493
✉ peter.heard@forest-heath.gov.uk

Leisure and Cultural Services: Mr Simon Phelan, Head of Community Development, District Offices, College Heath Road, Mildenhall IP28 7EY ☎ 01638 7194400 🖷 01638 716493
✉ simon.phelan@forest-heath.gov.uk

Leisure and Cultural Services: Mr Ian Shipp, Cultural Services Manager, District Offices, College Heath Road, Mildenhall IP28 7EY ☎ 01638 719219 🖷 01638 716493
✉ ian.shipp@forest-heath.gov.uk

Licensing: Mr Tom Wright, Licensing Manager, District Offices, College Heath Road, Mildenhall IP28 7EY ☎ 01638 719353 🖷 01638 716493 ✉ neil.vollenhoven@forest-heath.gov.uk

Lighting: Mr Nigel McCurdy, Strategic Director (Resources), District Offices, College Heath Road, Mildenhall IP28 7EY ☎ 01638 719000 🖷 01638 719310
✉ nigel.mccurdy@forest-heath.gov.uk

Parking: Mr Andrew Claydon, Strategic Director (Resources), District Offices, College Heath Road, Mildenhall IP28 7EY ☎ 01638 719701 🖷 01638 719310
✉ andrew.claydon@forest-heath.gov.uk

Personnel / HR: Mrs Ruth Littlechild, Head of Human Resources & Corporate Support Services, District Offices, College Heath Road, Mildenhall IP28 7EY ☎ 01638 719326 🖷 01638 716493 ✉ ruth.littlechild@forest-heath.gov.uk

Planning: Ms Nicola Baker, Head of Planning Services, District Offices, College Heath Road, Mildenhall IP28 7EY ☎ 01284 757306; 01638 719423 🖷 01284 757374; 01638 719493 ✉ nicola.baker@stedsbc.gov.uk; nicola.baker@forest-heath.gov.uk

Planning: Mr Nigel McCurdy, Strategic Director (Resources), District Offices, College Heath Road, Mildenhall IP28 7EY ☎ 01638 719000 🖷 01638 719310
✉ nigel.mccurdy@forest-heath.gov.uk

Recycling & Waste Minimisation: Mr Mark Christie, Environmental Services Manager, District Offices, College Heath Road, Mildenhall IP28 7EY ☎ 01638 719220 🖷 01638 716493
✉ mark.christie@forest-heath.gov.uk

Regeneration: Mr Simon Phelan, Head of Community Development, District Offices, College Heath Road, Mildenhall IP28 7EY ☎ 01638 719440 🖷 01638 716493
✉ simon.phelan@forest-heath.gov.uk

Staff Training: Mrs Ruth Littlechild, Head of Human Resources & Corporate Support Services, District Offices, College Heath Road, Mildenhall IP28 7EY ☎ 01638 719326 🖷 01638 716493
✉ ruth.littlechild@forest-heath.gov.uk

Street Scene: Mr Mark Christie, Environmental Services Manager, District Offices, College Heath Road, Mildenhall IP28 7EY ☎ 01638 719220 🖷 01638 716493
✉ mark.christie@forest-heath.gov.uk

Sustainable Communities: Mr Mark Christie, Environmental Services Manager, District Offices, College Heath Road, Mildenhall IP28 7EY ☎ 01638 719220 🖷 01638 716493
✉ mark.christie@forest-heath.gov.uk

Sustainable Development: Mr Mark Christie, Environmental Services Manager, District Offices, College Heath Road, Mildenhall IP28 7EY ☎ 01638 719220 🖷 01638 716493
✉ mark.christie@forest-heath.gov.uk

Tourism: Mr Simon Batey, Tourism Services Manager, District

Offices, College Heath Road, Mildenhall IP28 7EY ☎ 01638 667200 ✉ simon.batey@forest-heath.gov.uk

Town Centre: Ms Joanne Rogers, Town Centre Manager, District Offices, College Heath Road, Mildenhall IP28 7EY ☎ 01638 719399 ✉ joanne.rogers@forest-heath.gov.uk

Transport Planner: Mr Nigel McCurdy, Strategic Director (Resources), District Offices, College Heath Road, Mildenhall IP28 7EY ☎ 01638 719000 🖷 01638 719310 ✉ nigel.mccurdy@forest-heath.gov.uk

Waste Collection and Disposal: Mr Mark Christie, Environmental Services Manager, District Offices, College Heath Road, Mildenhall IP28 7EY ☎ 01638 719220 🖷 01638 716493 ✉ mark.christie@forest-heath.gov.uk

Waste Management: Mr Mark Christie, Environmental Services Manager, District Offices, College Heath Road, Mildenhall IP28 7EY ☎ 01638 719220 🖷 01638 716493 ✉ mark.christie@forest-heath.gov.uk

MEMBERS OF THE COUNCIL (27)

***Leader of the Council:* Waters**, James (CON - Eriswell and The Rows)
james.waters@forest-heath.gov.uk
***Deputy Leader of the Council:* Roman**, Nigel (CON - Great Heath)
nigel.roman@forest-heath.gov.uk
Anderson, Michael (CON - Severals)
michael.anderson@forest-heath.gov.uk
Barker, Chris (CON - St Mary's)
chris.barker@forest-heath.gov.uk
Bimson, David (CON - Brandon West)
david.bimson@forest-heath.gov.uk
Bishop, Bill (CON - Brandon East)
william.bishop@forest-heath.gov.uk
Bowman, David (CON - Eriswell and The Rows)
david.bowman@forest-heath.gov.uk
Burt, Rona (CON - Iceni)
rona.burt@forest-heath.gov.uk
Dicker, Roger (CON - Red Lodge)
roger.dicker@forest-heath.gov.uk
Drummond, Andy (CON - Red Lodge)
andy.drummond@forest-heath.gov.uk
Edwards, Stephen (CON - Brandon East)
stephen.edwards@forest-heath.gov.uk
Gathercole, David (CON - Lakenheath)
david.gathercole@forest-heath.gov.uk
Hirst, Warwick (O - Severals)
warwick.hirst@forest-heath.gov.uk
Hood, Rachel (CON - Severals)
rachel.hood@forest-heath.gov.uk
Huggan, Timothy (LD - Manor)
tim.huggan@forest-heath.gov.uk
Jaggard, Geoffrey (CON - All Saints)
geoffrey.jaggard@forest-heath.gov.uk
Jefferys, Michael (LAB - St Mary's)
michael.jefferys@forest-heath.gov.uk
Lynch, Carol (CON - South)
carol.lynch@forest-heath.gov.uk
McGhee, John (CON - Market)
john.mcghee@forest-heath.gov.uk
Millar, Robin (CON - All Saints)
robin.millar@forest-heath.gov.uk
Noble, Colin (CON - Lakenheath)
colin.noble@forest-heath.gov.uk
Sadler, William (CON - St Mary's)
bill.sadler@forest-heath.gov.uk
Simmons, Tony (CON - Brandon West)
tony.simmons@forest-heath.gov.uk
Smith, Malcolm (CON - Market)
malcolm.smith@forest-heath.gov.uk
Stewart, Edward (CON - Brandon East)
eddie.stewart@forest-heath.gov.uk
Wheble, Tony (CON - Great Heath)
tony.wheble@forest-heath.gov.uk
Williams, Neil (LD - Exning)
neilwilliams@onetel.com

POLITICAL COMPOSITION

CON: 23, LD: 2, O: 1, LAB: 1

FOREST OF DEAN — D

Forest of Dean District Council, Council Offices, High Street, Coleford GL16 8HG ☎ 01594 810000 🖷 01594 812590 ✉ council@fdean.gov.uk 🖳 www.fdean.gov.uk

FACTS & FIGURES

Police Authority: Gloucestershire Police Authority
Health Authority: NHS South West
Learning and Skills Council: South West
Parliamentary Constituencies: Forest of Dean
EU Constituencies: South West
Election Frequency: Elections are of whole council

PRINCIPAL OFFICERS

Chief Executive: Ms Sue Pangborne, Strategic Director, Council Offices, High Street, Coleford GL16 8HG ☎ 01594 812501 ✉ sue.pangborne@fdean.gov.uk

Senior Management: Mr Peter Hibberd, Strategic Director, Council Offices, High Street, Coleford GL16 8HG ☎ 01594 812640 ✉ peter.hibberd@fdean.gov.uk

Senior Management: Ms Sue Pangborne, Strategic Director, Council Offices, High Street, Coleford GL16 8HG ☎ 01594 812501 ✉ sue.pangborne@fdean.gov.uk

Building Control: Mr Peter Williams, Group Manager - Planning & Housing, Council Offices, Coleford GL16 8HG ☎ 01594 812300 ✉ peter.williams@fdean.gov.uk

Community Safety: Mrs Debbie Powell, Community Engagement Co-ordinator, Council Offices, Coleford GL16 8HG ☎ 01594 812613 ✉ debbie.powell@fdean.gov.uk

Computer Management: Mr Matthew Thomas, ICT Manager, Council Offices, High Street, Coleford GL16 8HG ☎ 01594 812471 ✉ matthew.thomas@fdean.gov.uk

E-Government: Mr Matthew Thomas, ICT Manager, Council Offices, High Street, Coleford GL16 8HG ☎ 01594 812471 ✉ matthew.thomas@fdean.gov.uk

Electoral Registration: Mrs Geraldine Randall-Wilce, Electoral Services Officer, Council Offices, Coleford GL16 8HG ☎ 01594 812626 🖷 01594 812470 ✉ geraldine.randall-wilce@fdean.gov.uk

Emergency Planning: Mrs Karen Rushworth, Pricipal Policy Officer, Forest of Dean District Councik, Council Offices, High Street, Coleford GL16 8HG ☎ 01594 812524 ✉ karen.rushworth@fdean.gov.uk

Environmental / Technical Services: Mr Roger Garbett, Group Manager - Environmental Health, Council Offices, High Street, Coleford GL16 8HG ☎ 01594 812431 ✉ roger.garbett@fdean.gov.uk

Environmental Health: Mr Roger Garbett, Group Manager - Environmental Health, Council Offices, High Street, Coleford GL16 8HG ☎ 01594 812431 ✉ roger.garbett@fdean.gov.uk

Estates, Property & Valuation: Mr Derek Broom, Group Manager - Finance & Property, Council Offices, High Street, Coleford GL16 8HG ☎ 01594 812540 ✉ derek.broom@fdean.gov.uk

Estates, Property & Valuation: Mr Chris Johns, Land & Property Manager, Council Offices, Gloucester Road, Tewkesbury GL20 5TT ☎ 01684 272274; 01594 810000 ✉ chris.johns@tewkesbury.gov.uk

Finance and Treasurer: Mr Derek Broom, Group Manager - Finance & Property, Council Offices, High Street, Coleford GL16 8HG ☎ 01594 812540 ✉ derek.broom@fdean.gov.uk

Grounds Maintenance: Mr Derek Broom, Group Manager - Finance & Property, Council Offices, High Street, Coleford GL16 8HG ☎ 01594 812540 ✉ derek.broom@fdean.gov.uk

Health and Safety: Mr Roger Garbett, Group Manager - Environmental Health, Council Offices, High Street, Coleford GL16 8HG ☎ 01594 812431 ✉ roger.garbett@fdean.gov.uk

Housing: Mr Peter Williams, Group Manager - Planning & Housing, Council Offices, Coleford GL16 8HG ☎ 01594 812300 ✉ peter.williams@fdean.gov.uk

Legal: Ms Marie Rosenthal, Group Manager - Legal & Democratic Services, Council Offices, High Street, Coleford GL16 8HG ☎ 01594 812510 🖷 01594 812470 ✉ marie.rosenthal@fdean.gov.uk

Leisure and Cultural Services: Mr Andy Barge, Group Manager - Customer Services, Council Offices, Coleford GL16 8HG ☎ 01594 812383 ✉ andy.barge@fdean.gov.uk

Licensing: Mr Roger Garbett, Group Manager - Environmental Health, Council Offices, High Street, Coleford GL16 8HG ☎ 01594 812431 ✉ roger.garbett@fdean.gov.uk

Member Services: Mrs Julie Jones, Democratic Services Manager, Council Offices, High Street, Coleford GL16 8HG ☎ 01594 812623 🖷 01594 812470 ✉ julie.jones@fdean.gov.uk

Personnel / HR: Ms Marie Rosenthal, Group Manager - Legal & Democratic Services, Council Offices, High Street, Coleford GL16 8HG ☎ 01594 812510 🖷 01594 812470 ✉ marie.rosenthal@fdean.gov.uk

Planning: Mr Peter Williams, Group Manager - Planning & Housing, Council Offices, Coleford GL16 8HG ☎ 01594 812300 ✉ peter.williams@fdean.gov.uk

Procurement: Mr Derek Broom, Group Manager - Finance & Property, Council Offices, High Street, Coleford GL16 8HG ☎ 01594 812540 ✉ derek.broom@fdean.gov.uk

Recycling & Waste Minimisation: Mr Roger Garbett, Group Manager - Environmental Health, Council Offices, High Street, Coleford GL16 8HG ☎ 01594 812431 ✉ roger.garbett@fdean.gov.uk

Staff Training: Ms Karen Gane, HR Manager, Council Offices, Coleford GL16 8HG ☎ 01594 812650 ✉ karen.gane@fdean.gov.uk

Street Scene: Mr Andy Barge, Group Manager - Customer Services, Council Offices, Coleford GL16 8HG ☎ 01594 812383 ✉ andy.barge@fdean.gov.uk

Sustainable Communities: Mr Alastair Chapman, Sustainability Team Leader, Council Offices, High Street, Coleford GL16 8HG ☎ 01594 812329 ✉ alastair.chapman@fdean.gov.uk

Sustainable Development: Mr Alastair Chapman, Sustainability Team Leader, Council Offices, High Street, Coleford GL16 8HG ☎ 01594 812329 ✉ alastair.chapman@fdean.gov.uk

Tourism: Ms Paula Burrows, Manager - Commercial Services, Council Offices, High Street, Coleford GL16 8HG ☎ 01594 812389 ✉ paula.burrows@fdean.gov.uk

Waste Collection and Disposal: Mr Roger Garbett, Group Manager - Environmental Health, Council Offices, High Street, Coleford GL16 8HG ☎ 01594 812431 ✉ roger.garbett@fdean.gov.uk

Waste Management: Mr Roger Garbett, Group Manager - Environmental Health, Council Offices, High Street, Coleford GL16 8HG ☎ 01594 812431 ✉ roger.garbett@fdean.gov.uk

MEMBERS OF THE COUNCIL (48)

***Chair:* Stephens**, Norman (IND - Newnham and Westbury)
Norman.Stephens@fdean.gov.uk

***Leader of the Council:* Molyneux**, Patrick (CON - Hewelsfield and Woolaston)
Patrick.Molyneux@fdean.gov.uk

***Deputy Leader of the Council:* Robinson**, Brian (CON - Mitcheldean and Drybrook)
Brian.Robinson@fdean.gov.uk

Allaway Martin, Carole (CON - Coleford Central)
Carole.Allawaymartin@fdean.gov.uk

Baynham, Frank (LAB - Coleford East)
Frank.Baynham@fdean.gov.uk

Bevan, James (CON - Lydney East)
James.Bevan@fdean.gov.uk

Birch, Roy (LD - Tidenham)
Roy.Birch@fdean.gov.uk

Burford, Philip (IND - Hartpury)
Philip.Burford@fdean.gov.uk
Coborn, Max (LAB - Cinderford East)
Max.Coborn@fdean.gov.uk
Connell, Jim (CON - Bromsberrow and Dymock)
Jim.Connell@fdean.gov.uk
Davies, Gethyn (CON - Tidenham)
Gethyn.Davies@fdean.gov.uk
Davis, Judy (CON - Lydney North)
Judy.Davis@fdean.gov.uk
East, David (IND - Blaisdon and Longhope)
David.East@fdean.gov.uk
Ede, Peter (CON - Redmarley)
Peter.Ede@fdean.gov.uk
Edey, Maria (IND - Coleford East)
Maria.Edey@fdean.gov.uk
Edwards, Brian (CON - Awre)
Brian.Edwards@fdean.gov.uk
Edwards, Diana (CON - Newnham and Westbury)
Diana.Edwards@fdean.gov.uk
Elsmore, Clive (IND - Coleford Central)
Clive.Elsmore@fdean.gov.uk
Evans, Frankie (CON - Pillowell)
Frankie.Evans@fdean.gov.uk
Evans, Bill (LAB - Bream)
Bill.Evans@fdean.gov.uk
Fraser, Jackie (LAB - Mitcheldean and Drybrook)
Jackie.Fraser@fdean.gov.uk
Gardiner, Andrew (IND - Lydbrook and Ruardean)
Andrew.Gardiner@fdean.gov.uk
Glastonbury, Terry (CON - Alvington, Aylburton and West Lydney)
Terry.Glastonbury@fdean.gov.uk
Gooch, Julia (IND - Newent Central)
Julia.Gooch@fdean.gov.uk
Hale, Terry (CON - Newland and St Briavels)
Terry.Hale@fdean.gov.uk
Hiett, Paul (LAB - Bream)
Paul.Hiett@fdean.gov.uk
Hobman, Val (LAB - Lydney East)
Val.Hobman@fdean.gov.uk
Hogan, Bruce (LAB - Lydbrook and Ruardean)
Bruce.Hogan@fdean.gov.uk
Horne, Jane (CON - Tibberton)
Jane.Horne@fdean.gov.uk
Jones, Brian (CON - Churcham and Huntley)
Brian.Jones@fdean.gov.uk
Kirkpatrick, Gabriella (IND - Tidenham)
Gabriella.Kirkpatrick@fdean.gov.uk
Lawton, Len (CON - Newent Central)
Len.Lawton@fdean.gov.uk
Martin, Di (LAB - Cinderford East)
Di.Martin@fdean.gov.uk
McMahon, Paul (LAB - Coleford East)
Paul.McMahon@fdean.gov.uk
Morgan, Graham (LAB - Cinderford West)
Graham.Morgan@fdean.gov.uk
O'Neill, Bernie (LAB - Littledean and Ruspidge)
Bernie.Oneill@fdean.gov.uk
Osborne, Bill (LAB - Lydney East)
Bill.Osborne@fdean.gov.uk
Pugh, Don (LAB - Pillowell)
Don.Pugh@fdean.gov.uk
Quaile, Martin (CON - Littledean and Ruspidge)
Martin.Quaile@fdean.gov.uk
Smart, Marrilyn (CON - Christchurch and English Bicknor)
Marrilyn.Smart@fdean.gov.uk
Sterry, Lynn (LAB - Cinderford West)
Lynn.Sterry@fdean.gov.uk
Sterry, Roger (LAB - Cinderford West)
roger.sterry@fdean.gov.uk
Stewart, Helen (LAB - Berry Hill)
Helen.Stewart@fdean.gov.uk
Thomas, Arthur (IND - Newland and St. Briavels)
Arthur.Thomas@fdean.gov.uk
Thomson, David (LAB - Lydbrook and Ruardean)
David.Thompson@fdean.gov.uk
Whitburn, Ian (IND - Mitcheldean and Drybrook)
Ian.Whitburn@fdean.gov.uk
Winship, Marion (IND - Alvington, Aylburton and West Lydney)
Marion.Winship@fdean.gov.uk
Yeates, Roger (CON - Oxenhall and Newent North East)
Roger.Yeates@fdean.gov.uk

POLITICAL COMPOSITION
CON: 19, LAB: 17, IND: 11, LD: 1

CABINET
Community: Mr Terry Hale
Deputy Leader/Efficient Council and Planning Policy: Mr Brian Robinson
Environment: Mr Martin Quaile
Leader/Regeneration: Mr Patrick Molyneux
Strategic Partnerships and Projects: Ms Diana Edwards

COMMITTEE CHAIRS
Audit: Mr Roy Birch
Licensing: Mr Len Lawton
Planning: Mr Terry Glastonbury
Strategic Overview & Scrutiny: Mr Philip Burford

FYLDE D
Fylde Borough Council, Town Hall, St. Annes Road West, St. Annes-on-Sea FY8 1LW ☎ 01253 658658 🖷 01253 713113 ✉ listening@fylde.gov.uk 🖳 www.fylde.gov.uk

FACTS & FIGURES
Police Authority: Lancashire Police Authority
Health Authority: North West Strategic Health Authority
Learning and Skills Council: North West
Parliamentary Constituencies: Fylde
EU Constituencies: North West
Election Frequency: Elections are of whole council

PRINCIPAL OFFICERS
Chief Executive: Mr Allan Oldfield, Chief Executive & Director - Customer and Operational Services, Town Hall, St. Annes Road West, St. Annes-on-Sea FY8 1LW ☎ 01253 658576 🖷 01253 713113 ✉ allano@fylde.gov.uk

Architect, Building / Property Services: Mr Paul Walker, Director - Strategic Development Services, Town Hall, Lytham St. Annes FY8 1LW ☎ 01253 658658 ✉ paulw@fylde.gov.uk

Building Control: Mr Andrew Dickson, Head of Technical Services, Town Hall, Lytham St. Annes FY8 1LW ☎ 01253 658675 ✉ andrewd@fylde.gov.uk

PR / Communications: Mr Neil Graham, Communcations and

Consultations Manager, Town Hall, St. Annes Road West, St. Annes-on-Sea FY8 1LW ☎ 01253 658499 ✉ neil.graham@fylde.gov.uk

Community Planning: Mr Paul Walker, Director - Strategic Development Services, Town Hall, Lytham St. Annes FY8 1LW ☎ 01253 658658 ✉ paulw@fylde.gov.uk

Community Safety: Mrs Tracy Scholes, Director of Corporate Resources, Town Hall, St. Annes Road West, St. Annes-on-Sea FY8 1LW ☎ 01253 658521 🖷 01253 713113 ✉ tracys@fylde.gov.uk

Computer Management: Mr Andrew Marriott, Computer Manager, Town Hall, Lytham St. Annes FY8 1LW ☎ 01253 658658 🖷 01253 713113 ✉ andrewm@fylde.gov.uk

Consumer Protection and Trading Standards: Mr Paul Walker, Director - Strategic Development Services, Town Hall, St. Annes Road West, St. Annes-on-Sea FY8 1LW ☎ 01253 658658 ✉ paulw@fylde.gov.uk

Customer Service: Mr Andrew Cain, Customer Services Manager, Town Hall, St. Annes Road West, St. Annes-on-Sea FY8 1LW ☎ 01253 658495 ✉ andrewc@fylde.gov.uk

Economic Development: Mr Paul Walker, Director - Strategic Development Services, Town Hall, St. Annes Road West, St. Annes-on-Sea FY8 1LW ☎ 01253 658658 ✉ paulw@fylde.gov.uk

E-Government: Mr Andrew Cain, Customer Services Manager, Town Hall, St. Annes Road West, St. Annes-on-Sea FY8 1LW ☎ 01253 658495 ✉ andrewc@fylde.gov.uk

Electoral Registration: Mr Roger Davies, Electoral Services Manager, Town Hall, St. Annes Road West, St. Annes-on-Sea FY8 1LW ☎ 01253 658658 🖷 01253 719113 ✉ roger.davies@fylde.gov.uk

Emergency Planning: Ms Clare Platt, Director - Community Services, Town Hall, St. Annes Road West, St. Annes-on-Sea FY8 1LW ☎ 01253 658602 🖷 01253 713113 ✉ clarep@fylde.gov.uk

Energy Management: Mr Andrew Loynd, Parking and Energy Officer, Town Hall, St. Annes Road West, St. Annes-on-Sea FY8 1LW ☎ 01253658527 ✉ andrewl@fylde.gov.uk

Environmental / Technical Services: Mr Andrew Dickson, Head of Technical Services, Town Hall, Lytham St. Annes FY8 1LW ☎ 01253 658675 ✉ andrewd@fylde.gov.uk

Environmental Health: Mr Paul Walker, Director - Strategic Development Services, Town Hall, St. Annes Road West, St. Annes-on-Sea FY8 1LW ☎ 01253 658658 ✉ paulw@fylde.gov.uk

Estates, Property & Valuation: Mr Gary Sams, Principal Estates Surveyor, Town Hall, St. Annes Road West, St. Annes-on-Sea FY8 1LW ☎ 01253 658462 ✉ gary.sams@fylde.gov.uk

Finance and Treasurer: Mr Paul O'Donoghue, Head of Finance, Town Hall, St. Annes Road West, St. Annes-on-Sea FY8 1LW ☎ 01253 658658 🖷 01253 713113 ✉ paul.o'donoghue@fylde.gov.uk

Grounds Maintenance: Mr Peter Graveson, Grounds Maintenance Officer, Town Hall, Lytham St. Annes FY8 1LW ☎ 01253 658471 🖷 01253 713113 ✉ peterg@fylde.gov.uk

Grounds Maintenance: Ms Clare Platt, Director - Community Services, Town Hall, St. Annes Road West, St. Annes-on-Sea FY8 1LW ☎ 01253 658602 🖷 01253 713113 ✉ clarep@fylde.gov.uk

Health and Safety: Mr Andrew Wilsdon, Insurance & Risk Management Officer, Town Hall, Lytham St. Annes FY8 1LW ☎ 01253 658412 🖷 01253 713113 ✉ andreww@fylde.gov.uk

Housing: Mr David Gillett, Head of Environmental Health & Housing, Town Hall, St. Annes Road West, St. Annes-on-Sea FY8 1LW ☎ 01253 658689 🖷 01253 713113 ✉ davidg@fylde.gov.uk

Legal: Mr Ian Curtis, Head of Governance, Town Hall, St. Annes Road West, St. Annes-on-Sea FY8 1LW ☎ 01253 658506 🖷 01253 713113 ✉ ianc@fylde.gov.uk

Leisure and Cultural Services: Ms Clare Platt, Director - Community Services, Town Hall, St. Annes Road West, St. Annes-on-Sea FY8 1LW ☎ 01253 658602 🖷 01253 713113 ✉ clarep@fylde.gov.uk

Licensing: Ms Clare Platt, Director - Community Services, Town Hall, St. Annes Road West, St. Annes-on-Sea FY8 1LW ☎ 01253 658602 🖷 01253 713113 ✉ clarep@fylde.gov.uk

Member Services: Mr Ian Curtis, Head of Governance, Town Hall, St. Annes Road West, St. Annes-on-Sea FY8 1LW ☎ 01253 658506 🖷 01253 713113 ✉ ianc@fylde.gov.uk

Parking: Mr Andrew Loynd, Parking and Energy Officer, Town Hall, St. Annes Road West, St. Annes-on-Sea FY8 1LW ☎ 01253658527 ✉ andrewl@fylde.gov.uk

Partnerships: Mrs Christine Miller, Head of Partnerships, Town Hall, Lytham St. Annes FY8 1LW ☎ 01253 658441 🖷 01253 713113 ✉ christinem@fylde.gov.uk

Partnerships: Mrs Tracy Scholes, Director of Corporate Resources, Town Hall, St. Annes Road West, St. Annes-on-Sea FY8 1LW ☎ 01253 658521 🖷 01253 713113 ✉ tracys@fylde.gov.uk

Personnel / HR: Mr Allan Oldfield, Chief Executive & Director - Customer and Operational Services, Town Hall, St. Annes Road West, St. Annes-on-Sea FY8 1LW ☎ 01253 658576 🖷 01253 713113 ✉ allano@fylde.gov.uk

Planning: Mr Paul Walker, Director - Strategic Development Services, Town Hall, Lytham St. Annes FY8 1LW ☎ 01253 658658 ✉ paulw@fylde.gov.uk

Procurement: Mr Allan Williams, Procurement Officer, Town Hall, Lytham St. Annes FY8 1LW ☎ 01253 658639 🖷 01253 713113 ✉ allanw@fylde.gov.uk

Recycling & Waste Minimisation: Ms Kathy Winstanley, Waste & Fleet Services Manager, Town Hall, St. Annes Road West, St. Annes-on-Sea FY8 1LW ☎ 01253 658576 🖷 01253 713113 ✉ kathyw@fylde.gov.uk

Regeneration: Mr Paul Walker, Director - Strategic Development Services, Town Hall, St. Annes Road West, St. Annes-on-Sea FY8 1LW ☎ 01253 658658 ✉ paulw@fylde.gov.uk

Tourism: Mrs Vivien Wood, Tourism Officer, Town Hall, Lytham St. Annes FY8 1LW ☎ 01253 658436 🖷 01253 713113 ✉ vivw@fylde.gov.uk

Transport: Ms Kathy Winstanley, Waste & Fleet Services Manager, Town Hall, St. Annes Road West, St. Annes-on-Sea FY8 1LW ☎ 01253 658576 🖷 01253 713113 ✉ kathyw@fylde.gov.uk

Waste Collection and Disposal: Ms Kathy Winstanley, Waste & Fleet Services Manager, Town Hall, St. Annes Road West, St. Annes-on-Sea FY8 1LW ☎ 01253 658576 🖷 01253 713113 ✉ kathyw@fylde.gov.uk

Waste Management: Ms Kathy Winstanley, Waste & Fleet Services Manager, Town Hall, St. Annes Road West, St. Annes-on-Sea FY8 1LW ☎ 01253 658576 🖷 01253 713113 ✉ kathyw@fylde.gov.uk

MEMBERS OF THE COUNCIL (50)

Leader of the Council: **Eaves**, David (CON - Ansdell)
cllr.deaves@fylde.gov.uk
Deputy Leader of the Council: **Fazackerley**, Susan (CON - Central)
cllr.sfazackerley@fylde.gov.uk
Ackers, Brenda (CON - St Johns)
cllr.backers@fylde.gov.uk
Aitken, Ben (CON - Ansdell)
cllr.baitken@fylde.gov.uk
Akeroyd, Christine (CON - Kilnhouse)
cllr.cakeroyd@fylde.gov.uk
Andrews, Frank (CON - Ribby-with-Wrea)
cllr.fandrews@fylde.gov.uk
Armit, Timothy (CON - Kilnhouse)
cllr.tarmit@fylde.gov.uk
Ashton, Timothy (CON - St Johns)
Tim.ashton@lancashire.gov.uk
Ashton, Susan Ann (CON - Warton and Westby)
cllr.sashton@fylde.gov.uk
Beckett, Keith (IND - Kirkham North)
cllr.kbeckett@fylde.gov.uk
Brickles, Julie (IND - Warton and Westby)
cllr.jbrickles@fylde.gov.uk
Buckley, Karen (CON - St Leonards)
cllr.kbuckley@fylde.gov.uk
Chedd, David (IND - Park)
cllr.dchedd@fylde.gov.uk
Chew, Maxine (IND - Singleton and Greenhalgh)
cllr.mchew@fylde.gov.uk
Clayton, Alan (IND - Medlar-with-Wesham)
cllr.aclayton@fylde.gov.uk
Collins, Peter (IND - Newton and Treales)
petercollins4568@aol.com
Cox, Simon (CON - Park)
cllr.scox@fylde.gov.uk
Craig-Wilson, Fabian (CON - Central)
cllr.fwilson@fylde.gov.uk
Cunningham, Susanne (CON - Warton and Westby)
cllr.scunningham@fylde.gov.uk
Davies, Leonard (CON - Clifton)
cllr.ldavies@fylde.gov.uk
Davies, John (R - Ashton)
cllr.jdavies@fylde.gov.uk
Donaldson, David (CON - Fairhaven)
cllr.ddonaldson@fylde.gov.uk
Duffy, Charlie (IND - Clifton)
cllr.cduffy@fylde.gov.uk
Eastham, Richard (R - Fairhaven)
cllr.keastham@fylde.gov.uk
Fiddler, Trevor (CON - Freckleton West)
cllr.tfiddler@fylde.gov.uk
Ford, Tony (LD - Ashton)
cllr.tford@fylde.gov.uk
Goodman, Gill (CON - Ashton)
cllr.ggoodman@fylde.gov.uk
Goodrich, Nigel (CON - Heyhouses)
cllr.ngoodrich@fylde.gov.uk
Hardy, Peter (IND - Kirkham South)
cllr.phardy@fylde.gov.uk
Harper, Kathleen (R - St Johns)
cllr.kharper@fylde.gov.uk
Hayhurst, Paul (INDNA - Elswick and Little Eccleston)
cllr.phayhurst@fylde.gov.uk
Henshaw, Howard (LD - St Leonards)
cllr.hhenshaw@fylde.gov.uk
Henshaw, Karen (LD - Kilnhouse)
cllr.khenshaw@fylde.gov.uk
Hodgson, Paul (IND - Kirkham North)
cllr.phodgson@fylde.gov.uk
Hopwood, Ken (IND - Clifton)
cllr.khopwood@fylde.gov.uk
Jacques, Angela (CON - St Leonards)
cllr.ajacques@fylde.gov.uk
Little, Cheryl (CON - Fairhaven)
cllr.clittle@fylde.gov.uk
Mulholland, James (INDNA - Freckleton East)
kiranmul@dsl.pipex.com
Nash, Edward (CON - Central)
cllr.enash@fylde.gov.uk
Nulty, Linda (IND - Medlar-with-Wesham)
cllr.lnulty@fylde.gov.uk
Oades, Elizabeth (IND - Kirkham South)
cllr.eoades@fylde.gov.uk
Pounder, Albert (CON - Staining and Weeton)
cllr.apounder@fylde.gov.uk
Prestwich, Dawn (CON - Park)
cllr.dprestwich@fylde.gov.uk
Redcliffe, Richard (CON - Ansdell)
cllr.rredcliffe@fylde.gov.uk
Rigby, Louis (IND - Freckleton West)
cllr.lrigby@fylde.gov.uk
Silverwood, Elaine (IND - Kirkham North)
cllr.esilverwood@fylde.gov.uk
Singleton, John (IND - Staining and Weeton)
cllr.jsingleton@fylde.gov.uk
Speak, Heather (IND - Newton and Treales)
cllr.hspeak@fylde.gov.uk
Threlfall, Thomas (CON - Freckleton East)
cllr.tthrelfall@fylde.gov.uk
Willder, Viv (CON - Heyhouses)
cllr.vwillder@fylde.gov.uk

POLITICAL COMPOSITION

CON: 26, IND: 16, LD: 3, R: 3, INDNA: 2

CABINET

Leader: Mr David Eaves
Deputy Leader / Leisure & Culture: Ms Susan Fazackerley
Customer & Operational Services: Mr Albert Pounder
Environment & Partnerships: Mr Thomas Threlfall
Finance & Resources: Ms Karen Buckley
Planning & Development: Mr Trevor Fiddler

GATESHEAD M

Gateshead Council, Civic Centre, Regent Street, Gateshead NE8 1HH ☎ 0191 433 3000 ✉ enquiries@gateshead.gov.uk
🖳 www.gateshead.gov.uk

FACTS & FIGURES

Police Authority: Northumbria Police Authority
Health Authority: North East Strategic Health Authority
Learning and Skills Council: North East
Parliamentary Constituencies: Blaydon, Gateshead, Jarrow, Tyne Bridge
EU Constituencies: North East
Election Frequency: Elections are by thirds
Twinning: St. Etienne-du-Rouvray (France); Komatsu City (Japan)

PRINCIPAL OFFICERS

Chief Executive: Mrs Jane Robinson, Chief Executive, Civic Centre, Regent Street, Gateshead NE8 1HH ☎ 0191 433 3000 🖷 0191 478 2755 ✉ janerobinson@gateshead.gov.uk

Assistant Chief Executive: Mrs Sheila Johnston, Assistant Chief Executive, Civic Centre, Regent Street, Gateshead NE8 1HH ☎ 0191433 3000 ✉ sheilajohnston@gateshead.gov.uk

Senior Management: Mr Mike Barker, Strategic Director, Legal & Corporate Services, Civic Centre, Regent Street, Gateshead NE8 1HH ☎ 01914332102 ✉ caroleshaw@gateshead.gov.uk

Senior Management: Mr Derek Coates, Strategic Director, Finance & ICT, Civic Centre, Regent Street, Gateshead NE8 1HH ☎ 0191 433 3580 ✉ carolsouter@gateshead.gov.uk

Senior Management: Ms Margaret Whellans, Director of Adult Care & Housing, Civic Centre, Regent Street, Gateshead NE8 1HH ☎ 0191 433 2602 ✉ margaretwhellans@gateshead.gov.uk

Access Officer / Social Services (Disability): Mr Michael Laing, Director of Adult Care & Housing, Civic Centre, Regent Street, Gateshead NE8 1HH ☎ 0191 433 2602 ✉ michaellaing@gateshead.gov.uk

Architect, Building / Property Services: Ms Victoria Beattie, Head of Construction, Civic Centre, Regent Street, Gateshead NE8 1HH ☎ 0191 433 7311 ✉ victoriabeattie@gateshead.gov.uk

Architect, Building / Property Services: Mr Chris Tearney, Head of Construction, Civic Centre, Regent Street, Gateshead NE8 1HH ☎ 0191 433 7201 ✉ christearney@gateshead.gov.uk

Architect, Building / Property Services: Mr Peter Udall, Head of Design, Civic Centre, Regent Street, Gateshead NE8 1HH ☎ 0191 433 2901 ✉ peterudall@gateshead.gov.uk

Best Value: Ms Marisa Jobling, Head of Service Improvement, Civic Centre, Regent Street, Gateshead NE8 1HH ☎ 0191 433 3000 ✉ marisajobling@gateshead.gov.uk

Building Control: Ms Victoria Beattie, Head of Construction, Civic Centre, Regent Street, Gateshead NE8 1HH ☎ 0191 433 7311 ✉ victoriabeattie@gateshead.gov.uk

Building Control: Mr Chris Tearney, Head of Construction, Civic Centre, Regent Street, Gateshead NE8 1HH ☎ 0191 433 7201 ✉ christearney@gateshead.gov.uk

Catering Services: Mr Dale Robson, Head of Transport, Catering & Cleaning Services, Civic Centre, Regent Street, Gateshead NE8 1HH ☎ 0191 433 5510 ✉ dalerobson@gateshead.gov.uk

Children / Youth Services: Ms Frances Powell, Head of Children, Families & Young Offenders, Civic Centre, Regent Street, Gateshead NE8 1HH ☎ 0191 433 3000 ✉ francespowell@gateshead.gov.uk

Children / Youth Services: Ms Alison Walton, Director - Children & Young People, Civic Centre, Regent Street, Gateshead NE8 1HH ☎ 0191 433 3000 ✉ alisonwalton@gateshead.gov.uk

Civil Registration: Ms Deborah Hill, Head of Litigation, Civic Centre, Regent Street, Gateshead NE8 1HH ☎ 0191 433 2110 ✉ deborahhill@gateshead.gov.uk

PR / Communications: Mr Robert Schopen, Head of Communications, Civic Centre, Regent Street, Gateshead NE8 1HH ☎ 0191 433 2070 ✉ robertschopen@gateshead.gov.uk

Community Planning: Mr Andrew Marshall, Environmental Regeneration Manager, Civic Centre, Regent Street, Gateshead NE8 1HH ☎ 0191 433 3000

Computer Management: Mr Derek Coates, Strategic Director, Finance & ICT, Civic Centre, Regent Street, Gateshead NE8 1HH ☎ 0191 433 3580 ✉ carolsouter@gateshead.gov.uk

Computer Management: Mr Roy Sheehan, Head of ICT Development, Civic Centre, Regent Street, Gateshead NE8 1HH ☎ 0191 433 3000 ✉ roysheehan@gateshead.gov.uk

Consumer Protection and Trading Standards: Mr Peter Wright, Environmental Health & Trading Standards, Civic Centre, Regent Street, Gateshead NE8 1HH ☎ 0191 433 3910 ✉ peterwright@gateshead.gov.uk

Contracts: Mrs Andrea Tickner, Head of Corporate Purchasing, Civic Centre, Regent Street, Gateshead NE8 1HH ☎ 0191 438 5995 ✉ andreatickner@gateshead.gov.uk

Corporate Services: Mr Jeff Dean, Head of Corporate Service, Civic Centre, Regent Street, Gateshead NE8 1HH ☎ 0191 433 2250 ✉ jeffdean@gateshead.gov.uk

Customer Service: Mr John Jopling, Head of Financial Services, Civic Centre, Regent Street, Gateshead NE8 1HH ☎ 0191 433 3000 ✉ johnjopling@gateshead.gov.uk

Education: Mr David Mitchell, Director - Learning & Schools, Civic Centre, Regent Street, Gateshead NE8 1HH ☎ 0191 433 3000 ✉ davidmitchell@gateshead.gov.uk

E-Government: Mr Derek Coates, Strategic Director, Finance & ICT, Civic Centre, Regent Street, Gateshead NE8 1HH ☎ 0191 433 3580 ✉ carolsouter@gateshead.gov.uk

E-Government: Mr Roy Sheehan, Head of ICT Development, Civic Centre, Regent Street, Gateshead NE8 1HH ☎ 0191 433 3000 ✉ roysheehan@gateshead.gov.uk

Electoral Registration: Ms Christine Thomas, Electoral Services Manager, Civic Centre, Regent Street, Gateshead NE8 1HH ☎ 0191 433 2152 ✉ christinethomas@gateshead.gov.uk

Emergency Planning: Ms Janet Kirton, Resilience Planning Manager, Civic Centre, Regent Street, Gateshead NE8 1HH ☎ 01914332279

Energy Management: Mr Peter Thompson, Head of Environmental Regeneration, Civic Centre, Regent Street, Gateshead NE8 1HH ☎ 0191 433 3000 ✉ peterthompson@gateshead.gov.uk

Environmental / Technical Services: Mr Anthony Alder, Director of Local Environmental Services, Civic Centre, Regent Street, Gateshead NE8 1HH ☎ 0191 433 3000 ✉ anthonyalder@gateshead.gov.uk

Environmental Health: Mr Peter Thompson, Head of Environmental Regeneration, Civic Centre, Regent Street, Gateshead NE8 1HH ☎ 0191 433 3000 ✉ peterthompson@gateshead.gov.uk

Estates, Property & Valuation: Mr Peter Udall, Head of Design, Civic Centre, Regent Street, Gateshead NE8 1HH ☎ 0191 433 2901 ✉ peterudall@gateshead.gov.uk

European Liaison: Mrs Lindsay Murray, Director of Policy & Improvement, Civic Centre, Regent Street, Gateshead NE8 1HH ☎ 0191 433 2794 ✉ lindsaymurray@gateshead.gov.uk

Events Manager: Mr Mick Laidler, Events Manager, Civic Centre, Regent Street, Gateshead NE8 1HH ☎ 0191 433 3000

Finance and Treasurer: Mr Derek Coates, Strategic Director, Finance & ICT, Civic Centre, Regent Street, Gateshead NE8 1HH ☎ 0191 433 3580 ✉ carolsouter@gateshead.gov.uk

Finance and Treasurer: Mr Darren Collins, Corporate Director Head of Finance, Civic Centre, Regent Street, Gateshead NE8 1HH ☎ 0191 433 3581 ✉ carolsouter@gateshead.gov.uk

Finance and Treasurer: Mr John Jopling, Head of Financial Services, Civic Centre, Regent Street, Gateshead NE8 1HH ☎ 0191 433 3000 ✉ johnjopling@gateshead.gov.uk

Finance and Treasurer: Mr Keith Purvis, Head of Financial Management, Civic Centre, Regent Street, Gateshead NE8 1HH ☎ 0191 433 3000 ✉ keithpurvis@gateshead.gov.uk

Fleet Management: Mr Graham Telfer, Fleet Manager, Civic Centre, Regent Street, Gateshead NE8 1HH ☎ 0191 533 7425 ✉ grahamtelfer@gateshead.gov.uk

Grounds Maintenance: Mr Colin Huntington, Head of Waste Services & Grounds Maintenance, Civic Centre, Regent Street, Gateshead NE8 1HH ☎ 0191 433 7402 ✉ colinhuntington@gateshead.gov.uk

Health and Safety: Ms Susan Smith, Occupational Health & Safety Manager, Civic Centre, Regent Street, Gateshead NE8 1HH ☎ 0191 433 3000

Highways: Mr Nick Clennett, Head of Transport & Highways, Civic Centre, Regent Street, Gateshead NE8 1HH ☎ 0191 433 2526 🖷 0191 478 8422 ✉ nickclennett@gateshead.gov.uk

Housing: Ms Jackie Park, Head of Housing Services, Civic Centre, Regent Street, Gateshead NE8 1HH ☎ 0191 433 3482 ✉ jackiepark@gateshead.gov.uk

Local Area Agreement: Mrs Lindsay Murray, Director of Policy & Improvement, Civic Centre, Regent Street, Gateshead NE8 1HH ☎ 0191 433 2794 ✉ lindsaymurray@gateshead.gov.uk

Legal: Ms Deborah Hill, Head of Litigation, Civic Centre, Regent Street, Gateshead NE8 1HH ☎ 0191 433 2110 ✉ deborahhill@gateshead.gov.uk

Leisure and Cultural Services: Ms Ann Borthwick, Head of Libraries & Arts, Civic Centre, Regent Street, Gateshead NE8 1HH ☎ 0191 433 3000 ✉ annborthwick@gateshead.gov.uk

Leisure and Cultural Services: Mr David Bunce, Director of Culture & Communities, Civic Centre, Regent Street, Gateshead NE8 1HH ☎ 0191 433 3250 ✉ davidbunce@gateshead.gov.uk

Leisure and Cultural Services: Ms Louise Rule, Head of Service, Sport & Leisure, Civic Centre, Regent Street, Gateshead NE8 1HH ☎ 0191 433 3000 ✉ louiserule@gateshead.gov.uk

Licensing: Ms Elaine Rudman, Environmental Health, Licensing & Enforcement Manager, Civic Centre, Regent Street, Gateshead NE8 1HH ☎ 0191 433 3911 ✉ licensing@gateshead.gov.uk

Lifelong Learning: Mr Paul Carvin, Head of Raising Achievement, Dryden Professional Development Centre, Evistones Road, Gateshead NE9 5UR ☎ 0191 433 8601 ✉ paulcarvin@gateshead.gov.uk

Lighting: Mr Nick Clennett, Head of Transport & Highways, Civic Centre, Regent Street, Gateshead NE8 1HH ☎ 0191 433 2526 🖷 0191 478 8422 ✉ nickclennett@gateshead.gov.uk

Lottery Funding, Charity and Voluntary: Mrs Lindsay Murray, Director of Policy & Improvement, Civic Centre, Regent Street, Gateshead NE8 1HH ☎ 0191 433 2794 ✉ lindsaymurray@gateshead.gov.uk

Member Services: Mr Martin Harrison, Head of Development Law & Democratic Services, Civic Centre, Regent Street, Gateshead NE8 1HH ☎ 0191 433 2101 ✉ martinharrison@gateshead.gov.uk

Parking: Mr Steve Donaldson, Parking Services Manager, Civic Centre, Regent Street, Gateshead NE8 1HH ☎ 0191 433 3000

Partnerships: Mrs Lindsay Murray, Director of Policy & Improvement, Civic Centre, Regent Street, Gateshead NE8 1HH ☎ 0191 433 2794 ✉ lindsaymurray@gateshead.gov.uk

Planning: Mr Andrew Hickie, Development Control Manager, Civic Centre, Regent Street, Gateshead NE8 1HH ☎ 0191 433 3747 ✉ andrewhickie@gateshead.gov.uk

Procurement: Mrs Andrea Tickner, Head of Corporate Purchasing, Civic Centre, Regent Street, Gateshead NE8 1HH ☎ 0191 438 5995 ✉ andreatickner@gateshead.gov.uk

Public Libraries: Ms Ann Borthwick, Head of Libraries & Arts, Civic Centre, Regent Street, Gateshead NE8 1HH ☎ 0191 433 3000 ✉ annborthwick@gateshead.gov.uk

Public Libraries: Mr David Bunce, Director of Culture & Communities, Civic Centre, Regent Street, Gateshead NE8 1HH ☎ 0191 433 3250 ✉ davidbunce@gateshead.gov.uk

Recycling & Waste Minimisation: Mr Jeff Moffitt, Waste, Recycling & Contract Manager, Park Road, Gateshead NE8 3HN ☎ 0191 433 7420 🖷 0191 478 1138 ✉ jeffmoffitt@gateshead.gov.uk

Regeneration: Mrs Sheila Johnston, Assistant Chief Executive, Civic Centre, Regent Street, Gateshead NE8 1HH ☎ 0191433 3000 ✉ sheilajohnston@gateshead.gov.uk

Social Services: Ms Margaret Whellans, Director of Adult Care & Housing, Civic Centre, Regent Street, Gateshead NE8 1HH ☎ 0191 433 2602 ✉ margaretwhellans@gateshead.gov.uk

Social Services (Adult): Mr David Bunce, Director of Culture & Communities, Civic Centre, Regent Street, Gateshead NE8 1HH ☎ 0191 433 3250 ✉ davidbunce@gateshead.gov.uk

Social Services (Adult): Mr Michael Laing, Director of Adult Care & Housing, Civic Centre, Regent Street, Gateshead NE8 1HH ☎ 0191 433 2602 ✉ michaellaing@gateshead.gov.uk

Social Services (Children): Ms Alison Walton, Director - Children & Young People, Civic Centre, Regent Street, Gateshead NE8 1HH ☎ 0191 433 3000 ✉ alisonwalton@gateshead.gov.uk

Social Services (Children): Ms Margaret Whellans, Director of Adult Care & Housing, Civic Centre, Regent Street, Gateshead NE8 1HH ☎ 0191 433 2602 ✉ margaretwhellans@gateshead.gov.uk

Staff Training: Mr Dennis Burnett, Organisation Development Manager, Civic Centre, Regent Street, Gateshead NE8 1HH ☎ 0191 4333000 ✉ dennisburnett@gateshead.gov.uk

Street Scene: Mr Colin Huntington, Head of Waste Services & Grounds Maintenance, Civic Centre, Regent Street, Gateshead NE8 1HH ☎ 0191 433 7402 ✉ colinhuntington@gateshead.gov.uk

Tourism: Mr David Bunce, Director of Culture & Communities, Civic Centre, Regent Street, Gateshead NE8 1HH ☎ 0191 433 3250 ✉ davidbunce@gateshead.gov.uk

Traffic Management: Mr Nick Clennett, Head of Transport & Highways, Civic Centre, Regent Street, Gateshead NE8 1HH ☎ 0191 433 2526 🖷 0191 478 8422 ✉ nickclennett@gateshead.gov.uk

Traffic Management: Mr Ian Gibson, Traffic Planning Manager, Civic Centre, Regent Street, Gateshead NE8 1HH ☎ 0191 433 3100 ✉ iangibson@gateshead.gov.uk

Traffic Management: Mr Andy Price, Team Leader & Network Manager, Civic Centre, Regent Street, Gateshead NE8 1HH ☎ 0191 433 3101 ✉ andyprice@gateshead.gov.uk

Transport: Mr Nick Clennett, Head of Transport & Highways, Civic Centre, Regent Street, Gateshead NE8 1HH ☎ 0191 433 2526 🖷 0191 478 8422 ✉ nickclennett@gateshead.gov.uk

Transport: Mr Andrew Haysey, Transport Planning Manager, Civic Centre, Regent Street, Gateshead NE8 1HH ☎ 0191 433 3124 ✉ andrewhaysey@gateshead.gov.uk

Total Place: Mrs Lindsay Murray, Director of Policy & Improvement, Civic Centre, Regent Street, Gateshead NE8 1HH ☎ 0191 433 2794 ✉ lindsaymurray@gateshead.gov.uk

Waste Collection and Disposal: Mr Colin Huntington, Head of Waste Services & Grounds Maintenance, Civic Centre, Regent Street, Gateshead NE8 1HH ☎ 0191 433 7402 ✉ colinhuntington@gateshead.gov.uk

Waste Management: Mr Colin Huntington, Head of Waste Services & Grounds Maintenance, Civic Centre, Regent Street, Gateshead NE8 1HH ☎ 0191 433 7402 ✉ colinhuntington@gateshead.gov.uk

Waste Management: Mr Jeff Moffitt, Waste, Recycling & Contract Manager, Park Road, Gateshead NE8 3HN ☎ 0191 433 7420 🖷 0191 478 1138 ✉ jeffmoffitt@gateshead.gov.uk

Children's Play Areas: Mr Colin Huntington, Head of Waste Services & Grounds Maintenance, Civic Centre, Regent Street, Gateshead NE8 1HH ☎ 0191 433 7402 ✉ colinhuntington@gateshead.gov.uk

MEMBERS OF THE COUNCIL (66)

***Mayor:* Brain**, Malcolm (LAB - Blaydon)
cllr.mbrain@gateshead.gov.uk

***Leader of the Council:* Henry**, Mick (LAB - Saltwell)
cllr.m.henry@gateshead.gov.uk

***Deputy Leader of the Council:* Gannon**, Martin (LAB - Deckham)
cllr.mgannon@gateshead.gov.uk

Beadle, Ron (LD - Low Fell)
cllr.rbeadle@gateshead.gov.uk

Bradley, Christine (LAB - Lamesley)
cllr.cbradley@gateshead.gov.uk

Caffrey, Lynne (LAB - Chopwell and Rowlands Gill)
cllr.lcaffrey@gateshead.gov.uk

Charlton, Marilyn (LAB - Winlaton and High Spen)
cllr.mcharlton@gateshead.gov.uk

Chatto, Alison (LAB - Dunston Hill and Whickham East)
cllr.achatto@gateshead.gov.uk

Clelland, Brenda (LAB - Dunston and Teams)
cllr.bclelland@gateshead.gov.uk

Coates, Brian (LAB - Deckham)
cllr.bcoates@gateshead.gov.uk

Craig, Peter (LD - Whickham North)
cllr.ptcraig@Gateshead.Gov.Uk
Craig, Susan (LD - Low Fell)
cllr.scraig@gateshead.gov.uk
Davidson, Doreen (LAB - High Fell)
cllr.ddavidson@gateshead.gov.uk
Dick, Bill (LAB - Felling)
cllr.wdick@gateshead.gov.uk
Dickie, Sonya (LAB - Felling)
cllr.sdickie@gateshead.gov.uk
Dillon, Pauline (LAB - Dunston and Teams)
cllr.pdillon@gateshead.gov.uk
Dodds, Kevin (LAB - Lobley Hill and Bensham)
cllr.k.dodds@gateshead.gov.uk
Donovan, Catherine (LAB - Lobley Hill and Bensham)
cllr.cdonovan@gateshead.gov.uk
Douglas, Angela (LAB - Bridges)
cllr.aarmstrong@gateshead.gov.uk
Eagle, John (LAB - Bridges)
cllr.jeagle@gateshead.gov.uk
Ferdinand, Kathryn (LAB - Blaydon)
cllr.k.ferdinand@gateshead.gov.uk
Foy, Mary (LAB - Lamesley)
cllr.mfoy@gateshead.gov.uk
Foy, Paul (LAB - Birtley)
cllr.pfoy@gateshead.gov.uk
Geddes, Alex (LAB - Ryton, Crookhill and Stella)
cllr.ageddes@gateshead.gov.uk
Goldsworthy, Bob (LAB - Bridges)
cllr.bgoldsworthy@gateshead.gov.uk
Goldsworthy, Maureen (LAB - Chowdene)
cllr.mgoldsworthy@gateshead.gov.uk
Graham, Malcolm (LAB - High Fell)
cllr.mgraham@gateshead.gov.uk
Graham, Jack (LAB - Crawcrook and Greenside)
cllr.jgraham@gateshead.gov.uk
Graham, Thomas (LAB - Windy Nook and Whitehills)
cllr.tgraham@gateshead.gov.uk
Green, Stuart (LAB - Wardley and Leam Lane)
cllr.sgreen@gateshead.gov.uk
Green, Linda (LAB - Wardley and Leam Lane)
cllr.lgreen@gateshead.gov.uk
Green, Jill (LAB - Pelaw and Heworth)
cllr.jgreen@gateshead.gov.uk
Haley, Gary (LAB - Dunston and Teams)
cllr.ghaley@gateshead.gov.uk
Hall, Maria (LAB - Winlaton and High Spen)
cllr.mhall@gateshead.gov.uk
Hamilton, John (LAB - Chopwell and Rowlands Gill)
cllr.jhamilton@gateshead.gov.uk
Hawkins, Sonya (LD - Whickham North)
cllr.shawkins@gateshead.gov.uk
Hindle, Frank (LD - Low Fell)
cllr.fhindle@gateshead.gov.uk
Holmes, Lee (LAB - Pelaw and Heworth)
cllr.lholmes@gateshead.gov.uk
Hood, Michael (LAB - Lamesley)
cllr.mhood@gateshead.gov.uk
Hughes, Helen (LAB - Crawcrook and Greenside)
cllr.hhughes@gateshead.gov.uk
Lee, Jean (LAB - High Fell)
cllr.jlee@gateshead.gov.uk
Maughan, Peter (LD - Dunston Hill and Whickham East)
cllr.pmaughan@gateshead.gov.uk
McCartney, Kathleen (LAB - Crawcrook and Greenside)
cllr.kmccartney@gateshead.gov.uk
McClurey, John (LD - Whickham South and Sunniside)
cllr.jmcclurey@gateshead.gov.uk
McElroy, John (LAB - Chowdene)
cllr.jmcelroy@gateshead.gov.uk
McHatton, Christine (LD - Ryton, Crookhill and Stella)
cllr.cmchatton@gateshead.gov.uk
McMaster, Eileen (LAB - Lobley Hill and Bensham)
cllr.emcmaster@gateshead.gov.uk
McNally, Paul (LAB - Felling)
cllr.pmcnally@gateshead.gov.uk
McNestry, Michael (LAB - Chopwell and Rowlands Gill)
cllr.mmcnestry@gateshead.gov.uk
McNicol, Yvonne (LAB - Dunston Hill and Whickham East)
cllr.ymcnichol@gateshead.gov.uk
Mitchinson, Joe (LAB - Saltwell)
cllr.jmitchinson@gateshead.gov.uk
Mole, Peter (LAB - Wardley and Leam Lane)
cllr.pmole@gateshead.gov.uk
Oliphant, Bernadette (LAB - Deckham)
cllr.boliphant@gateshead.gov.uk
Ord, Christopher (LD - Whickham North)
cllr.cord@gateshead.gov.uk
Ord, Marilynn (LD - Whickham South and Sunniside)
cllr.mord@gateshead.gov.uk
Robson, Denise (LAB - Saltwell)
cllr.drobson@gateshead.gov.uk
Ronan, Pat (LAB - Windy Nook and Whitehills)
cllr.pronan@gateshead.gov.uk
Ronchetti, Stephen (LAB - Blaydon)
cllr.sronchetti@gateshead.gov.uk
Simcox, Catherine (LAB - Birtley)
cllr.csimcox@gateshead.gov.uk
Simpson, Julie (LAB - Winlaton and High Spen)
cllr.jsimpson@gateshead.gov.uk
Turnbull, Jim (LAB - Windy Nook and Whitehills)
cllr.jturnbull@gateshead.gov.uk
Twist, Liz (LAB - Ryton, Crookhill and Stella)
cllr.ltwist@gateshead.gov.uk
Wallace, Jonathan (LD - Whickham South and Sunniside)
cllr.jwallace@gateshead.gov.uk
Weatherley, Neil (LAB - Birtley)
cllr.nweatherley@gateshead.gov.uk
Wheeler, Anne (LAB - Pelaw and Heworth)
cllr.awheeler@gateshead.gov.uk
Wood, Keith (LAB - Chowdene)
cllr.kwood@gateshead.gov.uk

POLITICAL COMPOSITION

LAB: 55, LD: 11

CABINET

Leader: Mr Mick Henry
Deputy Leader: Mr Martin Gannon
Adult Social Care: Mr Michael McNestry
Central Area: Ms Linda Green
Children & Young People: Ms Angela Douglas
Culture: Ms Linda Green
Employment & Skills: Mr Malcolm Graham
Neighbourhood Services: Mr Peter Mole
Transport & Environment: Mr John McElroy

GEDLING D

Gedling Borough Council, Civic Centre, Arnot Hill Park, Nottingham NG5 6LU ☎ 0115 901 3901 🖷 0115 901 3921
💻 www.gedling.gov.uk

FACTS & FIGURES

Police Authority: Nottinghamshire Police Authority
Health Authority: East Midlands Strategic Health Authority
Learning and Skills Council: East Midlands
Parliamentary Constituencies: Gedling, Sherwood
EU Constituencies: East Midlands
Election Frequency: Elections are of whole council
Twinning: Gedling: Rotenburg-A.D. Fulda (Germany); Messolonghi (Greece); Vandoeuvre (France); Calverton: Longue (France)

PRINCIPAL OFFICERS

Chief Executive: Mr John Robinson, Chief Executive, Civic Centre, Arnot Hill Park, Nottingham NG5 6LU ☎ 0115 901 3915 🖷 0115 901 3758 ✉ john.robinson@gedling.gov.uk

Senior Management: Mrs Paula Darlington, Corporate Director, Civic Centre, Arnot Hill Park, Nottingham NG5 6LU ☎ 0115 901 3951 🖷 0115 901 3921 ✉ paula.darlington@gedling.gov.uk

Senior Management: Mr Mark Kimberley, Head of Corporate Services, Civic Centre, Arnot Hill Park, Nottingham NG5 6LU ☎ 0115 901 3990 🖷 0115 901 3861 ✉ mark.kimberley@gedling.gov.uk

Best Value: Ms Stephen Bray, Corporate Director, Council Offices, Arnot Hill Park, Arnold, Nottingham NG5 6LU ☎ 0115 901 3808 🖷 0115 901 3920 ✉ stephen.bray@gedling.gov.uk

PR / Communications: Ms Stephen Bray, Corporate Director, Council Offices, Arnot Hill Park, Arnold, Nottingham NG5 6LU ☎ 0115 901 3808 🖷 0115 901 3920 ✉ stephen.bray@gedling.gov.uk

Computer Management: Mr Mark Lane, Service Manager, Civic Centre, Arnot Hill Park, Nottingham NG5 6LU ☎ 0115 901 3876 🖷 0115 9013921 ✉ mark.lane@gedling.gov.uk

Corporate Services: Mr Mark Kimberley, Head of Corporate Services, Civic Centre, Arnot Hill Park, Nottingham NG5 6LU ☎ 0115 901 3990 🖷 0115 901 3861 ✉ mark.kimberley@gedling.gov.uk

Customer Service: Mr Mark Lane, Service Manager, Civic Centre, Arnot Hill Park, Nottingham NG5 6LU ☎ 0115 901 3876 🖷 0115 9013921 ✉ mark.lane@gedling.gov.uk

E-Government: Mr Mark Kimberley, Head of Corporate Services, Civic Centre, Arnot Hill Park, Nottingham NG5 6LU ☎ 0115 901 3990 🖷 0115 901 3861 ✉ mark.kimberley@gedling.gov.uk

Emergency Planning: Mr David Wakelin, Corporate Director, Civic Centre, Arnot Hill Park, Nottingham NG5 6LU ☎ 0115 901 3952 🖷 0115 901 3920 ✉ david.wakelin@gedling.gov.uk

Energy Management: Mr Steve Wiseman, Architectural & Buildings Services Manager, Civic Centre, Arnot Hill Park, Arnold, Nottingham NG5 6LU ☎ 0115 901 3779 🖷 0115 901 3790 ✉ steve.wiseman@gedling.gov.uk

Environmental / Technical Services: Mr Andy Callingham, Service Manager, Civic Centre, Arnot Hill Park, Nottingham NG5 6LU ☎ 0115 901 3834 🖷 0115 901 3921 ✉ andy.callingham@gedling.gov.uk

Estates, Property & Valuation: Mr David Wakelin, Corporate Director, Civic Centre, Arnot Hill Park, Nottingham NG5 6LU ☎ 0115 901 3952 🖷 0115 901 3920 ✉ david.wakelin@gedling.gov.uk

Events Manager: Ms Lorraine Brown, Events & Play Officer, Civic Centre, Arnot Hill Park, Nottingham NG5 6LU ☎ 015 901 3602 ✉ lorraine.brown@gedling.gov.uk

Finance and Treasurer: Mr Mark Kimberley, Head of Corporate Services, Civic Centre, Arnot Hill Park, Nottingham NG5 6LU ☎ 0115 901 3990 🖷 0115 901 3861 ✉ mark.kimberley@gedling.gov.uk

Fleet Management: Mr Mark Hurst, Transport Services Manager, Civic Centre, Arnot Hill Park, Nottingham NG5 6LU ☎ 0115 901 3612 ✉ mark.hurst@gedling.gov.uk

Grounds Maintenance: Mr Melvyn Cryer, Service Manager, Civic Centre, Arnot Hill Park, Nottingham NG5 6LU ☎ 0115 901 3788 ✉ melvyn.cryer@gedling.gov.uk

Health and Safety: Mr Barry Saunders, Safety Officer, Civic Centre, Arnot Hill Park, Arnold, Nottingham NG5 6LU ☎ 0115 901 3940 🖷 0115 901 3807 ✉ barry.saunders@gedling.gov.uk

Legal: Mrs Helen Barrington, Head of Legal Services, Civic Centre, Arnot Hill Park, Nottingham NG5 6LU ☎ 0115 901 3901 🖷 0115 901 3920 ✉ helen.barrington@gedling.gov.uk

Leisure and Cultural Services: Mrs Paula Darlington, Corporate Director, Civic Centre, Arnot Hill Park, Nottingham NG5 6LU ☎ 0115 901 3951 🖷 0115 901 3921 ✉ paula.darlington@gedling.gov.uk

Licensing: Mr Andy Callingham, Service Manager, Civic Centre, Arnot Hill Park, Nottingham NG5 6LU ☎ 0115 901 3834 🖷 0115 901 3921 ✉ andy.callingham@gedling.gov.uk

Member Services: Mr Alec Dubberley, Service Manager, Civic Centre, Arnot Hill Park, Nottingham NG5 6LU ☎ 0115 901 3906 🖷 0115 901 3920 ✉ alec.dubberley@gedling.gov.uk

Personnel / HR: Mr David Archer, Service Manager, Civic Centre, Arnot Hill Park, Arnold, Nottingham NG5 6LU ☎ 0115 901 3937 🖷 0115 901 3807 ✉ david.archer@gedling.gov.uk

Planning: Mr Peter Baguley, Service Manager, Civic Centre, Arnot Hill Park, Nottingham NG5 6LU ☎ 0115 901 3751 🖷 0115 901 3758 ✉ peter.baguley@gedling.gov.uk

Procurement: Mr Vince Rimmington, Service Manager, Civic Centre, Arnot Hill Park, Nottingham NG5 6LU ☎ 0115 901 3850 🖷 0115 901 3861 ✉ vince.rimmington@gedling.gov.uk

Staff Training: Mr David Archer, Service Manager, Civic Centre,

Arnot Hill Park, Arnold, Nottingham NG5 6LU ☎ 0115 901 3937 🖷 0115 901 3807 ✉ david.archer@gedling.gov.uk

Sustainable Development: Mr Peter Baguley, Service Manager, Civic Centre, Arnot Hill Park, Nottingham NG5 6LU ☎ 0115 901 3751 🖷 0115 901 3758 ✉ peter.baguley@gedling.gov.uk

Tourism: Ms Jayne Cox, Service Manager, Civic Centre, Arnot Hill Park, Nottingham NG5 6LU ☎ 0115 901 3703 ✉ jayne.cox@gedling.gov.uk

Town Centre: Mr Peter Baguley, Service Manager, Civic Centre, Arnot Hill Park, Nottingham NG5 6LU ☎ 0115 901 3751 🖷 0115 901 3758 ✉ peter.baguley@gedling.gov.uk

Transport: Mr Mark Hurst, Transport Services Manager, Civic Centre, Arnot Hill Park, Nottingham NG5 6LU ☎ 0115 901 3612 ✉ mark.hurst@gedling.gov.uk

Waste Collection and Disposal: Mrs Caroline McKenzie, Service Manager, Civic Centre, Arnot Hill Park, Nottingham NG5 6LU ☎ 0115 901 3611 🖷 0115 901 3790 ✉ caroline.mckenzie@gedling.gov.uk

Waste Management: Mrs Caroline McKenzie, Service Manager, Civic Centre, Arnot Hill Park, Nottingham NG5 6LU ☎ 0115 901 3611 🖷 0115 901 3790 ✉ caroline.mckenzie@gedling.gov.uk

Children's Play Areas: Mr Melvyn Cryer, Service Manager, Civic Centre, Arnot Hill Park, Nottingham NG5 6LU ☎ 0115 901 3788 ✉ melvyn.cryer@gedling.gov.uk

MEMBERS OF THE COUNCIL (50)

***Mayor:* Barnes**, Sandra (LAB - Daybrook)
Cllr.Sandra.Barnes@gedling.gov.uk
***Deputy Mayor:* Collis**, Robert (LAB - Porchester)
bob.collis@ntlworld.com
***Leader of the Council:* Clarke**, William (LAB - Netherfield and Colwick)
Cllr.John.Clarke@gedling.gov.uk
***Deputy Leader of the Council:* Payne**, Michael (LAB - St Mary's)
Cllr.Michael.Payne@gedling.gov.uk
***Group Leader:* Gillam**, Anthony (LD - St James)
Cllr.Anthony.Gillam@gedling.gov.uk
***Group Leader:* Hughes**, Paul (LD - Valley)
paul.hughes@futuresnn.co.uk
Ainley, Steve (LAB - Carlton)
s.ainley1@ntlworld.com
Allan, Roy (LAB - Bonington)
Cllr.Roy.Allan@gedling.gov.uk
Allan, Pauline (LAB - St Mary's)
Cllr.Pauline.Allan@gedling.gov.uk
Andrews, Patricia (CON - Newstead)
Cllr.Patricia.Andrews@gedling.gov.uk
Andrews, Bruce (CON - Ravenshead)
bruce@nodnol.org
Bailey, Emily (LAB - Calverton)
Cllr.Emily.Bailey@gedling.gov.uk
Barnes, Peter (LAB - Daybrook)
Cllr.Peter.Barnes@gedling.gov.uk
Barnfather, Christopher (CON - Ravenshead)
Cllr.Chris.Barnfather@gedling.gov.uk
Beeston, Denis (LAB - Bestwood Village)
beeston972@btinternet.com
Bexon, Alan (CON - Woodthorpe)
Cllr.Alan.Bexon@gedling.gov.uk
Blair, Krista (LAB - Gedling)
cllr.krista.blair@gedling.gov.uk
Boot, Francis (CON - Woodborough)
Cllr.John.Boot@gedling.gov.uk
Brooks, Nicki (LAB - Carlton)
Cllr.Nicki.Brooks@gedling.gov.uk
Clarke, Gerald (CON - Mapperley Plains)
ged@derwent.go-plus.net
Creamer, Seamus (LAB - Carlton Hill)
Cllr.Seamus.Creamer@gedling.gov.uk
Ellis, Roxanne (LAB - Bonington)
Cllr.Roxanne.Ellis@gedling.gov.uk
Ellwood, Andrew (LD - Phoenix)
andrewmellwood@yahoo.gov.uk
Feeney, Paul (LAB - Carlton Hill)
Cllr.Paul.Feeney@gedling.gov.uk
Fox, Kathryn (LAB - St James)
Cllr.Kathryn.Fox@gedling.gov.uk
Glover, Mark (LAB - Carlton)
Cllr.Mark.Glover@gedling.gov.uk
Gregory, Gary (LAB - Valley)
Cllr.Gary.Gregory@gedling.gov.uk
Hewlett, Cheryl (LAB - Phoenix)
cherylhewlett44@hotmail.co.uk
Hewson, Sarah (CON - Kingswell)
sarah.hewson2@ntlworld.com
Hollingsworth, Jenny (LAB - Gedling)
Cllr.Jenny.Hollingsworth@gedling.gov.uk
Hope, Mike (LAB - Calverton)
Cllr.Mike.Hope@gedling.gov.uk
Key, Paul (LAB - Kingswell)
Cllr.Paul.Key@gedling.gov.uk
Lawrence, Meredith (LAB - Netherfield and Colwick)
Cllr.Meredith.Lawrence@gedling.gov.uk
McCauley, Phil (LAB - Bonington)
Miller, Barbara (LAB - Netherfield and Colwick)
Cllr.Barbara.Miller@gedling.gov.uk
Nicholson, Richard (CON - Woodthorpe)
Cllr.Richard.Nicholson@gedling.gov.uk
Paling, Marje (LAB - St Mary's)
Cllr.Marje.Paling@gedling.gov.uk
Parr, John (CON - Mapperley Plains)
Cllr.John.Parr@gedling.gov.uk
Pepper, Veronica (CON - Mapperley Plains)
Cllr.Carol.Pepper@gedling.gov.uk
Poole, Stephen (CON - Burton Joyce and Stoke Bardolph)
Cllr.Stephen.Poole@gedling.gov.uk
Powell, Colin (CON - Ravenshead)
Cllr.Colin.Powell@gedling.gov.uk
Prew-Smith, Suzanne (CON - Woodthorpe)
Cllr.suzanne.prew-smith@gedling.gov.uk
Pulk, Darrell (LAB - Carlton Hill)
Cllr.Darrell.Pulk@gedling.gov.uk
Quilty, Nick (LAB - Calverton)
qcoach@googlemail.com
Spencer, Roland (CON - Lambley)
Cllr.Roland.Spencer@gedling.gov.uk
Tomlinson, Sarah (CON - Burton Joyce and Stoke Bardolph)
sarahj_tomlinson@hotmail.co.uk
Truscott, John (LAB - Porchester)

Cllr.John.Truscott@gedling.gov.uk
Tunnicliffe, Gordon (LD - Gedling)
Cllr.Gordon.Tunnicliffe@gedling.gov.uk
Weisz, Muriel (LAB - Porchester)
Cllr.Muriel.Weisz@gedling.gov.uk
Wheeler, Henry (LAB - Killisick)
Cllr.Henry.Wheeler@gedling.gov.uk

POLITICAL COMPOSITION
LAB: 31, CON: 15, LD: 4

CABINET
Leader / Finance & Performance: Mr William Clarke
Deputy Leader / Communications & Public Protection: Mr Michael Payne
Economic & Strategic Development: Mr Roy Allan
Environment & Sustainability: Mr Paul Feeney
Health & Wellbeing: Ms Jenny Hollingsworth
Leisure & Culture: Mr Darrell Pulk

COMMITTEE CHAIRS
Audit: Mr Phil McCauley
Environment & Licensing: Ms Marje Paling
Housing: Mrs Veronica Pepper
Performance Review (Scrutiny): Mr Paul Hughes
Planning: Mr Peter Barnes
Policy Review (Scrutiny): Mr Colin Powell

GLASGOW, CITY OF S

Glasgow City Council, City Chambers, George Square, Glasgow G2 1DU ☎ 0141 287 2000 🖷 0141 287 5666 pr@glasgow.gov.uk
www.glasgow.gov.uk

FACTS & FIGURES
Police Authority: Strathclyde Police Authority
Health Authority: NHS Greater Glasgow & Clyde Health Board
Learning and Skills Council: Scotland
Parliamentary Constituencies: Glasgow Central, Glasgow East, Glasgow North, Glasgow North East, Glasgow North West, Glasgow South, Glasgow South West
EU Constituencies: Scotland
Election Frequency: Elections are of whole council
Twinning: Dalian (China), Havana (Cuba), Nuremberg (Germany), Rostov-on-Don (Russia), Turin (Italy)

PRINCIPAL OFFICERS
Chief Executive: Mr George Black, Chief Executive, City Chambers, George Square, Glasgow G2 1DU ☎ 0141 287 4739 🖷 0141 287 3627 george.black@ced.glasgow.gov.uk

Access Officer / Social Services (Disability): Ms Liz Oswald, Corporate Policy Officer, City Chambers, George Square, Glasgow G2 1DU ☎ 0141 287 3840 🖷 0141 287 5997 liz.oswald@glasgow.gov.uk

Architect, Building / Property Services: Mr Richard Brown, Executive Director - Development & Regeneration Services, Exchange House, 231 George Street, Glasgow G1 1RX ☎ 0141 287 6000 🖷 0141 287 6004 richard.brown@drs.glasgow.gov.uk

Architect, Building / Property Services: Mr Tom Turley, Assistant Director - Development & Regeneration Services, Exchange House, 229 George Street, Glasgow G1 1QU ☎ 0141 287 8751 tom.turley@glasgow.gov.uk

Best Value: Mr George Black, Chief Executive, City Chambers, George Square, Glasgow G2 1DU ☎ 0141 287 4739 🖷 0141 287 3627 george.black@ced.glasgow.gov.uk

Children / Youth Services: Ms Jill Miller, Director - Operations, Glasgow Life, 5th Floor, 220 High Street, Glasgow G4 0QW ☎ 0141 287 8900 🖷 0141 287 8909 jill.miller@glasgow.gov.uk

Civil Registration: Ms Fiona Borland, Chief Registrar, 1 Martha Street, Glasgow G1 1JJ ☎ 0141 287 7653 🖷 0141 287 7666 fiona.borland@glasgow.gov.uk

PR / Communications: Mr Chris Starrs, PR Manager, City Chambers, George Square, Glasgow G2 1DU ☎ 0141 287 5742 🖷 0141 287 0925 chris.starrs@glasgow.gov.uk

Community Safety: Mr Phil Walker, Managing Director - Glasgow Community & Safety Services, Eastgate, 727 London Road, Glasgow G40 3AP ☎ 0141 276 7627 🖷 0141 276 7499 phil.walker@glasgow.gov.uk

Computer Management: Ms Angela Murphy, Head - Information Technology, 350 Darnick Street, Glasgow G21 4BA ☎ 0141 287 2381 🖷 0141 287 2238 angela.murphy@glasgow.gov.uk

Corporate Services: Mr Ian Hooper, Director - Special Projects, Glasgow Life, 20 Trongate, Glasgow G1 5ES ☎ 0141 287 0961 🖷 0141 287 5151 ian.hooper@glasgowlife.org.uk

Corporate Services: Ms Anne Marie O'Donnell, Executive Director, City Chambers, George Square, Glasgow G2 1DU ☎ 0141 287 4522 🖷 0141 287 3627 annemarie.o'donnell@ced.glasgow.gov.uk

Corporate Services: Ms Sharon Wearing, Head - Service Development, Wheatley House, 25 Cochrane Street, Glasgow G1 1HL ☎ 0141 287 8838 🖷 0141 287 8840 sharon.wearing@sw.glasgow.gov.uk

Corporate Services: Mr Jim Wilson, Head - Performance & Asset Management, Wheatley House, 25 Cochrane Street, Glasgow G1 1HL ☎ 0141 287 4573 🖷 0141 287 4895 jim.wilson@education.glasgow.gov.uk

Customer Service: Ms Bernadette Cooklin, Corporate Customer Care Development Manager, Room 4, City Chambers, George Square, Glasgow G2 1DU ☎ 0141 276 1257 🖷 0141 287 4575 bernadette.cooklin@ced.glasgow.gov.uk

Economic Development: Mr Richard Brown, Executive Director - Development & Regeneration Services, Exchange House, 229 George Street, Glasgow G1 1QV ☎ 0141 287 6000 🖷 0141 287 6004 richard.brown@drs.glasgow.gov.uk

Education: Ms Maureen McKenna, Executive Director - Education, Wheatley House, 25 Cochrane Street, Glasgow G1 1HL ☎ 0141 287 4551 🖷 0141 287 4895 maureen.mckenna@education.glasgow.gov.uk

Electoral Registration: Mr Hugh Munro, Registration Officer, Richmond Square, 20 Cadogan Street, Glasgow G2 7AD ☎ 0141 287 7515 ✉ hugh.munro@fs.glasgow.gov.uk

Energy Management: Mr Sandy Gillon, Training & Environmental Manager, Development & Regeneration Services, 229 George Street, Glasgow G1 1RX ☎ 0141 287 8607 🖷 0141 287 6030 ✉ sandy.gillon@glasgow.gov.uk

Events Manager: Mr Keith Russell, Head - Sports & Events, Glasgow Life, 20 Trongate, Glasgow G1 5ES ☎ 0141 287 5975 🖷 0141 287 5151 ✉ keith.russell@glasgow.gov.uk

Finance and Treasurer: Ms Lynn Brown, Executive Director - Financial Services, City Chambers, George Square, Glasgow G2 1DU ☎ 0141 287 3837 🖷 0141 287 3917 ✉ lynn.brown@fs.glasgow.gov.uk

Highways: Mr Brian Devlin, Executive Director - Land & Environmental Services, Exchange House, 231 George Street, Glasgow G1 1RX ☎ 0141 287 9100 🖷 0141 287 9501 ✉ brian.devlin@glasgow.gov.uk

Housing Maintenance: Mr Graham Paterson, Director - Operations, 350 Darnick Street, Glasgow G21 4BA ☎ 0141 287 1786 🖷 0141 287 2159 ✉ graham.paterson@citybuildingglasgow.gov.uk

Legal: Ms Anne Marie O'Donnell, Executive Director, City Chambers, George Square, Glasgow G2 1DU ☎ 0141 287 4522 🖷 0141 287 3627 ✉ annemarie.o'donnell@ced.glasgow.gov.uk

Leisure and Cultural Services: Ms Bridget McConnell, Chief Executive - Glasgow Life, Glasgow Life, 20 Trongate, Glasgow G1 5ES ☎ 0141 287 5058 🖷 0141 287 5151 ✉ bridget.mcconnell@csglasgow.org

Leisure and Cultural Services: Mr Mark O'Neill, Director - Research & Development, Glasgow Life, 20 Trongate, Glasgow G1 5ES ☎ 0141 287 0446 🖷 0141 287 5151 ✉ mark.o'neill@csglasgow.org

Leisure and Cultural Services: Mr Keith Russell, Head - Sports & Events, Glasgow Life, 20 Trongate, Glasgow G1 5ES ☎ 0141 287 5975 🖷 0141 287 5151 ✉ keith.russell@glasgow.gov.uk

Lifelong Learning: Mrs Jane Edgar, Head - Learning, Glasgow Life, 20 Trongate, Glasgow G1 5ES ☎ 0141 287 8937 ✉ jane.edgar@glasgowlife.org.uk

Lighting: Mr George Gillespie, Assistant Director, 231 George Street, Glasgow G1 1RX ☎ 0141 287 9106 🖷 0141 287 9013 ✉ george.gillespie@glasgow.gov.uk

Lottery Funding, Charity and Voluntary: Ms Lynn Brown, Executive Director - Financial Services, City Chambers, George Square, Glasgow G2 1DU ☎ 0141 287 3837 🖷 0141 287 3917 ✉ lynn.brown@fs.glasgow.gov.uk

Member Services: Ms Carole Forrest, Assistant Director - Corporate Services, 40 Cochrane Street, Glasgow G1 1JT ☎ 0141 287 0467 🖷 0141 287 5589 ✉ carole.forrest@glasgow.gov.uk

Parking: Mr John Clarkin, Managing Director - City Parking, Cadogan Square, Glasgow G2 7PH ☎ 0141 276 1835 🖷 0141 276 1843 ✉ john.clarkin@cityparkingglasgow.co.uk

Planning: Mr Ian Manson, Chief Executive - Clyde Gateway, Clyde Gateway, 15 Bridgeton Cross, Glasgow G40 1BN ☎ 0141 276 1567 🖷 0141 276 1578 ✉ ian.manson@glasgow.gov.uk

Procurement: Ms Margaret McKechnie, Head - Corporate Procurement, 235 Geroge Street, Glasgow G2 1DU ☎ 0141 287 6400 🖷 0141 287 6444 ✉ margaret.mckechnie@glasgow.gov.uk

Public Libraries: Ms Karen Cunningham, Head - Libraries & Cultural Venues, Glasgow Life, 20 Trongate, Glasgow G1 5ES ☎ 0141 287 5114 🖷 0141 287 5151 ✉ karen.cunningham@glasgow.gov.uk

Recycling & Waste Minimisation: Mr Rolf Matthews, Waste Disposal Manager, Exchange House, 231 George Street, Glasgow G1 1RX ☎ 0141 287 2082 ✉ rolf.matthews@glasgow.gov.uk

Regeneration: Mr Richard Brown, Executive Director - Development & Regeneration Services, Exchange House, 231 George Street, Glasgow G1 1RX ☎ 0141 287 6000 🖷 0141 287 6004 ✉ richard.brown@drs.glasgow.gov.uk

Road Safety: Mr George Cairns, Engineering Officer, Richmond Exchange, 20 Cadogan Street, Glasgow G2 7AD ☎ 0141 287 9043 🖷 0141 287 9041 ✉ george.cairns@land.glasgow.gov.uk

Social Services: Mr David Crawford, Executive Director - Social Work Services, Wheatley House, 25 Cochrane Road, Glasgow G1 1HL ☎ 0141 287 8853 🖷 0141 287 4895 ✉ david.crawford@sw.glasgow.gov.uk

Social Services (Children): Ms Susanne Miller, Head - Children's Services, Centenary House, 100 Morrison Street, Glasgow G5 8LN ☎ 0141 420 5880 🖷 0141 420 5892 ✉ susanne.millar@glasgow.gov.uk

Sustainable Development: Mr Sandy Gillon, Training & Environmental Manager, Development & Regeneration Services, 229 George Street, Glasgow G1 1RX ☎ 0141 287 8607 🖷 0141 287 6030 ✉ sandy.gillon@glasgow.gov.uk

Tourism: Mr Scott Taylor, Chief Executive - Glasgow City Marketing Bureau, 11 George Square, Glasgow G2 1DY ☎ 0141 566 0809 🖷 0141 566 4073 ✉ scott.taylor@seeglasgow.com

Waste Collection and Disposal: Mr Brian Devlin, Executive Director - Land & Environmental Services, Exchange House, 231 George Street, Glasgow G1 1RX ☎ 0141 287 9100 ✉ brian.devlin@glasgow.gov.uk

MEMBERS OF THE COUNCIL (79)

Adams, James (LAB - Govan)
james.adams2@councillors.glasgow.gov.uk

Aitken, Susan (SNP - Langside)
susan.aitken@councillors.glasgow.gov.uk

Andrew, Ken (SNP - Hillhead)
ken.andrew@councillors.glasgow.gov.uk

Baker, Nina (SGP - Anderston/ City)

nina.baker@councillors.glasgow.gov.uk
Balfour, Malcolm (SNP - Drumchapel/Anniesland)
malcolm.balfour@councillors.glasgow.gov.uk
Bartos, Martin (SGP - Patrick West)
martin.bartos@councillors.glasgow.gov.uk
Boyle, Gerry (SNP - North East)
gerry.boyle2@councillors.glasgow.gov.uk
Braat, Philip (LAB - Anderston/ City)
philip.braat@councillors.glasgow.gov.uk
Burke, Maureen (LAB - North East)
maureen.burke@councillors.glasgow.gov.uk
Butler, Bill (LAB - Greater Pollok)
bill.butler@councillors.glasgow.gov.uk
Cameron, Liz (LAB - Garscadden/Scotstounhill)
liz.cameron@councillors.glasgow.gov.uk
Carey, Paul (LAB - Drumchapel/Anniesland)
paul.carey@councillors.glasgow.gov.uk
Clark, Margot (LD - Linn)
margot.clark@councillors.glasgow.gov.uk
Coleman, James (LAB - Baillieston)
james.coleman@councillors.glasgow.gov.uk
Colleran, Aileen (LAB - Partick West)
aileen.colleran@councillors.glasgow.gov.uk
Cunning, Malcolm (LAB - Linn)
malcolm.cunning@councillors.glasgow.gov.uk
Curran, Stephen (LAB - Newsland/Auldburn)
stephen.curran@councillors.glasgow.gov.uk
Dalton, Feargal (SNP - Patrick West)
feargal.dalton@councillors.glasgow.gov.uk
Davidson, Gilbert (LAB - Springburn)
gilbert.davidson@councillors.glasgow.gov.uk
Docherty, Josephine (SNP - Newlands/Auldburn)
josephine.docherty@councillors.glasgow.gov.uk
Docherty, Martin (SNP - Anderston/ City)
martin.docherty@councillors.glasgow.gov.uk
Docherty, Sadie (LAB - Linn)
sadie.docherty@councillors.glasgow.gov.uk
Docherty, Frank (LAB - East Centre)
frank.docherty@councillors.glasgow.gov.uk
Dornan, Stephen (LAB - Govan)
stephen.dornan@councillors.glasgow.gov.uk
Dunn, Jennifer (SNP - East Centre)
jennifer.dunn@councilors.glasgow.gov.uk
Elder, Glenn (SNP - Linn)
glenn.elder@councillors.glasgow.gov.uk
Findlay, Jonathan (LAB - Drumchapel/Anniesland)
jonathan.findlay@councillors.glasgow.gov.uk
Fisher, Judith (LAB - Drumchapel/Anniesland)
judith.fisher@councillors.glasgow.gov.uk
Garrity, Marie (LAB - Baillieston)
marie.garrity@councillors.glasgow.gov.uk
Gibson, Iris (SNP - Craigton)
iris.gibson@councillors.glasgow.gov.uk
Gillan, Emma (LAB - Newlands/Auldburn)
emma.gillan@councillors.glasgow.gov.uk
Graham, Archie (LAB - Langside)
archie.graham@councillors.glasgow.gov.uk
Greene, Phil (SNP - Springburn)
phil.greene@councillors.glasgow.gov.uk
Hainey, Liam (SGP - Langside)
liam.hainey@councillors.glasgow.gov.uk
Hanif, Jahangir (SNP - Southside Central)
jahangir.hanif@councillors.glasgow.gov.uk
Hendry, Graeme (SNP - Garscadden/Scotstounhill)
graeme.hendry@councillors.glasgow.gov.uk
Hunter, Alison (SNP - Govan)
alison.hunter@councillors.glasgow.gov.uk
Hunter, Mhairi (SNP - Southside Central)
mhairi.hunter@councillors.glasgow.gov.uk
Hussain, Rashid (LAB - Greater Pollok)
rashid.hussain@councillors.glasgow.gov.uk
Jaffri, Shabbar (SNP - Greater Pollok)
shabbar.jaffri@councillors.glasgow.gov.uk
Kelly, John (LAB - Garscadden/Scotstounhill)
john.kelly2@councillors.glasgow.gov.uk
Kelly, Chris (LAB - Canal)
chris.kelly@councillors.glasgow.gov.uk
Kerr, Matthew (LAB - Craigton)
matthew.kerr@councillors.glasgow.gov.uk
Kucuk, Yvonne (LAB - Calton)
yvonne.kucuk@councillors.glasgow.gov.uk
Leonard, Gerald (LAB - North East)
gerald.leonard@councillors.glasgow.gov.uk
Letford, John (SNP - Maryhill/Kelvin)
john.letford@councillors.glasgow.gov.uk
MacLeod, Norman (SNP - Pollokshields)
norman.macleod@councillors.glasgow.gov.uk
Matheson, Gordon (LAB - Anderston/ City)
gordon.matheson@councillors.glasgow.gov.uk
McAllister, Billy (SNP - Canal)
billy.mcallister@councillors.glasgow.gov.uk
McAveety, Frank (LAB - Shettleston)
frank.mcaveety@councillors.glasgow.gov.uk
McDonald, David (SNP - Greater Pollok)
david.mcdonald@councillors.glasgow.gov.uk
McDougall, Elaine (LAB - East Centre)
elaine.mcdougall@councillors.glasgow.gov.uk
McElroy, Martin (SNP - Hillhead)
martin.mcelroy@councillors.glasgow.gov.uk
McKeever, Pauline (LAB - Hilllhead)
paulineann.mckeever@councillors.glasgow.gov.uk
McLaughlin, John (SNP - Shettleston)
john.mclaughlin@councillors.glasgow.gov.uk
McLean, Kenny (SNP - Patrick West)
kenny.mclean@councillors.glasgow.gov.uk
Meikle, David (CON - Pollokshields)
david.meikle@councillors.glasgow.gov.uk
Raja, Hanif (LAB - Pollokshields)
hanif.raja@councillors.glasgow.gov.uk
Razaq, Mohammed (LAB - Maryhill/Kelvin)
mohammed.razaq@councillors.glasgow.gov.uk
Redmond, George (LAB - Calton)
george.redmond@councillors.glasgow.gov.uk
Rhodes, Martin (LAB - Maryhill/Kelvin)
martin.rhodes@councillors.glasgow.gov.uk
Roberts, George (SNP - Hilllhead)
george.roberts@councillors.glasgow.gov.uk
Robertson, Russell (LAB - East Centre)
russell.robertson@councillors.glasgow.gov.uk
Rooney, Paul (LAB - Garscadden/Scotstounhill)
paul.rooney@councillors.glasgow.gov.uk
Ryan, George (LAB - Shettleston)
george.ryan@councillors.glasgow.gov.uk
Scally, Franny (SNP - Maryhill/Kelvin)
franny.scally@councillors.glasgow.gov.uk
Scanlon, James (LAB - Southside Central)
james.scanlon@councillors.glasgow.gov.uk
Sheridan, Austin (SNP - Baillieston)
austin.sheridan@councillors.glasgow.gov.uk
Siddique, Soryia (LAB - Southside Central)

soryia.siddique@councillors.glasgow.gov.uk
Simpson, Anne (LAB - Shettleston)
anne.simpson@councillors.glasgow.gov.uk
Singh, Sohan (LAB - North East)
sohan.singh@councillors.glasgow.gov.uk
Stephen, Helen (LAB - Canal)
helen.stephen@councillors.glasgow.gov.uk
Stewart, Allan (LAB - Springburn)
allan.stewart@councillors.glasgow.gov.uk
Thewliss, Alison (SNP - Calton)
alison.thewliss@councillors.glasgow.gov.uk
Thomas, Fariha (LAB - Govan)
fariha.thomas@councillors.glasgow.gov.uk
Torrance, Jim (SNP - Craigton)
jim.torrance@councillors.glasgow.gov.uk
Turner, David (SNP - Baillieston)
david.turner@councillors.glasgow.gov.uk
Watson, Alistair (LAB - Craigton)
alistair.watson@councillors.glasgow.gov.uk
Wild, Kieran (GRN - Canal)
kieran.wild@councillors.glasgow.gov.uk

POLITICAL COMPOSITION

LAB: 44, SNP: 29, SGP: 3, CON: 1, LD: 1, GRN: 1

GLOUCESTER CITY D

Gloucester City Council, North Warehouse, The Docks, Gloucester GL1 2EP ☎ 01452 522232 🖷 01452 396140 ✉ thecouncil@gloucester.gov.uk 💻 www.gloucester.gov.uk

FACTS & FIGURES

Police Authority: Gloucestershire Police Authority
Health Authority: NHS South West
Learning and Skills Council: South West
Parliamentary Constituencies: Gloucester
EU Constituencies: South West
Election Frequency: Elections are by thirds
Twinning: Metz (France); Trier (Germany); Gouda (Netherlands); St. Ann (Jamaica)

PRINCIPAL OFFICERS

Chief Executive: Mr Julian Wain, Chief Executive, North Warehouse, The Docks, Gloucester GL1 2EP ☎ 01452 396201 🖷 01452 396212 ✉ julian.wain@gloucester.gov.uk

Best Value: Mr Martin Shields, Corporate Director of Services & Neighbourhoods, North Warehouse, The Docks, Gloucester GL1 2EP ☎ 01452 396745 ✉ martin.shields@gloucester.gov.uk

Building Control: Ms Tina Bromilow, Building Control Service Manager, Kimberley Warehouse, The Docks, Gloucester GL1 2EP ☎ 01452 396713 ✉ tina.bromilow@gloucester.gov.uk

Catering Services: Mr Richard Bywater, Catering Manager, North Warehouse, The Docks, Gloucester GL1 2EP ☎ 01452 396136 🖷 01452 396136 ✉ richardb@gloucester.gov.uk

PR / Communications: Mr Marcus Grodentz, Service Manager - Communications & Marketing, North Warehouse, The Docks, Gloucester GL1 2EP ☎ 01452 396133 🖷 01452 396133 ✉ marcus.grodentz@gloucester.gov.uk

Community Safety: Mr Edward Pomfret, Health & Safety Service Manager, North Warehouse, The Docks, Gloucester GL1 2EP ☎ 01452 396069 ✉ edward.pomfret@gloucester.gov.uk

Contracts: Ms Diana Mumford, Procurement Officer, North Warehouse, The Docks, Gloucester GL1 2EP ☎ 01452 396419 ✉ diana.mumford@gloucester.gov.uk

Corporate Services: Mr Terry Rodway, Group Manager - Audit & Assurance, Kimberley Warehouse, The Docks, Gloucester GL1 2EQ ☎ 01452 396430 ✉ terry.rodway@gloucester.gov.uk

Customer Service: Ms Wendy Jones, Senior Customer Service Manager, North Warehouse, The Docks, Gloucester GL1 2EP ☎ 01452 396101 ✉ wendy.jones@gloucester.gov.uk

Economic Development: Mr Philip Staddon, Corporate Director of Regeneration, Phillpotts Warehouse, The Docks, Gloucester GL1 2EQ ☎ 01452 396452 ✉ philips@gloucester.gov.uk

Electoral Registration: Mrs Kirsty Cox, Senior Electoral Services Officer, Legal and Democratic Services, Herbert Warehouse, The Docks, Gloucester GL1 2EP ☎ 01452 396203 ✉ kirsty.cox@gloucester.gov.uk

Emergency Planning: Ms Gill Ragon, Group Manager - Environmental Health & Regulatory Services, Herbert Warehouse, The Docks, Gloucester GL1 2EP ☎ 01452 396321 🖷 01452 396140 ✉ gill.ragon@gloucester.gov.uk

Environmental / Technical Services: Ms Gill Ragon, Group Manager - Environmental Health & Regulatory Services, Herbert Warehouse, The Docks, Gloucester GL1 2EP ☎ 01452 396321 🖷 01452 396140 ✉ gill.ragon@gloucester.gov.uk

Environmental Health: Ms Gill Ragon, Group Manager - Environmental Health & Regulatory Services, Herbert Warehouse, The Docks, Gloucester GL1 2EP ☎ 01452 396321 🖷 01452 396140 ✉ gill.ragon@gloucester.gov.uk

Events Manager: Ms Sheila McDaid, Markets & City Centre Services Manager, North Warehouse, The Docks, Gloucester GL1 2EP ☎ 01452 528796 ✉ sheila.mcdaid@gloucester.gov.uk

Facilities: Ms Julie Wells, Group Manager - Property & City Centre Services, Kimberley Warehouse, The Docks, Gloucester GL1 2EP ☎ 01452 396363 ✉ julie.wells@gloucester.gov.uk

Finance and Treasurer: Mr Peter Gillett, Corporate Director of Resources, North Warehouse, The Docks, Gloucester GL1 2EP ☎ 01452 396400 ✉ pete.gillett@gloucester.gov.uk

Health and Safety: Mr Edward Pomfret, Health & Safety Service Manager, North Warehouse, The Docks, Gloucester GL1 2EP ☎ 01452 396069 ✉ edward.pomfret@gloucester.gov.uk

Home Energy Conservation: Mr Stephen McDonnell, Environmental Co-ordinator, North Warehouse, The Docks, Gloucester GL1 2EP ☎ ; 01452 396209 🖷 01452 366899 ✉ stephen.mcdonnell@gloucester.gov.uk

Housing: Mr Ross Cook, Group Manager - Housing &

Neighbourhood Services, Herbert Warehouse, The Docks, Gloucester GL1 2EQ ☎ 01452 396355 ✉ ross.cook@gloucester.gov.uk

Housing Maintenance: Mr Ashley Green, Chief Executive - Gloucester City Homes, Southgate House, Southgate Street, Gloucester GL1 1UW ☎ 01452 396471 ✉ ashleyg@gloucester.gov.uk

Legal: Ms Sue Mullins, Group Manager of Legal & Democratic Services, North Warehouse, The Docks, Gloucester GL1 2EP ☎ 01452 396110 ✉ sue.mullins@gloucester.gov.uk

Leisure and Cultural Services: Ms Vicki Rowan, Group Manager - Cultural Services & Tourism, Southgate House, Gloucester GL1 2EQ ☎ 01452 396179 ✉ vickir@gloucester.gov.uk

Licensing: Ms Gill Ragon, Group Manager - Environmental Health & Regulatory Services, Herbert Warehouse, The Docks, Gloucester GL1 2EP ☎ 01452 396321 🖷 01452 396140 ✉ gill.ragon@gloucester.gov.uk

Member Services: Ms Tanya Davies, Democratic & Electoral Services Manager, Kimberley Warehouse, The Docks, Gloucester GL1 2EQ ☎ 01452 396127 ✉ tanya.davies@gloucester.gov.uk

Parking: Ms Heather Clarke, Parking Services Manager, Kimberley Warehouse, The Docks, Gloucester GL1 2EP ☎ 01452 396724

Personnel / HR: Mr Peter Gillett, Corporate Director of Resources, North Warehouse, The Docks, Gloucester GL1 2EP ☎ 01452 396400 ✉ pete.gillett@gloucester.gov.uk

Procurement: Ms Diana Mumford, Procurement Officer, North Warehouse, The Docks, Gloucester GL1 2EP ☎ 01452 396419 ✉ diana.mumford@gloucester.gov.uk

Recycling & Waste Minimisation: Mr Stephen McDonnell, Environmental Co-ordinator, North Warehouse, The Docks, Gloucester GL1 2EP ☎ ; 01452 396209 🖷 01452 366899 ✉ stephen.mcdonnell@gloucester.gov.uk

Regeneration: Mr Philip Staddon, Corporate Director of Regeneration, Phillpotts Warehouse, The Docks, Gloucester GL1 2EQ ☎ 01452 396452 ✉ philips@gloucester.gov.uk

Staff Training: Ms Tracy Kendrick, Apprenticeship Manager, North Warehouse, The Docks, Gloucester GL1 2EP ☎ 01452 39680 ✉ tracy.kendrick@gloucester.gov.uk

Street Scene: Mr Ross Cook, Group Manager - Housing & Neighbourhood Services, Herbert Warehouse, The Docks, Gloucester GL1 2EQ ☎ 01452 396355 ✉ ross.cook@gloucester.gov.uk

Sustainable Communities: Mr Stephen McDonnell, Environmental Co-ordinator, North Warehouse, The Docks, Gloucester GL1 2EP ☎ ; 01452 396209 🖷 01452 366899 ✉ stephen.mcdonnell@gloucester.gov.uk

Sustainable Development: Mr Stephen McDonnell, Environmental Co-ordinator, North Warehouse, The Docks, Gloucester GL1 2EP ☎ 01452 396209 🖷 01452 366899 ✉ stephen.mcdonnell@gloucester.gov.uk

Tourism: Ms Vicki Rowan, Group Manager - Cultural Services & Tourism, Bruton Way, Gloucester GL1 1DE ☎ 01452 396179 ✉ vickir@gloucester.gov.uk

Town Centre: Ms Sheila McDaid, Markets & City Centre Services Manager, Herbert Warehouse, The Docks, Gloucester GL1 2EQ ☎ 01452 528796 ✉ sheila.mcdaid@gloucester.gov.uk

Waste Collection and Disposal: Mr Ross Cook, Group Manager - Housing & Neighbourhood Services, North Warehouse, The Docks, Gloucester GL1 2EP ☎ 01452 396355 ✉ ross.cook@gloucester.gov.uk

MEMBERS OF THE COUNCIL (36)

***Mayor:* Brown**, David (LD - Hucclecote)
david.brown@gloucester.gov.uk

***Deputy Mayor:* McLellan**, Phil (LD - Barnwood)
philipm@gloucester.gov.uk

***Leader of the Council:* James**, Paul (CON - Longlevens)
psj@gloucester.gov.uk

***Deputy Leader of the Council:* Llewellyn**, Debbie (CON - Quedgeley Fieldcourt)
debbie.llewellyn@gloucester.gov.uk

***Group Leader:* Haigh**, Katie (LAB - Matson and Robinswood)
kate.haigh@gloucester.gov.uk

***Group Leader:* Hilton**, Jeremy (LD - Kingsholm and Wotton)
jeremy.hilton@gloucester.gov.uk

Beeley, James (LD - Hucclecote)
james.beeley@gloucester.gov.uk

Bhaimia, Usman (LD - Barton and Tredworth)
usman.bhaimia@gloucester.gov.uk

Chatterton, Chris (LAB - Grange)
chris.chatterton@gloucester.gov.uk

Dallimore, Jennie (CON - Podsmead)
jennie.dallimore@gloucester.gov.uk

Dee, Gerald (CON - Tuffley)
gerald.dee@gloucester.gov.uk

Durrant, Nicholas (LAB - Moreland)
nicholas.durrant@gloucester.gov.uk

Field, Sebastian (LD - Kingsholm and Wotton)
sebastian.field@gloucester.gov.uk

Gilson, Matthew (LAB - Moreland)
matthew.gilson@gloucester.gov.uk

Gravells, Andrew (CON - Abbey)
andrew.gravells@gloucester.gov.uk

Handot, Said (LAB - Barton and Tredworth)
ahmed.hansdot@gloucester.gov.uk

Hanman, Nigel (CON - Grange)
nigel.hanman@gloucester.gov.uk

Hobbs, Mark (LAB - Moreland)
mark.hobbs@gloucester.gov.uk

Lewis, Andrew (CON - Quedgeley Severn Vale)
andrew.lewis@gloucester.gov.uk

Lugg, Janet (LAB - Matson and Robinswood)
janet.lugg@gloucester.gov.uk

Mozol, Anna (LD - Quedgeley Severn Vale)
anna.mozol@gloucester.gov.uk

Noakes, Lise (CON - Barnwood)
lise.noakes@gloucester.gov.uk

Organ, Colin (CON - Tuffley)

colin.organ@gloucester.gov.uk
Patel, Sajid (CON - Barton and Tredworth)
sajid.patel@gloucester.gov.uk
Porter, Jim (CON - Longlevens)
kim.porter@gloucester.gov.uk
Randle, Tarren (CON - Barnwood)
tarren.randle@gloucester.gov.uk
Ravenhill, Norman (CON - Abbey)
norman.ravenhill@gloucester.gov.uk
Smith, Mary (LAB - Matson and Robinswood)
mary.smith@gloucester.gov.uk
Taylor, Gordon (CON - Abbey)
gordon.taylor@gloucester.gov.uk
Toleman, Paul (CON - Westgate)
paul.toleman@gloucester.gov.uk
Tracey, Pam (CON - Westgate)
pam.tracey@gloucester.gov.uk
Williams, Kathy (CON - Longlevens)
kathy.williams@gloucester.gov.uk
Wilson, Declan (LD - Hucclecote)
declan.wilson@gloucester.gov.uk
Witts, Susan (LD - Elmbridge)
susan.witts@gloucester.gov.uk
Witts, Chris (LD - Elmbridge)
chris.witts@gloucester.gov.uk
Wood, Frederick (CON - Quedgeley Fieldcourt)
frederick.wood@gloucester.gov.uk

POLITICAL COMPOSITION
CON: 18, LD: 10, LAB: 8

CABINET
Leader; Regeneration & Culture: Mr Paul James
Deputy Leader / Performance & Resources: Mrs Debbie Llewellyn
Communities & Neighbourhoods: Ms Jennie Dallimore
Environment: Mrs Kathy Williams
Housing, Health & Leisure: Mr Colin Organ

COMMITTEE CHAIRS
Audit & Governance: Mr Declan Wilson
Licensing and Enforcement: Ms Lise Noakes
Organisational Development: Mr Paul James
Overview & Scrutiny: Dr Janet Lugg
Planning: Mr Gordon Taylor

GLOUCESTERSHIRE C

Gloucestershire County Council, Shire Hall, Westgate Street, Gloucester GL1 2TG ☎ 01452 425000 🖷 01452 425850
💻 www.gloucestershire.gov.uk

FACTS & FIGURES
Police Authority: Gloucestershire Police Authority
Health Authority: NHS South West
Learning and Skills Council: South West
EU Constituencies: South West
Election Frequency: Elections are of whole council

PRINCIPAL OFFICERS
Chief Executive: Mr Peter Bungard, Chief Executive, Shire Hall, Westgate Street, Gloucester GL1 2TG ☎ 01452 425875 🖷 01452 425875 ✉ peter.bungard@gloucestershire.gov.uk

Deputy Chief Executive: Mr Peter Jones, Deputy Chief Executive - Enabling and Transition, Shire Hall, Gloucester GL1 2TG ☎ 01452 426347 🖷 01452 425876 ✉ peter.jones@gloucestershire.gov.uk

Assistant Chief Executive: Ms Jane Burns, Director: Strategy & Challenge, Shire Hall, Gloucester GL1 2TG ☎ 01452 425202 🖷 01452 425876 ✉ jane.burns@gloucestershire.gov.uk

Senior Management: Ms Jane Burns, Director: Strategy & Challenge, Shire Hall, Westgate Street, Gloucester GL1 2TG ☎ 01452 425202 🖷 01452 425876 ✉ jane.burns@gloucestershire.gov.uk

Senior Management: Mr Duncan Jordan, Group Director: Chief Operating Officer, Shire Hall, Westgate Street, Gloucester GL1 2TG ☎ 01452 425523 ✉ duncan.jordan@gloucestershire.gov.uk

Senior Management: Mr Stewart King, Head of Business Development, Shire Hall, Westgate Street, Gloucester GL1 2TG ☎ 01452 425441 ✉ stewart.king@gloucestershire.gov.uk

Senior Management: Mr Eugene O'Kane, Programme Manager, Shire Hall, Westgate Street, Gloucester GL1 2TG ☎ 01452 583591 ✉ eugene.okane@gloucestershire.gov.uk

Senior Management: Mr Mark Spilsbury, Head of Finance: Financial Management, Shire Hall, Westgate Street, Gloucester GL1 2TG ☎ 01452 426127 ✉ mark.spilsbury@gloucestershire.gov.uk

Senior Management: Ms Linda Uren, Commissioning Director: Children, Shire Hall, Westgate Street, Gloucester GL1 2TG ☎ 01452 427788 ✉ linda.uren@gloucestershire.gov.uk

Senior Management: Ms Jo Walker, Director: Strategic Finance, Shire Hall, Westgate Street, Gloucester GL1 2TG ☎ 01453 427492 ✉ jo.walker@gloucestershire.gov.uk

Senior Management: Ms Margaret Willcox, Commissioning Director: Adults, Shire Hall, Westgate Street, Gloucester GL1 2TG ☎ 01452 425102 🖷 01452 425101 ✉ margaret.willcox@gloucestershire.gov.uk

Senior Management: Mrs Dilys Wynn, Director of People Services, Shire Hall, Westgate Street, Gloucester GL1 2TG ☎ 01452 425824 ✉ dilys.wynn@gloucestershire.gov.uk

Architect, Building / Property Services: Mr Neil Corbett, Building Support Manager, Shire Hall, Westgate Street, Gloucester GL1 2TG ☎ 01452 425786 ✉ neil.corbett@gloucestershire.gov.uk

Best Value: Mr Rob Ayliffe, Head of Policy & Performance, Shire Hall, Westgate Street, Gloucester GL1 2TG ☎ 01452 426613 ✉ rob.ayliffe@gloucestershire.gov.uk

Building Control: Mr Mark Anderson, Shire Hall Support Officer, Shire Hall, Gloucester GL1 2TG ☎ 01452 425746 ✉ mark.anderson@gloucestershire.gov.uk

Building Control: Mr Neil Corbett, Building Support Manager,

Shire Hall, Westgate Street, Gloucester GL1 2TG ☎ 01452 425786 ✆ neil.corbett@gloucestershire.gov.uk

Children / Youth Services: Mr Tim Browne, Head of Service, Commissioning for Learning, Shire Hall, Westgate Street, Gloucester GL1 2TG ☎ 01452 425468 ✆ tim.browne@gloucestershire.gov.uk

Children / Youth Services: Mr Ian Godfrey, Children In Care Service Manager, Shire Hall, Westgate Street, Block 1, Gloucester GL2 5GH ☎ 01452 427650 ✆ ian.godfrey@gloucestershire.gov.uk

Children / Youth Services: Mr Duncan Jordan, Director of Children & Young People's Services, Shire Hall, Gloucester GL1 2TG ☎ 01452 426332 ✆ duncan.jordan@gloucestershire.gov.uk

Children / Youth Services: Mr Eugene O'Kane, Programme Manager, Shire Hall, Westgate Street, Gloucester GL1 2TG ☎ 01452 583591 ✆ eugene.okane@gloucestershire.gov.uk

Children / Youth Services: Ms Lynne Speak, Operations Manager, 92-96 Westgate Street, Gloucester GL1 2PF ☎ 01452 583791 ✆ lynne.speak@gloucestershire.gov.uk

Civil Registration: Ms Sally Bye, Registration & Coroner Services Manager, Hillfield House, Denmark Road, Gloucester GL1 3LD ☎ 01452 425227 ✆ sally.bye@gloucestershire.gov.uk

Consumer Protection and Trading Standards: Mr Eddie Coventry, Head of Trading Standards, Registration and Coroners, Hillfield House, Denmark Road, Gloucester GL1 3LD ☎ 01452 426786 ✆ eddie.coventry@gloucestershire.gov.uk

Contracts: Mr Simon Bilous, Head of Service Joint Commissioning, 1st Floor, Quayside House, Quay street , Gloucester GL1 2HY ☎ 01452 426653 ✆ simon.bilous@gloucestershire.gov.uk

Corporate Services: Ms Jane Burns, Director: Strategy & Challenge, Shire Hall, Gloucester GL1 2TG ☎ 01452 425202 🖷 01452 425876 ✆ jane.burns@gloucestershire.gov.uk

Corporate Services: Mr Stewart King, Head of Business Development, Shire Hall, Westgate Street, Gloucester GL1 2TG ☎ 01452 425441 ✆ stewart.king@gloucestershire.gov.uk

Corporate Services: Mrs Dilys Wynn, Director of People Services, Shire Hall, Westgate Street, Gloucester GL1 2TG ☎ 01452 425824 ✆ dilys.wynn@gloucestershire.gov.uk

Customer Service: Mrs Nicola Ratcliffe, Head of Customer Services, Shire Hall, Westgate Street, Gloucester GL1 2TG ☎ 01452 426944 ✆ nicola.ratcliffe@gloucestershire.gov.uk

Customer Service: Ms Margaret Willcox, Commissioning Director: Adults, Shire Hall, Westgate Street, Gloucester GL1 2TG ☎ 01452 425102 🖷 01452 425101 ✆ margaret.willcox@gloucestershire.gov.uk

Education: Ms Jo Grills, Director of Learning & Development, Shire Hall, Gloucester GL1 2TG ☎ 01452 425301 ✆ jo.grills@gloucestershire.gov.uk

Education: Mr Duncan Jordan, Director of Children & Young People's Services, Shire Hall, Gloucester GL1 2TG ☎ 01452 426332 ✆ duncan.jordan@gloucestershire.gov.uk

Environmental / Technical Services: Ms Jo Walker, Director: Strategic Finance, Shire Hall, Westgate Street, Gloucester GL1 2TG ☎ 01453 427492 ✆ jo.walker@gloucestershire.gov.uk

Environmental Health: Mr John Davison, Head of Safety, Health & Environment (SHE Unit), Shire Hall, Westgate Street, Gloucester GL1 2TG ☎ 01452 426762 ✆ john.davison@gloucestershire.gov.uk

Estates, Property & Valuation: Mr Neil Corbett, Building Support Manager, Shire Hall, Westgate Street, Gloucester GL1 2TG ☎ 01452 425786 ✆ neil.corbett@gloucestershire.gov.uk

European Liaison: Ms Susan Stoner, European Affairs & External Funding, Llanthony Warehouse, The Docks, Gloucester GL1 2EH ☎ 01452 328311 ✆ sue.stoner@gloucestershire.gov.uk

Facilities: Mr Mark Anderson, Shire Hall Support Officer, Shire Hall, Gloucester GL1 2TG ☎ 01452 425746 ✆ mark.anderson@gloucestershire.gov.uk

Facilities: Mr Neil Corbett, Building Support Manager, Shire Hall, Westgate Street, Gloucester GL1 2TG ☎ 01452 425786 ✆ neil.corbett@gloucestershire.gov.uk

Finance and Treasurer: Mr Graham Burrow, Head of Finance - Exchequer, Shire Hall, Westgate Street, Gloucester GL1 2TG ☎ 01452 425880 ✆ graham.burrow@gloucestershire.gov.uk

Finance and Treasurer: Mr Mark Spilsbury, Head of Finance: Financial Management, Shire Hall, Westgate Street, Gloucester GL1 2TG ☎ 01452 426127 ✆ mark.spilsbury@gloucestershire.gov.uk

Health and Safety: Mr John Davison, Head of Safety, Health & Environment (SHE Unit), Shire Hall, Westgate Street, Gloucester GL1 2TG ☎ 01452 426762 ✆ john.davison@gloucestershire.gov.uk

Highways: Mr Nigel Tomlinson, Head of Gloucestershire Highways, Imperial Gate, Corinium Avenue , Barnwood, Gloucester GL4 3BW ☎ 01452 583431 ✆ nigel.tomlinson@gloucestershire.gov.uk

Local Area Agreement: Mr Rob Ayliffe, Head of Performance and Need, Shire Hall, Westgate Street, Gloucester GL1 2TG ☎ 01452 426613 ✆ rob.ayliffe@gloucestershire.gov.uk

Local Area Agreement: Ms Jane Burns, Director: Strategy & Challenge, Shire Hall, Westgate Street, Gloucester GL1 2TG ☎ 01452 425202 🖷 01452 425876 ✆ jane.burns@gloucestershire.gov.uk

Legal: Mr Nigel Roberts, Director of Law & Administration, Quayside House, First Floor, Gloucester GL1 2TG ☎ 01452 425201 ✆ nigel.roberts@gloucestershire.gov.uk

Leisure and Cultural Services: Mr Chris Dee, Marketing Manager, Llanthony Warehouse, The Docks, Gloucester GL1 2EH ☎ 01452 328302 🖷 01452 426363 ✉ chris.dee@gloucestershire.gov.uk

Lifelong Learning: Mr Jim Austin, Head of Adult Education, Llanthony Warehouse, The Docks, Gloucester GL1 2EH ☎ 01452 583810 ✉ jim.austin@gloucestershire.gov.uk

Lifelong Learning: Mr David Grocott, Head of Lifelong Learning, Shire Hall, Gloucester GL1 2TG ☎ 01452 425801 🖷 01452 427576 ✉ david.grocott@gloucestershire.gov.uk

Lottery Funding, Charity and Voluntary: Mrs Rachel Wright, Voluntary Sector Manager, Shire Hall, Westgate Street, Gloucester GL1 2TG ☎ 01452 427615 🖷 01452 425850 ✉ rachel.wright@gloucestershire.gov.uk

Member Services: Ms Julie Hill, Democratic Services Unit Manager, Shire Hall, Westgate Street, Gloucester GL1 2TG ☎ 01452 425005 ✉ julie.hill@gloucestershire.gov.uk

Member Services: Mr Nigel Roberts, Director of Law & Administration, Quayside House, First Floor, Gloucester GL1 2TG ☎ 01452 425201 ✉ nigel.roberts@gloucestershire.gov.uk

Parking: Mr Jim Daniels, Parking Manager, Shire Hall, Westgate Street, Gloucester GL1 2TG ☎ 01452 425610 ✉ jim.daniels@gloucestershire.gov.uk

Partnerships: Ms Jane Burns, Director: Strategy & Challenge, Shire Hall, Westgate Street, Gloucester GL1 2TG ☎ 01452 425202 🖷 01452 425876 ✉ jane.burns@gloucestershire.gov.uk

Partnerships: Ms Linda Uren, Commissioning Director: Children, Shire Hall, Westgate Street, Gloucester GL1 2TG ☎ 01452 427788 ✉ linda.uren@gloucestershire.gov.uk

Personnel / HR: Ms Susan Scrivens, Change Management Advisor, Shire Hall, Gloucester GL1 2TG ☎ 01452 427683 🖷 01452 427683 ✉ sue.scrivens@gloucestershire.gov.uk

Personnel / HR: Mrs Dilys Wynn, Director of People Services, Shire Hall, Westgate Street, Gloucester GL1 2TG ☎ 01452 425824 ✉ dilys.wynn@gloucestershire.gov.uk

Procurement: Ms Claire Smart, Director of Strategic Procurement, Shire Hall, Westgate Street, Gloucester GL1 2TG ☎ 01452 425035 ✉ claire.smart@gloucestershire.gov.uk

Procurement: Mrs Dilys Wynn, Director of People Services, Shire Hall, Westgate Street, Gloucester GL1 2TG ☎ 01452 425824 ✉ dilys.wynn@gloucestershire.gov.uk

Public Libraries: Ms Margaret Willcox, Commissioning Director: Adults, Shire Hall, Westgate Street, Gloucester GL1 2TG ☎ 01452 425102 🖷 01452 425101 ✉ margaret.willcox@gloucestershire.gov.uk

Road Safety: Ms Sheila Jones, Lead Commissioner Highways Asset/Traffic Management, Shire Hall, Gloucester GL1 2TG ☎ 01452 426444 🖷 01452 425640 ✉ sheila.jones@gloucestershire.gov.uk

Social Services: Mr Ian Godfrey, Children In Care Service Manager, Shire Hall, Westgate Street, Block 1, Gloucester GL2 5GH ☎ 01452 427650 ✉ ian.godfrey@gloucestershire.gov.uk

Social Services: Ms Tina Reid, Head of Care Provision, Shire Hall, Westgate Street, Gloucester GL1 2TG ☎ 01452 427300 ✉ tina.reid@gloucestershire.gov.uk

Social Services: Ms Margaret Willcox, Commissioning Director: Adults, Shire Hall, Westgate Street, Gloucester GL1 2TG ☎ 01452 425102 🖷 01452 425101 ✉ margaret.willcox@gloucestershire.gov.uk

Social Services (Adult): Ms Margaret Willcox, Commissioning Director: Adults, Shire Hall, Westgate Street, Gloucester GL1 2TG ☎ 01452 425102 🖷 01452 425101 ✉ margaret.willcox@gloucestershire.gov.uk

Social Services (Children): Mr Duncan Jordan, Chief Operating Officer (Group Director), Shire Hall, Gloucester GL1 2TG ☎ 01452 425523 ✉ duncan.jordan@gloucestershire.gov.uk

Sustainable Communities: Mr Peter Wiggins, Corporate Sustainability Manager, Environment Directorate, Shire Hall, Westgate Street, Gloucester GL1 2TG ☎ 01452 425189 🖷 01452 541305 ✉ peter.wiggins@gloucestershire.gov.uk

Tourism: Mr Chris Dee, Marketing Manager, Llanthony Warehouse, The Docks, Gloucester GL1 2EH ☎ 01452 328302 🖷 01452 426363 ✉ chris.dee@gloucestershire.gov.uk

Traffic Management: Mr Lawrence Elcocks, Network & Traffic Manager, Environment Department, Shire Hall, Westgate Street, Gloucester GL1 2TG ☎ 01452 425564 ✉ lawrence.elcocks@gloucestershire.gov.uk

Waste Collection and Disposal: Mr Tony Childs, Waste Services and Sustainability Manager, Shire Hall, Westgate Street, Gloucester GL1 2TG ☎ 01452 425448 ✉ tony.childs@gloucestershire.gov.uk

Waste Management: Mr Tony Childs, Waste Services and Sustainability Manager, Shire Hall, Westgate Street, Gloucester GL1 2TG ☎ 01452 425448 ✉ tony.childs@gloucestershire.gov.uk

Waste Management: Mr Ian Mawdsley, Project Lead - Residual Waste Management, Shire Hall, Gloucester GL1 2TH ☎ 01452 425835 🖷 01452 425126 ✉ ian.mawdsley@gloucestershire.gov.uk

MEMBERS OF THE COUNCIL (62)

***Chair:* Hicks**, Tony (CON - Tetbury)
tony.hicks@gloucestershire.gov.uk
***Vice-Chair:* Nash**, Joan (CON - Upton St Leonards, Bisley and Painswick)
joan.nash@gloucestershire.gov.uk
***Leader of the Council:* Hawthorne**, Mark (CON - Moreland)
mark.hawthorne@gloucestershire.gov.uk
***Deputy Leader of the Council:* McLain**, Paul (CON - Charlton Kings)
paul.mclain@gloucestershire.gov.uk

Allen, Ron (CON - Winchcombe)
ron.allen@gloucestershire.gov.uk
Andrewartha, Dennis (LD - Cam and Dursley)
dennis.andrewartha@gloucestershire.gov.uk
Awford, Philip (CON - Severn Vale)
philip.awford@gloucestershire.gov.uk
Blackburn, Anthony (CON - North Stroud)
anthony.blackburn@gloucestershire.gov.uk
Booth, Basil (CON - Berkeley Vale)
basil.booth@gloucestsershire.gov.uk
Braidwood, Peter (CON - Cirencester)
peter.braidwood@gloucestershire.gov.uk
Burgess, John (CON - Cirencester)
john.burgess@gloucestershire.gov.uk
Collins, Michael (LD - Brockworth)
michael.collins2@gloucestershire.gov.uk
Cooksley, David (CON - Lydney)
david.cooksley@gloucestershire.gov.uk
Cordwell, John (LD - Wotton-under-Edge)
john.cordwell@gloucestershire.gov.uk
Crowther, Bill (LD - Hucclecote)
bill.crowther@gloucestershire.gov.uk
Dare, Barry (CON - Moreton-Stow)
barry.dare@gloucestershire.gov.uk
Dee, Gerald (CON - Podsmead)
gerald.dee@gloucestershire.gov.uk
Fellows, Charles (CON - Chalford)
chas.fellowes@gloucestershire.gov.uk
Friend, Sonia (LAB - Barton and Tredworth)
sonia.friend@gloucestershire.gov.uk
Garnham, Robert (CON - Lansdown, Park and Warden Hill)
rob.garnham@gloucestershire.gov.uk
Glastonbury, Terry (CON - West Dean)
terry.glastonbury@gloucestershire.gov.uk
Gravells, Andrew (CON - Abbey)
andrew.gravells@gloucestershire.gov.uk
Hale, Terry (CON - Coleford)
terry.hale@gloucestershire.gov.uk
Hall, Jackie (CON - Quedgeley)
jackie.hall@gloucestershire.gov.uk
Hibbert, Diane (O - Oakley, Pittville and Prestbury)
diane.hibbert@gloucestershire.gov.uk
Hilton, Jeremy (LD - Westgate)
jeremy.hilton@gloucestershire.gov.uk
Jones, Ceri (LD - Cleeve)
ceri.jones@gloucestershire.gov.uk
Lunnon, Sarah (GRN - Stroud East)
sarah.lunnon@gloucestershire.gov.uk
McHale, Steve (LAB - Robinswood)
steve.mchale@gloucestershire.gov.uk
McKenzie, Fiona (CON - Northleach)
fiona.mckenzie@gloucestershire.gov.uk
McLellan, Phillip (LD - Barnwood)
phillip.mclellan@gloucestershire.gov.uk
McMillan, Stephen (CON - Mid Dean)
stephen.mcmillan@gloucestershire.gov.uk
Morgan, Graham (LAB - Cinderford)
graham.morgan@gloucestershire.gov.uk
Noble, Antonia (CON - Lansdown, Park and Warden Hill)
antonia.noble@gloucestershire.gov.uk
Oosthuysen, Brian (CON - Rodborough)
stephen.glanfield@gloucestershire.gov.uk
Pallet, Christopher (LD - Hesters Way and Up Hatherley)
christopher.pallet@gloucestershire.gov.uk
Parsons, Shaun (CON - South Cotswold)
shaun.parsons@gloucestershire.gov.uk
Prince, David (O - Oakley, Pittville and Prestbury)
david.prince@gloucestershire.gov.uk
Quaile, Martin (CON - Pillowel and Littledean)
martin.quaile@gloucestershire.gov.uk
Rice, Vic (CON - Quedgeley)
vic.rice@gloucestershire.gov.uk
Robinson, Brian (CON - Brooksdean)
brian.robinson@gloucestershire.gov.uk
Sheppard, Charmian (LD - St Mark's, St Paul's and St Peter's)
charmian.sheppard@gloucestershire.gov.uk
Shurmer, Gordon (CON - Ashchurch, Cleeve and Oxenton Hill)
gordon.shurmer@gloucestershire.gov.uk
Skinner, Mike (LD - St Mark's, St Paul's and St Peter's)
mike.skinner@gloucestershire.gov.uk
Smith, Vernon (CON - Tewkesbury)
vernon.smith@gloucestershire.gov.uk
Smith, Duncan (CON - All Saints)
duncan.smith@gloucestershire.gov.uk
Stowe, Lynden (CON - North Cotswold)
lynden.stowe@gloucestershire.gov.uk
Sudbury, Klara (LD - All Saints)
klara.sudbury@gloucestershire.gov.uk
Sztymiak, Mike (IND - Tewkesbury)
mike.sztymiak@gloucestershire.gov.uk
Theodoulou, Raymond (CON - East Cotswold)
raymond.theodoulou@gloucestershire.gov.uk
Thornton, Brian (CON - Tidenham)
brian.thornton@gloucestershire.gov.uk
Thorpe, David (CON - Bourton)
david.thorpe@gloucestershire.gov.uk
Tipper, Brian (CON - Cam and Dursley)
brian.tipper@gloucestershire.gov.uk
Tracey, Pam (CON - Westgate)
pam.tracey@gloucestershire.gov.uk
Waddington, John (CON - Nailsworth and Minchinhampton)
john.waddington@gloucestershire.gov.uk
Wheeler, Simon (LD - Hesters Way and Up Hatherley)
simon.wheeler@gloucestershire.gov.uk
Whelan, Bill (LD - Churchdown St John's)
bill.whelan@gloucestershire.gov.uk
Williams, Kathy (CON - Longlevens)
kathy.williams@gloucestershire.gov.uk
Williams, Suzanne (LD - Springbank)
suzanne.williams@gloucestershire.gov.uk
Williams, Lesley (LAB - Stonehouse)
lesley.williams@gloucestershire.gov.uk
Williams, Mike (CON - Stroud West)
mike.williams2@gloucestershire.gov.uk
Windsor-Clive, Will (CON - Newent)
will.windsor-clive@gloucestershire.gov.uk

POLITICAL COMPOSITION

CON: 40, LD: 14, LAB: 4, O: 2, GRN: 1, IND: 1

CABINET

Leader: Mr Mark Hawthorne
Deputy Leader / Vulnerable Families: Mr Paul McLain
Communities: Mr Will Windsor-Clive
Economy & Environment: Mr Charles Fellows
Education & Skills: Ms Jackie Hall
Finance & Change: Mr Raymond Theodoulou
Health & Wellbeing: Mr Andrew Gravells
People with Long Term Support: Ms Antonia Noble

COMMITTEE CHAIRS

Audit: Mr Phillip McLellan
Budget & Performance (Scrutiny): Mr Dennis Andrewartha
Children & Young People (Scrutiny): Mr Philip Awford
Community Safety (Scrutiny): Ms Kathy Williams
Corporate Parenting: Mr Duncan Smith
Environment: Mr John Cordwell
Health, Community & Care (Scrutiny): Mr Gordon Shurmer
Overview & Scrutiny Management: Mr Robert Garnham
Planning: Mr Martin Quaile

GOSPORT D

Gosport Borough Council, Town Hall, High Street, Gosport PO12 1EB ☎ 023 9258 4242 🖷 023 9254 5587 ✉ enquiries@gosport.gov.uk 💻 www.gosport.gov.uk

FACTS & FIGURES

Police Authority: Hampshire Police Authority
Health Authority: South Central Strategic Health Authority
Learning and Skills Council: South East
Parliamentary Constituencies: Gosport
EU Constituencies: South East
Election Frequency: Elections are biennial
Twinning: Royan (France)

PRINCIPAL OFFICERS

Chief Executive: Mr Ian Lycett, Chief Executive, Town Hall, High Street, Gosport PO12 1EB ☎ 023 9251 5201 🖷 023 9251 1279 ✉ ian.lycett@gosport.gov.uk

Deputy Chief Executive: Ms Linda Edwards, Deputy Chief Executive & Borough Solicitor, Town Hall, High Street, Gosport PO12 1EB ☎ 023 9254 5401 🖷 023 9254 5587 ✉ linda.edwards@gosport.gov.uk

Access Officer / Social Services (Disability): Mr Richard Sturgess, Access Officer, Town Hall, High Street, Gosport PO12 1EB ☎ 023 9254 5535 🖷 023 9254 5588 ✉ rsturgess@fareham.gov.uk

Architect, Building / Property Services: Mr Mark Pam, Head of Property Services, Town Hall, High Street, Gosport PO12 1EB ☎ 023 9254 5563 🖷 023 9254 5588 ✉ mark.pam@gosport.gov.uk

Best Value: Mrs Julie Petty, Head of Corporate Policy & Performance, Town Hall, High Street, Gosport PO12 1EB ☎ 023 9254 5381 🖷 023 9254 5238 ✉ julie.petty@gosport.gov.uk

Building Control: Mr John Shaw, Building Control Manager, Civic Offices, Civic Way, Fareham PO16 7TT ☎ 01329 824823 🖷 01329 822732 ✉ john.shaw@fareham.gov.uk

PR / Communications: Mrs Brenda Brooker, Press Officer, Town Hall, High Street, Gosport PO12 1EB ☎ 023 9254 5255 🖷 023 9254 5229 ✉ brenda.brooker@gosport.gov.uk

Community Planning: Mrs Julie Petty, Head of Corporate Policy & Performance, Town Hall, High Street, Gosport PO12 1EB ☎ 023 9254 5381 🖷 023 9254 5238 ✉ julie.petty@gosport.gov.uk

Community Safety: Mrs Julie Petty, Head of Corporate Policy & Performance, Town Hall, High Street, Gosport PO12 1EB ☎ 023 9254 5381 🖷 023 9254 5238 ✉ julie.petty@gosport.gov.uk

Computer Management: Mr David Eland, Head of IT, Town Hall, High Street, Gosport PO12 1EB ☎ 023 9254 5309 ✉ david.eland@gosport.gov.uk

Contracts: Mr Stevyn Ricketts, Head of Streetscene, Town Hall, High Street, Gosport PO12 1EB ☎ 023 9254 5282 🖷 023 9258 8053 ✉ stevyn.ricketts@gosport.gov.uk

Corporate Services: Ms Kim Carron, Corporate & Customer Services Manager, Town Hall, High Street, Gosport PO12 1EB ☎ 023 9254 5512 🖷 023 9254 5724 ✉ kim.carron@gosport.gov.uk

Customer Service: Ms Kim Carron, Corporate & Customer Services Manager, Town Hall, High Street, Gosport PO12 1EB ☎ 023 9254 5512 🖷 023 9254 5724 ✉ kim.carron@gosport.gov.uk

Economic Development: Mrs Lynda Dine, Head of Economic Prosperity, Town Hall, High Street, Gosport PO12 1EB ☎ 023 9254 5231 🖷 023 9254 5238 ✉ lynda.dine@gosport.gov.uk

E-Government: Mr David Eland, Head of IT, Town Hall, High Street, Gosport PO12 1EB ☎ 023 9254 5309 ✉ david.eland@gosport.gov.uk

Electoral Registration: Ms Linda Edwards, Deputy Chief Executive & Borough Solicitor, Town Hall, High Street, Gosport PO12 1EB ☎ 023 9254 5401 🖷 023 9254 5587 ✉ linda.edwards@gosport.gov.uk

Emergency Planning: Mr Ken Lucking, Emergency Planning Officer, Town Hall, High Street, Gosport PO12 1EB ☎ 023 9254 5305 🖷 023 9254 5253 ✉ ken.lucking@gosport.gov.uk

Environmental Health: Mr Ian Rickman, Head of Environmental Health, Town Hall, High Street, Gosport PO12 1EB ☎ 023 9258 5517 🖷 023 9254 5360 ✉ irickman@fareham.gov.uk

Estates, Property & Valuation: Mr Mark Pam, Head of Property Services, Town Hall, High Street, Gosport PO12 1EB ☎ 023 9254 5563 🖷 023 9254 5588 ✉ mark.pam@gosport.gov.uk

European Liaison: Mrs Lynda Dine, Head of Economic Prosperity, Town Hall, High Street, Gosport PO12 1EB ☎ 023 9254 5231 🖷 023 9254 5238 ✉ lynda.dine@gosport.gov.uk

Finance and Treasurer: Mr Julian Bowcher, Borough Treasurer, Town Hall, High Street, Gosport PO12 1EB ☎ 023 9254 5301 🖷 023 9254 5341 ✉ julian.bowcher@gosport.gov.uk

Grounds Maintenance: Ms Caroline Smith, Landscape Management Officer, Town Hall, High Street, Gosport PO12 1EB ☎ 023 9258 4566 🖷 023 9258 8053 ✉ caroline.smith@gosport.gov.uk

Health and Safety: Mr Keith Perkins, Health & Safety Officer, Town Hall, High Street, Gosport PO12 1EB ☎ 023 9254 5547 🖷 023 9254 5360 ✉ keith.perkins@gosport.gov.uk

Highways: Mr Andy Peryer, Highways Manager, Hampshire County Council, Town Hall, Gosport PO12 1EB ☎ 023 9254 5417 🖷 023 9254 5436 ✉ andrew.peryer@hants.gov.uk

Housing Maintenance: Mr Charles Harman, Head of Operational Services, Town Hall, High Street, Gosport PO12 1EB ☎ 023 9254 5287 🖷 023 9254 5285 ✉ charles.harman@gosport.gov.uk

Legal: Ms Linda Edwards, Deputy Chief Executive & Borough Solicitor, Town Hall, High Street, Gosport PO12 1EB ☎ 023 9254 5401 🖷 023 9254 5587 ✉ linda.edwards@gosport.gov.uk

Licensing: Mr Ian Rickman, Head of Environmental Health, Town Hall, High Street, Gosport PO12 1EB ☎ 023 9258 5517 🖷 023 9254 5360 ✉ irickman@fareham.gov.uk

Member Services: Mr Geoff Rawling, Head of Democratic Services, Town Hall, High Street, Gosport PO12 1EB ☎ 023 9254 5215 🖷 023 9254 5587 ✉ geoff.rawling@gosport.gov.uk

Parking: Mr Graeme Mudge, Team Leader - Enforcement Officer, Town Hall, High Street, Gosport PO12 1EB ☎ 023 9254 5569 🖷 023 9258 8053 ✉ graeme.mudge@gosport.gov.uk

Personnel / HR: Mrs Kathy Inch, Head of Personnel, Town Hall, High Street, Gosport PO12 1EB ☎ 023 9251 5524 🖷 023 9254 5253 ✉ kathy.inch@gosport.gov.uk

Planning: Ms Linda Edwards, Deputy Chief Executive & Borough Solicitor, Town Hall, High Street, Gosport PO12 1EB ☎ 023 9254 5401 🖷 023 9254 5587 ✉ linda.edwards@gosport.gov.uk

Procurement: Mrs Maree Hall, Senior Procurement Officer, Town Hall, High Street, Gosport PO12 1EB ☎ 023 9254 5379 🖷 023 9254 5253 ✉ maree.hall@gosport.gov.uk

Recycling & Waste Minimisation: Mrs Angela Benneworth, Principal Contracts Officer, Town Hall, High Street, Gosport PO12 1EB ☎ 023 9254 8053 🖷 023 9254 5395 ✉ angela.benneworth@gosport.gov.uk

Regeneration: Mrs Lynda Dine, Head of Economic Prosperity, Town Hall, High Street, Gosport PO12 1EB ☎ 023 9254 5231 🖷 023 9254 5238 ✉ lynda.dine@gosport.gov.uk

Road Safety: Mr David Duckett, Head of Traffic Management, Town Hall, High Street, Gosport PO12 1EB ☎ 023 9254 5424 🖷 023 9254 5588 ✉ david.duckett@gosport.gov.uk

Staff Training: Mrs Kathy Inch, Head of Personnel, Town Hall, High Street, Gosport PO12 1EB ☎ 023 9251 5524 🖷 023 9254 5253 ✉ kathy.inch@gosport.gov.uk

Street Scene: Mr Stevyn Ricketts, Head of Streetscene, Town Hall, High Street, Gosport PO12 1EB ☎ 023 9254 5282 🖷 023 9258 8053 ✉ stevyn.ricketts@gosport.gov.uk

Sustainable Communities: Mrs Julie Petty, Head of Corporate Policy & Performance, Town Hall, High Street, Gosport PO12 1EB ☎ 023 9254 5381 🖷 023 9254 5238 ✉ julie.petty@gosport.gov.uk

Tourism: Mr David Martin, Leisure & Corporate Services Manager, Town Hall, High Street, Gosport PO12 1EB ☎ 023 9254 5512 🖷 023 9254 5724 ✉ david.martin@gosport.gov.uk

Traffic Management: Mr David Duckett, Head of Traffic Management, Town Hall, High Street, Gosport PO12 1EB ☎ 023 9254 5424 🖷 023 9254 5588 ✉ david.duckett@gosport.gov.uk

Transport: Mr David Duckett, Head of Traffic Management, Town Hall, High Street, Gosport PO12 1EB ☎ 023 9254 5424 🖷 023 9254 5588 ✉ david.duckett@gosport.gov.uk

Transport Planner: Mr David Duckett, Head of Traffic Management, Town Hall, High Street, Gosport PO12 1EB ☎ 023 9254 5424 🖷 023 9254 5588 ✉ david.duckett@gosport.gov.uk

Waste Collection and Disposal: Mr Stevyn Ricketts, Head of Streetscene, Town Hall, High Street, Gosport PO12 1EB ☎ 023 9254 5282 🖷 023 9258 8053 ✉ stevyn.ricketts@gosport.gov.uk

MEMBERS OF THE COUNCIL (34)

***Mayor:* Dickson**, Richard (CON - Christchurch)
richard.dickson@gosport.gov.uk

***Deputy Mayor:* Beavis**, John (CON - Lee West)
john.beavis@gosport.gov.uk

***Leader of the Council:* Hook**, Mark (CON - Alverstoke)
mark.hook@gosport.gov.uk

***Deputy Leader of the Council:* Burgess**, Graham (CON - Lee East)
graham.burgess@gosport.gov.uk

***Group Leader:* Chegwyn**, Peter (LD - Leesland)
peter.chegwyn@gosport.gov.uk

***Group Leader:* Wright**, Dennis (LAB - Bridgemary North)
dennis.wright@gosport.gov.uk

Allen, Roger (CON - Hardway)
roger.allen@gosport.gov.uk

Ballard, Susan (LD - Elson)
susan.ballard@gosport.gov.uk

Carter, Christopher (CON - Bridgemary South)
chrisk.carter@gosport.gov.uk

Carter, Chris (CON - Lee West)
chris.carter@gosport.gov.uk

Cully, June (LAB - Town)
june.cully@gosport.gov.uk

Diffey, Maria (LD - Leesland)
maria.diffey@gosport.gov.uk

Edgar, Peter (CON - Alverstoke)
peter.edgar@gosport.gov.uk

Farr, Keith (LAB - Forton)
keith.farr@gosport.gov.uk

Forder, Robert (O - Anglesey)
robert.forder@gosport.gov.uk

Foster-Reed, Clive (LD - Forton)
clive.foster-reed@gosport.gov.uk

Geddes, Michael (CON - Bridgemary South)
michael.geddes@gosport.gov.uk

Gill, Keith (CON - Privett)
keith.gill@gosport.gov.uk

Hazel, Craig (CON - Elson)
craig.hazel@gosport.gov.uk

Henshaw, Justin (CON - Brockhurst)
justin.henshaw@gosport.gov.uk

Hook, Lynn (CON - Peel Common)
lynn.hook@gosport.gov.uk

Hylands, Robert (LD - Brockhurst)
robert.hylands@gosport.gov.uk
Jacobs, Colin (CON - Privett)
colin.jacobs@gosport.gov.uk
Jessop, Tony (CON - Grange)
tony.jessop@gosport.gov.uk
Kimber, Derek (CON - Lee East)
derek.kimber@gosport.gov.uk
Lane, Michael (CON - Rowner and Holbrook)
michael.lane@gosport.gov.uk
Langdon, Peter (CON - Hardway)
peter.langdon@gosport.gov.uk
Morgan, Margaret (CON - Grange)
margaret.morgan@gosport.gov.uk
Murphy, Marcus (CON - Rowner and Holbrook)
marcus.murphy@gosport.gov.uk
Philpott, Stephen (CON - Peel Common)
stephen.philpott@gosport.gov.uk
Roynane, Wayne (CON - Christchurch)
wayne.roynane@gosport.gov.uk
Scard, Alan (CON - Anglesey)
alan.scard@gosport.gov.uk
Searle, Diane (LAB - Town)
diane.searle@gosport.gov.uk
Wright, Jill (LAB - Bridgemary North)
jill.wright@gosport.gov.uk

POLITICAL COMPOSITION
CON: 23, LAB: 5, LD: 5, O: 1

COMMITTEE CHAIRS
Community & Environment: Mr Graham Burgess
Economic Development: Mr Michael Lane
Licensing: Mr John Beavis
Overview & Scrutiny: Mr Robert Forder
Policy & Organisation: Mr Mark Hook
Regulatory: Mr Wayne Roynane

GRAVESHAM D

Gravesham Borough Council, Civic Centre, Windmill Street, Gravesend DA12 1AU ☎ 01474 564422 🖷 01474 337453
✉ forename.surname@gravesham.gov.uk
💻 www.gravesham.gov.uk

FACTS & FIGURES
Police Authority: Kent Police Authority
Health Authority: South East Coast Strategic Health Authority
Learning and Skills Council: South East
Parliamentary Constituencies: Gravesham
EU Constituencies: South East
Election Frequency: Elections are of whole council
Twinning: Cambrai (France); Neumunster (Germany); Meopham: Valkenisse (Netherlands); Virginia (USA)

PRINCIPAL OFFICERS
Chief Executive: Mr David Hughes, Chief Executive, Civic Centre, Windmill Street, Gravesend DA12 1AU ☎ 01474 337380 🖷 01474 351982 ✉ david.hughes@gravesham.gov.uk

Architect, Building / Property Services: Mr Simon Hookway, Service Manager (Economic Development), Civic Centre, Windmill Street, Gravesend DA12 1BQ ☎ 01474 337238 🖷 01474 337577 ✉ simon.hookway@gravesham.gov.uk

Best Value: Ms Michelle Parfitt, Performance & Policy Manager, Civic Centre, Windmill Street, Gravesend DA12 1AU ☎ 01474 337201 ✉ michelle.parfitt@gravesham.gov.uk

PR / Communications: Mrs Melanie Norris, Director (Communities), Civic Centre, Windmill Street, Gravesend DA12 1AU ☎ 01474 337324 🖷 01474 337944 ✉ melanie.norris@gravesham.gov.uk

Community Safety: Mrs Sarah Kilkie, Assistant Director (Communities), Civic Centre, Windmill Street, Gravesend DA12 1BQ ☎ 01474 337235 🖷 01474 337577 ✉ sarah.kilkie@gravesham.gov.uk

Computer Management: Mr Darren Everden, Service Manager (IT Services), Civic Centre, Windmill Street, Gravesend DA12 1AU ☎ 01474 337240 🖷 01474 334518 ✉ darren.everden@gravesham.gov.uk

Customer Service: Ms Anita Tysoe, Services Manager (Customer & Theatre Services), Civic Centre, Windmill Street, Gravesend DA12 1AU ☎ 01474 337360 ✉ anita.tysoe@gravesham.gov.uk

Direct Labour: Mr Nick Brown, Director (Finance & Environment), Brookvale, Springhead Road, Northfleet DA11 8HW ☎ 01474 337229 🖷 01474 337597 ✉ nick.brown@gravesham.gov.uk

Economic Development: Mr Simon Hookway, Service Manager (Economic Development), Civic Centre, Windmill Street, Gravesend DA12 1BQ ☎ 01474 337238 🖷 01474 337577 ✉ simon.hookway@gravesham.gov.uk

E-Government: Mr Darren Everden, Service Manager (IT Services), Civic Centre, Windmill Street, Gravesend DA12 1AU ☎ 01474 337240 🖷 01474 334518 ✉ darren.everden@gravesham.gov.uk

Electoral Registration: Mrs Sue Hill, Committee & Elections Manager, Civic Centre, Windmill Street, Gravesend DA12 1AU ☎ 01474 337247 🖷 01474 337947 ✉ sue.hill@gravesham.gov.uk

Emergency Planning: Mr Nick Brown, Director (Finance & Environment), Brookvale, Springhead Road, Northfleet DA11 8HW ☎ 01474 337229 🖷 01474 337597 ✉ nick.brown@gravesham.gov.uk

Environmental / Technical Services: Mrs Sarah Kilkie, Assistant Director (Communities), Civic Centre, Windmill Street, Gravesend DA12 1BQ ☎ 01474 337235 🖷 01474 337577 ✉ sarah.kilkie@gravesham.gov.uk

Environmental Health: Mrs Sarah Kilkie, Assistant Director (Communities), Civic Centre, Windmill Street, Gravesend DA12 1BQ ☎ 01474 337235 🖷 01474 337577 ✉ sarah.kilkie@gravesham.gov.uk

Estates, Property & Valuation: Mr Simon Hookway, Service Manager (Economic Development), Civic Centre, Windmill Street,

Gravesend DA12 1BQ ☎ 01474 337238 🖷 01474 337577 simon.hookway@gravesham.gov.uk

European Liaison: Mr Kevin Burbidge, Director (Housing & Regeneration), Civic Centre, Windmill Street, Gravesend DA12 1BQ ☎ 01474 337585 🖷 01474 337531 kevin.burbidge@gravesham.gov.uk

Events Manager: Mr Brian Tourle, Arts & Heritage Manager, Civic Centre, Windmill Street, Gravesend DA12 1AU ☎ 01474 337457 brian.tourle@gravesham.gov.uk

Facilities: Mrs Melanie Norris, Director (Communities), Civic Centre, Windmill Street, Gravesend DA12 1AU ☎ 01474 337324 🖷 01474 337944 melanie.norris@gravesham.gov.uk

Finance and Treasurer: Mr Nick Brown, Director (Finance & Environment), Civic Centre, Windmill Street, Gravesend DA12 1AU ☎ 01474 337229 🖷 01474 337597 nick.brown@gravesham.gov.uk

Fleet Management: Mr Nick Brown, Director (Finance & Environment), Brookvale, Springhead Road, Northfleet DA11 8HW ☎ 01474 337229 🖷 01474 337597 nick.brown@gravesham.gov.uk

Grounds Maintenance: Mr Nick Brown, Director (Finance & Environment), Brookvale, Springhead Road, Northfleet DA11 8HW ☎ 01474 337229 🖷 01474 337597 nick.brown@gravesham.gov.uk

Health and Safety: Mrs Sarah Kilkie, Assistant Director (Communities), Civic Centre, Windmill Street, Gravesend DA12 1BQ ☎ 01474 337235 🖷 01474 337577 sarah.kilkie@gravesham.gov.uk

Highways: Mr Kevin Burbidge, Director (Housing & Regeneration), Civic Centre, Windmill Street, Gravesend DA12 1BQ ☎ 01474 337585 🖷 01474 337531 kevin.burbidge@gravesham.gov.uk

Housing: Mr Wale Adetoro, Assistant Director (Housing), Civic Centre, Windmill Street, Gravesend DA12 1AU ☎ 01474 337816 🖷 01474 337453 wale.adetoro@gravesham.gov.uk

Housing Maintenance: Mr Wale Adetoro, Assistant Director (Housing), Civic Centre, Windmill Street, Gravesend DA12 1AU ☎ 01474 337816 🖷 01474 337453 wale.adetoro@gravesham.gov.uk

Legal: Mr Mike Hayley, Assistant Director (Governance & Law), Civic Centre, Windmill Street, Gravesend DA12 1AU ☎ 01474 337256 mike.hayley@gravesham.gov.uk

Leisure and Cultural Services: Mrs Melanie Norris, Director (Communities), Civic Centre, Windmill Street, Gravesend DA12 1AU ☎ 01474 337323 🖷 01474 337577 melanie.norris@gravesham.gov.uk

Licensing: Mrs Sarah Kilkie, Assistant Director (Communities), Civic Centre, Windmill Street, Gravesend DA12 1BQ ☎ 01474 337235 🖷 01474 337577 sarah.kilkie@gravesham.gov.uk

Member Services: Mrs Sue Hill, Committee & Elections Manager, Civic Centre, Windmill Street, Gravesend DA12 1AU ☎ 01474 337247 🖷 01474 337947 sue.hill@gravesham.gov.uk

Parking: Mr Paul Gibbons, Service Manager (Parking & Amenities), Civic Centre, Windmill Street, Gravesend DA12 1AU ☎ 01474 337820 paul.gibbons@gravesham.gov.uk

Partnerships: Mrs Melanie Norris, Director (Communities), Civic Centre, Windmill Street, Gravesend DA12 1AU ☎ 01474 337324 🖷 01474 337944 melanie.norris@gravesham.gov.uk

Personnel / HR: Mrs Melanie Norris, Director (Communities), Civic Centre, Windmill Street, Gravesend DA12 1AU ☎ 01474 337324 🖷 01474 337944 melanie.norris@gravesham.gov.uk

Planning: Mr Kevin Burbidge, Director (Housing & Regeneration), Civic Centre, Windmill Street, Gravesend DA12 1BQ ☎ 01474 337585 🖷 01474 337531 kevin.burbidge@gravesham.gov.uk

Procurement: Mr David Hollands, Procurement Manager, Civic Centre, Windmill Street, Gravesend DA12 1AU ☎ 01474 337446 david.hollands@gravesham.gov.uk

Recycling & Waste Minimisation: Mr Nick Brown, Director (Finance & Environment), Brookvale, Springhead Road, Northfleet DA11 8HW ☎ 01474 337229 🖷 01474 337597 nick.brown@gravesham.gov.uk

Regeneration: Mr Kevin Burbidge, Director (Housing & Regeneration), Civic Centre, Windmill Street, Gravesend DA12 1BQ ☎ 01474 337585 🖷 01474 337531 kevin.burbidge@gravesham.gov.uk

Staff Training: Mrs Melanie Norris, Director (Communities), Civic Centre, Windmill Street, Gravesend DA12 1AU ☎ 01474 337324 🖷 01474 337944 melanie.norris@gravesham.gov.uk

Sustainable Communities: Mr David Hughes, Chief Executive, Civic Centre, Windmill Street, Gravesend DA12 1AU ☎ 01474 337380 🖷 01474 351982 david.hughes@gravesham.gov.uk

Sustainable Development: Mrs Sarah Kilkie, Assistant Director (Communities), Civic Centre, Windmill Street, Gravesend DA12 1BQ ☎ 01474 337235 🖷 01474 337577 sarah.kilkie@gravesham.gov.uk

Tourism: Mr Simon Hookway, Service Manager (Economic Development), Civic Centre, Windmill Street, Gravesend DA12 1BQ ☎ 01474 337238 🖷 01474 337577 simon.hookway@gravesham.gov.uk

Town Centre: Mr Simon Hookway, Service Manager (Economic Development), Civic Centre, Windmill Street, Gravesend DA12 1BQ ☎ 01474 337238 🖷 01474 337577 simon.hookway@gravesham.gov.uk

Traffic Management: Mr Rob Bright, Senior Engineer, Civic Centre, Windmill Street, Gravesend DA12 1AU ☎ 01474 337580 🖷 01474 337546 rob.bright@gravesham.gov.uk

Transport Planner: Mr Tony Chadwick, Principal Planning Officer, Civic Centre, Windmill Street, Gravesend DA12 1AU ☎ 01474 337404 ✉ tony.chadwick@gravesham.gov.uk

Waste Collection and Disposal: Mr Nick Brown, Director (Finance & Environment), Brookvale, Springhead Road, Northfleet DA11 8HW ☎ 01474 337229 🖷 01474 337597 ✉ nick.brown@gravesham.gov.uk

Waste Management: Mr Nick Brown, Director (Finance & Environment), Brookvale, Springhead Road, Northfleet DA11 8HW ☎ 01474 337229 🖷 01474 337597 ✉ nick.brown@gravesham.gov.uk

MEMBERS OF THE COUNCIL (44)

***Mayor:* Milner**, Lyn (LAB - Riverside)
lyn.milner@gravesham.gov.uk
***Deputy Mayor:* Sales**, Derk (LAB - Central)
derek.sales@gravesham.gov.uk
***Leader of the Council:* Burden**, John (LAB - Northfleet South)
john.burden@gravesham.gov.uk
***Deputy Leader of the Council:* Croxton**, Lee (LAB - Riverside)
lee.croxton@gravesham.gov.uk
Ashenden, Valerie (LAB - Westcourt)
valerie.ashenden@gravesham.gov.uk
Averibou, Jean (LAB - Singlewell)
jean.averibou@gravesham.gov.uk
Boycott, Lesley (CON - Meopham South and Vigo)
lesley.boycott@gravesham.gov.uk
Bungar, Gurdip Ram (LAB - Central)
gurdip.bungar@gravesham.gov.uk
Caller, John (LAB - Westcourt)
john.caller@gravesham.gov.uk
Caller, Colin (LAB - Westcourt)
colin.caller@gravesham.gov.uk
Compton, Senja (CON - Whitehill)
senja.compton@gravesham.gov.uk
Craske, Harold (LAB - Higham)
harold.craske@gravesham.gov.uk
Cribbon, Jane (LAB - Pelham)
jane.cribbon@gravesham.gov.uk
Cubitt, John (CON - Meopham North)
john.cubitt@gravesham.gov.uk
Dennis, Colin (LAB - Painters Ash)
colin.dennis@gravesham.gov.uk
Dhesi, Tanmanjeet Singh (LAB - Northfleet North)
tanmanjeet.dhesi@gravesham.gov.uk
Francis, Brian (LAB - Singlewell)
brian.francis@gravesham.gov.uk
Goatley, Greta (CON - Central)
greta.goatley@gravesham.gov.uk
Halpin, Rob (LAB - Singlewell)
robert.halpin@gravesham.gov.uk
Handley, Glen (CON - Whitehill)
glen.handley@gravesham.gov.uk
Hills, Leslie (CON - Chalk)
leslie.hills@gravesham.gov.uk
Howes, Susan (LAB - Coldharbour)
susan.howes@gravesham.gov.uk
Howes, Les (LAB - Painters Ash)
les.howes@gravesham.gov.uk
Hurley, David (CON - Riverview)
david.hurley@gravesham.gov.uk
Lambert, William (CON - Riverview)
william.lambert@gravesham.gov.uk
Langdale, Sara (CON - Woodlands)
sara.langdale@gravesham.gov.uk
Leadley, Rosemary (LAB - Coldharbour)
rosemary.leadley@gravesham.gov.uk
Loughlin, John (LAB - Northfleet South)
john.loughlin@gravesham.gov.uk
Moore, Alex (CON - Shorne, Cobham and Luddesdown)
alex.moore@gravesham.gov.uk
Pearton, Leslie (CON - Higham)
leslie.pearton@graveshem.gov.uk
Pritchard, Anthony (CON - Woodlands)
anthony.pritchard@gravesham.gov.uk
Rayner, Peter (LAB - Northfleet North)
peter.rayner@gravesham.gov.uk
Sangha, Brian (LAB - Pelham)
brian.sangha@gravesham.gov.uk
Shelbrooke, Derek (CON - Meopham South and Vigo)
derek.shelbrooke@gravesham.gov.uk
Shelton, Caroline (LAB - Painters Ash)
caroline.shelton@gravesham.gov.uk
Singh, Makhan (LAB - Pelham)
makhan.singh@gravesham.gov.uk
Singh-Thandi, Narinderjit (LAB - Northfleet South)
narinderjit.singh.thandi@gravesham.gov.uk
Smith, Richard (LAB - Riverside)
richard.smith@gravesham.gov.uk
Snelling, Michael (CON - Meopham North)
michael.snelling@gravesham.gov.uk
Sweetland, Brian (CON - Istead Rise)
bryan.sweetland@gravesham.gov.uk
Theobald, Robin (CON - Shorne, Cobham and Luddesdown)
robin.theobald@gravesham.gov.uk
Turner, David (CON - Istead Rise)
david.turner@gravesham.gov.uk
Webb, Andrea (LAB - Northfleet North)
andrea.webb@gravesham.gov.uk
Wenban, Michael (CON - Woodlands)
michael.wenban@gravesham.gov.uk

POLITICAL COMPOSITION

LAB: 26, CON: 18

CABINET

Leader: Mr John Burden
Deputy/Planning Delivery: Mr Lee Croxton
Business and Partnerships: Mr Tanmanjeet Singh Dhesi
Community and The Environment: Ms Andrea Webb
Crime & Disorder: Mr Brian Sangha
Public and Private Section Housing: Ms Susan Howes

COMMITTEE CHAIRS

Finance & Audit: Mr Colin Caller
Licensing: Mr John Loughlin
Overview Scrutiny: Mr Michael Snelling
Regulatory Board: Ms Jane Cribbon

GREAT YARMOUTH D

Great Yarmouth Borough Council, Town Hall, Hall Plain, Great Yarmouth NR30 2QF ☎ 01493 856100 🖷 01493 846332
✉ gy@great-yarmouth.gov.uk
🖳 www.great-yarmouth.gov.uk

FACTS & FIGURES

Police Authority: Norfolk Police Authority
Health Authority: East of England Strategic Health Authority
Learning and Skills Council: Eastern
Parliamentary Constituencies: Great Yarmouth
EU Constituencies: Eastern
Election Frequency: Elections are by thirds
Twinning: Rambouillet (France)

PRINCIPAL OFFICERS

Deputy Chief Executive: Ms Jane Ratcliffe, Deputy Managing Director, Town Hall, Hall Plain, Great Yarmouth NR30 2QF ☎ 01493 846210 🖷 01496 846539 ✉ j.ratcliffe@great-yarmouth.gov.uk

Senior Management: Mrs Jen Beck, Head - Wellbeing Services, Trefalgar House, Hall Plain, Great Yarmouth NR30 2QF ☎ 01493 846418 ✉ jeb@great-yarmouth.gov.uk

Senior Management: Mr Sebastian Duncan, Head - Resources & Governance, Trafalgar House, Hall Plain, Great Yarmouth NR30 2QG ☎ 01493 856100 🖷 01493 846539 ✉ sgd@great-yarmouth.gov.uk

Senior Management: Mr Robert Read, Head - Housing Services, Greyfriars House, Greyfriars Way, Great Yarmouth NR30 2QE ☎ 01493 846278 ✉ rr@great-yarmouth.gov.uk

Senior Management: Mr Peter Warner, Head of Planning & Business Services, Maltings House, Malthouse Lane, Gorleston, Great Yarmouth NR31 0GY ☎ 01493 856104 ✉ pcw@great-yarmouth.gov.uk

Building Control: Mr Peter Warner, Head of Planning & Business Services, Trafalgar House, Hall Plain, Great Yarmouth NR30 2QG ☎ 01493 856104 ✉ pcw@great-yarmouth.gov.uk

PR / Communications: Mrs Karla Symonds, Service Manager - Communications, Town Hall, Hall Plain, Great Yarmouth NR30 2QF ☎ 01493 846512 🖷 01493 846513 ✉ krs@great-yarmouth.gov.uk

Computer Management: Mr Geoff Jones, Information Manager, Trafalgar House, Hall Plain, Great Yarmouth NR30 2QG ☎ 01493 846255 ✉ geoff@great-yarmouth.gov.uk

Customer Service: Mrs Jen Beck, Heaqd - Wellbeing Services, Trefalgar House, Hall Plain, Great Yarmouth NR30 2QF ☎ 01493 846418 ✉ jeb@great-yarmouth.gov.uk

Customer Service: Mrs Beverley Houghton, ITSS Services, Town Hall, Hall Plain, Great Yarmouth NR30 2QF ☎ 01493 846293 ✉ bev@great-yarmouth.gov.uk

Direct Labour: Mr Graham Jermyn, Director, GYB Services Ltd, 101 Churchill Road, Great Yarmouth NR30 4JJ ☎ 01493 742 187

E-Government: Ms Jane Ratcliffe, Deputy Managing Director, Town Hall, Hall Plain, Great Yarmouth NR30 2QF ☎ 01493 846210 🖷 01496 846539 ✉ j.ratcliffe@great-yarmouth.gov.uk

Electoral Registration: Mrs Linda Mockford, Licensing & Elections, Town Hall, Hall Plain, Great Yarmouth NR30 2QF ☎ 01493 846100 🖷 01493 646350

Emergency Planning: Ms Jane Ratcliffe, Deputy Managing Director, Town Hall, Hall Plain, Great Yarmouth NR30 2QF ☎ 01493 846210 🖷 01496 846539 ✉ j.ratcliffe@great-yarmouth.gov.uk

Environmental Health: Ms Kate Watts, Environmental Health Manager, Trafalgar House, Hall Plain, Great Yarmouth NR30 2QG ☎ 01493 856547 🖷 01493 846252 ✉ kaw@great-yarmouth.gov.uk

Estates, Property & Valuation: Mr Robin Neve, Service Manager, Trafalgar House, Hall Plain, Great Yarmouth NR30 2QG ☎ 01493 846399 🖷 01493 846405

Finance and Treasurer: Ms Jane Ratcliffe, Deputy Managing Director, Town Hall, Hall Plain, Great Yarmouth NR30 2QF ☎ 01493 846210 🖷 01496 846539 ✉ j.ratcliffe@great-yarmouth.gov.uk

Housing: Mr Robert Read, Head - Housing Services, Greyfriars House, Greyfriars Way, Great Yarmouth NR30 2QE ☎ 01493 846278 ✉ rr@great-yarmouth.gov.uk

Housing Maintenance: Mr Robert Read, Head - Housing Services, Greyfriars House, Greyfriars Way, Great Yarmouth NR30 2QE ☎ 01493 846278 ✉ rr@great-yarmouth.gov.uk

Licensing: Mrs Linda Mockford, Licensing & Elections, Town Hall, Hall Plain, Great Yarmouth NR30 2QF ☎ 01493 846100 🖷 01493 646350

Lighting: Mr Graham Jermyn, Director, GYB Services Ltd, 101 Churchill Road, Great Yarmouth NR30 4JJ ☎ 01493 742 187

Member Services: Mr Robin Hodds, Member Services Manager, Town Hall, Hall Plain, Great Yarmouth NR30 2QF ☎ 01493 856100 🖷 01493 846332 ✉ rh@great-yarmouth.gov.uk

Parking: Mr Andy Dyson, Service Manager, Town Hall, Hall Plain, Great Yarmouth NR30 2QF ☎ 01493 846399

Personnel / HR: Mr Barry Walton, Service Manager - Human Resources, Town Hall, Hall Plain, Great Yarmouth NR30 2QF ☎ 01493 846260 ✉ bjw@great-yarmouth.gov.uk

Planning: Mr Peter Warner, Head of Planning & Business Services, Town Hall, Hall Plain, Great Yarmouth NR30 2QF ☎ 01493 856104 ✉ pcw@great-yarmouth.gov.uk

Staff Training: Mr Barry Walton, Service Manager - Human Resources, Town Hall, Hall Plain, Great Yarmouth NR30 2QF ☎ 01493 846260 ✉ bjw@great-yarmouth.gov.uk

Street Scene: Mr Jonathan Newman, Town Centre Manager, Unit 5, Wilkinsons Yard, Marketgates, Great Yarmouth NR30 2AX ☎ 01493 745828 🖷 01493 335315

Tourism: Mr Alan Carr, Service Manager - Tourism, Town Hall, Hall Plain, Great Yarmouth NR30 2QF ☎ 01493 846345 🖷 01493

846221 ✉ aac@great-yarmouth.gov.uk

Town Centre: Mr Jonathan Newman, Town Centre Manager, Unit 5, Wilkinsons Yard, Marketgates, Great Yarmouth NR30 2AX ☎ 01493 745828 🖷 01493 335315

Transport Planner: Mr Jonathan Newman, Town Centre Manager, Unit 5, Wilkinsons Yard, Marketgates, Great Yarmouth NR30 2AX ☎ 01493 745828 🖷 01493 335315

Waste Collection and Disposal: Mr Graham Jermyn, Director, GYB Services Ltd, 101 Churchill Road, Great Yarmouth NR30 4JJ ☎ 01493 742 187

MEMBERS OF THE COUNCIL (39)

***Mayor:* Walker**, Colleen (LAB - Claydon)
colleen.walker@norfolk.gov.uk
***Leader of the Council:* Wainwright**, Trevor (LAB - Magdalen)
cllr.trevor.wainwright@great-yarmouth.gov.uk
***Deputy Leader of the Council:* Walker**, Brian (LAB - Magdalen)
cllr.brian.walker@great-yarmouth.gov.uk
Blyth, Anthony (LAB - Claydon)
cllr.anthony.blyth@great-yarmouth.gov.uk
Burroughs, John (CON - Gorleston)
cllr.john.burroughs@great-yarmouth.gov.uk
Castle, Michael (LAB - Central and Northgate)
cllr.michael.castle@great-yarmouth.gov.uk
Coleman, Mary (CON - West Flegg)
cllr.mary.coleman@great-yarmouth.gov.uk
Coleman, Barry (CON - West Flegg)
cllr.barry.coleman@great-yarmouth.gov.uk
Collins, Bert (CON - Gorleston)
cllr.bert.collins@great-yarmouth.gov.uk
Cunniffe, Barry (CON - Caister North)
cllr.barry.cunniffe@great-yarmouth.gov.uk
Fairhead, Marlene (LAB - St Andrews)
cllr.marlene.fairhead@great-yarmouth.gov.uk
Field, Marie (LAB - Central and Northgate)
cllr.marie.field@great-yarmouth.gov.uk
Fox, Colin (LAB - Yarmouth North)
Hacon, Sue (CON - Bradwell South and Hopton)
cllr.sue.hacon@great-yarmouth.gov.uk
Hanton, Ron (CON - Caister South)
cllr.ron.hanton@great-yarmouth.gov.uk
Holmes, John (LAB - Southtown and Cobholm)
cllr.john.holmes@great-yarmouth.gov.uk
Jeal, Michael (LAB - Nelson)
cllr.michael.jeal@great-yarmouth.gov.uk
Jermany, George (CON - East Flegg)
cllr.george.jermany@great-yarmouth.gov.uk
Linden, Penny (LAB - Southtown and Cobholm)
cllr.penny.linden@great-yarmouth.gov.uk
Marseden, Charles (LAB - Yarmouth North)
cllr.charles.marsden@great-yarmouth.gov.uk
Peck, Robert (CON - Caister South)
cllr.bob.peck@great-yarmouth.gov.uk
Pettit, Valerie (LAB - Nelson)
cllr.vale.pettit@great-yarmouth.gov.uk
Plane, Martin (CON - Bradwell South and Hopton)
cllr.martin.plane@great-yarmouth.gov.uk
Plant, Graham (CON - Bradwell North)
cllr.graham.plant@great-yarmouth.gov.uk
Pratt, Emma (LAB - Magdalen)
Reynolds, Charles (CON - Ormesby)
cllr.charles.reynolds@great-yarmouth.gov.uk
Robinson-Payne, Kerry (LAB - Nelson)
cllr.kelly.payne@great-yarmouth.gov.uk
Shrimplin, Jim (CON - Ormesby)
cllr.jim.shrimplin@great-yarmouth.gov.uk
Smith, Anthony (CON - Caister North)
cllr.anthony.smith@great-yarmouth.gov.uk
Smith, Jamie (LAB - Bradwell North)
smithjamie@me.com
Stone, Barry (CON - Lothingland)
cllr.barry.stone@great-yarmouth.gov.uk
Sutton, Lee (LAB - Central and Northgate)
cllr.lee.sutton@great-yarmouth.gov.uk
Tate, James (CON - Bradwell North)
cllr.james.tate@great-yarmouth.gov.uk
Thompson, David (CON - Fleggburgh)
cllr.david.thompson@great-yarmouth.gov.uk
Thompson, Mark (CON - Lothingland)
cllr.mark.thompson@great-yarmouth.gov.uk
Wainwright, Hilary (LAB - Bradwell South and Hopton)
Weymouth, Shirley (CON - East Flegg)
cllr.shirley.weymouth@great-yarmouth.gov.uk
Williamson, Bernard (LAB - Claydon)
cllr.bernard.williamson@great-yarmouth.gov.uk
Wright, Barbara (LAB - St Andrews)
cllr.barbara.wright@great-yarmouth.gov.uk

POLITICAL COMPOSITION

LAB: 20, CON: 19

CABINET

Leader: Mr Trevor Wainwright
Deputy Leader / Resources: Mr Brian Walker
Communities: Mrs Penny Linden
Environment: Mrs Valerie Pettit
Tourism & Business Services: Mr Michael Jeal
Transformation & Regeneration: Mr Bernard Williamson

COMMITTEE CHAIRS

Appeals: Mr Anthony Smith
Audit & Risk: Mr Lee Sutton
Community Housing: Mr Robert Peck
Development Control: Mr Ron Hanton
Housing Appeals: Mrs Mary Coleman
Licensing: Mr George Jermany
Standards: Mr Lee Sutton

GREENWICH L

Greenwich London Borough Council, The Woolwich Centre, 35 Wellington Street, Woolwich, London SE18 6HQ ☎ 020 8854 8888 🖷 020 8921 5074 🖳 www.greenwich.gov.uk

FACTS & FIGURES

Police Authority: Metropolitan Police Authority
Health Authority: NHS London
Learning and Skills Council: London
Parliamentary Constituencies: Eltham, Erith and Thamesmead, Greenwich and Woolwich
EU Constituencies: London
Election Frequency: Elections are of whole council
Twinning: Easington (County Durham, UK); Maribor (Slovenia); Reinickendorf (Germany); Tema (Ghana)

PRINCIPAL OFFICERS

Chief Executive: Ms Mary Ney, Chief Executive, The Woolwich Centre, 35 Wellington Street, Woolwich, London SE18 6HQ ☎ 020 8921 5000 🖷 020 8921 5943 ✉ mary.ney@greenwich.gov.uk

Deputy Chief Executive: Mr Chris Perry, Deputy Chief Executive, The Woolwich Centre, 35 Wellington Street, Woolwich, London SE18 6HQ ☎ 020 8921 5240 ✉ chris.perry@greenwich.gov.uk

Assistant Chief Executive: Mr Harcourt Alleyne, Assistant Chief Executive - Policy, Inclusion & Performance, The Woolwich Centre, 35 Wellington Street, Woolwich, London SE18 6HQ ☎ 020 8921 5002 🖷 020 8921 5943 ✉ harcourt.alleyne@greenwich.gov.uk

Assistant Chief Executive: Ms Katrina Delaney, Assistant Chief Executive, The Woolwich Centre, 35 Wellington Street, Woolwich, London SE18 6HQ ☎ 020 8921 6101 🖷 020 8921 5252 ✉ katrina.delaney@greenwich.gov.uk

Architect, Building / Property Services: Mr Laurence Smith, Assistant Director - Property, The Woolwich Centre, 35 Wellington Street, Woolwich, London SE18 6HQ ☎ 020 8921 5425 🖷 020 8921 5282 ✉ laurence.smith@greenwich.gov.uk

Building Control: Mr Chris Stevens, Head - Building Control, The Woolwich Centre, 35 Wellington Street, Woolwich, London SE18 6HQ ☎ 020 8921 5414 🖷 020 8921 5544 ✉ chris.stevens@greenwich.gov.uk

Catering Services: Ms Sue Butterfill, Principal Manager - Community Services & Civic Catering, The Woolwich Centre, 35 Wellington Street, Woolwich, London SE18 6HQ ☎ 020 8921 ✉ sue.butterfill@greenwich.gov.uk

Catering Services: Mr Gurmel Singh-Kandola, Managing Director - GS Plus, The Woolwich Centre, 35 Wellington Street, Woolwich, London SE18 6HQ ☎ 020 8921 8147 🖷 020 8921 6484 ✉ gurmel.singh-kandola@greenwich.gov.uk

Children / Youth Services: Ms Jenny Kavanagh, IYSS Manager-Health & Integrated Support, The Woolwich Centre, 35 Wellington Street, Woolwich, London SE18 6HQ ☎ 020 8921 8249 ✉ jenny.kavanagh@greenwich.gov.uk

Civil Registration: Ms Julia Newton, Head - Community Services, The Woolwich Centre, 35 Wellington Street, Woolwich, London SE18 6HQ ☎ 020 8921 8332 🖷 020 8921 8322 ✉ julia.newton@greenwich.gov.uk

PR / Communications: Ms Katrina Delaney, Assistant Chief Executive, The Woolwich Centre, 35 Wellington Street, Woolwich, London SE18 6HQ ☎ 020 8921 6101 🖷 020 8921 5252 ✉ katrina.delaney@greenwich.gov.uk

Community Planning: Mr Steve Pallett, Assistant Director - Planning, The Woolwich Centre, 35 Wellington Street, Woolwich, London SE18 6HQ ☎ 020 8921 5229 ✉ steve.pallett@greenwich.gov.uk

Community Safety: Mr Matthew Norwell, Director - Community Safety & Environment, The Woolwich Centre, 35 Wellington Street, Woolwich, London SE18 6HQ ☎ 020 8921 8291 🖷 020 8921 8080 ✉ matthew.norwell@greenwich.gov.uk

Computer Management: Mr Kevin Corbett, Director - IT & eGov, The Woolwich Centre, 35 Wellington Street, Woolwich, London SE18 6HQ ☎ 020 8921 2076 ✉ kevin.corbett@greenwich.gov.uk

Contracts: Mr Ian Tasker, Head - Financial Operations, The Woolwich Centre, 35 Wellington Street, Woolwich, London SE18 6HQ ☎ 020 8921 6189 ✉ ian.tasker@greenwich.gov.uk

Corporate Services: Mr Harcourt Alleyne, Assistant Chief Executive - Policy, Inclusion & Performance, The Woolwich Centre, 35 Wellington Street, Woolwich, London SE18 6HQ ☎ 020 8921 5002 🖷 020 8921 5943 ✉ harcourt.alleyne@greenwich.gov.uk

Economic Development: Mr Trevor Dorling, Assistant Director - Employment & Skills, The Woolwich Centre, 35 Wellington Street, Woolwich, London SE18 6HQ ☎ 020 8921 6147 🖷 020 8921 6283 ✉ trevor.dorling@greenwich.gov.uk

Education: Ms Gillian Palmer, Director - Children's Services, The Woolwich Centre, 35 Wellington Street, Woolwich, London SE18 6HQ ☎ 020 8921 8230 🖷 020 8921 8097 ✉ gillian.palmer@greenwich.gov.uk

E-Government: Mr Kevin Corbett, Director - IT & eGov, The Woolwich Centre, 35 Wellington Street, Woolwich, London SE18 6HQ ☎ 020 8921 2076 ✉ kevin.corbett@greenwich.gov.uk

Electoral Registration: Mr Stephen O'Hare, Electoral Service Manager, The Woolwich Centre, 35 Wellington Street, Woolwich, London SE18 6HQ ☎ 020 8921 6130 🖷 020 8921 6338 ✉ stephen.ohare@greenwich.gov.uk

Emergency Planning: Ms Lynette Russell, Head - Emergency Planning & Resilience, The Woolwich Centre, 35 Wellington Street, Woolwich, London SE18 6HQ ☎ 020 8921 6258 🖷 020 8921 6267 ✉ lynette.russell@greenwich.gov.uk

Energy Management: Ms Pippa Hack, Strategic Development Manager, The Woolwich Centre, 35 Wellington Street, Woolwich, London SE18 6HQ ☎ 020 8921 5519 🖷 020 8921 5950 ✉ pippa.hack@greenwich.gov.uk

Estates, Property & Valuation: Mr Laurence Smith, Assistant Director - Property, The Woolwich Centre, 35 Wellington Street, Woolwich, London SE18 6HQ ☎ 020 8921 5425 🖷 020 8921 5282 ✉ laurence.smith@greenwich.gov.uk

European Liaison: Ms Anna Carver, European Programmes & Partnership Officer, The Woolwich Centre, 35 Wellington Street, Woolwich, London SE18 6HQ ☎ 020 8921 5426 ✉ anna.carver@greenwich.gov.uk

Events Manager: Mr Bob Hills, Principal Communications Officer, The Woolwich Centre, 35 Wellington Street, Woolwich, London SE18 6HQ ☎ 020 8921 5077 🖷 020 8921 5252 ✉ bob.hills@greenwich.gov.uk

Facilities: Mr Gurmel Singh-Kandola, Managing Director - GS Plus, The Woolwich Centre, 35 Wellington Street, Woolwich, London SE18 6HQ ☎ 020 8921 8147 🖷 020 8921 6484 ✉ gurmel.singh-kandola@greenwich.gov.uk

Finance and Treasurer: Mr Chris Perry, Deputy Chief Executive, The Woolwich Centre, 35 Wellington Street, Woolwich, London SE18 6HQ ☎ 020 8921 5240 🖷 020 8316 6094 ✉ chris.perry@greenwich.gov.uk

Finance and Treasurer: Ms Debbie Warren, Director - Finance, The Woolwich Centre, 35 Wellington Street, Woolwich, London SE18 6HQ ☎ 020 8921 5201 ✉ debbie.warren@greenwich.gov.uk

Fleet Management: Mr Gurmel Singh-Kandola, Managing Director - GS Plus, The Woolwich Centre, 35 Wellington Street, Woolwich, London SE18 6HQ ☎ 020 8921 8147 🖷 020 8921 6484 ✉ gurmel.singh-kandola@greenwich.gov.uk

Grounds Maintenance: Mr Ray Collingham, Senior Assistant Director - Community Safety & Environment, The Woolwich Centre, 4th Floor, 35 Wellington Street, London SE18 6HQ ☎ 020 8921 8699 ✉ ray.collingham@greenwich.gov.uk

Grounds Maintenance: Mr Gurmel Singh-Kandola, Managing Director - GS Plus, The Woolwich Centre, 35 Wellington Street, Woolwich, London SE18 6HQ ☎ 020 8921 8147 🖷 020 8921 6484 ✉ gurmel.singh-kandola@greenwich.gov.uk

Health and Safety: Mr Al Parry, Manager - Health, Safety & Wellbeing, The Woolwich Centre, 35 Wellington Street, Woolwich, London SE18 6HQ ☎ ; 020 8921 5196 🖷 020 8921 6267 ✉ al.parry@greenwich.gov.uk

Highways: Mr Mike Freestone, Assistant Director - Strategic Transportation, The Woolwich Centre, 35 Wellington Street, Woolwich, London SE18 6HQ ☎ 020 8921 5453 ✉ mike.freestone@greenwich.gov.uk

Housing Maintenance: Mr Tim Derrik, Project Manager - Technical Services, The Woolwich Centre, 35 Wellington Street, Woolwich, London SE18 6HQ ☎ 020 8921 4275 ✉ tim.derrik@greenwich.gov.uk

Local Area Agreement: Mr Graham Verge, Head- Policy, Partnerships & Performance, The Woolwich Centre, 35 Wellington Street, Woolwich, London SE18 6HQ ☎ 020 8921 5038 ✉ graham.verge@greenwich.gov.uk

Legal: Ms Eileen Edwards, Head - Policy, Parnerships & Performance, The Woolwich Centre, 35 Wellington Street, Woolwich, London SE18 6HQ ☎ 020 8921 5132 ✉ eileen.edwards@greenwich.gov.uk

Legal: Mr Russell Power, Head - Law & Governance, The Woolwich Centre, 35 Wellington Street, Woolwich, London SE18 6HQ ☎ 020 8921 5105 🖷 020 8921 5556 ✉ russell.power@greenwich.gov.uk

Licensing: Mr Des Campbell, Licensing Officer, The Woolwich Centre, 35 Wellington Street, Woolwich, London SE18 6HQ ☎ 020 8921 8137 🖷 020 8921 8380 ✉ des.campbell@greenwich.gov.uk

Member Services: Mr Harcourt Alleyne, Assistant Chief Executive - Policy, Inclusion & Performance, The Woolwich Centre, 35 Wellington Street, Woolwich, London SE18 6HQ ☎ 020 8921 5002 🖷 020 8921 5943 ✉ harcourt.alleyne@greenwich.gov.uk

Partnerships: Mr Harcourt Alleyne, Assistant Chief Executive - Policy, Inclusion & Performance, The Woolwich Centre, 35 Wellington Street, Woolwich, London SE18 6HQ ☎ 020 8921 5002 🖷 020 8921 5943 ✉ harcourt.alleyne@greenwich.gov.uk

Planning: Mr John Clark, Director - Planning, The Woolwich Centre, 35 Wellington Street, Woolwich, London SE18 6HQ ☎ 020 8854 8888 ✉ john.clark@greenwich.gov.uk

Planning: Mr John Comber, Director - Regeneration, Enterprise & Skills, The Woolwich Centre, 35 Wellington Street, Woolwich, London SE18 6HQ ☎ ; 020 8921 6426 🖷 020 8371 0806 ✉ john.comber@greenwich.gov.uk

Planning: Mr Steve Pallett, Assistant Director - Planning, The Woolwich Centre, 35 Wellington Street, Woolwich, London SE18 6HQ ☎ 020 8921 5229 ✉ steve.pallett@greenwich.gov.uk

Procurement: Mr Ian Tasker, Head - Financial Operations, The Woolwich Centre, 35 Wellington Street, Woolwich, London SE18 6HQ ☎ 020 8921 6189 ✉ ian.tasker@greenwich.gov.uk

Public Libraries: Ms Julia Newton, Head - Community Services, The Woolwich Centre, 35 Wellington Street, Woolwich, London SE18 6HQ ☎ 020 8921 8332 🖷 020 8921 8322 ✉ julia.newton@greenwich.gov.uk

Recycling & Waste Minimisation: Mr Peter Dalley, Waste Services Operations Manager, The Woolwich Centre, 35 Wellington Street, Woolwich, London SE18 6HQ ☎ 020 8921 4641 🖷 020 8921 4636 ✉ peter.dalley@greenwich.gov.uk

Regeneration: Mr John Comber, Director - Regeneration, Enterprise & Skills, The Woolwich Centre, 35 Wellington Street, Woolwich, London SE18 6HQ ☎ ; 020 8921 6426 🖷 020 8371 0806 ✉ john.comber@greenwich.gov.uk

Road Safety: Ms Khair-un-nisa Simmonds, Safety Education Manager, The Woolwich Centre, 35 Wellington Street, Woolwich, London SE18 6HQ ☎ 020 8921 8075 🖷 020 8921 8080 ✉ khairunnisa.simmonds@greenwich.gov.uk

Social Services: Mr John Nawrockyi, Director - Adults & Older People's Services, The Woolwich Centre, 35 Wellington Street, Woolwich, London SE18 6HQ ☎ 020 8921 3000 🖷 020 8921 3112 ✉ john.nawrockyi@greenwich.gov.uk

Social Services (Adult): Mr John Nawrockyi, Director - Adults & Older People's Services, The Woolwich Centre, 35 Wellington Street, Woolwich, London SE18 6HQ ☎ 020 8921 3000 🖷 020 8921 3112 ✉ john.nawrockyi@greenwich.gov.uk

Social Services (Children): Mr Andrew O'Sullivan, Senior Assistant Director Children's Safeguarding & Social Care, The

Woolwich Centre, 35 Wellington Street, Woolwich, London SE18 6HQ ☎ 020 8921 3102 🖷 020 8921 3112 ✉ andrew.osullivan@greenwich.gov.uk

Staff Training: Mr Kosi Banga, Learning & Development Officer, The Woolwich Centre, 35 Wellington Street, Woolwich, London SE18 6HQ ☎ 020 8921 5640 ✉ kosi.banga@greenwich.gov.uk

Sustainable Communities: Mr Mike Hows, Assistant Director - Planning, The Woolwich Centre, 35 Wellington Street, Woolwich, London SE18 6HQ ☎ 020 8921 5363 🖷 020 8317 0806 ✉ mike.hows@greenwich.gov.uk

Sustainable Development: Ms Pippa Hack, Strategic Development Manager, The Woolwich Centre, 35 Wellington Street, Woolwich, London SE18 6HQ ☎ 020 8921 5519 🖷 020 8921 5950 ✉ pippa.hack@greenwich.gov.uk

Town Centre: Ms Alison Harris, Principal Regeneration Manger for Eldham, The Woolwich Centre, 35 Wellington Street, Woolwich, London SE18 6HQ ☎ 020 8850 3479 ✉ alison.harris@greenwich.gov.uk

Traffic Management: Mr Mike Freestone, Assistant Director - Strategic Transportation, The Woolwich Centre, 35 Wellington Street, Woolwich, London SE18 6HQ ☎ 020 8921 5453 ✉ mike.freestone@greenwich.gov.uk

Transport: Mr Gurmel Singh-Kandola, Managing Director - GS Plus, The Woolwich Centre, 35 Wellington Street, Woolwich, London SE18 6HQ ☎ 020 8921 8147 🖷 020 8921 6484 ✉ gurmel.singh-kandola@greenwich.gov.uk

Transport Planner: Mr Mike Freestone, Assistant Director - Strategic Transportation, The Woolwich Centre, 35 Wellington Street, Woolwich, London SE18 6HQ ☎ 020 8921 5453 ✉ mike.freestone@greenwich.gov.uk

Waste Collection and Disposal: Mr Peter Dalley, Waste Services Operations Manager, The Woolwich Centre, 35 Wellington Street, Woolwich, London SE18 6HQ ☎ 020 8921 4641 🖷 020 8921 4636 ✉ peter.dalley@greenwich.gov.uk

Waste Management: Mr Peter Dalley, Waste Services Operations Manager, The Woolwich Centre, 35 Wellington Street, Woolwich, London SE18 6HQ ☎ 020 8921 4641 🖷 020 8921 4636 ✉ peter.dalley@greenwich.gov.uk

MEMBERS OF THE COUNCIL (51)

***Deputy Mayor:* Cornforth**, Angela (LAB - Plumstead)
angela.cornforth@greenwich.gov.uk

***Leader of the Council:* Roberts**, Chris (LAB - Glyndon)
chris.roberts@greenwich.gov.uk

***Deputy Leader of the Council:* Brooks**, Peter (LAB - Thamesmead Moorings)
peter.brooks@greenwich.gov.uk

Adams, Norman (LAB - Kidbrooke and Hornfair)
norman.adams@greenwich.gov.uk

Austen, Don (LAB - Glyndon)
don.austen@greenwich.gov.uk

Barwick, Barbara (LAB - Woolwich Riverside)
barbara.barwick@greenwich.gov.uk

Brighty, Geoffrey (CON - Blackheath Westcombe)
geoffrey.brighty@greenwich.gov.uk

Brinkhurst, Mandy (CON - Coldharbour and New Eltham)
mandy.brinkhurst@greenwich.gov.uk

Clare, Matt (CON - Eltham South)
matt.clare@greenwich.gov.uk

Dickinson, Neil (CON - Coldharbour and New Eltham)
neil.dickinson@greenwich.gov.uk

Drury, Spencer (CON - Eltham North)
spencer.drury@greenwich.gov.uk

Fahy, John (LAB - Woolwich Riverside)
john.fahy@greenwich.gov.uk

Fletcher, Nigel (CON - Eltham North)
nigel.fletcher@greenwich.gov.uk

Fletcher, Hayley (LAB - Kidbrooke and Hornfair)
hayley.fletcher@greenwich.gov.uk

Freeman, Bill (LAB - Eltham West)
bill.freeman@greenwich.gov.uk

Gillman, Janet (LAB - Charlton)
janet.gillman@greenwich.gov.uk

Gillman, Jim (LAB - Kidbrooke and Hornfair)
jim.gillman@greenwich.gov.uk

Glover, Eileen (CON - Eltham South)
eileen.glover@greenwich.gov.uk

Grant, Alex (LAB - Blackheath Westcombe)
alex.grant@greenwich.gov.uk

Grant, David (LAB - Greenwich West)
david.grant@greenwich.gov.uk

Hayes, Mick (LAB - Eltham West)
mick.hayes@greenwich.gov.uk

Hills, John (CON - Coldharbour and New Eltham)
john.hills@greenwich.gov.uk

Hyland, Denise (LAB - Abbey Wood)
denise.hyland@greenwich.gov.uk

Iqbal, Mohammed (LAB - Woolwich Riverside)
mohammed.iqbal@greenwich.gov.uk

James, Mark (LAB - Middle Park and Sutcliffe)
mark.james@greenwich.gov.uk

Jawaid, Sajid (LAB - Plumstead)
sajid.jawaid@greenwich.gov.uk

Jones, Beverley (LAB - Woolwich Common)
beverley.jones@greenwich.gov.uk

Kotz, Peter (LAB - Thamesmead Moorings)
peter.kotz@greenwich.gov.uk

MacCarthy, Allan (LAB - Charlton)
allan.maccarthy@greenwich.gov.uk

Mardner, Clive (LAB - Abbey Wood)
clive.mardner@greenwich.gov.uk

May, Christine (LAB - Middle Park and Sutcliffe)
christine.may@greenwich.gov.uk

Mills, Mary (LAB - Peninsula)
mary.mills@greenwich.gov.uk

Morris, Clare (LAB - Middle Park and Sutcliffe)
clare.morris@greenwich.gov.uk

Morrow, Matthew (LAB - Plumstead)
matthew.morrow@greenwich.gov.uk

Offord, Steve (LAB - Abbey Wood)
steve.offord@greenwich.gov.uk

O'Mara, Maureen (LAB - Greenwich West)
maureen.omara@greenwich.gov.uk

Parker, Gary (LAB - Charlton)
gary.parker@greenwich.gov.uk

Pennycook, Matthew (LAB - Greenwich West)
matthew.pennycook@greenwich.gov.uk

Poston, Dermot (CON - Eltham North)

dermot.poston@greenwich.gov.uk
Quibell, Dick (LAB - Peninsula)
dick.quibell@greenwich.gov.uk
Rabadia, Radhna (LAB - Glyndon)
radha.rabadia@greenwich.gov.uk
Sekhon, Jagir (LAB - Shooters Hill)
jagir.sekhon@greenwich.gov.uk
Sidhu, Rajwant (LAB - Woolwich Common)
rajwant.sidhu@greenwich.gov.uk
Singh, Harry (LAB - Woolwich Common)
harpinder.singh@greenwich.gov.uk
Smith, Jackie (LAB - Thamesmead Moorings)
jackie.smith@greenwich.gov.uk
Taylor, Barry (LAB - Shooters Hill)
barry.taylor@greenwich.gov.uk
Thomas, Adam (CON - Eltham South)
adam.thomas@greenwich.gov.uk
Thorpe, Danny (LAB - Shooters Hill)
danny.thorpe@greenwich.gov.uk
Walker, Ray (LAB - Eltham West)
ray.walker@greenwich.gov.uk
Williams, Miranda (LAB - Peninsula)
miranda.williams@greenwich.gov.uk
Wilson, Alex (CON - Blackheath Westcombe)
alex.wilson@greenwich.gov.uk

POLITICAL COMPOSITION
LAB: 40, CON: 11

CABINET
Leader: Mr Chris Roberts
Deputy Leader: Mr Peter Brooks
Children's Services: Ms Jackie Smith
Community Safety & Environment: Ms Maureen O'Mara
Cultural & Creative Industries: Mr Peter Kotz
Customer & Community Services: Mr Sajid Jawaid
Greener Greenwich: Mr Harry Singh
Health, Adults & Older People: Mr John Fahy
Housing: Mr Steve Offord
Regeneration, Enterprise & Skills: Ms Denise Hyland

COMMITTEE CHAIRS
Children & Young People (Scrutiny): Mr Barry Taylor
Finance & Public Services (Scrutiny): Mr Danny Thorpe
Healthier Communities & Older People (Scrutiny): Ms Janet Gillman
Highways: Mr Jim Gillman
Licensing: Ms Maureen O'Mara
Overview & Scrutiny: Mr Mick Hayes
Pension Fund Investment & Administration: Mr Don Austen
Planning Board: Mr Ray Walker
Safer & Stronger Communities (Scrutiny): Mr Clive Mardner
Social Inclusion (Scrutiny): Mr Allan MacCarthy
Sustainable Communities & Transport (Scrutiny): Ms Hayley Fletcher

GUILDFORD — D

Guildford Borough Council, Millmead House, Millmead, Guildford GU2 4BB ☎ 01483 505050 🖷 01483 444444
enquiries@guildford.gov.uk
www.guildford.gov.uk

FACTS & FIGURES
Police Authority: Surrey Police Authority
Health Authority: South East Coast Strategic Health Authority
Learning and Skills Council: South East
Parliamentary Constituencies: Guildford
EU Constituencies: South East
Election Frequency: Elections are of whole council
Twinning: Freiburg (Germany)

PRINCIPAL OFFICERS
Chief Executive: Mr David Hill, Chief Executive, Millmead House, Millmead, Guildford GU2 4BB ☎ 01483 505050
david.hill@guildford.gov.uk

Senior Management: Mr Jim Miles, Director, Millmead House, Millmead, Guildford GU2 4BB ☎ 01483 444701 🖷 01483 444717

Senior Management: Ms Sue Reekie, Head of Financial Services, Millmead House, Millmead, Guildford GU2 4BB ☎ 01483 444829 🖷 01483 444828

Access Officer / Social Services (Disability): Mrs Judith Coslett, Head of Human Resources, Millmead House, Millmead, Guildford GU2 4BB ☎ 01483 444010 🖷 01483 444018

Architect, Building / Property Services: Mr John Weedon, Head of Property, Millmead House, Millmead, Guildford GU2 4BB ☎ 01483 444994 🖷 01483 444581

Building Control: Ms Jacqui Barr, Building Control Manager, Millmead House, Millmead, Guildford GU2 4BB ☎ 01483 444680 🖷 01483 444511

Community Safety: Ms Marie Clarke, Safer Guildford Partnership Manager, Millmead House, Millmead, Guildford GU2 4BB ☎ 01483 444510 🖷 01483 444511

Community Safety: Mr John Martin, Head of Community Care Services, Millmead House, Millmead, Guildford GU2 4BB ☎ 01483 444350

Computer Management: Mr Steve Wragge-Morley, Head of Business Systems, Millmead House, Millmead, Guildford GU2 4BB ☎ 01483 444900 🖷 01483 444844

Direct Labour: Mr James Whiteman, Head of Operational Services, Cleansing Department, Woking Road Depot, Woking Road, Guildford GU1 1QE ☎ 01483 445030 🖷 01483 445039
james.whiteman@guildford.gov.uk

Economic Development: Mr Chris Mansfield, Head of Economic Development, Millmead House, Millmead, Guildford GU2 4BB ☎ 01483 444550

E-Government: Ms Sue Reekie, Head of Financial Services, Millmead House, Millmead, Guildford GU2 4BB ☎ 01483 444829 🖷 01483 444828

Electoral Registration: Ms Lynda Murlewski, Electoral Services Manager, Millmead House, Millmead, Guildford GU2 4BB ☎ 01483 444101 🖷 01483 302221

Emergency Planning: Mr Mark Reed, Strategic Director, Millmead House, Millmead, Guildford GU2 4BB ☎ 01483 444370

Energy Management: Mr Garry Bosworth, Principal Climate Change Officer, Millmead House, Millmead, Guildford GU2 4BB ☎ 01483 444515 ✉ garry.bosworth@guildford.gov.uk

Energy Management: Mr Kevin Handley, Facilities Manager, Millmead House, Millmead, Guildford GU2 5BB ☎ 01483 444447 📠 01483 302221 ✉ kevin.handley@guildford.gov.uk

Environmental Health: Mr Chris Woodhatch, Principal Environmental Health Officer, Millmead House, Millmead, Guildford GU2 4BB ☎ 01483 444370; 01483 444370 📠 01483 444546; 01483 444546

Estates, Property & Valuation: Mr John Weedon, Head of Property, Millmead House, Millmead, Guildford GU2 4BB ☎ 01483 444994 📠 01483 444581

Facilities: Mr Kevin Handley, Facilities Manager, Millmead House, Millmead, Guildford GU2 5BB ☎ 01483 444447 📠 01483 302221 ✉ kevin.handley@guildford.gov.uk

Finance and Treasurer: Ms Sue Reekie, Head of Financial Services, Millmead House, Millmead, Guildford GU2 4BB ☎ 01483 444829 📠 01483 444828

Finance and Treasurer: Mr Steve White, Head of Revenues & Payments Services, Millmead House, Millmead, Guildford GU2 4BB ☎ 01483 444920 📠 01483 444874

Fleet Management: Mr Paul Wells, Waste and Fleet Operations Manager, Woking Road Depot, Woking Road, Guildford GU1 1QE ☎ 01483 445011

Grounds Maintenance: Mr Phil Newcombe, Head of Parks & Countryside Services, Millmead House, Millmead, Guildford GU2 4BB ☎ 01483 444702 📠 01483 444717 ✉ phil.newcombe@guildford.gov.uk

Health and Safety: Mr Paul Osborn, Occupational Health and Safety Officer, Millmead House, Millmead, Guildford GU2 4BB ☎ 01483 444025

Home Energy Conservation: Mr Garry Bosworth, Principal Climate Change Officer, Millmead House, Millmead, Guildford GU2 4BB ☎ 01483 444515 ✉ garry.bosworth@guildford.gov.uk

Housing: Ms Kim Rippett, Acting Head of Housing Advice, Millmead House, Millmead, Guildford GU2 4BB ☎ 01483 444240 ✉ kim.rippett@guildford.gov.uk

Housing Maintenance: Mr Philip O'Dwyer, Head of Neighbourhood & Housing Management, Millmead House, Millmead, Guildford GU2 4BB ☎ 01483 444318

Legal: Mr Stephan Gerrard, Interim Head of Legal & Democratic Services, Millmead House, Millmead, Guildford GU2 4BB ☎ 01483 444042 ✉ stephan.gerrard@guildford.gov.uk

Legal: Ms Glynis Mancini, Principal Solicitor, Millmead House, Millmead, Guildford GU2 4BB ☎ 01483 444060

Leisure and Cultural Services: Mr Jim Miles, Director, Millmead House, Millmead, Guildford GU2 4BB ☎ 01483 444701 📠 01483 444717

Licensing: Mr David Curtis-Botting, Licensing Services Manager, Millmead House, Millmead, Guildford GU2 4BB ☎ 01483 444387

Lottery Funding, Charity and Voluntary: Mrs Joan Poole, Audit Manager, Millmead House, Millmead, Guildford GU2 4BB ☎ 01483 444854 📠 01483 444828

Member Services: Mr Stephan Gerrard, Interim Head of Legal & Democratic Services, Millmead House, Millmead, Guildford GU2 4BB ☎ 01483 444042 ✉ stephan.gerrard@guildford.gov.uk

Parking: Mr James Whiteman, Head of Operational Services, Cleansing Department, Woking Road Depot, Woking Road, Guildford GU1 1QE ☎ 01483 445030 📠 01483 445039 ✉ james.whiteman@guildford.gov.uk

Personnel / HR: Mrs Judith Coslett, Head of Human Resources, Millmead House, Millmead, Guildford GU2 4BB ☎ 01483 444010 📠 01483 444018

Planning: Ms Carol Humphrey, Head of Planning & Development Services, Millmead House, Millmead, Guildford GU2 4BB ☎ 01483 444620

Procurement: Mr Simon Gregory, Procurement Officer, Millmead House, Millmead, Guildford GU2 4BB ☎ 01483 444421

Recycling & Waste Minimisation: Mr Ian Westgate, Recycling Officer, Millmead House, Millmead, Guildford GU2 4BB ☎ 01483 455088 📠 01483 445039

Regeneration: Mr Chris Mansfield, Head of Economic Development, Millmead House, Millmead, Guildford GU2 4BB ☎ 01483 444550

Social Services: Mr John Martin, Head of Community Care Services, Millmead House, Millmead, Guildford GU2 4BB ☎ 01483 444350

Staff Training: Ms Hannah Cornick, Training Officer, Millmead House, Millmead, Guildford GU2 4BB ☎ 01483 505050

Sustainable Development: Ms Carol Humphrey, Head of Planning & Development Services, Millmead House, Millmead, Guildford GU2 4BB ☎ 01483 444620

Tourism: Mr Chris Mansfield, Head of Economic Development, Millmead House, Millmead, Guildford GU2 4BB ☎ 01483 444550

Town Centre: Mr David Bott, Town Centre Officer, Millmead House, Millmead, Guildford GU2 4BB ☎ 01483 444331

Transport: Mr Tim Pilsbury, Transportation Projects Manager, Millmead House, Millmead, Guildford GU2 4BB ☎ 01483 444521

Waste Collection and Disposal: Mr James Whiteman, Head of Operational Services, Cleansing Department, Woking Road Depot,

LOCAL AUTHORITIES

Woking Road, Guildford GU1 1QE ☎ 01483 445030 🖷 01483 445039 ✉ james.whiteman@guildford.gov.uk

Waste Management: Mr James Whiteman, Head of Operational Services, Cleansing Department, Woking Road Depot, Woking Road, Guildford GU1 1QE ☎ 01483 445030 🖷 01483 445039 ✉ james.whiteman@guildford.gov.uk

MEMBERS OF THE COUNCIL (48)

***Mayor:* Jordan**, Jennifer (CON - Merrow)
Jennifer.Jordan@guildford.gov.uk
***Deputy Mayor:* Searle**, Pauline (LD - Stoughton)
Pauline.Searle@guildford.gov.uk
***Leader of the Council:* Rooth**, Tony (CON - Pilgrims)
Tony.Rooth@guildford.gov.uk
***Deputy Leader of the Council:* Wright**, David (CON - Tillingbourne)
David.Wright@guildford.gov.uk
Billington, Richard (CON - Tillingbourne)
richard.billington@guildford.gov.uk
Bright, Melanie (CON - Holy Trinity)
Melanie.Bright@guildford.gov.uk
Carpenter, David (CON - Merrow)
David.Carpenter@guildford.gov.uk
Chandler, Adrian (CON - Onslow)
adrian.chandles@guildford.gov.uk
Chapman, Mark (LD - Westborough)
mark.chapman@guildford.gov.uk
Creedy, Sarah (CON - Holy Trinity)
Sarah.Creedy@guildford.gov.uk
Ellwood, Graham (CON - Merrow)
graham.ellwood@guildford.gov.uk
Elms, David (CON - Worplesdon)
david.elms@guildford.gov.uk
Franklin, Zoe (LD - Stoke)
zoe.frankin@guildford.gov.uk
Freeman, Steven (LD - Onslow)
Steve.Freeman@guildford.gov.uk
French, Andrew (CON - Clandon and Horsley)
Andrew.French@guildford.gov.uk
Furniss, Matthew (CON - Christchurch)
Matt.Furniss@guildford.gov.uk
Garrett, John (CON - Lovelace)
John.Garrett@guildford.gov.uk
Gilliam, Christian (LAB - Westborough)
christian.gilliam@guildford.gov.uk
Goodwin, David (LD - Friary & St Nicolas)
David.Goodwin@guildford.gov.uk
Gunning, Angela (LAB - Stoke)
angela.gunning@guildford.gov.uk
Harwood, Gillian (LD - Stoughton)
Gillian.Harwood@guildford.gov.uk
Hewlett, Jayne (CON - Ash Wharf)
Jayne.Hewlett@guildford.gov.uk
Hogger, Liz (LD - Effingham)
Liz.Hogger@guildford.gov.uk
Holliday, Christian (CON - Burpham)
christian.holliday@guildford.gov.uk
Hooper, Philip (CON - Holy Trinity)
philip.hooper@guildford.gov.uk
Jackson, Gordon (CON - Pirbright)
gordon.jackson@guildford.gov.uk
Juneja, Monika (CON - Burpham)
monika.Juneja@guildford.gov.uk
Lockyer-Nibbs, Diana (CON - Normandy)
Diana.Lockyer-Nibbs@guildford.gov.uk
Manning, Nigel (CON - Ash Vale)
Nigel.Manning@guildford.gov.uk
Mansbridge, Stephen (CON - Ash South and Tongham)
Stephen.Mansbridge@guildford.gov.uk
May, Wendy (LD - Stoughton)
Wendy.May@guildford.gov.uk
McShame, Julia (LD - Westborough)
julia.mcshane@guildford.gov.uk
McShee, Bob (CON - Worplesdon)
bob.mcshee@guildford.gov.uk
Meredith, Anne (LD - Friary & St Nicolas)
Anne.Meredith@guildford.gov.uk
Moseley, Marsha (CON - Ash Vale)
Marsha.Moseley@guildford.gov.uk
Nelson-Smith, Nikki (CON - Christchurch)
nikki.nelson-smith@guildford.gov.uk
Palmer, James (CON - Shalford)
james.palmer@guildford.gov.uk
Patrick, Terence (CON - Send)
Terence.Patrick@guildford.gov.uk
Phillips, Tony (LD - Onslow)
Tony.Philips@guildford.gov.uk
Powell, Jennifer (CON - Clandon and Horsley)
Jennifer.Powell@guildford.gov.uk
Randall, John (CON - Ash Wharf)
john.randall@guildford.gov.uk
Reeves, Caroline (LD - Friary & St Nicolas)
Caroline.Reeves@guildford.gov.uk
Richards, Douglas (CON - Ash South and Tongham)
doug.richards@guildford.gov.uk
Roche, Iseult (CON - Worplesdon)
iseult.roche@guildford.gov.uk
Sutcliffe, Nicholas (CON - Ash South and Tongham)
Nick.Sutcliffe@guildford.gov.uk
Taylor, Keith (CON - Send)
Keith.Taylor@guildford.gov.uk
Ward, Neil (CON - Shalford)
Neil.Ward@guildford.gov.uk
Wicks, Jenny (CON - Clandon and Horsley)
Jenny.Wicks@guildford.gov.uk

POLITICAL COMPOSITION

CON: 34, LD: 12, LAB: 2

CABINET

Leader: Mr Tony Rooth
Deputy Leader/Finance & Resources: Mr David Wright
Culture & Leisure: Mrs Jennifer Powell
Environmental Services: Mr Nicholas Sutcliffe
Housing & Social Care: Mrs Sarah Creedy
Planning & Development: Mrs Jenny Wicks
Service Transformation: Mr Nigel Manning
Stronger Communities: Mr Stephen Mansbridge

COMMITTEE CHAIRS

Corporate Improvement Scrutiny: Mr Tony Phillips
Customer & Community Scrutiny: Mr Matthew Furniss
Licensing: Mr David Elms
Planning: Mr Gordon Jackson

GWYNEDD W

Gwynedd Council, (Cyngor Gwynedd), Swyddfa'r Cyngor, Stryd Y Jel, Caernarfon LL55 1SH ☎ 01286 672255 🖷 01286 673993 ✉ enquiries@gwynedd.gov.uk 💻 www.gwynedd.gov.uk

FACTS & FIGURES

Police Authority: North Wales Police Authority
Learning and Skills Council: Wales
Parliamentary Constituencies: Arfon, Dwyfor Meirionnydd
EU Constituencies: Wales
Election Frequency: Elections are of whole council

PRINCIPAL OFFICERS

Chief Executive: Mr Harry Thomas, Chief Executive, Swyddfa'r Cyngor, Stryd Y Jel, Caernarfon LL55 1SH ☎ 01286 679002 🖷 01286 679488 ✉ harrythomas@gwynedd.gov.uk

Senior Management: Mr Dafydd Lewis, Corporate Director, Swyddfa'r Cyngor, Stryd Y Jel, Caernarfon LL55 1SH ☎ 01286 679468 ✉ davidplewis@gwynedd.gov.uk

Senior Management: Mr Iwan Trefor Jones, Corporate Director, Swyddfa'r Cyngor, Stryd Y Jel, Caernarfon LL55 1SH ☎ 01286 679162 🖷 01286 673324 ✉ iwanj@gwynedd.gov.uk

Senior Management: Mr Dilwyn Owen Williams, Corporate Director, Swyddfa'r Cyngor, Stryd Y Jel, Caernarfon LL55 1SH ☎ 01286 679103 ✉ DilwynOwenWilliams@gwynedd.gov.uk

Access Officer / Social Services (Disability): Mrs Gwen Carrington, Head of Housing and Social Services, Swyddfa'r Cyngor, Stryd Y Jel, Caernarfon LL55 1SH ☎ 01286 679227 🖷 01286 677486 ✉ gwencarrington@gwynedd.gov.uk

Architect, Building / Property Services: Mr Huw Williams, Head of Gwynedd Consultancy, Swyddfa'r Cyngor, Stryd Y Jel, Caernarfon LL55 1SH ☎ 01286 679426 🖷 01286 679299 ✉ huwwilliams@gwynedd.gov.uk

Best Value: Mr Geraint George, Head of Strategic & Improvement, Swyddfa'r Cyngor, Stryd Y Jel, Caernarfon LL55 1SH ☎ 01286 679052 🖷 01286 676310 ✉ geraintg@gwynedd.gov.uk

Building Control: Mr Huw Williams, Head of Gwynedd Consultancy, Swyddfa'r Cyngor, Stryd Y Jel, Caernarfon LL55 1SH ☎ 01286 679426 🖷 01286 679299 ✉ huwwilliams@gwynedd.gov.uk

Catering Services: Mrs Morwenna Edwards, Head of Provider & Leisure, Swyddfa'r Cyngor, Stryd Y Jel, Caernarfon LL55 1SH ☎ 01286 679479 ✉ morwennaedwards@gwynedd.gov.uk

Children / Youth Services: Mrs Gwen Carrington, Head of Housing and Social Services, Swyddfa'r Cyngor, Stryd Y Jel, Caernarfon LL55 1SH ☎ 01286 679227 🖷 01286 677486 ✉ gwencarrington@gwynedd.gov.uk

Civil Registration: Mrs Dilys Phillips, Head of Democracy & Legal, Swyddfa'r Cyngor, Stryd Y Jel, Caernarfon LL55 1SH ☎ 01286 679011 ✉ dilysannphillips@gwynedd.gov.uk

PR / Communications: Ms Gwenan Parry, Head of Customer Care, Swyddfa'r Cyngor, Stryd Y Jel, Caernarfon LL55 1SH ☎ 01286 679003 🖷 01286 676998 ✉ gwenanparry@gwynedd.gov.uk

Community Planning: Mrs Sioned Williams, Head of Economy & Community, Swyddfa'r Cyngor, Stryd Y Jel, Caernarfon LL55 1SH ☎ 01286 679547 🖷 01286 673324 ✉ sionedewilliams@gwynedd.gov.uk

Community Safety: Ms Catherine Roberts, Senior Community Safety Officer, Mona Building, Gwynedd Council, Caernarfon LL55 1SH ☎ 01286 679047 ✉ catherineeroberts@gwynedd.gov.uk

Computer Management: Ms Gwenan Parry, Head of Customer Care, Swyddfa'r Cyngor, Stryd Y Jel, Caernarfon LL55 1SH ☎ 01286 679003 🖷 01286 676998 ✉ gwenanparry@gwynedd.gov.uk

Consumer Protection and Trading Standards: Mr Aled Davies, Head of Regulatory, Swyddfa'r Cyngor, Stryd Y Jel, Caernarfon LL55 1SH ☎ 01286 679370 🖷 01286 673324 ✉ aleddavies@gwynedd.gov.uk

Contracts: Mr Geraint George, Head of Strategic & Improvement, Swyddfa'r Cyngor, Stryd Y Jel, Caernarfon LL55 1SH ☎ 01286 679052 🖷 01286 676310 ✉ geraintg@gwynedd.gov.uk

Corporate Services: Mr Harry Thomas, Chief Executive, Swyddfa'r Cyngor, Stryd Y Jel, Caernarfon LL55 1SH ☎ 01286 679002 🖷 01286 679488 ✉ harrythomas@gwynedd.gov.uk

Customer Service: Ms Gwenan Parry, Head of Customer Care, Swyddfa'r Cyngor, Stryd Y Jel, Caernarfon LL55 1SH ☎ 01286 679003 🖷 01286 676998 ✉ gwenanparry@gwynedd.gov.uk

Direct Labour: Mr Gwyn Morris Jones, Head of Highways & Municipal Services, Swyddfa'r Cyngor, Stryd Y Jel, Caernarfon LL55 1SH ☎ 01286 679402 🖷 01286 675961 ✉ gwynmorrisjones@gwynedd.gov.uk

Economic Development: Mrs Sioned Williams, Head of Economy & Community, Swyddfa'r Cyngor, Stryd Y Jel, Caernarfon LL55 1SH ☎ 01286 679547 🖷 01286 673324 ✉ sionedewilliams@gwynedd.gov.uk

Education: Mr Dewi Jones, Head of Education, Swyddfa'r Cyngor, Stryd Y Jel, Caernarfon LL55 1SH ☎ 01286 679467 🖷 01286 677347 ✉ dewirjones@gwynedd.gov.uk

E-Government: Ms Gwenan Parry, Head of Customer Care, Swyddfa'r Cyngor, Stryd Y Jel, Caernarfon LL55 1SH ☎ 01286 679003 🖷 01286 676998 ✉ gwenanparry@gwynedd.gov.uk

Electoral Registration: Mrs Dilys Phillips, Head of Democracy & Legal, Swyddfa'r Cyngor, Stryd Y Jel, Caernarfon LL55 1SH ☎ 01286 679011 ✉ dilysannphillips@gwynedd.gov.uk

Emergency Planning: Ms Gwenan Parry, Head of Customer Care, Swyddfa'r Cyngor, Stryd Y Jel, Caernarfon LL55 1SH ☎ 01286 679003 🖷 01286 676998

✉ gwenanparry@gwynedd.gov.uk

Energy Management: Mr David Mark Lewis, Energy Conservation Officer, Swyddfa'r Cyngor, Stryd Y Jel, Caernarfon LL55 1SH ☎ 01286 679307 📠 01286 676998 ✉ davidmarklewis@gwynedd.gov.uk

Environmental Health: Mr Aled Davies, Head of Regulatory, Swyddfa'r Cyngor, Stryd Y Jel, Caernarfon LL55 1SH ☎ 01286 679370 📠 01286 673324 ✉ aleddavies@gwynedd.gov.uk

Estates, Property & Valuation: Ms Gwenan Parry, Head of Customer Care, Swyddfa'r Cyngor, Stryd Y Jel, Caernarfon LL55 1SH ☎ 01286 679003 📠 01286 676998 ✉ gwenanparry@gwynedd.gov.uk

European Liaison: Mrs Vivienne Pritchard, European Officer, Swyddfa'r Cyngor, Stryd Y Jel, Caernarfon LL55 1SH ☎ 01286 679487 ✉ viviennepritchard@gwynedd.gov.uk

Events Manager: Mr Hugh Edwin Jones, Events Manager, Swyddfa'r Cyngor, Stryd Y Jel, Caernarfon LL55 1SH ☎ 01286 679398 📠 01286 679338 ✉ hughedwinjones@gwynedd.gov.uk

Finance and Treasurer: Mr Dafydd Edwards, Head of Finance, Finance Service, Penrallt, Caernarfon LL55 1BN ☎ 01286 682682 📠 01286 682856 ✉ dafyddle@gwynedd.gov.uk

Fleet Management: Mr Gwyn Morris Jones, Head of Highways & Municipal Services, Swyddfa'r Cyngor, Stryd Y Jel, Caernarfon LL55 1SH ☎ 01286 679402 📠 01286 675961 ✉ gwynmorrisjones@gwynedd.gov.uk

Grounds Maintenance: Mr Gwyn Morris Jones, Head of Highways & Municipal Services, Swyddfa'r Cyngor, Stryd Y Jel, Caernarfon LL55 1SH ☎ 01286 679402 📠 01286 675961 ✉ gwynmorrisjones@gwynedd.gov.uk

Health and Safety: Mr Leigh Roberts, Health & Safety Manager, Swyddfa'r Cyngor, Stryd Y Jel, Caernarfon LL55 1SH ☎ 01286 679459 📠 01286 671072 ✉ leighroberts@gwynedd.gov.uk

Highways: Mr Gwyn Morris Jones, Head of Highways & Municipal Services, Swyddfa'r Cyngor, Stryd Y Jel, Caernarfon LL55 1SH ☎ 01286 679402 📠 01286 675961 ✉ gwynmorrisjones@gwynedd.gov.uk

Housing: Mrs Gwen Carrington, Head of Housing and Social Services, Swyddfa'r Cyngor, Stryd Y Jel, Caernarfon LL55 1SH ☎ 01286 679227 📠 01286 677486 ✉ gwencarrington@gwynedd.gov.uk

Legal: Mrs Dilys Phillips, Head of Democracy & Legal, Swyddfa'r Cyngor, Stryd Y Jel, Caernarfon LL55 1SH ☎ 01286 679011 ✉ dilysannphillips@gwynedd.gov.uk

Leisure and Cultural Services: Mrs Sioned Williams, Head of Economy & Community, Swyddfa'r Cyngor, Stryd Y Jel, Caernarfon LL55 1SH ☎ 01286 679547 📠 01286 673324 ✉ sionedewilliams@gwynedd.gov.uk

Licensing: Mr Aled Davies, Head of Regulatory, Swyddfa'r Cyngor, Stryd Y Jel, Caernarfon LL55 1SH ☎ 01286 679370 📠 01286 673324 ✉ aleddavies@gwynedd.gov.uk

Lighting: Mr Gwyn Morris Jones, Head of Highways & Municipal Services, Swyddfa'r Cyngor, Stryd Y Jel, Caernarfon LL55 1SH ☎ 01286 679402 📠 01286 675961 ✉ gwynmorrisjones@gwynedd.gov.uk

Lottery Funding, Charity and Voluntary: Ms Heather Wyn Williams, Senior Gwynedd Cist Officer, Plas Llanwnda, Castle Street, Caernarfon LL55 1SH ☎ 01286 679153 📠 01286 679338 ✉ heatherwilliams@gwynedd.gov.uk

Member Services: Mrs Dilys Phillips, Head of Democracy & Legal, Swyddfa'r Cyngor, Stryd Y Jel, Caernarfon LL55 1SH ☎ 01286 679011 ✉ dilysannphillips@gwynedd.gov.uk

Parking: Mr Aled Davies, Head of Regulatory, Swyddfa'r Cyngor, Stryd Y Jel, Caernarfon LL55 1SH ☎ 01286 679370 📠 01286 673324 ✉ aleddavies@gwynedd.gov.uk

Partnerships: Mr Geraint George, Head of Strategic & Improvement, Swyddfa'r Cyngor, Stryd Y Jel, Caernarfon LL55 1SH ☎ 01286 679052 📠 01286 676310 ✉ geraintg@gwynedd.gov.uk

Personnel / HR: Mr Alwyn Evans Jones, Head of Human Resources, Swyddfa'r Cyngor, Stryd Y Jel, Caernarfon LL55 1SH ☎ 01286 679072 📠 01286 671072 ✉ alwynevansjones@gwynedd.gov.uk

Planning: Mr Aled Davies, Head of Regulatory, Swyddfa'r Cyngor, Stryd Y Jel, Caernarfon LL55 1SH ☎ 01286 679370 📠 01286 673324 ✉ aleddavies@gwynedd.gov.uk

Procurement: Mr Geraint George, Head of Strategic & Improvement, Swyddfa'r Cyngor, Stryd Y Jel, Caernarfon LL55 1SH ☎ 01286 679052 📠 01286 676310 ✉ geraintg@gwynedd.gov.uk

Public Libraries: Mr Hywel James, Chief Librarian, Swyddfa'r Cyngor, Stryd Y Jel, Caernarfon LL55 1SH ☎ 01286 679504 📠 01286 677347 ✉ hyweljames@gwynedd.gov.uk

Recycling & Waste Minimisation: Mr Gwyn Morris Jones, Head of Highways & Municipal Services, Swyddfa'r Cyngor, Stryd Y Jel, Caernarfon LL55 1SH ☎ 01286 679402 📠 01286 675961 ✉ gwynmorrisjones@gwynedd.gov.uk

Regeneration: Mrs Sioned Williams, Head of Economy & Community, Swyddfa'r Cyngor, Stryd Y Jel, Caernarfon LL55 1SH ☎ 01286 679547 📠 01286 673324 ✉ sionedewilliams@gwynedd.gov.uk

Road Safety: Mr Colin Jones, Parking and Road Safety Manager, Swyddfa'r Cyngor, Stryd Y Jel, Caernarfon LL55 1SH ☎ 01286 679753 📠 01286 679823 ✉ colinjones@gwynedd.gov.uk

Social Services: Mrs Gwen Carrington, Head of Housing and Social Services, Swyddfa'r Cyngor, Stryd Y Jel, Caernarfon LL55 1SH ☎ 01286 679227 📠 01286 677486 ✉ gwencarrington@gwynedd.gov.uk

Social Services (Adult): Mrs Gwen Carrington, Head of Housing and Social Services, Swyddfa'r Cygor, Stryd Y Jel, Caernarfon LL55 1SH ☎ 01286 679227 🖷 01286 677486 🖰 gwencarrington@gwynedd.gov.uk

Social Services (Children): Mrs Gwen Carrington, Head of Housing and Social Services, Swyddfa'r Cygor, Stryd Y Jel, Caernarfon LL55 1SH ☎ 01286 679227 🖷 01286 677486 🖰 gwencarrington@gwynedd.gov.uk

Staff Training: Mr Alwyn Evans Jones, Head of Human Resources, Swyddfa'r Cygor, Stryd Y Jel, Caernarfon LL55 1SH ☎ 01286 679072 🖷 01286 671072 🖰 alwynevansjones@gwynedd.gov.uk

Street Scene: Mr Aled Davies, Head of Regulatory, Swyddfa'r Cygor, Stryd Y Jel, Caernarfon LL55 1SH ☎ 01286 679370 🖷 01286 673324 🖰 aleddavies@gwynedd.gov.uk

Sustainable Communities: Mrs Sioned Williams, Head of Economy & Community, Swyddfa'r Cygor, Stryd Y Jel, Caernarfon LL55 1SH ☎ 01286 679547 🖷 01286 673324 🖰 sionedewilliams@gwynedd.gov.uk

Sustainable Development: Mr Aled Davies, Head of Regulatory, Swyddfa'r Cygor, Stryd Y Jel, Caernarfon LL55 1SH ☎ 01286 679370 🖷 01286 673324 🖰 aleddavies@gwynedd.gov.uk

Tourism: Mrs Sian Jones, Tourism Marketing and Customer Care Service Manager, Swyddfa'r Cygor, Stryd Y Jel, Caernarfon LL55 1SH ☎ 01286 679963 🖷 01286 679338 🖰 sianpjones@gwynedd.gov.uk

Traffic Management: Mr Aled Davies, Head of Regulatory, Swyddfa'r Cygor, Stryd Y Jel, Caernarfon LL55 1SH ☎ 01286 679370 🖷 01286 673324 🖰 aleddavies@gwynedd.gov.uk

Transport: Mr Aled Davies, Head of Regulatory, Swyddfa'r Cygor, Stryd Y Jel, Caernarfon LL55 1SH ☎ 01286 679370 🖷 01286 673324 🖰 aleddavies@gwynedd.gov.uk

Transport Planner: Mr Dafydd Wyn Williams, Chief Engineer Transportation & Street Care, Swyddfa'r Cygor, Stryd Y Jel, Caernarfon LL55 1SH ☎ 01286 679422 🖷 01286 676119 🖰 davidwynwilliams@gwynedd.gov.uk

Total Place: Mr Iwan Trefor Jones, Corporate Director, Swyddfa'r Cygor, Stryd Y Jel, Caernarfon LL55 1SH ☎ 01286 679162 🖷 01286 673324 🖰 iwanj@gwynedd.gov.uk

Waste Collection and Disposal: Mr Gwyn Morris Jones, Head of Highways & Municipal Services, Swyddfa'r Cygor, Stryd Y Jel, Caernarfon LL55 1SH ☎ 01286 679402 🖷 01286 675961 🖰 gwynmorrisjones@gwynedd.gov.uk

Waste Management: Mr Gwyn Morris Jones, Head of Highways & Municipal Services, Swyddfa'r Cygor, Stryd Y Jel, Caernarfon LL55 1SH ☎ 01286 679402 🖷 01286 675961 🖰 gwynmorrisjones@gwynedd.gov.uk

Children's Play Areas: Mr Gwyn Morris Jones, Head of Highways & Municipal Services, Swyddfa'r Cygor, Stryd Y Jel, Caernarfon LL55 1SH ☎ 01286 679402 🖷 01286 675961 🖰 gwynmorrisjones@gwynedd.gov.uk

MEMBERS OF THE COUNCIL (75)

***Leader of the Council:* Edwards**, Dyfed (PC - Penygroes)
Cynghorydd.DyfedEdwards@gwynedd.gov.uk
***Deputy Leader of the Council:* Gwenllian**, Sian (PC - Y Felinheli)
cynghorydd.siangwenllian.gov.uk
Ab Iago, Craig (PC - Llanllyfni)
cynghorydd.craigabiago@gwynedd.gov.uk
Churchman, Stephen (LD - Dolbenmaen)
Cynghorydd.StephenChurchman@gwynedd.gov.uk
Davies, Anwen (O - Efailnewydd/Buan)
Cynghorydd.AnwenJaneDavies@gwynedd.gov.uk
Day, Lesley (IND - Garth)
cynghorydd@gwynedd.gov.uk
Dogan, Edward (PC - Dewi)
Edwards, Huw (PC - Cadnant)
Edwards, Gwynfor (LAB - Deiniol)
cynghord.gwynforedwards@gwynedd.gov.uk
Edwards, Trefor (IND - Llanberis)
Edwards, Elwyn (PC - Llandderfel)
Cynghorydd.ElwynEdwards@gwynedd.gov.uk
Ellis, Thomas (IND - Transfynydd)
Cynghorydd.TomEllis@gwynedd.gov.uk
Evans, Alan (PC - Llanuwchllyn)
Cynghorydd.AlanJonesEvans@gwynedd.gov.uk
Evans, Aled (PC - Llanystumdwy)
Cynghorydd.AledEvans@gwynedd.gov.uk
Forsyth, Jean (LD - Hirael)
Cynghorydd.Jean.Forsyth@gwynedd.gov.uk
Forsyth, Jean (O - Llanwnda)
Cynghorydd.AeronMaldwynJones@gwynedd.gov.uk
Glyn, Simon (O - Tudweiliog)
Cynghorydd.SimonGlyn@gwynedd.gov.uk
Glyn, Gweno (O - Botwnnog)
Cynghorydd.GwenoGlyn@gwynedd.gov.uk
Griffith, Gwen (LAB - Tregarth a Mynydd Llandegai)
Cynghorydd.gwengriffith@gwynedd.gov.uk
Griffiths, Selwyn (PC - Porthmadog)
Cynghorydd.SelwynGriffiths@gwynedd.gov.uk
Gruffydd, Alwyn (O - Porthmadog/Tremadog)
Cynghorydd.AlwynGruffydd@gwynedd.gov.uk
Gwynedd, Endaf (O - Seiont (1))
cynghorydd.endafcooke@gwynedd.gov.uk
Hughes, Chris (PC - Bontnewydd)
Hughes, John (O - Llanengan)
cynghorydd.JohnHughes@gwynedd.gov.uk
Hughes, Louise (O - Llangelynnin)
Cynghorydd.LouiseHughes@gwynedd.gov.uk
Hughes, Annwen (PC - Llanbedr)
Cynghorydd.AnwenHughes@gwynedd.gov.uk
Humphreys, Jason (O - Porthmadog)
Cynghorydd.JasonHumphreys@gwynedd.gov.uk
Jenkins, Peredur (PC - Brithdir + Llanfachreth)
Cynghorydd.PeredurJenkins@gwynedd.gov.uk
Jones, Llywarch (O - Llanaelhaearn)
Cynghorydd.LlywarchBowenJones@gwynedd.gov.uk
Jones, Dyfrig (PC - Gerlan)
cynghorydd.dyfrigjones@gwynedd.gov.uk
Jones, John Wynn (PC - Hendre)
johnwynnjones@hotmail.co.uk
Jones, Elin (PC - Glyder)

cynghorydd.elinwjones@gwynedd.gov.uk
Jones, Eric (IND - Groeslon)
cynghorydd.ericmerfynjones@gwynedd.gov.uk
Jones, Sion (LAB - Bethel)
cynghorydd.sionjones@gwynedd.gov.uk
Jones, Brian (LAB - Cwm y Glo)
Cynghorydd.BrianJones@gwynedd.gov.uk
Jones, Charles (PC - Llanrug)
Cynghorydd.CharlesWynJones@gwynedd.gov.uk
Jones, Anne (IND - Tywyn (1))
Cynghorydd.AnneLloyd-Jones@gwynedd.gov.uk
Jones, Linda (PC - Teigl)
Cynghorydd.LindaAnnJones@gwynedd.gov.uk
Jones-Williams, Eryl (IND - Dyffryn Ardudwy)
Cynghorydd.EarlJones-Williams@gwynedd.gov.uk
Lawton, Beth (IND - Bryncrug/Llanfihangel)
Cynhorydd.BethLawton@gwnedd.gov.uk
Lloyd, Ifor (IND - Talysarn)
dilwyn.lloyd@btopenworld.com
Marshall, June (LD - Menai (Bangor) (1))
junemarshall18@hotmail.com
Meurig, Dafydd (PC - Arllechwedd)
cynghorydd.dafyddmeurig@gwynedd.gov.uk
Morgan, Dilwyn (PC - Y Bala)
Cynghordd.DilwynMorgan@gwynedd.gov.uk
Morgan, Linda (PC - Dolgellau)
Cynghorydd.LindaLindaMorgan@gwynedd.gov.uk
O'Neal, Christopher (IND - Marchog (1))
cynghorydd.oneal@gwynedd.gov.uk
Owen, William Tudor (PC - Peblig)
Cynghorydd.WilliamTudorOwen@gwynedd.gov.uk
Owen, William (IND - Seoint (2))
cynghorydd.williamroyowen@gwynedd.gov.uk
Owen, Michael (PC - Pwllheli (Gogledd/North))
Cynghorydd.MichaelSolOwen@gwynedd.gov.uk
Owen, Dewi (IND - Aberdyfi)
Cynghorydd.DewiOwen@gwynedd.gov.uk
Pickavance, Nigel (IND - Marchog (2))
cynghorydd.nigelpickavance@gwynedd.gov.uk
Read, Peter (O - Abererch)
Cynghorydd@Peter.Read@gwynedd.gov.uk
Roberts, Liz (PC - Morfa Nefyn)
Cynghorydd.Liz.SavilleRoberts@gwynedd.gov.uk
Roberts, Caerwyn (PC - Harlech/Talsarnau)
Cynghorydd.CaerwynRoberts@gwynedd.gov.uk
Roberts, John (IND - Corris/ Mawddwy)
Cynghorydd.JohnPugheRoberts@gwynedd.gov.uk
Roberts, Gareth (PC - Aberdaron)
Cynghotydd.GarethRoberts@gwynedd.gov.uk
Rowlands, Mair (PC - Menai (Bangor) (2))
cynghorydd.mairrowlands@gwymedd.gov.uk
Russell, Angela (IND - Llanbedrog)
Cynghorydd.AngelaRussell@gwynedd.gov.uk
Siencyn, Dyfrig (PC - Dolgellau)
Cynghorydd.DyfrigLewisSiencyn@gwynedd.gov.uk
Stevens, Mike (IND - Tywyn (2))
Cynghorydd.Mike.Stevens@gwynedd.gov.uk
Thomas, Paul (PC - Bowydd + Rhiw)
Cynghorydd.PaulThomas@gwynedd.gov.uk
Thomas, Gareth (PC - Penrhyndeudraeth)
Cynghorydd.GarethThomas@gwynedd.gov.uk
Thomas, Ioan Caredig (PC - Menai (Caernarfon))
Cynghorydd.IoanThomas@gwynedd.gov.uk
Willaims, Hefin (PC - Penisarwaun)
cynghorydd.hefinwilliams@gwynedd.gov.uk
Williams, Ann (PC - Ogwen)
anngerlan@hotmail.co.uk
Williams, John (PC - Pentir)
john_wyn_williams@hotmail.com
Williams, Elfed (IND - Deiniolen)
cynghorydd.elfedwilliams@gwynedd.gov.uk
Williams, Hywel (PC - Abersoch)
cynghorydd.RHywellWynWilliams@gwynedd.gov.uk
Williams, Owain (O - Clynnog)
Cynghorydd.OwainWilliams@gwynedd.gov.uk
Williams, Eirwyn (IND - Cricieth)
Cynghorydd.EirwynWilliams@gwynedd.gov.uk
Williams, Gruffydd (O - Nefyn)
Cynghorydd.GruffyddWilliams@gwynedd.gov.uk
Williams, Gethin (PC - Abermaw)
cynghorydd.gethinglynwilliams@gwynedd.gov.uk
Williams-Davies, Mandy (PC - Diffwys + Maenofferen)
Cynghordd.MandyWDavies@gwynedd.gov.uk
Wright, Robert (O - Pwllheli (gogledd/North))
Cynghorydd.BobWright@gwynedd.gov.uk
Wyn, Eurig (PC - Waunfawr)
cynghorydd.eurigwyn@gwynedd.gov.uk

POLITICAL COMPOSITION

PC: 37, IND: 17, O: 14, LAB: 4, LD: 3

CABINET

Leader: Mr Dyfed Edwards
Deputy Leader/ Education: Ms Sian Gwenllian
Care: Mr Hywel Williams
Customer Care: Mr Ioan Caredig Thomas
Deprivation: Mr Brian Jones
Economy: Mr John Wynn Jones
Education: Ms Sian Gwenllian
Environment: Mr Gareth Roberts
Healthy Gwynedd: Mr Paul Thomas
Planning: Mr John Williams
Resources: Mr Peredur Jenkins

COMMITTEE CHAIRS

Audit: Mr Trevor Edwards
Central Licensing: Mr William Tudor Owen
Communities Scrutiny: Mr Eric Jones
Corporate Scrutiny: Mr Simon Glyn
Democratic Services: Mr Dewi Owen
Employment Appeals: Ms Jean Forsyth
Language: Ms Liz Roberts
Pensions: TBA
Planning: Ms Gwen Griffith
Services Scrutiny: Mr Dyfrig Siencyn

HACKNEY L

Hackney London Borough Council, Town Hall, Mare Street, London E8 1EA ☎ 020 8356 5000 🖷 020 8356 2080
💻 www.hackney.gov.uk

FACTS & FIGURES

Police Authority: Metropolitan Police Authority
Health Authority: NHS London
Learning and Skills Council: London
Parliamentary Constituencies: Hackney North and Stoke

Newington, Hackney South and Shoreditch
EU Constituencies: London
Election Frequency: Elections are of whole council
Twinning: Haifa (Israel); Landkreis Gottingen (Germany); Suresnes (France); St. George's (Grenada)

PRINCIPAL OFFICERS

Chief Executive: Mr Tim Shields, Chief Executive, Town Hall, Mare Street, London E8 1EA ☎ 020 8356 3210 🖷 020 8356 3047 ✉ tim.shields@hackney.gov.uk

Senior Management: Ms Gifty Edila, Corporate Director of Legal, HR and Regulatory Services, Town Hall, Mare Street, London E8 1EA ☎ 020 8356 3265 🖷 020 8536 3047 ✉ gifty.edila@hackney.gov.uk

Senior Management: Mr Charlie Foreman, Chief Officer Olympic and Paralympic Unit, 2 Hillman Street, London E8 1FB ☎ 020 8356 2012 ✉ charlie.foreman@hackney.gov.uk

Senior Management: Mr Ian Lewis, Chief Officer Policy and Partnership, Town Hall, Mare Street, London E8 1EA ☎ 020 8356 3388 ✉ ian.lewis@hackney.gov.uk

Senior Management: Ms Joanna Sumner, Chief Officer Programmes, Projects and Performance, Town Hall, Mare Street, London E8 1EA ☎ 020 8356 3135 ✉ joanna.sumner@hackney.gov.uk

Senior Management: Mr Ian Williams, Corporate Director of Finance & Resources, Town Hall, Mare Street, London E8 1EA ☎ 020 8356 3003 ✉ ian.williams@hackney.gov.uk

Senior Management: Mr Alan Wood, Corporate Director of Children & Young People's Services, The Learning Trust, 1 Reading Lane, London E8 1GQ ☎ 020 8820 7515 ✉ alan.wood@hackney.gov.uk

Senior Management: Ms Kim Wright, Corporate Director of Health and Community Services, Town Hall, Mare Street, London E8 1EA ☎ 020 8356 7347 🖷 020 8356 7544 ✉ kim.wright@hackney.gov.uk

Access Officer / Social Services (Disability): Mr Rob Blackstone, AD Adult Social Care, 1 Hillman Street, London E8 1DY ☎ 020 8356 4282

Building Control: Mr Alan Hawes, Interim Head of Building Control & Licensing, 1 Hillman Street, London E8 1DY ☎ 020 8356 8121 ✉ alan.hawes@hackney.gov.uk

Building Control: Mr Jim Paterson, Interim Divisional Head of Building Maintenance, 6-15 Florfield Street, London E8 1DT ☎ 020 8356 6899 🖷 020 8356 4740 ✉ jim.paterson@hackney.gov.uk

Civil Registration: Ms Christie Junor-Sheppard, Head of Registrational Services, Town Hall, Mare Street, London E8 1EA ☎ 020 8356 4382 ✉ christie.sheppard@hackney.gov.uk

PR / Communications: Ms Polly Cziok, Head of Communications & Consultation, Town Hall, Mare Street, London E8 1EA ☎ 020 8356 3323 ✉ polly.cziok@hackney.gov.uk

Community Safety: Ms Liz Hughes, Head of Safer Communities, Maurice Bishop House, 17 Reading Lane, London E8 1HH ☎ 020 8356 3164 🖷 020 8356 2241 ✉ liz.hughes@hackney.gov.uk

Computer Management: Ms Christine Peacock, Assistant Director - ICT, 6-15 Florfield Road, London E8 1DT ☎ 020 8356 2600 ✉ christine.peacock@hackney.gov.uk

Consumer Protection and Trading Standards: Mrs Josile Munroe, Head of Environment, Health & Consumer Protection, 1st Floor, 81 Downham Road, London N1 5TR ☎ 020 8356 4903 🖷 020 8356 4916 ✉ josile.munroe@hackney.gov.uk

Contracts: Mr Michael Robson, Head of Strategic Procurement, Town Hall, Mare Street, London E8 1EA ☎ 0208 356 3821 ✉ michael.robson@hackney.gov.uk

Education: Mr Alan Wood, Corporate Director of Children & Young People's Services, The Learning Trust, 1 Reading Lane, London E8 1GQ ☎ 020 8820 7515 ✉ alan.wood@hackney.gov.uk

Electoral Registration: Mr Michael Summerville, Head of Electoral & Member Services, Town Hall, Mare Street, London E8 1EA ☎ 020 8356 3115 ✉ michael.summerville@hackney.gov.uk

Emergency Planning: Mr Roy Hitching, CCTV & Emergency Planning Head of Service, Stoke Newington Municipal Offices, Stoke Newington Church Street, London N16 0JR ☎ 020 8356 2182 ✉ roy.hitching@hackney.gov.uk

Energy Management: Mr John Maloney, Head of Energy Management, 2 Hillman Street, London E8 1FB ☎ 020 8356 2764 ✉ john.maloney@hackney.gov.uk

Environmental / Technical Services: Mr Tom McCourt, Assistant Director of Public Realm, 263 Mare Street, London E8 3HT ☎ 020 8356 8219 ✉ tom.mccourt@hackney.gov.uk

Environmental Health: Ms Aleyne Fontenelle, Interim Environmental Health Manager, Town Hall, Mare Street, London E8 1EA ☎ 020 8356 4918 🖷 020 8356 4740 ✉ aleyne.fontenelle@hackney.gov.uk

Estates, Property & Valuation: Mr Philip Glascoe, Interim Head of Estates, Keltan House, 89-755 Mare Street, Hackney, London E8 4RU ☎ 020 8536 4034 🖷 020 8536 8261 ✉ philip.glascoe@hackney.gov.uk

Events Manager: Ms Donna Walsh, Corporate Events Manager, Town Hall, Mare Street, London E8 1EA ☎ 020 8356 3410 ✉ donna.walsh@hackney.gov.uk

Facilities: Mr Simon Miller, Campus Building Manager, 6-15 Florfield Road, London E8 1DT ☎ 020 8356 3329 ✉ simon.miller@hackney.gov.uk

Finance and Treasurer: Ms Jill Davys, Head of Financial Services, Keltan House, 89-155 Mare Street, Hackney, London E8 4RU ☎ 020 8356 2646 ✉ jill.davys@hackney.gov.uk

Finance and Treasurer: Mr Ian Williams, Corporate Director of Finance & Resources, Town Hall, Mare Street, London E8 1EA ☎ 020 8356 3003 ✉ ian.williams@hackney.gov.uk

Fleet Management: Mr Norman Harding, Corporate Fleet Management, Keltan House, 89-115 Mare Street, London E8 4RU ☎ 020 8356 3613 ✉ norman.harding@hackney.gov.uk

Health and Safety: Mr Keith Miller, Head of HR Policy & Occupational Health, 280 Mare Street, London E8 1EA ☎ 020 8356 3473 ✉ keith.miller@hackney.gov.uk

Highways: Mr Trevor Rawson, Head of Highways & Engineering, Keltan House, 89-115 Mare Street, London E8 4RU ☎ 020 8356 8312 🖷 020 8356 2863 ✉ trevor.rawson@hackney.gov.uk

Housing: Ms Charlotte Graves, Corporate Director of Housing/Chief Executive of Hackney Homes, Christopher Addison House, 72 Wilton Way, London E8 1BJ ☎ 020 8356 3670 🖷 ; 020 8356 2242 ✉ charlotte.graves@hackney.gov.uk

Local Area Agreement: Mr Bruce Devile, Head of Corporate Performance, Town Hall, Mare Street, London E8 1EA ☎ 020 8356 3418 ✉ bruce.devile@hackney.gov.uk

Legal: Ms Gifty Edila, Corporate Director of Legal, HR and Regulatory Services, Town Hall, Mare Street, London E8 1EA ☎ 020 8356 3265 🖷 020 8536 3047 ✉ gifty.edila@hackney.gov.uk

Legal: Mr Yinka Owa, Assistant Director - Legal and Democratic Services, Town Hall, Mare Street, London E8 1EA ☎ 020 8356 6234 ✉ yinka.owa@hackney.gov.uk

Licensing: Ms Pat Tuohy, Principal Licensing Officer, 1 Hillman Street, London E8 1DY ☎ 020 8356 4971 ✉ pat.tuohy@hackney.gov.uk

Member Services: Ms Suzanne Awotwi, Deputy Head of Member Services, Town Hall, Mare Street, London E8 1EA ☎ 020 8356 3091 ✉ suzanne.awotwi@hackney.gov.uk

Parking: Mr Seamus Adams, Head of Parking Services, 2 Hillman Street, London E8 1FB ☎ 020 8356 8333 ✉ seamus.adams@hackney.gov.uk

Partnerships: Mr Ian Lewis, Chief Officer Policy and Partnership, Town Hall, Mare Street, London E8 1EA ☎ 020 8356 3388 ✉ ian.lewis@hackney.gov.uk

Personnel / HR: Ms Caroline Anderson, Assistant Director - HR and OD, 280 Mare Street, London E8 1EA ☎ 020 8356 3110 ✉ caroline.anderson@hackney.gov.uk

Planning: Mr Graham Loveland, Interim Assistant Director (Planning), 2 Hillman Street, London E8 1FB ☎ 020 8356 8134 ✉ graham.loveland@hackney.gov.uk

Procurement: Mr Chris Hudson, Assistant Director of Procurement & Fleet, 3rd Floor Keltan House, E8 4RU ☎ 020 8356 2725 🖷 020 8356 3037 ✉ chris.hudson@hackney.gov.uk

Recycling & Waste Minimisation: Mr Richard Gilbert, Senior Recycling Officer, Keltan House, 89-115 Mare Street, London E8 4RU ☎ 020 8356 4946 🖷 020 8356 4740 ✉ richard.gilbert@hackney.gov.uk

Regeneration: Mr Stephen McDonald, Assistant Director - Housing Regeneration & Strategy, Town Hall, Mare Street, London E8 1EA ☎ 020 8356 3315 🖷 020 8356 4740 ✉ stephen.mcdonald@hackney.gov.uk

Road Safety: Ms Maryann Allen, Road Safety Team Leader, Keltan House, 89-115 Mare Street, London E8 4RU ☎ 020 8356 8184 🖷 020 8356 8263 ✉ maryann.allen@hackney.gov.uk

Social Services: Mr Stephen John, Head of MHCOP & Social Care Lead, 30 Felstead Street, London E9 5LG ☎ 020 8356 8500 ✉ stephen.john@hackney.gov.uk

Social Services (Adult): Ms Kim Wright, Corporate Director of Health and Community Services, Town Hall, Mare Street, London E8 1EA ☎ 020 8356 7347 🖷 020 8356 7544 ✉ kim.wright@hackney.gov.uk

Social Services (Children): Ms Sheila Durr, Head of Looked After Children, 1 Hillman Street, London E8 1DY ☎ 020 8356 4603 🖷 020 8356 4740 ✉ sheila.durr@hackney.gov.uk

Social Services (Children): Mr Steve Goodman, Deputy Director Children & Young Peoples Services, 1 Hillman Street, London E8 1DY ☎ 020 8356 4757 🖷 020 8356 4740 ✉ steve.goodman@hackney.gov.uk

Street Scene: Mr Andy Cunningham, Head of Streetscene, Keltan House, 89-115 Mare Street, London E8 4RU ☎ 020 8356 6657 ✉ andy.cunningham@hackney.gov.uk

Traffic Management: Mr Andy Cunningham, Head of Streetscene, Keltan House, 89-115 Mare Street, London E8 4RU ☎ 020 8356 6657 ✉ andy.cunningham@hackney.gov.uk

Transport: Mr Andy Cunningham, Head of Streetscene, Keltan House, 89-115 Mare Street, London E8 4RU ☎ 020 8356 6657 ✉ andy.cunningham@hackney.gov.uk

Transport: Mr Tom McCourt, Assistant Director of Public Realm, Keltan House, 89-115 Mare Street, London E8 4RU ☎ 020 8356 8219 ✉ tom.mccourt@hackney.gov.uk

Transport Planner: Satu Vaisanen, Transport Planner, 300 Mare Street, London E8 3HE ☎ 020 8356 8123 ✉ satu.vaisanen@hackney.gov.uk

Waste Collection and Disposal: Mr Jim Paterson, Interim Divisional Head of Building Maintenance, 6-15 Florfield Road, London E8 1DT ☎ 020 8356 6899 🖷 020 8356 4740 ✉ jim.paterson@hackney.gov.uk

Waste Management: Mr John Wheatley, Head of Waste, Millfields Depot, London E5 0AR ☎ 0208 356 6690 ✉ john.wheatley@hackney.gov.uk

MEMBERS OF THE COUNCIL (58)

***Directly Elected Mayor:* Pipe**, Jules (LAB -)
***Deputy Mayor:* Alcock**, Karen (LAB - Clissold)
karen.alcock@hackney.gov.uk
Akehurst, Luke (LAB - Chatham)
luke.akehurst@hackney.gov.uk
Akhoon, Dawood (LD - Cazenove)
dawood.akhoon@hackney.gov.uk
Aussenberg, Bernard (CON - Lordship)
bernard.aussenberg@hackney.gov.uk
Bell, Brian (LAB - Brownswood)
brian.bell@hackney.gov.uk
Bramble, Antoinette (LAB - Wick)
anntoinette.bramble@hackney.gov.uk
Brown, Edward (LAB - Lordship)
edward.brown@hackney.gov.uk
Buitekant, Barry (LAB - Haggerston)
barry.buitekant@hackney.gov.uk
Chapman, Robert (LAB - De Beauvoir)
robert.chapman@hackney.gov.uk
De Botton, Oli (LAB - Brownswood)
Oli.DeBotton@Hackney.gov.uk
Demirci, Feryal (LAB - Brownswood)
feryal.demirci@hackney.gov.uk
Desmond, Michael (LAB - Hackney Downs)
michael@desm.new.labour.org.uk
Ebbutt, Tom (LAB - De Beauvoir)
tom.ebbutt@hackney.gov.uk
Fajana, Susan (LAB - Stoke Newington Central)
susan.fajanathomas@hackney.gov.uk
Glanville, Philip (LAB - Hoxton)
philip.glanville@hackney.gov.uk
Gordon, Margaret (LAB - Springfield)
margaret.gordon@hackney.gov.uk
Gregory, Michelle (LAB - Dalston)
michelle.gregory@hackney.gov.uk
Hanson, Katie (LAB - Victoria)
katie.hanson@hackney.gov.uk
Icoz, Gulay (LAB - De Beauvoir)
gulay.icoz@hackney.gov.uk
Jacobson, Abraham (LD - Cazenove)
abraham.jacobson@hackney.gov.uk
Jones, Michael (LAB - New River)
michael.jones@hackney.gov.uk
Kelly, Linda (LAB - Leabridge)
linda.kelly@hackney.gov.uk
Kemp, Daniel (LAB - Victoria)
daniel.kemp@hackney.gov.uk
Kennedy, Christopher (LAB - Wick)
christopher.kennedy@hackney.gov.uk
Krishna, Rita (LAB - Stoke Newington Central)
rita.krishna@hackney.gov.uk
Laing, Alan (LAB - Hackney Central)
alan.laing@hackney.gov.uk
Levy, Michael (CON - Springfield)
Linden, Sophie (LAB - Dalston)
sophie.linden@hackney.gov.uk
Lloyd, Samantha (LAB - Hackney Central)
samantha.lloyd@hackney.gov.uk
McKenzie, Clayeon (LAB - Hoxton)
clayeon.mckenzie@hackney.gov.uk
McShane, Jonathan (LAB - Haggerston)
jonathan.mcshane@hackney.gov.uk
Mitchell, Wendy (LAB - Clissold)
wendy.mitchell@hackney.gov.uk
Muir, Rick (LAB - Hackney Downs)
rick.muir@hackney.gov.uk
Mulready, Sally (LAB - Chatham)
sally.mulready@hackney.gov.uk
Mulready, Ned (LAB - New River)
ned.mulready@hackney.gov.uk
Mulready-Jones, Angus (LAB - Dalston)
angus.mulready-jones@hackney.gov.uk
Munn, Ann (LAB - Haggerston)
ann.munn@hackney.gov.uk
Nicholson, Guy (LAB - Chatham)
guy.nicholson@hackney.gov.uk
Nkafu, Julius (LAB - Kings Park)
julius.nfaku@hackney.gov.uk
Oguzkanli, Deniz (LAB - Leabridge)
deniz.oguzkanli@hackney.gov.uk
Papier, Benzion (CON - New River)
Patrick, Sharon (LAB - Kings Park)
sharon.patrick@hackney.gov.uk
Plouviez, Emma (LAB - Queensbridge)
emma.plouviez@hackney.gov.uk
Price, Tom (LAB - Queensbridge)
tom.price@hackney.gov.uk
Rathbone, Ian (LAB - Leabridge)
ian.rathbone@hackney.gov.uk
Russell, Alex (LAB - Hackney Downs)
alex.russell@hackney.gov.uk
Sharer, Ian (LD - Cazenove)
ian.sharer@Hackney.gov.uk
Siddiqui, Saleem (LAB - Kings Park)
saleem.siddiqui@hackney.gov.uk
Smith, Linda (LAB - Clissold)
linda.smith@hackney.gov.uk
Steinberger, Simche (CON - Springfield)
simche.steinberger@hackney.gov.uk
Stevens, Daniel (LAB - Lordship)
daniel.stevens@hackney.gov.uk
Stops, Vincent (LAB - Hackney Central)
vincent.stops@hackney.gov.uk
Taylor, Geoffrey (LAB - Victoria)
geoffrey.taylor@hackney.gov.uk
Thomson, Louisa (LAB - Stoke Newington Central)
louisa.thomson@hackney.gov.uk
Vernon, Patrick (LAB - Queensbridge)
patrick.vernon@hackney.gov.uk
Webb, Jessica (LAB - Wick)
jessica.webb@hackney.gov.uk
Williams, Carole (LAB - Hoxton)
carole.williams@hackney.gov.uk

POLITICAL COMPOSITION

LAB: 51, CON: 4, LD: 3

CABINET

Children's Services: Ms Rita Krishna
Community Services: Mr Jonathan McShane
Crime, Sustainability & Customer Services: Ms Sophie Linden
Finance: Ms Samantha Lloyd
Neighbourhoods: Ms Feryal Demirci
Regeneration & 2012 Olympic & Paralympic Games: Mr Guy Nicholson

COMMITTEE CHAIRS

Appointments: Mr Jules Pipe

Audit Sub Committee: Mr Brian Bell
Better Homes Partnership Board: Ms Charlotte Graves
Better Homes Partnership Board: Ms Karen Alcock
Cabinet Procurement: Ms Samantha Lloyd
Cabinet: Mr Jules Pipe
Children & Young People Partnership Board: Ms Rita Krishna
Children & Young People Scrutiny Commission: Ms Gulay Icoz
Community Safety & Social Inclusion Scrutiny Commission: Ms Carole Williams
Council Joint Committee: Ms Karen Alcock
Economic Development Partnership Board: Mr Guy Nicholson
Economic Development Partnership Board: Mr Ian Ashman
Governance & Resources Scrutiny Commission (Scrutiny): Mr Robert Chapman
Health in Hackney Scrutiny Commission (Scrutiny): Mr Luke Akehurst
Homerton Neighbourhood Forum: Mr Geoffrey Taylor
Licensing: Mr Christopher Kennedy
Living in Hackney Scrutiny Commission: Mr Philip Glanville
North East Neighbourhood Committee: TBA
Overview & Scrutiny Board: Mr Simche Steinberger
Pensions Sub Committee: Ms Samantha Lloyd
Planning Sub Committee: Mr Vincent Stops
Regulatory: Mr Brian Bell
Safer Cleaner Partnership Board: Mr Tim Shields (External)
Shoreditch Neighbourhood: Ms Ann Munn
Standards: Mr George Gross (External)
Stoke Newington Neighbourhood Forum: TBA
Team Hackney Board: Mr Jules Pipe

HALTON U

Halton Borough Council, Municipal Building, Kingsway, Widnes WA8 7QF ☎ 0303 333 4300 🖷 0151 471 7301 hdl@halton.gov.uk www.halton.gov.uk

FACTS & FIGURES

Police Authority: Cheshire Police Authority
Health Authority: North West Strategic Health Authority
Learning and Skills Council: North West
Parliamentary Constituencies: Halton
EU Constituencies: North West
Election Frequency: Elections are by thirds
Twinning: Economic linkages: Leiria (Portugal); Marzahn, Berlin (Germany); Usti nad Labem (Czech Republic); Tongling City (China)

PRINCIPAL OFFICERS

Chief Executive: Mr David Parr, Chief Executive, Municipal Building, Kingsway, Widnes WA8 7QF ☎ 0303 333 4300 david.parr@halton.gov.uk

Senior Management: Mr Dwayne Johnson, Strategic Director - Health & Communtiy, Municipal Building, Kingsway, Widnes WA8 7QF ☎ 0303 333 4300 🖷 0151 471 7536 dwayne.johnson@halton.gov.uk

Senior Management: Mr Ian Leivesley, Strategic Director - Corporate & Policy, Municipal Building, Kingsway, Widnes WA8 7QF ☎ 0151 907 8300 ian.leivesley@halton.gov.uk

Senior Management: Mr Richard Tregea, Strategic Director - Environment, Municipal Building, Kingsway, Widnes WA8 7QF ☎ 0151 907 8300 🖷 0151 471 7304 richard.tregea@halton.gov.uk

Architect, Building / Property Services: Mr Wesley Rourke, Operational Director - Employment, Enterprise & Property, Corporate & Policy Directorate, Municipal Building, Kingsway, Widnes WA8 7QF ☎ 0303 333 4300 wesley.rourke@halton.gov.uk

Best Value: Mr Mike Foy, Senior Performance Management Officer, Corporate & Policy Directorate, Municipal Building, Kingsway, Widnes WA8 7QF ☎ 0151 511 8081 🖷 0151 471 7301 mike.foy@halton.gov.uk

Building Control: Mr Mick Noone, Operational Director - Policy, Planning & Transportation, Municipal Building, Kingsway, Widnes WA8 7QF ☎ 0151 471 7370 mick.noone@halton.gov.uk

Catering Services: Mr Chris Patino, Operational Director - Communities & Environment, Halton Stadium, Lowerhouse Lane, Widnes WA8 7DZ ☎ 0151 510 6000 chris.patino@halton.gov.uk

Children / Youth Services: Mr Gareth Jones, Head of Service - Youth Offenders, Grosvenor House, Halton Lea, Runcorn WA7 2WD ☎ 0151 511 7499 gareth.jones@halton.gov.uk

Children / Youth Services: Mr Gerald Meehan, Strategic Director - Children & Young People, Municipal Building, Kingsway, Widnes WA8 7QF ☎ 0151 907 8300 gerald.meehan@halton.gov.uk

Children / Youth Services: Mr Steve Nyakatawa, Operational Director - Children & Young People, Grosvenor House, Halton Lea, Runcorn WA7 2WD ☎ 0151 906 4846 steve.nyakatawa@halton.gov.uk

PR / Communications: Miss Michelle Baker, Operational Director - Communications & Marketing, Municipal Building, Kingsway, Widnes WA8 7QF ☎ 0151 471 7388 🖷 0151 471 7311 michelle.baker@halton.gov.uk

Community Safety: Mr Mick Andrews, Community Safety Officer, 6-8 Church Street, Runcorn WA8 7LT ☎ 0151 511 7695

Computer Management: Mr Simon Riley, Operational Director - ICT Services, Municipal Building, Kingsway, Widnes WA8 7QF ☎ 0151 424 2061 🖷 0151 471 7302 simon.riley@halton.gov.uk

Contracts: Ms Lorraine Cox, Operational Director - Procurement, Municipal Building, Kingsway, Widnes WA8 7QF ☎ 0151 907 8300 lorraine.cox@halton.gov.uk

Corporate Services: Mr Ian Leivesley, Strategic Director - Corporate & Policy, Municipal Building, Kingsway, Widnes WA8 7QF ☎ 0151 907 8300 ian.leivesley@halton.gov.uk

Education: Mr Gerald Meehan, Strategic Director - Children & Young People, Municipal Building, Kingsway, Widnes WA8 7QF ☎ 0151 907 8300 gerald.meehan@halton.gov.uk

E-Government: Mr Patrick Oliver, E-Government Development Team Leader, Municipal Building, Kingsway, Widnes WA8 7QF ☎ 0151 907 8390 ✉ pat.oliver@halton.gov.uk

Electoral Registration: Mrs Christine Lawley, Principal Electoral Services/ Elections Officer, Corporate & Policy Directorate, Municipal Building, Kingsway, Widnes WA8 7QF ☎ 0151 511 8328 🖷 0151 471 7301 ✉ christine.lawley@halton.gov.uk

Emergency Planning: Mr Stephen Rimmer, Head - Traffic Risk & Emergency Planning, Municipal Building, Kingsway, Widnes WA8 7QF ☎ 0151 907 8300 🖷 0151 471 7301 ✉ stephen.rimmer@halton.gov.uk

Environmental Health: Mr Richard Tregea, Strategic Director - Environment, Municipal Building, Kingsway, Widnes WA8 7QF ☎ 0151 907 8300 🖷 0151 471 7304 ✉ richard.tregea@halton.gov.uk

Estates, Property & Valuation: Mr Wesley Rourke, Operational Director - Employment, Enterprise & Property, Corporate & Policy Directorate, Municipal Building, Kingsway, Widnes WA8 7QF ☎ 0303 333 4300 ✉ wesley.rourke@halton.gov.uk

Events Manager: Ms Amy Covington, Events Officer, The Heath Business & Technical Park, Runcorn WA7 4QX ☎ 0151 511 8914 ✉ amy.covington@halton.gov.uk

Facilities: Mr Bill Seymour, Facilities Manager, Municipal Building, Kingsway, Widnes WA8 7QF ☎ 0151 907 8300 🖷 0151 471 7309 ✉ william.seymour@halton.gov.uk

Finance and Treasurer: Mr Bill Dodd, Operational Director - Financial Services, Municipal Building, Kingsway, Widnes WA8 7QF ☎ 0151 471 7336 ✉ bill.dodd@halton.gov.uk

Finance and Treasurer: Mr Peter McCann, Head - Halton Direct Link & Revenue & Benefits, Municipal Building, Kingsway, Widnes WA8 7QF ☎ 0151 471 7430 ✉ peter.mccann@halton.gov.uk

Fleet Management: Mr Chris Cullen, Head - Operational Support Services, Lowerhouse Lane Depot, Lowerhouse Lane, Widnes WA8 7AW ☎ 0151 424 2061 🖷 0151 471 7305 ✉ chris.cullen@halton.gov.uk

Grounds Maintenance: Mr Tim Ward-Dutton, Operational Spaces Manager, Municipal Building, Kingsway, Widnes WA8 7QF ☎ 01928 583913 ✉ tim.ward-dutton@halton.gov.uk

Highways: Mr Mick Noone, Operational Director - Policy, Planning & Transportation, Municipal Building, Kingsway, Widnes WA8 7QF ☎ 0151 471 7370 ✉ mick.noone@halton.gov.uk

Local Area Agreement: Ms Shelah Semoff, Partnership Officer, Municipal Building, Kingsway, Widnes WA8 7QF ☎ 0151 471 7528 ✉ shelah.semoff@halton.gov.uk

Legal: Mr Mark Reaney, Operational Director - Legal & Democratic Services, Municipal Building, Kingsway, Widnes WA8 7QF ☎ 0151 907 8300 🖷 0151 471 7301 ✉ mark.reaney@halton.gov.uk

Leisure and Cultural Services: Mr Chris Patino, Operational Director - Communities & Environment, Halton Stadium, Lowerhouse Lane, Widnes WA8 7DZ ☎ 0151 510 6000 ✉ chris.patino@halton.gov.uk

Licensing: Mr Mark Reaney, Operational Director - Legal & Democratic Services, Municipal Building, Kingsway, Widnes WA8 7QF ☎ 0151 907 8300 🖷 0151 471 7301 ✉ mark.reaney@halton.gov.uk

Lighting: Mr Stephen Rimmer, Head - Traffic Risk & Emergency Planning, Municipal Building, Kingsway, Widnes WA8 7QF ☎ 0151 907 8300 🖷 0151 471 7301 ✉ stephen.rimmer@halton.gov.uk

Lottery Funding, Charity and Voluntary: Mr Wesley Rourke, Operational Director - Employment, Enterprise & Property, Corporate & Policy Directorate, Municipal Building, Kingsway, Widnes WA8 7QF ☎ 0303 333 4300 ✉ wesley.rourke@halton.gov.uk

Member Services: Mrs Christine Lawley, Principal Electoral Services/ Elections Officer, Corporate & Policy Directorate, Municipal Building, Kingsway, Widnes WA8 7QF ☎ 0151 511 8328 🖷 0151 471 7301 ✉ christine.lawley@halton.gov.uk

Personnel / HR: Mr Jane Burgess, Divisional Manager - Human Resources & Learning Development, Municipal Building, Kingsway, Widnes WA8 7QF ☎ 0151 471 7522 ✉ jane.burgess@halton.gov.uk

Planning: Mr Mick Noone, Operational Director - Policy, Planning & Transportation, Municipal Building, Kingsway, Widnes WA8 7QF ☎ 0151 471 7370 ✉ mick.noone@halton.gov.uk

Procurement: Ms Lorraine Cox, Operational Director - Procurement, Municipal Building, Kingsway, Widnes WA8 7QF ☎ 0151 907 8300 ✉ lorraine.cox@halton.gov.uk

Public Libraries: Ms Paula Reilly-Cooper, Library Services Manager, Town Hall, Heath Road, Runcorn WA7 5TD ☎ 0151 907 8300 🖷 0151 471 7303 ✉ paula.reilly-cooper@halton.gov.uk

Recycling & Waste Minimisation: Mr Andy Horrocks, Recycling Officer, Lowerhouse Lane Depot, Lowerhouse Lane, Widnes WA8 7AW ☎ 0151 511 7520 🖷 0151 471 7305 ✉ andy.horrocks@halton.gov.uk

Road Safety: Mr Stephen Rimmer, Head - Traffic Risk & Emergency Planning, Municipal Building, Kingsway, Widnes WA8 7QF ☎ 0151 907 8300 🖷 0151 471 7301 ✉ stephen.rimmer@halton.gov.uk

Social Services: Mr Dwayne Johnson, Strategic Director - Health & Communtiy, Municipal Building, Kingsway, Widnes WA8 7QF ☎ 0303 333 4300 🖷 0151 471 7536 ✉ dwayne.johnson@halton.gov.uk

Staff Training: Mr Jane Burgess, Divisional Manager - Human Resources & Learning Development, Municipal Building, Kingsway, Widnes WA8 7QF ☎ 0151 471 7522 ✉ jane.burgess@halton.gov.uk

Town Centre: Mr Paul Smith, Town Centre Manager, Halton Business Forum, Victoria Square, Widnes WA8 7QZ ☎ 0151 907 8300 ✉ paul.smith@halton.gov.uk

Traffic Management: Mr Stephen Rimmer, Head - Traffic Risk & Emergency Planning, Municipal Building, Kingsway, Widnes WA8 7QF ☎ 0151 907 8300 🖷 0151 471 7301 ✉ stephen.rimmer@halton.gov.uk

Transport: Mr Mick Noone, Operational Director - Policy, Planning & Transportation, Municipal Building, Kingsway, Widnes WA8 7QF ☎ 0151 471 7370 ✉ mick.noone@halton.gov.uk

Transport Planner: Mr Mick Noone, Operational Director - Policy, Planning & Transportation, Municipal Building, Kingsway, Widnes WA8 7QF ☎ 0151 471 7370 ✉ mick.noone@halton.gov.uk

Waste Collection and Disposal: Mr Jimmy Unsworth, Head - Waste Management, Lowerhouse Lane Depot, Lowerhouse Lane, Widnes WA8 7AW ☎ 0151 907 8300 🖷 0151 471 7305 ✉ jimmy.Unsworth@halton.gov.uk

Waste Management: Mr Jimmy Unsworth, Head - Waste Management, Lowerhouse Lane Depot, Lowerhouse Lane, Widnes WA8 7AW ☎ 0151 907 8300 🖷 0151 471 7305 ✉ jimmy.Unsworth@halton.gov.uk

MEMBERS OF THE COUNCIL (56)

***Mayor:* McInerney**, Tom (LAB - Halton View)
tom.mcinerney@halton.gov.uk
***Deputy Mayor:* Ratcliffe**, Margaret (LD - Heath)
margaret.ratcliffe@halton.gov.uk
***Leader of the Council:* Polhill**, Rob (LAB - Halton View)
rob.polhill@halton.gov.uk
***Deputy Leader of the Council:* Wharton**, Mike (LAB - Hale)
mike.wharton@halton.gov.uk
***Group Leader:* Logan**, Geoffrey (LAB - Beechwood)
geoffrey.logan@halton.gov.uk
Baker, Sandra (LAB - Birchfield)
sandra.baker@halton.gov.uk
Bradshaw, Marjorie (CON - Daresbury)
marjorie.bradshaw@halton.gov.uk
Bradshaw, John (CON - Daresbury)
john.bradshaw@halton.gov.uk
Cargill, Dave (LAB - Norton South)
dave.cargill@halton.gov.uk
Cargill, Ellen (LAB - Halton Castle)
ellen.cargill@halton.gov.uk
Cassidy, Lauren (LAB - Norton North)
lauren.cassidy@halton.gov.uk
Cole, Arthur (LAB - Halton Castle)
arthur.cole@halton.gov.uk
Dennett, Mark (LAB - Grange)
mark.dennett@halton.gov.uk
Edge, Susan (LAB - Appleton)
sue.edge@halton.gov.uk
Fraser, Frank (LAB - Kingsway)
frank.fraser@halton.gov.uk
Fry, Mike (LAB - Birchfield)
michael.fry@halton.gov.uk
Gerrard, John (LAB - Mersey)
john.gerrard@halton.gov.uk
Gilligan, Robert (LAB - Broadheath)
robert.gilligan@halton.gov.uk
Harris, Phil (LAB - Hough Green)
phil.harris@halton.gov.uk
Hignett, Pauline (LAB - Windmill House)
pauline.hignett2@halton.gov.uk
Hignett, Ron (LAB - Norton South)
ron.hignett@halton.gov.uk
Hill, Valerie (LAB - Farnworth)
valerie.hill@halton.gov.uk
Hill, Stan (LAB - Riverside)
stan.hill@halton.gov.uk
Hodge, Miriam (LD - Kingsway)
miriam.hodge@halton.gov.uk
Horabin, Margaret (LAB - Kingsway)
margaret.horabin@halton.gov.uk
Howard, Harry (LAB - Halton Castle)
harry.howard@halton.gov.uk
Jones, Eddie (LAB - Appleton)
eddie.jones@halton.gov.uk
Lea, Darren (LAB - Grange)
darren.lea@halton.gov.uk
Lloyd-Jones, Martha (LAB - Norton South)
martha.lloydjones@halton.gov.uk
Lloyd-Jones, Peter (LAB - Norton North)
peter.lloydjones@halton.gov.uk
Loftus, Kath (LAB - Halton Lea)
kath.loftus@halton.gov.uk
Loftus, Chris (LAB - Beechwood)
chris.loftus@halton.gov.uk
Lowe, Alan (LAB - Halton Lea)
alan.lowe@halton.gov.uk
Lowe, Joan (LAB - Grange)
joan.lowe@halton.gov.uk
MacManus, Andrew (LAB - Farnworth)
andrew.macmanus@halton.gov.uk
McDermott, Tony (LAB - Broadheath)
tony.mcdermott@halton.gov.uk
McInerney, Angela (LAB - Farnworth)
angela.mcinerney@halton.gov.uk
Morley, Keith (LAB - Broadheath)
keith.morley@halton.gov.uk
Nelson, Steff (LAB - Halton Brook)
stef.nelson@halton.gov.uk
Nolan, Paul (LAB - Hough Green)
paul.nolan@halton.gov.uk
Osborne, Shaun (LAB - Ditton)
shaun.osborne@halton.gov.uk
Parker, Stan (LAB - Halton View)
stan.parker@halton.gov.uk
Philbin, Ged (LAB - Appleton)
ged.philbin@halton.gov.uk
Plumpton-Walsh, Carol (LAB - Halton Brook)
carol.plumptonwalsh@halton.gov.uk
Pumpton-Walsh, Norman (LAB - Mersey)
norman.plumptonwalsh@halton.gov.uk
Roberts, Joe (LAB - Ditton)
joe.roberts@halton.gov.uk
Rowe, Christopher (LD - Heath)
christopher.rowe@halton.gov.uk
Sinnott, Pauline (LAB - Mersey)
pauline.sinnott2@halton.gov.uk
Stockton, John (LAB - Halton Brook)
john.stockton@halton.gov.uk
Stockton, Gareth (LD - Heath)
gareth.stockton@halton.gov.uk

Thompson, Dave (LAB - Halton Lea)
dave.thompson@halton.gov.uk
Wainwright, Kevan (LAB - Hough Green)
kevan.wainwright@halton.gov.uk
Wallace, Pamela (LAB - Riverside)
pamela.wallace@halton.gov.uk
Woolfall, Bill (LAB - Birchfield)
bill.woolfall2@halton.gov.uk
Wright, Marie (LAB - Ditton)
marie.wright@halton.gov.uk
Zygadllo, Geoff (LAB - Norton North)
geoff.zygadllo@halton.gov.uk

POLITICAL COMPOSITION
LAB: 50, LD: 4, CON: 2

CABINET
Leader: Mr Rob Polhill
Deputy Leader / Resources: Mr Mike Wharton
Children, Young People & Families: Mr Ged Philbin
Community Safety: Mr Dave Cargill
Environmental Sustainability: Mr Steff Nelson
Health & Adults: Ms Marie Wright
Neighbourhood, Leisure & Sport: Mr Phil Harris
Physical Environment: Mr Ron Hignett
Transportation: Mr John Stockton

COMMITTEE CHAIRS
Children, Young People & Families: Mr Mark Dennett
Corporate Policy & Performance: Mr Robert Gilligan
Development Control: Mr Paul Nolan
Employment, Learning Skills & Community: Ms Susan Edge
Environment & Urban Renewal: Mr John Gerrard
Health Policy & Performance: Ms Ellen Cargill
Regulatory: Mrs Kath Loftus
Standards: Mr Peter Lloyd-Jones

HAMBLETON D
Hambleton District Council, Civic Centre, Stone Cross, Northallerton DL6 2UU ☎ 0845 121 1555 🖷 01609 767228
✉ info@hambleton.gov.uk 🖳 www.hambleton.gov.uk

FACTS & FIGURES
Police Authority: North Yorkshire Police Authority
Health Authority: NHS Yorkshire & the Humber
Learning and Skills Council: Yorkshire and the Humber
Parliamentary Constituencies: Richmond (Yorks)
EU Constituencies: Yorkshire and the Humber
Election Frequency: Elections are of whole council

PRINCIPAL OFFICERS
Chief Executive: Mr Phil Morton, Chief Executive, Civic Centre, Stone Cross, Northallerton DL6 2UU ☎ 01609 767022; 01609 767001 ✉ phil.morton@hambleton.gov.uk

Senior Management: Mr Dave Goodwin, Director of Leisure & Health, Civic Centre, Stone Cross, Northallerton DL6 2UU ☎ 01609 767147 🖷 01609 767228 ✉ dave.goodwin@hambleton.gov.uk

Senior Management: Mr Michael Jewitt, Director of Housing & Planning, Civic Centre, Stone Cross, Northallerton DL6 2UU ☎ 01609 757053 🖷 01609 767228 ✉ mick.jewitt@hambleton.gov.uk

Senior Management: Mr Martyn Richards, Director of Corporate Services, Civic Centre, Stone Cross, Northallerton DL6 2UU ☎ 01609 767010 🖷 01609 767228 ✉ martyn.richards@hambleton.gov.uk

Senior Management: Mrs Sandra Walbran, Director of Customer Services, Civic Centre, Stone Cross, Northallerton DL6 2UU ☎ 01609 767235 🖷 01609 767228 ✉ sandra.walbran@hambleton.gov.uk

Architect, Building / Property Services: Mr David McGloin, Assistant Director, Civic Centre, Stone Cross, Northallerton DL6 2UU ☎ 0845 121 1555 🖷 01609 767228 ✉ david.mcgloin@hambleton.gov.uk

Building Control: Mr Maurice Cann, Head of Services Development, Civic Centre, Stone Cross, Northallerton DL6 2UU ☎ 0845 121 1555 ✉ maurice.cann@richmondshire.gov.uk; maurice.cann@hambleton.gov.uk

PR / Communications: Mrs Aly Thompson, Communications Manager, Civic Centre, Stone Cross, Northallerton DL6 2UU ☎ 01609 767063 ✉ aly.thompson@hambleton.gov.uk

Community Planning: Mrs Sandra Walbran, Director of Customer Services, Civic Centre, Stone Cross, Northallerton DL6 2UU ☎ 01609 767235 🖷 01609 767228 ✉ sandra.walbran@hambleton.gov.uk

Community Safety: Mr Michael Jewitt, Director of Housing & Planning, Civic Centre, Stone Cross, Northallerton DL6 2UU ☎ 01609 757053 🖷 01609 767228 ✉ mick.jewitt@hambleton.gov.uk

Customer Service: Mr Simon Fletcher, Assistant Director, Swale House, Frenchgate, Richmond DL10 4JE

Economic Development: Mr David McGloin, Assistant Director, Civic Centre, Stone Cross, Northallerton DL6 2UU ☎ 0845 121 1555 🖷 01609 767228 ✉ david.mcgloin@hambleton.gov.uk

Electoral Registration: Mr Martyn Richards, Director of Corporate Services, Civic Centre, Stone Cross, Northallerton DL6 2UU ☎ 01609 767010 🖷 01609 767228 ✉ martyn.richards@hambleton.gov.uk

Emergency Planning: Mr Callum McKeon, Assistant Director, Civic Centre, Stone Cross, Northallerton DL6 2UU ☎ 01748 829100 🖷 01748 826186 ✉ callum.mckeon@richmondshire.gov.uk; callum.mckeon@hambleton.gov.uk

Environmental / Technical Services: Mr Maurice Cann, Head of Services Development, Civic Centre, Stone Cross, Northallerton DL6 2UU ✉ maurice.cann@hambleton.gov.uk

Environmental Health: Mr Philip Mepham, Environmental Health Manager, Swale House, Frenchgate, Richmond DL10 4JE ☎ 01748 829100 🖷 01748 826186

philip.mepham@richmondshire.gov.uk

Finance and Treasurer: Ms Claire Blackburn, Finance Manager, Swale House, Frenchgate, Richmond DL10 4JE ☎ 01748 829100 🖷 01748 826186 claire.blackburn@richmondshire.gov.uk

Grounds Maintenance: Mr David McGloin, Assistant Director, Civic Centre, Stone Cross, Northallerton DL6 2UU ☎ 0845 121 1555 🖷 01609 767228 david.mcgloin@hambleton.gov.uk

Health and Safety: Mr Tim Burrows, Health & Safety Advisor, Swale House, Frenchgate, Richmond DL10 4JE ☎ 01748 829100 🖷 01748 826186 tim.burrows@richmondshire.gov.uk

Housing: Mr Michael Jewitt, Director of Housing & Planning, Civic Centre, Stone Cross, Northallerton DL6 2UU ☎ 01609 757053 🖷 01609 767228 mick.jewitt@hambleton.gov.uk

Housing Maintenance: Mr Michael Jewitt, Director of Housing & Planning, Civic Centre, Stone Cross, Northallerton DL6 2UU ☎ 01609 757053 🖷 01609 767228 mick.jewitt@hambleton.gov.uk

Local Area Agreement: Mr Michael Jewitt, Director of Housing & Planning, Civic Centre, Stone Cross, Northallerton DL6 2UU ☎ 01609 757053 🖷 01609 767228 mick.jewitt@hambleton.gov.uk

Legal: Mr Martyn Richards, Director of Corporate Services, Civic Centre, Stone Cross, Northallerton DL6 2UU ☎ 01609 767010 🖷 01609 767228 martyn.richards@hambleton.gov.uk

Leisure and Cultural Services: Mr Dave Goodwin, Director of Leisure & Health, Civic Centre, Stone Cross, Northallerton DL6 2UU ☎ 01609 767147 🖷 01609 767228 dave.goodwin@hambleton.gov.uk

Licensing: Mr Maurice Cann, Head of Services Development, Civic Centre, Stone Cross, Northallerton DL6 2UU maurice.cann@hambleton.gov.uk

Lighting: Mr David McGloin, Assistant Director, Civic Centre, Stone Cross, Northallerton DL6 2UU ☎ 0845 121 1555 🖷 01609 767228 david.mcgloin@hambleton.gov.uk

Member Services: Mr Callum McKeon, Assistant Director, Civic Centre, Stone Cross, Northallerton DL6 2UU ☎ 01748 829100 🖷 01748 826186 callum.mckeon@richmondshire.gov.uk; callum.mckeon@hambleton.gov.uk

Parking: Mr David McGloin, Assistant Director, Civic Centre, Stone Cross, Northallerton DL6 2UU ☎ 0845 121 1555 🖷 01609 767228 david.mcgloin@hambleton.gov.uk

Partnerships: Mrs Sandra Walbran, Director of Customer Services, Civic Centre, Stone Cross, Northallerton DL6 2UU ☎ 01609 767235 🖷 01609 767228 sandra.walbran@hambleton.gov.uk

Personnel / HR: Ms Sheila Somerford, Head of People Services, Civic Centre, Stone Cross, Northallerton DL6 2UU ☎ 01609 767066; 01748 829100 🖷 01748 826186 sheila.somerford@hamledon.gov.uk; sheila.somerford@richmondshire.gov.uk

Planning: Mr Maurice Cann, Head of Services Development, Civic Centre, Stone Cross, Northallerton DL6 2UU maurice.cann@hambleton.gov.uk

Procurement: Mrs Sandra Walbran, Director of Customer Services, Civic Centre, Stone Cross, Northallerton DL6 2UU ☎ 01609 767235 🖷 01609 767228 sandra.walbran@hambleton.gov.uk

Recycling & Waste Minimisation: Mr Paul Staines, Operations Manager, Civic Centre, Stone Cross, Northallerton DL6 2UU ☎ 0845 121 1555 paul.staines@hambleton.gov.uk

Regeneration: Mr David McGloin, Assistant Director, Civic Centre, Stone Cross, Northallerton DL6 2UU ☎ 0845 121 1555 🖷 01609 767228 david.mcgloin@hambleton.gov.uk

Staff Training: Ms Sheila Somerford, Head of People Services, Civic Centre, Stone Cross, Northallerton DL6 2UU ☎ 01609 767066; 01748 829100 🖷 01748 826186 sheila.somerford@hamledon.gov.uk; sheila.somerford@richmondshire.gov.uk

Street Scene: Mr John Proud, Street Scene Manager, Civic Centre, Stone Cross, Northallerton DL6 2UU ☎ 0845 121 1555 john.proud@hambleton.gov.uk

Sustainable Communities: Mr Michael Jewitt, Director of Housing & Planning, Civic Centre, Stone Cross, Northallerton DL6 2UU ☎ 01609 757053 🖷 01609 767228 mick.jewitt@hambleton.gov.uk

Sustainable Development: Mr Michael Jewitt, Director of Housing & Planning, Civic Centre, Stone Cross, Northallerton DL6 2UU ☎ 01609 757053 🖷 01609 767228 mick.jewitt@hambleton.gov.uk

Tourism: Mr David McGloin, Assistant Director, Civic Centre, Stone Cross, Northallerton DL6 2UU ☎ 0845 121 1555 🖷 01609 767228 david.mcgloin@hambleton.gov.uk

Waste Collection and Disposal: Mr Paul Staines, Operations Manager, Civic Centre, Stone Cross, Northallerton DL6 2UU ☎ 0845 121 1555 paul.staines@hambleton.gov.uk

Waste Management: Mr Paul Staines, Operations Manager, Civic Centre, Stone Cross, Northallerton DL6 2UU ☎ 0845 121 1555 paul.staines@hambleton.gov.uk

Children's Play Areas: Ms Jo-Anne Simpson, Culture & Wellbeing Delivery Manager, Civic Centre, Stone Cross, Northallerton DL6 2UU ☎ 01748 829100 🖷 01748 826186 jo-anne.simpson@richmondshire.gov.uk; joanne.simpson@hambleton.gov.uk

MEMBERS OF THE COUNCIL (44)

***Leader of the Council:* Huxtable**, Neville (CON - Topcliffe)
cllr.neville.huxtable@hambleton.gov.uk
***Deputy Leader of the Council:* Kirk**, Ron (CON - Great Ayton)

cllr.ron.kirk@hambleton.gov.uk
Adamson, Derek (CON - Thirsk)
cllr.derek.adamson@hambleton.gov.uk
Baker, Robert (CON - The Thorntons)
cllr.bob.baker@hambleton.gov.uk
Bardon, Peter (CON - Sowerby)
cllr.peter.bardon@hambleton.gov.uk
Barker, Arthur (CON - Leeming)
cllr.arthur.barker@hambleton.gov.uk
Billings, Ken (CON - Northallerton North)
cllr.ken.billings@hambleton.gov.uk
Blades, David (CON - Northallerton Broomfield)
cllr.david.blades@hambleton.gov.uk
Clack, Nigel (CON - Whitestonecliffe)
cllr.nigel.clack@hambleton.gov.uk
Cookman, Christine (CON - Stillington)
cllr.christine.cookman@hambleton.gov.uk
Coulson, John (IND - Northallerton Central)
cllr.john.coulson@hambleton.gov.uk
Dadd, Gareth (CON - Thirsk)
cllr.gareth.dadd@hambleton.gov.uk
Dickins, Stephen (CON - Rudby)
cllr.stephen.dickins@hambleton.gov.uk
Ellis, Geoff (CON - Easingwold)
cllr.geoff.ellis@hambleton.gov.uk
Fortune, Bridget (CON - Rudby)
cllr.bridget.fortune@hambleton.gov.uk
Greenwell, Frances (CON - Great Ayton)
cllr.frances.greenwell@hambleton.gov.uk
Griffiths, Jackie (LD - Stokesley)
cllr.jackie.griffiths@hambleton.gov.uk
Griffiths, Bryn (LD - Stokesley)
cllr.bryn.griffiths@hambleton.gov.uk
Hall, Tony (CON - Northallerton Central)
cllr.tony.hall@hambleton.gov.uk
Hardisty, Kevin (CON - Romanby)
cllr.kevin.hardisty@hambleton.gov.uk
Hudson, Richard (CON - Great Ayton)
cllr.richard.hudson@hambleton.gov.uk
Hugill, David (CON - Swainby)
cllr.david.hugill@hambleton.gov.uk
Knapton, Nigel (CON - Tollerton)
cllr.nigel.knapton@hambleton.gov.uk
Les, Carl (CON - Bedale)
cllr.carl.les@hambleton.gov.uk
Noone, John (CON - Bedale)
cllr.john.noone@hambleton.gov.uk
Patmore, Caroline (CON - White Horse)
cllr.caroline.patmore@hambleton.gov.uk
Phillips, Brian (CON - Morton on Swale)
cllr.brian.phillips@hambleton.gov.uk
Prest, John (CON - Northallerton North)
cllr.john.prest@hambleton.gov.uk
Rigby, Mike (IND - Huby Sutton)
cllr.mike.rigby@hambleton.gov.uk
Robinson, Andrew (CON - Thirsk)
cllr.andrew.robinson@hambleton.gov.uk
Robson, Mark (CON - Sowerby)
cllr.mark.robson@hambleton.gov.uk
Rooke, Chris (CON - Shipton)
cllr.chris.rooke@hambleton.gov.uk
Sanderson, Isobel (CON - Brompton)
cllr.isobel.sanderson@hambleton.gov.uk
Shepherd, Shirley (CON - Easingwold)
cllr.shirley.shepherd@hambleton.gov.uk
Skilbeck, Margaret (CON - Broughton and Greenhow)
cllr.margaret.skilbeck@hambleton.gov.uk
Smith, John (CON - Romanby)
cllr.john.smith@hambleton.gov.uk
Smith, David (IND - Crakehall)
cllr.david.smith@hambleton.gov.uk
Sowray, Peter (CON - Helperby)
cllr.peter.sowray@hambleton.gov.uk
Swales, Timothy (CON - Osmotherley)
cllr.tim.swales@hambleton.gov.uk
Wake, Andy (CON - Stokesley)
cllr.andy.wake@hambleton.gov.uk
Watson, Stephen (CON - Cowtons)
cllr.stephen.watson@hambleton.gov.uk
Webster, David (CON - Tanfield)
cllr.david.webster@hambleton.gov.uk
Wilkinson, Peter (CON - Northallerton Broomfield)
cllr.peter.wilkinson@hambleton.gov.uk
Wood, Anthony (CON - Leeming Bar)
cllr.anthony.wood@hambleton.gov.uk

POLITICAL COMPOSITION

CON: 39, IND: 3, LD: 2

CABINET

Leader: Mr Neville Huxtable
Deputy Leader / Resources: Mr Ron Kirk
Corporate: Mr Brian Phillips
Customers: Mr Timothy Swales
Housing & Planning: Mr Mark Robson
Leisure & Health: Mr Peter Wilkinson

HAMMERSMITH & FULHAM L

Hammersmith & Fulham London Borough Council, 77 Glenthorne Road, Hammersmith, London W6 0LJ ☎ 020 8748 3020 🖷 020 8741 0307 ✉ information@lbhf.gov.uk 🖳 www.lbhf.gov.uk

FACTS & FIGURES

Police Authority: Metropolitan Police Authority
Health Authority: NHS London
Learning and Skills Council: London
Parliamentary Constituencies: Hammersmith
EU Constituencies: London
Election Frequency: Elections are of whole council
Twinning: Boulogne-Billancourt (France); Berlin-Neukolln (Germany); Marino-Rome (Italy); Zaanstad (Netherlands)

PRINCIPAL OFFICERS

Chief Executive: Mr Derek Myers, Chief Executive, Town Hall, King Street, London W6 9JU ☎ 020 8753 2001; 020 7361 2299 🖷 020 8741 0307; 020 7361 2764 ✉ derek.myers@lbhf.gov.uk; derek.myers@rbkc.gov.uk

Senior Management: Ms Lyn Carpenter, Executive Director of Environment Leisure & Residents' Services, 77 Glenthorne Road, Hammersmith, London W6 0LJ ☎ 020 8753 5710 ✉ lyn.carpenter@lbhf.gov.uk; lyn.carpenter@lbhf.gov.uk

Senior Management: Mr Andrew Christie, Tri-Borough Director of Children's Services, Cambridge House, London W6 0LE ☎ 020 8753 5002; 020 7361 2354; 020 7361 3300

🖷 020 7361 3300 ✉ andrew.christie@lbhf.gov.uk; andrew.christie@rbkc.gov.uk

Senior Management: Mr Nigel Pallace, Executive Director of Transport & Technical Services, Town Hall Extension, King Street, London W6 9JU ☎ 020 8753 3000 🖷 020 8753 3397 ✉ nigel.pallace@lbhf.gov.uk

Senior Management: Mr Andrew Webster, Executive Director of Adult Social Care, Westminster Council, London SW1E 6QP ☎ 020 8753 5000 ✉ andrew.webster@lbhf.gov.uk

Senior Management: Ms Jane West, Executive Director - Finance & Corporate Governance, Town Hall, King Street, London W6 9JU ☎ 020 8753 1900 🖷 020 8741 0307 ✉ jane.west@lbhf.gov.uk

Access Officer / Social Services (Disability): Ms Zena Deayton, Director of Adult Social Care Operations, 4th Floor, 77 Glenthorne Road, London W6 0LJ ☎ 020 7641 2262 ✉ zena.deayton@lbhf.gov.uk

Architect, Building / Property Services: Ms Maureen McDonald-Khan, Director - Building & Property Management, Town Hall Extension, King Street, London W6 9JU ☎ 020 8753 4701 ✉ maureen.mcdonald-khan@lbhf.gov.uk

Building Control: Mr Jay Jayaweera, Head of Building Control, Town Hall Extension, King Street, London W6 9JU ☎ 020 8753 3424 🖷 020 8753 3367 ✉ jay.jayaweera@lbhf.gov.uk

Civil Registration: Mr John Collins, Director - H&F Direct, Town Hall, King Street, London W6 9JU ☎ 020 8753 1544 ✉ john.collins@lbhf.gov.uk

PR / Communications: Mr Simon Jones, Assistant Director - Communications & Policy, Town Hall, King Street, London W6 9JU ☎ 020 8753 2086 ✉ simon.jones@lbhf.gov.uk

PR / Communications: Ms Louise Raisey, Corporate Communications Manager, Hammersmith Town Hall, King Street, London W6 9JT ☎ 020 8753 2012 ✉ louise.raisey@lbhf.gov.uk

PR / Communications: Mr David Ruse, Tri-Borough Director of Libraries & Archives, Westminster Reference Library, 35 St Martin's Street, London WC2H 7HP ☎ 020 7641 2496 🖷 020 7641 3406 ✉ druse@westminster.gov.uk

Community Safety: Mr David Page, Director of Safer Neighbourhoods, 77 Glenthorne Road, Hammersmith, London W6 0LJ ☎ 020 8753 2125 ✉ david.page@lbhf.gov.uk

Computer Management: Ms Jackie Hudson, Assistant Director - Procurement and IT Strategy, 77 Glenthorne Road, Hammersmith, London W6 0LJ ☎ 020 8753 2946 🖷 020 8741 0307 ✉ jackie.hudson@lbhf.gov.uk

Consumer Protection and Trading Standards: Mr Nick Austin, Director of Environmental Health, 77 Glenthorne Road, Hammersmith, London W6 0LJ ☎ 020 8753 3904 ✉ nick.austin@lbhf.gov.uk

Corporate Services: Ms Jane West, Executive Director - Finance & Corporate Governance, Town Hall, King Street, London W6 9JU ☎ 020 8753 1900 🖷 020 8741 0307 ✉ jane.west@lbhf.gov.uk

Economic Development: Ms Kim Dero, Head of Economic Development, Town Hall Extension, King Street, London W6 9JU ☎ 020 8748 3020 ✉ kim.dero@lbhf.gov.uk

Education: Mr Ian Heggs, Director of Schools Quality & Standards, Cambridge House, Cambridge Grove, Hammersmith, London W6 0LE ☎ 020 8753 2880 ✉ ian.heggs@lbhf.gov.uk

E-Government: Ms Jackie Hudson, Assistant Director - Procurement and IT Strategy, 77 Glenthorne Road, Hammersmith, London W6 0LJ ☎ 020 8753 2946 🖷 020 8741 0307 ✉ jackie.hudson@lbhf.gov.uk

Electoral Registration: Mr Steve Miller, Electoral Services Manager, Town Hall Extension, King Street, London W6 9JU ☎ 020 8753 2175 🖷 020 8753 2229 ✉ steve.miller@lbhf.gov.uk

Emergency Planning: Mr Adrian Price, Head of Emergency Services, Town Hall, King Street, London W6 9JU ☎ 020 8741 2260 🖷 020 8563 0732 ✉ adrian.price@lbhf.gov.uk

Environmental / Technical Services: Mr Nigel Pallace, Executive Director of Transport & Technical Services, Town Hall Extension, King Street, London W6 9JU ☎ 020 8753 3000 🖷 020 8753 3397 ✉ nigel.pallace@lbhf.gov.uk

Environmental Health: Mr Nick Austin, Director of Environmental Health, 77 Glenthorne Road, Hammersmith, London W6 0LJ ☎ 020 8753 3904 ✉ nick.austin@lbhf.gov.uk

Estates, Property & Valuation: Ms Maureen McDonald-Khan, Director - Building & Property Management, Town Hall Extension, King Street, London W6 9JU ☎ 020 8753 4701 ✉ maureen.mcdonald-khan@lbhf.gov.uk

Events Manager: Ms Helen Pinnington, Events Manager, 77 Glenthorne Road, Hammersmith, London W6 0LJ ☎ 020 8753 2104 ✉ helen.pinnington@lbhf.gov.uk

Facilities: Ms Adele Casey, Technical Services Manager, Town Hall Extension, King Street, London W6 9JU ☎ 020 8753 2106 ✉ adele.casey@lbhf.gov.uk

Finance and Treasurer: Mr Hitesh Jolapara, Deputy Director of Financial Services, Town Hall, Hornton Street, London W8 7NX ☎ 020 7361 2316 🖷 020 7361 3716 ✉ hitesh.jolapara@rbkc.gov.uk

Finance and Treasurer: Ms Jane West, Executive Director - Finance & Corporate Governance, Town Hall, King Street, London W6 9JU ☎ 020 8753 1900 🖷 020 8741 0307 ✉ jane.west@lbhf.gov.uk

Fleet Management: Mr Roy Finan, fleet manager cleaner greener and cultureal services, 25 Bagleys Lane, Fulham, London SW6 2QA ☎ 020 8753 3225 🖷 020 8753 3231 ✉ roy.finan@lbhf.gov.uk

Grounds Maintenance: Ms Sue Harris, Director of Cleaner, Greener & Cultural Services, 77 Glenthorne Road, Hammersmith, London W6 0LJ ☎ 020 8753 4295 ✉ sue.harris@lbhf.gov.uk

Health and Safety: Mr Nick Austin, Director of Environmental Health, 77 Glenthorne Road, Hammersmith, London W6 0LJ ☎ 020 8753 3904 ✉ nick.austin@lbhf.gov.uk

Highways: Mr Mahmood Siddiqi, Director of Transport & Highways, Town Hall, Hornton Street, London W8 7NX ☎ 020 7361 3589 ✉ mahmood.siddiqi@rbkc.gov.uk

Home Energy Conservation: Mr Nigel Pallace, Executive Director of Transport & Technical Services, Town Hall Extension, King Street, London W6 9JU ☎ 020 8753 3000 🖷 020 8753 3397 ✉ nigel.pallace@lbhf.gov.uk

Housing: Mr Melbourne Barrett, Executive Director - Housing and Regeneration, Town Hall Extension, King Street, London W6 9JU ☎ 020 8753 4228 ✉ melbourne.barrett@lbhf.gov.uk

Local Area Agreement: Mr Peter Smith, Strategy Manager, Room 39, Hammersmith Town Hall, London W6 9JT ☎ 020 8753 2206 ✉ peter.smith@lbhf.gov.uk

Leisure and Cultural Services: Ms Donna Pentelow, Head of Culture, 77 Glenthorne Road, Hammersmith, London W6 0LJ ☎ 020 8753 2358 🖷 020 8753 3713 ✉ donna.pentelow@lbhf.gov.uk

Licensing: Ms Sharon Baylis, Assistant Director Customer and Commercial, 77 Glenthorne Road, Hammersmith, London W6 0LJ ☎ 020 8753 1636 ✉ sharon.baylis@lbhf.gov.uk

Lottery Funding, Charity and Voluntary: Ms Sue Spiller, Head - Investment, 145 King Street, Hammersmith, London W6 9XY ☎ 020 8753 2483 🖷 020 8741 4448 ✉ sue.spiller@lbhf.gov.uk

Member Services: Ms Lyn Anthony, Head - Executive Services, 77 Glenthorne Road, Hammersmith, London W6 0LJ ☎ 020 8753 1011 ✉ lyn.anthony@lbhf.gov.uk

Parking: Mr David Taylor, Head - Parking Services, PO Box 3387, London SW6 2QF ☎ 020 8753 3251 ✉ david.taylor@lbhf.gov.uk

Personnel / HR: Ms Debbie Morris, Director of Human Resources, Town Hall, King Street, London W6 9JU ☎ 020 8753 3068 ✉ debbie.morris@lbhf.gov.uk

Planning: Mr Nigel Pallace, Executive Director of Transport & Technical Services, Town Hall Extension, King Street, London W6 9JU ☎ 020 8753 3000 🖷 020 8753 3397 ✉ nigel.pallace@lbhf.gov.uk

Public Libraries: Mr Chris Lloyd, Deputy Head of Libraries, Hammersmith Library, Shepherds Bush Road, London W6 7AT ☎ 020 8753 3811 🖷 020 8753 3815 ✉ chris.lloyd@lbhf.gov.uk

Public Libraries: Mr David Ruse, Tri-Borough Director of Libraries & Archives, Westminster Reference Library, 35 St Martin's Street, London WC2H 7HP ☎ 020 7641 2496 🖷 020 7641 3406 ✉ druse@westminster.gov.uk

Recycling & Waste Minimisation: Ms Sue Harris, Director of Cleaner, Greener & Cultural Services, 77 Glenthorne Road, Hammersmith, London W6 0LJ ☎ 020 8753 4295 ✉ sue.harris@lbhf.gov.uk

Regeneration: Mr Melbourne Barrett, Executive Director - Housing and Regeneration, Town Hall Extension, King Street, London W6 9JU ☎ 020 8753 4228 ✉ melbourne.barrett@lbhf.gov.uk

Social Services: Ms Stella Baillie, Director of Adult Social Care, Provided Services & Mental Health Partnerships, 77 Glenthorne Road, Hammersmith, London W6 0LJ ☎ 020 7361 2401 ✉ stella.baillie@rbkc.gov.uk

Social Services (Adult): Ms Zena Deayton, Director of Adult Social Care Operations, 4th Floor, 77 Glenthorne Road, London W6 0LJ ☎ 020 7641 2262 ✉ zena.deayton@lbhf.gov.uk

Social Services (Adult): Ms Zena Deayton, Director of Adult Social Care Operations, 4th Floor, 77 Glenthorne Road, London W6 0LJ ☎ 020 7641 2262 ✉ zena.deayton@lbhf.gov.uk

Social Services (Children): Mr Andrew Christie, Tri-Borough Director of Children's Services, Cambridge House, London W6 0LE ☎ 020 8753 5002 🖷 020 7361 3300 ✉ andrew.christie@lbhf.gov.uk

Staff Training: Ms Debbie Morris, Director of Human Resources, Town Hall, King Street, London W6 9JU ☎ 020 8753 3068 ✉ debbie.morris@lbhf.gov.uk

Street Scene: Ms Sue Harris, Director of Cleaner, Greener & Cultural Services, 77 Glenthorne Road, Hammersmith, London W6 0LJ ☎ 020 8753 4295 ✉ sue.harris@lbhf.gov.uk

Sustainable Communities: Mr Nigel Pallace, Executive Director of Transport & Technical Services, Town Hall Extension, King Street, London W6 9JU ☎ 020 8753 3000 🖷 020 8753 3397 ✉ nigel.pallace@lbhf.gov.uk; nigel.pallace@lbhf.gov.uk

Town Centre: Ms Kim Dero, Head of Economic Development, 145 King Street, Hammersmith, London W6 9JU ☎ 020 8748 3020 ✉ kim.dero@lbhf.gov.uk

Total Place: Mr Peter Smith, Strategy Manager, Room 39, Hammersmith Town Hall, London W6 9JT ☎ 020 8753 2206 ✉ Peter.smith@lbhf.gov.uk

Waste Collection and Disposal: Ms Sue Harris, Director of Cleaner, Greener & Cultural Services, 77 Glenthorne Road, Hammersmith, London W6 0LJ ☎ 020 8753 4295 ✉ sue.harris@lbhf.gov.uk

Waste Management: Ms Sue Harris, Director of Cleaner, Greener & Cultural Services, 77 Glenthorne Road, Hammersmith, London W6 0LJ ☎ 020 8753 4295 ✉ sue.harris@lbhf.gov.uk

Waste Management: Ms Kathy May, Head of Waste and Street Enforcement, Council Offices, 37 Pembroke Road, London W8 6PW ☎ 020 7341 5616 ✉ kathy.may@rbkc.gov.uk

MEMBERS OF THE COUNCIL (45)

***Mayor:* Donovan**, Belinda (CON - Addison)
belinda.donovan@lbhf.gov.uk
***Deputy Mayor:* Stainton**, Frances (CON - Parsons Green and Walham)
frances.stainton@lbhf.gov.uk
***Leader of the Council:* Botterill**, Nicholas (CON - Parsons Green and Walham)
nicholas.botterill@lbhf.gov.uk
***Deputy Leader of the Council:* Smith**, Gregg (CON - Town)
greg.smith@lbhf.gov.uk
***Group Leader:* Cowan**, Stephen (LAB - Hammersmith Broadway)
stephen.cowan@lbhf.gov.uk
Adam, Michael (CON - Munster)
michael.adam@lbhf.gov.uk
Aherne, Colin (LAB - Wormholt and White City)
colin.aherne@lbhf.gov.uk
Alford, Adronie (CON - Munster)
adronie.alford@lbhf.gov.uk
Binmore, Helen (CON - Avonmore and Brook Green)
helen.binmore@lbhf.gov.uk
Brocklebank-Fowler, Victoria (CON - Fulham Broadway)
victoria.brocklebank-fowler@lbhf.gov.uk
Brown, Daryl (LAB - North End)
daryl.brown@lbhf.gov.uk
Campbell, Jean (LAB - Wormholt and White City)
jean.campbell@lbhf.gov.uk
Carlebach, Joe (CON - Avonmore and Brook Green)
joe.carlebach@lbhf.gov.uk
Cartwright, Michael (LAB - Hammersmith Broadway)
michael.cartwight@lbhf.gov.uk
Chalk, Alex (CON - Addison)
alex.chalk@lbhf.gov.uk
Chumnery, Elaine (LAB - College Park and Old Oak)
elaine.chumnery@lbhf.gov.uk
Coleman, Iain (LAB - Shepherds Bush Green)
iain.coleman@lbhf.gov.uk
Cooney, Georgie (CON - North End)
georgie.cooney@lbhf.gov.uk
Craig, Oliver (CON - Town)
oliver.craig@lbhf.gov.uk
Crofts, Tom (CON - North End)
tom.crofts@lbhf.gov.uk
de Lisle, Ali (CON - Sands End)
Ali.deLisle@lbhf.gov.uk
Dewhirst, Charlie (CON - Ravenscourt Park)
charlie.dewhirst@lbhf.gov.uk
Donovan, Gavin (CON - Fulham Reach)
gavin.donovan@lbhf.gov.uk
Ford, Rachel (CON - Fulham Broadway)
rachel.ford@lbhf.gov.uk
Ginn, Marcus (CON - Palace Riverside)
marcus.ginn@lbhf.gov.uk
Graham, Peter (CON - Fulham Reach)
p.graham@lbhf.gov.uk
Hamilton, Steve (CON - Sands End)
steve.hamilton@lbhf.gov.uk
Harcourt, Wesley (LAB - College Park and Old Oak)
wesley.harcourt@lbhf.gov.uk
Homan, Lisa (LAB - Askew)
lisa.homan@lbhf.gov.uk
Iggulden, Robert (CON - Avonmore and Brook Green)
robert.iggulden@lbhf.gov.uk
Ivimy, Lucy (CON - Ravenscourt Park)
lucy.ivimy@lbhf.gov.uk
Johnson, Donald (CON - Palace Riverside)
donald.johnson@lbhf.gov.uk
Johnson, Andrew (CON - Fulham Reach)
andrew.johnson@lbhf.gov.uk
Jones, Andrew (LAB - Shepherds Bush Green)
andrew.jones@lbhf.gov.uk
Karmel, Alex (CON - Munster)
alex.karmel@lbhf.gov.uk
Law, Jane (CON - Sands End)
jane.law@lbhf.gov.uk
Loveday, Mark (CON - Parsons Green and Walham)
mark.loveday@lbhf.gov.uk
Murphy, P J (LAB - Hammersmith Broadway)
pj.murphy@lbhf.gov.uk
Needham, Caroline (LAB - Askew)
caroline.needham@lbhf.gov.uk
Phibbs, Harry (CON - Ravenscourt Park)
harry.phibbs@lbhf.gov.uk
Powell, Sally (LAB - Wormholt and White City)
sally.powell@lbhf.gov.uk
Thorley, Matt (CON - Fulham Broadway)
matt.thorley@lbhf.gov.uk
Tobias, Peter (CON - Addison)
peter.tobias@lbhf.gov.uk
Umeh, Mercy (LAB - Shepherds Bush Green)
mercy.umeh@lbhf.gov.uk
Vaughan, Rory (LAB - Askew)
rory.vaughan@lbhf.gov.uk

POLITICAL COMPOSITION

CON: 30, LAB: 15

CABINET

Leader: Mr Nicholas Botterill
Deputy Leader / Residents' Services: Mr Gregg Smith
Children's Services: Ms Helen Binmore
Communications: Mr Mark Loveday
Community Care: Mr Marcus Ginn
Housing: Mr Andrew Johnson
Transport & Technical Services: Ms Victoria Brocklebank-Fowler

COMMITTEE CHAIRS

Audit, Pensions & Standards: Mr Michael Adam
Education & Children's Services (Scrutiny): Mr Donald Johnson
Housing, Health & Adult Social Care (Scrutiny): Ms Lucy Ivimy
Licensing: Mr Matt Thorley
Overview & Scrutiny (Scrutiny): Mr Alex Karmel
Planning Applications: Mr Alex Chalk
Transport, Environment & Residents' Services: Ms Rachel Ford

HAMPSHIRE C

Hampshire County Council, The Castle, Winchester SO23 8UJ
☎ 01962 841841 🖷 01962 867273 ✉ info@hants.gov.uk
💻 www.hants.gov.uk

FACTS & FIGURES

Police Authority: Hampshire Police Authority
Health Authority: South Central Strategic Health Authority
Learning and Skills Council: South East
Parliamentary Constituencies: Aldershot, Basingstoke, Eastleigh, Fareham, Gosport, Havant, Meon Valley, New Forest East, New Forest West, Southampton, Test, Winchester
EU Constituencies: South East
Election Frequency: Elections are of whole council
Twinning: Partnership Link: Basse Normandie (France)

PRINCIPAL OFFICERS

Chief Executive: Mr Andrew Smith, Chief Executive, Elizabeth II Court South, Winchester SO23 8UJ ☎ 01962 847300 ✉ andrew.j.smith@hants.gov.uk

Deputy Chief Executive: Mr John Coughlan, Deputy Chief Executive, Director of Children's Services, Elizabeth II Court South, Winchester SO23 8UG ☎ 01962 846400 ✉ john.coughlan@hants.gov.uk

Assistant Chief Executive: Mr Paul Archer, Assistant Chief Executive, Elizabeth II Court South, Winchester SO23 8UJ ☎ 01962 846124 ✉ paul.archer@hants.gov.uk

Access Officer / Social Services (Disability): Ms Lucy Butler, Assistant Director - Integrated Learning Disabilities & Mental Health Services, Elizabeth II Court West, Winchester SO23 8UG ☎ 01962 845612 ✉ lucy.butler@hants.gov.uk

Access Officer / Social Services (Disability): Ms Ruth Dixon, Assistant Director - Older People & Physical Disabilities, Elizabeth II Court West, Winchester SO23 8UG ☎ 01962 847260 ✉ ruth.dixon@hants.gov.uk

Access Officer / Social Services (Disability): Mr Mohammed Mossadaq, Head of Inclusion & Engagement, Elizabeth II Court West, Winchester SO23 8UG ☎ 01962 845880 ✉ mohammed.mossadaq@hants.gov.uk

Architect, Building / Property Services: Mr Steve Clow, Assistant Director - Property Services, Three Minsters House, 76 High Street, Winchester SO23 8UL ☎ 01962 847858 ✉ steve.clow@hants.gov.uk

Best Value: Mr Gary Smith, Head of Policy, The Castle, Winchester SO23 8UJ ☎ 01962 847402 ✉ gary.smith@hants.gov.uk

Building Control: Mr Steve Clow, Assistant Director - Property Services, Three Minsters House, 76 High Street, Winchester SO23 8UL ☎ 01962 847858 ✉ steve.clow@hants.gov.uk

Catering Services: Ms Amanda Frost, Head of Catering Services, 27-29 Market Street, Eastleigh SO53 5RG ☎ 02380 627729 ✉ amanda.frost@hants.gov.uk

Children / Youth Services: Mr John Clarke, Deputy Director - Education & Inclusion, Elizabeth II Court East, Winchester SO23 8UG ☎ 01962 846459 ✉ john.clarke@hants.gov.uk

Children / Youth Services: Mr John Coughlan, Deputy Chief Executive & Director of Children's Services, Castle Avenue, Winchester SO23 8UG ☎ 01962 846400 🖷 01962 845648 ✉ john.coughlan@hants.gov.uk

Children / Youth Services: Mr Steve Crocker, Deputy Director of Children's Services (Children & Families), Elizabeth II Court East, Winchester SO23 8UG ☎ 01962 847991 ✉ steve.crocker@hants.gov.uk

Children / Youth Services: Mrs Felicity Roe, Assistant Director - Performance and Resources, Elizabeth II Court East, Winchester SO23 8UG ☎ 01962 846374 ✉ felicity.roe@hants.gov.uk

Civil Registration: Mrs Nicola Horsey, Assistant Director - Community, Mottisfont Court, High Street, Winchester SO23 8ZF ☎ 01962 845423 ✉ nicola.horsey@hants.gov.uk

PR / Communications: Ms Kate Ball, Communications Manager (Media), Elizabeth II Court South, Winchester SO23 8ZF ☎ 01962 847317 ✉ kate.ball@hants.gov.uk

PR / Communications: Ms Karen Mann, Head of Corporate Marketing & Public Relations, Elizabeth II Court South, Winchester SO23 8UJ ☎ 01962 846751 ✉ karen.mann@hants.gov.uk

Community Planning: Mr Robert Ormerod, Community Strategy Manager, Elizabeth II Court South, Winchester SO23 8UJ ☎ 01962 845122 ✉ robert.ormerod@hants.gov.uk

Community Safety: Mrs Nicola Horsey, Assistant Director - Community, Mottisfont Court, High Street, Winchester SO23 8ZF ☎ 01962 845423 ✉ nicola.horsey@hants.gov.uk

Computer Management: Mr Jos Creese, Head of IT, Elizabeth II Court South, Winchester SO23 8UJ ☎ 01962 847436 ✉ jos.creese@hants.gov.uk

Consumer Protection and Trading Standards: Mrs Nicola Horsey, Assistant Director - Community, Mottisfont Court, High Street, Winchester SO23 8ZF ☎ 01962 845423 ✉ nicola.horsey@hants.gov.uk

Contracts: Mr Neil Jones, Assistant Director of Business Services, Three Minsters House, 76 High Street, Winchester SO23 8UL ☎ 01962 846180 ✉ neil.jones@hants.gov.uk

Corporate Services: Mrs Barbara Beardwell, Monitoring Officer & Head of Governance, Elizabeth II Court South, The Castle, Winchester SO23 8UJ ☎ 01962 845157 ✉ barbara.beardwell@hants.gov.uk

Corporate Services: Mr Gordon Smith, Information Services Manager, Elizabeth II Court South, Winchester SO23 8UJ ☎ 01962 846971 ✉ gordon.smith@hants.gov.uk

Corporate Services: Mrs Debbie Vaughan, Head of Member Services, Elizabeth II Court South, Winchester SO23 8UJ ☎ 01962 847330 ✉ debbie.vaughan@hants.gov.uk

Customer Service: Mr Bob Wild, Corporate Customer Services

Manager, Parkway Offices, Wickham Road, Fareham PO16 7JL ☎ 01329 225329 ✆ bob.wild@hants.gov.uk

Economic Development: Ms Hazel Simmonds, Assistant Director - Economic Development, Elizabeth II Court West, Winchester SO23 8UG ☎ 01962 846125 ✆ hazel.simmonds@hants.gov.uk

Education: Mr John Coughlan, Deputy Chief Executive, Director of Children's Services, Elizabeth II Court East, Winchester SO23 8UD ☎ 01962 846400 ✆ john.coughlan@hants.gov.uk

E-Government: Mr Jos Creese, Head of IT, Elizabeth II Court, Winchester SO23 8UJ ☎ 01962 847436 ✆ jos.creese@hants.gov.uk

Emergency Planning: Mr Ian Hoult, County Emergency Planning Officer, Elizabeth II Court South, Winchester SO23 8UJ ☎ 01962 846840 📠 01962 855020 ✆ ian.hoult@hants.gov.uk

Energy Management: Mr Bryan Boult, Head of Energy & Environment Futures, Elizabeth II Court West, Winchester SO23 8UD ☎ 01962 846772 ✆ bryan.boult@hants.gov.uk

Environmental / Technical Services: Mr Stuart Jarvis, Director of Economy, Transport & Environment, Elizabeth II Court West, Winchester SO23 8UD ☎ 01962 845260 ✆ stuart.jarvis@hants.gov.uk

Environmental / Technical Services: Mr John Osborne, Deputy Director of Waste, Planning & Environment, Elizabeth II Court West, Winchester SO23 8UD ☎ 01962 845626 ✆ john.osborne@hants.gov.uk

Environmental / Technical Services: Mr James Strachan, Assistant Director - Research & Resources, Elizabeth II Court West, Winchester SO23 8UD ☎ 01962 846454 ✆ james.strachan@hants.gov.uk

Environmental / Technical Services: Mrs Linda Tartaglia-Kershaw, Head of Strategic Environmental Delivery, Elizabeth II Court West, Winchester SO23 8UD ☎ 01962 842342 ✆ linda.tartaglia-kershaw@hants.gov.uk

Estates, Property & Valuation: Mr Steve Clow, Assistant Director - Property Services, Three Minsters House, 76 High Street, Winchester SO23 8UL ☎ 01962 847858 ✆ steve.clow@hants.gov.uk

European Liaison: Ms Paddy Hillary, Corporate Policy Manager (Partnerships), Elizabeth II Court South, Winchester SO23 8UJ ☎ 01962 847391 ✆ paddy.hillary@hants.gov.uk

Facilities: Ms Vicky Jolly, Head of Facilities Management, Three Ministers House, 76 High Street, Winchester SO23 8UL ☎ 01962 841841 ✆ vicky.jolly@hants.gov.uk

Finance and Treasurer: Mr Rob Carr, Deputy County Treasurer, Elizabeth II Court South, Winchester SO23 8UJ ☎ 01962 847408 ✆ rob.carr@hants.gov.uk

Finance and Treasurer: Mr Nick Weaver, Head of Pension Services, Elizabeth II Court South, Winchester SO23 8UJ ☎ 01962 847587 ✆ nick.weaver@hants.gov.uk

Finance and Treasurer: Ms Carolyn Williamson, County Treasurer, Elizabeth II Court South, Winchester SO23 8UJ ☎ 01962 847400 ✆ carolyn.williamson@hants.gov.uk

Fleet Management: Mr Paul Leaves, Transport Management - Client, Hampshire Transport Management, Moorside Road, Winchester SO23 7RX ☎ 01962 873933 ✆ paul.leaves@hants.gov.uk

Grounds Maintenance: Mr Steve Clow, Assistant Director - Property Services, Three Minsters House, 76 High Street, Winchester SO23 8UL ☎ 01962 847858 ✆ steve.clow@hants.gov.uk

Health and Safety: Mr Peter Andrews, Corporate Risk Manager, Elizabeth II Court South, Winchester SO23 8UJ ☎ 01962 847309 ✆ peter.andrews@hants.gov.uk

Highways: Mr Adrian Gray, Head of Highways Area - North & East, Old College Street, Petersfield GU31 4AG ☎ 01256 382409 ✆ adrian.gray@hants.gov.uk

Highways: Mr Chris Lait, Head of Highways Area - South, Hampshire Highways Unit South, Fareham Borough Council, Civic Way, Fareham PO16 7TY ☎ 01329 824485 ✆ chris.lait@hants.gov.uk

Highways: Mr Tim Lawton, Head of Highways - West, Jacobs Gutter Lane, Totton, Southampton SO40 9QT ☎ 023 8042 7001 ✆ tim.lawton@hants.gov.uk

Highways: Mr Phil Samms, Head of Highways (HQ), Elizabeth II Court West, Winchester SO23 8UD ☎ 01962 846892 ✆ phil.samms@hants.gov.uk

Highways: Mr Colin Taylor, Assistant Director - Highways, Traffic & Transport, Elizabeth II Court West, Winchester SO23 8UD ☎ 01962 846753 ✆ colin.taylor@hants.gov.uk

Local Area Agreement: Mr Robert Ormerod, Community Strategy Manager, Elizabeth II Court South, Winchester SO23 8UJ ☎ 01962 845122 ✆ robert.ormerod@hants.gov.uk

Legal: Mr Kevin Gardner, Head of Legal Services, Elizabeth II Court South, Winchester SO23 8UJ ☎ 01962 847381 ✆ kevin.gardner@hants.gov.uk

Leisure and Cultural Services: Ms Janet Mein, Head of Hampshire Arts Service, Mottisfont Court, High Street, Winchester SO23 8ZF ☎ 01962 845468 ✆ janet.mein@hants.gov.uk

Leisure and Cultural Services: Ms Karen Murray, Director of Culture, Communities & Business Services, Three Minsters House, 76 High Street, Winchester SO23 8UL ☎ 01962 847876 ✆ karen.murray@hants.gov.uk

Leisure and Cultural Services: Dr Janet Owen, Head of Museums & Arts, Chilcomb House, Chilcomb Lane, Winchester

SO23 8RD ☎ 01962 826704 ✉ janet.owen@hants.gov.uk

Leisure and Cultural Services: Mr Andy Smith, Head of Countryside Service, Mottisfont Court, High Street, Winchester SR23 8ZF ☎ 01962 846003 ✉ andy.smith@hants.gov.uk

Leisure and Cultural Services: Mr John Tickle, Assistant Director - Culture & Heritage, Mottisfont Court, High Street, Winchester SO23 8ZF ☎ 01962 846000 ✉ john.tickle@hants.gov.uk

Lifelong Learning: Mr George Allen, Head of Adult & Community Learning, First Floor, South Side Offices, The Castle, Winchester SO23 8ZB ☎ 01962 846943 ✉ george.allen@hants.gov.uk

Lighting: Mr Julian Higgins, Policy & Communications Manager - Street Lighting, HCC Street Lighting, PFI Office, Unit 1 Royal London Park, Flanders Road, Hedge End, Southampton SO30 2LG ☎ ; 01489 771772 ✉ julian.higgins@hants.gov.uk

Lighting: Mr Jim Pendrey, Street Lighting Manager, HCC Street Lighting, PFI Office, Unit 1 Royal London Park, Flanders Road, Hedge End, Southampton SO30 2LG ☎ 01329 824809 ✉ jim.pendrey@hants.gov.uk

Member Services: Mrs Debbie Vaughan, Head of Member Services, Elizabeth II Court South, Winchester SO23 8UJ ☎ 01962 847330 ✉ debbie.vaughan@hants.gov.uk

Partnerships: Ms Paddy Hillary, Corporate Policy Manager (Partnerships), Elizabeth II Court South, Winchester SO23 8UJ ☎ 01962 847391 ✉ paddy.hillary@hants.gov.uk

Personnel / HR: Ms Christina Hefferon, Head of Employment Practice, Athelstan House, St. Clement Street, Winchester SO23 9DR ☎ ; 01962 813918 ✉ christina.hefferon@hants.gov.uk

Personnel / HR: Mr Gavin Wright, Director of Human Resources, Regency House, 13 St Clement Street, Winchester SO23 9HH ☎ ; 01962 833023 ✉ gavin.wright@hants.gov.uk

Planning: Mr Richard Read, Head of County Planning, Elizabeth II Court West, Winchester SO23 0UD ☎ 01962 846727 ✉ richard.read@hants.gov.uk

Procurement: Mr Neil Jones, Assistant Director - Business Services, Three Ministers House, 76 High Street, Winchester SO23 8UL ☎ 01962 846180 ✉ neil.jones@hants.gov.uk

Procurement: Mr Shaun Le Picq, Head of Procurement, County Supplies, Bar End Road, Winchester SO23 9NR ☎ 01962 846216 ✉ shaun.lepicq@hants.gov.uk

Public Libraries: Mrs Nicola Horsey, Assistant Director - Community, Mottisfont Court, High Street, Winchester SO23 8ZF ☎ 01962 845423 ✉ nicola.horsey@hants.gov.uk

Recycling & Waste Minimisation: Ms Clare Saunders, Head of Waste & Resource Management, Elizabeth II Court West, Winchester SO23 8UD ☎ 01962 832252 ✉ clare.saunders@hants.gov.uk

Regeneration: Mr John Osborne, Deputy Director of Waste, Planning & Environment, Elizabeth II Court West, Winchester SO23 8UD ☎ 01962 845626 ✉ john.osborne@hants.gov.uk

Road Safety: Mr Mark Samways, Traffic Management & Safety Manager, Capital House, 48-52 Andover Road, Winchester SO23 7BH ☎ 01962 832238 ✉ mark.samways@hants.gov.uk

Social Services (Adult): Ms Lucy Butler, Assistant Director of Adult Services, Integrated Learning Disabilities & Mental Health Services, Elizabeth II Court West, Winchester SO23 8UG ☎ 01962 845612 ✉ lucy.butler@hants.gov.uk

Social Services (Adult): Ms Ruth Dixon, Assistant Director, Older People & Physical Disabilities, Elizabeth II Court West, Winchester SO23 8UG ☎ 01962 847260 ✉ ruth.dixon@hants.gov.uk

Social Services (Adult): Mrs Gill Duncan, Director of Adult Services, Elizabeth II Court West, Winchester SO23 8UG ☎ 01962 847200 ✉ gill.duncan@hants.gov.uk

Social Services (Adult): Mr Richard Ellis, Deputy Director, Commissioning & Partnerships, Elizabeth II Court West, Winchester SO23 8UG ☎ 01962 847284 ✉ richard.ellis@hants.gov.uk

Social Services (Adult): Mr Mohammed Mossadaq, Head of Inclusion & Engagement, Elizabeth II Court West, Winchester SO23 8UG ☎ 01962 845880 ✉ mohammed.mossadaq@hants.gov.uk

Social Services (Adult): Mr Adrian Thorne, Assistant Director - Performance & Business Management, Elizabeth II Court West, Winchester SO23 8UG ☎ 01962 847259 ✉ adrian.thorne@hants.gov.uk

Social Services (Children): Mr John Coughlan, Deputy Chief Executive, Director of Children's Services, Elizabeth II Court East, Winchester SO23 8UD ☎ 01962 846400 ✉ john.coughlan@hants.gov.uk

Social Services (Children): Mr Steve Crocker, Deputy Director of Children's Services (Children & Families), Elizabeth II Court East, Winchester SO23 8UG ☎ 01962 847991 ✉ steve.crocker@hants.gov.uk

Social Services (Children): Mrs Felicity Roe, Assistant Director of Children's Services (Performance & Resources), Elizabeth II Court East, Winchester SO23 8UG ☎ 01962 846374 ✉ felicity.roe@hants.gov.uk

Staff Training: Ms Susan Baker, Head of Hampshire Learning Centre, Regency House, 13 St. Clement Street, Winchester SO23 9HH ☎ 01962 833019 ✉ susan.baker@hants.gov.uk

Sustainable Communities: Mr Robert Ormerod, Community Strategy Manager, Elizabeth II Court South, Winchester SO23 8UJ ☎ 01962 845122 ✉ robert.ormerod@hants.gov.uk

Sustainable Development: Mr Bryan Boult, Head of Energy & Environment Futures, Elizabeth II Court West, Winchester SO23

8UD ☎ 01962 846772 ✉ bryan.boult@hants.gov.uk

Tourism: Mr Andrew Bateman, Tourism Manager, Mottisfont Court, High Street, Winchester SO23 8ZF ☎ 01962 845478 ✉ andrew.bateman@hants.gov.uk

Traffic Management: Mr Colin Taylor, Assistant Director - Highways, Traffic & Transport, Elizabeth II Court West, Winchester SO23 8UD ☎ 01962 846753 ✉ colin.taylor@hants.gov.uk

Traffic Management: Mr Keith Willcox, Head of Strategic Transport, Elizabeth II Court West, Winchester SO23 8UD ☎ 01962 846997 ✉ keith.willcox@hants.gov.uk

Transport: Mr Adrian Gray, Head of Highways Area - North & East, Old College Street, Petersfield GU31 4AG ☎ 01256 382409 ✉ adrian.gray@hants.gov.uk

Transport: Mr Chris Lait, Head of Highways Area - South, Hampshire Highways Unit South, Fareham Borough Council, Civic Way, Fareham PO16 7TY ☎ 01329 824485 ✉ chris.lait@hants.gov.uk

Transport: Mr Tim Lawton, Head of Highways - West, Jacobs Gutter Lane, Totton, Southampton SO40 9QT ☎ 023 8042 7001 ✉ tim.lawton@hants.gov.uk

Transport: Mr Phil Samms, Head of Highways (HQ), Elizabeth II Court West, Winchester SO23 8UD ☎ 01962 846892 ✉ phil.samms@hants.gov.uk

Transport: Mr Peter Shelley, Head of Passenger Transport, Elizabeth II Court West, Winchester SO23 8UD ☎ 01962 846992 ✉ peter.shelley@hants.gov.uk

Transport Planner: Mr Keith Willcox, Head of Strategic Transport, Elizabeth II Court West, Winchester SO23 8UD ☎ 01962 846997 ✉ keith.willcox@hants.gov.uk

Waste Collection and Disposal: Ms Clare Saunders, Head of Waste & Resource Management, Elizabeth II Court West, Winchester SO23 8UD ☎ 01962 832252 ✉ clare.saunders@hants.gov.uk

Waste Management: Ms Clare Saunders, Head of Waste & Resource Management, Elizabeth II Court West, Winchester SO23 8UD ☎ 01962 832252 ✉ clare.saunders@hants.gov.uk

MEMBERS OF THE COUNCIL (78)

***Chair:* Joy**, Andrew (CON - Alton Town)
andrew.joy@hants.gov.uk
***Vice-Chair:* Mutton**, Pam (CON - Andover North)
pam.mutton@hants.gov.uk
***Leader of the Council:* Thornber**, Ken (CON - Brockenhurst)
ken.thornber@hants.gov.uk
***Deputy Leader of the Council:* Kendal**, Mel (CON - New Milton)
mel.kendal@hants.gov.uk
***Group Leader:* Hussey**, Ronald (LD - Basingstoke Central)
ronald.hussey@hants.gov.uk
Bailey, Charlotte (LD - Winchester Downlands)
charlotte.bailey@trafford.gov.uk
Beagley, Ian (CON - Waterloo and Stakes (North))
ian.beagley@hants.gov.uk
Bolton, Ray (CON - Emsworth and St Faith's)
ray.bolton@hants.gov.uk
Broadhurst, Alan (LD - Eastleigh West)
alan.broadhurst@hants.gov.uk
Bryant, John (CON - Fareham Town)
john.v.bryant@hants.gov.uk
Buckley, Ann (LD - Bedhampton and Leigh Park)
ann.buckley@hants.gov.uk
Burgess, Graham (CON - Lee)
Burgess, Rita (CON - Basingstoke South West)
rita.burgess@hants.gov.uk
Carew, Adam (LD - Bordon, Whitehill and Lindford)
adam.carew@hants.gov.uk
Carter, Christopher (CON - Leesland and Town)
christopher.carter@hants.gov.uk
Chadd, Roz (CON - Farnborough North)
roz.chadd@hants.gov.uk
Chapman, Keith (CON - Calleva and Kingsclere)
keith.chapman@hants.gov.uk
Chegwyn, Peter (LD - Hardway)
peter.chegwyn@hants.gov.uk
Clarke, Vaughan (CON - Petersfield Hangars)
vaughan.clarke@hants.gov.uk
Collett, Adrian (LD - Yateley East, Blackwater and Ancells)
adrian.collett@hants.gov.uk
Collin, Brian (LD - Winchester Eastgate)
brian.collin@hants.gov.uk
Cooper, Mark (LD - Romsey Town)
cllr.mark.cooper@hants.gov.uk
Darragh, Sam (LD - Catherington)
sam.darragh@hants.gov.uk
Dash, Brian (LD - Dibden And Hythe)
brian.dash@hants.gov.uk
Davidovitz, Colin (CON - Chandlers Ford)
colin.dav@hants.gov.uk
Dickens, Phrynette (LD - Winchester Westgate)
phrynette.dickens@hants.gov.uk
Dowden, Alan (LD - Baddesley)
alan.dowden@hants.gov.uk
Drew, David (CON - Andover South)
david.drew@hants.gov.uk
Edgar, Peter (CON - Leesland and Town)
peter.edgar@hants.gov.uk
Ellis, Raymond (CON - Fareham Town)
raymond.ellis@hants.gov.uk
Evans, Keith (CON - Fareham Warsash)
keith.evans@hants.gov.uk
Evans, Adrian (CON - Lymington)
adrian.evans@hants.gov.uk
Fairhurst, Liz (CON - Bedhampton and Leigh Park)
liz.fairhurst@hants.gov.uk
Ferris, Cowper (CON - Headley)
ferris.cowper@hants.gov.uk
Frankum, Jane (LAB - Basingstoke North)
jane.frankum@hants.gov.uk
Geddes, Michael (CON - Bridgemary)
michael.geddes@hants.gov.uk
Gibson, Andrew (CON - Test Valley Central)
andrew.gibson@hants.gov.uk
Glen, Jonathan (CON - Odiham)
jonathan.glen@hants.gov.uk
Gurden, Brian (LD - Basingstoke South East)

brian.gurden@hants.gov.uk
Harrison, David (LD - Totton South and Marchwood)
david.harrison@hants.gov.uk
Heron, Edward (CON - Fordingbridge)
edward.heron@hants.gov.uk
Hindson, Felicity (CON - Meon Valley)
felicity.hindson@hants.gov.uk
Hockley, Geoffrey (CON - Fareham Titchfield)
geoff.hockley@hants.gov.uk
House, Keith (LD - Hamble)
keith.house@hants.gov.uk
Keast, David (CON - Cowplain and Hart Plain)
david.keast@hants.gov.uk
Kemp-Gee, Mark (CON - Alton Rrual)
mark.kemp-gee@hants.gov.uk
Kimber, Roger (CON - Aldershot West)
roger.kimber@hants.gov.uk
Knight, Timothy (CON - Fareham Crofton)
tim.knight@hants.gov.uk
Kryle, Rupert (LD - Botley and Hedge End)
rupert.kyrle@hants.gov.uk
Leversha, Carol (CON - Farnborough West)
carol.leversha@hants.gov.uk
Mans, Keith (CON - Lyndhurst)
keith.mans@hants.gov.uk
Mason, Peter (LD - Bishops Waltham)
peter.mason@hants.gov.uk
McEvoy, Alexis (CON - South Waterside)
alexis.mcevoy@hants.gov.uk
McIntosh, Robin (CON - Purbrook and Stakes South)
robin.mcintosh@hants.gov.uk
McNair Scott, Anna (CON - Candovers)
anna.mcnairscott@hants.gov.uk
Neal, Eric (CON - Aldershot East)
eric.neal@hants.gov.uk
Pearce, Frank (CON - Hayling Island)
frank.pearce@hants.gov.uk
Perry, Roy (CON - Romsey Extra)
roy.perry@hants.gov.uk
Porter, Jacqueline (LD - Itchen Valley)
jackie.porter@hants.gov.uk
Price, Roger (LD - Fareham Portchester)
roger.price@hants.gov.uk
Radley, Jenny (IND - Church Crookham and Ewshot)
jenny.radley@hants.gov.uk
Reid, Stephen (CON - Basingstoke North West)
stephen.reid@hants.gov.uk
Rice, Alan (CON - Milford and Hordle)
alan.rice@hants.gov.uk
Rippon-Swaine, Steve (CON - Ringwood)
steve.rippon-swaine@hants.gov.uk
Roling, Angela (LD - Bishopstoke and Fair Oak)
angela.roling@hants.gov.uk
Simpson, David (LD - Hartley Wintney, Eversley and Yateley West)
david.simpson@hants.gov.uk
Stallard, Patricia (CON - Winchester Southern Parishes)
members.support@hants.gov.uk
Still, Elaine (CON - Loddon)
elaine.still@hants.gov.uk
Tennent, Bruce (LD - West End, Hedge End and Grange Park)
bruce.tennent@hants.gov.uk
Thacker, Tom (CON - Whitchurch and Clere)
tom.thacker@hants.gov.uk
Thomas, Christopher (LD - Eastleigh East)
chris.thomas@hants.gov.uk
Tucker, Marilyn (CON - Tadley and Baughurst)
marilyn.tucker@hants.gov.uk
Wall, John (CON - Farnborough South)
john.wall@hants.gov.uk
Weeks, Alan (LD - Totton North)
alan.weeks@hants.gov.uk
West, Pat (CON - Andover West)
pat.west@hants.gov.uk
West, John (CON - Peterefield Butser)
john.west@hants.gov.uk
Wheale, Sharyn (CON - Fleet)
sharyn.wheale@hants.gov.uk
Woodward, Seán D T (CON - Fareham Sarisbury)
sean.woodward@hants.gov.uk

POLITICAL COMPOSITION

CON: 51, LD: 25, IND: 1, LAB: 1

CABINET

Leader / Policy & Resources: Mr Ken Thornber
Deputy Leader / Environment & Transport: Mr Mel Kendal
Adult Social Care: Mrs Felicity Hindson
Children's Services: Mr Roy Perry
Communications & Efficiency: Mr Colin Davidovitz
Communities & International Relations: Mr Keith Mans
Culture & Recreation: Mr Keith Chapman
Strategic Development: Mr Stephen Reid

COMMITTEE CHAIRS

Audit: Mr Keith Evans
Buildings, Land & Procurement: Mr Ken Thornber
Children & Families: Mrs Marilyn Tucker
Culture, Communities & Rural Affairs (Scrutiny): Ms Elaine Still
Education Advisory: Mr Peter Edgar
Environment & Transportation Select (Scrutiny): Mrs Sharyn Wheale
Finance & General Purposes: Mr Ian Beagley
Health Overview & Scrutiny (Scrutiny): Mrs Pat West
Human Resources: Mr Adrian Evans
Pension Fund: Mr Mark Kemp-Gee
Policy & Resources Select (Scrutiny): Mrs Carol Leversha
Safe & Healthy People Select: Ms Liz Fairhurst

HARBOROUGH D

Harborough District Council, Council Offices, Adam & Eve Street, Market Harborough LE16 7AG ☎ 01858 828282 🖷 01858 821000 💻 www.harborough.gov.uk

FACTS & FIGURES

Police Authority: Leicestershire Police Authority
Health Authority: East Midlands Strategic Health Authority
Learning and Skills Council: East Midlands
Parliamentary Constituencies: Harborough, Leicestershire South, Rutland and Melton
EU Constituencies: East Midlands
Election Frequency: Elections are of whole council
Twinning: La Serte sous Jouarre (France)

PRINCIPAL OFFICERS

Chief Executive: Ms Anna Graves, Chief Executive, Council Offices, Adam & Eve Street, Market Harborough LE16 7AG

☎ 01858 828282 🖷 01858 821000 ✉ a.graves@harborough.gov.uk

Senior Management: Mrs Beverley Jolly, Assistant Director (Corporate Services), Council Offices, Adam & Eve Street, Market Harborough LE16 7AG ☎ 01858 828282 🖷 01858 821000 ✉ b.jolly@harborough.gov.uk

Senior Management: Mr Norman Proudfoot, Assistant Director (Community Services), Council Offices, Adam & Eve Street, Market Harborough LE16 7AG ☎ 01858 828282 🖷 01858 821000 ✉ n.proudfoot@harborough.gov.uk

Building Control: Mr Adrian Eastwood, Development Control Service Manager, Council Offices, Adam & Eve Street, Market Harborough LE16 7AG ☎ 01858 821142 🖷 01858 821097 ✉ a.eastwood@harborough.gov.uk

Children / Youth Services: Ms Stella Renwick, Children & Youth Officer, Council Offices, Adam & Eve Street, Market Harborough LE16 7AG ☎ 01858 828282 ✉ s.renwick@harborough.gov.uk

PR / Communications: Mrs Rachael Abbott, Media & PR Officer, Council Offices, Adam & Eve Street, Market Harborough LE16 7AG ☎ 01858 821217 🖷 01858 821041 ✉ r.abbott@harborough.gov.uk

Community Safety: Mr Thomas Day, Community Safety Officer, Council Offices, Adam & Eve Street, Market Harborough LE16 7AG ☎ 01858 828282 ✉ t.day@harborough.gov.uk

Computer Management: Mr Chris James, Information Systems Manager, Council Offices, Adam & Eve Street, Market Harborough LE16 7AG ☎ 01858 821311 🖷 01858 821311 ✉ c.james@harborough.gov.uk

Corporate Services: Mr Richard Ellis, Corporate Services Manager, Council Offices, Adam & Eve Street, Market Harborough LE16 7AG ☎ 01858 821370 🖷 01858 821000 ✉ r.ellis@harborough.gov.uk

Customer Service: Mrs Rachael Abbott, Media & PR Officer, Council Offices, Adam & Eve Street, Market Harborough LE16 7AG ☎ 01858 821217 🖷 01858 821041 ✉ r.abbott@harborough.gov.uk

Economic Development: Mrs Heather Wakefield, Economic Development & Tourism Officer, Council Offices, Adam & Eve Street, Market Harborough LE16 7AG ☎ 01858 828282 🖷 01858 821000 ✉ h.wakefield@harborough.gov.uk

E-Government: Mr Chris James, Information Systems Manager, Council Offices, Adam & Eve Street, Market Harborough LE16 7AG ☎ 01858 821311 🖷 01858 821311 ✉ c.james@harborough.gov.uk

Electoral Registration: Ms Sheena Mortimer, Electoral Services Manager, Council Offices, Adam & Eve Street, Market Harborough LE16 7AG 🖷 01858 821311 ✉ s.mortimer@harborough.gov.uk

Emergency Planning: Ms Anna Graves, Chief Executive, Council Offices, Adam & Eve Street, Market Harborough LE16 7AG ☎ 01858 828282 🖷 01858 821000 ✉ a.graves@harborough.gov.uk

Energy Management: Mr Graham Ladds, Energy Manager, Council Offices, Adam & Eve Street, Market Harborough LE16 7AG ☎ 01858 821036 🖷 01858 821002 ✉ g.ladds@harborough.gov.uk

Environmental / Technical Services: Ms Elaine Bird, Community Protection Manager, Council Offices, Adam & Eve Street, Market Harborough LE16 7AG ☎ 01858 821130 🖷 01858 821100 ✉ e.bird@harborough.gov.uk

Events Manager: Mr Chris Stewart, Town Development Officer, Council Offices, Adam & Eve Street, Market Harborough LE16 7AG ☎ 01858 828282

Facilities: Mr Matthew Bradford, Service Manager, Council Offices, Adam & Eve Street, Market Harborough LE16 7AG ☎ 01858 821290 ✉ m.bradford@harborough.gov.uk

Finance and Treasurer: Ms Kirsty Cowell, Financial Services Manager, Council Offices, Adam & Eve Street, Market Harborough LE16 7AG ☎ 01858 821220

Grounds Maintenance: Mr Matthew Bradford, Service Manager, Council Offices, Adam & Eve Street, Market Harborough LE16 7AG ☎ 01858 821290 ✉ m.bradford@harborough.gov.uk

Health and Safety: Mrs Jo-Anne Moore, Health & Safety Officer, Council Offices, Adam & Eve Street, Market Harborough LE16 7AG ☎ 01858 821185 🖷 01858 821100 ✉ j.moore@harborough.gov.uk

Home Energy Conservation: Mr Graham Ladds, Energy Manager, Council Offices, Adam & Eve Street, Market Harborough LE16 7AG ☎ 01858 821036 🖷 01858 821002 ✉ g.ladds@harborough.gov.uk

Legal: Mrs Verina Wenham, Head of Legal Services, Council Offices, Adam & Eve Street, Market Harborough LE16 7AG ☎ 01858 821360 🖷 01858 821000 ✉ v.wenham@harborough.gov.uk

Leisure and Cultural Services: Ms Jayne Wisely, Cultural Services Manager, Council Offices, Adam & Eve Street, Market Harborough LE16 7AG ☎ 01858 821288 🖷 01858 821000 ✉ j.wisely@harborough.gov.uk

Licensing: Ms Sarah Gledhill, Senior Licensing Officer, Council Offices, Adam & Eve Street, Market Harborough LE16 7AG ☎ 01858 821172 ✉ s.gledhill@harborough.gov.uk

Member Services: Ms Beth Murgatroyd, Principal Democratic Officer, Council Offices, Adam & Eve Street, Market Harborough LE16 7AG ☎ 01858 821370 🖷 01858 821000 ✉ b.murgatroyd@harborough.gov.uk

Personnel / HR: Mrs Kate Frow, Human Resources Manager, Council Offices, Adam & Eve Street, Market Harborough LE16 7AG ☎ 01858 828282 🖷 01858 821306 ✉ k.frow@harborough.gov.uk

Planning: Mr Adrian Eastwood, Development Control Service Manager, Council Offices, Adam & Eve Street, Market Harborough LE16 7AG ☎ 01858 821142 🖷 01858 821097 a.eastwood@harborough.gov.uk

Recycling & Waste Minimisation: Mr Russell Smith, Senior Waste Management Officer, Council Offices, Adam & Eve Street, Market Harborough LE16 7AG ☎ 01858 821177 r.smith@harborough.gov.uk

Regeneration: Mr Stephen Pointer, Head of Built Environment, Council Offices, Adam & Eve Street, Market Harborough LE16 7AG ☎ 01858 821146 🖷 01858 821159 s.pointer@harborough.gov.uk

Staff Training: Mrs Kate Frow, Human Resources Manager, Council Offices, Adam & Eve Street, Market Harborough LE16 7AG ☎ 01858 828282 🖷 01858 821306 k.frow@harborough.gov.uk

Street Scene: Mr Stephen Pointer, Head of Built Environment, Council Offices, Adam & Eve Street, Market Harborough LE16 7AG ☎ 01858 821146 🖷 01858 821159 s.pointer@harborough.gov.uk

Sustainable Communities: Mr Matthew Bradford, Service Manager, Council Offices, Adam & Eve Street, Market Harborough LE16 7AG ☎ 01858 821290 m.bradford@harborough.gov.uk

Tourism: Mr Stephen Pointer, Head of Built Environment, Council Offices, Adam & Eve Street, Market Harborough LE16 7AG ☎ 01858 821146 🖷 01858 821159 s.pointer@harborough.gov.uk

Waste Collection and Disposal: Mr Russell Smith, Senior Waste Management Officer, Council Offices, Adam & Eve Street, Market Harborough LE16 7AG ☎ 01858 821177 r.smith@harborough.gov.uk

Waste Management: Mr Russell Smith, Senior Waste Management Officer, Council Offices, Adam & Eve Street, Market Harborough LE16 7AG ☎ 01858 821177 r.smith@harborough.gov.uk

MEMBERS OF THE COUNCIL (37)

***Chair:* Everett**, John (CON - Misterton)
j.everett@harborough.gov.uk
***Vice-Chair:* Robinson**, Geraldine (CON - Lutterworth Orchard)
g.robinson@harborough.gov.uk
***Leader of the Council:* Rook**, Michael (CON - Tilton)
m.rook@harborough.gov.uk
***Deputy Leader of the Council:* Pain**, Blake (CON - Lubenham)
b.pain@harborough.gov.uk
Ackerley, Janette (CON - Lutterworth - Swift)
j.ackerley@harborough.gov.uk
Bannister, Neil (CON - Dunton)
Beaty, David (CON - Nevill)
d.beaty@harborough.gov.uk
Beesley-Reynolds, Lynne (CON - Kibworth)
l.beesley-reynolds@harborough.gov.uk
Birch, Alan (LD - Fleckney)
a.birch@harborough.gov.uk
Bremner, Paul (CON - Market Harborough - Logan)
p.bremner@harborough.gov.uk
Brodrick, Jo (CON - Market Harborough Welland)
j.brodrick@harborough.gov.uk
Burrell, Amanda (LD - Thurnby and Houghton)
a.burrell@harborough.gov.uk
Callis, Peter (LD - Market Harborough - Logan)
p.callis@harborough.gov.uk
Charlish, Steven (CON - Billesdon)
s.charlish@harborough.gov.uk
Dann, Paul (CON - Broughton Astley - Primethorpe)
p.dann@harborough.gov.uk
Dewes, Richard (CON - Lutterworth Springs)
r.dewes@harborough.gov.uk
Dunton, Roger (LD - Market Harborough Welland)
r.dunton@harborough.gov.uk
Evans, Derek (CON - Market Harborough - Little Bowden)
d.evans@harborough.gov.uk
Galton, Simon (LD - Thurnby and Houghton)
s.galton@harborough.gov.uk
Golding, Colin (CON - Broughton Astley - Broughton)
colingolding@btinternet.com
Graves, Mark (CON - Broughton Astley-Astley)
m.graves@harborough.gov.uk
Hall, Neville (CON - Peatling)
n.hall@harborough.gov.uk
Hallam, James (CON - Glen)
j.hallam@harborough.gov.uk
Hill, Sarah (LD - Market Harborough Great Bowden and Arden)
s.hill@harborough.gov.uk
Holyoak, Christopher (CON - Kibworth)
c.holyoak@harborough.gov.uk
Johnson, Barbara (LD - Market Harborough Great Bowden and Arden)
b.johnson@harborough.gov.uk
King, Phillip (CON - Kibworth)
p.king@harborough.gov.uk
Knowles, Phil (LD - Market Harborough Great Bowden and Arden)
p.knowles@harborough.gov.uk
Liquorish, Bill (CON - Broughton Astley - Sutton)
w.liquorish@harborough.gov.uk
McHugo, Francesca (CON - Market Harborough - Little Bowden)
f.mchugo@harborough.gov.uk
Page, Rosita (CON - Ullesthorpe)
r.page@harborough.gov.uk
Simpson, Julie (LD - Market Harborough Welland)
j.simpson@harborough.gov.uk
Smith, Brian (CON - Bosworth)
b.smith@harborough.gov.uk
Spendlove-Mason, Grahame (CON - Glen)
g.spendlove-mason@harborough.gov.uk
Tomlin, Richard (CON - Lutterworth Brookfield)
r.tomlin@harborough.gov.uk
Tooley, Jan (LD - Thurnby and Houghton)
j.tooley@harborough.gov.uk
Wood, Charmaine (CON - Fleckney)
c.wood@harborough.gov.uk

POLITICAL COMPOSITION

CON: 27, LD: 10

CABINET

Leader / Business: Mr Michael Rook

Deputy Leader / Health & Community: Mr Blake Pain
Community Engagement, Cohesion & Wellbeing: Dr Paul Bremner
Finance, Efficiency & Assets: Mr Grahame Spendlove-Mason
Planning, Environment & Conservation: Mrs Janette Ackerley
Regulatory & Safety: Mr Colin Golding

COMMITTEE CHAIRS

Places: Mr Phillip King
Planning: Mr Bill Liquorish
Resource Development: Mr Christopher Holyoak

HARINGEY L

Haringey London Borough Council, River Park House, 225 High Road, London N22 8HQ ☎ 020 8489 0000 customer.services@haringey.gov.uk www.haringey.gov.uk

FACTS & FIGURES

Police Authority: Metropolitan Police Authority
Health Authority: NHS London
Learning and Skills Council: London
Parliamentary Constituencies: Hornsey and Wood Green, Tottenham
EU Constituencies: London
Election Frequency: Elections are of whole council
Twinning: Arima (Trinidad & Tobago); Clarendon (Jamaica); Koblenz Stadt (Germany); Larnaca (Cyprus); Livry Gargan (France); Sundbyberg (Sweden);

PRINCIPAL OFFICERS

Chief Executive: Mr Kevin Crompton, Chief Executive, 5th Floor, River Park House, 225 High Road, London N22 8HQ ☎ 020 8489 2648 kevin.crompton@haringey.gov.uk

Assistant Chief Executive: Mr Stuart Young, Assistant Chief Executive, People, Organisation & Development, 5th Floor, River Park House, 225 High Road, London N22 8HQ ☎ 020 8489 1952

Access Officer / Social Services (Disability): Ms Eve Pelekanos, Head of Performance & Policy, 7th Floor, River Park Houser, 225 High Road, London N22 8HQ ☎ 020 8489 2508 eve.pelekanos@haringey.gov.uk

Architect, Building / Property Services: Mr S Barnes, Head of Property & Contracts, 1st Floor Civic Centre, Wood Green, London N22 8LE ☎ 020 8489 3805

Architect, Building / Property Services: Mr Dinesh Kotecha, Head of Property Services, 1st Floor, Alexandra House, 10 Station Road, London N22 7TR ☎ 020 8489 2101 dinesh.kotecha@haringey.gov.uk

Best Value: Ms Eve Pelekanos, Head of Performance & Policy, 7th Floor, River Park Houser, 225 High Road, London N22 8HQ ☎ 020 8489 2508 eve.pelekanos@haringey.gov.uk

Building Control: Mr Bob McIver, Head of Building Control, 639 High Road, London N17 8BD ☎ 020 8489 5500

Catering Services: Ms Marianna Clune-Georgiou, Head of Catering, Lea Valley Techno Park, London N17 9LN ☎ 020 8489 4643 marianna.clune-georgiou@haringey.gov.uk

Children / Youth Services: Ms Rachel Oakley, Head of Safeguarding, Quality Assurance & Practice Development, 1st Floor, 48 Station Road, London N22 7TY ☎ 020 8489 1177 rachel.oakley@haringey.gov.uk

Community Planning: Ms Claire Kowalska, Safer Stronger Communities, 4th Floor, River Park House, 225 Station Road, London N22 8HQ

Community Safety: Ms Jean Croot, Safer Communities, 3rd Floor, Alexandra House, 10 Station Road, London N22 7TR ☎ 020 8489 6934 🖷 020 8489 2992

Computer Management: Mr David Airey, Head of IT, 3rd Floor, River Park House, 225 High Road, London N22 8HQ ☎ 020 8489 4673 🖷 020 8489 3998 david.airey@haringey.gov.uk

Consumer Protection and Trading Standards: Mr Keith Betts, Service Manager for Commercial Enforcement, 1st Floor, Ashley Road, London N17 9LN ☎ 020 8849 5525

Contracts: Mr Michael Wood, Head of Procurement, Alexandra House, 5th Floor, 10 Station Road, London N22 7TR ☎ 020 8489 2120

Corporate Services: Ms Helen Constantine, Head of Governance & Partnerships, 40 Cumberland Road, Wood Green, London N22 7SG ☎ 020 8489 3905 helen.constantine@haringey.gov.uk

Corporate Services: Mr Michael Wood, Head of Procurement, Alexandra House, 5th Floor, 10 Station Road, London N22 7TR ☎ 020 8489 2120

Education: Mr Terry O'Reirdan, Head of Education Welfare, First Floor PDC, Downhills Park Road, London N17 6AR ☎ 020 8489 3872 terry.o'reirdan@haringey.gov.uk

Electoral Registration: Mr George Cooper, Electoral Registration Manager, Civic Centre, Wood Green, High Road, London N22 8LE ☎ 020 8489 2976

Emergency Planning: Mr Andrew Meek, Emergency Planning Officer, 6th Floor, Alexandra House, 10 Station Road, London N22 7TR ☎ 020 8489 1164 andrew.meek@haringey.gov.uk

Environmental / Technical Services: Ms Anne Lippit, Director of Place & Sustainability, 2nd Floor, River Park House, 225 High Road, London N22 8HQ ☎ 020 8489 4537 anne.lippit@haringey.gov.uk

Environmental Health: Mr Stephen McDonnell, Assistant Director - Enforcement, 4th Floor, River Park House, 225 Station Road, London N22 8HQ ☎ 020 8489 2485 stephen.mcdonnell@haringey.gov.uk

Events Manager: Ms Elena Pippou, Arts, Culture & Marketing Officer, Ground Floor, Hornsey Library, London N22 9JA ☎ 020 8489 1419 elena.pippou@haringey.gov.uk

Finance and Treasurer: Mr Kevin Bartle, Lead Finance Offier, Ground Floor, Ashley Road Depot, High Road, London N17 9AY ☎ 020 8489 2975 ✉ kevin.bartle@haringey.gov.uk

Fleet Management: Mr Darren Butterfield, Transport Manager, Ground Floor, Ashley Road Depot, High Road, London N17 9AY ☎ 020 8489 5786 ✉ darren.butterfield@haringey.gov.uk

Highways: Ms Joan Hancox, Head of Neighbourhood Services, 1st Floor, River Park House, 225 High Road, London N22 8HQ ☎ 020 8489 1777

Highways: Mr Olatunji Oladejo, Head of Highways Maintenance, River Park House, 225 High Road, London N22 8HQ ☎ 020 8489 1713 ✉ olatunji.oladejo@haringey.gov.uk

Housing: Mr Paul Bridge, Chief Executive Homes for Haringey, 6th Floor, River Park House, 225 High Road, London N22 8HQ ☎ 020 8489 4260 ✉ paul.bridge@haringey.gov.uk

Housing Maintenance: Mr Keith Carter, Director - Building Services, River Park House, 225 High Road, London N22 8HQ ☎ 020 8489 3272 ✉ keith.carter@haringey.gov.uk

Local Area Agreement: Ms Claire Kowalska, Safer Stronger Communities, 4th Floor, River Park House, 225 Station Road, London N22 8HQ

Legal: Ms E Featherstone, Principal Equalities Officer, 7th Floor, Wood Green Library, High Road, London N22 6XD ☎ 020 8489 2583

Legal: Mr Bernie Ryan, Head of Legal Services, 5th Floor, River Park House, 225 High Road, London N22 8HQ

Leisure and Cultural Services: Mr John Morris, Assistant Director - Recreation Services, 40 Cumberland Road, London N22 7SG ☎ 020 8489 5686 ✉ john.morris@haringey.gov.uk

Lighting: Mr Anthony Kennedy, Transport Policy & Projects Manager, 1st Floor, River Park House, 225 High Road, London N22 8HQ ☎ 020 8489 5351 ✉ tony.kennedy@haringey.gov.uk

Lottery Funding, Charity and Voluntary: Ms Elena Pippou, Arts, Culture & Marketing Officer, Ground Floor, Hornsey Library, London N22 9JA ☎ 020 8489 1419 ✉ elena.pippou@haringey.gov.uk

Member Services: Mr Clifford Hart, Cabinet Committees Manager, River Park House, 225 High Road, London N22 8HQ ☎ 020 8489 2922 ✉ clifford.hart@haringey.gov.uk

Personnel / HR: Mr Steve Davies, Head of Human Resources, Alexandra House, 10 Station Road, London N22 7TR ☎ 020 8489 3172 ✉ steve.davies@haringey.gov.uk

Personnel / HR: Mr Stuart Young, Assistant Chief Executive, People, Organisation & Development, Alexandra House, 10 Station Road, London N22 7TR ☎ 020 8489 1952

Planning: Mr Marc Dorfman, Assistant Director for Planning, Regeneration & Economy, 639 High Road, Tottenham, London N17 8BD ☎ 020 8489 5208 ✉ marc.dorfman@haringey.gov.uk

Procurement: Mr Michael Wood, Head of Procurement, Alexandra House, 5th Floor, 10 Station Road, London N22 7TR ☎ 020 8489 2120

Recycling & Waste Minimisation: Mr Steve MacDonnell, Head of Environmental Resources, Level 4, River Park House, 225 High Road, London N22 8HQ ☎ 020 8489 2485 ✉ steve.macdonnell@haringey.gov.uk

Regeneration: Mr Marc Dorfman, Assistant Director - Planning & Regeneration, River Park House, 225 High Road, London N22 8HQ ☎ 020 8489 5208 ✉ mark.dorfman@haringey.gov.uk

Road Safety: Ms Wendy Thorogood, Technical Support Officer, River Park House, 225 High Road, London N22 8HQ ☎ 020 8489 5351 ✉ wendy.thorogood@haringey.gov.uk

Social Services: Mr Thun Thong Phung, Director of Adult Culture Services, 40 Cumberland Road, London N22 7SG ☎ 020 8489 5919

Staff Training: Ms Philipa Morris, Head of OD, Wood Green Central Library, London N22 6XD ☎ 020 8489 1088 ✉ philipa.morris@haringey.gov.uk

Tourism: Ms Elena Pippou, Arts, Culture & Marketing Officer, Ground Floor, Hornsey Library, London N22 9JA ☎ 020 8489 1419 ✉ elena.pippou@haringey.gov.uk

Traffic Management: Mr Anthony Kennedy, Transport Policy & Projects Manager, 1st Floor, River Park House, 225 High Road, London N22 8HQ ☎ 020 8489 5351 ✉ tony.kennedy@haringey.gov.uk

Transport: Mr Pembe Hipolyte, Escort Supervisor, Ashley Road Depot, Ashley Road, London N17 9AY ☎ 020 8489 5629 🖷 020 8489 5647

Waste Collection and Disposal: Mr Steve MacDonnell, Head of Environmental Resources, Level 4, River Park House, 225 High Road, London N22 8HQ ☎ 020 8489 2485 ✉ steve.macdonnell@haringey.gov.uk

Waste Management: Mr Steve MacDonnell, Head of Environmental Resources, Level 4, River Park House, 225 High Road, London N22 8HQ ☎ 020 8489 2485 ✉ steve.macdonnell@haringey.gov.uk

MEMBERS OF THE COUNCIL (57)

***Mayor:* Browne**, David (LAB - St Ann's)
david.browne@haringey.gov.uk

***Deputy Mayor:* Peacock**, Sheila (LAB - Northumberland Park)
sheila.peacock@haringey.gov.uk

***Leader of the Council:* Kober**, Claire (LAB - Seven Sisters)
claire.kober@haringey.gov.uk

***Deputy Leader of the Council:* Reith**, Lorna (LAB - Tottenham Hale)
lorna.reith@haringey.gov.uk

***Deputy Leader of the Council:* Vanier**, Bernice (LAB - Tottenham Green)
bernice.vanier@haringey.gov.uk

***Group Leader:* Gorrie**, Robert (LD - Hornsey)
robert.gorrie@haringey.gov.uk
***Group Leader:* Wilson**, Richard (LD - Stroud Green)
richard.wilson@haringey.gov.uk
Adamou, Gina (LAB - Harringay)
gina.adamou@haringey.gov.uk
Adje, Charles (LAB - White Hart Lane)
charles.adje@haringey.gov.uk
Alexander, Karen (LD - Harringay)
karen.alexander@haringey.gov.uk
Allison, Rachel (LD - Highgate)
rachael.allison@haringey.gov.uk
Amin, Kaushika (LAB - Northumberland Park)
kaushika.amin@haringey.gov.uk
Basu, Dhiren (LAB - Seven Sisters)
dhiren.basu@haringey.gov.uk
Beacham, David (LD - Alexandra)
david.beacham@haringey.gov.uk
Bevan, John (LAB - Northumberland Park)
john.bevan@haringey.gov.uk
Bloch, Jonathan (LD - Muswell Hill)
jonathan.bloch@haringey.gov.uk
Brabazon, Zena (LAB - St Ann's)
zena.brabazon@haringey.gov.uk
Bull, Gideon (LAB - White Hart Lane)
gideon.bull@haringey.gov.uk
Butcher, Ed (LD - Stroud Green)
ed.butcher@haringey.gov.uk
Canver, Nilgun (LAB - St Ann's)
nilgun.canver@haringey.gov.uk
Christophides, Joanna (LAB - Bounds Green)
joanna.christophides@haringey.gov.uk
Cooke, Matt (LAB - Bounds Green)
matt.cooke@haringey.gov.uk
Davies, Matt (LD - Fortis Green)
matt.davies@haringey.gov.uk
Demirci, Ali (LAB - Bounds Green)
ali.demirci@haringey.gov.uk
Diakides, Isidoros (LAB - Tottenham Green)
isidoros.dialides@haringey.gov.uk
Dogus, Dilek (LAB - Bruce Grove)
dilek.dogus@haringey.gov.uk
Egan, Pat (LAB - Woodside)
pat.egan@haringey.gov.uk
Ejiofer, Joseph (LAB - Bruce Grove)
joseph.ejiofer@haringey.gov.uk
Engert, Gail (LD - Muswell Hill)
gail.engert@haringey.gov.uk
Erskine, Sophie (LD - Fortis Green)
sophie.erskine@haringey.gov.uk
Gibson, Pauline (LAB - Noel Park)
pauline.gibson@haringey.gov.uk
Goldberg, Joe (LAB - Seven Sisters)
joe.goldberg@haringey.gov.uk
Griffith, Eddie (LAB - West Green)
eddie.griffith@haringey.gov.uk
Hare, Bob (LD - Highgate)
bob.hare@haringey.gov.uk
Jenks, Jim (LD - Muswell Hill)
jim.jenks@haringey.gov.uk
Khan, Gmmh Rahman (LAB - West Green)
rahman.khan@haringey.gov.uk
Mallett, Toni (LAB - West Green)
toni.mallett@haringey.gov.uk
McNamara, Stuart (LAB - Bruce Grove)
stuart.mcnamara@haringey.gov.uk
Meehan, George (LAB - Woodside)
george.meehan@haringey.gov.uk
Newton, Martin (LD - Fortis Green)
martin.newton@haringey.gov.uk
Reece, Katherine (LD - Stroud Green)
katherine.reece@haringey.gov.uk
Reid, Errol (LD - Hornsey)
errol.reid@haringey.gov.uk
Rice, Reg (LAB - Tottenham Hale)
reg.rice@haringey.gov.uk
Schmitz, David (LD - Harringay)
david.schmitz@haringey.gov.uk
Scott, Nigel (LD - Alexandra)
nigel.scott@haringey.gov.uk
Soloman, Juliet (LD - Alexandra)
juliet.soloman@haringey.gov.uk
Stanton, Alan (LAB - Tottenham Hale)
alan.stanton@haringey.gov.uk
Stennett, Anne (LAB - White Hart Lane)
anne.stennett@haringey.gov.uk
Stewart, James (LAB - Noel Park)
james.stewart@haringey.gov.uk
Strang, Paul (LD - Crouch End)
paul.strang@haringey.gov.uk
Strickland, Alan (LAB - Noel Park)
alan.strickland@haringey.gov.uk
Waters, Ann (LAB - Woodside)
an.waters@haringey.gov.uk
Watson, Richard (LAB - Tottenham Green)
richard.watson@haringey.gov.uk
Weber, Lyn (LD - Crouch End)
lyn.weber@haringey.gov.uk
Whyte, Monica (LD - Hornsey)
monica.whyte@haringey.gov.uk
Williams, Neil (LD - Highgate)
neil.williams@haringey.gov.uk
Winskill, David (LD - Crouch End)
david.winskill@haringey.gov.uk

POLITICAL COMPOSITION

LAB: 34, LD: 23

CABINET

Leader: Ms Claire Kober
Deputy Leader / Health & Adult Services: Ms Bernice Vanier
Children: Ms Ann Waters
Communities: Mr Richard Watson
Economic Development and Social Inclusion: Mr Alan Strickland
Environment: Ms Nilgun Canver
Finance and Carbon Reduction: Mr Joe Goldberg
Housing: Mr John Bevan

COMMITTEE CHAIRS

Community Safety: Ms Bernice Vanier
Environment & Housing: Mr Stuart McNamara
Overview & Scrutiny (Scrutiny): Mr Reg Rice
Regulatory: Mr Ali Demirci

HARLOW D

Harlow District Council, Civic Centre, The Water Gardens, Harlow CM20 1WG ☎ 01279 446611 🖷 01279 446767
contact@harlow.gov.uk 💻 www.harlow.gov.uk

FACTS & FIGURES

Police Authority: Essex Police Authority
Health Authority: East of England Strategic Health Authority
Learning and Skills Council: Eastern
Parliamentary Constituencies: Harlow
EU Constituencies: Eastern
Election Frequency: Elections are by thirds
Twinning: Velizy-Villacoublay (France); Havirov (Czech Republic)

PRINCIPAL OFFICERS

Chief Executive: Mr Malcolm Morley, Chief Executive, Civic Centre, The Water Gardens, Harlow CM20 1WG ☎ 01279 446611 ✉ malcolm.morley@harlow.gov.uk

Assistant Chief Executive: Ms Cath Shaw, Assistant Chief Executive, Civic Centre, The Water Gardens, Harlow CM20 1WG ☎ 01279 446428 ✉ cath.shaw@harlow.gov.uk

Senior Management: Mr Graham Branchett, Strategic Director, Civic Centre, The Water Gardens, Harlow CM20 1WG ☎ 01279 446611 ✉ graham.branchett@harlow.gov.uk

Architect, Building / Property Services: Mr Graeme Bloomer, Head of Regulation, Civic Centre, The Water Gardens, Harlow CM20 1WG ☎ 01276 446270 ✉ graeme.bloomer@harlow.gov.uk

Building Control: Mr Graeme Bloomer, Head of Regulation, Civic Centre, The Water Gardens, Harlow CM20 1WG ☎ 01276 446270 ✉ graeme.bloomer@harlow.gov.uk

Civil Registration: Mr Mike White, Head of Governance, Civic Centre, The Water Gardens, Harlow CM20 1WG ☎ 01279 446037 ✉ mike.white@harlow.gov.uk

PR / Communications: Mr Mike White, Head of Governance, Civic Centre, The Water Gardens, Harlow CM20 1WG ☎ 01279 446037 ✉ mike.white@harlow.gov.uk

Community Planning: Ms Lynn Seward, Head of Community Services, Civic Centre, The Water Gardens, Harlow CM20 1WG ☎ 01279 446119 ✉ lynn.seward@harlow.gov.uk

Community Safety: Ms Lynn Seward, Head of Community Services, Civic Centre, The Water Gardens, Harlow CM20 1WG ☎ 01279 446119 ✉ lynn.seward@harlow.gov.uk

Computer Management: Mr Mike White, Head of Governance, Civic Centre, The Water Gardens, Harlow CM20 1WG ☎ 01279 446037 ✉ mike.white@harlow.gov.uk

Contracts: Mrs Lynn Seward, Head of Community Services, Civic Centre, The Water Gardens, Harlow CM20 1WG ☎ 01279 446119 ✉ lynn.seward@harlow.gov.uk

Corporate Services: Mr Mike White, Head of Governance, Civic Centre, The Water Gardens, Harlow CM20 1WG ☎ 01279 446037 ✉ mike.white@harlow.gov.uk

Customer Service: Ms Lynn Seward, Head of Community Services, Civic Centre, The Water Gardens, Harlow CM20 1WG ☎ 01279 446119 ✉ lynn.seward@harlow.gov.uk

Electoral Registration: Mr Mike White, Head of Governance, Civic Centre, The Water Gardens, Harlow CM20 1WG ☎ 01279 446037 ✉ mike.white@harlow.gov.uk

Emergency Planning: Ms Cath Shaw, Assistant Chief Executive, Civic Centre, The Water Gardens, Harlow CM20 1WG ☎ 01279 446428 ✉ cath.shaw@harlow.gov.uk

Energy Management: Mr Graeme Bloomer, Head of Regulation, Civic Centre, The Water Gardens, Harlow CM20 1WG ☎ 01276 446270 ✉ graeme.bloomer@harlow.gov.uk

Environmental / Technical Services: Mr Graeme Bloomer, Head of Regulation, Civic Centre, The Water Gardens, Harlow CM20 1WG ☎ 01276 446270 ✉ graeme.bloomer@harlow.gov.uk

Environmental Health: Mr Graeme Bloomer, Head of Regulation, Civic Centre, The Water Gardens, Harlow CM20 1WG ☎ 01279 446611 ✉ graeme.bloomer@harlow.gov.uk

Estates, Property & Valuation: Mr Graeme Bloomer, Head of Regulation, Civic Centre, The Water Gardens, Harlow CM20 1WG ☎ 01279 446611 ✉ graeme.bloomer@harlow.gov.uk

Facilities: Ms Cath Shaw, Assistant Chief Executive, Civic Centre, The Water Gardens, Harlow CM20 1WG ☎ 01279 446428 ✉ cath.shaw@harlow.gov.uk

Health and Safety: Mr Graeme Bloomer, Head of Regulation, Civic Centre, The Water Gardens, Harlow CM20 1WG ☎ 01276 446270 ✉ graeme.bloomer@harlow.gov.uk

Highways: Mr Graeme Bloomer, Head of Regulation, Civic Centre, The Water Gardens, Harlow CM20 1WG ☎ 01276 446270 ✉ graeme.bloomer@harlow.gov.uk

Home Energy Conservation: Mr Graeme Bloomer, Head of Regulation, Civic Centre, The Water Gardens, Harlow CM20 1WG ☎ 01276 446270 ✉ graeme.bloomer@harlow.gov.uk

Housing: Mr Andrew Murray, Head of Housing, Civic Centre, The Water Gardens, Harlow SM20 1WG ☎ 01279 446676 ✉ andrew.murray@harlow.gov.uk

Housing Maintenance: Mr Andrew Murray, Head of Housing, Civic Centre, The Water Gardens, Harlow SM20 1WG ☎ 01279 446676 ✉ andrew.murray@harlow.gov.uk

Legal: Mr Mike White, Head of Governance, Civic Centre, The Water Gardens, Harlow CM20 1WG ☎ 01279 446037 ✉ mike.white@harlow.gov.uk

Leisure and Cultural Services: Ms Lynn Seward, Head of Community Services, Civic Centre, The Water Gardens, Harlow CM20 1WG ☎ 01279 446119 ✉ lynn.seward@harlow.gov.uk

Licensing: Mr Graeme Bloomer, Head of Regulation, Civic Centre, The Water Gardens, Harlow CM20 1WG ☎ 01276 446270 ✉ graeme.bloomer@harlow.gov.uk

Member Services: Mr Mike White, Head of Governance, Civic Centre, The Water Gardens, Harlow CM20 1WG ☎ 01279 446037

✉ mike.white@harlow.gov.uk

Parking: Ms Cath Shaw, Assistant Chief Executive, Civic Centre, The Water Gardens, Harlow CM20 1WG ☎ 01279 446428 ✉ cath.shaw@harlow.gov.uk

Personnel / HR: Mr Mike White, Head of Governance, Civic Centre, The Water Gardens, Harlow CM20 1WG ☎ 01279 446037 ✉ mike.white@harlow.gov.uk

Planning: Mr Graeme Bloomer, Head of Regulation, Civic Centre, The Water Gardens, Harlow CM20 1WG ☎ 01276 446270 ✉ graeme.bloomer@harlow.gov.uk

Procurement: Ms Lynn Seward, Head of Community Services, Civic Centre, The Water Gardens, Harlow CM20 1WG ☎ 01279 446119 ✉ lynn.seward@harlow.gov.uk

Recycling & Waste Minimisation: Mr Graeme Bloomer, Head of Regulation, Civic Centre, The Water Gardens, Harlow CM20 1WG ☎ 01279 446611 ✉ graeme.bloomer@harlow.gov.uk

Regeneration: Ms Cath Shaw, Assistant Chief Executive, Civic Centre, The Water Gardens, Harlow CM20 1WG ☎ 01279 446428 ✉ cath.shaw@harlow.gov.uk

Staff Training: Mr Mike White, Head of Governance, Civic Centre, The Water Gardens, Harlow CM20 1WG ☎ 01279 446037 ✉ mike.white@harlow.gov.uk

Street Scene: Mr Graeme Bloomer, Head of Regulation, Civic Centre, The Water Gardens, Harlow CM20 1WG ☎ 01276 446270 ✉ graeme.bloomer@harlow.gov.uk

Town Centre: Ms Cath Shaw, Assistant Chief Executive, Civic Centre, The Water Gardens, Harlow CM20 1WG ☎ 01279 446428 ✉ cath.shaw@harlow.gov.uk

Waste Collection and Disposal: Mr Graeme Bloomer, Head of Regulation, Civic Centre, The Water Gardens, Harlow CM20 1WG ☎ 01276 446270 ✉ graeme.bloomer@harlow.gov.uk

Waste Management: Mr Graeme Bloomer, Head of Regulation, Civic Centre, The Water Gardens, Harlow CM20 1WG ☎ 01276 446270 ✉ graeme.bloomer@harlow.gov.uk

MEMBERS OF THE COUNCIL (33)

Chair: **Hulcoop**, Margaret (LAB - Harlow Common)
maggie.hulcoop@harlow.gov.uk

Leader of the Council: **Wilkinson**, Mark (LAB - Harlow Common)
mark.wilkinson@harlow.gov.uk

Deputy Leader of the Council: **Clark**, Jean (LAB - Little Parndon and Hare Street)
jean.clark@harlow.gov.uk

Deputy Leader of the Council: **Johnson**, Eddie (CON - Great Parndon)
eddie.johnson@harlow.gov.uk

Beckett, Ian (LAB - Bush Fair)
ian.beckett@harlow.gov.uk

Carter, Simon (CON - Church Langley)
simon.carter@harlow.gov.uk

Carter, David (CON - Great Parndon)
david.carter@harlow.gov.uk

Churchill, Nick (CON - Sumners and Kingsmoor)
nick.churchill@harlow.gov.uk

Clempner, Jon (LAB - Little Parndon and Hare Street)
jon.clempner@harlow.gov.uk

Cross, Jacqui (LAB - Mark Hall)
jacqui.cross@harlow.gov.uk

Danvers, Mike (LAB - Netteswell)
mike.danvers@harlow.gov.uk

Davis, Bob (LAB - Toddbrook)
bob.davis@harlow.gov.uk

Doku, Emmanuel (LAB - Bush Fair)
emmanuel.doku@harlow.gov.uk

Durcan, Tony (LAB - Little Parndon and Hare Street)
anthony.durcan@harlow.gov.uk

Forman, Waida (LAB - Netteswell)
waida.forman@harlow.gov.uk

Garnett, Michael (CON - Old Harlow)
michael.garnett@harlow.gov.uk

Hall, Tony (CON - Church Langley)
tony.hall@harlow.gov.uk

Johnson, Andrew (CON - Church Langley)
andrew.johnson@harlow.gov.uk

Jolles, Muriel (CON - Old Harlow)
muriel.jolles@harlow.gov.uk

Jolles, Joshua (CON - Great Parndon)
joshua.jolles@harlow.gov.uk

Livings, Sue (CON - Old Harlow)
sue.livings@harlow.gov.uk

McCabe, Patrick (LAB - Staple Tye)
patrick.mccabe@harlow.gov.uk

Mitchinson, Guy (CON - Staple Tye)
guy.mitchinson@essex.gov.uk

Pailing, Linda (CON - Sumners and Kingsmoor)
linda.pailing@harlow.gov.uk

Palmer, Dennis (LAB - Staple Tye)
dennis.palmer@harlow.gov.uk

Perrin, Russell (CON - Sumners and Kingsmoor)
russell.perrin@harlow.gov.uk

Pritchard, Daniella (LAB - Bush Fair)
daniella.pritchard@harlow.gov.u

Schroder, Paul (LAB - Mark Hall)
paul.schroder@harlow.gov.uk

Stevens, Edna (LAB - Netteswell)
edna.stevens@harlow.gov.uk

Sztumpf, Paul (LAB - Mark Hall)
paul.sztumpf@harlow.gov.uk

Toal, Emma (LAB - Harlow Common)
emma.toal@harlow.gov.uk

Truan, Rod (LAB - Toddbrook)
rod.truan@harlow.gov.uk

Waite, Phil (LAB - Toddbrook)
phil.waite@harlow.gov.uk

POLITICAL COMPOSITION

LAB: 20, CON: 13

CABINET

Leader / Governance: Mr Mark Wilkinson
Deputy Leader / Community & Inclusion: Ms Jean Clark
Environment: Mr Jon Clempner
Housing: Mr Rod Truan
Regeneration & Enterprise: Mr Tony Durcan

Resources: Mr Mike Danvers
Youth & Citizenship: Ms Emma Toal

HARROGATE D

Harrogate Borough Council, Council Offices, Crescent Gardens, Harrogate HG1 2SG ☎ 01423 500600 🖷 01423 556100
💻 www.harrogate.gov.uk

FACTS & FIGURES

Police Authority: North Yorkshire Police Authority
Health Authority: NHS Yorkshire & the Humber
Learning and Skills Council: Yorkshire and the Humber
Parliamentary Constituencies: Harrogate and Knaresborough
EU Constituencies: Yorkshire and the Humber
Election Frequency: Elections are by thirds
Twinning: Bagneres-de-Luchon (France); Wellington (New Zealand); Knaresborough: Bebra (Germany); Ripon: Ripon (USA); Foix (France)

PRINCIPAL OFFICERS

Chief Executive: Mr Wallace Sampson, Chief Executive, Council Offices, Crescent Gardens, Harrogate HG1 2SG ☎ 01423 556081 🖷 01423 556160 ✉ chiefexecutive@harrogate.gov.uk

Deputy Chief Executive: Mr John Sowden, Director of Resources/Deputy Chief Executive, Council Offices, Crescent Gardens, Harrogate HG1 2SG ☎ ; 01423 556121 🖷 01423 556120 ✉ john.sowden@harrogate.gov.uk

Assistant Chief Executive: Mrs Rachel Bowles, Assistant Chief Executive, Council Offices, Crescent Gardens, Harrogate HG1 2SG ☎ 01423 556705 ✉ rachel.bowles@harrogate.gov.uk

Senior Management: Mr Angus Houston, Director of Harrogate International Centre, Harrogate International Centre, King's Road, Harrogate HG1 5LA ☎ 01423 537209 🖷 01423 537210 ✉ angus.houston@harrogate.gov.uk

Senior Management: Mr Les Williamson, Director of Community Services, Springfield House, Kings Road, Harrogate HG1 5NX ☎ 01423 556846 🖷 01423 556810 ✉ les.williamson@harrogate.gov.uk

Access Officer / Social Services (Disability): Mr Nigel Thompson, Chief Facilities Manager, Knapping Mount, West Grove Road, Harrogate HG1 2AE ☎ 01423 556657 🖷 01423 556580 ✉ nigel.thompson-dts@harrogate.gov.uk

Architect, Building / Property Services: Mr Nigel Avison, Director of Development Services, Knapping Mount, West Grove Road, Harrogate HG1 2AE ☎ 01423 556536 🖷 01423 556530 ✉ nigel.avison@harrogate.gov.uk

Architect, Building / Property Services: Mrs Kathryn Daly, Acting Head of Property & Economic Development, Knapping Mount, West Grove Road, Harrogate HG1 2AE ☎ 01423 556054 🖷 01423 556530 ✉ kathryn.daly@harrogate.gov.uk

Building Control: Mr John Kirkman, Chief Building Control Officer, Knapping Mount, West Grove Road, Harrogate HG1 2AE ☎ 01423 556597 🖷 01423 556550 ✉ john.kirkman@harrogate.gov.uk

PR / Communications: Mrs Lynne Mee, Communications and Media Manager, Council Offices, Crescent Gardens, Harrogate HG1 2SG ☎ 01423 556022 🖷 ; 01423 556010 ✉ lynne.mee@harrogate.gov.uk

Community Planning: Mr Les Williamson, Director of Community Services, Springfield House, Kings Road, Harrogate HG1 5NX ☎ 01423 556846 🖷 01423 556810 ✉ les.williamson@harrogate.gov.uk

Community Safety: Mrs Nicky Garside, Head of Public Protection, Springfield House, Kings Road, Harrogate HG1 5NX ☎ 01423 556847 ✉ nicky.garside@harrogate.gov.uk

Community Safety: Mrs Julia Stack, Community Safety & CCTV Manager, Springfield House, Kings Road, Harrogate HG1 5NX ☎ 01423 556632 🖷 01423 556820 ✉ julia.stack@harrogate.gov.uk

Computer Management: Mr Mike Kenworthy, Director of ICT, Council Offices, Crescent Gardens, Harrogate HG1 2SG ☎ 01423 556073 ✉ mike.kenworthy@harrogate.gov.uk

Corporate Services: Mr Simon Kent, Head of Operations, Harrogate International Centre, Kings Road, Harrogate HG1 5LA ☎ 01423 537237 ✉ simon.kent@harrogate.gov.uk

Customer Service: Mrs Christine Pyatt, Customer Services Manager, Council Offices, Crescent Gardens, Harrogate HG1 2SG ☎ 01423 556845 🖷 01423 556810 ✉ simon.johnson@harrogate.gov.uk

Direct Labour: Mr Simon Johnson, Head of Environment, Springfield House, Kings Road, Harrogate HG1 5NX ☎ 01423 556845 🖷 01423 556810 ✉ simon.johnson@harrogate.gov.uk

Economic Development: Mr Nigel Avison, Director of Development Services, Knapping Mount, West Grove Road, Harrogate HG1 2AE ☎ 01423 556536 🖷 01423 556530 ✉ nigel.avison@harrogate.gov.uk

Economic Development: Mrs Kathryn Daly, Acting Head of Property & Economic Development, Knapping Mount, West Grove Road, Harrogate HG1 2AE ☎ 01423 556054 🖷 01423 556530 ✉ kathryn.daly@harrogate.gov.uk

E-Government: Mr Mike Kenworthy, Director of ICT, Council Offices, Crescent Gardens, Harrogate HG1 2SG ☎ 01423 556073 ✉ mike.kenworthy@harrogate.gov.uk

Electoral Registration: Mr Peter Jordan, Head of Legal & Democratic Services, Council Offices, Crescent Gardens, Harrogate HG1 2SG ☎ 01423 556049 ✉ peter.jordan@harrogate.gov.uk

Emergency Planning: Mr Ian Speirs, Civil Contingencies/Resilience Officer, Council Offices, Crescent Gardens, Harrogate HG1 2SG ☎ 01423 556014 ✉ ian.speirs@harrogate.gov.uk

Energy Management: Mr Simon Johnson, Head of Environment, Springfield House, Kings Road, Harrogate HG1 5NX ☎ 01423 556845 🖷 01423 556810 ✉ simon.johnson@harrogate.gov.uk

Environmental / Technical Services: Mr Simon Johnson, Head of Environment, Springfield House, Kings Road, Harrogate HG1 5NX ☎ 01423 556845 🖷 01423 556810 ✉ simon.johnson@harrogate.gov.uk

Environmental Health: Mrs Nicky Garside, Head of Public Protection, Springfield House, Kings Road, Harrogate HG1 5NX ☎ 01423 556847 ✉ nicky.garside@harrogate.gov.uk

Environmental Health: Mr Les Williamson, Director of Community Services, Springfield House, Kings Road, Harrogate HG1 5NX ☎ 01423 556846 🖷 ; 01423 556810 ✉ les.williamson@harrogate.gov.uk

Estates, Property & Valuation: Mr Nigel Avison, Director of Development Services, Knapping Mount, West Grove Road, Harrogate HG1 2AE ☎ 01423 556536 🖷 01423 556530 ✉ nigel.avison@harrogate.gov.uk

European Liaison: Ms Genevieve Gillies, Economic Development Officer (Regeneration), Knapping Mount, West Grove Road, Harrogate HG1 2AE ☎ 01423 556079 🖷 01423 556050 ✉ genevieve.gillies@harrogate.gov.uk

Finance and Treasurer: Mrs Val Hunter, Head of Financial Management, Council Offices, Crescent Gardens, Harrogate HG1 2SG ☎ 01423 556124 ✉ val.hunter@harrogate.gov.uk

Finance and Treasurer: Mr John Sowden, Director of Resources/Deputy Chief Executive, Council Offices, Crescent Gardens, Harrogate HG1 2SG ☎ ; 01423 556121 🖷 01423 556120 ✉ ; john.sowden@harrogate.gov.uk

Fleet Management: Mr Alan Smith, Transport Manager, Claro Road Depot, Claro Road, Harrogate HG1 4AT ☎ 01423 556877 🖷 01423 530174 ✉ alan.smith@harrogate.gov.uk

Grounds Maintenance: Mr Patrick Kilburn, Head of Parks & Open Spaces, Springfield House, Kings Road, Harrogate HG1 5NX ☎ 01423 551106 🖷 01423 556810 ✉ patrick.kilburn@harrogate.gov.uk

Health and Safety: Mrs Yvonne Wilman, Health & Safety Advisor, Council Offices, Crescent Gardens, Harrogate HG1 2SG ☎ 01423 556058 🖷 01423 556180 ✉ yvonne.wilman@harrogate.gov.uk

Home Energy Conservation: Mrs Jane Money, Environmental Strategy Manager, Springfield House, Kings Road, Harrogate HG1 5NX ☎ 01423 556801 🖷 01423 556720 ✉ jane.money@harrogate.gov.uk

Housing: Mr Alan Jenks, Head of Housing, Springfield House, Kings Road, Harrogate HG1 5NX ☎ 01423 556849 ✉ alan.jenks@harrogate.gov.uk

Housing: Mr Les Williamson, Director of Community Services, Springfield House, Kings Road, Harrogate HG1 5NX ☎ 01423 556846 🖷 ; 01423 556810 ✉ les.williamson@harrogate.gov.uk

Housing Maintenance: Mr Stephen Hargreaves, Property Services Manager, Scottsdale House, Springfield Avenue, Harrogate HG1 2SD ☎ 01423 556907 🖷 01423 556860 ✉ stephen.hargreaves@harrogate.gov.uk

Legal: Mr Peter Jordan, Head of Legal & Democratic Services, Council Offices, Crescent Gardens, Harrogate HG1 2SG ☎ 01423 556049 ✉ peter.jordan@harrogate.gov.uk

Leisure and Cultural Services: Ms Lois Toyne, Head of Culture, Tourism & Sports, Knapping Mount, West Grove Road, Harrogate HG1 2AE ☎ 01423 556187 ✉ lois.toyne@harrogate.gov.uk

Licensing: Mr Gareth Bentley, Licensing Manager, Springfield House, Kings Road, Harrogate HG1 5NX ☎ 01423 881027 🖷 01423 556820 ✉ gareth.bentley@harrogate.gov.uk

Lighting: Mr David Oliver, Street Lighting Engineer, Knapping Mount, West Grove Road, Harrogate HG1 2AE ☎ 01423 556544 ✉ david.oliver@harrogate.gov.uk

Lottery Funding, Charity and Voluntary: Mr Peter Jordan, Head of Legal & Democratic Services, Council Offices, Crescent Gardens, Harrogate HG1 2SG ☎ 01423 556049 ✉ peter.jordan@harrogate.gov.uk

Member Services: Mr Peter Jordan, Head of Legal & Democratic Services, Council Offices, Crescent Gardens, Harrogate HG1 2SG ☎ 01423 556049 ✉ peter.jordan@harrogate.gov.uk

Parking: Mr Nigel Avison, Director of Development Services, Knapping Mount, West Grove Road, Harrogate HG1 2AE ☎ 01423 556536 🖷 01423 556530 ✉ nigel.avison@harrogate.gov.uk

Partnerships: Mrs Ann Byrne, Corporate Improvement Officer (Partnerships), Council Offices, Crescent Gardens, Harrogate HG1 2SG ☎ 01423 556067 ✉ ann.byrne@harrogate.gov.uk

Personnel / HR: Mrs Dianne Kilburn, Head of Human Resources, Council Offices, Crescent Gardens, Harrogate HG1 2SG ☎ 01423 556062 🖷 01423 556180 ✉ dianne.kilburn@harrogate.gov.uk

Planning: Mr Gary Bell, Acting Head of Planning, Knapping Mount, West Grove Road, Harrogate HG1 2AE ☎ 01423 556542 🖷 01423 556630 ✉ gary.bell@harrogate.gov.uk

Recycling & Waste Minimisation: Mrs Alex Rankin, Recycling & Promotions Officer, Claro Road Depot, Claro Road, Harrogate HG1 4AT ☎ 01423 556906 🖷 01423 530174 ✉ alex.rankin@harrogate.gov.uk

Regeneration: Ms Genevieve Gillies, Economic Development Officer (Regeneration), Knapping Mount, West Grove Road, Harrogate HG1 2AE ☎ 01423 556079 🖷 01423 556050 ✉ genevieve.gillies@harrogate.gov.uk

Sustainable Communities: Mrs Jane Money, Environmental Strategy Manager, Springfield House, Kings Road, Harrogate HG1

5NX ☎ 01423 556801 🖷 01423 556720
🖰 jane.money@harrogate.gov.uk

Sustainable Development: Mrs Jane Money, Environmental Strategy Manager, Springfield House, Kings Road, Harrogate HG1 5NX ☎ 01423 556801 🖷 01423 556720
🖰 jane.money@harrogate.gov.uk

Tourism: Mr Angus Houston, Director of Harrogate International Centre, Harrogate International Centre, King's Road, Harrogate HG1 5LA ☎ 01423 537209 🖷 01423 537210
🖰 angus.houston@harrogate.gov.uk

Tourism: Ms Helen Suckling, Visitor Services Manager, Springfield House, Kings Road, Harrogate HG1 5NX ☎ 01423 537306 🖷 01423 537270 🖰 tourismteam@harrogate.gov.uk

Transport: Mr Alan Smith, Transport Manager, Claro Road Depot, Claro Road, Harrogate HG1 4AT ☎ 01423 556877 🖷 01423 530174 🖰 alan.smith@harrogate.gov.uk

Waste Collection and Disposal: Mr Simon Johnson, Head of Environment, Springfield House, Kings Road, Harrogate HG1 5NX ☎ 01423 556845 🖷 01423 556810
🖰 simon.johnson@harrogate.gov.uk

Waste Management: Mr Simon Johnson, Head of Environment, Springfield House, Kings Road, Harrogate HG1 5NX ☎ 01423 556845 🖷 01423 556810 🖰 simon.johnson@harrogate.gov.uk

MEMBERS OF THE COUNCIL (54)

Leader of the Council: **Alton**, Anthony (CON - Claro)
anthony.alton@harrogate.gov.uk
Deputy Leader of the Council: **Skidmore**, Alan (CON - Ripon Spa)
alan.skidmore@harrogate.gov.uk
Group Leader: **Williams**, Andrew (IND - Ripon Moorside)
andrewinripon@hotmail.com
Atkinson, Margaret (CON - Kirkby Malzeard)
margaret.atkinson@harrogate.gov.uk
Bateman, Bernard (CON - Wathvale)
bernard.bateman@harrogate.gov.uk
Batt, Barrington (CON - Knaresborough East)
john.batt@harrogate.gov.uk
Bayliss, Caroline (CON - Ribston)
caroline.bayliss@harrogate.gov.uk
Bentley, Sharon (CON - Pannal)
sharon.bentley@harrogate.gov.uk
Broadbank, Philip (LD - Starbeck)
philip.broadbank@harrogate.gov.uk
Brown, Nick (CON - Newby)
nick.brown@harrogate.gov.uk
Brown, Alec (CON - Bilton)
alec.brown@harrogate.gov.uk
Butterfield, Jean (CON - Low Harrogate)
jean.butterfield@harrogate.gov.uk
Chambers, Michael (CON - Ripon Spa)
mike.chambers@harrogate.gov.uk
Chapman, Trevor (LD - New Park)
trevor.chapman@harrogate.gov.uk
Clark, Jim (CON - Rossett)
jim.clark@harrogate.gov.uk
Cooper, Richard (CON - High Harrogate)
richard.cooper@harrogate.gov.uk
Ennis, John (CON - Low Harrogate)
john.ennis@harrogate.gov.uk
Fawcett, Shirley (CON - Spofforth with Lower Wharfedale)
Flynn, Helen (LD - Nidd Valley)
helen.flynn@harrogate.gov.uk
Fox, John (LD - Granby)
john.fox@harrogate.gov.uk
Fox, Ivor (CON - Knaresborough Scriven Park)
ivor.fox@harrogate.gov.uk
Galloway, Ian (CON - Bishop Monkton)
ian.galloway@harrogate.gov.uk
Goss, Andrew (LD - Woodfield)
andrew.goss@harrogate.gov.uk
Harrison, Michael (CON - Killinghall)
michael.harrison@harrogate.gov.uk
Hill, Matthew (CON - Pannal)
matt.hill@harrogate.gov.uk
Hill, Christine (CON - Lower Nidderdale)
christine.hill@harrogate.gov.uk
Hoult, Bill (LD - Knaresborough King James)
bill.hoult@harrogate.gov.uk
Ireland, Philip (CON - Knaresborough King James)
phil.ireland@harrogate.gov.uk
Jackson, Steven (CON - Saltergate)
steven.jackson@harrogate.gov.uk
Jones, Pat (CON - Stray)
Pat.Jones@harrogate.gov.uk
Jones, Anne (LD - Knaresborough Scriven Park)
anne.jones@harrogate.gov.uk
Knight, Greta (LD - Woodfield)
greta.knight@harrogate.gov.uk
Law, Janet (LD - Starbeck)
janet.law@harrogate.gov.uk
Lewis, Chris (IND - Ouseburn)
chris.lewis@harrogate.gov.uk
Lumley, Stanley (CON - Pateley Bridge)
stanley.lumley@harrogate.gov.uk
Mackenzie, Don (CON - Harlow Moor)
don.mackenzie@harrogate.gov.uk
Marsh, Pat (LD - Hookstone)
pat.marsh@harrogate.gov.uk
Marsh, Reg (LD - Hookstone)
reg.marsh@harrogate.gov.uk
Martin, Stuart (CON - Ripon Minster)
stuart.martin@harrogate.gov.uk
McKenzie, Clare (LD - Bilton)
cllrclare.mckenzie@harrogate.gov.uk
Newby, Michael (LD - Saltergate)
michael.newby@harrogate.gov.uk
Pickles, George (CON - Ripon Minster)
george.pickles@harrogate.gov.uk
Powell, Charlie (IND - Ripon Moorside)
cllr.powell@harrogate.gov.uk
Russell, Amanda (LD - High Harrogate)
amanda.russell@harrogate.gov.uk
Ryder, Christine (CON - Washburn)
christine.ryder@harrogate.gov.uk
Savage, John (LIB - Marston Moor)
john.savage@harrogate.gov.uk
Simms, Nigel (CON - Mashamshire)
nigel.simms@harrogate.gov.uk
Theakston, Simon (CON - Harlow Moor)
simon.theakston@theakstons.co.uk
Travena, Jennifer (LD - Granby)

jennifer.travena@harrogate.gov.uk
Trotter, Clifford (CON - Stray)
cliff.trotter@harrogate.gov.uk
Webber, Matthew (LD - New Park)
matthew.webber@harrogate.gov.uk
Willoughby, Christine (LD - Knaresborough East)
christine.willoughby@harrogate.gov.uk
Windass, Robert (CON - Boroughbridge)
cllr.windass@harrogate.gov.uk
Woolley, Michelle (CON - Rossett)
michelle.woolley@harrogate.gov.uk

POLITICAL COMPOSITION
CON: 33, LD: 17, IND: 3, LIB: 1

CABINET
Leader: Mr Anthony Alton
Deputy: Mr Alan Skidmore
Cultural Services: Ms Pat Jones
Environment: Mr Philip Ireland
Finance & Resources: Mr Ivor Fox
Housing: Mr Michael Chambers
Public Protection & Rural Affairs: Mrs Margaret Atkinson

COMMITTEE CHAIRS
Licensing: Mr Stuart Martin
Overview & Scrutiny: Mr Ivor Fox
Planning: Mr Nigel Simms

HARROW L

Harrow London Borough Council, Civic Centre, Station Road, Harrow HA1 2XF ☎ 020 8863 5611 🖷 020 8424 1134 ✉ info@harrow.gov.uk 🖳 www.harrow.gov.uk

FACTS & FIGURES
Police Authority: Metropolitan Police Authority
Health Authority: NHS London
Learning and Skills Council: London
Parliamentary Constituencies: Harrow East, Harrow West, Uxbridge and Ruislip South
EU Constituencies: London
Election Frequency: Elections are of whole council
Twinning: Douai (France)

PRINCIPAL OFFICERS
Chief Executive: Mr Michael Lockwood, Chief Executive, Civic Centre, Station Road, Harrow HA1 2XF ☎ 020 8424 1001 ✉ michael.lockwood@harrow.gov.uk

Assistant Chief Executive: Mr Tom Whiting, Assistant Chief Executive, Civic Centre, Station Road, Harrow HA1 2XF ☎ 020 8863 5611 ✉ tom.whiting@harrow.gov.uk

Senior Management: Ms Carol Cutler, Director of Business Transformation & Customer Service, Exchequer Building, Civic Centre, Station Road, Harrow HA1 2XF ☎ 020 8424 6701 ✉ carol.cutler@harrow.gov.uk

Children / Youth Services: Ms Wendy Beeton, Divisional Director - Integrated Early Years & Community Services, Civic Centre, Station Road, Harrow HA1 2XF ☎ 020 8416 8830 ✉ wendy.beeton@harrow.gov.uk

Children / Youth Services: Ms Catherine Doran, Corporate Director - Children's Services, Civic Centre, Station Road, Harrow HA1 2XF ☎ 020 8424 1356 ✉ catherine.doran@harrow.gov.uk

Children / Youth Services: Mr Richard Segalov, Divisional Director - Young People's Services, Civic Centre, Station Road, Harrow HA1 2XF ☎ 020 8420 9344 ✉ richard.segalov@harrow.gov.uk

Civil Registration: Ms Geraldine Sparrow, Registration & Support Services Manager, Civic Centre, Station Road, Harrow HA1 2XF ☎ 020 8424 1328 ✉ geraldine.sparrow@harrow.gov.uk

PR / Communications: Ms Lindsay Coulson, Head of Communications, Civic Centre, Station Road, Harrow HA1 2XF ☎ 020 8424 1292 ✉ linday.coulson@harrow.gov.uk

Community Planning: Ms Carol Yarde, Head of Adults & Housing Transformation, Civic Centre, Station Road, Harrow HA1 2XF ☎ 020 8420 9660 ✉ carol.yarde@harrow.gov.uk

Community Safety: Mr Andew Howe, Joint Director of Public Health, Civic Centre, Station Road, Harrow HA1 2XF ☎ 020 8966 1172 ✉ andrew.how@harrow.gov.uk

Corporate Services: Mr Andy Parsons, Head of Service - Business Management, Civic Centre, Station Road, Harrow HA1 2XF ☎ 020 8736 6106 ✉ andy.parsons@harrow.gov.uk

Corporate Services: Mr Anu Singh, Head of Development and Improvement, Civic Centre, Station Road, Harrow HA1 2XF ☎ 020 8420 9298 ✉ anu.singh@harrow.gov.uk

Corporate Services: Mr Andrew Trehern, Corporate Director for Place Shaping, Civic Centre, Station Road, Harrow HA1 2XF ☎ 020 8424 1590 ✉ andrew.trehern@harrow.gov.uk

Customer Service: Ms Carol Cutler, Director of Business Transformation & Customer Service, Exchequer Building, Civic Centre, Station Road, Harrow HA1 2XF ☎ 020 8424 6701 ✉ carol.cutler@harrow.gov.uk

Economic Development: Mr Mark Billington, Head of Service - Economic Development, Research & Enterprise, Civic Centre, Station Road, Harrow HA1 2XF ☎ 020 8736 6533 ✉ mark.billington@harrow.gov.uk

Education: Ms Leora Cruddes, Divisional Director, Civic Centre, Station Road, Harrow HA1 2XF ✉ leora.cruddes@harrow.gov.uk

Emergency Planning: Mr Kan Grover, Service Manager for Emergency Planning & Business Continuity, Civic Centre, Station Road, Harrow HA1 2XF ☎ 020 8420 9319 ✉ kan.grover@harrow.gov.uk

Environmental / Technical Services: Mr John Edwards, Divisional Director of Environmental Services, Civic Centre, Station Road, Harrow HA1 2XF ☎ 020 8736 6799 ✉ john.edwards@harrow.gov.uk

Finance and Treasurer: Ms Julie Alderson, Interim Director Finance (S151 Officer), Civic Centre, Station Road, Harrow HA1 2XF ☎ 020 8420 9269 ✉ julie.alderson@harrow.gov.uk

Finance and Treasurer: Ms Jennifer Hydari, Divisional Director - Finance (S151 Officer), Civic Centre, Station Road, Harrow HA1 2XF ☎ 020 8424 1393 ✉ jennifer.hydari@harrow.gov.uk

Housing: Mr Paul Najsarek, Corporate Director of Adults & Housing, Civic Centre, Station Road, Harrow HA1 2XF ☎ 020 8424 1361 ✉ paul.najsarek@harrow.gov.uk

Housing: Ms Lynne Pennington, Divisional Director - Housing Services, Civic Centre, Station Road, Harrow HA1 2XF ☎ 020 8424 1998 ✉ lynne.pennington@harrow.gov.uk

Legal: Ms Jessica Farmer, Head of Legal Practice, Civic Centre, Station Road, Harrow HA1 2XF ☎ 020 8424 1889 ✉ jessica.farmer@harrow.gov.uk

Legal: Mr Hugh Peart, Director of Legal & Governance Services, Civic Centre, Station Road, Harrow HA1 2XF ☎ 020 8424 1272 ✉ hugh.peart@harrow.gov.uk

Leisure and Cultural Services: Ms Marianne Locke, Divisional Director - Community & Cultural Services, Civic Centre, Station Road, Harrow HA1 2XF ☎ 020 8736 6530 ✉ marianne.locke@harrow.gov.uk

Member Services: Ms Pauline Ferris, Democratic & Electoral Services Manager, Civic Centre, Station Road, Harrow HA1 2XF ☎ 020 8424 1269 ✉ pauline.ferris@harrow.gov.uk

Partnerships: Mr Alex Dewsnap, Divisional Director - Partnership Development & Performance, Civic Centre, Station Road, Harrow HA1 2XF ☎ 020 8416 8250 ✉ alex.dewsnap@harrow.gov.uk

Personnel / HR: Mr Jon Turner, Divisional Director - HRD & Shared Services, Civic Centre, Station Road, Harrow HA1 2XF ☎ 020 8424 1225 ✉ jon.turner@harrow.gov.uk

Planning: Mr Phil Greenwood, Head of Service - Major Development Projects, Civic Centre, Station Road, Harrow HA1 2XF ☎ 020 8424 1166 ✉ phil.greenwood@harrow.gov.uk

Planning: Mr Stephen Kelly, Divisional Director - Planning Services, Civic Centre, Station Road, Harrow HA1 2XF ☎ 020 8736 6149 ✉ stephen.kelly@harrow.gov.uk

Procurement: Mr Richard Hawtin, Interim Head of Procurement, Civic Centre, Station Road, Harrow HA1 2XF ☎ 020 8416 8442 ✉ richard.hawtin@harrow.gov.uk

Social Services: Mr Roger Rickman, Divisional Director - Special Needs Services, Civic Centre, Station Road, Harrow HA1 2XF ☎ 020 8966 6334 ✉ roger.rickman@harrow.gov.uk

Social Services (Adult): Ms Bernie Flaherty, Divisional Director - Adult Social Care, Civic Centre, Station Road, Harrow HA1 2XF ☎ 020 8863 5611 ✉ bernie.flaherty@harrow.gov.uk

Social Services (Children): Ms Gail Hancock, Divisional Director - Safeguarding, Family Placement & Support, Civic Centre, Station Road, Harrow HA1 2XF ☎ 020 8736 6968 ✉ gail.hancock@harrow.gov.uk

Sustainable Communities: Mr John Edwards, Divisional Director of Environmental Services, Civic Centre, Station Road, Harrow HA1 2XF ☎ 020 8736 6799 ✉ john.edwards@harrow.gov.uk

MEMBERS OF THE COUNCIL (63)

Mayor: **Ismail**, Nizam (LAB - Queensbury)
nizam.ismail@harrow.gov.uk
Deputy Mayor: **Asante**, Nana (LAB - Edgware)
nana.asante@harrow.gov.uk
Leader of the Council: **Stephenson**, Bill (LAB - Headstone South)
bill.stephenson@harrow.gov.uk
Deputy Leader of the Council: **Idaikkadar**, Thaya (LAB - Roxeth)
thaya10@aol.com
Group Leader: **Hall**, Susan (CON - Hatch End)
susan.hall@harrow.gov.uk
Akhtar, Husain (CON - Canons)
husain.akhtar@harrow.gov.uk
Anderson, Susan (LAB - Greenhill)
sue.anderson@harrow.gov.uk
Ashton, Marilyn (CON - Stanmore Park)
Bath, Camilla (CON - Stanmore Park)
camilla.bath@harrow.gov.uk
Bednell, Christine (CON - Stanmore Park)
christine.bednell@harrow.gov.uk
Bond, James (IND - Headstone North)
james.bond@harrow.gov.uk
Champagnie, Lurline (CON - Pinner)
lurline.champagnie@harrow.gov.uk
Chana, Kamaljit (CON - Pinner South)
kamaljit.chana@harrow.gov.uk
Chauhan, Ramji (CON - Harrow Weald)
ramji.chauhan@harrow.gov.uk
Choudhury, Mrinal (LAB - Edgware)
mrinal.choudhury@harrow.gov.uk
Currie, Bob (LAB - Roxbourne)
bob.curie@harrow.gov.uk
Davine, Margaret (LAB - Edgware)
margaret.davine@harrow.gov.uk
Dharmarajah, Mano (LAB - Roxbourne)
mano.dharmarajah@harrow.gov.uk
Ferrari, Anthony (CON - Harrow Weald)
anthony.ferrari@harrow.gov.uk
Ferry, Keith (LAB - Wealdstone)
keith.ferry@harrow.gov.uk
Gate, Brian (LAB - West Harrow)
brian.gate@harrow.gov.uk
Gate, Anne (LAB - Harrow on the Hill)
ann.gate@harrow.gov.uk
Gawn, David (LAB - Harrow on the Hill)
david.gawn@harrow.gov.uk
Greek, Stephen (CON - Harrow Weald)
stephen.greek@harrow.gov.uk
Green, Mitzi (LAB - Kenton East)
mitzi.green@harrow.gov.uk
Henson, Graham (LAB - Roxbourne)
graham.henson@harrow.gov.uk
James, Krishna (LAB - Marlborough)

krishna.james@harrow.gov.uk
Kara, Manji (CON - Belmont)
maji.kara@harrow.gov.uk
Khalid, Zarina (LAB - Queensbury)
zarina.khalid@harrow.gov.uk
Lammiman, Jean (CON - Hatch End)
jean.lammiman@harrow.gov.uk
Macleod-Cullinane, Barry (CON - Belmont)
barry.macleod-cullinane@harrow.gov.uk
Marikar, Kairul (LAB - West Harrow)
kairul.marikar@harrow.gov.uk
Maru, Ajay (LAB - Kenton West)
ajay.maru@harrow.gov.uk
Miles, Jerry (LAB - Roxeth)
jerry.miles@harrow.gov.uk
Mithani, Vina (CON - Kenton West)
vina.mithani@harrow.gov.uk
Moshenson, Amir (CON - Canons)
amir.moshenson@harrow.gov.uk
Mote, Janet (CON - Headstone North)
janet.mote@harrow.gov.uk
Mote, Chris (CON - Pinner South)
chris.mote@harrow.gov.uk
Nickolay, John (CON - Pinner South)
john.nickolav@harrow.gov.uk
Nickolay, Joyce (CON - Rayners Lane)
jnickolay@hotmail.com
Noyce, Chris (LD - Rayners Lane)
chris.noyce@harrow.gov.uk
O'Dell, Phillip (LAB - Wealdstone)
phillip.odell@harrow.gov.uk
Omar, Asad (LAB - Headstone South)
asad.omar@harrow.gov.uk
Osborn, Paul (CON - Pinner)
paul.osborn@harrow.gov.uk
Parmar, Varsha (LAB - Marlborough)
varsha.parmar@harrow.gov.uk
Perry, David (LAB - Marlborough)
david.perry@harrow.gov.uk
Phillips, Bill (LAB - Greenhill)
bill.phillips@harrow.gov.uk
Ray, Raj (LAB - Roxeth)
raj.ray@harrow.gov.uk
Romain, Richard (CON - Canons)
richard.romain@harrow.gov.uk
Seymour, Anthony (CON - Headstone North)
anthony.seymour@harrow.gov.uk
Seymour, Lynda (CON - Belmont)
lynda.seymour@harrow.gov.uk
Shah, Sachin (LAB - Queensbury)
sachin.shah@harrow.gov.uk
Shah, Rekha (LAB - Wealdstone)
rekha.shah@harrow.gov.uk
Shah, Navin (LAB - Kenton East)
navin.shah@harrow.gov.uk
Sheinwald, Stanley (CON - Hatch End)
stanley.sheinwald@harrow.gov.uk
Silver, Victoria (LAB - Kenton East)
victoria.silver@harrow.gov.uk
Stoodley, William (LAB - West Harrow)
william.stoodley@harrow.gov.uk
Suresh, Krishna (LAB - Rayners Lane)
krishna.suresh@harrow.gov.uk
Suresh, Sasikala (LAB - Headstone South)
sasikala.suresh@harrow.gov.uk
Teli, Yogesh (CON - Kenton West)
yogesh.teli@harrow.gov.uk
Wealthy, Ben (LAB - Greenhill)
ben.wealthy@harrow.gov.uk
Williams, Simon (CON - Harrow on the Hill)
simon.williams@harrow.gov.uk
Wright, Stephen (CON - Pinner)
stephen.wright@harrow.gov.uk

POLITICAL COMPOSITION
LAB: 34, CON: 27, IND: 1, LD: 1

CABINET
Leader, Strategy, Partnership & Finance: Mr Bill Stephenson
Deputy Leader/Property and Major contracts: Mr Thaya Idaikkadar
Adult Social Care, Health and Wellbeing: Ms Margaret Davine
Community & Cultural Services: Mr David Perry
Environment & Community Safety: Mr Phillip O'Dell
Housing: Mr Bob Currie
Finance: Mr Sachin Shah
Planning and Regeneration: Mr Keith Ferry
Performance, Communication & Corporate Services: Mr Graham Henson

COMMITTEE CHAIRS
Audit: Mr John Cowan
Governance, Audit & Risk Management: Mr John Cowan
Licensing & General Purposes: Mr Mano Dharmarajah
Major Developments: Mr Bill Stephenson
Overview & Scrutiny (Scrutiny): Mr Jerry Miles
Planning: Mr Keith Ferry

HART D

Hart District Council, Civic Offices, Harlington Way, Fleet GU51 4AE ☎ 01252 622122 🖷 01252 626886 ✉ enquiries@hart.gov.uk 💻 www.hart.gov.uk

FACTS & FIGURES
Police Authority: Hampshire Police Authority
Health Authority: South Central Strategic Health Authority
Learning and Skills Council: South East
Parliamentary Constituencies: Hampshire North East
EU Constituencies: South East
Election Frequency: Elections are by thirds
Twinning: Hartley Wintney: St. Savin (France); Crookham Village: Levignen (France); Odiham: Sourdeval (France)

PRINCIPAL OFFICERS
Chief Executive: Mr Geoff Bonner, Chief Execuitve, Civic Offices, Harlington Way, Fleet GU51 4AE ☎ 01252 774108

Senior Management: Ms Patricia Hughes, Corporate Director, Civic Offices, Harlington Way, Fleet GU51 4AE ☎ 01252 622122 ✉ patricia.hughes@hart.gov.uk

Senior Management: Mr Daryl Phillips, Corporate Director and S151 Officer, Civic Offices, Harlington Way, Fleet GU51 4AE ☎ 01252 622122 ✉ daryl.phillips@hart.gov.uk

Architect, Building / Property Services: Mr John Elson, Head of Technical Services, Civic Offices, Harlington Way, Fleet GU51 4AE ☎ 01252 622122 ✉ john.elson@hart.gov.uk

Best Value: Mr Richard Menhinick, Performance & Innovation Officer, Civic Offices, Harlington Way, Fleet GU51 4AE ☎ 01252 622122 🖷 01252 774464 ✉ richard.menhinick@hart.gov.uk

Building Control: Mr Dave Harris, Building Control Manager, Civic Offices, Harlington Way, Fleet GU51 4AE ☎ 01252 774422 ✉ david.harris@hart.gov.uk

PR / Communications: Mr John Walton, Press Officer, Civic Offices, Harlington Way, Fleet GU51 4AE ☎ 01252 774461 🖷 01252 774464 ✉ john.walton@hart.gov.uk

Community Safety: Ms Caroline Ryan, Community Safety Manager, Civic Offices, Harlington Way, Fleet GU51 4AE ☎ 01252 622122

Contracts: Mr John Elson, Head of Technical Services, Civic Offices, Harlington Way, Fleet GU51 4AE ☎ 01252 622122 ✉ john.elson@hart.gov.uk

Corporate Services: Mr Andy Tiffin, Head of Democratic Services, Civic Offices, Harlington Way, Fleet GU51 4AE ☎ 01252 622122 ✉ andrew.tiffin@hart.gov.uk

Customer Service: Mrs Liz Marshall, Head of Revenues & Benefits, Civic Offices, Harlington Way, Fleet GU51 4AE ☎ 01252 622122 ✉ liz.marshall@hart.gov.uk

Direct Labour: Ms Sarah Incher, Waste & Recycling Manager, Springwell Lane Depot, Hartley Wintney RG27 8BW ☎ 01252 774173 ✉ sarah.incher@hart.gov.uk

Electoral Registration: Mr Andy Tiffin, Head of Democratic Services, Civic Offices, Harlington Way, Fleet GU51 4AE ☎ 01252 622122 ✉ andrew.tiffin@hart.gov.uk

Emergency Planning: Mr John Elson, Head of Technical Services, Civic Offices, Harlington Way, Fleet GU51 4AE ☎ 01252 622122 ✉ john.elson@hart.gov.uk

Energy Management: Mr John Elson, Head of Technical Services, Civic Offices, Harlington Way, Fleet GU51 4AE ☎ 01252 622122 ✉ john.elson@hart.gov.uk

Environmental / Technical Services: Mr John Elson, Head of Technical Services, Civic Offices, Harlington Way, Fleet GU51 4AE ☎ 01252 622122 ✉ john.elson@hart.gov.uk

Environmental Health: Mr Nick Steevens, Public Protection Manager, Civic Offices, Harlington Way, Fleet GU51 4AE ☎ 01252 774296 ✉ nick.steevens@hart.gov.uk

Estates, Property & Valuation: Mr John Elson, Head of Technical Services, Civic Offices, Harlington Way, Fleet GU51 4AE ☎ 01252 622122 ✉ john.elson@hart.gov.uk

Facilities: Mr Malcolm Harris, Building Manager, Civic Offices, Harlington Way, Fleet GU51 4AE ☎ 01252 774448 🖷 01252 774408 ✉ malcolm.harris@hart.gov.uk

Finance and Treasurer: Mr Tony Higgins, Head of Finance, Civic Offices, Harlington Way, Fleet GU51 4AE ☎ 01252 622122 ✉ tony.higgins@hart.gov.uk

Grounds Maintenance: Mr Adam Green, Grounds & Countryside Manager, Civic Offices, Harlington Way, Fleet GU51 4AE ☎ 01252 622122 ✉ adam.green@hart.gov.uk

Health and Safety: Mr Paul Beaumont, Principal Environmental Health Officer, Civic Offices, Harlington Way, Fleet GU51 4AE ☎ 01252 622122 ✉ paul.beaumont@hart.gov.uk

Highways: Mr John Elson, Head of Technical Services, Civic Offices, Harlington Way, Fleet GU51 4AE ☎ 01252 622122 ✉ john.elson@hart.gov.uk

Home Energy Conservation: Ms Carolyn Whistlecraft, Principal Environmental Health Officer, Civic Offices, Harlington Way, Fleet GU51 4AE ☎ 01252 622122 ✉ carolyn.whistlecraft@hart.gov.uk

Housing: Mr Nigel Preston, Head of Housing & Customer Services, Civic Offices, Harlington Way, Fleet GU51 4AE ☎ 01252 774488 ✉ nigel.preston@hart.gov.uk

Legal: Mr Chris Guy, Head of Legal & Democratic Services, Civic Offices, Harlington Way, Fleet GU51 4AE ☎ 01256 845402 ✉ chris.guy@basingstoke.gov.uk

Leisure and Cultural Services: Mr Carl Westby, Head of Leisure, Civic Offices, Harlington Way, Fleet GU51 4AE ☎ 01252 622122 ✉ carl.westby@hart.gov.uk

Licensing: Ms Caroline Ryan, Community Safety Manager, Civic Offices, Harlington Way, Fleet GU51 4AE ☎ 01252 622122

Member Services: Mr Andy Tiffin, Head of Democratic Services, Civic Offices, Harlington Way, Fleet GU51 4AE ☎ 01252 622122 ✉ andrew.tiffin@hart.gov.uk

Parking: Mr Geoff Hislop, Parking Manager, Civic Offices, Harlington Way, Fleet GU51 4AE ☎ 01252 622122 ✉ geoff.hislop@hart.gov.uk

Partnerships: Mr Geoff Bonner, Chief Execuitve, Civic Offices, Harlington Way, Fleet GU51 4AE ☎ 01252 774108

Planning: Mr Daryl Phillips, Corporate Director and S151 Officer, Civic Offices, Harlington Way, Fleet GU51 4AE ☎ 01252 622122 ✉ daryl.phillips@hart.gov.uk

Recycling & Waste Minimisation: Mr John Elson, Head of Technical Services, Civic Offices, Harlington Way, Fleet GU51 4AE ☎ 01252 622122 ✉ john.elson@hart.gov.uk

Road Safety: Mr John Elson, Head of Technical Services, Civic Offices, Harlington Way, Fleet GU51 4AE ☎ 01252 622122 ✉ john.elson@hart.gov.uk

Street Scene: Ms Sarah Incher, Waste & Recycling Manager, Springwell Lane Depot, Hartley Wintney RG27 8BW ☎ 01252 774173 ✉ sarah.incher@hart.gov.uk

Traffic Management: Mr John Elson, Head of Technical Services, Civic Offices, Harlington Way, Fleet GU51 4AE ☎ 01252 622122 ✉ john.elson@hart.gov.uk

Waste Collection and Disposal: Mr John Elson, Head of Technical Services, Civic Offices, Harlington Way, Fleet GU51 4AE ☎ 01252 622122 ✉ john.elson@hart.gov.uk

Waste Management: Ms Sarah Incher, Waste & Recycling Manager, Springwell Lane Depot, Hartley Wintney RG27 8BW ☎ 01252 774173 ✉ sarah.incher@hart.gov.uk

Children's Play Areas: Mr Adam Green, Grounds & Countryside Manager, Civic Offices, Harlington Way, Fleet GU51 4AE ☎ 01252 622122 ✉ adam.green@hart.gov.uk

MEMBERS OF THE COUNCIL (35)

***Chair:* Axam**, Chris (R - Fleet Courtmoor)
chris.axam@hart.gov.uk
***Vice-Chair:* Gorys**, Stephen (CON - Odiham)
stephen.gorys@hart.gov.uk
***Leader of the Council:* Crookes**, Kenneth (CON - Odiham)
kenneth.crookes@hart.gov.uk
***Deputy Leader of the Council:* Parker**, Stephen (CON - Fleet North)
stephen.parker@hart.gov.uk
***Group Leader:* Neighbour**, David (LD - Yateley North)
david.neighbour@hart.gov.uk
***Group Leader:* Radley**, James (O - Church Crookham East)
james.radley@hart.gov.uk
Ambler, Simon (O - Church Crookham West)
simon.ambler@hart.gov.uk
Appleton, Richard (CON - Fleet West)
richard.appleton@hart.gov.uk
Bailey, Stuart (LD - Yateley East)
stuart.bailey@hart.gov.uk
Barrell, Anthony (CON - Fleet North)
tony.barrell@hart.gov.uk
Bennison, John (R - Fleet Courtmoor)
john.bennison@hart.gov.uk
Billings, Myra (LD - Yateley West)
myra.billings@hart.gov.uk
Blewett, Brian (LD - Blackwater and Hawley)
brian.blewett@hart.gov.uk
Burchfield, Brian (CON - Hook)
brian.burchfield@hart.gov.uk
Butler, Gill (O - Church Crookham East)
gill.butler@hart.gov.uk
Clarke, Tony (O - Crondall)
tony.clarke@hart.gov.uk
Cockarill, Graham (LD - Yateley East)
graham.cockarill@hart.gov.uk
Collett, Adrian (LD - Blackwater and Hawley)
adrian.collett@hart.gov.uk
Crampton, Anne (CON - Eversley)
anne.crampton@hart.gov.uk
Evans, Gavin (CON - Fleet Central)
gavin.evans@hart.gov.uk
Gani, Akmal (CON - Fleet Central)
akmal.gani@hart.gov.uk
Glen, Jonathan (CON - Hook)
jonathan.glen@hart.gov.uk
Harward, Robert (LD - Frogmore and Darby Green)
robert.harward@hart.gov.uk
Ive, Colin (LD - Yateley North)
colin.ive@hart.gov.uk
Kennett, John (CON - Long Sutton)
john.kennett@hart.gov.uk
Kinnell, Sara (CON - Hartley Wintney)
sara.kinnell@hart.gov.uk
Lewis, Ian (CON - Fleet Pondtail)
ian.lewis@hart.gov.uk
Lit, Kulwant (LD - Frogmore and Darby Green)
kulwant.lit@hart.gov.uk
Morris, Mike (CON - Hook)
mike.morris@hart.gov.uk
Murphy, Mark (LD - Yateley West)
mark.murphy@hart.gov.uk
Oliver, Alan (IND - Fleet West)
alan.oliver@hart.gov.uk
Radley, Jenny (O - Church Crookham West)
jenny.radley@hart.gov.uk
Simmons, Chris (CON - Crondall)
chris.simmons@hart.gov.uk
Southern, Tim (CON - Hartley Wintney)
tim.southern@hart.gov.uk
Wheale, Sharyn (CON - Fleet Pondtail)
sharyn.wheale@hart.gov.uk

POLITICAL COMPOSITION

CON: 17, LD: 10, O: 5, R: 2, IND: 1

CABINET

Leader: Mr Kenneth Crookes
Deputy Leader / Planning & Regulation: Mr Stephen Parker
Community Safety: Mr John Kennett
Corporate Services: Mr Brian Burchfield
Environment: Mr Jonathan Glen
Fleet Town Centre: Mr Gavin Evans
Health & Housing: Ms Anne Crampton
Leisure & Recreation: Mrs Sara Kinnell

COMMITTEE CHAIRS

Audit: Mr David Neighbour
Licensing: Mr Colin Ive
Overview & Scrutiny (Scrutiny): Mr Kulwant Lit
Planning: Mr Graham Cockarill
Staffing: Mr Kenneth Crookes

HARTLEPOOL U

Hartlepool Borough Council, Civic Centre, Victoria Road, Hartlepool TS24 8AY ☎ 01429 266522 🖷 01429 523005 ✉ customer.service@hartlepool.gov.uk 💻 www.hartlepool.gov.uk

FACTS & FIGURES

Police Authority: Cleveland Police Authority
Health Authority: North East Strategic Health Authority
Learning and Skills Council: North East
Parliamentary Constituencies: Hartlepool
EU Constituencies: North East
Election Frequency: Elections are by thirds
Twinning: Hucklehoven (Germany)

PRINCIPAL OFFICERS

Chief Executive: Ms Nicola Bailey, Acting Chief Executive, Civic Centre, Victoria Road, Hartlepool TS24 8AY ☎ 01429 523001

🖷 01429 523865 ✉ nicola.bailey@hartlepool.gov.uk

Assistant Chief Executive: Mr Andrew Atkin, Assistant Chief Executive, Civic Centre, Victoria Road, Hartlepool TS24 8AY ☎ 01429 523003 🖷 01429 523856 ✉ andrew.atkin@hartlepool.gov.uk

Senior Management: Mrs Jill Harrison, Assistant Director of Adult & Social Care, Civic Centre, Victoria Road, Hartlepool TS24 8AY ☎ 01429 523911 🖷 01429 523908 ✉ jill.harrison@hartlepool.gov.uk

Senior Management: Ms Caroline O'Neil, Assistant Director of Performance & Achievement, Civic Centre, Victoria Road, Hartlepool TS24 8AY ☎ 01429 523914 🖷 01429 523908 ✉ caroline.oneil@hartlepool.gov.uk

Senior Management: Mr David Stubbs, Director of Regeneration & Neighbourhoods, Civic Centre, Victoria Road, Hartlepool TS24 8AY ☎ 01429 523301 🖷 01429 523344 ✉ dave.stubbs@hartlepool.gov.uk

Architect, Building / Property Services: Mr Graham Frankland, Assistant Director of Resources, Civic Centre, Level 3, Hartlepool TS24 8AY ☎ 01429 523211 🖷 01429 523899 ✉ graham.frankland@hartlepool.gov.uk

Best Value: Mr Andrew Atkin, Assistant Chief Executive, Civic Centre, Victoria Road, Hartlepool TS24 8AY ☎ 01429 523003 🖷 01429 523856 ✉ andrew.atkin@hartlepool.gov.uk

Children / Youth Services: Mr Mark Smith, Locality Officer, Civic Centre, Victoria Road, Hartlepool TS24 8AY ☎ 01429 523901 ✉ mark.smith@hartlepool.gov.uk

Civil Registration: Mrs Christine Armstrong, Customer & Support Services Manager, Civic Centre, Victoria Road, Hartlepool TS24 8AY ☎ 01429 523016 🖷 01429 523005 ✉ christine.armstrong@hartlepool.gov.uk

PR / Communications: Mr Alastair Rae, Public Relations Officer, Civic Centre, Victoria Road, Hartlepool TS24 8AY ☎ 01429 523510 🖷 01429 523355 ✉ alastair.rae@hartlepool.gov.uk

Community Planning: Mr Damien Wilson, Assistant Director of Regeneration & Planning, Civic Centre, Victoria Road, Hartlepool TS24 8AY ☎ 01429 523400 ✉ damien.wilson@hartlepool.gov.uk

Community Safety: Mrs Denise Ogden, Assistant Director of Neighbourhood Services, Civic Centre, Victoria Road, Hartlepool TS24 8AY ☎ 01429 523808 🖷 01429 523038 ✉ denise.ogden@hartlepool.gov.uk

Community Safety: Mr Damien Wilson, Assistant Director of Regeneration & Planning, Civic Centre, Victoria Road, Hartlepool TS24 8AY ☎ 01429 523400 ✉ damien.wilson@hartlepool.gov.uk

Computer Management: Mr Andrew Atkin, Assistant Chief Executive, Civic Centre, Victoria Road, Hartlepool TS24 8AY ☎ 01429 523003 🖷 01429 523856 ✉ andrew.atkin@hartlepool.gov.uk

Consumer Protection and Trading Standards: Mr Ian Harrison, Principal Trading Standards & Licensing Officer, Bryan Hanson House, Lynn Street, Hartlepool TS24 7BT ☎ 01429 523349 ✉ ian.harrison@hartlepool.gov.uk

Contracts: Mr Graham Frankland, Assistant Director of Resources, Civic Centre, Level 3, Hartlepool TS24 8AY ☎ 01429 523211 🖷 01429 523899 ✉ graham.frankland@hartlepool.gov.uk

Corporate Services: Mrs Christine Armstrong, Customer & Support Services Manager, Civic Centre, Victoria Road, Hartlepool TS24 8AY ☎ 01429 523016 🖷 01429 523005 ✉ christine.armstrong@hartlepool.gov.uk

Customer Service: Ms Joanne Machers, Chief Customer & Workforce Services Officer, Civic Centre, Victoria Road, Hartlepool TS24 8AY ☎ 01429 523003 🖷 01429 523856 ✉ joanne.machers@hartlepool.gov.uk

Direct Labour: Mr David Stubbs, Director of Regeneration & Neighbourhoods, Civic Centre, Victoria Road, Hartlepool TS24 8AY ☎ 01429 523301 🖷 01429 523344 ✉ dave.stubbs@hartlepool.gov.uk

Economic Development: Mr Damien Wilson, Assistant Director of Regeneration & Planning, Civic Centre, Victoria Road, Hartlepool TS24 8AY ☎ 01429 523400 ✉ damien.wilson@hartlepool.gov.uk

Education: Ms Nicola Bailey, Acting Chief Executive, Civic Centre, Victoria Road, Hartlepool TS24 8AY ☎ 01429 523001 🖷 01429 523865 ✉ nicola.bailey@hartlepool.gov.uk

E-Government: Mr Andrew Atkin, Assistant Chief Executive, Civic Centre, Victoria Road, Hartlepool TS24 8AY ☎ 01429 523003 🖷 01429 523856 ✉ andrew.atkin@hartlepool.gov.uk

Electoral Registration: Mr Peter Devlin, Chief Solicitor, Civic Centre, Victoria Road, Hartlepool TS24 8AY ☎ 01429 523003 🖷 01429 523856 ✉ peter.devlin@hartlepool.gov.uk

Emergency Planning: Mr Andy Summerbell, Head of Emergency Planning, Emergency Planning Unit, Aurora Court, Barton Road, Riverside Park, Middlesbrough TS2 1RY ☎ 01642 232442 🖷 01642 224926 ✉ andy.summerbell@hartlepool.gov.uk

Environmental / Technical Services: Mr Alastair Smith, Assistant Director of Transport & Engineering, Civic Centre, Victoria Road, Hartlepool TS24 8AY ☎ 01429 523802 🖷 01429 523038 ✉ alastair.smith@hartlepool.gov.uk

Environmental Health: Mr Adrian Hurst, Principal Environmental Health Officer, Bryan Hanson House, Lynn Street, Hartlepool TS24 8BT ☎ 01429 523323 ✉ adrian.hurst@hartlepool.gov.uk

Estates, Property & Valuation: Mr Graham Frankland, Assistant Director of Resources, Civic Centre, Level 3, Hartlepool TS24 8AY ☎ 01429 523211 🖷 01429 523899 ✉ graham.frankland@hartlepool.gov.uk

Events Manager: Mr John Mennear, Assistant Director of Adult & Community Services, Civic Centre, Victoria Road, Hartlepool

TS24 8AY ☎ 01429 523417 🖷 01429 523908
✉ john.mennear@hartlepool.gov.uk

Finance and Treasurer: Mr Chris Little, Chief Financial Officer, Civic Centre, Victoria Road, Hartlepool TS24 8AY ☎ 01429 523003 🖷 01429 523856 ✉ chris.little@hartlepool.gov.uk

Fleet Management: Mr Alastair Smith, Assistant Director of Transport & Engineering, Civic Centre, Victoria Road, Hartlepool TS24 8AY ☎ 01429 523802 🖷 01429 523038
✉ alastair.smith@hartlepool.gov.uk

Grounds Maintenance: Mrs Denise Ogden, Assistant Director of Neighbourhood Services, Civic Centre, Victoria Road, Hartlepool TS24 8AY ☎ 01429 523808 🖷 01429 523038
✉ denise.ogden@hartlepool.gov.uk

Grounds Maintenance: Mr David Stubbs, Director of Regeneration & Neighbourhoods, Civic Centre, Victoria Road, Hartlepool TS24 8AY ☎ 01429 523301 🖷 01429 523344
✉ dave.stubbs@hartlepool.gov.uk

Health and Safety: Mr Stuart Langston, Health, Safety & Wellbeing Manager, Civic Centre, Victoria Road, Hartlepool TS24 8AY ☎ 01429 523560 🖷 01429 5204036
✉ stuart.langston@hartlepool.gov.uk

Highways: Mr Alastair Smith, Assistant Director of Transport & Engineering, Bryan Hanson House, Lynn Street, Hartlepool TS24 8BT ☎ 01429 523802 🖷 01429 523038
✉ alastair.smith@hartlepool.gov.uk

Housing: Mr David Stubbs, Director of Regeneration & Neighbourhoods, Civic Centre, Victoria Road, Hartlepool TS24 8AY ☎ 01429 523301 🖷 01429 523344
✉ dave.stubbs@hartlepool.gov.uk

Local Area Agreement: Miss Joanne Smithson, Head of Community Strategy, Civic Centre, Victoria Road, Hartlepool TS24 8AY ☎ 01429 524161 🖷 01429 523599
✉ joanne.smithson@hartlepool.gov.uk

Legal: Mr Peter Devlin, Chief Solicitor, Civic Centre, Victoria Road, Hartlepool TS24 8AY ☎ 01429 523003 🖷 01429 523856
✉ peter.devlin@hartlepool.gov.uk

Leisure and Cultural Services: Ms Nicola Bailey, Acting Chief Executive, Civic Centre, Victoria Road, Hartlepool TS24 8AY ☎ 01429 523001 🖷 01429 523865
✉ nicola.bailey@hartlepool.gov.uk

Licensing: Mr Ian Harrison, Principal Trading Standards & Licensing Officer, Bryan Hanson House, Lynn Street, Hartlepool TS24 7BT ☎ 01429 523349 ✉ ian.harrison@hartlepool.gov.uk

Lifelong Learning: Ms Nicola Bailey, Acting Chief Executive, Civic Centre, Victoria Road, Hartlepool TS24 8AY ☎ 01429 523001 🖷 01429 523865 ✉ nicola.bailey@hartlepool.gov.uk

Lighting: Mr Bob Golightly, Street Lighting Controller, Church Street, Hartlepool TS24 7BT ☎ 01429 523254 🖷 01429 523599
✉ bob.golightly@hartlepool.gov.uk

Member Services: Mrs Christine Armstrong, Customer & Support Services Manager, Civic Centre, Victoria Road, Hartlepool TS24 8AY ☎ 01429 523016 🖷 01429 523005
✉ christine.armstrong@hartlepool.gov.uk

Parking: Mr Alastair Smith, Assistant Director of Transport & Engineering, Civic Centre, Victoria Road, Hartlepool TS24 8AY ☎ 01429 523802 🖷 01429 523038
✉ alastair.smith@hartlepool.gov.uk

Partnerships: Ms Catherine Frank, Local Strategic Partnership Manager, Civic Centre, Victoria Road, Hartlepool TS24 8AY ☎ 01429 284322 🖷 01429 523536
✉ catherine.frank@hartlepool.gov.uk

Partnerships: Mr Graham Frankland, Assistant Director of Resources, Civic Centre, Level 3, Hartlepool TS24 8AY ☎ 01429 523211 🖷 01429 523899 ✉ graham.frankland@hartlepool.gov.uk

Personnel / HR: Ms Joanne Machers, Chief Customer & Workforce Services Officer, Civic Centre, Victoria Road, Hartlepool TS24 8AY ☎ 01429 523003 🖷 01429 523856
✉ joanne.machers@hartlepool.gov.uk

Procurement: Mr Graham Frankland, Assistant Director of Resources, Civic Centre, Level 3, Hartlepool TS24 8AY ☎ 01429 523211 🖷 01429 523899 ✉ graham.frankland@hartlepool.gov.uk

Public Libraries: Ms Nicola Bailey, Acting Chief Executive, Civic Centre, Victoria Road, Hartlepool TS24 8AY ☎ 01429 523001 🖷 01429 523865 ✉ nicola.bailey@hartlepool.gov.uk

Recycling & Waste Minimisation: Mrs Denise Ogden, Assistant Director of Neighbourhood Services, Civic Centre, Victoria Road, Hartlepool TS24 8AY ☎ 01429 523808 🖷 01429 523038
✉ denise.ogden@hartlepool.gov.uk

Recycling & Waste Minimisation: Ms Fiona Srogi, Waste Services Officer, Church Street, Lynn Street Depot, Hartlepool TS24 7BT ☎ 01429 523 829 ✉ fiona.srogi@hartlepool.gov.uk

Regeneration: Mr Derek Gouldburn, Urban & Planning Policy Manager, Bryan Hanson House, Lynn Street, Hartlepool TS24 7BT ☎ 01429 523276 ✉ derek.gouldburn@hartlepool.gov.uk

Regeneration: Mr Damien Wilson, Assistant Director of Regeneration & Planning, Civic Centre, Victoria Road, Hartlepool TS24 8AY ☎ 01429 523400 ✉ damien.wilson@hartlepool.gov.uk

Road Safety: Mr Paul Watson, Road Safety Officer, Church Street, Lynn Street Depot, Hartlepool TS24 7BT ☎ 01429 523590 🖷 01429 860830 ✉ paul.watson@hartlepool.gov.uk

Social Services (Adult): Ms Nicola Bailey, Acting Chief Executive, Civic Centre, Victoria Road, Hartlepool TS24 8AY ☎ 01429 523001 🖷 01429 523865
✉ nicola.bailey@hartlepool.gov.uk

Social Services (Adult): Ms Geraldine Martin, Head of Adult Services, Civic Centre, Victoria Road, Hartlepool TS24 8AY ☎ 01429 266522 ✉ geraldine.martin@hartlepool.gov.uk

Social Services (Children): Mr Mark Smith, Locality Officer, Civic Centre, Victoria Road, Hartlepool TS24 8AY ☎ 01429 523901 ✉ mark.smith@hartlepool.gov.uk

Staff Training: Ms Joanne Machers, Chief Customer & Workforce Services Officer, Civic Centre, Victoria Road, Hartlepool TS24 8AY ☎ 01429 523003 🖷 01429 523856 ✉ joanne.machers@hartlepool.gov.uk

Street Scene: Mrs Denise Ogden, Assistant Director of Neighbourhood Services, Civic Centre, Victoria Road, Hartlepool TS24 8AY ☎ 01429 523808 🖷 01429 523038 ✉ denise.ogden@hartlepool.gov.uk

Sustainable Communities: Mr Damien Wilson, Assistant Director of Regeneration & Planning, Civic Centre, Victoria Road, Hartlepool TS24 8AY ☎ 01429 523400 ✉ damien.wilson@hartlepool.gov.uk

Sustainable Development: Miss Joanne Smithson, Head of Community Strategy, Civic Centre, Victoria Road, Hartlepool TS24 8AY ☎ 01429 524161 🖷 01429 523599 ✉ joanne.smithson@hartlepool.gov.uk

Tourism: Ms Jo Cole, Tourism Officer, Bryan Hanson House, Lynn Street, Hartlepool TS24 7BT ☎ 01429 523508 ✉ jo.cole@hartlepool.gov.uk

Town Centre: Mrs Denise Ogden, Assistant Director of Neighbourhood Services, Civic Centre, Victoria Road, Hartlepool TS24 8AY ☎ 01429 523808 🖷 01429 523038 ✉ denise.ogden@hartlepool.gov.uk

Traffic Management: Mr Alastair Smith, Assistant Director of Transport & Engineering, Bryan Hanson House, Lynn Street, Hartlepool TS24 8BT ☎ 01429 523802 🖷 01429 523038 ✉ alastair.smith@hartlepool.gov.uk

Transport: Mr Alastair Smith, Assistant Director of Transport & Engineering, Bryan Hanson House, Lynn Street, Hartlepool TS24 8BT ☎ 01429 523802 🖷 01429 523038 ✉ alastair.smith@hartlepool.gov.uk

Transport Planner: Mr David Stubbs, Director of Regeneration & Neighbourhoods, Civic Centre, Victoria Road, Hartlepool TS24 8AY ☎ 01429 523301 🖷 01429 523344 ✉ dave.stubbs@hartlepool.gov.uk

Waste Collection and Disposal: Mrs Denise Ogden, Assistant Director of Neighbourhood Services, Civic Centre, Victoria Road, Hartlepool TS24 8AY ☎ 01429 523808 🖷 01429 523038 ✉ denise.ogden@hartlepool.gov.uk

Waste Management: Mrs Denise Ogden, Assistant Director of Neighbourhood Services, Civic Centre, Victoria Road, Hartlepool TS24 8AY ☎ 01429 523808 🖷 01429 523038 ✉ denise.ogden@hartlepool.gov.uk

MEMBERS OF THE COUNCIL (34)

***Chair:* Akers-Belcher**, Stephen (LAB - Manor House)
stephen.akers-belcher@hartlepool.gov.uk
***Vice-Chair:* Cranney**, Kevin (LAB - Foggy Furze)
kevin.cranney@hartlepool.gov.uk
***Mayor:* Drummond**, Stuart (IND - Mayor Hartlepool)
stuart.drummond@hartlepool.gov.uk
***Deputy Mayor:* Hill**, Cath (IND - Seaton)
cath.hill@hartlepool.gov.uk
Ainslie, Jim (LAB - Headland & Harbour)
jim.ainslie@hartlepool.gov.uk
Akers-Belcher, Christopher (LAB - Foggy Furze)
christopher.akers-belcher@hartlepool.gov.uk
Beck, Paul (LAB - Hart)
paul.beck@hartlepool.gov.uk
Brash, Jonathan (LAB - Burn Valley)
jonathan.brash@hartlepool.gov.uk
Cook, Rob (LAB - De Bruce)
rob.cook@hartlepool.gov.uk
Dawkins, Keith (IND - Jesmond)
keith.dawkins@hartlepool.gov.uk
Fisher, Keith (IND - Hart)
keith.fisher@hartlepool.gov.uk
Fleet, Mary (LAB - Jesmond)
mary.fleet@hartlepool.gov.uk
Gibbon, Steve (IND - Fens & Rossmere)
steve.gibbon@hartlepool.gov.uk
Griffin, Sheila (LAB - De Bruce)
sheila.griffin@hartlepool.gov.uk
Hall, Gerald (LAB - Burn Valley)
gerard.hall@hartlepool.gov.uk
Hargreaves, Pamela (LAB - Victoria)
pamela.hargreaves@hartlepool.gov.uk
Jackson, Peter (LAB - Headland & Harbour)
peter.jackson@hartlepool.gov.uk
James, Marjorie (LAB - Manor House)
marjoriejames45@yahoo.co.uk
Lauderdale, John (IND - Burn Valley)
john.lauderdale@hartlepool.gov.uk
Lilley, Geoff (IND - Fens & Rossmere)
geoff.lilley@googlemail.com
Lilley, Alison (IND - Fens & Rossmere)
alison.lilley46@googlemail.com
Lyons, Brenda (CON - Rural West)
brenda.lyons@hartlepool.gov.uk
Morris, George (CON - Rural West)
george.morris@hartlepool.gov.uk
Payne, Robbie (LAB - Headland & Harbour)
robbie.payne@hartlepool.gov.uk
Richardson, Carl (LAB - Victoria)
carl.richardson@hartlepool.gov.uk
Robinson, Jean (LAB - Hart)
Shields, Linda (LAB - Jesmond)
linda.shields@hartlepool.gov.uk
Simmons, Chris (LAB - Victoria)
chris.simmons@hartlepool.gov.uk
Sirs, Kaylee (LAB - Foggy Furze)
kaylee.sirs@hartlepool.gov.uk
Tempest, Sylvia (LAB - De Bruce)
sylvia.tempest@hartlepool.gov.uk
Thompson, Paul (IND - Seaton)
paul.thompson@hartlepool.gov.uk
Turner, Michael (IND - Seaton)
michael.turner@hartlepool.gov.uk
Wells, Ray (CON - Rural West)
ray.wells@hartlepool.gov.uk
Wilcox, Angie (LAB - Manor House)
angie.wilcox@hartlepool.gov.uk

LOCAL AUTHORITIES

POLITICAL COMPOSITION
LAB: 21, IND: 10, CON: 3

CABINET
The Mayor / Neighbourhoods & Regeneration: Mr Stuart Drummond
Adult Services & Public Health: Mr John Lauderdale
Children's & Community Services: Mrs Cath Hill
Finance & Corporate Services: Mr Paul Thompson

COMMITTEE CHAIRS
Adult & Community Services: Mr Carl Richardson
Audit: Mr Christopher Akers-Belcher
General Purposes & Planning: Mr Rob Cook
Licensing: Mr George Morris
Neighbourhood Services: Ms Sylvia Tempest
Regeneration & Planning: Mr Gerald Hall
Scrutiny (Scrutiny): Ms Marjorie James

HASTINGS D

Hastings Borough Council, Town Hall, Queen's Road, Hastings TN34 1QR ☎ 01424 781066 🖷 01424 781743
💻 www.hastings.gov.uk

FACTS & FIGURES
Police Authority: Sussex Police Authority
Health Authority: South East Coast Strategic Health Authority
Learning and Skills Council: South East
Parliamentary Constituencies: Hastings and Rye
EU Constituencies: South East
Election Frequency: Elections are biennial
Twinning: Bethune (France); Dordrecht (Netherlands); Oudenaarde (Belgium); Schwerte (Germany); Sierra Leone (Africa)

PRINCIPAL OFFICERS
Building Control: Mr Brian Bristow, Building Control Manager, Rother District Council, Town Hall, Bexhill-on-Sea TN19 3JX ☎ 01424 783280 🖷 01424 783208 ✉ bbristow@rother.gov.uk

Children / Youth Services: Mr Simon Hubbard, Director of Regeneration, Aquila House, Breeds Place, Hastings TN34 3UY ☎ 01424 451753 ✉ shubbard@hastings.gov.uk

PR / Communications: Mr Kevin Boorman, Head of Marketing & Communications, Town Hall, Queen's Road, Hastings TN34 1QR ☎ 01424 451123 🖷 01424 781743 ✉ kboorman@hastings.gov.uk

Community Safety: Mr Mike Fagan, Community Safety Manager, Aquila House, Breeds Place, Hastings TN34 3UY ☎ 01424 451438 ✉ mfagan@hastings.gov.uk

Computer Management: Mr Mark Bourne, IT Manager, Aquila House, Breeds Place, Hastings TN34 3UY ☎ 01424 451414 🖷 01424 781401 ✉ mbourne@hastings.gov.uk

Corporate Services: Mr Neil Dart, Director of Corporate Resources, Aquila House, Breeds Place, Hastings TN34 3UY ☎ 01424 451502 ✉ ndart@hastings.gov.uk

Customer Service: Ms Julie Smee, Contact Centre Project Manager, Town Hall, Queen's Road, Hastings TN34 1QR ☎ 01424 451260 🖷 01424 451191 ✉ jsmee@hastings.gov.uk

Economic Development: Ms Monica Adams-Acton, Head of Regeneration & Planning Policy, Aquila House, Breeds Place, Hastings TN34 3UY ☎ 01424 451749 🖷 01424 451749 ✉ madams-acton@hastings.gov.uk

E-Government: Mr Mark Bourne, IT Manager, Aquila House, Breeds Place, Hastings TN34 3UY ☎ 01424 451414 🖷 01424 781401 ✉ mbourne@hastings.gov.uk

Electoral Registration: Mrs Katrina Silverson, Scrutiny & Electoral Services Officer, Aquila House, Breeds Place, Hastings TN34 3UY ☎ 01424 451747 🖷 01424 451732 ✉ ksilverson@hastings.gov.uk

Emergency Planning: Mr Charlie Sharrod, Emergency Planner, Aquila House, Breeds Place, Hastings TN34 3UY ☎ 01424 783226 ✉ csharrod@hastings.gov.uk

Environmental / Technical Services: Mr Richard Homewood, Director of Environmental Services, Aquila House, Breeds Place, Hastings TN34 3UY ☎ 01424 783200 ✉ rhomewood@hastings.gov.uk

Environmental Health: Mr Richard Homewood, Director of Environmental Services, Aquila House, Breeds Place, Hastings TN34 3UY ☎ 01424 783200 ✉ rhomewood@hastings.gov.uk

Estates, Property & Valuation: Ms Amy Terry, Estates Manager, Aquila House, Breeds Place, Hastings TN34 3UY ☎ 01424 451640 🖷 01424 781648 ✉ aterry@hastings.gov.uk

Finance and Treasurer: Mr Neil Dart, Director of Corporate Resources, Aquila House, Breeds Place, Hastings TN34 3UY ☎ 01424 451502 ✉ ndart@hastings.gov.uk

Finance and Treasurer: Mr Peter Grace, Head of Finance, Aquila House, Breeds Place, Hastings TN34 3UY ☎ 01424 451503 🖷 01424 781515 ✉ pgrace@hastings.gov.uk

Highways: Mr Mike Hepworth, Head of Environmental Health, Aquila House, Breeds Place, Hastings TN34 3UY ☎ 01424 783332 ✉ mhepworth@hastings.gov.uk

Home Energy Conservation: Ms Carol Hughes, Principal Environmental Health Officer, Aquila House, Breeds Place, Hastings TN34 3UY ☎ 01424 783345 🖷 01424 451345 ✉ chughes@hastings.gov.uk

Housing: Mr Andrew Palmer, Head of Housing & Development, Aqulia House, Breeds Place, Hastings TN34 3UY ☎ 01424 451316 🖷 01424 781305 ✉ apalmer@hastings.gov.uk

Legal: Ms Christine Barkshire-Jones, Chief Legal Officer, Aquila House, Breeds Place, Hastings TN34 3UY ☎ 01424 451733 🖷 01424 781743 ✉ cbarkshire-jones@hastings.gov.uk

Leisure and Cultural Services: Mrs Virginia Gilbert, Head of Amenities, Resorts & Leisure, Aquila House, Breeds Place, Hastings TN34 3UY ☎ 01424 451956 ✉ vgilbert@hastings.gov.uk

Licensing: Mr Bob Brown, Licensing Manager, Aquila House, Breeds Place, Hastings TN34 3UY ☎ 01424 783249 ✉ bbrown@hastings.gov.uk

Member Services: Ms Jane Hartnell, Head of Corporate Services, Aquila House, Breeds Place, Hastings TB34 3UY ☎ 01424 451718 🖷 01424 451482 ✉ jhartnell@hastings.gov.uk

Parking: Mr Mike Hepworth, Head of Environmental Health, Aquila House, Breeds Place, Hastings TN34 3UY ☎ 01424 783332 ✉ mhepworth@hastings.gov.uk

Personnel / HR: Mrs Verna Connolly, Executive Manager - People & Organisational Development, Town Hall, Queen's Road, Hastings TN34 1QR ☎ 01424 451707 🖷 01424 781769 ✉ vconnolly@hastings.gov.uk

Planning: Mr Tim Cookson, Strategic Planning Manager, Aquila House, Breeds Place, Hastings TN34 3UY ☎ 01424 783201 ✉ tcookson@hastings.gov.uk

Procurement: Mr Hugh Davidson, Procurement Officer, Aquila House, Breeds Place, Hastings TN34 3UY ☎ 01424 451504 🖷 01424 781515 ✉ hdavidson@hastings.gov.uk

Regeneration: Mr Simon Hubbard, Director of Regeneration, Aquila House, Breeds Place, Hastings TN34 3UY ☎ 01424 451753 ✉ shubbard@hastings.gov.uk

Staff Training: Ms Barbara Garlinge, Senior HR Partner, Town Hall, Queen's Road, Hastings TN34 1QR ☎ 01424 451455 🖷 01424 781743 ✉ bgarlinge@hastings.gov.uk

Street Scene: Mr Peter Mead, Waste & Streetscene Services Manager, Bulverhythe Depot, Bulverhythe Road, St Leonards-on-Sea TN38 8AF ☎ 01424 451385 🖷 01424 781515 ✉ pmead@hastings.gov.uk

Sustainable Communities: Mr Simon Hubbard, Director of Regeneration, Aquila House, Breeds Place, Hastings TN34 3UY ☎ 01424 451753 ✉ shubbard@hastings.gov.uk

Tourism: Mr Kevin Boorman, Head of Marketing & Communications, Aquila House, Breeds Place, Hastings TN34 3UY ☎ 01424 451123 🖷 01424 781743 ✉ kboorman@hastings.gov.uk

Town Centre: Mr Robert Woods, Town Centre Manager, Summerfields Business Centre, Bohemia Road, Hastings TN34 1UT ☎ 01424 205516 ✉ rwoods@hastings.gov.uk

Traffic Management: Mr Mike Hepworth, Head of Environmental Health, Aquila House, Breeds Place, Hastings TN34 3UY ☎ 01424 783332 ✉ mhepworth@hastings.gov.uk

Waste Management: Mr Richard Homewood, Director of Environmental Services, Aquila House, Breeds Place, Hastings TN34 3UY ☎ 01424 783200 ✉ rhomewood@hastings.gov.uk

MEMBERS OF THE COUNCIL (32)

***Mayor:* Roberts**, Alan (LAB - Wishing Tree)
cllr.alan.roberts@hastings.gov.uk

***Deputy Mayor:* Dowling**, Bruce (LAB - Hollington)
cllr.bruce.dowling@hastings.gov.uk

***Leader of the Council:* Birch**, Jeremy (LAB - Central St Leonards)
cllr.jeremy.birch@hastings.gov.uk

Batsford, Andy (LAB - St Helens)
cllr.andy.batsford@hastings.gov.uk

Cartwright, Andrew (LAB - Gensing)
cllr.andrew.cartwright@hastings.gov.uk

Charlesworth, Maureen (CON - Maze Hill)
cllr.maureen.charlesworth@hastings.gov.uk

Chowney, Peter (LAB - Tressell)
cllr.peter.chowney@hastings.gov.uk

Clark, Lee (LAB - Castle)
cllr.lee.clark@hastings.gov.uk

Cooke, Robert (CON - Ashdown)
cllr.robert.cooke@hastings.gov.uk

Corello, Simon (CON - St Helens)
cllr.simon.corello@hastings.gov.uk

Daniel, Godfrey (LAB - Braybrooke)
cllr.godfrey.daniel@hastings.gov.uk

Davies, Warren (LAB - Baird)
cllr.warren.davies@hastings.gov.uk

Finch, Pete (CON - West St Leonards)
cllr.peter.finch@hastings.gov.uk

Forward, Kim (LAB - Gensing)
cllr.kim.forward@hastings.gov.uk

Gurney, Andrew (CON - Silverhill)
cllr.andrew.gurney@hastings.gov.uk

Hodges, John (LAB - Old Hastings)
cllr.john.hodges@hastings.gov.uk

Howard, Mike (LAB - West St Leonards)
cllr.mike.howard@hastings.gov.uk

Kramer, Jay (LAB - Tressell)
cllr.jay.kramer@hastings.gov.uk

Martin, Eve (CON - Conquest)
cllr.eve.martin@hastings.gov.uk

Poole, Dawn (LAB - Old Hastings)
cllr.dawn.poole@hastings.gov.uk

Pragnell, Peter (CON - Conquest)
cllr.peter.pragnell@hastings.gov.uk

Rogers, Judy (LAB - Castle)
cllr.judy.rogers@hastings.gov.uk

Sabetian, Dominic (LAB - Braybrooke)
cllr.dominic.sabetian@hastings.gov.uk

Scott, Philip (LAB - Wishing Tree)
cllr.philip.scott@hastings.gov.uk

Sinden, Nigel (LAB - Silverhill)
cllr.nigel.sinden@hastings.gov.uk

Street, Richard (LAB - Ore)
cllr.richard.street@hastings.gov.uk

Turner, Mike (LAB - Baird)
cllr.mike.turner@hastings.gov.uk

Waite, Joy (CON - Maze Hill)
cllr.joy.waite@hastings.gov.uk

Webb, Trevor (LAB - Central St Leonards)
cllr.trevor.webb@hastings.gov.uk

Westley, Emily (LAB - Hollington)
cllr.emily.westley@hastings.gov.uk

Wilson, John (CON - Ashdown)
cllr.john.wilson@hastings.gov.uk

Wincott, Michael (LAB - Ore)
cllr.michael.wincott@hastings.gov.uk

POLITICAL COMPOSITION
LAB: 23, CON: 9

COMMITTEE CHAIRS
Audit: Mr Peter Pragnell
Employment: Mr Jeremy Birch
Environment & Safety: Mr Bruce Dowling
Licensing: Mr Dominic Sabetian
Overview & Scrutiny (Scrutiny): Mr Trevor Webb
Planning: Mr Godfrey Daniel

HAVANT D
Havant Borough Council, Civic Offices, Civic Centre Road, Havant PO9 2AX ☎ 023 9247 4174 🖷 023 9248 0263
💻 www.havant.gov.uk

FACTS & FIGURES
Police Authority: Hampshire Police Authority
Health Authority: South Central Strategic Health Authority
Learning and Skills Council: South East
Parliamentary Constituencies: Havant
EU Constituencies: South East
Election Frequency: Elections are by thirds
Twinning: Waterlooville: Wesermarsch LK (Germany); Maurepas (France); Emsworth: St. Aubin (France)

PRINCIPAL OFFICERS
Chief Executive: Ms Sandy Hopkins, Joint Chief Executive, Public Service Plaza, Civic Centre Road, Havant PO9 2AX ☎ 023 9244 6150 🖷 023 9248 0263 ✉ sandy.hopkins@havant.gov.uk

Senior Management: Mr Tom Horwood, Executive Director, Public Service Plaza, Civic Centre Road, Havant PO9 2AX ☎ 01730 234025; 023 9244 6151 🖷 01730 267760; 023 9248 0263 ✉ tom.horwood@easthants.gov.uk

Senior Management: Ms Gill Kneller, Executive Director, Public Service Plaza, Civic Centre Road, Havant PO9 2AX ☎ 01730 234004; 023 9244 6151 🖷 01730 234012; 023 9248 0263 ✉ gill.kneller@easthants.gov.uk

Access Officer / Social Services (Disability): Mrs Caren Ransom, Equalities & Access Officer, Public Service Plaza, Civic Centre Road, Havant PO9 2AX ☎ 023 9244 6007 ✉ caren.ransom@havant.gov.uk

Architect, Building / Property Services: Mr Jon Sanders, Service Manager - Property, Public Service Plaza, Civic Centre Road, Havant PO9 2AX ☎ 01730 234091; 023 9244 6241 🖷 023 9248 0263 ✉ jon_sanders@easthants.gov.uk

Building Control: Mr Chris Murray, Service Manager - Planning, Public Service Plaza, Civic Centre Road, Havant PO9 2AX ☎ 01730 234331; 023 9244 6512 ✉ chris.murray@easthants.gov.uk

PR / Communications: Mrs Dawn Adey, Service Manager - Communications, Public Service Plaza, Civic Centre Road, Havant PO9 2AX ☎ 023 9244 6491 🖷 023 9248 0263 ✉ dawn.adey@havant.gov.uk

Community Safety: Mr Tim Pointer, Community Team Leader, Public Service Plaza, Civic Centre Road, Havant PO9 2AX ☎ 023 9244 6606 🖷 023 8248 0263 ✉ tim.pointer@havant.gov.uk

Computer Management: Mr Keith Hoare, ICT Contracts Officer, Public Service Plaza, Civic Centre Road, Havant PO9 2AX ☎ 023 9244 6391 🖷 023 9244 6240 ✉ keith.hoare@havant.gov.uk

Corporate Services: Ms Sandy Hopkins, Joint Chief Executive, Public Service Plaza, Civic Centre Road, Havant PO9 2AX ☎ 023 9244 6150 🖷 023 9248 0263 ✉ sandy.hopkins@havant.gov.uk

Customer Service: Mrs Janice Newman, Customer Services Manager, Public Service Plaza, Civic Centre Road, Havant PO9 2AX ☎ 023 9244 6040 🖷 023 9248 0263 ✉ janice.newman@havant.gov.uk

Direct Labour: Mr Peter Vince, Environmental Quality Manager, Southmoor Depot, 2 Penner Road, Havant PO9 1QH ☎ 023 9244 5253 🖷 023 9249 8031 ✉ peter.vince@havant.gov.uk

Economic Development: Mr Jeff Crate, Business Development Officer - Team Leader, Public Service Plaza, Civic Centre Road, Havant PO9 2AX ☎ 023 9244 6615 🖷 023 9244 6545 ✉ jeff.crate@havant.gov.uk

E-Government: Mrs Susan Parker, Service Manager - Organisational Development, Public Service Plaza, Civic Centre Road, Havant PO9 2AX ☎ 023 9244 6493 🖷 023 9248 0263 ✉ susan.parker@havant.gov.uk

Electoral Registration: Mrs Jayne Day, Electoral Services Team Leader, Public Service Plaza, Civic Centre Road, Havant PO9 2AX ☎ 023 9244 6226 🖷 023 9248 0263 ✉ jayne.day@havant.gov.uk

Emergency Planning: Mr Stuart Pinkney, Safety & Emergency Planning Officer, Public Service Plaza, Civic Centre Road, Havant PO9 2AX ☎ 023 9244 6675 🖷 023 9244 6455 ✉ stuart.pinkney@havant.gov.uk

Energy Management: Mr Peter Gammage, Building Services Officer, Public Service Plaza, Civic Centre Road, Havant PO9 2AX ☎ 023 9248 6409 🖷 023 9248 0263 ✉ peter.gammage@havant.gov.uk

Environmental / Technical Services: Mrs Jackie Batchelor, Head of Development & Technical Services, Public Service Plaza, Civic Centre Road, Havant PO9 2AX ☎ 023 9244 6520 🖷 023 9244 6588 ✉ jackie.batchelor@havant.gov.uk

Environmental / Technical Services: Mr Peter Vince, Environmental Quality Manager, Southmoor Depot, 2 Penner Road, Havant PO9 1QH ☎ 023 9244 5253 🖷 023 9249 8031 ✉ peter.vince@havant.gov.uk

Environmental Health: Mr Stuart Wedgebury, Service Manager - Environmental Health, Public Service Plaza, Civic Centre Road, Havant PO9 2AX ☎ 023 9244 6651 🖷 023 9244 6659 ✉ stuart.wedgebury@easthants.gov.uk

Estates, Property & Valuation: Mr Jon Sanders, Service

Manager - Property, Public Service Plaza, Civic Centre Road, Havant PO9 2AX ☎ 01730 234091 🖷 023 9248 0263 ✉ jon_sanders@easthants.gov.uk

European Liaison: Miss Hannah Newbury, Senior Solicitor, Public Service Plaza, Civic Centre Road, Havant PO9 2AX ☎ 023 9244 6213 🖷 023 9248 0263 ✉ hannah.newbury@havant.gov.uk

Facilities: Mr Neil Payne, Facilities Team Leader, Public Service Plaza, Civic Centre Road, Havant PO9 2AX ☎ 023 9244 6646 🖷 023 9244 6240 ✉ neil.payne@havant.gov.uk

Finance and Treasurer: Mrs Jane Eaton, Executive Head - Governance & Logistics, Public Service Plaza, Civic Centre Road, Havant PO9 2AX ☎ 01730 234035; 023 9244 6151 🖷 023 9248 0263 ✉ jane.eaton@havant.gov.uk

Fleet Management: Mr Peter Vince, Environmental Quality Manager, Southmoor Depot, 2 Penner Road, Havant PO9 1QH ☎ 023 9244 5253 🖷 023 9249 8031 ✉ peter.vince@havant.gov.uk

Grounds Maintenance: Mr Andy Paffett, Open Spaces Manager, Southmoor Depot, 2 Penner Road, Havant PO9 1QH ☎ 023 9244 5258 🖷 023 9249 8031 ✉ andy.paffett@havant.gov.uk

Grounds Maintenance: Mr Peter Vince, Environmental Quality Manager, Southmoor Depot, 2 Penner Road, Havant PO9 1QH ☎ 023 9244 5253 🖷 023 9249 8031 ✉ peter.vince@havant.gov.uk

Health and Safety: Mr Stuart Pinkney, Safety & Emergency Planning Officer, Public Service Plaza, Civic Centre Road, Havant PO9 2AX ☎ 023 9244 6675 🖷 023 9244 6455 ✉ stuart.pinkney@havant.gov.uk

Highways: Mr Tony Cailes, Technical Services Manager, Public Service Plaza, Civic Centre Road, Havant Po9 2AX ☎ 023 9244 6462 🖷 023 9244 6455 ✉ tony.cailes@havant.gov.uk

Home Energy Conservation: Mrs Pennie Brown, Sustainability Adviser, Public Service Plaza, Civic Centre Road, Havant PO9 2AX ☎ 023 9244 6554 🖷 023 9248 0263 ✉ pennie.smith@havant.gov.uk

Housing: Ms Tracey Howard, Service Manager - Housing, Public Service Plaza, Civic Centre Road, Havant PO9 2AX ☎ 023 9244 6626 🖷 023 9248 0263 ✉ tracey.howard@easthants.gov.uk

Legal: Mrs Jo Barden-Hernandez, Solicitor to the Council, Public Service Plaza, Civic Centre Road, Havant PO9 2AX ☎ 01730 234068 🖷 023 9248 0263 ✉ jo_gabell@easthants.gov.uk

Leisure and Cultural Services: Mr Tim Slater, Executive Head - Economy & Community, Public Service Plaza, Civic Centre Road, Havant PO9 2AX ☎ 01730 234613 🖷 023 9248 0263 ✉ tim.slater@havant.gov.uk

Licensing: Mr Stuart Wedgebury, Service Manager - Environmental Health, Public Service Plaza, Civic Centre Road, Havant PO9 2AX ☎ 023 9244 6651 🖷 023 9244 6659 ✉ stuart.wedgebury@easthants.gov.uk

Lighting: Mr Tony Cailes, Technical Services Manager, Public Service Plaza, Civic Centre Road, Havant PO9 2AX ☎ 023 9244 6462 🖷 023 9244 6455 ✉ tony.cailes@havant.gov.uk

Lottery Funding, Charity and Voluntary: Mr David Harris, Economic Development/External Funding Officer, Public Service Plaza, Civic Centre Road, Havant PO9 2AX ☎ 023 9244 6460 🖷 023 9244 6545 ✉ david.harris@havant.gov.uk

Member Services: Mr Lee Abraham, Democratic Services Team Leader, Public Service Plaza, Civic Centre Road, Havant PO9 2AX ☎ 023 9244 6230 🖷 023 9248 0263 ✉ lee.abraham@havant.gov.uk

Parking: Ms Michelle Green, Parking & Traffic Management Team Leader, Public Service Plaza, Civic Centre Road, Havant PO9 2AX ☎ 023 9244 6437 🖷 023 9248 0263 ✉ michelle.green@havant.gov.uk

Partnerships: Mrs Nicki Conyard, Community Regeneration Team Leader, Public Service Plaza, Civic Centre Road, Havant PO9 2AX ☎ 023 9244 6114 ✉ nicki.conyard@havant.gov.uk

Personnel / HR: Ms Caroline Halsall, Service Manager - Human Resources, Public Service Plaza, Civic Centre Road, Havant PO9 2AX ☎ 023 9244 6160 🖷 023 9244 6684 ✉ caroline.halsall@havant.gov.uk

Planning: Mrs Julia Potter, Executive Head - Planning & Built Environment, Public Service Plaza, Civic Centre Road, Havant PO9 2AX ☎ 01730 234376 🖷 01730 234385 ✉ julia.potter@easthants.gov.uk

Procurement: Ms Hilda Jackson, Procurement Team Manager, Public Service Plaza, Civic Centre Road, Havant PO9 2AX ☎ 023 9244 6396 🖷 023 9244 6240 ✉ hilda.jackson@havant.gov.uk

Recycling & Waste Minimisation: Mrs Sally Smith, Waste Recycling Officer, Southmoor Depot, 2 Penner Road, Havant PO9 1QH ☎ 023 9244 5445 🖷 023 9249 8031 ✉ sally.smith@havant.gov.uk

Regeneration: Mrs Claire Hughes, Economic Development and Community Manager, Public Service Plaza, Civic Centre Road, Havant PO9 2AX ☎ 023 9244 5235 🖷 023 9249 8031 ✉ claire.hughes@havant.gov.uk

Road Safety: Mr Tony Cailes, Technical Services Manager, Public Service Plaza, Civic Centre Road, Havant PO9 2AX ☎ 023 9244 6462 🖷 023 9244 6455 ✉ tony.cailes@havant.gov.uk

Staff Training: Mr Spencer Drain, Learning & Development Adviser, Public Service Plaza, Civic Centre Road, Havant PO9 2AX ☎ 023 9244 6325 🖷 023 9244 6684 ✉ spencer.drain@havant.gov.uk

Sustainable Communities: Mrs Claire Hughes, Economic Development and Community Manager, Public Service Plaza, Civic Centre Road, Havant PO9 2AX ☎ 023 9244 5235 🖷 023 9249 8031 ✉ claire.hughes@havant.gov.uk

Tourism: Mr Jeff Crate, Business Development Officer - Team

Leader, Public Service Plaza, Civic Centre Road, Havant PO9 2AX ☎ 023 9244 6615 🖷 023 9244 6545 jeff.crate@havant.gov.uk

Town Centre: Mr Jeff Crate, Business Development Officer - Team Leader, Public Service Plaza, Civic Centre Road, Havant PO9 2AX ☎ 023 9244 6615 🖷 023 9244 6545 jeff.crate@havant.gov.uk

Traffic Management: Mr Tony Cailes, Technical Services Manager, Public Service Plaza, Civic Centre Road, Havant PO9 2AX ☎ 023 9244 6462 🖷 023 9244 6455 tony.cailes@havant.gov.uk

Transport: Mr Peter Vince, Environmental Quality Manager, Southmoor Depot, 2 Penner Road, Havant PO9 1QH ☎ 023 9244 5253 🖷 023 9249 8031 peter.vince@havant.gov.uk

Waste Collection and Disposal: Mr Peter Vince, Environmental Quality Manager, Southmoor Depot, 2 Penner Road, Havant PO9 1QH ☎ 023 9244 5253 🖷 023 9249 8031 peter.vince@havant.gov.uk

Waste Management: Mr Peter Vince, Environmental Quality Manager, Southmoor Depot, 2 Penner Road, Havant PO9 1QH ☎ 023 9244 5253 🖷 023 9249 8031 peter.vince@havant.gov.uk

MEMBERS OF THE COUNCIL (38)

***Mayor:* Shimbart**, Gerald (CON - Hart Plain)
gerald.shimbart@havant.gov.uk

***Deputy Mayor:* Buckley**, Paul (CON - Waterloo)
paul.buckley@havant.gov.uk

***Leader of the Council:* Briggs**, Anthony (CON - Cowplain)
tony.briggs@havant.gov.uk

***Deputy Leader of the Council:* Guest**, David (CON - St Faith's)
david.guest@havant.gov.uk

***Group Leader:* Smith**, George (CON - Bedhampton)
george.smith@havant.gov.uk

Bastin, Ray (CON - Waterloo)
ray.bastin@havant.gov.uk

Blackett, Gwendoline (CON - Purbrook)
gwen.blackett@havant.gov.uk

Bolton, Raymond (CON - St Faith's)
ray.bolton@havant.gov.uk

Branson, Jackie (CON - St Faith's)
jackie.branson@havant.gov.uk

Brown, Richard (LAB - Warren Park)
richard.brown@havant.gov.uk

Cheshire, Michael (CON - Hart Plain)
michael.cheshire@havant.gov.uk

Collins, David (CON - Hayling East)
david.collins@havant.gov.uk

Cousins, Ralph (LAB - Battins)
ralph.cousins@havant.gov.uk

Edwards, Frida (CON - Bondfields)
frida.edwards@havant.gov.uk

Fairhurst, Michael (CON - Barncroft)
mike.fairhurst@havant.gov.uk

Farrow, Hilary (CON - Purbrook)
hilary.farrow@havant.gov.uk

Galloway, Richard (CON - Emsworth)
richard.galloway@havant.gov.uk

Gibb-Gray, Brendan (CON - Emsworth)
brendan.gibb-gray@havant.gov.uk

Gillet, David (CON - Emsworth)
david.gillett@havant.gov.uk

Hart, Terence (LAB - Bondfields)
terry.hart@havant.gov.uk

Heard, Rory (CON - Stakes)
rory.heard@havant.gov.uk

Hilton, Cyril (CON - Stakes)
cyril.hilton@havant.gov.uk

Hunt, John (CON - Waterloo)
john.hunt@havant.gov.uk

Johnson, Mark (CON - Warren Park)
mark.johnson@havant.gov.uk

Keast, David (CON - Cowplain)
david.keast@havant.gov.uk

Kennedy, Olwyn (CON - Stakes)
olwyn.kennedy@havant.gov.uk

Lenaghan, Andrew (CON - Hayling West)
andrew.lenaghan@havant.gov.uk

Pierce-Jones, Victor (CON - Hayling West)
victor.pierce-jones@havant.gov.uk

Ray, Katie (LD - Battins)
katie.ray@havant.gov.uk

Shimbart, Elaine (CON - Hart Plain)
elaine.shimbart@havant.gov.uk

Smallcorn, Marjorie (CON - Cowplain)
marjorie.smallcorn@havant.gov.uk

Smith, Kenneth (CON - Bedhampton)
ken.smith@havant.gov.uk

Smith, John (CON - Hayling East)
john.smith@havant.gov.uk

Tarrant, Caren (CON - Stakes)
caren.tarrant@havant.gov.uk

Turner, Leah (CON - Hayling East)
leah.turner@havant.gov.uk

Weeks, Yvonne (CON - Barncroft)
yvonne.weeks@havant.gov.uk

Wilson, Michael (CON - Hayling West)
michael.wilson@havant.gov.uk

Wride, Jennifer (CON - Bedhampton)
jenny.wride@havant.gov.uk

POLITICAL COMPOSITION

CON: 34, LAB: 3, LD: 1

CABINET

Leader: Mr Anthony Briggs
Economy & Communities: Mrs Yvonne Weeks
Environment & Neighbourhood Quality: Mr David Collins
Governance & Logistics: Ms Jackie Branson
Marketing & Development: Mr Michael Cheshire
Planning & Built Environment: Mr David Guest

COMMITTEE CHAIRS

Development Management: Mr Paul Buckley
Licensing: Mr Mark Johnson
Scrutiny: Mr David Keast

HAVERING L

Havering London Borough Council, Town Hall, Main Road, Romford RM1 3BD ☎ 01708 434343 🖷 01708 432424 info@havering.gov.uk www.havering.gov.uk

FACTS & FIGURES

Police Authority: Metropolitan Police Authority
Health Authority: NHS London
Learning and Skills Council: London
Parliamentary Constituencies: Hornchurch and Upminster, Romford
EU Constituencies: London
Election Frequency: Elections are of whole council
Twinning: Ludwigshafen (Germany); Hesdin (France)

PRINCIPAL OFFICERS

Chief Executive: Ms Cheryl Coppell, Chief Executive, Town Hall, Main Road, Romford RM1 3BD ☎ 01708 432062 🖷 01708 432068 ✉ cheryl.coppell@havering.gov.uk

Assistant Chief Executive: Mr Ian Burns, Acting Assistant Chief Executive, Legal & Democratic Services, Town Hall, Main Road, Romford RM1 3BD ☎ 01708 432484 ✉ ian.burns@havering.gov.uk

Senior Management: Mr Andrew Blake-Herbert, Director of Finance & Commerce, Town Hall, Main Road, Romford RM1 3BD ☎ 01708 432218 ✉ andrew.blake-herbert@havering.gov.uk

Senior Management: Ms Sarah Bryant, Head of Internal Shared Services, Town Hall, Main Road, Romford RM1 3BD ☎ 01708 432434 ✉ sarah.bryant@havering.gov.uk

Senior Management: Mr Joe Coogan, Assistant Director - Commissioning, Town Hall, Main Road, Romford RM1 3BD ☎ 01708 431950 ✉ joe.coogan@havering.gov.uk

Architect, Building / Property Services: Mr Garry Green, Property Strategy Manager, Tollgate House, 96 - 98 Market Place, Romford RM1 3ER ☎ 01708 432566 ✉ garry.green@havering.gov.uk

Architect, Building / Property Services: Mr Andrew Skeggs, Technical & Facilities Group Manager, River Chambers, 36 High Street, Romford RM1 1HR ☎ 01708 433600 ✉ andy.skeggs@havering.gov.uk

Best Value: Ms Claire Thompson, Performance Manager, Town Hall, Main Road, Romford RM1 3BD ☎ 01708 431003 ✉ claire.thompson@havering.gov.uk

Building Control: Mr Martin Ramsey, Building Control Manager, 3rd Floor Mercury House, Mercury Gardens, Romford RM1 3SL ☎ 01708 432705 ✉ martin.ramsey@havering.gov.uk

Catering Services: Mr Gerry Clinton, Catering & Traded Services Manager, 7th Floor Mercury House, Mercury Gardens, Romford RM1 3AH ☎ 01708 433149 ✉ gerry.clinton@havering.gov.uk

Children / Youth Services: Ms Kathy Bundred, Head of Children & Young People's Services, Mercury House, Mercury Gardens, Romford RM1 3SL ☎ 01708 433002 ✉ kathy.bundred@havering.gov.uk

Children / Youth Services: Mr Steve Power, Manager - Youth Services, Mercury House, Mercury Gardens, Romford RM1 3SL ☎ 01708 433863 ✉ steve.power@havering.gov.uk

Civil Registration: Mrs Maggie Wright, Superintendent Registrar of Births, Deaths & Marriages, Langtons House, Billet Lane, Hornchurch RM1 1XL ☎ 01708 433498 ✉ maggie.wright@havering.gov.uk

PR / Communications: Mr Mark Leech, Head of Communications, Town Hall, Main Road, Romford RM1 3BD ☎ 01708 434373 ✉ mark.leech@havering.gov.uk

Community Planning: Mr Roger McFarland, Head of Regeneration & Strategic Planning, Town Hall, Main Road, Romford RM1 3BD ☎ 01708 432583 ✉ roger.mcfarland@havering.gov.uk

Community Safety: Ms Deborah Houston-MacBean, Community Safety Manager, Town Hall, Main Road, Romford RM1 3BD ☎ 01708 434960 🖷 01708 432448 ✉ deborah.houstonmacbean@havering.gov.uk

Computer Management: Mr Geoff Connell, Acting Head of Business Systems, Mercury House, Mercury Garden, Romford RM1 3SL ☎ 020 8430 4451 ✉ geoff.connell@havering.gov.uk

Consumer Protection and Trading Standards: Mr John Wade, Public Protection Manager, Mercury House, Mercury Gardens, Romford RM1 3SL ☎ 01708 432748 ✉ john.wade@havering.gov.uk

Contracts: Mr Hassan Iqbal, Senior Procurement Business Partner, Central Library, St Edwards Way, Romford RM1 3AR ☎ 01708 432541 ✉ hassan.iqbal@havering.gov.uk

Corporate Services: Mr Mark Butler, Head of Asset Management, River Chambers, High Street, Romford RM1 1JD ☎ 01708 432947 ✉ mark.butler@havering.gov.uk

Corporate Services: Ms Nikki Richardson, Corporate Support Services Manager, Town Hall, Main Road, Romford RM1 3BD ☎ 01708 432170 ✉ nikki.richardson@havering.gov.uk

Customer Service: Ms Penny Nugent, Customer Services Manager, Mercury House, Mercury Gardens, Romford RM1 3SL ☎ 01708 434225 ✉ penny.nugent@havering.gov.uk

Economic Development: Mr Roger McFarland, Head of Regeneration & Strategic Planning, Town Hall, Main Road, Romford RM1 3BD ☎ 01708 432583 ✉ roger.mcfarland@havering.gov.uk

Education: Ms Sue Butterworth, Group Director - Social Care & Learning, Town Hall, Main Road, Romford RM1 3BD ☎ 01708 432443 ✉ sue.butterworth@havering.gov.uk

E-Government: Mr Geoff Connell, Director of ICT, Mercury House, Mercury Gardens, Romford RM1 3SL ☎ 020 8430 2000; 020 8430 4451 ✉ geoff.connell@newham.gov.uk; geoff.connell@havering.gov.uk

Electoral Registration: Ms Sandra Cottle, Election Services Manager, Town Hall, Main Road, Romford RM1 3BD ☎ 01708 432446 ✉ sandra.cottle@havering.gov.uk

LOCAL AUTHORITIES

Emergency Planning: Mr Alan Clark, Emergency Planning & Business Continuity Manager, Mercury House, Mercury Gardens, Romford RM1 3SL ☎ 01708 433206 ✉ alan.clark@havering.gov.uk

Energy Management: Mr Mark Lowers, Energy Team Leader, Mercury House, Mercury Gardens, Romford RM1 3SL ☎ 01708 432884 ✉ mark.lowers@havering.gov.uk

Environmental / Technical Services: Mr John Wade, Public Protection Manager, Mercury House, Mercury Gardens, Romford RM1 3SL ☎ 01708 432748 ✉ john.wade@havering.gov.uk

Environmental Health: Mr John Wade, Public Protection Manager, Mercury House, Mercury Gardens, Romford RM1 3SL ☎ 01708 432748 ✉ john.wade@havering.gov.uk

Estates, Property & Valuation: Mr Garry Green, Property Strategy Manager, Tollgate House, 96 - 98 Market Place, Romford RM1 3ER ☎ 01708 432566 ✉ garry.green@havering.gov.uk

European Liaison: Mr Roger McFarland, Head of Regeneration & Strategic Planning, Town Hall, Main Road, Romford RM1 3BD ☎ 01708 432583 ✉ roger.mcfarland@havering.gov.uk

Events Manager: Mr Michael Thomas, Events & Campaign Officer, Town Hall, Main Road, Romford RM1 3BD ☎ 01708 432427 ✉ michael.thomas@havering.gov.uk

Facilities: Mr Andrew Skeggs, Technical & Facilities Group Manager, River Chambers, 36 High Street, Romford RM1 1HR ☎ 01708 433600 ✉ andy.skeggs@havering.gov.uk

Finance and Treasurer: Mr Andrew Blake-Herbert, Director of Finance & Commerce, Town Hall, Main Road, Romford RM1 3BD ☎ 01708 432218 ✉ andrew.blake-herbert@havering.gov.uk

Finance and Treasurer: Mr Jeff Potter, Head of Exchequer Services, Town Hall, Main Road, Romford RM1 3BD ☎ 01708 434139 ✉ jeff.potter@havering.gov.uk

Finance and Treasurer: Mr Mike Stringer, Head of Finance & Procurement, 1st Floor Central Library, St Edwards Way, Romford RM1 3AR ☎ 01708 432101 ✉ mike.stringer@havering.gov.uk

Fleet Management: Mr Mark Butler, Head of Asset Management, River Chambers, High Street, Romford RM1 1JD ☎ 01708 432947 ✉ mark.butler@havering.gov.uk

Grounds Maintenance: Mr Simon Parkinson, Head of Culture & Leisure Services, Stable Block, Langtons House, Billet Lane, Hornchurch RM11 1XJ ☎ 01708 432199 ✉ simon.parkinson@havering.gov.uk

Health and Safety: Mr Daniel Darkens, Corporate Health & Safety Officer, River Chambers, 36 High Street, Romford RM1 1HR ☎ 01708 432865 ✉ daniel.darkens@havering.gov.uk

Highways: Mr Bob Wenman, Head of Street Care, Mercury House, Mercury Gardens, Romford RM1 3RX ☎ 01708 432898 ✉ bob.wenman@havering.gov.uk

Home Energy Conservation: Mr Mark Lowers, Energy Team Leader, Mercury House, Mercury Gardens, Romford RM1 3SL ☎ 01708 432884 ✉ mark.lowers@havering.gov.uk

Housing: Mr Jonathan Geall, Housing Needs & Strategy Manager, 2nd Floor Mercury House, Mercury Gardens, Romford RM1 3SL ☎ 01708 434606 ✉ jonathan.geall@havering.gov.uk

Housing: Ms Sue Witherspoon, Head of Housing & Public Protection, Mercury House, Mercury Gardens, Romford RM1 3RX ☎ 01708 433747 ✉ sue.witherspoon@havering.gov.uk

Housing Maintenance: Mr Kevin Hazelwood, Director of Property Services, Homes in Havering, Chippenham Road, Harold Hill, Romford RM3 8YQ ☎ 01708 434091 ✉ kevin.hazelwood@havering.gov.uk

Local Area Agreement: Ms Claire Thompson, Performance Manager, Town Hall, Main Road, Romford RM1 3BD ☎ 01708 431003 ✉ claire.thompson@havering.gov.uk

Legal: Mr Ian Burns, Acting Assistant Chief Executive, Legal & Democratic Services, Town Hall, Main Road, Romford RM1 3BD ☎ 01708 432484 ✉ ian.burns@havering.gov.uk

Leisure and Cultural Services: Ms Cynthia Griffin, Group Director, Culture & Community, Town Hall, Main Road, Romford RM1 3BD ☎ 01708 432260 ✉ cynthia.griffin@havering.gov.uk

Leisure and Cultural Services: Mr Simon Parkinson, Head of Culture & Leisure Services, Stable Block, Langtons House, Billet Lane, Hornchurch RM11 1XJ ☎ 01708 432199 ✉ simon.parkinson@havering.gov.uk

Licensing: Ms Trudi Penman, Licensing Divisional Manager, Mercury House, Mercury Gardens, Romford RM1 3SL ☎ 01708 432718 ✉ trudi.penman@havering.gov.uk

Lifelong Learning: Ms Sue Butterworth, Group Director - Social Care & Learning, Scimitar House, 23 Eastern Road, Romford RM1 3NH ☎ 01708 432443 ✉ sue.butterworth@havering.gov.uk

Lifelong Learning: Mrs Mary Pattinson, Head of Learning & Achievement, Mercury House, Mercury Gardens, Romford RM1 3SL ☎ 01708 433808 ✉ mary.pattinson@havering.gov.uk

Lighting: Mr Bob Wenman, Head of Street Care, Mercury House, Mercury Gardens, Romford RM1 3RX ☎ 01708 432898 ✉ bob.wenman@havering.gov.uk

Lottery Funding, Charity and Voluntary: Mrs Amanda Lewsey, Regeneration Funding Team Manager, Mercury House, Mercury Gardens, Romford RM1 3SL ☎ 01708 432932 ✉ amanda.lewsey@havering.gov.uk

Member Services: Mr Ian Buckmaster, Manager of Committee & Member Support, Havering Town Hall, Main Road, Romford RM1 3BD ☎ 01708 432431 ✉ ian.buckmaster@havering.gov.uk

Parking: Mr David Pritchard, Parking Services Manager, Mercury House, Mercury Gardens, Romford RM1 3SL ☎ 01708 433123 ✉ david.pritchard@havering.gov.uk

Personnel / HR: Ms Joanna Ruffle, Interim Head of People & Change, Central Library, St Edwards Way, Romford RM1 3AR ☎ 01702 215393; 01708 432181 ✉ joannaruffle@southend.gov.uk; joanna.ruffle@havering.gov.uk

Planning: Mr Patrick Keyes, Head of Development Building Control, 7th Floor Mercury House, Romford RM1 3SL ☎ 01708 432720 ✉ patrick.keyes@havering.gov.uk

Procurement: Mr John Scowen, Operational Procurement Team Leader, Central Library, St Edwards Way, Romford RM1 3AR ☎ 01708 433165 ✉ john.scowen@havering.gov.uk

Public Libraries: Ms Ann Rennie, Library Service Manager, Central Library, St Edwards Way, Romford RM1 3AR ☎ 01708 432374 ✉ ann.rennie@havering.gov.uk

Recycling & Waste Minimisation: Mr Paul Ellis, Waste & Recycling Manager, Mercury House, Mercury Gardens, Romford RM1 3SL ☎ 01708 432966 ✉ paul.ellis@havering.gov.uk

Regeneration: Mr Nigel Young, Regeneration Manager, Town Hall, Main Road, Romford RM1 3BD ☎ 01708 432543 ✉ nigel.young@havering.gov.uk

Road Safety: Mr Ray Crane, Road Safety Manager, Town Hall, Main Road, Romford RM1 3BD ☎ 01708 432808 ✉ ray.crane@havering.gov.uk

Social Services: Ms Lorna Payne, Group Director - Adults & Health, Town Hall, Main Road, Romford RM1 3BD ☎ 01708 433203 ✉ lorna.payne@havering.gov.uk

Social Services (Adult): Mr David Cooper, Head of Adult Social Services, 6th Floor Mercury House, Mercury Gardens, Romford RM1 3SL ☎ 01708 433069 ✉ david.cooper@havering.gov.uk

Social Services (Children): Ms Kathy Bundred, Head of Children & Young People's Services, Mercury House, Mercury Gardens, Romford RM1 3SL ☎ 01708 433002 ✉ kathy.bundred@havering.gov.uk

Staff Training: Mr Mark Porter, Operational HR Team Leader, Central Library, St Edwards Way, Romford RM1 3AR ☎ 01708 432989 ✉ mark.porter@havering.gov.uk

Street Scene: Mr Bob Wenman, Head of Street Care, Mercury House, Mercury Gardens, Romford RM1 3RX ☎ 01708 432898 ✉ bob.wenman@havering.gov.uk

Sustainable Development: Ms Sheri Lim, Sustainability Officer, Town Hall, Main Road, Romford RM1 3BD ☎ 01708 432590 ✉ sheri.lim@havering.gov.uk

Tourism: Mrs Amanda Lewsey, Regeneration Funding Team Manager, Town Hall, Main Road, Romford RM1 3BD ☎ 01708 432932 ✉ amanda.lewsey@havering.gov.uk

Town Centre: Mr Perry Brooker, Town Centres Officer, Town Hall, Main Road, Romford RM1 3BD ☎ 01708 432577 ✉ perry.brooker@havering.gov.uk

Traffic Management: Ms Emma Cockburn, Transportation Planning Team Leader, Town Hall, Main Road, Romford RM1 3BD ☎ 01708 432850 ✉ emma.cockburn@havering.gov.uk

Transport: Mr Norman Webb, Transport Operations Manager, Central Depot, Rainham Road, Hornchurch RM12 5BF ☎ 01708 434316 ✉ norman.webb@havering.gov.uk

Transport Planner: Ms Emma Cockburn, Transportation Planning Team Leader, Town Hall, Main Road, Romford RM1 3BD ☎ 01708 432850 ✉ emma.cockburn@havering.gov.uk

Waste Collection and Disposal: Mr Paul Ellis, Waste & Recycling Manager, Mercury House, Mercury Gardens, Romford RM1 3SL ☎ 01708 432966 ✉ paul.ellis@havering.gov.uk

Waste Management: Mr Paul Ellis, Waste & Recycling Manager, Mercury House, Mercury Gardens, Romford RM1 3SL ☎ 01708 432966 ✉ paul.ellis@havering.gov.uk

Waste Management: Mr Bob Wenman, Head of Street Care, Mercury House, Mercury Gardens, Romford RM1 3RX ☎ 01708 432898 ✉ bob.wenman@havering.gov.uk

Children's Play Areas: Mr Simon Parkinson, Head of Culture & Leisure Services, Stable Block, Langtons House, Billet Lane, Hornchurch RM11 1XJ ☎ 01708 432199 ✉ simon.parkinson@havering.gov.uk

MEMBERS OF THE COUNCIL (54)

***Mayor:* Thorpe**, Lynden (CON - Squirrel's Heath)
lynden.thorpe@havering.gov.uk
***Deputy Mayor:* Munday**, Eric (CON - Squirrel's Heath)
eric.munday@havering.gov.uk
***Leader of the Council:* White**, Michael (CON - Squirrel's Heath)
michael.white@havering.gov.uk
***Deputy Leader of the Council:* Kelly**, Steven (CON - Emerson Park)
steven.kelly@havering.gov.uk
***Group Leader:* Barrett**, Clarence (R - Cranham)
clarence.barrett@havering.gov.uk
***Group Leader:* Darvill**, Keith (LAB - Heaton)
keith.darvill@havering.gov.uk
***Group Leader:* Tucker**, Jeffrey (R - Rainham and Wennington)
jeffrey.tucker@havering.gov.uk
Alexander, June (R - Cranham)
june.alexander@havering.gov.uk
Armstrong, Michael (CON - Pettits)
michael.armstrong@havering.gov.uk
Benham, Robert (CON - Brooklands)
robert.benham@havering.gov.uk
Bennett, Rebecca (CON - South Hornchurch)
rebbecca.bennett@havering.gov.uk
Binion, Sandra (CON - Havering Park)
sandra.binion@havering.gov.uk
Brace, Jeffrey (CON - Elm Park)
jeffrey.brace@havering.gov.uk
Breading, Denis (LAB - South Hornchurch)
denis.breading@havering.gov.uk
Brice-Thompson, Wendy (CON - Romford Town)
wendy.bricethompson@havering.gov.uk
Bull, Dennis (CON - Gooshays)
dennis.bull@havering.gov.uk

Burton, Michael Deon (R - South Hornchurch)
michaeldeon.burton@havering.gov.uk
Curtin, Andrew (CON - Romford Town)
andrew.curtin@havering.gov.uk
Dervish, Osman (CON - Mawneys)
osman.deverish@havering.gov.uk
Dodin, Nic (R - Hacton)
nic.dodin@havering.gov.uk
Durant, David (R - Rainham and Wennington)
david.durant@havering.gov.uk
Eagling, Brian (R - Harold Wood)
brian.eagling@havering.gov.uk
Eden, Ted (CON - Pettits)
ted.eden@havering.gov.uk
Evans, Roger (CON - Elm Park)
roger.evans@havering.gov.uk
Ford, Gillian (R - Cranham)
gillian.ford@havering.gov.uk
Galpin, Georgina (CON - Hylands)
georgina.galpin@havering.gov.uk
Gardner, Peter (CON - Hylands)
peter.gardner@havering.gov.uk
Hawthorn, Linda (R - Upminster)
linda.hawthorn@havering.gov.uk
Kelly, Lesley (CON - Harold Wood)
lesley.kelly@havering.gov.uk
Light, Pam (CON - Harold Wood)
pam.light@havering.gov.uk
Logan, Mark (R - Rainham and Wennington)
mark.logan@havering.gov.uk
Matthews, Barbara (R - Hacton)
barbara.matthews@havering.gov.uk
McGeary, Paul (LAB - Heaton)
paul.mcgeary@havering.gov.uk
Misir, Robby (CON - Pettits)
robby.misir@havering.gov.uk
Morgon, Ray (R - Hacton)
raymond.morgan@havering.gov.uk
Murray, Patrick (LAB - Gooshays)
pat.murray@havering.gov.uk
Mylod, John (R - Saint Andrews)
john.mylod@havering.gov.uk
Oddy, Barry (CON - Elm Park)
barry.oddy@havering.gov.uk
O'Flynn, Denis (LAB - Heaton)
denis.oflynn@havering.gov.uk
Osborne, Fred (CON - Brooklands)
fred.osborne@havering.gov.uk
Ower, Ron (R - Upminster)
ron.ower@havering.gov.uk
Pain, Garry (CON - Saint Andrews)
garry.pain@havering.gov.uk
Ramsey, Roger (CON - Emerson Park)
roger.ramsey@havering.gov.uk
Rochford, Paul (CON - Emerson Park)
paul.rochford@havering.gov.uk
Starns, Geoffrey (CON - Havering Park)
geoffrey.starns@havering.gov.uk
Taylor, Billy (CON - Havering Park)
billy.taylor@havering.gov.uk
Tebbutt, Barry (CON - Brooklands)
barry.tebbutt@havering.gov.uk
Thompson, Frederick (CON - Romford Town)
frederick.thompson@havering.gov.uk
Trew, Linda (CON - Mawneys)
linda.trew@havering.gov.uk
Van den Hende, Linda (R - Upminster)
linda.vandenhende@havering.gov.uk
Wallace, Melvin (CON - Mawneys)
melvin.wallace@havering.gov.uk
Wells, Keith (CON - Gooshays)
keith.wells@havering.gov.uk
White, Damien (CON - Hylands)
damian.white@havering.gov.uk
Wood, John (R - Saint Andrews)
john.wood@havering.gov.uk

POLITICAL COMPOSITION

CON: 33, R: 16, LAB: 5

CABINET

Leader: Mr Michael White
Deputy Leader / Individuals: Mr Steven Kelly
Children & Learning: Mr Paul Rochford
Community Empowerment: Mr Robert Benham
Community Safety: Mr Geoffrey Starns
Culture, Town & Communities: Mr Andrew Curtin
Environment: Mr Barry Tebbutt
Housing: Ms Lesley Kelly
Transformation: Mr Michael Armstrong
Value: Mr Roger Ramsey

COMMITTEE CHAIRS

Audit: Ms Georgina Galpin
Children & Learning Overview & Scrutiny: Ms Sandra Binion
Crime & Disorder: Mr Osman Dervish
Environment Overview & Scrutiny: Mr Jeffrey Brace
Governance: Mr Frederick Thompson
Health Overview & Scrutiny: Ms Pam Light
Highways Advisory: Mr Garry Pain
Licensing: Mr Peter Gardner
Overview & Scrutiny: Mr Fred Osborne
Pensions: Mr Melvin Wallace
Regulatory Services: Mr Barry Oddy

HEREFORDSHIRE U

Herefordshire Council, Brockington, 35 Hafod Road, Hereford HR1 1ZT ☎ 01432 260000 🖷 01432 260286
info@herefordshire.gov.uk 💻 www.herefordshire.gov.uk

FACTS & FIGURES

Police Authority: West Mercia Police Authority
Health Authority: NHS West Midlands
Learning and Skills Council: West Midlands
Parliamentary Constituencies: Hereford and Herefordshire South, Herefordshire North
EU Constituencies: West Midlands
Election Frequency: Elections are by thirds

PRINCIPAL OFFICERS

Chief Executive: Mr Chris Bull, Chief Executive, Brockington, 35 Hafod Road, Hereford HR1 1ZT ☎ 01432 260044 🖷 01432 340189
cjbull@herefordshire.gov.uk

Deputy Chief Executive: Mr Dean Taylor, Deputy Chief Executive &Director of Corporate Services, Brockington, 35

Hafod Road, Hereford HR1 1ZT ☎ 01432 260037 🖷 01432 340189 ✉ dtaylor@herefordshire.gov.uk

Senior Management: Mr Geoff Hughes, Director - Places and Communities, Brockington, 35 Hafod Road, Hereford HR1 1ZT ☎ 01432 260695 🖷 01568 340189 ✉ ghughes@herefordshire.gov.uk

Catering Services: Ms Rhian Brown, Catering Manager, Brockington, 35 Hafod Road, Hereford HR1 1ZT ☎ 01432 260000 ✉ rbrown@herefordshire.gov.uk

Children / Youth Services: Ms Jo Davidson, Director - People's Services, Brockington, 35 Hafod Road, Hereford HR1 1ZT ☎ 01432 260039 🖷 01432 340189 ✉ jdavidson@herefordshire.gov.uk

PR / Communications: Mr Richard Beavan-Pearson, Customer Assistant Director, Brockington, 35 Hafod Road, Hereford HR1 1ZT ☎ 01432 383510 🖷 04132 260384 ✉ rbeavan-pearson@herefordshire.gov.uk

Community Safety: Mr Shane Hancock, Community Protection Manager, 14/15 Blackfriars Street, Hereford HR4 9HS ☎ 01432 261752 ✉ shancock@herefordshire.gov.uk

Consumer Protection and Trading Standards: Mr Mike Pigrem, Interim Head - Consumer & Business Protection, County Offices, Bath Street, Hereford HR1 2HQ ☎ 01432 261658 🖷 01432 261982 ✉ mpigrem@herefordshire.gov.uk

Corporate Services: Ms Kathy Roberts, Assistant Community Youth Worker, Brockington, 35 Hafod Road, Hereford HR1 1ZT ☎ 01432 260000 ✉ kroberts@hereforshire.gov.uk

Economic Development: Mr Andrew Ashcroft, Assistant Director - Economic, Environment & Cultural Services, Blue School House, Blue School Street, Hereford HR1 2ZB ☎ 01432 383098 ✉ aashcroft@herefordshire.gov.uk

Education: Ms Bridget Knight, Senior Primary Advisor, Blackfriars, Blackfriars Street, Hereford HR4 9ZR ☎ 01432 260000 🖷 01432 260958

Electoral Registration: Ms Colette Maund, Electoral Registration Service Manager, Town Hall, St Owens Street, Hereford HR1 2PJ ☎ 01432 260110 🖷 01432 260114 ✉ cmaund@herefordshire.gov.uk

Emergency Planning: Mr Nigel Thomas, Acting Emergency Planning Manager, Brockington, 35 Hafod House, Hereford HR1 1SH ☎ 01432 261719 🖷 01432 260206 ✉ nthomas@herefordshire.gov.uk

Environmental / Technical Services: Mr Chris Jenner, Environmental Services Manager, Blue School House, Blue School Street, Hereford HR1 2ZB ☎ 01432 261941 ✉ cjenner@herefordshire.gov.uk

Estates, Property & Valuation: Mr Tony Featherstone, Strategic Asset Manager, Plough Lane, PO BOX 236, Hereford H4 0WZ ☎ 01432 261980 ✉ afeatherstone@herefordshire.gov.uk

European Liaison: Ms Vinia Abesamis, Senior Policy & Funding Officer, Plough Lane, PO Box 4, Hereford HR4 0XH ☎ 01432 383031 🖷 01432 610677 ✉ vabesamis@herefordshire.gov.uk

Finance and Treasurer: Mr David Powell, Chief Officer- Finance & Commercial, Brockington, 35 Hafod House, Hereford HR1 1SH ☎ 01432 383519 ✉ dpowell@herefordshire.gov.uk

Finance and Treasurer: Mr Mike Toney, Head - Benefit & Exchequer Services, Plough Lane, 35 Hafod Road, Hereford HR4 0SH ☎ 01432 260000 ✉ mtoney@herefordshire.gov.uk

Highways: Mr Richard Ball, Assistant Director - Placed Based Commissioning, Plough Lane, PO Box 236, Hereford HR4 0WZ ☎ 01432 260965 🖷 01432 383031 ✉ rball@herefordshire.gov.uk

Housing: Mr Richard Gabb, Assistant Director - Homes & Community Services, Plough Lane, PO Box 4, Hereford HR4 0XH ☎ 01432 261902 ✉ rgabb@herefordshire.gov.uk

Legal: Mr Chris Chapman, Assistant Director - Law, Governance & Resilience, Brockington, 35 Hafod Road, Hereford HR1 1ZT ☎ 01432 260200 ✉ cchapman@herefordshire.gov.uk

Leisure and Cultural Services: Mr Tony Featherstone, Strategic Asset Manager, Plough Lane, PO Box 236, Hereford HR4 0WZ ☎ 01568 798321 🖷 01568 798526 ✉ afeatherstone@herefordshire.gov.uk

Lifelong Learning: Mr Peter Ding, Lifelong Learning Development Manager, Plough Lane, PO Box 4, Hereford HR1 1SH ☎ 01432 260637 🖷 01432 383031 ✉ pding@herefordshire.gov.uk

Member Services: Ms Sally Cole, Governance Services, 35 Haford Road, Hereford HR1 1SH ☎ 01432 260249 ✉ scole@herefordshire.gov.uk

Personnel / HR: Ms Suzanne Penny, Interim Director - Human Resources, Plough Lane, PO Box 4, Hereford HR4 0XH ☎ 01432 383820 ✉ suzanne.penny@herefordpct.nhs.uk

Procurement: Mr Wayne Welsby, Head - Commercial Services, Brockington, 35 Hafod Road, Hereford HR1 1ZT ☎ 01432 260000 ✉ wwelsby@herefordshire.gov.uk

Recycling & Waste Minimisation: Mrs Laura Blackwell, Recycling Officer, Plough Lane, PO Box 167, Hereford HR4 0WY ☎ 01432 260520 ✉ lblackwell@herefordshire.gov.uk

Regeneration: Mr Nick Webster, Economic Development Manager, Plough Lane, PO Box 4, Hereford HR4 0XH ☎ 01432 260601 ✉ nwebster@herefordshire.gov.uk

Road Safety: Mrs Ann Mann, Road Safety Officer, PO Box 236, Plough Lane, Hereford HR4 0WZ ☎ 01432 260947 🖷 01432 383031 ✉ amann@herefordshire.gov.uk

Social Services: Ms Jo Davidson, Director - People's Services, Brockington, 35 Hafod Road, Hereford HR1 1ZT ☎ 01432 260039 🖷 01432 340189 ✉ jdavidson@herefordshire.gov.uk

Staff Training: Ms Lucy Marder, Organisational Development Manager, Plough Lane, PO Box 265, Hereford HR4 0ZF
☎ 01432 383198 🖷 01432 260020
lmarder@herefordshire.gov.uk

Transport: Mr Richard Ball, Assistant Director - Placed Based Commissioning, Plough Lane, PO Box 236, Hereford HR4 0WZ
☎ 01432 260965 🖷 01432 383031 rball@herefordshire.gov.uk

Waste Management: Mr Richard Wood, Senior Contracts Manager - Waste Management, Plough Lane, PO Box 167, Hereford HR4 0WY ☎ 01432 260992 rnwood@hereford.gov.uk

MEMBERS OF THE COUNCIL (58)

***Chair:* Barnett**, Olwyn (CON - Mortimer)
obarnett@herefordshire.gov.uk
***Deputy Chair:* Chappell**, Chris (LAB - St. Martins and Hinton)
cchappell@herefordshire.gov.uk
***Leader of the Council:* Jarvis**, John (CON - Kerne Bridge)
jjarvis@herefordshire.gov.uk
***Deputy Leader of the Council:* Price**, Philip (CON - Golden Valley North)
pprice@herefordshire.gov.uk
***Group Leader:* Hubbard**, Mark (IND - Central)
mhubbard@herefordshire.gov.uk
***Group Leader:* James**, Terry (LD - Kington Town)
tjames@herefordshire.gov.uk
Andrews, Polly (LD - Three Elms)
paandrews@herefordshire.gov.uk
Atkinson, A (CON - Ross-on-Wye East)
aatkinson@herefordshire.gov.uk
Attwood, C (IND - Hope End)
cattwood1@herefordshire.gov.uk
Bartrum, Chris (LD - Ross-on-Wye West)
cbartrum@herefordshire.gov.uk
Bettington, P (CON - Ledbury)
pbettington@herefordshire.gov.uk
Blackshaw, Adrian (CON - Wormsley Ridge)
ablackshaw@herefordshire.gov.uk
Bowen, Sebastian (IND - Bircher)
sbowen@herefordshire.gov.uk
Bramer, Harry (CON - Penyard)
hbramer@herefordshire.gov.uk
Bridges, A (IND - Belmont)
abridges@herefordshire.gov.uk
Chave, E (IND - Three Elms)
lchave@herefordshire.gov.uk
Cooper, M (CON - Golden Cross with Weobley)
mcooper2@herefordshire.gov.uk
Cutter, Phil (CON - Ross-on-Wye East)
pcutter@herefordshire.gov.uk
Durkin, Barry (CON - Old Gore)
bdurkin@herefordshire.gov.uk
Edwards, Phil (IND - Belmont)
pjedwards@herefordshire.gov.uk
Greenow, Dave (CON - Hagley)
dgreenow@herefordshire.gov.uk
Guthrie, Kema (CON - Sutton Walls)
kguthrie@herefordshire.gov.uk
Hamilton, R (CON - Pontrilas)
russellbhamilton@herefordshire.gov.uk
Hardwick, J (IND - Backbury)
jhardwick1@herefordshire.gov.uk
Harvey, E (IND - Ledbury)
Hempton-Smith, A (IND - Tupsley)
ahempton-smith@herefordshire.gov.uk
Hope, John (CON - Castle)
jhope@herefordshire.gov.uk
Hunt, Roger (CON - Leominster South)
Hyde, Jenny (CON - Llangarron)
jhyde@herefordshire.gov.uk
Johnson, A (CON - Hope End)
ajohnson@herefordshire.gov.uk
Jones, Peter (CON - Leominster North)
pjones2@herefordshire.gov.uk
Kenyon, J (IND - Tupsley)
jkenyon@herefordshire.gov.uk
Knipe, J (IND - Valletts)
jknipe@herefordshire.gov.uk
Lester, J (CON - Bromyard)
jlester@herefordshire.gov.uk
Lloyd-Hayes, Marcelle (LD - Tupsley)
mlloyd-hayes@herefordshire.gov.uk
Lucas, Gordon (CON - Ross-on-Wye West)
glucas@herefordshire.gov.uk
Matthews, Bob (IND - Credenhill)
rmatthews@herefordshire.gov.uk
McCaull, P J (IND - Leominster South)
pmccaull@herefordshire.gov.uk
Michael, S (IND - St. Nicholas)
smichael@herefordshire.gov.uk
Millar, J (CON - Hampton Court)
jmillar2@herefordshire.gov.uk
Morgan, Patricia (CON - Frome)
pmorgan@herefordshire.gov.uk
Nenadich, N (CON - Aylestone)
nnenadich@herefordshire.gov.uk
Nicholls, C (IND - Three Elms)
cnicholls@herefordshire.gov.uk
Norman, F (GRN - Leominster North)
fnorman@herefordshire.gov.uk
Phillips, Roger (CON - Pembridge and Lyonshall with Titley)
rjphillips@herefordshire.gov.uk
Powell, G (CON - Golden Valley South)
gjpowell@herefordshire.gov.uk
Powell, Glenda (IND - Belmont)
gpowell@herefordshire.gov.uk
Preece, R (IND - St. Martins and Hinton)
rpreece@herefordshire.gov.uk
Robertson, Sally (IND - Burghill, Holmer and Lyde)
srobertson@herefordshire.gov.uk
Rone, P (CON - St. Martins and Hinton)
prone@herefordshire.gov.uk
Seldon, Alan (IND - Bromyard)
aseldon@herefordshire.gov.uk
Sinclair-Knipe, P (CON - Hollington)
Stone, John (CON - Upton)
jstone@herefordshire.gov.uk
Swinford, G (IND - Bringsty)
gswinford@herefordshire.gov.uk
Taylor, David (IND - Stoney Street)
dctaylor@herefordshire.gov.uk
Watts, Peter (CON - Ledbury)
pwatts@herefordshire.gov.uk
Wilcox, Brian (CON - Aylestone)
bwilcox@herefordshire.gov.uk
Woodward, Julie (IND - St. Nicholas)
jwoodward@herefordshire.gov.uk

POLITICAL COMPOSITION
CON: 30, IND: 22, LD: 4, GRN: 1, LAB: 1

CABINET
Leader: Mr John Jarvis
Deputy Leader / Corporate Services: Mr Philip Price
Education & Infrastructure: Mr G Powell
Enterprise & Culture: Mr Roger Phillips
Environment & Planning: Mr R Hamilton
Health & Wellbeing: Ms Patricia Morgan
Major Contracts: Mr Harry Bramer

COMMITTEE CHAIRS
Audit & Governance: Mr John Stone
Overview & Scrutiny: Mr Alan Seldon
Planning: Mr Phil Cutter
Regulatory: Mr John Hope

HERTFORDSHIRE C
Hertfordshire County Council, County Hall, Pegs Lane, Hertford SG13 8DE ☎ 01992 555555 🖷 01992 555644 firstname.lastname@hertscc.gov.uk www.hertsdirect.org

FACTS & FIGURES
Police Authority: Hertfordshire Police Authority
Health Authority: East of England Strategic Health Authority
Learning and Skills Council: Eastern
Parliamentary Constituencies: Hertfordshire South West
EU Constituencies: Eastern
Election Frequency: Elections are of whole council
Twinning: Rheinland-Pfalz (Germany)

PRINCIPAL OFFICERS
Chief Executive: Mr John Wood, Chief Executive & Director of Environment, County Hall, Pegs Lane, Hertford SG13 8DF ☎ 01992 555601 🖷 01992 555505 john.wood@hertscc.gov.uk

Senior Management: Ms Jenny Coles, Director - Children's Safeguarding & Specialist Services, County Hall, Pegs Lane, Hertford SG13 8DE ☎ 01992 555755 🖷 01992 555719 jenny.coles@hertscc.gov.uk

Senior Management: Mr Justin Donovan, Director - Education & Early Intervention, County Hall, Pegs Lane, Hertford SG13 8DE ☎ 01992 555764 🖷 01992 555719 justin.donovan@hertscc.gov.uk

Senior Management: Mr Mike Parsons, Director - Resources & Performance, County Hall, Pegs Lane, Hertford SG13 8DE ☎ 01992 555601 🖷 01992 555505 mike.parsons@hertscc.gov.uk

Senior Management: Mrs Sarah Pickup, Director - Health & Community Services, County Hall, Pegs Lane, Hertford SG13 8DE ☎ 01992 556300 🖷 01992 556323 sarah.pickup@hertscc.gov.uk

Senior Management: Mr Roy Wilsher, Director - Community Protection & Chief Fire Officer, Service HQ, Old London Road, Hertford SG13 7LD ☎ 01992 507501 🖷 01992 503048 roy.wilsher@hertscc.gov.uk

Best Value: Ms Rebecca Price, Head of Performance Improvement, County Hall, Pegs Lane, Hertford SG13 8DE ☎ 01992 588746 rebecca.price@hertscc.gov.uk

Building Control: Ms Angela Bucksey, Assistant Director - Property & Technology, County Hall, Pegs Lane, Hertford SG13 8DE ☎ 01992 556397 🖷 01992 556206 angela.bucksey@hertscc.gov.uk

Catering Services: Ms Lin O'Brien, Head of Catering, Hertfordshire Business Services, The Mundells, Welwyn Garden City, Hertford AL7 1FT ☎ 01707 293510 lin.obrien@hertscc.gov.uk

Children / Youth Services: Mr Andrew Simmons, Deputy Director Services for Young People, County Hall, Pegs Lane, Hertford SG13 8DE ☎ 01992 901510 🖷 01992 555719

Civil Registration: Mr Steve Charteris, Head of Statutory Services, The Old Courthouse, St Albans Road East, Hatfield AL10 0ES ☎ 01707 897375 🖷 01707 897399 steve.charteris@hertscc.gov.uk

PR / Communications: Ms Nuala Milbourn, Head of Communications, County Hall, Pegs Lane, Hertford SG13 8DE ☎ 01992 588535 🖷 01992 555647 nuala.milbourn@hertscc.gov.uk

Computer Management: Ms Angela Bucksey, Assistant Director - Property & Technology, County Hall, Pegs Lane, Hertford SG13 8DE ☎ 01992 556397 🖷 01992 556206 angela.bucksey@hertscc.gov.uk

Consumer Protection and Trading Standards: Mr Guy Pratt, Head of Trading Standards, 45 Grosvenor Road, St. Albans AL1 3AW ☎ 01727 813849 🖷 01727 813829 guy.pratt@hertscc.gov.uk

Contracts: Mr Peter Maguire, Head of Strategic Procurement, County Hall, Pegs Lane, Hertford SG13 8DE ☎ 01992 588830 peter.maguire@hertscc.gov.uk

Corporate Services: Mr Jonathan Fisher, Head of Placement & Provider Services, County Hall, Pegs Lane, Hertford SG13 8DE ☎ 01992 556337 jonathan.fisher@hertscc.gov.uk

Customer Service: Mr Michael Franci, Customer Service Centre Manager, Customer Service Centre Manager, Kings Court, London Road, Stevenage SG1 2TP ☎ 01992 555603 michael.franci@hertscc.gov.uk

Economic Development: Ms Jan Hayes-Griffin, Assistant Director - Strategy & Communications, County Hall, Pegs Lane, Hertford SG13 8DE ☎ 01992 555203 🖷 01992 556169 jan.hayes-griffin@hertscc.gov.uk

Education: Ms Gillian Cawley, Head of Standards & School Effectiveness, County Hall, Pegs Lane, Hertford SG13 8DE ☎ 01483 844818 gillian.cawley@hertscc.gov.uk

Education: Mr Justin Donovan, Director - Education & Early Intervention, County Hall, Pegs Lane, Hertford SG13 8DE

☎ 01992 555764 🖷 01992 555719
✆ justin.donovan@hertscc.gov.uk

E-Government: Mr Michael Franci, Customer Service Centre Manager, Customer Service Centre Manager, Kings Court, London Road, Stevenage SG1 2TP ☎ 01992 555603
✆ michael.franci@hertscc.gov.uk

Electoral Registration: Mr David Roberts, Head of Democratic Services, County Hall, Pegs Lane, Hertford SG13 8DE ☎ 01992 555562 🖷 01992 555518 ✆ david.roberts@hertscc.gov.uk

Emergency Planning: Mr John Boulter, Head of Safety Emergency & Risk Management Unit, County Hall, Pegs Lane, Hertford SG13 8DE ☎ 01992 555951
✆ john.boulter@hertscc.gov.uk

Estates, Property & Valuation: Mr Simon Aries, Head of Access Heritage & Estates, County Hall, Pegs Lane, Hertford SG13 8DE ☎ 01992 555255 ✆ simon.aries@hertscc.gov.uk

Estates, Property & Valuation: Ms Angela Bucksey, Assistant Director - Property & Technology, County Hall, Pegs Lane, Hertford SG13 8DE ☎ 01992 556397 🖷 01992 556206
✆ angela.bucksey@hertscc.gov.uk

Facilities: Mr Chris Hinge, Head of Facilities & Operations, County Hall, Pegs Lane, Hertford SG13 8DE ☎ 01992 556282 🖷 01992 588717 ✆ chris.hinge@hertscc.gov.uk

Finance and Treasurer: Mr Mike Parsons, Director - Resources & Performance, County Hall, Pegs Lane, Hertford SG13 8DE ☎ 01992 555601 🖷 01992 555505
✆ mike.parsons@hertscc.gov.uk

Fleet Management: Mr Alan Smith, Head of Contract Management Services, Fleet Services, Unit 2 Mallow Park, Watchmead, Welwyn Garden City AL7 1LT ☎ 01707 343620
✆ alan.smith@hertscc.gov.uk

Health and Safety: Mr James Ottery, Hertfordshire Property Health & Safety Manager, County Hall, Pegs Lane, Hertford SG13 8DE ☎ 01992 556677 🖷 01992 555962
✆ james.ottery@hertscc.gov.uk

Highways: Mr Rob Smith, Assistant Director (Transport Management), County Hall, Pegs Lane, Hertford SG13 8DE ☎ 01992 556121 🖷 01992 556106 ✆ rob.smith@hertscc.gov.uk

Legal: Ms Kathryn Pettitt, Chief Legal Officer, County Hall, Pegs Lane, Hertford SG13 8DE ☎ 01992 555527
✆ kathryn.pettitt@hertscc.gov.uk

Leisure and Cultural Services: Mr Simon Aries, Head of Access Heritage & Estates, County Hall, Pegs Lane, Hertford SG13 8DE ☎ 01992 555255 ✆ simon.aries@hertscc.gov.uk

Lifelong Learning: Mr Andrew Bignell, Head of Information Services & Lifelong Learning, New Barnfield, Travellers Lane, Hatfield AL10 8XG ☎ 01707 281531 🖷 01707 281589
✆ andrew.bignell@hertscc.gov.uk

Lighting: Mr Dave Jackson, Strategy Development Manager (Lighting & Signals), Highways House, Broadwater Road, Welwyn Garden City, Hertford AL7 3AY ☎ 01707 356572 🖷 01707 356550 ✆ dave.jackson@hertshighways.org.uk

Member Services: Mr David Roberts, Head of Democratic Services, County Hall, Pegs Lane, Hertford SG13 8DE ☎ 01992 555562 🖷 01992 555518 ✆ david.roberts@hertscc.gov.uk

Partnerships: Ms Jan Hayes-Griffin, Assistant Director - Strategy & Communications, County Hall, Pegs Lane, Hertford SG13 8DE ☎ 01992 555203 🖷 01992 556169 ✆ jan.hayes-griffin@hertscc.gov.uk

Personnel / HR: Ms Louise Tibbert, Head of Human Resources & Organisational Development, County Hall, Pegs Lane, Hertford SG13 8DE ☎ 01992 556653 ✆ louise.tibbert@hertscc.gov.uk

Planning: Mr Richard Brown, Assistant Director - Strategic Planning & Environmental Management, County Hall, Pegs Lane, Hertford SG13 8DE ☎ 01992 555250 🖷 01992 555202
✆ richard.brown@hertscc.gov.uk

Procurement: Mr Peter Maguire, Head of Strategic Procurement, County Hall, Pegs Lane, Hertford SG13 8DE ☎ 01992 588830
✆ peter.maguire@hertscc.gov.uk

Public Libraries: Mr Taryn Pearson, Assistant Director - Customer Services & Libraries, County Hall, Pegs Lane, Hertford SG13 8DE ☎ 01707 281559 ✆ taryn.pearson@hertscc.gov.uk

Recycling & Waste Minimisation: Mr Matt King, Head of Waste Management, County Hall, Pegs Lane, Hertford SG13 8DE ☎ 01992 556160 🖷 01992 556180 ✆ matt.king@hertscc.gov.uk

Regeneration: Mr Jon Tiley, Head of Forward Planning, County Hall, Pegs Lane, Hertford SG13 8DE ☎ 01992 556292 🖷 01992 556290 ✆ jonathan.tiley@hertscc.gov.uk

Road Safety: Mr Trevor Mason, Head of Safe & Sustainable Journeys Team, County Hall, Pegs Lane, Hertford SG13 8DE ☎ 01992 556804 🖷 01992 556820
✆ trevor.mason@hertscc.gov.uk

Social Services: Mrs Sarah Pickup, Director - Health & Community Services, County Hall, Pegs Lane, Hertford SG13 8DE ☎ 01992 556300 🖷 01992 556323
✆ sarah.pickup@hertscc.gov.uk

Social Services: Ms Ann Ricketts, Head of Multi Agency & Psychology Service, County Hall, Pegs Lane, Hertford SG13 8DE ☎ 01992 555700 ✆ ann.ricketts@hertscc.gov.uk

Social Services (Adult): Mr Earl Dutton, Assistant Director - Older People & Physically Disabled People, County Hall, Pegs Lane, Hertford SG13 8DE ☎ 01992 556301 🖷 01992 556323
✆ earl.dutton@hertscc.gov.uk

Social Services (Adult): Ms Jess Lievesley, Assistant Director - Community Commissioning, County Hall, Pegs Lane, Hertford SG13 8DE ☎ 01992 556350 🖷 01992 556323
✆ jess.lievesley@hertscc.gov.uk

Social Services (Children): Ms Jenny Coles, Director - Children's Safeguarding & Specialist Services, County Hall, Pegs Lane, Hertford SG13 8DE ☎ 01992 555755 🖷 01992 555719 ✉ jenny.coles@hertscc.gov.uk

Staff Training: Ms Samantha Holliday, Head of HR Learning & Organisational Development, Herts HR Learning & Organisational Development, Farnham House, Six Hills Way, Stevenage SG1 2FQ ☎ 01438 845105 ✉ samantha.holliday@hertscc.gov.uk

Sustainable Communities: Mr John Rumble, Team Leader - Sustainability, County Hall, Pegs Lane, Hertford SG13 8DE ☎ 01992 556296 🖷 01992 556290 ✉ john.rumble@hertscc.gov.uk

Sustainable Development: Mr Jon Tiley, Head of Forward Planning, County Hall, Pegs Lane, Hertford SG13 8DE ☎ 01992 556292 🖷 01992 556290 ✉ jonathan.tiley@hertscc.gov.uk

Tourism: Ms Annie Hawkins, County Tourism Manager, County Hall, Pegs Lane, Hertford SG13 8DE ☎ 01992 556231 ✉ annie.hawkins@hertscc.gov.uk

Transport: Mr Rob Smith, Assistant Director (Transport Management), County Hall, Pegs Lane, Hertford SG13 8DE ☎ 01992 556121 🖷 01992 556106 ✉ rob.smith@hertscc.gov.uk

Transport Planner: Ms Glenda Hardy, Head of Admissions & Transport, County Hall, Pegs Lane, Hertford SG13 8DE ☎ 01438 737500 ✉ glenda.hardy@hertscc.gov.uk

Transport Planner: Mr John Sykes, Head of Transportation Planning & Policy, County Hall, Pegs Lane, Hertford SG13 8DE ☎ 01992 556112 🖷 01992 556106 ✉ john.sykes@hertscc.gov.uk

Waste Management: Mr Matt King, Head of Waste Management, County Hall, Pegs Lane, Hertford SG13 8DE ☎ 01992 556160 🖷 01992 556180 ✉ matt.king@hertscc.gov.uk

MEMBERS OF THE COUNCIL (77)

Chair: **Pitman**, Jane (CON - Braughing)
jane.pitman@hertscc.gov.uk

Leader of the Council: **Gordon**, Robert (CON - Goffs Oak and Bury Green)
robert.gordon@hertscc.gov.uk

Deputy Leader of the Council: **Lloyd**, David (CON - Bridgewater)
david.lloyd@hertscc.gov.uk

Group Leader: **Taylor**, Sharon (LAB - Bedwell)
sharon.taylor@stevenage.gov.uk

Andrews, David (CON - Ware North)
david.andrews@hertscc.gov.uk

Ashley, Derrick (CON - Hitchin South)
derrick.ashley@hertscc.gov.uk

Barfoot, John (CON - Bishop's Stortford East)
john.barfoot@hertscc.gov.uk

Beeching, Roger (CON - Sawbridgeworth)
roger.beeching@hertscc.gov.uk

Bell, Nigel (LAB - Vicarage Holywell)
nigel.bell@hertscc.gov.uk

Berry, Clare (CON - Hatfield North)
clare.berry@hertscc.gov.uk

Bibby, Philip (CON - St Nicholas)
philip.bibby@hertscc.gov.uk

Brandon, Ian (GRN - Callowland Leggatts)
ian.brandon@hertscc.gov.uk

Brazier, Chris (LD - The Colneys)
chris.brazier@hertscc.gov.uk

Bright, Morris (CON - Borehamwood South)
morris.bright@hertscc.gov.uk

Brook, Nigel (CON - Hitchin Rural)
nigel.brook@hertscc.gov.uk

Button, Frances (CON - Oxhey Park)
frances.button@hertscc.gov.uk

Cheswright, Rosemary (CON - Ware South)
rose.cheswright@hertscc.gov.uk

Churchard, Geoff (LD - Sandridge)
geoff.churchard@hertscc.gov.uk

Clapper, Caroline (CON - Watling)
caroline.clapper@hertscc.gov.uk

Cowan, Malcolm (LD - Handside and Peartree)
malcolm.cowan@hertscc.gov.uk

Crawley, Maxine (CON - St Albans Rural)
maxine.crawley@hertscc.gov.uk

Douris, Terry (CON - Hemel Hempstead North West)
terry.douris@hertscc.gov.uk

Drury, Steve (LD - Croxley)
david.drury@hertscc.gov.uk

Emsall, Keith (CON - Letchworth South)
keith.emsall@hertscc.gov.uk

Eynon, Wilf (CON - Hoddesdon North)
wilf.eynon@hertscc.gov.uk

Fraser, James (CON - Old Stevenage)
james.fraser@hertscc.gov.uk

Frearson, Martin (LD - St Albans South)
martin.frearson@hertscc.gov.uk

Gates, Deirdre (BNP - South Oxhey)
deirdre.gates@hertscc.gov.uk

Giles-Medhurst, Stephen (LD - Central Oxhey)
sgm@cix.co.uk

Goggins, Paul (LD - Abbots Langley)
paul.goggins@hertscc.gov.uk

Hammond, Bryan (CON - Hertford Rural)
bryan.hammond@hertscc.gov.uk

Hart, Dee (CON - Waltham Cross)
dee.hart@hertscc.gov.uk

Hastrick, Kareen (LD - Meriden Tudor)

Hayward, Chris (CON - Chorleywood)
christopher.hayward@hertscc.gov.uk

Heritage, Teresa (CON - Harpenden South West)
teresa.heritage@hertscc.gov.uk

Hewitt, David (CON - Cheshunt Central)
david.hewitt@hertscc.gov.uk

Hill, Fiona (CON - Royston)
fiona.hill@hertscc.gov.uk

Hollinghurst, Nicholas (LD - Tring)
nicholas.hollinghurst@hertscc.gov.uk

Hone, Terry (CON - Letchworth North West)
terry.hone@hertscc.gov.uk

Hunter, Tony (CON - North Herts Rural)
tony.hunter@hertscc.gov.uk

Hurst, Matthew (CON - Broadwater)
matthew.hurst@hertscc.gov.uk

Johnston, Sara (CON - Haldens)
sara.johnston@hertscc.gov.uk

Lamb, Barbara (CON - Rickmansworth)
barbara.lamb@hertscc.gov.uk

Lee, Aislinn (LD - St Stephen's)
aislinn.lee@hertscc.gov.uk

Lloyd, Bernard (CON - Harpenden North East)
bernard.lloyd@hertscc.gov.uk
Lloyd, John (LAB - Shephall)
john.lloyd@hertscc.gov.uk
Maddern, Jan (CON - Hemel Hempstead South East)
jan.maddern@hertscc.gov.uk
Markiewicz, Steven (CON - Welwyn Garden City South)
steven.markiewicz@hertscc.gov.uk
Mitchell, Chris (CON - Flamstead End and Turnford)
chris.mitchell@hertscc.gov.uk
Muir, Michael (CON - Letchworth East and Baldock)
michael.muir@hertscc.gov.uk
Newlyn, Leanda (CON - Bishop's Stortford Rural)
leanda.newlyn@hertscc.gov.uk
Newton, Sally (CON - All Saints)
sally.newton@hertscc.gov.uk
O'Brien, Steve (CON - Bushey North)
steve.obrien@hertscc.gov.uk
Parker, Robin (LD - Chells)
robin.parker@hertscc.gov.uk
Pile, Stuart (CON - Hatfield South)
stuart.pile@hertscc.gov.uk
Plancey, Alan (CON - Borehamwood North)
alan.plancey@hertscc.gov.uk
Prowse, Robert (LD - St Albans East)
robert.prowse@hertscc.gov.uk
Quilty, Seamus (CON - Bushey South)
seamus.quilty@hertscc.gov.uk
Reay, Ian (CON - Berkhamsted)
ian.reay@hertscc.gov.uk
Roach, Edwin (CON - Potters Bar East)
edwin.roach@hertscc.gov.uk
Roberts, Richard (CON - Kings Langley)
richard.roberts@hertscc.gov.uk
Ruffles, Peter (CON - St Andrews)
peter.ruffles@hertscc.gov.uk
Scudder, Derek (LD - Woodside Stanborough)
derek.scudder@hertscc.gov.uk
Searing, Alan (CON - Hoddesdon South)
alan.searing@hertscc.gov.uk
Shakespeare-Smith, Ray (CON - Hitchin North)
ray.shakespearesmith@hertscc.gov.uk
Smith, Richard (CON - Welwyn)
richard.smith@hertscc.gov.uk
Storey, Bill (CON - Hatfield Rural)
bill.storey@hertscc.gov.uk
Thake, Richard (CON - Knebworth and Codicote)
richard.thake@hertscc.gov.uk
Tindell, Ron (LD - Hemel Hempstead St Pauls)
ron.tindall@hertscc.gov.uk
Usher, John (CON - Potters Bar West and Shenley)
john.usher@hertscc.gov.uk
Watkin, Mark (LD - Nascot Park)
mark.watkin@hertscc.gov.uk
White, Chris (LD - St Albans Central)
chriswhite@cix.co.uk
Williams, Andrew (CON - Hemel Hempstead East)
andrew.williams@hertscc.gov.uk
Witherick, Alan (LD - St Albans North)
alan.witherick@hertscc.gov.uk
Woodward, Colin (CON - Bishop's Stortford West)
colin.woodward@hertscc.gov.uk
Wyatt-Lowe, Colette (CON - Hemel Hempstead North)
colette.wyatt-lowe@hertscc.gov.uk
Wyatt-Lowe, William (CON - Hemel Hempstead Town)

POLITICAL COMPOSITION
CON: 55, LD: 17, LAB: 3, GRN: 1, BNP: 1

CABINET
Leader: Mr Robert Gordon
Deputy Leader / Resources and Economic Wellbeing: Mr David Lloyd
Children's Services: Mr Richard Roberts
Education and Skills: Mr Frances Button
Environment and Community Safety: Mr Richard Thake
Health and Adult Care: Ms Colette Wyatt-Lowe
Highways and Transport: Mr Stuart Pile
Resources & Economic Wellbeing: Mr David Lloyd
Transformation, Performance and Waste Management: Mr Derrick Ashley

COMMITTEE CHAIRS
Audit: Mr Seamus Quilty
Development Control: Mr Richard Smith
Health: Ms Sally Newton
Overview & Scrutiny (Scrutiny): Mr Alan Searing

HERTSMERE — D

Hertsmere Borough Council, Civic Offices, Elstree Way, Borehamwood WD6 1WA ☎ 020 8207 2277 🖷 020 8207 7441 ✉ customer.services@hertsmere.gov.uk 💻 www.hertsmere.gov.uk

FACTS & FIGURES
Police Authority: Hertfordshire Police Authority
Health Authority: East of England Strategic Health Authority
Learning and Skills Council: Eastern
Parliamentary Constituencies: Hertsmere
EU Constituencies: Eastern
Election Frequency: Elections are by thirds
Twinning: Elstree, Borehamwood: Offenburg (Germany); Fontenay aux Roses (France); Potters Bar: Franconville (France); Viernheim (Germany); Radlett and Aldenham: Lautertal (Germany); Louveciennes (France); Bushey (educational and cultural agreement): Landsberg-am-Lech (Germany)

PRINCIPAL OFFICERS
Chief Executive: Mr Donald Graham, Chief Executive, Civic Offices, Elstree Way, Borehamwood WD6 1WA ☎ 020 8207 2277 🖷 020 8207 7441 ✉ donald.graham@hertsmere.gov.uk

Senior Management: Ms Sajida Bijle, Director of Resources, Civic Offices, Elstree Way, Borehamwood WD6 1WA ☎ 020 8207 2277 🖷 020 8207 7487 ✉ sajida.bijle@hertsmere.gov.uk

Senior Management: Mr Glen Wooldrige, Director of Environment, Civic Offices, Elstree Way, Borehamwood WD6 1WA ☎ 020 8207 2277 ✉ environment@hertsmere.gov.uk

Architect, Building / Property Services: Mr Richard Stubbs, Asset Manager, Civic Offices, Elstree Way, Borehamwood WD6 1WA ☎ 020 8207 2277 🖷 020 8207 7441

Building Control: Mrs Polly Harris-Gorf, Head of Planning & Building Control, Civic Offices, Elstree Way, Borehamwood WD6 1WA ☎ 020 8207 2277

PR / Communications: Ms Catherine Feast, Corporate Communications Manager, Civic Offices, Elstree Way, Borehamwood WD6 1WA ☎ 020 8207 2277 🖷 020 8207 7441 corporate.communications@hertsmere.gov.uk

Community Safety: Ms Valerie Kane, Community Safety Officer, Civic Offices, Elstree Way, Borehamwood WD6 1WA ☎ 020 8207 7462 🖷 020 8207 7478 community.services@hertsmere.gov.uk

Computer Management: Ms Sajida Bijle, Director of Resources, Civic Offices, Elstree Way, Borehamwood WD6 1WA ☎ 020 8207 2277 🖷 020 8207 7487 sajida.bijle@hertsmere.gov.uk

Computer Management: Mr Tom Jackson, Knowledge Manager, Hertsmere Borough Council, Borehamwood WD6 1WA ☎ 020 8207 2277 tom.jackson@hertsmere.gov.uk

Contracts: Mr Andrew Harper, Procurement Manager, Civic Offices, Elstree Way, Borehamwood WD6 1WA ☎ 020 8207 2277; 01707 357371 🖷 020 8207 7441 accountancy.finance@hertsmere.gov.uk; a.harper@welhat.gov.uk

Corporate Services: Ms Hilary Shade, Head of Corporate Support & Community Services, Civic Offices, Elstree Way, Borehamwood WD6 1WA ☎ 020 8207 7519 🖷 020 8207 7499 corporate.support@hertsmere.gov.uk

Customer Service: Ms Judith Fear, Head of HR & Customer Services, Civic Offices, Elstree Way, Borehamwood WD6 1WA ☎ 020 8207 7475 🖷 020 8207 7550 human.resources@hertsmere.gov.uk

Customer Service: Mr Lee Gallagher, Customer Service Operation Manager, Civic Offices, Elstree Way, Borehamwood WD6 1WA ☎ 020 8207 2277 🖷 020 8207 7424 customer.services@hertsmere.gov.uk

Economic Development: Mr Glen Wooldrige, Director of Environment, Civic Offices, Elstree Way, Borehamwood WD6 1WA ☎ 020 8207 2277 environment@hertsmere.gov.uk

Electoral Registration: Ms Jo Bateman, Electoral Services Manager, Civic Offices, Elstree Way, Borehamwood WD6 1WA ☎ 020 8207 7481 🖷 020 8207 7555 jo.bateman@hertsmere.gov.uk

Emergency Planning: Mr Chris Gascoigne, Chief Environmental Health Officer, Civic Offices, Elstree Way, Borehamwood WD6 1WA ☎ 020 8207 7433 🖷 020 8207 7441 environmental.health@hertsmere.gov.uk

Emergency Planning: Mr Glen Wooldrige, Director of Environment, Civic Offices, Elstree Way, Borehamwood WD6 1WA ☎ 020 8207 2277 environment@hertsmere.gov.uk

Environmental / Technical Services: Mr Simon Payton, Head of Engineering, Civic Offices, Elstree Way, Borehamwood WD6 1WA ☎ 020 8207 2277 🖷 020 8207 7441 engineering.services@hertsmere.gov.uk

Environmental Health: Mr Chris Gascoigne, Chief Environmental Health Officer, Civic Offices, Elstree Way, Borehamwood WD6 1WA ☎ 020 8207 7433 🖷 020 8207 7441 environmental.health@hertsmere.gov.uk

Environmental Health: Mr Glen Wooldrige, Director of Environment, Civic Offices, Elstree Way, Borehamwood WD6 1WA ☎ 020 8207 2277 environment@hertsmere.gov.uk

Estates, Property & Valuation: Mr Rob Ambler, Estates Valuer, Civic Offices, Elstree Way, Borehamwood WD6 1WA ☎ 020 8207 7486 🖷 020 8207 7499 estate.maintenance@hertsmere.gov.uk

Finance and Treasurer: Ms Sajida Bijle, Director of Resources, Civic Offices, Elstree Way, Borehamwood WD6 1WA ☎ 020 8207 2277 🖷 020 8207 7487 sajida.bijle@hertsmere.gov.uk

Finance and Treasurer: Mr D Gopal, Head of Finance, Revenues, Benefits & IS, Civic Offices, Elstree Way, Borehamwood WD6 1WA ☎ 020 8207 2277

Fleet Management: Mr Steve Burton, Head of Waste & Street Scene, Civic Offices, Elstree Way, Borehamwood WD6 1WA ☎ 020 8207 2277 waste.management@hertsmere.gov.uk

Grounds Maintenance: Mr Steve Burton, Head of Waste & Street Scene, Civic Offices, Elstree Way, Borehamwood WD6 1WA ☎ 020 8207 2277 waste.management@hertsmere.gov.uk

Health and Safety: Mr Geoff Schooling, Health & Safety Manager, Civic Offices, Elstree Way, Borehamwood WD6 1WA ☎ 020 8207 2277 geoff.schooling@hertsmere.gov.uk

Housing: Mr Glen Wooldrige, Director of Environment, Civic Offices, Elstree Way, Borehamwood WD6 1WA ☎ 020 8207 2277 environment@hertsmere.gov.uk

Legal: Ms Sajida Bijle, Director of Resources, Civic Offices, Elstree Way, Borehamwood WD6 1WA ☎ 020 8207 2277 🖷 020 8207 7487 sajida.bijle@hertsmere.gov.uk

Licensing: Ms Sue Hardy, Principal Licensing Officer, Civic Offices, Elstree Way, Borehamwood WD6 1WA ☎ 020 8207 7441 🖷 020 8207 7436 licensing.services@hertsmere.gov.uk

Licensing: Mr Glen Wooldrige, Director of Environment, Civic Offices, Elstree Way, Borehamwood WD6 1WA ☎ 020 8207 2277 environment@hertsmere.gov.uk

Member Services: Ms Sajida Bijle, Director of Resources, Civic Offices, Elstree Way, Borehamwood WD6 1WA ☎ 020 8207 2277 🖷 020 8207 7487 sajida.bijle@hertsmere.gov.uk

Parking: Mrs Clare Fensome, Parking Operations Manager, Civic Offices, Elstree Way, Borehamwood WD6 1WA ☎ 020 7208 2277 cpz.department@hertsmere.gov.uk

Parking: Mr Glen Wooldrige, Director of Environment, Civic Offices, Elstree Way, Borehamwood WD6 1WA ☎ 020 8207 2277 environment@hertsmere.gov.uk

Partnerships: Ms Hilary Shade, Head of Corporate Support & Community Services, Civic Offices, Elstree Way, Borehamwood

WD6 1WA ☏ 020 8207 7519 🖷 020 8207 7499
corporate.support@hertsmere.gov.uk

Personnel / HR: Ms Sajida Bijle, Director of Resources, Civic Offices, Elstree Way, Borehamwood WD6 1WA ☏ 020 8207 2277 🖷 020 8207 7487 sajida.bijle@hertsmere.gov.uk

Personnel / HR: Ms Judith Fear, Head of HR & Customer Services, Civic Offices, Elstree Way, Borehamwood WD6 1WA ☏ 020 8207 7475 🖷 020 8207 7550
human.resources@hertsmere.gov.uk

Planning: Mr Glen Wooldrige, Director of Environment, Civic Offices, Elstree Way, Borehamwood WD6 1WA ☏ 020 8207 2277
environment@hertsmere.gov.uk

Procurement: Mr Andrew Harper, Procurement Manager, Civic Offices, Elstree Way, Borehamwood WD6 1WA ☏ 020 8207 2277; 01707 357371 🖷 020 8207 7441
accountancy.finance@hertsmere.gov.uk; a.harper@welhat.gov.uk

Recycling & Waste Minimisation: Mr Steve Burton, Head of Waste & Street Scene, Civic Offices, Elstree Way, Borehamwood WD6 1WA ☏ 020 8207 2277
waste.management@hertsmere.gov.uk

Recycling & Waste Minimisation: Mr Glen Wooldrige, Director of Environment, Civic Offices, Elstree Way, Borehamwood WD6 1WA ☏ 020 8207 2277 environment@hertsmere.gov.uk

Staff Training: Ms Judith Fear, Head of HR & Customer Services, Civic Offices, Elstree Way, Borehamwood WD6 1WA ☏ 020 8207 7475 🖷 020 8207 7550
human.resources@hertsmere.gov.uk

Street Scene: Mr Steve Burton, Head of Waste & Street Scene, Civic Offices, Elstree Way, Borehamwood WD6 1WA
☏ 020 8207 2277 waste.management@hertsmere.gov.uk

Street Scene: Mr Glen Wooldrige, Director of Environment, Civic Offices, Elstree Way, Borehamwood WD6 1WA ☏ 020 8207 2277
environment@hertsmere.gov.uk

Sustainable Communities: Mr Chris Gascoigne, Chief Environmental Health Officer, Civic Offices, Elstree Way, Borehamwood WD6 1WA ☏ 020 8207 7433 🖷 020 8207 7441
environmental.health@hertsmere.gov.uk

Sustainable Development: Mrs Polly Harris-Gorf, Head of Planning & Building Control, Civic Offices, Elstree Way, Borehamwood WD6 1WA ☏ 020 8207 2277

Tourism: Mr Lee Gallagher, Customer Service Operation Manager, Civic Offices, Elstree Way, Borehamwood WD6 1WA ☏ 020 8207 2277 🖷 020 8207 7424
customer.services@hertsmere.gov.uk

Waste Collection and Disposal: Mr Steve Burton, Head of Waste & Street Scene, Civic Offices, Elstree Way, Borehamwood WD6 1WA ☏ 020 8207 2277
waste.management@hertsmere.gov.uk

Waste Collection and Disposal: Mr Glen Wooldrige, Director of Environment, Civic Offices, Elstree Way, Borehamwood WD6 1WA ☏ 020 8207 2277 environment@hertsmere.gov.uk

Waste Management: Mr Steve Burton, Head of Waste & Street Scene, Civic Offices, Elstree Way, Borehamwood WD6 1WA ☏ 020 8207 2277 waste.management@hertsmere.gov.uk

MEMBERS OF THE COUNCIL (39)

***Mayor:* Strack**, Pat (CON - Borehamwood Kenilworth)
cllr.pat.strack@hertsmere.gov.uk
***Deputy Mayor:* Griffin**, Dan (CON - Aldenham West)
cllr.dan.griffin@hertsmere.gov.uk
***Leader of the Council:* Bright**, Morris (CON - Elstree)
cllr.morris.bright@hertsmere.gov.uk
***Group Leader:* Harrison**, Ann (LAB - Borehamwood Cowley Hill)
cllr.ann.harrison@hertsmere.gov.uk
Batten, Brenda (CON - Bushey Heath)
cllr.brenda.batten@hertsmere.gov.uk
Butler, Richard (LAB - Borehamwood Kenilworth)
cllr.richard.butler@hertsmere.gov.uk
Butler, Ernie (LAB - Borehamwood Cowley Hill)
cllr.ernie.butler@hertsmere.gov.uk
Calcutt, Robert (CON - Potters Bar Oakmere)
cllr.bob.calcutt@hertsmere.gov.uk
Choudhury, Pervez (CON - Bushey St James)
cllr.pervez.choudhury@hertsmere.gov.uk
Clapper, Caroline (CON - Aldenham West)
cllr.caroline.clapper@hertsmere.gov.uk
Cohen, Harvey (CON - Borehamwood Brookmeadow)
cllr.harvey.cohen@hertsmere.gov.uk
Collins, David (CON - Bushey Park)
cllr.david.collins@hertsmere.gov.uk
David, Hannah (CON - Borehamwood Hillside)
cllr.hannah.david@hertsmere.gov.uk
Dobin, Sam (CON - Borehamwood Brookmeadow)
cllr.sam.dobin@hertsmere.gov.uk
Donne, John (CON - Potters Bar Parkfield)
cllr.john.donne@hertsmere.gov.uk
Gilligan, Rosemary (CON - Shenley)
cllr.rosemary.gilligan@hertsmere.gov.uk
Goldstein, Charles (CON - Aldenham East)
cllr.charles.goldstein@hertsmere.gov.uk
Graham, John (CON - Aldenham East)
cllr.john.graham@hertsmere.gov.uk
Gunasekera, Derrick (CON - Elstree)
cllr.derek.gunasekera@hertsmere.gov.uk
Heywood, Jean (CON - Borehamwood Hillside)
cllr.jean.heywood@hertsmere.gov.uk
Hodgson-Jones, Sarah (CON - Potters Bar Parkfield)
cllr.sarah.hosgson-jones@hertsmere.gov.uk
Hodgson-Jones, Paul (CON - Potters Bar Parkfield)
cllr.paul.hodgson-jones@hertsmere.gov.uk
Hoeksma, Di (LAB - Borehamwood Cowley Hill)
cllr.di.hoeksma@hertsmere.gov.uk
Keates, Carey (CON - Bushey St James)
cllr.carey.keates@hertsmere.gov.uk
Kieran, Denise (CON - Bushey St James)
cllr.denise.heywood@hertsmere.gov.uk
Knell, Peter (CON - Potters Bar Furzefield)
cllr.peter.knell@hertsmere.gov.uk
Legate, Brian (CON - Potters Bar Furzefield)
cllr.brian.legate@hertsmere.gov.uk
Maughan, Susan (LAB - Borehamwood Brookmeadow)

cllr.susan.maughan@hertsmere.gov.uk
Morris, Paul (CON - Bushey Heath)
cllr.paul.morris@hertsmere.gov.uk
O'Brien, Steve (CON - Bushey North)
cllr.steve.obrien@hertsmere.gov.uk
Parnell, Sandra (CON - Borehamwood Hillside)
cllr.sandra.parnell@hertsmere.gov.uk
Quilty, Seamus (CON - Bushey Heath)
cllr.seamus.quilty@hertsmere.gov.uk
Ricks, James (CON - Potters Bar Oakmere)
cllr.james.ricks@hertsmere.gov.uk
Silver, Linda (CON - Bushey Park)
cllr.linda.silver@hertsmere.gov.uk
Swallow, Penny (CON - Potters Bar Oakmere)
cllr.penny.swallow@hertsmere.gov.uk
Wayne, Peter (CON - Shenley)
cllr.peter.wayne@hertsmere.gov.uk
West, Jane (CON - Bushey North)
jane.west@hertsmere.gov.uk
Winters, Leslie (CON - Bushey North)
cllr.leslie.winters@hertsmere.gov.uk
Worster, Martin (CON - Potters Bar Furzefield)
cllr.martin.worster@hertsmere.gov.uk

POLITICAL COMPOSITION

CON: 34, LAB: 5

CABINET

Leader / Communications & Consultation: Mr Morris Bright
Community Safety & Performance: Mr Charles Goldstein
Environment & Transport: Mrs Jean Heywood
Finance & Property: Mr John Graham
Housing & Economic Development: Mr Seamus Quilty
Leisure, Culture & Health: Ms Brenda Batten
Planning & Localism: Dr Harvey Cohen

COMMITTEE CHAIRS

Audit: Mr Paul Hodgson-Jones
Environment (Scrutiny): Mr Dan Griffin
Licensing: Ms Rosemary Gilligan
Overview & Performance: Mr Paul Morris
Personnel: Mr John Donne
Planning Referrals: Mr Derrick Gunasekera
Resources (Scrutiny): Ms Di Hoeksma

HIGH PEAK D

High Peak Borough Council, Town Hall, Market Place, Buxton SK17 6EL ☎ 0845 129 7777 🖷 01663 751042
borough-council@highpeak.gov.uk 💻 www.highpeak.gov.uk

FACTS & FIGURES

Police Authority: Derbyshire Police Authority
Health Authority: East Midlands Strategic Health Authority
Learning and Skills Council: East Midlands
Parliamentary Constituencies: High Peak
EU Constituencies: East Midlands
Election Frequency: Elections are of whole council
Twinning: High Peak: Wetteraukries (Germany); Glossop: Bad Vilbel (Germany); Buxton: Oignies (France); Bad Nauheim (Germany); New Mills: Alsfeld (Germany); Whaley Bridge: Tymbark (Poland)

PRINCIPAL OFFICERS

Chief Executive: Mr Simon Baker, Chief Executive (in alliance with Staffordshire Moorlands DC), Town Hall, Buxton SK17 6EL simon.baker@highpeak.gov.uk

Senior Management: Mr Dai Larner, Executive Director, Town Hall, Buxton SK17 6EL ☎ 01538 395400 dai.larner@highpeak.gov.uk

Senior Management: Mr Andrew Stokes, Executive Director & Chief Financial Officer, Moorlands House, Stockwell Street, Leek ST13 6HQ ☎ 01538 395622 andrew.stokes@staffsmoorlands.gov.uk

Senior Management: Mr Mark Trillo, Executive Director & Monitoring Officer, Moorlands House, Stockwell Street, Leek ST13 6HQ ☎ 01538 395623 mark.trillo@highpeak.gov.uk

Architect, Building / Property Services: Ms Joanne Higgins, Property Services Manager, Moorlands House, Stockwell Street, Leek ST13 6HQ ☎ 01538 395400 joanne.higgins@highpeak.gov.uk

Best Value: Mr Chris Elliott, Transformation Manager, Moorlands House, Stockwell Street, Leek ST13 6HQ ☎ 01538 395400 chris.elliott@highpeak.gov.uk

Building Control: Mr Mike Green, Planning Applications Manager, Town Hall, Buxton SK17 6EL ☎ 01538 395400 mike.green@highpeak.gov.uk

Building Control: Mr Dai Larner, Executive Director, Town Hall, Market Place, Buxton SK17 6EL ☎ 01538 395400 dai.larner@highpeak.gov.uk

PR / Communications: Mr Peter Dunkley, Customer Services Manager, Moorlands House, Stockwell Street, Leek ST13 6HQ ☎ 01538 395614 peter.dunkley@highpeak.gov.uk

Community Planning: Mr Mark Forrester, Community and Cultural Services Manager, Moorlands House, Stockwell Street, Leek ST13 6HQ ☎ 01538 395768 mark.forrester@highpeak.gov.uk

Community Planning: Mr Dai Larner, Executive Director, Town Hall, Market Place, Buxton SK17 6EL ☎ 01538 395400 dai.larner@highpeak.gov.uk

Community Safety: Mr Mark Forrester, Community and Cultural Services Manager, Moorlands House, Stockwell Street, Leek ST13 6HQ ☎ 01538 395768 mark.forrester@highpeak.gov.uk

Computer Management: Mr Chris Elliott, Transformation Manager, Moorlands House, Stockwell Street, Leek ST13 6HQ ☎ 01538 395400 chris.elliott@highpeak.gov.uk

Customer Service: Mr Peter Dunkley, Customer Services Manager, Moorlands House, Stockwell Street, Leek ST13 6HQ ☎ 01538 395614 peter.dunkley@highpeak.gov.uk

Economic Development: Mr Perry Wardle, Regeneration Manager, Moorlands House, Stockwell Street, Leek ST13 6HQ

☎ 01538 395582 ✉ perry.wardle@highpeak.gov.uk

Environmental Health: Mr Dai Larner, Executive Director, Town Hall, Market Place, Buxton SK17 6EL ☎ 01538 395400 ✉ dai.larner@highpeak.gov.uk

Environmental Health: Mrs Tammy Towers, Environmental Health Manager, Town Hall, Buxton SK17 6EL ☎ 01298 284 00 ext. 4462 ✉ tammy.towers@highpeak.gov.uk

Estates, Property & Valuation: Ms Joanne Higgins, Property Services Manager, Moorlands House, Stockwell Street, Leek ST13 6HQ ☎ 01538 395400 ✉ joanne.higgins@highpeak.gov.uk

Facilities: Ms Joanne Higgins, Property Services Manager, Moorlands House, Stockwell Street, Leek ST13 6HQ ☎ 01538 395400 ✉ joanne.higgins@highpeak.gov.uk

Finance and Treasurer: Mr Chris Hartgrove, Finance and Performance Manager, Moorlands House, Stockwell Street, Leek ST13 6HQ ☎ 01538 395400 ✉ chris.hartgrove@highpeak.gov.uk

Finance and Treasurer: Mr Andrew Stokes, Executive Director & Chief Financial Officer, Moorlands House, Stockwell Street, Leek ST13 6HQ ☎ 01538 395622 ✉ andrew.stokes@staffsmoorlands.gov.uk

Grounds Maintenance: Ms Nicola Kemp, Waste Collection Manager, Moorlands House, Stockwell Street, Leek ST13 6HQ ☎ 01538 395400 ✉ nicola.kemp@highpeak.gov.uk

Home Energy Conservation: Mr Ian Young, Housing Strategy Manager, Moorlands House, Stockwell Street, Leek ST13 6HQ ☎ 01538 395400 ✉ ian.young@highpeak.gov.uk

Housing: Mr Dai Larner, Executive Director, Town Hall, Market Place, Buxton SK17 6EL ☎ ; 01538 395400 ✉ dai.larner@highpeak.gov.uk

Housing: Mr Ian Young, Housing Strategy Manager, Moorlands House, Stockwell Street, Leek ST13 6HQ ☎ 01538 395400 ✉ ian.young@highpeak.gov.uk

Housing Maintenance: Mr Dai Larner, Executive Director, Town Hall, Market Place, Buxton SK17 6EL ☎ 01538 395400 ✉ dai.larner@highpeak.gov.uk

Housing Maintenance: Mr Ian Young, Housing Strategy Manager, Moorlands House, Stockwell Street, Leek ST13 6HQ ☎ 01538 395400 ✉ ian.young@highpeak.gov.uk

Local Area Agreement: Mr Mark Forrester, Community and Cultural Services Manager, Moorlands House, Stockwell Street, Leek ST13 6HQ ☎ 01538 395768 ✉ mark.forrester@highpeak.gov.uk

Legal: Mr Mark Trillo, Executive Director & Monitoring Officer, Moorlands House, Stockwell Street, Leek ST13 6HQ ☎ 01538 395623 ✉ mark.trillo@highpeak.gov.uk

Legal: Mr Linden Vernon, Member Services Manager, Moorlands House, Stockwell Street, Leek ST13 6HQ ☎ 01538 395400 ✉ linden.vernon@highpeak.gov.uk

Leisure and Cultural Services: Mr Terry Crawford, Visitor Services Manager, Pavillion Gardens, St John's Road, Buxton SK17 6XN ☎ 01298 284 00 ext 4224 ✉ terry.crawford@highpeak.gov.uk

Leisure and Cultural Services: Mr Mark Forrester, Community and Cultural Services Manager, Moorlands House, Stockwell Street, Leek ST13 6HQ ☎ 01538 395768 ✉ mark.forrester@highpeak.gov.uk

Licensing: Mrs Tammy Towers, Environmental Health Manager, Town Hall, Buxton SK17 6EL ☎ 01298 284 00 ext. 4462 ✉ tammy.towers@highpeak.gov.uk

Member Services: Mr Linden Vernon, Member Services Manager, Moorlands House, Stockwell Street, Leek ST13 6HQ ☎ 01538 395400 ✉ linden.vernon@highpeak.gov.uk

Parking: Mr Terry Crawford, Visitor Services Manager, Pavilion Gardens, St John's Road, Buxton SK17 6XN ☎ 01298 284 00 ext 4224 ✉ terry.crawford@highpeak.gov.uk

Parking: Mr Mark Forrester, Community and Cultural Services Manager, Moorlands House, Stockwell Street, Leek ST13 6HQ ☎ 01538 395768 ✉ mark.forrester@highpeak.gov.uk

Partnerships: Mr Mark Forrester, Community and Cultural Services Manager, Moorlands House, Stockwell Street, Leek ST13 6HQ ☎ 01538 395768 ✉ mark.forrester@highpeak.gov.uk

Personnel / HR: Ms Julie Grime, HR Manager, Moorlands House, Stockwell Street, Leek ST13 6EL ☎ 01538 395690 ✉ julie.grime@highpeak.gov.uk

Planning: Mr Mike Green, Planning Applications Manager, Moorlands House, Stockwell Street, Leek ST13 6HQ ☎ 01538 395400 ✉ mike.green@highpeak.gov.uk

Planning: Mr Dai Larner, Executive Director, Town Hall, Market Place, Buxton SK17 6EL ☎ 01538 395400 ✉ dai.larner@highpeak.gov.uk

Procurement: Mr Chris Elliott, Transformation Manager, Moorlands House, Stockwell Street, Leek ST13 6HQ ☎ 01538 395400 ✉ chris.elliott@highpeak.gov.uk

Recycling & Waste Minimisation: Ms Nicola Kemp, Waste Collection Manager, Moorlands House, Stockwell Street, Leek ST13 6HQ ☎ 01538 395400 ✉ nicola.kemp@highpeak.gov.uk

Regeneration: Mr Perry Wardle, Regeneration Manager, Moorlands House, Stockwell Street, Leek ST13 6HQ ☎ 01538 395582 ✉ perry.wardle@highpeak.gov.uk

Staff Training: Ms Julie Grime, HR Manager, Moorlands House, Stockwell Street, Leek ST13 6EL ☎ 01538 395690 ✉ julie.grime@highpeak.gov.uk

Street Scene: Ms Nicola Kemp, Waste Collection Manager, Moorlands House, Stockwell Street, Buxton ST13 6HQ

☎ 01538 395400 ✉ nicola.kemp@highpeak.gov.uk

Street Scene: Mrs Joy Redfern, Street Scene Manager, Town Hall, Market Place, Buxton SK17 6EL ☎ 0845 129 7777 ✉ joy.redfern@highpeak.gov.uk

Sustainable Communities: Mr Mark Forrester, Community and Cultural Services Manager, Moorlands House, Stockwell Street, Leek ST13 6HQ ☎ 01538 395768 ✉ mark.forrester@highpeak.gov.uk

Tourism: Mr Terry Crawford, Visitor Services Manager, Pavilion Gardens, St John's Road, Buxton SK17 6XN ☎ 01298 284 00 ext 4224 ✉ terry.crawford@highpeak.gov.uk

Tourism: Mr Dai Larner, Executive Director, Town Hall, Market Place, Buxton SK17 6EL ☎ 01538 395400 ✉ dai.larner@highpeak.gov.uk

Town Centre: Mr Perry Wardle, Regeneration Manager, Moorlands House, Stockwell Street, Leek ST13 6HQ ☎ 01538 395582 ✉ perry.wardle@highpeak.gov.uk

Total Place: Mr Mark Forrester, Community and Cultural Services Manager, Moorlands House, Stockwell Street, Leek ST13 6HQ ☎ 01538 395768 ✉ mark.forrester@highpeak.gov.uk

Waste Collection and Disposal: Ms Nicola Kemp, Waste Collection Manager, Moorlands House, Stockwell Street, Leek ST13 6HQ ☎ 01538 395400 ✉ nicola.kemp@highpeak.gov.uk

Waste Management: Ms Nicola Kemp, Waste Collection Manager, Moorlands House, Stockwell Street, Leek ST13 6HQ ☎ 01538 395400 ✉ nicola.kemp@highpeak.gov.uk

MEMBERS OF THE COUNCIL (43)

***Mayor:* Jenner**, Pat (LAB - Tintwistle)
pat.jenner@highpeak.gov.uk
***Leader of the Council:* Bisknell**, Caitlin (LAB - Stone Bench)
caitlin.bisknell@highpeak.gov.uk
***Deputy Leader of the Council:* McKeown**, Anthony (LAB - Gamesley)
anthony.mckeown@highpeak.gov.uk
St John's: Vacant
Ashton, Tony (CON - Sett)
tony.ashton@highpeak.gov.uk
Atkins, Ray (LD - New Mills West)
ray.atkins@highpeak.gov.uk
Baldry, Linda (CON - Corbar)
linda.baldry@highpeak.gov.uk
Barrow, Alan (LAB - New Mills East)
alan.barrow@highpeak.gov.uk
Bramah, Audrey (CON - Blackbrook)
audrey.bramah@highpeak.gov.uk
Claff, Godfrey (LAB - Howard Town)
godfrey.claff@highpeak.gov.uk
Dowson, Lance (LAB - New Mills West)
lance.dowson@highpeak.gov.uk
Faulkner, John (CON - Burbage)
john.faulkner@highpeak.gov.uk
Favell, Anthony Rowland (CON - Hope Valley)
anthony.favell@highpeak.gov.uk
Haken, John (CON - Simmondley)
john.haken@highpeak.gov.uk
Huddlestone, Ian (LAB - New Mills East)
ian.huddlestone@highpeak.gov.uk
Kemp, Tony (CON - Corbar)
tony.kemp@highpeak.gov.uk
Leather, Linda (LD - Whaley Bridge)
linda.leather@highpeak.gov.uk
Lomax, David (LD - Whaley Bridge)
david.lomax@highpeak.gov.uk
Mann, Victoria (LAB - Hadfield North)
victoria.mann@highpeak.gov.uk
McCabe, Julie Ann (CON - Simmondley)
julie.mccabe@highpeak.gov.uk
McKeown, Robert (LAB - Hadfield South)
robert.mckeown@highpeak.gov.uk
Mellor, David (IND - Hayfield)
david.mellor@highpeak.gov.uk
Norton, Timothy Ian (LAB - Chapel West)
tim.norton@highpeak.gov.uk
Oakley, Graham (LAB - Whitfield)
graham.oakley@highpeak.gov.uk
Parvin, Garry Lawrence (LAB - Old Glossop)
garry.parvin@highpeak.gov.uk
Payne, Christopher (LAB - Central)
christopher.payne@highpeak.gov.uk
Pearson, Christopher (CON - Blackbrook)
Chris.Pearson@highpeak.gov.uk
Perkins, Jim (CON - Chapel East)
jim.perkins@highpeak.gov.uk
Pritchard, John Arthur Thomas (IND - Whaley Bridge)
john.pritchard@highpeak.gov.uk
Quinn, Rachael (LAB - Barms)
rachael.quinn@highpeak.gov.uk
Savage, Keith (LAB - Cote Heath)
keith.savage@highpeak.gov.uk
Siddall, Edward (LAB - Hadfield South)
edward.siddall@highpeak.gov.uk
Sloman, Fiona (LAB - Stone Bench)
fiona.sloman@highpeak.gov.uk
Stone, Lynn (LAB - Cote Heath)
lynn.stone@highpeak.gov.uk
Thrane, Emily (CON - Temple)
emily.thrane@highpeak.gov.uk
Todd, Jean (LAB - Central)
jean.todd@highpeak.gov.uk
Udale, Derek (CON - Limestone Peak)
derek.udale@highpeak.gov.uk
Walton, John (CON - Hope Valley)
john.walton@highpeak.gov.uk
Waude, Colin Peter (LAB - Howard Town)
colin.waude@highpeak.gov.uk
Webster, Christopher (IND - Old Glossop)
christopher.webster@highpeak.gov.uk
Wharmby, Jean (CON - Dinting)
jean.wharmby@highpeak.gov.uk
Wilcox, Ellie (LAB - Padfield)
ellie.wilcox@highpeak.gov.uk
Young, Stewart (CON - Chapel West)
stewart.young@highpeak.gov.uk

POLITICAL COMPOSITION

LAB: 21, CON: 15, IND: 3, LD: 3, Vacant: 1

CABINET

Leader: Ms Caitlin Bisknell

Deputy Leader; Community Services: Mr Anthony McKeown
Corporate Services: Mr Timothy Ian Norton
Regeneration Services: Mr Godfrey Claff

COMMITTEE CHAIRS

Audit and Regulatory: Mr John Arthur Thomas Pritchard
Community: Mr Garry Lawrence Parvin
Corporate: Mr Philip Ashmore
Development Control: Mr David Mellor
Licensing: Ms Fiona Sloman
Regeneration: Mr Christopher James Payne
Standards: Mr P Matthews (External)

HIGHLAND S

Highland Council, Council Offices, Glenurquhart Road, Inverness IV3 5NX ☎ 01463 702000 🖷 01463 702182
💻 www.highland.gov.uk

FACTS & FIGURES

Police Authority: Northern Joint Police Board
Health Authority: NHS Highland
Learning and Skills Council: Scotland
Parliamentary Constituencies: Caithness, Sutherland and Easter Ross, Inverness, Nairn, Badenoch and Strathspey, Ross, Skye and Lochaber
EU Constituencies: Scotland
Election Frequency: Elections are of whole council

PRINCIPAL OFFICERS

Chief Executive: Mr Alistair Dodds, Chief Executive, Council Offices, Glenurquhart Road, Inverness IV3 5NX ☎ 01463 702837 🖷 01463 702830 ✉ alistair.dodds@highland.gov.uk

Deputy Chief Executive: Mr Steve Barron, Depute Chief Executive & Director of Housing & Property, Council Offices, Glenurquhart Road, Inverness IV3 5NX ☎ 01463 702853 🖷 01463 702879 ✉ steve.barron@highland.gov.uk

Assistant Chief Executive: Ms Michelle Morris, Assistant Chief Executive, Council Offices, Glenurquhart Road, Inverness IV3 5NX ☎ 01463 702845 🖷 01463 702182
✉ michelle.morris@highland.gov.uk

Access Officer / Social Services (Disability): Ms Kateryna Zoryk, Senior Personnel Advisor, Council Offices, Glenurquhart Road, Inverness IV3 5NX ☎ 01463 702055 🖷 01463 702062
✉ kateryna.zoryk@highland.gov.uk

Architect, Building / Property Services: Mr Steve Barron, Depute Chief Executive & Director of Housing & Property, Council Offices, Glenurquhart Road, Inverness IV3 5NX ☎ 01463 702853 🖷 01463 702879 ✉ steve.barron@highland.gov.uk

Catering Services: Mrs Norma Murray, Catering & Cleaning Manager, Ness House, Drummond School, Drummond Road, Inverness IV2 4NZ ☎ 01463 663307 🖷 01463 702828
✉ norma.murray@highland.gov.uk

Children / Youth Services: Mr Jonathan King, Head of Intergrated Children's Services, Council Offices, Glenurquhart Road, Inverness IV3 5NX ☎ 01463 702876 🖷 01463 702855

PR / Communications: Mr Gordon Fyfe, Public Relations Manager, Council Offices, Glenurquhart Road, Inverness IV3 5NX ☎ 01463 702020 🖷 01463 702025
✉ gordon.fyfe@highland.gov.uk

Community Planning: Mr Malcolm MacLeod, Head of Planning & Building Standards, Council Offices, Glenurquhart Road, Inverness IV3 5NX ☎ 01463 702506 🖷 01463 702298
✉ malcolm.macleod@highland.gov.uk

Community Safety: Ms Isabelle Kaminiarz, Community Safety Officer, Council Offices, Glenurquhart Road, Inverness IV3 5NX ☎ 01463 702246 🖷 01463 702830
✉ isabelle.kaminiarz@highland.gov.uk

Computer Management: Mr John Grieve, Corporate ICT Manager, Council Offices, Glenurquhart Road, Inverness IV3 5NX ☎ 01463 702741 🖷 01463 702830 ✉ john.grieve@highland.gov.uk

Contracts: Mr Gary Westwater, Head of Property, Council Offices, Glenurquhart Road, Inverness IV3 5NX ☎ 01463 702235 🖷 01463 702222 ✉ gary.westwater@highland.gov.uk

Corporate Services: Mr Alistair Dodds, Chief Executive, Council Offices, Glenurquhart Road, Inverness IV3 5NX ☎ 01463 702837 🖷 01463 702830 ✉ alistair.dodds@highland.gov.uk

Corporate Services: Mr George McCaig, Head of Social Work Business Support, Kinmylies Building, Leachkin Road, Inverness IV3 8NN ☎ 01463 703526 ✉ george.mccaig@highland.gov.uk

Customer Service: Mr Keiron Scott, Customer Services Manager, Council Offices, Glenurquhart Road, Inverness IV3 5NX ☎ 01463 702707 🖷 01463 702830
✉ keiron.scott@highland.gov.uk

Education: Mr Hugh Fraser, Director of Education, Culture and Sport, Council Offices, Glenurquhart Road, Inverness IV3 5NX ☎ 01463 702801 🖷 01463 702828 ✉ hugh.fraser@highland.gov.uk

E-Government: Ms Vicki Nairn, Head of E-Government, Council Offices, Glenurquhart Road, Inverness IV3 5NX ☎ 01463 702848 🖷 01463 702830 ✉ vicki.nairn@highland.gov.uk

Electoral Registration: Mr John Bruce, Elections Manager, Council Offices, Dingwall IV15 9QN ☎ 01349 868524 🖷 01349 862465 ✉ john.bruce@highland.gov.uk

Emergency Planning: Mr Donald Norrie, Emergency Planning & Business Continuity Manager, Council Offices, Glenurquhart Road, Inverness IV3 5NX ☎ 01463 713479 🖷 01463 243583
✉ donald.norrie@highland.gov.uk

Energy Management: Mr Eddie Boyd, Head of Energy & Engineering Services, Council Offices, Glenurquhart Road, Inverness IV3 5NX ☎ 01463 703503
✉ eddie.boyd@highland.gov.uk

Environmental / Technical Services: Mr Neil Gillies, Director of Transport, Environmental & Community Services, Council Offices, Glenurquhart Road, Inverness IV3 5NX ☎ 01463 702601 🖷 01463 702606 ✉ neil.gillies@highland.gov.uk

Estates, Property & Valuation: Mr Allan Maguire, Head of Housing, Development & Estates, Council Offices, Glenurquhart Road, Inverness IV3 5NX ☎ 01463 702528 🖷 01463 702885 ✉ allan.maguire@highland.gov.uk

European Liaison: Mr Gordon Summers, Principal European Officer, Council Offices, Glenurquhart Road, Inverness IV3 5NX ☎ 01463 702508 🖷 01463 702830 ✉ gordon.summers@highland.gov.uk

Events Manager: Mr Gerry Reynolds, Events & Promotions Officer, Town House, Inverness IV2 4SF ☎ 01463 724216 ✉ gerry.reynolds@highlands.gov.uk

Finance and Treasurer: Mr Derek Yule, Director of Finance, Council Offices, Glenurquhart Road, Inverness IV3 5NX ☎ 01463 702301 🖷 01463 702310 ✉ derek.yule@highland.gov.uk

Fleet Management: Mr William MacPherson, Fleet & Maintenance Manager, Council Offices, Glenurquhart Road, Inverness IV3 5NX ☎ 01463 702665 🖷 01463 702606 ✉ william.macpherson@highland.gov.uk

Grounds Maintenance: Mr Ian Belford, Maintenance Manager, 30 Harbour Road, Inverness IV1 1VA ☎ 01463 251308 🖷 01463 715280 ✉ ian.belford@highland.gov.uk

Health and Safety: Ms Gena Falconer, Health, Safety & Wellbeing Manager, Dochfour Drive, Inverness IV3 5EB ☎ 01463 703094 🖷 01463 703090 ✉ gena.falconer@highland.gov.uk

Highways: Mr Neil Gillies, Director of Transport, Environmental & Community Services, Council Offices, Glenurquhart Road, Inverness IV3 5NX ☎ 01463 702601 🖷 01463 702606 ✉ neil.gillies@highland.gov.uk

Housing: Mr David Goldie, Head of Housing, Council Offices, Glenurquhart Road, Inverness IV3 5NX ☎ 01463 702864 🖷 01463 702222 ✉ david.goldie@highland.gov.uk

Leisure and Cultural Services: Mr Ian Murray, Chief Executive - High Life Highland, 12/13 Ardross Street, Inverness IV3 5NS ☎ 01463 663824 🖷 01463 663809 ✉ ian.murray@highland.gov.uk

Licensing: Mr Michael Elsey, Senior Licensing Officer, Town House, High Street, Inverness IV1 1JJ ☎ 01463 724298 🖷 01463 724300 ✉ michael.elsey@highland.gov.uk

Lottery Funding, Charity and Voluntary: Mrs Carron McDiarmid, Head of Policy & Performance, Council Offices, Glenurquhart Road, Inverness IV3 5NX ☎ 01463 702852 🖷 01463 702830 ✉ carron.mcdiarmid@highland.gov.uk

Member Services: Ms Julie MacLennan, Democratic Services Manager, Council Offices, Glenurquhart Road, Inverness IV3 5NX ☎ 01463 702118 🖷 01463 702182 ✉ julie.maclennan@highland.gov.uk

Personnel / HR: Mr John Batchelor, Head of Personnel, Council Offices, Glenurquhart Road, Inverness IV3 5NX ☎ 01463 702056 🖷 01463 702062 ✉ john.batchelor@highland.gov.uk

Personnel / HR: Mr Charlie MacCallum, Payroll & Pensions Manager, Council Offices, Glenurquhart Road, Inverness IV3 5NX ☎ 01463 702334 🖷 01463 715673 ✉ charlie.maccallum@highland.gov.uk

Planning: Mr Stuart Black, Director of Planning & Development, Council Offices, Glenurquhart Road, Inverness IV3 5NX ☎ 01463 702251 🖷 01463 702298 ✉ stuart.black@highland.gov.uk

Procurement: Mr Ashley Gould, Head of Procurement, Floor 3, 21/23 Church Street, Inverness IV1 1DY ☎ 01463 703989 ✉ ashley.gould@highland.gov.uk

Recycling & Waste Minimisation: Mr Colin Clark, Head of Waste Management, Council Offices, Glenurquhart Road, Inverness IV3 5NX ☎ 01463 702527 🖷 01463 702233 ✉ colin.clark@highland.gov.uk

Road Safety: Ms Isabelle Kaminiarz, Community Safety Officer, Council Offices, Glenurquhart Road, Inverness IV3 5NX ☎ 01463 702246 🖷 01463 702830 ✉ isabelle.kaminiarz@highland.gov.uk

Social Services: Mr Bill Alexander, Director of Social Work, Council Offices, Glenurquhart Road, Inverness IV3 5NX

Social Services (Adult): Mr Jonathan King, Head of Intergrated Children's Services, Council Offices, Glenurquhart Road, Inverness IV3 5NX ☎ 01463 702876 🖷 01463 702855

Social Services (Children): Ms Fiona Palin, Head of Social Care, Council Offices, Glenurquhart Road, Inverness IV3 5NX ☎ 01463 702874 🖷 01463 702855

Staff Training: Ms Catherine Christie, Employee Development Manager, Dochfour Drive, Inverness IV3 5EB ☎ 01463 703064 🖷 01463 703051 ✉ catherine.christie@highland.gov.uk

Sustainable Development: Ms Ailsa Villegas, Sustainable Development Manager, Council Offices, Glenurquhart Road, Inverness IV3 5NX ☎ 01463 702543 🖷 01463 702830 ✉ ailsa.villegas@highland.gov.uk

Tourism: Mr Gordon Ireland, Tourism Development Officer, Council Buildings, Glenurquhart Road, Inverness IV3 5NX ☎ 01463 702949 🖷 01463 710848 ✉ gordon.ireland@highland.gov.uk

Town Centre: Mr David Haas, City Manager, Town House, High Street, Inverness IV1 1JJ ☎ 01463 724201 ✉ david.haas@highland.gov.uk

Traffic Management: Mr Richard Guest, Head of Roads & Community Works, Council Offices, Glenurquhart Road, Inverness IV3 5NX ☎ 01463 702622 🖷 01463 702606 ✉ neil.gillies@highland.gov.uk

Transport: Mr Sam MacNaughton, Head of Transport & Infrastructure, Council Offices, Glenurquhart Road, Inverness IV3 5NX ☎ 01463 702607 🖷 01463 702506 ✉ sam.macnaughton@highland.gov.uk

Waste Collection and Disposal: Mr Colin Clark, Head of Waste

Management, Council Offices, Glenurquhart Road, Inverness IV3 5NX ☎ 01463 702527 🖷 01463 702233 ✉ colin.clark@highland.gov.uk

Waste Management: Mr Colin Clark, Head of Waste Management, Council Offices, Glenurquhart Road, Inverness IV3 5NX ☎ 01463 702527 🖷 01463 702233 ✉ colin.clark@highland.gov.uk

MEMBERS OF THE COUNCIL (80)

***Leader of the Council:* Hendry**, Drew (SNP - Aird and Loch Ness)
***Deputy Leader of the Council:* Alston**, David (LD - Black Isle)
***Group Leader:* Wilson**, Carolyn (IND - Cromarty Firth)
Balfour, Roderick (INDNA - Culloden and Ardersier)
Barclay, William (IND - Black Isle)
Baxter, Andrew (IND - Fort William and Ardnamurchan)
Bremner, David (INDNA - Landward Caithness)
Brown, Ian (SNP - Inverness Millburn)
Caddick, Carolyn (LD - Inverness South)
Campbell, Janet (LD - Inverness Central)
Campbell, Isabelle (LD - Wester Ross, Strathpeffer and Lochalsh)
Carmichael, Helen (IND - Aird and Loch Ness)
Christie, Alasdair (LD - Inverness West)
Clark, William (IND - Caol and Mallaig)
Cockburn, Ian (SNP - Wester Ross, Strathpeffer and Lochalsh)
Coghill, Robert (IND - Landward Caithness)
Crawford, Jim (IND - Inverness South)
Davidson, Margaret (IND - Aird and Loch Ness)
Donald, Norman (IND - Inverness Ness-side)
Douglas, Jaci (IND - Badenoch and Strathspey)
Duffy, Allan (SNP - Inverness West)
Fallows, David (SNP - Badenoch and Strathspey)
Farlow, George (SNP - North, West and Central Sutherland)
Fernie, William (IND - Wick)
Finlayson, Mike (IND - Cromarty Firth)
Ford, John (LAB - Culloden and Ardersier)
Fraser, Hamish (IND - Eilean a' Cheo)
Fraser, Laurie (IND - Nairn)
Fraser, Craig (SNP - Black Isle)
Gordon, John (IND - Eilean a' Cheo)
Gormley, Bren (SNP - Fort William and Ardnamurchan)
Gowans, Ken (SNP - Inverness South)
Graham, Alex (LD - Inverness West)
Gray, Jimmy (LAB - Inverness Millburn)
Green, Michael (IND - Nairn)
Greene, Richard (IND - Wester Ross, Strathpeffer and Lochalsh)
Henderson, Allan (IND - Caol and Mallaig)
Hunter, Edward (IND - Caol and Mallaig)
Kerr, Donnie (SNP - Inverness Central)
Laird, Richard (SNP - Inverness Central)
Lobban, Bill (SNP - Badenoch and Strathspey)
Macaulay, Colin (SNP - Nairn)
MacDonald, Neil (LAB - Wick)
MacDonald, Liz (SNP - Nairn)
Mackay, Donald (IND - Thurso)
MacKay, Deirdre (LAB - East Sutherland and Edderton)
MacKay, Willie (IND - Landward Caithness)
MacKenzie, Graham (SNP - Dingwall and Seaforth)
MacKinnon, Alister (IND - Dingwall and Seaforth)
MacLean, Angela (LD - Dingwall and Seaforth)
MacLennan, Thomas (IND - Fort William and Ardnamurchan)
MacLeod, Alex (SNP - Landward Caithness)
MacLeod, Kenneth (LD - Inverness Milburn)
McAlister, Bet (LAB - Inverness Central)
McCallum, Isobel (IND - Black Isle)
McGillivray, Jim (IND - East Sutherland and Edderton)
Millar, Andrew (LD - Eilean a' Cheo)
Morrison, Hugh (IND - North, West and Central Sutherland)
Munro, Linda (LD - North, West and Central Sutherland)
Murphy, Brian (LAB - Fort William and Ardnamurchan)
Parr, Fraser (LAB - Inverness Ness-side)
Paterson, Margaret (IND - Dingwall and Seaforth)
Phillips, Graham (SNP - East Sutherland and Edderton)
Prag, Thomas (LD - Inverness South)
Rattray, Martin (LD - Cromarty Firth)
Renwick, Ian (SNP - Eilean a' Cheo)
Rhind, Alasdair (IND - Tain and Easter Ross)
Rimell, Gregor (LD - Badenoch and Strathspey)
Robertson, Fiona (IND - Tain and Easter Ross)
Rosie, John (IND - Thurso)
Ross, Graham (IND - Inverness West)
Ross, Gail (SNP - Wick)
Saxon, Roger (LAB - Thurso)
Sinclair, Glynis (LD - Culloden and Ardersier)
Sinclair, Audrey (IND - Wester Ross, Strathpeffer and Lochalsh)
Slater, Jean (SNP - Inverness Ness-side)
Smith, Maxine (SNP - Cromarty Firth)
Stephen, Kate (LD - Culloden and Ardersier)
Stone, Jamie (LD - Tain and Easter Ross)
Wood, Hamish (LD - Aird and Loch Ness)

POLITICAL COMPOSITION

IND: 32, SNP: 21, LD: 17, LAB: 8, INDNA: 2

COMMITTEE CHAIRS

Adult & Children's Services: Mr Alasdair Christie
Audit & Scutiny (Scrutiny): Mrs Margaret Davidson
Community Safety, Public Engagemnet & Equalities: Mr Andrew Millar
Finance, Housing & Resources: Mr David Fallows
Planning Environment & Development (Scrutiny): Mr Thomas Prag
Transport, Environmental & Community Services (Scrutiny): Mr Graham Phillips

HILLINGDON — L

Hillingdon London Borough Council, (London Borough of Hillingdon Council), Civic Centre, High Street, Uxbridge UB8 1UW ☎ 01895 250111 🖷 01895 273636 💻 www.hillingdon.gov.uk

FACTS & FIGURES

Police Authority: Metropolitan Police Authority
Health Authority: NHS London
Learning and Skills Council: London
Parliamentary Constituencies: Hayes and Harlington, Ruislip-Northwood, Uxbridge and Ruislip South
EU Constituencies: London
Election Frequency: Elections are of whole council

Twinning: Emden and Schleswig (Germany); Mantes-la-Jolie (France)

PRINCIPAL OFFICERS

Chief Executive: Mr Hugh Dunnachie, Chief Executive, Civic Centre, High Street, Uxbridge UB8 1UW ☎ 01895 250569 🖷 01895 277047 ✉ hdunnachie@hillingdon.gov.uk

Deputy Chief Executive: Ms Fran Beasley, Deputy Chief Executive and Director of Central Services, Civic Centre, High Street, Uxbridge UB8 1UW ☎ 01895 250725 🖷 01895 277047 ✉ fbeasley@hillingdon.gov.uk

Deputy Chief Executive: Ms Jean Palmer, Deputy Chief Executive and Director of Planning, Environment, Education and Community Services, Civic Centre, Uxbridge UB8 1UW ☎ 01895 250622 🖷 01895 250223 ✉ jean.palmer@hillingdon.gov.uk

Senior Management: Mr David Holdstock, Head of Corporate Communications, Civic Centre, High Street, Uxbridge UB8 1UW ☎ 01895 556063 ✉ dholdstock@hillingdon.gov.uk

Senior Management: Ms Linda Sanders, Director of Social Care, Health & Housing, Civic Centre, High Street, Uxbridge UB8 1UW ☎ ; 01895 250506 ✉ lsanders@hillingdon.gov.uk

Senior Management: Mr Paul Whaymand, Deputy Director of Finance, Civic Centre, High Street, Uxbridge UB8 1UW ☎ 01895 556071 🖷 01895 250871 ✉ pwhaymand@hillingdon.gov.uk

Access Officer / Social Services (Disability): Mr Gary Collier, Commissioning Services Manager, Civic Centre, High Street, Uxbridge UB8 1UW ☎ 01895 250570 🖷 01895250204 ✉ gcollier@hillingdon.gov.uk

Architect, Building / Property Services: Mr Boe Williams-Obasi, Head of Corporate Property & Construction, Civic Centre, High Street, Uxbridge UB8 1UW ☎ 01895 250932 🖷 01895 277785 ✉ Bwilliams-Obasi@hillingdon.gov.uk

Building Control: Ms Jales Tippell, Head of Highways, Transportation and Planning Policy, Civic Centre, High Street, Uxbridge UB8 1UW ☎ 01895 277468 🖷 01895 277086 ✉ jtippel@hillingdon.gov.uk

Catering Services: Ms Gwen Terry, Contract Manager - FM Soft Services, Civic Centre, High Street, Uxbridge UB8 1UW ☎ 01895 250221 ✉ gterry@hillingdon.gov.uk

Children / Youth Services: Mr Tom Murphy, Service Manager - Early Intervention, Civic Centre, High Street, Uxbridge UB8 1UW ☎ 01895 558273 🖷 01895 250493 ✉ tmurphy@hillingdon.gov.uk

Civil Registration: Mr Steve Vincent, Acting Superintendent Registrar, Civic Centre, High Street, Uxbridge UB8 1UW ☎ 01895 250452 🖷 01895 250678

PR / Communications: Mr David Holdstock, Head of Corporate Communications, Civic Centre, High Street, Uxbridge UB8 1UW ☎ 01895 556063 ✉ dholdstock@hillingdon.gov.uk

Community Safety: Ms Tesa McKeer, Senior Community Safety Officer, Civic Centre, High Street, Uxbridge UB8 1UW ☎ 01895 556320 🖷 01895 250116 ✉ TMcKeer@hillingdon.gov.uk

Computer Management: Mr Steve Palmer, Deputy Director of ICT, Highways & Business Services, Civic Centre, Uxbridge UB8 1UW ☎ 01895 556033 🖷 01895 250869 ✉ spalmer@hillingdon.gov.uk

Consumer Protection and Trading Standards: Miss Sue Pollitt, Divisional Trading Standards Officer, Civic Centre, Uxbridge UB8 1UW ☎ 01895 277425 🖷 01895 277443 ✉ spollitt@hillingdon.gov.uk

Contracts: Mr Trevor Gibson, Contracts Officer, Civic Centre, High Street, Uxbridge UB8 1UW ☎ 01895 250883 ✉ tgibson@hillingdon.gov.uk

Customer Service: Ms Lynn Smith, Customer Services Manager, Civic Centre, High Street, Uxbridge UB8 1UW ☎ 01895 556027 🖷 01895 250869 ✉ lsmith@hillingdon.gov.uk

Economic Development: Ms Helena Webster, Economic Development Manager, Civic Centre, High Street, Uxbridge UB8 1UW ☎ 01895 250638 🖷 01895 250823 ✉ hwebster@hillingdon.gov.uk

Education: Ms Anna Crispin, Chief Education Officer, Civic Centre, High Street, Uxbridge UB8 1UW ☎ 01895 277970 🖷 01895 250831 ✉ acrispin@hillingdon.gov.uk

E-Government: Ms Julie Prior, E-Government Officer, Civic Centre, High Street, Uxbridge UB8 1UW ☎ 01895 558124 🖷 01895 250869 ✉ jprior@hillingdon.gov.uk

Electoral Registration: Mr Mike Liddiard, Electoral Services Manager, Civic Centre, High Street, Uxbridge UB8 1UW ☎ 01895 250962 🖷 01805 250812 ✉ mliddiard@hillingdon.gov.uk

Emergency Planning: Mr Mike Price, Civil Protection Manager, Civic Centre, High Street, Uxbridge UB8 1UW ☎ 01895 250515 🖷 01895 556419 ✉ mprice@hillingdon.gov.uk

Energy Management: Mr David Haygarth, Energy Manager, Civic Centre, High Street, Uxbridge UB8 1UW ☎ 01895 250338 🖷 01895 250619

Estates, Property & Valuation: Mr Boe Williams-Obasi, Head of Corporate Property & Construction, Civic Centre, High Street, Uxbridge UB8 1UW ☎ 01895 250932 🖷 01895 277785 ✉ Bwilliams-Obasi@hillingdon.gov.uk

Events Manager: Ms Lyn Summers, Project, Events & Improvements Officer, Civic Centre, High Street, Uxbridge UB8 1UW ☎ 01895 556640 ✉ lsummers@hillingdon.gov.uk

Facilities: Mr Steve Smith, Facilities Manager, Civic Centre, Uxbridge UB8 1UW ☎ 01895 250518 🖷 01895 250290 ✉ ssmith@hillingdon.gov.uk

Finance and Treasurer: Mr Paul Whaymand, Deputy Director of Finance, Civic Centre, High Street, Uxbridge UB8 1UW ☎ 01895 556071 🖷 01895 250871 ✉ pwhaymand@hillingdon.gov.uk

Fleet Management: Mr David Fisher, Transport Manager, Civic Centre, High Street, Uxbridge UB8 1UW ☎ 01895 250024 🖷 01895 277461 ⌂ dfisher@hillingdon.gov.uk

Grounds Maintenance: Mr Paul Richards, Green Spaces, Sport & Leisure Senior Manager, Civic Centre, High Street, Uxbridge UB8 1UW ☎ 01895 250814 ⌂ prichards@hillingdon.gov.uk

Health and Safety: Ms Christine Barker, Occupational Health & Safety Services Manager, Civic Centre, High Street, Uxbridge UB8 1UW ☎ 01895 277377 🖷 01895 250217 ⌂ cbarker@hillingdon.gov.uk

Highways: Mr John Ferns, Highways Inspector Manager, Civic Centre, High Street, Uxbridge UB8 1UW ☎ 01895 277557 🖷 01895 277086 ⌂ jfern@hillingdon.gov.uk

Home Energy Conservation: Ms Jo Gill, Energy Efficiency Co-ordinator, Civic Centre, High Street, Uxbridge UB8 1UW ☎ 01895 277436 🖷 01895 277340 ⌂ jgill@hillingdon.gov.uk

Housing: Ms Linda Sanders, Director of Social Care, Health & Housing, Civic Centre, High Street, Uxbridge UB8 1UW ☎ 01895 250506 ⌂ lsanders@hillingdon.gov.uk

Housing Maintenance: Mr Grant Walker, Head of Maintenance, Civic Centre, Uxbridge UB8 1UW ☎ 01895 277477 🖷 01895 250104 ⌂ gwalker@hillingdon.gov.uk

Legal: Mr Rajesh Alagh, Borough Solicitor, Civic Centre, Uxbridge UB8 1UW ☎ 01895 250617 🖷 01895 277373 ⌂ ralagh@hillingdon.gov.uk

Leisure and Cultural Services: Mr Nigel Dicker, Deputy Director, Public Safety and Environment, Civic Centre, High Street, Uxbridge UB8 1UW ☎ 01895 558215 ⌂ ndicker@hillingdon.gov.uk

Leisure and Cultural Services: Mr James Rodger, Head of Planning, Sport and Green Spaces, Civic Centre, High Street, Uxbridge UB8 1UW ☎ 01895 556255 ⌂ jrodger2@hillingdon.gov.uk

Licensing: Ms Stephanie Waterford, Licensing Services Manager, Civic Centre, High Street, Uxbridge UB8 1UW ☎ 01895 277232 🖷 01895 250223 ⌂ swaterford@hillingdon.gov.uk

Lifelong Learning: Ms Tricia Collis, Universal Service for Education and Skills, Civic Centre, High Street, Uxbridge UB8 1UW ☎ 01895 676690 ⌂ tcollis2@hillingdon.gov.uk

Lighting: Mr Tim Edwards, Public Lighting Manager, Civic Centre, High Street, Uxbridge UB8 1UW ☎ 01895 277511 🖷 01895 277508 ⌂ tedwards@hillingdon.gov.uk

Lottery Funding, Charity and Voluntary: Mr Nigel Cramb, Partnerships, Business & Community Engagement Manager, Civic Centre, Uxbridge UB8 1UW ☎ 01895 250394 🖷 01895 250823 ⌂ ncramb@hillingdon.gov.uk

Member Services: Mr Lloyd White, Head of Democratic Services, Civic Centre, High Street, Uxbridge UB8 1UW ☎ 01895 250636 🖷 01895 277373 ⌂ lwhite@hillingdon.gov.uk

Parking: Mr Roy Clark, Parking Services Manager, Civic Centre, High Street, Uxbridge UB8 1UW ☎ 01895 277776 ⌂ rclark@hillingdon.gov.uk

Partnerships: Mr Kevin Byrne, Head of Policy & Performance, Civic Centre, High Street, Uxbridge UB8 1UW ☎ 01895 556719 ⌂ kbyrne2@hillingdon.gov.uk

Personnel / HR: Ms Pauline Moore, Acting Head of Human Resources, Civic Centre, High Street, Uxbridge UB8 1UW ☎ 01895 556737 ⌂ pmoore2@hillingdon.gov.uk

Planning: Mr James Rodger, Head of Planning, Sport and Green Spaces, Civic Centre, High Street, Uxbridge UB8 1UW ☎ 01895 556255 ⌂ jrodger2@hillingdon.gov.uk

Procurement: Mr Matthew Kelly, Head of Procurement, Civic Centre, High Street, Uxbridge UB8 1UW ☎ 01895 556349 ⌂ mkelly2@hillingdon.gov.uk

Procurement: Mr Matthew Kelly, Head of Procurement, Civic Centre, High Street, Uxbridge UB8 1UW ☎ 01895 556349 ⌂ mkelly2@hillingdon.gov.uk

Public Libraries: Mr Nigel Dicker, Deputy Director, Public Safety and Environment, Civic Centre, High Street, Uxbridge UB8 1UW ☎ 01895 558215 ⌂ ndicker@hillingdon.gov.uk

Recycling & Waste Minimisation: Mr Colin Russell, Waste Division Manager, Harlington Road Depot, Harlington Road, Hillingdon UB8 3EY ☎ 01895 556217 🖷 01895 2500103 ⌂ crussell@hillingdon.gov.uk

Road Safety: Ms Mhairi Stephens, Road Safety and School Travel Manager, Civic Centre, High Street, Uxbridge UB8 1UW ☎ 01895 250484 🖷 01895 277208 ⌂ mstephens@hillingdon.gov.uk

Social Services: Ms Linda Sanders, Director of Social Care, Health & Housing, Civic Centre, High Street, Uxbridge UB8 1UW ☎ ; 01895 250506 ⌂ lsanders@hillingdon.gov.uk

Social Services (Adult): Ms Linda Sanders, Director of Social Care, Health & Housing, Civic Centre, High Street, Uxbridge UB8 1UW ☎ ; 01895 250506 ⌂ lsanders@hillingdon.gov.uk

Social Services (Children): Ms Merlin Joseph, Deputy Director Children & Families, Civic Centre, High Street, Uxbridge UB8 1UW ☎ 01895 250527 ⌂ mjoseph@hillingdon.gov.uk

Staff Training: Ms Gill McLean, Corporate Learning & Development Manager, Civic Centre, High Street, Uxbridge UB8 1UW ☎ 01895 277338 ⌂ gmclean@hillingdon.gov.uk

Street Scene: Mrs Maggie Allen, Street Scene Locality Team Manager, Civic Centre, High Street, Uxbridge UB8 1UW ☎ 01895 277704 ⌂ mallen1@hillingdon.gov.uk

Sustainable Communities: Mr Kevin Byrne, Head of Policy & Performance, Civic Centre, High Street, Uxbridge UB8 1UW

☎ 01895 556719 ✉ kbyrne2@hillingdon.gov.uk

Town Centre: Mr Nigel Cramb, Partnerships, Business & Community Engagement Manager, Civic Centre, Uxbridge UB8 1UW ☎ 01895 250394 🖷 01895 250823 ✉ ncramb@hillingdon.gov.uk

Traffic Management: Mr James Birch, Traffic Manager, Civic Centre, High Street, Uxbridge UB8 1UW ☎ 01895 556133 ✉ jbirch2@hillingdon.gov.uk

Transport: Mr David Fisher, Transport Manager, Civic Centre, High Street, Uxbridge UB8 1UW ☎ 01895 250024 🖷 01895 277461 ✉ dfisher@hillingdon.gov.uk

Transport Planner: Ms Jales Tippell, Head of Highways, Transportation and Planning Policy, Civic Centre, High Street, Uxbridge UB8 1UW ☎ 01895 277468 🖷 01895 277086 ✉ jtippel@hillingdon.gov.uk

Total Place: Mr Kevin Byrne, Head of Policy & Performance, Civic Centre, High Street, Uxbridge UB8 1UW ☎ 01895 556719 ✉ kbyrne2@hillingdon.gov.uk

Waste Collection and Disposal: Mr Colin Russell, Waste Division Manager, Harlington Road Depot, Harlington Road, Hillingdon UB8 3EY ☎ 01895 556217 🖷 01895 2500103 ✉ crussell@hillingdon.gov.uk

Waste Management: Mr Colin Russell, Waste Division Manager, Harlington Road Depot, Harlington Road, Hillingdon UB8 3EY ☎ 01895 556217 🖷 01895 2500103 ✉ crussell@hillingdon.gov.uk

Children's Play Areas: Mr Paul Richards, Green Spaces, Sport & Leisure Senior Manager, Civic Centre, High Street, Uxbridge UB8 1UW ☎ 01895 250814 ✉ prichards@hillingdon.gov.uk

MEMBERS OF THE COUNCIL (65)

***Mayor:* Markham**, Michael (CON - Manor)
mmarkham@hillingdon.gov.uk
***Deputy Mayor:* Kauffman**, Allan (CON - South Ruislip)
akauffman2@hillingdon.gov.uk
***Leader of the Council:* Puddifoot**, Ray (CON - Ickenham)
rpuddifoot@hillingdon.gov.uk
***Deputy Leader of the Council:* Simmonds**, David (CON - Ickenham)
dsimmonds@hillingdon.gov.uk
***Group Leader:* Curling**, Peter (LAB - Townfield)
PCurling@hillingdon.gov.uk
***Group Leader:* Khursheed**, Mo (LAB - Botwell)
mkhursheed@hillingdon.gov.uk
Allam, Dave (LAB - Yeading)
dallam@hillingdon.gov.uk
Allen, Lynne (LAB - Townfield)
lallen@hillingdon.gov.uk
Baker, Bruce (CON - Eastcote and East Ruislip)
bbaker@hillingdon.gov.uk
Barker, Tim (CON - Hillingdon East)
tbarker@hillingdon.gov.uk
Barnes, Richard (CON - Harefield)
rbarnes@hillingdon.gov.uk
Barrett, Josephine (CON - Uxbridge North)
jbarrett@hillingdon.gov.uk
Benson, David (CON - Heathrow Villages)
dbenson@hillingdon.gov.uk
Bianco, Jonathan (CON - Northwood Hills)
jbianco@hillingdon.gov.uk
Bliss, Lindsay (LAB - Barnhill)
lbliss@hillingdon.gov.uk
Brar, Sukhpal (CON - Heathrow Villages)
sbrar@hillingdon.gov.uk
Bridges, Wayne (CON - Hillingdon East)
w.bridges@hillingdon.gov.uk
Bull, Mike (CON - West Drayton)
mbull@hillingdon.gov.uk
Burrows, Keith (CON - Uxbridge South)
kburrows@hillingdon.gov.uk
Buttivant, Paul (CON - West Drayton)
PButtivant@hillingdon.gov.uk
Cooper, Judith (CON - Uxbridge South)
jcooper@hillingdon.gov.uk
Cooper, George (CON - Uxbridge North)
gcooper@hillingdon.gov.uk
Corthorne, Philip (CON - West Ruislip)
pcorthorne@hillingdon.gov.uk
Crowe, Brian (CON - West Ruislip)
bcrowe@hilingdon.gov.uk
Dann, Catherine (CON - Eastcote and East Ruislip)
cdann@hillingdon.gov.uk
Dhillon, Jazz (LAB - Pinkwell)
jdhillon@hillingdon.gov.uk
Duncan, Janet (LAB - Yeading)
JDuncan2@hillingdon.gov.uk
East, Beulah (LAB - Charville)
BeulahEast@hillingdon.gov.uk
Fyfe, Neil (CON - Charville)
nfyfe@hillingdon.gov.uk
Gardner, Janet (LAB - Botwell)
jgardner@hillingdon.gov.uk
Garg, Sid (LAB - Yeading)
sgarg@hillingdon.gov.uk
Ghei, Roshan Lal (LAB - Barnhill)
rghei@hillingdon.gov.uk
Gilham, Dominic (CON - Yiewsley)
dgilham@hillingdon.gov.uk
Graham, Raymond (CON - Cavendish)
RGraham@hillingdon.gov.uk
Harmsworth, Paul (LAB - Yiewsley)
pharmsworth@hillingdon.gov.uk
Harper-O'Neill, Shirley (CON - South Ruislip)
sharper-o'neill@hillingdon.gov.uk
Hensley, John (CON - Ickenham)
jhensley@hillingdon.gov.uk
Higgins, Henry (CON - Harefield)
hhiggins@hillingdon.gov.uk
Jackson, Pat (CON - Hillingdon East)
pjackson@hillingdon.gov.uk
Jarjussey, Phoday (LAB - Botwell)
pjarjussey@hillingdon.gov.uk
Jenkins, Sandra (CON - Brunel)
sjenkins@hillingdon.gov.uk
Kelly, Judy (CON - South Ruislip)
jkelly@hillingdon.gov.uk
Kemp, Peter (CON - Yiewsley)
pkemp@hillingdon.gov.uk
Lakhmana, Kuldeep (LAB - Pinkwell)
klakhmana@hillingdon.gov.uk
Lavery, Edward (CON - Cavendish)

elavery@hillingdon.gov.uk
Lewis, Richard (CON - Northwood)
rlewis@hillingdon.gov.uk
MacDonald, Anita (LAB - West Drayton)
CllrAMacDonald@hillingdon.gov.uk
Major, John (LAB - Barnhill)
jmajor@hillingdon.gov.uk
Melvin, Carol (CON - Northwood)
cmelvin@hillingdon.gov.uk
Mills, Douglas (CON - Manor)
dmills@hillingdon.gov.uk
Mills, Richard (CON - Brunel)
rmills2@hillingdon.gov.uk
Morgan, John (CON - Northwood Hills)
jmorgan2@hillingdon.gov.uk
Nelson, June (LAB - Heathrow Villages)
jnelson@hillingdon.gov.uk
O'Brien, Susan (CON - Manor)
so'brien@hillingdon.gov.uk
O'Connor, Mary (CON - Charville)
mo'connor@hillingdon.gov.uk
Payne, David (CON - Eastcote and East Ruislip)
dpayne@hillingdon.gov.uk
Retter, Andrew (CON - Northwood Hills)
aretter@hillingdon.gov.uk
Riley, John (CON - West Ruislip)
jriley@hillingdon.gov.uk
Routledge, David (CON - Uxbridge South)
droutledge@hillingdon.gov.uk
Sandhu, Avtar Singh (LAB - Pinkwell)
ASandhu@hillingdon.gov.uk
Sansarpuri, Robin (LAB - Townfield)
rsansarpuri@hillingdon.gov.uk
Seaman-Digby, Scott (CON - Northwood)
sseaman-digby@hillingdon.gov.uk
Stead, Brian (CON - Brunel)
bstead@hillingdon.gov.uk
White, Michael (CON - Cavendish)
mrwhite@hillingdon.gov.uk
Yarrow, David (CON - Uxbridge North)
dyarrow@hillingdon.gov.uk

POLITICAL COMPOSITION
CON: 46, LAB: 19

CABINET
Leader: Mr Ray Puddifoot
Deputy Leader / Education & Children's Services: Mr David Simmonds
Co-ordination & Central Services: Mr Scott Seaman-Digby
Culture, Sport & Leisure: Mr Henry Higgins
Finance, Property & Business Services: Mr Jonathan Bianco
Improvement, Partnerships & Community Safety: Mr Douglas Mills
Planning, Transportation & Recycling: Mr Keith Burrows
Social Services, Health & Housing: Mr Philip Corthorne

COMMITTEE CHAIRS
Appointments: Mr Ray Puddifoot
Audit: Mr John Morley (External)
Corporate Services & Partnerships Policy Overview (Scrutiny): Mr Richard Lewis
Education & Children's Services Policy Overview (Scrutiny): Ms Catherine Dann
Licensing: Mr Andrew Retter
Pensions: Mr Philip Corthorne
Registration & Appeals: Mr George Cooper
Residents & Enviromental Services Policy Overview: Mr Michael Markham
Social Services, Health & Housing Policy Overview (Scrutiny): Ms Judith Cooper
Standards: Mr Allan Edwards (External)

HINCKLEY & BOSWORTH D

Hinckley & Bosworth Borough Council, Council Offices, Argents Mead, Hinckley LE10 1BZ ☎ 01455 238141 🖷 01455 251172 🖳 www.hinckley-bosworth.gov.uk

FACTS & FIGURES
Police Authority: Leicestershire Police Authority
Health Authority: East Midlands Strategic Health Authority
Learning and Skills Council: East Midlands
Parliamentary Constituencies: Bosworth
EU Constituencies: East Midlands
Election Frequency: Elections are of whole council
Twinning: Herford (Germany); Le Grand Quevilly (France); Bihorel (France)

PRINCIPAL OFFICERS
Chief Executive: Mr Steve Atkinson, Chief Executive, Council Offices, Argents Mead, Hinckley LE10 1BZ ☎ 01455 255606 🖷 01455 251172 ✉ steve.atkinson@hinckley-bosworth.gov.uk

Deputy Chief Executive: Mr Bill Cullen, Deputy Chief Executive (Community Direction), Council Offices, Argents Mead, Hinckley LE10 1BZ ☎ 01455 255676 🖷 01455 251172 ✉ bill.cullen@hinckley-bosworth.gov.uk

Deputy Chief Executive: Mr Sanjiv Kohli, Deputy Chief Executive (Corporate Direction), Council Offices, Argents Mead, Hinckley LE10 1BZ ☎ 01455 255607 🖷 01455 251172 ✉ sanjiv.kohli@hinckley-bosworth.gov.uk

Building Control: Mr Simon Wood, Head of Planning, Council Offices, Argents Mead, Hinckley LE10 1BZ ☎ 01455 255692 🖷 01455 251172 ✉ simon.wood@hinckley-bosworth.gov.uk

Children / Youth Services: Ms Rebecca Ball, Children & Young People's Strategic Co-ordinator, Council Offices, Argents Mead, Hinckley LE10 1BZ ☎ 01455 255937 🖷 01455 891505 ✉ rebecca.ball@hickley-bosworth.gov.uk

PR / Communications: Mr David Potter, Communications & Promotions Officer, Council Offices, Argents Mead, Hinckley LE10 1BZ ✉ david.potter@hinckley-bosworth.gov.uk

PR / Communications: Mrs Jacqueline Puffett, Communications & Promotions Officer, Council Offices, Argents Mead, Hinckley LE10 1BZ ☎ 01455 255630 🖷 01455 635692 ✉ jacqueline.puffett@hinckley-bosworth.gov.uk

Community Planning: Ms Edwina Grant, Strategic & Community Planning Officer, Council Offices, Argents Mead, Hinckley LE10 1BZ ☎ 01455 255629 🖷 01455 255997 ✉ edwina.grant@hinckley-bosworth.gov.uk

Community Safety: Ms Sharon Stacey, Chief Officer for Housing, Community Safety & Partnerships, Council Offices, Argents Mead, Hinckley LE10 1BZ ☎ 01455 255636 🖷 01455 251172 ✉ sharon.stacey@hinckley-bosworth.gov.uk

Computer Management: Mr Paul Langham, ICT Manager, Council Offices, Argents Mead, Hinckley LE10 1BZ ☎ 01455 255995 🖷 01455 255632 ✉ paul.langham@hinckley-bosworth.gov.uk

Contracts: Mrs Julie Kenny, Chief Officer for Finance, ICT, Asset Management, Audit & Procurement, Council Offices, Argents Mead, Hinckley LE10 1BZ ☎ 01455 255985 🖷 01455 251172 ✉ julie.kenny@hinckley-bosworth.gov.uk

Corporate Services: Ms Louisa Horton, Chief Officer for Corporate & Customer Resources, Scrutiny & Ethical Standards (Monitoring Officer), Council Offices, Argents Mead, Hinckley LE10 1BZ ☎ 01455 255859 🖷 01455 635692 ✉ louisa.horton@hinckley-bosworth.gov.uk

Customer Service: Ms Lynn Fray, Customer Services Manager, Council Offices, Argents Mead, Hinckley LE10 1BZ ☎ 01455 255625 🖷 01455 251172 ✉ lynn.fray@hinckley-bosworth.gov.uk

Economic Development: Mrs Judith Sturley, Senior Economic Regeneration Officer, Council Offices, Argents Mead, Hinckley LE10 1BZ ☎ 01455 255855 🖷 01455 251172 ✉ judith.sturley@hinckley-bosworth.gov.uk

Electoral Registration: Mrs Yvonne Hughes, Electoral Services Officer, Council Offices, Argents Mead, Hinckley LE10 1BZ ☎ 01455 255835 🖷 01455 635692 ✉ yvonne.hughes@hinckley-bosworth.gov.uk

Energy Management: Mrs Jane Neachell, Environmental Co-ordinator, Council Offices, Argents Mead, Hinckley LE10 1BZ ☎ 01455 255968 🖷 01455 234590 ✉ jane.neachell@hinckley-bosworth.gov.uk

Environmental / Technical Services: Mr Rob Parkinson, Chief Officer for Environmental Health, Council Offices, Argents Mead, Hinckley LE10 1BZ ☎ 01455 255641 🖷 01455 234590 ✉ rob.parkinson@hinckley-bosworth.gov.uk

Environmental Health: Mr Steven Merry, Environmental Health Manager (Commercial), Council Offices, Argents Mead, Hinckley LE10 1BZ ☎ 01455 255735 🖷 01455 234590 ✉ steven.merry@hinckley-bosworth.gov.uk

Environmental Health: Mr Rob Parkinson, Chief Officer for Environmental Health, Council Offices, St Mary's Road, Hinckley LE10 1EQ ☎ 01455 255641 🖷 01455 234590 ✉ rob.parkinson@hinckley-bosworth.gov.uk

Estates, Property & Valuation: Mr Malcolm Evans, Estates & Assets Manager, Council Offices, Argents Mead, Hinckley LE10 1BZ ☎ 01455 255614 🖷 01455 251172 ✉ malcolm.evans@hinckley-bosworth.gov.uk

Events Manager: Ms Sherrilee Fahey, Events Assistant, Council Offices, Argents Mead, Hinckley LE10 1BZ ☎ 01455 255893 🖷 01455 891505 ✉ sherliee.fahey@hinckley-bosworth.gov.uk

Finance and Treasurer: Mr Malcolm Evans, Estates & Assets Manager, Council Offices, Argents Mead, Hinckley LE10 1BZ ☎ 01455 255614 🖷 01455 251172 ✉ malcolm.evans@hinckley-bosworth.gov.uk

Grounds Maintenance: Mrs Caroline Roffey, Public Space Manager, The Depot, Middlefield Lane, Hinckley LE10 0RA ☎ 01455 255782 🖷 01455 891428 ✉ caroline.roffey@hinckley-bosworth.gov.uk

Health and Safety: Mr Adrian Wykes, Principle Safety, Health & Resilience Officer (Environmental Health), Council Offices, Argents Mead, Hinckley LE10 1BZ ☎ 01455 238141 🖷 01455 234590 ✉ adrian.wykes@hinckley-bosworth.gov.uk

Housing: Ms Sharon Stacey, Chief Officer for Housing, Community Safety & Partnerships, Council Offices, St Mary's Road, Hinckley LE10 1EQ ☎ 01455 255636 🖷 01455 251172 ✉ sharon.stacey@hinckley-bosworth.gov.uk

Housing Maintenance: Ms Sharon Stacey, Chief Officer for Housing, Community Safety & Partnerships, Council Offices, St Mary's Road, Hinckley LE10 1EQ ☎ 01455 255636 🖷 01455 251172 ✉ sharon.stacey@hinckley-bosworth.gov.uk

Legal: Mr Adam Bottomley, Senior Solicitor, Council Offices, Argents Mead, Hinckley LE10 1BZ ☎ 01455 255621 🖷 01455 635692 ✉ adam.bottomley@hinckley-bosworth.gov.uk

Leisure and Cultural Services: Mr Simon Jones, Cultural Services Manager, Council Offices, Argents Mead, Hinckley LE10 1BZ ☎ 01455 255699 🖷 01455 891505 ✉ simon.jones@hinckley-bosworth.gov.uk

Licensing: Mr Mark Brymer, Principal Licensing Officer, Council Offices, Argents Mead, Hinckley LE10 1BZ ☎ 01455 255645 🖷 01455 234590 ✉ mark.brymer@hinckley-bosworth.gov.uk

Member Services: Miss Rebecca Owen, Democratic Services Officer, Council Offices, Argents Mead, Hinckley LE10 1BZ ☎ 01455 255879 🖷 01455 635692 ✉ rebecca.owen@hinckley-bosworth.gov.uk

Personnel / HR: Mrs Julie Stay, Human Resources & Transformation Manager, Council Offices, Argents Mead, Hinckley LE10 1BZ ☎ 01455 255688 🖷 01455 255997 ✉ julie.stay@hinckley-bosworth.gov.uk

Planning: Mr Simon Wood, Head of Planning, Council Offices, Argents Mead, Hinckley LE10 1BZ ☎ 01455 255692 🖷 01455 251172 ✉ simon.wood@hinckley-bosworth.gov.uk

Procurement: Mrs Julie Kenny, Chief Officer for Finance, ICT, Asset Management, Audit & Procurement, Council Offices, St Mary's Road, Hinckley LE10 1EQ ☎ 01455 255985 🖷 01455 251172 ✉ julie.kenny@hinckley-bosworth.gov.uk

Recycling & Waste Minimisation: Ms Sarah Elliott, Waste

Manager, The Depot, Middlefield Lane, Hinckley LE10 0RA ☏ 01455 255980 🖷 01455 891428 ✉ sarah.elliott@hinckley-bosworth.gov.uk

Regeneration: Mr Simon Wood, Head of Planning, Council Offices, Argents Mead, Hinckley LE10 1BZ ☏ 01455 238141 🖷 01455 251172 ✉ simon.wood@hinckley-bosworth.gov.uk

Staff Training: Mrs Julie Stay, Human Resources & Transformation Manager, Council Offices, St Mary's Road, Hinckley LE10 1EQ ☏ 01455 255688 🖷 01455 255997 ✉ julie.stay@hinckley-bosworth.gov.uk

Street Scene: Mr Michael Brymer, Chief Officer for Business, Contract & Streetscene Services, Council Offices, Argents Mead, Hinckley LE10 1BZ ☏ 01455 255852 🖷 01455 251172 ✉ michael.brymer@hinckley-bosworth.gov.uk

Tourism: Ms Lindsay Orton, Creative Communites & Tourism Officer, Council Offices, Argents Mead, Hinckley LE10 1BZ ☏ 01455 255833 🖷 01455 891505 ✉ linday.orton@hinckley-bosworth.gov.uk

Town Centre: Mr Mark Hyrniw, Town Centre Manager, Council Offices, Argents Mead, Hinckley LE10 1BZ ☏ 01455 255755 🖷 01455 891505 ✉ mark.hryniw@hinckley-bosworth.gov.uk

Waste Collection and Disposal: Ms Sarah Elliott, Waste Manager, The Depot, Middlefield Lane, Hinckley LE10 0RA ☏ 01455 255980 🖷 01455 891428 ✉ sarah.elliott@hinckley-bosworth.gov.uk

Waste Management: Ms Sarah Elliott, Waste Manager, The Depot, Middlefield Lane, Hinckley LE10 0RA ☏ 01455 255980 🖷 01455 891428 ✉ sarah.elliott@hinckley-bosworth.gov.uk

MEMBERS OF THE COUNCIL (34)

***Mayor:* Cartwright**, Martin (CON - Groby)
martin.cartwright@hinckley-bosworth.gov.uk
***Deputy Mayor:* Hodgkins**, Lynda (LD - Hinckley De Montfort)
lynda.hodgkins@hinckley-bosworth.gov.uk
***Leader of the Council:* Bray**, Stuart (LD - Hinckley Castle)
stuart.bray@hinckley-bosworth.gov.uk
***Deputy Leader of the Council:* Bill**, David (LD - Hinckley Clarendon)
david.bill@hinckley-bosworth.gov.uk
***Group Leader:* Bessant**, Paul (CON - Newbold Verdon with Desford & Peckleton)
paul.bessant@hinckley-bosworth.gov.uk
Allen, Richard (CON - Earl Shilton)
richard.allen@hinckley-bosworth.gov.uk
Bannister, Jeff (LD - Hinckley De Monfort)
jeffrey.bannister@hinckley-bosworth.gov.uk
Batty, Peter (CON - Groby)
peter.batty@hinckley-bosworth.gov.uk
Boothby, Chris (CON - Ratby, Bagworth & Thornton)
chris.boothby@hinckley-bosworth.gov.uk
Camamile, Ruth (CON - Newbold Verdon with Desford & Peckleton)
ruth.camamile@hinckley-bosworth.gov.uk
Chastney, Tina (CON - Cadeby, Carlton & Market Bosworth with Shackerstone)
tina.chastney@hinckley-bosworth.gov.uk
Cope, David (LD - Hinckley Trinity)
david.cope@hinckley-bosworth.gov.uk
Crooks, William (LD - Barlestone, Nailstone and Obaston)
bill.crooks@hotmail.co.uk
Gould, David (LD - Barwell)
david.gould@hinckley-bosworth.gov.uk
Hall, Peter (LD - Burbage, St Catherine's and Lash Hill)
peter.hall@hinckley-bosworth.gov.uk
Hall, Ann (LD - Burbage, St Catherine's and Lash Hill)
ann.hall@hinckley-bosworth.gov.uk
Hulbert, Matthew (LD - Barwell)
matthew.hulbert@hinckley-bosworth.gov.uk
Inman, David (LD - Burbage, Sketchley and Stretton)
david.inman@hinckley-bosworth.gov.uk
Ladkin, Chris (CON - Earl Shilton)
chris.ladkin@hinckley-bosworth.gov.uk
Lay, Matthew (LAB - Markfield, Stanton and Field Head)
matthew.lay@hinckley-bosworth.gov.uk
Lynch, Keith (LD - Hinckley Clarendon)
cllr.klynch@hinckley-bosworth.gov.uk
Mayne, Rob (LD - Burbage, Sketchley and Stretton)
rob.mayne@hinckley-bosworth.gov.uk
Moore, John (CON - Burbage, Sketchley and Stretton)
john.moore@hinckley-bosworth.gov.uk
Morrell, K (CON - Twycross & Witherley with Sheepy)
kevin.morrell@hinckley-bosworth.gov.uk
Mullaney, Michael (LD - Hinckley Trinity)
michael.mullaney@hinckley-bosworth.gov.uk
Nichols, Keith (LD - Hinckley De Montfort)
keith.nichols@hinckley-bosworth.gov.uk
O'Shea, Ozzy (CON - Ratby, Bagworth & Thornton)
ozzy.oshea@hinckley-bosworth.gov.uk
Richards, Janice (CON - Earl Shilton)
janice.richards@hinckley-bosworth.gov.uk
Smith, Hazel (CON - Barwell)
hazel.smith@hinckley-bosworth.gov.uk
Sprason, Sue (CON - Markfield, Stanton and Field Head)
sue.sprason@hinckley-bosworth.gov.uk
Sutton, B (CON - Newbold Verdon with Desford & Peckleton)
brian.sutton@hinckley-bosworth.gov.uk
Taylor, Diane (LD - Hinckley Clarendon)
diane.taylor@hinckley-bosworth.gov.uk
Ward, R (CON - Ambien)
reg.ward@hinckley-bosworth.gov.uk
Witherford, Bronwen (LD - Hinckley Castle)
bron.witherford@hinckley-bosworth.gov.uk

POLITICAL COMPOSITION

LD: 17, CON: 16, LAB: 1

CABINET

Leader: Mr Stuart Bray
Deputy Leader / Community Safety & Partnerships: Mr David Bill
Corporate Services: Ms Bronwen Witherford
Culture, Leisure, Parks & Open Spaces: Mr Michael Mullaney
Environment & Housing: Mr David Cope
Finance, ICT & Asset Management: Mr Keith Lynch
Refuse, Recycling & Rural Affairs: Mr William Crooks

COMMITTEE CHAIRS

Finance, Audit & Performance: Mr Peter Hall
Licensing: Mr Keith Nichols

Personnel: Mr Martin Cartwright
Planning: Mr Rob Mayne
Scrutiny Commission (Scrutiny): Mr Matthew Lay

HORSHAM D

Horsham District Council, Park North, North Street, Horsham RH12 1RL ☎ 01403 215100 🖷 01403 262985 contact@horsham.gov.uk www.horsham.gov.uk

FACTS & FIGURES

Police Authority: Sussex Police Authority
Health Authority: South East Coast Strategic Health Authority
Learning and Skills Council: South East
Parliamentary Constituencies: Arundel and South Downs, Horsham
EU Constituencies: South East
Election Frequency: Elections are of whole council
Twinning: Lage (Germany); St. Maixent (France)

PRINCIPAL OFFICERS

Chief Executive: Mr Tom Crowley, Chief Executive, Park North, North Street, Horsham RH12 1RL ☎ 01403 215102 🖷 01403 215145 tom.crowley@horsham.gov.uk

Senior Management: Mrs Natalie Brahma-Pearl, Director of Community Services, Park North, North Street, Horsham RH12 1RL ☎ 01403 215250

Senior Management: Mrs Katharine Eberhart, Director of Corporate Resources, Park North, North Street, Horsham RH12 1RL ☎ 01403 215301 🖷 01403 215371 katharine.eberhart@horsham.gov.uk

Access Officer / Social Services (Disability): Mr Stephen Shorrocks, Head of Building Control, Park North, North Street, Horsham RH12 1RL ☎ 01403 215500 🖷 01403 215198 stephen.shorrocks@horsham.gov.uk

Architect, Building / Property Services: Mr Peter Dawes, Head of Corporate Support Services, Park North, North Street, Horsham RH12 1RL ☎ 01403 215406 🖷 01403 215467 peter.dawes@horsham.gov.uk

Architect, Building / Property Services: Mr Stephen Shorrocks, Head of Building Control, Park North, North Street, Horsham RH12 1RL ☎ 01403 215500 🖷 01403 215198 stephen.shorrocks@horsham.gov.uk

Best Value: Mrs Jill Scarfield, Interim Head of Corporate Policy, Park North, North Street, Horsham RH12 1RL ☎ 01403 215303 🖷 01403 215266 jill.scarfield@horsham.gov.uk

Building Control: Mr Stephen Shorrocks, Head of Building Control, Park North, North Street, Horsham RH12 1RL ☎ 01403 215500 🖷 01403 215198 stephen.shorrocks@horsham.gov.uk

Children / Youth Services: Mr Trevor Beadle, Community Safety Officer, Park North, North Street, Horsham RH12 1RL ☎ 01403 215493 🖷 01403 262985 trevor.beadle@horsham.gov.uk

PR / Communications: Mr Richard Morris, Communications Manager, Park North, North Street, Horsham RH12 1RL ☎ 01403 215549 🖷 01403 262985 richard.morris@horsham.gov.uk

Community Planning: Mrs Jill Scarfield, Interim Head of Corporate Policy, Park North, North Street, Horsham RH12 1RL ☎ 01403 215303 🖷 01403 215266 jill.scarfield@horsham.gov.uk

Community Safety: Mr Trevor Beadle, Community Safety Officer, Park North, North Street, Horsham RH12 1RL ☎ 01403 215493 🖷 01403 262985 trevor.beadle@horsham.gov.uk

Community Safety: Mr Greg Charman, Community Safety Manager, Park North, North Street, Horsham RH12 1RL ☎ 01403 215124 greg.charman@horsham.gov.uk

Computer Management: Mr Peter Dawes, Head of Corporate Support Services, Park North, North Street, Horsham RH12 1RL ☎ 01403 215406 🖷 01403 215467 peter.dawes@horsham.gov.uk

Contracts: Mrs Katharine Eberhart, Director of Corporate Resources, Park North, North Street, Horsham RH12 1RL ☎ 01403 215301 🖷 01403 215371 katharine.eberhart@horsham.gov.uk

Corporate Services: Mr Peter Dawes, Head of Corporate Support Services, Park North, North Street, Horsham RH12 1RL ☎ 01403 215406 🖷 01403 215467 peter.dawes@horsham.gov.uk

Customer Service: Mr Richard Morris, Communications Manager, Park North, North Street, Horsham RH12 1RL ☎ 01403 215549 🖷 01403 262985 richard.morris@horsham.gov.uk

Direct Labour: Mr Ian Jopling, Head of Environmental Operational Services, Park North, North Street, Horsham RH12 1RL ☎ 01403 215556 🖷 01403 215553 ian.jopling@horsham.gov.uk

Economic Development: Mrs Christine Baister, Business Development Officer, Park North, North Street, Horsham RH12 1RL ☎ 01403 215542 🖷 01403 215266 chris.baister@horsham.gov.uk

E-Government: Mr Peter Dawes, Head of Corporate Support Services, Park North, North Street, Horsham RH12 1RL ☎ 01403 215406 🖷 01403 215467 peter.dawes@horsham.gov.uk

Electoral Registration: Mrs Judy Buckley, Elections Services Officer, Park North, North Street, Horsham RH12 1RL ☎ 01403 215126 🖷 01403 262985 judy.buckley@horsham.gov.uk

Emergency Planning: Mr Greg Charman, Community Safety Manager, Park North, North Street, Horsham RH12 1RL ☎ 01403 215124 greg.charman@horsham.gov.uk

Energy Management: Mr Tony Appleby, Principal Building Surveyor, Park North, North Street, Horsham RH12 1RL ☎ 01403 215068 🖷 01403 215371 tony.appleby@horsham.gov.uk

Environmental / Technical Services: Mr Rod Brown, Head of Planning & Environmental Services, Park North, North Street,

Horsham RH12 1RL ☎ 01403 215426
✉ rod.brown@horsham.gov.uk

Environmental Health: Mr Rod Brown, Head of Planning & Environmental Services, Park North, North Street, Horsham RH12 1RL ☎ 01403 215426 ✉ rod.brown@horsham.gov.uk

Estates, Property & Valuation: Mr Peter Dawes, Head of Corporate Support Services, Park North, North Street, Horsham RH12 1RL ☎ 01403 215406 🖷 01403 215467
✉ peter.dawes@horsham.gov.uk

Estates, Property & Valuation: Mr John Loxley, Estates Management & Valuation Surveyor, Park North, North Street, Horsham RH12 1RL ☎ 01403 215483 🖷 01403 215487
✉ john.loxley@horsham.gov.uk

European Liaison: Mrs Christine Baister, Business Development Officer, Park North, North Street, Horsham RH12 1RL
☎ 01403 215542 🖷 01403 215266
✉ chris.baister@horsham.gov.uk

Finance and Treasurer: Mr T Delaney, Head of Revenues, Park North, North Street, Horsham RH12 1RL ☎ 01403 215339

Finance and Treasurer: Mrs Katharine Eberhart, Director of Corporate Resources, Park North, North Street, Horsham RH12 1RL ☎ 01403 215301 🖷 01403 215371
✉ katharine.eberhart@horsham.gov.uk

Fleet Management: Mr Ian Jopling, Head of Environmental Operational Services, Park North, North Street, Horsham RH12 1RL ☎ 01403 215556 🖷 01403 215553
✉ ian.jopling@horsham.gov.uk

Grounds Maintenance: Mr Evan Giles, Parks Services Manager, Park North, North Street, Horsham RH12 1RL ☎ 01403 215257
🖷 01403 215268 ✉ evan.giles@horsham.gov.uk

Health and Safety: Mrs Carron Burton, Principal Personnel Officer, Park North, North Street, Horsham RH12 1RL
☎ 01403 215131 ✉ carron.burton@horsham.gov.uk

Home Energy Conservation: Miss Gill Daniel, Environmental Co-ordination Officer, Park North, North Street, Horsham RH12 1RL ☎ 01403 215281 🖷 01403 215467
✉ gill.daniel@horsham.gov.uk

Housing: Mr Trevor Beadle, Community Safety Officer, Park North, North Street, Horsham RH12 1RL ☎ 01403 215493
🖷 01403 262985 ✉ trevor.beadle@horsham.gov.uk

Legal: Mrs Sue McMillan, Head of Financial & Legal Services, Park North, North Street, Horsham RH12 1RL ☎ 01403 215302
✉ sue.mcmillan@horsham.gov.uk

Leisure and Cultural Services: Mrs Barbara Childs, Head of Leisure & Economic Development, Park North, North Street, Horsham RH12 1RL ☎ 01403 215181

Licensing: Mr Rod Brown, Head of Planning & Environmental Services, Park North, North Street, Horsham RH12 1RL
☎ 01403 215426

Lottery Funding, Charity and Voluntary: Mrs Jill Scarfield, Interim Head of Corporate Policy, Park North, North Street, Horsham RH12 1RL ☎ 01403 215303 🖷 01403 215266
✉ jill.scarfield@horsham.gov.uk

Member Services: Mrs Lesley Morgan, Democratic Services Officer, Park North, North Street, Horsham RH12 1RL ☎ 01403 215123 ✉ lesley.morgan@horsham.gov.uk

Parking: Mr Ian Jopling, Head of Environmental Operational Services, Park North, North Street, Horsham RH12 1RL ☎ 01403 215556 🖷 01403 215553 ✉ ian.jopling@horsham.gov.uk

Personnel / HR: Mrs Carron Burton, Principal Personnel Officer, Park North, North Street, Horsham RH12 1RL ☎ 01403 215131
✉ carron.burton@horsham.gov.uk

Planning: Mr Rod Brown, Head of Planning & Environmental Services, Park North, North Street, Horsham RH12 1RL ☎ 01403 215426

Procurement: Mr Peter Dawes, Head of Corporate Support Services, Park North, North Street, Horsham RH12 1RL ☎ 01403 215406 🖷 01403 215467 ✉ peter.dawes@horsham.gov.uk

Procurement: Mr Roger Dennis, Joint Procurement Advisor, Park North, North Street, Horsham RH12 1RL ☎ 01403 215299
✉ roger.dennis@horsham.gov.uk

Recycling & Waste Minimisation: Mr Ian Jopling, Head of Environmental Operational Services, Park North, North Street, Horsham RH12 1RL ☎ 01403 215556 🖷 01403 215553
✉ ian.jopling@horsham.gov.uk

Staff Training: Mrs Carron Burton, Principal Personnel Officer, Park North, North Street, Horsham RH12 1RL ☎ 01403 215131
✉ carron.burton@horsham.gov.uk

Street Scene: Mr Trevor Beadle, Community Safety Officer, Park North, North Street, Horsham RH12 1RL ☎ 01403 215493
🖷 01403 262985 ✉ trevor.beadle@horsham.gov.uk

Sustainable Communities: Mrs Jill Scarfield, Interim Head of Corporate Policy, Park North, North Street, Horsham RH12 1RL ☎ 01403 215303 🖷 01403 215266 ✉ jill.scarfield@horsham.gov.uk

Sustainable Development: Mr Peter Dawes, Head of Corporate Support Services, Park North, North Street, Horsham RH12 1RL ☎ 01403 215406 🖷 01403 215467
✉ peter.dawes@horsham.gov.uk

Tourism: Mrs Barbara Childs, Head of Leisure & Economic Development, Park North, North Street, Horsham RH12 1RL
☎ 01403 215181

Tourism: Mr Tom Leighton, Head of Leisure & Economic Development, Park North, North Street, Horsham RH12 1RL
☎ 01403 215260

Town Centre: Mr Garry Mortimer-Cook, Town Centres Manager,

Park Hosue, North Street, Horsham RH12 1RL ☎ 01403 215386 ✉ garry.mortimer-cook@horsham.gov.uk

Transport: Mr Ian Jopling, Head of Environmental Operational Services, Park North, North Street, Horsham RH12 1RL ☎ 01403 215556 🖷 01403 215553 ✉ ian.jopling@horsham.gov.uk

Transport Planner: Mrs Jill Scarfield, Interim Head of Corporate Policy, Park North, North Street, Horsham RH12 1RL ☎ 01403 215303 🖷 01403 215266 ✉ jill.scarfield@horsham.gov.uk

Waste Collection and Disposal: Mr Ian Jopling, Head of Environmental Operational Services, Park North, North Street, Horsham RH12 1RL ☎ 01403 215556 🖷 01403 215553 ✉ ian.jopling@horsham.gov.uk

Waste Management: Mr Ian Jopling, Head of Environmental Operational Services, Park North, North Street, Horsham RH12 1RL ☎ 01403 215556 🖷 01403 215553 ✉ ian.jopling@horsham.gov.uk

Children's Play Areas: Mr Evan Giles, Parks Services Manager, Park North, North Street, Horsham RH12 1RL ☎ 01403 215257 🖷 01403 215268 ✉ evan.giles@horsham.gov.uk

MEMBERS OF THE COUNCIL (45)

***Chair:* Crosbie**, Leonard (LD - Trafalgar (Horsham Town))
leonard.crosbie@horsham.gov.uk

***Vice-Chair:* Circus**, Philip (CON - Chanctonbury (Ashington, Thakeham, West Chiltington and Wiston))
Philip.Circus@horsham.gov.uk

***Leader of the Council:* Dawe**, Ray (CON - Chantry (Amberley, Parham, Storrington and Sullington and Washington))
Ray.Dawe@horsham.gov.uk

***Deputy Leader of the Council:* Arthur**, Roger (CON - Chanctonbury (Ashington, Thakeham, West Chiltington and Wiston))
roger.arthur@horsham.gov.uk

Ichingfield, Slinfold and Warnham: Vacant

Bailey, John (CON - Rudgwick)
John.Bailey%40horsham.gov.uk

Baldwin, Andrew (CON - Holbrook East (North Horsham))
Andrew.Baldwin@horsham.gov.uk

Breacher, Adam (CON - Billingshurst and Shipley)
adam.breacher@horsham.gov.uk

Burgess, Peter (CON - Holbrook West (Horsham Town and Holbrook West Ward of North Horsham))
peter.burgess@horsham.gov.uk

Chidlow, John (CON - Southwater)
john.chidlow@horsham.gov.uk

Chowen, Jonathan (CON - Cowfold, Shermanbury and West Grinstead)
Jonathan.Chowen@horsham.gov.uk

Cockman, George (IND - Steyning (Steyning and Ashurst))
George.Cockman@horsham.gov.uk

Coldwell, David (CON - Bramber, Upper Beeding and Woodmancote)
david.coldwell@horsham.gov.uk

Cornell, Roy (CON - Roffey South (Horsham Town and Roffey South Ward of North Horsham))
Roy.Cornell@horsham.gov.uk

Costin, Christine (LD - Trafalgar (Horsham Town))
Christine.Costin@horsham.gov.uk

Croft, Helena (CON - Roffey North (North Horsham))
Helena.Croft@horsham.gov.uk

Curnock, Malcolm (LD - Broadbridge Heath)
malcolm.curnock@horsham.gov.uk

Deakins, Laurence (CON - Denne (Horsham Town))
laurence.deakins@horsham.gov.uk

Donnelly, Brian (CON - Pulborough and Coldwaltham)
Brian.Donnelly@horsham.gov.uk

Dunlop, Andrew (CON - Cowfold, Shermanbury and West Grinstead)
andrew.dunlop@horsham.gov.uk

England, Duncan (CON - Nuthurst (Lower Beeding and Nuthurst))
duncan.england@horsham.gov.uk

Goddard, Jim (CON - Bramber, Upper Beeding and Woodmancote)
jim.goddard@horsham.gov.uk

Haigh, Frances (LD - Horsham Park (Horsham Town))
frances.haigh@horsham.gov.uk

Holmes, David (LD - Horsham Park (Horsham Town))
David.Holmes@horsham.gov.uk

Howard, Ian (CON - Southwater)
Ian.Howard@horsham.gov.uk

Jenkins, David (CON - Chanctonbury (Ashington, Thakeham, West Chiltington and Wiston))
David.Jenkins@horsham.gov.uk

Kitchen, Liz (CON - Rusper and Colgate)
Elizabeth.kitchen@horsham.gov.uk

Lindsay, Gordon (CON - Billingshurst and Shipley)
gordon.lindsay@horsham.gov.uk

Mason, Chris (CON - Chantry (Amberley, Parham, Storrington and Sullington and Washington))
Chris.Mason@horsham.gov.uk

Matthews, Sheila (IND - Henfield (Henfield Parish))
Sheila.Matthews@horsham.gov.uk

Mitchell, Christian (CON - Holbrook West (Horsham Town and Holbrook West Ward of North Horsham))
Christian.Mitchell@horsham.gov.uk

Murphy, Josh (CON - Horsham Park (Horsham Town))
josh.murphy@horsham.gov.uk

Newman, Godfrey (LD - Forest (Horsham Town))
godfrey.newman@horsham.gov.uk

O'Connell, Brian (CON - Henfield (Henfield Parish))
brian.oconnell@horsham.gov.uk

Paterson, Roger (CON - Pulborough and Coldwaltham)
Roger.Paterson@horsham.gov.uk

Rae, Jim (CON - Holbrook East (North Horsham))
jim.rae@horsham.gov.uk

Ritchie, Stuart (CON - Itchingfield, Slinfold and Warnham)
stuart.ritchie@horsham.gov.uk

Rogers, Sue (CON - Steyning (Steyning and Ashurst))
sue.rogers@horsham.gov.uk

Rowbottom, Kate (CON - Billingshurst and Shipley)
kate.rowbottom@horsham.gov.uk

Sanson, Jim (CON - Chantry (Amberley, Parham, Storrington and Sullington and Washington))
jim.sanson@horsham.gov.uk

Sheldon, David (LD - Denne (Horsham Town))
David.Sheldon@horsham.gov.uk

Skipp, David (LD - Roffey North (North Horsham))
David.Skipp@horsham.gov.uk

Torn, Simon (CON - Roffey South (Horsham Town and Roffey South Ward of North Horsham))
simon.torn@horsham.gov.uk

Vickers, Claire (CON - Southwater)
claire.vickers@horsham.gov.uk
Youtan, Tricia (CON - Itchingfield, Slinfold and Warnham)
tricia.youtan@horsham.gov.uk

POLITICAL COMPOSITION
CON: 34, LD: 8, IND: 2, Vacant: 1

CABINET
Leader: Mr Ray Dawe
Deputy Leader / Efficiency & Resources: Mr Roger Arthur
A Safer & Healthier District: Mrs Sue Rogers
Arts, Heritage & Leisure: Mr Jonathan Chowen
Communication, Special Projects & Horsham Town: Ms Helena Croft
Environment: Mr Andrew Baldwin
Living & Working Communities: Mr Ian Howard

HOUNSLOW L

Hounslow London Borough Council, Civic Centre, Lampton Road, Hounslow TW3 4DN ☎ 020 8583 2000 🖷 020 8583 2592 ✉ information.ced@hounslow.gov.uk 🖳 www.hounslow.gov.uk

FACTS & FIGURES
Police Authority: Metropolitan Police Authority
Health Authority: NHS London
Learning and Skills Council: London
Parliamentary Constituencies: Brentford and Isleworth, Feltham and Heston
EU Constituencies: London
Election Frequency: Elections are of whole council
Twinning: Issy-les-Moulineaux (France); Lahore (Pakistan); Ramallah-el-Birch (West Bank)

PRINCIPAL OFFICERS
Chief Executive: Ms Mary Harpley, Chief Executive, Civic Centre, Lampton Road, Hounslow TW3 4DN ☎ 020 8583 2012 🖷 020 8583 2013 ✉ mary.harpley@hounslow.gov.uk

Senior Management: Mr Richard Gruet, Assistant Director - Corporate Governance, Civic Centre, Lampton Road, Hounslow TW3 4DN ☎ 020 8583 2023 ✉ richard.gruet@hounslow.gov.uk

Senior Management: Mr Mike Jordan, Director of Environment, Civic Centre, Lampton Road, Hounslow TW3 4DN ☎ 020 8583 5331 🖷 020 8283 4900 ✉ michael.jordan@hounslow.gov.uk

Senior Management: Mr Anthony Kemp, Director of Corporate Services, Civic Centre, Lampton Road, Hounslow TW3 4DN ☎ 020 8583 2288 ✉ anthony.kemp@hounslow.gov.uk

Senior Management: Ms Mimi Konigsberg, Director of Community Services, Civic Centre, Lampton Road, Hounslow TW3 4DN ☎ 020 8583 3500 🖷 020 8583 3077 ✉ mimi.konigsberg@hounslow.gov.uk

Senior Management: Ms Judith Pettersen, Director of Children's Services & Lifelong Learning, Civic Centre, Lampton Road, Hounslow TW3 4DN ☎ 020 8583 2901 🖷 020 8583 2907 ✉ judith.pettersen@hounslow.gov.uk

Best Value: Mr David Allum, Director of Corporate Services, Hounslow Homes, St Catherines House, 2 Hanworth Road, Feltham TW13 5AB ☎ 020 8583 3938 🖷 020 8583 3730 ✉ david.allum@hounslowhomes.org.uk

Building Control: Ms Cathy Gallagher, Assistant Director - Regulatory & Development Services, Civic Centre, Lampton Road, Hounslow TW3 4DN ☎ 020 8583 4945 ✉ cathy.gallgher@hounslow.gov.uk

Building Control: Mr Simon Lawes, Head of Building Control, Civic Centre, Lampton Road, Hounslow TW3 4DN ☎ 020 8583 5402 🖷 020 8583 5405 ✉ simon.lawes@hounslow.gov.uk

Catering Services: Mr Nick Moore, Interim General Manager - DSO Catering, Spring Grove House, West Thames College, Isleworth TW7 4HS ☎ 020 8583 2932 ✉ nick.moore@hounslow.gov.uk

Children / Youth Services: Ms Judith Pettersen, Director of Children's Services & Lifelong Learning, Civic Centre, Lampton Road, Hounslow TW3 4DN ☎ 020 8583 2901 🖷 020 8583 2907 ✉ judith.pettersen@hounslow.gov.uk

Civil Registration: Ms Susan Hayter, Registration & Nationality Service Manager Superintendent Registrar, Civic Centre, Lampton Road, Hounslow TW3 4DN ☎ 020 8583 2086 ✉ susan.hayter@hounslow.gov.uk

PR / Communications: Mr Andy Allsopp, Head of Corporate Communications, Civic Centre, Lampton Road, Hounslow TW3 4DN ☎ 020 8583 2180 ✉ andy.allsopp@hounslow.gov.uk

Community Planning: Ms Merle Abbott, Head of Inclusion, Civic Centre, Lampton Road, Hounslow TW3 4DN ☎ 020 8583 2788 ✉ merle.abbott@hounslow.gov.uk

Community Safety: Ms Kirti Sisodia, Head of Community Safety & Crime Reduction, Civic Centre, Lampton Road, Hounslow TW3 4DN ☎ 020 8583 2464 🖷 020 8583 2466 ✉ kirti.sisodia@hounslow.gov.uk

Computer Management: Ms Barbara Munden, Head of ICT, Civic Centre, Lampton Road, Hounslow TW3 4DN ☎ 020 8583 5950 ✉ barbara.munden@hounslow.gov.uk

Consumer Protection and Trading Standards: Mr Nigel Farmer, Head of Business Regulations, Civic Centre, Lampton Road, Hounslow TW3 4DN ☎ 020 8583 5147 🖷 020 8583 5130 ✉ nigel.farmer@hounslow.gov.uk

Corporate Services: Ms Jini Amarasekara, Acting Head of Corporate Communications, Civic Centre, Lampton Road, Hounslow TW3 4DN ☎ 020 8583 2186 ✉ jini.amarasekara@hounslow.gov.uk

Corporate Services: Mr Anthony Kemp, Director of Corporate Services, Civic Centre, Lampton Road, Hounslow TW3 4DN ☎ 020 8583 2288 ✉ anthony.kemp@hounslow.gov.uk

Customer Service: Mr Robert Della-Sala, Head of Customer Services, Civic Centre, Lampton Road, Hounslow TW3 4DN

☎ 020 8583 2279 🖷 020 8583 2592
✉ robert.della-sala@hounslow.gov.uk

Customer Service: Mr David Palmer, Head of Business Support, Civic Centre, Lampton Road, Hounslow TW3 4DN ☎ 020 8583 5300 ✉ david.palmer@hounslow.gov.uk

Direct Labour: Mr Sayeed Kadir, Director of Property Services - Hounslow Homes, Hounslow Homes, Civic Centre, Lampton Road, Hounslow TW3 4DN ☎ 020 8583 4301 🖷 020 8583 3709 ✉ sayeed.kadir@hounslowhomes.org.uk

Economic Development: Ms Jan Henson, Principal Economic Development Officer, Civic Centre, Lampton Road, Hounslow TW3 4DN ☎ 020 8583 2420 🖷 202 8583 2106 ✉ jan.henson@hounslow.gov.uk

Education: Ms Judith Pettersen, Director of Children's Services & Lifelong Learning, Civic Centre, Lampton Road, Hounslow TW3 4DN ☎ 020 8583 2901 🖷 020 8583 2907 ✉ judith.pettersen@hounslow.gov.uk

E-Government: Ms Barbara Munden, Head of ICT, Civic Centre, Lampton Road, Hounslow TW3 4DN ☎ 020 8583 5950 ✉ barbara.munden@hounslow.gov.uk

Electoral Registration: Ms Angela Holden, Electoral Manager, Civic Centre, Lampton Road, Hounslow TW3 4DN ☎ 020 8583 2095 🖷 020 8583 2055 ✉ angela.holden@hounslow.gov.uk

Emergency Planning: Mr Andre Paul Lyons, Interim Head of Emergency Planning, Civic Centre, Lampton Road, Hounslow TW3 4DN ☎ 020 8583 5019 ✉ andre-paullyons@hounslow.gov.uk

Environmental Health: Mr Gerry McCarthy, Head of Pollution Control Team, Civic Centre, Lampton Road, Hounslow TW3 4DN ☎ 020 8583 5183 ✉ gerry.mccarthy@hounslow.gov.uk

Estates, Property & Valuation: Mrs Angela Rench, Head of Property Management in Corporate Property, Civic Centre, Lampton Road, Hounslow TW3 4DN ☎ 020 8583 2500 🖷 020 8583 2515 ✉ angela.rench@hounslow.gov.uk

Events Manager: Ms Andreea Fitzgerald, Events Manager, Civic Centre, Lampton Road, Hounslow TW3 4DN ☎ 020 8583 2547 ✉ andreea.fitzgerald@hounslow.gov.uk

Facilities: Ms Anna Harries, Head of Facilities, Civic Centre, Lampton Road, Hounslow TW3 4DN ☎ 020 8583 4079 🖷 020 8583 2488 ✉ anna.harries@hounslow.gov.uk

Finance and Treasurer: Mr David Burton, Head of Finance - Environment, Civic Centre, Lampton Road, Hounslow TW3 4DN ☎ 020 8583 5311 ✉ david.burton@hounslow.gov.uk

Finance and Treasurer: Mr Stephen Fitzgerald, Assistant Director - Finance, Civic Centre, Lampton Road, Hounslow TW3 4DN ☎ 020 8583 2300 ✉ stephen.fitzgerald@hounslow.gov.uk

Finance and Treasurer: Ms Christine Holland, Head of Central Finance (CED), Civic Centre, Lampton Road, Hounslow TW3 4DN ☎ 020 8583 2380 ✉ christine.holland@hounslow.gov.uk

Finance and Treasurer: Mr Alex Taylor, Head of Finance & Accountancy (CSLL), Civic Centre, Lampton Road, Hounslow TW3 4DN ☎ 020 8583 2836 ✉ alex.taylor@hounslow.gov.uk

Grounds Maintenance: Mr Andrew Smith, Leisure & Cultural Services, Civic Centre, Lampton Road, Hounslow TW3 4DN ☎ 020 8583 6794 ✉ andrew.smith1@hounslow.gov.uk

Health and Safety: Ms Geraldine Austen-Reed, Lead Occupational Health & Safety Advisor, Civic Centre, Lampton Road, Hounslow TW3 4DN

Highways: Mr Krishnan Radhakrishnan, Head of Street Care Services, Civic Centre, Lampton Road, Hounslow TW3 4DN ☎ 020 8583 5315 🖷 020 8583 4973 ✉ krishnan.radhakrishnan@hounslow.gov.uk

Home Energy Conservation: Mr Charles Pipe, Energy Efficiency Advisor, Civic Centre, Lampton Road, Hounslow TW3 4DN ☎ 020 8583 3963 🖷 020 8583 3990 ✉ charles.pipe@hounslow.gov.uk

Housing: Ms Alison Simmons, Assistant Director - Housing Strategy Services, Civic Centre, Lampton Road, Hounslow TW3 4DN ☎ 020 8583 3500 ✉ alison.simmons@hounslow.gov.uk

Housing Maintenance: Ms Bernadette O'Shea, Chief Executive - Hounslow Homes, St Catherine's House, 2 hanworth Road, Feltham TW13 5AB ☎ 020 8583 3707 🖷 020 8583 2592 ✉ bernadette.oshea@hounslow.gov.uk

Local Area Agreement: Ms Helen Wilson, Policy Officer, Civic Centre, Lampton Road, Hounslow TW3 4DN ☎ 020 8583 2461 ✉ helen.wilson@hounslow.gov.uk

Legal: Mr Richard Gruet, Assistant Director - Corporate Governance, Civic Centre, Lampton Road, Hounslow TW3 4DN ☎ 020 8583 2023 ✉ richard.gruet@hounslow.gov.uk

Leisure and Cultural Services: Mr Hamish Pringle, Assistant Director - Leisure and Cultural Services, Civic Centre, Lampton Road, Hounslow TW3 4DN ☎ 202 8583 4647 ✉ Hamish.pringle@gov.uk

Licensing: Mr Nigel Farmer, Head of Business Regulations, Civic Centre, Lampton Road, Hounslow TW3 4DN ☎ 020 8583 5147 🖷 020 8583 5130 ✉ nigel.farmer@hounslow.gov.uk

Lifelong Learning: Ms Judith Pettersen, Director of Children's Services & Lifelong Learning, Civic Centre, Lampton Road, Hounslow TW3 4DN ☎ 020 8583 2901 🖷 020 8583 2907 ✉ judith.pettersen@hounslow.gov.uk

Lighting: Mr Ian Goodger, Senior Street Lighting Engineer, Civic Centre, Lampton Road, Hounslow TW3 4DN ☎ 020 8583 4953 🖷 020 8583 4955 ✉ ian.goodger@hounslow.gov.uk

Lottery Funding, Charity and Voluntary: Ms Uttam Gujral, Head of Community Investment & Cohesion, Civic Centre, Lampton Road, Hounslow TW3 4DN ☎ 020 8583 2455 🖷 020 8583 2466 ✉ uttam.gujral@hounslow.gov.uk

Member Services: Mr Thomas Ribbits, Head of Democratic

Services, Civic Centre, Lampton Road, Hounslow TW3 4DN ☎ 020 8583 2251 🖷 020 8583 2252 ✉ thomas.ribbits@hounslow.gov.uk

Member Services: Ms Sunita Sharma, Head of Scrutiny & Performance, Civic Centre, Lampton Road, Hounslow TW3 4DN ☎ 020 8583 2470 ✉ sunita.sharma@hounslow.gov.uk

Parking: Mr Steve Prince, Head of Parking, Civic Centre, Lampton Road, Hounslow TW3 4DN ☎ 020 8583 6222 ✉ steve.prince@hounslow.gov.uk

Personnel / HR: Mr John Kitching, Head of Human Resources, Civic Centre, Lampton Road, Hounslow TW3 4DN ☎ 020 8583 2287 ✉ john.kitching@hounslow.gov.uk

Planning: Mr Mike Jordan, Director of Environment, Civic Centre, Lampton Road, Hounslow TW3 4DN ☎ 020 8583 5331 🖷 020 8283 4900 ✉ michael.jordan@hounslow.gov.uk

Procurement: Ms Christine Holland, Interim Procurement Supervisor, Civic Centre, Lampton Road, Hounslow TW3 4DN ☎ 020 8583 2380 ✉ christine.holland@hounslow.gov.uk

Public Libraries: Mr Tim Douglas, Leisure & Cultural Services Manager, Civic Centre, Lampton Road, Hounslow TW3 4DN ☎ 020 8583 3538 ✉ tim.douglas@hounslow.gov.uk

Recycling & Waste Minimisation: Ms Natasha Epstein, Head of Waste & Recycling, Civic Centre, Lampton Road, Hounslow TW3 4DN ☎ 020 8583 5065 🖷 020 8583 5134 ✉ natasha.epstein@hounslow.gov.uk

Regeneration: Ms Christel Dance, Head of Transformation & Programmes, Civic Centre, Lampton Road, Hounslow TW3 4DN ☎ 020 8583 2125 ✉ christel.dance@hounslow.gov.uk

Road Safety: Ms Liz Knight, Road Safety Manager, Civic Centre, Lampton Road, Hounslow TW3 4DN ☎ 020 8583 5034 🖷 020 8583 5044 ✉ elisabeth.knight@hounslow.gov.uk

Social Services: Mr Martin Elliott, Assistant Director - Adult Social Care, Civic Centre, Lampton Road, Hounslow TW3 4DN ☎ 020 8583 3593

Social Services (Adult): Ms Mimi Konigsberg, Director of Community Services, Civic Centre, Lampton Road, Hounslow TW3 4DN ☎ 020 8583 3500 🖷 020 8583 3077 ✉ mimi.konigsberg@hounslow.gov.uk

Social Services (Children): Ms Chris Hogan, Assistant Director - Specialist Services, Civic Centre, Lampton Road, Hounslow TW3 4DN ☎ 020 8583 3002 🖷 020 8583 2907 ✉ chris.hogan@hounslow.gov.uk

Staff Training: Ms Denise July, Head of Organisational Development, Civic Centre, Lampton Road, Hounslow TW3 4DN ☎ 020 8583 2150 🖷 020 8583 2130 ✉ denise.july@hounslow.gov.uk

Street Scene: Mr Krishnan Radhakrishnan, Head of Street Care Services, Civic Centre, Lampton Road, Hounslow TW3 4DN ☎ 020 8583 5315 🖷 020 8583 4973 ✉ krishnan.radhakrishnan@hounslow.gov.uk

Sustainable Development: Mr Rob Gibson, Head of Environmental Strategy, Civic Centre, Lampton Road, Hounslow TW3 4DN ☎ 020 8583 5217 🖷 020 8583 5233 ✉ rob.gibson@hounslow.gov.uk

Tourism: Mr Hamish Pringle, Assistant Director - Leisure and Cultural Services, Civic Centre, Lampton Road, Hounslow TW3 4DN ☎ 202 8583 4647 ✉ Hamish.pringle@gov.uk

Traffic Management: Mr Nick Woods, Head of Traffic Management, Civic Centre, Lampton Road, Hounslow TW3 4DN ☎ 020 8583 4870 🖷 020 8582 4880 ✉ nick.woods@hounslow.gov.uk

Transport: Mr Chris Calvi-Freeman, Head of Transport, Civic Centre, Lampton Road, Hounslow TW3 4DN ☎ 020 8583 5215 🖷 020 8583 5233 ✉ chris.calvi-freeman@hounslow.gov.uk

Transport Planner: Mr Chris Calvi-Freeman, Head of Transport, Civic Centre, Lampton Road, Hounslow TW3 4DN ☎ 020 8583 5215 🖷 020 8583 5233 ✉ chris.calvi-freeman@hounslow.gov.uk

Waste Collection and Disposal: Ms Natasha Epstein, Head of Waste & Recycling, Civic Centre, Lampton Road, Hounslow TW3 4DN ☎ 020 8583 5065 🖷 020 8583 5134 ✉ natasha.epstein@hounslow.gov.uk

Waste Management: Ms Natasha Epstein, Head of Waste & Recycling, Civic Centre, Lampton Road, Hounslow TW3 4DN ☎ 020 8583 5065 🖷 020 8583 5134 ✉ natasha.epstein@hounslow.gov.uk

MEMBERS OF THE COUNCIL (60)

***Mayor:* Grewal**, Pritam (LAB - Hounslow Central)
pritam.grewal@hounslow.gov.uk
***Deputy Mayor:* Bains**, Mindu (LAB - Isleworth)
mindu.bains@hounslow.gov.uk
***Leader of the Council:* Sharma**, Jagdish Rai (LAB - Hounslow West)
jagdish.sharma@hounslow.gov.uk
***Deputy Leader of the Council:* Cadbury**, Ruth (LAB - Brentford)
ruth.cadbury@hounslow.gov.uk
***Group Leader:* Bowen**, Mark (CON - Feltham North)
mark.bowen@hounslow.gov.uk
Barber, Alan (LAB - Hanworth)
alan.barber@hounslow.gov.uk
Barwood, Felicity (CON - Chiswick Riverside)
felicity.barwood@hounslow.gov.uk
Bath, Lily (LAB - Hounslow Central)
lily.bath@hounslow.gov.uk
Bath, Rajinder (LAB - Heston West)
rajinder.bath@hounslow.gov.uk
Botterill, Colin (CON - Feltham West)
colin.botterill@hounslow.gov.uk
Bruce, Tom (LAB - Bedfont)
tom.bruce@hounslow.gov.uk
Carey, Peter (CON - Osterley and Spring Grove)
peter.carey@hounslow.gov.uk
Chatt, John (LAB - Cranford)

john.chatt@hounslow.gov.uk
Collins, Melvin (LAB - Brentford)
mel.collins@hounslow.gov.uk
Cooper, John (LAB - Feltham West)
john.cooper@hounslow.gov.uk
Curran, Steve (LAB - Syon)
steve.curran@hounslow.gov.uk
Davies, Linda (CON - Hounslow South)
linda.davies@hounslow.gov.uk
Davies, Samantha (CON - Turnham Green)
samantha.davies@hounslow.gov.uk
Dennison, Theo (LAB - Syon)
theo.dennison@hounslow.gov.uk
Dhillon, Poonam (LAB - Cranford)
poonam.dhillon@hounslow.gov.uk
Dhillon, Gopal (LAB - Heston Central)
gopal.dhillon@hounslow.gov.uk
Dhillon, Ajmer (LAB - Hounslow West)
ajmer.dhillon@hounslow.gov.uk
Ellar, Colin (LAB - Hounslow Heath)
colin.ellar@hounslow.gov.uk
Ellar, Jason (LAB - Syon)
jason.ellar@hounslow.gov.uk
Fisher, Bradley (CON - Hounslow South)
bradley.fisher@hounslow.gov.uk
Fisher, Pamela (CON - Hounslow South)
pamela.fisher@hounslow.gov.uk
Gill, Mohinder (LAB - Heston Central)
mohinder.gill@hounslow.gov.uk
Grewal, Ajmer (LAB - Hounslow Central)
ajmer.grewal@hounslow.gov.uk
Grewal, Darshan (LAB - Hounslow Heath)
darhsan.grewal@hounslow.gov.uk
Gupta, Sachin (LAB - Bedfont)
sachin.gupta@hounslow.gov.uk
Harmer, Mat (LAB - Brentford)
matt.harmer@hounslow.gov.uk
Harris, Barbara (CON - Feltham West)
barbara.harris@hounslow.gov.uk
Hearn, Sam (CON - Chiswick Riverside)
sam.hearn@hounslow.gov.uk
Hughes, Elizabeth (LAB - Heston West)
elizabeth.hughes@hounslow.gov.uk
Hughes, David (LAB - Hanworth)
david.hughes@hounslow.gov.uk
Hutchison, Gill (CON - Feltham North)
gillian.hutchinson@hounslow.gov.uk
Jabbal, Paul (CON - Hanworth Park)
paul.jabbal@hounslow.gov.uk
Kaur, Kamaljit (LAB - Heston East)
kamaljit.kaur@hounslow.gov.uk
Lal, Gurmail Singh (LAB - Heston East)
gurmail.lal@hounslow.gov.uk
Lee, Adrian (CON - Turnham Green)
adrian.lee@hounslow.gov.uk
Lynch, Paul (CON - Chiswick Riverside)
paul.lynch@hounslow.gov.uk
Mammatt, Liz (CON - Bedfont)
liz.mammatt@hounslow.gov.uk
Mann, Amritpal (LAB - Heston East)
amit.mann@hounslow.gov.uk
Mayne, Ed (LAB - Isleworth)
ed.mayne@hounslow.gov.uk
McGregor, Gerald (CON - Chiswick Homefields)
gerald.mcgregor@hounslow.gov.uk
Morgan-Watts, Andy (CON - Hanworth)
andrew.morgan-watts@hounslow.gov.uk
O'Reilly, Sheila (CON - Osterley and Spring Grove)
sheilaoreilly6@hotmail.com
Oulds, Robert (CON - Chiswick Homefields)
robert.oulds@hounslow.gov.uk
Rajawat, Shantanu (LAB - Heston West)
Shantanu.Rajawat@hounslow.gov.uk
Reid, Barbara (CON - Osterley and Spring Grove)
barbara.reid@hounslow.gov.uk
Samson, Sue (LAB - Isleworth)
sue.sampson@hounslow.gov.uk
Sangha, Sohan Singh (LAB - Cranford)
sohan.sangha@hounslow.gov.uk
Smart, Corinna (LAB - Hounslow Heath)
corinna.smart@hounslow.gov.uk
Sond, Balvir (LAB - Hounslow West)
balvir.sond@hounslow.gov.uk
Stewart, Becky (CON - Hanworth Park)
councillorstewart44@fsmail.net
Thompson, Peter (CON - Turnham Green)
peter.thompson@hounslow.gov.uk
Todd, John (CON - Chiswick Homefields)
john.todd@hounslow.gov.uk
Vaught, Peta (LAB - Heston Central)
peta.vaught@hounslow.gov.uk
Williams, Beverley (CON - Hanworth Park)
beverley.williams@hounslow.gov.uk
Wilson, Allan (CON - Feltham North)
allan.wilson@hounslow.gov.uk

POLITICAL COMPOSITION
LAB: 35, CON: 25

CABINET
Leader: Mr Jagdish Rai Sharma
Deputy Leader: Ms Ruth Cadbury
Adult Social Care & Health: Mr Gurmail Singh Lal
Children, Youth & Families: Ms Lily Bath
Community Safety & Regulatory Services: Mr Ed Mayne
Communities: Mr Sachin Gupta
Education: Mr Sachin Gupta
Environment: Ms Corinna Smart
Finance & Performance: Mr Theo Dennison
Leisure & Well-Being: Mr Pritam Grewal

COMMITTEE CHAIRS
Audit: Mr John Chatt
Children & Young People: Ms Balvir Sond
Finance & Performance: Mr Rajinder Bath
Health & Adult Care: Ms Poonam Dhillon
Housing & Environment: Mr Mohinder Gill
Licensing: Mr Darshan Grewal
Overview & Scrutiny: Mr Sohan Singh Sangha
Pension Fund: Mr John Chatt
Planning: Mr Theo Dennison

HUNTINGDONSHIRE D

Huntingdonshire District Council, Pathfinder House, St. Mary's Street, Huntingdon PE29 3TN ☎ 01480 388388 🖷 01480 388099 mail@huntsdc.gov.uk 💻 www.huntsdc.gov.uk

LOCAL AUTHORITIES

FACTS & FIGURES

Police Authority: Cambridgeshire Police Authority
Health Authority: East of England Strategic Health Authority
Learning and Skills Council: Eastern
Parliamentary Constituencies: Cambridgeshire North West, Huntingdon
EU Constituencies: Eastern
Election Frequency: Elections are by thirds
Twinning: Huntingdonshire: Landkreis Marburg - Biedenkopf (Germany); Huntingdon and Godmanchester: Salon-de-Provence (France) and Werthein am Main (Germany); Szentendre (Hungary); St. Ives: Stadtallendorf (Germany); St. Neots: Faches Thumesnil (France); Sawtry: Gemeinde Weimar (Germany)

PRINCIPAL OFFICERS

Senior Management: Mr Terry Parker, Managing Director (Finance), Pathfinder House, St. Mary's Street, Huntingdon PE29 3TN ☎ 01480 388388 🖷 01480 388099 ✉ terry.parker@huntsdc.gov.uk

Senior Management: Mr Malcolm Sharp, Managing Director (Communities, Partnerships & Projects), Pathfinder House, St. Mary's Street, Huntingdon PE29 3TN ☎ 01480 388388 🖷 01480 388099 ✉ malcolm.sharp@huntsdc.gov.uk

Architect, Building / Property Services: Dr Paul Jose, Head of Environmental Management, Pathfinder House, St. Mary's Street, Huntingdon PE29 3TN ☎ 01480 388388 🖷 01480 388099 ✉ paul.jose@huntsdc.gov.uk

Building Control: Mr Graham Shipley, Building Control Manager, Pathfinder House, St. Mary's Street, Huntingdon PE29 3TN ☎ 01480 388388 🖷 01480 388099 ✉ graham.shipley@huntsdc.gov.uk

PR / Communications: Mrs Donna Rocket, Corporate Project Officer - Communications, Pathfinder House, St. Mary's Street, Huntingdon PE29 3TN ☎ 01480 388388 🖷 01480 388099 ✉ donna.rocket@huntsdc.gov.uk

Community Planning: Mr Dan Smith, Community Initiatives Manager, Pathfinder House, St. Mary's Street, Huntingdon PE29 3TN ☎ 01480 388388 🖷 01480 388099 ✉ dan.smith@huntsdc.gov.uk

Community Safety: Miss Claudia Waters, Team Leader - Community Safety, Pathfinder House, St. Mary's Street, Huntingdon PE29 3TN ☎ 01480 388388 🖷 01480 388099 ✉ claudia.waters@huntsdc.gov.uk

Computer Management: Mr Chris Hall, Head of Information Management Division, Pathfinder House, St. Mary's Street, Huntingdon PE29 3TN ☎ 01480 388388 🖷 01480 388099 ✉ chris.hall@huntsdc.gov.uk

Contracts: Mr Nigel Arkle, Procurement Manager, Pathfinder House, St. Mary's Street, Huntingdon PE29 3TN ☎ 01480 388388 🖷 01480 388099 ✉ nigel.arkle@huntsdc.gov.uk

Customer Service: Mrs Julia Barber, Head of Customer Services, Pathfinder House, St. Mary's Street, Huntingdon PE29 3TN ☎ 01480 388105 ✉ julie.barber@huntsdc.gov.uk

Economic Development: Mrs Helen Donellan, Corporate Team Manager, Pathfinder House, St. Mary's Street, Huntingdon PE29 3TN ☎ 01480 388388 🖷 01480 388099 ✉ helen.donnellan@huntsdc.gov.uk

E-Government: Mr Chris Hall, Head of Information Management Division, Pathfinder House, St. Mary's Street, Huntingdon PE29 3TN ☎ 01480 388388 🖷 01480 388099 ✉ chris.hall@huntsdc.gov.uk

Electoral Registration: Miss Laura Lock, Elections Manager, Pathfinder House, St. Mary's Street, Huntingdon PE29 3TN ☎ 01480 388388 🖷 01480 388099 ✉ laura.lock@huntsdc.gov.uk

Environmental / Technical Services: Dr Paul Jose, Head of Environmental Management, Pathfinder House, St. Mary's Street, Huntingdon PE29 3TN ☎ 01480 388388 🖷 01480 388099 ✉ paul.jose@huntsdc.gov.uk

Environmental Health: Dr Susan Lammin, Head of Environmental & Community Health Services, Pathfinder House, St. Mary's Street, Huntingdon PE29 3TN ☎ 01480 388388 🖷 01480 388099 ✉ susan.lammin@huntsdc.gov.uk

Estates, Property & Valuation: Mr Colin Meadowcroft, Head of Legal & Estates, Pathfinder House, St. Mary's Street, Huntingdon PE29 3TN ☎ 01480 388388 🖷 01480 388099 ✉ colin.meadowcroft@huntsdc.gov.uk

Finance and Treasurer: Mr Steve Couper, Head of Financial Services, Pathfinder House, St. Mary's Street, Huntingdon PE29 3TN ☎ 01480 388388 🖷 01480 388099 ✉ steve.couper@huntsdc.gov.uk

Fleet Management: Dr Paul Jose, Head of Environmental Management, Pathfinder House, St. Mary's Street, Huntingdon PE29 3TN ☎ 01480 388388 🖷 01480 388099 ✉ paul.jose@huntsdc.gov.uk

Grounds Maintenance: Mr Gareth Jakes, Supervising Inspector - Arboriculture, Pathfinder House, St. Mary's Street, Huntingdon PE29 3TN ☎ 01480 388388 ✉ gareth.jakes@huntingdonshire.gov.uk

Health and Safety: Mr Chris Lloyd, Health Protection Manager, Pathfinder House, St. Mary's Street, Huntingdon PE29 3TN ☎ 01480 388388 🖷 01480 388099 ✉ chris.lloyd@huntsdc.gov.uk

Home Energy Conservation: Ms Julia Blackwell, Energy Efficiency Officer, Pathfinder House, St. Mary's Street, Huntingdon PE29 3TN ☎ 01480 388388 🖷 01480 388099 ✉ julia.blackwell@huntsdc.gov.uk

Housing: Mrs Julia Barber, Head of Customer Services, Pathfinder House, St. Mary's Street, Huntingdon PE29 3TN ☎ 01480 388105 ✉ julie.barber@huntsdc.gov.uk

Housing Maintenance: Mrs Julia Barber, Head of Customer Services, Pathfinder House, St. Mary's Street, Huntingdon PE29 3TN ☎ 01480 388105 ✉ julie.barber@huntsdc.gov.uk

Legal: Mr Colin Meadowcroft, Head of Legal & Estates, Pathfinder House, St. Mary's Street, Huntingdon PE29 3TN ☏ 01480 388388 🖷 01480 388099 ✉ colin.meadowcroft@huntsdc.gov.uk

Leisure and Cultural Services: Mr Simon Bell, General Manager - Leisure, Pathfinder House, St. Mary's Street, Huntingdon PE29 3TN ☏ 01480 388388 🖷 01480 388099 ✉ simon.bell@huntsdc.gov.uk

Licensing: Mrs Christine Allison, Licensing Manager, Pathfinder House, St. Mary's Street, Huntingdon PE29 3TN ☏ 01480 388010 🖷 01480 388099 ✉ christine.allison@huntsdc.gov.uk

Member Services: Ms Christine Deller, Democratic Services Manager, Pathfinder House, St. Mary's Street, Huntingdon PE29 3TN ☏ 01480 388388 🖷 01480 388099 ✉ christine.deller@huntsdc.gov.uk

Parking: Dr Paul Jose, Head of Environmental Management, Pathfinder House, St. Mary's Street, Huntingdon PE29 3TN ☏ 01480 388388 🖷 01480 388099 ✉ paul.jose@huntsdc.gov.uk

Partnerships: Mrs Helen Donellan, Corporate Team Manager, Pathfinder House, St. Mary's Street, Huntingdon PE29 3TN ☏ 01480 388388 🖷 01480 388099 ✉ helen.donnellan@huntsdc.gov.uk

Personnel / HR: Mr Terry Parker, Managing Director (Finance), Pathfinder House, St. Mary's Street, Huntingdon PE29 3TN ☏ 01480 388388 🖷 01480 388099 ✉ terry.parker@huntsdc.gov.uk

Planning: Mr Steve Ingram, Head of Planning Services, Pathfinder House, St. Mary's Street, Huntingdon PE29 3TN ☏ 01480 388388 🖷 01480 388099 ✉ steve.ingram@huntsdc.gov.uk

Procurement: Mr Nigel Arkle, Procurement Manager, Pathfinder House, St. Mary's Street, Huntingdon PE29 3TN ☏ 01480 388388 🖷 01480 388099 ✉ nigel.arkle@huntsdc.gov.uk

Recycling & Waste Minimisation: Mr Chris Jablonski, Environment Team Leader, Pathfinder House, St. Mary's Street, Huntingdon PE29 3TN ☏ 01480 388388 🖷 01480 388099 ✉ chris.jablonski@huntsdc.gov.uk

Regeneration: Mr Steve Ingram, Head of Planning Services, Pathfinder House, St. Mary's Street, Huntingdon PE29 3TN ☏ 01480 388388 🖷 01480 388099 ✉ steve.ingram@huntsdc.gov.uk

Staff Training: Ms Suzanne Stefanelli, Training & Development Adviser, Pathfinder House, St. Mary's Street, Huntingdon PE29 3TN ☏ 01480 388388 🖷 01480 388099 ✉ suzanne.stefanelli@huntsdc.gov.uk

Street Scene: Mrs Sonia Hansen, Street Scene Manager, Pathfinder House, St. Mary's Street, Huntingdon PE29 3TN ☏ 01480 388360 🖷 01480 388099 ✉ sonia.hansen@huntsdc.gov.uk

Sustainable Communities: Mrs Helen Donellan, Corporate Team Manager, Pathfinder House, St. Mary's Street, Huntingdon PE29 3TN ☏ 01480 388388 🖷 01480 388099 ✉ helen.donnellan@huntsdc.gov.uk

Sustainable Development: Mr Paul Bland, Planning Services Manager (Policy), Pathfinder House, St. Mary's Street, Huntingdon PE29 3TN ☏ 01480 388388 🖷 01480 388099 ✉ paul.bland@huntsdc.gov.uk

Town Centre: Mrs Helen Donellan, Corporate Team Manager, Pathfinder House, St. Mary's Street, Huntingdon PE29 3TN ☏ 01480 388388 🖷 01480 388099 ✉ helen.donnellan@huntsdc.gov.uk

Transport: Mr Stuart Bell, Transportation Team Leader, Pathfinder House, St. Mary's Street, Huntingdon PE29 3TN ☏ 01480 388388 🖷 01480 388099 ✉ stuart.bell@huntsdc.gov.uk

Transport Planner: Mr Stuart Bell, Transportation Team Leader, Pathfinder House, St. Mary's Street, Huntingdon PE29 3TN ☏ 01480 388388 🖷 01480 388099 ✉ stuart.bell@huntsdc.gov.uk

Waste Collection and Disposal: Mrs Beth Gordon, Operations Manager, Pathfinder House, St. Mary's Street, Huntingdon PE29 3TN ☏ 01480 388720

MEMBERS OF THE COUNCIL (52)

***Chair:* Boddington**, Barbara (CON - Gransden and The Offords)
barbara.boddington@huntingdonshire.gov.uk

***Vice-Chair:* Baker**, Keith (CON - Alconbury and the Stukeleys)
keith.baker@huntingdonshire.gov.uk

***Leader of the Council:* Ablewhite**, Jason (CON - St Ives - East)
jason.ablewhite@huntingdonshire.gov.uk

***Deputy Leader of the Council:* Guyatt**, Nick (CON - Elton and Folksworth)
nick.guyatt@huntingdonshire.gov.uk

***Group Leader:* Downes**, Peter (LD - Brampton)
peter.downes@huntingdonshire.gov.uk

Akthar, Sid (CON - Huntingdon East)
Sid.Akthar@huntingdonshire.gov.uk

Baker, Mike (LD - Ellington)
mike.baker@huntingdonshire.gov.uk

Banerjee, Maddie (CON - Yaxley and Farcet)
maddie.banerjee@huntingdonshire.gov.uk

Bates, Ian (CON - The Hemingfords)
ian.bates@huntingdonshire.gov.uk

Bucknell, Peter (CON - Warboys and Bury)
peter.bucknell@huntingdonshire.gov.uk

Bull, Graham (CON - Somersham)
Graham.Bull@huntingdonshire.gov.uk

Butler, Eric (CON - Yaxley and Farcet)
eric.butler@huntsdc.gov.uk

Carter, Robin (CON - Earith)

Cawley, Stephen (CON - Huntingdon West)
stephen.cawley@huntingdonshire.gov.uk

Chapman, Barry (CON - St Neots - Priory Park)
barry.chapman@huntingdonshire.gov.uk

Churchill, Ken (CON - Little Paxton)
ken.churchill@huntingdonshire.gov.uk

Clough, Terry (LD - Buckden)
terry.clough@huntingdonshire.gov.uk

Criswell, Steve (CON - Somersham)

steve.criswell@huntingdonshire.gov.uk
Curtis, Ian (UKIP - Ramsey)
Ian.Curtis@huntingdonshire.gov.uk
Davies, John (CON - St Ives - South)
john.davies@huntingdonshire.gov.uk
Dew, Douglas (CON - St Ives - South)
douglas.dew@huntingdonshire.gov.uk
Duffy, Lisa (UKIP - Ramsey)
lisa.duffy@huntingdonshire.gov.uk
Farrer, Rodney (CON - St Neots - Eaton Ford)
bob.farrer@huntingdonshire.gov.uk
Fuller, Ryan (CON - St Ives - West)
ryan.fuller@huntingdonshire.gov.uk
Giles, Derek (O - St Neots - Eaton Socon)
derek.giles@huntingdonshire.gov.uk
Gray, Jonathan (CON - Kimbolton and Staughton)
jonathan.gray@huntingdonshire.gov.uk
Greenall, Stephen (LD - Huntingdon East)
ste.greenall@huntingdonshire.gov.uk
Hansard, Andrew (CON - St Neots - Eynesbury)
andrew.hansard@huntingdonshire.gov.uk
Harlock, Gregory (CON - Fenstanton)
Greg.Harlock@huntingdonshire.gov.uk
Harrison, Roger (CON - St Neots - Eaton Socon)
roger.harrison@huntingdonshire.gov.uk
Harty, David (CON - St Neots - Eaton Ford)
david.harty@huntingdonshire.gov.uk
Howe, Robin (CON - Upwood and The Raveleys)
robin.howe@huntingdonshire.gov.uk
Hyams, Colin (CON - Godmanchester)
colin.hyams@huntingdonshire.gov.uk
Jordan, Patricia (LD - Brampton)
patricia.jordan@huntingdonshire.gov.uk
Kadewere, Patrick (LAB - Huntingdon North)
patrick.kadewere@huntingdonshire.gov.uk
Kadic, Laine (CON - Godmanchester)
laine.kadic@huntingdonshire.gov.uk
Longford, Paula (CON - St Neots - Priory Park)
paula.longford@huntingdonshire.gov.uk
Mackender-Lawrence, Alan (CON - Huntingdon North)
Alan.Mackender@huntingdonshire.gov.uk
Mitchell, Peter (CON - Stilton)
peter.mitchell@huntingdonshire.gov.uk
Oliver, Mark (CON - Yaxley and Farcet)
mark.oliver@huntingdonshire.gov.uk
Pethard, John (CON - Warboys and Bury)
john.pethard@huntingdonshire.gov.uk
Reeve, Peter (UKIP - Ramsey)
reeve@ukip.org
Reynolds, Deborah (CON - St Ives - East)
deborah.reynolds@huntingdonshire.gov.uk
Rogers, Terence (CON - Earith)
terry.rogers@huntingdonshire.gov.uk
Sanderson, Tom (CON - Huntingdon West)
tom.sanderson@huntingdonshire.gov.uk
Shellens, Michael (LD - Huntingdon East)
mike.shellens@huntingdonshire.gov.uk
Tuplin, Dick (IND - Sawtry)
dick.tuplin@huntingdonshire.gov.uk
Tysoe, Darren (CON - Sawtry)
darren.tysoe@huntingdonshire.gov.uk
Ursell, Paul (CON - St Neots - Eynesbury)
paul.ursell@huntingdonshire.gov.uk
Van De Kerkhove, Steven (LD - St Neots - Eynesbury)
steve.vandkerkhove@huntingdonshire.gov.uk
West, Richard (CON - Gransden and The Offords)
richard.west@huntingdonshire.gov.uk
Williams, Alan (CON - The Hemingfords)
alan.williams@huntingdonshire.gov.uk

POLITICAL COMPOSITION

CON: 39, LD: 7, UKIP: 3, O: 1, IND: 1, LAB: 1

CABINET

Leader / Strategic Economic Development: Mr Jason Ablewhite
Deputy Leader / Strategic Planning & Housing: Mr Nick Guyatt
Customer Services: Mr Barry Chapman
Environment: Mr Darren Tysoe
Healthy & Active Communities: Mr Tom Sanderson
Resources: Mr Jonathan Gray

COMMITTEE CHAIRS

Corporate Governance: Mr Eric Butler
Development Management: Mr Douglas Dew
Employment: Mr Stephen Cawley
Licensing & Protection: Mr John Davies
Overview & Scrutiny - Environmental Wellbeing: Mr David Harty
Overview & Scrutiny - Social Wellbeing: Mr Steve Criswell
Overview & Scrutiny: Mr Terence Rogers

HYNDBURN D

Hyndburn Borough Council, Scaitcliffe House, Ormerod Street, Accrington BB5 0PF ☎ 01254 388111 🖷 01254 392597 💻 www.hyndburnbc.gov.uk

FACTS & FIGURES

Police Authority: Lancashire Police Authority
Health Authority: North West Strategic Health Authority
Learning and Skills Council: North West
Parliamentary Constituencies: Hyndburn
EU Constituencies: North West
Election Frequency: Elections are by thirds

PRINCIPAL OFFICERS

Chief Executive: Mr David Welsby, Chief Executive, Scaitcliffe House, Ormerod Street, Accrington BB5 0PF ☎ 01254 388111 🖷 01254 380637 ✉ dave.welsby@hyndburnbc.gov.uk

Deputy Chief Executive: Mr Joe McIntyre, Deputy Chief Executive (Resources), Scaitcliffe House, Ormerod Street, Accrington BB5 0PF ☎ 01254 388111 🖷 01254 380637 ✉ joe.mcintyre@hyndburnbc.gov.uk

Deputy Chief Executive: Mr Steve Tanti, Deputy Chief Executive, Scaitcliffe House, Ormerod Street, Accrington BB5 0PF ☎ 01254 388111 🖷 01254 380637 ✉ steve.tanti@hyndburnbc.gov.uk

Senior Management: Ms Jane Ellis, Executive Director (Legal & Democratic Services), Scaitcliffe House, Ormerod Street, Accrington BB5 0PF ☎ 01254 388111 🖷 01254 380637 ✉ jane.ellis@hyndburnbc.gov.uk

Architect, Building / Property Services: Mr Ian Hoole,

Corporate Property Manager, Scaitcliffe House, Ormerod Street, Accrington BB5 0PF ☎ 01254 388111 🖷 01254 380122 ✉ ian.hoole@hyndburnbc.gov.uk

Best Value: Mr Michael Walker, Corporate Performance Manager, Scaitcliffe House, Ormerod Street, Accrington BB5 0PF ☎ 01254 388111 🖷 01254 380637 ✉ michael.walker@hyndburnbc.gov.uk

Building Control: Mr Peter Boyes, Building Control Manager, Scaitcliffe House, Ormerod Street, Accrington BB5 0PF ☎ 01254 388111 🖷 01254 391625 ✉ peter.boyes@hyndburnbc.gov.uk

PR / Communications: Mrs Cathy Kierans, Senior Marketing & Communications Officer, Scaitcliffe House, Ormerod Street, Accrington BB5 0PF ☎ 01254 388111 🖷 01254 380637 ✉ cathy.kierans@hyndburnbc.gov.uk

Community Planning: Mr Rob Grigorjevs, Head of Policy, Partnerships & Performance, 20 Cannon Street, Accrington BB5 1NJ ☎ 01254 388111 🖷 01254 380981 ✉ rob.grigorjevs@hyndburnbc.gov.uk

Community Safety: Mr Michael Walker, Corporate Performance Manager, Scaitcliffe House, Ormerod Street, Accrington BB5 0PF ☎ 01254 388111 🖷 01254 380637 ✉ michael.walker@hyndburnbc.gov.uk

Computer Management: Mr Scott Gardner, ICT Manager, Scaitcliffe House, Ormerod Street, Accrington BB5 0PF ☎ 01254 388111 🖷 01254 380272 ✉ scott.gardner@hyndburnbc.gov.uk

Corporate Services: Mr David Welsby, Chief Executive, Scaitcliffe House, Ormerod Street, Accrington BB5 0PF ☎ 01254 388111 🖷 01254 380637 ✉ dave.welsby@hyndburnbc.gov.uk

Customer Service: Mrs Pauline Duckworth, Head of Customer Services & Benefits, Town Hall, Blackburn Road, Accrington BB5 1LA ☎ 01254 380200 ✉ pauline.duckworth@hyndburnbc.gov.uk

Customer Service: Mr Lee Middlehurst, Customer Services Manager, Town Hall, Blackburn Road, Accrington BB5 1LA ☎ 01254 388111 🖷 01254 392597 ✉ lee.middlehurst@hyndburnbc.gov.uk

E-Government: Mr Scott Gardner, ICT Manager, Scaitcliffe House, Ormerod Street, Accrington BB5 0PF ☎ 01254 388111 🖷 01254 380272 ✉ scott.gardner@hyndburnbc.gov.uk

Electoral Registration: Ms Rachel Wilkinson, Elections Officer, Scaitcliffe House, Ormerod Street, Accrington BB5 0PF ☎ 01254 388111 🖷 01254 392597 ✉ rachel.wilkinson@hyndburnbc.gov.uk

Emergency Planning: Mr Paul Fleck, Safety & Emergency Planning Officer, Willows Lane Depot, Willows Lane, Accrington BB5 0RT ☎ 01254 388111 🖷 01254 872250 ✉ paul.fleck@hyndburnbc.gov.uk

Energy Management: Mr Ian Hoole, Corporate Property Manager, Scaitcliffe House, Ormerod Street, Accrington BB5 0PF ☎ 01254 388111 🖷 01254 380122 ✉ ian.hoole@hyndburnbc.gov.uk

Environmental Health: Mr Tony Akrigg, Head of Environmental Health, 20 Cannon Street, Accrington BB5 1NJ ☎ 01254 388111 🖷 01254 386711 ✉ tony.akrigg@hyndburnbc.gov.uk

Estates, Property & Valuation: Mr Ian Hoole, Corporate Property Manager, Scaitcliffe House, Ormerod Street, Accrington BB5 0PF ☎ 01254 388111 🖷 01254 380122 ✉ ian.hoole@hyndburnbc.gov.uk

Events Manager: Mr Michael Hunt, Chief Executive, Town Hall, Blackburn Road, Accrington BB5 1LA ☎ 01254 388111 🖷 01254 380291 ✉ michael.hunt@hyndburnbc.gov.uk

Finance and Treasurer: Mr Joe McIntyre, Deputy Chief Executive (Resources), Scaitcliffe House, Ormerod Street, Accrington BB5 0PF ☎ 01254 388111 🖷 01254 380637 ✉ joe.mcintyre@hyndburnbc.gov.uk

Fleet Management: Mr David Allonby, Head of Environmental Services, Willows Lane Depot, Willows Lane, Accrington BB5 0RT ☎ 01254 388111 🖷 01254 872250 ✉ david.allonby@hyndburnbc.gov.uk

Grounds Maintenance: Mr Craig Haraben, Parks & Open Spaces Manager, Willows Lane Depot, Willows Lane, Accrington BB5 0RT ☎ 01254 388111 🖷 01254 872250 ✉ craig.haraben@hyndburndc.gov.uk

Health and Safety: Mr Paul Fleck, Safety & Emergency Planning Officer, Willows Lane Depot, Willows Lane, Accrington BB5 0RT ☎ 01254 388111 🖷 01254 872250 ✉ paul.fleck@hyndburnbc.gov.uk

Housing: Mrs Judith Hodgson, Housing Advice & Homelessness Manager, 20 Cannon Street, Accrington BB5 1NJ ☎ 01254 388111 🖷 01254 389599 ✉ judith.hodgson@hyndburnbc.gov.uk

Legal: Ms Jane Ellis, Executive Director (Legal & Democratic Services), Scaitcliffe House, Ormerod Street, Accrington BB5 0PF ☎ 01254 388111 🖷 01254 380637 ✉ jane.ellis@hyndburnbc.gov.uk

Leisure and Cultural Services: Mr Michael Hunt, Chief Executive, Town Hall, Blackburn Road, Accrington BB5 1LA ☎ 01254 388111 🖷 01254 380291 ✉ michael.hunt@hyndburnbc.gov.uk

Leisure and Cultural Services: Mr Steve Tanti, Deputy Chief Executive, Scaitcliffe House, Ormerod Street, Accrington BB5 0PF ☎ 01254 388111 🖷 01254 380637 ✉ steve.tanti@hyndburnbc.gov.uk

Licensing: Mr Howard Bee, Licensing Manager, Scaitcliffe House, Ormerod Street, Accrington BB5 0PF ☎ 01254 388111 🖷 01254 386711 ✉ howard.bee@hyndburnbc.gov.uk

Member Services: Mrs Helen Gee, Member Services Manager, Scaitcliffe House, Ormerod Street, Accrington BB5 0PF ☎ 01254 388111 🖷 01254 380122 ✉ helen.gee@hyndburnbc.gov.uk

Partnerships: Mr Michael Walker, Corporate Performance Manager, Scaitcliffe House, Ormerod Street, Accrington BB5 0PF ☎ 01254 388111 🖷 01254 380637

michael.walker@hyndburnbc.gov.uk

Personnel / HR: Mrs Kirsten Burnett, Head of Human Resources, Scaitcliffe House, Ormerod Street, Accrington BB5 0PF ☎ 01254 388111 ☏ 01254 392597 kirsten.burnett@hyndburnbc.gov.uk

Planning: Mr Simon Prideaux, Chief Planning & Transportation Officer, Scaitcliffe House, Ormerod Street, Accrington BB5 0PF ☎ 01254 388111 ☏ 01254 391625 simon.prideaux@hyndburnbc.gov.uk

Procurement: Mr Derek Rydeheard, Administration Services Manager, Scaitcliffe House, Ormerod Street, Accrington BB5 0PF ☎ 01254 388111 ☏ 01254 392597 derek.rydeheard@hyndburnbc.gov.uk

Recycling & Waste Minimisation: Mr David Allonby, Head of Environmental Services, Willows Lane Depot, Willows Lane, Accrington BB5 0RT ☎ 01254 388111 ☏ 01254 872250 david.allonby@hyndburnbc.gov.uk

Regeneration: Mr Vladimir Pejcinovic, Regeneration Co-ordinator, 20 Cannon Street, Accrington BB5 1NJ ☎ 01254 388111 ☏ 01254 389599 vladimir.pejcinovic@hyndburnbc.gov.uk

Staff Training: Ms Ivy Crossley, Principal Organisational Development Officer, Scaitcliffe House, Ormerod Street, Accrington BB5 0PF ☎ 01254 388111 ☏ 01254 392597 ivy.crossley@hyndburnbc.gov.uk

Sustainable Communities: Mr Simon Prideaux, Chief Planning & Transportation Officer, Scaitcliffe House, Ormerod Street, Accrington BB5 0PF ☎ 01254 388111 ☏ 01254 391625 simon.prideaux@hyndburnbc.gov.uk

Sustainable Development: Ms Anne Hourican, Senior Environmental Initiatives Officer, Scaitcliffe House, Ormerod Street, Accrington BB5 0PF ☎ 01254 388111 ☏ 01254 391625 anne.hourican@hyndburnbc.gov.uk

Tourism: Mr Michael Hunt, Chief Executive, Town Hall, Blackburn Road, Accrington BB5 1LA ☎ 01254 388111 ☏ 01254 380291 michael.hunt@hyndburnbc.gov.uk

Town Centre: Mr Rob Grigorjevs, Head of Policy, Partnerships & Performance, 20 Cannon Street, Accrington BB5 1NJ ☎ 01254 388111 ☏ 01254 380981 rob.grigorjevs@hyndburnbc.gov.uk

Waste Collection and Disposal: Mr David Allonby, Head of Environmental Services, Willows Lane Depot, Willows Lane, Accrington BB5 0RT ☎ 01254 388111 ☏ 01254 872250 david.allonby@hyndburnbc.gov.uk

Waste Management: Mr David Allonby, Head of Environmental Services, Willows Lane Depot, Willows Lane, Accrington BB5 0RT ☎ 01254 388111 ☏ 01254 872250 david.allonby@hyndburnbc.gov.uk

MEMBERS OF THE COUNCIL (35)

***Mayor:* Broadley**, John (LAB - Church)
john.broadley@hyndburnbc.gov.uk
***Deputy Mayor:* Addison**, Judith (CON - Immanuel)
judith.addison@hyndburnfc.gov.uk
***Leader of the Council:* Parkinson**, Miles (LAB - Altham)
miles.parkinson@hyndburnbc.gov.uk
***Deputy Leader of the Council:* Dad**, Munsif (LAB - Spring Hill)
munsif.dad@hyndburnbc.gov.uk
***Deputy Leader of the Council:* Pritchard**, Clare (LAB - Milnshaw)
clare.pritchard@hyndburnbc.gov.uk
Ayub, Mohammad (LAB - Central)
mohammad.ayub@hyndburnbc.gov.uk
Aziz, Noordad (LAB - Netherton)
noordad.aziz@hyndburnbc.gov.uk
Barton, Pam (LAB - Spring Hill)
pam.barton@hyndburnbc.gov.uk
Britcliffe, Peter (CON - St. Andrew's)
peter.britcliffe@hyndburnbc.gov.uk
Cleary, Clare (LAB - Rishton)
clare.cleary@hyndburnbc.gov.uk
Collingridge, Nick (IND - Clayton-le-Moors)
nick.collingridge@hyndburnbc.gov.uk
Cox, Paul (LAB - Milnshaw)
paul.cox@hyndburnbc.gov.uk
Dawson, Bernard (LAB - Peel)
b.dawson@btinternet.com
Dobson, Tony (CON - Barnfield)
tdob@aol.com
Dwyer, Wendy Beatrice (LAB - Peel)
wendy_dwyer35@talktalk.net
Fisher, Christopher (LAB - Altham)
chris.fisher@hyndburnbc.gov.uk
Grayson, Harry (LAB - Rishton)
harry.grayson@hyndburnbc.gov.uk
Harrison, June (LAB - Barnfield)
june.harrison@hyndburnbc.gov.uk
Haworth, Marlene (CON - St. Oswald's)
marlene.haworth@hyndburnbc.gov.uk
Hayes, Douglas (CON - St. Oswald's)
dougossy@msn.com
Hurn, Terry (CON - Baxenden)
terry.hurn@hyndburnbc.gov.uk
Khan, Abdul (LAB - Central)
abdul.khan@hyndburnbc.gov.uk
McCormack, Colette (LAB - Immanuel)
colette.mccormack@hyndburnbc.gov.uk
Molineux, Kerry-Anne (LAB - Overton)
kerry.molineux@hyndburnbc.gov.uk
Molineux, Gareth (LAB - Overton)
gareth.molineux@hyndburnbc.gov.uk
Moss, Ken (LAB - Rishton)
ken.moss@hyndburnfc.gov.uk
O'Kane, Tim (LAB - Clayton-le-Moors)
tim.okane@hyndburnbc.gov.uk
Parkins, David (IND - Huncoat)
dave.parkins@hyndburnbc.gov.uk
Pinder, William (LAB - St. Andrew's)
bill.pinder@hyndburnbc.gov.uk
Pratt, Kath (CON - Baxenden)
kathleen.pratt@hyndburnbc.gov.uk
Roberts, Brian (CON - St. Oswald's)
brian.roberts@hyndburnbc.gov.uk
Robinson, Ian (IND - Overton)
ian.robinson@hyndburnbc.gov.uk
Smith, Joan (LAB - Church)

cllrjoansmith@googlemail.com
Wells, Ciaran (LAB - Netherton)
ciaran.wells@hyndburnbc.gov.uk
Whittaker, Nick (CON - Huncoat)
nick.whittaker@hyndburnbc.gov.uk

POLITICAL COMPOSITION
LAB: 23, CON: 9, IND: 3

CABINET
Leader: Mr Miles Parkinson
Deputy Leader: Mr Munsif Dad
Deputy Leader: Ms Clare Pritchard
Health & Communities: Mrs Pam Barton
Resources: Mrs Joan Smith
Education, Leisure & Arts: Mr Ciaran Wells

COMMITTEE CHAIRS
Area Councils: Mr Harry Grayson
Audit: Mr Harry Grayson
Communities & Wellbeing (Scrutiny): Mr Tim O'Kane
Development Plan: Mr Bernard Dawson
Health & Communites: Mrs Pam Barton
Judicial: Mrs Pam Barton
Learning & Development: Ms Clare Pritchard
Planning: Mr Bernard Dawson
Regeneration & Housing Market Renewal: Ms Clare Pritchard
Resources (Scrutiny): Mr Ken Moss

INVERCLYDE S

Inverclyde Council, Municipal Buildings, Clyde Square, Greenock PA15 1LY ☎ 01475 717171 🖷 01475 712777
💻 www.inverclyde.gov.uk

FACTS & FIGURES
Police Authority: Strathclyde Police Authority
Learning and Skills Council: Scotland
Parliamentary Constituencies: Inverclyde
EU Constituencies: Scotland
Election Frequency: Elections are of whole council

PRINCIPAL OFFICERS
Chief Executive: Mr John Mundell, Chief Executive, Municipal Buildings, Clyde Square, Greenock PA15 1LY ☎ 01475 712701 🖷 01475 712777 ✉ chief.executive@inverclyde.gov.uk

Senior Management: Mr Aubrey Fawcett, Corporate Director - Environment, Regeneration & Resources, Municipal Buildings, Clyde Square, Greenock PA15 1LY ☎ 01475 712761 ✉ aubrey.fawcett@inverclyde.gov.uk

Senior Management: Mr Albert Henderson, Corporate Director - Community Health & Care Partnership, Municipal Buildings, Clyde Square, Greenock PA15 1LY ☎ 01475 712761 ✉ albert.henderson@inverclyde.gov.uk

Senior Management: Mr Robert Murphy, Corporate Director - Community Health & Care Partnership, Municipal Buildings, Clyde Square, Greenock PA15 1LY ☎ 01475 712762 ✉ robert.murphy@inverclyde.gov.uk

Senior Management: Mr Robert Stoakes, Transitional Head of ICT, Municipal Buildings, Clyde Square, Greenock PA15 1LY ☎ 01475 712765 ✉ robert.stoakes@inverclyde.gov.uk

Access Officer / Social Services (Disability): Mr Stuart Jamieson, Head of Regeneration & Planning, 6 Cathcart Square, Greenock PA15 1LS ☎ 01475 712402 🖷 01475 712468 ✉ stuart.jamieson@inverclyde.gov.uk

Architect, Building / Property Services: Mr Andrew Gerard, Head of Property Assets & Facilities Management, 6 Cathcart Square, Greenock PA15 1LS ☎ 01475 712456 ✉ andrew.gerard@inverclyde.gov.uk

Building Control: Mr Nicolas McLaren, Building Control Manager, Cathcart House, Cathcart Sqaure, Greenock PA15 1LS ☎ 01475 712403 🖷 01475 712465 ✉ nicolas.mclaren@inverclyde.gov.uk

Catering Services: Ms Elspeth Tierney, Facilities Services Manager, Municipal Buildings, Greenock PA15 1LY ☎ 01475 712449 ✉ elspeth.tierney@inverclyde.gov.uk

Civil Registration: Mr Ian Kearns, Registration Manager, 40 West Stewart Street, Greenock PA15 1YA ☎ 01475 714256 ✉ ian.kearns@inverclyde.gov.uk

PR / Communications: Mrs Elaine Dyer, Corporate Communications Manager, Municipal Buildings, Clyde Square, Greenock PA15 1LY ☎ 01475 712385 ✉ elaine.dyer@inverclyde.gov.uk

Community Planning: Mr Aubrey Fawcett, Corporate Director - Environment, Regeneration & Resources, Municipal Buildings, Clyde Square, Greenock PA15 1LY ☎ 01475 712761 ✉ aubrey.fawcett@inverclyde.gov.uk

Community Planning: Ms Miriam McKenna, Strategic Partnership Manager, Municipal Buildings, Clyde Square, Greenock PA15 1LY ☎ 01475 712042 ✉ miriam.mckenna@inverclyde.gov.uk

Computer Management: Mr Robert Stoakes, Transitional Head of ICT, Municipal Buildings, Clyde Square, Greenock PA15 1LY ☎ 01475 712765 ✉ robert.stoakes@inverclyde.gov.uk

Consumer Protection and Trading Standards: Mr John Arthur, Head of Safer & Inclusive Communities, West Stewart Street, Greenock PA15 1SN ☎ 01475 714263 🖷 01475 714253 ✉ john.arthur@inverclyde.gov.uk

Customer Service: Mr Robert Stoakes, Transitional Head of ICT, Municipal Buildings, Clyde Square, Greenock PA15 1LY ☎ 01475 712765 ✉ robert.stoakes@inverclyde.gov.uk

Direct Labour: Mr Andrew Gerard, Head of Property Assets & Facilities Management, 6 Cathcart Square, Greenock PA15 1LS ☎ 01475 712456 ✉ andrew.gerard@inverclyde.gov.uk

Economic Development: Mr Stuart Jamieson, Head of Regeneration & Planning, 6 Cathcart Square, Greenock PA15 1LS ☎ 01475 712402 🖷 01475 712468

✉ stuart.jamieson@inverclyde.gov.uk

Education: Mrs Wilma Bain, Head of Education, 105 Dalrymple Street, Greenock PA15 1LS ☎ 01475 712850 ✉ wilma.bain@inverclyde.gov.uk

Education: Ms Angela Edwards, Head of Educational Planning & Culture, 105 Dalrymple Street, Greenock PA15 1LS ✉ angela.edwards@inverclyde.gov.uk

E-Government: Mr Robert Stoakes, Transitional Head of ICT, Municipal Buildings, Clyde Square, Greenock PA15 1LY ☎ 01475 712765 ✉ robert.stoakes@inverclyde.gov.uk

Emergency Planning: Mr Colin Pearson, Civil Contingencies Officer, West Stewart Street, Greenock PA15 1SN ☎ 01475 714222 ✉ colin.pearson@inverclyde.gov.uk

Energy Management: Mr Andrew Gerard, Head of Property Assets & Facilities Management, 6 Cathcart Square, Greenock PA15 1LS ☎ 01475 712456 ✉ andrew.gerard@inverclyde.gov.uk

Environmental Health: Mr John Arthur, Head of Safer & Inclusive Communities, West Stewart Street, Greenock PA15 1SN ☎ 01475 714263 🖷 01475 714253 ✉ john.arthur@inverclyde.gov.uk

Estates, Property & Valuation: Mrs Audrey Galloway, Asset Management Planning Manager, Cathcart House, Cathcart Sqaure, Greenock PA15 1LS ☎ 01475 712508 ✉ audrey.greenwood@inverclyde.gov.uk

European Liaison: Mr Stuart Jamieson, Head of Regeneration & Planning, 6 Cathcart Square, Greenock PA15 1LS ☎ 01475 712402 🖷 01475 712468 ✉ stuart.jamieson@inverclyde.gov.uk

Events Manager: Mr Stuart Jamieson, Head of Regeneration & Planning, 6 Cathcart Square, Greenock PA15 1LS ☎ 01475 712402 🖷 01475 712468 ✉ stuart.jamieson@inverclyde.gov.uk

Finance and Treasurer: Mr Alan Puckrin, Chief Financial Officer, Municipal Buildings, Clyde Square, Greenock PA15 1LY ☎ 01475 712223 🖷 01475 712288 ✉ alan.puckrin@inverclyde.gov.uk

Fleet Management: Mr John Williams, Transport Manager, Municipal Buildings, Clyde Square, Greenock PA15 1LY ☎ 01475 717171

Grounds Maintenance: Mr William Rennie, Grounds Services Manager, Pottery Street, Greenock PA15 2UD ☎ 01475 714761 ✉ willie.rennie@inverclyde.gov.uk

Health and Safety: Ms Pauline Ramsay, Senior Health & Safety Officer, Personnel Services, Municipal Buildings, Clyde Square, Greenock PA15 1LY ☎ 01475 712717 🖷 01475 712726 ✉ pauline.ramsay@inverclyde.gov.uk

Highways: Mr Robert Graham, Environmental Services Manager Roads, Transport & Waste Services, 71 East Hamilton Street, Greenock PA15 2UA ☎ 01475 714800 🖷 01475 714825 ✉ robert.graham@inverclyde.gov.uk

Home Energy Conservation: Mr Willie Rice, Senior Grants Officer, Wallace Place, Greenock PA15 1LZ ☎ 01475 712542 🖷 01475 712573 ✉ willie.rice@inverclyde.gov.uk

Legal: Ms Elaine Paterson, Head of Legal & Democratic Services, Municipal Buildings, Clyde Square, Greenock PA15 1LY ☎ 01475 712139 🖷 01475 712137 ✉ elaine.paterson@inverclyde.gov.uk

Leisure and Cultural Services: Mr Stuart Jamieson, Head of Regeneration & Planning, 6 Cathcart Square, Greenock PA15 1LS ☎ 01475 712402 🖷 01475 712468 ✉ stuart.jamieson@inverclyde.gov.uk

Licensing: Ms Elaine Paterson, Head of Legal & Democratic Services, Municipal Buildings, Clyde Square, Greenock PA15 1LY ☎ 01475 712139 🖷 01475 712137 ✉ elaine.paterson@inverclyde.gov.uk

Lighting: Mr Robert Graham, Environmental Services Manager Roads, Transport & Waste Services, 71 East Hamilton Street, Greenock PA15 2UA ☎ 01475 714800 🖷 01475 714825 ✉ robert.graham@inverclyde.gov.uk

Lottery Funding, Charity and Voluntary: Mr Stuart Jamieson, Head of Regeneration & Planning, 6 Cathcart Square, Greenock PA15 1LS ☎ 01475 712402 🖷 01475 712468 ✉ stuart.jamieson@inverclyde.gov.uk

Personnel / HR: Mr Alasdair Moore, Head of Organisational Development & Human Resources, Municipal Buildings, Clyde Square, Greenock PA15 1LY ☎ 01475 712015 🖷 01475 712726 ✉ alasdair.moore@inverclyde.gov.uk

Planning: Mr Stuart Jamieson, Head of Regeneration & Planning, 6 Cathcart Square, Greenock PA15 1LS ☎ 01475 712402 🖷 01475 712468 ✉ stuart.jamieson@inverclyde.gov.uk

Public Libraries: Mr Stuart Jamieson, Head of Regeneration & Planning, 6 Cathcart Sqaure, Greenock PA15 1LS ☎ 01475 712402 🖷 01475 712468 ✉ stuart.jamieson@inverclyde.gov.uk

Public Libraries: Ms Alana Ward, Libraries Manager, Central Library, Clyde Square, Greenock PA15 1NB ☎ 01475 712347 ✉ alana.ward@inverclyde.gov.uk

Recycling & Waste Minimisation: Mr Drew Hall, Energy Manager, Environmental & Consumer Services, 40 West Stewart Street, Greenock PA15 1SN ☎ 01475 714272 🖷 01475 714216 ✉ drew.hall@inverclyde.gov.uk

Road Safety: Ms Margaret Dickson, Road Safety Training Officer, 71 East Hamilton Street, Greenock PA15 2UA ☎ 01475 714811 🖷 01475 714825 ✉ margaret.dickson@inverclyde.gov.uk

Social Services: Mr Robert Murphy, Corporate Director, Community Health & Care Partnership, Municipal Buildings, Clyde Square, Greenock PA15 1LY ☎ 01475 714011 🖷 01475 714060 ✉ robert.murphy@inverclyde.gov.uk

Social Services (Adult): Mr Brian Moore, Head of Community Care & Health, Dalrymple House, Dalrymple Street, Greenock

PA15 1HT ☎ 01475 714015 🖷 01475 714060
✉ brian.moore@inverclyde.gov.uk

Social Services (Children): Ms Sharon McAlees, Head of Children & Criminal Justic Services, Dalrymple House, Dalrymple Street, Greenock PA15 1UN ☎ 01475 714006 🖷 01475 712726
✉ robert.murphy@inverclyde.gov.uk

Staff Training: Mrs Carol Reid, Project Manager, Municipal Buildings, Clyde Square, Greenock PA15 1LY ☎ 01475 712027 🖷 01475 712726 ✉ carol.reid@inverclyde.gov.uk

Street Scene: Mr William Rennie, Grounds Services Manager, Pottery Street, Greenock PA15 2UD ☎ 01475 714761
✉ willie.rennie@inverclyde.gov.uk

Sustainable Development: Mr Drew Hall, Energy Manager, Environmental & Consumer Services, 40 West Stewart Street, Greenock PA15 1SN ☎ 01475 714272 🖷 01475 714216
✉ drew.hall@inverclyde.gov.uk

Tourism: Mr Stuart Jamieson, Head of Regeneration & Planning, Business Store, Greenock PA15 1DE ☎ 01475 712402 🖷 01475 712468 ✉ stuart.jamieson@inverclyde.gov.uk

Traffic Management: Mr Robert Graham, Environmental Services Manager Roads, Transport & Waste Services, 71 East Hamilton Street, Greenock PA15 2UA ☎ 01475 714800 🖷 01475 714825 ✉ robert.graham@inverclyde.gov.uk

Transport: Mr John Williams, Transport Manager, Pottery Street, Greenock PA15 2UH ☎ 01475 717171

Waste Collection and Disposal: Mr Ian Moffat, Head of Environmental & Commercial Services, Pottery Street, Greenock PA15 2UH ☎ 01475 714760 🖷 01475 714770
✉ ian.moffat@inverclyde.gov.uk

Waste Management: Mr Ian Moffat, Head of Environmental & Commercial Services, Pottery Street, Greenock PA15 2UH
☎ 01475 714760 🖷 01475 714770 ✉ ian.moffat@inverclyde.gov.uk

MEMBERS OF THE COUNCIL (20)

Ahlfeld, Ronnie (IND - Inverclyde West)
ronnie.ahlfeld@inverclyde.gov.uk
Brennan, Martin (LAB - Inverclyde North)
Brooks, Keith (SNP - Inverclyde South)
keith.brooks@inverclyde.gov.uk
Campbell-Sturgess, Math (SNP - Inverclyde North)
Clocherty, Jim (LAB - Inverclyde North)
jim.clocherty@inverclyde.gov.uk
Dorrian, Gerry (LAB - Inverclyde South West)
gerry.dorrain@linverclyde.gov.uk
Grieve, Jim (SNP - Inverclyde East Central)
jim.grieve@inverclyde.gov.uk
Jones, Vaughan (LAB - Inverclyde South)
Loughran, Terry (LAB - Inverclyde West)
terry.loughran@linverclyde.gov.uk
MacLeod, Jim (SNP - Inverclyde East)
jim.macleod@inverclyde.gov.uk
McCabe, Stephen (LAB - Inverclyde East)
stephen.mccabe@inverclyde.gov.uk
McColgan, James (LAB - Inverclyde East)
McCormick, Michael (LAB - Inverclyde East Central)
michael.mccormick@inverclyde.gov.uk
McEleny, Chris (SNP - Inverclyde West)
McIlwee, Joe (LAB - Inverclyde South)
joe.mcilwee@inverclyde.gov.uk
Moran, Robert (LAB - Inverclyde East Central)
robert.moran@inverclyde.gov.uk
Nelson, Innes (SNP - Inverclyde South West)
innes.nelson@inverclyde.gov.uk
Rebecchi, Luciano (LD - Inverclyde South West)
luciano.rebecchi@inverclyde.gov.uk
Shepherd, Kenny (LD - Inverclyde North)
Wilson, David (CON - Inverclyde East)
david.wilson@inverclyde.gov.uk

POLITICAL COMPOSITION

LAB: 10, SNP: 6, LD: 2, CON: 1, IND: 1

COMMITTEE CHAIRS

Education & Communities: Mr Terry Loughran
Environment & Regeneration: Mr Michael McCormick
Health & Social Care: Mr Joe McIlwee
Planning: Mr David Wilson
Policy & Resources: Mr Stephen McCabe

IPSWICH D

Ipswich Borough Council, Grafton House, 15-17 Russell Road, Ipswich IP1 2DE ☎ 01473 432000 🖷 01473 432522
✉ enquiries@ipswich.gov.uk 💻 www.ipswich.gov.uk

FACTS & FIGURES

Police Authority: Suffolk Police Authority
Health Authority: East of England Strategic Health Authority
Learning and Skills Council: Eastern
Parliamentary Constituencies: Ipswich
EU Constituencies: Eastern
Election Frequency: Elections are by thirds
Twinning: Arras (France)

PRINCIPAL OFFICERS

Chief Executive: Mr Russell Williams, Chief Executive, Grafton House, 15-17 Russell Road, Ipswich IP1 2DE ☎ 01473 433501 🖷 01473 432033 ✉ russell.williams@ipswich.gov.uk

Senior Management: Mr Laurence Collins, Director, Grafton House, 15-17 Russell Road, Ipswich IP1 2DE ☎ 01473 432012 🖷 01473 432033 ✉ laurence.collins@ipswich.gov.uk

Senior Management: Mr Jonathan Owen, Director, Grafton House, 15-17 Russell Road, Ipswich IP1 2DE ☎ 01473 432002 🖷 01473 432033 ✉ jonathan.owen@ipswich.gov.uk

Access Officer / Social Services (Disability): Mr Colin Hook, Operations Manager - Building Control, Grafton House, 15-17 Russell Road, Ipswich IP1 2DE ☎ 01473 432962
✉ colin.hook@ipswich.gov.uk

Architect, Building / Property Services: Mr John Parling, Operations Manager - Asset, Property & Economic Development, Grafton House, 15-17 Russell Road, Ipswich IP1 2DE ☎ 01473 432203 ✉ john.parling@ipswich.gov.uk

Best Value: Mrs Vicky Moseley, Senior Performance & Projects Officer, Grafton House, 15-17 Russell Road, Ipswich IP1 2DE ☎ 01473 432044 ✉ vicky.moseley@ipswich.gov.uk

Building Control: Mr Colin Hook, Operations Manager - Building Control, Grafton House, 15-17 Russell Road, Ipswich IP1 2DE ☎ 01473 432962 ✉ colin.hook@ipswich.gov.uk

PR / Communications: Mr Max Stocker, Head of Communications & Design, Grafton House, 15-17 Russell Road, Ipswich IP1 2DE ☎ 01473 432035 ✉ max.stocker@ipswich.gov.uk

Community Planning: Ms Renu Mandal, Operations Manager - Community Development, Grafton House, 15-17 Russell Road, Ipswich IP1 2DE ☎ 01473 433504 🖷 01473 432105 ✉ renu.mandal@ipswich.gov.uk

Community Safety: Mr Jim Manning, Operations Manager - Safer Ipswich, Grafton House, 15-17 Russell Road, Ipswich IP1 2DE ☎ 01473 432702 ✉ jim.manning@ipswich.gov.uk

Computer Management: Mr Howard Gaskin, IT Infrastructure Manager, Grafton House, 15-17 Russell Road, Ipswich IP1 2DE ☎ 01473 433891 ✉ howard.gaskin@ipswich.gov.uk

Contracts: Mr Kevin Oxborrow, Operations Manager - Maintenance & Contracts, Gipping House, 7 Whittle Road, Hadleigh Road Industrial Estate, Ipswich IP1 2DE ☎ 01473 432414 ✉ kevin.oxborrow@ipswich.gov.uk

Corporate Services: Mr David Field, Head of Corporate Development, Grafton House, 15-17 Russell Road, Ipswich IP1 2DE ☎ 01473 433859 ✉ david.field@ipswich.gov.uk

Customer Service: Mr Paul Farrer, Operations Manager - Customer Services, Grafton House, 15-17 Russell Road, Ipswich IP1 2DE ☎ 01473 432360 ✉ paul.farrer@ipswich.gov.uk

Economic Development: Mr John Parling, Operations Manager - Asset, Property & Economic Development, Grafton House, 15-17 Russell Road, Ipswich IP1 2DE ☎ 01473 432203 ✉ john.parling@ipswich.gov.uk

Electoral Registration: Mrs Emily Yule, Team Leader - Business & Democratic Support, Grafton House, 15-17 Russell Road, Ipswich IP1 2DE ☎ 01473 432305 ✉ emily.yule@ipswich.gov.uk

Emergency Planning: Ms Karen Chambers, Emergency Planning Officer, Grafton House, 15-17 Russell Road, Ipswich IP1 2DE ☎ 01473 433434 🖷 01473 433898 ✉ karen.chambers@ipswich.gov.uk

Energy Management: Mr Matthew Ling, Head of Environmental Services, Grafton House, 15-17 Russell Road, Ipswich IP1 2DE ☎ 01473 432095 ✉ matthew.ling@ipswich.gov.uk

Environmental / Technical Services: Mr Matthew Ling, Head of Environmental Services, Grafton House, 15-17 Russell Road, Ipswich IP1 2DE ☎ 01473 432095 ✉ matthew.ling@ipswich.gov.uk

Environmental Health: Mr Matthew Ling, Head of Environmental Services, Grafton House, 15-17 Russell Road, Ipswich IP1 2DE ☎ 01473 432095 ✉ matthew.ling@ipswich.gov.uk

Estates, Property & Valuation: Mr Simon Unthank, Principal Valuation Surveyor, Grafton House, 15-17 Russell Road, Ipswich IP1 2DE ☎ 01473 432212 🖷 01473 432974 ✉ simon.unthank@ipswich.gov.uk

Events Manager: Mr James Young, Events Officer, Grafton House, 15-17 Russell Road, Ipswich IP1 2DE ☎ 01473 432869 ✉ james.young@ipswich.gov.uk

Finance and Treasurer: Mr Ian Blofield, Head of Resource Management (Interim), Grafton House, 15-17 Russell Road, Ipswich IP1 2DE ☎ 01473 433710; 01206 282350 🖷 01206 282358 ✉ ian.blofield@ipswich.gov.uk; ian.blofield@colchester.gov.uk

Fleet Management: Ms Ondraya Plowman, Vehicle Fleet Manager, Grafton House, 15-17 Russell Road, Ipswich IP1 2DE ☎ 01473 432430 ✉ ondraya.plowman@ipswich.gov.uk

Grounds Maintenance: Mr Eddie Peters, Operations Manager - Streetcare, Gipping House, 7 Whittle Road, Hadleigh Road Industrial Estate, Ipswich IP2 0UH ☎ 01473 432412 ✉ eddie.peters@ipswich.gov.uk

Health and Safety: Mr Malcolm Earl, Corporate Health & Safety Mananger, Grafton House, 15-17 Russell Road, Ipswich IP1 2DE ☎ 01473 433435 ✉ malcolm.earl@ipswich.gov.uk

Highways: Mr Mike Tee, Head of Planning, Transport & Regeneration, Grafton House, 15-17 Russell Road, Ipswich IP1 2DE ☎ 01473 432932 ✉ mike.tee@ipswich.gov.uk

Home Energy Conservation: Mr Joe Howarth, Head of Housing Services, Grafton House, 15-17 Russell Road, Ipswich IP1 2DE ☎ 01473 433014 ✉ joe.howarth@ipswich.gov.uk

Housing: Mr Joe Howarth, Head of Housing Services, Grafton House, 15-17 Russell Road, Ipswich IP1 2DE ☎ 01473 433014 ✉ joe.howarth@ipswich.gov.uk

Housing Maintenance: Mr Joe Howarth, Head of Housing Services, Grafton House, 15-17 Russell Road, Ipswich IP1 2DE ☎ 01473 433014 ✉ joe.howarth@ipswich.gov.uk

Legal: Ms Claire Barritt, Head of Legal & Democratic Services, Grafton House, 15-17 Russell Road, Ipswich IP1 2DE ☎ 01473 432320 ✉ claire.barritt@ipswich.gov.uk

Leisure and Cultural Services: Mr Billy Brennan, Head of Cultural & Leisure Services, Grafton House, 15-17 Russell Road, Ipswich IP1 2DE ☎ 01473 432060 ✉ billy.brennan@ipswich.gov.uk

Licensing: Mr Mike Grimwood, Operations Manager - Licensing, Enforcement and Bereavement Services, Grafton House, 15-17 Russell Road, Ipswich IP1 2DE ☎ 01473 433052 ✉ mike.grimwood@ipswich.gov.uk

Lighting: Mr Mike Tee, Head of Planning, Transport & Regeneration, Grafton House, 15-17 Russell Road, Ipswich IP1 2DE ☎ 01473 432932 ✉ mike.tee@ipswich.gov.uk

Member Services: Mr Stephen McGrath, Senior Committee Services Officer, Grafton House, 15-17 Russell Road, Ipswich IP1 2DE ☎ 01473 432510 ✉ stephen.mcgrath@ipswich.gov.uk

Parking: Ms Mandy Chapman, Assistant Manager Car Parks, Gipping House, 7 Whittle Road, Hadleigh Road Industrial Estate, Ipswich IP2 0UH ☎ 01473 432849 ✉ mandy.chapman@ipswich.gov.uk

Partnerships: Ms Renu Mandal, Operations Manager - Community Development, Grafton House, 15-17 Russell Road, Ipswich IP1 2DE ☎ 01473 433504 🖷 01473 432105 ✉ renu.mandal@ipswich.gov.uk

Personnel / HR: Ms Faye Hendin, Human Resources Manager - Operations, Grafton House, 15-17 Russell Road, Ipswich IP1 2DE ☎ 01473 433405 ✉ faye.hendin@ipswich.gov.uk

Planning: Mr Mike Tee, Head of Planning, Transport & Regeneration, Grafton House, 15-17 Russell Road, Ipswich IP1 2DE ☎ 01473 432932 ✉ mike.tee@ipswich.gov.uk

Procurement: Mr Andrew Beschizza, Procurement Manager, Grafton House, 15-17 Russell Road, Ipswich IP1 2DE ☎ 01473 433906 ✉ andrew.beschizza@ipswich.gov.uk

Recycling & Waste Minimisation: Ms Debbie Reeve, Operational Manager - Waste and Environment, Grafton House, 15-17 Russell Road, Ipswich IP1 2DE ☎ 01473 432427 ✉ debbie.reeve@ipswich.gov.uk

Regeneration: Mr Mike Tee, Head of Planning, Transport & Regeneration, Grafton House, 15-17 Russell Road, Ipswich IP1 2DE ☎ 01473 432932 ✉ mike.tee@ipswich.gov.uk

Road Safety: Mr Mike Tee, Head of Planning, Transport & Regeneration, Grafton House, 15-17 Russell Road, Ipswich IP1 2DE ☎ 01473 432932 ✉ mike.tee@ipswich.gov.uk

Staff Training: Ms Katie Coupe, Employee Development Advisor, Grafton House, 15-17 Russell Road, Ipswich IP1 2DE ☎ 01473 433425 ✉ katie.coupe@ipswich.gov.uk

Street Scene: Ms Ondraya Plowman, Vehicle Fleet Manager, Gipping House, 7 Whittle Road, Hadleigh Road Industrial Estate, Ipswich IP2 0UH ☎ 01473 432430 ✉ ondraya.plowman@ipswich.gov.uk

Sustainable Communities: Mr Mike Tee, Head of Planning, Transport & Regeneration, Grafton House, 15-17 Russell Road, Ipswich IP1 2DE ☎ 01473 432932 ✉ mike.tee@ipswich.gov.uk

Tourism: Mr David Stainer, Tourist Centre Manager, Tourist Information Centre, St Stephens Church, St Stephens Lane, Ipswich IP1 1DP ☎ 01473 43078

Town Centre: Mr Mike Tee, Head of Planning, Transport & Regeneration, Grafton House, 15-17 Russell Road, Ipswich IP1 2DE ☎ 01473 432932 ✉ mike.tee@ipswich.gov.uk

Traffic Management: Mr Mike Tee, Head of Planning, Transport & Regeneration, Grafton House, 15-17 Russell Road, Ipswich IP1 2DE ☎ 01473 432932 ✉ mike.tee@ipswich.gov.uk

Transport: Mr Mike Tee, Head of Planning, Transport & Regeneration, Grafton House, 15-17 Russell Road, Ipswich IP1 2DE ☎ 01473 432932 ✉ mike.tee@ipswich.gov.uk

Transport Planner: Mr Mike Tee, Head of Planning, Transport & Regeneration, Grafton House, 15-17 Russell Road, Ipswich IP1 2DE ☎ 01473 432932 ✉ mike.tee@ipswich.gov.uk

Waste Collection and Disposal: Ms Debbie Reeve, Operational Manager - Waste and Environment, Gipping House, 7 Whittle Road, Hadleigh Road Industrial Estate, Ipswich IP2 0UH ☎ 01473 432427 ✉ debbie.reeve@ipswich.gov.uk

Waste Management: Mr Matthew Ling, Head of Environmental Services, Grafton House, 15-17 Russell Road, Ipswich IP1 2DE ☎ 01473 432095 ✉ matthew.ling@ipswich.gov.uk

Children's Play Areas: Mr Eddie Peters, Operations Manager - Streetcare, Gipping House, 7 Whittle Road, Hadleigh Road Industrial Estate, Ipswich IP2 0UH ☎ 01473 432412 ✉ eddie.peters@ipswich.gov.uk

MEMBERS OF THE COUNCIL (48)

***Mayor:* Blake**, Mary (LAB - Westgate)
mary.blake@councillors.ipswich.gov.uk
***Deputy Mayor:* Le Grys**, John (LAB - Priory Heath)
john.legrys@councillors.ipswich.gov.uk
***Leader of the Council:* Ellesmere**, David (LAB - Gipping)
david.ellesmere@councillors.ipswich.gov.uk
***Deputy Leader of the Council:* Macdonald**, Neil (LAB - St John's)
neil.macdonald@councillors.ipswich.gov.uk
***Group Leader:* Carnall**, John (CON - Bixley)
john.carnall@councillors.ipswich.gov.uk
Ball, David (LAB - Whitehouse)
david.ball@councillors.ipswich.gov.uk
Bates, Ken (LD - Alexandra)
ken.bates@councillors.ipswich.gov.uk
Cann, Andrew (LD - St Margaret's)
andrew.cann@councillors.ipswich.gov.uk
Cenci, Nadia (CON - Stoke Park)
nadia.cenci@councillors.ipswich.gov.uk
Chisholm, Glen (LAB - Stoke Park)
glen.chisholm@councillors.ipswich.gov.uk
Clarke, Hamil (LAB - Sprites)
hamil.clarke@councillors.ipswich.gov.uk
Connelly, Stephen (LAB - Whitton)
stephen.connelly@councillors.ipswich.gov.uk
Cook, Martin (LAB - Gainsborough)
martin.cook@councillors.ipswich.gov.uk
Crane, Harvey (LAB - Alexandra)
harvey.crane@councillors.ipswich.gov.uk
Debman, George (CON - Holywells)
george.debman@councillors.ipswich.gov.uk
Fern, Roger (LAB - Sprites)
roger.fern@councillors.ipswich.gov.uk
French, Cathy (LD - St Margaret's)
cathy.french@councillors.ipswich.gov.uk
Gardiner, Peter (LAB - Gipping)
peter.gardiner@councillors.ipswich.gov.uk
Gibbs, Julian (LAB - Westgate)
julian.gibbs@councillors.ipswich.gov.uk
Goldsmith, David (CON - Castle Hill)

david.goldsmith@councillors.ipswich.gov.uk
Goonan, Martin (LAB - Whitehouse)
martin.goonan@councillors.ipswich.gov.uk
Grant, Tracy (LAB - Rushmere)
tracy.grant@councillors.ipswich.gov.uk
Grant, Albert (LAB - Whitehouse)
albert.grant@councillors.ipswich.gov.uk
Harsant, Elizabeth (CON - Holywells)
elizabeth.harsant@councillors.ipswich.gov.uk
Jones, Carole (LAB - Westgate)
carole.jones@councillors.ipswich.gov.uk
Kirby, Richard (LAB - Sprites)
richard.kirby@councillors.ipswich.gov.uk
Knowles, Bill (LAB - Priory Heath)
bill.knowles@councillors.ipswich.gov.uk
Leeder, Adam (LAB - Alexandra)
adam.leeder@councillors.ipswich.gov.uk
Lockington, Inga (LD - St Margaret's)
inga.lockington@councillors.ipswich.gov.uk
Macartney, Jeanette (LAB - Gipping)
jeanette.macartney@councillors.ipswich.gov.uk
Martin, Sandy (LAB - St John's)
sandy.martin@councillors.ipswich.gov.uk
Meudec, Sophie (LAB - Whitton)
sophie.meudec@councillors.ipswich.gov.uk
Mowles, John (LAB - Gainsborough)
john.mowles@councillors.ipswich.gov.uk
Pope, Richard (CON - Bixley)
richard.pope@ipswich.gov.uk
Powell, Jim (LAB - Bridge)
jim.powell@councillors.ipswich.gov.uk
Quinton, Bill (LAB - Priory Heath)
bill.quinton@councillors.ipswich.gov.uk
Rawlingson, Keith (LAB - Gainsborough)
keith.rawlingson@councillors.ipswich.gov.uk
Ross, Alasdair (LAB - Rushmere)
alasdair.ross@councillors.ipswich.gov.uk
Rudkin, Bryony (LAB - Bridge)
bryony.rudkin@councillors.ipswich.gov.uk
Smart, Phil (LAB - Bridge)
phil.smart@councillors.ipswich.gov.uk
Stewart, Pam (CON - Holywells)
pam.stewart@councillors.ipswich.gov.uk
Stewart, Christopher (CON - Whitton)
christopher.stewart@councillors.ipswich.gov.uk
Stimson, Jennifer (LAB - St John's)
jennifer.stimson@councillors.ipswich.gov.u
Stroet, Kym (CON - Bixley)
kym.stroet@councillors.ipswich.gov.uk
Studd, Barry (LAB - Stoke Park)
barry.studd@councillors.ipswich.gov.uk
Terry, Judy (CON - Rushmere)
judy.terry@councillors.ipswich.gov.uk
Vickery, Robin (CON - Castle Hill)
robin.vickery@councillors.ipswich.gov.uk
Young, Mary (CON - Castle Hill)
mary.young@councillors.ipswich.gov.uk

POLITICAL COMPOSITION
LAB: 32, CON: 12, LD: 4

CABINET
Leader: Mr David Ellesmere
Deputy Leader / Safer Ipswich: Mr Neil Macdonald
Culture: Ms Bryony Rudkin
Economic Development & Planning: Ms Carole Jones
Fairer & Greener Ipswich: Mr Sandy Martin
Housing: Mr John Mowles
Resources: Mr Martin Cook
Transport: Mr Phil Smart

COMMITTEE CHAIRS
Council: Mrs Elizabeth Harsant
Human Resources: Mr David Hale
Licensing & Regulatory: Ms Eileen Smith
Overview & Scrutiny (Scrutiny): Mr Gavin Maclure
Planning & Development: Mr John Cooper

ISLE OF ANGLESEY — W

Isle of Anglesey County Council, (Cyngor Sir Ynys Môn), County Offices, Llangefni LL77 7TW ☎ 01248 750057 🖷 01248 750839 ✉ gjxce@anglesey.gov.uk 💻 www.anglesey.gov.uk

FACTS & FIGURES
Police Authority: North Wales Police Authority
Learning and Skills Council: Wales
Parliamentary Constituencies: Ynys Mon
EU Constituencies: Wales
Election Frequency: Elections are of whole council

PRINCIPAL OFFICERS
Chief Executive: Mr Richard Parry Jones, Chief Executive, Swyddfa'r Sir, Llangefni LL77 7TW ☎ 01248 752102 🖷 01248 750839 ✉ rpjed@ynysmon.gov.uk

Senior Management: Ms Lynn Ball, Head of Function: Legal & Administration / Monitoring Officer, Swyddfa'r Sir, Llangefni LL77 7TW ☎ 01248 752586 🖷 01248 752132 ✉ lbxcs@anglesey.gov.uk

Senior Management: Mr Richard Parry Jones, Chief Executive, Swyddfa'r Sir, Llangefni LL77 7TW ☎ 01248 752102 🖷 01248 750839 ✉ rpjed@ynysmon.gov.uk

Senior Management: Mr Stephen Sloss, Interim Director of Community, Swyddfa'r Sir, Llangefni LL77 7TW ☎ 01248 752703 🖷 01248 752705 ✉ sgsss@ynysmon.gov.uk

Access Officer / Social Services (Disability): Mrs Glenys Williams, Team Leader - Disability Service, Swyddfa'r Sir, Llangefni LL7 7TW ☎ 01248 752771 🖷 01248 750107 ✉ gwxss@ynysmon.gov.uk

Architect, Building / Property Services: Mr Rhys Griffiths, Principal Surveyor, Swyddfa'r Sir, Llangefni LL77 7TW ☎ 01248 752161 🖷 01248 724839 ✉ rhghp@ynysmon.gov.uk

Best Value: Mr Gethin Morgan, Business Planning & Programme Manager, Swyddfa'r Sir, Llangefni LL77 7TW ☎ 01248 752111 🖷 01248 750839 ✉ grmce@ynysmon.gov.uk

Building Control: Mr Gareth Jones, Senior Property Officer, Swyddfa'r Sir, Llangefni LL77 7TW ☎ 01248 752253 🖷 01248 752232 ✉ rgjhp@anglesey.gov.uk

Children / Youth Services: Mr Stephen Sloss, Interim Director of Community, Swyddfa'r Sir, Llangefni LL77 7TW ☎ 01248 752703 🖷 01248 752705 ✉ sgsss@ynysmon.gov.uk

Civil Registration: Ms Marian Wyn Griffiths, Superintendent Registrar, Shire Hall, Llangefni LL77 7TW ☎ 01248 752564 🖷 01248 723459 ✉ mgxcs@anglesey.gov.uk

PR / Communications: Mr Gethin Jones, Communication Officer, Swyddfa'r Sir, Llangefni LL77 7TW ☎ 01248 752130 🖷 01248 750839 ✉ gjxce@anglesey.gov.uk

Community Safety: Mr Tony Jones, Community Safety Co-ordinator, Swyddfa'r Sir, Llangefni LL77 7TW ☎ 01248 752816 🖷 01248 752880 ✉ twjpp@ynysmon.gov.uk

Computer Management: Mr Dave Gardner, Head of IT Services, Swyddfa'r Sir, Llangefni LL77 7TW ☎ 01248 752671 🖷 01248 752887

Consumer Protection and Trading Standards: Mr David Riley, Chief Trading Standards Officer, Swyddfa'r Sir, Llangefni LL77 7TW ☎ 01248 752841 🖷 01248 752880 ✉ davidriley@ynysmon.gov.uk

Contracts: Mr Stephen Sloss, Interim Director of Community, Swyddfa'r Sir, Llangefni LL77 7TW ☎ 01248 752703 🖷 01248 752705 ✉ sgsss@ynysmon.gov.uk

Corporate Services: Ms Carys Edwards, Interim Head of Human Resources, Swyddfa'r Sir, Llangefni LL77 7TW ☎ 01248 752502 🖷 01248 752583 ✉ cexcs@ynysmon.gov.uk

Economic Development: Mr Dylan Williams, Interim Head of Economic Development, Anglesey Business Centre, Bryn Cefni Business Park, Llangefni LL77 7XA ☎ 01248 752499 🖷 01248 752192 ✉ dwxpl@ynysmon.gov.uk

Education: Dr Gwynne Jones, Director of Lifelong Learning, Parc Mount, Glanhwfa Road, Llangefni LL77 7EY ☎ 01248 752921

Education: Mr Gwyn Parri, Head of Service - Education, Parc Mount, Glanhwfa Road, Llangefni LL77 7TW ☎ 01248 752923 ✉ gxped@anglesey.gov.uk

E-Government: Mr Barry Eaton, ICT Infrastructure Manager, Swyddfa'r Sir, Llangefni LL77 7TW ☎ 01248 752622 🖷 01248 752887 ✉ bexfi@ynysmon.gov.uk

Electoral Registration: Ms Haulwen Ann Hughes, Electoral Services Officer, Anglesey Business Centre, Bryn Cefni Business Park, Llangefni LL77 7XA ☎ 01248 752519

Emergency Planning: Mr Alan Williams, Emergency Planning Officer, Anglesey Business Centre, Bryn Cefni Business Park, Llangefni LL77 7TW ☎ 01248 752815 🖷 01248 752880 ✉ awxpp@anglesey.gov.uk

Energy Management: Mr Adrian Williams, Energy Manager, Swyddfa'r Sir, Llangefni LL77 7TW ☎ 01248 752249 🖷 01248 724839 ✉ awxht@anglesey.gov.uk

Environmental / Technical Services: Mr Arthur Owen, Director of Sustainable Development, Swyddfa'r Sir, Llangefni LL77 7TW ☎ 01248 752401 🖷 01248 752412 ✉ awopl@ynysmon.gov.uk

Environmental Health: Mr Tony Burgess, Chief Environmental Health Officer, Swyddfa'r Sir, Llangefni LL77 7TW ☎ 01248 752821 🖷 01248 752880 ✉ acburgess@anglesey.gov.uk

Estates, Property & Valuation: Mr Gareth Jones, Senior Property Officer, Swyddfa'r Sir, Llangefni LL77 7TW ☎ 01248 752253 🖷 01248 752232 ✉ rgjhp@anglesey.gov.uk

European Liaison: Mr Aled Prys Davies, Principal Development Officer (European Support), Anglesey Business Centre, Bryn Cefni Business Park, Llangefni LL77 7XA ☎ 01248 752479 🖷 01248 752192 ✉ apdpl@ynysmon.gov.uk

Events Manager: Mr Michael Thomas, Senior Development Officer Toursim & Marketing, Anglesey Business Centre, Bryn Cefni Business Park, Llangefni LL77 7XA ☎ 01248 752492 ✉ mptpl@anglesey.gov.uk

Finance and Treasurer: Mrs Gill Lewis, Interim Deputy Chief Executive, Swyddfa'r Sir, Llangefni LL77 7TW ☎ 01248 752620 🖷 01248 752696 ✉ glxfi@ynysmon.gov.uk

Fleet Management: Mr Noel Roberts, Fleet & Driver Manager, Swyddfa'r Sir, Llangefni LL77 7TW ☎ 01248 752375 🖷 01248 724839 ✉ rnrht@ynysmon.gov.uk

Grounds Maintenance: Mr Colin Edwards, Principal Engineer: Highway Maintenance, Swyddfa'r Sir, Llangefni LL77 7TW ☎ 01248 752350 🖷 01248 724839 ✉ cjeht@ynysmon.gov.uk

Health and Safety: Mr Stephen Nicol, Health & Safety Team Leader, Swyddfa'r Sir, Llangefni LL77 7TW ☎ 01248 751884 🖷 01248 752880 ✉ snxpp@anglesey.gov.uk

Highways: Mr Colin Edwards, Principal Engineer: Highway Maintenance, Swyddfa'r Sir, Llangefni LL77 7TW ☎ 01248 752350 🖷 01248 724839 ✉ cjeht@ynysmon.gov.uk

Housing: Ms Shan Williams, Head of Housing, Swyddfa'r Sir, Llangefni LL77 7TW ☎ 01248 725201 🖷 01248 752243; 01248 752233 ✉ slwhp@ynysmon.gov.uk

Legal: Ms Lynn Ball, Head of Function: Legal & Administration / Monitoring Officer, Swyddfa'r Sir, Llangefni LL77 7TW ☎ 01248 752586 🖷 01248 752132 ✉ lbxcs@anglesey.gov.uk

Leisure and Cultural Services: Mr John Rees Thomas, Head of Leisure & Lifelong Learning, Parc Mount, Glanhwfa Road, Llangefni LL77 7EY ☎ 01248 752908 🖷 01248 752999 ✉ jrtlh@ynysmon.gov.uk

Licensing: Mr John Lloyd, Senior Enforcement Officer (Licensing), Swyddfa'r Sir, Llangefni LL77 7TW ☎ 01248 752852 🖷 01248 752884 ✉ jelpp@anglesey.gov.uk

Licensing: Mr Dafydd Merfyn Jones, Principal Licensing Officer, Swyddfa'r Sir, Llangefni LL77 7TW ☎ 01248 752847 🖷 01248 752884 ✉ dmjpp@anglesey.gov.uk

Lifelong Learning: Mr John Rees Thomas, Head of Leisure & Lifelong Learning, Parc Mount, Glanhwfa Road, Llangefni LL77 7EY ☎ 01248 752908 🖷 01248 752999 ✉ jrtlh@ynysmon.gov.uk

Lighting: Mr Arwel Roberts, Senior Engineer (Lighting), Swyddfa'r Sir, Llangefni LL77 7TW ☎ 01248 752392 🖷 01248 724839 ✉ arxht@ynysmon.gov.uk

Lottery Funding, Charity and Voluntary: Mr John Rees Thomas, Head of Leisure & Lifelong Learning, Parc Mount, Glanhwfa Road, Llangefni LL77 7EY ☎ 01248 752908 🖷 01248 752999 ✉ jrtlh@ynysmon.gov.uk

Member Services: Mr Huw Jones, Head of Policy, Swyddfa'r Sir, Llangefni LL77 7TW ☎ 01248 752109 🖷 01248 750839 ✉ jhjce@ynysmon.gov.uk

Parking: Mr Alun Roberts, Decriminalised Parking Officer, Swyddfa'r Sir, Llangefni LL77 7TW ☎ 01248 752244 ✉ jarht@anglesey.gov.uk

Partnerships: Mr John Rees Thomas, Head of Leisure & Lifelong Learning, Parc Mount, Glanhwfa Road, Llangefni LL77 7EY ☎ 01248 752908 🖷 01248 752999 ✉ jrtlh@ynysmon.gov.uk

Personnel / HR: Ms Carys Edwards, Interim Head of Human Resources, Swyddfa'r Sir, Llangefni LL77 7TW ☎ 01248 752502 🖷 01248 752583 ✉ cexcs@ynysmon.gov.uk

Planning: Mr Arthur Owen, Director of Sustainable Development, Swyddfa'r Sir, Llangefni LL77 7TW ☎ 01248 752401 🖷 01248 752412 ✉ awopl@ynysmon.gov.uk

Procurement: Mrs Sioned Rowlands, Procurement Officer, Swyddfa'r Sir, Llangefni LL77 7TW ☎ 01248 752136 ✉ srxce@anglesey.gov.uk

Public Libraries: Mr John Rees Thomas, Head of Leisure & Lifelong Learning, Parc Mount, Glanhwfa Road, Llangefni LL77 7EY ☎ 01248 752908 🖷 01248 752999 ✉ jrtlh@ynysmon.gov.uk

Recycling & Waste Minimisation: Mr Meirion Edwards, Principal Waste Management Officer, Swyddfa'r Sir, Llangefni LL77 7TW ☎ 01248 752818 ✉ mpepp@anglesey.gov.uk

Regeneration: Mr Dylan Williams, Interim Head of Economic Development, Anglesey Business Centre, Bryan Cefni Business Park, Llangefni LL77 7TW ☎ 01248 752499 🖷 01248 752192 ✉ dwxpl@ynysmon.gov.uk

Road Safety: Mr Huw Percy, Chief Engineer (Network), Swyddfa'r Sir, Llangefni LL77 7TW ☎ 01248 752371 🖷 01248 724839 ✉ hmpht@ynysmon.gov.uk

Social Services: Mr Stephen Sloss, Interim Director of Community, Swyddfa'r Sir, Llangefni LL77 7TW ☎ 01248 752703 🖷 01248 752705 ✉ sgsss@ynysmon.gov.uk

Social Services (Adult): Ms Anwen Davies, Head of Adult Services, Syddfa'r Sir, Llangefni LL77 7TW ☎ 01248 752707 ✉ adxss@ynysmon.gov.uk

Social Services (Children): Ms Anwen Huws, Head of Children's Services, Swyddfa'r Sir, Llangefni LL77 7TW ☎ 01248 752797 ✉ amhss@ynysmon.gov.uk

Staff Training: Ms Carys Edwards, Interim Head of Human Resources, Swyddfa'r Sir, Llangefni LL77 7TW ☎ 01248 752502 🖷 01248 752583 ✉ cexcs@ynysmon.gov.uk

Sustainable Development: Mr Arthur Owen, Director of Sustainable Development, Swyddfa'r Sir, Llangefni LL77 7TW ☎ 01248 752401 🖷 01248 752412 ✉ awopl@ynysmon.gov.uk

Tourism: Mr Iwan Huws, Principal Tourism Development Officer, Anglesey Business Centre, Bryn Cefni Business Park, Llangefni LL77 7TW ☎ 01248 752493 ✉ gihpl@anglesey.gov.uk

Traffic Management: Mr Huw Percy, Chief Engineer (Network), Swyddfa'r Sir, Llangefni LL77 7TW ☎ 01248 752371 🖷 01248 724839 ✉ hmpht@ynysmon.gov.uk

Transport: Mr Dewi Roberts, Principal Officer (Transportation), Swyddfa'r Sir, Llangefni LL77 7TW ☎ 01248 752457 🖷 01248 724839 ✉ dwrpl@ynysmon.gov.uk

Transport Planner: Mr Huw Percy, Chief Engineer (Network), Swyddfa'r Sir, Llangefni LL77 7TW ☎ 01248 752371 🖷 01248 724839 ✉ hmpht@ynysmon.gov.uk

Waste Collection and Disposal: Mr Meirion Edwards, Principal Waste Management Officer, Swyddfa'r Sir, Llangefni LL77 7TW ☎ 01248 752860 🖷 01248 752880 ✉ mpepp@ynysmon.gov.uk

Waste Collection and Disposal: Ms Carys Wyn Roberts, Contract Supervisor, Swyddfa'r Sir, Llangefni LL77 7TW ☎ 01248 752860 🖷 01248 752880 ✉ cwrpp@anglesey.gov.uk

Waste Management: Mr Meirion Edwards, Principal Waste Management Officer, Swyddfa'r Sir, Llangefni LL77 7TW ☎ 01248 752860 🖷 01248 752880 ✉ mpepp@ynysmon.gov.uk

MEMBERS OF THE COUNCIL (40)

***Chair:* Jones**, Robert (INDNA - Porthyfelln)
rljau@ynysmon.gov.uk
***Deputy Chair:* Davies**, Eurfryn (PC - Cwm Cadnant)
egdau@ynysmon.gov.uk
***Leader of the Council:* Owen**, Bryan (IND - Tudur)
boxau@ynysmon.gov.uk
***Deputy Leader of the Council:* Hughes**, Kenneth (IND - Llanfaethlu)
KennethHughes@anglesey.gov.uk
Chorlton, John (LAB - Kingsland)
JohnChorlton@anglesey.gov.uk
Davies, Lewis (PC - Llangoed)
LewisDavies@anglesey.gov.uk
Davies, Lewis (PC - Cefni)
fmhau@ynysmon.gov.uk
Dew, Richard (IND - Rhosneigr)
RichardDew@anglesey.gov.uk
Evans, Keith (INDNA - Cadnant)
Evans, Jim (IND - Braint)
JimEvans@anglesey.gov.uk
Evans, Keith (IND - Biwmares / Beaumaris)
rloau@ynysmon.gov.uk

Everett, Clifford (LAB - Tref Caergybl / Holyhead Town)
CliffordEverett@anglesey.gov.uk
Hughes, Derlwyn (IND - Moelfre)
Hughes, Robert (IND - Bodorgan)
rlhau@ynysmon.gov.uk
Hughes, William (IND - Llanbadrig)
WilliamTHughes@anglesey.gov.uk
Hughes, William (PC - Bodffordd)
WilliamIHughes@anglesey.gov.uk
Hughes, Trefor Lloyd (PC - Maeshyfryd)
tlhau@ynysmon.gov.uk
Hughes, Vaughan (PC - Llanbedrgoch)
Jones, Raymond (LAB - Fford Llundain/London Road)
RaymondJones@anglesey.gov.uk
Jones, Dylan (LAB - Porth Amlwch)
rdjau@ynysmon.gov.uk
Jones, Eric (IND - Llanfihangel Esceifiog)
ejxau@ynysmon.gov.uk
Jones, H Eifion (IND - Llanidan)
HywelEifionJones@anglesey.gov.uk
Jones, Owen Glyn (IND - Aberffraw)
GlynJones@anglesey.gov.uk
Jones, Gwilym (IND - Llanfair yn Neubwll)
GwilymJones@anglesey.gov.uk
Jones, Thomas (IND - Llanfechell)
thjau@ynysmon.gov.uk
McGreggor, Clive (IND - Llanddfnan)
cmxau@ynysmon.gov.uk
Medi, Rhian (PC - Cyngar)
RhianMedi@anglesey.gov.uk
Mummery, Alun (IND - Gwyngyll)
Owen, John Victor (IND - Parc a'r Mynydd)
jvoau@ynysmon.gov.uk
Parry, Robert (PC - Trewalchmai)
BobParry@anglesey.gov.uk
Parry, Goronwy (CON - Valley)
gopau@ynysmon.gov.uk
Roberts, Gareth (IND - Amlwch Rural)
gwrau@ynysmon.gov.uk
Roberts, J Arwel (LAB - Morawelon)
JArwellRoberts@anglesey.gov.uk
Roberts, Eric (CON - Trearddur)
EricRoberts@anglesey.gov.uk
Rogers, Peter (INDNA - Rhosyr)
PeterRogers@anglesey.gov.uk
Schofield, Elwyn (IND - Llannerchymedd)
esxau@ynysmon.gov.uk
Thomas, Hefin Wyn (IND - Pentraeth)
hwtau@ynysmon.gov.uk
Thomas, Hefin (LD - Llaneilian)
amjau@ynysmon.gov.uk
Williams, Selwyn (LD - Tysilio)
SelwynWilliams@anglesey.gov.uk
Williams, Selwyn (IND - Brynteg)
IleuanWilliams@anglesey.gov.uk

POLITICAL COMPOSITION

IND: 20, PC: 8, LAB: 5, INDNA: 3, LD: 2, CON: 2

CABINET

Leader / Economic Development, Tourism & Leisure: Mr Bryan Owen
Deputy Leader / Social Services: Mr Kenneth Hughes
Education, Welsh Language, Children & Young People: Mr Goronwy Parry
Finance, IT & Human Resources: Mr Thomas Jones
Property, Highways & Waste Management: Mr Robert Parry
Housing & Community Safety: Mr William Hughes
Planning: Mr Robert Hughes

COMMITTEE CHAIRS

Audit (Scrutiny): Mr Hefin Thomas
Corporate Scrutiny (Scrutiny): Mr Selwyn Williams
Economic Development, Tourism & Property: Mr John Victor Owen
Education & Leisure (Scrutiny): Mr Derlwyn Hughes
Environment & Technical Services (Scrutiny): Mr Keith Evans
Housing & Social Services (Scrutiny): Mr Lewis Davies
Licensing: Mr J Arwel Roberts
Planning & Orders: Mr J Arwel Roberts

ISLE OF WIGHT U

Isle of Wight Council, County Hall, High Street, Newport PO30 1UD ☎ 01983 821000 🖷 01983 823333
customer.services@iow.gov.uk 💻 www.iwight.com

FACTS & FIGURES

Police Authority: Hampshire Police Authority
Health Authority: South Central Strategic Health Authority
Learning and Skills Council: South East
Parliamentary Constituencies: Isle of Wight
EU Constituencies: South East
Election Frequency: Elections are of whole council
Twinning: Ostholstein, (Germany); Puenteareas (Spain); Coburg (Bavaria)

PRINCIPAL OFFICERS

Chief Executive: Mr Steve Beynon, Chief Executive, County Hall, High Street, Newport PO30 1UD ☎ 01983 821000
steve.beynon@iow.gov.uk

Architect, Building / Property Services: Mr Barry Cooke, Head - Strategic Asset Management, County Hall, High Street, Newport PO30 1UD ☎ 01983 823266 🖷 01983 822763
barry.cooke@iow.gov.uk

Building Control: Mr John Lutas, Building Control Manager, Seaclose, Fairlee Road, Newport PO30 2QS ☎ 01983 821000 🖷 01983 823851 john.lutas@iow.gov.uk

Catering Services: Ms Jo Ewell, Client Catering Officer, Thompson House, Newport PO30 3ED ☎ 01983 821000
jo.ewell@iow.gov.uk

PR / Communications: Miss Claire Robertson, Strategic Manager - Communications, County Hall, High Street, Newport PO30 1UD ☎ 01983 823747 🖷 01983 823109
claire.robertson@iow.gov.uk

Community Planning: Mr Ian Anderson, Director - Communitites, Wellbeing & Social Care, County Hall, High Street, Newport PO30 1UD ☎ 01983 821 000 ian.anderson@iow.gov.uk

Community Planning: Mrs Sue Chilton, Members Services Manager, County Hall, High Street, Newport PO30 1UD ☎ 01983

823632 🖷 01983 823535 🖰 sue.chilton@iow.gov.uk

Community Safety: Mrs Zoryna O'Donnell, Lead - Strengthening Families Programme, Charter House, 14 St. Thomas' Square, Newport PO30 1SL ☎ 01983 821000 🖷 01983 814390 🖰 zoryna.odonnell@iow.gov.uk

Computer Management: Mr Richard Williams, Head - ICT, County Hall, High Street, Newport PO30 1UD ☎ 01983 821000 🖷 01983 823501 🖰 richard.williams@iow.gov.uk

Contracts: Miss Lucy Hebditch, Senior Procurement Officer, County Hall, High Street, Newport PO30 1UD ☎ 01983 821000 🖰 lucy.hebditch@iow.gov.uk

Corporate Services: Ms Davina Fiore, Deputy Director - Resources, County Hall, High Street, Newport PO30 1UD ☎ 01983 823203 🖰 davina.fiore@iow.gov.uk

Economic Development: Mr Stuart Love, Director - Economy & Environment, County Hall, High Street, Newport PO30 1UD ☎ 01983 821000 🖰 stuart.love@iow.gov.uk

Economic Development: Mr John Metcalfe, Assistant Director - Economic Development Tourism & Leisure, County Hall, High Street, Newport PO30 1UD ☎ 01983 821000 🖰 john.metcalf@iow.gov.uk

E-Government: Mr Richard Williams, Head - ICT, County Hall, High Street, Newport PO30 1UD ☎ 01983 821000 🖷 01983 823501 🖰 richard.williams@iow.gov.uk

Electoral Registration: Mr Clive Joynes, Election & Land Charges Manager, County Hall, High Street, Newport PO30 1UD ☎ 01983 823341 🖷 01983 823344 🖰 clive.joynes@iow.gov.uk

Emergency Planning: Mr Ian Collins, Resilience Manager, County Hall, High Street, Newport PO30 1UD ☎ 01983 823314 🖷 01983 521636 🖰 ian.collins@iow.gov.uk

Energy Management: Mr Timothy Watson, Energy Manager, County Hall, High Street, Newport PO30 1UD ☎ 01983 821000 🖷 01983 822763 🖰 timothy.watson@iow.gov.uk

Environmental / Technical Services: Mr Stuart Love, Director - Economy & Environment, County Hall, High Street, Newport PO30 1UD ☎ 01983 821000 🖰 stuart.love@iow.gov.uk

Estates, Property & Valuation: Miss Andrea Jenkins, Senior Estates Manager, County Hall, High Street, Newport PO30 1UD ☎ 01983 823263 🖷 01983 822763 🖰 andrea.jenkins@iow.gov.uk

Events Manager: Miss Elaine Cesar, Senior Events Officer, County Hall, High Street, Newport PO30 1UD ☎ 01983 821000 🖰 elaine.cesar@iow.gov.uk

Finance and Treasurer: Mr David Burbage, Director of Resources, County Hall, High Street, Newport PO30 1UD ☎ 01983 823606 🖷 01983 823603 🖰 david.burbage@iow.gov.uk

Fleet Management: Mr Nick Symes, Fleet Manager, Cemetery Hill, Carisbrooke, Newport PO30 1YS ☎ 01983 823786 🖰 nick.symes@iow.gov.uk

Grounds Maintenance: Mr Matthew Chatfield, Parks & Countryside Manager, Enterprise House, St Cross Business Park, Newport PO30 5WB ☎ 01983 821000 🖷 01983 823841 🖰 matthew.chatfield@iow.gov.uk

Highways: Mr Peter Hayward, Strategy Manager - Highways & Public Realm, Enterprise House, St Cross Business Park, PO30 5WB ☎ 01983 821000 🖷 01983 520563 🖰 peter.hayward@iow.gov.uk

Housing: Mr Mark Howell, Head - Commissioning, Housing & Community Support, County Hall, High Street, Newport PO30 1UD ☎ 01983 821000 🖰 mark.howell@iow.gov.uk

Legal: Ms Davina Fiore, Deputy Director - Resources, County Hall, High Street, Newport PO30 1UD ☎ 01983 823203 🖰 davina.fiore@iow.gov.uk

Legal: Mrs Helen Miles, Service Manager - Legal Services, County Hall, High Street, Newport PO30 1UD ☎ 01983 821000 🖰 helen.miles@iow.gov.uk

Leisure and Cultural Services: Mr Lee Matthews, Recreation & Public Spaces Manager, Guildhall, Newport PO30 1TY ☎ 01983 823815 🖷 01983 823841 🖰 lee.matthews@iow.gov.uk

Licensing: Mr Kevin Winchcombe, Principal Licensing Officer, Jubilee Stores, The Quay, Newport PO30 2EH ☎ 01983 821000 🖷 01983 823171 🖰 kevin.winchcombe@iow.gov.uk

Lifelong Learning: Mrs Sarah Teague, Manager - Community & Family Learning, Carnival Learning Centre, Westridge, PO33 1QS ☎ 01983 817280 🖰 sarah.teague@iow.gov.uk

Lighting: Mr Geoff Woodhouse, Principal Engineer - Lighting / Electrical, Street Lightning Store, Bennett Street, Ryde PO33 2BJ ☎ 01983 565552 🖰 geoff.woodhouse@iow.gov.uk

Member Services: Mrs Sue Chilton, Members Services Manager, County Hall, High Street, Newport PO30 1UD ☎ 01983 823632 🖷 01983 823535 🖰 sue.chilton@iow.gov.uk

Parking: Mr Mark Downer, Parking Operations Manager, 17a Riverway, Newport PO30 5UX ☎ 01983 821000 🖰 mark.downer@iow.gov.uk

Partnerships: Ms Astrid Davies, Commissioning Manager, County Hall, High Street, Newport PO30 1UD ☎ 01983 823804 🖷 01983 823535 🖰 astrid.davies@iow.gov.uk

Personnel / HR: Mrs Claire Shand, Head - Human Resources, County Hall, High Street, Newport PO30 1UD ☎ 01983 823120 🖷 01983 823012 🖰 claire.shand@iow.gov.uk

Planning: Mr Bill Murphy, Head - Planning & Regulatory Services, Seaclose, Fairlee Road, Newport PO30 2QS ☎ 01983 821000 🖷 01983 823563 🖰 bill.murphy@iow.gov.uk

Procurement: Miss Lucy Hebditch, Senior Procurement Officer, County Hall, High Street, Newport PO30 1UD ☎ 01983 821000

 lucy.hebditch@iow.gov.uk

Public Libraries: Mr Rob Jones, Libraries Officer, 5 Mariners Way, Somerton Industrial Estate, Cowes PO31 8PD ☎ 01983 203885 rob.jones@iow.gov.uk

Recycling & Waste Minimisation: Ms Laura Kay, Principal Waste Policy & Delivery Manager, County Hall, High Street, Newport PO30 1UD ☎ 01983 823777 🖷 01983 520563 laura.kay@iow.gov.uk

Regeneration: Mr Peter Hopkins, Commissioning Manager - Safe & Secure Homes, County Hall, High Street, Newport PO30 1UD ☎ 01983 821000

Road Safety: Mr Kevin Burton, Group Manager - Transport Strategy, Enterprise House, St Cross Business Park, Newport PO30 5WB ☎ 01983 821000 🖷 01983 523291 kevin.burton@iow.gov.uk

Social Services: Mr Ian Anderson, Director - Communitites, Wellbeing & Social Care, County Hall, High Street, Newport PO30 1UD ☎ 01983 821 000 ian.anderson@iow.gov.uk

Social Services: Mr Mark Howell, Head - Commissioning, Housing & Community Support, County Hall, High Street, Newport PO30 1UD ☎ 01983 821000 mark.howell@iow.gov.uk

Social Services (Adult): Ms Suzanne Wixey, Head - Adult Social Care, 17 Fairlee Road, Newport PO30 2EA ☎ 01983 821000 (Phone)

Staff Training: Ms Jenni Charity, Lead Officer - Learning & Development, County Hall, High Street, Newport PO30 1UD ☎ 01983 823629 jenni.charity@iow.gov.uk

Sustainable Communities: Ms Suzanne Wixey, Head - Adult Social Care, 17 Fairlee Road, Newport PO30 2EA ☎ 01983 821000 (Phone)

Tourism: Ms Amanda Gregory, Regular Tourist Service Manager, County Hall, High Street, Newport PO30 1UD ☎ 01983 821000 amanda.gregory@iow.gov.uk

Tourism: Mr John Metcalfe, Assistant Director - Economic Development Tourism & Leisure, County Hall, High Street, Newport PO30 1UD ☎ 01983 821000 john.metcalf@iow.gov.uk

Tourism: Miss Liz Walker, Tourism Development Officer & Strategic Tourism Officer, County Hall, High Street, Newport PO30 1UD ☎ 01983 821000 liz.walker@iow.gov.uk

Town Centre: Mr Simon Dennis, Team Leader - Community & Environment, Charter House, 14 St. Thomas' Square, Newport PO30 1SL ☎ 01983 821000 simon.dennis@iow.gov.uk

Transport Planner: Mr Chris Wells, Principal Policy Planning Officer - Highways & Transport, Enterprise House, St Cross Business Park, Newport PO30 5WB ☎ 01983 821000 chris.wells@iow.gov.uk

Waste Collection and Disposal: Mr Mike Ackrill, Principal Waste & Contracts Officer, County Hall, High Street, Newport PO30 1UD ☎ 01983 821000 mike.ackrill@iow.gov.uk

Waste Management: Mr Mike Ackrill, Principal Waste & Contracts Officer, County Hall, High Street, Newport PO30 1UD ☎ 01983 821000 mike.ackrill@iow.gov.uk

MEMBERS OF THE COUNCIL (39)

***Chair:* Stephens**, Ian (IND - Ryde West)
ian.stephens@iow.gov.uk
***Leader of the Council:* Pugh**, David (CON - Shanklin South)
david.pugh@iow.gov.uk
***Deputy Leader of the Council:* Brown**, George (CON - Cowes North)
george.brown@iow.gov.uk
Abraham, Barry (CON - Wootton Bridge)
barry.abraham@iow.gov.uk
Bacon, Jonathan (IND - Brading, St.Helens and Bembridge)
Jonathan.Bacon@iow.gov.uk
Barry, Reginald (LD - Nettlestone and Seaview)
Reg.Barry@iow.gov.uk
Bingham, Peter (CON - Central Wight)
Peter.Bingham@iow.gov.uk
Cameron, George (CON - Freshwater South)
george.cameron@iow.gov.uk
Churchman, Vanessa (IND - Havenstreet, Ashey and Haylands)
vanessa.churchman@iow.gov.uk
Cousins, Dawn (CON - Newport North)
dawn.cousins@iow.gov.uk
Dixcey, Roger (CON - Newport South)
roger.dixcey@iow.gov.uk
Downer, Rodney (IND - Godshill and Wroxhall)
rodney.downer@iow.gov.uk
Fuller, Paul (IND - Cowes West and Gurnard)
paulfulleriw@gmail.com
Giles, Edward (CON - Whippingham and Osborne)
Edward.Giles@iow.gov.uk
Hobart, John (CON - Carisbrooke)
john.hobart@iow.gov.uk
Hollis, Richard (CON - Parkhurst)
Richard.Hollis@iow.gov.uk
Howe, John (LD - Totland)
John.Howe@iow.gov.uk
Humby, Heather (IND - Sandown North)
heather.humby@iow.gov.uk
Hunter-Henderson, Tim (CON - Lake South)
tim.hunter-henderson@iow.gov.uk
Jones-Evans, Julie (CON - Newport Central)
Julie.Jones-Evans@iow.gov.uk
Joyce, Patrick (IND - Brading, St Helens and Bembridge)
patrick.joyce@iow.gov.uk
Knowles, David (LD - Ryde East)
david.knowles@iow.gov.uk
Lumley, Geoff (LAB - Newport East)
geofflumley2@gmail.com
Mazillius, Roger (CON - Cowes South and Northwood)
roger.mazillius@iow.gov.uk
Peacey-Wilcox, Lora (CON - Cowes Medina)
lora@onwight.net
Richards, Colin (LD - Arreton and Newchurch)
colin.richards@iow.gov.uk
Scoccia, Susan (CON - Ventnor West)
susan.soccia@iow.gov.uk
Stewart, David (CON - Chale Niton and Whitwell)

david.stewart@iow.gov.uk
Sutton, Andy (CON - Freshwater Nortth)
andy.sutton@iow.gov.uk
Taylor, Gary (CON - Ryde South)
gary.taylor@iow.gov.uk
Taylor, Arthur (CON - Ryde North West)
arthur.taylor@iow.gov.uk
Ward, Ian (CON - Sandown South)
ian.ward@iow.gov.uk
Warlow, Ivor (IND - Binstead and Fishbourne)
mary.warlow@tiscali.co.uk
Webster, Margaret (CON - East Cowes)
margaret.webster@iow.gov.uk
Welsford, Chris (IND - Ventnor East)
Chris.Welsford@iow.gov.uk
White, Jerry (CON - Lake North)
Gerard.White@iow.gov.uk
Whittaker, David (CON - Newport West)
david.whittaker@iow.gov.uk
Whittle, Wayne (IND - Ryde North East)
Wayne.Whittle@iow.gov.uk
Williams, David (CON - Shanklin Central)
david.williams@iow.gov.uk

POLITICAL COMPOSITION
CON: 24, IND: 10, LD: 4, LAB: 1

CABINET
Leader / Resources: Mr David Pugh
Deputy Leader / Economy & Environment: Mr George Brown
Adult Social Care, Housing & Community Safety: Mr Roger Mazillius
Children's Services & Education: Mrs Dawn Cousins
Fire, Culture & Residents' Services: Mr Barry Abraham
Highways, Transport & Waste: Mr Edward Giles

COMMITTEE CHAIRS
Audit (Scrutiny): Mrs Julie Jones-Evans
Children & Young People (Scrutiny): Mr George Cameron
Economy & Environment (Scrutiny): Mr Ian Ward
Ethical Standards: Mr Mark Southwell (External)
Health & Community Wellbeing (Scrutiny): Mrs Margaret Webster
Isle of Wight Pension Fund (Scrutiny): Mr Peter Bingham
Licensing & General Purposes: Ms Susan Scoccia
Overview & Scrutiny (Scrutiny): Mr Wayne Whittle
Planning Committee (Scrutiny): Mr Richard Hollis

ISLINGTON L
Islington London Borough Council, Town Hall, Upper Street, London N1 2UD ☎ 020 7527 2000 🖷 020 7527 5001 contact@islington.gov.uk www.islington.gov.uk

FACTS & FIGURES
Police Authority: Metropolitan Police Authority
Health Authority: NHS London
Learning and Skills Council: London
Parliamentary Constituencies: Islington North, Islington South and Finsbury
EU Constituencies: London
Election Frequency: Elections are of whole council

PRINCIPAL OFFICERS
Chief Executive: Ms Lesley Seary, Chief Executive, Town Hall, Upper Street, London N1 2UD ☎ 020 7527 3062 lesley.seary@islington.gov.uk

Senior Management: Mr Mike Curtis, Director of Finance, 7 Newington Barrow Way, London N7 7EP ☎ 020 7527 2294 🖷 020 7527 2407 mike.curtis@islington.gov.uk

Senior Management: Ms Lela Kogbara, Director - Strategy & Partnerships, Room G16, Town Hall, Upper Street, London N1 2UD ☎ 020 7527 3120 🖷 020 7527 3013 lela.kogbara@islington.gov.uk

Senior Management: Mr Sean McLaughlin, Corporate Director - Housing & Adult Social Services, 338-346 Goswell Road, London EC1V 7LQ ☎ 020 7527 8178 🖷 020 7527 8362 sean.mclaughlin@islington.gov.uk

Senior Management: Mr Kevin O'Leary, Corporate Director - Environment & Regeneration, 222 Upper Street, London N1 1XR ☎ 020 7527 2350 🖷 020 7527 2731 kevin.oleary@islington.gov.uk

Senior Management: Ms Louise Round, Corporate Director - Corporate Resources, Town Hall, Upper Street, London N1 2UD ☎ 020 7527 3174 louise.round@islington.gov.uk

Senior Management: Ms Eleanor Schooling, Corporate Director - Children's Services, 222 Upper Street, London N1 1YA ☎ 020 7527 5624 eleanor.schooling@islington.gov.uk

Access Officer / Social Services (Disability): Mr Sean McLaughlin, Corporate Director - Housing & Adult Social Services, 338-346 Goswell Road, London EC1V 7LQ ☎ 020 7527 8178 🖷 020 7527 8362 sean.mclaughlin@islington.gov.uk

Building Control: Ms Jan Hart, Service Director - Public Protection & Development Management, 222 Upper Street, London N1 1XR ☎ 020 7527 3193 🖷 020 7527 3375 jan.hart@islington.gov.uk

Children / Youth Services: Ms Eleanor Schooling, Corporate Director - Children's Services, 222 Upper Street, London N1 1YA ☎ 020 7527 5624 eleanor.schooling@islington.gov.uk

Children / Youth Services: Ms Jane Winterbone, Service Director - Young People, 222 Upper Street, London N1 NXR ☎ 020 7527 5880 jane.winterbone@islington.gov.uk

Civil Registration: Mr Besserat Atsehaba, Superintendent Registrar, Town Hall, Upper Street, London N1 2UD ☎ 020 7527 6357 🖷 020 7527 6308 besserat.atsehaba@islington.gov.uk

PR / Communications: Ms Emma Marinos, Director of Communications & Technology, Town Hall, Upper Street, London N1 2UD ☎ 020 7527 3467 🖷 020 7527 3291 emma.marinos@islington.gov.uk

Community Safety: Mr Alva Bailey, Head of Service - Community Safety, Room 116, 222 Upper Street, London N1 1XR ☎ 020 7527 3135 🖷 020 7527 3098

alva.bailey@islington.gov.uk

Computer Management: Ms Emma Marinos, Director of Communications & Technology, Town Hall, Upper Street, London N1 2UD ☎ 020 7527 3467 fax 020 7527 3291 emma.marinos@islington.gov.uk

Consumer Protection and Trading Standards: Ms Jan Hart, Service Director - Public Protection & Development Management, 222 Upper Street, London N1 1XR ☎ 020 7527 3193 fax 020 7527 3375 jan.hart@islington.gov.uk

Corporate Services: Mr Tony MacMamara, Audit Manager, 7 Newington Barrow Way, London N7 7EP ☎ 020 7527 2000 tony.macmamara@islington.gov.uk

Customer Service: Mr Martin Bevis, Director of Customer Services, Town Hall, Upper Street, London N1 2UD ☎ 020 7527 2000 fax 0207 527 5454 martin.bevis@islington.gov.uk

Economic Development: Ms Lela Kogbara, Director - Strategy & Partnerships, Room G16, Town Hall, Upper Street, London N1 2UD ☎ 020 7527 3120 fax 020 7527 3013 lela.kogbara@islington.gov.uk

Education: Ms Eleanor Schooling, Corporate Director - Children's Services, 222 Upper Street, London N1 1YA ☎ 020 7527 5624 eleanor.schooling@islington.gov.uk

E-Government: Ms Emma Marinos, Director of Communications & Technology, Town Hall, Upper Street, London N1 2UD ☎ 020 7527 3467 fax 020 7527 3291 emma.marinos@islington.gov.uk

Electoral Registration: Mr Andrew Smith, Electoral Services Manager, Town Hall, Upper Street, London N1 2UD ☎ 020 7527 3085 fax 020 7527 3289 andrew.smith@islington.gov.uk

Emergency Planning: Mr Andy French, Principal Emergency Planning Officer, 222 Upper Street, London N1 1XE ☎ 020 7527 3195 fax 020 7527 3375 andy.french@islington.gov.uk

Environmental / Technical Services: Mr Kevin O'Leary, Corporate Director - Environment & Regeneration, 222 Upper Street, London N1 1XR ☎ 020 7527 2350 fax 020 7527 2731 kevin.oleary@islington.gov.uk

Environmental Health: Ms Jan Hart, Service Director - Public Protection & Development Management, 222 Upper Street, London N1 1XE ☎ 020 7527 3193 fax 020 7527 3375 jan.hart@islington.gov.uk

Facilities: Mr John Roberts, Head of Accommodation & Facilities, Town Hall, Upper Street, London N1 2UD ☎ 020 7527 3173 fax 020 7527 3021 john.roberts@islington.gov.uk

Finance and Treasurer: Mr Mike Curtis, Director of Finance, 222 Upper Street, London N1 1XR ☎ 020 7527 2294 fax 020 7527 2407 mike.curtis@islington.gov.uk

Finance and Treasurer: Mr Alan Layton, Director of Financial Management, 222 Upper Street, London N1 1XR ☎ 020 7527 2835 fax 020 7527 2407 alan.layton@islington.gov.uk

Fleet Management: Mr Chris Rutherford, Transport & Depot Manager, 1 Cottage Road, London N7 8TP ☎ 020 7527 7539 chris.rutherford@islington.gov.uk

Grounds Maintenance: Mr Andrew Bedford, Principal Parks Manager, Clocktower Office, 36 North Road, London N7 9TU ☎ 020 7527 3287 andrew.bedford@islington.gov.uk

Health and Safety: Mr John Roberts, Head of Accommodation & Facilities, Town Hall, Upper Street, London N1 2UD ☎ 020 7527 3173 fax 020 7527 3021 john.roberts@islington.gov.uk

Highways: Mr Bram Kainth, Director - Public Realm, 222 Upper Street, London N1 1XR ☎ 020 7527 2949 fax 020 7527 2145 bram.kainth@islington.gov.uk

Home Energy Conservation: Ms Lucy Padfield, Energy Services Manager, Energy Centre, 222 Upper Street, London N1 1RE ☎ 020 7527 2501 fax 020 7527 2332 lucy.padfield@islington.gov.uk

Housing: Mr Patrick Odling-Smee, Service Director - Housing, 338-346 Goswell Road, London EC1V 7LQ ☎ 020 7527 8190 patrick.odling-smee@islington.gov.uk

Local Area Agreement: Ms Anette Hobart, ISP Support Manager, Town Hall, Upper Street, London N1 2UD ☎ 020 7527 3244 annette.hobart@islington.gov.uk

Legal: Ms Debra Norman, Director - Legal & HR Services, Town Hall, Upper Street, London N1 2UD ☎ 020 7527 6096 fax 020 7527 3267 debra.norman@islington.gov.uk

Licensing: Ms Jan Hart, Service Director - Public Protection & Development Management, 222 Upper Street, London N1 1RE ☎ 020 7527 3193 fax 020 7527 3375 jan.hart@islington.gov.uk

Lighting: Mr Bram Kainth, Director - Public Realm, 222 Upper Street, London N1 1XR ☎ 020 7527 2949 fax 020 7527 2145 bram.kainth@islington.gov.uk

Member Services: Mr John Lynch, Head of Democratic Services, Town Hall, Upper Street, London N1 2UD ☎ 020 7527 3002 fax 020 7527 3092 john.lynch@islington.gov.uk

Parking: Mr Bram Kainth, Director - Public Realm, 222 Upper Street, London N1 1XR ☎ 020 7527 2949 fax 020 7527 2145 bram.kainth@islington.gov.uk

Personnel / HR: Ms Debra Norman, Director - Legal & HR Services, Town Hall, Upper Street, London N1 2UD ☎ 020 7527 6096 fax 020 7527 3267 debra.norman@islington.gov.uk

Planning: Ms Jan Hart, Service Director - Public Protection & Development Management, 222 Upper Street, London N1 1XR ☎ 020 7527 3193 fax 020 7527 3375 jan.hart@islington.gov.uk

Public Libraries: Ms Rosemary Doyle, Head of Library & Cultural Services, Fieldway Crescent, London N5 1PF ☎ 020 7619 6903 fax 020 7619 6906 rosemary.doyle@islington.gov.uk

Recycling & Waste Minimisation: Mr Bram Kainth, Director -

Public Realm, 222 Upper Street, London N1 1XR ☎ 020 7527 2949 🖷 020 7527 2145 ✉ bram.kainth@islington.gov.uk

Road Safety: Mr Bram Kainth, Director - Public Realm, 222 Upper Street, London N1 1XR ☎ 020 7527 2949 🖷 020 7527 2145 ✉ bram.kainth@islington.gov.uk

Social Services (Adult): Mr Sean McLaughlin, Corporate Director - Housing & Adult Social Services, 338-346 Goswell Road, London EC1V 7LQ ☎ 020 7527 8178 🖷 020 7527 8362 ✉ sean.mclaughlin@islington.gov.uk

Social Services (Children): Ms Eleanor Schooling, Corporate Director - Children's Services, 222 Upper Street, London N1 1YA ☎ 020 7527 5624 ✉ eleanor.schooling@islington.gov.uk

Street Scene: Mr Bram Kainth, Director - Public Realm, 222 Upper Street, London N1 1XR ☎ 020 7527 2949 🖷 020 7527 2145 ✉ bram.kainth@islington.gov.uk

Traffic Management: Mr Bram Kainth, Director - Public Realm, 222 Upper Street, London N1 1XR ☎ 020 7527 2949 🖷 020 7527 2145 ✉ bram.kainth@islington.gov.uk

Transport: Mr Bram Kainth, Director - Public Realm, 222 Upper Street, London N1 1XR ☎ 020 7527 2949 🖷 020 7527 2145 ✉ bram.kainth@islington.gov.uk

Transport Planner: Ms Karen Sullivan, Head of Transport Planning Services, 222 Upper Street, London N1 1XR ☎ 020 7527 2730 ✉ karen.sullivan@islington.gov.uk

Waste Collection and Disposal: Mr Bram Kainth, Director - Public Realm, 222 Upper Street, London N1 1XR ☎ 020 7527 2949 🖷 020 7527 2145 ✉ bram.kainth@islington.gov.uk

Waste Management: Mr Bram Kainth, Director - Public Realm, 222 Upper Street, London N1 1XR ☎ 020 7527 2949 🖷 020 7527 2145 ✉ bram.kainth@islington.gov.uk

MEMBERS OF THE COUNCIL (48)

***Mayor:* Chowdhury**, Jilani (LAB - Barnsbury)
jiliani.chowdhury@islington.gov.uk
***Deputy Mayor:* Edwards**, Barry (LAB - Holloway)
barry.edwards@islington.gov.uk
***Leader of the Council:* West**, Catherine (LAB - Tollington)
catherine.west@islington.gov.uk
***Deputy Leader of the Council:* Greening**, Richard (LAB - Highbury West)
richard.greening@islington.gov.uk
***Group Leader:* Stacy**, Terry (LD - Highbury East)
terry.stacy@islington.gov.uk
Allan, George (LD - Clerkenwell)
george.allan@islington.gov.uk
Andrews, Raphael (LAB - Clerkenwell)
raphael.andrews@islington.gov.uk
Asato, Jessica (LAB - St. Georges)
jessica.asato@islington.gov.uk
Belford, Paula (LD - Canonbury)
paula.belford@islington.gov.uk
Buchanan, Susan (LD - St. Mary's)
susan.buchanan@islington.gov.uk
Burgess, Janet (LAB - Junction)
janet.burgess@islington.gov.uk
Burgess, Wally (LAB - Canonbury)
wally.burgess@islington.gov.uk
Caluori, Joe (LAB - Mildmay)
joe.caluori@islington.gov.uk
Charalambous, Steph (LAB - Clerkenwell)
steph.charalambous@islington.gov.uk
Constantinou, Lorraine (LD - Hillrise)
lorraine.constantinou@islington.gov.uk
Convery, Paul (LAB - Caledonian)
paul.convery@islington.gov.uk
Davis, Rhiannon (LAB - St. Marys)
rhiannon.davis@islington.gov.uk
Debono, Theresa (LAB - Highbury West)
theresa.debono@islington.gov.uk
Doolan, Gary (LAB - St. Peters)
gary.doolan@islington.gov.uk
Foxsmith, Greg (LD - Hillrise)
greg.foxsmith@islington.gov.uk
Gallagher, Troy (LAB - Bunhill)
troy.gallagher@islington.gov.uk
Gilbert, John (LD - Highbury East)
john.gilbert@islington.gov.uk
Graves, Arthur (LD - Junction)
arthur.graves@islington.gov.uk
Groucutt, Kate (LAB - Mildmay)
kate.groucutt@islington.gov.uk
Hamitouche, Mouna (LAB - Barnsbury)
mouna.hamitouche@islington.gov.uk
Horten, Julie (LD - Highbury East)
julie.horten@islington.gov.uk
Hull, Andy (LAB - Highbury West)
andy.hull@islington.gov.uk
Ismail, Rakhia (LAB - Holloway)
rakhia.ismail@islington.gov.uk
Ismail, Tracy (LD - St. George's)
tracy.ismail@islington.gov.uk
Jamieson-Ball, Rhodri (LD - Mildmay)
rhodri.jamieson-ball@islington.gov.uk
Kaseki, Jean Roger (LAB - Tollington)
jean.kaseki@islington.gov.uk
Kelly, Phil (LAB - Finsbury Park)
phil.kelly@islington.gov.uk
Khan, Robert (LAB - Bunhill)
robert.khan@islington.gov.uk
Klute, Martin (LAB - St. Peters)
martin.klute@islington.gov.uk
Murray, James (LAB - Barnsbury)
james.murray@islington.gov.uk
O'Sullivan, Michael (LAB - Finsbury Park)
michael.osullivan@islington.gov.uk
Perry, Rupert (LAB - Caledonian)
rupert.perry@islington.gov.uk
Perry, Alice (LAB - St. Peters)
alice.perry@islington.gov.uk
Poole, Gary (LAB - St. Mary's)
gary.poole@islington.gov.uk
Pullen, Charlynne (LAB - Caledonian)
charlynne.pullen@islington.gov.uk
Sidnell, Barbara (LAB - Finsbury Park)
barbara.sidnell@islington.gov.uk
Smith, Paul (LAB - Holloway)
paul.smith@islington.gov.uk
Spall, Marian (LAB - Hillrise)
marian.spall@islington.gov.uk

Watts, Richard (LAB - Tollington)
richard.watts@islington.gov.uk
Webbe, Claudia (LAB - Bunhill)
claudia.webbe@islington.gov.uk
Whaley, Faye (LAB - Canonbury)
faye.whaley@islington.gov.uk
Wilson, David (LD - St. George's)
david.wilson@islington.gov.uk
Woolley, Ursula (LD - Junction)
ursula.woolley@islington.gov.uk

POLITICAL COMPOSITION
LAB: 35, LD: 13

CABINET
Leader: Ms Catherine West
Deputy Leader; Finance: Mr Richard Greening
Children & Families: Mr Richard Watts
Community Safety: Mr Paul Convery
Environment: Mr Paul Smith
Health & Wellbeing: Ms Janet Burgess
Housing & Development: Mr James Murray
Tenants, Residents & Communities: Ms Barbara Sidnell

COMMITTEE CHAIRS
Audit: Mr Phil Kelly
Health & Wellbeing: Mr Martin Klute
Licensing: Mr Joe Caluori
Overview: Mr Troy Gallagher
Planning: Mr Robert Khan
Regeneration & Employment: Mr Greg Foxsmith

KENSINGTON & CHELSEA L
The Royal Borough of Kensington & Chelsea Council, Town Hall, Hornton Street, London W8 7NX ☎ 020 7361 3000 🖷 020 7938 1445 💻 www.rbkc.gov.uk

FACTS & FIGURES
Police Authority: Metropolitan Police Authority
Health Authority: NHS London
Learning and Skills Council: London
Parliamentary Constituencies: Chelsea and Fulham, Kensington
EU Constituencies: London
Election Frequency: Elections are of whole council
Twinning: Ville de Cannes (France)

PRINCIPAL OFFICERS
Chief Executive: Mr Derek Myers, Chief Executive, Town Hall, Hornton Street, London W8 7NX ☎ 020 8753 2001; 020 7361 2299 🖷 020 8741 0307; 020 7361 2764
✉ derek.myers@lbhf.gov.uk; derek.myers@rbkc.gov.uk

Assistant Chief Executive: Ms Tot Brill, Assistant Chief Executive, Council Offices, Pembroke Road, London W8 6PW ☎ 020 7341 5101 🖷 020 7341 5155 ✉ tot.brill@rbkc.gov.uk

Senior Management: Mr Jonathan Bore, Executive Director of Planning & Borough Development, Town Hall, Hornton Street, London W8 7NX ☎ 020 7361 2944 ✉ jonathan.bore@rbkc.gov.uk

Senior Management: Ms Lyn Carpenter, Executive Director of Environment Leisure & Residents' Services, Town Hall, Hornton Street, London W8 7NX ☎ 020 8753 5710
✉ lyn.carpenter@lbhf.gov.uk; lyn.carpenter@lbhf.gov.uk

Senior Management: Mr Andrew Christie, Tri-Borough Director of Children's Services, Town Hall, Hornton Street, London W8 7NX ☎ 020 8753 5002; 020 7361 2354; 020 7361 3300
🖷 020 7361 3300 ✉ andrew.christie@lbhf.gov.uk; andrew.christie@rbkc.gov.uk

Senior Management: Mr Nicholas Holgate, Town Clerk & Executive Director of Finance, Town Hall, Hornton Street, London W8 7NX ☎ 020 7361 2384 🖷 020 7361 3716
✉ nicholas.holgate@rbkc.gov.uk

Senior Management: Mr Nigel Pallace, Executive Director of Transport & Technical Services, Town Hall, Hornton Street, London W8 7NX ☎ 020 8753 3000 🖷 020 8753 3397
✉ nigel.pallace@lbhf.gov.uk

Senior Management: Mr Tony Redpath, Director of Strategy & Local Services, Town Hall, Hornton Street, London W8 7NX
☎ 020 7361 3174 ✉ tony.redpath@rbkc.gov.uk

Senior Management: Mr Andrew Webster, Executive Director of Adult Social Care, Westminster Council, London SW1E 6QP
☎ 020 8753 5000 ✉ awebster@westminster.gov.uk

Access Officer / Social Services (Disability): Mr Richard Holden, Head of Complex Needs & Disabilities, Town Hall, Hornton Street, London W8 7NX ☎ 020 7361 3751
✉ richard.holden@rbkc.gov.uk

Best Value: Ms Milisa Savic, Service Improvement Manager, Town Hall, Hornton Street, London W8 7NX ☎ 020 7361 3691
🖷 020 7361 2764 ✉ milisa.savic@rbkc.gov.uk

Building Control: Mr Jonathan Bore, Executive Director of Planning & Borough Development, Town Hall, Hornton Street, London W8 7NX ☎ 020 7361 2075 🖷 020 7361 3463
✉ jonathan.bore@rbkc.gov.uk

Building Control: Mr John Jackson, Head of Building Control, Town Hall, Hornton Street, London W8 7NX ☎ 020 7361 3822
🖷 020 7361 3820 ✉ john.jackson@rbkc.gov.uk

Children / Youth Services: Mr Andrew Christie, Tri-Borough Director of Children's Services, Town Hall, Hornton Street, London W8 7NX ☎ 020 8753 5002🖷 020 7361 3300 ✉ andrew.christie@lbhf.gov.uk; andrew.christie@rbkc.gov.uk

Civil Registration: Mr Andrew Kenyon, Superintendent Registrar, Chelsea Registrar Office, Kings Road, London SW3 5EE
☎ 020 7361 4107 ✉ andrew.kenyon@rbkc.gov.uk

PR / Communications: Mr Martin Fitzpatrick, Head of Media & Communications, Town Hall, Hornton Street, London W8 7NX
☎ 020 7361 3585 🖷 020 7937 9670
✉ martin.fitzpatrick@rbkc.gov.uk

Community Safety: Mr David Page, Director of Safer

Neighbourhoods, Town Hall, Hornton Street, London W8 7NX ☎ 020 8753 2125 ✉ david.page@lbhf.gov.uk

Computer Management: Mr Barry Holloway, Head of Information Systems, Town Hall, Hornton Street, London W8 7NX ☎ 020 7361 2042 🖷 020 7361 2754 ✉ barry.holloway@rbkc.gov.uk

Contracts: Mr Roger van Goethem, Procurement & Commercial Manager, Town Hall, Hornton Street, London W8 7NX ☎ 020 7361 3345 ✉ roger.vangoethem@rbkc.gov.uk

Corporate Services: Ms Debbie Morris, Director of Human Resources, Town Hall, Hornton Street, London W8 7NX ☎ 020 8753 3068; 020 7361 2172 ✉ debbie.morris@lbhf.gov.uk; debbie.morris@rbkc.gov.uk

Customer Service: Mr Ray Brown, Head of Business Management & Customer Access, Town Hall, Hornton Street, London W8 7NX ☎ 020 7361 3291 🖷 020 7368 0246 ✉ ray.brown@rbkc.gov.uk

Economic Development: Mr Graham Hart, Regeneration Manager, Town Hall, Hornton Street, London W8 7NX ☎ 020 7631 3336 🖷 020 7361 2764 ✉ graham.hart@rbkc.gov.uk

Education: Mr Andrew Christie, Tri-Borough Director of Children's Services, Town Hall, Hornton Street, London W8 7NX ☎ 020 8753 5002; 020 7361 2354; 020 7361 3300 🖷 020 7361 3300 ✉ andrew.christie@lbhf.gov.uk; andrew.christie@rbkc.gov.uk

Education: Mr Ian Heggs, Director of Schools Quality & Standards, Town Hall, Hornton Street, London W8 7NX ☎ 020 8753 2880; 020 7361 3332 ✉ ian.heggs@lbhf.gov.uk; ian.heggs@rbkc.gov.uk

E-Government: Mr Barry Holloway, Head of Information Systems, Town Hall, Hornton Street, London W8 7NX ☎ 020 7361 2042 🖷 020 7361 2754 ✉ barry.holloway@rbkc.gov.uk

Electoral Registration: Mrs Susan Loynes, Electoral Services Manager, Town Hall, Hornton Street, London W8 7NX ☎ 020 7361 3931 ✉ susan.loynes@rbkc.gov.uk

Emergency Planning: Mr David Kerry, Contingency Planning Manager, Town Hall, Hornton Street, London W8 7NX ☎ 020 7361 2139 🖷 020 7361 2573 ✉ david.kerry@rbkc.gov.uk

Energy Management: Ms Sue Cooper, Head of Facilities Management, Town Hall, Hornton Street, London W8 7NX ☎ 020 7361 2110 🖷 020 7361 3164 ✉ sue.cooper@rbkc.gov.uk

Environmental / Technical Services: Mr Nigel Pallace, Executive Director of Transport & Technical Services, Town Hall, Hornton Street, London W8 7NX ☎ 020 8753 3000 🖷 020 8753 3397 ✉ nigel.pallace@lbhf.gov.uk

Environmental Health: Mr Nick Austin, Director of Environmental Health, Council Offices, 37 Pembroke Road, London W6 6PW ☎ 020 8753 3904; 020 7341 5600 ✉ nick.austin@lbhf.gov.uk; nick.austin@brkc.gov.uk

Estates, Property & Valuation: Mr Michael Clark, Director of Corporate Property, Town Hall, Hornton Street, London W8 7NX ☎ 020 7361 3888 🖷 020 7361 2008 ✉ michael.clark@rbkc.gov.uk

Events Manager: Mr David Scott, Conference & Events Manager, Town Hall, Hornton Street, London W8 7NX ☎ 020 7361 2635 ✉ david.scott@rbkc.gov.uk

Facilities: Ms Sue Cooper, Head of Facilities Management, Town Hall, Hornton Street, London W8 7NX ☎ 020 7361 2110 🖷 020 7361 3164 ✉ sue.cooper@rbkc.gov.uk

Finance and Treasurer: Mr Nicholas Holgate, Town Clerk & Executive Director of Finance, Town Hall, Hornton Street, London W8 7NX ☎ 020 7361 2384 🖷 020 7361 3716 ✉ nicholas.holgate@rbkc.gov.uk

Finance and Treasurer: Mr Hitesh Jolapara, Deputy Director of Financial Services, Town Hall, Hornton Street, London W8 7NX ☎ 020 7361 2316; 020 8748 3020 🖷 020 7361 3716 ✉ hitesh.jolapara@rbkc.gov.uk

Health and Safety: Mr Gary Mann, Health & Safety Officer, Town Hall, Hornton Street, London W8 7NX ☎ 020 7361 3733 🖷 020 7361 2676 ✉ gary.mann@rbkc.gov.uk

Highways: Mr Mahmood Siddiqi, Director of Transport & Highways, Town Hall, Hornton Street, London W8 7NX ☎ 020 7361 3589; 020 8748 3020 ✉ mahmood.siddiqi@rbkc.gov.uk

Housing: Ms Laura Johnson, Director of Housing, Town Hall, Hornton Street, London W8 7NX ☎ 020 7361 2362 ✉ laura.johnson@rbkc.gov.uk

Housing Maintenance: Mr Nick Austin, Director of Environmental Health, Council Offices, 37 Pembroke Road, London W6 6PW ☎ 020 8753 3904; 020 7341 5600 ✉ nick.austin@lbhf.gov.uk; nick.austin@brkc.gov.uk

Leisure and Cultural Services: Mr Ullash Karia, Head of Leisure & Parks, The Stableyard, Holland Park, Ilchester Place, London W8 6LU ☎ 020 7938 8171 ✉ ullash.karia@rbkc.gov.uk

Leisure and Cultural Services: Ms Donna Pentelow, Head of Culture, Town Hall, King Street, London W6 0LJ ☎ 020 8753 2358 🖷 020 8753 3713 ✉ donna.pentelow@lbhf.gov.uk

Licensing: Mr Patrick Crowley, Licensing Team Manager, Council Offices, 37 Pembroke Road, London W8 6PW ☎ 020 7341 5601 🖷 020 7368 0231 ✉ patrick.crowley@rbkc.gov.uk

Lighting: Mr Derek Mahon, Senior Lighting Engineer, Council Offices, 37 Pembroke Road, London W8 6PW ☎ 020 7341 5254 ✉ derek.mahon@rbkc.gov.uk

Lottery Funding, Charity and Voluntary: Ms Lucy Ashall, Voluntary Sector Manager, Town Hall, Hornton Street, London W8 7NX ☎ 020 7361 5853 ✉ lucy.ashall@rbkc.gov.uk

Parking: Mr David Taylor, Head of Parking Services, PO Box 3387, London SW6 2QF ☎ 020 8753 3251 ✉ david.taylor@lbhf.gov.uk

Partnerships: Mr Stephen Morgan, Community Engagement Manager, Westway Centre, 2-4 Malton Road, London W10 5UP ☎ 020 7854 5852 stephen.morgan@rbkc.gov.uk

Personnel / HR: Ms Debbie Morris, Director of Human Resources, Town Hall, Hornton Street, London W8 7NX ☎ 020 8753 3068; 020 7361 2172 debbie.morris@lbhf.gov.uk; debbie.morris@rbkc.gov.uk

Planning: Mr Jonathan Bore, Executive Director of Planning & Borough Development, Town Hall, Hornton Street, London W8 7NX ☎ 020 7361 2944 jonathan.bore@rbkc.gov.uk

Procurement: Mr Andrew Lee, Head of Strategic Procurement, Town Hall, Hornton Street, London W8 7NX ☎ 020 7361 2674 andrew.lee@rbkc.gov.uk

Public Libraries: Mr David Ruse, Tri-Borough Director of Libraries & Archives, Westminster Reference Library, 35 St Martin's Street, London WC2H 7HP ☎ 020 7641 2496; 020 7641 2199 🖷 020 7641 3406 druse@westminster.gov.uk

Recycling & Waste Minimisation: Ms Sue Harris, Director of Cleaner, Greener & Cultural Services, Town Hall, King Street, London W6 0LJ ☎ 020 8753 4295 sue.harris@lbhf.gov.uk

Regeneration: Mr Graham Hart, Regeneration Manager, Town Hall, Hornton Street, London W8 7NX ☎ 020 7631 3336 🖷 020 7361 2764 graham.hart@rbkc.gov.uk

Road Safety: Ms Kathryn King, Road Safety Manager, Council Offices, 37 Pembroke Road, London W8 6PW ☎ 020 7361 2736 🖷 020 73613766 kathryn.king@brkc.gov.uk

Social Services: Ms Stella Baillie, Director of Adult Social Care, Provided Services & Mental Health Partnerships, Town Hall, Hornton Street, London W8 7NX ☎ 020 7361 2401 stella.baillie@rbkc.gov.uk

Social Services (Adult): Ms Zena Deayton, Director of Adult Social Care Operations, 4th Floor, 77 Glenthorne Road, London W6 0LJ ☎ 020 7641 2262; 020 8753 5004 zdeayton@westminster.gov.uk; zena.deayton@lbhf.gov.uk

Social Services (Children): Mr Andrew Christie, Tri-Borough Director of Children's Services, Town Hall, Hornton Street, London W8 7NX ☎ 020 8753 5002 🖷 020 7361 3300 andrew.christie@lbhf.gov.uk; andrew.christie@rbkc.gov.uk

Staff Training: Mr Nick Alcock, Corporate Learning & Development Manager, Council Offices, 37 Pembroke Road, London W8 6PW ☎ 020 7341 5130 nick.alcock@rbkc.gov.uk

Sustainable Communities: Mr Tony Redpath, Director of Strategy & Local Services, Town Hall, Hornton Street, London W8 7NX ☎ 020 7361 3174 tony.redpath@rbkc.gov.uk

Sustainable Development: Ms Joan McGarvey, Senior Policy Officer, Transport, Environment and Leisure Services, Council Offices, 37 Pembroke Road, London W8 6PW ☎ 020 7341 5173 🖷 020 7341 5145 joan.mcgarvey@rbkc.gov.uk

Town Centre: Mr Jonathan Bore, Executive Director of Planning & Borough Development, Town Hall, Hornton Street, London W8 7NX ☎ 020 7361 2075 🖷 020 7361 3463 jonathan.bore@rbkc.gov.uk

Town Centre: Ms Joanna Hammond, Town Centre Initiatives Manager, Town Hall, Hornton Street, London W8 7NX ☎ 020 7361 2061 joanna.hammond@rbkc.gov.uk

Transport Planner: Mr Geoff Burrage, Senior Transport Planner, Town Hall, Hornton Street, London W8 7NX ☎ 0207 361 2557 geoff.burrage@rbkc.gov.uk

Waste Management: Ms Kathy May, Head of Waste and Street Enforcement, Council Offices, 37 Pembroke Road, London W8 6PW ☎ 020 7341 5616; 020 7341 5616 kathy.may@rbkc.gov.uk; kathy.may@rbkc.gov.uk

MEMBERS OF THE COUNCIL (54)

***Mayor:* Buckmaster**, Christopher (CON - Campden)
mayor@rbkc.gov.uk
***Deputy Mayor:* Borwick**, Victoria (CON - Abingdon)
cllr.borwick@rbkc.gov.uk
***Leader of the Council:* Cockell**, Merrick (CON - Stanley)
leader@rbkc.gov.uk
Ahern, Tim (CON - Campden)
cllr.ahern@rbkc.gov.uk
Atkinson, Robert (LAB - Notting Barns)
cllr.r.atkinson@rbkc.gov.uk
Barkhordar, Abbas (CON - Brompton)
cllr.barkhordar@rbkc.gov.uk
Blakeman, Judith (LAB - Notting Barns)
cllr.blakeman@rbkc.gov.uk
Buxton, Terence (CON - Earl's Court)
cllr.buxton@rbkc.gov.uk
Buxton, Fiona (CON - Queen's Gate)
cllr.f.buxton@rbkc.gov.uk
Campbell, Elizabeth (CON - Royal Hospital)
cllr.e.campbell@rbkc.gov.uk
Campbell, Barbara (CON - Pembridge)
cllr.campbell@rbkc.gov.uk
Campion, David (CON - Pembridge)
cllr.campion@rbkc.gov.uk
Caruana, Carol (LD - Colville)
Cllr.Caruana@rbkc.gov.uk
Coates, Anthony (CON - Courtfield)
cllr.coates@rbkc.gov.uk
Coleridge, Timothy (CON - Hans Town)
cllr.coleridge@rbkc.gov.uk
Collinson, Deborah (CON - Holland)
cllr.collinson@rbkc.gov.uk
Condon-Simmonds, Maighread (CON - Cremorne)
cllr.condon-simmonds@rbkc.gov.uk
Dent Coad, Emma (LAB - Golborne)
cllr.dentcoad@rbkc.gov.uk
Donaldson, Ian (CON - Royal Hospital)
cllr.donaldson@rbkc.gov.uk
Faulks, Catherine (CON - Norland)
cllr.faulks@rbkc.gov.uk
Feilding-Mellen, Rock (CON - Holland)
cllr.feilding-mellen@rbkc.gov.uk
Foreman, Todd (LAB - Notting Barns)
cllr.foreman@rbkc.gov.uk
Freeman, Robert (CON - Campden)

cllr.freeman@rbkc.gov.uk
Gardner, Joanna (CON - Abingdon)
cllr.gardner@rbkc.gov.uk
Hargreaves, Gerard (CON - Cremorne)
cllr.hargreaves@rbkc.gov.uk
Healy, Pat (LAB - St. Charles)
cllr.healy@rbkc.gov.uk
Hoier, Bridget (LAB - Golborne)
cllr.b.hoier@rbkc.gov.uk
Holt, Tony (CON - Courtfield)
cllr.holt@rbkc.gov.uk
Husband, James (CON - Abingdon)
cllr.husband@rbkc.gov.uk
Jones, Tim (LD - Colville)
cllr.jones@rbkc.gov.uk
Lightfoot, Warwick (CON - Holland)
cllr.lightfoot@rbkc.gov.uk
Lindsay, David (CON - Norland)
cllr.lindsay@rbkc.gov.uk
Mackover, Sam (CON - Queen's Gate)
Cllr.mackover@rbkc.gov.uk
Marshall, Quentin (CON - Brompton)
cllr.marshall@rbkc.gov.uk
Mason, Pat (LAB - Golborne)
cllr.mason@rbkc.gov.uk
Mills, Julie (CON - Norland)
cllr.mills@rbkc.gov.uk
Mingay, Bob (LAB - St. Charles)
cllr.mingay@rbkc.gov.uk
Mosley, Loius (CON - Brompton)
Cllr.mosley@rbkc.gov.uk
Moylan, Daniel (CON - Queen's Gate)
cllr.moylan@rbkc.gov.uk
Neal, Matthew (CON - Cremorne)
cllr.neal@rbkc.gov.uk
O'Neill, Dez (LAB - Colville)
cllr.o'neill@rbkc.gov.uk
Paget-Brown, Nicholas (CON - Hans Town)
cllr.paget-brown@rbkc.gov.uk
Palmer, Matthew (CON - St. Charles)
cllr.palmer@rbkc.gov.uk
Pascall, Will (CON - Stanley)
cllr.pascall@rbkc.gov.uk
Read, Jonathon (CON - Earl's Court)
cllr.read@rbkc.gov.uk
Rossi, Marie-Therese (CON - Redcliffe)
cllr.rossi@rbkc.gov.uk
Rutherford, Elizabeth (CON - Courtfield)
cllr.rutherford@rbkc.gov.uk
Taylor, Frances (CON - Redcliffe)
cllr.taylor@rbkc.gov.uk
Wade, Linda (LD - Earl's Court)
cllr.wade@rbkc.gov.uk
Warrick, Paul (CON - Stanley)
cllr.warrick@rbkc.gov.uk
Weale, Mary (CON - Hans Town)
cllr.weale@rbkc.gov.uk
Weatherhead, Doreen (CON - Pembridge)
cllr.weatherhead@rbkc.gov.uk
Will, Emma (CON - Royal Hospital)
cllr.will@rbkc.gov.uk
Williams, Charles
(CON - Redcliffe)
cllr.williams@rbkc.gov.uk

POLITICAL COMPOSITION

CON: 42, LAB: 9, LD: 3

CABINET

Leader: Mr Merrick Cockell
Deputy Leader: Mr Nicholas Paget-Brown
Adult Social Care, Public Health & Environmental Health: Mrs Fiona Buxton
Civil Society: Mr Rock Feilding-Mellen
Family & Children's Services & Education & Libraries: Mrs Elizabeth Campbell
Finance & IT: Mr Warwick Lightfoot
Housing & Property: Mr Timothy Coleridge
Planning Policy: Mr Tim Ahern
Transportation, Environment & Leisure: Mr Nicholas Paget-Brown

COMMITTEE CHAIRS

Appeals: Ms Barbara Campbell
Audit: Mr Paul Warrick
Corporate Services Scrutiny: Ms Emma Dent Coad
Family & Chidren's Services Scrutiny: Mr David Lindsay
Health, Environmental Health & Adult Social Care Scrutiny: Mrs Mary Weale
Housing & Property Scrutiny: Mr Quentin Marshall
Licensing: Ms Julie Mills
Major Planning Development: Mr Terence Buxton
Planning Applications: Mr Terence Buxton
Public Realm Scrutiny: Mrs Joanna Gardner

KENT C

Kent County Council, Sessions House, County Hall, Maidstone ME14 1XQ ☎ 0845 824 7247 🖷 01622 759905
🖳 www.kent.gov.uk

FACTS & FIGURES

Police Authority: Kent Police Authority
Health Authority: South East Coast Strategic Health Authority
Learning and Skills Council: South East
Parliamentary Constituencies: Thanet North, Thanet South
EU Constituencies: South East
Election Frequency: Elections are of whole council

PRINCIPAL OFFICERS

Deputy Chief Executive: Mr David Cockburn, Corporate Director of Business Strategy & Support, Sessions House, County Hall, Maidstone ME14 1XQ ☎ 01622 694386
✉ david.cockburn@kent.gov.uk

Assistant Chief Executive: Ms Amanda Beer, Corporate Director of Human Resources, Sessions House, County Hall, Maidstone ME14 1XQ ☎ 01622 694136 ✉ amanda.beer@kent.gov.uk

Senior Management: Mr Mike Austerberry, Corporate Director of Enterprise & Environment, Sessions House, County Hall, Maidstone ME14 1XQ ☎ 01622 694130 🖷 01622 675155
✉ mike.austerberry@kent.gov.uk

Senior Management: Ms Amanda Honey, Corporate Director of Customer & Communities, Sessions House, County Hall,

Maidstone ME14 1XQ ☎ 01622 694600 🖷 01732 221764 ✉ amanda.honey@kent.gov.uk

Senior Management: Mr Andrew Ireland, Corporate Director of Families & Social Care, Sessions House, County Hall, Maidstone ME14 1XQ ☎ 01622 696083 ✉ andrew.ireland@kent.gov.uk

Senior Management: Mr Patrick Leeson, Corporate Director of Education, Learning & Skills, Sessions House, County Hall, Maidstone ME14 1XQ ☎ 01622 694372 ✉ patrick.leeson@kent.gov.uk

Senior Management: Mr Andy Wood, Corporate Director of Finance & Procurement, Sessions House, County Hall, Maidstone ME14 1XQ ☎ 01622 694622 ✉ andy.wood@kent.gov.uk

Architect, Building / Property Services: Mr Paul Kennedy, Resources Manager, Sessions House, County Hall, Maidstone ME14 1XQ ☎ 01622 221388 ✉ paul.kennedy@kent.gov.uk

Building Control: Ms Rebecca Spore, Director of Property & Infrastructure Support, Sessions House, County Hall, Maidstone ME14 1XQ ☎ 01622 221151 ✉ rebecca.spore@kent.gov.uk

Children / Youth Services: Ms Karen Graham, Head of Children's Services - East Kent, St. Peters House, Danes Valley Road, St. Peters, Broadstairs CT10 3JJ ☎ 0845 824 7247 ✉ karen.graham@kent.gov.uk

Children / Youth Services: Ms Angela Slaven, Director for Service Improvement, 3rd Floor Invicta House, County Hall, Maidstone ME14 1XQ ☎ 01622 221696 ✉ angela.slaven@kent.gov.uk

Civil Registration: Mr Giles Adey, Head of Registration, Coroners & Property Officer, Invicta House, County Hall, Maidstone ME14 1XX ☎ 01622 221003 ✉ giles.adey@kent.gov.uk

PR / Communications: Mr Matt Burrows, Director of Communications & Engagement, Sessions House, County Hall, Maidstone ME14 1XQ ☎ 01622 694015 ✉ matt.burrows@kent.gov.uk

Community Safety: Mr Stuart Beaumont, Head of Community Safety & Emergency Planning, First Floor, Invicta House, Maidstone ME14 1XX ☎ 01622 694878 🖷 01622 696035 ✉ stuart.beaumont@kent.gov.uk

Community Safety: Ms Lorraine Goodsell, Associate Director of Commissioning, Child Health & Maternity NHS Kent & Medway, Sessions House, County Hall, Maidstone ME14 1XQ ☎ 01622 221196; 01233 618119 ✉ larraine.goodsell@nhs.net

Computer Management: Mr Peter Boyle, Director of ICT, Sessions House, County Hall, Maidstone ME14 1XQ ☎ 01622 696174 ✉ peter.boyle@kent.gov.uk

Contracts: Ms Anne Tidmarsh, Director of Commissioning & Provision, Brenchley House, Maidstone ME14 1RF ✉ anne.tidmarsh@kent.gov.uk

Corporate Services: Ms Theresa Bruton, Head of Regeneration Projects, 2nd Floor, Invicta House, Maidstone ME14 1XX ☎ 01622 221957 ✉ theresa.bruton@kent.gov.uk

Economic Development: Mr David Cockburn, Corporate Director of Business Strategy & Support, Sessions House, County Hall, Maidstone ME14 1XQ ☎ 01622 694386 ✉ david.cockburn@kent.gov.uk

Economic Development: Ms Barbara Cooper, Director of Economic & Spatial Development, Invicta House, County Hall, Maidstone ME14 1XX ☎ 01622 221856 ✉ barbara.cooper@kent.gov.uk

Education: Mr Keith Abbott, Director of Resources & Planning, Sessions House, County Hall, Maidstone ME14 1XQ ☎ 01622 696588 🖷 01622 696665 ✉ keith.abbott@kent.gov.uk

Education: Mr Scott Bagshaw, Head of Admissions & Transport, Sessions House, County Hall, Maidstone ME14 1XQ ☎ 01622 694185 🖷 01622 696665 ✉ scott.bagshaw@kent.gov.uk

Education: Ms Sue Rogers, Director of Education, Quality & Standards, Sessions House, County Hall, Maidstone ME14 1XQ ☎ 01622 694983 🖷 01622 696665 ✉ sue.rogers@kent.gov.uk

Emergency Planning: Mr David Cloake, Head of Emergency Planning, Invicta House, County Hall, Maidstone ME14 1XX ☎ 01622 694809 🖷 01622 694805 ✉ david.cloake@kent.gov.uk

Environmental Health: Ms Meradin Peachey, Director of Public Health, Sessions House, County Hall, Maidstone ME14 1XQ ☎ 01622 694293 ✉ meradin.peachey@kent.gov.uk

European Liaison: Mr Dafydd Pugh, Head of Brussels Office, Kent Brussels Office, International House, 45 Rue du Commerce, Brussels, B- 1000 ☎ 00322 504 0750 ✉ dafydd.pugh@kent.gov.uk

Events Manager: Mrs Deborah Malthouse, Events Manager, Sessions House, County Hall, Maidstone ME14 1XQ ☎ 01622 694119 🖷 01622 761538 ✉ deborah.malthouse@kent.gov.uk

Facilities: Mr Edward Trimmer, Kent Facilities Business Manager, Invicta House, Maidstone ME14 1XX ☎ 01622 694655 🖷 01622 696223 ✉ edward.trimmer@kent.gov.uk

Fleet Management: Mr Garry Mitchell, Kent Fleet Manager, The Forstal, Beddow Way, Aylesford ME20 7HB ☎ 01622 605893 ✉ garry.mitchell@kent.gov.uk

Grounds Maintenance: Mr Richard Kilvington, Business Manager, Aylesford Depot, Aylesford ME20 7HB ☎ 01622 605025 ✉ richard.kilvington@kent.gov.uk

Health and Safety: Ms Helen Bale, Corporate Health & Safety Manager, Sessions House, County Hall, Maidstone ME14 1XQ ☎ 01622 694273 🖷 01622 694538 ✉ helen.bale@kent.gov.uk

Highways: Mr John Burr, Director of Highways & Transportation, Invicta House, County Hall, Maidstone ME14 1XX ☎ 01622 694192 ✉ john.burr@kent.gov.uk

Legal: Mr Geoff Wild, Director of Governance & Law, Sessions House, County Hall, Maidstone ME14 1XQ ☎ 01622 694302 ✉ geoff.wild@kent.gov.uk

Leisure and Cultural Services: Mr Des Crilley, Director of Customer Services, 3rd Floor Invicta House, County Hall, Maidstone ME14 1XX ☎ 01622 696630 🖷 01622 694448 ✉ des.crilley@kent.gov.uk

Leisure and Cultural Services: Mr Chris Hespe, Head of Culture & Sport Group, Gibson Drive, Commercial Services Building, West Malling ME19 4QG ☎ 01622 605002 🖷 01732 874836 ✉ chris.hespe@kent.gov.uk

Lifelong Learning: Ms Amanda Honey, Corporate Director of Customer & Communities, Invicta House, County Hall, Maidstone ME14 1XX ☎ 01622 694600 🖷 01732 221764 ✉ amanda.honey@kent.gov.uk

Member Services: Mr Peter Sass, Head of Democratic Services & Local Leadership, Sessions House, County Hall, Maidstone ME14 1XQ ☎ 01622 694002 🖷 01622 694383 ✉ peter.sass@kent.gov.uk

Personnel / HR: Ms Amanda Beer, Corporate Director of Human Resources, Sessions House, County Hall, Maidstone ME14 1XQ ☎ 01622 694136 ✉ amanda.beer@kent.gov.uk

Planning: Mr Paul Crick, Director of Planning & Environment, Invicta House, County Hall, Maidstone ME14 1XX ☎ 01622 221527 ✉ paul.crick@kent.gov.uk

Planning: Ms Anne-Marie Hannam, Senior Transport Planner, 2 Beer Cart Lane, Canterbury CT1 2NN ✉ anne-marie.hannam@kent.gov.uk

Planning: Ms Lillian Harrison, Minerals & Waste LDF Manager, Invicta House, County Hall, Maidstone ME14 1XX ☎ 01622 221318 ✉ lillian.harrison@kent.gov.uk

Planning: Mr Tim Martin, Strategy Manager, Invicta House, County Hall, Maidstone ME14 1XX ☎ 01622 221618 ✉ tim.martin@kent.gov.uk

Planning: Mr Robert Smith, Senior Transport Planner, Invicta House, County Hall, Maidstone ME14 1XX ☎ 01622 221050 ✉ robert.smith3@kent.gov.uk

Planning: Mrs Sharon Thompson, Head of Planning Applications, Invicta House, County Hall, Maidstone ME14 1XX ☎ 01622 696131 ✉ sharon.thompson@kent.gov.uk

Procurement: Mr Nick Vickers, Head of Financial Management, Sessions House, County Hall, Maidstone ME14 1XQ ☎ 01622 694603 ✉ nick.vickers@kent.gov.uk

Public Libraries: Ms Cath Anley, Head of Libraries, Registration & Archives, Kent History & Library Centre, Springfield, Royal Engineers Road, Maidstone ME14 2LH ☎ 01622 696496 🖷 01622 696450 ✉ cath.anley@kent.gov.uk

Recycling & Waste Minimisation: Mr Peter Horn, Waste Operations Manager, Waste Management, Block H, The Forstal, Beddow Way, Aylesford ME20 7BT ☎ 01622 605996 ✉ peter.horn@kent.gov.uk

Social Services: Mr Andrew Ireland, Corporate Director of Families & Social Care, Sessions House, County Hall, Maidstone ME14 1XQ ☎ 01622 696083 ✉ andrew.ireland@kent.gov.uk

Social Services: Mr Mark Lobban, Director of Strategic Commissioning, 3rd Floor, Brenchley House, Week Street, Maidstone ME14 1RF ☎ 01622 694934 ✉ mark.lobban@kent.gov.uk

Social Services: Ms Penny Southern, Director of Learning Disability & Mental Health FSC, Brenchley House, Week Street, Maidstone ME14 1RF ☎ 01622 694888 ✉ penny.southern@kent.gov.uk

Social Services (Adult): Ms Anne Tidmarsh, Director of Commissioning & Provision, Brenchley House, Maidstone ME14 1RF ✉ anne.tidmarsh@kent.gov.uk

Social Services (Children): Ms Jean Imray, Director of Specialist Children's Services, Sessions House, County Hall, Maidstone ME14 1XQ ☎ 01622 221573 🖷 01622 694091 ✉ jean.imray@kent.gov.uk

Staff Training: Mrs Coral Ingleton, Training Manager, Sessions House, County Hall, Maidstone ME14 1XQ ☎ 01622 694532 ✉ coral.ingleton@kent.gov.uk

Tourism: Ms Fran Warrington, Head of Tourism, Invicta House, County Hall, Maidstone ME14 1XX ☎ 01622 221923 🖷 01622 691418 ✉ frances.warrington@kent.gov.uk

Transport: Mr David Hall, Future Highways Manager, 1st Floor, Invicta House, County Hall, Maidstone ME14 1XX ☎ 01622 221081 🖷 01622 691028 ✉ david.hall@kent.gov.uk

Transport: Mr Ian McPherson, Managing Director of Commercial Services, 30 Gibson Drive, Kings Hill, West Malling ME19 4QG ☎ 01622 605352 ✉ ian.mcpherson@kent.gov.uk

Waste Management: Ms Caroline Arnold, Head of Waste Management, Waste Management, Block H, The Forstal, Beddow Way, Maidstone ME20 7BT ☎ 01622 605990 🖷 01622 605999 ✉ caroline.arnold@kent.gov.uk

MEMBERS OF THE COUNCIL (84)

Leader of the Council: **Carter**, Paul (CON - Maidstone Rural North)
paul.carter@kent.gov.uk

Allen, Ann (CON - Wilmington)
ann.allen@kent.gov.uk

Angell, Mike (CON - Ashford Rural South)
mike.angell@kent.gov.uk

Bayford, Robert (CON - Broadstairs and Sir Moses Montefiore)
bob.bayford@kent.gov.uk

Bowles, Andrew (CON - Swale East)
andrew.bowles@kent.gov.uk

Brazier, David (CON - Sevenoaks North East)
david.brazier@kent.gov.uk

Brookbank, Robert (CON - Swanley)
robert.brookbank@kent.gov.uk
Bullock, Roy (CON - Tunbridge Wells North)
roy.bullock@kent.gov.uk
Burgess, Robert (CON - Margate West)
robert.burgess@kent.gov.uk
Capon, Chris (CON - Hythe)
christopher.capon@kent.gov.uk
Carey, Susan (CON - Elham Valley)
susan.carey@kent.gov.uk
Chard, Nick (CON - Sevenoaks East)
nick.chard@kent.gov.uk
Chell, Alan (CON - Maidstone South)
alan.chell@kent.gov.uk
Chittenden, Ian (LD - Maidstone North East)
ian.chittenden@kent.gov.uk
Christie, Leslie (LAB - Northfleet and Gravesend West)
leslie.christie@kent.gov.uk
Cole, Penny (CON - Dartford East)
penny.cole@kent.gov.uk
Collor, Nigel (CON - Dover Town)
nigel.collor@kent.gov.uk
Cooke, Gary (CON - Maidstone South East)
gary.cooke@kent.gov.uk
Cope, Bryan (CON - Dover West)
bryan.cope@kent.gov.uk
Cowan, Gordon (LAB - Dover Town)
gordon.cowan@kent.gov.uk
Craske, Harold (CON - Northfleet and Gravesend West)
harold.craske@kent.gov.uk
Crowther, Adrian (CON - Sheppey)
adrian.crowther@kent.gov.uk
Cubitt, John (CON - Gravesham East)
john.cubitt@kent.gov.uk
Dagger, Valerie (CON - Malling West)
valerie.dagger@kent.gov.uk
Daley, Dan (LD - Maidstone Central)
dan.daley@kent.gov.uk
Dance, Mark (CON - Whitstable)
mark.dance@kent.gov.uk
Davies, John (CON - Tunbridge Wells West)
john.davies@kent.gov.uk
Dean, Trudy (LD - Malling Central)
trudy.dean@kent.gov.uk
Ferrin, Keith (CON - Swale West)
keith.ferrin@kent.gov.uk
Gates, Tom (CON - Faversham)
tom.gates@kent.gov.uk
Gibbens, Graham (CON - Canterbury City North East)
graham.gibbens@kent.gov.uk
Gough, Roger (CON - Darent Valley)
roger.gough@kent.gov.uk
Green, Elizabeth (LAB - Ramsgate)
elizabeth.green@kent.gov.uk
Harrison, Mike (CON - Whitstable)
mike.harrison@kent.gov.uk
Hayton, Bill (CON - Broadstairs and Sir Moses Montefiore)
bill.hayton@kent.gov.uk
Hibberd, Charles (CON - Birchington and Villages)
charles.hibberd@kent.gov.uk
Hill, Michael (CON - Tenterden)
michael.hill@kent.gov.uk
Hirst, David (CON - Herne Bay)
david.hirst@kent.gov.uk
Hohler, Sarah (CON - Malling North)
sarah.hohler@kent.gov.uk
Hohler, Alice (CON - Tonbridge)
alice.hohler@kent.gov.uk
Homewood, Peter (CON - Malling Rural North East)
peter.homewood@kent.gov.uk
Hotson, Eric (CON - Maidstone Rural South)
eric.hotson@kent.gov.uk
Jarvis, Michael (CON - Margate and Cliftonville)
michael.jarvis@kent.gov.uk
King, Alex (CON - Tunbridge Wells Rural)
alex.king@kent.gov.uk
King, Richard (CON - Ashford Rural West)
richard.king@kent.gov.uk
Kirby, John (CON - Ramsgate)
john.kirby@kent.gov.uk
Kite, Jeremy (CON - Dartford Rural)
jeremy.kite@kent.gov.uk
Koowaree, George (LD - Ashford East)
george.koowaree@kent.gov.uk
Lake, Peter (CON - Sevenoaks South)
peter.lake@kent.gov.uk
Law, Jean (CON - Herne Bay)
jean.law@kent.gov.uk
Lees, Richard (R - Swanscombe and greenhithe)
richard.lees@kent.gov.uk
London, John (CON - Sevenoaks Central)
john.london@kent.gov.uk
Long, Richard (CON - Malling Rural East)
richard.long1@kent.gov.uk
Manion, Steve (CON - Dover North)
steve.manion@kent.gov.uk
Manning, Roger (CON - Cranbrook)
roger.manning@kent.gov.uk
Marsh, Alan (CON - Herne and Sturry)
alan.marsh@kent.gov.uk
Northey, Michael (CON - Canterbury South East)
michael.northey@kent.gov.uk
Ozog, Jan (CON - Dartford West)
jan.ozog@kent.gov.uk
Parry, Richard (CON - Sevenoaks West)
richard.parry@kent.gov.uk
Pascoe, Richard (CON - Folkestone North East)
richard.pascoe@kent.gov.uk
Prater, Tim (LD - Folkestone West)
tim.prater@kent.gov.uk
Pugh, Ken (CON - Sheerness)
ken.pugh@kent.gov.uk
Ridings, Leyland (CON - Sandwich)
leyland.ridings@kent.gov.uk
Robertson, Malcolm (LD - Maidstone Central)
malcolm.robertson@kent.gov.uk
Rook, Julie (CON - Deal)
julie.rook@kent.gov.uk
Sandhu, Avtar (CON - Dartford North East)
avtar.sandhu@kent.gov.uk
Scholes, James (CON - Tunbridge Wells South)
james.scholes@kent.gov.uk
Simmonds, John (CON - Canterbury West)
john.simmonds@kent.gov.uk
Smith, Kit (CON - Deal)
kit.smith@kent.gov.uk
Smith, Christopher (CON - Tonbridge)
chris.smith@kent.gov.uk
Snelling, Michael (CON - Gravesham Rural)
michael.snelling@kent.gov.uk

Stockell, Paulina (CON - Maidstone Rural West)
paulina.stockell@kent.gov.uk
Sweetland, Bryan (CON - Gravesham East)
bryan.sweetland@kent.gov.uk
Tansley, James (CON - Tunbridge Wells East)
james.tansley@kent.gov.uk
Tolputt, Roland (CON - Folkestone South)
roland.tolputt@kent.gov.uk
Tweed, Elizabeth (CON - Ashford Central)
elizabeth.tweed@kent.gov.uk
Vye, Martin (LD - Canterbury City South West)
martin.vye@kent.gov.uk
Waters, Carole (CON - Romney Marsh)
carole.waters@kent.gov.uk
Wedgbury, Jim (CON - Ashford South)
jim.wedgbury@kent.gov.uk
Wells, Chris (CON - Margate and Cliftonville)
chris.wells@kent.gov.uk
Whiting, Mike (CON - Swale Central)
mike.whiting@kent.gov.uk
Whittle, Jenny (CON - Maidstone Rural East)
jenny.whittle2@kent.gov.uk
Wickham, Andrew (CON - Ashford Rural East)
andrew.wickham@kent.gov.uk
Willicombe, Alan (CON - Swale Central)
alan.willicombe@kent.gov.uk

POLITICAL COMPOSITION
CON: 73, LD: 7, LAB: 3, R: 1

CABINET
Leader: Mr Paul Carter
Deputy Leader: Mr Richard King
Adult Social Care & Public Health: Mr Graham Gibbens
Business Strategy, Performance & Health Reform: Mr Roger Gough
Customer & Communities: Brig Michael Hill
Education, Learning & Skills: Mr Mike Whiting
Environment, Highways & Waste: Mr Bryan Sweetland
Finance & Business Support: Mr John Simmonds
Regeneration & Economic Development: Mr Mark Dance
Specialist Children's Services: Ms Jenny Whittle

COMMITTEE CHAIRS
Communities: Ms Alice Hohler
Economic Development: Mr Andrew Wickham
Education: Mr Gary Cooke
Environment, Highways & Waste: Mr David Brazier
Govenor Appointments Panel: Mr David Brazier
Governance & Audit: Mr Richard Long
Health Overview & Scrutiny: Mr Michael Snelling
Personnel: Mr Paul Carter
Planning Applications: Mr John Davies
Policy & Resources: Mr Eric Hotson
Regulation: Mr Mike Harrison
Scrutiny: Mr Roger Manning
Social Care & Public Health: Mr Christopher Smith
Superannuation Fund: Mr James Scholes

KETTERING D

Kettering Borough Council, Municipal Offices, Bowling Green Road, Kettering NN15 7QX ☎ 01536 410333 🖷 01536 410795
💻 www.kettering.gov.uk

FACTS & FIGURES
Police Authority: Northamptonshire Police Authority
Health Authority: East Midlands Strategic Health Authority
Learning and Skills Council: East Midlands
Parliamentary Constituencies: Kettering
EU Constituencies: East Midlands
Election Frequency: Elections are of whole council
Twinning: Burton Latimer: Altendiez (Germany); Desborough: Neuville de Poitou (France); Kettering: Ohio (USA); Lahnstein (Germany); Rothwell: Droue (France)

PRINCIPAL OFFICERS
Chief Executive: Mr David Cook, Chief Executive, Municipal Offices, Bowling Green Road, Kettering NN15 7QX ☎ 01536 534205 🖷 01536 534218 ✉ davidcook@kettering.gov.uk

Deputy Chief Executive: Ms Julia Beckett, Deputy Chief Executive, Municipal Offices, Bowling Green Road, Kettering NN15 7QX ☎ 01536 534342 🖷 01536 315116 ✉ juliabeckett@kettering.gov.uk

Deputy Chief Executive: Mr Martin Hammond, Deputy Chief Executive, Municipal Offices, Bowling Green Road, Kettering NN15 7QX ☎ 01536 534210 🖷 01536 315116 ✉ martinhammond@kettering.gov.uk

Deputy Chief Executive: Mr Graham Soulsby, Deputy Chief Executive, Municipal Offices, Bowling Green Road, Kettering NN15 7QX ☎ 01536 532413 🖷 01536 315116 ✉ grahamsoulsby@kettering.gov.uk

Best Value: Mr Guy Holloway, Head - Corporate Development, Municipal Offices, Bowling Green Road, Kettering NN15 7QX ☎ 01536 534243 ✉ guyholloway@kettering.gov.uk

Building Control: Ms Cath Bicknell, Head - Development Services, Municipal Offices, Bowling Green Road, Kettering NN15 7QX ☎ 01536 534216 ✉ cathbicknell@kettering.gov.uk

PR / Communications: Mr Guy Holloway, Head - Corporate Development, Municipal Offices, Bowling Green Road, Kettering NN15 7QX ☎ 01536 534243 ✉ guyholloway@kettering.gov.uk

Community Planning: Ms Cath Bicknell, Head - Development Services, Municipal Offices, Bowling Green Road, Kettering NN15 7QX ☎ 01536 534216 ✉ cathbicknell@kettering.gov.uk

Community Safety: Ms Valerie Hitchman, Head - Community Services, Municipal Offices, Bowling Green Road, Kettering NN15 7QX ☎ 01536 534392 ✉ valeriehitchman@kettering.gov.uk

Computer Management: Mr Guy Holloway, Head - Corporate Development, Municipal Offices, Bowling Green Road, Kettering NN15 7QX ☎ 01536 534243 ✉ guyholloway@kettering.gov.uk

Corporate Services: Mr Guy Holloway, Head - Corporate Development, Municipal Offices, Bowling Green Road, Kettering NN15 7QX ☎ 01536 534243 ✉ guyholloway@kettering.gov.uk

Customer Service: Mrs Julie Trahern, Head - Income & Debt

Management, Municipal Offices, Bowling Green Road, Kettering NN15 7QX ☎ 01536 532428 ✉ julietrahern@kettering.gov.uk

Direct Labour: Ms Sarah Rodmell, HR Manager, Municipal Offices, Bowling Green Road, Kettering NN15 7QX ☎ 01536 534329 ✉ sarahrodmell@kettering.gov.uk

Economic Development: Ms Valerie Hitchman, Head - Community Services, Municipal Offices, Bowling Green Road, Kettering NN15 7QX ☎ 01536 534392 ✉ valeriehitchman@kettering.gov.uk

E-Government: Mr Guy Holloway, Head - Corporate Development, Municipal Offices, Bowling Green Road, Kettering NN15 7QX ☎ 01536 534342 ✉ guyholloway@kettering.gov.uk

Electoral Registration: Ms Sue Lyons, Head - Democratic & Legal Services, Municipal Offices, Bowling Green Road, Kettering NN15 7QX ☎ 01536 534209; 01536 543209 🖷 01933 231542 ✉ suelyons@kettering.gov.uk

Emergency Planning: Mr Brendan Coleman, Head - Environmental Care Services, 4 Robinson Way, Telford Way Industrial Estate, Kettering NN16 8PP ☎ 01536 534460 ✉ brendancoleman@kettering.gov.uk

Environmental Health: Mrs Shirley Plenderleith, Head - Environmental Health, Municipal Offices, Bowling Green Road, Kettering NN15 7QX ☎ 01536 535696 ✉ shirleyplenderleith@kettering.gov.uk

Estates, Property & Valuation: Ms Sue Lyons, Head - Democratic & Legal Services, Municipal Offices, Bowling Green Road, Kettering NN15 7QX ☎ 01536 534209 🖷 01933 231542 ✉ suelyons@kettering.gov.uk;

Facilities: Mr Guy Holloway, Head - Corporate Development, Municipal Offices, Bowling Green Road, Kettering NN15 7QX ☎ 01536 534342 ✉ guyholloway@kettering.gov.uk

Finance and Treasurer: Mr Paul Sutton, Head - Finance, Municipal Offices, Bowling Green Road, Kettering NN15 7QX ☎ 01536 534330 ✉ paulsutton@kettering.gov.uk

Fleet Management: Mr Brendan Coleman, Head - Environmental Care Services, 4 Robinson Way, Telford Way Industrial Estate, Kettering NN16 8PP ☎ 01536 534460 ✉ brendancoleman@kettering.gov.uk

Grounds Maintenance: Mr Brendan Coleman, Head - Environmental Care Services, 4 Robinson Way, Telford Way Industrial Estate, Kettering NN16 8PP ☎ 01536 534460 ✉ brendancoleman@kettering.gov.uk

Health and Safety: Mr Brendan Coleman, Head - Environmental Care Services, 4 Robinson Way, Telford Way Industrial Estate, Kettering NN16 8PP ☎ 01536 534460 ✉ brendancoleman@kettering.gov.uk

Home Energy Conservation: Mrs Shirley Plenderleith, Head - Environmental Health, Municipal Offices, Bowling Green Road, Kettering NN15 7QX ☎ 01536 535696 ✉ shirleyplenderleith@kettering.gov.uk

Housing: Mr John Conway, Head - Housing, Municipal Offices, Bowling Green Road, Kettering NN15 7QX ☎ 01536 534288 ✉ johnconway@kettering.gov.uk

Housing Maintenance: Mr John Conway, Head - Housing, Municipal Offices, Bowling Green Road, Kettering NN15 7QX ☎ 01536 534288 ✉ johnconway@kettering.gov.uk

Legal: Ms Sue Lyons, Head - Democratic & Legal Services, Municipal Offices, Bowling Green Road, Kettering NN15 7QX ☎ 01536 534209 🖷 01933 231542 ✉ suelyons@kettering.gov.uk

Leisure and Cultural Services: Ms Valerie Hitchman, Head - Community Services, Municipal Offices, Bowling Green Road, Kettering NN15 7QX ☎ 01536 534392 ✉ valeriehitchman@kettering.gov.uk

Licensing: Mrs Shirley Plenderleith, Head - Environmental Health, Municipal Offices, Bowling Green Road, Kettering NN15 7QX ☎ 01536 535696 ✉ shirleyplenderleith@kettering.gov.uk

Lighting: Mr Brendan Coleman, Head - Environmental Care Services, 4 Robinson Way, Telford Way Industrial Estate, Kettering NN16 8PP ☎ 01536 534460 ✉ brendancoleman@kettering.gov.uk

Lottery Funding, Charity and Voluntary: Ms Valerie Hitchman, Head - Community Services, Municipal Offices, Bowling Green Road, Kettering NN15 7QX ☎ 01536 534392 ✉ valeriehitchman@kettering.gov.uk

Member Services: Ms Sue Lyons, Head - Democratic & Legal Services, Municipal Offices, Bowling Green Road, Kettering NN15 7QX ☎ 01536 534209 🖷 01933 231542 ✉ suelyons@kettering.gov.uk

Parking: Mrs Shirley Plenderleith, Head - Environmental Health, Municipal Offices, Bowling Green Road, Kettering NN15 7QX ☎ 01536 535696 ✉ shirleyplenderleith@kettering.gov.uk

Personnel / HR: Ms Sam Maher, Interim Head - HR, Municipal Offices, Bowling Green Road, Kettering NN15 7QX ☎ 01536 534214 ✉ sammaher@kettering.gov.uk

Planning: Ms Cath Bicknell, Head - Development Services, Municipal Offices, Bowling Green Road, Kettering NN15 7QX ☎ 01536 534216 ✉ cathbicknell@kettering.gov.uk

Procurement: Mr Guy Holloway, Head - Corporate Development, Municipal Offices, Bowling Green Road, Kettering NN15 7QX ☎ 01536 534243 ✉ guyholloway@kettering.gov.uk

Recycling & Waste Minimisation: Mr Brendan Coleman, Head - Environmental Care Services, 4 Robinson Way, Telford Way Industrial Estate, Kettering NN16 8PP ☎ 01536 534460 ✉ brendancoleman@kettering.gov.uk

Staff Training: Ms Sam Maher, Interim Head - HR, Municipal Offices, Bowling Green Road, Kettering NN15 7QX ☎ 01536 534214 ✉ sammaher@kettering.gov.uk

Street Scene: Mr Brendan Coleman, Head - Environmental Care Services, 4 Robinson Way, Telford Way Industrial Estate, Kettering NN16 8PP ☎ 01536 534460 🖱 brendancoleman@kettering.gov.uk

Sustainable Communities: Ms Cath Bicknell, Head - Development Services, Municipal Offices, Bowling Green Road, Kettering NN15 7QX ☎ 01536 534216 🖱 cathbicknell@kettering.gov.uk

Sustainable Development: Ms Cath Bicknell, Head - Development Services, Municipal Offices, Bowling Green Road, Kettering NN15 7QX ☎ 01536 534216 🖱 cathbicknell@kettering.gov.uk

Tourism: Ms Valerie Hitchman, Head - Community Services, Municipal Offices, Bowling Green Road, Kettering NN15 7QX ☎ 01536 534392 🖱 valeriehitchman@kettering.gov.uk

Town Centre: Ms Valerie Hitchman, Head of Community Services, Municipal Offices, Bowling Green Road, Kettering NN15 7QX ☎ 01536 534392 🖱 valeriehitchman@kettering.gov.uk

Waste Collection and Disposal: Mr Brendan Coleman, Head - Environmental Care Services, 4 Robinson Way, Telford Way Industrial Estate, Kettering NN16 8PP ☎ 01536 534460 🖱 brendancoleman@kettering.gov.uk

Waste Management: Mr Brendan Coleman, Head - Environmental Care Services, 4 Robinson Way, Telford Way Industrial Estate, Kettering NN16 8PP ☎ 01536 534460 🖱 brendancoleman@kettering.gov.uk

MEMBERS OF THE COUNCIL (36)

***Mayor:* Hakewill**, James (CON - Slade)
jimhakewill@kettering.gov.uk
***Deputy Mayor:* Watts**, Keli (LAB - William Knibb)
keliwatts@kettering.gov.uk
***Leader of the Council:* Roberts**, Russell (CON - Barton)
russellroberts@kettering.gov.uk
***Group Leader:* West**, Jonathan (LAB - All Saints)
jonathanwest@kettering.gov.uk
Adams, Linda (LAB - Avondale Grange)
lindaadams@kettering.gov.uk
Bain, Duncan (CON - Pipers Hill)
duncanbain@kettering.gov.uk
Bayes, Maurice (CON - Brambleside)
mauricebayes@kettering.gov.uk
Bellamy, Steve (CON - Pipers Hill)
stevebellamy@kettering.gov.uk
Bishop, David (LAB - William Knibb)
davidbishop@kettering.gov.uk
Brown, Michael (CON - All Saints)
michaelbrown@kettering.gov.uk
Bullock, Jonathan (CON - Queen Eleanor and Buccleuch)
jonathanbullock@kettering.gov.uk
Bunday, Lloyd (CON - Ise Lodge)
lloydbunday@kettering.gov.uk
Corazzo, Paul (LAB - Avondale Grange)
paulcorazzo@kettering.gov.uk
Dearing, Mark (CON - Desborough Loatland)
markdearing@kettering.gov.uk
Derbyshire, June (CON - Desborough Loatland)
junederbyshire@kettering.gov.uk
Don, Maggie (LAB - St Michaels and Wicksteed)
maggiedon2@kettering.gov.uk
Edwards, Scott (CON - St Michaels and Wicksteed)
scottedwards@kettering.gov.uk
Freer, Terry (CON - St Peter's)
terryfreer@kettering.gov.uk
George, Michelle (LAB - All Saints)
michellegeorge@kettering.gov.uk
Groome, Ruth (IND - Burton Latimer)
ruthgroome@kettering.gov.uk
Henson, Jenny (CON - St Michaels and Wicksteed)
jennyhenson@kettering.gov.uk
Hollobone, Philip (CON - Ise Lodge)
philip.hollobone.mp@parliament.uk
Jelley, Ian (CON - Rothwell)
ianjelley@kettering.gov.uk
Lamb, Christopher (CON - Barton)
christopherlamb@kettering.gov.uk
Lynch, Shirley (CON - Ise Lodge)
shirleylynch@kettering.gov.uk
Malin, Mary (CON - St Peter's)
marymalin@kettering.gov.uk
Manns, Ellie (LAB - Northfield)
elliemanns@kettering.gov.uk
Marks, Paul (CON - Brambleside)
paulmarks@kettering.gov.uk
Mills, Alan (LAB - Rothwell)
alanmills@kettering.gov.uk
Moreton, Cliff (CON - Slade)
cliffmoreton@kettering.gov.uk
Smith, Jan (CON - Burton Latimer)
jansmith@kettering.gov.uk
Soans, Dave (CON - Desborough St Giles)
davidsoans@kettering.gov.uk
Talbot, Margaret (CON - Rothwell)
margarettalbot@kettering.gov.uk
Tebbutt, Mike (CON - Desborough St Giles)
miketebbutt@kettering.gov.uk
Wiley, Alison (CON - Welland)
alisonwiley@kettering.gov.uk
Zanger, Derek (CON - Burton Latimer)
derekzanger@kettering.gov.uk

POLITICAL COMPOSITION

CON: 26, LAB: 9, IND: 1

CABINET

Leader: Mr Russell Roberts
Deputy Leader: Mrs Mary Malin
Community & Culture: Mr Steve Bellamy
Community & Rural: Mr Jonathan Bullock
Environment: Mr Ian Jelley
Finance: Ms Alison Wiley
Housing: Mr Derek Zanger
Planning, Enterprise & Growth: Mr Terry Freer
Regeneration: Mr Mark Dearing

COMMITTEE CHAIRS

Licensing: Mr Christopher Lamb
Monitoring & Audit: Mr David Bishop
Planning Policy: Mr Mike Tebbutt
Planning: Mrs Shirley Lynch

Research & Development: Mr Paul Marks

KING'S LYNN & WEST NORFOLK D

Borough Council of King's Lynn & West Norfolk, Chapel Street, King's Lynn PE30 1EX ☎ 01553 616200 🖷 01553 691663 contact@west-norfolk.gov.uk www.west-norfolk.gov.uk

FACTS & FIGURES

Police Authority: Norfolk Police Authority
Health Authority: East of England Strategic Health Authority
Learning and Skills Council: Eastern
EU Constituencies: Eastern
Election Frequency: Elections are of whole council
Twinning: Downham Market: Civray (France); King's Lynn: Emmerich (Germany); King's Lynn & West Norfolk: 'Sister City' Bayside (Australia); Jicin (Czech Rep); Mlada Boleslav (Czech Rep)

PRINCIPAL OFFICERS

Chief Executive: Mr Ray Harding, Chief Executive, King's Court, Chapel Street, King's Lynn PE30 1EX ☎ 01553 616245 🖷 01553 616736 ray.harding@west-norfolk.gov.uk

Deputy Chief Executive: Mr David Thomason, Executive Director - Finance & Resources, King's Court, Chapel Street, King's Lynn PE30 1EX ☎ 01553 616246 🖷 01553 616565 david.thomason@west-norfolk.gov.uk

Access Officer / Social Services (Disability): Mrs Allison Bingham, Building Technician, King's Court, Chapel Street, King's Lynn PE30 1EX ☎ 01553 616743 allison.bingham@west-norfolk.gov.uk

Architect, Building / Property Services: Mr Matthew Henry, Property Services Manager, King's Court, Chapel Street, King's Lynn PE30 1EX ☎ 01553 616272 🖷 01553 616682 matthew.henry@west-norfolk.gov.uk

Best Value: Mr Ian Burbidge, Policy & Performance Manager, King's Court, Chapel Street, King's Lynn PE30 1EX ☎ 01553 616722 🖷 01553 616680 ian.burbidge@west-norfolk.gov.uk

Building Control: Mr Geoff Hall, Executive Director - Regeneration & Development Services, King's Court, Chapel Street, King's Lynn PE30 1EX ☎ 01553 616618 🖷 01553 616652 geoff.hall@west-norfolk.gov.uk

PR / Communications: Mrs Sharon Burbidge, Communications Manager, King's Court, Chapel Street, King's Lynn PE30 1EX ☎ 01553 616711 🖷 01553 616680 sharon.burbidge@west-norfolk.gov.uk

Community Planning: Mrs Debbie Gates, Executive Director - Central Services, King's Court, Chapel Street, King's Lynn PE30 1EX ☎ 01553 616605 🖷 01553 616728 debbie.gates@west-norfolk.gov.uk

Community Safety: Mr Andy Piper, Executive Director - Environmental Health & Housing, King's Court, Chapel Street, King's Lynn PE30 1EX ☎ 01553 616365 🖷 01553 775142 andy.piper@west-norfolk.gov.uk

Computer Management: Mr David Thomason, Executive Director - Finance & Resources, King's Court, Chapel Street, King's Lynn PE30 1EX ☎ 01553 616246 🖷 01553 616565 david.thomason@west-norfolk.gov.uk

Contracts: Mrs Nicola Leader, Legal Services Manager, King's Court, Chapel Street, King's Lynn PE30 1EX ☎ 01553 616270 🖷 01553 616728 nicola.leader@west-norfolk.gov.uk

Corporate Services: Mr Ray Harding, Chief Executive, King's Court, Chapel Street, King's Lynn PE30 1EX ☎ 01553 616245 🖷 01553 616736 ray.harding@west-norfolk.gov.uk

Customer Service: Mrs Debbie Gates, Executive Director - Central Services, King's Court, Chapel Street, King's Lynn PE30 1EX ☎ 01553 616605 🖷 01553 616728 debbie.gates@west-norfolk.gov.uk

Economic Development: Mr Geoff Hall, Executive Director - Regeneration & Development Services, King's Court, Chapel Street, King's Lynn PE30 1EX ☎ 01553 616618 🖷 01553 616652 geoff.hall@west-norfolk.gov.uk

E-Government: Mr David Thomason, Executive Director - Finance & Resources, King's Court, Chapel Street, King's Lynn PE30 1EX ☎ 01553 616246 🖷 01553 616565 david.thomason@west-norfolk.gov.uk

Electoral Registration: Mrs Sam Winter, Democratic Services Manager, King's Court, Chapel Street, King's Lynn PE30 1EX ☎ 01553 616327 🖷 01553 616758 sam.winter@west-norfolk.gov.uk

Emergency Planning: Mr Andy Piper, Executive Director - Environmental Health & Housing, King's Court, Chapel Street, King's Lynn PE30 1EX ☎ 01553 616365 🖷 01553 775142 andy.piper@west-norfolk.gov.uk

Energy Management: Mr Andy Piper, Executive Director - Environmental Health & Housing, King's Court, Chapel Street, King's Lynn PE30 1EX ☎ 01553 616365 🖷 01553 775142 andy.piper@west-norfolk.gov.uk

Environmental Health: Mr Andy Piper, Executive Director - Environmental Health & Housing, King's Court, Chapel Street, King's Lynn PE30 1EX ☎ 01553 616365 🖷 01553 775142 andy.piper@west-norfolk.gov.uk

Estates, Property & Valuation: Mr Matthew Henry, Property Services Manager, King's Court, Chapel Street, King's Lynn PE30 1EX ☎ 01553 616272 🖷 01553 616682 matthew.henry@west-norfolk.gov.uk

European Liaison: Mr Ostap Paparega, Regeneration & Economic Development Manager, King's Court, Chapel Street, King's Lynn PE30 1EX ☎ 01553 616890 🖷 01553 775726 ostap.paparega@west-norfolk.gov.uk

Events Manager: Mr Les Miller, General Manager - Corn Exchange, Chapel Street, King's Lynn PE30 1EX ☎ 01553 779106 les.miller@west-norfolk.gov.uk

Finance and Treasurer: Mr David Thomason, Executive Director - Finance & Resources, King's Court, Chapel Street, King's Lynn PE30 1EX ☎ 01553 616246 🖷 01553 616565 ✉ david.thomason@west-norfolk.gov.uk

Grounds Maintenance: Mr Nathan Johnson, Public & Open Space Manager, King's Court, Chapel Street, King's Lynn PE30 1EX ☎ 01553 780780 🖷 01553 771657 ✉ nathan.johnson@west-norfolk.gov.uk

Health and Safety: Mr Dave Clack, Safety & Welfare Adviser, King's Court, Chapel Street, King's Lynn PE30 1EX ☎ 01553 616368 🖷 01553 616680 ✉ dave.clack@west-norfolk.gov.uk

Health and Safety: Mr Andy Piper, Executive Director - Environmental Health & Housing, King's Court, Chapel Street, King's Lynn PE30 1EX ☎ 01553 616365 🖷 01553 775142 ✉ andy.piper@west-norfolk.gov.uk

Home Energy Conservation: Mr Tony Howell, Housing Officer, King's Court, Chapel Street, King's Lynn PE30 1EX ☎ 01553 616469 🖷 01553 775142 ✉ tony.howell@west-norfolk.gov.uk

Housing: Mr Andy Piper, Executive Director - Environmental Health & Housing, King's Court, Chapel Street, King's Lynn PE30 1EX ☎ 01553 616365 🖷 01553 775142 ✉ andy.piper@west-norfolk.gov.uk

Legal: Mrs Nicola Leader, Legal Services Manager, King's Court, Chapel Street, King's Lynn PE30 1EX ☎ 01553 616270 🖷 01553 616728 ✉ nicola.leader@west-norfolk.gov.uk

Leisure and Cultural Services: Mr Chris Bamfield, Executive Director - Leisure & Public Space, King's Court, Chapel Street, King's Lynn PE30 1EX ☎ 01553 616648 🖷 01553 616640 ✉ chris.bamfield@west-norfolk.gov.uk

Licensing: Mr Andy Piper, Executive Director - Environmental Health & Housing, King's Court, Chapel Street, King's Lynn PE30 1EX ☎ 01553 616365 🖷 01553 775142 ✉ andy.piper@west-norfolk.gov.uk

Lottery Funding, Charity and Voluntary: Mr Ian Burbidge, Policy & Performance Manager, King's Court, Chapel Street, King's Lynn PE30 1EX ☎ 01553 616722 🖷 01553 616680 ✉ ian.burbidge@west-norfolk.gov.uk

Member Services: Mrs Sam Winter, Democratic Services Manager, King's Court, Chapel Street, King's Lynn PE30 1EX ☎ 01553 616327 🖷 01553 616758 ✉ sam.winter@west-norfolk.gov.uk

Parking: Mr Chris Bamfield, Executive Director - Leisure & Public Space, King's Court, Chapel Street, King's Lynn PE30 1EX ☎ 01553 616648 🖷 01553 616640 ✉ chris.bamfield@west-norfolk.gov.uk

Partnerships: Mr Ian Burbidge, Policy & Performance Manager, King's Court, Chapel Street, King's Lynn PE30 1EX ☎ 01553 616722 🖷 01553 616680 ✉ ian.burbidge@west-norfolk.gov.uk

Personnel / HR: Mrs Debbie Gates, Executive Director - Central Services, King's Court, Chapel Street, King's Lynn PE30 1EX ☎ 01553 616605 🖷 01553 616728 ✉ debbie.gates@west-norfolk.gov.uk

Planning: Mr Geoff Hall, Executive Director - Regeneration & Development Services, King's Court, Chapel Street, King's Lynn PE30 1EX ☎ 01553 616618 🖷 01553 616652 ✉ geoff.hall@west-norfolk.gov.uk

Procurement: Mr Toby Cowper, Principal Accountant, King's Court, Chapel Street, King's Lynn PE30 1EX ☎ 01553 616248 🖷 01553 616565 ✉ toby.cowper@west-norfolk.gov.uk

Recycling & Waste Minimisation: Mr Chris Bamfield, Executive Director - Leisure & Public Space, King's Court, Chapel Street, King's Lynn PE30 1EX ☎ 01553 616648 🖷 01553 616640 ✉ chris.bamfield@west-norfolk.gov.uk

Recycling & Waste Minimisation: Mr Barry Branford, Environmental Services Manager, Council Offices, Holt Road, Cromer NR27 9EN ☎ 01263 516308 🖷 01263 514627 ✉ barry.branford@north-norfolk.gov.uk

Regeneration: Mr Geoff Hall, Executive Director - Regeneration & Development Services, King's Court, Chapel Street, King's Lynn PE30 1EX ☎ 01553 616618 🖷 01553 616652 ✉ geoff.hall@west-norfolk.gov.uk

Staff Training: Miss Becky Box, Personnel Manager, King's Court, Chapel Street, King's Lynn PE30 1EX ☎ 01553 616502 🖷 01553 616680 ✉ becky.box@west-norfolk.gov.uk

Street Scene: Mr Chris Bamfield, Executive Director - Leisure & Public Space, King's Court, Chapel Street, King's Lynn PE30 1EX ☎ 01553 616648 🖷 01553 616640 ✉ chris.bamfield@west-norfolk.gov.uk

Sustainable Communities: Mr Geoff Hall, Executive Director - Regeneration & Development Services, King's Court, Chapel Street, King's Lynn PE30 1EX ☎ 01553 616618 🖷 01553 616652 ✉ geoff.hall@west-norfolk.gov.uk

Sustainable Development: Mr Geoff Hall, Executive Director - Regeneration & Development Services, King's Court, Chapel Street, King's Lynn PE30 1EX ☎ 01553 616618 🖷 01553 616652 ✉ geoff.hall@west-norfolk.gov.uk

Tourism: Mr Tim Humphreys, Tourism Manager, King's Court, Chapel Street, King's Lynn PE30 1EX ☎ 01553 616643 🖷 01553 775726 ✉ tim.humphreys@west-norfolk.gov.uk

Town Centre: Mr Alistair Cox, Town Centre Manager, King's Court, Chapel Street, King's Lynn PE30 1EX ☎ 01553 616739 🖷 01553 775726 ✉ alistair.cox@west-norfolk.gov.uk

Transport: Mr Geoff Hall, Executive Director - Regeneration & Development Services, King's Court, Chapel Street, King's Lynn PE30 1EX ☎ 01553 616618 🖷 01553 616652 ✉ geoff.hall@west-norfolk.gov.uk

Waste Collection and Disposal: Mr Chris Bamfield, Executive

Director - Leisure & Public Space, King's Court, Chapel Street, King's Lynn PE30 1EX ☎ 01553 616648 🖷 01553 616640
✉ chris.bamfield@west-norfolk.gov.uk

Waste Management: Mr Chris Bamfield, Executive Director - Leisure & Public Space, King's Court, Chapel Street, King's Lynn PE30 1EX ☎ 01553 616648 🖷 01553 616640
✉ chris.bamfield@west-norfolk.gov.uk

MEMBERS OF THE COUNCIL (62)

***Deputy Mayor:* Sandell**, Garry (CON - Burnham)
cllr.garry.sandell@west-norfolk.gov.uk
***Leader of the Council:* Daubney**, Nick (CON - South Wootton)
cllr.nick.daubney@west-norfolk.gov.uk
***Deputy Leader of the Council:* Long**, Brian (CON - Marshland)
cllr.brian.long@west-norfolk.gov.uk
Allen, Lori (GRN - Airfield)
cllr.lori.allen@west-norfolk.gov.uk
Ayres, Barry (CON - St Lawrence)
cllr.barry.ayres@west-norfolk.gov.uk
Back, Mark (LAB - St Margarets with St Nicholas)
cllr.mark.back@west-norfolk.gov.uk
Bambridge, Lesley (CON - St Margarets with St Nicholas)
cllr.lesley.bambridge@west-norfolk.gov.uk
Beal, Paul (CON - Hunstanton)
cllr.paul.beal@west-norfolk.gov.uk
Beales, Alistair (CON - Gayton)
cllr.alistair.beales@west-norfolk.gov.uk
Bird, Richard (LAB - Hunstanton)
cllr.richard.bird@west-norfolk.gov.uk
Bubb, Anthony (LD - Dersingham)
cllr.tony.bubb@west-norfolk.gov.uk
Chenery, Michael (CON - East Rudham)
cllr.baron.horsbrugh@west-norfolk.gov.uk
Christopher, Zipha (CON - Snettisham)
cllr.zipha.christopher@west-norfolk.gov.uk
Collingham, Judy (CON - Dersingham)
cllr.judith.collingham@west-norfolk.gov.uk
Collis, David (LAB - Lynn North)
cllr.david.collis@west-norfolk.gov.uk
Collop, Sandra (LAB - Gaywood Chase)
cllr.sandra.collop@west-norfolk.gov.uk
Collop, John (LAB - Gaywood Chase)
cllr.john.collop@west-norfolk.gov.uk
Cousins, Peter (CON - Spellowfields)
cllr.peter.cousins@west-norfolk.gov.uk
Crofts, Chris (CON - Emneth with Outwell)
cllr.chris.crofts@west-norfolk.gov.uk
De Winton, Tom (CON - Brancaster)
cllr.tom.dewinton@west-norfolk.gov.uk
Foster, Paul (CON - West Winch)
cllr.paul.foster@west-norfolk.gov.uk
Gourlay, Ian (LAB - Fairstead)
cllr.ian.gourlay@west-norfolk.gov.uk
Groom, Roy (CON - Walton)
cllr.roy.groom@west-norfolk.gov.uk
Harwood, David (CON - Spellowfields)
cllr.david.harwood@west-norfolk.gov.uk
Hopkins, Marcus (IND - Wiggenhall)
cllr.marcus.hopkins@west-norfolk.gov.uk
Howard, Greville (CON - North Wootton)
cllr.greville.howard@west-norfolk.gov.uk
Howland, Michael (CON - Airfield)
cllr.michael.howland@west-norfolk.gov.uk
Howman, Gary (LAB - Gaywood Old)
cllr.gary.howman@west-norfolk.gov.uk
Humphrey, Harry (CON - Emneth with Outwell)
cllr.harry.humphrey@west-norfolk.gov.uk
Johnson, David (CON - Snettisham)
cllr.david.johnson@west-norfolk.gov.uk
Joyce, Charles (LAB - Lynn, South & West)
cllr.charles.joyce@west-norfolk.gov.uk
Langwade, Michael (CON - Gaywood North Bank)
cllr.michael.langwade@west-norfolk.gov.uk
Lawrence, Adrian (CON - Denton)
cllr.adrian.lawrence@west-norfolk.gov.uk
Leamon, June (IND - West Winch)
cllr.june.leamon@west-norfolk.gov.uk
Loveless, John (LD - Springwood)
cllr.john.loveless@west-norfolk.gov.uk
Lovett, Anthony (CON - East Downham)
cllr.anthony.lovett@west-norfolk.gov.uk
Mack, Ian (LD - Watlington)
cllr.ian.mack@west-norfolk.gov.uk
Manley, Trevor (CON - Wimbotsham with Fincham)
cllr.trevor.manley@west-norfolk.gov.uk
Manning, Colin (CON - Heacham)
cllr.colin.manning@west-norfolk.gov.uk
McGuinness, Gary (LAB - Lynn, South & West)
cllr.gary.mcguinness@west-norfolk.gov.uk
Mellish, Kathy (CON - Downham Old Town)
cllr.kathy.mellish@west-norfolk.gov.uk
Moriarty, James (LAB - Priory)
cllr.james.moriarty@west-norfolk.gov.uk
Morrison, Andrew (CON - Docking)
cllr.andrew.morrison@west-norfolk.gov.uk
Nockolds, Elizabeth (CON - South Wootton)
cllr.elizabeth.nockolds@west-norfolk.gov.uk
Peake, Mick (CON - Denton)
cllr.mick.peake@west-norfolk.gov.uk
Pitcher, Michael (CON - Grimston)
cllr.michael.pitcher@west-norfolk.gov.uk
Pope, David (CON - Upwell and Delph)
cllr.david.pope@west-norfolk.gov.uk
Sampson, Colin (CON - Wissey)
cllr.colin.sampson@west-norfolk.gov.uk
Scott, Laurence (LAB - Gaywood North Bank)
cllr.laurence.scott@west-norfolk.gov.uk
Shorting, Mark (CON - Gaywood North Bank)
cllr.mark.shorting@west-norfolk.gov.uk
Smeaton, Stephanie (CON - Heacham)
cllr.stephanie.smeaton@west-norfolk.gov.uk
Spikings, Vivienne (CON - Upwell and Delph)
cllr.vivienne.spikings@west-norfolk.gov.uk
Storey, Martin (CON - Denton)
cllr.martin.storey@west-norfolk.gov.uk
Tilbury, Mike (IND - Valley Hill)
cllr.mike.tilbury@west-norfolk.gov.uk
Tyler, Donald (CON - South Downham)
cllr.donald.tyler@west-norfolk.gov.uk
Tyler, Andy (LAB - Lynn North)
cllr.andy.tyler@west-norfolk.gov.uk
Wareham, Geoff (CON - North Downham)
cllr.geoff.wareham@west-norfolk.gov.uk
Watson, Elizabeth (CON - Hunstanton)
cllr.elizabeth.watson@west-norfolk.gov.uk
Whitby, David (CON - Clenchwarton)
cllr.david.whitby@west-norfolk.gov.uk
White, Anthony (CON - Hilgay with Denver)

cllr.tony.white@west-norfolk.gov.uk
Wilkinson, Margaret (LAB - Fairstead)
cllr.margaret.wilkinson@west-norfolk.gov.uk
Wright, Anthony (CON - Walpole)
cllr.anthony.wright@west-norfolk.gov.uk

POLITICAL COMPOSITION

CON: 42, LAB: 13, LD: 3, IND: 3, GRN: 1

CABINET

Leader/ Resources: Mr Nick Daubney
Deputy Leader: Mr Brian Long
Development: Mrs Vivienne Spikings
Environment & Community: Mr Brian Long
Health & Wellbeing: Mrs Elizabeth Nockolds
Leisure & Operational Assets: Mr David Pope
Regeneration & Commercial Services: Mr Alistair Beales
Special Projects: Lord Greville Howard

COMMITTEE CHAIRS

Appointments Board: Mr Nick Daubney
Audit & Risk: Mrs Kathy Mellish
Licensing Appeals: Mr Roy Groom
Licensing: Mr Roy Groom
Planning: Mrs Vivienne Spikings
Regeneration, Environment & Community Panel: Mr Colin Sampson
Resources & Performance: Mr Paul Beal

KINGSTON UPON HULL CITY U

Kingston upon Hull City Council, (Hull City Council), Guildhall, Alfred Gelder Street, Hull HU1 2AA ☎ 01482 609100 info@hullcc.gov.uk www.hullcc.gov.uk

FACTS & FIGURES

Police Authority: Humberside Police Authority
Health Authority: NHS Yorkshire & the Humber
Learning and Skills Council: Yorkshire and the Humber
Parliamentary Constituencies: Hull East, Hull North, Hull West and Hessle
EU Constituencies: Yorkshire and the Humber
Election Frequency: Elections are by thirds
Twinning: Freetown (Sierra Leone)

PRINCIPAL OFFICERS

Chief Executive: Mrs Nicola Yates, Chief Executive, Guildhall, Alfred Gelder Street, Hull HU1 2AA ☎ 01482 616320 🖷 01482 613111 nicola.yates@hullcc.gov.uk

Deputy Chief Executive: Ms Adrienne Kelbie, Corporate Director - Business Support, The Guildhall, Alfred Gelder Street, Hull HU1 2AA ☎ 01482 614812 🖷 01482 613111 adrienne.kelbie@hullcc.gov.uk

Senior Management: Miss Trish Dalby, Corporate Director - Neighbourhoods & Families, The Guildhall, Alfred Gelder Street, Hull HU1 2AA ☎ 01482 615000 🖷 01482 613111 trish.dalby@hullcc.gov.uk

Senior Management: Mrs Pauline Davis, Corporate Director - Regeneration, The Guildhall, Alfred Gelder Street, Hull HU1 2AA ☎ 01482 613232 🖷 01482 613111 pauline.davis@hullcc.gov.uk

Senior Management: Ms Adrienne Kelbie, Corporate Director - Business Support, The Guildhall, Alfred Gelder Street, Hull HU1 2AA ☎ 01482 614812 adrienne.kelbie@hullcc.gov.uk

Senior Management: Ms Adrienne Kelbie, Corporate Director - Business Support, The Guildhall, Alfred Gelder Street, Hull HU1 2AA ☎ 01482 614812 🖷 01482 613111 adrienne.kelbie@hullcc.gov.uk

Senior Management: Mr John Readman, Corporate Director - Children & Young People's Services, The Guildhall, Alfred Gelder Street, Hull HU1 2AA ☎ 01482 616324 john.readman@hullcc.gov.uk

Access Officer / Social Services (Disability): Miss Trish Dalby, Corporate Director - Neighbourhoods & Families, The Guildhall, Alfred Gelder Street, Hull HU1 2AA ☎ 01482 615000 🖷 01482 613111 trish.dalby@hullcc.gov.uk

Access Officer / Social Services (Disability): Ms Angela Dunn, Head of Social Care, Brunswick House, Strand Close, Bevereley Road, Hull HU2 9DB ☎ 01482 616308 🖷 01482 616162 angela.dunn@hullcc.gov.uk

Access Officer / Social Services (Disability): Ms Tracy Harsley, Head of Citysafe, 3rd Floor, Kingston House, Bond Street, Hull HU1 3ER ☎ 01482 615022 tracy.harsley@hullcc.go.uk

Architect, Building / Property Services: Mrs Pauline Davis, Corporate Director - Regeneration, The Guildhall, Alfred Gelder Street, Hull HU1 2AA ☎ 01482 613232 🖷 01482 613111 pauline.davis@hullcc.gov.uk

Best Value: Mr Alistair Doxat-Purser, Head of Partnership Working, Guildhall, Alfred Gelder Street, Hull HU1 2AA ☎ 01482 615126 🖷 01482 613235 alistair.doxatpurser@hullcc.gov.uk

Building Control: Mrs Pauline Davis, Corporate Director - Regeneration, The Guildhall, Alfred Gelder Street, Hull HU1 2AA ☎ 01482 613232 🖷 01482 613111 pauline.davis@hullcc.gov.uk

Building Control: Mr Mark Jones, Head of Economic Development & Regeneration, 1st Floor, Kingston House, Bond Street, Hull HU1 3ER ☎ 01482 612162 🖷 01482 612160 mark.jones@hullcc.gov.uk

Catering Services: Mrs Pauline Davis, Corporate Director - Regeneration, The Guildhall, Alfred Gelder Street, Hull HU1 2AA ☎ 01482 613232 🖷 01482 613111 pauline.davis@hullcc.gov.uk

Children / Youth Services: Miss Vanessa Harvey-Samuel, Head of Children & Young People's Localities & Learning, Brunswick House, Strand Close, Bevereley Road, Hull HU2 9DB ☎ 01482 616019 vanessa.harvey-samuel@hullcc.gov.uk

Children / Youth Services: Mr John Readman, Corporate Director - Children & Young People's Services, The Guildhall, Alfred Gelder Street, Hull HU1 2AA ☎ 01482 616324 john.readman@hullcc.gov.uk

Civil Registration: Mr Andy Brown, Head of Customer Services, Guildhall, Alfred Gelder Street, Hull HU1 2AA ☎ 01482 613444 🖷 01482 613562 ✉ andy.brown@hullcc.gov.uk

Civil Registration: Miss Trish Dalby, Corporate Director - Neighbourhoods & Families, The Guildhall, Alfred Gelder Street, Hull HU1 2AA ☎ 01482 615000 🖷 01482 613111 ✉ trish.dalby@hullcc.gov.uk

PR / Communications: Mr Eddie Coates-Madden, Assistant Head of Service, The Guildhall, Alfred Gelder Street, Hull HU1 2AA ☎ 01482 613754 ✉ eddie.coates-madden@hullcc.gov.uk

PR / Communications: Ms Adrienne Kelbie, Corporate Director - Business Support, The Guildhall, Alfred Gelder Street, Hull HU1 2AA ☎ 01482 614812 ✉ adrienne.kelbie@hullcc.gov.uk

PR / Communications: Ms Adrienne Kelbie, Corporate Director - Business Support, The Guildhall, Alfred Gelder Street, Hull HU1 2AA ☎ 01482 614812 🖷 01482 613111 ✉ adrienne.kelbie@hullcc.gov.uk

Community Planning: Miss Trish Dalby, Corporate Director - Neighbourhoods & Families, The Guildhall, Alfred Gelder Street, Hull HU1 2AA ☎ 01482 615000 🖷 01482 613111 ✉ trish.dalby@hullcc.gov.uk

Community Safety: Miss Trish Dalby, Corporate Director - Neighbourhoods & Families, The Guildhall, Alfred Gelder Street, Hull HU1 2AA ☎ 01482 615000 🖷 01482 613111 ✉ trish.dalby@hullcc.gov.uk

Community Safety: Ms Tracy Harsley, Head of Citysafe, 3rd Floor, Kingston House, Bond Street, Hull HU1 3ER ☎ 01482 615022 ✉ tracy.harsley@hullcc.go.uk

Computer Management: Ms Adrienne Kelbie, Corporate Director - Business Support, The Guildhall, Alfred Gelder Street, Hull HU1 2AA ☎ 01482 614812 🖷 01482 613111 ✉ adrienne.kelbie@hullcc.gov.uk

Computer Management: Ms Adrienne Kelbie, Corporate Director - Business Support, The Guildhall, Alfred Gelder Street, Hull HU1 2AA ☎ 01482 614812 ✉ adrienne.kelbie@hullcc.gov.uk

Computer Management: Mr Stuart Ross, Head of Procurement, ICT and Facilities, The Guildhall, Alfred Gelder Street, Hull HU1 2AA ☎ 01482 616337 ✉ stuart.ross@hullcc.gov.uk

Consumer Protection and Trading Standards: Miss Trish Dalby, Corporate Director - Neighbourhoods & Families, The Guildhall, Alfred Gelder Street, Hull HU1 2AA ☎ 01482 615000 🖷 01482 613111 ✉ trish.dalby@hullcc.gov.uk

Consumer Protection and Trading Standards: Ms Tracy Harsley, Head of Citysafe, 3rd Floor, Kingston House, Bond Street, Hull HU1 3ER ☎ 01482 615022 ✉ tracy.harsley@hullcc.go.uk

Contracts: Ms Adrienne Kelbie, Corporate Director - Business Support, The Guildhall, Alfred Gelder Street, Hull HU1 2AA ☎ 01482 614812 ✉ adrienne.kelbie@hullcc.gov.uk

Contracts: Ms Adrienne Kelbie, Corporate Director - Business Support, The Guildhall, Alfred Gelder Street, Hull HU1 2AA ☎ 01482 614812 🖷 01482 613111 ✉ adrienne.kelbie@hullcc.gov.uk

Contracts: Mr Stuart Ross, Head of Procurement, ICT & Facilities, The Guildhall, Alfred Gelder Street, Hull HU1 2AA ☎ 01482 616337 ✉ stuart.ross@hullcc.gov.uk

Corporate Services: Mr Alistair Doxat-Purser, Head of Partnership Working, Guildhall, Alfred Gelder Street, Hull HU1 2AA ☎ 01482 615126 🖷 01482 613235 ✉ alistair.doxatpurser@hullcc.gov.uk

Customer Service: Mr Andy Brown, Head of Customer Services, Guildhall, Alfred Gelder Street, Hull HU1 2AA ☎ 01482 613444 🖷 01482 613562 ✉ andy.brown@hullcc.gov.uk

Customer Service: Miss Trish Dalby, Corporate Director - Neighbourhoods & Families, The Guildhall, Alfred Gelder Street, Hull HU1 2AA ☎ 01482 615000 🖷 01482 613111 ✉ trish.dalby@hullcc.gov.uk

Economic Development: Mrs Pauline Davis, Corporate Director - Regeneration, The Guildhall, Alfred Gelder Street, Hull HU1 2AA ☎ 01482 613232 🖷 01482 613111 ✉ pauline.davis@hullcc.gov.uk

Economic Development: Mr Mark Jones, Head of Economic Development & Regeneration, 1st Floor, Kingston House, Bond Street, Hull HU1 3ER ☎ 01482 612162 🖷 01482 612160 ✉ mark.jones@hullcc.gov.uk

Education: Miss Vanessa Harvey-Samuel, Head of Children & Young People's Localities & Learning, Brunswick House, Strand Close, Bevereley Road, Hull HU2 9DB ☎ 01482 616019 ✉ vanessa.harvey-samuel@hullcc.gov.uk

Education: Mr John Readman, Corporate Director - Children and Young People's Services, The Guildhall, Alfred Gelder Street, Hull HU1 2AA ☎ 01482 616324 ✉ john.readman@hullcc.gov.uk

Education: Mr Ken Sainty, Interim Head of Children & Young People's Localities & Learning, Brunswick House, Strand Close, Bevereley Road, Hull HU2 9DB ☎ 01482 616255 ✉ ken.sainty@hullcc.gov.uk

E-Government: Ms Adrienne Kelbie, Corporate Director - Business Support, The Guildhall, Alfred Gelder Street, Hull HU1 2AA ☎ 01482 614812 ✉ adrienne.kelbie@hullcc.gov.uk

E-Government: Ms Adrienne Kelbie, Corporate Director - Business Support, The Guildhall, Alfred Gelder Street, Hull HU1 2AA ☎ 01482 614812 🖷 01482 613111 ✉ adrienne.kelbie@hullcc.gov.uk

E-Government: Mr Stuart Ross, Head of Procurement, ICT and Facilities, The Guildhall, Alfred Gelder Street, Hull HU1 2AA ☎ 01482 616337 ✉ stuart.ross@hullcc.gov.uk

Electoral Registration: Mr Ian Anderson, Head of Legal & Democratic Services (& Monitoring Officer), Guildhall, Alfred Gelder Street, Hull HU1 2AA ☎ 01482 613233 🖷 01482 613081 ✉ ian.anderson@hullcc.gov.uk

Electoral Registration: Ms Adrienne Kelbie, Corporate Director - Business Support, The Guildhall, Alfred Gelder Street, Hull HU1 2AA ☎ 01482 614812 ✉ adrienne.kelbie@hullcc.gov.uk

Electoral Registration: Ms Adrienne Kelbie, Corporate Director - Business Support, The Guildhall, Alfred Gelder Street, Hull HU1 2AA ☎ 01482 614812 🖷 01482 613111 ✉ adrienne.kelbie@hullcc.gov.uk

Emergency Planning: Mr Andy Brown, Head of Customer Services, Guildhall, Alfred Gelder Street, Hull HU1 2AA ☎ 01482 613444 🖷 01482 613562 ✉ andy.brown@hullcc.gov.uk

Emergency Planning: Miss Trish Dalby, Corporate Director - Neighbourhoods & Families, The Guildhall, Alfred Gelder Street, Hull HU1 2AA ☎ 01482 615000 🖷 01482 613111 ✉ trish.dalby@hullcc.gov.uk

Energy Management: Ms Adrienne Kelbie, Corporate Director - Business Support, The Guildhall, Alfred Gelder Street, Hull HU1 2AA ☎ 01482 614812 🖷 01482 613111 ✉ adrienne.kelbie@hullcc.gov.uk

Energy Management: Ms Adrienne Kelbie, Corporate Director - Business Support, The Guildhall, Alfred Gelder Street, Hull HU1 2AA ☎ 01482 614812 ✉ adrienne.kelbie@hullcc.gov.uk

Energy Management: Mr Stuart Ross, Head of Procurement, ICT & Facilities, The Guildhall, Alfred Gelder Street, Hull HU1 2AA ☎ 01482 616337 ✉ stuart.ross@hullcc.gov.uk

Environmental / Technical Services: Mr Andy Burton, Head of Streetscene, Kingston House, Bond Street, Hull HU1 3ER ☎ 01482 614002 ✉ andy.burton@hullcc.gov.uk

Environmental / Technical Services: Ms Angela Dunn, Head of Social Care, Brunswick House, Strand Close, Bevereley Road, Hull HU2 9DB ☎ 01482 616308 🖷 01482 616162 ✉ angela.dunn@hullcc.gov.uk

Environmental / Technical Services: Ms Tracy Harsley, Head of Citysafe, 3rd Floor, Kingston House, Bond Street, Hull HU1 3ER ☎ 01482 615022 ✉ tracy.harsley@hullcc.go.uk

Environmental Health: Miss Trish Dalby, Corporate Director - Neighbourhoods & Families, The Guildhall, Alfred Gelder Street, Hull HU1 2AA ☎ 01482 615000 🖷 01482 613111 ✉ trish.dalby@hullcc.gov.uk

Environmental Health: Ms Angela Dunn, Head of Social Care, Brunswick House, Strand Close, Bevereley Road, Hull HU2 9DB ☎ 01482 616308 🖷 01482 616162 ✉ angela.dunn@hullcc.gov.uk

Environmental Health: Ms Tracy Harsley, Head of Citysafe, 3rd Floor, Kingston House, Bond Street, Hull HU1 3ER ☎ 01482 615022 ✉ tracy.harsley@hullcc.go.uk

Estates, Property & Valuation: Mrs Laura Carr, Head of Physical Regeneration, 5th Floor, Kingston House, Bond Street, Hull HU1 3ER ☎ 01482 612643 ✉ laura.carr@hullcc.gov.uk

Estates, Property & Valuation: Mrs Pauline Davis, Corporate Director - Regeneration, The Guildhall, Alfred Gelder Street, Hull HU1 2AA ☎ 01482 613232 🖷 01482 613111 ✉ pauline.davis@hullcc.gov.uk

European Liaison: Mrs Pauline Davis, Corporate Director - Regeneration, The Guildhall, Alfred Gelder Street, Hull HU1 2AA ☎ 01482 613232 🖷 01482 613111 ✉ pauline.davis@hullcc.gov.uk

European Liaison: Mr Mark Jones, Head of Economic Development & Regeneration, 1st Floor, Kingston House, Bond Street, Hull HU1 3ER ☎ 01482 612162 🖷 01482 612160 ✉ mark.jones@hullcc.gov.uk

Events Manager: Mrs Pauline Davis, Corporate Director - Regeneration, The Guildhall, Alfred Gelder Street, Hull HU1 2AA ☎ 01482 613232 🖷 01482 613111 ✉ pauline.davis@hullcc.gov.uk

Events Manager: Mr Mark Jones, Head of Economic Development & Regeneration, 1st Floor, Kingston House, Bond Street, Hull HU1 3ER ☎ 01482 612162 🖷 01482 612160 ✉ mark.jones@hullcc.gov.uk

Facilities: Ms Adrienne Kelbie, Corporate Director - Business Support, The Guildhall, Alfred Gelder Street, Hull HU1 2AA ☎ 01482 614812 ✉ adrienne.kelbie@hullcc.gov.uk

Facilities: Ms Adrienne Kelbie, Corporate Director - Business Support, The Guildhall, Alfred Gelder Street, Hull HU1 2AA ☎ 01482 614812 🖷 01482 613111 ✉ adrienne.kelbie@hullcc.gov.uk

Facilities: Mr Stuart Ross, Head of Procurement, ICT & Facilities, The Guildhall, Alfred Gelder Street, Hull HU1 2AA ☎ 01482 616337 ✉ stuart.ross@hullcc.gov.uk

Finance and Treasurer: Mr Brendan Arnold, Head of Corporate Planning & Finance, Treasury Building, Guildhall Road, Hull HU1 2AB ☎ 01482 613001 ✉ brendan.arnold@hullcc.gov.uk

Finance and Treasurer: Ms Adrienne Kelbie, Corporate Director - Business Support, The Guildhall, Alfred Gelder Street, Hull HU1 2AA ☎ 01482 614812 🖷 01482 613111 ✉ adrienne.kelbie@hullcc.gov.uk

Finance and Treasurer: Ms Adrienne Kelbie, Corporate Director - Business Support, The Guildhall, Alfred Gelder Street, Hull HU1 2AA ☎ 01482 614812 ✉ adrienne.kelbie@hullcc.gov.uk

Fleet Management: Mr Andy Burton, Head of Streetscene, Kingston House, Bond Street, Hull HU1 3ER ☎ 01482 612725 ✉ andy.burton@hullcc.gov.uk

Fleet Management: Mr Andy Burton, Head of Streetscene, Kingston House, Bond Street, Hull HU1 3ER ☎ 01482 614002 ✉ andy.burton@hullcc.gov.uk

Fleet Management: Miss Trish Dalby, Corporate Director - Neighbourhoods & Families, The Guildhall, Alfred Gelder Street, Hull HU1 2AA ☎ 01482 615000 🖷 01482 613111 ✉ trish.dalby@hullcc.gov.uk

Grounds Maintenance: Mr Andy Burton, Head of Streetscene, Kingston House, Bond Street, Hull HU1 3ER ☎ 01482 614002

✉ andy.burton@hullcc.gov.uk

Grounds Maintenance: Mr Andy Burton, Head of Streetscene, Kingston House, Bond Street, Hull HU1 3ER ☎ 01482 612725 ✉ andy.burton@hullcc.gov.uk

Grounds Maintenance: Miss Trish Dalby, Corporate Director - Neighbourhoods & Families, The Guildhall, Alfred Gelder Street, Hull HU1 2AA ☎ 01482 615000 🖷 01482 613111 ✉ trish.dalby@hullcc.gov.uk

Health and Safety: Ms Adrienne Kelbie, Corporate Director - Business Support, The Guildhall, Alfred Gelder Street, Hull HU1 2AA ☎ 01482 614812 🖷 01482 613111 ✉ adrienne.kelbie@hullcc.gov.uk

Health and Safety: Ms Adrienne Kelbie, Corporate Director - Business Support, The Guildhall, Alfred Gelder Street, Hull HU1 2AA ☎ 01482 614812 ✉ adrienne.kelbie@hullcc.gov.uk

Health and Safety: Mr Stuart Ross, Head of Procurement, ICT & Facilities, The Guildhall, Alfred Gelder Street, Hull HU1 2AA ☎ 01482 616337 ✉ stuart.ross@hullcc.gov.uk

Highways: Mr Andy Burton, Head of Streetscene, Kingston House, Bond Street, Hull HU1 3ER ☎ 01482 612725 ✉ andy.burton@hullcc.gov.uk

Highways: Mr Andy Burton, Head of Streetscene, Kingston House, Bond Street, Hull HU1 3ER ☎ 01482 614002 ✉ andy.burton@hullcc.gov.uk

Highways: Miss Trish Dalby, Corporate Director - Neighbourhoods & Families, The Guildhall, Alfred Gelder Street, Hull HU1 2AA ☎ 01482 615000 🖷 01482 613111 ✉ trish.dalby@hullcc.gov.uk

Home Energy Conservation: Miss Trish Dalby, Corporate Director - Neighbourhoods & Families, The Guildhall, Alfred Gelder Street, Hull HU1 2AA ☎ 01482 615000 🖷 01482 613111 ✉ trish.dalby@hullcc.gov.uk

Home Energy Conservation: Mrs Pauline Davis, Corporate Director - Regeneration, The Guildhall, Alfred Gelder Street, Hull HU1 2AA ☎ 01482 613232 🖷 01482 613111 ✉ pauline.davis@hullcc.gov.uk

Home Energy Conservation: Ms Angela Dunn, Head of Social Care, Brunswick House, Strand Close, Bevereley Road, Hull HU2 9DB ☎ 01482 616308 🖷 01482 616162 ✉ angela.dunn@hullcc.gov.uk

Housing: Miss Trish Dalby, Corporate Director - Neighbourhoods & Families, The Guildhall, Alfred Gelder Street, Hull HU1 2AA ☎ 01482 615000 🖷 01482 613111 ✉ trish.dalby@hullcc.gov.uk

Housing: Mrs Pauline Davis, Corporate Director - Regeneration, The Guildhall, Alfred Gelder Street, Hull HU1 2AA ☎ 01482 613232 🖷 01482 613111 ✉ pauline.davis@hullcc.gov.uk

Housing Maintenance: Mrs Pauline Davis, Corporate Director - Regeneration, The Guildhall, Alfred Gelder Street, Hull HU1 2AA ☎ 01482 613232 🖷 01482 613111 ✉ pauline.davis@hullcc.gov.uk

Local Area Agreement: Mr Alistair Doxat-Purser, Head of Partnership Working, Guildhall, Alfred Gelder Street, Hull HU1 2AA ☎ 01482 615126 🖷 01482 613235 ✉ alistair.doxatpurser@hullcc.gov.uk

Legal: Mr Ian Anderson, Head of Legal & Democratic Services (& Monitoring Officer), Guildhall, Alfred Gelder Street, Hull HU1 2AA ☎ 01482 613233 🖷 01482 613081 ✉ ian.anderson@hullcc.gov.uk

Legal: Ms Adrienne Kelbie, Corporate Director - Business Support, The Guildhall, Alfred Gelder Street, Hull HU1 2AA ☎ 01482 614812 🖷 01482 613111 ✉ adrienne.kelbie@hullcc.gov.uk

Legal: Ms Adrienne Kelbie, Corporate Director - Business Support, The Guildhall, Alfred Gelder Street, Hull HU1 2AA ☎ 01482 614812 ✉ adrienne.kelbie@hullcc.gov.uk

Leisure and Cultural Services: Mrs Pauline Davis, Corporate Director - Regeneration, The Guildhall, Alfred Gelder Street, Hull HU1 2AA ☎ 01482 613232 🖷 01482 613111 ✉ pauline.davis@hullcc.gov.uk

Leisure and Cultural Services: Mr Mark Jones, Head of Economic Development & Regeneration, 1st Floor, Kingston House, Bond Street, Hull HU1 3ER ☎ 01482 612162 🖷 01482 612160 ✉ mark.jones@hullcc.gov.uk

Licensing: Miss Trish Dalby, Corporate Director - Neighbourhoods & Families, The Guildhall, Alfred Gelder Street, Hull HU1 2AA ☎ 01482 615000 🖷 01482 613111 ✉ trish.dalby@hullcc.gov.uk

Licensing: Ms Tracy Harsley, Head of Citysafe, 3rd Floor, Kingston House, Bond Street, Hull HU1 3ER ☎ 01482 615022 ✉ tracy.harsley@hullcc.go.uk

Lifelong Learning: Miss Vanessa Harvey-Samuel, Head of Children & Young People's Localities & Learning, Brunswick House, Strand Close, Bevereley Road, Hull HU2 9DB ☎ 01482 616019 ✉ vanessa.harvey-samuel@hullcc.gov.uk

Lifelong Learning: Mr John Readman, Corporate Director - Children & Young People's Services, The Guildhall, Alfred Gelder Street, Hull HU1 2AA ☎ 01482 616324 ✉ john.readman@hullcc.gov.uk

Lifelong Learning: Mr Ken Sainty, Interim Head of Children & Young People's Localities & Learning, Brunswick House, Strand Close, Bevereley Road, Hull HU2 9DB ☎ 01482 616255 ✉ ken.sainty@hullcc.gov.uk

Lighting: Mr Andy Burton, Head of Streetscene, Kingston House, Bond Street, Hull HU1 3ER ☎ 01482 614002 ✉ andy.burton@hullcc.gov.uk

Lighting: Mr Andy Burton, Head of Streetscene, Kingston House, Bond Street, Hull HU1 3ER ☎ 01482 612725 ✉ andy.burton@hullcc.gov.uk

Lighting: Miss Trish Dalby, Corporate Director - Neighbourhoods

& Families, The Guildhall, Alfred Gelder Street, Hull HU1 2AA ☎ 01482 615000 🖷 01482 613111 ✉ trish.dalby@hullcc.gov.uk

Member Services: Ms Adrienne Kelbie, Corporate Director - Business Support, The Guildhall, Alfred Gelder Street, Hull HU1 2AA ☎ 01482 614812 🖷 01482 613111 ✉ adrienne.kelbie@hullcc.gov.uk

Member Services: Ms Adrienne Kelbie, Corporate Director - Business Support, The Guildhall, Alfred Gelder Street, Hull HU1 2AA ☎ 01482 614812 ✉ adrienne.kelbie@hullcc.gov.uk

Parking: Mr Andy Burton, Head of Streetscene, Kingston House, Bond Street, Hull HU1 3ER ☎ 01482 612725 ✉ andy.burton@hullcc.gov.uk

Parking: Mr Andy Burton, Head of Streetscene, Kingston House, Bond Street, Hull HU1 3ER ☎ 01482 614002 ✉ andy.burton@hullcc.gov.uk

Parking: Miss Trish Dalby, Corporate Director - Neighbourhoods & Families, The Guildhall, Alfred Gelder Street, Hull HU1 2AA ☎ 01482 615000 🖷 01482 613111 ✉ trish.dalby@hullcc.gov.uk

Partnerships: Mr Alistair Doxat-Purser, Head of Partnership Working, Guildhall, Alfred Gelder Street, Hull HU1 2AA ☎ 01482 615126 🖷 01482 613235 ✉ alistair.doxatpurser@hullcc.gov.uk

Personnel / HR: Mrs Jacqui Blesic, Head of Human Resources, The Guildhall, Alfred Gelder Street, Hull HU1 2AA ☎ 01482 613260 ✉ jacqui.blesic@hullcc.gov.uk

Personnel / HR: Ms Adrienne Kelbie, Corporate Director - Business Support, The Guildhall, Alfred Gelder Street, Hull HU1 2AA ☎ 01482 614812 🖷 01482 613111 ✉ adrienne.kelbie@hullcc.gov.uk

Personnel / HR: Ms Adrienne Kelbie, Corporate Director - Business Support, The Guildhall, Alfred Gelder Street, Hull HU1 2AA ☎ 01482 614812 ✉ adrienne.kelbie@hullcc.gov.uk

Planning: Mrs Pauline Davis, Corporate Director - Regeneration, The Guildhall, Alfred Gelder Street, Hull HU1 2AA ☎ 01482 613232 🖷 01482 613111 ✉ pauline.davis@hullcc.gov.uk

Planning: Mr Mark Jones, Head of Economic Development & Regeneration, 1st Floor, Kingston House, Bond Street, Hull HU1 3ER ☎ 01482 612162 🖷 01482 612160 ✉ mark.jones@hullcc.gov.uk

Procurement: Ms Adrienne Kelbie, Corporate Director - Business Support, The Guildhall, Alfred Gelder Street, Hull HU1 2AA ☎ 01482 614812 ✉ adrienne.kelbie@hullcc.gov.uk

Procurement: Ms Adrienne Kelbie, Corporate Director - Business Support, The Guildhall, Alfred Gelder Street, Hull HU1 2AA ☎ 01482 614812 🖷 01482 613111 ✉ adrienne.kelbie@hullcc.gov.uk

Procurement: Mr Stuart Ross, Head of Procurement, ICT & Facilities, The Guildhall, Alfred Gelder Street, Hull HU1 2AA ☎ 01482 616337 ✉ stuart.ross@hullcc.gov.uk

Public Libraries: Mr Andy Brown, Head of Customer Services, Guildhall, Alfred Gelder Street, Hull HU1 2AA ☎ 01482 613444 🖷 01482 613562 ✉ andy.brown@hullcc.gov.uk

Public Libraries: Miss Trish Dalby, Corporate Director - Neighbourhoods & Families, The Guildhall, Alfred Gelder Street, Hull HU1 2AA ☎ 01482 615000 🖷 01482 613111 ✉ trish.dalby@hullcc.gov.uk

Recycling & Waste Minimisation: Mr Andy Burton, Head of Streetscene, Kingston House, Bond Street, Hull HU1 3ER ☎ 01482 614002 ✉ andy.burton@hullcc.gov.uk

Recycling & Waste Minimisation: Mr Andy Burton, Head of Streetscene, Kingston House, Bond Street, Hull HU1 3ER ☎ 01482 612725 ✉ andy.burton@hullcc.gov.uk

Recycling & Waste Minimisation: Miss Trish Dalby, Corporate Director - Neighbourhoods & Families, The Guildhall, Alfred Gelder Street, Hull HU1 2AA ☎ 01482 615000 🖷 01482 613111 ✉ trish.dalby@hullcc.gov.uk

Recycling & Waste Minimisation: Miss Trish Dalby, Corporate Director - Neighbourhoods & Families, The Guildhall, Alfred Gelder Street, Hull HU1 2AA ☎ 01482 615000 🖷 01482 613111 ✉ trish.dalby@hullcc.gov.uk

Regeneration: Mrs Pauline Davis, Corporate Director - Regeneration, The Guildhall, Alfred Gelder Street, Hull HU1 2AA ☎ 01482 613232 🖷 01482 613111 ✉ pauline.davis@hullcc.gov.uk

Regeneration: Mr Mark Jones, Head of Economic Development & Regeneration, 1st Floor, Kingston House, Bond Street, Hull HU1 3ER ☎ 01482 612162 🖷 01482 612160 ✉ mark.jones@hullcc.gov.uk

Road Safety: Mr Andy Burton, Head of Streetscene, Kingston House, Bond Street, Hull HU1 3ER ☎ 01482 612725 ✉ andy.burton@hullcc.gov.uk

Road Safety: Mr Andy Burton, Head of Streetscene, Kingston House, Bond Street, Hull HU1 3ER ☎ 01482 614002 ✉ andy.burton@hullcc.gov.uk

Road Safety: Miss Trish Dalby, Corporate Director - Neighbourhoods & Families, The Guildhall, Alfred Gelder Street, Hull HU1 2AA ☎ 01482 615000 🖷 01482 613111 ✉ trish.dalby@hullcc.gov.uk

Road Safety: Miss Trish Dalby, Corporate Director - Neighbourhoods & Families, The Guildhall, Alfred Gelder Street, Hull HU1 2AA ☎ 01482 615000 🖷 01482 613111 ✉ trish.dalby@hullcc.gov.uk

Social Services: Miss Trish Dalby, Corporate Director - Neighbourhoods & Families, The Guildhall, Alfred Gelder Street, Hull HU1 2AA ☎ 01482 615000 🖷 01482 613111 ✉ trish.dalby@hullcc.gov.uk

Social Services: Mr John Readman, Corporate Director - Children & Young People's Services, The Guildhall, Alfred Gelder Street, Hull HU1 2AA ☎ 01482 616324

john.readman@hullcc.gov.uk

Social Services (Adult): Miss Trish Dalby, Corporate Director - Neighbourhoods & Families, The Guildhall, Alfred Gelder Street, Hull HU1 2AA ☎ 01482 615000 🖷 01482 613111 trish.dalby@hullcc.gov.uk

Social Services (Adult): Ms Angela Dunn, Head of Social Care, Brunswick House, Strand Close, Bevereley Road, Hull HU2 9DB ☎ 01482 616308 🖷 01482 616162 angela.dunn@hullcc.gov.uk

Social Services (Children): Mr Jon Plant, Head of Children and Young People's Localities & Safeguarding, Brunswick House, Strand Close, Bevereley Road, Hull HU2 9DB ☎ 01482 616004 🖷 01482 616107 jon.plant@hullcc.gov.uk

Social Services (Children): Mr John Readman, Corporate Director - Children & Young People's Services, The Guildhall, Alfred Gelder Street, Hull HU1 2AA ☎ 01482 616324 john.readman@hullcc.gov.uk

Staff Training: Mrs Jacqui Blesic, Head of Human Resources, The Guildhall, Alfred Gelder Street, Hull HU1 2AA ☎ 01482 613809 jacqui.blesic@hullcc.gov.uk

Staff Training: Mrs Jacqui Blesic, Head of Human Resources, The Guildhall, Alfred Gelder Street, Hull HU1 2AA ☎ 01482 613260 jacqui.blesic@hullcc.gov.uk

Staff Training: Ms Adrienne Kelbie, Corporate Director - Business Support, The Guildhall, Alfred Gelder Street, Hull HU1 2AA ☎ 01482 614812 🖷 01482 613111 adrienne.kelbie@hullcc.gov.uk

Street Scene: Mr Andy Burton, Head of Streetscene, Kingston House, Bond Street, Hull HU1 3ER ☎ 01482 614002 andy.burton@hullcc.gov.uk

Street Scene: Mr Andy Burton, Head of Streetscene, Kingston House, Bond Street, Hull HU1 3ER ☎ 01482 612725 andy.burton@hullcc.gov.uk

Street Scene: Miss Trish Dalby, Corporate Director - Neighbourhoods & Families, The Guildhall, Alfred Gelder Street, Hull HU1 2AA ☎ 01482 615000 🖷 01482 613111 trish.dalby@hullcc.gov.uk

Sustainable Communities: Mrs Pauline Davis, Corporate Director - Regeneration, The Guildhall, Alfred Gelder Street, Hull HU1 2AA ☎ 01482 613232 🖷 01482 613111 pauline.davis@hullcc.gov.uk

Sustainable Communities: Mr Mark Jones, Head of Economic Development & Regeneration, 1st Floor, Kingston House, Bond Street, Hull HU1 3ER ☎ 01482 612162 🖷 01482 612160 mark.jones@hullcc.gov.uk

Sustainable Development: Mrs Pauline Davis, Corporate Director - Regeneration, The Guildhall, Alfred Gelder Street, Hull HU1 2AA ☎ 01482 613232 🖷 01482 613111 pauline.davis@hullcc.gov.uk

Sustainable Development: Mr Mark Jones, Head of Economic Development & Regeneration, 1st Floor, Kingston House, Bond Street, Hull HU1 3ER ☎ 01482 612162 🖷 01482 612160 mark.jones@hullcc.gov.uk

Tourism: Mrs Pauline Davis, Corporate Director - Regeneration, The Guildhall, Alfred Gelder Street, Hull HU1 2AA ☎ 01482 613232 🖷 01482 613111 pauline.davis@hullcc.gov.uk

Tourism: Mr Mark Jones, Head of Economic Development & Regeneration, 1st Floor, Kingston House, Bond Street, Hull HU1 3ER ☎ 01482 612162 🖷 01482 612160 mark.jones@hullcc.gov.uk

Town Centre: Mrs Pauline Davis, Corporate Director - Regeneration, The Guildhall, Alfred Gelder Street, Hull HU1 2AA ☎ 01482 613232 🖷 01482 613111 pauline.davis@hullcc.gov.uk

Town Centre: Mr Mark Jones, Head of Economic Development & Regeneration, 1st Floor, Kingston House, Bond Street, Hull HU1 3ER ☎ 01482 612162 🖷 01482 612160 mark.jones@hullcc.gov.uk

Traffic Management: Mr Andy Burton, Head of Streetscene, Kingston House, Bond Street, Hull HU1 3ER ☎ 01482 612725 andy.burton@hullcc.gov.uk

Traffic Management: Mr Andy Burton, Head of Streetscene, Kingston House, Bond Street, Hull HU1 3ER ☎ 01482 614002 andy.burton@hullcc.gov.uk

Traffic Management: Miss Trish Dalby, Corporate Director - Neighbourhoods & Families, The Guildhall, Alfred Gelder Street, Hull HU1 2AA ☎ 01482 615000 🖷 01482 613111 trish.dalby@hullcc.gov.uk

Transport: Mrs Pauline Davis, Corporate Director - Regeneration, The Guildhall, Alfred Gelder Street, Hull HU1 2AA ☎ 01482 613232 🖷 01482 613111 pauline.davis@hullcc.gov.uk

Transport: Mr Mark Jones, Head of Economic Development & Regeneration, 1st Floor, Kingston House, Bond Street, Hull HU1 3ER ☎ 01482 612162 🖷 01482 612160 mark.jones@hullcc.gov.uk

Transport Planner: Mrs Pauline Davis, Corporate Director - Regeneration, The Guildhall, Alfred Gelder Street, Hull HU1 2AA ☎ 01482 613232 🖷 01482 613111 pauline.davis@hullcc.gov.uk

Transport Planner: Mr Mark Jones, Head of Economic Development & Regeneration, 1st Floor, Kingston House, Bond Street, Hull HU1 3ER ☎ 01482 612162 🖷 01482 612160 mark.jones@hullcc.gov.uk

Waste Collection and Disposal: Mr Andy Burton, Head of Streetscene, Kingston House, Bond Street, Hull HU1 3ER ☎ 01482 614002 andy.burton@hullcc.gov.uk

Waste Collection and Disposal: Mr Andy Burton, Head of Streetscene, Kingston House, Bond Street, Hull HU1 3ER ☎ 01482 612725 andy.burton@hullcc.gov.uk

Waste Collection and Disposal: Miss Trish Dalby, Corporate Director - Neighbourhoods & Families, The Guildhall, Alfred Gelder Street, Hull HU1 2AA ☎ 01482 615000 🖷 01482 613111
✉ trish.dalby@hullcc.gov.uk

Waste Management: Mr Andy Burton, Head of Streetscene, Kingston House, Bond Street, Hull HU1 3ER ☎ 01482 612725
✉ andy.burton@hullcc.gov.uk

Waste Management: Miss Trish Dalby, Corporate Director - Neighbourhoods & Families, The Guildhall, Alfred Gelder Street, Hull HU1 2AA ☎ 01482 615000 🖷 01482 613111
✉ trish.dalby@hullcc.gov.uk

Children's Play Areas: Mr John Readman, Corporate Director - Children & Young People's Services, The Guildhall, Alfred Gelder Street, Hull HU1 2AA ☎ 01482 616324
✉ john.readman@hullcc.gov.uk

MEMBERS OF THE COUNCIL (59)

***Mayor:* Brown**, Danny (LAB - Kings Park)
councillor.brown@hullcc.gov.uk
***Deputy Mayor:* Fudge**, Nadine (LAB - St Andrews)
councillor.fudge@hullcc.gov.uk
***Group Leader:* Bell**, Abigail (LD - Pickering)
councillor.bell@hullcc.gov.uk
***Group Leader:* Fareham**, John (CON - Bricknell)
councillor.fareham@hullcc.gov.uk
Abbott, John (CON - Bricknell)
councillor.abbott@hullcc.gov.uk
Allen, Pete (LAB - Pickering)
councillor.allen@hullcc.gov.uk
Armstrong, Suzanne (LAB - Ings)
councillor.armstrong@hullcc.gov.uk
Baker, Stephen (LD - Boothferry)
councillor.baker@hullcc.gov.uk
Bayes, Steven (LAB - Orchard Park and Greenwood)
steven.bayes@hullcc.gov.uk
Black, John (LAB - Longhill)
councillor.black@hullcc.gov.uk
Brady, Stephen (LAB - Southcoates West)
councillor.brady@hullcc.gov.uk
Butterworth, Simone (LD - Avenue)
councillor.butterworth@hullcc.gov.uk
Chambers, Linda (LD - Drypool)
councillor.chambers@hullcc.gov.uk
Chaytor, Sean (LAB - Marfleet)
councillor.chaytor@hullcc.gov.uk
Clark, Alan (LAB - Newington)
councillor.clark@hullcc.gov.uk
Clark, Peter (LAB - Bransholme East)
councillor.p.clark@hullcc.gov.uk
Clarkson, Carol (LAB - Longhill)
councillor.clarkson@hullcc.gov.uk
Conner, Julia (LAB - Orchard Park and Greenwood)
councillor.conner@hullcc.gov.uk
Craker, Dave (LAB - Sutton)
councillor.craker@hullcc.gov.uk
Dorton, Andy (LAB - Avenue)
councillor.dorton@hullcc.gov.uk
Elizabeth, Karen (LD - Beverely)
councillor.mathieson@hullcc.gov.uk
Gardiner, Alan (LAB - Ings)
councillor.gardiner@hullcc.gov.uk
Gemmell, David (LAB - Southcoates East)
councillor.gemmell@hullcc.gov.uk
Geraghty, Terry (LAB - Orchard Park and Greenwood)
councillor.geraghty@hullcc.gov.uk
Glew, Mary (LAB - Southcoates West)
councillor.glew@hullcc.gov.uk
Hale, Daren (LAB - St Andrews)
councillor.hale@hullcc.gov.uk
Harrison, Anita (O - Bransholme East)
councillor.harrison@hullcc.gov.uk
Hewitt, John (LAB - Longhill)
councillor.j.hewitt@hullcc.gov.uk
Hornby, Jan (LD - Holderness)
councillor.hornby@hullcc.gov.uk
Hull, Stephen (LD - Derringham)
councillor.hull@hullcc.gov.uk
Inglis, Colin (LAB - Myton)
Councillor.Inglis@hullcc.gov.uk
Inglis, Colin (LAB - Myton)
councillor.inglis@hullcc.gov.uk
Jones, Rilba (LAB - Myton)
councillor.jones@hullcc.gov.uk
Keal, Terry (LD - Sutton)
councillor.keal@hullcc.gov.uk
Kennett, Gill (LAB - Holderness)
councillor.kennett@hullcc.gov.uk
Kirk, Dean (LAB - Derringham)
councillor.kirk@hullcc.gov.uk
Korczak Fields, Joyce (LAB - University)
councillor.KorczakFields@hullcc.gov.uk
Mancey, Martin (LAB - Myton)
councillor.mancey@hullcc.gov.uk
Mann, Eliza (LD - Derringham)
councillor.mann@hullcc.gov.uk
McCobb, David (LD - Beverley)
councillor.mccobb@hullcc.gov.uk
McEvoy, Tom (LD - University)
councillor.mcevoy@hullcc.gov.uk
McVie, Tom (LAB - Southcoates East)
councillor.mcvie@hullcc.gov.uk
Nicola, Rosie (LAB - Avenue)
councillor.nicola@hullcc.gov.uk
O'Mullane, Helene (LAB - Bransholme West)
councillor.o'mullane@hullcc.gov.uk
Pantelakis, Rosemary (LAB - Marfleet)
councillor.pantelakis@hullcc.gov.uk
Petrini, Lynn (LAB - Newington)
councillor.petrini@hullcc.gov.uk
Quinn, Charles (LD - Kings Park)
councillor.quinn@hullcc.gov.uk
Ross, Michael (LD - Newland)
councillor.ross@hullcc.gov.uk
Shipley, John (LAB - Newland)
councillor.shipley@hullcc.gov.uk
Spencer, Helena (LAB - Newington)
councillor.spencer@hullcc.gov.uk
Sumpton, Christopher (LAB - Holderness)
councillor.sumpton@hullcc.gov.uk
Thomas, Claire (LD - Pickering)
councillor.thomas@hullcc.gov.uk
Turner, Ken (LAB - Sutton)
councillor.turner@hullcc.gov.uk
Walker, Steve (LAB - Ings)
councillor.s.walker@hullcc.gov.uk
Wareing, Gary (LAB - Drypool)

councillor.wareing@hullcc.gov.uk
Waudby, Shiela (LAB - Marfleet)
Councillor.Waudby@hullcc.gov.uk
Waudby, Shiela (LAB - Marfleet)
councillor.waudby@hullcc.gov.uk
Webster, Phil (LAB - Bransholme West)
councillor.webster@hullcc.gov.uk
Williams, Adam (LD - Drypool)
councillor.williams@hullcc.gov.uk
Woods, Karen (LD - Boothferry)
councillor.k.woods@hullcc.gov.uk
Woods, Helena (LD - Boothferry)
councillor.woods@hullcc.gov.uk

POLITICAL COMPOSITION
LAB: 39, LD: 17, CON: 2, O: 1

CABINET
Leader/ Personnel: Mr Stephen Brady
Deputy Leader/ Finance: Mr Daren Hale
Children's Services: Ms Helene O'Mullane
Economic Regeneration & Employement: Mr Steven Bayes
Environment, Transport & Emergency Planning: Mr Martin Mancey
Finance, Business Support & Procurement: Mr Phil Webster
Health & Equalities: Mrs Rilba Jones
Leisure & Culture: Mr Terry Geraghty
Neighbourhoods & Communities: Mr John Hewitt
Strategic & Operational Housing: Mr John Black

COMMITTEE CHAIRS
Appeals: Mr Peter Clark
Civic: Mr Danny Brown
Community Safety Overview & Scrutiny: Mr Pete Allen
Environment & Transport Overview & Scrutiny: Mr Terry Keal
Health & Social Wellbeing: Mr Danny Brown
Housing, Economic Development & Regeneration Overview & Scrutiny: Mr Dave Craker
Licensing: Mrs Nadine Fudge
Overview & Scrutiny Management: Mr Tom McVie
Park Area: Ms Shiela Waudby
Planning: Mr Sean Chaytor

KINGSTON UPON THAMES L

Royal Borough of Kingston upon Thames Council, (Kingston Council), Guildhall 2, High Street, Kingston upon Thames KT1 1EU ☎ 020 8547 5757 🖳 www.kingston.gov.uk

FACTS & FIGURES
Police Authority: Metropolitan Police Authority
Health Authority: NHS London
Learning and Skills Council: London
Parliamentary Constituencies: Kingston and Surbiton, Richmond Park
EU Constituencies: London
Election Frequency: Elections are of whole council

PRINCIPAL OFFICERS
Chief Executive: Mr Bruce McDonald, Chief Executive, Guildhall, Kingston upon Thames KT1 1EU ☎ 020 8547 5150 🖷 020 8547 5012 ✉ bruce.mcdonald@rbk.kingston.gov.uk

Senior Management: Mr David Smith, Director - Health & Adult Services / Chief Executive NHS Kingston, Guildhall 2, High Street, Kingston upon Thames KT1 1EU ☎ 020 8547 6000 🖷 020 8547 6086 ✉ david.smith@rbk.kingston.gov.uk

Senior Management: Mr Roy Thompson, Director - Planning & Transportation, Guildhall 2, High Street, Kingston upon Thames KT1 1EU ☎ 020 8547 5343 ✉ roy.thompson@rbk.kingston.gov.uk

Senior Management: Mrs Sheila West, Executive Head - Organisational Development & Strategic Business, Guildhall 2, Kingston upon Thames KT1 1EU ☎ 020 8547 5153 🖷 020 8547 5188 ✉ sheila.west@rbk.kingston.gov.uk

Senior Management: Mr Leigh Whitehouse, Director - Finance, Guildhall 2, Kingston upon Thames KT1 1EU ☎ 020 8547 5570 🖷 020 8547 5925 ✉ leigh.whitehouse@rbk.kingston.gov.uk

Architect, Building / Property Services: Mr Peter Cordy, Interim Head - Property, Guildhall 2, High Street, Kingston upon Thames KT1 1EU ☎ 020 8547 5670 🖷 020 8547 5925 ✉ peter.cordy@rbk.kingston.gov.uk

Best Value: Mr Chris Morgan, Capability Lead - Commissioning, Guildhall 2, High Street, Kingston upon Thames KT1 1EU ☎ 020 8547 5300 ✉ chris.morgan@rbk.kingston.gov.uk

Civil Registration: Mr Dennis Mulligan, Registration Manager & Superintendent Registrar, The Register Office, 35 Coombe Road, Kingston upon Thames KT2 7BA ☎ 020 8547 6191 🖷 020 8547 6188 ✉ dennis.mulligan@rbk.kingston.gov.uk

PR / Communications: Mr Jack Taylor, Capability Lead - Communications, Guildhall, Kingston upon Thames KT1 1EU ☎ 020 8547 4614 🖷 020 8547 5012 ✉ jack.taylor@rbk.kingston.gov.uk

Community Planning: Mr Gary Walsh, Capability Lead - Community, Guildhall 2, High Street, Kingston upon Thames KT1 1EU ☎ 020 8547 4698 ✉ gary.walsh@rbk.kingston.gov.uk

Community Safety: Ms Marion Todd, Safer Kingston Partnership Manager, Guildhall 2, High Street, Kingston upon Thames KT1 1EU ☎ 020 8547 5039 ✉ marion.todd@rbk.kingston.gov.uk

Computer Management: Mr Mike Fogaty, Interim Head - ICT, Guildhall 2, High Street, Kingston upon Thames KT1 1EU ☎ 020 8547 5093 ✉ mike.fogaty@rbk.kingston.gov.uk

Consumer Protection and Trading Standards: Mr David Booker, Group Manager - Environmental Health & Trading Standards, Guildhall 2, High Street, Kingston upon Thames KT1 1EU ☎ 020 8547 5513 🖷 020 8547 5515 ✉ david.booker@rbk.kingston.gov.uk

Contracts: Mr Chris Morgan, Capability Lead - Commissioning, Guildhall 2, High Street, Kingston upon Thames KT1 1EU ☎ 020 8547 5300 ✉ chris.morgan@rbk.kingston.gov.uk

Customer Service: Mr Russell Anthony, Transitional Service Manager - Customer Contact, Guildhall 2, High Street, Kingston upon Thames KT1 1EU ☎ 020 8547 5393

russell.anthony@rbk.kingston.gov.uk

Economic Development: Ms Jill Darling, Team Leader - Voluntary Sector & Business Community, Guildhall 2, High Street, Kingston upon Thames KT1 1EU ☎ 020 8547 5124 fax 020 8547 5125 jill.darling@rbk.kingston.gov.uk

E-Government: Mr Mike Fogaty, Interim Head - ICT, Guildhall 2, High Street, Kingston upon Thames KT1 1EU ☎ 020 8547 5093 mike.fogaty@rbk.kingston.gov.uk

Electoral Registration: Mr Andrew Bessant, Head - Corporate Governance, Guildhall 2, High Street, Kingston upon Thames KT1 1EU ☎ 020 8547 4628 fax 020 8547 5125 andrew.bessant@rbk.kingston.gov.uk

Electoral Registration: Mr Gareth Harrington, Manager - Electoral Services, Guildhall, High Street, Kingston upon Thames KT1 1EU ☎ 020 8547 5035 fax 020 8547 5099 gareth.harrington@rbk.kingston.gov.uk

Emergency Planning: Mr Robert Bell, Contingency Planning Manager, Guildhall, Kingston upon Thames KT1 1EU ☎ 020 8547 5400 fax 020 8547 6224 rob.bell@rbk.kingston.gov.uk

Environmental / Technical Services: Mr David Booker, Group Manager - Environmental Health & Trading Standards, Guildhall 2, High Street, Kingston upon Thames KT1 1EU ☎ 020 8547 5513 fax 020 8547 5515 david.booker@rbk.kingston.gov.uk

Environmental / Technical Services: Mr Tom Jeffrey, Executive Head - Environment, Guildhall 2, High Street, Kingston upon Thames KT1 1EU ☎ 020 8547 4705 tom.jeffrey@rbk.kingston.gov.uk

Estates, Property & Valuation: Mr Peter Cordy, Interim Head - Property, Guildhall 2, High Street, Kingston upon Thames KT1 1EU ☎ 020 8547 5670 fax 020 8547 5925 peter.cordy@rbk.kingston.gov.uk

European Liaison: Ms Brigitte Pfender, International Partnerships Co-ordinator, Guildhall, Kingston upon Thames KT1 1EU ☎ 020 8547 5009 fax 020 8547 5125 brigitte.pfender@rbk.kingston.gov.uk

Facilities: Mr Steve Manners, Facilities Manager, Guildhall, Kingston upon Thames KT1 1EU ☎ 020 8547 5067 fax 020 8547 5065 steve.manners@rbk.kingston.gov.uk

Finance and Treasurer: Mr Iain Millar, Head - Treasury Services, Guildhall 2, High Street, Kingston upon Thames KT1 1EU ☎ 020 8547 5757 iain.millar@rbk.kingston.gov.uk

Finance and Treasurer: Mr Jeremy Randall, Head - Financial Services, Guildhall 2, High Street, Kingston upon Thames KT1 1EU ☎ 020 8547 5572 jeremy.randall@rbk.kingston.gov.uk

Finance and Treasurer: Mr Leigh Whitehouse, Director - Finance, Guildhall 2, Kingston upon Thames KT1 1EU ☎ 020 8547 5570 fax 020 8547 5925 leigh.whitehouse@rbk.kingston.gov.uk

Grounds Maintenance: Ms Marie-Claire Edwards, Service Manager - Green Spaces, Guildhall 2, Kingston upon Thames KT1 1EU ☎ 020 8547 5372 marie-claire.edwards@rbk.kingston.gov.uk

Health and Safety: Ms Lorna Mansell, Occupational Health & Safety Manager, Guildhall, Kingston upon Thames KT1 1EU ☎ 020 8547 5187 fax 020 8547 5186 lorna.mansell@rbk.kingston.gov.uk

Highways: Mr Roy Thompson, Director - Planning & Transportation, Guildhall 2, Kingston upon Thames KT1 1EU ☎ 020 8547 5343 roy.thompson@rbk.kingston.gov.uk

Housing: Mr Keith Broxup, Interim Head - Housing, Guildhall 1, Kingston upon Thames KT1 1EU ☎ 020 8547 5430 keith.broxup@rbk.kingston.gov.uk

Housing Maintenance: Mr Keith Broxup, Interim Head - Housing, Guildhall 1, Kingston upon Thames KT1 1EU ☎ 020 8547 5430 keith.broxup@rbk.kingston.gov.uk

Housing Maintenance: Mr Simon Oelman, Head - Housing Operations, Guildhall 1, Kingston upon Thames KT1 1EU ☎ 020 8547 5479 fax 020 8547 5524 simon.oelman@rbk.kingston.gov.uk

Local Area Agreement: Mr Kevin Mitchell, Capability Lead Strategy, Guildhall 2, High Street, Kingston upon Thames KT1 1EU ☎ 020 8547 5982 kevin.mitchell@rbk.kingston.gov.uk

Legal: Mr Nick Bishop, Head - Legal Services, Guildhall, Kingston upon Thames KT1 1EU ☎ 020 8547 5110 fax 020 8547 5127 nick.bishop@rbk.kingston.gov.uk

Leisure and Cultural Services: Mr Scott Herbertson, Head - Cultural Services & Lifelong Learning, Guildhall 2, Kingston upon Thames KT1 1EU ☎ 020 8547 5267 fax 020 8547 5213 scott.herbertson@rbk.kingston.gov.uk

Lifelong Learning: Mr Scott Herbertson, Head - Cultural Services & Lifelong Learning, Guildhall 2, Room 146, Kingston upon Thames KT1 1EU ☎ 020 8547 5267 fax 020 8547 5213 scott.herbertson@rbk.kingston.gov.uk

Lottery Funding, Charity and Voluntary: Ms Jill Darling, Team Leader - Voluntary Sector & Business Community, Guildhall 2, High Street, Kingston upon Thames KT1 1EU ☎ 020 8547 5124 fax 020 8547 5125 jill.darling@rbk.kingston.gov.uk

Member Services: Mr Andrew Bessant, Head - Corporate Governance, Guildhall, Kingston upon Thames KT1 1EU ☎ 020 8547 4628 fax 020 8547 5125 andrew.bessant@rbk.kingston.gov.uk

Parking: Mr John Bolland, Service Manager - Traffic Management & Design, Guildhall 2, High Street, Kingston upon Thames KT1 1EU ☎ 020 8547 4691 john.bolland@rbk.kingston.gov.uk

Partnerships: Mr Andrew Bessant, Head - Corporate Governance, Guildhall 2, High Street, Kingston upon Thames KT1

1EU ☎ 020 8547 4628 🖷 020 8547 5125
✉ andrew.bessant@rbk.kingston.gov.uk

Personnel / HR: Mrs Sheila West, Executive Head - Organisational Development & Strategic Business, Guildhall 2, Kingston upon Thames KT1 1EU ☎ 020 8547 5153 🖷 020 8547 5188 ✉ sheila.west@rbk.kingston.gov.uk

Procurement: Mr Chris Morgan, Capability Lead - Commissioning, Guildhall 2, High Street, Kingston upon Thames KT1 1EU ☎ 020 8547 5300 ✉ chris.morgan@rbk.kingston.gov.uk

Public Libraries: Mr Scott Herbertson, Head - Cultural Services & Lifelong Learning, Guildhall 2, Kingston upon Thames KT1 1EU ☎ 020 8547 5267 🖷 020 8547 5213
✉ scott.herbertson@rbk.kingston.gov.uk

Public Libraries: Ms Grace McElwee, Strategic Manager of Libraries & Heritage Services, Kingston Library, Fairfield Road, Kingston upon Thames KT1 2PS ☎ 020 8547 6423 🖷 020 8547 6426 ✉ grace.mcelwee@rbk.kingston.gov.uk

Recycling & Waste Minimisation: Mr Tom Jeffrey, Executive Head - Environment, Guildhall 2, High Street, Kingston upon Thames KT1 1EU ☎ 020 8547 4705
✉ tom.jeffrey@rbk.kingston.gov.uk

Regeneration: Mr Kevin Mitchell, Capability Lead - Strategy, Guildhall 2, High Street, Kingston upon Thames KT1 1EU ☎ 020 8547 5982 ✉ kevin.mitchell@rbk.kingston.gov.uk

Road Safety: Mr John Bolland, Service Manager - Traffic Management & Design, Guildhall 2, High Street, Kingston upon Thames KT1 1EU ☎ 020 8547 4691
✉ john.bolland@rbk.kingston.gov.uk

Social Services: Mr David Smith, Director - Health & Adult Services / Chief Executive NHS Kingston, Guildhall 2, High Street, Kingston upon Thames KT1 1EU ☎ 020 8547 6000 🖷 020 8547 6086 ✉ david.smith@rbk.kingston.gov.uk

Social Services (Adult): Mr Simon Pearce, Executive Head - Adult Care, 22 Hollyfield Road, Surbiton KT5 9AL ☎ 020 8547 6052 🖷 020 8547 6100 ✉ simon.pearce@rbk.kingston.gov.uk

Social Services (Adult): Mr David Smith, Director - Health & Adult Services / Chief Executive NHS Kingston, Guildhall 2, High Street, Kingston upon Thames KT1 1EU ☎ 020 8547 6000
🖷 020 8547 6086 ✉ david.smith@rbk.kingston.gov.uk

Staff Training: Mrs Sheila West, Executive Head - Organisational Development & Strategic Business, Guildhall 2, Kingston upon Thames KT1 1EU ☎ 020 8547 5153 🖷 020 8547 5188 ✉ sheila.west@rbk.kingston.gov.uk

Street Scene: Mr Matthew Jezzard, Service Manager - Street Scene, Guildhall 2, High Street, Kingston upon Thames KT1 1EU ☎ 020 8547 5895 ✉ matthew.jezzard@rbk.kingston.gov.uk

Sustainable Communities: Ms Helen Wagner, Strategic Relationship Manager - Places & Environment, Guildhall 2, High Street, Kingston upon Thames KT1 1EU ☎ 020 8547 5981
✉ helen.wagner@rbk.kingston.gov.uk

Tourism: Mr Jack Taylor, Capability Lead - Communications, Guildhall, Kingston upon Thames KT1 1EU ☎ 020 8547 4614 🖷 020 8547 5012 ✉ jack.taylor@rbk.kingston.gov.uk

Town Centre: Ms Ros Morgan, Kingston Town Centre Manager, 3rd Floor, Neville House, 55 Eden Street, Kingston upon Thames KT1 1EU ☎ 020 8547 1221

Traffic Management: Mr John Bolland, Service Manager - Traffic Management & Design, Guildhall 2, High Street, Kingston upon Thames KT1 1EU ☎ 020 8547 4691
✉ john.bolland@rbk.kingston.gov.uk

Transport: Mr Roy Thompson, Director - Planning & Transportation, Guildhall 2, High Street, Kingston upon Thames KT1 1EU ☎ 020 8547 5343 ✉ roy.thompson@rbk.kingston.gov.uk

Transport Planner: Mr Roy Thompson, Director - Planning & Transportation, Guildhall 2, High Street, Kingston upon Thames KT1 1EU ☎ 020 8547 5343 ✉ roy.thompson@rbk.kingston.gov.uk

Waste Collection and Disposal: Mr Tom Jeffrey, Executive Head - Environment, Guildhall 2, High Street, Kingston upon Thames KT1 1EU ☎ 020 8547 4705
✉ tom.jeffrey@rbk.kingston.gov.uk

Waste Management: Ms Rachel Sherman, Service Manager - Waste, Guildhall 2, High Street, Kingston upon Thames KT1 1EU ☎ 020 8547 5757 🖷 020 8547 4602
✉ rachel.sherman@rbk.kingston.gov.uk

MEMBERS OF THE COUNCIL (48)

***Chair:* Codd**, Patrick (CON - Coombe Hill)
patrick.codd@councillors.kingston.gov.uk
***Deputy Mayor:* O'Mahony**, Barry (LD - Grove)
barry.omahony@councillors.kingston.gov.uk
***Leader of the Council:* Osbourne**, Derek (LD - Beverley)
derek.osbourne@councillors.kingston.gov.uk
***Deputy Leader of the Council:* Green**, Elizabeth (LD - St Marks)
liz.green@councillors.kingston.gov.uk
Grove: Vacant
Amson, Mick (CON - Old Malden)
mick.amson@councillors.kingston.gov.uk
Austin, Geoff (CON - Canbury)
geoffrey.Austin@councillors.kingston.gov.uk
Ayles, John (LD - Surbiton Hill)
john.ayles@councillors.kingston.gov.uk
Bamford, Patricia (LD - Chessington South)
patricia.bamford@councillors.kingston.gov.uk
Brister, Stephen (LD - Norbiton)
stephen.brister@councillors.kingston.gov.uk
Burden, Michael (CON - Alexandra)
michael.burden@councillors.kingston.gov.uk
Burgess, John (LD - Alexandra)
john.burgess@councillors.kingston.gov.uk
Craig, Andrea (CON - Canbury)
andrea.craig@councillors.kingston.gov.uk
Cunningham, David (CON - Tudor)
david.cunningham@councillors.kingston.gov.uk
Davies, Rolson (LD - Tolworth and Hook Rise)

rolson.davies@councillors.kingston.gov.uk
Day, Andrew (CON - Chessington North and Hook)
andrew.day@councillors.kingston.gov.uk
Dean, Alan (LD - Chessington North and Hook)
alan.dean@councillors.kingston.gov.uk
Dennen, Tim (IND - Canbury)
timothy.dennen@councillors.kingston.gov.uk
Doe, Dennis (CON - Tudor)
dennis.doe@councillors.kingston.gov.uk
Finnerty, Lynne (CON - Coombe Vale)
lynne.finnerty@councillors.kingston.gov.uk
Fraser, David (CON - Old Malden)
david.fraser@councillors.kingston.gov.uk
George, Karen (CON - Berrylands)
karen.george@councillors.kingston.gov.uk
Harris, Vicki (LD - Tolworth and Hook Rise)
vicki.harris@councillors.kingston.gov.uk
Hartley, Sharon (LD - Tolworth and Hook Rise)
sharon.hartley@councillors.kingston.gov.uk
Heap, Trevor (LD - Beverley)
trevor.heap@councillors.kingston.gov.uk
Heathcote, Mary (LD - St Marks)
mary.heathcote@councillors.kingston.gov.uk
Hitchcock, Chrissie (LD - Grove)
chrissie.hitchcock@councillors.kingston.gov.uk
Holder, Adrian (CON - Coombe Vale)
adrian.holder@councillors.kingston.gov.uk
Houston, Neil (LD - Surbiton Hill)
neil.houston@councillors.kingston.gov.uk
Hudson, Richard (CON - Alexandra)
richard.hudson@councillors.kingston.gov.uk
Humphrey, Eric (CON - Coombe Hill)
eric.humphrey@councillors.kingston.gov.uk
James, Simon (LD - Beverley)
simon.james@councillors.kingston.gov.uk
Jones, Howard (CON - St James's)
howard.jones@councillors.kingston.gov.uk
Mirza, Shiraz (LD - Chessington South)
shiraz.mirza@councillors.kingston.gov.uk
Moseley, Frances (LD - Berrylands)
frances.moseley@councillors.kingston.gov.uk
Patel, Priyen (CON - St James's)
priyen.patel@councillors.kingston.gov.uk
Pickering, Julie (CON - Coombe Vale)
julie.pickering@councillors.kingston.gov.uk
Reid, Rachel (LD - Chessington South)
rachel.reid@councillors.kingston.gov.uk
Ryder-Mills, David (LD - Norbiton)
david.ryder-mills@councillors.kingston.gov.uk
Self, Malcolm (LD - Surbiton Hill)
malcolm.self@councillors.kingston.gov.uk
Shelton, Penny (LD - Norbiton)
penny.shelton@councillors.kingston.gov.uk
Smith, Ken (CON - St James's)
ken.smith@councillors.kingston.gov.uk
Steed, Robert (LD - Berrylands)
bob.steed@councillors.kingston.gov.uk
Stinton, Kate (CON - Old Malden)
kate.stinton@councillors.kingston.gov.uk
Thompson, Margaret (LD - Chessington North and Hook)
margaret.thompson@councillors.kingston.gov.uk
Thompson, Frank (CON - Tudor)
frank.thompson@councillors.kingston.gov.uk
Wallooppillai, Gaj (CON - Coombe Hill)
gaj.wallooppillai@councillors.kingston.gov.uk
Yoganathan, Yogan (LD - St Marks)
yogan.yoganathan@councillors.kingston.gov.uk

POLITICAL COMPOSITION
LD: 25, CON: 21, IND: 1, Vacant: 1

CABINET
Leader: Mr Derek Osbourne
Deputy Leader: Ms Elizabeth Green
Better Homes: Ms Frances Moseley
Children & Young People: Ms Patricia Bamford
Finance & Resources: Mr Rolson Davies
Healthy Living & Adult Support: Ms Penny Shelton
Sustainability & Sport: Ms Sharon Hartley
Sustainable Place: Mr Simon James

COMMITTEE CHAIRS
Audit: Mr Trevor Heap
Development Control: Ms Vicki Harris
Health Overview & Scrutiny: Ms Margaret Thompson
Kingston Town Neighbourhood: Mr Tim Dennen
Licensing: Ms Chrissie Hitchcock
Pension Fund: Mr Derek Osbourne
People's Services: Ms Patricia Bamford
Place & Sustainability: Ms Sharon Hartley
Policy & Resources: Mr Rolson Davies
Scrutiny: Mr Dennis Doe
Standards: Mr Hiraral Banerjee (External)

KIRKLEES M

Kirklees Metropolitan Council, (Kirklees Council), Civic Centre 3, Market Street, Huddersfield HD1 1WG ☎ 01484 221000
🖷 01484 221777 ✉ performance.communication@kirklees.gov.uk
💻 www.kirklees.gov.uk

FACTS & FIGURES
Police Authority: West Yorkshire Police Authority
Health Authority: NHS Yorkshire & the Humber
Learning and Skills Council: Yorkshire and the Humber
Parliamentary Constituencies: Batley and Spen, Colne Valley, Dewsbury, Huddersfield, Wakefield
EU Constituencies: Yorkshire and the Humber
Election Frequency: Elections are by thirds
Twinning: Besancon (France); Bielsko-Biata (Poland); Kostani (Kazakhstan); Kreis Unna (Germany)

PRINCIPAL OFFICERS
Chief Executive: Mr Adrian Lythgo, Chief Executive, 1st Floor, Civic Centre 3, Market Street, Huddersfield HD1 2TG
☎ 01484 226600 🖷 01484 221065
✉ adrian.lythgo@kirklees.gov.uk

Senior Management: Ms Jacqui Gedman, Interim Director of Place, Civic Centre 3, Market Street, Huddersfield HD1 1WG
☎ 01484 221641 🖷 01484 221645
✉ jacqui.gedman@kirklees.gov.uk

Senior Management: Ms Merran McRae, Director of Well-being & Communities, Civic Centre 3, Market Street, Huddersfield HD1 1WG ☎ 01484 221248 🖷 01484 221777 merran.mcrae@kirklees.gov.uk

Senior Management: Mrs Alison O'Sullivan, Director for Children & Young People, Ground Floor, Civic Centre 1, High Street, Huddersfield HD1 2NF ☎ 01484 225242 🖷 01484 225237 alison.o'sullivan@kirklees.gov.uk

Senior Management: Mr David Smith, Director of Resources, Civic Centre 3, Market Street, Huddersfield HD1 1WG ☎ 01484 221124 david.smith@kirklees.gov.uk

Access Officer / Social Services (Disability): Ms Sally McIvor, Assistant Director of Well-being & Integration, Gateway to Care, 3rd Floor, Market Street, Huddersfield HD1 2HG ☎ 01484 225145 sally.mcivor@kirklees.gov.uk

Catering Services: Ms Annette Bird, Schools FM Manager, Civic Centre 3, Market Street, Huddersfield HD1 1WG ☎ 01484 226162 annette.bird@kirklees.gov.uk

Children / Youth Services: Mrs Alison O'Sullivan, Director for Children & Young People, Children & Young People Service, Oldgate House, 2 Oldgate, Huddersfield HD1 6QW ☎ 01484 225242 🖷 01484 225237 alison.o'sullivan@kirklees.gov.uk

Civil Registration: Ms Lesley Hewitson, Superintendent Registrar, Register Office, Wellington Street, Dewsbury WF13 1LY ☎ 01924 324880

PR / Communications: Mr Alun Ireland, Publicity & Media Manager, Civic Centre 3, Market Street, Huddersfield HD1 1WG ☎ 01484 225319

Community Planning: Ms Merran McRae, Director of Well-being & Communities, Civic Centre 3, Market Street, Huddersfield HD1 1WG ☎ 01484 221248 🖷 01484 221777 merran.mcrae@kirklees.gov.uk

Community Safety: Ms Merran McRae, Director of Well-being & Communities, Civic Centre 3, Market Street, Huddersfield HD1 1WG ☎ 01484 221248 🖷 01484 221777 merran.mcrae@kirklees.gov.uk

Computer Management: Mrs Laura Rawnsley, Assistant Director of Change & Technology, IT Civic Centre 1, High Street, Huddersfield HD1 1SP ☎ 01484 225910 🖷 01484 225916 laura.rawnsley@kirklees.gov.uk

Consumer Protection and Trading Standards: Mr Graham Hebblethwaite, Chief Officer, West Yorkshire Joint Services, West Yorkshire Joint Services, PO Box 5, Nepshaw Lane South, Morley LS27 0QP ☎ 0113 253 0241

Contracts: Mr Keith Smith, Assistant Director of Personalisation & Commissioning, Gateway to Care, 3rd Floor, Market Street, Huddersfield HD1 2HG ☎ 01484 225321 keith.smith@kirklees.gov.uk

Corporate Services: Ms Susan Betteridge, Assistant Director of Innovation & Efficiency, Civic Centre 3, Market Street, Huddersfield HD1 1WG susan.betteridge@kirkless.gov.uk

Corporate Services: Ms Julie Fothergill, Policy Unit Manager, Civic Centre 3, Market Street, Huddersfield HD1 1WG ☎ 01484 221783 julie.fothergill@kirklees.gov.uk

Corporate Services: Mr John Heneghan, Policy Unit Manager, Civic Centre 3, Market Street, Huddersfield HD1 1WG ☎ 01484 221779 john.henegham@kirklees.gov.uk

Customer Service: Ms Jane Brady, Assistant Director of Customer & Exchequer Services, Civic Centre 1, High Street, Huddersfield HD1 2NF ☎ 01484 221193 jane.brady@kirklees.gov.uk

Electoral Registration: Ms Susan Hutson, Electoral Services Manager, 49-51 Huddersfield Road, Holmfirth HD9 3ER ☎ 01484 222403 🖷 01484 222450 susan.hutson@kirklees.gov.uk

Emergency Planning: Mr Sean Westerby, Corporate Safety / Resilience Team Manager, Emergency Planning, Kirkgate Buildings, Byram Street, Huddersfield HD1 1BY ☎ 01484 226414 🖷 01484 224883 sean.westerby@kirklees.gov.uk

Environmental / Technical Services: Mr Rob Dalby, Environmental Protection Manager, Flint Street, Fartown, Huddersfield HD1 6LG ☎ 01484 226403 🖷 01484 226409 rob.dalby@kirkless.gov.uk

Environmental Health: Mr Rob Dalby, Environmental Protection Manager, Flint Street, Fartown, Huddersfield HD1 6LG ☎ 01484 226403 🖷 01484 226409 rob.dalby@kirkless.gov.uk

Estates, Property & Valuation: Ms Joanne Bartholomew, Assistant Director of Physical Resources & Procurement, Design & Property Service, Kirkgate Buildings, Byram street, Huddersfield HD1 4SA ☎ 01484 226052 joanne.bartholomew@kirklees.gov.uk

Facilities: Ms Joanne Bartholomew, Assistant Director of Physical Resources & Procurement, Design & Property Service, Kirkgate Buildings, Byram street, Huddersfield HD1 4SA ☎ 01484 226052 joanne.bartholomew@kirklees.gov.uk

Facilities: Ms Rebecca Jones, Support Services, High Street Buildings, High Street, Huddersfield HD1 2NQ ☎ 01484 416584 rebecca.jones@kirklees.gov.uk

Grounds Maintenance: Mr John Fletcher, Assistant Head of Service, Parks & Open Spaces, Culture & Leisure Services, The Stadium Business and Leisure Complex, Stadium Way, Huddersfield HD1 6PG ☎ 01484 234132 🖷 01484 234144 john.fletcher@kirklees.gov.uk

Health and Safety: Ms Jan Paley, Health & Safety Officer, Civic Centre 3, Market Street, Huddersfield HD1 1WG ☎ 01484 221000

Highways: Ms Jacqui Gedman, Interim Director of Place, E & T Highways & Transportation, Flint Street, Huddersfield HD1 6LG ☎ 01484 221641 🖷 01484 221645 jacqui.gedman@kirklees.gov.uk

Home Energy Conservation: Mr Chris Moorhouse, Energy Team Manager, Investment Team, Perseverance House, St Andrew's

Road, Huddersfield HD1 6RW ☎ 01484 416732 ✉ chris.moorhouse@kirklees.gov.uk

Housing: Ms Kim Brear, Assistant Director of Streetscene & Housing, Civic Centre 1, 4th Floor South, High Street, Huddersfield HD1 2NF ☎ 01484 221487 📠 01484 221250 ✉ kim.brear@kirklees.gov.uk

Housing Maintenance: Mr Noel Chambers, Director of Investment, Kirklees Neighbourhood Housing, Perseverance House, St Andrew's Road, Huddersfield HD1 6RY ☎ 01484 416648 ✉ noel.chambers@kirklees.gov.uk

Local Area Agreement: Ms Julie Fothergill, Policy Unit Manager, Civic Centre 3, Market Street, Huddersfield HD1 1WG ☎ 01484 221783 ✉ julie.fothergill@kirklees.gov.uk

Legal: Ms Vanessa Redfern, Assistant Director of Legal, Governance & Monitoring, 2nd Floor, Civic Centre 3, Market Street, Huddersfield HD1 2TG ☎ 01484 221720 ✉ vanessa.redfern@kirklees.gov.uk

Leisure and Cultural Services: Ms Kimiyo Rickett, Assistant Director of Communities & Leisure, The Stadium Business and Leisure Complex, Stadium Way, Huddersfield HD1 6PG ☎ 01484 234002 📠 01484 234014 ✉ kimiyo.rickett@kirklees.gov.uk

Licensing: Mr Peter Swallow, Acting Licensing Manager, Queensgate Market, Princess Alexandra Walk, Huddersfield HD1 2UJ 📠 01484 223465 ✉ peter.swallow@kirklees.gov.uk

Lifelong Learning: Mr John Edwards, Assistant Director of Learning, Ground Floor, Civic Centre 1, High Street, Huddersfield HD1 2NF ☎ 01484 416678 ✉ john.edwards@kirklees.gov.uk

Lighting: Mr Richard Bunney, Highway Network Manager, Flint Street, Fartown, Huddersfield HD1 6LG ☎ 01484 225519 📠 01484 225599 ✉ richard.bunney@kirklees.gov.uk

Member Services: Ms Vanessa Redfern, Assistant Director of Legal, Governance & Monitoring, 2nd Floor, Civic Centre 3, Market Street, Huddersfield HD1 2TG ☎ 01484 221720 ✉ vanessa.redfern@kirklees.gov.uk

Parking: Mr Neil Tootill, Operational Manager, Corporation Yard, Mayman Lane, Batley WF17 7TA ☎ 01484 222858 ✉ neil.tootill@kirklees.gov.uk

Partnerships: Mr Ken Gillespie, Director of Place, Civic Centre 3, Market Street, Huddersfield HD1 2TG ☎ 01484 221641 📠 01484 221645 ✉ ken.gillespie@kirklees.gov.uk

Planning: Mr Andrew Pennington, Assistant Director of Commissioning & Safeguarding Assurance, Ground Floor, Civic Centre 1, High Street, Huddersfield HD1 2NF ☎ 01484 225284 ✉ andrew.pennington@kirklees.gov.uk

Planning: Mr Keith Smith, Assistant Director of Personalisation & Commissioning, Gateway to Care, 3rd Floor, Market Street, Huddersfield HD1 2HG ☎ 01484 225321 ✉ keith.smith@kirklees.gov.uk

Procurement: Ms Joanne Bartholomew, Assistant Director of Physical Resources & Procurement, Kirkgate Buildings, Byram Street, Huddersfield HD1 1BY ☎ 01484 226052 ✉ joanne.bartholomew@kirklees.gov.uk

Public Libraries: Ms Kimiyo Rickett, Assistant Director of Communities & Leisure, The Stadium Business and Leisure Complex, Stadium Way, Huddersfield HD1 6PG ☎ 01484 234002 📠 01484 234014 ✉ kimiyo.rickett@kirklees.gov.uk

Recycling & Waste Minimisation: Mr Dave McMahon, Environmental Projects Manager, Vine Street Depot, Leeds Road, Huddersfield HD1 6NT ☎ 01484 223116 📠 01484 223155 ✉ dave.mcmahon@kirklees.gov.uk

Regeneration: Ms Jacqui Gedman, Interim Director of Place, Civic Centre 3, Market Street, Huddersfield HD1 1WG ☎ 01484 221641 📠 01484 221645 ✉ jacqui.gedman@kirklees.gov.uk

Road Safety: Ms Cath Bottomley, Unit Manager - Business Support, Flint Street, Fartown, Huddersfield HD1 6LG ☎ 01484 225552 ✉ cath.bottomley@kirklees.gov.uk

Social Services: Mr Paul Johnson, Assistant Director of Family Support & Protection Services, Ground Floor, Civic Centre 1, High Street, Huddersfield HD1 2NF ☎ 01484 225331 📠 01484 225188 ✉ paul.johnson@kirklees.gov.uk

Social Services (Adult): Ms Sally McIvor, Assistant Director of Well-being & Integration, Gateway to Care, 3rd Floor, Market Street, Huddersfield HD1 2HG ☎ 01484 225145 ✉ sally.mcivor@kirklees.gov.uk

Social Services (Children): Mrs Alison O'Sullivan, Director for Children & Young People, Ground Floor, Civic Centre 1, High Street, Huddersfield HD1 2NF ☎ 01484 225242 📠 01484 225237 ✉ alison.o'sullivan@kirklees.gov.uk

Staff Training: Ms Heather Paul, Corporate Learning & Development Manager, Corporate HR Service, Oldgate House, 2 Oldgate, Huddersfield HD1 6QW ☎ 01484 416209 📠 01484 225217 ✉ heather.paul@kirklees.gov.uk

Street Scene: Ms Kim Brear, Assistant Director of Streetscene & Housing, Civic Centre 1, 4th Floor South, High Street, Huddersfield HD1 2NF ☎ 01484 221487 📠 01484 221250 ✉ kim.brear@kirklees.gov.uk

Sustainable Communities: Ms Karen Johnson, Head of Safer Stronger Communities, The Deighton Centre, Deighton Road, Huddersfield HD2 1JP ☎ 01484 221109 ✉ karen.johnson@kirklees.gov.uk

Tourism: Ms Jess Newbould, Senior Tourism Officer, Economic Development Service, Civic Centre 3, Huddersfield HD1 2EY ☎ 01484 221675 ✉ jess.newbould@kirklees.gov.uk

Town Centre: Ms Jayne Pearson, Town Centre Manager, Queensgate Market, Princess Alexandra Walk, Huddersfield HD1 2SU ☎ 01484 223357 ✉ jayne.pearson@kirklees.gov.uk

Waste Collection and Disposal: Mr Roger Wilson, Head of

Waste, Recycling & Transport, Riverbank Court, Wakefield Road, Huddersfield HD5 9AA ☎ 01484 223146 🖷 01484 223155
✉ roger.wilson@kirklees.gov.uk

MEMBERS OF THE COUNCIL (69)

***Mayor:* Ridgway**, David (LD - Colne Valley)
david.ridgway@kirklees.gov.uk

***Deputy Mayor:* Bolt**, Martyn (CON - Mirfield)
martyn.bolt@kirklees.gov.uk

***Leader of the Council:* Khan**, Mehboob (LAB - Greenhead)
mehboob.khan@kirklees.gov.uk

***Group Leader:* Cooper**, Andrew (IND - Newsome)
andrew.cooper@kirklees.gov.uk

***Group Leader:* Dodds**, Jim (CON - Denby Dale)
jim.dodds@kirklees.gov.uk

***Group Leader:* Light**, Robert (CON - Birstall and Birkenshaw)
robert.light@kirklees.gov.uk

***Group Leader:* Pinnock**, Kath (LD - Cleckheaton)
kath.pinnock@kirklees.gov.uk

Ahmed, Masood (LAB - Dewsbury South)
masoodg.ahmed@kirklees.gov.uk

Akhtar, Mahmood (LAB - Batley East)
mahmood.akhtar@kirklees.gov.uk

Barraclough, Robert (IND - Kirkburton)
robertw.barraclough@kirklees.gov.uk

Bates, Margaret (CON - Liversedge and Gomersal)
margaret.bates@kirklees.gov.uk

Bellamy, Donna (CON - Colne Valley)
donna.bellamy@kirklees.gov.uk

Blanchard, James (LD - Almondbury)
james.blanchard@kirklees.gov.uk

Brice, Tony (CON - Lindley)
tony.brice@kirklees.gov.uk

Burke, Cahal (LD - Lindley)
cahal.burke@kirklees.gov.uk

Calvert, Jean (LAB - Ashbrow)
jean.calvert@kirklees.gov.uk

Firth, Eric (LAB - Dewsbury East)
eric.firth@kirklees.gov.uk

Firth, Donald (CON - Holme Valley South)
donald.firth@kirklees.gov.uk

Greaves, Charles (IND - Holme Valley North)
charles.greaves@kirklees.gov.uk

Hall, Steve (LAB - Heckmondwike)
steve.hall@kirklees.gov.uk

Hall, David (CON - Liversedge and Gomersal)
david.hall@kirklees.gov.uk

Hardcastle, Derek (IND - Kirkburton)
derek.hardcastle@kirklees.gov.uk

Harris, Cath (LAB - Ashbrow)
cath.harris@kirklees.gov.uk

Hemingway, Mark (CON - Lindley)
mark.hemingway@kirklees.gov.uk

Holmes, Lisa (CON - Liversedge and Gomersal)
lisa.holmes@kirklees.gov.uk

Holroyd-Doveton, Edgar (IND - Holme Valley North)
edgar.holroyd-doveton@kirklees.gov.uk

Hughes, Judith (LAB - Greenhead)
judith.hughes@kirklees.gov.uk

Hussain, Mumtaz (LAB - Dewsbury West)
mumtaz.hussain@kirklees.gov.uk

Kane, Paul (LAB - Dewsbury East)
paul.kane@kirklees.gov.uk

Kendrick, Viv (LAB - Heckmondwike)
viv.kendrick@kirklees.gov.uk

Lawson, John Craig (LD - Cleckheaton)
john.lawson@kirklees.gov.uk

Lees-Hamilton, Vivien (CON - Mirfield)
vivien.lees-hamilton@kirklees.gov.uk

Lowe, Gwen (LAB - Batley West)
gwen.lowe@kirklees.gov.uk

Lyons, Terry (IND - Holme Valley North)
terry.lyons@kirklees.gov.uk

Marchington, Andrew (LD - Golcar)
andrew.marchington@kirklees.gov.uk

Mather, Naheed (LAB - Dalton)
naheed.mather@kirklees.gov.uk

Mayet, Hanif (LAB - Batley East)
hanif.mayet@kirklees.gov.uk

McBride, Peter (LAB - Dalton)
peter.mcbride@kirklees.gov.uk

O'Donovan, Darren (LAB - Dewsbury West)
darren.odonovan@kirklees.gov.uk

O'Neill, Peter (LAB - Batley West)
peter.o'neill@kirklees.gov.uk

Palfreeman, Andrew (CON - Birstall and Birkenshaw)
andrew.palfreeman@kirklees.gov.uk

Pandor, Shabir (LAB - Batley West)
shabir.pandor@kirklees.gov.uk

Patel, Abdul (LAB - Dewsbury South)
abdul.patel@kirklees.gov.uk

Patel, Salim (CON - Dewsbury South)
salim.patel@kirklees.gov.uk

Patrick, Nigel (CON - Holme Valley South)
nigel.patrick@kirklees.gov.uk

Pattison, Carole (LAB - Crosland Moor and Netherton)
carole.pattison@kirklees.gov.uk

Pinnock, Andrew (LD - Cleckheaton)
andrew.pinnock@kirklees.gov.uk

Preest, Cliff (LAB - Dalton)
cliff.preest@kirklees.gov.uk

Richards, Hilary (LAB - Golcar)
hilary.richards@kirklees.gov.uk

Rowling, Karen (LAB - Dewsbury West)
karen.rowling@kirklees.gov.uk

Salveson, Paul (LAB - Golcar)
paul.salveson@kirklees.gov.uk

Sarwar, Mohammad (LAB - Crosland Moor and Netherton)
mohammad.sarwar@kirklees.gov.uk

Scott, Phil (LD - Almondbury)
phil.scott@kirklees.gov.uk

Scott, Cathy (LAB - Dewsbury East)
cathy.scott@kirklees.gov.uk

Sheard, David (LAB - Heckmondwike)
david.sheard@kirklees.gov.uk

Simpson, Graham (GRN - Newsome)
graham.simpson@kirklees.gov.uk

Sims, Ken (CON - Holme Valley South)
kenneth.sims@kirklees.gov.uk

Smaje, Liz (CON - Birstall and Birkenshaw)
elizabeth.smaje@kirklees.gov.uk

Smith, Ken (LAB - Ashbrow)
ken.smith@kirklees.gov.uk

Smith, Christine (CON - Kirkburton)
christine.smith@kirklees.gov.uk

Sokhal, Mohan (LAB - Greenhead)
mohan.sokhal@kirklees.gov.uk

Stewart-Turner, Julie (GRN - Newsome)
julie.stewart-turner@kirklees.gov.uk

Stubley, Amanda (LAB - Batley East)

amanda.stubley@kirklees.gov.uk
Taylor, Kathleen (CON - Mirfield)
kath.taylor@kirklees.gov.uk
Turner, Nicola (LD - Colne Valley)
nicola.turner@kirklees.gov.uk
Turner, Graham (LAB - Denby Dale)
graham.turner@kirklees.gov.uk
Walton, Molly (LAB - Crosland Moor and Netherton)
molly.walton@kirklees.gov.uk
Ward, Elaine (CON - Denby Dale)
elaine.ward@kirklees.gov.uk
Wilkinson, Linda (LD - Almondbury)
linda.wilkinson@kirklees.gov.uk

POLITICAL COMPOSITION

LAB: 32, CON: 19, LD: 10, IND: 6, GRN: 2

CABINET

Leader: Mr Mehboob Khan
Deputy Leader/ Resources: Mr David Sheard
Children's Services: Ms Cath Harris
Children's Services: Mr Peter O'Neill
Health, Wellbeing & Communities: Ms Jean Calvert
Health, Wellbeing & Communities: Ms Molly Walton
Place (Investment & Housing): Mr Peter McBride
Place (Investment & Housing): Ms Cathy Scott
Resources: Mr Shabir Pandor

COMMITTEE CHAIRS

Children & Young People Overview & Scrutiny: Mr Cahal Burke
Development & Environment Overview & Scrutiny: Mr Ken Sims
Resources Overview & Scrutiny: Mr Donald Firth
Wellbeing & Communitites Overview & Scrutiny: Ms Viv Kendrick

KNOWSLEY M

Knowsley Metropolitan Borough Council, Municipal Buildings, Archway Road, Huyton L36 9UX ☎ 0151 489 6000 🖷 0151 443 3507 🖳 www.knowsley.gov.uk

FACTS & FIGURES

Police Authority: Merseyside Police Authority
Health Authority: North West Strategic Health Authority
Learning and Skills Council: North West
Parliamentary Constituencies: Garston and Halewood, Knowsley
EU Constituencies: North West
Election Frequency: Elections are by thirds
Twinning: Stadt Moers (Germany), Friendship Agreement with Montana (Bulgaria).

PRINCIPAL OFFICERS

Chief Executive: Ms Sheena Ramsey, Chief Executive Knowsley MBC, MD NHS Knowsley and Interim Director of Children & Families Services, PO Box 21, Municipal Buildings, Archway Road, Huyton L36 9YU ☎ 0151 443 3772 🖷 0151 443 3030

Deputy Chief Executive: Mr Mike Harden, Deputy Chief Executive, PO Box 24, Municipal Buildings, Archway Road, Huyton L36 9UX ☎ 0151 443 3566 🖷 0151 443 3557 mike.harden@knowsley.gov.uk

Senior Management: Mr David Coulson, Executive Director - Neighbourhood Services, Municipal Buildings, Archway Road, Huyton L36 9UX ☎ 0151 443 3009 david.coulson@knowsley.gov.uk

Senior Management: Mr Mike Harden, Deputy Chief Executive, PO Box 24, Municipal Buildings, Archway Road, Huyton L36 9UX ☎ 0151 443 3566 🖷 0151 443 3557 mike.harden@knowsley.gov.uk

Architect, Building / Property Services: Mr Stuart Barnes, Head of Planning, Housing & Transportation, PO Box 26, Municipal Buildings, Archway Road, Huyton L36 9FB ☎ 0151 443 2303 stuart.barnes@knowsley.gov.uk

Architect, Building / Property Services: Mr Ian Capper, Head of Property Asset Management & Construction, Municipal Buildings, Archway Road, Huyton L36 9UX ☎ 0151 443 2323 ian.capper@knowsley.gov.uk

Building Control: Mr Geoff Baskett, Development Control Manager, Yorkon Building, Archway Road, Huyton L36 9FB ☎ 0151 443 2362 geoff.baskett@knowsley.gov.uk

Catering Services: Mrs Julie Mallon, Head of Commercial Services, Stretton Way, Archway Road, Huyton L36 6JF ☎ 0151 443 2410 🖷 0151 443 2467 julie.mallon@knowsley.gov.uk

Civil Registration: Ms Pauline Douglas, Superintendent Registrar, Council Offices, High Street, Prescot L34 3LH ☎ 0151 443 5299 pauline.douglas@knowsley.gov.uk

Community Planning: Mr Justin Thompson, Service Director - Neighbourhoods, PO Box 21, Municipal Buildings, Archway Road, Huyton L36 9YU ☎ 0151 443 3397 🖷 0151 443 3030 justin.thompson@knowsley.gov.uk

Community Safety: Mr Mark Harrison, Head of Crime & Disorder Strategy Unit, Municipal Buildings, Archway Road, Huyton L36 9UX ☎ 0151 443 3930 🖷 0151 443 3077 mark.harrison@knowsley.gov.uk

Community Safety: Mr Paul Johnson, Head of Police Support Unit, West House, Mercury Court, Tithebarn Street, Liverpool L69 2UN ☎ 0151 489 6000 paul.johnson@knowsley.gov.uk

Computer Management: Mr Andrew Garden, Head of IT, Civic Way, Westmoreland Road, Huyton L36 9GD ☎ 0151 443 3487 🖷 0151 4433814 andrew.garden@knowsley.gov.uk

Consumer Protection and Trading Standards: Mr Mike Leyden, Trading Standards Manager, Municipal Buildings, Cherryfield Drive, Kirkby L32 1TX ☎ 0151 443 4744 mike.leyden@knowsley.gov.uk

Contracts: Ms Deborah Lee, Assistant Borough Treasurer, Exchequer Services, Kirkby Municipal Buildings, Cherryfield Drive, Kirkby L32 1TX ☎ 0151 443 4126 🖷 0151 443 5407 deborah.lee@knowsley.gov.uk

Corporate Services: Mrs Dawn Boyer, Service Director - Business Transformation, Nutgrove Villa, Westmorland Road, Huyton, Liverpool L36 6GA ☎ 0151 443 3476 ✉ dawn.boyer@knowsley.gov.uk

Corporate Services: Ms Nita Cresswell, Director - Community Services Commissioning, Nutgrove Villa, Westmorland Road, Huyton, Liverpool L36 6GA ☎ 0151 443 3448 ✉ nita.cresswell@knowsley.gov.uk

Customer Service: Mr Phil Aspinall, One Stop Shop Manager, Municipal Buildings, Archway Road, Huyton L36 9UX ☎ 0151 443 3378 ✉ phil.aspinall@knowsley.gov.uk

Economic Development: Mr Barry Fawcett, Head of Business Liasion & Investment, Yorkon Building, Archway Road, Huyton L36 9UX ☎ 0151 443 2251 ✉ barry.fawcett@knowsley.gov.uk

E-Government: Mr Andrew Garden, Head of IT, Civic Way, Westmoreland Road, Huyton L36 9GD ☎ 0151 443 3487 🖷 0151 4433814 ✉ andrew.garden@knowsley.gov.uk

Electoral Registration: Ms Cheryl Ryder, Elections Officer, Democratic Services, Municipal Buildings, Archway Road, Huyton L36 9UX ☎ 0151 489 6000

Emergency Planning: Mr Brian Toolan, Head of Risk & Resilience, Civic Way, Westmorland Road, Huyton L36 9GD ☎ 0151 443 3601 ✉ brian.toolan@knowsley.gov.uk

Energy Management: Mr John Burns, Energy Consrvation Officer, Municipal Buildings, Archway Road, Huyton L36 9UX ☎ 0151 443 2201 ✉ john.burns@knowsley.gov.uk

Environmental / Technical Services: Mr John Flaherty, Service Director Environmental Services & Sustainability, Stretton Way, Archway Road, Huyton L36 6JF ☎ 0151 443 2410 🖷 0151 443 2467 ✉ john.flaherty@knowsley.gov.uk

Environmental Health: Ms Tracy Dickinson, Head of Environmental Health & Consumer Protection, Kirkby Municipal Buildings, Cherryfield Drive, Kirkby L32 1TX ☎ 0151 443 4732 🖷 0151 289 7488 ✉ tracy.dickinson@knowsley.gov.uk

Facilities: Mrs Julie Mallon, Head of Commercial Services, Stretton Way, Archway Road, Huyton L36 6JF ☎ 0151 443 2410 🖷 0151 443 2467 ✉ julie.mallon@knowsley.gov.uk

Finance and Treasurer: Mr James Duncan, Borough Treasurer, PO Box 24, Municipal Buildings, Archway Road, Huyton L36 9YZ ☎ 0151 443 3407 🖷 0151 443 3661 ✉ james.duncan@knowsley.gov.uk

Fleet Management: Mr Andy Millar, Transportation, Road Safety & Travel Plans Manager, PO Box 26, Municipal Buildings, Archway Road, Huyton L36 9FB ☎ 0151 443 2235 ✉ andy.millar@knowsley.gov.uk

Fleet Management: Mr Damian Walshe, Head of Fleet & Logistics, Stretton Way, Archway Road, Huyton L36 6JF ☎ 0151 443 2416 🖷 0151 443 2457 ✉ damian.walshe@knowsley.gov.uk

Grounds Maintenance: Mr David Barkley, Street Scene Operations Manager, Stretton Way, Archway Road, Huthwaite L36 6JF ☎ 0151 443 2829 🖷 0151 443 2447 ✉ dave.barkley@knowsley.gov.uk

Health and Safety: Mr Mike Williams, Principal Court Health & Safety Advisor, PO Box 24, Municipal Buildings, Archway Road, Huyton L36 9YZ ☎ 0151 443 3611 🖷 0151 4433661 ✉ mike.williams@knowsley.gov.uk

Highways: Mr Andy Millar, Transportation, Road Safety & Travel Plans Manager, PO Box 26, Municipal Buildings, Archway Road, Huyton L36 9FB ☎ 0151 443 2235 ✉ andy.millar@knowsley.gov.uk

Home Energy Conservation: Mr John Burns, Energy Consrvation Officer, Municipal Buildings, Archway Road, Huyton L36 9UX ☎ 0151 443 2201 ✉ john.burns@knowsley.gov.uk

Housing: Ms Steph Byrne, Head of Regeneration, PO Box 26, Municipal Buildings, Archway Road, Huyton L36 9FB ☎ 0151 443 5960 ✉ steph.byrne@knowsley.gov.uk

Local Area Agreement: Mr Justin Thompson, Service Director - Neighbourhood Delivery, PO Box 21, Municipal Buildings, Archway Road, Huyton L36 9YU ☎ 0151 443 3397 🖷 0151 4433030 ✉ justin.thompson@knowsley.gov.uk

Legal: Mr Mike Dearing, Head of Legal Services, PO Box 21, Municipal Buildings, Archway Road, Huyton L36 9YU ☎ 0151 443 3762 ✉ mike.dearing@knowsley.gov.uk

Leisure and Cultural Services: Mr Derek Jones, Leisure & Culture Operations, Leisure & Culture Park, Longview Drive, Huyton L36 6EG ☎ 0151 443 3470 ✉ derek.jones@knowsley.gov.uk

Leisure and Cultural Services: Mr Andrew McCormick, Service Director - Leisure & Culture, 1st Floor, Nutgrove Villa, Westmorland Road, Huyton L36 6GA ☎ 0151 443 3951 ✉ andrew.mccormick@knowsley.gov.uk

Leisure and Cultural Services: Ms Paula Williams, Head of Leisure & Culture Development, Nutgrove Villa, Westmorland Road, Huyton L36 6GA ☎ 0151 443 3468 ✉ paula.williams@knowsley.gov.uk

Licensing: Mr Alan Shone, Consumer Protection Manager, Municipal Buildings, Cherryfield Drive, Kirkby L32 1TX ☎ 0151 443 2789 🖷 0151 443 5438 ✉ alan.shone@knowsley.gov.uk

Lighting: Ms Sue Callister, Team Leader of Lighting, PO Box 26, Municipal Buildings, Archway Road, Huyton L36 9FB ☎ 0151 443 5819 ✉ susan.callister@knowsley.gov.uk

Member Services: Ms Yvonne Ledgerton, Head of Democratic Services, PO Box 21, Municipal Buildings, Archway Road, Huyton L36 9UX ☎ 0151 443 3609 🖷 0151 482 1262 ✉ yvonne.ledgerton@knowsley.gov.uk

Partnerships: Mr Justin Thompson, Service Director - Neighbourhoods, PO Box 21, Municipal Buildings, Archway Road,

Huyton L36 9YU ☎ 0151 443 3397 🖷 0151 4433030
✉ justin.thompson@knowsley.gov.uk

Personnel / HR: Mr Dave Turner, Head of Human Resources, Civic Way, Westmorland Road, Huyton L36 9GD ☎ 0151 443 2951
✉ dave.turner@knowsley.gov.uk

Planning: Mr Stuart Barnes, Head of Planning, Housing & Transportation, PO Box 26, Municipal Buildings, Archway Road, Huyton L36 9FB ☎ 0151 443 2303
✉ stuart.barnes@knowsley.gov.uk

Procurement: Mr Ian Capper, Head of Property Asset Management & Construction, Municipal Buildings, Archway Road, Huyton L36 9UX ☎ 0151 443 2323
✉ ian.capper@knowsley.gov.uk

Procurement: Mr Kevin McGlone, Assistant Borough Treasurer, Exchequer Services, Kirkby Municipal Buildings, Cherryfield Drive, Kirkby L32 1TX ☎ 0151 443 5400 🖷 0151 443 5407
✉ kevin.mcglone@knowsley.gov.uk

Public Libraries: Mr Peter Marchant, Head of Libraries Services, Huyton Library, Civic Way, Huyton L36 9GD ☎ 0151 443 3680
🖷 0151 443 3729 ✉ peter.marchant@knowsley.gov.uk

Recycling & Waste Minimisation: Mr Jon Dyson, Head of Waste & Streetscene, Stretton Way, Archway Road, Huyton L36 6JF ☎ 0151 443 2415 🖷 01514 432467
✉ jon.dyson@knowsley.gov.uk

Regeneration: Ms Lisa Harris, Service Director - Regeneration, Economy & Skills, Yorkon Building, Archway Road, Huyton L36 9FB ☎ 0151 443 2377 ✉ lisa.harris@knowsley.gov.uk

Road Safety: Mr Andy Millar, Transportation, Road Safety & Travel Plans Manager, PO Box 26, Municipal Buildings, Archway Road, Huyton L36 9FB ☎ 0151 443 2235
✉ andy.millar@knowsley.gov.uk

Social Services (Adult): Ms Jan Coulter, Director of Health & Social Care, PO Box 23, Nutgrove Villa, Westmoorland Road, L36 6GA ☎ 0151 443 3440 🖷 0151 443 3670
✉ jan.coulter@knowsley.gov.uk

Social Services (Children): Ms Kitty Ferris, Service Director - Safeguarding & Specialist Services, Municipal Buildings, Archway Road, Huyton L36 9UX ☎ 0151 443 3244 🖷 0151 443 5627
✉ kitty.ferris@knowsley.gov.uk

Staff Training: Ms Sue Williams, Workforce & Business Manager, Municipal Buildings, Archway Road, Huyton L36 9UX
☎ 0151 443 2706 🖷 0151 480 4411
✉ sue.c.williams@knowsley.gov.uk

Street Scene: Mr Jon Dyson, Head of Waste & Streetscene, Stretton Way, Archway Road, Huyton L36 6JF ☎ 0151 443 2415
🖷 01514 432467 ✉ jon.dyson@knowsley.gov.uk

Sustainable Communities: Mr Philip Monaghan, Head of Sustainable Resources, Stretton Way, Archway Road, Huyton L36 6JF ☎ 0151 443 2835 ✉ philip.monaghan@knowsley.gov.uk

Sustainable Development: Mr Philip Monaghan, Head of Sustainable Resources, Stretton Way, Archway Road, Huyton L36 6JF ☎ 0151 443 2835 ✉ philip.monaghan@knowsley.gov.uk

Tourism: Ms Alison Riley, Creative Industries Manager, Municipal Buildings, Archway Road, Huyton L36 9UX ☎ 0151 443 5592
✉ alison.riley@knowsley.gov.uk

Town Centre: Mr Dale Milburn, Head of Property Development, PO Box 26, Municipal Buildings, Archway Road, Huyton L36 9FB
☎ 0151 443 2290 ✉ dale.milburn@knowsley.gov.uk

Traffic Management: Mr Sean Traynor, Group Manager - Site Development & Traffic Management, Municipal Buildings, Archway Road, Huyton L36 9UX ☎ 0151 443 2332
✉ sean.traynor@knowsley.gov.uk

Transport: Mr Andy Millar, Transportation, Road Safety & Travel Plans Manager, PO Box 26, Municipal Buildings, Archway Road, Huyton L36 9FB ☎ 0151 443 2235
✉ andy.millar@knowsley.gov.uk

Waste Management: Mr Jon Dyson, Head of Waste & Streetscene, Stretton Way, Archway Road, Huyton L36 6JF
☎ 0151 443 2415 🖷 01514 432467 ✉ jon.dyson@knowsley.gov.uk

MEMBERS OF THE COUNCIL (63)

***Mayor:* Hogg**, Norman (LAB - Halewood West)
norman.hogg@knowsley.gov.uk
***Leader of the Council:* Round**, Ron (LAB - Swanside)
ron.round@knowsley.gov.uk
Allen, Denise (LAB - Prescot East)
denise.allen@knowsley.gov.uk
Arnall, Del (LAB - Park)
del.arnall@knowsley.gov.uk
Arnall, Shannon (LAB - Prescot East)
shannon.arnall@knowsley.gov.uk
Arnall, Robert (LAB - Prescot West)
robert.arnall@knowsley.gov.uk
Aston, Jayne (LAB - Cherryfield)
jayne.aston@knowsley.gov.uk
Bannon, Christine (LAB - Roby)
christine.bannon@knowsley.gov.uk
Baum, Dennis (LAB - Stockbridge)
dennis.baum@knowsley.gov.uk
Boland, Peter (LAB - St Gabriel's)
peter.boland@knowsley.gov.uk
Brennan, Bill (LAB - Kirby Central)
bill.brennan@knowsley.gov.uk
Byron, Terry (LAB - Whiston South)
terry.byron@knowsley.gov.uk
Connor, Edward (LAB - Northwood)
eddie.connor@knowsley.gov.uk
Cunningham, Tony (LAB - St Bartholomew's)
tony.cunningham@knowsley.gov.uk
Dobbie, Dave (LAB - Park)
dave.dobbie@knowsley.gov.uk
Fearns, Thomas (LAB - Halewood West)
tommy.fearns@knowsley.gov.uk
Finneran, Edna (LAB - Halewood North)
edna.finneran@knowsley.gov.uk
Gaffney, Sandra (LAB - Whiston North)
sandra.gaffney@knowsley.gov.uk

Gaffney, Ron (LAB - Whiston North)
ron.gaffney@knowsley.gov.uk
Garland, Terence (LAB - Northwood)
terence.garland@knowsley.gov.uk
Grannell, Ted (LAB - Cherryfield)
ted.grannell@knowsley.gov.uk
Greer, John (LAB - Park)
john.greer@knowsley.gov.uk
Grierson, Thomas (LAB - Shevington)
thomas.grierson@knowsley.gov.uk
Halpin, Ray (LAB - Shevington)
ray.halpin@knowsley.gov.uk
Harris, Jackie (LAB - Kirkby Central)
jackie.harris@knowsley.gov.uk
Harris, Tina (LAB - Halewood South)
tina.harris@knowsley.gov.uk
Harvey, Allan (LAB - Halewood South)
allan.harvey@knowsley.gov.uk
Harvey, Margaret (LAB - St Bartholomew's)
margaret.harvey@knowsley.gov.uk
Harvey, Tony (LAB - Longview)
tony.harvey@knowsley.gov.uk
Kearns, Mike (LAB - Prescot West)
mike.kearns@knowsley.gov.uk
Keats, Jean (LAB - Whitefield)
jean.keats@knowsley.gov.uk
Keats, Norman (LAB - Whitefield)
norman.keats@knowsley.gov.uk
Keith, Ken (LAB - St Michael's)
ken.keith@knowsley.gov.uk
Kelly, Pauline (LAB - Whiston North)
pauline.kelly@knowsley.gov.uk
Lee, Samuel (LAB - Longview)
sammy.lee@knowsley.gov.uk
Lilly, Joan (LAB - St Michael's)
joan.lilly@knowsley.gov.uk
Lonergan, David (LAB - Cherryfield)
david.lonergan@knowsley.gov.uk
Maguire, Bob (LAB - Swanside)
bob.maguire@knowsley.gov.uk
Mcegan, Derek (LAB - Prescot East)
derek.mcegan@knowsley.gov.uk
McGlashan, Ken (LAB - Page Moss)
ken.mcglashan@knowsley.gov.uk
McNeill, Veronica (LAB - Page Moss)
veronica.mcneill@knowsley.gov.uk
Moorhead, Kay (LAB - St Michael's)
kay.moorhead@knowsley.gov.uk
Moorhead, Andy (LAB - St Bartholomew's)
andy.moorhead@knowsley.gov.uk
Morgan, Graham (LAB - Roby)
graham.morgan@knowsley.gov.uk
Murphy, Michael (LAB - Northwood)
michael.murphy@knowsley.gov.uk
Newman, Tony (LAB - Whiston South)
tony.newman@knowsley.gov.uk
O'Hare, Christina (LAB - Roby)
christina.ohare@knowsley.gov.uk
O'Hare, Brian (LAB - St Gabriel's)
brian.o'hare@knowsley.gov.uk
Powell, Terry (LAB - Halewood North)
terry.powell@knowsley.gov.uk
Powell, Shelley (LAB - Halewood North)
shelley.powell@knowsley.gov.uk
Reid, Diane (LAB - Longview)
diane.reid@knowsley.gov.uk
See, Gary (LAB - Halewood South)
gary.see@knowsley.gov.uk
Sharp, Malcolm (LAB - Shevington)
malcolm.sharp@knowsley.gov.uk
Smith, Ros (LAB - Whitefield)
ros.smith@knowsley.gov.uk
Stuart, Marie (LAB - Kirkby Central)
marie.stuart@knowsley.gov.uk
Swann, Bob (LAB - Halewood West)
bob.swann@knowsley.gov.uk
Tully, Dave (LAB - Page Moss)
dave.tully@knowsley.gov.uk
Walsh, Frank (LD - St Gabriel's)
frank.walsh@knowsley.gov.uk
Weightman, Heather (LAB - Stockbridge)
heather.weightman@knowsley.gov.uk
Weightman, Bill (LAB - Stockbridge)
bill.weightman@knowsley.gov.uk
Whiley, Bob (LAB - Prescot West)
bob.whiley@knowsley.gov.uk
Williams, David (LAB - Whiston South)
david.williams@knowsley.gov.uk
Wright, Graham (LAB - Swanside)
graham.wright@knowsley.gov.uk

POLITICAL COMPOSITION
LAB: 62, LD: 1

CABINET
Leader: Mr Ron Round
Children & Family Services: Mr Graham Wright
Community Safety & Social Inclusion: Mrs Jackie Harris
Corporate & Customer Services: Mr Ken Keith
Finance & IT: Mr Norman Keats
Health & Social Care: Ms Jayne Aston
Human Resources: Mr Ron Gaffney
Leisure, Community & Culture: Mr Edward Connor
Neighbourhood Delivery: Mr Graham Morgan
Regeneration, Economy & Skills: Mr David Lonergan

COMMITTEE CHAIRS
Appeals: Mrs Heather Weightman
Children & Families: Mr Graham Wright
Employment & Appeals: Mr Ron Round
Governance & Audit: Mr Bob Swann
Health & Wellbeing: Ms Jayne Aston
Human Resources Appeals: Mrs Jean Keats
Licensing: Mr Thomas Fearns
Overview & Scrutiny: Mr Bob Swann
Planning: Mrs Margaret Harvey
Town Centre Management: Mr Thomas Fearns

LAMBETH L

London Borough of Lambeth, Lambeth Town Hall, Brixton Hill, London SW2 1RW ☎ 020 7926 1000 🖳 www.lambeth.gov.uk

FACTS & FIGURES
Police Authority: Metropolitan Police Authority
Health Authority: NHS London
Learning and Skills Council: London
Parliamentary Constituencies: Dulwich and West Norwood,

Streatham, Vauxhall
EU Constituencies: London
Election Frequency: Elections are of whole council
Twinning: Bluefields (Nicaragua); Moskvoretsky (Russia); Spanish Town (Jamaica); Vincennes (France)

PRINCIPAL OFFICERS

Chief Executive: Mr Derrick Anderson, Chief Executive, Lambeth Town Hall, Brixton Hill, London SW2 1RW ☎ 020 7926 1000 ✉ danderson@lambeth.gov.uk

Senior Management: Mr Derrick Anderson, Chief Executive, Lambeth Town Hall, Brixton Hill, London SW2 1RW ☎ 020 7926 1000 ✉ danderson@lambeth.gov.uk

Senior Management: Ms Jo Cleary, Executive Director of Adults & Community Services, 6th Floor, Phoenix House, 10 Wandsworth Road, London SW8 2LL ☎ 020 7926 4787 🖷 020 7926 4783 ✉ jcleary@lambeth.gov.uk

Senior Management: Ms Debbie Jones, Executive Director of Children & Young People's Services, 7th Floor, International House, 6 Canterbury Crescent, London SW9 7QE ☎ 020 7926 9771 🖷 020 7926 9778

Senior Management: Mr Mike Suarez, Executive Director of Finance & Resources, Olive Morris House, 18 Brixton Hill, London SW2 1RL ☎ 020 7926 9337 🖷 020 7926 9748

Access Officer / Social Services (Disability): Mr Dominic Stanton, Assistant Director - Adult Social Care, 6th Floor, Phoenix House, 10 Wandsworth Road, London SW8 2LL ☎ 020 7926 4515 ✉ dstanton@lambeth.gov.uk

Architect, Building / Property Services: Mr Andy Gutherson, Interim Head of Development Management, Phoenix House, 10 Wandsworth Road, London SW8 2LL ☎ 020 7926 1109 🖷 020 7926 1155 ✉ agutherson@lambeth.gov.uk

Building Control: Mr Andy Gutherson, Interim Head of Development Management, Phoenix House, 10 Wandsworth Road, London SW8 2LL ☎ 020 7926 1109 🖷 020 7926 1155 ✉ agutherson@lambeth.gov.uk

Children / Youth Services: Ms Debbie Jones, Executive Director of Children & Young People's Services, Lambeth Town Hall, Brixton Hill, London SW2 1RW ☎ 020 7926 9771 🖷 020 7926 9778

PR / Communications: Mr Julian Ellerby, Divisional Director - Campaigns & Communications, Lambeth Town Hall, Brixton Hill, London SW2 1RW ☎ 020 7926 1273 🖷 020 7926 2839 ✉ jellerby@lambeth.gov.uk

Community Planning: Ms Alison Young, Divisional Director - Planning, Regeneration & Enterprise, Phoenix House, 10 Wandsworth Road, London SW8 2LL ☎ 020 7926 9225 🖷 020 7926 9778 ✉ ayoung5@lambeth.gov.uk

Community Safety: Ms Ann Corbett, Assistant Director - Community Safety, 205 Stockwell Road, Brixton, London SW9 9SL ☎ 020 7926 2898 ✉ acorbett@lambeth.gov.uk

Computer Management: Mr Ed Garcez, Divisional Director - ICT Services, Ivor House, 1 Acre Lane, London SW2 5BF ☎ 020 7926 0070 🖷 020 7926 2843 ✉ egarcez@lambeth.gov.uk

Consumer Protection and Trading Standards: Mr Robert Gardner, Head of Trading Standards, 2 Herne Hill Road, Brixton Hill, London SE24 0AU ☎ 020 7926 1000

Corporate Services: Ms S Looney, Divisional Director of Policy, Equalities & Performance, Lambeth Town Hall, Brixton Hill, London SW2 1RW ☎ 020 7926 2960 ✉ slooney@lambeth.gov.uk

Economic Development: Mr Leonard Igbodo, Energy Manager, Lambeth Town Hall, Brixton Hill, London SW2 1RW ☎ 020 7926 3591 ✉ ligbodo@lambeth.gov.uk

Education: Ms Debbie Jones, Executive Director of Children & Young People's Services, Lambeth Town Hall, Brixton Hill, London SW2 1RW ☎ 020 7926 9771 🖷 020 7926 9778

E-Government: Mr Ed Garcez, Head of IT Strategy & E-Government, Lambeth Town Hall, Brixton Hill, London SW2 1RW ☎ 020 7926 9133 🖷 020 7926 9104 ✉ egarcez@lambeth.gov.uk

Electoral Registration: Mr Len Lewis, Electoral Services Manager, Lambeth Town Hall, Brixton Hill, London SW2 1RW ☎ 020 7926 2307 🖷 020 7926 2688 ✉ llewis@lambeth.gov.uk

Emergency Planning: Mr Paul Randall, Emergency Response Planning Officer, Lambeth Town Hall, Brixton Hill, London SW2 1RW ☎ 020 7926 6148 🖷 020 7926 6150 ✉ prandall@lambeth.gov.uk

Energy Management: Mr Leonard Igbodo, Energy Manager, Lambeth Town Hall, Brixton Hill, London SW2 1RW ☎ 020 7926 3591 ✉ ligbodo@lambeth.gov.uk

Environmental / Technical Services: Ms Sue Foster, Executive Director - Housing, Regeneration & Environment, Hambrook House, Porden Road, London SW2 5RW ✉ sfoster1@lambeth.gov.uk

Estates, Property & Valuation: Mr Uzo Nwanze, Head of Assets Strategy, Lambeth Town Hall, Brixton Hill, London SW2 1RW ☎ 020 7926 9929 🖷 020 7926 9357 ✉ unwanze@lambeth.gov.uk

Finance and Treasurer: Mr Mike Suarez, Executive Director of Finance & Resources, Olive Morris House, London SW2 1WB ☎ 020 7926 9337 🖷 020 7926 9748

Highways: Mr Doug Perry, Head of Environmental Services & Highways, 1st Floor, Service Team House, 185 - 205 Shakespeare, London SE24 0PZ ☎ 020 7926 1255 ✉ dperry@lambeth.gov.uk

Home Energy Conservation: Mr Leonard Igbodo, Energy Manager, Lambeth Town Hall, Brixton Hill, London SW2 1RW ☎ 020 7926 3591 ✉ ligbodo@lambeth.gov.uk

Housing: Ms Sue Foster, Executive Director - Housing, Regeneration & Environment, Hambrook House, Porden Road, London SW2 5RW ✉ sfoster1@lambeth.gov.uk

Legal: Mr Mark Hynes, Director of Governance & Democracy, Lambeth Town Hall, Brixton Hill, London SW2 1RW ☎ 020 7926 2433

Leisure and Cultural Services: Ms Jo Cleary, Executive Director of Adults & Community Services, 3rd Floor, Phoenix House, 10 Wandsworth Road, London SW8 2LL ☎ 020 7926 4787 🖷 020 7926 4783 ✉ jcleary@lambeth.gov.uk

Licensing: Mr Dave Bright, Head of Consumer Protection & Sustainability, 2 Herne Hill Road, London SE24 0AU ☎ 020 7926 6131 🖷 020 7926 6130 ✉ dbright@lambeth.gov.uk

Member Services: Mr David Burn, Head of Democratic Services & Scrutiny, Lambeth Town Hall, Brixton Hill, London SW2 1RW ☎ 020 7926 2186 🖷 020 7929 2755 ✉ dburn@lambeth.gov.uk

Parking: Mr Raj Mistry, Head of Parking, 234 - 244 Stockwell Road, Brixton, London SW9 9SP ☎ 020 7926 6263 ✉ rmistry@lambeth.gov.uk

Personnel / HR: Ms Nana Amoa-Buahin, Divisional Director - HR & OD, Phoenix House, 10 Wandsworth Road, London SW2 1RW ☎ 020 7926 0068 🖷 020 7926 9518 ✉ namoa-buahin@lambeth.gov.uk

Regeneration: Ms Sue Foster, Executive Director - Housing, Regeneration & Environment, Hambrook House, Porden Road, London SW2 5RW ✉ sfoster1@lambeth.gov.uk

Regeneration: Ms Alison Young, Divisional Director - Planning, Regeneration & Enterprise, Phoenix House, 10 Wandsworth Road, London SW2 1RW ☎ 020 7926 9225 🖷 020 7926 9778 ✉ ayoung5@lambeth.gov.uk

Social Services (Adult): Ms Jo Cleary, Executive Director of Adults & Community Services, 3rd Floor, Phoenix House, 10 Wandsworth Road, London SW8 2LL ☎ 020 7926 4787 🖷 020 7926 4783 ✉ jcleary@lambeth.gov.uk

Social Services (Children): Ms Debbie Jones, Executive Director of Children & Young People's Services, International House, 6 Canterbury Crescent, London SW9 7QE ☎ 020 7926 9771 🖷 020 7926 9778

Street Scene: Mr Doug Perry, Head of Environmental Services & Highways, Lambeth Town Hall, Brixton Hill, London SW2 1RW ☎ 020 7926 1255 ✉ dperry@lambeth.gov.uk

MEMBERS OF THE COUNCIL (63)

***Mayor:* Bennett**, Clive (LD - St. Leonard's)
CllrCliveBennett@LambethLibDems.org.uk

***Deputy Mayor:* Bennett**, Mark (LAB - Streatham South)
MEbennett@lambeth.gov.uk

***Leader of the Council:* Reed**, Steve (LAB - Brixton Hill)
sreed@lambeth.gov.uk

***Deputy Leader of the Council:* Meldrum**, Jackie (LAB - Knight's Hill)
jmeldrum@lambeth.gov.uk

***Group Leader:* Lumsden**, Ashley (LD - Streatham Hill)
CllrAshleyLumsden@LambethLibDems.org.uk

Abrams, Kingsley (LAB - Vassall)
Kingsleyabrams@hotmail.com

Aminu, Adedamola (LAB - Tulse Hill)
aaminu@lambeth.gov.uk

Anyanwu, Donatus (LAB - Coldharbour)
DAnyanwu@lambeth.gov.uk

Barratt, Christine (LD - Clapham Common)
CllrChristineBarratt@LambethLibDems.org.uk

Bennett, Matthew (LAB - Gipsy Hill)
mpbennett@lambeth.gov.uk

Best, Judith (LD - Streatham Wells)
CllrJudyBest@LambethLibDems.org.uk

Bigham, Alex (LAB - Stockwell)
abigham@lambeth.gov.uk

Boucher, Carol (LAB - Herne Hill)
cboucher@lambeth.gov.uk

Bowyer, Peter (LAB - Stockwell)
pbowyer@lambeth.gov.uk

Bradley, Steve (LD - Vassall)
CllrSteveBradley@LambethLibDems.org.uk

Braithwaite, Diana (LD - Bishop's)
CllrDianaBraithwaite@LambethLibDems.org.uk

Brathwaite, Jennifer (LAB - Gipsy Hill)
jbrathwaite@lambeth.gov.uk

Brown, Ishabel (LD - Oval)
CllrIshbelBrown@LambethLibDems.org.uk

Cameron, Marcia (LAB - Tulse Hill)
mcameron@lambeth.gov.uk

Campbell, Lorna (LAB - Prince's)
lcampbell@lambeth.gov.uk

Clyne, Jeremy (LD - Streatham Hill)
CllrJeremyClyne@LambethLibDems.org.uk

Cosgrave, Shirley (CON - Clapham Common)
scosgrave@lambeth.gov.uk

Davie, Edward (LAB - Thornton)
edavie@lambeth.gov.uk

Davies, Alexander (LD - Streatham Wells)
CllrAlexDavies@LambethLibDems.org.uk

Dickson, Jim (LAB - Herne Hill)
jdickson@lambeth.gov.uk

Dodsworth, Gavin (LD - Bishop's)
CllrGavinDodsworth@LambethLibDems.org.uk

Edbrooke, Jane (LAB - Oval)
cllr.jane.edbrooke@gmail.com

Francis, Niranjan (LAB - Gipsy Hill)
nrfrancis@lambeth.gov.uk

Garden, Adrian (LAB - Vassall)
agarden@lambeth.gov.uk

Giess, Roger (LD - St. Leonard's)
CllrRogerGiess@LambethLibDems.org.uk

Harrison, Mark (LAB - Prince's)
mharrison@lambeth.gov.uk

Haselden, Nigel (LAB - Clapham Town)
nhaselden@lambeth.gov.uk

Heywood, Rachel (LAB - Coldharbour)
rheywood@lambeth.gov.uk

Holland, Alexander (LAB - Brixton Hill)
aholland@lambeth.gov.uk

Hopkins, Jack (LAB - Oval)
jhopkins@lambeth.gov.uk

Kazantzis, John (LAB - Streatham South)
JKazantzis@lambeth.gov.uk

Kingsbury, Ann (LAB - Thurlow Park)
akingsbury@lambeth.gov.uk

Ling, Ruth (LAB - Tulse Hill)
council.ruth@gmail.com

Malley, Dave (LAB - Streatham South)
DMalley@lambeth.gov.uk

Marchant, Daphne (LD - Streatham Wells)
CllrDaphneMarchant@LambethLibDems.org.uk
McGlone, Paul (LAB - Ferndale)
pmcglone@lambeth.gov.uk
Memery, Julia (CON - Clapham Common)
jmemery@lambeth.gov.uk
Morgan, Stephen (LAB - Prince's)
srmorgan@lambeth.gov.uk
Morris, Diana (LAB - Thornton)
dmmorris@lambeth.gov.uk
Nosegbe, Florence (LAB - Brixton Hill)
fnosegbe@lambeth.gov.uk
Ogden, Kita (LD - Streatham Hill)
CllrKitaOgden@LambethLibDems.org.uk
O'Malley, Helen (LAB - Clapham Town)
HOMalley@lambeth.gov.uk
Palmer, Brian (LD - St. Leonard's)
CllrBrianPalmer@LambethLibDems.org.uk
Parr, Matt (LAB - Coldharbour)
mparr1@lambeth.gov.uk
Patil, Neeraj (LAB - Larkhall)
npatil@lambeth.gov.uk
Peck, Lib (LAB - Thornton)
lpeck@lambeth.gov.uk
Pickard, Jane (LAB - Knight's Hill)
jpickard@lambeth.gov.uk
Prentice, Sally (LAB - Ferndale)
SPrentice@lambeth.gov.uk
Robbins, Peter (LAB - Larkhall)
probbins@lambeth.gov.uk
Sabharwal, Neil (LAB - Ferndale)
nsabharwal@lambeth.gov.uk
Smith, Mike (LAB - Knight's Hill)
msmith10@lambeth.gov.uk
Targett-Parker, Leanne (LAB - Herne Hill)
ltargett-parker@lambeth.gov.uk
Truesdale, Peter (LD - Bishop's)
CllrPeterTruesdale@LambethLibDems.org.uk
Valcarcel, Christiana (LAB - Larkhall)
cvalcarcel@lambeth.gov.uk
Walker, Imogen (LAB - Stockwell)
cllr.imogenwalker@gmail.com
Wellbelove, Christopher (LAB - Clapham Town)
cllrwellbelove@gmail.com
Whelan, Clare (CON - Thurlow Park)
cwhelan@lambeth.gov.uk
Whelan, John (CON - Thurlow Park)
jwhelan@lambeth.gov.uk

POLITICAL COMPOSITION

LAB: 44, LD: 15, CON: 4

CABINET

Leader: Mr Steve Reed
Deputy Leader: Ms Jackie Meldrum
Children & Families: Ms Rachel Heywood
Culture, Leisure and the Olympics: Ms Sally Prentice
Equalities & Communities: Ms Lorna Campbell
Finance & Resources: Mr Paul McGlone
Health & Wellbeing: Mr Jim Dickson
Neighbourhood Services: Mr Peter Robbins
Public Protection: Mr Jack Hopkins
Regeneration & Strategic Housing: Ms Lib Peck

LANCASHIRE — C

Lancashire County Council, PO Box 78, County Hall, Preston PR1 8XJ ☎ 0845 053 0000 🖷 01722 533553 ✉ enquiries@lancashire.gov.uk 🖳 www.lancashire.gov.uk

FACTS & FIGURES

Police Authority: Lancashire Police Authority
Health Authority: North West Strategic Health Authority
Learning and Skills Council: North West
Parliamentary Constituencies: Burnley, Chorley, Fylde, Hyndburn, Morecambe and Lunesdale, Pendle, Preston, Ribble Valley, Rossendale and Darwen, South Ribble
EU Constituencies: North West
Election Frequency: Elections are of whole council

PRINCIPAL OFFICERS

Chief Executive: Mr Phil Halsall, Chief Executive, PO Box 78, County Hall, Preston PR1 8XJ ✉ phill.halsall@lancashire.gov.uk

Assistant Chief Executive: Mr Eddie Sutton, Assistant Chief Executive, PO Box 78, County Hall, Preston PR1 8XJ ☎ 01772 535171 ✉ eddie.sutton@lancashire.gov.uk

Senior Management: Mr Steve Browne, Director of Strategy & Policy, PO Box 78, County Hall, Preston PR1 8XJ ☎ 01772 534121 🖷 01722 534178 ✉ steve.browne@lancashire.gov.uk

Senior Management: Ms Olive Carroll, Director of Personal Social Care, County Hall, Preston PR1 0LD ☎ 01772 534393 🖷 01772 534425 ✉ olive.carroll@lancashire.gov.uk

Senior Management: Mrs Helen Denton, Executive Director for Children & Young People, PO Box 61, County Hall, Preston PR1 8RJ ☎ 01772 531646 ✉ helen.denton@lancashire.gov.uk

Senior Management: Mr Ian Fisher, County Secretary & Solicitor, PO Box 78, County Hall, Preston PR1 8XJ ☎ 01772 533386 🖷 01772 535171 ✉ ian.fisher@lancashire.gov.uk

Senior Management: Mr Michael Hart, Director for Resources, Planning & Business Services, PO Box 78, County Hall, Preston PR1 8XJ ☎ 01772 31652 ✉ mike.hart@lancashire.gov.uk

Senior Management: Mr Richard Jones, Executive Director for Adult & Community Services, County Hall, Preston PR1 0LD ☎ 01772 534390 ✉ richard.jones@lancashire.gov.uk

Senior Management: Ms Faith Mann, Director for Targeted & Early Intervention Services, PO Box 78, County Hall, Preston PR1 8XJ ☎ 01772 534237

Senior Management: Ms Ann Pennell, Director for Targeted Assessment Services, PO Box 78, County Hall, Preston PR1 8XJ ☎ 01772 535237 ✉ ann.pennell@lancashire.gov.uk

Senior Management: Mr Bob Stott, Director for Universal & Early Support Services, PO Box 78, County Hall, Preston PR1 8XJ ☎ 01772 531652 ✉ bob.stott@lancashire.gov.uk

Senior Management: Ms Jo Turton, Executive Director for the Environment, PO Box 61, County Hall, Preston PR1 0LD ☎ 01772

534450 🖷 01772 533381 ✉ jo.turton@lancashire.gov.uk

Best Value: Mr Habib Patel, Head of Health & Wellbeing Partnership, PO Box 78, County Hall, Preston PR1 8XJ ☎ 01772 536099 ✉ habib.patel@lancashire.gov.uk

Building Control: Ms Clare Joynson, Facilities Manager, PO Box 100, County Hall, Preston PR1 0LD ☎ 01772 533403 ✉ clare.joynson@lancashire.gov.uk

Catering Services: Mr Nigel Finnamore, Director of Lancashire County Commercial Group, LCCG, Headquarters Office, Dewhurst Row, Bamber Bridge, Preston PR5 6BB ☎ 01772 536942 ✉ nigel.finnamore@lancashire.gov.uk

Catering Services: Ms Catherine Parker, Food & Beverage Manager, PO Box 61, County Hall, Preston PR1 0LD ☎ 01772 533342 ✉ catherine.parker@lancashire.gov.uk

Children / Youth Services: Mr Paul Armitage, Head of Children's Social Care, Chaddesley House, 155 Green Bank Street, Burnley BB11 1HW ☎ 01282 470138 ✉ paul.armitage@lancashire.gov.uk

Children / Youth Services: Mrs Helen Denton, Executive Director for Children & Young People, PO Box 61, County Hall, Preston PR1 8RJ ☎ 01772 531646 ✉ helen.denton@lancashire.gov.uk

Children / Youth Services: Ms Louise Taylor, Director of Specialist Services, PO Box 78, County Hall, Preston PR1 8XJ ☎ 01772 536126 ✉ louise.taylor@lancashire.gov.uk

Civil Registration: Mr Ian Watson, Head of Cultural Services, County Hall, Preston PR1 0LD ☎ 01772 534009 ✉ ian.watson@lancashire.gov.uk

PR / Communications: Mr Tim Seamans, Head of Communications, Corporate Communications Group, County Hall, Preston PR1 8XJ ☎ 01772 530760 🖷 01772 533553 ✉ tim.seamans@lancashire.gov.uk

Community Safety: Mr Tom Daniels, Head of Personal Social Care (East), 4 Blackburn Road, Rishton, Blackburn BB1 4BS ☎ 01254 220827 ✉ tom.daniels@lancashire.gov.uk

Community Safety: Ms Colleen Martin, Community Safety Manager, PO Box 78, County Hall, Preston PR1 8XJ ☎ 01772 530690 🖷 01772 533353 ✉ colleen.martin@lancashire.gov.uk

Computer Management: Mr Mark Orford, Director of ICT, County Hall, Preston PR1 0LD ☎ 01772 534000 ✉ mark.orford@oneconnectlimited.co.uk

Consumer Protection and Trading Standards: Mr Paul Noone, Head of Trading Standards Service, County Hall, Preston PR1 0LD ☎ 01772 534123 ✉ paul.noone@lancashire.gov.uk

Contracts: Miss Andrea Johnson, Head of Procurement, County Hall, Preston PR1 0LD ☎ 01772 533838 ✉ andrea.johnson@lancashire.gov.uk

Corporate Services: Mr Roger Hulme, Director of Community Services & Resources, County Hall, Preston PR1 0LD ☎ 01772 534286 ✉ roger.hulme@lancashire.gov.uk

Corporate Services: Ms Ruth Lowry, Head of Internal Audit, PO Box 78, County Hall, Preston PR1 8XJ ☎ 01772 534898 ✉ ruth.lowry@lancashire.gov.uk

Direct Labour: Mr Nigel Finnamore, Director of Lancashire County Commercial Group, LCCG, Headquarters Office, Dewhurst Row, Bamber Bridge, Preston PR5 6BB ☎ 01772 536942 ✉ nigel.finnamore@lancashire.gov.uk

Economic Development: Mr Martin Kelly, Director of Economic Development, PO Box 78, County Hall, Preston PR1 8XJ ☎ 01772 536197 ✉ martin.kelly@lancashire.gov.uk

Education: Mrs Helen Denton, Executive Director for Children & Young People, PO Box 61, County Hall, Preston PR1 8RJ ☎ 01772 531646 ✉ helen.denton@lancashire.gov.uk

Electoral Registration: Mr Roy Jones, Assistant County Secretary, PO Box 78, County Hall, Preston PR1 8XJ ☎ 01772 533619 🖷 01772 533465 ✉ roy.jones@lancashire.gov.uk

Emergency Planning: Mr Bernard Kershaw, Principal Emergency Planning Officer, County Offices, Marsh Lane, Preston PR1 8NL ☎ 01772 537913 🖷 01772 733378 ✉ bernard.kershaw@lancashire.gov.uk

Energy Management: Mr Matthew Tidmarsh, Head of Building Services Engineering, Lancashire County Property Group, PO Box 27, County Hall, Preston PR1 0LD ☎ 01772 533243 🖷 01772 533184 ✉ matthew.tidmarsh@lancashire.gov.uk

Environmental / Technical Services: Ms Jo Turton, Executive Director for the Environment, PO Box 61, County Hall, Preston PR1 0LD ☎ 01772 534450 🖷 01772 533381 ✉ jo.turton@lancashire.gov.uk

Estates, Property & Valuation: Ms Suzy Jeffrey, Head of Estates, County Hall, Preston PR1 0LD ☎ 01772 536834 ✉ suzy.jeffrey@lancashire.gov.uk

European Liaison: Mr Sean McGrath, Manager - External Relations, PO Box 78, County Hall, Preston PR1 8XJ ☎ 01772 531053 ✉ sean.mcgrath@lancashire.gov.uk

Events Manager: Ms Mercia Woest, Events & Marketing Manager, County Hall, Preston PR1 0LD ☎ 01772 537311 ✉ mercia.woest@oneconnectlimited.co.uk

Facilities: Ms Clare Joynson, Facilities Manager, PO Box 100, County Hall, Preston PR1 0LD ☎ 01772 533403 ✉ clare.joynson@lancashire.gov.uk

Finance and Treasurer: Mr Paul Williams, Director of Finance, County Hall, Preston PR1 0LD ☎ 01772 537922 ✉ paul.williams2@lancashire.gov.uk

Fleet Management: Mr Eddie Hart, Principal Fleet Manager, Holme Road, Lostock Lane, Bamber Bridge, Preston PR5 6BQ

☎ 01772 532385 🖷 01772 532392
✉ eddie.hart@lancashire.gov.uk

Health and Safety: Ms Jill Cornwell, Principal HR Manager - Health, Safety and Wellbeing, County Hall, Preston PR1 0LD ☎ 07831 871511 ✉ jill.cornwell@lancashire.gov.uk

Highways: Mr Shaun Capper, Assistant Director of Environmental Services (Area South), Cuerdan Way, Bamber Bridge, Preston PR5 6BF ☎ 01772 530251 🖷 01772 531022 ✉ shaun.capper@lancashire.gov.uk

Legal: Mr Ian Fisher, County Secretary & Solicitor, PO Box 78, County Hall, Preston PR1 8XJ ☎ 01772 533386 🖷 01772 532050 ✉ ian.fisher@lancashire.gov.uk

Leisure and Cultural Services: Mr Ian Watson, Head of Cultural Services, County Hall, Preston PR1 0LD ☎ 01772 534009 ✉ ian.watson@lancashire.gov.uk

Lifelong Learning: Ms Julie Bell, County Libraries Manager, Park Hotel, East Cliff, Preston PR1 3EA ☎ 01772 536727 ✉ julie.bell@lancashire.gov.uk

Lottery Funding, Charity and Voluntary: Mr Jason Crausby, Voluntary, Community & Faith Sector (VCFS) Manager, County Hall, Preston PR1 0LD ☎ 01772 533544 ✉ jason.crausby@lancashire.gov.uk

Member Services: Mr Ian Young, Deputy County Secretary & Solicitor, PO Box 78, County Hall, Preston PR1 8XJ ☎ 01772 533531 ✉ ian.young@lancashire.gov.uk

Parking: Mr Vali Birang, Director of Transportation & Strategic Highway, County Hall, Preston PR1 0LD ☎ 01772 534788 🖷 01772 534766 ✉ vali.birang@lancashire.gov.uk

Personnel / HR: Ms Katie Dunne, Head of HR (Directorates/LCCG), County Hall, Preston PR1 0LD ☎ 01772 530360 ✉ katie.dunne@oneconnectlimited.co.uk

Personnel / HR: Ms Pam Goulding, Head of HR (People), County Hall, Preston PR1 0LD ☎ 01772 532345 ✉ pam.goulding@lancashire.gov.uk

Personnel / HR: Mr Dave Hewitt, Head of HR (Schools), County Hall, Preston PR1 0LD ☎ 01772 531758 ✉ dave.hewitt@lancashire.gov.uk

Planning: Mr Marcus Hudson, Head of Planning, County Hall, Preston PR1 0LD ☎ 01772 530696 ✉ marcus.hudson@lancashire.gov.uk

Procurement: Miss Andrea Johnson, Head of Procurement, PO Box 100, County Hall, Preston PR1 0LD ☎ 01772 533838 ✉ andrea.johnson@lancashire.gov.uk

Public Libraries: Ms Julie Bell, County Libraries Manager, Park Hotel, East Cliff, Preston PR1 3EA ☎ 01772 536727 ✉ julie.bell@lancashire.gov.uk

Recycling & Waste Minimisation: Ms Sue Procter, Assistant Director - Environmental Services (Area East), LCC Highways Office, Highways Depot, Willows Lane, Accrington BB5 0RT ☎ 01254 770985 ✉ susan.procter@lancashire.gov.uk

Road Safety: Mr Steve Whitehouse, Lancashire Partnership for Road Safety Manager, County Hall, Preston PR1 0LD ☎ 01772 532411 ✉ stephen.whitehouse@lancashire.gov.uk

Social Services: Mr Richard Jones, Executive Director for Adult & Community Services, County Hall, Preston PR1 0LD ☎ 01772 534390 ✉ richard.jones@lancashire.gov.uk

Social Services (Adult): Ms Olive Carroll, Director of Personal Social Care, County Hall, Preston PR1 0LD ☎ 01772 534393 🖷 01772 534425 ✉ olive.carroll@lancashire.gov.uk

Social Services (Adult): Mr Stephen Gross, Director of Commissioning, County Hall, Preston PR1 0LD ☎ 01772 536287 ✉ stephen.gross@lancashire.gov.uk

Social Services (Children): Mrs Helen Denton, Executive Director for Children & Young People, PO Box 61, County Hall, Preston PR1 8RJ ☎ 01772 531646 ✉ helen.denton@lancashire.gov.uk

Traffic Management: Mr Vali Birang, Director of Transportation & Strategic Highway, County Hall, Preston PR1 0LD ☎ 01772 534788 🖷 01772 534766 ✉ vali.birang@lancashire.gov.uk

Transport Planner: Mr Mike Kirby, Transportation & Strategic Highway, PO Box 78, County Hall, Preston PR1 8XJ ☎ 01772 534660 ✉ mike.kirby@lancashire.gov.uk

Waste Management: Mr Steve Scott, Head of Waste Management, County Hall, Preston PR1 0LD ☎ 01772 533755 ✉ steve.scott@lancashire.gov.uk

MEMBERS OF THE COUNCIL (84)

Deputy Leader of the Council: **Atkinson**, Albert (CON - Ribble Valley North East)
albert.atkinson@lancashire.gov.uk
Group Leader: **Mein**, Jennifer (LAB - Preston South East)
jennifer.mein@lancashire.gov.uk
Group Leader: **Winlow**, Bill (LD - Preston West)
bill.winlow@lancashire.gov.uk
Adam, George (LAB - Nelson South)
george.adam@lancashire.gov.uk
Aldridge, Terence (LAB - Skelmersdale Central)
terry.aldridge@lancashire.gov.uk
Ashton, Timothy (CON - Lytham)
tim.ashton@lancashire.gov.uk
Askew, George (CON - Pendal Central)
george.askew@lancashire.gov.uk
Bailey, Rob (CON - Ormskirk West)
rob.bailey@lancashire.gov.uk
Bailey, Keith (CON - West Craven)
keith.bailey@lancashire.gov.uk
Barron, Malcolm (CON - West Lancashire North)
malcolm.barron@lancashire.gov.uk
Blow, Renee (CON - Penwortham South)
renee.blow@lancashire.gov.uk
Briggs, Charlie (LD - Burnley Central West)
charlie.briggs@lancashire.gov.uk

Brindle, Margaret (LD - Burnley Rural)
margaret.brindle@lancashire.gov.uk
Britcliffe, Peter (CON - Oswaldtwistle)
peter.britcliffe@lancashire.gov.uk
Brown, Terry (LAB - Chorley East)
terry.brown@lancashire.gov.uk
Brown, Ken (CON - Heysham)
ken.brown@lancashire.gov.uk
Calvert, Mike (CON - Pendle East)
mike.calvert@lancashire.gov.uk
Case, Pat (CON - Chorley Rural East)
pat.case@lancashire.gov.uk
Chapman, Sam (CON - Chorley South)
sam.chapman@lancashire.gov.uk
Charles, Susie (CON - Lancaster Rural East)
susie.charles@lancashire.gov.uk
Coates, Christopher (GRN - Lancaster Central)
christopher.coates@lancashire.gov.uk
Craig-Wilson, Fabian (CON - St Annes South)
fabian.craig-wilson@lancashire.gov.uk
Crompton, Carl (LAB - Preston Central South)
carl.crompton@lancashire.gov.uk
Cropper, William (CON - West Lancashire West)
william.cropper@lancashire.gov.uk
De Molfetta, Francesco (LAB - Preston Central North)
francesco.demolfetta@lancashire.gov.uk
Derwent, Shelagh (CON - Pendle West)
shelagh.derwent@lancashire.gov.uk
Devaney, Michael (CON - Chorley Rural North)
michael.devaney@lancashire.gov.uk
Driver, Geoff (CON - Preston North)
geoff.driver@lancashire.gov.uk
Eaton, James (CON - Rossendale East)
james.eaton@lancashire.gov.uk
Ellard, Kevin (LAB - Preston East)
kevin.ellard@lancashire.gov.uk
Evans, Peter (CON - Rossendale West)
peter.evans@lancashire.gov.uk
Evans, Carolyn (CON - Skelmersdale East)
carolyn.evans@lancashire.gov.uk
Fishwick, Sarah (CON - Lancaster Rural North)
sarah.fishwick@lancashire.gov.uk
France, Mike (CON - Leyland Central)
mike.france@lancashire.gov.uk
Green, Michael (CON - Leyland South West)
mike.france@lancashire.gov.uk
Grunshaw, Clive (LAB - Fleetwood East)
clive.grunshaw@lancashire.gov.uk
Hanson, Janice (LAB - Morecambe West)
janice.hanson@lancashire.gov.uk
Hassan, Misfar (LAB - Burnley Central East)
misfar.hassan@lancashire.gov.uk
Hayhurst, Paul (IND - Fylde West)
paul.hayhurst@lancashire.gov.uk
Henshaw, Howard (LD - St Annes North)
Holtom, Chris (CON - Ribble Valley South West)
chris.holtom@lancashire.gov.uk
Iddon, Keith (CON - Chorley Rural West)
keith.iddon@lancashire.gov.uk
Iqbal, Mohammed (LAB - Brierfield and Nelson North)
mohammed.iqbal@lancashire.gov.uk
Jackson, Joan (CON - Lancaster South East)
joan.jackson@lancashire.gov.uk
Jewell, Mark (LD - Preston North West)
mark.jewell@lancashire.gov.uk
Jones, Anthony (CON - Morecambe North)
anthony.jones@lancashire.gov.uk
Jones, Graham (LAB - Accrington South)
graham.jones@lancashire.gov.uk
Kay, Andrea (CON - Thornton Cleveleys North)
andrea.kay@lancashire.gov.uk
Knox, Allan (LD - Clitheroe)
allan.knox@lancashire.gov.uk
Lawrenson, Jim (CON - Thornton Cleveleys Central)
jim.lawrenson@lancashire.co.uk
Leadbetter, Stan (CON - Fleetwood West)
stan.leadbetter@lancashire.gov.uk
Malpas, Peter (CON - Chorley West)
peter.malpas@lancashire.gov.uk
McCann, Pete (LD - Burnley North East)
peter.mccann@lancashire.gov.uk
Motala, Yousuf (LAB - Preston City)
yousuf.motala@lancashire.gov.uk
Mulineaux, Peter (CON - Bamber Bridge and Walton le Dale)
peter.mulineaux@lancashire.gov.uk
Oades, Liz (IND - Fylde East)
liz.oades@lancashire.gov.uk
O'Toole, David (CON - West Lancashire South)
david.o'toole@lancashire.gov.uk
Otter, Mike (CON - Farington)
mike.otter@lancashire.gov.uk
Parkinson, Miles (LAB - Rishton and Clayton-Le-Moors)
miles.parkinson@lancashire.gov.uk
Penney, Nicola (LAB - Skerton)
niki.penney@lancashire.gov.uk
Perks, Mark (CON - Chorley North)
mark.perks@lancashire.gov.uk
Pimblett, Anthony (LD - Penwortham North)
tony.pimblett@lancashire.gov.uk
Pritchard, Malcolm (IND - Accrington North)
malcolm.pritchard@lancashire.gov.uk
Riches, Sam (GRN - Lancaster East)
sam.riches@lancashire.gov.uk
Rigby, Paul (CON - Fylde South)
paul.rigby@lancashire.gov.uk
Roper, Geoffrey (CON - Poulton-le-Fylde)
geoffrey.roper@lancashire.gov.uk
Sharratt, Thomas (O - South Ribble Rural West)
thomas.sharratt@lancashire.gov.uk
Shedwick, John (CON - Amounderness)
john.shedwick@lancashire.gov.uk
Skilling, Maggie (LAB - Skelmersdale West)
maggie.skilling@lancashire.gov.uk
Smith, David (CON - Longridge with Bowland)
david.smith@lancashire.gov.uk
Smith, Darryl (CON - Rossendale South)
darryl.smith@lancashire.gov.uk
Steen, Peter (CON - Whitworth)
peter.steen@lancashire.gov.uk
Sumner, Jeff (LD - Burnley South West)
jeff.sumner@lancashire.gov.uk
Taylor, Vivien (CON - Wyre Side)
vivien.taylor@lancashire.gov.uk
Thornton, Albert (CON - Morecambe South)
albert.thornton@lancashire.gov.uk
Wells, Ciaran (LAB - Great Harwood)
ciaran.wells@lancashire.gov.uk
Welsh, Michael (CON - Preston North East)
watercrook@btinernet.com
Westley, David (CON - West Lancashire East)

david.westley@lancashire.gov.uk
Wilkins, George (CON - Preston Rural)
george.wilkins@lancashire.gov.uk
Wilkinson, Sharon (BNP - Padiham and Burnley West)
sharon.wilkinson@lancashire.gov.uk
Wilson, Valerie (CON - Garstang)
valerie.wilson@lancashire.gov.uk
Winder, Tony (CON - Rossendale North)
tony.winder@lancashire.gov.uk
Young, Keith (CON - South Ribble Rural West)
keith.young@lancashire.gov.uk
Younis, Mohammed (CON - Accrington West)
mohammed.younis@lancashire.gov.uk

POLITICAL COMPOSITION
CON: 51, LAB: 17, LD: 9, IND: 3, GRN: 2, BNP: 1, O: 1

CABINET
Leader: Mr Geoff Driver
Deputy Leader: Mr Albert Atkinson
Adult & Community Services: Mr Mike Calvert
Children & Schools: Mr Keith Iddon
Economic Development, Environment & Planning: Mr Michael Green
Health & Wellbeing: Mrs Valerie Wilson
Highways & Transport: Mr Timothy Ashton
Young People: Mr Mark Perks

COMMITTEE CHAIRS
Audit: Mr Sam Chapman
Development Control: Mr Michael Devaney
Education (Scrutiny): Mrs Pat Case
Employment: Mr Geoff Driver
Health (Scrutiny): Ms Maggie Skillling
Pension Fund: Mr David Westley
Regulatory: Mr Anthony Jones
Scrutiny (Scrutiny): Mr Peter Britcliffe

LANCASTER CITY D

Lancaster City Council, Town Hall, Dalton Square, Lancaster LA1 1PJ ☎ 01524 582000 🖷 01524 582979 customerservices@lancaster.gov.uk 💻 www.lancaster.gov.uk

FACTS & FIGURES
Police Authority: Lancashire Police Authority
Health Authority: North West Strategic Health Authority
Learning and Skills Council: North West
Parliamentary Constituencies: Lancaster and Fleetwood
EU Constituencies: North West
Election Frequency: Elections are of whole council
Twinning: Aalborg (Denmark); Perpignan (France); Rendsburg (Germany); Lublin (Poland); Vaxjo (Sweden); Wray and Hornby: Grez-Neuville (France); Carnforth: Saill Sur La Lys

PRINCIPAL OFFICERS
Chief Executive: Mr Mark Cullinan, Chief Executive, Town Hall, Dalton Square, Lancaster LA1 1PJ ☎ 01524 582011 🖷 01524 582042 chiefexecutive@lancaster.gov.uk

Senior Management: Mr Mark Davies, Head of Environmental Services, White Lund Depot, White Lund Industrial Estate, Morecambe LA3 3DT ☎ 01524 582401 🖷 01524 582401 mdavies@lancaster.gov.uk

Senior Management: Mr Andrew Dobson, Head of Regeneration & Policy, Town Hall, Marine Road, Morecambe LA4 4AF ☎ 01524 582303 🖷 01524 582323 adobson@lancaster.gov.uk

Senior Management: Ms Suzanne Lodge, Head of Health & Housing Services, Town Hall, Marine Road, Morecambe LA4 4AF ☎ 01524 582709 🖷 01524 582701 slodge@lancaster.gov.uk

Senior Management: Ms Nadine Muschamp, Head of Financial Services, Town Hall, Dalton Square, Lancaster LA1 1PJ ☎ 01524 582117 🖷 ; 01524 582160 nmuschamp@lancaster.gov.uk

Senior Management: Mrs Sarah Taylor, Head of Governance, Town Hall, Dalton Square, Lancaster LA1 1PJ ☎ 01524 582025 🖷 01524 582030 staylor@lancaster.gov.uk

Senior Management: Mr Richard Tulej, Head of Community Engagement, St. Leonard's House, St. Leonardgate, Lancaster LA1 1NN ☎ 01524 582079 🖷 01524 582689 rtulej@lancaster.gov.uk

Access Officer / Social Services (Disability): Mr Rob Bracewell, Access Officer, Town Hall, Marine Road, Morecambe LA4 4AF ☎ 01524 582372 🖷 01524 582323 rbracewell@lancaster.gov.uk

Architect, Building / Property Services: Mr Graham Cox, Head of Property Services, Town Hall, Dalton Square, Lancaster LA1 1PJ ☎ 01524 582504 🖷 01524 582505 gcox@lancaster.gov.uk

Building Control: Mr Andrew Dobson, Head of Regeneration & Policy, Town Hall, Marine Road, Morecambe LA4 4AF ☎ 01524 582303 🖷 01524 582323 adobson@lancaster.gov.uk

PR / Communications: Mrs Gill Haigh, Assistant Head of Community Engagement (Communications), Town Hall, Dalton Square, Lancaster LA1 1PJ ☎ 01524 582178 🖷 01524 582159 ghaigh@lancaster.gov.uk

Community Planning: Mr Andrew Dobson, Head of Regeneration & Policy, Town Hall, Marine Road, Morecambe LA4 4AF ☎ 01524 582303 🖷 01524 582323 adobson@lancaster.gov.uk

Community Safety: Mr Richard Tulej, Head of Community Engagement, Town Hall, Dalton Square, Lancaster LA1 1PJ ☎ 01524 582079 🖷 01524 582689 rtulej@lancaster.gov.uk

Computer Management: Mr Chris Riley, Applications Manager for ICT Services, Town Hall, Dalton Square, Lancaster LA1 1PJ ☎ 01524 582106 🖷 01524 582171 cjriley@lancaster.gov.uk

Consumer Protection and Trading Standards: Ms Suzanne Lodge, Head of Health & Housing Services, Town Hall, Marine Road, Morecambe LA4 4AF ☎ 01524 582709 🖷 01524 582701 slodge@lancaster.gov.uk

Contracts: Mr Mark Davies, Head of Environmental Services, White Lund Depot, White Lund Industrial Estate, Morecambe LA3

3DT ☎ 01524 582401 🖷 01524 582401
🖱 mdavies@lancaster.gov.uk

Corporate Services: Mr Richard Tulej, Head of Community Engagement, Town Hall, Dalton Square, Lancaster LA1 1PJ ☎ 01524 582079 🖷 01524 582689 🖱 rtulej@lancaster.gov.uk

Customer Service: Ms Heather Armstrong, Customer Service & Visitor Information Centre Manager, Town Hall, Dalton Square, Lancaster LA1 1PJ ☎ 01524 582399 🖷 01524 582979
🖱 harmstrong@lancaster.gov.uk

Direct Labour: Mr Mark Davies, Head of Environmental Services, White Lund Depot, White Lund Industrial Estate, Morecambe LA3 3DT ☎ 01524 582401 🖷 01524 582401
🖱 mdavies@lancaster.gov.uk

Economic Development: Mr Richard Tulej, Head of Community Engagement, Town Hall, Dalton Square, Lancaster LA1 1PJ ☎ 01524 582079 🖷 01524 582689 🖱 rtulej@lancaster.gov.uk

E-Government: Mr Richard Tulej, Head of Community Engagement, St. Leonard's House, St. Leonardgate, Lancaster LA1 1NN ☎ 01524 582079 🖷 01524 582689
🖱 rtulej@lancaster.gov.uk

Electoral Registration: Mrs Sarah Taylor, Head of Governance, Town Hall, Dalton Square, Lancaster LA1 1PJ ☎ 01524 582025 🖷 01524 582030 🖱 staylor@lancaster.gov.uk

Emergency Planning: Mr Mark Bartlett, Civil Contingencies Officer, Town Hall, Marine Road, Morecambe LA4 4AF ☎ 01524 582680 🖷 01524 582709 🖱 mbartlett@lancaster.gov.uk

Energy Management: Ms Suzanne Lodge, Head of Health & Housing Services, Town Hall, Marine Road, Morecambe LA4 4AF ☎ 01524 582709 🖷 01524 582701 🖱 slodge@lancaster.gov.uk

Environmental / Technical Services: Mr Mark Davies, Head of Environmental Services, White Lund Depot, White Lund Industrial Estate, Morecambe LA3 3DT ☎ 01524 582401 🖷 01524 582401
🖱 mdavies@lancaster.gov.uk

Environmental Health: Ms Suzanne Lodge, Head of Health & Housing Services, Town Hall, Marine Road, Morecambe LA4 4AF ☎ 01524 582709 🖷 01524 582701 🖱 slodge@lancaster.gov.uk

Estates, Property & Valuation: Mr Graham Cox, Head of Property Services, Town Hall, Dalton Square, Lancaster LA1 1PJ ☎ 01524 582504 🖷 01524 582505 🖱 gcox@lancaster.gov.uk

European Liaison: Mrs Sarah Taylor, Head of Governance, Town Hall, Dalton Square, Lancaster LA1 1PJ ☎ 01524 582025 🖷 01524 582030 🖱 staylor@lancaster.gov.uk

Events Manager: Mr Richard Tulej, Head of Community Engagement, Town Hall, Dalton Square, Lancaster LA1 1PJ ☎ 01524 582079 🖷 ; 01524 582689 🖱 rtulej@lancaster.gov.uk

Facilities: Mr Graham Cox, Head of Property Services, Town Hall, Dalton Square, Lancaster LA1 1PJ ☎ 01524 582504 🖷 01524 582505 🖱 gcox@lancaster.gov.uk

Finance and Treasurer: Ms Nadine Muschamp, Head of Financial Services, Town Hall, Dalton Square, Lancaster LA1 1PJ ☎ 01524 582117 🖷 01524 582160
🖱 nmuschamp@lancaster.gov.uk

Fleet Management: Mr Mark Davies, Head of Environmental Services, White Lund Depot, White Lund Industrial Estate, Morecambe LA3 3DT ☎ 01524 582401 🖷 01524 582401
🖱 mdavies@lancaster.gov.uk

Grounds Maintenance: Mr Mark Davies, Head of Environmental Services, White Lund Depot, White Lund Industrial Estate, Morecambe LA3 3DT ☎ 01524 582401 🖷 01524 582401
🖱 mdavies@lancaster.gov.uk

Health and Safety: Ms Suzanne Lodge, Head of Health & Housing Services, Town Hall, Marine Road, Morecambe LA4 4AF ☎ 01524 582709 🖷 01524 582701 🖱 slodge@lancaster.gov.uk

Highways: Mr Mark Davies, Head of Environmental Services, White Lund Depot, White Lund Industrial Estate, Morecambe LA3 3DT ☎ 01524 582401 🖷 01524 582401
🖱 mdavies@lancaster.gov.uk

Housing: Ms Suzanne Lodge, Head of Health & Housing Services, Town Hall, Marine Road, Morecambe LA4 4AF ☎ 01524 582709 🖷 01524 582701 🖱 slodge@lancaster.gov.uk

Housing Maintenance: Ms Suzanne Lodge, Head of Health & Housing Services, Town Hall, Marine Road, Morecambe LA4 4AF ☎ 01524 582709 🖷 01524 582701 🖱 slodge@lancaster.gov.uk

Legal: Mrs Sarah Taylor, Head of Governance, Town Hall, Dalton Square, Lancaster LA1 1PJ ☎ 01524 582025 🖷 01524 582030
🖱 staylor@lancaster.gov.uk

Leisure and Cultural Services: Mr Richard Tulej, Head of Community Engagement, Town Hall, Dalton Square, Lancaster LA1 1PJ ☎ 01524 582079 🖷 01524 582689
🖱 rtulej@lancaster.gov.uk

Licensing: Mrs Sarah Taylor, Head of Governance, Town Hall, Dalton Square, Lancaster LA1 1PJ ☎ 01524 582025 🖷 01524 582030 🖱 staylor@lancaster.gov.uk

Lighting: Mr Mark Davies, Head of Environmental Services, White Lund Depot, White Lund Industrial Estate, Morecambe LA3 3DT ☎ 01524 582401 🖷 01524 582401
🖱 mdavies@lancaster.gov.uk

Member Services: Mrs Sarah Taylor, Head of Governance, Town Hall, Dalton Square, Lancaster LA1 1PJ ☎ 01524 582025 🖷 01524 582030 🖱 staylor@lancaster.gov.uk

Parking: Mr Graham Cox, Head of Property Services, Town Hall, Dalton Square, Lancaster LA1 1PJ ☎ 01524 582504 🖷 01524 582505 🖱 gcox@lancaster.gov.uk

Partnerships: Mr James Sommerville, Partnerships Officer, Town Hall, Dalton Square, Lancaster LA1 1PJ ☎ 01524 582588
🖱 jsommerville@lancaster.gov.uk

Personnel / HR: Mrs Sarah Taylor, Head of Governance, Town Hall, Dalton Square, Lancaster LA1 1PJ ☎ 01524 582025 🖷 01524 582030 ✉ staylor@lancaster.gov.uk

Planning: Mr Andrew Dobson, Head of Regeneration & Policy, Town Hall, Marine Road, Morecambe LA4 4AF ☎ 01524 582303 🖷 01524 582323 ✉ adobson@lancaster.gov.uk

Procurement: Ms Nadine Muschamp, Head of Financial Services, Town Hall, Dalton Square, Lancaster LA1 1PJ ☎ 01524 582117 🖷 01524 582160 ✉ nmuschamp@lancaster.gov.uk

Recycling & Waste Minimisation: Mr Mark Davies, Head of Environmental Services, White Lund Depot, White Lund Industrial Estate, Morecambe LA3 3DT ☎ 01524 582401 🖷 01524 582401 ✉ mdavies@lancaster.gov.uk

Regeneration: Mr Andrew Dobson, Head of Regeneration & Policy, Town Hall, Marine Road, Morecambe LA4 4AF ☎ 01524 582303 🖷 01524 582323 ✉ adobson@lancaster.gov.uk

Staff Training: Mrs Sarah Taylor, Head of Governance, Town Hall, Dalton Square, Lancaster LA1 1PJ ☎ 01524 582025 🖷 01524 582030 ✉ staylor@lancaster.gov.uk

Street Scene: Mr Mark Davies, Head of Environmental Services, White Lund Depot, White Lund Industrial Estate, Morecambe LA3 3DT ☎ 01524 582401 🖷 01524 582401 ✉ mdavies@lancaster.gov.uk

Sustainable Development: Ms Jill Wesolowski, Environmental Co-ordinator, Town Hall, Dalton Square, Lancaster LA1 1PJ ☎ 01524 582061 🖷 01524 582020 ✉ jwesolowski@lancaster.gov.uk

Tourism: Mr Richard Tulej, Head of Community Engagement, Town Hall, Dalton Square, Lancaster LA1 1PJ ☎ 01524 582079 🖷 01524 582689 ✉ rtulej@lancaster.gov.uk

Town Centre: Mr Graham Cox, Head of Property Services, Town Hall, Dalton Square, Lancaster LA1 1PJ ☎ 01524 582504 🖷 01524 582505 ✉ gcox@lancaster.gov.uk

Waste Collection and Disposal: Mr Mark Davies, Head of Environmental Services, White Lund Depot, White Lund Industrial Estate, Morecambe LA3 3DT ☎ 01524 582401 🖷 01524 582401 ✉ mdavies@lancaster.gov.uk

Waste Management: Mr Mark Davies, Head of Environmental Services, White Lund Depot, White Lund Industrial Estate, Morecambe LA3 3DT ☎ 01524 582401 🖷 01524 582401 ✉ mdavies@lancaster.gov.uk

MEMBERS OF THE COUNCIL (60)

***Mayor:* Denwood**, Sheila (LAB - Scotforth West)
sdenwood@lancaster.gov.uk
***Deputy Mayor:* Redfern**, Robert (LAB - Skerton East)
rredfern@lancaster.gov.uk
***Leader of the Council:* Blamire**, Eileen (LAB - John O'Gaunt)
eblamire@lancaster.gov.uk
***Deputy Leader of the Council:* Hanson**, Janice (LAB - Harbour)
jhanson@lancaster.gov.uk

Aitchson, Paul (LAB - University)
paitchison@lancaster.gov.uk
Anderson, Tony (IND - Bare)
tanderson@lancaster.gov.uk
Ashworth, June (IND - Bare)
jashworth@lancaster.gov.uk
Bancroft, Josh (LAB - Scotforth West)
jbancroft@lancaster.gov.uk
Barry, Jon (GRN - Castle)
jbarry@lancaster.gov.uk
Bevan, Mark (LAB - Poulton)
mbevan@lancaster.gov.uk
Brooks, Dave (GRN - Dukes)
dbrookes@lancaster.gov.uk
Bryning, Abbott (LAB - Skerton East)
abryning@lancaster.gov.uk
Budden, Keith (IND - Bolton-le-Sands)
kbudden@lancaster.gov.uk
Burns, Shirley (IND - Poulton)
sburns@lancaster.gov.uk
Charles, Susan (CON - Ellel)
scharles@lancaster.gov.uk
Coates, Chris (GRN - Scotforth West)
ccoates@lancaster.gov.uk
Dennison, Roger (IND - Torrisholme)
rdennison@lancaster.gov.uk
Dixon, Jonathan (LAB - University)
jdixon@lancaster.gov.uk
Forrest, Melanie (GRN - Castle)
mforrest@lancaster.gov.uk
Gardner, Paul (LAB - Carnforth)
pgardner@lancaster.gov.uk
Graham, Kathleen (CON - Silverdale)
kgraham@lancaster.gov.uk
Greenall, Michael (IND - Heysham South)
mgreenall@lancaster.gov.uk
Hall, Janet (LAB - Skerton East)
jhall@lancaster.gov.uk
Hamilton-Cox, Tim (GRN - Bulk)
thamiltoncox@lancaster.gov.uk
Harrison, John (LAB - Skerton West)
jharrison@lancaster.gov.uk
Helme, Helen (CON - Ellel)
hhelme@lancaster.gov.uk
Hill, Billy (CON - Scotforth East)
bhill@lancaster.gov.uk
Histed, Val (CON - Bolton-le-Sands)
vhisted@lancaster.gov.uk
Jackson, Joan (CON - Lower Lune Valley)
jjackson@lancaster.gov.uk
James, Alycia (CON - Warton)
ajames@lancaster.gov.uk
Johnson, Anthony (CON - Carnforth)
ajohnson@lancaster.gov.uk
Kay, Andrew (GRN - Bulk)
akay@lancaster.gov.uk
Kennedy, Tracey (GRN - Castle)
tkennedy@lancaster.gov.uk
Kerr, David (IND - Westgate)
dkerr@lancaster.gov.uk
Knight, Geoff (IND - Heysham Central)
gknight@lancaster.gov.uk
Leytham, Karen (LAB - Skerton West)
k.leytham@lancaster.gov.uk
Mace, Roger (CON - Kellet)

rmace@lancaster.gov.uk
Marsland, Geoff (IND - Torrisholme)
gmarsland@lancaster.gov.uk
Metcalfe, Terrie (LAB - Poulton)
tmetcalfe@lancaster.gov.uk
Mumford, Ceri (GRN - Bulk)
cmumford@lancaster.gov.uk
Newman-Thompson, Richard (LAB - John O'Gaunt)
rnewman-thompson@lancaster.gov.uk
Parkinson, Jane (CON - Lower Lune Valley)
japarkinson@lancaster.gov.uk
Pattison, Ian (LAB - Harbour)
ipattison@lancaster.gov.uk
Pattison, Margaret (LAB - Heysham North)
mpattison@lancaster.gov.uk
Pickles, Pam (LAB - Scotforth East)
ppickles@lancaster.gov.uk
Price, Vikki (LAB - Westgate)
vprice@lancaster.gov.uk
Rogerson, Sylvia (CON - Slyne-with-Hest)
srogerson@lancaster.gov.uk
Rollins, Richard (CON - Heysham South)
rrollins@lancaster.gov.uk
Sands, Ronald (LAB - Heysham North)
rsands@lancaster.gov.uk
Scott, Elizabeth (LAB - John O'Gaunt)
lscott@lancaster.gov.uk
Sherlock, Roger (LAB - Skerton West)
rsherlock@lancaster.gov.uk
Smith, David (LAB - Westgate)
dasmith@lancaster.gov.uk
Smith, Emma (CON - Heysham South)
elsmith@lancaster.gov.uk
Sowden, Keith (INDNA - Overton)
ksowden@lancaster.gov.uk
Sykes, Susan (CON - Torrisholme)
ssykes@lancaster.gov.uk
Taylor, Joyce (IND - Heysham Central)
jtaylor@lancaster.gov.uk
Thomas, Malcolm (CON - Slyne-with-Hest)
mthomas@lancaster.gov.uk
Whitaker, David (LAB - Harbour)
dwhitaker@lancaster.gov.uk
Williamson, Peter (CON - Upper Lune Valley)
pwilliamson@lancaster.gov.uk
Woodruff, Paul
(INDNA - Halton-with-Aughton)
pwoodruff@lancaster.gov.uk

POLITICAL COMPOSITION

LAB: 24, CON: 16, IND: 10, GRN: 8, INDNA: 2

CABINET

Leader: Mrs Eileen Blamire
Deputy Leader / Economic Regeneration & Planning: Ms Janice Hanson
Children & Young People / Culture & Tourism: Mr Ronald Sands
Climate Change & Property Services: Mr Tim Hamilton-Cox
Communities & Older People: Mr Jon Barry
Community Safety and Clean & Green: Mr David Smith
Finance, Revenues & Benefits: Mr Abbott Bryning
Housing & Environmental Health: Ms Karen Leytham

COMMITTEE CHAIRS

Appeals: Mrs Helen Helme
Audit: Mr Malcolm Thomas
Budget & Performance: Ms Susan Sykes
Licensing Act: Mrs Joyce Taylor
Licensing Regulatory: Mr John Harrison
Overview & Scrutiny (Scrutiny): Mr David Kerr
Planning & Highways Regulatory: Mr Keith Budden

LARNE N

Larne Borough Council, Smiley Buildings, Victoria Road, Larne BT40 1RU ☎ 028 2827 2313 🖷 028 2826 0660 admin@larne.gov.uk www.larne.gov.uk

FACTS & FIGURES

Police Authority: Northern Ireland Policing Board
Health Authority: Health & Social Care Board
Learning and Skills Council: Northern Ireland
Parliamentary Constituencies: Antrim East
EU Constituencies: Northern Ireland
Election Frequency: Elections are of whole council
Twinning: Larne: Clover, South Carolina (USA)

PRINCIPAL OFFICERS

Chief Executive: Mrs Geraldine McGahey, Chief Executive, Smiley Buildings, Victoria Road, Larne BT40 1RU ☎ 028 2827 2313 mcgaheyg@larne.gov.uk

Senior Management: Mrs Linda McCullough, Director of Development, Smiley Buildings, Victoria Road, Larne BT40 1RU ☎ 028 2827 2313 🖷 028 2826 0660 mcculloughl@larne.gov.uk

Architect, Building / Property Services: Mr Stephen Hipkins, Head of Building Control, Smiley Buildings, Victoria Road, Larne BT40 1RU ☎ 028 2827 2313 🖷 028 2826 0660 hipkinss@larne.gov.uk

Best Value: Mrs Sandra McDonald, Best Value Officer, Smiley Buildings, Victoria Road, Larne BT40 1RU ☎ 028 2827 2313 🖷 028 2826 0660 mcdonalds@larne.gov.uk

Building Control: Mr Stephen Hipkins, Head of Building Control, Smiley Buildings, Victoria Road, Larne BT40 1RU ☎ 028 2827 2313 🖷 028 2826 0660 hipkinss@larne.gov.uk

Civil Registration: Mrs Jackie Tennant, Registrar, Smiley Buildings, Victoria Road, Larne BT40 2HH ☎ 028 2827 2313 🖷 028 2826 0660 tennantj@larne.gove.uk

Community Safety: Ms Wendy Carson, Community Safety Manager, Smiley Buildings, Victoria Road, Larne BT40 1RU ☎ 028 2827 2313 🖷 028 2826 0660 carsonw@larne.gov.uk

Computer Management: Ms Maria Young, IT Officer, Smiley Buildings, Victoria Road, Larne BT40 1RU ☎ 028 2827 2313 🖷 028 2826 0660 youngm@larne.gov.uk

Economic Development: Mr Ken Nelson, Economic Development Officer, LEDCOM Industrial Estate, Bank Road, Larne BT40 3AW ☎ 028 2827 2313

Emergency Planning: Mrs Julie Parkinson, Senior Environmental Health Officer, Smiley Buildings, Victoria Road, Larne BT40 1RU ☎ 028 2827 2313 🖷 028 2826 0660 ✉ parkinsonj@larne.gov.uk

Energy Management: Mr Stephen Hipkins, Head of Building Control, Smiley Buildings, Victoria Road, Larne BT40 1RU ☎ 028 2827 2313 🖷 028 2826 0660 ✉ hipkinss@larne.gov.uk

Environmental / Technical Services: Mr Philip Thompson, Director of Environmental Services, Smiley Buildings, Victoria Road, Larne BT40 1RU ☎ 028 2827 2313 🖷 028 2826 0660

Environmental Health: Mr Sean Martin, Head of Environmental Health, Smiley Buildings, Victoria Road, Larne BT40 1RU ☎ 028 2827 2313 🖷 028 2826 0660 ✉ martins@larne.gov.uk

Events Manager: Ms Rachael McMaster, Arts & Events Officer, Smiley Buildings, Victoria Road, Larne BT40 1RU ☎ 028 2826 3086 ✉ mcmasterr@larne.gov.uk

Facilities: Mr Philip Thompson, Director of Environmental Services, Smiley Buildings, Victoria Road, Larne BT40 1RU ☎ 028 2827 2313 🖷 028 2826 0660

Finance and Treasurer: Mr George Boyd, Financial Controller, Smiley Buildings, Victoria Road, Larne BT40 1RU ☎ 028 2827 2313 🖷 028 2826 0660 ✉ boydg@larne.gov.uk

Grounds Maintenance: Mr Christopher Hogg, Head of Parks, Smiley Buildings, Victoria Road, Larne BT40 1RU ☎ 028 2827 2313 ✉ hoggc@larne.gov.uk

Leisure and Cultural Services: Mrs Linda McCullough, Director of Development, Smiley Buildings, Victoria Road, Larne BT40 1RU ☎ 028 2827 2313 🖷 028 2820 0660 ✉ mcculloughl@larne.gov.uk

Licensing: Mr Sean Martin, Head of Environmental Health, Smiley Buildings, Victoria Road, Larne BT40 1RU ☎ 028 2827 2313 🖷 028 2826 0660 ✉ martins@larne.gov.uk

Member Services: Mrs Lorraine Hunter, Head of Democratic & Administrative Services, Smiley Buildings, Victoria Road, Larne BT40 1RU ☎ 028 2827 2313 🖷 028 2826 0660 ✉ hunterl@larne.gov.uk

Personnel / HR: Mr Stephen Burns, Acting HR Manager, Sir Thomas Dixon Building, Victoria Road, Larne BT40 1RU ☎ 028 2827 2313 🖷 028 2826 3088 ✉ burnss@larne.gov.uk

Procurement: Mrs Sandra McDonald, Best Value Officer, Smiley Buildings, Victoria Road, Larne BT40 1RU ☎ 028 2827 2313 🖷 028 2826 0660 ✉ mcdonalds@larne.gov.uk

Recycling & Waste Minimisation: Mrs Elaine Smith, Environmental Services Officer, Smiley Buildings, Victoria Road, Larne BT40 1RU ☎ 028 2827 2313 ✉ smithe@larne.gov.uk

Tourism: Mrs Ainsley McWilliams, Tourism Manager, Smiley Buildings, Victoria Road, Larne BT40 1RU ☎ 028 2827 2313 ✉ mcwilliamsa@larne.gov.uk

Town Centre: Mrs Hazel Bell, Town Development Manager, Sir Thomas Dixon Buildings, Victoria Road , Larne BT40 1RU ☎ 028 2827 2313 🖷 028 2826 0660 ✉ bellh@larne.gov.uk

Waste Collection and Disposal: Mrs Elaine Smith, Environmental Services Officer, Smiley Buildings, Victoria Road, Larne BT40 1RU ☎ 028 2827 2313 ✉ smithe@larne.gov.uk

Waste Management: Mr Philip Thompson, Director of Environmental Services, Smiley Buildings, Victoria Road, Larne BT40 1RU ☎ 028 2827 2313 🖷 028 2826 0660

MEMBERS OF THE COUNCIL (15)

***Mayor:* Mulvenna**, Gerardine (ALL - Coast Road)
gerardine.mulvenna@larne.gov.uk
***Deputy Mayor:* McKinty**, Mark (UUP - Larne Lough)
mark.mckinty@larne.gov.uk
***Alderman:* Beggs**, Roy (UUP - Larne Lough)
roy.beggs@larne.gov.uk
***Alderman:* Fulton**, Winston (DUP - Coast Road)
winston.fulton@larne.gov.uk
***Alderman:* McKee**, Jack (O - Larne Town)
jack.mckee@larne.gov.uk
Craig, Roy (IND - Larne Town)
roy.craig@larne.gov.uk
Dunn, Brian (UUP - Coast Road)
brian.dunn@larne.gov.uk
Lynch, Michael (IND - Larne Town)
michael.lynch@larne.gov.uk
Mathews, John (ALL - Larne Lough)
john.mathews@larne.gov.uk
McKee, Bobby (DUP - Larne Lough)
robert.mckee@larne.gov.uk
McKeen, Gregg (DUP - Larne Lough)
gregg.mckeen@larne.gov.uk
McKeown, James (SF - Coast Road)
james.mckeown@larne.gov.uk
Morrow, Maureen (UUP - Coast Road)
maureen.morrow@larne.gov.uk
Niblock, Drew (DUP - Larne Town)
drew.niblock@larne.gov.uk
Wilson, Martin (SDLP - Larne Town)
martin.wilson@larne.gov.uk

POLITICAL COMPOSITION

DUP: 4, UUP: 4, ALL: 2, IND: 2, O: 1, SF: 1, SDLP: 1

LEEDS CITY — M

Leeds City Council, Civic Hall, Leeds LS1 1UR
☎ 0113 222 4444
🖳 www.leeds.gov.uk

FACTS & FIGURES

Police Authority: West Yorkshire Police Authority
Health Authority: NHS Yorkshire & the Humber
Learning and Skills Council: Yorkshire and the Humber
Parliamentary Constituencies: Elmet and Rothwell, Leeds Central, Leeds East, Leeds North East, Leeds North West, Leeds West, Morley and Outwood, Normanton, Pontefract and Castleford, Pudsey
EU Constituencies: Yorkshire and the Humber
Election Frequency: Elections are by thirds
Twinning: Dortmund Siegen (Germany), Lille (France)

PRINCIPAL OFFICERS

Chief Executive: Mr Tom Riordan, Chief Executive, Chief Executive's Office, 3rd Floor East, Civic Hall, Leeds LS1 1UR ☎ 0113 247 4328 ✉ tom.riordan@leeds.gov.uk

Assistant Chief Executive: Mr James Rogers, Assistant Chief Executive (Planning, Policy & Improvement), 3rd Floor East, Civic Hall, Calverley Street, Leeds LS1 1UR ☎ 0113 224 3579 🖷 0113 247 4870 ✉ james.rogers@leeds.gov.uk

Senior Management: Mr Neil Evans, Director of Environment & Neighbourhoods, 4th Floor West, Merrion House, Leeds LS1 1UR ☎ 0113 247 4721 🖷 0113 247 4721 ✉ neil.evans@leeds.gov.uk

Senior Management: Mr Martin Farrington, Director of Development, The Leonardo Building, 2 Rossington Street, Leeds LS2 8HB ☎ 0113 224 3816 🖷 0113 247 7748 ✉ martin.farrington@leeds.gov.uk

Senior Management: Mr Alan Gay, Director of Resources, Civic Hall, Calverley Street, Leeds LS1 1UR ☎ 0113 247 4226 🖷 0113 247 4346 ✉ alan.gay@leeds.gov.uk

Access Officer / Social Services (Disability): Ms Lelir Yeung, Head of Equality, Civic Hall, Calverley Street, Leeds LS1 1UR ☎ 0113 247 4152 ✉ lelir.yeung@leeds.gov.uk

Architect, Building / Property Services: Mr David Graham, Head of Building Maintenance, Merrion House, 110 Merrion Centre, Leeds LS2 8DT ☎ 0113 247 8756 ✉ david.graham@leeds.gov.uk

Architect, Building / Property Services: Mr David Little, Head of Service - Building Control, Civic Hall, Leeds LS1 1UR ☎ 0113 247 8097 🖷 0113 247 8230 ✉ david.little@leeds.gov.uk

Best Value: Mr James Rogers, Assistant Chief Executive (Planning, Policy & Improvement), 3rd Floor East, Civic Hall, Calverley Street, Leeds LS1 1UR ☎ 0113 224 3579 🖷 0113 247 4870 ✉ james.rogers@leeds.gov.uk

Building Control: Mr David Little, Head of Service - Building Control, Planning Services, Leonardo Building, Level 4, Leeds LS2 8DT ☎ 0113 247 8097 🖷 0113 247 8230 ✉ david.little@leeds.gov.uk

Catering Services: Mr Nigel Crossland, Catering Manager, Seacroft Ring Road Depot, Seacroft Ring Road, Leeds LS14 1NZ ☎ 0113 214 4037

Catering Services: Ms Helen Franklin, Head of Highways Services, Civic Hall, Leeds LS1 1UR ☎ 0113 247 5318 ✉ helen.franklin@leeds.gov.uk

Children / Youth Services: Mr Jim Hopkinson, Head of Service Youth Offending, 31 Moor Road, Headingley, Leeds LS6 4BG ☎ 0113 214 5300 ✉ jim.hopkinson@leeds.gov.uk

Children / Youth Services: Mr John Paxton, Head of Youth Service, Merrion House, 110 Merrion Centre, Leeds LS2 8DT ☎ 0113 247 7592 🖷 0113 247 6519 ✉ john.paxton@leeds.gov.uk

Children / Youth Services: Mr Nigel Richardson, Director of Children's Services, Childrens Services, 6th Floor East, Civic Hall, Leeds LS2 8DT ☎ 0113 395 0925 ✉ eleanor.brazil@leeds.gov.uk

Civil Registration: Ms Brenda Knott, Head of Civic & Ceremonial Support, Democratic Services, 2nd Floor East, Civic Hall, Leeds LS1 1UR ☎ 0113 247 4572 ✉ brenda.knott@leeds.gov.uk

PR / Communications: Ms Dee Reid, Head of Communications, Communications Team, 4th Floor West, Civic Hall, Leeds LS1 1UR ☎ 0113 247 5427; 0113 247 5427 ✉ dee.reid@leeds.gov.uk; dee.reid@leeds.gov.uk

Community Planning: Mr Neil Evans, Director of Environment & Neighbourhoods, 4th Floor West, Merrion House, Leeds LS1 1UR ☎ 0113 247 4721 🖷 0113 247 4721 ✉ neil.evans@leeds.gov.uk

Computer Management: Mr Dylan Roberts, Chief ICT Officer, Apex Centre, Apex Way, Leeds LS11 5LT ☎ 0113 395 1515 ✉ dylan.roberts@leeds.gov.uk

Corporate Services: Mr Paul Broughton, Chief Customer Services Officer, Civic Hall, Leeds LS1 1JF ☎ 0113 376 0001 ✉ paul.broughton@leeds.gov.uk

Corporate Services: Mr Alan Gay, Director of Resources, Civic Hall, Calverley Street, Leeds LS1 1UR ☎ 0113 247 4226 🖷 0113 247 4346 ✉ alan.gay@leeds.gov.uk

Corporate Services: Mr Lee Hemsworth, Chief Officer - Intelligence & Improvement, Information Knowledge Management, 2nd Floor West, Civic Hall, Leeds LS1 1UR ☎ 0113 247 4411 ✉ lee.hemsworth@leeds.gov.uk

Corporate Services: Mr John Lennon, Chief Officer - Access & Inclusion, Merrion House, Leeds LS2 8QB ☎ 0113 247 8665

Customer Service: Mr Paul Broughton, Chief Customer Services Officer, Civic Hall, Leeds LS1 1JF ☎ 0113 376 0001 ✉ paul.broughton@leeds.gov.uk

Customer Service: Mr Arfan Hanif, Head of Strategy & Development, Business Transformation, 4th Floor East, Civic Hall, Leeds LS1 1UR ☎ 0113 395 0386 ✉ arfan.hanif@leeds.gov.uk

Customer Service: Ms Susan Murray, Head of Face to Face Contact, Westgate, 6 Grace Street, Leeds LS1 2RP ☎ 0113 376 0023 ✉ susan.murray@leeds.gov.uk

Economic Development: Ms Sue Burgess, Manager - Leeds Market, Civic Hall, Leeds LS1 1UR

Economic Development: Mr Martin Farrington, Director of Development, The Leonardo Building, 2 Rossington Street, Leeds LS2 8HB ☎ 0113 224 3816 🖷 0113 247 7748 ✉ martin.farrington@leeds.gov.uk

Economic Development: Mr Thomas Holvey, Economic Policy Manager, Level 6, Leonardo, 2 Rossington Street, Leeds LS2 8HD ☎ 0113 247 8073 ✉ tom.holvey@leeds.gov.uk

LOCAL AUTHORITIES

Electoral Registration: Ms Susanna Benton, Electoral Services Manager, Town Hall, The Headrow, Leeds LS1 3AD ☎ 0113 247 4339 ⌨ susanna.benton@leeds.gov.uk

Emergency Planning: Mr Roger Carter, Principal Emergency Planning Officer, Civic Hall, Leeds LS1 1UR ☎ 0113 247 4339 🖷 0113 247 4338 ⌨ roger.carter@leeds.gov.uk

Energy Management: Mr Peter Lynes, Group Manager, Thoresby House, Level 5SE, 2 Rossington Street, Leeds LS2 8HD ☎ 0113 247 5539 🖷 0113 395 1461 ⌨ peter.lynes@leeds.gov.uk

Environmental / Technical Services: Ms Helen Freeman, Chief Officer (HEAS), 4th Floor West, Merrion House, Leeds LS2 8BB ☎ 0113 247 6397 🖷 0113 224 3543 ⌨ helen.freeman@leeds.gov.uk

Environmental Health: Mr Andy Beattie, Head of Service - Housing & Pollution Control, Limewood, 1st Floor, 2-5 Limewood Approach, Leeds LS14 1NG ☎ 0113 247 6141 🖷 0113 224 3543 ⌨ andy.beattie@leeds.gov.uk

Estates, Property & Valuation: Mr Martin Farrington, Director of Development, The Leonardo Building, 2 Rossington Street, Leeds LS2 8HB ☎ 0113 224 3816 🖷 0113 247 7748 ⌨ martin.farrington@leeds.gov.uk

European Liaison: Mr Martin Dean, Head of Leeds Initiative & International Partnerships, Leeds Initiative, 1st Floor West, Civic Hall, Leeds LS1 1UR ☎ 0113 247 4154 ⌨ martin.dean@leeds.gov.uk

Events Manager: Mr Paul Footitt, Events Manager, 1st Floor, Town Hall, Headrow, Leeds LS1 3AD ☎ 0113 224 3600 ⌨ paul.footitt@leeds.gov.uk

Finance and Treasurer: Mr Alan Gay, Director of Resources, Civic Hall, Calverley Street, Leeds LS1 1UR ☎ 0113 247 4226 🖷 0113 247 4346 ⌨ alan.gay@leeds.gov.uk

Fleet Management: Mr Terence Pycroft, Head of Fleet Services, 255a York Road, Leeds LS9 7QQ ☎ 0113 214 3170

Grounds Maintenance: Ms Sarah Martin, Property Maintenance Manager, Commercial Services, Seacroft Ring Road Depot, Ring Road, Seacroft, Leeds LS14 1NZ ☎ 0113 214 9501 ⌨ sarah.martin@leeds.gov.uk

Highways: Mr Martin Farrington, Director of Development, The Leonardo Building, 2 Rossington Street, Leeds LS2 8HB ☎ 0113 224 3816 🖷 0113 247 7748 ⌨ martin.farrington@leeds.gov.uk

Highways: Ms Helen Franklin, Head of Highways Services, Middleton Highways, 1st Floor Room 222, Ring Road, Leeds LS10 4AX ☎ 0113 247 5318 ⌨ helen.franklin@leeds.gov.uk

Home Energy Conservation: Mr George Munson, Climate Change Manager, Planning and sustainable development, Thoresby House, 4th Floor, 2 Rossington Street, Leeds LS2 8HD ☎ 0113 395 1767 ⌨ george.munson@leeds.gov.uk

Housing: Mr Neil Evans, Director of Environment & Neighbourhoods, 4th Floor West, Merrion House, Leeds LS1 1UR ☎ 0113 247 4721 🖷 0113 247 4721 ⌨ neil.evans@leeds.gov.uk

Housing Maintenance: Mr Paul Langford, Chief Housing Services Officer, 4th Floor West, Merrion House, Leeds LS2 8BB ☎ 0113 247 4721 🖷 0113 224 3543 ⌨ paul.langford@leeds.gov.uk

Local Area Agreement: Ms Jane Stageman, Senior Project Manager, Human Resources, 3rd Floor East, Civic Hall, Leeds LS1 1UR ☎ 0113 2474352 ⌨ jane.stageman@leeds.gov.uk

Legal: Mr Ian Spafford, Head of Community Services & Litigation, St Georges House, 40 Great George Street, Leeds LS1 3DL ☎ 0113 247 4409 ⌨ ian.spafford@leeds.gov.uk

Leisure and Cultural Services: Mr Mark Allman, Head of Sport & Active Recreation, John Charles Centre for Sport, Middleton Grove, Leeds LS11 5DJ ☎ 0113 247 8323 🖷 0113 247 8430 ⌨ mark.allman@leeds.gov.uk

Licensing: Mr Stuart Turnock, Chief Officer (Legal, Licensing & Registration), St George House, Great George Street, Leeds LS1 3DL ☎ 0113 247 4666 ⌨ stuart.turnock@leeds.gov.uk

Lighting: Mr Martin Farrington, Director of Development, The Leonardo Building, 2 Rossington Street, Leeds LS2 8HB ☎ 0113 224 3816 🖷 0113 247 7748 ⌨ martin.farrington@leeds.gov.uk

Lottery Funding, Charity and Voluntary: Mr Stephen Boyle, Chief Regeneration Officer, 4th Floor West, Merrion House, Leeds LS2 8BB ☎ 0113 395 0924 🖷 0113 224 3543 ⌨ stephen.boyle@leeds.gov.uk

Member Services: Mr Nick De La Taste, Chief Democratic Services Officer, Civic Hall, Calverley Street, Leeds LS1 1UR ☎ 0113 247 4560

Member Services: Mr Andy Hodson, Head of Governance Services, Corporate Governance, 4th Floor West, Civic Hall, Leeds LS1 1UR ☎ 0113 224 3208 ⌨ andy.hodson@leeds.gov.uk

Member Services: Mr Peter Marrington, Head of Scrutiny & Member Development, Civic Hall, Leeds LS1 1UR ☎ 0113 395 1151 ⌨ peter.marrington@leeds.gov.uk

Personnel / HR: Ms Lorraine Hallam, Chief Officer (Human Resources), Civic Hall, Calverley Street, Leeds LS1 1UR ☎ 0113 395 1600

Planning: Mr Martin Farrington, Director of Development, The Leonardo Building, 2 Rossington Street, Leeds LS2 8HB ☎ 0113 224 3816 🖷 0113 247 7748 ⌨ martin.farrington@leeds.gov.uk

Procurement: Mr Dean Backhouse, Procurement Compliance & Regulations Manager, Procurement, 4th Floor West, Civic Hall, Leeds LS1 1UR ☎ 0113 224 3702 ⌨ dean.backhouse@leeds.gov.uk

Public Libraries: Miss Catherine Blanshard, Chief Libraries, Arts & Heritage Officer, 7th Floor West, Merrion House, Leeds LS2 1DT ☎ 0113 247 8331 🖷 0113 247 7747

catherine.blanshard@leeds.gov.uk

Recycling & Waste Minimisation: Mr David Bailey, Recycling & Waste Minimisation Officer, Knowsthorpe Gate, Cross Green, Leeds LS9 0NP ☎ 0113 2477858 🖷 0113 2478307 david.bailey@leeds.gov.uk

Regeneration: Mr Martin Farrington, Director of Development, The Leonardo Building, 2 Rossington Street, Leeds LS2 8HB ☎ 0113 224 3816 🖷 0113 247 7748 martin.farrington@leeds.gov.uk

Road Safety: Mr Martin Farrington, Director of Development, The Leonardo Building, 2 Rossington Street, Leeds LS2 8HB ☎ 0113 224 3816 🖷 0113 247 7748 martin.farrington@leeds.gov.uk

Social Services (Adult): Ms Sandie Keene, Director of Adult Social Services, Merrion House, 110 Merrion Centre, Leeds LS2 8DT sandie.keene@leeds.gov.uk

Social Services (Children): Ms Jean Davey, Principal Youth Officer, Childrens Services, 6th Floor East, Civic Hall, Leeds LS2 8DT ☎ 0113 231 9903 jean.davey@leeds.gov.uk

Staff Training: Ms Lorraine Hallam, Chief Officer (Human Resources), 3rd Floor West, Civic Hall, Leeds LS1 1UR ☎ 0113 395 1600 lorraine.hallam@leeds.gov.uk

Street Scene: Mr Stephen Smith, Head of Environmental Services, Civic Hall, Calverley Street, Leeds LS1 1UR ☎ 0113 247 4249 🖷 0113 247 4984 stephen.smith@leeds.gov.uk

Sustainable Communities: Mr Stephen Boyle, Chief Regeneration Officer, 4th Floor West, Merrion House, Leeds LS2 8BB ☎ 0113 395 0924 🖷 0113 224 3543 stephen.boyle@leeds.gov.uk

Sustainable Development: Mr Steve Speak, Chief Strategy & Policy Officer, The Leonardo Building, 2 Rossington Street, Leeds LS2 8HD ☎ 0113 247 8086 🖷 0113 247 4736

Town Centre: Ms Cath Follin, Head of City Centre & Markets, Leonardo Building, 2 Rossington Street, Leeds LS2 8HD ☎ 0113 247 4474 🖷 0113 244 3600 cath.follin@leeds.gov.uk

Traffic Management: Mr Martin Farrington, Director of Development, The Leonardo Building, 2 Rossington Street, Leeds LS2 8HB ☎ 0113 224 3816 🖷 0113 247 7748 martin.farrington@leeds.gov.uk

Transport: Ms Julie Meakin, Chief Commercial Services Officer, Seacroft Ring Road Depot, Ring Road, Seacroft, Leeds LS14 1NZ ☎ 0113 214 9568 julie.meakin@leeds.gov.uk

Transport Planner: Ms Julie Meakin, Chief Commercial Services Officer, Seacroft Ring Road Depot, Ring Road, Seacroft, Leeds LS14 1NZ ☎ 0113 214 9568 julie.meakin@leeds.gov.uk

Waste Collection and Disposal: Mr Stephen Smith, Head of Environmental Services, Civic Hall, Calverley Street, Leeds LS1 1UR ☎ 0113 247 4249 🖷 0113 247 4984 stephen.smith@leeds.gov.uk

Waste Management: Ms Amanda Pitt, Project Manager (Waste Strategy), Knowsthorpe Gate, Cross Green, Leeds LS9 0NP ☎ 0113 247 5609 🖷 0113 247 8862 amanda.pitt@leeds.gov.uk

Waste Management: Mr Stephen Smith, Head of Environmental Services, Civic Hall, Calverley Street, Leeds LS1 1UR ☎ 0113 247 4249 🖷 0113 247 4984 stephen.smith@leeds.gov.uk

MEMBERS OF THE COUNCIL (99)

***Mayor:* Castle**, Ann (CON - Harewood)
ann.castle@leeds.gov.uk

***Leader of the Council:* Wakefield**, Keith (LAB - Kippax and Methley)
keith.wakefield@leeds.gov.uk

***Deputy Leader of the Council:* Blake**, Judith (LAB - Middleton Park)
judith.blake@leeds.gov.uk

***Group Leader:* Blackburn**, Ann (GRN - Farnley and Wortley)
ann.blackburn@leeds.gov.uk

***Group Leader:* Carter**, Andrew (CON - Calverley and Farsley)
andrew.carter@leeds.gov.uk

***Group Leader:* Finnigan**, Robert (IND - Morley North)
robert.finnigan@leeds.gov.uk

***Group Leader:* Golton**, Stewart (LD - Rothwell)
stewart.golton@leeds.gov.uk

***Group Leader:* McKenna**, James (LAB - Armley)
james.mckenna@leeds.gov.uk

Akhtar, Javaid (LAB - Hyde Park and Woodhouse)
javaid.akhtar@leeds.gov.uk

Anderson, Barry (CON - Adel and Wharfedale)
barry.anderson@leeds.gov.uk

Armitage, Suzi (LAB - Cross Gates and Whinmoor)
suzi.armitage@leeds.gov.uk

Atha, Bernard (LAB - Kirkstall)
bernard.atha@leeds.gov.uk

Bentley, Sue (LD - Weetwood)
sue.bentley@leeds.gov.uk

Bentley, Jonathan (LD - Weetwood)
jonathan.bentley@leeds.gov.uk

Blackburn, David (GRN - Farnley and Wortley)
cllr.david.blackburn@leeds.gov.uk

Bruce, Karen (LAB - Rothwell)
karen.bruce@leeds.gov.uk

Buckley, Neil (CON - Alwoodley)
neil.buckley@leeds.gov.uk

Campbell, Colin (LD - Otley and Yeadon)
colin.campbell@leeds.gov.uk

Carter, John (CON - Adel and Wharfedale)
les.carter@leeds.gov.uk

Chapman, Judith (LD - Weetwood)
judith.m.chapman@leeds.gov.uk

Charlwood, Rebecca (LAB - Moortown)
rebecca.charlwood@leeds.gov.uk

Cleasby, Brian (LD - Horsforth)
brian.cleasby@leeds.gov.uk

Cohen, Daniel (CON - Alwoodley)
daniel.cohen@leeds.gov.uk

Collins, Dawn (CON - Horsforth)
dawn.collins2@leeds.gov.uk

Congreve, David (LAB - Beeston and Holbeck)
david.congreve@leeds.gov.uk

Coulson, Mick (LAB - Pudsey)
mick.coulson@leeds.gov.uk

Cummins, Judith (LAB - Temple Newsam)

judith.cummins@leeds.gov.uk
Davey, Patrick (LAB - City and Hunslet)
patrick.davey@leeds.gov.uk
Dawson, Neil (LAB - Morley South)
neil.dawson@leeds.gov.uk
Dobson, Mark (LAB - Garforth and Swillington)
mark.dobson@leeds.gov.uk
Downes, Ryk (LD - Otley and Yeadon)
ryk.downes@leeds.gov.uk
Dowson, Jane (LAB - Chapel Allerton)
jane.dowson@leeds.gov.uk
Dunn, Jack (LAB - Ardsley and Robin Hood)
jack.dunn@leeds.gov.uk
Elliott, Judith (IND - Morley South)
judith.elliott@leeds.gov.uk
Fox, Clive (CON - Adel and Wharfedale)
clive.fox@leeds.gov.uk
Gabriel, Angela (LAB - Beeston and Holbeck)
angela.gabriel@leeds.gov.uk
Gettings, Bob (IND - Morley North)
robert.gettings@leeds.gov.uk
Grahame, Ronald (LAB - Burmantofts and Richmond Hill)
ronald.grahame@leeds.gov.uk
Grahame, Pauleen (LAB - Cross Gates and Whinmoor)
pauleen.grahame@leeds.gov.uk
Groves, Kim (LAB - Middleton Park)
kim.groves@leeds.gov.uk
Gruen, Peter (LAB - Cross Gates and Whinmoor)
peter.gruen@leeds.gov.uk
Gruen, Caroline (LAB - Bramley and Stanningley)
Hamilton, Martin (LD - Headingley)
martin.hamilton@leeds.gov.uk
Hamilton, Sharon (LAB - Moortown)
sharon.hamilton@leeds.gov.uk
Hanley, Ted (LAB - Bramley and Stanningley)
ted.hanley@leeds.gov.uk
Hardy, John (LAB - Farnley and Wortley)
john.hardy@leeds.gov.uk
Harland, Mary (LAB - Kippax and Methley)
Harper, Gerry (LAB - Hyde Park and Woodhouse)
gerald.harper@leeds.gov.uk
Harper, Janet (LAB - Armley)
janet.harper@leeds.gov.uk
Harrand, Peter (CON - Alwoodley)
peter.harrand@leeds.gov.uk
Harrington, Roger (LAB - Gipton and Harehills)
Hussain, Arif (LAB - Gipton and Harehills)
arif.hussain@leeds.gov.uk
Hussain, Ghulam (LAB - Roundhay)
ghulam.hussain@leeds.gov.uk
Hyde, Graham (LAB - Killingbeck and Seacroft)
graham.hyde@leeds.gov.uk
Illingworth, John (LAB - Kirkstall)
john.illingworth@leeds.gov.uk
Ingham, Maureen (LAB - Burmantofts and Richmond Hill)
Iqbal, Mohammed (LAB - City and Hunslet)
mohammed.iqbal@leeds.gov.uk
Jarosz, Josephine (LAB - Pudsey)
josephine.jarosz@leeds.gov.uk
Khan, Asghar (LAB - Burmantofts and Richmond Hill)
asghar.khan@leeds.gov.uk
Lamb, Alan (CON - Wetherby)
alan.lamb@leeds.gov.uk
Latty, Pat (CON - Guiseley and Rawdon)
patricia.latty@leeds.gov.uk
Latty, Graham (CON - Guiseley and Rawdon)
graham.latty@leeds.gov.uk
Lay, Sandy (LD - Otley and Yeadon)
sandy.lay@leeds.gov.uk
Leadley, Tom (IND - Morley North)
thomas.leadley@leeds.gov.uk
Lewis, James (LAB - Kippax and Methley)
james.lewis@leeds.gov.uk
Lewis, Richard (LAB - Pudsey)
richard.lewis@leeds.gov.uk
Lowe, Alison (LAB - Armley)
alison.lowe@leeds.gov.uk
Lyons, Michael (LAB - Temple Newsam)
michael.lyons@leeds.gov.uk
Macniven, Christine (LAB - Roundhay)
christine.macniven@leeds.gov.uk
Magsood, Kamila (LAB - Gipton and Harehills)
kamila.maqsood@leeds.gov.uk
Marjoram, Joseph (CON - Calverley and Farsley)
joe.marjoram@leeds.gov.uk
McKenna, Andrea (LAB - Garforth and Swillington)
andrea.mckenna@leeds.gov.uk
Mitchell, Katherine (LAB - Temple Newsam)
katherine.mitchell@leeds.gov.uk
Morgan, Vonnie (LAB - Killingbeck and Seacroft)
veronica.morgan@leeds.gov.uk
Mulherin, Lisa (LAB - Ardsley and Robin Hood)
lisa.mulherin@leeds.gov.uk
Murray, Thomas (LAB - Garforth and Swillington)
thomas.murray@leeds.gov.uk
Nagle, David (LAB - Rothwell)
david.nagle@leeds.gov.uk
Nash, Elizabeth (LAB - City and Hunslet)
elizabeth.nash@leeds.gov.uk
Ogilvie, Adam (LAB - Beeston and Holbeck)
adam.ogilvie@leeds.gov.uk
Procter, Rachael (CON - Harewood)
rachael.procter@leeds.gov.uk
Procter, John (CON - Wetherby)
john.procter@leeds.gov.uk
Rafique, Mohammed (LAB - Chapel Allerton)
cllr.mohammed.rafique@leeds.gov.uk
Renshaw, Karen (LAB - Ardsley and Robin Hood)
karen.renshaw@leeds.gov.uk
Robinson, Matthew (CON - Harewood)
matthew.robinson@leeds.gov.uk
Selby, Brian (LAB - Killingbeck and Seacroft)
brian.selby@leeds.gov.uk
Sobel, Alex (LAB - Moortown)
alex.sobel@leeds.gov.uk
Taggart, Neil (LAB - Brmaley and Stanningley)
neil.taggart.@leeds.gov.uk
Taylor, Eileen (LAB - Chapel Allerton)
eileen.taylor@leeds.gov.uk
Towler, Christine (LAB - Hyde Park and Woodhouse)
Townsley, Christopher (LD - Horsforth)
christopher.townsley@leeds.gov.uk
Truswell, Paul (LAB - Middleton Park)
paul.truswell@leeds.gov.uk
Urry, Bill (LAB - Roundhay)
bill.urry@leeds.gov.uk
Varley, Shirley (IND - Morley South)
shirley.varley@leeds.gov.uk
Wadsworth, Paul (CON - Guiseley and Rawdon)

paul.wadsworth@leeds.gov.uk
Walker, Janette (LAB - Headingley)
Walshaw, Neil (LAB - Headingley)
neil.walshaw@leeds.gov.uk
Wilkinson, Gerald (CON - Wetherby)
gerald.wilkinson@leeds.gov.uk
Wood, Rod (CON - Calverley and Farsley)
roderic.wood@leeds.gov.uk
Yeadon, Lucinda (LAB - Kirkstall)
lucinda.yeadon@leeds.gov.uk

POLITICAL COMPOSITION

LAB: 63, CON: 19, LD: 10, IND: 5, GRN: 2

CABINET

Leader: Mr Keith Wakefield
Deputy Leader / Children's Services: Ms Judith Blake
Deputy Leader / Neighbourhood, Housing & Regeneration: Mr Peter Gruen
Adult Health & Social Care: Ms Lucinda Yeadon
Development: Mr Richard Lewis
Environmental Services: Mr Mark Dobson
Leisure: Mr Adam Ogilvie

COMMITTEE CHAIRS

Development: Mr Neil Taggart
General Purposes: Mr Keith Wakefield
Scrutiny - Children & Families: Ms Judith Chapman
Scrutiny - Health, Wellbeing & Adult Social Care: Mr John Illingworth
Scrutiny - Housing & Regeneration: Mr John Procter
Scrutiny - Resources: Mrs Pauleen Grahame
Scrutiny - Safer & Stronger Communities: Mr Barry Anderson
Scrutiny - Sustainable Economy & Culture: Mr Mohammed Rafique

LEICESTER CITY U

Leicester City Council, New Walk Centre, Welford Place, Leicester LE1 6ZG ☎ 0116 254 9922 🖷 0116 254 5531
🖳 www.leicester.gov.uk

FACTS & FIGURES

Police Authority: Leicestershire Police Authority
Health Authority: East Midlands Strategic Health Authority
Learning and Skills Council: East Midlands
Parliamentary Constituencies: Leicester East, Leicester South, Leicester West
EU Constituencies: East Midlands
Election Frequency: Elections are of whole council
Twinning: Chongqing (China); Krefeld (Germany); Masaya (Nicaragua); Rajkot (India); Strasbourg (France)

PRINCIPAL OFFICERS

Deputy Chief Executive: Mr Andy Keeling, Chief Operating Officer, New Walk Centre, Welford Place, Leicester LE1 6ZG ☎ 0116 252 7380 ✉ andy.keeling@leicester.gov.uk

Senior Management: Mr Adrian Russell, Director of Environmental Services, New Walk Centre, Welford Place, Leicester LE1 6ZG ☎ 0116 252 7295 🖷 0116 254 3720 ✉ adrian.russell@leicester.gov.uk

Access Officer / Social Services (Disability): Mr Ashraf Osman, Interim Director of Care Services, New Walk Centre, Welford Place, Leicester LE1 6ZG ☎ 0116 252 8303 🖷 0116 224 7147

Architect, Building / Property Services: Mr Andrew Smith, Director of Planning, Transport & Economic Development, New Walk Centre, Welford Place, Leicester LE1 6ZG ☎ 0116 252 7201 ✉ andrewl.smith@leicester.gov.uk

Best Value: Mr Simon Sadler, Head of Partnership, Planning & Performance, New Walk Centre, Welford Place, Leicester LE1 6ZG ☎ 0116 252 6788 🖷 0116 255 2451 ✉ simon.sadler@leicester.gov.uk

Children / Youth Services: Ms Rachel Dickinson, Strategic Director - Children, New Walk Centre, Welford Place, Leicester LE1 6ZG ☎ 0116 252 7700 ✉ rachel.dickinson@leicester.gov.uk

Children / Youth Services: Ms Margaret Librari, Director of Learning Services, New Walk Centre, Welford Place, Leicester LE1 6ZG ☎ 0116 252 7701 🖷 0116 285 6241 ✉ margaret.librari@leicester.gov.uk

Civil Registration: Mr Kevin Lewis, Registration Service Manager, Town Hall, Town Hall Square, Leicester LE1 9BG ☎ 0845 045 0901 ✉ lewk001@leicester.gov.uk

PR / Communications: Mr Mark Bentley, Head of Communications, New Walk Centre, Welford Place, Leicester LE1 6ZG ☎ 0116 252 6397 🖷 0116 254 5391 ✉ mark.bentley@leicester.gov.uk

Community Safety: Mr Kelvin Bates, Community Safety Team Leader, New Walk Centre, Welford Place, Leicester LE1 6ZG ☎ 0116 252 6032 🖷 0116 285 6241

Computer Management: Mrs Jill Craig, Director of Information & Customer Access, New Walk Centre, Welford Place, Leicester LE1 6ZG ☎ 0116 252 7407 🖷 0116 255 1843 ✉ jill.craig@leicester.gov.uk

Consumer Protection and Trading Standards: Mr Roman Leszczyszyn, Head of Business Regulation, New Walk Centre, Welford Place, Leicester LE1 6ZG ☎ 0116 252 6576 🖷 0116 224 8009

Corporate Services: Ms Miranda Cannon, Director of Delivery & Political Governance, New Walk Centre, Welford Place, Leicester LE1 6ZG ☎ 0116 252 6079 ✉ miranda.cannon@leicester.gov.uk

Customer Service: Mrs Pat Jones, Head of Customer Service, New Walk Centre, Welford Place, Leicester LE1 6ZG ☎ 0116 252 6497 🖷 0116 252 6499 ✉ pat.jones@leicester.gov.uk

Economic Development: Mr Andrew Smith, Director of Planning, Transport & Economic Development, New Walk Centre, Welford Place, Leicester LE1 6ZG ☎ 0116 252 7201 ✉ andrewl.smith@leicester.gov.uk

Education: Ms Margaret Librari, Director of Learning Services, New Walk Centre, Welford Place, Leicester LE1 6ZG ☎ 0116 252

7701 🖷 0116 285 6241 ✉ margaret.librari@leicester.gov.uk

E-Government: Mrs Jill Craig, Director of Information & Customer Access, New Walk Centre, Welford Place, Leicester LE1 6ZG ☎ 0116 252 7407 🖷 0116 255 1843 ✉ jill.craig@leicester.gov.uk

Electoral Registration: Ms Alison Scott, Electoral Services Manager, Town Hall, Town Hall Square, Leicester LE1 9BG ☎ 0116 299 5965 🖷 0116 247 0863 ✉ alison.scott@leicester.gov.uk

Emergency Planning: Mr Martin Halse, Resilience Manager, New Walk Centre, Welford Place, Leicester LE1 6ZG ☎ 0116 238 5001 🖷 0116 252 6749 ✉ martin.halse@leicester.gov.uk

Environmental Health: Mr Adrian Russell, Director of Environmental Services, New Walk Centre, Welford Place, Leicester LE1 6ZG ☎ 0116 252 7295 🖷 0116 254 3720 ✉ adrian.russell@leicester.gov.uk

Estates, Property & Valuation: Mr Neil Gamble, Head of Estates & Asset Management, New Walk Centre, Welford Place, Leicester LE1 6ZG ☎ 0116 299 5001 ✉ neil.gamble@leicester.gov.uk

European Liaison: Mrs Joanne Ives, Regeneration Programs Manager, New Walk Centre, Welford Place, Leicester LE1 6ZG ☎ 0116 252 6524 🖷 0116 254 3720 ✉ joanne.ives@leicester.gov.uk

Events Manager: Ms Maggie Shutt, Festivals & Events Manager, Wellington House, Wellington Street, Leicester LE1 6HL ☎ 0116 238 5079 🖷 0116 299 5979

Facilities: Mr Azim Mohamed, Facilities Manager, 16 New Walk, Leicester LE1 6UB ☎ 0116 252 7073 ✉ moha001@leicester.gov.uk

Finance and Treasurer: Mr Colin Sharpe, Acting Director of Finance, New Walk Centre, Welford Place, Leicester LE1 6ZG ☎ 0116 252 7401 🖷 0116 255 1843 ✉ colin.sharpe@leicester.gov.uk

Health and Safety: Mr Frank Imms, Head of Health & Safety & Wellbeing, New Walk Centre, Welford Place, Leicester LE1 6ZG ☎ 0116 252 8099 ✉ frank.imms@leicester.gov.uk

Highways: Mr Andy Thomas, Head of Traffic Management, York House, Granby Street, Leicester LE1 6FB ☎ 0116 252 6540 🖷 0116 229 4100 ✉ andrew.thomas@leicester.gov.uk

Home Energy Conservation: Mr Mike Richardson, Home Energy Team Leader, 35 Rowsley Street, Leicester LE5 5JP ☎ 0116 299 5123 🖷 0116 221 1180 ✉ richm002@leicester.gov.uk

Housing: Ms Ann Branson, Director of Housing, Ian Marlow Centre, Blackbird Road, Leicester LE4 0AR ☎ 0116 252 6802 ✉ ann.branson@leicester.gov.uk

Housing Maintenance: Ms Ann Branson, Director of Housing, Ian Marlow Centre, Blackbird Road, Leicester LE4 0AR ☎ 0116 252 6802 ✉ ann.branson@leicester.gov.uk

Housing Maintenance: Mr Ian Craig, Head of Direct Services, Housing Department, Blackbird Road, Leicester LE4 0AR ☎ 0116 252 6106 🖷 0116 251 8998 ✉ craii001@leicester.gov.uk

Local Area Agreement: Mr Adam Archer, Lead Officer - Partnerships, Planning & Performance, New Walk Centre, Welford Place, Leicester LE1 6ZG ☎ 0116 252 6070 ✉ adam.archer@leicester.gov.uk

Legal: Mr Kamal Adatia, City Barrister & Head of Standards, New Walk Centre, Welford Place, Leicester LE1 6ZG ✉ kamal.adatia@leicester.gov.uk

Leisure and Cultural Services: Ms Liz Blyth, Acting Director of Cultural Services, New Walk Centre, Welford Place, Leicester LE1 6ZG ☎ 0116 252 7301 🖷 0116 255 4894 ✉ liz.blyth@leicester.gov.uk

Leisure and Cultural Services: Mr Paul Edwards, Head of Sports Services, New Walk Centre, Welford Place, Leicester LE1 6ZG ☎ 0116 252 7323 🖷 0116 255 2451 ✉ paul.edwards@leicester.gov.uk

Leisure and Cultural Services: Ms Sarah Levitt, Head of Arts & Museums, New Walk Centre, Welford Place, Leicester LE1 6ZG ☎ 0116 252 8912 ✉ sarah.levitt@leicester.gov.uk

Licensing: Mr Mike Broster, Head of Licensing & Pollution Control, New Walk Centre, Welford Place, Leicester LE1 6ZG ☎ 0116 252 6408 🖷 0116 255 3773 ✉ mike.broster@leicester.gov.uk

Lifelong Learning: Ms Helen Ryan, Director - Learning Environment, B Block, King Street, Leicester LE1 6ZG ☎ 0116 221 1656 ✉ helen.ryan@leicester.gov.uk

Partnerships: Mr Adam Archer, Lead Officer - Partnerships, Planning & Performance, New Walk Centre, Welford Place, Leicester LE1 6ZG ☎ 0116 252 6070 ✉ adam.archer@leicester.gov.uk

Personnel / HR: Ms Fiona Skene, Director of HR & Workforce Development, New Walk Centre, Welford Place, Leicester LE1 6ZG ☎ 0116 252 6003 ✉ fiona.skene@leicester.gov.uk

Planning: Ms Margaret Librari, Director of Learning Services, New Walk Centre, Welford Place, Leicester LE1 6ZG ☎ 0116 252 7701 🖷 0116 285 6241 ✉ margaret.librari@leicester.gov.uk

Planning: Mr Andrew Smith, Director of Planning, Transport & Economic Development, New Walk Centre, Welford Place, Leicester LE1 6ZG ☎ 0116 252 7201 ✉ andrewl.smith@leicester.gov.uk

Procurement: Mr Jayesh Joshi, Head of Corporate Procurement, New Walk Centre, Welford Place, Leicester LE1 6ZG ☎ 0116 252 6304 🖷 0116 222 1504 ✉ jayesh.joshi@leicester.gov.uk

Public Libraries: Mr Adrian Wills, Head of Libraries, New Walk Centre, Welford Place, Leicester LE1 6ZG ☎ 0116 252 6762

☞ adrian.wills@leicester.gov.uk

Recycling & Waste Minimisation: Mr Steve Weston, Head of Waste Management, New Walk Centre, Welford Place, Leicester LE1 6ZG ☎ 0116 252 8582 🖷 0116 252 8592 ☞ steve.weston@leicester.gov.uk

Social Services: Ms Tracie Rees, Director of Care Services & Commissioning, New Walk Centre, Welford Place, Leicester LE1 6ZG ☎ 0116 252 8305 ☞ tracie.rees@leicester.gov.uk

Social Services: Mr Andy Smith, Director of Children's Social Care & Safeguarding, New Walk Centre, Welford Place, Leicester LE1 6ZG ☎ 0116 252 5213 ☞ andy.smith@leicester.gov.uk

Social Services (Adult): Ms Ruth Lake, Director of Adult Social Care & Safeguarding, New Walk Centre, Welford Place, Leicester LE1 6ZG ☎ 0116 252 8302 ☞ ruth.lake@leicester.gov.uk

Social Services (Children): Mr Trevor Pringle, Director of Young People's Services, New Walk Centre, Welford Place, Leicester LE1 6ZG ☎ 0116 252 7702 🖷 0116 285 6241 ☞ trevor.pringle@leicester.gov.uk

Social Services (Children): Mr Andy Smith, Director of Children's Social Care & Safeguarding, New Walk Centre, Welford Place, Leicester LE1 6ZG ☎ 0116 252 5213 ☞ andy.smith@leicester.gov.uk

Staff Training: Mr Paul McChrystal, Head of Learning and Development, New Walk Centre, Welford Place, Leicester LE1 6ZG ☎ 0116 252 8620 ☞ paul.mcchrystal@leicester.gov.uk

Street Scene: Mr Adrian Russell, Director of Environmental Services, New Walk Centre, Welford Place, Leicester LE1 6ZG ☎ 0116 252 7295 🖷 0116 254 3720 ☞ adrian.russell@leicester.gov.uk

Sustainable Communities: Ms Carol Brass, Team Leader - Environment Team, New Walk Centre, Welford Place, Leicester LE1 6ZG ☎ 0116 252 6732 🖷 0116 255 9053 ☞ carol.brass@leicester.gov.uk

Sustainable Communities: Ms Anna Dodd, Team Leader - Environment Team, New Walk Centre, Welford Place, Leicester LE1 6ZG ☎ 0116 252 6732 🖷 0116 255 9053 ☞ anna.dodd@leicester.gov.uk

Sustainable Development: Ms Carol Brass, Team Leader - Environment Team, New Walk Centre, Welford Place, Leicester LE1 6ZG ☎ 0116 252 6732 🖷 0116 255 9053 ☞ carol.brass@leicester.gov.uk

Sustainable Development: Ms Anna Dodd, Team Leader - Environment Team, New Walk Centre, Welford Place, Leicester LE1 6ZG ☎ 0116 252 6732 🖷 0116 255 9053 ☞ anna.dodd@leicester.gov.uk

Town Centre: Ms Sarah Harrison, Director of City Centre, York House, Granby Street, Leicester LE1 6FB ☎ 0116 222 3329 ☞ sarahmharrison@leicester.gov.uk

Transport: Mr David Ison, Group Manager, New Walk Centre, Welford Place, Leicester LE1 6ZG ☎ 0116 225 2425 🖷 0116 225 2423 ☞ david.ison@leicester.gov.uk

Transport: Mr Andy Thomas, Head of Traffic Management, York House, Granby Street, Leicester LE1 6FB ☎ 0116 252 6540 🖷 0116 229 4100 ☞ andrew.thomas@leicester.gov.uk

Waste Management: Mr Steve Weston, Head of Waste Management, New Walk Centre, Welford Place, Leicester LE1 6ZG ☎ 0116 252 8582 🖷 0116 252 8592 ☞ steve.weston@leicester.gov.uk

MEMBERS OF THE COUNCIL (55)

***Mayor:* Soulsby**, Peter (LAB - City Mayor)
peter.soulsby@leicester.gov.uk

***Deputy Mayor:* Palmer**, Rory (LAB - Eyres Monsell)
rory.palmer@leicester.gov.uk

Alfonso, Dawn (LAB - New Parks)
dawn.alfonso@leicester.gov.uk

Aqbany, Hanif-Jussab (LAB - Spinney Hills)
hanif.aqbany@leicester.gov.uk

Bajaj, Deepak (LAB - Evington)
deepak.bajaj@leicester.gov.uk

Barton, Susan (LAB - Western Park)
susan.barton@leicester.gov.uk

Bhatti, Culdipp (LAB - Rushey Mead)
members.services@leicester.gov.uk

Bhavsar, Harshad (LAB - Abbey)
harshad.bhavsar@leicester.gov.uk

Byrne, Annette (LAB - Abbey)
annette.byrne@leicester.gov.uk

Cassidy, Ted (LAB - Fosse)

Chapman, Lucy (LAB - Stoneygate)

Chowdhury, Shofiqul (LAB - Spinney Hills)
shofiqul.chowdhury@leicester.gov.uk

Clair, Piara (LAB - Rushey Mead)
piara.singhclair@leicester.gov.uk

Clarke, Adam (LAB - Aylestone)
adam.clarke@leicester.gov.uk

Clayton, Neil (LAB - Castle)
neil.clayton@leicester.gov.uk

Cleaver, Virginia (LAB - Eyres Monsell)
virginia.cleaver@leicester.gov.uk

Cole, George (LAB - Western Park)
george.cole@leicester.gov.uk

Connelly, Andrew (LAB - Westcotes)
andy.connelly@leicester.gov.uk

Cooke, Michael (LAB - Braunstone Park and Rowley Fields)
michael.cooke@leicester.gov.uk

Corrall, Stephen (LAB - New Parks)
stephen.corrall@leicester.gov.uk

Cutkelvin, Elly (LAB - Freeman)

Dawood, Mohammed (LAB - Spinney Hills)
councillor.mohammed.dawood@leicester.gov.uk

Dempster, Vi (LAB - Beaumont Leys)
vi.dempster@leicester.gov.uk

Desai, Iqbal (LAB - Stoneygate)
iqbal.desai@leicester.gov.uk

Fonseca, Luis (LAB - Thurncourt)
luis.fonseca@leicester.gov.uk

Glover, Anne (LAB - Braunstone Park and Rowley Fields)
anne.glover@leicester.gov.uk

Grant, Ross (CON - Knighton)

ross.grant@leicester.gov.uk
Gugnani, Inderjit (LAB - Knighton)
inderjit.gugnani@leicester.gov.uk
Joshi, Rashmikant (LAB - Belgrave)
rashmikant.joshi@leicester.gov.uk
Kamal, Mustafa (LAB - Stoneygate)
mustafa.kamal@leicester.gov.uk
Kitterick, Patrick (LAB - Castle)
patrick.kitterick@btinternet.com
Marriott, Colin (LAB - Abbey)
colin.marriott@leicester.gov.uk
Mayat, Mian (LAB - Coleman)
members.services@leicester.gov.uk
Meghani, Sundip (LAB - Beaumont Leys)
sundip.meghani@leicester.gov.uk
Moore, Lynn (LAB - Knighton)
councillor.lynn.moore@leicester.gov.uk
Naylor, Wayne (LAB - Braunstone Park and Rowley Fields)
wayne.naylor@leicester.gov.uk
Newcombe, Paul (LAB - Charnwood)
paul.newcombe@leicester.gov.uk
Osman, Abdul (LAB - Charnwood)
abdul.osman@leicester.gov.uk
Patel, Rita (LAB - Humberstone and Hamilton)
Patel, Veejay (LAB - Latimer)
veejay.patel@leicester.gov.uk
Porter, Nigel (CON - Aylestone)
nigel.porter@leicester.gov.uk
Potter, Barbara (LAB - Humberstone and Hamilton)
members.services@leicester.gov.uk
Russell, Sarah (LAB - Westcotes)
sarah.russell@leicester.gov.uk
Sandhu, Gurinder Singh (LAB - Humberstone and Hamilton)
Sangster, Deborah (LAB - Coleman)
Senior, Lynn (LAB - Castle)
lynn.senior@leicester.gov.uk
Shelton, Bill (LAB - Freeman)
bill.shelton@leicester.gov.uk
Singh, Baljit (LAB - Evington)
Sood, Manjula (LAB - Latimer)
manjula.sood@leicester.gov.uk
Thomas, John (LAB - Belgrave)
john.thomas@leicester.gov.uk
Unsworth, Malcolm (LAB - New Parks)
malcolm.unsworth@leicester.gov.uk
Waddington, Susan (LAB - Fosse)
Wann, Rob (LAB - Thurncourt)
rob.wann@leicester.gov.uk
Westley, Paul (LAB - Beaumont Leys)
members.services@leicester.gov.uk
Willmott, Ross (LAB - Rushey Mead)
members.services@leicester.gov.uk

POLITICAL COMPOSITION

LAB: 53, CON: 2

COMMITTEE CHAIRS

Audit & Risk: Ms Rita Patel
Children, Young People & Schools: Mr Andrew Connelly
Health & Community: Mr Michael Cooke
Licensing: Mr John Thomas
Neighbourhood Services: Ms Anne Glover
Planning & Development: Mr Patrick Kitterick

LEICESTERSHIRE C

Leicestershire County Council, County Hall, Glenfield, Leicester LE3 8TF ☎ 0116 232 3232 🖷 0116 305 6260; 0116 265 6260 ✉ information@leics.gov.uk 🖳 www.leics.gov.uk

FACTS & FIGURES

Police Authority: Leicestershire Police Authority
Health Authority: East Midlands Strategic Health Authority
Learning and Skills Council: East Midlands
EU Constituencies: East Midlands
Election Frequency: Elections are of whole council

PRINCIPAL OFFICERS

Chief Executive: Mr John Sinnott, Chief Executive, County Hall, Glenfield, Leicester LE3 8RA ☎ 0116 305 6001 🖷 0116 305 6221 ✉ john.sinnott@leics.gov.uk

Assistant Chief Executive: Mr Andy Robinson, Assistant Chief Executive - Community Planning, County Hall, Glenfield, Leicester LE3 8RA ☎ 0116 305 7017 🖷 0116 305 7271 ✉ andy.robinson@leics.gov.uk

Senior Management: Mr Mick Connell, Director of Adults & Communities, County Hall, Glenfield, Leicester LE3 8RA ☎ 0116 305 7454 🖷 0116 305 7460 ✉ mick.connell@leics.gov.uk

Senior Management: Mr Matthew Lugg, Director of Environment & Transport, County Hall, Glenfield, Leicester LE3 8RJ ☎ 0116 305 7000 🖷 0116 305 7962 ✉ matthew.lugg@leics.gov.uk

Senior Management: Mr Brian Roberts, Director of Corporate Resources, County Hall, Glenfield, Leicester LE3 8RA ☎ 0116 305 7830 🖷 0116 305 7833 ✉ brian.roberts@leic.gov.uk

Senior Management: Mr Gareth Williams, Director of Children & Young People's Services, County Hall, Glenfield, Leicester LE3 8RL ☎ 0116 305 6300 🖷 0116 305 6332 ✉ gareth.williams@leics.gov.uk

Access Officer / Social Services (Disability): Ms Heather Pick, Head of Service (Promoting Independence), County Hall, Glenfield, Leicester LE3 8TF ☎ 0116 305 7458 🖷 0116 305 7460 ✉ heather.pick@leics.gov.uk

Architect, Building / Property Services: Mr David Cragg, Building Design Manager, County Hall, Glenfield, Leicester LE3 8RE ☎ 0116 305 6809 🖷 0116 305 6722 ✉ david.cragg@leics.gov.uk

Catering Services: Mr Ian Boyd-Stevenson, Catering Manager, County Hall, Glenfield, Leicester LE3 8TF ☎ 0116 305 6115

Catering Services: Ms Carol Harris, Principle Assistant - Food & Nutrition, County Hall, Glenfield, Leicester LE3 8TF ☎ 0116 305 9242 ✉ carol.harris@leics.gov.uk

Catering Services: Ms Wendy Philp, School Food Service Manager, The Courtyard, Whitwick Business Park, Coalville LE67 3NR ☎ 0116 305 5770 ✉ wendy.philp@leics.gov.uk

Catering Services: Ms Ros Speight, Business Support Manager, County Hall, Glenfield, Leicester LE3 8TF ☎ 0116 305 7534 ✉ ros.speight@leics.gov.uk

Children / Youth Services: Mr Phil Hawkins, Head of Youth Justice & Safer Communities, County Hall, Glenfield, Leicester LE3 8RA ☎ 0116 305 6780 🖷 0116 305 6260 ✉ phil.hawkins@leics.gov.uk

Children / Youth Services: Mr Walter McCulloch, Assistant Director of Specialist Services, County Hall, Glenfield, Leicester LE3 8TF ☎ 0116 3057441 ✉ walter.mcculloch@leics.gov.uk

Children / Youth Services: Mr Gareth Williams, Director of Children & Young People's Services, County Hall, Glenfield, Leicester LE3 8RL ☎ 0116 305 6300 🖷 0116 305 6332 ✉ gareth.williams@leics.gov.uk

Civil Registration: Mrs Amanda Bettany, County Superintendent Registrar, County Hall, Glenfield, Leicester LE3 8TF ☎ 0116 605 6585 🖷 0116 305 6580 ✉ jackie.pope@leics.gov.uk

PR / Communications: Ms Joanna Morrison, Head of Communications, County Hall, Glenfield, Leicester LE3 8TF ☎ 0116 305 5850 🖷 0116 305 6266 ✉ joanna.morrison@leics.gov.uk

Community Planning: Mr Andy Robinson, Assistant Chief Executive - Community Planning, County Hall, Glenfield, Leicester LE3 8RA ☎ 0116 305 7017 🖷 0116 305 7271 ✉ andy.robinson@leics.gov.uk

Community Safety: Mrs Gurjit Samra-Rai, Community Safety Manger, County Hall, Glenfield, Leicester LE3 8RA ☎ 0116 305 6056 🖷 0116 305 6260 ✉ grai@leics.gov.uk

Computer Management: Mr Andy Roberts, Head of ICT Services, County Hall, Glenfield, Leicester LE3 8RA ☎ 0116 305 7800 🖷 0116 305 7721 ✉ andy.roberts@leics.gov.uk

Consumer Protection and Trading Standards: Mr David Bull, Head of Regulatory Services, County Hall, Glenfield, Leicester LE3 8RN ☎ 0116 305 7572 🖷 0116 305 7370 ✉ david.bull@leics.gov.uk

Consumer Protection and Trading Standards: Mr Paul Love, Project Manager - Property Services Improvement, County Hall, Glenfield, Leicester LE3 8TF ☎ 0116 305 7376 ✉ paul.love@leics.gov.uk

Customer Service: Mrs Rachael Stone-Browning, Customer Services Manager, County Hall, Glenfield, Leicester LE3 8RA ☎ 0116 305 6227 🖷 0116 305 0006 ✉ rachael.stone-browning@leics.gov.uk

Economic Development: Mr Tom Purnell, Group Manager - Policy, Performance & Research, County Hall, Glenfield, Leicester LE3 8RA ☎ 0116 305 7019 🖷 0116 305 7271 ✉ tom.purnell@leics.gov.uk

Education: Mr David Atterbury, Education Officer - Strategic Services, County Hall, Glenfield, Leicester LE3 8TF ☎ 0116 305 7729 🖷 0116 305 6332 ✉ david.atterbury@leics.gov.uk

Education: Ms Lesley Hagger, Assistant Director - Strategic Initiatives, County Hall, Glenfield, Leicester LE3 8RA ☎ 0116 305 6340 🖷 0116 305 6310 ✉ lesley.hagger@leics.gov.uk

Education: Mr Tony Mulhearn, Assistant Director - Universal Services, County Hall, Glenfield, Leicester LE3 8TF ☎ 0116 305 6505 ✉ tony.mulhearn@leics.gov.uk

Education: Mr Gareth Williams, Director of Children & Young People's Services, County Hall, Glenfield, Leicester LE3 8RL ☎ 0116 305 6300 🖷 0116 305 6332 ✉ gareth.williams@leics.gov.uk

E-Government: Mr Andy Roberts, Head of ICT Services, County Hall, Glenfield, Leicester LE3 8RA ☎ 0116 305 7800 🖷 0116 305 7721 ✉ andy.roberts@leics.gov.uk

Electoral Registration: Mr David Pitt, Head of Democratic Services & Administration, County Hall, Glenfield, Leicester LE3 8RA ☎ 0116 305 6034 🖷 0116 305 6260 ✉ david.pitt@leics.gov.uk

Energy Management: Mr David Cragg, Building Design Manager, County Hall, Glenfield, Leicester LE3 8RE ☎ 0116 305 6809 🖷 0116 305 6722 ✉ david.cragg@leics.gov.uk

Environmental / Technical Services: Ms Holly Fields, Assistant Director - Environment, County Hall, Glenfield, Leicester LE3 8TF ☎ 0116 305 8101 ✉ holly.field@leics.gov.uk

Estates, Property & Valuation: Mrs Elaine Derrick, Estates Practise Manager, County Hall, Glenfield, Leicester LE3 8RE ☎ 0116 265 6991 🖷 0116 265 6722 ✉ elaine.derrick@leics.gov.uk

Estates, Property & Valuation: Mr Steve Siddons, Head of Property Services & Asset Management, County Hall, Glenfield, Leicester LE3 8RE ☎ 0116 305 6800 🖷 0116 305 6722 ✉ steve.siddons@leics.gov.uk

European Liaison: Ms Nicole Rickard, Team Leader - Policy & Partnerships, County Hall, Glenfield, Leicester LE3 8RA ☎ 0116 305 6977 🖷 0116 305 7271 ✉ nicole.rickard@leics.gov.uk

Facilities: Mr Graham Read, County Hall Facilities Manager, County Hall, Glenfield, Leicester LE3 8RA ☎ 0116 305 6724 🖷 0116 305 6722 ✉ graham.read@leics.gov.uk

Finance and Treasurer: Mr Brian Roberts, Director of Corporate Resources, County Hall, Glenfield, Leicester LE3 8RA ☎ 0116 305 7830 🖷 0116 305 7833 ✉ brian.roberts@leic.gov.uk

Finance and Treasurer: Mr Chris Tambini, Head of Strategic Finance, County Hall, Glenfield, Leicester LE3 8TF ☎ 0116 305 6199 ✉ chris.tambini@leics.gov.uk

Fleet Management: Mr David Atterbury, Education Officer - Strategic Services, County Hall, Glenfield, Leicester LE3 8TF ☎ 0116 305 7729 🖷 0116 305 6332 ✉ david.atterbury@leics.gov.uk

Fleet Management: Mr Tony Kirk, Group Manager - Passenger

Transport Unit, County Hall, Glenfield, Leicester LE3 8TF ☎ 0116 305 6270 🖷 0116 305 7181 ✉ tony.kirk@leics.gov.uk

Grounds Maintenance: Mr Graham Read, County Hall Corporate Facilities Manager, County Hall, Glenfield, Leicester LE3 8TF ☎ 0116 305 6278 🖷 0116 288 1674 ✉ graham.read@leics.gov.uk

Health and Safety: Mr Colin Jones, Health, Safety & Wellbeing Manager, County Hall, Glenfield, Leicester LE3 8TF ☎ 0116 305 7552 ✉ colin.jones@leics.gov.uk

Highways: Mr Matthew Lugg, Director of Environment & Transport, County Hall, Glenfield, Leicester LE3 8RJ ☎ 0116 305 7000 🖷 0116 305 7962 ✉ matthew.lugg@leics.gov.uk

Highways: Mr Mark Stevens, Assistant Director of Highways, County Hall, Glenfield, Leicester LE3 8RA ☎ 0116 305 7966 🖷 0116 305 7962 ✉ mark.stevens@leics.gov.uk

Local Area Agreement: Mr John Wright, Senior Policy & Performance Officer, County Hall, Glenfield, Leicester LE3 8TF ☎ 0116 305 7041 ✉ john.r.wright@leics.gov.uk

Legal: Mr David Morgan, Head of Legal Services, County Hall, Glenfield, Leicester LE3 8RA ☎ 0116 305 6007 🖷 0116 305 6161 ✉ david.morgan@leics.gov.uk

Leisure and Cultural Services: Mrs Heather Broughton, Assistant Director - Communities & Wellbeing, County Hall, Glenfield, Leicester LE3 8TF ☎ 0116 305 6781 ✉ heather.broughton@leics.gov.uk

Leisure and Cultural Services: Mr John Byrne, Sports Co-ordinator, County Hall, Glenfield, Leicester LE3 8RA ☎ 01509 564852 ✉ j.byrne2@lboro.ac.uk

Lifelong Learning: Mrs Heather Broughton, Head of Communities & Wellbeing, County Hall, Glenfield, Leicester LE3 8TF ☎ 0116 305 7378 🖷 0116 305 7370 ✉ heather.broughton@leics.gov.uk

Lighting: Mr Mark Stevens, Assistant Director of Highways, County Hall, Glenfield, Leicester LE3 8RA ☎ 0116 305 7966 🖷 0116 305 7962 ✉ mark.stevens@leics.gov.uk

Member Services: Ms Liz Clark, Head of Organisational Development, County Hall, Glenfield, Leicester LE3 8TF ☎ 0116 305 6236 ✉ liz.clark@leics.gov.uk

Member Services: Mr David Pitt, Head of Democratic Services & Administration, County Hall, Glenfield, Leicester LE3 8RA ☎ 0116 305 6034 🖷 0116 305 6260 ✉ david.pitt@leics.gov.uk

Partnerships: Mr Andy Robinson, Assistant Chief Executive - Community Planning, County Hall, Glenfield, Leicester LE3 8RA ☎ 0116 305 7017 🖷 0116 305 7271 ✉ andy.robinson@leics.gov.uk

Personnel / HR: Mr Simon Nearney, Head of Strategic Human Resources, County Hall, Glenfield, Leicester LE3 8RA ☎ 0116 305 6123 ✉ simon.nearney@leics.gov.uk

Planning: Mr Lonek Wojtulewicz, Head of Planning Historic & Natural Environment, County Hall, Glenfield, Leicester LE3 8TE ☎ 0116 305 7040 🖷 0116 305 7297 ✉ lonek.wojtulewicz@leics.gov.uk

Procurement: Ms Fiona Holbourn, Head of Procurement, County Hall, Glenfield, Leicester LE3 8RB ☎ 0116 305 6185 ✉ fiona.holbourn@leics.gov.uk

Public Libraries: Mrs Heather Broughton, Head of Communities & Wellbeing, County Hall, Glenfield, Leicester LE3 8TF ☎ 0116 305 7378 🖷 0116 305 7370 ✉ heather.broughton@leics.gov.uk

Public Libraries: Mr Nigel Thomas, Service Delivery Manager, County Hall, Glenfield, Leicester LE3 8TF ☎ 0116 305 7379 🖷 0116 305 7370 ✉ nigel.thomas@leics.gov.uk

Recycling & Waste Minimisation: Ms Holly Field, Assistant Director - Environment, County Hall, Glenfield, Leicester LE3 8RJ ☎ 0116 305 8101 🖷 0116 305 8128 ✉ holly.field@leics.gov.uk

Regeneration: Mr Simon McIntosh, Group Manager - Communities & Places, County Hall, Glenfield, Leicester LE3 8TF ☎ 0116 305 5700 🖷 0116 305 7271 ✉ simon.mcintosh@leics.gov.uk

Road Safety: Mr Nigel Horsley, Team Manager, Road Safety & Travel Awareness, County Hall, Glenfield, Leicester LE3 8TF ☎ 0116 305 7227 ✉ nigel.horsley@leics.gov.uk

Social Services: Mr Mick Connell, Director of Adults & Communities, County Hall, Glenfield, Leicester LE3 8RA ☎ 0116 305 7454 🖷 0116 305 7460 ✉ mick.connell@leics.gov.uk

Social Services (Adult): Ms Sue Disley, Assistant Director - Personal Care & Support, County Hall, Glenfield, Leicester LE3 8RA ☎ 0116 305 7456 🖷 0116 305 7460

Social Services (Children): Mr Walter McCulloch, Assistant Director - Children's Social Care, County Hall, Glenfield, Leicester LE3 8TF ☎ 0116 305 7441 ✉ walter.mcculloch@leics.gov.uk

Staff Training: Ms Jennifer Penfold, Learning & Development Manager, County Hall, Glenfield, Leicester LE3 8TF ☎ 0116 305 5615 🖷 0116 305 6285 ✉ jennifer.penfold@leics.gov.uk

Sustainable Communities: Mr Hetal Patel, Development Officer - Environment Action, County Hall, Glenfield, Leicester LE3 8RA ☎ 0116 305 7068 🖷 0116 305 7965 ✉ hetal.patel@leics.gov.uk

Sustainable Development: Mr Hetal Patel, Development Officer - Environment Action, County Hall, Glenfield, Leicester LE3 8RA ☎ 0116 305 7068 🖷 0116 305 7965 ✉ hetal.patel@leics.gov.uk

Tourism: Ms Joanna Morrison, Head of Communications, County Hall, Glenfield, Leicester LE3 8TF ☎ 0116 305 5850 🖷 0116 305 6266 ✉ joanna.morrison@leics.gov.uk

Transport: Mr Ian Drummond, Assistant Director - Environment & Transport, County Hall, Glenfield, Leicester LE3 8TF ☎ 0116 305 5990 ✉ ian.drummond@leics.gov.uk

Transport: Mr Matthew Lugg, Director of Environment &

Transport, County Hall, Glenfield, Leicester LE3 8RJ ☎ 0116 305 7000 🖷 0116 305 7962 ✉ matthew.lugg@leics.gov.uk

Transport Planner: Mr Paul Sheard, Group Manager - Transport Planning, County Hall, Glenfield, Leicester LE3 8RJ ☎ 0116 305 7191 ✉ paul.sheard@leics.gov.uk

Total Place: Mr Simon Lawrence, Programme Manager, County Hall, Glenfield, Leicester LE3 8TF ☎ 0116 305 7243 ✉ simon.lawrence@leics.gov.uk

Waste Collection and Disposal: Ms Holly Field, Assistant Director - Environment, County Hall, Glenfield, Leicester LE3 8RJ ☎ 0116 305 8101 🖷 0116 305 8128 ✉ holly.field@leics.gov.uk

Waste Management: Ms Holly Field, Assistant Director - Environment, County Hall, Glenfield, Leicester LE3 8RJ ☎ 0116 305 8101 🖷 0116 305 8128 ✉ holly.field@leics.gov.uk

Waste Management: Mr Matthew Lugg, Director of Environment & Transport, County Hall, Glenfield, Leicester LE3 8RJ ☎ 0116 305 7000 🖷 0116 305 7962 ✉ matthew.lugg@leics.gov.uk

MEMBERS OF THE COUNCIL (55)

***Chair:* Lewis**, Peter (CON - Loughborough South West)
peter.lewis@leics.gov.uk
***Leader of the Council:* Parsons**, David (CON - Kirby Muxloe and Leicester Forest)
david.parsons@leics.gov.uk
***Deputy Leader of the Council:* Rushton**, Nicholas (CON - Valley)
nicholas.rushton@leics.gov.uk
***Group Leader:* Galton**, Simon (LD - Launde)
simon.galton@leics.gov.uk
***Group Leader:* Hunt**, Max (LAB - Loughborough North West)
max.hunt@leics.gov.uk
Bailey, Alan (LD - Blaby and Glen Parva)
alan.bailey@leics.gov.uk
Bill, David (LD - Hinckley)
david.bill@leics.gov.uk
Blunt, Richard (CON - Ibstock & Appleby)
richard.blunt@leics.gov.uk
Boulter, Bill (LD - Wigston South)
bill.boulter@leics.gov.uk
Bray, Stuart (LD - Burbage Castle)
stuart.bray@leics.gov.uk
Camamile, Ruth (CON - Mallory)
ruth.camamile@leics.gov.uk
Charlesworth, Michael (LD - Wigston Busloe)
michael.charlesworth@leics.gov.uk
Coxon, John (CON - Ashby de la Zouch)
john.coxon@leics.gov.uk
Dickinson, Jackie (CON - Enderby Meridian)
jackie.dickinson@leics.gov.uk
Feltham, Kevin (CON - Gartree)
kevin.feltham@leics.gov.uk
Fox, Jo (LAB - Braunstone Town)
jo.fox@leics.gov.uk
Fraser, Rob (CON - Groby and Ratby)
rob.fraser@leics.gov.uk
Gamble, Dean (LD - Oadby)
dean.gamble@leics.gov.uk
Garner, Barry (CON - Narborough & Whetstone)
barry.garner@leics.gov.uk
Gillard, Tony (CON - Whitwick)
tony.gillard@leics.gov.uk
Griffiths, Michael (LD - Oadby)
michael.griffiths@leics.gov.uk
Hampson, Stephen (CON - Syston Ridgeway)
stephen.hampson@leics.gov.uk
Harley, Paul (CON - Thurmaston)
paul.harley@leics.gov.uk
Hart, Graham (CON - Bruntingthorpe)
graham.hart@leics.gov.uk
Hill, Sarah (LD - Market Harborough East)
sarah.hill@leics.gov.uk
Houseman, David (CON - Syston Fosse)
dave.houseman@leics.gov.uk
Jennings, David (CON - Cosby & Countesthorpe)
david.jennings@leics.gov.uk
Jones, Geraint (CON - Forest & Measham)
geraint.jones@leics.gov.uk
Kershaw, Tony (CON - Quorn and Barrow)
tony.kershaw@leics.gov.uk
Liquorish, Bill (CON - Broughton Astley)
bill.liquorish@leics.gov.uk
Lloydall, Helen (LD - Wigston Poplars)
helen.lloydall@leics.gov.uk
Lynch, Keith (LD - Burbage Castle)
keith.lynch@leics.gov.uk
Miah, Jewel (LAB - Loughborough East)
jewel.miah@leics.gov.uk
Newton, Betty (LAB - Loughborough North)
betty.newton@leics.gov.uk
Orson, Joseph (CON - Asfordby)
joe.orson@leics.gov.uk
Osborne, Peter (CON - Rothley & Mountsorrel)
peter.osborne@leics.gov.uk
Ould, Ivan (CON - Market Bosworth)
ivan.ould@leics.gov.uk
Page, Brian (CON - Glenfields)
brian.page@leics.gov.uk
Page, Rosita (CON - Lutterworth)
rosita.page@leics.gov.uk
Pain, Blake (CON - Market Harborough West & Foxton)
blake.pain@leics.gov.uk
Partner, Graham (BNP - Coalville)
graham.partner@leics.gov.uk
Pendleton, Lesley (CON - Castle Donington)
lesley.pendleton@leics.gov.uk
Posnett, Pam (CON - Melton North)
pam.posnett@leics.gov.uk
Radford, Christine (CON - Shepshed)
christine.radford@leics.gov.uk
Rhodes, Byron (CON - Belvoir)
byron.rhodes@leics.gov.uk
Richards, Janice (CON - Earl Shilton)
janice.richards@leics.gov.uk
Roffey, Peter (CON - Melton South)
peter.roffey@leics.gov.uk
Shepherd, Richard (CON - Sileby and The WOlds)
richard.shepherd@leics.gov.uk
Slater, David (CON - Loughborough South)
david.slater@leics.gov.uk
Snartt, David (CON - Bradgate)
david.snartt@leics.gov.uk
Sprason, David (CON - Markfield Desford & Thornton)
david.sprason@leics.gov.uk
White, Ernie (CON - Stanton Croft & Normanton)

ernie.white@leics.gov.uk
Wilson, Roger (LD - Birstall)
roger.wilson@leics.gov.uk
Wright, Don (LD - Hinckley)
don.wright@leics.gov.uk
Wyatt, Michael (LD - Warren Hills)
michael.wyatt@leics.gov.uk

POLITICAL COMPOSITION

CON: 36, LD: 14, LAB: 4, BNP: 1

CABINET

Leader: Mr David Parsons
Deputy Leader: Mr Nicholas Rushton
Adult Social Care: Mr David Sprason
Children & Young People: Mr Ivan Ould
Climate Action: Mr Peter Osborne
Environment & Transport / Equalities / Chair of Leicestershire Rural Partnership: Mrs Lesley Pendleton
Health: Mr Ernie White
Regulatory Services, Planning & Historic, Natural Environment & Resources: Mr Byron Rhodes
Safer Communitites: Mr Joseph Orson
Waste Management: Mr Richard Blunt

COMMITTEE CHAIRS

Adults, Communities & Health (Scrutiny): Mrs Ruth Camamile
Budget & Performance: Mr Tony Kershaw
Children & Young People: Mr Bill Liquorish
Corporate Governance: Mr David Snartt
Development Control: Mr David Jennings
Employment: Mr Nicholas Rushton
Pension Fund: Mr Brian Page
Scrutiny (Scrutiny): Mr Simon Galton

LEWES D

Lewes District Council, Lewes House, 32 High Street, Lewes BN7 2LX ☎ 01273 471600 🖳 www.lewes.gov.uk

FACTS & FIGURES

Police Authority: Sussex Police Authority
Health Authority: South East Coast Strategic Health Authority
Learning and Skills Council: South East
Parliamentary Constituencies: Lewes
EU Constituencies: South East
Election Frequency: Elections are of whole council
Twinning: Lewes: Blois (France); Waldshut-Tiengen (Germany); Peacehaven: Epinay-sous-Senart (France); Isernhagen (Germany); Seaford: Bonningstedt (Germany)

PRINCIPAL OFFICERS

Chief Executive: Ms Jenny Rowlands, Chief Executive, Lewes House, 32 High Street, Lewes BN7 2LX
🖰 jenny.rowlands@lewes.gov.uk

Senior Management: Mr Lindsay Frost, Director - Planning & Building Control, Southover House, Southover Road, Lewes BN7 1AB ☎ 01273 484468 🖰 lindsay.frost@lewes.gov.uk

Senior Management: Mr John Magness, Director - Finance, Southover House, Southover Road, Lewes BN7 1AB ☎ 01273 484467 🖷 01273 484233 🖰 john.magness@lewes.gov.uk

Access Officer / Social Services (Disability): Ms Sue Dunkley, Access Officer, Southover House, Southover Road, Lewes BN7 1AB ☎ 01273 484409 🖷 01273 484452
🖰 sue.dunkley@lewes.gov.uk

Architect, Building / Property Services: Mr Andy Chequers, Corporate Head - Housing Services, Lewes House, 32 High Street, Lewes BN7 2LX ☎ 01273 484380 🖷 01273 484431
🖰 andy.chequers@lewes.gov.uk

Best Value: Mr David Heath, Head of Audit & Performance, 4 Fisher Street, Lewes BN7 2DQ ☎ 01273 471600 🖷 01273 484090
🖰 david.heath@lewes.gov.uk

Building Control: Mr Roger Carsons, Head - Building Control, Planning and Environment Services, PO Box 2707, Southover House, Southover Road, Lewes BN7 1AB ☎ 01273 484414
🖷 01273 484442 🖰 roger.carsons@lewes.gov.uk

Building Control: Mr Martin Stallard, Head - Development & Management, Lewes House, 32 High Street, Lewes BN7 2LX
☎ 01273 484434 🖰 martin.stallard@lewes.gov.uk

PR / Communications: Ms Liz Lacon, Communications Manager, Lewes House, 32 High Street, Lewes BN7 2LX ☎ 01273 484141
🖷 01273 484254 🖰 liz.lacon@lewes.gov.uk

Community Planning: Ms Nilam Popat, Corporate Head - Property, Regeneration & Enterprise, PO Box 2708, Southover House, Southover Road, Lewes BN7 1AB ☎ 01273 484404
🖰 nilam.popat@lewes.gov.uk

Computer Management: Ms Jane Amos-Davidson, Interim Head - Human Resources, Lewes House, 32 High Street, Lewes BN7 2LX ☎ 01273 484237 🖰 jane.amos-davidson@lewes.gov.uk

Computer Management: Mr Owen Brady, Interim Manager - IT, Lewes House, 32 High Street, Lewes BN7 2LX ☎ 01273 484049
🖰 owen.brady@lewes.gov.uk

Contracts: Mr John Magness, Director - Finance, Southover House, Southover Road, Lewes BN7 1AB ☎ 01273 484467
🖷 01273 484233 🖰 john.magness@lewes.gov.uk

Corporate Services: Mrs Deborah Lade, Corporate Support Manager, Lewes House, 32 High Street, Lewes BN7 2LX
☎ 01273 484142 🖰 deborah.lade@lewes.gov.uk

Customer Service: Mr David Parry, Senior Customer Services Assistant, Southover House, Southover Road, Lewes BN7 1AB
☎ 01273 484392 🖰 david.parry@lewes.gov.uk

Economic Development: Mr Lindsay Frost, Director - Planning & Building Control, Southover House, Southover Road, Lewes BN7 1AB ☎ 01273 484468 🖰 lindsay.frost@lewes.gov.uk

Economic Development: Ms Claire Onslow, Tourism & Economic Development Manager, Lewes House, 32 High Street, Lewes BN7 2LX ☎ 01273 484401 🖰 claire.onslow@lewes.gov.uk

E-Government: Ms Jane Amos-Davidson, Interim Head - Human Resources, Lewes House, 32 High Street, Lewes BN7 2LX ☎ 01273 484237 ✉ jane.amos-davidson@lewes.gov.uk

Electoral Registration: Mr Steven Andrews, Electoral Services Manager, Lewes House, 32 High Street, Lewes BN7 2LX ☎ 01273 484117 ✉ steven.andrews@lewes.gov.uk

Emergency Planning: Mr Lindsay Frost, Director - Planning & Building Control, Southover House, Southover Road, Lewes BN7 1AB ☎ 01273 484468 ✉ lindsay.frost@lewes.gov.uk

Emergency Planning: Mr Ian Hodgson, Emergency Planning Officer, Southover House, Southover Road, Lewes BN7 1AB ☎ 01273 484485 ✉ ian.hodgson@lewes.gov.uk

Energy Management: Ms Rebecca Ritchie, Environment & Energy Officer, Lewes House, 32 High Street, Lewes BN7 2LX ☎ 01279 486617 ✉ rebecca.ritchie@lewes.gov.uk

Environmental / Technical Services: Mr Ian Kedge, Head - Environmental Health, Southover House, Southover Street, Lewes BN7 1AB ☎ 01273 484353 🖷 01273 484451 ✉ ian.kedge@lewes.gov.uk

Environmental Health: Mr Tim Bartlett, Principal Environmental Health Officer, Lewes House, 32 High Street, Lewes BN7 2LX ☎ 01273 484345 ✉ tim.bartlett@lewes.gov.uk

Environmental Health: Mr Ian Kedge, Head - Environmental Health, Southover House, Southover Street, Lewes BN7 1AB ☎ 01273 484353 🖷 01273 484451 ✉ ian.kedge@lewes.gov.uk

Estates, Property & Valuation: Mr Peter Buck-Bouchard, Estates Officer, Southover House, Southover Road, Lewes BN7 1AB ☎ 01273 484405 🖷 01273 484499 ✉ peter.buck-bouchard@lewes.gov.uk

European Liaison: Mr Greg McDonald, Economic Regeneration Development Officer, Lewes House, 32 High Street, Lewes BN7 2LX ☎ 01273 471600 ✉ greg.mcdonald@lewes.gov.uk

Finance and Treasurer: Mr John Magness, Director - Finance, Southover House, Southover Road, Lewes BN7 1AB ☎ 01273 484467 🖷 01273 484233 ✉ john.magness@lewes.gov.uk

Finance and Treasurer: Mr Ian Morris, Head - Revenues & Benefits, Lewes House, 32 High Street, Lewes BN7 2LX ☎ 01273 484079 ✉ ian.morris@lewes.gov.uk

Fleet Management: Mr Andrew Bryce, Head - District Services, Robinson Road, Newhaven BN9 9BL ☎ 01273 471600 🖷 01273 484292 ✉ andy.bryce@lewes.gov.uk

Grounds Maintenance: Mr Andy Frost, Parks Manager, Southover House, Southover Road, Lewes BN7 1AB ☎ 01273 484398 ✉ andy.frost@lewes.gov.uk

Health and Safety: Mr Matthew Britnell, Safety Officer, Lewes House, 32 High Street, Lewes BN7 2LX ☎ 01273 484 229 ✉ matthew.britnell@lewes.gov.uk

Home Energy Conservation: Mr Matthew Bird, Sustainability Officer, Community Recycling Centre, 20 North Street, Lewes BN7 2PE ☎ 01273 474968 🖷 01273 480082 ✉ matthew.bird@lewes.gov.uk

Housing: Ms Jo Jacks, Principal Housing Needs Officer, Fisher Street, Lewes BN7 2DQ ☎ 01273 484095 ✉ jo.jacks@lewes.gov.uk

Housing: Mr John Magness, Director - Finance, Southover House, Southover Road, Lewes BN7 1AB ☎ 01273 484467 🖷 01273 484233 ✉ john.magness@lewes.gov.uk

Housing Maintenance: Mr Andy Chequers, Corporate Head - Housing Services, Lewes House, 32 High Street, Lewes BN7 2LX ☎ 01273 484380 🖷 01273 484431 ✉ andy.chequers@lewes.gov.uk

Housing Maintenance: Mr Tony Johnson, Housing Maintenance Manager, Southover House, Southover Street, Lewes BN7 1AB ☎ 01273 484378 ✉ tony.johnson@lewes.gov.uk

Legal: Ms Catherine Knight, Corporate Head - Legal & Democratic Services, Lewes House, 32 High Street, Lewes BN7 2LX ☎ 01273 484118 🖷 01273 484121 ✉ catherine.knight@lewes.gov.uk

Licensing: Mr Lindsay Frost, Director - Planning & Building Control, Southover House, Southover Road, Lewes BN7 1AB ☎ 01273 484468 ✉ lindsay.frost@lewes.gov.uk

Member Services: Ms Rachel Allan, Scrutiny & Committee Officer, Lewes House, 32 High Street, Lewes BN7 2LX ☎ 01273 484174 ✉ rachel.allan@lewes.gov.uk

Personnel / HR: Ms Jane Amos-Davidson, Interim Head - Human Resources, Lewes House, 32 High Street, Lewes BN7 2LX ☎ 01273 484237 ✉ jane.amos-davidson@lewes.gov.uk

Planning: Mr Lindsay Frost, Director - Planning & Building Control, Southover House, Southover Road, Lewes BN7 1AB ☎ 01273 484468 ✉ lindsay.frost@lewes.gov.uk

Recycling & Waste Minimisation: Ms Julia Black, Community Recycling Officer, Community Recycling Centre, 20 North Street, Lewes BN7 2PE ☎ 01273 488937 🖷 01273 486619 ✉ julia.black@lewes.gov.uk

Regeneration: Mr Greg McDonald, Economic Regeneration Development Officer, Lewes House, 32 High Street, Lewes BN7 2LX ☎ 01273 471600 ✉ greg.mcdonald@lewes.gov.uk

Staff Training: Ms Justine Klemenz, Personnel Officer, Lewes House, 32 High Street, Lewes BN7 2LX ☎ 01273 484239 🖷 01273 484233 ✉ justine.klemenz@lewes.gov.uk

Staff Training: Ms Helen Knight, Personnel Officer, Lewes House, 32 High Street, Lewes BN7 2LX ☎ 01273 484239 ✉ helen.knight@lewes.gov.uk

Staff Training: Ms Jill Yeates, Personnel Officer, Lewes House, 32 High Street, Lewes BN7 2LX ☎ 01273 484239 🖷 01273

484233 jill.yeates@lewes.gov.uk

Street Scene: Mr Ian Stratton, Street Services Manager, Lewes House, 32 High Street, Lewes BN7 2LX ☎ 01273 484369 ian.stratton@lewes.gov.uk

Sustainable Communities: Mr Ian Kedge, Head - Environmental Health, Southover House, Southover Street, Lewes BN7 1AB ☎ 01273 484353 🖷 01273 484451 ian.kedge@lewes.gov.uk

Sustainable Development: Mr Trevor Watson, Assistant Head - Waste & Recycling & Sustainability Manager, Community Recycling Centre, 20 North Street, Lewes BN7 2PE ☎ 01273 486423 🖷 01273 486827 trevor.watson@lewes.gov.uk

Tourism: Ms Claire Onslow, Tourism & Economic Development Manager, Lewes House, 32 High Street, Lewes BN7 2LX ☎ 01273 484401 claire.onslow@lewes.gov.uk

Waste Collection and Disposal: Mr Andrew Bryce, Head - District Services, Robinson Road, Newhaven BN9 9BL ☎ 01273 471600 🖷 01273 484292 andy.bryce@lewes.gov.uk

Waste Management: Mr Andrew Bryce, Head - District Services, Robinson Road, Newhaven BN9 9BL ☎ 01273 471600 🖷 01273 484292 andy.bryce@lewes.gov.uk

MEMBERS OF THE COUNCIL (41)

Chair: **Nicholson**, Tony (CON - Seaford East)
tony.nicholson@lewes.gov.uk
Leader of the Council: **Page**, James (CON - East Saltdean and Telscombe Cliffs)
james.page@lewes.gov.uk
Group Leader: **MacCleary**, James (LD - Lewes Bridge)
james.maccleary@lewes.gov.uk
Adeniji, Sam (CON - Seaford South)
sam.adeniji@lewes.gov.uk
Allen, Bob (LD - Seaford South)
b.allen@lewes.gov.uk
Amy, Graham (LD - Newhaven Denton and Meeching)
graham.amy@lewes.gov.uk
Blackman, Rob (CON - Seaford East)
rob.blackman@lewes.gov.uk
Bowers, Chris (LD - Ouse Valley and Ringmer)
cbowers@gn.apc.org
Butler, Carla (LD - Newhaven Denton and Meeching)
carlabutler@btinternet.com
Carr, Julie (LD - Newhaven Valley)
julie.carr@lewes.gov.uk
Chartier, Michael (LD - Lewes Castle)
michael.cartier@lewes.gov.uk
Cutress, Melanie (LD - Kingston)
melanie.cutress@lewes.gov.uk
Davy, Sharon (CON - Chailey and Wivelsfield)
sharon.davy@lewes.gov.uk
Dean, Amanda (LD - Lewes Priory)
amanda.dean@lewes.gov.uk
Edmunds, Donna (CON - Barcombe and Hamsey)
donna.edmunds@lewes.gov.uk
Eiloart, Ian (LD - Lewes Priory)
cllr@eiloart.com
Franklin, Paul (CON - Seaford North)
paul.franklin@lewes.gov.uk
Gander, Paul (CON - Ouse Valley and Ringmer)
paul.gander@lewes.gov.uk
Gardiner, Peter (LD - Ouse Valley and Ringmer)
peter.gardiner@lewes.gov.uk
Gauntlett, Stephen (LD - Seaford Central)
stephen.gauntlett@lewes.gov.uk
Gray, David (LD - Lewes Castle)
david.gray@lewes.gov.uk
Groves, Barry (CON - Seaford West)
barry.groves@lewes.gov.uk
Harris, Job (CON - Peacehaven West)
job.harris@lewes.gov.uk
Harrison-Hicks, Jacqueline (CON - Peacehaven East)
jmharricks@btinternet.com
Howson, Philip (CON - East Saltdean and Telscombe Cliffs)
cllr.philip.howson@eastsussex.gov.uk
Jones, Tom (CON - Ditchling and Westmerton)
tom.jones@lewes.gov.uk
Lambert, Carolyn (LD - Seaford Central)
cllr.caryolyn.lambert@eastsussex.gov.uk
Main, Rod (LD - Newhaven Denton and Meeching)
roderick.main@tiscali.co.uk
Maskell, Ron (CON - East Saltdean and Telscombe Cliffs)
cllr.ronmaskell@gmail.com
Merry, Elayne (CON - Peacehaven North)
elayne.merry@lewes.gov.uk
O'Keeffe, Ruth (IND - Lewes Priory)
rok@supanet.com
Osborne, Sarah (LD - Plumpton Streat East Chiltington & St John Without)
sarah.osborne2@lewes.gov.uk
Robertson, Robbie (CON - Newhaven Valley)
robbie.robertson@lewes.gov.uk
Russel, Eileen (CON - Peacehaven West)
eileen.russel@lewes.gov.uk
Saunders, Steve (LD - Newhaven Valley)
steve.saunders@lewes.gov.uk
Sheppard, Jim (CON - Newick)
j.sheppard3@btinternet.com
Smith, Andy (CON - East Saltdean and Telscombe Cliffs)
cllr.andysmith.ldc@gmail.com
Stockdale, John (LD - Lewes Bridge)
john@plantpress.com
Sugarman, Cyril (CON - Chailey and Wivelsfield)
cyril.sugarman@lewes.gov.uk
Warren, Benjamin (CON - Seaford North)
benjamin.warren@lewes.gov.uk
White, Ian (CON - Seaford West)
ian.white@lewes.gov.uk

POLITICAL COMPOSITION

CON: 22, LD: 18, IND: 1

COMMITTEE CHAIRS

Audit: Mr Ian Eiloart
Licensing: Mr Philip Howson
Planning: Ms Jacqueline Harrison-Hicks
Scrutiny (Scrutiny): Ms Sarah Osborne

LEWISHAM

L

Lewisham London Borough Council, Civic Suite, Town Hall, London SE6 4RU ☎ 020 8314 6000 🖳 www.lewisham.gov.uk

FACTS & FIGURES

Police Authority: Metropolitan Police Authority
Health Authority: NHS London
Learning and Skills Council: London
Parliamentary Constituencies: Lewisham Deptford, Lewisham East, Lewisham West and Penge
EU Constituencies: London
Election Frequency: Elections are of whole council
Twinning: Antony (France); Charlottenburg-Wilmersdorf (Germany); Matagalpa (Nicaragua)

PRINCIPAL OFFICERS

Chief Executive: Mr Barry Quirk, Chief Executive, Lewisham Town Hall, London SE6 4RU ☎ 020 8314 6445 🖷 020 8314 3028 ✉ barry.quirk@lewisham.gov.uk

Architect, Building / Property Services: Ms Fresia Campbell, Head of Property Services, 2nd Floor, Laurence House, 1 Catford Road, London SE6 4RU ☎ 020 8314 9247 🖷 020 8314 3126 ✉ fresia.campbell@lewisham.gov.uk

Best Value: Mr Barrie Neal, Head of Corporate Policy & Governance, Town Hall, London SE6 4RU ☎ 020 8314 9852 ✉ barrie.neal@lewisham.gov.uk

Building Control: Mr Tony Mottram, District Surveyor, Town Hall Chambers, London SE6 4RU ☎ 020 8314 8063 🖷 020 8314 3138 ✉ tony.mottram@lewisham.gov.uk

Children / Youth Services: Mr Vic Campbell-Macdonald, Head of Services for Student & Pupil Support, Civic Suite, Town Hall, London SE6 4RU ☎ 020 8314 8527 ✉ vic.campbell-macdonald@lewisham.gov.uk

Children / Youth Services: Ms Frankie Sulke, Executive Director for Children & Young People, Laurence House, 1 Catford Road, London SE6 4RU ☎ 020 8314 6301 🖷 020 8314 3151 ✉ frankie.sulke@lewisham.gov.uk

Civil Registration: Mr Glynne Harris, Superintendent Registrar, Registrar Office, Lewisham High Street, London SE13 4RU ☎ 020 8690 2128 🖷 020 8314 1078 ✉ glynne.harris@lewisham.gov.uk

Civil Registration: Ms D Verona, Head of Land Charges, 5th Floor, Laurence House, 1 Catford Road, London SE6 4RU ☎ 020 8314 6262

PR / Communications: Mr Adrian Wardle, Head of Communications, Room 412, Town Hall, London SE6 4RU ☎ 020 8314 6087 🖷 020 8314 3120 ✉ adrian.wardle@lewisham.gov.uk

Community Planning: Ms S Jones, Head of Community Sector Team, 38/39 Winslade Way, Catford, London SE6 4RU ☎ 020 8314 6579

Community Safety: Mr Gary Connors, Strategic Safety Services Manager, Mercia Grove, Lewisham, London SE13 7EZ ☎ 020 8314 9773 ✉ gary.connors@lewisham.gov.uk

Community Safety: Ms Geeta Subramaniam, Head of Crime Reduction & Supporting People, Civic Suite, Town Hall, London SE6 4RU ☎ 020 8314 9509 ✉ geeta.subramaniam@lewisham.gov.uk

Consumer Protection and Trading Standards: Mr John Pye, Chief Trading Standards Officer, Town Hall Chambers, Rushy Green, London SE6 4RY ☎ 020 8314 9259 🖷 020 8314 3138 ✉ john.pye@lewisham.gov.uk

Contracts: Mr Andy Murray, Procurement Strategy Manager, Directorate of Resources, Lewisham Town Hall, London SE6 4RU ☎ 020 8314 8133 🖷 020 8314 3092 ✉ andy.murray@lewisham.gov.uk

Customer Service: Mr Kevin Sheehan, Executive Director for Customer Services, Civic Suite, Town Hall, London SE6 4RU ✉ kevin.sheehan@lewisham.gov.uk

Economic Development: Mr Kevin Turner, Economic Development Manager, Laurence House, 1 Catford Road, London SE6 4RU ☎ 020 8314 8229 🖷 020 8314 3129 ✉ kevin.turner@lewisham.gov.uk

Education: Ms Louise Comely, Head of Inclusion Service, Kaleidoscope, 4th Floor, 32 Rushey Green, London SE6 4JF ☎ 020 7138 1432 ✉ louise.comely@lewisham.gov.uk

Education: Ms Frankie Sulke, Executive Director for Children & Young People, Laurence House, 1 Catford Road, London SE6 4RU ☎ 020 8314 6301 🖷 020 8314 3151 ✉ frankie.sulke@lewisham.gov.uk

E-Government: Mr Simon Berlin, Head of E-Government, Lewisham Town Hall, London SE6 4RU ☎ 020 8314 6999 🖷 020 8314 3046 ✉ simon.berlin@lewisham.gov.uk

Electoral Registration: Ms Kath Nicholson, Head of Law, Lewisham Town Hall, London SE6 4RU ☎ 020 8314 7648 🖷 020 8314 3107 ✉ kath.nicholson@lewisham.gov.uk

Emergency Planning: Mr John Brown, Principal Emergency Planning Officer, 5th Floor, Laurence House, 1 Catford Road , London SE6 4RU ☎ 020 8314 8579 🖷 020 8314 3155

Energy Management: Mr Martin O'Brien, Sustainability Officer, Civic Suite, Town Hall, London SE6 4RU ☎ 020 8314 6605 ✉ martin.o'brien@lewisham.gov.uk

Environmental / Technical Services: Mr Nigel Tyrell, Head of Environment, Lewisham Town Hall, London SE6 4RU ☎ 020 8314 6000 ✉ nigel.tyrell@lewisham.gov.uk

Estates, Property & Valuation: Mr Steve Gough, Head of Programme Management & Property, 3rd Floor, Laurence House, 1 Catford Road, London SE6 4RU ☎ 020 8314 9428 🖷 020 8314 8885 ✉ steve.gough@lewisham.gov.uk

Estates, Property & Valuation: Ms Marilyn Hale, Service Unit Manager - Estate Management, 3rd Floor, Laurance House, 1 Catford Road, London SE6 4RU ☎ 020 8695 6000

European Liaison: Ms Katie Wood, International Partnerships &

Projects Officer, Civic Suite, Town Hall, London SE6 4RU ☎ 0208 324 7227 🖷 0208 314 3111 🖱 katie.wood@lewisham.gov.uk

Events Manager: Ms Carmel Langstaff, Head of Arts & Entertainment, Lewisham Town Hall, London SE6 4RU ☎ 020 8314 7729 🖱 liz.dart@lewisham.gov.uk

Events Manager: Ms Hilary Renwick, Head of Cultural Services, Lewisham Town Hall, London SE6 4RU ☎ 020 8314 6359 🖱 hilary.renwick@lewisham.gov.uk

Facilities: Ms Fresia Campbell, Head of Property Services, 2nd Floor, Laurence House, 1 Catford Road, London SE6 4RU ☎ 020 8314 9247 🖷 020 8314 3126 🖱 fresia.campbell@lewisham.gov.uk

Finance and Treasurer: Ms Janet Senior, Executive Director for Resources & Regeneration, Lewisham Town Hall, London SE6 4RU ☎ 020 8314 8013 🖷 020 8314 3046 🖱 janet.senior@lewisham.gov.uk

Fleet Management: Mr Martin Champkins, Service Unit Manager for Lewisham Door to Door, Lewisham Town Hall, London SE6 4RU ☎ 020 8314 0991 🖷 020 8314 2190 🖱 martin.champkins@lewisham.gov.uk

Health and Safety: Mr David Austin, Health & Safety Manager, 3rd Floor, Town Hall, London SE6 4RU ☎ 020 8314 8914 🖷 020 8314 3448 🖱 david.austin@lewisham.gov.uk

Highways: Ms Linda Swinburne, Acting Head of Transport, Laurence House, 1 Catford Road, London SE6 4RU ☎ 020 8314 9956 🖷 020 8314 3642 🖱 linda.swinburne@lewisham.gov.uk

Housing: Ms Genevieve Macklin, Head of Strategic Housing, Civic Suite, Town Hall, London SE6 4RU ☎ 020 8314 6057 🖱 genevieve.macklin@lewisham.gov.uk

Local Area Agreement: Ms Fenella Beckman, Strategic Partnership Manager, Civic Suite, Town Hall, London SE6 4RU ☎ 020 8314 8632 🖱 Fenella.Beckman@lewisham.gov.uk

Legal: Ms Kath Nicholson, Head of Law, Lewisham Town Hall, London SE6 4RU ☎ 020 8314 7648 🖷 020 8314 3107 🖱 kath.nicholson@lewisham.gov.uk

Leisure and Cultural Services: Ms Annette Stead, Head of Sports & Active Recreation, Town Hall Chambers, Catford Broadway, London SE6 4RU ☎ 020 8314 8496 🖷 020 8314 3333 🖱 annette.stead@lewisham.gov.uk

Licensing: Ms Cheryl Collins, Head of Licensing Team, Laurence House, 1 Catford Road, London SE6 4RU ☎ 020 8314 6338 🖷 020 8314 3143 🖱 cheryl.collins@lewisham.gov.uk

Lifelong Learning: Ms Frankie Sulke, Executive Director for Children & Young People, Laurence House, 1 Catford Road, London SE6 4RU ☎ 020 8314 6301 🖷 020 8314 3151 🖱 frankie.sulke@lewisham.gov.uk

Lottery Funding, Charity and Voluntary: Mr Paul Hadfield, Enterprise Development Manager, 5th Floor, Laurence House, 1 Catford Road, London SE6 4RU ☎ 020 8314 8022 🖷 020 8314 3129 🖱 paul.hadfield@lewisham.gov.uk

Member Services: Mr Kevin Flaherty, Head of Business & Committee, Lewisham Town Hall, London SE6 4RU ☎ 020 8314 8824 🖷 020 8314 3111 🖱 kevin.flaherty@lewisham.gov.uk

Member Services: Mr Derek Johnson, Business & Civic Co-ordinator, Lewisham Town Hall, London SE6 4RU ☎ 020 8314 8636 🖷 020 8314 3111 🖱 derek.johnson@lewisham.gov.uk

Parking: Ms Lesley Brooks, Service Group Manager - Travel Demand, Wearside Depot, Lewisham, London SE13 7EZ ☎ 020 8314 6000 🖷 020 8690 6083 🖱 lesley.brooks@lewisham.gov.uk

Partnerships: Mr Paul Aladenika, Head of Policy & Partnerships, Civic Suite, Town Hall, London SE6 4RU ☎ 020 8314 7148 🖱 paul.aladenika@lewisham.gov.uk

Personnel / HR: Mr Andreas Ghosh, Head of Personnel & Development, Lewisham Town Hall, London SE6 4RU ☎ 020 8314 7519 🖷 020 8314 3071 🖱 andreas.ghosh@lewisham.gov.uk

Planning: Mr John Miller, Head of Planning Services, Town Hall Chambers, Rushy Green, London SE6 4RY ☎ 020 8314 8706 🖷 020 8314 3127 🖱 john.miller@lewisham.gov.uk

Procurement: Mr Andy Murray, Procurement Strategy Manager, Directorate of Resources, Lewisham Town Hall, London SE6 4RU ☎ 020 8314 8133 🖷 020 8314 3092 🖱 andy.murray@lewisham.gov.uk

Public Libraries: Ms Helen Hammond, Head of Community Education, 2nd Floor, Laurence House, 1 Catford Road, London SE6 4RU ☎ 020 8314 6189 🖱 helen.hammond@lewisham.gov.uk

Public Libraries: Mr Antonio Rizzo, Head of Libraries, 2nd Floor, Laurence House, 1 Catford Road, London SE13 6LG ☎ 020 8314 8025 🖱 antonio.rizzo@lewisham.gov.uk

Recycling & Waste Minimisation: Ms Sam Kirk, Strategic Waste & Environment Manager, Wearside Service Centre, Wearside Road, London SE13 7EZ ☎ 020 8314 2076 🖷 020 8314 2128 🖱 sam.kirk@lewisham.gov.uk

Road Safety: Ms Lesley Brooks, Service Group Manager - Travel Demand, Wearside Depot, Lewisham, London SE13 7EZ ☎ 020 8314 6000 🖷 020 8690 6083 🖱 lesley.brooks@lewisham.gov.uk

Social Services: Ms S Bishop, Head of Bereavement Services, Lewisham Crematorium, Verdant Lane, London SE6 1JX ☎ 020 8697 2555

Social Services: Ms Aileen Buckton, Executive Director for Community Services, Town Hall Chambers, Rushey Green, London SE6 4RX ☎ 020 8314 8107 🖷 020 8314 3023 🖱 aileen.buckton@lewisham.gov.uk

Social Services: Mr Alan Docksey, Head of Resources - Social Care, Civic Suite, Town Hall, London SE6 4RU ☎ 020 8314 3582 🖱 alan.docksey@lewisham.gov.uk

Social Services: Ms Sarah Wainer, Head of Performance & Strategy in Adult Care & Health, Lewisham Town Hall, London SE6 4RU ☎ 020 8314 9611 🖷 020 8314 3023 ✉ sarah.wainer@lewisham.gov.uk

Social Services (Adult): Mr Greg Russell, Occupational Therapist Locum, 2nd Floor, Laurence House, 1 Catford Road, London SE6 4RU ☎ 020 7206 3244 ✉ greg.russell@lewisham.gov.uk

Social Services (Children): Mr Ian Smith, Director of Children's Social Care, Laurence House, 1 Catford Road, London SE6 4RU ☎ 020 8314 8140 🖷 020 8314 3024 ✉ alastair.pettigrew@lewisham.gov.uk

Staff Training: Ms Devora Wolfson, Acting Learning & Development Manager, Lewisham Town Hall, London SE6 4RU ☎ 020 8314 6181 🖷 020 8314 3065 ✉ devora.wolfson@lewisham.gov.uk

Street Scene: Mr Bob Quatresols, Highway Design & Maintenance Manager, Wearside Depot, London SE13 7EZ ☎ 020 8314 2036 🖷 020 8690 4905 ✉ bob.quatresols@lewisham.gov.uk

Sustainable Communities: Mr Martin O'Brien, Sustainability Officer, Civic Suite, Town Hall, London SE6 4RU ☎ 020 8314 6605 ✉ martin.o'brien@lewisham.gov.uk

Sustainable Development: Mr Martin O'Brien, Sustainability Officer, Civic Suite, Town Hall, London SE6 4RU ☎ 020 8314 6605 ✉ martin.o'brien@lewisham.gov.uk

Tourism: Mr Kevin Turner, Economic Development Manager, Laurence House, 1 Catford Road, London SE6 4RU ☎ 020 8314 8229 🖷 020 8314 3129 ✉ kevin.turner@lewisham.gov.uk

Traffic Management: Mr Paul Stewart, Transport Planning Manager, Wearside Depot, Lewisham, London SE13 7EZ ☎ 020 8314 2269 🖷 020 8314 2066 ✉ paul.stewart@lewisham.gov.uk

Transport: Ms Linda Swinburne, Acting Head of Transport, Laurence House, 1 Catford Road, London SE6 4RU ☎ 020 8314 9956 🖷 020 8314 3642 ✉ linda.swinburne@lewisham.gov.uk

Transport Planner: Ms Linda Swinburne, Acting Head of Transport, Laurence House, 1 Catford Road, London SE6 4RU ☎ 020 8314 9956 🖷 020 8314 3642 ✉ linda.swinburne@lewisham.gov.uk

Total Place: Mr Joel Hartfield, Principal Policy Officer, Civic Suite, Town Hall, London SE6 4RU ☎ 020 8314 9941 ✉ joel.hartfield@lewisham.gov.uk

Total Place: Mr Kevin Sheehan, Executive Director for Customer Services, Civic Suite, Town Hall, London SE6 4RU ✉ kevin.sheehan@lewisham.gov.uk

Waste Collection and Disposal: Mr Michael Bryan, Group Service Manager Refuse, Wearside Service Centre, Wearside Road, London SE13 7EZ ☎ 020 8314 2113 🖷 020 8314 2043 ✉ michael.bryan@lewisham.gov.uk

Waste Collection and Disposal: Ms Sam Kirk, Strategic Waste & Environment Manager, Wearside Service Centre, Wearside Road, London SE13 7EZ ☎ 020 8314 2076 🖷 020 8314 2128 ✉ sam.kirk@lewisham.gov.uk

Waste Management: Ms Sam Kirk, Strategic Waste & Environment Manager, Wearside Service Centre, Wearside Road, London SE13 7EZ ☎ 020 8314 2076 🖷 020 8314 2128 ✉ sam.kirk@lewisham.gov.uk

MEMBERS OF THE COUNCIL (55)

***Directly Elected Mayor:* Bullock**, Steve (O -)
steve.bullock@lewisham.gov.uk

***Chair:* Long**, Madeliene (LAB - New Cross)
cllr_madeliene.long@lewisham.gov.uk

***Deputy Mayor:* Smith**, Alan (LAB - Catford South)
cllr_alan.smith@lewisham.gov.uk

Addison, Jacqueline (LAB - Crofton Park)
cllr_jackie.addison@lewisham.gov.uk

Adefiranye, Obajimi (LAB - Brockley)
cllr_obajimi.adefiranye@lewisham.gov.uk

Affiku, Anne (LAB - Forest Hill)
cllr_anne.affiku@lewisham.gov.uk

Allinson, Christine (CON - Grove Park)
cllr_christine.allinson@lewisham.gov.uk

Amrani, Abdeslam (LAB - Catford South)
cllr_abdeslam.amrani@lewisham.gov.uk

Beck, Pauline (LD - Lee Green)
cllr_pauline.beck@lewisham.gov.uk

Bell, Paul (LAB - Telegraph Hill)
cllr_paul.bell@lewisham.gov.uk

Best, Chris (LAB - Sydenham)
cllr_chris.best@lewisham.gov.uk

Bonavia, Kevin (LAB - Blackheath)
cllr_kevin.bonavia@lewisham.gov.uk

Bowen, John (LD - Crofton Park)
cllr_john.bowen@lewisham.gov.uk

Britton, David (CON - Grove Park)
david.britton17@hotmail.com

Brooks, Duwayne (LD - Downham)
cllr_duwayne.brooks@lewisham.gov.uk

Clarke, Suzannah (LAB - Grove Park)
cllr_suzannah.clarke@lewisham.gov.uk

Clutten, Jenni (LD - Downham)
cllr_jenni.clutten@lewisham.gov.uk

Curran, Liam (LAB - Sydenham)
cllr_liam.curran@lewisham.gov.uk

Daby, Janet (LAB - Whitefoot)
cllr_janet.daby@lewisham.gov.uk

Davis, Vincent (LAB - Ladywell)
cllr_vincent.davis@lewisham.gov.uk

De Ryk, Amanda (LD - Blackheath)
cllr_amanda.deryk@lewisham.gov.uk

Egan, Damien (LAB - Lewisham Central)
damien.egan@lewisham.gov.uk

Feakes, Alex (LD - Forest Hill)
cllr_alex.feakes@lewisham.gov.uk

Fitzsimmons, Peggy (LAB - Rushey Green)
cllr_peggy.fitzsimmons@lewisham.gov.uk

Fletcher, Julia (LD - Downham)
cllr_julia.fletcher@lewisham.gov.uk

Folorunso, Joseph (LAB - Evelyn)
cllr_joseph.folorunso@lewisham.gov.uk

Foreman, Patsy (LD - Whitefoot)

cllr_patsy.foreman@lewisham.gov.uk
Foxcroft, Vicky (LAB - Brockley)
cllr_vicky.foxcroft@lewisham.gov.uk
Gibson, Helen (LAB - Ladywell)
cllr_helen.gibson@lewisham.gov.uk
Griesenbeck, Sven (LD - Lee Green)
cllr_sven.griesenbeck@lewisham.gov.uk
Hall, Alan (LAB - Bellingham)
cllr_alan.hall@lewisham.gov.uk
Handley, Carl (LAB - Ladywell)
cllr_carlrichard.handley@lewisham.gov.uk
Harris, Michael (LAB - Lewisham Central)
cllr_michael.harris@lewisham.gov.uk
Ibitson, Ami (LAB - Bellingham)
cllr_ami.ibitson@lewisham.gov.uk
Jeffrey, Stella (LAB - Lewisham Central)
cllr_stella.jeffrey@lewisham.gov.uk
Johnson, Darren (GRN - Brockley)
cllr_darren.johnson@lewisham.gov.uk
Klier, Helen (LAB - Rushey Green)
cllr_helen.klier@lewisham.gov.uk
Maines, Chris (LD - Blackheath)
cllr_chris.maines@lewisham.gov.uk
Mallory, Jim (LAB - Lee Green)
cllr_jim.mallory@lewisham.gov.uk
Maslin, Paul (LAB - New Cross)
cllr_paul.maslin@lewisham.gov.uk
Millbank, Joan (LAB - Telegraph Hill)
cllr_joan.millbank@lewisham.gov.uk
Morrison, Pauline (LAB - Crofton Park)
cllr_pauline.morrison@lewisham.gov.uk
Muldoon, John (LAB - Rushey Green)
cllr_john.muldoon@lewisham.gov.uk
Nisbet, Marion (LAB - Sydenham)
cllr_marion.nisbet@lewisham.gov.uk
Onuegbu, Crada (LAB - Evelyn)
cllr_crada.onuegbu@lewisham.gov.uk
Owolabi-Oluyole, Sam (LAB - Evelyn)
cllr_sam.owolabi-oluyole@lewisham.gov.uk
Padmore, Stephen (LAB - New Cross)
cllr_stephen.padmore@lewisham.gov.uk
Paschoud, John (LAB - Perry Vale)
cllr_john.paschoud@lewisham.gov.uk
Paschoud, Jacq (LAB - Bellingham)
cllr_jacq.paschoud@lewisham.gov.uk
Pattisson, Pete (LD - Whitefoot)
pete.pattisson@lewisham.gov.uk
Peake, Philip (LD - Forest Hill)
cllr_philip.peake@lewisham.gov.uk
Stamirowski, Eva (LAB - Catford South)
cllr_eva.stamirowski@lewisham.gov.uk
Till, Alan (LAB - Perry Vale)
cllr_alan.till@lewisham.gov.uk
Whittle, Dan (LAB - Telegraph Hill)
cllr_dan.whittle@lewisham.gov.uk
Wise, Susan (LAB - Perry Vale)
cllr_susan.wise@lewisham.gov.uk

POLITICAL COMPOSITION
LAB: 39, LD: 12, CON: 2, O: 1, GRN: 1

CABINET
Children & Young People: Ms Helen Klier
Community Safety: Ms Janet Daby
Community Services & Older People: Ms Chris Best
Customer Services: Ms Susan Wise
Regeneration: Mr Alan Smith
Resources: Mr Paul Maslin
Strategy & Communication: Mr Damien Egan
Youth: Ms Crada Onuegbu

COMMITTEE CHAIRS
Audit: Mr Michael Harris
Children & Young People: Mr John Paschoud
Healthier Communities: Mr John Muldoon
Licensing: Ms Eva Stamirowski
Overview & Scrutiny: Mr Alan Hall
Pensions Investment: Mr Dan Whittle
Safer & Stronger Communities: Ms Pauline Morrison
Strategic Planning: Mr John Paschoud
Sustainable Development: Mr Liam Curran

LICHFIELD — D

Lichfield District Council, District Council House, Frog Lane, Lichfield WS13 6ZB ☎ 01543 308000 🖷 01543 309899 ✉ enquiries@lichfielddc.gov.uk 🖳 www.lichfielddc.gov.uk

FACTS & FIGURES
Police Authority: Staffordshire Police Authority
Health Authority: NHS West Midlands
Learning and Skills Council: West Midlands
Parliamentary Constituencies: Lichfield, Tamworth
EU Constituencies: West Midlands
Election Frequency: Elections are of whole council

PRINCIPAL OFFICERS
Chief Executive: Ms Nina Dawes, Chief Executive, District Council House, Frog Lane, Lichfield WS13 6ZB ☎ 01543 308001 🖷 01543 308049 ✉ nina.dawes@lichfielddc.gov.uk

Senior Management: Mr Richard King, Strategic Director - Democratic, Development & Legal Services, District Council House, Frog Lane, Lichfield WS13 6YU ☎ 01543 308060 🖷 01543 308200 ✉ richard.king@lichfielddc.gov.uk

Architect, Building / Property Services: Mr John Brown, Land & Property Manager, District Council House, Frog Lane, Lichfield WS13 6YU ☎ 01543 308061 🖷 01543 309899 ✉ john.brown@lichfielddc.gov.uk

Architect, Building / Property Services: Mr Richard King, Strategic Director - Democratic Development & Legal Services, District Council House, Frog Lane, Lichfield WS13 6YU ☎ 01543 308060 🖷 01543 309899 ✉ richard.king@lichfielddc.gov.uk

Building Control: Mr Ged Cooper, Building Control Manager, District Council House, Frog Lane, Lichfield WS13 6YZ ☎ 01543 308155 🖷 01543 308161 ✉ ged.cooper@lichfielddc.gov.uk

Building Control: Mr Richard King, Strategic Director - Democratic, Development & Legal Services, District Council House, Frog Lane, Lichfield WS13 6YU ☎ 01543 308060 🖷 01543 308200 ✉ richard.king@lichfielddc.gov.uk

Building Control: Mr Richard King, Strategic Director -

Democratic Development & Legal Services, District Council House, Frog Lane, Lichfield WS13 6YU ☎ 01543 308060 🖷 01543 309899 ✉ richard.king@lichfielddc.gov.uk

PR / Communications: Mr Richard King, Strategic Director - Democratic Development & Legal Services, District Council House, Frog Lane, Lichfield WS13 6YU ☎ 01543 308060 🖷 01543 309899 ✉ richard.king@lichfielddc.gov.uk

PR / Communications: Ms Elizabeth Thatcher, PR Manager, District Council House, Frog Lane, Lichfield WS13 6ZD ☎ 01543 308781 🖷 01543 308780 ✉ elizabeth.thatcher@lichfielddc.gov.uk

Community Planning: Ms Lesley Bovington, Regeneration Manager, Donegal House, Bore Street, Lichfield WS13 6NE ☎ 01543 308170 🖷 01543 308211 ✉ lesley.bovington@lichfielddc.gov.uk

Community Planning: Mr Richard King, Strategic Director - Democratic Development & Legal Services, District Council House, Frog Lane, Lichfield WS13 6YU ☎ 01543 308060 🖷 01543 309899 ✉ richard.king@lichfielddc.gov.uk

Community Safety: Ms Jenni Coleman, Community Safety Officer, Donegal House, Bore Street, Lichfield WS13 6NE ☎ 01543 308005 🖷 01543 308211 ✉ jenni.coleman@lichfielddc.gov.uk

Computer Management: Mr Kevin Sleeman, E-Business & Information Strategy Manager, District Council House, Frog Lane, Lichfield WS13 6ZF ☎ 01543 308000

Contracts: Mr Richard King, Strategic Director - Democratic Development & Legal Services, District Council House, Frog Lane, Lichfield WS13 6YU ☎ 01543 308060 🖷 01543 309899 ✉ richard.king@lichfielddc.gov.uk

Contracts: Mrs Ruth Plant, Operational Services - Director, Off Ring Road, Zone 2, Burntwood Business Park, Chase Terrace, Burntwood WS7 3JQ ☎ 01543 687540 🖷 01543 308955 ✉ ruth.plant@lichfielddc.gov.uk

Corporate Services: Mr Richard King, Strategic Director - Democratic Development & Legal Services, District Council House, Frog Lane, Lichfield WS13 6YU ☎ 01543 308060 🖷 01543 309899 ✉ richard.king@lichfielddc.gov.uk

Customer Service: Ms Helen Spearey, Strategic Director - Community, Housing & Health, District Council House, Frog Lane, Lichfield WS13 6ZE ☎ 01543 308700 🖷 01543 308712 ✉ helen.spearey@lichfielddc.gov.uk

Customer Service: Mrs Ysanne Williams, Customer Services Manager, District Council House, Frog Lane, Lichfield WS13 6ZF ☎ 01543 308738 ✉ ysanne.williams@lichfielddc.gov.uk

Direct Labour: Mrs Ruth Plant, Operational Services - Director, Off Ring Road, Zone 2, Burntwood Business Park, Chase Terrace, Burntwood WS7 3JQ ☎ 01543 687540 🖷 01543 308955 ✉ ruth.plant@lichfielddc.gov.uk

Economic Development: Ms Lesley Bovington, Regeneration Manager, Donegal House, Bore Street, Lichfield WS13 6NE ☎ 01543 308170 🖷 01543 308211 ✉ lesley.bovington@lichfielddc.gov.uk

Economic Development: Mr Richard King, Strategic Director - Democratic, Development & Legal Services, District Council House, Frog Lane, Lichfield WS13 6YU ☎ 01543 308060 🖷 01543 308200 ✉ richard.king@lichfielddc.gov.uk

Economic Development: Mr James Roberts, Economic Development & Enterprise Manager, Marmion House, Lichfield Street, Tamworth B79 7BZ ☎ 01827 709204 🖷 01827 709271 ✉ james-roberts@tamworth.gov.uk

E-Government: Mr Kevin Sleeman, E-Business & Information Strategy Manager, District Council House, Frog Lane, Lichfield WS13 6ZF ☎ 01543 308000

Electoral Registration: Mr Richard King, Strategic Director - Democratic Development & Legal Services, District Council House, Frog Lane, Lichfield WS13 6YU ☎ 01543 308060 🖷 01543 309899 ✉ richard.king@lichfielddc.gov.uk

Electoral Registration: Ms Sarah Pearce, Licensing & Electoral Services Manager, District Council House, Frog Lane, Lichfield WS13 6YU ☎ 01543 308008 🖷 01543 309899 ✉ sarah.pearce@lichfielddc.gov.uk

Emergency Planning: Mrs Ruth Plant, Operational Services - Director, Off Ring Road, Zone 2, Burntwood Business Park, Chase Terrace, Burntwood WS7 3JQ ☎ 01543 687540 🖷 01543 308955 ✉ ruth.plant@lichfielddc.gov.uk

Emergency Planning: Mr Nigel Walker, Resilience Manager, District Council House, Frog Lane, Lichfield WS13 6YU ☎ 01543 308070 🖷 01543 309899 ✉ nigel.walker@lichfielddc.gov.uk

Energy Management: Mr Richard King, Strategic Director - Democratic Development & Legal Services, District Council House, Frog Lane, Lichfield WS13 6YU ☎ 01543 308060 🖷 01543 309899 ✉ richard.king@lichfielddc.gov.uk

Energy Management: Ms Helen Spearey, Strategic Director - Community, Housing & Health, District Council House, Frog Lane, Lichfield WS13 6ZE ☎ 01543 308700 🖷 01543 308712 ✉ helen.spearey@lichfielddc.gov.uk

Environmental / Technical Services: Ms Helen Spearey, Strategic Director - Community, Housing & Health, District Council House, Frog Lane, Lichfield WS13 6ZE ☎ 01543 308700 🖷 01543 308712 ✉ helen.spearey@lichfielddc.gov.uk

Environmental Health: Mr Tim Matthews, Environmental Health Manager, District Council House, Frog Lane, Lichfield WS13 6ZE ☎ 01543 308755 🖷 01543 308728 ✉ tim.matthews@lichfielddc.gov.uk

Estates, Property & Valuation: Mr John Brown, Land & Property Manager, District Council House, Frog Lane, Lichfield WS13 6YU ☎ 01543 308061 🖷 01543 309899 ✉ john.brown@lichfielddc.gov.uk

Estates, Property & Valuation: Mr Richard King, Strategic Director - Democratic Development & Legal Services, District Council House, Frog Lane, Lichfield WS13 6YU ☎ 01543 308060 🖷 01543 309899 ✉ richard.king@lichfielddc.gov.uk

European Liaison: Ms Lesley Bovington, Regeneration Manager, Donegal House, Bore Street, Lichfield WS13 6NE ☎ 01543 308170 🖷 01543 308211 ✉ lesley.bovington@lichfielddc.gov.uk

Finance and Treasurer: Mrs Jane Kitchen, Director - Finance, Revenues & Benefits, District Council House, Frog Lane, Lichfield WS13 6YU ☎ 01543 308770 ✉ jane.kitchen@lichfielddc.gov.uk

Health and Safety: Mr Steve Langston, Health & Safety Manager, District Council House, Frog Lane, Lichfield WS13 6ZF ☎ 01543 308107; 01827 709224 🖷 01543 308103; 01827 709271 ✉ steven.langston@lichfielddc.gov.uk

Health and Safety: Mr Neil Turner, Leisure, Parks & Play Director, District Council House, Frog Lane, Lichfield WS13 6ZD ☎ 01543 308761

Home Energy Conservation: Ms Helen Spearey, Strategic Director - Community, Housing & Health, District Council House, Frog Lane, Lichfield WS13 6ZE ☎ 01543 308700 🖷 01543 308712 ✉ helen.spearey@lichfielddc.gov.uk

Housing: Ms Helen Spearey, Strategic Director - Community, Housing & Health, District Council House, Frog Lane, Lichfield WS13 6ZE ☎ 01543 308700 🖷 01543 308712 ✉ helen.spearey@lichfielddc.gov.uk

Legal: Mr Richard King, Strategic Director - Democratic Development & Legal Services, District Council House, Frog Lane, Lichfield WS13 6YU ☎ 01543 308060 🖷 01543 309899 ✉ richard.king@lichfielddc.gov.uk

Legal: Mr Richard King, Strategic Director Democratic, Development & Legal Services, District Council House, Frog Lane, Lichfield WS13 6YU ☎ 01543 308060 🖷 01543 308200 ✉ richard.king@lichfielddc.gov.uk

Leisure and Cultural Services: Mr Neil Turner, Leisure, Parks & Play Director, District Council House, Frog Lane, Lichfield WS13 6ZD ☎ 01543 308761

Licensing: Mr Richard King, Strategic Director - Democratic, Development & Legal Services, District Council House, Frog Lane, Lichfield WS13 6YU ☎ 01543 308060 🖷 01543 308200 ✉ richard.king@lichfielddc.gov.uk

Licensing: Mr Richard King, Strategic Director - Democratic Development & Legal Services, District Council House, Frog Lane, Lichfield WS13 6YU ☎ 01543 308060 🖷 01543 309899 ✉ richard.king@lichfielddc.gov.uk

Licensing: Ms Sarah Pearce, Licensing & Electoral Services Manager, District Council House, Frog Lane, Lichfield WS13 6YU ☎ 01543 308008 🖷 01543 309899 ✉ sarah.pearce@lichfieddc.gov.uk

Lottery Funding, Charity and Voluntary: Mr Richard King, Strategic Director - Democratic Development & Legal Services, District Council House, Frog Lane, Lichfield WS13 6YU ☎ 01543 308060 🖷 01543 309899 ✉ richard.king@lichfielddc.gov.uk

Member Services: Mrs Sharon Ashton, Democratic Services Manager, District Council House, Frog Lane, Lichfield WS13 6YU ☎ 01543 308062 🖷 01543 309899 ✉ sharon.ashton@lichfielddc.gov.uk

Member Services: Mr Richard King, Strategic Director - Democratic, Development & Legal Services, District Council House, Frog Lane, Lichfield WS13 6YU ☎ 01543 308060 🖷 01543 308200 ✉ richard.king@lichfielddc.gov.uk

Member Services: Mr Richard King, Strategic Director - Democratic Development & Legal Services, District Council House, Frog Lane, Lichfield WS13 6YU ☎ 01543 308060 🖷 01543 309899 ✉ richard.king@lichfielddc.gov.uk

Parking: Mrs Ruth Plant, Operational Services - Director, Off Ring Road, Zone 2, Burntwood Business Park, Chase Terrace, Burntwood WS7 3JQ ☎ 01543 687540 🖷 01543 308955 ✉ ruth.plant@lichfielddc.gov.uk

Personnel / HR: Ms Nina Dawes, Chief Executive, District Council House, Frog Lane, Lichfield WS13 6ZB ☎ 01543 308001 🖷 01543 308049 ✉ nina.dawes@lichfielddc.gov.uk

Personnel / HR: Mrs Cathy Pepper, Personnel Manager, District Council House, Frog Lane, Lichfield WS13 6ZF ☎ 01543 308112 🖷 01543 308103 ✉ cathy.pepper@lichfielddc.gov.uk

Planning: Mr Richard King, Strategic Director - Democratic Development & Legal Services, District Council House, Frog Lane, Lichfield WS13 6YU ☎ 01543 308060 🖷 01543 309899 ✉ richard.king@lichfielddc.gov.uk

Procurement: Mrs Jane Kitchen, Director - Finance, Revenues & Benefits, District Council House, Frog Lane, Lichfield WS13 6YU ☎ 01543 308770 ✉ jane.kitchen@lichfielddc.gov.uk

Regeneration: Ms Lesley Bovington, Regeneration Manager, Donegal House, Bore Street, Lichfield WS13 6NE ☎ 01543 308170 🖷 01543 308211 ✉ lesley.bovington@lichfielddc.gov.uk

Regeneration: Mr Richard King, Strategic Director - Democratic, Development & Legal Services, District Council House, Frog Lane, Lichfield WS13 6YU ☎ 01543 308060 🖷 01543 308200 ✉ richard.king@lichfielddc.gov.uk

Regeneration: Mr Richard King, Strategic Director - Democratic Development & Legal Services, District Council House, Frog Lane, Lichfield WS13 6YU ☎ 01543 308060 🖷 01543 309899 ✉ richard.king@lichfielddc.gov.uk

Sustainable Communities: Ms Lesley Bovington, Regeneration Manager, Donegal House, Bore Street, Lichfield WS13 6NE ☎ 01543 308170 🖷 01543 308211 ✉ lesley.bovington@lichfielddc.gov.uk

Sustainable Development: Mr Richard King, Strategic Director - Democratic, Development & Legal Services, District Council

House, Frog Lane, Lichfield WS13 6YU ☎ 01543 308060 🖷 01543 308200 ✉ richard.king@lichfielddc.gov.uk

Sustainable Development: Mr Richard King, Strategic Director - Democratic Development & Legal Services, District Council House, Frog Lane, Lichfield WS13 6YU ☎ 01543 308060 🖷 01543 309899 ✉ richard.king@lichfielddc.gov.uk

Tourism: Mr Richard King, Strategic Director - Democratic Development & Legal Services, District Council House, Frog Lane, Lichfield WS13 6YU ☎ 01543 308060 🖷 01543 309899 ✉ richard.king@lichfielddc.gov.uk

Waste Collection and Disposal: Mrs Ruth Plant, Operational Services - Director, Off Ring Road, Zone 2, Burntwood Business Park, Chase Terrace, Burntwood WS7 3JQ ☎ 01543 687540 🖷 01543 308955 ✉ ruth.plant@lichfielddc.gov.uk

Waste Management: Mrs Ruth Plant, Operational Services - Director, Off Ring Road, Zone 2, Burntwood Business Park, Chase Terrace, Burntwood WS7 3JQ ☎ 01543 687540 🖷 01543 308955 ✉ ruth.plant@lichfielddc.gov.uk

Children's Play Areas: Mr Neil Turner, Leisure, Parks & Play Director, District Council House, Frog Lane, Lichfield WS13 6ZD ☎ 01543 308761

MEMBERS OF THE COUNCIL (56)

Leader of the Council: **Wilcox**, Michael (CON - Alrewas and Fradley)
michael.wilcox@lichfielddc.gov.uk

Deputy Leader of the Council: **Richards**, Valerie (CON - Hammerwich)
val.richards@lichfielddc.gov.uk

Allsopp, Jeanette (CON - Boley Park)
jeanette.allsopp@lichfielddc.gov.uk

Arnold, Susan (CON - Mease and Tame)
susan.arnold@lichfielddc.gov.uk

Awty, Bob (CON - Leomansley)
bob.awty@lichfielddc.gov.uk

Bacon, Brian (CON - Curborough)
brain.bacon@lochfielddc.gov.uk

Bacon, Norma (CON - Curborough)
norma.bacon@lichfielddc.gov.uk

Barnett, Shirley Ann (CON - Colton and Mavesyn Ridware)
shirley.barnett@lichfielddc.gov.uk

Boyle, Gwyneth (CON - St. John's)
gwyneth.boyle@lichfielddc.gov.uk

Constable, Douglas (CON - Highfield)
douglas.constable@lichfielddc.gov.uk

Constable, Brenda (CON - All Saints)
brenda.constable@lichfielddc.gov.uk

Cox, Richard (CON - Armitage with Handsacre)
richard.cox@lichfielddc.gov.uk

Derrick, Bernard (CON - Stowe)
bernard.derrick@lichfielddc.gov.uk

Drinkwater, Eric (LAB - Chase Terrace)
eric.drinkwater@lichfielddc.gov.uk

Eadie, Iain (CON - Leomansley)
iain.eadie@lichfielddc.gov.uk

Eagland, Janet (CON - Boley Park)
janet.eagland@lichfielddc.gov.uk

Evans, Diane (LAB - Boney Hay)
diane.evans@lichfielddc.gov.uk

Fisher, Helen (CON - Highfield)
helen.fisher@lichfielddc.gov.uk

Flowith, Louise (CON - Little Aston)
louise.flowith@lichfielddc.gov.uk

Fryers, Michael (CON - Chadsmead)
michael.fryers@lichfielddc.gov.uk

Greatorex, Colin (CON - Stowe)
colin.greatorex@lichfielddc.gov.uk

Hancocks, Rita (CON - Shenstone)
rita.hancocks@lichfielddc.gov.uk

Heath, Russell (LAB - Boney Hay)
russell.heath@lichfielddc.gov.uk

Hogan, Paul (CON - Alrewas and Fradley)
paul.hogan@lichfielddc.gov.uk

Humphreys, Ken (CON - All Saints)
kenneth.humphreys@lichfielddc.gov.uk

Isaacs, Donald (LAB - Summerfield)
donald.isaacs@lichfielddc.gov.uk

Lewin, Ian (CON - Fazeley)
ian.lewin@lichfield.gov.uk

Leytham, David (CON - Curborough)
david.leytham@lichfielddc.gov.uk

Marshall, Thomas (CON - Armitage with Handsacre)
thomas.marshall@lichfielddc.gov.uk

Mosson, Richard (CON - Burntwood Central)
richard.mosson@lichfielddc.gov.uk

Mynott, Glen (LAB - Fazeley)
glen.mynott@lichfielddc.gov.uk

Norman, Steven (LAB - Summerfield)
steven.norman@lichfielddc.gov.uk

Pearce, Alan (CON - Fazeley)
alan.pearce@lichfielddc.gov.uk

Perkins, Ellen (CON - Mease and Tame)
ellen.perkins@lichfielddc.gov.uk

Powell, Joseph (CON - Little Aston)
joseph.powell@lichfielddc.gov.uk

Pritchard, Ian (CON - Kings Bromley)
ian.pritchard@lichfielddc.gov.uk

Roberts, Neil (CON - Longdon)
neil.roberts@lichfielddc.gov.uk

Salter, David (CON - Shenstone)
david.salter@lichfielddc.gov.uk

Smedley, David (CON - Stowe)
david.smedley@lichfielddc.gov.uk

Smith, David (CON - Stonnall)
david.smith@lichfielddc.gov.uk

Smith, Andrew (CON - Leomansley)
andrew.smith@lichfielddc.gov.uk

Spruce, Christopher (CON - St. John's)
christopher.spruce@lichfielddc.gov.uk

Stanhope, Margaret (CON - Alrewas and Fradley)
margaret.stanhope@lichfielddc.gov.uk

Strachan, Robert (CON - Whittington)
cllr.robertstrachan@lichfielddc.gov.uk

Taylor, Stephen (LAB - Chasetown)
stephen.taylor@lichfielddc.gov.uk

Thomas, Terry (CON - CHadsmead)
terry.thomas@lichfielddc.gov.uk

Tittley, Martyn (CON - Armitage with Handsacre)
martyn.tittley@lichfielddc.gov.uk

Tranter, Heather (CON - Burntwood Central)
heather.tranter@lichfielddc.gov.uk

Walker, John (LAB - Chase Terrace)
johnthomas.walker@lichfielddc.gov.uk

Warfield, Mark (CON - Boley Park)
mark.warfield@lichfielddc.gov.uk
White, Alan (CON - Whittington)
alan.white@lichfielddc.gov.uk
Wilks, John (CON - St. John's)
john.wilks@lichfielddc.gov.uk
Willis-Croft, Keith (LAB - Chasetown)
keith.willis-croft@lichfielddc.gov.uk
Wilson, Brett (CON - Hammerwich)
brett.wilson@lichfielddc.gov.uk
Woodward, Susan (LAB - Chase Terrace)
susan.woodward@lichfielddc.gov.uk
Yeates, Brian (CON - Bourne Vale)
brian.yeates@lichfielddc.gov.uk

POLITICAL COMPOSITION
CON: 46, LAB: 10

CABINET
Leader / Finance, Revenues & Benefits: Mr Michael Wilcox
Deputy Leader / Leisure Services & Communications: Mrs Valerie Richards
Community & Organisational Development: Mr Colin Greatorex
Democratic & Legal Services: Mrs Margaret Stanhope
Development Services: Mr Alan White
Housing, Health & Environmental Protection: Mr Ian Pritchard
Operational Services & Tourism: Mrs Louise Flowith

LIMAVADY N
Limavady Borough Council, 7 Connell Street, Limavady BT49 0HA ☎ 028 7772 2226 🖷 028 7772 2010 💻 www.limavady.gov.uk

FACTS & FIGURES
Police Authority: Northern Ireland Policing Board
Health Authority: Western Local Commissioning Group
Learning and Skills Council: Northern Ireland
Parliamentary Constituencies: Londonderry East
EU Constituencies: Northern Ireland
Election Frequency: Elections are by thirds
Twinning: Westport, Co. Mayo: Vigneux-sur-Seine

PRINCIPAL OFFICERS
Chief Executive: Mr Liam Flanigan, Chief Executive, 7 Connell Street, Limavady BT49 0HA ☎ 028 7776 0300 🖷 028 7776 5241 ✉ liam.flanigan@limavady.gov.uk

Deputy Chief Executive: Mr Gerry McCourt, Head - Finance, 7 Connell Street, Limavady BT49 0HA ☎ 028 7772 2226 🖷 028 7772 2010 ✉ gerry.mccourt@limavady.gov.uk

Senior Management: Mr Noel Crawford, Director - Environmental Services, 7 Connell Street, Limavady BT49 0HA ☎ 028 7776 0302 ✉ noel.crawford@limavady.gov.uk

Architect, Building / Property Services: Mr Noel Crawford, Director - Environmental Services, 7 Connell Street, Limavady BT49 0HA ☎ 028 7776 0302 ✉ noel.crawford@limavady.gov.uk

Best Value: Mr Gerry McCourt, Head - Finance, 7 Connell Street, Limavady BT49 0HA ☎ 028 7772 2226 🖷 028 7772 2010 ✉ gerry.mccourt@limavady.gov.uk

Building Control: Mr Noel Crawford, Director - Environmental Services, 7 Connell Street, Limavady BT49 0HA ☎ 028 7776 0302 ✉ noel.crawford@limavady.gov.uk

Community Safety: Mrs Bridget McCaughan, Community Safety Officer, 7 Connell Street, Limavady BT49 0HA ☎ 028 7776 0314 🖷 028 777 22010 ✉ bridget.mccaughan@limavady.gov.uk

Computer Management: Mr Darren Maynes, IT Officer, 7 Connell Street, Limavady BT49 0HA ☎ 028 7772 2226 🖷 028 7772 2010 ✉ darren.maynes@limavady.gov.uk

Consumer Protection and Trading Standards: Mr Noel Crawford, Director - Environmental Services, 7 Connell Street, Limavady BT49 0HA ☎ 028 7776 0302 ✉ noel.crawford@limavady.gov.uk

Economic Development: Mr Paul Beattie, Development Services Manager, 7 Connell Street, Limavady BT49 0HA ☎ 028 7772 2226 🖷 028 7772 2010 ✉ paul.beattie@limavady.gov.uk

E-Government: Mr Gerry McCourt, Head - Finance, 7 Connell Street, Limavady BT49 0HA ☎ 028 7772 2226 🖷 028 7772 2010 ✉ gerry.mccourt@limavady.gov.uk

Emergency Planning: Mr Noel Crawford, Director - Environmental Services, 7 Connell Street, Limavady BT49 0HA ☎ 028 7776 0302 ✉ noel.crawford@limavady.gov.uk

Environmental Health: Mr Noel Crawford, Director - Environmental Services, 7 Connell Street, Limavady BT49 0HA ☎ 028 7776 0302 ✉ noel.crawford@limavady.gov.uk

European Liaison: Mr Paul Beattie, Development Services Manager, 7 Connell Street, Limavady BT49 0HA ☎ 028 7772 2226 🖷 028 7772 2010 ✉ paul.beattie@limavady.gov.uk

Events Manager: Ms Geraldine Smyth, Events Officer, 7 Connell Street, Limavady BT49 0HA ☎ 028 7772 0651 ✉ geraldine.smyth@limavady.gov.uk

Finance and Treasurer: Mr Gerry McCourt, Head - Finance, 7 Connell Street, Limavady BT49 0HA ☎ 028 7772 2226 🖷 028 7772 2010 ✉ gerry.mccourt@limavady.gov.uk

Grounds Maintenance: Mr Jimmy McArthur, Operations Manager, 7 Connell Street, Limavady BT49 0HA ☎ 028 7776 0305 ✉ james.mcarthur@limavady.gov.uk

Health and Safety: Miss Orla Dowd, Health & Safety Advisor, 7 Connell Street, Limavady BT49 0HA ☎ 028 7776 0302 🖷 028 7772 2010 ✉ orla.dowd@limavady.gov.uk

Leisure and Cultural Services: Mrs Valerie Richmond, Director - Development Services, 7 Connell Street, Limavady BT49 0HA ☎ 028 7776 0304 🖷 028 777 68107 ✉ valerie.richmond@limavady.gov.uk

Member Services: Mrs Edwina McCaul, Committee Clerk, 7 Connell Street, Limavady BT49 0HA ☎ 028 7776 0300 🖷 028 7776 5241 ✉ edwina.mccaul@limavady.gov.uk

Personnel / HR: Mrs Sandra Kelly, Human Resources Manager, 7 Connell Street, Limavady BT49 0HA ☎ 028 7772 2226 🖷 028 7772 2010 🖱 sandra.kelly@limavady.gov.uk

Procurement: Mr Gerry McCourt, Head - Finance, 7 Connell Street, Limavady BT49 0HA ☎ 028 7772 2226 🖷 028 7772 2010 🖱 gerry.mccourt@limavady.gov.uk

Regeneration: Mr Paul Beattie, Development Services Manager, 7 Connell Street, Limavady BT49 0HA ☎ 028 7772 2226 🖷 028 7772 2010 🖱 paul.beattie@limavady.gov.uk

Staff Training: Mrs Sandra Kelly, Human Resources Manager, 7 Connell Street, Limavady BT49 0HA ☎ 028 7772 2226 🖷 028 7772 2010 🖱 sandra.kelly@limavady.gov.uk

Sustainable Communities: Mrs Valerie Richmond, Director - Development Services, 7 Connell Street, Limavady BT49 0HA ☎ 028 7776 0304 🖷 028 777 68107 🖱 valerie.richmond@limavady.gov.uk

Sustainable Development: Mr Paul Beattie, Development Services Manager, 7 Connell Street, Limavady BT49 0HA ☎ 028 7772 2226 🖷 028 7772 2010 🖱 paul.beattie@limavady.gov.uk

Tourism: Mrs Clare Quinn, Tourism Development Officer, 7 Connell Street, Limavady BT49 0HA ☎ 028 7776 0654 🖷 028 7772 2010 🖱 clare.quinn@limavady.gov.uk

Waste Management: Mr John McCarron, Waste Management Manager, 7 Connell Street, Limavady BT49 0HA ☎ 028 7772 2226 🖱 john.mccarron@limavady.gov.uk

MEMBERS OF THE COUNCIL (15)

***Mayor:* McLaughlin**, Cathal (SF - Bellarena)
cathal.mclaughin@limavady.gov.uk

***Deputy Mayor:* Robinson**, Alan (DUP - Limavady Town)
limavadyhq@dup.org.uk

***Alderman:* Coyle**, Michael (SDLP - Benbradagh)
michael.coyle@Limavady.gov.uk

***Alderman:* Robinson**, George (DUP - Bellarena)
limavadyhq@dup.org.uk

Beattie, Orla (SDLP - Bellarena)
orla.beattie@limavady.gov.uk

Brolly, Anne (SF - Limavady Town)
anne.brolly@Limavady.gov.uk

Chivers, Brenda (SF - Bellarena)
brenda.chivers@limavady.gov.uk

Douglas, Boyd (O - Benbradagh)
boyd.douglas@limavady.gov.uk

McCaul, Tony (SF - Benbradagh)
emailto:tony.mccaul@limavady.gov.uk

McCorkell, James (DUP - Limavady Town)
james.mccorkell@limavady.gov.uk

McGlinchley, Sean (SF - Benbradagh)
sean.mcglinchey@limavady.gov.uk

Mullan, Gerry (SDLP - Limavady Town)
gerry.mullan@Limavady.gov.uk

Nicholl, Dermot (SF - Bellarena)
dermot.nicholl@limavady.gov.uk

Rankin, Jack (UUP - Limavady Town)
jack.rankin@limavady.gov.uk

Stevenson, Edwin (UUP - Bellarena)
Edwin.Stevenson@limavady.gov.uk

POLITICAL COMPOSITION

SF: 6, SDLP: 3, DUP: 3, UUP: 2, O: 1

COMMITTEE CHAIRS

Development: Mr Michael Coyle
Environmental Services: Mr Cathal McLaughlin
Planning & Development Services: Mr Dermot Nicholl
Support Services: Mr Tony McCaul

LINCOLN CITY — D

Lincoln City Council, (City of Lincoln Council), City Hall, Beaumont Fee, Lincoln LN1 1DD ☎ 01522 881188 🖷 01522 521736 🖱 email@lincoln.gov.uk 💻 www.lincoln.gov.uk

FACTS & FIGURES

Police Authority: Lincolnshire Police Authority
Health Authority: East Midlands Strategic Health Authority
Learning and Skills Council: East Midlands
Parliamentary Constituencies: Lincoln
EU Constituencies: East Midlands
Election Frequency: Elections are by thirds
Twinning: Neustadt an der Weinstrasse (Germany); Port Lincoln (Australia); Tangshan (China)

PRINCIPAL OFFICERS

Chief Executive: Mr Andrew Taylor, Chief Executive & Town Clerk, City Hall, Beaumont Fee, Lincoln LN1 1DD ☎ 01522 873303 🖷 01522 521736

Senior Management: Mrs Angela Andrews, Director of Resources, City Hall, Beaumont Fee, Lincoln LN1 1DD ☎ 01522 873292 🖷 01522 542569 🖱 angela.andrews@lincoln.gov.uk

Senior Management: Mr John Bibby, Director of Housing & Community Services, City Hall, Beaumont Fee, Lincoln LN1 1DE ☎ 01522 873201 🖷 01522 510822 🖱 john.bibby@lincoln.gov.uk

Senior Management: Mr John Latham, Director of Development & Environmental Services, City Hall, Beaumont Fee, Lincoln LN1 1DD ☎ 01522 873471 🖷 01522 567934 🖱 john.latham@lincoln.gov.uk

Building Control: Mr Philip King, Service Manager - Building Control, City Hall, Beaumont Fee, Lincoln LN1 1DD ☎ 01522 873425 🖷 01522 567934 🖱 phil.king@lincoln.gov.uk

PR / Communications: Mr Chris Dunbar, Communications Manager, City Hall, Beaumont Fee, Lincoln LN1 1DD ☎ 01522 873318 🖷 01522 521736 🖱 chris.dunbar@lincoln.gov.uk

Community Planning: Mr John Latham, Director of Development & Environmental Services, City Hall, Beaumont Fee, Lincoln LN1 1DD ☎ 01522 873471 🖷 01522 567934 🖱 john.latham@lincoln.gov.uk

Community Safety: Mr John Latham, Director of Development & Environmental Services, City Hall, Beaumont Fee, Lincoln LN1 1DD ☎ 01522 873471 🖷 01522 567934 🖱 john.latham@lincoln.gov.uk

Computer Management: Mr Matt Smith, Business Development & IT Manager, City Hall, Beaumont Fee, Lincoln LN1 1DD ☎ 01522 873308 🖷 01522 560049 ✉ matt.smith@lincoln.gov.uk

Corporate Services: Mr Simon Walters, Assistant Director of Corporate Review & Development, City Hall, Beaumont Fee, Lincoln LN1 1DD ☎ 01522 873866 🖷 01522 521736 ✉ simon.walters@lincoln.gov.uk

Corporate Services: Mrs Carolyn Wheater, Assistant Director of Legal & Corporate Support Services, City Hall, Beaumont Fee, Lincoln LN1 1DD ☎ 01522 873323 🖷 01522 542569 ✉ carolyn.wheater@lincoln.gov.uk

Customer Service: Ms Joanne Crookes, Customer Services Manager, City Hall, Beaumont Fee, Lincoln LN1 1DD ☎ 01522 873407 🖷 01522 542569 ✉ joanne.crookes@lincoln.gov.uk

Economic Development: Ms Kate Ellis, Economic Sustainability & Tourism Programme Manager, City Hall, Beaumont Fee, Lincoln LN1 1DD ☎ 01522 873824 🖷 01522 560049 ✉ kate.ellis@lincoln.gov.uk

E-Government: Mr Matt Smith, Business Development & IT Manager, City Hall, Beaumont Fee, Lincoln LN1 1DD ☎ 01522 873308 🖷 01522 560049 ✉ matt.smith@lincoln.gov.uk

Electoral Registration: Mr Steve Swain, Principal Democratic Services Officer, City Hall, Beaumont Fee, Lincoln LN1 1DD ☎ 01522 873439 🖷 01522 542569 ✉ steve.swain@lincoln.gov.uk

Emergency Planning: Mr John Latham, Director of Development & Environmental Services, City Hall, Beaumont Fee, Lincoln LN1 1DD ☎ 01522 873471 🖷 01522 567934 ✉ john.latham@lincoln.gov.uk

Energy Management: Mr David Bowskill, Housing Energy Officer, City Hall, Beaumont Fee, Lincoln LN1 1DD ☎ 01522 873377 🖷 01522 510822 ✉ david.bowskill@lincoln.gov.uk

Environmental Health: Ms Sara Boothright, Food, Health & Safety Manager, City Hall, Beaumont Fee, Lincoln LN1 1DD ☎ 01522 873314 🖷 01522 546702 ✉ sara.boothright@lincoln.gov.uk

Estates, Property & Valuation: Mr John Morris, Tenancy Management Team Leader, City Hall, Beaumont Fee, Lincoln LN1 1DD ☎ 01522 881188 🖷 01522 510822 ✉ john.morris@lincoln.gov.uk

European Liaison: Ms Michelle Smith, Senior Programme Managements Officer, City Hall, Beaumont Fee, Lincoln LN1 1DD ☎ 01522 873329 🖷 01522 567934 ✉ michelle.smith@lincoln.gov.uk

Events Manager: Ms Kate Ellis, Economic Sustainability & Tourism Programme Manager, City Hall, Beaumont Fee, Lincoln LN1 1DD ☎ 01522 873824 🖷 01522 560049 ✉ kate.ellis@lincoln.gov.uk

Finance and Treasurer: Mrs Angela Andrews, Director of Resources, City Hall, Beaumont Fee, Lincoln LN1 1DD ☎ 01522 873292 🖷 01522 542569 ✉ angela.andrews@lincoln.gov.uk

Grounds Maintenance: Mr Dave Charysz, Open Spaces Officer, City Hall, Beaumont Fee, Lincoln LN1 1DE ☎ 01522 873414 🖷 01522 560049 ✉ dave.charysz@lincoln.gov.uk

Health and Safety: Ms Sara Boothright, Food, Health & Safety Manager, City Hall, Beaumont Fee, Lincoln LN1 1DD ☎ 01522 873314 🖷 01522 546702 ✉ sara.boothright@lincoln.gov.uk

Home Energy Conservation: Mr David Bowskill, Housing Energy Officer, City Hall, Beaumont Fee, Lincoln LN1 1DD ☎ 01522 873377 🖷 01522 510822 ✉ david.bowskill@lincoln.gov.uk

Housing: Mr Tim Whitworth, Assistant Director of Housing, City Hall, Beaumont Fee, Lincoln LN1 1DD ☎ 01522 873532 🖷 01522 510822 ✉ tim.whitworth@lincoln.gov.uk

Housing Maintenance: Mr John Morris, Tenancy Management Team Leader, City Hall, Beaumont Fee, Lincoln LN1 1DD ☎ 01522 881188 🖷 01522 510822 ✉ john.morris@lincoln.gov.uk

Legal: Ms Carolyn Wheater, Head of Corporate Support Services, City Hall, Beaumont Fee, Lincoln LN1 1DD ☎ 01522 873323 🖷 01522 521736 ✉ carolyn.wheater@lincoln.gov.uk

Leisure and Cultural Services: Mr John Bibby, Director of Housing & Community Services, City Hall, Beaumont Fee, Lincoln LN1 1DE ☎ 01522 873201 🖷 01522 510822 ✉ john.bibby@lincoln.gov.uk

Leisure and Cultural Services: Mr Steve Bird, Assistant Director of Communities & Street Scene, City Hall, Beaumont Fee, Lincoln LN1 1DH ☎ 01522 873421 🖷 01522 546702 ✉ steve.bird@lincoln.gov.uk

Licensing: Mr Kevin Barron, Licensing Manager, City Hall, Beaumont Fee, Lincoln LN1 1DD ☎ 01522 873564 🖷 01522 542569 ✉ kevin.barron@lincoln.gov.uk

Lifelong Learning: Mr Richard Linder, Training Advisor, City Hall, Beaumont Fee, Lincoln LN1 1DD ☎ 01522 873306 🖷 01522 521736 ✉ richard.linder@lincoln.gov.uk

Lottery Funding, Charity and Voluntary: Ms Michelle Smith, Senior Programme Managements Officer, City Hall, Beaumont Fee, Lincoln LN1 1DD ☎ 01522 873329 🖷 01522 567934 ✉ michelle.smith@lincoln.gov.uk

Member Services: Mr Steve Swain, Principal Democratic Services Officer, City Hall, Beaumont Fee, Lincoln LN1 1DD ☎ 01522 873439 🖷 01522 542569 ✉ steve.swain@lincoln.gov.uk

Parking: Mr Steve Lockwood, Leisure, Sport & City Services Manager, City Hall, Beaumont Fee, Lincoln LN1 1DD ☎ 01522 873520 ✉ steve.lockwood@lincoln.gov.uk

Partnerships: Mr Andrew Taylor, Chief Executive & Town Clerk, City Hall, Beaumont Fee, Lincoln LN1 1DD ☎ 01522 873303 🖷 01522 521736

Personnel / HR: Ms Sally Zubic, Human Resources Manager, City Hall, Beaumont Fee, Lincoln LN1 1DD ☎ 01522 873279 🖷 01522 521736 ✉ sally.zubic@lincoln.gov.uk

Procurement: Ms Jaclyn Gibson, Assistant Director of Business Development & Finance, City Hall, Beaumont Fee, Lincoln LN1 1DD ☎ 01522 873258 🖷 01522 542569 ✉ jaclyn.gibson@lincoln.gov.uk

Staff Training: Mr Richard Linder, Training Advisor, City Hall, Beaumont Fee, Lincoln LN1 1DD ☎ 01522 873306 🖷 01522 521736 ✉ richard.linder@lincoln.gov.uk

Street Scene: Ms Caroline Pritchard, Community Services Manager, City Hall, Beaumont Fee, Lincoln LN1 1DD ☎ 01522 873422 🖷 01522 546702 ✉ caroline.pritchard@lincoln.gov.uk

Sustainable Communities: Ms Jennie Chapman, Partnership Manager, City Hall, Beaumont Fee, Lincoln LN1 1DD ☎ 01522 873343 🖷 01522 567934 ✉ jennie.chapman@lincoln.gov.uk

Waste Collection and Disposal: Mr Steve Bird, Assistant Director of Communities & Street Scene, City Hall, Beaumont Fee, Lincoln LN1 1DH ☎ 01522 873421 🖷 01522 546702 ✉ steve.bird@lincoln.gov.uk

Waste Management: Ms Caroline Pritchard, Community Services Manager, City Hall, Beaumont Fee, Lincoln LN1 1DD ☎ 01522 873422 🖷 01522 546702 ✉ caroline.pritchard@lincoln.gov.uk

MEMBERS OF THE COUNCIL (33)

***Deputy Mayor:* Vaughan**, Patrick (LAB - Glebe)
pat.vaughan@lincoln.gov.uk
***Leader of the Council:* Metcalfe**, Richard (LAB - Glebe)
richard.metcalfe@lincoln.gov.uk
***Deputy Leader of the Council:* Nannestad**, Donald (LAB - Castle)
donald.nannestad@lincoln.gov.uk
Bilton, Bill (LAB - Bracebridge)
bill.bilton@lincoln.gov.uk
Bodger, Yvonne (CON - Minster)
yvonne.bodger@lincoln.gov.uk
Brothwell, Kathleen (LAB - Abbey)
kathleen.brothwell@lincoln.gov.uk
Burke, Chris (LAB - Park)
chris.burke@lincoln.gov.uk
Burke, Sue (LAB - Minster)
sue.burke@lincoln.gov.uk
Bushell, Bob (LAB - Moorland)
bob.bushell@lincoln.gov.uk
Charlesworth, Brent (LAB - Park)
brent.charlesworth@lincoln.gov.uk
Clark, Jane (CON - Birchwood)
jane.clark@lincoln.gov.uk
Clayton-Hewson, Gill (LAB - Boultham)
gill.clayton-hewson@lincoln.gov.uk
Ellis, Adrianna (LAB - Moorland)
adrianna.ellis@lincoln.gov.uk
Ellis, Geoff (LAB - Moorland)
geoff.ellis@lincoln.gov.uk
Gratrick, David (CON - Minster)
david.gratrick@lincoln.gov.uk
Grice, Darren (CON - Bracebridge)
darren.grice@lincoln.gov.uk
Hanrahan, Jim (LAB - Castle)
jim.hanrahan@lincoln.gov.uk
Hewson, Gary (LAB - Boultham)
garythewson@hotmail.com
Hills, Ronald (CON - Hartsolme)
ronald.hills@lincoln.gov.uk
Jackson, David (LAB - Park)
david.jackson@lincoln.gov.uk
Kerry, Andrew (CON - Hartsolme)
andrew.kerry@lincoln.gov.uk
Kirk, Jackie (LAB - Glebe)
jackie.kirk@lincoln.gov.uk
Kirk, Rosanne (LAB - Birchwood)
rosanne.kirk@lincoln.gov.uk
Kirkby, Geoffrey (CON - Hartsolme)
geoffrey.kirby@lincoln.gov.uk
Lee, Karen (LAB - Carholme)
karen.lee@lincoln.gov.uk
Murray, Neil (LAB - Carholme)
neilmurraymis@hotmail.com
Smith, Fay (LAB - Abbey)
fay.smith@lincoln.gov.uk
Speakman, Tony (LAB - Carholme)
tony.speakman@lincoln.gov.uk
Spratt, Hilton (CON - Bracebridge)
members@lincoln.gov.uk
Strengiel, Edmund (CON - Birchwood)
estrengiel@phoenix-ifa.co.uk
Toofany, Ralph (LAB - Boultham)
ralph.toofany@lincoln.gov.uk
West, Peter (LAB - Abbey)
peter.west@lincoln.gov.uk
Woolley, Loraine (LAB - Castle)
loraine.woolley@lincoln.gov.uk

POLITICAL COMPOSITION

LAB: 24, CON: 9

CABINET

Leader / Corporate Management: Mr Richard Metcalfe
Deputy Leader / Recreational Services & Health: Mr Donald Nannestad
Environmental Services & Public Protection: Ms Fay Smith
Housing: Mr Peter West
Planning Policy & Economic Regeneration: Mr Neil Murray
Social Inclusion & Community Cohesion: Mr Brent Charlesworth

COMMITTEE CHAIRS

Audit: Mr Geoff Ellis
Planning: Mr Peter West
Policy Scrutiny: Mr David Jackson
Standards: Mr Geoff Ellis

LINCOLNSHIRE C

Lincolnshire County Council, County Offices, Newland, Lincoln LN1 1YL ☎ 01522 552222 🖷 01522 516137 ✉ customer_services@lincolnshire.gov.uk 💻 www.lincolnshire.gov.uk

FACTS & FIGURES

Police Authority: Lincolnshire Police Authority
Health Authority: East Midlands Strategic Health Authority
Learning and Skills Council: East Midlands
EU Constituencies: East Midlands

Election Frequency: Elections are of whole council

PRINCIPAL OFFICERS

Chief Executive: Mr Tony McArdle, Chief Executive, County Offices, Newland, Lincoln LN1 1YL ☎ 01522 552222 🖷 01522 552004 🖱 tony.mcardle@lincolnshire.gov.uk

Senior Management: Ms Debbie Barnes, Director of Children's Services, County Offices, Newland, Lincoln LN1 1YL ☎ 01552 553201 🖱 debbie.barnes@lincolnshire.gov.uk

Senior Management: Dr Tony Hill, Director of Public Health, 15 - 17 The Avenue, Lincoln LN1 1PD ☎ 01552 553960 🖱 tony.hill@lincolnshire.gov.uk

Senior Management: Mr Pete Moore, Executive Director - Resources & Community Safety, County Offices, Newland, Lincoln LN1 1YL ☎ 01522 553602 🖷 01522 553962 🖱 pete.moore@lincolnshire.gov.uk

Senior Management: Mr David O'Connor, Executive Director - Performance & Governance, County Offices, Newland, Lincoln LN1 1YL ☎ 01522 552316 🖱 david.oconnor@lincolnshire.gov.uk

Senior Management: Mr Richard Wills, Executive Director - Communities, City Hall, Beaumont Fee, Lincoln LN1 1DN ☎ 01522 553000 🖷 01522 512335 🖱 richard.wills@lincolnshire.gov.uk

Access Officer / Social Services (Disability): Mr Glen Garrod, Assistant Director - Adult Social Care Commissioning, Orchard House, Orchard Street, Lincoln LN1 1BA ☎ 01522 552808 🖱 glen.garrod@lincolnshire.gov.uk

Architect, Building / Property Services: Mr Kevin Kendall, Chief Property Officer, 51 Newland, Lincoln LN1 1YL ☎ 01552 553099 🖷 01522 541561 🖱 kevin.kendall@lincolnshire.gov.uk

Best Value: Mr George Spiteri, Programme Manager (Value for Money & Performance), County Offices, Newland, Lincoln LN1 1YL ☎ 01522 552120 🖱 george.spiteri@lincolnshire.gov.uk

Catering Services: Mrs Claire Blackbourn, Assistant Catering Services Manager, Mill House (3rd Floor), Brayford Wharf North, Lincoln LN1 1YT ☎ 01522 830032 🖷 01522 516061 🖱 claire.blackbourn@mouchel-lincoln.com

Children / Youth Services: Mr Stuart Carlton, Assistant Director - Children's Services, County Offices, Newland, Lincoln LN1 1YL ☎ 01552 554051 🖱 stuart.carlton@lincolnshire.gov.uk

Civil Registration: Ms Donna Sharp, County Services Manager, Lindum Road, Lincoln LN2 1NN ☎ 01522 554052 🖷 01522 589524 🖱 donna.sharp@lincolnshire.gov.uk

PR / Communications: Ms Karen Spencer, Communications Manager, County Offices, Newland, Lincoln LN1 1YL ☎ 01522 552303 🖱 karen.spencer@lincolnshire.gov.uk

Community Safety: Mrs Sara Barry, Head of Safer Communities, Witham Park House, Waterside South, Lincoln LN5 7JN ☎ 01522 552499 🖱 sara.barry@lincolnshire.gov.uk

Computer Management: Ms Judith Hetherington-Smith, Chief Information Officer, Business Modernisation Unit, County Offices, Newland, Lincoln LN1 1YL ☎ 01522 553603 🖱 judith.hetheringtonsmith@lincolnshire.gov.uk

Consumer Protection and Trading Standards: Mrs Sara Barry, Head of Safer Communities, Witham Park House, Waterside South, Lincoln LN5 7JN ☎ 01522 552499 🖱 sara.barry@lincolnshire.gov.uk

Contracts: Mrs Sharon Cuff, Head of Procurement Lincolnshire, Orchard House, Orchard Street, Lincoln LN1 1YL ☎ 01522 553281 🖷 01522 554234 🖱 sharon.cuff@lincolnshire.gov.uk

Corporate Services: Mr Pete Moore, Executive Director - Resources & Community Safety, County Offices, Newland, Lincoln LN1 1YL ☎ 01522 553602 🖷 01522 553962 🖱 pete.moore@lincolnshire.gov.uk

Customer Service: Mr Mark Haynes, Head of Customer Operations, Witham Park House, Waterside South, Lincoln LN5 7JN ☎ 01522 550002 🖱 mark.haynes@lincolnshire.gov.uk

Economic Development: Ms Jenny Gammon, Assistant Director - Economy & Culture Services, Ground Floor, City Hall, Beaumont Fee, Lincoln LN1 1DD ☎ 01552 550511 🖷 01522 516720 🖱 jenny.gammon@lincolnshire.gov.uk

Education: Mr Andy Breckon, Director of Education Services, The Vicarage, West Parade, Lincoln LN1 1NU ☎ 01522 553286 🖱 andy.breckon@lincolnshire.gov.uk

E-Government: Ms Judith Hetherington-Smith, Chief Information Officer, Business Modernisation Unit, County Offices, Newland, Lincoln LN1 1YL ☎ 01522 553603 🖱 judith.hetheringtonsmith@lincolnshire.gov.uk

Emergency Planning: Mr David Powell, Head of Emergency Planning, Fire and Rescue Headquarters, South Park Avenue, Lincoln LN5 8EL ☎ 01522 582224 🖷 01522 519318 🖱 david.powell@lincoln.fire-uk.org

Energy Management: Mr Jim Hogg, Property Manager - Operations, 51 Newland, Lincoln LN1 1YL ☎ 01522 553664 🖷 01522 541651 🖱 jim.hogg@lincolnshire.gov.uk

Environmental / Technical Services: Mr Richard Wills, Executive Director - Communities, City Hall, Beaumont Fee, Lincoln LN1 1DN ☎ 01522 553000 🖷 01522 512335 🖱 richard.wills@lincolnshire.gov.uk

Estates, Property & Valuation: Mr Jim Hogg, Property Manager - Operations, Orchard House, Orchard Street, Lincoln LN1 1BA ☎ 01522 553664 🖷 01522 541651 🖱 jim.hogg@lincolnshire.gov.uk

European Liaison: Mr Justin Brown, Head of Enterprise, Ground Floor, City Hall, Beaumont Fee, Lincoln LN1 1DD ☎ 01522 550630 🖷 01522 516720 🖱 justin.brown@lincolnshire.gov.uk

Events Manager: Mr Mark Stoneham, Events Manager, County Offices, Newland, Lincoln LN1 1YL ☎ 01522 552118 🖷 01522 552323 🖱 mark.stoneham@lincolnshire.gov.uk

Facilities: Mr Phil Foster, Business Services Manager, Mouchel, Mill House, Brayford Wharf North, Lincoln LN1 1YT ☎ 01522 836053 🖷 01522 516079 ✉ phil.foster@mouchel-lincoln.com

Finance and Treasurer: Mr David Forbes, Assistant Director - Finance & Resources, County Offices, Newland, Lincoln LN1 1YL ☎ 01522 553642 🖷 01522 541651 ✉ david.forbes@lincolnshire.gov.uk

Fleet Management: Mr David J Davies, Principal Maintenance Engineer, City Hall, Beaumont Fee, Lincoln LN1 1DN ☎ 01522 553080 🖷 01522 553149 ✉ davidj.davies@lincolnshire.gov.uk

Health and Safety: Ms Sarah Tennant, Strategic Risk Manager, County Offices, Newland, Lincoln LN1 1YL ☎ 01522 552206 🖷 01522 554930 ✉ sarah.tennant@lincolnshire.gov.uk

Highways: Mr Paul Coathup, Assistant Director - Highways & Transportation, City Hall, Beaumont Fee, Lincoln LN1 1DN ☎ 01522 553086 🖷 01522 512335 ✉ paul.coathup@lincolnshire.gov.uk

Local Area Agreement: Mr David O'Connor, Executive Director - Performance & Governance, County Offices, Newland, Lincoln LN1 1YL ☎ 01522 552316 ✉ david.oconnor@lincolnshire.gov.uk

Legal: Mr David Coleman, Joint Head of Legal Services, 45 - 49 Newland, Lincoln LN1 1XZ ☎ 01522 552542 🖷 01522 552588 ✉ david.coleman@lincolnshire.gov.uk

Legal: Ms Eleanor Hoggart, Joint Head of Legal Services, 45 - 49 Newland, Lincoln LN1 1XZ ☎ 01522 552542 🖷 01522 552588 ✉ eleanor.hoggart@lincolnshire.gov.uk

Leisure and Cultural Services: Ms Jenny Gammon, Assistant Director - Economy & Culture Services, Beech House, Witham Park, Waterside South, Lincoln LN5 7JH ☎ 01552 550511 🖷 01522 516720 ✉ jenny.gammon@lincolnshire.gov.uk

Lifelong Learning: Ms Thea Croxall, Delivery Manager - Learning, Eastgate Centre, 105 Eastgate, Sleaford NG34 7EN ☎ 01522 550381 ✉ thea.croxall@lincolnshire.gov.uk

Lighting: Mr Stan Hall, Principal Engineer Street Lighting, Technical Services, Witham Park, Waterside South, Lincoln LN5 7JN ☎ 01522 555572 🖷 01522 553068 ✉ stan.hall@lincolnshire.gov.uk

Lottery Funding, Charity and Voluntary: Mr Justin Brown, Head of Enterprise, Ground Floor, City Hall, Beaumont Fee, Lincoln LN1 1DD ☎ 01522 550630 🖷 01522 516720 ✉ justin.brown@lincolnshire.gov.uk

Member Services: Mr Nigel West, Democratic Services Manager, County Offices, Newland, Lincoln LN1 1YL ☎ 01522 552840 🖷 01522 552004 ✉ nigel.west@lincolnshire.gov.uk

Personnel / HR: Mrs Fiona Thompson, Head of People Management, Orchard House, Orchard Street, Lincoln LN1 1BA ☎ 01522 552207 🖷 01522 516010 ✉ fiona.thompson@lincolnshire.gov.uk

Personnel / HR: Mr David Vickers, Pensions Manager, Mill House (3rd Floor), Brayford Wharf North, Lincoln LN1 1YT ☎ 01522 836462 🖷 01522 516050 ✉ dave.vickers@mouchel-lincoln.com

Planning: Mr Alan Freeman, Head of Spatial Planning, Witham Park House, Waterside South, Lincoln LN5 7JN ☎ 01522 554840 🖷 01522 554829 ✉ alan.freeman@lincolnshire.gov.uk

Procurement: Mrs Sharon Cuff, Head of Procurement Lincolnshire, Orchard House, Orchard Street, Lincoln LN1 1YL ☎ 01522 553281 🖷 01522 554234 ✉ sharon.cuff@lincolnshire.gov.uk

Public Libraries: Mr Jonathan Platt, Head of Libraries & Heritage, Ground Floor, City Hall, Beaumont Fee, Lincoln LN1 1DD ☎ 01522 550586 ✉ jonathan.platt@lincolnshire.gov.uk

Recycling & Waste Minimisation: Mr Sean Kent, Head of Environmental Management, Witham Park House, Waterside South, Lincoln LN5 7JN ☎ 01522 554833 🖷 01522 554840 ✉ sean.kent@lincolnshire.gov.uk

Regeneration: Ms Jenny Gammon, Assistant Director - Economy & Culture Services, Beech House, Witham Park, Waterside South, Lincoln LN5 7JH ☎ 01552 550511 🖷 01522 516720 ✉ jenny.gammon@lincolnshire.gov.uk

Regeneration: Mr Paul Wheatley, Head of Regeneration, Ground Floor, City Hall, Beaumont Fee, Lincoln LN1 1DD ☎ 01522 550600 ✉ paul.wheatley@lincolnshire.gov.uk

Road Safety: Mr Richard Greener, Partnership Development Manager, 2nd Floor, Witham House, Pelham Bridge Centre, Pelham Bridge, Lincoln LN5 8HE ☎ 01522 805801 🖷 01522 805803 ✉ richard.greener@lincolnshire.gov.uk

Social Services: Mr Glen Garrod, Assistant Director - Adult Social Care Commissioning, Orchard House, Orchard Street, Lincoln LN1 1BA ☎ 01522 552808 ✉ glen.garrod@lincolnshire.gov.uk

Social Services (Adult): Mr Glen Garrod, Assistant Director - Adult Social Care Commissioning, Orchard House, Orchard Street, Lincoln LN1 1BA ☎ 01522 552808 ✉ glen.garrod@lincolnshire.gov.uk

Social Services (Adult): Mr Tony McGinty, Assistant Director - Healthier Communities, Orchard House, Orchard Street, Lincoln LN1 1BA ☎ 01522 554229 ✉ tony.mcginty@lincolnshire.gov.uk

Staff Training: Mrs Fiona Thompson, Head of People Management, Orchard House, Orchard Street, Lincoln LN1 1BA ☎ 01522 552207 🖷 01522 516010 ✉ fiona.thompson@lincolnshire.gov.uk

Sustainable Communities: Mr Richard Wills, Executive Director - Communities, City Hall, Beaumont Fee, Lincoln LN1 1DN ☎ 01522 553000 🖷 01522 512335 ✉ richard.wills@lincolnshire.gov.uk

Sustainable Development: Mr Douglas Robinson, Sustainability & Climate Change Team Leader, Witham Park, Waterside South,

Lincoln LN5 7JN ☎ 01522 554816 🖷 01522 554840
✉ douglas.robinson@lincolnshire.gov.uk

Tourism: Ms Mary Powell, Tourism Development Officer, Ground Floor, City Hall, Beaumont Fee, Lincoln LN1 1DD ☎ 01522 550612 🖷 01522 516720 ✉ mary.powell@lincolnshire.gov.uk

Traffic Management: Mr Paul Coathup, Assistant Director - Highways & Transportation, City Hall, Beaumont Fee, Lincoln LN1 1DN ☎ 01522 553086 🖷 01522 512335
✉ paul.coathup@lincolnshire.gov.uk

Transport: Mr Chris Briggs, Head of Transportation, County Offices, Newland, Lincoln LN1 1YL ☎ 01522 553050 🖷 01522 516098 ✉ chris.briggs@lincolnshire.gov.uk

Transport Planner: Mr Chris Briggs, Head of Transportation, County Offices, Newland, Lincoln LN1 1YL ☎ 01522 553050 🖷 01522 516098 ✉ chris.briggs@lincolnshire.gov.uk

Waste Collection and Disposal: Mr Sean Kent, Head of Environmental Management, Witham Park House, Waterside South, Lincoln LN5 7JN ☎ 01522 554833 🖷 01522 554840
✉ sean.kent@lincolnshire.gov.uk

Waste Management: Mr Sean Kent, Head of Environmental Management, Witham Park House, Waterside South, Lincoln LN5 7JN ☎ 01522 554833 🖷 01522 554840
✉ sean.kent@lincolnshire.gov.uk

MEMBERS OF THE COUNCIL (77)

***Chair:* Palmer**, Robert (CON - Louth Marsh)
cllrr.palmer@lincolnshire.gov.uk
***Vice-Chair:* Farquharson**, Charlotte (CON - Bourne Castle)
cllrc.farquharson@lincolnshire.gov.uk
***Leader of the Council:* Hill**, Martin (CON - Folkingham Rural)
cllrm.hill@lincolnshire.gov.uk
***Deputy Leader of the Council:* Bradwell**, Patricia (CON - Billinghay and Metheringham)
cllrp.bradwell@lincolnshire.gov.uk
***Deputy Leader of the Council:* Przyszlak**, Paul (CON - Crowland and Whaplode)
cllrp.przyszlak@lincolnshire.gov.uk
***Group Leader:* Marriott**, John (LD - Hykeham Forum)
cllrj.marriott@lincolnshire.gov.uk
***Group Leader:* Overton**, Marianne (IND - Branston and Navenby)
cllrm.overton@lincolnshire.gov.uk
***Group Leader:* Parker**, Robert (LAB - Lincoln West)
cllrr.parker@lincolnshire.gov.uk
Lincoln East: Vacant
Aron, Bill (IND - Horncastle and Tetford)
cllrb.aron@lincolnshire.gov.uk
Bauer, Eran (CON - Ruskington and Cranwell)
cllre.bauer@lincolnshire.gov.uk
Bedford, Peter (CON - Boston Coastal)
cllrp.bedford@lincolnshire.gov.uk
Bosworth, Pam (CON - Grantham Barrowby)
cllrp.bosworth@lincolnshire.gov.uk
Brailsford, David (CON - Stamford West)
cllrd.brailsford@lincolnshire.gov.uk
Brewis, Christopher (IND - Sutton Elloe)
cllrcbrewis@lincolnshire.gov.uk
Brookes, Michael (CON - Boston Rural)
cllrm.brookes@lincolnshire.gov.uk
Carpenter, Paul (CON - Grantham East)
cllrp.carpenter@lincolnshire.gov.uk
Chapman, Edward (CON - Colsterworth Rural)
cllre.chapman@lincolnshire.gov.uk
Clarke, Kevin (LAB - Lincoln Boultham)
cllrk.clarke@lincolnshire.gov.uk
Cooper, Neil (CON - Wainfleet and Burgh)
cllrn.cooper@lincolnshire.gov.uk
Dark, Graham (IND - Spalding South)
cllrg.dark@lincolnshire.gov.uk
Davie, Colin (CON - Ingoldmells Rural)
cllrc.davie@lincolnshire.gov.uk
Davies, Richard (CON - Grantham North West)
cllrr.davies@lincolnshire.gov.uk
Dickinson, David (CON - Sleaford)
cllrd.dickinson@lincolnshire.gov.uk
Exton, Mike (CON - Deeping St. James)
cllrm.exton@lincolnshire.gov.uk
Farrar, Christopher (CON - Hough)
cllrc.farrar@lincolnshire.gov.uk
Fleetwood, Ian (CON - Bardney and Cherry Willingham)
cllri.fleetwood@lincolnshire.gov.uk
Gilbert, Mike (CON - Boston East)
cllrm.gilbert@lincolnshire.gov.uk
Gooding, Graham (CON - Mablethorpe)
cllrg.gooding@lincolnshire.gov.uk
Hagues, Andrew (CON - Sleaford West and Leasingham)
Harvey, Betty (CON - Tattershall Castle)
cllrb.harvey@lincolnshire.gov.uk
Hicks, John (IND - Stamford North)
cllrj.hicks@lincolnshire.gov.uk
Hills, Ron (CON - Lincoln Hartsholme)
cllrr.hills@lincolnshire.gov.uk
Hough, John (LAB - Louth South)
cllrj.hough@lincolnshire.gov.uk
Hoyes, Denis (CON - Woodhall Spa and Wragby)
cllrd.hoyes@lincolnshire.gov.uk
Hubbard, Rachel (CON - Lincoln Bracebridge)
cllrr.hubbard@lincolnshire.gov.uk
Jackson, Nev (LAB - Lincoln Park)
cllrn.jackson@lincolnshire.gov.uk
Jenkyns, Andrea (CON - Boston North West)
cllra.jenkyns@lincolnshire.gov.uk
Johnson, Howard (CON - Spalding West)
cllrh.johnson@lincolnshire.gov.uk
Johnson, Jean (CON - Louth Rural North)
cllrj.johnson@lincolnshire.gov.uk
Keimach, Burt (CON - Market Rasen Wolds)
cllrb.keimach@lincolnshire.gov.uk
Kinch, Stuart (CON - Gainsborough Rural South)
cllrs.kinch@lincolnshire.gov.uk
Marfleet, Hugo (CON - Louth Wolds)
cllrh.marfleet@lincolnshire.gov.uk
Marsh, Graham (CON - Alford and Sutton)
cllrg.marsh@lincolnshire.gov.uk
Mathers, Pauline (CON - Lincoln Glebe)
cllrp.mathers@lincolnshire.gov.uk
Milner, Ken (CON - Skegness South)
cllrk.milner@lincolnshire.gov.uk
Newell, Ray (IND - Boston West)
cllrr.newell@lincolnshire.gov.uk
O'Connor, Pat (LD - Gainsborough Trent)

cllrp.oconnor@lincolnshire.gov.uk
Oxby, Ron (CON - Heighington and Washingborough)
cllrr.oxby@lincolnshire.gov.uk
Phillips, Raymond (CON - Bassingham Rural)
cllrr.phillips@lincolnshire.gov.uk
Poll, Eddy (CON - Spalding East and Moulton)
cllre.poll@lincolnshire.gov.uk
Puttick, Amanda (CON - Donington Rural)
cllra.puttick@lincolnshire.gov.uk
Rawlins, Sue (CON - Welton Rural)
cllrs.rawlins@lincolnshire.gov.uk
Robinson, Peter (CON - Market Deeping, West Deeping and Langtoft)
cllrp.robinson@lincolnshire.gov.uk
Sellars, Ray (LD - Nettleham and Saxilby)
cllrr.sellars@lincolnshire.gov.uk
Shore, Reg (LD - Skellingthorpe and Hykeham South)
cllrr.shore@lincolnshire.gov.uk
Singleton-McGuire, Raymond (CON - Boston Fishtoft)
cllrr.singleton-mcguire@lincolnshire.gov.uk
Skinner, Paul (CON - Boston South)
cllrp.skinner@lincolnshire.gov.uk
Smith, Mark (CON - Skegness North)
cllrm.smith@lincolnshire.gov.uk
Smith, Kelly (CON - Lincoln Moorland)
cllrk.smith@lincolnshire.gov.uk
Stokes, Adam (CON - Grantham South)
cllra.stokes@lincolnshire.gov.uk
Strange, Charles (CON - Ancholme Cliff)
cllrc.strange@lincolnshire.gov.uk
Strengiel, Eddie (CON - Lincoln Birchwood)
cllre.strengiel@lincolnshire.gov.uk
Swanson, Jim (IND - Spilsby Fen)
cllrj.swanson@lincolnshire.gov.uk
Talbot, Christine (CON - Bracebridge Heath and Waddington)
cllrc.talbot@lincolnshire.gov.uk
Tinker, Michael (LD - Gainsborough Hill)
cllrm.tinker@lincolnshire.gov.uk
Trollope-Bellew, Martin (CON - Stamford Rural)
cllrt.trollopebellew@lincolnshire.gov.uk
Turner, Tony (CON - North Wolds)
cllra.turner@lincolnshire.gov.uk
Underwood-Frost, Chris (CON - Scotter Rural)
cllrc.underwoodfrost@lincolnshire.gov.uk
Watson, Pauline (CON - Louth North)
cllrp.watson@lincolnshire.gov.uk
Webb, William (CON - Holbeach Rural)
cllrw.webb@lincolnshire.gov.uk
Williams, Stephen (CON - Spalding Elloe)
cllrs.williams@lincolnshire.gov.uk
Williams, Alister (CON - Lincoln North)
cllra.williams@lincolnshire.gov.uk
Woolley, Sue (CON - Bourne Abbey)
cllrs.woolley@lincolnshire.gov.uk
Wootten, Ray (CON - Grantham North)
cllrr.wootten@lincolnshire.gov.uk
Worth, Nick (CON - Holbeach)
cllrn.worth@lincolnshire.gov.uk
Young, Barry
(CON - Sleaford Rural South)
cllrb.young@lincolnshire.gov.uk

POLITICAL COMPOSITION

CON: 60, IND: 7, LD: 5, LAB: 4, Vacant: 1

CABINET

Leader / Policy, Strategy & Communications: Mr Martin Hill
Adult Social Care: Mr Graham Marsh
Children's Services & Lifelong Learning: Mrs Patricia Bradwell
Community Safety, Cohesion & Diversity: Mr Peter Robinson
Economic Development: Mr Eddy Poll
Finance & HR: Mr Kelly Smith
Health, Housing & Community: Mrs Sue Woolley
Highways & Transport: Mr William Webb
Waste Services & Green Issues: Mr Charles Strange

COMMITTEE CHAIRS

Adults (Scrutiny): Mrs Amanda Puttick
Appointments: Mr Martin Hill
Audit: Mr Barry Young
Children & Young People (Scrutiny): Mr Stephen Williams
Communites (Scrutiny): Mr Christopher Brewis
Economic (Scrutiny): Mr Pat O'Connor
Environmental (Scrutiny): Mr Colin Davie
Flood & Drainage (Scrutiny): Mr Colin Davie
Health (Scrutiny): Mrs Christine Talbot
Highways, Transport & Technology (Scrutiny): Mr Richard Davies
Overview & Scrutiny Management (Scrutiny): Mr Howard Johnson
Pensions: Mr Christopher Farrar
Planning & Regulation: Mr Ian Fleetwood
Standards: Mr Jerzy Krawiec (External)
Value For Money (Scrutiny): Mr Robert Parker

LISBURN N

Lisburn City Council, Island Civic Centre, The Island, Lisburn BT27 4RL ☎ 028 9250 9250 🖷 028 9250 9288
✉ enquiries@lisburn.gov.uk 💻 www.lisburncity.gov.uk

FACTS & FIGURES

Police Authority: Northern Ireland Policing Board
Health Authority: Eastern Health & Social Services Board
Learning and Skills Council: Northern Ireland
Parliamentary Constituencies: Belfast West, Lagan Valley
EU Constituencies: Northern Ireland
Election Frequency: Elections are of whole council

PRINCIPAL OFFICERS

Chief Executive: Mr Norman Davidson, Chief Executive, Island Civic Centre, The Island, Lisburn BT27 4RL ☎ 028 9250 9206 🖷 028 9250 9208 ✉ normand@lisburn.gov.uk

Senior Management: Mr Colin McClintock, Director of Environmental Services, Island Civic Centre, The Island, Lisburn BT27 4RL ☎ 028 9250 9350 🖷 028 9250 9349 ✉ colinm@lisburn.gov.uk

Senior Management: Mr Jim Rose, Director of Leisure Services, Island Civic Centre, The Island, Lisburn BT27 4RL ☎ 028 9250 9203 🖷 028 9250 9564 ✉ jimr@lisburn.gov.uk

Best Value: Mrs Janet Burns, Policy & Co-ordination Officer, Island Civic Centre, The Island, Lisburn BT27 4RL ☎ 028 9250 9213 🖷 028 9250 9208 ✉ janet.burns@lisburn.gov.uk

Building Control: Mr Ian Wilson, Assistant Director of Environmental Services, Island Civic Centre, The Island, Lisburn BT27 4RL ☎ 028 9250 9361 🖷 028 9250 9375 ✉ ian.wilson@lisburn.gov.uk

Civil Registration: Mrs Carmel Connolly, Assistant Director of Corporate Services, Island Civic Centre, The Island, Lisburn BT27 4RL ☎ 028 9250 9259 🖷 028 9250 9257 ✉ carmel.connolly@lisburn.gov.uk

PR / Communications: Mrs Claire Bethel, Assistant Director of Corporate Services, Island Civic Centre, The Island, Lisburn BT27 4RL ☎ 028 9250 9214 🖷 028 9250 9459 ✉ mcuassistantdirector@lisburn.gov.uk

PR / Communications: Mrs Alison Goddard, Assistant Director of Corporate Services, Island Civic Centre, The Island, Lisburn BT27 4RL ☎ 028 9250 9215 🖷 028 9250 9459 ✉ mcuassistantdirector@lisburn.gov.uk

Computer Management: Mr David Mayers, Information Technology Manager, Island Civic Centre, The Island, Lisburn BT27 4RL ☎ 028 9250 9239 🖷 028 9250 9234 ✉ david.mayers@lisburn.gov.uk

Consumer Protection and Trading Standards: Mrs Sally Courtney, Senior Environmental Health Officer, Island Civic Centre, The Island, Lisburn BT27 4RL ☎ 028 9250 9401 🖷 028 9250 9378 ✉ sally.courtney@lisburn.gov.uk

Contracts: Mr Norman Davidson, Chief Executive, Island Civic Centre, The Island, Lisburn BT27 4RL ☎ 028 9250 9206 🖷 028 9250 9208 ✉ normand@lisburn.gov.uk

Corporate Services: Mr Adrian Donaldson, Director of Corporate Services, Island Civic Centre, The Island, Lisburn BT27 4RL ☎ 028 9250 9258 🖷 028 9250 9257 ✉ adriand@lisburn.gov.uk

Economic Development: Mr Paul McCormick, Assistant Director of Environmental Services, Island Civic Centre, The Island, Lisburn BT27 4RL ☎ 028 9250 9480 🖷 028 9250 9227 ✉ paul.mccormick@lisburn.gov.uk

Electoral Registration: Mrs Carmel Connolly, Assistant Director of Corporate Services, Island Civic Centre, The Island, Lisburn BT27 4RL ☎ 028 9250 9259 🖷 028 9250 9257 ✉ carmel.connolly@lisburn.gov.uk

Emergency Planning: Mr Maurice Woods, Assistant Director of Environmental Services, Island Civic Centre, The Island, Lisburn BT27 4RL ☎ 028 9250 9400 🖷 028 9250 9378 ✉ maurice.woods@lisburn.gov.uk

Environmental / Technical Services: Mr Colin McClintock, Director of Environmental Services, Island Civic Centre, The Island, Lisburn BT27 4RL ☎ 028 9250 9350 🖷 028 9250 9349 ✉ colinm@lisburn.gov.uk

Environmental Health: Mr Maurice Woods, Assistant Director of Environmental Services, Island Civic Centre, The Island, Lisburn BT27 4RL ☎ 028 9250 9400 🖷 028 9250 9378 ✉ maurice.woods@lisburn.gov.uk

European Liaison: Miss Hazel King, Assistant Economic Development Officer, Island Civic Centre, The Island, Lisburn BT27 4RL ☎ 028 9250 9484 🖷 028 9250 9227 ✉ hazel.king@lisburn.gov.uk

Finance and Treasurer: Mrs Leah Scott, Assistant Director of Corporate Services, Island Civic Centre, The Island, Lisburn BT27 4RL ☎ 028 9250 9245 🖷 028 9250 9234 ✉ leah.scott@lisburn.gov.uk

Grounds Maintenance: Mr Roy Hanna, Assistant Director of Environmental Services (Acting), Central Services Depot, Altona Industrial Estate, Altona Road, Lisburn BT27 5QB ☎ 028 9267 3417 🖷 028 9266 2731 ✉ roy.hanna@lisburn.gov.uk

Health and Safety: Mr Maurice Woods, Assistant Director of Environmental Services, Island Civic Centre, The Island, Lisburn BT27 4RL ☎ 028 9250 9400 🖷 028 9250 9378 ✉ maurice.woods@lisburn.gov.uk

Legal: Mrs Carmel Connolly, Assistant Director of Corporate Services, Island Civic Centre, The Island, Lisburn BT27 4RL ☎ 028 9250 9259 🖷 028 9250 9257 ✉ carmel.connolly@lisburn.gov.uk

Leisure and Cultural Services: Mr Brian Mackey, Assistant Director of Leisure Services (Cultural Services), Irish Linen Centre and Lisburn Museum, Market Square, Lisburn BT28 1AG ☎ 028 9266 3377 🖷 028 9267 2624 ✉ brian.mackey@lisburn.gov.uk

Leisure and Cultural Services: Mr Robert McKnight, Assistant Director of Leisure Services, Island Civic Centre, The Island, Lisburn BT27 4RL ☎ 028 9250 9568 🖷 028 9250 9564 ✉ robert.mcknight@lisburn.gov.uk

Leisure and Cultural Services: Mr Jim Rose, Director of Leisure Services, Island Civic Centre, The Island, Lisburn BT27 4RL ☎ 028 9250 9203 🖷 028 9250 9564 ✉ jimr@lisburn.gov.uk

Member Services: Mrs Carmel Connolly, Assistant Director of Corporate Services, Island Civic Centre, The Island, Lisburn BT27 4RL ☎ 028 9250 9259 🖷 028 9250 9257 ✉ carmel.connolly@lisburn.gov.uk

Personnel / HR: Miss Sinead Clarke, Assistant Director of Corporate Services, Island Civic Centre, The Island, Lisburn BT27 4RL ☎ 028 9250 9379 🖷 028 9250 9478 ✉ sinead.clarke@lisburn.gov.uk

Planning: Mr Ian Wilson, Assistant Director of Environmental Services, Island Civic Centre, The Island, Lisburn BT27 4RL ☎ 028 9250 9361 🖷 028 9250 9375 ✉ ian.wilson@lisburn.gov.uk

Procurement: Mrs Carmel Connolly, Assistant Director of Corporate Services, Island Civic Centre, The Island, Lisburn BT27 4RL ☎ 028 9250 9259 🖷 028 9250 9257 ✉ carmel.connolly@lisburn.gov.uk

Recycling & Waste Minimisation: Mrs Noeleen O'Malley, Assistant Director of Environmental Services (Acting), Island Civic Centre, The Island, Lisburn BT27 4RL ☎ 028 9250 9455 🖷 028

9250 9432 noeleen.omalley@lisburn.gov.uk

Recycling & Waste Minimisation: Mr Albert Reynolds, Assistant Director of Environmental Services (Acting), Island Civic Centre, The Island, Lisburn BT27 4RL ☎ 028 9250 9450 🖷 028 9250 9432 albert.reynolds@lisburn.gov.uk

Regeneration: Miss Suzanne Lutton, Lagan Corridor Programme Manager, Island Civic Centre, The Island, Lisburn BT27 4RL ☎ 028 9250 9489 🖷 028 9250 9227 suzanne.lutton@lisburn.gov.uk

Staff Training: Mrs Caroline Magee, Human Resources Manager (Employee Relations & Training), Island Civic Centre, The Island, Lisburn BT27 4RL ☎ 028 9250 9305 🖷 028 9250 9285 caroline.magee@lisburn.gov.uk

Tourism: Mr Andrew Kennedy, Tourism Development Manager, Island Civic Centre, The Island, Lisburn BT27 4RL ☎ 028 9250 9483 🖷 028 9250 9227 andrew.kennedy@lisburn.gov.uk

Town Centre: Mr Alan Clarke, City Centre Manager, Lisburn City Centre Management, Rawdon House, 45-47 Market Square, Lisburn BT28 1AD ☎ 028 9266 0625 🖷 028 9266 0192 alanclarke@lisburnccm.co.uk

Waste Collection and Disposal: Mrs Noeleen O'Malley, Assistant Director of Environmental Services (Acting), Island Civic Centre, The Island, Lisburn BT27 4RL ☎ 028 9250 9455 🖷 028 9250 9432 noeleen.omalley@lisburn.gov.uk

Waste Collection and Disposal: Mr Albert Reynolds, Assistant Director of Environmental Services (Acting), Island Civic Centre, The Island, Lisburn BT27 4RL ☎ 028 9250 9450 🖷 028 9250 9432 albert.reynolds@lisburn.gov.uk

Waste Management: Mrs Noeleen O'Malley, Assistant Director of Environmental Services (Acting), Island Civic Centre, The Island, Lisburn BT27 4RL ☎ 028 9250 9455 🖷 028 9250 9432 noeleen.omalley@lisburn.gov.uk

Waste Management: Mr Albert Reynolds, Assistant Director of Environmental Services (Acting), Island Civic Centre, The Island, Lisburn BT27 4RL ☎ 028 9250 9450 🖷 028 9250 9432 albert.reynolds@lisburn.gov.uk

MEMBERS OF THE COUNCIL (30)

***Mayor:* Leathem**, William (DUP - Lisburn Town North)
william.leathem@lisburn.gov.uk

***Alderman:* Craig**, Jonathan (DUP - Lisburn Town North)
jonathan.craig@lisburn.gov.uk

***Alderman:* Dillon**, Jim (UUP - Killultagh)

***Alderman:* Given**, Paul (DUP - Lisburn Town North)
paul.given@lisburn.gov.uk

***Alderman:* Porter**, Paul (DUP - Lisburn Town South)
paul.porter@lisburn.gov.uk

Baird, James (UUP - Downshire)
james.baird@lisburn.gov.uk

Beckett, Thomas (DUP - Killultagh)
thomas.beckett@lisburn.gov.uk

Bell, David (SF - Dunmurry Cross)
daithi3@hotmail.com

Bloomfield, Brian (UUP - Lisburn Town North)
brian.bloomfield@lisburn.gov.uk

Carlisle, Alan (UUP - Lisburn Town South)
alan.carlisle@lisburn.gov.uk

Carson, Arthur (SF - Dunmurry Cross)

Catney, Patrick (SDLP - Killultagh)
pat.catney@lisburn.gov.uk

Coulter, Jennifer (ALL - Downshire)
jennifer.coulter@lisburn.gov.uk

Crawford, Ronnie (UUP - Lisburn Town North)
roncrawford@btinternet.com

Dornan, Brian (ALL - Lisburn Town North)
brian.dornan@lisburn.gov.uk

Drake, John (SDLP - Lisburn Town North)
john.drake@lisburn.gov.uk

Ewart, Allan (DUP - Downshire)
allan.ewart@lisburn.gov.uk

Ewing, Andrew (DUP - Lisburn Town South)
andrew.ewing@lisburn.gov.uk

Heading, Brian (SDLP - Dunmurry Cross)
cllrheading@ireland.com

Mackin, Uel (DUP - Downshire)
uel.mackin@lisburn.gov.uk

Magennis, Stephen (SF - Dunmurry Cross)
stephenmagennis@btinternet.com

Martin, Stephen (ALL - Lisburn Town South)
stephen.martin@lisburn.gov.uk

Nelson, Angela (SF - Dunmurry Cross)
angela.nelson@lisburn.gov.uk

O'Hara, Charlene (SF - Dunmurry Cross)
charlene.ohara@lisburn.gov.uk

Palmer, John (DUP - Killultagh)
john.palmer@lisburn.gov.uk

Palmer, Jennifer (DUP - Lisburn Town South)
jenny.palmer@lisburn.gov.uk

Stewart, Paul (DUP - Downshire)
paul.stewart@lisburn.gov.uk

Tinsley, James (DUP - Killultagh)
james.tinsley@lisburn.gov.uk

Tolerton, Margaret (DUP - Dunmurry Cross)
margaret.tolerton@lisburn.gov.uk

Young, Roy (DUP - Lisburn Town South)
roy.young@lisburn.gov.uk

POLITICAL COMPOSITION

DUP: 14, SF: 5, UUP: 5, ALL: 3, SDLP: 3

COMMITTEE CHAIRS

Corporate Services: Mr Stephen Martin
Economic Development: Mr Jim Dillon
Environmental Services: Mr Andrew Ewing
Leisure Services: Mr Thomas Beckett
Planning: Mr James Tinsley
Strategic Policy: Mr Arthur Carson

LIVERPOOL CITY M

Liverpool City Council, Labour Group Office, Municipal Buildings, Dale Street, Liverpool L69 2DH ☎ 0151 233 3000 liverpool.direct@liverpool.gov.uk www.liverpool.gov.uk

FACTS & FIGURES

Police Authority: Merseyside Police Authority
Health Authority: North West Strategic Health Authority

Learning and Skills Council: North West
Parliamentary Constituencies: Liverpool, Riverside, Liverpool, Walton, Liverpool, Wavertree, Liverpool, West Derby
EU Constituencies: North West
Election Frequency: Elections are by thirds
Twinning: Dublin (Ireland); Cologne (Germany); Odessa (Ukraine); Shanghai (China)

PRINCIPAL OFFICERS

Chief Executive: Mr Ged Fitzgerald, Chief Executive, Labour Group Office, Municipal Buildings, Dale Street, Liverpool L69 2DH ☎ 0151 225 3602 ✉ ged.fitzgerald@liverpool.gov.uk

Senior Management: Mr Bob Clark, Interim Director of Education & Children's Services, 2nd Floor, Millennium House, 60 Victoria Street, Liverpool L1 6JF ☎ 0151 233 2799 🖷 0151 233 8200 ✉ bob.clark@liverpool.gov.uk

Senior Management: Mr Samih Kalakeche, Director of Adult Services & Health, 2nd Floor, Millennium House, Victoria Street, Liverpool L1 6LD ☎ 0151 223 4213 ✉ samih.kalakeche@liverpool.gov.uk

Senior Management: Mr Nick Kavanagh, Director of Regeneration & Employment, 3rd Floor Millennium House, Victoria Street, Liverpool L1 6LD ☎ 0151 233 6715 ✉ nick.kavanagh@liverpool.gov.uk

Senior Management: Mr Peter Timmins, Interim Director of Finance & Resources, Room 14 Municipal Buildings, Dale Street, Liverpool L69 2DH ☎ 0151 225 2347 ✉ peter.timmins@liverpool.gov.uk

Catering Services: Ms Suzanne Halsall, Catering Business Manager, Municipal Buildings, Dale Street, Liverpool L69 2DH ☎ 0151 225 5021 🖷 0151 225 5148 ✉ suzanne.halsall@liverpool.gov.uk

Children / Youth Services: Mr Bob Clark, Interim Director of Education & Children's Services, 2nd Floor, Millennium House, 60 Victoria Street, Liverpool L1 6JF ☎ 0151 233 2799 🖷 0151 233 8200 ✉ bob.clark@liverpool.gov.uk

Civil Registration: Ms Patricia Dobie, Registration Service Manager, The Register Office, Heritage Entrance, St. George's Hall, St. George's Place, Liverpool L1 1JJ ☎ 0151 225 5719 🖷 0151 707 8793 ✉ patricia.dobie@liverpool.gov.uk

PR / Communications: Mr Paul Johnston, Communications Manager, Municipal Buildings, Dale Street, Liverpool LR 2DH ☎ 0151 225 5517 🖷 0151 225 5510 ✉ paul.johnston@liverpool.gov.uk

Community Planning: Mr Mark Kitts, Acting Assistant Director of Planning, Housing & Development, Municipal Buildings, Dale Street, Liverpool L2 2DH ☎ 0151 233 4202 🖷 0151 225 3959 ✉ mark.kitts@liverpool.gov.uk

Community Safety: Mrs Jan Rowley, Acting Director of Community Safety, 2nd Floor Management Suite, Millennium House, Victoria Street, Liverpool L1 6LD ☎ 0151 233 3000 ✉ jan.rowley@liverpool.gov.uk

Consumer Protection and Trading Standards: Mr Dale Willis, Acting Divisional Manager of Environmental Protection & Licensing, 3rd Floor, Millennium House, Victoria Street, Liverpool L1 6LD ☎ 0151 233 4202 ✉ dale.willis@liverpool.gov.uk

Economic Development: Mr Nick Kavanagh, Director of Regeneration & Employment, 3rd Floor Millennium House, Victoria Street, Liverpool L1 6LD ☎ 0151 233 6715 ✉ nick.kavanagh@liverpool.gov.uk

Education: Mr Bob Clark, Interim Director of Education & Children's Services, 2nd Floor, Millennium House, 60 Victoria Street, Liverpool L1 6JF ☎ 0151 233 2799 🖷 0151 233 8200 ✉ bob.clark@liverpool.gov.uk

Electoral Registration: Mr Stephen Barker, Interim Elections Manager, Room 230, Municipal Buildings, Dale Street, Liverpool L2 2DH ☎ 0151 225 3519 🖷 0151 225 2365 ✉ stephen.barker@liverpool.gov.uk

Emergency Planning: Mr Jamie Riley, Emergency Planning Officer, Brougham Terrace, West Derby Road, Liverpool L6 1AE ☎ 0151 225 6017 🖷 0151 225 6039 ✉ jamie.riley@liverpool.gov.uk

Environmental Health: Mr Chris Lomas, Head of Public Protection, Municipal Buildings, Dale Street, Liverpool L2 2DH ☎ 0151 225 6056 ✉ chris.lomas@liverpool.gov.uk

European Liaison: Mr Martin Eyres, Head of European Programmes, Chief Executive's Office, Municipal Buildings, Dale Street, Liverpool L2 2DH ☎ 0151 225 3023 🖷 0151 233 6386 ✉ martin.eyres@liverpool.gov.uk

Events Manager: Mrs Judith Feather, Head of Events, The Capital Building, 10th Floor, 39 Old Hall Street, Liverpool L3 9PP ☎ 0151 600 2909 ✉ judith.feather@liverpool.gov.uk

Facilities: Mr Tony Wylie, Premises Manager, Ground Floor, Mucipal Buildings, Dale Street, Liverpool L2 2DH ☎ 0151 225 2217 🖷 0151 225 2218 ✉ tony.wylie@liverpool.gov.uk

Finance and Treasurer: Mr Tim Povall, Head of Finance, Ground Floor, Municipal Buildings, Dale Street, Liverpool L2 2DH ☎ 0151 225 2345 ✉ tim.povall@liverpool.gov.uk

Finance and Treasurer: Mr Peter Timmins, Interim Director of Finance & Resources, Room 14 Municipal Buildings, Dale Street, Liverpool L69 2DH ☎ 0151 225 2347 ✉ peter.timmins@liverpool.gov.uk

Fleet Management: Mr John Carrington, Fleet Services Manager, Newton Road Depot, Liverpool L2 2DH ☎ 0151 233 6504 🖷 0151 233 6517 ✉ john.carrington@liverpool.gov.uk

Health and Safety: Mr Stephen Hall, Corporate Health & Safety Manager, Ground Floor, Municipal Buildings, Dale Street, Liverpool L2 2DH ☎ 0151 225 2677 🖷 0151 225 2300 ✉ steve.hall@liverpool.gov.uk

Highways: Mr Steven Holcroft, Transportation Divisional

Manager, 4th Floor, Millennium House, 60 Victoria Street, Liverpool L2 2DH ☎ 0151 233 8130 🖰 steven.holcroft@liverpool.gov.uk

Home Energy Conservation: Mr Brendan Peurcell, Head of Energy Management, Room 106, Municipal Buildings, Dale Street, Liverpool L69 2DH ☎ 0151 225 2473 🖷 0151 225 2218 🖰 brendan.purcell@liverpool.gov.uk

Housing: Mr Mark Kitts, Acting Assistant Director of Planning, Housing & Development, Municipal Buildings, Dale Street, Liverpool L2 2DH ☎ 0151 233 4202 🖷 0151 225 3959 🖰 mark.kitts@liverpool.gov.uk

Legal: Mrs Jeanette McLoughlin, Interim City Solicitor, Labour Group Office, Municipal Buildings, Dale Street, Liverpool L69 2DH ☎ 0151 225 6795 🖷 0151 225 2392 🖰 jeanette.mcloughlin@liverpool.gov.uk

Leisure and Cultural Services: Mrs Claire McColgan, Assistant Director of Culture & Tourism, The Capital Building, 10th Floor, 39 Old Hall Street, Liverpool L3 9PP ☎ 0151 600 2956 🖰 claire.mccolgan@liverpool.gov.uk

Licensing: Mr John McHale, Head of Licensing, Room 216, Municipal Buildings, Dale Street, Liverpool L2 2DH ☎ 0151 233 4415 🖰 john.mchale@liverpool.gov.uk

Lighting: Mr Steven Holcroft, Transportation Divisional Manager, 4th Floor, Millennium House, 60 Victoria Street, Liverpool L2 2DH ☎ 0151 233 8130 🖰 steven.holcroft@liverpool.gov.uk

Member Services: Mr Chris Walsh, Head of Democratic, Municipal Buildings, Dale Street, Liverpool L2 2DH ☎ 0151 225 2432 🖷 0151 225 2427 🖰 chris.walsh@liverpool.gov.uk

Parking: Mr Roy Tunstall, Parking Services Manager, 5 Crosshall Street, Liverpool L2 2DH ☎ 0151 233 3011 🖷 0151 225 2488 🖰 roy.tunstall@liverpool.gov.uk

Partnerships: Ms Catherine Garnell, Divisional Manager of Policy & Partnerships, Municipal Buildings, Dale Street, Liverpool L2 2DH ☎ 0151 225 2877 🖷 0151 255 6313 🖰 catherine.garnell@liverpool.gov.uk

Personnel / HR: Ms Colette Hannay, Head of Human Resources & Payroll Services, 6th Floor, Venture Place, 13 - 17 Sir Thomas Street, Liverpool L1 6BW ☎ 0151 233 3000 🖰 colette.hannay@liverpool.gov.uk

Planning: Mr Mark Loughran, Interim Manager of Development Control, 3rd Floor Millennium House, 60 Victoria Street, Liverpool L1 6AJ ☎ 0151 233 6749 🖰 mark.loughran@liverpool.gov.uk

Procurement: Mrs Jane Christopher, Corporate Procurement Unit Manager, 4th Floor, Venture Place, Liverpool L1 6AJ ☎ 0151 225 2426 🖰 jane.christopher@liverpool.gov.uk

Public Libraries: Ms Joyce Little, Head of Libraries & Information Services, Municipal Buildings, Dale Street, Liverpool L2 2DH ☎ 0151 233 6346 🖷 0151 233 6399 🖰 joyce.little@liverpool.gov.uk

Recycling & Waste Minimisation: Mr Andrew McCartan, Environmental Services Manager (Interim), 1st Floor, Millennium House, Victoria Street, Liverpool L69 1JB ☎ 0151 233 6380 🖰 andrew.mccartan@liverpool.gov.uk

Regeneration: Mr Nick Kavanagh, Director of Regeneration & Employment, 3rd Floor Millennium House, Victoria Street, Liverpool L1 6LD ☎ 0151 233 6715 🖰 nick.kavanagh@liverpool.gov.uk

Road Safety: Mr David Ng, Team Leader, Road Safety Services, PO Box 981, Municipal Buildings, Liverpool L69 1JB ☎ 0151 233 2386 🖷 0151 233 2384 🖰 david.ng@liverpool.gov.uk

Social Services: Mrs Bernie Brown, Assistant Director of Education & Children's Services, 2nd Floor, Millennium House, 60 Victoria Street, Liverpool L1 6JF ☎ 0151 233 2747 🖷 0151 233 4222 🖰 bernie.brown@liverpool.gov.uk

Social Services (Adult): Mr Samih Kalakeche, Director of Adult Services & Health, 2nd Floor, Millennium House, Victoria Street, Liverpool L1 6JQ ☎ 0151 223 4213 🖰 samih.kalakeche@liverpool.gov.uk

Social Services (Children): Ms Liz Mekki, Divisional Manager of Children's Safeguarding, Team 2, 2nd Floor, Millennium House, 60 Victoria Street, Liverpool L1 6JF ☎ 0151 233 4174 🖷 0151 233 4222 🖰 liz.mekki@liverpool.gov.uk

Sustainable Development: Mr Mark Kitts, Acting Assistant Director of Planning, Housing & Development, Municipal Buildings, Dale Street, Liverpool L2 2DH ☎ 0151 233 4202 🖷 0151 225 3959 🖰 mark.kitts@liverpool.gov.uk

Tourism: Mr Keith Blundell, Head of Tourism, The Capital Building, 39 Old Hall Street, Liverpool L3 9PP ☎ 0151 233 6363 🖷 0151 233 6333

Town Centre: Mr Mike Cockburn, City Centre Manager, 1st Floor, Millennium House, 60 Victoria Street, Liverpool L1 6JE ☎ 0151 233 5327 🖰 mike.cockburn@liverpool.gov.uk

Traffic Management: Mr Steven Holcroft, Transportation Divisional Manager, 4th Floor, Millennium House, 60 Victoria Street, Liverpool L2 2DH ☎ 0151 233 8130 🖰 steven.holcroft@liverpool.gov.uk

Transport: Mr Steven Holcroft, Transportation Divisional Manager, 4th Floor, Millennium House, 60 Victoria Street, Liverpool L2 2DH ☎ 0151 233 8130 🖰 steven.holcroft@liverpool.gov.uk

Transport Planner: Mr Steven Holcroft, Transportation Divisional Manager, 4th Floor, Millennium House, 60 Victoria Street, Liverpool L2 2DH ☎ 0151 233 8130 🖰 steven.holcroft@liverpool.gov.uk

Waste Collection and Disposal: Mr Chris Lomas, Head of Public Protection, Municipal Buildings, Dale Street, Liverpool L2 2DH ☎ 0151 225 6056 🖰 chris.lomas@liverpool.gov.uk

Waste Management: Mr Chris Lomas, Head of Public

Protection, Municipal Buildings, Dale Street, Liverpool L2 2DH
☎ 0151 225 6056 chris.lomas@liverpool.gov.uk

MEMBERS OF THE COUNCIL (89)

***The Lord Mayor:* Sullivan**, Sharon (LAB - Central)
sharon.sullivan@liverpool.gov.uk
***Deputy Mayor:* Brant**, Paul (LAB - Riverside)
paul.brant@liverpool.gov.uk
***Deputy Mayor:* Millar**, Gary (LD - Old Swan)
gary.millar@liverpool.gov.uk
***Leader of the Council:* Anderson**, Joe (LAB - No Ward)
***Group Leader:* Aspinall**, Mary (LAB - Cressington)
mary.aspinall@liverpool.gov.uk
***Group Leader:* Jennings**, Sarah (GRN - St Michaels)
sarah.jennings@liverpool.gov.uk
***Group Leader:* Morrison**, Tom (LD - Church)
tom.morrison@liverpool.gov.uk
***Group Leader:* Radford**, Steve (LIB - Tuebrook and Stoneycroft)
northwestliberalparty@hotmail.co.uk
Allen, Elaine (LD - Greenbank)
elaine.allen@liverpool.gov.uk
Ashton-Armstrong, Louise (LAB - Fazakerley)
louise.ashton-armstrong@liverpool.gov.uk
Baldock, Louise (LAB - Kensington and Fairfield)
louise.baldock@liverpool.gov.uk
Banks, Christine (LAB - Central)
christine.banks2@liverpool.gov.uk
Barrington, Daniel (LAB - West Derby)
daniel.barrington@liverpool.gov.uk
Beaumont, Tim (LAB - Picton)
tim.beaumont@liverpool.gov.uk
Bebb, Violet (LAB - Norris Green)
violet.bebb@liverpool.gov.uk
Brennan, Peter (LAB - Old Swan)
peter.brennan2@liverpool.gov.uk
Calvert, Joanne (LAB - Old Swan)
joanne.calvert@liverpool.gov.uk
Casstles, Helen (LAB - Wavertree)
helen.casstles@liverpool.gov.uk
Clarke, Peter (LAB - Fazakerley)
peter.clarke@liverpool.gov.uk
Concepcion, Tony (LAB - Yew Tree)
Corbett, Jane (LAB - Everton)
jane.corbett@liverpool.gov.uk
Coyne, John (GRN - St Michaels)
john.coyne@liverpool.gov.uk
Crofts, Nick (LAB - Knotty Ash)
nick.crofts@liverpool.gov.uk
Cummins, Martin (LAB - Croxteth)
martin.cummins@liverpool.gov.uk
Dean, Alan (LAB - Princes Park)
alan.dean@liverpool.gov.uk
Dowling, Adele (LAB - Anfield)
adele.dowling@liverpool.gov.uk
Dowling, Brian (LAB - Anfield)
brian.dowling@liverpool.gov.uk
Fraenkel, Beatrice (LAB - Kirkdale)
beatrice.fraenkel@liverpool.gov.uk
Francis, Ian (LAB - Anfield)
ian.francis@liverpool.gov.uk
Gale, Claire (LAB - Belle Vale)
claire.wilner@liverpool.gov.uk
Gladden, Roz (LAB - Clubmoor)
roz.gladden@liverpool.gov.uk
Gladden, Roy (LAB - County)
roy.gladden@liverpool.gov.uk
Gould, Tina (LD - Mossley Hill)
tina.gould@liverpool.gov.uk
Green, Sharon (LD - St Michaels)
sharon.green@liverpool.gov.uk
Hanratty, Dave (LAB - Fazakerley)
dave.hanratty@liverpool.gov.uk
Hanson, Joseph (LAB - Kirkdale)
joseph.hanson@liverpool.gov.uk
Hirschfield, Ruth (LAB - Childwall)
ruth.hirschfield@liverpool.gov.uk
Hughes, Dan (LAB - Allerton and Hunts Cross)
dan.hughes@liverpool.gov.uk
Hurley, Patrick (LAB - Mossley Hill)
patrick.hurley@liverpool.gov.uk
Jobling, Ian (LAB - Allerton and Hunts Cross)
ian.jobling@liverpool.gov.uk
Jolly, Rosie (LD - Wavertree)
rosie.jolly@liverpool.gov.uk
Jones, Bill (LAB - Cressington)
bill.jones@liverpool.gov.uk
Kelly, Malcolm (LD - Woolton)
malcolm.kelly@liverpool.gov.uk
Kemp, Richard (LD - Church)
richard.kemp@liverpool.gov.uk
Kemp, Erica (LD - Church)
erica.kemp@liverpool.gov.uk
Kennedy, Malcolm (LAB - Kirkdale)
malcolm.kennedy@liverpool.gov.uk
Kent, Janet (LAB - Belle Vale)
janet.kent@liverpool.gov.uk
Knight, Doreen (LAB - Speke-Garston)
doreen.knight@liverpool.gov.uk
Kushner, Barry (LAB - Norris Green)
barry.kushner@liverpool.gov.uk
Lenton, Chris (LIB - Tuebrook and Stoneycroft)
chris.lenton@liverpool.gov.uk
Mace, Barbara (LD - Woolton)
barbara.mace@liverpool.gov.uk
McEvoy, Maria (LAB - Warbreck)
maria.mcevoy2@liverpool.gov.uk
McIntosh, John (LAB - Everton)
john.mcintosh@liverpool.gov.uk
McLinden, Richard (LAB - Warbreck)
richard.mclinden@liverpool.gov.uk
Mitchell, Peter (LAB - Croxteth)
Moloney, Pat (LD - Childwall)
pat.moloney@liverpool.gov.uk
Moore, Timothy (LAB - Princes Park)
timothy.moore@liverpool.gov.uk
Morrison, Jake (LAB - Wavertree)
jake.morrison@liverpool.gov.uk
Munby, Steve (LAB - Riverside)
stephen.munby@liverpool.gov.uk
Murray, Barbara (LAB - Yew Tree)
barbara.murray@liverpool.gov.uk
Nasuh, Jacqui (LAB - Knotty Ash)
jacqueline.nasuh@liverpool.gov.uk
Nicholas, Nathalie (LAB - Picton)
nathalie.nicholas@liverpool.gov.uk
Noakes, James (LAB - Clubmoor)
james.noakes@liverpool.gov.uk
Norris, Mark (LAB - Woolton)

mark.norris@liverpool.gov.uk
O'Byrne, Ann (LAB - Warbreck)
ann.o'byrne@liverpool.gov.uk
Oglethorpe, Richard (LD - Cressington)
richard.oglethorpe@liverpool.gov.uk
Orr, Lana (LAB - West Derby)
lana.orr@liverpool.gov.uk
Owen, Eryl (LAB - County)
eryl.owen@liverpool.gov.uk
Prendergast, Frank (LAB - Everton)
frank.prendergast@liverpool.gov.uk
Prince, John (LAB - Yew Tree)
john.prince@liverpool.gov.uk
Qadir, Abdul (LAB - Picton)
abdul.qadir@liverpool.gov.uk
Rainey, Irene (LAB - Clubmoor)
irene.rainey@liverpool.gov.uk
Rasmussen, Mary (LAB - Speke-Garston)
mary.rasmussen@liverpool.gov.uk
Roberts, James (LAB - Greenbank)
james.roberts2@liverpool.gov.uk
Robertson-Collins, Laura (LAB - Greenbank)
laura.robertson-collins@liverpool.gov.uk
Robinson, Liam (LAB - Kensington and Fairfield)
liam.robinson@liverpool.gov.uk
Rothery, Anna (LAB - Princes Park)
anna.rothery@liverpool.gov.uk
Simon, Wendy (LAB - Kensington and Fairfield)
wendy.simon@liverpool.gov.uk
Small, Nick (LAB - Central)
nick.small@liverpool.gov.uk
Spurrell, Emily (LAB - Mossley Hill)
emily.spurrell@liverpool.gov.uk
Strickland, Colin (LAB - Speke-Garston)
colin.strickland@liverpool.gov.uk
Thomas, Pam (LAB - West Derby)
pamela.thomas@liverpool.gov.uk
Till, Stephanie (LAB - Croxteth)
stephanie.till@liverpool.gov.uk
Todd, Hayley (LAB - Knotty Ash)
hayley.todd@liverpool.gov.uk
Walker, Alan (LAB - Norris Green)
alan.walker@liverpool.gov.uk
Walton, Pauline (LAB - Belle Vale)
pauline.walton@liverpool.gov.uk
Williams, Hazel (LIB - Tuebrook and Stoneycroft)
hazel.williams@liverpool.gov.uk
Wolfson, Jeremy (LAB - Childwall)
jeremy.wolfson@liverpool.gov.uk
Woodhouse, Gerard (LAB - County)
gerard.woodhouse@liverpool.gov.uk

POLITICAL COMPOSITION

LAB: 72, LD: 12, LIB: 3, GRN: 2

CABINET

Leader: Mr Joseph Anderson
Deputy Leader / Finance & Resources: Mr Paul Brant
Adult Social Care & Health: Ms Roz Gladden
Culture & Tourism: Ms Wendy Simon
Education & Children's Services: Ms Jane Corbett
Employment, Enterprise & Skills: Mr Nick Small
Environment & Climate Change: Mr Timothy Moore
Housing & Community Safety: Ms Ann O'Byrne
Neighbourhoods: Mr Steve Munby
Regeneration & Transport: Mr Malcolm Kennedy

COMMITTEE CHAIRS

Adult Social Care & Health: Mr Richard McLinden
Audit & Accounts: Mr Liam Robinson
Culture & Tourism: Ms Anna Rothery
Education & Children's Services: Mr John Prince
Employment, Enterprise & Skills: Mr Gary Millar
Environment & Climate Change: Mr James Noakes
Finance & Resources: Ms Louise Baldock
Housing & Community Safety: Mr Tony Concepcion
Licensing: Ms Christine Banks
Neighbourhood Services: Ms Pam Thomas
Overview & Scrutiny (Scrutiny): Ms Sarah Jennings
Planning: Mr John McIntosh
Regeneration & Transport: Ms Beatrice Fraenkel

LUTON U

Luton Borough Council, Town Hall, Luton LU1 2BQ
☎ 01582 546000 🖷 01582 546680 💻 www.luton.gov.uk

FACTS & FIGURES

Police Authority: Bedfordshire Police Authority
Health Authority: East of England Strategic Health Authority
Learning and Skills Council: Eastern
Parliamentary Constituencies: Luton North, Luton South
EU Constituencies: Eastern
Election Frequency: Elections are of whole council
Twinning: Bourgoin Jallieu (France); Bergisch Gladbach (Germany); Berlin-Spandau (Germany); Eskilstuna (Sweden); Wolfsburg (Germany)

PRINCIPAL OFFICERS

Chief Executive: Mr Trevor Holden, Chief Executive, Town Hall, Luton LU1 2BQ ☎ 01582 546015 🖷 01582 546680 ✉ chiefexec@luton.gov.uk

Senior Management: Mr Colin Chick, Corporate Director of Environment & Regeneration, 2nd Floor, Town Hall, Luton LU1 2BQ ☎ 01582 546301 🖷 01582 546975 ✉ colin.chick@luton.gov.uk

Senior Management: Ms Pam Garraway, Corporate Director of Housing, Community Living & Adult Services (Interim), 3rd Floor, Unity House, 111 Stuart Street, Luton LU1 5NP ☎ 01582 547500 🖷 01582 547733 ✉ pam.garraway@luton.gov.uk

Senior Management: Mr Steve Heappey, Director of Customer & Corporate Services, Apex House, Luton LU1 2RD ☎ 01582 546281 🖷 01582 546451 ✉ steve.heappey@luton.gov.uk

Senior Management: Mr Martin Pratt, Corporate Director of Children & Learning, 3rd Floor, Unity House, 111 Stuart Street, Luton LU1 2NP ☎ 01582 548400 🖷 01582 548454 ✉ debbie.jones@luton.gov.uk

Architect, Building / Property Services: Mr Michael Scorer, Interim Head of Capital & Asset Management, 2nd Floor, Apex House, 30-34 Upper George Street, Luton LU1 2RD ☎ 01582 548268 ✉ michael.scorer@luton.gov.uk

Best Value: Mr Dean Stokes, Head of Citizen Engagement & Strategic Policy, Ground Floor, Town Hall, Luton LU1 2BQ ☎ 01582 546073 🖷 01582 546680 🖱 dean.stokes@luton.gov.uk

Building Control: Mr Chris Pagdin, Head of Planning, Town Hall, Luton LU1 2BQ ☎ 01582 546329 🖷 01582 547138 🖱 chris.pagdin@luton.gov.uk

Catering Services: Mr Ferri Fassihi, General Catering Manager, Luton Learning and Resource Centre, Strangers Way, Luton LU1 ☎ 01582 538211 🖷 01582 538226 🖱 feraidoun.fassihi@luton.gov.uk

Children / Youth Services: Mr Nick Chamberlain, Early Intervention Service Manager, 1st Floor, Unity House, 111 Stuart Street, Luton LU1 5NP ☎ 01582 548057 🖷 01582 548232 🖱 nicholas.chamberlain@luton.gov.uk

Children / Youth Services: Mr Martin Pratt, Corporate Director of Children & Learning, Unity House, Luton LU1 2NP ☎ 01582 548400 🖷 01582 548454 🖱 debbie.jones@luton.gov.uk

Civil Registration: Ms Angela Claridge, Head of HR & Monitoring Officer, 2nd Floor, Apex House, 30-34 Upper George Street, Luton LU1 2RD ☎ 01582 546291 🖷 01582 546994 🖱 angela.claridge@luton.gov.uk

PR / Communications: Mr Rob Leigh, Head of Communications, 1st Floor, Town Hall Annexe, Luton LU1 2BQ ☎ 01582 546035 🖱 rob.leigh@luton.gov.uk

Community Planning: Ms Laura Church, Head of Regeneration Services, 2nd Floor, Town Hall, Luton LU1 2BQ ☎ 01582 546433 🖷 01582 546971 🖱 laura.church@luton.gov.uk

Community Safety: Ms Vicky Hayes, Community Safety & Anti-Social Behaviour Officer, Luton Police Station, Buxton Road, Luton LU4 8AU ☎ 01582 556628 🖷 01582 556630 🖱 vicky.hayes@luton.gov.uk

Contracts: Mr Chris Addey, Corporate Procurement Manager, 2nd Floor - Stuart House, Upper George Street, Luton LU1 2RD ☎ 01582 546867 🖷 01582 546850 🖱 addeyc@luton.gov.uk

Corporate Services: Mr Robin Porter, Director of Commercial & Transformation Service, Ground Floor, Unity House, 111 Stuart Street, Luton LU1 2NP ☎ 01582 548205 🖱 robin.porter@luton.gov.uk

Customer Service: Mr Robin Porter, Director of Commercial & Transformation Service, Ground Floor, Unity House, 111 Stuart Street, Luton LU1 2NP ☎ 01582 548205 🖱 robin.porter@luton.gov.uk

Direct Labour: Ms Mo Harkin, Head of Housing, 2nd Floor, Unity House, 111 Stuart Street, Luton LU1 5NP ☎ 01582 546202 🖷 01582 547733 🖱 HOHSG@luton.gov.uk

Economic Development: Ms Laura Church, Head of Regeneration Services, 1st Floor - Stuart House, Upper George Street, Luton LU1 2RD ☎ 01582 546433 🖷 01582 546971 🖱 laura.church@luton.gov.uk

Education: Mr Martin Pratt, Corporate Director of Children & Learning, Unity House, Luton LU1 2NP ☎ 01582 548400 🖷 01582 548454 🖱 debbie.jones@luton.gov.uk

Emergency Planning: Mr Robert Marshall, Civil Protection Manager, 1st Floor, Town Hall Annexe, Luton LU1 2BQ ☎ 01582 546071 🖷 01582 547058 🖱 robert.marshall@luton.gov.uk

Environmental / Technical Services: Mr Colin Chick, Corporate Director of Environment & Regeneration, 2nd Floor, Town Hall, Luton LU1 2BQ ☎ 01582 546301 🖷 01582 546975 🖱 colin.chick@luton.gov.uk

Environmental Health: Ms Laura Church, Head of Regeneration Services, 1st Floor - Stuart House, Upper George Street, Luton LU1 2RD ☎ 01582 546433 🖷 01582 546971 🖱 laura.church@luton.gov.uk

Finance and Treasurer: Mr David Kempson, Head of Corporate Finance, 2nd Floor, Wesley House, Chapel Street, Luton LU1 2SE ☎ 01582 546087 🖱 david.kempson@luton.gov.uk

Fleet Management: Mr Simon Smith, Transport Manager, Central Depot, Kingsway, Luton LU4 8AU ☎ 01582 546877 🖷 01582 546883 🖱 simon.smith@luton.gov.uk

Grounds Maintenance: Mr Barry Timms, Parks & Cemeteries Manager, Wardown Park Offices, Luton LU2 7HA ☎ 01582 546702 🖷 01582 546894 🖱 barry.timms@luton.gov.uk

Health and Safety: Ms Caron Owens, Corporate Health & Safety Manager, 2nd Floor, Clemiston House, 14 Upper George Street, Luton LU1 2RP ☎ 01582 546299 🖷 01582 546350 🖱 caron.owens@luton.gov.uk

Highways: Mr Mehmood Khan, Head of Engineering & Transportation, Town Hall, Luton LU1 2BQ ☎ 01582 546172 🖷 01582 546649 🖱 mehmood.khan@luton.gov.uk

Housing: Ms Pam Garraway, Corporate Director of Housing, Community Living & Adult Services (Interim), Unity House, 111 Stuart Street, Luton LU1 5NP ☎ 01582 547500 🖷 01582 547733 🖱 pam.garraway@luton.gov.uk

Housing: Ms Mo Harkin, Head of Housing, 2nd Floor, Unity House, 111 Stuart Street, Luton LU1 5NP ☎ 01582 546202 🖷 01582 547733 🖱 HOHSG@luton.gov.uk

Local Area Agreement: Mr Dean Stokes, Head of Citizen Engagement & Strategic Policy, Town Hall Annexe, Luton LU1 2BQ ☎ 01582 546073 🖷 01582 546680 🖱 dean.stokes@luton.gov.uk

Legal: Ms Angela Claridge, Head of HR & Monitoring Officer, Apex House, Luton LU1 2RD ☎ 01582 546291 🖷 01582 546994 🖱 angela.claridge@luton.gov.uk

Leisure and Cultural Services: Ms Maggie Appleton, Lesiure & Cultural Services Manager, Central Library, Luton LU1 2BQ ☎ 01582 546000 🖱 maggie.appleton@luton.gov.uk

Licensing: Ms Laura Church, Head of Regeneration Services, 1st

Floor - Stuart House, Upper George Street, Luton LU1 2RD ☎ 01582 546433 🖷 01582 546971 🖱 laura.church@luton.gov.uk

Lifelong Learning: Mr Martin Pratt, Corporate Director of Children & Learning, Unity House, Luton LU1 2NP ☎ 01582 548400 🖷 01582 548454 🖱 debbie.jones@luton.gov.uk

Lighting: Mrs Celia Robb, Head of Engineering & Street Services, Central Depot, Kingsway, Luton LU4 8AU ☎ 01582 546248 🖷 01582 546806 🖱 celia.robb@luton.gov.uk

Lighting: Mr Graham Turner, Highways Maintenance Services Manager, 4th Floor, Town Hall, Luton LU1 2BQ ☎ 01582 546257 🖷 01582 547177 🖱 graham.turner@luton.gov.uk

Member Services: Ms Debbie Janes, Democratic Services Manager, Town Hall, Luton LU1 2BQ ☎ 01582 546038 🖷 01582 547143 🖱 deborah.janes@luton.gov.uk

Member Services: Mr Dean Stokes, Head of Citizen Engagement & Strategic Policy, Town Hall Annexe, Luton LU1 2BQ ☎ 01582 546073 🖷 01582 546680 🖱 dean.stokes@luton.gov.uk

Parking: Mr Tony Stefano, Parking Operations Manager, Town Hall, Luton LU1 2BQ ☎ 01582 548521 🖷 01582 548522 🖱 tony.stefano@luton.gov.uk

Personnel / HR: Ms Angela Claridge, Head of HR & Monitoring Officer, 2nd Floor, Apex House, 30-34 Upper George Street, Luton LU1 2RD ☎ 01582 546291 🖷 01582 546994 🖱 angela.claridge@luton.gov.uk

Planning: Mr Chris Pagdin, Head of Planning, Town Hall, Luton LU1 2BQ ☎ 01582 546329 🖷 01582 547138 🖱 chris.pagdin@luton.gov.uk

Procurement: Mr Chris Addey, Corporate Procurement Manager, 2nd Floor, Wesley House, Chapel Street, Luton LU1 2SE ☎ 01582 546867 🖷 01582 546850 🖱 addeyc@luton.gov.uk

Regeneration: Ms Laura Church, Head of Regeneration Services, 2nd Floor, Town Hall, George Street, Luton LU1 2RD ☎ 01582 546433 🖷 01582 546971 🖱 laura.church@luton.gov.uk

Road Safety: Mrs Celia Robb, Head of Engineering & Street Services, Kingsway Depot, Luton LU4 8AU ☎ 01582 546248 🖷 01582 546806 🖱 celia.robb@luton.gov.uk

Social Services (Adult): Ms Pam Garraway, Corporate Director of Housing, Community Living & Adult Services (Interim), Unity House, 111 Stuart Street, Luton LU1 5NP ☎ 01582 547500 🖷 01582 547733 🖱 pam.garraway@luton.gov.uk

Social Services (Adult): Mr Graham Wrycroft, Interim Head of Adult Social Care, Unity House, 111 Stuart House, Luton LU1 5NP ☎ 01582 547503 🖷 01582 547733 🖱 graham.wrycroft@luton.gov.uk

Social Services (Children): Ms Anne Futcher, Head of Area Integrated Services, Unity House, 111 Stuart House, Luton LU1 5NP ☎ 01582 547502 🖷 01582 547141 🖱 anne.futcher@luton.gov.uk

Social Services (Children): Ms Pam Garraway, Corporate Director of Housing, Community Living & Adult Services (Interim), Unity House, 111 Stuart Street, Luton LU1 5NP ☎ 01582 547500 🖷 01582 547733 🖱 pam.garraway@luton.gov.uk

Staff Training: Ms Lesley McNeill, Learning & Development Manager, Ground Floor, Apex House, 30 - 34 George Street, Luton LU1 2RD ☎ 01582 547556 🖷 01582 547753 🖱 lesley.mcneill@luton.gov.uk

Street Scene: Mrs Celia Robb, Head of Engineering & Street Services, Central Depot, Kingsway, Luton LU4 8AU ☎ 01582 546248 🖷 01582 546806 🖱 celia.robb@luton.gov.uk

Sustainable Communities: Mr Colin Chick, Corporate Director of Environment & Regeneration, Town Hall, Luton LU1 2BQ ☎ 01582 546301 🖷 01582 546975 🖱 colin.chick@luton.gov.uk

Sustainable Communities: Ms Laura Church, Head of Regeneration Services, 2nd Floor, Town Hall, Luton LU1 2BQ ☎ 01582 546433 🖷 01582 546971 🖱 laura.church@luton.gov.uk

Sustainable Development: Mr Colin Chick, Corporate Director of Environment & Regeneration, Town Hall, Luton LU1 2BQ ☎ 01582 546301 🖷 01582 546975 🖱 colin.chick@luton.gov.uk

Sustainable Development: Ms Laura Church, Head of Regeneration Services, 2nd Floor, Town Hall, Luton LU1 2BQ ☎ 01582 546433 🖷 01582 546971 🖱 laura.church@luton.gov.uk

Tourism: Ms Laura Church, Head of Regeneration Services, 2nd Floor, Town Hall, Luton LU1 2BQ ☎ 01582 546433 🖷 01582 546971 🖱 laura.church@luton.gov.uk

Town Centre: Mr Mal Hussain, Team Leader, 2nd Floor, 2 - 12 Victoria Street, Luton LU1 2UA ☎ 01582 547227 🖷 01582 546971

Traffic Management: Mr Jonathan Palmer, Traffic & Asset Manager, 4th Floor, Town Hall, Luton LU1 2BQ ☎ 01582 546686 🖷 01582 547177 🖱 jonathan.palmer@luton.gov.uk

Transport: Mr Simon Smith, Transport Manager, Central Depot, Kingsway, Luton LU4 8AU ☎ 01582 546877 🖷 01582 546883 🖱 simon.smith@luton.gov.uk

Transport Planner: Mr Mehmood Khan, Head of Engineering & Transportation, Town Hall, Luton LU1 2BQ ☎ 01582 546172 🖷 01582 546649 🖱 mehmood.khan@luton.gov.uk

Total Place: Mr Robin Porter, Director of Commercial & Transformation Service, Ground Floor, Unity House, 111 Stuart Street, Luton LU1 2NP ☎ 01582 548205 🖱 robin.porter@luton.gov.uk

Waste Management: Mrs Celia Robb, Head of Engineering & Street Services, Central Depot, Kingsway, Luton LU4 8AU ☎ 01582 546248 🖷 01582 546806 🖱 celia.robb@luton.gov.uk

MEMBERS OF THE COUNCIL (48)

Mayor: **Knight**, Syd (LAB - Sundon Park)

syd.knight@luton.gov.uk
***Leader of the Council:* Simmons**, Hazel (LAB - Lewsey)
hazel.simmons@luton.gov.uk
***Deputy Leader of the Council:* Timoney**, Sian (LAB - Farley)
sian.timoney@luton.gov.uk
Akbar, Waheed (LAB - Leagrave)
waheed.akbar@luton.gov.uk
Ashraf, Mohammed (LAB - Dallow)
mohammed.ashraf@luton.gov.uk
Ayub, Naseem (LAB - Biscot)
Ayub, Mohammed (LAB - Biscot)
mohammed.ayub@luton.gov.uk
Bailey, Joan (LAB - Lewsey)
joan.bailey@luton.gov.uk
Burnett, Jacqui (LAB - Limbury)
jacqueline.burnett@luton.gov.uk
Campbell, Gilbert (CON - Bramingham)
gilbert.campbell@luton.gov.uk
Cato, Malvin (LAB - Crawley)
melvin.cato@luton.gov.uk
Chapman, Peter (LD - Wigmore)
peter.chapman@luton.gov.uk
Davies, Jenny (LD - Stopsley)
jenny.davies@luton.gov.uk
Davies, Roy (LD - Wigmore)
roy.davies@luton.gov.uk
Davis, Roy J (LAB - Northwell)
roy.davis@luton.gov.uk
Dolling, Michael (LD - Stopsley)
michael.dolling@luton.gov.uk
Farooq, Mohammed (LAB - Dallow)
mohammed.farooq@luton.gov.uk
Foord, Katie (CON - Bramingham)
katie.foord@luton.gov.uk
Franks, David (LD - Crawley)
david.franks@luton.gov.uk
Gale, Keir (LAB - South)
keir.gale@luton.gov.uk
Garrett, Michael (CON - Icknield)
michael.garrett@luton.gov.uk
Hanif, Yaqub (LAB - Round Green)
yaqub.hanif@luton.gov.uk
Harris, Robin (LAB - Farley)
robin.harris@luton.gov.uk
Hinkley, Doris (LD - Sundon Park)
doris.hinckley@luton.gov.uk
Hopkins, Rachel (LAB - Barnfield)
rachel.hopkins@luton.gov.uk
Hussain, Mahmood (LAB - Farley)
mahmood.hussain@luton.gov.uk
Khan, Tahir (LAB - Biscot)
tahir.khan@luton.gov.uk
Khan, Aslam (LAB - Lewsey)
aslam.khan@luton.gov.uk
Lewis, Stephen (LAB - Limbury)
stephen.lewis@luton.gov.uk
Malcolm, Andrew (LAB - High Town)
andrew.malcolm@luton.gov.uk
Malik, Tahir (LAB - Challney)
tahir.malik@luton.gov.uk
Malik, Khtija (LAB - Challney)
khtija.malik@luton.gov.uk
Moles, Diane (LD - Wigmore)
diane.moles@luton.gov.uk
O'Callaghan, Amy (LAB - South)
amy.o'callaghan@luton.gov.uk
Pantling, Martin (LD - Barnfield)
martin.pantling@luton.gov.uk
Rathore, Asma (LAB - Saints)
asma.rathore@luton.gov.uk
Riaz, Mohammed (LAB - Saints)
mohammed.riaz@luton.gov.uk
Rivers, Mark (LAB - Round Green)
mark.rivers@luton.gov.uk
Roden, Sheila (LAB - Leagrave)
sheila.roden@luton.gov.uk
Saleem, Raja (LAB - Saints)
raja.saleem@luton.gov.uk
Sharif, Tafheen (LAB - Dallow)
tafheen.sharif@luton.gov.uk
Shaw, Tom (LAB - Challney)
tom.shaw@luton.gov.uk
Stewart, Desline (LAB - Leagrave)
desline.stewart@luton.gov.uk
Taylor, Dave (LAB - South)
dave.taylor@luton.gov.uk
Titmuss, John (CON - Icknield)
john.titmuss@luton.gov.uk
Whittaker, Roxanna (LAB - High Town)
roxanna.whittaker@luton.gov.uk
Worlding, Don (LAB - Northwell)
don.worlding@luton.gov.uk
Zia, Mohammed (LAB - Round Green)
mohammed.zia@luton.gov.uk

POLITICAL COMPOSITION

LAB: 36, LD: 8, CON: 4

CABINET

Leader: Ms Hazel Simmons
Deputy Leader / Finance: Mrs Sian Timoney
Adult Social Care: Mr Mahmood Hussain
Children's Services: Mr Tahir Khan
Children's Social Care: Ms Sheild Roden
Community Engagement: Ms Joan Bailey
Environment: Mr Dave Taylor
Housing: Mr Waheed Akbar
Leisure, Community & Community Safety: Mr Mohammed Ashraf
Regeneration: Mr Roy Davis

COMMITTEE CHAIRS

Audit & Governance (Scrutiny): Mr Mohammed Farooq
Development Control: Mr Waheed Akbar
Licensing: Mr Mahmood Hussain
Overview & Scrutiny Board: Mrs Doris Hinkley

MAGHERAFELT N

Magherafelt District Council, Council Offices, 50 Ballyronan Road, Magherafelt BT45 6EN ☎ 028 7939 7979 🖷 028 7939 7980 ✉ info@magherafelt.gov.uk 💻 www.magherafelt.gov.uk

FACTS & FIGURES

Police Authority: Northern Ireland Policing Board
Health Authority: Health & Social Care Board
Learning and Skills Council: Northern Ireland
EU Constituencies: Northern Ireland

Election Frequency: Elections are of whole council

PRINCIPAL OFFICERS

Chief Executive: Mr John McLaughlin, Chief Executive, 50 Ballyronan Road, Magherafelt BT45 6EN ☎ 028 7939 7979 🖷 028 7939 7980

Deputy Chief Executive: Mr JJ Tohill, Director of Finance & Administration, 50 Ballyronan Road, Magherafelt BT45 6EN ☎ 028 7939 7979 🖷 028 7939 7980 jjtohill@magherafelt.gov.uk

Senior Management: Mr Andrew Cassells, Director of Operations, Council Offices, 50 Ballyronan Road, Magherafelt BT45 6EN ☎ 028 7939 7979 🖷 028 7939 7980 andrew.cassells@magherafelt.gov.uk

Senior Management: Mr Ian Glendinning, Director of Building Control, 50 Ballyronan Road, Magherafelt BT45 6EN ☎ 028 7939 7979 🖷 028 7939 7980 ian.glendinning@magherafelt.gov.uk

Senior Management: Mr Maurice Young, Director of Environmental Health, 50 Ballyronan Road, Magherafelt BT45 6EN ☎ 028 7939 7979 🖷 028 7939 7980 maurice.young@magherafelt.gov.uk

Architect, Building / Property Services: Mr Ian Glendinning, Director of Building Control, 50 Ballyronan Road, Magherafelt BT45 6EN ☎ 028 7939 7979 🖷 028 7939 7980 ian.glendinning@magherafelt.gov.uk

Best Value: Mr JJ Tohill, Director of Finance & Administration, 50 Ballyronan Road, Magherafelt BT45 6EN ☎ 028 7939 7979 🖷 028 7939 7980 jjtohill@magherafelt.gov.uk

Building Control: Mr Ian Glendinning, Director of Building Control, 50 Ballyronan Road, Magherafelt BT45 6EN ☎ 028 7939 7979 🖷 028 7939 7980 ian.glendinning@magherafelt.gov.uk

PR / Communications: Mr John McLaughlin, Chief Executive, 50 Ballyronan Road, Magherafelt BT45 6EN ☎ 028 7939 7979 🖷 028 7939 7980

Community Planning: Mrs Anne-Marie Campbell, Director of Development & Implementation, 50 Ballyronan Road, Magherafelt BT45 6EN ☎ 028 7939 7979 🖷 028 7939 7980 anne-marie.campbell@magherafelt.gov.uk

Community Safety: Mrs Anne-Marie Campbell, Director of Development & Implementation, 50 Ballyronan Road, Magherafelt BT45 6EN ☎ 028 7939 7979 🖷 028 7939 7980 anne-marie.campbell@magherafelt.gov.uk

Computer Management: Mr JJ Tohill, Director of Finance & Administration, 50 Ballyronan Road, Magherafelt BT45 6EN ☎ 028 7939 7979 🖷 028 7939 7980 jjtohill@magherafelt.gov.uk

Consumer Protection and Trading Standards: Mr Maurice Young, Director of Environmental Health, 50 Ballyronan Road, Magherafelt BT45 6EN ☎ 028 7939 7979 🖷 028 7939 7980 maurice.young@magherafelt.gov.uk

Contracts: Mr John McLaughlin, Chief Executive, 50 Ballyronan Road, Magherafelt BT45 6EN ☎ 028 7939 7979 🖷 028 7939 7980

Corporate Services: Mr JJ Tohill, Director of Finance & Administration, 50 Ballyronan Road, Magherafelt BT45 6EN ☎ 028 7939 7979 🖷 028 7939 7980 jjtohill@magherafelt.gov.uk

Direct Labour: Mr Andrew Cassells, Director of Operations, Council Offices, 50 Ballyronan Road, Magherafelt BT45 6EN ☎ 028 7939 7979 🖷 028 7939 7980 andrew.cassells@magherafelt.gov.uk

Economic Development: Mr John McLaughlin, Chief Executive, 50 Ballyronan Road, Magherafelt BT45 6EN ☎ 028 7939 7979 🖷 028 7939 7980

Emergency Planning: Mr John McLaughlin, Chief Executive, 50 Ballyronan Road, Magherafelt BT45 6EN ☎ 028 7939 7979 🖷 028 7939 7980

Energy Management: Mr JJ Tohill, Director of Finance & Administration, 50 Ballyronan Road, Magherafelt BT45 6EN ☎ 028 7939 7979 🖷 028 7939 7980 jjtohill@magherafelt.gov.uk

Environmental / Technical Services: Mr Andrew Cassells, Director of Operations, Council Offices, 50 Ballyronan Road, Magherafelt BT45 6EN ☎ 028 7939 7979 🖷 028 7939 7980 andrew.cassells@magherafelt.gov.uk

Environmental Health: Mr Maurice Young, Director of Environmental Health, 50 Ballyronan Road, Magherafelt BT45 6EN ☎ 028 7939 7979 🖷 028 7939 7980 maurice.young@magherafelt.gov.uk

European Liaison: Mr John McLaughlin, Chief Executive, 50 Ballyronan Road, Magherafelt BT45 6EN ☎ 028 7939 7979 🖷 028 7939 7980

Finance and Treasurer: Mr A Hogg, Head of Finance, 50 Ballyronan Road, Magherafelt BT45 6EN ☎ 028 7939 7979 ahogg@magherafelt.gov.uk

Finance and Treasurer: Mr JJ Tohill, Director of Finance & Administration, 50 Ballyronan Road, Magherafelt BT45 6EN ☎ 028 7939 7979 🖷 028 7939 7980 jjtohill@magherafelt.gov.uk

Fleet Management: Mr Andrew Cassells, Director of Operations, Council Offices, 50 Ballyronan Road, Magherafelt BT45 6EN ☎ 028 7939 7979 🖷 028 7939 7980 andrew.cassells@magherafelt.gov.uk

Grounds Maintenance: Mr Andrew Cassells, Director of Operations, Council Offices, 50 Ballyronan Road, Magherafelt BT45 6EN ☎ 028 7939 7979 🖷 028 7939 7980 andrew.cassells@magherafelt.gov.uk

Health and Safety: Mr Maurice Young, Director of Environmental Health, 50 Ballyronan Road, Magherafelt BT45 6EN ☎ 028 7939

7979 🖷 028 7939 7980 ✉ maurice.young@magherafelt.gov.uk

Leisure and Cultural Services: Mr Laurence Hastings, Head of Leisure Services, 50 Ballyronan Road, Magherafelt BT45 6EN ☎ 028 7963 2796 🖷 028 7930 1261

Licensing: Miss Ann Boyle, Licensing Officer, 50 Ballyronan Road, Magherafelt BT45 6EN ☎ 028 7939 7979 🖷 028 7939 7980

Lottery Funding, Charity and Voluntary: Mr Michael Browne, Head of Communication Services, 50 Ballyronan Road, Magherafelt BT45 6EN ☎ 028 7939 7979 🖷 028 7939 7980

Member Services: Miss Ann Boyle, Licensing Officer, 50 Ballyronan Road, Magherafelt BT45 6EN ☎ 028 7939 7979 🖷 028 7939 7980

Personnel / HR: Mrs Florence Wilson, Head of Administration & Personnel, 50 Ballyronan Road, Magherafelt BT45 6EN ☎ 028 7939 7979 ext. 3216 🖷 028 7939 7980 ✉ florence.wilson@magherafelt.gov.uk

Procurement: Mr JJ Tohill, Director of Finance & Administration, 50 Ballyronan Road, Magherafelt BT45 6EN ☎ 028 7939 7979 🖷 028 7939 7980 ✉ jjtothill@magherafelt.gov.uk

Recycling & Waste Minimisation: Mr Andrew Cassells, Director of Operations, Council Offices, 50 Ballyronan Road, Magherafelt BT45 6EN ☎ 028 7939 7979 🖷 028 7939 7980 ✉ andrew.cassells@magherafelt.gov.uk

Staff Training: Mrs Florence Wilson, Head of Administration & Personnel, 50 Ballyronan Road, Magherafelt BT45 6EN ☎ 028 7939 7979 ext. 3216 🖷 028 7939 7980 ✉ florence.wilson@magherafelt.gov.uk

Sustainable Development: Mr John McLaughlin, Chief Executive, 50 Ballyronan Road, Magherafelt BT45 6EN ☎ 028 7939 7979 🖷 028 7939 7980

Tourism: Mrs Anne-Marie Campbell, Director of Development & Implementation, 50 Ballyronan Road, Magherafelt BT45 6EN ☎ 028 7939 7979 🖷 028 7939 7980 ✉ anne-marie.campbell@magherafelt.gov.uk

Transport: Mr Andrew Cassells, Director of Operations, Council Offices, 50 Ballyronan Road, Magherafelt BT45 6EN ☎ 028 7939 7979 🖷 028 7939 7980 ✉ andrew.cassells@magherafelt.gov.uk

Waste Collection and Disposal: Mr Andrew Cassells, Director of Operations, Council Offices, 50 Ballyronan Road, Magherafelt BT45 6EN ☎ 028 7939 7979 🖷 028 7939 7980 ✉ andrew.cassells@magherafelt.gov.uk

Waste Management: Mr Andrew Cassells, Director of Operations, Council Offices, 50 Ballyronan Road, Magherafelt BT45 6EN ☎ 028 7939 7979 🖷 028 7939 7980 ✉ andrew.cassells@magherafelt.gov.uk

MEMBERS OF THE COUNCIL (16)

Chair: **McLean**, Paul (DUP - Magherafelt Town)
paul@mclean-clan.co.uk
Bateson, Peter (SF - Magherafelt Town)
southderrysinnfein@ireland.com
Campbell, James (SDLP - Magherafelt Town)
jimcampbell10@hotmail.com
Catherwood, Thomas (DUP - Moyola)
Crawford, John (UUP - Moyola)
john.crawford12@googlemail.com
Elattar, Catherine (SF - Magherafelt Town)
celattar@yahoo.ie
Forde, Elizabeth Anne (DUP - Sperrin)
cllr.forde@magherafelt.gov.uk
Kerr, John (SF - Sperrin)
seankerr@lineone.net
Lagan, Kathleen (SDLP - Sperrin)
kate.lagan@btopenworld.com
McEldowney, Kathleen (SF - Sperrin)
southderrysinnfein@ireland.com
McGuigan, Brian (SF - Sperrin)
bmcguigan52@yahoo.ie
McPeake, Sean (SF - Moyola)
seanmcpeake@hotmail.com
Milne, Ian (SF - Moyola)
southderrysinnfein@ireland.com
Ni Shiadhail, Deborah (SF - Magherafelt Town)
deborahnishiadhail@yahoo.ie
Scullion, Caoimhe (SF - Moyola)
caoimhe.scullion@yahoo.com
Shiels, George (UUP - Magherafelt Town)
george.shiels@magherafelt.gov.uk

POLITICAL COMPOSITION

SF: 9, DUP: 3, SDLP: 2, UUP: 2

MAIDSTONE D

Maidstone Borough Council, Maidstone House, King Street, Maidstone ME15 6JQ ☎ 01622 602000 💻 www.maidstone.gov.uk

FACTS & FIGURES

Police Authority: Kent Police Authority
Health Authority: South East Coast Strategic Health Authority
Learning and Skills Council: South East
Parliamentary Constituencies: Faversham & Mid Kent, Maidstone and the Weald
EU Constituencies: South East
Election Frequency: Elections are by thirds
Twinning: Beauvais (France)

PRINCIPAL OFFICERS

Chief Executive: Mrs Alison Broom, Chief Executive, Maidstone House, King Street, Maidstone ME15 6JQ ☎ 01622 602019 🖷 01622 602226 ✉ alisonbroom@maidstone.gov.uk

Senior Management: Mr David Edwards, Director of Change, Planning & Environment, Maidstone House, King Street, Maidstone ME15 6JQ ☎ 01622 602797 🖷 01622 602974 ✉ davidedwards@maidstone.gov.uk

Access Officer / Social Services (Disability): Ms Sarah Robson, Community Development Manager, Maidstone House, King Street, Maidstone ME15 6JQ ☎ 01622 602750 ✉ sarahrobson@maidstone.gov.uk

Architect, Building / Property Services: Mr David Tibbit, Property, Projects & Procurement Manager, Maidstone House, King Street, Maidstone ME15 6JQ ☎ 01622 602361 🖷 01622 602029 ✉ davidtibbit@maidstone.gov.uk

Best Value: Miss Georgia Hawkes, Head of Business Improvement, Maidstone House, King Street, Maidstone ME15 6JQ ☎ 01622 602168 ✉ georgiahawkes@maidstone.gov.uk

Building Control: Mr David Harrison, Emergency Planning Officer, Maidstone House, King Street, Maidstone ME12 6JQ ☎ 01622 602034 ✉ davidharrison@maidstone.gov.uk

Children / Youth Services: Mr Jim Boot, Community Development Manager, Maidstone House, King Street, Maidstone ME15 6JQ ☎ 01622 602246 🖷 01622 602970 ✉ jimboot@maidstone.gov.uk

PR / Communications: Mr Roger Adley, Head of Communications, Maidstone House, King Street, Maidstone ME15 6JQ ☎ 01622 602758 🖷 01622 602226

Community Planning: Ms Sarah Robson, Community Development Manager, Maidstone House, King Street, Maidstone ME15 6JQ ☎ 01622 602750 ✉ sarahrobson@maidstone.gov.uk

Community Safety: Mr John Littlemore, Head of Housing & Community Safety, Maidstone House, King Street, Maidstone ME15 6JQ ☎ 01622 602207 🖷 01622 602974 ✉ johnlittlemore@maidstone.gov.uk

Computer Management: Mr Dave Lindsay, IT Manager, Maidstone House, King Street, Maidstone ME15 6JQ ☎ 01622 602156 🖷 01622 602970 ✉ davelindsay@maidstone.gov.uk

Contracts: Ms Georgia Hawkes, Head of Business Improvement, Maidstone House, King Street, Maidstone ME15 6JQ ☎ 01622 602168 🖷 01622 602970 ✉ georgiahawkes@maidstone.gov.uk

Corporate Services: Mr Paul Riley, Head of Finance & Customer Service, Maidstone House, King Street, Maidstone ME15 6JQ ☎ 01622 602032 ✉ paulriley@maidstone.gov.uk

Economic Development: Mr John Foster, Economic Development Manager, Maidstone House, King Street, Maidstone ME15 6JQ ☎ 01622 602394 ✉ johnfoster@maidstone.gov.uk

E-Government: Mr Dave Lindsay, IT Manager, Maidstone House, King Street, Maidstone ME15 6JQ ☎ 01622 602156 🖷 01622 602970 ✉ davelindsay@maidstone.gov.uk

Electoral Registration: Mrs Gill Gymer, Registration & Democratic Services Manager, Maidstone House, King Street, Maidstone ME15 6JQ ☎ 01622 602023 ✉ gillgymer@maidstone.gov.uk

Emergency Planning: Mr David Harrison, Emergency Planning Officer, Maidstone House, King Street, Maidstone ME12 6JQ ☎ 01622 602034 ✉ davidharrison@maidstone.gov.uk

Energy Management: Mr Chris Finch, Corporate Property Manager, Maidstone House, King Street, Maidstone ME15 6JQ ☎ 01622 602720 🖷 01622 602974 ✉ christopherfinch@maidstone.gov.uk

Environmental Health: Mr Ron Wallis, Environmental Health Manager, Maidstone House, King Street, Maidstone ME15 6JQ ☎ 01622 602145 🖷 01622 602972 ✉ ronwallis@maidstone.gov.uk

Estates, Property & Valuation: Mr David Tibbit, Property, Projects & Procurement Manager, Maidstone House, King Street, Maidstone ME15 6JQ ☎ 01622 602361 🖷 01622 602029 ✉ davidtibbit@maidstone.gov.uk

Events Manager: Miss Mandy Hare, Theatre & Events Manager, Hazlitt Theatre, Earl Street, Maidstone ME14 1PL ☎ 01622 602178 🖷 01622 602194 ✉ mandyhare@maidstone.gov.uk

Facilities: Ms Lisa Cook, Facilities Manager, Maidstone House, King Street, Maidstone ME15 6JQ ☎ 01622 602509 ✉ lisacook@maidstone.gov.uk

Finance and Treasurer: Mr Paul Riley, Head of Finance & Customer Service, Maidstone House, King Street, Maidstone ME15 6JQ ☎ 01622 602032 ✉ paulriley@maidstone.gov.uk

Fleet Management: Ms Lisa Cook, Facilities Manager, Maidstone House, King Street, Maidstone ME15 6JQ ☎ 01622 602509 ✉ lisacook@maidstone.gov.uk

Health and Safety: Mr Alistair Barker, Corporate Health & Safety Manager, Maidstone House, King Street, Maidstone ME15 6JQ ☎ 01622 605308 🖷 01622 602972 ✉ alastairbarker@maidstone.gov.uk

Housing: Mr John Littlemore, Head of Housing & Community Safety, Maidstone House, King Street, Maidstone ME15 6JQ ☎ 01622 602207 🖷 01622 602974 ✉ johnlittlemore@maidstone.gov.uk

Legal: Mr Paul Fisher, Head of Corporate Law & Legal Services, Maidstone House, King Street, Maidstone ME15 6JQ ☎ 01622 602006 🖷 01622 602974 ✉ paulfisher@maidstone.gov.uk

Leisure and Cultural Services: Mr Brian Morgan, Assistant Director of Development & Community Services, Maidstone House, King Street, Maidstone ME15 6JQ ☎ 01622 602236 ✉ brianmorgan@maidstone.gov.uk

Licensing: Ms Lorraine Neale, Licensing Enforcement Officer, Maidstone House, King Street, Maidstone ME15 6JQ ☎ 01622 602028 ✉ lorraineneale@maidstone.gov.uk

Licensing: Mrs Claire Perry, Licensing Partnership Manager, Council Offices, Argyle Road, Sevenoaks TN13 1HG ☎ 01732 227325; 07970 731616 ✉ claire.perry@sevenoaks.gov.uk; claire.perry@tunbridgewells.gov.uk

Member Services: Mr Neil Harris, Head of Democratic Services, Maidstone House, King Street, Maidstone ME15 6JQ ☎ 01622 602020 🖷 01622 692246 ✉ neilharris@maidstone.gov.uk

Parking: Mr Jeff Kitson, Parking Services Manager, Maidstone House, King Street, Maidstone ME15 6JQ ☎ 01622 602376

jeffkitson@maidstone.gov.uk

Partnerships: Ms Zena Cooke, Director of Regeneration, Maidstone House, King Street, Maidstone ME15 6JQ

Personnel / HR: Ms Dena Smart, Head of Human Resources, Maidstone House, King Street, Maidstone ME15 6JQ ☎ 01622 602712 🖷 01622 602974 denasmart@maidstone.gov.uk

Planning: Mr Rob Jarman, Head of Planning, Maidstone House, King Street, Maidstone ME15 6JQ ☎ 01622 602214 🖷 01622 602974 robjarman@maidstone.gov.uk

Procurement: Mr Stephen Trigg, Procurement Manager, Maidstone House, King Street, Maidstone ME15 6JQ ☎ 01622 602811 stephentrigg@maidstone.gov.uk

Recycling & Waste Minimisation: Mrs Jennifer Gosling, Waste Collection Manager, Maidstone House, King Street, Maidstone ME15 6JQ ☎ 01622 602400 🖷 01622 602972 jennifergosling@maidstone.gov.uk

Regeneration: Mr Brian Morgan, Assistant Director of Development & Community Services, Maidstone House, King Street, Maidstone ME15 6JQ ☎ 01622 602236 brianmorgan@maidstone.gov.uk

Staff Training: Ms Tina Edwards, Learning & Development Manager, Maidstone House, King Street, Maidstone ME15 6JQ ☎ 01622 602219 🖷 01622 602974 tinaedwards@maidstone.gov.uk

Sustainable Communities: Mr Brian Morgan, Assistant Director of Development & Community Services, Maidstone House, King Street, Maidstone ME15 6JQ ☎ 01622 602236 brianmorgan@maidstone.gov.uk

Sustainable Development: Mr Jim Boot, Community Development Manager, Maidstone House, King Street, Maidstone ME15 6JQ ☎ 01622 602246 🖷 01622 602970 jimboot@maidstone.gov.uk

Tourism: Mrs Laura Dickson, Tourism Manager, Maidstone House, King Street, Maidstone ME15 6JQ ☎ 01622 602510 🖷 01622 602970 lauradickson@maidstone.gov.uk

Town Centre: Mr Bill Moss, Town Centre Manager, The Management Suite, Chequers Centre, Pads Hill, Maidstone ME15 6AL ☎ 01622 678777

Transport: Mr Clive Cheeseman, Transport Policy Officer, Maidstone House, King Street, Maidstone ME15 6JQ ☎ 01622 602365 🖷 01622 602970 clivecheeseman@maidstone.gov.uk

Transport Planner: Mr Bill Moss, Town Centre Manager, The Management Suite, Chequers Centre, Pads Hill, Maidstone ME15 6AL ☎ 01622 678777

Waste Collection and Disposal: Mrs Jennifer Gosling, Waste Collection Manager, Maidstone House, King Street, Maidstone ME15 6JQ ☎ 01622 602400 🖷 01622 602972 jennifergosling@maidstone.gov.uk

MEMBERS OF THE COUNCIL (55)

***Mayor:* Nelson-Gracie**, Rodd (CON - Marden and Yalding)
roddnelson-gracie@maidstone.gov.uk

***Leader of the Council:* Garland**, Christopher (CON - Shepway North)
christophergarland@maidstone.gov.uk

Ash, Richard (CON - Bearsted)
richardash@maidstone.gov.uk

Barned, John (CON - Harrietsham and Lenham)
JohnBarned@maidstone.gov.uk

Beerling, Stephen (LD - Fant)
stephenbeerling@maidstone.gov.uk

Black, Alistair (CON - Fant)
alistairblack@maidstone.gov.uk

Blackmore, Annabelle (CON - Marden and Yalding)
annabelleblackmore@maidstone.gov.uk

Brindle, Adrian (CON - Shepway South)
AdrianBrindle@maidstone.gov.uk

Burton, David (CON - Park Wood)
david.burton@burtons.uk.com

Butler, Derek (CON - Boxley)
derekbutler@maidstone.gov.uk

Chittenden, Ian (LD - South)
inachittenden@maidstone.gov.uk

Collins, Dennis (CON - Coxheath and Hunton)
denniscollins@maidstone.gov.uk

Cox, Martin (LD - East)
martincox@maidstone.gov.uk

Cuming, Mike (CON - Bearsted)
mikecuming@maidstone.gov.uk

Daley, Dan (LD - Allington)
dandaley@maidstone.gov.uk

de Wiggondene, Nick (CON - Detling and Thurnham)
nickdewiggondene@maidstone.gov.uk

English, Clive (LD - HIgh Street)
cliveenglish@maidstone.gov.uk

Gibson, Jenefer (CON - Headcorn)
jenefergibson@maidstone.gov.uk

Gooch, Fay (IND - Barming)
faygooch@maidstone.gov.uk

Greer, Malcolm (CON - Boxley)
malcolmgreer@hazelwoodbox.fsnet.co.uk

Griffin, Jane (LD - East)
janegriffin@maidstone.gov.uk

Grigg, Susan (LD - Loose)
susangrigg@maidstone.gov.uk

Harwood, Tony (LD - North)
tonyharwood@maidstone.gov.uk

Hinder, Wendy (CON - Boxley)
wendyhinder@maidstone.gov.uk

Hogg, Mike (CON - South)
mikehogg@maidstone.gov.uk

Hotson, Eric (CON - Staplehurst)
erichotson@maidstone.gov.uk

Joy, Denise (LD - HIgh Street)
denisejoy@maidstone.gov.uk

Lusty, Richard (CON - Staplehurst)
richardlusty@maidstone.gov.uk

Mckay, Malcolm (LAB - Shepway South)
malcolmmckay@maidstone.gov.uk

McLoughlin, Steve (CON - Marden and Yalding)
stevemcloughlin@maidstone.gov.uk

Moriarty, Daniel (IND - Park Wood)
danielmoriarty@maidstone.gov.uk

Mortimer, Derek (LD - South)
DerekMortimer@maidstone.gov.uk
Mortimer, Brian (LD - Coxheath and Hunton)
brianmortimer@maidstone.gov.uk
Moss, Brian (CON - Heath)
brianmoss@maidstone.gov.uk
Munford, Steve (IND - Boughton Monchelsea and Chart Sutton)
stevemunford@maidstone.gov.uk
Naghi, David (LD - East)
davidnaghi@maidstone.gov.uk
Newton, Gordon (IND - Downswood and Otham)
gordonnewton@maidstone.gov.uk
Paine, Stephen (CON - Fant)
stephenpaine@maidstone.gov.uk
Parvin, Daphne (CON - North Downs)
daphneparvin@maidstone.gov.uk
Parvin, Peter (CON - Leeds)
peterparvin@maidstone.gov.uk
Paterson, Jenni (LD - North)
Pickett, David (LD - Bridge)
davidpickett@maidstone.gov.uk
Ring, Marion (CON - Shepway North)
marionring@maidstone.gov.uk
Robertson, Cynthia (LD - Allington)
cynthiarobertson@maidstone.gov.uk
Robertson, Malcolm (LD - Allington)
malcolmroberts@maidstone.gov.uk
Ross, James (CON - Bridge)
jamesross@maidstone.gov.uk
Sams, Tom (IND - Harrietsham and Lenham)
tomsams@maidstone.gov.uk
Springett, Val (CON - Bearsted)
valspringett@maidstone.gov.uk
Stockell, Pauline (CON - Sutton Valence and Langley)
paulinastockell@maidstone.gov.uk
Thick, Richard (CON - Headcorn)
richardthick@maidstone.gov.uk
Vizzard, Bryan (LD - Heath)
bryanvizzard@maidstone.gov.uk
Warner, Mervyn (LD - North)
mervynwarner@maidstone.gov.uk
Wilson, Fran (LD - High Street)
franwilson@maidstone.gov.uk
Wilson, John A (CON - Coxheath and Hunton)
johnawilson@maidstone.gov.uk
Yates, Michael (CON - Shepway North)
michaelyates@maidstone.co.uk

POLITICAL COMPOSITION

CON: 30, LD: 19, IND: 5, LAB: 1

CABINET

Leader: Mr Christopher Garland
Community & Leisure Services: Mr John A Wilson
Corporate Services: Mr Eric Hotson
Economic & Commercial Development: Mr Malcolm Greer
Environment: Ms Marion Ring
Planning, Transport & Development: Mr Stephen Paine

COMMITTEE CHAIRS

Audit: Mr Derek Butler
Planning: Mr Richard Lusty

MALDON D

Maldon District Council, District Council Offices, Princes Road, Maldon CM9 7DL ☎ 01621 854477 🖷 01621 852575
💻 www.maldon.gov.uk

FACTS & FIGURES

Police Authority: Essex Police Authority
Health Authority: East of England Strategic Health Authority
Learning and Skills Council: Eastern
Parliamentary Constituencies: Maldon
EU Constituencies: Eastern
Election Frequency: Elections are of whole council
Twinning: Old Town of Maldon: Cuijk-en-St. Agatha (Netherlands); Burnham on Crouch: L'Aiguillon-sur-Mer (France)

PRINCIPAL OFFICERS

Chief Executive: Ms Fiona Marshall, Chief Executive, Council Offices, Princes Road, Maldon CM9 5DL ☎ 01621 854477 🖷 01621 852575 ✉ fiona.marshall@maldon.gov.uk

Senior Management: Mrs Hazel Berrett, Strategic Director, Council Offices, Princes Road, Maldon CM9 5DL ☎ 01621 854477 ✉ hazel.berrett@maldon.gov.uk

Senior Management: Ms Fiona Marshall, Chief Executive, Council Offices, Princes Road, Maldon CM9 5DL ☎ 01621 854477 🖷 01621 852575 ✉ fiona.marshall@maldon.gov.uk

Access Officer / Social Services (Disability): Mr Colin Miles, Part-Time Access Officer, Princes Road, Maldon CM9 5DL ☎ 01621 854477 ✉ colin.miles@maldon.gov.uk

PR / Communications: Mr Russell Dawes, Communications Manager, Council Offices, Princes Road, Maldon CM9 5DL ☎ 01621 854477 ✉ russell.dawes@maldon.gov.uk

PR / Communications: Mr Peter Wyatt, Head of Organisational Development, Council Offices, Princes Road, Maldon CM9 5DL ☎ 01621 854477 ✉ peter.wyatt@maldon.gov.uk

Community Safety: Mr Richard Holmes, Head of Lesiure & Liveability, District Council Offices, Princes Road, Maldon CM9 7DL ☎ 01621 875752 ✉ richard.holmes@maldon.gov.uk

Community Safety: Mrs Chris Rust, Community Safety & LSP Co-ordinator, District Council Offices, Princes Road, Maldon CM9 7DL ☎ 01621 854477 ✉ chris.rust@maldon.gov.uk

Computer Management: Mr Simon Mitchell, IT Team Leader, Council Offices, Princes Road, Maldon CM9 5DL ☎ 01621 854477 ✉ simon.mitchell@maldon.gov.uk

Corporate Services: Mr Peter Wyatt, Head of Organisational Development, Council Offices, Princes Road, Maldon CM9 5DL ☎ 01621 854477 ✉ peter.wyatt@maldon.gov.uk

Customer Service: Mr Ben Brown, Head of Customers & Facilities, Council Offices, Princes Road, Maldon CM9 5DL ☎ 01621 854477 ✉ ben.brown@maldon.gov.uk

Direct Labour: Mr Steve Krolzig, Maintenance Officer, District Council Offices, Princes Road, Maldon CM9 7DL ☎ 01621 875826

steve.krolzig@maldon.gov.uk

Economic Development: Mrs Jenny Lewsey, Economic Development Officer, District Council Offices, Princes Road, Maldon CM9 7DL ☎ 01621 875853 🖷 01621 842665 jenny.lewsey@maldon.gov.uk

E-Government: Mr Simon Mitchell, IT Team Leader, Council Offices, Princes Road, Maldon CM9 5DL ☎ 01621 854477 simon.mitchell@maldon.gov.uk

Electoral Registration: Mr Ben Brown, Head of Customers & Facilities, Council Offices, Princes Road, Maldon CM9 5DL ☎ 01621 854477 ben.brown@maldon.gov.uk

Electoral Registration: Ms Lynda Elsegood, Elections Management Officer, Council Offices, Princes Road, Maldon CM9 5DL ☎ 01621 854477 🖷 01621 852575 lynda.elsegood@maldon.gov.uk

Electoral Registration: Mrs Alex Hallam, Essex County Council Legal Services, Council Offices, Princes Road, Maldon CM9 5DL ☎ 01621 854477 🖷 01621 852575 simon.quelch@maldon.gov.uk

Emergency Planning: Mr Richard Holmes, Head of Lesiure & Liveability, District Council Offices, Princes Road, Maldon CM9 7DL ☎ 01621 875752 richard.holmes@maldon.gov.uk

Energy Management: Mrs Shirley Hall, Environment Team Leader, Council Offices, Princes Road, Maldon CM9 7DL ☎ 01621 854477 🖷 01621 852575 shirley.hall@maldon.gov.uk

Environmental / Technical Services: Mrs Gill Gibson, Environmental Health Team Leader - Commercial, Council Offices, Princes Road, Maldon CM9 5DL ☎ 01621 854477 gillian.gibson@maldon.gov.uk

Environmental / Technical Services: Mr Ian Haines, Head of Environmental Services, Council Offices, Princes Road, Maldon CM9 5DL ☎ 01621 854477 🖷 01621 852575 ian.haines@maldon.gov.uk

Environmental Health: Mrs Gill Gibson, Environmental Health Team Leader - Commercial, Council Offices, Princes Road, Maldon CM9 5DL ☎ 01621 854477 gillian.gibson@maldon.gov.uk

Environmental Health: Mr Ian Haines, Head of Environmental Services, Council Offices, Princes Road, Maldon CM9 5DL ☎ 01621 854477 🖷 01621 852575 ian.haines@maldon.gov.uk

Estates, Property & Valuation: Mr Ben Brown, Head of Customers & Facilities, Council Offices, Princes Road, Maldon CM9 5DL ☎ 01621 854477 ben.brown@maldon.gov.uk

Events Manager: Mr Richard Heard, Leisure & Commmunity Team Leader, District Council Offices, Princes Road, Maldon CM9 7DL ☎ 01621 875838 richard.heard@maldon.gov.uk

Facilities: Mr Ben Brown, Head of Customers & Facilities, Council Offices, Princes Road, Maldon CM9 5DL ☎ 01621 854477 ben.brown@maldon.gov.uk

Finance and Treasurer: Mr Jon Cooke, Head of Financial Services, Council Offices, Princes Road, Maldon CM9 5DL ☎ 01621 854477 🖷 01621 852575 jon.cooke@maldon.gov.uk

Finance and Treasurer: Ms Fiona Marshall, Chief Executive, Council Offices, Princes Road, Maldon CM9 5DL ☎ 01621 854477 🖷 01621 852575 fiona.marshall@maldon.gov.uk

Grounds Maintenance: Mr Richard Holmes, Head of Lesiure & Liveability, District Council Offices, Princes Road, Maldon CM9 7DL ☎ 01621 875752 richard.holmes@maldon.gov.uk

Grounds Maintenance: Mr Steve Krolzig, Maintenance Officer, District Council Offices, Princes Road, Maldon CM9 7DL ☎ 01621 875826 steve.krolzig@maldon.gov.uk

Health and Safety: Mrs Gill Gibson, Environmental Health Team Leader - Commercial, Council Offices, Princes Road, Maldon CM9 5DL ☎ 01621 854477 gillian.gibson@maldon.gov.uk

Home Energy Conservation: Miss Julie-Anne Hogbin, Energy Efficiency Officer, Council Offices, Princes Road, Maldon CM9 7DL ☎ 01621 854477 🖷 01621 852575 julie-anne.hogbin@maldon.gov.uk

Housing: Mrs Hazel Cybyk, Director of Community Services, Council Offices, Princes Road, Maldon CM9 7DL ☎ 01621 854477 hazel.cybyk@maldon.gov.uk

Housing: Ms Fiona Marshall, Chief Executive, Council Offices, Princes Road, Maldon CM9 5DL ☎ 01621 854477 🖷 01621 852575 fiona.marshall@maldon.gov.uk

Legal: Mrs Alex Hallam, Essex County Council Legal Services, Council Offices, Princes Road, Maldon CM9 5DL ☎ 01621 854477 🖷 01621 852575 simon.quelch@maldon.gov.uk

Leisure and Cultural Services: Mr Richard Heard, Leisure & Commmunity Team Leader, District Council Offices, Princes Road, Maldon CM9 7DL ☎ 01621 875838 richard.heard@maldon.gov.uk

Leisure and Cultural Services: Mr Richard Holmes, Head of Lesiure & Liveability, District Council Offices, Princes Road, Maldon CM9 7DL ☎ 01621 875752 richard.holmes@maldon.gov.uk

Lottery Funding, Charity and Voluntary: Ms Fiona Marshall, Chief Executive, Council Offices, Princes Road, Maldon CM9 5DL ☎ 01621 854477 🖷 01621 852575 fiona.marshall@maldon.gov.uk

Member Services: Mrs Val Downes, PA to the Leader, Council Offices, Princes Road, Maldon CM9 7DL ☎ 01621 854477 🖷 01621 875757 val.downes@maldon.gov.uk

Member Services: Mrs Alex Hallam, Essex County Council Legal Services, Council Offices, Princes Road, Maldon CM9 5DL ☎ 01621 854477 🖷 01621 852575 simon.quelch@maldon.gov.uk

Parking: Mr Ben Brown, Head of Customers & Facilities, Council Offices, Princes Road, Maldon CM9 5DL ☎ 01621 854477

ben.brown@maldon.gov.uk

Parking: Mr Richard Holmes, Head of Lesiure & Liveability, District Council Offices, Princes Road, Maldon CM9 7DL ☎ 01621 875752 richard.holmes@maldon.gov.uk

Partnerships: Mrs Hazel Cybyk, Director of Community Services, Council Offices, Princes Road, Maldon CM9 7DL ☎ 01621 854477 hazel.cybyk@maldon.gov.uk

Personnel / HR: Mrs Gill Gibson, Environmental Health Team Leader - Commercial, Council Offices, Princes Road, Maldon CM9 5DL ☎ 01621 854477 gillian.gibson@maldon.gov.uk

Personnel / HR: Mr Peter Wyatt, Head of Organisational Development, Council Offices, Princes Road, Maldon CM9 5DL ☎ 01621 854477 peter.wyatt@maldon.gov.uk

Planning: Mrs Jennifer Candler, Acting Head of Planning Services, District Council Offices, Princes Road, Maldon CM9 7DL ☎ 01621 875870 jennifer.candler@maldon.gov.uk

Recycling & Waste Minimisation: Mr Ian Haines, Head of Environmental Services, Council Offices, Princes Road, Maldon CM9 5DL ☎ 01621 854477 🖷 01621 852575 ian.haines@maldon.gov.uk

Staff Training: Mrs Gill Gibson, Environmental Health Team Leader - Commercial, Council Offices, Princes Road, Maldon CM9 5DL ☎ 01621 854477 gillian.gibson@maldon.gov.uk

Street Scene: Mr Gerald Lewsey, Contract Liaison & Enforcement Officer, District Council Offices, Princes Road, Maldon CM9 7DL ☎ 01621 854477 gerald.lewsey@maldon.gov.uk

Sustainable Communities: Mrs Hazel Cybyk, Director of Community Services, Council Offices, Princes Road, Maldon CM9 7DL ☎ 01621 854477 hazel.cybyk@maldon.gov.uk

Sustainable Communities: Mr Richard Holmes, Head of Lesiure & Liveability, District Council Offices, Princes Road, Maldon CM9 7DL ☎ 01621 875752 richard.holmes@maldon.gov.uk

Waste Management: Mr Ian Haines, Head of Environmental Services, Council Offices, Princes Road, Maldon CM9 5DL ☎ 01621 854477 🖷 01621 852575 ian.haines@maldon.gov.uk

Waste Management: Mr Christopher Quilter, Business Development Officer, Economic Development, Council Offices, Princes Road, Maldon CM9 7DL ☎ 01621 854477 🖷 01621 842665

MEMBERS OF THE COUNCIL (31)

***Chair:* Williams**, David (CON - Maldon West)
cllr.david.williams@maldon.gov.uk
***Vice-Chair:* Delderfield**, Frank (CON - Great Totham)
cllr.frank.delderfield@maldon.gov.uk
***Leader of the Council:* Boyce**, Robert (CON - Althorne)
cllr.bob.boyce@maldon.gov.uk
***Deputy Leader of the Council:* Bass**, Henry (CON - Wickham Bishops and Woodham)
cllr.henry.bass@maldon.gov.uk
Tollesbury: Vacant
Archer, John (CON - Purleigh)
cllr.john.archer@maldon.gov.uk
Beale, Brian (IND - Southminster)
cllr.brian.beale@maldon.gov.uk
Beale, Anne (CON - Heybridge East)
cllr.anne.beale@maldon.gov.uk
Cain, Andrew (CON - Maldon South)
cllr.andrew.cain@maldon.gov.uk
Channer, Penny (CON - Mayland)
cllr.penny.channer@maldon.gov.uk
Cheshire, Alan (CON - Heybridge West)
cllr.alan.cheshire@maldon.gov.uk
Cussen, Antony (CON - Althorne)
cllr.anthony.cussen@maldon.gov.uk
Dewick, Richard (CON - Tillingham)
cllr.richard.dewick@maldon.gov.uk
Durham, Mark (CON - Wickham Bishops and Woodham)
cllr.mark.durham@maldon.gov.uk
Elliott, Peter (CON - Burnham South)
cllr.peter.elliott@maldon.gov.uk
Fluker, Adrian (CON - Southminster)
cllr.adrian.fluker@maldon.gov.uk
Harker, Brenda (CON - Maldon South)
cllr.brenda.harker@maldon.gov.uk
Harker, Bryan (CON - Heybridge East)
cllr.bryan.harker@maldon.gov.uk
Heard, Mark (IND - Maldon West)
cllr.mark.heard@maldon.gov.uk
Horner, David (CON - Mayland)
cllr.david.horner@maldon.gov.uk
Lewis, Miriam (CON - Heybridge West)
cllr.miriam.lewis@maldon.gov.uk
Long, Robert (CON - Tolleshunt D'Arcy)
cllr.robert.long@maldon.gov.uk
Pearlman, Michael (CON - Maldon North)
cllr.michael.pearlman@maldon.gov.uk
Pratt, Ron (CON - Burnham South)
cllr.ron.pratt@maldon.gov.uk
Pudney, Neil (CON - Burnham North)
cllr.neil.pudney@maldon.gov.uk
Savage, Stephen (CON - Maldon East)
cllr.stephen.savage@maldon.gov.uk
Shrimpton, Anthony (CON - Maldon North)
cllr.tony.shrimpton@maldon.gov.uk
Sismey, David (CON - Great Totham)
cllr.david.sismey@maldon.gov.uk
Thompson, Maddie (CON - Tolleshunt D'Arcy)
cllr.maddie.thompson@maldon.gov.uk
White, Sue (CON - Purleigh)
cllr.sue.white@maldon.gov.uk
Wood, Mike (IND - Burnham North)
cllr.mike.wood@maldon.gov.uk

POLITICAL COMPOSITION

CON: 27, IND: 3, Vacant: 1

CABINET

Leader: Mr Robert Boyce
Deputy Leader: Mr Henry Bass

COMMITTEE CHAIRS

Audit Committee: Mr David Horner
Community Services: Mrs Brenda Harker

Finance & Corporate Services: Mr David Sismey
Overview & Scrutiny (Scrutiny): Mr Antony Cussen
Planning & Licensing: Mrs Penny Channer
Standards Committee: Rev Anthony Shrimpton

MALVERN HILLS D

Malvern Hills District Council, Council House, Avenue Road, Malvern WR14 3AF ☎ 01684 862151 🖷 01684 862473 ✉ contactus@malvernhills.gov.uk 💻 www.malvernhills.gov.uk

FACTS & FIGURES

Police Authority: West Mercia Police Authority
Health Authority: NHS West Midlands
Learning and Skills Council: West Midlands
EU Constituencies: West Midlands
Election Frequency: Elections are of whole council
Twinning: Tenbury Wells: Frenkeneck (Germany); Pont-du-Casse (France)

PRINCIPAL OFFICERS

Chief Executive: Mr Chris Bocock, Chief Executive, Council House, Avenue Road, Malvern WR14 3AF ☎ 01684 862338 🖷 01684 862398 ✉ chris.bocock@malvernhills.gov.uk

Senior Management: Mr Andy Baldwin, Head of Resources, Council House, Avenue Road, Malvern WR14 3AF ☎ 01684 862235 ✉ andy.baldwin@malvernhills.gov.uk

Best Value: Mr John Williams, Head of Policy & Governance, Council House, Avenue Road, Malvern WR14 3AF ☎ 01684 862227 🖷 01684 862367 ✉ john.williams@malvernhills.gov.uk

Building Control: Mr Reza Saneie, Building Control Partnership Manager, Council House, Avenue Road, Malvern WR14 3AF ☎ 01684 862146; 01905 722233 ✉ reza.saneie@malvernhills.gov.uk

PR / Communications: Ms Jeanette Covington, Corporate Communications Officer, Council House, Avenue Road, Malvern WR14 3AF ☎ 01684 862333 ✉ jeanette.covington@malverhills.gov.uk

Community Planning: Mr Gary Williams, Head of Planning, Economy & Housing, Council House, Avenue Road, Malvern WR14 2TB ☎ 01684 862293 🖷 01684 862367 ✉ gary.williams@malvernhills.gov.uk

Contracts: Mr John Williams, Head of Policy & Governance, Council House, Avenue Road, Malvern WR14 3AF ☎ 01684 862227 🖷 01684 862367 ✉ john.williams@malvernhills.gov.uk

Corporate Services: Mr John Williams, Head of Policy & Governance, Council House, Avenue Road, Malvern WR14 3AF ☎ 01684 862227 🖷 01684 862367 ✉ john.williams@malvernhills.gov.uk

Customer Service: Mr Ivor Pumfrey, Head of Community Services, Council House, Avenue Road, Malvern WR14 3AF ☎ 01684 862296 🖷 01684 862367 ✉ ivor.pumfrey@malvernhills.gov.uk

Direct Labour: Mr Alex Bill, Operations Manager, Council House, Avenue Road, Malvern WR14 3AF ☎ 01684 862401 🖷 01684 576781 ✉ alex.bill@malvernhills.gov.uk

E-Government: Mr Andy Baldwin, Head of Resources, Council House, Avenue Road, Malvern WR14 3AF ☎ 01684 862235 ✉ andy.baldwin@malvernhills.gov.uk

Electoral Registration: Ms Mary Wood, Electoral Services Manager, Council House, Avenue Road, Malvern WR14 3AF ☎ 01684 862212 🖷 01684 862367 ✉ mary.wood@malvernhills.gov.uk

Emergency Planning: Mr John Williams, Head of Policy & Governance, Council House, Avenue Road, Malvern WR14 3AF ☎ 01684 862227 🖷 01684 862367 ✉ john.williams@malvernhills.gov.uk

Energy Management: Mr David Hawley, Technical Services Manager, Council House, Avenue Road, Malvern WR14 3AF ☎ 01684 862365 🖷 01684 862367 ✉ dave.hawley@malvernhills.gov.uk

Environmental / Technical Services: Mr David Hawley, Technical Services Manager, Council House, Avenue Road, Malvern WR14 3AF ☎ 01684 862365 🖷 01684 862367 ✉ dave.hawley@malvernhills.gov.uk

Environmental Health: Mr Ivor Pumfrey, Head of Community Services, Council House, Avenue Road, Malvern WR14 3AF ☎ 01684 862296 🖷 01684 862367 ✉ ivor.pumfrey@malvernhills.gov.uk

Estates, Property & Valuation: Mr Nigel Snape, Head of Legal & Governance, Council House, Avenue Road, Malvern WR14 3AF ☎ 01684 892213 🖷 ; 01684 862367 ✉ nigel.snape@malvernhills.gov.uk

Facilities: Mr Nigel Snape, Head of Legal & Governance, Council House, Avenue Road, Malvern WR14 3AF ☎ 01684 892213 🖷 01684 862367 ✉ nigel.snape@malvernhills.gov.uk

Finance and Treasurer: Mr Andy Baldwin, Head of Resources, Council House, Avenue Road, Malvern WR14 3AF ☎ 01684 862235 ✉ andy.baldwin@malvernhills.gov.uk

Fleet Management: Mr Alex Bill, Operations Manager, Council House, Avenue Road, Malvern WR14 3AF ☎ 01684 862401 🖷 01684 576781 ✉ alex.bill@malvernhills.gov.uk

Grounds Maintenance: Mr Alex Bill, Operations Manager, Council House, Avenue Road, Malvern WR14 3AF ☎ 01684 862401 🖷 01684 576781 ✉ alex.bill@malvernhills.gov.uk

Health and Safety: Mr Philip Bowles, Health & Safety Officer, Council House, Avenue Road, Malvern WR14 3AF ☎ 01684 862747 🖷 01684 862367 ✉ philip.bowles@malvernhills.gov.uk

Housing: Mr Gary Williams, Head of Planning, Economy & Housing, Council House, Avenue Road, Malvern WR14 2TB ☎ 01684 862293 🖷 01684 862367 ✉ gary.williams@malvernhills.gov.uk

Legal: Mr Nigel Snape, Head of Legal & Governance, Council House, Avenue Road, Malvern WR14 3AF ☎ 01684 892213 🖷 01684 862367 ✉ nigel.snape@malvernhills.gov.uk

Leisure and Cultural Services: Mr Ivor Pumfrey, Head of Community Services, Council House, Avenue Road, Malvern WR14 3AF ☎ 01684 862296 🖷 01684 862367 ✉ ivor.pumfrey@malvernhills.gov.uk

Licensing: Mr Niall McMenamin, Licensing Officer, Worcestershire Regulatory Services, Wyatt House, Farrier Street, Worcester WR1 3BH ☎ 07970 145044 ✉ niall.mcmenamin@malvernhills.gov.uk

Lifelong Learning: Miss Tina Beckett, Learning & Development Officer, Council House, Avenue Road, Malvern WR14 3AF ☎ 01684 862363 🖷 01684 862367 ✉ tina.beckett@malvernhills.gov.uk

Member Services: Mr David Hawley, Technical Services Manager, Council House, Avenue Road, Malvern WR14 3AF ☎ 01684 862365 🖷 01684 862474 ✉ dave.hawley@malvernhills.gov.uk

Member Services: Mr Nigel Snape, Head of Legal & Governance, Council House, Avenue Road, Malvern WR14 3AF ☎ 01684 892213 🖷 01684 862367 ✉ nigel.snape@malvernhills.gov.uk

Parking: Mr Ivor Pumfrey, Head of Community Services, Council House, Avenue Road, Malvern WR14 3AF ☎ 01684 862296 🖷 01684 862367 ✉ ivor.pumfrey@malvernhills.gov.uk

Personnel / HR: Mr Andy Baldwin, Head of Resources, Council House, Avenue Road, Malvern WR14 3AF ☎ 01684 862235 ✉ andy.baldwin@malvernhills.gov.uk

Personnel / HR: Ms Kim Stallard, Personnel Manager, Council House, Avenue Road, Malvern WR14 3AF ☎ 01684 862379 🖷 01684 862367 ✉ kim.stallard@malvernhills.gov.uk

Planning: Mr Gary Williams, Head of Planning, Economy & Housing, Council House, Avenue Road, Malvern WR14 2TB ☎ 01684 862293 🖷 01684 862367 ✉ gary.williams@malvernhills.gov.uk

Procurement: Mr Dave Billings, Business Support Manager, Council House, Avenue Road, Malvern WR14 3AF ☎ 01684 862352 ✉ dave.billings@malvernhills.gov.uk

Recycling & Waste Minimisation: Mr Alex Bill, Operations Manager, Council House, Avenue Road, Malvern WR14 3AF ☎ 01684 862401 🖷 01684 576781 ✉ alex.bill@malvernhills.gov.uk

Staff Training: Miss Tina Beckett, Learning & Development Officer, Council House, Avenue Road, Malvern WR14 3AF ☎ 01684 862363 🖷 01684 862367 ✉ tina.beckett@malvernhills.gov.uk

Street Scene: Mr Ivor Pumfrey, Head of Community Services, Council House, Avenue Road, Malvern WR14 3AF ☎ 01684 862296 🖷 01684 862367 ✉ ivor.pumfrey@malvernhills.gov.uk

Tourism: Mr Simon Smith, Economic Development Manager, Council House, Avenue Road, Malvern WR14 3AF ☎ 01684 862199 🖷 ; 01684 862367 ✉ simon.smith@malvernhills.gov.uk

Transport: Mr Simon Smith, Economic Development Manager, Council House, Avenue Road, Malvern WR14 3AF ☎ 01684 862199 🖷 ; 01684 862367 ✉ simon.smith@malvernhills.gov.uk

Waste Collection and Disposal: Mr Alex Bill, Operations Manager, Council House, Avenue Road, Malvern WR14 3AF ☎ 01684 862401 🖷 01684 576781 ✉ alex.bill@malvernhills.gov.uk

Waste Management: Mr Alex Bill, Operations Manager, Council House, Avenue Road, Malvern WR14 3AF ☎ 01684 862401 🖷 01684 576781 ✉ alex.bill@malvernhills.gov.uk

MEMBERS OF THE COUNCIL (38)

***Chair:* Tuthill**, Paul (CON - Link)
paul.tuthill@malvernhills.gov.uk
***Vice-Chair:* Sutton**, Roger (IND - Ripple)
roger.sutton@malvernhills.gov.uk
***Leader of the Council:* Hughes**, David (CON - Alfrick and Leigh)
david.hughes@malvernhills.gov.uk
***Deputy Leader of the Council:* Swinburn**, Paul (CON - Broadheath)
paul.swinburn@malvernhills.gov.uk
***Group Leader:* Wells**, Tom (LD - Powick)
tom.wells@malvernhills.gov.uk
Bass, Roger (CON - Broadheath)
roger.bass@malvernhills.gov.uk
Behan, Bronwen (CON - Longdon)
bronwen.behan@malvernhills.gov.uk
Brown, Steve (LD - Chase)
steve.brown@malvernhills.gov.uk
Campbell, Jill (CON - Wells)
jill.campbell@malvernhills.gov.uk
Campbell, Hannah (CON - Priory)
hannah.campbell@malvernhills.gov.uk
Cheeseman, Chris (CON - Wells)
chris.cheeseman@malvernhills.gov.uk
Clarke, Dean (LD - Hallow)
dean.clarke@malvernhills.gov.uk
Cousins, Roger (LD - Morton)
roger.cousins@malvernhills.gov.uk
Cumming, Paul (CON - Woodbury)
paul.cumming@malvernhills.gov.uk
Farmer, Gill (CON - Teme Valley)
gill.farmer@malvernhills.gov.uk
Gill, Susan (CON - Baldwin)
susan.gill@malvernhills.gov.uk
Grove, Phillip (CON - Tenbury)
phillip.grove@malvernhills.gov.uk
Hall-Jones, Roger (CON - Priory)
roger.hall-jones@malvernhills.gov.uk
Harding, Roy (CON - Chase)
roy.harding@malvernhills.gov.uk
Harrison, David (IND - Kempsey)
david.harrison@malvernhills.gov.uk
Marriott, Janet (LD - Dyson Perrins)
janet.marriott@malvernhills.gov.uk
Massey, Rebecca (CON - Chase)
rebecca.massey@malvernhills.gov.uk
Morgan, Mike (CON - Upton and Hanley)

mike.morgan@malvernhills.gov.uk
Myatt, Valerie (LD - Pickersleigh)
valerie.myatt@malvernhills.gov.uk
Myatt, Graham (LD - Dyson Perrins)
graham.myatt@malvernhills.gov.uk
Newman, Elaine (LD - Powick)
elaine.newman@malvernhills.gov.uk
Penn, Tony (CON - Tenbury)
tony.penn@malvernhills.gov.uk
Perry, Tim (IND - Upton and Hanley)
timothy.perry@malvernhills.gov.uk
Pilcher, Brian (LD - Pickersliegh)
brian.pilcher@malvernhills.gov.uk
Raine, John (GRN - West)
john.raine@malvernhills.gov.uk
Rea, Adam (IND - Kempsey)
adam.rea@malvernhills.gov.uk
Redman, Will (CON - Lindbridge)
Roskams, Julian (GRN - West)
julian.roskams@malvernhills.gov.uk
Smith, Clive (LD - Link)
clive.smith@malvernhills.gov.uk
Soley, Michael (CON - Link)
michael.soley@malvernhills.gov.uk
Warburton, Anthony (CON - Alfrick and Leigh)
anthony.warburton@malvernhills.gov.uk
Williams, Barbara (CON - Martley)
barbara.williams@malvernhills.gov.uk
Young, Sheila (LD - Pickersleigh)
sheila.young@malvernhills.gov.uk

POLITICAL COMPOSITION

CON: 21, LD: 11, IND: 4, GRN: 2

COMMITTEE CHAIRS

Licensing & Appeals: Ms Gill Farmer
Licensing: Ms Gill Farmer
Overview & Scrutiny: Mr Tom Wells
Planning: Mr Tony Penn
Standards: Mr T Lyons (TBC July 2010) (External)
Waste Management: Mrs Bronwen Behan

MANCHESTER CITY — M

Manchester City Council, PO Box 532, Town Hall, Albert Square, Manchester M60 2AF ☎ 0161 234 5000
manchester@manchester.gov.uk www.manchester.gov.uk

FACTS & FIGURES

Police Authority: Greater Manchester Police Authority
Health Authority: North West Strategic Health Authority
Learning and Skills Council: North West
Parliamentary Constituencies: Blackley and Broughton, Manchester Central, Manchester, Gorton, Manchester, Withington, Wythenshawe and Sale East
EU Constituencies: North West
Election Frequency: Elections are by thirds
Twinning: Wuhan (China), Chemnitz (Germany), Rohovot (Israel), St Petersburg (Russia), Bilwi (Nicaragua)

PRINCIPAL OFFICERS

Chief Executive: Sir Howard Bernstein, Chief Executive, PO Box 532 , Town Hall, Albert Square, Manchester M60 2LA ☎ 0161 234 3006 🖷 0161 234 3098 h.bernstein@manchester.gov.uk

Deputy Chief Executive: Mr Geoff Little, Deputy Chief Executive (Performance), PO Box 532, Town Hall, Albert Square, Manchester M60 2AF ☎ 0161 234 3280 🖷 0161 236 2959 g.little@manchester.gov.uk

Deputy Chief Executive: Ms Vicky Rosin, Deputy Chief Executive (Neighbourhoods), PO Box 532, Town Hall, Albert Square, Manchester M60 2AF ☎ 0161 234 3718 🖷 0161 274 7005 v.rosin@manchester.gov.uk

Assistant Chief Executive: Ms Carol Culley, Assistant Chief Executive (Finance & Performance), PO Box 532, Town Hall, Albert Square, Manchester M60 2AF ☎ 0161 234 3406 🖷 0161 234 3435 c.culley@manchester.gov.uk

Assistant Chief Executive: Ms Sharon Kemp, Assistant Chief Executive (People), PO Box 532, Town Hall, Albert Square, Manchester M60 2AF ☎ 0161 234 1145 s.kemp@manchester.gov.uk

Assistant Chief Executive: Mr Sean McGonigle, Assistant Chief Executive (Neighbourhood Strategy & Delivery), PO Box 532, Town Hall, Albert Square, Manchester M60 2AF ☎ 0161 234 4821 🖷 0161 274 7117 s.mcgonigle@manchester.gov.uk

Assistant Chief Executive: Ms Sara Todd, Assistant Chief Executive (Regeneration), PO Box 532, Town Hall, Albert Square, Manchester M60 2AF ☎ 0161 234 3286 🖷 0161 274 7003 s.todd@manchester.gov.uk

Assistant Chief Executive: Ms Sara Tomkins, Assistant Chief Executive (Communications, Customer & ICT), PO Box 532, Town Hall, Albert Square, Manchester M60 2AF ☎ 0161 234 3706 🖷 0161 274 0034 s.tomkins@manchester.gov.uk

Senior Management: Ms Jenny Andrews, Deputy Director (Children's Services), Town Hall, Albert Square, Manchester M60 2LA ☎ 0161 234 3804 🖷 0161 276 7629 j.andrews@manchester.gov.uk

Senior Management: Mrs Liz Bruce, Strategic Director (Adults, Health & Wellbeing), Town Hall, Albert Square, Manchester M60 2LA ☎ 0161 234 3952 🖷 0161 234 7058 l.bruce@manchester.gov.uk

Senior Management: Mr Mike Livingstone, Strategic Director (Children's Services), Town Hall, Albert Square, Manchester M60 2LA ☎ 0161 234 3804 🖷 0161 276 7629 m.livingstone@manchester.gov.uk

Senior Management: Ms Susan Orrell, City Solicitor, PO Box 532, Town Hall, Albert Square, Manchester M60 2LA ☎ 0161 234 3087 🖷 0161 234 3098 s.orrell@manchester.gov.uk

Senior Management: Mr Richard Paver, City Treasurer, PO Box 314, Town Hall, Albert Square, Manchester M60 2JR ☎ 0161 234 3564 🖷 0161 274 7015 r.paver@manchester.gov.uk

Senior Management: Mr Eddie Smith, Chief Executive of New East Manachester Ltd, 187 Grey Mare Lane, Beswick, Manchester

M11 3ND ☎ 0161 223 1155 🖷 0161 230 8966 ✉ e.smith@manchester.gov.uk

Building Control: Mr David Lea, Director (Commercial Serivces), PO Box 536, Town Hall Extension, Albert Square, Manchester M60 2AF ☎ 0161 234 4808 🖷 0161 274 7047 ✉ d.lea@manchester.gov.uk

Children / Youth Services: Ms Jenny Andrews, Deputy Director (Children's Services), 5th Floor, Overseas House, Quay Street, Manchester M3 3BB ☎ 0161 234 3804 🖷 0161 276 7629 ✉ j.andrews@manchester.gov.uk

Children / Youth Services: Mr Mike Livingstone, Strategic Director (Children's Services), Overseas House, Quay Street, Manchester M3 3BB ☎ 0161 234 3804 🖷 0161 276 7629 ✉ m.livingstone@manchester.gov.uk

Civil Registration: Ms Susan Orrell, City Solicitor, PO Box 532, Town Hall, Albert Square, Manchester M60 2LA ☎ 0161 234 3087 🖷 0161 234 3098 ✉ s.orrell@manchester.gov.uk

PR / Communications: Ms Sara Tomkins, Assistant Chief Executive (Communications, Customer & ICT), PO Box 532, Town Hall, Albert Square, Manchester M60 2AF ☎ 0161 234 3706 🖷 0161 274 0034 ✉ s.tomkins@manchester.gov.uk

Community Safety: Ms Vicky Charles, Strategic Lead (Crime & Disorder), Bootle Street Police Station, Bootle Street, Manchester M2 5GU ☎ 0161 856 9269 ✉ v.charles@manchester.gov.uk

Computer Management: Ms Karen Johnson, Head of Information & Communication Technology Service, PO Box 532, Town Hall, Albert Square, Manchester M60 2AF ☎ 0161 234 5997 ✉ karen.johnson@manchester.gov.uk

Consumer Protection and Trading Standards: Ms Janet Shaw, Citywide Support Team Lead - Trading Standards, Hammerstone Road Depot, Gorton, Manchester M18 8EQ ☎ 0161 234 1587 🖷 0161 274 7239 ✉ j.shaw@manchester.gov.uk

Contracts: Mr Ian Brown, Head of Corporate Procurement, Manchester City Council, Town Hall, Albert Square, Manchester M60 2JR ☎ 0161 234 3255 🖷 0161 274 7015 ✉ i.brown1@manchester.gov.uk

Corporate Services: Mr John Lorimer, Capital Programme Director, Manchester City Council, 5th Floor, Heron House, 47 Lloyd Street, Manchester M2 5LE ☎ 0161 219 6501 🖷 0161 274 7106 ✉ j.lorimer@manchester.gov.uk

Corporate Services: Mr Richard Paver, City Treasurer, PO Box 314, Town Hall, Albert Square, Manchester M60 2JR ☎ 0161 234 3564 🖷 0161 274 7015 ✉ r.paver@manchester.gov.uk

Customer Service: Mr Lee Owen, Head of Customer Services, Manchester City Council, Level 4, One First Street, Manchester M1 5DE ☎ 0161 245 7525 ✉ l.owen@manchester.gov.uk

Customer Service: Ms Sara Tomkins, Assistant Chief Executive (Communications, Customer & ICT), PO Box 532, Town Hall, Albert Square, Manchester M60 2AF ☎ 0161 234 3706 🖷 0161 274 0034 ✉ s.tomkins@manchester.gov.uk

Direct Labour: Mr Mike Brogan, Operations Manager, Manchester City Council, Hopper Street Depot, Ardwick, Manchester M12 6LA ☎ 0161 908 5840 🖷 0161 908 5858 ✉ m.brogan@manchester.gov.uk

Economic Development: Ms Sara Todd, Assistant Chief Executive (Regeneration), PO Box 532, Town Hall, Albert Square, Manchester M60 2LA ☎ 0161 234 3286 🖷 0161 274 7003 ✉ s.todd@manchester.gov.uk

Electoral Registration: Ms Michelle Chard, Head of Democratic Services, PO Box 536, Town Hall Extension, Manchester M60 2AF ☎ 0161 234 4098 🖷 0161 274 7007 ✉ m.chard@manchester.gov.uk

Emergency Planning: Ms Lucy Kennon, Head of Civil Contingencies, PO Box 532, Town Hall, Albert Square, Manchester M60 2AF ☎ 0161 234 4444 🖷 0161 274 7143 ✉ l.kennon@manchester.gov.uk

Energy Management: Mr Walter Dooley, Energy Manager, Energy Management Unit, Town Hall, Albert Square, Manchester M60 3NY ☎ 0161 234 3633 🖷 0161 236 0357 ✉ w.dooley@manchester.gov.uk

Environmental / Technical Services: Mr Richard Sharland, Head of Environmental Strategy (Neighbourhood Services), PO Box 532, Town Hall, Albert Square, Manchester M60 2AF ☎ 0161 234 3232 ✉ r.sharland@manchester.gov.uk

Environmental Health: Ms Louise Barton, Project Manager (Environmental Strategy Manager), PO Box 532, Town Hall, Albert Square, Manchester M60 2AF ☎ 0161 234 4234 ✉ l.barton@manchester.gov.uk

Estates, Property & Valuation: Ms Helen Jones, Head of Corporate Property, Town Hall Extension, Manchester M60 2AX ☎ 0161 234 3701 🖷 0161 234 1257 ✉ h.jones4@manchester.gov.uk

Events Manager: Mr Mike Parrott, Head of Events, Floor 4, 1 First Street, Manchester M15 4FN ☎ 0161 234 5242 ✉ m.parrott@manchester.gov.uk

Finance and Treasurer: Mr Richard Paver, City Treasurer, PO Box 314, Town Hall, Albert Square, Manchester M60 2JR ☎ 0161 234 3564 🖷 0161 274 7015 ✉ r.paver@manchester.gov.uk

Fleet Management: Ms Elaine Heggie, Head of Business Units, PO Box 532, Town Hall, Albert Square, Manchester M60 2AF ☎ 0161 234 1290 🖷 0161 274 7336 ✉ e.heggie@manchester.gov.uk

Health and Safety: Mr Simon Gardiner, Personnel Manager, Health, Safety & Welfare, PO Box 532, Town Hall, Albert Square, Manchester M60 2AF ☎ 0161 234 1851 🖷 0161 274 7229 ✉ s.gardiner@manchester.gov.uk

Health and Safety: Mr David Regan, Director of Public Health for Manchester, PO Box 532, Town Hall, Albert Square,

Manchester M60 2LA ☎ 0161 234 3981 🖷 0161 234 3269 ⌂ d.regan@manchester.gov.uk

Highways: Mr Kevin Gillham, Citywide Highway Manager, Hammerstone Road, Gorton, Manchester M18 8EQ ☎ 0161 234 5148 🖷 0161 908 5716 ⌂ k.gillham@manchester.gov.uk

Housing: Mr Paul Beardmore, Director (Housing), Town Hall Extension, Manchester M60 2JX ☎ 0161 234 4811 🖷 0161 234 4232 ⌂ p.beardmore@manchester.gov.uk

Local Area Agreement: Mr Geoff Little, Deputy Chief Executive (Performance), PO Box 532, Town Hall, Albert Square, Manchester M60 2LA ☎ 0161 234 3280 🖷 0161 236 2959 ⌂ g.little@manchester.gov.uk

Legal: Ms Susan Orrell, City Solicitor, PO Box 532, Town Hall, Albert Square, Manchester M60 2LA ☎ 0161 234 3087 🖷 0161 234 3098 ⌂ s.orrell@manchester.gov.uk

Legal: Ms Liz Treacy, Head of Legal Services, PO Box 532, Town Hall, Albert Square, Manchester M2 5DB ☎ 0161 234 3339 🖷 0161 274 0041 ⌂ l.treacy@manchester.gov.uk

Leisure and Cultural Services: Ms Maria Balshaw, Director of Manchester City Galleries, Manchester City Art Galleries, Mosley Street, Manchester M2 3JL ☎ 0161 235 8801 🖷 0161 274 7146 ⌂ m.balshaw@manchester.gov.uk

Leisure and Cultural Services: Mr Eamonn O'Rourke, Head of Community & Cultural Services, PO Box 532, Town Hall, Albert Square, Manchester M60 2AF ☎ 0161 219 6946 ⌂ e.orourke@manchester.gov.uk

Leisure and Cultural Services: Ms Fran Toms, Head of Culture, Town Hall, Albert Square, Manchester M60 2LA ☎ 0161 234 4256 🖷 0161 234 4202 ⌂ f.toms@manchester.gov.uk

Licensing: Ms Jenette Hicks, Licensing Unit Manager, Hammerstone Road, Gorton, Manchester M18 8YU ☎ 0161 234 4962 🖷 0161 234 8396 ⌂ j.hicks@manchester.gov.uk

Member Services: Mr Donald Connolly, Governance & Scrutiny Support Unit Manager, PO Box 532, Town Hall, Albert Square, Manchester M60 2LA ☎ 0161 234 3336 🖷 0161 274 7017 ⌂ d.connolly@manchester.gov.uk

Member Services: Ms Nicola Fernley, Head of Member Services, PO Box 532, Town Hall, Albert Square, Manchester M60 2AF ☎ 0161 234 4289 🖷 0161 274 7009 ⌂ n.fernley@manchester.gov.uk

Partnerships: Ms Sarah Henry, Head of Research & Performance, PO Box 532, Town Hall, Albert Square, Manchester M60 2AF ☎ 0161 234 7650 ⌂ s.henry@manchester.gov.uk

Partnerships: Mr Geoff Little, Deputy Chief Executive (Performance), PO Box 532, Town Hall, Albert Square, Manchester M60 2LA ☎ 0161 234 3280 🖷 0161 236 2959 ⌂ g.little@manchester.gov.uk

Partnerships: Ms Nicky Parker, Head of Transformation, PO Box 532, Town Hall, Albert Square, Manchester M60 2AF ☎ 0161 219 6948 🖷 0161 274 7029 ⌂ n.parker@manchester.gov.uk

Personnel / HR: Ms Sharon Kemp, Assistant Chief Executive (People), PO Box 532, Town Hall, Albert Square, Manchester M60 2AF ☎ 0161 234 1145 ⌂ s.kemp@manchester.gov.uk

Planning: Ms Julie Roscoe, Head of Planning, PO Box 532, Town Hall, Albert Square, Manchester M60 2AF ☎ 0161 234 4552 🖷 0161 234 4508 ⌂ j.roscoe@manchester.gov.uk

Procurement: Mr Ian Brown, Head of Corporate Procurement, Manchester City Council, Town Hall, Albert Square, Manchester M60 2JR ☎ 0161 234 3255 🖷 0161 274 7015 ⌂ i.brown1@manchester.gov.uk

Public Libraries: Mr Neil MacInnes, Libraries Strategic Lead, City Library, Elliot House, 151 Deansgate, Manchester M3 3WD ☎ 0161 234 1392 🖷 0161 274 7053 ⌂ n.macinnes@libraries.manchester.gov.uk

Recycling & Waste Minimisation: Mr Paul Castle, Acting Head of Waste Management, New East Manchester, 187 Grey Mare Lane, Beswick, Manchester M11 3ND ☎ 0161 223 1155 ⌂ p.castle@manchester.gov.uk

Regeneration: Ms Sara Todd, Assistant Chief Executive (Regeneration), PO Box 532, Town Hall, Albert Square, Manchester M60 2LA ☎ 0161 234 3286 🖷 0161 274 7003 ⌂ s.todd@manchester.gov.uk

Road Safety: Mr Mel Kirby, Road Safety Officer, Level 7, Wenlock Way Office, Wenlock Way, Manchester M12 5DH ☎ 0161 953 2666 🖷 0151 274 7027 ⌂ m.kirby@manchester.gov.uk

Social Services (Adult): Mrs Liz Bruce, Strategic Director (Adults, Health & Wellbeing), PO Box 532, Town Hall, Albert Square, Manchester M60 2AF ☎ 0161 234 3952 🖷 0161 234 7058 ⌂ l.bruce@manchester.gov.uk

Social Services (Adult): Mrs Diane Eaton, Assistant Director (Integrated Community Provision), PO Box 532, Town Hall, Albert Square, Manchester M60 2AF ☎ 0161 234 3909 ⌂ diane.eaton@manchester.gov.uk

Social Services (Adult): Mrs Fionnuala Stringer, Assistant Director (Integration & Partnerships), PO Box 536, Town Hall Exentsion, Manchester M60 2AF ☎ 0161 234 3806 🖷 0161 274 7058 ⌂ fionnuala.stringer@manchester.gov.uk

Staff Training: Mr Andrew Wales, Operations Manager - Learning & Events Team, PO Box 532, Town Hall, Albert Square, Manchester M60 2AF ☎ 0161 234 3260 🖷 0161 274 7132 ⌂ a.wales@manchester.gov.uk

Street Scene: Mr Erle Gardner, Group Manager - Street Scene Services, Hooper Street Depot, Off Midland Street, Manchester M12 6LA ☎ 0161 908 5806 🖷 0161 908 5858 ⌂ e.gardner@manchester.gov.uk

Sustainable Communities: Mr Paul Castle, Acting Head of Waste Management, New East Manchester, 187 Grey Mare Lane,

Manchester M11 3NQ ☎ 0161 223 1155
✉ p.castle@manchester.gov.uk

Sustainable Communities: Ms Rachel Christie, Strategic Area Manager - City Wide & Wythenshawe, Hammerstone Road, Gorton, Manchester M18 8EQ ☎ 0161 234 4916 🖷 0161 234 4872
✉ r.christie@manchester.gov.uk

Sustainable Communities: Mr Mark Glynn, Strategic Area Manager - South Manager, Level One, Number One First Street, Manchester M15 4FN ☎ 0161 245 7580 🖷 0161 274 0023
✉ m.glynn@manchester.gov.uk

Sustainable Communities: Ms Fiona Sharkey, Strategic Area Manager - North Manchester, Harpurhey District Office, 8 Moston Lane, Manchester M9 4DP ☎ 0161 234 1567 🖷 0161 274 7245
✉ f.sharkey@machester.gov.uk

Sustainable Development: Ms Beverley Taylor, Head of Community & Customer Engagement, Level 3, Pink Bank Lane, Manchester M12 5QN ☎ 0161 234 4234 🖷 0161 274 7068
✉ b.taylor@manchester.gov.uk

Traffic Management: Mr Kevin Gillham, Citywide Highway Manager, Hammerstone Road, Gorton, Manchester M18 8EQ
☎ 0161 234 5148 🖷 0161 908 5716 ✉ k.gillham@manchester.gov.uk

Transport: Mr Gary Campin, Fleet Services Manager, Fleet Services, Hammerstone Road, Gorton, Manchester M18 8EQ
☎ 0161 957 8418 🖷 0161 274 8239 ✉ g.campin@manchester.gov.uk

Transport Planner: Ms Penny Boothman, Head of Greater Manchester Integrated Support Team & Deputy Clerk of TFGMC, PO Box 532, Town Hall, Albert Square, Manchester M60 2LA
☎ 0161 234 3124 🖷 0161 234 4021
✉ p.boothman@manchester.gov.uk

Total Place: Mr Geoff Little, Deputy Chief Executive (Performance), PO Box 532, Town Hall, Albert Square, Manchester M60 2AF ☎ 0161 234 3280 🖷 0161 236 2959
✉ g.little@manchester.gov.uk

MEMBERS OF THE COUNCIL (96)

***The Lord Mayor:* Boyes**, Elaine (LD - City Centre)
cllr.e.boyes@manchester.gov.uk
***Leader of the Council:* Leese**, Richard (LAB - Crumpsall)
cllr.r.leese@manchester.gov.uk
***Deputy Leader of the Council:* Murphy**, Sue (LAB - Brooklands)
cllr.s.murphy@manchester.gov.uk
Adams, Bridie (LAB - Didsbury East)
cllr.b.adams@manhester.gov.uk
Ahmed, Aftab (LAB - Levenshulme)
cllr.a.ahmed@manchester.gov.uk
Akbar, Rabnawaz (LAB - Rusholme)
cllr.r.akbar@manchester.gov.uk
Ali, Ahmed (LAB - Rusholme)
cllr.a.ali@manchester.gov.uk
Ali, Shaukat (LAB - Cheetham)
cllr.shaukat.ali@manchester.gov.uk
Ali, Sameem (LAB - Moss Side)
cllr.s.ali@manchester.gov.uk
Amesbury, Michael Lee (LAB - Fallowfield)
cllr.m.amesbury@manchester.gov.uk
Andrews, Paul (LAB - Baguley)
cllr.p.andrews@manchester.gov.uk
Austin, Carl (LAB - Burnage)
cllr.c.austin@manchester.gov.uk
Barrett, Hugh (LAB - Sharston)
cllr.h.barrett@manchester.gov.uk
Battle, Jim (LAB - Ancoats and Clayton)
cllr.j.battle@manchester.gov.uk
Battle, Rosa (LAB - Bradford)
cllr.r.battle@manchester.gov.uk
Carmody, Mike (LAB - Ancoats and Clayton)
cllr.m.carmody@manchester.gov.uk
Chamberlain, Victor (LD - Chorlton)
cllr.v.chamberlain@manchester.gov.uk
Chappell, Kate (LAB - Rusholme)
cllr.k.chappell@manchester.gov.uk
Chohan, Abid (LAB - Longsight)
cllr.a.chohan@manchester.gov.uk
Clayton, Mark (LD - Didsbury West)
cllr.m.clayton@manchester.gov.uk
Cookson, Peter (LAB - Gorton South)
cllr.p.cookson@manchester.gov.uk
Cooley, Susan (LAB - Brooklands)
cllr.s.cooley@manchester.gov.uk
Cooper, Henry (LAB - Moston)
cllr.h.cooper@manchester.gov.uk
Cowell, Richard (LAB - Northenden)
cllr.r.cowell@manchester.gov.uk
Cox, Alistair (LAB - Moss Side)
cllr.a.cox@manchester.gov.uk
Craig, Bev (LAB - Burnage)
cllr.b.craig@manchester.gov.uk
Curley, Basil (LAB - Charlestown)
cllr.b.curley@manchester.gov.uk
Davies, Joan (LAB - City Centre)
cllr.j.davies@mamchester.gov.uk
Di Mauro, Mary (LD - Northenden)
cllr.m.dimauro@manchester.gov.uk
Ellison, David (LAB - Didsbury West)
cllr.d.ellison@manchester.gov.uk
Evans, Glynn (LAB - Brooklands)
cllr.g.evans@manchester.gov.uk
Fairweather, Paul (LAB - Harpurhey)
cllr.p.fairweather@manchester.gov.uk
Fender, Andrew (LAB - Old Moat)
cllr.a.fender@manchester.gov.uk
Fisher, Bill (LD - Burnage)
cllr.b.fisher@manchester.gov.uk
Flanagan, John (LAB - Miles Platting and Newton Heath)
cll.j.flanagan@manchester.gov.uk
Fletcher-Hackwood, Grace (LAB - Fallowfield)
cllr.g.fletcher-hackwood@manchester.gov.uk
Gillard, Daniel (LAB - Withington)
cllr.d.gillard@manchester.gov.uk
Green, Joanne (LAB - Harpurhey)
cllr.j.green@manchester.gov.uk
Grimshaw, Carmine (LAB - Miles Platting and Newton Heath)
cllr.c.grimshaw@manchester.gov.uk
Hackett, Mark (LAB - Charlestown)
cllr.m.hackett@manchester.gov.uk
Hennigan, James (LD - Levenshulme)
cllr.j.hennigan@manchester.gov.uk
Hitchen, June (LAB - Miles Platting and Newton Heath)
cllr.j.hitchen@manchester.gov.uk

Hughes, Jon (LAB - Gorton North)
cllr.j.hughes@manchester.gov.uk
Hyde, Ian (LAB - Chorlton Park)
cllr.i.hyde@manchester.gov.uk
Judge, Thomas (LAB - Sharston)
cllr.t.judge@manchester.gov.uk
Kamal, Afia (LAB - Gorton North)
cllr.a.kamal@manchester.gov.uk
Karney, Patrick (LAB - Harpurhey)
cllr.p.karney@manchester.gov.uk
Keegan, Con (LAB - Crumpsall)
cllr.c.keegan@manchester.gov.uk
Keller, Joyce (LAB - Sharston)
cllr.j.keller@manchester.gov.uk
Khan, Afzal (LAB - Cheetham)
cllr.a.khan@manchester.gov.uk
Kirkpartick, Veronica (LAB - Charlestown)
cllr.v.kirkpatrick@manchester.gov.uk
Lanchbury, Shelley (LAB - Higher Blackley)
cllr.s.lanchbury@machester.gov.uk
Lewis, Norman (LD - Chorlton Park)
cllr.n.lewis@manchester.gov.uk
Lone, Amina (LAB - Hulme)
cllr.a.lone@manchester.gov.uk
Longsden, John (LAB - Bradford)
cllr.j.longsden@manchester.gov.uk
Loughman, Mick (LAB - Ancoats and Clayton)
cllr.m.loughman@manchester.gov.uk
Lyons, Harold (LAB - Higher Blackley)
cllr.h.lyons@manchester.gov.uk
Midgley, Joanna (LAB - Chorlton Park)
cllr.j.midgley@manchester.gov.uk
Murphy, Paul (LAB - Moston)
cllr.p.murphy@manchester.gov.uk
Murphy, Mary (LAB - Hulme)
cllr.m.murphy@manchester.gov.uk
Murphy, Nigel (LAB - Hulme)
cllr.n.murphy@manchester.gov.uk
Newman, Sheila (LAB - Chorlton)
cllr.s.newman@manchester.gov.uk
Newman, Eddy (LAB - Woodhouse Park)
cllr.e.newman@manchester.gov.uk
O'Callaghan, Tom (LAB - Ardwick)
cllr.t.o'callaghan@manchester.gov.uk
Ollerhead, Carl (LAB - Didsbury West)
Cllr.c.ollerhead@manchester.gov.uk
O'Neil, Brian (LAB - Woodhouse Park)
cllr.brian.oneil@manchester.gov.uk
O'Neil, Barbara (LAB - Woodhouse Park)
cllr.barbara.oneil@manchester.gov.uk
Paul, Chris (LAB - Withington)
cllr.c.paul@manchester.gov.uk
Peel, Kevin (LAB - City Centre)
cllr.k.peel@manchester.gov.uk
Priest, Bernard (LAB - Ardwick)
cllr.b.priest@manchester.gov.uk
Pritchard, Jon-Leigh (LAB - Crumpsall)
cllr.j.pritchard@manchester.gov.uk
Rahman, Luthfur (LAB - Longsight)
cllr.l.rahman@manchester.gov.uk
Raikes, Luke (LAB - Baguley)
cllr.l.raikes@manchester.gov.uk
Rawlins, Tracey (LAB - Baguley)
cllr.t.rawlins@manchester.gov.uk
Razaq, Aftab (LAB - Whalley Range)
cllr.a.razaq@manchester.gov.uk
Reeves, Suzannah (LAB - Old Moat)
cllr.s.reeves@manchester.gov.uk
Reid, Julie (LAB - Gorton South)
cllr.j.reid@manchester.gov.uk
Richards, Suzanne (LAB - Longsight)
cllr.s.richards@manchester.gov.uk
Royle, David (LAB - Fallowfield)
cllr.d.royle@manchester.gov.uk
Shone, Fran (LAB - Northenden)
cllr.f.shone@manchester.gov.uk
Siddiqi, Nilofar (LAB - Gorton North)
cllr.n.siddiqi@manchester.gov.uk
Simcock, Andrew (LAB - Didsbury East)
cllr.a.simcock@manchester.gov.uk
Smith, Jeff (LAB - Old Moat)
cllr.jeff.smith@manchester.gov.uk
Smitheman, Mavis (LAB - Ardwick)
mave@smitheman1.demon.co.uk
Stogia, Angeliki (LAB - Whalley Range)
cllr.a.stogia@manchester.gov.uk
Stone, Bernard (LAB - Gorton South)
cllr.b.stone@manchester.gov.uk
Strong, Matt (LAB - Chorlton)
cllr.m.strong@manchester.gov.uk
Swannick, Neil (LAB - Bradford)
cllr.n.swannick@manchester.gov.uk
Tavernor, Rita (LAB - Moston)
cllr.r.tavernor@manchester.gov.uk
Taylor, Andrew (LD - Didsbury East)
cllr.a.taylor@manchester.gov.uk
Trotman, Anna (LAB - Higher Blackley)
cllr.a.trotman@manchester.gov.uk
Ul-Hassan, Naeem (LAB - Cheetham)
cllr.n.hassan@manchester.gov.uk
Walters, Roy (LAB - Moss Side)
cllr.r.walters@manchester.gov.uk
Ward, Nasrin (LAB - Levenshulme)
cllr.n.ali@manchester.gov.uk
Watson, Mary (LAB - Whalley Range)
cllr.m.watson@manchester.gov.uk
Wheale, Simon (LD - Withington)
cllr.s.wheale@manchester.gov.uk

POLITICAL COMPOSITION

LAB: 87, LD: 9

CABINET

Leader: Sir Richard Leese
Deputy Leader: Ms Sue Murphy
Adult Services: Mr Glynn Evans
Children's Services: Mr Afzal Khan
Culture & Leisure: Ms Rosa Battle
Environment: Mr Nigel Murphy
Finance & Human Resources: Mr Jeff Smith
Neighbourhood Services: Mr Bernard Priest

COMMITTEE CHAIRS

Audit: Mr John Flanagan
Children & Young People (Scrutiny): Mr Mike Carmody
Communities & Neighbourhoods (Scrutiny): Mr Basil Curley
Communities: Mr Victor Chamberlain
Economy, Employment & Skills (Scrutiny): Ms Joanne Green

Economy: Ms Joanne Green
Health & Wellbeing (Scrutiny): Mr Eddy Newman
Licensing & Appeals: Ms June Hitchen
Licensing: Ms June Hitchen
Personnel: Mr Jeff Smith
Planning & Highways: Mr Mick Loughman
Standards: Mr J Snadden (External)

MANSFIELD D

Mansfield District Council, Civic Centre, Chesterfield Road South, Mansfield NG19 7BH ☎ 01623 463463 🖷 01623 463900 ✉ mdc@mansfield.gov.uk 💻 www.mansfield.gov.uk

FACTS & FIGURES

Police Authority: Nottinghamshire Police Authority
Health Authority: East Midlands Strategic Health Authority
Learning and Skills Council: East Midlands
Parliamentary Constituencies: Mansfield
EU Constituencies: East Midlands
Election Frequency: Elections are of whole council
Twinning: Heiligenhaus (Germany); Mansfield, Ohio (USA); Reutov (Russia); Stryj (Ukraine)

PRINCIPAL OFFICERS

Chief Executive: Mrs Ruth Marlow, Managing Director, Civic Centre, Chesterfield Road South, Mansfield NG19 7BH ☎ 01623 463045 🖷 01623 463999 ✉ rmarlow@mansfield.gov.uk

Architect, Building / Property Services: Mr Philip Colledge, Principal General Practice Surveyor & Corporate Asset Manager, Civic Centre, Chesterfield Road South, Mansfield NG19 7BH ☎ 01623 463463 🖷 01623 463900 ✉ pcolledge@mansfield.gov.uk

Architect, Building / Property Services: Mr Brian Holmes, Architecture & Facilities Manager, Civic Centre, Chesterfield Road South, Mansfield NG19 7BH ☎ 01623 463463 ✉ bholmes@mansfield.gov.uk

Architect, Building / Property Services: Mr Steve Melhuish, Group Architect, Civic Centre, Chesterfield Road South, Mansfield NG19 7BH ☎ 01623 463463 ✉ smelhuish@mansfield.gov.uk

Building Control: Mr Martyn Saxton, Head of Planning, Community Safety & Regulatory Services, Civic Centre, Chesterfield Road South, Mansfield NG19 7BH ☎ 01623 463208 ✉ msaxton@mansfield.gov.uk

PR / Communications: Ms Carrie McMurdo, Senior Public Relations Officer, Civic Centre, Chesterfield Road South, Mansfield NG19 7BH ☎ 01623 463463 🖷 01623 463900 ✉ cmcmurdo@mansfield.gov.uk

Community Planning: Mr M Robinson, Head of Regeneration, Leisure & Marketing, Civic Centre, Chesterfield Road South, Mansfield NG19 7BH ☎ 01623 463900 ✉ mrobinson@mansfield.gov.uk

Community Safety: Mrs Bev Smith, Corporate Director - Regeneration & Regulation, Civic Centre, Chesterfield Road South, Mansfield NG19 7BH ☎ 01623 463463 🖷 01623 463900 ✉ bsmith@mansfield.gov.uk

Computer Management: Mrs Christine Marsh, ICT Manager, Civic Centre, Chesterfield Road South, Mansfield NG19 7BH ☎ 01623 463463 🖷 01623 463900 ✉ cmarsh@mansfield.gov.uk

Contracts: Mr Ajman Ali, Corporate Director - Housing & Environment, Civic Centre, Chesterfield Road South, Mansfield NG19 7BH ☎ 01623 463463 🖷 01623 463900 ✉ aali@mansfield.gov.uk

Contracts: Ms Anita Bradley, Head of Corporate Administration, Civic Centre, Chesterfield Road South, Mansfield NG19 7BH ☎ 01623 463463 🖷 01623 463900 ✉ abradley@mansfield.gov.uk

Corporate Services: Ms Anita Bradley, Head of Corporate Administration, Civic Centre, Chesterfield Road South, Mansfield NG19 7BH ☎ 01623 463463 ✉ abradley@mansfield.gov.uk

Customer Service: Mr Mick Andrews, Head of Finance, Property & Revenue Services, Civic Centre, Chesterfield Road South, Mansfield NG19 7BH ☎ 01623 463031 🖷 01623 463900 ✉ mandrews@mansfield.gov.uk

Direct Labour: Mr Martyn Thurman, Head of Neighbourhood Services, Civic Centre, Chesterfield Road South, Mansfield NG19 7BH ☎ 01623 463463 🖷 01623 463900 ✉ mthurman@mansfield.gov.uk

Economic Development: Mr M Robinson, Head of Regeneration, Leisure & Marketing, Civic Centre, Chesterfield Road South, Mansfield NG19 7BH ☎ 01623 463900 ✉ mrobinson@mansfield.gov.uk

E-Government: Mrs Christine Marsh, ICT Manager, Civic Centre, Chesterfield Road South, Mansfield NG19 7BH ☎ 01623 463463 🖷 01623 463900 ✉ cmarsh@mansfield.gov.uk

Electoral Registration: Ms Julie Jevons, Electoral Services Manager, Civic Centre, Chesterfield Road South, Mansfield NG19 7BH ☎ 01623 463463 Extn 3394 🖷 01623 463900 ✉ jjevons@mansfield.gov.uk

Emergency Planning: Mrs Bev Smith, Corporate Director - Regeneration & Regulation, Civic Centre, Chesterfield Road South, Mansfield NG19 7BH ☎ 01623 463463 🖷 01623 463900 ✉ bsmith@mansfield.gov.uk

Energy Management: Mr Ajman Ali, Corporate Director - Housing & Environment, Civic Centre, Chesterfield Road South, Mansfield NG19 7BH ☎ 01623 463463 🖷 01623 463900 ✉ aali@mansfield.gov.uk

Environmental / Technical Services: Mr Ajman Ali, Corporate Director - Housing & Environment, Civic Centre, Chesterfield Road South, Mansfield NG19 7BH ☎ 01623 463463 🖷 01623 463900 ✉ aali@mansfield.gov.uk

Environmental / Technical Services: Mr Martyn Thurman, Head of Neighbourhood Services, Civic Centre, Chesterfield Road South, Mansfield NG19 7BH ☎ 01623 463463 🖷 01623 463900 ✉ mthurman@mansfield.gov.uk

Environmental Health: Mr Chris Rowlston, Environmental Health

Manager, Civic Centre, Chesterfield Road South, Mansfield NG19 7BH ☎ 01623 463038 ✉ crowlston@mansfield.gov.uk

Estates, Property & Valuation: Mr Philip Colledge, Principal General Practice Surveyor & Corporate Asset Manager, Civic Centre, Chesterfield Road South, Mansfield NG19 7BH ☎ 01623 463463 🖷 01623 463900 ✉ pcolledge@mansfield.gov.uk

Events Manager: Mr Nick Turner, Town Centre Manager, Civic Centre, Chesterfield Road South, Mansfield NG19 7BH ☎ 01623 653350 ✉ nturner@mansfield.gov.uk

Finance and Treasurer: Mr Mick Andrews, Head of Finance, Property & Revenue Services, Civic Centre, Chesterfield Road South, Mansfield NG19 7BH ☎ 01623 463031 🖷 01623 463900 ✉ mandrews@mansfield.gov.uk

Fleet Management: Mr Nick Farrow, Fleet Manager, Hermitage Lane Depot, Hermitage Lane, Mansfield NG18 5GU ☎ 01623 463093 ✉ nfarrow@mansfield.gov.uk

Grounds Maintenance: Mr Martyn Thurman, Head of Neighbourhood Services, Civic Centre, Chesterfield Road South, Mansfield NG19 7BH ☎ 01623 463463 🖷 01623 463900 ✉ mthurman@mansfield.gov.uk

Health and Safety: Mrs Bev Smith, Corporate Director - Regeneration & Regulation, Civic Centre, Chesterfield Road South, Mansfield NG19 7BH ☎ 01623 463463 🖷 01623 463900 ✉ bsmith@mansfield.gov.uk

Highways: Mr Martyn Thurman, Head of Neighbourhood Services, Civic Centre, Chesterfield Road South, Mansfield NG19 7BH ☎ 01623 463463 🖷 01623 463900 ✉ mthurman@mansfield.gov.uk

Home Energy Conservation: Mr Ajman Ali, Corporate Director - Housing & Environment, Civic Centre, Chesterfield Road South, Mansfield NG19 7BH ☎ 01623 463463 🖷 01623 463900 ✉ aali@mansfield.gov.uk

Housing: Ms Hayley Barsby, Head of Housing, Civic Centre, Chesterfield Road South, Mansfield NG19 7BH ☎ 01623 463463 🖷 01623 463900 ✉ hbarsby@mansfield.gov.uk

Housing Maintenance: Mr Andrew Johnson, Housing Repairs, Civic Centre, Chesterfield Road South, Mansfield NG19 7BH ☎ 01623 463463 (extn 1)

Legal: Ms Anita Bradley, Head of Corporate Administration, Civic Centre, Chesterfield Road South, Mansfield NG19 7BH ☎ 01623 463463 🖷 01623 463900 ✉ abradley@mansfield.gov.uk

Leisure and Cultural Services: Mr M Robinson, Head of Regeneration, Leisure & Marketing, Civic Centre, Chesterfield Road South, Mansfield NG19 7BH ☎ 01623 463900 ✉ mrobinson@mansfield.gov.uk

Licensing: Mr Chris Rowlston, Environmental Health Manager, Civic Centre, Chesterfield Road South, Mansfield NG19 7BH ☎ 01623 463038 ✉ crowlston@mansfield.gov.uk

Lighting: Mr Martyn Thurman, Head of Neighbourhood Services, Civic Centre, Chesterfield Road South, Mansfield NG19 7BH ☎ 01623 463463 🖷 01623 463900 ✉ mthurman@mansfield.gov.uk

Member Services: Mr Mark Pemberton, Democratic Services Manager, Civic Centre, Chesterfield Road South, Mansfield NG19 7BH ☎ 01623 463463 🖷 01623 463900 ✉ mpemberton@mansfield.gov.uk

Parking: Mr Martyn Thurman, Head of Neighbourhood Services, Civic Centre, Chesterfield Road South, Mansfield NG19 7BH ☎ 01623 463463 🖷 01623 463900 ✉ mthurman@mansfield.gov.uk

Parking: Mr Nick Turner, Town Centre Manager, Civic Centre, Chesterfield Road South, Mansfield NG19 7BH ☎ 01623 653350 ✉ nturner@mansfield.gov.uk

Partnerships: Mr M Robinson, Head of Regeneration, Leisure & Marketing, Civic Centre, Chesterfield Road South, Mansfield NG19 7BH ☎ 01623 463900 ✉ mrobinson@mansfield.gov.uk

Personnel / HR: Ms Mariam Amos, HR Manager, Civic Centre, Chesterfield Road South, Mansfield NG19 7BH ☎ 01623 663032 🖷 01623 420197 ✉ mamos@mansfield.gov.uk

Planning: Mr Martyn Saxton, Head of Planning, Community Safety & Regulatory Services, Civic Centre, Chesterfield Road South, Mansfield NG19 7BH ☎ 01623 463208 ✉ msaxton@mansfield.gov.uk

Procurement: Mr Mick Andrews, Head of Finance, Property & Revenue Services, Civic Centre, Chesterfield Road South, Mansfield NG19 7BH ☎ 01623 463031 🖷 01623 463900 ✉ mandrews@mansfield.gov.uk

Recycling & Waste Minimisation: Mr Martyn Thurman, Head of Neighbourhood Services, Civic Centre, Chesterfield Road South, Mansfield NG19 7BH ☎ 01623 463463 🖷 01623 463900 ✉ mthurman@mansfield.gov.uk

Regeneration: Mr M Robinson, Head of Regeneration, Leisure & Marketing, Civic Centre, Chesterfield Road South, Mansfield NG19 7BH ☎ 01623 463900 ✉ mrobinson@mansfield.gov.uk

Staff Training: Mrs Lorraine Powney, Principal Learning & Development Adviser, Civic Centre, Chesterfield Road South, Mansfield NG19 7BH ☎ 01623 463463 🖷 01623 463900 ✉ lpowney@mansfield.gov.uk

Street Scene: Mr Martyn Thurman, Head of Neighbourhood Services, Civic Centre, Chesterfield Road South, Mansfield NG19 7BH ☎ 01623 463463 🖷 01623 463900 ✉ mthurman@mansfield.gov.uk

Sustainable Communities: Mrs Ruth Marlow, Managing Director, Civic Centre, Chesterfield Road South, Mansfield NG19 7BH ☎ 01623 463045 🖷 01623 463999 ✉ rmarlow@mansfield.gov.uk

Town Centre: Mr Nick Turner, Town Centre Manager, Civic Centre, Chesterfield Road South, Mansfield NG19 7BH ☎ 01623

653350 nturner@mansfield.gov.uk

Waste Collection and Disposal: Mr Martyn Thurman, Head of Neighbourhood Services, Civic Centre, Chesterfield Road South, Mansfield NG19 7BH ☎ 01623 463463 🖷 01623 463900 mthurman@mansfield.gov.uk

Waste Management: Mr Martyn Thurman, Head of Neighbourhood Services, Civic Centre, Chesterfield Road South, Mansfield NG19 7BH ☎ 01623 463463 🖷 01623 463900 mthurman@mansfield.gov.uk

MEMBERS OF THE COUNCIL (37)

Mayor: **Egginton**, Tony
Adey, Sharron (LAB - Abbott)
sadey@mansfield.gov.uk
Allsop, Kate (IND - Oakham)
kallsop@mansfield.gov.uk
Atherton, Katrina (LAB - Manor)
katherton@mansfield.gov.uk
Barton, Mick (IND - Maun Valley)
mbarton@mansfield.gov.uk
Bennet, Nicholas (LAB - Kingsway)
nbennett@mansfield.gov.uk
Bosnjak, Joyce (LAB - Hornby)
jbosnjak@mansfield.gov.uk
Clay, Terry (LAB - Brick Kiln)
tclay@mansfield.gov.uk
Clayton, Colin (LAB - Kingswalk)
cclayton@mansfield.gov.uk
Colley, Mick (LAB - Bull Farm & Pleasley Hill)
mcolley@mansfield.gov.uk
Crawford, Peter (LAB - Warsop Carrs)
pcrawford@mansfield.gov.uk
Evans, Derek (IND - Netherfield)
djevans@mansfield.gov.uk
Fisher, Amanda (LAB - Woodhouse)
afisher@mansfield.gov.uk
Garner, Stephen (IND - Racecourse)
sgarner@mansfield.gov.uk
Hammersley, Charles (LAB - Ling Forest)
chammersley@mansfield.gov.uk
Harpham, Adrian (LAB - Sandhurst)
aharpham@mansfield.gov.uk
Henshaw, Paul (LAB - Newgate)
phenshaw@mansfield.gov.uk
Higgins, Sally (LAB - Ladybrook)
shiggins@mansfield.gov.uk
Hopewel, Vaughan (LAB - Oak Tree)
vhopewell@mansfield.gov.uk
Jelley, Ron (IND - Grange Farm)
rjelley@mansfield.gov.uk
Kerr, John (LAB - Market Warsop)
jkerr@mansfield.gov.uk
Lee, Martin (LAB - Eakring)
mlee@mansfield.gov.uk
Lohan, Brian (LAB - Portland)
blohan@mansfield.gov.uk
Moody, Denise (LAB - Newlands)
dmoody@mansfield.gov.uk
Norman, Ann (LAB - Park Hall)
anorman@mansfield.gov.uk
O'Neill, Dennis (LAB - Broomhill)
doneill@mansfield.gov.uk
Richardson, Stuart (LAB - Penniment)
srichardson@mansfield.gov.uk
Shields, Philip (LAB - Yeoman Hill)
pshields@mansfield.gov.uk
Smart, John (LAB - Ransom Wood)
jsmart@mansfield.gov.uk
Smith, David (IND - Woodlands)
dmsmith@mansfield.gov.uk
Smith, Christine (IND - Carr Bank)
cjsmith@mansfield.gov.uk
Sutcliffe, Roger (IND - Lindhurst)
rsutcliffe@mansfield.gov.uk
Tristram, Andrew (IND - Berry Hill)
atristram@mansfield.gov.uk
Ward, Sonja (LAB - Peafields)
sward@mansfield.gov.uk
Wetton, Andy (LAB - Meden)
awetton@mansfield.gov.uk
Wright, Martin (IND - Holly)
mwright@mansfield.gov.uk
Yemm, Julia (LAB - Sherwood)
jyemm@mansfield.gov.uk

POLITICAL COMPOSITION

LAB: 26, IND: 10, UKWN: 1

CABINET

Mayor: Mr Tony Egginton
Corporate Issues: Mr Andrew Tristram
Economic Regeneration: Mrs Kate Allsop
Environment: Mr Philip Shields
Housing: Mr Derek Evans
Public Protection: Mr Mick Barton
Resources: Mr Roger Sutcliffe
Tenancy Services & Special needs: Mr Mick Colley

COMMITTEE CHAIRS

Licensing: Mr John Smart
Personnel: Mr Tony Egginton
Planning: Mrs Sally Higgins
Select Commission 1 (Housing & Environment): Mr Adrian Harpham
Select Commission 2 (Crime & Regeneration): Ms Charles Hammersley
Select Commission 3 (Corporate Issues): Mr Paul Henshaw
Standards & Appeals: Ms Joyce Bosnjak

MEDWAY U

Medway Council, Civic Headquarters, Gun Wharf, Dock Road, Chatham ME4 4TR ☎ 01634 306000 🖷 01634 332756
info@medway.gov.uk
www.medway.gov.uk

FACTS & FIGURES

Police Authority: Kent Police Authority
Health Authority: South East Coast Strategic Health Authority
Learning and Skills Council: South East
Parliamentary Constituencies: Chatham and Aylesford, Gillingham and Rainham, Rochester and Strood
EU Constituencies: South East
Election Frequency: Elections are of whole council

PRINCIPAL OFFICERS

Chief Executive: Mr Neil Davies, Chief Executive, Civic Headquarters, Gun Wharf, Dock Road, Chatham ME4 4TR ☎ 01634 332705 🖷 01634 332743 ✉ neil.davies@medway.gov.uk

Senior Management: Ms Rose Collinson, Director - Children & Adults, Civic Headquarters, Gun Wharf, Dock Road, Chatham ME4 4TR ☎ 01634 331011 🖷 01634 332848 ✉ rose.collinson@medway.gov.uk

Senior Management: Mr Robin Cooper, Director - Regeneration, Community & Culture, Civic Headquarters, Gun Wharf, Dock Road, Chatham ME4 4TR ☎ 01634 331323 🖷 01634 331729 ✉ robin.cooper@medway.gov.uk

Senior Management: Mr Mick Hayward, Chief Finance Officer, Civic Headquarters, Gun Wharf, Dock Road, Chatham ME4 4TR ☎ 01634 332220 🖷 01634 332876 ✉ mick.hayward@medway.gov.uk

Access Officer / Social Services (Disability): Ms Jackie Challis, Joint Physical Disability Manager, Civic Headquarters, Gun Wharf, Dock Road, Chatham ME4 4TR ☎ 01634 331272 ✉ jackie.challis@medway.gov.uk

Access Officer / Social Services (Disability): Ms Amanda Dean, Joint Physical Disability Manager, Civic Headquarters, Gun Wharf, Dock Road, Chatham ME4 4TR ☎ 01634 331272 ✉ amanda.dean@medway.gov.uk

Architect, Building / Property Services: Mr Nick Anthony, Head - Property Services, Civic Headquarters, Gun Wharf, Dock Road, Chatham ME4 4TR ☎ 01634 332294 ✉ nick.anthony@medway.gov.uk

Building Control: Mr Tony Van Veghel, South Thames Gateway Building Control Partnership Director, Compass Centre, Chatham Maritime, Chatham ME4 4YH ☎ 01634 331552 🖷 01634 331624 ✉ tony.vanveghel@medway.gov.uk

Children / Youth Services: Ms Rose Collinson, Director - Children & Adults, Civic Headquarters, Gun Wharf, Dock Road, Chatham ME4 4TR ☎ 01634 331011 🖷 01634 332848 ✉ rose.collinson@medway.gov.uk

Civil Registration: Mr Paul Edwards, Bereavement & Registration Services Manager, Medway Crematorium, Upper Robin Hood Lane, Blue Bell Hill, Chatham ME5 9QU ☎ 01634 331352 ✉ paul.edwards@medway.gov.uk

PR / Communications: Ms Stephanie Goad, Assistant Director - Communications, Performance & Partnerships, Civic Headquarters, Gun Wharf, Dock Road, Chatham ME4 4TR ☎ 01634 332737 🖷 01634 332743 ✉ stephanie.goad@medway.gov.uk

PR / Communications: Mr Simon Wakeman, Head - Communications & Marketing, Civic Headquarters, Gun Wharf, Dock Road, Chatham ME4 4TR ☎ 01634 332776 ✉ simon.wakeman@medway.gov.uk

Community Safety: Mr Tim England, Head - Safer Communities, Civic Centre, Strood, Rochester ME2 4AU ☎ 01634 333534 🖷 01634 333117 ✉ tim.england@medway.gov.uk

Computer Management: Ms Moira Bragg, Head - ICT, Civic Headquarters, Gun Wharf, Dock Road, Chatham ME4 4TR ☎ 01634 332087 🖷 01634 332881 ✉ moira.bragg@medway.gov.uk

Customer Service: Mr Martin Garlick, Head - Customer First & Libraries, Civic Headquarters, Gun Wharf, Dock Road, Chatham ME4 4TR ☎ 01634 338771 ✉ martin.garlick@medway.gov.uk

Economic Development: Mr Clem Smith, Head - Economic Development & Social Regeneration, Civic Headquarters, Gun Wharf, Dock Road, Chatham ME4 4TR ☎ 01634 338119 ✉ clem.smith@medway.gov.uk

Education: Ms Rose Collinson, Director - Children & Adults, Civic Headquarters, Gun Wharf, Dock Road, Chatham ME4 4TR ☎ 01634 331011 🖷 01634 332848 ✉ rose.collinson@medway.gov.uk

E-Government: Ms Moira Bragg, Head - ICT, Civic Headquarters, Gun Wharf, Dock Road, Chatham ME4 4TR ☎ 01634 332087 🖷 01634 332881 ✉ moira.bragg@medway.gov.uk

Electoral Registration: Ms Jane Ringham, Head - Elections & Member Services, Civic Headquarters, Gun Wharf, Dock Road, Chatham ME4 4TR ☎ 01634 332864 🖷 01634 332862 ✉ jane.ringham@medway.gov.uk

Emergency Planning: Ms Angela Wilkins, Emergency Planning Manager, Civic Centre, Strood, Rochester ME2 4AU ☎ 01634 333542 🖷 01634 331720 ✉ angela.wilkins@medway.gov.uk

Environmental / Technical Services: Mr Robin Cooper, Director - Regeneration, Community & Culture, Civic Headquarters, Gun Wharf, Dock Road, Chatham ME4 4TR ☎ 01634 331323 🖷 01634 331729 ✉ robin.cooper@medway.gov.uk

Estates, Property & Valuation: Mr Nick Anthony, Head - Property Services, Civic Headquarters, Gun Wharf, Dock Road, Chatham ME4 4TR ☎ 01634 332294 ✉ nick.anthony@medway.gov.uk

Estates, Property & Valuation: Ms Angela Drum, Head - Legal Services, Civic Headquarters, Gun Wharf, Dock Road, Chatham ME4 4TR ☎ 01634 332774 ✉ angela.drum@medway.gov.uk

European Liaison: Mr Clem Smith, Head - Economic Development & Social Regeneration, Civic Headquarters, Gun Wharf, Dock Road, Chatham ME4 4TR ☎ 01634 338119 ✉ clem.smith@medway.gov.uk

Events Manager: Mr Carl Madjitey, Head - Festivals, Arts, Theatres & Events, Civic Headquarters, Gun Wharf, Dock Road, Chatham ME4 4TR ☎ 01634 338114 ✉ carl.madjitey@medway.gov.uk

Finance and Treasurer: Mr Stuart Bull, Operations Manager, Civic Headquarters, Gun Wharf, Dock Road, Chatham ME4 4TR ☎ 01634 332210 🖷 01634 332858 ✉ stuart.bull@medway.gov.uk

Finance and Treasurer: Mr Mick Hayward, Chief Finance Officer, Civic Headquarters, Gun Wharf, Dock Road, Chatham ME4 4TR ☎ 01634 332220 🖷 01634 332876 mick.hayward@medway.gov.uk

Finance and Treasurer: Mr Jon Poulson, Medway Revenues & Benefits Service Contract Manager, Civic Headquarters, Gun Wharf, Dock Road, Chatham ME4 4TR ☎ 01634 333700 jon.poulson@medway.gov.uk

Grounds Maintenance: Mr Simon Swift, Head - Greenspace Services, Heritage & Libraries, Civic Headquarters, Gun Wharf, Dock Road, Chatham ME4 4TR ☎ 01634 331276 simon.swift@medway.gov.uk

Health and Safety: Ms Lynette Rispoli, Corporate Health & Safety Manager, Civic Headquarters, Gun Wharf, Dock Road, Chatham ME4 4TR ☎ 01634 333011 lynette.rispoli@medway.gov.uk

Highways: Mr Phil Moore, Head - Highways & Parking Services, Civic Centre, Rochester ME2 4AU ☎ 01634 331146 🖷 01634 331759 phil.moore@medway.gov.uk

Housing: Mr Matthew Gough, Head - Strategic Housing, Civic Headquarters, Gun Wharf, Dock Road, Chatham ME4 4TR ☎ 01634 333177 matthew.gough@medway.gov.uk

Housing Maintenance: Mr Matthew Gough, Head - Strategic Housing, Civic Headquarters, Gun Wharf, Dock Road, Chatham ME4 4TR ☎ 01634 333177 matthew.gough@medway.gov.uk

Local Area Agreement: Ms Stephanie Goad, Assistant Director - Communications, Performance & Partnerships, Civic Headquarters, Gun Wharf, Dock Road, Chatham ME4 4TR ☎ 01634 332737 🖷 01634 332743 stephanie.goad@medway.gov.uk

Legal: Mr Glenn Watson, Legal Development Officers, Civic Headquarters, Gunwharf, Dock Road, Chatham ME2 4AU ☎ 01634 333179 🖷 01634 331720 glenn.watson@medway.gov.uk

Leisure and Cultural Services: Mr Richard Hicks, Assistant Director - Customer First, Civic Headquarters, Gun Wharf, Dock Road, Chatham ME4 4TR ☎ 01634 332764 🖷 01634 332743 richard.hicks@medway.gov.uk

Licensing: Ms Alison Poulson, Local Land Charges & Licensing Manager, Civic Headquarters, Gun Wharf, Dock Road, Chatham ME4 4TR ☎ 01634 332774 alison.poulson@medway.gov.uk

Lifelong Learning: Ms Sue Hopkins, Service Manager - Adult Learning Services, Medway Adult Learning Service, Eastgate, Rochester ME1 1EW ☎ 01634 338442 sue.hopkins@medway.gov.uk

Lighting: Mr Phil Moore, Head - Highways & Parking Services, Civic Centre, Rochester ME2 4AU ☎ 01634 331146 🖷 01634 331759 phil.moore@medway.gov.uk

Member Services: Ms Jane Ringham, Head - Elections & Member Services, Civic Headquarters, Gun Wharf, Dock Road, Chatham ME4 4TR ☎ 01634 332864 🖷 01634 332862 jane.ringham@medway.gov.uk

Parking: Ms Rubena Hafizi, Parking Manager, Civic Centre, Strood, Rochester ME2 4AU ☎ 01634 331725 🖷 01634 331777 rubena.hafizi@medway.gov.uk

Partnerships: Ms Stephanie Goad, Assistant Director - Communications, Performance & Partnerships, Civic Headquarters, Gun Wharf, Dock Road, Chatham ME4 4TR ☎ 01634 332737 🖷 01634 332743 stephanie.goad@medway.gov.uk

Personnel / HR: Ms Tricia Palmer, Assistant Director - Organisational Services, Civic Headquarters, Gun Wharf, Dock Road, Chatham ME4 4TR ☎ 01634 332343 🖷 01634 332858 tricia.palmer@medway.gov.uk

Planning: Mr Stephen Gaimster, Assistant Director - Housing, Development & Transport, Civic Headquarters, Gun Wharf, Dock Road, Chatham ME4 4TR ☎ 01634 331192 🖷 01634 331184 stephen.gaimster@medway.gov.uk

Planning: Mr Dave Harris, Development Manager, Civic Headquarters, Gun Wharf, Dock Road, Chatham ME4 4TR ☎ 01634 331575 🖷 01634 331184 dave.harris@medway.gov.uk

Public Libraries: Mr Martin Garlick, Head - Customer First & Libraries, Civic Headquarters, Gun Wharf, Dock Road, Chatham ME4 4TR ☎ 01634 338771 martin.garlick@medway.gov.uk

Recycling & Waste Minimisation: Ms Sarah Dagwell, Head - Waste Services, Civic Centre, Rochester ME2 4AU ☎ 01634 331597 🖷 01634 331720 sarah.dagwell@medway.gov.uk

Regeneration: Mr Robin Cooper, Director - Regeneration, Community & Culture, Civic Headquarters, Gun Wharf, Dock Road, Chatham ME4 4TR ☎ 01634 331323 🖷 01634 331729 robin.cooper@medway.gov.uk

Road Safety: Mr Ian Wilson, Service Manager - Regeneration, Community & Culture & Head of Frontline, Capital Projects, Road Safety & Networks, Civic Centre, Rochester ME2 4AU ☎ 01634 331543 ian.wilson@medway.gov.uk

Social Services: Mr David Quirke-Thornton, Assistant Director - Adult Services, Civic Headquarters, Gun Wharf, Dock Road, Chatham ME4 4TR ☎ 01634 331212 david.quirkethornton@medway.gov.uk

Social Services (Adult): Ms Genette Laws, Interim Head - Category Manager, Civic Headquarters, Gun Wharf, Dock Road, Chatham ME4 4TR ☎ 01634 331345 genette.laws@medway.gov.uk

Social Services (Adult): Mrs Liz Nicholas, Learning Disability Service Manager, Lordswood Healthy Living Centre, Sultan Road, Chatham ME5 8TJ ☎ 01634 337567 🖷 liz.nicholas@medway.gov.uk

Social Services (Adult): Mr David Quirke-Thornton, Assistant

Director - Adult Services, Civic Headquarters, Gun Wharf, Dock Road, Chatham ME4 4TR ☎ 01634 331212 ✆ david.quirkethornton@medway.gov.uk

Social Services (Adult): Mr Jeremy Shannon, Older People Policy & Service Manager, Civic Headquarters, Gun Wharf, Dock Road, Chatham ME4 4TR ☎ 01634 331071 ✆ jeremy.shannon@medway.gov.uk

Social Services (Children): Mr James Malthus, Children's Care Business Support Manager, Civic Headquarters, Gun Wharf, Dock Road, Chatham ME4 4TR ☎ 01634 334023 🖷 01634 332848 ✆ james.malthus@medway.gov.uk

Social Services (Children): Mr Paul Munday, Service Manager, Woodlands Place, Woodlands Road, Gillingham ME7 2DT ☎ 01634 334101 🖷 01634 334170 ✆ paul.munday@medway.gov.uk

Social Services (Children): Mrs Liz Nicholas, Learning Disability Service Manager, Lordswood Healthy Living Centre, Sultan Road, Chatham ME5 8TJ ☎ 01634 337567 🖷 ✆ liz.nicholas@medway.gov.uk

Social Services (Children): Ms Karen Reardon, Service Manager, Redvers Centre, Redvers Road, Chatham ME4 5UU ☎ 01634 337311 🖷 01634 337293 ✆ karen.reardon@medway.gov.uk

Social Services (Children): Ms Clare Wilkes, Local Authority Designated Officer, Civic Headquarters, Gun Wharf, Dock Road, Chatham ME4 4TR ☎ 01634 331229 🖷 01634 332848 ✆ clare.wilkes@medway.gov.uk

Street Scene: Mr Andy McGrath, Assistant Director, Civic Centre, Rochester ME2 4AU ☎ 01634 331376 🖷 01634 331613 ✆ andy.mcgrath@medway.gov.uk

Sustainable Communities: Mr Stephen Gaimster, Assistant Director - Housing, Development & Transport, Civic Headquarters, Gun Wharf, Dock Road, Chatham ME4 4TR ☎ 01634 331192 🖷 01634 331184 ✆ stephen.gaimster@medway.gov.uk

Sustainable Development: Mr Stephen Gaimster, Assistant Director - Housing, Development & Transport, Civic Headquarters, Gun Wharf, Dock Road, Chatham ME4 4TR ☎ 01634 331192 🖷 01634 331184 ✆ stephen.gaimster@medway.gov.uk

Town Centre: Mr Stephen Gaimster, Assistant Director - Housing, Development & Transport, Civic Headquarters, Gun Wharf, Dock Road, Chatham ME4 4TR ☎ 01634 331192 🖷 01634 331184 ✆ stephen.gaimster@medway.gov.uk

Traffic Management: Mr Martin Morris, Traffic Management Manager, Civic Centre, Rochester ME2 4AU ☎ 01634 331148 ✆ martin.morris@medway.gov.uk

Transport: Mr Steve Hewlett, Head - Intergrated Transport, Civic Headquarters, Gun Wharf, Dock Road, Chatham ME4 4TR ☎ 01634 331103 🖷 01634 331729 ✆ steve.hewlett@medway.gov.uk

Transport Planner: Mr Steve Hewlett, Head - Intergrated Transport, Civic Headquarters, Gun Wharf, Dock Road, Chatham ME4 4TR ☎ 01634 331103 🖷 01634 331729 ✆ steve.hewlett@medway.gov.uk

Waste Collection and Disposal: Ms Michelle Chambers, Contract Services Manager, Civic Centre, Rochester ME2 4AU ☎ 01634 333008 🖷 01634 331720 ✆ michelle.chambers@medway.gov.uk

Waste Collection and Disposal: Ms Sarah Dagwell, Head - Waste Services, Civic Centre, Rochester ME2 4AU ☎ 01634 331597 🖷 01634 331720 ✆ sarah.dagwell@medway.gov.uk

Waste Management: Ms Sarah Dagwell, Head - Waste Services, Civic Centre, Rochester ME2 4AU ☎ 01634 331597 🖷 01634 331720 ✆ sarah.dagwell@medway.gov.uk

Children's Play Areas: Mr Simon Swift, Head - Greenspace Services, Heritage & Libraries, Civic Headquarters, Gun Wharf, Dock Road, Chatham ME4 4TR ☎ 01634 331276 ✆ simon.swift@medway.gov.uk

MEMBERS OF THE COUNCIL (55)

***Mayor:* Hewett**, Vaughan (CON - Rainham North)
vaughan.hewett@medway.gov.uk

***Deputy Mayor:* Iles**, Josie (CON - Strood South)
josie_iles@blueyonder.co.uk

Avey, John (CON - Strood South)
johnavey@tiscali.co.uk

Baker, Ted (CON - Rochester West)
cllrtedbaker@aol.com

Bowler, Nicholas (LAB - Rochester East)
nickbowler89@btinternet.com

Brake, David (CON - Walderslade)
david.brake@medway.gov.uk

Bright, Matt (CON - Princes Park)
mjbright76@yahoo.co.uk

Carr, David (CON - Rainham North)
davidcarr@rya-online.net

Chambers, Rodney (CON - Hempstead and Wigmore)
rodney.chambers@medway.gov.uk

Chambers, Diane (CON - Hempstead and Wigmore)
diane.chambers@medway.gov.uk

Chishti, Rehman (CON - Rainham Central)
rehman@rehmanchishti.com

Chitty, Jane (CON - Strood North)
jane.chitty@medway.gov.uk

Clarke, Trevor (CON - Rochester South and Horsted)
trevor.clarke@blueyonder.co.uk

Colman, David (LAB - Gillingham South)
davidcolman@blueyonder.co.uk

Cooper, Pat (IND - Gillingham North)
patecooper@virginmedia.com

Craven, Sam (LAB - Luton and Wayfield)
sam.craven@medway.gov.uk

Doe, Howard (CON - Rainham South)
howard.doe@medway.gov.uk

Etheridge, Jane (CON - Strood North)
jane.etheridge@medway.gov.uk

Filmer, Philip (CON - Peninsula)
phil.filmer@medway.gov.uk

Gilry, Dorte (LAB - Twydall)
dorte.gilry@btinternet.com

Godwin, Paul (LAB - Chatham Central)
paul.godwin@medway.gov.uk
Goodwin, Christine (LAB - Luton and Wayfield)
christine.godwin@medway.gov.uk
Griffin, Sylvia (CON - Rochester South and Horsted)
sylvia.griffin@medway.gov.uk
Griffiths, Glyn (LAB - Twydall)
glyn.griffiths@medway.gov.uk
Gulvi, Adrian (CON - Walderslade)
avhgulvin@btinternet.com
Gulvin, Pat (CON - Princes Park)
patgulvin@yahoo.co.uk
Harriott, Paul (LAB - Twydall)
harriott.paul@googlemail.com
Hicks, Peter (CON - Strood Rural)
peter.hicks@medway.gov.uk
Hubbard, Stephen (LAB - Strood North)
stephen.hubbard@medway.gov.uk
Igwe, Isaac (LAB - Strood South)
isaac.igwe@medway.gov.uk
Irvine, Chris (CON - Peninsula)
cg.irvine@virginmedia.com
Jarrett, Alan (CON - Lordswood and Capstone)
alan.jarrett@medway.gov.uk
Juby, Geoff (LD - Gillingham South)
geoff.juby@medway.gov.uk
Kearney, Sheila (LD - Gillingham South)
sheila.kearney@medway.gov.uk
Kemp, Barry (CON - Rainham Central)
barryjkemp@hotmail.com
Mackinlay, Craig (CON - River)
c@riverward.co.uk
Mackness, Andrew (CON - River)
andrew@riverward.co.uk
Maisey, Raymond (CON - Cuxton and Halling)
ray.maisey@medway.gov.uk
Maple, Vince (LAB - Chatham Central)
vince.maple@medway.gov.uk
Mason, Tom (CON - Strood Rural)
tmason358@aol.com
Murray, Teresa (LAB - Rochester East)
teresamurraytm@aol.com
O'Brien, Mike (CON - Rainham Central)
mike.obrien@medway.gov.uk
Osbourne, Tristan (LAB - Luton and Wayfield)
tris.osborne@gmail.com
Price, Adam (LAB - Gillingham North)
adam.price@medway.gov.uk
Purdy, Wendy (CON - Watling)
Johnpurdy@btinternet.com
Rodberg, Peter (CON - Strood Rural)
fern.rodberg@talktalk.net
Royle, David (CON - Rainham South)
droyle7@aol.com
Shaw, Julie (LAB - Chatham Central)
shaw9089@btinternet.com
Smith, Diana (LD - Watling)
diana.smith@medway.gov.uk
Stamp, Andy (IND - Gillingham North)
andy.stamp@medway.gov.uk
Tolhurst, Kelly (CON - Rochester West)
kellytolhurst@hotmail.co.uk
Turpin, Rupert (CON - Rochester South and Horsted)
rupert.turpin@gmail.com
Watson, Tony (CON - Peninsula)
tonywatson2006@btinternet.com
Wickes, Les (CON - Rainham South)
les.wicks@medway.gov.uk
Wildey, David (CON - Lordswood and Capstone)
david.wiley@medway.gov.uk

POLITICAL COMPOSITION

CON: 35, LAB: 15, LD: 3, IND: 2

CABINET

Leader: Mr Rodney Chambers
Deputy Leader / Finance: Mr Alan Jarrett
Adult Services: Mr David Brake
Children's Services: Mr Leslie Wicks
Children's Social Care: Mr David Wildey
Community Safety & Customer Support: Mr Mike O'Brien
Corporate Services: Mr Tom Mason
Front Line Services: Mr Phil Filmer
Housing & Community Services: Mr Howard Doe
Strategic Development & Economic Growth: Mrs Jane Chitty

COMMITTEE CHAIRS

Audit: Mr Trevor Clarke
Business Support (Scrutiny): Mr David Carr
Children & Adults: Mr David Royle
Employment Matters: Mr David Carr
Health & Adult Social Care: Mr John Avey
Licensing & Safety: Mrs Diane Chambers
Planning: Mrs Diane Chambers
Regeneration, Community & Culture (Scrutiny): Mr Matt Bright
School Transport & Curriculum Appeals: Mr David Royle

MELTON D

Melton Borough Council, Council Offices, Nottingham Road, Melton Mowbray LE13 0UL ☎ 01664 502502 🖷 01664 410283
💻 www.melton.gov.uk

FACTS & FIGURES

Police Authority: Leicestershire Police Authority
Health Authority: East Midlands Strategic Health Authority
Learning and Skills Council: East Midlands
Parliamentary Constituencies: Rutland and Melton
EU Constituencies: East Midlands
Election Frequency: Elections are of whole council
Twinning: Kapelle (Holland), Sochaczew (Poland)

PRINCIPAL OFFICERS

Chief Executive: Mrs Lynn Aisbett, Chief Executive, Council Offices, Nottingham Road, Melton Mowbray LE13 0UL ☎ 01664 502502 ✉ laisbett@melton.gov.uk

Assistant Chief Executive: Mr Keith Aubrey, Strategic Director, Council Offices, Nottingham Road, Melton Mowbray LE13 0UL ☎ 01664 502502 ✉ kaubrey@melton.gov.uk

Assistant Chief Executive: Ms Christine Marshall, Strategic Director, Council Offices, Nottingham Road, Melton Mowbray LE13 0UL ☎ 01664 502502 🖷 01664 410283 ✉ cmarshall@melton.gov.uk

Architect, Building / Property Services: Mr David Blanchard,

Corporate Property Officer, Council Offices, Nottingham Road, Melton Mowbray LE13 0UL ☎ 01664 502502 ✉ dblanchard@melton.gov.uk

Building Control: Mr Jim Worley, Head of Regulatory Services, Council Offices, Nottingham Road, Melton Mowbray LE13 0UL ☎ 01664 502502 🖷 01664 410283 ✉ jworley@melton.gov.uk

PR / Communications: Mrs Angela Tebbutt, Head of Communications, Council Offices, Nottingham Road, Melton Mowbray LE13 0UL ☎ 01664 502502 🖷 01664 410283 ✉ atebbutt@melton.gov.uk

Community Planning: Mr Harrinder Rai, Head of Communities & Neighbourhoods, Council Offices, Nottingham Road, Melton Mowbray LE13 0UL ☎ 01664 502502 🖷 01664 410283 ✉ hrai@melton.gov.uk

Community Safety: Mr Kevin Quinn, Community Safety Officer, Council Offices, Nottingham Road, Melton Mowbray LE13 0UL ☎ 01664 502502 ✉ kquinn@melton.gov.uk

Computer Management: Mr Chris Stone, IT Client Manager, Council Offices, Nottingham Road, Melton Mowbray LE13 0UL ☎ 01664 502502 ✉ cstone@melton.gov.uk

Contracts: Mr Tony Hall, Head of Welland Procurement, Parkside, Station Approach, Burton Street, Melton Mowbray LE13 1GH ☎ 01664 502502 ✉ thall@melton.gov.uk

Customer Service: Mrs Angela Tebbutt, Head of Communications, Council Offices, Nottingham Road, Melton Mowbray LE13 0UL ☎ 01664 502502 🖷 01664 410283 ✉ atebbutt@melton.gov.uk

Economic Development: Mr Harrinder Rai, Head of Communities & Neighbourhoods, Council Offices, Nottingham Road, Melton Mowbray LE13 0UL ☎ 01664 502502 🖷 01664 410283 ✉ hrai@melton.gov.uk

E-Government: Mr Chris Stone, IT Client Manager, Council Offices, Nottingham Road, Melton Mowbray LE13 0UL ☎ 01664 502502 ✉ cstone@melton.gov.uk

Electoral Registration: Ms Sally Renwick, Elections Officer, Council Offices, Nottingham Road, Melton Mowbray LE13 0UL ☎ 01664 502502 ✉ srenwick@melton.gov.uk

Emergency Planning: Mr Jim Worley, Head of Regulatory Services, Council Offices, Nottingham Road, Melton Mowbray LE13 0UL ☎ 01664 502502 🖷 01664 410283 ✉ jworley@melton.gov.uk

Environmental Health: Mrs Victoria Clarke, Environment Protection & Safety Manager, Council Offices, Nottingham Road, Melton Mowbray LE13 0UL ☎ 01664 502502 🖷 01664 410283 ✉ vclarke@melton.gov.uk

Estates, Property & Valuation: Mr David Blanchard, Corporate Property Officer, Council Offices, Nottingham Road, Melton Mowbray LE13 0UL ☎ 01664 502502 ✉ dblanchard@melton.gov.uk

Events Manager: Ms Lisa Hammond, Joint Town Centre Manager, Council Offices, Nottingham Road, Melton Mowbray LE13 0UL ☎ 01664 502502 ✉ lhammond@melton.gov.uk

Facilities: Mr Gerald Royston, Facilities Manager, Parkside, Station Approach, Burton Street, Melton Mowbray LE13 1GH ☎ 01664 502502 ✉ groyston@melton.gov.uk

Finance and Treasurer: Mrs Dawn Garton, Head of Central Services, Council Offices, Nottingham Road, Melton Mowbray LE13 0UL ☎ 01664 502502 ✉ dgarton@melton.gov.uk

Grounds Maintenance: Mr Ramon Selvon, Principal Assistant Environment, Council Offices, Nottingham Road, Melton Mowbray LE13 0UL ☎ 01664 502502 ✉ rselvon@melton.gov.uk

Health and Safety: Ms Sarah Burton, Health & Safety Advisor, Council Offices, Nottingham Road, Melton Mowbray LE13 0UL ☎ 01664 502502 ✉ sburton@melton.gov.uk

Housing: Mr Harrinder Rai, Head of Communities & Neighbourhoods, Council Offices, Nottingham Road, Melton Mowbray LE13 0UL ☎ 01664 502502 🖷 01664 410283 ✉ hrai@melton.gov.uk

Housing Maintenance: Mr Harrinder Rai, Head of Communities & Neighbourhoods, Council Offices, Nottingham Road, Melton Mowbray LE13 0UL ☎ 01664 502502 🖷 01664 410283 ✉ hrai@melton.gov.uk

Legal: Ms Verina Wenham, Solicitor to the Council, Council Offices, Nottingham Road, Melton Mowbray LE13 0UL ☎ 01664 502502 🖷 01664 410283 ✉ vwenham@melton.gov.uk

Leisure and Cultural Services: Mr Ronan Browne, People Manager, Council Offices, Nottingham Road, Melton Mowbray LE13 0UL ☎ 01664 502502 🖷 01664 410283 ✉ rbrowne@melton.gov.uk

Licensing: Mrs E Holdsworth, Licensing Officer, Council Offices, Nottingham Road, Melton Mowbray LE13 0UL ☎ 01664 502502 ✉ eholdsworth@melton.gov.uk

Licensing: Mr Jim Worley, Head of Regulatory Services, Council Offices, Nottingham Road, Melton Mowbray LE13 0UL ☎ 01664 502502 🖷 01664 410283 ✉ jworley@melton.gov.uk

Lottery Funding, Charity and Voluntary: Mr Harrinder Rai, Head of Communities & Neighbourhoods, Council Offices, Nottingham Road, Melton Mowbray LE13 0UL ☎ 01664 502502 🖷 01664 410283 ✉ hrai@melton.gov.uk

Member Services: Mrs Angela Tebbutt, Head of Communications, Council Offices, Nottingham Road, Melton Mowbray LE13 0UL ☎ 01664 502502 🖷 01664 410283 ✉ atebbutt@melton.gov.uk

Parking: Mr David Blanchard, Corporate Property Officer, Parkside, Station Approach, Burton Street, Melton Mowbray LE13 1GH ☎ 01664 502502 ✉ dblanchard@melton.gov.uk

Personnel / HR: Mrs Angela Tebbutt, Head of Communications,

Council Offices, Nottingham Road, Melton Mowbray LE13 0UL ☎ 01664 502502 🖷 01664 410283 ✉ atebbutt@melton.gov.uk

Planning: Mr Jim Worley, Head of Regulatory Services, Council Offices, Nottingham Road, Melton Mowbray LE13 0UL ☎ 01664 502502 🖷 01664 410283 ✉ jworley@melton.gov.uk

Procurement: Mr Tony Hall, Head of Welland Procurement, Council Offices, Nottingham Road, Melton Mowbray LE13 0UL ☎ 01664 502502 ✉ thall@melton.gov.uk

Recycling & Waste Minimisation: Ms Amanda Hume, Environmental Services Officer, Council Offices, Nottingham Road, Melton Mowbray LE13 0UL ☎ 01664 502502 🖷 01664 410283 ✉ ahume@melton.gov.uk

Recycling & Waste Minimisation: Mr Ramon Selvon, Principal Assistant Environment, Council Offices, Nottingham Road, Melton Mowbray LE13 0UL ☎ 01664 502502 ✉ rselvon@melton.gov.uk

Regeneration: Mr Harrinder Rai, Head of Communities & Neighbourhoods, Council Offices, Nottingham Road, Melton Mowbray LE13 0UL ☎ 01664 502502 🖷 01664 410283 ✉ hrai@melton.gov.uk

Staff Training: Mrs Sarah-Jane O'Connor, HR & Communications Manager, Council Offices, Nottingham Road, Melton Mowbray LE13 0UL ☎ 01664 502502 🖷 01664 410283 ✉ soconnor@melton.gov.uk

Sustainable Communities: Mr Harrinder Rai, Head of Communities & Neighbourhoods, Council Offices, Nottingham Road, Melton Mowbray LE13 0UL ☎ 01664 502502 🖷 01664 410283 ✉ hrai@melton.gov.uk

Sustainable Development: Mr Harrinder Rai, Head of Communities & Neighbourhoods, Council Offices, Nottingham Road, Melton Mowbray LE13 0UL ☎ 01664 502502 🖷 01664 410283 ✉ hrai@melton.gov.uk

Tourism: Mr Harrinder Rai, Head of Communities & Neighbourhoods, Council Offices, Nottingham Road, Melton Mowbray LE13 0UL ☎ 01664 502502 🖷 01664 410283 ✉ hrai@melton.gov.uk

Town Centre: Ms Shelagh Core, Joint Town Centre Manager, Council Offices, Nottingham Road, Melton Mowbray LE13 0UL ☎ 01664 502502 ✉ score@melton.gov.uk

Town Centre: Ms Lisa Hammond, Joint Town Centre Manager, Council Offices, Nottingham Road, Melton Mowbray LE13 0UL ☎ 01664 502502 ✉ lhammond@melton.gov.uk

Transport: Mr Jim Worley, Head of Regulatory Services, Council Offices, Nottingham Road, Melton Mowbray LE13 0UL ☎ 01664 502502 🖷 01664 410283 ✉ jworley@melton.gov.uk

Waste Collection and Disposal: Mr Jim Worley, Head of Regulatory Services, Council Offices, Nottingham Road, Melton Mowbray LE13 0UL ☎ 01664 502502 🖷 01664 410283 ✉ jworley@melton.gov.uk

Waste Management: Mr Ramon Selvon, Principal Assistant Environment, Council Offices, Nottingham Road, Melton Mowbray LE13 0UL ☎ 01664 502502 ✉ rselvon@melton.gov.uk

Waste Management: Mr Jim Worley, Head of Regulatory Services, Council Offices, Nottingham Road, Melton Mowbray LE13 0UL ☎ 01664 502502 🖷 01664 410283 ✉ jworley@melton.gov.uk

MEMBERS OF THE COUNCIL (28)

***Mayor:* Illingworth**, John (CON - Sysonby)

***Leader of the Council:* Rhodes**, Byron (CON - Long Clawson and Stathern)
brhodes@leics.gov.uk

***Deputy Leader of the Council:* Posnett**, Pam (CON - Newport)
pposnett@melton.gov.uk

Baguley, Pam (CON - Long Clawson and Stathern)
pbaguley@melton.gov.uk

Barnes, Mark (CON - Somerby)
mbarnes@melton.gov.uk

Botterill, Gerald (CON - Croxton Kerrial)
gbotterill@melton.gov.uk

Bush, Gary (LAB - Craven)
gbush@melton.gov.uk

Chandler, Pru (CON - Bottesford)
pchandler@melton.gov.uk

Cumbers, Pat (CON - Dorian)
pcumbers@melton.gov.uk

Douglas, Jeanne (CON - Craven)
jdouglas@melton.gov.uk

Dungworth, Steve (LAB - Egerton)
sdungworth@melton.gov.uk

Freer, Alison (CON - Warwick)
afreer@melton.gov.uk

Gordon, Marilyn (LAB - Dorian)
mgordon@melton.gov.uk

Graham, Malise (CON - Wymondham)
mgraham@melton.gov.uk

Holmes, Elaine (IND - Waltham on the Wolds)
eholmes@melton.gov.uk

Horton, Laura (LAB - Egerton)
laurahorton@melton.gov.uk

Hutchinson, Edward (IND - Frisby on the Wreake)
ehutchinson@melton.gov.uk

Lumley, Simon (CON - Newport)
slumley@melton.gov.uk

Manderson, Val (CON - Sysonby)
vmanderson@melton.gov.uk

Moncrieff, Trevor (LAB - Ashfordby)
tmoncrieff@melton.gov.uk

Moulding, John (LAB - Dorian)
jmoulding@melton.gov.uk

O'Callaghan, Matthew (LAB - Newport)
mocallaghan@melton.gov.uk

Orson, Joe (CON - Old Dalby)
jorson@melton.gov.uk

Sheldon, Mal (CON - Ashfordby)
msheldon@melton.gov.uk

Simpson, Janet (CON - Gaddesby)
janetsimpson@melton.gov.uk

Slater, Norman (CON - Warwick)
nslater@melton.gov.uk

Wright, David (CON - Bottesford)
dwright@melton.gov.uk

Wyatt, John (CON - Sysonby)
jwyatt@melton.gov.uk

POLITICAL COMPOSITION

CON: 19, LAB: 7, IND: 2

COMMITTEE CHAIRS

Appeals: Mrs Pat Cumbers
Community & Social Affairs: Mr David Wright
Development: Mrs Pru Chandler
Licensing: Mr Mark Barnes
Policy, Finance & Administration: Mr Byron Rhodes
Rural, Economic & Environmental Affairs: Mr Joe Orson

MENDIP D

Mendip District Council, Council Offices, Cannards Grave Road, Shepton Mallet BA4 5BT ☎ 01749 648999 🖷 01749 344050 customerservices@mendip.gov.uk www.mendip.gov.uk

FACTS & FIGURES

Police Authority: Avon & Somerset Police Authority
Health Authority: NHS South West
Learning and Skills Council: South West
Parliamentary Constituencies: Wells
EU Constituencies: South West
Election Frequency: Elections are of whole council
Twinning: Chilcompton: Montsurs (France); Frome: Chateau Gontier (France); Murrhardt (Germany); Shepton Mallet: Bollnas (Sweden); Misburg (Germany); Oissel (France); Street: Notre Dame-de-Gravenchon (France); Isny-im-Allgau (Germany); Wells: Paray-le-Monial (France); Bad Durkheim (Germany)

PRINCIPAL OFFICERS

Chief Executive: Mr Stuart Brown, Chief Executive, Mendip District Council, Cannards Grave Road, Shepton Mallet BA4 5BT ☎ 01749 341364 stuart.brown@mendip.gov.uk

Senior Management: Mr Stuart Brown, Chief Executive, Mendip District Council, Cannards Grave Road, Shepton Mallet BA4 5BT ☎ 01749 341364 stuart.brown@mendip.gov.uk

Access Officer / Social Services (Disability): Mr Keith Bush, Quality & Diversity Officer, Council Offices, Cannards Grave Road, Shepton Mallet BA4 5BT ☎ 01749 341386 keith.bush@mendip.gov.uk

Building Control: Mrs Tracy Aarons, Places Group Manager, Council Offices, Cannards Grave Road, Shepton Mallet BA4 5BT ☎ 01749 341448 🖷 01749 344050 tracy.aarons@mendip.gov.uk

PR / Communications: Ms Laura Thomas, Senior Communications Officer, Council Offices, Cannards Grave Road, Shepton Mallet BA4 5BT ☎ 01749 341205 laura.thomas@mendip.gov.uk

Community Planning: Mrs Sara Skirton, Community Planning & Partners Team Leader, Council Offices, Cannards Grave Road, Shepton Mallet BA4 5BT ☎ 01749 341340 🖷 01749 344050 sara.skirton@mendip.gov.uk

Contracts: Mrs Chris Atkinson, Access to Services Group Manager, Council Offices, Cannards Grave Road, Shepton Mallet BA4 5BT ☎ 01749 341217 🖷 01749 341542 chris.atkinson@mendip.gov.uk

Corporate Services: Mrs Chris Atkinson, Access to Services Group Manager, Council Offices, Cannards Grave Road, Shepton Mallet BA4 5BT ☎ 01749 341217 🖷 01749 341542 chris.atkinson@mendip.gov.uk

Customer Service: Mrs Chris Atkinson, Access to Services Group Manager, Council Offices, Cannards Grave Road, Shepton Mallet BA4 5BT ☎ 01749 341217 🖷 01749 341542 chris.atkinson@mendip.gov.uk

Economic Development: Mr Stuart Cave, Enforcement & Compliance Group Manager, Mendip District Council, Cannards Grave Road, Shepton Mallet BA4 5BT ☎ 01749 341331 stuart.cave@mendip.gov.uk

Electoral Registration: Mr Steve Lake, Electoral Services Manager, Mendip District Council, Cannards Grave Road, Shepton Mallet BA4 5BT ☎ 01749 341236 steven.lake@capita.co.uk

Environmental Health: Mrs Claire Malcolmson, Environmental Health Manager, Mendip District Council, Cannards Grave Road, Shepton Mallet BA4 5BT ☎ 01749 341350 claire.malcolmson@mendip.gov.uk

Health and Safety: Mr Geoff Thompson, Corporate Services Team Manager, Council Offices, Cannards Grave Road, Shepton Mallet BA4 5BT ☎ 01749 341396 geoff.thompson@mendip.gov.uk

Housing: Mrs Tracy Aarons, Places Group Manager, Council Offices, Cannards Grave Road, Shepton Mallet BA4 5BT ☎ 01749 341448 🖷 01749 344050 tracy.aarons@mendip.gov.uk

Legal: Mrs Donna Nolan, Governance & Resources Group Manager, Mendip District Council, Cannards Grave Road, Shepton Mallet BA4 5BT ☎ 01749 341210 donna.nolan@mendip.gov.uk

Licensing: Mr Jason Kirkwood, Licensing Manager, Council Offices, Cannards Grave Road, Shepton Mallet BA4 5BT ☎ 01749 341445 🖷 01749 344050 jason.kirkwood@mendip.gov.uk

Lottery Funding, Charity and Voluntary: Mrs Sally Gubb, Voluntary Sector Grants Officer, Council Offices, Cannards Grave Road, Shepton Mallet BA4 5BT ☎ 01749 341411 🖷 01749 344050 sally.gubb@mendip.gov.uk

Member Services: Mrs Claire Dicken, Member Support Officer, Council Offices, Cannards Grave Road, Shepton Mallet BA4 5BT ☎ 01749 341341 🖷 01749 341542 claire.dicken@mendip.gov.uk

Planning: Mrs Tracy Aarons, Places Group Manager, Council Offices, Cannards Grave Road, Shepton Mallet BA4 5BT ☎ 01749 341448 🖷 01749 344050 tracy.aarons@mendip.gov.uk

Procurement: Mr Geoff Thompson, Corporate Services Team Manager, Council Offices, Cannards Grave Road, Shepton Mallet BA4 5BT ☎ 01749 341396 geoff.thompson@mendip.gov.uk

Staff Training: Ms Dawn Carbin, Personnel Officer, Council Offices, Cannards Grave Road, Shepton Mallet BA4 5BT
☎ 01749 341244 🖷 01749 344050 ✉ dawn.carbin@mendip.gov.uk

MEMBERS OF THE COUNCIL (47)

***Chair:* Forrest**, Ronald (CON - St. Cuthbert Out North)
cllr.forrest@mendip.gov.uk
***Vice-Chair:* Coles**, John (CON - Glastonbury St John's)
cllr.coles@mendip.gov.uk
***Leader of the Council:* Siggs**, Harvey (CON - Wells St Cuthberts)
cllr.siggs@mendip.gov.uk
***Deputy Leader of the Council:* Killen**, Tom (CON - Chewton Mendip and Ston Easton)
cllr.killen@mendip.gov.uk
Baker, Julie (CON - Rodney & Westbury)
Cllr.Baker@mendip.gov.uk
Beha, Bryan (LD - Street South)
Cllr.Beha@mendip.gov.uk
Boyden, Adam (LD - Frome College)
Cllr.Boyden@mendip.gov.uk
Bradshaw, Peter (CON - Creech)
Cllr.Bradshaw@mendip.gov.uk
Brunsdon, John (CON - Glastonbury St Edmund's)
cllr.brunsdon@mendip.gov.uk
Bullen, Carole (CON - Frome College)
Cllr. Bullen@mendip.gov.uk
Carter, John (CON - Street North)
Cllr.Carter@mendip.gov.uk
Cawood, Gloria (LD - Cranmore, Doulting and Nunney)
cllr.cawood@mendip.gov.uk
Closier, Wayne (CON - Ashwick, Chilcompton & Stratton)
Cllr.Closier@mendip.gov.uk
Cook, Sue (LD - Shepton West)
Cllr.Cook@mendip.gov.uk
Cottle, Nick (LD - Glastonbury St Edmund's)
Cllr.Cottle@mendip.gov.uk
Crossley, John (CON - The Pennards & Ditcheat)
Cllr.Crossley@mendip.gov.uk
Denison, Andy (CON - Wells St Thomas')
Cllr.Denison@mendip.gov.uk
Dobinson, Adrian (LD - Frome Berkley Down)
cllr.dobinson@mendip.gov.uk
Drewe, Edward (CON - Ammerdown)
Cllr.Drewe@mendip.gov.uk
Ellis, Matthew (CON - Rode & Norton St Philip)
Cllr.Ellis@mendip.gov.uk
Ham, Philip (CON - Coleford and Holcombe)
cllr.ham@mendip.gov.uk
Height, Bente (CON - Shepton East)
Cllr.Height@mendip.gov.uk
Henderson, Steve (CON - Glastonbury St Benedict's)
Cllr.Henderson@mendip.gov.uk
Hewitt-Cooper, Nigel (CON - Croscombe and Pilton)
cllr.hewitt-cooper@mendip.gov.uk
Hooton, Damon (LD - Frome Park)
cllr.hooton@mendip.gov.uk
Horler, Valerie (CON - Coleford and Holcombe)
Cllr.Horler@mendip.gov.uk
Horsfall, Alvin (LD - Frome Keyford)
cllr.horsfall@mendip.gov.uk
Hudson, Claire (LD - Frome Park)
cllr.hudson@mendip.gov.uk
Hughes, Lloyd (IND - Street South)
cllr.hughes@mendip.gov.uk
Knibbs, Peter (CON - Beckington and Selwood)
Cllr.Knibbs@mendip.gov.uk
Marsh, Jeannette (CON - Shepton East)
cllr.marsh@mendip.gov.uk
Napper, Terry (CON - Street West)
Cllr.Napper@mendip.gov.uk
Noel, Graham (CON - Moor)
Cllr.Noel@mendip.gov.uk
North, John (CON - Wells Central)
Cllr.North@mendip.gov.uk
Osman, John (CON - Wells St Cuthburts)
Cllr.Osman@mendip.gov.uk
Parham, John (CON - Shepton West)
cllr.parham@mendip.gov.uk
Phripp, Sam (LD - Frome Berkley Down)
Cllr.Phripp@mendip.gov.uk
Pinnock, Richard (LD - Frome Keyford)
Cllr.Pinnock@mendip.gov.uk
Priscott, Steven (CON - Ashwick, Chilcompton and Stratton)
cllr.priscott@mendip.gov.uk
Snook, Sharon (LD - Frome Market)
Cllr.Snook@mendip.gov.uk
Spawson-White, Helen (LD - Frome Oakfield)
Cllr.Sprawson-White@mendip.gov.uk
Steer, George (CON - Street North)
Cllr.Steer@mendip.gov.uk
Stevens, David (CON - Postlebury)
Cllr.Stevens@mendip.gov.uk
Tanswell, Derek (LD - Frome Market)
Cllr.Tanswell@mendip.gov.uk
Taylor, Nigel (CON - Wookey and St Cuthbert Out West)
Cllr.Taylor@mendip.gov.uk
Unwin, Daniel (LD - Wells St Thomas')
cllr.unwin@mendip.gov.uk
Woollcombe-Adams, Nigel (CON - Butleigh and Baltonsborough)
Cllr.Woollcombe-Adams@mendip.gov.uk

POLITICAL COMPOSITION

CON: 31, LD: 15, IND: 1

CABINET

Leader: Mr Harvey Siggs
Deputy Leader: Mr Tom Killen
Access to Services: Mr Graham Noel (Mr Sam Phripp)
Built Environment: Mr Nigel Woollcombe-Adams (Mr Derek Tanswell)
Finance: Mr Steven Priscott (Mr Richard Pinnock)
Governance, Assets & Public Places: Mr Philip Ham (Mr Adam Boyden)
People & Places: Mr Nigel Taylor (Mr Nick Cottle)
Regulatory Services: Mr Nigel Taylor (Ms Helen Spawson-White)

COMMITTEE CHAIRS

Audit: Mr John Carter
Independent Remuneration Panel: Mr Paul Oddie (External)
Licensing: Ms Jeannette Marsh
Planning: Mr Nigel Woollcombe-Adams
Scrutiny (Scrutiny): Mr Damon Hooton
Standards: Mr Mike Hillman (External)

MERTHYR TYDFIL W

Merthyr Tydfil County Borough Council, (Cyngor Bwrdeistref Sirol Merthyr Tudful), Civic Centre, Castle Street, Merthyr Tydfil CF47 8AN ☎ 01685 725000 🖷 01685 722146 ✉ customer.care@merthyr.gov.uk 💻 www.merthyr.gov.uk

FACTS & FIGURES

Police Authority: South Wales Police Authority
Learning and Skills Council: Wales
Parliamentary Constituencies: Merthyr Tydfil and Rhymney
EU Constituencies: Wales
Election Frequency: Elections are of whole council
Twinning: Clichy La Garenne (France)

PRINCIPAL OFFICERS

Chief Executive: Mr Gareth Chapman, Chief Executive, Civic Centre, Castle Street, Merthyr Tydfil CF47 8AN ☎ 01685 725208 ✉ gareth.chapman@merthyr.gov.uk

Deputy Chief Executive: Mr Gareth Chapman, Chief Executive, Civic Centre, Castle Street, Merthyr Tydfil CF47 8AN ☎ 01685 725208 ✉ gareth.chapman@merthyr.gov.uk

Senior Management: Mr Giovanni Isingrini, Director - Community Services, Civic Centre, Castle Street, Merthyr Tydfil CF47 8AN ☎ 01685 724680 🖷 01685 384868 ✉ giovanni.isingrini@merthyr.gov.uk

Senior Management: Mr Steve Jones, Director - Finance, Civic Centre, Castle Street, Merthyr Tydfil CF47 8AN ☎ 01685 725000 ✉ steve.jones@merthyr.gov.uk

Senior Management: Mr Gary Thomas, Director - Customer Services, Civic Centre, Castle Street, Merthyr Tydfil CF47 8AN ☎ 01685 725253 🖷 01685 387740 ✉ gary.thomas@merthyr.gov.uk

Access Officer / Social Services (Disability): Ms Lisa Emerson, Access Manager, Ty Keir Hardie, Riverside Court, Avenue de Clichy, Merthyr Tydfil CF47 8XD ☎ 01685 726237 ✉ lisa.emerson@merthyr.gov.uk

Architect, Building / Property Services: Ms Cheryllee Evans, Principal Technical Officer - Property Services, Civic Centre, Castle Street, Merthyr Tydfil CF47 8AN ☎ 01685 725290 ✉ cheryllee.evans@merthyr.gov.uk

Building Control: Mr Ken Bateman, Group Leader - Building Control, Ty Keir Hardie, Riverside Court, Avenue de Clichy, Merthyr Tydfil CF47 8XD ☎ 01685 726257 🖷 01685 382698 ✉ ken.bateman@merthyr.gov.uk

Catering Services: Ms Edwina Pickering, Acting Team Leader - Catering Service, Civic Centre, Castle Street, Merthyr Tydfil CF47 8AN ☎ 01685 725000 ✉ edwina.pickering@merthyr.gov.uk

Children / Youth Services: Mr Ian Benbow, Head - Adult & Family Social Regeneration, Ty Keir Hardie, Riverside Court, Avenue de Clichy, Merthyr Tydfil CF47 8XD ☎ 01685 724602 ✉ ian.benbow@merthyr.gov.uk

Children / Youth Services: Mr Chris Hole, Head - Youth Service, Ty Keir Hardie, Riverside Court, Avenue de Clichy, Merthyr Tydfil CF47 8XD ☎ 01685 725000 🖷 01685 721795 ✉ chris.hole@merthyr.gov.uk

Civil Registration: Mrs Dianne Green, Superintendent Registrar, Register Office, Ty Penderyn, 26 High Street, Merthyr Tydfil CF47 8DP ☎ ; 01685 725000 ✉ dianne.green@merthyr.gov.uk

PR / Communications: Mrs Lee-Anne Leyshon, Team Leader - Corporate Communications, Civic Centre, Castle Street, Merthyr Tydfil CF47 8AN ☎ 01685 725483 🖷 01685 374397 ✉ corporate.communications@merthyr.gov.uk

Community Planning: Mr Gary Thomas, Director - Customer Services, Civic Centre, Castle Street, Merthyr Tydfil CF47 8AN ☎ 01685 725253 🖷 01685 387740 ✉ gary.thomas@merthyr.gov.uk

Community Safety: Mr Gary Thomas, Director - Customer Services, Civic Centre, Castle Street, Merthyr Tydfil CF47 8AN ☎ 01685 725253 🖷 01685 387740 ✉ gary.thomas@merthyr.gov.uk

Computer Management: Mr Ellis Cooper, Assistant Director - Customer Services, Civic Centre, Castle Street, Merthyr Tydfil CF47 8AN ☎ 01685 726295 ✉ ellis.cooper@merthyr.gov.uk

Consumer Protection and Trading Standards: Mr Steve Peters, Public Protection & Housing Manager, Civic Centre, Castle Street, Merthyr Tydfil CF47 8AN ☎ 01685 725030 🖷 01685 374201 ✉ steve.peters@merthyr.gov.uk

Contracts: Ms Sharon Phillips, Procurement & Efficiency Officer, Unit 5, Triangle Business Park, Pentrebach, Merthyr Tydfil CF48 4TQ ☎ 01685 725264 ✉ sharon.phillips@merthyr.gov.uk

Corporate Services: Mr Mark Thomas, Assistant Director - Audit, Performance & Partnership Manager, Civic Centre, Castle Street, Merthyr Tydfil CF47 8AN ☎ 01685 725204 ✉ mark.thomas@merthyr.gov.uk

Customer Service: Mr Gary Thomas, Director - Customer Services, Civic Centre, Castle Street, Merthyr Tydfil CF47 8AN ☎ 01685 725253 🖷 01685 387740 ✉ gary.thomas@merthyr.gov.uk

Direct Labour: Mr Gary Thomas, Director - Customer Services, Civic Centre, Castle Street, Merthyr Tydfil CF47 8AN ☎ 01685 725253 🖷 01685 387740 ✉ gary.thomas@merthyr.gov.uk

Economic Development: Mr Alyn Owen, Head - Regeneration, Unit 5, Triangle Business Park, Pentrebach, Merthyr Tydfil CF48 4TQ ☎ 01625 725303 🖷 01685 723751 ✉ alyn.owen@merthyr.gov.uk

Education: Mr Mike Southcoat, Chief Education Officer, Ty Keir Hardie, Riverside Court, Avenue de Clichy, Merthyr Tydfil CF47 8XD ☎ 01685 724621 ✉ mike.southcoat@merthyr.gov.uk

E-Government: Mr Ellis Cooper, Assistant Director - Customer Services, Civic Centre, Castle Street, Merthyr Tydfil CF47 8AN ☎ 01685 726295 ✉ ellis.cooper@merthyr.gov.uk

Electoral Registration: Ms Ann Taylor, Team Leader - Democratic Services, Civic Centre, Castle Street, Merthyr Tydfil CF47 8AN ☎ 01685 725202 🖷 01685 374397 ✉ ann.taylor@merthyr.gov.uk

Emergency Planning: Mr Ray Davies, Rapid Response Officer, Civic Centre, Castle Street, Merthyr Tydfil CF47 8AN ☎ 01685 724438 ✉ ray.davies@merthyr.gov.uk

Emergency Planning: Mr Robert Gough, Emergency Planning/ Local Resilience Unit Manager, Civic Centre, Castle Street, Merthyr Tydfil CF47 8AN ☎ 01685 725162 🖷 01685 387740 ✉ robert.gough@merthyr.gov.uk

Energy Management: Mr James Edwards, Energy Officer, Civic Centre, Castle Street, Merthyr Tydfil CF47 8AN ☎ 01685 726208 🖷 01685 383168 ✉ james.edwards@merthyr.gov.uk

Environmental / Technical Services: Mr Mike Thomas, Waste Services Manager, Civic Centre, Castle Street, Merthyr Tydfil CF47 8AN ☎ 01685 725345 🖷 01685 725024 ✉ mike.thomas@merthyr.gov.uk

Estates, Property & Valuation: Mr Mark Taylor, Head - Corporate Property & Physical Regeneration, Unit 5, Triange Business Park, Pentrebach, Merthyr Tydfil CF48 4TQ ☎ 01685 725319 🖷 01685 725060 ✉ mark.taylor@merthyr.gov.uk

European Liaison: Mr Alyn Owen, Head - Regeneration, Unit 5, Triangle Business Park, Pentrebach, Merthyr Tydfil CF48 4TQ ☎ 01625 725303 🖷 01685 723751 ✉ alyn.owen@merthyr.gov.uk

Events Manager: Mr Richard Marsh, Manager - Leisure, Culture & Environment, Civic Centre, Castle Street, Merthyr Tydfil CF47 8AN ☎ 01685 725273 ✉ richard.marsh@merthyr.gov.uk

Finance and Treasurer: Mr Steve Jones, Director - Finance, Civic Centre, Castle Street, Merthyr Tydfil CF47 8AN ☎ 01685 725000 ✉ steve.jones@merthyr.gov.uk

Fleet Management: Mr Paul Davies, Fleet Manager, Unit 20, Merthyr Industrial Estate, Pentrebach, Merthyr Tydfil CF48 4DR ☎ ; 01685 725000 🖷 01685 387982 ✉ paul.davies@merthyr.gov.uk

Grounds Maintenance: Mr Gary Thomas, Director - Customer Services, Civic Centre, Castle Street, Merthyr Tydfil CF47 8AN ☎ 01685 725253 🖷 01685 387740 ✉ gary.thomas@merthyr.gov.uk

Health and Safety: Mr Alyn Dinham, Occupational Health & Safety Officer, Civic Centre, Castle Street, Merthyr Tydfil CF47 8AN ☎ 01685 724677 🖷 01685 725055 ✉ alyn.dinham@merthyr.gov.uk

Highways: Mr Jeremy Morgan, Head - Engineering, Unit 20, Merthyr Industrial Park, Pentrebach, Merthyr Tydfil CF48 4DR ☎ 01685 726253 ✉ jeremy.morgan@merthyr.gov.uk

Housing: Mr Steve Peters, Public Protection & Housing Manager, Civic Centre, Castle Street, Merthyr Tydfil CF47 8AN ☎ 01685 725030 🖷 01685 374201 ✉ steve.peters@merthyr.gov.uk

Housing Maintenance: Ms Cheryllee Evans, Principal Technical Officer - Property Services, Civic Centre, Castle Street, Merthyr Tydfil CF47 8AN ☎ 01685 725290 ✉ cheryllee.evans@merthyr.gov.uk

Housing Maintenance: Mr Gary Thomas, Director - Customer Services, Civic Centre, Castle Street, Merthyr Tydfil CF47 8AN ☎ 01685 725253 🖷 01685 387740 ✉ gary.thomas@merthyr.gov.uk

Legal: Mrs Carys Kennedy, Head - Legal Services, Ty Kier Hardie, Riverside Court, Avenue de Clichy, Merthyr Tydfil CF47 8XD ☎ 01685 725454 🖷 01685 725060 ✉ carys.kennedy@merthyr.gov.uk

Leisure and Cultural Services: Mr Richard Marsh, Manager - Leisure, Culture & Environment, Civic Centre, Castle Street, Merthyr Tydfil CF47 8AN ☎ 01685 725273 ✉ richard.marsh@merthyr.gov.uk

Licensing: Mr Alyn Owen, Head - Regeneration, Unit 5, Triangle Business Park, Pentrebach, Merthyr Tydfil CF48 4QT ☎ 01625 725303 🖷 01685 723751 ✉ alyn.owen@merthyr.gov.uk

Lifelong Learning: Mr Giovanni Isingrini, Director - Community Services, Civic Centre, Castle Street, Merthyr Tydfil CF47 8AN ☎ 01685 724680 🖷 01685 384868 ✉ giovanni.isingrini@merthyr.gov.uk

Parking: Mr Jeremy Morgan, Head - Engineering, Unit 20, Merthyr Industrial Park, Pentrebach, Merthyr Tydfil CF48 4DR ☎ 01685 726253 ✉ jeremy.morgan@merthyr.gov.uk

Personnel / HR: Mr David Jones, Payroll Officer, Civic Centre, Castle Street, Merthyr Tydfil CF47 8AN ☎ 01685 725325 ✉ david.jones@merthyr.gov.uk

Personnel / HR: Mr Mark Tuson, HR & Communications Manager, Civic Centre, Castle Street, Merthyr Tydfil CF47 8AN ☎ 01685 724674 ✉ mark.tuson@merthyr.gov.uk

Planning: Ms Judith Jones, Planning Manager, Ty Keir Hardie, Riverside Court, Avenue de Clichy, Merthyr Tydfil CF47 8XD ☎ 01685 725000 ✉ judith.jones@merthyr.gov.uk

Procurement: Mrs Sharon Phillips, Procurement & Efficiency Officer, Unit 5, Triangle Business Park, Pentrebach, Merthyr Tydfil CF48 4TQ ☎ 01685 725264 ✉ sharon.phililps@merthyr.gov.uk

Public Libraries: Ms Sian Antony, Libraries Manager, Central Library, High Street, Merthyr Tydfil CF47 8AF ☎ 01685 353480 ✉ sian.antony@merthyr.gov.uk

Public Libraries: Ms Jane Selwood, Libraries Manager, Central Library, High Street, Merthyr Tydfil CF47 8AF ☎ 01685 353480 ✉ jane.selwood@merthyr.gov.uk

Recycling & Waste Minimisation: Ms Valerie Steel, Waste Services Officer, Civic Centre, Castle Street, Merthyr Tydfil CF47 8AN ☎ 01685 725478 🖷 01685 725024 ✉ val.steel@merthyr.gov.uk

Regeneration: Mr Alyn Owen, Head - Regeneration, Unit 5, Triangle Business Park, Pentrebach, Merthyr Tydfil CF48 4QT ☎ 01625 725303 🖷 01685 723751 ✉ alyn.owen@merthyr.gov.uk

Road Safety: Ms Lisa Clement-Williams, Road Safety Officer, Unit 20, Merthyr Industrial Estate, Pentrebach, Merthyr Tydfil CF48 4DR ☎ 01685 726286 ✉ lisa.clement-williams@merthyr.gov.uk

Social Services: Mr Richard Warrilow, Assistant Director - Social Services, Ty Keir Hardie, Riverside Court, Avenue de Clichy, Merthyr Tydfil CF47 8XD ☎ 01685 724693 ✉ richard.warrilow@merthyr.gov.uk

Social Services (Adult): Mr Giovanni Isingrini, Director - Community Services, Civic Centre, Castle Street, Merthyr Tydfil CF47 8AN ☎ 01685 724680 🖷 01685 384868 ✉ giovanni.isingrini@merthyr.gov.uk

Social Services (Adult): Mr Richard Warrilow, Assistant Director - Social Services, Ty Keir Hardie, Riverside Court, Avenue de Clichy, Merthyr Tydfil CF47 8XD ☎ 01685 724693 ✉ richard.warrilow@merthyr.gov.uk

Social Services (Children): Mr Martin Price, Head - Children's Services, Civic Centre, Castle Street, Merthyr Tydfil CF47 8AN ☎ 01685 724694 ✉ martin.price@merthyr.gov.uk

Staff Training: Ms Tracy Jones, Training Co-ordinator, Civic Centre, Castle Street, Merthyr Tydfil CF47 8AN ☎ 01685 725000 ✉ tracy.jones@merthyr.gov.uk

Street Scene: Mr Mike Thomas, Waste Services Manager, Civic Centre, Castle Street, Merthyr Tydfil CF47 8AN ☎ 01685 725345 🖷 01685 725024 ✉ mike.thomas@merthyr.gov.uk

Tourism: Mr Chris Long, Business Support & Tourism Manager, Civic Centre, Castle Street, Merthyr Tydfil CF47 8AN ☎ 01685 725079 🖷 01685 723751 ✉ chris.long@merthyr.gov.uk

Tourism: Mr Gary Thomas, Director - Customer Services, Civic Centre, Castle Street, Merthyr Tydfil CF47 8AN ☎ 01685 725253 🖷 01685 387740 ✉ gary.thomas@merthyr.gov.uk

Town Centre: Mrs Rhian Prosser, Town Centre Manager, Civic Centre, Castle Street, Merthyr Tydfil CF47 8AN ☎ 01685 725106 ✉ rhian.prosser@merthyr.gov.uk

Traffic Management: Mr Martin Stark, Traffic Management Engineer, Unit 20, Merthyr Industrial Park, Pentrebach, Merthyr Tydfil CF48 4DR ☎ 01685 726287 🖷 01685 387982 ✉ martin.stark@merthyr.gov.uk

Transport: Mr Martin Stark, Traffic Management Engineer, Unit 20, Merthyr Industrial Park, Pentrebach, Merthyr Tydfil CF48 4DR ☎ 01685 726287 🖷 01685 387982 ✉ martin.stark@merthyr.gov.uk

Waste Collection and Disposal: Mr Mike Thomas, Waste Services Manager, Civic Centre, Castle Street, Merthyr Tydfil CF47 8AN ☎ 01685 725345 🖷 01685 725024 ✉ mike.thomas@merthyr.gov.uk

Waste Management: Mr Mike Thomas, Waste Services Manager, Civic Centre, Castle Street, Merthyr Tydfil CF47 8AN ☎ 01685 725345 🖷 01685 725024 ✉ mike.thomas@merthyr.gov.uk

MEMBERS OF THE COUNCIL (33)

***Mayor:* Mytton**, Lisa (IND - Vaynor)
lisa.mytton@merthyr.gov.uk

***Deputy Mayor:* Davies**, Graham (LAB - Town)
democratic@merthyr.gov.uk

***Leader of the Council:* Toomey**, Brendan (LAB - Park)
brendan.toomey@merthyr.gov.uk

Barrett, Howard (IND - Vaynor)
howard.barrett@merthyr.gov.uk

Barry, Chris (LAB - Park)
chris.barry@merthyr.gov.uk

Braithwaite, Rhonda (LAB - Gurnos)
democratic@merthyr.gov.uk

Brown, Paul (IND - Cyfarthfa)
paul.brown@merthyr.gov.uk

Carter, Brent (LAB - Plymouth)
brent.carter@merthyr.gov.uk

Chaplin, Tony (LAB - Cyfarthfa)
democratic@merthyr.gov.uk

Davies, David (LAB - Town)
david.davies3@merthyr.gov.uk

Elliott, Les (O - Cyfarthfa)
les.elliott@merthyr.gov.uk

Galsworthy, Ernie (LAB - Treharris)
democratic@merthyr.gov.uk

Greer, Neil (IND - Penydarren)
neil.greer@merthyr.gov.uk

Isaac, David (LAB - Penydarren)
david.isaac@merthyr.gov.uk

Jarrett, David (LAB - Gurnos)
democtraic@merthyr.gov.uk

Jones, Harvey (LAB - Plymouth)
harvey.jones@merthyr.gov.uk

Jones, David (LAB - Town)
david.jones2@merthyr.gov.uk

Jones, Clive (LAB - Park)
clive.jones@merthyr.gov.uk

Jones, Gareth (IND - Bedlinog)
gareth.jones1@merthyr.gov.uk

Jones, Allan (IND - Penydarren)
allan.jones@merthyr.gov.uk

Lewis, Gareth (LAB - Plymouth)
gareth.lewis@merthyr.gov.uk

Lewis, Tom (LAB - Dowlais)
tom.lewis@merthyr.gov.uk

Mansbridge, Brian (LAB - Merthyr Vale)
brian.mansbridge@merthyr.gov.uk

Matthews, Linda (LAB - Town)
linda.matthews@merthyr.gov.uk

Morgan, Kate (LAB - Treharris)
democratic@merthyr.gov.uk

Roberts, Darren (LAB - Merthyr Vale)
darren.roberts@merthyr.gov.uk

Smart, Leighton (IND - Bedlinog)
leighton.smart@merthyr.gov.uk

Smith, Bill (LAB - Gurnos)
bill.smith@merthyr.gov.uk

Thomas, Raymond (LAB - Dowlais)
ray.thomas@merthyr.gov.uk

Thomas, Richard (IND - Treharris)

richard.thomas@merthyr.gov.uk
Tovey, Clive (IND - Gurnos)
clive.tovey@merthyr.gov.uk
Williams, Phil (LAB - Dowlais)
phil.williams@merthyr.gov.uk
Williams, Simon (LAB - Dowlais)
democratic@merthyr.gov.uk

POLITICAL COMPOSITION
LAB: 23, IND: 9, O: 1

CABINET
Leader: Mr Brendan Toomey
Deputy Leader: Mr Phil Williams
Business Reglatory Services: Mr Chris Barry
Chief Executive & Corporate Centre Services: Mr Julian Amos
Schools: Mr Harvey Jones
Social Services & Social Regeneration: Mr Brent Carter
Technical & Enviromental Services: Mr David Jones

COMMITTEE CHAIRS
Audit: Mr Richard Thomas
Chief Executive Services: Mr Phil Williams
Customer Services: Mr Darren Roberts
Licensing: Mr Clive Jones
Planning & Regulatory: Mr Clive Jones
Schools, Governance & Technical Services (Scrutiny): Mr Paul Brown
Social Services & Social Regeneration: Mr Bill Smith

MERTON L
London Borough of Merton, Merton Civic Centre, London Road, Morden SM4 5DX ☎ 020 8274 4901 🖷 020 8545 0446
communications@merton.gov.uk www.merton.gov.uk

FACTS & FIGURES
Police Authority: Metropolitan Police Authority
Health Authority: NHS London
Learning and Skills Council: London
Parliamentary Constituencies: Mitcham and Morden, Wimbledon
EU Constituencies: London
Election Frequency: Elections are of whole council

PRINCIPAL OFFICERS
Chief Executive: Mr Ged Curran, Chief Executive, Merton Civic Centre, London Road, Morden SM4 5DX ☎ 020 8545 3332 ged.curran@merton.gov.uk

Senior Management: Ms Caroline Holland, Director - Corporate Services, Merton Civic Centre, London Road, Morden SM4 5DX ☎ 020 8545 3450 🖷 020 8543 3952 caroline.holland@merton.gov.uk

Senior Management: Mr Chris Lee, Director - Environment & Regeneration, Merton Civic Centre, London Road, Morden SM4 5DX ☎ 020 8545 3050 🖷 020 8545 4105 chris.lee@merton.gov.uk

Senior Management: Ms Yvette Stanley, Director - Children, Schools & Families, Merton Civic Centre, London Road, Morden SM4 5DX ☎ 020 8545 3251 🖷 020 8545 3443 yvette.stanley@merton.gov.uk

Senior Management: Mr Simon Williams, Director - Community & Housing, Merton Civic Centre, London Road, Morden SM4 5DX ☎ 020 8545 3680 simon.williams@merton.gov.uk

Access Officer / Social Services (Disability): Mrs Kate Martyn, Head - Policy, Strategy & Partnerships, Merton Civic Centre, London Road, Morden SM4 5DX ☎ 020 8545 4632 🖷 020 8545 0446 kate.martyn@merton.gov.uk

Architect, Building / Property Services: Mr Howard Joy, Property Management & Review Manager, Merton Civic Centre, London Road, Morden SM4 5DX ☎ 020 8545 3083 howard.joy@merton.gov.uk

Architect, Building / Property Services: Mr James McGinlay, Head - Sustainable Communities, Merton Civic Centre, London Road, Morden SM4 5DX ☎ 020 8545 4154 james.mcginlay@merton.gov.uk

Best Value: Ms Kate Martyn, Head - Policy, Strategy & Partnerships, Merton Civic Centre, London Road, Morden SM4 5DX ☎ 020 8545 4632 kate.martyn@merton.gov.uk

Building Control: Mr John Hill, Head - Public Protection & Development, Merton Civic Centre, London Road, Morden SM4 5DX ☎ 020 8545 3052 🖷 020 8545 4105 john.hill@merton.gov.uk

Building Control: Mr Chris Lee, Director - Environment & Regeneration, Merton Civic Centre, London Road, Morden SM4 5DX ☎ 020 8545 3050 🖷 020 8545 4105 chris.lee@merton.gov.uk

Building Control: Mr Trevor McIntosh, Building Control Liaison Officer, Merton Civic Centre, London Road, Morden SM4 5DX ☎ 020 8545 3121 🖷 020 8545 6085 trevor.mcintosh@merton.gov.uk

Catering Services: Mrs Christine Humphries, Corporate Contracts & Administration Manager, Merton Civic Centre, London Road, Morden SM4 5DX ☎ 020 8545 3510 🖷 020 8545 3572 christine.humphries@merton.gov.uk

Children / Youth Services: Mr Paul Ballatt, Head - Commissioning, Strategy & Performance, Merton Civic Centre, London Road, Morden SM4 5DX ☎ 020 8274 4901 paul.ballatt@merton.gov.uk

Children / Youth Services: Ms Kaye Beeson, Service Manger – SEN & Disabilites Integrated Service, Merton Civic Centre, London Road, Morden SM4 5DX ☎ 020 8545 4800 kaye.beeson@merton.gov.uk

Children / Youth Services: Mrs Sheila Caie, Service Manager - LAC Permanency & Placements, Merton Civic Centre, London Road, Morden SM4 5DX ☎ 020 8545 4658 sheila.caie@merton.gov.uk

Children / Youth Services: Ms Melissa Caslake, Head - Social

Care & Youth Inclusion, Merton Civic Centre, London Road, Morden SM4 5DX ☎ 020 8545 3253 ✉ melissa.caslake@merton.gov.uk

Children / Youth Services: Ms Allison Jones, Service Manager – Early Years, Merton Civic Centre, London Road, Morden SM4 5DX ☎ 020 8545 3796 ✉ allison.jones@merton.gov.uk

Children / Youth Services: Mrs Theresa Leavy, Interim Head - Social Care & Youth Inclusion, Merton Civic Centre, London Road, Morden SM4 5DX ☎ 020 8545 3253 ✉ theresa.leavey@merton.gov.uk

Children / Youth Services: Ms Janet Martin, Head - Education, Merton Civic Centre, London Road, Morden SM4 5DX ☎ 020 8545 4060 ✉ janet.martin@merton.gov.uk

Children / Youth Services: Ms Kate Saksena, Manager - School Standards & Quality, Merton Civic Centre, London Road, Morden SM4 5DX ☎ 020 8545 3806 ✉ kate.saksena@merton.gov.uk

Children / Youth Services: Ms Yvette Stanley, Director - Children, Schools & Families, Merton Civic Centre, London Road, Morden SM4 5DX ☎ 020 8545 3251 🖷 020 8545 3443 ✉ yvette.stanley@merton.gov.uk

Civil Registration: Ms Virginia Morris, Service Manager - Registration, Merton Civic Centre, London Road, Morden SM4 5DX ☎ 020 8648 0414 ✉ virginia.morris@merton.gov.uk

PR / Communications: Ms Sophie Poole, Head - Communications, Merton Civic Centre, London Road, Morden SM4 5DX ☎ 020 8545 3181 🖷 020 8545 0446 ✉ sophie.poole@merton.gov.uk

Community Planning: Mrs Kate Martyn, Head - Policy, Strategy & Partnerships, Merton Civic Centre, London Road, Morden SM4 5DX ☎ 020 8545 4632 🖷 020 8545 0446 ✉ kate.martyn@merton.gov.uk

Community Safety: Ms Annalise Elliott, Head - Safer Merton, Merton Civic Centre, London Road, Morden SM4 5DX ☎ 020 8545 3240 ✉ annalise.elliott@merton.gov.uk

Community Safety: Mr Chris Lee, Director - Environment & Regeneration, Merton Civic Centre, London Road, Morden SM4 5DX ☎ 020 8545 3050 🖷 020 8545 4105 ✉ chris.lee@merton.gov.uk

Consumer Protection and Trading Standards: Mr John Hill, Head - Public Protection & Development, Merton Civic Centre, London Road, Morden SM4 5DX ☎ 020 8545 3052 🖷 020 8545 4105 ✉ john.hill@merton.gov.uk

Consumer Protection and Trading Standards: Mr Chris Lee, Director - Environment & Regeneration, Merton Civic Centre, London Road, Morden SM4 5DX ☎ 020 8545 3050 🖷 020 8545 4105 ✉ chris.lee@merton.gov.uk

Consumer Protection and Trading Standards: Mr Ian Murrell, Environmental Health, Trading Standards & Licensing Manager, Merton Civic Centre, London Road, Morden SM4 5DX ☎ 020 8545 3929 ✉ ian.murrell@merton.gov.uk

Contracts: Mr Paul Ballatt, Head - Commissioning, Strategy & Performance, Merton Civic Centre, London Road, Morden SM4 5DX ☎ 020 8274 4901 ✉ paul.ballatt@merton.gov.uk

Contracts: Mrs Christine Humphries, Corporate Contracts & Administration Manager, Merton Civic Centre, London Road, Morden SM4 5DX ☎ 020 8545 3510 🖷 020 8545 3572 ✉ christine.humphries@merton.gov.uk

Corporate Services: Ms Caroline Holland, Director - Corporate Services, Merton Civic Centre, London Road, Morden SM4 5DX ☎ 020 8545 3450 🖷 020 8543 3952 ✉ caroline.holland@merton.gov.uk

Corporate Services: Mr Dean Shoesmith, Joint Executive Head - Human Resources, Merton Civic Centre, London Road, Morden SM4 5DX ☎ 020 8545 3370 ✉ dean.shoesmith@merton.gov.uk

Customer Service: Mr Anthony Hopkins, Head - Libraries & Heritage Services, Merton Civic Centre, London Road, Morden SM4 5DX ☎ 020 8545 3770 ✉ anthony.hopkins@merton.gov.uk

Economic Development: Mr Chris Lee, Director - Environment & Regeneration, Merton Civic Centre, London Road, Morden SM4 5DX ☎ 020 8545 3050 🖷 020 8545 4105 ✉ chris.lee@merton.gov.uk

Education: Mr Paul Evans, Assistant Director - Corporate Governance / Joint Head - Legal, Clifford House, 67C St Helier Avenue, Morden SM4 6HY ☎ 020 8545 3338 ✉ paul.evans@merton.gov.uk

Education: Ms Janet Martin, Head - Education, Merton Civic Centre, London Road, Morden SM4 5DX ☎ 020 8545 4060 ✉ janet.martin@merton.gov.uk

Education: Ms Yvette Stanley, Director - Children, Schools & Families, Merton Civic Centre, London Road, Morden SM4 5DX ☎ 020 8545 3251 🖷 020 8545 3443 ✉ yvette.stanley@merton.gov.uk

Education: Ms Yvonne Tomlin, Head - Merton Adult Education, Merton Civic Centre, London Road, Morden SM4 5DX ☎ 020 8545 3711 ✉ yvonne.tomlin@merton.gov.uk

Electoral Registration: Mr Paul Evans, Assistant Director - Corporate Governance / Joint Head - Legal, Clifford House, 67C St Helier Avenue, Morden SM4 6HY ☎ 020 8545 3338 ✉ paul.evans@merton.gov.uk

Energy Management: Mr John Hill Clark, Head - Public Protection & Development, Merton Civic Centre, London Road, Morden SM4 5DX ☎ 020 8545 3052 🖷 020 8545 4105 ✉ john.hill@merton.gov.uk

Environmental / Technical Services: Mr John Hill, Head - Public Protection & Development, Merton Civic Centre, London Road, Morden SM4 5DX ☎ 020 8545 3052 🖷 020 8545 4105 ✉ john.hill@merton.gov.uk

Environmental / Technical Services: Mr Chris Lee, Director - Environment & Regeneration, Merton Civic Centre, London Road, Morden SM4 5DX ☎ 020 8545 3050 🖷 020 8545 4105 ✉ chris.lee@merton.gov.uk

Environmental / Technical Services: Mr Cormac Stokes, Head - Street Scene & Waste, Merton Civic Centre, London Road, Morden SM4 5DX ☎ 020 8545 3190 🖷 020 8545 4105 ✉ cormac.stokes@merton.gov.uk

Environmental Health: Mr Paul Evans, Assistant Director - Corporate Governance / Joint Head - Legal, Clifford House, 67C St Helier Avenue, Morden SM4 6HY ☎ 020 8545 3338 ✉ paul.evans@merton.gov.uk

Environmental Health: Mr John Hill, Head - Public Protection & Development, Merton Civic Centre, London Road, Morden SM4 5DX ☎ 020 8545 3052 🖷 020 8545 4105 ✉ john.hill@merton.gov.uk

Environmental Health: Mr Chris Lee, Director - Environment & Regeneration, Merton Civic Centre, London Road, Morden SM4 5DX ☎ 020 8545 3050 🖷 020 8545 4105 ✉ chris.lee@merton.gov.uk

Environmental Health: Mr Ian Murrell, Environmental Health, Trading Standards & Licensing Manager, Merton Civic Centre, London Road, Morden SM4 5DX ☎ 020 8545 3929 ✉ ian.murrell@merton.gov.uk

Estates, Property & Valuation: Mr Paul Evans, Assistant Director - Corporate Governance / Joint Head - Legal, Clifford House, 67C St Helier Avenue, Morden SM4 6HY ☎ 020 8545 3338 ✉ paul.evans@merton.gov.uk

Estates, Property & Valuation: Mr John Hill, Head - Public Protection & Development, Merton Civic Centre, London Road, Morden SM4 5DX ☎ 020 8545 3052 🖷 020 8545 4105 ✉ john.hill@merton.gov.uk

Estates, Property & Valuation: Mr Howard Joy, Property Management & Review Manager, Merton Civic Centre, London Road, Morden SM4 5DX ☎ 020 8545 3083 ✉ howard.joy@merton.gov.uk

Estates, Property & Valuation: Mr Chris Lee, Director - Environment & Regeneration, Merton Civic Centre, London Road, Morden SM4 5DX ☎ 020 8545 3050 🖷 020 8545 4105 ✉ chris.lee@merton.gov.uk

European Liaison: Mr Paul Evans, Assistant Director - Corporate Governance / Joint Head - Legal, Clifford House, 67C St Helier Avenue, Morden SM4 6HY ☎ 020 8545 3338 ✉ paul.evans@merton.gov.uk

European Liaison: Mr Chris Lee, Director - Environment & Regeneration, Merton Civic Centre, London Road, Morden SM4 5DX ☎ 020 8545 3050 🖷 020 8545 4105 ✉ chris.lee@merton.gov.uk

Events Manager: Mr Chris Lee, Director - Environment & Regeneration, Merton Civic Centre, London Road, Morden SM4 5DX ☎ 020 8545 3050 🖷 020 8545 4105 ✉ chris.lee@merton.gov.uk

Events Manager: Ms Sophie Poole, Head - Communications, Merton Civic Centre, London Road, Morden SM4 5DX ☎ 020 8545 3181 🖷 020 8545 0446 ✉ sophie.poole@merton.gov.uk

Facilities: Mrs Christine Humphries, Corporate Contracts & Administration Manager, Merton Civic Centre, London Road, Morden SM4 5DX ☎ 020 8545 3510 🖷 020 8545 3572 ✉ christine.humphries@merton.gov.uk

Finance and Treasurer: Mr Paul Dale, Interim Assistant Director - Resources, Merton Civic Centre, London Road, Morden SM4 5DX ☎ 020 8545 3325 ✉ paul.dale@merton.gov.uk

Fleet Management: Mr Chris Lee, Director - Environment & Regeneration, Merton Civic Centre, London Road, Morden SM4 5DX ☎ 020 8545 3050 🖷 020 8545 4105 ✉ chris.lee@merton.gov.uk

Fleet Management: Mr Cormac Stokes, Head - Street Scene & Waste, Merton Civic Centre, London Road, Morden SM4 5DX ☎ 020 8545 3190 🖷 020 8545 4105 ✉ cormac.stokes@merton.gov.uk

Grounds Maintenance: Mr Chris Lee, Director - Environment & Regeneration, Merton Civic Centre, London Road, Morden SM4 5DX ☎ 020 8545 3050 🖷 020 8545 4105 ✉ chris.lee@merton.gov.uk

Grounds Maintenance: Mr Cormac Stokes, Head - Street Scene & Waste, Merton Civic Centre, London Road, Morden SM4 5DX ☎ 020 8545 3190 🖷 020 8545 4105 ✉ cormac.stokes@merton.gov.uk

Health and Safety: Mr Paul Evans, Assistant Director - Corporate Governance / Joint Head - Legal, Clifford House, 67C St Helier Avenue, Morden SM4 6HY ☎ 020 8545 3338 ✉ paul.evans@merton.gov.uk

Health and Safety: Mr Chris Lee, Director - Environment & Regeneration, Merton Civic Centre, London Road, Morden SM4 5DX ☎ 020 8545 3050 🖷 020 8545 4105 ✉ chris.lee@merton.gov.uk

Highways: Mr Paul Evans, Assistant Director - Corporate Governance / Joint Head - Legal, Clifford House, 67C St Helier Avenue, Morden SM4 6HY ☎ 020 8545 3338 ✉ paul.evans@merton.gov.uk

Highways: Mr Mario Lecordier, Traffic & Highways Service Manager, Merton Civic Centre, London Road, Morden SM4 5DX ☎ 020 8545 3202 🖷 020 8545 3199 ✉ mario.lecordier@merton.gov.uk

Highways: Mr Cormac Stokes, Head - Street Scene & Waste, Merton Civic Centre, London Road, Morden SM4 5DX ☎ 020 8545 3190 🖷 020 8545 4105 ✉ cormac.stokes@merton.gov.uk

Home Energy Conservation: Mr John Hill Clark, Head - Public Protection & Development, Merton Civic Centre, London Road,

Morden SM4 5DX ☎ 020 8545 3052 🖷 020 8545 4105 john.hill@merton.gov.uk

Home Energy Conservation: Mr Chris Lee, Director - Environment & Regeneration, Merton Civic Centre, London Road, Morden SM4 5DX ☎ 020 8545 3050 🖷 020 8545 4105 chris.lee@merton.gov.uk

Housing: Mr Simon Williams, Director - Community & Housing, Merton Civic Centre, London Road, Morden SM4 5DX ☎ 020 8545 3680 simon.williams@merton.gov.uk

Legal: Mr Paul Evans, Assistant Director - Corporate Governance / Joint Head - Legal, Clifford House, 67C St Helier Avenue, Morden SM4 6HY ☎ 020 8545 3338 paul.evans@merton.gov.uk

Leisure and Cultural Services: Mr Anthony Hopkins, Head - Libraries & Heritage Services, Merton Civic Centre, London Road, Morden SM4 5DX ☎ 020 8545 3770 anthony.hopkins@merton.gov.uk

Leisure and Cultural Services: Mr Chris Lee, Director - Environment & Regeneration, Merton Civic Centre, London Road, Morden SM4 5DX ☎ 020 8545 3050 🖷 020 8545 4105 chris.lee@merton.gov.uk

Licensing: Mr John Hill, Head - Public Protection & Development, Merton Civic Centre, London Road, Morden SM4 5DX ☎ 020 8545 3052 🖷 020 8545 4105 john.hill@merton.gov.uk

Licensing: Mr John Hill Clark, Head - Public Protection & Development, Merton Civic Centre, London Road, Morden SM4 5DX ☎ 020 8545 3052 🖷 020 8545 4105 john.hill@merton.gov.uk

Licensing: Mr Ian Murrell, Environmental Health, Trading Standards & Licensing Manager, Merton Civic Centre, London Road, Morden SM4 5DX ☎ 020 8545 3929 ian.murrell@merton.gov.uk

Lifelong Learning: Ms Yvette Stanley, Director - Children, Schools & Families, Merton Civic Centre, London Road, Morden SM4 5DX ☎ 020 8545 3251 🖷 020 8545 3443 yvette.stanley@merton.gov.uk

Lifelong Learning: Ms Yvonne Tomlin, Head - Merton Adult Education, Merton Civic Centre, London Road, Morden SM4 5DX ☎ 020 8545 3711 yvonne.tomlin@merton.gov.uk

Lifelong Learning: Mr Simon Williams, Director - Community & Housing, Merton Civic Centre, London Road, Morden SM4 5DX ☎ 020 8545 3680 simon.williams@merton.gov.uk

Lighting: Mr Mario Lecordier, Traffic & Highways Service Manager, Merton Civic Centre, London Road, Morden SM4 5DX ☎ 020 8545 3202 🖷 020 8545 3199 mario.lecordier@merton.gov.uk

Lighting: Mr Cormac Stokes, Head - Street Scene & Waste, Merton Civic Centre, London Road, Morden SM4 5DX ☎ 020 8545 3190 🖷 020 8545 4105 cormac.stokes@merton.gov.uk

Lottery Funding, Charity and Voluntary: Mr Chris Lee, Director - Environment & Regeneration, Merton Civic Centre, London Road, Morden SM4 5DX ☎ 020 8545 3050 🖷 020 8545 4105 chris.lee@merton.gov.uk

Member Services: Mr Paul Evans, Assistant Director - Corporate Governance / Joint Head - Legal, Clifford House, 67C St Helier Avenue, Morden SM4 6HY ☎ 020 8545 3338 paul.evans@merton.gov.uk

Parking: Mr John Hill, Head - Public Protection & Development, Merton Civic Centre, London Road, Morden SM4 5DX ☎ 020 8545 3052 🖷 020 8545 4105 john.hill@merton.gov.uk

Parking: Mr John Hill Clark, Head - Public Protection & Development, Merton Civic Centre, London Road, Morden SM4 5DX ☎ 020 8545 3052 🖷 020 8545 4105 john.hill@merton.gov.uk

Parking: Mr Cormac Stokes, Head - Street Scene & Waste, Merton Civic Centre, London Road, Morden SM4 5DX ☎ 020 8545 3190 🖷 020 8545 4105 cormac.stokes@merton.gov.uk

Partnerships: Mrs Kate Martyn, Head - Policy, Strategy & Partnerships, Merton Civic Centre, London Road, Morden SM4 5DX ☎ 020 8545 4632 🖷 020 8545 0446 kate.martyn@merton.gov.uk

Partnerships: Mr Dean Shoesmith, Joint Executive Head - Human Resources, Merton Civic Centre, London Road, Morden SM4 5DX ☎ 020 8545 3370 dean.shoesmith@merton.gov.uk

Personnel / HR: Mr John Hill, Head - Public Protection & Development, Merton Civic Centre, London Road, Morden SM4 5DX ☎ 020 8545 3052 🖷 020 8545 4105 john.hill@merton.gov.uk

Personnel / HR: Mr Dean Shoesmith, Joint Executive Head - Human Resources, Merton Civic Centre, London Road, Morden SM4 5DX ☎ 020 8545 3370 dean.shoesmith@merton.gov.uk

Planning: Ms Hilary Di Salvo, Programme Manager - Customer Contact Programme, Merton Civic Centre, London Road, Morden SM4 5DX ☎ 020 8274 4901 hilary.disalvo@merton.gov.uk

Planning: Mr John Hill, Head - Public Protection & Development, Merton Civic Centre, London Road, Morden SM4 5DX ☎ 020 8545 3052 🖷 020 8545 4105 john.hill@merton.gov.uk

Procurement: Mr Kevin Churchill, Head - Procurement, Merton Civic Centre, London Road, Morden SM4 5DX ☎ 020 8545 3736 terry.ireland@merton.gov.uk

Procurement: Mr John Hill, Head - Public Protection & Development, Merton Civic Centre, London Road, Morden SM4 5DX ☎ 020 8545 3052 🖷 020 8545 4105 john.hill@merton.gov.uk

Procurement: Mr Tom Procter, Manager - Contracts, Procurement & School Organisation, Merton Civic Centre, London

Road, Morden SM4 5DX ☎ 020 8545 3306
✉ tom.procter@merton.gov.uk

Public Libraries: Mr Anthony Hopkins, Head - Libraries & Heritage Services, Merton Civic Centre, London Road, Morden SM4 5DX ☎ 020 8545 3770 ✉ anthony.hopkins@merton.gov.uk

Public Libraries: Mr Simon Williams, Director - Community & Housing, Merton Civic Centre, London Road, Morden SM4 5DX ☎ 020 8545 3680 ✉ simon.williams@merton.gov.uk

Recycling & Waste Minimisation: Mr Cormac Stokes, Head - Street Scene & Waste, Merton Civic Centre, London Road, Morden SM4 5DX ☎ 020 8545 3190 🖷 020 8545 4105 ✉ cormac.stokes@merton.gov.uk

Regeneration: Mr John Hill, Head - Public Protection & Development, Merton Civic Centre, London Road, Morden SM4 5DX ☎ 020 8545 3052 🖷 020 8545 4105 ✉ john.hill@merton.gov.uk

Regeneration: Mr Chris Lee, Director - Environment & Regeneration, Merton Civic Centre, London Road, Morden SM4 5DX ☎ 020 8545 3050 🖷 020 8545 4105 ✉ chris.lee@merton.gov.uk

Regeneration: Mr James McGinlay, Head - Sustainable Communities, Merton Civic Centre, London Road, Morden SM4 5DX ☎ 020 8545 4154 ✉ james.mcginlay@merton.gov.uk

Road Safety: Mr Cormac Stokes, Head - Street Scene & Waste, Merton Civic Centre, London Road, Morden SM4 5DX ☎ 020 8545 3190 🖷 020 8545 4105 ✉ cormac.stokes@merton.gov.uk

Social Services: Ms Marcia Whitehall-Smith, Service Manager – Community Support, Merton Civic Centre, London Road, Morden SM4 5DX ☎ 020 8545 4631 ✉ marcia.whitehall-smith@merton.gov.uk

Social Services: Mr Simon Williams, Director - Community & Housing, Merton Civic Centre, London Road, Morden SM4 5DX ☎ 020 8545 3680 ✉ simon.williams@merton.gov.uk

Social Services (Adult): Mr Simon Williams, Director - Community & Housing, Merton Civic Centre, London Road, Morden SM4 5DX ☎ 020 8545 3680 ✉ simon.williams@merton.gov.uk

Social Services (Children): Ms Kaye Beeson, Service Manger – SEN & Disabilites Integrated Service, Merton Civic Centre, London Road, Morden SM4 5DX ☎ 020 8545 4800 ✉ kaye.beeson@merton.gov.uk

Social Services (Children): Mrs Sheila Caie, Service Manager - LAC Permanency & Placements, Merton Civic Centre, London Road, Morden SM4 5DX ☎ 020 8545 4658 ✉ sheila.caie@merton.gov.uk

Social Services (Children): Ms Melissa Caslake, Head - Social Care & Youth Inclusion, Merton Civic Centre, London Road, Morden SM4 5DX ☎ 020 8545 3253 ✉ melissa.caslake@merton.gov.uk

Social Services (Children): Mr Lee Hopkins, Service Manger - Safeguarding & Partnerships, Merton Civic Centre, London Road, Morden SM4 5DX ☎ 020 8274 4901 ✉ lee.hopkins@merton.gov.uk

Social Services (Children): Mrs Theresa Leavy, Interim Head - Social Care & Youth Inclusion, Merton Civic Centre, London Road, Morden SM4 5DX ☎ 020 8545 3253 ✉ theresa.leavey@merton.gov.uk

Social Services (Children): Mr Keith Shipman, Manager - Education Youth & Inclusion, Merton Civic Centre, London Road, Morden SM4 5DX ☎ 020 8545 3546 ✉ keith.shipman@merton.gov.uk

Social Services (Children): Ms Yvette Stanley, Director - Children, Schools & Families, Merton Civic Centre, London Road, Morden SM4 5DX ☎ 020 8545 3251 🖷 020 8545 3443 ✉ yvette.stanley@merton.gov.uk

Social Services (Children): Mr Michael Sutherland, Service Manager - Policy, Planning & Performance, Merton Civic Centre, London Road, Morden SM4 5DX ☎ 020 8545 4090 ✉ michael.sutherland@merton.gov.uk

Social Services (Children): Ms Leanne Wallder, Joint Commissioning Manager - Children & Families, Merton Civic Centre, London Road, Morden SM4 5DX ☎ 020 8545 3591 ✉ leanne.wallder@merton.gov.uk

Staff Training: Mr Dean Shoesmith, Joint Executive Head - Human Resources, Merton Civic Centre, London Road, Morden SM4 5DX ☎ 020 8545 3370 ✉ dean.shoesmith@merton.gov.uk

Street Scene: Mr Cormac Stokes, Head - Street Scene & Waste, Merton Civic Centre, London Road, Morden SM4 5DX ☎ 020 8545 3190 🖷 020 8545 4105 ✉ cormac.stokes@merton.gov.uk

Sustainable Communities: Mr James McGinlay, Head - Sustainable Communities, Merton Civic Centre, London Road, Morden SM4 5DX ☎ 020 8545 4154 ✉ james.mcginlay@merton.gov.uk

Sustainable Development: Mr John Hill, Head - Public Protection & Development, Merton Civic Centre, London Road, Morden SM4 5DX ☎ 020 8545 3052 🖷 020 8545 4105 ✉ john.hill@merton.gov.uk

Sustainable Development: Mr James McGinlay, Head - Sustainable Communities, Merton Civic Centre, London Road, Morden SM4 5DX ☎ 020 8545 4154 ✉ james.mcginlay@merton.gov.uk

Town Centre: Mr John Hill, Head - Public Protection & Development, Merton Civic Centre, London Road, Morden SM4 5DX ☎ 020 8545 3052 🖷 020 8545 4105 ✉ john.hill@merton.gov.uk

Traffic Management: Mr Cormac Stokes, Head - Street Scene & Waste, Merton Civic Centre, London Road, Morden SM4 5DX ☎ 020 8545 3190 🖷 020 8545 4105 ✉ cormac.stokes@merton.gov.uk

Transport: Mr Cormac Stokes, Head - Street Scene & Waste, Merton Civic Centre, London Road, Morden SM4 5DX ☎ 020 8545 3190 🖷 020 8545 4105 ✉ cormac.stokes@merton.gov.uk

Transport Planner: Mr Cormac Stokes, Head - Street Scene & Waste, Merton Civic Centre, London Road, Morden SM4 5DX ☎ 020 8545 3190 🖷 020 8545 4105 ✉ cormac.stokes@merton.gov.uk

Total Place: Mr John Hill, Head - Public Protection & Development, Merton Civic Centre, London Road, Morden SM4 5DX ☎ 020 8545 3052 🖷 020 8545 4105 ✉ john.hill@merton.gov.uk

Waste Collection and Disposal: Mr Brian McLoughlin, Waste Operations Manager, Merton Civic Centre, London Road, Morden SM4 5DX ☎ 020 8545 4779 🖷 020 8545 3942 ✉ brian.mcloughlin@merton.gov.uk

Waste Collection and Disposal: Mr Cormac Stokes, Head - Street Scene & Waste, Merton Civic Centre, London Road, Morden SM4 5DX ☎ 020 8545 3190 🖷 020 8545 4105 ✉ cormac.stokes@merton.gov.uk

Waste Management: Mr Brian McLoughlin, Waste Operations Manager, Merton Civic Centre, London Road, Morden SM4 5DX ☎ 020 8545 4779 🖷 020 8545 3942 ✉ brian.mcloughlin@merton.gov.uk

Waste Management: Mr Cormac Stokes, Head - Street Scene & Waste, Merton Civic Centre, London Road, Morden SM4 5DX ☎ 020 8545 3190 🖷 020 8545 4105 ✉ cormac.stokes@merton.gov.uk

MEMBERS OF THE COUNCIL (60)

Leader of the Council: **Alambritis**, Stephen (LAB - Ravensbury)
stephen.alambritis@merton.gov.uk
Deputy Leader of the Council: **Betteridge**, Mark (LAB - Lavender Fields)
mark.betteridge@merton.gov.uk
Ahmad, Tariq (CON - Wimbledon Park)
tariq.ahmad@merton.gov.uk
Akyigyina, Agatha (LAB - Figge's Marsh)
agatha.akyigyina@merton.gov.uk
Allison, Mark (LAB - Lavender Fields)
mark.allison@merton.gov.uk
Anderson, Stan (LAB - St. Helier)
stan.anderson@merton.gov.uk
Attawar, Laxmi (LAB - Colliers Wood)
laxmi.attawar@merton.gov.uk
Bowcott, John (CON - Village)
john.bowcott@merton.gov.uk
Brierly, Margaret (CON - Raynes Park)
margaret.brierly@merton.gov.uk
Chellew, Richard (CON - Village)
richard.chellew@merton.gov.uk
Chung, David (LAB - Longthornton)
david.chung@merton.gov.uk
Dean, David (CON - Dundonald)
david.dean@merton.gov.uk
Dehaney, John (LAB - Graveney)
john.dehaney@merton.gov.uk
Draper, Nick (LAB - Colliers Wood)
nick.draper@merton.gov.uk
Dysart, Iain (LD - West Barnes)
iain.dysart@merton.gov.uk
Edge, Chris (CON - Dundonald)
chris.edge@merton.gov.uk
Evans, Suzanne (CON - Hillside)
suzanne.evans@merton.gov.uk
Forbes, Karin (R - Merton Park)
karin.forbes@merton.gov.uk
Fraser, Brenda (LAB - Longthornton)
brenda.fraser@merton.gov.uk
George, Samantha (CON - Village)
samantha.george@merton.gov.uk
Grocott, Suzanne (CON - Dundonald)
suzanne.grocott@merton.gov.uk
Groves, Maurice (CON - Lower Morden)
maurice.groves@merton.gov.uk
Gurung, Gam (LAB - Colliers Wood)
gam.gurung@merton.gov.uk
Hanna, Jeff (LAB - Pollards Hill)
jeff.hanna@merton.gov.uk
Hannah, Jeff (LAB - St. Helier)
dennis.pearce@merton.gov.uk
Hilton, Richard (CON - Lower Morden)
richard.hilton@merton.gov.uk
Holmes, James (CON - Trinity)
james.holmes@merton.gov.uk
Howard, Janice (CON - Wimbledon Park)
janice.howard@merton.gov.uk
Jeanes, Mary-Jane (LD - West Barnes)
mary-jane.jeanes@merton.gov.uk
Jones, Philip (LAB - Ravensbury)
philip.jones@merton.gov.uk
Judge, Andrew (LAB - Abbey)
andrew.judge@merton.gov.uk
Kirby, Linda (LAB - Graveney)
linda.kirby@merton.gov.uk
Lewis-Lavender, Gilli (CON - West Barnes)
gill.lewis-lavender@merton.gov.uk
Lohendran, Logie (CON - Cannon Hill)
logie.lohendran@merton.gov.uk
Macauley, Edith (LAB - Lavender Fields)
edith.macauley@merton.gov.uk
Makin, Russell (LAB - Cricket Green)
russell.makin@merton.gov.uk
Martin, Maxi (LAB - St. Helier)
maxi.martin@merton.gov.uk
McCabe, Peter (LAB - Ravensbury)
peter.mccabe@merton.gov.uk
Miller, Krystal (CON - Trinity)
krystal.miller@merton.gov.uk
Moulton, Oonagh (CON - Wimbledon Park)
oonagh.moulton@merton.gov.uk
Munn, Ian (LAB - Cricket Green)
ian.munn@merton.gov.uk
Neil Mills, Diane (CON - Abbey)
diane.neilmills@merton.gov.uk
Nelless, Henry (CON - Abbey)
henry.nelless@merton.gov.uk
Sargeant, John (R - Merton Park)
john.sargeant@merton.gov.uk
Saunders, Judy (LAB - Cricket Green)
judy.saunders@merton.gov.uk
Scott, Roderick (CON - Raynes Park)
rod.scott@merton.gov.uk

Scott, Linda (CON - Raynes Park)
linda.scott@merton.gov.uk
Shears, Deborah (CON - Cannon Hill)
deborah.shears@merton.gov.uk
Simpson, David (CON - Hillside)
david.simpson@merton.gov.uk
Southgate, Peter (R - Merton Park)
peter.southgate@merton.gov.uk
Stanford, Geraldine (LAB - Figge's Marsh)
geraldine.stanord@merton.gov.uk
Thomas, Sam (LAB - Longthornton)
sam.thomas@merton.gov.uk
Tindle, Ray (CON - Lower Morden)
ray.tindle@merton.gov.uk
Udeh, Gregory (LAB - Graveney)
gregory.udeh@merton.gov.uk
Walker, Peter (LAB - Figges Marsh)
peter.walker@merton.gov.uk
Whelton, Martin (LAB - Pollards Hill)
martin.whelton@merton.gov.uk
Williams, Richard (LAB - Pollards Hill)
richard.williams@merton.gov.uk
Williams, David (CON - Hillside)
david.williams@merton.gov.uk
Windsor, Miles (CON - Cannon Hill)
miles.windsor@merton.gov.uk
Withey, Simon (CON - Trinity)
simon.withey@merton.go.uk

POLITICAL COMPOSITION
LAB: 28, CON: 27, R: 3, LD: 2

CABINET
Leader: Mr Stephen Alambritis
Deputy Leader / Performance & Implementation: Mr Mark Betteridge
Adult Social Care & Health: Ms Linda Kirby
Children's Services: Ms Maxi Martin
Community & Culture: Mr Nick Draper
Community Safety, Engagement & Equalities: Ms Edith Macauley
Education: Mr Martin Whelton
Environmental Sustainability & Regeneration: Mr Andrew Judge
Finance: Mr Mark Allison

COMMITTEE CHAIRS
Appointments: Mr Stephen Alambritis
Audit: Mr Dave Roberts (External)
Children & Young People (Scrutiny): Mr Jeff Hannah
Conservation & Design: Mr Maurice Groves
General Purposes: Mr Peter McCabe
Healthier Communities & Older People: Ms Suzanne Evans
Joint Consultative Committee with Ethnic Minority Organisations: Ms Edith Macauley
Licensing: Mr David Simpson
Overview & Scrutiny Commission: Mr Peter Southgate
Planning Applications: Mr Philip Jones
Standards (Scrutiny): Mr Simon Sapper (External)
Sustainable Communities (Scrutiny): Mr Russell Makin

MID DEVON — D

Mid Devon District Council, Phoenix House, Phoenix Lane, Tiverton EX16 6PP ☎ 01884 255255 🖷 01884 234318 chiefexec@middevon.gov.uk www.middevon.gov.uk

FACTS & FIGURES
Police Authority: Devon & Cornwall Police Authority
Health Authority: NHS South West
Learning and Skills Council: South West
Parliamentary Constituencies: Devon Central, Tiverton and Honiton
EU Constituencies: South West
Election Frequency: Elections are of whole council
Twinning: Bampton: Villers Bocage (France); Bow: St Martin-du-Bienfaite (France); Bradninch: Landunveg (France); Chawleigh: St. Martin-du-Mailloc (France); Cheriton Fitzpaine: Pre d'auge (France); Copplestone: St Cyr du Ronceray (France); Cullompton: Ploudalmezeau (France); Lapford: Grainville-Langannerie (France); Morchard Bishop: St Gatien-des-Bois (France); Poughill: Sept Vents (France); Sandford: Demouville (France); Tiverton: Chinon (France) and Hofheim (Germany); Uffculme: Caumont L'Evente (France)

PRINCIPAL OFFICERS
Chief Executive: Mr Kevin Finan, Chief Executive, Phoenix House, Phoenix Lane, Tiverton EX16 6PP ☎ 01884 234201 kfinan@middevon.gov.uk

Senior Management: Mrs Christina Cross, Head of ICT, Phoenix House, Phoenix Lane, Tiverton EX16 6PP ☎ 01884 234912 🖷 01884 234318 ccross@middevon.gov.uk

Senior Management: Mr Jonathan Guscott, Head of Planning & Regeneration, Phoenix House, Phoenix Lane, Tiverton EX16 6PP ☎ 01884 234273 🖷 01884 234306 jguscott@middevon.gov.uk

Senior Management: Mr Andrew Jarrett, Financial Services Manager, Phoenix House, Phoenix Lane, Tiverton EX16 6PP ☎ 01884 234242 🖷 01884 234318 ajarrett@middevon.gov.uk

Senior Management: Mr Simon Johnson, Legal Services Manager, Phoenix House, Phoenix Lane, Tiverton EX16 6PP ☎ 01884 234210 sjohnson@middevon.gov.uk

Senior Management: Ms Jill Stimpson, Human Resources Manager, Phoenix House, Phoenix Lane, Tiverton EX16 6PP ☎ 01884 234381 🖷 01884 234395 jstimpson@middevon.gov.uk

Senior Management: Miss Amy Tregellas, Audit Manager, Phoenix House, Phoenix Lane, Tiverton EX16 6PP ☎ 01884 234246 atregellas@middevon.gov.uk

Best Value: Miss Amy Tregellas, Audit Manager, Phoenix House, Phoenix Lane, Tiverton EX16 6PP ☎ 01884 234246 atregellas@middevon.gov.uk

Building Control: Mr Ken McLaren, Building Control Officer, Phoenix House, Phoenix Lane, Tiverton EX16 6PP ☎ 01884 234347 🖷 01884 234256 kmclaren@middevon.gov.uk

Children / Youth Services: Mr John Bodley-Scott, Community

Development Officer, Phoenix House, Phoenix Lane, Tiverton EX16 6PP ☎ 01884 234363 🖷 01884 234908 ✉ jbodleyscott@middevon.gov.uk

PR / Communications: Mr Andrew Lacey, Communications Manager, Phoenix House, Phoenix Lane, Tiverton EX16 6PP ☎ 01884 234232 🖷 01884 234318 ✉ alacey@middevon.gov.uk

Community Planning: Mr John Bodley-Scott, Community Development Officer, Phoenix House, Phoenix Lane, Tiverton EX16 6PP ☎ 01884 234363 🖷 01884 234908 ✉ jbodleyscott@middevon.gov.uk

Community Safety: Mrs Julia Ryder, Community Safety Officer, Phoenix House, Phoenix Lane, Tiverton EX16 6PP ☎ 01884 234997 🖷 01884 234931 ✉ jryder@middevon.gov.uk

Computer Management: Mrs Christina Cross, Head of ICT, Phoenix House, Phoenix Lane, Tiverton EX16 6PP ☎ 01884 234912 🖷 01884 234318 ✉ ccross@middevon.gov.uk

Customer Service: Ms Liz Reeves, Customer First Manager, Phoenix House, Phoenix Lane, Tiverton EX16 6PP ☎ 01884 234371 🖷 01884 234335 ✉ lreeves@middevon.gov.uk

Direct Labour: Mrs Chanelle White, Procurement Manager, Phoenix House, Phoenix Lane, Tiverton EX16 6PP ☎ 01884 234228 🖷 01884 234318 ✉ cwhite@middevon.gov.uk

Economic Development: Mr Gordon Cleaver, Regeneration Manager, Phoenix House, Phoenix Lane, Tiverton EX16 6PP ☎ 01884 234368 🖷 01884 234908 ✉ gcleaver@middevon.gov.uk

Electoral Registration: Miss Jackie Stoneman, Electoral Services Officer, Phoenix House, Phoenix Lane, Tiverton EX16 6PP ☎ 01884 234214 🖷 01884 234318 ✉ jstoneman@middevon.gov.uk

Emergency Planning: Mr Paul Williams, Emergency Planning Officer, Phoenix House, Phoenix Lane, Tiverton EX16 6PP ☎ 01884 244606 🖷 01884 234318 ✉ pnwilliams@middevon.gov.uk

Energy Management: Mr Andrew Busby, Corporate Buildings Manager, Phoenix House, Phoenix Lane, Tiverton EX16 6PP ☎ 01884 234948 ✉ abusby@middevon.gov.uk

Environmental Health: Mr Jayme Carme, Environmental Health Officer, Phoenix House, Phoenix Lane, Tiverton EX16 6PP ☎ 01884 244621 ✉ jcarne@middevon.gov.uk

Environmental Health: Mr Paul Williams, Health Services Manager, Phoenix House, Phoenix Lane, Tiverton EX16 6PP ☎ 01884 244606 ✉ pwilliams@middevon.gov.uk

Estates, Property & Valuation: Mr Nick Sanderson, Estates Manager, Phoenix House, Phoenix Lane, Tiverton EX16 6PP ☎ 01884 234960 ✉ nsanderson@middevon.gov.uk

European Liaison: Mr Gordon Cleaver, Regeneration Manager, Phoenix House, Phoenix Lane, Tiverton EX16 6PP ☎ 01884 234368 🖷 01884 234908 ✉ gcleaver@middevon.gov.uk

Finance and Treasurer: Mr Andrew Jarrett, Financial Services Manager, Phoenix House, Phoenix Lane, Tiverton EX16 6PP ☎ 01884 234242 🖷 01884 234318 ✉ ajarrett@middevon.gov.uk

Fleet Management: Mr Gary Pilling, Cleansing & Transport Manager, Old Road, Tiverton EX16 4LA ☎ 01884 234241 🖷 01884 256014 ✉ gpilling@middevon.gov.uk

Grounds Maintenance: Mr Nick Sanderson, Estates Manager, Phoenix House, Phoenix Lane, Tiverton EX16 6PP ☎ 01884 234960 ✉ nsanderson@middevon.gov.uk

Housing: Mrs Claire Fry, Housing Services Manager, Phoenix House, Phoenix Lane, Tiverton EX16 6PP ☎ 01884 234386 ✉ cfry@middevon.gov.uk

Housing Maintenance: Mr Stephen Bennett, Planned Maintenance Manager, Phoenix House, Phoenix Lane, Tiverton EX16 6PP ☎ 01884 233036 🖷 01884 233024 ✉ sbennett@middevon.gov.uk

Legal: Mr Simon Johnson, Legal Services Manager, Phoenix House, Phoenix Lane, Tiverton EX16 6PP ☎ 01884 234210 ✉ sjohnson@middevon.gov.uk

Leisure and Cultural Services: Miss Samantha Bennion, Leisure Services Manager, Phoenix House, Phoenix Lane, Tiverton EX16 6PP ☎ 01884 234902 ✉ sbennion@middevon.gov.uk

Licensing: Mrs Marjory Parish, Licensing Manager, Phoenix House, Phoenix Lane, Tiverton EX16 6PP ☎ 01884 234618 🖷 01884 234256 ✉ mparish@middevon.gov.uk

Lottery Funding, Charity and Voluntary: Mr Paul Tucker, Grants Officer, Phoenix House, Phoenix Lane, Tiverton EX16 6PP ☎ 01884 234930 🖷 01884 234908 ✉ ptucker@middevon.gov.uk

Member Services: Mr Simon Coombs, Member Services Manager, Phoenix House, Phoenix Lane, Tiverton EX16 6PP ☎ 01844 234209 🖷 01844 234318 ✉ scoombs@middevon.gov.uk

Parking: Mr Nick Sanderson, Estates Manager, Phoenix House, Phoenix Lane, Tiverton EX16 6PP ☎ 01884 234960 ✉ nsanderson@middevon.gov.uk

Personnel / HR: Ms Jill Stimpson, Human Resources Manager, Phoenix House, Phoenix Lane, Tiverton EX16 6PP ☎ 01884 234381 🖷 01884 234395 ✉ jstimpson@middevon.gov.uk

Planning: Mr Jonathan Guscott, Head of Planning & Regeneration, Phoenix House, Phoenix Lane, Tiverton EX16 6PP ☎ 01884 234273 🖷 01884 234306 ✉ jguscott@middevon.gov.uk

Procurement: Mrs Chanelle White, Procurement Manager, Phoenix House, Phoenix Lane, Tiverton EX16 6PP ☎ 01884 234228 🖷 01884 234318 ✉ cwhite@middevon.gov.uk

Recycling & Waste Minimisation: Mr Simon Hill, Waste Strategy Recycling Officer, Phoenix House, Phoenix Lane, Tiverton EX16 6PP ☎ 01884 234917 🖷 01884 256014 ✉ sphill@middevon.gov.uk

Regeneration: Mr Gordon Cleaver, Regeneration Manager, Phoenix House, Phoenix Lane, Tiverton EX16 6PP ☎ 01884 234368 🖷 01884 234908 ✉ gcleaver@middevon.gov.uk

Staff Training: Mrs Julia Licorish, Learning & Development Officer, Phoenix House, Phoenix Lane, Tiverton EX16 6PP ☎ 01884 234381 🖷 01884 234202 ✉ jlicorish@middevon.gov.uk

Street Scene: Mr Nick Sanderson, Estates Manager, Phoenix House, Phoenix Lane, Tiverton EX16 6PP ☎ 01884 234960 ✉ nsanderson@middevon.gov.uk

Sustainable Communities: Mr John Bodley-Scott, Community Development Officer, Phoenix House, Phoenix Lane, Tiverton EX16 6PP ☎ 01884 234363 🖷 01884 234908 ✉ jbodleyscott@middevon.gov.uk

Waste Collection and Disposal: Mr Gary Pilling, Cleansing & Transport Manager, Old Road, Tiverton EX16 4LA ☎ 01884 234241 🖷 01884 256014 ✉ gpilling@middevon.gov.uk

Waste Management: Mr Gary Pilling, Cleansing & Transport Manager, Old Road, Tiverton EX16 4LA ☎ 01884 234241 🖷 01884 256014 ✉ gpilling@middevon.gov.uk

MEMBERS OF THE COUNCIL (43)

***Chair:* Hull**, Brenda (CON - Lower Culme)
bhull@middevon.gov.uk
***Leader of the Council:* Hare-Scott**, Peter (CON - Newbrook Road)
pharescott@middevon.gov.uk
***Deputy Leader of the Council:* Colthorpe**, Polly (CON - Clare and Shuttern)
pcolthorpe@middevon.gov.uk
Clare and Shuttern: Vacant
Andrews, Eileen (IND - Cullompton South)
eandrews@middevon.gov.uk
Bainbridge, Heather (CON - Canonsleigh)
hbainbridge@middevon.gov.uk
Berry, John (CON - Bradninch)
jberry@middevon.gov.uk
Binks, Martin (LD - Lawrence)
mbinks@middevon.gov.uk
Brandon, Diane (IND - Lower Culme)
dbrandon@middevon.gov.uk
Chesterton, Richard (CON - Lower Culme)
rchesterton@middevon.gov.uk
Coren, Derek (CON - Yeo)
dcoren@middevon.gov.uk
Davey, Neal (CON - 7 Amory Road)
ndavey@middevon.gov.uk
Daw, John (IND - Taw)
jdaw@middevon.gov.uk
Deed, Bob (CON - Cadbury)
bdeed@middevon.gov.uk
Downes, John (LD - Boniface)
jdownes@middevon.gov.uk
Eginton, Clive (CON - Taw Vale)
ceginton@middevon.gov.uk
Evans, Bob (CON - Lower Culme)
revans@middevon.gov.uk
Fox, Sarah (CON - Way)
sfox@middevon.gov.uk
Griffiths, Alan (CON - Westexe South)
griffithsalan@aol.com
Griggs, Sue (CON - Cranmore)
sgriggs@middevon.gov.uk
Heal, Peter (CON - Yeo)
pheal@middevon.gov.uk
Holloway, Linda (IND - Cullompton North)
lholloway@middevon.gov.uk
Hughes, Glanmor (CON - Upper Culm)
ghughes@middevon.gov.uk
Knowles, Dennis (IND - Lowman)
dknowles@middevon.gov.uk
Lee, Michael (CON - Sandford and Creedy)
michael.lee@devon.gov.uk
Lucas, Mel (IND - Canonsleigh)
mlucas@middevon.gov.uk
Luxton, Gerald (IND - Westexe North)
gluxton@middevon.gov.uk
Pugsley, David (IND - Cullompton Outer)
dpugsley@middevon.gov.uk
Radford, Ray (CON - Halberton and Uplowman)
rradford@middevon.gov.uk
Rendle, Janet (CON - Castle)
jrendle@middevon.gov.uk
Roach, Jenny (LIB - Silverton)
jroach@middevon.gov.uk
Rosamond, Frank (IND - Upper Culm)
frosamond@middevon.gov.uk
Slade, Colin (CON - Cullompton Town)
cslade@middevon.gov.uk
Snow, Terry (IND - Cullompton South)
tsnow@middevon.gov.uk
Squire, John (CON - Upper Yeo)
jsquire@middevon.gov.uk
Squires, Margaret (CON - Sandford and Creedy)
msquires@middevon.gov.uk
Stanley, Raymond (CON - Clare and Shuttern)
rstanley@middevon.gov.uk
Turner, Mary (IND - Westexe South)
mturner@eclipse.co.uk
Way, Nick (LD - Boniface)
nway@middevon.gov.uk
Williams, Paul (LD - Canal)
paulwillie@aol.com
Wilson, Kevin (LD - Cranmore)
kwilson@middevon.go.vuk
Woollatt, Nikki (IND - Cullompton North)
nwoollatt@middevon.gov.uk
Wright, Bob (LD - Lawrence)
bwright@middevon.gov.uk

POLITICAL COMPOSITION

CON: 23, IND: 12, LD: 6, Vacant: 1, LIB: 1

CABINET

Leader: Mr Peter Hare-Scott
Deputy Leader: Mrs Polly Colthorpe
Community Well-Being: Mrs Jane Campbell
Finance: Mr Neal Davey
Housing: Mr Raymond Stanley
Street Scene: Mr Ray Radford
Working Environment & Support Services: Mr Dennis Knowles

COMMITTEE CHAIRS

Audit: Ms Sarah Fox
Executive: Mr Peter Hare-Scott
Licensing: Mr Glanmor Hughes
Planning: Mrs Margaret Squires
Scrutiny: Mr Nick Way

MID SUFFOLK D

Mid Suffolk District Council, Council Offices, 131 High Street, Needham Market IP6 8DL ☎ 01449 724500 🖷 01449 724696 💻 www.midsuffolk.gov.uk

FACTS & FIGURES

Police Authority: Suffolk Police Authority
Health Authority: East of England Strategic Health Authority
Learning and Skills Council: Eastern
Parliamentary Constituencies: Bury St. Edmunds
EU Constituencies: Eastern
Election Frequency: Elections are of whole council
Twinning: Eye: Pouzauges (France); Framsden: St. Etienne-de-Lisse (France); Haughley and Wetherden: Noyelles-les-Seclin (France); Redgrave, Botesdale, Rickinghall: Tinteniac (France); Stowmarket: Verneuil-sur-Avre (France); Wortham: Hede (France)

PRINCIPAL OFFICERS

Chief Executive: Mr Charlie Adan, Chief Executive, Council Offices, 131 High Street, Needham Market, Ipswich IP6 8DL ☎ 01449 724802 🖷 01443 724696 ✉ charlie.adan@midsuffolk.gov.uk

Senior Management: Ms Lindsay Barker, Strategic Director - Place, Council Offices, 131 High Street, Needham Market IP6 8DL ☎ 01449 724697 🖷 01449 724696 ✉ lindsay.barker@midsuffolk.gov.uk

Senior Management: Mr Mike Evans, Strategic Director - People, Council Offices, 131 High Street, Needham Market IP6 8DL ☎ 01449 724803 🖷 01449 724696 ✉ mike.evans@midsuffolk.gov.uk

Senior Management: Mr Mike Hammond, Interim Director - Transformation, Council Offices, 131 High Street, Needham Market IP6 8DL ☎ 01449 724670 🖷 01449 724696 ✉ mike.hammond@babergh.gov.uk

Senior Management: Mr Andrew Hunkin, Strategic Director - Corporate, Council Offices, 131 High Street, Needham Market IP6 8DL ☎ 01449 724526 🖷 01449 724696 ✉ andrew.hunkin@babergh.gov.uk

Best Value: Mr Peter Quirk, Head - Corporate Organisation, Council Offices, 131 High Street, Needham Market IP6 8DL ☎ 01449 724656 🖷 01449 724696 ✉ peter.quirk@babergh.gov.uk

Building Control: Mr Peter Burrows, Head - Economy, Council Offices, 131 High Street, Needham Market IP6 8DL ☎ 01449 724503 🖷 01449 724514 ✉ peter.burrows@midsuffolk.gov.uk

Building Control: Mr Gary Starling, Corporate Manager - Building Control, Council Offices, 131 High Street, Needham Market IP6 8DL ☎ 01449 724502 🖷 01449 724514 ✉ gary.starling@midsuffolk.gov.uk

PR / Communications: Mr Paul Simon, Corporate Manager - Communications, Council Offices, Corks Lane, Hadleigh IP7 6SJ ☎ 01473 826634 🖷 01473 825742 ✉ paul.simon@babergh.gov.uk

Community Planning: Mr Tom Barker, Corporate Manager - Strong Communities, Council Offices, 131 High Street, Needham Market IP6 8DL ☎ 01449 724647 🖷 01449 724655 ✉ tom.baker@midsuffolk.gov.uk

Community Safety: Ms Peta Jones, Corporate Manager - Safe Communities, Council Offices, 131 High Street, Needham Market IP6 8DL ☎ 01449 724642 🖷 01449 724655 ✉ peta.jones@midsuffolk.gov.uk

Computer Management: Mr Carl Reeder, Corporate Manager - Information Management & ICT, Council Offices, 131 High Street, Needham Market IP6 8DL ☎ 01449 724695 ✉ carl.reeder@babergh.gov.uk

Contracts: Mrs Rachel Hodson - Gibbons, Procurement Consultant, Council Offices, 131 High Street, Needham Market IP6 8DL ☎ 01449 724587 ✉ rachel.hodson-gibbons@midsuffolk.gov.uk

Corporate Services: Mr Peter Quirk, Head - Corporate Organisation, Council Offices, 131 High Street, Needham Market IP6 8DL ☎ 01449 724656 🖷 01449 724696 ✉ peter.quirk@babergh.gov.uk

Corporate Services: Ms Kathryn Saward, Monitoring Officer, Council Offices, 131 High Street, Needham Market IP6 8DL ☎ 01449 724803; 01449 724679 🖷 01449 727345; 01449 724696 ✉ catherine.saward@midsuffolk.gov.uk; kathryn.saward@babergh.gov.uk

Corporate Services: Ms Katherine Steel, Head - Corporate Resources, Council Offices, 131 High Street, Needham Market IP6 8DL ☎ 01449 724806 🖷 01449 724696 ✉ katherine.steel@midsuffolk.gov.uk; kathryn.steel@babergh.gov.uk

Customer Service: Mr David Cleary, Corporate Manager - Customer Services, Council Offices, 131 High Street, Needham Market IP6 8DL ☎ 01449 724581; 01449 724581 🖷 01473 823594 ✉ david.cleary@midsuffolk.gov.uk; david.cleary@midsuffolk.gov.uk

Direct Labour: Mr Ryan Jones, Corporate Manager - Asset Management Operations, Council Offices, 131 High Street, Needham Market IP6 8DL ☎ 01449 724733; 01449 724733 🖷 01449 724745 ✉ ryan.jones@babergh.gov.uk

Economic Development: Mr David Benham, Corporate Manager - Economic Development & Tourism, Council Offices, 131 High Street, Needham Market IP6 8DL ☎ 01449 724649 🖷 01449 724655 ✉ david.benham@midsuffolk.gov.uk

E-Government: Mr Carl Reeder, Corporate Manager - Information Management & ICT, Council Offices, 131 High Street, Needham Market IP6 8DL ☎ 01449 724695 ✉ carl.reeder@babergh.gov.uk

Electoral Registration: Mr Philip Tallent, Corporate Manager -

Elections & Electoral Management, Council Offices, 131 High Street, Needham Market IP6 8DL ☎ 01449 724694 🖷 01449 724696 ✉ philip.tallent@midsuffolk.gov.uk

Emergency Planning: Mr Steve Pinion, District Emergency Planning Officer, Council Offices, 131 High Street, Needham Market IP6 8DL ☎ 01449 724858 🖷 01449 724655 ✉ steve.pinion@suffolk.gov.uk

Energy Management: Mr Chris Fry, Head - Environment, Council Offices, 131 High Street, Needham Market IP6 8DL ☎ 01449 724805 🖷 01449 724696 ✉ chris.fry@midsuffolk.gov.uk

Environmental / Technical Services: Mr Ryan Jones, Corporate Manager - Asset Management Operations, Council Offices, 131 High Street, Needham Market IP6 8DL ☎ 01449 724733 🖷 01449 724745 ✉ ryan.jones@babergh.gov.uk

Environmental Health: Mr James Buckingham, Corporate Manager - Environmental Protection, Council Offices, 131 High Street, Needham Market IP6 8DL ☎ 01449 724705 🖷 01449 724727 ✉ james.buckingham@midsuffolk.gov.uk

Estates, Property & Valuation: Mr Ryan Jones, Corporate Manager - Asset Management Operations, Council Offices, 131 High Street, Needham Market IP6 8DL ☎ 01449 724733 🖷 01449 724745 ✉ ryan.jones@babergh.gov.uk

European Liaison: Mr Jonathan Free, Head - Communities, Council Offices, 131 High Street, Needham Market IP6 8DL ☎ 01449 724648 🖷 01449 724655 ✉ jonathan.free@midsuffolk.gov.uk

Facilities: Mr Ryan Jones, Corporate Manager - Asset Management Operations, Council Offices, 131 High Street, Needham Market IP6 8DL ☎ 01449 724733 🖷 01449 724745 ✉ ryan.jones@babergh.gov.uk

Finance and Treasurer: Ms Katherine Steel, Head - Corporate Resources, Council Offices, 131 High Street, Needham Market IP6 8DL ☎ 01449 724806 🖷 01449 724696 ✉ katherine.steel@midsuffolk.gov.uk

Fleet Management: Mr Ryan Jones, Corporate Manager - Asset Management Operations, Council Offices, 131 High Street, Needham Market IP6 8DL ☎ 01449 724733 🖷 01449 724745 ✉ ryan.jones@babergh.gov.uk

Grounds Maintenance: Mr Ryan Jones, Corporate Manager - Asset Management Operations, Council Offices, 131 High Street, Needham Market IP6 8DL ☎ 01449 724733; 01449 724733 🖷 01449 724745 ✉ ryan.jones@babergh.gov.uk

Health and Safety: Ms Jeanette Bray, Corporate Manager - Organisational Development, Council Offices, Corks Lane, Hadleigh IP7 6SJ ☎ 01473 825744 🖷 01473 825742 ✉ jeanette.bray@babergh.gov.uk

Home Energy Conservation: Mr James Buckingham, Corporate Manager - Environmental Protection, Council Offices, 131 High Street, Needham Market IP6 8DL ☎ 01449 724705 🖷 01449 724727 ✉ james.buckingham@midsuffolk.gov.uk

Housing: Mr Martin King, Head - Housing, Council Offices, 131 High Street, Needham Market IP6 8DL ☎ 01449 724769 ✉ martin.king@midsuffolk.gov.uk

Housing Maintenance: Mr Ryan Jones, Corporate Manager - Asset Management Operations, Council Offices, 131 High Street, Needham Market IP6 8DL ☎ 01449 724733 🖷 01449 724745 ✉ ryan.jones@babergh.gov.uk

Legal: Mrs Kathryn Saward, Head - Legal Services, Council Offices, 131 High Street, Needham Market IP6 8DL ☎ 01449 724679 🖷 01449 724696 ✉ kathryn.saward@babergh.gov.uk

Leisure and Cultural Services: Mr Jonathan Free, Head - Communities, Council Offices, 131 High Street, Needham Market IP6 8DL ☎ 01449 724648 🖷 01449 724655 ✉ jonathan.free@midsuffolk.gov.uk

Leisure and Cultural Services: Mr Jonathan Seed, Corporate Manager - Healthy Communities, Council Offices, 131 High Street, Needham Market IP6 8DL ☎ 01449 724643 🖷 01449 724655 ✉ jonathan.seed@midsuffolk.gov.uk

Licensing: Mr Lee Carvell, Corporate Manager - Licensing, Council Offices, 131 High Street, Needham Market IP6 8DL ☎ 01449 724685 ✉ lee.carvell@babergh.gov.uk

Lottery Funding, Charity and Voluntary: Mr Tom Barker, Corporate Manager - Strong Communities, Council Offices, 131 High Street, Needham Market IP6 8DL ☎ 01449 724647 🖷 01449 724655 ✉ tom.baker@midsuffolk.gov.uk

Member Services: Mr Peter Quirk, Head - Corporate Organisation, Council Offices, 131 High Street, Needham Market IP6 8DL ☎ 01449 724656 🖷 01449 724696 ✉ peter.quirk@babergh.gov.uk

Parking: Mr Chris Fry, Head - Environment, Council Offices, 131 High Street, Needham Market IP6 8DL ☎ 01449 724805 🖷 01449 724696 ✉ chris.fry@midsuffolk.gov.uk

Partnerships: Mr Tom Barker, Corporate Manager - Strong Communities, Council Offices, 131 High Street, Needham Market IP6 8DL ☎ 01449 724647 🖷 01449 724655 ✉ tom.baker@midsuffolk.gov.uk

Personnel / HR: Ms Jeanette Bray, Corporate Manager - Organisational Development, Council Offices, Corks Lane, Hadleigh IP7 6SJ ☎ 01473 825744; 01473 825744 🖷 01473 825742 ✉ jeanette.bray@babergh.gov.uk

Planning: Mr Philip Isbell, Corporate Manager - Development Control, Council Offices, 131 High Street, Needham Market IP6 8DL ☎ 01449 724537 ✉ philip.isbell@midsuffolk.gov.uk

Procurement: Mrs Rachel Hodson - Gibbons, Procurement Consultant, Council Offices, 131 High Street, Needham Market IP6 8DL ☎ 01449 724587 ✉ rachel.hodson-gibbons@midsuffolk.gov.uk

Recycling & Waste Minimisation: Ms Brigitte Dawson, Corporate Manager - Waste, Council Offices, 131 High Street,

Needham Market IP6 8DL ☎ 01449 778621
✉ brigitte.dawson@midsuffolk.gov.uk

Regeneration: Mr David Benham, Corporate Manager - Economic Development & Tourism, Council Offices, 131 High Street, Needham Market IP6 8DL ☎ 01449 724649
🖷 01449 724655 ✉ david.benham@midsuffolk.gov.uk

Staff Training: Ms Jeanette Bray, Corporate Manager - Organisational Development, Council Offices, Corks Lane, Hadleigh IP7 6SJ ☎ 01473 825744 🖷 01473 825742
✉ jeanette.bray@babergh.gov.uk

Sustainable Communities: Mr Rich Cooke, Corporate Manager - Spatial Planning Policy, Council Offices, Corks Lane, Hadleigh IP7 6SJ ☎ 01473 825775 ✉ rich.cooke@babergh.gov.uk

Sustainable Development: Mr Chris Fry, Head - Environment, Council Offices, 131 High Street, Needham Market IP6 8DL
☎ 01449 724805 🖷 01449 724696 ✉ chris.fry@midsuffolk.gov.uk

Tourism: Mr David Benham, Corporate Manager - Economic Development & Tourism, Council Offices, 131 High Street, Needham Market IP6 8DL ☎ 01449 724649; 01449 724649
🖷 01449 724655 ✉ david.benham@midsuffolk.gov.uk

Waste Collection and Disposal: Ms Brigitte Dawson, Corporate Manager - Waste, Council Offices, 131 High Street, Needham Market IP6 8DL ☎ 01449 778621
✉ brigitte.dawson@midsuffolk.gov.uk

Waste Management: Ms Brigitte Dawson, Corporate Manager - Waste, Council Offices, 131 High Street, Needham Market IP6 8DL ☎ 01449 778621 ✉ brigitte.dawson@midsuffolk.gov.uk

Children's Play Areas: Mr Chris Fry, Head - Environment, Council Offices, 131 High Street, Needham Market IP6 8DL
☎ 01449 724805 🖷 01449 724696 ✉ chris.fry@midsuffolk.gov.uk

MEMBERS OF THE COUNCIL (75)

***Chair:* Pembroke**, Jeremy (CON - Cosford)
jeremy.pembroke@suffolk.gov.uk
***Vice-Chair:* Whybrow**, Anne (CON - Stowmarket South)
anne.whybrow@suffolk.gov.uk
***Leader of the Council:* Bee**, Mark (CON - Beccles)
mark.bee@suffolk.gov.uk
***Deputy Leader of the Council:* Storey**, Jane (CON - Elmswell and Norton)
jane.storey@midsuffolk.gov.uk
Alcock, Eddy (CON - Thredling)
eddy.alcock@suffolk.gov.uk
Barber, Nick (CON - Felixstowe Coastal)
nick.barber@suffolk.gov.uk
Barnard, Mike (CON - Oulton)
mike.barnard@suffolk.gov.uk
Beckwith, Trevor (IND - Eastgate and Moreton Hall)
trevor.beckwith@suffolk.gov.uk
Beer, Peter (CON - Great Cornard)
peter.beer@suffolk.gov.uk
Bellfield, Peter (CON - Carlford)
peter.bellfield@suffolk.gov.uk
Bishop, Bill (CON - Brandon)
bill.bishop@suffolk.gov.uk
Bond, Michael (CON - Wickham)
michael.bond@suffolk.gov.uk
Cann, Andrew (LD - St Margaret's and Westgate)
andrew.cann@suffolk.gov.uk
Chambers, Jane (LD - St Helens)
jane.chambers@suffolk.gov.uk
Chambers, Lisa (CON - Newmarket and Red Lodge)
lisa.chambers@suffolk.gov.uk
Clements, Terry (CON - Thingoe South)
terry.clements@suffolk.gov.uk
Dearden-Pillips, Craig (LD - Hardwick)
craig.dearden-phillips@suffolk.gov.uk
Debman, Carol (CON - Gainsborough)
carol.debman@suffolk.gov.uk
Ereira, Mark (GRN - Tower)
mark.ereira@suffolk.gov.uk
Field, John (LD - Gripping Valley)
john.field@midsuffolk.gov.uk
Finch, James (CON - Stour Valley)
james.finch@suffolk.gov.uk
French, Phillip (CON - Haverhill Cangle)
phillip.french@suffolk.gov.uk
Frost, Stephen (CON - Mildenhall)
stephen.frost@suffolk.gov.uk
Gardiner, Peter (LAB - Chantry)
peter.gardiner@suffolk.gov.uk
Goldsmith, John (CON - Kessingland and Southwold)
john.goldsmith@suffolk.gov.uk
Goldson, Tony (CON - Halesworth)
tony.goldson@suffolk.gov.uk
Goodwin, John (CON - Felixstowe North and Trimley)
john.goodwin@suffolk.gov.uk
Gosling, Kathy (CON - Pakefield)
kathy.gosling@suffolk.gov.uk
Gower, Anne (CON - Haverhill East and Kedington)
anne.gower@suffolk.gov.uk
Green, Gary (CON - Stowmarket North and Stowupland)
gary.green@midsuffolk.gov.uk
Grutchfield, David (LD - Hadleigh)
david.grutchfield@suffolk.gov.uk
Hart, Colin (CON - Framlingham)
colin.hart@suffolk.gov.uk
Hopfensperger, Beccy (CON - Thingoe North)
rebecca.hopfensperger@suffolk.gov.uk
Hudson, Christopher (CON - Kesgrave and Rushmere St Andrew)
christopher.hudson@suffolk.gov.uk
Hudson, Steven (CON - Kesgrave and Rushmere St Andrew)
steven.hudson@suffolk.gov.uk
Kemp, Richard (IND - Melford)
richard.kemp@suffolk.gov.uk
Law, Colin (CON - Oulton)
colin.law@suffolk.gov.uk
Law, Deanna (CON - Lowestoft South)
deanna.law@suffolk.gov.uk
Leighton, Rae (CON - Blything)
rae.leighton@suffolk.gov.uk
Lockington, Inga (LD - St Margaret's and Westgate)
inga.lockington@suffolk.gov.uk
Maguire, Susan (LAB - Priory Heath)
susan.maguire@suffolk.gov.uk
Marks, Tim (CON - Haverhill Cangle)
tim.marks@suffolk.gov.uk
Martin, Sandy (LAB - St John's)
sandy.martin@suffolk.gov.uk
McGregor, Guy (CON - Hoxne and Eye)

guy.mcgregor@suffolk.gov.uk
Michell, Charles (CON - Hartismere)
charles.michell@suffolk.gov.uk
Midwood, Jane (CON - Clare)
jane.midwood@suffolk.gov.uk
Mountford, Bill (UKIP - Lowestoft South)
bill.mountford@suffolk.gov.uk
Murray, Alan (CON - Bixley)
alan.murray@suffolk.gov.uk
Newman, Graham (CON - Felixstowe Coastal)
graham.newman@suffolk.gov.uk
Noble, Colin (CON - Row Heath)
colin.noble@suffolk.gov.uk
O'Brien, Patricia (CON - Martlesham)
patricia.obrien@suffolk.gov.uk
Oliver, Stefan (CON - Tower)
stefan.oliver@suffolk.gov.uk
Otton, Penelope (LD - Rattlesden)
penny.otton@midsuffolk.gov.uk
Page, Caroline (LD - Woodbridge)
caroline.page@suffolk.gov.uk
Pollard, Kathy (LD - Belstead Brook)
kathy.pollard@suffolk.go.uk
Provan, Bruce (CON - Gunton)
bruce.provan@suffolk.gov.uk
Punt, Chris (CON - Beccles)
chris.punt@suffolk.gov.uk
Reid, Andrew (CON - Wilford)
andrew.reid@suffolk.gov.uk
Ritchie, David (CON - Bungay)
david.ritchie@suffolk.gov.uk
Rudd, Mary (CON - Gunton)
mary.rudd@suffolk.gov.uk
Rudkin, Bryony (LAB - Bridge)
bryony.rudkin@suffolk.gov.uk
Sadler, Bill (CON - Exning and Newmarket)
bill.sadler@suffolk.gov.uk
Sale, Ken (CON - Pakefield)
kan.sale@suffolk.gov.uk
Sayers, John (CON - Sudbury)
john.sayers@suffolk.gov.uk
Smith, Richard (CON - Aldeburgh and leiston)
richard.smith@suffolk.gov.uk
Spence, Colin (CON - Sudbury East and Waldingfield)
colin.spence@suffolk.gov.uk
Spicer, Joanna (CON - Blackbourn)
joanna.spicer@suffolk.gov.uk
Stringer, Andrew (GRN - Mendlesham)
andrew.stringer@midsuffolk.gov.uk
Terry, Judy (CON - Rushmere)
judy.terry@suffolk.gov.uk
Truelove, Julia (LD - Bosmere)
julia.truelove@suffolk.gov.uk
Vickery, Robin (CON - whitehouse and Whitton)
robin.vickery@suffolk.gov.uk
West, Paul (CON - Chantry)
paul.west@suffolk.gov.uk
Wood, David (LD - Peninsula)
david.wood@suffolk.gov.uk
Yorke-Edwards, David (CON - Samford)
david.yorke-edwards@suffolk.gov.uk
Young, Mary
(CON - Whitehouse and Whitton)
mary.young@suffolk.gov.uk

POLITICAL COMPOSITION
CON: 55, LD: 11, LAB: 4, GRN: 2, IND: 2, UKIP: 1

CABINET
Leader: Mr Mark Bee
Deputy Leader: Mrs Jane Storey
Economic Development: Ms Judy Terry
Education & Young People: Mr Graham Newman
Environment & Property Management: Ms Lisa Chambers
Health & Adult Care: Mr Colin Noble
Puplic Protection: Mr Colin Spence
Roads & Transport: Mr Guy McGregor

COMMITTEE CHAIRS
Audit: Mr Richard Smith
Development Control: Mr Charles Michell
Education & Transport Appeals: Mr Nick Barber
Health Scrutiny: Ms Kathy Gosling
Licensing: Mr Ramon Melvin
Pension Fund: Mr Peter Bellfield
Scrutiny: Mr Colin Hart

MID SUSSEX D

Mid Sussex District Council, Oaklands, Oaklands Road, Haywards Heath RH16 1SS ☎ 01444 458166 🖷 01444 450027 ✉ enquiries@midsussex.gov.uk 🖳 www.midsussex.gov.uk

FACTS & FIGURES
Police Authority: Sussex Police Authority
Health Authority: South East Coast Strategic Health Authority
Learning and Skills Council: South East
EU Constituencies: South East
Election Frequency: Elections are of whole council
Twinning: Abbeville (France); Burgess Hill: Schmallenberg (Germany); East Grinstead: Bourge-de-Peage (France); Mindelheim (Germany); San Felieu de Guixols (Spain); Schwaz (Austria); Verbania (Italy); Hassocks: Wald-Michelbach (Germany); Mount Mirail (France); Haywards Heath: Traunstein (Bavaria); Horsted Keynes: Cahagnes (France); Slaugham: St. Martin-des-Besaus (France)

PRINCIPAL OFFICERS
Chief Executive: Ms Kathryn Hall, Chief Executive, Mid Sussex District Council, Oaklands, Oaklands Road, Haywards Heath RH16 1SS ☎ 01444 477498 🖷 01444 477507 ✉ Kathryn.hall@midsussex.gov.uk

Assistant Chief Executive: Mr Richard Hodson, Assistant Chief Executive, Oaklands, Oaklands Road, Haywards Heath RH16 1SS ☎ 01444 477015 ✉ Richard.hodson@midsussex.gov.uk

Building Control: Mrs Yvonne Leddy, Environmental Health Manager, Oaklands, Oaklands Road, Haywards Heath RH16 1SS ☎ 01444 477300 ✉ yvonne.leddy@midsussex.gov.uk

Children / Youth Services: Ms Susannah Conway, Young Persons' Development Officer, Oaklands, Oaklands Road, Haywards Heath RH16 1SS ☎ 01444 477518 ✉ susannah.conway@midsussex.gov.uk

PR / Communications: Mr Richard Hodson, Assistant Chief

Executive, Oaklands, Oaklands Road, Haywards Heath RH16 1SS ☎ 01444 477015 Richard.hodson@midsussex.gov.uk

Community Planning: Ms Ioni Sullivan, Community Partnership Officer, Oaklands, Oaklands Road, Haywards Heath RH16 1SS ☎ 01444 477204 🖷 01444 477507 ioni.sullivan@midsussex.gov.uk

Community Safety: Ms Nicolette Russell, Community Safety Officer, Oaklands, Oaklands Road, Haywards Heath RH16 1SS ☎ 01444 477550 🖷 01444 417965 nicoletter@midsussex.gov.uk

Computer Management: Mr Mark Gawley, CenSus IT Operations Manager, Oaklands, Oaklands Road, Haywards Heath RH16 1SS ☎ 01903 221197 Mark.Gawley@adur-worthing.gov.uk

Contracts: Ms Emma Grundy, Property & Asset Manager, Oaklands, Oaklands Road, Haywards Heath RH16 1SS ☎ 01444 477490 emma.grundy@midsussex.gov.uk

Corporate Services: Mr Richard Hodson, Assistant Chief Executive, Oaklands, Oaklands Road, Haywards Heath RH16 1SS ☎ 01444 477015 ; Richard.hodson@midsussex.gov.uk

Customer Service: Ms Karen Pyke, Senior Customer Services Officer, Oaklands, Oaklands Road, Haywards Heath RH16 1SS ☎ 01444 477510 karen.pyke@midsussex.gov.uk

Economic Development: Ms Claire Tester, Head of Planning & Economic Promotion, Oaklands, Oaklands Road, Haywards Heath RH16 1SS ☎ 01444 477322 claire.tester@midsussex.gov.uk

Electoral Registration: Mr David Peake, Senior Elections Officer, Oaklands, Oaklands Road, Haywards Heath RH16 1SS ☎ 01444 477415 david.peake@midsussex.gov.uk

Emergency Planning: Mr Ben Toogood, Emergency Planning & Outdoor Services Manager, Oaklands, Oaklands Road, Haywards Heath RH16 1SS ☎ 01444 477379 ben.toogood@midsussex.gov.uk

Energy Management: Ms Emma Grundy, Property & Asset Manager, Oaklands, Oaklands Road, Haywards Heath RH16 1SS ☎ 01444 477490 emma.grundy@midsussex.gov.uk

Environmental Health: Mrs Yvonne Leddy, Environmental Health Manager, Oaklands, Oaklands Road, Haywards Heath RH16 1SS ☎ 01444 477300 yvonne.leddy@midsussex.gov.uk

Estates, Property & Valuation: Ms Emma Grundy, Property & Asset Manager, Oaklands, Oaklands Road, Haywards Heath RH16 1SS ☎ 01444 477490 emma.grundy@midsussex.gov.uk

Events Manager: Ms Gill Lake, Leisure Manager, Oaklands, Oaklands Road, Haywards Heath RH16 1SS ☎ 01444 477539 🖷 01444 477464 gill.lake@midsussex.gov.uk

Facilities: Mr David Harper, Waste & Outdoor Services Manager, Oaklands, Oaklands Road, Haywards Heath RH16 1SS ☎ 01444 477487 🖷 01444 450027 david.harper@midsussex.gov.uk

Finance and Treasurer: Mr Peter Stuart, Head of Finance, ICT & Personnel, Oaklands, Oaklands Road, Haywards Heath RH16 1SS ☎ 01444 477315 peter.stuart@midsussex.gov.uk

Grounds Maintenance: Mr Rupert Browning, Landscapes Manager, Oaklands, Oaklands Road, Haywards Heath RH16 1SS ☎ 01444 477374 🖷 01444 477464 rupert.browning@midsussex.gov.uk

Health and Safety: Mr Ian Allsobrook, Corporate Safety & Technical Services Officer, Oaklands, Oaklands Road, Haywards Heath RH16 1SS ☎ 01444 477002 ian.allsobrook@midsussex.gov.uk

Home Energy Conservation: Ms Celia Austin, Sustainability Officer, Oaklands, Oaklands Road, Haywards Heath RH16 1SS ☎ 01444 477370 celia.austin@midsussex.gov.uk

Housing: Mrs Lynne Standing, Head of Housing, Environmental Health & Building Control, Oaklands, Oaklands Road, Haywards Heath RH16 1SS ☎ 01444 477411 🖷 01444 417965 lynne.standing@midsussex.gov.uk

Legal: Mr Tom Clark, Solicitor to the Council, Mid Sussex District Council, Oaklands, Oaklands Road, Haywards Heath RH16 1SS ☎ 01444 477459 tom.clark@midsussex.gov.uk

Leisure and Cultural Services: Mr Mark Fisher, Head of Leisure & Sustainability, Oaklands, Oaklands Road, Haywards Heath RH16 1SS ☎ 01444 477367 mark.fisher@midsussex.gov.uk

Licensing: Mr Paul Thornton, Senior Licensing Officer, Oaklands, Oaklands Road, Haywards Heath RH16 1SS ☎ 01444 477428 paul.thornton@midsussex.gov.uk

Member Services: Mr Daniel Kington, Senior Member Services Officer, Oaklands, Oaklands Road, Haywards Heath RH16 1SS ☎ 01444 477111 daniel.kington@midsussex.gov.uk

Parking: Mrs Sue Rees, Parking Services Manager, Mid Sussex District Council, Oaklands, Oaklands Road, Haywards Heath RH16 1SS ☎ 01444 477586 sue.rees@midsussex.gov.uk

Partnerships: Mrs Jo Harper, Business Unit Leader for Member Support & Partnerships, Oaklands, Oaklands Road, Haywards Heath RH16 1SS ☎ 01444 477514 jo.harper@midsussex.gov.uk

Personnel / HR: Mr Peter Stuart, Head of Finance, ICT & Personnel, Oaklands, Oaklands Road, Haywards Heath RH16 1SS ☎ 01444 477315 peter.stuart@midsussex.gov.uk

Planning: Ms Claire Tester, Head of Planning & Economic Promotion, Oaklands, Oaklands Road, Haywards Heath RH16 1SS ☎ 01444 477322 claire.tester@midsussex.gov.uk

Procurement: Mr Roger Dennis, Joint Procurement Officer, Oaklands, Oaklands Road, Haywards Heath RH16 1SS ☎ 01444 477254 rogerd@horsham.gov.uk

Recycling & Waste Minimisation: Mr David Harper, Waste & Outdoor Services Manager, Oaklands, Oaklands Road, Haywards Heath RH16 1SS ☎ 01444 477487 🖷 01444 450027 david.harper@midsussex.gov.uk

Staff Training: Ms Emma Jackson, Personnel & Training Assistant, Oaklands, Oaklands Road, Haywards Heath RH16 1SS ☎ 01444 477276 🖷 01444 450027 ✉ emma.jackson@midsussex.gov.uk

Sustainable Communities: Mr Simon Hardy, Principal Development Manager, Oaklands, Oaklands Road, Haywards Heath RH16 1SS ☎ 01444 477454 🖷 01444 477461 ✉ simon.hardy@midsussex.gov.uk

Sustainable Development: Ms Celia Austin, Sustainability Officer, Oaklands, Oaklands Road, Haywards Heath RH16 1SS ☎ 01444 477370 ✉ celia.austin@midsussex.gov.uk

Waste Collection and Disposal: Mr David Harper, Waste & Outdoor Services Manager, Oaklands, Oaklands Road, Haywards Heath RH16 1SS ☎ 01444 477487 🖷 01444 450027 ✉ david.harper@midsussex.gov.uk

Waste Management: Mr David Harper, Waste & Outdoor Services Manager, Oaklands, Oaklands Road, Haywards Heath RH16 1SS ☎ 01444 477487 🖷 01444 450027 ✉ david.harper@midsussex.gov.uk

MEMBERS OF THE COUNCIL (54)

***Leader of the Council:* Wall**, Garry (CON - Haywards Heath - Franklands)
rry.wall@midsussex.gov.uk

***Deputy Leader of the Council:* Marsh**, Gary (CON - Ardingly and Balcombe)
gary.marsh@midsussex.gov.uk

Ash-Edwards, Jonathan (CON - Haywards Heath - Heath)
jonathan.ash-edwards@midsussex.gov.uk

Banham, Simon (CON - Hurstpierpoint and Downs)
Simon.Banham@midsussex.gov.uk

Barnett, Stephen (LD - Ashurst Wood)
stephen.barnett@midsussex.gov.uk

Barrett-Miles, Andrew (CON - Burgess Hill - Dunstall)

Bates, Richard (LD - Haywards Heath - Ashenground)
richard.bates@midsussex.gov.uk

Belsey, Edward (CON - East Grinstead - Herontye)
Edward.Belsey@midsussex.gov.uk

Belsey, Margaret (CON - East Grinstead - Baldwins)
Margaret.Belsey@midsussex.gov.uk

Bennett, Liz (CON - East Grinstead - Ashplats)
liz.bennett@midsussex.gov.uk

Bourne, Katy (CON - Cuckfield)
Katy.Bourne@midsussex.gov.uk

Brunsdon, Heidi (CON - East Grinstead - Imberhorne)
heidi.brunsdon@midsussex.gov.uk

Callaghan, Jack (CON - Hurstpierpoint and Downs)
jack.callaghan@midsussex.gov.uk

Catherine, Cherry (CON - Burgess Hill - Leylands)
Cherry.Catharine@midsussex.gov.uk

Coote, Philip (CON - Crawley Down and Turners Hill)
Phillip.Coote@midsussex.gov.uk

Davies, Mims (CON - Haywards Heath - Lucastes)
Mims.Davies@midsussex.gov.uk

De Mierre, John (CON - Haywards Heath - Franklands)
john.demierre@midsussex.gov.uk

Dorking, David (CON - Haywards Heath - Bentswood)
David.Dorking@midsussex.gov.uk

Dumbovic, Kathleen (LD - Burgess Hill - Meeds)
kathleen.dumbovic@midsussex.gov.uk

Farmer, Tim (CON - Haywards Heath - Lucastes)
Tim.Farmer@midsussex.gov.uk

Forbes, Bruce (CON - Crawley Down and Turners Hill)
Bruce.Forbes@midsussex.gov.uk

Goddard, Richard (LAB - Haywards Heath - Bentwood)
Richard.Goddard@midsussex.gov.uk

Hatton, Susan (LD - Hassocks)
sue.hatton@midsussex.gov.uk

Heard, Ginny (CON - Burgess Hill - Franklands)
Ginny.Heard@midsussex.gov.uk

Hersey, Margaret (CON - Lindfield)
margaret.hersey@midsussex.gov.uk

Hersey, Christopher (CON - High Weald)
chris.hersey@midsussex.gov.uk

Ingham, Catrin (LD - East Grinstead - Town)
Catrin.Ingham@midsussex.gov.uk

Jones, Denis (LD - Burgess Hill - St Andrews)
Denis.Jones@midsussex.gov.uk

Jones, Anne (CON - Burgess Hill - Meeds)
anne.jones@midsussex.gov.uk

Knight, Graham (LD - Burgess Hill - St Andrews)
graham.knight@midsussex.gov.uk

Knight, Jim (CON - Haywards Heath - Ashenground)
Jim.Knight@midsussex.gov.uk

Landriani, Jacqui (CON - Burgess Hill - Dunstall)

Lea, Andrew (CON - Lindfield)
andrew.lea@midsussex.gov.uk

Livesey, Mike (CON - Copthorne and Worth)
mike.livesey@midsussex.gov.uk

MacNaughton, Andrew (CON - Ardingly and Balcombe)
andrew.macnaughton@midsussex.gov.uk

Mainstone, Bob (LD - East Grinstead - Imberhorne)
Bob.Mainstone@midsussex.gov.uk

March, Natalie (CON - Haywards Heath - Heath)
Natalie.March@midsussex.gov.uk

Marples, Gordon (CON - Hassocks)
gordon.marples@midsussex.gov.uk

Martin, Peter (CON - Hassocks)
peter.martin@midsussex.gov.uk

Matthews, Edward (CON - Copthorne and Worth)
edward.matthews@midsussex.gov.uk

McMenemy, Simon (CON - High Weald)
simon.mcmenemy@midsussex.gov.uk

Moore, Pru (CON - Burgess Hill - Leylands)
pru.moore@midsussex.gov.uk

O'Brien, John (CON - East Grinstead - Town)
John.O'Brien@midsussex.gov.uk

Reed, Peter (CON - East Grinstead - Ashplats)
peter.reed@midsussex.gov.uk

Salisbury, Robert (CON - Cuckfield)
robert.salisbury@midsussex.gov.uk

Seward, Sue (CON - Bolney)
susan.seward@midsussex.gov.uk

Simpson, Ian (CON - Burgess Hill - Franklands)
Ian.Simpson@midsussex.gov.uk

Snowling, Christopher (CON - Lindfield)
christopher.snowling@midsussex.gov.uk

Sweatman, Dick (CON - East Grinstead - Herontye)
Dick.Sweatman@midsussex.gov.uk

Thomas-Atkin, Mandy (CON - Burgess Hill - Victoria)
mandy.thomas-atkin@midsussex.gov.uk

Trumble, Colin (CON - Hurstpierpoint and Downs)
Colin.Trumble@midsussex.gov.uk

Walker, Neville (CON - Crawley Down and Turners Hill)
Neville.Walker@midsussex.gov.uk

Webster, Norman (CON - East Grinstead - Baldwins)
Norman.Webster@midsussex.gov.uk
White, Emily (CON - Burgess Hill - Victoria)
Emily.White@midsussex.gov.uk

POLITICAL COMPOSITION

CON: 45, LD: 8, LAB: 1

CABINET

Leader, Corporate / Strategic Issues: Mr Garry Wall
Deputy Leader / Planning & Regeneration: Mr Gary Marsh
Economic Development: Mr John De Mierre
Finance & Service Delivery: Mr Jonathan Ash-Edwards
Health & Communities: Mr Christopher Snowling
Leisure & Outdoor Services: Mrs Pru Moore

COMMITTEE CHAIRS

Audit (Scrutiny): Mr Andrew Lea
Better Environment Advisory Group: Mr Peter Martin
Licensing: Mr Christopher Hersey
Performance & Scruntiny: Mrs Sue Seward

MIDDLESBROUGH U

Middlesbrough Council, Town Hall, Middlesbrough TS1 2QQ
☎ 01642 245432 🖳 www.middlesbrough.gov.uk

FACTS & FIGURES

Police Authority: Cleveland Police Authority
Health Authority: North East Strategic Health Authority
Learning and Skills Council: North East
Parliamentary Constituencies: Middlesbrough
EU Constituencies: North East
Election Frequency: Elections are of whole council
Twinning: Dunkerque (France); Masvingo (Zimbabwe); Oberhausen (Germany);

PRINCIPAL OFFICERS

Chief Executive: Mr Ian Parker, Chief Executive, Town Hall, Middlesbrough TS1 2QQ ☎ 01642 729101 🖷 01642 729973 ✉ ian_parker@middlesbrough.gov.uk

Assistant Chief Executive: Mrs Karen Whitmore, Assistant Chief Executive, Civic Centre, Middlesbrough TS1 9FT ☎ 01642 729117 ✉ karen_whitmore@middlesbrough.gov.uk

Senior Management: Mr Richard Long, Director of Legal & Democratic Services, Town Hall, Middlesbrough TS1 2QQ ☎ 01642 729781 🖷 01642 729877 ✉ richard_long@middlesbrough.gov.uk

Senior Management: Ms Sandra Philips, Managing Director of West Middlesbrough Neighbourhood Trust, 99 Acklam Road, Acklam, Middlesbrough TS5 5HR ☎ 01642 856030 🖷 01642 827770 ✉ sandra.philips@wmnt.co.uk

Senior Management: Mr Mike Robinson, Director of Environment & Adult Social Care, Civic Centre, Middlesbrough TS1 9FT ☎ 01642 729500 🖷 01642 729969 ✉ mike_robinson@middlesbrough.gov.uk

Senior Management: Ms Gill Rollings, Executive Director of Children, Families & Learning, Vancouver House, Gurney Street, Middlesbrough TA1 1EL ☎ 01642 728700 🖷 01642 728970 ✉ gill_rollings@middlesbrough.gov.uk

Access Officer / Social Services (Disability): Mrs Ruth Hicks, Assistant Director of Assesment & Care Management, Civic Centre, Middlesbrough TS1 2QQ ☎ 01642 729034 ✉ ruth_hicks@middlesbrough.gov.uk

Architect, Building / Property Services: Mr Ian McConville, Highway Management, Maintenance & Design Manager, PO Box 502, Vancouver House, Gurney Street, Middlesbrough TS1 9FW ☎ 01642 728160 ✉ ian_mcconville@middlebrough.gov.uk

Building Control: Mr Paul Clark, Planning Services Manager, Civic Centre, Middlesbrough TS1 9FY ☎ 01642 729063 ✉ paul_clarke@middlesbrough.gov.uk

Catering Services: Mrs Angela Blower, Catering Manager, First Floor, Vancouver House, Gurney Street, Middlesbrough TS1 1EL ☎ 01642 728030 🖷 01642 728965 ✉ angela_blower@middlesbrough.gov.uk

Children / Youth Services: Ms Gill Rollings, Executive Director of Children, Families & Learning, Vancouver House, Gurney Street, Middlesbrough TA1 1EL ☎ 01642 728700 🖷 01642 728970 ✉ gill_rollings@middlesbrough.gov.uk

Civil Registration: Mr Mike Robinson, Executive Director of Environment & Adult Social Care, PO Box 99A, Town Hall, Middlesbrough TS1 2QQ ☎ 01642 729500 🖷 01642 729969 ✉ mike_robinson@middlebrough.gov.uk

PR / Communications: Mrs Debbie Robinson, Communications Manager, Civic Centre, Middlesbrough TS1 2QQ ☎ 01642 729205 🖷 01642 729660 ✉ debbie_robinson@servicemiddlesbrough.org

Community Safety: Mr Ed Chicken, Assistant Director of Community Protection, Vancouver House, Gurney Street, Middlesbrough TS1 1QP ☎ 01642 728057 🖷 01642 728938 ✉ ed_chicken@middlesbrough.gov.uk

Computer Management: Mr Andy Evans, IT Manager, Rede House, Middlesbrough TS1 1LY ☎ 01642 727801

Consumer Protection and Trading Standards: Mr Ed Chicken, Assistant Director of Community Protection, Vancouver House, Gurney Street, Middlesbrough TS1 1QP ☎ 01642 728057 🖷 01642 728938 ✉ ed_chicken@middlesbrough.gov.uk

Contracts: Mrs Janice Chapman, Strategic Commissioning Manager, Civic Centre, Middlesbrough TS1 9FT ☎ 01642 729180 ✉ janice_chapman@middlesbrough.gov.uk

Contracts: Mr Ian Featherstone, Strategic Commissioning Manager, Civic Centre, Middlesbrough TS1 9FT ☎ 01642 729176 ✉ ian_featherstone@middlesbrough.gov.uk

Corporate Services: Mrs Karen Whitmore, Assistant Chief Executive, Town Hall, Middlesbrough TS1 2QQ ☎ 01642 729117 ✉ karen_whitmore@middlesbrough:gov.uk

Customer Service: Mr Andy Unsworth, Customer Services Manager, Middlebrough House, 50 Corporation Road, Middlesbrough TS1 2RH ☎ 01642 726104 ✉ andy.unsworth@mouchel-middlesbrough.gov.uk

Direct Labour: Mr Tom Punton, Assistant Director of Environment, Vancouver House, Gurney Street, Middlesbrough TS1 1QP ☎ 01642 728300 🖷 01642 728987 ✉ tom_punton@middlesbrough.gov.uk

Economic Development: Ms Sandra Cartlidge, Assistant Director of Economic Development, Culture & Communities, Civic Centre, Middlesbrough TS1 2QQ ☎ 01642 729538 🖷 01642 729978 ✉ sandra_cartlidge@middlesbrough.gov.uk

Education: Ms Gill Rollings, Executive Director of Children, Families & Learning, Vancouver House, Gurney Street, Middlesbrough TA1 1EL ☎ 01642 728700 🖷 01642 728970 ✉ gill_rollings@middlesbrough.gov.uk

Education: Mr Paul Wilson, Head of Education ICT, Rede House, Middlesbrough TS1 1LY ☎ 01642 727609

E-Government: Ms Julia Coxon, ICT Strategy & Projects Manager, Civic Centre, Middlesbrough TS1 2QQ ☎ 01642 729628 ✉ julia_coxon@middlesbrough.gov.uk

Electoral Registration: Mr John Stuart, Electoral Services Manager, PO Box 506, Civic Centre, Middlesbrough TS1 9GA ☎ 01642 729771 🖷 01642 729877 ✉ john_stuart@middlesbrough.gov.uk

Emergency Planning: Ms Claire Storey, Senior Emergency Planning Officer, Cleveland Emergency Planning Unit, PO Box 194, Middlesbrough TS5 6YF ☎ 01642 301526 🖷 01642 821016 ✉ claire.storey@hartlepool.gov.uk

Energy Management: Mr Mike Knox, Energy Manager, Civic Centre, Middlesbrough TS1 9FT ☎ 01642 729271 ✉ mike_knox@middlesbrough.gov.uk

Environmental Health: Mr Jeff Duffield, Public Health & Development Manager, Vancouver House, Gurney Street, Middlesbrough TS1 1QP ☎ 01642 728197 🖷 01642 728960 ✉ jeff_duffield@middlesbrough.gov.uk

Estates, Property & Valuation: Mr Tim Wake, Head of Valuation Estates & Enterprise Network, Civic Centre, Middlesbrough TS1 9FT ☎ 01642 727076 🖷 01642 727973 ✉ tim.wake@mouchel-middlesbrough.gov.uk

Events Manager: Ms Judith Croft, Festivals & Events Manager, Civic Centre, Middlesbrough TS1 2QQ ☎ 01642 729137 🖷 01462 729964 ✉ judith_croft@middlesbrough.gov.uk

Finance and Treasurer: Mr Paul Slocombe, Director of Strategic Resources, Civic Centre, Middlesbrough TS1 2QQ ☎ 01642 729032 🖷 01642 729983 ✉ paul_slocombe@middlesbrough.gov.uk

Fleet Management: Mr Tom Punton, Assistant Director of Environment, Vancouver House, Gurney Street, Middlesbrough TS1 1QP ☎ 01642 728300 🖷 01642 728987 ✉ tom_punton@middlesbrough.gov.uk

Grounds Maintenance: Mr Tom Punton, Assistant Director of Environment, Town Hall, Middlesbrough TS1 2QQ ☎ 01642 728300 🖷 01642 728987 ✉ tom_punton@middlesbrough.gov.uk

Health and Safety: Mr Ian Campbell, Health & Safety Adviser, Rede House, Corporation Road, Middlesbrough TS1 1LY ☎ 01642 727414 🖷 01642 727967 ✉ ian.campbell@mouchel-middlesbrough.com

Highways: Mr Derek Gittens, Highways & Transportation Manager, Vancouver House, Gurney Street, Middlesbrough TS1 9FW ☎ 01642 728638 🖷 01642 728962 ✉ derek_gittens@middlesbrough.gov.uk

Housing: Mrs Sharon Thomas, Assistant Director of Development, Civic Centre, Middlesbrough TS1 9FY ☎ 01642 729600 ✉ sharon_thomas@middlesbrough.gov.uk

Legal: Mr Richard Long, Director of Legal & Democratic Services, Town Hall, Middlesbrough TS1 2QQ ☎ 01642 729781 🖷 01642 729877 ✉ richard_long@middlesbrough.gov.uk

Leisure and Cultural Services: Ms Kate Brindley, Director of Museums & Galleries, Middlesbrough Institute of Modern Art, Centre Square, Middlesbrough TS1 2AZ ☎ 01642 245432 ✉ kate.brindley@middlesbrough.gov.uk

Leisure and Cultural Services: Ms Sandra Cartlidge, Assistant Director of Economic Development, Culture & Communities, Civic Centre, Middlesbrough TS1 2QQ ☎ 01642 729538 🖷 01642 729978 ✉ sandra_cartlidge@middlesbrough.gov.uk

Leisure and Cultural Services: Mr Jeff Duffield, Public Health & Development Manager, Vancouver House, Gurney Street, Middlesbrough TS1 1QP ☎ 01642 728197 🖷 01642 728960 ✉ jeff_duffield@middlesbrough.gov.uk

Licensing: Mr Tim Hodgkinson, Principal Licensing Officer, PO Box 65, Vancouver House, Gurney Street, Middlesbrough TS1 1QP ☎ 01642 728720 🖷 01642 728902 ✉ tim_hodgkinson@middlesbrough.gov.uk

Lifelong Learning: Ms Gill Rollings, Executive Director of Children, Families & Learning, Vancouver House, Gurney Street, Middlesbrough TA1 1EL ☎ 01642 728700 🖷 01642 728970 ✉ gill_rollings@middlesbrough.gov.uk

Lighting: Mr Ron Dawson, Principal Engineer, PO Box 65, Vancouver House, Gurney Street, Middlesbrough TS1 1QP ☎ 01642 728163 🖷 01642 728964 ✉ ron_dawson@middlesbrough.gov.uk

Lottery Funding, Charity and Voluntary: Mr Martin Harvey, Community Regeneration Manager, Civic Centre, Middlesbrough TS1 9FT ☎ 01642 729254 ✉ martin_harvey@middlesbrough.gov.uk

Member Services: Mr Chris Davies, Members' Office Manager, Town Hall, Middlesbrough TS1 2QQ ☎ 01642 729704

🖷 01642 729882 ✉ chris_davies@middlesbrough.gov.uk

Parking: Mr Derek Gittens, Highways & Transportation Manager, Vancouver House, Gurney Street, Middlesbrough TS1 9FW ☎ 01642 728638 🖷 01642 728962 ✉ derek_gittens@middlesbrough.gov.uk

Partnerships: Mr John Polson, Partnership Manager, Civic Centre, Middlesbrough TS1 9FT ☎ 01642 729017 ✉ john_polson@middlesbrough.gov.uk

Personnel / HR: Mrs Karen Whitmore, Assistant Chief Executive, Town Hall, Middlesbrough TS1 2QQ ☎ 01642 729117 ✉ karen_whitmore@middlesbrough.gov.uk

Planning: Mrs Sharon Thomas, Assistant Director of Development, Civic Centre, Middlesbrough TS1 9FY ☎ 01642 729600 ✉ sharon_thomas@middlesbrough.gov.uk

Procurement: Mr Paul Slocombe, Director of Strategic Resources, Civic Centre, Middlesbrough TS1 2QQ ☎ 01642 729032 🖷 01642 729983 ✉ paul_slocombe@middlesbrough.gov.uk

Public Libraries: Ms Jen Brittain, Head of Libraries, Central Library, Victoria Square, Middlesbrough TS1 2AY ☎ 01642 729418 ✉ jen_brittain@middlesbrough.gov.uk

Recycling & Waste Minimisation: Mr Ken Sherwood, Waste Policy & Performance Manager, PO Box 65, Vancouver House, Gurney Street, Middlesbrough TS1 1QP ☎ 01642 728514 🖷 01642 728987 ✉ ken_sherwood@middlesbrough.gov.uk

Regeneration: Mr Kevin Parkes, Executive Director of Regeneration, Civic Centre, Middlesbrough TS1 2QQ ☎ 01642 729601 ✉ kevin_parkes@middlesbrough.gov.uk

Road Safety: Mr Derek Gittens, Highways & Transportation Manager, Vancouver House, Gurney Street, Middlesbrough TS1 9FW ☎ 01642 728638 🖷 01642 728962 ✉ derek_gittens@middlesbrough.gov.uk

Social Services (Adult): Mr Tony Parkinson, Assistant Director of Business, Development & Commissioning, Civic Centre, Middlesbrough TS1 9FT ☎ 01642 245432 ✉ tony_parkinson@middlesbrough.gov.uk

Social Services (Adult): Mr Mike Robinson, Executive Director of Environment & Adult Social Care, PO Box 99A, Town Hall, Middlesbrough TS1 2QQ ☎ 01642 729500 🖷 01642 729969 ✉ mike_robinson@middlebrough.gov.uk

Social Services (Children): Ms Gill Rollings, Executive Director of Children, Families & Learning, Vancouver House, Gurney Street, Middlesbrough TA1 1EL ☎ 01642 728700 🖷 01642 728970 ✉ gill_rollings@middlesbrough.gov.uk

Street Scene: Mr Tom Punton, Assistant Director of Environment, Town Hall, Middlesbrough TS1 2QQ ☎ 01642 728300 🖷 01642 728987 ✉ tom_punton@middlesbrough.gov.uk

Sustainable Development: Mr Jeff Duffield, Public Health & Development Manager, Vancouver House, Gurney Street, Middlesbrough TS1 1QP ☎ 01642 728197 🖷 01642 728960 ✉ jeff_duffield@middlesbrough.gov.uk

Tourism: Mrs Yaffa Philips, Tourism Officer, Civic Centre, Middlesbrough TS1 9FY ☎ 01642 729139 ✉ yaffa_phillips@middlesbrough.gov.uk

Town Centre: Mr Alan Weston, Town Centre Manager, Captain Cook Management Suite, 16 Newport Crescent, Middlesbrough TS1 5UA ☎ 01642 226622 🖷 01642 226623 ✉ alan_weston@middlesbrough.gov.uk

Traffic Management: Mr Derek Gittens, Highways & Transportation Manager, Vancouver House, Gurney Street, Middlesbrough TS1 9FW ☎ 01642 728638 🖷 01642 728962 ✉ derek_gittens@middlesbrough.gov.uk

Transport: Mr Derek Gittens, Highways & Transportation Manager, Vancouver House, Gurney Street, Middlesbrough TS1 9FW ☎ 01642 728638 🖷 01642 728962 ✉ derek_gittens@middlesbrough.gov.uk

Transport Planner: Mr Derek Gittens, Highways & Transportation Manager, Vancouver House, Gurney Street, Middlesbrough TS1 9FW ☎ 01642 728638 🖷 01642 728962 ✉ derek_gittens@middlesbrough.gov.uk

Total Place: Mr Martin Harvey, Community Regeneration Manager, Civic Centre, Middlesbrough TS1 9FT ☎ 01642 729254 ✉ martin_harvey@middlesbrough.gov.uk

Waste Collection and Disposal: Mr Ken Sherwood, Waste Policy & Performance Manager, PO Box 65, Vancouver House, Gurney Street, Middlesbrough TS1 1QP ☎ 01642 728514 🖷 01642 728987 ✉ ken_sherwood@middlesbrough.gov.uk

Waste Management: Mr Ken Sherwood, Waste Policy & Performance Manager, PO Box 65, Vancouver House, Gurney Street, Middlesbrough TS1 1QP ☎ 01642 728514 🖷 01642 728987 ✉ ken_sherwood@middlesbrough.gov.uk

MEMBERS OF THE COUNCIL (48)

***Directly Elected Mayor:* Mallon**, Ray (NP - Mayors)
ray_mallon@middlesbrough.gov.uk

***Chair:* Bloundele**, Stephen (LAB - Linthorpe)
stephen_bloundele@middlesbrough.gov.uk

***Deputy Mayor:* Budd**, David (LAB - Ladgate)
david_budd@middlesbrough.gov.uk

Arundale, Ronald (CON - Kader)
ronald_arundale@middlesbrough.gov.uk

Biswas, Shamal (LAB - Acklam)
shamal_biswas@middlesbrough.gov.uk

Brady, Bob (LAB - Gresham)
bob_brady@middlesbrough.gov.uk

Brunton, Janice (LAB - Coulby Newham)
janice_brunton@middlesbrough.gov.uk

Carr, Mike (LAB - Ladgate)
mike_carr@middlesbrough.gov.uk

Clark, Garry (LAB - Beechwood)
garry_clark@middlesbrough.gov.uk

Cole, John (LAB - Coulby Newham)
john_cole@middlesbrough.gov.uk

Coppinger, Barry (LAB - Pallister)

barry_coppinger@middlesbrough.gov.uk
Cox, Peter (IND - Beckfield)
peter_cox@middlesbrough.gov.uk
Davison, Dorothy (IND - Marton)
dorothy_davison@middlesbrough.gov.uk
Dryden, Eddie (LAB - Pallister)
eddie_dryden@middlesbrough.gov.uk
Hanif, Mohammed (LAB - University)
mohammed_hanif@middlesbrough.gov.uk
Harvey, Tracy (LD - Stainton and Thornton)
maelor_williams@middlesbrough.gov.uk
Harvey, Tracy (LAB - Gresham)
cllrtracy_harvey@middlesbrough.gov.uk
Hawthorne, Bill (IND - Ayresome)
bill_hawthorne@middlesbrough.gov.uk
Hobson, Chris (CON - Marton West)
chris_hobson@middlesbrough.gov.uk
Hobson, John (CON - Marton West)
john_hobson@middlesbrough.gov.uk
Hubbard, Brian (IND - Beckfield)
brian_hubbard@middlesbrough.gov.uk
Hudson, Michael (IND - Coulby Newham)
michael_hudson@middlesbrough.gov.uk
Hussain, Naweed (LAB - Linthorpe)
naweed_hussain@middlesbrough.gov.uk
Junier, Len (LAB - North Ormesby and Brambles Farm)
len_junier@middlesbrough.gov.uk
Kerr, Bob (LAB - Clairville)
bob_kerr@middlesbrough.gov.uk
Khan, Sajaad (LAB - Gresham)
sajaad_khan@middlesbrough.gov.uk
Khan, Pervaz (LAB - Middlehaven)
pervaz_khan@middlesbrough.gov.uk
Lowes, Ron (IND - Acklam)
ron_lowes@middlesbrough.gov.uk
Mawston, Tom (IND - Marton)
tom_mawston@middlesbrough.gov.uk
McIntyre, Frances (LAB - Park)
frances_mcintyre@middlesbrough.gov.uk
McPartland, John (LAB - Middlehaven)
john_mcpartland@middlesbrough.gov.uk
McTigue, Joan (IND - Beechwood)
joan_mctigue@middlesbrough.gov.uk
Michna, Joe (GRN - Park)
joe_michna@middlesbrough.gov.uk
Morby, Kevin (IND - Park End)
kevin_morby@middlesbrough.gov.uk
Pearson, Hazel (CON - Kader)
hazel_pearson@middlesbrough.gov.uk
Purvis, Geraldine (LAB - Thorntree)
geraldine_purvis@middlesbrough.gov.uk
Purvis, Peter (LAB - Thorntree)
peter_purvis@middlesbrough.gov.uk
Rehman, Habib (LAB - University)
habib_rehman@middlesbrough.gov.uk
Rostron, Julia (LAB - Linthorpe)
julia_rostron@middlesbrough.gov.uk
Sanderson, Peter (IND - Nunthorpe)
peter_sanderson@middlesbrough.gov.uk
Saunders, Michael (IND - Park End)
michael_saunders@middlesbrough.gov.uk
Sharrocks, Jean (LAB - Brookfield)
jean_sharrocks@middlesbrough.gov.uk
Sharrocks, Peter (LAB - Brookfield)
peter_sharrocks@middlesbrough.gov.uk
Sharrocks, Peter (LAB - Clairville)
charles_rooney@middlesbrough.gov.uk
Taylor, Bernie (LAB - Ayresome)
bernie_taylor@middlesbrough.gov.uk
Thompson, Brenda (IND - Nunthorpe)
brenda_thompson@middlesbrough.gov.uk
Walker, Nicky (LAB - Hemlington)
nichola_walker@middlesbrough.gov.uk
Walker, Jeanette (LAB - Hemlington)
jeanette_walker@middlesbrough.gov.uk

POLITICAL COMPOSITION

LAB: 29, IND: 12, CON: 4, LD: 1, NP: 1, GRN: 1

CABINET

Elected Mayor: Mr Ray Mallon
Deputy Mayor / Resources: Mr David Budd
Children, Families & Learning: Mr Mike Carr
Community Protection: Ms Julia Rostron
Public Health & Sport: Ms Brenda Thompson
Regeneration & Economic Development: Mr Peter Sharrocks
Social Care: Mr Barry Coppinger
Streetscene Services & Transport: Ms Nicky Walker

COMMITTEE CHAIRS

Audit & Governance: Mr Len Junier
Chief Officers Appointment: Mr David Budd
Children & Learning (Scrutiny): Ms Jeanette Walker
Constitution: Mr Stephen Bloundele
Corporate Affairs: Mr Garry Clark
Corporate Health & Safety: Mr Peter Sharrocks
Corporate Parenting Board: Mr Mike Carr
Economic Regeneration & Transport (Scrutiny): Ms Tracy Harvey
Environment (Scrutiny): Mr Bob Kerr
Health (Scrutiny): Mr Eddie Dryden
Licensing: Mr Bernie Taylor
Planning & Development: Mr John Cole
Social Care & Adult Services (Scrutiny): Mr Peter Purvis
Social Services Appeals: Mr John McPartland
Teesside Pension Fund & Investment Panel: Mr Stephen Bloundele

MIDLOTHIAN — S

Midlothian Council, Midlothian House, Buccleuch Street, Dalkeith EH22 1DN ☎ 0131 270 7500 🖷 0131 271 3050
enquiries@midlothian.gov.uk www.midlothian.gov.uk

FACTS & FIGURES

Police Authority: Lothian & Borders Police Board
Health Authority: NHS Lothian
Learning and Skills Council: Scotland
Parliamentary Constituencies: Midlothian
EU Constituencies: Scotland
Election Frequency: Elections are of whole council

PRINCIPAL OFFICERS

Chief Executive: Mr Kenneth Lawrie, Chief Executive, Midlothian House, Buccleuch Street, Dalkeith EH22 1DN ☎ 0131 270 7500 🖷 0131 271 3050

Senior Management: Mr John Blair, Director of Corporate Resources, Midlothian House, Buclleuch Street, Dalkeith EH22 1DJ ☎ 0131 270 7500 🖷 0131 654 2797

Senior Management: Mr Don Ledingham, Joint Director of Education & Children's Services, Fairfield House, 8 Lothian Road, Dalkeith EH22 3ZG ☎ 01620 827596; 0131 270 7500 🖷 0131 271 3751 ✉ dledingham@eastlothian.gov.uk

Architect, Building / Property Services: Mr John Blair, Director of Corporate Resources, Midlothian House, Buclleuch Street, Dalkeith EH22 1DJ ☎ 0131 270 7500 🖷 0131 654 2797

Building Control: Mr John Delamar, Building Standards Manager, Fairfield House, 8 Lothian Road, Dalkeith EH22 1DJ ☎ 0131 270 7500 🖷 0131 271 3050 ✉ john.delamar@midlothian.gov.uk

Building Control: Mr Ian Johnson, Head of Planning & Development, Fairfield House, 8 Lothian Road, Dalkeith EH22 3ZQ ☎ 0131 270 7500

Catering Services: Mr John Blair, Director of Corporate Resources, Midlothian House, Buclleuch Street, Dalkeith EH22 1DJ ☎ 0131 270 7500 🖷 0131 654 2797

Catering Services: Mr Norman Catto, Business Manager, Catering/Cleaning, Commercial Services, Dundas Buildings, 62a Polton Street, Bonnyrigg EH19 3YD ☎ 0131 561 5263

Civil Registration: Mr John Blair, Director of Corporate Resources, Midlothian House, Buclleuch Street, Dalkeith EH22 1DJ ☎ 0131 270 7500 🖷 0131 654 2797

Civil Registration: Mrs Hillary Kelly, Head of Customer Services, Midlothian House, Buccleuch Street, Dalkeith EH22 1DN ☎ 0131 270 7500 🖷 0131 271 3252

PR / Communications: Mr Stephen Fraser, Communications Manager, Midlothian House, Buccleuch Street, Dalkeith EH22 1DN ☎ 0131 271 3531 ✉ stephen.fraser@midlothian.gov.uk

Community Safety: Mr Kevin Anderson, Head of Community Safety & Housing, Fairfield House, 8 Lothian Road, Dalkeith EH22 3ZH ☎ 0131 271 3670

Computer Management: Mr John Blair, Director of Corporate Resources, Midlothian House, Buclleuch Street, Dalkeith EH22 1DJ ☎ 0131 270 7500 🖷 0131 654 2797

Consumer Protection and Trading Standards: Mr Kevin Anderson, Head of Community Safety & Housing, Fairfield House, 8 Lothian Road, Dalkeith EH22 3ZH ☎ 0131 271 3670

Contracts: Mr John Blair, Director of Corporate Resources, Midlothian House, Buclleuch Street, Dalkeith EH22 1DJ ☎ 0131 270 7500 🖷 0131 654 2797

Corporate Services: Mr John Blair, Director of Corporate Resources, Midlothian House, Buclleuch Street, Dalkeith EH22 1DJ ☎ 0131 270 7500 🖷 0131 654 2797

Customer Service: Mrs Hillary Kelly, Head of Customer Services, Midlothian House, Buccleuch Street, Dalkeith EH22 1DN ☎ 0131 270 7500 🖷 0131 271 3252

Economic Development: Mr Ian Johnson, Head of Planning & Development, Fairfield House, 8 Lothian Road, Dalkeith EH22 3ZQ ☎ 0131 270 7500

Education: Mr Don Ledingham, Joint Director of Education & Children's Services, Fairfield House, 8 Lothian Road, Dalkeith EH22 3ZG ☎ 01620 827596; 0131 270 7500 🖷 0131 271 3751 ✉ dledingham@eastlothian.gov.uk

Electoral Registration: Mr John Blair, Director of Corporate Resources, Midlothian House, Buclleuch Street, Dalkeith EH22 1DJ ☎ 0131 270 7500 🖷 0131 654 2797

Electoral Registration: Mr Allan Brown, Electoral Officer, Midlothian House, Buccleuch Street, Dalkeith EH22 1DN ☎ 0131 271 3156

Emergency Planning: Mr John Blair, Director of Corporate Resources, Midlothian House, Buclleuch Street, Dalkeith EH22 1DJ ☎ 0131 270 7500 🖷 0131 654 2797

Emergency Planning: Mrs Jane Young, Emergency Planning Officer, Midlothian House, Buccleuch Street, Dalkeith EH22 1DJ ☎ 0131 271 3078 🖷 0131 271 3077

Environmental Health: Mr Kevin Anderson, Head of Community Safety & Housing, Fairfield House, 8 Lothian Road, Dalkeith EH22 3ZH ☎ 0131 271 3670

Estates, Property & Valuation: Mr Ian Johnson, Head of Planning & Development, Fairfield House, 8 Lothian Road, Dalkeith EH22 3ZQ ☎ 0131 270 7500

Finance and Treasurer: Mr Gary Fairley, Head of Finance and Human Resources, Midlothian House, Buccleuch Street, Dalkeith EH22 1DN ☎ 0131 270 7500 🖷 0131 654 2797

Fleet Management: Mr Phil Riddell, Business Manager - Waste & Fleet Services, Dundas Buildings, 62a Polton Street, Bonnyrigg EH19 3YD ☎ 0131 660 9840 🖷 0131 654 2797

Health and Safety: Mr Chris Lawson, Senior Health & Safety Officer, Midlothian House, Buccleuch Street, Dalkeith EH22 1DN ☎ 0131 270 7500 🖷 0131 271 3050

Highways: Mr Ricky Moffat, Head of Commercial Operations, Midlothian House, Buccleuch Street, Dalkeith EH22 1DN ☎ 0131 270 7500 🖷 0131 654 2797

Home Energy Conservation: Mr William Jackson, Service Provision Manager, Dundas Buildings, 62a Polton Street, Bonnyrigg EH19 3YD ☎ 0131 270 7500

Housing: Mr Kevin Anderson, Head of Community Safety & Housing, Fairfield House, 8 Lothian Road, Dalkeith EH22 3ZH ☎ 0131 271 3670

Housing Maintenance: Mr William Jackson, Service Provision

Manager, Dundas Buildings, 62a Polton Street, Bonnyrigg EH19 3YD ☎ 0131 270 7500

Licensing: Mr John Blair, Director of Corporate Resources, Midlothian House, Buccleuch Street, Dalkeith EH22 1DJ ☎ 0131 270 7500 🖷 0131 654 2797

Lighting: Mr Keith Slight, Lighting Manager, Midlothian House, Buccleuch Street, Dalkeith EH22 1DN ☎ 0131 561 5222 🖷 0131 654 2797

Member Services: Mr James Clifford, Council Secretary, Midlothian House, Buccleuch Street, Dalkeith EH22 1DJ ☎ 0131 270 7500 🖷 0131 271 3050

Member Services: Mrs Hillary Kelly, Head of Customer Services, Midlothian House, Buccleuch Street, Dalkeith EH22 1DN ☎ 0131 270 7500 🖷 0131 271 3252

Personnel / HR: Mr Gary Fairley, Head of Finance & Human Resources, Midlothian House, Buccleuch Street, Dalkeith EH22 1DN ☎ 0131 270 7500

Personnel / HR: Mr Ian Pilbeam, HR Policy & Strategy Manager, Buccleuch Street, Dalkeith EH22 1YH ☎ 0131 270 7500 🖷 0131 271 3050

Planning: Mr Ian Johnson, Head of Planning, Fairfield House, 8 Lothian Road, Dalkeith EH22 3ZQ ☎ 0131 270 7500

Recycling & Waste Minimisation: Mr John Blair, Director of Corporate Resources, Midlothian House, Buccleuch Street, Dalkeith EH22 1DJ ☎ 0131 270 7500 🖷 0131 654 2797

Road Safety: Mr John Blair, Director of Corporate Resources, Midlothian House, Buclleuch Street, Dalkeith EH22 1DJ ☎ 0131 270 7500 🖷 0131 654 2797

Road Safety: Mr Ian Johnson, Head of Planning & Development, Fairfield House, 8 Lothian Road, Dalkeith EH22 3ZQ ☎ 0131 270 7500

Social Services: Ms Eibhlin McHugh, Director of Communities & Wellbeing, Fairfield House, 8 Lothian Road, Dalkeith EH22 3ZH ☎ 0131 270 7500 🖷 0131 271 3624 ✉ eibhlin.mchugh@midlothian.gov.uk

Social Services (Adult): Ms Alison White, Head of Adult & Community Care, Fairfield House, 8 Lothian Road, Dalkeith EH22 3ZH ☎ 0131 271 3670

Social Services (Children): Mrs Mary Smith, Head of Children & Families, Fairfield House, 8 Lothian Road, Dalkeith EH22 3ZH ☎ 0131 270 7500 🖷 0131 271 3751

Sustainable Communities: Mr Alasdair Mathers, Regeneration & Social Policy Manager, 1 Eskdail Court, Dalkeith EH22 1AG ☎ 0131 270 7500 🖷 0131 271 3535 ✉ alasdair.mathers@midlothian.gov.uk

Tourism: Mr John Blair, Director of Corporate Resources, Midlothian House, Buccleuch Street, Dalkeith EH22 1DJ ☎ 0131 270 7500 🖷 0131 654 2797

Waste Collection and Disposal: Mr John Blair, Director of Corporate Resources, Midlothian House, Buccleuch Street, Dalkeith EH22 1DJ ☎ 0131 270 7500 🖷 0131 654 2797

Waste Management: Mr John Blair, Director of Corporate Resources, Midlothian House, Buccleuch Street, Dalkeith EH22 1DJ ☎ 0131 270 7500 🖷 0131 654 2797

MEMBERS OF THE COUNCIL (18)

Baxter, Ian (SGP - Bonnyrigg)
ian.baxter@midlothian.gov.uk
Beattie, Lisa (SNP - Midlothian East)
lisa.beattie@midlothian.gov.uk
Bennett, Alex (LAB - Dalkeith)
alex.bennett@midlothian.gov.uk
Boyes, Peter (LAB - Midlothian East)
peter.boyes@midlothian.gov.uk
Bryant, Jim (SNP - Dalkeith)
jim.bryant@midlothian.gov.uk
Constable, Bob (SNP - Bonnyrigg)
bob.constable@midlothian.gov.uk
Coventry, Andrew (SNP - Midlothian West)
de Vink, Peter (IND - Midlothian East)
peter.deVink@midlothian.gov.uk
Imrie, Russell (LAB - Midlothian West)
russell.imrie@midlothian.gov.uk
Johnstone, Cath (SNP - Midlothian South)
cath.johnstone@midlothian.gov.uk
Milligan, Derek (LAB - Bonyrigg)
derek.milligan@midlothian.gov.uk
Montgomery, Adam (LAB - Penicuik)
adam.montgomery@midlothian.gov.uk
Muirhead, James (LAB - Midlothian South)
jim.muirhead@midlothian.gov.uk
Pottinger, Bryan (LAB - Midlothian South)
Rosie, Derek (SNP - Penicuik)
derek.rosie@midlothian.gov.uk
Russell, Margot (LAB - Dalkeith)
margot.russell@midlothian.gov.uk
Thompson, Owen (SNP - Midlothian West)
owen.thompson@midlothian.gov.uk
Wallace, Joe (SNP - Penicuik)
joe.wallace@midlothian.gov.uk

POLITICAL COMPOSITION

LAB: 8, SNP: 8, IND: 1, SGP: 1

MILTON KEYNES U

Milton Keynes Council, Civic Offices, 1 Saxon Gate East, Milton Keynes MK9 3EJ ☎ 01908 691691 🖷 01908 252456
✉ firstname.lastname@milton-keynes.gov.uk
💻 www.milton-keynes.gov.uk

FACTS & FIGURES

Police Authority: Thames Valley Police Authority
Learning and Skills Council: South East
Parliamentary Constituencies: Milton Keynes North, Milton Keynes South
EU Constituencies: South East
Election Frequency: Elections are by thirds

PRINCIPAL OFFICERS

Chief Executive: Mr David Hill, Chief Executive, Civic Offices, 1 Saxon Gate East, Milton Keynes MK9 3EJ ☎ 01908 252200 ✉ david.hill@milton-keynes.gov.uk

Access Officer / Social Services (Disability): Ms Maurica Legg, Joint Services Manager, Tower Drive Centre, Tower Drive, Neath Hill, Milton Keynes MK14 6NA ☎ 01908 253042 🖷 01908 253185 ✉ maurica.legg@milton-keynes.gov.uk

Best Value: Mr Mike Hood, Assistant Director - Partnerships, Civic Offices, 1 Saxon Gate East, Milton Keynes MK9 3EJ ☎ 01908 254612 🖷 01908 252768 ✉ mike.hood@milton-keynes.gov.uk

Building Control: Mr Neil Allen, Head of Building Control & Sustainability, Civic Offices, 1 Saxon Gate East, Milton Keynes MK9 3EJ ☎ 01908 252365 🖷 01908 252319 ✉ neil.allen@milton-keynes.gov.uk

Children / Youth Services: Ms Gail Tolley, Corporate Director - Children & Young People's Services, Civic Offices, 1 Saxon Gate East, Milton Keynes MK9 3EJ ☎ 01908 254062 🖷 01908 252456 ✉ gail.tolley@milton-keynes.gov.uk

Civil Registration: Ms Sharon Taylor, Superintendent Registrar, Bracknell House, Aylesbury Street, Bletchley, Milton Keynes MK2 2BE ☎ 01908 372101 ✉ sharon.taylor@milton-keynes.gov.uk

PR / Communications: Ms Kellie Evans, Corporate Communications Manager, Civic Offices, 1 Saxon Gate East, Milton Keynes MK9 3EJ ☎ 01908 252413 🖷 01908 252768 ✉ kellie.evans@milton-keynes.gov.uk

Community Planning: Ms Sarah Gonsalves, Head of Policy & Performance, Civic Offices, 1 Saxon Gate East, Milton Keynes MK9 3EJ ☎ 01908 252309 🖷 01908 252768

Community Safety: Mr Richard Solly, Community Safety Manager, Lloyds Court, North 10th Street, Milton Keynes MK9 3EE ☎ 01908 254429 🖷 01908 254810 ✉ richard.solly@milton-keynes.gov.uk

Computer Management: Mr Steven Jewell, Head of IT, Saxon Court, 502 Avebury Boulevard, Milton Keynes MK9 3HS ☎ 01908 254141 🖷 01908 252456 ✉ steven.jewell@milton-keynes.gov.uk

Consumer Protection and Trading Standards: Ms Karen Ford, Head of Trading Standards, Civic Offices, 1 Saxon Gate East, Milton Keynes MK9 3EJ ☎ 01908 252267 ✉ karen.ford@milton-keynes.gov.uk

Contracts: Mr Christopher Edwards, Head of Commissioning & Customer Care, Saxon Court, 502 Avebury Boulevard, Milton Keynes MK9 3HS ☎ ; 01908 254779 ✉ christopher.edwards@milton-keynes.gov.uk

Contracts: Mr Andrew Potter, Contracts & Procurement Manager, Saxon Court, 502 Avebury Boulevard, Milton Keynes MK9 3HS ☎ 01908 253216 ✉ andrew.potter@milton-keynes.gov.uk

Corporate Services: Mr Geoff Snelson, Director - Strategy, Civic Offices, 1 Saxon Gate East, Milton Keynes MK9 3EJ ☎ 01908 252665 🖷 01908 252768 ✉ geoff.snelson@milton-keynes.gov.uk

Customer Service: Mr Christopher Edwards, Head of Commissioning & Customer Care, Saxon Court, 502 Avebury Boulevard, Milton Keynes MK9 3HS ☎ 01908 254779 ✉ christopher.edwards@milton-keynes.gov.uk

Customer Service: Mrs Norma Evans, Complaints & Information Governance Manager, Civic Offices, 1 Saxon Gate East, Milton Keynes MK9 3EJ ☎ 01908 252752 ✉ norma.evans@milton-keynes.gov.uk

Direct Labour: Mr Mike Brown, Assistant Director - Environmental Services, Civic Offices, 1 Saxon Gate East, Milton Keynes MK9 3EJ ☎ 01908 254180 ✉ mike.brown@milton-keynes.gov.uk

Economic Development: Ms Pam Gosal, Corporate Head of Economic Development, Civic Offices, 1 Saxon Gate East, Milton Keynes MK9 3EJ ☎ 01908 252192 ✉ pam.gosal@milton-keynes.gov.uk

Education: Mr Michael Bracey, Assistant Director - Education, Effectiveness & Participation, Saxon Court, 502 Avebury Boulevard, Milton Keynes MK9 3HS ☎ 01908 258041 🖷 01908 252456 ✉ michael.bracey@milton-keynes.gov.uk

E-Government: Mr Steven Jewell, Head of IT, Saxon Court, 502 Avebury Boulevard, Milton Keynes MK9 3HS ☎ 01908 254141 🖷 01908 252456 ✉ steven.jewell@milton-keynes.gov.uk

Electoral Registration: Mr John Moffoot, Assistant Director - Democratic Services, Civic Offices, 1 Saxon Gate East, Milton Keynes MK9 3EJ ☎ 01908 252314 🖷 01908 252511 ✉ john.moffoot@milton-keynes.gov.uk

Emergency Planning: Mr John Godwin, Corporate Health & Safety Officer, Civic Offices, 1 Saxon Gate East, Milton Keynes MK9 3EJ ☎ 01908 253495 🖷 01908 252456 ✉ john.godwin@milton-keynes.gov.uk

Energy Management: Mr Jeremy Draper, Energy Manager, Civic Offices, 1 Saxon Gate East, Milton Keynes MK9 3EJ ☎ 01908 252652 🖷 01908 252575 ✉ jeremy.draper@milton-keynes.gov.uk

Environmental / Technical Services: Mr Alex Constantinides, Assistant Director - Transport, PO Box 113, Civic Offices, 1 Saxon Gate East, Milton Keynes MK9 3HN ☎ 01908 254258 ✉ alex.constantinides@milton-keynes.gov.uk

Environmental Health: Mr Philip Winsor, Assistant Director - Regulatory Services, PO Box 105, Civic Offices, 1 Saxon Gate East, Milton Keynes MK9 3HH ☎ 01908 252405 ✉ philip.winsor@milton-keynes.gov.uk

Estates, Property & Valuation: Mr Peter Smettem, Head of Property & Estates, Civic Offices, 1 Saxon Gate East, Milton Keynes MK9 3EJ ☎ 01908 252334 🖷 01908 252751 ✉ peter.smettem@milton-keynes.gov.uk

Facilities: Ms Yvonne Mullens, Facilities Manager, Saxon Court,

502 Avebury Boulevard, Milton Keynes MK9 3HS ☎ 01908 253627 🖷 01908 252456 ✉ yvonne.mullens@milton-keynes.gov.uk

Finance and Treasurer: Mr Tim Hannam, Corporate Director - Resources, Saxon Court, 502 Avebury Boulevard, Milton Keynes MK9 3HS ☎ 01908 252756 ✉ tim.hannam@milton-keynes.gov.uk

Grounds Maintenance: Mr Mike Brown, Assistant Director - Environmental Services, Civic Offices, 1 Saxon Gate East, Milton Keynes MK9 3EJ ☎ 01908 254180 ✉ mike.brown@milton-keynes.gov.uk

Health and Safety: Mr Philip Winsor, Assistant Director - Regulatory Services, PO Box 105, Civic Offices, 1 Saxon Gate East, Milton Keynes MK9 3HH ☎ 01908 252405 ✉ philip.winsor@milton-keynes.gov.uk

Highways: Mr Brian Matthews, Head of Transportation Services, Council Offices, The Gateway, Gatehouse Road, Aylesbury HP19 8FF ☎ 01908 252064 🖷 01908 252456 ✉ brian.matthews@milton-keynes.gov.uk

Home Energy Conservation: Mr Jeremy Draper, Energy Manager, Civic Offices, 1 Saxon Gate East, Milton Keynes MK9 3EJ ☎ 01908 252652 🖷 01908 252575 ✉ jeremy.draper@milton-keynes.gov.uk

Housing: Ms Lynda Bull, Corporate Director - Community Wellbeing, Civic Offices, 1 Saxon Gate East, Milton Keynes MK9 3EJ ☎ 01908 253357 ✉ lynda.bull@milton-keynes.gov.uk

Housing Maintenance: Mr Anthony Hodson-Curran, Head of Assets & Strategy, Civic Offices, 1 Saxon Gate East, Milton Keynes MK9 3EJ ☎ 01908 253951 ✉ anthony.hodson-curran@milton-keynes.gov.uk

Local Area Agreement: Mr Mike Hood, Assistant Director - Partnerships, Civic Offices, 1 Saxon Gate East, Milton Keynes MK9 3EJ ☎ 01908 254612 🖷 01908 252768 ✉ mike.hood@milton-keynes.gov.uk

Legal: Mr Philip McCourt, Assistant Director - Law & Governance, Civic Offices, 1 Saxon Gate East, Milton Keynes MK9 3EJ ☎ 01908 252962 🖷 01908 252600 ✉ philip.mccourt@milton-keynes.gov.uk

Leisure and Cultural Services: Mr Paul Sanders, Assistant Director - Community Facilities Unit, Community Wellbeing, Saxon Court, 502 Avebury Avenue, Milton Keynes MK9 3HS ☎ 01908 253639 🖷 01908 253304 ✉ paul.sanders@milton-keynes.gov.uk

Licensing: Mr Philip Winsor, Assistant Director - Regulatory Services, Civic Offices, 1 Saxon Gate East, Milton Keynes MK9 3EJ ☎ 01908 252405 ✉ philip.winsor@milton-keynes.gov.uk

Lifelong Learning: Mr Michael Bracey, Assistant Director - Education, Effectiveness & Participation, Saxon Court, 502 Avebury Boulevard, Milton Keynes MK9 3HS ☎ 01908 258041 🖷 01908 252456 ✉ michael.bracey@milton-keynes.gov.uk

Lighting: Mr Chris Hales, Street Lighting Engineer, Saxon Court, 502 Avebury Boulevard, Milton Keynes MK6 1HS ☎ 01908 252825 🖷 01908 252822 ✉ chris.hales@milton-keynes.gov.uk

Lottery Funding, Charity and Voluntary: Mr Paul Sanders, Assistant Director - Community Facilities Unit, Saxon Court, 502 Avebury Boulevard, Milton Keynes MK6 1NE ☎ 01908 253639 🖷 01908 253304 ✉ paul.sanders@milton-keynes.gov.uk

Member Services: Mr John Moffoot, Assistant Director - Democratic Services, Civic Offices, 1 Saxon Gate East, Milton Keynes MK9 3EJ ☎ 01908 252314 🖷 01908 252511 ✉ john.moffoot@milton-keynes.gov.uk

Parking: Ms Sara Bailey, CMK Parking Change Manager, Civic Offices, 1 Saxon Gate East, Milton Keynes MK9 3EJ ☎ 01908 252198 🖷 01908 252456 ✉ sara.bailey@milton-keynes.gov.uk

Partnerships: Mr Mike Hood, Assistant Director - Partnerships, Saxon Court, 502 Avebury Boulevard, Milton Keynes MK9 3HS ☎ 01908 254612 🖷 01908 252768 ✉ mike.hood@milton-keynes.gov.uk

Personnel / HR: Ms Morag Shaw, Assistant Director - HR Strategy, Human Resources, Saxon Court, 502 Avebury Boulevard, Milton Keynes MK9 3HS ☎ 01908 253857 🖷 01908 253867 ✉ morag.shaw@milton-keynes.gov.uk

Planning: Mr Nick Fenwick, Assistant Director - Planning, Economy & Development, Civic Offices, 1 Saxon Gate East, Milton Keynes MK9 3EJ ☎ 01908 252492 🖷 01908 252456 ✉ nick.fenwick@milton-keynes.gov.uk

Procurement: Mr Andrew Potter, Contracts & Procurement Manager, Saxon Court, 502 Avebury Boulevard, Milton Keynes MK9 3HS ☎ 01908 253216 ✉ andrew.potter@milton-keynes.gov.uk

Public Libraries: Mr Paul Sanders, Assistant Director - Community Facilities Unit, Saxon Court, 502 Avebury Boulevard, Milton Keynes MK6 1NE ☎ 01908 253639 🖷 01908 253304 ✉ paul.sanders@milton-keynes.gov.uk

Recycling & Waste Minimisation: Mr Andy Hudson, Head of Environment & Waste, Civic Offices, 1 Saxon Gate East, Milton Keynes MK9 3EJ ☎ 01908 252577 🖷 01908 252575 ✉ andy.hudson@milton-keynes.gov.uk

Regeneration: Ms Jan Phillips, Regeneration Co-ordinator, Civic Offices, 1 Saxon Gate East, Milton Keynes MK9 3EJ ☎ 01908 631783 🖷 01908 253304 ✉ jan.phillips@milton-keynes.gov.uk

Road Safety: Mr Adrian Carden, Road Safety Team Leader, Civic Offices, 1 Saxon Gate East, Milton Keynes MK9 3EJ ☎ 01908 252764 ✉ adrian.carden@milton-keynes.gov.uk

Social Services: Mr David Hill, Chief Executive, Civic Offices, 1 Saxon Gate East, Milton Keynes MK9 3EJ ☎ 01908 252200 ✉ david.hill@milton-keynes.gov.uk

Social Services (Adult): Ms Lyn Scott, Assistant Director - Adult Social Care, Civic Offices, 1 Saxon Gate East, Milton Keynes MK9

3EJ ☎ 01908 257973 🖷 01908 252456 ✉ lyn.scott@milton-keynes.gov.uk

Social Services (Children): Ms Gail Tolley, Corporate Director - Children & Young People's Services, Civic Offices, 1 Saxon Gate East, Milton Keynes MK9 3EJ ☎ 01908 254062 🖷 01908 252456 ✉ gail.tolley@milton-keynes.gov.uk

Staff Training: Ms Jacky Hart, Learning & Development Team Leader, Human Resources, Saxon Court, 502 Avebury Boulevard, Milton Keynes MK9 3HS ☎ 01908 253604 🖷 01908 253867 ✉ jacky.hart@milton-keynes.gov.uk

Street Scene: Mr Mike Brown, Assistant Director - Environmental Services, Synergy Park, Chesney Wood, Milton Keynes MK6 1NE ☎ 01908 254180 ✉ mike.brown@milton-keynes.gov.uk

Sustainable Communities: Mr Geoff Snelson, Director - Strategy, Civic Offices, 1 Saxon Gate East, Milton Keynes MK9 3EJ ☎ 01908 252665 🖷 01908 252768 ✉ geoff.snelson@milton-keynes.gov.uk

Sustainable Development: Mr Alan Mills, Joint Head of Development Management, Civic Offices, 1 Saxon Gate East, Milton Keynes MK9 3EJ ☎ 01908 252412 ✉ alan.mills@milton-keynes.gov.uk

Traffic Management: Mr Alex Constantinides, Assistant Director - Transport, Civic Offices, 1 Saxon Gate East, Milton Keynes MK9 3EJ ☎ 01908 254258 ✉ alex.constantinides@milton-keynes.gov.uk

Transport: Mr Andrew Coleman, Passenger Transport Manager, Civic Offices, 1 Saxon Gate East, Milton Keynes MK9 3EJ ☎ 01908 254739 🖷 01908 252302 ✉ andrew.coleman@milton-keynes.gov.uk

Transport: Mr Brian Matthews, Head of Transportation Services, Council Offices, The Gateway, Gatehouse Road, Aylesbury HP19 8FF ☎ 01908 252064 🖷 01908 252456 ✉ brian.matthews@milton-keynes.gov.uk

Transport Planner: Mr David Lawson, Transport Policy & Programme Manager, Civic Offices, 1 Saxon Gate East, Milton Keynes MK9 3EJ ☎ 01908 252510 🖷 01908 252302 ✉ david.lawson@milton-keynes.gov.uk

Waste Collection and Disposal: Mr Andy Hudson, Head of Environment & Waste, Civic Offices, 1 Saxon Gate East, Milton Keynes MK9 3EJ ☎ 01908 252577 🖷 01908 252575 ✉ andy.hudson@milton-keynes.gov.uk

Waste Management: Mr Andy Hudson, Head of Environment & Waste, Civic Offices, 1 Saxon Gate East, Milton Keynes MK9 3EJ ☎ 01908 252577 🖷 01908 252575 ✉ andy.hudson@milton-keynes.gov.uk

MEMBERS OF THE COUNCIL (51)

***Mayor:* Morris**, Catriona (CON - Linford South)
catriona.morris@milton-keynes.gov.uk
***Deputy Mayor:* Brackenbury**, Ric (LAB - Stantonbury)
brian.white@milton-keynes.gov.uk
***Leader of the Council:* Geary**, Andrew (CON - Hanslope Park)
andrew.geary@milton-keynes.gov.uk
Alexander, Paul (LD - Newport Pagnell North)
Paul.Alexander@milton-keynes.gov.uk
Bald, Edith (CON - Emerson Valley)
edith.bald@milton-keynes.gov.uk
Barney, Lee (UKIP - Walton Park)
lee.barney@milton-keynes.gov.uk
Brackenbury, Rick (LD - Linford South)
rick.brackenbury@milton-keynes.gov.uk
Bradburn, Robin (LD - Bradwell)
robin.bradburn@milton-keynes.gov.uk
Bradburn, Robin (CON - Loughton Park)
andy.dransfield@milton-keynes.gov.uk
Bramall, Alice (CON - Walton Park)
alice.bramall@milton-keynes.gov.uk
Brock, Debbie (CON - Olney)
mayorsoffice@milton-keynes.gov.uk
Brunning, Denise (CON - Stony Stratford)
Denise.Brunning@milton-keynes.gov.uk
Burke, Margaret (LAB - Stantonbury)
margaret.burke@milton-keynes.gov.uk
Burke, Stuart (LD - Emerson Valley)
stuart.burke@milton-keynes.gov.uk
Coventry, Stephen (LAB - Woughton)
steve.coventry@milton-keynes.gov.uk
Eastman, Derek (LD - Newport Pagnell North)
derek.eastman@milton-keynes.gov.uk
Edwards, Reg (LAB - Eaton Manor)
reg.edwards@milton-keynes.gov.uk
Exon, Robert (LD - Bradwell)
robert.exon@milton-keynes.gov.uk
Ferrans, Jennie (LD - Furzton)
jenni.ferans@milton-keynes.gov.uk
Geary, Peter (CON - Olney)
peter.geary@milton-keynes.gov.uk
Hawthorn, John (CON - Stony Stratford)
john.hawthorn@milton-keynes.gov.uk
Hopkins, David (CON - Danesborough)
david.hopkins@milton-keynes.gov.uk
Hoyle, Donald (CON - Loughton Park)
donald.hoyle@milton-keynes.gov.uk
Jury, Ruth (CON - Loughton Park)
ruth.jury@milton-keynes.gov.uk
Kennedy, Angela (CON - Bletchley and Fenny Stratford)
angela.kennedy@milton-keynes.gov.uk
Klein, Mick (CON - Bletchley and Fenny Stratford)
mick.klein@milton-keynes.gov.uk
Legg, Mick (LAB - Denbigh)
michael.legg@yahoo.com
Long, Nigel (LAB - Denbigh)
nigel.long@milton-keynes.gov.uk
Maric, Andy (LD - Newport Pagnell South)
andy.maric@milton-keynes.gov.uk
Marland, Peter (LAB - Wolverton)
peter.marland@milton-keynes.gov.uk
McCall, Douglas (LD - Newport Pagnell South)
douglas.mccall@milton-keynes.gov.uk
McCall, Isobel (LD - Campbell Park)
isobel.mccall@milton-keynes.gov.uk
McCdonald, Peter (CON - Middleton)
peter.mcdonald@milton-keynes.gov.uk
McKenzie, Gladstone (LAB - Whaddon)
gladstone.mckenzie@milton-keynes.gov.uk

McLean, Keith (CON - Sherington)
keith.mclean@milton-keynes.gov.uk
Middleton, Robert (LAB - Wolverton)
robert.middleton@milton-keynes.gov.uk
Miles, Norman (LAB - Wolverton)
norman.miles@milton-keynes.gov.uk
O'Neill, Hannah (LAB - Woughton)
hannah.o'neill@milton-keynes.gov.uk
Richards, Alan (LD - Linford North)
alan.richards@milton-keynes.gov.uk
Shafiq, Subhan (LD - Walton Park)
subhan.shafiq@milton-keynes.gov.uk
Small, Gerald (CON - Emerson Valley)
gerald.small@milton-keynes.gov.uk
Tallack, Cec (LD - Campbell Park)
cec.tallack@milton-keynes.gov.uk
Venn, Rita (LAB - Bletchley and Fenny Stratford)
rita.venn@milton-keynes.gov.uk
Wales, Elaine (LAB - Whaddon)
elaine.wales@milton-keynes.gov.uk
Wallis, Pauline (LAB - Bradwell)
Pauline.Wallis@milton-keynes.gov.uk
Webb, Alan (LAB - Eaton Manor)
alan.webb@milton-keynes.gov.uk
Wharton, Philip (CON - Stony Stratford)
phil.wharton@milton-keynes.gov.uk
Williams, Paul (LAB - Campbell Park)
Paul.Williams@milton-keynes.gov.uk
Williams, Chris (LD - Furzton)
chris.williams1@milton-keynes.gov.uk
Williams, Chris (CON - Middleton)
john.bint@milton-keynes.gov.uk
Zealley, Christine (LD - Linford North)
christine.zealley@milton-keynes.gov.uk

POLITICAL COMPOSITION
CON: 19, LAB: 16, LD: 15, UKIP: 1

CABINET
Leader: Mr Andrew Geary
Deputy Leader / Economic Development: Mr David Hopkins
Adult, Older Years & Health: Ms Debbie Brock
Children & Young People: Mr Robin Bradburn
Communities, Corporate Services & Transformation: Mr Peter Geary
Finance: Ms Edith Bald
Transport & Highways: Mr Chris Williams

COMMITTEE CHAIRS
Audit: Mr Ric Brackenbury
Children & Young People's Select: Mr Robin Bradburn
Development Control: Mr Brian White
Economy, Growth & Regeneration: Ms Isobel McCall
Environment & Transport: Mr Cec Tallack
Executive Scrutiny Panel: Mr Chris Williams
Health & Community Wellbeing Select: Mr Nigel Long
Housing & Communities: Mr Stephen Coventry
Licensing: Mr Stuart Burke
Overview & Scrutiny Management: Mr Norman Miles
Regulatory: Mr Stuart Burke
Standards: Mr Christopher Fogden (External)

MOLE VALLEY — D

Mole Valley District Council, Pippbrook, Dorking RH4 1SJ
☎ 01306 885001 🖷 01306 876821 ✉ info@molevalley.gov.uk
🖳 www.molevalley.gov.uk

FACTS & FIGURES
Police Authority: Surrey Police Authority
Health Authority: South East Coast Strategic Health Authority
Learning and Skills Council: South East
Parliamentary Constituencies: Mole Valley
EU Constituencies: South East
Election Frequency: Elections are by thirds
Twinning: Dorkingt: Gouvieux (France), Guglingen (Germany). Leatherhead; Triel (France)

PRINCIPAL OFFICERS
Chief Executive: Mr Darren Mepham, Chief Executive, Pippbrook, Dorking RH4 1SJ ☎ 01306 879101 🖷 01306 879302
✉ darren.mepham@molevalley.gov.uk

Senior Management: Mr Nick Gray, Strategic Director, Pippbrook, Dorking RH4 1SJ ☎ 01306 879307 🖷 01306 876821
✉ nick.gray@molevalley.gov.uk

Senior Management: Ms Laura Taylor, Strategic Director, Pippbrook, Dorking RH4 1SJ ☎ 01306 879190
✉ laura.taylor@molevalley.gov.uk

Access Officer / Social Services (Disability): Mrs Rachel O'Reilly, Corporate Head of Service, Pippbrook, Dorking RH4 1SJ ☎ 01306 879358 🖷 01306 876821
✉ rachel.o'reilly@molevalley.gov.uk

Architect, Building / Property Services: Mr Richard Burrows, Corporate Head of Service, Pippbrook, Dorking RH4 1SJ ☎ 01306 879156 ✉ richard.burrows@molevalley.gov.uk

Building Control: Mr Malcolm Dean, Building Control Manager, Pippbrook, Dorking RH4 1SJ ☎ 01306 879252 🖷 01306 876821
✉ malcolm.dean@molevalley.gov.uk

Children / Youth Services: Mrs Rachel O'Reilly, Corporate Head of Service, Pippbrook, Dorking RH4 1SJ ☎ 01306 879358
🖷 01306 876821 ✉ rachel.o'reilly@molevalley.gov.uk

PR / Communications: Mrs Louise Bircher, Customer Service & Communications Manager, Pippbrook, Dorking RH4 1SJ ☎ 01306 879155 🖷 01306 876821 ✉ louise.bircher@molevalley.gov.uk

Community Planning: Mrs Rachel O'Reilly, Corporate Head of Service, Pippbrook, Dorking RH4 1SJ ☎ 01306 879358 🖷 01306 876821 ✉ rachel.o'reilly@molevalley.gov.uk

Community Safety: Mrs Rachel O'Reilly, Corporate Head of Service, Pippbrook, Dorking RH4 1SJ ☎ 01306 879358 🖷 01306 876821 ✉ rachel.o'reilly@molevalley.gov.uk

Computer Management: Mr Robert Thomas, Head of Information Technology, Pippbrook, Dorking RH4 1SJ ☎ 01306 879171 🖷 01306 876821 ✉ bob.thomas@molevalley.gov.uk

Corporate Services: Mr Darren Mepham, Chief Executive,

Pippbrook, Dorking RH4 1SJ ☎ 01306 879101 🖷 01306 879302 ✉ darren.mepham@molevalley.gov.uk

Customer Service: Mrs Louise Bircher, Customer Service & Communications Manager, Pippbrook, Dorking RH4 1SJ ☎ 01306 879155 🖷 01306 876821 ✉ louise.bircher@molevalley.gov.uk

Economic Development: Ms Sandra Grant, Economic Unit Manager, Pippbrook, Dorking RH4 1SJ ☎ 01306 655017 🖷 01306 742359 ✉ sandra.grant@molevalley.gov.uk

Electoral Registration: Mrs Arabella Davies, Democratic Services Manager, Pippbrook, Dorking RH4 1SJ ☎ 01306 879137 🖷 01306 879302 ✉ arabella.davies@molevalley.gov.uk

Emergency Planning: Mr Paul Anderson, Policy Manager, Pippbrook, Dorking RH4 1SJ ☎ 01306 870613 🖷 01306 876821 ✉ paul.anderson@molevalley.gov.uk

Energy Management: Mr Graeme Kane, Sustainability Manager, Pippbrook, Dorking RH4 1SJ ☎ 01306 870622 🖷 01306 876321 ✉ graeme.kane@molevalley.gov.uk

Environmental / Technical Services: Mr Graeme Kane, Sustainability Manager, Pippbrook, Dorking RH4 1SJ ☎ 01306 870622 🖷 01306 876321 ✉ graeme.kane@molevalley.gov.uk

Environmental Health: Mr Graeme Kane, Sustainability Manager, Pippbrook, Dorking RH4 1SJ ☎ 01306 870622 🖷 01306 876321 ✉ graeme.kane@molevalley.gov.uk

Estates, Property & Valuation: Mr Richard Burrows, Corporate Head of Service, Pippbrook, Dorking RH4 1SJ ☎ 01306 879156 ✉ richard.burrows@molevalley.gov.uk

Facilities: Mr Jason Hughes, Senior Engineer & IT Co-ordinator, Pippbrook, Dorking RH4 1SJ ☎ 01306 879184 🖷 01306 876821 ✉ jason.hughes@molevalley.gov.uk

Finance and Treasurer: Mr Nick Gray, Strategic Director, Pippbrook, Dorking RH4 1SJ ☎ 01306 879307 🖷 01306 876821 ✉ nick.gray@molevalley.gov.uk

Grounds Maintenance: Mr Graeme Kane, Sustainability Manager, Pippbrook, Dorking RH4 1SJ ☎ 01306 870622 🖷 01306 876321 ✉ graeme.kane@molevalley.gov.uk

Health and Safety: Ms Laura Taylor, Strategic Director, Pippbrook, Dorking RH4 1SJ ☎ 01306 879190 ✉ laura.taylor@molevalley.gov.uk

Home Energy Conservation: Mr Graeme Kane, Sustainability Manager, Pippbrook, Dorking RH4 1SJ ☎ 01306 870622 🖷 01306 876321 ✉ graeme.kane@molevalley.gov.uk

Housing: Ms Alison Wilks, Strategic Housing Manager, Pippbrook, Dorking RH4 1SJ ☎ 01306 870645 🖷 01306 876321 ✉ alison.wilks@molevalley.gov.uk

Housing Maintenance: Ms Alison Wilks, Strategic Housing Manager, Pippbrook, Dorking RH4 1SJ ☎ 01306 870645 🖷 01306 876321 ✉ alison.wilks@molevalley.gov.uk

Legal: Mr Chris Harris, Services Manager, Pippbrook, Dorking RH4 1SJ ☎ 01306 879130 🖷 01306 876821 ✉ christopher.harris@molevalley.gov.uk

Leisure and Cultural Services: Mr Richard Burrows, Corporate Head of Service, Pippbrook, Dorking RH4 1SJ ☎ 01306 879156 ✉ richard.burrows@molevalley.gov.uk

Licensing: Mr John Pleasance, Senior Licensing Officer, Pippbrook, Dorking RH4 1SJ ☎ 01306 879351 🖷 01306 876321 ✉ john.pleasance@molevalley.gov.uk

Lottery Funding, Charity and Voluntary: Mrs Rachel O'Reilly, Corporate Head of Service, Pippbrook, Dorking RH4 1SJ ☎ 01306 879358 🖷 01306 876821 ✉ rachel.o'reilly@molevalley.gov.uk

Member Services: Mrs Angela Griffiths, Corporate Head of Service, Pippbrook, Dorking RH4 1SJ ☎ 01306 879133 🖷 01306 879302 ✉ angela.griffiths@molevalley.gov.uk

Parking: Mr Stuart Clark, Parking Manager, Pippbrook, Dorking RH4 1SJ ☎ 01306 879369 🖷 01306 876821 ✉ stuart.clark@molevalley.gov.uk

Partnerships: Ms Laura Taylor, Strategic Director, Pippbrook, Dorking RH4 1SJ ☎ 01306 879190 ✉ laura.taylor@molevalley.gov.uk

Personnel / HR: Mr Darren Mepham, Chief Executive, Pippbrook, Dorking RH4 1SJ ☎ 01306 879101 🖷 01306 879302 ✉ darren.mepham@molevalley.gov.uk

Planning: Mr Andrew Bircher, Corporate Head of Service with Responsibility for Planning, Pippbrook, Dorking RH4 1SJ ☎ 01306 879237 🖷 01306 876821 ✉ andrew.bircher@molevalley.gov.uk

Planning: Mr Jack Straw, Planning Policy Manager, Pippbrook, Dorking RH4 1SJ ☎ 01306 879246 🖷 01306 876821 ✉ jack.straw@molevalley.gov.uk

Procurement: Mr Richard Burrows, Corporate Head of Service, Pippbrook, Dorking RH4 1SJ ☎ 01306 879156 ✉ richard.burrows@molevalley.gov.uk

Recycling & Waste Minimisation: Mr Graeme Kane, Sustainability Manager, Pippbrook, Dorking RH4 1SJ ☎ 01306 870622 🖷 01306 876321 ✉ graeme.kane@molevalley.gov.uk

Staff Training: Mr Darren Mepham, Chief Executive, Pippbrook, Dorking RH4 1SJ ☎ 01306 879101 🖷 01306 879302 ✉ darren.mepham@molevalley.gov.uk

Street Scene: Mr Rod Shaw, Prinicipal Conservation Officer, Pippbrook, Dorking RH4 1SJ ☎ 01306 879247 ✉ rod.shaw@molevalley.gov.uk

Sustainable Communities: Ms Laura Taylor, Strategic Director, Pippbrook, Dorking RH4 1SJ ☎ 01306 879190 ✉ laura.taylor@molevalley.gov.uk

Sustainable Development: Mr Graeme Kane, Sustainability Manager, Pippbrook, Dorking RH4 1SJ ☎ 01306 870622 🖷 01306

876321 ✉ graeme.kane@molevalley.gov.uk

Town Centre: Ms Sandra Grant, Dorking Town Centre Manager, Dorking Town Centre Management, c/o Barclays Bank Plc, 87/99 High Street, Dorking RH4 1AN ☎ 01306 655017 🖷 01306 742359 ✉ sandra.grant@molevalley.gov.uk

Town Centre: Mrs Lucy Hanson, Leatherhead Town Centre Manager, 25-29 High Street, Leatherhead KT22 8AB ☎ 01372 363652 🖷 01372 363652 ✉ lucy.hanson@molevalley.gov.uk

Waste Collection and Disposal: Mr Graeme Kane, Sustainability Manager, Pippbrook, Dorking RH4 1SJ ☎ 01306 870622 🖷 01306 876321 ✉ graeme.kane@molevalley.gov.uk

Waste Management: Mr Graeme Kane, Sustainability Manager, Pippbrook, Dorking RH4 1SJ ☎ 01306 870622 🖷 01306 876321 ✉ graeme.kane@molevalley.gov.uk

Children's Play Areas: Mr Graeme Kane, Sustainability Manager, Pippbrook, Dorking RH4 1SJ ☎ 01306 870622 🖷 01306 876321 ✉ graeme.kane@molevalley.gov.uk

MEMBERS OF THE COUNCIL (41)

***Chair:* Northcott**, John (LD - Holmwoods)
cllr.salmon@molevalley.gov.uk
***Leader of the Council:* Townsend**, Chris (IND - Ashtead Park)
cllr.townsend@molevalley.gov.uk
***Deputy Leader of the Council:* Friend**, James (CON - Westcott)
cllr.friend@molevalley.gov.uk
Aboud, Emile (CON - Fetcham West)
cllr.aboud@molevalley.gov.uk
Brooke, Richard (IND - Ashtead Park)
cllr.brooke@molevalley.gov.uk
Brooks, Lynne (CON - Fetcham East)
Cllr.LynneBrooks@molevalley.gov.uk
Brooks, Stella (LD - Bookham South)
cllr.brooks@molevalley.gov.uk
Burt, Derrick (SD - Dorking North)
cllr.burt@molevalley.gov.uk
Chandler, John (NP - Bookham South)
cllr.chandler@molevalley.gov.uk
Cooksey, Stephen (LD - Dorking South)
cllr.cooksey@molevalley.gov.uk
Cooksey, Margaret (LD - Dorking South)
cllr.margaretcooksey@molevalley.gov.uk
Cooper, Mary (IND - Ashtead Village)
cllr.cooper@molevalley.gov.uk
Curran, Clare (CON - Bookham North)
cllr.curran@molevalley.gov.uk
Dickson, Rosemary (CON - Leatherhead South)
cllr.dickson@molevalley.gov.uk
Elderton, Paul (LD - Dorking North)
paul.elderton@virgin.net
Hancock, Paula (IND - Ashtead Common)
cllr.hancock@molevalley.gov.uk
Haque, Raj (LD - Fetcham West)
cllr.haque@molevalley.gov.uk
Harris, Phil (CON - Bookham South)
cllr.harris@molevalley.gov.uk
Homewood, Valerie (LD - Beare Green)
cllr.valeriehomewood@molevalley.gov.uk
Howarth, Dave (LD - Leatherhead North)
cllr.howarth@molevalley.gov.uk
Hunt, Chris (CON - Ashtead Village)
cllr.hunt@molevalley.gov.uk
Hurworth, Tessa (CON - Bookham North)
cllr.hurworth@molevalley.gov.uk
Lewis-Carr, Bridget (LD - Leatherhead North)
cllr.lewis-carr@molevalley.gov.uk
Ling, Simon (IND - Ashtead Village)
cllr.ling@molevalley.gov.uk
Longhurst, Mick (LD - Holmwoods)
cllr.longhurst@molevalley.gov.uk
Loretto, Tim (LD - Dorking South)
cllr.loretto@molevalley.gov.uk
McCheyne, Rebecca (LD - Mickleham, Westhumble and Pixham)
cllr.mccheyne@molevalley.gov.uk
Michael, Vivienne (CON - Okewood)
cllr.michael@molevalley.gov.uk
Mir, David (CON - Leith Hill)
cllr.mir@molevalley.gov.uk
Monkman, Wayne (LD - Holmwoods)
cllr.monkman@molevalley.gov.uk
Muggeridge, John (CON - Brockham, Betchwood and Buckland)
cllr.muggeridge@molevalley.gov.uk
Murdoch, Iain (LD - Capel, Leigh and Newdigate)
cllr.murdoch@molevalley.gov.uk
Newman, Paul (CON - Bookham North)
cllr.newman@molevalley.gov.uk
Northcott, John (IND - Ashtead Common)
cllr.northcott@molevalley.gov.uk
Osborne-Patterson, Corinna (CON - Capel, Leigh and Newdigate)
Cllr.Osborne-Patterson@molevalley.gov.uk
Potter, Paul (LD - Brockham, Betchworth and Buckland)
cllr.potter@molevalley.gov.uk
Preedy, David (LD - Box Hill and Headley)
cllr.preedy@molevalley.gov.uk
Sharland, David (CON - Leatherhead South)
cllr.sharland@molevalley.gov.uk
Shimmin, Philippa (LD - Leatherhead North)
cllr.shimmin@molevalley.gov.uk
Westwood, Kathryn (IND - Fetcham East)
cllr.westwood@molevalley.gov.uk
Yarwood, Charles (CON - Charlwood)
cllr.yarwood@molevalley.gov.uk

POLITICAL COMPOSITION

LD: 17, CON: 15, IND: 7, NP: 1, SD: 1

CABINET

Leader: Mr Stephen Cooksey
Deputy Leader / Environment: Mr James Friend
Customer Service & Wellbeing: Ms Vivienne Michael
Communities & Assets: Mr Charles Yarwood
Finance: Mr Simon Ling
Planning: Mr John Northcott

COMMITTEE CHAIRS

Audit: Mrs Clare Curran
Development Control: Mr John Northcott
Licensing: Mr Paul Elderton
Scrutiny: Mr Stephen Cooksey
Standards: Mr Tim Prideux (External)

MONMOUTHSHIRE W

Monmouthshire County Council, County Hall, Cwmbran NP44 2XH ☎ 01633 644644 🖷 01633 644666 ✉ feedback@monmouthshire.gov.uk 💻 www.monmouthshire.gov.uk

FACTS & FIGURES

Police Authority: Gwent Police Authority
Learning and Skills Council: Wales
Parliamentary Constituencies: Monmouth
EU Constituencies: Wales
Election Frequency: Elections are of whole council
Twinning: Abergavenny: Oestringen (Germany); Sarno (Italy); Caldicot: Waghausel (Germany); Chepstow: Cormeilles (France); Monmouth: Carbonne (France); Waldbrown (Germany); Usk: Graben (Germany); Neudorf (Germany); Landkreis Karlsruhe (Germany)

PRINCIPAL OFFICERS

Chief Executive: Mr Paul Matthews, Chief Executive, County Hall, Cwmbran NP44 2XH ☎ 01633 644644 ✉ paulmatthews@monmouthshire.gov.uk

Deputy Chief Executive: Ms Moyna Wilkinson, Deputy Chief Executive, County Hall, Cwmbran NP44 2XH ☎ 01633 644644 ✉ moynawilkinson@monmouthshire.gov.uk

Senior Management: Mr Steve Greenslade, Director - Transition, County Hall, Cwmbran NP44 2XH ☎ 01633 644266 ✉ stevegreenslade@monmouthshire.gov.uk

Architect, Building / Property Services: Mr Rob O'Dwyer, Head - Property Services, County Hall, Cwmbran NP44 2XH ☎ 01633 644452 ✉ roberto'dwyer@monmouthshire.gov.uk

Building Control: Mr Philip Thomas, Manager - Planning, County Hall, Cwmbran NP44 2XH ☎ 01633 644644 ✉ philipthomas@monmouthshire.gov.uk

Catering Services: Ms Jackie Tudor, Contracts Manager, County Hall, Cwmbran NP44 2XH ☎ 01633 644150 ✉ jackietudor@monmouthshire.gov.uk

Children / Youth Services: Ms Tracy Allison, Head of Children's Services, County Hall, Cwmbran NP44 2HX ☎ 01633 644571 🖷 01633 644577 ✉ tracyallison@monmouthshire.gov.uk

Civil Registration: Ms Julie Hole, Chief Registrar, Coed Glas, Rockfield Road, Abergavenny NP7 5LE ☎ ; 01873 735468 ✉ juliehole@monmouthshire.gov.uk

Consumer Protection and Trading Standards: Mr David Jones, Head - Regeneration & Culture, County Hall, Cwmbran NP44 2XH ☎ 01633 644101 🖷 01633 644105 ✉ davidjones@monmouthshire.gov.uk

Contracts: Mr Roger Hoggins, Head - Infrastructure & Sustainability, County Hall, Cwmbran NP44 2XH ☎ 01633 644134 🖷 01633 644144 ✉ rogerhoggins@monmouthshire.gov.uk

Corporate Services: Ms Moyna Wilkinson, Deputy Chief Executive, County Hall, Cwmbran NP44 2XH ☎ 01633 644644 ✉ moynawilkinson@monmouthshire.gov.uk

Customer Service: Ms Moyna Wilkinson, Deputy Chief Executive, County Hall, Cwmbran NP44 2XH ☎ 01633 644644 ✉ moynawilkinson@monmouthshire.gov.uk

Direct Labour: Mr Roger Hoggins, Head - Infrastructure & Sustainability, County Hall, Cwmbran NP44 2XH ☎ 01633 644134 🖷 01633 644144 ✉ rogerhoggins@monmouthshire.gov.uk

Education: Mr Andrew Keep, Chief Officer - Children & Young People, County Hall, Cwmbran NP44 2XH ☎ 01633 644644 🖷 01633 644488 ✉ andrewkeep@monmouthshire.gov.uk

Education: Mr Jon Murphy, Head - School Improvement, County Hall, Cwmbran NP44 2XH ☎ 01633 644644 ✉ jonmurphy@monmouthshire.gov.uk

Electoral Registration: Mr John Pearson, Local Democracy Manager, County Hall, Cwmbran NP44 2XH ☎ 01633 644247 🖷 01633 644216 ✉ johnpearson@monmouthshire.gov.uk

Emergency Planning: Ms Julia Detheridge, Emergency Planning Officer, County Hall, Cwmbran NP44 2XH ☎ 01633 644091 🖷 01633 644090 ✉ juliadetheridge@monmouthshire.gov.uk

Emergency Planning: Mr Ian Hardman, Manager - Emergency Planning, County Hall, Cwmbran NP44 2XH ☎ 01633 644644 ✉ ianhardman@monmouthshire.gov.uk

Emergency Planning: Ms Julie Pinnell, Emergency Planning Officer, County Hall, Cwmbran NP44 2XH ☎ 01633 644644 ✉ juliepinnell@monmouthshire.gov.uk

Energy Management: Mr Roger Hoggins, Head - Infrastructure & Sustainability, County Hall, Cwmbran NP44 2XH ☎ 01633 644134 🖷 01633 644144 ✉ rogerhoggins@monmouthshire.gov.uk

Environmental Health: Mr David Jones, Head - Regeneration & Culture, County Hall, Cwmbran NP44 2XH ☎ 01633 644101 🖷 01633 644105 ✉ davidjones@monmouthshire.gov.uk

Estates, Property & Valuation: Ms Debra Hill-Howells, Head - Asset Management, County Hall, Cwmbran NP44 2XH ☎ 01633 644281 🖷 01633 644666 ✉ debrahill-howells@monmouthshire.gov.uk

Facilities: Mr Morley Sims, Facilities Manager, County Hall, Cwmbran NP44 2XH ☎ 01873 73590 ✉ morleysims@monmouthshire.gov.uk

Finance and Treasurer: Mrs Joy Robson, Head - Finance & Section 151 Officer, County Hall, Cwmbran NP44 2XH ☎ 01633 644644 🖷 01633 644270 ✉ joyrobson@monmouthshire.gov.uk

Fleet Management: Mr Lyndon Knight, Head - Transport, County Hall, Cwmbran NP44 2XH ☎ 01291 691312 ✉ lyndonknight@monmouthshire.gov.uk

Grounds Maintenance: Mr Roger Hoggins, Head - Infrastructure & Sustainability, County Hall, Cwmbran NP44 2XH ☎ 01633 644134 🖷 01633 644144 ✉ rogerhoggins@monmouthshire.gov.uk

Health and Safety: Mr Laurence Dawkins, Safety Manager, County Hall, Cwmbran NP44 2XH ☎ 01633 644196 🖷 01633 644666 ✉ laurencedawkins@monmouthshire.gov.uk

Highways: Mr Glyn Edmunds, Head - Highways & Waste, County Hall, Cwmbran NP44 2XH ☎ 01633 644644 ✉ glynedmunds@monmouthshire.gov.uk

Home Energy Conservation: Mr John Parfitt, Housing Renewals & Careline Manager, County Hall, Cwmbran NP44 2XH ☎ 01633 644681 ✉ johnparfitt@monmouthshire.gov.uk

Housing: Mr Ian Blakewell, Head - Housing, County Hall, Cwmbran NP44 2XH ☎ 01633 644479 🖷 01633 644577 ✉ ian.blakewell@monmouthshire.gov.uk

Housing Maintenance: Mr Ian Blakewell, Head - Housing, County Hall, Cwmbran NP44 2XH ☎ 01633 644479 🖷 01633 644577 ✉ ian.blakewell@monmouthshire.gov.uk

Legal: Mr Murray Andrews, Monitoring Officer, County Hall, Cwmbran NP44 2XH ☎ 01633 644058 🖷 01633 644061 ✉ murrayandrews@monmouthshire.gov.uk

Leisure and Cultural Services: Mr David Jones, Head - Regeneration & Culture, County Hall, Cwmbran NP44 2XH ☎ 01633 644101 🖷 01633 644105 ✉ davidjones@monmouthshire.gov.uk

Licensing: Ms Linda O'Gorman, Principal Licensing Officer, County Hall, Cwmbran NP44 2XH ☎ 01633 644214 ✉ lindaogorman@monmouthshire.gov.uk

Lifelong Learning: Mr Andrew Keep, Chief Officer - Children & Young People, County Hall, Cwmbran NP44 2XH ☎ 01633 644644 🖷 01633 644488 ✉ andrewkeep@monmouthshire.gov.uk

Lottery Funding, Charity and Voluntary: Mrs Denise Wilson, Licensing Administrating Officer, County Hall, Cwmbran NP44 2XH ☎ 01633 644644

Member Services: Mr Peter Evans, Manager - Democratic Services, County Hall, Cwmbran NP44 2XH ☎ 01633 644229 🖷 01633 644216 ✉ peterevans@monmouthshire.gov.uk

Parking: Mr Glyn Edmunds, Head - Highways & Waste, County Hall, Cwmbran NP44 2XH ☎ 01633 644644 ✉ glynedmunds@monmouthshire.gov.uk

Partnerships: Mr David Jones, Head - Regeneration & Culture, County Hall, Cwmbran NP44 2XH ☎ 01633 644101 🖷 01633 644105 ✉ davidjones@monmouthshire.gov.uk

Personnel / HR: Ms Sian Hayward, Manager - Strategic Personnel, County Hall, Cwmbran NP44 2XH ☎ 01633 644644 ✉ sianhayward@monmouthshire.gov.uk

Planning: Mr George Ashworth, Head of Planning, County Hall, Cwmbran NP44 2XH ☎ 01633 644803 🖷 01633 644800 ✉ georgeashworth@monmouthshire.gov.uk

Procurement: Mr Scott James, Strategic Procurement Manager, County Hall, Cwmbran NP44 2XH ☎ 01633 644068 ✉ scottjames@monmouthshire.gov.uk

Recycling & Waste Minimisation: Mr Glyn Edmunds, Head - Highways & Waste, County Hall, Cwmbran NP44 2XH ☎ 01633 644644 ✉ glynedmunds@monmouthshire.gov.uk

Regeneration: Ms Kellie Beirne, Director - Regeneration & Culture, County Hall, Cwmbran NP44 2XH ☎ 01633 644468 ✉ kelliebeirne@monmouthshire.gov.uk

Road Safety: Mr Simon Burch, Chief Officer - Health & Social Care, County Hall, Cwmbran NP44 2XH ☎ 01633 644601 🖷 01633 644577 ✉ simonburch@monmouthshire.gov.uk

Social Services: Mr Simon Burch, Chief Officer - Health & Social Care, County Hall, Cwmbran NP44 2XH ☎ 01633 644601 🖷 01633 644577 ✉ simonburch@monmouthshire.gov.uk

Social Services (Adult): Ms Julie Boothroyd, Head - Adult Services, County Hall, Cwmbran NP44 2XH ☎ 01633 644601 🖷 01633 644577 ✉ julieboothroyd@monmouthshire.gov.uk

Social Services (Children): Ms Tracy Allison, Head of Children's Services, County Hall, Cwmbran NP44 2HX ☎ 01633 644571 🖷 01633 644577 ✉ tracyallison@monmouthshire.gov.uk

Staff Training: Mr John McConnachie, Staff Development Officer, County Hall, Cwmbran NP44 2XH ☎ 01873 735453 ✉ johnmcconnachie@monmouthshire.gov.uk

Sustainable Development: Ms Hazel Clatworthy, Sustainable Development Co-ordinator, County Hall, Cwmbran NP44 2XH ☎ 01633 644843 🖷 01633 644200 ✉ hazelclatworthy@monmouthshire.gov.uk

Tourism: Ms Nicola Smith, Tourism Officer, County Hall, Cwmbran NP44 2XH ☎ 01633 644847 🖷 01633 644800 ✉ nicolasmith@monmouthshire.gov.uk

Traffic Management: Mr Paul Keeble, Traffic & Network Manager, County Hall, Cwmbran NP44 2XH ☎ 01633 644644 ✉ paulkeeble@monmouthshire.gov.uk

Transport: Mr Richard Cope, Passenger Transport Unit Manager, County Hall, Cwmbran NP44 2XH ☎ 01633 644745 ✉ richardcope@monmouthshire.gov.uk

Transport Planner: Mr Glyn Edmunds, Head - Highways & Waste, County Hall, Cwmbran NP44 2XH ☎ 01633 644644 ✉ glynedmunds@monmouthshire.gov.uk

Waste Collection and Disposal: Mr Glyn Edmunds, Head - Highways & Waste, County Hall, Cwmbran NP44 2XH ☎ 01633 644644 ✉ glynedmunds@monmouthshire.gov.uk

Waste Collection and Disposal: Mr Roger Hoggins, Head - Infrastructure & Sustainability, County Hall, Cwmbran NP44 2XH ☎ 01633 644134 🖷 01633 644144 ✉ rogerhoggins@monmouthshire.gov.uk

Waste Management: Mr Glyn Edmunds, Head - Highways &

Waste, County Hall, Cwmbran NP44 2XH ☏ 01633 644644
glynedmunds@monmouthshire.gov.uk

MEMBERS OF THE COUNCIL (43)

***Chair:* Powell**, Maureen (CON - Castle)
maureenpowell@monmouthshire.gov.uk
***Vice-Chair:* Dovey**, David (CON - St. Kingsmark)
daviddovey@monmouthshire.gov.uk
***Leader of the Council:* Fox**, Peter (CON - Portskewett)
peterfox@monmouthshire.gov.uk
***Deputy Leader of the Council:* Greenland**, Robert (CON - Devauden)
robertgreenland@monmouthshire.gov.uk
***Deputy Leader of the Council:* Murphy**, Philip (CON - Caerwent)
philmurphy@monmouthshire.gov.uk
Batrouni, Dimitri (LAB - St. Christopher's)
dimitribatrouni@monmouthshire.gov.uk
Blakebrough, Debby (IND - Trellech United)
debbyblakebrough@monmouthshire.gov.uk
Burrows, Geoffrey (CON - Mitchel Troy)
geoffburrows@monmouthsire.gov.uk
Chapman, Ralph (IND - Mardy)
ralphchapman@monmouthshire.gov.uk
Clarke, Peter (CON - Llangybi Fawr)
peterclarke@monmouthshire.gov.uk
Crook, Jessica (LAB - The Elms)
jessicacrook@monmouthshire.gov.uk
Down, Graham (IND - Shirenewton)
grahamdown@monmouthshire.gov.uk
Easson, Anthony (LAB - Dewstow)
anthonyeasson@monmouthshire.gov.uk
Edwards, Douglas (LD - Grofield)
douglasedwards@monmouthshire.gov.uk
Edwards, Ruth (CON - Llantilio Crossenny)
ruthedwards@monmouthshire.gov.uk
Evans, David (LAB - West End)
davidevans2@monmouthshire.gov.uk
Farley, Peter (LAB - Chepstow, St Mary's)
peterfarley@monmouhshire.gov.uk
George, James (LD - Lansdown)
jamesgeorge@monmouthshire.gov.uk
Guppy, Linda (LD - Rogiet)
lindaguppy@monmouthshire.gov.uk
Hacket Pain, Elizabeth (CON - Wyesham)
lizhacketpain@monmouthshire.gov.uk
Harris, Roger (LAB - Croesonen)
rogerharris@monmouthshire.gov.uk
Hayward, Robert (CON - Dixton with Osbaston)
bobhayward@monmouthshire.gov.uk
Hickman, Martin (CON - Llanfoist Fawr)
martinhickman@monmouthshire.gov.uk
Higginson, Jim (LAB - Severn)
ronhigginson@monmouthshire.gov.uk
Hobson, Phil (LD - Chepstow, Larkfield)
philhobson@monmouthshire.gov.uk
Howard, Giles (CON - Llanelly Hill)
gileshoward@monmouthsire.gov.uk
Howarth, Simon (IND - Llanelly Hill)
simonhowarth@monmouthshire.gov.uk
Jones, Sara (CON - Llanover)
sarajones2@monmouthshire.gov.uk
Jones, Bryan (CON - Goytre Fawr)
bryanjones@monmouthshire.gov.uk
Jones, Penny (CON - Raglan)
pennyjones@monmouthshire.gov.uk
Jones, David (IND - Crucorney)
davidhughesjones@monmouthshire.gov.uk
Jordan, Paul (CON - Cantref)
pauljordan@monmouthshire.gov.uk
Marshall, John (IND - Green Lane)
johnmarshall@monmouthshire.gov.uk
Prosser, John (CON - Priory - Abergavenny)
johnprosser@monmouthshire.gov.uk
Smith, Val (CON - Llanbadoc)
valsmith@monmouthshire.gov.uk
Strong, Brian (CON - Usk)
brianstrong@monmouthshire.gov.uk
Taylor, Frances (IND - Mill)
francestaylor@monmouthdhire.gov.uk
Watts, Pauline (LAB - Caldicot Castle)
wattspauline@monmouthshire.gov.uk
Watts, Armand (LAB - Thornwell)
armandwatts@monmouthshire.gov.uk
Webb, Ann (CON - St. Arvans)
annwebb@monmouthshire.gov.uk
White, Susan (CON - Overmonnow)
susanwhite@monmouthshire.gov.uk
Williams, Kevin (LAB - Llanwenarth Ultra)
kevinwilliams@monmouthshire.gov.uk
Wintle, Alan (CON - Drybirdge)
alanwintle@monmouthshire.gov.uk

POLITICAL COMPOSITION

CON: 22, LAB: 10, IND: 7, LD: 4

CABINET

Leader / Corporate Services & Organisational Development: Mr Peter Fox
Deputy Leader / Modernisation, Enterprise & Communications: Mr Robert Greenland
Children, Young People & Learning: Ms Elizabeth Hacket Pain
County Operations: Mr Bryan Jones
Culture & Environment: Mr Giles Howard
Finance & Performance Improvement: Mr Philip Murphy
Social Care, Health & Housing: Mr Geoffrey Burrows

COMMITTEE CHAIRS

Audit: Mr Paul Jordan
Economy & Development: Mr Anthony Easson
Planning: Ms Ruth Edwards
Strong Communities Select: Ms Ann Webb

MORAY S

Moray Council, Council Offices, High Street, Elgin IV30 1BX
☏ 01343 543451 🖷 01343 540399 💻 www.moray.gov.uk

FACTS & FIGURES

Police Authority: Grampian Joint Police Board
Health Authority: NHS Grampian
Learning and Skills Council: Scotland
Parliamentary Constituencies: Moray
EU Constituencies: Scotland
Election Frequency: Elections are of whole council
Twinning: Elgin-Landshut, Lossiemouth-Hersburck, Forres-Vienenburg, Royal Burgh of Forres-Mount Dora (Flora),

Fochabers-Magnac-sur-Touvre

PRINCIPAL OFFICERS

Chief Executive: Mr Roddy Burns, Acting Chief Executive, Council Offices, High Street, Elgin IV30 1BX ☎ 01343 563011 🖷 01343 540183 🖱 roddy.burns@moray.gov.uk

Senior Management: Mr Jim Grant, Head of Development Services, Council Offices, High Street, Elgin IV30 1BX ☎ 01343 563262 🖷 01343 563260 🖱 jim.grant@moray.gov.uk

Senior Management: Mrs Rhona Gunn, Head of Legal & Democratic Services, Council Offices, High Street, Elgin IV30 1BX ☎ 01343 563152 🖷 01343 540183 🖱 rhona.gunn@moray.gov.uk

Senior Management: Mr Mark Palmer, Corporate Director (Corporate Services), Council Offices, High Street, Elgin IV30 1BX ☎ 01343 563103 🖷 01343 563221 🖱 palmerm@finance.moray.gov.uk

Senior Management: Mr Sandy Riddell, Corporate Director (Education & Social Care), Council Offices, High Street, Elgin IV30 1BX ☎ 01343 563530 🖷 01343 563134 🖱 sandy.riddell@moray.gov.uk

Access Officer / Social Services (Disability): Mr Kevan Sturgeon, Building Standards Manager, Council Offices, High Street, Elgin IV30 1BX ☎ 01343 563269 🖷 01343 563263 🖱 kevan.sturgeon@moray.gov.uk

Architect, Building / Property Services: Mr Ron Phillips, Property Manager (Contracts), Property Services, Commerce House Annexe, South Street, Elgin IV30 1JE ☎ 01343 557102 🖱 ron.phillips@moray.gov.uk

Best Value: Mrs Bridget Mustard, Corporate Policy Unit Manager, Council Offices, High Street, Elgin IV30 1BX ☎ 01343 563048 🖷 01343 540399 🖱 mustarb@moray.gov.uk

Building Control: Mr Kevan Sturgeon, Building Standards Manager, Council Offices, High Street, Elgin IV30 1BX ☎ 01343 563269 🖷 01343 563263 🖱 kevan.sturgeon@moray.gov.uk

Catering Services: Ms Pearl Gray, Catering Officer, Council Offices, High Street, Elgin IV30 1BX ☎ 01343 557086 🖱 pearl.gray@moray.gov.uk

Children / Youth Services: Mr John Carney, Head of Children, Families & Criminal Justice Services, Council Offices, High Street, Elgin IV30 1BX ☎ 01343 563534 🖱 john.carney@moray.gov.uk

Civil Registration: Ms Jill Addison, Registrar, Buckie Office, 13 Cluny Square, Elgin AB56 1AJ ☎ 01542 832691 🖱 jill.addison@moray.gov.uk

PR / Communications: Mr Peter Jones, PR & Communications Officer, Council Offices, High Street, Elgin IV30 1BX ☎ 01343 563601 🖷 01343 563311 🖱 peter.jones@moray.gov.uk

Community Planning: Mrs Bridget Mustard, Corporate Policy Unit Manager, Council Offices, High Street, Elgin IV30 1BX ☎ 01343 563048 🖱 bridget.mustard@moray.gov.uk

Community Safety: Mrs Jane Mackie, Head of Community Care, The Moray Council, Spynie Hospital, Elgin IV30 5PW ☎ 01343 567127 🖱 jane.mackie@moray.gov.uk

Community Safety: Mr Adrian Moar, Local Authority Liaison Officer, Council Offices, High Street, Elgin IV30 1BX ☎ 01343 563407 🖱 adrian.moar@moray.gov.uk

Computer Management: Mrs Denise Whitworth, Head of Human Resources and ICT, Council Offices, High Street, Elgin IV30 1BX ☎ 01343 563060 🖱 denise.whitworth@moray.gov.uk

Consumer Protection and Trading Standards: Mr David Owen, Trading Standards Manager, 232 High Street, Elgin IV30 1DJ ☎ 01343 554617 🖱 david.owen@moray.gov.uk

Contracts: Mr Ian Bruce, Environmental Protection Manager, Ashgrove Depot, Ashgrove Road, Elgin IV30 1UU ☎ 01343 557040 🖱 brucei@moray.gov.uk

Direct Labour: Mr Michael Rollo, General Manager - Building Services, The DLO Depot, Mosstodloch, IV30 1TY ☎ 01343 823043 🖱 mike.rollo@moray.gov.uk

Economic Development: Mr Richard Hartland, Corporate Director (Environmental Services), Council Offices, High Street, Elgin IV30 1BX ☎ 01343 563097 🖱 richard.hartland@moray.gov.uk

Education: Mr Richard Donald, Head of Additional Support Services, Council Offices, High Street, Elgin IV30 1BX ☎ 01343 563182 🖱 richard.donald@moray.gov.uk

Education: Mr Alistair Farquar, Head of Educational Resources, Council Offices, High Street, Elgin IV30 1BX ☎ 01343 563339 🖱 alistair.farquhar@moray.gov.uk

Education: Mr Sandy Riddell, Corporate Director (Education & Social Care), Council Offices, High Street, Elgin IV30 1BX ☎ 01343 563530 🖷 01343 563134 🖱 sandy.riddell@moray.gov.uk

Education: Mr George Sinclair, Head of Educational Development Services, Council Offices, High Street, Elgin IV30 1BX ☎ 01343 563519 🖱 george.sinclair@moray.gov.uk

Electoral Registration: Mr Roddy Burns, Acting Chief Executive, Council Offices, High Street, Elgin IV30 1BX ☎ 01343 563011 🖷 01343 540183 🖱 roddy.burns@moray.gov.uk

Energy Management: Mr Moray MacLeod, Design Manager, Commerce House, South Street, Elgin IV30 1JE ☎ 01343 557123 🖱 moray.macleod@moray.gov.uk

Environmental / Technical Services: Mr Jim Grant, Head of Development Services, Council Offices, High Street, Elgin IV30 1BX ☎ 01343 563262 🖷 01343 563260 🖱 jim.grant@moray.gov.uk

Environmental Health: Mr Donnie Mackay, Environmental Health Manager, Council Offices, High Street, Elgin IV30 1BX ☎ 01343 563358 🖷 01343 563483

donnie.mackay@moray.gov.uk

Estates, Property & Valuation: Mr Moray MacLeod, Design Manager, Commerce House, South Street, Elgin IV30 1JE ☎ 01343 557123 moray.macleod@moray.gov.uk

Finance and Treasurer: Mr Mark Palmer, Corporate Director (Corporate Services), Council Offices, High Street, Elgin IV30 1BX ☎ 01343 563103 🖷 01343 563221 palmerm@finance.moray.gov.uk

Finance and Treasurer: Ms Margaret Wilson, Head of Financial Services, Council Offices, High Street, Elgin IV30 1BX ☎ 01343 563102 margaret.wilson@moray.gov.uk

Fleet Management: Mr Leslie Thomson, Fleet Services Manager, Ashgrove Depot, Ashgrove Road, Elgin IV30 1UU ☎ 01343 557306 leslie.thomson@moray.gov.uk

Health and Safety: Mr Doug Reid, Senior Health & Safety Adviser, Council Offices, High Street, Elgin IV30 1BX ☎ 01343 563073 doug.reid@moray.gov.uk

Housing: Mrs Jill Stewart, Head of Housing & Property, Council Offices, High Street, Elgin IV30 1BX ☎ 01343 563532 jill.stewart@moray.gov.uk

Housing Maintenance: Mrs Jill Stewart, Head of Housing & Property, Council Offices, High Street, Elgin IV30 1BX ☎ 01343 563532 jill.stewart@moray.gov.uk

Legal: Mrs Rhona Gunn, Head of Legal & Democratic Services, Council Offices, High Street, Elgin IV30 1BX ☎ 01343 563152 🖷 01343 540183 rhona.gunn@moray.gov.uk

Leisure and Cultural Services: Mr Nick Goodchild, Educational Resources Manager, Council Offices, High Street, Elgin IV30 1BX ☎ 01343 563401 goodchn@moray.gov.uk

Licensing: Mrs Rhona Gunn, Head of Legal & Democratic Services, Council Offices, High Street, Elgin IV30 1BX ☎ 01343 563152 🖷 01343 540183 rhona.gunn@moray.gov.uk

Lifelong Learning: Mr Alistair Campbell, Libraries & Museums Manager, Council Offices, High Street, Elgin IV30 1BX ☎ 01343 563398 campbea@moray.gov.uk

Lighting: Mr John Phillips, Area Engineer Lighting, Roads Service, Ashgrove Depot, Elgin IV30 1UU ☎ 01343 557343 🖷 01343 545628 john.phillips@moray.gov.uk

Member Services: Mr Roddy Burns, Acting Chief Executive, Council Offices, High Street, Elgin IV30 1BX ☎ 01343 563011 🖷 01343 540183 roddy.burns@moray.gov.uk

Partnerships: Mr Peter Jones, PR & Communications Officer, Council Offices, High Street, Elgin IV30 1BX ☎ 01343 563601 🖷 01343 563311 peter.jones@moray.gov.uk

Partnerships: Mrs Bridget Mustard, Corporate Policy Unit Manager, Council Offices, High Street, Elgin IV30 1BX ☎ 01343 563048 🖷 01343 540399 mustarb@moray.gov.uk

Personnel / HR: Ms Denise Whitworth, Head of Human Resources & ICT, Council Offices, High Street, Elgin IV30 1BX ☎ 01343 563060 denise.whitworth@moray.gov.uk

Planning: Mr Jim Grant, Head of Development Services, Council Offices, High Street, Elgin IV30 1BX ☎ 01343 563262 🖷 01343 563260 jim.grant@moray.gov.uk

Planning: Mr Jim Grant, Head of Development Services, Council Offices, High Street, Elgin IV30 1BX ☎ 01343 563262 🖷 01343 563260 jim.grant@moray.gov.uk

Procurement: Mrs Diane Law, Payments Manager, Council Offices, High Street, Elgin IV30 1BX ☎ 01343 563136 lawd@moray.gov.uk

Public Libraries: Mr Alistair Campbell, Libraries & Museums Manager, Council Offices, High Street, Elgin IV30 1BX ☎ 01343 563398 campbea@moray.gov.uk

Recycling & Waste Minimisation: Mr Ian Bruce, Environmental Protection Manager, Ashgrove Depot, Ashgrove Road, Elgin IV30 1UU ☎ 01343 557040 brucei@moray.gov.uk

Road Safety: Mr Gordon Holland, Transportation Manager, Council Offices, Academy Street, Elgin IV30 1LL ☎ 01343 562514 gordon.holland@moray.gov.uk

Social Services: Mr John Carney, Head of Children, Families & Criminal Justice Services, Council Offices, High Street, Elgin IV30 1BX ☎ 01343 563534 john.carney@moray.gov.uk

Social Services (Adult): Mrs Jane Mackie, Head of Community Care, The Moray Council, Spynie Hospital, Elgin IV30 5PW ☎ 01343 567127 jane.mackie@moray.gov.uk

Social Services (Children): Mr John Carney, Head of Children, Families & Criminal Justice Services, Council Offices, High Street, Elgin IV30 1BX ☎ 01343 563534 john.carney@moray.gov.uk

Staff Training: Ms Carol Sheridan, Senior Employee Development Adviser, Council Offices, 149 High Street, Elgin IV30 1BX ☎ 01343 563070 carol.sheridan@moray.gov.uk

Sustainable Development: Mr Richard Hartland, Corporate Director (Environmental Services), Council Offices, High Street, Elgin IV30 1BX ☎ 01343 563097 richard.hartland@moray.gov.uk

Tourism: Mr Pierre Masson, Business Projects Officer, Council Offices, High Street, Elgin IV30 1BX ☎ 01343 563485 pierre.masson@moray.gov.uk

Traffic Management: Mr Gordon Holland, Transportation Manager, Council Offices, Academy Street, Elgin IV30 1LL ☎ 01343 562514 gordon.holland@moray.gov.uk

Transport: Mr Peter Findlay, Public Transport Manager, Council Offices, Academy Street, Elgin IV30 1LL ☎ 01343 562541 peter.findlay@moray.gov.uk

Transport: Mr Gordon Holland, Transportation Manager, Council Offices, Academy Street, Elgin IV30 1LL ☎ 01343 562514 ✉ gordon.holland@moray.gov.uk

Waste Collection and Disposal: Mr Ian Bruce, Environmental Protection Manager, Ashgrove Depot, Ashgrove Road, Elgin IV30 1UU ☎ 01343 557040 ✉ brucei@moray.gov.uk

Waste Management: Mr Ian Bruce, Environmental Protection Manager, Ashgrove Depot, Ashgrove Road, Elgin IV30 1UU ☎ 01343 557040 ✉ brucei@moray.gov.uk

MEMBERS OF THE COUNCIL (26)

***Convener:* Ross**, Douglas (IND - Keith and Cullen)
stewart.cree@moray.gov.uk
***Leader of the Council:* Wright**, Allan (CON - Heldon and Laich)
allan.wright@moray.gov.uk
Alexander, George (IND - Forres)
george.alexander@moray.gov.uk
Allan, James (CON - Elgin City South)
james.allan@moray.gov.uk
Coull, Gary (SNP - Keith and Cullen)
gary.coull@moray.gov.uk
Creswell, Lorna (IND - Forres)
lorna.creswell@moray.gov.uk
Divers, John (SNP - Elgin City South)
john.divers@moray.gov.uk
Gowans, Patsy (SNP - Elgin City North)
patsy.gowans@moray.gov.uk
Howe, Margo (SNP - Fochabers Lhanbryde)
margo.howe@moray.gov.uk
Jarvis, Barry (LAB - Elgin City North)
barry.a.jarvis@moray.gov.uk
Leadbitter, Graham (SNP - Elgin City South)
graham.leadbitter@moray.gov.uk
Mackay, Joseph (IND - Buckie)
joe.mackay@moray.gov.uk
McConachie, Michael (SNP - Speyside Glenlivet)
michael.mcconachie@moray.gov.uk
McDonald, Gordon (SNP - Buckie)
gordon.mcdonald@moray.gov.uk
McGillivray, Eric (IND - Heldon and Laich)
eric.mcgillivray@moray.gov.uk
McKay, Anne (IND - Buckie)
anne.mckay@moray.gov.uk
McLean, Aaron (SNP - Forres)
aaron.mclean@moray.gov.uk
Morton, Sean (LAB - Fochabers Lhanbryde)
sean.morton@moray.gov.uk
Murdoch, Fiona (IND - Speyside Glenlivet)
fiona.murdoch@moray.gov.uk
Paul, Pearl (SNP - Speyside Glenlivet)
pearl.paul@moray.gov.uk
Ralph, Carolle (SNP - Heldon and Laich)
carolle.ralph@moray.gov.uk
Ross, Douglas (CON - Fochabers Lhanbryde)
douglas.ross@moray.gov.uk
Shand, Michael (SNP - Elgin City North)
mike.shand@moray.gov.uk
Shepherd, Ronald (IND - Keith and Cullen)
ronald.shepherd@moray.gov.uk
Skene, Anne (IND - Forres)
anne.skene@moray.gov.uk
Tuke, Chris (IND - Heldon and Laich)
chris.tuke@moray.gov.uk

POLITICAL COMPOSITION

SNP: 11, IND: 10, CON: 3, LAB: 2

CABINET

Leader of Administration Group: Mr Allan Wright
Convener: Mr Douglas Ross

COMMITTEE CHAIRS

Appeals: Mr Douglas Ross
Children & Young People: Ms Anne Skene
Communities: Mr Eric McGillivray
Economic Development & Infrastructure: Ms Fiona Murdoch
Health & Social Care: Ms Anne Mckay
Licensing: Mr Ronald Shepherd
Planning & Regulatory Services: Mr Douglas Ross
Policy & Resources: Mr Allan Wright
Scrutiny (Audit & Performance Review): Mr Gordon McDonald

MOYLE N

Moyle District Council, Sheskburn House, 7 Mary Street, Ballycastle BT54 6QH ☎ 028 2076 2225 🖷 028 2076 2515 ✉ info@moyle-council.org 🖳 www.moyle-council.org

FACTS & FIGURES

Police Authority: Northern Ireland Policing Board
Health Authority: Health & Social Care Board
Learning and Skills Council: Northern Ireland
Parliamentary Constituencies: Antrim North
EU Constituencies: Northern Ireland
Election Frequency: Elections are of whole council

PRINCIPAL OFFICERS

Chief Executive: Mr Richard Lewis, Clerk & Chief Executive, Sheskburn House, 7 Mary Street, Ballycastle BT54 6QH ☎ 028 2076 2225 🖷 028 2076 2515 ✉ rlewis@moyle-council.org

Assistant Chief Executive: Mrs Moira Quinn, Assistant Chief Executive / Head of Corporate Services, Sheskburn House, 7 Mary Street, Ballycastle BT54 6QH ☎ 028 2076 2225 🖷 028 2076 2515 ✉ mquinn@moyle-council.org

Senior Management: Mr Peter Mawdsley, Head of Environmental Health & Enforcement, Sheskburn House, 7 Mary Street, Ballycastle BT54 6QH ☎ 028 2076 2225 🖷 028 2076 2515 ✉ pmawdsley@moyle-council.org

Best Value: Mrs Esther Mulholland, Head of Development, Sheskburn House, 7 Mary Street, Ballycastle BT54 6QH ☎ 028 2076 2225 🖷 028 2076 2515 ✉ emulholland@moyle-council.org

Building Control: Mr David Kelly, Head of Building Control, Sheskburn House, 7 Mary Street, Ballycastle BT54 6QH ☎ 028 2076 2225 🖷 028 2076 2515

PR / Communications: Mrs Esther Mulholland, Head of Development, Sheskburn House, 7 Mary Street, Ballycastle BT54 6QH ☎ 028 2076 2225 🖷 028 2076 2515 ✉ emulholland@moyle-council.org

Community Safety: Ms Bridgeen Butler, Policing Community Safety Partnership Manager, Sheskburn House, 7 Mary Street , Ballycastle BT54 6QH ☎ 028 2076 2225 🖷 028 2076 2515 ✉ bbutler@moyle-council.org

Consumer Protection and Trading Standards: Mr Peter Mawdsley, Head of Environmental Health & Enforcement, Sheskburn House, 7 Mary Street, Ballycastle BT54 6QH ☎ 028 2076 2225 🖷 028 2076 2515 ✉ pmawdsley@moyle-council.org

Contracts: Mr Aidan McPeake, Head of Technical Services, Sheskburn House, 7 Mary Street, Ballycastle BT54 6QH ☎ 028 2076 2225 🖷 028 2076 2515 ✉ amcpeake@moyle-council.org

Contracts: Mrs Moira Quinn, Assistant Chief Executive / Head of Corporate Services, Sheskburn House, 7 Mary Street, Ballycastle BT54 6QH ☎ 028 2076 2225 🖷 028 2076 2515 ✉ mquinn@moyle-council.org

Corporate Services: Mrs Moira Quinn, Assistant Chief Executive / Head of Corporate Services, Sheskburn House, 7 Mary Street, Ballycastle BT54 6QH ☎ 028 2076 2225 🖷 028 2076 2515 ✉ mquinn@moyle-council.org

Direct Labour: Mr Aidan McPeake, Head of Technical Services, Sheskburn House, 7 Mary Street, Ballycastle BT54 6QH ☎ 028 2076 2225 🖷 028 2076 2515 ✉ amcpeake@moyle-council.org

Economic Development: Ms Margaret Craig, Economic Development Officer, Sheskburn House, 7 Mary Street, Ballycastle BT54 6QH ☎ 028 2076 2225 🖷 028 2076 2515 ✉ mcraig@moyle-council.org

E-Government: Mrs Moira Quinn, Assistant Chief Executive / Head of Corporate Services, Sheskburn House, 7 Mary Street, Ballycastle BT54 6QH ☎ 028 2076 2225 🖷 028 2076 2515 ✉ mquinn@moyle-council.org

Emergency Planning: Mr Peter Mawdsley, Head of Environmental Health & Enforcement, Sheskburn House, 7 Mary Street, Ballycastle BT54 6QH ☎ 028 2076 2225 🖷 028 2076 2515 ✉ pmawdsley@moyle-council.org

Environmental / Technical Services: Mr Aidan McPeake, Head of Technical Services, Sheskburn House, 7 Mary Street, Ballycastle BT54 6QH ☎ 028 2076 2225 🖷 028 2076 2515 ✉ amcpeake@moyle-council.org

Environmental Health: Mr Peter Mawdsley, Head of Environmental Health & Enforcement, Sheskburn House, 7 Mary Street, Ballycastle BT54 6QH ☎ 028 2076 2225 🖷 028 2076 2515 ✉ pmawdsley@moyle-council.org

Estates, Property & Valuation: Mrs Moira Quinn, Assistant Chief Executive / Head of Corporate Services, Sheskburn House, 7 Mary Street, Ballycastle BT54 6QH ☎ 028 2076 2225 🖷 028 2076 2515 ✉ mquinn@moyle-council.org

Finance and Treasurer: Mrs Moira Quinn, Assistant Chief Executive / Head of Corporate Services, Sheskburn House, 7 Mary Street, Ballycastle BT54 6QH ☎ 028 2076 2225 🖷 028 2076 2515 ✉ mquinn@moyle-council.org

Fleet Management: Mr Aidan McPeake, Head of Technical Services, Sheskburn House, 7 Mary Street, Ballycastle BT54 6QH ☎ 028 2076 2225 🖷 028 2076 2515 ✉ amcpeake@moyle-council.org

Grounds Maintenance: Mr Aidan McPeake, Head of Technical Services, Sheskburn House, 7 Mary Street, Ballycastle BT54 6QH ☎ 028 2076 2225 🖷 028 2076 2515 ✉ amcpeake@moyle-council.org

Health and Safety: Mrs Deborah O'Neill, Lead Officer Health & Safety, Sheskburn House, 7 Mary Street, Ballycastle BT54 6QH ☎ 028 2076 2225 🖷 028 2076 2515 ✉ doneill@moyle-council.org

Lottery Funding, Charity and Voluntary: Ms Una Hamill, Development Assistant, Sheskburn House, 7 Mary Street, Ballycastle BT54 6QH ☎ 028 2076 2225 🖷 028 2076 2515

Personnel / HR: Mrs Brid Lofthouse, Human Resources Manager, Sheskburn House, 7 Mary Street, Ballycastle BT54 6QH ☎ 028 2076 2225 🖷 028 2076 2515 ✉ blofthouse@moyle-council.org

Procurement: Mrs K McCaw, Administration Officer, Sheskburn House, 7 Mary Street, Ballycastle BT54 6QH ☎ 028 2076 2225 🖷 028 2076 2515 ✉ kmccaw@moyle-council.org

Recycling & Waste Minimisation: Mr Aidan McPeake, Head of Technical Services, Sheskburn House, 7 Mary Street, Ballycastle BT54 6QH ☎ 028 2076 2225 🖷 028 2076 2515 ✉ amcpeake@moyle-council.org

Staff Training: Mrs K McCaw, Administration Officer, Sheskburn House, 7 Mary Street, Ballycastle BT54 6QH ☎ 028 2076 2225 🖷 028 2076 2515 ✉ kmccaw@moyle-council.org

Sustainable Development: Mrs Esther Mulholland, Head of Development, Sheskburn House, 7 Mary Street, Ballycastle BT54 6QH ☎ 028 2076 2225 🖷 028 2076 2515 ✉ emulholland@moyle-council.org

Tourism: Mr Kevin McGarry, Head of Tourism & Leisure Services, Sheskburn House, 7 Mary Street, Ballycastle BT54 6QH ☎ 028 2076 2225 🖷 028 2076 2515 ✉ kmcgarry@moyle-council.org

Transport: Mr Aidan McPeake, Head of Technical Services, Sheskburn House, 7 Mary Street, Ballycastle BT54 6QH ☎ 028 2076 2225 🖷 028 2076 2515 ✉ amcpeake@moyle-council.org

Transport Planner: Mr Aidan McPeake, Head of Technical Services, Sheskburn House, 7 Mary Street, Ballycastle BT54 6QH ☎ 028 2076 2225 🖷 028 2076 2515 ✉ amcpeake@moyle-council.org

Waste Collection and Disposal: Mr Aidan McPeake, Head of Technical Services, Sheskburn House, 7 Mary Street, Ballycastle BT54 6QH ☎ 028 2076 2225 🖷 028 2076 2515 ✉ amcpeake@moyle-council.org

Waste Management: Mr Aidan McPeake, Head of Technical Services, Sheskburn House, 7 Mary Street, Ballycastle BT54 6QH

☎ 028 2076 2225 🖷 028 2076 2515
✉ amcpeake@moyle-council.org

MEMBERS OF THE COUNCIL (15)

Baird, Joan (UUP - Ballycastle)
cllr.jbaird@moyle-council.org
Blaney, Seamus (IND - Ballycastle)

Cunningham, Donnal (SDLP - Ballycastle)
cllr.dcunningham@moyle-council.org
Graham, Willie (UUP - Giant's Causeway)
cllr.wgraham@moyle-council.org
Hunter, Sandra (UUP - Giant's Causeway)
cllr.shunter@moyle-council.org
McAllister, David (DUP - Giant's Causeway)
cllr.dmcallister@moyle-council.org
McAllister, Noreen (SF - The Glens)
cllr.nmcallister@moyle-council.org
McCambridge, Catherine (SDLP - The Glens)
cllr.cmccambridge@moyle-council.org
McDonnell, Randal (IND - The Glens)
McIlroy, Robert (DUP - Giant's Causeway)
cllr.rmcilroy@moyle-council.org
McKillip, Margaret (SF - The Glens)
cllr.mamckillop@moyle-council.org
McKillop, Sharon (O - Giant's Causeway)
cllr.smckillop@moyle-council.org
McShane, Padraig (SF - Ballycastle)
mcshaneshar@aol.com
McShane, Cara (SF - Ballycastle)
cllr.cmcshane@moyle-council.org
Thompson, Colum (IND - The Glens)
cllr.mamckillop@moyle-council.org

POLITICAL COMPOSITION

SF: 4, IND: 3, UUP: 3, DUP: 2, SDLP: 2, O: 1

NEATH PORT TALBOT W

Neath Port Talbot County Borough Council, (Cyngor Bwrdeistref Sirol Castell-nedd Port Talbot), Civic Centre, Port Talbot SA13 1PJ ☎ 01639 763333 🖷 01639 763444 🖳 www.npt.gov.uk

FACTS & FIGURES

Police Authority: South Wales Police Authority
Learning and Skills Council: Wales
Parliamentary Constituencies: Aberavon, Neath
EU Constituencies: Wales
Election Frequency: Elections are of whole council
Twinning: Albacete (Spain); Bagneux (France); Esslingen (Germany); Hellbronn (Germany); Schiedam (Netherlands); Velenje (Slovenia); Vienne (France); Piotrkow Trybunalski (Poland) Udine (Italy)

PRINCIPAL OFFICERS

Chief Executive: Mr Steven Phillips, Chief Executive, Civic Centre, Port Talbot SA13 1PJ

Architect, Building / Property Services: Mr Gareth Nutt, Head of Property & Regeneration, The Quays, Brunel Way, Baglan Energy Park, Neath SA11 2GG ☎ 01639 686370 🖷 01639 686103 ✉ g.nutt@npt.gov.uk

Building Control: Mr Geoff White, Head of Planning, The Quays, Brunel Way, Baglan Energy Park, Neath SA11 2GG ☎ 01639 686681 🖷 01639 686101 ✉ g.white@npt.gov.uk

Catering Services: Mr Andrew Thomas, Head of Support Services & Commissioning Development, Civic Centre, Port Talbot SA13 1PJ ☎ 01639 763791 🖷 01639 763150 ✉ a.d.thomas@npt.gov.uk

Children / Youth Services: Mr Russell Ward, Head of Partnerships & Community Development, Civic Centre, Port Talbot SA13 1PJ ☎ 01639 763475; 01639 763333 🖷 01639 763150 ✉ r.ward@npt.gov.uk

Civil Registration: Mr David Michael, Head of Legal & Democratic Services & Monitoring Officer, Civic Centre, Port Talbot SA13 1PJ ☎ 01639 763368 🖷 01639 763165 ✉ d.michael@npt.gov.uk

PR / Communications: Mr Owen Jenkins, Corporate Communications & Marketing Manager, Civic Centre, Port Talbot SA13 1PJ ☎ 01639 763207 🖷 01639 763751 ✉ o.jenkins1@npt.gov.uk

Community Planning: Mr Philip Graham, Head of Corporate Strategy, Civic Centre, Port Talbot SA13 1PJ ☎ 01639 763171 🖷 01639 899930 ✉ p.graham@npt.gov.uk

Community Safety: Mr Philip Graham, Head of Corporate Strategy, Chief Executive's Directorate, Civic Centre, Port Talbot SA13 1PJ ☎ 01639 763171 🖷 01639 899930 ✉ p.graham@npt.gov.uk

Computer Management: Mr Stephen John, Head of ICT, The Quays, Brunel Way, Baglan Energy Park, Neath SA11 2GG ☎ 01639 686218 🖷 01639 686123 ✉ s.john@npt.gov.uk

Consumer Protection and Trading Standards: Ms Angela Thomas, Head of Business Strategy & Public Protection, Civic Centre, Port Talbot SA13 1PJ ☎ 01639 763794 🖷 01639 763269 ✉ a.j.thomas@npt.gov.uk

Contracts: Mr Hywel Jenkins, Head of Financial Services, Aberavon House, Port Talbot SA13 1PJ ☎ 01639 763646 🖷 01639 763645 ✉ h.jenkins@npt.gov.uk

Corporate Services: Mr Derek Davies, Corporate Director of Finance & Corporate Services, Civic Centre, Port Talbot SA13 1PJ ☎ 01639 763252 🖷 01639 763469 ✉ d.w.davies@npt.gov.uk

Corporate Services: Mr Philip Graham, Head of Corporate Strategy, Civic Centre, Port Talbot SA13 1PJ ☎ 01639 763171 🖷 01639 899930 ✉ p.graham@npt.gov.uk

Customer Service: Mr Philip Graham, Head of Corporate Strategy, Civic Centre, Port Talbot SA13 1PJ ☎ 01639 763171 🖷 01639 899930 ✉ p.graham@npt.gov.uk

Economic Development: Mr Gareth Nutt, Head of Property & Regeneration, The Quays, Brunel Way, Baglan Energy Park, Neath SA11 2GG ☎ 01639 686370 🖷 01639 686103 ✉ g.nutt@npt.gov.uk

Education: Mr Karl Napieralla, Corporate Director of Education, Leisure & Lifelong Learning, Civic Centre, Port Talbot SA13 1PJ ☎ 01639 763298 🖷 01639 763000 k.napieralla@npt.gov.uk

E-Government: Mr Derek Davies, Corporate Director of Finance & Corporate Services, Civic Centre, Port Talbot SA13 1PJ ☎ 01639 763252 🖷 01639 763469 d.w.davies@npt.gov.uk

Electoral Registration: Mr Rhys George, Electoral Registration Officer, Civic Centre, Port Talbot SA13 1PJ ☎ 01639 763719; 01639 763323 🖷 01639 899930 r.j.george@npt.gov.uk

Emergency Planning: Mr Graham Jones, Head of Human Resources, Civic Centre, Port Talbot SA13 1PJ ☎ 01639 763315; 01639 763177 🖷 01639 763377 g.jones@npt.gov.uk

Energy Management: Mr John Flower, Corporate Director of Environment, Civic Centre, Port Talbot SA13 1PJ ☎ 01639 686668 🖷 01639 686667 w.watson@npt.gov.uk

Environmental / Technical Services: Mr John Flower, Corporate Director of Environment, Civic Centre, Port Talbot SA13 1PJ ☎ 01639 686668 🖷 01639 686667 w.watson@npt.gov.uk

Environmental Health: Ms Angela Thomas, Head of Business Strategy & Public Protection, Civic Centre, Port Talbot SA13 1PJ ☎ 01639 763794 🖷 01639 763269 a.j.thomas@npt.gov.uk

Estates, Property & Valuation: Mr Gareth Nutt, Head of Property & Regeneration, The Quays, Brunel Way, Baglan Energy Park, Neath SA11 2GG ☎ 01639 686370 🖷 01639 686103 g.nutt@npt.gov.uk

European Liaison: Mr Gareth Nutt, Head of Property & Regeneration, The Quays, Brunel Way, Baglan Energy Park, Neath SA11 2GG ☎ 01639 686370 🖷 01639 686103 g.nutt@npt.gov.uk

Events Manager: Mr Russell Ward, Head of Partnerships & Community Development, Civic Centre, Port Talbot SA13 1PJ ☎ 01639 763475; 01639 763333 🖷 01639 763150 r.ward@npt.gov.uk

Facilities: Mr Gareth Nutt, Head of Property & Regeneration, The Quays, Brunel Way, Baglan Energy Park, Neath SA11 2GG ☎ 01639 686370 🖷 01639 686103 g.nutt@npt.gov.uk

Finance and Treasurer: Mr Derek Davies, Corporate Director of Finance & Corporate Services, Civic Centre, Port Talbot SA13 1PJ ☎ 01639 763252 🖷 01639 763469 d.w.davies@npt.gov.uk

Fleet Management: Mr Mike Roberts, Head of Streetcare, The Quays, Brunel Way, Baglan Energy Park, Neath SA11 2GG ☎ 01639 686966 🖷 01639 686103 m.roberts@npt.gov.uk

Grounds Maintenance: Mr Mike Roberts, Head of Streetcare, The Quays, Brunel Way, Baglan Energy Park, Neath SA11 2GG ☎ 01639 686966 🖷 01639 686103 m.roberts@npt.gov.uk

Health and Safety: Mr Graham Jones, Head of Human Resources, Civic Centre, Port Talbot SA13 1PJ ☎ 01639 763315 🖷 01639 763377 g.jones@npt.gov.uk

Highways: Mr David Griffiths, Head of Engineering & Transport, The Quays, Brunel Way, Baglan Energy Park, Neath SA11 2GG ☎ 01639 686340 🖷 01639 686108 d.w.griffiths@npt.gov.uk

Housing: NPT Homes, Llys Penrhys, Off Curwen Close, Pontrhydyfen, Port Talbot SA12 9UT ☎ 0300 777 0000 ask@npthomes.co.uk

Legal: Mr David Michael, Head of Legal & Democratic Services & Monitoring Officer, Civic Centre, Port Talbot SA13 1PJ ☎ 01639 763368 🖷 01639 763165 d.michael@npt.gov.uk

Leisure and Cultural Services: Mr Russell Ward, Head of Partnerships & Community Development, Civic Centre, Port Talbot SA13 1PJ ☎ 01639 763475; 01639 763333 🖷 01639 763150 r.ward@npt.gov.uk

Licensing: Mr David Michael, Head of Legal & Democratic Services & Monitoring Officer, Civic Centre, Port Talbot SA13 1PJ ☎ 01639 763368 🖷 01639 763165 d.michael@npt.gov.uk

Lifelong Learning: Mr Russell Ward, Head of Partnerships & Community Development, Civic Centre, Port Talbot SA13 1PJ ☎ 01639 763475 🖷 01639 763150 r.ward@npt.gov.uk

Lighting: Mr Mike Roberts, Head of Streetcare, The Quays, Brunel Way, Baglan Energy Park, Neath SA11 2GG ☎ 01639 686966 🖷 01639 686103 m.roberts@npt.gov.uk

Lottery Funding, Charity and Voluntary: Mr Russell Ward, Head of Partnerships & Community Development, Civic Centre, Port Talbot SA13 1PJ ☎ 01639 763475; 01639 763333 🖷 01639 763150 r.ward@npt.gov.uk

Member Services: Mr David Michael, Head of Legal & Democratic Services & Monitoring Officer, Civic Centre, Port Talbot SA13 1PJ ☎ 01639 763368 🖷 01639 763165 d.michael@npt.gov.uk

Parking: Mr David Griffiths, Head of Engineering & Transport, The Quays, Brunel Way, Baglan Energy Park, Neath SA11 2GG ☎ 01639 686340 🖷 01639 686108 d.w.griffiths@npt.gov.uk

Partnerships: Mr Russell Ward, Head of Partnerships & Community Development, Civic Centre, Port Talbot SA13 1PJ ☎ 01639 763475 🖷 01639 763150 r.ward@npt.gov.uk

Personnel / HR: Mr Graham Jones, Head of Human Resources, Civic Centre, Port Talbot SA13 1PJ ☎ 01639 763315 🖷 01639 763377 g.jones@npt.gov.uk

Planning: Mr Geoff White, Head of Planning, The Quays, Brunel Way, Baglan Energy Park, Neath SA11 2GG ☎ 01639 686681 🖷 01639 686101 g.white@npt.gov.uk

Procurement: Mr Hywel Jenkins, Head of Financial Services, Aberavon House, Port Talbot SA13 1PJ ☎ 01639 763646 🖷 01639 763645 h.jenkins@npt.gov.uk

Public Libraries: Mr Russell Ward, Head of Partnerships & Community Development, Civic Centre, Port Talbot SA13 1PJ ☎ 01639 763475 🖷 01639 763150 r.ward@npt.gov.uk

Recycling & Waste Minimisation: Mr Mike Roberts, Head of Streetcare, The Quays, Brunel Way, Baglan Energy Park, Neath SA11 2GG ☎ 01639 686966 🖷 01639 686103 ✉ m.roberts@npt.gov.uk

Regeneration: Mr Gareth Nutt, Head of Property & Regeneration, The Quays, Brunel Way, Baglan Energy Park, Neath SA11 2GG ☎ 01639 686370 🖷 01639 686103 ✉ g.nutt@npt.gov.uk

Road Safety: Mr David Griffiths, Head of Engineering & Transport, The Quays, Brunel Way, Baglan Energy Park, Neath SA11 2GG ☎ 01639 686340 🖷 01639 686108 ✉ d.w.griffiths@npt.gov.uk

Social Services: Mr Tony Clements, Director of Social Services, Health & Housing, Port Talbot Civic Centre, Port Talbot SA13 1PJ ☎ 01639 763333 🖷 01639 763176 ✉ t.clements@npt.gov.uk

Social Services (Adult): Ms Claire Marchant, Head of Community Care & Housing Services, Civic Centre, Port Talbot SA13 1PJ ☎ 01639 763287 ✉ c.marchant@npt.gov.uk

Social Services (Children): Mrs Karen Jones, Interim Head of Children & Young People Services, Civic Centre, Port Talbot SA13 1PJ ☎ 01639 763283 ✉ k.jones3@npt.gov.uk

Staff Training: Mr Graham Jones, Head of Human Resources, Civic Centre, Port Talbot SA13 1PJ ☎ 01639 763315 🖷 01639 763377 ✉ g.jones@npt.gov.uk

Street Scene: Mr Mike Roberts, Head of Streetcare, The Quays, Brunel Way, Baglan Energy Park, Neath SA11 2GG ☎ 01639 686966 🖷 01639 686103 ✉ m.roberts@npt.gov.uk

Sustainable Communities: Ms Claire Marchant, Head of Community Care & Housing Services, Civic Centre, Port Talbot SA13 1PJ ☎ 01639 763287 ✉ c.marchant@npt.gov.uk

Sustainable Communities: Mr Geoff White, Head of Planning, The Quays, Brunel Way, Baglan Energy Park, Neath SA11 2GG ☎ 01639 686681 🖷 01639 686101 ✉ g.white@npt.gov.uk

Sustainable Development: Mr Geoff White, Head of Planning, The Quays, Brunel Way, Baglan Energy Park, Neath SA11 2GG ☎ 01639 686681 🖷 01639 686101 ✉ g.white@npt.gov.uk

Tourism: Mr Russell Ward, Head of Partnerships & Community Development, Civic Centre, Port Talbot SA13 1PJ ☎ 01639 763475; 01639 763333 🖷 01639 763150 ✉ r.ward@npt.gov.uk

Town Centre: Ms Gemma Nesbitt, Neath Town Centre Manager, The Quays, Brunel Way, Baglan Energy Park, Neath SA11 1PJ ☎ 01639 686413

Traffic Management: Mr David Griffiths, Head of Engineering & Transport, The Quays, Brunel Way, Baglan Energy Park, Neath SA11 2GG ☎ 01639 686340 🖷 01639 686108 ✉ d.w.griffiths@npt.gov.uk

Transport: Mr David Griffiths, Head of Engineering & Transport, The Quays, Brunel Way, Baglan Energy Park, Neath SA11 2GG ☎ 01639 686340 🖷 01639 686108 ✉ d.w.griffiths@npt.gov.uk

Waste Collection and Disposal: Mr Mike Roberts, Head of Streetcare, The Quays, Brunel Way, Baglan Energy Park, Neath SA11 2GG ☎ 01639 686966 🖷 01639 686103 ✉ m.roberts@npt.gov.uk

Waste Management: Mr Mike Roberts, Head of Streetcare, The Quays, Brunel Way, Baglan Energy Park, Neath SA11 2GG ☎ 01639 686966 🖷 01639 686103 ✉ m.roberts@npt.gov.uk

MEMBERS OF THE COUNCIL (64)

***Mayor:* Peters**, Martyn (PC - Dyffryn)
cllr.d.m.peters@npt.gov.uk

***Deputy Mayor:* Lewis**, Marian (LAB - Bryn and Cwmavon)
cllr.m.a.lewis@npt.gov.uk

***Leader of the Council:* Thomas**, Alun (LAB - Onllwyn)
leader@npt.gov.uk

***Deputy Leader of the Council:* Rees**, Peter (LAB - Neath South)
peter.rees@ntlworld.com

Bebell, Harry (LAB - Coedffranc West)
cllr.h.m.bebell@npt.gov.uk

Bebell, Paula (LAB - Coedffranc Central)
cllr.p.bebell@npt.gov.uk

Bryant, John (PC - Bryncoch North)
cllr.j.r.bryant@npt.gov.uk

Carter, Alan (LAB - Cimla)
cllr.a.carter@npt.gov.uk

Chaves, Audrey (LAB - Sandfields West)
cllr.a.chaves@npt.gov.uk

Clement, Carol (LAB - Baglan)
cllr.c.clement@npt.gov.uk

Crowley, Colin (LAB - Sandfields East)
cllr.c.crowley@npt.gov.uk

Davies, Rosalyn (PC - Godre'r Graig)
cllr.r.davies@npt.gov.uk

Davies, Arthur (LAB - Coedffranc Central)
cllr.a.p.h.davies@npt.gov.uk

Davies, Des (LAB - Resolven)
cllr.d.w.davies@npt.gov.uk

Dudley, Janice (PC - Bryncoch South)
cllr.j.dudley@npt.gov.uk

Ellis, Martin (IND - Pelenna)
cllr.m.ellis@npt.gov.uk

Evans, James (LAB - Sandfields West)
cllr.j.s.evans@npt.gov.uk

Golding, Ceri (LAB - Aberavon)
cllr.c.p.golding@npt.gov.uk

Greenaway, Paul (LAB - Baglan)
cllr.p.greenaway@npt.gov.uk

Gunter, Malcolm (LAB - Neath South)
cllr.m.b.gunter@npt.gov.uk

Harvey, Mike (LAB - Coedffranc North)
cllr.m.harvey@npt.gov.uk

Hunt, Steve (IND - Seven Sisters)
cllr.s.k.hunt@npt.gov.uk

James, Ian (LAB - Port Talbot)
cllr.i.b.james@npt.gov.uk

James, Rob (LAB - Bryncoch South)
cllr.r.james@npt.gov.uk

James, Hugh (LAB - Briton Ferry West)
cllr.h.n.james@npt.gov.uk

James, Lella (IND - Sandfields East)

cllr.l.h.james@npt.gov.uk
James, Mike (LAB - Pontardawe)
cllr.m.l.james@npt.gov.uk
Jones, Doreen (LAB - Aberdulais)
cllr.d.jones@npt.gov.uk
Jones, Eddie (LAB - Glynneath)
cllr.e.e.jones@npt.gov.uk
Jones, Mark (LAB - Aberavon)
cllr.m.jones@npt.gov.uk
Jones, Rob (LAB - Margam)
cllr.r.g.jones@npt.gov.uk
Jones, Scott (LAB - Cymmer)
cllr.s.jones@npt.gov.uk
Keogh, Dennis (LAB - Port Talbot)
cllr.d.keogh@npt.gov.uk
Latham, Ted (LAB - Sandfields East)
cllr.e.v.latham@npt.gov.uk
Lewis, David (LAB - Allt-Wen)
cllr.d.lewis@npt.gov.uk
Lewis, Rebecca (PC - Trebanos)
cllr.r.lewis@npt.gov.uk
Llewellyn, Alun (PC - Ystalyfera)
cllr.a.llewellyn@npt.gov.uk
Lockyer, Alan Richard (LAB - Neath North)
cllr.a.r.lockyer@npt.gov.uk
Miller, John (LAB - Neath East)
cllr.j.miller@npt.gov.uk
Miller, Sandra (LAB - Neath East)
cllr.s.miller@npt.gov.uk
Morgan, Del (PC - Glynneath)
cllr.j.d.morgan@npt.gov.uk
Morgan, Colin (LAB - Briton Ferry East)
cllr.c.morgan@npt.gov.uk
Morgans, Cari (LAB - Tonna)
cllr.c.morgans@npt.gov.uk
Paddison, Suzanne (LAB - Sandfields West)
cllr.s.paddison@npt.gov.uk
Pearson, Karen (LAB - Crynant)
cllr.k.pearson@npt.gov.uk
Penry, Sheila (LAB - Neath East)
cllr.s.m.penry@npt.gov.uk
Prothoe, Mark (LAB - Neath North)
cllr.m.protheroe@npt.gov.uk
Purcell, Linet (PC - Pontardawe)
cllr.l.purcell@npt.gov.uk
Rahaman, Saifur (LAB - Port Talbot)
cllr.s.rahaman@npt.gov.uk
Rawlings, Glyn (LAB - Glyncorrwg)
cllr.h.g.rawlings@npt.gov.uk
Richards, Eirion (LAB - Cwmllynfell)
cllr.c.e.richards@npt.gov.uk
Richards, Peter (LAB - Baglan)
cllr.p.d.richards@npt.gov.uk
Rogers, John (LAB - Tai-Bach)
cllr.j.rogers@npt.gov.uk
Siddley, Alf (LAB - Blaengwrach)
cllr.a.j.siddley@npt.gov.uk
Taylor, Anthony (SD - Aberavon)
cllr.a.taylor@npt.gov.uk
Taylor, Anthony J (LAB - Tai-Bach)
cllr.a.j.taylor@npt.gov.uk
Thomas, Alex (LAB - Rhos)
cllr.a.l.thomas@npt.gov.uk
Thomas, Ralph (LAB - Gwynfi)
cllr.r.thomas@npt.gov.uk
Warman, John (LD - Cimla)
cllr.j.warman@npt.gov.uk
Whitelock, Dave (LAB - Bryn and Cwmavon)
cllr.d.whitelock@npt.gov.uk
Williams, Lynda (LAB - Gwaun-Cae-Gurwen)
cllr.l.g.williams@npt.gov.uk
Williams, David (LAB - Bryn and Cwmavon)
cllr.i.d.williams@npt.gov.uk
Wingrave, Annette (LAB - Cadoxton)
cllr.a.wingrave@npt.gov.uk
Woolcock, Arwyn (LAB - Lower Brynamman)
cllr.a.n.woolcock@npt.gov.uk

POLITICAL COMPOSITION
LAB: 51, PC: 8, IND: 3, SD: 1, LD: 1

CABINET
Leader / Community & Strategic Leadership: Mr Alun Thomas
Deputy Leader / Finance, Transformation & Corporate Services: Mr Peter Rees
Children & Young People: Mr Peter Richards
Community & Leisure Services: Mr Mike James
Economic Development & Property Services: Mr Colin Morgan
Education & Lifelong Learning: Mr David Lewis
Environment: Mr Ted Latham
Social Care, Health & Housing: Mr John Rogers
Streetcare & Highway Services: Mrs Sandra Miller

COMMITTEE CHAIRS
Appeals: Mrs Lynda Williams
Audit: Mrs Lella James
Licensing & Gambling Acts: Mr Colin Crowley
Personnel: Mrs Andrea Davies
Planning & Development Control: Mr Arwyn Woolcock
Registration & Licensing: Mr Colin Crowley
Standards: Mr G Pullen (External)

NEW FOREST — D

New Forest District Council, Appletree Court, Beaulieu Road, Lyndhurst SO43 7PA ☎ 023 8028 5000 🖷 023 8028 5555
💻 www.newforest.gov.uk

FACTS & FIGURES
Police Authority: Hampshire Police Authority
Health Authority: South Central Strategic Health Authority
Learning and Skills Council: South East
Parliamentary Constituencies: New Forest East, New Forest West
EU Constituencies: South East
Election Frequency: Elections are of whole council

PRINCIPAL OFFICERS
Chief Executive: Mr Dave Yates, Chief Executive, Appletree Court, Beaulieu Road, Lyndhurst SO43 7PA ☎ 023 8028 5588 🖷 023 8028 5555 ✉ dave.yates@nfdc.gov.uk

Senior Management: Mr Robert Jackson, Executive Director, Appletree Court, Beaulieu Road, Lyndhurst SO43 7PA ☎ 023 8028 5588 🖷 023 8028 5555 ✉ bob.jackson@nfdc.gov.uk

Senior Management: Mr John Mascall, Executive Director,

Appletree Court, Beaulieu Road, Lyndhurst SO43 7PA
☎ 023 8028 5588 🖷 023 8028 5555 ✉ john.mascall@nfdc.gov.uk

Access Officer / Social Services (Disability): Mrs Catherine Granville, Equalities Officer, Appletree Court, Beaulieu Road, Lyndhurst SO43 7PA ☎ 023 8028 5588 🖷 023 8028 5555 ✉ catherine.granville@nfdc.gov.uk

Architect, Building / Property Services: Mr Geoff Bettle, Head of Property Services, Marsh Lane Depot, Marsh Lane, Lymington SO41 9BX ☎ 023 8028 5588 🖷 023 8028 5076 ✉ geoff.bettle@nfdc.gov.uk

Best Value: Mr Robert Jackson, Executive Director, Appletree Court, Beaulieu Road, Lyndhurst SO43 7PA ☎ 023 8028 5588 🖷 023 8028 5555 ✉ bob.jackson@nfdc.gov.uk

Building Control: Mr John Brian, Building Control Manager, Appletree Court, Beaulieu Road, Lyndhurst SO43 7PA ☎ 023 8028 5588 🖷 023 8028 5370 ✉ john.brian@nfdc.gov.uk

PR / Communications: Ms Davina Staples, Corporate Communication Officer, Appletree Court, Beaulieu Road, Lyndhurst SO43 7PA ☎ 023 8028 5588 🖷 023 8028 5555 ✉ davina.staples@nfdc.gov.uk

Community Safety: Ms Stephanie Bennett, Community Safety Officer, Appletree Court, Beaulieu Road, Lyndhurst SO43 7PA ☎ 023 8028 5588 🖷 023 8028 5370 ✉ stephanie.bennett@nfdc.gov.uk

Computer Management: Mr Ken Connolly, Head of ICT Services, Appletree Court, Beaulieu Road, Lyndhurst SO43 7PA ☎ 023 8028 5588 🖷 023 8028 5555 ✉ ken.connolly@nfdc.gov.uk

Customer Service: Mr Glynne Miles, Head of Customer Services, Town Hall, Avenue Road, Lymington SO41 9ZG ☎ 023 8028 5588 🖷 023 8028 5555 ✉ glynne.miles@nfdc.gov.uk

Direct Labour: Mr Colin Read, Head of Environment Services, Marsh Lane Depot, Marsh Lane, Lymington SO41 9BX ☎ 023 8028 5588 🖷 023 8028 5052 ✉ colin.read@nfdc.gov.uk

Economic Development: Mr Martin Devine, Head of Communities & Employment, Appletree Court, Beaulieu Road, Lyndhurst SO43 7PA ☎ 023 8028 5588 🖷 023 8028 5555 ✉ martin.devine@nfdc.gov.uk

E-Government: Mr Ken Connolly, Head of ICT Services, Appletree Court, Beaulieu Road, Lyndhurst SO43 7PA ☎ 023 8028 5588 🖷 023 8028 5555 ✉ ken.connolly@nfdc.gov.uk

Electoral Registration: Mrs Rosemary Rutins, Democratic Services Manager, Appletree Court, Beaulieu Road, Lyndhurst SO43 7PA ☎ 023 8028 5588 🖷 023 8028 5555 ✉ rosemary.rutins@nfdc.gov.uk

Emergency Planning: Mrs Annie Righton, Head of Public Health & Community Safety, Appletree Court, Beaulieu Road, Lyndhurst SO43 7PA ☎ 023 8028 5588 🖷 023 8028 5370 ✉ annie.righton@nfdc.gov.uk

Energy Management: Ms Emma Waterman, Energy & Environment Officer, Appletree Court, Beaulieu Road, Lyndhurst SO43 7PA ☎ 023 8028 5588 🖷 023 8028 5370 ✉ emma.waterman@nfdc.gov.uk

Environmental / Technical Services: Mr Colin Read, Head of Environment Services, Marsh Lane Depot, Marsh Lane, Lymington SO41 9BX ☎ 023 8028 5588 🖷 023 8028 5052 ✉ colin.read@nfdc.gov.uk

Environmental Health: Mrs Annie Righton, Head of Public Health & Community Safety, Appletree Court, Beaulieu Road, Lyndhurst SO43 7PA ☎ 023 8028 5588 🖷 023 8028 5370 ✉ annie.righton@nfdc.gov.uk

Estates, Property & Valuation: Mr Andy Groom, Valuer, Appletree Court, Beaulieu Road, Lyndhurst SO43 7PA ☎ 023 8028 5588 🖷 023 8028 5370 ✉ andy.groom@nfdc.gov.uk

Facilities: Mr Peter Hughes, Property Manager, Appletree Court, Beaulieu Road, Lyndhurst SO43 7PA ☎ 023 8028 5588 🖷 023 8028 5370 ✉ peter.hughes@nfdc.gov.uk

Finance and Treasurer: Mr Robert Jackson, Executive Director, Appletree Court, Beaulieu Road, Lyndhurst SO43 7PA ☎ 023 8028 5588 🖷 023 8028 5555 ✉ bob.jackson@nfdc.gov.uk

Fleet Management: Mr Colin Read, Head of Environment Services, Marsh Lane Depot, Marsh Lane, Lymington SO41 9BX ☎ 023 8028 5588 🖷 023 8028 5052 ✉ colin.read@nfdc.gov.uk

Grounds Maintenance: Mr Colin Read, Head of Environment Services, Marsh Lane Depot, Marsh Lane, Lymington SO41 9BX ☎ 023 8028 5588 🖷 023 8028 5052 ✉ colin.read@nfdc.gov.uk

Health and Safety: Miss Helen Woodvine, Corporate Health & Safety Risk Manager, Appletree Court, Beaulieu Road, Lyndhurst SO43 7PA ☎ 023 8028 5588 🖷 023 8028 5555 ✉ helen.woodvine@nfdc.gov.uk

Highways: Mr Nick Hunt, Principal Engineer - Transportation, Appletree Court, Beaulieu Road, Lyndhurst SO43 7PA ☎ 023 8028 5588 🖷 023 8028 5370 ✉ nick.hunt@nfdc.gov.uk

Home Energy Conservation: Ms Emma Waterman, Energy & Environment Officer, Appletree Court, Beaulieu Road, Lyndhurst SO43 7PA ☎ 023 8028 5588 🖷 023 8028 5370 ✉ emma.waterman@nfdc.gov.uk

Housing: Mr Dave Brown, Head of Housing, Appletree Court, Beaulieu Road, Lyndhurst SO43 7PA ☎ 023 8028 5588 🖷 023 8028 5386 ✉ dave.brown@nfdc.gov.uk

Housing Maintenance: Mr Dave Brown, Head of Housing, Appletree Court, Beaulieu Road, Lyndhurst SO43 7PA ☎ 023 8028 5588 🖷 023 8028 5386 ✉ dave.brown@nfdc.gov.uk

Legal: Ms Grainne O'Rourke, Head of Legal & Democratic Services, Appletree Court, Beaulieu Road, Lyndhurst SO43 7PA ☎ 023 8028 5588 🖷 023 8028 5555 ✉ grainne.o'rourke@nfdc.gov.uk

Leisure and Cultural Services: Mr Martin Devine, Head of Communities & Employment, Appletree Court, Beaulieu Road, Lyndhurst SO43 7PA ☎ 023 8028 5588 🖷 023 8028 5555 ✉ martin.devine@nfdc.gov.uk

Leisure and Cultural Services: Mr Bob Millard, Head of Leisure Services, Appletree Court, Beaulieu Road, Lyndhurst SO43 7PA ☎ 023 8028 5588 🖷 023 8028 5555 ✉ bob.millard@nfdc.gov.uk

Licensing: Mr Paul Weston, Licensing Manager, Appletree Court, Beaulieu Road, Lyndhurst SO43 7PA ☎ 023 8028 5588 🖷 023 8028 5370 ✉ paul.weston@nfdc.gov.uk

Lighting: Mr Allan Ellis, Assistant Engineer, Appletree Court, Beaulieu Road, Lyndhurst SO43 7PA ☎ 023 8028 5588 🖷 023 8028 5370 ✉ allan.ellis@nfdc.gov.uk

Lottery Funding, Charity and Voluntary: Mr Martin Devine, Head of Communities & Employment, Appletree Court, Beaulieu Road, Lyndhurst SO43 7PA ☎ 023 8028 5588 🖷 023 8028 5555 ✉ martin.devine@nfdc.gov.uk

Member Services: Ms Grainne O'Rourke, Head of Legal & Democratic Services, Appletree Court, Beaulieu Road, Lyndhurst SO43 7PA ☎ 023 8028 5588 🖷 023 8028 5555 ✉ grainne.o'rourke@nfdc.gov.uk

Parking: Mr John Bull, Parking Manager, Town Hall, Avenue Road, Lymington SO41 9ZG ☎ 023 8028 5588 🖷 023 8028 5755 ✉ john.bull@nfdc.gov.uk

Personnel / HR: Mrs Manjit Sandhu, Head of Human Resources, Appletree Court, Beaulieu Road, Lyndhurst SO43 7PA ☎ 023 8028 5482 🖷 023 8028 5405 ✉ manjit.sandhu@nfdc.gov.uk

Planning: Mr Chris Elliott, Head of Planning & Transportation, Appletree Court, Beaulieu Road, Lyndhurst SO43 7PA ☎ 023 8028 5588 🖷 023 8028 5370 ✉ chris.elliott@nfdc.gov.uk

Procurement: Mr Ian Smoker, Procurement Manager, Marsh Lane Depot, Marsh Lane, Lymington SO41 9BX ☎ 023 8028 5588 🖷 023 8028 5076 ✉ ian.smoker@nfdc.gov.uk

Recycling & Waste Minimisation: Mr Colin Read, Head of Environment Services, Marsh Lane Depot, Marsh Lane, Lymington SO41 9BX ☎ 023 8028 5588 🖷 023 8028 5052 ✉ colin.read@nfdc.gov.uk

Road Safety: Mr Nick Hunt, Principal Engineer - Transportation, Appletree Court, Beaulieu Road, Lyndhurst SO43 7PA ☎ 023 8028 5588 🖷 023 8028 5370 ✉ nick.hunt@nfdc.gov.uk

Staff Training: Mrs Zoe Ormerod, Human Resources Advisor, Appletree Court, Beaulieu Road, Lyndhurst SO43 7PA ☎ 023 8028 5588 🖷 023 8028 5555 ✉ zoe.ormerod@nfdc.gov.uk

Street Scene: Mr Colin Read, Head of Environment Services, Marsh Lane Depot, Marsh Lane, Lymington SO41 9BX ☎ 023 8028 5588 🖷 023 8028 5052 ✉ colin.read@nfdc.gov.uk

Tourism: Mr Anthony Climpson, Employment & Tourism Manager, Appletree Court, Beaulieu Road, Lyndhurst SO43 7PA ☎ 023 8028 5588 🖷 023 8028 5555 ✉ anthony.climpson@nfdc.gov.uk

Traffic Management: Mr Nick Hunt, Principal Engineer - Transportation, Appletree Court, Beaulieu Road, Lyndhurst SO43 7PA ☎ 023 8028 5588 🖷 023 8028 5370 ✉ nick.hunt@nfdc.gov.uk

Transport: Mr Nick Hunt, Principal Engineer - Transportation, Appletree Court, Beaulieu Road, Lyndhurst SO43 7PA ☎ 023 8028 5588 🖷 023 8028 5370 ✉ nick.hunt@nfdc.gov.uk

Transport Planner: Mr Nick Hunt, Principal Engineer - Transportation, Appletree Court, Beaulieu Road, Lyndhurst SO43 7PA ☎ 023 8028 5588 🖷 023 8028 5370 ✉ nick.hunt@nfdc.gov.uk

Waste Collection and Disposal: Mr Colin Read, Head of Environment Services, Marsh Lane Depot, Marsh Lane, Lymington SO41 9BX ☎ 023 8028 5588 🖷 023 8028 5052 ✉ colin.read@nfdc.gov.uk

Waste Management: Mr Colin Read, Head of Environment Services, Marsh Lane Depot, Marsh Lane, Lymington SO41 9BX ☎ 023 8028 5588 🖷 023 8028 5052 ✉ colin.read@nfdc.gov.uk

MEMBERS OF THE COUNCIL (60)

***Chair:* McEvoy**, Alexis (CON - Fawley, Blackfield and Langley)
alexis.mcevoy@newforest.gov.uk

***Vice-Chair:* Ford**, Christine (CON - Ringwood North)
christine.ford@newforest.gov.uk

***Leader of the Council:* Rickman**, Barry (CON - Boldre and Sway)
barry.rickman@newforest.gov.uk

***Deputy Leader of the Council:* Heron**, Edward (CON - Downlands and Forest)
edward.heron@newforest.gov.uk

Milford: Vacant

Alvey, Alan (CON - Holbury and North Blackfield)
alan.alvey@newforest.gov.uk

Andrews, Diane (CON - Bramshaw, Copythorne North and Minstead)
diane.andrews@newforest.gov.uk

Beck, Goff (CON - Barton)
goff.beck@newforest.gov.uk

Bellows, Roxy (CON - Fordingbridge)
roxanne.bellows@newforest.gov.uk

Bennison, Sue (CON - Marchwood)
sue.bennison@newforest.gov.uk

Binns, James (CON - Butts Ash and Dibden Purlieu)
james.binns@newforest.gov.uk

Britton, Dean (CON - Totton East)
dean.britton@newforest.gov.uk

Brooks, Di (CON - Totton West)
di.brooks@newforest.gov.uk

Clarke, Steve (CON - Milton)
steve.clarke@newforest.gov.uk

Cleary, Jill (CON - Fernhill)
jill.cleary@newforest.gov.uk

Dart, George (CON - Totton North)
george.dart@newforest.gov.uk

Davies, Steve (CON - Milton)
stevep.davies@newforest.gov.uk

Dow, Bill (CON - Forest North West)

bill.dow@newforest.gov.uk
Glass, Allan (CON - Holbury and North Blackfield)
allan.glass@newforest.gov.uk
Harris, Michael (CON - Furzedown and Hardley)
michael.harris@newforest.gov.uk
Harrison, David (LD - Totton South)
david.harrison@newforest.gov.uk
Harrison, Chris (LD - Dibden and Hythe East)
chris.harrison@newforest.gov.uk
Heron, Jeremy (CON - Ringwood South)
jeremy.heron@newforest.gov.uk
Hickman, Ann (CON - Bransgore and Burley)
ann.hickman@newforest.gov.uk
Hoare, Alison (CON - Marchwood)
alison.hoare@newforest.gov.uk
Holding, Maureen (CON - Brockenhurst and Forest South East)
maureen.holding@newforest.gov.uk
Jackman, Penny (CON - Pennington)
penny.jackman@newforest.gov.uk
Kendal, Mel (CON - Milford)
melville.kendal@newforest.gov.uk
Kilgour, Alexander (CON - Pennington)
alexander.kilgour@newforest.gov.uk
Lagdon, Chris (CON - Totton East)
chris.lagdon@newforest.gov.uk
Lewis, Elizabeth (CON - Lymington Town)
elizabeth.lewis@newforest.gov.uk
Lovelace, Penny (CON - Hordle)
penny.lovelace@newforest.gov.uk
Lucas, Brian (CON - Totton Central)
brian.lucas@newforest.gov.uk
McLean, Maureen (LD - Hythe West and Langdown)
maureen.mclean@newforest.gov.uk
O'Sullivan, Alan (CON - Barton)
alan.osullivan@newforest.gov.uk
Penman, Neville (CON - Totton North)
neville.penman@newforest.gov.uk
Penwarden, John (CON - Bransgore and Burley)
john.penwarden@newforest.gov.uk
Puttock, Leslie (CON - Ashurst, Copythorne South and Netley Marsh)
leslie.puttock@newforest.gov.uk
Rice, Alan (CON - Bashley)
alan.rice@newforest.gov.uk
Rippon-Swaine, Steve (CON - Ringwood South)
steve.rippon-swain@newforest.gov.uk
Robinson, Maureen (LD - Hythe West and Langdown)
maureen.robinson@newforest.gov.uk
Rostand, Anna (CON - Lymington Town)
anna.rostand@newforest.gov.uk
Russell, David (CON - Totton West)
david.russell@newforest.gov.uk
Scrivens, Ronald (CON - Totton Central)
ron.scrivens@newforest.gov.uk
Sevier, Ann (CON - Fordingbridge)
ann.sevier@newforest.gov.uk
Southgate, Michael (CON - Totton South)
michael.southgate@newforest.gov.uk
Swain, Tony (CON - Buckland)
tony.swain@newforest.gov.uk
Thierry, Michael (CON - Ringwood North)
michael.thierry@newforest.gov.uk
Tinsley, Andrew (CON - Hordle)
andrew.tinsley@newforest.gov.uk
Tipp, Derek (CON - Ashurst, Copythorne South and Netley Marsh)
derek.tipp@newforest.gov.uk
Vickers, Paul (CON - Brockenhurst and Forest South East)
paul.vickers@newforest.gov.uk
Wade, Stan (LD - Dibden and Hythe East)
stan.wade@newforest.gov.uk
Wade, Malcolm (LD - Butts Ash and Dibden Purlieu)
malcolm.wade@newforest.gov.uk
Wappet, Bob (CON - Fawley, Blackfield and Langley)
bob.wappet@newforest.gov.uk
Ward, Christine (CON - Becton)
christine.ward@newforest.gov.uk
Ward, John (CON - Fernhill)
johngward@newforest.gov.uk
Wise, Colin (CON - Boldre and Sway)
colin.wise@newforest.gov.uk
Woodifield, Barbara (CON - Ringwood East and Sopley)
barbara.woodifield@newforest.gov.uk
Woods, Paul (CON - Becton)
paul.woods@newforest.gov.uk
Wyeth, Pat (CON - Lyndhurst)
pat.wyeth@newforest.gov.uk

POLITICAL COMPOSITION
CON: 53, LD: 6, Vacant: 1

CABINET
Leader: Mr Barry Rickman
Deputy Leader / Environment: Mr Edward Heron
Finance & Efficiency: Mr Colin Wise
Health & Leisure: Mrs Di Brooks
Housing & Communities: Mrs Jill Cleary
Planning & Transportation: Mr Paul Vickers

COMMITTEE CHAIRS
Appeals: Mr Bob Wappet
Audit: Mr Alan O'Sullivan
Community Overview & Scrutiny: Mrs Penny Jackman
Corporate Overview Panel (Scrutiny): Mr John Ward
Environment Review Panel (Scrutiny): Ms Christine Ford
General Purposes & Licensing: Mr Goff Beck
Planning Development Control: Mrs Alison Hoare

NEWARK & SHERWOOD D

Newark & Sherwood District Council, Kelham Hall, Newark NG23 5QX ☎ 01636 650000 🖷 01636 655229
corporate@nsdc.info 💻 www.newark-sherwooddc.gov.uk

FACTS & FIGURES
Police Authority: Nottinghamshire Police Authority
Health Authority: East Midlands Strategic Health Authority
Learning and Skills Council: East Midlands
Parliamentary Constituencies: Newark, Sherwood
EU Constituencies: East Midlands
Election Frequency: Elections are of whole council
Twinning: Collingham: Villeneuve-sur-Yonne (France); Farnsfield: Andouille (France); Newark: Emmendingen (Germany); Southwell: Sees (France); Ceskybrod (Czech Rep);

PRINCIPAL OFFICERS
Chief Executive: Mr Andrew Muter, Chief Executive, Kelham Hall, Newark NG23 5QX ☎ 01636 650000

✉ andrew.muter@nsdc.info

Deputy Chief Executive: Mrs Kirsty Cole, Deputy Chief Executive, Kelham Hall, Newark NG23 5QX ☎ 01636 650000 ✉ kirsty.cole@nsdc.info

Architect, Building / Property Services: Miss Leanne Baines, Business Manager - Asset Management, Kelham Hall, Newark NG23 5QX ☎ 01636 650000 ✉ leanne.baines@nsdc.info

Building Control: Mr David Jones, Building Control Manager, Kelham Hall, Newark NG23 5QX ☎ 01636 650000 ✉ david.jones@nsdc.info

PR / Communications: Mrs Sally Dunbar, Business Manager - Communications & Marketing, Kelham Hall, Newark NG23 5QX ☎ 01636 650000 ✉ sally.dunbar@nsdc.info

Community Safety: Ms Lisa Lancaster, Business Manager - Community Safety, Kelham Hall, Newark NG23 5QX ☎ 01636 650000 ✉ lisa.lancaster@nsdc.info

Computer Management: Mrs Sharon Parkinson, Business Manager - ICT, Kelham Hall, Newark NG23 5QX ☎ 01636 650000 ✉ sharon.parkinson@nsdc.info

Corporate Services: Mrs Kirsty Cole, Deputy Chief Executive, Kelham Hall, Newark NG23 5QX ☎ 01636 650000 ✉ kirsty.cole@nsdc.info

Customer Service: Ms Jill Simpson, Business Manager - Customer Services, Kelham Hall, Newark NG23 5QX ☎ 01636 650000 ✉ jill.simpson@nsdc.info

Electoral Registration: Mr Mark Jurejko, Elections Manager, Kelham Hall, Newark NG23 5QX ☎ 01636 650000 ✉ mark.jurejko@nsdc.info

Emergency Planning: Ms Lisa Lancaster, Business Manager - Community Safety, Kelham Hall, Newark NG23 5QX ☎ 01636 650000 ✉ lisa.lancaster@nsdc.info

Environmental / Technical Services: Mr Andy Statham, Director - Community, Kelham Hall, Newark NG23 5QX ☎ 01636 650000 ✉ andy.statham@nsdc.info

Environmental Health: Mr Alan Batty, Business Manager - Environmental Health, Kelham Hall, Newark NG23 5QX ☎ 01636 650000 ✉ alan.batty@nsdc.info

Estates, Property & Valuation: Miss Leanne Baines, Business Manager - Asset Management, Kelham Hall, Newark NG23 5QX ☎ 01636 650000 ✉ leanne.baines@nsdc.info

Finance and Treasurer: Mr David Dickinson, Director - Resources, Kelham Hall, Newark NG23 5QX ☎ 01636 650000 ✉ david.dickinson@nsdc.info

Fleet Management: Mr Andrew Kirk, Business Manager - Waste, Litter & Recycling, Kelham Hall, Newark NG23 5QX ☎ 01636 650000 ✉ andrew.kirk@nsdc.info

Grounds Maintenance: Mr Philip Beard, Business Manager - Parks & Amenities, Kelham Hall, Newark NG23 5QX ☎ 01636 650000 🖷 01636 655705 ✉ philip.beard@nsdc.info

Health and Safety: Ms Lisa Lancaster, Business Manager - Community Safety, Kelham Hall, Newark NG23 5QX ☎ 01636 650000 ✉ lisa.lancaster@nsdc.info

Housing: Mr Rob Main, Strategic Housing Manager, Kelham Hall, Newark NG23 5QX ☎ 01636 650000 ✉ rob.main@nsdc.info

Legal: Mrs Karen White, Director - Safety, Kelham Hall, Newark NG23 5QX ☎ 01636 650000 ✉ karen.white@nsdc.info

Leisure and Cultural Services: Mr Andy Carolan, Principal Manager - Leisure Centres, Kelham Hall, Newark NG23 5QX ☎ 01636 650000 ✉ andy.carolan@nsdc.info

Licensing: Mr Alan Batty, Business Manager - Environmental Health, Kelham Hall, Newark NG23 5QX ☎ 01636 650000 ✉ alan.batty@nsdc.info

Lifelong Learning: Mrs Tracey Mellors, Business Manager - Human Resources, Kelham Hall, Newark NG23 5QX ☎ 01636 650000 ✉ tracey.mellors@nsdc.info

Lottery Funding, Charity and Voluntary: Mr Andrew Hardy, Business Manager - Community, Arts & Sports, Kelham Hall, Newark NG23 5QX ☎ 01636 650000 ✉ andrew.hardy@nsdc.info

Member Services: Mr Nigel Hill, Bunsiness Manager - Democratic Services, Kelham Hall, Newark NG23 5QX ☎ 01636 650000 ✉ nigel.hill@nsdc.info

Personnel / HR: Mrs Tracey Mellors, Business Manager - Human Resources, Kelham Hall, Newark NG23 5QX ☎ 01636 650000 ✉ tracey.mellors@nsdc.info

Planning: Mr Colin Walker, Director - Growth, Kelham Hall, Newark NG23 5QX ☎ 01636 650000 ✉ colin.walker@nsdc.info

Procurement: Mr John King, Business Manager - Procurement, Kelham Hall, Newark NG23 5QX ☎ 01636 650000 ✉ john.king@nsdc.gov.uk

Recycling & Waste Minimisation: Mr Andrew Kirk, Business Manager - Waste, Litter & Recycling, Kelham Hall, Newark NG23 5QX ☎ 01636 650000 ✉ andrew.kirk@nsdc.info

Regeneration: Mr Mike Robinson, Economic Development Manager, Kelham Hall, Newark NG23 5QX ☎ 01636 650000 ✉ mike.robinson@nsdc.info

Staff Training: Mrs Tracey Mellors, Business Manager - Human Resources, Kelham Hall, Newark NG23 5QX ☎ 01636 650000 ✉ tracey.mellors@nsdc.info

Tourism: Mr John Briggs, Tourism Manager, Kelham Hall, Newark NG23 5QX ☎ 01636 650000 ✉ john.briggs@nsdc.info

Transport: Mr Andrew Kirk, Business Manager - Waste, Litter & Recycling, Kelham Hall, Newark NG23 5QX ☎ 01636 650000

andrew.kirk@nsdc.info

Waste Collection and Disposal: Mr Andrew Kirk, Business Manager - Waste, Litter & Recycling, Kelham Hall, Newark NG23 5QX ☎ 01636 650000 andrew.kirk@nsdc.info

Waste Management: Mr Andrew Kirk, Business Manager - Waste, Litter & Recycling, Kelham Hall, Newark NG23 5QX ☎ 01636 650000 andrew.kirk@nsdc.info

MEMBERS OF THE COUNCIL (46)

***Chair:* Tribe**, Marika (CON - Beacon)
***Leader of the Council:* Blaney**, Roger (CON - Trent)
roger.blaney@nsdc.info
***Deputy Leader of the Council:* Roberts**, Tony (CON - Magnus)
tony.roberts@newark-sherwooddc.gov.uk
Allsopp, Neil (CON - Balderton (North))
neilallsopp@ntlworld.com
Armstrong, Nora (CON - Farnsfield & Bilsthorpe)
nora.armstrong@nsdc.info
Bickley, Thomas (CON - Castle)
thomas.bickley@nsdc.info
Bradbury, John (LAB - Rainworth)
cllr.jb@j-brad.org.uk
Bradbury, Robert (CON - Farnsfield & Bilsthorpe)
Brooks, Betty (CON - Balderton (West))
Brooks, Celia (LAB - Edwinstowe)
brooks209@btinternet.com
Brooks, Gordon (CON - Balderton (West))
Brown, Irene (IND - Bridge)
Crawford, Stan (LAB - Ollerton)
Crowe, Rita (CON - Magnus)
Dawn, Gill (IND - Bridge)
Dobson, Maureen (CON - Winthorpe)
Duncan, Peter (CON - Beacon)
peter.duncan@nsdc.info
Gurney, Trish (LAB - Devon)
trish.gurney@newark-sherwooddc.gov.uk
Hamilton, Julian (LD - Southwell East)
enquiries@jobtelmanda.co.uk
Handley, Paul (CON - Southwell North)
Harris, Peter (LD - Southwell West)
peter.harris@nsdc.info
Jackson, Roger (CON - Lowdham)
rjac900@aol.com
Jones, Dennis (LAB - Devon)
dennis.jones1@ntlworld.com
Laughton, Robert (CON - Farnsfield & Bilsthorpe)
bruce.laughton@btinternet.com
Lloyd, David (CON - Beacon)
davidlloyd@newarkconservatives.com
Logue, Declan (IND - Farndon)
declanlogue@btinternet.com
Merry, Geoffrey (IND - Blidworth)
cllr.geoff.merry@nottscc.gov.uk
Michael, Sylvia (CON - Caunton)
Middleton, Arthur (LAB - Rainworth)
jjmid@hotmail.co.uk
Osborne, Jason (CON - Balderton (North))
jlosborne@live.co.uk
Payne, David (CON - Castle)
davidpayne@paynegamage.com
Peck, John (LAB - Edwinstowe)
johnmpeck4@aol.com
Rontree, Kevin (CON - Collingham and Meering)
kevr4@fsmail.net
Rose, Christine (LD - Sutton-on-Trent)
chrisivyfarm@googlemail.com
Saddington, Susan (CON - Muskham)
cllr.susan.saddington@nottscc.gov.uk
Shaw, Melvyn (CON - Collingham and Meering)
mel@melshaw.co.uk
Shilling, Linda (LAB - Boughton)
lindaandrayo1@aol.com
Soar, Sheila (LAB - Clipstone)
sheilasoar@yahoo.co.uk
Staples, David (LAB - Boughton)
david.staples@newark-sherwooddc.gov.uk
Thompson, David (LAB - Clipstone)
ncbdave@ntlworld.com
Tift, Linda (LAB - Rainworth)
tifty2@msn.com
Truswell, Abbie (LAB - Ollerton)
abbie.truswell@nsdc.info
Walker, Ivor (CON - Farndon)
ivor.walker@surfree.co.uk
Wells, Benjamin (LAB - Ollerton)
benjaminwells@hotmail.co.uk
Wendels, Tim (CON - Lowdham)
timwendels@lineone.net
Woodhead, Yvonne (LAB - Blidworth)

POLITICAL COMPOSITION

CON: 24, LAB: 15, IND: 4, LD: 3

CABINET

Leader / Strategy & Prosperity: Mr Roger Blaney
Deputy Leader / People & Communities: Mr Tony Roberts
Clean & Green: Ms Nora Armstrong
Finance & Property: Mr David Lloyd
Health & Homes: Mr Robert Laughton
Leisure & Culture: Mr Roger Jackson

COMMITTEE CHAIRS

Audit & Accounts: Ms Rita Crowe
General Purposes: Mr Ivor Walker
Licensing: Mr Ivor Walker
Planning: Mr David Payne
Policy (Scrutiny): Mr Stan Crawford
Services (Scrutiny): Mrs Yvonne Woodhead

NEWCASTLE UPON TYNE CITY M

Newcastle upon Tyne City Council, (Newcastle City Council), Civic Centre, Newcastle upon Tyne NE99 2BN ☎ 0191 232 8520 🖷 0191 211 4942 www.newcastle.gov.uk

FACTS & FIGURES

Police Authority: Northumbria Police Authority
Health Authority: North East Strategic Health Authority
Learning and Skills Council: North East
Parliamentary Constituencies: Newcastle Central, Newcastle East, Newcastle North
EU Constituencies: North East
Election Frequency: Elections are by thirds
Twinning: Atlanta (USA); Bergen (Norway); Gelsenkirchen (Germany); Groningen (Netherlands); Haifa (Israel); Nancy

(France); Newcastle (Australia); Taiyuan (China);

PRINCIPAL OFFICERS

Chief Executive: Mr Barry Rowland, Chief Executive, Room 258, Civic Centre, Newcastle upon Tyne NE99 2BN ☎ 0191 211 5000 🖷 0191 211 4908 ✉ barry.rowland@newcastle.gov.uk

Senior Management: Mr John Collings, Executive Director of Children's Services, Civic Centre, Newcastle upon Tyne NE99 2BN ☎ 0191 232 8520 extn 24997 ✉ john.collings@newcastle.gov.uk

Senior Management: Mr Steve Evans, Director of Corporate Services, Civic Centre, Newcastle upon Tyne NE99 2BN ☎ 0191 232 8520 ext. 25200 🖷 0191 211 5252 ✉ steve.evans@newcastle.gov.uk

Senior Management: Mr Andrew Lewis, Director of Policy, Strategy & Communications, Civic Centre, Newcastle upon Tyne NE99 2BN ☎ 0191 232 8520 extn 25681 ✉ andrew.lewis@newcastle.gov.uk

Senior Management: Mr David Slater, Executive Director of Environment & Regeneration, Civic Centre, Newcastle upon Tyne NE99 2BN ☎ 0191 277 8900 🖷 0191 2114935 ✉ david.slater@newcastle.gov.uk

Senior Management: Mr Ewen Weir, Executive Director of Adult & Culture Services, Civic Centre, Newcastle upon Tyne NE99 1RD ☎ 0191 211 6300 🖷 0191 211 4955 ✉ ewen.weir@newcastle.gov.uk

Senior Management: Mr Paul Woods, Director of Finance & Resources, Civic Centre, Newcastle upon Tyne NE99 1RD ☎ 0191 277 7527 🖷 0191 211 4901 ✉ paul.v.woods@newcastle.gov.uk

Access Officer / Social Services (Disability): Mr Neil Swinney, Access Officer, Civic Centre, Newcastle upon Tyne NE99 2BN ☎ 0191 211 6804 ✉ neil.swinney@newcastle.gov.uk

Architect, Building / Property Services: Mr Stuart Turnbull, Head of Architecture & Building Design Services, Civic Centre, Newcastle upon Tyne NE99 2BN ☎ 0191 278 3277 ✉ stuart.turnbull@newcastle.gov.uk

Building Control: Mr David Ewles, Head of Building Control, Civic Centre, Newcastle upon Tyne NE99 2BN ☎ 0191 211 6180 🖷 0191 211 4889 ✉ david.n.ewles@newcastle.gov.uk

Catering Services: Mr David Moffat, Hospitality Services Manager, Civic Centre, Newcastle upon Tyne NE99 2BN ☎ 0191 232 8520 extn 26969 ✉ david.moffat@newcastle.gov.uk

Children / Youth Services: Mr John Collings, Executive Director of Children's Services, Civic Centre, Newcastle upon Tyne NE99 2BN ☎ 0191 232 8520 extn 24997 ✉ john.collings@newcastle.gov.uk

Civil Registration: Mr Ron Grey, Superintendent Registrar, Civic Centre, Newcastle upon Tyne NE99 2BN ☎ 0191 232 8520 extn 25081 🖷 0191 211 4970 ✉ ronald.grey@newcastle.gov.uk

PR / Communications: Mr Steve Park, Head of Communications & Marketing, Civic Centre, Newcastle upon Tyne NE99 2BN ☎ 0191 232 8520 extn 25071 🖷 0191 211 4888 ✉ steve.park@newcastle.gov.uk

Community Planning: Ms Jan Cromarty, Head of Community Engagement & Empowerment, Civic Centre, Newcastle upon Tyne NE99 2BN ☎ 0191 277 7020 🖷 0191 211 5862 ✉ jan.cromarty@newcastle.gov.uk

Community Safety: Ms Robyn Thomas, Head of Community Safety, Community Safety Team, Civic Centre, Newcastle upon Tyne NE99 2BN ☎ 0191 277 7835 🖷 0191 277 7834 ✉ robyn.thomas@newcastle.gov.uk

Computer Management: Mr James Lowden, ICT Services Manager, Civic Centre, Newcastle upon Tyne NE99 2BN ☎ 0191 232 8520 extn 27282 ✉ james.lowden@newcastle.gov.uk

Consumer Protection and Trading Standards: Mr Stephen Savage, Director of Regulatory Services & Public Protection, Civic Centre, Newcastle upon Tyne NE1 8PB ☎ 0191 211 6101 🖷 0191 211 6060 ✉ stephen.savage@newcastle.gov.uk

Contracts: Ms Christine Herriot, Head of Efficiency & Procurement, Room 207, Civic Centre, Newcastle upon Tyne NE99 2BN ☎ 0191 277 7665 🖷 0191 277 7662 ✉ christine.herriot@newcastle.gov.uk

Corporate Services: Mr Steve Evans, Director of Corporate Services, Civic Centre, Newcastle upon Tyne NE99 2BN ☎ 0191 232 8520 ext. 25200 🖷 0191 211 5252 ✉ steve.evans@newcastle.gov.uk

Customer Service: Ms Diane Scott, Head of Customer Services, PO Box 766, Civic Centre, Newcastle upon Tyne NE99 1FR ☎ 0191 277 7580 🖷 0191 211 4835 ✉ diane.scott@newcastle.gov.uk

Direct Labour: Mr Nigel Hails, Director of Neighbourhood Services, Civic Centre, Newcastle upon Tyne NE99 2BN ☎ 0191 277 3500 ✉ nigel.hails@newcastle.gov.uk

Economic Development: Mr Rob Hamilton, Head of Economic Policy, Civic Centre, Newcastle upon Tyne NE99 2BN ☎ 0191 277 8947 ✉ rob.hamilton@newcastle.gov.uk

Education: Mr John Collings, Executive Director of Children's Services, Civic Centre, Newcastle upon Tyne NE99 2BN ☎ 0191 232 8520 extn 24997 ✉ john.collings@newcastle.gov.uk

Education: Mr Martin Surtees, Director of Performance, Outcomes & Commissioning, Civic Centre, Newcastle upon Tyne NE99 2BN ☎ 0191 211 5300 ✉ martin.surtees@newcastle.gov.uk

E-Government: Mr James Lowden, ICT Services Manager, Civic Centre, Newcastle upon Tyne NE99 2BN ☎ 0191 232 8520 extn 27282 ✉ james.lowden@newcastle.gov.uk

Electoral Registration: Mr Ian Poll, Head of Democratic Services, Civic Centre, Newcastle upon Tyne NE99 2BN ☎ 0191 211 5159 🖷 0191 211 5149 ✉ ian.poll@newcastle.gov.uk

Emergency Planning: Mr Stephen Savage, Director of Regulatory Services & Public Protection, Civic Centre, Newcastle upon Tyne NE1 8PB ☎ 0191 211 6101 🖷 0191 211 6060 ✉ stephen.savage@newcastle.gov.uk

Energy Management: Mr Simon Johnson, Energy Services Team Manager, Allendale House, Newcastle upon Tyne NE6 2SZ ☎ 0191 278 3449 🖷 0191 278 3311 ✉ simon.johnson@newcastle.gov.uk

Environmental / Technical Services: Mr Rob Nichols, Head of Environmental Services, Civic Centre, Newcastle upon Tyne NE99 2BN ☎ 0191 277 3501 🖷 0191 277 3686 ✉ rob.nichols@newcastle.gov.uk

Environmental Health: Mr Stephen Savage, Director of Regulatory Services & Public Protection, Civic Centre, Newcastle upon Tyne NE1 8PB ☎ 0191 211 6101 🖷 0191 211 6060 ✉ stephen.savage@newcastle.gov.uk

Estates, Property & Valuation: Mr Mark Lloyd, Head of Strategic Property and Asset Management, Civic Centre, Newcastle upon Tyne NE99 2BN ☎ 0191 211 5516 🖷 0191 2115521 ✉ mark.lloyd@newcastle.gov.uk

European Liaison: Mr Kevin Richardson, Policy, Research & Scrutiny Team Manager, Civic Centre, Newcastle upon Tyne NE1 8QN ☎ 0191 211 5675 🖷 0191 211 5687 ✉ kevin.richardson@newcastle.gov.uk

Events Manager: Mr Stephen Savage, Director of Regulatory Services & Public Protection, Civic Centre, Newcastle upon Tyne NE1 8PB ☎ 0191 211 6101 🖷 0191 211 6060 ✉ stephen.savage@newcastle.gov.uk

Facilities: Mr Steve Boon, Head of Facility Services, Allendale Road, Byker, Newcastle upon Tyne NE64 2SZ ☎ 0191 278 3210 🖷 0191 278 3101 ✉ steve.boon@newcastle.gov.uk

Finance and Treasurer: Mr Paul Woods, Director of Finance & Resources, Civic Centre, Newcastle upon Tyne NE99 1RD ☎ 0191 277 7527 🖷 0191 211 4901 ✉ paul.v.woods@newcastle.gov.uk

Fleet Management: Mr Peter Morton, Fleet Manager, Newington Road West, Newcastle upon Tyne NE5 6BD ☎ 0191 278 3901 🖷 0191 278 3924 ✉ peter.morton@newcastle.gov.uk

Grounds Maintenance: Mr Rob Nichols, Head of Environmental Services, Civic Centre, Newcastle upon Tyne NE99 2BN ☎ 0191 277 3501 🖷 0191 277 3686 ✉ rob.nichols@newcastle.gov.uk

Health and Safety: Mr Peter Jesson, Head of Health & Safety, Civic Centre, Newcastle upon Tyne NE99 2BN ☎ 0191 232 8520 Extn 25223 🖷 0191 211 5252 ✉ peter.jesson@newcastle.gov.uk

Highways: Mr Michael Murphy, Director of Technical Services, Civic Centre, Newcastle upon Tyne NE99 2BN ☎ 0191 211 5950 🖷 0191 211 5909 ✉ michael.murphy@newcastle.gov.uk

Home Energy Conservation: Mr Simon Johnson, Energy Services Team Manager, Room FF2, Allendale Road, Newcastle upon Tyne NE64 2SZ ☎ 0191 278 3449 🖷 0191 278 3311 ✉ simon.johnson@newcastle.gov.uk

Housing: Mr Harvey Emms, Director of Strategic Housing, Planning & Transportation, Civic Centre, Newcastle upon Tyne NE99 2BN ☎ 0191 211 6036 🖷 0191 211 4810 ✉ harvey.emms@newcastle.gov.uk

Housing Maintenance: Mr Nigel Hails, Director of Neighbourhood Services, Civic Centre, Newcastle upon Tyne NE99 2BN ☎ ; 0191 277 3500 ✉ nigel.hails@newcastle.gov.uk

Local Area Agreement: Mr Phil Hunter, Head of Policy & Research, Civic Centre, Newcastle upon Tyne NE99 2BN ☎ 0191 277 7802 ✉ philip.hunter@newcastle.gov.uk

Legal: Mr Stuart Ovens, Head of Corporate Law, Civic Centre, Newcastle upon Tyne NE99 2BN ☎ 0191 277 7122 🖷 0191 277 7127 ✉ stuart.ovens@newcastle.gov.uk

Leisure and Cultural Services: Mr Anthony McKenna, Head of Leisure Services, Civic Centre, Newcastle upon Tyne NE1 8PD ☎ 0191 277 3591 ✉ tony.mckenna@newcastle.gov.uk

Licensing: Mr Stephen Savage, Director of Regulatory Services & Public Protection, Civic Centre, Newcastle upon Tyne NE1 8PB ☎ 0191 211 6101 🖷 0191 211 6060 ✉ stephen.savage@newcastle.gov.uk

Lifelong Learning: Mr Tony Durcan, Director of Culture, Libraries & Lifelong Learning, Civic Centre, Newcastle upon Tyne NE99 2BN ☎ 0191 211 5383 🖷 0191 277 4137 ✉ tony.durcan@newcastle.gov.uk

Lighting: Mr Michael Murphy, Director of Technical Services, Civic Centre, Newcastle upon Tyne NE99 2BN ☎ 0191 211 5950 🖷 0191 211 5909 ✉ michael.murphy@newcastle.gov.uk

Member Services: Ms Elaine Dobinson, Senior Admin Assistant, Room 150, Civic Centre, Newcastle upon Tyne NE99 2BN ☎ 0191 211 5042 ✉ elaine.dobson@newcastle.gov.uk

Parking: Mr Stephen Savage, Director of Regulatory Services & Public Protection, Civic Centre, Newcastle upon Tyne NE1 8PB ☎ 0191 211 6101 🖷 0191 211 6060 ✉ stephen.savage@newcastle.gov.uk

Personnel / HR: Ms Pam Perry, Head of Strategic HR, Civic Centre, Newcastle upon Tyne NE99 2BN ☎ 0191 232 8520 extn 25246 ✉ pam.perry@newcastle.gov.uk

Planning: Mr Harvey Emms, Director of Strategic Housing, Planning & Transportation, Civic Centre, Newcastle upon Tyne NE1 8PD ☎ 0191 211 6036 🖷 0191 211 4810 ✉ harvey.emms@newcastle.gov.uk

Procurement: Ms Christine Herriot, Head of Efficiency & Procurement, Civic Centre, Newcastle upon Tyne NE99 2BN ☎ 0191 277 7665 🖷 0191 277 7662 ✉ christine.herriot@newcastle.gov.uk

Public Libraries: Mr Tony Durcan, Director of Culture, Libraries & Lifelong Learning, Civic Centre, Newcastle upon Tyne NE99

2BN ☎ 0191 211 5383 🖷 0191 277 4137
✉ tony.durcan@newcastle.gov.uk

Recycling & Waste Minimisation: Mr Rob Nichols, Head of Environmental Services, Civic Centre, Newcastle upon Tyne NE99 2BN ☎ 0191 277 3501 🖷 0191 277 3686
✉ rob.nichols@newcastle.gov.uk

Regeneration: Mr David Slater, Executive Director of Environment & Regeneration, Civic Centre, Newcastle upon Tyne NE99 2BN ☎ 0191 277 8900 🖷 0191 2114935
✉ david.slater@newcastle.gov.uk

Road Safety: Mr Michael Murphy, Director of Technical Services, Civic Centre, Newcastle upon Tyne NE99 2BN ☎ 0191 211 5950 🖷 0191 211 5909 ✉ michael.murphy@newcastle.gov.uk

Social Services: Mr Ewen Weir, Executive Director of Adult & Culture Services, Civic Centre, Newcastle upon Tyne NE99 1RD ☎ 0191 211 6300 🖷 0191 211 4955 ✉ ewen.weir@newcastle.gov.uk

Social Services (Adult): Ms Cathy Bull, Director of Adult Social Care, Civic Centre, Newcastle upon Tyne NE99 2BN ☎ 0191 211 6318 🖷 0191 211 4955 ✉ cathy.bull@newcastle.gov.uk

Social Services (Children): Mr Mick McCracken, Director of Children's Safeguarding & Social Care, Civic Centre, Newcastle upon Tyne NE99 2BN ☎ 0191 211 6307
✉ mick.mccracken@newcastle.gov.uk

Staff Training: Ms Jan Kincaid, Senior Human Resources Consultant, Civic Centre, Newcastle upon Tyne NE99 2BN
☎ 0191 277 7689 🖷 0191 211 5252
✉ jan.kincaid@newcastle.gov.uk

Street Scene: Mr Rob Nichols, Head of Environmental Services, Cypress Avenue, Fenham, Newcastle upon Tyne NE4 9JJ ☎ 0191 277 3501 🖷 0191 277 3686 ✉ rob.nichols@newcastle.gov.uk

Sustainable Communities: Ms Jan Cromarty, Head of Community Engagement & Empowerment, Civic Centre, Newcastle upon Tyne NE99 2BN ☎ 0191 277 7020
🖷 0191 211 5862 ✉ jan.cromarty@newcastle.gov.uk

Sustainable Development: Mr Harvey Emms, Director of Strategic Housing, Planning & Transportation, Civic Centre, Newcastle upon Tyne NE99 2BN ☎ 0191 211 6036 🖷 0191 211 4810 ✉ harvey.emms@newcastle.gov.uk

Tourism: Mr Andrew Rothwell, Culture & Tourism Manager, Civic Centre, Newcastle upon Tyne NE99 2BN ☎ 0191 211 5610
🖷 0191 277 5602 ✉ andrew.rothwell@newcastle.gov.uk

Town Centre: Mr Sean Bullick, Director of City Centre Partnership, Provincial House, Northumberland Street, Newcastle upon Tyne NE1 7DQ ☎ 0191 277 1922 🖷 0191 277 1923
✉ sean.bullick@newcastle.gov.uk

Traffic Management: Mr Michael Murphy, Director of Technical Services, Civic Centre, Newcastle upon Tyne NE99 2BN ☎ 0191 211 5950 🖷 0191 211 5909 ✉ michael.murphy@newcastle.gov.uk

Transport: Mr Rob Nichols, Head of Environmental Services, Civic Centre, Newcastle upon Tyne NE99 2BN ☎ 0191 277 3501
🖷 0191 277 3686 ✉ rob.nichols@newcastle.gov.uk

Transport Planner: Mr Harvey Emms, Director of Strategic Housing, Planning & Transportation, Civic Centre, Newcastle upon Tyne NE99 2BN ☎ 0191 211 6036 🖷 0191 211 4810
✉ harvey.emms@newcastle.gov.uk

Total Place: Mr Andrew Lewis, Director of Policy, Strategy & Communications, Civic Centre, Newcastle upon Tyne NE99 2BN
☎ 0191 232 8520 extn 25681 ✉ andrew.lewis@newcastle.gov.uk

Waste Collection and Disposal: Mr Rob Nichols, Head of Environmental Services, Civic Centre, Newcastle upon Tyne NE99 2BN ☎ 0191 277 3501 🖷 0191 277 3686
✉ rob.nichols@newcastle.gov.uk

Waste Management: Mr Rob Nichols, Head of Environmental Services, Civic Centre, Newcastle upon Tyne NE99 2BN ☎ 0191 277 3501 🖷 0191 277 3686 ✉ rob.nichols@newcastle.gov.uk

Children's Play Areas: Mr Mick McCracken, Director of Children's Safeguarding & Social Care, Civic Centre, Newcastle upon Tyne NE99 2BN ☎ 0191 211 6307
✉ mick.mccracken@newcastle.gov.uk

MEMBERS OF THE COUNCIL (78)

***The Lord Mayor:* Slesenger**, Jaqueline (LD - West Gosforth)
jacqueline.slesenger@newcastle.gov.uk

***Leader of the Council:* Forbes**, Nick (LAB - Westgate)
nick.forbes@newcastle.gov.uk

***Deputy Leader of the Council:* McCarty**, Joyce (LAB - Wingrove)
joyce.mccarty@newcastle.gov.uk

***Group Leader:* Faulkner**, David (LD - Fawdon)
david.faulkner@newcastle.gov.uk

Ahad, Dipu (LAB - Elswick)
dipu.ahad@newcastle.gov.uk

Ali, Irim (LAB - Wingrove)
irim.ali@newcastle.gov.uk

Allen, Pauline (LD - Parklands)
pauline.allen@newcastle.gov.uk

Allison, George (LAB - Byker)
george.allison@newcastle.gov.uk

Andras, Peter (LD - North Jesmond)
peter.andras@newcastle.gov.uk

Armstrong, Tania (LAB - Walkergate)
tania.armstrong@newcastle.gov.uk

Bartlett, Christopher (LAB - South Heaton)
christopher.bartlett@newcastle.gov.uk

Beecham, Jeremy (LAB - Benwell and Scotswood)
jeremybeecham@blueyonder.co.uk

Bell, Ged (LAB - Kenton)
ged.bell@newcastle.gov.uk

Bird, Simon (LAB - Denton)
simon.bird@newcastle.gov.uk

Breakey, Peter (LD - North Jesmond)
peter.breakey@newcastle.gov.uk

Burke, Michael (LAB - Denton)
michael.burke@newcastle.gov.uk

Cook, David (LAB - Lemington)
david.cook@newcastle.gov.uk

Cott, Nick (LD - West Gosforth)
nick.cott@newcastle.gov.uk
Cross, Sarah Ann (LD - Denton)
sarah.ann.cross@newcastle.gov.uk
Denholm, David (LAB - Walkergate)
david.denholm@newcastle.gov.uk
Donnelly, Marc (IND - Westerhope)
marc.donnelly@newcastle.gov.uk
Down, David (LD - Parklands)
david.down@newcastle.gov.uk
Dunn, Veronica (LAB - Byker)
veronica.dunn@newcastle.gov.uk
Fairlie, Stephen (LAB - Newburn)
steve.fairlie@newcastle.gov.uk
Franks, Hilary (LAB - Newburn)
hilary.franks@newcastle.gov.uk
Gallagher, Henry (LD - East Gosforth)
henry.gallagher@newcastle.gov.uk
Graham, Ian (LD - Castle)
ian.graham@newcastle.gov.uk
Graham, Kevin (LAB - Woolsington)
kevin.graham@newcastle.gov.uk
Hardman, David (LAB - South Jesmond)
david.hardman@newcastle.gov.uk
Higgins, Robert (LAB - Benwell and Scotswood)
rob.higgins@newcastle.gov.uk
Hindmarsh, Brenda (LD - Fawdon)
brenda.hindmarsh@newcastle.gov.uk
Hobson, Linda (LAB - Westerhope)
linda.hobson@newcastle.gov.uk
Huddart, Doreen (LD - North Heaton)
doreen.huddart@newcastle.gov.uk
Hunter, Brian (LAB - Westerhope)
brian.hunter@newcastle.gov.uk
Johnson, Michael (LAB - North Heaton)
michael.johnson@newcastle.gov.uk
Kane, Gareth (LD - Ouseburn)
gareth.kane@newcastle.gov.uk
Kemp, Nick (LAB - Byker)
nick.kemp@newcastle.gov.uk
Kingsland, Joanne (LAB - Westgate)
joanne.kingsland@newcastle.gov.uk
Lambert, Stephen (LAB - Kenton)
stephen.lambert@newcastle.gov.uk
Laverick, Ian (LD - Castle)
ian.laverick@newcastle.gov.uk
Leggott, Peter (LD - East Gosforth)
peter.leggott@newcastle.gov.uk
Lower, Anita (LD - Castle)
anita.lower@newcastle.gov.uk
Lowson, Maureen (LAB - Walkergate)
maureen.lowson@newcastle.gov.uk
McStravick, Helen (LAB - Fenham)
helen.mcstravick@newcastle.gov.uk
Mendelson, Felicity (LAB - South Jesmond)
felicity.mendelson@newcastle.gov.uk
Murison, Henri (LAB - South Heaton)
henri.murison@newcastle.gov.uk
Myers, Matthew (LAB - Fenham)
matthew.myers@newcastle.gov.uk
O'Brien, Geoff (LAB - Westgate)
geoff.obrien@newcastle.gov.uk
Packham, Diane (LD - Parklands)
diane.packham@newcastle.gov.uk
Pagan, Catherine (LD - North Jesmond)
catherine.pagan@newcastle.gov.uk
Pattison, Sharon (LAB - Woolsington)
sharon.pattison@newcastle.gov.uk
Pattison, George (LAB - Woolsington)
george.pattison@newcastle.gov.uk
Pearson, Sue (LAB - Blakelaw)
sue.pearson@newcastle.gov.uk
Phillipson, Barry (LAB - Lemington)
barry.phillipson@newcastle.gov.uk
Preston, Ian (LAB - Ouseburn)
ian.preston@newcastle.gov.uk
Psallidas, Stephen (LD - Ouseburn)
stephen.psallidas@newcastle.gov.uk
Rahman, Habib (LAB - Elswick)
habib.rahman@newcastle.gov.uk
Renton, Bob (LD - Dene)
bob.renton@newcastle.gov.uk
Risk, Phil (LAB - Blakelaw)
phil.risk@newcastle.gov.uk
Robinson, Karen (LD - Dene)
Schofield, Ann (LAB - Elswick)
ann.schofield@newcastle.gov.uk
Shepherd, Bill (LD - West Gosforth)
william.shepherd@newcastle.gov.uk
Slesenger, David (LD - East Gosforth)
david.slesenger@newcastle.gov.uk
Stephenson, Hazel (LAB - Benwell and Scotswood)
hazel.stephenson@newcastle.gov.uk
Stockdale, David (LAB - Blakelaw)
david.stockdale@newcastle.gov.uk
Stokel-Walker, John (LAB - Walker)
john.stokel-walker@newcastle.gov.uk
Stone, Greg (LD - North Heaton)
greg.stone@newcastle.gov.uk
Streather, Jane (LAB - Kenton)
jane.streather@newcastle.gov.uk
Sutcliffe, Louise (LAB - Lemington)
louise.sutcliffe@newcastle.gov.uk
Talbot, Marion (LAB - Fenham)
marion.talbot@newcastle.gov.uk
Taylor, Wendy (LD - Dene)
wendy.taylor@newcastle.gov.uk
Tinnion, Antoine (LAB - Fawdon)
antoine.tinnion@newcastle.gov.uk
Todd, Nigel (LAB - Wingrove)
nigel.todd@newcastle.gov.uk
White, Sophie (LAB - South Heaton)
sophie.white@newcastle.gov.uk
Wood, Margaret (LAB - Walker)
margaret.wood@newcastle.gov.uk
Wood, Dave (LAB - Walker)
dave.wood@newcastle.gov.uk
Woodwark, Tom (LD - South Jesmond)
tom.woodwark@newcastle.gov.uk
Wright, Linda (LAB - Newburn)
linda.wright@newcastle.gov.uk

POLITICAL COMPOSITION

LAB: 51, LD: 26, IND: 1

CABINET

Leader: Mr Nick Forbes
Deputy Leader: Ms Joyce McCarty
Adult Services: Mrs Veronica Dunn

Chief Executive's Directorate: Ms Hazel Stephenson
Children's Services: Ms Joanne Kingsland
Quality of Life: Mr Henri Murison

NEWCASTLE-UNDER-LYME D

Newcastle-under-Lyme Borough Council, Civic Offices, Merrial Street, Newcastle-under-Lyme ST5 2AG ☎ 01782 717717 🖷 01782 711032 🖳 www.newcastle-staffs.gov.uk

FACTS & FIGURES

Police Authority: Staffordshire Police Authority
Health Authority: NHS West Midlands
Learning and Skills Council: West Midlands
Parliamentary Constituencies: Newcastle-under-Lyme, Stoke-on-Trent North, Stone
EU Constituencies: West Midlands
Election Frequency: Elections are by thirds

PRINCIPAL OFFICERS

Chief Executive: Mr John Sellgren, Chief Executive, Civic Offices, Merrial Street, Newcastle-under-Lyme ST5 2AG

Senior Management: Mr Dave Adams, Executive Director - Operational Services, Civic Offices, Merrial Street, Newcastle-under-Lyme ST5 2AG ☎ 01782 742504 🖷 01782 713252 ✉ dave.adams@newcastle-staffs.gov.uk

Senior Management: Mr Neale Clifton, Executive Director - Regeneration & Development, Civic Offices, Merrial Street, Newcastle-under-Lyme ST5 2AG ☎ 01782 742401 🖷 01782 714303 ✉ neale.clifton@newcastle-staffs.gov.uk

Senior Management: Mr Kelvin Turner, Executive Director - Resources & Support Services, Civic Offices, Merrial Street, Newcastle-under-Lyme ST5 2AG ☎ 01782 742106 ✉ kelvin.turner@newcastle-staffs.gov.uk

Architect, Building / Property Services: Mr Graham Williams, Engineering & Facilities Manager, Civic Offices, Merrial Street, Newcastle-under-Lyme ST5 2AG ☎ 01782 742311 🖷 01782 714303 ✉ graham.williams@newcastle-staffs.gov.uk

Building Control: Mr Guy Benson, Head of Planning and Development, Civic Offices, Merrial Street, Newcastle-under-Lyme ST5 2AG ☎ 01782 744440 ✉ guy.benson@newcastle-staffs.gov.uk

PR / Communications: Mr Phil Jones, Head of Communications, Civic Offices, Merrial Street, Newcastle-under-Lyme ST5 2AG ☎ 01782 742271 ✉ phil.jones@newcastle-staffs.gov.uk

Community Safety: Mr Rob Avann, Community Safety Partnership Manager, Civic Offices, Merrial Street, Newcastle-under-Lyme ST5 2AG ☎ 01782 742251 🖷 01782 714303 ✉ rob.avann@newcastle-staffs.gov.uk

Computer Management: Mrs Jeannette Hilton, Head of Customer Services & ICT Services, Civic Offices, Merrial Street, Newcastle-under-Lyme ST5 2AG ☎ 01782 742470 ✉ jeannette.hilton@newcastle-staffs.gov.uk

Contracts: Mr Roger Tait, Head of Operations, Civic Offices, Merrial Street, Newcastle-under-Lyme ST5 2AG ☎ 01782 742632 🖷 01782 713251 ✉ roger.tait@newcastle-staffs.gov.uk

Corporate Services: Mr Kelvin Turner, Executive Director - Resources & Support Services, Civic Offices, Merrial Street, Newcastle-under-Lyme ST5 2AG ☎ 01782 742106 ✉ kelvin.turner@newcastle-staffs.gov.uk

Customer Service: Mrs Jeannette Hilton, Head of Customer Services & ICT Services, Civic Offices, Merrial Street, Newcastle-under-Lyme ST5 2AG ☎ 01782 742470 ✉ jeannette.hilton@newcastle-staffs.gov.uk

Direct Labour: Mr Paul Pickerill, Streetscene Manager, Civic Offices, Merrial Street, Newcastle-under-Lyme ST5 2AG ☎ 01782 744760

Economic Development: Mr Simon Smith, Regeneration & Economic Development Manager, Civic Offices, Merrial Street, Newcastle-under-Lyme ST5 2AG ☎ 01782 742460 🖷 01782 714303 ✉ simon.smith@newcastle-staffs.gov.uk

Electoral Registration: Miss Julia Cleary, Elections & Licensing Manager, Civic Offices, Merrial Street, Newcastle-under-Lyme ST5 2AG ☎ 01782 742227 🖷 01782 711032 ✉ julia.cleary@newcastle-staffs.gov.uk

Emergency Planning: Mr Graham Williams, Engineering & Facilities Manager, Civic Offices, Merrial Street, Newcastle-under-Lyme ST5 2AG ☎ 01782 742311 🖷 01782 714303 ✉ graham.williams@newcastle-staffs.gov.uk

Energy Management: Mr Graham Williams, Engineering & Facilities Manager, Civic Offices, Merrial Street, Newcastle-under-Lyme ST5 2AG ☎ 01782 742311 🖷 01782 714303 ✉ graham.williams@newcastle-staffs.gov.uk

Environmental Health: Mr Neale Clifton, Executive Director - Regeneration & Development, Civic Offices, Merrial Street, Newcastle-under-Lyme ST5 2AG ☎ 01782 742401 🖷 01782 714303 ✉ neale.clifton@newcastle-staffs.gov.uk

Estates, Property & Valuation: Mr Neale Clifton, Executive Director - Regeneration & Development, Civic Offices, Merrial Street, Newcastle-under-Lyme ST5 2AG ☎ 01782 742401 🖷 01782 714303 ✉ neale.clifton@newcastle-staffs.gov.uk

Estates, Property & Valuation: Mr Jeff Hamnett, Head of Assets & Regeneration, Civic Offices, Merrial Street, Newcastle-under-Lyme ST5 2AG ☎ 01782 742371 🖷 01782 714303 ✉ jeff.hamnett@newcastle-staffs.gov.uk

European Liaison: Mr Simon Smith, Regeneration & Economic Development Manager, Civic Offices, Merrial Street, Newcastle-under-Lyme ST5 2AG ☎ 01782 742460 🖷 01782 714303 ✉ simon.smith@newcastle-staffs.gov.uk

Events Manager: Mrs Janet Baddeley, Communications Manager, Civic Offices, Merrial Street, Newcastle-under-Lyme ST5 2AG ☎ 01782 742605 ✉ janet.baddeley@newcastle-staffs.gov.uk

Facilities: Mr Julian Lythgo, Facilities Manager, Civic Offices, Merrial Street, Newcastle-under-Lyme ST5 2AG ☎ 01782 742368 ✉ julian.lythgo@newcastle-staff.gov.uk

Finance and Treasurer: Mr Dave Baker, Head of Revenues & Benefits, Civic Offices, Merrial Street, Newcastle-under-Lyme ST5 2AG ☎ 01782 742131 ✉ dave.baker@newcastle-staffs.gov.uk

Finance and Treasurer: Mr Dave Roberts, Head of Finance, Civic Offices, Merrial Street, Newcastle-under-Lyme ST5 2AG ☎ 01782 742111 ✉ dave.roberts@newcastle-staffs.gov.uk

Finance and Treasurer: Mr Kelvin Turner, Executive Director - Resources & Support Services, Civic Offices, Merrial Street, Newcastle-under-Lyme ST5 2AG ☎ 01782 742106 ✉ kelvin.turner@newcastle-staffs.gov.uk

Fleet Management: Mr Dave Adams, Executive Director - Operational Services, Civic Offices, Merrial Street, Newcastle-under-Lyme ST5 2AG ☎ 01782 742504 🖷 01782 713252 ✉ dave.adams@newcastle-staffs.gov.uk

Grounds Maintenance: Mr Dave Adams, Executive Director - Operational Services, Civic Offices, Merrial Street, Newcastle-under-Lyme ST5 2AG ☎ 01782 742504 🖷 01782 713252 ✉ dave.adams@newcastle-staffs.gov.uk

Health and Safety: Ms Jane Kent, Corporate Health & Safety Officer, Civic Offices, Merrial Street, Newcastle-under-Lyme ST5 2AG ☎ 01782 742262 ✉ jane.kent@newcastle-staffs.gov.uk

Home Energy Conservation: Mr Michael O'Connor, Principal Environmental Health Officer, Civic Offices, Merrial Street, Newcastle-under-Lyme ST5 2AG ☎ 01782 742564 🖷 01782 713252 ✉ mike.o'connor@newcastle-staffs.gov.uk

Housing: Miss Joanne Basnett, Head of Housing, Civic Offices, Merrial Street, Newcastle-under-Lyme ST5 2AG ☎ 01782 742451 🖷 01782 714303 ✉ joanne.basnett@newcastle-staffs.gov.uk

Housing: Mr Neale Clifton, Executive Director - Regeneration & Development, Civic Offices, Merrial Street, Newcastle-under-Lyme ST5 2AG ☎ 01782 742401 🖷 01782 714303 ✉ neale.clifton@newcastle-staffs.gov.uk

Legal: Mr Paul Clisby, Head of Central Services, Civic Offices, Merrial Street, Newcastle-under-Lyme ST5 2AG ☎ 01782 742201 ✉ paul.clisby@newcastle-staffs.gov.uk

Leisure and Cultural Services: Mr Robert Foster, Head of Leisure & Cultural Services, Civic Offices, Merrial Street, Newcastle-under-Lyme ST5 2AG ☎ 01782 742636 🖷 01782 713252 ✉ robert.foster@newcastle-staffs.gov.uk

Licensing: Mr Paul Clisby, Head of Central Services, Civic Offices, Merrial Street, Newcastle-under-Lyme ST5 2AG ☎ 01782 742201 ✉ paul.clisby@newcastle-staffs.gov.uk

Lottery Funding, Charity and Voluntary: Mr Robert Foster, Head of Leisure & Cultural Services, Civic Offices, Merrial Street, Newcastle-under-Lyme ST5 2AG ☎ 01782 742636 🖷 01782 713252 ✉ robert.foster@newcastle-staffs.gov.uk

Parking: Mr Graham Williams, Engineering & Facilities Manager, Civic Offices, Merrial Street, Newcastle-under-Lyme ST5 2AG ☎ 01782 742311 🖷 01782 714303 ✉ graham.williams@newcastle-staffs.gov.uk

Personnel / HR: Mr Richard Durrant, Human Resources Manager, Civic Offices, Merrial Street, Newcastle-under-Lyme ST5 2AG ☎ 01782 742260 🖷 01782 711032 ✉ richard.durrant@newcastle-staffs.gov.uk

Planning: Mr Neale Clifton, Executive Director - Regeneration & Development, Civic Offices, Merrial Street, Newcastle-under-Lyme ST5 2AG ☎ 01782 742401 🖷 01782 714303 ✉ neale.clifton@newcastle-staffs.gov.uk

Procurement: Mr Simon Sowerby, Procurement Officer, Civic Offices, Merrial Street, Newcastle-under-Lyme ST5 2AG ☎ 01782 742756 🖷 01782 711032

Recycling & Waste Minimisation: Mr Dave Adams, Executive Director - Operational Services, Civic Offices, Merrial Street, Newcastle-under-Lyme ST5 2AG ☎ 01782 742504 🖷 01782 713252 ✉ dave.adams@newcastle-staffs.gov.uk

Regeneration: Mr Neale Clifton, Executive Director - Regeneration & Development, Civic Offices, Merrial Street, Newcastle-under-Lyme ST5 2AG ☎ 01782 742401 🖷 01782 714303 ✉ neale.clifton@newcastle-staffs.gov.uk

Staff Training: Mr Richard Durrant, Human Resources Manager, Civic Offices, Merrial Street, Newcastle-under-Lyme ST5 2AG ☎ 01782 742260 🖷 01782 711032 ✉ richard.durrant@newcastle-staffs.gov.uk

Street Scene: Mr Dave Adams, Executive Director - Operational Services, Civic Offices, Merrial Street, Newcastle-under-Lyme ST5 2AG ☎ 01782 742504 🖷 01782 713252 ✉ dave.adams@newcastle-staffs.gov.uk

Street Scene: Mr Paul Pickerill, Streetscene Manager, Civic Offices, Merrial Street, Newcastle-under-Lyme ST5 2AG ☎ 01782 744760

Sustainable Communities: Mr Neale Clifton, Executive Director - Regeneration & Development, Civic Offices, Merrial Street, Newcastle-under-Lyme ST5 2AG ☎ 01782 742401 🖷 01782 714303 ✉ neale.clifton@newcastle-staffs.gov.uk

Sustainable Development: Mr Neale Clifton, Executive Director - Regeneration & Development, Civic Offices, Merrial Street, Newcastle-under-Lyme ST5 2AG ☎ 01782 742401 🖷 01782 714303 ✉ neale.clifton@newcastle-staffs.gov.uk

Tourism: Mr Phil Jones, Head of Communications, Civic Offices, Merrial Street, Newcastle-under-Lyme ST5 2AG ☎ 01782 742271 ✉ phil.jones@newcastle-staffs.gov.uk

Transport: Mr Stephen Gee, Transport Manager, Central Depot, Knutton Lane, Newcastle-under-Lyme ST5 2SL ☎ 01782 742712 🖷 01782 713179 ✉ stephen.gee@newcastle-staffs.gov.uk

Transport Planner: Mr Stephen Gee, Transport Manager, Central

Depot, Knutton Lane, Newcastle-under-Lyme ST5 2SL ☎ 01782 742712 🖷 01782 713179 ✉ stephen.gee@newcastle-staffs.gov.uk

Waste Collection and Disposal: Mr Dave Adams, Executive Director - Operational Services, Civic Offices, Merrial Street, Newcastle-under-Lyme ST5 2AG ☎ 01782 742504 🖷 01782 713252 ✉ dave.adams@newcastle-staffs.gov.uk

Waste Management: Mr Dave Adams, Executive Director - Operational Services, Civic Offices, Merrial Street, Newcastle-under-Lyme ST5 2AG ☎ 01782 742504 🖷 01782 713252 ✉ dave.adams@newcastle-staffs.gov.uk

Waste Management: Mr Paul Pickerill, Streetscene Manager, Civic Offices, Merrial Street, Newcastle-under-Lyme ST5 2AG ☎ 01782 744760

MEMBERS OF THE COUNCIL (60)

***Mayor:* Becket**, David (LD - Halmer End)
david.becket@newcastle-staffs.gov.uk
***Leader of the Council:* Snell**, Gareth (LAB - Knutton and Silverdale)
gareth.snell@newcastle-staffs.gov.uk
***Deputy Leader of the Council:* Boden**, Eddie (LAB - Chesterton)
eddie.boden@newcastle-staffs.gov.uk
Allport, David (LAB - Talke)
david.allport@newcastle-staffs.gov.uk
Astle, Margaret (LAB - Kidsgrove)
margaret.astle@kidsgrove.info
Bailey, Reginald (LAB - Kidsgrove)
reg.bailey44@yahoo.co.uk
Baker, Sophia (LAB - Holditch)
sophia.baker@newcastle-staffs.gov.uk
Bannister, James (CON - May Bank)
james.bannister@newcastle-staffs.gov.uk
Bates, Elsie (LAB - Newchapel)
elsie.bates@newcastle-staffs.gov.uk
Beech, Ann (LAB - Audley and Bignall End)
ann.beech@newcastle-staffs.gov.uk
Burgess, Silvia (LAB - Butt Lane)
silvia.burgess@newcastle-staffs.gov.uk
Burnett, Gillian (LAB - Ravenscliffe)
gillian.burnett@newcastle-staffs.gov.uk
Cairns, George (LAB - Silverdale and Parksite)
george.cairns@newcastle-staffs.gov.uk
Clarke, Michael (LAB - Holditch)
michael.clarke@newcastle-staffs.gov.uk
Cooper, Julie (CON - Porthill)
julie.cooper@newcastle-staffs.gov.uk
Cooper, John (CON - Porthill)
john.cooper@newcastle-staffs.gov.uk
Cornes, Dylis (LD - Audley and Bignall End)
dylis.cornes@newcastle-staffs.gov.uk
Eagles, Tony (LAB - Knutton and Silverdale)
anthony.eagles@newcastle.staffs.gov.uk
Eastwood, Colin (LAB - Wolstanton)
colin.eastwood@newcastle-staffs.gov.uk
Fear, Andrew (CON - Seabridge)
andrew.fear@newcastle-staffs.gov.uk
Hailstones, Linda (CON - Westlands)
linda.hailstones@newcastle-staffs.gov.uk
Hailstones, Peter (CON - Seabridge)
peter.hailstones@newcastle-staffs.gov.uk
Hambleton, Sandra (LAB - Bradwell)
sandra.hambleton@newcastle-staffs.gov.uk
Hambleton, Trevor (LAB - Bradwell)
trevor.hambleton@newcastle-staffs.gov.uk
Heames, Ann (CON - Clayton)
ann.heames@newcastle-staffs.gov.uk
Heesom, Gillian (CON - Westlands)
gillian.heesom@newcastle-staffs.gov.uk
Holland, Mark (CON - Westlands)
mark.holland@newcastle-staffs.gov.uk
Howells, Ashley (CON - Loggerheads and Whitmore)
ashley.howells@newcastle-staffs.gov.uk
Johnson, Hilda (LAB - Chesterton)
hilda.johnson@newcastle-staffs.gov.uk
Jones, Nigel (LD - Thistleberry)
williamnigel.jones@newcastle-staffs.gov.uk
Kearon, Tony (LAB - Keele)
tony.kearon@newcastle-staffs.gov.uk
Lawton, Thomas (LAB - Silverdale and Parksite)
thomas.lawton@newcastle-staffs.gov.uk
Loades, David (CON - Loggerheads and Whitmore)
david.loades@newcastle-staffs.gov.uk
Mancey, Chloe (CON - Seabridge)
chloe.mancey@newcastle-staffs.gov.uk
Matthews, Ian (CON - May Bank)
ian.matthews@newcastle-staffs.gov.uk
Olszewski, Sophie (LAB - Wolstanton)
sophie.olszewski@newcastle-staffs.gov.uk
Olszewski, Mark (LAB - Wolstanton)
mark.olszewski@newcastle-staffs.gov.uk
Peers, Tracey (CON - Loggerheads and Whitmore)
tracey.peers@newcastle-staffs.gov.uk
Plant, Glyn (LAB - Bradwell)
glyn.plant@newcastle-staffs.gov.uk
Reddish, Marion (LD - Thistleberry)
marion.reddish@newcastle-staffs.gov.uk
Robinson, Kyle (LAB - Butt Lane)
kyle.robinson@newcastle-staffs.gov.uk
Shenton, Elizabeth (LD - Town)
elizabeth.shenton@newcastle-staffs.gov.uk
Simpson, Sandra (LAB - Chesterton)
sandra.simpson@newcastle-staffs.gov.uk
Stringer, David (LAB - Ravenscliffe)
david.stringer@newcastle-staffs.gov.uk
Stubbs, Mike (LAB - Talke)
mike.stubbs@newcastle-staffs.gov.uk
Studd, Robin (LD - Keele)
robin.studd@newcastle-staffs.gov.uk
Sweeney, Stephen (CON - Clayton)
stephen.sweeney@newcastle-staffs.gov.uk
Tagg, Simon (CON - May Bank)
simon.tagg@newcastle-staffs.gov.uk
Taylor, Matt (LAB - Town)
matt.taylor@newcastle-staffs.gov.uk
Taylor, John (LAB - Butt Lane)
john.taylor@newcastle-staffs.gov.uk
Turner, Terry (LAB - Kidsgrove)
Walklate, June (LD - Thistleberry)
june.walklate@newcastle-staffs.gov.uk
Waring, Paul (LAB - Newchapel)
paul.waring@newcastle-staffs.gov.uk
Welsh, Billy (LD - Madeley)
billy.welsh@newcastle-staffs.gov.uk
Wemyss, Andrew (LD - Halmer End)

andrew.wemyss@newcastle-staffs.gov.uk
White, Simon (LD - Madeley)
simon.white@newcastle-staffs.gov.uk
Wilkes, Ian (LD - Audley and Bignall End)
ian.wilkes@newcastle-staffs.gov.uk
Williams, Gillian (LAB - Cross Heath)
gillian.williams@newcastle-staffs.gov.uk
Williams, John (LAB - Cross Heath)
john.williams@newcastle-staffs.gov.uk
Winfield, Joan (LAB - Cross Heath)
joan.winfield@newcastle-staffs.gov.uk

POLITICAL COMPOSITION
LAB: 33, CON: 16, LD: 11

CABINET
Leader / Communications, Transformation & Partnerships: Mr Gareth Snell
Deputy Leader / Regeneration, Planning & Town Centres: Mr Eddie Boden
Culture & Leisure: Mrs Elsie Bates
Environment & Recycling: Mrs Ann Beech
Finance & Budget Management: Mr Mike Stubbs
Safer Communities: Mr Tony Kearon
Stronger & Active Neighbourhoods: Mr John Williams

COMMITTEE CHAIRS
Active & Cohesive Communities (Scrutiny): Mr George Cairns
Cleaner, Greener & Safer Communities (Scrutiny): Mrs Gillian Williams
Economic Development & Enterprise (Scrutiny): Mr Ian Matthews
Health Scrutiny (Scrutiny): Mr Colin Eastwood
Licensing: Mr Trevor Hambleton
Planning: Mr Andrew Fear
Transformation & Resources: Mrs Elizabeth Shenton

NEWHAM L

Newham London Borough Council, Newham Dockside, 1000 Dockside Road, Royal Albert Dock, London E16 2QU ☎ 020 8430 2000 firstname.lastname@newham.gov.uk
www.newham.gov.uk

FACTS & FIGURES
Police Authority: Metropolitan Police Authority
Health Authority: NHS London
Learning and Skills Council: London
Parliamentary Constituencies: East Ham, West Ham
EU Constituencies: London
Election Frequency: Elections are of whole council
Twinning: Kaiserslautern (Germany)

PRINCIPAL OFFICERS
Chief Executive: Mr Kim Bromley-Derry, Chief Executive, Newham Dockside, 1000 Dockside Road, Royal Albert Dock, London E16 2QU ☎ 020 8430 2000
kim.bromley-derry@newham.gov.uk

Access Officer / Social Services (Disability): Miss Grainne Siggins, Director of Adult Social Care, Newham Dockside, 1000 Dockside Road, Royal Albert Dock, London E16 2QU
grainne.siggins@newham.gov.uk

Architect, Building / Property Services: Mr Michael Flanagan, Director of Business Systems, Property & Commercial Development, Newham Dockside, 1000 Dockside Road, Royal Albert Dock, London E16 2QU ☎ 020 8430 2000
michael.flanagan@newham.gov.uk

Building Control: Mr Tim Gillooly, Head of Building Control, Newham Dockside, 1000 Dockside Road, Royal Albert Dock, London E16 2QU ☎ 020 3373 9739
tim.gillooly@newham.gov.uk

Catering Services: Mr John Ledgley, Head of Newham Catering & Cleaning Services, Newham Catering, 242 Fernhill Street , London E16 2HZ ☎ 020 8430 2000
john.ledgley@newham.gov.uk

Children / Youth Services: Ms Linzi Roberts-Egan, Director of Early Intervention & Progression, Newham Dockside, 1000 Dockside Road, Royal Albert Dock, London E16 2QU ☎ 020 8430 2000 linzi.robertsegan@newham.gov.uk

Civil Registration: Ms Lynne Cummings, Superintendent Registrar, Newham Register Office, 207 Plashet Grove, London E6 1BT ☎ 020 8430 3616 lynne.cummings@newham.gov.uk

PR / Communications: Mrs Sue Meiners, Head of Events & Sponsorship, Newham Dockside, 1000 Dockside Road, Royal Albert Dock, London E16 2QU ☎ 020 8430 2000
sue.meiners@newham.gov.uk

PR / Communications: Mr Douglas Trainer, Head of Communications, Newham Dockside, 1000 Dockside Road, Royal Albert Dock, London E16 2QU ☎ 020 8430 2000
douglas.trainer@newham.gov.uk

Community Planning: Ms Jenny Wilmott, Head of Community Leaders & Engagement, Newham Dockside, 1000 Dockside Road, Royal Albert Dock, London E16 2QU ☎ 020 8430 2000
jenny.wilmott@newham.gov.uk

Community Safety: Mr Nick Bracken, Director of Community Safety, Newham Dockside, 1000 Dockside Road, Royal Albert Dock, London E16 2QU ☎ 020 8430 2000
nick.bracken@newham.gov.uk

Computer Management: Mr Geoff Connell, Director of ICT, Newham Dockside, 1000 Dockside Road, Royal Albert Dock, London E16 2QU ☎ 020 8430 2000; 020 8430 4451
geoff.connell@newham.gov.uk; geoff.connell@havering.gov.uk

Consumer Protection and Trading Standards: Ms Shiela Roberts, Operational Manager, Newham Dockside, 1000 Dockside Road, Royal Albert Dock, London E16 2QU ☎ 020 3373 7914
shiela.roberts@newham.gov.uk

Contracts: Mr David Pridmore, Head of Procurement, Newham Dockside, 1000 Dockside Road, Royal Albert Dock, London E16 2QU ☎ 020 8430 2000 david.pridmore@newham.gov.uk

Customer Service: Mr Chris Boylett, Head of Customer

Transactions, Newham Dockside, 1000 Dockside Road, Royal Albert Dock, London E16 2QU ☎ 020 8430 2000 ✉ chris.boylett@newham.gov.uk

Economic Development: Ms Jo Negrini, Director of Strategic Regeneration Planning & Olympic Legacy, Newham Dockside, 1000 Dockside Road, Royal Albert Dock, London E16 2QU ☎ 020 8430 2000 ✉ jo.negrini@newham.gov.uk

Education: Mr Trevor Matthews, Head of Schools Traded Services, Newham Dockside, 1000 Dockside Road, Royal Albert Dock, London E16 2QU ☎ 020 8430 2000 ✉ trevor.matthews@newham.gov.uk

E-Government: Mr Barry Ray, Head of Committees & Partnerships, Newham Dockside, 1000 Dockside Road, Royal Albert Dock, London E16 2QU ☎ 020 8430 2000 ✉ barry.ray@newham.gov.uk

Electoral Registration: Mr Paul Libreri, Head of Registration & Electoral Services, East Ham Town Hall, 324 Barking Road, London E6 2RP ☎ 020 8430 2000 ✉ paul.libreri@newham.gov.uk

Emergency Planning: Mr Russel Bryan, Operations Manager, Newham Dockside, 1000 Dockside Road, Royal Albert Dock, London E16 2QU ☎ 020 8430 2000 ✉ russel.bryan@newham.gov.uk

Emergency Planning: Mr Jason Dear, Resilience Manager, Newham Dockside, 1000 Dockside Road, Royal Albert Dock, London E16 2QU ☎ 020 8430 2000 ✉ jason.dear@newham.gov.uk

Energy Management: Mr Bernie Carney, Mechanical Service Manager, Newham Dockside, 1000 Dockside Road, Royal Albert Dock, London E16 2QU ☎ 020 8430 2000 ✉ bernie.carney@newham.gov.uk

Environmental / Technical Services: Ms Jackie Belton, Executive Director of Operations, Newham Dockside, 1000 Dockside Road, Royal Albert Dock, London E16 2QU ☎ 020 8430 2000 ✉ jackie.belton@newham.gov.uk

Environmental Health: Mr Russel Bryan, Operations Manager, Newham Dockside, 1000 Dockside Road, Royal Albert Dock, London E16 2QU ☎ 020 8430 2000 ✉ russel.bryan@newham.gov.uk

Environmental Health: Ms Shiela Roberts, Operational Manager, Newham Dockside, 1000 Dockside Road, Royal Albert Dock, London E16 2QU ☎ 020 3373 7914 ✉ shiela.roberts@newham.gov.uk

Estates, Property & Valuation: Mr Michael Flanagan, Director of Business Systems, Property & Commercial Development, Newham Dockside, 1000 Dockside Road, Royal Albert Dock, London E16 2QU ☎ 020 8430 2000 ✉ michael.flanagan@newham.gov.uk

European Liaison: Ms Emma Lindsell, External Funding Team Leader, Newham Dockside, 1000 Dockside Road, Royal Albert Dock, London E16 2QU ☎ 020 8430 2000 ✉ emma.lindsell@newham.gov.uk

Events Manager: Mrs Sue Miners, Head of Events & Sponsorship, Newham Dockside, 1000 Dockside Road, Royal Albert Dock, London E16 2QU ☎ 020 8430 2000 ✉ sue.miners@newham.gov.uk

Facilities: Mr Liam Keaveney, Head of Facilities Management, Newham Dockside, 1000 Dockside Road, Royal Albert Dock, London E16 2QU ☎ 020 8430 2000 ✉ liam.keaveney@newham.gov.uk

Finance and Treasurer: Mrs Deborah Hindson, Director of Corporate Finance, Newham Dockside, 1000 Dockside Road, Royal Albert Dock, London E16 2QU ☎ 020 8430 2000 ✉ deborah.hindson@newham.gov.uk

Finance and Treasurer: Mrs Vera White, Exchequer Services Manager, Newham Dockside, 1000 Dockside Road, Royal Albert Dock, London E16 2QU ☎ 020 8430 2000 ✉ vera.white@newham.gov.uk

Fleet Management: Mr Tony Silk, Fleet Management Officer, Central Depot Folkestone Road, London E6 4BX ☎ 020 8430 2000 ✉ tony.silk@newham.gov.uk

Grounds Maintenance: Mr Peter Gay, Head of Greenspace, Newham Dockside, 1000 Dockside Road, Royal Albert Dock, London E16 2QU ☎ 020 3373 1996 ✉ peter.gay@newham.gov.uk

Health and Safety: Mr Garry Fisher, Assistant Head of HR (Health & Safety), Newham Dockside, 1000 Dockside Road, Royal Albert Dock, London E16 2QU ☎ 020 8430 2000 ✉ garry.fisher@newham.gov.uk

Highways: Mr Steve Moore, Director of Environmental Services, Newham Dockside, 1000 Dockside Road, Royal Albert Dock, London E16 2QU ☎ 020 8430 2000 ✉ steve.moore@newham.gov.uk

Home Energy Conservation: Mrs Catherine Illingworth, Head of Property Services, Bridge House, 320 High Street North, London E15 1EP ☎ 020 8430 2000 ✉ catherine.illingworth@newham.gov.uk

Housing: Mr John East, Director of Community Infrastructure, Newham Dockside, 1000 Dockside Road, Royal Albert Dock, London E16 2QU ☎ 020 8430 2000 ✉ john.east@newham.gov.uk

Housing Maintenance: Mr John East, Director of Community Infrastructure, Newham Dockside, 1000 Dockside Road, Royal Albert Dock, London E16 2QU ☎ 020 8430 2000 ✉ john.east@newham.gov.uk

Local Area Agreement: Mr David Hodgkins, Head of Strategy, Newham Dockside, 1000 Dockside Road, Royal Albert Dock, London E16 2QU ☎ 020 8430 2000 ✉ david.hodgkins@newham.gov.uk

Legal: Ms Helen Sidwell, Director of Legal, People & Change, Newham Dockside, 1000 Dockside Road, Royal Albert Dock, London E16 2QU ☎ 020 8430 2000 ✉ helen.sidwell@newham.gov.uk

Leisure and Cultural Services: Mr Grant Aitken, Managing

Director - Transition for Newham Leisure Cultural Enterprise (FT), Newham Dockside, 1000 Dockside Road, Royal Albert Dock, London E16 2QU ☎ 020 8430 2000 ✉ grant.aitken@newham.gov.uk

Licensing: Ms Shiela Roberts, Operational Manager, Newham Dockside, 1000 Dockside Road, Royal Albert Dock, London E16 2QU ☎ 020 3373 7914 ✉ shiela.roberts@newham.gov.uk

Lifelong Learning: Mr Steve Cameron, Head of Employability & Skills, Connexions, 51 Broadway, London E15 4BQ ☎ 020 8430 2000 ✉ steve.cameron@newham.gov.uk

Lighting: Mr Jaspal Sehmi, Head of Asset Maintenance, Newham Dockside, 1000 Dockside Road, Royal Albert Dock, London E16 2QU ☎ 020 8430 2000 ✉ jaspal.sehmi@newham.gov.uk

Lottery Funding, Charity and Voluntary: Mr David Hodgkins, Head of Strategy, Newham Dockside, 1000 Dockside Road, Royal Albert Dock, London E16 2QU ☎ 020 8430 2000 ✉ david.hodgkins@newham.gov.uk

Member Services: Mr Barry Ray, Head of Committees & Partnerships, Newham Dockside, 1000 Dockside Road, Royal Albert Dock, London E16 2QU ☎ 020 8430 2000 ✉ barry.ray@newham.gov.uk

Parking: Mr Laurence Courtney, Head of Parking, Newham Dockside, 1000 Dockside Road, Royal Albert Dock, London E16 2QU ☎ 020 8430 2000 ✉ laurence.courtney@newham.gov.uk

Partnerships: Mr David Hodgkins, Head of Strategy, Newham Dockside, 1000 Dockside Road, Royal Albert Dock, London E16 2QU ☎ 020 8430 2000 ✉ david.hodgkins@newham.gov.uk

Personnel / HR: Mr Steve Whitehead, Deputy Divisional Director of Human Resources, Newham Dockside, 1000 Dockside Road, Royal Albert Dock, London E16 2QU ☎ 020 8430 2000 ✉ steve.whitehead@newham.gov.uk

Personnel / HR: Ms Beverley Williams, Deputy Divisional Director of Human Resources, Newham Dockside, 1000 Dockside Road, Royal Albert Dock, London E16 2QU ☎ 020 8430 2000 ✉ beverley.williams@newham.gov.uk

Planning: Ms Jo Negrini, Director of Strategic Regeneration Planning & Olympic Legacy, Newham Dockside, 1000 Dockside Road, Royal Albert Dock, London E16 2QU ☎ 020 8430 2000 ✉ jo.negrini@newham.gov.uk

Procurement: Mr David Pridmore, Head of Procurement, Newham Dockside, 1000 Dockside Road, Royal Albert Dock, London E16 2QU ☎ 020 8430 2000 ✉ david.pridmore@newham.gov.uk

Public Libraries: Mrs Alexis Wainwright, Customer Services Support Manager, Newham Dockside, 1000 Dockside Road, Royal Albert Dock, London E16 2QU ☎ 020 8430 2000 ✉ alexis.wainwright@newham.gov.uk

Recycling & Waste Minimisation: Mr Steve Moore, Director of Environmental Services, Newham Dockside, 1000 Dockside Road, Royal Albert Dock, London E16 2QU ☎ 020 8430 2000 ✉ steve.moore@newham.gov.uk

Regeneration: Mr Clive Dutton, Executive Director of Regeneration & Inward Investment, Newham Dockside, 1000 Dockside Road, Royal Albert Dock, London E16 2QU ☎ 020 8430 2000 ✉ clive.dutton@newham.gov.uk

Regeneration: Ms Jo Negrini, Director of Strategic Regeneration Planning & Olympic Legacy, Newham Dockside, 1000 Dockside Road, Royal Albert Dock, London E16 2QU ☎ 020 8430 2000 ✉ jo.negrini@newham.gov.uk

Road Safety: Mr John Bidden, Head of Traffic & Transportation, Newham Dockside, 1000 Dockside Road, Royal Albert Dock, London E16 2QU ☎ 020 8430 2000 ✉ john.biden@newham.gov.uk

Social Services (Adult): Miss Grainne Siggins, Director of Adult Social Care, Newham Dockside, 1000 Dockside Road, Royal Albert Dock, London E16 2QU ✉ grainne.siggins@newham.gov.uk

Social Services (Children): Mrs Vivien Lines, Director of Children's Social Care & Safeguarding, Newham Dockside, 1000 Dockside Road, Royal Albert Dock, London E16 2QU ☎ 020 8430 2000 ✉ vivien.lines@newham.gov.uk

Staff Training: Mr Steve Whitehead, Deputy Divisional Director of Human Resources, Newham Dockside, 1000 Dockside Road, Royal Albert Dock, London E16 2QU ☎ 020 8430 2000 ✉ steve.whitehead@newham.gov.uk

Staff Training: Ms Beverley Williams, Deputy Divisional Director of Human Resources, Newham Dockside, 1000 Dockside Road, Royal Albert Dock, London E16 2QU ☎ 020 8430 2000 ✉ beverley.williams@newham.gov.uk

Street Scene: Miss Angela Agyei, Service Monitoring Group Leader - Street Scene, Newham Dockside, 1000 Dockside Road, Royal Albert Dock, London E16 2QU ☎ 020 8430 2000 ✉ angela.agyei@newham.gov.uk

Sustainable Communities: Ms Milly Camley, Director of Strategic Commissioning & Partnership Development, Newham Dockside, 1000 Dockside Road, Royal Albert Dock, London E16 2QU ☎ 020 8430 2000 ✉ milly.camley@newham.gov.uk

Town Centre: Ms Jo Negrini, Director of Strategic Regeneration Planning & Olympic Legacy, Newham Dockside, 1000 Dockside Road, Royal Albert Dock, London E16 2QU ☎ 020 8430 2000 ✉ jo.negrini@newham.gov.uk

Traffic Management: Mr John Bidden, Head of Traffic & Transportation, Newham Dockside, 1000 Dockside Road, Royal Albert Dock, London E16 2QU ☎ 020 8430 2000 ✉ john.biden@newham.gov.uk

Transport: Mr John Bidden, Head of Traffic & Transportation, Newham Dockside, 1000 Dockside Road, Royal Albert Dock, London E16 2QU ☎ 020 8430 2000 ✉ john.biden@newham.gov.uk

Transport Planner: Mr Dominic West, Group Leader Transportation, Newham Dockside, 1000 Dockside Road, Royal Albert Dock, London E16 2QU ☎ 020 8430 2000
✉ dominic.west@newham.gov.uk

Waste Collection and Disposal: Mr Jarlath Griffin, Head of Operations, Newham Dockside, 1000 Dockside Road, Royal Albert Dock, London E16 2QU ☎ 020 8430 2000
✉ jarlath.griffin@newham.gov.uk

Waste Management: Mr Steve Moore, Director of Environmental Services, Newham Dockside, 1000 Dockside Road, Royal Albert Dock, London E16 2QU ☎ 020 8430 2000
✉ steve.moore@newham.gov.uk

MEMBERS OF THE COUNCIL (61)

***Directly Elected Mayor:* Wales**, Robin (LAB -)
robin.wales@newham.gov.uk
***Chair:* Singh**, Amarjit (LAB - Manor Park)
amarjit.singh@newham.gov.uk
***Vice-Chair:* Nicholas**, Michael (LAB - Canning Town South)
michael.nicholas@newham.gov.uk
***Deputy Mayor:* Baikie**, Andrew (LAB - Little Ilford)
andrew.baikie@newham.gov.uk
Ahmad, Shama (LAB - Forest Gate North)
shama.ahmad@newham.gov.uk
Alexander, Jose (LAB - East Ham North)
jose.alexander@newham.gov.uk
Bourne, Freda (LAB - West Ham)
freda.bourne@newham.gov.uk
Brayshaw, Stephen (LAB - Royal Docks)
steve.brayshaw@newham.gov.uk
Brickell, Paul (LAB - Forest Gate North)
paul.brickell@newham.gov.uk
Cameron, Leanora (LAB - Forest Gate South)
leanora.cameron@newham.gov.uk
Chadha, Nirmal Kaur (LAB - Green Street East)
nirmal.chadha@newham.gov.uk
Chaudhary, Akbar (LAB - Forest Gate South)
akbar.chaudhary@newham.gov.uk
Chowdhury, Ayesha (LAB - Beckton)
ayesha.chowdhury@newham.gov.uk
Christie, David (LAB - Beckton)
david.christie@newham.gov.uk
Collier, Bryan (LAB - Canning Town South)
bryan.collier@newham.gov.uk
Collier, Marie (LAB - Canning Town North)
marie.collier@newham.gov.uk
Corbett, Ian (LAB - East Ham Central)
ian.corbett@newham.gov.uk
Corbett, Jo (LAB - Boleyn)
jo.corbett@newham.gov.uk
Crawford, Richard (LAB - Stratford and New Town)
richard.crawford@newham.gov.uk
Desai, Unmesh (LAB - East Ham Central)
unmesh.desai@newham.gov.uk
Fiberesima, Charity (LAB - Plaistow South)
charity.fiberesima@newham.gov.uk
Furness, Clive (LAB - Canning Town North)
clive.furness@newham.gov.uk
Gangadharan, Omana (LAB - Wall End)
omana.gangadharan@newham.gov.uk
Gray, John (LAB - West Ham)
john.gray@newham.gov.uk
Griffiths, Alan (LAB - Plaistow North)
alan.griffiths@newham.gov.uk
Holland, Patricia (LAB - Custom House)
patricia.holland@newham.gov.uk
Hudson, Lester (LAB - Wall End)
lester.hudson@newham.gov.uk
Hussain, Forhad (LAB - Plaistow North)
forhad.hussain@newham.gov.uk
Jenkins, Kevin (LAB - East Ham South)
kevin.jenkins@newham.gov.uk
Kazi, Khalil (LAB - Little Ilford)
khalil.kazi@newham.gov.uk
Kellaway, Alec (LAB - Beckton)
alec.kellaway@newham.gov.uk
Laguda, Joy (LAB - Plaistow North)
joy.laguda@newham.gov.uk
Mahmood, Sharaf (LAB - Green Street East)
sharaf.mahmood@newham.gov.uk
Manley, Ron (LAB - West Ham)
ron.manley@newham.gov.uk
McAlmont, Anthony (LAB - Royal Docks)
anthony.mcalmont@newham.gov.uk
McAuley, Conor (LAB - Custom House)
conor.mcauley@newham.gov.uk
McLean, Charlene (LAB - Stratford and New Town)
charlene.mclean@newham.gov.uk
Mirza, Riaz Ahmed (LAB - Boleyn)
riaz.mirza@newham.gov.uk
Murphy, Patrick (LAB - Royal Docks)
patrick.murphy@newham.gov.uk
Nazeer, Farah (LAB - Little Ilford)
farah.nazeer@newham.gov.uk
Nekiwala, Firoza (LAB - East Ham North)
firoza.nekiwala@newham.gov.uk
Patel, Salim (LAB - Manor Park)
salim.patel@newham.gov.uk
Patel, Mukesh (LAB - Green Street West)
mukesh.patel@newham.gov.uk
Paul, Terence (LAB - Stratford and New Town)
terence.paul@newham.gov.uk
Pearson, Gavin (LAB - Custom House)
gavin.pearson@newham.gov.uk
Peppiatt, Quintin (LAB - East Ham South)
quintin.peppiatt@newham.gov.uk
Rahman, Rohima (LAB - Green Street East)
rohima.rahman@newham.gov.uk
Robinson, Ellie (LAB - Forest Gate North)
ellie.robinson@newham.gov.uk
Sathianesan, Paul (LAB - East Ham North)
paul.sathianesan@newham.gov.uk
Schafer, Paul (LAB - Canning Town North)
paul.schafer@newham.gov.uk
Scoresby, Kay (LAB - Manor Park)
kay.scoresby@newham.gov.uk
Shah, Lakmini (LAB - East Ham South)
lakmini.shah@newham.gov.uk
Shillingford, Pearson (LAB - Boleyn)
pearson.shillingford@newham.gov.uk
Skyers, Mary (LAB - East Ham Central)
mary.skyers@newham.gov.uk
Sparrowhawk, Ted (LAB - Wall End)
ted.sparrowhawk@newham.gov.uk
Talati, Rustam (O - Green Street West)
rustam.talati@newham.gov.uk
Taylor, Alan (LAB - Canning Town South)

alan.taylor@newham.gov.uk
Thomas, Sheila (LAB - Plaistow South)
sheila.thomas@newham.gov.uk
Vaughan, Winston (LAB - Forest Gate South)
winston.vaughan@newham.gov.uk
Virdee, Harvinder (LAB - Green Street West)
harvinder.virdee@newham.gov.uk
Wilson, Neil (LAB - Plaistow South)
neil.wilson@newham.gov.uk

POLITICAL COMPOSITION

LAB: 60, O: 1

CABINET

Business & Skills: Mr Alec Kellaway
Children & Young People: Rev Quintin Peppiatt
Community Affairs: Mr Richard Crawford
Crime & Anti-Social Behaviour: Mr Unmesh Desai
Equalities & Social Inclusion: Mr Neil Wilson
Finance, Property & Support Services: Mr Lester Hudson
Games Times & Public Affairs: Mr Paul Brickell
Health & Adults Commissioning: Mr Clive Furness
Housing & Customer Services: Mr Andrew Baikie
Infrastructure & Environment: Mr Ian Corbett
Regeneration & Strategic Planning: Mr Conor McAuley
Safeguarding, Corporate Parenting & Adults' Services: Mr Riaz Ahmed Mirza

COMMITTEE CHAIRS

Audit: Mr Lester Hudson
Children & Young People (Scrutiny): Ms Ellie Robinson
Crime & Disorder (Scrutiny): Mr Terence Paul
Health & Social Care (Scrutiny): Mr Winston Vaughan
Licensing: Mr Ian Corbett
Local Development: Mr Ron Manley
Overview & Scrutiny (Scrutiny): Mr Ted Sparrowhawk
Regeneration & Employment (Scrutiny): Mr Ted Sparrowhawk

NEWPORT CITY W

Newport City Council, Civic Centre, Newport NP20 4UR
☎ 01633 656656 🖷 01633 656611 info@newport.gov.uk
www.newport.gov.uk

FACTS & FIGURES

Police Authority: Gwent Police Authority
Learning and Skills Council: Wales
Parliamentary Constituencies: Newport East , Newport West
EU Constituencies: Wales
Election Frequency: Elections are of whole council
Twinning: Guangxi (China); Heidenheim (Germany); Kutaisi (Georgia)

PRINCIPAL OFFICERS

Chief Executive: Ms Tracey Lee, Managing Director, Civic Centre, Newport NP20 4UR ☎ 01633 232002 🖷 01633 232001 tracey.lee@newport.gov.uk

Assistant Chief Executive: Ms Sheila Davies, Corporate Director - Regeneration & Environment, Civic Centre, Newport NP20 4UR ☎ 01633 656656 🖷 01633 232379 sheila.davies@newport.gov.uk

Assistant Chief Executive: Mr Stewart Greenwell, Corporate Director - Care & Customers, Civic Centre, Newport NP20 4UR ☎ 01633 656656 🖷 01633 232379 stewart.greenwell@newport.gov.uk

Assistant Chief Executive: Ms Debra Wood-Lawson, Interim Corporate Director - Corporate Services, Civic Centre, Newport NP20 4UR ☎ 01633 232020 🖷 01633 232025 debra.wood-lawson@newport.gov.uk

Building Control: Ms Susan Bolter, Head of Regeneration & Regulatory Services, Civic Centre, Newport NP20 4UR ☎ 01633 232504 susan.bolter@newport.gov.uk

Children / Youth Services: Ms Jane Lavelle, Youth & Community Manager, Rivermead Centre, Fuscia Way, Rogerstone, Newport NP10 9LZ ☎ 01633 414650 jane.lavelle@newport.gov.uk

Civil Registration: Ms Shan Jenkins, Registration Services Manager, Register Office, The Mansion House, 4 Stow Park Circle, Newport NP20 4HE ☎ 01633 414770

PR / Communications: Mr Jonathan Hollins, Communications & Marketing Manager, Civic Centre, Newport NP20 4UR ☎ 01633 232887 jonathan.hollins@newport.gov.uk

Community Safety: Ms Helen Wilkie, Public Protection Manager, Civic Centre, Newport NP20 4UR ☎ 01633 232805 helen.wilkie@newport.gov.uk

Computer Management: Mr Mark Neilson, Head of Customer & Information Services, Civic Centre, Newport NP20 4UR ☎ 01633 851563 mark.neilson@newport.gov.uk

Consumer Protection and Trading Standards: Ms Helen Wilkie, Public Protection Manager, Civic Centre, Newport NP20 4UR ☎ 01633 232805 helen.wilkie@newport.gov.uk

Customer Service: Mr Kit Wilson, Customer Services Manager, Civic Centre, Newport NP20 4UR ☎ 01633 851560 kit.wilson@newport.gov.uk

Economic Development: Ms Susan Bolter, Head of Regeneration & Regulatory Services, Civic Centre, Newport NP20 4UR ☎ 01633 232504 susan.bolter@newport.gov.uk

Education: Dr Brett Pugh, Chief Education Officer, Civic Centre, Newport NP20 4UR ☎ 01633 232257 brett.pugh@newport.gov.uk

E-Government: Mr Mark Neilson, Head of Customer & Information Services, Civic Centre, Newport NP20 4UR ☎ 01633 851563 mark.neilson@newport.gov.uk

Electoral Registration: Mr Phillip Johnson, Electoral Registration Manager, Civic Centre, Newport NP20 4UR ☎ 01633 232007 phillip.johnson@newport.gov.uk

Emergency Planning: Mr Alan Young, Civil Contingencies Manager, Civic Centre, Newport NP20 4UR ☎ 01633 414513 alan.young@newport.gov.uk

Energy Management: Mr Carl Touhig, Sustainability Manager, Civic Centre, Newport NP20 4UR ☎ 01633 232452 ✉ carl.touhig@newport.gov.uk

Environmental Health: Ms Helen Wilkie, Public Protection Manager, Civic Centre, Newport NP20 4UR ☎ 01633 232805 ✉ helen.wilkie@newport.gov.uk

Estates, Property & Valuation: Mr Don Waters, Corporate Property Officer, Civic Centre, Newport NP20 4UR ☎ 01633 232600 ✉ don.waters@newport.gov.uk

European Liaison: Ms Sarah Armstrong, European Officer, Civic Centre, Newport NP20 4UR ☎ 01633 233285 ✉ sarah.armstrong@newport.gov.uk

Events Manager: Mr Jonathan Hollins, Communications & Marketing Manager, Civic Centre, Newport NP20 4UR ☎ 01633 232887 ✉ jonathan.hollins@newport.gov.uk

Finance and Treasurer: Mr Chris Barton, Head of Finance, Civic Centre, Newport NP20 4UR ☎ 01633 232205 ✉ chris.barton@newport.gov.uk

Grounds Maintenance: Mr Andrew Morris, Head of Streetscene, Civic Centre, Newport NP20 4UR ☎ 01633 232692 ✉ andrew.morris@newport.gov.uk

Health and Safety: Ms Debra Wood-Lawson, Interim Corporate Director - Corporate Services, Civic Centre, Newport NP20 4UR ☎ 01633 232020 🖷 01633 232025 ✉ debra.wood-lawson@newport.gov.uk

Highways: Mr Andrew Morris, Head of Streetscene, Civic Centre, Newport NP20 4UR ☎ 01633 232692 ✉ andrew.morris@newport.gov.uk

Housing: Mr Mike Jones, Housing & Community Regeneration Manager, Civic Centre, Newport NP20 4UR ☎ 01633 232494 ✉ mike.jones@newport.gov.uk

Legal: Mr Gareth Price, Head of Law & Standards, Civic Centre, Newport NP20 4UR ☎ 01633 232123 🖷 01633 244721 ✉ gareth.price@newport.gov.uk

Leisure and Cultural Services: Ms Ffion Lloyd, Head of Continuing Learning & Leisure, Civic Centre, Newport NP20 4UR ☎ 01633 233342 🖷 01633 232808 ✉ ffion.lloyd@newport.gov.uk

Licensing: Ms Helen Wilkie, Public Protection Manager, Civic Centre, Newport NP20 4UR ☎ 01633 232805 ✉ helen.wilkie@newport.gov.uk

Lifelong Learning: Ms Ffion Lloyd, Head of Continuing Learning & Leisure, Civic Centre, Newport NP20 4UR ☎ 01633 233342 🖷 01633 232808 ✉ ffion.lloyd@newport.gov.uk

Lighting: Mr Andrew Morris, Head of Streetscene, Civic Centre, Newport NP20 4UR ☎ 01633 232692 ✉ andrew.morris@newport.gov.uk

Member Services: Mr Richard Jefferies, Chief Democratic Services Officer, Civic Centre, Newport NP20 4UR ☎ 01633 232381 🖷 01633 233462 ✉ richard.jefferies@newport.gov.uk

Personnel / HR: Ms Debra Wood-Lawson, Interim Corporate Director - Corporate Services, Civic Centre, Newport NP20 4UR ☎ 01633 232020 🖷 01633 232025 ✉ debra.wood-lawson@newport.gov.uk

Planning: Mr Mark Hand, Development Services Manager, Civic Centre, Newport NP20 4UR ☎ 01633 232506 ✉ mark.hand@newport.gov.uk

Procurement: Ms Sheila Powell, Strategic Procurement Officer, Civic Centre, Newport NP20 4UR ☎ 01633 232216 ✉ sheila.powell@newport.gov.uk

Public Libraries: Ms Gill John, Community Learning & Libraries Manager, Central Library, John Frost Square, Newport NP20 1PA ☎ 01633 414706 🖷 01633 222615 ✉ gill.john@newport.gov.uk

Recycling & Waste Minimisation: Ms Susan Bolter, Head of Regeneration & Regulatory Services, Civic Centre, Newport NP20 4UR ☎ 01633 232504 ✉ susan.bolter@newport.gov.uk

Regeneration: Mr Andy Evans, Head of Regeneration & Regulatory Services, Civic Centre, Newport NP20 4UR ☎ 01633 232504 🖷 01633 232496 ✉ andy.evans@newport.gov.uk

Social Services: Mr Stewart Greenwell, Corporate Director - Care & Customers, Civic Centre, Newport NP20 4UR ☎ 01633 656656 🖷 01633 232379 ✉ stewart.greenwell@newport.gov.uk

Social Services (Adult): Mr Robert Sainsbury, Head of Integrated Services - Social Care & Health, Civic Centre, Newport NP20 4UR ☎ 01633 233447 ✉ robert.sainsbury@newport.gov.uk

Social Services (Children): Mr Mike Nicholson, Head of Children & Family Services, Civic Centre, Newport NP20 4UR ☎ 01633 233297 ✉ mike.nicholson@newport.gov.uk

Staff Training: Ms Debra Wood-Lawson, Interim Corporate Director - Corporate Services, Civic Centre, Newport NP20 4UR ☎ 01633 232020 🖷 01633 232025 ✉ debra.wood-lawson@newport.gov.uk

Street Scene: Mr Andrew Morris, Head of Streetscene, Civic Centre, Newport NP20 4UR ☎ 01633 232692 ✉ andrew.morris@newport.gov.uk

Sustainable Development: Mr Carl Touhig, Sustainability Manager, Civic Centre, Newport NP20 4UR ☎ 01633 232452 ✉ carl.touhig@newport.gov.uk

Tourism: Ms Lynne Richards, Tourism Officer, Civic Centre, Newport NP20 4UR ☎ 01633 233327 ✉ lynne.richards@newport.gov.uk

Waste Collection and Disposal: Mr Malcolm Lane, Environment Manager, Civic Centre, Newport NP20 4UR ☎ 01633 232709 ✉ malcolm.lane@newport.gov.uk

Waste Management: Mr Malcolm Lane, Environment Manager,

Civic Centre, Newport NP20 4UR ☎ 01633 232709
malcolm.lane@newport.gov.uk

MEMBERS OF THE COUNCIL (50)

***Mayor:* Guy**, John (LAB - Alway)
john.guy@newport.gov.uk
***Deputy Mayor:* Suller**, Cliff (LAB - Caerleon)
cliff.suller@newport.gov.uk
***Leader of the Council:* Bright**, Bob (LAB - Ringland)
bob.bright@newport.gov.uk
***Deputy Leader of the Council:* Truman**, Ray (LAB - Alway)
ray.truman@newport.gov.uk
Al-Nuaimi, Miqdad (LAB - Stow Hill)
miqdad.al-nuaimi@newport.gov.uk
Atwell, David (CON - Langstone)
david.atwell@newport.gov.uk
Bond, Tom (LAB - Rogerstone)
tom.bond@newport.gov.uk
Cockeram, Paul (LAB - Shaftesbury)
paul.cokeram@newport.gov.uk
Cornelious, Margaret (CON - Graig)
margaret.cornelious@newport.gov.uk
Corten, Emma (LAB - Ringland)
emma.corten@newport.gov.uk
Critchley, Ken (LAB - Liswerry)
ken.critchley@newport.gov.uk
Davies, Deb (LAB - Beechwood)
deb.davies@newport.gov.uk
Delahaye, Val (LAB - Bettws)
valerie.delahaye@newport.gov.uk
Evans, Matthew (CON - Allt-yr-yn)
matthew.evans@newport.gov.uk
Evans, Chris (LAB - Rogerstone)
chris.evans@newport.gov.uk
Ferris, Charles (CON - Allt-yr-yn)
charles.ferris@newport.gov.uk
Fouweather, David (CON - Allt-yr-yn)
david.fouweather@newport.gov.uk
Garland, Emma (LAB - St. Julians)
emma.garland@newport.gov.uk
Giles, Gail (LAB - Caerleon)
gail.giles@newport.gov.uk
Hannon, Paul (LAB - Beechwood)
paul.hannon@newport.gov.uk
Harvey, Debbie (LAB - Alway)
debbie.harvey@newport.gov.uk
Hayat, Ibrahim (LAB - Pillgwenlly)
ibrahim.hayat@newport.gov.uk
Huntley, Paul (LAB - Caerleon)
paul.huntley@newport.gov.uk
Hutchings, Rhys (LAB - St. Julians)
rhys.hutchings@newport.gov.uk
Jeavons, Roger (LAB - Liswerry)
roger.jeavons@newport.gov.uk
Jenkins, Christine (LAB - Victoria)
christine.jenkins@newport.gov.uk
Jones, Ron (LAB - Pillgwenlly)
ron.jones@newport.gov.uk
Kellaway, Martyn (CON - Llanwern)
martyn.kellaway@newport.gov.uk
Linton, Malcolm (LAB - Ringland)
malcolm.linton@newport.gov.uk
Maxfield, Christine (LAB - Malpas)
christine.maxfield@newport.gov.uk
Mayer, David (LAB - Malpas)
david.mayer@newport.gov.uk
Mlewa, Sally (LAB - Rogerstone)
sally.mlewa@newport.gov.uk
Mogford, Ray (CON - Langstone)
ray.mogford@newport.gov.uk
Morris, Allan (LAB - Liswerry)
allan.morris@newport.gov.uk
Mudd, Jane (LAB - Malpas)
jane.mudd@newport.gov.uk
Poole, Bob (LAB - Shaftesbury)
bob.poole@newport.gov.uk
Rahman, Majid (LAB - Victoria)
majid.rahman@newport.gov.uk
Richards, John (LAB - Liswerry)
john.richards@newport.gov.uk
Spencer, Mark (LAB - Beechwood)
mark.spencer@newport.gov.uk
Suller, Tom (CON - Marshfield)
tom.suller@newport.gov.uk
Thomas, Kate (LAB - Stow Hill)
kate.thomas@newport.gov.uk
Thomas, Herbert (LAB - Gaer)
herbert.thomas@newport.gov.uk
Townsend, Ed (LD - St. Julians)
ed.townsend@newport.gov.uk
Trigg, Noel (IND - Bettws)
noel.trigg@newport.gov.uk
Watkins, Trevor (LAB - Tredegar Park)
trevor.watkins@newport.gov.uk
Whitcutt, Mark (LAB - Gaer)
mark.whitcutt@newport.gov.uk
White, Richard (CON - Marshfield)
richard.white@newport.gov.uk
Whitehead, Kevin (IND - Bettws)
kevin.whitehead@newport.gov.uk
Wilcox, Deborah (LAB - Gaer)
debbie.wilcox@newport.gov.uk
Williams, David (CON - Graig)
david.williams@newport.gov.uk

POLITICAL COMPOSITION

LAB: 37, CON: 10, IND: 2, LD: 1

CABINET

Leader: Mr Bob Bright
Deputy Leader: Mr Ray Truman
Education & Young People: Mr Bob Poole
Human Resources & Assets: Mr Mark Whitcutt
Infrastructure: Mr Ken Critchley
Leisure & Culture: Ms Deborah Wilcox
Licensing & Statutory Functions: Ms Gail Giles
Regeneration & Development: Mr John Richards
Skills & Work: Ms Deb Davies
Social Care & Wellbeing: Mr Paul Cockeram

COMMITTEE CHAIRS

Community Planning & Development Scrutiny: Mr David Atwell
Democratic Services: Mr Charles Ferris
Learning, Caring & Leisure: Mr David Mayer
Licensing: Mr Allan Morris
Planning: Mr Ron Jones
Street Scene, Regeneration & Scrutiny: Mr Roger Jeavons

NEWRY & MOURNE N

Newry & Mourne District Council, (Comhairle an Iúir Agus Mhúrn), O'Hagan House, Monaghan Row, Newry BT35 8DL
☎ 028 3031 3031 🖷 028 3031 3077
✉ administration@newryandmourne.gov.uk
💻 www.newryandmourne.gov.uk

FACTS & FIGURES

Police Authority: Northern Ireland Policing Board
Health Authority: Southern Health & Social Care Board
Learning and Skills Council: Northern Ireland
Parliamentary Constituencies: Down South, Newry and Armagh
EU Constituencies: Northern Ireland
Election Frequency: Elections are of whole council

PRINCIPAL OFFICERS

Chief Executive: Mr Tom McCall, Clerk & Chief Executive, O'Hagan House, Monaghan Row, Newry BT35 8DL ☎ 028 3031 3031 🖷 028 3031 3077 ✉ tom.mccall@newryandmourne.gov.uk

Senior Management: Mr Edwin Curtis, Director - Administration, O'Hagan House, Monaghan Row, Newry BT35 8DL ☎ 028 3031 3031 🖷 028 3031 3077

Senior Management: Mr Robert Dowey, Director - Finance, O'Hagan House, Monaghan Row, Newry BT35 8DJ ☎ 028 3031 3031 🖷 028 3031 3077

Senior Management: Mr John Farrell, Director - Environmental Health & Building Services, District Council Offices, Monaghan Row, Newry BT35 8DJ ☎ 028 3031 3031

Senior Management: Mr Gerard McGivern, Director - District Development, Haughey House, Rampart Road, Greenbank Industrial Estate, Newry BT34 2QU ☎ 028 3031 3233

Access Officer / Social Services (Disability): Mrs Ciara Lowe, Disability Liaison Officer, Sports Centre, Patrick Street, Newry BT35 8TR ☎ 028 3025 6428 🖷 028 3025 1718

Architect, Building / Property Services: Mr David Shanks, Assistant Director - Environmental Health & Building Services, O'Hagan House, Monghan Row, Newry BT35 8DJ ☎ 028 3031 3000 🖷 028 3031 3020 ✉ david.shanks@newryandmourne.gov.uk

Best Value: Mrs Regina Mackin, Assistant Director - Administration Equality, O'Hagan House, Monaghan Row, Newry BT35 8DJ ☎ 028 3031 3095 🖷 028 3031 3077
✉ regina.mackin@newryandmourne.gov.uk

Building Control: Mr David Shanks, Assistant Director - Environmental Health & Building Services, O'Hagan House, Monghan Row, Newry BT35 8DJ ☎ 028 3031 3000 🖷 028 3031 3020 ✉ david.shanks@newryandmourne.gov.uk

Civil Registration: Mrs Carmel McKenna, Assistant Director - Administration General Services, O'Hagan House, Monaghan Row, Newry BT35 8DL ☎ 028 3031 3031
✉ carmel.mckenna@newryandmourne.gov.uk

PR / Communications: Mrs Regina Mackin, Assistant Director - Administration Equality, O'Hagan House, Monaghan Row, Newry BT35 8DJ ☎ 028 3031 3095 🖷 028 3031 3077
✉ regina.mackin@newryandmourne.gov.uk

Community Safety: Mrs Heather McKee, Community Safety Officer, O'Hagan House, Monaghan Row, Newry BT35 8DL ☎ 028 3031 3073 🖷 028 3031 3077
✉ heather.mckee@newryandmourne.gov.uk

Computer Management: Mr Seamus McGivern, Assistant Director - Finance, Information Technology & Purchasing, O'Hagan House, Monaghan Row, Newry BT35 8DJ ☎ 028 3031 3146 🖷 028 3031 3077
✉ seamus.mcgivern@newryandmourne.gov.uk

Consumer Protection and Trading Standards: Mr John Farrell, Director - Environmental Health & Building Services, District Council Offices, Monaghan Row, Newry BT35 8DJ ☎ 028 3031 3031

Contracts: Mr Jim McCorry, Director - Technical & Leisure Services, Haughey House, Rampart Road, Greenbank Industrial Estate, Newry BT34 2QU ☎ 028 3031 3233 🖷 028 3031 3299

Corporate Services: Mr Tom McCall, Clerk & Chief Executive, O'Hagan House, Monaghan Row, Newry BT35 8DL ☎ 028 3031 3031 🖷 028 3031 3077 ✉ tom.mccall@newryandmourne.gov.uk

Customer Service: Mrs Regina Mackin, Assistant Director - Administration Equality, O'Hagan House, Monaghan Row, Newry BT35 8DJ ☎ 028 3031 3095 🖷 028 3031 3077
✉ regina.mackin@newryandmourne.gov.uk

Economic Development: Mr Jonathan McGilly, Assistant Director - District Development & Economic Regeneration, Haughey House, Rampart Road, Greenbank Industrial Estate, Newry BT34 2QU ☎ 028 3031 3233 🖷 028 3031 3299
✉ jonathan.mcgilly@newryandmourne.gov.uk

E-Government: Mr Robert Dowey, Director - Finance, O'Hagan House, Monaghan Row, Newry BT35 8DJ ☎ 028 3031 3031
🖷 028 3031 3077

Electoral Registration: Mr Tom McCall, Clerk & Chief Executive, O'Hagan House, Monaghan Row, Newry BT35 8DL ☎ 028 3031 3031 🖷 028 3031 3077 ✉ tom.mccall@newryandmourne.gov.uk

Emergency Planning: Mr Tom McCall, Clerk & Chief Executive, O'Hagan House, Monaghan Row, Newry BT35 8DL ☎ 028 3031 3031 🖷 028 3031 3077 ✉ tom.mccall@newryandmourne.gov.uk

Energy Management: Mr John Farrell, Director - Environmental Health & Building Services, District Council Offices, Monaghan Row, Newry BT35 8DJ ☎ 028 3031 3031

Energy Management: Mr David Shanks, Assistant Director - Environmental Health & Building Services, O'Hagan House, Monghan Row, Newry BT35 8DJ ☎ 028 3031 3000 🖷 028 3031 3020 ✉ david.shanks@newryandmourne.gov.uk

Environmental / Technical Services: Mr John Farrell, Director - Environmental Health & Building Services, District Council

Offices, Monaghan Row, Newry BT35 8DJ ☎ 028 3031 3031

Environmental Health: Mr John Farrell, Director - Environmental Health & Building Services, District Council Offices, Monaghan Row, Newry BT35 8DJ ☎ 028 3031 3031

Estates, Property & Valuation: Mr Robert Dowey, Director - Finance, O'Hagan House, Monaghan Row, Newry BT35 8DJ ☎ 028 3031 3031 🖷 028 3031 3077

European Liaison: Mr Jonathan McGilly, Assistant Director - District Development & Economic Regeneration, Haughey House, Rampart Road, Greenbank Industrial Estate, Newry BT34 2QU ☎ 028 3031 3233 🖷 028 3031 3299 ✉ jonathan.mcgilly@newryandmourne.gov.uk

Events Manager: Mrs Regina Mackin, Assistant Director - Administration Equality, O'Hagan House, Monaghan Row, Newry BT35 8DJ ☎ 028 3031 3095 🖷 028 3031 3077 ✉ regina.mackin@newryandmourne.gov.uk

Finance and Treasurer: Mr Robert Dowey, Director - Finance, O'Hagan House, Monaghan Row, Newry BT35 8DJ ☎ 028 3031 3031 🖷 028 3031 3077

Fleet Management: Mr Jim McCorry, Director - Technical & Leisure Services, Haughey House, Rampart Road, Greenbank Industrial Estate, Newry BT34 2QU ☎ 028 3031 3233 🖷 028 3031 3299

Grounds Maintenance: Mr Jim McCorry, Director - Technical & Leisure Services, Haughey House, Rampart Road, Greenbank Industrial Estate, Newry BT34 2QU ☎ 028 3031 3233 🖷 028 3031 3299

Health and Safety: Mr Ian Sands, Health & Safety Officer, O'Hagan House, Monaghan Row, Newry BT35 8DL ☎ 028 3031 3082 🖷 028 3031 3098 ✉ ian.sands@newryandmourne.gov.uk

Home Energy Conservation: Mr John Farrell, Director - Environmental Health & Building Services, District Council Offices, Monaghan Row, Newry BT35 8DJ ☎ 028 3031 3031

Leisure and Cultural Services: Mr Jim McCorry, Director - Technical & Leisure Services, Haughey House, Rampart Road, Greenbank Industrial Estate, Newry BT34 2QU ☎ 028 3031 3233 🖷 028 3031 3299

Licensing: Mr David Shanks, Assistant Director - Environmental Health & Building Services, O'Hagan House, Monghan Row, Newry BT35 8DJ ☎ 028 3031 3000 🖷 028 3031 3020 ✉ david.shanks@newryandmourne.gov.uk

Lottery Funding, Charity and Voluntary: Mr Jonathan McGilly, Assistant Director - District Development & Economic Regeneration, Haughey House, Rampart Road, Greenbank Industrial Estate, Newry BT34 2QU ☎ 028 3031 3233 🖷 028 3031 3299 ✉ jonathan.mcgilly@newryandmourne.gov.uk

Member Services: Mr Edwin Curtis, Director - Administration, O'Hagan House, Monaghan Row, Newry BT35 8DL ☎ 028 3031 3031 🖷 028 3031 3077

Partnerships: Mr Tom McCall, Clerk & Chief Executive, O'Hagan House, Monaghan Row, Newry BT35 8DL ☎ 028 3031 3031 🖷 028 3031 3077 ✉ tom.mccall@newryandmourne.gov.uk

Personnel / HR: Mr Edwin Curtis, Director - Administration, O'Hagan House, Monaghan Row, Newry BT35 8DL ☎ 028 3031 3031 🖷 028 3031 3077

Procurement: Mr David Barter, Purchasing Officer, District Council Offices, Unit 19, Rampart Road, Greenbank Industrial Estate, Newry BT34 2QU ☎ 028 3031 3233 🖷 028 3031 3299 ✉ david.barter@newryandmourne.gov.uk

Recycling & Waste Minimisation: Mr Jim McCorry, Director - Technical & Leisure Services, Haughey House, Rampart Road, Greenbank Industrial Estate, Newry BT34 2QU ☎ 028 3031 3233 🖷 028 3031 3299

Regeneration: Mr Jonathan McGilly, Assistant Director - District Development & Economic Regeneration, Haughey House, Rampart Road, Greenbank Industrial Estate, Newry BT34 2QU ☎ 028 3031 3233 🖷 028 3031 3299 ✉ jonathan.mcgilly@newryandmourne.gov.uk

Staff Training: Mr Edwin Curtis, Director - Administration, O'Hagan House, Monaghan Row, Newry BT35 8DL ☎ 028 3031 3031 🖷 028 3031 3077

Sustainable Development: Mr Patrick McShane, Environmental Co-ordinator, O'Hagan House, Monaghan Row, Newry BT35 8DJ ☎ 028 3031 3100 🖷 028 3036 4482

Tourism: Mr Gerard McGivern, Director - District Development, Haughey House, Rampart Road, Greenbank Industrial Estate, Newry BT34 2QU ☎ 028 3031 3233

Transport: Mr Jim McCorry, Director - Technical & Leisure Services, Haughey House, Rampart Road, Greenbank Industrial Estate, Newry BT34 2QU ☎ 028 3031 3233 🖷 028 3031 3299

Transport Planner: Mr Jim McCorry, Director - Technical & Leisure Services, Haughey House, Rampart Road, Greenbank Industrial Estate, Newry BT34 2QU ☎ 028 3031 3233 🖷 028 3031 3299

Waste Collection and Disposal: Mr Jim McCorry, Director - Technical & Leisure Services, Haughey House, Rampart Road, Greenbank Industrial Estate, Newry BT34 2QU ☎ 028 3031 3233 🖷 028 3031 3299

Waste Management: Mr Jim McCorry, Director - Technical & Leisure Services, Haughey House, Rampart Road, Greenbank Industrial Estate, Newry BT34 2QU ☎ 028 3031 3233 🖷 028 3031 3299

MEMBERS OF THE COUNCIL (30)

***Mayor:* McArdle**, John (SDLP - Newry Town)
john.mcardle@newryandmourne.gov.uk

***Deputy Mayor:* McDonald**, Patrick (SF - Slieve Gullion)
patrick.mcdonald@newryandmourne.gov.uk

Burns, Colman (SF - Slieve Gullion)
colman.burns@newryandmourne.gov.uk

Burns, William (DUP - The Mournes)
william.burns@newryandmourne.gov.uk
Carr, Michael (SDLP - Crotlieve)
michael.carr@newryandmourne.gov.uk
Casey, Charlie (SF - Newry Town)
charlie.casey@newryandmourne.gov.uk
Curran, Brendan (SF - Newry Town)
brendan.curran@newryandmourne.gov.uk
Donnelly, Geraldine (SDLP - Slieve Gullion)
geraldine.donnelly@newryandmourne.gov.uk
Doran, Sean (SF - The Mournes)
sean.doran@newryandmourne.gov.uk
Feehan, John (SDLP - Fews)
john.feehan@newryandmourne.gov.uk
Feely, Frank (SDLP - Newry Town)
frank.feely@newryandmourne.gov.uk
Flynn, A (SF - Slieve Gullion)
Harte, Valerie (SF - Newry Town)
valerie.harte@newryandmourne.gov.uk
Hearty, Terry (SF - Slieve Gullion)
terry.hearty@newryandmourne.gov.uk
Hyland, David (IND - Newry Town)
david.hyland@newryandmourne.gov.uk
Kearney, Peter (SF - Crotlieve)
peter.kearney@newryandmourne.gov.uk
McAteer, Declan (SDLP - Crotlieve)
declan.mcateer@newryandmourne.gov.uk
McCreesh, J (SF - Fews)
McGinn, Pat (SF - Fews)
pat.mcginn@newryandmourne.gov.uk
McGreevy, Connaire (SDLP - Crotlieve)
connaire.mcgreevy@newryandmourne.gov.uk
McKee, Harold (UUP - The Mournes)
harold.mckee@newryandmourne.gov.uk
Moffett, Andy (UUP - Fews)
Murphy, Turlough (SF - Fews)
turlough.murphy@newryandmourne.gov.uk
Murphy, Mick (SF - Crotlieve)
mick.murphy@newryandmourne.gov.uk
O'Hare, Sean (SDLP - Crotlieve)
sean.ohare@newryandmourne.gov.uk
Patterson, Jackie (IND - Newry Town)
jackie.patterson@newryandmourne.gov.uk
Quinn, (SDLP - The Mournes)
brian.quinn@newryandmourne.gov.uk
Reilly, Henry (IND - The Mournes)
henry.reilly@newryandmourne.gov.uk
Ruane, Michael (SF - Crotlieve)
michael.ruane@newryandmourne.gov.uk
Taylor, David (UUP - Fews)
david.taylor@newryandmourne.gov.uk

POLITICAL COMPOSITION

SF: 14, SDLP: 9, UUP: 3, IND: 3, DUP: 1

NEWTOWNABBEY N

Newtownabbey Borough Council, Mossley Mill, Newtownabbey BT36 5QA ☎ 028 9034 0000 🖷 028 9034 0200 ✉ info@newtownabbey.gov.uk 💻 www.newtownabbey.gov.uk

FACTS & FIGURES

Police Authority: Northern Ireland Policing Board
Health Authority: Health & Social Care Board
Learning and Skills Council: Northern Ireland
Parliamentary Constituencies: Antrim South, Belfast North
EU Constituencies: Northern Ireland
Election Frequency: Elections are normally held every 4 years
Twinning: Dorsten (Germany); Gilbert, Arizona (USA); Rybnik (Poland)

PRINCIPAL OFFICERS

Chief Executive: Mrs Jacqui Dixon, Chief Executive, Mossley Mill, Newtownabbey BT36 5QA ☎ 028 9034 0001 🖷 028 9034 0004 ✉ jdixon@newtownabbey.gov.uk

Senior Management: Mr Hugh Kelly, Director - Environmental & Leisure Services, Mossley Mill, Newtownabbey BT36 5QA ☎ 028 9034 0000 ✉ hkelly@newtownabbey.gov.uk

Senior Management: Mr Peter McCabe, Director - Financial Services, Mossley Mill, Newtownabbey BT36 5QA ☎ 028 9034 0111 🖷 028 9034 0200 ✉ pmccabe@newtownabbey.gov.uk

Senior Management: Ms Andrea McCooke, Head - Corporate Services, Mossley Mill, Newtownabbey BT36 5QA ☎ 028 9034 0088 ✉ amcooke@newtownabbey.gov.uk

Best Value: Mrs Helen McBride, Corporate Improvement Manager, Mossley Mill, Newtownabbey BT36 5QA ☎ 028 9034 0038 🖷 028 9034 0043 ✉ hmcbride@newtownabbey.gov.uk

Building Control: Mr David Blair, Property Services Manager, Mossley Mill, Newtownabbey BT36 5QA ☎ 028 9034 0000 ✉ dblair@newtownabbey.gov.uk

Children / Youth Services: Mr Dean Holmes, Sport & Play Development Officer, Mossley Mill, Newtownabbey BT36 5QA ☎ 028 9034 0065 🖷 028 9034 0062 ✉ dholmes@newtownabbey.gov.uk

Civil Registration: Mrs Claire Lipsett, Registrar, Mossley Mill, Newtownabbey BT36 5QA ☎ 028 9034 0180 🖷 028 9034 0179 ✉ clipsett@newtownabbey.gov.uk

PR / Communications: Mrs Tracey White, Marketing & PR Manager, Mossley Mill, Newtownabbey BT36 5QA ☎ 028 9034 0028 🖷 028 9034 0043 ✉ twhite@newtownabbey.gov.uk

Computer Management: Mr Paul Allan, IT Manager, Mossley Mill, Newtownabbey BT36 5QA ☎ 028 9034 0035 🖷 028 9034 0043 ✉ pallan@newtownabbey.gov.uk

Customer Service: Ms Lisa Hall, Customer Relations Officer, Mossley Mill, Newtownabbey BT36 5QA ☎ 028 9034 0031 🖷 028 9034 0043 ✉ lhall@newtownabbey.gov.uk

Direct Labour: Mr Hugh Kelly, Director - Environmental Services, Mossley Mill, Newtownabbey BT36 5QA ☎ 028 9034 0044 🖷 028 9034 0062 ✉ hkelly@newtownabbey.gov.uk

Economic Development: Ms Nadean Lowe, Economic Development Officer, Mossley Mill, Newtownabbey BT36 5QA ☎ 028 9034 0072 ✉ nlowe@newtownabbey.gov.uk

Electoral Registration: Ms Andrea McCooke, Head - Corporate

Services, Mossley Mill, Newtownabbey BT36 5QA ☎ 028 9034 0088 ✉ amcooke@newtownabbey.gov.uk

Emergency Planning: Mrs Jacqui Dixon, Chief Executive, Mossley Mill, Newtownabbey BT36 5QA ☎ 028 9034 0001 🖷 028 9034 0004 ✉ jdixon@newtownabbey.gov.uk

Environmental Health: Mr Hugh Kelly, Director - Environmental Services, Mossley Mill, Newtownabbey BT36 5QA ☎ 028 9034 0044 🖷 028 9034 0062 ✉ hkelly@newtownabbey.gov.uk

Finance and Treasurer: Mr Peter McCabe, Director - Financial Services, Mossley Mill, Newtownabbey BT36 5QA ☎ 028 9034 0111 🖷 028 9034 0200 ✉ pmccabe@newtownabbey.gov.uk

Fleet Management: Mr Jim Gurney, Waste Management Manager, Mossley Mill, Newtownabbey BT36 5QA ☎ 028 9034 0047 🖷 028 9034 0062 ✉ jgurney@newtownabbey.gov.uk

Grounds Maintenance: Mr Hugh Kelly, Director - Environmental & Leisure Services, Mossley Mill, Newtownabbey BT36 5QA ☎ 028 9034 0000 ✉ hkelly@newtownabbey.gov.uk

Health and Safety: Mr John Whinnery, Health & Safety Manager, Mossley Mill, Newtownabbey BT36 5QA ☎ 028 9034 0000 ✉ jwhinnery@newtownabbey.gov.uk

Leisure and Cultural Services: Mrs Ursula Fay, Manager - Leisure & Culture Development, Mossley Mill, Newtownabbey BT36 5QA ☎ 028 9034 0020 🖷 028 9034 0150 ✉ ufay@newtownabbey.gov.uk

Member Services: Mr Alan Clements, Council Business & Administrative Manager, Mossley Mill, Newtownabbey BT36 5QA ☎ 028 9034 0099 ✉ aclements@newtownabbey.gov.uk

Personnel / HR: Ms Andrea McCooke, Head - Corporate Services, Mossley Mill, Newtownabbey BT36 5QA ☎ 028 9034 0088 ✉ amcooke@newtownabbey.gov.uk

Procurement: Mrs Sharon Logue, Procurement Manager, Mossley Mill, Newtownabbey BT36 5QA ☎ 028 9034 0090 🖷 028 9034 0200 ✉ slogue@newtownabbey.gov.uk

Recycling & Waste Minimisation: Mr Hugh Kelly, Director - Environmental Services, Mossley Mill, Newtownabbey BT36 5QA ☎ 028 9034 0044 🖷 028 9034 0062 ✉ hkelly@newtownabbey.gov.uk

Regeneration: Miss Majella McAlister, Director - Development, Mossley Mill, Newtownabbey BT36 5QA ☎ 028 9034 0050 ✉ mmcalister@newtownabbey.gov.uk

Staff Training: Mrs Helen Hall, Learning & Development Manager, Mossley Mill, Newtownabbey BT36 5QA ☎ 028 9034 0083 🖷 028 9034 0200 ✉ hhall@newtownabbey.gov.uk

Sustainable Development: Ms Andrea McCooke, Head - Corporate Services, Mossley Mill, Newtownabbey BT36 5QA ☎ 028 9034 0000 ✉ amccooke@newtownabbey.gov.uk

Tourism: Mrs Lisa O'Kane, Tourism & Events Manager, Mossley Mill, Newtownabbey BT36 5QA ☎ 028 9034 0052 🖷 028 9034 0062 ✉ lokane@newtownabbey.gov.uk

Town Centre: Mrs Lisa O'Kane, Tourism & Events Manager, Mossley Mill, Newtownabbey BT36 5QA ☎ 028 9034 0052 🖷 028 9034 0062 ✉ lokane@newtownabbey.gov.uk

Waste Collection and Disposal: Mr Jim Gurney, Waste Management Manager, Mossley Mill, Newtownabbey BT36 5QA ☎ 028 9034 0047 🖷 028 9034 0062 ✉ jgurney@newtownabbey.gov.uk

Waste Collection and Disposal: Mr Hugh Kelly, Director - Environmental Services, Mossley Mill, Newtownabbey BT36 5QA ☎ 028 9034 0044 🖷 028 9034 0062 ✉ hkelly@newtownabbey.gov.uk

Waste Management: Mr Hugh Kelly, Director - Environmental Services, Mossley Mill, Newtownabbey BT36 5QA ☎ 028 9034 0044 🖷 028 9034 0062 ✉ hkelly@newtownabbey.gov.uk

MEMBERS OF THE COUNCIL (25)

***Mayor:* Robinson**, Victor (DUP - Macedon)
vrobinson@newtownabbey.gov.uk

***Deputy Mayor:* Agnew**, Frazer (IND - University)
fagnew@newtownabbey.gov.uk

***Alderman:* Ball**, William (DUP - University)
wball@newtownabbey.gov.uk

***Alderman:* Blair**, John (ALL - Antrim Line)
jblair@newtownabbey.gov.uk

***Alderman:* DeCourcy**, Billy (DUP - Macedon)
wdecourcy@newtownabbey.gov.uk

***Alderman:* Girvan**, Paul (DUP - Ballyclare)
paul.girvan@mla.niassembly.gov.uk

Ball, Audrey (DUP - Antrim Line)
aball@newtownabbey.gov.uk

Barr, Pamela (DUP - University)
pbarr@newtownabbey.gov.uk

Bingham, Jim (UUP - Ballyclare)
jbingham@newtownabbey.gov.uk

Bradley, Paula (DUP - Antrim Line)
pbradley@newtownabbey.gov.uk

Campbell, Tom (ALL - University)
tomcampbell@campbellstafford.com

Cosgrove, Mark (UUP - Antrim Line)
mcosgrove@newtownabbey.gov.uk

Frazer, Lynn (ALL - University)
lfraser@newtownabbey.gov.uk

Girvan, Mandy (DUP - Ballyclare)
mgirvan@newtownabbey.gov.uk

Hill, Robert (DUP - University)
rhill@newtownabbey.gov.uk

Hogg, Thomas (DUP - Macedon)
thogg@newtownabbey.gov.uk

Mackessy, Marie (SF - Antrim Line)
mmackessy@newtownabbey.gov.uk

Mann, Jackie (DUP - Ballyclare)
jmann@newtownabbey.gov.uk

McClelland, Noreen (SDLP - Antrim Line)
nmcclelland@newtownabbey.gov.uk

McCudden, Pat (ALL - Ballyclare)
pmccudden@newtownabbey.gov.uk

O'Reilly, Gerard (SF - Antrim Line)
goreilly@newtownabbey.gov.uk

Robinson, Ken (UUP - University)
krobinson@newtownabbey.gov.uk
Scott, John (UUP - Macedon)
jscott@newtownabbey.gov.uk
Walker, Dineen (DUP - Macedon)
dwalker@newtownabbey.gov.uk
Webb, Billy (ALL - Macedon)
wjwebb@newtownabbey.gov.uk

POLITICAL COMPOSITION
DUP: 12, ALL: 5, UUP: 4, SF: 2, SDLP: 1, IND: 1

COMMITTEE CHAIRS
Audit: Mr Mark Cosgrove
Development: Ms Pamela Barr
Environment: Mr Robert Hill
Leisure: Mr John Scott
Planning & Consultation: Mr Jackie Mann
Policy & Governance: Ms Mandy Girvan

NORFOLK C

Norfolk County Council, County Hall, Martineau Lane, Norwich NR1 2DH ☎ 0844 800 8020 🖷 0844 800 8012
information@norfolk.gov.uk www.norfolk.gov.uk

FACTS & FIGURES
Police Authority: Norfolk Police Authority
Health Authority: East of England Strategic Health Authority
Learning and Skills Council: Eastern
Parliamentary Constituencies: Broadland, Great Yarmouth, Norfolk Mid, Norfolk North, Norfolk North West, Norfolk South, Norfolk South West, Norwich North, Norwich South
EU Constituencies: Eastern
Election Frequency: Elections are of whole council
Twinning: Strategic alliance: Noord Holland Province (Netherlands); South Trondelag (Norway) Trondheim (Norway)

PRINCIPAL OFFICERS
Chief Executive: Mr David White, Chief Executive, County Hall, Martineau Lane, Norwich NR1 2DH ☎ 01603 222001 🖷 01603 223232 david.white@norfolk.gov.uk

Senior Management: Mr Michael Britch, Managing Director - NPS Group, Lancaster House, 16 Central Avenue, St Andrews Business Park, Norwich NR7 0HR ☎ 01603 706100 🖷 01603 706102 mike.britch@nps.co.uk

Access Officer / Social Services (Disability): Mr Harold Bodmer, Director - Community Services, County Hall, Martineau Lane, Norwich NR1 2DH ☎ 01603 223175 🖷 01603 222301 harold.bodmer@norfolk.gov.uk

Architect, Building / Property Services: Mr John Greenfield, Architectural Director, Lancaster House, 16 Central Avenue, St Andrews Business Park, Norwich NR7 0HR ☎ 01603 706624 john.greenfield@nps.co.uk

Best Value: Ms Pippa Bestwick, Head - Programme Office, County Hall, Martineau Lane, Norwich NR1 2DH ☎ 01603 222200 pippa.bestwick@norfolk.gov.uk

Building Control: Mr Jeff Clarke, Estates Manager, Lancaster House, 16 Central Avenue, St Andrews Business Park, Norwich NR7 0HR ☎ 0344 800 8020 jeff.clarke@nps.gov.uk

Catering Services: Mr Peter Hawes, Managing Director - NORSE Commercial Services, Fifers Lane, 280 Fifers Lane, Norwich NR6 6EQ ☎ 01603 894270 peter.hawes@ncsgrp.co.uk

Children / Youth Services: Ms Lisa Christensen, Director - Children's Services, County Hall, Martineau Lane, Norwich NR1 2DL ☎ 01603 222601 🖷 01603 222688 lisa.christensen@norfolk.gov.uk

Civil Registration: Mrs Caroline Clarke, Strategy & Regulatory Manager, County Hall, Martineau Lane, Norwich NR1 2DH ☎ 01603 222949 caroline.clarke@norfolk.gov.uk

PR / Communications: Ms Christine Birchall, Manager - Corporate Communications & Marketing, County Hall, Martineau Lane, Norwich NR1 2DH ☎ 01603 222843 🖷 01603 222602 christine.birchall@norfolk.gov.uk

PR / Communications: Mrs Joanna Hannam, Head - Customer Service & Communications, County Hall, Martineau Lane, Norwich NR1 2DH ☎ 01603 224471 joanna.hannam@norfolk.gov.uk

PR / Communications: Mr Mark Langlands, Media & Public Affairs Manager, County Hall, Martineau Lane, Norwich NR1 2DH ☎ 01603 222973 🖷 01603 222602 mark.langlands@norfolk.gov.uk

Community Planning: Ms Jo Richardson, Manager - Planning, Performance & Partnerships, County Hall, Martineau Lane, Norwich NR1 2DH ☎ 01603 223816 jo.richardson@norfolk.gov.uk

Community Safety: Mr Peter Burnham, Head - Community Safety, Police HQ, Jubilee House, Falconer's Chase, Wymondham NR18 0WW ☎ 01953 423994 burnhamp@norfolk.pnn.police.uk

Computer Management: Miss Karen O'Kane, Head - ICT, 2nd Floor, North Wing, County Hall, Martineau Lane, Norwich NR1 2DH ☎ 01603 222100 🖷 01603 224474 karen.okane@norfolk.gov.uk

Consumer Protection and Trading Standards: Mr David Collinson, Assistant Director - Public Protection, County Hall, Martineau Lane, Norwich NR1 2DH ☎ 0344 800 8020 🖷 01603 222889 david.collinson@norfolk.gov.uk

Contracts: Mr Colin Bottjer, Category Manager, County Hall, Martineau Lane, Norwich NR1 2DH ☎ 01603 222025 colin.bottjer@norfolk.gov.uk

Contracts: Mr Al Collier, Head - Procurement, County Hall, Martineau Lane, Norwich NR1 2DH ☎ 01603 223372 al.collier@norfolk.gov.uk

Corporate Services: Mrs Debbie Bartlett, Head - Planning, Policy & Performance, County Hall, Martineau Lane, Norwich NR1 2DH ☎ 0344 800 8020 debbie.bartlett@norfolk.gov.uk

Corporate Services: Ms Amanda Gray, Business Support & Development Manager, County Hall, Martineau Lane, Norwich NR1 2DH ☎ 01603 223184 ✉ amanda.gray@norfolk.gov.uk

Customer Service: Mrs Joanna Hannam, Head - Customer Service & Communications, County Hall, Martineau Lane, Norwich NR1 2DH ☎ 01603 224471 ✉ joanna.hannam@norfolk.gov.uk

Direct Labour: Mr Peter Hawes, Managing Director - NORSE Commercial Services, The Annex, County Hall, Norwich NR1 2UQ ☎ 01603 894270 ✉ peter.hawes@ncsgrp.co.uk

Economic Development: Ms Fiona McDiarmid, Assistant Director - Economic Development & Strategy, County Hall, Martineau Lane, Norwich NR1 2DH ☎ 01603 223810 🖷 01603 223345 ✉ fiona.mcdiarmid@norfolk.gov.uk

Education: Ms Lisa Christensen, Director - Children's Services, County Hall, Martineau Lane, Norwich NR1 2DL ☎ 01603 222601 🖷 01603 222688 ✉ lisa.christensen@norfolk.gov.uk

Education: Mr Richard Snowden, Head - Admissions, County Hall, Martineau Lane, Norwich NR1 2DH ☎ 01603 223489 ✉ richard.snowden@norfolk.gov.uk

E-Government: Miss Karen O'Kane, Head - ICT, 2nd Floor, North Wing, County Hall, Martineau Lane, Norwich NR1 2DH ☎ 01603 222100 🖷 01603 224474 ✉ karen.okane@norfolk.gov.uk

Emergency Planning: Mr John Ellis, Resiliance Manager, County Hall, Martineau Lane, Norwich NR1 2DH ☎ 01603 222014 🖷 01603 223010 ✉ john.ellis@norfolk.gov.uk

Energy Management: Mr Phil Bennett-Lloyd, Climate Change Manager, County Hall, Martineau Lane, Norwich NR1 2DH ☎ 01603 222754 ✉ philip.bennett-lloyd@norfolk.gov.uk

Environmental / Technical Services: Mr Mike Jackson, Director - Environment, Transport & Development, County Hall, Martineau Lane, Norwich NR1 2DH ☎ 01603 222500 🖷 01603 222240 ✉ mike.jackson@norfolk.gov.uk

Environmental Health: Ms Jenny Harris, Joint Director - Public Health, County Hall, Martineau Lane, Norwich NR1 2DH ☎ 0344 800 8020 ✉ jenny.harris@norfolk.gov.uk

Estates, Property & Valuation: Mr Michael Britch, Managing Director - NPS Group, Lancaster House, 16 Central Avenue, St Andrews Business Park, Norwich NR7 0HR ☎ 01603 706100 🖷 01603 706102 ✉ mike.britch@nps.co.uk

Estates, Property & Valuation: Mr Peter Weavers, Asset Management Director, NPS County Hall, Martineau Lane, Norwich NR1 2SF ☎ 01603 222561 ✉ peter.weavers@nps.co.uk

European Liaison: Ms Karen Gibson, Partnership & Delivery Manager, County Hall, Martineau Lane, Norwich NR1 2DH ☎ 01603 222302 ✉ karen.gibson@norfolk.gov.uk

Events Manager: Mrs Joanna Hannam, Head - Customer Service & Communications, County Hall, Martineau Lane, Norwich NR1 2DH ☎ 01603 224471 ✉ joanna.hannam@norfolk.gov.uk

Facilities: Mr Graham Wray, Facilities Manager, NPS Property Consultants Ltd, Building Surveying Group, Martineau Lane, Norwich NR1 1DH ☎ 01603 222554 ✉ graham.wray@nps.gov.uk

Finance and Treasurer: Mr Paul Brittain, Head - Finance, County Hall, Martineau Lane, Norwich NR1 2DH ☎ 01603 222400 🖷 01603 222694 ✉ paul.brittain@norfolk.gov.uk

Fleet Management: Ms Cheryl Hewett, Business Travel Manager, County Hall, Martineau Lane, Norwich NR1 2DH ☎ 0344 800 8020 ✉ cheryl.hewett@norfolk.gov.uk

Grounds Maintenance: Mr Jonathan Hyam, Senior Facilities Operations Manager, County Hall, Martineau Lane, Norwich NR1 2DH ☎ 01603 638101 ✉ jonathan.hyam@ncsgrp.co.uk

Health and Safety: Ms Derryth Wright, Corporate Health & Safety Manager, County Hall, Martineau Lane, Norwich NR1 2DH ☎ 01603 222912 ✉ derryth.wright@norfolk.gov.uk

Highways: Mr Laurie Egan, Travel Network Manager, County Hall, Martineau Lane, Norwich NR1 2SG ☎ 01603 222893 🖷 01603 223207 ✉ laurie.egan@norfolk.gov.uk

Local Area Agreement: Ms Jo Richardson, Manager - Planning, Performance & Partnerships, County Hall, Martineau Lane, Norwich NR1 2DH ☎ 01603 223 816 ✉ jo.richardson@norfolk.gov.uk

Legal: Ms Victoria McNeill, Practice Director, County Hall, Martineau Lane, Norwich NR1 2DH ☎ 01603 223415 🖷 01603 222899 ✉ victoria.mcneill@norfolk.gov.uk

Leisure and Cultural Services: Ms Mari Martin, Head - Arts & Events, County Hall, Martineau Lane, Norwich NR1 2DH ☎ 01603 222269 ✉ mari.martin@norfolk.gov.uk

Leisure and Cultural Services: Mrs Vanessa Trevelyan, Head - Museums & Archaeology Service, Shirehall, Norwich NR1 3JQ ☎ 01603 493620 ✉ vanessa.trevelyan@norfolk.gov.uk

Licensing: Mr Chris Walton, Head - Democratic Services, County Hall, Martineau Lane, Norwich NR1 2DH ☎ 01603 222620 ✉ chris.walton@norfolk.gov.uk

Lifelong Learning: Ms Beverley Evans, Head - Adult Education, Wensum Lodge, 169 King Street, Norwich NR1 1QW ☎ 01603 306583 ✉ beverley.evans@norfolk.gov.uk

Lifelong Learning: Ms Kerry Furness, Head - Community Learning & Development, County Hall, Martineau Lane, Norwich NR1 2DH ☎ 01603 275350 ✉ kerry.furness@norfolk.gov.uk

Lighting: Mr Stephen Littleboy, Street Lighting Manager, County Hall, Martineau Lane, Norwich NR1 2DH ☎ 01603 222476 ✉ stephen.littleboy@norfolk.gov.uk

Member Services: Mrs Christine Byles, Member Support Officer, County Hall, Martineau Lane, Norwich NR1 2DH ☎ 01603 223237 🖷 01603 222419 ✉ christine.byles@norfolk.gov.uk

Partnerships: Ms Caroline Money, Senior Planning, Performance

& Partnership Officer, County Hall, Martineau Lane, Norwich NR1 2DH ☎ 01603 228961 ✉ caroline.money@norfolk.gov.uk

Personnel / HR: Ms Kathy Bonney, Lead HR & OD Business Partner, County Hall, Martineau Lane, Norwich NR1 2DH ☎ 01603 228952 ✉ kathy.bonney@norfolk.gov.uk

Personnel / HR: Ms Anne Gibson, Head - Human Resources & OD, County Hall, Martineau Lane, Norwich NR1 2DH ☎ 01603 222796 🖷 01603 222970 ✉ anne.gibson@norfolk.gov.uk

Personnel / HR: Ms Nicola Mark, Head - Pensions & Investments, Laurence House, 5 St Andrews Hill, Norwich NR2 1AD ☎ 01603 222171 ✉ nicola.mark@norfolk.gov.uk

Planning: Mr Mike Jackson, Director - Environment, Transport & Development, County Hall, Martineau Lane, Norwich NR1 2DH ☎ 01603 222500 🖷 01603 222240 ✉ mike.jackson@norfolk.gov.uk

Procurement: Mr Al Collier, Head - Procurement, County Hall, Martineau Lane, Norwich NR1 2DH ☎ 01603 223372 ✉ al.collier@norfolk.gov.uk

Public Libraries: Mrs Jennifer Holland, Assistant Director - Community Services / Head - Library & Information Services, County Hall, Martineau Lane, Norwich NR1 2UA ☎ 01603 222272 🖷 01603 222422 ✉ jennifer.holland@norfolk.gov.uk

Recycling & Waste Minimisation: Mr Mark Allen, Assistant Director - Environment & Waste Management, County Hall, Martineau Lane, Norwich NR1 2SG ☎ 01603 223222 🖷 01603 223219 ✉ mark.allen@norfolk.gov.uk

Regeneration: Ms Fiona McDiarmid, Assistant Director - Economic Development & Strategy, County Hall, Martineau Lane, Norwich NR1 2DH ☎ 01603 223810 🖷 01603 223345 ✉ fiona.mcdiarmid@norfolk.gov.uk

Road Safety: Mr Iain Temperton, Team Manager - Casualty Reduction, Education & Development, County Hall, Martineau Lane, Norwich NR1 2SG ☎ 01603 223348 🖷 01603 222024 ✉ iain.temperton@norfolk.gov.uk

Social Services (Adult): Mr Harold Bodmer, Director - Community Services, County Hall, Martineau Lane, Norwich NR1 2DH ☎ 01603 223175 🖷 01603 222301 ✉ harold.bodmer@norfolk.gov.uk

Social Services (Children): Ms Lisa Christensen, Director - Children's Services, County Hall, Martineau Lane, Norwich NR1 2DL ☎ 01603 222601 🖷 01603 222688 ✉ lisa.christensen@norfolk.gov.uk

Sustainable Communities: Mr Dominic Allen, Manager - Sustainability, County Hall, Martineau Lane, Norwich NR1 2SG ☎ 01603 224463 🖷 01603 223219 ✉ dominic.allen@norfolk.gov.uk

Sustainable Development: Mr Dominic Allen, Manager - Sustainability, County Hall, Martineau Lane, Norwich NR1 2SG ☎ 01603 224463 🖷 01603 223219 ✉ dominic.allen@norfolk.gov.uk

Tourism: Ms Lydia Smith, Director - Norfolk Tourism Team, County Hall, Martineau Lane, Norwich NR1 2DH ☎ 01603 222727 ✉ lsmith@visit.norfolk.gov.uk

Traffic Management: Mr Laurie Egan, Travel Network Manager, County Hall, Martineau Lane, Norwich NR1 2SG ☎ 01603 222893 🖷 01603 223207 ✉ laurie.egan@norfolk.gov.uk

Transport: Mr Paul Elliott, Transport Programme Manager, County Hall, Martineau Lane, Norwich NR1 2DH ☎ 01603 222210 ✉ paul.elliott@norfolk.gov.uk

Transport Planner: Mr David Cumming, Principal Infrastructure & Economic Growth Planner, County Hall, Martineau Lane, Norwich NR1 2DH ☎ 01603 224225 ✉ david.cumming@norfolk.gov.uk

Transport Planner: Ms Tracy Jessop, Assistant Director - Passenger Transport Unit, County Hall, Martineau Lane, Norwich NR1 2DH ☎ 01603 223831 ✉ tracy.jessop@norfolk.gov.uk

Waste Collection and Disposal: Mr Paul Borrett, Waste Resource Manager, County Hall, Martineau Lane, Norwich NR1 2SG ☎ 01603 222197 ✉ paul.borrett@norfolk.gov.uk

Waste Management: Mr Mark Allen, Assistant Director - Environment & Waste Management, County Hall, Martineau Lane, Norwich NR1 2DH ☎ 01603 223222 ✉ mark.allen@norfolk.gov.uk

MEMBERS OF THE COUNCIL (84)

***Chair:* Monson**, Ian (CON - The Brecks)
ian.monson@norfolk.gov.uk

***Vice-Chair:* Shrimplin**, James (CON - East Flegg)
james.shrimplin@norfolk.gov.uk

***Leader of the Council:* Murphy**, Derrick (CON - Freebridge Lynn)
derrick.murphy@norfolk.gov.uk

***Deputy Leader of the Council:* Mackie**, Ian (CON - Thorpe St Andrew)
ian.mackie@norfolk.gov.uk

***Group Leader:* Bearman**, Richard (GRN - Mancroft)
richard.bearman@norfolk.gov.uk

***Group Leader:* Brindle**, Mike (LD - Thetford West)
mike.brindle@norfolk.gov.uk

***Group Leader:* Nobbs**, George (LAB - Crome)
george.nobbs@norfolk.gov.uk

Adams, Anthony (CON - Drayton and Horsford)
anthony.adams@norfolk.gov.uk

Bett, Stephen (CON - North Coast)

Borrett, Bill (CON - Elmham and Mattishall)
bill.borrett@norfolk.gov.uk

Boswell, Andrew (GRN - Nelson)
andrew.boswell@norfolk.gov.uk

Bremner, Bert (LAB - University)
bert.bremner@norfolk.gov.uk

Byrne, Alexander (CON - Attleborough)
alexander.byrne@norfolk.gov.uk

Callaby, David (LD - Fakenham)
david.callaby@norfolk.gov.uk

Carswell, James (CON - Wroxham)
james.carswell@norfolk.gov.uk

Carttiss, Michael (CON - West Flegg)

Casimir, Charlotte (CON - Catton Grove)
charlotte.casimir@norfolk.gov.uk

Chamberlin, Jennifer (CON - Diss and Roydon)

jennifer.chamberlin@norfolk.gov.uk
Chapman-Allen, Marion (CON - Thetford East)
marion.chapman-allen@norfolk.gov.uk
Chenery of Horsbrugh, Michael (CON - Docking)
michael.chenery@norfolk.gov.uk
Clancy, Stuart (CON - Taverham)
stuart.clancy@norfolk.gov.uk
Clarke, Diana (LD - North Walsham West and Erpingham)
diana.clarke@norfolk.gov.uk
Collins, Bertie (CON - Gorleston St Andrews)
bjc@great-yarmouth.gov.uk
Dixon, Nigel (CON - Hoveton and Stalham)
nigel.dixon@norfolk.gov.uk
Dobson, John (CON - Dersingham)
john.dobson@norfolk.gov.uk
Dorrington, Steven (CON - Hingham)
steve.dorrington@norfolk.gov.uk
Duigan, Phillip (CON - Dereham South)
phillip.duigan@norfolk.gov.uk
East, Tim (LD - Costessey)
tim.east@norfolk.gov.uk
Edwards, Richard (GRN - Mile Cross)
richard.edwards@norfolk.gov.uk
Garrod, Thomas (CON - Yarmouth North and Central)
thomas.garrod@norfolk.gov.uk
Gunson, Adrian (CON - Loddon)
adrian.gunson@norfolk.gov.uk
Gurney, Shelagh (CON - Hellesdon)
shelagh.gurney@norfolk.gov.uk
Hannah, Brian (LD - Sheringham)
brian.hannah@norfolk.gov.uk
Hanton, Ronald (CON - Caister-on-Sea)
ronald.hanton@norfolk.gov.uk
Hardy, Philip (GRN - Thorpe Hamlet)
philip.hardy@norfolk.gov.uk
Harrison, David (LD - Aylsham)
david.harrison@norfolk.gov.uk
Harwood, David (CON - Clenchwarton and King's Lynn South)
david.harwood@norfolk.gov.uk
Hemsley, Marcus (GRN - Wensum)
marcus.hemsley@norfolk.gov.uk
Herbert, Jon (CON - Forehoe)
jon.herbert@norfolk.gov.uk
Humphrey, Harry (CON - Marshland South)
harry.humphrey@norfolk.gov.uk
Hutson, Shelagh (CON - Downham Market)
shelagh.hutson@norfolk.gov.uk
Iles, Brian (CON - Acle)
brian.iles@norfolk.gov.uk
Irving, Diana (CON - Dereham North)
diana.irving@norfolk.gov.uk
Jones, Graham (LD - Mundesley)
graham.jones@norfolk.gov.uk
Jordan, Cliff (CON - Yare and All Saints)
cliff.jordan@norfolk.gov.uk
Joyce, James (LD - Reepham)
james.joyce@norfolk.gov.uk
Kiddle-Morris, Mark (CON - Necton and Launditch)
mark.kiddle-morris@norfolk.gov.uk
Langwade, Michael (CON - Gaywood South)
michael.langwade@norfolk.gov.uk
Leggett, Judy (CON - Old Catton)
judy.leggett@norfolk.gov.uk
Little, Stephen (GRN - Town Close)
stephen.little@norfolk.gov.uk
Long, Brian (CON - King's Lynn North and Central)
brian.long@norfolk.gov.uk
Mickleburgh, Jean (CON - Gaywood North and Central)
jean.mickleburgh@norfolk.gov.uk
Mooney, Joe (CON - Wymondham)
joe.mooney@norfolk.gov.uk
Morse, Paul (LD - North Walsham East)
paul.morse@norfolk.gov.uk
Murphy, Janet (CON - Gayton and Nar Valley)
janet.murphy@norfolk.gov.uk
Nunn, William (CON - Guiltcross)
william.nunn@norfolk.gov.uk
Parkinson-Hare, Rex (UKIP - Yarmouth Nelson and Southtown)
rex.parkinson-hare@norfolk.gov.uk
Perry-Warnes, John (CON - Holt)
john.perry-warnes@norfolk.gov.uk
Plant, Graham (CON - Breydon)
graham.plant@norfolk.gov.uk
Proctor, Andrew (CON - Blofield and Brundall)
andrew.proctor@norfolk.gov.uk
Rice, Paul (LD - South Smallburgh)
paul.rice@norfolk.gov.uk
Rockcliffe, Richard (CON - Fincham)
richard.rockcliffe@norfolk.gov.uk
Rogers, John (CON - Watton)
john.rogers@norfolk.gov.uk
Scutter, Mervyn (LD - Eaton)
mervyn.scutter@norfolk.gov.uk
Shaw, Nigel (CON - Woodside)
nigel.shaw@norfolk.gov.uk
Smith, Roger (CON - Henstead)
roger.smith@norfolk.gov.uk
Spratt, Beverley (CON - West Depwade)
beverley.spratt@norfolk.gov.uk
Steward, Ann (CON - Swaffham)
ann.steward@norfolk.gov.uk
Stone, Barry (CON - Lothingland)
barry.stone@norfolk.gov.uk
Strong, Marie (LD - Wells)
marie.strong@norfolk.gov.uk
Thomas, Alison (CON - Long Stratton)
alison.thomas@norfolk.gov.uk
Thompson, Hilary (CON - Cromer)
hilary.thompson@norfolk.gov.uk
Tomkinson, Tony (CON - Clavering)
anthony.tomkinson@norfolk.gov.uk
Toms, Jennifer (GRN - Sewell)
jennifer.toms@norfolk.gov.uk
Virgo, Judith (CON - Humbleyard)
judith.virgo@norfolk.gov.uk
Walker, Colleen (LAB - Magdalen)
colleen.walker@norfolk.gov.uk
Ward, John (CON - Sprowston)
john.ward@norfolk.gov.uk
Wells, Paul (CON - Bowthorpe)
paul.wells@norfolk.gov.uk
Whitaker, Sue (LAB - Lakenham)
sue.whitaker@norfolk.gov.uk
White, Anthony (CON - Feltwell)
anthony.white@norfolk.gov.uk
Wilby, Martin (CON - East Depwade)
martin.wilby@norfolk.gov.uk
Williams, Tony (CON - Hevingham and Spixworth)
tony.williams@norfolk.gov.uk
Wright, Anthony (CON - Marshland North)

anthony.wright@norfolk.gov.uk
Wright, Russell (CON - Melton Constable)
russell.wright@norfolk.gov.uk

POLITICAL COMPOSITION
CON: 60, LD: 12, GRN: 7, LAB: 4, UKIP: 1

CABINET
Leader: Mr Derrick Murphy
Deputy Leader / Finance & Performance: Mr Ian Mackie
Adult & Community Services: Mr David Harwood
Children's Services: Ms Alison Thomas
Community Protection: Mr Harry Humphrey
Cultural Services, Customer Services & Communications: Mr Barry Stone
Economic Development: Ms Ann Steward
Efficiency: Mr Cliff Jordan
Environment & Waste: Mr Bill Borrett
Planning & Transportation: Mr Graham Plant

COMMITTEE CHAIRS
Audit: Mr Roger Smith
Children's Services (Scrutiny): Miss Charlotte Casimir
Community Services (Scrutiny): Mrs Jean Mickleburgh
Corporate Resources (Scrutiny): Mr Andrew Proctor
Environment Transport & Development (Scrutiny): Mr Alexander Byrne
Health: Mr Michael Carttiss
Pensions: Mr Derrick Murphy
Personnel: Mr Derrick Murphy
Planning: Mr John Rogers

NORTH AYRSHIRE S

North Ayrshire Council, Cunninghame House, Irvine KA12 8EE
☎ 0845 603 0590 🖷 01294 324144
contactus@north-ayrshire.gov.uk 💻 www.north-ayrshire.gov.uk

FACTS & FIGURES
Police Authority: Strathclyde Police Authority
Health Authority: NHS Ayrshire & Arran
Learning and Skills Council: Scotland
Parliamentary Constituencies: Ayrshire North and Arran
EU Constituencies: Scotland
Election Frequency: Elections are of whole council

PRINCIPAL OFFICERS
Chief Executive: Ms Elma Murray, Chief Executive, Cunninghame House, Irvine KA12 8EE ☎ 01294 324124 🖷 01294 324114 asproul@north-ayrshire.gov.uk

Senior Management: Ms Laura Friel, Corporate Director - Finance & Infrastructure, Cunninghame House, Irvine KA12 8EE ☎ 01294 324152 🖷 01294 324544 lfriel@north-ayrshire.gov.uk

Senior Management: Mr Murray Macfarlane, Head of Human Resources, Cunninghame House, Irvine KA12 8EE ☎ 01294 324651 🖷 01294 324664 mmacfarlane@north-ayrshire.gov.uk

Access Officer / Social Services (Disability): Ms Louise Kirk, Access Officer, Cunninghame House, Irvine KA12 8EE ☎ 01294 324766 🖷 01294 324372 lkirk@north-ayrshire.gov.uk

Architect, Building / Property Services: Mr Alex Kirk, Manager - Design & Property, Perceton House, Irvine KA11 2AL ☎ 01294 225122 🖷 01294 225044 akirk@north-ayrshire.gov.uk

Best Value: Mr James Montgomery, General Manager, Cunninghame House, Irvine KA12 8EE ☎ 01294 324125 🖷 01294 324144 jmontgomery@north-ayrshire.gov.uk

Building Control: Mr James Delury, Chief Building Standards Officer, Cunninghame House, Irvine KA12 8EE ☎ 01294 324346 🖷 01294 324304 jdelury@north-ayrshire.gov.uk

Catering Services: Ms Catherine Nelson, General Manager Environment & Related Services, Montgomerie House, 2A Byrehill Drive, West Byrehill Industrial Estate, Kilwinning KA13 6HN ☎ 01294 541522 🖷 01294 541564 cnelson@north-ayrshire.gov.uk

Children / Youth Services: Mr John McKnight, Manager - Community Development, St. John's Primary School Base, Morrison Avenue, Stevenston, KA20 4HH ☎ 01294 468035 🖷 01294 602938 jmcknight@north-ayrshire.gov.uk

Children / Youth Services: Dr Audrey Sutton, Head of Community & Culture, Cunninghame House, Irvine KA12 8EE ☎ 01294 324414 🖷 01294 324444 asutton@north-ayrshire.gov.uk

Civil Registration: Ms Sandra McGregor, Chief Registrar & Administration Officer, Cunninghame House, Irvine KA12 8EE ☎ 01294 324989 🖷 01294 324985 smcgregor@north-ayrshire.gov.uk

PR / Communications: Ms Lynne McEwan, Communications Manager, Cunninghame House, Irvine KA12 8EE ☎ 01294 324117 🖷 01294 324154 lmcewan@north-ayreshire.gov.uk

Community Planning: Ms Morna Rae, Community Planning Officer, Cunninghame House, Irvine KA12 8EE ☎ 01294 324117 🖷 01294 324144 annetodd@north-ayrshire.gov.uk

Community Safety: Mr Alastair Osborne, Policy & Performance Officer, Cunninghame House, Irvine KA12 8EE ☎ 01294 324126 🖷 01294 324144 aosborne@north-ayrshire.gov.uk

Computer Management: Mr Alan Blakely, IT Manager, Cunninghame House, Irvine KA12 8EE ☎ 01294 324272 🖷 01294 324274 ablakely@north-ayrshire.gov.uk

Consumer Protection and Trading Standards: Mr Andy Moynihan, Team Manager (Trading Standards), Bridgegate House, Bridgegate, Irvine KA12 8BD ☎ 01294 324959 🖷 01294 324914 amoynihan@north-ayrshire.gov.uk

Contracts: Mr Ian Mackay, Solicitor to the Council, Cunninghame House, Irvine KA12 8EE ☎ 01294 324386 🖷 01294 324394 imackay@north-ayrshire.gov.uk

Corporate Services: Mr Ian Mackay, Solicitor to the Council, Cunninghame House, Irvine KA12 8EE ☎ 01294 324386 🖷 01294 324394 imackay@north-ayrshire.gov.uk

Customer Service: Ms Esther Gunn, Customer Services Manager, Bridgegate House, Irvine KA12 8DB ☎ 01294 323690 🖷 01294 323974 ↰ egunn@north-ayrshire.gov.uk

Economic Development: Mr Alex Anderson, Economic Development Manager, Perceton House, Irvine KA11 2DE ☎ 01294 225165 🖷 01295 225184 ↰ aanderson@north-ayrshire.gov.uk

Education: Mr Mark Armstrong, Head of Logistics & Infrastructure, Cunninghame House, Irvine KA12 8EE ☎ 01294 324413 🖷 01294 324444 ↰ marmstrong@north-ayrshire.gov.uk

Education: Ms Carol Kirk, Corporate Director - Education & Skills, Cunninghame House, Irvine KA12 8EE ☎ 01294 324412 🖷 01294 324444 ↰ ckirk@north-ayrshire.gov.uk

Electoral Registration: Ms Elma Murray, Chief Executive, Cunninghame House, Irvine KA12 8EE ☎ 01294 324124 🖷 01294 324114 ↰ asproul@north-ayrshire.gov.uk

Emergency Planning: Ms Jane McGeorge, Civil Contingencies Co-ordinator, Ayrshire Civil Contingencies Team, Building 372, Alpha Freight Area, Robertson Road, Glasgow Prestwick Airport, Prestwick KA9 2PL ☎ 01292 692182 🖷 01292 692184 ↰ jmcgeorge@north-ayrshire.gov.uk

Energy Management: Ms Jennifer Wraith, Energy Officer, Perceton House, Irvine KA11 2AL ↰ jwraith@north-ayrshire.gov.uk

Environmental / Technical Services: Mr C Hatton, Head of Environment & Related Services, Montgomerie House, 2A Byrehill Drive, West Byrehill Industrial Estate, Kilwinning KA13 6HN ☎ 01294 541514 🖷 01294 541504 ↰ chatton@north-ayrshire.gov.uk

Environmental Health: Mr Kevin McMunn, Senior Environmental Health & Trading Standards Manager, Cunninghame House, Irvine KA12 8EE ☎ 01294 324354 🖷 01294 324360 ↰ kmcmunn@north-ayrshire.gov.uk

Estates, Property & Valuation: Mr Tom Burns, Asset Manager, Perceton House, Irvine KA11 2AL ↰ tburns@north-ayrshire.gov.uk

European Liaison: Ms Linda Aird, European Officer, Perceton House, Irvine KA11 2AL ☎ 01294 225195 🖷 01294 225184 ↰ lindaaird@north-ayrshire.gov.uk

Events Manager: Mr Garry Hamilton, Festivals & Events Officer, Cunningham House, Friars Croft, Irvine KA12 8EE ☎ 01294 324123 🖷 01294 324154 ↰ ghamilton@north-ayrshire.gov.uk

Finance and Treasurer: Ms Laura Friel, Corporate Director - Finance & Infrastructure, Cunninghame House, Irvine KA12 8EE ☎ 01294 324152 🖷 01294 324544 ↰ lfriel@north-ayrshire.gov.uk

Fleet Management: Mr Gordon Mitchell, Transport Manager, Montgomerie House, 2A Byrehill Drive, West Byrehill Industrial Estate, Kilwinning KA13 6HN ☎ 01294 541601 🖷 01294 551604 ↰ gmitchell@north-ayreshire.gov.uk

Grounds Maintenance: Mr Wallace Turpie, Operations Manager - Sreetscene, Montgomerie House, 2A Byrehill Drive, West Byrehill Industrial Estate, Kilwinning KA13 6HN ☎ 01294 541546 🖷 01294 541504 ↰ chatton@north-ayreshire.gov.uk

Health and Safety: Mr Malcolm Reid, Team Manager - Health & Safety, Cunninghame House, Irvine KA12 8EE ☎ 01294 324688 🖷 01294 324664 ↰ mreid@north-ayreshire.gov.uk

Highways: Mr Angus Bodie, Head of Service - Finance & Infrastructure, Perceton House, Irvine KA11 2AL ☎ 01294 225211 🖷 01294 225244 ↰ headofroads@north-ayreshire.gov.uk

Home Energy Conservation: Ms Jennifer Wraith, Energy Officer, Perceton House, Irvine KA11 2AL ↰ jwraith@north-ayrshire.gov.uk

Housing: Ms Olga Clayton, Head of Service - Community Care & Housing, Cunninghame House, Irvine KA12 8EE ↰ oclayton@north-ayrshire.gov.uk

Housing Maintenance: Mr Hugh Cunning, Inspection Supervisor, Perceton House, Irvine KA11 2AL ☎ 01294 225138 🖷 01294 225044 ↰ hcunning@north-ayrshire.gov.uk

Legal: Mr Ian Mackay, Solicitor to the Council, Cunninghame House, Irvine KA12 8EE ☎ 01294 324386 🖷 01294 324394 ↰ imackay@north-ayrshire.gov.uk

Licensing: Mr William O'Brien, Senior Solicitor - Licensing, District Court & Licensing Office, Townshouse, Irvine KA12 0AZ ☎ 01294 311998 🖷 01294 312170 ↰ nalexander@north-ayreshire.gov.uk

Lifelong Learning: Ms Carol Kirk, Corporate Director - Education & Skills, Cunninghame House, Irvine KA12 8EE ☎ 01294 324412 🖷 01294 324444 ↰ ckirk@north-ayrshire.gov.uk

Lighting: Mr Angus Bodie, Head of Service - Finance & Infrastructure, Perceton House, Irvine KA11 2AL ☎ 01294 225211 🖷 01294 225244 ↰ headofroads@north-ayreshire.gov.uk

Lottery Funding, Charity and Voluntary: Mr Alastair Osborne, Policy & Performance Officer, Cunninghame House, Irvine KA12 8EE ☎ 01294 324126 🖷 01294 324144 ↰ aosborne@north-ayrshire.gov.uk

Member Services: Ms Karen Swayne, Senior Administration Assistant, Cunninghame House, Irvine KA12 8EE ☎ 01294 324171 🖷 01294 324114 ↰ kswayne@north-ayrshire

Parking: Mr Angus Bodie, Head of Service - Finance & Infrastructure, Perceton House, Irvine KA11 2AL ☎ 01294 225211 🖷 01294 225244 ↰ headofroads@north-ayreshire.gov.uk

Personnel / HR: Mr Murray Macfarlane, Head of Human Resources, Cunninghame House, Irvine KA12 8EE ☎ 01294 324651 🖷 01294 324664 ↰ mmacfarlane@north-ayrshire.gov.uk

Planning: Mr Ian Mackay, Solicitor to the Council, Cunninghame House, Irvine KA12 8EE ☎ 01294 324386 🖷 01294 324394 ↰ imackay@north-ayrshire.gov.uk

Planning: Mr James Miller, Chief Development Management

Officer, Cunninghame House, Irvine KA12 8EE ☎ 01294 324315 🖷 01294 324372 ✉ jmiller@north-ayrshire.gov.uk

Procurement: Ms Laura Friel, Corporate Director - Finance & Infrastructure, Cunninghame House, Irvine KA12 8EE ☎ 01294 324152 🖷 01294 324544 ✉ lfriel@north-ayrshire.gov.uk

Public Libraries: Ms Carol Kirk, Corporate Director - Education & Skills, Cunninghame House, Irvine KA12 8EE ☎ 01294 324412 🖷 01294 324444 ✉ ckirk@north-ayrshire.gov.uk

Recycling & Waste Minimisation: Mr Robert Robb, Waste Collection & Recycling Manager, Montgomerie House, 2a Byrehill, West Byrehill Industrial Estate, Kilwinning KA13 6HN ☎ 01294 541535 🖷 01294 541544 ✉ rrobb@north-ayrshire.gov.uk

Regeneration: Mr Alex Anderson, Economic Development Manager, Perceton House, Irvine KA11 2DE ☎ 01294 225165 🖷 01295 225184 ✉ aanderson@north-ayrshire.gov.uk

Road Safety: Mr Angus Bodie, Head of Service - Finance & Infrastructure, Perceton House, Irvine KA11 2AL ☎ 01294 225211 🖷 01294 225244 ✉ headofroads@north-ayreshire.gov.uk

Social Services: Ms Iona Colvin, Corporate Director - Social Services & Health, Cunninghame House, Irvine KA12 8EE ☎ 01294 317725 🖷 01294 317702 ✉ icolvin@north-ayrshire.gov.uk

Social Services (Adult): Ms Olga Clayton, Head of Service - Community Care & Housing, Cunninghame House, Irvine KA12 8EE ✉ oclayton@north-ayrshire.gov.uk

Social Services (Children): Ms Sheena Gault, Head of Service - Children, Families & Criminal Justice, Cunninghame House, Irvine KA12 8EE ☎ 01294 317733 🖷 01294 317701 ✉ sgault@north-ayrshire.gov.uk

Staff Training: Mr Murray Macfarlane, Head of Human Resources, Cunninghame House, Irvine KA12 8EE ☎ 01294 324651 🖷 01294 324664 ✉ mmacfarlane@north-ayrshire.gov.uk

Street Scene: Mr Craig Hatton, Head of Environment & Related Services, Montgomerie House, 2A Byrehill Drive, West Byrehill Industrial Estate, Kilwinning KA13 6HN ☎ 01294 541514 🖷 01294 541504 ✉ chatton@north-ayrshire.gov.uk

Sustainable Communities: Mr Alex Anderson, Economic Development Manager, Perceton House, Irvine KA11 2DE ☎ 01294 225165 🖷 01295 225184 ✉ aanderson@north-ayrshire.gov.uk

Sustainable Development: Mr Alex Anderson, Economic Development Manager, Perceton House, Irvine KA11 2DE ☎ 01294 225165 🖷 01295 225184 ✉ aanderson@north-ayrshire.gov.uk

Tourism: Mr Alex Anderson, Economic Development Manager, Perceton House, Irvine KA11 2DE ☎ 01294 225165 🖷 01295 225184 ✉ aanderson@north-ayrshire.gov.uk

Town Centre: Mr Alex Anderson, Economic Development Manager, Perceton House, Irvine KA11 2DE ☎ 01294 225165 🖷 01295 225184 ✉ aanderson@north-ayrshire.gov.uk

Traffic Management: Mr Angus Bodie, Head of Service - Finance & Infrastructure, Perceton House, Irvine KA11 2AL ☎ 01294 225211 🖷 01294 225244 ✉ headofroads@north-ayreshire.gov.uk

Transport: Mr Craig Hatton, Head of Environment & Related Services, Montgomerie House, 2A Byrehill Drive, West Byrehill Industrial Estate, Kilwinning KA13 6HN ☎ 01294 541514 🖷 01294 541504 ✉ chatton@north-ayrshire.gov.uk

Transport Planner: Mr Angus Bodie, Head of Service - Finance & Infrastructure, Perceton House, Irvine KA11 2AL ☎ 01294 225211 🖷 01294 225244 ✉ headofroads@north-ayreshire.gov.uk

Waste Collection and Disposal: Mr Craig Hatton, Head of Environment & Related Services, Montgomerie House, 2A Byrehill Drive, West Byrehill Industrial Estate, Kilwinning KA13 6HN ☎ 01294 541514 🖷 01294 541504 ✉ chatton@north-ayrshire.gov.uk

Waste Management: Mr Craig Hatton, Head of Environment & Related Services, Montgomerie House, 2A Byrehill Drive, West Byrehill Industrial Estate, Kilwinning KA13 6HN ☎ 01294 541514 🖷 01294 541504 ✉ chatton@north-ayrshire.gov.uk

MEMBERS OF THE COUNCIL (30)

***Deputy Leader of the Council:* Hill**, Alan (SNP - North Coast and Cumbraes)
alanhill@north-ayrshire.gov.uk

Barr, Robert (IND - Dalry and West Kilbride)
rbarr@north-ayrshire.gov.uk

Bell, John (LAB - Kilbirnie and Beith)
jbell@north-ayrshire.gov.uk

Brown, Matthew (SNP - Irvine West)
matthewbrown@north-ayrshire.gov.uk

Bruce, John (SNP - Ardrossan and Arran)
johnbruce@north-ayrshire.gov.uk

Burns, Marie (SNP - Irvine East)
marieburns@north-ayrshire.gov.uk

Clarkson, Ian (LAB - Irvine West)
Iclarkson@north-ayrshire.gov.uk

Cullinane, Joe (LAB - Kilwinning)
joecullinane@north-ayrshire.gov.uk

Dickson, Anthea (SNP - Kilbirnie and Beith)
antheadickson@north-ayrshire.gov.uk

Easdale, John (LAB - Irvine East)
johneasdale@north-ayrshire.gov.uk

Ferguson, John (SNP - Kilwinning)
fergusonjohn@north-ayrshire.gov.uk

Gallagher, Alex (LAB - North Coast and Cumbraes)
agallagher@north-ayrshire.gov.uk

Gibson, Willie (SNP - Saltcoats and Stevenston)
wjrgibson@north-ayrshire.gov.uk

Gurney, Anthony (SNP - Ardrossan and Arran)
agurney@north-ayrshire.gov.uk

Highgate, Jean (IND - Kilbirnie and Beith)
jhighgate@north-ayrshire.gov.uk

Hunter, John (IND - Ardrossan and Arran)
jhunter@north-ayrshire.gov.uk

Maguire, Ruth (SNP - Irvine West)
ruthmaguire@north-ayrshire.gov.uk

Marshall, Tom (O - North Coast and Cumbraes)

tommarshall@north-ayrshire.gov.uk
McLardy, Elizabeth (IND - Dalry and West Kilbride)
emclardy@north-ayrshire.gov.uk
McLean, Alex (SNP - North Coast and Cumbraes)
alexmclean@north-ayrshire.gov.uk
McMillan, Catherine (SNP - Dalry and West Kilbride)
catherinemcmillan@north-ayrshire.gov.uk
McNamara, Peter (LAB - Ardrossan and Arran)
pmcnamara@north-ayrshire.gov.uk
McNichol, Ronnie (IND - Saltcoats and Stevenston)
rmcnicol@north-ayrshire.gov.uk
Montgomerie, Jim (LAB - Saltcoats and Stevenston)
jimmontgomerie@north-ayrshire.gov.uk
Munro, Alan (LAB - Saltcoats and Stevenston)
amunro@north-ayrshire.gov.uk
Oldfather, Irene (LAB - Irvine East)
ireneoldfather@north-ayrshire.gov.uk
O'Neill, David (LAB - Irvine West)
do'neill@north-ayrshire.gov.uk
Reid, John (LAB - Dalry and West Kilbride)
jreid@north-ayrshire.gov.uk
Steel, Robert (IND - Kilwinning)
robertsteel@north-ayrshire.gov.uk
Sturgeon, Joan (SNP - Irvine East)
jsturgeon@north-ayrshire.gov.uk

POLITICAL COMPOSITION
SNP: 12, LAB: 11, IND: 6, O: 1

NORTH DEVON — D

North Devon District Council, Civic Centre, North Walk, Barnstaple EX31 1EA ☎ 01271 327711 🖷 01271 388451 ✉ info@northdevon.gov.uk 💻 www.northdevon.gov.uk

FACTS & FIGURES
Police Authority: Devon & Cornwall Police Authority
Health Authority: NHS South West
Learning and Skills Council: South West
EU Constituencies: South West
Election Frequency: Elections are of whole council
Twinning: Barnstaple: Trouville (France); Uelzen (Germany); Barnstable (USA); Bratton Fleming: St. Martin-de-Sallon (France); Braunton: Plouescat (France); Burrington: Cormolain (France); Chulmleigh: Fontenay-le-Marmion (France); Combe Martin: Cormelles-le-Royal (France); Fremington: Colombelles (France); Goodleigh: Rosel (France); Ilfracombe: Herxheim (Germany); Iff (France); Instow: Arromanches (France); South Molton: Livarot (France); Swimbridge: St. Honorine-du-Fay (France); Witheridge: Cambremer (France)

PRINCIPAL OFFICERS
Chief Executive: Mr Mike Mansell, Chief Executive, Civic Centre, North Walk, Barnstaple EX31 1EA ☎ 01271 327711 🖷 01271 374312 ✉ mike.mansell@northdevon.gov.uk

Assistant Chief Executive: Ms Anne Cowley, Assistant Chief Executive - Policy & Performance Improvement, Civic Centre, North Walk, Barnstaple EX31 1EA ☎ 01271 327711 🖷 01271 324280 ✉ anne.cowley@northdevon.gov.uk

Senior Management: Mr Mike Mansell, Chief Executive, Civic Centre, North Walk, Barnstaple EX31 1EA ☎ 01271 327711 🖷 01271 374312 ✉ mike.mansell@northdevon.gov.uk

Access Officer / Social Services (Disability): Mrs Emily Poyner, Diversity Officer, Civic Centre, North Walk, Barnstaple EX31 1EA ☎ 01271 388773 🖷 01271 388451 ✉ emily.poyner@northdevon.gov.uk

Architect, Building / Property Services: Ms Diana Hill, Head of Property & Technical Services, Civic Centre, North Walk, Barnstaple EX31 1EA ☎ 01271 388377 🖷 01271 388268 ✉ diana.hill@northdevon.gov.uk

Building Control: Mr Steve Peers, Building Control Manager, Civic Centre, North Walk, Barnstaple EX33 1EA ☎ 01271 388400 🖷 01271 388201 ✉ steve.peers@northdevon.gov.uk

PR / Communications: Mrs Claire Holm, Communications Manager, Civic Centre, North Walk, Barnstaple EX31 1EA ☎ 01271 388239 🖷 01271 329433 ✉ claire.holm@northdevon.gov.uk

Community Planning: Mr Brian Holme, Head of Corporate & Community Services, Civic Centre, North Walk, Barnstaple EX31 1EA ☎ 01271 388315 ✉ brian.holme@northdevon.gov.uk

Community Safety: Ms Amanda Palmer, Community Safety Officer, Civic Centre, North Walk, Barnstaple EX31 1EA ☎ 01271 335241 ✉ amanda.palmer@northdevon.gov.uk

Computer Management: Mrs Sue Button, ICT Manager, Civic Centre, North Walk, Barnstaple EX31 1EA ☎ 01271 388338 ✉ sue.button@northdevon.gov.uk

Contracts: Mr Mike Mansell, Chief Executive, Civic Centre, North Walk, Barnstaple EX31 1EA ☎ ; 01271 327711 🖷 01271 374312 ✉ mike.mansell@northdevon.gov.uk

Corporate Services: Mr John Patrinos, Corporate & Community Support Manager, Civic Centre, North Walk, Barnstaple EX31 1EA ☎ 01271 388238 🖷 01271 343968 ✉ john.patrinos@northdevon.gov.uk

Customer Service: Mrs Sharon Harrison, Customer Services Manager, Civic Centre, North Walk, Barnstaple EX31 1EA ☎ 01271 388422 🖷 01271 388451 ✉ sharon.harrison@northdevon.gov.uk

Economic Development: Ms Ellen Vernon, Economic Regeneration Officer, Civic Centre, North Walk, Barnstaple EX31 1EA ☎ 01271 388368 ✉ ellen.vernon@northdevon.gov.uk

E-Government: Mrs Sue Button, ICT Manager, Civic Centre, North Walk, Barnstaple EX31 1EA ☎ 01271 388338 ✉ sue.button@northdevon.gov.uk

Electoral Registration: Mrs Judith Dark, Electoral Services Officer, Civic Centre, North Walk, Barnstaple EX31 1EA ☎ 01271 388277 ✉ judith.dark@northdevon.gov.uk

Emergency Planning: Mr Andrew Millie, Environmental Protection & Emergency Planning Manager, Civic Centre, North Walk, Barnstaple EX31 1EA ☎ 01271 388334 🖷 01271 388328 ✉ andrew.millie@northdevon.gov.uk

Energy Management: Ms Diana Hill, Head of Property &

Technical Services, Civic Centre, North Walk, Barnstaple EX31 1EA ☎ 01271 388377 🖷 01271 388268 ✉ diana.hill@northdevon.gov.uk

Environmental Health: Mr Jeremy Mann, Head of Environmental Health & Housing Services, Civic Centre, North Walk, Barnstaple EX31 1EA ☎ 01271 388341 🖷 01271 388328 ✉ jeremy.mann@northdevon.gov.uk

Estates, Property & Valuation: Ms Diana Hill, Head of Property & Technical Services, Civic Centre, North Walk, Barnstaple EX31 1EA ☎ 01271 388377 🖷 01271 388268 ✉ diana.hill@northdevon.gov.uk

Events Manager: Mr Brian Holme, Head of Corporate & Community Services, Civic Centre, North Walk, Barnstaple EX31 1EA ☎ 01271 388315 ✉ brian.holme@northdevon.gov.uk

Facilities: Ms Diana Hill, Head of Property & Technical Services, Civic Centre, North Walk, Barnstaple EX31 1EA ☎ 01271 388377 🖷 01271 388268 ✉ diana.hill@northdevon.gov.uk

Finance and Treasurer: Mr Steve Hearse, Head of Financial Services, Civic Centre, North Walk, Barnstaple EX31 1EA ☎ 01271 388218 ✉ steve.hearse@northdevon.gov.uk

Fleet Management: Mr Steve Hearse, Head of Financial Services, Civic Centre, North Walk, Barnstaple EX31 1EA ☎ 01271 388218 ✉ steve.hearse@northdevon.gov.uk

Grounds Maintenance: Mr Mark Kenteel, Contracts Delivery Manager, Civic Centre, North Walk, Barnstaple EX31 1EA ☎ 01271 327711 ✉ mark.kenteel@northdevon.gov.uk

Health and Safety: Mr Mike Ballard, Health & Safety Advisor, Civic Centre, North Walk, Barnstaple EX31 1EA ☎ 01271 327711 ✉ mike.ballard@northdevon.gov.uk

Home Energy Conservation: Mr Jeremy Mann, Head of Environmental Health & Housing Services, Civic Centre, North Walk, Barnstaple EX31 1EA ☎ 01271 388341 🖷 01271 388328 ✉ jeremy.mann@northdevon.gov.uk

Housing: Mr Jeremy Mann, Head of Environmental Health & Housing Services, Civic Centre, North Walk, Barnstaple EX31 1EA ☎ 01271 388341 🖷 01271 388328 ✉ jeremy.mann@northdevon.gov.uk

Legal: Mr Mark Smart, Legal Services Manager, Civic Centre, North Walk, Barnstaple EX31 1EA ☎ 01271 388267 ✉ mark.smart@northdevon.gov.uk

Leisure and Cultural Services: Mr Brian Holme, Head of Corporate & Community Services, Civic Centre, North Walk, Barnstaple EX31 1EA ☎ 01271 388315 ✉ brian.holme@northdevon.gov.uk

Licensing: Miss Katy Nicholls, Licensing Manager, Civic Centre, North Walk, Barnstaple EX31 1EA ☎ 01271 388312 🖷 01271 388328 ✉ katy.nicholls@northdevon.gov.uk

Lifelong Learning: Ms Angela Gizzi, Human Resources Manager, 16 Castle Street, Barnstaple EX31 1DR ☎ 01271 327711 🖷 01271 328421 ✉ angela.gizzi@northdevon.gov.uk

Lottery Funding, Charity and Voluntary: Mrs Lorna Jones, Community Grants & Funding Officer, Civic Centre, North Walk, Barnstaple EX31 1EA ☎ 01271 388327 🖷 01271 324280 ✉ lorna.jones@northdevon.gov.uk

Member Services: Mr John Patrinos, Corporate & Community Support Manager, Civic Centre, North Walk, Barnstaple EX31 1EA ☎ 01271 388238 🖷 01271 343968 ✉ john.patrinos@northdevon.gov.uk

Parking: Mr Martin Williams, Procurement & Service Delivery Manager, Lynton House, Commercial Road, Barnstaple EX31 1DG ☎ 01271 388273 ✉ martin.williams@northdevon.gov.uk

Partnerships: Mr Mark Harper, Partnership Sergeant, Civic Centre, North Walk, Barnstaple EX31 1EA ☎ 01271 335241 ✉ mark.harper@northdevon.gov.uk

Personnel / HR: Ms Angela Gizzi, Human Resources Manager, 16 Castle Street, Barnstaple EX31 1DR ☎ 01271 327711 🖷 01271 328421 ✉ angela.gizzi@northdevon.gov.uk

Planning: Ms Kate Little, Joint Head of Strategic Development & Planning, Civic Centre, North Walk, Barnstaple EX31 1EA ☎ 01271 388297; 01271 388297 🖷 01271 343968; 01271 343968 ✉ kate.little@northdevon.gov.uk

Procurement: Mr Martin Williams, Procurement & Service Delivery Manager, Lynton House, Commercial Road, Barnstaple EX31 1DG ☎ 01271 388273 ✉ martin.williams@northdevon.gov.uk

Staff Training: Ms Angela Gizzi, Human Resources Manager, 16 Castle Street, Barnstaple EX31 1DR ☎ 01271 327711 🖷 01271 328421 ✉ angela.gizzi@northdevon.gov.uk

Sustainable Communities: Mr Brian Holme, Head of Corporate & Community Services, Civic Centre, North Walk, Barnstaple EX31 1EA ☎ 01271 388315 ✉ brian.holme@northdevon.gov.uk

Sustainable Development: Mr Brian Holme, Head of Corporate & Community Services, Civic Centre, North Walk, Barnstaple EX31 1EA ☎ 01271 388315 ✉ brian.holme@northdevon.gov.uk

Town Centre: Mr Craig Bulley, CCTV & Town Centre Co-ordinator, Yeo Suite, Barum House, The Square, Barnstaple EX32 8LS ☎ 01271 321049 ✉ craig.bulley@northdevon.gov.uk

Transport Planner: Ms Kate Little, Joint Head of Strategic Development & Planning, Civic Centre, North Walk, Barnstaple EX31 1EA ☎ 01271 388297 🖷 01271 343968 ✉ kate.little@northdevon.gov.uk

MEMBERS OF THE COUNCIL (43)

***Chair:* Haywood**, Sue (LD - Barnstaple (Forches and Whiddon Valley))
suzanne.haywood@northdevon.gov.uk

***Vice-Chair:* Fowler**, Geoffery (LD - Ilfracombe (West))
geoffrey.fowler@northdevon.gov.uk

***Leader of the Council:* Greenslade**, Brian (LD - Barnstaple (Pilton))

brian.greenslade@northdevon.gov.uk
***Deputy Leader of the Council:* Cann**, Rodney (INDNA - Bickington and Roundswell)
rodney.cann@northdevon.gov.uk
Barker, Pat (CON - Georgeham and Mortehoe)
pat.barker@northdevon.gov.uk
Biederman, Frank (INDNA - Fremington)
frank.biederman@northdevon.gov.uk
Bradford, Adam (LD - Barnstaple (Central))
adam.bradford@northdevon.gov.uk
Brailey, David (CON - Barnstaple (Longbridge))
david.brailey@northdevon.gov.uk
Brown, Lesley (LD - Barnstaple (Yeo Valley))
lesley.brown@northdevon.gov.uk
Chesters, Jasmine (CON - Braunton (West))
jasmine.chesters@northdevon.gov.uk
Chugg, Caroline (CON - Braunton (West))
caroline.chugg@northdevon.gov.uk
Clark, Julia (INDNA - Combe Martin)
julia.clark@northdevon.gov.uk
Crabb, Paul (CON - Ilfracombe (Central))
paul.crabb@northdevon.gov.uk
Croft, Sue (CON - Chulmleigh)
sue.croft@northdevon.gov.uk
Davis, Andrea (CON - Heanton Punchardon)
andrea.davis@northdevon.gov.uk
Edgell, Richard (CON - North Molton)
richard.edgell@northdevon.gov.uk
Edmunds, Mike (IND - Ilfracombe (East))
mike.edmunds@northdevon.gov.uk
Flynn, Jaqueline (CON - Barnstaple (Longbridge))
jacqueline.flynn@northdevon.gov.uk
Gubb, Yvette (LD - Combe Martin)
yvette.gubb@northdevon.gov.uk
Gurney, Julian (LD - Lynton and Lynmouth)
julian.gurney@northdevon.gov.uk
Harrison, Michael (CON - Barnstaple (Newport))
henry.harrison@northdevon.gov.uk
Hockin, Brian (INDNA - Bickington and Roundswell)
brian.hockin@northdevon.gov.uk
Hunt, Julie (LD - Barnstaple (Forches and Whiddon Valley))
julie.hunt@northdevon.gov.uk
Lane, Glyn (CON - Landkey, Swimbridge and Taw)
glyn.lane@northdevon.gov.uk
Ley, Eric (IND - Bishops Nympton)
eric.ley@northdevon.gov.uk
Lucas, Roy (CON - Brauton East)
douglas.lucas@northdevon.gov.uk
Luggar, David (CON - Landkey, Swimbridge and Taw)
david.luggar@northdevon.gov.uk
Manuel, Mair (LD - Barnstaple (Pilton))
mair.manuel@northdevon.gov.uk
Mathews, John (CON - Barnstaple (Newport))
john.mathews@northdevon.gov.uk
Moore, John (INDNA - South Molton)
john.moore@northdevon.gov.uk
Moores, Brian (CON - Instow)
brian.moores@northdevon.gov.uk
Payne, Colin (LD - Barnstaple (Yeo Valley))
colin.payne@northdevon.gov.uk
Prowse, Malcolm (LD - Bratton Fleming)
malcolm.prowse@northdevon.gov.uk
Spear, Derrick (LD - Braunton East)
derrick.spear@northdevon.gov.uk
Tucker, Frederick (LD - Marwood)
frederick.tucker@northdevon.gov.uk
Turner, Christopher (IND - Fremington)
chris.turner@northdevon.gov.uk
Webb, Philip (CON - Ilfracombe (West))
philip.webb@northdevon.gov.uk
Webber, Faye (LD - Barnstaple (Central))
faye.webber@northdevon.gov.uk
White, Walter (IND - Chittlehampton)
walter.white@northdevon.gov.uk
Wilkinson, Malcolm (LD - Georgeham and Mortehoe)
malcolm.wilkinson@northdevon.gov.uk
Worden, David (LD - South Molton)
david.worden@northdevon.gov.uk
Yabsley, Paul (CON - Ilfracombe (Central))
paul.yabsley@northdevon.gov.uk
Yabsley, Jeremy (CON - Witheridge Ward)
jeremy.yabsley@northdevon.gov.uk

POLITICAL COMPOSITION

CON: 18, LD: 16, INDNA: 5, IND: 4

CABINET

Leader: Mr Brian Greenslade
Deputy Leader: Mr Rodney Cann
Without Portfolio: Mr Mike Edmunds , Mrs Yvette Gubb , Mrs Mair Manuel , Mr Malcolm Prowse , Mr Derrick Spear , Ms Faye Webber

COMMITTEE CHAIRS

Audit: Mr Adam Bradford
Crime & Disorder Overview & Scrutiny: Mr Frank Biederman
Ethics: Mr Walter White
Licensing: Mr Frederick Tucker
Overview & Scrutiny: Mr Frank Biederman
Personnel: Mr Malcolm Wilkinson
Planning: Mr Eric Ley
Standards: Mr Philip Loft (External)

NORTH DORSET D

North Dorset District Council, Nordon, Salisbury Road, Blandford Forum DT11 7LL ☎ 01258 454111 🖷 01258 480179 💻 www.north-dorset.gov.uk

FACTS & FIGURES

Police Authority: Dorset Police Authority
Health Authority: NHS South West
Learning and Skills Council: South West
Parliamentary Constituencies: Dorset North
EU Constituencies: South West
Election Frequency: Elections are of whole council
Twinning: Blandford: Preetz (Germany); Mortain (France); Gillingham: Le Neubourg (France); Shaftesbury: Brionne (France); Lindlar (Germany)

PRINCIPAL OFFICERS

Chief Executive: Mrs Liz Goodall, Chief Executive, Nordon, Salisbury Road, Blandford Forum DT11 7LL ☎ 01258 484140 🖷 01258 484007 ✉ lgoodall@north-dorset.gov.uk

Senior Management: Mrs Joyce Guest, General Manager, Nordon, Sailsbury Road, Blandford Forum DT11 7LL ☎ 01258 484048 🖷 01258 484007 ✉ jguest@north-dorset.gov.uk

Senior Management: Mr Stephen Hill, General Manager, Nordon, Salisbury Road, Blandford Forum DT11 7LL ☎ 01258 484034 🖷 01258 484007 ✉ shill@north-dorset.gov.uk

Best Value: Mr Drystan Gatrell, Policy Officer - Performance & Review, Nordon, Salisbury Road, Blandford Forum DT11 7LL ☎ 01258 484056 🖷 01258 480007 ✉ dgatrell@north-dorset.gov.uk

Building Control: Mr Mike Crisp, Building Control Team Leader, Nordon, Sailsbury Road, Blandford Forum DT11 7LL ☎ 01258 484261 🖷 01258 484265 ✉ mcrisp@north-dorset.gov.uk

PR / Communications: Mr Peter Hyde, Marketing & Communications Manager, Nordon, Salisbury Road, Blandford Forum DT11 7LL ☎ 01258 484100 ✉ phyde@north-dorset.gov.uk

Community Planning: Mrs Hilary Ritchie, Policy Manager - Regeneration, Nordon, Salisbury Road, Blandford Forum DT11 7LL ☎ 01258 484005 🖷 01258 480179 ✉ hritchie@north-dorset.gov.uk

Community Safety: Mr Derek Hardy, Housing & Community Safety Policy Manager, Nordon, Salisbury Road, Blandford Forum DT11 7LL ☎ 01258 484041 🖷 01258 480179 ✉ dhardy@north-dorset.gov.uk

Computer Management: Mr Bryan Alford, Business Technology Solutions Advisor, Nordon, Salisbury Road, Blandford Forum DT11 7LL ☎ 01258 484073 🖷 01258 480007 ✉ balford@north-dorset.gov.uk

Customer Service: Mrs Lisa Wickham, Customer Services Manager, Nordon, Salisbury Road, Blandford Forum DT11 7LL ☎ 01258 484186 🖷 01258 480179 ✉ lwickham@north-dorset.gov.uk

Economic Development: Mrs Hilary Ritchie, Policy Manager - Regeneration, Nordon, Salisbury Road, Blandford Forum DT11 7LL ☎ 01258 484005 🖷 01258 480179 ✉ hritchie@north-dorset.gov.uk

E-Government: Mr Bryan Alford, Business Technology Solutions Advisor, Nordon, Salisbury Road, Blandford Forum DT11 7LL ☎ 01258 484073 🖷 01258 480007 ✉ balford@north-dorset.gov.uk

Electoral Registration: Ms Jacqui Andrews, Democratic Services Manager, Nordon, Salisbury Road, Blandford Forum DT11 7LL ☎ 01258 484325 🖷 01258 480179 ✉ jandrews@north-dorset.gov.uk

Emergency Planning: Mrs Liz Goodall, Chief Executive, Nordon, Salisbury Road, Blandford Forum DT11 7LL ☎ 01258 484140 🖷 01258 484007 ✉ lgoodall@north-dorset.gov.uk

Energy Management: Mr Kevin Morris, Environment, Land & Property Manager, Nordon, Salisbury Road, Blandford Forum DT11 7LL ☎ 01258 484276 🖷 01258 480179 ✉ kmorris@north-dorset.gov.uk

Environmental / Technical Services: Mr Mike Coker, Principal Technical Officer, Nordon, Salisbury Road, Blandford Forum DT11 7LL ☎ 01258 484275 🖷 01258 480179 ✉ mcoker@north-dorset.gov.uk

Environmental Health: Mr Roger Frost, Food Safety & Licensing Manager, Nordon, Salisbury Road, Blandford Forum DT11 7LL ☎ 01258 484316 🖷 01258 480179 ✉ rfrost@north-dorset.gov.uk

Environmental Health: Mr Kerry Pitt-Kerby, Environmental Protection & Private Sector Housing Manager, Nordon, Salisbury Road, Blandford Forum DT11 7LL ☎ 01258 484311 🖷 01258 480179 ✉ kpittkerby@north-dorset.gov.uk

Facilities: Mrs Janice Burgess, Facilities Team Leader, Nordon, Salisbury Road, Blandford Forum DT11 7LL ☎ 01258 484051 🖷 01258 480179 ✉ jburgess@north-dorset.gov.uk

Finance and Treasurer: Mr Andy Smith, Finance & Resources Manager, Nordon, Salisbury Road, Blandford Forum DT11 7LL ☎ 01258 454114 🖷 01258 484007 ✉ asmith@north-dorset.gov.uk

Health and Safety: Mr Roger Frost, Food Safety & Licensing Manager, Nordon, Salisbury Road, Blandford Forum DT11 7LL ☎ 01258 484316 🖷 01258 480179 ✉ rfrost@north-dorset.gov.uk

Home Energy Conservation: Mr Kerry Pitt-Kerby, Environmental Protection & Private Sector Housing Manager, Nordon, Salisbury Road, Blandford Forum DT11 7LL ☎ 01258 484311 🖷 01258 480179 ✉ kpittkerby@north-dorset.gov.uk

Housing: Mr Derek Hardy, Housing & Community Safety Policy Manager, Nordon, Salisbury Road, Blandford Forum DT11 7LL ☎ 01258 484041 🖷 01258 480179 ✉ dhardy@north-dorset.gov.uk

Legal: Mr Stuart Caundle, Solicitor to the Council & General Manager, Nordon, Salisbury Road, Blandford Forum DT11 7LL ☎ 01258 484010 🖷 01258 480179 ✉ scaundle@north-dorset.gov.uk

Licensing: Mrs Loretto Dennigan, Licensing Officer, Nordon, Salisbury Road, Blandford Forum DT11 7LL ☎ 01258 484014 🖷 01258 480179 ✉ ldennigan@north-dorset.gov.uk

Member Services: Ms Jacqui Andrews, Democratic Services Manager, Nordon, Salisbury Road, Blandford Forum DT11 7LL ☎ 01258 484325 🖷 01258 480179 ✉ jandrews@north-dorset.gov.uk

Parking: Mrs Bernice Deakin, Car Parks Services Officer, Nordon, Salisbury Road, Blandford Forum DT11 7LL ☎ 01258 484315 🖷 01258 480179 ✉ bdeakin@north-dorset.gov.uk

Partnerships: Mrs Joyce Guest, General Manager, Nordon, Sailsbury Road, Blandford Forum DT11 7LL ☎ 01258 484048 🖷 01258 484007 ✉ jguest@north-dorset.gov.uk

Personnel / HR: Ms Bobbie Bragg, Senior Personnel Advisor, Nordon, Salisbury Road, Blandford Forum DT11 7LL ☎ 01258 454032 🖷 01258 484037 ✉ bbragg@north-dorset.gov.uk

Planning: Mr John Hammond, Development Services Manager, Nordon, Salisbury Road, Blandford Forum DT11 7LL ☎ 01258 484202 🖷 01258 480179 ✉ jhammond@north-dorset.gov.uk

Regeneration: Mrs Hilary Ritchie, Policy Manager - Regeneration, Nordon, Salisbury Road, Blandford Forum DT11 7LL ☎ 01258 484005 🖷 01258 480179 ✉ hritchie@north-dorset.gov.uk

Staff Training: Ms Jane Jeffs, Workforce Development Officer, Nordon, Salisbury Road, Blandford Forum DT11 7LL ☎ 01258 484036 🖷 01258 484037 ✉ jjeffs@north-dorset.gov.uk

Sustainable Communities: Mr Kevin Morris, Environment, Land & Property Manager, Nordon, Salisbury Road, Blandford Forum DT11 7LL ☎ 01258 484276 🖷 01258 480179 ✉ kmorris@north-dorset.gov.uk

Sustainable Development: Mr Paul McIntosh, Sustainability Officer, Nordon, Salisbury Road, Blandford Forum DT11 7LL ☎ 01258 484019 🖷 01258 480179 ✉ pmcintosh@north-dorset.gov.uk

Waste Management: Mrs Joyce Guest, General Manager, Nordon, Sailsbury Road, Blandford Forum DT11 7LL ☎ 01258 484048 🖷 01258 484007 ✉ jguest@north-dorset.gov.uk

MEMBERS OF THE COUNCIL (33)

***Chair:* Oliver**, Michael (IND - Cranborne Chase)
mdo@nmsigrp.com
***Vice-Chair:* Hunt**, Su (CON - Milton)
hunt.su@tiscali.co.uk
***Leader of the Council:* Webb**, Peter (CON - The Stours)
pwebb@north-dorset.gov.uk
Batstone, Pauline (CON - Lydden Vale)
p.batstone@virgin.net
Batty-Smith, Bill (CON - Blackmore)
w.battysmith@readingfans.co.uk
Beer, Derek (LD - Shaftesbury Central)
Burch, Audrey (CON - Bulbarrow)
audreyburch01@googlemail.com
Butler, Esme (IND - Blandford Damory Down)
esbutler@sky.com
Carr-Jones, Graham (CON - Blackmore)
grahamcarrjones@aol.com
Cooper, Barrie (LD - Blandford Langton St Leonards)
Croney, Deborah (CON - Hill Forts)
hillfortsward@hotmail.co.uk
Dowden, Charles (CON - Marnhull)
charles.dowden010@btinternet.com
Fox, Victor (CON - Stour Valley)
victorfox187@btinternet.com
Harrocks, Anthony (CON - Blandford Hilltop)
Hickish, Joe (LD - Blandford Old Town)
joehickish@hotmail.com
Jefferson, Gary (CON - Shaftesbury Underhill)
gpjefferson@gmail.com
Jeffery, Mervyn (LD - Shaftesbury Christy's)
mervynjeffery@uwclub.net
Jespersen, Sherry (CON - Hill Forts)
cllr.jespersen@btinternet.com
Miller, Geoffrey (IND - Bourton and District)
gmiller@hollyfieldsschool.co.uk
Milstead, David (LD - Gillingham Town)
david.milsted@virgin.net
Moyle, Richard (CON - Riversdale)
remoyle@aol.com
Parker, Emma (CON - Abbey)
emmaparker77@hotmail.co.uk
Pothecary, Val (CON - Wyke)
vpothecary@tiscali.co.uk
Pritchard, Simon (IND - Shaftesbury Grosvenor)
cllrpritchard@hotmail.co.uk
Roake, Michael (CON - Stour Valley)
mroake5179@aol.com
Shaw, Adrian (CON - Motcombe and Ham)
awshaw@rocketmail.com
Skipwith, Deirdre (CON - Lower Tarrants)
Somper, Jane (CON - Abbey)
janesomper@hotmail.co.uk
Speers, Julian (CON - The Beacon)
cjl_speers@hotmail.com
Stayt, John (CON - Portman)
john.stayt@btinternet.com
Tanner, John (LD - Blandford Station)
jjtanners@hotmail.com
Walsh, David (CON - Wyke)
cllr.davidwalsh@talktalk.net
Webb, Helen (CON - Lodbourne)
helenwebbwyke@sky.com

POLITICAL COMPOSITION

CON: 23, LD: 6, IND: 4

CABINET

Leader / Finance: Mr Peter Webb
Deputy Leader: Ms Deborah Croney
Access & Affordable Housing: Mr Graham Carr-Jones
Community & Regeneration: Mrs Val Pothecary
Development: Mr David Walsh
Environment & Leisure: Mr Michael Roake

COMMITTEE CHAIRS

Accounts & Audit: Mr John Stayt
Development Control: Mr Bill Batty-Smith
Licensing & Orders: Mr Derek Beer
Planning: Mr David Walsh

NORTH DOWN

N

North Down Borough Council, Town Hall, The Castle, Bangor BT20 4BT ☎ 028 9127 0371 🖷 028 9127 1370 ✉ enquiries@northdown.gov.uk 🖳 www.northdown.gov.uk

FACTS & FIGURES

Police Authority: Northern Ireland Policing Board
Health Authority: Eastern Health & Social Services Board
Learning and Skills Council: Northern Ireland
Parliamentary Constituencies: Down North
EU Constituencies: Northern Ireland
Election Frequency: Elections are of whole council
Twinning: Bregenz (Austria); Sister Cities Agreement: Virginia Beach (Virginia, USA)

PRINCIPAL OFFICERS

Chief Executive: Mr Trevor Polley, Chief Executive & Town Clerk, Town Hall, The Castle, Bangor BT20 4BT ☎ 028 9127 0371 🖷 028 9127 1370 ✉ trevor.polley@northdown.gov.uk

Deputy Chief Executive: Mr Jackie Snodden, Director of Amenities & Technical Services / Deputy Chief Executive, Waste Transfer Station, 15A Balloo Drive, Bangor BT19 7QY ☎ 028 9127 0302 🖷 028 9127 1370 ✉ jackie.snodden@northdown.gov.uk

Access Officer / Social Services (Disability): Ms Shirley Poxon, Equality Officer, Town Hall, The Castle, Bangor BT20 4BT ☎ 028

9127 0371 ☎ 028 9127 1370 ✉ shirley.poxon@northdown.gov.uk

Architect, Building / Property Services: Mr David Howard, Principal Lands & Property Officer, Town Hall, The Castle, Bangor BT20 4BT ☎ 028 9127 0371 ☎ 028 9127 1370 ✉ david.howard@northdown.gov.uk

Building Control: Mr Richard McCracken, Principal Building Control Officer, Town Hall, The Castle, Bangor BT20 4BT ☎ 028 9127 0371 ☎ 028 9127 1370 ✉ richard.mccracken@northdown.gov.uk

Civil Registration: Mrs Pauline Mossey, Registrar, Town Hall, The Castle, Bangor BT20 4BT ☎ 028 9127 0371 ✉ registration@northdown.gov.uk

PR / Communications: Ms Claire Jackson, Corporate Communication Officer, Town Hall, The Castle, Bangor BT20 4BT ☎ 028 9127 0371 ☎ 028 9127 1370 ✉ claire.jackson@northdown.gov.uk

Community Safety: Mr Martin Magee, Community Safety Officer, Town Hall, The Castle, Bangor BT20 4BT ☎ 028 9127 0371 ✉ martin.magee@northdown.gov.uk

Computer Management: Mrs Moira McVeigh, Information Technology Manager, Town Hall, The Castle, Bangor BT20 4BT ☎ 028 9127 0371 ☎ 028 9127 1370 ✉ moira.mcveigh@northdown.gov.uk

Consumer Protection and Trading Standards: Mr Graham Yarr, Director of Environmental Services, Town Hall, The Castle, Bangor BT20 4BT ☎ 028 9127 0371 ☎ 028 9127 1370 ✉ graham.yarr@northdown.gov.uk

Contracts: Mrs Debbie Bolton, Procurement Officer, Town Hall, The Castle, Bangor BT20 4BT ☎ 028 9127 0371 ☎ 028 9127 1370 ✉ debbie.bolton@northdown.gov.uk

Customer Service: Ms Claire Jackson, Corporate Communication Officer, Town Hall, The Castle, Bangor BT20 4BT ☎ 028 9127 0371 ☎ 028 9127 1370 ✉ claire.jackson@northdown.gov.uk

Economic Development: Ms Clare McGill, Economic Development Manager, SIGNAL Centre of Business Excellence, 2 Innotec Drive, Balloo Road, Bangor BY19 7PD ☎ 028 9147 3788 ☎ 028 9147 3485 ✉ clare.mcgill@northdown.gov.uk

E-Government: Mrs Moira McVeigh, Information Technology Manager, Town Hall, The Castle, Bangor BT20 4BT ☎ 028 9127 0371 ☎ 028 9127 1370 ✉ moira.mcveigh@northdown.gov.uk

Electoral Registration: Mrs Moira McVeigh, Information Technology Manager, Town Hall, The Castle, Bangor BT20 4BT ☎ 028 9127 0371 ☎ 028 9127 1370 ✉ moira.mcveigh@northdown.gov.uk

Emergency Planning: Ms Jill Hunter, Health & Safety Officer, Town Hall, The Castle, Bangor BT20 4BT ☎ 028 9127 0371 ☎ 028 9127 1370 ✉ jill.hunter@northdown.gov.uk

Energy Management: Mr Tommy Taylor, Principal Technical Officer, Waste Transfer Station, 15A Balloo Drive, Bangor BT19 7QY ☎ 028 9127 0302 ✉ tommy.taylor@northdown.gov.uk

Environmental / Technical Services: Mr Graham Yarr, Director of Environmental Services, Town Hall, The Castle, Bangor BT20 4BT ☎ 028 9127 0371 ☎ 028 9127 1370 ✉ graham.yarr@northdown.gov.uk

Environmental Health: Mr Graham Yarr, Director of Environmental Services, Town Hall, The Castle, Bangor BT20 4BT ☎ 028 9127 0371 ☎ 028 9127 1370 ✉ graham.yarr@northdown.gov.uk

Estates, Property & Valuation: Mr David Howard, Principal Lands & Property Officer, Town Hall, The Castle, Bangor BT20 4BT ☎ 028 9127 0371 ☎ 028 9127 1370 ✉ david.howard@northdown.gov.uk

Events Manager: Mrs Wendy Smith, Events Officer, Tower House, 34 Quay Street, Bangor BT20 5ED ☎ 028 9127 0069 ☎ 028 9127 4466 ✉ wendy.smith@northdown.gov.uk

Finance and Treasurer: Ms Sharon McCullough, Chief Finance Officer, Town Hall, The Castle, Bangor BT20 4BT ☎ 028 9127 0371 ☎ 028 9127 1370 ✉ sharon.mccullough@northdown.gov.uk

Grounds Maintenance: Mr Ian Beaney, Ground Maintenance Officer, Waste Transfer Station, 15A Balloo Drive, Bangor BT19 7QY ☎ 028 9127 0302 ✉ ian.beaney@northdown.gov.uk

Health and Safety: Ms Jill Hunter, Health & Safety Officer, Town Hall, The Castle, Bangor BT20 4BT ☎ 028 9127 0371 ☎ 028 9127 1370 ✉ jill.hunter@northdown.gov.uk

Leisure and Cultural Services: Mr David Warden, Head of Leisure & Community, Town Hall, The Castle, Bangor BT20 4BT ☎ 028 9127 0371 ☎ 028 9127 1370 ✉ david.warden@northdown.gov.uk

Licensing: Mr David Brown, Borough Inspector, Town Hall, The Castle, Bangor BT20 4BT ☎ 028 9127 0371 ☎ 028 9127 1370 ✉ david.brown@northdown.gov.uk

Member Services: Ms Jayne Taylor, Senior Administrative Officer, Town Hall, The Castle, Bangor BT20 4BT ☎ 028 9127 0371 ☎ 028 9127 1370 ✉ jayne.taylor@northdown.gov.uk

Personnel / HR: Mrs Wendy Monson, Head of Human Resources & Admin, Town Hall, The Castle, Bangor BT20 4BT ☎ 028 9127 0371 ☎ 028 9127 1370 ✉ wendy.monson@northdown.gov.uk

Procurement: Mrs Debbie Bolton, Procurement Officer, Town Hall, The Castle, Bangor BT20 4BT ☎ 028 9127 0371 ☎ 028 9127 1370 ✉ debbie.bolton@northdown.gov.uk

Recycling & Waste Minimisation: Ms Alison Curtis, Waste Services Officer, Waste Transfer Station, 15A Balloo Drive, Bangor BT19 7QY ☎ 029 9127 0302 ✉ alison.curtis@northdown.gov.uk

Recycling & Waste Minimisation: Mr Jackie Snodden, Director of Amenities & Technical Services / Deputy Chief Executive, Waste Transfer Station, 15A Balloo Drive, Bangor BT19 7QY ☎ 028 9127 0302 🖷 028 9127 1370 jackie.snodden@northdown.gov.uk

Staff Training: Ms Christine Robinson, Human Resources Officer, Town Hall, The Castle, Bangor BT20 4BT ☎ 028 9127 0371 🖷 028 9127 1370 christine.robinson@northdown.gov.uk

Sustainable Development: Ms Betsy Gray, Policy Officer, Town Hall, The Castle, Bangor BT20 4BT ☎ 028 9127 0371 🖷 028 9127 1370 betsy.gray@northdown.gov.uk

Tourism: Ms Alison Stobie, Tourism Manager, Tower House, 34 Quay Street, Bangor BT20 5ED ☎ 028 9127 0069 🖷 028 9127 4466 alison.stobie@northdown.gov.uk

Town Centre: Mr Stephen Dunlop, Bangor & Holywood Town Centre Manager, 65b Main Street, Bangor BT20 5AF ☎ 028 9147 9651

Waste Collection and Disposal: Mr Peter McCoy, Operations Manager, Waste Transfer Station, 15A Balloo Drive, Bangor BT19 7QY ☎ 028 9127 0302 peter.mccoy@northdown.gov.uk

Waste Management: Mr Peter McCoy, Operations Manager, Waste Transfer Station, 15A Balloo Drive, Bangor BT19 7QY ☎ 028 9127 0302 peter.mccoy@northdown.gov.uk

MEMBERS OF THE COUNCIL (25)

***Mayor:* Irvine**, Wesley (DUP - Abbey)
wesley.irvine@northdown.gov.uk
***Deputy Mayor:* Smith**, Marion (UUP - Bangor West)
marion.smith@northdown.gov.uk
***Alderman:* Cooling**, Ruby (DUP - Abbey)
ruby.cooling@northdown.gov.uk
***Alderman:* Dunne**, Gordon (DUP - Holywood)
gordon.dunne@northdown.gov.uk
***Alderman:* Graham**, Alan (DUP - Bangor West)
alan.graham@northdown.gov.uk
***Alderman:* McKay**, Ellie (UUP - Holywood)
ellie.mckay@northdown.gov.uk
***Alderman:* Wilson**, Brian (GRN - Bangor West)
aldermanwilson@hotmail.com
Barry, John (GRN - Abbey)
john.barry@northdown.gov.uk
Bower, Christine (ALL - Ballyholme and Groomsport)
christine.bower@northdown.gov.uk
Bower, Michael (ALL - Abbey)
michael.bower@northdown.gov.uk
Chambers, Alan (IND - Ballyholme and Groomsport)
alan.chambers@northdown.gov.uk
Dunlop, Harry (UUP - Abbey)
harry.dunlop@northdown.gov.uk
Easton, Alex (DUP - Ballyholme and Groomsport)
alexander.easton@northdown.gov.uk
Gilmour, Jennifer (DUP - Holywood)
jennifer.gilmour@northdown.gov.uk
Harbinson, Adam (ALL - Bangor West)
adam.harbinson@northdown.gov.uk
Henry, Ian (UUP - Ballyholme and Groomsport)
ian.henry@northdown.gov.uk
Lennon, Austen (IND - Ballyholme and Groomsport)
info@austenlennon.co.uk
Leslie, Alan (DUP - Bangor West)
alan.leslie@northdown.gov.uk
Martin, Peter (DUP - Ballyholme and Groomsport)
peter.martin@northdown.gov.uk
McKerrow, James (UUP - Bangor West)
james.mckerrow@northdown.gov.uk
Montgomery, John (DUP - Abbey)
info@wjmontgomery.co.uk
Muir, Andrew (ALL - Holywood)
andrew.muir@northdown.gov.uk
Thompson, Larry (ALL - Holywood)
larry.thompson@northdown.gov.uk
Weir, Peter (DUP - Ballyholme and Groomsport)
pjweir@hotmail.com
Wilson, Anne (ALL - Bangor West)
anne.wilson@northdown.gov.uk

POLITICAL COMPOSITION

DUP: 10, ALL: 6, UUP: 5, IND: 2, GRN: 2

NORTH EAST DERBYSHIRE D

North East Derbyshire District Council, (North East Derbyshire District Council), Council House, Chesterfield S40 1LF ☎ 01246 231111 🖷 01246 550213 enquiries@ne-derbyshire.gov.uk www.ne-derbyshire.gov.uk

FACTS & FIGURES

Police Authority: Derbyshire Police Authority
Health Authority: East Midlands Strategic Health Authority
Learning and Skills Council: East Midlands
Parliamentary Constituencies: Derbyshire North East
EU Constituencies: East Midlands
Election Frequency: Elections are of whole council
Twinning: Darmstadt-Dieburg, Germany

PRINCIPAL OFFICERS

Chief Executive: Mr Wes Lumley, Joint Chief Executive Officer, Council House, Chesterfield S40 1LF ☎ 01246 242462 🖷 01246 242423 wes.lumley@bolsover.gov.uk

Senior Management: Mr Paul Hackett, Joint Director - Health & Wellbeing, Sherwood Lodge, Bolsover S44 6NF ☎ 01246 242566 🖷 01246 242423 paul.hackett@ne-derbyshire.gov.uk

Senior Management: Mr Kevin Hopkinson, Joint Director - Development, Council House, Chesterfield S40 1LF ☎ 01246 242585 🖷 01246 242423 kevin.hopkinson@bolsover.gov.uk

Senior Management: Mr Bryan Mason, Joint Director - Corporate Resources, Sherwood Lodge, Bolsover S44 6NF ☎ 01246 242431 🖷 01246 242423 bryan.mason@ne-derbyshire.gov.uk

Senior Management: Mr Stuart Tomlinson, Joint Director - Neighbourhoods, Riverside Depot, Mansfield Road, Doe Lea, Chesterfield S44 5NY ☎ 01246 593099 🖷 01246 242423 stuart.tomlinson@bolsover.gov.uk

Architect, Building / Property Services: Mr Gary Goodrich, Estates & Valuation Officer, Council House, Saltergate,

Chesterfield S40 1LF ☎ 01246 217193 🖷 01246 217446 ✉ gary.goodrich@ne-derbyshire.gov.uk

Best Value: Mrs Jane Foley, Joint Assistant Director - Strategy & Performance, Council House, Chesterfield S40 1LF ☎ 01246 242343; 01246 217804 🖷 01246 242423; 01246 217442 ✉ jane.foley@bolsover.gov.uk

Building Control: Mr Malcolm Clinton, Business Manager, Council House, Chesterfield S40 1LF ☎ 01246 345817 ✉ malcolm.clinton@ne-derbyshire.gov.uk

Children / Youth Services: Mrs Rebecca Slack, Housing Strategy & Enabling Manager, Council House, Chesterfield S40 1LF ☎ 01246 217289 ✉ rebecca.slack@ne-derbyshire.gov.uk

PR / Communications: Mr Chris Taylor, Communications & Marketing Manager, Council House, Saltergate, Chesterfield S40 1LF ☎ 01246 217823 ✉ chris.taylor@ne-derbyshire.gov.uk

Community Planning: Mr Adrian Kirkham, Planning Services Manager, Council House, Chesterfield S40 1LF ☎ 01246 217591 ✉ adrian.kirkham@ne-derbyshire.gov.uk

Community Planning: Mr Wes Lumley, Joint Chief Executive Officer, Council House, Chesterfield S40 1LF ☎ 01246 242462 🖷 01246 242423 ✉ wes.lumley@bolsover.gov.uk

Community Safety: Ms Faye Green, Community Safety Manager, Council House, Chesterfield S40 1LF ☎ 01246 217015 ✉ faye.green@ne-derbyshire.gov.uk

Community Safety: Mr Stuart Tomlinson, Joint Director - Neighbourhoods, Council House, Chesterfield S40 1LF ☎ 01246 217160 🖷 01246 217442 ✉ stuart.tomlinson@ne-derbyshire.gov.uk

Computer Management: Mr Nick Blaney, Joint IT Services Manager, Council House, Chesterfield S40 1LF ☎ 01246 217103 🖷 01246 242423 ✉ nick.blaney@ne-derbyshire.gov.uk

Contracts: Mr John Hall, Procure to Pay Manager, Council House, Chesterfield S40 1LF ☎ 01246 217215 🖷 01246 217442 ✉ john.hall@ne-derbyshire.gov.uk

Contracts: Mr Bob Trusswell, Head - Procurement, Sherwood Lodge, Bolsover S44 6NF ☎ 01246 242311 ✉ bob.trusswell@bolsover.gov.uk

Corporate Services: Mrs Sarah Sternberg, Solicitor to the Council, Council House, Chesterfield S40 1LF ☎ 01246 217057 🖷 01246 217442 ✉ sarah.sternberg@ne-derbyshire.gov.uk

Corporate Services: Mrs Allison Westray-Chapman, Joint Assistant Director - Resources, Sherwood Lodge, Bolsover S44 6NF ✉ allison.westray-chapman@ne-derbyshire.gov.uk

Customer Service: Ms Rachel Pope, Customer Services Operational Manager, Council House, Chesterfield S40 1LF ☎ 01246 217658 ✉ rachael.pope@ne-derbyshire.gov.uk

Customer Service: Mrs Allison Westray-Chapman, Joint Assistant Director - Resources, Sherwood Lodge, Bolsover S44 6NF ✉ allison.westray-chapman@ne-derbyshire.gov.uk

Economic Development: Mr Dave Eccles, Joint Assistant Director - Regeneration, Sherwood Lodge, Bolsover S44 6NF ☎ 01246 242421 🖷 01246 242423 ✉ dave.eccles@bolsover.gov.uk

Economic Development: Mr Kevin Hopkinson, Joint Director - Development, Council House, Chesterfield S40 1LF ☎ 01246 217165 ✉ kevin.hopkinson@ne-derbyshire.gov.uk

E-Government: Mrs Sarah Sternberg, Solicitor to the Council, Council House, Chesterfield S40 1LF ☎ 01246 217057 🖷 01246 217442 ✉ sarah.sternberg@ne-derbyshire.gov.uk

Electoral Registration: Mrs Sarah Sternberg, Solicitor to the Council, Council House, Chesterfield S40 1LF ☎ 01246 217057 🖷 01246 217442 ✉ sarah.sternberg@ne-derbyshire.gov.uk

Emergency Planning: Mr Paul Hackett, Joint Director - Health & Wellbeing, Sherwood Lodge, Bolsover S44 6NF ☎ 01246 242566 🖷 01246 242423 ✉ paul.hackett@ne-derbyshire.gov.uk

Emergency Planning: Ms Gael Hepburn, Joint Assistant Director - Environmental Services, Council House, Chesterfield S40 1LF ☎ 01246 217804 🖷 01246 217442 ✉ gael.hepburn@ne-derbyshire.gov.uk

Energy Management: Mr Paul Hackett, Joint Director - Health & Wellbeing, Council House, Chesterfield S40 1LF ☎ 01246 217543 ✉ paul.hackett@ne-derbyshire.gov.uk

Environmental / Technical Services: Mrs Gael Hepburn, Joint Assistant Director - Environmental Services, Council House, Chesterfield S40 1LF ☎ 01246 242254 🖷 01246 242423 ✉ gael.hepburn@ne-derbyshire.gov.uk

Environmental Health: Ms Gael Hepburn, Joint Assistant Director - Environmental Services, Council House, Chesterfield S40 1LF ☎ 01246 217804 🖷 01246 217442 ✉ gael.hepburn@ne-derbyshire.gov.uk

Estates, Property & Valuation: Mr Dave Eccles, Joint Assistant Director - Regeneration, Sherwood Lodge, Bolsover S44 6NF ☎ 01246 242421 🖷 01246 242423 ✉ dave.eccles@bolsover.gov.uk

Estates, Property & Valuation: Mr Gary Goodrich, Estates & Valuation Officer, Council House, Saltergate, Chesterfield S40 1LF ☎ 01246 217193 🖷 01246 217446 ✉ gary.goodrich@ne-derbyshire.gov.uk

Estates, Property & Valuation: Mr Kevin Hopkinson, Joint Director - Development, Council House, Chesterfield S40 1LF ☎ 01246 217165 ✉ kevin.hopkinson@ne-derbyshire.gov.uk

European Liaison: Mr Wes Lumley, Joint Chief Executive Officer, Council House, Chesterfield S40 1LF ☎ 01246 242462 🖷 01246 242423 ✉ wes.lumley@bolsover.gov.uk

Facilities: Mr Kevin Hopkinson, Joint Director - Development, Council House, Chesterfield S40 1LF ☎ 01246 217165 ✉ kevin.hopkinson@ne-derbyshire.gov.uk

Facilities: Mr Robert Walker, Property Services Officer, Council House, Chesterfield S40 1LF ☎ 01246 217588 🖷 01246 217446 ✉ robert.walker@ne-derbyshire.gov.uk

Finance and Treasurer: Mr Geoff Bagnal, Financial Services Manager, Council House, Chesterfield S40 1LF ☎ 01246 217078 🖷 01246 217442 ✉ dawn.edwards@ne-derbyshire.gov.uk

Finance and Treasurer: Mr Bryan Mason, Joint Director - Corporate Resources, Council House, Chesterfield S40 1LF ☎ 01246 242431 🖷 01246 242423 ✉ bryan.mason@ne-derbyshire.gov.uk

Fleet Management: Mr Steve Brunt, Streetscene Manager, Council House, Chesterfield S40 1LF ☎ 01246 217264 ✉ steve.brunt@ne-derbyshire.gov.uk

Grounds Maintenance: Mr Steve Brunt, Streetscene Manager, Council House, Chesterfield S40 1LF ☎ 01246 217264 ✉ steve.brunt@ne-derbyshire.gov.uk

Grounds Maintenance: Mr Stuart Tomlinson, Joint Director - Neighbourhoods, Council House, Chesterfield S40 1LF ☎ 01246 217160 🖷 01246 217442 ✉ stuart.tomlinson@ne-derbyshire.gov.uk

Health and Safety: Mrs Angela Grundy, Joint Assistant Director - Human Resources & Payroll, Sherwood Lodge, Bolsover S44 6NF ☎ 01246 242411 🖷 01246 242423 ✉ angela.grundy@ne-derbyshire.gov.uk

Health and Safety: Mr Paul Hackett, Joint Director - Health & Wellbeing, Council House, Chesterfield S40 1LF ☎ 01246 217543 ✉ paul.hackett@ne-derbyshire.gov.uk

Health and Safety: Mr Mick Roddy, Health & Safety Advisor, Council House, Saltergate, Chesterfield S40 1LF ☎ 01246 217242 🖷 01246 217447 ✉ mick.roddy@ne-derbyshire.gov.uk

Home Energy Conservation: Ms Gael Hepburn, Joint Assistant Director - Environmental Services, Council House, Chesterfield S40 1LF ☎ 01246 217804 🖷 01246 217442 ✉ gael.hepburn@ne-derbyshire.gov.uk

Housing: Ms Lorraine Shaw, Managing Director - Rykneld Homes, Rykneld Homes, Pioneer House, Mill Lane, Wingerworth, Chesterfield S42 6NT ☎ 01246 217808 ✉ lorraine.shaw@rykneldhomes.org.uk

Housing Maintenance: Mr Lee Bloomfield, Director of Operations, Rykneld Homes, Pioneer House, Mill Lane, Wingerworth, Chesterfield S42 6NT ☎ 01246 217808 ✉ lee.bloomfield@rykneldhomes.org.uk

Legal: Mrs Naomi Smith, Principal Solicitor, Council House, Chesterfield S40 1LF ☎ 01246 237141 ✉ naomi.smith@ne-derbyshire.gov.uk

Leisure and Cultural Services: Mr Lee Hickin, Head - Leisure, Riverside Depot, Doe Lea, Bolsover S44 5NY ☎ 01246 593056 🖷 01246 242423 ✉ lee.hickin@bolsover.gov.uk

Leisure and Cultural Services: Ms Kelly Massey, Health & Well-Being Officer, Council House, Chesterfield S40 1LF ☎ 01246 217219 ✉ kelly.massey@ne-derbyshire.gov.uk

Licensing: Mr John Chambers, Office Manager, Council House, Saltergate, Chesterfield S40 1LF ☎ 01246 217216 🖷 01246 217447 ✉ john.chambers@ne-derbyshire.gov.uk

Lottery Funding, Charity and Voluntary: Ms Dawn Clarke, Chief Accountant, Council House, Chesterfield S40 1LF ☎ 01246 217658 ✉ dawn.clarke@ne-derbyshire.gov.uk

Member Services: Mrs Sarah Sternberg, Solicitor to the Council, Council House, Chesterfield S40 1LF ☎ 01246 217057 🖷 01246 217442 ✉ sarah.sternberg@ne-derbyshire.gov.uk

Partnerships: Mr Sam Ulyatt, Policy Officer, Council House, Chesterfield S40 1LF ☎ 01246 217014 ✉ sam.ulyatt@ne-derbyshire.gov.uk

Personnel / HR: Mrs Angela Grundy, Joint Assistant Director - Human Resources & Payroll, Sherwood Lodge, Bolsover S44 6NF ☎ 01246 242411 🖷 01246 242423 ✉ angela.grundy@ne-derbyshire.gov.uk

Planning: Mr James Arnold, Head - Planning & Environmental Health, Sherwood Lodge, Bolsover S44 6NF ☎ 01246 242254 🖷 01246 242423 ✉ james.arnold@bolsover.gov.uk

Planning: Mr Kevin Hopkinson, Joint Director - Development, Council House, Chesterfield S40 1LF ☎ 01246 217165 ✉ kevin.hopkinson@ne-derbyshire.gov.uk

Planning: Mr Adrian Kirkham, Planning Services Manager, Council House, Chesterfield S40 1LF ☎ 01246 217591 ✉ adrian.kirkham@ne-derbyshire.gov.uk

Procurement: Mr John Hall, Procure to Pay Manager, Council House, Chesterfield S40 1LF ☎ 01246 217215 🖷 01246 217442 ✉ john.hall@ne-derbyshire.gov.uk

Procurement: Mr Bob Trusswell, Head - Procurement, Sherwood Lodge, Bolsover S44 6NF ☎ 01246 242311 ✉ bob.trusswell@bolsover.gov.uk

Recycling & Waste Minimisation: Mr Stuart Tomlinson, Joint Director - Neighbourhoods, Council House, Chesterfield S40 1LF ☎ 01246 217160 🖷 01246 217442 ✉ stuart.tomlinson@ne-derbyshire.gov.uk

Regeneration: Mr Dave Eccles, Joint Assistant Director - Regeneration, Council House, Chesterfield S40 1LF ☎ 01246 242421 🖷 01246 242423 ✉ dave.eccles@bolsover.gov.uk

Regeneration: Mr Kevin Hopkinson, Joint Director - Development, Council House, Chesterfield S40 1LF ☎ 01246 217165 ✉ kevin.hopkinson@ne-derbyshire.gov.uk

Staff Training: Mrs Angela Grundy, Joint Assistant Director - Human Resources, Council House, Chesterfield S40 1LF ☎ 01246 217009 ✉ angela.grundy@ne-derbyshire.gov.uk

Street Scene: Mr Steve Brunt, Streetscene Manager, Council

House, Chesterfield S40 1LF ☎ 01246 217264
✉ steve.brunt@ne-derbyshire.gov.uk

Street Scene: Mr Stuart Tomlinson, Joint Director - Neighbourhoods, Council House, Chesterfield S40 1LF ☎ 01246 217160 🖷 01246 217442 ✉ stuart.tomlinson@ne-derbyshire.gov.uk

Sustainable Communities: Mr Andrew Towlerton, Assistant Director - Sustainable Communities, Council House, Chesterfield S40 1LF ☎ 01246 217658 ✉ andrew.towlerton@ne-derbyshire.gov.uk

Sustainable Development: Mr Phillip Spurr, Director of Housing, Council House, Chesterfield S40 1LF ☎ 01246 217089 ✉ phillip.spurr@ne-derbyshire.gov.uk

Tourism: Mr David Eccles, Joint Assistant Director - Regeneration, Council House, Chesterfield S40 1LF ☎ 01246 217199 🖷 01246 217446 ✉ david.eccles@ne-derbyshire.gov.uk

Tourism: Mr Paul Hackett, Joint Director - Health & Wellbeing, Council House, Chesterfield S40 1LF ☎ 01246 217543 ✉ paul.hackett@ne-derbyshire.gov.uk

Transport: Mr Steve Brunt, Streetscene Manager, Council House, Chesterfield S40 1LF ☎ 01246 217264 ✉ steve.brunt@ne-derbyshire.gov.uk

Transport: Mr Gary Snowden, Workshop Manager, Rotherside Road, Eckington, Chesterfield S31 9FH ☎ 01246 217275 🖷 01246 217461 ✉ gary.snowden@ne-derbyshire.gov.uk

Waste Collection and Disposal: Mr Steve Brunt, Streetscene Manager, Council House, Chesterfield S40 1LF ☎ 01246 217264 ✉ steve.brunt@ne-derbyshire.gov.uk

Waste Management: Mr Steve Brunt, Streetscene Manager, Council House, Chesterfield S40 1LF ☎ 01246 217624 ✉ steve.brunt@ne-derbyshire.gov.uk

MEMBERS OF THE COUNCIL (53)

***Chair:* Savidge**, Ken (LAB - Clay Cross North)
cllr.savidge@ne-derbyshire.gov.uk
***Vice-Chair:* Hill**, Janet (LAB - Unstone)
***Leader of the Council:* Baxter**, Graham (LAB - Dronfield North)
cllr.baxter@ne-derbyshire.gov.uk
***Group Leader:* Thacker**, Martin (CON - Brampton and Walton)
martin.thacker@ne-derbyshire.gov.uk
Antcliff, Pat (CON - Wingerworth)
Austen, Jane (LAB - Eckington North)
Barker, Nigel (LAB - North Wingfield Central)
nigel.barker@ne-derbyshire.gov.uk
Barnes, Barry (LAB - Shirland)
Blackburn, Adele (CON - Gosforth Valley)
Blackburn, Philip (CON - Coal Aston)
cllr.blackburn@ne-derbyshire.gov.uk
Butler, Geoff (LAB - North Wingfield Central)
geoffrey.butler@ne-derbyshire.gov.uk
Cooper, Andrew (IND - Pilsley and Morton)
andrew.cooper@ne-derbyshire.gov.uk
Dargue, Jack (LAB - Eckington North)
jack.dargue@ne-derbyshire.gov.uk
Dolby, Norma (LAB - Sutton)
norma.dolby@ne-derbyshire.gov.uk
Elliott, Peter (CON - Brampton and Walton)
peter.elliot@ne-derbyshire.gov.uk
Ellis, Stuart (CON - Wingerworth)
stuart.ellis@ne-derbyshire.gov.uk
Ellis, Frances (CON - Wingerworth)
Emmens, Michelle (CON - Gosforth Valley)
Emmens, Michael (CON - Coal Aston)
cllr.emmens@ne-derbyshire.gov.uk
Foster, Angelique (CON - Dronfield South)
Foster, Nick (LAB - Dronfield South)
Garrett, Alan (LAB - Killamarsh West)
alan.garrett@ne-derbyshire.gov.uk
Gillot, Kevin (LAB - North Wingfield Central)
Gordon, Michael (LAB - Ridgeway and Marsh Lane)
cllr.gordon@ne-derbyshire.gov.uk
Hall, Roger (CON - Dronfield Woodhouse)
Hemsley, Pamela (LAB - Grassmoor)
pamela.hemsley@ne-derbyshire.gov.uk
Hill, Elizabeth (LAB - Grassmoor)
cllr.hill@ne-derbyshire.gov.uk
Holmes, Patricia (LAB - Pilsley and Morton)
patricia.holmes@ne-derbyshire.gov.uk
Huckerby, Carol (CON - Barlow and Holmesfield)
carol.huckerby@ne-derbyshire.gov.uk
Hunt, Clive (LAB - Eckington South)
clive.hunt@ne-derbyshire.gov.uk
Kerry, Patrick (LAB - Sutton)
patrick.kerry@ne-derbyshire.gov.uk
Laws, Harold (LAB - Killamarsh East)
Lewis, Barry (CON - Shirland)
Lilleyman, Wayne (LAB - Tupton)
McGory, John (CON - Gosforth Valley)
Moon, Terence (IND - Pilsley and Morton)
terence.moon@ne-derbyshire.gov.uk
Morley, Geoff (LAB - Clay Cross North)
cllr.morley@ne-derbyshire.gov.uk
Oxspring, Doug (LD - Dronfield South)
doug.oxspring@ne-derbyshire.gov.uk
Peters, Stephen (LAB - Tupton)
Ramshaw, George (CON - Ashover)
cllr.ramshaw@ne-derbyshire.gov.uk
Reader, Tracy (LAB - Clay Cross North)
Rice, William (LAB - Killamarsh West)
billy.rice@ne-derbyshire.gov.uk
Ridgway, Jacqueline (LAB - Eckington South)
Ridgway, Brian (LAB - Renishaw)
brian.ridgway@ne-derbyshire.gov.uk
Riggott, Peter (LAB - Clay Cross South)
peter.riggott@ne-derbyshire.gov.uk
Robinson, Lilian (LAB - Killamarsh West)
Skinner, Derrick (LAB - Shirland)
Smith, Christine (LAB - Dronfield North)
christine.smith@ne-derbyshire.gov.uk
Stone, Lee (LAB - Holmewood and Heath)
lee.stone@ne-derbyshire.gov.uk
Widdowson, Paul (CON - Dronfield Woodhouse)
Williams, Patricia (LAB - Holmewood and Heath)
patricia.williams@ne-derbyshire.gov.uk
Windle, John (LAB - Killamarsh East)
john.windle@ne-derbyshire.gov.uk
Wright, Brian (LAB - Clay Cross South)
brian.wright@ne-derbyshire.gov.uk

POLITICAL COMPOSITION
LAB: 34, CON: 16, IND: 2, LD: 1

CABINET
Leader / Building a Better Council: Mr Graham Baxter
Deputy Leader / Housing Strategy & Social Inclusion: Mrs Elizabeth Hill
Community Safety & Health: Ms Lilian Robinson
Economy, Finance, Regeneration & CHART LSP: Mr Patrick Kerry
Environment: Mr Nick Foster
Human Resources, Training & Member Development: Mr Jack Dargue
IT, e-Government & Asset Management: Ms Patricia Williams
Licensing & Planning: Mr Harold Laws
Social Inclusion: Ms Patricia Williams

COMMITTEE CHAIRS
Audit & Corporate Governance (Scrutiny): Mr David Mortimer
Economic Regeneration, Skills & Environment (Scrutiny): Mr Michael Emmens
Ethical Standards: Ms Maggie Kellman (External)
Healthy Communities & Wellbeing (Scrutiny): Mr Michael Gordon
Licensing: Mrs Dorothy Ward
Overview & Scrutiny Board: Mr Frank Taylor
Planning: Mrs Dorothy Ward
Safer Homes & Neighbourhoods (Scrutiny): Mr Harold Laws

NORTH EAST LINCOLNSHIRE U
North East Lincolnshire Council, Municipal Offices, Town Hall Square, Grimsby DN31 1HU ☎ 01472 313131
💻 www.nelincs.gov.uk

FACTS & FIGURES
Police Authority: Humberside Police Authority
Health Authority: NHS Yorkshire & the Humber
Learning and Skills Council: Yorkshire and the Humber
Parliamentary Constituencies: Cleethorpes, Great Grimsby
EU Constituencies: Yorkshire and the Humber
Election Frequency: Elections are by thirds

PRINCIPAL OFFICERS
Chief Executive: Mr Tony Hunter, Chief Executive, Municipal Offices, Town Hall Square, Grimsby DN31 1HU ☎ 01472 324700 ✉ tony.hunter@nelincs.gov.uk

Deputy Chief Executive: Ms Liz Jones, Deputy Chief Executive, Municipal Offices, Town Hall Square, Grimsby DN31 1HU ☎ 01472 324200 🖷 01472 324203 ✉ elizabeth.jones@nelincs.gov.uk

Senior Management: Mr Marc Cole, Strategic Director - Economy, Environment & Housing, Municipal Offices, Town Hall Square, Grimsby DN31 1HU ☎ 01472 324710 ✉ marc.cole@nelincs.gov.uk

Architect, Building / Property Services: Mr Peter Tomlinson, Head of Architecture, Origin 2, Origin Way, Europarc, Grimsby DN37 9TZ ☎ 01472 326593 ✉ peter.tomlinson@nelincs.gov.uk

Building Control: Mr Dean Oglesby, Business Manager, Origin 2, Origin Way, Europarc, Grimsby DN37 9TZ ☎ 01472 323203 🖷 01472 324223 ✉ dean.oglesby@nelincs.gov.uk

Children / Youth Services: Ms Shelly Andrews, Youth Counsellor, Queen Street, Grimsby DN31 1JA ☎ 01472 323220 ✉ shelly.andrews@nelincs.gov.uk

Civil Registration: Mrs Tracy Frisby, Registration & Celebratory Services Manager, Cleethorpes Town Hall, Knoll Street, Grimsby DN35 8LN ☎ 01472 324860 ✉ tracy.riley@nelincs.gov.uk

PR / Communications: Ms Amy Wood, Head of Communications, Municipal Offices, Town Hall Square, Grimsby DN31 1HU ☎ 01472 325965 ✉ amy.wood@nelincs.gov.uk

Community Planning: Mr Jamie Dunn, Policy & Partnership Manager, Municipal Offices, Town Hall Square, Grimsby DN31 1HU ☎ 01472 325952 ✉ jamie.dunn@nelincs.gov.uk

Community Safety: Mr Spencer Hunt, Service Manager Safer Communities, The Elms, 22 Abbey Road, Grimsby DN32 0HW ☎ 01472 325939 ✉ spencer.hunt@neclincs.gov.uk

Consumer Protection and Trading Standards: Mr John Seale, Public Protection Manager, Thrunscoe Centre, Highgate, Cleethorpes DN35 8NX ☎ 01472 324811 🖷 01472 324823 ✉ john.seale@nelincs.gov.uk

Contracts: Ms Rachel Devaney, Technical Specialist, St James House, Grimsby DN31 1EP ☎ 01472 324153 ✉ rachel.devaney@nelincs.gov.uk

Corporate Services: Mr Rob Woollatt, Head of Corporate Finance, Cleethorpes Civic Offices, Knoll Street, Cleethorpes DN35 8LN ☎ 01472 323886 🖷 01472 323921 ✉ rob.woollatt@nelincs.gov.uk

Customer Service: Ms Mary Vessey, Head of Customer Services, Municipal Offices, Town Hall Square, Grimsby DN31 1HU ☎ 01472 323775 🖷 01472 324141 ✉ mary.vessey@nelincs.gov.uk

Economic Development: Mr Damien Jaines-White, Economic Development Manager, Acorn Business Park, Unit 5, Moss Road, Grimsby DN32 0LT ☎ 01472 324674 🖷 01472 326402 ✉ damien.jaines-white@nelincs.gov.uk

Education: Ms Janet Thompson, SEN Assessment & Review Team Manager, Ground Floor, Freeman House, Freeman Way, Grimsby DN32 7AU ☎ 01472 323165 🖷 01472 324398 ✉ janet.thompson@nelincs.gov.uk

E-Government: Ms Sally Jack, Head of Commissioning & Information Systems, Municipal Offices, Town Hall Square, Grimsby DN31 1HU ☎ 01472 325631 🖷 01472 323030 ✉ sally.jack@nelincs.gov.uk

Electoral Registration: Ms Jenny Fenton, Electoral Services Officer, Municipal Offices, Town Hall Square, Grimsby DN31 1HU ☎ 01472 324160 🖷 01472 324132 ✉ jenny.fenton@nelincs.gov.uk

Emergency Planning: Mr James Mason, Assistant Emergency Planning Manager, Doughty Road Depot, Grimsby DN32 0LL ☎ 01472 324829 🖷 01472 324411 ✉ james.mason@nelincs.gov.uk

Energy Management: Mr Tony Neul, Head of Neighbourhood Services, Municipal Offices, Town Hall Square, Grimsby DN31 1HU ☎ 01472 323989 ✉ tony.neul@nelincs.gov.uk

Environmental / Technical Services: Mr Neil Beeken, Food Health Manager, Thrunscoe Centre, Highgate, Cleethorpes DN35 8NX ☎ 01472 324773 🖷 01472 324767 ✉ neil.beeken@nelincs.gov.uk

Environmental Health: Mr Neil Beeken, Food Health Manager, Municipal Offices, Town Hall Square, Grimsby DN31 1HU ☎ 01472 324773 🖷 01472 324767 ✉ neil.beeken@nelincs.gov.uk

Estates, Property & Valuation: Mr Damien Jaines-White, Economic Development Manager, Origin 2, Origin Way, Europarc, Grimsby DN37 9TZ ☎ 01472 324674 🖷 01472 326402 ✉ damien.jaines-white@nelincs.gov.uk

Events Manager: Mr Richard Topliss, Cultural Services Performance Manager, Thrunscoe Centre, Highgate, Cleethorpes DN35 8NX ☎ 01472 324361 🖷 01472 325733 ✉ richard.topliss@nelincs.gov.uk

Facilities: Mr Paul Thorpe, Building & Facilities Operation Manager, Origin 2, Origin Way, Europarc, Grimsby DN37 9TZ ☎ 01472 324782 ✉ paul.thorpe@nelincs.gov.uk

Finance and Treasurer: Ms Liz Jones, Deputy Chief Executive, Municipal Offices, Town Hall Square, Grimsby DN31 1HU ☎ 01472 324200 🖷 01472 324203 ✉ elizabeth.jones@nelincs.gov.uk

Fleet Management: Mr Glenn Greetham, Interim Deputy Director of Neighbourhood Operations, Doughty Road Depot, Grimsby DN32 0LL ☎ 01472 325709 ✉ glenn.greetham@nelincs.gov.uk

Grounds Maintenance: Mr Glenn Greetham, Interim Deputy Director of Neighbourhood Operations, Doughty Road Depot, Grimsby DN32 0LL ☎ 01472 325709 ✉ glenn.greetham@nelincs.gov.uk

Health and Safety: Mr Mike Breeze, HR Officer - Health & Safety, Municipal Offices, Town Hall Square, Grimsby DN31 1HU ☎ 01472 324072 ✉ mike.breeze@nelincs.gov.uk

Highways: Mr Marcus Asquith, Head of Highways & Transport, Origin 2, Origin Way, Europarc, Grimsby DN37 9TZ ☎ 01472 336676 🖷 01472 325657 ✉ marcus.asquith@nelincs.gov.uk

Home Energy Conservation: Ms Debra Fox, Home Energy Promotions Officer, Origin 2, Origin Way, Europarc, Grimsby DN37 9TZ ☎ 01472 324782 ✉ debra.fox@nelincs.gov.uk

Local Area Agreement: Mr Jamie Dunn, Policy & Partnership Manager, Municipal Offices, Town Hall Square, Grimsby DN31 1HU ☎ 01472 325952 ✉ jamie.dunn@nelincs.gov.uk

Local Area Agreement: Ms Liz Jones, Deputy Chief Executive, Municipal Offices, Town Hall Square, Grimsby DN31 1HU ☎ 01472 324200 🖷 01472 324203 ✉ elizabeth.jones@nelincs.gov.uk

Legal: Mr Rob Walsh, Strategic Director - Government & Transformation, Municipal Offices, Town Hall Square, Grimsby DN31 1HU ☎ 01472 323870 🖷 01472 323917 ✉ rob.walsh@nelincs.gov.uk

Leisure and Cultural Services: Mrs Sue Wells, Head of Culture, Leisure & Sport, Municipal Offices, Town Hall Square, Grimsby DN31 1HU ☎ 01472 323674 ✉ sue.wells@nelincs.gov.uk

Licensing: Mr Adrian Moody, Licensing Manager, Thrunscoe Centre, Highgate, Cleethorpes DN35 8NX ☎ 01472 324759 ✉ adrian.moody@nelincs.gov.uk

Lighting: Mr Marcus Asquith, Head of Highways & Transport, Municipal Offices, Town Hall Square, Grimsby DN31 1HU ☎ 01472 336676 🖷 01472 325657 ✉ marcus.asquith@nelincs.gov.uk

Member Services: Ms Elizabeth Lidster, Head of Democratic Services, Municipal Offices, Town Hall Square, Grimsby DN31 1HU ☎ 01472 324123 🖷 01472 324132 ✉ elizabeth.lidster@nelincs.gov.uk

Parking: Mr Michael Phoenix, Parking Services Manager, Origin 1, Europarc, Grimsby DN37 9TZ ☎ 01472 325850 🖷 01472 325857 ✉ michael.phoenix@nelincs.gov.uk

Personnel / HR: Ms Jackie Andrews, Head of Human Resources, Civic Offices, Knoll Street, Cleethorpes DN35 8LN ☎ 01472 323259 🖷 01472 326110 ✉ jackie.andrews@nelincs.gov.uk

Planning: Mr Marcus Asquith, Head of Highways & Transport, Municipal Offices, Town Hall Square, Grimsby DN31 1HU ☎ 01472 336676 🖷 01472 325657 ✉ marcus.asquith@nelincs.gov.uk

Procurement: Ms Andrea Fitzgerald, Group Manager - Commissioning & Delivery, St James House, Grimsby DN31 1EP ☎ 01472 325925 ✉ andrea.fitzgerald@nelincs.gov.uk

Public Libraries: Mr Steve Hipkins, Head of Cultural Services, Central Library, Town Hall Square, Grimsby DN31 1HG ☎ 01472 323611 🖷 01472 323618 ✉ steve.hipkins@nelincs.gov.uk

Recycling & Waste Minimisation: Mr Tony Neul, Head of Neighbourhood Services, Origin 1, Europarc, Grimsby DN37 9TZ ☎ 01472 323989 ✉ tony.neul@nelincs.gov.uk

Regeneration: Mr Marc Cole, Strategic Director - Economy, Environment & Housing, Municipal Offices, Town Hall Square, Grimsby DN31 1HU ☎ 01472 324710 ✉ marc.cole@nelincs.gov.uk

Regeneration: Mr Dean Oglesby, Business Manager, Origin 2, Origin Way, Europarc, Grimsby DN37 9TZ ☎ 01472 323203 🖷 01472 324223 ✉ dean.oglesby@nelincs.gov.uk

Road Safety: Mr Dave Poucher, Principal Traffic Engineer, Origin 1, Europarc, Grimsby DN37 9TZ ☎ 01472 324497 🖷 01472 324517 ✉ dave.poucher@nelincs.gov.uk

Social Services: Mr Jack Blackmore, Strategic Director - People

& Communities, Municipal Offices, Town Hall Square, Grimsby DN31 1HU ☎ 01472 323021 ✉ jack.blackmore@nelincs.gov.uk

Social Services (Adult): Mr Jack Blackmore, Strategic Director - People & Communities, Municipal Offices, Town Hall Square, Grimsby DN31 1HU ☎ 01472 323021 ✉ jack.blackmore@nelincs.gov.uk

Social Services (Children): Mr Paul Cordy, Head of Vulnerable Children, Western Technology Site, Cambridge Road, Grimsby DN34 5TD ☎ 01472 323255 🖷 01472 323030 ✉ paul.cordy@nelincs.gov.uk

Staff Training: Ms Laura Bennett, Learning & Development Manager, Civic Offices, Knoll Street, Cleethorpes DN34 5TD ☎ 01472 325985 ✉ laura.bennett@nelincs.gov.uk

Sustainable Communities: Mr Jack Blackmore, Strategic Director - People & Communities, Municipal Offices, Town Hall Square, Grimsby DN31 1HU ☎ 01472 323021 ✉ jack.blackmore@nelincs.gov.uk

Tourism: Mrs Sue Wells, Head of Culture, Leisure & Sport, Municipal Offices, Town Hall Square, Grimsby DN31 1HU ☎ 01472 323674 ✉ sue.wells@nelincs.gov.uk

Traffic Management: Mr Dave Poucher, Principal Traffic Engineer, Origin 1, Europarc, Grimsby DN37 9TZ ☎ 01472 324497 🖷 01472 324517 ✉ dave.poucher@nelincs.gov.uk

Transport: Mr Marcus Asquith, Head of Highways & Transport, Municipal Offices, Town Hall Square, Grimsby DN31 1HU ☎ 01472 336676 🖷 01472 325657 ✉ marcus.asquith@nelincs.gov.uk

Transport Planner: Mr Marcus Asquith, Head of Highways & Transport, Municipal Offices, Town Hall Square, Grimsby DN31 1HU ☎ 01472 336676 🖷 01472 325657 ✉ marcus.asquith@nelincs.gov.uk

Waste Collection and Disposal: Mr Michael Brown, Waste Management Technical Officer, Thrunscoe Centre, Highgate, Cleethorpes DN35 8NX ☎ 01472 325825 ✉ michael.brown@nelincs.gov.uk

Waste Management: Mr Michael Brown, Waste Management Technical Officer, Thrunscoe Centre, Highgate, Cleethorpes DN35 8NX ☎ 01472 325825 ✉ michael.brown@nelincs.gov.uk

MEMBERS OF THE COUNCIL (42)

Leader of the Council: **Shaw**, Christopher (LAB - Sidney Sussex)
chris.shaw@nelincs.gov.uk

Deputy Leader of the Council: **Burnett**, Michael (LAB - Croft Baker)
michael.burnett@nelincs.gov.uk

Barber, Clifford (LD - Freshney)
cliff.barber@nelincs.gov.uk

Barrow, Matthew (LAB - Park)
matthew.barrow@nelincs.gov.uk

Baxter, Alex (CON - Scartho)
alex.baxter@nelincs.gov.uk

Beasant, Stephen (LD - East Marsh)
steve.beasant@nelincs.gov.uk

Billard, Darren (LAB - West Marsh)
darren.billard@nelincs.gov.uk

Bolton, David (LAB - Immingham)
david.bolton@nelincs.gov.uk

Bramley, Jane (LAB - South)
jane.bramley@nelincs.gov.uk

Brookes, Keith (CON - Haverstoe)
keith.brookes@nelincs.gov.uk

Brown, Matthew (LAB - Croft Baker)
matthew.brown@nelincs.gov.uk

Burton, Mike (LAB - Immingham)
mike.burton@nelincs.gov.uk

Chase, Hazel (LAB - Sidney Sussex)
hazel.chase@nelincs.gov.uk

Colebrook, John (CON - Humberston and New Waltham)
john.colebrook@nelincs.gov.uk

Colquhoun, Iain (CON - Waltham)
iain.colquhoun@nelincs.gov.uk

Cracknell, Margaret (CON - Haverstoe)
margaret.cracknell@nelincs.gov.uk

Darby, Anne (LD - Yarborough)
annie.darby@nelincs.gov.uk

De Freitas, Andrew (LD - Park)
andrew.defreitas@nelincs.gov.uk

Dickerson, Melanie (CON - Wolds)
melaine.dickerson@nelincs.gov.uk

Elliott, Peggy (LAB - Freshney)
peggy.elliott@nelincs.gov.uk

Fenty, John (CON - Humberston and New Waltham)
john.fenty@ntlworld.com

Hornby, David (CON - Scartho)
david.hornby@nelincs.gov.uk

Howarth, Jon-Paul (LAB - East Marsh)
Jon-Paul.Howarth@nelincs.gov.uk

Hyldon-King, Jane (LAB - Yarborough)
jane.hyldon-king@nelincs.gov.uk

Jackson, Philip (CON - Waltham)
philip.jackson@nelincs.gov.uk

James, Rosalind (LD - Heneage)
ros.james@nelincs.gov.uk

Lincoln, Norma (LAB - South)
norma.lincoln@nelincs.gov.uk

Lindley, Ian (LAB - West Marsh)
ian.lindley@nelincs.gov.uk

McGilligan-Fell, Christina (LD - Park)
christina.mcgilliganfell@nelincs.gov.uk

Mills, Peter (CON - Wolds)
peter.mills@nelincs.gov.uk

Norton, Steve (CON - Humberston and New Waltham)
steve.norton@nelincs.gov.uk

Oxby, Ray (LAB - South)
ray.oxby@nelincs.gov.uk

Parkinson, Bill (CON - Haverstoe)
bill.parkinson@nelincs.gov.uk

Patrick, Matthew (LAB - Heneage)
matthew.patrick@nelincs.gov.uk

Scartho, Ron (UKIP - Scartho)
ronald.shepherd@nelincs.gov.uk

Sutton, Ray (LAB - Freshney)
ray.sutton@nelincs.gov.uk

Thurogood, Terry (LAB - Croft Baker)
terry.thurogood@nelincs.gov.uk

Walker, Terry (LAB - East Marsh)

terry.walker@nelincs.gov.uk
Wallace, Alex (LAB - Sidney Sussex)
alex.wallace@nelincs.gov.uk
Watson, David (LAB - Immingham)
dave.watson@nelincs.gov.uk
Wheatley, Peter (LAB - Yarborough)
peter.wheatley@nelincs.gov.uk
Wilson, Karl (LAB - Heneage)
karl.wilson@nelincs.gov.uk

POLITICAL COMPOSITION
LAB: 23, CON: 12, LD: 6, UKIP: 1

CABINET
Leader: Mr Christopher Shaw
Deputy Leader / Tourism & Culture: Mr Michael Burnett
Community Safety & Neighbourhoods: Mr David Bolton
Citizens & Partnerships: Ms Hazel Chase
Finance, Governance & Support Services: Mr Darren Billard
Housing & Wellbeing: Mrs Rosalind James
People Services: Mr Ian Lindley
Regeneration & Environment: Mr Peter Wheatley

COMMITTEE CHAIRS
Children & Young People (Scrutiny): Mr Matthew Brown
Community Protection: Mrs Norma Lincoln
Health, Housing & Wellbeing (Scrutiny): Ms Peggy Elliott
Licensing: Mr Clifford Barber
Planning: Mr Alex Wallace
Policy, Performance & Resources: Mr Ray Sutton
Regeneration & Environment (Scrutiny): Mr Karl Wilson
Safer & Stronger Communities (Scrutiny): Mr Jon-Paul Howarth
Tourism, Leisure & Culture (Scrutiny): Mr Terry Walker

NORTH HERTFORDSHIRE D

North Hertfordshire District Council, Council Offices, Gernon Road, Letchworth SG6 3JF ☎ 01462 474000 🖷 01462 474559; 01462 474227 🖳 www.north-herts.gov.uk

FACTS & FIGURES
Police Authority: Hertfordshire Police Authority
Health Authority: East of England Strategic Health Authority
Learning and Skills Council: Eastern
Parliamentary Constituencies: Hertfordshire North East, Hitchin and Harpenden
EU Constituencies: Eastern
Election Frequency: Elections are by thirds
Twinning: Baldock: Eisenberg (Germany); Sanvignes-Les-Mines (France); Hitchin: Bingen-am-Rhein (Germany); Nuits St. Georges (France); Knebworth: Chatelaillon Plage (France); Letchworth: Chagny (France); Kristiansand (Norway); Wissen (Germany); Royston: Grossalmerode (Germany); La Loupe (France)

PRINCIPAL OFFICERS
Chief Executive: Mr David Scholes, Interim Chief Executive & Strategic Director of Planning, Housing & Enterprise, Council Offices, Gernon Road, Letchworth SG6 3JF ☎ 01462 474836 ✉ david.scholes@north-herts.gov.uk

Senior Management: Mrs Norma Atlay, Strategic Director of Finance, Policy & Governance, Council Offices, Gernon Road, Letchworth SG6 3JF ☎ 01462 474297 🖷 01462 474396 ✉ norma.atlay@north-herts.gov.uk

Senior Management: Mr John Robinson, Strategic Director of Customer Services, Council Offices, Gernon Road, Letchworth SG6 3JF ☎ 01462 474655 🖷 01462 474633 ✉ john.robinson@north-herts.gov.uk

Senior Management: Mr David Scholes, Interim Chief Executive & Strategic Director of Planning, Housing & Enterprise, Council Offices, Gernon Road, Letchworth SG6 3JF ☎ 01462 474836 ✉ david.scholes@north-herts.gov.uk

Best Value: Ms Fiona Timms, Performance & Risk Manager, Council Offices, Gernon Road, Letchworth SG6 3JF ☎ 01462 474251 🖷 01462 474396 ✉ fiona.timms@north-herts.gov.uk

Building Control: Mr Ian Fullstone, Head of Development & Building Control, Council Offices, Gernon Road, Letchworth SG6 3HU ☎ 01462 474480 ✉ ian.fullstone@north-herts.gov.uk

Children / Youth Services: Ms Helen Turner, Children's & Young People's Development Manager, Council Offices, Gernon Road, Letchworth SG6 3JF ☎ 01462 474333 ✉ helen.turner@north-herts.gov.uk

PR / Communications: Ms Sarah Dobor, Communications Manager, Council Offices, Gernon Road, Letchworth SG6 3JF ☎ 01462 474552 ✉ sarah.dobor@north-herts.gov.uk

Community Safety: Ms Rebecca Coates, Community Safety Manager, Council Offices, Gernon Road, Letchworth SG6 3JF ☎ 01462 474504 ✉ rebecca.coates@north-herts.gov.uk

Computer Management: Mr Vic Godfrey, Information Technology Manager, Town Lodge, Gernon Road, Letchworth SG6 3HN ☎ 01462 474455 🖷 01462 474396 ✉ vic.godfrey@north-herts.gov.uk

Corporate Services: Ms Liz Green, Head of Policy & Community Services, Council Offices, Gernon Road, Letchworth SG6 3JF ☎ 01462 474230 ✉ liz.green@north-herts.gov.uk

Corporate Services: Mr John Robinson, Strategic Director of Customer Services, Council Offices, Gernon Road, Letchworth SG6 3JF ☎ 01462 474655 🖷 01462 474633 ✉ john.robinson@north-herts.gov.uk

Customer Service: Ms Johanne Dufficy, Customer Services Manager, Council Offices, Gernon Road, Letchworth SG6 3JF ☎ 01462 474555 ✉ johanne.dufficy@north-herts.gov.uk

E-Government: Mr Gavin Midgley, Website Manager, Council Offices, Gernon Road, Letchworth SG6 3JF ✉ gavin.midgley@north-herts.gov.uk

Electoral Registration: Mr David Miley, Democratic Services Manager, Council Offices, Gernon Road, Letchworth SG6 3JF ☎ 01462 474208 🖷 01462 474227 ✉ david.miley@north-herts.gov.uk

Emergency Planning: Mr Derek Wootton, Emergency Planning Officer, Council Offices, Gernon Road, Letchworth SG6 3JF ☎ 01462 474246 ✉ derek.wootton@north-herts.gov.uk

Environmental / Technical Services: Mr Vaughan Watson, Head of Leisure & Environmental Services, Council Offices, Gernon Road, Letchworth SG6 3JF ☎ 01462 474641 🖷 01462 474500 ✉ vaughan.watson@north-herts.gov.uk

Environmental Health: Mr Andrew Godman, Head of Housing & Public Protection, Council Offices, Gernon Road, Letchworth SG6 3JF ☎ 01462 474293 ✉ andrew.godman@north-herts.gov.uk

Finance and Treasurer: Mrs Norma Atlay, Strategic Director of Finance, Policy & Governance, Council Offices, Gernon Road, Letchworth SG6 3JF ☎ 01462 474297 🖷 01462 474396 ✉ norma.atlay@north-herts.gov.uk

Finance and Treasurer: Mr Andrew Cavanagh, Head of Finance Performance & Asset Management, Council Offices, Gernon Road, Letchworth SG6 3JF ☎ 01462 474247 ✉ andrew.cavanagh@north-herts.gov.uk

Fleet Management: Mr Daniel Kingsley, Service Manager - Waste Management, Council Offices, Gernon Road, Letchworth SG6 3JF ☎ 01462 474304 ✉ daniel.kingsley@north-herts.gov.uk

Grounds Maintenance: Mr Andrew Mills, Service Manager - Grounds Maintenance, Council Offices, Gernon Road, Letchworth SG6 3TR ☎ 01462 474272 ✉ andrew.mills@north-herts.gov.uk

Health and Safety: Mr Les Davidson, Health & Safety Officer, Council Offices, Gernon Road, Letchworth SG6 3TR ☎ 01462 474600 ✉ les.davidson@north-herts.gov.uk

Legal: Ms Katie White, Corporate Legal Manager & Monitoring Officer, Council Offices, Gernon Road, Letchworth SG6 3JF ☎ 01462 474315 ✉ katie.white@north-herts.gov.uk

Leisure and Cultural Services: Mrs Ros Allwood, Cultural Services Manager, Council Offices, Gernon Road, Letchworth SG6 3JF ☎ 01462 435197 ✉ ros.allwood@north-herts.gov.uk

Leisure and Cultural Services: Mr Vaughan Watson, Head of Leisure & Environmental Services, Council Offices, Gernon Road, Letchworth SG6 3JF ☎ 01462 474641 🖷 01462 474500 ✉ vaughan.watson@north-herts.gov.uk

Licensing: Ms Giovanna Silverio, Licensing & Enforcement Manager, Council Offices, Gernon Road, Letchworth SG6 3JF ☎ 01462 474370 🖷 01462 474409 ✉ giovanna.silverio@north-herts.gov.uk

Member Services: Mr Ian Gourlay, Senior Committee & Member Services Officer, Council Offices, Gernon Road, Letchworth SG6 3JF ☎ 01462 474641 ✉ ian.gourlay@north-herts.gov.uk

Member Services: Mr David Miley, Democratic Services Manager, Council Offices, Gernon Road, Letchworth SG6 3JF ☎ 01462 474208 🖷 01462 474227 ✉ david.miley@north-herts.gov.uk

Parking: Mr Steve Crowley, Contracts & Projects Manager, Council Offices, Gernon Road, Letchworth SG6 3JF ☎ 01462 474211 ✉ steve.crowley@north-herts.gov.uk

Partnerships: Ms Liz Green, Head of Policy & Community Services, Council Offices, Gernon Road, Letchworth SG6 3JF ☎ 01462 474230 ✉ liz.green@north-herts.gov.uk

Personnel / HR: Mrs Kerry Shorrocks, Corporate Human Resources Manager, Council Offices, Gernon Road, Letchworth SG6 3JF ☎ 01462 474224 ✉ kerry.shorrocks@north-herts.gov.uk

Planning: Mr Andy Beavan, Corporate Strategy Planning & Enterprise Manager, Council Offices, Gernon Road, Letchworth SG6 3JF ☎ 01462 474836 ✉ andy.beavan@north-herts.gov.uk

Recycling & Waste Minimisation: Mr Daniel Kingsley, Service Manager - Waste Management, Council Offices, Gernon Road, Letchworth SG6 3JF ☎ 01462 474304 ✉ daniel.kingsley@north-herts.gov.uk

Staff Training: Mrs Liz Goddard, Learning & Development Manager, Council Offices, Gernon Road, Letchworth SG6 3JF ☎ 01462 474580 ✉ liz.goddard@north-herts.gov.uk

Sustainable Communities: Mr Stuart Izzard, Community Development Manager, Council Offices, Gernon Road, Letchworth SG6 3JF ☎ 01462 474439 ✉ stuart.izzard@north-herts.gov.uk

Waste Collection and Disposal: Mr Daniel Kingsley, Service Manager - Waste Management, Council Offices, Gernon Road, Letchworth SG6 3JF ☎ 01462 474304 ✉ daniel.kingsley@north-herts.gov.uk

MEMBERS OF THE COUNCIL (49)

***Chair:* Kirby**, Joan (LAB - Hitchin Oughton)

***Vice-Chair:* Gray**, Jane (CON - Knebworth)
jeg@oldknebworth.com

***Leader of the Council:* Needham**, Lynda (CON - Letchworth South West)
lynda.needham@north-herts.gov.uk

***Group Leader:* Jarvis**, Steve (LD - Weston and Sandon)
steve.jarvis@north-herts.gov.uk

Ashley, Allison (CON - Hitchin Priory)
allison_priory@yahoo.co.uk

Bardett, Alan (CON - Knebworth)
alanbardett1@btinternet.com

Barnard, David (CON - Hitchwood, Offa and Hoo)
david.barnard@north-herts.gov.uk

Billing, David (LAB - Hitchin Oughton)
david.billing@north-herts.gov.uk

Billing, Clare (LAB - Letchworth Grange)
clare.billing@north-herts.gov.uk

Billing, Judi (LAB - Hitchin Bearton)
judi.billing@north-herts.gov.uk

Bishop, John (CON - Kimpton)
john.bishop@north-herts.gov.uk

Booth, John (CON - Letchworth South East)
john.booth@north-herts.gov.uk

Brindley, Thomas (CON - Codicote)
nhdc@todeka.co.uk

Burt, Peter (CON - Royston Heath)
peter.burt@north-herts.gov.uk

Chambers, Dave (CON - Letchworth Grange)
dave.chambers@north-herts.gov.uk
Clark, Paul (LD - Hitchin Highbury)
paul.clark@north-herts.gov.uk
Courts, Lisa (LD - Hitchin Bearton)
lisa.courts@north-herts.gov.uk
Cowley, Tricia (CON - Cadwell (Holwell, Ickleford))
patriciagibbs249@btinternet.com
Davidson, Bill (CON - Royston Meridian)
Green, Jean (CON - Royston Palace)
jean.green@north-herts.gov.uk
Grindal, Gary (LAB - Letchworth Wilbury)
gary.grindal@north-herts.gov.uk
Harman, Richard (CON - Letchworth South East)
richard.harman@north-herts.gov.uk
Harris, John (CON - Baldock East)
john.harris@north-herts.gov.uk
Henry, Cathryn (CON - Chesfield)
cathryn.henry@north-herts.gov.uk
Hill, Fiona (CON - Royston Heath)
fiona.hill@north-herts.gov.uk
Hone, Terry (CON - Letchworth South West)
terry.hone@north-herts.gov.uk
Hunter, Tony (CON - Royston Meridian)
tony.hunter@hertscc.gov.uk
Inwood, Robert (LD - Royston Palace)
robert.inwood@north-herts.gov.uk
Jarvis, Sal (LD - Chesfield)
sal.jarvis@north-herts.gov.uk
Kearns, David (LAB - Letchworth Grange)
david.kearns@north-herts.gov.uk
Kercher, Lorna (LAB - Letchworth East)
lorna.kercher@north-herts.gov.uk
Knighton, Ian (CON - Baldock Town)
ian.knighton@north-hearts.gov.uk
Leal-Bennett, David (CON - Hitchin Highbury)
david.leal-bennett@north-herts.gov.uk
Levett, David (CON - Letchworth South East)
david@dlevett.co.uk
Lovewell, Bernard (CON - Hitchin Walsworth)
bernard.lovewell@north-herts.gov.uk
Mantle, Ian (LAB - Letchworth East)
ian.mantle@north-herts.gov.uk
Millard, Alan (CON - Hitchin Walsworth)
alanjmillard@yahoo.com
Miller, David (CON - Hitchwood, Offa and Hoo)
david.miller@north-herts.gov.uk
Morris, Gerald (CON - Ermine)
gerald.morris@north-herts.gov.uk
Muir, Michael (CON - Baldock Town)
michael.muir@hertscc.gov.uk
Oliver, Lawrence (LD - Hitchin Highbury)
lawrence.oliver@north-herts.gov.uk
Rice, Mike (CON - Letchworth South West)
mike.rice@ntlworld.com
Sangha, Deepak (LAB - Hitchin Bearton)
deepak.sangha@north-herts.gov.uk
Segalini, Deborah (LAB - Hitchin Bearton)
deborah.segalini@north-herts.gov.uk
Shakespeare-Smith, Raymond (CON - Hitchin Walsworth)
rayss83@hotmail.com
Strong, Claire (CON - Hitchwood, Offa and Hoo)
Thake, Richard (CON - Hitchin Priory)
richard.thake@north-herts.gov.uk
Weeks, Michael (CON - Baldock Town)
michael.weeks@north-herts.gov.uk
Young, Andrew (CON - Arbury)
andrew.young@north-herts.gov.uk

POLITICAL COMPOSITION

CON: 33, LAB: 10, LD: 6

CABINET

Leader: Mrs Lynda Needham
Deputy Leader / Finance & IT: Mr Terry Hone
Community Engagement & Rural Affairs: Mrs Tricia Cowley
Housing & Environmental Health: Mr Bernard Lovewell
Leisure: Mr Ian Knighton
Planning, Transport & Enterprise: Mr Thomas Brindley
Policy: Mrs Claire Strong
Waste Management, Recycling & Environment: Mr Peter Burt

COMMITTEE CHAIRS

Finance, Audit & Risk (Scrutiny): Mr David Levett
Licensing & Appeals: Mr David Barnard
Overview & Scrutiny: Mr Raymond Shakespeare-Smith
Planning Control: Mrs Jane Gray

NORTH KESTEVEN — D

North Kesteven District Council, District Council Offices, Kesteven Street, Sleaford NG34 7EF ☎ 01529 414155 🖷 01529 413956 ✉ customer_services@n-kesteven.gov.uk 💻 www.n-kesteven.gov.uk

FACTS & FIGURES

Police Authority: Lincolnshire Police Authority
Health Authority: East Midlands Strategic Health Authority
Learning and Skills Council: East Midlands
Parliamentary Constituencies: Sleaford and North Hykeham
EU Constituencies: East Midlands
Election Frequency: Elections are of whole council

PRINCIPAL OFFICERS

Chief Executive: Mr Ian Fytche, Chief Executive, District Council Offices, Kesteven Street, Sleaford NG34 7EF ☎ 01529 414155 ✉ ian_fytche@n-kesteven.gov.uk

Deputy Chief Executive: Mr Alan Thomas, Deputy Chief Executive, District Council Offices, Kesteven Street, Sleaford NG34 7EF ☎ 01529 414155 ✉ alan_thomas@n-kesteven.gov.uk

Senior Management: Ms Karen Bradford, Monitoring Officer, District Council Offices, Kesteven Street, Sleaford NG34 7EF ☎ 01529 414155 ✉ karen_bradford@n-kesteven.gov.uk

Access Officer / Social Services (Disability): Mr Paul Weldon, Building Control Manager & Access Officer, District Council Offices, Kesteven Street, Sleaford NG34 7EF ☎ 01529 414155 ✉ paul_weldon@n-kesteven.gov.uk

Architect, Building / Property Services: Mr Michael Gadd, Property Services Manager, District Council Offices, Kesteven Street, Sleaford NG34 7EF ☎ 01529 414155 ✉ michael_gadd@n-kesteven.gov.uk

Building Control: Mr Paul Weldon, Building Control Manager & Access Officer, District Council Offices, Kesteven Street, Sleaford NG34 7EF ☎ 01529 414155 ✉ paul_weldon@n-kesteven.gov.uk

Children / Youth Services: Ms Sharon Bark, Communities Initiative Co-ordinator, District Council Offices, Kesteven Street, Sleaford NG34 7EF ☎ 01529 414155 ✉ sharon_bark@n-kesteven.gov.uk

PR / Communications: Ms Pip Batty, Communications & Media Manager, District Council Offices, Kesteven Street, Sleaford NG34 7EF ☎ 01529 414155 ✉ pip_batty@n-kesteven.gov.uk

Community Planning: Ms Luisa McIntosh, Community Partnerships Manager, District Council Offices, Kesteven Street, Sleaford NG34 7EF ☎ 01529 414155 ✉ luisa_mcintosh@n-kesteven.gov.uk

Community Safety: Mrs Heidi Ryder, Community Safety Officer, District Council Offices, Kesteven Street, Sleaford NG34 7EF ☎ 01529 414155 ✉ heidi_ryder@n-kesteven.gov.uk

Computer Management: Ms Michelle Carrington, Head of Corporate & Customer Services, District Council Offices, Kesteven Street, Sleaford NG34 7EF ☎ 01529 414155 ✉ michelle_carrington@n-kesteven.gov.uk

Computer Management: Mr Gareth Kinton, Information Technology Manager, District Council Offices, Kesteven Street, Sleaford NG34 7EF ☎ 01529 414155 ✉ gareth_kinton@n-kesteven.gov.uk

Contracts: Mr Michael Gadd, Property Services Manager, District Council Offices, Kesteven Street, Sleaford NG34 7EF ☎ 01529 414155 ✉ michael_gadd@n-kesteven.gov.uk

Corporate Services: Ms Michelle Carrington, Head of Corporate & Customer Services, District Council Offices, Kesteven Street, Sleaford NG34 7EF ☎ 01529 414155 ✉ michelle_carrington@n-kesteven.gov.uk

Customer Service: Ms Michelle Carrington, Head of Corporate & Customer Services, District Council Offices, Kesteven Street, Sleaford NG34 7EF ☎ 01529 414155 ✉ michelle_carrington@n-kesteven.gov.uk

Direct Labour: Ms Nina Camm, Environmental Manager, District Council Offices, Kesteven Street, Sleaford NG34 7EF ☎ 01529 414155 ✉ nina_camm@n-kesteven.gov.uk

Economic Development: Mr Alan Gray, Economic Development Manager, District Council Offices, Kesteven Street, Sleaford NG34 7EF ☎ 01529 414155 ✉ alan.gray@n-kesteven.gov.uk

E-Government: Mr Alan Thomas, Deputy Chief Executive, District Council Offices, Kesteven Street, Sleaford NG34 7EF ☎ 01529 414155 ✉ alan_thomas@n-kesteven.gov.uk

Electoral Registration: Mrs Gill Hopkins, Electoral Services Manager, District Council Offices, Kesteven Street, Sleaford NG34 7EF ☎ 01529 414155 ✉ gill_hopkins@n-kesteven.gov.uk

Emergency Planning: Ms Sarah Golembiewski, Corporate Health, Safety & Emergency Planning Officer, District Council Offices, Kesteven Street, Sleaford NG34 7EF ☎ 01529 414155 ✉ sarah_golembiewski@n-kesteven.gov.uk

Energy Management: Mr Michael Gadd, Property Services Manager, District Council Offices, Kesteven Street, Sleaford NG34 7EF ☎ 01529 414155 ✉ michael_gadd@n-kesteven.gov.uk

Environmental / Technical Services: Mr Mark Taylor, Head of Environment & Public Protection, District Council Offices, Kesteven Street, Sleaford NG34 7EF ☎ 01529 414155 🖷 01476 406000 ✉ mark_taylor@n-kesteven.gov.uk

Environmental Health: Mr Mark Taylor, Head of Environment & Public Protection, District Council Offices, Kesteven Street, Sleaford NG34 7EF ☎ 01529 414155 🖷 01476 406000 ✉ mark_taylor@n-kesteven.gov.uk

Estates, Property & Valuation: Mr Michael Gadd, Property Services Manager, District Council Offices, Kesteven Street, Sleaford NG34 7EF ☎ 01529 414155 ✉ michael_gadd@n-kesteven.gov.uk

Finance and Treasurer: Mr Robert Dickens, Accountancy Manager, District Council Offices, Kesteven Street, Sleaford NG34 7EF ☎ 01529 414155 ✉ robert_dickens@n-kesteven.gov.uk

Finance and Treasurer: Mr Jason Jarvis, Head of Business Management, District Council Offices, Kesteven Street, Sleaford NG34 7EF ☎ 01529 414155 ✉ jason_jarvis@n-kesteven.gov.uk

Fleet Management: Ms Nina Camm, Environmental Manager, District Council Offices, Kesteven Street, Sleaford NG34 7EF ☎ 01529 414155 ✉ nina_camm@n-kesteven.gov.uk

Grounds Maintenance: Ms Nina Camm, Environmental Manager, District Council Offices, Kesteven Street, Sleaford NG34 7EF ☎ 01529 414155 ✉ nina_camm@n-kesteven.gov.uk

Health and Safety: Ms Sarah Golembiewski, Corporate Health, Safety & Emergency Planning Officer, District Council Offices, Kesteven Street, Sleaford NG34 7EF ☎ 01529 414155 ✉ sarah_golembiewski@n-kesteven.gov.uk

Home Energy Conservation: Mr Sean Johnson, Housing Renewal Manager, District Council Offices, Kesteven Street, Sleaford NG34 7EF ☎ 01529 414155 ✉ sean_johnson@n-kesteven.gov.uk

Housing: Mr Philip Roberts, Head of Housing Partnerships & Communities, District Council Offices, Kesteven Street, Sleaford NG34 7EF ☎ 01529 414155 ✉ philip_roberts@n-kesteven.gov.uk

Housing Maintenance: Mr Michael Gadd, Property Services Manager, District Council Offices, Kesteven Street, Sleaford NG34 7EF ☎ 01529 414155 ✉ michael_gadd@n-kesteven.gov.uk

Legal: Ms Karen Bradford, Monitoring Officer, District Council Offices, Kesteven Street, Sleaford NG34 7EF ☎ 01529 414155 ✉ karen_bradford@n-kesteven.gov.uk

Leisure and Cultural Services: Mr Mike Lock, Client Officer, District Council Offices, Kesteven Street, Sleaford NG34 7EF ☎ 01529 414155 ✉ mike_lock@n-kesteven.gov.uk

Licensing: Mr John Gibson, Principal Environmental Health Officer, District Council Offices, Kesteven Street, Sleaford NG34 7EF ☎ 01529 414155 ✉ john_gibson@n-kesteven.gov.uk

Lighting: Mr Russell Shortland, Design & Maintenance Manager, District Council Offices, Kesteven Street, Sleaford NG34 7EF ☎ 01529 414155 ✉ russell_shortland@n-kesteven.gov.uk

Lottery Funding, Charity and Voluntary: Ms Karen Bradford, Monitoring Officer, District Council Offices, Kesteven Street, Sleaford NG34 7EF ☎ 01529 414155 ✉ karen_bradford@n-kesteven.gov.uk

Member Services: Mrs Pauline Collett, Civic Officer, District Council Offices, Kesteven Street, Sleaford NG34 7EF ☎ 01529 414155 ✉ pauline_collett@n-kesteven.gov.uk

Member Services: Ms Marcella Heath, Democratic Services Manager, District Council Offices, Kesteven Street, Sleaford NG34 7EF ☎ 01529 414155 ✉ marcella_heath@n-kesteven.gov.uk

Personnel / HR: Mr Jason Jarvis, Head of Business Management, District Council Offices, Kesteven Street, Sleaford NG34 7EF ☎ 01529 414155 ✉ jason_jarvis@n-kesteven.gov.uk

Personnel / HR: Ms Christine Richardson, Human Resources Manager, District Council Offices, Kesteven Street, Sleaford NG34 7EF ☎ 01529 414155 ✉ christine_richardson@n-kesteven.gov.uk

Planning: Mrs Jane Wells, Head of Planning, Economic & Cultural Services, District Council Offices, Kesteven Street, Sleaford NG34 7EF ☎ 01529 414155 ✉ jane_wells@n-kesteven.gov.uk

Procurement: Mr Jason Jarvis, Head of Business Management, District Council Offices, Kesteven Street, Sleaford NG34 7EF ☎ 01529 414155 ✉ scrutiny@n-kesteven.gov.uk

Recycling & Waste Minimisation: Ms Nina Camm, Environmental Manager, District Council Offices, Kesteven Street, Sleaford NG34 7EF ☎ 01529 414155 ✉ nina_camm@n-kesteven.gov.uk

Staff Training: Ms Christine Richardson, Human Resources Manager, District Council Offices, Kesteven Street, Sleaford NG34 7EF ☎ 01529 414155 ✉ christine_richardson@n-kesteven.gov.uk

Street Scene: Ms Nina Camm, Environmental Manager, District Council Offices, Kesteven Street, Sleaford NG34 7EF ☎ 01529 414155 ✉ nina_camm@n-kesteven.gov.uk

Sustainable Communities: Mrs Jane Wells, Head of Planning, Economic & Cultural Services, District Council Offices, Kesteven Street, Sleaford NG34 7EF ☎ 01529 414155 ✉ jane_wells@n-kesteven.gov.uk

Sustainable Development: Ms Bonnie Fricker, Sustainability Co-ordination Officer, District Council Offices, Kesteven Street, Sleaford NG34 7EF ☎ 01529 414155 ✉ bonnie_fricker@n-kesteven.gov.uk

Tourism: Mrs Jane Wells, Head of Planning, Economic & Cultural Services, District Council Offices, Kesteven Street, Sleaford NG34 7EF ☎ ; 01529 414155 ✉ jane_wells@n-kesteven.gov.uk

Transport: Ms Nina Camm, Environmental Manager, District Council Offices, Kesteven Street, Sleaford NG34 7EF ☎ 01529 414155 ✉ nina_camm@n-kesteven.gov.uk

Waste Collection and Disposal: Ms Nina Camm, Environmental Manager, District Council Offices, Kesteven Street, Sleaford NG34 7EF ☎ 01529 414155 ✉ nina_camm@n-kesteven.gov.uk

Waste Collection and Disposal: Mr Mark Taylor, Head of Environment & Public Protection, District Council Offices, Kesteven Street, Sleaford NG34 7EF ☎ 01529 414155 🖷 01476 406000 ✉ mark_taylor@n-kesteven.gov.uk

Waste Management: Ms Nina Camm, Environmental Manager, District Council Offices, Kesteven Street, Sleaford NG34 7EF ☎ 01529 414155 ✉ nina_camm@n-kesteven.gov.uk

MEMBERS OF THE COUNCIL (43)

***Chair:* Cucksey**, Ray (CON - Branston)
cllr_ray_cucksey@n-kesteven.gov.uk

***Vice-Chair:* Boston**, Terry (CON - Ruskington)
cllr_terry_boston@n-kesteven.gov.uk

***Leader of the Council:* Brighton**, Marion (CON - Heighington and Washingborough)
cllr_marion_brighton@n-kesteven.gov.uk

***Deputy Leader of the Council:* Gallagher**, Mike (CON - Bracebridge Heath and Waddington East)
cllr_mike_gallagher@n-kesteven.gov.uk

Allen, Mark (CON - Sleaford Quarrington and Mareham)
Cllr_Mark_Allan@n-kesteven.gov.uk

Appleby, Sally (CON - Eagle, Swinderby and Witham St Hughs)
Cllr_Sally_Appleby@n-kesteven.gov.uk

Barrett, Kay (LD - North Hykeham Forum)
cllr_kay_barrett@n-kesteven.gov.uk

Bishop, John (LD - North Hykeham Moor)
Cllr_John_Bishop@n-kesteven.gov.uk

Burley, Peter (IND - Bracebridge Heath and Waddington East)
Cllr_Peter_Burley@n-kesteven.gov.uk

Carrington, Ian (CON - Heighington and Washingborough)
cllr_ian_carrington@n-kesteven.gov.uk

Cartwright, Ian (CON - Ashby De La Launde and Cranwell)
cllr_ian_cartwright@n-kesteven.gov.uk

Cawrey, Lindsey (CON - Bracebridge Heath and Waddington East)
Cllr_Lindsey_Cawrey@n-kesteven.gov.uk

Clark, Helen (IND - North Hykeham Mill)
Cllr_Helen_Clark@n-kesteven.gov.uk

Clarke, Andrea (CON - North Hykeham Mill)
Cllr_Andrea_Clarke@n-kesteven.gov.uk

Conway, Laura (IND - Cliff Villages)
Cllr_Laura_Conway@n-kesteven.gov.uk

Cook, Jim (IND - Osbournby)
Cllr_Jim_Cook@n-kesteven.gov.uk

Dickinson, David (CON - Kirkby la Thorpe and South Kyme)

cllr_david_dickinson@n-kesteven.gov.uk
Dolby, Ian (INDNA - Sleaford Quarrington and Mareham)
Cllr_Ian_Dolby@n-kesteven.gov.uk
Dolby, Keith (INDNA - Sleaford Castle)
Cllr_Keith_Dolby@n-kesteven.gov.uk
Flint, Shirley (IND - Skellingthorpe)
cllr_shirley_flint@n-kesteven.gov.uk
Frost, Joyce (CON - Branston)
cllr_joyce_frost@n-kesteven.gov.uk
Goldson, Chris (IND - Skellingthorpe)
cllr_chris_goldson@n-kesteven.gov.uk
Haysum, Peter (IND - Sleaford Holdingham)
cllr_peter_haysum@n-kesteven.gov.uk
Hazelwood, Geoff (CON - Sleaford Quarrington and Mareham)
Cllr_Geoffrey_Hazelwood@n-kesteven.gov.uk
Howe, Sue (CON - Bassingham and Brant Broughton)
Cllr_Sue_Howe@n-kesteven.gov.uk
Kendrick, Rob (CON - Metheringham)
Cllr_Rob_Kendrick@n-kesteven.gov.uk
Lee, Wallace (LD - North Hykeham Memorial)
Cllr_Wallace_Lee@n-kesteven.gov.uk
Little, Ross (CON - North Hykeham Witham)
Cllr_Ross_Little@n-kesteven.gov.uk
Money, John (CON - Metheringham)
cllr_john_money@n-kesteven.gov.uk
Ogden, Stewart (CON - Heckington Rural)
cllr_stewart_ogden@n-kesteven.gov.uk
Ogden, Gill (CON - Billinghay, Martin and North Kyme)
cllr_gill_ogden@n-kesteven.gov.uk
Overton, Marianne (IND - Cliff Villages)
cllr_marianne_overton@n-kesteven.gov.uk
Oxby, Ron (CON - Heighington and Washingborough)
cllr_ron_oxby@n-kesteven.gov.uk
Pennell, Lance (CON - Waddington West)
cllr_lance_pennell@n-kesteven.gov.uk
Powell, Mike (IND - Billinghay, Martin and North Kyme)
cllr_mike_powell@n-kesteven.gov.uk
Suiter, David (IND - Sleaford Navigation)
Cllr_David_Suiter@n-kesteven.gov.uk
Tarry, Sally (CON - Heckington Rural)
cllr_sally_tarry@n-kesteven.gov.uk
Waring, Susan (CON - Leasingham and Rauceby)
Cllr_Susan_Waring@n-kesteven.gov.uk
Watson, Brian (IND - Sleaford Westholme)
cllr_brian_watson@n-kesteven.gov.uk
Wells, Barbara (IND - Eagle, Swinderby and Witham St Hughs)
cllr_barbara_wells@n-kesteven.gov.uk
Whittle, Geoffrey (CON - Ashby De La Launde and Cranwell)
Cllr_Geoffrey_Whittle@n-kesteven.gov.uk
Woodman, Pat (IND - Bassingham and Brant Broughton)
cllr_pat_woodman@n-kesteven.gov.uk
Wright, Richard (CON - Ruskington)
Cllr_Richard_Wright@n-kesteven.gov.uk

POLITICAL COMPOSITION

CON: 25, IND: 13, LD: 3, INDNA: 2

CABINET

Leader: Mrs M Brighton
Deputy Leader: Mr M Gallagher

COMMITTEE CHAIRS

Audit: Mrs Sue Howe
Communities & Economy: Mr Peter Burley
Environment & Communities (Scrutiny): Mr Chris Goldson
Licensing: Mr Terry Boston
Performance & Resources (Scrutiny): Mr Geoffrey Whittle
Planning: Mrs Pat Woodman
Standards: Miss Andrea Clarke

NORTH LANARKSHIRE S

North Lanarkshire Council, Civic Centre, Motherwell ML1 1AB
☎ 01698 302222 🖷 01698 275125 🖳 www.northlan.gov.uk

FACTS & FIGURES

Police Authority: Strathclyde Police Authority
Health Authority: NHS Lanarkshire
Parliamentary Constituencies: Airdrie and Shotts, Coatbridge, Chryston & Bellshill, Cumbernauld, Kilsyth and Kirkintilloch East, Motherwell & Wishaw
Election Frequency: Elections are of whole council
Twinning: Bron (France); Campi Bisenzio (Italy); Gatchina (Russia); Les Marches (France); Medlan (France); Schweinfurt (Germany); St. Denis (France)

PRINCIPAL OFFICERS

Chief Executive: Mr Gavin Whitefield, Chief Executive, Civic Centre, Windmillhill Street, Motherwell ML1 1AB ☎ 01698 302452 🖷 01698 230265 ✉ whitefieldg@northlan.gov.uk

Senior Management: Ms Mary Castles, Executive Director of Housing & Social Work Services, Civic Centre, Motherwell ML1 1AB ☎ 01698 302350 🖷 01698 302537 ✉ castlesm@northlan.gov.uk

Senior Management: Mr Alistair Crichton, Executive Director of Finance & Customer Service, Civic Centre, Motherwell ML1 1AB ☎ 01698 302200 🖷 01698 264116 ✉ crichtona@northlan.gov.uk

Senior Management: Mr Paul Jukes, Executive Director of Environmental Services, Civic Centre, Motherwell ML1 1AB ☎ 01698 302746 🖷 01698 264116 ✉ jukesp@northlan.gov.uk

Senior Management: Mr John O'Hagan, Executive Director of Corporate Services, Civic Centre, Motherwell ML1 1AB ☎ 01698 302344 🖷 01698 276101 ✉ ohaganj@northlan.gov.uk

Senior Management: Ms Christine Pollock, Executive Director of Learning & Leisure Services, Civic Centre, Motherwell ML1 1AB ☎ ; 01698 302222 ✉ pollockc@northlan.gov.uk

Access Officer / Social Services (Disability): Mr Dilini Wilkinson, Community Care Senior (Older Adults), 122 Bank Street, Coatbridge ML5 1ET ☎ 01236 622202 🖷 01698 332179 ✉ wilkinsondi@northlan.gov.uk

Architect, Building / Property Services: Mr William Hope, Head of Deisgn & Property Services, Civic Centre, Motherwell ML1 1AB ☎ 01698 504001 ✉ hopew@northlan.gov.uk

Best Value: Ms Mary Castles, Executive Director of Housing & Social Work Services, Civic Centre, Motherwell ML1 1AB ☎ 01698 302350 🖷 01698 302537 ✉ castlesm@northlan.gov.uk

Building Control: Mr David Provan, Business Building Standards Manager, Fleming House , 2 Tryst Road, Cumbernauld G67 1JW

☎ 01698 812369 🖷 01236 618099 ✉ provand@northlan.gov.uk

Catering Services: Mr Brian Dunbar, First Stop Shop Manager, Buchanan Tower, Stepps, Glasgow G33 6HR ☎ 01698 302222 ✉ dunbarb@northlan.gov.uk

Children / Youth Services: Ms Mary Fegan, Head of Social Work Services, Scott House, 73-77 Merry Street, Motherwell ML1 1JE ☎ 01698 332001 🖷 01698 332095 ✉ feganm@northlan.gov.uk

Civil Registration: Mr John O'Hagan, Executive Director of Corporate Services, Civic Centre, Motherwell ML1 1AB ☎ 01698 302344 🖷 01698 276101 ✉ ohaganj@northlan.gov.uk

PR / Communications: Mr Stephen Penman, Head of Corporate Communications & Marketing, Civic Centre, Motherwell ML1 1AB ☎ 01698 302591 ✉ penmanste@northlan.gov.uk

Community Safety: Sgt Mark Milligan, Community Safety Officer, Civic Centre, Motherwell ML1 1AB ☎ 01698 302222

Computer Management: Mrs Irene McKelvey, Head of E-Government & Service Development, Civic Centre, Motherwell ML1 1AB ☎ 01698 302532 🖷 01698 403011 ✉ mckelveyi@northlan.gov.uk

Consumer Protection and Trading Standards: Mr Dave Roderick, Trading Standards Manager, Fleming House, 2 Tryst Road, Cumbernauld G67 1JW ☎ 01236 616415 ✉ roderickd@northlan.gov.uk

Corporate Services: Mr Brian Cook, Head of Revenue Services, Dalziel Building, 7 Scott Street, Motherwell ML1 1PN ☎ 01698 403929 ✉ cookb@northlan.gov.uk

Corporate Services: Mr John O'Hagan, Executive Director of Corporate Services, Civic Centre, Motherwell ML1 1AB ☎ 01698 302344 🖷 01698 276101 ✉ ohaganj@northlan.gov.uk

Economic Development: Mr Eric Hislop, Head of Regeneration & Infrastructure, Civic Centre, Motherwell ML1 1AB ☎ 01236 616305 ✉ hislope@snorthlan.gov.uk

Education: Ms J Liddell, Head of Education Quality & Development, Municipal Buildings, Kildonan Street, Coatbridge ML5 3BT ☎ 01236 812279 ✉ liddellj@northlan.gov.uk

Education: Mr Murdo MacIver, Head of Educational Provision, Municipal Buildings, Kildonan Street, Coatbridge ML5 3BT ☎ 01236 812269 ✉ maciverm@northlan.gov.uk

Education: Ms Christine Pollock, Executive Director of Learning & Leisure Services, Civic Centre, Motherwell ML1 1AB ☎ 01698 302222 ✉ pollockc@northlan.gov.uk

E-Government: Mrs Irene McKelvey, Head of E-Government & Service Development, Civic Centre, Motherwell ML1 1AB ☎ 01698 302532 🖷 01698 403011 ✉ mckelveyi@northlan.gov.uk

Emergency Planning: Ms Erin McCann, Emergency Planning Officer, Civic Centre, Motherwell ML1 1AB ☎ 01698 302561 ✉ mccanne@northlan.gov.uk

Environmental / Technical Services: Mr Paul Jukes, Executive Director of Environmental Services, Civic Centre, Motherwell ML1 1AB ☎ 01698 302746 🖷 01698 264116 ✉ jukesp@northlan.gov.uk

Environmental Health: Mr Paul Jukes, Executive Director of Environmental Services, Civic Centre, Motherwell ML1 1AB ☎ 01698 302746 🖷 01698 264116 ✉ jukesp@northlan.gov.uk

Estates, Property & Valuation: Mr Eric Hislop, Head of Regeneration & Infrastructure, Civic Centre, Motherwell ML1 1AB ☎ 01236 616305 ✉ hislope@snorthlan.gov.uk

European Liaison: Mr Eric Hislop, Head of Regeneration & Infrastructure, Civic Centre, Motherwell ML1 1AB ☎ 01236 616305 ✉ hislope@snorthlan.gov.uk

Facilities: Mr Graham Patrick, Head of Facility Support Services, Buchanan Tower, Stepps, Glasgow G33 6HR ☎ 01698 302222 ✉ patrickg@northlan.gov.uk

Finance and Treasurer: Mr Alistair Crichton, Executive Director of Finance & Customer Service, Civic Centre, Motherwell ML1 1AB ☎ 01698 302200 🖷 01698 264116 ✉ crichtona@northlan.gov.uk

Finance and Treasurer: Mr Paul Hughes, Head of Financial Services, Civic Centre, Motherwell ML1 1AB ☎ 01698 302275 ✉ hughesp@northlan.gov.uk

Grounds Maintenance: Mr Paul Duncan, Grounds Maintenance Manager, Old Edinburgh Road, Belshill ML4 3JS ☎ 01698 506268 🖷 01698 506249 ✉ duncanp@northlan.gov.uk

Health and Safety: Mr Stuart Hamilton, Principal Health & Safety Officer, Civic Centre, Motherwell ML1 1AB ☎ 01698 302368 🖷 01698 230278 ✉ hamiltonst@northlan.gov.uk

Health and Safety: Mr John O'Hagan, Executive Director of Corporate Services, Civic Centre, Motherwell ML1 1AB ☎ 01698 302344 🖷 01698 276101 ✉ ohaganj@northlan.gov.uk

Housing: Ms Mary Castles, Executive Director of Housing & Social Work Services, Civic Centre, Motherwell ML1 1AB ☎ 01698 302350 🖷 01698 302537 ✉ castlesm@northlan.gov.uk

Housing: Ms Elaine McHugh, Head of Housing Services, Civic Centre, Motherwell ML1 1AB ☎ 01698 302222 ✉ elaine.mchugh@northlan.gov.uk

Housing: Mr Ronald Paul, Head of Housing & Social Work Resources, Scott House, 73-77 Merry Street, Motherwell ML1 1JE ☎ 01698 332023 ✉ paulr@northlan.gov.uk

Housing Maintenance: Ms Mary Castles, Executive Director of Housing & Social Work Services, Civic Centre, Motherwell ML1 1AB ☎ 01698 302350 🖷 01698 302537 ✉ castlesm@northlan.gov.uk

Legal: Ms June Murray, Head of Legal Services, Civic Centre, Motherwell ML1 1AB ☎ 01698 302295 ✉ murrayjune@northlan.gov.uk

Leisure and Cultural Services: Ms Christine Pollock, Executive Director of Learning & Leisure Services, Civic Centre, Motherwell ML1 1AB ☎ ; 01698 302222 pollockc@northlan.gov.uk

Licensing: Ms Eileen Howson, Chief Solicitor, Civic Centre, Motherwell ML1 1AB ☎ 01698 302526 howsone@northlan.gov.uk

Licensing: Mr Mitch Kerr, Chief Solicitor, Civic Centre, Motherwell ML1 1AB ☎ 01698 302371 🖷 01698 302211 kerrm@northlan.gov.uk

Lifelong Learning: Ms L McMurrich, Head of Community Information & Learning, Municipal Buildings, Kildonan Street, Coatbridge ML5 3BT ☎ 01236 812338 mcmurrichl@northlan.gov.uk

Lifelong Learning: Ms Christine Pollock, Executive Director of Learning & Leisure Services, Civic Centre, Motherwell ML1 1AB ☎ 01698 302222 pollockc@northlan.gov.uk

Lighting: Mr Colin Nimmo, Lighting Design Manager, Civic Centre, Motherwell ML1 1AB ☎ 01236 616217 nimmoc@northlan.gov.uk

Member Services: Mr John Fleming, Head of Central Services, Civic Centre, Motherwell ML1 1AB ☎ 01698 302222 🖷 01698 275125 flemingj@northlan.gov.uk

Personnel / HR: Ms Iris Wylie, Head of Human Resources, Civic Centre, Motherwell ML1 1AB ☎ 01698 302215 🖷 01698 230387 wyliei@northlan.gov.uk

Planning: Mr Paul Jukes, Executive Director of Environmental Services, Civic Centre, Motherwell ML1 1AB ☎ 01698 302746 🖷 01698 264116 jukesp@northlan.gov.uk

Planning: Mr Patrick Kelly, Head of Planning & Development, Buchanan Tower, Buchanan Business Park, Stepps, Glasgow G33 6HR ☎ 01698 302222 kellyp@northlan.gov.uk

Procurement: Ms Audrey Telfer, Senior Procurement Officer, Dalziel House, 7 Scott Street, Motherwell ML1 1PN ☎ 01698 403954 telfera@northlan.gov.uk

Public Libraries: Ms Gemma Alexander, Libraries & Information Manager, Civic Centre, Motherwell ML1 1AB ☎ 01698 332604 alexanderg@northlan.gov.uk

Regeneration: Mr Eric Hislop, Head of Regeneration & Infrastructure, Civic Centre, Motherwell ML1 1AB ☎ 01236 616305 hislope@snorthlan.gov.uk

Social Services: Ms Mary Fegan, Head of Social Work Services, Scott House, 73-77 Merry Street, Motherwell ML1 1JE ☎ 01698 332001 🖷 01698 332095 feganm@northlan.gov.uk

Social Services: Mr Duncan Mackay, Head of Social Work Development, Scott House, 73-77 Merry Street, Motherwell ML1 1JE ☎ 01698 332024 mackayd@northlan.gov.uk

Social Services: Mr Crawford Morgan, Head of Protective Services, Fleming House, Tryst Road, Cumbernauld G67 1JW ☎ 01698 302222 morganc@northlan.gov.uk

Social Services: Mr Ronald Paul, Head of Housing & Social Work Resources, Scott House, 73-77 Merry Street, Motherwell ML1 1JE ☎ 01698 332023 paulr@northlan.gov.uk

Social Services (Adult): Ms Mary Fegan, Head of Social Work Services, Scott House, 73-77 Merry Street, Motherwell ML1 1JE ☎ 01698 332001 🖷 01698 332095 feganm@northlan.gov.uk

Social Services (Children): Ms Mary Fegan, Head of Social Work Services, Scott House, 73-77 Merry Street, Motherwell ML1 1JE ☎ 01698 332001 🖷 01698 332095 feganm@northlan.gov.uk

Staff Training: Ms Heather Liddle, Principal Training Officer, Civic Centre, Motherwell ML1 1AB ☎ 01698 302097 🖷 01698 230278 liddleh@northlan.gov.uk

Street Scene: Mr David Cullen, Joint Cleansing Services Manager, Bellshill Complex, Old Edinburgh Road, Bellshill ML4 3JF ☎ 01698 506271 🖷 01698 302044 cullend@northlan.gov.uk

Street Scene: Mr Harry Morgan, Joint Cleansing Services Manager, Bellshill Complex, Old Edinburgh Road, Bellshill ML4 3JF ☎ 01698 506271 🖷 01698 302044 morganh@northlan.gov.uk

Sustainable Development: Mr David Baxter, Assistant Business Manager, Fleming House, 2 Tryst Road, Cumbernauld G67 1JW ☎ 01236 616243 🖷 01236 616232 baxterd@northlan.gov.uk

Town Centre: Mr Jack Duffy, Town Centre Manager (Cumbernauld), Town Centre Initiatives Ltd, Coatbridge ML5 3EL ☎ 01263 638444 duffyja@northlan.gov.uk

Town Centre: Ms Anne Flood, Town Centre Manager, Town Centre Initiatives Ltd, Coatbridge ML5 3EL ☎ 01263 638443 flooda@northlan.gov.uk

Traffic Management: Mr John Marran, Business Manager (Road Strategy & Assets), Fleming House, 2 Tryst Road, Cumbernauld G67 1JW ☎ 01236 616253 🖷 01236 616232 marranj@northlan.gov.uk

Transport: Mr Graham Mackay, Head of Roads & Transportation, Fleming House, 2 Tryst Road, Cumbernauld G67 1JW ☎ 01236 616202 🖷 01236 616232 mackaygd@northlan.gov.uk

Transport Planner: Mr Graham Mackay, Head of Roads & Transportation, Buchanan Tower, Stepps, Glasgow G33 6HR ☎ 01236 616202 🖷 01236 616232 mackaygd@northlan.gov.uk

Waste Collection and Disposal: Mr Kenneth Wilson, Head of Land Services, Buchanan Business Park, Stepps , Glasgow G33 6HR ☎ 01698 302222 wilsonk@northlan.gov.uk

Waste Management: Mr Kenneth Wilson, Head of Land Services, Buchanan Business Park, Stepps , Glasgow G33 6HR ☎ 01698 302222 wilsonk@northlan.gov.uk

MEMBERS OF THE COUNCIL (70)

***Provost:* Robertson**, James (LAB - Fortissat)
robertsonj@northlan.gov.uk

***Deputy Provost:* Jones**, Jean (LAB - Kilsyth)
jonesj@northlan.gov.uk

***Leader of the Council:* Lyle**, Marina (SNP - Belshill)
lylem@northlan.gov.uk

***Leader of the Council:* McCabe**, James (LAB - Thorniewood)
mccabej@northlan.gov.uk

Baird, David (SNP - Mossend and Holytown)
bairdda@northlan.gov.uk

Beveridge, Alan (SNP - Airdrie North)
beveridgeal@northlan.gov.uk

Brooks, James (LAB - Coatbridge South)
brooksj@northlan.gov.uk

Burrows, Robert (LAB - Thorniewood)
BurrowsR@northlan.gov.uk

Cefferty, Charles (IND - Fortissat)
ceffertyc@northlan.gov.uk

Chadha, Balwant Singh (LAB - Cumbernauld North)
chadhab@northlan.gov.uk

Clinch, Alan (LAB - Murdostoun)
clincha@northlan.gov.uk

Cochrane, Thomas (SNP - Fortissat)
cochraneth@northlan.gov.uk

Coyle, Michael (SNP - Airdrie South)
coylem@northlan.gov.uk

Coyle, Agnes (SNP - Airdrie South)
coylea@northlan.gov.uk

Coyle, James (LAB - Mossend and Holytown)
coylej@northlan.gov.uk

Coyle, Sophia (SNP - Airdrie North)
CoyleS@northlan.gov.uk

Curley, Thomas (LAB - Airdrie South)
curleyt@northlan.gov.uk

Curran, Harry (LAB - Belshill)
curranh@northlan.gov.uk

Fagan, David (LAB - Airdrie South)
cllr.david.fagan@googlemail.com

Farooq, Shahid (SNP - Motherwell North)
farooqs@northlan.gov.uk

Fellows, Marion (SNP - Wishaw)
fellowsm@northlan.gov.uk

Goldie, William (SNP - Cumbernauld South)
GoldieW@northlan.gov.uk

Graham, Alan (LAB - Cumbernauld South)
grahamallan@northlan.gov.uk

Grant, Stephen (LAB - Abronhill, Kildrum and the Village)
grantst@northlan.gov.uk

Harmon, Kaye (LAB - Motherwell South East and Ravenscraig)
harmonk@northlan.gov.uk

Higgins, John (LAB - Coatbridge South)
higginsjoh@northlan.gov.uk

Hogg, Paddy (SNP - Cumbernauld South)
hoggp@northlan.gov.uk

Hogg, William (LAB - Strathkelvin)
hoggw@northlan.gov.uk

Hume, Jim (SNP - Wishaw)
humej@northlan.gov.uk

Irvine, Elizabeth (SNP - Abronhill, Kildrum and the Village)
irvinee@northlan.gov.uk

Johnston, Tom (SNP - Abronhill, Kildrum and the Village)
johnstont@northlan.gov.uk

Kelly, Paul (LAB - Motherwell West)
kellyp2@northlan.gov.uk

Logue, James (LAB - Airdrie Central)
loguej@northlan.gov.uk

Love, Samuel (LAB - Wishaw)
lovesam@northlan.gov.uk

Lunny, Thomas (LAB - Motherwell South East and Ravenscraig)
lunnyt@northlan.gov.uk

MacGregor, Fulton (SNP - Coatbridge North and Glenboig)
macgregorful@northlan.gov.uk

Maginnis, Thomas (LAB - Coatbridge West)
maginnist@northlan.gov.uk

Majid, Imtiaz (SNP - Coatbridge South)
majidi@northlan.gov.uk

Masterton, Alan (SNP - Cumbernauld North)
mastertona@northlan.gov.uk

McAnulty, Julie (SNP - Coatbridge North and Glenboig)
macnultyj@northlan.oov.uk

McAuley, Annita (LAB - Motherwell North)
McAuleyAn@northlan.gov.uk

McCulloch, Barry (LAB - Cumbernauld North)
mccullochb@northlan.gov.uk

McGlinchey, Frances (SNP - Strathkelvin)
mcglincheyf@northlan.gov.uk

McGuigan, Harry (LAB - Belshill)
mcguiganh@northlan.gov.uk

McKay, Frank (LAB - Wishaw)
mckayf@northlan.gov.uk

McKendrick, Robert (IND - Murdostoun)
mckendrickr@northlan.gov.uk

McKenna, Helen (LAB - Motherwell North)
McKennaH@northlan.gov.uk

McLaren, John (LAB - Strathkelvin)
mclarenjohn@northlan.gov.uk

McNally, Frank (LAB - Mossend and Holytown)
mcnallyf@northlan.gov.uk

McPake, Michael (LAB - Coatbridge North and Glenboig)
mcpakemi@northlan.gov.uk

McShannon, Duncan (SNP - Thorniewood)
mcshannond@northlan.gov.uk

McVey, Heather (LAB - Kilsyth)
mcveyh@northlan.gov.uk

Morgan, Thomas (LAB - Airdrie North)
morgant@northlan.gov.uk

Muir, Stephanie (LAB - Cumbernauld South)
muirsteph@northlan.gov.uk

Nolan, Peter (LAB - Motherwell North)
nolanp@northlan.gov.uk

O'Brien, Alan (SNP - Cumbernauld North)
obrienal@northlan.gov.uk

O'Rorke, Gary (LAB - Motherwell South East and Ravenscraig)
ororkeg@northlan.gov.uk

Ross, Michael (LAB - Motherwell West)
rossm@northlan.gov.uk

Shevlin, Nicky (LAB - Murdostoun)
shevlinn@northlan.gov.uk

Shields, William (LAB - Coatbridge North and Glenboig)
shieldsb@northlan.gov.uk

Smith, James (LAB - Coatbridge West)
smithjam@northlan.gov.uk

Spowart, Andrew (LAB - Airdrie North)
spowarta@northlan.gov.uk

Stevenson, Alan (SNP - Kilsyth)
stevensonal@northlan.gov.uk

Stocks, David (SNP - Airdrie Central)
stocksd@northlan.gov.uk

Sullivan, Peter (LAB - Airdrie Central)
sullivanp@northlan.gov.uk
Taggart, John (SNP - Murdostoun)
taggartjo@northlan.gov.uk
Valentine, Annette (SNP - Motherwell West)
valentinean@northlan.gov.uk
Valentine, Alan (SNP - Motherwell South East and Ravenscraig)
valentinea@northlan.gov.uk
Wallace, Brian (LAB - Strathkelvin)
wallaceb@northlan.gov.uk
Welsh, Paul (SNP - Coatbridge West)
welshp@northlan.gov.uk

POLITICAL COMPOSITION
LAB: 41, SNP: 27, IND: 2

COMMITTEE CHAIRS
Audit & Governance: Mr Thomas Morgan
Environmental Services: Ms Helen McKenna
Housing & Social Work Services: Mr Samuel Love
Leisure & Learning Services: Mr James Logue
Licensing: Mr Peter Nolan
Planning & Transportation: Mr James Coyle

NORTH LINCOLNSHIRE U

North Lincolnshire Council, Pittwood House, Ashby Road, Scunthorpe DN16 1AB ☎ 01724 296296 🖷 01724 296079 ✉ pittwoodreception@northlincs.gov.uk 💻 www.northlincs.gov.uk

FACTS & FIGURES
Police Authority: Humberside Police Authority
Health Authority: NHS Yorkshire & the Humber
Learning and Skills Council: East Midlands
Parliamentary Constituencies: Brigg and Goole, Scunthorpe
EU Constituencies: East Midlands
Election Frequency: Elections are of whole council

PRINCIPAL OFFICERS
Chief Executive: Mr Simon Driver, Chief Executive, Civic Centre, Ashby Road, Scunthorpe DN16 1AB ☎ 01724 296000 🖷 01724 296005 ✉ simon.driver@northlincs.gov.uk

Access Officer / Social Services (Disability): Ms Denise Hyde, Director - People, Civic Centre, Ashby Road, Scunthorpe DN16 1AB ☎ 01724 296406 🖷 01724 296404 ✉ denise.hyde@northlincs.gov.uk

Architect, Building / Property Services: Mr Peter Williams, Director - Places, Civic Centre, Ashby Road, Scunthorpe DN16 1AB ☎ 01724 296710 🖷 01724 296770 ✉ peter.williams@northlincs.gov.uk

Best Value: Mr Jason Whaler, Assistant Director - Business Support, Civic Centre, Ashby Road, Scunthorpe DN16 1AB ☎ 01724 296018 🖷 01724 296030 ✉ jason.whaler@northlincs.gov.uk

Building Control: Mr Martin Salmon, Building Control Team Manager, Church Square House, PO Box 42, Scunthorpe DN15 6XQ ☎ 01724 297400 🖷 01724 297872 ✉ martin.salmon@northlincs.gov.uk

Catering Services: Mrs Sharon Seddon, Head - Catering & Cleaning, Church Square House, Scunthorpe DN15 6NL ☎ 01724 297922 ✉ sharon.seddon@northlincs.gov.uk

Children / Youth Services: Mr Mick Gibbs, Assistant Director - Specialist Services, Hewson House, Station Road, Brigg DN20 8XJ ☎ 01724 296410 ✉ mick.gibbs@northlincs.gov.uk

Children / Youth Services: Ms Denise Hyde, Director - People, Civic Centre, Ashby Road, Scunthorpe DN16 1AB ☎ 01724 296406 🖷 01724 296404 ✉ denise.hyde@northlincs.gov.uk

Civil Registration: Mrs Alison Prestwood, Head - Registration, Civic Centre, Ashby Road, Scunthorpe DN16 1AB ☎ 01724 842425 ✉ alison.prestwood@northlincs.gov.uk

PR / Communications: Mr Chris Skinner, Head - Communications, Civic Centre, Ashby Road, Scunthorpe DN16 1AB ☎ 01724 296301 ✉ chris.skinner@northlincs.gov.uk

Community Planning: Mr David Hey, Head - Stronger Communities, Civic Centre, Ashby Road, Scunthorpe DN16 1AB ☎ 01724 296646 ✉ dave.hey@northlincs.gov.uk

Community Safety: Mr Stuart Minto, Head - Safer Neighbourhoods, Shelford House, Scunthorpe DN15 6NU ☎ 01724 244654 ✉ stuart.minto@northlincs.gov.uk

Computer Management: Mr Martin Oglesby, Head - IT Services, Cary Lane, Brigg DN15 6XQ ☎ 01724 296266 ✉ martin.oglesby@northlincs.gov.uk

Consumer Protection and Trading Standards: Mr Simon Talbot, Head - Trading Standards, Church Square House, Scunthorpe DL15 6QX ☎ 01724 297660 ✉ simon.talbot@northlincs.gov.uk

Contracts: Mr Jason Whaler, Assistant Director - Business Support, Civic Centre, Ashby Road, Scunthorpe DN16 1AB ☎ 01724 296018 🖷 01724 296030 ✉ jason.whaler@northlincs.gov.uk

Corporate Services: Mr Chris Ellerby, Head - Asset Management, Hewson House, Station Road, Brigg DN20 8XJ ☎ 01724 296763 ✉ chris.ellerby@northlincs.gov.uk

Customer Service: Miss Helen Rowe, Assistant Director - Customer Services, Civic Centre, Ashby Road, Scunthorpe DN16 1AB ☎ 01724 297667 ✉ helen.rowe@northlincs.gov.uk

Economic Development: Mr Marcus Walker, Assistant Director - Planning & Regeneration, Civic Centre, Ashby Road, Scunthorpe DN16 1AB ☎ 01724 297305 🖷 01724 297899 ✉ marcus.walker@northlincs.gov.uk

Education: Mr Peter Thorpe, Assistant Director - School Improvement, Hewson House, Brigg DN20 8HX ☎ 01724 297096 ✉ peter.thorpe@northlincs.gov.uk

E-Government: Mr Jason Whaler, Assistant Director - Business Support, Civic Centre, Ashby Road, Scunthorpe DN16 1AB ☎ 01724 296018 🖷 01724 296030 ✉ jason.whaler@northlincs.gov.uk

Electoral Registration: Mrs Anthia Taylor, Electoral Registrations Officer, Civic Centre, Ashby Road, Scunthorpe DN16 1AB ☎ 01724 296248 🖱 anthia.taylor@northlincs.gov.uk

Emergency Planning: Mr John Whiteman, Emergency Planning Manager, Humber Emergency Planning Service, County Hall, Beverley HU17 9BA ☎ 01482 884140 🖷 01482 882901 🖱 john.whiteman@eastriding.gov.uk

Energy Management: Mr Craig Stapleton, Energy Manager, Hewson House, Brigg DN20 8XY ☎ 01724 296514 🖱 craig.stapleton@northlincs.gov.uk

Environmental / Technical Services: Mr Trevor Laming, Assistant Director - Technical & Environmental Services, The Angel, Brigg DN20 8LD ☎ 01724 297603 🖷 01724 297333 🖱 trevor.laming@northlincs.gov.uk

Environmental Health: Mr Barry Hutchinson, Assistant Service Director - Neighbourhood & Environmental Services, The Angel, Brigg DN20 8LD ☎ 01724 297802 🖷 01724 297909 🖱 barry.hutchinson@northlincs.gov.uk

Estates, Property & Valuation: Mr Paul Nicholson, Estates & Valuations Manager, Hewson House, Station Road, Brigg DN20 8XY ☎ 01724 296789 🖱 paul.nicholson@northlincs.gov.uk

European Liaison: Mr Marcus Walker, Assistant Director - Planning & Regeneration, Civic Centre, Ashby Road, Scunthorpe DN16 1AB ☎ 01724 297305 🖷 01724 297899 🖱 marcus.walker@northlincs.gov.uk

Events Manager: Mrs Christine Edwards, Tourism & Town Centre Manager, Hewson House, Station Road, Brigg DN20 8XY ☎ 01724 297350 🖱 christine.edwards@northlincs.gov.uk

Facilities: Miss Helen Rowe, Assistant Director - Customer Services, Civic Centre, Ashby Road, Scunthorpe DN16 1AB ☎ 01724 297667 🖱 helen.rowe@northlincs.gov.uk

Facilities: Mr Peter Williams, Director - Places, Civic Centre, Ashby Road, Scunthorpe DN16 1AB ☎ 01724 296710 🖷 01724 296770 🖱 peter.williams@northlincs.gov.uk

Finance and Treasurer: Mr Mike Wedgewood, Director - Policy & Resources, Civic Centre, Ashby Road, Scunthorpe DN16 1AB ☎ 01724 296012 🖷 01724 296030 🖱 mike.wedgewood@northlincs.gov.uk

Fleet Management: Mr Chris Matthews, Assistant Director - Community Services, Hewson House, Station Road, Brigg DN20 8XJ ☎ 01724 297366 🖷 01724 297880 🖱 chris.matthews@northlincs.gov.uk

Grounds Maintenance: Mr Chris Matthews, Assistant Director - Community Services, Hewson House, Station Road, Brigg DN20 8XJ ☎ 01724 297366 🖷 01724 297880 🖱 chris.matthews@northlincs.gov.uk

Health and Safety: Mr John Rennison, Head - Health, Safety & Welfare, 92 Oswald Road, Scunthorpe DN15 7PA ☎ 01724 297605 🖱 john.rennison@northlincs.gov.uk

Highways: Mr Chris Matthews, Assistant Director - Community Services, Hewson House, Station Road, Brigg DN20 8XJ ☎ 01724 297366 🖷 01724 297880 🖱 chris.matthews@northlincs.gov.uk

Home Energy Conservation: Mr Trevor Laming, Assistant Director - Technical & Environmental Services, Church Square House, Scunthorpe DN15 6XG ☎ 01724 297603 🖷 01724 297333 🖱 trevor.laming@northlincs.gov.uk

Housing: Mr Trevor Laming, Assistant Director - Technical & Environmental Services, Church Square House, Scunthorpe DN15 6XG ☎ 01724 297603 🖷 01724 297333 🖱 trevor.laming@northlincs.gov.uk

Legal: Mr Will Bell, Assistant Director - Legal & Democratic, Civic Centre, Ashby Road, Scunthorpe DN16 1AB ☎ 01724 296204 🖱 will.bell@northlincs.gov.uk

Leisure and Cultural Services: Miss Helen Rowe, Assistant Director - Customer Services, Civic Centre, Ashby Road, Scunthorpe DN16 1AB ☎ 01724 297667 🖱 helen.rowe@northlincs.gov.uk

Leisure and Cultural Services: Miss Helen Rowe, Assistant Director - Customer Services, Civic Centre, Ashby Road, Scunthorpe DN16 1AB ☎ 01724 297667 🖱 helen.rowe@northlincs.gov.uk

Licensing: Mr Trevor Laming, Assistant Director - Technical & Environmental Services, Church Square House, Scunthorpe DN15 6XG ☎ 01724 297603 🖷 01724 297333 🖱 trevor.laming@northlincs.gov.uk

Lifelong Learning: Miss Helen Rowe, Assistant Director - Customer Services, Civic Centre, Ashby Road, Scunthorpe DN16 1AB ☎ 01724 297667 🖱 helen.rowe@northlincs.gov.uk

Lighting: Mr Chris Matthews, Assistant Director - Community Services, Hewson House, Station Road, Brigg DN20 8XJ ☎ 01724 297366 🖷 01724 297880 🖱 chris.matthews@northlincs.gov.uk

Member Services: Mr Mel Holmes, Head - Democratic Services, Civic Centre, Ashby Road, Scunthorpe DN16 1AB ☎ 01724 296230 🖷 01724 281705 🖱 mel.holmes@northlincs.gov.uk

Parking: Mr Marcus Walker, Assistant Director - Planning & Regeneration, Civic Centre, Ashby Road, Scunthorpe DN16 1AB ☎ 01724 297305 🖷 01724 297899 🖱 marcus.walker@northlincs.gov.uk

Partnerships: Miss Rachel Johnson, Strategy Development Manager, Civic Centre, Ashby Road, Scunthorpe DN16 1AB ☎ 01724 296391 🖱 rachel.johnson@northlincs.gov.uk

Personnel / HR: Mrs Helen Manderson, Assistant Director - Human Resources, Civic Centre, Ashby Road, Scunthorpe DN16 1AB ☎ 01724 296460 🖷 01724 296339 🖱 helen.manderson@northlincs.gov.uk

Planning: Mr Phil Wallis, Head - Development Management,

Civic Centre, Ashby Road, Scunthorpe DN16 1AB ☎ 01724 297492 ✉ philip.wallis@northlincs.gov.uk

Procurement: Mr Jason Whaler, Assistant Director - Business Support, Civic Centre, Ashby Road, Scunthorpe DN16 1AB ☎ 01724 296018 🖷 01724 296030 ✉ jason.whaler@northlincs.gov.uk

Public Libraries: Miss Helen Rowe, Assistant Director - Customer Services, Civic Centre, Ashby Road, Scunthorpe DN16 1AB ☎ 01724 297667 ✉ helen.rowe@northlincs.gov.uk

Recycling & Waste Minimisation: Mr Chris Matthews, Assistant Director - Community Services, Hewson House, Station Road, Brigg DN20 8XJ ☎ 01724 297366 🖷 01724 297880 ✉ chris.matthews@northlincs.gov.uk

Regeneration: Mr Marcus Walker, Assistant Director - Planning & Regeneration, Civic Centre, Ashby Road, Scunthorpe DN16 1AB ☎ 01724 297305 🖷 01724 297899 ✉ marcus.walker@northlincs.gov.uk

Road Safety: Mr Chris Matthews, Assistant Director - Community Services, Hewson House, Station Road, Brigg DN20 8XJ ☎ 01724 297366 🖷 01724 297880 ✉ chris.matthews@northlincs.gov.uk

Social Services (Adult): Ms Karen Pavey, Assistant Director - Adult Services, Civic Centre, Ashby Road, Scunthorpe DN16 1AB ☎ 01724 296420 ✉ karen.pavey@northlincs.gov.uk

Social Services (Children): Ms Denise Hyde, Director - People, Civic Centre, Ashby Road, Scunthorpe DN16 1AB ☎ 01724 296406 🖷 01724 296404 ✉ denise.hyde@northlincs.gov.uk

Staff Training: Mrs Christine Wilkinson, Head - Organisational Development, Civic Centre, Ashby Road, Scunthorpe DN16 1AB ☎ 01724 296322 🖷 01724 296339 ✉ christine.wilkinson@northlincs.gov.uk

Street Scene: Mr Chris Matthews, Assistant Director - Community Services, Hewson House, Station Road, Brigg DN20 8XJ ☎ 01724 297366 🖷 01724 297880 ✉ chris.matthews@northlincs.gov.uk

Sustainable Communities: Mr David Hey, Head - Stronger Communities, Civic Centre, Ashby Road, Scunthorpe DN16 1AB ☎ 01724 296646 ✉ dave.hey@northlincs.gov.uk

Sustainable Development: Mr Tim Allen, Environment Team Manager, Church Square House, PO Box 42, Scunthorpe DN15 6XQ ☎ 01724 297387 🖷 01724 297870 ✉ tim.allen@northlincs.gov.uk

Tourism: Mrs Christine Edwards, Tourism & Town Centre Manager, Hewson House, Station Road, Brigg DN20 8XY ☎ 01724 297350 ✉ christine.edwards@northlincs.gov.uk

Town Centre: Mrs Christine Edwards, Tourism & Town Centre Manager, Hewson House, Station Road, Brigg DN20 8XY ☎ 01724 297350 ✉ christine.edwards@northlincs.gov.uk

Traffic Management: Mr Chris Matthews, Assistant Director - Community Services, Hewson House, Station Road, Brigg DN20 8XJ ☎ 01724 297366 🖷 01724 297880 ✉ chris.matthews@northlincs.gov.uk

Transport: Miss Jodie Booth, Team Manager - Transport Planning, Hewson House, Station Road, Scunthorpe DN20 8XJ ☎ 01724 297373 🖷 01724 297899 ✉ jodie.booth@northlincs.gov.uk

Transport Planner: Mrs Gwyneth McInn, Transport Planning Officer, Hewson House, Station Road, Scunthorpe DN20 8XJ ☎ 01724 297312 🖷 01724 297899 ✉ gwyneth.mcinn@northlincs.gov.uk

Waste Collection and Disposal: Mr John Coates, Project Director - Waste Contracts, North Linc Council, Cottage Beck Road, Scunthorpe DN16 1TS ☎ 01724 297901 ✉ john.coates@northlincs.gov.uk

Waste Management: Mr John Coates, Project Director - Waste Contracts, North Linc Council, Cottage Beck Road, Scunthorpe DN16 1TS ☎ 01724 297901 ✉ john.coates@northlincs.gov.uk

Children's Play Areas: Mr Tom Coburn, Head - Sport, Leisure & Culture, Hewson House, Station Road, Brigg DN20 8XJ ☎ 01724 297260 ✉ tom.coburn@northlincs.gov.uk

MEMBERS OF THE COUNCIL (43)

***Mayor:* Glover**, Ivan (CON - Broughton and Appleby)
antjeo1@btinternet.com

***Deputy Mayor:* Clark**, Peter (CON - Ferry)
peterclark777@btinternet.com

***Leader of the Council:* Redfern**, Liz (CON - Axholme Central)
cllr.lizredfern@northlincs.gov.uk

Ali, Mashook (LAB - Town)
cllr.mashookali@northlincs.gov.uk

Allcock, Ron (CON - Axholme South)
Cllr.RonAllcock@northlincs.gov.uk

Armitage, Susan (LAB - Brumby)
cllr.suearmitage@northlincs.gov.uk

Bainbridge, Sandra (LAB - Frodingham)
cllr.sandrabainbridge@northlincs.gov.uk

Barker, Trevor (LAB - Axholme North)
cllr.trevorbarker@northlincs.gov.uk

Briggs, John (CON - Axholme North)
cllr.johnbriggs@northlincs.gov.uk

Bromby, Jean (CON - Bottesford)
cllr.jeanbromby@northlincs.gov.uk

Bunyan, Arthur (CON - Broughton and Appleby)
cllr.arthurbunyan@northlincs.gov.uk

Carlile, Pauline (LAB - Brumby)
paulinecarlile@aol.com

Collinson, John (LAB - Ashby)
cllr.johncollinson@northlincs.gov.uk

Davison, Andrea (LAB - Ashby)
cllandreadavison@aol.com

Eckhardt, Charles (CON - Axholme South)
cllr.williameckhardt@northlincs.gov.uk

Ellerby, Anthony (LAB - Frodingham)
cllr.tonyellerby@northlincs.gov.uk

England, John (CON - Ridge)
cllr.johnengland@northlincs.gov.uk

Evison, Jonathan (CON - Barton)
Cllr.JonathanEvison@northlincs.gov.uk
Foster, Trevor (CON - Ridge)
cllr.trevorfoster@northlincs.gov.uk
Foster, Leonard (LAB - Brumby)
len.k.foster@northlincs.gov.uk
Godfrey, Susan (LAB - Kingsway with Lincoln Gardens)
Cllr.SusanGodfrey@northlincs.gov.uk
Gosling, Antony (LAB - Kingsway with Lincoln Gardens)
cllr.tonygosling@northlincs.gov.uk
Grant, Michael (LAB - Ashby)
cllr.mickgrant@northlincs.gov.uk
Jawaid, Ishaq (LAB - Crosby and Park)
cllrjawaidishaq@northlincs.gov.uk
Kataria, Haque Nawaz (LAB - Town)
cllr.haquekataria@northlincs.gov.uk
Kirk, Mark (LAB - Crosby and Park)
mark.kirk@northlincs.gov.uk
Marper, Elaine (CON - Burton Upon Stather and Winterton)
Cllr.ElaineMarper@northlincs.gov.uk
Ogg, Ralph (CON - Burton Upon Stather and Winterton)
Cllr.RalphOgg@northlincs.gov.uk
Oldfield, David (LAB - Burringham and Gunness)
cllr.daveoldfield@northlincs.gov.uk
O'Sullivan, Christine (LAB - Crosby and Park)
cllr.christineo'sullivan@northlincs.gov.uk
Poole, Neil (CON - Ridge)
cllr.neilpoole@northlincs.gov.uk
Robinson, David (CON - Axholme Central)
Cllr.DavidRobinson@northlincs.gov.uk
Rowson, Helen (CON - Burton Upon Stather and Winterton)
Cllr.HelenRowson@northlincs.gov.uk
Sherwood, Nigel (CON - Brigg and Wolds)
cllr.nigelsherwood@northlincs.gov.uk
Sherwood, Carl (CON - Brigg and Wolds)
cllr.carlsherwood@northlincs.gov.uk
Swift, Stephen (LAB - Bottesford)
cllr.steveswift@northlincs.gov.uk
Vickers, Keith (CON - Barton)
cllr.keithvickers@northlincs.gov.uk
Vickers, Paul (CON - Barton)
cllr.paulvickers@northlincs.gov.uk
Waltham, Rob (CON - Brigg and Wolds)
rob.waltham@northlincs.gov.uk
Wardle, John (CON - Ferry)
Wells, David (CON - Ferry)
cllr.davidwells@northlincs.gov.uk
Whiteley, David (LAB - Bottesford)
cllr.davidwhiteley@northlincs.gov.uk
Wilson, Stuart (LAB - Kingsway with Lincoln Gardens)
cllr.stuartwilson@northlincs.gov.uk

POLITICAL COMPOSITION

CON: 23, LAB: 20

CABINET

Leader / Regeneration: Ms Liz Redfern
Asset Management, Culture & Housing: Mr John Briggs
Customer Services, Sport & Leisure: Mr Carl Sherwood
Highways & Neighbourhoods: Mr Nigel Sherwood
People: Mr Rob Waltham

COMMITTEE CHAIRS

Audit: Mr Charles Eckhardt
Corporate Scrutiny: Mr David Robinson
Health Scrutiny: Mrs Jean Bromby
Licensing: Mr Keith Vickers
Places: Mr Trevor Foster
Planning: Mr Arthur Bunyan
Standards: Mr Neil Poole

NORTH NORFOLK — D

North Norfolk District Council, Council Offices, Holt Road, Cromer NR27 9EN ☎ 01263 513811 🖷 01263 515042
✉ districtcouncil@north-norfolk.gov.uk 💻 www.northnorfolk.org

FACTS & FIGURES

Police Authority: Norfolk Police Authority
Health Authority: East of England Strategic Health Authority
Learning and Skills Council: Eastern
Parliamentary Constituencies: Norfolk North
EU Constituencies: Eastern
Election Frequency: Elections are of whole council
Twinning: Cromer: Crest (France), Nidda (Germany); Fakenham: Olivet (France); North Walsham: Friesenried (Germany); Sheringham: Otterndorf (Germany); Aldborough: Villiers St Dennis (France)

PRINCIPAL OFFICERS

Chief Executive: Mrs Sheila Oxtoby, Chief Executive, Council Offices, Holt Road, Cromer NR27 9EN ☎ 01263 513811 🖷 01263 515042 ✉ sheila.oxtoby@north-norfolk.gov.uk

Senior Management: Mr Nick Baker, Corporate Director, Council Offices, Holt Road, Cromer NR27 9EN ☎ 01263 516221 🖷 01263 514627 ✉ nick.baker@north-norfolk.gov.uk

Senior Management: Mr Steve Blatch, Corporate Director, Council Offices, Holt Road, Cromer NR27 9EN ☎ 01263 516232 🖷 01263 515042 ✉ steve.blatch@north-norfolk.gov.uk

Access Officer / Social Services (Disability): Mr Mike Radley, Building Control & Access Manager, Council Offices, Holt Road, Cromer NR27 9EN ☎ 01263 513811 🖷 01263 514802 ✉ mike.radley@north-norfolk.gov.uk

Building Control: Mr Mike Radley, Building Control & Access Manager, Council Offices, Holt Road, Cromer NR27 9EN ☎ 01263 513811 🖷 01263 514802 ✉ mike.radley@north-norfolk.gov.uk

PR / Communications: Mr Peter Battrick, Communications Manager, Council Offices, Holt Road, Cromer NR27 9EN ☎ 01263 516344 🖷 01263 515042 ✉ peter.battrick@north-norfolk.gov.uk

Community Safety: Mr Steve Blatch, Corporate Director, Council Offices, Holt Road, Cromer NR27 9EN ☎ 01263 516232 🖷 01263 515042 ✉ steve.blatch@north-norfolk.gov.uk

Computer Management: Mrs Helen Mitchell, ICT Manager, Council Offices, Holt Road, Cromer NR27 9EN ☎ 01263 516118 ✉ helen.mitchell@north-norfolk.gov.uk

Corporate Services: Mr Tony Ing, Strategic Director -

Information, Council Offices, Holt Road, Cromer NR27 9EN ☎ 01263 516080 🖷 01263 515042 ✉ tony.ing@north-norfolk.gov.uk

Customer Service: Ms Estelle Bawden, Customer Services Manager, Council Offices, Holt Road, Cromer NR27 9EN ☎ 01263 516080 🖷 01263 515042 ✉ estelle.bawden@north-norfolk.gov.uk

Economic Development: Mr Robin Smith, Economic & Tourism Development Manager, Council Offices, Holt Road, Cromer NR27 9EN ☎ 01263 516236 🖷 01263 515042 ✉ robin.smith@north-norfolk.gov.uk

E-Government: Mr Peter Battrick, Communications Manager, Council Offices, Holt Road, Cromer NR27 9EN ☎ 01263 516344 🖷 01263 515042 ✉ peter.battrick@north-norfolk.gov.uk

Electoral Registration: Mrs Emma Duncan, Legal & Democratic Services Manager, Council Offices, Holt Road, Cromer NR27 9EN ☎ 01263 516045 🖷 01263 515042 ✉ emma.duncan@north-norfolk.gov.uk

Emergency Planning: Mr Stephen Hems, Environmental Health Manager, Council Offices, Holt Road, Cromer NR27 9EN ☎ 01263 516182 ✉ steve.hems@north-norfolk.gov.uk

Energy Management: Mr Nick Baker, Corporate Director, Council Offices, Holt Road, Cromer NR27 9EN ☎ 01263 516221 🖷 01263 514627 ✉ nick.baker@north-norfolk.gov.uk

Environmental / Technical Services: Mr Nick Baker, Corporate Director, Council Offices, Holt Road, Cromer NR27 9EN ☎ 01263 516221 🖷 01263 514627 ✉ nick.baker@north-norfolk.gov.uk

Environmental / Technical Services: Mr Stephen Hems, Environmental Health Manager, Council Offices, Holt Road, Cromer NR27 9EN ☎ 01263 516182 ✉ steve.hems@north-norfolk.gov.uk

Environmental Health: Mr Nick Baker, Corporate Director, Council Offices, Holt Road, Cromer NR27 9EN ☎ 01263 516221 🖷 01263 514627 ✉ nick.baker@north-norfolk.gov.uk

Environmental Health: Mr Stephen Hems, Environmental Health Manager, Council Offices, Holt Road, Cromer NR27 9EN ☎ 01263 516187 ✉ steve.hems@north-norfolk.gov.uk

European Liaison: Mr Robin Smith, Economic & Tourism Development Manager, Council Offices, Holt Road, Cromer NR27 9EN ☎ 01263 516236 🖷 01263 515042 ✉ robin.smith@north-norfolk.gov.uk

Facilities: Mr Tony Turner, Property Manager, Council Offices, Holt Road, Cromer NR27 9EN ☎ 01263 516196 🖷 01263 515042 ✉ tony.turner@north-norfolk.gov.uk

Finance and Treasurer: Miss Karen Sly, Corporate Finance Manager, Council Offices, Holt Road, Cromer NR27 9EN ☎ 01263 516243 🖷 01263 515042 ✉ karen.sly@north-norfolk.gov.uk

Fleet Management: Mrs Julie Cooke, Organisational Development Manager, Council Offices, Holt Road, Cromer NR27 9EN ☎ 01263 516040 ✉ julie.cooke@north-norfolk.gov.uk

Grounds Maintenance: Mr Karl Read, Leisure & Cultural Services Manager, Council Offices, Holt Road, Cromer NR27 9EN ☎ 01263 516002 🖷 01263 515042 ✉ karl.read@north-norfolk.gov.uk

Health and Safety: Mr Nick Baker, Corporate Director, Council Offices, Holt Road, Cromer NR27 9EN ☎ 01263 516221 🖷 01263 514627 ✉ nick.baker@north-norfolk.gov.uk

Housing: Ms Karen Hill, Strategic Housing Manager, Council Offices, Holt Road, Cromer NR27 9EN ☎ 01263 516183 ✉ karen.hill@north-norfolk.gov.uk

Legal: Mrs Emma Duncan, Legal & Democratic Services Manager, Council Offices, Holt Road, Cromer NR27 9EN ☎ 01263 516045 🖷 01263 515042 ✉ emma.duncan@north-norfolk.gov.uk

Leisure and Cultural Services: Mr Karl Read, Leisure & Cultural Services Manager, Council Offices, Holt Road, Cromer NR27 9EN ☎ 01263 516002 🖷 01263 515042 ✉ karl.read@north-norfolk.gov.uk

Licensing: Mr Stephen Hems, Environmental Health Manager, Council Offices, Holt Road, Cromer NR27 9EN ☎ 01263 516182 ✉ steve.hems@north-norfolk.gov.uk

Lifelong Learning: Mr Robin Smith, Economic & Tourism Development Manager, Council Offices, Holt Road, Cromer NR27 9EN ☎ 01263 516236 🖷 01263 515042 ✉ robin.smith@north-norfolk.gov.uk

Member Services: Mrs Emma Duncan, Legal & Democratic Services Manager, Council Offices, Holt Road, Cromer NR27 9EN ☎ 01263 516045 🖷 01263 515042 ✉ emma.duncan@north-norfolk.gov.uk

Partnerships: Mrs Beatrix Ward, Community Partnerships Manager, Council Offices, Holt Road, Cromer NR27 9EN ☎ 01263 516248 ✉ beatrix.ward@north-norfolk.gov.uk

Personnel / HR: Mrs Julie Cooke, Organisational Development Manager, Council Offices, Holt Road, Cromer NR27 9EN ☎ 01263 516040 ✉ julie.cooke@north-norfolk.gov.uk

Planning: Mr Steve Oxenham, Head of Planning & Building Control, Council Offices, Holt Road, Cromer NR27 9EN ☎ 01263 516135 🖷 01263 514802 ✉ steve.oxenham@north-norfolk.gov.uk

Procurement: Mr Duncan Ellis, Procurement Officer, Council Offices, Holt Road, Cromer NR27 9EN ☎ 01263 516330 🖷 01263 515042 ✉ duncan.ellis@north-norfolk.gov.uk

Recycling & Waste Minimisation: Mr Barry Branford, Environmental Services Manager, Council Offices, Holt Road, Cromer NR27 9EN ☎ 01263 516308; 01263 516308 🖷 01263 514627; 01263 514627 ✉ barry.branford@north-norfolk.gov.uk; barry.branford@north-norfolk.gov.uk

Regeneration: Mr Robin Smith, Economic & Tourism Development Manager, Council Offices, Holt Road, Cromer NR27 9EN ☎ 01263 516236 🖷 01263 515042 ✉ robin.smith@north-norfolk.gov.uk

Staff Training: Mrs Julie Cooke, Organisational Development Manager, Council Offices, Holt Road, Cromer NR27 9EN ☎ 01263 516040 ✉ julie.cooke@north-norfolk.gov.uk

Sustainable Communities: Mrs Maureen Clarke, Active Communities Manager, Council Offices, Holt Road, Cromer NR27 9EN ☎ 01263 516340 🖷 01263 515042 ✉ maureen.clarke@north-norfolk.gov.uk

Tourism: Mr Robin Smith, Economic & Tourism Development Manager, Council Offices, Holt Road, Cromer NR27 9EN ☎ 01263 516236 🖷 01263 515042 ✉ robin.smith@north-norfolk.gov.uk

Waste Collection and Disposal: Mr Barry Branford, Environmental Services Manager, Council Offices, Holt Road, Cromer NR27 9EN ☎ 01263 516308 🖷 01263 514627 ✉ barry.branford@north-norfolk.gov.uk

Waste Management: Mr Barry Branford, Environmental Services Manager, Council Offices, Holt Road, Cromer NR27 9EN ☎ 01263 516308 🖷 01263 514627 ✉ barry.branford@north-norfolk.gov.uk

MEMBERS OF THE COUNCIL (48)

Chair: **Perry-Warnes**, John (CON - Corpusty)
john.perry-warnes@norfolk.gov.uk
Leader of the Council: **Johnson**, Keith (CON - Cromer Town)
keith.johnson@north-norfolk.gov.uk
Deputy Leader of the Council: **FitzPatrick**, Tom (CON - Walsingham)
tom.fitzpatrick@north-norfolk.gov.uk
Arnold, Sue (CON - Roughton)
sue.arnold@north-norfolk.gov.uk
Baker, Mike (UKIP - Holt)
mjm.baker@ukonline.co.uk
Brettle, Lindsay (CON - Glaven Hill)
lindsay.brettle@north-norfolk.gov.uk
Cabbell Manners, Benjamin (CON - Cromer Town)
cabman@clara.net
Claussen-Reynolds, Annie (CON - Lancaster North)
annie.claussen-reynolds@north-norfolk.gov.uk
Dixon, Nigel (CON - Hoveton)
NigelNDD@aol.com
Eales, Helen (CON - The Runtons)
helen.eales@north-norfolk.gov.uk
Fitch-Tillett, Angie (CON - Poppyland)
angie.tillett@north-norfolk.gov.uk
Gay, Virginia (LD - North Walsham West)
v.gay@virgin.net
Green, Ann (CON - Wensum)
ann.green@north-norfolk.gov.uk
Grove-Jones, Pauline (LD - Stalham and Sutton)
pauline.grove-jones@north-norfolk.gov.uk
Hannah, Brian (LD - Sheringham North)
brian.hannah@north-norfolk.gov.uk
High, Philip (LD - Holt)
philip.high@north-norfolk.gov.uk
Ivory, Trevor (CON - Scottow)
trevor@trevorivory.com
Jarvis, Ben (CON - Waterside)
benjamin.jarvis@north-norfolk.gov.uk
Jones, Graham (LD - Gaunt)
grahamjones128@btinernet.com
Lee, John (CON - Suffield Park)
john.lee@north-norfolk.gov.uk
Lloyd, Nigel (LD - North Walsham)
nigel.lloyd@north-norfolk.gov.uk
McGoun, Barbara (LD - St Benet)
barbara.mcgoun@north-norfolk.gov.uk
Moore, Ann (LD - North Walsham North)
cllrannmoore@aol.com
Moore, Peter (LD - North Walsham East)
cllrpetermoore@aol.com
Northam, Wyndham (CON - Mundesley)
wyndham.northam@north-norfolk.gov.uk
Oliver, Rhodri (CON - Sheringham South)
rhodri.oliver@btinternet.com
Palmer, Becky (CON - The Raynhams)
becky.palmer@north-norfolk.gov.uk
Price, Richard (CON - Waxham)
richardpri@freenetname.co.uk
Punchard, Jeremy (CON - Lancaster South)
jeremy.punchard@north-norfolk.gov.uk
Reynolds, Roy (CON - Lancaster North)
roy.reynolds@north-norfolk.gov.uk
Savory, Jonathan (CON - Priory)
jds@thelaurels.plus.com
Seward, Eric (LD - North Walsham North)
eric.seward@north-norfolk.gov.uk
Shepherd, Richard (CON - Sheringham South)
richard.shepherd@north-norfolk.gov.uk
Smith, Richard (LD - Sheringham North)
richard.smith@north-norfolk.gov.uk
Smith, Norman (CON - Erpingham)
norman.smith@north-norfolk.gov.uk
Smith, Barry (CON - Mundesley)
barry.smith@north-norfolk.gov.uk
Stevens, Robert (CON - Stalham and Sutton)
Sweeney, Anthea (LD - Chaucer)
anthea.sweeney@north-norfolk.gov.uk
Terrington, Peter (IND - Priory)
peter.terrington@north-norfolk.gov.uk
Thompson, Hilary (CON - Suffield Park)
hilary.thompson@norfolk.gov.uk
Uprichard, Vivienne (LD - North Walsham East)
vivienne.uprichard@north-norfolk.gov.uk
Walker, Lee (LD - Happisburgh)
gbeachkidz@btinternet.com
Ward, Steven (CON - Lancaster South)
steven.ward@north-norfolk.gov.uk
Williams, Glyn (LD - Worstead)
glyn.williams@north-norfolk.gov.uk
Williams, Paul (LD - Waterside)
waterside.dc@btinternet.com
Wright, Russell (CON - Astley)
russell.wright@norfolk.gov.uk
Wyatt, John (LD - Briston)
john.wyatt@north-norfolk.gov.uk
Young, David
(LD - High Heath)
david.young@north-norfolk.gov.uk

POLITICAL COMPOSITION

CON: 28, LD: 18, UKIP: 1, IND: 1

CABINET

Leader / Organisation Development: Mr Keith Johnson
Deputy Leader / Customer & Democratic Services: Mr Tom FitzPatrick
Coastal, Health & Wellbeing: Mrs Angie Fitch-Tillett
Environmental Services, Tourism, Leisure & Cultural Services: Mr John Lee
Financial Services, Corporate Assets, Revenues & Benefits: Mr Wyndham Northam
Localism and the Big Society, Communication, Legal Services & Licensing: Mr Trevor Ivory

NORTH SOMERSET U

North Somerset Council, Town Hall, Walliscote Grove Road, Weston-super-Mare BS23 1UJ ☎ 01934 888888 🖷 01934 888822
✉ firstname.surname@n-somerset.gov.uk
🖳 www.n-somerset.gov.uk

FACTS & FIGURES

Police Authority: Avon & Somerset Police Authority
Health Authority: NHS South West
Learning and Skills Council: South West
Parliamentary Constituencies: Weston-super-Mare
EU Constituencies: South West
Election Frequency: Elections are of whole council
Twinning: North Somerset: Stadt Hildesheim (Germany)

PRINCIPAL OFFICERS

Chief Executive: Mr Graham Turner, Chief Executive Officer, Town Hall, Walliscote Grove Road, Weston-super-Mare BS23 1DZ ☎ 01934 634972 🖷 01934 888822 ✉ graham.turner@n-somerset.gov.uk

Senior Management: Ms Jane Smith, Director - Adult Social Services & Housing, Town Hall, Walliscote Grove Road, Weston-super-Mare BS23 1AE ☎ 01934 634803 🖷 01934 888832 ✉ jane.smith@n-somerset.gov.uk

Senior Management: Ms Sheila Smith, Director - Children & Young People's Services, Town Hall, Walliscote Grove Road, Weston-super-Mare BS23 1ZZ ☎ 01934 888830 🖷 01934 888834 ✉ sheila.smith@n-somerset.gov.uk

Senior Management: Mr David Turner, Director - Development & Environment, Somerset House, Oxford Street, Weston-super-Mare BS23 1TG ☎ 01934 888885 🖷 01275 884280 ✉ david.turner@n-somerset.gov.uk

Access Officer / Social Services (Disability): Mr Anthony Rylands, Disability Equality Access Officer, Town Hall, Walliscote Grove Road, Weston-super-Mare BS23 1UJ ☎ 01934 634989 ✉ anthony.rylands@n-somerset.gov.uk

Architect, Building / Property Services: Mr Mark McSweeney, Property Services Manager, Zone A, Floor 2, Castlewood, Clevedon BS21 6FW ☎ 01275 882920 ✉ mark.mcsweeney@n-somerset.gov.uk

Best Value: Mr Paul Morris, Head - Performance Improvement & Human Resources, Town Hall, Walliscote Grove Road, Weston-super-Mare BS23 1AE ☎ 01934 888843 🖷 01934 888822 ✉ paul.morris@n-somerset.gov.uk

Building Control: Ms Mandy Bishop, Head - Community & Consumer Services, Town Hall, Walliscote Grove Road, Weston-super-Mare BS23 1UJ ☎ 01275 882806 🖷 01934 634280 ✉ mandy.bishop@n-somerset.gov.uk

Catering Services: Mrs Lynda Mitchell, Commissioning & Contracts Manager, Town Hall, Walliscote Grove Road, Weston-super-Mare BS23 1UJ ☎ 01275 888319 🖷 01275 884058 ✉ lynda.mitchell@n-somerset.gov.uk

Children / Youth Services: Ms Sheila Smith, Director - Children & Young People's Services, Town Hall, Walliscote Grove Road, Weston-super-Mare BS23 1ZZ ☎ 01934 888830 🖷 01934 888834 ✉ sheila.smith@n-somerset.gov.uk

Civil Registration: Mr Richard Tucker, Superintendent Registrar, Registrars Office, Boulevard, Weston-super-Mare BS23 1UJ ☎ 01934 627552 ✉ richard.tucker@n-somerset.gov.uk

PR / Communications: Ms Vanessa Setterington, Customer Service Officer, Town Hall, Walliscote Grove Road, Weston-super-Mare BS23 1UJ ☎ 01275 888728 ✉ vanessa.setterington@n-somerset.gov.uk

Community Planning: Mr Michael Reep, Planning Policy Manager, Somerset House, Oxford Street, Weston-super-Mare BS23 1TG ☎ 01934 426775 🖷 01934 426678 ✉ michael.reep@n-somerset.gov.uk

Community Safety: Mr Derek Carter, Community Involvement Group Manager, 59-61 Oxford Street, Weston-super-Mare BS23 1TR ☎ 01275 888391 🖷 01275 888386 ✉ derek.carter@n-somerset.gov.uk

Community Safety: Ms Jo Mercer, Community Safety & DAT Manager, 59-61 Oxford Street, Weston-super-Mare BS23 1TR ☎ 01275 888394 🖷 01275 888386 ✉ jo.mercer@n-somerset.gov.uk

Computer Management: Mr David Wild, Strategic ICT Client Manager, Floor 2 - Zone A, Castlewood, Clevedon BS21 6AB ☎ 01934 426385 🖷 01934 427639 ✉ david.wild@agilisys.co.uk

Consumer Protection and Trading Standards: Ms Mandy Bishop, Head - Community & Consumer Services, Somerset House, Oxford Street, Weston-super-Mare BS23 1TG ☎ 01275 882806 🖷 01934 634280 ✉ mandy.bishop@n-somerset.gov.uk

Contracts: Mr Simon Farnsworth, Commercial & Contracts Manager, Floor 1, Zone 3, Castlewood, Clevedon BS21 6FW ☎ 01275 882963 ✉ simon.farnsworth@n-somerset.gov.uk

Customer Service: Ms Vanessa Setterington, Customer Service Officer, Town Hall, Walliscote Grove Road, Weston-super-Mare BS23 1UJ ☎ 01275 888728 ✉ vanessa.setterington@n-somerset.gov.uk

Economic Development: Mr Simon Gregory, Economic Development Service Manager, Town Hall, Walliscote Grove Road, Weston-super-Mare BS23 1UJ ☎ 01934 426327 🖷 01934 612006 ✉ simon.gregory@n-somerset.gov.uk

Education: Mr Paul Jacobs, Head - School Improvement, Town Hall, Walliscote Grove Road, Weston-super-Mare BS23 1UJ ☎ 01275 884381 ✉ paul.jacobs@n-somerset.gov.uk

Electoral Registration: Mr Mike Jones, Electoral Services Manager, Corporate Services Unit, Town Hall, Weston-super-Mare BS23 1DY ☎ 01934 634903 🖷 01934 418194 ✉ mike.jones@n-somerset.gov.uk

Emergency Planning: Mr Ian Wilson, Emergency Management Officer, Corporate Services Unit, Town Hall, Weston-super-Mare BS23 1DZ ☎ 01934 426706 🖷 01934 888831 ✉ ian.wilson@n-somerset.gov.uk

Energy Management: Mr Steve Hodges, Mechanical, Electrical & Energy Manager, Finance and Resources, Town Hall, Weston-super-Mare BS23 1UJ ☎ 01934 634710 🖷 01934 426605 ✉ steve.hodges@n-somerset.gov.uk

Environmental Health: Ms Mandy Bishop, Head - Community & Consumer Services, Town Hall, Walliscote Grove Road, Weston-super-Mare BS23 1UJ ☎ 01275 882806 🖷 01934 634280 ✉ mandy.bishop@n-somerset.gov.uk

Estates, Property & Valuation: Mr Lyndon Watkins, Head - Property & Asset Management, Zone A, Floor 2, Castlewood, Clevedon BS21 6FW ☎ 01934 427468 🖷 01275 884419 ✉ lyndon.watkins@n-somerset.gov.uk

Events Manager: Mr Darren Fairchild, Seafront, Events & Concessions Manager, Town Hall, Walliscote Grove Road, Weston-super-Mare BS23 1UJ ☎ 01934 427274 🖷 01934 612323 ✉ darren.fairchild@n-somerset.gov.uk

Facilities: Mr Daniel Owen, Service Line Manager, Zone A, Floor 2, Castlewood, Clevedon BS21 6FW ☎ 01934 882895 ✉ daniel.owen@agilisys.co.uk

Finance and Treasurer: Mr Peter Sloman, Head - Financial Management, Town Hall, Walliscote Grove Road, Weston-super-Mare BS23 1UJ ☎ 01275 884353 ✉ peter.sloman@n-somerset.gov.uk

Grounds Maintenance: Mr Ed McKay, Contracts Officer, Zone B, Ground Floor, Castlewood, Clevedon BS21 6BD ☎ 01934 427681 ✉ edward.mckay@n-somerset.gov.uk

Health and Safety: Ms Cate Sampson, Health & Safety Advisor Corporate, Town Hall, Walliscote Grove Road, Weston-super-Mare BS23 1UJ ☎ 01934 888632 ✉ cate.sampson@n-somerset.gov.uk

Highways: Mr Frank Cox, Highway Service Manager, Zone C, Ground Floor, Castlewood, Clevedon BS21 6BD ☎ 01934 426784 🖷 01934 426884 ✉ frank.cox@n-somerset.gov.uk

Highways: Mr Colin Medus, Head - Highways & Transport, Floor 1 - Zone C, Castlewood, Clevedon BS21 6BD ☎ 01934 426498 🖷 01934 426678 ✉ colin.medus@n-somerset.gov.uk

Home Energy Conservation: Ms Kim Herivel, Home Energy Efficiency Officer, Town Hall, Walliscote Grove Road, Weston-super-Mare BS23 1UJ ☎ 01934 634807 ✉ kim.herivel@n-somerset.gov.uk

Housing: Mr Mark Hughes, Head - Housing, Town Hall, Weston-super-Mare BS23 1HB ☎ 01934 426320 ✉ mark.hughes@n-somerset.gov.uk

Local Area Agreement: Mr James Foster, Strategic Policy Development Manager, Town Hall, Walliscote Grove Road, Weston-super-Mare BS23 1UJ ☎ 01934 634897 ✉ james.foster@n-somerset.gov.uk

Local Area Agreement: Ms Rhiannon Jones, Policy Development Officer, Town Hall, Walliscote Grove Road, Weston-super-Mare BS23 1UJ ☎ 01275 884733 ✉ rhiannon.jones@n-somerset.gov.uk

Legal: Mr Nick Brain, Head - Legal & Democratic Services, Town Hall, Walliscote Grove Road, Weston-super-Mare BS23 1UJ ☎ 01934 634929 🖷 01934 634884 ✉ nick.brain@n-somerset.gov.uk

Leisure and Cultural Services: Ms Mandy Bishop, Head - Community & Consumer Services, Town Hall, Walliscote Grove Road, Weston-super-Mare BS23 1UJ ☎ 01275 882806 🖷 01934 634280 ✉ mandy.bishop@n-somerset.gov.uk

Licensing: Ms Mandy Bishop, Head - Community & Consumer Services, Town Hall, Walliscote Grove Road, Weston-super-Mare BS23 1UJ ☎ 01275 882806 🖷 01934 634280 ✉ mandy.bishop@n-somerset.gov.uk

Lifelong Learning: Ms Jill Croskell, Community Learning Team Manager, Town Hall, Walliscote Grove Road, Weston-super-Mare BS23 1UJ ☎ 01934 426105 ✉ jill.croskell@n-somerset.gov.uk

Lighting: Mr Colin Medus, Head - Highways & Transport, Zone C, Ground Floor, Castlewood, Clevedon BS21 6BD ☎ 01934 426498 🖷 01934 426678 ✉ colin.medus@n-somerset.gov.uk

Lottery Funding, Charity and Voluntary: Mr Phil Humphries, Senior Development Officer, 59-61 Oxford Street, Weston-super-Mare BS23 1TR ☎ ; 01934 426727 🖷 01275 888386 ✉ phil.humphries@n-somerset.gov.uk

Member Services: Ms Fiona Robertson, Deputy Head - Legal & Democratic Services, Town Hall, Walliscote Grove Road, Weston-super-Mare BS23 1UJ ☎ 01934 634686 ✉ fiona.robertson@n-somerset.gov.uk

Parking: Mr Allan Taylor, Car Parking Manager, Town Hall, Walliscote Grove Road, Weston-super-Mare BS23 1UJ ☎ 01394 427293 ✉ allan.taylor@n-somerset.gov.uk

Partnerships: Mr Richard Penska, Assistant Director, Zone A, Floor 2, Castlewood, Clevedon BS21 6FW ☎ 01275 884256 ✉ richard.penska@n-somerset.gov.uk

Personnel / HR: Mr Paul Morris, Head - Performance Improvement & Human Resources, Town Hall, Weston-super-Mare BS23 1AE ☎ 01934 888843 🖷 01934 888822 paul.morris@n-somerset.gov.uk

Planning: Mr Richard Kent, Head - Development Management, Town Hall, Walliscote Grove Road, Weston-super-Mare BS23 1UJ ☎ 01934 426732 🖷 01275 888693 richard.kent@n-somerset.gov.uk

Procurement: Mr Stuart Anstead, Commercial & Commissioning Manager, Zone A, Floor 2, Castlewood, Clevedon BS21 6BD ☎ 01934 427532 stuart.ainstead@n-somerset.gov.uk

Public Libraries: Mr Andy Brisley, Libraries Manager, Town Hall, Walliscote Grove Road, Weston-super-Mare BS23 1UJ ☎ 01934 426658 🖷 01934 612182 andy.brisley@n-somerset.gov.uk

Recycling & Waste Minimisation: Mr Colin Russell, Recycling & Waste Service Manager, Zone C, Ground Floor, Castlewood, Clevedon BS21 6BD ☎ 01934 888802 colin.russell@n-somerset.gov.uk

Regeneration: Mr Richard Kent, Head - Development Management, Town Hall, Walliscote Grove Road, Weston-super-Mare BS23 1UJ ☎ 01934 426732 🖷 01275 888693 richard.kent@n-somerset.gov.uk

Regeneration: Mr Karuna Tharmananthar, Deputy Director, Town Hall, Walliscote Grove Road, Weston-super-Mare BS23 1UJ ☎ 01275 888886 🖷 01934 634280 karuna.tharmananthar@n-somerset.gov.uk

Road Safety: Mr Frank Cox, Highway Service Manager, Zone C, Ground Floor, Castlewood, Clevedon BS21 6BD ☎ 01934 426784 🖷 01934 426884 frank.cox@n-somerset.gov.uk

Social Services (Adult): Ms Claire Leandro, Assistant Director - Adult Care, Town Hall, Walliscote Grove Road, Weston-super-Mare BS23 1UJ ☎ 01934 634803 🖷 01934 888832 claire.leandro@n-somerset.gov.uk

Social Services (Adult): Ms Jane Smith, Director - Adult Social Services & Housing, Town Hall, Weston-super-Mare BS23 1AE ☎ 01934 634803 🖷 01934 888832 jane.smith@n-somerset.gov.uk

Social Services (Children): Mr Eifion Price, Assistant Director - Support & Safeguarding, Town Hall, Walliscote Grove Road, Weston-super-Mare BS23 1UJ ☎ 01275 884392 eifion.price@n-somerset.gov.uk

Staff Training: Mr Paul Morris, Head - Performance Improvement & Human Resources, Town Hall, Weston-super-Mare BS23 1AE ☎ 01934 888843 🖷 01934 888822 paul.morris@n-somerset.gov.uk

Street Scene: Mr John Carson, Waste Contracts Manager, Zone C, Ground Floor, Castlewood, Clevedon BS21 6BD ☎ 01934 427401 john.carson@n-somerset.gov.uk

Sustainable Communities: Mr David Turner, Director - Development & Environment, Town Hall, Walliscote Grove Road, Weston-super-Mare BS23 1UJ ☎ 01934 888885 🖷 01275 884280 david.turner@n-somerset.gov.uk

Sustainable Development: Mr Michael Reep, Planning Policy Manager, Town Hall, Walliscote Grove Road, Weston-super-Mare BS23 1UJ ☎ 01934 426775 🖷 01934 426678 michael.reep@n-somerset.gov.uk

Tourism: Mr Simon Gregory, Economic Development Service Manager, Town Hall, Walliscote Grove Road, Weston-super-Mare BS23 1UJ ☎ 01934 426327 🖷 01934 612006 simon.gregory@n-somerset.gov.uk

Town Centre: Mr Mark MacGregor, Head - Streets & Open Spaces, Zone C, Ground Floor, Castlewood, Clevedon BS21 6BD ☎ 01934 888802 🖷 01934 888810 mark.macgregor@n-somerset.gov.uk

Traffic Management: Mr Frank Cox, Highway Service Manager, Zone C, Ground Floor, Castlewood, Clevedon BS21 6BD ☎ 01934 426784 🖷 01934 426884 frank.cox@n-somerset.gov.uk

Transport: Mr Colin Medus, Head - Highways & Transport, Zone C, Ground Floor, Castlewood, Clevedon BS21 6BD ☎ 01934 426498 🖷 01934 426678 colin.medus@n-somerset.gov.uk

Transport Planner: Mr Colin Medus, Head - Highways & Transport, Zone C, Ground Floor, Castlewood, Clevedon BS21 6BD ☎ 01934 426498 🖷 01934 426678 colin.medus@n-somerset.gov.uk

Waste Collection and Disposal: Mr John Carson, Waste Contracts Manager, Zone C, Ground Floor, Castlewood, Clevedon BS21 6BD ☎ 01934 427401 john.carson@n-somerset.gov.uk

Waste Management: Mr Colin Russell, Recycling & Waste Service Manager, Zone C, Ground Floor, Castlewood, Clevedon BS21 6BD ☎ 01934 888802 colin.russell@n-somerset.gov.uk

Children's Play Areas: Mr Ed McKay, Contracts Officer, Zone B, Ground Floor, Castlewood, Clevedon BS21 6BD ☎ 01934 427681 edward.mckay@n-somerset.gov.uk

MEMBERS OF THE COUNCIL (61)

***Chair:* Porter**, Terry (CON - Hutton and Locking)
terry.porter@n-somerset.gov.uk

***Leader of the Council:* Ashton**, Nigel (CON - Gordano)
nigel.ashton@n-somerset.gov.uk

***Deputy Leader of the Council:* Ap Rees**, Elfan (CON - Hutton and Locking)
elfan.ap.rees@n-somerset.gov.uk

Baker, Felicity (CON - Portishead Redcliffe Bay)
felicity.baker@n-somerset.gov.uk

Barber, Jan (CON - Nailsea East)
jan.barber@n-somerset.gov.uk

Barclay, Karen (IND - Backwell)
karen.barclay@n-somerset.gov.uk

Bateman, Bob (LAB - Weston-super-Mare South)
bob.bateman@n-somerset.gov.uk

Bell, Mike (LD - Weston-super-Mare Central)
mike.bell@n-somerset.gov.uk

Blades, Chris (CON - Clevedon West)
christopher.blades@n-somerset.gov.uk

Blatchford, Jeremy (CON - Nailsea North and West)
jeremy.blatchford@n-somerset.gov.uk
Blatchford, Mary (CON - Nailsea North and West)
marymjblatchford@blueyonder.co.uk
Bryant, Peter (CON - Weston-super-Mare Clarence and Uphill)
p.bryant@n-somerset.gov.uk
Canniford, Mark (LD - Weston-super-Mare West)
mark.canniford@n-somerset.gov.uk
Cave, Charles (CON - Wraxall and Long Ashton)
charles.cave@n-somerset.gov.uk
Cleland, Robert (CON - Weston-super-Mare South Worle)
robert.cleland@n-somerset.gov.uk
Cole, Andrew (LD - Nailsea East)
andy.cole@n-somerset.gov.uk
Cook, Bob (CON - Wraxall and Long Ashton)
bob.cook@n-somerset.gov.uk
Coombs, Geoff (IND - Backwell)
geoff.coombs@n-somerset.gov.uk
Crew, Peter (CON - Weston-super-Mare South Worle)
peter.crew@n-somerset.gov.uk
Crockford-Hawley, John (LD - Weston-super-Mare West)
john.crockford-hawley@n-somerset.gov.uk
Davies, Donald (IND - Pill)
donald.davies@n-somerset.gov.uk
Francis-Pester, Carl (CON - Easton-in-Gordano)
carl.francis-pester@n-somerset.gov.uk
Fudge, Stephen (CON - Weston-super-Mare Milton and Old Worle)
stephen.fudge@n-somerset.gov.uk
Garner, Bob (CON - Clevedon North)
bob.garner@n-somerset.gov.uk
Gibbons, Catherine (LAB - Weston-super-Mare East)
catherine.gibbons@n-somerset.gov.uk
Gregor, Hugh (IND - Winford)
hugh.gregor@n-somerset.gov.uk
Hall, Colin (CON - Clevedon Yeo)
colin.hall@n-somerset.gov.uk
Harley, Ann (CON - Banwell and Winscombe)
anne.harley@n-somerset.gov.uk
Hitchins, David (CON - Weston-super-Mare South Worle)
david.hitchins@n-somerset.gov.uk
Iles, Jill (CON - Yatton)
jill.iles@n-somerset.gov.uk
Jolley, David (CON - Portishead West)
david.jolley@n-somerset.gov.uk
Judd, Philip (CON - Weston-super-Mare North Worle)
philip.judd@n-somerset.gov.uk
Kemp, Anne (CON - Nailsea North and West)
anne.kemp@n-somerset.gov.uk
Kingsbury-Bell, Clare (LD - Weston-super-Mare Central)
clare.kingsbury-bell@n-somerset.gov.uk
Knight, Reyna (CON - Portishead Central)
reyna.knight@n-somerset.gov.uk
Knott, Linda (CON - Clevedon South)
linda.knott@n-somerset.gov.uk
Lake, Tony (CON - Banwell and Winscombe)
tony.lake@n-somerset.gov.uk
Leimdorfer, Tom (GRN - Congresbury)
tom.leimdorfer@n-somerset.gov.uk
Marter, Tim (CON - Banwell and Winscombe)
tim.marter@n-somerset.gov.uk
McMurray, Alan (CON - Portishead South and North Weston)
alan.mcmurray@n-somerset.gov.uk
Moulin, Tony (IND - Yatton)
tony.moulin@n-somerset.gov.uk
Norton-Sealey, John (CON - Clevedon Walton)
john.norton-sealey@n-somerset.gov.uk
Parker, Ian (LAB - Weston-super-Mare South)
ian.parker@n-somerset.gov.uk
Pasley, David (CON - Portishead Coast)
david.pasley@n-somerset.gov.uk
Payne, Robert (LD - Weston-super-Mare West)
robert.payne@n-somerset.gov.uk
Payne, Dawn (CON - Weston-super-Mare East)
dawn.payne@n-somerset.gov.uk
Pennycott, Nick (CON - Clevedon Central)
nick.pennycott@n-somerset.gov.uk
Pepperall, Marcia (CON - Weston-super-Mare North Worle)
marcia.pepperall@n-somerset.gov.uk
Pilgrim, Lisa Jane (CON - Weston-super-Mare Milton and Old Worle)
lisa.pilgrim@n-somerset.gov.uk
Poole, David (CON - Weston-super-Mare Clarence and Uphill)
david.poole@n-somerset.gov.uk
Porter, Ian (CON - Kewstoke)
ian.porter@n-somerset.gov.uk
Russe, Sonia (CON - Weston-super-Mare North Worle)
sonia.russe@n-somerset.gov.uk
Shopland, David (IND - Clevedon East)
david.shopland@n-somerset.gov.uk
Stone, Debbie (LAB - Weston-super-Mare South)
debbie.stone@n-somerset.gov.uk
Tall, Annabel (CON - Yatton)
annabel.tall@n-somerset.gov.uk
Terry, Arthur (CON - Portishead East)
arthur.terry@n-somerset.gov.uk
Tucker, Richard (LAB - Weston-super-Mare East)
richard.tucker@n-somerset.gov.uk
Webb, Clive (CON - Weston-super-Mare Clarence and Uphill)
clive.webb@n-somerset.gov.uk
Wells, Elizabeth (CON - Blagdon and Churchill)

Willis, Rosslyn (CON - Weston-super-Mare Milton and Old Worle)
roz.willis@n-somerset.gov.uk
Yamanaka, Deborah (LD - Wrington)
deborah.yamanaka@n-somerset.gov.uk

POLITICAL COMPOSITION

CON: 42, LD: 7, IND: 6, LAB: 5, GRN: 1

CABINET

Leader: Mr Nigel Ashton
Deputy Leader / Strategic Planning, Highways & Transportation: Mr Elfan Ap Rees
Children & Young People's Services: Mr Jeremy Blatchford
Community Services, Safety, Tourism & Leisure: Ms Felicity Baker
Human Resources, Asset Management & Finance: Mr Tony Lake
Waste & Recycling / Environmental Protection: Mr Peter Bryant

COMMITTEE CHAIRS

Adult Services & Housing (Scrutiny): Mrs Anne Kemp
Children & Young People's Services (Scrutiny): Ms Jan Barber
Community Services (Scrutiny): Mr Andrew Cole

Environmental Services (Scrutiny): Mr Bob Garner
Finance & Performance (Scrutiny): Mr Andrew Horler
Health (Scrutiny): Mrs Reyna Knight
Licensing: Ms Felicity Baker
Planning & Regulatory: Mrs Nan Kirsen
Standards: Mr Peter Barrett (External)
Strategic Planning & Economic Development (Scrutiny): Mr Clive Webb

NORTH TYNESIDE M

North Tyneside Metropolitan Borough Council, Quadrant, The Silverlink North, Cobalt Business Park, North Tyneside, NE27 0BY ☎ 0845 200 0101 💻 www.northtyneside.gov.uk

FACTS & FIGURES

Police Authority: Northumbria Police Authority
Health Authority: North East Strategic Health Authority
Learning and Skills Council: North East
Parliamentary Constituencies: Tynemouth, Tyneside North
EU Constituencies: North East
Election Frequency: Elections are by thirds
Twinning: Oer Erkenschwick (Germany); Frederikshavn (Denmark); Klaipeda (Lithuania); Monchengladbach (Germany); Halluin (France)

PRINCIPAL OFFICERS

Chief Executive: Mr Graham Haywood, Interim Chief Executive, Quadrant, The Silverlink North, Cobalt Business Park, North Tyneside, NE27 0BY ☎ 0191 643 2001 🖷 0191 643 2431 ✉ graham.haywood@northtyneside.gov.uk

Senior Management: Ms Gill Alexander, Strategic Director - Children, Young People & Learning, Quadrant, The Silverlink North, Cobalt Business Park, NE27 0BY ☎ 0191 643 8001 🖷 0191 643 2431 ✉ gill.alexander@northtyneside.gov.uk

Senior Management: Mr Paul Hanson, Strategic Director - Community Services, Quadrant, The Silverlink North, Cobalt Business Park, NE27 0BY ☎ 0191 643 7000 🖷 0191 643 2431 ✉ paul.hanson@northtyneside.gov.uk

Senior Management: Mrs Fiona Rooney, Strategic Director - Finance & Resources, Quadrant, The Silverlink North, Cobalt Business Park, North Tyneside, NE27 0BY ☎ 0191 643 5724 🖷 0191 643 2431 ✉ fiona.rooney@northtyneside.gov.uk

Senior Management: Mr Ken Wilson, Head of Regeneration, Development & Regulatory Services, Quadrant, The Silverlink North, Cobalt Business Park, NE27 0BY ☎ 0191 643 6091 🖷 0191 643 2426 ✉ ken.wilson@northtyneside.gov.uk

Access Officer / Social Services (Disability): Mrs Jacqui Old, Head of Adult Social Care, Quadrant, The Silverlink North, Cobalt Business Park, North Tyneside, NE27 0BY ☎ 0191 643 7317 🖷 0191 643 3413 ✉ jacqui.old@northtyneside.gov.uk

Architect, Building / Property Services: Mr Paul Green, Senior Manager of Strategic Property Estates & Valuation, Quadrant, The Silverlink North, Cobalt Business Park, North Tyneside, NE27 0BY ☎ 0191 643 6516 🖷 0191 643 2429 ✉ paul.green@northtyneside.gov.uk

Best Value: Mrs Alison Stanners, Performance & Scrutiny Manager, Quadrant, The Silverlink North, Cobalt Business Park, North Tyneside, NE27 0BY ☎ 0191 643 5617 ✉ alison.stanners@northtyneside.gov.uk

Building Control: Mr Michael Clarkson, Building Control Manager, Quadrant, The Silverlink North, Cobalt Business Park, NE27 0BY ☎ 0191 643 6012 ✉ michael.clarkson@northtyneside.gov.uk

Catering Services: Ms Barbara Patterson, Catering Manager, Quadrant, The Silverlink North, Cobalt Business Park, North Tyneside, NE27 0BY ☎ 0191 643 8340 🖷 0191 643 2408 ✉ barbara.patterson@northtyneside.gov.uk

Children / Youth Services: Ms Gill Alexander, Strategic Director - Children, Young People & Learning, Quadrant, The Silverlink North, Cobalt Business Park, NE27 0BY ☎ 0191 643 8001 🖷 0191 643 2431 ✉ gill.alexander@northtyneside.gov.uk

Civil Registration: Ms Christine Lois, Superintendent Registrar, Maritime Chambers, Howard Street, North Shields NE30 1LZ ☎ 0191 200 6164 🖷 0191 200 6382 ✉ christine.lois@northtyneside.gov.uk

PR / Communications: Mrs Jeanette Hedley, Senior Communications Officer, Quadrant, The Silverlink North, Cobalt Business Park, North Tyneside, NE27 0BY ☎ 0191 643 5077 🖷 0191 643 2431 ✉ jeanette.hedley@northtyneside.gov.uk

Community Safety: Ms Lynne Crowe, Community Safety Officer, Quadrant, The Silverlink North, Cobalt Business Park, North Tyneside, NE27 0BY ☎ 0191 643 6433 ✉ lynne.crowe@northtyneside.gov.uk

Computer Management: Mr Barry Jackson, ICT Services Manager, Quadrant, The Silverlink North, Cobalt Business Park, North Tyneside, NE27 0BY ☎ 0191 643 5104 🖷 0191 643 2425 ✉ barry.jackson@northtyneside.gov.uk

Consumer Protection and Trading Standards: Mr Colin MacDonald, Consumer Protection Group Manager, Quadrant, The Silverlink North, Cobalt Business Park, North Tyneside, NE27 0BY ☎ 0191 643 6620 🖷 0191 643 2391 ✉ colin.macdonald@northtyneside.gov.uk

Corporate Services: Ms Vivienne Geary, Head of Legal Governance & Commercial Services, Quadrant, The Silverlink North, Cobalt Business Park, North Tyneside, NE27 0BY ☎ 0191 643 5339 🖷 0191 643 2431 ✉ vivienne.geary@northtyneside.gov.uk

Customer Service: Mr Paul Gowans, Head of Cultural Services & Customer Services, Quadrant, The Silverlink North, Cobalt Business Park, North Tyneside, NE27 0BY ☎ 0191 643 7401 🖷 0191 643 2406 ✉ paul.gowans@northtyneside.gov.uk

Economic Development: Mr Sean Collier, Business & Enterprise Manager, Quadrant, The Silverlink North, Cobalt Business Park, North Tyneside, NE27 0BY ☎ 0191 643 6409 🖷 0191 643 2408 ✉ sean.collier@northtyneside.gov.uk

Education: Ms Gill Alexander, Strategic Director - Children,

Young People & Learning, Quadrant, The Silverlink North, Cobalt Business Park, NE27 0BY ☎ 0191 643 8001 🖷 0191 643 2431 ✉ gill.alexander@northtyneside.gov.uk

E-Government: Mr Barry Jackson, ICT Services Manager, Quadrant, The Silverlink North, Cobalt Business Park, North Tyneside, NE27 0BY ☎ 0191 643 5104 🖷 0191 643 2425 ✉ barry.jackson@northtyneside.gov.uk

Electoral Registration: Ms Vivienne Geary, Head of Legal Governance & Commercial Services, Quadrant, The Silverlink North, Cobalt Business Park, North Tyneside, NE27 0BY ☎ 0191 643 5339 🖷 0191 643 2431 ✉ vivienne.geary@northtyneside.gov.uk

Emergency Planning: Mr Phil Scott, Head of Environmental Services, Quadrant, The Silverlink North, 2nd Floor, Quadrant West, Cobalt Business Park, NE27 0BY ☎ 0191 643 7295 🖷 0191 643 2414 ✉ phil.scott@northtyneside.gov.uk

Energy Management: Mr Phil Scott, Head of Environmental Services, Quadrant, The Silverlink North, 2nd Floor, Quadrant West, Cobalt Business Park, NE27 0BY ☎ 0191 643 7295 🖷 0191 643 2414 ✉ phil.scott@northtyneside.gov.uk

Environmental / Technical Services: Mr Ken Wilson, Head of Regeneration, Development & Regulatory Services, Quadrant, The Silverlink North, Cobalt Business Park, NE27 0BY ☎ 0191 643 6091 🖷 0191 643 2426 ✉ ken.wilson@northtyneside.gov.uk

Environmental Health: Mr Colin MacDonald, Consumer Protection Group Manager, Quadrant, The Silverlink North, Cobalt Business Park, North Tyneside, NE27 0BY ☎ 0191 643 6620 🖷 0191 643 2391 ✉ colin.macdonald@northtyneside.gov.uk

Estates, Property & Valuation: Mr John Rutherford, Valuation & Asset Manager, Quadrant, The Silverlink North, Cobalt Business Park, NE27 0BY ☎ 0191 643 6519 🖷 0191 643 2429 ✉ john.rutherford@northtyneside.gov.uk

European Liaison: Mr David Workman, Principal Regeneration Officer (Europe), Quadrant, The Silverlink North, Cobalt Business Park, NE27 0BY ☎ 0191 643 6412 ✉ david.workman@northtyneside.gov.uk

Events Manager: Mr Peter Warne, Tourism & Events Development Manager, Town Hall, High Street East, Wallsend NE28 7RR ☎ 0191 643 7411 🖷 0191 643 2406 ✉ pete.warne@northtyneside.gov.uk

Facilities: Mr Paul Green, Senior Manager of Strategic Property Estates & Valuation, Quadrant, The Silverlink North, Cobalt Business Park, North Tyneside, NE27 0BY ☎ 0191 643 6516 🖷 0191 643 2429 ✉ paul.green@northtyneside.gov.uk

Finance and Treasurer: Mrs Fiona Rooney, Strategic Director - Finance & Resources, Quadrant, The Silverlink North, Cobalt Business Park, NE27 0BY ☎ 0191 643 5724 🖷 0191 643 2431 ✉ fiona.rooney@northtyneside.gov.uk

Fleet Management: Mr Steve Helyer, Senior Management - Fleet, Security & Building Cleaning, Quadrant, The Silverlink North, Cobalt Business Park, North Tyneside, NE27 0BY ☎ 0191 643 6490 🖷 0191 643 2414 ✉ steve.helyer@northtyneside.gov.uk

Grounds Maintenance: Mr Phil Scott, Head of Environmental Services, Quadrant, The Silverlink North, 2nd Floor, Quadrant West, Cobalt Business Park, NE27 0BY ☎ 0191 643 7295 🖷 0191 643 2414 ✉ phil.scott@northtyneside.gov.uk

Health and Safety: Mr Steve Quinlan, Manager - Occupational Health & Safety, Quadrant, The Silverlink North, Cobalt Business Park, North Tyneside, NE27 0BY ☎ 0191 643 5029 🖷 0191 643 2431 ✉ steve.quinlan@northtyneside.gov.uk

Highways: Mr Kevin Ridpath, Network & Transport Manager, Quadrant, The Silverlink North, Cobalt Business Park, NE27 0BY ☎ 0191 643 6089 🖷 0191 643 2426 ✉ kevin.ridpath@northtyneside.gov.uk

Home Energy Conservation: Mr Phil Scott, Head of Environmental Services, Quadrant, The Silverlink North, 2nd Floor, Quadrant West, Cobalt Business Park, NE27 0BY ☎ 0191 643 7295 🖷 0191 643 2414 ✉ phil.scott@northtyneside.gov.uk

Housing: Mr Ian Conway, Head of North Tyneside Homes, Quadrant, The Silverlink North, 2nd Floor, Quadrant West, Cobalt Business Park, NE27 0BY ☎ 0191 643 7501 🖷 0191 643 7575 ✉ ian.conway@northtyneside.gov.uk

Housing Maintenance: Mr Paul Worth, Housing Operations Manager, Quadrant, The Silverlink North, Cobalt Business Park, North Tyneside, NE27 0BY ☎ 0191 643 7554 🖷 0191 643 2412 ✉ paul.worth@northtyneside.gov.uk

Local Area Agreement: Mr Craig Anderson, Policy Officer, Quadrant, The Silverlink North, Cobalt Business Park, North Tyneside, NE27 0BY ☎ 0191 643 5621 🖷 0191 643 2431

Legal: Ms Vivienne Geary, Head of Legal Governance & Commercial Services, Quadrant, The Silverlink North, Cobalt Business Park, North Tyneside, NE27 0BY ☎ 0191 643 5339 🖷 0191 643 2431 ✉ vivienne.geary@northtyneside.gov.uk

Leisure and Cultural Services: Mr Paul Gowans, Head of Cultural Services & Customer Services, Quadrant, The Silverlink North, Cobalt Business Park, North Tyneside, NE27 0BY ☎ 0191 643 7401 🖷 0191 643 2406 ✉ paul.gowans@northtyneside.gov.uk

Leisure and Cultural Services: Mr Paul Youlden, Sport & Leisure Manager, Quadrant, The Silverlink North, Cobalt Business Park, North Tyneside, NE27 0BY ☎ 0191 643 7430 🖷 0191 200 6696 ✉ paul.youlden@northtyneside.gov.uk

Licensing: Mr Colin MacDonald, Consumer Protection Group Manager, Quadrant, The Silverlink North, Cobalt Business Park, North Tyneside, NE27 0BY ☎ 0191 643 6620 🖷 0191 643 2391 ✉ colin.macdonald@northtyneside.gov.uk

Lifelong Learning: Ms Gill Alexander, Strategic Director - Children, Young People & Learning, Quadrant, The Silverlink North, Cobalt Business Park, NE27 0BY ☎ 0191 643 8001 🖷 0191 643 2431 ✉ gill.alexander@northtyneside.gov.uk

Lifelong Learning: Mrs Jean Griffiths, Head of Schools, Learning & Skills, Quadrant, The Silverlink North, Cobalt Business Park, North Tyneside, NE27 0BY ☎ 0191 643 8783 🖷 0191 643 2408 ✉ jean.griffiths@northtyneside.gov.uk

Lighting: Mr Andrew Gate, Senior Manager: Strategic Projects, Quadrant, The Silverlink North, Cobalt Business Park, North Tyneside, NE27 0BY ☎ 0191 643 6450 ✉ andrew.gate@northtyneside.gov.uk

Lottery Funding, Charity and Voluntary: Mrs Felicity Shoesmith, Manager - Engagement, Quadrant, The Silverlink North, Cobalt Business Park, North Tyneside, NE27 0BY ☎ 0191 643 7071 🖷 0191 643 2431 ✉ felicity.shoesmith@northtyneside.gov.uk

Member Services: Ms Yvette Monaghan, Manager of Member Services & Customer Liaison, Quadrant, The Silverlink North, Cobalt Business Park, North Tyneside, NE27 0BY ☎ 0191 643 5341 🖷 0191 643 2415 ✉ yvette.monaghan@northtyneside.gov.uk

Parking: Mr Garry Hoyle, Parking Team Leader - Car Parks, Town Hall, High Street West, Wallsend NE28 8HX ☎ 0191 643 6599 ✉ garry.hoyle@northtyneside.gov.uk

Partnerships: Mrs Jackie Laughton, Strategic Manager - Policy & Partnerships, Quadrant, The Silverlink North, Cobalt Business Park, North Tyneside, NE27 0BY ☎ 0191 643 7070 🖷 0191 643 2427 ✉ jacqueline.laughton@northtyneside.gov.uk

Personnel / HR: Ms Alison Lazazzera, Strategic HR Manager, Quadrant, The Silverlink North, Cobalt Business Park, NE27 0BY ☎ 0191 643 5012 🖷 0191 643 2431 ✉ alison.lazazzera@northtyneside.gov.uk

Planning: Mr Peter Brown, Planning Manager, Quadrant, The Silverlink North, Cobalt Business Park, NE27 0BY ☎ 0191 643 6326 ✉ peter.brown@northtyneside.gov.uk

Planning: Mr Ken Wilson, Head of Regeneration, Development & Regulatory Services, Quadrant, The Silverlink North, Cobalt Business Park, NE27 0BY ☎ 0191 643 6091 🖷 0191 643 2426 ✉ ken.wilson@northtyneside.gov.uk

Procurement: Mr Andrew Lowe, Procurement Manager, Quadrant, The Silverlink North, Cobalt Business Park, NE27 0BY ☎ 0191 643 5651 🖷 0191 643 2430 ✉ andrew.lowe@northtyneside.gov.uk

Public Libraries: Ms Andrea Stephenson, Group Manager (East) Libraries, Community Centres & TICs, Quadrant, The Silverlink North, Cobalt Business Park, North Tyneside, NE27 0BY ☎ 0191 643 5291 🖷 0191 643 5821 ✉ andrea.stephenson@northtyneside.gov.uk

Recycling & Waste Minimisation: Mrs Catherine Lyons, Senior Manager - Waste & Environmental Sustainability, Quadrant, The Silverlink North, Cobalt Business Park, North Tyneside, NE27 0BY ☎ 0191 643 7780 🖷 0191 643 2414 ✉ catherine.lyons@northtyneside.gov.uk

Regeneration: Mr Francis Lowes, Senior Manager - Investment & Regeneration, Quadrant, The Silverlink North, Cobalt Business Park, North Tyneside, NE27 0BY ☎ 0191 643 6421 ✉ francis.lowes@northtyneside.gov.uk

Road Safety: Ms Liz Moore, Road Safety Officer, Quadrant, The Silverlink North, 2nd Floor, Quadrant West, Cobalt Business Park, NE27 0BY ☎ 0191 643 6104 🖷 0191 643 2426 ✉ liz.moore@northtyneside.gov.uk

Social Services (Adult): Mrs Jacqui Old, Head of Adult Social Care, Quadrant, The Silverlink North, Cobalt Business Park, North Tyneside, NE27 0BY ☎ 0191 643 7317 🖷 0191 643 3413 ✉ jacqui.old@northtyneside.gov.uk

Social Services (Children): Mr Paul Cook, Head of Preventative & Safeguarding Services, Quadrant, The Silverlink North, Cobalt Business Park, North Tyneside, NE27 0BY ☎ 0191 643 7381 🖷 0191 643 2409 ✉ paul.cook@northtyneside.gov.uk

Staff Training: Ms Alison Lazazzera, Strategic HR Manager, Quadrant, The Silverlink North, Cobalt Business Park, NE27 0BY ☎ 0191 643 5012 🖷 0191 643 2431 ✉ alison.lazazzera@northtyneside.gov.uk

Street Scene: Mr Phil Scott, Head of Environmental Services, Quadrant, The Silverlink North, Cobalt Business Park, North Tyneside, NE27 0BY ☎ 0191 643 7295 🖷 0191 643 2414 ✉ phil.scott@northtyneside.gov.uk

Sustainable Communities: Mr Phil Scott, Head of Environmental Services, Quadrant, The Silverlink North, 2nd Floor, Quadrant West, Cobalt Business Park, NE27 0BY ☎ 0191 643 7295 🖷 0191 643 2414 ✉ phil.scott@northtyneside.gov.uk

Sustainable Development: Mrs Catherine Lyons, Senior Manager - Waste & Environmental Sustainability, Quadrant, The Silverlink North, Cobalt Business Park, North Tyneside, NE27 0BY ☎ 0191 643 7780 🖷 0191 643 2414 ✉ catherine.lyons@northtyneside.gov.uk

Sustainable Development: Mr Paul Nelson, Environmental Sustainability Manager, Quadrant, The Silverlink North, Cobalt Business Park, North Tyneside, NE27 0BY ☎ 0191 643 6467 🖷 0191 643 2141 ✉ paul.nelson@northtyneside.gov.uk

Tourism: Mr Paul Gowans, Head of Cultural Services & Customer Services, Quadrant, The Silverlink North, Cobalt Business Park, North Tyneside, NE27 0BY ☎ 0191 643 7401 🖷 0191 643 2406 ✉ paul.gowans@northtyneside.gov.uk

Town Centre: Mr John Fleet, Town Centres Manager, Quadrant, The Silverlink North, Cobalt Business Park, NE27 0BY ☎ 0191 643 6419 ✉ john.fleet@northtyneside.gov.uk

Traffic Management: Mr Kevin Ridpath, Network & Transport Manager, Quadrant, The Silverlink North, Cobalt Business Park, NE27 0BY ☎ 0191 643 6089 🖷 0191 643 2426 ✉ kevin.ridpath@northtyneside.gov.uk

Transport Planner: Mr Steve Bland, Transport Team Leader, Quadrant, The Silverlink North, Cobalt Business Park, NE27 0BY ☎ 0191 643 6117 ✉ steve.bland@northtyneside.gov.uk

Total Place: Mrs Jackie Laughton, Strategic Manager - Policy & Partnerships, Quadrant, The Silverlink North, Cobalt Business Park, North Tyneside, NE27 0BY ☎ 0191 643 7070 🖷 0191 643 2427 ✉ jacqueline.laughton@northtyneside.gov.uk

Waste Collection and Disposal: Mr Phil Scott, Head of Environmental Services, Quadrant, The Silverlink North, Cobalt Business Park, North Tyneside, NE27 0BY ☎ 0191 643 7295 🖷 0191 643 2414 ✉ phil.scott@northtyneside.gov.uk

Waste Management: Mr Phil Scott, Head of Environmental Services, Quadrant, The Silverlink North, Cobalt Business Park, North Tyneside, NE27 0BY ☎ 0191 643 7295 🖷 0191 643 2414 ✉ phil.scott@northtyneside.gov.uk

Children's Play Areas: Mr Keith Hardy, Play & Urban Games Manager, Elm House, Riverside Centre, Minton Lane, North Shields NE28 6DQ ☎ 0191 643 8384 🖷 0191 643 8035 ✉ keith.hardy@northtyneside.gov.uk

MEMBERS OF THE COUNCIL (61)

***Directly Elected Mayor:* Arkley**, Linda
linda.arkley@northtyneside.gov.uk
***Chair:* Lott**, Frank (LAB - Riverside)
frank.lott@northtyneside.gov.uk
***Deputy Mayor:* Wallace**, Judith (CON - St Mary's)
judith.wallace@northtyneside.gov.uk
***Deputy Chair:* Hunter**, Janet (LAB - Benton)
janet.hunter@northtyneside.gov.uk
Allan, Jim (LAB - Camperdown)
jim.allan@ea-direct.com
Arkle, Anne (LAB - Camperdown)
anne.arkle@northtyneside.gov.uk
Austin, Alison (CON - Monkseaton North)
alison.austin@northtyneside.gov.uk
Barrie, Ken (CON - Cullercoats)
ken.barrie@northtyneside.gov.uk
Bell, Gary (LAB - Killingworth)
gary.bell@northtyneside.gov.uk
Brooks, Pamela (LAB - Whitley Bay)
pamela.brooks@northtyneside.gov.uk
Burdis, Brian (LAB - Valley)
valleycllrs@hotmail.com
Cairhness, Bill (LAB - Monkseaton South)
bill.caithness@northtyneside.gov.uk
Conroy, Kevin (LAB - Longbenton)
Corkey, David (LAB - Chirton)
david.corkey@northtyneside.gov.uk
Cowie, Alex (LAB - Weetslade)
alex.cowie@northtyneside.gov.uk
Cox, Steve (LAB - Collingwood)
cllrstevecox@gmail.com
Darke, Linda (LAB - Killingworth)
linda.darke@northtyneside.gov.uk
Darke, Eddie (LAB - Longbenton)
eddie.darke@northtyneside.gov.uk
Davis, Cath (LAB - Preston)
cath.davis@northtyneside.gov.uk
Day, Sarah (LAB - Tynemouth)
sarah.day@northtyneside.gov.uk
Finlay, Margaret (LD - Wallsend)
margyfinlay@yahoo.co.uk
Gambling, Carole (LAB - Valley)
valleycllrs@hotmail.com
Glindon, Ray (LAB - Camperdown)
ray.glindon@northtyneside.gov.uk
Graham, Sandra (LAB - Whitley Bay)
sandra.graham@northtyneside.gov.uk
Grayson, Ian (CON - Monkseaton South)
igrayson@hotmail.com
Green, Muriel (LAB - Weetslade)
muriel.green@northtyneside.gov.uk
Harrison, John (LAB - Howdon)
john.harrison@northtyneside.gov.uk
Hill, Stuart (LAB - Benton)
stuart.hill@northtyneside.gov.uk
Hodson, Edwin (CON - St Mary's)
edwin.hodson@northtyneside.gov.uk
Hunter, John (LAB - Howdon)
john.hunter@northtyneside.gov.uk
Huscroft, Marian (LD - Northumberland)
Huscroft, Nigel (LD - Northumberland)
Johnson, Carl (LAB - Battle Hill)
carl.johnson@northtyneside.gov.uk
Lilly, David (CON - Tynemouth)
david.lilly@nothtyneside.gov.uk
Madden, Gary (LAB - Wallsend)
gary.madden@northtyneside.gov.uk
Madden, Maureen (LAB - Howdon)
maureen.madden@northtyneside.gov.uk
Mason, Paul (CON - Monkseaton North)
paul.mason@northtyneside.gov.uk
McGarr, David (LAB - Battle Hill)
david.mcgarr@northtyneside.gov.uk
McIntyre, Pam (CON - St Mary's)
pam.mcintyre@northtyneside.gov.uk
McLaughlin, Jean (CON - Tynemouth)
jean.mclaughlin@northtyneside.gov.uk
McMullen, Anthony (LAB - Weetslade)
anthony.mcmullen@northtyneside.gov.uk
Miller, Leslie (CON - Monkseaton North)
les.miller@northtyneside.gov.uk
Mortimer, Shirley (CON - Cullercoats)
shirley.mortimer@northtyneside.gov.uk
Mulvenna, Tommy (LAB - Valley)
tommy.mulvenna@northtyneside.gov.uk
Munby, Joan (LAB - Monkseaton South)
joan.munby@northtyneside.gov.uk
Normand, Amanda (LAB - Chirton)
amanda.normand@northtyneside.gov.uk
Oliver, Pat (LAB - Benton)
pat.oliver@northtyneside.gov.uk
Ord, David (LD - Northumberland)
david.ord@northtyneside.gov.uk
Osborne, Kate (LAB - Preston)
kate.osborne@northtyneside.gov.uk
O'Shea, John (LAB - Whitley Bay)
john.o'shea@northtyneside.gov.uk
Pickard, Bruce (LAB - Riverside)
bruce.pickard@northtyneside.gov.uk
Pickard, Jeanette (LAB - Collingwood)
jeanette.pickard@northtyneside.gov.uk
Rankin, Martin (LAB - Collingwood)
martin.rankin@northtyneside.gov.uk
Redfearn, Norma (LAB - Riverside)
norma.redfearn@northtyneside.gov.uk
Rutherford, Jules (LAB - Wallsend)
jules.rutherford@northtyneside.gov.uk
Sarin, David (CON - Preston)

david.sarin@northtyneside.gov.uk
Spillard, Lesley (LAB - Battle Hill)
lesley.spillard@northtyneside.gov.uk
Stirling, John (LAB - Chirton)
john.stirling@northtyneside.gov.uk
Waggott-Fairley, Alison (LAB - Killingworth)
alison.waggott-fairley@northtyneside.gov.uk
Walker, Joan (LAB - Longbenton)
joan.walker@northtyneside.gov.uk
Westwater, George (CON - Cullercoats)
george.westwater@northtyneside.gov.uk

POLITICAL COMPOSITION

LAB: 43, CON: 14, LD: 4

CABINET

Mayor: Ms Linda Arkley
Deputy Mayor / Finance: Mrs Judith Wallace
Children, Young People & Learning: Mr David Lilly
Community & Regulatory Services: Mr George Westwater
Housing: Mr Paul Mason
Public Health & Adult Social Care: Mr Les Miller
Transport & the Environment: Mr Edwin Hodson

NORTH WARWICKSHIRE D

North Warwickshire Borough Council, The Council House, South Street, Atherstone CV9 1DE ☎ 01827 715341 🖷 01827 719225 ✉ customerservices@northwarks.gov.uk 💻 www.northwarks.gov.uk

FACTS & FIGURES

Police Authority: Warwickshire Police Authority
Health Authority: NHS West Midlands
Learning and Skills Council: West Midlands
Parliamentary Constituencies: Warwickshire North
EU Constituencies: West Midlands
Election Frequency: Elections are of whole council

PRINCIPAL OFFICERS

Chief Executive: Mr Jerry Hutchinson, Chief Executive, Old Bank House, 129 Long Street, Atherstone CV9 1DE ☎ 01827 715341 ✉ jerryhutchinson@northwarks.gov.uk

Deputy Chief Executive: Mr Chris Brewer, Deputy Chief Executive, The Council House, South Street, Atherstone CV9 1DE ☎ 01827 715341 ✉ chrisbrewer@northwarks.gov.uk

Assistant Chief Executive: Mr Steve Maxey, Assistant Chief Executive & Solicitor to the Council, Old Bank House, South Street, Atherstone CV9 1DE ☎ 01827 719438; 01827 715341 ✉ stevemaxey@northwarks.gov.uk

Assistant Chief Executive: Mr Bob Trahern, Assistant Chief Executive - Community Services, The Council House, South Street, Atherstone CV9 1DE ☎ 01827 715341 🖷 01827 719225 ✉ bobtrahern@northwarks.gov.uk

Building Control: Mr Kevin Bunsell, Head of Building Control, Town Hall, Nuneaton CV11 5AA ☎ 024 7637 6521 ✉ kevin.bunsell@nuneatonandbedworth.gov.uk

Children / Youth Services: Ms Jessica Grove, Community Development Officer (Young People & Intergeneration), The Council House, South Street, Atherstone CV9 1DE ☎ 01827 719220 ✉ jessicagrove@northwarks.gov.uk

PR / Communications: Miss Karen Barrow, Communications/PR Officer, The Council House, South Street, Atherstone CV9 1DE ☎ 01827 719309 ✉ karenbarrow@northwarks.gov.uk

Community Planning: Mr Jerry Hutchinson, Chief Executive, Old Bank House, 129 Long Street, Atherstone CV9 1DE ☎ 01827 715341 ✉ jerryhutchinson@northwarks.gov.uk

Community Safety: Mr Robert Beggs, Policy Support Manager, Old Bank House, 129 Long Street, Atherstone CV9 1DE ☎ 01827 719238 ✉ robertbeggs@northwarks.gov.uk

Computer Management: Ms Linda Bird, Assistant Director - Corporate Services, The Council House, South Street, Atherstone CV9 1DE ☎ 01827 719327 🖷 01827 719225 ✉ lindabird@northwarks.gov.uk

Corporate Services: Ms Linda Bird, Assistant Director - Corporate Services, The Council House, South Street, Atherstone CV9 1DE ☎ 01827 719327 🖷 01827 719225 ✉ lindabird@northwarks.gov.uk

Customer Service: Mr Bob Trahern, Assistant Chief Executive - Community Services, The Council House, South Street, Atherstone CV9 1DE ☎ 01827 715341 🖷 01827 719225 ✉ bobtrahern@northwarks.gov.uk

E-Government: Ms Linda Bird, Assistant Director - Corporate Services, The Council House, South Street, Atherstone CV9 1DE ☎ 01827 719327 🖷 01827 719225 ✉ lindabird@northwarks.gov.uk

Electoral Registration: Mr David Harris, Democratic Services Manager, Old Bank House, 129 Long Street, Atherstone CV9 1DE ☎ 01827 719222 ✉ davidharris@northwarks.gov.uk

Emergency Planning: Mr Robert Beggs, Policy Support Manager, The Council House, South Street, Atherstone CV9 1DE ☎ 01827 719238 ✉ robertbeggs@northwarks.gov.uk

Energy Management: Mr David Baxendale, Environmental Health Manager, The Council House, South Street, Atherstone CV9 1DE ☎ 01827 719322 ✉ davidbaxendale@northwarks.gov.uk

Environmental / Technical Services: Mr Richard Dobbs, Assistant Director - Streetscape, The Council House, South Street, Atherstone CV9 1DE ☎ 01827 719440 ✉ richarddobbs@northwarks.gov.uk

Environmental Health: Mr Steve Whiles, Environmental Health Manager, Old Bank House, South Street, Atherstone CV9 1DE ☎ 01827 715341 ✉ stephenwhiles@northwarks.gov.uk

Facilities: Mr Chris Jones, Facilities Management Manager, The Council House, South Street, Atherstone CV9 1DE ☎ 01827 719265 ✉ chrisjones@northwarks.gov.uk

Finance and Treasurer: Mr Chris Brewer, Deputy Chief Executive, The Council House, South Street, Atherstone CV9 1DE

☎ 01827 715341 ✉ chrisbrewer@northwarks.gov.uk

Fleet Management: Mr Richard Dobbs, Assistant Director - Streetscape, The Council House, South Street, Atherstone CV9 1DE ☎ 01827 719440 ✉ richarddobbs@northwarks.gov.uk

Grounds Maintenance: Mr Richard Dobbs, Assistant Director - Streetscape, The Council House, South Street, Atherstone CV9 1DE ☎ 01827 719440 ✉ richarddobbs@northwarks.gov.uk

Health and Safety: Miss Kerry Drakeley, HR Officer, The Council House, South Street, Atherstone CV9 1DE ☎ 01827 719300 ✉ kerrydrakeley@northwarks.gov.uk

Home Energy Conservation: Mr David Baxendale, Environmental Health Manager, The Council House, South Street, Atherstone CV9 1DE ☎ 01827 719322 ✉ davidbaxendale@northwarks.gov.uk

Housing: Ms Angela Coates, Assistant Director - Housing, The Council House, South Street, Atherstone CV9 1DE ☎ 01827 715341 ✉ angelacoates@northwarks.gov.uk

Housing Maintenance: Mr Peter Collins, Housing Maintenance Officer, The Council House, South Street, Atherstone CV9 1DE ☎ 01827 719308 ✉ petercollins@northwarks.gov.uk

Legal: Mr Steve Maxey, Assistant Chief Executive & Solicitor to the Council, Old Bank House, South Street, Atherstone CV9 1DE ☎ 01827 719438; 01827 715341 ✉ stevemaxey@northwarks.gov.uk

Leisure and Cultural Services: Mr Simon Powell, Assistant Director - Leisure & Community Development, The Council House, South Street, Atherstone CV9 1DE ☎ 01827 715341 ✉ simonpowell@northwarks.gov.uk

Licensing: Mr Phil Wortley, Licensing Enforcement Officer, Old Bank House, 129 Long Street, Atherstone CV9 1DE ☎ 01827 719482 ✉ philwortley@northwarks.gov.uk

Lottery Funding, Charity and Voluntary: Ms Jaki Douglas, Partnership & Development Manager, The Council House, South Street, Atherstone CV9 1DE ☎ 01827 719492 ✉ jakidouglas@northwarks.gov.uk

Member Services: Mr David Harris, Democratic Services Manager, Old Bank House, 129 Long Street, Atherstone CV9 1DE ☎ 01827 719222 ✉ davidharris@northwarks.gov.uk

Partnerships: Ms Jaki Douglas, Partnership & Development Manager, The Council House, South Street, Atherstone CV9 1DE ☎ 01827 719492 ✉ jakidouglas@northwarks.gov.uk

Personnel / HR: Ms Sue Garner, Assistant Director - Finance & HR, The Council House, South Street, Atherstone CV9 1DE ☎ 01827 719374 🖷 01827 719225 ✉ suegarner@northwarks.gov.uk

Personnel / HR: Ms Janis McCulloch, HR Manager, The Council House, South Street, Atherstone CV9 1DE ☎ 01827 719236 🖷 01827 719225 ✉ janismcculloch@northwarks.gov.uk

Planning: Mr Jeff Brown, Head of Development Control, The Council House, South Street, Atherstone CV9 1DE ☎ 01827 719310 🖷 01827 719363 ✉ jeffbrown@northwarks.gov.uk

Procurement: Mrs Elayne Cooper, Procurement Manager, The Council House, South Street, Atherstone CV9 1DE ☎ 01827 719203 🖷 01827 719225 ✉ elaynecooper@northwarks.gov.uk

Recycling & Waste Minimisation: Mr Richard Dobbs, Assistant Director - Streetscape, The Council House, South Street, Atherstone CV9 1DE ☎ 01827 719440 ✉ richarddobbs@northwarks.gov.uk

Recycling & Waste Minimisation: Mr Richard Dobbs, Assistant Director - Streetscape, The Council House, South Street, Atherstone CV9 1DE ☎ 01827 719440 ✉ richarddobbs@northwarks.gov.uk

Regeneration: Mrs Rachel Stephens, Community Development Officer (Rural Regeneration), The Council House, South Street, Atherstone CV9 1DE ☎ 01827 719301 ✉ rachelstephens@northwarks.gov.uk

Staff Training: Ms Sue Garner, Assistant Director - Finance & HR, The Council House, South Street, Atherstone CV9 1DE ☎ 01827 719374 🖷 01827 719225 ✉ suegarner@northwarks.gov.uk

Street Scene: Mr Richard Dobbs, Assistant Director - Streetscape, The Council House, South Street, Atherstone CV9 1DE ☎ 01827 719440 ✉ richarddobbs@northwarks.gov.uk

Sustainable Communities: Mrs Julie Taylor, Senior Policy Support Officer, Old Bank House, 129 Long Street, Atherstone CV9 1DE ☎ 01827 719437 ✉ julietaylor@northwarks.gov.uk

Sustainable Development: Mrs Julie Taylor, Senior Policy Support Officer, Old Bank House, 129 Long Street, Atherstone CV9 1DE ☎ 01827 719437 ✉ julietaylor@northwarks.gov.uk

Waste Collection and Disposal: Mr Richard Dobbs, Assistant Director - Streetscape, The Council House, South Street, Atherstone CV9 1DE ☎ 01827 719440 ✉ richarddobbs@northwarks.gov.uk

Waste Management: Mr Richard Dobbs, Assistant Director - Streetscape, The Council House, South Street, Atherstone CV9 1DE ☎ 01827 719440 ✉ richarddobbs@northwarks.gov.uk

MEMBERS OF THE COUNCIL (35)

***Mayor:* Dirveiks**, Lorna (LAB - Atherstone Central)
lornadirveiks@northwarks.gov.uk

***Deputy Mayor:* Ferro**, Dominic (LAB - Coleshill North)
dominicferro@northwarks.gov.uk

***Leader of the Council:* Stanley**, Michael (LAB - Polesworth East)
mickstanley@northwarks.gov.uk

***Deputy Leader of the Council:* Sweet**, Ray (LAB - Baddesley Ensor and Grendon)
raysweet@northwarks.gov.uk

Barber, Karen (CON - Arley and Whitacre)
karenbarber@northwarks.gov.uk

Butcher, Dave (LAB - Polesworth West)
davebutcher@northwarks.gov.uk

Davis, Martin (CON - Atherstone South and Mancetter)

martindavis@northwarks.gov.uk
Dirveiks, Neil (LAB - Atherstone Central)
neildirveiks@northwarks.gov.uk
Forwood, Anne (LAB - Atherstone North)
anneforwood@northwarks.gov.uk
Fowler, Peter (CON - Coleshill North)
peterfowler@northwarks.gov.uk
Fox, Carol (CON - Arley and Whitacre)
carolfox@northwarks.gov.uk
Freer, Lorraine (CON - Atherstone South and Mancetter)
lorrainefreer@northwarks.gov.uk
Hayfield, Colin (CON - Fillongley)
colinhayfield@northwarks.gov.uk
Holland, Alan (CON - Water Orton)
allanholland@northwarks.gov.uk
Humphreys, David (CON - Newton Regis and Warton)
davidhumphreys@northwarks.gov.uk
Johnston, Kath (CON - Hartshill)
kathjohnston@northwarks.gov.uk
Lea, Joan (CON - Curdworth)
joanlea@northwarks.gov.uk
Lewis, Ann (LAB - Hurley and Wood End)
annlewis@northwarks.gov.uk
May, Matilda (CON - Newton Regis and Warton)
matildamay@northwarks.gov.uk
Moore, John (LAB - Baddesley Ensor and Grendon)
johnmoore@northwarks.gov.uk
Morson, Peter (LAB - Dordon)
petermorson@northwarks.gov.uk
Moss, Brian (LAB - Kingsbury)
brianmoss@northwarks.gov.uk
Moss, Margaret (LAB - Kingsbury)
margaretmoss@northwarks.gov.uk
Payne, Raymond (CON - Water Orton)
raymondpayne@northwarks.gov.uk
Phillips, Hayden (LAB - Hurley and Wood End)
haydenphillips@northwarks.gov.uk
Pickard, Derek (LAB - Atherstone North)
derekpickard@northwarks.gov.uk
Sherratt, Gordon (CON - Coleshill South)
gordonsherratt@northwarks.gov.uk
Simpson, Mark (CON - Curdworth)
marksimpson@northwarks.gov.uk
Smith, Leslie (CON - Fillongley)
lessmith@northwarks.gov.uk
Stanley, Alison (LAB - Polesworth West)
alisonstanley@northwarks.gov.uk
Stanley, Yvette (LAB - Polesworth East)
yvettestanley@northwarks.gov.uk
Turley, Nigel (LAB - Arley and Whitacre)
nigelturley@northwarks.gov.uk
Watkins, Andrew (CON - Coleshill South)
andrewwatkins@northwarks.gov.uk
Winter, John (LAB - Dordon)
johnwinter@northwarks.gov.uk
Wykes, Tim (CON - Hartshill)
timwykes@northwarks.gov.uk

POLITICAL COMPOSITION

LAB: 18, CON: 17

NORTH WEST LEICESTERSHIRE D

North West Leicestershire District Council, Council Offices, Coalville LE67 3FJ ☎ 01530 454545 🖷 01530 454506
customer.services@nwleicestershire.gov.uk
www.nwleics.gov.uk

FACTS & FIGURES

Police Authority: Leicestershire Police Authority
Health Authority: East Midlands Strategic Health Authority
Learning and Skills Council: East Midlands
Parliamentary Constituencies: Leicestershire North West
EU Constituencies: East Midlands
Election Frequency: Elections are of whole council
Twinning: Ashby-de-la-Zouch: Pithiviers (France); Coalville: Romans-sur-Isere (France); Kegworth: Bois Guillaume, Plateau Nord de Rouen (France); Castle Donington: Gasny (France)

PRINCIPAL OFFICERS

Chief Executive: Miss Christine Fisher, Chief Executive, Council Offices, Coalville LE67 3FJ ☎ 01530 454502 🖷 01530 454504
christine.fisher@nwleicestershire.gov.uk

Deputy Chief Executive: Mr Steve Bambrick, Director of Services / Deputy Chief Executive, Council Offices, Coalville LE67 3FJ ☎ 01530 454555 🖷 01530 454506
steve.bambrick@nwleicestershire.gov.uk

Senior Management: Mr Steve Bambrick, Director of Services / Deputy Chief Executive, Council Offices, Coalville LE67 3FJ ☎ 01530 454555 🖷 01530 454506
steve.bambrick@nwleicestershire.gov.uk

Senior Management: Mr Ray Bowmer, Head of Finance, Council Offices, Coalville LE67 3FJ ☎ 01530 454520
ray.bowmer@nwleicestershire.gov.uk

Senior Management: Mrs Sue Haslett, Head of Planning & Engagement, Council Offices, Coalville LE67 3FJ ☎ 01530 454661 sue.haslett@nwleicestershire.gov.uk

Senior Management: Mr Christopher Lambert, Head of Housing & Customer Services, Council Offices, Coalville LE67 3FJ ☎ 01530 454780 chris.lambert@nwleicestershire.gov.uk

Senior Management: Mr John Richardson, Head of Community Services, Council Offices, Coalville LE67 3FJ ☎ 01530 454832 🖷 01530 454506 john.richardson@nwleicestershire.gov.uk

Senior Management: Miss Elizabeth Warhurst, Head of Legal & Democratic Services, Council Offices, Coalville LE67 3FJ ☎ 01530 454762 🖷 01530 454506
elizabeth.warhurst@nwleicestershire.gov.uk

Building Control: Mr Steve Bambrick, Director of Services / Deputy Chief Executive, Council Offices, Coalville LE67 3FJ ☎ 01530 454555 🖷 01530 454506
steve.bambrick@nwleicestershire.gov.uk

Building Control: Mr David Darlington, Building Control Manager, Council Offices, Coalville LE67 3FJ ☎ 01530 454691
david.darlington@nwleicestershire.gov.uk

Building Control: Mr Chris Elston, Planning & Development Team Manager, Council Offices, Coalville LE67 3FJ ☎ 01530 454668 chris.elston@nwleicestershire.gov.uk

Building Control: Mrs Sue Haslett, Head of Planning & Engagement, Council Offices, Coalville LE67 3FJ ☎ 01530 454661

Children / Youth Services: Mr John Richardson, Head of Community Services, Council Offices, Coalville LE67 3FJ ☎ 01530 454832 🖷 01530 454506 🖰 john.richardson@nwleicestershire.gov.uk

Community Planning: Mrs Sue Haslett, Head of Planning & Engagement, Council Offices, Coalville LE67 3FJ ☎ 01530 454661 🖰 sue.haslett@nwleicestershire.gov.uk

Community Safety: Ms Karen Talbot, Stronger & Safer Communities Team Manager, Council Offices, Coalville LE67 3FJ ☎ 01530 454696 🖰 karen.talbot@nwleicestershire.gov.uk

Computer Management: Mr Phil Clark, ICT Team Manager, Council Offices, Coalville LE67 3FJ ☎ 01530 454716 🖷 01530 454506 🖰 phil.clark@nwleicestershire.gov.uk

Corporate Services: Miss Anna Wright, Senior Auditor, Whitwick Road, Coalville LE67 3FJ ☎ 01530 454728 🖰 anna.wright@nwleicestershire.gov.uk

Customer Service: Mr Steve Bambrick, Director of Services / Deputy Chief Executive, Council Offices, Coalville LE67 3FJ ☎ 01530 454555 🖷 01530 454506 🖰 steve.bambrick@nwleicestershire.gov.uk

Customer Service: Mr Christopher Lambert, Head of Housing & Customer Services, Council Offices, Coalville LE67 3FJ ☎ 01530 454780 🖰 chris.lambert@nwleicestershire.gov.uk

Customer Service: Miss Emma Sparkes, Performance & Business Support Team Manager, Council Offices, Coalville LE67 3FJ ☎ 01530 454781 🖰 emma.sparkles@nwleicestershire.gov.uk

Economic Development: Mr Barrie Walford, Economic Development Officer, Council Offices, Coalville LE67 3FJ ☎ 01530 454822 🖰 barrie.walford@nwleicestershire.gov.uk

Electoral Registration: Mrs Louise Beeston, Senior Electoral Services Officer, Council Offices, Coalville LE67 3FJ ☎ 01530 454512 🖷 01530 454574 🖰 louise.beeston@nwleicestershire.gov.uk

Electoral Registration: Miss Christine Fisher, Chief Executive, Council Offices, Coalville LE67 3FJ ☎ 01530 454502 🖷 01530 454504 🖰 christine.fisher@nwleicestershire.gov.uk

Electoral Registration: Mrs Melanie Phillips, Democratic & Support Services Team Manager, Whitwick Road, Coalville LE67 3FJ ☎ 01530 454511 🖷 01530 454589 🖰 melaine.phillips@nwleicestershire.gov.uk

Emergency Planning: Miss Christine Fisher, Chief Executive, Council Offices, Coalville LE67 3FJ ☎ 01530 454502 🖷 01530 454504 🖰 christine.fisher@nwleicestershire.gov.uk

Environmental Health: Mr Steve Bambrick, Director of Services / Deputy Chief Executive, Council Offices, Coalville LE67 3FJ ☎ 01530 454555 🖷 01530 454506 🖰 steve.bambrick@nwleicestershire.gov.uk

Environmental Health: Mr Lee Mansfield, Environmental Health Team Manager, Council Offices, Coalville LE67 3FJ ☎ 01530 454610 🖷 01530 454506 🖰 lee.mansfield@nwleicestershire.gov.uk

Environmental Health: Mr John Richardson, Head of Community Services, Council Offices, Coalville LE67 3FJ ☎ 01530 454832 🖷 01530 454506 🖰 john.richardson@nwleicestershire.gov.uk

Estates, Property & Valuation: Mr Simon Harvey, Property Asset Manager, Council Offices, Coalville LE67 3FJ ☎ 01530 454550 🖰 simon.harvey@nwleicestershire.gov.uk

Finance and Treasurer: Mr Ray Bowmer, Head of Finance, Council Offices, Coalville LE67 3FJ ☎ 01530 454520 🖰 ray.bowmer@nwleicestershire.gov.uk

Housing: Mr Steve Bambrick, Director of Services / Deputy Chief Executive, Council Offices, Coalville LE67 3FJ ☎ 01530 454555 🖷 01530 454506 🖰 steve.bambrick@nwleicestershire.gov.uk

Housing: Mrs Sue Hallam, Strategic Housing Team Manager, Council Offices, Coalville LE67 3FJ ☎ 01530 454612 🖰 sue.hallam@nwleicestershire.gov.uk

Housing: Ms Amanda Harper, Housing Management Team Manager, Council Offices, Coalville LE67 3FJ ☎ 01530 454808 🖰 amanda.harper@nwleicestershire.gov.uk

Housing: Mr Christopher Lambert, Head of Housing & Customer Services, Council Offices, Coalville LE67 3FJ ☎ 01530 454780 🖰 chris.lambert@nwleicestershire.gov.uk

Housing: Clive Taylor, Housing (Older Persons) Team Manager, Whitwick Road, Coalville LE67 3FJ ☎ 01530 454699 🖰 clive.taylor@nwleicestershire.gov.uk

Housing Maintenance: Mr Mark Tuff, Housing Maintenance Manager, Whitwick Road, Coalville LE67 3FJ ☎ 01530 454849 🖰 mark.tuff@nwleicestershire.gov.uk

Legal: Miss Elizabeth Warhurst, Head of Legal & Democratic Services, Council Offices, Coalville LE67 3FJ ☎ 01530 454762 🖷 01530 454506 🖰 elizabeth.warhurst@nwleicestershire.gov.uk

Leisure and Cultural Services: Mr Steve Bambrick, Director of Services / Deputy Chief Executive, Council Offices, Coalville LE67 3FJ ☎ 01530 454555 🖷 01530 454506 🖰 steve.bambrick@nwleicestershire.gov.uk

Leisure and Cultural Services: Mr Jason Knight, Leisure Services Team Manager, Whitwick Road, Coalville LE67 3FJ ☎ 01530 454602

Leisure and Cultural Services: Mr Goff Lewis, Cultural Services Team Manager, Council Offices, Coalville LE67 3FJ ☎ 01530 454601 🖰 goff.lewis@nwleicestershire.gov.uk

Leisure and Cultural Services: Mr John Richardson, Head of Community Services, Council Offices, Coalville LE67 3FJ ☎ 01530 454832 🖷 01530 454506 ✉ john.richardson@nwleicestershire.gov.uk

Licensing: Mr Lee Mansfield, Environmental Health Team Manager, Council Offices, Coalville LE67 3FJ ☎ 01530 454610 🖷 01530 454506 ✉ lee.mansfield@nwleicestershire.gov.uk

Member Services: Mrs Melanie Phillips, Democratic & Support Services Team Manager, Whitwick Road, Coalville LE67 3FJ ☎ 01530 454511

Member Services: Miss Elizabeth Warhurst, Head of Legal & Democratic Services, Council Offices, Coalville LE67 3FJ ☎ 01530 454762 🖷 01530 454506 ✉ elizabeth.warhurst@nwleicestershire.gov.uk

Partnerships: Ms Sue Oliver, Procurement & Partnership Manager, Council Offices, Coalville LE67 3FJ ☎ 01530 454492 ✉ sue.oliver@neleicestershire.gov.uk

Personnel / HR: Mr Mike Murphy, Human Resources Manager, Council Offices, Coalville LE67 3FJ ☎ 01530 454518 🖷 01530 454506 ✉ mike.murphy@nwleicestershire.gov.uk

Planning: Mr Steve Bambrick, Director of Services / Deputy Chief Executive, Council Offices, Coalville LE67 3FJ ☎ 01530 454555 🖷 01530 454506 ✉ steve.bambrick@nwleicestershire.gov.uk

Planning: Mr Chris Elston, Planning & Development Team Manager, Council Offices, Coalville LE67 3FJ ☎ 01530 454668 ✉ chris.elston@nwleicestershire.gov.uk

Planning: Mrs Sue Haslett, Head of Planning & Engagement, Council Offices, Coalville LE67 3FJ ☎ 01530 454661 ✉ sue.haslett@nwleicestershire.gov.uk

Procurement: Ms Sue Oliver, Procurement & Partnership Manager, Council Offices, Coalville LE67 3FJ ☎ 01530 454492 ✉ sue.oliver@neleicestershire.gov.uk

Recycling & Waste Minimisation: Mr Paul Coates, Waste Services Team Manager, Council Offices, Coalville LE67 3FJ ☎ 01530 454663 ✉ paul.coates@nwleicestershire.gov.uk

Regeneration: Mr Steve Bambrick, Director of Services / Deputy Chief Executive, Council Offices, Coalville LE67 3FJ ☎ 01530 454555 🖷 01530 454506 ✉ steve.bambrick@nwleicestershire.gov.uk

Regeneration: Mr Ian Nelson, Head of Planning Policy & Regeneration, Council Offices, Coalville LE67 3FJ ☎ 01530 454676 ✉ ian.nelson@nwleicestershire.gov.uk

Street Scene: Mr John Richardson, Head of Community Services, Council Offices, Coalville LE67 3FJ ☎ 01530 454832 🖷 01530 454506 ✉ john.richardson@nwleicestershire.gov.uk

Sustainable Communities: Ms Karen Talbot, Stronger & Safer Communities Team Manager, Council Offices, Coalville LE67 3FJ ☎ 01530 454696 ✉ karen.talbot@nwleicestershire.gov.uk

Town Centre: Ms Emily Todd, Business Focus Team Leader, Council Offices, Coalville LE67 3FJ ☎ 01530 454678 ✉ emily.todd@nwleicestershire.gov.uk

Waste Collection and Disposal: Mr Paul Coates, Waste Services Team Manager, Council Offices, Coalville LE67 3FJ ☎ 01530 454545

Waste Management: Mr Paul Coates, Waste Services Team Manager, Council Offices, Coalville LE67 3FJ ☎ 01530 454663 ✉ paul.coates@nwleicestershire.gov.uk

Waste Management: Mr John Richardson, Head of Community Services, Council Offices, Coalville LE67 3FJ ☎ 01530 454832 🖷 01530 454506 ✉ john.richardson@nwleicestershire.gov.uk

MEMBERS OF THE COUNCIL (38)

***Chair:* Specht**, Michael (CON - Bardon)
michael.specht@nwleicestershire.gov.uk
***Deputy Chair:* Jones**, Geraint (CON - Ashby Ivanhoe)
geraint.jones@neleicestershire.gov.uk
***Leader of the Council:* Blunt**, Richard (CON - Appleby)
richard.blunt@nwleicestershire.gov.uk
***Deputy Leader of the Council:* Smith**, Alison (CON - Kegworth and Whatton)
alison.smith@nwleicestershire.gov.uk
Adams, Ron (LAB - Greenhill)
ronnie.adams@nwleicestershire.gov.uk
Allman, Graham (CON - Ashby Holywell)
graham.allman@nwleicestershire.gov.uk
Bayliss, Roger (CON - Ashby Holywell)
roger.bayliss@nwleicestershire.gov.uk
Bridges, John (CON - Moira)
john.bridges@nwleicestershire.gov.uk
Bridges, Annette (CON - Moira)
annette.bridges@nwleicestershire.gov.uk
Clarke, Nick (LAB - Greenhill)
nick.clarke@nwleicestershire.gov.uk
Clayfield, Pam (LAB - Coalville)
pam.clayfield@nwleicestershire.gov.uk
Cotterill, John (CON - Hugglescote)
john.cotterill@nwleicestershire.gov.uk
Coxon, John (CON - Ashby Castle)
john.coxon@nwleicestershire.gov.uk
De Lacy, Dave (LAB - Ibstock and Heather)
dave.delacy@nwleicestershire.gov.uk
Everitt, David (LAB - Thringstone)
david.everitt@nwleicestershire.gov.uk
Geary, John (LAB - Snibston)
john.geary@nwleicestershire.gov.uk
Gillard, Tony (CON - Whitwick)
tony.gillard@nwleicestershire.gov.uk
Holland, Rowena (CON - Valley)
Hoult, Jim (CON - Ashby Ivanhoe)
jim.hoult@nwleicestershire.gov.uk
Howe, Derek (LAB - Whitwick)
derek.howe@nwleicestershire.gov.uk
Hyde, Paul (LAB - Hugglescote)
paul.hyde@nwleicestershire.gov.uk
Johnson, Russell (LAB - Snibston)
russell.johnson@nwleicestershire.gov.uk
Large, Caroline (CON - Castle Donington)
caroline.large@nwleicestershire.gov.uk
Legrys, John (LAB - Coalville)

john.legrys@nwleicestershire.gov.uk
Massey, Lesley (LAB - Oakthorpe and Donisthorpe)
lesley.massey@nwleicestershire.gov.uk
Meynell, Charles (CON - Castle Donington)
charles.meynell@nwleicestershire.gov.uk
Neilson, Tom (LAB - Measham)
tom.neilson@nwleicestershire.gov.uk
Pendleton, Trevor (CON - Kegworth and Whatton)
trevor.pendleton@nwleicestershire.gov.uk
Richichi, Virginio (CON - Ibstock and Heather)
virge.richichi@nwleicestershire.gov.uk
Ruff, Janet (LAB - Ibstock and Heather)
janet.ruff@nwleicestershire.gov.uk
Rushton, Nick (CON - Breedon)
nicholas.rushton@nwleicestershire.gov.uk
Saffell, Anthony (CON - Castle Donington)
tony.saffell@nwleicestershire.gov.uk
Sheahan, Sean (LAB - Measham)
sean.sheahan@nwleicestershire.gov.uk
Smith, Nigel (CON - Ravenstone and Packington)
nigel.smith@nwleicestershire.gov.uk
Spence, Leon (LAB - Thringstone)
leon.spence@nwleicestershire.gov.uk
Stevenson, David (CON - Valley)
david.stevenson@nwleicestershire.gov.uk
Woodward, Ray (LAB - Whitwick)

Wyatt, Michael (LD - Greenhill)
michael.wyatt@nwleicestershire.gov.uk

POLITICAL COMPOSITION

CON: 21, LAB: 16, LD: 1

CABINET

Leader: Mr Richard Blunt
Deputy Leader / Community Services: Mrs Alison Smith
Corporate: Mr Nick Rushton
Housing & Customer Services: Mr Roger Bayliss
Planning & Engagement: Mr Trevor Pendleton

COMMITTEE CHAIRS

Licensing: Mr Nigel Smith
Planning: Mr David Stevenson

NORTH YORKSHIRE C

North Yorkshire County Council, County Hall, Northallerton DL7 8AD ☎ 0845 872 7374 🖷 01609 778199
💻 www.northyorks.gov.uk

FACTS & FIGURES

Police Authority: North Yorkshire Police Authority
Health Authority: NHS Yorkshire & the Humber
Learning and Skills Council: Yorkshire and the Humber
Parliamentary Constituencies: Harrogate and Knaresborough, Richmond (Yorks), Scarborough and Whitby, Skipton and Ripon
EU Constituencies: Yorkshire and the Humber
Election Frequency: Elections are of whole council

PRINCIPAL OFFICERS

Chief Executive: Mr Richard Flinton, Chief Executive, County Hall, Northallerton DL7 8AD ☎ 01609 532444 🖷 01609 778199
✉ richard.flinton@northyorks.gov.uk

Assistant Chief Executive: Mrs Justine Brooksbank, Assistant Chief Executive - Human Resources & Organisational Development Services, County Hall, Northallerton DL7 8AD ☎ 01609 532103 🖷 01609 779938
✉ justine.brooksbank@northyorks.gov.uk

Assistant Chief Executive: Mr Gary Fielding, Assistant Chief Executive - Policy, Performance & Partnerships, County Hall, Northallerton DL7 8AD ☎ 01609 533304 🖷 01609 778199
✉ gary.fielding@northyorks.gov.uk

Senior Management: Mr John Moore, Corporate Director - Financial & Central Services, County Hall, Northallerton DL7 8AL ☎ 01609 532114 🖷 01609 777567
✉ john.moore@northyorks.gov.uk

Architect, Building / Property Services: Mr Peter Bright, Assistant Director - Corporate Property Management, County Hall, Northallerton DL7 8AD ☎ 01609 532105 🖷 01609 532484
✉ peter.bright@northyorks.gov.uk

Catering Services: Mr Nick Postma, Client Catering Manager, County Hall, Northallerton DL7 8AD ☎ 01609 532167
✉ nick.postma@northyorks.gov.uk

Civil Registration: Mrs Lesley Willetts, General Manager - Registration, Archives & Coroners, Library Headquarters, 21 Grammar School Lane, DL7 8AD ☎ 01609 533877 🖷 01609 780793 ✉ lesley.willetts@northyorks.gov.uk

PR / Communications: Ms Helen Edwards, Head of Communications, County Hall, Northallerton DL7 8AD ☎ 01609 532104 ✉ helen.edwards@northyorks.gov.uk

Community Planning: Mr Neil Irving, Assistant Director - Policy & Partnerships, County Hall, Northallerton DL7 8AD ☎ 01609 533489 🖷 01609 778199 ✉ neil.irving@northyorks.gov.uk

Community Safety: Mr Neil Irving, Assistant Director - Policy & Partnerships, County Hall, Northallerton DL7 8AD ☎ 01609 533489 🖷 01609 778199 ✉ neil.irving@northyorks.gov.uk

Computer Management: Mr David Sadler, Head of ICT Services, County Hall, Northallerton DL7 8AD ☎ 01609 532116 🖷 01609 532020 ✉ david.sadler@northyorks.gov.uk

Consumer Protection and Trading Standards: Mr Graham Venn, Head of Trading Standards & Regulatory Services, Thornfield Business Park, Standard Way, Northallerton DL6 2XQ ☎ 01609 766408 🖷 01609 780970
✉ graham.venn@northyorks.gov.uk

Contracts: Mr Ian Beverley, Director of Procurement, 50 South Parade, Northallerton DL7 8SL ☎ 01609 538458
✉ ian.beverley@northyorks.gov.uk

Customer Service: Mr Gary Fielding, Assistant Chief Executive - Policy, Performance & Partnerships, County Hall, Northallerton DL7 8AD ☎ 01609 533304 🖷 01609 778199
✉ gary.fielding@northyorks.gov.uk

Economic Development: Mr James Farrar, Assistant Director -

Economic & Partnerships Unit, County Hall, Northallerton DL7 8AD ☎ 01609 533598 ✉ james.farrar@northyorks.gov.uk

Education: Ms Cynthia Welbourn, Corporate Director - Children & Young People's Services, County Hall, Northallerton DL7 8AE ☎ 01609 532146 🖷 01609 773756 ✉ cynthia.welbourn@northyorks.gov.uk

E-Government: Ms Lucy Darwin, Systems Manager, County Hall, Northallerton DL7 8AD ☎ 01609 533337

Electoral Registration: Ms Josie O'Dowd, Democratic Services Manager, County Hall, Northallerton DL7 8AD ☎ 01609 532591 🖷 01609 532343 ✉ josie.o'dowd@northyorks.gov.uk

Emergency Planning: Mr Mark Wilkinson, Head of Emergency Planning, County Hall, Northallerton DL7 8AD ☎ 01609 532110 🖷 01609 780733 ✉ mark.wilkinson@northyorks.gov.uk

Energy Management: Ms Karen Atkinson, Energy Officer, County Hall, Northallerton DL7 8AD ☎ 01609 535775 ✉ karen.p.atkinson@northyorks.gov.uk

European Liaison: Mr Jochen Werres, Funding, Strategy & Performance Team Leader, County Hall, Northallerton DL7 8AD ☎ 01609 532832 🖷 01609 532022 ✉ jochen.werres@northyorks.gov.uk

Facilities: Mr Peter Bright, Assistant Director - Corporate Property Management, County Hall, Northallerton DL7 8AD ☎ 01609 532105 🖷 01609 532484 ✉ peter.bright@northyorks.gov.uk

Finance and Treasurer: Mr John Burrows, Head of Central Finance Business Unit, County Hall, Northallerton DL7 8AD ☎ 01609 780780 ✉ john.burrows@northyorks.gov.uk

Finance and Treasurer: Mr John Moore, Corporate Director - Financial & Central Services, County Hall, Northallerton DL7 8AL ☎ 01609 532114 🖷 01609 777567 ✉ john.moore@northyorks.gov.uk

Grounds Maintenance: Mr Peter Bright, Assistant Director - Corporate Property Management, County Hall, Northallerton DL7 8AD ☎ 01609 532105 🖷 01609 532484 ✉ peter.bright@northyorks.gov.uk

Health and Safety: Mr Dominic Passman, Head of Health & Safety Risk Management, County Hall, Northallerton DL7 8AD ☎ ; 01609 532594 🖷 01609 780733 ✉ dominic.passman@northyorks.gov.uk

Highways: Mr David Bowe, Corporate Director - BES, County Hall, Northallerton DL7 8AD ☎ 01609 532128 🖷 01609 760794 ✉ david.bowe@northyorks.gov.uk

Local Area Agreement: Mr Kevin Brown, Performance, Research & Intelligence Officer, County Hall, Northallerton DL7 8AD ☎ 01609 532996 ✉ kevin.brown@northyorks.gov.uk

Local Area Agreement: Mr Hugh Williamson, Head of Scrutiny & Corporate Performance, County Hall, Northallerton DL7 8AD ☎ 01609 532352 🖷 01609 778199 ✉ hugh.williamson@northyorks.gov.uk

Legal: Ms Carole Dunn, Assistant Chief Executive - Legal & Democratic Services, County Hall, Northallerton DL7 8AD ☎ 01609 532173 🖷 01609 780447 ✉ carole.dunn@northyorks.gov.uk

Lifelong Learning: Mr Chris McGee, Assistant Director - Learning, Youth & Skills, County Hall, Northallerton D27 8AE ☎ 01609 532149 🖷 01609 780098 ✉ chris.mcgee@northyorks.gov.uk

Lighting: Mr Paul Gilmore, Road Lighting Team Leader, County Hall, Northallerton DL7 8AD ☎ 01609 532946 🖷 01609 532772 ✉ paul.gilmore@northyorks.gov.uk

Lottery Funding, Charity and Voluntary: Mr Neil Irving, Assistant Director - Policy & Partnerships, County Hall, Northallerton DL7 8AD ☎ 01609 533489 🖷 01609 778199 ✉ neil.irving@northyorks.gov.uk

Member Services: Mrs Amanda Fry, Staff Officer to Chief Executive, County Hall, Northallerton DL7 8AD ☎ 01609 532705 🖷 01609 778199 ✉ amanda.fry@northyorks.gov.uk

Personnel / HR: Mrs Justine Brooksbank, Assistant Chief Executive - Human Resources & Organisational Development Services, County Hall, Northallerton DL7 8AD ☎ 01609 532103 🖷 01609 779938 ✉ justine.brooksbank@northyorks.gov.uk

Personnel / HR: Mr Colin Parkin, Head of Workforce Planning & Performance, County Hall, Northallerton DL7 8AD ☎ 01609 532115 ✉ colin.parkin@northyorks.gov.uk

Personnel / HR: Ms Penny Yeadon, Head of Human Resources, County Hall, Northallerton DL7 8AD ☎ 01609 533302 ✉ penny.yeadon@northyorks.gov.uk

Planning: Mr James Farrar, Assistant Director - Economic & Partnerships Unit, County Hall, Northallerton DL7 8AD ☎ 01609 533598 ✉ james.farrar@northyorks.gov.uk

Procurement: Mr Ian Beverley, Director of Procurement, 50 South Parade, Northallerton DL7 8SL ☎ 01609 538458 ✉ ian.beverley@northyorks.gov.uk

Public Libraries: Ms Julie Blaisdale, Assistant Director - Information Services, County Hall, Northallerton DL7 8AD ☎ 01609 533494 🖷 01609 780793 ✉ julie.blaisdale@northyorks.gov.uk

Recycling & Waste Minimisation: Mr Ian Fielding, Assistant Director - Waste Management, County Hall, Northallerton DL7 8AD ☎ 01609 532161 🖷 01609 532474 ✉ ian.fielding@northyorks.gov.uk

Regeneration: Mr Gary Fielding, Assistant Chief Executive - Policy, Performance & Partnerships, County Hall, Northallerton DL7 8AD ☎ 01609 533304 🖷 01609 778199 ✉ gary.fielding@northyorks.gov.uk

Road Safety: Mr Allan McVeigh, Traffic Management & Road

Safety Group Manager, County Hall, Northallerton DL7 8AD ☎ 01609 532847 🖷 01609 779838 ✉ allan.mcveigh@northyorks.gov.uk

Social Services: Ms Kathryn Smith, Head of Social Care Provision & Regulation, County Hall, Northallerton DL7 8AD ☎ 01609 780780 ✉ kathryn.smith@northyorks.gov.uk

Social Services: Ms Helen Taylor, Director - Health & Adult Services, County Hall, Northallerton DL7 8AD

Social Services (Adult): Mr Michael Hunt, Assistant Director - Commissioning & Partnerships, County Hall, Northallerton DL7 8AD ☎ 01609 534480 🖷 01609 532025 ✉ michael.hunt@northyorks.gov.uk

Social Services (Children): Mr Paul Nixon, Head of Children & Families, County Hall, Northallerton DL7 8DD ☎ 01609 532140 🖷 01609 532025 ✉ paul.nixon@northyorks.gov.uk

Staff Training: Ms Sarah Watson, Adoption Social Worker, County Hall, Northallerton DL7 8AD ☎ 01609 538835 🖷 01609 779938 ✉ sarah.watson@northyorks.gov.uk

Sustainable Communities: Mr Neil Irving, Assistant Director - Policy & Partnerships, County Hall, Northallerton DL7 8AD ☎ 01609 533489 🖷 01609 778199 ✉ neil.irving@northyorks.gov.uk

Sustainable Development: Mr Tom Bryant, Senior Policy & Partnerships Officer, County Hall, Northallerton DL7 8AD ☎ 01609 533749 🖷 01609 778199 ✉ tom.bryant@northyorks.gov.uk

Tourism: Mr James Farrar, Assistant Director - Economic & Partnerships Unit, County Hall, Northallerton DL7 8AD ☎ 01609 533598 ✉ james.farrar@northyorks.gov.uk

Town Centre: Mr James Farrar, Assistant Director - Economic & Partnerships Unit, County Hall, Northallerton DL7 8AD ☎ 01609 533598 ✉ james.farrar@northyorks.gov.uk

Traffic Management: Mr Barrie Mason, Assistant Director - Highways, County Hall, Northallerton DL7 8AD ☎ 01609 532137 🖷 01609 779838 ✉ barrie.mason@northyorks.gov.uk

Transport: Mr David Bowe, Corporate Director - BES, County Hall, Northallerton DL7 8AD ☎ 01609 532128 🖷 01609 760794 ✉ david.bowe@northyorks.gov.uk

Waste Collection and Disposal: Mr Ian Fielding, Assistant Director - Waste Management, County Hall, Northallerton DL7 8AD ☎ 01609 532161 🖷 01609 532474 ✉ ian.fielding@northyorks.gov.uk

Waste Management: Mr Ian Fielding, Assistant Director - Waste Management, County Hall, Northallerton DL7 8AD ☎ 01609 532161 🖷 01609 532474 ✉ ian.fielding@northyorks.gov.uk

MEMBERS OF THE COUNCIL (72)

***Chair:* Trotter**, Cliff (CON - Pannal and Lower Wharfedale)
cllr.cliff.trotter@northyorks.gov.uk

***Leader of the Council:* Weighell**, John (CON - Bedale)
cllr.john.weighell@northyorks.gov.uk

***Deputy Leader of the Council:* Les**, Carl (CON - Catterick Bridge)
cllr.carl.les@northyorks.gov.uk

***Group Leader:* Arthur**, Karl (CON - Selby Barlby)
cllr.karl.arthur@northyorks.gov.uk

***Group Leader:* Hoult**, Bill (LD - Knaresborough)
cllr.bill.hoult@northyorks.gov.uk

Arnold, Val (CON - Kirkbymoorside)
cllr.val.arnold@northyorks.gov.uk

Backhouse, Andrew (CON - Newby)
cllr.andrew.backhouse@northyorks.gov.uk

Barker, Arthur (CON - Swale)
cllr.arthur.barker@northyorks.gov.uk

Barnes, Keith (LD - Harrogate Oatlands)
cllr.keith.barnes@northyorks.gov.uk

Barrett, Philip (IND - South Craven)
cllr.philip.barrett@northyorks.gov.uk

Bateman, Bernard (CON - Ripon North)
cllr.bernard.bateman@northyorks.gov.uk

Batt, John (CON - Knaresborough)
cllr.john.batt@northyorks.gov.uk

Blackburn, John (CON - Hertford and Cayton)
cllr.john.blackburn@scarborough.gov.uk

Blackie, John (IND - Upper Dales)
cllr.john.blackie@northyorks.gov.uk

Blades, David (CON - Romanby and Broomfield)
cllr.david.blades@northyorks.gov.uk

Casling, Elizabeth (CON - Escrick)
cllr.elizabeth.casling@northyorks.gov.uk

Chatt, William (IND - Woodlands)
cllr.bill.chatt@northyorks.gov.uk

Clark, Jim (CON - Harrogate Harlow)
cllr.jim.clark@northyorks.gov.uk

Clark, John (LIB - Pickering)
cllr.john.clark@northyorks.gov.uk

Cockerill, Michael (IND - Filey)
cllr.mike.cockerill@northyorks.gov.uk

Dadd, Gareth (CON - Thirsk)
cllr.gareth.dadd@northyorks.gov.uk

de Courcey-Bayley, Margaret-Ann (LD - Harrogate Starbeck)
cllr.margaret-ann.decourcey-bayley@northyorks.gov.uk

English, Polly (LD - Skipton West)
cllr.polly.english@northyorks.gov.uk

Fort, John (CON - Pateley Bridge)
cllr.john.fort@northyorks.gov.uk

Fox, John (LD - Harrogate Central)
cllr.john.fox@northyorks.gov.uk

Garnett, Heather (CON - Lower Nidderdale and Bishop Monkton)
cllr.heather.garnett@northyorks.gov.uk

Goss, Andrew (LD - Harrogate Bilton and Nidd Gorge)
cllr.andrew.goss@northyorks.gov.uk

Grant, Helen (IND - Central Richmondshire)
cllr.helen.grant@northyorks.gov.uk

Hall, Tony (CON - Northallerton)
cllr.tony.hall@northyorks.gov.uk

Harrison-Topham, Roger (CON - Middle Dales)
cllr.roger.harrison-topham@btinternet.com

Heseltine, Michael (CON - Richmondshire North)
cllr.michael.heseltine@northyorks.gov.uk

Heseltine, Robert (IND - Skipton East)
cllr.robert.heseltine@northyorks.gov.uk

Hulme, Margaret (CON - South Selby)
cllr.margaret.hulme@northyorks.gov.uk

Huxtable, Neville (CON - Sowerby)

cllr.neville.huxtable@northyorks.gov.uk
Ireton, David (CON - North Craven)
cllr.david.ireton@northyorks.gov.uk
Jeffels, David (CON - Seamer and Derwent Valley)
cllr.david.jeffles@scarborough.gov.uk
Jefferson, Janet (IND - Castle)
cllr.janet.jefferson@northyorks.gov.uk
Jordan, Mike (CON - Sherburn in Elmet)
cllr.mike.jordan@northyorks.gov.uk
Kenyon, Jane (CON - Whitby / Mayfield cum Mulgrave)
cllr.jane.kenyon@scarborough.gov.uk
Knaggs, Michael (CON - Malton)
cllr.michael.knaggs@northyorks.gov.uk
Lee, Andrew (CON - Cawood and Saxton)
cllr.andrew.lee@northyorks.gov.uk
Mackenzie, Don (CON - Harrogate Saltergate)
cllr.don.mackenzie@northyorks.gov.uk
Marsburg, Patricia (IND - Falsgrave and Stepney)
cllr.pat.marsburg@northyorks.gov.uk
Marsden, Penny (IND - Weaponness and Ramshill)
cllr.penny.marsden@northyorks.gov.uk
Marshall, Brian (LAB - Selby Barlby)
cllr.brian.marshall@northyorks.gov.uk
Marshall, John (LD - Harrogate Central)
Marshall, Shelagh (CON - Mid-Craven)
cllr.shelagh.marshall@northyorks.gov.uk
McCartney, John (IND - Osgoldcross)
cllr.john.mccartney@northyorks.gov.uk
Metcalfe, Chris (CON - Tadcaster)
cllr.chris.metcalfe@northyorks.gov.uk
Moorehouse, Heather (CON - Great Ayton)
cllr.heather.moorehouse@northyorks.gov.uk
Mulligan, Patrick (CON - Airedale)
cllr.patrick.mulligan@northyorks.gov.uk
Parsons, Stuart (LD - Richmond)
cllr.stuart.parsons@northyorks.gov.uk
Patmore, Caroline (CON - Stillington)
cllr.caroline.patmore@northyorks.gov.uk
Pearson, Christopher (CON - Mid Selby)
cllr.chris.pearson@northyorks.gov.uk
Peart, David (CON - Selby Brayton)
cllr.dave.peart@northyorks.gov.uk
Plant, Joe (CON - Whiteley / Streonshalh)
cllr.joe.plant@northyorks.gov.uk
Popple, Peter (IND - Northstead)
cllr.peter.popple@northyorks.gov.uk
Richardson, Paul (CON - Masham and Fountains)
cllr.paul.richardson@northyorks.gov.uk
Sanderson, Janet (CON - Thornton Dale and The Wolds)
cllr.janet.sanderson@northyorks.gov.uk
Savage, John (LIB - Ainsty)
cllr.john.savage@northyorks.gov.uk
Seymour, Caroline (LD - Stokesley)
cllr.caroline.seymour@northyorks.gov.uk
Shaw, Stephen (CON - Norton)
cllr.stephen.shaw@northyorks.gov.uk
Simpson, Brian (LD - Eastfield and Osgodby)
cllr.brian.simpson@northyorks.gov.uk
Sowray, Peter (CON - Easingwold)
cllr.peter.sowray@northyorks.gov.uk
Swales, Timothy (CON - North Hambleton)
cllr.tim.swales@northyorks.gov.uk
Swiers, Helen (CON - Scalby and The Coast)
cllr.helen.swiers@northyorks.gov.uk
Tindall, Herbert (CON - Esk Valley)
cllr.herbert.tindall@northyorks.gov.uk
Watson, John (CON - Boroughbridge)
cllr.john.watson@northyorks.gov.uk
Webber, Geoffrey (LD - Harrogate Bilton and Nidd Gorge)
cllr.geoff.webber@northyorks.gov.uk
Welch, Richard (CON - Ribblesdale)
cllr.richard.welch@northyorks.gov.uk
Williams, Andrew (IND - Ripon South)
cllr.andrew.williams@northyorks.gov.uk
Wood, Clare (CON - Hovingham and Sheriff Hutton)
cllr.clare.wood@northyorks.gov.uk

POLITICAL COMPOSITION

CON: 46, IND: 12, LD: 11, LIB: 2, LAB: 1

CABINET

Leader / Budget & External Organisations: Mr John Weighell
Deputy Leader / Children's Services: Mr Carl Les
Adult Services: Mrs Clare Wood
Financial Services & IT: Mr John Watson
Highways & Planning Services: Mr Gareth Dadd
Rural Services, Waste Disposal, Transport & Economic Development: Mr Chris Metcalfe
Schools & Youth Service: Mr Arthur Barker

NORTHAMPTON D

Northampton Borough Council, The Guildhall, St Giles Square, Northampton NN1 1DE ☎ 01604 837837 🖷 01604 837395 ✉ enquiries@northampton.gov.uk 💻 www.northampton.gov.uk

FACTS & FIGURES

Police Authority: Northamptonshire Police Authority
Health Authority: East Midlands Strategic Health Authority
Learning and Skills Council: East Midlands
Parliamentary Constituencies: Northampton North, Northampton South
EU Constituencies: East Midlands
Election Frequency: Elections are of whole council
Twinning: Marburg (Germany); Poitiers (France)

PRINCIPAL OFFICERS

Chief Executive: Mr David Kennedy, Chief Executive, The Guildhall, St Giles Square, Northampton NN1 1DE ☎ 01604 837726 ✉ dkennedy@northampton.gov.uk

Architect, Building / Property Services: Mr Simon Dougall, Corporate Asset Manager, Clifton House, Bedford Road, Northampton NN4 7NR ☎ 01604 838177 ✉ sdougall@northampton.gov.uk

Building Control: Mr Lee Hunter, Building Control Manager, NBC, Cliftonville House, Ground Floor, Cliftonville Road, Northampton NN4 7NR ☎ 01604 838926 ✉ lhunter@northampton.gov.uk

PR / Communications: Ms Deborah Denton, Communications Manager, The Guildhall, St Giles Square, Northampton NN1 1DE ☎ 01604 837393 ✉ ddenton@northampton.gov.uk

Community Safety: Mr Steve Elsey, Head of Public Protection, Westbridge Depot, St James Mill Road, Northampton NN5 5HW ☎ 01604 837508 ✉ selsey@northampton.gov.uk

Computer Management: Ms Marion Goodman, Head of Customer & Cultural Services, The Guildhall, St Giles Square, Northampton NN1 1DE ☎ 01604 838273 ✉ mgoodman@northampton.gov.uk

Corporate Services: Ms Cassie Triggs, Democratic & Chief Executive Services Manager, The Guildhall, St Giles Square, Northampton NN1 1DE ☎ 01604 837680 ✉ ctriggs@northampton.gov.uk

Customer Service: Ms Marion Goodman, Head of Customer & Cultural Services, The Guildhall, St Giles Square, Northampton NN1 1DE ☎ 01604 838273 ✉ mgoodman@northampton.gov.uk

Economic Development: Mr Christopher Cavanagh, Head of Regeneration & Development, The Guildhall, St Giles Square, Northampton NN1 1DE ☎ 01604 838461 ✉ ccavanagh@northampton.gov.uk

E-Government: Ms Marion Goodman, Head of Customer & Cultural Services, The Guildhall, St Giles Square, Northampton NN1 1DE ☎ 01604 838273 ✉ mgoodman@northampton.gov.uk

Electoral Registration: Ms Cassie Triggs, Democratic & Chief Executive Services Manager, The Guildhall, St Giles Square, Northampton NN1 1DE ☎ 01604 837680 ✉ ctriggs@northampton.gov.uk

Emergency Planning: Mr Aaron Goddard, Emergency Planning Officer, The Guildhall, St Giles Square, Northampton NN1 1DE ☎ 01604 837589 ✉ agoddard@northampton.gov.uk

Energy Management: Ms Julie Seddon, Director of Customers & Communities, Westbridge Depot, St James Mill Road, Northampton NN5 5JW ✉ julieseddon@northampton.gov.uk

Environmental / Technical Services: Ms Julie Seddon, Director of Customers & Communities, Westbridge Depot, St James Mill Road, Northampton NN5 5JW ✉ julieseddon@northampton.gov.uk

Environmental Health: Ms Ruth Austen, Environment Health Manager - Environment Protection, The Guildhall, St Giles Square, Northampton NN1 1DE ☎ 01604 837794 ✉ rausten@northampton.gov.uk

Estates, Property & Valuation: Mr Simon Dougall, Corporate Asset Manager, Clifton House, Bedford Road, Northampton NN4 7NR ☎ 01604 838177 ✉ sdougall@northampton.gov.uk

European Liaison: Mr Mick Lorkins, Economic Intelligence Manager, The Guildhall, St Giles Square, Northampton NN1 1DE ☎ 01604 838033 ✉ mlorkins@northampton.gov.uk

Events Manager: Mr Matt Parsons, Senior Events Manager, St Johns Car Park, PO Box 5432, Northampton NN1 1ZE ☎ 01604 837720 ✉ mparsons@northampton.gov.uk

Facilities: Ms Catherine Kimmet, Facilities Manager, The Guildhall, St Giles Square, Northampton NN1 1DE ☎ 01604 837378 ✉ ckimmet@northampton.gov.uk

Finance and Treasurer: Mr Robin Bates, Head of Finance & Resources, The Guildhall, St Giles Square, Northampton NN1 1DE ☎ 01604 837119 ✉ rbates@northampton.gov.uk

Finance and Treasurer: Mr Bill Lewis, Assistant Head of Finance, The Guildhall, St Giles Square, Northampton NN1 1DE ☎ 01604 837167 ✉ blewis@northampton.gov.uk

Finance and Treasurer: Ms Isabell Proctor, Director of Resources, The Guildhall, St Giles Square, Northampton NN1 1DE ☎ 01604 838757 ✉ iproctor@northampton.gov.uk

Health and Safety: Mrs Kennie Bassey, Health, Safety & Wellbeing Manager, The Guildhall, St Giles Square, Northampton NN1 1DE ☎ 01604 838100

Housing: Lesley Wearing, Director of Housing, The Guildhall, St Giles Square, Northampton NN1 1DE ☎ 01604 837837 ✉ lwearing@northampton.gov.uk

Housing Maintenance: Ms Mary Wood, Interim Head of Landlord Services, Westbridge Depot, St James Mill Road, Northampton NN5 5JW ☎ 01604 838955 ✉ mwood@northampton.gov.uk

Legal: Mr Francis Fernandes, Borough Secretary, The Guildhall, Northampton NN1 1DE ☎ 01604 837334 ✉ ffernandes@northampton.gov.uk

Leisure and Cultural Services: Ms Julie Seddon, Director of Customers & Communities, Westbridge Depot, St James Mill Road, Northampton NN5 5JW ✉ julieseddon@northampton.gov.uk

Licensing: Mr Steve Elsey, Head of Public Protection, Cliftonville House, Bedford Road, Northampton NN4 7NR ☎ 01604 837508 ✉ selsey@northampton.gov.uk

Lottery Funding, Charity and Voluntary: Ms Nicci Marzec, Head of Partnership Support, The Guildhall, St Giles Square, Northampton NN1 1DE ☎ 01604 837431 ✉ nmarzec@northampton.gov.uk

Member Services: Mr Frazer McGown, Democratic Services Manager, The Guildhall, Northampton NN1 1DE ☎ 01604 837101 ✉ fmcgown@northampton.gov.uk

Parking: Mr Derrick Simpson, Town Centre Manager, St. John's, Northampton NN1 1DE ☎ 01604 838514 ✉ dsimpson@northampton.gov.uk

Partnerships: Ms Nicci Marzec, Head of Partnership Support, Fish Street, Northampton NN1 1DE ☎ 01604 837431 ✉ nmarzec@northampton.gov.uk

Personnel / HR: Ms Catherine Wilson, Head of Business Change, The Guildhall, St Giles Square, Northampton NN1 1DE ☎ 01604 837377 ✉ cwilson@northampton.gov.uk

Planning: Ms Sue Bridge, Head of Planning, The Guildhall, St Giles Square, Northampton NN1 1DE ☎ 01604 837837 ✉ sbridge@northampton.gov.uk

Planning: Ms Marie Fallon, Director of Regeneration, Enterprise

& Planning, The Guildhall, St Giles Square, Northampton NN1 1DE ☎ 01604 837287 ✉ mfallon@northampton.gov.uk

Procurement: Mr Stuart Taylor, Procurement Manager, The Guildhall, St Giles Square, Northampton NN1 1DE ☎ 01604 838660 ✉ staylor@northampton.gov.uk

Recycling & Waste Minimisation: Ms Julie Seddon, Director of Customers & Communities, Westbridge Depot, St James Mill Road, Northampton NN5 5JW ✉ julieseddon@northampton.gov.uk

Regeneration: Mr Christopher Cavanagh, Head of Regeneration & Development, The Guildhall, St Giles Square, Northampton NN1 1DE ☎ 01604 838461 ✉ ccavanagh@northampton.gov.uk

Staff Training: Ms Renee Bullock, HR & Organisational Development Manager, The Guildhall, St Giles Square, Northampton NN1 1DE ☎ 01604 838100 ✉ rbullock@northampton.gov.uk

Sustainable Development: Ms Marie Fallon, Director of Regeneration, Enterprise & Planning, The Guildhall, St Giles Square, Northampton NN1 1DE ☎ 01604 837287 ✉ mfallon@northampton.gov.uk

Town Centre: Mr Derrick Simpson, Town Centre Manager, St. John's, Northampton NN1 1DE ☎ 01604 838514 ✉ dsimpson@northampton.gov.uk

Waste Collection and Disposal: Ms Julie Seddon, Director of Customers & Communities, Westbridge Depot, St James Mill Road, Northampton NN5 5JW ✉ julieseddon@northampton.gov.uk

Waste Management: Ms Julie Seddon, Director of Customers & Communities, Westbridge Depot, St James Mill Road, Northampton NN5 5JW ✉ julieseddon@northampton.gov.uk

Children's Play Areas: Ms Julie Seddon, Director of Customers & Communities, Westbridge Depot, St James Mill Road, Northampton NN5 5JW ✉ julieseddon@northampton.gov.uk

MEMBERS OF THE COUNCIL (45)

***Mayor:* Conroy**, Roger (LD - Kings Heath)
cllr.rconroy@northampton.gov.uk

***Deputy Mayor:* Marriott**, Les (LAB - Semilong)
cllr.lmarriott@northampton.gov.uk

***Leader of the Council:* Mackintosh**, David (CON - Rectory Farm)
cllr.dmackintosh@northampton.gov.uk

***Deputy Leader of the Council:* Caswell**, John (CON - New Duston)
cllr.jcaswell@northampton.gov.uk

***Group Leader:* Beardsworth**, Sally (LD - Kingsthorpe)
cllr.sbeardsworth@northampton.gov.uk

***Group Leader:* Mason**, Lee (LAB - Brookside)
cllr.lmason@northampton.gov.uk

***Group Leader:* Wire**, Terry (LAB - St James)
cllr.twire@northampton.gov.uk

Ansell, Tony (CON - Abington)
cllr.tansell@northampton.gov.uk

Begum, Nahar (LAB - Trinity)
cllr.nbegum@northampton.gov.uk

Bottwood, Alan (CON - Upton)
cllr.abottwood@northampton.gov.uk

Capstick, Joy (LAB - Talavera)
joychope1@aol.com

Choudary, Nazim (LAB - St Davids)
cllr.nchoudary@northampton.gov.uk

Choudary, Iftikhar Ahmed (LAB - Abington)
cllr.ichoudary@northampton.gov.uk

Davies, Geraldine (LAB - Delapre & Briar Hill)
cllr.gdavies@northampton.gov.uk

Duncan, Norman (CON - Park)
cllr.nduncan@northampton.gov.uk

Eales, Gareth (LAB - Spencer)
cllr.geales@northampton.gov.uk

Eldred, Brandon (CON - East Hunsbury)
cllr.beldred@northampton.gov.uk

Flavell, Penelope (CON - Rushmills)
cllr.pflavell@northampton.gov.uk

Ford, Michael (CON - Delapre & Briar Hill)
cllr.mford@northampton.gov.uk

Glynane, Brendon (LD - Delapre & Briar Hill)
cllr.bglynane@northampton.gov.uk

Golby, Matthew (CON - New Duston)
cllr.mgolby@northampton.gov.uk

Gowen, Elizabeth (LAB - Eastfield)
cllr.egowen@northampton.gov.uk

Hadland, Tim (CON - Old Duston)
hadlandtj@gmail.com

Hallam, Mike (CON - Parklands)
cllr.mhallam@northampton.gov.uk

Hibbert, Stephen (CON - Riverside)
cllr.shibbert@northampton.gov.uk

Hill, Michael (CON - Nene Valley)
northamptonhill@yahoo.com

King, Anna (CON - Phippsville)
cllr.aking@northampton.gov.uk

Lane, Jamie (CON - Boothville)
cllr.jlane@northampton.gov.uk

Larratt, Phil (CON - East Hunsbury)
cllr.plarratt@northampton.gov.uk

Lynch, Matthew (CON - Westone)
matt.lynch@talk21.com

Malpas, Christopher (CON - Billing)
cllr.cmalpas@northampton.gov.uk

Markham, Mary (CON - Obelisk)
cllr.mmarkham@northampton.gov.uk

Mennell, Beverley-Anne (LAB - Kingsley)
cllr.bmennell@northampton.gov.uk

Meredith, Dennis (LD - Talavera)
cllr.dmeredith@northampton.gov.uk

Nunn, Jonathan (CON - Nene Valley)

Oldham, Brian (CON - West Hunsbury)
bvoldham@talktalk.net

Palethorpe, David (CON - Billing)
cllr.davidpalethorpe@hotmail.co.uk

Parekh, Nilesh (CON - Sunnyside)
cllr.nparekh@northampton.gov.uk

Patel, Suresh (CON - Old Duston)
cllr.spatel@northampton.gov.uk

Rahman, Mohammed Azizur (LAB - Castle)
cllr.maziz@northampton.gov.uk

Sargeant, Brian (CON - Upton)
cllr.bsargeant@northampton.gov.uk

Stone, Danielle (LAB - Castle)
daniellevstone@gmail.com

Strachan, Winston (LAB - Castle)
cllr.wstrachan@northampton.gov.uk

Subbarayan, Sivaramen (LAB - Headlands)
cllr.ssubbarayan@northampton.gov.uk
Yates, John (CON - Spring Park)
cllr.jyates@northampton.gov.uk

POLITICAL COMPOSITION
CON: 26, LAB: 15, LD: 4

CABINET
Leader: Mr David Mackintosh
Deputy Leader / Environment: Mr John Caswell
Community Engagement: Mr Brandon Eldred
Finance: Mr Alan Bottwood
Housing: Ms Mary Markham
Planning, Regeneration & Enterprise: Mr Tim Hadland

COMMITTEE CHAIRS
Appointments & Appeals: Mr David Mackintosh
Audit: Mr Phil Larratt
General Purposes: Mr Suresh Patel
Licensing: Mr Christopher Malpas
Overview & Scrutiny: Mr Les Marriott
Planning: Ms Penelope Flavell
Standards: Mr John Yates

NORTHAMPTONSHIRE C

Northamptonshire County Council, County Hall, Northampton NN1 1AN ☎ 01604 236236 🖷 01604 236223
💻 www.northamptonshire.gov.uk

FACTS & FIGURES
Police Authority: Northamptonshire Police Authority
Health Authority: East Midlands Strategic Health Authority
Learning and Skills Council: East Midlands
EU Constituencies: East Midlands
Election Frequency: Elections are of whole council

PRINCIPAL OFFICERS
Chief Executive: Mr Paul Blantern, Chief Executive, PO Box 93, County Hall, Northampton NN1 1AN ☎ 01604 237100 🖷 01604 236652 ✉ pblantern@northamptonshire.gov.uk

Assistant Chief Executive: Mr Alex Hopkins, Assistant Chief Executive - Policy & Partnership, PO Box 93, County Hall, Northampton NN1 1AN ☎ 01604 236359 🖷 01604 236652 ✉ aghopkins@northamptonshire.gov.uk

Senior Management: Mr Paul Blantern, Chief Executive, PO Box 93, County Hall, Northampton NN1 1AN ☎ 01604 237100 🖷 01604 236652 ✉ pblantern@northamptonshire.gov.uk

Senior Management: Mr Paul Burnett, Corporate Director of Children & Young People's Services, PO Box 93, County Hall, Northampton NN1 1AN ☎ 01604 236252 🖷 01604 236550 ✉ pburnett@northamptonshire.gov.uk

Senior Management: Mr Tony Ciaburro, Corporate Director of Environment, Growth & Commissioning, PO Box 93, County Hall, Northampton NN1 1AN ☎ 01604 236740 🖷 01604 236652 ✉ tciaburro@northamptonshire.gov.uk

Senior Management: Mr Charlie MacNally, Corporate Director of Health & Adult Social Services, PO Box 93, County Hall, Northampton NN1 1AN ☎ 01604 236024 🖷 01604 237160 ✉ cmacnally@northamptonshire.gov.uk

Access Officer / Social Services (Disability): Ms Janet Doran, Head of Policy, County Hall, Northampton NN1 1AN ☎ 01604 236023 🖷 01604 236223 ✉ jdoran@northamptonshire.gov.uk

Architect, Building / Property Services: Mr Richard Beeby, Head of Asset Management, County Hall, Northampton NN1 1AN ☎ 01604 236447 🖷 01604 236979 ✉ rbeeby@northamptonshire.gov.uk

Best Value: Mr John Jenkins, Corporate Planning & Consultation Team, Room 91, County Hall, Northampton NN1 1AN ☎ 01604 236827 🖷 01604 237255 ✉ jjenkins@northamptonshire.gov.uk

Building Control: Mr Richard Beeby, Head of Asset Management, County Hall, Northampton NN1 1AN ☎ 01604 236447 🖷 01604 236979 ✉ rbeeby@northamptonshire.gov.uk

Children / Youth Services: Mr Tim O'Neill, Head of Extended Services to Children, Young People & Families, PO Box 93, County Hall, Northampton NN1 1AN ☎ 01604 237652 ✉ toneill@northamptonshire.gov.uk

Children / Youth Services: Ms M Phillips, Head of Children, Young People & Families, County Hall, Northampton NN1 1AN ☎ 01604 236004 ✉ mephillips@northamptonshire.gov.uk

Civil Registration: Mr Robert Chadwick, Registration Service Manager, Trading Standards, Wootton Hall Park, Northampton NN4 0GB ☎ 01604 707923 🖷 01604 707901 ✉ rchadwick@northamptonshire.gov.uk

PR / Communications: Mrs Faye Scadden, Head of Communications & Marketing, Room 90, County Hall, Northampton NN1 1AN ☎ 01604 237111 🖷 01604 237255 ✉ fscadden@northamptonshire.gov.uk

Community Planning: Mr Roy Boulton, Head of Spatial, Environmental & Economical Planning, PO Box 93, County Hall, Northampton NN1 1AN ☎ 01604 236056 ✉ rboulton@northamptonshire.gov.uk

Community Planning: Ms Grace Kempster, Head of Community Information & Access, John Dryden House, 8-10 The Lakes, Northampton NN4 7DD ☎ 01604 237952 ✉ gkempster@northamptonshire.gov.uk

Community Safety: Ms Jane Taylor, Head of Community Safety, Room 232, County Hall, Northampton NN1 1AN ☎ 01604 236046 ✉ jataylor@northamptonshire.gov.uk

Computer Management: Mr Rocco Labellorte, Head of IT, County Hall, Northampton NN1 1AN ☎ 01604 236009 ✉ rlabellorte@northamptonshire.gov.uk

Consumer Protection and Trading Standards: Mr David Hedger, Assistant Head of Trading Standards, Trading Standards, Wootton Hall Park, Northampton NN4 0GB ☎ 01604 707957

🖷 01604 707901 ✉ dhedger@northamptonshire.gov.uk

Contracts: Mr Matt Bowmer, Head of Finance, County Hall, Northampton NN1 1AN ✉ m.bowmer@northamptonshire.gov.uk

Corporate Services: Mr Paul Blantern, Chief Executive, PO Box 93, County Hall, Northampton NN1 1AN ☎ 01604 237100 🖷 01604 236652 ✉ pblantern@northamptonshire.gov.uk

Corporate Services: Ms Alison Parry, Head of Commercial Management, County Hall, Northampton NN1 1AN ☎ 01604 236838 ✉ aparry@northamptonshire.gov.uk

Customer Service: Mr Paul Blantern, Chief Executive, PO Box 93, County Hall, Northampton NN1 1AN ☎ 01604 237100 🖷 01604 236652 ✉ pblantern@northamptonshire.gov.uk

Economic Development: Mr Tony Ciaburro, Corporate Director of Environment, Growth & Commissioning, PO Box 93, County Hall, Northampton NN1 1AN ☎ 01604 236740 🖷 01604 236652 ✉ tciaburro@northamptonshire.gov.uk

Education: Mr Paul Burnett, Corporate Director of Children & Young People's Services, PO Box 93, County Hall, Northampton NN1 1AN ☎ 01604 236252 🖷 01604 236550 ✉ pburnett@northamptonshire.gov.uk

E-Government: Mr Matt Bowmer, Head of Finance, County Hall, Northampton NN1 1AN ✉ m.bowmer@northamptonshire.gov.uk

Electoral Registration: Mr Adam Simmonds, Head of Strategy & Business Administration, PO Box 93, County Hall, Northampton NN1 1AN ☎ 01604 236963 🖷 01604 237840 ✉ asimmonds@northamptonshire.gov.uk

Emergency Planning: Mr Matthew Hoy, Emergency Planning Manager, PO Box 93, County Hall, Northampton NN1 1AN ☎ 01604 236380 ✉ mhoy@northamptonshire.gov.uk

Energy Management: Dr Darren Perry, Strategic Leader - Energy & Carbon Management, County Hall, Northampton NN1 1AN ☎ 01604 236948 ✉ daperry@northamptonshire.gov.uk

Estates, Property & Valuation: Mr Richard Beeby, Head of Asset Management, County Hall, Northampton NN1 1AN ☎ 01604 236447 🖷 01604 236979 ✉ rbeeby@northamptonshire.gov.uk

European Liaison: Mr Tony Ciaburro, Corporate Director of Environment, Growth & Commissioning, PO Box 93, County Hall, Northampton NN1 1AN ☎ 01604 236740 🖷 01604 236652 ✉ tciaburro@northamptonshire.gov.uk

Facilities: Mrs Susan Hird, Facilities Manager, County Hall, Northampton NN1 1AN ☎ 01604 236766 🖷 01604 236903 ✉ shird@northamptonshire.gov.uk

Finance and Treasurer: Mr Matt Bowmer, Head of Finance, County Hall, Northampton NN1 1AN ✉ m.bowmer@northamptonshire.gov.uk

Fleet Management: Mr Michael Jones, Fleet Transport Manager, 4th Floor, Riverside House, Rivreside Way, Bedford Road, Northampton NN1 5NX ☎ 01604 654469 ✉ mrjones@northamptonshire.gov.uk

Grounds Maintenance: Mr Richard Beeby, Head of Asset Management, PO Box 128, County Hall, Northampton NN1 1AS ☎ 01604 236447 🖷 01604 236979 ✉ rbeeby@northamptonshire.gov.uk

Health and Safety: Ms Sue Stagg, Health & Safety Manager, PO Box 179, John Dryden House, 8-10 The Lakes, Northampton NN4 7DA ☎ 01604 236016 🖷 01604 237359 ✉ sstagg@northamptonshire.gov.uk

Highways: Mr David Farquhar, Head of Transport & Highways, Riverside House, Riverside Way, Bedford Road, Northampton NN1 5NX ☎ 01604 654401 🖷 01604 654455 ✉ dfarquhar@northamptonshire.gov.uk

Local Area Agreement: Mr Peter McLaren, Head of Partnership Support Unit, PO Box 93, County Hall, Northampton NN1 1AN ☎ 01604 237106 🖷 01604 237675 ✉ pmclaren@northamptonshire.gov.uk

Leisure and Cultural Services: Ms Sue Grace, Head of Customer & Cultural Services, PO Box 93, County Hall, Northampton NN1 1AN ☎ 01604 237960 🖷 01604 237600 ✉ sgrace@northamptonshire.gov.uk

Licensing: Mr David Hedger, Assistant Head of Trading Standards, Trading Standards, Wootton Hall Park, Northampton NN4 0GB ☎ 01604 707957 🖷 01604 707901 ✉ dhedger@northamptonshire.gov.uk

Lifelong Learning: Ms Sue Grace, Head of Customer & Cultural Services, PO Box 93, County Hall, Northampton NN1 1AN ☎ 01604 237960 🖷 01604 237600 ✉ sgrace@northamptonshire.gov.uk

Lighting: Mr Geoff Emmins, Highways Maintenance Manager, Riverside House, Riverside Way, Bedford Road, Northampton NN1 5NX ☎ 01604 654481 ✉ gemmins@northamptonshire.gov.uk

Lottery Funding, Charity and Voluntary: Mr Tony Ciaburro, Corporate Director of Environment, Growth & Commissioning, PO Box 93, County Hall, Northampton NN1 1AN ☎ 01604 236740 🖷 01604 236652 ✉ tciaburro@northamptonshire.gov.uk

Member Services: Mr Adam Simmonds, Head of Strategy & Business Administration, PO Box 93, County Hall, Northampton NN1 1AN ☎ 01604 236963 🖷 01604 237840 ✉ asimmonds@northamptonshire.gov.uk

Parking: Mr David Farquhar, Head of Transport & Highways, Riverside House, Riverside Way, Bedford Road, Northampton NN1 5NX ☎ 01604 654401 🖷 01604 654455 ✉ dfarquhar@northamptonshire.gov.uk

Partnerships: Mr Peter McLaren, Head of Partnership Support Unit, PO Box 93, County Hall, Northampton NN1 1AN ☎ 01604 237106 🖷 01604 237675 ✉ pmclaren@northamptonshire.gov.uk

Personnel / HR: Mrs Christine Reed, Head of Human

Resources, PO Box 93, County Hall, Northampton NN1 1AN ☎ 01604 237291 ✉ creed@northamptonshire.gov.uk

Planning: Mr Roy Boulton, Head of Spatial, Environmental & Economical Planning, PO Box 93, County Hall, Northampton NN1 1AN ☎ 01604 236056 ✉ rboulton@northamptonshire.gov.uk

Procurement: Mr Paul White, Head of Shared Services & Procurement, PO Box 93, County Hall, Northampton NN1 1DN ☎ 01604 236465 ✉ pwhite@northamptonshire.gov.uk

Public Libraries: Ms Sue Grace, Head of Customer & Cultural Services, PO Box 93, County Hall, Northampton NN1 1AN ☎ 01604 237960 🖷 01604 237600 ✉ sgrace@northamptonshire.gov.uk

Recycling & Waste Minimisation: Mr Wade Siddiqui, Head of Waste Management (Interim), County Hall, Northampton NN1 1AN ☎ 01604 237147 🖷 01604 237331 ✉ wsiddiqui@northamptonshire.gov.uk

Regeneration: Mr Tony Ciaburro, Corporate Director of Environment, Growth & Commissioning, PO Box 93, County Hall, Northampton NN1 1AN ☎ 01604 236740 🖷 01604 236652 ✉ tciaburro@northamptonshire.gov.uk

Road Safety: Mr John Spencer, Casualty Reduction Manager, Riverside Way, Bedford Road, Northampton NN1 5NX ☎ 01604 654430 🖷 01604 654455 ✉ jspencer@northamptonshire.gov.uk

Social Services: Mr Charlie MacNally, Corporate Director of Health & Adult Social Services, PO Box 93, County Hall, Northampton NN1 1AN ☎ 01604 236024 🖷 01604 237160 ✉ cmacnally@northamptonshire.gov.uk

Social Services (Adult): Mrs Fiona Seymour, Head of Strategic Planning & Commissioning, County Hall, Northampton NN1 1AN ☎ 01604 236770 🖷 01604 237160 ✉ fseymour@northamptonshire.gov.uk

Social Services (Children): Mr Paul Burnett, Corporate Director of Children & Young People's Services, PO Box 93, County Hall, Northampton NN1 1AN ☎ 01604 236252 🖷 01604 236550 ✉ pburnett@northamptonshire.gov.uk

Staff Training: Ms Barbara Barrett, Learning & Organisational Development Manager, John Dryden House, Northampton NN4 7YD ☎ 01604 236630 🖷 01604 237377 ✉ bbarrett@northamptonshire.gov.uk

Sustainable Communities: Mr Tony Ciaburro, Corporate Director of Environment, Growth & Commissioning, PO Box 93, County Hall, Northampton NN1 1AN ☎ 01604 236740 🖷 01604 236652 ✉ tciaburro@northamptonshire.gov.uk

Sustainable Development: Mr Tony Ciaburro, Corporate Director of Environment, Growth & Commissioning, PO Box 93, County Hall, Northampton NN1 1AN ☎ 01604 236740 🖷 01604 236652 ✉ tciaburro@northamptonshire.gov.uk

Tourism: Ms Sue Grace, Head of Customer & Cultural Services, PO Box 93, County Hall, Northampton NN1 1AN ☎ 01604 237960 🖷 01604 237600 ✉ sgrace@northamptonshire.gov.uk

Traffic Management: Mr David Farquhar, Head of Transport & Highways, Riverside House, Riverside Way, Bedford Road, Northampton NN1 5NX ☎ 01604 654401 🖷 01604 654455 ✉ dfarquhar@northamptonshire.gov.uk

Transport: Mr David Farquhar, Head of Transport & Highways, Riverside House, Riverside Way, Bedford Road, Northampton NN1 5NX ☎ 01604 654401 🖷 01604 654455 ✉ dfarquhar@northamptonshire.gov.uk

Transport Planner: Mr David Farquhar, Head of Transport & Highways, Riverside House, Riverside Way, Bedford Road, Northampton NN1 5NX ☎ 01604 654401 🖷 01604 654455 ✉ dfarquhar@northamptonshire.gov.uk

Waste Collection and Disposal: Mr Wade Siddiqui, Head of Waste Management (Interim), County Hall, Northampton NN1 1AN ☎ 01604 237147 🖷 01604 237331 ✉ wsiddiqui@northamptonshire.gov.uk

Waste Management: Mr Wade Siddiqui, Head of Waste Management (Interim), County Hall, Northampton NN1 1AN ☎ 01604 237147 🖷 01604 237331 ✉ wsiddiqui@northamptonshire.gov.uk

MEMBERS OF THE COUNCIL (73)

***Leader of the Council:* Harker**, Jim (CON - Kettering Rural)
jharker@northamptonshire.gov.uk
Bailey, John (CON - Finedon)
jobailey@northamptonshire.gov.uk
Beardsworth, Sally (LD - Kingsthorpe)
sbeardsworth@northamptonshire.gov.uk
Bell, Paul (CON - Swanspool)
pbell@northamptonshire.gov.uk
Blackwell, George (LAB - Earls Barton)
gblackwell@northamptonshire.gov.uk
Boardman, Catherine (CON - Uplands)
cboardman@northamptonshire.gov.uk
Brookfield, Julie (LAB - Shire Lodge)
jbrookfield@northamptonshire.gov.uk
Brown, Robin (CON - Braunston)
rwbrown@northamptonshire.gov.uk
Bullock, Mark (LAB - Corby Central)
mbullock@northamptonshire.gov.uk
Church, Richard (LD - Kingsley)
rchurch@northamptonshire.gov.uk
Civil, Robert (CON - Ise)
rcivil@northamptonshire.gov.uk
Clarke, Michael (CON - Hackleton)
mclarke@northamptonshire.gov.uk
Clarke, Tony (IND - Castle)
tclarke@northamptonshire.gov.uk
Conroy, Jenny (LD - Spencer)
jeconroy@northamptonshire.gov.uk
Dean, David (CON - Queensway)
dean982@btinternet.com
Edwards, Donald (CON - Old Duston)
dedwards@northamptonshire.gov.uk
Edwards, Scott (CON - Wicksteed)
saedwards@northamptonshire.gov.uk
Giddings, Richard (LD - Lumbertubs)

rgiddings@northamptonshire.gov.uk
Glynane, Brendan (LD - Delapre)
bglynane@northamptonshire.gov.uk
Golby, Matthew (CON - New Duston)
mgolby@northamptonshire.gov.uk
Gonzalez De Savage, Andre (CON - East Hunsbury)
agdesavage@northamptonshire.gov.uk
Grant, Andrew (CON - Brackley East)
agrant@northamptonshire.gov.uk
Groome, Christopher (IND - Burton)
cgroome@northamptonshire.gov.uk
Hallam, Mike (CON - Parklands)
Harding, Rebecca (CON - Abington)
rharding@northamptonshire.gov.uk
Heggs, Stanley (CON - Corby Rural)
sheggs@northamptonshire.gov.uk
Henson, Larry (CON - Kettering Central)
lhenson@northamptonshire.gov.uk
Hills, Alan (CON - Daventry East)
ahills@northamptonshire.gov.uk
Hollis, Jane (LD - St David)
jshollis@northamptonshire.gov.uk
Homer, Sue (CON - Irchester)
shomer@northamptonshire.gov.uk
Hughes, Dudley (CON - Raunds)
dhuges@northamptonshire.gov.uk
Hugheston-Roberts, David (CON - West Hunsbury)
dhugheston-roberts@northamptonshire.gov.uk
Humfrey, Belinda (CON - Desborough)
bhumfrey@northamptonshire.gov.uk
Ingram, Bernard (CON - Roade)
bingram@northamptonshire.gov.uk
Kirkbride, Joan (CON - Bugbrooke)
jkirkbridge@northamptonshire.gov.uk
Langley, Andrew (CON - Irthlingborough)
alangley@northamptonshire.gov.uk
Larratt, Phil (CON - Nene Valley)
cllr.plarratt@northampton.gov.uk
Lawman, Graham (CON - Boughton Green)
gmlawman@northamptonshire.gov.uk
Lawson, Derek (CON - Higham Ferrers)
dlawson@northamptonshire.gov.uk
Legg, Stephen (CON - Weston)
slegg@northamptonshire.gov.uk
Lofts, Chris (LD - Towcester)
Long, Chris (CON - Daventry West)
clong@northamptonshire.gov.uk
Lynch, Matt (CON - St Andrew's and St Peter's)
matt.lynch@talk21.com
Mackintosh, David (CON - Ecton Brook)
dmackintosh@northamptonshire.gov.uk
Malpas, Christopher (CON - Billing)
cmalpas@northamptonshire.gov.uk
Maxted, Carolyn (CON - Grange)
cmaxted@northamptonshire.gov.uk
McGhee, John (LAB - Kingswood)
jmcghee@northamptonshire.gov.uk
Melling, Ken (CON - Middleton Cheney)
kmelling@northamptonshire.gov.uk
Mercer, Andy (CON - Rushden East)
amercer@northamptonshire.gov.uk
Meredith, Dennis (LD - Thorplands)
dmeredith@northamptonshire.gov.uk
Millar, Chris (CON - Brixworth)
cmillar@northamptonshire.gov.uk
Minney, Marion (LD - Headlands)
mminney@northamptonshire.gov.uk
Ogden, Gina (CON - Weedon Bec & Woodford)
gogden@northamptonshire.gov.uk
Osborne, Steve (CON - Long Buckby)
sjosborne@northamptonshire.gov.uk
Parker, Bill (CON - Brambleside)
bparker@northamptonshire.gov.uk
Patel, Bhupendra (CON - Hemmingwell)
bpatel@northamptonshire.gov.uk
Patel, Suresh (CON - St James)
supatel@northamptonshire.gov.uk
Pinnock, Ron (CON - Rushden West)
rpinnock@northamptonshire.gov.uk
Pote, Alan (CON - Rothwell)
apote@northamptonshire.gov.uk
Reichhold, Rupert (CON - Oundle)
rreichold@northamptonshire.gov.uk
Sawbridge, Ron (CON - Brackley West)
rsawbridge@northamptonshire.gov.uk
Scott, Bob (LAB - Lloyds)
bob.scott@unitetheunion.com
Seery, Bob (CON - Thrapston)
bseery@northamptonshire.gov.uk
Shephard, Judy (CON - Moulton)
jshepherd@northamptonshire.gov.uk
Smith, Ben (CON - Greens Norton)
benz@btinternet.com
Smith, Heather (CON - Prebendal)
hsmith@northamptonshire.gov.uk
Stanbra, Chris (LD - Danesholme)
stanbra@btinternet.com
Strachan, Winston (LAB - St Crispin)
wstrachan@northamptonshire.gov.uk
Tye, Michael (CON - Rushden South)
mtye@northamptonshire.gov.uk
Walia, Jay (CON - Croyland)
jwalia@northamptonshire.gov.uk
Walker, Allen (CON - Deanshanger)
awalker@northamptonshire.gov.uk
Waters, Malcolm (CON - Redwell)
mwaters@northamptonshire.gov.uk
Wright, Alan (CON - Eastfield)
alanwright14@ntlworld.com

POLITICAL COMPOSITION

CON: 55, LD: 10, LAB: 6, IND: 2

CABINET

Leader: Mr Jim Harker
Children & Young People: Mrs Joan Kirkbride
Commercial & Asset Management: Mr Andrew Langley
Health & Adult Social Services: Mr Robin Brown
Highways, Minerals & Waste: Mr Heather Smith
Regeneration & Growth: Mr Ben Smith
Revenue Finance: Mr Bill Parker

COMMITTEE CHAIRS

Customers & Communities (Scrutiny): Mr Phil Larratt
Customers, Communities & Education: Mr Bernard Ingram
Development Control: Mr Michael Clarke
Environment, Development & Transport: Ms Marion Minney
Finance & Performance Scrutiny: Mr Chris Long
Health & Adult Social Services: Mrs Gina Ogden

Health & Social Care: Mrs Judy Shephard
Healthier Communities (Scrutiny): Mr Robin Brown

NORTHUMBERLAND U

Northumberland Council, County Hall, Morpeth NE61 2EF
☎ 0845 600 6400 🖷 01670 534117 ✉ ask@northumberland.gov.uk
💻 www.northumberland.gov.uk

FACTS & FIGURES

Learning and Skills Council: North East
Parliamentary Constituencies: Berwick-upon-Tweed, Blyth Valley, Hexham, Wansbeck
EU Constituencies: North East
Election Frequency: Elections are of whole council

PRINCIPAL OFFICERS

Chief Executive: Mr Steve Stewart, Chief Executive, County Hall, Morpeth NE61 2EF ☎ 0845 600 6400 🖷 01670 511413 ✉ steve.stewart@northumberland.gov.uk

Deputy Chief Executive: Ms Kate Roe, Deputy Chief Executive, County Hall, Morpeth NE61 2EF ☎ 0845 600 6400 🖷 01670 511413

Senior Management: Mrs Caroline Bruce, Corporate Director of Local Services, County Hall, Morpeth NE61 2EF ☎ 0845 600 6400 🖷 01670 511413 ✉ caroline.bruce@northumberland.gov.uk

Senior Management: Mrs Daljit Lally, Corporate Director of Adult Services & Housing, County Hall, Morpeth NE61 2EF ☎ 0845 600 6400 🖷 01670 511413 ✉ daljit.lally@northumberland.gov.uk

Senior Management: Mr Steve Mason, Corporate Director of Finance, County Hall, Morpeth NE61 2EF ☎ 01670 533000 🖷 01670 511413 ✉ steven.mason@northumberland.gov.uk

Senior Management: Ms Sue Milner, Director of Public Health & Protection, County Hall, Morpeth NE61 2EF ☎ 0845 600 6400 🖷 01670 511413 ✉ smilner@northumberland.gov.uk

Senior Management: Mr Paul Moffat, Corporate Director of Children's Services, County Hall, Morpeth NE61 2EF ☎ 0845 600 6400 🖷 01670 511413 ✉ paul.moffat@northumberland.gov.uk

Architect, Building / Property Services: Mr Frank Jordan, Head of Commercial & Property Services, County Hall, Morpeth NE61 2EF ☎ 0845 600 6400 🖷 01670 511413 ✉ frank.jordan@northumberland.gov.uk

Building Control: Mrs Vickie Barrington, Head of Public Protection, County Hall, Morpeth NE61 2EF ☎ 0845 600 6400 🖷 01670 511413 ✉ victoria.barrington@northumberland.gov.uk

Catering Services: Mr Frank Jordan, Head of Commercial & Property Services, County Hall, Morpeth NE61 2EF ☎ 0845 600 6400 🖷 01670 511413 ✉ frank.jordan@northumberland.gov.uk

Children / Youth Services: Mr Tony Mays, Head of Early Years & Schools, County Hall, Morpeth NE61 2EF ☎ 0845 600 6400 🖷 01670 511413 ✉ tony.mays@northumberland.gov.uk

Children / Youth Services: Mrs Elaine O'Connor, Head of Employability & Skills, County Hall, Morpeth NE61 2EF ☎ 0845 600 6400 🖷 01670 511413 ✉ elaine.o'connor@northumberland.gov.uk

Civil Registration: Mrs Lorraine Dewison, Services Manager - Customer Services, Libraries, Registrars and Coroners, County Hall, Morpeth NE61 2EF ☎ 0845 600 6400 🖷 01670 511413 ✉ lorraine.dewison@northumberland.gov.uk

PR / Communications: Mr Ross Wigham, Head of Communications, County Hall, Morpeth NE61 2EF ☎ 0845 600 6400 🖷 01670 511413 ✉ ross.wigham@northumberland.gov.uk

Community Safety: Mr Alex Bennett, Chief Fire Officer, Fire & Rescue Service Headquarters, West Hartford Business Park, Cramlington NE23 3JP ☎ 01670 591110 ✉ alex.bennett@northumberland.gov.uk

Computer Management: Mr Steve Somerfield, Head of Information Services, County Hall, Morpeth NE61 2EF ☎ 0845 600 6400 🖷 01670 511413 ✉ steve.somerfield@northumberland.gov.uk

Consumer Protection and Trading Standards: Mrs Vickie Barrington, Head of Public Protection, County Hall, Morpeth NE61 2EF ☎ 0845 600 6400 🖷 01670 511413 ✉ victoria.barrington@northumberland.gov.uk

Contracts: Mr Frank Jordan, Head of Commercial & Property Services, County Hall, Morpeth NE61 2EF ☎ 0845 600 6400 🖷 01670 511413 ✉ frank.jordan@northumberland.gov.uk

Customer Service: Mrs Stacey Burlet, Head of Customer & Cultural Services, County Hall, Morpeth NE61 2EF ☎ 0845 600 6400 🖷 01670 511413 ✉ stacey.burlet@northumberland.gov.uk

Direct Labour: Mr Andy Rutherford, Head of Highways & Neighbourhood Services, County Hall, Morpeth NE61 2EF ☎ 0845 600 6400 🖷 01670 511413 ✉ andy.rutherford@northumberland.gov.uk

Economic Development: Ms Annie Faulder, Interim Director of Regeneration & Economic Development, County Hall, Morpeth NE61 2EF ☎ 0845 600 6400 🖷 01670 511413 ✉ annie.faulder@northumberland.gov.uk

Education: Mr Robin Casson, Director of Schools, Enterprise & Lifelong Learning, County Hall, Morpeth NE61 2EF ☎ 0845 600 6400 🖷 01670 511413 ✉ robin.casson@northumberland.gov.uk

Education: Mr John Clark, Head of Planning & Organisation, County Hall, Morpeth NE61 2EF ☎ 0845 600 6400 🖷 01670 511413 ✉ john.clark@northumberland.gov.uk

Education: Mr Paul Moffat, Corporate Director of Children's Services, County Hall, Morpeth NE61 2EF ☎ 0845 600 6400 🖷 01670 511413 ✉ paul.moffat@northumberland.gov.uk

E-Government: Mr Steve Somerfield, Head of Information Services, County Hall, Morpeth NE61 2EF ☎ 0845 600 6400 🖷 01670 511413 ✉ steve.somerfield@northumberland.gov.uk

Electoral Registration: Mr Paddy Gascoigne, Service Manager - Democratic Services, County Hall, Morpeth NE61 2EF ☎ 0845 600 6400 🖷 01670 511413 ✉ paddy.gascoigne@northumberland.gov.uk

Emergency Planning: Mr Alex Bennett, Chief Fire Officer, Fire & Rescue Service Headquarters, West Hartford Business Park, Cramlington NE23 3JP ☎ 01670 591110 ✉ alex.bennett@northumberland.gov.uk

Energy Management: Mr Peter McArdle, Energy Officer, County Hall, Morpeth NE61 2EF ☎ 0845 600 6400 🖷 01670 511413 ✉ peter.mcardle@northumberland.gov.uk

Environmental / Technical Services: Mrs Vickie Barrington, Head of Public Protection, County Hall, Morpeth NE61 2EF ☎ 0845 600 6400 🖷 01670 511413 ✉ victoria.barrington@northumberland.gov.uk

Environmental Health: Mrs Vickie Barrington, Head of Public Protection, County Hall, Morpeth NE61 2EF ☎ 0845 600 6400 🖷 01670 511413 ✉ victoria.barrington@northumberland.gov.uk

Estates, Property & Valuation: Mr Frank Jordan, Head of Commercial & Property Services, County Hall, Morpeth NE61 2EF ☎ 0845 600 6400 🖷 01670 511413 ✉ frank.jordan@northumberland.gov.uk

Facilities: Mr Frank Jordan, Head of Commercial & Property Services, County Hall, Morpeth NE61 2EF ☎ 0845 600 6400 🖷 01670 511413 ✉ frank.jordan@northumberland.gov.uk

Finance and Treasurer: Mr Steve Mason, Corporate Director of Finance, County Hall, Morpeth NE61 2EF ☎ 0845 600 6400 🖷 01670 511413 ✉ steven.mason@northumberland.gov.uk

Fleet Management: Mr Frank Jordan, Head of Commercial & Property Services, County Hall, Morpeth NE61 2EF ☎ 0845 600 6400 🖷 01670 511413 ✉ frank.jordan@northumberland.gov.uk

Grounds Maintenance: Mr Andy Rutherford, Head of Highways & Neighbourhood Services, County Hall, Morpeth NE61 2EF ☎ 0845 600 6400 🖷 01670 511413 ✉ andy.rutherford@northumberland.gov.uk

Health and Safety: Mrs Vickie Barrington, Head of Public Protection, County Hall, Morpeth NE61 2EF ☎ 0845 600 6400 🖷 01670 511413 ✉ victoria.barrington@northumberland.gov.uk

Highways: Mr Andy Rutherford, Head of Highways & Neighbourhood Services, County Hall, Morpeth NE61 2EF ☎ 0845 600 6400 🖷 01670 511413 ✉ andy.rutherford@northumberland.gov.uk

Housing: Mr Kevin Lowry, Head of Housing Services, County Hall, Morpeth NE61 2EF ☎ 0845 600 6400 🖷 01670 511413 ✉ kevin.lowry@northumberland.gov.uk

Housing Maintenance: Mr Kevin Lowry, Head of Housing Services, County Hall, Morpeth NE61 2EF ☎ 0845 600 6400 🖷 01670 511413 ✉ kevin.lowry@northumberland.gov.uk

Legal: Mr Andy Thom, Chief Legal Officer, County Hall, Morpeth NE61 2EF ☎ 0845 600 6400 🖷 01670 533238 ✉ andy.thom@northumberland.gcsx.gov.uk

Leisure and Cultural Services: Mrs Lynn Turner, Service Manager - Culture, Leisure & Tourism, County Hall, Morpeth NE61 2EF ☎ 0845 600 6400 🖷 01670 511413 ✉ lynn.turner@northumberland.gov.uk

Licensing: Mr Phil Soderquest, Public Safety Unit Manager, County Hall, Morpeth NE61 2EF ☎ 0845 600 6400 🖷 01670 511413 ✉ phil.soderquest@northumberland.gov.uk

Lifelong Learning: Mr Robin Casson, Director of Schools, Enterprise & Lifelong Learning, County Hall, Morpeth NE61 2EF ☎ 0845 600 6400 🖷 01670 511413 ✉ robin.casson@northumberland.gov.uk

Lifelong Learning: Ms Heather Thomas, Senior Adult Learning Manager, County Hall, Morpeth NE61 2EF ☎ 0845 600 6400 🖷 01670 511413 ✉ heather.thomas@northumberland.gov.uk

Lighting: Mr Andy Rutherford, Head of Highways & Neighbourhood Services, County Hall, Morpeth NE61 2EF ☎ 0845 600 6400 🖷 01670 511413 ✉ andy.rutherford@northumberland.gov.uk

Member Services: Mr Paddy Gascoigne, Service Manager - Democratic Services, County Hall, Morpeth NE61 2EF ☎ 0845 600 6400 🖷 01670 511413 ✉ paddy.gascoigne@northumberland.gov.uk

Parking: Mr Mike Scott, Head of Sustainable Transport, County Hall, Morpeth NE61 2EF ☎ 0845 600 6400 🖷 01670 511413 ✉ mike.scott@northumberland.gov.uk

Personnel / HR: Ms Janice Barclay, Lead Business Partner - Human Resources, County Hall, Morpeth NE61 2EF ☎ 0845 600 6400 🖷 01670 511413 ✉ janice.barclay@northumberland.gov.uk

Planning: Mrs Karen Ledger, Head of Development Services, County Hall, Morpeth NE61 2EF ☎ 0845 600 6400 🖷 01670 511413 ✉ karen.ledger@northumberland.gov.uk

Procurement: Mr Frank Jordan, Head of Commercial & Property Services, County Hall, Morpeth NE61 2EF ☎ 0845 600 6400 🖷 01670 511413 ✉ frank.jordan@northumberland.gov.uk

Public Libraries: Mrs Stacey Burlet, Head of Customer & Cultural Services, County Hall, Morpeth NE61 2EF ☎ 0845 600 6400 🖷 01670 511413 ✉ stacey.burlet@northumberland.gov.uk

Recycling & Waste Minimisation: Mr Paul Jones, Head of Waste Management, County Hall, Morpeth NE61 2EF ☎ 0845 600 6400 🖷 01670 511413 ✉ paul.jones01@northumberland.gov.uk

Regeneration: Ms Annie Faulder, Interim Director of Regeneration & Economic Development, County Hall, Morpeth NE61 2EF ☎ 0845 600 6400 🖷 01670 511413 ✉ annie.faulder@northumberland.gov.uk

Road Safety: Mr Mike Scott, Head of Sustainable Transport,

County Hall, Morpeth NE61 2EF ☎ 0845 600 6400 🖷 01670 511413 ✉ mike.scott@northumberland.gov.uk

Social Services (Adult): Mrs Daljit Lally, Corporate Director of Adult Services & Housing, County Hall, Morpeth NE61 2EF ☎ 0845 600 6400 🖷 01670 511413 ✉ daljit.lally@northumberland.gov.uk

Social Services (Children): Mr Mark Douglas, Head of Safeguarding & Looked After Children, County Hall, Morpeth NE61 2EF ☎ 0845 600 6400 🖷 01670 511413 ✉ mark.douglas@northumberland.gov.uk

Staff Training: Mr Paul Brooks, Learning & OD Manager, County Hall, Morpeth NE61 2EF ☎ 0845 600 6400 🖷 01670 511413 ✉ paul.brooks@northumberland.gov.uk

Street Scene: Mr Andy Rutherford, Head of Highways & Neighbourhood Services, County Hall, Morpeth NE61 2EF ☎ 0845 600 6400 🖷 01670 511413 ✉ andy.rutherford@northumberland.gov.uk

Sustainable Development: Mrs Karen Ledger, Head of Development Services, County Hall, Morpeth NE61 2EF ☎ 0845 600 6400 🖷 01670 511413 ✉ karen.ledger@northumberland.gov.uk

Tourism: Mrs Lynn Turner, Service Manager - Culture, Leisure & Tourism, County Hall, Morpeth NE61 2EF ☎ 0845 600 6400 🖷 01670 511413 ✉ lynn.turner@northumberland.gov.uk

Traffic Management: Mr Mike Scott, Head of Sustainable Transport, County Hall, Morpeth NE61 2EF ☎ 0845 600 6400 🖷 01670 511413 ✉ mike.scott@northumberland.gov.uk

Transport: Mr Mike Scott, Head of Sustainable Transport, County Hall, Morpeth NE61 2EF ☎ 0845 600 6400 🖷 01670 511413 ✉ mike.scott@northumberland.gov.uk

Transport Planner: Mr Mike Scott, Head of Sustainable Transport, County Hall, Morpeth NE61 2EF ☎ 0845 600 6400 🖷 01670 511413 ✉ mike.scott@northumberland.gov.uk

Waste Collection and Disposal: Mr Paul Jones, Head of Waste Management, County Hall, Morpeth NE61 2EF ☎ 0845 600 6400 🖷 01670 511413 ✉ paul.jones01@northumberland.gov.uk

Waste Management: Mr Paul Jones, Head of Waste Management, County Hall, Morpeth NE61 2EF ☎ 0845 600 6400 🖷 01670 511413 ✉ paul.jones01@northumberland.gov.uk

Children's Play Areas: Mr Andy Rutherford, Head of Highways & Neighbourhood Services, County Hall, Morpeth NE61 2EF ☎ 0845 600 6400 🖷 01670 511413 ✉ andy.rutherford@northumberland.gov.uk

MEMBERS OF THE COUNCIL (66)

***Chair:* Smith**, James (LD - Berwick East)
James.Smith@northumberland.gov.uk
***Leader of the Council:* Reid**, Jeff (LD - Plessey)
Jeff.Reid@northumberland.gov.uk
Arckless, George (LAB - Amble)
Robert.Arckless99@northumberland.gov.uk
Armstrong, Alan (LD - Cramlington Village)
Alan.Armstrong@northumberland.gov.uk
Armstrong, Eileen (CON - Ponteland East)
Eileen.Armstrong@northumberland.gov.uk
Bircham, Marcia (LD - Haydon)
marcia.bircham@northumberland.gov.uk
Bradbury, Neil (LD - Prudhoe West)
Neil.Bradbury@northumberland.gov.uk
Brechany, Thomas (LD - Cramlington South East)
Thomas.Brechany@northumberland.gov.uk
Bridgett, Steven (LD - Rothbury)
Steven.Bridgett@northumberland.gov.uk
Brook, Ingrid (CON - Hexham East)
ingrid.brook@northumberland.gov.uk
Brown, Maureen (LAB - Cramlington West)
Maureen.Brown@northumberland.gov.uk
Campbell, Deirdre (LAB - Newsham)
Castle, Gordon (IND - Alnwick)
Gordon.Castle@northumberland.gov.uk
Coils, Vince (INDNA - Croft)
Vince.Coils@northumberland.gov.uk
Crowther, Barrie (LD - Cramlington Eastfield)
Barrie.Crowther@northumberland.gov.uk
Dale, Anne (CON - Stocksfield and Broomhaugh)
Anne.Dale@northumberland.gov.uk
Daley, Wayne (CON - Cramlington North)
Wayne.Daley@northumberland.gov.uk
Davey, Susan (LAB - Cowpen)
Susan.Davey@northumberland.gov.uk
Davey, Grant (LAB - Kitty Brewster)
jgrant.davey@googlemail.com
Dodd, Richard (CON - Ponteland North)
Richard.Dodd@northumberland.gov.uk
Douglas, Milburn (IND - Lynemouth)
Milburn.Douglas@northumberland.gov.uk
Douglas, Brian (IND - Berwick North)
Brian.Douglas@northumberland.gov.uk
Fearon, Jean (CON - Corbridge)
Jean.Fearon@northumberland.gov.uk
Foster, Julie (LAB - Stakeford)
julie.rowe@northumberland.gov.uk
Garrett, William (IND - Prudhoe East)
William.Garrett@northumberland.gov.uk
Gobin, Jeff (LAB - Sleekburn)
Heslop, Edward (CON - Humshaugh)
Edward.Heslop@northumberland.gov.uk
Horncastle, Colin (CON - South Tynedale)
Colin.Horncastle@northumberland.gov.uk
Hunter, Elizabeth (LD - Berwick West with Ord)
Isabel.Hunter@northumberland.gov.uk
Hutchinson, Ian (CON - Haltwhistle)
Ian.Hutchinson@northumberland.gov.uk
Jackson, Peter (CON - Ponteland South with Heddon)
Peter.Jackson@northumberland.gov.uk
Jones, Veronica (CON - Ponteland West)
Veronica.Jones@northumberland.gov.uk
Kelly, Paul (IND - Bywell)
Paul.Kelly@northumberland.gov.uk
Kennedy, Derek (LD - Hexham West)
Derek.Kennedy@northumberland.gov.uk
Lang, Jim (LAB - Seaton and Newbiggin West)
jim.lang@northumberland.gov.uk
Ledger, David (LAB - Choppington)

david.ledger@northumberland.gov.uk
Lindley, Ian (LD - Morpeth Stobhill)
Ian.Lindley@northumberland.gov.uk
Moore, David (LD - Morpeth North)
David.Moore@northumberland.gov.uk
Murray, Anthony (CON - Wooler)
Anthony.Murray99@northumberland.gov.uk
Nixon, Bobby (LD - Holywell)
Bobby.Nixon@northumberland.gov.uk
Parry, Ken (LAB - Hirst)
ken.parry@northumberland.gov.uk
Pegg, Arthur (LD - Bedlington Central)
arthur.pegg@northumberland.gov.uk
Reed, Simon (LD - Bothal)
simon.reed@northumberland.gov.uk
Richards, Margaret (LAB - Seghill with Seaton Delaval)
Margaret.Richards01@northumberland.gov.uk
Rickerby, Lesley (LD - South Blyth)
Lesley.Rickerby@northumberland.gov.uk
Riddle, John (CON - Bellingham)
John.Riddle@northumberland.gov.uk
Robson, Terry (CON - Hexham Central with Acomb)
Terry.Robson@northumberland.gov.uk
Romer, Anita (LD - Hartley)
Anita.Romer@northumberland.gov.uk
Sanderson, Glen (CON - Chevington with Longhorsley)
Glen.Sanderson@northumberland.gov.uk
Sawyer, Jimmy (LAB - College)
jimmy.sawyer@northumberland.gov.uk
Scott, Patricia (LD - Bamburgh)
Patricia.Scott@northumberland.gov.uk
Sharp, Alan (LD - Haydon and Hadrian)
Alan.Sharp@northumberland.gov.uk
Sinclair, Thomas (LAB - Ashington Central)
thomas.wilson@northumberland.gov.uk
Styring, Roger (LD - Lesbury)
Roger.Styring@northumberland.gov.uk
Swithenbank, Ian (LAB - Cramlington East)
Ian.Swithenbank@northumberland.gov.uk
Taylor, John (IND - Longhoughton)
John.Taylor@northumberland.gov.uk
Tebbutt, Andrew (LD - Morpeth Kirkhill)
Andrew.Tebbutt@northumberland.gov.uk
Thorne, Trevor (CON - Shilbottle)
embletonhall@btinternet.com
Todd, George (LD - Bedlington West)
george.todd@northumberland.gov.uk
Tompkins, Ian (LD - Wensleydale)
Ian.Tompkins@northumberland.gov.uk
Towns, David (CON - Ulgham)
David.Towns@northumberland.gov.uk
Tyler, Valerie (LAB - Bedlington East)
valerie.tyler@northumberland.gov.uk
Watkin, Richard (LD - Norham and Islandshires)
DouWatkin@aol.com
Watson, Jeffrey (IND - Amble West and Warkworth)
Jeffrey.Watson@northumberland.gov.uk
Webb, Gordon (LAB - Isabella)
Gordon.Webb@northumberland.gov.uk
Woodard, David (LD - Pegswood)
David.Woodard@northumberland.gov.uk

POLITICAL COMPOSITION

LD: 25, CON: 17, LAB: 16, IND: 7, INDNA: 1

CABINET

Leader: Mr Jeff Reid
Deputy Leader: Mr Roger Styring
Adult Care & Well Being: Mr Ian Lindley
Children & Young People: Mrs Lesley Rickerby
Corporate Resources: Mr Andrew Tebbutt
Customer Relations & Culture: Mr Neil Bradbury
Health & Public Protection: Dr Anita Romer
Infrastructure & Environment: Ms Elizabeth Hunter
Neighbourhood Services, Highways & Transportation: Mr Alan Thompson
Planning, Housing & Regeneration: Mr Thomas Brechany

COMMITTEE CHAIRS

Audit: Mr Terry Robson
Care & Well-Being (Scrutiny): Ms Margaret Richards
Climate Change & Environmental Sustainability: Mr Roger Styring
Communities & Place (Scrutiny): Mr Glen Sanderson
Economic Prosperity & Strategic Services (Scrutiny): Mr Gordon Castle
Family & Children's Services (Scrutiny): Mr Richard Dodd
Housing & Care: Mr Gordon Webb
Licensing & Regulatory: Mr Jeffrey Watson
Local Development: Mr Richard Watkin
Pension Fund: Mr Derek Kennedy
Planning & Environment: Mr Trevor Thorne

NORWICH CITY D

Norwich City Council, City Hall, St. Peter's Street, Norwich NR2 1NH ☎ 0344 980 3333 ✉ info@norwich.gov.uk
🖳 www.norwich.gov.uk

FACTS & FIGURES

Police Authority: Norfolk Police Authority
Health Authority: East of England Strategic Health Authority
Learning and Skills Council: Eastern
Parliamentary Constituencies: Norwich North, Norwich South
EU Constituencies: Eastern
Election Frequency: Elections are by thirds
Twinning: Rouen (France); Koblenz Stadt (Germany); Novi Sad (Serbia); El Viejo (Nicaragua)

PRINCIPAL OFFICERS

Chief Executive: Ms Laura McGillivray, Chief Executive, City Hall, St. Peter's Street, Norwich NR2 1NH ☎ 01603 212000 🖷 01603 213001 ✉ lauramcgillivray@norwich.gov.uk

Deputy Chief Executive: Ms Bridget Buttinger, Deputy Chief Executive - Strategic Director of Corporate Resources, City Hall, St. Peter's Street, Norwich NR2 1NH ☎ 01603 212066 🖷 01603 213001 ✉ bridgetbuttinger@norwich.gov.uk

Assistant Chief Executive: Ms Bridget Buttinger, Deputy Chief Executive - Strategic Director of Corporate Resources, City Hall, St. Peter's Street, Norwich NR2 1NH ☎ 01603 212066 🖷 01603 213001 ✉ bridgetbuttinger@norwich.gov.uk

Senior Management: Ms Anne Bonsor, Assistant Director - City Development, Norwich City Council, St. Peter's Street, Norwich

NR2 1NH ☎ 01603 212353. ✉ annebonser@norwich.gov.uk

Senior Management: Ms Angela Hadley, Assistant Director - Community & Neighbourhoods, City Hall, St. Peter's Street, Norwich NR2 1NH ☎ 01603 212160 ✉ angelahadley@norwich.gov.uk

Senior Management: Mr Jerry Massey, Deputy Chief Executive - Operations, City Hall, St. Peter's Street, Norwich NR2 1NH ☎ 01603 212225 ✉ jerrymassey@norwich.gov.uk

Senior Management: Ms Nikki Rotsos, Head of Communications & Cultural Services, City Hall, St. Peter's Street, Norwich NR2 1NH ☎ 01603 212211 🖷 01603 212010 ✉ nikkirotsos@norwich.gov.uk

Access Officer / Social Services (Disability): Ms Bridget Buttinger, Deputy Chief Executive - Strategic Director of Corporate Resources, City Hall, St. Peter's Street, Norwich NR2 1NH ☎ 01603 212066 🖷 01603 213001 ✉ bridgetbuttinger@norwich.gov.uk

Architect, Building / Property Services: Mr Jerry Massey, Deputy Chief Executive - Operations, City Hall, St. Peter's Street, Norwich NR2 1NH ☎ 01603 212225 ✉ jerrymassey@norwich.gov.uk

Best Value: Ms Bridget Buttinger, Deputy Chief Executive - Strategic Director of Corporate Resources, City Hall, St. Peter's Street, Norwich NR2 1NH ☎ 01603 212066 🖷 01603 213001 ✉ bridgetbuttinger@norwich.gov.uk

Best Value: Mr O'Keefe Russell, Head of Strategy & Programme Management, Norwich City Council, City Hall, St Peter's Street, Norwich NR2 1NH ☎ 01603 765348 ✉ jackierodger@norwich.gov.uk

Best Value: Mr Paul Spencer, Director of Transformation, City Hall, St. Peter's Street, Norwich NR2 1NH ☎ 01603 212238 ✉ paulspencer@norwich.gov.uk

Building Control: Mr Jerry Massey, Director of Regeneration & Development, City Hall, St. Peter's Street, Norwich NR2 1NH ☎ 01603 212225 ✉ jerrymassey@norwich.gov.uk

Building Control: Mr Graham Nelson, Head of Planning, City Hall, St. Peter's Street, Norwich NR2 1NH ☎ 01603 212530 ✉ grahamnelson@norwich.gov.uk

Community Planning: Mr Bob Cronk, Head of Community Services, City Hall, St Peter's Street, Norwich NR2 1NH ☎ 01603 212373 🖷 01603 212380 ✉ bobcronk@norwich.gov.uk

Community Planning: Mr Jerry Massey, Director of Regeneration & Development, City Hall, St. Peter's Street, Norwich NR2 1NH ☎ 01603 212225 ✉ jerrymassey@norwich.gov.uk

Community Safety: Mr Bob Cronk, Head of Community Services, City Hall, St Peter's Street, Norwich NR2 1NH ☎ 01603 212373 🖷 01603 212380 ✉ bobcronk@norwich.gov.uk

Community Safety: Mr Barry Marshall, Head of Finance, City Hall, St. Peter's Street, Norwich NR2 1NH ☎ 01603 212556 ✉ barrymarshall@norwich.gov.uk

Community Safety: Mr Jerry Massey, Director of Regeneration & Development, City Hall, St. Peter's Street, Norwich NR2 1NH ☎ 01603 212225 ✉ jerrymassey@norwich.gov.uk

Computer Management: Mr Anthony Bull, Head of Procurement & Service Improvement, City Hall, St. Peter's Street, Norwich NR2 1NH ☎ 01603 212326 ✉ anthonybull@norwich.gov.uk

Contracts: Mr Adrian Akester, Head of Citywide Services, City Hall, St. Peter's Street, Norwich NR2 1NH ☎ 01603 213521 ✉ adrianakester@norwich.gov.uk

Contracts: Mr Anthony Bull, Executive Head of Business Relationship Management, City Hall, St. Peter's Street, Norwich NR2 1NH ☎ 01603 212326 ✉ anthonybull@norwich.gov.uk

Corporate Services: Mr Russell O'Keefe, Executive Head of Strategy, People & Democracy, Norwich City Council, City Hall, St Peter's Street, Norwich NR2 1NH ☎ 01603 212908 ✉ jackierodger@norwich.gov.uk

Customer Service: Ms Tina Bailey, Head of Customer Contact, City Hall, St. Peter's Street, Norwich NR2 1NH ☎ 01603 212759 ✉ tinabailey@norwich.gov.uk

Customer Service: Ms Nikki Rotsos, Head of Customers, Communications & Culture, City Hall, St. Peter's Street, Norwich NR2 1NH ☎ 01603 212211 🖷 01603 212010 ✉ nikkirotsos@norwich.gov.uk

Economic Development: Mr Jerry Massey, Director of Regeneration & Development, City Hall, St. Peter's Street, Norwich NR2 1NH ☎ 01603 212225 ✉ jerrymassey@norwich.gov.uk

E-Government: Ms Jane Rogers, Systems Support Team Leader, City Hall, St. Peter's Street, Norwich NR2 1NH ☎ 0344 980 3333

Electoral Registration: Mr Philip Hyde, Head of Legal Regulatory & Democratic Services, Norwich City Council, City Hall, St Peter's Street, Norwich NR2 1NH ☎ 01603 212440 ✉ philiphyde@norwich.gov.uk

Emergency Planning: Mr Adrian Akester, Head of Citywide Services, City Hall, St. Peter's Street, Norwich NR2 1NH ☎ 01603 213521 ✉ adrianakester@norwich.gov.uk

Emergency Planning: Mr Philip Hyde, Head of Legal Regulatory & Democratic Services, Norwich City Council, City Hall, St Peter's Street, Norwich NR2 1NH ☎ 01603 212440 ✉ philiphyde@norwich.gov.uk

Energy Management: Mr Jerry Massey, Director of Regeneration & Development, City Hall, St. Peter's Street, Norwich NR2 1NH ☎ 01603 212225 ✉ jerrymassey@norwich.gov.uk

Environmental / Technical Services: Mr Adrian Akester, Head of Citywide Services, City Hall, St. Peter's Street, Norwich NR2 1NH ☎ 01603 213521 ✉ adrianakester@norwich.gov.uk

Environmental / Technical Services: Mr Philip Hyde, Head of Legal Regulatory & Democratic Services, Norwich City Council, City Hall, St Peter's Street, Norwich NR2 1NH ☎ 01603 212440 ✉ philiphyde@norwich.gov.uk

Environmental Health: Mr Philip Hyde, Head of Legal Regulatory & Democratic Services, Norwich City Council, City Hall, St Peter's Street, Norwich NR2 1NH ☎ 01603 212440 ✉ philiphyde@norwich.gov.uk

Estates, Property & Valuation: Mr Jerry Massey, Director of Regeneration & Development, City Hall, St. Peter's Street, Norwich NR2 1NH ☎ 01603 212225 ✉ jerrymassey@norwich.gov.uk

Events Manager: Ms Nikki Rotsos, Head of Customers, Communications & Culture, City Hall, St. Peter's Street, Norwich NR2 1NH ☎ 01603 212211 🖷 01603 212010 ✉ nikkirotsos@norwich.gov.uk

Facilities: Mr Eamonn Pellican, Facilities Manager, City Hall, St. Peter's Street, Norwich NR2 1NH ☎ 0344 980 3333 ✉ eamonn.pellican@norwich.gov.uk

Finance and Treasurer: Mr Barry Marshall, Head of Finance, City Hall, St. Peter's Street, Norwich NR2 1NH ☎ 01603 212556 ✉ barrymarshall@norwich.gov.uk

Finance and Treasurer: Ms Caroline Ryba, Chief Finance Officer (Section 151 Officer), City Hall, Norwich NR2 1NH ☎ 01603 212064 ✉ caroline.ryba@cambridgeshire.co.uk

Grounds Maintenance: Mr Adrian Akester, Head of Citywide Services, City Hall, St. Peter's Street, Norwich NR2 1NH ☎ 01603 213521 ✉ adrianakester@norwich.gov.uk

Grounds Maintenance: Mr Jerry Massey, Director of Regeneration & Development, City Hall, St. Peter's Street, Norwich NR2 1NH ☎ 01603 212225 ✉ jerrymassey@norwich.gov.uk

Health and Safety: Mr Adrian Akester, Head of Citywide Services, City Hall, St. Peter's Street, Norwich NR2 1NH ☎ 01603 213521 ✉ adrianakester@norwich.gov.uk

Health and Safety: Mr Philip Hyde, Head of Legal Regulatory & Democratic Services, Norwich City Council, City Hall, St Peter's Street, Norwich NR2 1NH ☎ 01603 212440 ✉ philiphyde@norwich.gov.uk

Highways: Mr Jerry Massey, Director of Regeneration & Development, City Hall, St. Peter's Street, Norwich NR2 1NH ☎ 01603 212225 ✉ jerrymassey@norwich.gov.uk

Housing: Mrs Tracy John, Head of Neigbouhood & Strategic Housing, Norwich City Council, City Hall, St Peter's Street, Norwich NR2 1NH ☎ 01603 212939 ✉ tracyjohn@norwich.gov.uk

Housing: Mr Jerry Massey, Director of Regeneration & Development, City Hall, St. Peter's Street, Norwich NR2 1NH ☎ 01603 212225 ✉ jerrymassey@norwich.gov.uk

Housing: Mr Jerry Massey, Deputy Chief Executive - Operations, City Hall, St. Peter's Street, Norwich NR2 1NH ☎ 01603 212225 ✉ jerrymassey@norwich.gov.uk

Housing: Mr Chris Rayner, Head of Housing Property Services, Norwich City Council, City Hall, St Peter's Street, Norwich NR2 1NH ☎ 01603 213298 ✉ chrisrayner@norwich.gov.uk

Housing: Mr Doug Wilkinson, Assistant Director - Neighbourhoods, Norwich City Council, City Hall, St Peter's Street, Norwich NR2 1NH ☎ 01603 212775 ✉ dougwilkinson@norwich.gov.uk

Housing Maintenance: Ms Angela Hadley, Assistant Director - Community & Neighbourhoods, City Hall, St. Peter's Street, Norwich NR2 1NH ☎ 01603 212160 ✉ angelahadley@norwich.gov.uk

Housing Maintenance: Mr Jerry Massey, Director of Regeneration & Development, City Hall, St. Peter's Street, Norwich NR2 1NH ☎ 01603 212225 ✉ jerrymassey@norwich.gov.uk

Housing Maintenance: Mr Chris Rayner, Head of Housing Property Services, Norwich City Council, City Hall, St Peter's Street, Norwich NR2 1NH ☎ 01603 213298 ✉ chrisrayner@norwich.gov.uk

Housing Maintenance: Mr Doug Wilkinson, Assistant Director of Neighbourhoods, Norwich City Council, City Hall, St Peter's Street, Norwich NR2 1NH ☎ 01603 212775 ✉ dougwilkinson@norwich.gov.uk

Legal: Mr Philip Hyde, Head of Legal Regulatory & Democratic Services, Norwich City Council, City Hall, St Peter's Street, Norwich NR2 1NH ☎ 01603 212440 ✉ philiphyde@norwich.gov.uk

Leisure and Cultural Services: Ms Nikki Rotsos, Head of Communications & Cultural Services, City Hall, St. Peter's Street, Norwich NR2 1NH ☎ 01603 212211 🖷 01603 212010 ✉ nikkirotsos@norwich.gov.uk

Licensing: Mr Adrian Akester, Head of Citywide Services, City Hall, St. Peter's Street, Norwich NR2 1NH ☎ 01603 213521 ✉ adrianakester@norwich.gov.uk

Licensing: Mr Philip Hyde, Head of Legal Regulatory & Democratic Services, Norwich City Council, City Hall, St Peter's Street, Norwich NR2 1NH ☎ 01603 212440 ✉ philiphyde@norwich.gov.uk

Lighting: Mr Eric Dugdale, Urban Highways Engineer, City Hall, St. Peter's Street, Norwich NR2 1NH ☎ 0344 980 3333 ✉ eric.dugdale@norwich.gov.uk

Lottery Funding, Charity and Voluntary: Mr Bob Cronk, Head of Community Services, City Hall, St Peter's Street, Norwich NR2 1NH ☎ 01603 212373 🖷 01603 212380 ✉ bobcronk@norwich.gov.uk

Lottery Funding, Charity and Voluntary: Ms Angela Hadley, Assistant Director of Community & Neighbourhoods, City Hall, St. Peter's Street, Norwich NR2 1NH ☎ 01603 212160 ✉ angelahadley@norwich.gov.uk

Lottery Funding, Charity and Voluntary: Ms Nikki Rotsos, Head of Customers, Communications & Culture, City Hall, St. Peter's Street, Norwich NR2 1NH ☎ 01603 212211 🖷 01603 212010 ✉ nikkirotsos@norwich.gov.uk

Member Services: Mr Philip Hyde, Head of Legal Regulatory & Democratic Services, Norwich City Council, City Hall, St Peter's Street, Norwich NR2 1NH ☎ 01603 212440 ✉ philiphyde@norwich.gov.uk

Parking: Mr Jerry Massey, Director of Regeneration & Development, City Hall, St. Peter's Street, Norwich NR2 1NH ☎ 01603 212225 ✉ jerrymassey@norwich.gov.uk

Parking: Mr Andy Watt, Head of Transportation & Landscape, City Hall, St. Peter's Street, Norwich NR2 1NH ☎ 01603 212396 ✉ andywatt@norwich.gov.uk

Partnerships: Ms Laura McGillivray, Chief Executive, City Hall, St. Peter's Street, Norwich NR2 1NH ☎ 01603 212000 🖷 01603 213001 ✉ lauramcgillivray@norwich.gov.uk

Partnerships: Mr O'Keefe Russell, Head of Strategy & Programme Management, Norwich City Council, City Hall, St Peter's Street, Norwich NR2 1NH ☎ 01603 765348 ✉ jackierodger@norwich.gov.uk

Partnerships: Mr Doug Wilkinson, Assistant Director of Neighbourhoods, Norwich City Council, City Hall, St Peter's Street, Norwich NR2 1NH ☎ 01603 212775 ✉ dougwilkinson@norwich.gov.uk

Personnel / HR: Ms Nadia Harrington, Head of Learning & Organisational Development, City Hall, St. Peter's Street, Norwich NR2 1NH ☎ 01603 212428 ✉ nadiaharrington@norwich.gov.uk

Personnel / HR: Mr Russell O'Keefe, Executive Head of Strategy, People & Democracy, Norwich City Council, St. Peter's Street, Norwich NR2 1NH ☎ 01603 212908 ✉ jackierodger@norwich.gov.uk

Planning: Mr Jerry Massey, Deputy Chief Executive - Operations, City Hall, St. Peter's Street, Norwich NR2 1NH ☎ 01603 212225 ✉ jerrymassey@norwich.gov.uk

Planning: Mr Graham Nelson, Head of Planning, City Hall, St. Peter's Street, Norwich NR2 1NH ☎ 01603 212530 ✉ grahamnelson@norwich.gov.uk

Procurement: Mr Anthony Bull, Executive Head of Business Relationship Management, City Hall, St. Peter's Street, Norwich NR2 1NH ☎ 01603 212326 ✉ anthonybull@norwich.gov.uk

Recycling & Waste Minimisation: Mr Adrian Akester, Head of Citywide Services, City Hall, St. Peter's Street, Norwich NR2 1NH ☎ 01603 213521 ✉ adrianakester@norwich.gov.uk

Recycling & Waste Minimisation: Ms Angela Hadley, Assistant Director of Community & Neighbourhoods, City Hall, St. Peter's Street, Norwich NR2 1NH ☎ 01603 212160 ✉ angelahadley@norwich.gov.uk

Regeneration: Mr Jerry Massey, Deputy Chief Executive - Operations, City Hall, St. Peter's Street, Norwich NR2 1NH ☎ 01603 212225 ✉ jerrymassey@norwich.gov.uk

Regeneration: Mr Graham Nelson, Head of Planning, City Hall, St. Peter's Street, Norwich NR2 1NH ☎ 01603 212530 ✉ grahamnelson@norwich.gov.uk

Road Safety: Mr Andy Watt, Head of Transportation & Landscape, City Hall, St. Peter's Street, Norwich NR2 1NH ☎ 01603 212396 ✉ andywatt@norwich.gov.uk

Street Scene: Mr Adrian Akester, Head of Citywide Services, City Hall, St. Peter's Street, Norwich NR2 1NH ☎ 01603 213521 ✉ adrianakester@norwich.gov.uk

Street Scene: Ms Anne Bonsor, Assistant Director - City Development, Norwich City Council, St. Peter's Street, Norwich NR2 1NH ☎ 01603 212353 ✉ annebonsor@norwich.gov.uk

Street Scene: Mr Jerry Massey, Director of Regeneration & Development, City Hall, St. Peter's Street, Norwich NR2 1NH ☎ 01603 212225 ✉ jerrymassey@norwich.gov.uk

Street Scene: Mr Andy Watt, Head of Transportation & Landscape, City Hall, St. Peter's Street, Norwich NR2 1NH ☎ 01603 212396 ✉ andywatt@norwich.gov.uk

Sustainable Communities: Mr Jerry Massey, Director of Regeneration & Development, City Hall, St. Peter's Street, Norwich NR2 1NH ☎ 01603 212225 ✉ jerrymassey@norwich.gov.uk

Sustainable Communities: Mr Doug Wilkinson, Assistant Director of Neighbourhoods, Norwich City Council, City Hall, St Peter's Street, Norwich NR2 1NH ☎ 01603 212775 ✉ dougwilkinson@norwich.gov.uk

Sustainable Development: Mr Jerry Massey, Deputy Chief Executive - Operations, City Hall, St. Peter's Street, Norwich NR2 1NH ☎ 01603 212225 ✉ jerrymassey@norwich.gov.uk

Sustainable Development: Mr Doug Wilkinson, Assistant Director of Neighbourhoods, Norwich City Council, City Hall, St Peter's Street, Norwich NR2 1NH ☎ 01603 212775 ✉ dougwilkinson@norwich.gov.uk

Tourism: Ms Nikki Rotsos, Head of Communications & Cultural Services, City Hall, St. Peter's Street, Norwich NR2 1NH ☎ 01603 212211 🖷 01603 212010 ✉ nikkirotsos@norwich.gov.uk

Town Centre: Mr Jerry Massey, Director of Regeneration & Development, City Hall, St. Peter's Street, Norwich NR2 1NH ☎ 01603 212225 ✉ jerrymassey@norwich.gov.uk

Traffic Management: Ms Anne Bonsor, Assistant Director - City Development, Norwich City Council, St. Peter's Street, Norwich

NR2 1NH ☎ 01603 212353 ✉ annebonsor@norwich.gov.uk

Traffic Management: Mr Andy Watt, Head of Transportation & Landscape, City Hall, St. Peter's Street, Norwich NR2 1NH ☎ 01603 212396 ✉ andywatt@norwich.gov.uk

Transport: Mr Jerry Massey, Director of Regeneration & Development, City Hall, St. Peter's Street, Norwich NR2 1NH ☎ 01603 212225 ✉ jerrymassey@norwich.gov.uk

Transport: Mr Andy Watt, Head of Transportation & Landscape, City Hall, St. Peter's Street, Norwich NR2 1NH ☎ 01603 212396 ✉ andywatt@norwich.gov.uk

Transport Planner: Mr Jerry Massey, Director of Regeneration & Development, City Hall, St. Peter's Street, Norwich NR2 1NH ☎ 01603 212225 ✉ jerrymassey@norwich.gov.uk

Transport Planner: Mr Andy Watt, Head of Transportation & Landscape, City Hall, St. Peter's Street, Norwich NR2 1NH ☎ 01603 212396 ✉ andywatt@norwich.gov.uk

Waste Collection and Disposal: Mr Adrian Akester, Head of Citywide Services, City Hall, St. Peter's Street, Norwich NR2 1NH ☎ 01603 213521 ✉ adrianakester@norwich.gov.uk

Waste Collection and Disposal: Mr Jerry Massey, Director of Regeneration & Development, City Hall, St. Peter's Street, Norwich NR2 1NH ☎ 01603 212225 ✉ jerrymassey@norwich.gov.uk

Waste Collection and Disposal: Mr Doug Wilkinson, Assistant Director - Neighbourhoods, Norwich City Council, City Hall, St Peter's Street, Norwich NR2 1NH ☎ 01603 212775 ✉ dougwilkinson@norwich.gov.uk

Waste Management: Mr Adrian Akester, Head of Citywide Services, City Hall, St. Peter's Street, Norwich NR2 1NH ☎ 01603 213521 ✉ adrianakester@norwich.gov.uk

Waste Management: Mr Jerry Massey, Director of Regeneration & Development, City Hall, St. Peter's Street, Norwich NR2 1NH ☎ 01603 212225 ✉ jerrymassey@norwich.gov.uk

Waste Management: Mr Doug Wilkinson, Assistant Director of Neighbourhoods, Norwich City Council, City Hall, St Peter's Street, Norwich NR2 1NH ☎ 01603 212775 ✉ dougwilkinson@norwich.gov.uk

Children's Play Areas: Mr Adrian Akester, Head of Citywide Services, City Hall, St. Peter's Street, Norwich NR2 1NH ☎ 01603 213521 ✉ adrianakester@norwich.gov.uk

MEMBERS OF THE COUNCIL (39)

The Lord Mayor: **Gayton**, Ralph (LAB - Mile Cross)
r.gayton@cllr.norwich.gov.uk
Leader of the Council: **Arthur**, Brenda (LAB - University)
b.arthur@cllr.norwich.gov.uk
Ackroyd, Carolyne (LD - Eaton)
c.ackroyd@cllr.norwich.gov.uk
Barker, Kevin (LAB - Sewell)
k.barker@cllr.norwich.gov.uk
Blunt, Neil (GRN - Wensum)
n.blunt@cllr.norwich.gov.uk
Bradford, David (LAB - Crome)
d.bradford@cllr.norwich.gov.uk
Bremner, Bert (LAB - University)
b.bremner@cllr.norwich.gov.uk
Brimblecombe, Caroline (GRN - Wensum)
c.brimblecombe@cllr.norwich.gov.uk
Brociek-Coulton, Julie (LAB - Sewell)
j.brociekcoulton@cllr.norwich.gov.uk
Button, Sally (LAB - Bowthorpe)
s.button@cllr.norwich.gov.uk
Carlo, Denise (GRN - Nelson)
d.carlo@cllr.norwich.gov.uk
Driver, Keith (LAB - Lakenham)
k.driver@cllr.norwich.gov.uk
Galvin, Lucy (GRN - Wensum)
l.galvin@cllr.norwich.gov.uk
Gee, Graeme (GRN - Mancroft)
g.gee@cllr.norwich.gov.uk
Gihawi, Deborah (LAB - Mile Cross)
d.gihawi@cllr.norwich.gov.uk
Graham, Lesley (GRN - Thorpe Hamlet)
l.grahame@cllr.norwich.gov.uk
Grenville, Sarah (LAB - University)
s.grenville@cllr.norwich.gov.uk
Harris, Gail (LAB - Catton Grove)
g.harris@cllr.norwich.gov.uk
Haynes, Ash (GRN - Town Close)
a.haynes@cllr.norwich.gov.uk
Henderson, Jo (GRN - Thorpe Hamlet)
j.henderson@cllr.norwich.gov.uk
Howard, Lucy (GRN - Mancroft)
l.howard@cllr.norwich.gov.uk
Kendrick, Paul (LAB - Catton Grove)
p.kendrick@cllr.norwich.gov.uk
Lay, Jenny (LAB - Crome)
j.lay@cllr.norwich.gov.uk
Little, Stephen (GRN - Town Close)
s.little@cllr.norwich.gov.uk
Lubbock, Judith (LD - Eaton)
j.lubbock@cllr.norwich.gov.uk
MacDonald, Victoria (LAB - Lakenham)
v.macdonald@cllr.norwich.gov.uk
Manning, Patrick (LAB - Lakenham)
p.manning@cllr.norwich.gov.uk
Neale, Paul (GRN - Town Close)
p.neale@cllr.norwich.gov.uk
Price, Ben (GRN - Thorpe Hamlet)
b.price@cllr.norwich.gov.uk
Rogers, David (GRN - Nelson)
d.rogers@cllr.norwich.gov.uk
Sands, Mike (LAB - Bowthorpe)
m.sands@cllr.norwich.gov.uk
Sands, Sue (LAB - Sewell)
s.sands@cllr.norwich.gov.uk
Stammers, Amy (GRN - Mancroft)
a.stammers@cllr.norwich.gov.uk
Stephenson, Claire (GRN - Nelson)
Stonard, Mike (LAB - Catton Grove)
m.stonard@cllr.norwich.gov.uk
Storie, Jo (LAB - Bowthorpe)
j.storie@cllr.norwich.gov.uk
Thomas, Viv (LAB - Mile Cross)
v.thomas@cllr.norwich.gov.uk
Waters, Alan (LAB - Crome)

a.waters@cllr.norwich.gov.uk
Wright, James (LD - Eaton)
j.wright@cllr.norwich.gov.uk

POLITICAL COMPOSITION
LAB: 21, GRN: 15, LD: 3

CABINET
Leader / Strategy & Policy: Ms Brenda Arthur
Deputy Leader / Resources: Mr Alan Waters
Customer Access: Ms Julie Brociek-Coulton
Housing: Ms Victoria McDonald
Neighbourhood Development & Community Engagement: Mr Keith Driver
Planning & Transport: Mr Bert Bremner
Play Areas, Parks & Open Spaces: Mr Deborah Gihawi

COMMITTEE CHAIRS
Audit: Mr Stephen Little
Licensing: Mr Paul Kendrick
Planning Applications: Mr David Bradford
Regulatory: Mr Roy Blower
Scrutiny (Scrutiny): Ms Claire Stephenson
Standards: Mr Peter Franzen (External)

NOTTINGHAM CITY U

Nottingham City Council, Loxley House, Station Street, Nottingham NG2 3NG ☎ 0115 915 5555 🖷 0115 915 4636
💻 www.nottinghamcity.gov.uk

FACTS & FIGURES
Police Authority: Nottinghamshire Police Authority
Health Authority: East Midlands Strategic Health Authority
Learning and Skills Council: East Midlands
Parliamentary Constituencies: Nottingham East, Nottingham North, Nottingham South
EU Constituencies: East Midlands
Election Frequency: Elections are of whole council
Twinning: Ghent (Belgium); Harare (Zimbabwe); Karlsruhe (Germany); Ljubljana (Slovenia); Minsk (Belarus)

PRINCIPAL OFFICERS
Chief Executive: Mrs Carole Mills-Evans, Acting Chief Executive & Corporate Director - Resources, Loxley House, Station Street, Nottingham NG2 3NG ☎ 0115 876 3838 ✉ carole.mills-evans@nottinghamcity.gov.uk

Deputy Chief Executive: Ms Angela Probert, Director - Human Resources, Loxley House, Station Street, Nottingham NG2 3NG ☎ 0115 876 3440 ✉ angela.probert@nottinghamcity.gov.uk

Senior Management: Mr David Bishop, Corporate Director - Development, Loxley House, Station Street, Nottingham NG2 3NG ☎ 0115 915 5555 ✉ david.bishop@nottinghamcity.gov.uk

Senior Management: Mr Ian Curryer, Corporate Director - Children & Families, Loxley House, Station Street, Nottingham NG2 3NG ☎ 0115 876 3374 ✉ ian.curryer@nottinghamcity.gov.uk

Senior Management: Mrs Carole Mills-Evans, Acting Chief Executive & Corporate Director - Resources, Loxley House, Station Street, Nottingham NG2 3NG ☎ 0115 876 3838 ✉ carole.mills-evans@nottinghamcity.gov.uk

Building Control: Mr Robert De Rosa, Head - Building Control, Loxley House, Station Street, Nottingham NG2 3NG ☎ 0115 915 5363 ✉ robert.derosa@nottinghamcity.gov.uk

Catering Services: Ms Liz Dobson, Head - Catering & Facilities, Medway Building, Eastcroft Depot, London Road, Nottingham NG2 3AH ☎ 0115 915 2028 🖷 0115 915 2024 ✉ liz.dobson@nottinghamcity.gov.uk

Children / Youth Services: Mr Ken Beaumont, Head - Family Community Team South, Loxley House, Station Street, Nottingham NG2 3NG ☎ 0115 876 4912 ✉ ken.beaumont@nottinghamcity.gov.uk

Children / Youth Services: Ms Justine Darke, Service Manager - Youth, Loxley House, Station Street, Nottingham NG2 3NG ☎ 0115 915 8635 ✉ justine.darke@nottinghamcity.gov.uk

Civil Registration: Ms Lucy Lee, Service Manager - Registry Service, 50 Shakespeare Street, Nottingham NG1 4BT ☎ 0115 915 5817 ✉ lucy.lee@nottinghamcity.gov.uk

PR / Communications: Mrs Claire Richmond, Director - Policy, Partnership, Communications & Marketing, Loxley House, Station Street, Nottingham NG2 3NG ☎ 0115 876 3327 ✉ claire.richmond@nottinghamcity.gov.uk

Community Safety: Ms Emma Orrock, Service Improvement Manager, Loxley House, Station Street, Nottingham NG2 3NG ☎ 0115 876 5034 ✉ emma.orrock@nottinghamcity.gov.uk

Computer Management: Mr Paul Martin, Director - Information Technology, Loxley House, Station Street, Nottingham NG2 3NG ☎ 0115 876 2008 ✉ paul.martin@nottinghamcity.gov.uk

Customer Service: Ms Lynne North, Customer Liaison Officer, Loxley House, Station Street, Nottingham NG2 3NG ☎ 0115 876 4921 ✉ lynne.north@nottinghamcity.gov.uk

Education: Mr Ian Curryer, Corporate Director - Children & Families, Loxley House, Station Street, Nottingham NG2 3NG ☎ 0115 876 3374 ✉ ian.curryer@nottinghamcity.gov.uk

Electoral Registration: Ms Sarah Wilson, Manager - Electoral Services, Loxley House, Station Street, Nottingham NG2 3NG ☎ 0115 876 4308 ✉ sarah.wilson@nottinghamcity.gov.uk

Emergency Planning: Mr Paul Millward, Head - Resilience, Island Block, The Guildhall, Nottingham NG1 4BT ☎ 0115 915 4501 🖷 0115 915 4195 ✉ paul.millward@nottinghamcity.gov.uk

Energy Management: Ms Gail Scholes, Head - Sustainability & Climate Change, Tamar Building, Eastcroft Depot, London Road, Nottingham NG2 3AH ☎ 0115 915 2154 ✉ gail.scholes@nottinghamcity.gov.uk

Environmental Health: Mr Andy Vaughan, Director - Neighbourhood Services, The Clocktower, Eastcroft Depot, London Road, Nottingham NG1 4BT ☎ 0115 915 2206

↻ andy.vaughan@nottinghamcity.gov.uk

Estates, Property & Valuation: Mr Nick Quinsey, Head of Service - Estates, Loxley House, Station Street, Nottingham NG2 3NG ☎ 0115 915 5555 ↻ nick.quinsey@nottinghamcity.gov.uk

European Liaison: Mr John Connelly, Head - Regional & International Team, Loxley House, Station Street, Nottingham NG2 3NG ☎ 0115 915 5091 🖷 0115 915 5349 ↻ john.connelly@nottinghamcity.gov.uk

Finance and Treasurer: Mr Tony Kirkham, Director - Strategic Finance, Loxley House, Station Street, Nottingham NG2 3NG ☎ 0115 876 4157 ↻ tony.kirkham@nottinghamcity.gov.uk

Fleet Management: Mr Andy Vaughan, Director - Neighbourhood Services, The Clocktower, Eastcroft Depot, London Road, Nottingham NG1 4BT ☎ 0115 915 2206 ↻ andy.vaughan@nottinghamcity.gov.uk

Highways: Mr Chris Keane, Manager - Highway Services, Humber Building, Eastcroft Depot, London Road, Nottingham NG2 3AH ☎ 0115 915 2081 ↻ chris.keane@nottinghamcity.gov.uk

Housing: Ms Gill Moy, Director - Housing, NCH, 14 Houndsgate, Nottingham NG1 7BA ☎ 0115 915 7430 🖷 0115 915 5349 ↻ gill.moy@nottinghamcityhomes.org.uk

Local Area Agreement: Ms Liz Jones, Head - Partnership Policy, Loxley House, Station Street, Nottingham NG2 3NG ☎ 0115 876 3367 ↻ liz.jones@nottinghamcity.gov.uk

Legal: Mr Glen O'Connell, Director - Legal & Democratic Services & Monitoring Officer, Loxley House, Station Street, Nottingham NG2 3NG ☎ 0115 876 4330 🖷 0115 915 4179 ↻ glen.oconnell@nottinghamcity.gov.uk

Leisure and Cultural Services: Mr Nigel Hawkins, Head - Culture & Business Management, Loxley House, Station Street, Nottingham NG2 3NG ☎ 0115 876 4969 ↻ nigel.hawkins@nottinghamcity.gov.uk

Member Services: Ms Debra La Mola, Head - Democratic Services, Loxley House, Station Street, Nottingham NG2 3NG ☎ 0115 876 4292 🖷 0115 915 4812 ↻ debra.lamola@nottinghamcity.gov.uk

Parking: Mr Pete Mitchell, Head - Licensing, Permits & Regulations, Central Police Station, North Church Street, Nottingham NG1 4BH ☎ 0300 300 9999 🖷 0115 915 2258 ↻ pete.mitchell@nottinghamshire.pnn.police.uk

Personnel / HR: Ms Angela Probert, Director - Human Resources, Loxley House, Station Street, Nottingham NG2 3NG ☎ 0115 876 3440 ↻ angela.probert@nottinghamcity.gov.uk

Planning: Ms Rachel Gaskell, Principal Planning Officer, Loxley House, Station Street, Nottingham NG2 3NG ☎ 0115 915 5555 ↻ rachel.gaskell@nottinghamcity.gov.uk

Procurement: Ms Sue Tongue, Head - Project Finance Management, Loxley House, Station Street, Nottingham NG2 3NG ☎ 0115 876 3578 ↻ sue.tongue@nottinghamcity.gov.uk

Recycling & Waste Minimisation: Mr Daniel Ayrton, Manager - Waste & Recycling, Tyne Building, Eastcroft Depot, London Road, Nottingham NG2 3AH ☎ 0115 915 2136 ↻ daniel.ayrton@nottinghamcity.gov.uk

Regeneration: Ms Gill Callingham, Regeneration Co-ordination Manager, Loxley House, Station Street, Nottingham NG2 3NG ☎ 0115 876 3954 ↻ gill.callingham@nottinghamcity.gov.uk

Road Safety: Mr Francis Ashton, Service Manager - Road Safety & Traffic Services, Loxley House, Station Street, Nottingham NG2 3NG ☎ 0115 876 5224 ↻ francis.ashton@nottinghamcity.gov.uk

Social Services: Ms Elaine Yardley, Director - Adult Provision & Health Integration, Loxley House, Station Street, Nottingham NG2 3NG ☎ 0115 876 3502 ↻ elaine.yardley@nottinghamcity.gov.uk

Social Services (Adult): Ms Helen Jones, Director - Adult Assessment, Loxley House, Station Street, Nottingham NG2 3NG ☎ 0115 876 3504 ↻ helen.jones@nottinghamcity.gov.uk

Staff Training: Ms Rebecca Baxendale, Head - Organisational Development, Loxley House, Station Street, Nottingham NG2 3NG ☎ 0115 876 3463 ↻ rebecca.baxendale@nottinghamcity.gov.uk

Staff Training: Ms Denise Willis, Head - Organisational Development, Loxley House, Station Street, Nottingham NG2 3NG ☎ 0115 876 3463 ↻ denise.willis@nottinghamcity.gov.uk

Street Scene: Mr Dave Halstead, Head - City Services, The Clocktower, Eastcroft Depot, London Road, Nottingham NG2 3AH ☎ 0115 915 2247 ↻ dave.halstead@nottinghamcity.gov.uk

Traffic Management: Ms Caroline Stylianou, Service Manager - Traffic Management, Loxley House, Station Street, Nottingham NG2 3NG ☎ 0115 876 5243 🖷 0115 915 6550 ↻ caroline.stylianou@nottinghamcity.gov.uk

Transport: Mr Adrian Hill, Head - Commercial & Transport Services, Humber Building, Eastcroft Depot, London Road, Nottingham NG2 3AH ☎ 0115 915 2261 ↻ adrian.hill@nottinghamcity.gov.uk

Transport Planner: Mr Andrew Gregory, Head - Development, Loxley House, Station Street, Nottingham NG2 3NG ☎ 0115 915 5555 ↻ andrew.gregory@nottinghamcity.gov.uk

Waste Collection and Disposal: Mr Paul Marshall, Manager - Waste Operations, Tyne House, Eastcroft Depot, London Road, Nottingham NG2 3AH ☎ 0115 915 2059 ↻ paul.marshall@nottinghamcity.gov.uk

Waste Management: Mr Paul Marshall, Manager - Waste Operations, Tyne House, Eastcroft Depot, London Road, Nottingham NG2 3AH ☎ 0115 915 2059 ↻ paul.marshall@nottinghamcity.gov.uk

MEMBERS OF THE COUNCIL (55)

***The Lord Mayor:* Unczur**, Leon (LAB - Aspley)
leon.unczur@nottinghamcity.gov.uk
***Leader of the Council:* Collins**, Jon (LAB - St Ann's)
jon.collins@nottinghamcity.gov.uk
***Deputy Leader of the Council:* Chapman**, Graham (LAB - Aspley)
graham.chapman@nottinghamcity.gov.uk
Ali, Liaqat (LAB - Radford and Park)
liaqat.ali@nottinghamcity.gov.uk
Arnold, Cat (LAB - Basford)
cat.arnold@nottinghamcity.gov.uk
Aslam, Mohammad (LAB - Radford and Park)
mohammad.aslam@nottinghamcity.gov.uk
Ball, Alex (LAB - Sherwood)
alex.ball@nottinghamcity.gov.uk
Bryan, Merlita (LAB - Arboretum)
merlita.bryan@nottinghamcity.gov.uk
Campbell, Eunice (LAB - Bulwell Forest)
eunice.campbell@nottinghamcity.gov.uk
Choudhry, Azad (LAB - Arboretum)
azad.choudhry@nottinghamcity.gov.uk
Clark, Alan (LAB - Bulwell Forest)
alan.clark@nottinghamcity.gov.uk
Cresswell, Derek (LAB - Bilborough)
derek.cresswell@nottinghamcity.gov.uk
Culley, Georgina (CON - Wollaton West)
georgina.culley@nottinghamcity.gov.uk
Dewinton, Emma (LAB - Mapperley)
emma.dewinton@nottinghamcity.gov.uk
Edwards, Michael (LAB - Bridge)
michael.edwards@nottinghamcity.gov.uk
Fox, Stuart (LAB - Wollaton East and Lenton Abbey)
stuart.fox@nottinghamcity.gov.uk
Gibson, Chris (LAB - Clifton South)
chris.gibson@nottinghamcity.gov.uk
Grocock, Brian (LAB - Bestwood)
brian.grocock@nottinghamcity.gov.uk
Hartshorne, John (LAB - Bulwell)
john.hartshorne@nottinghamcity.gov.uk
Healy, Rosemary (LAB - Mapperley)
rosemary.healy@nottinghamcity.gov.uk
Heaton, Nicola (LAB - Bridge)
nicola.heaton@nottinghamcity.gov.uk
Ibrahim, Mohammed (LAB - Berridge)
mohammed.ibrahim@nottinghamcity.gov.uk
Jeffery, Lee (LAB - Clifton North)
lee.jeffery@nottinghamcity.gov.uk
Jenkins, Glyn (LAB - Leen Valley)
glyn.jenkins@nottinghamcity.gov.uk
Johnson, Sue (LAB - St Ann's)
sue.johnson@nottinghamcity.gov.uk
Jones, Carole-Ann (LAB - Berridge)
carole-ann.jones@nottinghamcity.gov.uk
Khan, Gul (LAB - Dales)
gul.khan@nottinghamcity.gov.uk
Klein, Ginny (LAB - Bulwell)
ginny.klein@nottinghamcity.gov.uk
Liversidge, David (LAB - St Ann's)
dave.liversidge@nottinghamcity.gov.uk
Longford, Sally (LAB - Wollaton East and Lenton Abbey)
sally.longford@nottinghamcity.gov.uk
Malcolm, Ian (LAB - Clifton South)
McCulloch, Carole (LAB - Aspley)
carole.mcculloch@nottinghamcity.gov.uk
McDonald, Nick (LAB - Bulwell Forest)
nick.mcdonald@nottinghamcity.gov.uk
Mellen, David (LAB - Dales)
david.mellen@nottinghamcity.gov.uk
Molife, Thulani (LAB - Mapperley)
thulani.molife@nottinghamcity.gov.uk
Morley, Eileen (CON - Wollaton West)
eileen.morley@nottinghamcity.gov.uk
Morris, Jackie (LAB - Bulwell)
jackie.morris@nottinghamcity.gov.uk
Neal, Toby (LAB - Berridge)
toby.neal@nottinghamcity.gov.uk
Norris, Alex (LAB - Basford)
alex.norris@nottinghamcity.gov.uk
Ottewell, Bill (LAB - Basford)
bill.ottewell@nottinghamcity.gov.uk
Packer, Jeannie (LAB - Clifton South)
jeannie.packer@nottinghamcity@nottinghamcity.gov.uk
Parbutt, Brian (LAB - Sherwood)
brian.parbutt@nottinghamcity.gov.uk
Parton, Steve (CON - Wollaton West)
steve.parton@nottinghamcity.gov.uk
Piper, Sarah (LAB - Dunkirk and Lenton)
sarah.piper@nottinghamcity.gov.uk
Saghir, Mohammed (LAB - Leen Valley)
cllrmohammed.saghir@nottinghamcity.gov.uk
Smith, David (LAB - Bestwood)
cllr-david smith@nottinghamcity.gov.uk
Spencer, Timothy (CON - Clifton North)
timothy.spencer@nottinghamcity.gov.uk
Steel, Roger (CON - Clifton North)
roger.steel@nottinghamcity.gov.uk
Trimble, David (LAB - Dunkirk and Lenton)
dave.trimble@nottinghamcity.gov.uk
Urquhart, Jane (LAB - Sherwood)
jane.arquhart@nottinghamcity.gov.uk
Watson, Marcia (LAB - Bilborough)
marcia.watson@nottinghamcity.gov.uk
Wildgust, Mick (LAB - Bestwood)
mick.wildgust@nottinghamcity.gov.uk
Williams, Kenneth (LAB - Dales)
ken.williams@nottinghamcity.gov.uk
Williams, Steph (LAB - Radford and Park)
steph.williams@nottinghamcity.gov.uk
Wood, Malcolm (LAB - Bilborough)
malcolm.wood@nottinghamcity.gov.uk

POLITICAL COMPOSITION

LAB: 50, CON: 5

CABINET

Leader / Health, Commissioning & Human Resources: Mr Jon Collins
Deputy Leader / Economic Development, Resources & Regeneration: Mr Graham Chapman
Adults & Health: Ms Eunice Campbell
Area Working, Cleansing & Community Safety: Mr Alex Norris
Children's Services: Mr David Mellen
Energy & Sustainability: Mr Alan Clark
Housing, Adults & Community Sector: Mr David Liversidge
Jobs, Skills & Business: Mr Nick McDonald
Leisure, Culture & Tourism: Mr Dave Trimble

Planning & Transportation: Ms Jane Urquhart

COMMITTEE CHAIRS

Audit: Mr Kenneth Williams
Corporate Parenting: Mr David Mellen
Development Control: Mr Chris Gibson
Licensing: Mr Brian Grocock
Overview & Scrutiny: Mr Brian Parbutt

NOTTINGHAMSHIRE C

Nottinghamshire County Council, County Hall, West Bridgford NG2 7QP ☎ 0115 982 3823 🖷 0115 971 7945 ✉ enquiries@nottscc.gov.uk 💻 www.nottinghamshire.gov.uk

FACTS & FIGURES

Police Authority: Nottinghamshire Police Authority
Health Authority: East Midlands Strategic Health Authority
Learning and Skills Council: East Midlands
EU Constituencies: East Midlands
Election Frequency: Elections are of whole council
Twinning: Poznan (Poland)

PRINCIPAL OFFICERS

Chief Executive: Mr Mick Burrows, Chief Executive, County Hall, West Bridgford NG2 7QP ☎ 0115 977 2045 🖷 0115 977 3490 ✉ michael.burrows@nottscc.gov.uk

Assistant Chief Executive: Ms Jayne Francis-Ward, Corporate Director - Policy, Planning & Corporate Services, County Hall, West Bridgford NG2 7QP ☎ 0115 977 3582 ✉ jayne.francis-ward@nottscc.gov.uk

Assistant Chief Executive: Mr David Pearson, Corporate Director - Adult Social Care, Health & Public Protection, County Hall, West Bridgford, Nottingham, Nottingham NG2 7QP ☎ 0115 977 4636 🖷 0115 977 2420 ✉ david.pearson@nottscc.gov.uk

Senior Management: Ms Jayne Francis-Ward, Corporate Director - Policy, Planning & Corporate Services, County Hall, West Bridgford NG2 7QP ☎ 0115 977 3582 ✉ jayne.francis-ward@nottscc.gov.uk

Senior Management: Mr Tim Gregory, Corporate Director - Environment & Resources, County Hall, West Bridgford NG2 7QP ☎ 0115 977 3404 ✉ tim.gregory@nottscc.gov.uk

Senior Management: Mr Anthony May, Corporate Director - Children, Families & Cultural Services, County Hall, West Bridgford NG2 7QP ☎ 0115 977 3353 ✉ anthony.may@nottscc.gov.uk

Senior Management: Mr David Pearson, Corporate Director - Adult Social Care, Health & Public Protection, County Hall, West Bridgford NG2 7QP ☎ 0115 977 4636 🖷 0115 977 2420 ✉ david.pearson@nottscc.gov.uk

Access Officer / Social Services (Disability): Mr Jon Wilson, Service Director - Personal Care & Support (Younger Adults), County Hall, West Bridgford NG2 7QP ☎ 0115 977 3985 ✉ jon.wilson@nottscc.gov.uk

Architect, Building / Property Services: Mr Tim Gregory, Corporate Director - Environment & Resources, County Hall, West Bridgford NG2 7QP ☎ 0115 977 3404 ✉ tim.gregory@nottscc.gov.uk

Architect, Building / Property Services: Mr Jas Hundal, Service Director - Transport, Property & Environment, County Hall, West Bridgford NG2 7QP ☎ 0115 977 4257 ✉ jas.hundal@nottscc.gov.uk

Best Value: Ms Celia Morris, Group Manager - Policy, Performance, Complaints & Research, County Hall, West Bridgford NG2 7QP ☎ 0115 977 2043 ✉ celia.morris@nottscc.gov.uk

Catering Services: Mr Jas Hundal, Service Director - Transport, Property & Environment, County Hall, West Bridgford NG2 7QP ☎ 0115 977 4257 ✉ jas.hundal@nottscc.gov.uk

Catering Services: Mr Kevin McKay, Group Manager - Catering & Facilities Management, County Hall, West Bridgford NG2 7QP ☎ 0115 977 4369 ✉ kevin.mckay@nottscc.gov.uk

Children / Youth Services: Ms Rachel Coombs, Group Manager - Children's Regulated & Corporate Parenting, West Bridgford House, Loughborough Road, West Bridgford NG2 7UN ☎ 0115 878 3590 ✉ rachel.coombs@nottscc.gov.uk

Children / Youth Services: Mr Anthony May, Corporate Director - Children, Families & Cultural Services, County Hall, West Bridgford NG2 7QP ☎ 0115 977 3353 ✉ anthony.may@nottscc.gov.uk

Children / Youth Services: Mr Chris Warren, Group Manager - Young People's Service, County Hall, West Bridgford NG2 7QP ☎ 0115 977 4430 ✉ christopher.warren@nottscc.gov.uk

Civil Registration: Mr Rob Fisher, Group Manager - Emergency Management & Registration, County Hall, West Bridgford NG2 7QP ☎ 0115 977 3681 ✉ rob.fisher@nottscc.gov.uk

Civil Registration: Mr Paul McKay, Service Director - Promoting Independence & Public Protection, County Hall, West Bridgford NG2 7QP ☎ 0115 977 3909 🖷 0115 977 2420 ✉ paul.mckay@nottscc.gov.uk

PR / Communications: Mr Martin Done, Service Director - Communications & Marketing, County Hall, West Bridgford NG2 7QP ☎ 0115 977 2026 ✉ martin.done@nottscc.gov.uk

Community Safety: Mr Christopher Walker, Community Safety Manager, County Hall, West Bridgford NG2 7QP ☎ 0115 977 4331 🖷 0115 977 3859 ✉ christopher.walker@nottscc.gov.uk

Computer Management: Mr Tim Gregory, Corporate Director - Environment & Resources, County Hall, West Bridgford NG2 7QP ☎ 0115 977 3404 ✉ tim.gregory@nottscc.gov.uk

Computer Management: Mr Ivor Nicholson, Service Director - ICT, County Hall, West Bridgford NG2 7QP ☎ 0115 977 3300 🖷 0115 981 4621 ✉ ivor.nicholson@nottscc.gov.uk

Consumer Protection and Trading Standards: Mr Paul McKay, Service Director - Promoting Independence & Public Protection, County Hall, West Bridgford NG2 7QP ☎ 0115 977 3909 🖷 0115 977 2420 ✉ paul.mckay@nottscc.gov.uk

Contracts: Ms Susan Travis, Strategy & Performance Team Manager, County Hall, West Bridgford NG2 7QP ☎ 0115 977 3828 🖷 0115 977 2745 ✉ susan.travis@nottscc.gov.uk

Corporate Services: Ms Linda Bayliss, Service Director - Strategic Services, County Hall, West Bridgford NG2 7QP ☎ 0115 977 4676 ✉ linda.bayliss@nottscc.gov.uk

Corporate Services: Ms Jayne Francis-Ward, Corporate Director - Policy, Planning & Corporate Services, County Hall, West Bridgford NG2 7QP ☎ 0115 977 3582 ✉ jayne.francis-ward@nottscc.gov.uk

Corporate Services: Mr Chris Holmes, Head of Governance & Scrutiny, County Hall, West Bridgford NG2 7QP ☎ 0115 977 3714 ✉ chris.holmes@nottscc.gov.uk

Corporate Services: Ms Liz Lambert, Service Head for Equalities & Business Performance, County Hall, West Bridgford NG2 7QP ☎ 0115 977 2566 ✉ liz.lambert@nottscc.gov.uk

Corporate Services: Ms Celia Morris, Group Manager - Policy, Performance, Complaints & Research, Trent Bridge House, Fox Road, West Bridgford NG2 6BJ ☎ 0115 977 2043 ✉ celia.morris@nottscc.gov.uk

Customer Service: Mr Martin Done, Service Director - Communications & Marketing, County Hall, West Bridgford NG2 7QP ☎ 0115 977 2026 ✉ martin.done@nottscc.gov.uk

Customer Service: Ms Celia Morris, Group Manager - Policy, Performance, Complaints & Research, County Hall, West Bridgford NG2 7QP ☎ 0115 977 2043 ✉ celia.morris@nottscc.gov.uk

Education: Mr Anthony May, Strategic Director - Children's & Young People's Services, County Hall, West Bridgford NG2 7QP ☎ 0115 977 3353 ✉ anthony.may@nottscc.gov.uk

Education: Mr Anthony May, Corporate Director - Children, Families & Cultural Services, County Hall, West Bridgford NG2 7QP ☎ ; 0115 977 3353 ✉ anthony.may@nottscc.gov.uk

Education: Mr John Slater, Service Director - Education Standards & Inclusion, County Hall, West Bridgford NG2 7QP ☎ 0115 977 3589 🖷 0115 981 2824 ✉ john.slater@nottscc.gov.uk

Education: Ms Gill Thackrey, Group Manager - Business Development & Support, County Hall, West Bridgford NG2 7QP ☎ 0115 977 3644 ✉ gill.thackrey@nottscc.gov.uk

E-Government: Mr Ivor Nicholson, Service Director - ICT, County Hall, West Bridgford NG2 7QP ☎ 0115 977 3300 🖷 0115 981 4621 ✉ ivor.nicholson@nottscc.gov.uk

Electoral Registration: Mr David Ellis, Service Manager - Member Support, County Hall, West Bridgford NG2 7QP ☎ 0115 977 2899 🖷 0115 977 3813 ✉ david.ellis@nottscc.gov.uk

Emergency Planning: Mr Rob Fisher, Group Manager - Emergency Management & Registration, County Hall, West Bridgford NG2 7QP ☎ 0115 977 3681 ✉ rob.fisher@nottscc.gov.uk

Emergency Planning: Mr Paul McKay, Service Director - Promoting Independence & Public Protection, County Hall, West Bridgford NG2 7QP ☎ 0115 977 3909 🖷 0115 977 2420 ✉ paul.mckay@nottscc.gov.uk

Energy Management: Mr Mick Allen, Group Manager - Waste & Energy Management, Trent Bridge House, Fox Road, West Bridgford NG2 6BJ ☎ 0115 977 4684 🖷 0115 945 4329 ✉ mick.allen@nottscc.gov.uk

Estates, Property & Valuation: Mr Jas Hundal, Service Director - Transport, Property & Environment, County Hall, West Bridgford NG2 7QP ☎ 0115 977 4257 ✉ jas.hundal@nottscc.gov.uk

Facilities: Mr Kevin McKay, Group Manager - Catering & Facilities Management, County Hall, West Bridgford NG2 7QP ☎ 0115 977 4369 ✉ kevin.mckay@nottscc.gov.uk

Fleet Management: Mr Andy Warrington, Service Director - Highways, Trent Bridge House, Fox Road, West Bridgford NG2 6BJ ☎ 0115 977 4681

Grounds Maintenance: Mr Andy Warrington, Service Director - Highways, Trent Bridge House, Fox Road, West Bridgford NG2 6BJ ☎ 0115 977 4681

Health and Safety: Mr Peter Roddis, Team Manager - Health & Safety, 41 Loughborough Road, West Bridgford NG2 7LJ ☎ 0115 977 3445 🖷 0115 977 2403 ✉ peter.roddis@nottscc.gov.uk

Highways: Mr Andy Warrington, Service Director - Highways, Trent Bridge House, Fox Road, West Bridgford NG2 6BJ ☎ 0115 977 4681

Legal: Ms Jayne Francis-Ward, Corporate Director - Policy, Planning & Corporate Services, County Hall, West Bridgford NG2 7QP ☎ 0115 977 3582 ✉ jayne.francis-ward@nottscc.gov.uk

Legal: Ms Liz Lambert, Service Head for Equalities & Business Performance, County Hall, West Bridgford NG2 7QP ☎ 0115 977 2566 ✉ liz.lambert@nottscc.gov.uk

Leisure and Cultural Services: Mr Steve Bradley, Group Manager - Cultural & Enrichment Services, County Hall, West Bridgford NG2 7QP ☎ 0115 977 4206 ✉ steve.bradley@nottscc.gov.uk

Leisure and Cultural Services: Mr Derek Higton, Service Director - Youth, Families & Culture, County Hall, West Bridgford NG2 7QP ☎ 0115 977 4430

Lifelong Learning: Ms Sue Green, Adult & Community Learning Services Manager, County Hall, West Bridgford NG2 7QP ☎ 0115 977 2875 🖷 0115 981 2824 ✉ sue.green@nottscc.gov.uk

Lighting: Mr Andy Warrington, Service Director - Highways, Trent Bridge House, Fox Road, West Bridgford NG2 6BJ ☎ 0115 977 4681

Lighting: Mr Gary Wood, Group Manager - Transport Policy & Programmes, County Hall, West Bridgford NG2 7QP ☎ 0115 977 4270 🖷 0115 945 4329 ✉ gary.wood@nottscc.gov.uk

Lottery Funding, Charity and Voluntary: Ms Wendy Young, Head of Service - Adult Social Care & Health, County Hall, West Bridgford NG2 7QP ☎ 0115 977 4967 ✉ wendy.young@nottscc.gov.uk

Member Services: Mr David Ellis, Service Manager - Member Support, County Hall, West Bridgford NG2 7QP ☎ 0115 977 2899 🖷 0115 977 3813 ✉ david.ellis@nottscc.gov.uk

Partnerships: Mr Martin Done, Service Director - Communications & Marketing, County Hall, West Bridgford NG2 7QP ☎ 0115 977 2026 ✉ martin.done@nottscc.gov.uk

Partnerships: Ms Ann Marie Hawkins, Group Manager - Localism & Partnerships, County Hall, West Bridgford NG2 7QP ☎ 0115 977 2460 ✉ annmarie.hawkins@nottscc.gov.uk

Personnel / HR: Mr Tim Gregory, Corporate Director - Environment & Resources, County Hall, West Bridgford NG2 7QP ☎ 0115 977 3404 ✉ tim.gregory@nottscc.gov.uk

Personnel / HR: Ms Marjorie Toward, Service Director - HR & Customer Services, County Hall, West Bridgford NG2 7QP ☎ 0115 977 4404 ✉ marje.toward@nottscc.gov.uk

Planning: Ms Sally Gill, Group Manager - Planning, County Hall, West Bridgford NG2 7QP ☎ 0115 969 6536 ✉ sally.gill@nottscc.gov.uk

Procurement: Ms Susan Travis, Strategy & Performance Team Manager, County Hall, West Bridgford NG2 7QP ☎ 0115 977 3828 🖷 0115 977 2745 ✉ susan.travis@nottscc.gov.uk

Public Libraries: Mr Peter Gaw, Group Manager - Libraries, Archives & Information Services, County Hall, West Bridgford NG2 7QP ☎ 0115 977 4201 ✉ peter.gaw@nottscc.gov.uk

Recycling & Waste Minimisation: Mr Mick Allen, Group Manager - Waste & Energy Management, Trent Bridge House, Fox Road, West Bridgford NG2 6BJ ☎ 0115 977 4684 🖷 0115 945 4329 ✉ mick.allen@nottscc.gov.uk

Regeneration: Mr Matthew Lockley, Team Manager - Economic Development, County Hall, West Bridgford NG2 7QP ☎ 0115 977 2446 ✉ matthew.lockley@nottscc.gov.uk

Road Safety: Ms Suzanne Heydon, Group Manager - Highway Safety, Trent Bridge House, Fox Road, West Bridgford NG2 6BJ ☎ 0115 977 4487 🖷 0115 945 4329 ✉ suzanne.heydon@nottscc.gov.uk

Social Services: Mr David Pearson, Corporate Director - Adult Social Care, Health & Public Protection, County Hall, West Bridgford NG2 7QP ☎ 0115 977 4636 🖷 0115 977 2420 ✉ david.pearson@nottscc.gov.uk

Social Services (Adult): Ms Caroline Baria, Service Director – Joint Commissioning Quality and Business Change, County Hall, West Bridgford NG2 7QP ☎ 0115 977 3985 ✉ caroline.baria@nottscc.gov.uk

Social Services (Adult): Mr David Hamilton, Service Director - Personal Care and Support (Older Adults), County Hall, West Bridgford NG2 7QP ☎ ; 0115 977 3909 🖷 0115 977 2420 ✉ david.hamilton@nottscc.gov.uk

Social Services (Adult): Mr Paul McKay, Service Director - Promoting Independence & Public Protection, County Hall, West Bridgford, Nottingham, Nottingham NG2 ☎ 0115 977 3909 🖷 0115 977 2420 ✉ paul.mckay@nottscc.gov.uk

Social Services (Adult): Mr Jon Wilson, Service Director - Personal Care & Support (Younger Adults), County Hall, West Bridgford NG2 7QP ☎ 0115 977 3985 ✉ jon.wilson@nottscc.gov.uk

Social Services (Children): Mr Steve Edwards, Service Director - Children's Social Care, County Hall, West Bridgford NG2 7QP ☎ 0115 977 4782 🖷 0115 977 2420 ✉ steve.edwards@nottscc.gov.uk

Social Services (Children): Mr Anthony May, Corporate Director - Children's & Young People's Services, County Hall, West Bridgford NG2 7QP ☎ 0115 982 3823 ✉ anthony.may@nottscc.gov.uk

Social Services (Children): Mr Anthony May, Corporate Director - Children, Families & Cultural Services, County Hall, West Bridgford NG2 7QP ☎ 0115 977 3353 ✉ anthony.may@nottscc.gov.uk

Social Services (Children): Ms Pam Rosseter, Group Manager - Safeguarding & Independent Review, County Hall, West Bridgford NG2 7QP ☎ 0115 977 3921 ✉ pam.rosseter@nottscc.gov.uk

Staff Training: Ms Marjorie Toward, Service Director - HR & Customer Services, County Hall, West Bridgford NG2 7QP ☎ 0115 977 4404 ✉ marje.toward@nottscc.gov.uk

Tourism: Mr Steve Bradley, Group Manager - Cultural & Enrichment Services, County Hall, West Bridgford NG2 7QP ☎ 0115 977 4206 ✉ steve.bradley@nottscc.gov.uk

Tourism: Mr Derek Higton, Service Director - Youth, Families & Culture, County Hall, West Bridgford NG2 7QP ☎ 0115 977 4430

Traffic Management: Mr Gary Wood, Group Manager - Transport Policy & Programmes, County Hall, West Bridgford NG2 7QP ☎ 0115 977 4270 🖷 0115 945 4329 ✉ gary.wood@nottscc.gov.uk

Transport: Mr Andy Warrington, Service Director - Highways, Trent Bridge House, Fox Road, West Bridgford NG2 6BJ ☎ 0115 977 4681

Transport: Mr Andy Warrington, Service Director - Highways,

Trent Bridge House, Fox Road, West Bridgford NG2 6BJ ☎ 0115 977 4681

Transport Planner: Mr Gary Wood, Group Manager - Transport Policy & Programmes, County Hall, West Bridgford NG2 7QP ☎ 0115 977 4270 🖷 0115 945 4329 ✉ gary.wood@nottscc.gov.uk

MEMBERS OF THE COUNCIL (66)

Chair: **Pepper**, Carol (CON - Arnold North)
cllr.carol.pepper@nottscc.gov.uk
Leader of the Council: **Cutts**, Kay (CON - Radcliffe-on-Trent)
cllr.katherine.cutts@nottscc.gov.uk
Deputy Leader of the Council: **Suthers**, Martin (CON - Bingham)
cllr.martin.suthers@nottscc.gov.uk
Adair, Reg (CON - Ruddington)
cllr.reg.adair@nottscc.gov.uk
Allin, John (LAB - Warsop)
cllr.john.allin@nottscc.gov.uk
Asbury, Fiona (LD - Sutton in Ashfield West)
cllr.fiona.asbury@nottscc.gov.uk
Barnfather, Chris (CON - Newstead)
cllr.chris.barnfather@nottscc.gov.uk
Bobo, Victor (CON - Mansfield West)
cllr.victor.bobo@nottscc.gov.uk
Bosnjak, Joyce (LAB - Mansfield North)
cllr.joyce.bosnjak@nottscc.gov.uk
Butler, Richard (CON - Cotgrave)
cllr.richard.butler@nottscc.gov.uk
Carr, Steve (LD - Beeston North)
cllr.steve.carr@nottscc.gov.uk
Carroll, Steve (LAB - Sutton in Ashfield East)
cllr.steven.carroll@nottscc.gov.uk
Clarke, Allen (CON - Carlton East)
cllr.allen.clarke@nottscc.gov.uk
Clarke, John (LAB - Carlton East)
cllr.john.clarke@nottscc.gov.uk
Clarke, Gerald (CON - Arnold North)
cllr.ged.clarke@nottscc.gov.uk
Cooper, Barrie (CON - West Bridgford Central and South)
cllr.barrie.coopers@nottscc.gov.uk
Cottee, John (CON - Keyworth)
cllr.john.cottee@nottscc.gov.uk
Cox, Michael (CON - West Bridgford Central and South)
cllr.michael.cox@nottscc.gov.uk
Creamer, Jim (LAB - Carlton West)
cllr.jim.creamer@nottscc.gov.uk
Cross, Bob (IND - Mansfield East)
bob.cross@nottscc.gov.uk
Dobson, Vincent (CON - Collingham)
conservative.group@nottscc.gov.uk
Doddy, John (CON - Chilwell and Toton)
Fielding, Sybil (LAB - Worksop North)
cllr.sybil.fielding@nottscc.gov.uk
Garner, Stephen (IND - Mansfield South)
cllr.stephen.garner@nottscc.gov.uk
Gent, Michelle (LD - Sutton in Ashfield Central)
cllr.michelle.gent@nottscc.gov.uk
Gilfoyle, Glynn (LAB - Worksop East)
cllr.glyn.gilfoyle@nottscc.gov.uk
Girling, Keith (CON - Newark West)
cllr.keith.girling@nottscc.gov.uk
Greaves, Kevin (LAB - Worksop West)
cllr.kevin.greaves@nottscc.gov.uk
Hempsall, John (CON - Tuxford)
cllr.john.hempsall@nottscc.gov.uk
Heptinstall, Stan (LD - Bramcote and Stapleford)
cllr.stan.heptinstall@nottscc.gov.uk
Irvine, Tom (UKIP - Hucknall)
cllr.tom.irvine@nottscc.gov.uk
Jackson, Richard (CON - Chilwell and Toton)
cllr.richard.jackson@nottscc.gov.uk
Kempster, Rod (CON - Arnold South)
cllr.rod.kempster@nottscc.gov.uk
Kerry, Eric (CON - Beeston South and Attenborough)
cllr.eric.kerry@nottscc.gov.uk
Knight, John (LAB - Kirkby in Ashfield North)
cllr.john.knight@nottscc.gov.uk
Laughton, Bruce (CON - Southwell and Caunton)
cllr.bruce.laughton@nottscc.gov.uk
Longdon, Keith (LD - Eastwood)
cllr.keith.longdon@nottscc.gov.uk
Madden, Rachel (LD - Kirkby in Ashfield South)
cllr.rachel.madden@nottscc.gov.uk
Merry, Geoff (IND - Blidworth)
cllr.geoff.merry@nottscc.gov.uk
Murphy, Mick (CON - Hucknall)
cllr.mick.murphy@nottscc.gov.uk
Owen, Philip (CON - Nuthall)
cllr.philip.owen@nottscc.gov.uk
Place, Sheila (LAB - Blyth and Harworth)
cllr.sheila.place@nottscc.gov.uk
Pulk, Darrell (LAB - Carlton West)
cllr.darrell.pulk@nottscc.gov.uk
Quigley, Wendy (CON - Retford East)
Quigley, Mike (CON - Retford West)
cllr.mike.quigley@nottscc.gov.uk
Rhodes, Alan (LAB - Worksop North East and Carlton)
cllr.alan.rhodes@nottscc.gov.uk
Rigby, Ken (LD - Kimberley and Trowell)
cllr.ken.rigby@nottscc.gov.uk
Rostance, Kevin (CON - Hucknall)
cllr.kevin.rostance@nottscc.gov.uk
Saddington, Sue (CON - Farndon and Muskham)
cllr.susan.saddington@nottscc.gov.uk
Shepherd, Melvyn (CON - Arnold South)
cllr.melvyn.shepherd@nottscc.gov.uk
Smedley, Stella (LAB - Ollerton)
cllr.stella.smedley@nottscc.gov.uk
Spencer, Mark (CON - Calverton)
cllr.mark.spencer@nottscc.gov.uk
Stendall, June (IND - Mansfield West)
cllr.june.stendall@nottscc.gov.uk
Stewart, Andy (CON - Farnsfield and Lowdham)
cllr.andy.stewart@nottscc.gov.uk
Sykes, Lynn (CON - Soar Valley)
cllr.lynn.sykes@nottscc.gov.uk
Taylor, David (CON - Beauvale)
cllr.david.taylor@nottscc.gov.uk
Tsimbiridis, Parry (LAB - Mansfield North)
cllr.parry.tsimbiridis@nottscc.gov.uk
Turner, Gail (IND - Selston)
cllr.gail.turner@nottscc.gov.uk
Walker, Keith (CON - Balderton)
cllr.keith.walker@nottscc.gov.uk
Wallace, Stuart (CON - Newark East)
cllr.stuart.wallace@nottscc.gov.uk
Wheeler, Gordon (CON - West Bridgford West)

cllr.gordon.wheeler@nottscc.gov.uk
Winterton, Chris (LAB - Mansfield South)
cllr.chris.winterton@nottscc.gov.uk
Wombwell, Brian (LD - Bramcote and Stapleford)
cllr.brian.wombwell@nottscc.gov.uk
Wright, Martin (IND - Mansfield East)
cllr.martin.wright@nottscc.gov.uk
Yates, Liz (CON - Misterton)
cllr.liz.yates@nottscc.gov.uk
Zadrozny, Jason (LD - Sutton in Ashfield North)
cllr.jason.zadrozny@nottscc.gov.uk

POLITICAL COMPOSITION
CON: 35, LAB: 15, LD: 9, IND: 6, UKIP: 1

COMMITTEE CHAIRS
Adult Social Care & Health: Mr Kevin Rostance
Children & Young People: Mr Philip Owen
Community Safety: Mr Mick Murphy
Culture: Mr John Cottee
Early Years & Youth Services: Ms Lynn Sykes
Economic Development: Mr Keith Girling
Environment & Sustainability: Mr Richard Butler
Finance & Property: Mr Reg Adair
Health & Wellbeing: Mr Gerald Clarke
Overview & Scrutiny: Ms Joyce Bosnjak
Pensions: Mr Michael Cox
Performance Management: Mr Gordon Wheeler
Personnel: Mr Andy Stewart
Planning & Licensing: Mr Chris Barnfather

NUNEATON & BEDWORTH D

Nuneaton & Bedworth Borough Council, Town Hall, Nuneaton CV11 5AA ☎ 024 7637 6376 🖷 024 7637 6583
💻 www.nuneatonandbedworth.gov.uk

FACTS & FIGURES
Police Authority: Warwickshire Police Authority
Health Authority: NHS West Midlands
Learning and Skills Council: West Midlands
Parliamentary Constituencies: Nuneaton
EU Constituencies: West Midlands
Election Frequency: Elections are biennial
Twinning: Roanne (France); Guadalajara (Spain); Cottbus (Germany)

PRINCIPAL OFFICERS
Chief Executive: Mr Alan Franks, Managing Director, Town Hall, Nuneaton CV11 5AA ☎ 024 7637 6438
🖱 alan.franks@nuneatonandbedworth.gov.uk

Senior Management: Mrs Dawn Dawson, Assistant Director - Housing & Communities, Town Hall, Nuneaton CV11 5AA
☎ 024 7637 6408 🖱 dawn.dawson@nuneatonandbedworth.gov.uk

Senior Management: Mrs Simone Donaghy, Assistant Director - Corporate Finance & Procurement, Town Hall, Nuneaton CV11 5AA ☎ 024 7637 6264
🖱 simone.donaghy@nuneatonandbedworth.gov.uk

Architect, Building / Property Services: Mr Brent Davis, Assistant Director - Assets & Street Services, Council House, Nuneaton CV11 5AA ☎ 024 7637 6347 🖷 024 7637 6465
🖱 brent.davis@nuneatonandbedworth.gov.uk

Building Control: Mr Kevin Bunsell, Head of Building Control, Town Hall, Nuneaton CV11 5AA ☎ 024 7637 6521; 024 7637 6521
🖱 kevin.bunsell@nuneatonandbedworth.gov.uk

PR / Communications: Mr Ben Coates, Communications Officer, Town Hall, Nuneaton CV11 5AA ☎ 024 7637 6321
🖱 ben.coates@nuneatonandbedworth.gov.uk

Corporate Services: Mrs Linda Downes, Head of Internal Audit, Town Hall, Nuneaton CV11 5AA ☎ 024 7637 6260
🖱 linda.downes@nuneatonandbedworth.gov.uk

Economic Development: Mr Les Snowdon, Head of Estates & Town Centres, Town Hall, Nuneaton CV11 5AA ☎ 024 7637 6376
🖱 les.snowdon@nuneatonandbedworth.gov.uk

Electoral Registration: Mrs Debbie Davies, Principal Democratic Services Offices, Town Hall, Nuneaton CV11 5AA ☎ 024 7637 6320 🖱 debbie.davies@nuneatonandbedworth.gov.uk

Environmental Health: Mr Ian Powell, Assistant Director - Regeneration & Public Protection, Town Hall, Nuneaton CV11 5AA
☎ 024 7637 6396 🖷 0870 608 9492
🖱 ian.powell@nuneatonandbedworth.gov.uk

Estates, Property & Valuation: Mr Les Snowdon, Head of Estates & Town Centres, Town Hall, Nuneaton CV11 5AA
☎ 024 7637 6376 🖱 les.snowdon@nuneatonandbedworth.gov.uk

Events Manager: Mr Andrew Daw, Communication & Civic Events Manager, Town Hall, Nuneaton CV11 5AA ☎ 024 7637 6372 🖱 andrew.daw@nuneatonandbedworth.gov.uk

Fleet Management: Mr George Harvey, Transport Engineer, St. Mary's Road Depot, Nuneaton CV11 5AR ☎ 024 7637 6029
🖷 024 7637 6032 🖱 george.harvey@nuneatonandbedworth.gov.uk

Health and Safety: Mr Paul Lynch, Head of Human Resources, Town Hall, Nuneaton CV11 5AA ☎ 024 7637 6190 🖷 0870 608 9463 🖱 paul.lynch@nuneatonandbedworth.gov.uk

Housing Maintenance: Mr Brent Davis, Assistant Director - Assets & Street Services, Council House, Nuneaton CV11 5AA
☎ 024 7637 6347 🖷 024 7637 6465
🖱 brent.davis@nuneatonandbedworth.gov.uk

Legal: Mr Philip Richardson, Assistant Director - Governance & Recreation, Town Hall, Nuneaton CV11 5AA ☎ 024 7637 6376
🖷 0870 608 9457 🖱 philip.richardson@nuneatonandbedworth.gov.uk

Licensing: Mr Ian Powell, Assistant Director - Regeneration & Public Protection, Town Hall, Nuneaton CV11 5AA ☎ 024 7637 6396 🖷 0870 608 9492 🖱 ian.powell@nuneatonandbedworth.gov.uk

Member Services: Mrs Pam Matthews, Senior Democratic Services Officer, Town Hall, Nuneaton CV11 5AA ☎ 024 7637 6204 🖱 pam.matthews@nuneatonandbedworth.gov.uk

Recycling & Waste Minimisation: Ms Sue Cummine, Recycling Officer, St. Mary's Road Depot, Nuneaton CV11 5AR ☎ 024 7637 6025 ✉ sue.cummine@nuneatonandbedworth.gov.uk

Tourism: Ms Rose Selwyn, Economic Development Officer, Town Hall, Nuneaton CV11 5AA ☎ 024 7637 6490 🖷 0870 608 5124 ✉ rose.selwyn@nuneatonandbedworth.gov.uk

Waste Collection and Disposal: Mrs Sarah Elliot, Waste & Cleansing Manager, Town Hall, Nuneaton CV11 5AA ☎ 024 7637 6049 ✉ sarah.elliot@nuneatonandbedworth.gov.uk

Waste Management: Mrs Sarah Elliot, Waste & Cleansing Manager, Town Hall, Nuneaton CV11 5AA ☎ 024 7637 6049 ✉ sarah.elliot@nuneatonandbedworth.gov.uk

MEMBERS OF THE COUNCIL (34)

***Mayor:* Haynes**, John (LAB - Bede)
john.haynes@nuneatonandbedworth.gov.uk
***Leader of the Council:* Harvey**, Dennis (LAB - Camp Hill)
dennis.harvey@nuneatonandbedworth.gov.uk
***Deputy Leader of the Council:* Jackson**, Julie (LAB - Wem Brook)
julie.jackson@nuneatonandbedworth.gov.uk
Aldington, Danny (LAB - Heath)
danny.aldington@nuneatonandbedworth.gov.uk
Beaumont, John (LAB - Bulkington)
john.beaumont@nuneatonandbedworth.gov.uk
Carr, David (CON - St Nicholas)
david.carr@nuneatonandbedworth.gov.uk
Copland, Robert (LAB - Poplar)
bob.copland@nuneatonandbedworth.gov.uk
Doughty, Sara (LAB - Exhall)
sara.doughty@nuneatonandbedworth.gov.uk
Foster, James (CON - St Nicholas)
james.foster@nuneatonandbedworth.gov.uk
Fowler, Dianne (LAB - Slough)
dianne.fowler@nuneatonandbedworth.gov.uk
Fowler, Victoria (LAB - Bar Pool)
victoria.fowler@nuneatonandbedworth.gov.uk
Gilbert, Peter (CON - Attleborough)
peter.gilbert@nuneatonandbedworth.gov.uk
Glass, John (LAB - Poplar)
john.glass@nuneatonandbedworth.gov.uk
Grant, Matthew (CON - Galley Common)
matthew.grant@nuneatonandbedworth.gov.uk
Grant, Nicholas (CON - Whitestone)
nick.grant@nuneatonandbedworth.gov.uk
Hancox, William (LAB - Bede)
bill.hancox@nuneatonandbedworth.gov.uk
Hawkes, Brian (LAB - Heath)
brian.hawkes@nuneatonandbedworth.gov.uk
Hickling, Paul (LAB - Galley Common)
paul.hickling@nuneatonandbedworth.gov.uk
Kondakor, Keith (GRN - Weddington)
keith.kondakor@nuneatonandbedworth.gov.uk
Lloyd, Anthony (LAB - Slough)
anthony.lloyd@nuneatonandbedworth.gov.uk
Lloyd, Ian (LAB - Camp Hill)
ian.lloyd@nuneatonandbedworth.gov.uk
Longden, Barry (LAB - Kingswood)
barry.longden@nuneatonandbedworth.gov.uk
Navarro, Don (LAB - Arbury)
don.navarro@nuneatonandbedworth.gov.uk
O'Brien, Desmond (CON - Bulkington)
des.o'brien@nuneatonandbedworth.gov.uk
Philips, Neil (LAB - Abbey)
neil.phillips@nuneatonandbedworth.gov.uk
Pomfrett, Gwynne (LAB - Bar Pool)
gwynne.pomfrett@nuneatonandbedworth.gov.uk
Sheppard, William (LAB - Wem Brook)
william.sheppard@nuneatonandbedworth.gov.uk
Sheppard, Jill (LAB - Abbey)
jill.sheppard@nuneatonandbedworth.gov.uk
Smith, Gerald (CON - Weddington)
gerald.smith@nuneatonandbedworth.gov.uk
Tandy, June (LAB - Attleborough)
june.tandy@nuneatonandbedworth.gov.uk
Taylor, Roma Ann (LAB - Exhall)
roma.taylor@nuneatonandbedworth.gov.uk
Watkins, Christopher (LAB - Kingswood)
christopher.watkins@nuneatonandbedworth.gov.uk
Wilson, Kristofer (CON - Whitestone)
kristofer.wilson@nuneatonandbedworth.gov.uk
Young, Kevin (LAB - Arbury)
kevin.young@nuneatonandbedworth.gov.uk

POLITICAL COMPOSITION

LAB: 25, CON: 8, GRN: 1

COMMITTEE CHAIRS

Arts & Leisure: Mr Ian Lloyd
Audit: Mr John Haynes
Economic & Corporate Overview & Scrutiny (Scrutiny): Mr Brian Hawkes
Finance & Civic Affairs: Mr Dennis Harvey
Health & Environment (Scrutiny): Mr Neil Philips
Housing, Health & Communities: Ms Sara Doughty
Licensing: Mr Robert Copland
Planning & Development: Mr Danny Aldington
Planning & Environment: Mr Don Navarro
Planning Applications: Mr William Hancox

OADBY & WIGSTON D

Oadby & Wigston Borough Council, Council Offices, Station Road, Wigston LE18 2DR ☎ 0116 288 8961 🖷 0116 288 7828 💻 www.oadby-wigston.gov.uk

FACTS & FIGURES

Police Authority: Leicestershire Police Authority
Health Authority: East Midlands Strategic Health Authority
Learning and Skills Council: East Midlands
Parliamentary Constituencies: Harborough
EU Constituencies: East Midlands
Election Frequency: Elections are of whole council
Twinning: Maromme (France); Norderstedt (Germany)

PRINCIPAL OFFICERS

Chief Executive: Mr Mark Hall, Chief Executive, Council Offices, Station Road, Wigston LE18 2DR ☎ 0116 257 2600 🖷 0116 288 7828 ✉ mark.hall@oadby-wigston.gov.uk

Deputy Chief Executive: Mr David Walton, Interim Director of Resources, Council Offices, Station Road, Wigston LE18 2DR ☎ 0116 257 2621 🖷 0116 257 2757 ✉ david.walton@oadby-wigston.gov.uk

Senior Management: Mrs Anne Court, Director of Service Delivery, Council Offices, Station Road, Wigston LE18 2DR ☎ 0116 257 2602 🖷 0116 288 7828 ✉ anne.court1@oadby-wigston.gov.uk

Building Control: Mr Rob Harbour, Director of Regulation & Regeneration, Council Offices, Station Road, Wigston LE18 2DR ☎ 0116 257 2733 🖷 0116 288 7828 ✉ rob.harbour@oadby-wigston.gov.uk

PR / Communications: Mrs Gurpreet Santini, Public Relations Officer, Council Offices, Station Road, Wigston LE18 2DR ☎ 0116 257 2712 🖷 0116 288 7828 ✉ gurpreet.santini@oadby-wigston.gov.uk

Community Safety: Mrs Tracy Gaskin, Community Safety Organiser, Council Offices, Station Road, Wigston LE18 2DR ☎ 0116 257 2735 🖷 0116 288 7828 ✉ tracy.gaskin@oadby-wigston.gov.uk

Computer Management: Mr Paul Langham, ICT Manager, Council Offices, Station Road, Wigston LE18 2DR ☎ 01455 255995 🖷 0116 288 7828 ✉ paul.langham@oadby-wigston.gov.uk

Contracts: Mr Nick Ainsworth-Smith, Senior Contracts Manager, The Depot, Wigston Road, Oadby LE2 5JE ☎ 0116 257 2835 🖷 0116 271 1459 ✉ nick.ainsworth-smith@oadby-wigston.gov.uk

Customer Service: Mr Nick Ainsworth-Smith, Senior Contracts Manager, The Depot, Wigston Road, Oadby LE2 5JE ☎ 0116 257 2835 🖷 0116 271 1459 ✉ nick.ainsworth-smith@oadby-wigston.gov.uk

Economic Development: Mr Duncan Elliott, Joint Economic Development Officer, Council Offices, Station Road, Wigston LE18 2DR ☎ 0116 257 2644 ✉ duncan.elliott@oadby-wigston.gov.uk

Economic Development: Mr Rob Harbour, Director of Regulation & Regeneration, Council Offices, Station Road, Wigston LE18 2DR ☎ 0116 257 2733 🖷 0116 288 7828 ✉ rob.harbour@oadby-wigston.gov.uk

Economic Development: Ms Claire Peters, Joint Economic Development Officer, Council Offices, Station Road, Wigston LE18 2DR ☎ 0116 257 2644 ✉ claire.peters@oadby-wigston.gov.uk

Economic Development: Ms Judith Sturley, Joint Economic Development Officer, Council Offices, Station Road, Wigston LE18 2DR ☎ 0116 257 2644 ✉ judith.sturley@oadby-wigston.gov.uk

Electoral Registration: Mr Gary Waterfield, Senior Legal & Lisencing Officer, Council Offices, Station Road, Wigston LE18 2DR ☎ 0116 257 2604 🖷 0117 288 7828 ✉ gary.waterfield@oadby-wigston.gov.uk

Environmental Health: Mr Rob Harbour, Director of Regulation & Regeneration, Council Offices, Station Road, Wigston LE18 2DR ☎ 0116 257 2733 🖷 0116 288 7828 ✉ rob.harbour@oadby-wigston.gov.uk

Estates, Property & Valuation: Mr Dean Allen, Principal Legal & Administration Officer, Council Offices, Station Road, Wigston LE18 2DR ☎ 0116 257 2605 🖷 0116 288 7828 ✉ dean.allen@oadby-wigston.gov.uk

Finance and Treasurer: Mr Sanjiv Kohli, 151 Officer, Council Offices, Station Road, Wigston LE18 2DR ☎ 0116 257 8961 ✉ sanjiv.kohli@oadby-wigston.gov.uk

Fleet Management: Mr Jez Crooks, Contracts Operations Manager, The Depot, Wigston Road, Oadby LE2 5JE ☎ 0116 257 2834 🖷 0116 271 1459 ✉ jez.crooks@oadby-wigston.gov.uk

Grounds Maintenance: Mr Simon Lucas, Grounds Maintenance Supervisor, The Depot, Wigston Road, Oadby LE2 5JE ☎ 0116 257 2839 🖷 0116 271 1459 ✉ simon.lucas@oadby-wigston.gov.uk

Housing: Mr Simon Folwell, Head of Housing, Council Offices, Station Road, Wigston LE18 2DR ☎ 0116 257 2692 🖷 0116 288 7828 ✉ simon.folwell@oadby-wigston.gov.uk

Housing Maintenance: Mr Alan Purdie, Senior Maintenance Officer, Council Offices, Station Road, Wigston LE18 2DR ☎ 0116 257 2613 🖷 0116 288 7828 ✉ alan.purdie@oadby-wigston.gov.uk

Legal: Mrs Anne Court, Director of Service Delivery, Council Offices, Station Road, Wigston LE18 2DR ☎ 0116 257 2602 🖷 0116 288 7828 ✉ anne.court1@oadby-wigston.gov.uk

Leisure and Cultural Services: Ms Avril Lennox, Leisure Development Officer, Council Offices, Station Road, Wigston LE18 2DR ☎ 0116 257 2735 🖷 0116 288 7828 ✉ avril.lennox@oadby-wigston.gov.uk

Licensing: Mr Rob Harbour, Director of Regulation & Regeneration, Council Offices, Station Road, Wigston LE18 2DR ☎ 0116 257 2733 🖷 0116 288 7828 ✉ rob.harbour@oadby-wigston.gov.uk

Licensing: Mr Gary Waterfield, Senior Legal & Lisencing Officer, Council Offices, Station Road, Wigston LE18 2DR ☎ 0116 257 2604 🖷 0117 288 7828 ✉ gary.waterfield@oadby-wigston.gov.uk

Parking: Mr Jez Crooks, Contracts Operations Manager, The Depot, Wigston Road, Oadby LE2 5JE ☎ 0116 257 2834 🖷 0116 271 1459 ✉ jez.crooks@oadby-wigston.gov.uk

Planning: Mr Rob Harbour, Director of Regulation & Regeneration, Council Offices, Station Road, Wigston LE18 2DR ☎ 0116 257 2733 🖷 0116 288 7828 ✉ rob.harbour@oadby-wigston.gov.uk

Procurement: Mr Paul Loveday, Head of Finance, Council Offices, Station Road, Wigston LE18 2DR ☎ 0116 257 2750 🖷 0116 288 7828 ✉ paul.loveday@oadby-wigston.gov.uk

Recycling & Waste Minimisation: Mrs Reshma Vanza-Adam, Waste Management Officer, The Depot, Wigston Road, Oadby LE2 5JE ☎ 0116 257 2848 🖷 0116 271 1459 ✉ reshma.vanza-adam@oadby-wigston.gov.uk

Regeneration: Mr Rob Harbour, Director of Regulation &

Regeneration, Council Offices, Station Road, Wigston LE18 2DR ☎ 0116 257 2733 🖷 0116 288 7828 ✉ rob.harbour@oadby-wigston.gov.uk

Street Scene: Mr Jez Crooks, Contracts Operations Manager, The Depot, Wigston Road, Oadby LE2 5JE ☎ 0116 257 2834 🖷 0116 271 1459 ✉ jez.crooks@oadby-wigston.gov.uk

Town Centre: Mr Rob Harbour, Director of Regulation & Regeneration, Council Offices, Station Road, Wigston LE18 2DR ☎ 0116 257 2733 🖷 0116 288 7828 ✉ rob.harbour@oadby-wigston.gov.uk

Transport: Mr Jez Crooks, Contracts Operations Manager, The Depot, Wigston Road, Oadby LE2 5JE ☎ 0116 257 2834 🖷 0116 271 1459 ✉ jez.crooks@oadby-wigston.gov.uk

Waste Collection and Disposal: Mr Neil Smith, Refuse Collection & Recycling Supervisor, Council Offices, Station Road, Wigston LE18 2DR ☎ 0116 257 2843 🖷 0116 271 1459 ✉ neil.smith@oadby-wigston.gov.uk

Waste Management: Mr Nick Ainsworth-Smith, Senior Contracts Manager, The Depot, Wigston Road, Oadby LE2 5JE ☎ 0116 257 2835 🖷 0116 271 1459 ✉ nick.ainsworth-smith@oadby-wigston.gov.uk

MEMBERS OF THE COUNCIL (26)

Bentley, Lee (LD - All Saints)
lee.bentley@oadby-wigston.gov.uk
Boulter, Bill (LD - Wigston Fields)
bill.boulter@oadby-wigston.gov.uk
Boyce, John (LD - South Wigston)
john.boyce@oadby-wigston.gov.uk
Broadley, Linda (LD - St Wolstans)
linda.broadley@oadby-wigston.gov.uk
Broadley, Frank (LD - St Wolstans)
frank.broadley@oadby-wigston.gov.uk
Carter, David (LD - Oadby St Peters)
david.carter@oadby-wigston.gov.uk
Chamberlain, Marie (LD - Meadowcourt)
marie.chamberlain@oadby-wigston.gov.uk
Charlesworth, Michael (LD - All Saints)
michael.charlesworth@oadby-wigston.gov.uk
Connell, Liz (LD - All Saints)
liz.connell@oadby-wigston.gov.uk
Darr, Latif (LD - Brocks Hill)
latif.darr@oadby-wigston.gov.uk
Dave, Bhupendra (CON - Woodlands)
bhupendra.dave@oadby-wigston.gov.uk
Dickinson, Sarah (LD - Grange)
sarah.dickingson@oadby-wigston.gov.uk
Eaton, Robert (LD - Meadowcourt)
robert.eaton@oadby-wigston.gov.uk
Eaton, Lynda (LD - St Wolstans)
lynda.eaton@oadby-wigston.gov.uk
Gamble, Dean (LD - Oadby Uplands)
dean.gamble@oadby-wigston.gov.uk
Gore, Jillian (CON - Meadowcourt)
jillian.gore@oadby-wigston.gov.uk
Haq, Samia Zaffar (LD - Oadby Uplands)
samia.haq@oadby-wigston.gov.uk
Kanabar, Rupa (LD - Woodlands)
rupa.kanabar@oadby-wigston.gov.uk
Kaufman, Jeffrey (LD - Brocks Hill)
jeffrey.kaufman@oadby-wigston.gov.uk
Kaufman, Lily (LD - Oadby St Peters)
lily.kaufman@oadby-wigston.gov.uk
Loydall, Kevin (LD - Wigston Fields)
kevin.loydall@oadby-wigston.gov.uk
Loydall, Helen (LD - Wigston Fields)
helen.loydall@oadby-wigston.gov.uk
Morris, Richard (LD - South Wigston)
richard.morris@oadby-wigston.gov.uk
Morris, Sharon (LD - South Wigston)
sharon.morris@oadby-wigston.gov.uk
Swift, Peter (CON - Grange)
peter.swift@oadby-wigston.gov.uk
Thakor, Ravendra (CON - Grange)
ravendra.thakor@oadby-wigston.gov.uk

POLITICAL COMPOSITION

LD: 22, CON: 4

COMMITTEE CHAIRS

Children & Young People: Mr Richard Morris
Development Control: Mr Lee Bentley
Licensing & Regulatory: Mrs Helen Loydall
Overview & Scrutiny: Mr Jeffrey Kaufman
Policy, Finance & Development: Mrs Sharon Morris
Resources & Regeneration: Mrs Sharon Morris
Service Delivery: Mr Bill Boulter
Service Development: Mrs Sharon Morris
Standards: Mr Michael Charlesworth

OLDHAM M

Oldham Metropolitan Borough Council, Civic Centre, West Street, Oldham OL1 1UG ☎ 0161 770 3000 🖷 0161 770 5185 💻 www.oldham.gov.uk

FACTS & FIGURES

Police Authority: Greater Manchester Police Authority
Health Authority: North West Strategic Health Authority
Learning and Skills Council: North West
Parliamentary Constituencies: Ashton under Lyne, Oldham East and Saddleworth, Oldham West and Royton
EU Constituencies: North West
Election Frequency: Elections are by thirds
Twinning: Kranj (former Yugoslavia); Chadderton: Geesthacht (Germany); Failsworth: Landsberg (Germany)

PRINCIPAL OFFICERS

Chief Executive: Mr Charlie Parker, Chief Executive, Civic Centre, West Street, Oldham OL1 1UG ☎ 0161 770 4190 🖷 0161 770 4045 ✉ charlie.parker@oldham.gov.uk

Assistant Chief Executive: Ms Carolyn Wilkins, Assistant Chief Executive, Civic Centre, West Street, Oldham OL1 1UG ☎ 0161 770 5532 ✉ carolyn.wilkins@oldham.gov.uk

Senior Management: Ms Emma Alexander, Executive Director - Performance Capacity & Services, Civic Centre, West Street, Oldham OL1 1UW ☎ 0161 770 5157 ✉ emma.alexander@oldham.gov.uk

Senior Management: Mrs Clare Fish, Chief of Staff, Civic Centre, West Street, Oldham OL1 1UG ☎ 0161 770 5442 ✉ clare.fish@oldham.gov.uk

Senior Management: Mr Michael Jameson, Interim Executive Director - People, Communities & Society, Civic Centre, West Street, Oldham OL1 1UG ☎ 0161 770 4200 ✉ michael.jameson@oldham.gov.uk

Senior Management: Ms Elaine McLean, Executive Director - Economy, Place & Skills, Civic Centre, West Street, Oldham OL1 1UW ☎ 0161 770 4079 ✉ elaine.mclean@oldham.gov.uk

Catering Services: Ms Anne Burns, Catering Manager, Civic Centre, West Street, Oldham OL1 1UG ☎ 0116 770 3000

Children / Youth Services: Mr Neil Consterdine, Head of Integrated Youth, Civic Centre, West Street, Oldham OL1 1UG ☎ 0161 770 8734 ✉ neil.consterdine@oldham.gov.uk

Children / Youth Services: Mr Michael Jameson, Interim Executive Director - People, Communities & Society, Civic Centre, West Street, Oldham OL1 1UG ☎ 0161 770 4200 ✉ michael.jameson@oldham.gov.uk

Civil Registration: Ms Carole Baggaley, Senior Registrar, Chadderton Town Hall, Oldham OL9 6PP ☎ 0161 770 8960 ✉ carole.baggaley@oldham.gov.uk

PR / Communications: Mrs Shelley Kipling, Senior Internal Communications Officer, Room 437, Civic Centre, West Street, Oldham OL1 1UG ☎ 0161 770 3792 🖷 0161 770 4045 ✉ shelley.kipling@oldham.gov.uk

PR / Communications: Mr Carl Marsden, Senior Media & Communications Officer, Room 437, Civic Centre, West Street, Oldham OL1 1UG ☎ 0161 770 4323 🖷 0161 770 4045 ✉ carl.marsden@oldham.gov.uk

Community Safety: Ms Colette Kelly, Assistant Executive Director - Neighbourhoods, Level 11, Civic Centre, Oldham OL1 1UT ☎ 0161 770 3103 ✉ colette.kelly@oldham.gov.uk

Computer Management: Mr Andrew Kendall, Managing Director - Unity Partnership, Henshaw House, Cheapside, Oldham OL1 1NY ☎ 0161 770 5170 ✉ andrew.kendall@unitypartnership.com

Consumer Protection and Trading Standards: Mr Mark Reynolds, Assistant Executive Director - Housing & Public Protection, Civic Centre, West Street, Oldham OL1 1UG ☎ 0161 770 5147 ✉ mark.reynolds@oldham.gov.uk

Contracts: Mrs Karen Lowes, Acting Head of Procurement, Civic Centre, West Street, Oldham OL1 1UG ☎ 0161 770 4936 ✉ karen.lowes@oldham.gov.uk

Corporate Services: Ms Clare Fish, Chief of Staff, Civic Centre, West Street, Oldham OL1 1UG ☎ 0161 770 5442 ✉ clare.fish@oldham.gov.uk

Corporate Services: Mr Ben Spinks, Assistant Executive Director - Policy, Communications & Customer Services, Civic Centre, West Street, Oldham OL1 1UG ☎ 0161 770 1085 ✉ ben.spinks@oldham.gov.uk

Customer Service: Ms Suzanne Heywood, Head of Customer Services, PO Box 160, Civic Centre, West Street, Oldham OL1 1UG ☎ 0161 770 4905 ✉ suzanne.heywood@oldham.gov.uk

Economic Development: Ms Michelle Carr, Assistant Executive Director - Economy, Skills & Place Shaping, Oldham Business Centre, Cromwell Street, Oldham OL1 1BB ☎ 0161 770 4475 ✉ michelle.carr@oldham.gov.uk

Education: Mr Michael Jameson, Assistant Executive Director - Children & Young People, Civic Centre, West Street, Oldham OL1 1XL ☎ 0161 770 4200 ✉ michael.jameson@oldham.gov.uk

Electoral Registration: Ms Julie Bruce, Deputy Electoral & Land Charges Manager, Civic Centre, West Street, Oldham OL1 1UG ☎ 0161 770 4712 ✉ julie.bruce@oldham.gov.uk

Emergency Planning: Mr Gary May, Civil Resilience Officer, Sir Robert Peacock House, Vulcan Street, Oldham OL1 4LA ☎ 0161 770 4699 ✉ gary.may@oldham.gov.uk

Environmental / Technical Services: Ms Elaine McLean, Executive Director - Economy, Place & Skills, Civic Centre, West Street, Oldham OL1 1UW ☎ 0161 770 4079 ✉ elaine.mclean@oldham.gov.uk

Environmental Health: Mr Graham Boundy, Acting Head of Public Protection, Sir Robert Peacock House, Vulcan Street, Oldham OL4 1LA ☎ 0161 770 4494 ✉ graham.boundy@oldham.gov.uk

Facilities: Mr Graham Dixon, Facilities Manager, Civic Centre, West Street, Oldham OL1 1UG ☎ 0161 770 4028 ✉ graham.dixon@oldham.gov.uk

Finance and Treasurer: Mr Steven Mair, Borough Treasurer, Civic Centre, West Street, Oldham OL1 1UG ☎ 0161 770 4900 ✉ steven.mair@oldham.gov.uk

Finance and Treasurer: Ms Anne Ryans, Assistant Director - Finance, PO Box 196, Civic Centre, West Street, Oldham OL1 1UG ☎ 0161 770 4902 ✉ anne.ryans@oldham.gov.uk

Fleet Management: Mr Martin Hamer, Fleet Manager, Civic Centre, West Street, Oldham OL1 1UG ☎ 0161 770 3000

Grounds Maintenance: Mr Steven Smith, Parks Manager, Henshaw House, Cheapside, Oldham OL1 1NY ☎ 0161 770 4642 🖷 0161 770 3069 ✉ steve.smith@oldham.gov.uk

Health and Safety: Ms Julie Wood, Group Manager - Health, Safety & Wellbeing, Civic Centre, West Street, Oldham OL1 1UG ☎ 0161 770 8989 ✉ julie.wood@oldham.gov.uk

Highways: Mr Christopher Tunstall, Interim Service Director - Highways, Henshaw House, Cheapside, Oldham OL1 1NY ☎ 0161 770 8898 🖷 0161 770 3410 ✉ christopher.tunstall@oldham.gov.uk

Housing: Mr Mark Reynolds, Assistant Executive Director - Housing & Public Protection, Level 11, Civic Centre, West Street, Oldham OL1 1UG ☎ 0161 770 5147 ✉ mark.reynolds@oldham.gov.uk

Legal: Mr Paul Entwistle, Borough Solicitor, PO Box 33, Civic Centre, West Street, Oldham OL1 1UL ☎ 0161 770 4822 ✉ paul.entwistle@oldham.gov.uk

Leisure and Cultural Services: Ms Sheena MacFarlane, Head of Heritage Libraries & Art, PO Box 335, Civic Centre, West Street, Oldham OL1 1XJ ☎ 0161 770 4664 🖷 0161 770 4652 ✉ sheena.macfarlane@oldham.gov.uk

Licensing: Mr John Garforth, Principal Licensing Officer, Sir Robert Peacock House, Vulcan Street, Oldham OL1 4LA ☎ 0161 770 5026 ✉ john.garforth@oldham.gov.uk

Lifelong Learning: Ms Lynda Fairhurst, Head of Lifelong Learning, Civic Centre, West Street, Oldham OL1 1UG ☎ 0161 770 4278 ✉ lynda.fairhurst@oldham.gov.uk

Lighting: Mr John McAuley, Street Lighting Manager, Lees Road Depot, Lees Road, Oldham OL4 1HD ☎ 0161 770 1669 ✉ john.mcauley@oldham.gov.uk

Member Services: Mrs Clare Fish, Chief of Staff, Civic Centre, West Street, Oldham OL1 1UG ☎ 0161 770 5442 ✉ clare.fish@oldham.gov.uk

Partnerships: Mr Darren Jones, Assistant Executive Director - Strategic Projects & Investment, Civic Centre, West Street, Oldham OL1 1UG

Partnerships: Mr Ben Spinks, Assistant Executive Director - Policy, Communications & Customer Services, Civic Centre, West Street, Oldham OL1 1UG ☎ 0161 770 1085 ✉ ben.spinks@oldham.gov.uk

Personnel / HR: Ms Dianne Frost, Head of People Services, Civic Centre, West Street, Oldham OL1 1UG ☎ 0161 770 4965 ✉ dianne.frost@oldham.gov.uk

Planning: Mr Philip Jobling, Head of Planning & Transport, Civic Centre, West Street, Oldham OL1 1UG ☎ 0161 770 4014 ✉ philip.jobling@oldham.gov.uk

Procurement: Mrs Karen Lowes, Acting Head of Procurement, Civic Centre, West Street, Oldham OL1 1UG ☎ 0161 770 4936 ✉ karen.lowes@oldham.gov.uk

Public Libraries: Ms Sheena MacFarlane, Head of Heritage Libraries & Art, PO Box 335, Civic Centre, West Street, Oldham OL1 1XJ ☎ 0161 770 4664 🖷 0161 770 4652 ✉ sheena.macfarlane@oldham.gov.uk

Recycling & Waste Minimisation: Ms Carol Brown, Assistant Executive Director - Environment, Civic Centre, West Street, Oldham OL1 1UG ☎ 0161 770 4452 ✉ carol.brown@oldham.gov.uk

Regeneration: Ms Imogen Fuller, Principal Regeneration Officer, 1st Floor, Oldham Business Centre, Oldham OL1 1BB ☎ 0161 770 4165 ✉ imogen.fuller@oldham.gov.uk

Road Safety: Ms Julie Williams, Road Safety Officer, Henshaw House, Cheapside, Oldham OL1 1NY ☎ 0161 770 4343 🖷 0161 770 3411 ✉ julie.e.williams@oldham.gov.uk

Social Services (Adult): Mr Paul Cassidy, Director - Adult Services, Level 10, Civic Centre, West Street, Oldham OL1 1UG ☎ 0161 770 4215 🖷 0161 770 4782 ✉ paul.cassidy@oldham.gov.uk

Social Services (Children): Mr Michael Jameson, Assistant Executive Director - Children & Young People, Civic Centre, West Street, Oldham OL1 1XL ☎ 0161 770 4200 ✉ michael.jameson@oldham.gov.uk

Staff Training: Mr John Fraine, Head of Workforce & Organisational Development, Ashwood House, Ellen Street, Oldham OL9 6QR ☎ 0161 770 8700 ✉ john.fraine@oldham.gov.uk

Street Scene: Ms Carol Brown, Assistant Executive Director - Environment, Civic Centre, West Street, Oldham OL1 1UG ☎ 0161 770 4452 ✉ carol.brown@oldham.gov.uk

Town Centre: Ms Sara Hewitt, Town Centre Manager, Level 3, Business Centre, Cromwell Street, Oldham OL1 1BB ☎ 0161 770 4516 🖷 0161 770 8306 ✉ sara.hewitt@oldham.gov.uk

Waste Collection and Disposal: Ms Carol Brown, Assistant Executive Director - Environment, West End House, Oldham OL1 1NY ☎ 0161 770 4452 ✉ carol.brown@oldham.gov.uk

Waste Management: Mr Craig Dale, Waste Management Service Manager, Moorhey Street Depot, Moorhey Street, Oldham OL4 1JF ☎ 0161 770 4441 ✉ craig.dale@oldham.gov.uk

MEMBERS OF THE COUNCIL (60)

***Mayor:* Chadderton**, Olwen (LAB - Royton North)
olwen.chadderton@oldham.gov.uk

***Leader of the Council:* McMahon**, James (LAB - Failsworth East)
cllr.j.mcmahon@oldham.gov.uk

Akhtar, Shoab (LAB - Werneth)
shoab.akhtar@oldham.gov.uk

Alcock, Mark (LD - Shaw)
mark.alcock@oldham.gov.uk

Alexander, Adrian (LAB - Saddleworth West & Lees)
cllr.a.alexander@oldham.gov.uk

Ames, Brian (LAB - Hollinwood)
brian.ames@oldham.gov.uk

Azad, Montaz Ali (LAB - Coldhurst)
cllr.m.azad@oldham.gov.uk

Ball, Cath (LAB - St. James)
cath.ball@oldham.gov.uk

Bashforth, Steven (LAB - Royton South)
steven.bashforth@oldham.gov.uk

Battye, John (LAB - Failsworth West)
john.battye@oldham.gov.uk

Beeley, Barbara (LD - Saddleworth West & Lees)
barbara.beeley@oldham.gov.uk

Blyth, Rod (LD - Shaw)
rod.blyth@oldham.gov.uk

Briggs, Norman (LAB - Failsworth East)
norman.briggs@oldham.gov.uk

Brownridge, Barbara (LAB - Chadderton North)
barbara.brownridge@oldham.gov.uk
Butterworth, Glenys (LAB - Failsworth West)
glenys.butterworth@oldham.gov.uk
Chadderton, Amanda (LAB - Royton South)
amanda.chadderton@oldham.gov.uk
Dawson, David (LAB - Failsworth East)
david.dawson@oldham.gov.uk
Dean, Peter (LAB - Waterhead)
cllr.p.dean@oldham.gov.uk
Dearden, Susan (LAB - Chadderton Central)
susan.dearden@oldham.gov.uk
Dillon, John (LD - Crompton)
john.dillon@oldham.gov.uk
Dillon, Philomena (LD - Crompton)
philomena.dillon@oldham.gov.uk
Fielding, Sean (LAB - Failsworth West)
sean.fielding@oldham.gov.uk
Fletcher, Dilys (LAB - Alexandra)
dilys.fletcher@oldham.gov.uk
Haque, Fazlul (LAB - Chadderton North)
fazlul.haque@oldham.gov.uk
Harkness, Gareth (LD - Saddleworth North)
garth.harkness@oldham.gov.uk
Harrison, Philip (LAB - Royton South)
philip.harrison@oldham.gov.uk
Harrison, Jenny (LAB - Alexandra)
Cllr.J.Harrison@oldham.gov.uk
Heffernan, Derek (LD - Saddleworth North)
derek.heffenan@oldham.gov.uk
Hibbert, David (LAB - Chadderton South)
david.hibbert@oldham.gov.uk
Hindle, Roger (LD - St. James)
roger.hindle@oldham.gov.uk
Houle, Dave (LAB - Chadderton North)
cllr.d.houle@oldham.gov.uk
Hudson, John (CON - Saddleworth South)
john.hudson@oldham.gov.uk
Hussain, Fida (LAB - Werneth)
fida.hussain@oldham.gov.uk
Iqbal, Javid (LAB - Werneth)
javid.iqbal@oldham.gov.uk
Jabbar, Abdul (LAB - Coldhurst)
abdul.jabbar@oldham.gov.uk
Judge, Bernard (LAB - Royton North)
bernard.judge@oldham.gov.uk
Larkin, Tony (LAB - Royton North)
tony.larkin@oldham.gov.uk
Malik, Abdul (LAB - Coldhurst)
McCann, John (LD - Saddleworth South)
john.mccann@oldham.gov.uk
McDonald, Hugh (LAB - Alexandra)
hugh.mcdonald@oldham.gov.uk
McLaren, Colin (LAB - Chadderton Central)
colin.mclaren@oldham.gov.uk
Moores, Eddie (LAB - Chadderton Central)
cllr.e.moores@oldham.gov.uk
Newton, Nigel (LAB - St. James)
cllr.n.newton@oldham.gov.uk
Price, Vita (LAB - Waterhead)
vita.price@oldham.gov.uk
Qumer, Shadab (LAB - St. Mary's)
shadab.qumer@oldham.gov.uk
Rehman, Kaiser (LAB - Medlock Vale)
cllr.k.rehman@oldham.gov.uk
Roughley, Alan (LD - Saddleworth North)
alanroughley@talktalk.net
Salamat, Ali Aqueel (LAB - St. Mary's)
a.a.salamat@oldham.gov.uk
Sedgwick, Valerie (LD - Saddleworth West & Lees)
val.sedgwick@oldham.gov.uk
Shah, Arooj (LAB - St. Mary's)
arooj.shah@oldham.gov.uk
Sheldon, Graham (CON - Saddleworth South)
cllr.g.sheldon@oldham.gov.uk
Shuttleworth, Graham (LAB - Chadderton South)
cllr.g.shuttleworth@oldham.gov.uk
Stretton, Jean (LAB - Hollinwood)
jean.stretton@oldham.gov.uk
Sykes, Howard (LD - Shaw)
howard.sykes@oldham.gov.uk
Thompson, Lynne (LD - Waterhead)
lynne.thompson@oldham.gov.uk
Toor, Yasmin (LAB - Medlock Vale)
yasmin.toor@oldham.gov.uk
Ur-Rehman, Ateeque (LAB - Medlock Vale)
ateeque.urrehman@oldham.gov.uk
Williams, Steve (LAB - Hollinwood)
cllr.s.williams@oldham.gov.uk
Williamson, Diane (LD - Crompton)
diane.williamson@oldham.gov.uk
Wrigglesworth, Joy (LAB - Chadderton South)
joy.wrigglesworth@oldham.gov.uk

POLITICAL COMPOSITION
LAB: 44, LD: 14, CON: 2

CABINET
Leader/ Strategic Projects & External Relations: Mr James McMahon
Deputy Leader/ Business, Skills & Town Centre: Mr Shoab Akhtar
Co-operatives & Community: Ms Barbara Brownridge
Education & Safeguarding: Mr Hugh McDonald
Finance, Human Resources & Strategic Partnerships: Mr Abdul Jabbar
Housing, Transport & Planning: Mr David Hibbert
Neighbourhoods & Devolved Services: Ms Jean Stretton
Social Services & Community Health: Mr Philip Harrison

COMMITTEE CHAIRS
Licensing: Mr Fida Hussain
Overview & Scrutiny: Mr Colin McLaren
Performance & Value for Money Overview & Scrutiny: Ms Joy Wrigglesworth
Planning: Mr John Battye

OMAGH N

Omagh District Council, Council Offices, The Grange, Mountjoy Road, Omagh BT79 7BL ☎ 028 8224 5321 🖷 028 8224 3888 ✉ info@omagh.gov.uk 💻 www.omagh.gov.uk

FACTS & FIGURES
Police Authority: Northern Ireland Policing Board
Health Authority: Western Local Commissioning Group
Learning and Skills Council: Northern Ireland
Parliamentary Constituencies: Tyrone West

EU Constituencies: Northern Ireland
Election Frequency: Elections are of whole council
Twinning: L'Haÿ Les Roses (France)

PRINCIPAL OFFICERS

Chief Executive: Mr Daniel McSorley, Interim Clerk & Chief Executive, Council Offices, The Grange, Mountjoy Road, Omagh BT79 7BL ☎ 028 8225 6206; 028 7138 2204 🖷 028 8225 2380 daniel.mcsorley@omagh.gov.uk; dmcsorley@strabanedc.com

Architect, Building / Property Services: Mr Kevin O'Gara, Chief Client Services Officer, Council Offices, The Grange, Mountjoy Road, Omagh BT79 7BL ☎ 028 8225 6200 🖷 028 8224 3888 kevin.ogara@omagh.gov.uk

Building Control: Mr Sean Kelly, District Chief Building Control Surveyor, Council Offices, The Grange, Mountjoy Road, Omagh BT79 7BL ☎ 028 8225 6201 🖷 028 8224 3888 sean.kelly@omagh.gov.uk

Civil Registration: Mrs Amy Smyton, Registrar, Council Offices, The Grange, Mountjoy Road, Omagh BT79 7BL ☎ 028 8225 6212 amy.smyton@omagh.gov.uk

PR / Communications: Mrs Elizabeth Harkin, Public Relations Officer, Council Offices, The Grange, Mountjoy Road, Omagh BT79 7BL ☎ 028 8224 5321 🖷 028 8225 2380 elizabeth.harkin@omagh.gov.uk

Community Planning: Ms Alison McCullagh, Head of Development, Council Offices, The Grange, Mountjoy Road, Omagh BT79 7BL ☎ 028 8225 6211 🖷 028 8224 3888 alison.mccullagh@omagh.gov.uk

Community Safety: Ms Sandra Armstrong, Community Safety Officer, Council Offices, The Grange, Mountjoy Road, Omagh BT79 7BL ☎ 028 8224 5321 🖷 028 8224 3888 sandra.armstrong@omagh.gov.uk

Computer Management: Ms Joan McCaffrey, Chief Finance Officer, Council Offices, The Grange, Mountjoy Road, Omagh BT79 7BL ☎ 028 8225 6210 🖷 028 8224 3888 joan.mccaffrey@omagh.gov.uk

Consumer Protection and Trading Standards: Mr Barny Heywood, Chief Environmental Health Officer, Lianamallard House, 11 Old Mountfield Road, Lisnamallard, Olney BT79 7EG ☎ 028 8225 6202 barny.heywood@omagh.gov.uk

Contracts: Mr Kevin O'Gara, Chief Client Services Officer, Council Offices, The Grange, Mountjoy Road, Omagh BT79 7BL ☎ 028 8225 6200 🖷 028 8224 3888 kevin.ogara@omagh.gov.uk

Corporate Services: Mrs Bronagh Brown, Business Manager, Council Offices, The Grange, Mountjoy Road, Omagh BT79 7BL ☎ 028 8225 6206 🖷 028 8225 2380 bronagh.brown@omagh.gov.uk

Customer Service: Mrs Elizabeth Harkin, Public Relations Officer, Council Offices, The Grange, Mountjoy Road, Omagh BT79 7BL ☎ 028 8224 5321 🖷 028 8225 2380 elizabeth.harkin@omagh.gov.uk

Economic Development: Ms Alison McCullagh, Head of Development, Council Offices, The Grange, Mountjoy Road, Omagh BT79 7BL ☎ 028 8225 6211 🖷 028 8224 3888 alison.mccullagh@omagh.gov.uk

E-Government: Ms Joan McCaffrey, Chief Finance Officer, Council Offices, The Grange, Mountjoy Road, Omagh BT79 7BL ☎ 028 8225 6210 🖷 028 8224 3888 joan.mccaffrey@omagh.gov.uk

Emergency Planning: Mr Barny Heywood, Chief Environmental Health Officer, Lianamallard House, 11 Old Mountfield Road, Lisnamallard, Olney BT79 7EG ☎ 028 8225 6202 barny.heywood@omagh.gov.uk

Emergency Planning: Mr Daniel McSorley, Interim Clerk & Chief Executive, Council Offices, The Grange, Mountjoy Road, Omagh BT79 7BL ☎ 028 8225 6206; 028 7138 2204 🖷 028 8225 2380 daniel.mcsorley@omagh.gov.uk; dmcsorley@strabanedc.com

Energy Management: Mr Sean Kelly, District Chief Building Control Surveyor, Council Offices, The Grange, Mountjoy Road, Omagh BT79 7BL ☎ 028 8225 6201 🖷 028 8224 3888 sean.kelly@omagh.gov.uk

Environmental / Technical Services: Mr Kevin O'Gara, Chief Client Services Officer, Council Offices, The Grange, Mountjoy Road, Omagh BT79 7BL ☎ 028 8225 6200 🖷 028 8224 3888 kevin.ogara@omagh.gov.uk

Environmental Health: Mr Barny Heywood, Chief Environmental Health Officer, Lianamallard House, 11 Old Mountfield Road, Lisnamallard, Olney BT79 7EG ☎ 028 8225 6202 barny.heywood@omagh.gov.uk

Estates, Property & Valuation: Mr Sean Kelly, District Chief Building Control Surveyor, Council Offices, The Grange, Mountjoy Road, Omagh BT79 7BL ☎ 028 8225 6201 🖷 028 8224 3888 sean.kelly@omagh.gov.uk

European Liaison: Mrs Elizabeth Harkin, Public Relations Officer, Council Offices, The Grange, Mountjoy Road, Omagh BT79 7BL ☎ 028 8224 5321 🖷 028 8225 2380 elizabeth.harkin@omagh.gov.uk

Events Manager: Ms Jean Brennan, Arts Officer, Strule Arts Centre, Townhall Square, Omagh ST78 1BL ☎ 028 8224 7831 jean.brennan@omagh.gov.uk

Facilities: Mr Sean Kelly, District Chief Building Control Surveyor, Council Offices, The Grange, Mountjoy Road, Omagh BT79 7BL ☎ 028 8225 6201 🖷 028 8224 3888 sean.kelly@omagh.gov.uk

Finance and Treasurer: Ms Joan McCaffrey, Chief Finance Officer, Council Offices, The Grange, Mountjoy Road, Omagh BT79 7BL ☎ 028 8225 6210 🖷 028 8224 3888 joan.mccaffrey@omagh.gov.uk

Grounds Maintenance: Mr Kevin O'Gara, Chief Client Services

Officer, Council Offices, The Grange, Mountjoy Road, Omagh BT79 7BL ☎ 028 8225 6200 🖷 028 8224 3888 ✉ kevin.ogara@omagh.gov.uk

Health and Safety: Mr Gerry Donnelly, Client Services Officer, Council Offices, The Grange, Mountjoy Road, Omagh BT79 7BL ☎ 028 8225 6200 🖷 028 8224 3888 ✉ gerry.donnelly@omagh.gov.uk

Leisure and Cultural Services: Mr Conor McGarvey, Leisure Manager, Omagh Leisure Complex, Old Mountfield Road, Omagh BT79 7EG ☎ 028 8224 6711 🖷 028 8225926 ✉ conor.mcgarvey@omagh.gov.uk

Licensing: Mr Kevin O'Gara, Chief Client Services Officer, Council Offices, The Grange, Mountjoy Road, Omagh BT79 7BL ☎ 028 8225 6200 🖷 028 8224 3888 ✉ kevin.ogara@omagh.gov.uk

Lifelong Learning: Mrs Rosemary Rafferty, Head of Human Resources, Council Offices, The Grange, Mountjoy Road, Omagh BT79 7BL ☎ 028 8225 6204 🖷 028 8224 3888 ✉ rosemary.rafferty@omagh.gov.uk

Lottery Funding, Charity and Voluntary: Ms Alison McCullagh, Head of Development, Council Offices, The Grange, Mountjoy Road, Omagh BT79 7BL ☎ 028 8225 6211 🖷 028 8224 3888 ✉ alison.mccullagh@omagh.gov.uk

Member Services: Mrs Bronagh Brown, Business Manager, Council Offices, The Grange, Mountjoy Road, Omagh BT79 7BL ☎ 028 8225 6206 🖷 028 8225 2380 ✉ bronagh.brown@omagh.gov.uk

Partnerships: Mr Daniel McSorley, Interim Clerk & Chief Executive, Council Offices, The Grange, Mountjoy Road, Omagh BT79 7BL ☎ 028 8225 6206; 028 7138 2204 🖷 028 8225 2380 ✉ daniel.mcsorley@omagh.gov.uk; dmcsorley@strabanedc.com

Personnel / HR: Mrs Rosemary Rafferty, Head of Human Resources, Council Offices, The Grange, Mountjoy Road, Omagh BT79 7BL ☎ 028 8225 6204 🖷 028 8224 3888 ✉ rosemary.rafferty@omagh.gov.uk

Procurement: Ms Nuala Conlan, Procurement Officer, Council Offices, The Grange, Mountjoy Road, Omagh BT79 7BL ☎ 028 8225 6210 🖷 028 8224 3888 ✉ nuala.conlan@omagh.gov.uk

Recycling & Waste Minimisation: Mr Kevin O'Gara, Chief Client Services Officer, Council Offices, The Grange, Mountjoy Road, Omagh BT79 7BL ☎ 028 8225 6200 🖷 028 8224 3888 ✉ kevin.ogara@omagh.gov.uk

Regeneration: Ms Alison McCullagh, Head of Development, Council Offices, The Grange, Mountjoy Road, Omagh BT79 7BL ☎ 028 8225 6211 🖷 028 8224 3888 ✉ alison.mccullagh@omagh.gov.uk

Staff Training: Mrs Rosemary Rafferty, Head of Human Resources, Council Offices, The Grange, Mountjoy Road, Omagh BT79 7BL ☎ 028 8225 6204 🖷 028 8224 3888 ✉ rosemary.rafferty@omagh.gov.uk

Sustainable Development: Mr Barny Heywood, Chief Environmental Health Officer, Lianamallard House, 11 Old Mountfield Road, Lisnamallard, Olney BT79 7EG ☎ 028 8225 6202 ✉ barny.heywood@omagh.gov.uk

Tourism: Mr George Bradshaw, Tourism Officer, Strule Arts Centre, Townhall Square, Omagh BT78 1BL ☎ 028 8224 7831 🖷 028 8224 0774 ✉ george.bradshaw@omagh.gov.uk

Town Centre: Ms Oonagh Donnelly, Urban Regeneration Officer, Public Services Centre, 16 High Street, Omagh BT79 7BL ☎ 028 824 6220 ✉ oonagh.donnelly@omagh.gov.uk

Transport: Mr Kevin O'Gara, Chief Client Services Officer, Council Offices, The Grange, Mountjoy Road, Omagh BT79 7BL ☎ 028 8225 6200 🖷 028 8224 3888 ✉ kevin.ogara@omagh.gov.uk

Transport Planner: Mr Kevin O'Gara, Chief Client Services Officer, Council Offices, The Grange, Mountjoy Road, Omagh BT79 7BL ☎ 028 8225 6200 🖷 028 8224 3888 ✉ kevin.ogara@omagh.gov.uk

Waste Collection and Disposal: Mr Kevin O'Gara, Chief Client Services Officer, Council Offices, The Grange, Mountjoy Road, Omagh BT79 7BL ☎ 028 8225 6200 🖷 028 8224 3888 ✉ kevin.ogara@omagh.gov.uk

Waste Management: Mr Kevin O'Gara, Chief Client Services Officer, Council Offices, The Grange, Mountjoy Road, Omagh BT79 7BL ☎ 028 8225 6200 🖷 028 8224 3888 ✉ kevin.ogara@omagh.gov.uk

MEMBERS OF THE COUNCIL (21)

***Chair:* Thompson**, Errol (DUP - Omagh Town)
cllrerrol.thompson@omagh.gov.uk
***Vice-Chair:* Kelly**, Peter (SF - West Tyrone)
CllrPete.Kelly@omagh.gov.uk
Begley, Sean (SF - Omagh Town)
CllrSean.Begley@omagh.gov.uk
Buchanan, Thomas (DUP - West Tyrone)
cllrtom.buchanan@omagh.gov.uk
Campbell, Glenn (SF - West Tyrone)
cllrglenn.campbell@omagh.gov.uk
Chittick, Charles (DUP - Mid Tyrone)
CllrCharlie.Chittick@omagh.gov.uk
Clarke, Sean (SF - Mid Tyrone)
CllrSean.Clarke@omagh.gov.uk
Deehan, Josephine (SDLP - Omagh Town)
CllrJosephine.Deehan@omagh.gov.uk
Donnelly, Sean (SF - Mid Tyrone)
cllrsean.donnelly@omagh.gov.uk
Donnelly, Frankie (SF - West Tyrone)
cllrfrankie.donnelly@omagh.gov.uk
Fitzgerald, Anne Marie (SF - Mid Tyrone)
CllrAM.Fitzgerald@omagh.gov.uk
Hussey, Ross (UUP - Omagh Town)
CllrRoss.Hussey@omagh.gov.uk
McAleer, Declan (SF - Mid Tyrone)
cllr.declan.mcaleer@omagh.gov.uk
McAnespy, Sorcha (SF - Omagh Town)
cllrsorcha.mcanespy@omagh.gov.uk
McDonnell, Patrick (SDLP - West Tyrone)

cllrpat.mcdonnell@omagh.gov.uk
McGowan, Patrick (IND - Omagh Town)
CllrPatrick.McGowan@omagh.gov.uk
McLaughlin, Johnny (IND - Omagh Town)
CllrJohnny.McLaughlin@omagh.gov.uk
Quinn, Ann (SF - West Tyrone)
CllrAnn.Quinn@omagh.gov.uk
Rainey, Allan (UUP - West Tyrone)
CllrAllan.Rainey@omagh.gov.uk
Shields, Seamus (SDLP - Mid Tyrone)
cllrseamus.shields@omagh.gov.uk
Wilson, Bert (UUP - Mid Tyrone)
CllrBert.Wilson@omagh.gov.uk

POLITICAL COMPOSITION
SF: 10, SDLP: 3, UUP: 3, DUP: 3, IND: 2

ORKNEY S
Orkney Islands Council, Council Offices, School Place, Kirkwall KW15 1NY ☎ 01856 873535 🖷 01856 874615 🖱 customerservice@orkney.gov.uk 💻 www.orkney.gov.uk

FACTS & FIGURES
Police Authority: Northern Joint Police Board
Learning and Skills Council: Scotland
Parliamentary Constituencies: Orkney and Shetland
EU Constituencies: Scotland
Election Frequency: Elections are of whole council
Twinning: Hordaland (Norway); Friendship Treaties: Moena, Trentu Province (Italy); Province of Manitoba (Canada)

PRINCIPAL OFFICERS
Chief Executive: Mr Albert Tait, Chief Executive, Council Offices, School Place, Kirkwall KW15 1NY ☎ 01856 873535 🖷 01856 876158 🖱 albert.tait@orkney.gov.uk

Deputy Chief Executive: Mr Leslie Manson, Deputy Chief Executive & Director of Education, Leisure & Housing, Council Offices, School Place, Kirkwall KW15 1NY ☎ 01856 873535 🖷 01856 870302 🖱 leslie.manson@orkney.gov.uk

Access Officer / Social Services (Disability): Mr Derek Aiken, Service Improvement Manager, Council Offices, School Place, Kirkwall KW15 1NY ☎ 01856 873535 🖱 derek.aiken@orkney.gov.uk

Best Value: Mr Jim Love, Corporate Services Officer, Council Offices, School Place, Kirkwall KW15 1NY ☎ 01856 873535 🖱 jim.love@orkney.gov.uk

Building Control: Mr Jack Leslie, Principal Building Standards Officer, Council Offices, School Place, Kirkwall KW15 1NY ☎ 01856 873535 🖷 01856 886451 🖱 jack.leslie@orkney.gov.uk

Catering Services: Ms Anne Harrison, Catering Manager, St Rognvald Street, Kirkwall KW15 1PR ☎ 01856 879238 🖷 01856 879239 🖱 anne.harrison@orkney.gov.uk

Children / Youth Services: Ms Marie O'Sullivan, Head of Children, Families & Criminal Justice, Council Offices, School Place, Kirkwall KW15 1NY ☎ 01856 873535 🖱 marie.osullivan@nhs.net

Civil Registration: Ms Patricia Breck, Senior Registrar, Council Offices, School Place, Kirkwall KW15 1NY ☎ 01856 873535 🖱 patricia.breck@orkney.gov.uk

PR / Communications: Mr David Hartley, Communications Officer, Council Offices, School Place, Kirkwall KW15 1NY ☎ 01856 873535 🖷 01856 874615 🖱 david.hartley@orkney.gov.uk

Community Planning: Ms Hannah Thomson, Community Planning Officer, Council Offices, School Place, Kirkwall KW15 1NY ☎ 01856 873535 🖱 hannah.thomson@orkney.gov.uk

Computer Management: Mr Robert Horrobin, Head of Information Services, 9 King Street, Kirkwall, Orkney KW15 1JF ☎ 01856 873535 🖷 01856 876158 🖱 robert.horrobin@orkney.gov.uk

Consumer Protection and Trading Standards: Mr Gary Foubister, Trading Standards Manager, Council Offices, School Place, Kirkwall KW15 1NY ☎ 01856 873535 🖷 01856 886450 🖱 gary.foubister@orkney.gov.uk

Contracts: Mr Gavin Barr, Executive Director of Development & Infrastructure, Council Offices, School Place, Kirkwall KW15 1NY ☎ 01856 873535 🖷 01856 876094 🖱 gavin.barr@orkney.gov.uk

Corporate Services: Mrs Gillian Morrison, Executive Director of Corporate Services, Council Offices, School Place, Kirkwall KW15 1NY ☎ 01856 873535 🖱 gillian.morrison@orkney.gov.uk

Corporate Services: Ms Dawn Sherwood, Head of IT & Support Services, Council Offices, School Place, Kirkwall KW15 1NY ☎ 01856 873535 🖱 dawn.sherwood@orkney.gov.uk

Customer Service: Mrs Catherine Foubister, Customer Services Manager, Council Offices, School Place, Kirkwall KW15 1NY ☎ 01856 873535 🖱 catherine.foubister@orkney.gov.uk

Direct Labour: Mr Gavin Barr, Executive Director of Development & Infrastructure, Council Offices, School Place, Kirkwall KW15 1NY ☎ 01856 873535 🖷 01856 876094 🖱 gavin.barr@orkney.gov.uk

Economic Development: Ms Evelyn Mathershaw, Head of Strategic Development & Regeneration, Council Offices, School Place, Kirkwall KW15 1NY ☎ 01856 873535 🖷 01856 875846 🖱 evelyn.mathershaw@orkney.gov.uk

Education: Mr Leslie Manson, Deputy Chief Executive & Director of Education, Leisure & Housing, Council Offices, School Place, Kirkwall KW15 1NY ☎ 01856 873535 🖷 01856 870302 🖱 leslie.manson@orkney.gov.uk

E-Government: Mr Robert Horrobin, Head of Information Services, 9 King Street, Kirkwall, Orkney KW15 1JF ☎ 01856 873535 🖷 01856 876158 🖱 robert.horrobin@orkney.gov.uk

Electoral Registration: Mr Michael Forbes, Electoral Registration Officer, Charlotte House, Commercial Road, Lerwick, Shetland ZE1 0LX ☎ 01595 745700; 01595 745700 🖷 01595 745710; 01595 745710 🖱 ero@shetland.gov.uk

Emergency Planning: Mrs Margaret Walters, Emergency

Planning Officer, Council Offices, School Place, Kirkwall KW15 1NY ☎ 01856 873535 🖷 01856 873319 ✉ margaret.walters@orkney.gov.uk

Energy Management: Mr Alistair Morton, Energy & Utilities Officer, Council Offices, School Place, Kirkwall KW15 1NY ☎ 01856 873535 🖷 01856 876094 ✉ alistair.morton@orkney.gov.uk

Environmental / Technical Services: Mr Gavin Barr, Executive Director of Development & Infrastructure, Council Offices, School Place, Kirkwall KW15 1NY ☎ 01856 873535 🖷 01856 876094 ✉ gavin.barr@orkney.gov.uk

Environmental Health: Mr David Brown, Environmental Health Manager, Council Offices, School Place, Kirkwall KW15 1NY ☎ 01856 873535 🖷 01856 876450 ✉ david.brown@orkney.gov.uk

Estates, Property & Valuation: Mr Graeme Christie, Estates Manager, Council Offices, School Place, Kirkwall KW15 1NY ☎ 01856 873535 🖷 01856 876094 ✉ graeme.christie@orkney.gov.uk

European Liaison: Miss Phyllis Harvey, European Liaison Officer, Council Offices, School Place, Kirkwall KW15 1NY ☎ 01856 873535 🖷 01856 875846 ✉ phyllis.harvey@orkney.gov.uk

Facilities: Mr Gwyn Evans, Facilities Manager, Council Offices, School Place, Kirkwall KW15 1NY ☎ 01856 873535 🖷 01856 876094 ✉ gwyn.evans@orkney.gov.uk

Finance and Treasurer: Mr Gareth Waterson, Head of Finance, Council Offices, School Place, Kirkwall KW15 1NY ✉ finance@orkney.gov.uk

Grounds Maintenance: Mr David Rendall, Head of Buildings & Facilities, Council Offices, School Place, Kirkwall KW15 1NY ☎ 01856 873535 🖷 01856 870302 ✉ developmentandenvironment@orkney.gov.uk

Health and Safety: Mr Malcolm Russell, Health & Safety Officer, Council Offices, School Place, Kirkwall KW15 1NY ☎ 01856 873535 🖷 01856 874615 ✉ malcolm.russell@orkney.gov.uk

Highways: Mr Brian Archibald, Head of Transport & Amenities, Council Offices, School Place, Kirkwall KW15 1NY ☎ 01856 873535 🖷 01856 876094 ✉ brian.archibald@orkney.gov.uk

Housing: Ms Frances Troup, Head of Housing & Homelessness, Council Offices, School Place, Kirkwall KW15 1NY ✉ frances.troup@orkney.gov.uk

Housing Maintenance: Ms Frances Troup, Head of Housing & Homelessness, Council Offices, School Place, Kirkwall KW15 1NY ✉ frances.troup@orkney.gov.uk

Legal: Mr Fraser Bell, Head of Legal Services, Council Offices, School Place, Kirkwall KW15 1NY ☎ 01856 873535 🖷 01856 874615 ✉ fraser.bell@orkney.gov.uk

Leisure and Cultural Services: Ms Karen Greaves, Head of Leisure & Lifelong Learning, Council Offices, School Place, Kirkwall KW15 1NY ☎ 01856 873535 🖷 01856 870302 ✉ karen.greaves@orkney.gov.uk

Licensing: Mr Fraser Bell, Head of Legal Services, Council Offices, School Place, Kirkwall KW15 1NY ☎ 01856 873535 🖷 01856 874615 ✉ fraser.bell@orkney.gov.uk

Lifelong Learning: Ms Karen Greaves, Head of Leisure & Lifelong Learning, Council Offices, School Place, Kirkwall KW15 1NY ☎ 01856 873535 🖷 01856 870302 ✉ karen.greaves@orkney.gov.uk

Lighting: Mr Gavin Barr, Executive Director of Development & Infrastructure, Council Offices, School Place, Kirkwall KW15 1NY ☎ 01856 873535 🖷 01856 876094 ✉ gavin.barr@orkney.gov.uk

Member Services: Mrs Maureen Spence, Democratic Services Manager, Council Offices, School Place, Kirkwall KW15 1NY ☎ 01856 873535 🖷 01856 871604 ✉ maureen.spence@orkney.gov.uk

Parking: Mr Gavin Barr, Executive Director of Development & Infrastructure, Council Offices, School Place, Kirkwall KW15 1NY ☎ 01856 873535 🖷 01856 876094 ✉ gavin.barr@orkney.gov.uk

Personnel / HR: Mr Andrew Groundwater, Head of HR & Performance, Council Offices, School Place, Kirkwall KW15 1NY ☎ 01856 873535 🖷 01856 888779 ✉ andrew.groundwater@orkney.gov.uk

Planning: Mr Roddy Mackay, Head of Planning & Regulatory Services, Council Offices, School Place, Kirkwall KW15 1NX ☎ 01856 873535 🖷 01856 886451 ✉ roddy.mackay@orkney.gov.uk

Procurement: Mr Gary Butler, Joint Head of Procurement, Council Offices, School Place, Kirkwall KW15 1NY ☎ 01856 873535 ✉ gary.butler@orkney.gov.uk

Public Libraries: Mr Gary Amos, Library & Archive Manager, The Orkney Library & Archive, Junction Road, Kirkwall KW15 1AG ☎ 01856 873166 🖷 01856 875260 ✉ gary.amos@orkneylibrary.org.uk

Recycling & Waste Minimisation: Ms Maria Cuthbertson, Waste Professional Adviser, Council Offices, School Place, Kirkwall KW15 1NY ☎ 01856 873535 ext 2702 ✉ maria.cuthbertson@orkney.gov.uk

Regeneration: Ms Evelyn Mathershaw, Head of Strategic Development & Regeneration, Council Offices, School Place, Kirkwall KW15 1NY ☎ 01856 873535 🖷 01856 875846 ✉ evelyn.mathershaw@orkney.gov.uk

Road Safety: Mrs Yvonne Scott, Community Safety Officer, Council Offices, School Place, Kirkwall KW15 1NY ☎ 01856 873535 ✉ yvonne.scott@orkney.gov.uk

Social Services: Mrs Cathie Cowan, Interim Director of Orkney Health & Care, Council Offices, School Place, Kirkwall KW15 1NY ☎ 01856 873535 🖷 01856 886453 ✉ social.services@orkney.gov.uk

Social Services (Adult): Ms Caroline Sinclair, Head of Health & Community Care, Council Offices, School Place, Kirkwall KW15 1NY ☎ 01856 873535 🖷 01856 876453 ✉ caroline.sinclair@orkney.gov.uk

Social Services (Children): Ms Marie O'Sullivan, Head of Children, Families & Criminal Justice, Council Offices, School Place, Kirkwall KW15 1NY ☏ 01856 873535 ✉ marie.osullivan@nhs.net

Staff Training: Mrs Alison Skea, Learning & Development Manager, Council Offices, School Place, Kirkwall KW15 1NY ✉ alison.skea@orkney.gov.uk

Sustainable Development: Mr Roddy Mackay, Head of Planning & Regulatory Services, Council Offices, School Place, Kirkwall KW15 1NX ☏ 01856 873535 🖷 01856 886451 ✉ roddy.mackay@orkney.gov.uk

Sustainable Development: Ms Evelyn Mathershaw, Head of Strategic Development & Regeneration, Council Offices, School Place, Kirkwall KW15 1NY ☏ 01856 873535 🖷 01856 875846 ✉ evelyn.mathershaw@orkney.gov.uk

Traffic Management: Mr Brian Archibald, Head of Transport & Amenities, Council Offices, School Place, Kirkwall KW15 1NY ☏ 01856 873535 🖷 01856 876094 ✉ brian.archibald@orkney.gov.uk

Transport: Mr Brian Archibald, Head of Transport & Amenities, Council Offices, School Place, Kirkwall KW15 1NY ☏ 01856 873535 🖷 01856 876094 ✉ brian.archibald@orkney.gov.uk

Transport Planner: Ms Phyllis Towrie, Transport Planner, Council Offices, School Place, Kirkwall KW15 1NY ☏ 01856 873535 🖷 01856 886466 ✉ phyllis.towrie@orkney.gov.uk

Waste Collection and Disposal: Ms Maria Cuthbertson, Waste Professional Adviser, Council Offices, School Place, Kirkwall KW15 1NY ☏ 01856 873535 ext 2702 ✉ maria.cuthbertson@orkney.gov.uk

Waste Management: Ms Maria Cuthbertson, Waste Professional Adviser, Council Offices, School Place, Kirkwall KW15 1NY ☏ 01856 873535 ext 2702 ✉ maria.cuthbertson@orkney.gov.uk

MEMBERS OF THE COUNCIL (22)

***Vice Convener:* Foubister**, Jim (IND - East Midland, South Ronaldsay & Burray)
james.foubister@orkney.gov.uk
Annal, Janice (IND - Kirkwall East)
janice.annal@orkney.gov.uk
Clackson, Stephen (IND - North Isles)
stephen.clackson@orkney.gov.uk
Clouston, Alan (IND - Kirkwall West & Orphir)
alan.clouston@orkney.gov.uk
Crichton, Robin (IND - West Mainland)
rob.critchon@orkney.gov.uk
Davidson, Maurice (IND - Stromness & South Isles)
maurice.davidson@orkney.gov.uk
Drever, Andrew (IND - East Mainland, South Ronaldsay & Burray)
andrew.drever@orkney.com
Eccles, John (IND - Stromness & South Isles)
john.eccles@orkney.gov.uk
Gordon, Alistair (IND - West Mainland)
alistair.gordon@orkney.com
Hagan, Stephen (IND - North Isles)
stephen.hagan@orkney.com
Heddle, Steven (IND - Kirkwall East)
steven.heddle@orkney.gov.uk
Johnston, Harvey (IND - West Mainland)
harvey.johnstone@orkney.gov.uk
Madge, Russ (IND - East Mainland, South Ronaldsay & Burray)
russ.madge@orkney.gov.uk
Moar, Jimmy (IND - West Mainland)
james.moar@orkney.gov.uk
Moodie, Jack (IND - Kirkwall West & Orphir)
jack.moodie@orkney.gov.uk
Richards, John (IND - Kirkwall West & Orphir)
john.richards@orkney.gov.uk
Shearer, Gwenda (IND - Kirkwall East)
gwenda.shearer@orkney.gov.uk
Sinclair, Graham (IND - North Isles)
graham.sinclair@orkney.gov.uk
Stockan, James (IND - Stromness & South Isles)
james.stockan@orkney.gov.uk
Stout, Bill (IND - Kirkwall East)
bill.stout@orkney.gov.uk
Tierney, Owen (IND - West Mainland)
owen.tierney@orkney.gov.uk
Tullock, David (IND - Kirkwall West & Orphir)
david.tullock@orkney.gov.uk

POLITICAL COMPOSITION

IND: 22

COMMITTEE CHAIRS

Development & Infrastructure: Mr James Stockan
Education, Leisure & Housing: Ms Janice Annal
Monitoring & Audit: Mr David Tullock
Planning: Mr Robin Crichton
Policy & Resources: Mr Steven Heddle

OXFORD CITY — D

Oxford City Council, Town Hall, St. Aldate's, Oxford OX1 1BX ☏ 01865 249811 🖳 www.oxford.gov.uk

FACTS & FIGURES

Police Authority: Thames Valley Police Authority
Health Authority: South Central Strategic Health Authority
Learning and Skills Council: South East
Parliamentary Constituencies: Oxford East, Oxford West and Abingdon
EU Constituencies: South East
Election Frequency: Elections are biennial
Twinning: Bonn (Germany); Grenoble (France); Leiden (Netherlands); Leon (Nicaragua)

PRINCIPAL OFFICERS

Chief Executive: Mr Peter Sloman, Chief Executive, Town Hall, St. Aldate's, Oxford OX1 1BX ☏ 01865 252400 ✉ psloman@oxford.gov.uk

Senior Management: Mr David Edwards, Executive Director - Regeneration & Housing, Town Hall, St. Aldate's, Oxford OX1 1BX ☏ 01865 252463 ✉ dedwards@oxford.gov.uk

Senior Management: Mr Tim Sadler, Executive Director - City

Services, Town Hall, St. Aldate's, Oxford OX1 1BX ☎ 01865 252101 🖷 01865 252256 ✉ tsadler@oxford.gov.uk

Access Officer / Social Services (Disability): Ms Lynne Hooper, Access Officer, Ramsay House, 10 St Ebbe's Street, Oxford OX1 1PT ☎ 01865 252531 ✉ lhooper@oxford.gov.uk

Architect, Building / Property Services: Mr Steve Sprason, Head - Corporate Property, Town Hall, St. Aldate's, Oxford OX1 1BX ☎ 01865 252802 ✉ ssprason@oxford.gov.uk

Best Value: Ms Jane Lubbock, Head - Business Improvement & Technology, Town Hall, St. Aldate's, Oxford OX1 1BX ☎ 01865 252218 ✉ jlubbock@oxford.gov.uk

Building Control: Mr Michael Crofton Briggs, Head - City Development, Ramsay House, 10 St. Ebbe's Street, Oxford OX1 1PT ☎ 01865 252360 🖷 01865 252198 ✉ mcrofton-briggs@oxford.gov.uk

PR / Communications: Mr Peter McQuitty, Head - Policy, Culture & Communications, Town Hall, St. Aldate's, Oxford OX1 1BX ☎ 01865 252780 ✉ pmcquitty@oxford.gov.uk

Community Safety: Mr Richard Adams, Community Safety Manager, Town Hall, St. Aldate's, Oxford OX1 1BX ☎ 01865 252283 🖷 01865 252066 ✉ rjadams@oxford.gov.uk

Customer Service: Ms Helen Bishop, Head - Customer Services, Town Hall, St. Aldate's, Oxford OX1 1BX ☎ 01865 858650 ✉ hbishop@oxford.gov.uk

Direct Labour: Mr Graham Bourton, Head - Direct Services, Cowley Marsh Depot, Marsh Road, Oxford OX4 2HH ☎ 01865 252974 ✉ gbourton@oxford.gov.uk

E-Government: Mr Christopher Lee, Web Contact Manager, Town Hall, St. Aldate's, Oxford OX1 1BX ☎ 01865 249811 ✉ clee@oxford.gov.uk

Electoral Registration: Mr Martin John, Electoral Services Manager, Town Hall, St. Aldate's, Oxford OX1 1BX ☎ 01865 252518 ✉ mjohn@oxford.gov.uk

Emergency Planning: Mr Richard Gosling, Emergency Planning Officer, Town Hall, Blue Boar Street, Oxford OX1 4EY ☎ 01865 252093 🖷 01865 252765 ✉ rgosling@oxford.gov.uk

Environmental Health: Mr John Copley, Head - Environmental Development, Ramsay House, 10 St. Ebbe's Street, Oxford OX1 1PT ☎ 01865 252386 ✉ jcopley@oxford.gov.uk

Estates, Property & Valuation: Mr Steve Sprason, Head - Corporate Property, Town Hall, St. Aldate's, Oxford OX1 1BX ☎ 01865 252802 ✉ ssprason@oxford.gov.uk

Events Manager: Mr Peter McQuitty, Head - Policy, Culture & Communications, Town Hall, St. Aldate's, Oxford OX1 1BX ☎ 01865 252780 ✉ pmcquitty@oxford.gov.uk

Facilities: Mr Steve Sprason, Head - Corporate Property, Town Hall, St. Aldate's, Oxford OX1 1BX ☎ 01865 252802 ✉ ssprason@oxford.gov.uk

Finance and Treasurer: Mr Nigel Kenedy, Head of Finance, Town Hall, St. Aldate's, Oxford OX1 1BX ☎ 01865 252708 ✉ nkennedy@oxford.gov.uk

Fleet Management: Mr Phil Dunsdon, Waste & Fleet Manager, Cowley Marsh Depot, Marsh Road, Cowley OX4 2HH ☎ 01865 252901 ✉ pdunsdon@oxford.gov.uk

Grounds Maintenance: Mr Stuart Fitzsimmons, Parks & Open Spaces Manager, Cutteslowe Park, Oxford OX2 8ES ☎ 01865 467270 ✉ sfitzsimmons@oxford.gov.uk

Health and Safety: Mr Mark Preston, Safety Adviser, Human Resources, Town Hall, St. Aldate's, Oxford OX1 1BX ☎ 01865 252486 🖷 01865 252276 ✉ mpreston@oxford.gov.uk

Highways: Mr Shaun Hatton, Highways Manager, Town Hall, St. Aldate's, Oxford OX1 1BX ☎ 01865 249811 ✉ shatton@oxford.gov.uk

Home Energy Conservation: Mr Paul Robinson, Team Leader, Energy & Climate Change, St Aldate's Chambers, St Aldate's, Oxford OX1 1DS ☎ 01865 252541 🖷 01865 252344 ✉ probinson@oxford.gov.uk

Housing Maintenance: Mr Graham Bourton, Head - Direct Services, Cowley Marsh Depot, Marsh Road, Oxford OX4 2HH ☎ 01865 252974 ✉ gbourton@oxford.gov.uk

Legal: Mr Jeremy Thomas, Head - Law & Governance, Town Hall, St. Aldate's, Oxford OX1 1BX ☎ 01865 252224 ✉ jthomas@oxford.gov.uk

Leisure and Cultural Services: Mr Ian Brooke, Head - Leisure & Parks, Bury Knowle House, Oxford OX3 9RG ☎ 01865 467232 ✉ ibrooke@oxford.gov.uk

Licensing: Mr John Copley, Head - Environmental Development, Ramsay House, 10 St. Ebbe's Street, Oxford OX1 1PT ☎ 01865 252386 ✉ jcopley@oxford.gov.uk

Parking: Mr Jason Munroe, Car Parks Manager, Town Hall, St. Aldate's, Oxford OX1 1BX ☎ 01865 252125 ✉ jmunroe@oxford.gov.uk

Partnerships: Mrs Val Johnson, Partnership Development Manager, Town Hall, St. Aldate's, Oxford OX1 1BX ☎ 01865 252209 ✉ vjohnson@oxford.gov.uk

Personnel / HR: Mr Simon Howick, Head of People & Equalities, Town Hall, St. Aldate's, Oxford OX1 1BX ☎ 01865 252354 ✉ showick@oxford.gov.uk

Planning: Mr Michael Crofton Briggs, Head - City Development, Ramsay House, 10 St. Ebbe's Street, Oxford OX1 1PT ☎ 01865 252360 🖷 01865 252198 ✉ mcrofton-briggs@oxford.gov.uk

Procurement: Ms Jane Lubbock, Head - Business Improvement & Technology, Town Hall, St. Aldate's, Oxford OX1 1BX ☎ 01865 252218 ✉ jlubbock@oxford.gov.uk

Recycling & Waste Minimisation: Mr Robert Brown, Waste & Recycling Development Officer, Cowley Marsh Depot, Marsh Road, Oxford OX4 2HH ☎ 01865 252955 ✉ Rbrown@oxford.gov.uk

Regeneration: Mr David Edwards, Executive Director - Regeneration & Housing, Town Hall, St. Aldate's, Oxford OX1 1BX ☎ 01865 252463 ✉ dedwards@oxford.gov.uk

Staff Training: Mr Simon Howick, Head of People & Equalities, Town Hall, St. Aldate's, Oxford OX1 1BX ☎ 01865 252354 ✉ showick@oxford.gov.uk

Street Scene: Mr Andrew Wright, Street Scene Area Manager, Cowley Marsh Depot, Marsh Road, Oxford OX4 2HH ☎ 01865 282967 ✉ awright@oxford.gov.uk

Tourism: Mr Michael Crofton Briggs, Head - City Development, Ramsay House, 10 St. Ebbe's Street, Oxford OX1 1PT ☎ 01865 252360 🖷 01865 252198 ✉ mcrofton-briggs@oxford.gov.uk

Transport: Mr Paul Eimon, Fleet & Maintenance Manager, Town Hall, St. Aldate's, Oxford OX1 1BX ☎ 01865 252928 ✉ peimon@oxford.gov.uk

Transport Planner: Mr Paul Eimon, Fleet & Maintenance Manager, Town Hall, St. Aldate's, Oxford OX1 1BX ☎ 01865 252928 ✉ peimon@oxford.gov.uk

Waste Collection and Disposal: Mr David Hoddle, Street Scene Area Manager, Cowley Marsh Depot, Marsh Road, Oxford OX4 2HH ☎ 01865 252955 ✉ dhoddle@oxford.gov.uk

Waste Management: Mr Robert Brown, Waste & Recycling Development Officer, Cowley Marsh Depot, Marsh Road, Oxford OX4 2HH ☎ 01865 282955 ✉ rbrown@oxfor.gov.uk

MEMBERS OF THE COUNCIL (48)

***Deputy Lord Mayor:* Abbasi**, Mohammed Niaz (LAB - Cowley Marsh)
cllrmabbasi@oxford.gov.uk
***Mayor:* Armitage**, Alan (LD - North)
cllraarmitage@oxford.gov.uk
***Sheriff:* Sinclair**, Delia (LAB - Quarry and Risinghurst)
cllrdsinclair@oxford.gov.uk
***Leader of the Council:* Williams**, David (GRN - Iffley Fields)
cllrdwilliams@oxford.gov.uk
***Group Leader:* Fooks**, Jean (LD - Summertown)
cllrjfooks@oxford.gov.uk
Altaf-Khan, Mohammed (LD - Headington Hill and Northway)
cllrmaltaf-khan@oxford.gov.uk
Bance, Antonia (LAB - Rose Hill and Iffley)
cllrabance@oxford.gov.uk
Baxter, Laurence (LAB - Quarry & Risinghurst)
cllrbaxter@oxford.gov.uk
Benjamin, Elise (GRN - Iffley Fields)
cllrebenjamin@oxford.gov.uk
Brett, Tony (LD - Carfax)
tony.brett@oxfordlibdems.org.uk
Campbell, Jim (LD - St. Margaret's)
cllrjcampbell@oxford.gov.uk
Canning, Anne-Marie (LAB - Carfax)
cllramcanning@oxford.gov.uk
Clark, Bev (LAB - St. Clement's)
cllrbclack@oxford.gov.uk
Clarkson, Mary (LAB - Marston)
cllrmclarkson@oxford.gov.uk
Cook, Colin (LAB - Jericho and Osney)
cllrccook@oxford.gov.uk
Coulter, Van (LAB - Barton and Sandhills)
cllrvcoulter@oxford.gov.uk
Curran, Steve (LAB - Northfield Brook)
cllrscurran@oxford.gov.uk
Darke, Roy (LAB - Headington Hill & Northway)
cllrrdarke@oxford.gov.uk
Fry, James (LAB - North)
cllrjfry@oxford.gov.uk
Goddard, John (LD - Wolvercote)
cllrjgoddard@oxford.gov.uk
Gotch, Mike (LD - Wolvercote)
cllrmgotch@oxford.gov.uk
Haines, Mick (IND - Marston)
cllrmhaines@oxford.gov.uk
Hollick, Sam (GRN - Holywell)
cllrshollick@oxford.gov.uk
Humberstone, Rae (LAB - Blackbird Leys)
cllrrhumberstone@oxford.gov.uk
Jones, Graham (LD - St. Clement's)
cllrgjones@oxford.gov.uk
Kennedy, Pat (LAB - Lye Valley)
cllrpkennedy@oxford.gov.uk
Khan, Shah Jahan (LAB - Cowley)
cllrsjkhan@oxford.gov.uk
Lloyd-Shogbesan, Ben (LAB - Lye Valley)
cllrblloyd-shogbesan@oxford.gov.uk
Lygo, Mark (LAB - Churchill)
cllrmlygo@oxford.gov.uk
Malik, Sajjad-Hussain (LAB - Cowley Marsh)
cllrsmalik@oxford.gov.uk
McCready, Stuart (LD - Summertown)
cllrsmccready@oxford.gov.uk
McManners, Joe (LAB - Churchill)
cllrjmcmanners@oxford.gov.uk
Mills, Mark (LD - Holywell)
cllrmmills@oxford.govr.uk
O'Hara, Helen (LAB - Cowley)
cllrhohara@oxford.gov.uk
Pressel, Susanna (LAB - Jericho and Osney)
cllrspressel@oxford.gov.uk
Price, Robert (LAB - Hinksey Park)
cllrbprice@oxford.gov.uk
Rowley, Mike (LAB - Barton and Sandhills)
cllrmrowley@oxford.gov.uk
Royce, Gwynneth (LD - St. Margaret's)
cllrgroyce@oxford.gov.uk
Rundle, David (LD - Headington)
cllrdrundle@oxford.gov.uk
Sanders, Gillian (LAB - Littlemore)
cllrgsanders@oxford.gov.uk
Seamons, Scott (LAB - Northfield Brook)
cllrsseamons@oxford.gov.uk
Simmons, Craig (GRN - St. Mary's)
cllrcsimmons@oxford.gov.uk
Smith, Val (LAB - Blackbird Leys)
cllrvsmith@oxford.gov.uk
Tanner, John (LAB - Littlemore)
cllrjtanner@oxford.gov.uk
Turner, Edward (LAB - Rose Hill and Iffley)

cllreturner@oxford.gov.uk
van Nooijen, Oscar (LAB - Hinksey Park)
cllrovannooijen@oxford.gov.uk
Wilkinson, Ruth (LD - Headington)
cllrrwilkinson@oxford.gov.uk
Wolff, Dick (GRN - St. Mary's)
cllrdwolff@oxford.gov.uk

POLITICAL COMPOSITION

LAB: 29, LD: 13, GRN: 5, IND: 1

CABINET

Leader/ Corporate Governance & Strategic Planning: Mr Robert Price
Deputy Leader/ Finance & Efficiency: Mr Edward Turner
City Development: Mr Colin Cook
Cleaner, Greener Oxford: Mr John Tanner
Crime & Community Safety: Ms Delia Sinclair
Customer Services & Regeneration: Mrs Val Smith
Housing: Mr Joe McManners
Leisure Services: Mr Van Coulter
Parks & Sports: Mr Mark Lygo
Young People, Education & Community Development: Mr Steve Curran

COMMITTEE CHAIRS

Audit & Governance: Mr Mike Rowley
Communities & Partnership Scrutiny: Mr Mohammed Altaf-Khan
General Purposes Licensing: Mr Colin Cook
Planning Review: Ms Antonia Bance
Value & Performance: Mr Mark Mills

OXFORDSHIRE C

Oxfordshire County Council, County Hall, New Road, Oxford OX1 1ND ☎ 01865 792422 ✉ online@oxfordshire.gov.uk
🖳 www.oxfordshire.gov.uk

FACTS & FIGURES

Police Authority: Thames Valley Police Authority
Health Authority: South Central Strategic Health Authority
Learning and Skills Council: South East
Parliamentary Constituencies: Banbury, Henley, Oxford East, Oxford West and Abingdon, Wantage, Witney
EU Constituencies: South East
Election Frequency: Elections are of whole council

PRINCIPAL OFFICERS

Chief Executive: Ms Joanna Simons, Chief Executive, County Hall, New Road, Oxford OX1 1ND ☎ 01865 815330 🖷 01865 815199 ✉ joanna.simons@oxfordshire.gov.uk

Assistant Chief Executive: Ms Sue Scane, Assistant Chief Executive & Chief Finance Officer, County Hall, New Road, Oxford OX1 1ND ☎ 01865 816399 ✉ sue.scane@oxfordshire.gov.uk

Senior Management: Mr David Etheridge, Chief Fire Officer & Head of Community, County Hall, New Road, Oxford OX1 1ND ☎ 01865 855205 🖷 01865 855242 ✉ david.etheridge@oxfordshire.gov.uk

Senior Management: Mr John Jackson, Director for Social & Community Services, County Hall, New Road, Oxford OX1 1ND ☎ 01865 323574 ✉ john.jackson@oxfordshire.gov.uk

Senior Management: Mr Huw Jones, Director for Environment & Economy, Speedwell House, Speedwell Street, Oxford OX1 1NE ☎ 01865 815827 🖷 01865 810308 ✉ huw.jones@oxfordshire.gov.uk

Senior Management: Mr Jim Leivers, Director for Children's Services, County Hall, New Road, Oxford OX1 1ND ☎ 01865 815122 ✉ jim.lievers@oxfordshire.gov.uk

Senior Management: Mr Jonathan McWilliam, Director for Public Health, County Hall, New Road, Oxford OX1 1ND

Access Officer / Social Services (Disability): Mr John Jackson, Director for Social & Community Services, County Hall, New Road, Oxford OX1 1ND ☎ 01865 323574 ✉ john.jackson@oxfordshire.gov.uk

Architect, Building / Property Services: Mr Martin Tugwell, Deputy Director for Environment & Economy - Growth & Infrastructure, Speedwell House, Speedwell Street, Oxford OX1 1NE ☎ 01865 815113 ✉ martin.tugwell@oxfordshire.gov.uk

Children / Youth Services: Ms Frances Craven, Deputy Director for Children's Services - Education & Early Intervention, County Hall, New Road, Oxford OX1 1ND ☎ 01865 815498 ✉ frances.craven@oxfordshire.gov.uk

Children / Youth Services: Mr Jim Leivers, Director for Children's Services, County Hall, New Road, Oxford OX1 1ND ☎ 01865 815122 ✉ jim.lievers@oxfordshire.gov.uk

Civil Registration: Mrs Jacquie Bugeja, Head of Registration & Coroners, 1 Tidmarsh Lane, Oxford OX1 1NS ☎ 01865 816288 ✉ jacquie.bugeja@oxfordshire.gov.uk

PR / Communications: Mr Vincenzo Rampulla, Senior Public Affairs & Campaigns Officer, County Hall, New Road, Oxford OX1 1ND ☎ 01865 328590 ✉ vincenzo.rampulla@oxfordshire.gov.uk

Community Safety: Mr David Etheridge, Chief Fire Officer & Head of Community, County Hall, New Road, Oxford OX1 1ND ☎ 01865 855205 🖷 01865 855242 ✉ david.etheridge@oxfordshire.gov.uk

Computer Management: Mr Martyn Ward, ICT Operations Manager, Clarendon House, 52 Cornmarket Street, Oxford OX1 3EJ ☎ 01865 328879 ✉ martyn.ward@oxfordshire.gov.uk

Consumer Protection and Trading Standards: Mr Richard Webb, Acting Head of Trading Standards & Community Safety, Graham Hill House, Electric Avenue, Ferry Hinksey Road, Oxford OX2 0BY ☎ 01865 815791 ✉ richard.webb@oxfordshire.gov.uk

Contracts: Ms Sara Livadeas, Deputy Director - Joint Commissioning, County Hall, New Road, Oxford OX1 1ND ☎ 01865 323968 ✉ sara.livadeas@oxfordshire.gov.uk

Customer Service: Mr Graham Shaw, Acting Deputy Director for

Oxfordshire Customer Services, Clarendon House, 52 Cornmarket Street, Oxford OX1 3EJ ☎ 01865 816593 ✉ graham.shaw@oxfordshire.gov.uk

Economic Development: Mr Dave Waller, Economy, Spatial Planning & Climate Change Manager, Speedwell House, Speedwell, Oxford OX1 ☎ 01865 810813 ✉ dave.waller@oxfordshire.gov.uk

Education: Ms Frances Craven, Deputy Director for Children's Services - Education & Early Intervention, County Hall, New Road, Oxford OX1 1ND ☎ 01865 815498 ✉ frances.craven@oxfordshire.gov.uk

E-Government: Mr Graham Shaw, Acting Deputy Director for Oxfordshire Customer Services, Clarendon House, 52 Cornmarket Street, Oxford OX1 3EJ ☎ 01865 816593 ✉ graham.shaw@oxfordshire.gov.uk

Emergency Planning: Ms Bethan Morgan, County Emergency Planning Officer, Woodeaton Manor, Oxford OX3 9GU ☎ 01865 323760 ✉ bethan.morgan@oxfordshire.gov.uk

Energy Management: Ms Susan Halliwell, Environment & Climate Change Manager, Speedwell House, Speedwell, Oxford OX1 1NE ☎ 01865 815089 ✉ susan.halliwell@oxfordshire.gov.uk

Environmental / Technical Services: Mr Martin Tugwell, Deputy Director for Environment & Economy - Growth & Infrastructure, Speedwell House, Speedwell Street, Oxford OX1 1NE ☎ 01865 815113 ✉ martin.tugwell@oxfordshire.gov.uk

Estates, Property & Valuation: Mr Martin Tugwell, Deputy Director for Environment & Economy - Growth & Infrastructure, Speedwell House, Speedwell Street, Oxford OX1 1NE ☎ 01865 815113 ✉ martin.tugwell@oxfordshire.gov.uk

Facilities: Mr Martin Tugwell, Deputy Director for Environment & Economy - Growth & Infrastructure, Speedwell House, Speedwell Street, Oxford OX1 1NE ☎ 01865 815113 ✉ martin.tugwell@oxfordshire.gov.uk

Finance and Treasurer: Ms Lorna Baxter, Deputy Chief Finance Officer, County Hall, New Road, Oxford OX1 1ND ☎ 01865 323971 ✉ lorna.baxter@oxfordshire.gov.uk

Health and Safety: Mr Graham Shaw, Acting Deputy Director for Oxfordshire Customer Services, Clarendon House, 52 Cornmarket Street, Oxford OX1 3EJ ☎ 01865 816593 ✉ graham.shaw@oxfordshire.gov.uk

Highways: Mr Mark Kemp, Deputy Director for Environment & Economy - Highways & Transport, Speedwell House, Speedwell Street, Oxford OX1 1NE ☎ 01865 815845 ✉ markj.kemp@oxfordshire.gov.uk

Legal: Mr Peter Clark, Head of Law & Cultural Services, County Hall, New Road, Oxford OX1 1ND ☎ 01865 323907 ✉ peter.clark@oxfordshire.gov.uk

Leisure and Cultural Services: Mr Peter Clark, Head of Law & Cultural Services, County Hall, New Road, Oxford OX1 1ND ☎ 01865 323907 ✉ peter.clark@oxfordshire.gov.uk

Lifelong Learning: Mr Graham Shaw, Acting Deputy Director for Oxfordshire Customer Services, Clarendon House, 52 Cornmarket Street, Oxford OX1 3EJ ☎ 01865 816593 ✉ graham.shaw@oxfordshire.gov.uk

Lottery Funding, Charity and Voluntary: Ms Alexandra Bailey, Senior Performance & Improvement Manager, County Hall, New Road, Oxford OX1 1ND ☎ 01865 816384 ✉ alexandra.bailey@oxfordshire.gov.uk

Member Services: Mr Peter Clark, Head of Law & Cultural Services, County Hall, New Road, Oxford OX1 1ND ☎ 01865 323907 ✉ peter.clark@oxfordshire.gov.uk

Partnerships: Ms Alexandra Bailey, Senior Performance & Improvement Manager, County Hall, New Road, Oxford OX1 1ND ☎ 01865 816384 ✉ alexandra.bailey@oxfordshire.gov.uk

Personnel / HR: Mr Steve Munn, Head of Human Resources, County Hall, New Road, Oxford OX1 1ND ☎ 01865 815191 ✉ steve.munn@oxfordshire.gov.uk

Planning: Mr Martin Tugwell, Deputy Director for Environment & Economy - Growth & Infrastructure, Speedwell House, Speedwell Street, Oxford OX1 1NE ☎ 01865 815113 ✉ martin.tugwell@oxfordshire.gov.uk

Procurement: Mr Graham Shaw, Acting Deputy Director for Oxfordshire Customer Services, Clarendon House, 52 Cornmarket Street, Oxford OX1 3EJ ☎ 01865 816593 ✉ graham.shaw@oxfordshire.gov.uk

Public Libraries: Ms Karen Warren, Acting County Librarian, Library Headquarters, Holton, Oxford HP20 1UU ☎ 01865 322580 ✉ karen.warren@oxfordshire.gov.uk

Recycling & Waste Minimisation: Mr Martin Tugwell, Deputy Director for Environment & Economy - Growth & Infrastructure, Speedwell House, Speedwell Street, Oxford OX1 1NE ☎ 01865 815113 ✉ martin.tugwell@oxfordshire.gov.uk

Road Safety: Mr Mark Kemp, Deputy Director for Environment & Economy - Highways & Transport, Speedwell House, Speedwell Street, Oxford OX1 1NE ☎ 01865 815845 ✉ markj.kemp@oxfordshire.gov.uk

Social Services: Mr John Jackson, Director for Social & Community Services, County Hall, New Road, Oxford OX1 1ND ☎ 01865 323574 ✉ john.jackson@oxfordshire.gov.uk

Social Services (Adult): Mr John Dixon, Interim Deputy Director - Adult Social Care, County Hall, New Road, Oxford OX1 1ND ☎ 01865 322576 ✉ john.dixon@oxfordshire.gov.uk

Social Services (Children): Mr Jim Leivers, Director for Children's Services, County Hall, New Road, Oxford OX1 1ND ☎ 01865 815122 ✉ jim.lievers@oxfordshire.gov.uk

Sustainable Communities: Mr Martin Tugwell, Deputy Director for Environment & Economy - Growth & Infrastructure, Speedwell

House, Speedwell Street, Oxford OX1 1NE ☎ 01865 815113
✉ martin.tugwell@oxfordshire.gov.uk

Sustainable Development: Mr Huw Jones, Director for Environment & Economy, Speedwell House, Speedwell Street, Oxford OX1 1NE ☎ 01865 815827 🖷 01865 810308
✉ huw.jones@oxfordshire.gov.uk

Sustainable Development: Mr Martin Tugwell, Deputy Director for Environment & Economy - Growth & Infrastructure, Speedwell House, Speedwell Street, Oxford OX1 1NE ☎ 01865 815113
✉ martin.tugwell@oxfordshire.gov.uk

Traffic Management: Mr Mark Kemp, Deputy Director for Environment & Economy - Highways & Transport, Speedwell House, Speedwell Street, Oxford OX1 1NE ☎ 01865 815845
✉ markj.kemp@oxfordshire.gov.uk

Transport: Mr Mark Kemp, Deputy Director for Environment & Economy - Highways & Transport, Speedwell House, Speedwell Street, Oxford OX1 1NE ☎ 01865 815845
✉ markj.kemp@oxfordshire.gov.uk

Transport Planner: Mr Mark Kemp, Deputy Director for Environment & Economy - Highways & Transport, Speedwell House, Speedwell Street, Oxford OX1 1NE ☎ 01865 815845
✉ markj.kemp@oxfordshire.gov.uk

Waste Management: Mr Andrew Pau, Head of Waste Management, Speedwell House, Speedwell Street, Oxford OX1 1UJ ☎ 01865 815867 ✉ andrew.pau@oxfordshire.gov.uk

MEMBERS OF THE COUNCIL (74)

Chair: **Seale**, Donald (CON - Bampton)
don.seale@oxfordshire.gov.uk
Ahmed, Alyas (CON - Banbury Neithrop)
alyas.ahmed@oxfordshire.gov.uk
Altaf-Khan, Mohammed (LD - Headington and Marston)
altaf.khan@oxfordshire.gov.uk
Armitage, Alan (LD - West Central Oxford)
alan.armitage@oxfordshire.gov.uk
Atkins, Lynda (IND - Wallingford)
lynda.atkins@oxfordshire.gov.uk
Badcock, Marilyn (CON - Abdingdon West)
marilyn.badcock@oxfordshire.gov.uk
Badcock, Michael (CON - Abingdon West)
michael.badcock@oxfordshire.gov.uk
Billington, Maurice (CON - Kidlington and Yarnton)
maurice.billington@oxfordshire.gov.uk
Bolster, Norman (CON - Bicester)
norman.bolster@oxfordshire.gov.uk
Bonner, Ann (CON - Banbury, Grimsbury and Castle)
ann.bonner@oxfordshire.gov.uk
Brighouse, Elizabeth (LAB - Barton and Churchill)
liz.brighouse@oxfordshire.gov.uk
Brown, Iain (CON - Hanneys and Hendeds)
iain.brown@oxfordshire.gov.uk
Carter, Nick (CON - Thame and Chinnor)
nick.carter@oxfordshire.gov.uk
Chapman, Louise (CON - Hanborough)
louise.chapman@oxfordshire.gov.uk
Couchman, Jim (CON - Burford and Carterton North East)
jim.couchman@oxfordshire.gov.uk
Crabbe, Anthony (CON - Benson)
tony.crabbe@oxfordshire.gov.uk
Darke, Roy (LAB - Headington and Marston)
roy.darke@oxfordshire.gov.uk
Fatemian, Arash (CON - Kennington and Radley)
arash.fatemian@oxfordshire.gov.uk
Fitzgerald-O'Connor, Anda (CON - Shrivenham)
anda.fitzgerald@oxfordshire.gov.uk
Fooks, Jean (LD - Summertown and Wolvercote)
jean.fooks@oxfordshire.gov.uk
Fulljames, Catherine (CON - Ploughley)
catherine.fulljames@oxfordshire.gov.uk
Gearing, Anthony (CON - Wootton)
anthony.gearing@oxfordshire.gov.uk
Gibbard, Michael (CON - Kidlington and Yarnton)
michael.gibbard@oxfordshire.gov.uk
Goddard, John (LD - Summertown and Wolvercote)
john.goddard@oxfordshire.gov.uk
Godden, Janet (LD - North Hinksey and Wytham)
janet.gooden@oxfordshire.gov.uk
Greene, Patrick (CON - Moreton)
patrick.greene@oxfordshire.gov.uk
Hallchurch, Timothy (CON - Otmoor and Kirtlington)
timothy.hallchurch@oxfordshire.gov.uk
Handley, Pete (CON - Carterton South West)
peter.handley@oxfordshire.gov.uk
Hannaby, Jenny (LD - Grove and Wantage)
jenny.hannaby@oxfordshire.gov.uk
Harbour, Tony (CON - Didcot South)
tony.harbour@oxfordshire.gov.uk
Harvey, David (CON - Witney West)
david.harvey@oxfordshire.gov.uk
Hayward, Stephen (CON - Witney West)
steve.hayward@oxfordshire.gov.uk
Heathcoat, Judith (CON - Faringdon)
judith.heathcoat@oxfordshire.gov.uk
Hibbert-Biles, Hilary (CON - Chipping Norton)
hilary.biles@oxfordshire.gov.uk
Hudspeth, Ian (CON - Woodstock)
ian.hudspeth@oxfordshire.gov.uk
Jelf, Ray (CON - Deddington)
ray.jelf@oxfordshire.gov.uk
Jones, Peter (CON - Abingdon East)
peter.jones@oxfordshire.gov.uk
Lilly, Stewart (CON - Sutton Courtenay and Harwell)
stewart.lilly@oxfordshire.gov.uk
Lindsay-Gale, Lorraine (CON - Dorchester and Berinsfield)
lorraine.lindsay-gale@oxfordshire.gov.uk
Lovatt, Sandy (CON - Abingdon North)
sandy.lovatt@oxfordshire.gov.uk
Malik, Sajjad Hussain (LAB - East Oxford)
sajjad.malik@oxfordshire.gov.uk
Mallon, Keiron (CON - Banbury Easington)
Mathew, Charles (CON - Eynsham)
charles.mathew@oxforshire.gov.uk
Mitchell, Keith (CON - Bloxham)
keith.mitchell@oxfordshire.gov.uk
Newton, Caroline (CON - Watlington)
caroline.newton@oxfordshire.gov.uk
Nimmo-Smith, David (CON - Henley North and Chilterns)
david.nimmo-smith@oxfordshire.gov.uk
Owen, Neil (CON - Charlbury)
neil.owen@oxfordshire.gov.uk
Patrick, Zoe (LD - Grove and Wantage)
zoe.patrick@oxfordshire.gov.uk

Pressel, Susanna (LAB - West Central Oxford)
susanna.pressel@oxfordshire.gov.uk
Purse, Anne (LD - Wheatley)
anne.purse@oxfordshire.gov.uk
Reynolds, George (CON - Wroxton)
george.reynolds@oxfordshire.gov.uk
Robertson, David (CON - Witney East)
david.robertson@oxfordshire.gov.uk
Rose, Rodney (CON - Wychwood)
rodney.rose@oxfordshire.gov.uk
Sanders, Gill (LAB - Cowley and Littlemore)
gill.sanders@oxfordshire.gov.uk
Sanders, Jon (LAB - Cowley and Littlemore)
john.sanders@oxfordshire.gov.uk
Sanders, Larry (GRN - East Oxford)
larry.sanders@oxfordshire.gov.uk
Service, Bill (CON - Didcot Ladygrove)
bill.service@oxfordshire.gov.uk
Sexon, Dave (CON - Goring)
dave.sexon@oxfordshire.gov.uk
Sherwood, Chip (GRN - Isis)
chip.sherwood@oxfordshire.gov.uk
Shouler, Charles (CON - Bicester South)
charles.shouler@oxfordshire.gov.uk
Skolar, Peter (CON - Henley South)
peter.skolar@oxfordshire.gov.uk
Smith, Rosalind (LD - Barton and Churchill)
roz.smith@oxfordshire.gov.uk
Smith, Valerie (LAB - Leys and Lye)
val.smith@oxfordshire.gov.uk
Stevens, Richard (LAB - Leys and Lye)
richard.stevens@oxfordshire.gov.uk
Strangwood, Keith (CON - Banbury Ruscote)
keith.strangwood@oxfordshire.gov.uk
Stratford, Lawrie (CON - Bicester)
lawrie.stratford@oxfordshire.gov.uk
Tanner, John (LAB - Isis)
john.tanner@oxfordshire.gov.uk
Thompson, Alan (CON - Didcot South)
alan.thompson@oxfordshire.gov.uk
Tilley, Melinda (CON - Kingston Bagpuize)
melinda.tilley@oxfordshire.gov.uk
Turner, Nicholas (CON - Banbury Hardwick)
nicholas.turner@oxfordshire.gov.uk
Turner, David (LD - Chalgrove)
david.turner@oxfordshire.gov.uk
Viney, Carol (CON - Sonning Common)
carol.viney@oxfordshire.gov.uk
Waine, Michael (CON - Bicester)
michael.waine@oxfordshire.gov.uk
Wilmshurst, David (CON - Thame and Chinnor)
david.wilmshurst@oxfordshire.gov.uk

POLITICAL COMPOSITION
CON: 52, LD: 10, LAB: 9, GRN: 2, IND: 1

CABINET
Leader: Mr Ian Hudspeth
Deputy Leader: Mr Rodney Rose
Adult Services: Mr Arash Fatemian
Business & Communications: Mr Nick Carter
Children & Voluntary Sector: Ms Louise Chapman
Education: Ms Melinda Tilley
Finance & Police: Mr Keiron Mallon
Growth & Infrastructure: Ms Hilary Hibbert-Biles
Safer & Stronger Communities: Mrs Judith Heathcoat

COMMITTEE CHAIRS
Adult Services Scrutiny: Mr Jim Couchman
Audit & Governance: Mr David Wilmshurst
Children Services Scrutiny: Mr Michael Waine
Growth & Infrastructure: Mr David Nimmo-Smith
Pension Fund: Mr David Harvey
Planning & Regulation: Mr Stephen Hayward
Safer & Stronger Communities: Mr Lawrie Stratford
Strategy & Partnerships Scrutiny: Ms Lorraine Lindsay-Gale

PEMBROKESHIRE W

Pembrokeshire County Council, County Hall, Haverfordwest SA61 1TP ☎ 01437 764551 🖷 01437 775303 enquiries@pembrokeshire.gov.uk www.pembrokeshire.gov.uk

FACTS & FIGURES
Police Authority: Dyfed Powys Police Authority
Learning and Skills Council: Wales
Parliamentary Constituencies: Carmarthen West and South Pembrokeshire, Preseli Pembrokeshire
EU Constituencies: Wales
Election Frequency: Elections are of whole council

PRINCIPAL OFFICERS
Chief Executive: Mr Bryn Parry-Jones, Chief Executive, County Hall, Haverfordwest SA61 1TP ☎ 01437 764551 🖷 01437 775303 chief.executive@pembrokeshire.gov.uk

Assistant Chief Executive: Dr Ben Pykett, Assistant Chief Executive, County Hall, Haverfordwest SA61 1TP ☎ 01437 764551 ben.pykett@pembrokeshire.gov.uk

Senior Management: Dr Steven Jones, Director of Development, County Hall, Haverfordwest SA61 1TP ☎ 01437 764551 steven_jones@pembrokeshire.gov.uk

Senior Management: Mr Mark Lewis, Director of Finance & Leisure, County Hall, Haverfordwest SA61 1TP ☎ 01437 764551 🖷 01437 775303 mark.lewis@pembrokeshire.gov.uk

Senior Management: Mr Graham Longster, Director of Education & Children's Services, County Hall, Haverfordwest SA61 1TP ☎ 01437 764551 graham.longster@pembrokeshire.gov.uk

Senior Management: Mr Jake Morgan, Director of Social Services, County Hall, Haverfordwest SA61 1TP ☎ 01437 764551 jake.morgan@pembrokeshire.gov.uk

Senior Management: Mr Jon Skone, Director of Social Care & Housing, County Hall, Haverfordwest SA61 1TP ☎ 01437 764551 🖷 01437 775303 jon.skone@pembrokeshire.gov.uk

Senior Management: Mr Ian Westley, Director of Transportation & Environment, County Hall, Haverfordwest SA61 1TP ☎ 01437 764551 ian.westley@pembrokeshire.gov.uk

Access Officer / Social Services (Disability): Mr Alan Hunt,

Access Officer, County Hall, Haverfordwest SA61 1TP ☎ 01437 764551 🖷 01437 775008 🖱 alan.hunt@pembrokeshire.gov.uk

Architect, Building / Property Services: Mr Neville Henstredge, Head of Property & Asset Management, County Hall, Haverfordwest SA61 1TP ☎ 01437 764551 🖷 01437 775394 🖱 neville.henstredge@pembrokeshire.gov.uk

Best Value: Dr Ben Pykett, Assistant Chief Executive, County Hall, Haverfordwest SA61 1TP ☎ 01437 764551 🖱 ben.pykett@pembrokeshire.gov.uk

Building Control: Mr Hywel Jones, Head of Planning, County Hall, Haverfordwest SA61 1TP ☎ 01437 764551 🖱 hywel.jones@pembrokeshire.gov.uk

Catering Services: Mrs Rosemary Griffiths, Catering Manager, County Hall, Haverfordwest SA61 1TP ☎ 01437 764551 🖱 rosemary.griffiths@pembrokeshire.gov.uk

Civil Registration: Mr Ceri Davies, Head of Personnel, County Hall, Haverfordwest SA61 1TP ☎ 01437 764551

PR / Communications: Mr Len Mullins, Press & Public Relations Officer, County Hall, Haverfordwest SA61 1TP ☎ 01437 764551 🖱 len.mullins@pembrokeshire.gov.uk

PR / Communications: Mr David Thomas, Head of Marketing & Communications, County Hall, Haverfordwest SA61 1TP ☎ 01437 764551 🖷 01437 775303 🖱 david.thomas@pembrokeshire.gov.uk

Community Planning: Dr Ben Pykett, Assistant Chief Executive, County Hall, Haverfordwest SA61 1TP ☎ 01437 764551 🖱 ben.pykett@pembrokeshire.gov.uk

Community Safety: Mr Jake Morgan, Director of Social Services, County Hall, Haverfordwest SA61 1TP ☎ 01437 764551 🖱 jake.morgan@pembrokeshire.gov.uk

Community Safety: Mr Jon Skone, Director of Social Care & Housing, County Hall, Haverfordwest SA61 1TP ☎ 01437 764551 🖷 01437 775303 🖱 jon.skone@pembrokeshire.gov.uk

Computer Management: Mr John Roberts, Head of IT, County Hall, Haverfordwest SA61 1TP ☎ 01437 764551 🖱 john.roberts@pembrokeshire.gov.uk

Consumer Protection and Trading Standards: Mr Mark Elliott, Head of Public Protection, County Hall, Haverfordwest SA61 1TP ☎ 01437 764551

Contracts: Mr Paul Ashley-Jones, Head of Procurement, County Hall, Haverfordwest SA61 1TP ☎ 01437 764551 🖷 01437 776510 🖱 paul.ashley-jones@pembrokeshire.gov.uk

Corporate Services: Dr Ben Pykett, Assistant Chief Executive, County Hall, Haverfordwest SA61 1TP ☎ 01437 764551 🖱 ben.pykett@pembrokeshire.gov.uk

Customer Service: Dr Ben Pykett, Assistant Chief Executive, County Hall, Haverfordwest SA61 1TP ☎ 01437 764551 🖱 ben.pykett@pembrokeshire.gov.uk

Customer Service: Mr John Roberts, Head of IT, County Hall, Haverfordwest SA61 1TP ☎ 01437 764551 🖱 john.roberts@pembrokeshire.gov.uk

Economic Development: Mr Martin White, Head of Regeneration, County Hall, Haverfordwest SA61 1TP ☎ 01437 764551

Education: Mr Graham Longster, Director of Education & Children's Services, County Hall, Haverfordwest SA61 1TP ☎ 01437 764551 🖱 graham.longster@pembrokeshire.gov.uk

E-Government: Mr John Roberts, IT Manager, County Hall, Haverfordwest SA61 1TP ☎ 01437 764551 🖱 john.roberts@pembrokeshire.gov.uk

E-Government: Mr John Roberts, Head of IT, County Hall, Haverfordwest SA61 1TP ☎ 01437 764551 🖱 john.roberts@pembrokeshire.gov.uk

Electoral Registration: Mr Glynne Morgan, Electoral Services Manager, County Hall, Haverfordwest SA61 1TP ☎ 01437 764551 🖱 glynne.morgan@pembrokeshire.gov.uk

Emergency Planning: Mr Richard Brown, Civil Contingencies Manager, County Hall, Haverfordwest SA61 1TP ☎ 01437 764551 🖱 richard.brown@pembrokeshire.gov.uk

Energy Management: Mr Darren Thomas, Head of Highways & Construction, County Hall, Haverfordwest SA61 1TP ☎ 01437 764551 🖷 01437 775008 🖱 darren.thomas@pembrokeshire.gov.uk

Environmental / Technical Services: Mr Ian Westley, Director of Transportation & Environment, County Hall, Haverfordwest SA61 1TP ☎ 01437 764551 🖱 ian.westley@pembrokeshire.gov.uk

Environmental Health: Mr Mark Elliott, Head of Public Protection, County Hall, Haverfordwest SA61 1TP ☎ 01437 764551

Estates, Property & Valuation: Mr Neville Henstredge, Head of Property & Asset Management, County Hall, Haverfordwest SA61 1TP ☎ 01437 764551 🖷 01437 775394 🖱 neville.henstredge@pembrokeshire.gov.uk

European Liaison: Mr Gwyn Evans, European Officer, County Hall, Haverfordwest SA61 1TP ☎ 01437 764551 🖷 01437 776184 🖱 gwyn.evans@pembrokeshire.gov.uk

Events Manager: Ms Rosemary Roach, Events & Admin Assistant, County Hall, Haverfordwest SA61 1TP ☎ 01437 764551 🖱 rosemary.roach@pembrokeshire.gov.uk

Facilities: Mr Gareth Howells, Facilities Manager, County Hall, Haverfordwest SA61 1TP ☎ 01437 764551 🖷 01437 775303 🖱 gareth.howells@pembrokeshire.gov.uk

Finance and Treasurer: Mr Mark Lewis, Director of Finance & Leisure, County Hall, Haverfordwest SA61 1TP ☎ 01437 764551 🖷 01437 775303 🖱 mark.lewis@pembrokeshire.gov.uk

Fleet Management: Mr Hubert Mathias, Transport & Fleet

Manager, County Hall, Haverfordwest SA61 1TP ☎ 01437 764551 🖱 hubert.mathias@pembrokeshire.gov.uk

Grounds Maintenance: Mr Brian Maddocks, Head of Maintenance, County Hall, Haverfordwest SA61 1TP ☎ 01437 764551 🖱 brian.maddocks@pembrokeshire.gov.uk

Health and Safety: Mr Paul Eades, Risk Manager & Business Continuity, County Hall, Haverfordwest SA61 1TP ☎ 01437 764551 🖱 paul.eades@pembrokeshire.gov.uk

Highways: Mr Darren Thomas, Head of Highways & Construction, County Hall, Haverfordwest SA61 1TP ☎ 01437 764551 📠 01437 775008 🖱 darren.thomas@pembrokeshire.gov.uk

Home Energy Conservation: Mr Steven Keating, Energy Manager, County Hall, Haverfordwest SA61 1TP ☎ 01437 764551 🖱 steve.keating@pembrokeshire.gov.uk

Housing: Mrs Lyn Hambidge, Head of Housing Commissioning, County Hall, Haverfordwest SA61 1TP ☎ 01437 764551 🖱 lyn.hambidge@pembrokeshire.gov.uk

Housing Maintenance: Mr Brian Maddocks, Head of Maintenance, County Hall, Haverfordwest SA61 1TP ☎ 01437 764551 🖱 brian.maddocks@pembrokeshire.gov.uk

Local Area Agreement: Dr Ben Pykett, Assistant Chief Executive, County Hall, Haverfordwest SA61 1TP ☎ 01437 764551 🖱 ben.pykett@pembrokeshire.gov.uk

Legal: Mr Huw Miller, Head of Legal & Committee Services, County Hall, Haverfordwest SA61 1TP ☎ 01437 764551 📠 01437 775303 🖱 huw.miller@pembrokeshire.gov.uk

Leisure and Cultural Services: Mr Neil Bennett, Head of Information & Cultural Services, County Hall, Haverfordwest SA61 1TP ☎ 01437 764551 🖱 neil.bennett@pembrokehire.gov.uk

Leisure and Cultural Services: Mr Mike Cavanagh, Head of Cultural Services, County Hall, Haverfordwest SA61 1TP ☎ 01437 764551

Leisure and Cultural Services: Mr Mark Lewis, Director of Finance & Leisure, County Hall, Haverfordwest SA61 1TP ☎ 01437 764551 📠 01437 775303 🖱 mark.lewis@pembrokeshire.gov.uk

Licensing: Mr Mark Elliott, Head of Public Protection, County Hall, Haverfordwest SA61 1TP ☎ 01437 764551

Lifelong Learning: Mrs Anne Wakefield, Head of Lifelong Learning & Youth Services, County Hall, Haverfordwest SA61 1TP ☎ 01437 764551 🖱 anne.wakefield@pembrokeshire.gov.uk

Lighting: Mr Darren Thomas, Head of Highways & Construction, County Hall, Haverfordwest SA61 1TP ☎ 01437 764551 📠 01437 775008 🖱 darren.thomas@pembrokeshire.gov.uk

Lottery Funding, Charity and Voluntary: Dr Ben Pykett, Assistant Chief Executive, County Hall, Haverfordwest SA61 1TP ☎ 01437 764551 🖱 ben.pykett@pembrokeshire.gov.uk

Member Services: Mr Roy Griffiths, Committee Services Officer, County Hall, Haverfordwest SA61 1TP ☎ 01437 764551 📠 01437 775303 🖱 roy.griffiths@pembrokeshire.gov.uk

Parking: Mr Ian Westley, Director of Transportation & Environment, County Hall, Haverfordwest SA61 1TP ☎ 01437 764551 🖱 ian.westley@pembrokeshire.gov.uk

Partnerships: Dr Ben Pykett, Assistant Chief Executive, County Hall, Haverfordwest SA61 1TP ☎ 01437 764551 🖱 ben.pykett@pembrokeshire.gov.uk

Personnel / HR: Mr Ceri Davies, Head of Personnel, County Hall, Haverfordwest SA61 1TP ☎ 01437 764551

Planning: Dr Steven Jones, Director of Development, County Hall, Haverfordwest SA61 1TP ☎ 01437 764551 🖱 steven_jones@pembrokeshire.gov.uk

Planning: Mr Hywel Jones, Head of Planning, County Hall, Haverfordwest SA61 1TP ☎ 01437 764551 🖱 hywel.jones@pembrokeshire.gov.uk

Procurement: Mr Paul Ashley-Jones, Head of Procurement, County Hall, Haverfordwest SA61 1TP ☎ 01437 764551 📠 01437 776510 🖱 paul.ashley-jones@pembrokeshire.gov.uk

Public Libraries: Mr Neil Bennett, Head of Information & Cultural Services, County Hall, Haverfordwest SA61 1TP ☎ 01437 764551 🖱 neil.bennett@pembrokehire.gov.uk

Public Libraries: Mr Mike Cavanagh, Head of Cultural Services, County Hall, Haverfordwest SA61 1TP ☎ 01437 764551

Recycling & Waste Minimisation: Mr Ian Westley, Director of Transportation & Environment, County Hall, Haverfordwest SA61 1TP ☎ 01437 764551 🖱 ian.westley@pembrokeshire.gov.uk

Regeneration: Mr Martin White, Head of Regeneration, County Hall, Haverfordwest SA61 1TP ☎ 01437 764551

Road Safety: Mr John Gobbi, Road Safety Officer, County Hall, Haverfordwest SA61 1TP ☎ 01437 764551 📠 01437 775008 🖱 john.gobbi@pembrokeshire.gov.uk

Social Services: Mr Jake Morgan, Director of Social Services, County Hall, Haverfordwest SA61 1TP ☎ 01437 764551 🖱 jake.morgan@pembrokeshire.gov.uk

Social Services: Mr Jon Skone, Director of Social Care & Housing, County Hall, Haverfordwest SA61 1TP ☎ 01437 764551 📠 01437 775303 🖱 jon.skone@pembrokeshire.gov.uk

Social Services (Adult): Mrs Angela Watwood, Head of Community Care Commissioning, County Hall, Haverfordwest SA61 1TP ☎ 01437 754551 🖱 angela.watwood@pembrokeshire.gov.uk

Social Services (Children): Ms Nicola Francis, Head of Child Care Commissioning, County Hall, Haverfordwest SA61 1TP ☎ 01437 764551

Staff Training: Mr Ceri Davies, Head of Personnel, County Hall, Haverfordwest SA61 1TP ☎ 01437 764551

Street Scene: Mr Darren Thomas, Head of Highways & Construction, County Hall, Haverfordwest SA61 1TP ☎ 01437 764551 🖷 01437 775008 ✉ darren.thomas@pembrokeshire.gov.uk

Sustainable Communities: Dr Steven Jones, Director of Development, County Hall, Haverfordwest SA61 1TP ☎ 01437 764551 ✉ steven_jones@pembrokeshire.gov.uk

Sustainable Development: Mr Ian Westley, Director of Transportation & Environment, County Hall, Haverfordwest SA61 1TP ☎ 01437 764551 ✉ ian.westley@pembrokeshire.gov.uk

Tourism: Mr Martin White, Head of Regeneration, County Hall, Haverfordwest SA61 1TP ☎ 01437 764551

Town Centre: Dr Steven Jones, Director of Development, County Hall, Haverfordwest SA61 1TP ☎ 01437 764551 ✉ steven_jones@pembrokeshire.gov.uk

Traffic Management: Mr Darren Thomas, Head of Highways & Construction, County Hall, Haverfordwest SA61 1TP ☎ 01437 764551 🖷 01437 775008 ✉ darren.thomas@pembrokeshire.gov.uk

Transport: Mr Hubert Mathias, Transport & Fleet Manager, County Hall, Haverfordwest SA61 1TP ☎ 01437 764551 ✉ hubert.mathias@pembrokeshire.gov.uk

Transport Planner: Mr Darren Thomas, Head of Highways & Construction, County Hall, Haverfordwest SA61 1TP ☎ 01437 764551 🖷 01437 775008 ✉ darren.thomas@pembrokeshire.gov.uk

Total Place: Dr Ben Pykett, Assistant Chief Executive, County Hall, Haverfordwest SA61 1TP ☎ 01437 764551 ✉ ben.pykett@pembrokeshire.gov.uk

Waste Collection and Disposal: Mr Richard Brown, Civil Contingencies Manager, County Hall, Haverfordwest SA61 1TP ☎ 01437 764551 ✉ richard.brown@pembrokeshire.gov.uk

Waste Management: Mr Ian Westley, Director of Transportation & Environment, County Hall, Haverfordwest SA61 1TP ☎ 01437 764551 ✉ ian.westley@pembrokeshire.gov.uk

Children's Play Areas: Mr Brian Maddocks, Head of Maintenance, County Hall, Haverfordwest SA61 1TP ☎ 01437 764551 ✉ brian.maddocks@pembrokeshire.gov.uk

MEMBERS OF THE COUNCIL (60)

Leader of the Council: **Adams**, James (IND - Camrose)
cllr.jamie.adams@pembrokeshire.gov.uk
Deputy Leader of the Council: **George**, Huw (IND - Maenclochog)
cllr.huw.george@pembrokeshire.gov.uk
Deputy Leader of the Council: **Lewis**, Robert (IND - Martletwy)
cllr.rob.lewis@pembrokeshire.gov.uk
Allen-Mirehouse, John (IND - Hundleton)
cllr.john.allen-mirehouse@pembrokeshire.gov.uk
Baker, Philip (O - Saundersfoot)
cllr.phil.baker@pembrokeshire.gov.uk
Bowen, Roderick (PC - Clydau)
cllr.rod.bowen@pembrokeshire.gov.uk
Brinsden, John Anthony (O - Amroth)
brinsden-2@supanet.com
Bush, Daphne (IND - Pembroke St. Mary: South)
cllr.daphne.bush@pembrokeshire.gov.uk
Davies, John Thomas (IND - Cilgerran)
john.cwmbetws@virgin.net
Davies, Pat (LAB - Fishguard: North West)
cllr.pat.davies@pembrokeshire.gov.uk
Edwards, David Mark (IND - Haverfordwest: Prendergast)
cllr.mark.edwards@pembrokeshire.gov.uk
Evans, Wynne (IND - Narberth)
cllr.wynne.evans@pembrokeshire.gov.uk
Evans, Mike (IND - Tenby South)
cllr.mike.evans@pembrokeshire.gov.uk
Frayling, Lyndon (IND - Haverfordwest: Garth)
cllr.lyndon.frayling@pembrokeshire.gov.uk
Hall, Brian (IND - Pembroke Dock: Market)
cllr.brian.hall@pembrokeshire.gov.uk
Hancock, Simon (LAB - Neyland: East)
simon615@btinternet.com
Harries, Paul (IND - Newport)
cllr.paul.harries@pembrokeshire.gov.uk
Havard, Umelda (IND - Merlins Bridge)
cllr.umelda.havard@pembrokeshire.gov.uk
Hodgson, Tessa (NP - Lamphey)
cllr.tessa.hodgson@pembrokeshire.gov.uk
Howlett, David (IND - Haverfordwest: Priory)
cllr.david.bryan@pembrokeshire.gov.uk
Howlett, David (CON - Wiston)
Hudson, Stanley (CON - Milford: North)
cllr.stanley.hudson@pembrokeshire.gov.uk
James, Owen (CON - Scleddau)
cllr.owen.james@pembrokeshire.gov.uk
James, Mike (IND - St Dogmaels)
Jenkins, Lyn (IND - Solva)
cllr.lyn.jenkins@pembrokeshire.gov.uk
John, Michael (IND - Llangwm)
cllr.michael.john@pembrokeshire.gov.uk
Joseph, Stephen (PC - Milford: Central)
cllr.stephen.joseph@pembrokeshire.gov.uk
Kidney, Phillip (NP - Manorbier)
cllr.phillip.kidney@pembrokeshire.gov.uk
Kilmister, Bob (LD - Dinas Cross)
cllr.bob.kilmister@pembrokeshire.gov.uk
Lee, Alison (LAB - Pembroke Dock: Central)
cllr.alison.lee@pembrokeshire.gov.uk
Lewis, Keith (IND - Pembroke St. Mary: North)
cllr.arwyn.williams@pembrokeshire.gov.uk
Lewis, Keith (IND - Crymych)
cllr.keith.lewis@pembrokeshire.gov.uk
Llewellyn, Pearl (IND - Pembroke: Monkton)
cllr.pearl.llewellyn@pembrokeshire.gov.uk
Lloyd, David (NP - St. Davids)
cllr.david.lloyd@pembrokeshire.gov.uk
Miller, Paul (LAB - Neyland: West)
cllr.paul.miller@pembrokeshire.gov.uk
Morgan, Peter (IND - The Havens)
cllr.peter.morgan@pembrokeshire.gov.uk
Morse, Elwyn (IND - Narberth Rural)
cllr.elwyn.morse@pembrokeshire.gov.uk
Neale, David (IND - Carew)
cllr.david.neale@pembrokeshire.gov.uk
Nutting, Jonathan (NP - Pembroke St Michael)
cllr.jonathan.nutting@pembrokeshire.gov.uk

Owens, Reg (IND - St. Ishmaels)
cllr.reg.owens@pembrokeshire.gov.uk
Pepper, Myles (IND - Fishguard: North East)
cllr.myles.pepper@pembrokeshire.gov.uk
Pepper, Myles (IND - Letterston)
Perkins, Susan (LAB - Pembroke Dock: Llanion)
cllr.susan.perkins@pembrokeshire.gov.uk
Preston, Jonathan (PC - Penally)
cllr.jonathan.preston@pembrokeshire.gov.uk
Price, Gwilym (LAB - Goodwick)
cllr.gwilym.price@pembrokeshire.gov.uk
Pugh, David (IND - Kilgetty / Begelly)
cllr.david.pugh@pembrokeshire.gov.uk
Rees, David (IND - Llanrhian)
cllr.david.rees@pembrokeshire.gov.uk
Rowlands, Kenneth (IND - Johnston)
cllr.ken.rowlands@pembrokeshire.gov.uk
Simpson, David (IND - Lampeter Velfrey)
cllr.david.simpson@pembrokeshire.gov.uk
Sinnett, Rhys (PC - Milford: West)
cllr.rhys.sinnett@pembrokeshire.gov.uk
Stock, Peter (IND - Haverfordwest: Portfield)
cllr.peter.stock@pembrokeshire.gov.uk
Stoddart, Mike (O - Milford: Hakin)
cllr.mike.stoddart@pembrokeshire.gov.uk
Stoddart, Viv (O - Milford: Hubberston)
vivien.stoddart@virgin.net
Tudor, Thomas (LAB - Haverfordwest: Castle)
cllr.thomas.tudor@pembrokeshire.gov.uk
Wilcox, Anthony (LAB - Pembroke Dock: Pennar)
cllr.tony.wilcox@pembrokeshire.gov.uk
Wildman, David (IND - Burton)
david@davidwildman.com
Williams, Michael (PC - Tenby: North)
cllr.michael.williams@pembrokeshire.gov.uk
Williams, Jacob (NP - East Williamston)
jw@jacobwilliams.com
Woodham, Guy (LAB - Milford: East)
cllr.guy.woodham@pembrokeshire.gov.uk
Yelland, Steve (IND - Rudbaxton)
cllr.steve.yelland@pembrokeshire.gov.uk

POLITICAL COMPOSITION

IND: 33, LAB: 9, NP: 5, PC: 5, O: 4, CON: 3, LD: 1

CABINET

Leader / Corporate Matters & Finance: Mr James Adams
Deputy Leader / Highways & Planning: Mr Robert Lewis
Deputy Leader / Education & the Welsh Language: Mr Huw George
Adult Services, Health & Well-being, & the Voluntary Sector: Mr David Wildman
Adult Services & Equalities: Mr Simon Hancock
Children's Services: Mrs Susan Perkins
Culture, Sports & Leisure: Mr Elwyn Morse
Economy, Tourism & Regulatory Services: Mr David Pugh
Environmental & Regulatory Services: Mr Kenneth Rowlands
Housing & Sustainability: Mr David Simpson
Safeguarding, Child Protection & The Well-being of Children & Young People: Mrs Anne Hughes

COMMITTEE CHAIRS

Children & Families (Scrutiny): Mr Thomas Tudor
Economy (Scrutiny): Mr Keith Lewis
Environment (Scrutiny): Mr Brian Hall
Licensing: Mrs pearl Llewellyn
Older Persons, Health & Well-Being (Scrutiny): Mr David Howlett
Planning: Mr Myles Pepper
Safeguarding & Scrutiny: Mr Rhys Sinnett
Standards: Mr J L Edge (External)

PENDLE D

Pendle Borough Council, Town Hall, Market Street, Nelson BB9 7LG ☎ 01282 661661 🖷 01282 661630 🖳 www.pendle.gov.uk

FACTS & FIGURES

Police Authority: Lancashire Police Authority
Health Authority: North West Strategic Health Authority
Learning and Skills Council: North West
Parliamentary Constituencies: Pendle
EU Constituencies: North West
Election Frequency: Elections are by thirds
Twinning: Creil (France); Marl (Germany)

PRINCIPAL OFFICERS

Chief Executive: Mr Stephen Barnes, Chief Executive, Town Hall, Market Street, Nelson BB9 7LG ☎ 01282 661602 🖷 01282 661601 stephen.barnes@pendle.gov.uk

Deputy Chief Executive: Mr Philip Mousdale, Deputy Chief Executive & Director (Services), Town Hall, Market Street, Nelson BB9 7LG ☎ 01282 661634 🖷 01282 661601 philip.mousdale@pendle.gov.uk

Senior Management: Mr Brian Cookson, Director (Regeneration), Town Hall, Market Street, Nelson BB9 7LG ☎ 01282 661605 🖷 01282 661601 brian.cookson@pendle.gov.uk

Architect, Building / Property Services: Ms Sharon Livesey, Property Services Manager, Number One Market Street, Nelson BB9 7LJ ☎ 01282 878937 🖷 01282 661940 sharon.livesey@liberata.com

Building Control: Mr Jerry Mannion, Principal Building Control Manager, Town Hall, Market Street, Nelson BB9 7LG ☎ 01283 661721 🖷 01283 661305 jerry.mannion@pendle.gov.uk

PR / Communications: Mr Paul Hussey, Head of Policy, Town Hall, Market Street, Nelson BB9 7LG ☎ 01282 661667 🖷 01282 661630 paul.hussey@pendle.gov.uk

Community Planning: Mr Paul Hussey, Head of Policy, Town Hall, Market Street, Nelson BB9 7LG ☎ 01282 661667 🖷 01282 661630 paul.hussey@pendle.gov.uk

Community Safety: Mr Geoff Whitehead, Localities, Communities and Policy Supervisor, Town Hall, Market Street, Nelson BB9 7LG ☎ 01282 661660 🖷 01282 661367 geoff.whitehead@pendle.gov.uk

Computer Management: Mr Peter Rushton, ICT Account Manager, Number One Market Street, Nelson BB9 7LJ ☎ 01282 878984 🖷 01282 661811 peterrushton@liberata.com

Corporate Services: Mr Paul Hussey, Head of Policy, Town Hall, Market Street, Nelson BB9 7LG ☎ 01282 661667 🖷 01282 661630 ✉ paul.hussey@pendle.gov.uk

Customer Service: Ms Wendy Liddell, Pendle Service Delivery Manager, Liberata UK Ltd, Manor Lane, Sheffield S2 1TR ☎ 07837 187997 ✉ wendyliddell@liberata.com

Economic Development: Ms Dorothy Morris, Economic Development & Tourism Manager, Pendle Business Centre, Trafalgar Court, Commercial Road, Nelson BB9 9BT ☎ 01282 661681 🖷 01282 661680 ✉ dorothy.morris@pendle.gov.uk

E-Government: Mr Peter Rushton, ICT Account Manager, Number One Market Street, Nelson BB9 7LJ ☎ 01282 878984 🖷 01282 661811 ✉ peterrushton@liberata.com

Electoral Registration: Mr Stephen Barnes, Chief Executive, Town Hall, Market Street, Nelson BB9 7LG ☎ 01282 661602 🖷 01282 661601 ✉ stephen.barnes@pendle.gov.uk

Electoral Registration: Mr Richard Townson, Democratic & Legal Manager, Town Hall, Market Street, Nelson BB9 7LG ☎ 01282 661650 🖷 01282 661630 ✉ richard.townson@pendle.gov.uk

Emergency Planning: Mr Philip Mousdale, Deputy Chief Executive & Director (Services), Town Hall, Market Street, Nelson BB9 7LG ☎ 01282 661634 🖷 01282 661601 ✉ philip.mousdale@pendle.gov.uk

Energy Management: Ms Sharon Livesey, Property Services Manager, Number One Market Street, Nelson BB9 7LJ ☎ 01282 878937 🖷 01282 661940 ✉ sharon.livesey@liberata.com

Environmental Health: Mr Stuart Arnott, Public Health Manager, Fleet Street Depot, Nelson BB9 7YQ ☎ 01282 661124 🖷 01282 661750 ✉ stuart.arnott@pendle.gov.uk

Estates, Property & Valuation: Ms Sharon Livesey, Property Services Manager, Number One Market Street, Nelson BB9 7LJ ☎ 01282 878937 🖷 01282 661940 ✉ sharon.livesey@liberata.com

European Liaison: Mr Paul Hussey, Head of Policy, Town Hall, Market Street, Nelson BB9 7LG ☎ 01282 661667 🖷 01282 661630 ✉ paul.hussey@pendle.gov.uk

Events Manager: Mr Vaughan Jones, Tourism & Community Initiatives Manager, Elliott House, 9 Market Square, Nelson BB9 0LX ☎ 01282 661962 🖷 01282 661881 ✉ vaughan.jones@pendle.gov.uk

Finance and Treasurer: Mr Dean Langton, Head of Central Services, Elliott House, Market Square, Nelson BB9 0LX ☎ 01282 661866 🖷 01282 661811 ✉ dean.langton@pendle.gov.uk

Health and Safety: Ms Michelle Molly, Health & Safety Officer, Number One Market Street, Nelson BB9 7LJ ☎ 01282 878801 🖷 01282 661700 ✉ michelle.molly@liberata.com

Home Energy Conservation: Ms Julie Whittaker, Economic & Housing Regeneration Manager, Elliott House, 9 Market Square, Nelson BB9 0LX ☎ 01282 661038 🖷 01282 661043 ✉ julie.whittaker@pendle.gov.uk

Legal: Mr Richard Townson, Democratic & Legal Manager, Town Hall, Market Street, Nelson BB9 7LG ☎ 01282 661650 🖷 01282 661630 ✉ richard.townson@pendle.gov.uk

Leisure and Cultural Services: Mr Phil Storey, Chief Executive - Pendle Leisure Trust, Town Hall, Market Street, Nelson BB9 7LG ☎ 01282 661224 🖷 01282 661221 ✉ phil.storey@pendle.gov.uk

Licensing: Mr Richard Townson, Democratic & Legal Manager, Town Hall, Market Street, Nelson BB9 7LG ☎ 01282 661650 🖷 01282 661630 ✉ richard.townson@pendle.gov.uk

Member Services: Mr Richard Townson, Democratic & Legal Manager, Town Hall, Market Street, Nelson BB9 7LG ☎ 01282 661650 🖷 01282 661630 ✉ richard.townson@pendle.gov.uk

Partnerships: Mr Paul Hussey, Head of Policy, Town Hall, Market Street, Nelson BB9 7LG ☎ 01282 661667 🖷 01282 661630 ✉ paul.hussey@pendle.gov.uk

Personnel / HR: Ms Susan Tyer, Human Resources Manager, Number One Market Street, Nelson BB9 7LJ ☎ 01282 878800 🖷 01282 661700 ✉ susan.tyer@liberata.com

Planning: Mr Neil Watson, Planning & Building Control Manager, Town Hall, Market Street, Nelson BB9 7LG ☎ 01282 661706 🖷 01282 661720 ✉ neil.watson@pendle.gov.uk

Procurement: Mr Kevin Stansfield, Audit & Performance Manager, Elliott House, 9 Market Square, Nelson BB9 0LX ☎ 01282 661879 ✉ kevin.stansfield@pendle.gov.uk

Recycling & Waste Minimisation: Mr David Walker, Waste Services Manager, Fleet Street Depot, Nelson BB9 7YQ ☎ 01282 661746 🖷 01282 661750 ✉ david.walker@pendle.gov.uk

Regeneration: Mr Brian Cookson, Director (Regeneration), Town Hall, Market Street, Nelson BB9 7LG ☎ 01282 661605 🖷 01282 661601 ✉ brian.cookson@pendle.gov.uk

Staff Training: Ms Susan Tyer, Human Resources Manager, Number One Market Street, Nelson BB9 7LJ ☎ 01282 878800 🖷 01282 661700 ✉ susan.tyer@liberata.com

Sustainable Communities: Mr Brian Cookson, Director (Regeneration), Town Hall, Market Street, Nelson BB9 7LG ☎ 01282 661605 🖷 01282 661601 ✉ brian.cookson@pendle.gov.uk

Tourism: Mr Vaughan Jones, Tourism & Community Initiatives Manager, Elliott House, 9 Market Square, Nelson BB9 0LX ☎ 01282 661962 🖷 01282 661881 ✉ vaughan.jones@pendle.gov.uk

Town Centre: Ms Dorothy Morris, Economic Development & Tourism Manager, Pendle Business Centre, Trafalgar Court, Commercial Road, Nelson BB9 9BT ☎ 01282 661681 🖷 01282 661680 ✉ dorothy.morris@pendle.gov.uk

Waste Collection and Disposal: Mr David Walker, Waste Services Manager, Fleet Street Depot, Nelson BB9 7YQ ☎ 01282

661746 🖷 01282 661750 ✉ david.walker@pendle.gov.uk

Waste Management: Mr David Walker, Waste Services Manager, Fleet Street Depot, Nelson BB9 7YQ ☎ 01282 661746 🖷 01282 661750 ✉ david.walker@pendle.gov.uk

Children's Play Areas: Mr Keith Higson, Parks Officer, Fleet Street Depot, Nelson BB9 7YQ ☎ 01282 661597 ✉ keith.higson@pendle.gov.uk

MEMBERS OF THE COUNCIL (49)

***Mayor:* Mahmood**, Asjad (LAB - Whitefield)
asjad.mahmood@pendle.gov.uk
***Leader of the Council:* Cooney**, Joe (CON - Vivary Bridge)
joe.cooney@pendle.gov.uk
***Deputy Leader of the Council:* David**, John (LD - Old Laund Booth)
john.david@pendle.gov.uk
Adams, Marjorie (LD - Coates)
marjorie.adams@pendle.gov.uk
Ahmed, Nadeem (LD - Whitefield)
nadeem.ahmed@pendle.gov.uk
Ahmed, Nawaz (LAB - Brierfield)
nawaz.ahmed@pendle.gov.uk
Allen, Robert (LAB - Reedley)
Arshad, Mohammed (LAB - Brierfield)
mohammed.arshad@pendle.gov.uk
Ashraf, Naeem (LAB - Brierfield)
naeem.ashraf@pendle.gov.uk
Aziz, Abdul (LAB - Walverden)
abdul.aziz@pendle.gov.uk
Beckett, Anthony (CON - Barrowford)
anthony.beckett@pendle.gov.uk
Benson, Smith (CON - Horsfield)
Butterworth, Neil (CON - Horsfield)
neil.butterworth@pendle.gov.uk
Carroll, Rosemary (CON - Earby)
rosemary.carroll@pendle.gov.uk
Carroll, Rosemary (LAB - Clover Hill)
eileen.ansar@pendle.gov.uk
Clegg, David (LD - Vivary Bridge)
david.clegg@pendle.gov.uk
Cooney, Tommy (CON - Marsden)
tommy.cooney@pendle.gov.uk
Crossley, Linda (CON - Barrowford)
linda.crossley@pendle.gov.uk
Derwent, Shelagh (CON - Blacko and Higherford)
shelagh.derwent@pendle.gov.uk
Dunn, Sheena (LAB - Southfield)
sheena.dunn@pendle.gov.uk
Eyre, Jonathan (CON - Barrowford)
jonathan.eyre@pendle.gov.uk
Foxley, Margaret (CON - Boulsworth)
margaret.foxley@pendle.gov.uk
Gaskell, Lindsay (LD - Coates)
lindsay.gaskell@pendle.gov.uk
Greaves, Tony (LD - Waterside)
tonygreaves@cix.co.uk
Hanif, Mohammad (LAB - Reedley)
mohammad.hanif@pandle.gov.uk
Hartley, Ken (LD - Craven)
ken.hartley@pendle.gov.uk
Henderson, Julie (LAB - Walverden)
julie.henderson@pendle.gov.uk
Horsfield, Morris (CON - Earby)
morris.horsfield@pendle.gov.uk
Kerrigan, Ann (LD - Horsfield)
ann.kerrigan@pendle.gov.uk
Lord, Dorothy (LD - Waterside)
dorothy.lord@pendle.gov.uk
McBeth, John (CON - Boulsworth)
john.mcbeth@pendle.gov.uk
McCormick, Pauline (CON - Reedley)
pauline.mccormick@pendle.gov.uk
Parker, Brian (BNP - Marsden)
bnparker@pendle.gov.uk
Purcell, Jennifer (CON - Craven)
cllrjenniferpurcell@tiscali.co.uk
Roach, Graham (LD - Waterside)
graham.roach@pendle.gov.uk
Sakib, Mohammad (LAB - Bradley)
mohammad.sakib@pendle.gov.uk
Shore, Kathleen (LAB - Clover Hill)
kathleen.shore@pendle.gov.uk
Smith, Richard (LAB - Clover Hill)
Starkie, James (CON - Higham and Pendleside)
james.starkie@pendle.gov.uk
Starkie, James (LAB - Bradley)
mohammed.iqbal@pendle.gov.uk
Tennant, Christopher (CON - Earby)
christopher.tennant@pendle.gov.uk
Throupe, Janine (LD - Coates)
janinethroupe@talktalk.net
Tweedie, Ian (LAB - Vivary Bridge)
ian.tweedie@pendle.gov.uk
Waugh, Graham (CON - Foulridge)
Whalley, David (LAB - Southfield)
whalleydavid@yahoo.com
Whipp, David (LD - Craven)
david.whipp@pendle.gov.uk
White, Paul (CON - Boulsworth)
paul@ewsporting.co.uk
Wicks, Sheila (LAB - Southfield)
sheila.wicks@pendle.gov.uk
Younis, Nadeem (LAB - Bradley)
nadeem.younis@pendle.gov.uk

POLITICAL COMPOSITION

CON: 18, LAB: 18, LD: 12, BNP: 1

CABINET

Leader / Housing & Regeneration: Mr Joe Cooney
Deputy Leader / Environmental Services: Mr John David
Central Services: Ms Linda Crossley
Chief Executive's Policy Unit: Mr Anthony Beckett
Communications & Engagement: Mr James Starkie
Community Safety & Enginering: Mr David Whipp
Devolved Services: Mr Christopher Tennant
Economic Developmant, Enterprise & Growth: Mr Paul White
Parks & Recreation: Mr Nadeem Ahmed
Planning Policy & Climate Change: Mr Tony Greaves

COMMITTEE CHAIRS

Accounts & Audit: Ms Shelagh Derwent
Development Management: Mr James Starkie
Licensing: Ms Rosemary Carroll
Scrutiny Management Team: Mr Graham Roach

PERTH & KINROSS S

Perth & Kinross Council, Perth & Kinross Council, 2 High Street, Perth PH1 5PH ☎ 01738 475000 🖷 01738 475710 ✉ enquiries@pkc.gov.uk 🖥 www.pkc.gov.uk

FACTS & FIGURES

Police Authority: Tayside Joint Police Board
Health Authority: NHS Tayside
Learning and Skills Council: Scotland
Parliamentary Constituencies: Ochil and Perthshire South, Perth and Perthshire North
EU Constituencies: Scotland
Election Frequency: Elections are of whole council
Twinning: Aschaffenburg (Germany); Bydgoszcz (Poland); Cognac (France); Haikou (China); Perth, Ontario (Canada); Pskov (Russia)

PRINCIPAL OFFICERS

Chief Executive: Ms Bernadette Malone, Chief Executive, Council Buildings, 2 High Street, Perth PH1 5PH ☎ 01738 475009 🖷 01738 475008 ✉ chiefexec@pkc.gov.uk

Deputy Chief Executive: Mr Jim Irons, Depute Chief Executive, 2 High Street, Perth PH1 5PH ☎ 01738c475003

Architect, Building / Property Services: Mr Russell Thomson, Head of Property, Council Buildings, 2 High Street, Perth PH1 5PH ☎ 01738 475901 🖷 01738 475949 ✉ jrthomson@pkc.gov.uk

Best Value: Mrs Tina Yule, Head of Business Transformation & Improvement, Perth & Kinross Council, 2 High Street, Perth PH1 5PH ☎ 01738 475002 🖷 01738 475008 ✉ tlyule@pkc.gov.uk

Children / Youth Services: Mr Bill Atkinson, Depute Director, Pullar House, 35 Kinnoull Street, Perth PH1 5GD ☎ 01738 476204 🖷 01738 476210 ✉ batkinson@pkc.gov.uk

Children / Youth Services: Ms Alison Irvine, Head of Children & Families, Pullar House, 35 Kinnoull Street, Perth PH1 5GD ☎ 01738 476205 ✉ AIrvine@pkc.gov.uk

Civil Registration: Mrs Gillian Taylor, Head of Democratic Services, Council Buildings, 2 High Street, Perth PH1 5PH ☎ 01738 475135 🖷 01738 475008 ✉ gataylor@pkc.gov.uk

PR / Communications: Mrs Gillian Taylor, Head of Democratic Services, Council Buildings, 2 High Street, Perth PH1 5PH ☎ 01738 475135 🖷 01738 475008 ✉ gataylor@pkc.gov.uk

Community Planning: Mrs Tina Yule, Head of Business Transformation & Improvement, Perth & Kinross Council, 2 High Street, Perth PH1 5PH ☎ 01738 475002 🖷 01738 475008 ✉ tlyule@pkc.gov.uk

Community Safety: Mr David Burke, Executive Director of Housing & Community Care, Perth & Kinross Council, 2 High Street, Perth PH1 5PH ☎ 01738 475101 🖷 01738 475110 ✉ dburke@pkc.gov.uk

Computer Management: Mrs Tina Yule, Head of Business Transformation & Improvement, Perth & Kinross Council, 2 High Street, Perth PH1 5PH ☎ 01738 475002 🖷 01738 475008 ✉ tlyule@pkc.gov.uk

Consumer Protection and Trading Standards: Mr Keith McNamara, Head of Environmental & Consumer Services, Pullar House, 35 Pullar House, Perth PH1 5GD ☎ 01738 476404 🖷 01738 475310 ✉ kdmcnamara@pkc.gov.uk

Contracts: Mr Ian Innes, Head of Legal Services, Council Buildings, 2 High Street, Perth PH1 5PH ☎ 01738 475103 🖷 01738 475910 ✉ iinnes@pkc.gov.uk

Customer Service: Mr John Walker, Deputy Director of Housing & Community Care, Pullar House, 35 Kinnoull Street, Perth PH1 5GD ☎ 01738 476001 ✉ jwalker@pkc.gov.uk

Economic Development: Mr David Littlejohn, Head of Planning & Regeneration, 3-5 High Street, Perth PH1 5JS ☎ 01738 477942 🖷 01738 475955 ✉ dlittlejohn@pkc.gov.uk

Education: Ms S Devlin, Head of Education Services (Primary), Pullar House, 35 Kinnoull Street, Perth PH1 5GD ☎ 01738 476312 ✉ sdevlin@pkc.gov.uk

Education: Mr John Fyffe, Executive Director of Education & Children's Services, Perth & Kinross Council, 2 High Street, Perth PH1 5PH ☎ 01738 475445 🖷 01738 475510 ✉ jfyffe@pkc.gov.uk

Education: Mr P McAvoy, Head of Education Services (Secondary), Pullar House, 35 Kinnoull Street, Perth PH1 5GD ☎ 01738 476387 ✉ pmcavoy@pkc.gov.uk

E-Government: Mrs Tina Yule, Head of Business Transformation & Improvement, Perth & Kinross Council, 2 High Street, Perth PH1 5PH ☎ 01738 475002 🖷 01738 475008 ✉ tlyule@pkc.gov.uk

Electoral Registration: Ms Bernadette Malone, Chief Executive, Council Buildings, 2 High Street, Perth PH1 5PH ☎ 01738 475009 🖷 01738 475008 ✉ chiefexec@pkc.gov.uk

Emergency Planning: Mr Jim Valentine, Executive Director of Environment, Pullar House, 35 Kinnoull Street, Perth PH1 5GD ☎ 01738 476502 🖷 01738 475310 ✉ jvalentine@pkc.gov.uk

Energy Management: Mr Russell Thomson, Head of Property, Council Buildings, 2 High Street, Perth PH1 5PH ☎ 01738 475901 🖷 01738 475949 ✉ jrthomson@pkc.gov.uk

Environmental / Technical Services: Mr Jim Valentine, Executive Director of Environment, Pullar House, 35 Kinnoull Street, Perth PH1 5GD ☎ 01738 476502 🖷 01738 475310 ✉ jvalentine@pkc.gov.uk

Environmental Health: Mr Keith McNamara, Head of Environmental & Consumer Services, Pullar House, 35 Pullar House, Perth PH1 5GD ☎ 01738 476404 🖷 01738 475310 ✉ kdmcnamara@pkc.gov.uk

Estates, Property & Valuation: Mr Russell Thomson, Head of Property, Council Buildings, 2 High Street, Perth PH1 5PH ☎ 01738 475901 🖷 01738 475949 ✉ jrthomson@pkc.gov.uk

Finance and Treasurer: Mr Stewart McKenzie, Acting Head of Finance, Council Buildings, 2 High Street, Perth PH1 5PH ☎ 01738 475504 🖷 01738 475110 ✉ smckenzie@pkc.gov.uk

Finance and Treasurer: Mr Alan Taylor, Head of Finance & Support Services, 5 Whitefriars Crescent, Perth PH2 0PA ☎ 01738 476702

Fleet Management: Mrs Barbara Renton, Head of Performance & Resources, Pullar House, 35 Pullar House, Perth PH1 5GD ☎ 01738 476505 🖷 01738 476510 ✉ brenton@pkc.gov.uk

Grounds Maintenance: Mrs Barbara Renton, Head of Performance & Resources, Pullar House, 35 Pullar House, Perth PH1 5GD ☎ 01738 476505 🖷 01738 476510 ✉ brenton@pkc.gov.uk

Health and Safety: Mrs Barbara Renton, Head of Performance & Resources, Pullar House, 35 Pullar House, Perth PH1 5GD ☎ 01738 476505 🖷 01738 476510 ✉ brenton@pkc.gov.uk

Housing: Mr David Burke, Executive Director of Housing & Community Care, Perth & Kinross Council, 2 High Street, Perth PH1 5PH ☎ 01738 475101 🖷 01738 475110 ✉ dburke@pkc.gov.uk

Housing: Ms Lorna Cameron, Head of Housing & Strategic Commissioning, 5 Whitefriars Crescent, Perth PH2 0PA ☎ 01738 476705

Housing Maintenance: Mr David Burke, Executive Director of Housing & Community Care, Perth & Kinross Council, 2 High Street, Perth PH1 5PH ☎ 01738 475101 🖷 01738 475110 ✉ dburke@pkc.gov.uk

Housing Maintenance: Ms Lorna Cameron, Head of Strategy & Support Services, Perth & Kinross Council, 5 Whitefriars Crescent, Perth PH2 0PA ☎ 01738 476705 ✉ lecameron@pkc.gov.uk

Legal: Mr Ian Innes, Head of Legal Services, Council Buildings, 2 High Street, Perth PH1 5PH ☎ 01738 475103 🖷 01738 475910 ✉ iinnes@pkc.gov.uk

Leisure and Cultural Services: Mr Jim Moyes, Chief Executive Officer, Bells Sports Centre, Hay Street, Perth PH1 5HS ☎ 01738 492411 ✉ jmoyes@pkc.gov.uk

Licensing: Mr Ian Innes, Head of Legal Services, Council Buildings, 2 High Street, Perth PH1 5PH ☎ 01738 475103 🖷 01738 475910 ✉ iinnes@pkc.gov.uk

Lifelong Learning: Mrs Heather Stuart, Head of Communities & Cultural Services, Pullar House, 35 Pullar House, Perth PH1 5GD ☎ 01738 476313 🖷 01738 476210 ✉ hstuart@pkc.gov.uk

Lottery Funding, Charity and Voluntary: Mr David Littlejohn, Head of Planning & Regeneration, 3-5 High Street, Perth PH1 5JS ☎ 01738 477942 🖷 01738 475955 ✉ dlittlejohn@pkc.gov.uk

Member Services: Mrs Gillian Taylor, Head of Democratic Services, Council Buildings, 2 High Street, Perth PH1 5PH ☎ 01738 475135 🖷 01738 475008 ✉ gataylor@pkc.gov.uk

Partnerships: Mrs Tina Yule, Head of Business Transformation & Improvement, Perth & Kinross Council, 2 High Street, Perth PH1 5PH ☎ 01738 475002 🖷 01738 475008 ✉ tlyule@pkc.gov.uk

Personnel / HR: Mr Hugh Mackenzie, Head of Human Resources, Council Buildings, 2 High Street, Perth PH1 5PH ☎ 01738 475402 🖷 01738 475410 ✉ hlmackenzie@pkc.gov.uk

Procurement: Ms Lorna Cameron, Head of Strategy & Support Services, Perth & Kinross Council, 5 Whitefriars Crescent, Perth PH2 0PA ☎ 01738 476705 ✉ lecameron@pkc.gov.uk

Public Libraries: Mrs Heather Stuart, Head of Communities & Cultural Services, Pullar House, 35 Pullar House, Perth PH1 5GD ☎ 01738 476313 🖷 01738 476210 ✉ hstuart@pkc.gov.uk

Recycling & Waste Minimisation: Mrs Barbara Renton, Head of Performance & Resources, Pullar House, 35 Pullar House, Perth PH1 5GD ☎ 01738 476505 🖷 01738 476510 ✉ brenton@pkc.gov.uk

Regeneration: Mr David Littlejohn, Head of Planning & Regeneration, 3-5 High Street, Perth PH1 5JS ☎ 01738 477942 🖷 01738 475955 ✉ dlittlejohn@pkc.gov.uk

Social Services: Mr John Gilruth, Head of Community Care, 5 Whitefriars Crescent, Perth PH2 0PA ☎ 01738 476711 🖷 01738 476010 ✉ jgilruth@pkc.gov.uk

Social Services (Adult): Mr John Gilruth, Head of Community Care, 5 Whitefriars Crescent, Perth PH2 0PA ☎ 01738 476711 🖷 01738 476010 ✉ jgilruth@pkc.gov.uk

Social Services (Adult): Mr John Gilruth, Head of Community Care, Pullar House, 35 Pullar House, Perth PH1 5GD ☎ 01738 476711

Social Services (Children): Mr Bill Atkinson, Depute Director, Pullar House, 35 Kinnoull Street, Perth PH1 5GD ☎ 01738 476204 🖷 01738 476210 ✉ batkinson@pkc.gov.uk

Social Services (Children): Mr John Gilruth, Head of Community Care, Pullar House, 35 Pullar House, Perth PH1 5GD ☎ 01738 476711

Social Services (Children): Ms Alison Irvine, Head of Children & Families, Pullar House, 35 Kinnoull Street, Perth PH1 5GD ☎ 01738 476205 ✉ AIrvine@pkc.gov.uk

Staff Training: Mr Hugh Mackenzie, Head of Human Resources, Council Buildings, 2 High Street, Perth PH1 5PH ☎ 01738 475402 🖷 01738 475410 ✉ hlmackenzie@pkc.gov.uk

Sustainable Communities: Mr David Burke, Executive Director of Housing & Community Care, Perth & Kinross Council, 2 High Street, Perth PH1 5PH ☎ 01738 475101 🖷 01738 475110 ✉ dburke@pkc.gov.uk

Tourism: Mr David Littlejohn, Head of Planning & Regeneration, 3-5 High Street, Perth PH1 5JS ☎ 01738 477942 🖷 01738 475955 ✉ dlittlejohn@pkc.gov.uk

Town Centre: Mr David Littlejohn, Head of Planning & Regeneration, 3-5 High Street, Perth PH1 5JS ☎ 01738 477942 🖷 01738 475955 ✉ dlittlejohn@pkc.gov.uk

Total Place: Ms Alison Irvine, Head of Children & Families, Pullar House, 35 Kinnoull Street, Perth PH1 5GD ☎ 01738 476205 ✉ AIrvine@pkc.gov.uk

Waste Collection and Disposal: Mrs Barbara Renton, Head of Performance & Resources, Pullar House, 35 Pullar House, Perth PH1 5GD ☎ 01738 476505 🖷 01738 476510 ✉ brenton@pkc.gov.uk

Waste Management: Mrs Barbara Renton, Head of Performance & Resources, Pullar House, 35 Pullar House, Perth PH1 5GD ☎ 01738 476505 🖷 01738 476510 ✉ brenton@pkc.gov.uk

MEMBERS OF THE COUNCIL (41)

***Provost:* Grant**, Elizabeth (SNP - Blairgowrie and Glens)
eagrant@pkc.gov.uk
***Deputy Provost:* Band**, Bob (SNP - Perth City South)
bband@pkc.gov.uk
***Leader of the Council:* Miller**, Ian (SNP - Strathmore)
imiller@pkc.gov.uk
***Deputy Leader of the Council:* Stewart**, Alexander (CON - Perth City South)
astewart@pkc.gov.uk
Anderson, Henry (SNP - Almond and Earn)
handerson@pkc.gov.uk
Barnacle, Michael (IND - Kinross shire)
mbarnacle@pkc.gov.uk
Barrett, Peter (LD - Perth City Centre)
pabarrett@pkc.gov.uk
Brock, Rhona (IND - Strathearn)
rbrock@pkc.gov.uk
Campbell, Ian (CON - Highland)
icampbell@pkc.gov.uk
Coburn, Jack (SNP - Perth City Centre)
jcoburn@pkc.gov.uk
Cowan, Ann (CON - Strathearn)
acowan@pkc.gov.uk
Cuthbert, Dave (IND - Kinross shire)
dcuthbert@pkc.gov.uk
Doogan, Dave (SNP - Perth City North)
ddoogan@pkc.gov.uk
Ellis, Bob (SNP - Blairgowrie and Glens)
rellis@pkc.gov.uk
Flynn, John (LAB - Perth City North)
jmflynn@pkc.gov.uk
Gaunt, Ann (LD - Strathallan)
agaunt@pkc.gov.uk
Giacopazzi, Joe (SNP - Kinross shire)
jgiacopazzi@pkc.gov.uk
Gillies, Callum (LAB - Perth City North)
cgillies@pkc.gov.uk
Grant, Alan (SNP - Strathmore)
adgrant@pkc.gov.uk
Gray, Tom (SNP - Strathallan)
tomgray@pkc.gov.uk
Howie, Kate (SNP - Highland)
ejhowie@pkc.gov.uk
Jack, Alan (IND - Almond and Earn)
hajack@pkc.gov.uk
Kellas, John (SNP - Strathtay)
jkellas@pkc.gov.uk
Laing, Grant (SNP - Strathtay)
glaing@pkc.gov.uk
Livingstone, Alan (CON - Almond and Earn)
alivingstone@pkc.gov.uk
Lyle, Murray (CON - Strathallan)
mlyle@pkc.gov.uk
Maclachlan, Elspeth (SNP - Perth City North)
emaclachlan@pkc.gov.uk
MacLellan, Archibald (LAB - Perth City Centre)
aamaclellan@pkc.gov.uk
Melloy, Dennis (CON - Strathmore)
dmelloy@pkc.gov.uk
Munro, Alistair (LAB - Perth City South)
alistairmunro@pkc.gov.uk
Pover, Douglas (SNP - Carse of Gowrie)
dpover@pkc.gov.uk
Roberts, Mac (CON - Carse of Gowrie)
mroberts@pkc.gov.uk
Robertson, William (LD - Kinross shire)
wbrobertson@pkc.gov.uk
Shiers, Caroline (CON - Blairgowrie and Glens)
cshiers@pkc.gov.uk
Simpson, Lewis (LD - Strathmore)
lddsimpson@pkc.gov.uk
Stewart, Heather (CON - Perth City Centre)
hstewart@pkc.gov.uk
Vaughan, Barbara (CON - Strathtay)
bvaughan@pkc.gov.uk
Walker, Gordon (SNP - Carse of Gowrie)
gordonwalker@pkc.gov.uk
Williamson, Mike (SNP - Highland)
mwilliamson@pkc.gov.uk
Wilson, Willie (LD - Perth City South)
wowilson@pkc.gov.uk
Younger, Anne (SNP - Strathearn)
ayounger@pkc.gov.uk

POLITICAL COMPOSITION

SNP: 18, CON: 10, LD: 5, IND: 4, LAB: 4

COMMITTEE CHAIRS

Community Safety: Mr William Robertson
Development Control: Mr Willie Wilson
Enterprise & Infrastructure: Mr John Kellas
Environment: Mr Alan Grant
Housing & Health: Mr Peter Barrett
Licensing: Mr Peter Mulheron
Lifelong Learning: Mrs Elizabeth Grant
Scrutiny (Scrutiny): Ms Kathleen Baird
Strategic Policy & Resources: Mr Ian Miller

PETERBOROUGH CITY U

Peterborough City Council, Town Hall, Bridge Street, Peterborough PE1 1HG ☎ 01733 747474 🖷 01733 452537 ✉ ask@peterborough.gov.uk 💻 www.peterborough.gov.uk

FACTS & FIGURES

Police Authority: Cambridgeshire Police Authority
Health Authority: East of England Strategic Health Authority
Learning and Skills Council: Eastern
Parliamentary Constituencies: Cambridgeshire North West,

Peterborough
EU Constituencies: Eastern
Election Frequency: Elections are by thirds
Twinning: Bourges (France); Viersen (Germany); Alcala de Henares (Spain); Forli (Italy); Vinnitsa (Ukraine)

PRINCIPAL OFFICERS

Chief Executive: Mrs Gillian Beasley, Chief Executive, Town Hall, Bridge Street, Peterborough PE1 1HL ☎ 01733 452390 🖷 01733 452694 ✉ gillian.beasley@peterborough.gov.uk

Access Officer / Social Services (Disability): Mr Gerald Reilly, Access Officer, Stuart House (East Wing), St Johns Street, Peterborough PE1 5DD ☎ 01733 453539 🖷 01733 453539 ✉ gerald.reilly@peterborough.gov.uk

Architect, Building / Property Services: Ms Julie Robinson-Judd, Head of Asset Management, Peterborough City Council, Manor Drive House, Manor Drive, Paston Parkway, Peterborough PE4 7AP ☎ 01733 384544 🖷 0870 238 8338 ✉ julie.robinson.judd@peterborough.gov.uk

Building Control: Mr Kevin Dawson, Building Control Manager, Stuart House, East Wing, St. John's Street, Peterborough PE1 5DD ☎ 01733 453464 🖷 01733 453505 ✉ kevin.dawson@peterborough.gov.uk

Building Control: Mr Simon Machen, Head of Planning, Transport & Engineering Services, Town Hall, Bridge Street, Peterborough PE1 1HG ☎ 01733 453475 🖷 01733 453444 ✉ simon.machen@peterborough.gov.uk

Catering Services: Ms Joolz Wright, Senior Catering Contracts Manager, Enterprise Peterborough, Nursery Lane, Fengate, Peterborough PE1 5BG ☎ 01733 425324 🖷 01733 425395 ✉ joolz.wright@peterborough.gov.uk

Children / Youth Services: Mr Iain Easton, Head of Youth Offending Service, 13-15 Cavell Court, Bridge Street, Peterborough PE1 1RJ ☎ 01733 864237 ✉ iain.easton@peterborough.gov.uk

Children / Youth Services: Mr Malcolm Newsam, Interim Executive Director for Children's Services, Bayard Place, Broadway, Peterborough PE1 1FB ☎ 01733 863601 🖷 01733 863602 ✉ malcolm.newsam@peterborough.gov.uk

Civil Registration: Ms Ruth Hodson, Interim Registration Manager, Register Office, 33 Thorpe Road, Peterborough PE3 6AB ☎ 01733 864640 ✉ ruth.hodson@peterborough.gov.uk

PR / Communications: Ms Claire Hughes, Head of Strategic Communications, Town Hall, Bridge Street, Peterborough PE1 1HG ☎ 01733 452313 ✉ claire.hughes@peterborough.gov.uk

Community Planning: Mr Adrian Chapman, Head of Neighbourhood Services, Bayard Place, Broadway, Peterborough PE1 1HZ ☎ 01733 863887 ✉ adrian.chapman@peterborough.gov.uk

Community Safety: Mr Adrian Chapman, Head of Neighbourhood Services, Bayard Place, Broadway, Peterborough PE1 1HZ ☎ 01733 863887 ✉ adrian.chapman@peterborough.gov.uk

Computer Management: Mr Paul Tonks, Interim Head of Business Transformation, Town Hall, Bridge Street, Peterborough PE1 1HG ☎ 01733 452471 ✉ paul.tonks@peterborough.gov.uk

Contracts: Mrs Margaret Welton, Principal Lawyer for Contracts & Procurement, Town Hall, Bridge Street, Peterborough PE1 1HG ☎ 01733 452226 🖷 01733 452524 ✉ margaret.welton@peterborough.gov.uk

Corporate Services: Mr Steve Crabtree, Head of Internal Audit, Lion House, Lion Yard, Cambridge CB2 3NA ☎ 01223 458181; 01223 458181 ✉ steve.crabtree@cambridge.gov.uk

Corporate Services: Mr John Harrison, Executive Director for Strategic Resources, Manor Drive, Paston Parkway, Peterborough PE4 7AP ☎ 01733 452398 🖷 01733 452664 ✉ john.harrison@peterborough.gov.uk

Corporate Services: Mr Richard Hodgson, Head of Strategic Projects, Stuart House (East Wing), St Johns Street, Peterborough PE1 5DD ☎ 01733 384535 ✉ richard.hodgson@peterborough.gov.uk

Corporate Services: Mr Steven Pilsworth, Head of Corporate Services, Manor Drive, Paston Parkway, Peterborough PE4 7AP ☎ 01733 384564 ✉ steven.pilsworth@peterborough.gov.uk

Customer Service: Mr Mark Sandhu, Head of Customer Services, Customer Service Centre, Bayard Place, Broadway, Peterborough PE1 1FZ ☎ 01733 296321 🖷 01733 354396 ✉ mark.sandhu@peterborough.gov.uk

Economic Development: Mr Adrian Chapman, Head of Neighbourhood Services, Bayard Place, Broadway, Peterborough PE1 1HZ ☎ 01733 863887 ✉ adrian.chapman@peterborough.gov.uk

E-Government: Mr Paul Tonks, Interim Head of Business Transformation, Town Hall, Bridge Street, Peterborough PE1 1HG ☎ 01733 452471 ✉ paul.tonks@peterborough.gov.uk

Electoral Registration: Mrs Diane Baker, Head of Governance, Town Hall, Bridge Street, Peterborough PE1 1HG ☎ 01733 452559 🖷 01733 452403 ✉ diane.baker@peterborough.gov.uk

Electoral Registration: Ms Sally Crawford, Electoral Services Officer, Town Hall, Bridge Street, Peterborough PE1 1HG ☎ 01733 452339 ✉ sally.crawford@peterborough.gov.uk

Emergency Planning: Mr Stuart Hamilton, Resilience Team Manager, 11 Commerce Road, Lynchwood, Peterborough PE2 6LR ☎ 01733 207207 🖷 01733 236395 ✉ stuart.hamilton@peterborough.gov.uk

Environmental / Technical Services: Mr Paul Philipson, Executive Director - Operations, Bridge House, Town Bridge, Peterborough PE1 1HB ☎ 01733 453455 🖷 01733 453484 ✉ paul.philipson@peterborough.gov.uk

Environmental Health: Mr Paul Philipson, Executive Director - Operations, Bridge House, Town Bridge, Peterborough PE1 1HB ☎ 01733 453455 🖷 01733 453484 ✉ paul.philipson@peterborough.gov.uk

Estates, Property & Valuation: Ms Julie Robinson-Judd, Head of Asset Management, Peterborough City Council, Manor Drive House, Manor Drive, Paston Parkway, Peterborough PE4 7AP ☎ 01733 384544 🖷 0870 238 8338 ✉ julie.robinson.judd@peterborough.gov.uk

Events Manager: Ms Annette Joyce, City Centre Director, Town Hall, Bridge Street, Peterborough PE1 1HG ☎ 01733 452283 ✉ annette.joyce@peterborough.gov.uk

Finance and Treasurer: Mr John Harrison, Executive Director for Strategic Resources, Manor Drive, Paston Parkway, Peterborough PE4 7AP ☎ 01733 452398 🖷 01733 452664 ✉ john.harrison@peterborough.gov.uk

Highways: Mr Simon Machen, Head of Planning, Transport & Engineering Services, Town Hall, Bridge Street, Peterborough PE1 1HG ☎ 01733 453475 🖷 01733 453444 ✉ simon.machen@peterborough.gov.uk

Home Energy Conservation: Mr Adrian Chapman, Head of Neighbourhood Services, Bayard Place, Broadway, Peterborough PE1 1HZ ☎ 01733 863887 ✉ adrian.chapman@peterborough.gov.uk

Housing: Mr Adrian Chapman, Head of Neighbourhood Services, Bayard Place, Broadway, Peterborough PE1 1HZ ☎ 01733 863887 ✉ adrian.chapman@peterborough.gov.uk

Local Area Agreement: Mr Richard Astle, Director - GPP, 25 Priestgate, Peterborough PE1 1JL ☎ 01733 865040 ✉ richard@gpp-peterborough.org.uk

Legal: Ms Helen Edwards, Solicitor to the Council, Town Hall, Bridge Street, Peterborough PE1 1HG ☎ 01733 452539 ✉ helen.edwards@peterborough.gov.uk

Leisure and Cultural Services: Mr Kevin Tighe, Chief Executive, Vivacity, Central Library, Broadway, Peterborough PE1 1HZ ☎ 01733 863784 ✉ kevin.tighe@peterborough.gov.uk

Licensing: Mr Adrian Day, Licensing Manager, Bridge House, Town Bridge, Peterborough PE1 1HB ☎ 01733 454437 🖷 01733 453518 ✉ adrian.day@peterborough.gov.uk

Lighting: Mr Martin Medlock, Street Lighting Manager, Bridge House, Town Bridge, Peterborough PE1 1HB ☎ 01733 453525 🖷 01733 453444 ✉ martin.medlock@peterborough.gov.uk

Member Services: Mrs Diane Baker, Head of Governance, Town Hall, Bridge Street, Peterborough PE1 1HG ☎ 01733 452559 🖷 01733 452403 ✉ diane.baker@peterborough.gov.uk

Parking: Mr Robert Saunders, Parking Services Manager, City Centre Services, Chauffeur's Cottage, St. Peters Road, Peterborough PE1 1HG ☎ 01733 452380 ✉ robert.saunders@peterborough.gov.uk

Personnel / HR: Mr Mike Kealey, Acting Head of Human Resources, Manor Drive, Paston Parkway, Peterborough PE4 7AP ☎ 01733 384500 ✉ mike.kealey@peterborough.gov.uk

Planning: Mr Simon Machen, Head of Planning Services, Stuart House (East Wing), St Johns Street, Peterborough PE1 5DD ☎ 01733 453475 🖷 01733 890348 ✉ simon.machen@peterborough.gov.uk

Procurement: Mr Adam Jacobs, Procurement Project Director, Town Hall, Bridge Street, Peterborough PE1 1HG ☎ 01733 317960 ✉ adam.jacobs@peterborough.gov.uk

Public Libraries: Ms Heather Walton, Library & Customer Services Manager, Central Library, Broadway, Peterborough PE1 1RX ☎ 01733 864271 🖷 01733 319140 ✉ heather.walton@peterborough.gov.uk

Road Safety: Ms Clair George, Road Safety Officer, Bridge House, Town Bridge, Peterborough PE1 1HB ☎ 01733 453576 🖷 01733 453444 ✉ clair.george@peterborough.gov.uk

Road Safety: Mr Peter Tebb, Traffic Manager, Bridge House, Town Bridge, Peterborough PE1 1HB ☎ 01733 453519 🖷 01733 453444 ✉ peter.tebb@peterborough.gov.uk

Social Services: Mr Terry Rich, Director of Adult Social Services, Town Hall, Bridge Street, Peterborough PE1 1HG ☎ 01733 758444 🖷 01733 758555 ✉ terry.rich@peterboroughpct.nhs.uk

Social Services (Adult): Mr Terry Rich, Director of Adult Social Services, Town Hall, Bridge Street, Peterborough PE1 1HG ☎ 01733 758444 🖷 01733 758555 ✉ terry.rich@peterboroughpct.nhs.uk

Social Services (Children): Mr Terry Rich, Director of Adult Social Services, Town Hall, Bridge Street, Peterborough PE1 1HG ☎ 01733 758444 🖷 01733 758555 ✉ terry.rich@peterboroughpct.nhs.uk

Staff Training: Mr Colin Wilson, Training & Development Manager, Midgate House, Midgate, Peterborough PE1 1TN ☎ 01733 864626 🖷 01733 384511 ✉ colin.wilson@peterborough.gov.uk

Sustainable Communities: Ms Julia Chatterton, Sustainability Infrastructure Officer, Town Hall, Bridge Street, Peterborough PE1 1HG ☎ 01733 747474 ✉ julia.chatterton@opportunitypeterborough.co.uk

Sustainable Development: Mr Paul Philipson, Executive Director - Operations, Bridge House, Town Bridge, Peterborough PE1 1HB ☎ 01733 453455 🖷 01733 453484 ✉ paul.philipson@peterborough.gov.uk

Town Centre: Ms Annette Joyce, City Centre Director, Bridge House, Town Bridge, Peterborough PE1 1HB ☎ 01733 452283 ✉ annette.joyce@peterborough.gov.uk

Traffic Management: Mr Simon Machen, Head of Planning, Transport & Engineering Services, Town Hall, Bridge Street, Peterborough PE1 1HG ☎ 01733 453475 🖷 01733 453444

🖰 simon.machen@peterborough.gov.uk

Transport: Mr Barry Kirk, Transportation Group Manager, Stuart House (East Wing), St. Johns Street, Peterborough PE1 5DD ☎ 01733 317450 🖰 barry.kirk@peterborough.gov.uk

Transport Planner: Mr Mark Speed, Transport Planning Team Manager, Stuart House (East Wing), St. Johns Street, Peterborough PE1 5DD ☎ 01733 317471 🖰 mark.speed@peterborough.gov.uk

MEMBERS OF THE COUNCIL (57)

***Chair:* Simons**, George (CON - Paston)
george.simons@peterborough.gov.uk
***Deputy Mayor:* Stokes**, June (CON - Orton Waterville)
june.stokes@peterborough.gov.uk
***Leader of the Council:* Fitzgerald**, Wayne (CON - Stanground Central)
marco.cereste@peterborough.gov.uk
Allen, Sue (CON - Orton Waterville)
sue.allen@peterborough.gov.uk
Arculus, Nick (CON - West)
nick.arculus@peterborough.gov.uk
Ash, Chris (LIB - Dogsthorpe)
chris.ash@peterborough.gov.uk
Boast, Steve (CON - West)
matthew.dalton@peterborough.gov.uk
Casey, Graham (CON - Orton Longueville)
graham.casey@peterborough.gov.uk
Davidson, Julia (LD - Werrington South)
julia.davidson@peterborough.gov.uk
Day, Susan (CON - Paston)
sue.day@peterborough.gov.uk
Day, Sue (CON - Werrington South)
paula.thacker@peterborough.gov.uk
Elsey, Gavin (CON - Orton Waterville)
gavin.elsey@peterborough.gov.uk
Fitzgerald, Wayne (CON - Bretton North)
wayne.fitzgerald@peterborough.gov.uk
Forbes, Lisa (LAB - Orton Longueville)
lisa.forbes@peterborough.gov.uk
Fower, Darren (LD - Werrington South)
darren.fower@peterborough.gov.uk
Fox, Judith (IND - Werrington North)
judy.fox@peterborough.gov.uk
Fox, John (IND - Werrington North)
john.fox@peterborough.gov.uk
Goodwin, Janet (CON - Orton Longueville)
janet.goodwin@peterborough.gov.uk
Harper, Chris (CON - Stanground East)
chris.harper@peterborough.gov.uk
Harrington, David (IND - Newborough)
david.harrington@peterborough.gov.uk
Hiller, Peter (CON - Northborough)
peter.hiller@peterborough.gov.uk
Holdich, John (CON - Glinton and Wittering)
john.holdich@peterborough.gov.uk
Jamil, Mohammed (LAB - Central)
mohammed.jamil@peterborough.gov.uk
Johnson, Jo (LAB - East)
jo.johnson@peterborough.gov.uk
Khan, Nazim (LAB - Central)
nazim.khan@peterborough.gov.uk
Knowles, John (LAB - Paston)
john.knowles@peterborough.gov.uk
Kreling, Pam (CON - Park)
pam.kreling@peterborough.gov.uk
Lamb, Diane (CON - Glinton and Witering)
diane.lamb@peterborough.gov.uk
Lane, Stephen (IND - Werrington North)
stephen.lane@peterborough.gov.uk
Lee, Matthew (CON - Fletton and Woodston)
matthew.lee@peterborough.gov.uk
Maqbool, Yasmeen (CON - West)
yasmeen.maqbool@peterborough.gov.uk
Martin, Stuart (LAB - Bretton North)
stuart.martin@peterborough.gov.uk
Mckean, Dale (CON - Eye and Thorney)
dale.mckean@peterborough.gov.uk
Miners, Adrian (LIB - Dogsthorpe)
adrian.miners@peterborough.gov.uk
Murphy, Ed (LAB - Ravensthorpe)
ed.murphy@peterborough.gov.uk
Nadeem, Mohammed (CON - Central)
mohammed.nadeem@peterborough.gov.uk
Nawaz, Gul (CON - Ravensthorpe)
gul.nawaz@peterborough.gov.uk
Over, David (CON - Barnack)
david.over@peterborough.gov.uk
Peach, John (CON - Park)
john.peach@peterborough.gov.uk
Rush, Brian (CON - Stanground Central)
brian.rush@peterborough.gov.uk
Saltmarsh, Bella (LIB - Dogsthorpe)
bella.saltmarsh@peterborough.gov.uk
Sanders, David (CON - Eye and Thorney)
david.sanders@peterborough.gov.uk
Sandford, Nick (LD - Walton)
nick.sandford@peterborough.gov.uk
Scott, Sheila (CON - Orton with Hampton)
sheila.scott@peterborough.gov.uk
Seaton, David (CON - Orton with Hampton)
david.seaton@peterborough.gov.uk
Serluca, Lucia (CON - Fletton and woodston)
lucia.serluca@peterborough.gov.uk
Serulca, Lucia (CON - Orton with Hampton)
nigel.north@peterborough.gov.uk
Shabbir, Nabil (LAB - East)
nabil.shabbir@peterborough.gov.uk
Shaheed, Asif (LD - Walton)
asif.shaheed@peterborough.gov.uk
Sharp, Keith (IND - North)
keith.sharp@peterborough.gov.uk
Shearman, John (LAB - Park)
john.shearman@peterborough.gov.uk
Swift, Charles (IND - North)
charles.swift@peterborough.gov.uk
Sylvester, Ann (LAB - Bretton North)
ann.sylvester@peterborough.gov.uk
Thulbourn, Nick (LAB - Fletton and Woodston)
nick.thulbourn@peterborough.gov.uk
Todd, Marion (CON - Bretton South)
michael.fletcher@peterborough.gov.uk
Todd, Marion (CON - East)
marion.todd@peterborough.gov.uk
Walsh, Irene
(CON - Stanground Central)
irene.walsh@peterborough.gov.uk

POLITICAL COMPOSITION
CON: 33, LAB: 11, IND: 6, LD: 4, LIB: 3

CABINET
Leader of the Council / Growth, Strategic Planning & Economic Development: Mr Wayne Fitzgerald
Deputy Leader / Culture, Recreation & Strategic Commissioning: Mr Matthew Lee
Adult Social Care: Mr Wayne Fitzgerald
Cabinet Advisor to the Deputy Leader: Mr Gavin Elsey
Children's Services: Ms Sheila Scott
Communications: Mr Steve Boast
Community Cohesion, Safety & Women's Enterprise: Ms Irene Walsh
Education, Skills & University: Mr John Holdich
Housing, Neighbourhoods & Planning: Mr Peter Hiller
Resources: Mr David Seaton

COMMITTEE CHAIRS
Audit: Ms Diane Lamb
Creating Opportunities & Tackling Inequalities (Scrutiny): Ms Sue Day
Employment: Mr Wayne Fitzgerald
Licensing: Ms Paula Thacker
Planning & Environmental Protection: Ms Lucia Serulca
Scrutiny Commission for Health Issues: Mr Brian Rush
Scrutiny Commission for Rural Communities: Mr David Over
Standards: Mr Steve Boast
Sustainable Growth (Scrutiny): Ms Marion Todd

PLYMOUTH CITY U

Plymouth City Council, Civic Centre, Royal Parade, Plymouth PL1 2AA ☎ 01752 668000 🖷 01752 304880 ✉ info@plymouth.gov.uk
💻 www.plymouth.gov.uk

FACTS & FIGURES
Police Authority: Devon & Cornwall Police Authority
Health Authority: NHS South West
Learning and Skills Council: South West
EU Constituencies: South West
Election Frequency: Elections are by thirds
Twinning: Brest (France); Gdynia (Poland); San Sebastian (Spain); Novorossisk (Russia) Plymouth (Massachusetts, USA)

PRINCIPAL OFFICERS
Chief Executive: Mr Bob Coomber, Interim Chief Executive, Civic Centre, Royal Parade, Plymouth PL1 2AA
✉ bob.coomber@plymouth.gov.uk

Senior Management: Mr Pete Aley, Assistant Director for Safer Communities, Civic Centre, Royal Parade, Plymouth PL1 2AA
☎ 01752 304321 🖷 01752 304536 ✉ pete.aley@plymouth.gov.uk

Senior Management: Mr Adam Broome, Director for Corporate Support, Civic Centre, Royal Parade, Plymouth PL1 2AA ☎ 01752 304940 🖷 01752 304923 ✉ adam.broome@plymouth.gov.uk

Senior Management: Mrs Carol Burgoyne, Director for People, Civic Centre, Royal Parade, Plymouth PL1 2AA ☎ 01752 307463
✉ carol.burgoyne@plymouth.gov.uk

Senior Management: Mr David Draffan, Assistant Director for Economic Development, Civic Centre, West Paddock, Leyland PR25 1DH ☎ 01752 306747 ✉ david.draffan@plymouth.gov.uk

Architect, Building / Property Services: Mr Anthony Payne, Director for Place, Civic Centre, Royal Parade, Plymouth PL1 2AA
☎ 01752 304170 🖷 01752 304536
✉ anthony.payne@plymouth.gov.uk

Building Control: Mr Paul Barnard, Assistant Director for Planning Services, Civic Centre, Royal Parade, Plymouth PL1 2AA
☎ 01752 304077 🖷 01752 304852
✉ paul.barnard@plymouth.gov.uk

Civil Registration: Ms Karen Ward, Superintendent Registrar, Registrars Office, Lockyer Street, Plymouth PL1 2AA
☎ 01752 307223 🖷 01752 256046
✉ karen.ward@plymouth.gov.uk

PR / Communications: Mr Richard Longford, Head of Communications, Civic Centre, Royal Parade, Plymouth PL1 2AA
☎ 01752 307816 🖷 01752 304933
✉ richard.longford@plymouth.gov.uk

Community Planning: Mr Paul Barnard, Assistant Director for Planning Services, Civic Centre, Royal Parade, Plymouth PL1 2AA
☎ 01752 304077 🖷 01752 304852
✉ paul.barnard@plymouth.gov.uk

Community Safety: Mr Pete Aley, Assistant Director for Safer Communities, Civic Centre, Royal Parade, Plymouth PL1 2AA
☎ 01752 304321 🖷 01752 304536 ✉ pete.aley@plymouth.gov.uk

Computer Management: Mr Neville Cannon, Programe Director for ICT Shared Services, Civic Centre, Royal Parade, Plymouth PL1 2AA ☎ 01752 304522 🖷 01752 304997
✉ neville.cannon@plymouth.gov.uk

Consumer Protection and Trading Standards: Mr Robin Carton, Public Protection Service Manager, Civic Centre, Plymouth PL1 2AA ☎ 01752 304141
✉ robin.carton@plymouth.gov.uk

Contracts: Ms Jane Keeley, Strategic Procurement Manager, Civic Centre, Royal Parade, Plymouth PL1 2AA ☎ 01752 307967
✉ jane.keeley@plymouth.gov.uk

Corporate Services: Mr Giles Perritt, Head of Policy, Performance & Partnership, Civic Centre, Royal Parade, Plymouth PL1 2AA ☎ 01752 304388 ✉ giles.peritt@plymouth.gov.uk

Customer Service: Mr John Paul Sanders, Assistant Director for Customer Services & Business Transformation, Civic Centre, Royal Parade, Plymouth PL1 2AA ☎ 01752 304003
✉ johnpaul.sanders@plymouth.gov.uk

Economic Development: Mr David Draffan, Assistant Director for Economic Development, Civic Centre, Royal Parade, Plymouth PL1 2AA ☎ 01752 306747 ✉ david.draffan@plymouth.gov.uk

E-Government: Mr Neville Cannon, Programe Director for ICT Shared Services, Civic Centre, Royal Parade, Plymouth PL1 2AA

☎ 01752 304522 🖷 01752 304997
✉ neville.cannon@plymouth.gov.uk

Electoral Registration: Mr Nigel Spilsbury, Electoral Services Manager, Civic Centre, Royal Parade, Plymouth PL1 2AA ☎ 01752 304861 🖷 01752 304819 ✉ nigel.spilsbury@plymouth.gov.uk

Emergency Planning: Mr Scott Senior, Civil Protection Manager, Civic Centre, Royal Parade, Plymouth PL1 2AA ☎ 01752 307723 🖷 01752 305519 ✉ scott.senior@plymouth.gov.uk

Energy Management: Mr Robin Carton, Public Protection Service Manager, Civic Centre, Royal Parade, Plymouth PL1 2AA ☎ 01752 304141 ✉ robin.carton@plymouth.gov.uk

Environmental Health: Ms Jayne Donovan, Assistant Director for Environmental Services, Civic Centre, Royal Parade, Plymouth PL1 2AA ☎ 01752 304754 ✉ jayne.donovan@plymouth.gov.uk

Finance and Treasurer: Mr Adam Broome, Director for Corporate Support, Civic Centre, Royal Parade, Plymouth PL1 2AA ☎ 01752 304940 🖷 01752 304923
✉ adam.broome@plymouth.gov.uk

Fleet Management: Mr Garry Stainer, Fleet & Garage Manager, Prince Rock Depot, Macadam Road, Plymouth PL4 0RZ ☎ 01752 304682 🖷 01752 304680 ✉ garry.stainer@plymouth.gov.uk

Grounds Maintenance: Mr Nick Jones, Principal Parks Manager, Central Park Depot, 90-92 Outland Road, Plymouth PL1 2AA ☎ 01752 304617 🖷 01752 509006 ✉ nick.jones@plymouth.gov.uk

Health and Safety: Mr Malcolm Fieldsend, Senior Health, Safety & Well-Being Adviser, Civic Centre, Royal Parade, Plymouth PL1 2AA ☎ 01752 312505 ✉ malcolm.fieldsend@plymouth.gov.uk

Home Energy Conservation: Mr Colin Anderson, Home Energy Co-ordinator, Civic Centre, Plymouth PL1 2AA ☎ 01752 307571 🖷 01752 307091 ✉ colin.anderson@plymouth.gov.uk

Housing: Mr Stuart Palmer, Assistant Director for Strategic Housing, Civic Centre, Royal Parade, Plymouth PL1 2AA ☎ 01752 306747 ✉ stuart.palmer@plymouth.gov.uk

Legal: Mr Tim Howes, Assistant Director for Democracy & Governance, Civic Centre, Royal Parade, Plymouth PL1 2AA ☎ 01752 305403 🖷 01752 306082 ✉ tim.howes@plymouth.gov.uk

Licensing: Mr Robin Carton, Public Protection Service Manager, Civic Centre, Plymouth PL1 2AA ☎ 01752 304141
✉ robin.carton@plymouth.gov.uk

Lighting: Ms Nicola Bleasdale, Street Care Co-ordinator, Civic Centre, Royal Parade, Plymouth PL1 2AA ☎ 01752 668000
✉ nicola.bleasdale@amey.co.uk

Member Services: Ms Judith Shore, Democractic & Members' Support Manager, Civic Centre, Royal Parade, Plymouth PL1 2AA ☎ 01752 304494 ✉ judith.shore@plymouth.gov.uk

Parking: Mr Mike Artherton, Parking & CCTV Manager, Civic Centre, Royal Parade, Plymouth PL1 2AA ☎ 01752 305582
✉ mike.artherton@plymouth.gov.uk

Partnerships: Mr Giles Perritt, Head of Policy, Performance & Partnership, Civic Centre, Royal Parade, Plymouth PL1 2AA ☎ 01752 304388 ✉ giles.peritt@plymouth.gov.uk

Personnel / HR: Mr Mark Grimley, Assistant Director for Human Resources & Organisational Development, Civic Centre, Royal Parade, Plymouth PL1 2AA ☎ 01752 304890 🖷 01752 304900
✉ mark.grimley@plymouth.gov.uk

Planning: Mr Paul Barnard, Assistant Director for Planning Services, Civic Centre, Royal Parade, Plymouth PL1 2AA ☎ 01752 304077 🖷 01752 304852 ✉ paul.barnard@plymouth.gov.uk

Procurement: Ms Jane Keeley, Strategic Procurement Manager, Civic Centre, Royal Parade, Plymouth PL1 2AA ☎ 01752 307967
✉ jane.keeley@plymouth.gov.uk

Recycling & Waste Minimisation: Ms Jayne Donovan, Assistant Director for Environmental Services, Civic Centre, Royal Parade, Plymouth PL1 2AA ☎ 01752 304754
✉ jayne.donovan@plymouth.gov.uk

Regeneration: Mr Anthony Payne, Director for Place, Civic Centre, Royal Parade, Plymouth PL1 2AA ☎ 01752 304170
🖷 01752 304536 ✉ anthony.payne@plymouth.gov.uk

Road Safety: Ms Susan Keith, Road Safety Team Manager, Civic Centre, Royal Parade, Plymouth PL1 2AA ☎ 01752 307729
✉ susan.keith@plymouth.gov.uk

Social Services (Adult): Ms Pam Marsden, Assistant Director forJoint Comisioning & Adult Health & Social Care, Civic Centre, Royal Parade, Plymouth PL1 2AA ☎ 01752 307344
✉ pamela.marsden@plymouth.gov.uk

Sustainable Development: Mr Paul Elliott, Sustainable Energy Officer, Civic Centre, Royal Parade, Plymouth PL1 2AA ☎ 01752 307571 ✉ paul.elliott@plymouth.gov.uk

Tourism: Mr David Draffan, Assistant Director for Economic Development, Civic Centre, West Paddock, Leyland PR25 1DH ☎ 01752 306747 ✉ david.draffan@plymouth.gov.uk

Town Centre: Mr Clint Jones, City Centre Manager, Civic Centre, Royal Parade, Plymouth PL1 2AA ☎ 01752 305468
✉ clint.jones@plymouth.gov.uk

MEMBERS OF THE COUNCIL (57)

***The Lord Mayor:* Wright**, Mike (LAB - Moor View)
mike.wright@plymouth.gov.uk
***Deputy Lord Mayor:* Singh**, Chaz (LAB - Drake)
chaz.singh@plymouth.gov.uk
***Leader of the Council:* Evans**, Tudor (LAB - Ham)
tudor.evans@plymouth.gov.uk
Aspinall, Mary (LAB - Sutton and Mount Gould)
mary.aspinall@plymouth.gov.uk
Aspinall, Mary (CON - Plympton St Mary)
david.j.james@plymouth.gov.uk
Aspinall, Mary (CON - Eggbuckland)
lynda.bowyer@plymouth.gov.uk

Ball, Richard (CON - Compton)
richard.ball@plymouth.gov.uk
Beer, Terri (CON - Plympton Erle)
terri.beer@plymouth.gov.uk
Berrow, Peter (CON - Southway)
peter.berrow@plymouth.gov.uk
Bowie, Sally (LAB - St Budeaux)
sally.bowie@plymouth.gov.uk
Bowyer, Ian (CON - Eggbuckland)
ian.bowyer@plymouth.gov.uk
Casey, Alison (LAB - Moor View)
alison.casey@plymouth.gov.uk
Churchill, Nigel (CON - Plymstock Dunstone)
nigel.churchill@plymouth.gov.uk
Coker, Mark (LAB - Devonport)
mark.coker@plymouth.gov.uk
Damarell, Danny (LAB - St Budeaux)
Darcy, Ian (CON - Plympton Erle)
ian.darcy@plymouth.gov.uk
Davey, Sam (LAB - Stoke)
sam.davey@plymouth.gov.uk
Davey, Philippa (LAB - Stoke)
Dolan, Jill (CON - Stoke)
jill.dolan@plymouth.gov.uk
Drean, Jonathan (CON - Budshead)
jonathan.drean@plymouth.gov.uk
Foster, Wendy (CON - Plymstock Radford)
wendy.foster@plymouth.gov.uk
Foster, Ken (CON - Plymstock Radford)
kenneth.foster@plymouth.gov.uk
Fox, Mike (LAB - Moor View)
`mike.fox@plymouth.gov.uk
Fry, Ted (CON - Compton)
ted.fry@plymouth.gov.uk
Gordon, Ian (LAB - Ham)
ian.gordon@plymouth.gov.uk
Haydon, David (LAB - Efford and Lipson)
david.haydon@plymouth.gov.uk
Jarvis, Paul (LAB - Eggbuckland)
paul.jarvis@plymouth.gov.uk
Jordan, Glenn (CON - Plympton Chaddlewood)
glenn.jordan@plymouth.gov.uk
Leaves, Martin (CON - Peverell)
martin.leaves@plymouth.gov.uk
Leaves, Michael (CON - Plymstock Radford)
michael.leaves@plymouth.gov.uk
Leaves, Samantha (CON - Plympton St Mary)
samantha.leaves@plymouth.gov.uk
Lowry, Mark (LAB - Honicknowle)
mark.lowry@plymouth.gov.uk
McDonald, Susan (LAB - St Peter and the Waterfront)
susan.mcdonald@plymouth.gov.uk
Monahan, Grant (CON - Budshead)
grant.monahan@plymouth.gov.uk
Murphy, Pauline (LAB - Efford and Lipson)
pauline.murphy@plymouth.gov.uk
Nelder, Jean (LAB - Sutton and Mount Gould)
jean.nelder@plymouth.gov.uk
Nicholson, Patricia (CON - Peverell)
patricia.nicholson@plymouth.gov.uk
Nicholson, Patrick (CON - Plympton St Mary)
patrick.nicholson@plymouth.gov.uk
Parker, Lorraine (LAB - Southway)
lorraine.parker@plymouth.gov.uk
Penberthy, Chris (LAB - St Peter and the Waterfront)
chris.penberthy@plymouth.gov.uk
Pengelly, Vivien (CON - Plymstock Dunstone)
vivien.pengelly@plymouth.gov.uk
Rennie, Eddie (LAB - Sutton and Mount Gould)
eddie.rennie@plymouth.gov.uk
Ricketts, Steven (CON - Drake)
steven.ricketts@plymouth.gov.uk
Salter, David (CON - Plympton Chaddlewood)
david.salter@plymouth.gov.uk
Smith, John (LAB - Southway)
john.smith@plymouth.gov.uk
Smith, Peter (LAB - Honicknowle)
peter.smith@plymouth.gov.uk
Stark, David (CON - Compton)
david.stark@plymouth.gov.uk
Stevens, William (LAB - Devonport)
william.stevens@plymouth.gov.uk
Taylor, Kate (LAB - Devonport)
Kate.taylor@plymouth.gov.uk
Taylor, John (LAB - Budshead)
jon.taylor@plymouth.gov.uk
Tuffin, Ian (LAB - St Peter and the Waterfront)
ian.tuffin@plymouth.gov.uk
Tuohy, Tina (LAB - Ham)
tina.tuohy@plymouth.gov.uk
Vincent, Brian (LAB - Efford and Lipson)
brian.vincent@plymouth.gov.uk
Wheeler, George (LAB - St Budeaux)
george.wheeler@plymouth.gov.uk
Wheeler, George (CON - Peverell)
john.mahony@plymouth.gov.uk
Wigens, Kevin (CON - Plymstock Dunstone)
kevin.wigens@plymouth.gov.uk
Williams, Nicky (LAB - Honicknowle)
nicky.williams@plymouth.gov.uk

POLITICAL COMPOSITION

LAB: 31, CON: 26

CABINET

Leader: Mr Tudor Evans
Deputy Leader: Mr Peter Smith
Adult Health & Social Care: Ms Susan McDonald
Children & Young People: Ms Nicky Williams
Environment: Mr Brian Vincent
Finance: Mr Ian Bowyer
Transport: Mr Mark Coker

COMMITTEE CHAIRS

Audit: Mr George Wheeler
Children & Young People (Scrutiny): Ms Sally Bowie
Customers & Communities (Scrutiny): Mr Ian Tuffin
Growth & Prosperity (Scrutiny): Mr Patrick Nicholson
Health & Adult Social Care (Scrutiny): Ms Mary Aspinall
Licensing: Mr Eddie Rennie
Overview & Scrutiny Commission (Scrutiny): Ms Mary Aspinall
Planning: Mr Bill Stevens
Standards: Mr Pearce

POOLE U

Borough of Poole, Civic Centre Annexe, Poole BH15 2RU
☎ 01202 633633 🖷 01202 633706 ✉ enquiries@poole.gov.uk
💻 www.boroughofpoole.com

FACTS & FIGURES

Police Authority: Dorset Police Authority
Health Authority: NHS South West
Learning and Skills Council: South West
Parliamentary Constituencies: Dorset Mid and Poole North, Poole
EU Constituencies: South West
Election Frequency: Elections are of whole council
Twinning: Cherbourg

PRINCIPAL OFFICERS

Chief Executive: Mr John McBride, Chief Executive, Civic Centre, Poole BH15 2RU ☎ 01202 633001 🖷 01202 633899 ✉ j.mcbride@poole.gov.uk

Architect, Building / Property Services: Mr Jim Bright, Acting Head of Asset Management & Property Services, Civic Centre Annexe, Poole BH15 2RU ☎ 01202 261200 🖷 01202 261211 ✉ j.bright@poole.gov.uk

Best Value: Ms Bridget West, Corporate Performance Manager, Civic Centre, Poole BH15 2RU ☎ 01202 633085 🖷 01202 633899 ✉ bridget.west@poole.gov.uk

Building Control: Mr Stephen Thorne, Head of Planning & Regeneration Services, Civic Centre Annexe, Poole BH15 2RU ☎ 01202 633327 🖷 01202 633345 ✉ s.thorne@poole.gov.uk

Catering Services: Ms Tina Hayter, Executive Catering Manager, Crown Buildings 4th Floor, Civic Centre, Poole BH15 2RU ☎ 01202 261178 🖷 01202 261001 ✉ t.hayter@poole.gov.uk

Children / Youth Services: Mrs Vicky Wales, Head of Children & Young People's Integrated Services, The Dolphin Centre, Poole BH15 1SZ ☎ 01202 262251 ✉ v.wales@poole.gov.uk

Civil Registration: Mr Tim Martin, Head of Legal & Democratic Services, Civic Centre, Poole BH15 2RU ☎ 01202 633021 🖷 01202 633040 ✉ t.martin@poole.gov.uk

PR / Communications: Mr Chris Owens, Head of Customer Services & Communications, Civic Centre, Poole BH15 2RU ☎ 01202 633487 ✉ chris.owens@poole.gov.uk

Community Planning: Mr Stephen Thorne, Head of Planning & Regeneration Services, Civic Centre Annexe, Poole BH15 2RU ☎ 01202 633327 🖷 01202 633345 ✉ s.thorne@poole.gov.uk

Community Safety: Mrs Anthi Minhinnick, Community Safety Partnership Manager, Joint Emergency Services Building, Wimbourne Road, Poole BH15 2RU ☎ 01202 223320 ✉ a.minhinnick@poole.gov.uk

Computer Management: Mrs Katie Lacey, Head of ICT & Business Support, Civic Centre, Poole BH15 2RU ☎ 01202 633186 🖷 01202 633163 ✉ k.lacey@poole.gov.uk

Consumer Protection and Trading Standards: Mr Shaun Robson, Head of Environmental & Consumer Protection, Unit 1, Newfields Business Park, 2 Stinsford Road, Poole BH17 0NF ☎ 01202 261701 🖷 01202 262240 ✉ s.robson@poole.gov.uk

Contracts: Mr Jeremy Richardson, Strategic Procurement Manager, Civic Centre, Poole BH15 2RU ☎ 01202 633208 🖷 01202 261241 ✉ j.richardson@poole.gov.uk

Customer Service: Mr Chris Owens, Head of Customer Services & Communications, Civic Centre, Poole BH15 2RU ☎ 01202 633487 ✉ chris.owens@poole.gov.uk

Economic Development: Mr Stephen Thorne, Head of Planning & Regeneration Services, Civic Centre Annexe, Poole BH15 2RU ☎ 01202 633327 🖷 01202 633345 ✉ s.thorne@poole.gov.uk

Education: Mr Stuart Twiss, Head of Children & Young People's Strategy, Quality & Improvement Services, Crown Buildings, 7th Floor, Civic Centre, Poole BH15 2RU ☎ 01202 633769 ✉ s.twiss@poole.gov.uk

Education: Mrs Vicky Wales, Head of Children & Young People's Integrated Services, The Dolphin Centre, Poole BH15 1SZ ☎ 01202 262251 ✉ v.wales@poole.gov.uk

Electoral Registration: Mr Paul Morris, Registration Services Manager, Room 157, Civic Centre, Poole BH15 2RH ☎ 01202 633028 🖷 01202 633094 ✉ p.morris@poole.gov.uk

Emergency Planning: Mr Simon Young, Business Continuity & Resilience Manager, Civic Centre, Poole BH15 2RU ☎ 01202 633450 ✉ simon.young@poole.gov.uk

Energy Management: Mr Julian Collins, Corporate Energy Conservation Officer, Civic Centre Annexe, Poole BH15 2RU ☎ 01202 261219 🖷 01202 261211 ✉ j.collins@poole.gov.uk

Environmental / Technical Services: Mr Shaun Robson, Head of Environmental & Consumer Protection, Unit 1, Newfields Business Park, 2 Stinsford Road, Poole BH17 0NF ☎ 01202 261701 🖷 01202 262240 ✉ s.robson@poole.gov.uk

Environmental Health: Mr Shaun Robson, Head of Environmental & Consumer Protection, Unit 1, Newfields Business Park, 2 Stinsford Road, Poole BH17 0NF ☎ 01202 261701 🖷 01202 262240 ✉ s.robson@poole.gov.uk

Estates, Property & Valuation: Mr Jim Bright, Acting Head of Asset Management & Property Services, Civic Centre Annexe, Poole BH15 2RU ☎ 01202 261200 🖷 01202 261211 ✉ j.bright@poole.gov.uk

European Liaison: Mr Stephen Thorne, Head of Planning & Regeneration Services, Civic Centre Annexe, Poole BH15 2RU ☎ 01202 633327 🖷 01202 633345 ✉ s.thorne@poole.gov.uk

Events Manager: Mr Chris Owens, Head of Customer Services & Communications, Civic Centre, Poole BH15 2RU ☎ 01202 633487 ✉ chris.owens@poole.gov.uk

Facilities: Mr Fred Painter, Facilities Manager, Civic Centre Annexe, Park Road, Poole BH15 2RN ☎ 01202 261231 ✉ f.painter@poole.gov.uk

Finance and Treasurer: Mr Adam Richens, Acting Head of Financial Services, Civic Centre, Poole BH15 2RU ☎ 01202

633105 🖷 01202 633811 ✉ a.richens@poole.gov.uk

Fleet Management: Mr Shaun Robson, Head of Environmental & Consumer Protection, Unit 1, Newfields Business Park, 2 Stinsford Road, Poole BH17 0NF ☎ 01202 261701 🖷 01202 262240 ✉ s.robson@poole.gov.uk

Grounds Maintenance: Mr Clive Smith, Head of Leisure Services, Creekmoor Centre, Northmead Drive, Poole BH17 7RP ☎ 01202 261380 🖷 01202 261381 ✉ c.smith@poole.gov.uk

Health and Safety: Mr Vincent Axford, Health & Safety Officer, Unit 1, Newfields Business Park, 2 Stinsford Road, Poole BH17 0NF ☎ 01202 633463 🖷 01202 633477 ✉ v.axford@poole.gov.uk

Highways: Mr Julian McLaughlin, Head of Transportation Services, St Johns House, Serpentine Road, Poole BH15 2DX ☎ 01202 262100 🖷 01202 262230 ✉ julian.mclaughlin@poole.gov.uk

Home Energy Conservation: Mr Julian Collins, Corporate Energy Conservation Officer, Civic Centre Annexe, Poole BH15 2RU ☎ 01202 261219 🖷 01202 261211 ✉ j.collins@poole.gov.uk

Housing: Ms Cally Antill, Head of Housing & Community Services, Civic Centre, Poole BH15 2RU ☎ 01202 633440 ✉ c.antill@poole.gov.uk

Local Area Agreement: Ms Hilary Evans, Community Strategy Manager, Civic Centre, Poole BH15 2RU ☎ 01202 633067 ✉ h.evans@poole.gov.uk

Legal: Mr Tim Martin, Head of Legal & Democratic Services, Civic Centre, Poole BH15 2RU ☎ 01202 633021 🖷 01202 633040 ✉ t.martin@poole.gov.uk

Leisure and Cultural Services: Mr Clive Smith, Head of Leisure Services, Creekmoor Centre, Northmead Drive, Poole BH17 7RP ☎ 01202 261380 🖷 01202 261381 ✉ c.smith@poole.gov.uk

Licensing: Mr Shaun Robson, Head of Environmental & Consumer Protection, Unit 1, Newfields Business Park, 2 Stinsford Road, Poole BH17 0NF ☎ 01202 261701 🖷 01202 262240 ✉ s.robson@poole.gov.uk

Lifelong Learning: Mr Kevin McErlane, Head of Culture & Community Learning, Poole Central Library, The Dolphin Centre, Poole BH15 1QE ☎ 01202 262400 🖷 01202 262431 ✉ k.mcerlane@poole.gov.uk

Lighting: Mr Steven Norcliffe, Engineer (Street Lighting), Hatchpond Depot, Hatchpond Road, Poole BH17 7LQ ☎ 01202 262248 🖷 01202 262029 ✉ s.norcliffe@poole.gov.uk

Lottery Funding, Charity and Voluntary: Ms Karen Naylor, Principal Officer Planning & Quality Assurance, Crown Buildings 3rd Floor, Poole BH15 2RU ☎ 01202 261130 🖷 01202 261161 ✉ k.naylor@poole.gov.uk

Lottery Funding, Charity and Voluntary: Mr Anthony Rogers, Recreation Manager, Creekmoor Centre, Northmead Drive, Poole BH17 7RP ☎ 01202 261345 🖷 01202 261342 ✉ a.rogers@poole.gov.uk

Member Services: Miss Pauline Gill, Democratic Services Manager, Civic Centre, Poole BH15 2RU ☎ 01202 633043 🖷 01202 633040 ✉ p.gill@poole.gov.uk

Parking: Mr Jason Benjamin, Parking Services Manager, St John's House, Serpentine Road, Poole BH15 2DX ☎ 01202 262150 🖷 01202 265259 ✉ j.benjamin@poole.gov.uk

Partnerships: Ms Hilary Evans, Community Strategy Manager, Civic Centre, Poole BH15 2RU ☎ 01202 633067 ✉ h.evans@poole.gov.uk

Personnel / HR: Mr Carl Wilcox, Head of Human Resources, Civic Centre, Poole BH15 2RU ☎ 01202 633452 🖷 01202 633477 ✉ c.wilcox@poole.gov.uk

Planning: Mr Stephen Thorne, Head of Planning & Regeneration Services, Civic Centre Annexe, Poole BH15 2RU ☎ 01202 633327 🖷 01202 633345 ✉ s.thorne@poole.gov.uk

Procurement: Mr Jeremy Richardson, Strategic Procurement Manager, Civic Centre, Poole BH15 2RU ☎ 01202 633208 🖷 01202 261241 ✉ j.richardson@poole.gov.uk

Public Libraries: Mr Kevin McErlane, Head of Culture & Community Learning, Poole Central Library, The Dolphin Centre, Poole BH15 1QE ☎ 01202 262400 🖷 01202 262431 ✉ k.mcerlane@poole.gov.uk

Recycling & Waste Minimisation: Mr Tom Gaze, Waste Management Officer, Unit 1 New Fields Business Park, Stinsford Road, Poole BH17 0NF ☎ 01202 261742 🖷 01202 261717 ✉ t.gaze@poole.gov.uk

Regeneration: Mr Stephen Thorne, Head of Planning & Regeneration Services, Civic Centre Annexe, Poole BH15 2RU ☎ 01202 633327 🖷 01202 633345 ✉ s.thorne@poole.gov.uk

Road Safety: Mr Martin Baker, Senior Road Safety Engineer, St John's House, Serpentine Road, Poole BH15 2DX ☎ 01202 262073 🖷 01202 262230 ✉ m.baker@poole.gov.uk

Social Services: Ms Jan Thurgood, Strategic Director, Civic Centre, Poole BH15 2RU ☎ 01202 633207 ✉ j.thurgood@poole.gov.uk

Social Services (Adult): Mr John Dermody, Head of Adult Social Services (Commissioning), Civic Centre Annexe, Poole BH15 2RU ☎ 01202 261132 ✉ j.dermody@poole.gov.uk

Social Services (Adult): Mr David Vitty, Head of Adult Social Care, Commissioning & Improvement, Crown Buildings 4th Floor, Civic Centre, Poole BH15 2RU ☎ 01202 261030 🖷 01202 261001 ✉ d.vitty@poole.gov.uk

Social Services (Children): Ms Gerry Moore, Head of Children & Young People's Social Care, 14a Commercial Road, Poole BH15 0JW ☎ 01202 714715 🖷 01202 715589 ✉ gerry.moore@poole.gov.uk

Staff Training: Mr Carl Wilcox, Head of Human Resources, Civic Centre, Poole BH15 2RU ☎ 01202 633452 🖷 01202 633477

c.wilcox@poole.gov.uk

Street Scene: Mr Shaun Robson, Head of Environmental & Consumer Protection, Unit 1, Newfields Business Park, 2 Stinsford Road, Poole BH17 0NF ☎ 01202 261701 🖷 01202 262240 s.robson@poole.gov.uk

Sustainable Communities: Ms Jan Thurgood, Strategic Director, Civic Centre, Poole BH15 2RU ☎ 01202 633207 j.thurgood@poole.gov.uk

Tourism: Mr Graham Richardson, Tourism Manager, Enefco House, Visitor Welcome Centre, 19 Strand Street, The Quay, Poole BH15 1HE ☎ 01202 262539 🖷 01202 262684 g.richardson@pooletourism.com

Town Centre: Mr Graham Richardson, Tourism Manager, Enefco House, Visitor Welcome Centre, 19 Strand Street, The Quay, Poole BH15 1HE ☎ 01202 262539 🖷 01202 262684 g.richardson@pooletourism.com

Traffic Management: Mr Julian McLaughlin, Head of Transportation Services, St Johns House, Serpentine Road, Poole BH15 2DX ☎ 01202 262100 🖷 01202 262230 julian.mclaughlin@poole.gov.uk

Transport: Mr Julian McLaughlin, Head of Transportation Services, St Johns House, Serpentine Road, Poole BH15 2DX ☎ 01202 262100 🖷 01202 262230 julian.mclaughlin@poole.gov.uk

Transport Planner: Mr Julian McLaughlin, Head of Transportation Services, St Johns House, Serpentine Road, Poole BH15 2DX ☎ 01202 262100 🖷 01202 262230 julian.mclaughlin@poole.gov.uk

Waste Collection and Disposal: Mr Shaun Robson, Head of Environmental & Consumer Protection, Unit 1, Newfields Business Park, 2 Stinsford Road, Poole BH17 0NF ☎ 01202 261701 🖷 01202 262240 s.robson@poole.gov.uk

Waste Management: Mr Shaun Robson, Head of Environmental & Consumer Protection, Unit 1, Newfields Business Park, 2 Stinsford Road, Poole BH17 0NF ☎ 01202 261701 🖷 01202 262240 s.robson@poole.gov.uk

MEMBERS OF THE COUNCIL (42)

Leader of the Council: **Atkinson**, Elaine (CON - Penn Hill)
elaine.atkinson@poole.gov.uk
Deputy Leader of the Council: **White**, Michael (CON - Hamworthy East)
mike.white@poole.gov.uk
Adams, Peter (CON - Oakdale)
p.adams@poole.gov.uk
Brooke, Michael (LD - Broadstone)
m.brooke@poole.gov.uk
Brown, David (LD - Merley and Bearwood)
d.brown@poole.gov.uk
Burden, Les (CON - Creekmoor)
l.burden@poole.gov.uk
Butt, Judy (CON - Creekmoor)
j.butt@poole.gov.uk
Carpenter, Sally (CON - Parkstone)
s.carpenter@poole.gov.uk
Chandler, Graham (CON - Hamworthy West)
g.chandler@poole.gov.uk
Clements, Jo (LD - Newtown)
Clements, Brian (LD - Newtown)
b.clements@poole.gov.uk
Cox, Sandra (LD - Merley and Bearwood)
s.cox@poole.gov.uk
Dion, Xena (CON - Penn Hill)
x.dion@poole.gov.uk
Eades, Phillip (LD - Branksome West)
p.eades@poole.gov.uk
Evans, Carol (CON - Poole Town)
c.evans@poole.gov.uk
Godfrey, Roy (LD - Broadstone)
Goodall, Phil (LD - Canford Heath West)
p.goodall@poole.gov.uk
Haines, May (CON - Canford Cliffs)
m.haines@poole.gov.uk
Hodges, Jennie (LD - Canford Heath East)
j.hodges@poole.gov.uk
Howell, Mark (IND - Poole Town)
m.howel@poole.gov.uk
Le Poidevin, Marion (LD - Branksome West)
m.lepoidevin@gov.uk
Maiden, Peter (LD - Merley and Bearwood)
p.maiden@poole.gov.uk
Matthews, Christopher (LD - Canford Heath West)
c.matthews@poole.gov.uk
Meachin, Charles (LD - Alderney)
c.meachin@poole.gov.uk
Moore, Sandra (LD - Canford Heath East)
s.moore@poole.gov.uk
Parker, Ron (CON - Penn Hill)
r.parker@poole.gov.uk
Parkinson, Charmaine (IND - Hamworthy East)
c.parkinson@poole.gov.uk
Pawlowski, Peter (CON - Canford Cliffs)
p.pawlowski@poole.gov.uk
Potter, Ian (CON - Oakdale)
i.potter@poole.gov.uk
Rampton, John (CON - Creekmoor)
j.rampton@poole.gov.uk
Rampton, Karen (CON - Branksome East)
k.rampton@poole.gov.uk
Rollo-Smith, Stephen (CON - Branksome East)
s.rollo-smith@poole.gov.uk
Slade, Vikki (LD - Broadstone)
v.slade@poole.gov.uk
Sorton, Neil (CON - Canford Cliffs)
n.sorton@poole.gov.uk
Stribley, Ann (CON - Parkstone)
a.stribley@poole.gov.uk
Trent, Tony (LD - Alderney)
t.trent@poole.gov.uk
Walton, Janet (CON - Oakdale)
j.walton@poole.gov.uk
Wilkins, Michael (CON - Hamworthy West)
m.wilkins@poole.gov.uk
Wilson, Chris (IND - Poole Town)
c.wilson@poole.gov.uk
Wilson, Lindsay (LD - Alderney)
lindsay.wilson@poole.gov.uk

Wilson, Graham (LD - Newtown)
g.wilson@poole.gov.uk
Woodcock, Tony (CON - Parkstone)
t.woodcock@poole.gov.uk

POLITICAL COMPOSITION
CON: 21, LD: 18, IND: 3

CABINET
Leader: Ms Elaine Atkinson
Deputy Leader: Mr Michael White
Budget & Finance, Customer Services & Communications: Ms Elaine Atkinson
Children, Families & Youth Services: Mrs Janet Walton
Communities, Public Engagement & Participation: Mrs Judy Butt
Environment & Local Economy: Mrs Xena Dion
Health & Wellbeing: Mr Peter Adams
Planning & Regeneration: Mr Michael White
Resources: Mr Neil Sorton

COMMITTEE CHAIRS
Audit: Mrs May Haines
Emergency: Mr Les Burden
Licensing: Mr John Rampton
Planning: Mr Phillip Eades

PORTSMOUTH CITY U

Portsmouth City Council, Civic Offices, Guildhall Square, Portsmouth PO1 2AL ☎ 023 9282 2251 🖷 023 9282 8441
💻 www.portsmouth.gov.uk

FACTS & FIGURES
Police Authority: Hampshire Police Authority
Health Authority: South Central Strategic Health Authority
Learning and Skills Council: South East
Parliamentary Constituencies: Portsmouth North, Portsmouth South
EU Constituencies: South East
Election Frequency: Elections are by thirds

PRINCIPAL OFFICERS
Chief Executive: Mr David Williams, Chief Executive, Civic Offices, Guildhall Square, Portsmouth PO1 2AL ☎ 023 9283 4009 david.williams@portsmouthcc.gov.uk

Senior Management: Ms Margaret Geary, Strategic Director - Housing, Health & Social Care, Civic Offices, Guildhall Square, Portsmouth PO1 2AL ☎ 023 9284 1150 margaret.geary@portsmouthcc.gov.uk

Senior Management: Mr Julian Wooster, Strategic Director - Children, Families & Learning, Civic Offices, Guildhall Square, Portsmouth PO1 2AL ☎ 023 9284 1202 🖷 023 9284 1208 julian.wooster@portsmouthcc.gov.uk

Architect, Building / Property Services: Mr Alan Langridge, Team Leader - Quantity Surveyors, Civic Offices, Guildhall Square, Portsmouth PO1 2AL ☎ 023 9283 4731 🖷 023 9283 4966 alan.langridge@portsmouthcc.gov.uk

Best Value: Mr Jeff Short, Business Development Manager, Civic Offices, Guildhall Square, Portsmouth PO1 2AL ☎ 023 9284 1737 jeff.short@portsmouthcc.gov.uk

Building Control: Mr Geoff Hill, Building Control Manager, Civic Offices, Guildhall Square, Portsmouth PO1 2AL ☎ 023 9283 4585 🖷 023 9283 4103 geoff.hill@portsmouthcc.gov.uk

Catering Services: Mr Clive Marshall, Guildhall Entertainments Manager, Guildhall, Guildhall Square, PO1 2AL ☎ 023 9283 4179 clive.marshall@dcleisure.co.uk

Catering Services: Mr David Pointon, Head of Procurement, Civic Offices, Guildhall Square, Portsmouth PO1 2BJ ☎ 023 9283 4406 🖷 023 9283 4996 david.pointon@portsmouthcc.gov.uk

Children / Youth Services: Ms Sharon George, Youth Support Commissioning Manager, Civic Offices, Guildhall Square, Portsmouth PO1 2AL ☎ 023 9268 8339 🖷 023 9286 5486 sharon.george@portsmouthcc.gov.uk

Civil Registration: Ms Lorraine Porter, Superintendent Registrar, Births, Deaths & Marriages, Milldam House, Burnaby Road, Portsmouth PO1 3AF ☎ 023 9282 9041 🖷 023 9283 1996 lorraine.porter@portsmouthcc.gov.uk

PR / Communications: Ms Louise Wilders, Head of Customer, Community & Democratic Services, Civic Offices, Guildhall Square, Portsmouth PO1 2AL ☎ 023 9268 8545 louise.wilders@portsmouthcc.gov.uk

Community Planning: Mr Paddy May, Corporate Strategy Manager, Civic Offices, Guildhall Square, Portsmouth PO1 2AL ☎ 023 9283 4020 paddy.may@portsmouthcc.gov.uk

Community Safety: Ms Rachael Dalby, Head of Community Safety, Civic Offices, Guildhall Square, Portsmouth PO1 2AL ☎ 023 9283 4040 rachael.dalby@portsmouthcc.gov.uk

Computer Management: Mr Andrew Mills, Head of Information & Resources, Civic Offices, Guildhall Square, Portsmouth PO1 2AL ☎ 023 9283 4414 🖷 023 9283 4198 andrew.mills@portsmouthcc.gov.uk

Consumer Protection and Trading Standards: Mr Paul Hunt, Head of Environment & Public Protection, Civic Offices, Guildhall Square, Portsmouth PO1 2BJ ☎ 023 9283 4213 🖷 023 9283 4519 paul.hunt@portsmouthcc.gov.uk

Contracts: Mr David Pointon, Head of Procurement, Civic Offices, Guildhall Square, Portsmouth PO1 2BJ ☎ 023 9283 4406 🖷 023 9283 4996 david.pointon@portsmouthcc.gov.uk

Corporate Services: Mr Jon Bell, Head of Audit & Performance Improvement, Civic Offices, Guildhall Square, Portsmouth PO1 2AL ☎ 023 8782 jon.bell@portsmouthcc.gov.uk

Customer Service: Ms Louise Wilders, Head of Customer, Community & Democratic Services, Civic Offices, Guildhall Square, Portsmouth PO1 2AL ☎ 023 9268 8545 louise.wilders@portsmouthcc.gov.uk

Economic Development: Mr Mike Stroud, Interim Strategic Director, Civic Offices, Guildhall Square, Portsmouth PO1 2AL ☎ 023 9283 4295 ✉ mike.stroud@portsmouthcc.gov.uk

Education: Mr Mike Fowler, Head of Transforming Education Services, Civic Offices, Guildhall Square, Portsmouth PO1 2AL ☎ 023 9284 1703 ✉ mike.fowler@portsmouthcc.gov.uk

Education: Mr Stephen Kitchman, Head of Children & Families Social Care & Safeguarding, Civic Offices, Guildhall Square, Portsmouth PO1 2AL ☎ 023 9284 1154 🖷 023 9284 1158 ✉ stephen.kitchman@portsmouthcc.gov.uk

E-Government: Mr Derrick Hawkes, Project Manager, Civic Offices, Guildhall Square, Portsmouth PO1 2AL ☎ 023 9284 1784 ✉ derrick.hawkes@portsmouthcc.gov.uk

Emergency Planning: Mr Michael Lawther, City Solicitor, Civic Offices, Guildhall Square, Portsmouth PO1 2AL ☎ 023 9283 4123 ✉ michael.lawther@portsmouthcc.gov.uk

Environmental / Technical Services: Mr David Maxted, Interim Strategic Director, Civic Offices, Guildhall Square, Portsmouth PO1 2AL ☎ 023 9268 8600 🖷 023 9283 4174 ✉ david.maxted@portsmouthcc.gov.uk

Environmental Health: Mr Paul Hunt, Head of Environment & Public Protection, Civic Offices, Guildhall Square, Portsmouth PO1 2BJ ☎ 023 9283 4213 🖷 023 9283 4519 ✉ paul.hunt@portsmouthcc.gov.uk

Events Manager: Mr Stephen Baily, Head of Cultural Services, Civic Offices, Guildhall Square, Portsmouth PO1 2AL ☎ 023 9283 4399 ✉ stephen.baily@portsmouthcc.gov.uk

Facilities: Mr Darren Thirlwell, Transformation Project Co-ordinator, Civic Offices, Guildhall Square, Portsmouth PO1 2AL ☎ 023 9283 4992 🖷 023 9283 4808 ✉ darren.thirlwell@portsmouthcc.gov.uk

Finance and Treasurer: Ms Valerie Lane, Head of Financial Services, Civic Offices, Guildhall Square, Portsmouth PO1 2AL ☎ 023 9283 4447 ✉ valerie.lane@portsmouthcc.gov.uk

Finance and Treasurer: Mr Tony Nicholas, Interim Head of Asset Management, Civic Offices, Guildhall Square, Portsmouth PO1 2AL ☎ 023 9284 1739 ✉ tony.nicholas@portsmouthcc.gov.uk

Grounds Maintenance: Mr Seamus Meyer, Parks & Recreation Manager, Civic Offices, Guildhall Square, Portsmouth PO1 2AL ☎ 023 9283 4163 ✉ seamus.meyer@portsmouthcc.gov.uk

Health and Safety: Mr Bob Briggs, Trading Standards Manager, Civic Offices, Guildhall Square, Portsmouth PO1 2AL ☎ 023 9284 4208 🖷 023 9283 4021 ✉ bob.briggs@portsmouthcc.gov.uk

Housing: Mr Owen Buckwell, Head of Housing Management, Civic Offices, Guildhall Square, Portsmouth PO1 2AL ☎ 023 9283 4503 ✉ owen.buckwell@portsmouthcc.gov.uk

Housing: Ms Margaret Geary, Strategic Director - Housing, Health & Social Care, Civic Offices, Guildhall Square, Portsmouth PO1 2AL ☎ 023 9284 1150 ✉ margaret.geary@portsmouthcc.gov.uk

Local Area Agreement: Mr Paddy May, Corporate Strategy Manager, Civic Offices, Guildhall Square, Portsmouth PO1 2AL ☎ 023 9283 4020 ✉ paddy.may@portsmouthcc.gov.uk

Legal: Mr Michael Lawther, City Solicitor, Civic Offices, Guildhall Square, Portsmouth PO1 2AL ☎ 023 9283 4123 ✉ michael.lawther@portsmouthcc.gov.uk

Leisure and Cultural Services: Mr Stephen Baily, Head of Cultural Services, Civic Offices, Guildhall Square, Portsmouth PO1 2AL ☎ 023 9283 4399 ✉ stephen.baily@portsmouthcc.gov.uk

Licensing: Mrs Nicki Humphreys, Licensing Manager, Civic Offices, Guildhall Square, Portsmouth PO1 2AL ☎ 023 9283 4604 ✉ licensing@portsmouthcc.gov.uk

Lifelong Learning: Mr Alan Cufley, Head of Community, Housing & Regeneration, Civic Offices, Guildhall Square, Portsmouth PO1 2AL ☎ 023 9283 4450 ✉ alan.cufley@portsmouthcc.gov.uk

Lifelong Learning: Ms Kathy Wadsworth, Strategic Director, Civic Offices, Guildhall Square, Portsmouth PO1 2AL ☎ 023 9283 4295 ✉ kathy.wadsworth@portsmouthcc.gov.uk

Lighting: Mr Ray Privett, PFI Contract Manager, Civic Offices, Guildhall Square, Portsmouth PO1 2AS ☎ 023 9283 4667 🖷 023 9287 6414 ✉ ray.privett@portsmouthcc.gov.uk

Member Services: Mr Stewart Agland, Local Democracy Manager, Civic Offices, Guildhall Square, Portsmouth PO1 2AL ☎ 023 9283 4055 🖷 023 9283 4076 ✉ stewart.agland@portsmouthcc.gov.uk

Parking: Mr Ken Ellcome, Parking Manager, Parking Office, Isambard Brunel MSCP, Portsmouth PO1 2BX ☎ 023 9268 8295 ✉ ken.ellcome@portsmouthcc.gov.uk

Parking: Mr David Maxted, Interim Strategic Director, Civic Offices, Guildhall Square, Portsmouth PO1 2AL ☎ 023 9268 8600 🖷 023 9283 4174 ✉ david.maxted@portsmouthcc.gov.uk

Personnel / HR: Mrs Kay White, Head of Human Resources, Civic Offices, Guildhall Square, Portsmouth PO1 2AL ☎ 023 9283 4196 🖷 023 9283 4021 ✉ kay.white@portsmouthcc.gov.uk

Planning: Mr John Slater, Head of Planning Services, Civic Offices, Guildhall Square, Portsmouth PO1 2AL ☎ 023 9283 4297 ✉ john.slater@portsmouthcc.gov.uk

Procurement: Mr David Pointon, Head of Procurement, Civic Offices, Guildhall Square, Portsmouth PO1 2BJ ☎ 023 9283 4406 🖷 023 9283 4996 ✉ david.pointon@portsmouthcc.gov.uk

Public Libraries: Mr Mike Stroud, Interim Strategic Director, Civic Offices, Guildhall Square, Portsmouth PO1 2AL ☎ 023 9283 4295 ✉ mike.stroud@portsmouthcc.gov.uk

Recycling & Waste Minimisation: Mr Paul Fielding, Strategic Waste Manager, Civic Offices, Guildhall Square, Portsmouth PO1

2AL ☏ 023 9283 4625 🖷 023 9284 1561
✉ paul.fielding@portsmouthcc.gov.uk

Regeneration: Ms Denise Vine, Regeneration Manager, Civic Offices, Guildhall Square, Portsmouth PO1 2AL ☏ 023 9268 8352
✉ denise.vine@portsmouthcc.gov.uk

Road Safety: Ms Angela Gill, Transport Planning Manager, Civic Offices, Guildhall Square, Portsmouth PO1 2AL ☏ 023 9268 8261
✉ angela.gill@portsmouthcc.gov.uk

Social Services: Ms Margaret Geary, Strategic Director - Housing, Health & Social Care, Civic Offices, Guildhall Square, Portsmouth PO1 2AL ☏ 023 9284 1150
✉ margaret.geary@portsmouthcc.gov.uk

Social Services (Adult): Mr Robert Watt, Head of Adult Social Care, Civic Offices, Guildhall Square, Portsmouth PO1 2AL
☏ 023 9284 1160 ✉ robert.watt@portsmouthcc.gov.uk

Social Services (Children): Mr Stephen Kitchman, Head of Children & Families Social Care & Safeguarding, Civic Offices, Guildhall Square, Portsmouth PO1 2AL ☏ 023 9284 1154
🖷 023 9284 1158 ✉ stephen.kitchman@portsmouthcc.gov.uk

Street Scene: Mr Paul Hunt, Head of Environment & Public Protection, Civic Offices, Guildhall Square, Portsmouth PO1 2BJ
☏ 023 9283 4213 🖷 023 9283 4519
✉ paul.hunt@portsmouthcc.gov.uk

Sustainable Communities: Ms Hazel Hine, Corporate Initiatives Manager, Chaucer House, 2nd Floor, Portsmouth PO1 2AX
☏ 023 9283 4729 🖷 023 9283 4523
✉ hazel.hine@portsmouthcc.gov.uk

Sustainable Development: Mr David Maxted, Interim Strategic Director, Civic Offices, Guildhall Square, Portsmouth PO1 2AL
☏ 023 9268 8600 🖷 023 9283 4174
✉ david.maxted@portsmouthcc.gov.uk

Town Centre: Mr Barry Walker, City Centre Manager, Civic Offices, Guildhall Square, Portsmouth PO1 2AL ☏ 023 6133 4529
✉ barry.walker@portsmouthcc.gov.uk

Transport: Mr David Maxted, Interim Strategic Director, Civic Offices, Guildhall Square, Portsmouth PO1 2AL ☏ 023 9268 8600
🖷 023 9283 4174 ✉ david.maxted@portsmouthcc.gov.uk

Waste Collection and Disposal: Mr Paul Fielding, Strategic Waste Manager, Civic Offices, Guildhall Square, Portsmouth PO1 2AL ☏ 023 9283 4625 🖷 023 9284 1561
✉ paul.fielding@portsmouthcc.gov.uk

Waste Collection and Disposal: Mrs Karen Rutter, Efficiency Project Manager, Civic Offices, Guildhall Square, Portsmouth PO1 2AS ☏ 023 9284 1344 🖷 023 9284 1561
✉ karen.rutter@portsmouthcc.gov.uk

Waste Collection and Disposal: Mr Vincent Venus, Waste Collection Manager, Civic Offices, Guildhall Square, Portsmouth PO1 2AS ☏ 023 9283 1210 🖷 023 9284 1561
✉ vincent.venus@portsmouthcc.gov.uk

Waste Management: Mr Paul Hunt, Head of Environment & Public Protection, Civic Offices, Guildhall Square, Portsmouth PO1 2BJ ☏ 023 9283 4213 🖷 023 9283 4519
✉ paul.hunt@portsmouthcc.gov.uk

MEMBERS OF THE COUNCIL (42)

***The Lord Mayor:* Jonas**, Frank (CON - Hilsea)
cllr.frank.jonas@portsmouthcc.gov.uk
***Leader of the Council:* Vernon-Jackson**, Gerald (LD - Milton)
cllr.gerald.vernon-jackson@portsmouthcc.gov.uk
***Deputy Leader of the Council:* Mason**, Hugh (LD - St Jude)
cllr.hugh.mason@portsmouthcc.gov.uk
Adair, Margaret (LD - Central Southsea)
cllr.margaret.adair@portsmouthcc.gov.uk
Andrewes, Michael (LD - St Jude)
Cllr.Michael.Andrewes@portsmouthcc.gov.uk
Bosher, Simon (CON - Drayton and Farlington)
cllr.simon.bosher@portsmouthcc.gov.uk
Eddis, Peter (LD - St Jude)
cllr.peter.eddis@portsmouthcc.gov.uk
Ellcome, Ken (CON - Drayton and Farlington)
Fazackarley, Jason (LD - Nelson)
cllr.jason.fazackarley@portsmouthcc.gov.uk
Ferrett, John (LAB - Paulsgrove)
Cllr.John.Ferrett@portsmouthcc.gov.uk
Ferrett, Ken (LAB - Nelson)
cllr.ken.ferrett@portsmouthcc.gov.uk
Foster, Margaret (LD - Charles Dickens)
cllr.margaret.foster@portsmouthcc.gov.uk
Fuller, David (LD - Fratton)
cllr.david.fuller@portsmouthcc.gov.uk
Gray, Aiden (LD - Cosham)
Cllr.Aiden.Gray@portsmouthcc.gov.uk
Hall, Terry (LD - Eastney and Craneswater)
cllr.terry.hall@portsmouthcc.gov.uk
Hancock, Mike (LD - Fratton)
cllr.mike.hancock@portsmouthcc.gov.uk
Hancock, Jacqui (LD - Charles Dickens)
cllr.jacqui.hancock@portsmouthcc.gov.uk
Horne, David (LAB - Paulsgrove)
cllr.david.horne@portsmouthcc.gov.uk
Hunt, Lee (LD - Central Southsea)
cllr.lee.hunt@portsmouthcc.gov.uk
Hunt, Lee (LD - Baffins)
cllr.darron.phillips@portsmouthcc.gov.uk
Jones, Donna (CON - Hilsea)
cllr.donna.jones@portsmouthcc.gov.uk
Madden, Leo (LD - Nelson)
cllr.leo.madden@portsmouthcc.gov.uk
Mason, Lee (CON - Cosham)
cllr.mason.lee@portsmouthcc.gov.uk
New, Robert (CON - Copnor)
Cllr.Robert.New@portsmouthcc.gov.uk
Park, Mike (CON - Copnor)
cllr.mike.park@portsmouthcc.gov.uk
Patey, Jim (LAB - Paulsgrove)
cllr.jim.patey@portsmouthcc.gov.uk
Purvis, Will (LD - Milton)
Cllr.Will.Purvis@portsmouthcc.gov.uk
Sanders, Darren (LD - Baffins)
Cllr.Darren.Sanders@portsmouthcc.gov.uk
Scott, Eleanor (LD - Fratton)
cllr.eleanor.scott@portsmouthcc.gov.uk
Scott, Caroline (LD - Milton)

cllr.caroline.scott@portsmouthcc.gov.uk
Smith, Phil (LD - Central Southsea)
cllr.phil.smith@portsmouthcc.gov.uk
Stagg, Lynne (LD - Baffins)
cllr.lynne.stag@portsmouthcc.gov.uk
Stevens, Les (LD - St Thomas)
cllr.les.stevens@portsmouthcc.gov.uk
Stockdale, Sandra (LD - St Thomas)
cllr.Sandra.Stockdale@portsmouthcc.gov.uk
Stubbs, Luke (CON - Eastney and Craneswater)
cllr.luke.stubbs@portsmouthcc.gov.uk
Thompson, Alistair (CON - Hilsea)
cllr.alastair.thompson@portsmouthcc.gov.uk
Wemyss, Steve (CON - Drayton and Farlington)
cllr.steve.wemyss@portsmouthcc.gov.uk
Windebank, April (CON - Cosham)
cllr.april.windebank@portsmouthcc.gov.uk
Winnington, Matthew (LD - Eastney and Craneswater)
Cllr.Matthew.Winnington@portsmouthcc.gov.uk
Wood, Rob (LD - St Thomas)
cllr.rob.wood@portsmouthcc.gov.uk
Wylie, Steven (LD - Charles Dickens)
cllr.steven.wylie@portsmouthcc.gov.uk
Young, Neil
(CON - Copnor)
cllr.neil.young@portsmouhtcc.gov.uk

POLITICAL COMPOSITION

LD: 26, CON: 12, LAB: 4

CABINET

Leader: Mr Gerald Vernon-Jackson
Deputy Leader / Resources: Mr Hugh Mason
Children & Education: Mr Rob Wood
Community Safety: Mr Aiden Gray
Culture, Leisure & Sport: Mr Lee Hunt
Environment: Ms Eleanor Scott
Health & Social Care: Mr Leo Madden
Housing: Mr Steven Wylie
Planning, Regeneration & Economic Development: Mr Mike Hancock
Traffic & Transportation: Mr Jason Fazackarley

COMMITTEE CHAIRS

Economic Development, Culture & Leisure (Scrutiny): Ms Terry Hall
Education, Children & Young People (Scrutiny): Mr Steve Wemyss
Employment: Mr Gerald Vernon-Jackson
Governance & Audit: Ms Terry Hall
Health (Scrutiny): Mr Peter Eddis
Housing & Social Care (Scrutiny): Mr James Williams
Licensing: Mr Les Stevens
Planning: Mr Lee Hunt
Scrutiny Management (Scrutiny): Mr Michael Andrewes
Standards: Mr Peter Wyles (External)

POWYS — W

Powys County Council, (Cyngor Sir Powys), County Hall, Llandrindod Wells LD1 5LG ☎ 01597 826000 🖷 01597 826230
💻 www.powys.gov.uk

FACTS & FIGURES

Police Authority: Dyfed Powys Police Authority
Health Authority: Powys Teaching Health Board
Learning and Skills Council: Wales
Parliamentary Constituencies: Brecon and Radnorshire, Montgomeryshire
EU Constituencies: Wales
Election Frequency: Elections are of whole council

PRINCIPAL OFFICERS

Chief Executive: Mr Jeremy Patterson, Chief Executive, County Hall, Llandrindod Wells LD1 5LG ☎ 01597 826082 🖷 01597 826220 ✉ jeremy.patterson@powys.gov.uk

Architect, Building / Property Services: Ms Sarah Jowett, Property Manager, County Hall, Llandrindod Wells LD1 5LG ☎ 01597 826553 ✉ sarah.jowett@powys.gov.uk

Best Value: Mr Nick Philpott, Head of ICT & Customer Services, County Hall, Llandrindod Wells Ld1 5LG ☎ 01597 826486 ✉ nick.philpott@powys.gov.uk

Building Control: Mr Christopher Jones, Senior Manager - Building Control, Neuadd Brycheiniog, Brecon LD3 7HR ☎ 01874 612290 ✉ christopher.jones@powys.gov.uk

Civil Registration: Ms Julie Nicholas-Humphreys, Customer Services Manager, County Hall, Llandrindod Wells LD1 5LG ☎ 01597 826036 ✉ julie.nicholas-humphreys@powys.gov.uk

PR / Communications: Ms Anya Richards, Senior Communications Manager, County Hall, Llandrindod Wells LD1 5LG ☎ 01597 826089 ✉ anya.richards@powys.gov.uk

Community Planning: Ms Melanie Jones, Senior Community Participation Officer, County Hall, Llandrindod Wells LD1 5LG ☎ 01597 826000 ✉ melanie.jones@powys.gov.uk

Community Safety: Mr Ian Fraser, Interim Head of Housing, Neuadd Maldwyn, Severn Road, Welshpool SY21 7AS ☎ 01597 826659 ✉ ian.fraser@powys.gov.uk

Community Safety: Ms Louisa Kerr, Community Safety Officer, The Gwalia, Llandrindod Wells LD1 6AA ☎ 01597 826000 ✉ louisa.kerr@powys.gov.uk

Computer Management: Mr Nick Philpott, Head of ICT & Customer Services, County Hall, Llandrindod Wells LD1 5LG ☎ 01597 826486 ✉ nick.philpott@powys.gov.uk

Consumer Protection and Trading Standards: Mr Ken Yorston, Trading Standards Manager, The Gwalia, Llandrindod Wells LD1 6AA ☎ 01597 826032 ✉ ken.yorston@powys.gov.uk

Contracts: Mr Steve Holdaway, Head of Local & Environmental Services, County Hall, Llandrindod Wells LD1 5LG ☎ 01597 826613 ✉ steve.holdaway@powys.gov.uk

Customer Service: Ms Julie Nicholas-Humphreys, Customer Services Manager, County Hall, Llandrindod Wells LD1 5LG ☎ 01597 826036 ✉ julie.nicholas-humphreys@powys.gov.uk

Direct Labour: Mr Steve Holdaway, Head of Local & Environmental Services, County Hall, Llandrindod Wells LD1 5LG ☎ 01597 826613 ✉ steve.holdaway@powys.gov.uk

Economic Development: Ms Lesley Kirkpatrick, Head of Regeneration & Development, County Hall, Llandrindod Wells LD1 5LG ☎ 01597 826676 ✉ lesley.kirkpatrick@powys.gov.uk

Education: Mr Stephen Rogers, Head of Schools & Inclusion, County Hall, Llandrindod Wells LD1 5LG ☎ 01597 826985 ✉ stephen.rogers@powys.gov.uk

Electoral Registration: Ms Sandra Matthews, Principal Elections Officer, County Hall, Llandrindod Wells LD1 5LG ☎ 01597 826747 ☏ 01597 826220 ✉ sandra.matthews@powys.gov.uk

Emergency Planning: Mr Wayne Jones, Prinicpal Emergency Planning Officer, County Hall, Llandrindod Wells LD1 5LG ☎ 01597 826000

Energy Management: Mr Gareth Richards, Energy Manager, County Hall, Llandrindod Wells LD1 5LG ☎ 01597 826629 ✉ garethr@powys.gov.uk

Environmental Health: Mr Steve Holdaway, Head of Local & Environmental Services, County Hall, Llandrindod Wells LD1 5LG ☎ 01597 826613 ✉ steve.holdaway@powys.gov.uk

Estates, Property & Valuation: Mr Steve Holdaway, Head of Local & Environmental Services, County Hall, Llandrindod Wells LD1 5LG ☎ 01597 826613 ✉ steve.holdaway@powys.gov.uk

Estates, Property & Valuation: Mr Geoff Petty, Strategic Director - Finance & Infrastructure, County Hall, Llandrindod Wells LD1 5LG ☎ 01597 826363 ✉ geoff.petty@powys.gov.uk

European Liaison: Mr Filippo Compagni, European Policy & External Funding Manager, County Hall, Llandrindod Wells LD1 5LG ☎ 01597 826641 ✉ filippo.compagni@powys.gov.uk

Finance and Treasurer: Mr Geoff Petty, Strategic Director - Finance & Infrastructure, County Hall, Llandrindod Wells LD1 5LG ☎ 01597 826363 ✉ geoff.petty@powys.gov.uk

Fleet Management: Mr Steve Holdaway, Head of Local & Environmental Services, County Hall, Llandrindod Wells LD1 5LG ☎ 01597 826613 ✉ steve.holdaway@powys.gov.uk

Grounds Maintenance: Mr Steve Holdaway, Head of Local & Environmental Services, County Hall, Llandrindod Wells LD1 5LG ☎ 01597 826613 ✉ steve.holdaway@powys.gov.uk

Highways: Mr Steve Holdaway, Head of Local & Environmental Services, County Hall, Llandrindod Wells LD1 5LG ☎ 01597 826613 ✉ steve.holdaway@powys.gov.uk

Housing: Mr Ian Fraser, Interim Head of Housing, Neuadd Maldwyn, Severn Road, Welshpool SY21 7AS ☎ 01597 826659 ✉ ian.fraser@powys.gov.uk

Housing Maintenance: Mr Ian Fraser, Housing Services Manager, Neuadd Maldwyn, Severn Road, Welshpool SY21 7AS ☎ 01938 551214 ✉ ian.fraser@powys.gov.uk

Legal: Ms Janet Kealey, Head of Legal & Democratic Services, County Hall, Llandrindod Wells LD1 5LG ☎ 01597 826385

Legal: Mr Clarence Meredith, Strategic Director - Law & Governance, County Hall, Llandrindod Wells LD1 5LG ☎ 01597 826365 ✉ clarence.meredith@powys.gov.uk

Leisure and Cultural Services: Mr Paul Griffiths, Strategic Director - Communities, Skills & Learning, County Hall, Llandrindod Wells LD1 5LG ☎ 01597 826464 ✉ paul.griffiths@powys.gov.uk

Leisure and Cultural Services: Mr Chris Jones, Head of Lesiure & Recreation, The Gwalia, Ithon Road, Llandrindod Wells LD1 6AA ☎ 01597 827615 ✉ chris.jones@powys.gov.uk

Licensing: Mr Steve Clinton, Environmental Health Manager, Neuadd Maldwyn, Severn Road, Welshpool SY21 7AS ☎ 01938 551246 ☏ 01938 551248 ✉ steve.clinton@powys.gov.uk

Lighting: Mr Steve Holdaway, Head of Local & Environmental Services, County Hall, Llandrindod Wells LD1 5LG ☎ 01597 826613 ✉ steve.holdaway@powys.gov.uk

Member Services: Mr Stephen Boyd, Cabinet Business Manager, County Hall, Llandrindod Wells LD1 5LG ☎ 01597 826374 ✉ stephen.boyd@powys.gov.uk

Personnel / HR: Ms Karen Williams, Head of Human Resources, County Hall, Llandrindod Wells LD1 5LG ☎ 01597 826743 ☏ 01597 826215 ✉ karen.williams@powys.gov.uk

Planning: Ms Lesley Kirkpatrick, Head of Regeneration & Development, County Hall, Llandrindod Wells LD1 5LG ☎ 01597 826676 ✉ lesley.kirkpatrick@powys.gov.uk

Procurement: Mr Mike Green, Procurement Manager, County Hall, Llandrindod Wells LD1 5LG ☎ 01597 826378 ☏ 01597 826231 ✉ mike.green@powys.gov.uk

Regeneration: Ms Lesley Kirkpatrick, Head of Regeneration & Development, County Hall, Llandrindod Wells LD1 5LG ☎ 01597 826676 ✉ lesley.kirkpatrick@powys.gov.uk

Road Safety: Mr Tony Caine, Road Safety & Traffic Systems Manager, County Hall, Llandrindod Wells LD1 5LG ☎ 0845 607 6060 ☏ 01597 826651 ✉ tony.caine@powys.gov.uk

Social Services: Mr Parry Davies, Strategic Director - Care & Well Being, County Hall, Llandrindod Wells LD1 5LG ☎ 01597 826906 ✉ parry.davies@powys.gov.uk

Social Services (Adult): Ms Nygaire Bevan, Head of Adult Services & Commissioning, County Hall, Llandrindod Wells LD1 5LG ☎ 01597 826657 ✉ nygaire.bevan@powys.gov.uk

Social Services (Children): Ms Amanda Lewis, Head of Children's Services, 1 High Street, Llandrindod Wells LD1 6AG ☎ 01597 827084 ✉ amanda.lewis@powys.gov.uk

LOCAL AUTHORITIES

Staff Training: Ms Sarah Powell, Principal Learning & Development Officer, Neuadd Bycheiniog, Brecon LD3 7HR ☎ 01874 612237 ✉ sarah.powell@powys.gov.uk

Sustainable Development: Ms Heather Delonnette, Sustainable Development Co-ordinator, County Hall, Llandrindod Wells LD1 5LG ☎ 01597 827481 ✉ heather.delonnette@powys.gov.uk

Traffic Management: Mr Tony Caine, Road Safety & Traffic Systems Manager, County Hall, Llandrindod Wells LD1 5LG ☎ 0845 607 6060 🖷 01597 826651 ✉ tony.caine@powys.gov.uk

Transport: Mr John Forsey, Transport Passenger Manager, County Hall, Llandrindod Wells LD1 5LG ☎ 01597 826642 ✉ john.forsey@powys.gov.uk

Transport Planner: Mr John Forsey, Transport Passenger Manager, County Hall, Llandrindod Wells LD1 5LG ☎ 01597 826642 ✉ john.forsey@powys.gov.uk

Waste Collection and Disposal: Mr Steve Holdaway, Head of Local & Environmental Services, County Hall, Llandrindod Wells LD1 5LG ☎ 01597 826613 ✉ steve.holdaway@powys.gov.uk

Waste Management: Mr Steve Holdaway, Head of Local & Environmental Services, County Hall, Llandrindod Wells LD1 5LG ☎ 01597 826613 ✉ steve.holdaway@powys.gov.uk

MEMBERS OF THE COUNCIL (72)

***Leader of the Council:* Jones**, David (IND - Guilsfield)
cllr.david.jones@powys.gov.uk
Alexander, Myfanwy (IND - Banwy)
cllr.myfanwy.alexander@powys.gov.uk
Ashton, Paul (LD - St Mary)
cllr.paul.ashton@powys.gov.uk
Bailey, Dawn (IND - Trewern)
cllr.dawn.bailey@powys.gov.uk
Banks, Garry (LD - Presteigne)
cllr.garry.banks@powys.gov.uk
Bowker, Gemma (LD - Newton Llanwchaiarn North)
cllr.gemma.jane.bowker@powys.gov.uk
Brown, Graham (IND - Llandrinio)
cllr.graham.brown@powys.gov.uk
Brunt, John (IND - Beguildy)
cllr.john.brunt@powys.gov.uk
Corfield, Linda (IND - Forden)
cllr.linda.corfield@powys.gov.uk
Curry, Kelvyn (LD - Rhayader)
cllr.kelvyn.curry@powys.gov.uk
Davies, Dai (IND - Berriew)
cllr.dai.davies@powys.gov.uk
Davies, Aled (CON - Llanrhaeadr-ym-Mochnant / Llansilin)
cllr.aled.davies@powys.gov.uk
Davies, Chris (CON - Glasbury)
cllr.chris.davies@powys.gov.uk
Davies, Stephen (IND - Bronllys)
cllr.stephen.davies@powys.gov.uk
Davies, Rachel (IND - Caersws)
cllr.rachel.davies@powys.gov.uk
Davies, Roche (IND - Llandinam)
cllr.roche.davies@powys.gov.uk
Davies, Sandra (LAB - Cwm-Twrch)
cllr.sandra.davies@powys.gov.uk
Davies, Melanie (IND - Llangors)
cllr.melanie.davies@powys.gov.uk
Dorrance, Matthew (LAB - St John)
cllr.matthew.dorrance@powys.gov.uk
Evans, Viola (IND - Llanfair Caereinion)
cllr.viola.evans@powys.gov.uk
Evans, David (IND - Nantmel)
cllr.david.evans@powys.gov.uk
Evans, John (IND - Llanyre)
cllr.john.evans@powys.gov.uk
Fitzpatrick, Liam (LD - Talybont-on-Usk)
cllr.liam.fitzpatrick@powys.gov.uk
George, Russell (CON - Newtown Central)
cllr.russell.george@powys.gov.uk
Harris, Rosemarie (NP - Llangynidr)
cllr.rosemarie.harris@powys.gov.uk
Harris, Peter (CON - Newtown Llanllwchaiarn West)
cllr.peter.harris@powys.gov.uk
Hayes, Stephen (IND - Montgomery)
cllr.stephen.hayes@powys.gov.uk
Holloway, Ann (IND - Welshpool Llanerchyddol)
cllr.ann.holloway@powys.gov.uk
Holmes, Jeff (LD - Llangattock)
cllr.jeff.holmes@powys.gov.uk
Jones, Wynne (IND - Dolforwyn)
cllr.wynne.jones@powys.gov.uk
Jones, Dai (IND - Llanbrynmair)
cllr.dai.jones@powys.gov.uk
Jones, Graham (CON - Blaen Hafren)
cllr.graham.jones@powys.gov.uk
Jones, Joy (LD - Newtown East)
cllr.joy.jones@powys.gov.uk
Jones, Michael (IND - Churchstoke)
Jones, Arwel (IND - Llandysilio)
cllr.arwel.jones@powys.gov.uk
Jones, Michael (IND - Old Radnor)
cllr.michael.jones@powys.gov.uk
Jones, Eldrydd (IND - Meifod)
cllr.eldrydd.jones@powys.gov.uk
Jump, Francesca (LD - Welshpool Gungrog)
cllr.francesca.jump@powys.gov.uk
Lewis, Peter (CON - Llanfyllin)
cllr.peter.lewis@powys.gov.uk
Lewis, Hywel (IND - Llangunllo)
cllr.hywel.lewis@powys.gov.uk
Mackenzie, Maureen (LD - Llanelwedd)
cllr.maureen.mackenzie@powys.gov.uk
Mayor, Darren (NP - Llanwddyn)
cllr.darren.mayor@powys.gov.uk
McNicholas, Susan (LAB - Ynescedwyn)
cllr.susan.mcnicholas@powys.gov.uk
Medicott, Peter (IND - Knighton)
cllr.peter.medlicott@powys.gov.uk
Meredith, David (IND - St John)
cllr.david.meredith@powys.gov.uk
Mills, Bob (IND - Newtown South)
cllr.bob.mills@powys.gov.uk
Morgan, Evan (IND - Maescar / Llywel)
cllr.evan.morgan@powys.gov.uk
Morgan, Bob (IND - Llanbrynmair)
cllr.bob.morgan@powys.gov.uk
Morgan, Gareth (IND - Llanidloes)
cllr.gareth.morgan@powys.gov.uk
Morris, John (LD - Crickhowell)

cllr.john.morris@powys.gov.uk
Powell, William (LD - Talgarth)
cllr.william.powell@powys.gov.uk
Powell, John (IND - Llanbadarn Fawr)
cllr.john.powell@powys.gov.uk
Price, David (IND - Llanafanfawr)
cllr.david.price@powys.gov.uk
Price, Gary (PC - Llandrindod East / Llandrindod West)
cllr.gary.price@powys.gov.uk
Pritchard, Philip (IND - Welshpool Castle)
cllr.phil.pritchard@powys.gov.uk
Ratcliffe, Gareth (CON - Hay)
cllr.gareth.ratcliffe@powys.gov.uk
Roberts-Jones, Kath (IND - Kerry)
cllr.kath.roberts-jones@powys.gov.uk
Shearer, Joy (IND - Rhiwcynon)
cllr.joy.shearer@powys.gov.uk
Silk, Kathryn (LD - Bwlch)
cllr.kathryn.silk@powys.gov.uk
Tampkin, Keith (IND - Llandrindod East/Llandrindod West)
cllr.keith.tampin@powys.gov.uk
Thomas, David (LAB - Tawe Uchaf)
cllr.david.thomas@powys.gov.uk
Thomas, Gwynfor (CON - Llansanffraid)
cllr.gwynfor.thomas@powys.gov.uk
Thomas, Tony (IND - Felin-fach)
cllr.tony.thomas@powys.gov.uk
Thomas, Gillian (IND - Yscir)
cllr.gillian.thomas@powys.gov.uk
Thomas, Barry (IND - Llanfihangel)
cllr.barry.thomas@powys.gov.uk
Turner, Tom (CON - Llandrindod)
cllr.tom.turner@powys.gov.uk
Van-Rees, Tim (IND - Llanwrtyd Wells)
cllr.tim.van-rees@powys.gov.uk
Vaughan, Gwilym (IND - Glantwymyn)
cllr.gwilym.vaughan@powys.gov.uk
Williams, Michael (IND - Machynlleth)
cllr.michael.williams@powys.gov.uk
Williams, Huw (NP - Ystradgynlais)
cllr.huw.williams@powys.gov.uk
Williams, Sarah (LAB - Aber-craf)
cllr.sarah.williams@powys.gov.uk
York, Avril (IND - Builth)
cllr.avril.york@powys.gov.uk

POLITICAL COMPOSITION
IND: 42, LD: 12, CON: 9, LAB: 5, NP: 3, PC: 1

CABINET
Leader: Mr David Jones
Children & Partnerships: Ms Melanie Davies
Corporate Governance: Mr Gary Price
Finance: Mr Dai Davies
Human Resources: Mr Gareth Ratcliffe
Planning: Mr Graham Brown
Property & Assets: Mr Garry Banks
Social Services, Care, Health & Housing: Ms Rosemarie Harris

COMMITTEE CHAIRS
Audit: Mrs Sandra Davies
Corporate Governance Policy & Scrutiny: Mr Aled Davies
Licensing: Mr Michael Williams
People Policy & Scrutiny: Mrs Kath Roberts-Jones
Planning: Mr Bob Mills
Principal Scrutiny: Mr John Morris
Regeneration & Environment Policy & Scrutiny: Mr John Brunt

PRESTON D

Preston City Council, Town Hall, Lancaster Road, Preston PR1 2RL ☎ 01772 906900 🖷 01772 906901 ✉ info@preston.gov.uk
💻 www.preston.gov.uk

FACTS & FIGURES
Police Authority: Lancashire Police Authority
Health Authority: North West Strategic Health Authority
Learning and Skills Council: North West
Parliamentary Constituencies: Preston
EU Constituencies: North West
Election Frequency: Elections are by thirds
Twinning: Nimes (France); Recklinghausen (Germany); Almelo (Netherlands); Kalisz (Poland)

PRINCIPAL OFFICERS
Chief Executive: Ms Lorraine Norris, Chief Executive, Town Hall, Lancaster Road, Preston PR1 2RL ☎ 01772 906101 🖷 01772 906366 ✉ l.norris@preston.gov.uk

Deputy Chief Executive: Mr Bernard Hayes, Deputy Chief Executive & Corporate Director, Community & Business Services, Town Hall, Lancaster Road, Preston PR1 2RL ☎ 01772 906002 🖷 01772 906366 ✉ b.p.hayes@preston.gov.uk

Best Value: Mrs Anne Nicholas, Assistant Director (Head of Policy), Town Hall, Lancaster Road, Preston PR1 2RL ☎ 01772 906811 🖷 01772 906822 ✉ a.nicholas@preston.gov.uk

Building Control: Mr D Tomlinson, Head of Building Services, Lancastria House, Lancastria Road, Preston PR1 2RH ☎ 01772 906536 ✉ d.tomlinson@preston.gov.uk

PR / Communications: Mr Stephen Parkinson, Head of Communications, Town Hall, Lancaster Road, Preston PR1 2RL ☎ 01772 906464 🖷 01771 906822 ✉ s.parkinson@preston.gov.uk

Community Safety: Mrs Michelle Pilling, Community Safety Manager, MAPS Team, Preston Police Preston, Lancaster Road North, Preston PR1 2SA ☎ 01772 209638
✉ m.pilling@preston.gov.uk

Computer Management: Mr Neil Fairhurst, Assistant Director (Head of ICT Services), PO Box 10, Town Hall, Lancaster Road, Preston PR1 2RL ☎ 01772 906017 ✉ n.fairhurst@preston.gov.uk

Contracts: Mrs Angela Harrison, Governance Director, Town Hall, Lancaster Road, Preston PR1 2RL ☎ 01772 906104
✉ a.harrison@preston.gov.uk

Corporate Services: Ms Lorraine Norris, Chief Executive, Town Hall, Lancaster Road, Preston PR1 2RL ☎ 01772 906101
🖷 01772 906366 ✉ l.norris@preston.gov.uk

Customer Service: Mr Peter Kerry, Call Centre Manager, Town Hall, Lancaster Road, Preston PR1 2RL ☎ 01772 906939
🖷 01772 906336 ✉ p.kerry@preston.gov.uk

Direct Labour: Mr Mick Lovatt, Corporate Director of Environment, Town Hall, Lancaster Road, Preston PR1 2RL ☎ 01772 906171 🖷 01772 906366 ✉ m.lovatt@preston.gov.uk

Economic Development: Mr Derek Whyte, Assistant Director (Head of Economic Regeneration), Town Hall, Lancaster Road, Preston PR1 2RL ☎ 01772 903401 ✉ d.whyte@preston.gov.uk

E-Government: Mr Neil Fairhurst, Assistant Director (Head of ICT Services), PO Box 10, Town Hall, Lancaster Road, Preston PR1 2RL ☎ 01772 906017 ✉ n.fairhurst@preston.gov.uk

Electoral Registration: Mr Peter Welsh, Head of Electoral Services, Town Hall, Lancaster Road, Preston PR1 2RL ☎ 01772 906115 ✉ p.welsh@preston.gov.uk

Emergency Planning: Mr Alan Murray, Emergency Planning Officer, PO Box 10, Town Hall, Lancaster Road, Preston PR1 2RL ☎ 01772 906162 🖷 01772 906822 ✉ a.murray@preston.gov.uk

Energy Management: Mr Mick Lovatt, Corporate Director of Environment, Town Hall, Lancaster Road, Preston PR1 2RL ☎ 01772 906171 🖷 01772 906366 ✉ m.lovatt@preston.gov.uk

Environmental Health: Mr Craig Sharp, Assistant Director (Chief Environmental Health Officer), Lancastria House, Lancaster Road, Preston PR1 2RH ☎ 01772 906302 ✉ c.sharp@preston.gov.uk

Estates, Property & Valuation: Mr Derek Woods, Head of Property Management, Lancastria House, Lancaster Road, Preston PR1 2RH ☎ 01772 906519 ✉ d.woods@preston.gov.uk

European Liaison: Mr Gordon Benson, European Procurement Officer, Town Hall, Lancaster Road, Preston PR1 2RL ☎ 01772 903410 🖷 01772 202167 ✉ g.benson@preston.gov.uk

Events Manager: Mr Tim Joel, Events Manager, Guild Hall, Lancaster Road, Preston PR1 1HT ☎ 01772 903663 ✉ t.joel@preston.gov.uk

Facilities: Mr Mick Lovatt, Corporate Director of Environment, Town Hall, Lancaster Road, Preston PR1 2RL ☎ 01772 906171 🖷 01772 906366 ✉ m.lovatt@preston.gov.uk

Finance and Treasurer: Mr Bernard Hayes, Deputy Chief Executive & Corporate Director, Community & Business Services, Town Hall, Lancaster Road, Preston PR1 2RL ☎ 01772 906002 🖷 01772 906366 ✉ b.p.hayes@preston.gov.uk

Finance and Treasurer: Mr A Robinson, Assistant Director (Head of Revenues & Benefits), Town Hall, Lancaster Road, Preston PR1 2RL ☎ 01772 906023 ✉ a.robinson@preston.gov.uk

Fleet Management: Mr Adrian Phillips, Deputy Director of Environment, Lancastria House, Lancaster House, Preston PR1 2RH ☎ 01772 906230 🖷 01772 906239 ✉ a.phillips@preston.gov.uk

Fleet Management: Mr R Rees, Head of Engineering, Lancastria House, Lancaster Road, Preston PR1 2RH ☎ 01772 906792 ✉ r.rees@preston.gov.uk

Grounds Maintenance: Mr Matt Kelly, Head of Parks & Horticultural Services, Argyll Road, Preston PR1 6JY ☎ 01772 906141 🖷 01772 558488 ✉ m.kelly@preston.gov.uk

Health and Safety: Ms Lesley Routh, Health & Safety Manager, PO Box 10, Town Hall, Lancaster Road, Preston PR1 2RL ☎ 01772 906385 🖷 01772 906822 ✉ l.routh@preston.gov.uk

Home Energy Conservation: Mr Derek Whyte, Assistant Director (Head of Economic Regeneration), Town Hall, Lancaster Road, Preston PR1 2RL ☎ 01772 903401 ✉ d.whyte@preston.gov.uk

Housing: Mr Derek Whyte, Assistant Director (Head of Economic Regeneration), Town Hall, Lancaster Road, Preston PR1 2RL ☎ 01772 903401 ✉ d.whyte@preston.gov.uk

Legal: Mrs Angela Harrison, Governance Director, Town Hall, Lancaster Road, Preston PR1 2RL ☎ 01772 906104 ✉ a.harrison@preston.gov.uk

Legal: Ms C Parmenter, Head of Legal Services, Town Hall, Lancaster Road, Preston PR1 2RL ☎ 01772 906373 ✉ c.parmenter@preston.gov.uk

Leisure and Cultural Services: Ms A M Walker, Head of Arts & Heritage Services, Lancastria House, Lancaster Road, Preston PR1 2RH ☎ 01772 906105 ✉ a.walker@preston.gov.uk

Leisure and Cultural Services: Mr Phil Walsh, Assistant Director (Head of Leisure, Sports & Arts), Guild Hall, Lancaster Road, Preston PR1 1HT ☎ 01772 903605 🖷 01772 881716 ✉ p.walsh@preston.gov.uk

Licensing: Mr Mike Thorpe, Head of Licensing Services, Lancastria House, Lancaster Road, Preston PR1 2RH ☎ 01772 906114 ✉ m.thorpe@preston.gov.uk

Lottery Funding, Charity and Voluntary: Mr Peter Bargh, Assistant Director (Head of Community Engagement), Lancastria House, Lancaster Road, Preston PR1 2RH ☎ 01772 903403 ✉ p.bargh@preston.gov.uk

Member Services: Ms Julie Grundy, Head of Member & Civic Services, PO Box 10, Town Hall, Lancaster Road, Preston PR1 2RL ☎ 01772 906112 ✉ j.grundy@preston.gov.uk

Parking: Mr Mick Tickle, Bus Station & Cleaning Manager, Lancastria House, Lancaster Road, Preston PR1 2RH ☎ 01772 906880 ✉ m.tickle@preston.gov.uk

Partnerships: Ms Ruth Bowen, Performance Adviser (Partnerships), Town Hall, Lancaster Road, Preston PR1 2RL ☎ 01772 906623 🖷 01772 906822 ✉ r.bowen@preston.gov.uk

Personnel / HR: Mrs Alison Brown, Assistant Director (Head of Human Resources), Town Hall, Lancaster Road, Preston PR1 2RL ☎ 01772 906399 🖷 01772 906822 ✉ a.brown@preston.gov.uk

Planning: Mr Chris Hayward, Assistant Director (City Planning Officer), Lancastria House, Preston PR1 2RH ☎ 01772 906719 ✉ c.hayward@preston.gov.uk

Procurement: Mrs Angela Harrison, Governance Director, Town Hall, Lancaster Road, Preston PR1 2RL ☎ 01772 906104 ✉ a.harrison@preston.gov.uk

Recycling & Waste Minimisation: Ms Amy Troner, Senior Waste Management Officer, Argyll Road, Preston PR1 6JY ☎ 01772 906267 🖷 01772 906762 ✉ a.troner@preston.gov.uk

Regeneration: Mr Derek Whyte, Assistant Director (Head of Economic Regeneration), Town Hall, Lancaster Road, Preston PR1 2RL ☎ 01772 903401 ✉ d.whyte@preston.gov.uk

Staff Training: Mrs Steph Hayes, Training & Development Manager, Town Hall, Lancaster Road, Preston PR1 2RL ☎ 01772 906399 🖷 01772 906822 ✉ s.hayes@preston.gov.uk

Sustainable Communities: Mr Peter Bargh, Assistant Director (Head of Community Engagement), Town Hall, Lancastria Road, Preston PR1 2RL ☎ 01772 903403 ✉ p.bargh@preston.gov.uk

Sustainable Communities: Ms Ruth Bowen, Performance Adviser (Partnerships), Town Hall, Lancaster Road, Preston PR1 2RL ☎ 01772 906623 🖷 01772 906822 ✉ r.bowen@preston.gov.uk

Sustainable Development: Ms Ruth Bowen, Performance Adviser (Partnerships), Town Hall, Lancaster Road, Preston PR1 2RL ☎ 01772 906623 🖷 01772 906822 ✉ r.bowen@preston.gov.uk

Tourism: Mrs Gayle Hewitt, Head of Destination Marketing, Guild Hall, Lancaster Road, Preston PR1 1HT ☎ 01772 903424 🖷 01772 881716 ✉ ; g.hewitt@preston.gov.uk

Transport: Mr Adrian Phillips, Deputy Director of Environment, Lancastria House, Lancaster Road, Preston PR1 2RH ☎ 01772 906230 🖷 01772 906239 ✉ a.phillips@preston.gov.uk

Waste Collection and Disposal: Mr Adrian Phillips, Deputy Director of Environment, Lancastria House, Lancaster Road, Preston PR1 2RH ☎ 01772 906230 🖷 01772 906239 ✉ a.phillips@preston.gov.uk

Waste Management: Mr Adrian Phillips, Deputy Director of Environment, Lancastria House, Lancaster Road, Preston PR1 2RH ☎ 01772 906230 🖷 01772 906239 ✉ a.phillips@preston.gov.uk

MEMBERS OF THE COUNCIL (57)

***Mayor:* Crompton**, Carl (LAB - University)
cllr.c.crompton@preston.gov.uk

***Deputy Mayor:* Afrin**, Veronica (LAB - St Matthew's)
cllr.v.afrin@preston.gov.uk

***Leader of the Council:* Rankin**, Peter John (LAB - Tulketh)

***Deputy Leader of the Council:* Swindells**, John (LAB - University)
cllr.j.swindells@preston.gov.uk

***Group Leader:* Hudson**, Kenneth (CON - Preston Rural North)
cllr.k.hudson@preston.gov.uk

Abram, Christine (LD - Lea)
cllr.c.abram@preston.gov.uk

Bax, Ismail (LAB - Deepdale)
cllr.i.bax@preston.gov.uk

Borrow, David (LAB - Moor Park)
cllr.d.borrow@preston.gov.uk

Boswell, Robert (LAB - Tulketh)
cllr.r.boswell@preston.gov.uk

Brown, Pauline (LD - Ingol)
cllr.p.brown@preston.gov.uk

Brown, Matthew (LAB - Tulketh)
cllr.m.brown@preston.gov.uk

Browne, John (LAB - Brookfield)
cllr.j.browne@preston.gov.uk

Bruton, John (LD - Cadley)
cllr.j.bruton@preston.gov.uk

Burns, Tom (LAB - Fishwick)
cllr.t.burns@preston.gov.uk

Buttle, Julie (CON - Lea)
cllr.j.buttle@preston.gov.uk

Cartwright, Neil (CON - Preston Rural East)
cllr.n.cartwright@preston.gov.uk

Cartwright, Terrence (IND - Deepdale)
cllr.t.cartwright@preston.gov.uk

Cartwright, Kathleen (CON - College)
cllr.b.cartwright@preston.gov.uk

Collins, John (LAB - Moor Park)

Corker, Philip (LAB - Brookfield)
cllr.p.corker@preston.gov.uk

Crompton, Linda (LAB - Riversway)
cllr.l.crompton@preston.gov.uk

Crowe, Phil (LAB - Larches)
cllr.p.crowe@preston.gov.uk

Davies, Thomas (CON - Preston Rural East)
cllr.t.davies@preston.gov.uk

Eaves, Nerys (LAB - Brookfield)
cllr.n.eaves@preston.gov.uk

Faruki, Anis (LAB - St George's)
cllr.a.faruki@preston.gov.uk

Fazackerley, Eric (CON - Sharoe Green)
cllr.e.fazackerley@preston.gov.uk

Gale, Drew (LAB - Town Centre)
cllr.d.gale@preston.gov.uk

Gardner, Samuel (LAB - Larches)
cllr.s.gardiner@preston.gov.uk

Greenhalgh, Stuart (CON - Garrison)
cllr.s.greenhalgh@preston.gov.uk

Greenhalgh, Jennifer (CON - Garrison)

Hammond, David (CON - Greyfriars)
cllr.d.hammond@preston.gov.uk

Hart, Trevor (CON - Lea)

Hull, James (LAB - St George's)
cllr.j.hull@preston.gov.uk

Iqbal, Javed (LAB - St. Matthew's)
cllr.j.iqbal@preston.gov.uk

Lavalette, Michael (IND - Town Centre)
cllr.m.lavalette@preston.gov.uk

McManus, Margaret (CON - Sharoe Green)
cllr.m.mcmanus@preston.gov.uk

Moore, Damien (CON - Greyfriars)
cllr.d.moore@preston.gov.uk

Patel, Yakub (LAB - Town Centre)
cllr.y.patel@preston.gov.uk

Patel, Bhikhu (LAB - Riversway)
cllr.b.patel@preston.gov.uk

Pomfret, Nicholas (LAB - Ribbleton)
cllr.n.pomfret@preston.gov.uk

Potter, John (LD - Cadley)

Pringle, Peter (LD - Ingol)
cllr.p.pringle@preston.gov.uk
Rawlinson, Martyn (LAB - Fishwick)
cllr.m.rawlinson@preston.gov.uk
Richardson, Albert (LAB - St Matthew's)
albirch2002@yahoo.co.uk
Rollo, Brian (LAB - Ribbleton)
cllr.b.rollo@preston.gov.uk
Routeledge, Mark (LAB - Ashton)
cllr.m.routledge@preston.gov.uk
Saksena, Jonathan (LAB - Ribbleton)
cllr.j.saksena@preston.gov.uk
Seddon, Harry (CON - College)
cllr.h.seddon@preston.gov.uk
Shannon, William (LD - Ingol)
cllr.b.shannon@preston.gov.uk
Smith, Lona (CON - Preston Rural North)
cllr.l.smith@preston.gov.uk
Thomas, Christine (CON - Garrison)
cllr.c.thomas@preston.gov.uk
Thompson, Stephen (CON - Greyfriars)
cllr.s.thompson@preston.gov.uk
Thomson-Ortega, Alexandra (CON - Preston Rural North)
cllr.a.thompson-ortega@preston.gov.uk
Walker, David (CON - Sharoe Green)
cllr.d.walker@preston.gov.uk
Wildgoose, Elizabeth (LAB - Ashton)
cllr.e.wildgoose@preston.gov.uk
Wilson, Dave (CON - Riversway)
cllr.d.wilson@preston.gov.uk
Yates, Mark (LAB - Larches)
cllr.m.yates@preston.gov.uk

POLITICAL COMPOSITION
LAB: 30, CON: 19, LD: 6, IND: 2

CABINET
Leader: Mr Peter John Rankin
Deputy Leader / Planning & Regulation: Mr John Swindells
Advice Services, Culture & Leisure: Mr Tom Burns
Resources: Mr Martyn Rawlinson
Community & Environment: Mr Robert Boswell
Community Engagement & Inclusion: Mr Matthew Brown
Planning & Regulations: Mr John Swindells

COMMITTEE CHAIRS
Audit: Mr Eric Fazackerley
Crime & Disorder: Mrs Veronica Afrin
Employment: Mr Dave Wilson
Environmental Protection & Licensing: Mr John Browne
Overview & Scrutiny Management: Mr Kenneth Hudson
Planning: Mr Brian Rollo

PURBECK D

Purbeck District Council, Westport House, Worgret Road, Wareham BH20 4PP ☎ 01929 556561 🖷 01929 552688
enquiries@purbeck-dc.gov.uk www.purbeck.gov.uk

FACTS & FIGURES
Police Authority: Dorset Police Authority
Learning and Skills Council: South West
Parliamentary Constituencies: Dorset Mid and Poole North, Dorset South
EU Constituencies: South West
Election Frequency: Elections are by thirds
Twinning: Hemsbach (Germany); Swanage: Rudesheim am Rhein (Germany); Wareham: Conches (France); Wareham (USA)

PRINCIPAL OFFICERS
Chief Executive: Mr Steven Mackenzie, Chief Executive, Westport House, Worgret Road, Wareham BH20 4PP ☎ 01929 557233 🖷 01929 557305 stevemackenzie@purbeck-dc.gov.uk

Senior Management: Ms Bridget Downton, General Manager - Planning & Community Services, Westport House, Worgret Road, Wareham BH20 4PP ☎ 01929 557268 🖷 01929 557348
bridgetdownton@purbeck-dc.gov.uk

Senior Management: Mrs Susan Joyce, General Manager - Financial Services, Westport House, Worgret Road, Wareham BH20 4PP ☎ 01929 557321 🖷 01929 557288
suejoyce@purbeck-dc.gov.uk

Senior Management: Mr Philip McStraw, General Manager - Central Services, Westport House, Worgret Road, Wareham BH20 4PP ☎ 01929 557208 🖷 01929 557360
philmcstraw@purbeck-dc.gov.uk

Senior Management: Mr Terry Peterson, Purbeck Sports Centre Manager, Purbeck Sports Centre, Worgret Road, Wareham, BH20 4PH ☎ 01929 500000 🖷 01929 554614
terrypeterson@purbeck-dc.gov.uk

Senior Management: Ms Frances West, General Manager - Public Health & Housing Services, Westport House, Worgret Road, Wareham BH20 4PP ☎ 01929 557215 🖷 01929 557351
franceswest@purbeck-dc.gov.uk

Best Value: Ms Jane Hay, Performance Officer, Westport House, Worgret Road, Wareham BH20 4PP ☎ 01929 557325 🖷 01929 557305 janehay@purbeck-dc.gov.uk

Building Control: Mr Rob Blake, Senior Building Control Officer, Westport House, Worgret Road, Wareham BH20 4PP ☎ 01929 557225 🖷 01929 557338 robblake@purbeck-dc.gov.uk

Building Control: Mr Paul Taylor, Senior Building Control Officer, Westport House, Worgret Road, Wareham BH20 4PP ☎ 01929 557272 🖷 01929 557338
paultaylor@purbeck-dc.gov.uk

PR / Communications: Miss Claire Lodge, Communications Officer, Westport House, Worgret Road, Wareham BH20 4PP ☎ 01929 557201 🖷 01929 557305
clairelodge@purbeck-dc.gov.uk

Community Planning: Ms Bridget Downton, General Manager - Planning & Community Services, Westport House, Worgret Road, Wareham BH20 4PP ☎ 01929 557268 🖷 01929 557348
bridgetdownton@purbeck-dc.gov.uk

Community Safety: Ms Kat Rowe, Democratic Services Manager, Westport House, Worgret Road, Wareham BH20 4PP ☎ 01929 557221 🖷 01929 557360

katrinarowe@purbeck-dc.gov.uk

Computer Management: Mr Paul Gammon, IT Manager, Westport House, Worgret Road, Wareham BH20 4PP ☎ 01929 577316 🖷 01929 557360 paulgammon@purbeck-dc.gov.uk

Contracts: Mrs Jacquie Hall, Property & Procurement Team Leader, Westport House, Worgret Road, Wareham BH20 4PP ☎ 01929 557299 🖷 01929 557360 jacquiehall@purbeck-dc.gov.uk

Corporate Services: Ms Jane Hay, Performance Officer, Westport House, Worgret Road, Wareham BH20 4PP ☎ 01929 557325 🖷 01929 557305 janehay@purbeck-dc.gov.uk

Customer Service: Mr Philip McStraw, General Manager - Central Services, Westport House, Worgret Road, Wareham BH20 4PP ☎ 01929 557208 🖷 01929 557360 philmcstraw@purbeck-dc.gov.uk

Economic Development: Mr Richard Wilson, Environmental Design Manager, Westport House, Worgret Road, Wareham BH20 4PP ☎ 01929 557320 🖷 01929 557348 richardwilson@purbeck-dc.gov.uk

E-Government: Mr Paul Gammon, IT Manager, Westport House, Worgret Road, Wareham BH20 4PP ☎ 01929 577316 🖷 01929 557360 paulgammon@purbeck-dc.gov.uk

Electoral Registration: Ms Kat Rowe, Democratic Services Manager, Westport House, Worgret Road, Wareham BH20 4PP ☎ 01929 557221 🖷 01929 557360 katrinarowe@purbeck-dc.gov.uk

Emergency Planning: Ms Kat Rowe, Democratic Services Manager, Westport House, Worgret Road, Wareham BH20 4PP ☎ 01929 557221 🖷 01929 557360 katrinarowe@purbeck-dc.gov.uk

Environmental / Technical Services: Ms Frances West, General Manager - Public Health & Housing Services, Westport House, Worgret Road, Wareham BH20 4PP ☎ 01929 557215 🖷 01929 557351 franceswest@purbeck-dc.gov.uk

Environmental Health: Mr Richard Conway, Environment & Health Manager (Private Sector Housing), Westport House, Worgret Road, Wareham BH20 4PP ☎ 01929 557267 🖷 01929 557351 susaneady@purbeck-dc.gov.uk

Environmental Health: Ms Susan Eady, Public Health Manager, Westport House, Worgret Road, Wareham BH20 4PP ☎ 01929 557275 🖷 01929 557351 susaneady@purbeck-dc.gov.uk

Estates, Property & Valuation: Mrs Jacquie Hall, Property & Procurement Team Leader, Westport House, Worgret Road, Wareham BH20 4PP ☎ 01929 557299 🖷 01929 557360 jacquiehall@purbeck-dc.gov.uk

Facilities: Mrs Jacquie Hall, Property & Procurement Team Leader, Westport House, Worgret Road, Wareham BH20 4PP ☎ 01929 557299 🖷 01929 557360 jacquiehall@purbeck-dc.gov.uk

Finance and Treasurer: Mrs Susan Joyce, General Manager - Financial Services, Westport House, Worgret Road, Wareham BH20 4PP ☎ 01929 557321 🖷 01929 557288 suejoyce@purbeck-dc.gov.uk

Grounds Maintenance: Ms Frances West, General Manager - Public Health & Housing Services, Westport House, Worgret Road, Wareham BH20 4PP ☎ 01929 557215 🖷 01929 557351 franceswest@purbeck-dc.gov.uk

Health and Safety: Mr Alfred Agbonlahor, Health & Safety Adviser, Westport House, Worgret Road, Wareham BH20 4PP ☎ 01929 557390 🖷 01929 557305 alfredagbonlahor@purbeck-dc.gov.uk

Housing: Ms Fiona Brown, Housing Manager, Westport House, Worgret Road, Wareham BH20 4PP ☎ 01929 557310 🖷 01929 557351 fionabrown@purbeck-dc.gov.uk

Legal: Mr John Hart, Legal Manager, Westport House, Worgret Road, Wareham BH20 4PP ☎ 01929 557217 🖷 01929 557360 johnhart@purbeck-dc.gov.uk

Leisure and Cultural Services: Mr Terry Peterson, Purbeck Sports Centre Manager, Purbeck Sports Centre, Worgret Road, Wareham, BH20 4PH ☎ 01929 500000 🖷 01929 554614 terrypeterson@purbeck-dc.gov.uk

Licensing: Ms Clare Stratford, Licensing Officer, Westport House, Worgret Road, Wareham BH20 4PP ☎ 01929 557220 🖷 01929 557360 clarestratford@purbeck-dc.gov.uk

Member Services: Ms Kat Rowe, Democratic Services Manager, Westport House, Worgret Road, Wareham BH20 4PP ☎ 01929 557221 🖷 01929 557360 katrinarowe@purbeck-dc.gov.uk

Parking: Mr Philip McStraw, General Manager - Central Services, Westport House, Worgret Road, Wareham BH20 4PP ☎ 01929 557208 🖷 01929 557360; philmcstraw@purbeck-dc.gov.uk

Partnerships: Mr Philip McStraw, General Manager - Central Services, Westport House, Worgret Road, Wareham BH20 4PP ☎ 01929 557208 🖷 01929 557360; philmcstraw@purbeck-dc.gov.uk

Personnel / HR: Mrs Christine Dewey, Human Resources Manager, Westport House, Worgret Road, Wareham BH20 4PP ☎ 01929 557204 🖷 01929 557305 christinedewey@purbeck-dc.gov.uk

Planning: Ms Bridget Downton, General Manager - Planning & Community Services, Westport House, Worgret Road, Wareham BH20 4PP ☎ 01929 557268 🖷 01929 557348 bridgetdownton@purbeck-dc.gov.uk

Procurement: Mrs Jacquie Hall, Property & Procurement Team Leader, Westport House, Worgret Road, Wareham BH20 4PP ☎ 01929 557299 🖷 01929 557360 jacquiehall@purbeck-dc.gov.uk

Regeneration: Mr Richard Wilson, Environmental Design Manager, Westport House, Worgret Road, Wareham BH20 4PP

☎ 01929 557320 🖷 01929 557348
✉ richardwilson@purbeck-dc.gov.uk

Staff Training: Mrs Christine Dewey, Human Resources Manager, Westport House, Worgret Road, Wareham BH20 4PP ☎ 01929 557204 🖷 01929 557305 ✉ christinedewey@purbeck-dc.gov.uk

Sustainable Communities: Mr Steve Dring, Planning Policy Section Manager, Westport House, Worgret Road, Wareham BH20 4PP ☎ 01929 557339 🖷 01929 55738
✉ stevedring@purbeck-dc.gov.uk

Sustainable Development: Mr Steve Dring, Planning Policy Section Manager, Westport House, Worgret Road, Wareham BH20 4PP ☎ 01929 557339 🖷 01929 55738
✉ stevedring@purbeck-dc.gov.uk

Tourism: Ms Alison Turnock, Natural Heritage & Tourism Section Manager, Westport House, Worgret Road, Wareham BH20 4PP ☎ 01929 557337 🖷 01929 557348 ✉ alisonturnock@purbeck-dc.gov.uk

MEMBERS OF THE COUNCIL (24)

***Leader of the Council:* Suttle**, Gary (CON - Swanage South)
gmsut@lineone.net
***Deputy Leader of the Council:* Quinn**, Barry (CON - West Purbeck)
Cllr.Quinn@purbeck-dc.gov.uk
Barnes, Malcolm (CON - Winfrith)
Cllr.Barnes@purbeck-dc.gov.uk
Budd, David (LD - Wareham)
a.budd@dorsetcc.gov.uk
Cake, Nick (CON - Creech Barrow)
Cllr.Cake@purbeck-dc.gov.uk
Critchley, Keith (LD - Wareham)
Cllr.Critchley@purbeck-dc.gov.uk
Dragon, Nigel (IND - Castle)
Cllr.Dragon@purbeck-dc.gov.uk
Drane, Fred (LD - Lytchett Minster and Upton East)
f.h.drane@dorsetcc.gov.uk
Ezzard, Beryl (LD - St. Martin)
beryle@homecall.co.uk
Goldsack, Simon (LD - Wool)
srbgoldsack@aol.com
Green, Keith (LD - St. Martin)
Cllr.Green@purbeck-dc.gov.uk
Holmes, Graham (LD - Wool)
Graham30kwk@talktalk.net
Johns, Paul (CON - Lytchett Minster and Upton West)
paul.johns12@btinternet.com
Lovell, Mike (CON - Langton)
mwjlovell@gmail.com
Marsh, Gloria (CON - Swanage North)
Cllr.Marsh@purbeck-dc.gov.uk
Osmond, Eric (LD - Wareham)
cllrosmond@gmail.com
Patrick, Ali (CON - Swanage South)
Cllr.Patrick@purbeck-dc.gov.uk
Pipe, Bill (CON - Lytchett Minster and Upton West)
magpiebillpipe@freeuk.com
Pratt, Mike (CON - Swanage South)
Marmike24@hotmail.com
Taylor, John (LD - Lytchett Matravers)
Cllr.Taylor@purbeck-dc.gov.uk
Tilling, Carol (LD - Lytchett Minster and Upton East)

Trite, Bill (CON - Swanage North)
swanbase.w@virgin.net
Webb, Peter (CON - Lytchett Matravers)
Peter4Lytchett@gmail.com
Wharf, Peter (IND - Bere Regis)
peter.wharf@btopenworld.com

POLITICAL COMPOSITION

CON: 12, LD: 10, IND: 2

COMMITTEE CHAIRS

Audit & Governance Panel: Mr Nigel Dragon
Licensing Board: Mrs Wendy Starr
Overview & Scrutiny Group: Mr Malcolm Barnes
Planning Board: Mr Peter Wharf
Policy Group: Mr David Budd
Standards: Mr Andrew Smetham (External)

READING U

Reading Borough Council, Civic Centre, Reading RG1 7TD
☎ 0118 937 3737 🖷 0118 958 9770
✉ forename.surname@reading.gov.uk 🖳 www.reading.gov.uk

FACTS & FIGURES

Police Authority: Thames Valley Police Authority
Health Authority: South Central Strategic Health Authority
Learning and Skills Council: South East
Parliamentary Constituencies: Reading East, Reading West
EU Constituencies: South East
Election Frequency: Elections are by thirds
Twinning: Clonmel (Republic of Ireland); Dusseldorf (Germany); San Francisco Libre (Nicaragua); Speightstown (Barbados)

PRINCIPAL OFFICERS

Senior Management: Mr Amar Dave, Interim Director of Environment, Culture & Sport, Civic Centre, Reading RG1 7TD ☎ 0118 937 2457 🖷 0118 939 0472 ✉ amar.dave@reading.gov.uk

Senior Management: Mr David Peasley, Director & Council Manager, Civic Centre, Reading RG1 7TD ☎ 0118 937 2741 🖷 0118 937 2278 ✉ dave.peasley@reading.gov.uk

Senior Management: Ms Avril Wilson, Director of Education, Social Services & Housing, Civic Centre, Reading RG1 7TD ☎ 0118 937 2094 🖷 0118 937 2323 ✉ avril.wilson@reading.gov.uk

Access Officer / Social Services (Disability): Mrs Zoe Hanim, Head of Policy, Performance & Community, Civic Centre, Reading RG1 7TD ☎ 0118 937 2173 🖷 0118 937 2155
✉ zoe.hanim@reading.gov.uk

Best Value: Mrs Zoe Hanim, Head of Policy, Performance & Community, Civic Centre, Reading RG1 7TD ☎ 0118 937 2173 🖷 0118 937 2155 ✉ zoe.hanim@reading.gov.uk

Building Control: Mr Neil Uzzell, Building Control & Fire Safety Manager, Civic Centre, Reading RG1 7TD ☎ 0118 937 2846

🖷 0118 937 2103 ✉ neil.uzzell@reading.gov.uk

Civil Registration: Mr Matthew Golledge, Trading Standards Manager, Civic Centre, Reading RG1 7TD ☎ 0118 937 2497 🖷 0118 937 2557 ✉ matthew.golledge@reading.gov.uk

PR / Communications: Mr Derek Plews, Head of Communications, Civic Centre, Reading RG1 7TD ☎ 0118 937 2333 🖷 0118 937 2282 ✉ derek.plews@reading.gov.uk

Community Planning: Mr Grant Thornton, Head of Transformation, Civic Centre, Reading RG1 7TD ☎ 0118 937 2416 🖷 0118 937 2155 ✉ grant.thornton@reading.gov.uk

Computer Management: Mr Mike Ibbitson, ICT Manager, Civic Centre, Reading RG1 7TD ☎ 0118 937 4240 🖷 0118 937 2675 ✉ mike.ibbitson@reading.gov.uk

Consumer Protection and Trading Standards: Mr Pollen Exeter, Consumer Protection Manager, Civic Centre, Reading RG1 7TD ☎ 0118 937 2245 🖷 0118 937 2557 ✉ pol.exeter@reading.gov.uk

Contracts: Mr Andy Allen, Finance Manager, Civic Centre, Reading RG1 7TD ☎ 0118 937 2748 🖷 0118 958 0278 ✉ andy.allen@reading.gov.uk

Economic Development: Mr Richard Byard, Economic & Development Manager, Davidson House, Forbury Square, Reading RG1 3EU ☎ 0118 900 1622 🖷 0118 900 1621 ✉ richard.byard@reading.gov.uk

Education: Ms Kim Bergamasco, Head of School Improvement & Inclusion, Civic Centre, Reading RG1 7TD ☎ 0118 937 2273 🖷 0118 937 2761 ✉ kim.bergamasco@reading.gov.uk

Education: Ms Avril Wilson, Director of Education, Social Services & Housing, Civic Centre, Reading RG1 7TD ☎ 0118 937 2094 🖷 0118 937 2323 ✉ avril.wilson@reading.gov.uk

E-Government: Mrs Zoe Hanim, Head of Policy, Performance & Community, Civic Centre, Reading RG1 7TD ☎ 0118 937 2173 🖷 0118 937 2155 ✉ zoe.hanim@reading.gov.uk

Electoral Registration: Mrs Julie Kempen, Electoral Services Manager, Civic Centre, Reading RG1 7TD ☎ 0118 937 2731 🖷 0118 937 2591 ✉ julie.kempen@reading.gov.uk

Emergency Planning: Mr Brett Dyson, Emergency Planning & Risk Officer, Civic Centre, Reading RG1 7TD ☎ 0118 937 2235 🖷 0118 397 2559 ✉ brett.dyson@reading.gov.uk

Energy Management: Mr Ben Burfoot, Sustainability Manager, Civic Centre, Reading RG1 7TD ☎ 0118 937 2232 🖷 0118 937 2155 ✉ ben.burfoot@reading.ac.uk

Environmental / Technical Services: Mr Kevin Holyer, Head of Environment & Consumer Services, Civic Centre, Reading RG1 7TD ☎ 0118 937 2324 🖷 0118 937 2435 ✉ kevin.holyer@reading.gov.uk

Environmental Health: Mr Pollen Exeter, Consumer Protection Manager, Civic Centre, Reading RG1 7TD ☎ 0118 937 2245 🖷 0118 937 2557 ✉ pol.exeter@reading.gov.uk

Estates, Property & Valuation: Mr Bruce Tindall, Head of Development, Civic Centre, Reading RG1 7TD ☎ 0118 937 2594 🖷 0118 937 2767 ✉ bruce.tindall@reading.gov.uk

European Liaison: Mr Grant Thornton, Head of Transformation, Civic Centre, Reading RG1 7TD ☎ 0118 937 2416 🖷 0118 937 2155 ✉ grant.thornton@reading.gov.uk

Events Manager: Ms Lucy Burgess, Events Officer, Civic Centre, Reading RG1 7TD ☎ 0118 937 2771 🖷 0118 937 2282 ✉ lucy.burgess@reading.gov.uk

Facilities: Ms Jan Sagoo, Head of Civic Services/New Civic Project, Civic Centre, Reading RG1 7TD ☎ 0118 937 2304 🖷 0118 937 2591 ✉ jan.sagoo@reading.gov.uk

Finance and Treasurer: Mr Andy Allen, Finance Manager, Civic Centre, Reading RG1 7TD ☎ 0118 937 2748 🖷 0118 958 0278 ✉ andy.allen@reading.gov.uk

Finance and Treasurer: Mr Alan Cross, Head of Finance, Civic Centre, Reading RG1 7TD ☎ 0118 937 2058 🖷 0118 937 2278 ✉ alan.cross@reading.gov.uk

Finance and Treasurer: Mr Dave Fisher, Chief Accountant, Civic Centre, Reading RG1 7TD ☎ 0118 937 2747 🖷 0118 937 2278 ✉ dave.fisher@reading.gov.uk

Finance and Treasurer: Mr David Peasley, Director & Council Manager, Civic Centre, Reading RG1 7TD ☎ 0118 937 2741 🖷 0118 937 2278 ✉ dave.peasley@reading.gov.uk

Fleet Management: Ms Michelle Crick, Street Care Business Support Manager, 6 Darwin Close, Reading RG2 0RB ☎ 0118 937 3993 ✉ peter.butler@reading.gov.uk

Grounds Maintenance: Mr Amar Dave, Interim Director of Environment, Culture & Sport, Civic Centre, Reading RG1 7TD ☎ 0118 937 2457 🖷 0118 939 0472 ✉ amar.dave@reading.gov.uk

Health and Safety: Mr Robin Pringle, Corporate Safety & Workforce Development, Civic Centre, Reading RG1 7TD ☎ 0118 937 2519 ✉ robin.pringle@reading.gov.uk

Highways: Mr Vaughan Norris, Highways Manager, Civic Centre, Reading RG1 7TD ☎ 0118 937 2669 🖷 0119 937 2609 ✉ vaughan.norris@reading.gov.uk

Home Energy Conservation: Mr Paul Taylor, Housing Stock Regeneration Manager, 6 Darwin Close, Reading RG2 0RB ☎ 0118 939 0224 🖷 0118 975 3334 ✉ paul.taylor@reading.gov.uk

Housing: Mr Phil Eldridge, Property Services Manager, Civic Centre, Reading RG1 7TD ☎ 0118 937 2266 🖷 0118 937 2052 ✉ phil.eldridge@reading.gov.uk

Housing Maintenance: Mr Phil Eldridge, Property Services Manager, Civic Centre, Reading RG1 7TD ☎ 0118 937 2266 🖷 0118 937 2052 ✉ phil.eldridge@reading.gov.uk

Local Area Agreement: Mrs Zoe Hanim, Head of Policy, Performance & Community, Civic Centre, Reading RG1 7TD ☎ 0118 937 2173 🖷 0118 937 2155 ✉ zoe.hanim@reading.gov.uk

Legal: Mr Christopher Brooks, Head of Legal & Democratic Services, Civic Centre, Reading RG1 7TD ☎ 0118 937 2602 🖷 0118 937 2767 ✉ chris.brooks@reading.gov.uk

Leisure and Cultural Services: Mr Amar Dave, Interim Director of Environment, Culture & Sport, Civic Centre, Reading RG1 7TD ☎ 0118 937 2457 🖷 0118 939 0472 ✉ amar.dave@reading.gov.uk

Leisure and Cultural Services: Mr Rhodri Thomas, Museum & Town Hall General Manager, Reading Central Library, Abbey Sqaure, Reading RG1 3BQ ☎ 0118 937 3943 🖷 0118 956 6719 ✉ rhodri.thomas@reading.gov.uk

Licensing: Ms Clare Bradley, Environmental Health Manager (Licensing & Environmental Protection), Civic Centre, Reading RG1 7TD ☎ 0118 937 2322 🖷 0118 937 2557 ✉ clare.bradley@reading.gov.uk

Lighting: Mr Vaughan Norris, Highways Manager, Civic Centre, Reading RG1 7TD ☎ 0118 937 2669 🖷 0119 937 2609 ✉ vaughan.norris@reading.gov.uk

Lottery Funding, Charity and Voluntary: Ms Irene Cameron, Team Leader - Funding Services, Civic Centre, Reading RG1 7TD ☎ 0118 937 2387 🖷 0118 939 0155 ✉ irene.cameron@reading.gov.uk

Member Services: Ms Jan Sagoo, Head of Civic Services/New Civic Project, Civic Centre, Reading RG1 7TD ☎ 0118 937 2304 🖷 0118 937 2591 ✉ jan.sagoo@reading.gov.uk

Parking: Mr Anthony Bolton, Head of Transport, Civic Centre, Reading RG1 7TD ☎ 0118 937 2813 🖷 0118 937 2633 ✉ pat.baxter@reading.gov.uk

Partnerships: Ms Sarah Gee, Head of Housing, Neighbourhoods & Communities, Civic Centre, Reading RG1 7TD ☎ 0118 937 2973 🖷 0118 937 2786 ✉ sarah.gee@reading.gov.uk

Personnel / HR: Ms Anne Burton, Head of Human Resources, Civic Centre, Reading RG1 7TD ☎ 0118 937 2492 🖷 0118 937 2484 ✉ anne.burton@reading.gov.uk

Planning: Ms Alison Bell, Head of Planning & Building Control, Civic Centre, Reading RG1 7TD ☎ 0118 937 2604 🖷 0118 937 2435 ✉ alison.bell@reading.gov.uk

Procurement: Mr John Littlefair, Procurement & Partnership Manager, Civic Centre, Reading RG1 7TD ☎ 0118 937 2748 🖷 0118 958 0278 ✉ andy.allen@reading.gov.uk

Public Libraries: Mr Amar Dave, Interim Director of Environment, Culture & Sport, Civic Centre, Reading RG1 7TD ☎ 0118 937 2457 🖷 0118 939 0472 ✉ amar.dave@reading.gov.uk

Recycling & Waste Minimisation: Mr Oliver Burt, Waste Disposal Manager, 2-4 Darwin Close, Reading RG2 0RB ☎ 0118 937 3990 ✉ oliver.burt@reading.gov.uk

Regeneration: Mr Chris Bloomfield, Neighbourhood Regeneration Manager, Civic Centre, Reading RG1 7TD ☎ 0118 937 2176 🖷 0118 937 2155 ✉ chris.bloomfield@reading.gov.uk

Road Safety: Mr Simon Beasley, UTMC Network Manager, Civic Centre, Reading RG1 7TD ☎ 0118 937 2228 🖷 0118 937 2633 ✉ simon.beasley@reading.gov.uk

Social Services: Ms Sue Gosling, CRT Business Support Team Leader, Civic Centre, Reading RG1 7TD ☎ 0118 937 3676 🖷 0118 955 3744 ✉ sue.gosling@reading.gov.uk

Social Services: Ms Avril Wilson, Director of Education, Social Services & Housing, Civic Centre, Reading RG1 7TD ☎ 0118 937 2094 🖷 0118 937 2323 ✉ avril.wilson@reading.gov.uk

Social Services (Adult): Ms Suzanne Westhead, Head of Adult Care, Civic Centre, Reading RG1 7TD ☎ 0118 937 4164 🖷 0118 937 2939 ✉ suzanne.westhead@reading.gov.uk

Social Services (Children): Ms Karen Reeve, Head of Children's Social Care, Civic Centre, Reading RG1 7TD ☎ 0118 937 4163 🖷 0118 937 2675 ✉ karen.reeve@reading.gov.uk

Staff Training: Mr Reg Friddle, Senior Learning & Development Officer, Civic Centre, Reading RG1 7TD ☎ 0118 937 2115 🖷 0118 937 2484 ✉ reg.friddle@reading.gov.uk

Street Scene: Mr Chris Camfield, Street Environment Manager, 19 Bennetts Road, Reading RG2 0QX ☎ 0118 937 2040 ✉ chris.camfield@reading.gov.uk

Sustainable Communities: Mr Ben Burfoot, Sustainability Manager, Civic Centre, Reading RG1 7TD ☎ 0118 937 2232 🖷 0118 937 2155 ✉ ben.burfoot@reading.ac.uk

Sustainable Development: Mr Ben Burfoot, Sustainability Manager, Civic Centre, Reading RG1 7TD ☎ 0118 937 2232 🖷 0118 937 2155 ✉ ben.burfoot@reading.ac.uk

Tourism: Ms Sue Brackley, Destination Manager, Reading UK CIC, Davidson House, Forbury Square, Reading RG1 3EY ☎ 0118 900 1624 🖷 0118 939 9885 ✉ sue.brackley@reading.gov.uk

Town Centre: Mr Guy Douglas, Business Improvement District Manager, Reading UK CIC, Davidson House, Forbury Square, Reading RG1 3EY ☎ 0118 900 1623 ✉ bid@livingreading.co.uk

Traffic Management: Mr Simon Beasley, UTMC Network Manager, Civic Centre, Reading RG1 7TD ☎ 0118 937 2228 🖷 0118 937 2633 ✉ simon.beasley@reading.gov.uk

Transport: Mr Anthony Bolton, Head of Transport, Civic Centre, Reading RG1 7TD ☎ 0118 937 2813 🖷 0118 937 2633 ✉ pat.baxter@reading.gov.uk

Transport Planner: Mr Anthony Bolton, Head of Transport, Civic Centre, Reading RG1 7TD ☎ 0118 937 2813 🖷 0118 937 2633 ✉ pat.baxter@reading.gov.uk

Waste Collection and Disposal: Mr Oliver Burt, Waste Disposal Manager, 2-4 Darwin Close, Reading RG2 0RB ☎ 0118 937 3990

oliver.burt@reading.gov.uk

Waste Collection and Disposal: Mr Chris Green, Waste Operations Manager, 2-4 Darwin Close, Reading RG2 0RB
☎ 0118 937 3950 chris.green@reading.gov.uk

MEMBERS OF THE COUNCIL (46)

***Mayor:* Rynn**, Jennifer (CON - Kentwood)
jenny.rynn@reading.gov.uk
***Deputy Mayor:* Edwards**, Deborah (LAB - Southcote)
deborah.edwards@reading.gov.uk
***Leader of the Council:* Lovelock**, Jo (LAB - Norcot)
lo.lovelock@reading.gov.uk
***Group Leader:* Harris**, Tim (CON - Church)
tim.harris@reading.gov.uk
***Group Leader:* White**, Rob (GRN - Park)
rob.white@reading.gov.uk
Anderson, James (CON - Kentwood)
james.anderson@reading.gov.uk
Ayub, Mohammed (LAB - Abbey)
mohammed.ayub@reading.gov.uk
Ballsdon, Isobel (CON - Mapledurham)
isobel.ballsdon@reading.gov.uk
Benson, Daisy (LD - Redlands)
daisy.benson@reading.gov.uk
Cumpsty, Andrew (CON - Caversham)
andrew.cumpsty@reading.gov.uk
Davies, Richard (LAB - Caversham)
richard.davies@reading.gov.uk
Duveen, Ricky (LD - Tilehurst)
ricky.duveen@reading.gov.uk
Eastwood, Melanie (GRN - Park)
melanie.eastwood@reading.gov.uk
Eden, Rachel (LAB - Whitley)
rachel.eden@reading.gov.uk
Edwards, Kelly (LAB - Whitley)
kelly.edwards@reading.gov.uk
Ennis, John (LAB - Southcote)
john.ennis@reading.gov.uk
Gavin, Jan (LAB - Redlands)
jan.gavin@reading.gov.uk
Gittings, Paul (LAB - Minster)
paul.gittings@reading.gov.uk
Hacker, Sarah (LAB - Battle)
sarah.hacker@reading.gov.uk
Hopper, Ed (CON - Thames)
ed.hopper@reading.gov.uk
Hoskin, Graeme (LAB - Norcot)
graeme.hoskin@reading.gov.uk
Jones, Tony (LAB - Redlands)
tony.jones@reading.gov.uk
Jones, Peter (LAB - Norcot)
peter.jones@reading.gov.uk
Khan, Gul (LAB - Battle)
gul.khan@reading.gov.uk
Livingston, Marian (LAB - Minster)
marian.livingston@reading.gov.uk
Maskell, Chris (LAB - Battle)
chris.maskell@reading.gov.uk
McElligott, Eileen (LAB - Church)
eileen.mcelligott@reading.gov.uk
O'Connell, Meri (LD - Tilehurst)
Orton, Mike (LAB - Whitley)
mike.orton@reading.gov.uk
Page, Tony (LAB - Abbey)
tony.page@reading.gov.uk
Ralph, Mark (IND - Peppard)
mark.ralph@reading.gov.uk
Rodda, Matt (LAB - Katesgrove)
matt.rodda@reading.gov.uk
Ruhemann, Pete (LAB - Southcote)
pete.ruhemann@reading.gov.uk
Rye, Rebecca (LD - Katesgrove)
rebecca.rye@reading.gov.uk
Singh, Daya Pal (LAB - Kentwood)
Skeats, Jeanette (CON - Thames)
jeanette.skeats@reading.gov.uk
Stanford-Beale, Jane (CON - Peppard)
Stanway, Tom (CON - Caversham)
tom.stanway@reading.gov.uk
Stevens, David (CON - Thames)
david.stevens@reading.gov.uk
Terry, Liz (LAB - Minster)
liz.terry@reading.gov.uk
Tickner, Bet (LAB - Abbey)
bet.tickner@reading.gov.uk
Vickers, Sandra (CON - Tilehurst)
sandra.vickers@reading.gov.uk
Whitham, Jamie (GRN - Park)
jamie.whitham@reading.gov.uk
Williams, Rose (LAB - Katesgrove)
rose.williams@reading.gov.uk
Willis, Richard (CON - Peppard)
richard.willis@reading.gov.uk
Woodward, Paul (LAB - Church)
paul.woodward@reading.gov.uk

POLITICAL COMPOSITION

LAB: 26, CON: 12, LD: 4, GRN: 3, IND: 1

CABINET

Leader: Ms Jo Lovelock
Deputy Leader; Regeneration, Transport & Planning: Mr Tony Page
Adult Social Care: Mr Mike Orton
Culture & Sport: Ms Marian Livingston
Education & Children's Services: Mr John Ennis
Environment & Climate Change: Mr Paul Gittings
Housing & Neighbourhoods: Ms Rachel Eden
Health & Wellbeing: Ms Bet Tickner
Community Involvement & Service Improvement: Ms Jan Gavin

COMMITTEE CHAIRS

Environment (Scrutiny): Mr Chris Maskell
Licensing Applications: Mr Peter Jones
Personnel: Ms Jo Lovelock
Planning Applications: Mr Pete Ruhemann
Standards: Ms Tina Barnes

REDBRIDGE L

Redbridge London Borough Council, (London Borough of Redbridge), Town Hall, High Road, Ilford IG1 1DD
☎ 020 8554 5000 customer.cc@redbridge.gov.uk
www.redbridge.gov.uk

LOCAL AUTHORITIES

FACTS & FIGURES

Police Authority: Metropolitan Police Authority
Health Authority: NHS London
Learning and Skills Council: London
Parliamentary Constituencies: Chingford and Woodford, Ilford North, Ilford South, Leyton and Wanstead
EU Constituencies: London
Election Frequency: Elections are of whole council
Twinning: 'Declaration of Friendship' with Genas, France

PRINCIPAL OFFICERS

Chief Executive: Mr Roger Hampson, Chief Executive, Town Hall, High Road, Ilford IG1 1DD ☎ 020 8708 2100 🖷 020 8478 2356 ✉ roger.hampson@redbridge.gov.uk

Senior Management: Mr Simon Barry, Director of Environment & Community Services, Lynton House, 255 - 259 High Road, Ilford IG1 1NY ☎ 020 8708 3411 🖷 020 8708 4224 ✉ simon.barry@redbridge.gov.uk

Senior Management: Mr Simon Goodwin, Borough Solicitor & Secretary, Town Hall, High Road, Ilford IG1 1DD ☎ 020 8708 2201 🖷 020 8708 2981 ✉ simon.goodwin@redbridge.gov.uk

Senior Management: Mr Geoff Pearce, Director of Finance & Resources, Town Hall, High Road, Ilford IG1 1DD ☎ 020 8708 3588 🖷 020 8708 3185 ✉ geoff.pearce@redbridge.gov.uk

Senior Management: Mr John Powell, Director of Adult Social Services & Housing, Ley Street House, 497-499 Ley Street, Ilford IG2 7QX ☎ 020 8708 5535 🖷 020 8708 5332 ✉ john.powell@redbridge.gov.uk

Senior Management: Ms Pat Reynolds, Director of Children's Services, Lynton House, 255-259 High Road, Ilford IG1 1NY ☎ 020 8708 3100 🖷 020 8708 3894 ✉ pat.reynolds@redbridge.gov.uk

Access Officer / Social Services (Disability): Ms Pauline Brown, Principal Officer - Access, Personalisation & Care, Ley Street House, 497-499 Ley Street, Ilford IG2 7QX ☎ 020 8708 5169 🖷 020 8708 5075 ✉ pauline.brown@redbridge.gov.uk

Access Officer / Social Services (Disability): Ms Sheenagh Burgess, Chief Officer, Ley Street, 497 - 499 Ley Street, Ilford IG2 7QZ ☎ 020 8708 5332 ✉ sheenagh.burgess@redbridge.gov.uk

Architect, Building / Property Services: Mr Fred Steel, Head of Building Services, Lynton House, 255-259 High Road, Ilford IG1 1NY ☎ 020 8708 3514 🖷 020 8708 3987 ✉ fred.steel@redbridge.gov.uk

Building Control: Mr Amrik Notta, Head of Building Control, Town Hall, High Road, Ilford IG1 1DD ☎ 020 8708 2521 🖷 020 8708 2985 ✉ amrik.notta@redbridge.gov.uk

Catering Services: Ms Therese Knight, Catering Manager, PO Box 2, Town Hall, High Road, Ilford IG1 1DD ☎ 020 8708 2003 🖷 020 8708 2405 ✉ therese.knight@redbridge.gov.uk

Children / Youth Services: Ms Pat Reynolds, Director of Children's Services, Lynton House, 255 - 299 High Road, Ilford IG1 1NY ☎ 020 8708 3100 🖷 020 8708 3894 ✉ pat.reynolds@redbridge.gov.uk

Civil Registration: Mrs Val Gilfillan, Head of Registration & Celebratory, Queen Victoria House, 794 Cranbrook Road, Barkingside, Ilford IG6 1JS ☎ 020 8708 7209 🖷 020 8708 7161 ✉ val.gilfillan@redbridge.gov.uk

PR / Communications: Mr Eddie Gibb, Head of Marketing & Communications, Town Hall, High Road, Ilford IG1 1DD ☎ 020 8708 3763 ✉ eddie.gibb@redbridge.gov.uk

Community Safety: Ms Kathy Nixon, Chief Community Safety Officer, 8 Perth Terrace, Perth Road, Ilford IG2 6AT ☎ 020 8708 5996 🖷 020 8708 5984 ✉ kathy.nixon@redbridge.gov.uk

Computer Management: Mr Lee Edwards, Chief ICT Officer, 17/23 Clements Road, Ilford IG1 1AG ☎ 020 8708 4100 🖷 020 8708 4983 ✉ lee.edwards@redbridge.gov.uk

Consumer Protection and Trading Standards: Mr Alan Drake, Head of Community Protection & Enforcement, 8 Perth Terrace, Perth Road, Ilford IG2 6AT ☎ 020 8708 5490 🖷 020 8708 5984 ✉ alan.drake@redbridge.gov.uk

Contracts: Mr Dave Wood, Head of Strategic Procurement, Lynton House, 255 - 259, High Road, Ilford IG1 1NY ☎ 020 8708 3268 ✉ dave.wood@redbridge.gov.uk

Corporate Services: Mr Kevin Wackett, Head of Parks & Open Spaces, 210 Wash Lodge, Cranbrook Road, Ilford IG1 4TG ☎ 020 8708 3223 ✉ kevin.wackett@visionrcl.org.uk

Customer Service: Mr Simon Barry, Director of Environment & Community Services, Lynton House, 255 - 259 High Road, Ilford IG1 1NY ☎ 020 8708 3411 🖷 020 8708 4224 ✉ simon.barry@redbridge.gov.uk

Direct Labour: Mr Dave Cuthell, Chief Highways & Cleansing Officer, Ley Street Depot, Ley Street, Ilford IG2 7QX ☎ 020 8708 5019 🖷 020 8708 5118 ✉ david.cuthell@redbridge.gov.uk

Economic Development: Mr Mark Lucas, Head of Inward Investment & Enterprise, Town Hall, High Road, Ilford IG1 1DD ☎ 020 8708 2143 🖷 020 8708 2379 ✉ mark.lucas@redbridge.gov.uk

Education: Ms Ronke Martins-Taylor, Chief Services to Young People Officer, Lynton House, 255-259 High Road, Ilford IG1 1NY ☎ 020 8708 3378 🖷 020 8708 3894 ✉ ronke.martins-taylor@redbridge.gov.uk

Education: Mr John O'Keefe, Chief Education Planning & Resources Officer, Lynton House, 255-259 High Road, Ilford IG1 1NY ☎ 020 8708 3117 🖷 020 8708 3894 ✉ john.okeefe@redbridge.gov.uk

Education: Ms Pat Reynolds, Director of Children's Services, Lynton House, 255-259 High Road, Ilford IG1 1NY ☎ 020 8708 3100 🖷 020 8708 3894 ✉ pat.reynolds@redbridge.gov.uk

Education: Mr Peter Shephard, Chief Officer - Learning & School Improvement, Lynton House, 255-259 High Road, Ilford IG1 1NY ☎ 020 8708 3056 🖷 020 8708 3894 peter.shephard@redbridge.gov.uk

E-Government: Mr Lee Edwards, Chief ICT Officer, 17-23 Clements Road, Ilford IG1 1AG ☎ 020 8708 4100 🖷 020 8708 4983 lee.edwards@redbridge.gov.uk

Electoral Registration: Mr George Sullivan, Electoral Services Manager, Queen Victoria House, 794 Cranbrook Road, Barkingside, Ilford IG6 1JS ☎ 020 8708 7170 🖷 020 8708 7150 george.sullivan@redbridge.gov.uk

Emergency Planning: Mr Derek Hobday, Emergency Planning & Business Continuity Manager, Redbridge Control Centre, Ley Street Depot, Ley Street, Ilford IG2 7QX ☎ 020 8708 5520 🖷 020 8708 5521 derek.hobday@redbridge.gov.uk

Energy Management: Mr John Mitchinson, Group Manager Environmental, Lynton House, 255-259 High Road, Ilford IG1 1NY ☎ 020 8708 3301 john.mitchinson@redbridge.gov.uk

Environmental Health: Mr Themis Skouros, Team Manager - Pollution, Public Health & Pest Control, 8 Perth Terrace, Perth Road, Ilford IG2 6AT themis.skouros@redbridge.gov.uk

Estates, Property & Valuation: Mr David Pethen, Head of Estates & Asset Management, Lynton House, 255-259 High Road, Ilford IG1 1NY ☎ 020 8708 3215 🖷 020 8708 3985 david.pethen@redbridge.gov.uk

Facilities: Mr Andrew Dalrymple, Head of Facilities Management, Lynton House, 255-259 High Road, Ilford IG1 1NY ☎ 020 8708 3345 🖷 020 8708 3985 andrew.dalrymple@redbridge.gov.uk

Finance and Treasurer: Mr Mark Green, Chief Financial Services Officer, Lynton House, 255-259 High Road, Ilford IG1 1NY ☎ 020 8708 3013 🖷 020 8708 3185 mark.green@redbridge.gov.uk

Finance and Treasurer: Mr Geoff Pearce, Director of Finance & Resources, Lynton House, 255-259 High Road, Ilford IG1 1NY ☎ 020 8708 3588 🖷 020 8708 3185 geoff.pearce@redbridge.gov.uk

Fleet Management: Mr Eddie Cross, Engineering Manager, Ley Street Depot, Ley Street, Ilford IG2 7QX ☎ 020 8708 5212 🖷 020 8708 5118 eddie.cross@redbridge.gov.uk

Grounds Maintenance: Mr Mark Fuller, Technical Manager, Ley Street Depot, Ley Street, Ilford IG2 7QX ☎ 020 8708 5315 🖷 020 8708 5378 mark.fuller@redbridge.gov.uk

Health and Safety: Mr Ian Wringe, Health & Safety Officer, Lynton House, 255 - 259 High Road, Ilford IG1 1NY ☎ 020 8708 3152 ian.wringe@redbridge.gov.uk

Highways: Mr Cliff Woolnoth, Head of Engineering, Lynton House, 255-259 High Road, Ilford IG1 1NY ☎ 020 8708 3570 🖷 020 8708 3970 cliff.woolnoth@redbridge.gov.uk

Home Energy Conservation: Mr John Mitchinson, Group Manager Environmental, Lynton House, 255-259 High Road, Ilford IG1 1NY ☎ 020 8708 3301 john.mitchinson@redbridge.gov.uk

Housing: Ms Lisa Marston, Chief Housing Officer, 17 - 23 Clements Road, Ilford IG1 1AG ☎ 020 8708 4156 🖷 020 8708 4119 lisa.marston@redbridge.gov.uk

Housing Maintenance: Mr Mark Easton, Redbridge Homes Interim Chief Executive, West Housing Office, 152 Broadmead Road, Woodford Green, Ilford IG8 0AG ☎ 020 8708 7610 🖷 020 8708 7627 mark.easton@redbridgehomes.org

Housing Maintenance: Mr Fred Steel, Head of Building Services, Lynton House, 255-259 High Road, Ilford IG1 1NY ☎ 020 8708 3514 fred.steel@redbridge.gov.uk

Local Area Agreement: Mr John Turkson, Partnerships Manager, Ley Street House, 497 - 499 Ley Street, Ilford IG2 7QX ☎ 020 8708 2381 john.turkson@redbridge.gov.uk

Legal: Mr Simon Goodwin, Borough Solicitor & Secretary, Town Hall, High Road, Ilford IG1 1DD ☎ 020 8708 2201 🖷 020 8708 2981 simon.goodwin@redbridge.gov.uk

Leisure and Cultural Services: Mr Iain Varah, Chief Executive, Central Library, Clements Road, Ilford IG1 1EA ☎ 020 8708 2012 🖷 020 8708 3178 iain.varah@visionrcl.org.uk

Licensing: Mr Alan Drake, Head of Community Protection & Enforcement, 8 Perth Terrace, Perth Road, Ilford IG2 6AT ☎ 020 8708 5490 🖷 020 8708 5984 alan.drake@redbridge.gov.uk

Lifelong Learning: Mr Iain Varah, Chief Executive, Central Library, Clements Road, Ilford IG1 1EA ☎ 020 8708 2012 🖷 020 8708 3178 iain.varah@visionrcl.org.uk

Lighting: Mr Cliff Woolnoth, Head of Engineering, Lynton House, 255-259 High Road, Ilford IG1 1NY ☎ 020 8708 3570 🖷 020 8708 3970 cliff.woolnoth@redbridge.gov.uk

Member Services: Mr Stephen Wastell, Head of Constitutional Services, Town Hall, High Road, Ilford IG1 1DD ☎ 020 8708 2162 🖷 020 8708 2356 steve.wastell@redbridge.gov.uk

Parking: Mr Mike Woodward, Business Manager, Lynton House, 255-259 High Road, Ilford IG1 1NY ☎ 020 8708 3461 🖷 020 8708 3987 mike.woodward@redbridge.gov.uk

Partnerships: Mr John Turkson, Partnerships Manager, Ley Street House, 497 - 499 Ley Street, Ilford IG2 7QX ☎ 020 8708 2381 john.turkson@redbridge.gov.uk

Personnel / HR: Ms Marj Keddy, Chief Human Resources Officer, Lynton House, 255-259 High Road, Ilford IG1 1NY ☎ 020 8708 3974 🖷 020 8708 3038 marj.keddy@redbridge.gov.uk

Personnel / HR: Mr Geoff Pearce, Director of Finance & Resources, Lynton House, 255-259 High Road, Ilford IG1 1NY ☎ 020 8708 3588 🖷 020 8708 3185 geoff.pearce@redbridge.gov.uk

Planning: Mr Stewart Murray, Chief Planning & Regeneration Officer, Town Hall, High Road, Ilford IG1 1DD ☎ 020 8708 2067 🖷 020 8708 2985 🖱 stewart.murray@redbridge.gov.uk

Procurement: Mr Dave Wood, Head of Strategic Procurement, Lynton House, 255 - 259 High Road, Ilford IG1 1NY ☎ 020 8708 3268 🖱 dave.wood@redbridge.gov.uk

Public Libraries: Mr Gareth Morley, Head of Culture & Libraries, Lynton House, 255-259 High Road, Ilford IG1 1NY ☎ 020 8708 3426 🖷 020 8708 2431 🖱 gareth.morley@visionrcl.org.uk

Recycling & Waste Minimisation: Mr Tom Lawrence, Recycling Manager, Ley Street Depot, Ley Street, Ilford IG2 7QX ☎ 020 8708 5517 🖷 020 8708 5987 🖱 tom.lawrence@redbridge.gov.uk

Regeneration: Mr Simon Barry, Director of Environment & Community Services, Lynton House, 255 - 259 High Road, Ilford IG1 1NY ☎ 020 8708 3411 🖷 020 8708 4224 🖱 simon.barry@redbridge.gov.uk

Regeneration: Mr Mark Lucas, Head of Inward Investment & Enterprise, Town Hall, High Road, Ilford IG1 1DD ☎ 020 8708 2143 🖷 020 8708 2379 🖱 mark.lucas@redbridge.gov.uk

Road Safety: Ms Jane Arthur, Group Manager, Road Safety, Lynton House, 255-259 High Road, Ilford IG1 1NY ☎ 020 8708 3971 🖷 020 8708 3970 🖱 jane.arthur@redbridge.gov.uk

Social Services: Mr John Powell, Director of Adult Social Services & Housing, Ley Street House, 497-499 Ley Street, Ilford IG2 7QX ☎ 020 8708 5535 🖷 020 8708 5332 🖱 john.powell@redbridge.gov.uk

Social Services (Adult): Mr John Powell, Director of Adult Social Services & Housing, Ley Street House, 497-499 Ley Street, Ilford IG2 7QX ☎ 020 8708 5535 🖷 020 8708 5332 🖱 john.powell@redbridge.gov.uk

Social Services (Children): Ms Sheenagh Burgess, Chief Officer, Ley Street House, 497-499 Ley Street, Ilford IG2 7QX ☎ ; 020 8708 5332 🖱 sheenagh.burgess@redbridge.gov.uk

Social Services (Children): Mr Patrick Power, Managing Director Children's Trust, Ley Street House, 497-499 Ley Street, Ilford IG2 7QX ☎ 020 8708 5752 🖷 020 8708 8708 🖱 patrick.power@redbridge.gov.uk

Staff Training: Ms Ann Butler, Workforce Development Manager, Lynton House, 255-259 High Road, Ilford IG1 1NY ☎ 020 8708 3446 🖷 020 8708 3038 🖱 ann.butler@redbridge.gov.uk

Street Scene: Mr Russell Ward, Head of Environmental Services, Ley Street Depot, Ley Street, Ilford IG2 7QX ☎ 020 8708 5511 🖷 020 8708 5981 🖱 russell.ward@redbridge.gov.uk

Sustainable Communities: Ms Una McCarthy, Head of Policy & Performance, Town Hall, High Road, Ilford IG1 1DD ☎ 020 8708 2228 🖷 020 8708 2376 🖱 una.mccarthy@redbridge.gov.uk

Sustainable Development: Mr Stewart Murray, Chief Planning & Regeneration Officer, Town Hall, High Road, Ilford IG1 1DD ☎ 020 8708 2067 🖷 020 8708 2985 🖱 stewart.murray@redbridge.gov.uk

Town Centre: Mr Neil Davis, Ilford Town Centre Manager, The Management Suite, The Exchange Mall, High Road, Ilford IG1 1RS ☎ 020 8478 3534 🖱 neil.davis@ilfordtown.co.uk

Town Centre: Mrs Beverley Stratton, Town Centre & BID Manager, Planning & Regeneration, Room 21, Town Hall, High Road, Ilford IG1 1DD ☎ 020 8708 2079 🖷 020 8708 2379 🖱 beverley.stratton@redbridge.gov.uk

Traffic Management: Mr Syed Hussain, Traffic Manager (Group Manager), Lynton House, 255-259 High Road, Ilford IG1 1NY ☎ 020 8708 3651 🖷 020 8708 3473 🖱 syed.hussain@redbridge.gov.uk

Transport: Mr Cliff Woolnoth, Head of Engineering, Lynton House, 255-259 High Road, Ilford IG1 1NY ☎ 020 8708 3570 🖷 020 8708 3970 🖱 cliff.woolnoth@redbridge.gov.uk

Transport Planner: Mr Cliff Woolnoth, Head of Engineering, Lynton House, 255-259 High Road, Ilford IG1 1NY ☎ 020 8708 3570 🖷 020 8708 3970 🖱 cliff.woolnoth@redbridge.gov.uk

Waste Collection and Disposal: Mr Dave Cuthell, Chief Highways & Cleansing Officer, Ley Street Depot, Ley Street, Ilford IG2 7QX ☎ 020 8708 5019 🖷 020 8708 5118 🖱 david.cuthell@redbridge.gov.uk

Waste Management: Mr Dave Cuthell, Chief Highways & Cleansing Officer, Ley Street Depot, Ley Street, Ilford IG2 7QX ☎ 020 8708 5019 🖷 020 8708 5118 🖱 david.cuthell@redbridge.gov.uk

MEMBERS OF THE COUNCIL (63)

***Mayor:* Javed**, Muhammed (LAB - Clementswood)
muhammed.javed@redbridge.gov.uk
***Deputy Mayor:* Norman**, Elaine (LAB - Newbury)
elaine.norman@redbridge.gov.uk
***Leader of the Council:* Prince**, Keith (CON - Barkingside)
cllr.prince@redbridge.gov.uk
***Group Leader:* Athwal**, Jas (LAB - Mayfield)
jas.athwal@redbridge.gov.uk
Ahmed, Mushtaq (LAB - Cranbrook)
mushtaq.ahmed@redbridge.gov.uk
Banks, Felicity (LD - Roding)
felicity.banks@redbridge.gov.uk
Bellwood, Stuart (LAB - Seven Kings)
stuart.bellwood@redbridge.gov.uk
Bhamra, Gurdial (LAB - Clayhall)
cllr.bhamra@redbridge.gov.uk
Bond, Ian (LD - Roding)
ian.bond@redbridge.gov.uk
Canal, Paul (CON - Bridge)
cllr.canal@redbridge.gov.uk
Candy, Ann (CON - Fullwell)
ann.candy@redbridge.gov.uk
Chan, Thomas (CON - Wanstead)
thomas.chan@redbridge.gov.uk
Chaudhary, Mahboob (CON - Cranbrook)
mahboob.chaudhary@redbridge.gov.uk
Choudhury, Aziz (LAB - Valentines)

aziz.choudhury@redbridge.gov.uk
Clark, Ruth (CON - Aldborough)
cllr.clark@redbridge.gov.uk
Cleaver, Hugh (LD - Church End)
cllr.cleaver@redbridge.gov.uk
Cole, Vanessa (CON - Aldborough)
cllr.v.cole@redbridge.gov.uk
Cole, Robert (CON - Clayhall)
cllr.r.cole@redbridge.gov.uk
Coomb, Helen (LAB - Clementswood)
helen.coomb@redbridge.gov.uk
Cummins, Christopher (CON - Snaresbrook)
christopher.cummins@redbridge.gov.uk
Deakins, Gwyneth (LD - Roding)
gwyneth.deakins@redbridge.gov.uk
Dunn, Michelle (CON - Wanstead)
michelle.dunn@redbridge.gov.uk
Fairley-Churchill, John (CON - Bridge)
cllr.fairley-churchill@redbridge.gov.uk
Flint, Kay (LAB - Mayfield)
kay.flint@redbridge.gov.uk
Goody, Peter (CON - Snaresbrook)
peter.goody@redbridge.gov.uk
Gray, Thomas (CON - Hainault)
thomas.gray@redbridge.gov.uk
Griffin, Edward (CON - Hainault)
edward.griffin@redbridge.gov.uk
Hai, Ali (IND - Goodmayes)
ali.hai@redbridge.gov.uk
Hatfull, Ross (LAB - Valentines)
ross.hatfull@redbridge.gov.uk
Hayes, Nicholas (CON - Fullwell)
nicholas.hayes@redbridge.gov.uk
Hoskins, Richard (LD - Church End)
cllr.r.hoskins@redbridge.gov.uk
Huggett, Linda (CON - Monkhams)
linda.huggett@redbridge.gov.uk
Hussain, Zulfi (LAB - Clementswood)
zulfiger.hussain@redbridge.gov.uk
Jeyaranjan, Thavathuray (LAB - Newbury)
thavathuray.jeyaranjan@redbridge.gov.uk
Jones, Bert (LAB - Goodmayes)
bert.jones@redbridge.gov.uk
Kaur-Thiara, Debbie (LAB - Aldborough)
cllr.kaur-thiara@redbridge.gov.uk
Kissin, Ashley (CON - Barkingside)
cllr.kissin@redbridge.gov.uk
Kumar, Ashok (CON - Cranbrook)
ashok.kumar@redbridge.gov.uk
Lambert, Brian (CON - Fairlop)
brian.lambert@redbridge.gov.uk
Littlewood, Robert (LAB - Seven Kings)
bob.littlewood@redbridge.gov.uk
Maravala, Filly (LAB - Loxford)
filly.maravala@redbridge.gov.uk
Moth, Harold (IND - Fullwell)
harold.moth@redbridge.gov.uk
Nijjar, Baldesh (LAB - Chadwell)
cllr.nijjar@redbridge.gov.uk
Nolan, Suzanne (CON - Snaresbrook)
suzanne.nolan@redbridge.gov.uk
O'Shea, James (CON - Monkhams)
cllr.o'shea@redbridge.gov.uk
Parkash, Ayodhiya (LAB - Mayfield)
ayodhiya.parkash@redbridge.gov.uk
Patel, Shoaib (LD - Valentines)
shoaib.patel@redbridge.gov.uk
Phillips, Alex (CON - Fairlop)
alex.phillips@redbridge.gov.uk
Poole, David (CON - Hainault)
david.poole@redbridge.gov.uk
Rashid, Taifur (LAB - Loxford)
taifur.rashid@redbridge.gov.uk
Ryan, Joyce (CON - Fairlop)
joyce.ryan@redbridge.gov.uk
Saund, Balvinder (LAB - Seven Kings)
balvinder.saund@redbridge.gov.uk
Sharma, Dev (LAB - Newbury)
dev.sharma@redbridge.gov.uk
Sinclair, Nicola (LD - Church End)
cllr.sinclair@redbrigde.gov.uk
Solomon, Tania (CON - Barkingside)
cllr.solomon@redbridge.gov.uk
Stark, Michael (CON - Monkhams)
michael.stark@redbridge.gov.uk
Streeting, Wes (LAB - Chadwell)
cllr.streeting@redbridge.gov.uk
Tewari, Virendra (LAB - Loxford)
virendra.tewari@redbridge.gov.uk
Turbefield, Robin (CON - Bridge)
cllr.turbefield@redbridge.gov.uk
Walker, Andy (LAB - Chadwell)
cllr.walker@redbridge.gov.uk
Weinberg, Alan (CON - Clayhall)
cllr.weinberg@redbridge.gov.uk
White, Barbara (LAB - Goodmayes)
barbara.white@redbridge.gov.uk
Wilson, Alex (CON - Wanstead)
alex.wilson@redbridge.gov.uk

POLITICAL COMPOSITION
CON: 29, LAB: 25, LD: 7, IND: 2

CABINET
Leader, Finance: Mr Keith Prince
Deputy Leader, Resources: Mr Ian Bond
Adult Social Services & Health: Mr John Fairley-Churchill
Children's Services: Mr Alan Weinberg
Environment & Community Safety: Mr Shoaib Patel
Transport: Mrs Suzanne Nolan
Housing: Mrs Michelle Dunn
Leisure & Youth Services: Mr Robin Turbefield
Regeneration & Property: Mr Thomas Chan

COMMITTEE CHAIRS
Area 1: Mr Christopher Cummins
Area 2: Mr Paul Canal
Area 2: Ms Gwyneth Deakins
Area 3: Mr Alex Phillips
Area 4: Mr Ashley Kissin
Area 5: Ms Barbara White
Area 6: Ms Helen Coomb
Area 7: Mr Mushtaq Ahmed
Conservation Advisory Panel: Mr Christopher Cummins
Cycling Liason Group: Mr Paul Canal
Health Scrutiny Panel (Scrutiny): Mrs Joyce Ryan
Licensing: Mrs Ruth Clark
Overview (Scrutiny): Mr Jas Athwal

Regulatory: Mr Richard Hoskins
Standards: Mrs S Barrow (External)
Statement of Accounts: Mr Ian Bond

REDCAR & CLEVELAND U

Redcar & Cleveland Borough Council, Town Hall, Fabian Road, South Bank, Redcar TS6 9AR ☎ 01642 774774
💻 www.redcar-cleveland.gov.uk

FACTS & FIGURES

Police Authority: Cleveland Police Authority
Health Authority: North East Strategic Health Authority
Learning and Skills Council: North East
Parliamentary Constituencies: Middlesbrough South and Cleveland East, Redcar
EU Constituencies: North East
Election Frequency: Elections are of whole council
Twinning: Troisdorf (Germany)

PRINCIPAL OFFICERS

Chief Executive: Ms Amanda Skelton, Chief Executive, Town Hall, Fabian Road, South Bank, Redcar TS6 9AR
☎ 01642 444003 🖷 01642 444004
🖰 amanda.skelton@redcar-cleveland.gov.uk

Access Officer / Social Services (Disability): Mrs Pauline Kavanagh, Head of Human Resources, Redcar and Cleveland House, Kirkleatham Street, Redcar TS10 1RT ☎ 01642 444021 🖷 01642 771284 🖰 pauline.kavanagh@redcar-cleveland.gov.uk

Architect, Building / Property Services: Mrs Caroline Blackburn, Strategic Property Manager, Redcar and Cleveland House, Kirkleatham Street, Redcar TS10 1YA ☎ 01642 771131
🖰 caroline.blackburn@redcar-cleveland.gov.uk

Building Control: Mr Kevin Johnson, Building Control Manager, Belmont House, Rectory Lane, Guisborough TS14 7SD
☎ 01287 612358 🖷 01287 612367
🖰 kevin.johnson@redcar-cleveland.gov.uk

Catering Services: Ms Eileen Robinson, Manager of Education Catering Services, Cooper Centre, Beech Grove, South Bank, Middlesbrough TS6 6SU ☎ 01642 495367
🖰 eileen.robinson@redcar-cleveland.gov.uk

Children / Youth Services: Mr Mark Gray, Integrated Youth Support Manager, Redcar Youth Centre, Coatham Road, Redcar TS10 1RP ☎ 01642 777544 🖰 mark.gray@redcar-cleveland.gov.uk

Civil Registration: Mrs Rachel Dooris, Head of Legal & Governance, Redcar and Cleveland House, Kirkleatham Street, Redcar TS10 1RT ☎ 01642 444648
🖰 rachel.dooris@redcar-cleveland.gov.uk

Computer Management: Mr Gary Flynn, Head of Operations & IT, Redcar and Cleveland House, Kirkleatham Street, Redcar TS10 1RT ☎ 01642 612456 🖰 gary.flynn@redcar-cleveland.gov.uk

Consumer Protection and Trading Standards: Mr Julian Sorrell, Principal Trading Standards Officer, Belmont House, Rectory Lane, Guisborough TS14 7FD ☎ 01287 612322
🖰 julian.sorrell@redcar-cleveland.gov.uk

Contracts: Ms Michelle Gray, Procurement & Projects Officer, Redcar & Cleveland House, Lirkleatham Street, Redcar TS10 1RT ☎ 01642 771257 🖰 michelle.gray@redcar-cleveland.gov.uk

Corporate Services: Mr Richard Frankland, Director of Corporate Resources, Redcar and Cleveland House, Kirkleatham Street, Redcar TS10 1RT ☎ 01642 444405 🖷 01642 771284
🖰 richard.frankland@redcar-cleveland.gov.uk

Customer Service: Mrs Catherine Adams, Customer Services Manager, Redcar and Cleveland House, Kirkleatham Street, Redcar TS10 1RT ☎ 01642 495380
🖰 cath.adams@redcar-cleveland.gov.uk

Economic Development: Mr Ian Wardle, Director of Regeneration Services, Redcar & Cleveland House, Kirkleatham Street, Redcar TS10 1RT ☎ 01642 444258
🖰 ian.wardle@redcar-cleveland.gov.uk

Education: Mr John Anthony, Chief Education Officer, Seafield House, Kirkleatham Street, Redcar TS10 1SP
🖰 john.anthony@redcar-cleveland.gov.uk

Electoral Registration: Mrs Rachel Dooris, Head of Legal & Governance, Redcar and Cleveland House, Kirkleatham Street, Redcar TS10 1RT ☎ 01642 444648
🖰 rachel.dooris@redcar-cleveland.gov.uk

Emergency Planning: Mr Stuart Marshall, Emergency Planning Officer, Redcar & Cleveland House, Kirkleatham Street, Redcar TS10 1RT ☎ 01642 444202
🖰 stuart.marshall@redcar-cleveland.gov.uk

Energy Management: Mrs Caroline Blackburn, Strategic Property Manager, The Innovation Centre, Vienna Court, Kirkleatham Business Park, Redcar TS10 1RT ☎ 01642 771131
🖰 caroline.blackburn@redcar-cleveland.gov.uk

Environmental / Technical Services: Mr Paul Taylor, Environmental Sustainability Specialist, Redcar & Cleveland House, Kirkleatham Street, Redcar TS10 1RT ☎ 01642 771225
🖰 paul.taylor@redcar-cleveland.gov.uk

Environmental Health: Mrs Vikki Bell, Principal Environmental Health Officer, Belmont House, Rectory Lane, Guisborough TS14 7FD ☎ 01287 612404 🖰 vikki.bell@redcar-cleveland.gov.uk

Estates, Property & Valuation: Mrs Caroline Blackburn, Strategic Property Manager, The Innovation Centre, Vienna Court, Kirkleatham Business Park, Redcar TS10 1RT ☎ 01642 771131
🖰 caroline.blackburn@redcar-cleveland.gov.uk

Events Manager: Ms Zohrah Zancudi, Head of Cultural Development, Redcar and Cleveland House, Kirkham Street, Redcar TS10 1RT ☎ 01642 444322
🖰 zohrah.zancudi@redcar-cleveland.gov.uk

Finance and Treasurer: Mr John Sampson, Head of Financial Services, Redcar and Cleveland House, Kirkleatham Street, Redcar TS10 1RT ☎ 01642 771144

john.sampson@redcar-cleveland.gov.uk

Fleet Management: Mr Simon Dale, Director of Area Management, Belmont House, Rectory Lane, Guisborough TS10 1RT ☎ 01642 612398 simon.dale@redcar-cleveland.gov.uk

Grounds Maintenance: Mr Anthony Smith, Waste Technical Manager, Central Depot, Limerick Road, Dormanston, Redcar TS10 5JU ☎ 08456 126126 anthony.smith@redcar-cleveland.gov.uk

Health and Safety: Mr John Summers, Health & Safety Manager, Belmont House, Rectory Lane, Guisborough TS14 7FD ☎ 01642 444064 john.summers@redcar-cleveland.gov.uk

Highways: Mr Andrew Mollon, Engineering Manager, Belmont House, Rectory Lane, Guisborough TS14 7FD ☎ 01287 612581 andrew.mollon@redcar-cleveland.gov.uk

Home Energy Conservation: Mrs Wendi Wheeler, Energy Manager, Redcar & Cleveland House, Kirkleatham Street, Redcar TS6 9AR ☎ 01642 771290 wendi.wheeler@redcar-cleveland.gov.uk

Housing: Miss Erika Grunert, Housing Services Manager, Belmont House, Rectory Lane, Guisborough TS14 7FD ☎ 01287 612457 erika.grunert@redcar-cleveland.gov.uk

Local Area Agreement: Mr Rob Mitchell, Policy, Performance & Partnership Manager, Redcar and Cleveland House, Kirkleatham Street, Redcar TS10 1RT ☎ 01642 444507 rob.mitchell@redcar-cleveland.gov.uk

Legal: Mrs Rachel Dooris, Head of Legal & Governance, Redcar and Cleveland House, Kirkleatham Street, Redcar TS10 1RT ☎ 01642 444648 rachel.dooris@redcar-cleveland.gov.uk

Leisure and Cultural Services: Ms Zohrah Zancudi, Head of Cultural Development, Redcar and Cleveland House, Kirkham Street, Redcar TS10 1RT ☎ 01642 444322 zohrah.zancudi@redcar-cleveland.gov.uk

Licensing: Mr Stephen Brown, Principal Licensing Officer, Belmont House, Rectory Lane, Guisborough TS14 7FD ☎ 01287 612402 licensing.admin@redcar-cleveland.gov.uk

Lighting: Mr Andrew Mollon, Engineering Manager, Belmont House, Rectory Lane, Guisborough TS14 7FD ☎ 01287 612581 andrew.mollon@redcar-cleveland.gov.uk

Lottery Funding, Charity and Voluntary: Ms Lynn Watson, Regeneration Funding Advisor, Redcar and Cleveland House, Kirkleatham Street, Redcar TS10 1RT ☎ 01642 444350 lynn.watson@redcar-cleveland.gov.uk

Member Services: Mrs Rachel Dooris, Head of Legal & Governance, Town Hall, Fabian Road, South Bank, Redcar TS6 9AR ☎ 01642 444648 rachel.dooris@redcar-cleveland.gov.uk

Parking: Mr Simon Dale, Director of Area Management, Belmont House, Rectory Lane, Guisborough TS14 7FD ☎ 01642 612398 simon.dale@redcar-cleveland.gov.uk

Partnerships: Ms Val Mitchell, Partnerships Officer, Cleveland Police HQ, Troisworf Way, Kirkleatham Business Park, Redcar TS6 9AR ☎ 01642 444238 val.mitchell@redcar-cleveland.gov.uk

Personnel / HR: Mrs Pauline Kavanagh, Head of Human Resources, Redcar and Cleveland House, Kirkleatham Street, Redcar TS10 1RT ☎ 01642 444021 🖷 01642 771284 pauline.kavanagh@redcar-cleveland.gov.uk

Planning: Mr Phil Jones, Strategic Planning Manager, Redcar and Cleveland House, Kirkleatham Street, Redcar TS10 1YA ☎ 01287 612355 phil.jones@redcar-cleveland.gov.uk

Procurement: Mrs Deborah Thorne, Strategic Procurement Officer, Redcar & Cleveland House, Kirkleatham Street, Redcar TS10 1RT ☎ 01642 771256 🖷 01642 771143 deborah.thorne@redcar-cleveland.gov.uk

Public Libraries: Mr Brian McLean, Head of Neighbourhoods, Belmont House, Rectory Lane, Guisborough TS14 7FD ☎ 01642 776902 brian.mclean@redcar-cleveland.gov.uk

Recycling & Waste Minimisation: Mr Anthony Smith, Waste Technical Manager, Fairway House, Limerick Road, Dormanstown, Redcar TS10 5JU ☎ 08456 126126 anthony.smith@redcar-cleveland.gov.uk

Regeneration: Mr Ian Wardle, Director of Regeneration Services, Redcar & Cleveland House, Kirkleatham Street, Redcar TS10 1RT ☎ 01642 444258 ian.wardle@redcar-cleveland.gov.uk

Road Safety: Mr Michael Hall, Promotions & Training Manager, Belmont House, Rectory Lane, Guisborough TS14 7SD ☎ 01287 612368 michael.hall@redcar-cleveland.gov.uk

Social Services: Ms Barbara Shaw, Director of Adult & Children's Services, Seafield House, Kirkleatham Street, Redcar TS10 1SP ☎ 01642 771674 🖷 01642 771670 barbara.shaw@redcar-cleveland.gov.uk

Social Services (Adult): Ms Carole Dodd, Acting Head of Social Services, Seafield House, Kirkleatham Street, Redcar TS10 1SP ☎ 01642 771676 carole.dodd@redcar-cleveland.gov.uk

Social Services (Adult): Ms Barbara Shaw, Director of Adult & Children's Services, Seafield House, Kirkleatham Street, Redcar TS10 1SP ☎ 01642 771674 🖷 01642 771670 barbara.shaw@redcar-cleveland.gov.uk

Social Services (Children): Mrs Linda McCalmont, Acting Head of Children's Services, Seafield House, Kirkleatham Street, Redcar TS10 1SP ☎ 01642 771529 🖷 01642 771670 linda.mccalmont@redcar-cleveland.gov.uk

Staff Training: Mrs Pauline Kavanagh, Head of Human Resources, Redcar and Cleveland House, Kirkleatham Street, Redcar TS10 1RT ☎ 01642 444021 🖷 01642 771284 pauline.kavanagh@redcar-cleveland.gov.uk

Street Scene: Mr Simon Dale, Director of Area Management, Belmont House, Rectory Lane, Guisborough TS14 7FD ☎ 01642

612398 ✉ simon.dale@redcar-cleveland.gov.uk

Sustainable Communities: Mr Ian Wardle, Director of Regeneration Services, Redcar & Cleveland House, Kirkleatham Street, Redcar TS10 1RT ☎ 01642 444258 ✉ ian.wardle@redcar-cleveland.gov.uk

Sustainable Development: Mr Ian Wardle, Director of Regeneration Services, Redcar & Cleveland House, Kirkleatham Street, Redcar TS10 1RT ☎ 01642 444258 ✉ ian.wardle@redcar-cleveland.gov.uk

Tourism: Ms Zohrah Zancudi, Head of Cultural Development, Redcar and Cleveland House, Kirkham Street, Redcar TS10 1RT ☎ 01642 444322 ✉ zohrah.zancudi@redcar-cleveland.gov.uk

Traffic Management: Mr Colin Bowley, Integrated Transport Manager, Fleet Depot, Limerick Road, Dormanstown, Redcar TS10 5JU ☎ 01642 776909 ✉ colin.bowley@redcar-cleveland.gov.uk

Transport: Mr Colin Bowley, Integrated Transport Manager, Fleet Depot, Limerick Road, Dormanstown, Redcar TS10 5JU ☎ 01642 776909 ✉ colin.bowley@redcar-cleveland.gov.uk

Transport Planner: Mr Colin Bowley, Integrated Transport Manager, Fleet Depot, Limerick Road, Dormanstown, Redcar TS10 5JU ☎ 01642 776909 ✉ colin.bowley@redcar-cleveland.gov.uk

Total Place: Mr Rob Mitchell, Policy, Performance & Partnership Manager, Town Hall, Fabian Road, South Bank, Redcar TS6 9AR ☎ 01642 444507 ✉ rob.mitchell@redcar-cleveland.gov.uk

Waste Collection and Disposal: Mr Simon Dale, Director of Area Management, Belmont House, Rectory Lane, Guisborough TS14 7FD ☎ 01642 612398 ✉ simon.dale@redcar-cleveland.gov.uk

Waste Management: Mr Simon Dale, Director of Area Management, Belmont House, Rectory Lane, Guisborough TS10 7FD ☎ 01642 612398 ✉ simon.dale@redcar-cleveland.gov.uk

MEMBERS OF THE COUNCIL (59)

***Mayor:* Bunn**, Denise (LAB - Guisborough)
denise_bunn@redcar-cleveland.gov.uk
***Deputy Mayor:* Jeffries**, Vic (LAB - Longbeck)
vic.jeffries@redcar-cleveland.gov.uk
***Leader of the Council:* Dunning**, George (LAB - Teesville)
george_dunning@redcar-cleveland.gov.uk
***Deputy Leader of the Council:* Clarke**, Sheelagh (LAB - Teesville)
sheelagh_clarke@redcar-cleveland.gov.uk
Abbott, Christopher (LD - Newcomen)
chris_abbott@redcar-cleveland.gov.uk
Ayre, Billy (LAB - Normanby)
billy_ayre@redcar-cleveland.gov.uk
Briggs, Brian (LAB - Skelton)
brian_briggs@redcar-cleveland.gov.uk
Carling, Michael (LD - West Dyke)
Michael_carling@redcar-cleveland.gov.uk
Cooney, Norah (CON - Longbeck)
norah_cooney@redcar-cleveland.gov.uk
Crawford, Josie (LD - Coatham)
josie_crawford@redcar-cleveland.gov.uk
Curr, Irene (LD - Coatham)
Irene_curr@redacr-cleveland.gov.uk
Dunlop, Peter (LAB - Grangetown)
peter_dunlop@redcar-cleveland.gov.uk
Earl, John (LD - Dormanstown)
john.earl@redcar-cleveland.gov.uk
Fitzpatrick, David (O - Loftus)
david_fitzpatrick@redcar-cleveland.gov.uk
Forster, Brenda (LAB - Kirkleatham)
Brenda_forster@redcar-cleveland.gov.uk
Glodswain, Steven (LAB - Eston)
steven.goldswain@redcar-cleveland.gov.uk
Goddard, Ray (LAB - Dormanstown)
ray_goddard@redcar-cleveland.gov.uk
Guy, Joan (LAB - Saltburn)
joan_guy@redcar-cleveland.gov.uk
Halton, Valerie (CON - Hutton)
Valerie_halton@redcar-cleveland.gov.uk
Hannon, Mark (LAB - Kirkleatham)
mark_hannon@redcar-cleveland.gov.uk
Hannon, John (LAB - Newcomen)
john.p.hannon@redcar-cleveland.gov.uk
Harrison, Ron (LD - Zetland)
ron.harrison@redcar-cleveland.gov.uk
Helm, Kay (LD - West Dyke)
kay.helm@redcar-cleveland.gov.uk
Hogg, Brian (LAB - Brotton)
brian_hogg@redcar-cleveland.gov.uk
Howden, Eric (LD - Dormanstown)
eric.howden@redcar-cleveland.gov.uk
Hunt, Barry (IND - Brotton)
barry.hunt@redcar-cleveland.gov.uk
Jackson, Eric (LAB - Loftus)
eric_jackson@redcar-cleveland.gov.uk
Jeffery, Carole (CON - Westworth)
carole_jeffery@redcar-cleveland.gov.uk
Jeffery, Graham (CON - Hutton)
graham_jeffery@redcar-cleveland.gov.uk
Jeffrey, Ian (LAB - South Bank)
ian_jeffrey@redcar-cleveland.gov.uk
Jeffrey, Sue (LAB - South Bank)
sue_jeffrey@redcar-cleveland.gov.uk
Kay, Steve (O - Lockwood)
steve_kay@redcar-cleveland.gov.uk
Keenan, Joe (LAB - Guisborough)
joe_keenan@redcar-cleveland.gov.uk
Lanigan, Mary (IND - Loftus)
mary_lanigan@redcar-cleveland.gov.uk
Learoyd, Tristan (LAB - St Germains)
tristan.learoyd@redcar-cleveland.gov.uk
Mason, Josh (LD - Zetland)
josh.mason@redcar-cleveland.gov.uk
Massey, Christopher (LAB - Eston)
christopher_massey@redcar-cleveland.gov.uk
McLuckie, Dave (LAB - Skelton)
dave_mcluckie@redcar-cleveland.gov.uk
McLuckie, Helen (LAB - Skelton)
Helen_mcluckie@redcar-cleveland.gov.uk
Moses, Marjorie (LD - St Germains)
madge_moses@redcar-cleveland.gov.uk
Nightingale, Glyn (LD - Ormesby)
glyn_nightingale@redcar-cleveland.gov.uk
Nightingale, Irene (LD - Ormesby)
Irene_nightingale@redcar-cleveland.gov.uk
Ovens, Mary (LD - West Dyke)

mary_ovens@redcar-cleveland.gov.uk
Pallister, Lynn (LAB - Grangetown)
lynn_pallister@redcar-cleveland.gov.uk
Peters, Olwyn (LAB - Eston)
olwyn_peters@redcar-cleveland.gov.uk
Pickthall, Norman (LAB - Teesville)
Norman_pickthall@redcar-cleveland.gov.uk
Pryce, Sean (LAB - St Germains)
sean.pryce@redcar-cleveland.gov.uk
Quigley, Dale (LAB - Kirkleatham)
dale.quigley@redcar-cleveland.gov.uk
Reyer, Victoria (LD - Longbeck)
victoria.reyer@redcar-cleveland.gov.uk
Rudland, Doreen (LAB - Brotton)
doreen_rudland@redcar-cleveland.gov.uk
Simms, Carole (LAB - Normanby)
carole.simms@redcar-cleveland.gov.uk
Smith, Stuart (IND - Saltburn)
stuart.smith@redcar-cleveland.gov.uk
Spencer, Peter (CON - Hutton)
peter_spencer@redcar-cleveland.gov.uk
Suthers, Bill (LAB - Guisborough)
bill.suthers@redcar-cleveland.gov.uk
Szintai, Sylvia (LAB - South Bank)
Sylvia_szintai@redcar-cleveland.gov.uk
Thomson, Philip (CON - Saltburn)
Philip_thomson@redcar-cleveland.gov.uk
Wall, Wendy (LAB - Normanby)
wendy_wall@redcar-cleveland.gov.uk
Williams, David (LAB - Westworth)
david_williams@redcar-cleveland.gov.uk
Wilson, Ann (LD - Ormesby)
ann_wilson@redcar-cleveland.gov.uk

POLITICAL COMPOSITION
LAB: 33, LD: 15, CON: 6, IND: 3, O: 2

CABINET
Culture, Leisure & Tourism: Mrs Olwyn Peters
Leader: Mr George Dunning
Deputy Leader: Mrs Sheelagh Clarke
Children's Services & Education: Ms Joan Guy
Community Protection: Mr Dave McLuckie
Economic Development: Mr Mark Hannon
Corporate Resources: Mr Norman Pickthall
Environment & Rural Affairs: Mr Christopher Massey
Health & Social Well-Being: Mrs Sheelagh Clarke
Highways, Transportation & Planning: Ms Helen McLuckie
Housing & Neighbourhood Renewal: Ms Lyn Pallister

COMMITTEE CHAIRS
Corporate Parenting Board: Mrs Wendy Wall
Employment Issues Panel: Mrs Carole Simms
Health (Scrutiny): Mrs Wendy Wall
Licensing: Mr David Williams
Planning: Mr Brian Hogg
Scrutiny Board: Ms Brenda Forster
Standards: Mr Les Manship (External)

REDDITCH D
Redditch, Town Hall, Walter Stranz Square, Redditch B98 8AH
☎ 01527 64252 🖷 01527 65216 ✉ corporate@redditch.gov.uk
💻 www.redditchbc.gov.uk

FACTS & FIGURES
Police Authority: West Mercia Police Authority
Health Authority: NHS West Midlands
Learning and Skills Council: West Midlands
Parliamentary Constituencies: Redditch
EU Constituencies: West Midlands
Election Frequency: Elections are by thirds
Twinning: Auxerre (France); Gruchet-le-Valasse (France); Gujar Khan (Pakistan); Mtwara (Tanzania); St. Elizabeth (Jamaica)

PRINCIPAL OFFICERS
Chief Executive: Mr Kevin Dicks, Chief Executive, Town Hall, Walter Stranz Square, Redditch B98 8AH ☎ 01527 881400 🖷 01527 881212 ✉ k.dicks@bromsgroveandredditch.gov.uk

Deputy Chief Executive: Mrs Susan Hanley, Executive Director & Deputy Chief Executive, Town Hall, Walter Stranz Square, Redditch B98 8AH ☎ 01527 64252 Extn 3601 🖷 01527 65216 ✉ s.hanley@bromsgroveandredditch.gov.uk

Senior Management: Ms Jayne Pickering, Director of Finance & Corporate Resources, Town Hall, Walter Stranz Square, Redditch B98 8AH ☎ 01527 64252 🖷 01527 65216 ✉ j.pickering@bromsgroveandredditch.gov.uk

Senior Management: Mr John Staniland, Executive Director of Planning, Regeneration, Regulatory & Housing, Town Hall, Walter Stranz Square, Redditch B98 8AH ☎ 01527 64252 Extn 3702 🖷 01527 65216 ✉ j.staniland@bromsgroveandredditch.gov.uk

Building Control: Mr Adrian Wyre, Principle Building Control Surveyor, The Council House, Burcot Lane, Bromsgrove B60 1AA ☎ 01527 881350 🖷 01527 881313 ✉ a.wyre@bromsgrove.gov.uk

Children / Youth Services: Mr John Godwin, Head of Leisure, Town Hall, Walter Stranz Square, Redditch B98 8AH ☎ 01527 64252 🖷 01527 65216 ✉ j.godwin@bromsgroveandredditch.gov.uk

PR / Communications: Mrs Anne-Marie Darroch, Communications & Publicity Manager, Town Hall, Walter Stranz Square, Redditch B98 8AH ☎ 01527 881651 🖷 01527 881212 ✉ a.darroch@bromsgroveandredditch.gov.uk

Community Planning: Ms Ruth Bamford, Head of Planning & Regeneration Services, Town Hall, Walter Stranz Square, Redditch B98 8AH ☎ 01527 64252 Extn 3201; 01527 64252 ext. 3201 🖷 01527 65216 ✉ r.bamford@bromsgroveandredditch.gov.uk

Community Safety: Ms Angie Heighway, Head of Community Services, Town Hall, Walter Stranz Square, Redditch B98 8AH ☎ 01527 64252 🖷 01527 65216 ✉ a.heighway@bromsgroveandredditch.gov.uk

Contracts: Ms Teresa Kristunas, Head of Finance & Corporate Resources, Town Hall, Walter Stranz Square, Redditch B98 8AH ☎ 01527 64252 🖷 01527 65216 ✉ t.kristunas@bromsgroveandredditch.gov.uk

Corporate Services: Ms Jayne Pickering, Director of Finance & Corporate Resources, Town Hall, Walter Stranz Square, Redditch B98 8AH ☎ 01527 64252; 01527 881207 🖷 01527 65216 ✉ j.pickering@bromsgroveandredditch.gov.uk

Customer Service: Ms Amanda de Warr, Head of Customer Services, Town Hall, Walter Stranz Square, Redditch B98 8AH ☎ 01527 64252 🖷 01527 65216 ✉ a.dewarr@bromsgroveandredditch.gov.uk

Economic Development: Ms Ruth Bamford, Head of Planning & Regeneration Services, Town Hall, Walter Stranz Square, Redditch B98 8AH ☎ 01527 64252 Extn 3201 🖷 01527 65216 ✉ r.bamford@bromsgroveandredditch.gov.uk

E-Government: Mrs Deb Poole, Head of Business Transformation, Town Hall, Walter Stranz Square, Redditch B98 8AH ☎ 01527 64252 🖷 01527 65216 ✉ d.poole@bromsgroveandredditch.gov.uk

Electoral Registration: Mrs Susan Mould, Electoral Services Manager, The Council House, Burcot Lane, Bromsgrove B60 1AA ☎ 01527 881462 🖷 01527 881414 ✉ s.mould@bromsgroveandredditch.gov.uk

Emergency Planning: Ms Ruth Bamford, Head of Planning & Regeneration Services, Town Hall, Walter Stranz Square, Redditch B98 8AH ☎ 01527 64252 Extn 3201 🖷 01527 65216 ✉ r.bamford@bromsgroveandredditch.gov.uk

Emergency Planning: Mr Andrew Coel, Strategic Housing Manager, The Council House, Burcot Lane, Bromsgrove B60 1AA ☎ 01527 881270 🖷 01527 881414 ✉ a.coel@bromsgroveandredditch.gov.uk

Emergency Planning: Mr Richard Davis-Leech, North Worcestershire Civil Contingencies Resilience Manager, Civic Centre, New Street, Stourport-on-Severn DY13 8UJ ☎ 01562 732711 ✉ richard.davis-leech@wyreforestdc.gov.uk

Energy Management: Ms Teresa Kristunas, Head of Finance & Corporate Resources, Town Hall, Walter Stranz Square, Redditch B98 8AH ☎ 01527 64252 🖷 01527 65216 ✉ t.kristunas@bromsgroveandredditch.gov.uk

Environmental / Technical Services: Mr Guy Revans, Head of Environmental Services, Town Hall, Walter Stranz Square, Redditch B98 8AH ☎ 01527 64252 🖷 01527 65216 ✉ g.revans@bromsgroveandredditch.gov.uk

Environmental Health: Mr Guy Revans, Head of Environmental Services, Town Hall, Walter Stranz Square, Redditch B98 8AH ☎ 01527 64252 🖷 01527 65216 ✉ g.revans@bromsgroveandredditch.gov.uk

Events Manager: Mr Ray Cooke, Leisure Services Manager, Town Hall, Walter Stranz Square, Redditch B98 8AH ☎ 01527 64252 Extn 3248 🖷 01527 65216 ✉ r.cooke@redditchbc.gov.uk

Events Manager: Mr Hugh Moseley, Arts Development & Special Events Officer, The Council House, Burcot Lane, Bromsgrove B60 1AA ☎ 01527 881381 ✉ h.mosley@bromsgroveandredditch.gov.uk

Finance and Treasurer: Ms Jayne Pickering, Director of Finance & Corporate Resources, Town Hall, Walter Stranz Square, Redditch B98 8AH ☎ 01527 64252 🖷 01527 65216 ✉ j.pickering@bromsgroveandredditch.gov.uk

Fleet Management: Mr Paul Mills, Transport & Supplies Manager, Town Hall, Walter Stranz Square, Redditch B98 8AH ☎ 01527 64252 🖷 01527 65216 ✉ p.mills@bromsgroveandredditch.gov.uk

Grounds Maintenance: Mr Guy Revans, Head of Environmental Services, Town Hall, Walter Stranz Square, Redditch B98 8AH ☎ 01527 64252 🖷 01527 65216 ✉ g.revans@bromsgroveandredditch.gov.uk

Health and Safety: Mrs Dawn Ibbitson, Health & Safety Advisor, The Council House, Burcot Lane, Bromsgrove B60 1AA ☎ 01527 881398 🖷 01527 881313 ✉ d.ibbitson@bromsgroveandredditch.gov.uk

Health and Safety: Mr John Walker, Health & Safety Adviser, Town Hall, Walter Stranz Square, Redditch B98 8AH ☎ 01527 64252 🖷 01527 65216 ✉ john.walker@bromsgroveandredditch.gov.uk

Home Energy Conservation: Ms Ceridwen John, Climate Change Manager, c/o Central Depot, Aston Road, Aston Fields, Bromsgrove B60 3EX ☎ 01527 64252 ext. 3046 ✉ ceridwen.john@bromsgroveandredditch.gov.uk

Home Energy Conservation: Mr Guy Revans, Head of Environmental Services, Town Hall, Walter Stranz Square, Redditch B98 8AH ☎ 01527 64252 🖷 01527 65216 ✉ g.revans@bromsgroveandredditch.gov.uk

Housing: Mrs Liz Tompkin, Head of Housing, Town Hall, Walter Stranz Square, Redditch B98 8AH ☎ 01527 64252 ext. 3304 🖷 01527 65216 ✉ l.tompkin@bromsgrove.gov.uk

Housing Maintenance: Mrs Liz Tompkin, Head of Housing, Town Hall, Walter Stranz Square, Redditch B98 8AH ☎ 01527 64252 ext. 3304 🖷 01527 65216 ✉ l.tompkin@bromsgrove.gov.uk

Legal: Mrs Claire Felton, Head of Legal, Equalities & Democratic Services, Town Hall, Walter Stranz Square, Redditch B98 8AH ☎ 01572 64252 🖷 01527 65216 ✉ c.felton@redditchbc.gov.uk

Leisure and Cultural Services: Mr John Godwin, Head of Leisure, Town Hall, Walter Stranz Square, Redditch B98 8AH ☎ 01527 64252 🖷 01527 65216 ✉ j.godwin@bromsgroveandredditch.gov.uk

Licensing: Mr Steve Jorden, Head of Regulatory Services, Town Hall, Walter Stranz Square, Redditch B98 8AH ☎ 01527 64252 🖷 01527 65216 ✉ s.jorden@redditchbc.gov.uk

Lottery Funding, Charity and Voluntary: Ms Angie Heighway, Head of Community Services, Town Hall, Walter Stranz Square, Redditch B98 8AH ☎ 01527 64252 🖷 01527 65216 ✉ a.heighway@bromsgroveandredditch.gov.uk

Member Services: Mrs Trish Buckley, Members' Services Officer, Town Hall, Walter Stranz Square, Redditch B98 8AH ☎ 01527 64252 Extn 3265 🖷 01527 65216

🖰 trish.buckley@bromsgroveandredditch.gov.uk

Member Services: Ms Karen Firth, Committee Group Leader, The Council House, Burcot Lane, Bromsgrove B60 1AA ☎ 01527 881625 🖷 01527 881414 🖰 k.firth@bromsgroveandredditch.gov.uk

Parking: Mr Peter Liddington, Civil Enforcement Parking Officer, Town Hall, Walter Stranz Square, Redditch B98 8AH ☎ 01527 64252 🖷 01527 65216 🖰 p.liddington@redditchbc.gov.uk

Partnerships: Mrs Rebecca Dunn, Policy Manager, Bromsgrove District Council, The Council House, Burcot Lane, Bromsgrove B66 1AA ☎ 01527 881616; 01527 881616 🖰 r.dunn@bromsgroveandredditch.gov.uk

Personnel / HR: Ms Becky Talbot, Human Resources Manager, Town Hall, Walter Stranz Square, Redditch B98 8AH ☎ 01527 64252 🖷 01527 65216 🖰 b.talbot@redditchbc.gov.uk

Planning: Ms Ruth Bamford, Head of Planning & Regeneration Services, Town Hall, Walter Stranz Square, Redditch B98 8AH ☎ 01527 64252 Extn 3201 🖷 01527 65216 🖰 r.bamford@bromsgroveandredditch.gov.uk

Procurement: Mr Alex Haslam, Procurement Officer, Town Hall, Walter Stranz Square, Redditch B98 8AH ☎ 01527 64252 ext. 3010 🖷 01527 881414 🖰 a.haslam@bromsgroveandredditch.gov.uk

Recycling & Waste Minimisation: Mr Guy Revans, Head of Environmental Services, Town Hall, Walter Stranz Square, Redditch B98 8AH ☎ 01527 64252 🖷 01527 65216 🖰 g.revans@bromsgroveandredditch.gov.uk

Regeneration: Ms Ruth Bamford, Head of Planning & Regeneration Services, Town Hall, Walter Stranz Square, Redditch B98 8AH ☎ 01527 64252 Extn 3201; 01527 64252 ext. 3201 🖷 01527 65216 🖰 r.bamford@bromsgroveandredditch.gov.uk; r.bamford@bromsgroveandredditch.gov.uk

Staff Training: Ms Becky Talbot, Human Resources Manager, Town Hall, Walter Stranz Square, Redditch B98 8AH ☎ 01527 64252 🖷 01527 65216 🖰 b.talbot@redditchbc.gov.uk

Street Scene: Mr Guy Revans, Head of Environmental Services, Town Hall, Walter Stranz Square, Redditch B98 8AH ☎ 01527 64252 🖷 01527 65216 🖰 g.revans@bromsgroveandredditch.gov.uk

Sustainable Development: Mr John Staniland, Executive Director of Planning, Regeneration, Regulatory & Housing, Town Hall, Walter Stranz Square, Redditch B98 8AH ☎ 01527 64252 Extn 3702 🖷 01527 65216 🖰 j.staniland@bromsgroveandredditch.gov.uk

Town Centre: Ms Ruth Bamford, Head of Planning & Regeneration Services, Town Hall, Walter Stranz Square, Redditch B98 8AH ☎ 01527 64252 Extn 3201 🖷 01527 65216 🖰 r.bamford@bromsgroveandredditch.gov.uk

Transport: Mr Paul Mills, Transport & Supplies Manager, Town Hall, Walter Stranz Square, Redditch B98 8AH ☎ 01527 64252 🖷 01527 65216 🖰 p.mills@bromsgroveandredditch.gov.uk

Transport Planner: Mr Paul Mills, Transport & Supplies Manager, Town Hall, Walter Stranz Square, Redditch B98 8AH ☎ 01527 64252 🖷 01527 65216 🖰 p.mills@bromsgroveandredditch.gov.uk

Waste Collection and Disposal: Mr Guy Revans, Head of Environmental Services, Town Hall, Walter Stranz Square, Redditch B98 8AH ☎ 01527 64252 🖷 01527 65216 🖰 g.revans@bromsgroveandredditch.gov.uk

Waste Management: Mr Guy Revans, Head of Environmental Services, Town Hall, Walter Stranz Square, Redditch B98 8AH ☎ 01527 64252 🖰 g.revans@bromsgroveandredditch.gov.uk

Children's Play Areas: Mr John Godwin, Head of Leisure, Town Hall, Walter Stranz Square, Redditch B98 8AH ☎ 01527 64252 🖷 01527 65216 🖰 j.godwin@bromsgroveandredditch.gov.uk

MEMBERS OF THE COUNCIL (29)

***Mayor:* Mason**, Alan (LAB - Abbey)
alan.mason@redditchbc.gov.uk
***Deputy Mayor:* King**, Wanda (LAB - Greenlands)
wanda.king@redditchbc.gov.uk
***Leader of the Council:* Hartnett**, Bill (LAB - Church Hill)
bill.hartnett@redditchbc.gov.uk
***Deputy Leader of the Council:* Chance**, Greg (LAB - Central)
greg.chance@redditchbc.gov.uk
***Group Leader:* Gandy**, Carole (CON - Headless Cross and Oakenshaw)
carole.gandy@redditchbc.gov.uk
Baker, Joe (LAB - Greenlands)
Bennett, Roger (CON - Headless Cross ad Oakenshaw)
roger.bennett@redditchbc.gov.uk
Blake, Rebecca (LAB - Greenlands)
rebecca.blake@redditchbc.gov.uk
Braley, Michael (CON - West)
michael.braley@redditchbc.gov.uk
Brazier, Andrew (CON - Crabbs Cross)
andrew.brazier@redditchbc.gov.uk
Brunner, Juliet (CON - Matchborough)
juliet.brunner@redditchbc.gov.uk
Bush, David (CON - West)
david.bush@redditchbc.gov.uk
Chalk, Simon (CON - Abbey)
simon.chalk@redditchbc.gov.uk
Chalk, Michael (CON - Astwood Bank and Feckenham)
mike.chalk@redditchbc.gov.uk
Clayton, Brandon (CON - Astwood Bank and Feckenham)
brandon.clayton@redditchbc.gov.uk
Fisher, John (LAB - Matchborough)
john.fisher@redditchbc.gov.uk
Fry, Andy (LAB - Lodge Park)
andy.fry@redditchbc.gov.uk
Griffin, Adam (CON - Winyates)
adam.griffin@redditchbc.gov.uk
Hill, Roger (CON - Church Hill)
roger.hill@redditchbc.gov.uk
Hill, Patty (LAB - Batchley and Brockhill)
Hopkins, Gay (CON - Headless Cross and Oakenshaw)
gay.hopkins@redditchbc.gov.uk
Mould, Phil (LAB - Winyates)
phil.mould@redditchbc.gov.uk
Quinney, Brenda (CON - Batchley and Brockhill)
brenda.quinney@redditchbc.gov.uk

Shurmer, Mark (LAB - Lodge Park)
mark.shurmer@redditchbc.gov.uk
Smith, Yvonne (LAB - Winyates)
yvonne.smith@redditchbc.gov.uk
Stephens, Luke (LAB - Batchley and Brockhill)
luke.stephens@redditchbc.gov.uk
Taylor, Debbie (LAB - Central)
debbie.taylor@redditchbc.gov.uk
Taylor, Derek (CON - Crabbs Cross)
derek.taylor@redditchbc.gov.uk
Witherspoon, Pat (LAB - Church Hill)

POLITICAL COMPOSITION
LAB: 15, CON: 14

CABINET
Leader: Cllr Bill Hartnett
Deputy Leader; Planning, Regeneration, Economic Development & Transport: Cllr Greg Chance
Community Safety & Regulatory Services: Ms Rebecca Blake
Housing: Cllr Mark Shurmer
Leisure & Tourism: Mr Luke Stephens
Local Environment & Health: Cllr Debbie Taylor
Corporate Management: Cllr Michael Braley

COMMITTEE CHAIRS
Audit & Governance: Mr Derek Taylor
Licensing: Cllr Andy Fry
Overview & Scrutiny: Cllr Juliet Brunner
Planning: Cllr Michael Chalk
Standards: Mrs Pat Witherspoon

REIGATE & BANSTEAD D

Reigate & Banstead Borough Council, Town Hall, Castlefield Road, Reigate RH2 0SH ☎ 01737 276000 🖷 01737 276718
customer.services@reigate-banstead.gov.uk
www.reigate-banstead.gov.uk

FACTS & FIGURES
Police Authority: Surrey Police Authority
Health Authority: South East Coast Strategic Health Authority
Learning and Skills Council: South East
Parliamentary Constituencies: Reigate
EU Constituencies: South East
Election Frequency: Elections are by thirds
Twinning: Brunoy (France); Eschweiler (Germany)

PRINCIPAL OFFICERS
Chief Executive: Mr John Jory, Chief Executive, Town Hall, Castlefield Road, Reigate RH2 0SH ☎ 01737 276151
mary.nicholls@reigate-banstead.gov.uk

Deputy Chief Executive: Mr Graham Cook, Deputy Chief Executive, Town Hall, Castlefield Road, Reigate RH2 0SH ☎ 01737 276503 shirley.parker-jones@reigate-banstead.gov.uk

Senior Management: Mr Graham Cook, Deputy Chief Executive, Town Hall, Castlefield Road, Reigate RH2 0SH ☎ 01737 276503
shirley.parker-jones@reigate-banstead.gov.uk

Architect, Building / Property Services: Mr John Reed, Building & Facilities Manager, Town Hall, Castlefield Road, Reigate RH2 0SH ☎ 01737 276571 🖷 01737 276070
john.reed@reigate-banstead.gov.uk

Building Control: Mr John Branchett, Building Control Manager, Town Hall, Castlefield Road, Reigate RH2 0SH ☎ 01737 276161
john.branchett@reigate-banstead.gov.uk

Building Control: Mr Mark Harbottle, Head of Service, Town Hall, Castlefield Road, Reigate RH2 0SH ☎ 01737 276165
🖷 01737 276018 mark.harbottle@reigate-banstead.gov.uk

PR / Communications: Ms Fiona Cullen, Communications & Information Manager, Town Hall, Castlefield Road, Reigate RH2 0SH ☎ 01737 276296
communications@reigate-banstead.gov.uk

Community Planning: Mr Simon Bland, Community Liaison Manager, Town Hall, Castlefield Road, Reigate RH2 0SH
☎ 01737 276303 🖷 01737 276404
simon.bland@reigate-banstead.gov.uk

Community Safety: Mr Mark Harbottle, Head of Service, Town Hall, Castlefield Road, Reigate RH2 0SH ☎ 01737 276165
🖷 01737 276018 mark.harbottle@reigate-banstead.gov.uk

Community Safety: Mrs Debbie Stitt, Community Safety Manager, Town Hall, Castlefield Road, Reigate RH2 0SH
☎ 01737 276305 🖷 01737 276739
debbie.stitt@reigate-banstead.gov.uk

Computer Management: Ms Sara Taylor, ICT Manager, Town Hall, Castlefield Road, Reigate RH2 0SH ☎ 01737 276454
🖷 01737 276586 sara.taylor@reigate-banstead.gov.uk

Contracts: Mr Nick Bennett, Legal Services Manager, Town Hall, Castlefield Road, Reigate RH2 0SH ☎ 01737 276057
nick.bennett@reigate-banstead.gov.uk

Corporate Services: Ms Margaret Quine, Head of Corporate Development, Town Hall, Castlefield Road, Reigate RH2 0SH
☎ 01737 276023 🖷 01737 276013
margaret.quine@reigate-banstead.gov.uk

Customer Service: Ms Lindsey Baxter, Customer Services Manager, Town Hall, Castlefield Road, Reigate RH2 0SH
☎ 01737 276252 lindsey.baxter@reigate-banstead.gov.uk

Customer Service: Mrs Anne Ebbett, Head of Community Services, Town Hall, Castlefield Road, Reigate RH2 0SH
☎ 01737 276430 🖷 01737 276260
anne.ebbett@reigate-banstead.gov.uk

Economic Development: Ms Kathy O'Leary, Head of Policy & Regeneration, Town Hall, Castlefield Road, Reigate RH2 0SH
☎ 07373 276512 kathy.oleary@reigate-banstead.gov.uk

E-Government: Ms Sara Taylor, ICT Manager, Town Hall, Castlefield Road, Reigate RH2 0SH ☎ 01737 276454
🖷 01737 276586 sara.taylor@reigate-banstead.gov.uk

Electoral Registration: Mr Chris Cook, Democratic Services

Manager, Town Hall, Castlefield Road, Reigate RH2 0SH ☎ 01737 276024 🖷 01737 276013 🖰 chris.cook@reigate-banstead.gov.uk

Emergency Planning: Mr Steve Williams, Head of Personnel, Housing & Support Services, Town Hall, Reigate RH2 0SH ☎ 01737 276088 🖷 01737 276755 🖰 steve.williams@reigate-banstead.gov.uk

Energy Management: Mr John Reed, Building & Facilities Manager, Town Hall, Castlefield Road, Reigate RH2 0SH ☎ 01737 276571 🖷 01737 276070 🖰 john.reed@reigate-banstead.gov.uk

Environmental / Technical Services: Mr Nic Martlew, Head of Neighbourhood & Parking Services, Town Hall, Castlefield Road, Reigate RH2 0SH ☎ 01737 276218 🖷 01737 276610 🖰 nic.martlew@reigate-banstead.gov.uk

Environmental Health: Mr Mark Harbottle, Head of Service, Town Hall, Castlefield Road, Reigate RH2 0SH ☎ 01737 276165 🖷 01737 276018 🖰 mark.harbottle@reigate-banstead.gov.uk

Estates, Property & Valuation: Mr Steve McLeod, Senior Asset Manager, Town Hall, Castlefield Road, Reigate RH2 0SH ☎ 01737 276074 🖷 01737 276070 🖰 steve.mcleod@reigate-banstead.gov.uk

Facilities: Mr John Reed, Building & Facilities Manager, Town Hall, Castlefield Road, Reigate RH2 0SH ☎ 01737 276571 🖷 01737 276070 🖰 john.reed@reigate-banstead.gov.uk

Finance and Treasurer: Mr Bill Pallett, Accountancy Manager, Town Hall, Castlefield Road, Reigate RH2 0SH ☎ 01737 276560 🖷 01737 276513 🖰 bill.pallett@reigate-banstead.gov.uk

Fleet Management: Mr Ken Dodds, Fleet Manager, Town Hall, Castlefield Road, Reigate RH2 0SH ☎ 01737 276614 🖷 01737 276641 🖰 ken.dodds@reigate-banstead.gov.uk

Grounds Maintenance: Mr Robin Davis, Parks & Countryside Manager, Town Hall, Castlefield Road, Reigate RH2 0SH ☎ 01737 276461 🖷 01737 276610 🖰 robin.davis@reigate-banstead.gov.uk

Health and Safety: Mr Steve Williams, Head of Personnel, Housing & Support Services, Town Hall, Reigate RH2 0SH ☎ 01737 276088 🖷 01737 276755 🖰 steve.williams@reigate-banstead.gov.uk

Home Energy Conservation: Mr Raymond Dill, Environmental Initiatives Officer, Town Hall, Castlefield Road, Reigate RH2 0SH ☎ 01737 276211 🖷 01737 276018 🖰 raymond.dill@reigate-banstead.gov.uk

Housing: Mr Steve Williams, Head of Personnel, Housing & Support Services, Town Hall, Reigate RH2 0SH ☎ 01737 276088 🖷 01737 276755 🖰 steve.williams@reigate-banstead.gov.uk

Legal: Mr Nick Bennett, Legal Services Manager, Town Hall, Castlefield Road, Reigate RH2 0SH ☎ 01737 276057 🖰 nick.bennett@reigate-banstead.gov.uk

Leisure and Cultural Services: Mr Tom Kealey, Manager - Harlequin, Town Hall, Castlefield Road, Reigate RH2 0SH ☎ 01737 276840 🖰 tom.kealey@reigate-banstead.gov.uk

Licensing: Ms Dianne Mitchell, Licensing Manager, Town Hall, Castlefield Road, Reigate RH2 0SH ☎ 01737 276411 🖷 01737 276404 🖰 dianne.mitchell@reigate-banstead.gov.uk

Lottery Funding, Charity and Voluntary: Mr Simon Bland, Community Liaison Manager, Town Hall, Castlefield Road, Reigate RH2 0SH ☎ 01737 276303 🖷 01737 276404 🖰 simon.bland@reigate-banstead.gov.uk

Member Services: Ms Margaret Quine, Head of Corporate Development, Town Hall, Castlefield Road, Reigate RH2 0SH ☎ 01737 276023 🖷 01737 276013 🖰 margaret.quine@reigate-banstead.gov.uk

Parking: Mr Nic Martlew, Head of Neighbourhood & Parking Services, Town Hall, Castlefield Road, Reigate RH2 0SH ☎ 01737 276218 🖷 01737 276610 🖰 nic.martlew@reigate-banstead.gov.uk

Partnerships: Mr Simon Bland, Community Liaison Manager, Town Hall, Castlefield Road, Reigate RH2 0SH ☎ 01737 276303 🖷 01737 276404 🖰 simon.bland@reigate-banstead.gov.uk

Personnel / HR: Mr Steve Williams, Head of Personnel, Housing & Support Services, Town Hall, Reigate RH2 0SH ☎ 01737 276088 🖷 01737 276755 🖰 steve.williams@reigate-banstead.gov.uk

Planning: Mr Mark Harbottle, Head of Service, Town Hall, Castlefield Road, Reigate RH2 0SH ☎ 01737 276165 🖷 01737 276018 🖰 mark.harbottle@reigate-banstead.gov.uk

Procurement: Mr Taofeeq Ladega, Procurement Assistant - Legal, Town Hall, Castlefield Road, Reigate RH2 0SH ☎ 01737 276094 🖰 taofeeq.ladega@reigate-banstead.gov.uk

Recycling & Waste Minimisation: Mr Frank Etheridge, Function Manager, Town Hall, Castlefield Road, Reigate RH2 0SH ☎ 01737 276219 🖰 frank.etheridge@reigate-banstead.gov.uk

Recycling & Waste Minimisation: Mr Nic Martlew, Head of Neighbourhood Services, Town Hall, Castlefield Road, Reigate RH2 0SH ☎ 01737 276218 🖷 01737 276010 🖰 nic.martlew@reigate-banstead.gov.uk

Regeneration: Ms Kathy O'Leary, Head of Policy & Regeneration, Town Hall, Castlefield Road, Reigate RH2 0SH ☎ 07373 276512 🖰 kathy.oleary@reigate-banstead.gov.uk

Staff Training: Mr Steve Williams, Head of Personnel, Housing & Support Services, Town Hall, Reigate RH2 0SH ☎ 01737 276088 🖷 01737 276755 🖰 steve.williams@reigate-banstead.gov.uk

Street Scene: Mr Nic Martlew, Head of Neighbourhood & Parking Services, Town Hall, Castlefield Road, Reigate RH2 0SH ☎ 01737 276218 🖷 01737 276610 🖰 nic.martlew@reigate-banstead.gov.uk

LOCAL AUTHORITIES

Sustainable Communities: Ms Kathy O'Leary, Head of Policy & Regeneration, Town Hall, Castlefield Road, Reigate RH2 0SH ☎ 07373 276512 ✉ kathy.oleary@reigate-banstead.gov.uk

Sustainable Development: Ms Kathy O'Leary, Head of Policy & Regeneration, Town Hall, Castlefield Road, Reigate RH2 0SH ☎ 07373 276512 ✉ kathy.oleary@reigate-banstead.gov.uk

Waste Collection and Disposal: Mr Nic Martlew, Head of Neighbourhood & Parking Services, Town Hall, Castlefield Road, Reigate RH2 0SH ☎ 01737 276218 📠 01737 276610 ✉ nic.martlew@reigate-banstead.gov.uk

Waste Management: Mr Phil Humphrey, Waste and Recycling Operations Manager, Town Hall, Castlefield Road, Reigate RH2 0SH ☎ 01737 276502 📠 01737 276610 ✉ phil.humphrey@reigate-banstead.gov.uk

MEMBERS OF THE COUNCIL (51)

***Mayor:* Newstead**, Roger (CON - Reigate Hill)
cllr.newstead@reigate-banstead.gov.uk
***Deputy Mayor:* Horwood**, Alexander (CON - Horley West)
Cllr.Horwood@reigate-banstead.gov.uk
***Leader of the Council:* Spiers**, Joan (CON - Kingswood with Burgh Heath)
cllr.spiers@reigate-banstead.gov.uk
***Deputy Leader of the Council:* Broad**, Victor (CON - Tadworth and Walton)
cllr.broad@reigate-banstead.gov.uk
Banwait, Surrinder (CON - Horley Central)
cllr.banwait@reigate-banstead.gov.uk
Bramhall, Natalie (CON - Redhill West)
Cllr.MrsBramhall@reigate-banstead.gov.uk
Bramhall, Stephen (CON - South Park and Woodhatch)
cllr.bramhall@reigate-banstead.gov.uk
Bray, Jill (R - Tattenhams)
cllr.bray@reigate-banstead.gov.uk
Brunt, Lisa (CON - Reigate Hill)
cllr.mrsbrunt@reigate-banstead.gov.uk
Brunt, Mark (CON - Merstham)
cllr.brunt@reigate-banstead.gov.uk
Crome, Graeme (CON - Merstham)
cllr.crome@reigate-banstead.gov.uk
De Save, Adam (CON - Reigate Central)
cllr.desave@reigate-banstead.gov.uk
Durrant, James (CON - Earlswood and Whitbushes)
Cllr.Durrant@reigate-banstead.gov.uk
Ellacott, Julian (CON - Redhill West)
cllr.ellacott@reigate-banstead.gov.uk
Essex, Jonathan (GRN - Redhill East)
Cllr.Essex@reigate-banstead.gov.uk
Farrer, Steve (CON - Reigate Central)
cllr.farrer@reigate-banstead.gov.uk
Finch, Sarah (GRN - Redhill East)
Cllr.Finch@reigate-banstead.gov.uk
Foreman, Keith (CON - Chipstead Hooley and Woodmansterne)
Cllr.Foreman@reigate-banstead.gov.uk
Hack, Lynne (CON - Banstead Village)
Cllr.hack@reigate-banstead.gov.uk
Harper, Robert (R - Tattenhams)
cllr.harper@reigate-banstead.gov.uk
Harper-Adamson, Gemma (R - Preston)
Cllr.Harper-Adamson@reigate-banstead.gov.uk
Harris, Norman (R - Nork)
cllr.norman.harris@reigate-banstead.gov.uk
Harrison, Nicholas (R - Tattenhams)
cllr.harrison@reigate-banstead.gov.uk
Humphreys, Eddy (CON - Banstead Village)
Cllr.Humphreys@reigate-banstead.gov.uk
Kay, Allen (CON - Horley Central)
cllr.kay@reigate-banstead.gov.uk
Kelly, Frank (CON - Merstham)
Cllr.Kelly@reigate-banstead.gov.uk
King, Frances (CON - South Park and Woodhatch)
cllr.king@reigate-banstead.gov.uk
Knight, Graham (CON - Horley East)
Cllr.Knight@reigate-banstead.gov.uk
Kulka, Stephen (LD - Meadvale and St John's)
cllr.kulka@reigate-banstead.gov.uk
Lynch, Andrew (CON - Horley Central)
cllr.lynch@reigate-banstead.gov.uk
Mantle, Richard (IND - Chipstead, Hooley and Woodmansterne)
cllr.mantle@reigate-banstead.gov.uk
Mill, Rosalind (CON - Kingswood with Burgh Heath)
cllr.mill@reigate-banstead.gov.uk
Miller, Mike (CON - Horley West)
cllr.miller@reigate-banstead.gov.uk
Norman, Graham (LD - Meadvale and St John's)
cllr.norman@reigate-banstead.gov.uk
Parnall, Simon (CON - Kingswood with Burgh Heath)
Cllr.Parnall@reigate-banstead.gov.uk
Pay, David (CON - Redhill West)
cllr.pay@reigate-banstead.gov.uk
Poulter, Carol (CON - South Park and Woodhatch)
cllr.poulter@reigate-banstead.gov.uk
Powell, David (CON - Horley West)
Cllr.Powell@reigate-banstead.gov.uk
Renton, Rita (CON - Earlswood and Whitebushes)
Cllr.Renton@reigate-banstead.gov.uk
Ross-Tomlin, Dorothy (CON - Salfords and Sidlow)
cllr.ross-tomlin@reigate-banstead.gov.uk
Schofield, Tony (CON - Horley East)
Selby, Michael (R - Nork)
cllr.selby@reigate-banstead.gov.uk
Shillinglaw, Patsy (CON - Meadvale and St Johns)
Cllr.Shillinglaw@reigate-banstead.gov.uk
Stead, Brian (R - Nork)
cllr.stead@reigate-banstead.gov.uk
Stephenson, John (CON - Chipstead, Hooley and Woodmansterne)
Cllr.Stephenson@reigate-banstead.gov.uk
Thompson, Barbara (CON - Earlswood and Whitebushes)
Cllr.Thomson@reigate-banstead.gov.uk
Truscott, Bryan (GRN - Redhill East)
Cllr.Trusctoo@reigate-banstead.gov.uk
Turner, Rachel (CON - Tadworth and Walton)
cllr.turner@reigate-banstead.gov.uk
Vivona, Michael (CON - Tadworth and Walton)
Cllr.Vivona@reigate-banstead.gov.uk
Walsh, Samuel (CON - Banstead Village)
cllr.walsh@reigate-banstead.gov.uk
Whinney, Christopher (IND - Reigate Central)
cllr.whinney@reigate-banstead.gov.uk

POLITICAL COMPOSITION

CON: 37, R: 7, GRN: 3, IND: 2, LD: 2

CABINET

Leader: Mrs Joan Spiers
Deputy Leader: Mr Victor Broad
Communities: Ms Rosalind Mill
Health: Ms Rita Renton
Housing & Welfare: Mr Julian Ellacott
Recycling & Street Services: Mr Allen Kay
Property & Regeneration: Mrs Natalie Bramhall
Planning & Development: Mr Mike Miller
Leisure: Mr Adam De Save
Economy & Jobs: Mr Samuel Walsh

COMMITTEE CHAIRS

Employment: Mr Julian Ellacott
Licensing: Mr Andrew Lynch
Overview and Scrutiny (Scrutiny): Mr Nicholas Harrison
Planning: Mr Mark Brunt
Regulatory: Mr Graeme Crome
Standards: Mr J Broadbent (External)

RENFREWSHIRE S

Renfrewshire Council, Renfrewshire House, Cotton Street, Paisley PA1 1UJ ☎ 0141 842 5000 🖷 0141 840 3335 ✉ chiefexec@renfrewshire.gov.uk 💻 www.renfrewshire.gov.uk

FACTS & FIGURES

Police Authority: Strathclyde Police Authority
Learning and Skills Council: Scotland
Parliamentary Constituencies: Paisley and Renfrewshire North, Paisley and Renfrewshire South
EU Constituencies: Scotland
Election Frequency: Elections are of whole council
Twinning: Furth (Germany); Gladsaxe (Denmark)

PRINCIPAL OFFICERS

Chief Executive: Mr David Martin, Chief Executive, Renfrewshire House, Cotton Street, Paisley PA1 1WB ☎ 0141 840 3601 🖷 0141 840 3349 ✉ david.martin@renfrewshire.gov.uk

Access Officer / Social Services (Disability): Mr Peter McCulloch, Joint Manager - Learning Disability Services, Renfrewshire House, Cotton Street, Paisley PA1 1UJ ☎ 0141 842 5000

Architect, Building / Property Services: Mr Frank Hughes, Estates & Property Services Manager, Renfrewshire House, Cotton Street, Paisley PA1 1UJ ☎ 0141 842 5000

Architect, Building / Property Services: Mr Joe Lynch, Head of Property Services, Renfrewshire House, Cotton Street, Paisley PA1 1UJ ☎ 0141 842 5642 ✉ joe.lynch@renfrewshire.gov.uk

Best Value: Mr Oliver Reid, Service Manager, Renfrewshire House, Cotton Street, Paisley PA1 1WU ☎ 0141 840 3298 🖷 0141 840 3349 ✉ oliver.reid@renfrewshire.gov.uk

Catering Services: Mr Robert Steenson, Head of Community Care, Renfrewshire House, Cotton Street, Paisley PA1 1WU ☎ 0141 842 5164 🖷 0141 840 3232 ✉ robert.steenson@renfrewshire.gov.uk

Children / Youth Services: Ms Dorothy Hawthorn, Head of Child Care & Criminal Justice, Renfrewshire House, Cotton Street, Paisley PA1 1UJ ☎ 0141 842 5161 ✉ dorothy.hawthorn@renfrewshire.gsx.gov.uk

Children / Youth Services: Ms Liz Jamieson, Head of Children's Services, Renfrewshire House, Cotton Street, Paisley PA1 1UJ ☎ 0141 842 5603 ✉ liz.jamieson@renfrewshire.gov.uk

Children / Youth Services: Mr Ian Simpson, Acting Head of Planning & Community Services, Renfrewshire House, Cotton Street, Paisley PA1 1TR ☎ 0141 842 5602 🖷 0141 842 5655 ✉ ian.simpson@renfrewshire.gov.uk

PR / Communications: Mr Oliver Reid, Service Manager, Renfrewshire House, Cotton Street, Paisley PA1 1WU ☎ 0141 840 3298 🖷 0141 840 3349 ✉ oliver.reid@renfrewshire.gov.uk

Community Planning: Mr John Paterson, Head of Community Care, Renfrewshire House, Cotton Street, Paisley PA1 1UJ ☎ 0141 842 5168 ✉ john.paterson@renfrewshire.gsx.gov.uk

Community Planning: Mr Oliver Reid, Service Manager, Renfrewshire House, Cotton Street, Paisley PA1 1WU ☎ 0141 840 3298 🖷 0141 840 3349 ✉ oliver.reid@renfrewshire.gov.uk

Community Planning: Mr Ian Simpson, Acting Head of Planning & Community Services, Renfrewshire House, Cotton Street, Paisley PA1 1TR ☎ 0141 842 5602 🖷 0141 842 5655 ✉ ian.simpson@renfrewshire.gov.uk

Community Safety: Mr Oliver Reid, Service Manager, Renfrewshire House, Cotton Street, Paisley PA1 1WU ☎ 0141 840 3298 🖷 0141 840 3349 ✉ oliver.reid@renfrewshire.gov.uk

Computer Management: Ms Liz McDonald, Technical and Support Services Manager, Renfrewshire House, Cotton Street, Paisley PA1 1HY ☎ 0141 842 5093 🖷 0141 842 5366 ✉ liz.mcdonald@renfrewshire.gov.uk

Consumer Protection and Trading Standards: Mrs Shona MacDougall, Director of Environmental Services, Renfrewshire House, Cotton Street, Paisley PA1 1BU ☎ 0141 840 3104 🖷 0141 840 3233 ✉ shona.i.macdougall@renfrewshire.gov.uk

Contracts: Mr Ken Graham, Head of Legal & Administrative Services, Renfrewshire House, Cotton Street, Paisley PA1 1TR ☎ 0141 840 3221 🖷 0141 840 3635 ✉ ken.graham@renfrewshire.gov.uk

Corporate Services: Ms Sandra Black, Director of Finance & Corporate Services, Renfrewshire House, Cotton Street, Paisley PA1 1TR ☎ 0141 842 5051 🖷 0141 842 5055 ✉ sandra.black@renfrewshire.gov.uk

Customer Service: Mr Gary Innes, Customer Service Operations Manager, Renfrewshire House, Cotton Street, Paisley PA1 1TR ☎ 0141 842 5410 ✉ gary.innes@renfrewshire.gov.uk

Economic Development: Ms Ruth Cooper, Economic Development Manager, Renfrewshire House, Cotton Street, Paisley PA1 1LL ☎ 0141 842 5000

ruth.cooper@renfrewshire.gov.uk

Education: Ms Liz Jamieson, Head of Children's Services, Renfrewshire House, Cotton Street, Paisley PA1 1UJ ☎ 0141 842 5603 liz.jamieson@renfrewshire.gov.uk

Education: Mr Robert Naylor, Director of Education & Leisure Services, Renfrewshire House, Cotton Street, Paisley PA1 1TR ☎ 0141 842 5601 🖷 0141 842 5655 robert.naylor@renfrewshire.gov.uk

Education: Mr Ian Simpson, Acting Head of Planning & Community Services, Renfrewshire House, Cotton Street, Paisley PA1 1TR ☎ 0141 842 5602 🖷 0141 842 5655 ian.simpson@renfrewshire.gov.uk

E-Government: Ms Sandra Black, Director of Finance & Corporate Services, Renfrewshire House, Cotton Street, Paisley PA1 1TR ☎ 0141 842 5051 🖷 0141 842 5055 sandra.black@renfrewshire.gov.uk

Emergency Planning: Mr John Donlin, Civil Contingencies Manager, Renfrewshire House, Cotton Street, Paisley PA1 1WB ☎ 0141 842 5690 🖷 0141 840 3697 john.donlin@renfrewshire.gov.uk

Energy Management: Mr Craig Doogan, Energy Manager, Renfrewshire House, Cotton Street, Paisley PA1 1JD ☎ 0141 840 3267 🖷 0141 842 5552

Environmental / Technical Services: Mrs Shona MacDougall, Director of Environmental Services, Renfrewshire House, Cotton Street, Paisley PA1 1BU ☎ 0141 840 3104 🖷 0141 840 3233 shona.i.macdougall@renfrewshire.gov.uk

Environmental Health: Mrs Shona MacDougall, Director of Environmental Services, Renfrewshire House, Cotton Street, Paisley PA1 1BU ☎ 0141 840 3104 🖷 0141 840 3233 shona.i.macdougall@renfrewshire.gov.uk

Environmental Health: Mr Robert Steenson, Head of Community Care, Renfrewshire House, Cotton Street, Paisley PA1 1WU ☎ 0141 842 5164 🖷 0141 840 3232 robert.steenson@renfrewshire.gov.uk

Environmental Health: Mr David Walls, Head of Resource Services, Renfrewshire House, Cotton Street, Paisley PA1 1UJ ☎ 0141 840 3101 david.walls@renfrewshire.gov.uk

Estates, Property & Valuation: Mr Frank Hughes, Estates & Property Services Manager, Renfrewshire House, Cotton Street, Paisley PA1 1UJ ☎ 0141 842 5000

European Liaison: Ms Ruth Cooper, Economic Development Manager, Renfrewshire House, Cotton Street, Paisley PA1 1LL ☎ 0141 842 5000 ruth.cooper@renfrewshire.gov.uk

Finance and Treasurer: Ms Sandra Black, Director of Finance & Corporate Services, Renfrewshire House, Cotton Street, Paisley PA1 1TR ☎ 0141 842 5051 🖷 0141 842 5055 sandra.black@renfrewshire.gov.uk

Finance and Treasurer: Mr Alan Russell, Head of Corporate Finance, Renfrewshire House, Cotton Street, Paisley PA1 1UJ ☎ 0141 842 5407 alan.russell@renfrewshire.gov.uk

Finance and Treasurer: Mr David Walls, Head of Resource Services, Renfrewshire House, Cotton Street, Paisley PA1 1UJ ☎ 0141 840 3101 david.walls@renfrewshire.gov.uk

Fleet Management: Mr Scott Allan, Head of Roads & Transportation, Renfrewshire House, Cotton Street, Paisley PA1 1UJ ☎ 0141 842 5000 scott.allan@renfrewshire.gov.uk

Grounds Maintenance: Mrs Shona MacDougall, Director of Environmental Services, Renfrewshire House, Cotton Street, Paisley PA1 1BU ☎ 0141 840 3104 🖷 0141 840 3233 shona.i.macdougall@renfrewshire.gov.uk

Health and Safety: Mr David Marshall, Head of Personnel Services, Renfrewshire House, Cotton Street, Paisley PA1 1TS ☎ 0141 840 3520 🖷 0141 848 5420 david.marshall@renfrewshire.gov.uk

Highways: Mr Scott Allan, Head of Roads & Transportation, Renfrewshire House, Cotton Street, Paisley PA1 1UJ ☎ 0141 842 5000 scott.allan@renfrewshire.gov.uk

Home Energy Conservation: Mr John Ritchie, Energy Officer, Renfrewshire House, Cotton Street, Paisley PA1 1BU ☎ 0141 840 3704 🖷 0141 840 3421 john.ritchie@renfrewshire.gov.uk

Housing: Ms Mary Crearie, Director of Housing & Property Services, Renfrewshire House, Cotton Street, Paisley PA1 1JD ☎ 0141 842 5616 🖷 0141 842 5552 mary.cerarie@renfrewshire.gov.uk

Housing: Mr Joe Lynch, Head of Property Services, Renfrewshire House, Cotton Street, Paisley PA1 1UJ ☎ 0141 842 5642 joe.lynch@renfrewshire.gov.uk

Housing: Ms Eileen MacLean, Head of Housing Services, Renfrewshire House, Cotton Street, Paisley PA1 1UJ ☎ 0141 842 5015 eileen.maclean@renfrewshire.gsx.gov.uk

Housing Maintenance: Mr Frank Hughes, Estates & Property Services Manager, Renfrewshire House, Cotton Street, Paisley PA1 1UJ ☎ 0141 842 5000

Legal: Mr Ken Graham, Head of Legal & Administrative Services, Renfrewshire House, Cotton Street, Paisley PA1 1TR ☎ 0141 840 3221 🖷 0141 840 3635 ken.graham@renfrewshire.gov.uk

Leisure and Cultural Services: Mr Robert Naylor, Director of Education & Leisure Services, Renfrewshire House, Cotton Street, Paisley PA1 1TR ☎ 0141 842 5601 🖷 0141 842 5655 robert.naylor@renfrewshire.gov.uk

Licensing: Mr Ken Graham, Head of Legal & Administrative Services, Renfrewshire House, Cotton Street, Paisley PA1 1TR ☎ 0141 840 3221 🖷 0141 840 3635 ken.graham@renfrewshire.gov.uk

Lifelong Learning: Mr Robert Naylor, Director of Education &

Leisure Services, Renfrewshire House, Cotton Street, Paisley PA1 1TR ☎ 0141 842 5601 🖷 0141 842 5655 🖰 robert.naylor@renfrewshire.gov.uk

Lighting: Mr Scott Allan, Head of Roads & Transportation, Renfrewshire House, Cotton Street, Paisley PA1 1UJ ☎ 0141 842 5000 🖰 scott.allan@renfrewshire.gov.uk

Lottery Funding, Charity and Voluntary: Ms Ruth Cooper, External Funding Manager, Renfrewshire House, Cotton Street, Paisley PA1 1TR ☎ 0141 842 5875 🖰 ruth.cooper@renfrewshire.gov.uk

Member Services: Mr Ken Graham, Head of Legal & Administrative Services, Renfrewshire House, Cotton Street, Paisley PA1 1TR ☎ 0141 840 3221 🖷 0141 840 3635 🖰 ken.graham@renfrewshire.gov.uk

Parking: Mr Scott Allan, Head of Roads & Transportation, Renfrewshire House, Cotton Street, Paisley PA1 1UJ ☎ 0141 842 5000 🖰 scott.allan@renfrewshire.gov.uk

Personnel / HR: Mr David Marshall, Head of Personnel Services, Renfrewshire House, Cotton Street, Paisley PA1 1TS ☎ 0141 840 3520 🖷 0141 848 5420 🖰 david.marshall@renfrewshire.gov.uk

Planning: Mr Bob Darracott, Director of Planning & Transport, Renfrewshire House, Cotton Street, Paisley PA1 1LL ☎ 0141 842 5811 🖷 0141 842 5833 🖰 bob.darracott@renfrewshire.gov.uk

Procurement: Ms Sandra Black, Director of Finance & Corporate Services, Renfrewshire House, Cotton Street, Paisley PA1 1TR ☎ 0141 842 5051 🖷 0141 842 5055 🖰 sandra.black@renfrewshire.gov.uk

Public Libraries: Mr Robert Naylor, Director of Education & Leisure Services, Renfrewshire House, Cotton Street, Paisley PA1 1TR ☎ 0141 842 5601 🖷 0141 842 5655 🖰 robert.naylor@renfrewshire.gov.uk

Recycling & Waste Minimisation: Mrs Shona MacDougall, Director of Environmental Services, Renfrewshire House, Cotton Street, Paisley PA1 1BU ☎ 0141 840 3104 🖷 0141 840 3233 🖰 shona.i.macdougall@renfrewshire.gov.uk

Regeneration: Mr Oliver Reid, Service Manager, Renfrewshire House, Cotton Street, Paisley PA1 1WU ☎ 0141 840 3298 🖷 0141 840 3349 🖰 oliver.reid@renfrewshire.gov.uk

Road Safety: Mr Scott Allan, Head of Roads & Transportation, Renfrewshire House, Cotton Street, Paisley PA1 1UJ ☎ 0141 842 5000 🖰 scott.allan@renfrewshire.gov.uk

Social Services: Mr Peter Macleod, Director of Social Work, Renfrewshire House, Cotton Street, Paisley PA1 1TZ ☎ 0141 842 5167 🖷 0141 842 5144 🖰 peter.macleod@renfrewshire.gov.uk

Social Services: Ms Anne McMillan, Head of Resources, Renfrewshire House, Cotton Street, Paisley PA1 1UJ ☎ 0141 840 3310 🖷 0141 842 5144 🖰 anne.mcmillan@renfrewshire.gsx.gov.uk

Social Services: Mr John Paterson, Head of Community Care, Renfrewshire House, Cotton Street, Paisley PA1 1UJ ☎ 0141 842 5168 🖰 john.paterson@renfrewshire.gsx.gov.uk

Social Services (Adult): Mr Peter Macleod, Director of Social Work, Renfrewshire House, Cotton Street, Paisley PA1 1TZ ☎ 0141 842 5167 🖷 0141 842 5144 🖰 peter.macleod@renfrewshire.gov.uk

Social Services (Children): Mr Peter Macleod, Director of Social Work, Renfrewshire House, Cotton Street, Paisley PA1 1TZ ☎ 0141 842 5167 🖷 0141 842 5144 🖰 peter.macleod@renfrewshire.gov.uk

Staff Training: Mr David Marshall, Head of Personnel Services, Renfrewshire House, Cotton Street, Paisley PA1 1TS ☎ 0141 840 3520 🖷 0141 848 5420 🖰 david.marshall@renfrewshire.gov.uk

Street Scene: Mr Scott Allan, Head of Roads & Transportation, Renfrewshire House, Cotton Street, Paisley PA1 1UJ ☎ 0141 842 5000 🖰 scott.allan@renfrewshire.gov.uk

Sustainable Development: Mr Bob Darracott, Director of Planning & Transport, Renfrewshire House, Cotton Street, Paisley PA1 1LL ☎ 0141 842 5811 🖷 0141 842 5833 🖰 bob.darracott@renfrewshire.gov.uk

Sustainable Development: Mrs Shona MacDougall, Director of Environmental Services, Renfrewshire House, Cotton Street, Paisley PA1 1BU ☎ 0141 840 3104 🖷 0141 840 3233 🖰 shona.i.macdougall@renfrewshire.gov.uk

Town Centre: Ms Amanda Moulson, Town Centre's Project Manager, Renfrewshire House, Cotton Street, Paisley PA1 1LL ☎ 0141 842 5421 🖷 0141 842 5833 🖰 amanda.moulson@renfrewshire.gov.uk

Traffic Management: Mr Scott Allan, Head of Roads & Transportation, Renfrewshire House, Cotton Street, Paisley PA1 1UJ ☎ 0141 842 5000 🖰 scott.allan@renfrewshire.gov.uk

Transport: Mr Scott Allan, Head of Roads & Transportation, Renfrewshire House, Cotton Street, Paisley PA1 1UJ ☎ 0141 842 5000 🖰 scott.allan@renfrewshire.gov.uk

Transport: Mr Bob Darracott, Director of Planning & Transport, Renfrewshire House, Cotton Street, Paisley PA1 1LL ☎ 0141 842 5811 🖷 0141 842 5833 🖰 bob.darracott@renfrewshire.gov.uk

Transport Planner: Mr Scott Allan, Head of Roads & Transportation, Renfrewshire House, Cotton Street, Paisley PA1 1UJ ☎ 0141 842 5000 🖰 scott.allan@renfrewshire.gov.uk

Waste Collection and Disposal: Mrs Shona MacDougall, Director of Environmental Services, Renfrewshire House, Cotton Street, Paisley PA1 1BU ☎ 0141 840 3104 🖷 0141 840 3233 🖰 shona.i.macdougall@renfrewshire.gov.uk

Waste Management: Mrs Shona MacDougall, Director of Environmental Services, Renfrewshire House, Cotton Street, Paisley PA1 1BU ☎ 0141 840 3104 🖷 0141 840 3233 🖰 shona.i.macdougall@renfrewshire.gov.uk

MEMBERS OF THE COUNCIL (40)

***Provost:* Hall**, Anne (LAB - Houston, Crosslee and Linwood)
cllr.anne.hall@renfrewshire.gov.uk

***Deputy Provost:* Caldwell**, John (LAB - Johnstone South, Elderslie and Howwood)
cllr.john.caldwell@renfrewshire.gov.uk

***Leader of the Council:* Macmillan**, Mark (LAB - Paisley South West)
cllr.mark.macmillan@renfrewshire.gov.uk

Bibby, Derek (LAB - Johnstone North, Kilbarchan and Lochwinnoch)
cllr.derek.bibby@renfrewshire.gov.uk

Brown, Maria (SNP - Bishopton, Bridge of Weir and Langbank)
cllr.maria.brown@renfrewshire.gov.uk

Brown, Bill (LAB - Renfrew North)
cllr.bill.brown@renfrewshire.gov.uk

Cameron, Lorraine (SNP - Paisley South West)
cllr.lorraine.cameron@renfrewshire.gov.uk

Clark, Stuart (LAB - Houston, Crosslee and Linwood)
cllr.stuart.clark@renfrewshire.gov.uk

Devin, Margaret (LAB - Renfrew South and Gallowhill)
cllr.margaret.devine@renfrewshire.gov.uk

Devine, Eddie (LAB - Paisley South)
cllr.eddie.devine@renfrewshire.gov.uk

Doig, Audrey (SNP - Houston, Crosslee and Linwood)
cllr.audrey.doig@renfrewshire.gov.uk

Doig, Andy (SNP - Johnstone North, Kilbarchan and Lochwinnoch)
cllr.andy.doig@renfrewshire.gov.uk

Gilmour, Christopher (LAB - Johnstone North, Kilbarchan and Lochwinnoch)
cllr.christopher.gilmour@renfrewshire.gov.uk

Glen, Roy (LAB - Paisley South)
cllr.roy.glen@renfrewshire.gov.uk

Grady, Eddie (LAB - Renfrew South and Gallowhill)
cllr.eddie.grady@renfrewshire.gov.uk

Harte, James (LAB - Erskine and Inchinnan)
cllr.james.harte@renfrewshire.gov.uk

Henry, Jacqueline (LAB - Paisley South West)
cllr.jacqueline.henry@renfrewshire.gov.uk

Holmes, Michael (LAB - Bishopton, Bridge of Weir and Langbank)
cllr.michael.holmes@renfrewshire.gov.uk

Hood, John (LAB - Johnstone South, Elderslie and Howwood)
cllr.john.hood@renfrewshire.gov.uk

Kelly, Terence (LAB - Paisley North West)
cllr.terry.kelly@renfrewshire.gov.uk

Lawson, Brian (SNP - Paisley East and Ralston)
cllr.brian.lawson@renfrewshire.gov.uk

Mack, Paul (IND - Paisley South)
cllr.paul.mack@renfrewshire.gov.uk

MacLaren, Kenny (SNP - Paisley North West)
cllr.kenny.maclaren@renfrewshire.gov.uk

MacLaren, Mags (SNP - Paisley North West)
cllr.mags.maclaren@renfrewshire.gov.uk

Maclaren, James (CON - Bishopton, Bridge of Weir and Lanbank)
cllr.james.maclaren@renfrewshire.gov.uk

McCartin, Eileen (LD - Paisley South West)
cllr.eileen.mccartin@renfrewshire.gov.uk

McEwan, Cathy (SNP - Renfrew South and Gallowhill)
cllr.cathy.mcewan@renfrewshire.gov.uk

McGee, Stephen (SNP - Johnstone South, Elderslie and Howwood)
cllr.stephen.mcgee@renfrewshire.gov.uk

McGurk, Marie (SNP - Paisley South)
cllr.marie.mcgurk@renfrewshire.gov.uk

McMillan, Iain (LAB - Johnstone South, Elderslie and Howwood)
cllr.iain.mcmillan@renfrewshire.gov.uk

McQuade, Jim (SNP - Erskine and Inchinnan)
cllr.jim.mcquade@renfrewshire.gov.uk

Mullin, Sam (LAB - Erskine and Inchinnan)
cllr.sam.mullin@renfrewshire.gov.uk

Murrin, Alexander (LAB - Renfrew North)
cllr.alex.murrin@renfrewshire.gov.uk

Mylet, Will (SNP - Paisley East and Ralston)
cllr.will.mylet@renfrewshire.gov.uk

Nicolson, Iain (SNP - Erskine and Inchinnan)
cllr.iain.nicholson@renfrewshire.gov.uk

Noon, Allan (SNP - Houston, Crosslee and Linwood)
cllr.allan.noon@renfrewshire.gov.uk

Perrie, Bill (SNP - Renfrew North)
cllr.bill.perrie@renfrewshire.gov.uk

Sharkey, Jim (LAB - Paisley East and Ralston)
cllr.jim.sharkey@renfrewshire.gov.uk

Sharkey, Maureen (LAB - Paisley East and Ralston)
cllr.maureen.sharkey@renfrewshire.gov.uk

Williams, Thomas (LAB - Paisley North West)
cllr.tommy.williams@renfrewshire.gov.uk

POLITICAL COMPOSITION

LAB: 22, SNP: 15, LD: 1, CON: 1, IND: 1

COMMITTEE CHAIRS

Appeals Board: Mr Sam Mullin
Community & Family Care Policy: Mr Iain McMillan
Education: Mrs Jacqueline Henry
Environment & Infrastructure Policy: Mr James Harte
General Management & Finance: Mr Michael Holmes
Housing & Community Safety: Mr Thomas Williams
Planning & Economic Development Policy Board: Mr Terence Kelly
Regulatory Functions: Mr John Hood
Scrutiny & Petitions: Mr Jim Sharkey

RHONDDA CYNON TAFF — W

Rhondda Cynon Taff County Borough Council, (Cyngor Bwrdeistref Sirol Rhondda Cynon Taf), The Pavilions, Cambrian Park, Clydach Vale, Tonypandy CF40 2XX ☎ 01443 424000
🖷 01443 424034; 01443 424034
🖳 www.rhondda-cynon-taff.gov.uk

FACTS & FIGURES

Police Authority: South Wales Police Authority
Health Authority: R.C.T Teaching Local Health Board
Learning and Skills Council: Wales
Parliamentary Constituencies: Cynon Valley, Pontypridd, Rhondda
EU Constituencies: Wales
Election Frequency: Elections are of whole council
Twinning: Nurtingen (Germany); Wolfenbuttel (Germany); Ravensburg (Germany); Montelimar (France).

PRINCIPAL OFFICERS

Chief Executive: Mr Keith Griffiths, Chief Executive, The Pavilions, Cambrian Park, Clydach Vale, Tonypandy CF40 2XX

☎ 01443 424026 🖷 01443 424027 ✉ keith.griffiths@rhondda-cynon-taff.gov.uk

Access Officer / Social Services (Disability): Ms Catherine Boulton, Senior Intermediate Car and Rehabilitation Co-ordinator, Bronllwyn Home for the Elderly, Colwyn Road, Gelli, Pentre CF41 7NW ☎ 01443 424999 🖷 01443 424990 ✉ catherine.boulton@rhondda-cynon-taff.gov.uk

Architect, Building / Property Services: Mr Colin Atyeo, Director of Corporate Estates, Valleys Innovation Centre, Navigation Park, Abercynon, Mountain Ash CF44 4SN ☎ 01443 665775 🖷 01443 665757 ✉ colin.m.atyeo@rhondda-cynon-taff.gov.uk

Building Control: Mr Stephen Long, Building Control Manager, Sardis House, Sardis Road, Pontypridd CF37 1DU ☎ 01443 494748 🖷 01443 494774 ✉ stephen.j.long@rhondda-cynon-taff.gov.uk

Catering Services: Mrs Anne Bull, Head of Catering Services & Schools Facilities Services, Ty Trevithick, Abercynon, Mountain Ash CF45 4UQ ☎ 01443 744155 🖷 01443 744290 ✉ anne.bull@rhondda-cynon-taff.gov.uk

Children / Youth Services: Ms Louise Cook, Acting Head of Youth Services to Young People, Ty Trevithick, Abercynon, Mountain Ash CF45 4UQ ☎ 01443 744105 🖷 01443 744023 ✉ louise.cook@rhondda-cynon-taff.gov.uk

Children / Youth Services: Mr Andrew Gwynn, Head of Youth Offending, Unit 2-Fairway Court, Tonteg Road, Treforest Industrial Estate, Pontypridd CF37 5UA ☎ 01443 827300 🖷 01443 827301 ✉ andrew.v.gwynn@rhondda-cynon-taff.gov.uk

PR / Communications: Mr Christian Hanagan, Head of Strategy, PR and Tourism, The Pavilions, Cambrian Park, Clydach Vale, Tonypandy CF40 2XX ☎ 01443 424005 🖷 01443 424004 ✉ christian.sj.hanagan@rhondda-cynon-taff.gov.uk

Community Safety: Mr Phil Bevan, Head of Community Safety Service, Unit 2, Fairway Court, Tonteg Road, Treforest Industrial Estate, Pontypridd CF37 5UA ☎ 01443 827351 🖷 01443 743820 ✉ phil.bevan@rhondda-cynon-taff.gov.uk

Computer Management: Mr Leigh Gripton, Director of Customer Care & ICT, Ty Elai, Dinas Isaf Industrial Estate, Williamstown, Tonypandy CF40 1NY ☎ 01443 444400 🖷 01443 444419 ✉ leigh.f.gripton@rhondda-cynon-taff.gov.uk

Computer Management: Mr Tim Jones, Head of ICT, Ty Elai, Dinas Isaf Industrial Estate, Williamstown, Tonypandy CF40 1NY ☎ 01443 444458 🖷 01443 444419 ✉ tim.d.jones@rhondda-cynon-taff.gov.uk

Consumer Protection and Trading Standards: Mr Paul Mee, Service Director - Public Health & Protection, Ty Elai, Dinas Isaf Industrial Estate, Williamstown, Tonypandy CF40 1NY ☎ 01443 445513 🖷 01443 425580 ✉ paul.j.mee@rhondda-cynon-taff.gov.uk

Corporate Services: Mr Steve Merritt, Group Director - Corporate Services, The Pavilions, Cambrian Park, Clydach Vale, Tonypandy CF40 2XX ☎ 01443 424026 🖷 01443 424027 ✉ steve.j.merritt@rhondda-cynon-taff.gov.uk

Customer Service: Mrs Roseann Edwards, Head of Customer Care, Ty Elai, Dinas Isaf Industrial Estate, Williamstown, Tonypandy CF40 1NY ☎ 01443 444402 🖷 01443 444419 ✉ roseann.edwards@rhondda-cynon-taff.gov.uk

Economic Development: Ms Jane Cook, Director of Regeneration & Planning, Floor 5, Unit 3, Ty Pennant, Catherine Street, Pontypridd CF37 2TB ☎ 01443 495161 🖷 01443 407725 ✉ jane.cook@rhondda-cynon-taff.gov.uk

Education: Mr Chris Bradshaw, Director of Education & Lifelong Learning, Ty Trevithick, Abercynon, Tonypandy CF45 4UQ ☎ 01443 744009 🖷 01443 744023 ✉ christopher.d.bradshaw@rhondda-cynon-taff.gov.uk

Education: Mr Gareth Rees, Acting Service Director for Planning Resources & Community Learning, Ty Trevithick, Abercynon, Mountain Ash CF45 4UQ ☎ 01443 744004 🖷 01443 744023 ✉ gareth.o.rees@rhondda-cynon-taff.gov.uk

E-Government: Mr Leigh Gripton, Director of Customer Care & ICT, Ty Elai, Dinas Isaf Industrial Esate, Williamstown, Tonypandy CF40 1NY ☎ 01443 444400 🖷 01443 444419 ✉ leigh.f.gripton@rhondda-cynon-taff.gov.uk

Electoral Registration: Mr Mark Green, Business Support Manager, The Pavilions, Cambrian Park, Clydach Vale, Tonypandy CF40 2XX ☎ 01443 424032 🖷 01443 424114 ✉ william.m.green@rhnodda-cynon-taff.gov.uk

Emergency Planning: Mr Brian Houston, Emergency Planning & Sustainability Manager, Sardis House, Sardis Road, Pontypridd CF37 1DU ☎ 01443 494877 ✉ brian.houston@rhondda-cynon-taff.gov.uk

Energy Management: Mr Gerald Israel, Energy Manager, Valleys Innovation Centre, Navigation Park, Abercynon CF45 4SN ☎ 01443 744419 🖷 01443 744466 ✉ gerald.a.israel@rhondda-cynon-taff.gov.uk

Environmental / Technical Services: Mr George Jones, Group Director of Environmental Services, The Pavilions, Cambrian Park, Clydach Vale, Tonypandy CF40 2XX ☎ 01443 424147 🖷 01443 424027 ✉ d.george.jones@rhondda-cynon-taff.gov.uk

Environmental Health: Mr Clive Osmond, Senior Environmental Health Officer, Ty Elai, Dina Isaf Industrial Estate, Williamstown, Tonypandy CF40 1NY ☎ 01443 425380 🖷 01443 425301 ✉ clive.g.osmond@rhondda-cynon-taff.gov.uk

Estates, Property & Valuation: Mr Colin Atyeo, Director of Corporate Estates, Valleys Innovation Centre, Navigation Park, Abercynon, Mountain Ash CF45 4SN ☎ 01443 665775 🖷 01443 665757 ✉ colin.m.atyeo@rhondda-cynon-taff.gov.uk

Events Manager: Mr Ian Christopher, Marketing & Strategic Events Officer, The Pavilions, Cambrian Park, Clydach Vale, Tonypandy CF40 2XX ☎ 0143 424017 ✉ ian.christopher@rhondda-cynon-taff.gov.uk

Finance and Treasurer: Mr Christopher Lee, Director of Financial Services, Bronwydd House, Porth CF39 9DL ☎ 01443 680616 🖷 01443 680504 christopher.d.lee@rhondda-cynon-taff.gov.uk

Fleet Management: Mrs Julie Waites, Fleet Manager, Ty Glantaf, Unit B23, Taff Falls Road, Treforest Industrial Estate, Pontypridd CF37 5TT ☎ 01443 827730 🖷 01443 827760 julie.y.waites@rhondda-cynon-taff.gov.uk

Grounds Maintenance: Mr Dave Batten, Head of Leisure, Parks & Countryside, Llwyncastan, Library Road, Pontypridd CF37 2YA ☎ 01443 490256 🖷 01443 490257 david.c.batten@rhondda-cynon-taff.gov.uk

Health and Safety: Mr Mike Murphy, Health & Safety Advisor, Ty Elai, Dinas Isaf Industrial Estate, Williamstown, Tonypandy CF40 1NY ☎ 01443 425536 🖷 01443 444534 mike.murphy@rhondda-cynon-taff.gov.uk

Highways: Mr Nigel Brinn, Service Director - Highways, Transportation & Strategic Projects, Sardis House, Sardis Road, Pontypridd CF37 1DU ☎ 01443 494861 🖷 01443 494799 nigel.brinn@rhondda-cynon-taff.gov.uk

Home Energy Conservation: Mr Paul Mee, Service Director - Public Health & Protection, Ty Elai, Dinas Isaf Industrial Estate, Williamstown, Tonypandy CF40 1NY ☎ 01443 445513 🖷 01443 425580 paul.j.mee@rhondda-cynon-taff.gov.uk

Local Area Agreement: Ms Nicola Gulley, Spatial Development Manager, Floor 5, Unit 3, Ty Pennant, Catherine Street, Pontypridd CF37 2TB ☎ 01443 494730 🖷 01443 407725 nicola.gulley@rhondda-cynon-taff.gov.uk

Legal: Mr Paul Lucas, Director of Legal & Democratic Services, The Pavilions, Cambrian Park, Clydach Vale, Tonypandy CF40 2XX ☎ 01443 424105 🖷 01443 424027 paul.j.lucas@rhondda-cynon-taff.gov.uk

Leisure and Cultural Services: Mr Dave Batten, Head of Leisure, Parks & Countryside, Llwyncastan, Library Road, Pontypridd CF37 2YA ☎ 01443 490256 🖷 01443 490257 david.c.batten@rhondda-cynon-taff.gov.uk

Licensing: Mrs Meryl Williams, Licensing Manager, Ty Elai, Dinas Isaf Industrial Estate, Williamstown, Tonypandy CF40 1NY ☎ 01443 425361 🖷 01443 425301 meryl.d.williams@rhondda-cynon-taff.gov.uk

Lifelong Learning: Mr Chris Bradshaw, Director of Education & Lifelong Learning, Ty Trevithick, Abercynon, Tonypandy CF45 4UQ ☎ 01443 744009 🖷 01443 744023 christopher.d.bradshaw@rhondda-cynon-taff.gov.uk

Lighting: Mr Howard Thomas, Highways & Technical Services Manager, Sardis House, Sardis Road, Pontypridd CF37 1DU ☎ 01443 494801 🖷 01443 494705 howard.j.thomas@rhondda-cynon-taff.gov.uk

Lottery Funding, Charity and Voluntary: Mr Peter Mortimer, Regeneration & Resources Manager, Level 5, Unit 3, Ty Pennant, Catherine Street, Pontypridd CF37 2TB ☎ 01443 490407 🖷 01443 407725 peter.j.mortimer@rhondda-cynon-taff.gov.uk

Member Services: Mrs Karyl May, Committee Services Manager, The Pavilions, Cambrian Park, Clydach Vale, Tonypandy CF40 2XX ☎ 01443 424045 🖷 01443 424114 karyl.may@rhondda-cynon-taff.gov.uk

Parking: Mr Andrew Carter, Parking Services Manager, Sardis House, Sardis Road, Pontypridd CF37 1DU ☎ 01443 494711 🖷 01443 494778 andrew.d.carter@rhondda-cynon-taff.gov.uk

Personnel / HR: Mr Tony Wilkins, Director of Human Resources, The Pavilions, Cambrian Park, Clydach Vale, CF40 2XX ☎ 01443 424166 🖷 01443 424025 tony.wilkins@rhondda-cynon-taff.gov.uk

Planning: Mr Simon Gale, Service Director Planning, Sardis House, Sardis Road, Pontypridd CF37 1DU ☎ 01443 494716 🖷 01443 494799 simon.gale@rhondda-cynon-taff.gov.uk

Procurement: Mr Vince Hanly, Service Director Procurement, Bronwydd, Porth CF39 9DL ☎ 01443 680538 🖷 01443 680787 vince.hanly@rhondda-cynon-taff.gov.uk

Public Libraries: Ms Rosalind Williams, Principal Officer - Libraries, Treorchy Library, Station Road, Treorchy CF42 6NW ☎ 01443 778952 🖷 01443 777047 ros.williams@rhondda-cynon-taff.gov.uk

Recycling & Waste Minimisation: Mr Nigel Wheeler, Service Director - Street Care, Ty Glantaf, Unit B23, Taff Falls Road, Treforest Industrial Estate, Pontypridd CF37 5TT ☎ 01443 827707 🖷 01443 827730 nigel.wheeler@rhondda-cynon-taff.gov.uk

Regeneration: Ms Jane Cook, Director of Regeneration & Planning, Floor 5, Unit 3, Ty Pennant, Catherine Street, Pontypridd CF37 2TB ☎ 01443 495161 🖷 01443 407725 jane.cook@rhondda-cynon-taff.gov.uk

Road Safety: Ms Paula Perry, Road Safety Manager, Sardis House, Sardis Road, Pontypridd CF37 1DU ☎ 01443 494789 🖷 01443 494748 paula.c.perry@rhondda-cynon-taff.gov.uk

Social Services: Ms Virginia Board, Principal Education & Child Psychologist, Ty Trevithick, Abercynon, Mountain Ash CF45 4UQ ☎ 01443 744326 🖷 01443 744125 virginia.e.board@rhondda-cynon-taff.gov.uk

Social Services: Mr Wynne Vaughan, Service Director - Health & Social Care, Ty Elai, Dinas Isaf East Industrial Estate, Williamstown, Tonypandy CF40 1NY ☎ 01443 425539 🖷 01443 425440 wynne.t.vaughan@rhondda-cynon-taff.gov.uk

Social Services: Mr Ellis Williams, Group Director - Community & Children's Services, The Pavilions, Cambrian Park, Clydach Vale, Tonypandy CF40 2XX ☎ 01443 424140 🖷 01443 424027 ellis.williams@rhondda-cynon-taff.gov.uk

Social Services (Adult): Mr Bob Gatis, Service Director - Community Care, Ty Elai, Dinas Isaf Industrial Estate,

Williamstown, Tonypandy CF40 1NY ☎ 01443 425401 🖷 01443 425440 ✉ robert.e.gatis@rhondda-cynon-taff.gov.uk

Social Services (Children): Mr Tony Young, Service Director - Children's Services, Unit 3, Ty Pennant, Catherine Street, Pontypridd CH37 2TB ☎ 01443 495118 🖷 01443 406290 ✉ tony.m.young@rhondda-cynon-taff.gov.uk

Staff Training: Mrs Liz James, Head of Organisational Development, The Pavilions, Cambrian Park, Clydach Vale, Tonypandy CF40 2XX ☎ 01443 424053 🖷 01443 424025 ✉ liz.a.james@rhondda-cynon-taff.gov.uk

Street Scene: Mr Steve Owen, Head of Street Care, Ty Glantaf, Unit B23, Taff Falls Road, Treforest Industrial Estate, Pontypridd CF37 5TT ☎ 01443 827702 🖷 01443 844310 ✉ steve.owen@rhondda-cynon-taff.gov.uk

Sustainable Development: Mr Brian Houston, Emergency Planning & Sustainability Manager, Sardis House, Sardis Road, Pontypridd CF37 1DU ☎ 01443 494877 ✉ brian.houston@rhondda-cynon-taff.gov.uk

Tourism: Ms Luan Oestrich, Tourism Manager, The Pavilions, Cambrian Park, Clydach Vale, Tonypandy CF40 2XX ☎ 01443 490237 🖷 01443 490257 ✉ luan.oestrich@rhondda-cynon-taff.gov.uk

Town Centre: Mr Chris Edwards, Co-ordinator and Business Club Manager, Floor 5, Unit 3, Ty Pennant, Catherine Street, Pontypridd CF32 2TB ☎ 01443 495189 🖷 01443 494774 ✉ chris.edwards@rhondda-cynon-taff.gov.uk

Traffic Management: Mr Jeff Higgins, Principal Engineer Traffic Management, Sardis House, Sardis Road, Pontypridd CF37 1DU ☎ 01443 494810 🖷 01443 494811 ✉ jeff.m.higgins@rhondda-cynon-taff.gov.uk

Transport: Mr Robert Harper, Transportation Strategy Manager, Sardis House, Sardis Road, Pontypridd CF37 1DU ☎ 01443 494856 🖷 01443 494852 ✉ robert.l.harper@rhondda-cynon-taff.gov.uk

Transport: Mr Roger Waters, Head of Highways, Transportation & Strategic Projects, Sardis House, Sardis Road, Pontypridd CF37 1DU ☎ 01443 494703 🖷 01443 494799 ✉ roger.j.waters@rhondda-cynon-taff.gov.uk

Transport Planner: Mr Tim Phillips, Transport Planner, Sardis House, Sardis Road, Pontypridd CF37 1DU ☎ 01443 494858 🖷 01443 494875 ✉ tim.dj.phillips@rhondda-cynon-taff.gov.uk

Waste Collection and Disposal: Mr Nigel Wheeler, Service Director - Street Care, Ty Glantaf, Unit B23, Taff Falls Road, Treforest Industrial Estate, Pontypridd CF37 5TT ☎ 01443 827707 🖷 01443 827730 ✉ nigel.wheeler@rhondda-cynon-taff.gov.uk

Waste Management: Mr Nigel Wheeler, Service Director - Street Care, Ty Glantaf, Unit B23, Taff Falls Road, Treforest Industrial Estate, Pontypridd CF37 5TT ☎ 01443 827707 🖷 01443 827730 ✉ nigel.wheeler@rhondda-cynon-taff.gov.uk

Children's Play Areas: Ms Lisa Austin, Playgrounds Officer, Llwyncastan, Library Road, Pontypridd CF37 2YA ☎ 01443 490227 🖷 01443 405184 ✉ lisa.austin@rhondda-cynon-taff.gov.uk

MEMBERS OF THE COUNCIL (75)

***Mayor:* Jones**, Sylvia (LAB - Llwynpia)
sylvia.j.jones@rhondda-cynon-taff.gov.uk

***Deputy Mayor:* Williams**, Doug (LAB - Glyncoch)
doug.williams@rhondda-cynon-taff.gov.uk

***Leader of the Council:* Christopher**, Anthony (LAB - Aberaman North)
anthony.christopher@rhondda-cynon-taff.gov.uk

***Deputy Leader of the Council:* Cannon**, Paul (LAB - Ystrad)
paul.cannon@rhondda-cynon-taff.gov.uk

Adams, Mark (LAB - Tylorstown)
lewis.m.adams@rhondda-cynon-taff.gov.uk

Baccara, Paul (IND - Talbot Green)
paul.baccara@rhondda-cynon-taff.gov.uk

Bates, Teressa (LAB - Hawthorn)
teressa.a.bates@rhondda-cynon-taff.gov.uk

Bevan, Robert (LAB - Tylorstown)
robert.bevan@rhondda-cynon-taff.gov.uk

Boggis, Helen (LAB - Penywaun)
Helen.Boggis@rhondda-cynon-taff.gov.uk

Bonetto, Jill (LAB - Taffs Well)
Jill.Bonetto@rhondda-cynon-taff.gov.uk

Bradwick, Steven (LAB - Aberdare East)
steven.a.bradwick@rhondda-cynon-taff.gov.uk

Bunnage, Jacqui (LAB - Llantwit Fardre)
Jacqui.Bunnage@rhondda-cynon-taff.gov.uk

Carter, Steve Laurence (LAB - Pontypridd Town)

Cass, Joyce (LAB - Graig)
joyce.cass@rhondda-cynon-taff.gov.uk

Crimmings, Ann (LAB - Aberdare West with Llwydcoed)
ann.crimmings@rhondda-cynon-taff.gov.uk

Culvert, Anita (LAB - Aberaman South)
Anita.Calvert@rhondda-cynon-taff.gov.uk

David, John (LAB - Tonteg)
john.david@rhondda-cynon-taff.gov.uk

Davies, Annette (LAB - Ferndale)
annette.davies@rhondda-cynon-taff.gov.uk

Davies, Margaret (LAB - Porth)
margaret.davies2@rhondda-cynon-taff.gov.uk

Davies, Albert (LAB - Abercynon)
alby.davies@rhondda-cynon-taff.gov.uk

Davies, Cennard (PC - Treorchy)

Davies, John (LAB - Aberdare West with Llwydcoed)
John.Davies2@rhondda-cynon-taff.gov.uk

Davies, Geraint (PC - Treherbert)
geraint.r.davies@btconnect.com

De Vet, Linda (LAB - Aberaman North)
linda.devet@rhondda-cynon-taff.gov.uk

Elliott, Jeffrey (LAB - Cwmbach)
Jeffrey.Elliott@rhondda-cynon-taff.gov.uk

Evans-Fear, Sera (PC - Treorchy)
treorci@yahoo.com

Forey, Michael (LAB - Aberdare East)
mike.forey@rhondda-cynon-taff.gov.uk

Fox, Adam (LAB - Penrhiwceiber)
adam.s.fox@rhondda-cynon-taff.gov.uk

Griffiths, Margaret (LAB - Pontyclun)
Margaret.Griffiths@rhondda-cynon-taff.gov.uk

Griffiths, Paul (LAB - Pontyclun)

Paul.Griffiths@rhondda-cynon-taff.gov.uk
Hanagan, Eudine (LAB - Tonyrefail West)
eudine.hanagan@rhondda-cynon-taff.gov.uk
Holmes, Glynne (LAB - Llantrisant Town)
glynne.holmes@rhondda-cynon-taff.gov.uk
Hopkins, Geraint (LAB - Llanharan)
geraint.e.hopkins@rhondda-cynon-taff.gov.uk
Howe, Philip (IND - Ferndale)
Philip.Howe@rhondda-cynon-taff.gov.uk
James, Joel (CON - Llantwit Fardre)
joel.s.james@rhondda-cynon-taff.gov.uk
Jarman, Pauline (PC - Mountain Ash East)
Langford, Lionel (LAB - Ynyshir)
lionel.langford@rhondda-cynon-taff.gov.uk
Lewis, Rhys (LAB - Abercynon)
Rhys.Lewis@rhondda-cynon-taff.gov.uk
Leyshon, Christina (LAB - Rhondda)
christina.leyshon@rhondda-cynon-taff.gov.uk
Lloyd, Simon (LAB - Mountain Ash West)
simon.lloyd@rhondda-cynon-taff.gov.uk
McDonald, Robert (LAB - Tonyrefail East)
robert.mcdonald@rhondda-cynon-taff.gov.uk
Middle, Craig (LAB - Tonypandy)
craig.j.middle@rhondda-cynon-taff.gov.uk
Montague, Keiron (LAB - Maerdy)
Morgan, Karen (PC - Hirwaun)
karen.morgan2@rhondda-cynon-taff.gov.uk
Morgan, Barrie (LAB - Cilfynydd)
barrie.j.morgan@rhondda-cynon-taff.gov.uk
Morgan, Andrew (LAB - Mountain Ash West)
andrew.morgan2@rhondda-cynon-taff.gov.uk
Norris, Mark (LAB - Cwm Clydach)
mark.a.norris@rhondda-cynon-taff.gov.uk
Pearce, Irene Elizabeth (PC - Treherbert)
Irene.E.Pearce@rhondda-cynon-taff.gov.uk
Pickering, Sue (LAB - Ynysybwl)
Sue.Pickering@rhondda-cynon-taff.gov.uk
Powderhill, Steve (LAB - Treforest)
Steve.Powderhill@rhondda-cynon-taff.gov.uk
Powell, Michael (LD - Trallwng)
michael.j.powell@rhondda-cynon-taff.gov.uk
Privett, Kenneth (LAB - Penygraig)
Rees, Sharon (LAB - Aberdare with Llwydcoed)
Sharon.Rees2@rhondda-cynon-taff.gov.uk
Rees-Owen, Shelley (PC - Pentre)
Shelley.Rees-Owen@rhondda-cynon-taff.gov.uk
Roberts, Aurfron (LAB - Gilfach Goch)
aurfron.roberts@rhondda-cynon-taff.gov.uk
Rosser, Joy (LAB - Trealaw)
Smith, Graham (LAB - Porth)
Graham.Smith@rhondda-cynon-taff.gov.uk
Smith, Robert (LAB - Rhondda)
robert.w.smith@rhondda-cynon-taff.gov.uk
Stacey, Graham (LAB - Church Village)
graham.stacey@rhondda-cynon-taff.gov.uk
Stephens, Barry (LAB - Llanharry)
Barry.Stephens2@rhondda-cynon-taff.gov.uk
Tegg, Margaret (LAB - Cymmer)
margaret.tegg@rhondda-cynon-taff.gov.uk
Thomas, Graham (LAB - Rhigos)
Graham.P.Thomas@rhondda-cynon-taff.gov.uk
Turner, Roger (LAB - Brynna)
roger.k.turner@rhondda-cynon-taff.gov.uk
Walker, Lyndon (IND - Tonteg)
Lyndon.Walker@rhondda-cynon-taff.gov.uk
Ward, Jane (LAB - Penrhiwceiber)
jane.ward@rhondda-cynon-taff.gov.uk
Wasley, Paul (IND - Tonyrefail East)
Paul.Wasley@rhondda-cynon-taff.gov.uk
Watts, John (LAB - Ystrad)
malcolm.j.watts@rhondda-cynon-taff.gov.uk
Weaver, Maureen (PC - Pentre)
Maureenowen54@gmail.com
Webber, Maureen (LAB - Rhydfelin Central)
maureen.webber@rhondda-cynon-taff.gov.uk
Webster, Emyr John (PC - Treorchy)
Emry.J.Webster@rhondda-cynon-taff.gov.uk
Weeks, Dennis (LAB - Penygraig)
william.d.weeks@rhondda-cynon-taff.gov.uk
Williams, Christopher (LAB - Cymmer)
christopher.j.williams3@rhondda-cynon-taff.gov.uk
Williams, Tina (LAB - Aberaman South)
Tina.Williams@rhondda-cynon-taff.gov.uk
Willis, Clayton (LAB - Tyn-y-Nant)
clayton.j.willis@rhondda-cynon-taff.gov.uk
Yeo, Richard (LAB - Beddau)
Richard.Yeo@rhondda-cynon-taff.gov.uk

POLITICAL COMPOSITION

LAB: 60, PC: 9, IND: 4, CON: 1, LD: 1

CABINET

Frontline Services: Mr Andrew Morgan
Leader of the Council: Mr Anthony Christopher
Deputy Leader, Economic Development & Community Safety: Mr Paul Cannon
Children's Social Services: Mrs Annette Davies
Council Business & Public Relations: Mrs Maureen Webber
Sustainable Development, Leisure & Tourism: Mr Robert Bevan
Education, Skills & Lifelong Learning: Ms Eudine Hanagan
Partnerships & Adults' Social Services: Mr Michael Forey
Human Resources & Service Improvement: Mr Clayton Willis
Social Justice: Mr Craig Middle

COMMITTEE CHAIRS

Appeals/Employee Appeals/Chief Officer Appeals: Mr Glynne Holmes
Appointments: Mrs Teressa Bates
Audit:
Community & Children's Services (Scrutiny): Ms Margaret Davies
Corporate Services (Scrutiny): Mr Graham Stacey
Development Control: Mr Robert McDonald
Education & Lifelong Learning (Scrutiny): Mrs Joyce Cass
Environmental Services (Scrutiny): Mr Geraint Davies
Licensing: Mr Adam Fox
Overview & Scrutiny: Mr Roger Turner

RIBBLE VALLEY D

Ribble Valley Borough Council, Council Offices, Church Walk, Clitheroe BB7 2RA ☎ 01200 425111 🖷 01200 414488
contact@ribblevalley.gov.uk 💻 www.ribblevalley.gov.uk

FACTS & FIGURES

Police Authority: Lancashire Police Authority

Health Authority: North West Strategic Health Authority
Learning and Skills Council: North West
Parliamentary Constituencies: Ribble Valley
EU Constituencies: North West
Election Frequency: Elections are of whole council

PRINCIPAL OFFICERS

Chief Executive: Mr Marshal Scott, Chief Executive, Council Offices, Church Walk, Clitheroe BB7 2RA ☎ 01200 425111 🖷 01200 414488

Deputy Chief Executive: Mr John Heap, Director of Community Services, Council Offices, Church Walk, Clitheroe BB7 2RA ☎ 01200 425111 🖷 01200 414488 ✉ john.heap@ribblevalley.gov.uk

Architect, Building / Property Services: Mr Terry Longden, Head of Engineering, Council Offices, Church Walk, Clitheroe BB7 2RA ☎ 0120042511

Architect, Building / Property Services: Mr Tim Lynas, Energy and Environment Manager, Council Offices, Church Walk, Clitheroe BB7 2RA ☎ 01200 413212 ✉ tim.lynas@ribblevalley.gov.uk

Best Value: Ms Jane Pearson, Director of Resources, Council Offices, Church Walk, Clitheroe BB7 2RA ☎ 01200 414430 ✉ jane.pearson@ribblevalley.gov.uk

Building Control: Mr James Russell, Head of Environmental Health, Council Offices, Church Walk, Clitheroe BB7 2RA ☎ 01200 425111 🖷 01200 414488 ✉ james.russell@ribblevalley.gov.uk

PR / Communications: Ms Theresa Robson, Communications Officer, Council Offices, Church Walk, Clitheroe BB7 2RA ☎ 01200 425111 🖷 01200 414488 ✉ theresa.robson@ribblevalley.gov.uk

PR / Communications: Mrs Michelle Smith, Head of HR, Council Offices, Church Walk, Clitheroe BB7 2RA ☎ 01200 425111 🖷 01200 414488 ✉ michelle.smith@ribblevalley.gov.uk

Community Planning: Mr Colin Hirst, Head of Regeneration & Housing, Council Offices, Church Walk, Clitheroe BB7 2RA ☎ 01200 425111 🖷 01200 414487 ✉ colin.hirst@ribblevalley.gov.uk

Community Safety: Mr William Alker, Policy Development Officer, Council Offices, Church Walk, Clitheroe BB7 2RA ☎ 01200 425111 🖷 01200 414488 ✉ bill.alker@ribblevalley.gov.uk

Computer Management: Mr Stuart Haworth, ICT Manager, Council Offices, Church Walk, Clitheroe BB7 2RA ☎ 01200 425111

Consumer Protection and Trading Standards: Mr James Russell, Head of Environmental Health, Council Offices, Church Walk, Clitheroe BB7 2RA ☎ 01200 425111 🖷 01200 414488 ✉ james.russell@ribblevalley.gov.uk

Contracts: Mr John Heap, Director of Community Services, Council Offices, Church Walk, Clitheroe BB7 2RA ☎ 01200 425111 🖷 01200 414488 ✉ john.heap@ribblevalley.gov.uk

Contracts: Mr Terry Longden, Head of Engineering, Council Offices, Church Walk, Clitheroe BB7 2RA ☎ 0120042511

Direct Labour: Mr Terry Longden, Head of Engineering, Council Offices, Church Walk, Clitheroe BB7 2RA ☎ 0120042511

Electoral Registration: Mrs Diane Rice, Head of Legal & Democratic Services, Council Offices, Church Walk, Clitheroe BB7 2RA ☎ 01200 425111 🖷 01200 414488 ✉ diane.rice@ribblevalley.gov.uk

Emergency Planning: Mr Chris Shuttleworth, Building Control Surveyor, Council Offices, Church Walk, Clitheroe BB7 2RA ☎ 01200 425111 🖷 01200 414488 ✉ chris.shuttleworth@ribblevalley.gov.uk

Energy Management: Mr Tim Lynas, Energy and Environment Manager, Council Offices, Church Walk, Clitheroe BB7 2RA ☎ 01200 413212 ✉ tim.lynas@ribblevalley.gov.uk

Environmental Health: Mr James Russell, Head of Environmental Health, Council Offices, Church Walk, Clitheroe BB7 2RA ☎ 01200 425111 🖷 01200 414488 ✉ james.russell@ribblevalley.gov.uk

Events Manager: Mr Tom Pridmore, Tourism & Events Officer, Council Offices, Church Walk, Clitheroe BB7 2RA ☎ 01200 425111

Finance and Treasurer: Ms Jane Pearson, Director of Resources, Council Offices, Church Walk, Clitheroe BB7 2RA ☎ 01200 414430 ✉ jane.pearson@ribblevalley.gov.uk

Grounds Maintenance: Mr Alan Boyer, Amenity Cleansing Manager, Council Offices, Church Walk, Clitheroe BB7 2RA ☎ 01200 425111 🖷 01200 414488 ✉ alan.boyer@ribblevalley.gov.uk

Health and Safety: Mr Phil Dodd, Health & Safety Officer, Council Offices, Church Walk, Clitheroe BB7 2RA ☎ 01200 425111 🖷 01200 414488 ✉ phil.dodd@ribblevalley.gov.uk

Health and Safety: Mrs Michelle Smith, Head of HR, Council Offices, Church Walk, Clitheroe BB7 2RA ☎ 01200 425111 🖷 01200 414488 ✉ michelle.smith@ribblevalley.gov.uk

Housing: Mr Colin Hirst, Head of Regeneration & Housing, Council Offices, Church Walk, Clitheroe BB7 2RA ☎ 01200 425111 🖷 01200 414487 ✉ colin.hirst@ribblevalley.gov.uk

Local Area Agreement: Mr Colin Hirst, Head of Regeneration & Housing, Council Offices, Church Walk, Clitheroe BB7 2RA ☎ 01200 425111 🖷 01200 414487 ✉ colin.hirst@ribblevalley.gov.uk

Legal: Mrs Diane Rice, Head of Legal & Democratic Services, Council Offices, Church Walk, Clitheroe BB7 2RA ☎ 01200 425111 🖷 01200 414488 ✉ diane.rice@ribblevalley.gov.uk

Leisure and Cultural Services: Mr Chris Hughes, Head of Cultural & Leisure Services, Council Offices, Church Walk, Clitheroe BB7 2RA ☎ 01200 425111 🖷 01200 414488 ✉ chris.hughes@ribblevalley.gov.uk

Licensing: Mrs Diane Rice, Head of Legal & Democratic Services, Council Offices, Church Walk, Clitheroe BB7 2RA ☎ 01200 425111 🖷 01200 414488 ✉ diane.rice@ribblevalley.gov.uk

Lifelong Learning: Mrs Michelle Smith, Head of HR, Council Offices, Church Walk, Clitheroe BB7 2RA ☎ 01200 425111 🖷 01200 414488 ✉ michelle.smith@ribblevalley.gov.uk

Lottery Funding, Charity and Voluntary: Mr Chris Hughes, Head of Cultural & Leisure Services, Council Offices, Church Walk, Clitheroe BB7 2RA ☎ 01200 425111 🖷 01200 414488 ✉ chris.hughes@ribblevalley.gov.uk

Member Services: Mrs Diane Rice, Head of Legal & Democratic Services, Council Offices, Church Walk, Clitheroe BB7 2RA ☎ 01200 425111 🖷 01200 414488 ✉ diane.rice@ribblevalley.gov.uk

Personnel / HR: Mrs Michelle Smith, Head of HR, Council Offices, Church Walk, Clitheroe BB7 2RA ☎ 01200 425111 🖷 01200 414488 ✉ michelle.smith@ribblevalley.gov.uk

Planning: Mr John Macholc, Head of Planning Services, Ribble Valley Borough Council, Church Walk, Clitheroe BB7 2RA ☎ 01200 425111 🖷 01200 414488 ✉ contact@ribblevalley.gov.uk

Procurement: Ms Jane Pearson, Director of Resources, Council Offices, Church Walk, Clitheroe BB7 2RA ☎ 01200 414430 ✉ jane.pearson@ribblevalley.gov.uk

Recycling & Waste Minimisation: Mr John Heap, Director of Community Services, Council Offices, Church Walk, Clitheroe BB7 2RA ☎ 01200 425111 🖷 01200 414488 ✉ john.heap@ribblevalley.gov.uk

Recycling & Waste Minimisation: Mr Terry Longden, Head of Engineering, Council Offices, Church Walk, Clitheroe BB7 2RA ☎ 01200425111

Recycling & Waste Minimisation: Mr Peter McGeorge, Waste Management Officer, Council Offices, Church Walk, Clitheroe BB7 2RA ☎ 01200 425111 🖷 01200 414488 ✉ peter.mcgeorge@ribblevalley.gov.uk

Staff Training: Mrs Michelle Smith, Head of HR, Council Offices, Church Walk, Clitheroe BB7 2RA ☎ 01200 425111 🖷 01200 414488 ✉ michelle.smith@ribblevalley.gov.uk

Street Scene: Mr Terry Longden, Head of Engineering, Council Offices, Church Walk, Clitheroe BB7 2RA ☎ 01200425111

Sustainable Communities: Mr Colin Hirst, Head of Regeneration & Housing, Council Offices, Church Walk, Clitheroe BB7 2RA ☎ 01200 425111 🖷 01200 414487 ✉ colin.hirst@ribblevalley.gov.uk

Tourism: Mr Chris Hughes, Head of Cultural & Leisure Services, Council Offices, Church Walk, Clitheroe BB7 2RA ☎ 01200 425111 🖷 01200 414488 ✉ chris.hughes@ribblevalley.gov.uk

Tourism: Mr Tom Pridmore, Tourism & Events Officer, Council Offices, Church Walk, Clitheroe BB7 2RA ☎ 01200 425111

Waste Collection and Disposal: Mr John Heap, Director of Community Services, Council Offices, Church Walk, Clitheroe BB7 2RA ☎ 01200 425111 🖷 01200 414488 ✉ john.heap@ribblevalley.gov.uk

Waste Collection and Disposal: Mr Terry Longden, Head of Engineering, Council Offices, Church Walk, Clitheroe BB7 2RA ☎ 01200425111

Waste Management: Mr John Heap, Director of Community Services, Council Offices, Church Walk, Clitheroe BB7 2RA ☎ 01200 425111 🖷 01200 414488 ✉ john.heap@ribblevalley.gov.uk

Waste Management: Mr Terry Longden, Head of Engineering, Council Offices, Church Walk, Clitheroe BB7 2RA ☎ 01200425111

Waste Management: Mr Peter McGeorge, Waste Management Officer, Council Offices, Church Walk, Clitheroe BB7 2RA ☎ 01200 425111 🖷 01200 414488 ✉ peter.mcgeorge@ribblevalley.gov.uk

Children's Play Areas: Mr Terry Longden, Head of Engineering, Council Offices, Church Walk, Clitheroe BB7 2RA ☎ 01200425111

MEMBERS OF THE COUNCIL (40)

***Mayor:* Sayers**, Ian (CON - Ribchester)
cllr.sayers@ribblevalley.gov.uk
***Deputy Mayor:* Sherras**, Richard (CON - Gisburn and Rimington)
cllr.sherras@ribblevalley.gov.uk
***Leader of the Council:* Ranson**, Michael (CON - Waddington and West Bradford)
cllr.ranson@ribblevalley.gov.uk
***Group Leader:* Knox**, Allan (LD - Primrose)
cllr.knox@ribblevalley.gov.uk
Ainsworth, Peter (CON - Clayton-le-Dale with Ramsgreave)
cllr.ainsworth@ribblevalley.gov.uk
Alcock, Janet (CON - Aighton, Bailey and Chaigley)
Bennett, Richard (CON - Read and Simonstone)
cllr.bennett@ribblevalley.gov.uk
Bibby, Susan (CON - Wilpshire)
cllr.bibby@ribblevalley.gov.uk
Brown, Ian (CON - Salthill)
cllr.brown@ribblevalley.gov.uk
Brunskill, Stella (CON - Mellor)
cllr.brunskill@ribblevalley.gov.uk
Carefoot, Stuart (CON - Derby and Thornley)
cllr.carefoot@ribblevalley.gov.uk
Conner, Christine (CON - Littlemoor)
cllr.conner@ribblevalley.gov.uk
Dowson, Pamela (CON - Salthill)
cllr.dowson@ribblevalley.gov.uk
Elms, Rosemary (CON - Bowland, Newton and Slaidburn)
cllr.elms@ribblevalley.gov.uk
Hargreaves, Ruth (LD - Edisford and Low Moor)
cllr.hargreaves@ribblevalley.gov.uk
Hill, Terry (CON - Whalley)
cllr.thill@ribblevalley.gov.uk
Hill, John (CON - Read and Simonstone)
cllr.hill@ribblevalley.gov.uk
Hilton, Bridget (CON - Waddington and West Bradford)
cllr.hilton@ribblevalley.gov.uk
Hind, Ken (CON - Dilworth)
cllr.hind@ribblevalley.gov.uk

Hirst, Stuart (CON - Wilpshire)
cllr.hirst@ribblevalley.gov.uk
Holgate, Joyce (CON - Whalley)
cllr.holgate@ribblevalley.gov.uk
Hore, Simon (CON - Chipping)
cllr.hore@ribblevalley.gov.uk
Horkin, Kevin (CON - St Marys)
cllr.horkin@ribblevalley.gov.uk
Knox, Susan (LD - Littlemoor)
cllr.sknox@ribblevalley.gov.uk
Mirfin, Ged (CON - Billington and Old Langho)
cllr.mirfin@ribblevalley.gov.uk
Moores, Ruth (CON - St Marys)
cllr.moores@ribblevalley.gov.uk
Newmark, Richard (CON - Sabden)
cllr.newmark@ribblevalley.gov.uk
Rimmer, Lois (CON - Langho)
cllr.rimmer@ribblevalley.gov.uk
Robinson, Mary (LD - Primrose)
cllr.robinson@ribblevalley.gov.uk
Rogerson, James (IND - Alston and Hothersall)
cllr.rogerson@ribblevalley.gov.uk
Ross, Carl (CON - Billington and Old Langho)
cllr.ross@ribblevalley.gov.uk
Scott, Gary (CON - Chatburn)
cllr.scott@ribblevalley.gov.uk
Smith, David (CON - Alston and Hothersall)
cllr.smith@ribblevalley.gov.uk
Swarbrick, Rupert (CON - Dilworth)
cllr.swarbrick@ribblevalley.gov.uk
Taylor, Doreen (CON - Clayton-le-Dale with Ramsgreave)
cllr.dtaylor@ribblevalley.gov.uk
Thomas, Mike (CON - Langho)
cllr.thomas@ribblevalley.gov.uk
Thompson, Robert (CON - Wiswell and Pendleton)
cllr.thompson@ribblevalley.gov.uk
Walsh, Noel (CON - Mellor)
cllr.walsh@ribblevalley.gov.uk
White, Jim (CON - Derby and Thornley)
cllr.white@ribblevalley.gov.uk
Yearing, Alan (LD - Edisford and Low Moor)
cllr.yearing@ribblevalley.gov.uk

POLITICAL COMPOSITION
CON: 34, LD: 5, IND: 1

COMMITTEE CHAIRS
Accounts & Audit: Mr Richard Sherras
Community Services: Mr Robert Thompson
Health & Housing: Mr Stuart Hirst
Licensing: Ms Janet Alcock
Personnel: Ms Rosemary Elms
Planning & Development: Mr Richard Sherras
Policy & Finance: Mr Michael Ranson

RICHMOND UPON THAMES L

Richmond upon Thames London Borough Council, Civic Centre, 44 York Street, Twickenham TW1 3BZ ☎ 020 8891 1411
press-pr@richmond.gov.uk www.richmond.gov.uk

FACTS & FIGURES
Police Authority: Metropolitan Police Authority
Health Authority: NHS London
Learning and Skills Council: London
Parliamentary Constituencies: Richmond Park, Twickenham
EU Constituencies: London
Election Frequency: Elections are of whole council
Twinning: Fontainebleau (France); Konstanz (Germany); Richmond (Virginia, USA)

PRINCIPAL OFFICERS
Chief Executive: Ms Gillian Norton, Chief Executive, Civic Centre, 44 York Street, Twickenham TW1 3BZ ☎ 020 8891 1411 🖷 020 8891 7703 g.norton@richmond.gov.uk

Senior Management: Mr Paul Chadwick, Director of Environment, Civic Centre, 44 York Street, Twickenham TW1 3BZ ☎ 020 8891 7870 🖷 020 8891 7361 p.chadwick@richmond.gov.uk

Senior Management: Ms Cathy Kerr, Director of Adult & Community Services, Civic Centre, 44 York Street, Twickenham TW1 3BZ ☎ 020 8891 7360 🖷 020 8891 7703 cathy.kerr@richmond.gov.uk

Senior Management: Mr Mark Maidment, Director of Finance & Corporate Services, York House Annexe, York House, Twickenham TW1 3AA ☎ 020 8891 7171 🖷 020 8891 7333 m.maidment@richmond.gov.uk

Senior Management: Mr Nick Whitfield, Director of Education, Children's Services & Culture, Civic Centre, 44 York Street, Twickenham TW1 3BZ ☎ 020 8891 7906 🖷 020 8831 6216 nick.whitfield@richmond.gov.uk

Architect, Building / Property Services: Mr Paul Chadwick, Director of Environment, Civic Centre, 44 York Street, Twickenham TW1 3BZ ☎ 020 8891 7870 🖷 020 8891 7361 p.chadwick@richmond.gov.uk

Best Value: Ms Gill Ford, Head of Performance & Quality Assurance, Civic Centre, 44 York Street, Twickenham TW1 3BZ ☎ 020 8487 5016 🖷 020 8487 5026 g.ford@richmond.gov.uk

Building Control: Mr David Batsford, Chief Building Surveyor, 2nd Floor, Civic Centre, 44 York Street, Twickenham TW1 3BZ ☎ 020 8891 7346 🖷 020 8891 7347 d.batsford@richmond.gov.uk

Children / Youth Services: Ms Barbara Murray, Assistant Director - Specialist Children's Services, Room 1, First Floor, 42 York Street, Twickenham TW1 3BW ☎ 020 8891 7678 🖷 020 8891 7719 b.murray@richmond.gov.uk

Civil Registration: Miss Alison Parr, Superintendent Registrar, Register Office, 1 Spring Terrace, Richmond TW9 1LW ☎ 020 8940 2853 🖷 020 8940 8226 alison.parr@richmond.gov.uk

PR / Communications: Ms Elinor Ridgeway, Head of Communications, Civic Centre, 44 York Street, Twickenham TW1 3BZ ☎ 020 8487 5159 🖷 020 8891 7718 e.ridgeway@richmond.gov.uk

PR / Communications: Ms Katrina Waite, Community Engagement Manager, Civic Centre, 44 York Street, Twickenham

TW1 3BZ ☎ 020 8831 6289 ✉ katrina.waite@richmond.gov.uk

Community Planning: Ms Mandy Skinner, Assistant Director - Commissioning, Corporate Policy & Strategy, Civic Centre, 44 York Street, Twickenham TW1 3BZ ☎ 020 8891 7929 🖷 020 8891 7703 ✉ mandy.skinner@richmond.gov.uk

Community Planning: Ms Katrina Waite, Community Engagement Manager, Civic Centre, 44 York Street, Twickenham TW1 3BZ ☎ 020 8831 6289 ✉ katrina.waite@richmond.gov.uk

Computer Management: Mr Adrian Boylan, Head of ICT, Civic Centre, 44 York Street, Twickenham TW1 3BZ ☎ 020 8891 7917 ✉ a.boylan@richmond.gov.uk

Computer Management: Mr Mike Gravatt, Assistant Director of Finance & Corporate Services, Civic Centre, 44 York Street, Twickenham TW1 3BZ ☎ 020 8891 7238 🖷 020 8891 7233 ✉ m.gravatt@richmond.gov.uk

Consumer Protection and Trading Standards: Ms Laura Aston, Head of Consumer Protection, Civic Centre, 44 York Street, Twickenham TW1 3BZ ☎ 020 8891 7988 🖷 020 8891 7451 ✉ l.aston@richmond.gov.uk

Consumer Protection and Trading Standards: Ms Pauline Kirby, Head of Consumer Protection, Civic Centre, 44 York Street, Twickenham TW1 3BZ ☎ 020 8891 7988 🖷 020 8891 7451 ✉ p.kirby@richmond.gov.uk

Corporate Services: Ms Gill Ford, Head of Performance & Quality Assurance, Civic Centre, 44 York Street, Twickenham TW1 3BZ ☎ 020 8487 5016 🖷 020 8487 5026 ✉ g.ford@richmond.gov.uk

Corporate Services: Mr Mark Maidment, Director of Finance & Corporate Services, York House Annexe, York House, Twickenham TW1 3AA ☎ 020 8891 7171 🖷 020 8891 7333 ✉ m.maidment@richmond.gov.uk

Corporate Services: Ms Carol McBean, Head of Corporate Partnership, Civic Centre, 44 York Street, Twickenham TW1 3BZ ☎ 020 8831 6231 ✉ c.macbean@richmond.gov.uk

Customer Service: Ms Dawn Cooper, Head of Customer Services, Civic Centre, 44 York Street, Twickenham TW1 3BZ ☎ 020 8487 5180 ✉ dawn.cooper@richmond.gov.uk

Direct Labour: Mr Andrew Darvill, Assistant Director - Highways & Transport, Civic Centre, 44 York Street, Twickenham TW1 3BZ ☎ 020 8891 7070 🖷 020 8891 7923 ✉ a.darvill@richmond.gov.uk

Economic Development: Mr Sean Gillen, Economic Development Manager, Civic Centre, 44 York Street, Twickenham TW1 3BZ ☎ 020 8831 6219 🖷 020 8891 7347 ✉ sean.gillen@richmond.gov.uk

Education: Mr Nick Whitfield, Director of Education, Children's Services & Culture, Civic Centre, 44 York Street, Twickenham TW1 3BZ ☎ 020 8891 7906 🖷 020 8831 6216 ✉ nick.whitfield@richmond.gov.uk

E-Government: Mr Mike Gravatt, Assistant Director of Finance & Corporate Services, Civic Centre, 44 York Street, Twickenham TW1 3BZ ☎ 020 8891 7238 🖷 020 8891 7233 ✉ m.gravatt@richmond.gov.uk

Electoral Registration: Mrs Stephanie Bishop, Acting Electoral Services Manager, 1-3 Richmond Road, Twickenham TW1 3AB ☎ 020 8891 7196 🖷 020 8891 7184 ✉ s.bishop@richmond.gov.uk

Emergency Planning: Mr Joe Halanen, Resilience Manager, Thames Link House, 1 Church Road, Richmond TW9 2QE ☎ 020 8891 7817 🖷 020 8332 1474

Energy Management: Miss Ishbel Murray, Assistant Director of Environment - Property, Parks & Sustainability, Civic Centre, 44 York Street, Twickenham TW1 3BZ ☎ 020 8891 7310 ✉ ishbel.murray@richmond.gov.uk

Environmental / Technical Services: Mr Paul Chadwick, Director of Environment, Civic Centre, 44 York Street, Twickenham TW1 3BZ ☎ 020 8891 7870 🖷 020 8891 7361 ✉ p.chadwick@richmond.gov.uk

Environmental Health: Mr Robert Angus, Head of Development & Enforcement, Civic Centre, 44 York Street, Twickenham TW1 3BZ ☎ 020 8891 7271 🖷 020 8891 7789 ✉ r.angus@richmond.gov.uk

Estates, Property & Valuation: Mr Paul Chadwick, Director of Environment, Civic Centre, 44 York Street, Twickenham TW1 3BZ ☎ 020 8891 7870 🖷 020 8891 7361 ✉ p.chadwick@richmond.gov.uk

Estates, Property & Valuation: Mr Peter Southcombe, Head of Estates & Valuation, Civic Centre, 44 York Street, Twickenham TW1 3BZ ☎ 020 8487 5118 🖷 020 8487 5125 ✉ p.southcombe@richmond.gov.uk

Facilities: Mr Paul Cook, Corporate Facilities Manager, Civic Centre, 44 York Street, Twickenham TW1 3BZ ☎ 020 8891 7463 🖷 020 8891 7858 ✉ p.cook@richmond.gov.uk

Finance and Treasurer: Mr Mike Gravatt, Assistant Director of Finance & Corporate Services, Civic Centre, 44 York Street, Twickenham TW1 3BZ ☎ 020 8891 7238 🖷 020 8891 7233 ✉ m.gravatt@richmond.gov.uk

Finance and Treasurer: Mr Mark Maidment, Director of Finance & Corporate Services, York House Annexe, York House, Twickenham TW1 3AA ☎ 020 8891 7171 🖷 020 8891 7333 ✉ m.maidment@richmond.gov.uk

Fleet Management: Mr Andrew Darvill, Assistant Director - Highways & Transport, Civic Centre, 44 York Street, Twickenham TW1 3BZ ☎ 020 8891 7070 🖷 020 8891 7923 ✉ a.darvill@richmond.gov.uk

Grounds Maintenance: Mr Paul Chadwick, Director of Environment, Civic Centre, 44 York Street, Twickenham TW1 3BZ ☎ 020 8891 7870 🖷 020 8891 7361 ✉ p.chadwick@richmond.gov.uk

Health and Safety: Mr Jon Robinson, Corporate Health & Safety Manager, Civic Centre, 44 York Street, Twickenham TW1 3BZ ☎ 020 8891 7330 🖷 020 8891 7858 ✉ jonathan.robinson@richmond.gov.uk

Highways: Mr Andrew Darvill, Assistant Director - Highways & Transport, Civic Centre, 44 York Street, Twickenham TW1 3BZ ☎ 020 8891 7070 🖷 020 8891 7923 ✉ a.darvill@richmond.gov.uk

Highways: Mr Aurang Zeb, Head of Highways & Transport, Civic Centre, 44 York Street, Twickenham TW1 3BZ ☎ 020 8487 5432 ✉ aurang.zeb@richmond.gov.uk

Home Energy Conservation: Mr Colin Coomber, Energy Efficiency Co-ordinator, Civic Centre, 44 York Street, Twickenham TW1 3BZ ☎ 020 8891 7663 🖷 020 8831 6404 ✉ c.coomber@richmond.gov.uk

Housing: Mr Brian Castle, Assistant Director - Community Service Operations, Civic Centre, 44 York Street, Twickenham TW1 3BZ ☎ 020 8891 7482 🖷 020 8891 7792 ✉ b.castle@richmond.gov.uk

Housing: Mr Ken Emerson, Head of Housing Operations, Civic Centre, 44 York Street, Twickenham TW1 3BZ ☎ 020 8831 6406 🖷 020 8891 7403 ✉ k.emerson@richmond.gov.uk

Local Area Agreement: Ms Carol MacBean, Head of Strategy and Policy, Civic Centre, 44 York Street, Twickenham TW1 3BZ ☎ 020 8831 6231 ✉ c.macbean@richmond.gov.uk

Legal: Mr Paul Evans, Assistant Director of Corporate Governance and Head of Shared Legal Services Richmond and Merton, 1st Floor, Gifford House Legal Services, 67c St Helier Avenue, Morden SM4 6HY ☎ 020 8545 3338 ✉ paul.evans@merton.gov.uk.cjsm.net

Leisure and Cultural Services: Mr Colin Sinclair, Head of Sport & Fitness, Regal House, London Road, Twickenham TW1 3QB ☎ 020 8831 6140 🖷 020 8891 7904 ✉ c.sinclair@richmond.gov.uk

Leisure and Cultural Services: Mr Nick Whitfield, Director of Education, Children's Services & Culture, Civic Centre, 44 York Street, Twickenham TW1 3BZ ☎ 020 8891 7906 🖷 020 8831 6216 ✉ nick.whitfield@richmond.gov.uk

Licensing: Ms Laura Aston, Head of Consumer Protection, Civic Centre, 44 York Street, Twickenham TW1 3BZ ☎ 020 8891 7988 🖷 020 8891 7451 ✉ l.aston@richmond.gov.uk

Licensing: Ms Pauline Kirby, Head of Consumer Protection, Civic Centre, 44 York Street, Twickenham TW1 3BZ ☎ 020 8891 7988 🖷 020 8891 7451 ✉ p.kirby@richmond.gov.uk

Lifelong Learning: Mr Ian Dodds, Head of Culture and Service Improvement, Regal House, London Road, Twickenham TW1 3BQ ☎ 020 8831 6116 🖷 020 8891 7714 ✉ ian.dodds@richmond.gov.uk

Lighting: Mr Andrew Darvill, Assistant Director - Highways & Transport, Civic Centre, 44 York Street, Twickenham TW1 3BZ ☎ 020 8891 7070 🖷 020 8891 7923 ✉ a.darvill@richmond.gov.uk

Member Services: Ms Kathryn Thomas, Head of Democratic Services, York House, Richmond Road, Twickenham TW1 3AA ☎ 020 8891 7860 🖷 020 8891 7701 ✉ kathryn.thomas@richmond.gov.uk

Parking: Mr Andrew Darvill, Assistant Director - Highways & Transport, Civic Centre, 44 York Street, Twickenham TW1 3BZ ☎ 020 8891 7070 🖷 020 8891 7923 ✉ a.darvill@richmond.gov.uk

Personnel / HR: Ms Sheila West, Corporate Head of Human Resources for Kingston and Richmond, Guildhall 2, High Street, Kingston upon Thames KT1 1EU ☎ 020 8547 5153 ✉ sheila.west@rbk.kingston.gov.uk

Planning: Mr Robert Angus, Head of Development & Enforcement, Civic Centre, 44 York Street, Twickenham TW1 3BZ ☎ 020 8891 7271 🖷 020 8891 7789 ✉ r.angus@richmond.gov.uk

Public Libraries: Mr Ian Dodds, Head of Culture and Service Improvement, Regal House, London Road, Twickenham TW1 3BQ ☎ 020 8831 6116 🖷 020 8891 7714 ✉ ian.dodds@richmond.gov.uk

Recycling & Waste Minimisation: Ms Eve Risbridger, Head of Street Scene, Central Depot, Langhorn Drive, Twickenham TW2 7SG ☎ 020 8891 6334 🖷 020 8891 7787 ✉ e.risbridger@richmond.gov.uk

Regeneration: Mr Philip Wealthy, Head of Policy & Design, Civic Centre, 44 York Street, Twickenham TW1 3BZ ☎ 020 8891 7320 🖷 020 8891 7703 ✉ p.wealthy@richmond.gov.uk

Road Safety: Mr Sam Merison, Principal Safety Education Officer, Civic Centre, 44 York Street, Twickenham TW1 3BZ ☎ 020 8487 5356 ✉ sam.merison@richmond.gov.uk

Social Services: Ms Cathy Kerr, Director of Adult & Community Services, Civic Centre, 44 York Street, Twickenham TW1 3BZ ☎ 020 8891 7360 🖷 020 8891 7703 ✉ cathy.kerr@richmond.gov.uk

Social Services (Adult): Mr Derek Oliver, Assistant Director of Community Care Services, Civic Centre, 44 York Street, Twickenham TW1 3BZ ☎ 020 8891 7608 ✉ derek.oliver@richmond.gov.uk

Social Services (Children): Ms Barbara Murray, Assistant Director - Specialist Children's Services, Room 1, First Floor, 42 York Street, Twickenham TW1 3BW ☎ 020 8891 7678 🖷 020 8891 7719 ✉ b.murray@richmond.gov.uk

Street Scene: Ms Eve Risbridger, Head of Street Scene, Central Depot, Langhorn Drive, Twickenham TW2 7SG ☎ 020 8891 6334 🖷 020 8891 7787 ✉ e.risbridger@richmond.gov.uk

Sustainable Communities: Mr Robert Angus, Head of Development & Enforcement, Civic Centre, 44 York Street, Twickenham TW1 3BZ ☎ 020 8891 7271 🖷 020 8891 7789 ✉ r.angus@richmond.gov.uk

Sustainable Development: Miss Ishbel Murray, Assistant Director of Environment - Property, Parks & Sustainability, Civic Centre, 44 York Street, Twickenham TW1 3BZ ☎ 020 8891 7310 ✉ ishbel.murray@richmond.gov.uk

Tourism: Ms Angela Ivey, Principal Tourism & Marketing Manager, Civic Centre, 44 York Street, Twickenham TW1 3BZ ☎ 020 8487 5047 🖷 020 8891 7347 a.ivey@richmond.gov.uk

Traffic Management: Mr Andrew Darvill, Assistant Director - Highways & Transport, Civic Centre, 44 York Street, Twickenham TW1 3BZ ☎ 020 8891 7070 🖷 020 8891 7923 a.darvill@richmond.gov.uk

Transport: Mr Andrew Darvill, Assistant Director - Highways & Transport, Civic Centre, 44 York Street, Twickenham TW1 3BZ ☎ 020 8891 7070 🖷 020 8891 7923 a.darvill@richmond.gov.uk

Transport: Mr Aurang Zeb, Head of Highways & Transport, Civic Centre, 44 York Street, Twickenham TW1 3BZ ☎ 020 8487 5432 aurang.zeb@richmond.gov.uk

Transport Planner: Mr Aurang Zeb, Head of Highways & Transport, Civic Centre, 44 York Street, Twickenham TW1 3BZ ☎ 020 8487 5432 aurang.zeb@richmond.gov.uk

Waste Collection and Disposal: Ms Eve Risbridger, Head of Street Scene, Central Depot, Langhorn Drive, Twickenham TW2 7SG ☎ 020 8891 6334 🖷 020 8891 7787 e.risbridger@richmond.gov.uk

Waste Management: Ms Eve Risbridger, Head of Street Scene, Central Depot, Langhorn Drive, Twickenham TW2 7SG ☎ 020 8891 6334 🖷 020 8891 7787 e.risbridger@richmond.gov.uk

Children's Play Areas: Mr David Allister, Head of Parks & Open Spaces, Civic Centre, 44 York Street, Twickenham TW1 3BZ ☎ 020 8831 6135 d.allister@richmond.gov.uk

MEMBERS OF THE COUNCIL (54)

***Mayor:* Palmer**, Rita (CON - Barnes)
cllr.rpalmer@richmond.gov.uk
***Deputy Mayor:* Blakemore**, Lisa (CON - North Richmond)
cllr.lblakemore@richmond.gov.uk
***Leader of the Council:* True**, Nicholas (CON - East Sheen)
cllr.lordtrue@richmond.gov.uk
***Deputy Leader of the Council:* Samuel**, Geoffrey (CON - Hampton North)
cllr.gsamuel@richmond.gov.uk
***Group Leader:* Knight**, Stephen (LD - Teddington)
cllr.sknight@richmond.gov.uk
Acton, Geoff (LD - St Margaret's and North Twickenham)
cllr.gacton@richmond.gov.uk
Allen, Piers (LD - West Twickenham)
cllr.pallen@richmond.gov.uk
Arbour, Tony (CON - Hampton Wick)
cllr.tarbour@richmond.gov.uk
Avon, Paul (CON - Mortlake and Barnes Common)
cllr.pavon@richmond.gov.uk
Bond, Meena (CON - Kew)
cllr.mbond@richmond.gov.uk
Bouchier, Frances (CON - South Richmond)
cllr.fbouchier@richmond.gov.uk
Burford, Jean-Francois (LD - Kew)
cllr.jburford@richmond.gov.uk
Butler, Alan (CON - Heathfield)
cllr.abutler@richmond.gov.uk
Cardy, Jonathan (LD - Fulwell and Hampton Hill)
cllr.jcardy@richmond.gov.uk
Chappell, Susan (CON - Twickenham Riverside)
cllr.schappell@richmond.gov.uk
Churchill, Jennifer (LD - Teddington)
cllr.jchurchill@richmond.gov.uk
Coombs, John (LD - Heathfield)
cllr.jcoombs@richmond.gov.uk
Day, Ellen (LD - Hampton North)
cllr.eday@richmond.gov.uk
Eady, Malcolm (LD - Fulwell and Hampton Hill)
cllr.meady@richmond.gov.uk
Elengorn, Martin (LD - Teddington)
cllr.melengorn@richmond.gov.uk
Elliot, Gareth (CON - Whitton)
cllr.gelliot@richmond.gov.uk
Elloy, Jerry (LD - Fulwell and Hampton Hill)
cllr.jelloy@richmond.gov.uk
Evans, Gareth (CON - Hampton Wick)
cllr.gevans@richmond.gov.uk
Fleming, Pamela (CON - South Richmond)
cllr.pfleming@richmond.gov.uk
Gibbons, Arnie (LD - Whitton)
cllr.agibbons@richmond.gov.uk
Harborne, Katharine (CON - North Richmond)
cllr.kharborne@richmond.gov.uk
Harrison, Chris (CON - St Margaret's and North Twickenham)
cllr.charrison@richmond.gov.uk
Head, Clare (CON - South Twickenham)
cllr.chead@richmond.gov.uk
Hodgins, Paul (CON - Barnes)
cllr.phodgins@richmond.gov.uk
Jaeger, Liz (LD - Whitton)
cllr.ljaeger@richmond.gov.uk
Jones, Sue (LD - Ham, Petersham and Richmond Riverside)
cllr.sjones@richmond.gov.uk
Khosa, Ben (LD - St Margaret's and North Twickenham)
cllr.bkhosa@richmond.gov.uk
Langhorne, Janet (LD - Hampton)
cllr.jlanghorne@richmond.gov.uk
Lee-Parsons, Helen (LD - West Twickenham)
cllr.hlee-parsons@richmond.gov.uk
Linnette, David (CON - Kew)
cllr.dlinnette@richmond.gov.uk
Marlow, David (CON - South Twickenham)
cllr.dmarlow@richmond.gov.uk
Martin, Richard (CON - Mortlake and Barnes Common)
cllr.rmartin@richmond.gov.uk
Mathias, Tania (CON - Hampton Wick)
cllr.tmathias@richmond.gov.uk
Miller, Brian (LD - Ham, Petersham and Richmond Riverside)
cllr.bmiller@richmond.gov.uk
Morris, Virginia (CON - East Sheen)
cllr.vmorris@richmond.gov.uk
Naylor, Scott (CON - Twickenham Riverside)
cllr.snaylor@richmond.gov.uk
Nicholson, Suzette (LD - Hampton)
cllr.snicholson@richmond.gov.uk
O'Malley, Thomas (CON - South Richmond)
cllr.tomalley@richmond.gov.uk
Percival, Christine (CON - Barnes)
cllr.cpercival@richmond.gov.uk
Pollesche, Lesley (LD - West Twickenham)
cllr.lpollesche@richmond.gov.uk
Porter, David (CON - South Twickenham)
cllr.dporter@richmond.gov.uk

Roberts, Gareth (LD - Hampton)
cllr.groberts@richmond.gov.uk
Salvoni, Samantha (CON - Twickenham Riverside)
cllr.ssalvoni@richmond.gov.uk
Speak, Stephen (CON - North Richmond)
democratic.services@richmond.gov.uk
Stockley, Gemma (CON - Mortlake and Barnes Common)
cllr.gstockley@richmond.gov.uk
Thornton, Darren (LD - Hampton North)
cllr.dthornton@richmond.gov.uk
Treble, Bill (LD - Heathfield)
cllr.wtreble@richmond.gov.uk
Urquhart, Nicola (CON - East Sheen)
cllr.nurquhart@richmond.gov.uk
Williams, David (LD - Ham, Petersham and Richmond Riverside)
cllr.dwilliams@richmond.gov.uk

POLITICAL COMPOSITION
CON: 30, LD: 24

CABINET
Community Development: Mr David Marlow
Leader: Lord Nicholas True
Deputy; Resources: Mr Geoffrey Samuel
Adult Services, Health & Housing: Ms Nicola Urquhart
Community Development: Mr David Marlow
Education, Youth & Children's Services: Ms Christine Percival
Environment, Planning, Parks & Highways: Ms Virginia Morris
Performance: Mr Tony Arbour
Schools: Mr Paul Hodgins
Community, Business & Culture: Ms Pamela Fleming
Highways & Street Scene: Mr Chris Harrison

COMMITTEE CHAIRS
Audit: Mr Jonathan Cardy
Education & Children's Services (Scrutiny): Mr Gareth Evans
Environment, Sustainability & Community (Scrutiny): Mr David Porter
Finance & Performance (Scrutiny): Mr Brian Miller
Health, Housing & Adult Services (Scrutiny): Ms Sue Jones
Pension Fund: Mr Geoff Acton
Planning: Mr David Linnette
Regulatory: Ms Susan Chappell
Statutory Accounts: Lord Nicholas True

RICHMONDSHIRE D

Richmondshire District Council, Swale House, Frenchgate, Richmond DL10 4JE ☎ 01748 829100 🖷 01748 825071 ✉ enquiries@richmondshire.gov.uk 🖳 www.richmondshire.gov.uk

FACTS & FIGURES
Police Authority: North Yorkshire Police Authority
Health Authority: NHS Yorkshire & the Humber
Learning and Skills Council: Yorkshire and the Humber
Parliamentary Constituencies: Richmond (Yorks)
EU Constituencies: Yorkshire and the Humber
Election Frequency: Elections are of whole council

PRINCIPAL OFFICERS
Deputy Chief Executive: Mr Tony Clark, Deputy Chief Executive, Swale House, Frenchgate, Richmond DL10 4JE ☎ 01748 829100 🖷 01748 829132 ✉ tony.clark@richmondshire.gov.uk

Senior Management: Mr Colin Dales, Assistant Director, Frenchgate House, Richmond DL10 7AF ☎ 01748 829100 🖷 01748 826186 ✉ colin.dales@richmondshire.gov.uk

Senior Management: Mr Callum McKeon, Assistant Director, Swale House, Frenchgate, Richmond DL10 4JE ☎ 01748 829100 🖷 01748 826186 ✉ callum.mckeon@richmondshire.gov.uk

Community Safety: Ms Pat Wilson, Community Safety Manager, Swale House, Frenchgate, Richmond DL10 4JE ☎ 01748 829100 🖷 01748 826186 ✉ pat.wilson@richmondshire.gov.uk

Customer Service: Ms Carole Dew, Customer Services Manager, Swale House, Frenchgate, Richmond DL10 4JE ☎ 01748 829100 🖷 01748 826186 ✉ carole.dew@richmondshire.gov.uk

Electoral Registration: Ms Sandra Hullah, Electoral Services Officer, Swale House, Frenchgate, Richmond DL10 4JE ☎ 01748 829100 🖷 01748 826186 ✉ sandra.hullah@richmondshire.gov.uk

Emergency Planning: Mr Callum McKeon, Assistant Director, Swale House, Frenchgate, Richmond DL10 4JE ☎ 01748 829100 🖷 01748 826186 ✉ callum.mckeon@richmondshire.gov.uk

Environmental Health: Mr Philip Mepham, Environmental Health Manager, Swale House, Frenchgate, Richmond DL10 4JE ☎ 01748 829100 🖷 01748 826186 ✉ philip.mepham@richmondshire.gov.uk

Finance and Treasurer: Ms Claire Blackburn, Finance Manager, Swale House, Frenchgate, Richmond DL10 4JE ☎ 01748 829100; 01748 829100 🖷 01748 826186; 01748 826186 ✉ claire.blackburn@richmondshire.gov.uk

Grounds Maintenance: Mr Gary Hudson, Head of Open Spaces, Swale House, Frenchgate, Richmond DL10 4JE ☎ 01748 829100 🖷 01748 826186 ✉ gary.hudson@richmondshire.gov.uk

Health and Safety: Mr Tim Burrows, Health & Safety Advisor, Swale House, Frenchgate, Richmond DL10 4JE ☎ 01748 829100; 01748 829100 🖷 01748 826186; 01748 826186 ✉ tim.burrows@richmondshire.gov.uk

Housing: Mr Colin Dales, Assistant Director, Frenchgate House, Richmond DL10 7AF ☎ 01748 829100 🖷 01748 826186 ✉ colin.dales@richmondshire.gov.uk

Housing Maintenance: Ms Sara Smith, Landlord Services Manager, Swale House, Frenchgate, Richmond DL10 4JE ☎ 01748 829100 🖷 01748 826186 ✉ sara.smith@richmondshire.gov.uk

Leisure and Cultural Services: Mr Colin Dales, Assistant Director, Frenchgate House, Richmond DL10 7AF ☎ 01748 829100 🖷 01748 826186 ✉ colin.dales@richmondshire.gov.uk

Licensing: Mr Philip Mepham, Environmental Health Manager, Swale House, Frenchgate, Richmond DL10 4JE ☎ 01748 829100 🖷 01748 826186 ✉ philip.mepham@richmondshire.gov.uk

Lottery Funding, Charity and Voluntary: Ms Jo-Anne Simpson, Culture & Wellbeing Delivery Manager, Swale House, Frenchgate, Richmond DL10 4JE ☎ 01748 829100 🖷 01748 826186 ✉ jo-anne.simpson@richmondshire.gov.uk

Member Services: Mr Michael Dowson, Democratic Services Manager, Swale House, Frenchgate, Richmond DL10 4JE ☎ 01748 829100 🖷 01748 826186 ✉ michael.dowson@richmondshire.gov.uk

Parking: Mr Gary Hudson, Head of Open Spaces, Swale House, Frenchgate, Richmond DL10 4JE ☎ 01748 829100 🖷 01748 826186 ✉ gary.hudson@richmondshire.gov.uk

Personnel / HR: Ms Sheila Somerford, Head of People Services, Swale House, Frenchgate, Richmond DL10 4JE ☎ 01609 767066; 01748 829100 🖷 01748 826186 ✉ sheila.somerford@richmondshire.gov.uk

Planning: Mr Peter Featherstone, Head of Development Management, Environment Services, Springwell House, Frenchgate, Richmond DL10 4LG ☎ 01748 829100 🖷 01748 826186 ✉ peter.featherstone@richmondshire.gov.uk

Staff Training: Ms Sheila Somerford, Head of People Services, Swale House, Frenchgate, Richmond DL10 4JE ☎ 01609 767066 🖷 01748 826186 ✉ sheila.somerford@richmondshire.gov.uk

Children's Play Areas: Mr Gary Hudson, Head of Open Spaces, Swale House, Frenchgate, Richmond DL10 4JE ☎ 01748 829100 🖷 01748 826186 ✉ gary.hudson@richmondshire.gov.uk

MEMBERS OF THE COUNCIL (34)

***Chair:* World**, Clive (LD - Richmond Central)
cllr.c.world@richmondshire.gov.uk
***Vice-Chair:* Johnson**, Rob (CON - Catterick)
cllr.r.johnson@richmondshire.gov.uk
***Leader of the Council:* Blackie**, John (IND - Hawes and High Abbotside)
cllr.j.blackie@richmondshire.gov.uk
***Deputy Leader of the Council:* Griffiths**, Mick (CON - Newsham with Eppleby)
cllr.m.griffiths@richmondshire.gov.uk
***Group Leader:* Butler**, Fleur (CON - Leyburn)
cllr.f.butler@richmondshire.gov.uk
***Group Leader:* Parlour**, Jane (LD - Croft)
cllr.j.parlour@richmondshire.gov.uk
Allen, Rachel (CON - Middleham)
cllr.r.allen@richmondshire.gov.uk
Amsden, John (IND - Bolton Castle)
cllr.j.amsden@richmondshire.gov.uk
Blythman, Muriel (CON - Richmond East)
cllr.m.blythman@richmondshire.gov.uk
Bradbury, Mark (IND - Scotton)
cllr.m.bradbury@richmondshire.gov.uk
Clarkson, Lin (CON - Hornby Castle)
cllr.l.clarkson@richmondshire.gov.uk
Cullen, Paul (IND - Hipswell)
cllr.p.cullen@richmondshire.gov.uk
Curran DL, Linda (IND - Richmond West)
cllr.l.curran@richmondshire.gov.uk
Dale, Angie (IND - Colburn)
cllr.a.dale@richmondshire.gov.uk
Dawson, Campbell (CON - Barton)
cllr.c.dawson@richmondshire.gov.uk
Duff, Tony (CON - Leyburn)
cllr.t.duff@richmondshire.gov.uk
Gale, Bob (IND - Reeth and Arkengarthdale)
cllr.b.gale@richmondshire.gov.uk
Gardner, Malcolm (IND - Swaledale)
cllr.m.gardner@richmondshire.gov.uk
Gill, Danny (CON - Brompton on Swale and Scorton)
cllr.d.gill@richmondshire.gov.uk
Glover, William (CON - Colburn)
cllr.w.glover@richmondshire.gov.uk
Heslop, William (IND - Gilling West)
cllr.w.heslop@richmondshire.gov.uk
Lambert, Ken (IND - Scotton)
cllr.k.lambert@richmondshire.gov.uk
Loadman, Keith (CON - Lower Wensleydale)
cllr.k.loadman@richmondshire.gov.uk
Lord, Russel (IND - Richmond East)
cllr.r.lord@richmondshire.gov.uk
McMullon, Jill (IND - Middleton Tyas)
cllr.j.mcmullon@richmondshire.gov.uk
Parsons, Stuart (LD - Richmond West)
cllr.s.parsons@richmondshire.gov.uk
Peacock, Yvonne (CON - Addlebrough)
cllr.y.peacock@richmondshire.gov.uk
Pelton, Tony (IND - Catterick)
cllr.t.pelton@richmondshire.gov.uk
Robinson, John (LD - Richmond Central)
cllr.j.robinson@richmondshire.gov.uk
Threlfall, Ian (CON - Brompton on Swale and Scorton)
cllr.i.threlfall@richmondshire.gov.uk
Todd, Stephanie (CON - Hipswell)
cllr.s.todd@richmondshire.gov.uk
Wilkes, Matthew (IND - Penhill)
cllr.m.wilkes@richmondshire.gov.uk
Wilson-Petch, Jimmy (CON - Melsonby)
cllr.j.wilson-petch@richmondshire.gov.uk
Wood, Peter (IND - Colburn)
cllr.p.wood@richmondshire.gov.uk

POLITICAL COMPOSITION

CON: 15, IND: 15, LD: 4

COMMITTEE CHAIRS

Audit & Governance: Mr Stuart Parsons
Licensing: Ms Jill McMullon
Overview & Scrutiny 1: Mr Paul Cullen
Overview & Scrutiny 2: Mr John Robinson
Planning: Ms Jane Parlour

ROCHDALE M

Rochdale Metropolitan Borough Council, Municipal Offices, Smith Street, Rochdale OL16 1LQ ☎ 01706 647474 ✉ council@rochdale.gov.uk 💻 www.rochdale.gov.uk

FACTS & FIGURES

Police Authority: Greater Manchester Police Authority
Health Authority: North West Strategic Health Authority
Learning and Skills Council: North West
Parliamentary Constituencies: Heywood and Middleton, Rochdale
EU Constituencies: North West

Election Frequency: Elections are by thirds
Twinning: Bielfeld (Germany); Tourcoing (France); Sahiwal (Pakistan)

PRINCIPAL OFFICERS

Chief Executive: Mr Jim Taylor, Chief Executive, PO Box 39, Floor 5, Rochdale OL16 1LQ ☎ 01706 925401 🖷 01706 925450 ✉ jim.taylor@rochdale.gov.uk

Senior Management: Ms Pam Smith, Executive Director for Transformation, Floor 6, Telegraph House, Bailloe Street, Rochdale OL15 1JA ☎ 01706 925204 ✉ pam.smith@rochdale.gov.uk

Access Officer / Social Services (Disability): Ms Sheila Downey, Executive Director of Adult Social Care, Brook House, Oldham Road, Middleton M24 1AY ☎ 01706 922975 ✉ sheila.downey@rochdale.gov.uk

Best Value: Ms Marie Basting, Improvement & Development Manager, Floor 6, Telegraph House, Baillie Street, Rochdale OL16 1JH ☎ 01706 925602 ✉ marie.basting@rochdale.gov.uk

Building Control: Mr Mark Dalzell, Building Control Manager, Telegraph House, Baillie Street, Rochdale OL16 1JH ☎ 01706 924328 ✉ mark.dalzell@rochdale.gov.uk

Catering Services: Mr Mark Widdup, Service Director, Green Lane, Heywood OL10 2DY ☎ 01706 922048 ✉ mark.widdup@rochdale.gov.uk

Children / Youth Services: Ms Sandra Bowness, Service Director, PO Box 70, Floor 7, Municipal Offices, Smith Street, Rochdale OL16 1YD ☎ 01706 925105 ✉ sandra.bowness@rochdale.gov.uk

Civil Registration: Mrs Aileen Bollard, Superindendent Registrar, PO Box 15, Ground Floor, Town Hall, Rochdale OL16 1AB ☎ 01706 924779 ✉ aileen.bollard@rochdale.gov.uk

PR / Communications: Ms Julia Youd, Marketing and Communications Manager, Floor 4, Municipal Offices, Smith Street, Rochdale OL16 1XU ☎ 01706 925725 ✉ julia.youd@rochdale.gov.uk

Community Planning: Mr Andy Zuntz, Executive Director, PO Box 39, Floor 4, Municipal Offices, Smith Street, Rochdale OL16 1LQ ☎ 01706 924005 🖷 01706 926648 ✉ andy.zuntz@rochdale.gov.uk

Community Safety: Ms Jeanette Staley, Safer Communities Manager, Floor 4, Municipal Offices, Smith Street, Rochdale OL16 1LQ ☎ 01706 924987 ✉ jeanette.staley@rochdale.gov.uk

Computer Management: Mr Andrew Kendall, Managing Director, Floor 11, Municipal Offices, Rochdale OL16 1LQ ☎ 01706 647474 ✉ andrew.kendall@rochdale.gov.uk

Consumer Protection and Trading Standards: Mr Andy Glover, Consumer Protection & Registration Manager, Floor 7, Telegraph House, Baille Street, Rochdale OL16 1JH ☎ 01706 924105 🖷 01706 924185 ✉ andy.glover@rochdale.gov.uk

Corporate Services: Ms Linda Fisher, Service Director - Corporate Services, PO Box 15, Town Hall, Rochdale OL16 1AB ☎ 01706 924703 ✉ linda.fisher@rochdale.gov.uk

Customer Service: Ms Kate Lindley, Head of Customer Access, Floor 10, Municipal Offices, Smith Street, Rochdale OL16 1LQ ☎ 01706 925685 ✉ kate.lindley@rochdale.gov.uk

Economic Development: Mr Andy Zuntz, Executive Director, PO Box 39, Floor 4, Municipal Offices, Smith Street, Rochdale OL16 1LQ ☎ 01706 924005 🖷 01706 926648 ✉ andy.zuntz@rochdale.gov.uk

Education: Ms Cheryl Eastwood, Executive Director of Children's Services, Municipal Offices, Smith Street, Rochdale OL16 1LQ ☎ 01706 925000 ✉ cheryl.eastwood@rochdale.gov.uk

E-Government: Mr Darren Wild, Customer and Business Services Director, Floor 12, Municipal Offices, Rochdale OL16 1LQ ☎ 01706 923392 🖷 01706 924626 ✉ darren.wild@rochdale.gov.uk

Electoral Registration: Mrs Clare Poole, Electoral Services Officer & Senior Administration Assistant, PO Box 15, Floor 2, Town Hall, Rochdale OL16 1AB ☎ 01706 924759 🖷 01706 924848 ✉ clare.poole@rochdale.gov.uk

Emergency Planning: Mr David Wolstenholme, Emergency Planning Officer, PO Box 15, Town Hall, Rochdale OL16 1AB ☎ 01706 924757 🖷 01706 929475 ✉ david.wolstenholme@rochdale.gov.uk

Energy Management: Ms Donna Bowler, Strategic Housing Manager, PO Box 446, Floor 4, Municipal Offices, Rochdale OL16 1WU ☎ 01706 745123 ✉ donna.bowler@rochdale.gov.uk

Energy Management: Mr Michael Crompton, Property Director, St Alban's House, Drake Street, Rochdale OL16 1UZ ☎ 01706 923321 🖷 01706 923321 ✉ michael.crompton@rochdale.gov.uk

Environmental / Technical Services: Mr Mark Widdup, Service Director, Green Lane, Heywood OL10 2DY ☎ 01706 922048 ✉ mark.widdup@rochdale.gov.uk

Environmental Health: Mr Peter Rowlinson, Service Director, Telegraph House, Baillie Street, Rochdale OL16 1JH ☎ 01706 924307 🖷 01706 924185 ✉ peter.rowlinson@rochdale.gov.uk

Estates, Property & Valuation: Ms Janet Butterworth, Asset Manager, Telegraph House, Baillie Street, Rochdale OL16 1JH ☎ 01706 923271 ✉ janet.butterworth@rochdale.gov.uk

European Liaison: Ms Penny Sharp, Service Director, PO Box 446, Floor 4, Municipal Offices, Rochdale OL16 1WU ☎ 01706 924676 🖷 ; 01706 926648 ✉ penny.sharp@rochdale.gov.uk

Events Manager: Ms Penny Sharp, Service Director, PO Box 446, Floor 4, Municipal Offices, Rochdale OL16 1WU ☎ 01706 924676 🖷 ; 01706 926648 ✉ penny.sharp@rochdale.gov.uk

Facilities: Mr Mark Widdup, Service Director, Green Lane, Heywood OL10 2DY ☎ 01706 922048

✆ mark.widdup@rochdale.gov.uk

Finance and Treasurer: Ms Pauline Kane, Service Director, Municipal Offices, Smith Street, Rochdale OL16 1ZR ☎ 01706 925002 ✆ pauline.kane@rochdale.gov.uk

Fleet Management: Mr Mark Widdup, Service Director, Green Lane, Heywood OL10 2DY ☎ 01706 922048 ✆ mark.widdup@rochdale.gov.uk

Grounds Maintenance: Mr Mark Widdup, Service Director, Green Lane, Heywood OL10 2DY ☎ 01706 922048 ✆ mark.widdup@rochdale.gov.uk

Highways: Mr David Nicholson, Director of Highways and Engineering, PO Box 50, Floor 3, Municipal Offices, Rochdale OL16 1FL ☎ 07719 208404 ✆ david.nicholson@rochdale.gov.uk

Home Energy Conservation: Ms Donna Bowler, Strategic Housing Manager, PO Box 446, Floor 4, Municipal Offices, Rochdale OL16 1WU ☎ 01706 745123 ✆ donna.bowler@rochdale.gov.uk

Housing: Ms Donna Bowler, Strategic Housing Manager, PO Box 446, Floor 4, Municipal Offices, Rochdale OL16 1WU ☎ 01706 745123 ✆ donna.bowler@rochdale.gov.uk

Local Area Agreement: Ms Jane Silvester, Interim Service Director, Telegraph House, Baillie Street, Rochdale OL16 1JH ☎ 01706 924301 ✆ jane.silvester@rochdale.gov.uk

Legal: Ms Linda Fisher, Service Director - Corporate Services, Town Hall, Rochdale OL16 1AB ☎ 01706 924703 ✆ linda.fisher@rochdale.gov.uk

Leisure and Cultural Services: Ms Pauline Kane, Service Director, Municipal Offices, Smith Street, Rochdale OL16 1ZR ☎ 01706 925002 ✆ pauline.kane@rochdale.gov.uk

Leisure and Cultural Services: Mr Craig McAteer, Managing Director, Link 4 Life, PO Box 428, Floor 6, Municipal Offices, Rochdale OL16 1ZL ☎ 01706 924345 🖷 01706 924104 ✆ craig.mcateer@rochdale.gov.uk

Licensing: Mr Peter Rowlinson, Service Director, Telegraph House, Baillie Street, Rochdale OL16 1JH ☎ 01706 924307 🖷 01706 924185 ✆ peter.rowlinson@rochdale.gov.uk

Lifelong Learning: Ms Sandra Bowness, Service Director, PO Box 70, Floor 7, Municipal Offices, Smith Street, Rochdale OL16 1YD ☎ 01706 925105 ✆ sandra.bowness@rochdale.gov.uk

Lighting: Mr David Nicholson, Director of Highways and Engineering, PO Box 50, Floor 3, Municipal Offices, Rochdale OL16 1FL ☎ 07719 208404 ✆ david.nicholson@rochdale.gov.uk

Lottery Funding, Charity and Voluntary: Ms Penny Sharp, Service Director, PO Box 446, Floor 4, Municipal Offices, Rochdale OL16 1WU ☎ 01706 924676 🖷 01706 926648 ✆ penny.sharp@rochdale.gov.uk

Member Services: Ms Linda Fisher, Service Director - Corporate Services, Town Hall, Rochdale OL16 1AB ☎ 01706 924703 ✆ linda.fisher@rochdale.gov.uk

Parking: Ms Julie Rushton, Parking Team Leader, PO Box 39, Floor 3, Municipal Offices, Rochdale OL16 1FL ☎ 01706 924464 ✆ julie.rushton@rochdale.gov.uk

Partnerships: Ms Jane Silvester, Interim Service Director, Telegraph House, Baillie Street, Rochdale OL16 1JH ☎ 01706 924301 ✆ jane.silvester@rochdale.gov.uk

Personnel / HR: Mr Stephen Harper, Service Director, PO Box 427, Floor 9, Municipal Offices, Smith Street, Rochdale OL16 1ZR ☎ 01706 925603 🖷 01706 925656 ✆ stephen.harper@rochdale.gov.uk

Planning: Mr Mark Robinson, Development Control Manager, Telegraph House, Baillie Street, Rochdale OL16 1JH ☎ 01706 924308 🖷 01706 924185 ✆ mark.robinson@rochdale.gov.uk

Procurement: Ms Pauline Kane, Service Director, Municipal Offices, Smith Street, Rochdale OL16 1ZR ☎ 01706 925002 ✆ pauline.kane@rochdale.gov.uk

Public Libraries: Ms Kate Lindley, Head of Customer Access, Floor 10, Municipal Offices, Smith Street, Rochdale OL16 1LQ ☎ 01706 925685 ✆ kate.lindley@rochdale.gov.uk

Public Libraries: Mr Paul Young, Head of Customers & Communications, PO Box 109, Floor 10, Municipal Offices, Smith Street, Rochdale OL16 1YR ☎ 01706 925535 🖷 01706 924185 ✆ paul.young@rochdale.gov.uk

Recycling & Waste Minimisation: Mr Andy Shaw, Waste Minimisation & Recycling Manager, Green Lane, Heywood OL10 2DY ☎ 01706 922023 ✆ andy.shaw@rochdale.gov.uk

Regeneration: Ms Penny Sharp, Service Director, PO Box 446, Floor 4, Municipal Offices, Rochdale OL16 1WU ☎ 01706 924676 🖷 01706 926648 ✆ penny.sharp@rochdale.gov.uk

Road Safety: Mr Tony Lees, Road Safety Team Leader, PO Box 50, Floor 3, Municipal Offices, Rochdale OL16 1FL ☎ 01706 924582 🖷 01706 921666 ✆ tony.lees@rochdale.gov.uk

Road Safety: Mr David Nicholson, Director of Highways and Engineering, PO Box 50, Floor 3, Municipal Offices, Rochdale OL16 1FL ☎ 07719 208404 ✆ david.nicholson@rochdale.gov.uk

Social Services: Ms Jane Rossini, Director of Public Health, Municipal Offices, Smith Street, Rochdale OL16 1LQ

Social Services (Adult): Ms Sheila Downey, Executive Director of Adult Social Care, Brook House, Oldham Road, Middleton M24 1AY ☎ 01706 922975 ✆ sheila.downey@rochdale.gov.uk

Social Services (Children): Mr Steve Garner, Head of Children's Social Care, Floor 10, Municipal Offices, Smith Street, Rochdale OL16 1YP ☎ 01706 925203 ✆ steve.garner@rochdale.gov.uk

Sustainable Communities: Ms Penny Sharp, Service Director, PO Box 446, Floor 4, Municipal Offices, Rochdale OL16 1WU

☎ 01706 924676 🖷 01706 926648
✉ penny.sharp@rochdale.gov.uk

Sustainable Development: Mr Paul Simpson, Strategic Planning Manager, Telegraph House, Baillie Street, Rochdale OL16 1JH
☎ 01706 516815 ✉ paul.simpson@rochdale.gov.uk

Tourism: Ms Susan Ayres, Economic Affairs Manager, PO Box 446, Floor 4, Municipal Offices, Rochdale OL16 1WU
☎ 01706 925636 ✉ susan.ayres@rochdale.gov.uk

Town Centre: Ms Debbie O'Brien, Town Centre Manager, 5 South Parade, Rochdale OL16 1LR ☎ 01706 926676
🖷 01706 718848 ✉ debbie@rochdaletcm.co.uk

Traffic Management: Mr John Grahamslaw, Traffic Team Leader, PO Box 50, Floor 3, Municipal Offices, Rochdale OL16 1FL ☎ 01706 924581 ✉ john.grahamslaw@rochdale.gov.uk

Transport: Mr Mark Widdup, Service Director, Green Lane, Heywood OL10 2DY ☎ 01706 922048
✉ mark.widdup@rochdale.gov.uk

Transport Planner: Mr David Nicholson, Director of Highways and Engineering, PO Box 50, Floor 3, Municipal Offices, Rochdale OL16 1FL ☎ 07719 208404 ✉ david.nicholson@rochdale.gov.uk

Waste Collection and Disposal: Mr Dennis Pennill, Waste Services Manager, Green Lane, Heywood OL10 2DY
☎ 01706 692006 ✉ dennis.pennill@rochdale.gov.uk

Waste Management: Mr Mark Widdup, Service Director, PO Box 39, Floor 10, Municipal Offices, Rochdale OL16 1LQ
☎ 01706 922048 ✉ mark.widdup@rochdale.gov.uk

MEMBERS OF THE COUNCIL (60)

***Mayor:* Gartside**, James (CON - Norden)
james.gartside@rochdale.gov.uk
***Deputy Mayor:* Rush**, Peter (LD - North Heywood)
peter.rush@rochdale.gov.uk
***Leader of the Council:* Lambert**, Colin (LAB - West Heywood)
colin.lambert@rochdale.gov.uk
***Deputy Leader of the Council:* Williams**, Peter (LAB - South Middleton)
peter.williams@rochdale.gov.uk
***Group Leader:* Dearnley**, Ashley (CON - Wardle and West Littleborough)
ashley.dearnley@rochdale.gov.uk
***Group Leader:* Kelly**, Andy (LD - Milnrow and Newhey)
andrew.kelly@rochdale.gov.uk
Ahmed, Iftikhar (LAB - Central Rochdale)
iftikhar.ahmed@rochdale.gov.uk
Ahmed, Shakil (LAB - Kingsway)
shakil.ahmed@rochdale.gov.uk
Ahmed, Farooq (LAB - Central Rochdale)
farooq.ahmed@rochdale.gov.uk
Ali, Daalat (LAB - Kingsway)
daalat.ali@rochdale.gov.uk
Ali, Sultan (LAB - Central Rochdale)
sultan.ali@rochdale.gov.uk
Begum, Shefali (LAB - Spotland and Falinge)
shefali.begum@rochdale.gov.uk
Beswick, Jacqueline (LAB - West Heywood)
Bethell, Philip (LAB - Balderstone and Kirkholt)
phillip.bethell@rochdale.gov.uk
Biant, Surinder (LAB - Spotland and Falinge)
surinder.biant@rochdale.gov.uk
Biant, Cecile (LAB - Spotland and Falinge)
cecile.biant@rochdale.gov.uk
Boriss, Malcolm (LAB - East Middleton)
malcolm.boriss@rochdale.gov.uk
Brett, Allen (LAB - Milnrow and Newhey)
allen.brett@rochdale.gov.uk
Burke, Philip (LAB - West Middleton)
philip.burke@rochdale.gov.uk
Burke, Martin (LAB - Smallbridge and Firgrove)
martin.burke@rochdale.gov.uk
Burns, Jonathan (LAB - North Middleton)
jonathan.burns@rochdale.gov.uk
Clegg, Robert (CON - Wardle and West Littleborough)
robert.clegg@rochdale.gov.uk
Danczuk, Karen (LAB - Kingsway)
karen.burke@rochdale.gov.uk
Darnbrough, Joyce (CON - Wardle and West Littleborough)
janet.darnbrough@rochdale.gov.uk
Davison, Peter (LAB - Castleton)
peter.davison@rochdale.gov.uk
Duckworth, Ian (CON - Bamford)
ian.duckworth@rochdale.gov.uk
Dutton, Raymond (LAB - North Heywood)
raymond.dutton@rochdale.gov.uk
Emmott, Neil (LAB - West Middleton)
neil.emmott@rochdale.gov.uk
Emmott, Susan (LAB - Hopwood Hall)
susan.emmott@rochdale.gov.uk
Farnell, Richard (LAB - Balderstone and Kirkholt)
richard.farnell@rochdale.gov.uk
Gartside, Jane (CON - Bamford)
jane.gartside@rochdale.gov.uk
Godson, Alan (LAB - North Middleton)
alan.godson@rochdale.gov.uk
Greenall, Pat (LAB - North Middleton)
pat.greenall@rochdale.gov.uk
Hartley, John (LAB - Littleborough Lakeside)
john.hartley@rochdale.gov.uk
Hobhouse, Wera (LD - Norden)
wera.hobhouse@rochdale.gov.uk
Holly, Michael (CON - South Middleton)
michael.holly@rochdale.gov.uk
Hornby, Jean (LAB - Castleton)
jean.hornby@rochdale.gov.uk
Hussain, Aftab (LAB - Smallbridge and Firgrove)
aftab.hussain2@rochdale.gov.uk
Joinson, Peter (LAB - South Middleton)
peter.joinson@rochdale.gov.uk
Linden, Terry (LAB - Milkstone and Deeplish)
terry.linden@rochdale.gov.uk
Martin, Donna (LAB - East Middleton)
donna.martin@rochdale.gov.uk
McCarthy, Alan (LAB - West Heywood)
alanmmccarthy@btinternet.com
Metcalfe, Ann (CON - Norden)
ann.metcalfe@rochdale.gov.uk
Mills, Stephanie (CON - Littleborough Lakeside)
stephanie.mills@rochdale.gov.uk
Mir, Amna (LAB - Smallbridge and Firgrove)
amna.mir@rochdale.gov.uk
Mulgrew, Dale (LD - Balderstone and Kirkholt)

dale.mulgrew@rochdale.gov.uk
Murphy, Lily (LAB - West Middleton)
lil.murphy@rochdale.gov.uk
Neilson, Andrew (CON - Healey)
andrew.neilson@rochdale.gov.uk
O'Neill, Shaun (LAB - Healey)
shaun.o'neill@rochdale.gov.uk
O'Rourke, Liam (LAB - North Heywood)
liam.o'rourke@rochdale.gov.uk
Robinson, Linda (LAB - Hopwood Hall)
linda.robinson@rochdale.gov.uk
Rodgers, Martin (LAB - Milnrow and Newhey)
martin.rodgers@rochdale.gov.uk
Rodgers, Hilary (LD - Healey)
hilary.rodgers@rochdale.gov.uk
Sheerin, Billy (LAB - Castleton)
billy.sheerin@rochdale.gov.uk
Stott, Ann (CON - Littleborough Lakeside)
ann.stott2@rochdale.gov.uk
Sullivan, Patricia (CON - Bamford)
patricia.sullivan@rochdale.gov.uk
Wardle, Carol (LAB - Hopwood Hall)
carolwardle1@gmail.com
Wazir, Shah (CON - Milkstone and Deeplish)
shah.wazir@rochdale.gov.uk
West, June (LAB - East Middleton)
june.west@rochdale.gov.uk
Zaman, Mohammed (LAB - Milkstone and Deeplish)
mohammed.zaman@rochdale.gov.uk

POLITICAL COMPOSITION
LAB: 42, CON: 13, LD: 5

CABINET
IT, Highway Services, Culture & Leisure: Ms Jacqueline Beswick
Leader: Mr Colin Lambert
Deputy Leader; Economic Development & Customer Services: Mr Peter Williams
Children, Schools & Families: Ms Donna Martin
Adult Care: Ms Jean Hornby
Environmental & Operational Services: Mr Martin Burke
Finance: Mr Farooq Ahmed
Corporate Services & Townships: Mr Richard Farnell

COMMITTEE CHAIRS
Health (Scrutiny): Ms Linda Robinson
Licensing & Regulatory: Ms Carol Wardle

ROCHFORD D

Rochford District Council, Council Offices, South Street, Rochford SS4 1BW ☎ 01702 546366 🖷 01702 545737 ✉ information@rochford.gov.uk 💻 www.rochford.gov.uk

FACTS & FIGURES
Police Authority: Essex Police Authority
Health Authority: East of England Strategic Health Authority
Learning and Skills Council: Eastern
Parliamentary Constituencies: Rayleigh and Wickford, Rochford and Southend East
EU Constituencies: Eastern
Election Frequency: Elections are by thirds
Twinning: Haltern (Germany)

PRINCIPAL OFFICERS
Chief Executive: Mr Paul Warren, Chief Executive, Council Offices, South Street, Rochford SS4 1BW ☎ 01702 546366 🖷 01702 545737 ✉ paul.warren@rochford.gov.uk

Architect, Building / Property Services: Mr Alan Thomas, Asset Manager, Council Offices, South Street, Rochford SS4 1BW ☎ 01702 546366 ✉ alan.thomas@rochford.gov.uk

Best Value: Ms Yvonne Woodward, Head of Finance, Council Offices, South Street, Rochford SS4 1BW ☎ 01702 546366 🖷 01702 545737 ✉ yvonne.woodward@rochford.gov.uk

Building Control: Mr Allan Taylor, Building Control Manager, Council Offices, South Street, Rochford SS4 1BW ☎ 01702 546366 🖷 01702 318181 ✉ allan.taylor@rochford.gov.uk

PR / Communications: Mrs Janet Cox, People and Policy Unit Manager, Council Offices, South Street, Rochford SS4 1BW ☎ 01702 546366 ✉ janet.cox@rochford.gov.uk

PR / Communications: Mrs Claudia McClellan, People and Policy Unit Manager, Council Offices, South Street, Rochford SS4 1BW ☎ 01702 546366 ✉ claudia.mcclellan@rochford.gov.uk

Community Safety: Mr Jeremy Bourne, Head of Community Services, Council Offices, South Street, Rochford SS4 1BW ☎ 01702 546366 🖷 01702 545737 ✉ jeremy.bourne@rochford.gov.uk

Computer Management: Ms Sarah Fowler, Head of Information & Customer Services, Council Offices, South Street, Rochford SS4 1BW ☎ ; 01702 546366 🖷 01702 545737 ✉ sarah.fowler@rochford.gov.uk

Corporate Services: Ms Sarah Fowler, Head of Information & Customer Services, Council Offices, South Street, Rochford SS4 1BW ☎ ; 01702 546366 🖷 01702 545737 ✉ sarah.fowler@rochford.gov.uk

Customer Service: Ms Sarah Fowler, Head of Information & Customer Services, Council Offices, South Street, Rochford SS4 1BW ☎ ; 01702 546366 🖷 01702 545737 ✉ sarah.fowler@rochford.gov.uk

Economic Development: Mr Shaun Scrutton, Head of Planning & Transportation, Council Offices, South Street, Rochford SS4 1BW ☎ ; 01702 546366 ✉ shaun.scrutton@rochford.gov.uk

E-Government: Ms Sarah Fowler, Head of Information & Customer Services, Council Offices, South Street, Rochford SS4 1BW ☎ ; 01702 546366 🖷 01702 545737 ✉ sarah.fowler@rochford.gov.uk

Electoral Registration: Ms Sarah Fowler, Head of Information & Customer Services, Council Offices, South Street, Rochford SS4 1BW ☎ ; 01702 546366 🖷 01702 545737 ✉ sarah.fowler@rochford.gov.uk

Emergency Planning: Mr Peter McKenzie, Emergency Planning

& Business Continuity Officer, Council Offices, South Street, Rochford SS4 1BW ☎ ; 01702 546366 🖷 01702 318183 ✉ peter.mckenzie@rochford.gov.uk

Energy Management: Mr Alan Thomas, Asset Manager, Council Offices, South Street, Rochford SS4 1BW ☎ 01702 546366 ✉ alan.thomas@rochford.gov.uk

Environmental / Technical Services: Mr Richard Evans, Head of Environmental Services, Council Offices, South Street, Rochford SS4 1BW ☎ 01702 546366 ✉ richard.evans@rochford.gov.uk

Environmental Health: Mr Richard Evans, Head of Environmental Services, Council Offices, South Street, Rochford SS4 1BW ☎ 01702 546366 ✉ richard.evans@rochford.gov.uk

Estates, Property & Valuation: Mr Alan Thomas, Asset Manager, Council Offices, South Street, Rochford SS4 1BW ☎ 01702 546366 ✉ alan.thomas@rochford.gov.uk

Finance and Treasurer: Ms Yvonne Woodward, Head of Finance, Council Offices, South Street, Rochford SS4 1BW ☎ 01702 546366 🖷 01702 545737 ✉ yvonne.woodward@rochford.gov.uk

Grounds Maintenance: Mr Richard Evans, Head of Environmental Services, Council Offices, South Street, Rochford SS4 1BW ☎ 01702 546366 ✉ richard.evans@rochford.gov.uk

Health and Safety: Mr David Connnor, Health and Safety Officer, Council Offices, South Street, Rochford SS4 1BW ☎ 01702 546366 ✉ david.connor@rochford.gov.uk

Home Energy Conservation: Mr Steve Neville, Strategic Housing Manager, Council Offices, South Street, Rochford SS4 1BW ☎ 01702 546366 ✉ steve.neville@rochford.gov.uk

Housing: Mr Jeremy Bourne, Head of Community Services, Council Offices, South Street, Rochford SS4 1BW ☎ 01702 546366 🖷 01702 545737 ✉ jeremy.bourne@rochford.gov.uk

Legal: Mr Albert Bugeja, Head of Legal, Estates and Member Services, Council Offices, South Street, Rochford SS4 1BW ☎ 01702 318130 🖷 01702 545737 ✉ albert.bugeja@rochford.gov.uk

Leisure and Cultural Services: Mr Jeremy Bourne, Head of Community Services, Council Offices, South Street, Rochford SS4 1BW ☎ 01702 546366 🖷 01702 545737 ✉ jeremy.bourne@rochford.gov.uk

Licensing: Mr Richard Evans, Head of Environmental Services, Council Offices, South Street, Rochford SS4 1BW ☎ 01702 546366 ✉ richard.evans@rochford.gov.uk

Member Services: Mr John Bostock, Member Services Manager, Council Offices, South Street, Rochford SS4 1BW ☎ 01702 546366 🖷 01702 545737 ✉ john.bostock@rochford.gov.uk

Parking: Mr Shaun Scrutton, Head of Planning & Transportation, Council Offices, South Street, Rochford SS4 1BW ☎ 01702 546366 ✉ shaun.scrutton@rochford.gov.uk

Personnel / HR: Mrs Janet Cox, People and Policy Unit Manager, Council Offices, South Street, Rochford SS4 1BW ☎ 01702 546366 ✉ janet.cox@rochford.gov.uk

Personnel / HR: Mrs Claudia McClellan, People and Policy Unit Manager, Council Offices, South Street, Rochford SS4 1BW ☎ 01702 546366 ✉ claudia.mcclellan@rochford.gov.uk

Planning: Mr Shaun Scrutton, Head of Planning & Transportation, Council Offices, South Street, Rochford SS4 1BW ☎ ; 01702 546366 ✉ shaun.scrutton@rochford.gov.uk

Procurement: Ms Yvonne Woodward, Head of Finance, Council Offices, South Street, Rochford SS4 1BW ☎ 01702 546366 🖷 01702 545737 ✉ yvonne.woodward@rochford.gov.uk

Recycling & Waste Minimisation: Mr Richard Evans, Head of Environmental Services, Council Offices, South Street, Rochford SS4 1BW ☎ 01702 546366 ✉ richard.evans@rochford.gov.uk

Regeneration: Mr Shaun Scrutton, Head of Planning & Transportation, Council Offices, South Street, Rochford SS4 1BW ☎ ; 01702 546366 ✉ shaun.scrutton@rochford.gov.uk

Staff Training: Mrs Janet Cox, People and Policy Unit Manager, Council Offices, South Street, Rochford SS4 1BW ☎ 01702 546366 ✉ janet.cox@rochford.gov.uk

Staff Training: Mrs Claudia McClellan, People and Policy Unit Manager, Council Offices, South Street, Rochford SS4 1BW ☎ 01702 546366 ✉ claudia.mcclellan@rochford.gov.uk

Street Scene: Mr Richard Evans, Head of Environmental Services, Council Offices, South Street, Rochford SS4 1BW ☎ 01702 546366 ✉ richard.evans@rochford.gov.uk

Waste Collection and Disposal: Mr Richard Evans, Head of Environmental Services, Council Offices, South Street, Rochford SS4 1BW ☎ 01702 546366 ✉ richard.evans@rochford.gov.uk

Waste Management: Mr Richard Evans, Head of Environmental Services, Council Offices, South Street, Rochford SS4 1BW ☎ 01702 546366 ✉ richard.evans@rochford.gov.uk

MEMBERS OF THE COUNCIL (39)

***Chair:* Mockford**, Joan (CON - Sweyne Park)
cllrjoan.mockford@rochford.gov.uk

***Vice-Chair:* Wilkins**, Barbara (CON - Foulness and Great Wakering)
cllrbarbara.wilkins@rochford.gov.uk

***Leader of the Council:* Cutmore**, Terry (CON - Ashingdon and Canewdon)
cllrterry.cutmore@rochford.gov.uk

***Deputy Leader of the Council:* Hudson**, Keith (CON - Hockley Central)
cllrkeith.hudson@rochford.gov.uk

Aves, Patricia (CON - Rayleigh Central)
cllrpatricia.aves@rochford.gov.uk

Black, Chris (LD - Downhall and Rawreth)
cllrchris.black@rochford.gov.uk

Capon, Tracey (CON - Ashingdon and Canewdon)

cllrtracy.capon@rochford.gov.uk
Capon, Phil (CON - Hawkwell South)
Carter, Michael (CON - Hockley North)
cllrmichael.carter@rochford.gov.uk
Cottis, James (CON - Rochford)
cllrjames.cottis@rochford.gov.uk
Glynn, Heather (CON - Hawkwell South)
Goodwin, Trevor (CON - Foulness and Great Wakering)
cllrtrevor.goodwin@rochford.gov.uk
Gordon, Keith (CON - Rochford)
cllrkeith.gordon@rochford.gov.uk
Grey, Jim (CON - Trinity)
cllrjim.grey@rochford.gov.uk
Griffin, John (CON - Wheatley)
cllrjohn.griffin@rochford.gov.uk
Hale, Angela (CON - Hullbridge)
cllrangela.hale@rochford.gov.uk
Hazlewood, Brian (CON - Hockley Central)
cllrbrian.hazlewood@rochford.gov.uk
Hoy, Diane (GRN - Hullbridge)
cllrdiane.hoy@rochford.gov.uk
Hoy, Michael (GRN - Hullbridge)
cllr.michael.hoy@rochford.gov.uk
Lucas-Gill, Gillian (CON - Rochford)
cllrgillian.lucas-gill@rochford.gov.uk
Lumley, June (LD - Grange)
cllrjune.lumley@rochford.gov.uk
Lumley, Chris (LD - Grange)
cllrchris.lumley@rochford.gov.uk
Maddocks, Malcolm (CON - Hockley West)
cllrmalcolm.maddocks@rochford.gov.uk
Mason, Christine (R - Hawkwell West)
cllrchristine.mason@rochford.gov.uk
Mason, John (R - Hawkwell West)
cllrjohn.mason@rochford.gov.uk
McPherson, Jo (CON - Hawkwell North)
cllrjo.mcpherson@rochford.gov.uk
Merrick, David (CON - Lodge)
cllrdavid.merrick@rochford.gov.uk
Mountain, Toby (CON - Sweyne Park)
cllrtoby.mountain@rochford.gov.uk
Oatham, Ron (LD - Downhall and Rawreth)
cllrron.oatham@rochford.gov.uk
Pointer, Bob (CON - Hawkwell North)
cllrbob.pointer@rochford.gov.uk
Roe, Cheryl (CON - Rayleigh Central)
cllrcheryl.roe@rochford.gov.uk
Seagers, Colin (CON - Foulness and Great Wakering)
cllrcolin.seagers@rochford.gov.uk
Smith, Simon (CON - Whitehouse)
cllrsimon.smith@rochford.gov.uk
Sperring, Dave (CON - Trinity)
cllrdave.sperring@rochford.gov.uk
Steptoe, Mike (CON - Barling and Sutton)
cllrmike.steptoe@rochford.gov.uk
Ward, Ian (CON - Lodge)
cllrian.ward@rochford.gov.uk
Webster, Mavis (CON - Wheatley)
cllrmavis.webster@rochford.gov.uk
Webster, Peter (CON - Whitehouse)
cllrpeter.webster@rochford.gov.uk
Weston, Carole
(CON - Hockley Central)
cllrcarole.weston@rochford.gov.uk

POLITICAL COMPOSITION
CON: 31, LD: 4, R: 2, GRN: 2

CABINET
Leader: Mr Terry Cutmore
Deputy Leader; Leisure, Tourism, Heritage, the Arts, Culture & Business: Mr Keith Gordon
Council Tax Collection, Benefits & Stategic Housing Functions: Mr Malcolm Maddocks
Environment: Mr Mike Steptoe
Finance & Resources: Mr Colin Seagers
Service Development/Improvement & Performance Management: Ms Gillian Lucas-Gill
Young Persons, Adult Services, Community Care & Safety, Health & Well-Being: Mrs Jo McPherson

COMMITTEE CHAIRS
Appeals: Mr Jim Grey
Audit: Mrs Joan Mockford
Development Control: Mr Simon Smith
Licensing: Mrs Carole Weston
Review: Mrs June Lumley
Standards: Mrs Mavis Webster

ROSSENDALE D

Rossendale Borough Council, Business Centre, Futures Park, Newchurch Road, Bacup OL13 0BB ☎ 01706 217777 🖷 01706 224504 ✉ enquiries@rossendale.gov.uk 💻 www.rossendale.gov.uk

FACTS & FIGURES
Police Authority: Lancashire Police Authority
Health Authority: North West Strategic Health Authority
Learning and Skills Council: North West
Parliamentary Constituencies: Hyndburn, Rossendale and Darwen
EU Constituencies: North West
Election Frequency: Elections are by thirds
Twinning: Bocholt (Germany); Whitworth: Kandel (Germany)

PRINCIPAL OFFICERS
Chief Executive: Mrs Helen Lockwood, Chief Executive, The Business Centre, Futures Park, Newchurch Road, Bacup OL13 0BB ☎ 01706 252430 ✉ helenlockwood@rossendalebc.gov.uk

Senior Management: Mr Stephen Jackson, Head of Health, Housing & Regeneration, The Business Centre, Futures Park, Newchurch Road, Bacup OL13 0BB ☎ 01706 252404 🖷 01706 873577 ✉ stephenjackson@rossendalebc.gov.uk

Senior Management: Mrs Liz Sandiford, Head of People & Policy, Stubbylee Hall, Stubbylee Lane, Bacup OL13 0DE ☎ 01706 252452 🖷 01706 873577 ✉ lizsandiford@rossendalebc.gov.uk

Senior Management: Mr Phil Seddon, Head of Finance & Property, The Business Centre, Futures Park, Newchurch Road, Bacup OL13 0BB ☎ 01706 252465 🖷 01706 873577 ✉ philseddon@rossendalebc.gov.uk

Architect, Building / Property Services: Mr Mike Forster,

Property Services Manager, The Business Centre, Futures Park, Newchurch Road, Bacup OL13 0BB ☎ 01706 252442 michael.forster@rossendalebc.gov.uk

Best Value: Mrs Liz Sandiford, Head of People & Policy, Stubbylee Hall, Stubbylee Lane, Bacup OL13 0DE ☎ 01706 252452 🖷 01706 873577 lizsandiford@rossendalebc.gov.uk

Building Control: Mr Keith Bell, Building Control Manager, Town Centre Offices, Lord Street , Rawtenstall, Rossendale BB4 7LZ ☎ 01706 252526 🖷 01706 871618 keithbell@rossendalebc.gov.uk

PR / Communications: Mrs Liz Sandiford, Head of People & Policy, Stubbylee Hall, Stubbylee Lane, Bacup OL13 0DE ☎ 01706 252452 🖷 01706 873577 lizsandiford@rossendalebc.gov.uk

Community Planning: Mr Michael Riley, Communities Manager, Stubbylee Hall, Stubbylee Lane, Bacup OL13 0DE ☎ 01706 252412 michaelriley@rossendalebc.gov.uk

Community Safety: Mr Michael Riley, Communities Manager, Stubbylee Hall, Stubbylee Lane, Bacup OL13 0DE ☎ 01706 252412 michaelriley@rossendalebc.gov.uk

Computer Management: Mr Andrew Buckle, Head of Customer Services & ICT, The Business Centre, Futures Park, Newchurch Road, Bacup OL13 0BB ☎ 01706 238606 andrewbuckle@rossendalebc.gov.uk

Contracts: Mr Stuart Sugarman, Director of Business, The Business Centre, Futures Park, Newchurch Road, Bacup OL13 0BB ☎ 01706 252440 🖷 01706 873577 stuartsugarman@rossendalebc.gov.uk

Customer Service: Mr Andrew Buckle, Head of Customer Services & ICT, The Business Centre, Futures Park, Newchurch Road, Bacup OL13 0BB ☎ 01706 238606 andrewbuckle@rossendalebc.gov.uk

Economic Development: Mr Stephen Jackson, Head of Health, Housing & Regeneration, The Business Centre, Futures Park, Newchurch Road, Bacup OL13 0BB ☎ 01706 252404 🖷 01706 873577 stephenjackson@rossendalebc.gov.uk

E-Government: Mr Andrew Buckle, Head of Customer Services & ICT, The Business Centre, Futures Park, Newchurch Road, Bacup OL13 0BB ☎ 01706 238606 andrewbuckle@rossendalebc.gov.uk

Electoral Registration: Ms Joanne Smith, Elections Manager, The Business Centre, Futures Park, Newchurch Road, Bacup OL13 0BB ☎ 01706 252445 joannesmith@rossendalebc.gov.uk

Emergency Planning: Mr Michael Riley, Communities Manager, Stubbylee Hall, Stubbylee Lane, Bacup OL13 0DE ☎ 01706 252412 michaelriley@rossendalebc.gov.uk

Energy Management: Mr Lee Childs, Electric Engineer, The Busniess Centre, Futures Park, Bacup OL13 0BB ☎ 01706 252527 leechilds@rossendalebc.gov.uk

Environmental / Technical Services: Mr Michael Riley, Communities Manager, Stubbylee Hall, Stubbylee Lane, Bacup OL13 0DE ☎ 01706 252412 michaelriley@rossendalebc.gov.uk

Environmental Health: Mr Stephen Jackson, Head of Health, Housing & Regeneration, The Business Centre, Futures Park, Newchurch Road, Bacup OL13 0BB ☎ 01706 252404 🖷 01706 873577 stephenjackson@rossendalebc.gov.uk

Estates, Property & Valuation: Mr Mike Forster, Property Services Manager, The Business Centre, Futures Park, Newchurch Road, Bacup OL13 0BB ☎ 01706 252442 michael.forster@rossendalebc.gov.uk

Events Manager: Mr Michael Riley, Communities Manager, Stubbylee Hall, Stubbylee Lane, Bacup OL13 0DE ☎ 01706 252412 michaelriley@rossendalebc.gov.uk

Facilities: Mr Mike Forster, Property Services Manager, The Business Centre, Futures Park, Newchurch Road, Bacup OL13 0BB ☎ 01706 252442 michael.forster@rossendalebc.gov.uk

Finance and Treasurer: Mr Phil Seddon, Head of Finance & Property, The Business Centre, Futures Park, Newchurch Road, Bacup OL13 0BB ☎ 01706 252465 🖷 01706 873577 philseddon@rossendalebc.gov.uk

Fleet Management: Ms Christine Chadderton, Transport Co-ordinator, Henrietta Street Depot, Bacup OL13 0AR ☎ 01706 878660 christinechadderton@rossendalebc.gov.uk

Health and Safety: Mr D Lawrence, Health & Safety Adviser, Stubbylee Hall, Stubbylee Lane, Bacup OL13 0DE ☎ 01282 425011; 01706 252655 🖷 01282 455464 davidlawrence@rossendalebc.gov.uk

Home Energy Conservation: Mr Stephen Jackson, Head of Health, Housing & Regeneration, The Business Centre, Futures Park, Newchurch Road, Bacup OL13 0BB ☎ 01706 252404 🖷 01706 873577 stephenjackson@rossendalebc.gov.uk

Housing: Mr Stephen Jackson, Head of Health, Housing & Regeneration, The Business Centre, Futures Park, Newchurch Road, Bacup OL13 0BB ☎ 01706 252404 🖷 01706 873577 stephenjackson@rossendalebc.gov.uk

Legal: Mr Stuart Sugarman, Director of Business, The Business Centre, Futures Park, Newchurch Road, Bacup OL13 0BB ☎ 01706 252440 🖷 01706 873577 stuartsugarman@rossendalebc.gov.uk

Leisure and Cultural Services: Mr Martin Kay, Chief Executive, Rossendale Leisure Trust, 32 Kay Street, Rawtenstall, Rossendale BB4 7LS ☎ 01706 242311 martin.kay@rltrust.co.uk

Licensing: Ms Tracy Brzozowski, Licensing & Enforcement Manager, Town Centre Offices, Rawtenstall, Rossendale BB4 7LZ ☎ 01706 238602 tracybrzozowski@rossendalebc.gov.uk

Lifelong Learning: Mrs Liz Sandiford, Head of People & Policy, Stubbylee Hall, Stubbylee Lane, Bacup OL13 0DE ☎ 01706 252452 🖷 01706 873577 lizsandiford@rossendalebc.gov.uk

Lottery Funding, Charity and Voluntary: Mr Michael Riley, Communities Manager, Stubbylee Hall, Stubbylee Lane, Bacup OL13 0DE ☎ 01706 252412 ✉ michaelriley@rossendalebc.gov.uk

Member Services: Mrs Carolyn Sharples, Committee & Member Services Manager, The Business Centre, Futures Park, Newchurch Road, Bacup OL13 0BB ☎ 01706 252422 🖷 01706 873577 ✉ carolynsharples@rossendalebc.gov.uk

Partnerships: Mr Michael Riley, Communities Manager, Stubbylee Hall, Stubbylee Lane, Bacup OL13 0DE ☎ 01706 252412 ✉ michaelriley@rossendalebc.gov.uk

Personnel / HR: Mrs Liz Sandiford, Head of People & Policy, Stubbylee Hall, Stubbylee Lane, Bacup OL13 0DE ☎ 01706 252452 🖷 01706 873577 ✉ lizsandiford@rossendalebc.gov.uk

Planning: Mr Stephen Stray, Planning Manager, Town Centre Offices, Rawtenstall, Rossendale BB4 7LZ ☎ 01706 252420 ✉ stephenstray@rossendalebc.gov.uk

Procurement: Mrs Gillian Hampson, Corporate Procurement Assistant, The Business Centre, Futures Park, Newchurch Road, Bacup OL13 0BB ☎ 01706 252444 ✉ gillianhampson@rossendalebc.gov.uk

Regeneration: Mr Stephen Jackson, Head of Health, Housing & Regeneration, The Business Centre, Futures Park, Newchurch Road, Bacup OL13 0BB ☎ 01706 252404 🖷 01706 873577 ✉ stephenjackson@rossendalebc.gov.uk

Staff Training: Mrs Liz Sandiford, Head of People & Policy, Stubbylee Hall, Stubbylee Lane, Bacup OL13 0DE ☎ 01706 252452 🖷 01706 873577 ✉ lizsandiford@rossendalebc.gov.uk

Street Scene: Mr Michael Riley, Communities Manager, Stubbylee Hall, Stubbylee Lane, Bacup OL13 0DE ☎ 01706 252412 ✉ michaelriley@rossendalebc.gov.uk

Sustainable Communities: Mr Michael Riley, Communities Manager, Stubbylee Hall, Stubbylee Lane, Bacup OL13 0DE ☎ 01706 252412 ✉ michaelriley@rossendalebc.gov.uk

Tourism: Mr David Presto, Economic Development Manager, Business Centre, Futures Park, Newchurch Road, Bacup OL13 0BB ☎ 01706 252477 🖷 01706 873577 ✉ davidpresto@rossendalebc.gov.uk

Town Centre: Mr Stephen Jackson, Head of Health, Housing & Regeneration, The Business Centre, Futures Park, Newchurch Road, Bacup OL13 0BB ☎ 01706 252404 🖷 01706 873577 ✉ stephenjackson@rossendalebc.gov.uk

Transport: Ms Christine Chadderton, Transport Co-ordinator, Henrietta Street Depot, Bacup OL13 0AR ☎ 01706 878660 ✉ christinechadderton@rossendalebc.gov.uk

MEMBERS OF THE COUNCIL (36)

***Mayor:* Essex**, Brian (CON - Helmshore)
brianessex@rossendalebc.gov.uk
***Leader of the Council:* Barnes**, Alyson (LAB - Goodshaw)
alysonbarnes@rossendalebc.gov.uk
***Deputy Leader of the Council:* Serridge**, Sean (LAB - Healey and Whitworth)
seanserridge@rossendalebc.gov.uk
***Group Leader:* Smith**, Darryl (CON - Eden)
darrylsmith@rossendalebc.gov.uk
Aldred, Thomas (LAB - Facit and Shawforth)
thomasaldred@rossendalebc.gov.uk
Ashworth, Barbara (LAB - Greensclough)
barbaraashworth@rossendalebc.gov.uk
Bleakley, Caroline (LAB - Hareholme)
carolinebleakley@rossendalebc.gov.uk
Cheetham, Anne (CON - Eden)
annecheetham@rossendalebc.gov.uk
Crawforth, Colin (LAB - Hareholme)
colincrawforth@rossendalebc.gov.uk
Creaser, Karen (LAB - Whitewell)
karencreaser@rossendalebc.gov.uk
de Souza, Madeline (IND - Facit and Shawforth)
madelinedesouza@rossendalebc.gov.uk
Eaton, James (CON - Greensclough)
jameseaton@rossendalebc.gov.uk
Evans, Peter (CON - Helmshore)
peterevans@rossendalebc.gov.uk
Farrington, Dorothy (LAB - Goodshaw)
dorothyfarrington@rossendalebc.gov.uk
Fletcher, Andrea (LAB - Cribden)
andreafletcher@rossendalebc.gov.uk
Gill, Christine (LAB - Cribden)
christinegill@rossendalebc.gov.uk
Hughes, Steve (LAB - Irwell)
stevehughes@rossendalebc.gov.uk
Jackson, Helen (LAB - Irwell)
helenjackson@rossendalebc.gov.uk
Kenyon, Ann (LAB - Worsley)
annkenyon@rossendalebc.gov.uk
Knowles, Roy (LAB - Longholme)
royknowles@rossendalebc.gov.uk
Lamb, Christine (LAB - Stacksteads)
christinelamb@rossendalebc.gov.uk
MacNae, Andrew (LAB - Greensclough)
andrewmacnae@rossendalebc.gov.uk
Marriott, Patrick (LAB - Hareholme)
patrickmarriott@rossendalebc.gov.uk
McInnes, Liz (LAB - Longholme)
lizmcinnes@rossendalebc.gov.uk
Milling, Amanda (CON - Helmshore)
amandamilling@rossendalebc.gov.uk
Morris, Granville (CON - Greenfield)
granvillemorris@rossendalebc.gov.uk
Neal, Ronald (IND - Healey and Whitworth)
alanneal@rossendalebc.gov.uk
Oakes, Jackie (LAB - Stacksteads)
jackieoakes@rossendalebc.gov.uk
Pilling, Jim (LD - Whitewell)
jimpilling23@btinternet.com
Procter, Marilyn (LAB - Worsley)
marilynprocter@rossendalebc.gov.uk
Roberts, Peter (LAB - Longholme)
peterroberts@rossendalebc.gov.uk
Robertson, Amanda (LAB - Whitewell)
amandarobertson@rossendalebc.gov.uk
Sandiford, Gladys (CON - Greenfield)
gladyssandiford@rossendalebc.gov.uk
Shipley, Annabel (CON - Greenfield)

annabelshipley@rossendalebc.gov.uk
Smith, Michelle (LAB - Irwell)
michellesmith@rossendalebc.gov.uk
Wilkinson, Robert (LAB - Worsley)
robertwilkinson@rossendalebc.gov.uk

POLITICAL COMPOSITION
LAB: 24, CON: 9, IND: 2, LD: 1

CABINET
Deputy Leader: Customers, Legal and Licensing: Mr Sean Serridge
Housing and Environmental Health: Ms Helen Jackson
Leader: Communities and Partnerships: Ms Alyson Barnes
Operational Services and Development Control: Ms Christine Lamb
Regeneration, Tourism and Leisure: Mr Andrew MacNae
Finance & Resources: Mr Patrick Marriott

COMMITTEE CHAIRS
Development Control (Scrutiny): Ms Amanda Robertson
Licensing: Ms Christine Gill
Overview (Scrutiny): Mrs Liz McInnes
Performance (Scrutiny): Mrs Liz McInnes
Policy Overview (Scrutiny): Ms Christine Lamb

ROTHER D
Rother District Council, Town Hall, Bexhill-on-Sea TN39 3JX
☎ 01424 787878 🖷 01424 787879 ✉ chiefexec@rother.gov.uk
🖳 www.rother.gov.uk

FACTS & FIGURES
Police Authority: Sussex Police Authority
Health Authority: South East Coast Strategic Health Authority
Learning and Skills Council: South East
Parliamentary Constituencies: Bexhill and Battle
EU Constituencies: South East
Election Frequency: Elections are of whole council
Twinning: Battle: St. Valery-sur-Somme (France); Hurst Green: Ellerhoop (Germany)

PRINCIPAL OFFICERS
Chief Executive: Mr Derek Stevens, Chief Executive, Town Hall, Bexhill-on-Sea TN39 3JX ☎ 01424 787801 🖷 01424 787879 ✉ chiefexec@rother.gov.uk

Best Value: Ms Joanne Wright, Policy Officer, Town Hall, Bexhill-on-Sea TN39 3JX ☎ 01424 787000 🖷 01424 787879 ✉ joanne.wright@rother.gov.uk.

Building Control: Mr Jonathan Cornell, Chief Building Control Officer, Town Hall, Bexhill-on-Sea TN39 3JX ☎ 01424 787878 ✉ jonathan.cornell@rother.gov.uk

PR / Communications: Mr Daniel Collins, Senior Communications Officer, Town Hall, Bexhill-on-Sea TN39 3JX ☎ 01424 787000 🖷 01424 787879 ✉ daniel.collins@rother.gov.uk

Community Planning: Mrs Brenda Mason, Head of Policy & Performance, Town Hall, Bexhill-on-Sea TN39 3JX ☎ 01424 787000 🖷 01424 787520 ✉ brenda.mason@rother.gov.uk

Computer Management: Mr John Collins, Head of HR and Technology, Town Hall, Bexhill-on-Sea TN39 3JX ☎ 01424 787701 🖷 01424 787000 ✉ john.collins@rother.gov.uk

Corporate Services: Ms Suzanne Collins, Head of Corporate Resources, Town Hall, Bexhill-on-Sea TN39 3JX ☎ 01424 787000 🖷 01424 787879 ✉ suzanne.collins@rother.gov.uk

Customer Service: Ms Jo Morris, Manager of Customer Services & Development, Town Hall, Bexhill-on-Sea TN39 3JX ☎ 01424 787000 ✉ jo.morris@rother.gov.uk

Economic Development: Mr Graham Burgess, Head of Regeneration, Town Hall, Bexhill-on-Sea TN39 3JX ☎ 01424 787000 ✉ graham.burgess@rother.gov.uk

E-Government: Mr Derek Stevens, Chief Executive, Town Hall, Bexhill-on-Sea TN39 3JX ☎ 01424 787801 🖷 01424 787879 ✉ chiefexec@rother.gov.uk

Electoral Registration: Ms Suzanne Collins, Head of Corporate Resources, Town Hall, Bexhill-on-Sea TN39 3JX ☎ 01424 787000 🖷 01424 787879 ✉ suzanne.collins@rother.gov.uk

Emergency Planning: Mr Derek Stevens, Chief Executive, Town Hall, Bexhill-on-Sea TN39 3JX ☎ 01424 787801 🖷 01424 787879 ✉ chiefexec@rother.gov.uk

Environmental Health: Mr Richard Parker-Harding, Head of Environmental Health, 14 Beeching Road, Bexhill-on-Sea TN39 3LG ☎ 01424 787551 🖷 01424 787520 ✉ richard.parker-harding@ rother.gov.uk

Estates, Property & Valuation: Ms Suzanne Collins, Head of Corporate Resources, Town Hall, Bexhill-on-Sea TN39 3JX ☎ 01424 787000 🖷 01424 787879 ✉ suzanne.collins@rother.gov.uk

Facilities: Ms Kim Ross, Head of Amenities, Town Hall, Bexhill-on-Sea TN39 3JX ☎ 01424 787000 ✉ kim.ross@rother.gov.uk

Finance and Treasurer: Mr Malcolm Johnston, Director of Resources, Town Hall, Bexhill-on-Sea TN39 3JX ☎ 01424 787000 🖷 01424 787879 ✉ malcolm.johnston@rother.gov.uk

Finance and Treasurer: Mr Robin Vennard, Head of Finance, Town Hall, Bexhill-on-Sea TN39 3JX ☎ 01424 787000 ✉ robin.vennard@rother.gov.uk

Health and Safety: Mr John Collins, Head of HR and Technology, Town Hall, Bexhill-on-Sea TN39 3JX ☎ 01424 787701 🖷 01424 787000 ✉ john.collins@rother.gov.uk

Home Energy Conservation: Ms Fiona Berry, Home Energy Efficiency Officer, 14 Beeching Road, Bexhill-on-Sea TN39 3LG ☎ 01424 787000 ✉ fiona.berry@rother.gov.uk

Housing: Mrs Anne Fennessy, Head of Housing, Town Hall, Bexhill-on-Sea TN39 3JX ☎ 01424 787000 🖷 01424 787520 ✉ anne.fennessy@rother.gov.uk

Legal: Ms Suzanne Collins, Head of Corporate Resources, Town

Hall, Bexhill-on-Sea TN39 3JX ☎ 01424 787716 🖷 01424 787879 ✉ suzanne.collins@rother.gov.uk

Leisure and Cultural Services: Ms Kim Ross, Head of Amenities, Town Hall, Bexhill-on-Sea TN39 3JX ☎ 01424 787000 ✉ kim.ross@rother.gov.uk

Licensing: Mr Richard Parker-Harding, Head of Environmental Health, 14 Beeching Road, Bexhill-on-Sea TN39 3LG ☎ 01424 787551 🖷 01424 787520 ✉ richard.parker-harding@ rother.gov.uk

Member Services: Ms Suzanne Collins, Head of Corporate Resources, Town Hall, Bexhill-on-Sea TN39 3JX ☎ 01424 787000 🖷 01424 787879 ✉ suzanne.collins@rother.gov.uk

Parking: Ms Kim Ross, Head of Amenities, Town Hall, Bexhill-on-Sea TN39 3JX ☎ 01424 787000 ✉ kim.ross@rother.gov.uk

Personnel / HR: Mr John Collins, Head of HR and Technology, Town Hall, Bexhill-on-Sea TN39 3JX ☎ 01424 787701 🖷 01424 787000 ✉ john.collins@rother.gov.uk

Planning: Mr Tim Hickling, Head of Planning, Town Hall, Bexhill-on-Sea TN39 3JX ☎ 01424 787000 ✉ tim.hickling@rother.gov.uk

Recycling & Waste Minimisation: Ms Kim Ross, Head of Amenities, 14 Beeching Road, Bexhill-on-Sea TN39 3LG ☎ 01424 787000 ✉ kim.ross@rother.gov.uk

Regeneration: Mr Graham Burgess, Head of Regeneration, Town Hall, Bexhill-on-Sea TN39 3JX ☎ 01424 787000 ✉ graham.burgess@rother.gov.uk

Staff Training: Mr John Collins, Head of HR and Technology, Town Hall, Bexhill-on-Sea TN39 3JX ☎ 01424 787701 🖷 01424 787000 ✉ john.collins@rother.gov.uk

Sustainable Communities: Mrs Brenda Mason, Head of Policy & Performance, Town Hall, Bexhill-on-Sea TN39 3JX ☎ 01424 787000 🖷 01424 787520 ✉ brenda.mason@rother.gov.uk

Sustainable Development: Mrs Brenda Mason, Head of Policy & Performance, Town Hall, Bexhill-on-Sea TN39 3JX ☎ 01424 787000 🖷 01424 787520 ✉ brenda.mason@rother.gov.uk

Tourism: Mr Graham Burgess, Head of Regeneration, Town Hall, Bexhill-on-Sea TN39 3JX
☎ 01424 787000
✉ graham.burgess@rother.gov.uk

MEMBERS OF THE COUNCIL (38)

***Mayor:* Gadd**, Joanne (CON - Bexhill St Marks)
cllr.joanne.gadd@rother.gov.uk

***Deputy Mayor:* Winterborn**, Frances (LD - Bexhill Old Town)
cllr.frances.winterborn@rother.gov.uk

***Leader of the Council:* Maynard**, Carl (CON - Brede Valley)
cllr.carl.maynard@rother.gov.uk

***Deputy Leader of the Council:* Patten**, Robin (CON - Marsham)
cllr.robin.patten@rother.gov.uk

***Group Leader:* Dixon**, Kevin (LD - Battle)
cllr.kevin.dixon@rother.gov.uk

***Group Leader:* Earl**, Stuart (IND - Bexhill St Marks)
cllr.stuart.earl@rother.gov.uk

***Group Leader:* Souster**, Samuel (LAB - Rye)
cllr.sam.souster@rother.gov.uk

Ampthill, (CON - Rye)
cllr.david.russell@rother.gov.uk

Barnes, Mary (CON - Ticehurst & Etchingham)
cllr.mary.barnes@rother.gov.uk

Bird, Roger (CON - Marsham)
cllr.roger.bird@rother.gov.uk

Browne, Graham (CON - Salehurst)
cllr.graham.browne@rother.gov.uk

Carroll, Richard (CON - Bexhill Central)
cllr.richard.carroll@rother.gov.uk

Carroll, James (CON - Bexhill Sidley)
cllr.jim.carroll@rother.gov.uk

Clark, Charles (IND - Bexhill St Michaels)
cllr.charles.clark@rother.gov.uk

Davies, Angharad (CON - Crowhurst)
cllr.angharad.davies@rother.gov.uk

Douart, Patrick (CON - Bexhill Sackville)
cllr.patrick.douart@rother.gov.uk

Elford, Simon (CON - Bexhill St Michaels)
cllr.simon.elford@rother.gov.uk

Elliston, Robert (CON - Ticehurst and Etchingham)
cllr.robert.elliston@rother.gov.uk

Field, Kathryn (LD - Battle)
cllr.kathryn.field@rother.ac.uk

Ganly, Anthony (CON - Ewhurst and Sedlescombe)
cllr.tony.ganly@rother.gov.uk

George, Bridget (CON - Bexhill St Stephens)
cllr.bridget.george@rother.gov.uk

Hughes, Joyce (CON - Bexhill Central)
cllr.joy.hughes@rother.gov.uk

Jenkins, Ian (CON - Rother Levels)
cllr.ian.jenkins@rother.gov.uk

Johnson, Jonathan (CON - Brede Valley)
cllr.jonathon.johnson@rother.gov.uk

Kentfield, Brian (CON - Bexhill Kewhurst)
cllr.brian.kentfield@rother.gov.uk

Kenward, Martin (CON - Bexhill Kewhurst)
cllr.martin.kenward@rother.gov.uk

Lee, John (IND - Bexhill Collington)
cllr.john.lee@rother.gov.uk

Lendon, Paul (IND - Bexhill St Stephens)
cllr.paul.lendon@rother.gov.uk

Mansi, Tony (IND - Bexhill Collington)
cllr.tony.mansi@rother.gov.uk

Mooney, Martin (CON - Rother Levels)
cllr.martin.mooney@rother.gov.uk

Osborne, Paul (CON - Eastern Rother)
cllr.paul.osborne@rother.gov.uk

Prochak, Susan (LD - Salehurst)
cllr.susan.prochak@rother.gov.uk

Ramus, Charles (CON - Eastern Rother)
cllr.nicholas.ramus@rother.gov.uk

Vereker, David (CON - Darwell)
cllr.david.vereker@rother.gov.uk

Watson, Maurice (LAB - Bexhill Sidley)
cllr.maurice.watson@rother.gov.uk

White, Robert (CON - Darwell)
cllr.bob.white@rother.gov.uk

Williams, Deirdre (CON - Bexhill Sackville)
cllr.deirdre.williams@rother.gov.uk

Wood, James (LD - Bexhill Old Town)
cllr.stuart.wood@rother.gov.uk

POLITICAL COMPOSITION
CON: 26, IND: 5, LD: 5, LAB: 2

CABINET
Finance & Value for Money: Mr Robin Patten
Leader: Mr Carl Maynard
Deputy Leader: Mr Robin Patten
Recycling and Waste, Rural Affairs & Town Council Liaison: Mr Anthony Ganly
Strategic Planning: Mrs Bridget George
Transport, Communications & Working in Partnership: Lord Ampthill
Young People, Sport & Equalities: Mr Jonathan Johnson
Culture, Tourism & Leisure: Mr Martin Kenward
Housing & Older People: Mr Robert White

COMMITTEE CHAIRS
Licensing & General Purposes: Mr Robin Patten
Planning: Mr Brian Kentfield
Resources (Scrutiny): Mr Martin Mooney
Services (Scrutiny): Mr Paul Osborne
Standards: Mr Stuart Earl

ROTHERHAM M

Rotherham Metropolitan Borough Council, Riverside House, Main Street, Rotherham S60 1AE ☎ 01709 382121
💻 www.rotherham.gov.uk

FACTS & FIGURES
Police Authority: South Yorkshire Police Authority
Health Authority: NHS Yorkshire & the Humber
Learning and Skills Council: Yorkshire and the Humber
Parliamentary Constituencies: Rother Valley, Rotherham, Wentworth and Dearne
EU Constituencies: Yorkshire and the Humber
Election Frequency: Elections are by thirds
Twinning: St. Quentin (France)

PRINCIPAL OFFICERS
Chief Executive: Mr Martin Kimber, Chief Executive, Riverside House, Main Street, Rotherham S60 1AE ☎ 01709 822770 🖷 01709 822794

Assistant Chief Executive: Mr Phil Howe, Director- HR, Norfolk House, Walker Place, Rotherham S65 1ES ☎ 01709 823714 🖷 01709 823744 🖰 phil.howe@rotherham.gov.uk

Access Officer / Social Services (Disability): Mr Stuart Carr, Disability Co-ordinator, Riverside House, Main Street, Rotherham S60 1AE ☎ 01709 254022 🖰 stuart.carr@rotherham.gov.uk

Building Control: Mr Bruce Carter, Building Control Manager, Riverside House, Main Street, Rotherham S60 1AE ☎ 01709 829841 🖰 bruce.carter@rotherham.gov.uk

Catering Services: Mr Ron Parry, Principal Catering Officer, Riverside House, Main Street, Rotherham S60 1AE ☎ 01709 822300 🖰 ron.parry@rotherham.gov.uk

Children / Youth Services: Ms Dorothy Smith, Director - Schools and life long Learning, Norfolk House, Walker Place, Rotherham S65 1AS ☎ 01709 822678 🖰 dorothy.smith@rotherham.gov.uk

Children / Youth Services: Mrs Joyce Thacker, Strategic Director - Children & Young People's Services, Norfolk House, Walker Place, Rotherham S65 1AB ☎ 01709 822506 🖷 01709 822501 🖰 joyce.thacker@rotherham.gov.uk

Civil Registration: Ms Louise Sennit, Superintendant Registrar, Bailey House, Rawmarsh Road, Rotherham S60 1TD ☎ 01709 822896

PR / Communications: Mrs Tracy Holmes, Head - Communications, Riverside House, Main Street, Rotherham S60 1AE ☎ 01709 822735 🖷 01709 822730 🖰 tracy.holmes@rotherham.gov.uk

Community Safety: Mr Steve Parry, Safer Rotherham Partnership Co-ordinator, Riverside House, Main Street, Rotherham S60 1AE ☎ 01709 334565 🖷 01709 334568 🖰 steve.parry@rotherham.gov.uk

Consumer Protection and Trading Standards: Mrs Janice Manning, Principal Officer - Environmental Health, Reresby House, Bow Lane, Templeborough, Rotherham S60 1BY ☎ 01709 823126 🖷 01709 823150 🖰 janice.manning@rotherham.gov.uk

Contracts: Ms Chrissy Wright, Strategic Commissioning Manager, 2nd Floor Norfolk House, Walker Place, Rotherham S65 1ES ☎ 01709 823905 🖰 kim.curry@rotherham.gov.uk

Corporate Services: Mr Matt Gladstone, Director - Community, Policy and Performance, Riverside House, Main Street, Rotherham S60 1AE ☎ 01709 822775 🖰 matthew.gladstone@rotherham.gov.uk

Corporate Services: Ms Carole Haywood, Head - Policy & Partnerships, Riverside House, Main Street, Rotherham S60 1AE ☎ 01709 254435 🖰 Carole.haywood@rotherham.gov.uk

Corporate Services: Mrs Tracy Holmes, Head - Communications, Riverside House, Main Street, Rotherham S60 1AE ☎ 01709 822735 🖷 01709 822730 🖰 tracy.holmes@rotherham.gov.uk

Customer Service: Ms Zoe Oxley, Customer & Cultural Services Officer, Riverside House, Main Street, Rotherham S60 1AE ☎ 01709 382121 🖰 zoe.oxley@rotherham.gov.uk

Economic Development: Mr Karl Battersby, Strategic Director - Environemnt & Development Services, Riverside House, Main Street, Rotherham S60 1AE ☎ 01709 823801 🖷 01709 379419 🖰 karl.battersby@rotherham.gov.uk

Economic Development: Mr Paul Woodcock, Director - Planning & Regeneration, Bailey House, Rawmarsh Road, Rotherham S60 1QT ☎ 01709 822971 🖷 01709 823810 🖰 paul.woodcock@rotherham.gov.uk

Education: Ms Dorothy Smith, Director - Schools and life long Learning, Norfolk House, Walker Place, Rotherham S65 1AS ☎ 01709 822678 🖰 dorothy.smith@rotherham.gov.uk

Education: Mrs Joyce Thacker, Strategic Director - Children & Young People's Services, Norfolk House, Walker Place, Rotherham S65 1AB ☎ 01709 822506 🖷 01709 822501 ✉ joyce.thacker@rotherham.gov.uk

Electoral Registration: Ms Mags Evers, Elections & Registration Officer, Riverside House, Main Street, Rotherham S60 1AE ☎ 01709 823521 🖷 01709 367343 ✉ mags.evers@rotherham.gov.uk

Emergency Planning: Mr Anthony McDermott, Emergency & Safety Manager, Bailey House, Rawmarsh Road, Rotherham S65 1QT ☎ 01709 823878 ✉ anthony.mcdermott@rotherham.gov.uk

Energy Management: Mr David Rhodes, Corperative Environmental Officer, Bailey House, Rawmarsh Road, Rotherham S65 1QT ☎ 01709 822166 ✉ david.rhodes@rotherham.gov.uk

Environmental / Technical Services: Mr Tom Cray, Strategic Director - Neighbourhoods & Adult Services, Riverside House, Main Street, Rotherham S60 1AE ☎ 01709 823400 🖷 01709 823430 ✉ tom.cray@rotherham.gov.uk

Environmental Health: Mr Mark Ford, Safer Neighbourhoods Manager, Riverside House, Main Street, Rotherham S60 1AE ☎ 01709 254951 🖷 01709 823430 ✉ mark.ford@rotherham.gov.uk

Estates, Property & Valuation: Mr Colin Earl, Director - Internal Audit & Governance, Riverside House, Main Street, Rotherham S60 1AE ☎ 01709 822022 ✉ colin.earl@rotherham.gov.uk

Estates, Property & Valuation: Mr Dave Stimpson, Valuation Manager, Riverside House, Main Street, Rotherham S60 1AE ☎ 01709 254057 ✉ dave.stimpson@rotherham.gov.uk

European Liaison: Mr Paul Woodcock, Director - Planning & Regeneration, Bailey House, Rawmarsh Road, Rotherham S60 1QT ☎ 01709 822971 🖷 01709 823810 ✉ paul.woodcock@rotherham.gov.uk

Events Manager: Mrs Tracy Holmes, Head - Communications, Riverside House, Main Street, Rotherham S60 1AE ☎ 01709 822735 🖷 01709 822730 ✉ tracy.holmes@rotherham.gov.uk

Finance and Treasurer: Mr Andrew Bedford, Strategic Director - Finance, Riverside House, Main Street, Rotherham S60 1AE ☎ 01709 822002 🖷 01709 822792 ✉ andrew.bedford@rotherham.gov.uk

Finance and Treasurer: Mr Stuart Booth, Director - Finance, Council Offices, Grove Road, Rotherham S60 2ER ☎ 01709 822034 ✉ stuart.booth@rotherham.gov.uk

Finance and Treasurer: Mr Colin Earl, Director - Internal Audit & Governance, Riverside House, Main Street, Rotherham S60 1AE ☎ 01709 822022 ✉ colin.earl@rotherham.gov.uk

Finance and Treasurer: Mr Colin Earl, Director - Internal Audit & Governance, Riverside House, Main Street, Rotherham S60 1AE ☎ 01709 822022 ✉ colin.earl@rotherham.gov.uk

Finance and Treasurer: Mr Pete Hudson, Chief Finance Officer, Riverside House, Main Street, Rotherham S60 1AE ☎ 01709 822032 ✉ peter.hudson@rotherham.gov.uk

Health and Safety: Mrs Janice Manning, Principal Officer - Environmental Health, Reresby House, Bow Lane, Templeborough, Rotherham S60 1BY ☎ 01709 823126 🖷 01709 823150 ✉ janice.manning@rotherham.gov.uk

Highways: Mr David Burton, Director - Streetpride, Bailey House, Rawmarsh Road, Rotherham S65 1QT ☎ 01709 382121 ✉ david.burton@rotherham.gov.uk

Home Energy Conservation: Mr Paul Maplethorpe, Manager - Affordable Warmth & Sustainable Energy Co-ordinator, Reresby House, Bow Bridge Close, Templeborough, Rotherham S60 1BY ☎ 01709 334964 🖷 01709 334972 ✉ paul.maplethorpe@rotherham.gov.uk

Housing: Ms Teresa Butler, Director - Business Development, Riverside House, Main Street, Rotherham S60 1AE ☎ 01709 255642 ✉ teresa.butler@rotherham.gov.uk

Housing: Mr Tom Cray, Strategic Director - Neighbourhoods & Adult Services, Riverside House, Main Street, Rotherham S60 1AE ☎ 01709 823400 🖷 01709 823430 ✉ tom.cray@rotherham.gov.uk

Housing: Mr Dave Richmond, Director - Housing & Neighbourhood Services, 2nd Floor, Norfolk House, Walker Place, Rotherham S60 1HX ☎ 01709 823100 ✉ dave.richmond@rotherham.gov.uk

Housing: Mr Paul Webb, Director - Neighbourhood Management, Eastwood Depot, Chesterton Road, Rotherham S65 1SZ ☎ 01709 822296

Housing Maintenance: Ms Teresa Butler, Director - Business Development, Riverside House, Main Street, Rotherham S60 1AE ☎ 01709 255642 ✉ teresa.butler@rotherham.gov.uk

Legal: Mr Matt Gladstone, Director - Community, Policy and Performance, Riverside House, Main Street, Rotherham S60 1AE ☎ 01709 822775 ✉ matthew.gladstone@rotherham.gov.uk

Leisure and Cultural Services: Ms Helena Fisher, Head - Cultural Services, Riverside House, Main Street, Rotherham S60 1AE ☎ 01709 823623 ✉ helena.fisher@rotherham.gov.uk

Leisure and Cultural Services: Mr Steve Hallsworth, Lesiure Services Manager, Riverside House, Main Street, Rotherham S60 1AE ☎ 01709 382121

Lifelong Learning: Ms Helena Fisher, Head - Cultural Services, Riverside House, Main Street, Rotherham S60 1AE ☎ 01709 823623 ✉ helena.fisher@rotherham.gov.uk

Lifelong Learning: Ms Dorothy Smith, Director - Schools and life long Learning, Norfolk House, Walker Place, Rotherham S65 1AS ☎ 01709 822678 ✉ dorothy.smith@rotherham.gov.uk

Lifelong Learning: Mrs Joyce Thacker, Strategic Director - Children & Young People's Services, Norfolk House, Walker Place, Rotherham S65 1AB ☎ 01709 822506 🖷 01709 822501

joyce.thacker@rotherham.gov.uk

Lighting: Mr David Burton, Director - Streetpride, Bailey House, Rawmarsh Road, Rotherham S65 1QT ☎ 01709 382121 david.burton@rotherham.gov.uk

Lottery Funding, Charity and Voluntary: Mrs Deborah Fellowes, Manager - Policy, External & Regional Affairs, The Eric Manns Building, Council Offices, Doncaster Gate, Doncaster Road, Rotherham S65 1DJ ☎ 01709 822769 🖷 01709 822794 deborah.fellowes@rotherham.gov.uk

Parking: Mr Martin Beard, Parking Services Manager, Riverside House, Main Street, Rotherham S60 1AN ☎ 01709 822929 🖷 01709 373987 martin.beard@rotherham.gov.uk

Partnerships: Mr Mark Gannon, Transformation & Strategic Partnerships Manager, Riverside House, Main Street, Rotherham S60 1AE ☎ 01709 336536 mark.gannon@rotherham.gov.uk

Partnerships: Mrs Carole Haywood, Rotherham Partnership Manager, Council Offices, Doncaster Gate, Doncaster Road, Rotherham S60 1DJ ☎ 01709 254435 🖷 01709 254435 carole.haywood@rotherham.gov.uk

Personnel / HR: Mr Phil Howe, Director- HR, Norfolk House, Walker Place, Rotherham S65 1ES ☎ 01709 823714 🖷 01709 823744 phil.howe@rotherham.gov.uk

Planning: Mr Karl Battersby, Strategic Director - Environemnt & Development Services, Riverside House, Main Street, Rotherham S60 1AN ☎ 01709 823801 🖷 01709 379419 karl.battersby@rotherham.gov.uk

Procurement: Mr Mark Gannon, Transformation & Strategic Partnerships Manager, Riverside House, Main Street, Rotherham S60 1AE ☎ 01709 336536 mark.gannon@rotherham.gov.uk

Public Libraries: Ms Helena Fisher, Head - Cultural Services, Riverside House, Main Street, Rotherham S60 1AE ☎ 01709 823623 helena.fisher@rotherham.gov.uk

Recycling & Waste Minimisation: Mr Adrian Gabriel, Waste Strategy Manager, Hellaby Depot, Sandbeck Way, Hellaby, Rotherham S66 8QL ☎ 01709 823108 🖷 01709 823120 adrian.gabriel@rotherham.gov.uk

Regeneration: Mr Karl Battersby, Strategic Director - Environemnt & Development Services, Riverside House, Main Street, Rotherham S60 1AN ☎ 01709 823801 🖷 01709 379419 karl.battersby@rotherham.gov.uk

Regeneration: Mr Paul Woodcock, Director - Planning & Regeneration, Bailey House, Rawmarsh Road, Rotherham S60 1QT ☎ 01709 822971 🖷 01709 823810 paul.woodcock@rotherham.gov.uk

Social Services: Mr Tom Cray, Strategic Director - Neighbourhoods & Adult Services, Riverside House, Main Street, Rotherham S60 1AE ☎ 01709 823400 🖷 01709 823430 tom.cray@rotherham.gov.uk

Social Services (Adult): Mr Tom Cray, Strategic Director - Neighbourhoods & Adult Services, Riverside House, Main Street, Rotherham S60 1AE ☎ 01709 823400 🖷 01709 823430 tom.cray@rotherham.gov.uk

Social Services (Adult): Ms Sam Newton, Director - Asset & Care Management, Crinoline House, Effingham Square, Rotherham S65 1AW ☎ 01709 824062 sam.newton@rotherham.gov.uk

Social Services (Children): Mrs Gani Martins, Director - Locality Services, Norfolk House, Walker Place, Rotherham S65 1HX ☎ 01709 823905 🖷 01709 822398 gani.martins@rotherham.gov.uk

Staff Training: Mr Phil Howe, Director- HR, Coumcil Offices, Doncaster Gate, Doncaster Road, Rotherham S65 1DJ ☎ 01709 823714 🖷 01709 823744 phil.howe@rotherham.gov.uk

Street Scene: Mr David Burton, Director - Streetpride, Bailey House, Rawmarsh Road, Rotherham S65 1QT ☎ 01709 382121 david.burton@rotherham.gov.uk

Sustainable Communities: Mr Tom Cray, Strategic Director - Neighbourhoods & Adult Services, Riverside House, Main Street, Rotherham S60 1AE ☎ 01709 823400 🖷 01709 823430 tom.cray@rotherham.gov.uk

Town Centre: Ms Bernadette Rushton, Town Centre Manager, Riverside House, Main Street, Rotherham S60 1AE ☎ 01709 254888 bernadette.rushton@rotherham.gov.uk

Traffic Management: Mr Ian Ashmore, Principal Traffic Office, Riverside House, Main Street, Rotherham S60 1AN ☎ 01709 822825 🖷 01709 822370 ian.ashmore@rotherham.gov.uk

Transport: Mr David Burton, Director - Streetpride, Bailey House, Rawmarsh Road, Rotherham S65 1QT ☎ 01709 382121 david.burton@rotherham.gov.uk

Transport Planner: Mr David Burton, Director - Streetpride, Bailey House, Rawmarsh Road, Rotherham S65 1QT ☎ 01709 382121 david.burton@rotherham.gov.uk

Waste Collection and Disposal: Mr David Burton, Director - Streetpride, Bailey House, Rawmarsh Road, Rotherham S65 1QT ☎ 01709 382121 david.burton@rotherham.gov.uk

Waste Collection and Disposal: Mr Adrian Gabriel, Waste Strategy Manager, Hellaby Depot, Sandbeck Way, Hellaby, Rotherham S66 8QL ☎ 01709 823108 🖷 01709 823120 adrian.gabriel@rotherham.gov.uk

Waste Management: Mr Adrian Gabriel, Waste Strategy Manager, Hellaby Depot, Sandbeck Way, Hellaby, Rotherham S66 8QL ☎ 01709 823108 🖷 01709 823120 adrian.gabriel@rotherham.gov.uk

MEMBERS OF THE COUNCIL (63)

***Mayor:* Pickering**, Dave (LAB - Valley)
dave.pickering@rotherham.gov.uk

***Deputy Mayor:* Foden**, John (LAB - Rotherham West)

john.foden@rotherham.gov.uk
***Leader of the Council:* Stone**, Roger (LAB - Silverwood)
leader@rotherham.gov.uk
***Deputy Leader of the Council:* Akhtar**, Jahangir (LAB - Rotherham West)
jahangir.akhtar@rotherham.gov.uk
Ahmed, Shabana (LAB - Brinsworth and Catcliffe)
shabana.ahmed@rotherham.gov.uk
Ali, Shaukat (LAB - Rotherham East)
shaukat.ali@rotherham.gov.uk
Andrews, Jenny (LAB - Hellaby)
jenny.andrews@rotherham.gov.uk
Astbury, Lauren (LAB - Hellaby)
lauren.astbury@rotherham.gov.uk
Atkin, Alan (LAB - Wath)
alan.aitken@rotherham.gov.uk
Barron, Ian (LAB - Keppel)
ian.barron@rotherham.gov.uk
Beaumont, Christine (LAB - Maltby)
christine.beaumont@rotherham.gov.uk
Beck, Dominic (LAB - Wales)
dominic.beck@rotherham.gov.uk
Buckley, Alan (LAB - Brinsworth and Catcliffe)
alan.buckley@rotherham.gov.uk
Burton, Josephine (LAB - Anston and Woodsetts)
josephine.burton@rotherham.gov.uk
Clark, Maggi (LAB - Keppel)
maggi.clark@rotherham.gov.uk
Currie, Simon (LAB - Valley)
simon.currie@rotherham.gov.uk
Dalton, Judith (LAB - Anston and Woodsetts)
judith.dalton@rotherham.gov.uk
Dodson, Barry (LAB - Rotherham East)
barry.dodson@rotherham.gov.uk
Donaldson, Lynda (CON - Hellaby)
lynda.donaldson@rotherham.gov.uk
Doyle, John (LAB - Swinton)
john.doyle@rotherham.gov.uk
Ellis, Sue (LAB - Wickersley)
sue.ellis@rotherham.gov.uk
Falvey, Jacquie (LAB - Dinnington)
jacquie.falvey@rotherham.gov.uk
Gilding, John (CON - Sitwell)
john.gilding@rotherham.gov.uk
Godfrey, Maggie (LAB - Maltby)
maggie.godfrey@rotherham.gov.uk
Gosling, Alan (LAB - Wath)
alan.gosling@rotherham.gov.uk
Goulty, Kevin (LAB - Wingfield)
kevin.goulty@rotherham.gov.uk
Hamilton, Neil (LAB - Rawmarsh)
neil.hamilton@rotherham.gov.uk
Hamilton, Jane (LAB - Hoober)
jane.hamilton@rotherham.gov.uk
Havenhand, Jane (LAB - Dinnington)
jane.havenhand@rotherham.gov.uk
Hoddinott, Emma (LAB - Wickersley)
emma.hoddinott@rotherham.gov.uk
Hussain, Mahroof (LAB - Boston Castle)
mahroof.hussain@rotherham.gov.uk
Jepson, Clive (IND - Anston and Woodsetts)
clive.jepson@rotherham.gov.uk
Johnson, Lindsay (LAB - Wingfield)
lindsay.johnston@rotherham.gov.uk
Kaye, Barry (LAB - Keppel)
barry.kaye@rotherham.gov.uk
Lakin, Paul (LAB - Valley)
paul.lakin@rotherham.gov.uk
Lelliott, Denise (LAB - Rother Valley)
denise.lelliott@rotherham.gov.uk
License, Neil (LAB - Swinton)
neil.license@rotherham.gov.uk
Mannion, Anthony (CON - Sitwell)
anthony.mannion@rotherham.gov.uk
McNeely, Rose (LAB - Boston Castle)
rose.mcneely@rotherham.gov.uk
Middleton, Christopher (CON - Sitwell)
christopher.middleton@rotherham.gov.uk
Pitchley, Lyndsay (LAB - Holderness)
lyndsay.pitchley@rotherham.gov.uk
Read, Chris (LAB - Wickersley)
chris.read@rotherham.gov.uk
Robinson, Christopher (LAB - Holderness)
chris-cllr.robinson@rotherham.gov.uk
Roche, David (LAB - Hoober)
david.roche@rotherham.gov.uk
Roddison, Andrew (LAB - Brinsworth and Catcliffe)
andrew.roddison@rotherham.gov.uk
Rushforth, Amy (LAB - Maltby)
amy.rushworth@rotherham.gov.uk
Russell, Patricia (LAB - Silverwood)
patricia.russell@rotherham.gov.uk
Russell, Gwendoline (LAB - Silverwood)
ann.russell@rotherham.gov.uk
Russell, Richard (LAB - Rother Vale)
richard.russell@rotherham.gov.uk
Sangster, Alex (LAB - Wath)
alex.sangster@rotherham.gov.uk
Sharman, Terry (LAB - Wingfield)
terry.sharman@rotherham.gov.uk
Sims, Kath (LAB - Rotherham West)
kath.sims@rotherham.gov.uk
Smith, Gerald (LAB - Holderness)
gerald.smith@rotherham.gov.uk
Steele, Brian (LAB - Hoober)
brian.steele@rotherham.gov.uk
Swift, John (LAB - Rother Vale)
john.swift@rotherham.gov.uk
Tweed, Simon (LAB - Dinnington)
simon.tweed@rotherham.gov.uk
Wallis, Emma (LAB - Rotherham East)
emma.wallis@rotherham.gov.uk
Watson, Gordon (LAB - Wales)
gordon.watson@rotherham.gov.uk
Whelbourn, Glyn (LAB - Rawmarsh)
glyn.whelbourn@rotherham.gov.uk
Whysall, Jennifer (LAB - Wales)
jennifer.whysall@rotherham.gov.uk
Wootton, Peter (LAB - Boston Castle)
peter.wootton@rotherham.gov.uk
Wright, Shaun (LAB - Rawmarsh)
shaun.wright@rotherham.gov.uk
Wyatt, Ken
(LAB - Swinton)
ken.wyatt@rotherham.gov.uk

POLITICAL COMPOSITION

LAB: 58, CON: 4, IND: 1

CABINET

Safe & Attractive Neighbourhoods: Ms Rose McNeely
Leader: Mr Roger Stone
Adult Independence, Health & Wellbeing: Mr John Doyle
Health & Wellbeing: Mr Ken Wyatt
Safeguarding & Developing Learning Opportunities: Mr Paul Lakin
Culture & Tourism: Ms Amy Rushforth
Regeneration & Development: Mr Gerald Smith
Resources & Commissioning: Mr Ken Wyatt

COMMITTEE CHAIRS

Audit: Mr Alex Sangster
Children, Young People & Families Services (Scrutiny): Mr Paul Lakin
Licensing: Mr Peter Wootton
Planning: Mr Dave Pickering

RUGBY D

Rugby Borough Council, Town Hall, Evreux Way, Rugby CV21 2RR ☎ 01788 533533 🖷 01788 533565 the.council@rugby.gov.uk 💻 www.rugby.gov.uk

FACTS & FIGURES

Police Authority: Warwickshire Police Authority
Health Authority: NHS West Midlands
Learning and Skills Council: West Midlands
Parliamentary Constituencies: Nuneaton, Rugby
EU Constituencies: West Midlands
Election Frequency: Elections are by thirds
Twinning: Evreux (France); Russelsheim (Germany)

PRINCIPAL OFFICERS

Chief Executive: Mr Ian Davis, Executive Director, Town Hall, Evreux Way, Rugby CV21 2RR ☎ 01788 533700 ian.davis@rugby.gov.uk

Deputy Chief Executive: Mr Andrew Gabbitas, Executive Director, PO Box 16, Evreux Way, Town Hall, Rugby CV21 2RR ☎ 01788 533550 🖷 01788 533409 andrew.gabbitas@rugby.gov.uk

Access Officer / Social Services (Disability): Mr Tim Margerison, Corporate Property & Building Control Manager, PO Box 16, Evreux Way, Town Hall, Rugby CV21 2RR ☎ 01788 533407 tim.margerison@rugby.gov.uk

Architect, Building / Property Services: Mr Tim Margerison, Corporate Property & Building Control Manager, PO Box 16, Evreux Way, Town Hall, Rugby CV21 2RR ☎ 01788 533407 tim.margerison@rugby.gov.uk

Best Value: Mr Doug Jones, Head of Business Transformation, Town Hall, Evreux Way, Rugby CV21 2LB ☎ 01788 533668 doug.jones@rugby.gov.uk

Building Control: Mr Tim Margerison, Corporate Property & Building Control Manager, PO Box 16, Evreux Way, Town Hall, Rugby CV21 2RR ☎ 01788 533407 tim.margerison@rugby.gov.uk

PR / Communications: Mr Matthew Deaves, Communication, Consultation & Information Manager, Town Hall, Evreux Way, Rugby CV21 2RR ☎ 01788 533562 matthew.deaves@rugby.gov.uk

Community Planning: Mrs Raj Chand, Head of Customer & Information Services, Town Hall, Evreux Way, Rugby CV21 2RR ☎ 01788 533870 raj.chand@rugby.gov.uk

Community Safety: Mr David Burrows, Regulatory Services Manager, Town Hall, Evreux Way, Rugby CV21 2RR ☎ 01788 533806 david.burrows@rugby.gov.uk

Computer Management: Mr Doug Jones, Head of Business Transformation, Town Hall, Evreux Way, Rugby CV21 2RR ☎ 01788 533668 doug.jones@rugby.gov.uk

Customer Service: Mrs Raj Chand, Head of Customer & Information Services, Town Hall, Evreux Way, Rugby CV21 2RR ☎ 01788 533870 raj.chand@rugby.gov.uk

Direct Labour: Mr Sean Lawson, Head of Environmental Services, Town Hall, Evreux Way, Rugby CV21 2RR ☎ 01788 533737 sean.lawson@rugby.gov.uk

Economic Development: Mr Robert Back, Forward Planning & Economic Development Manager, Town Hall, Evreux Way, Rugby CV21 2RR ☎ 01788 533752 robert.back@rugby.gov.uk

E-Government: Mr Doug Jones, Head of Business Transformation, Town Hall, Evreux Way, Rugby CV21 2RR ☎ 01788 533668 doug.jones@rugby.gov.uk

Electoral Registration: Mr Anthony Bingham, Elections Officer, Town Hall, Evreux Way, Rugby CV21 2RR ☎ 01788 533595 tony.bingham@rugby.gov.uk

Electoral Registration: Mr Mark Neale, Legal & Elections Manager, Town Hall, Evreux Way, Rugby CV21 2RR ☎ 01788 533510 mark.neale@rugby.gov.uk

Emergency Planning: Mr Sean Lawson, Head of Environmental Services, Town Hall, Evreux Way, Rugby CV21 2RR ☎ 01788 533737 sean.lawson@rugby.gov.uk

Energy Management: Mr Tim Margerison, Corporate Property & Building Control Manager, PO Box 16, Evreux Way, Town Hall, Rugby CV21 2RR ☎ 01788 533407 tim.margerison@rugby.gov.uk

Environmental / Technical Services: Mr Ian Davis, Deputy Chief Executive, PO Box 123, Town Hall, Evreux Way, Rugby CV21 2RR ☎ 01788 533700 🖷 01788 533778 ian.davis@rugby.gov.uk

Environmental / Technical Services: Mr Sean Lawson, Head of Environmental Services, Town Hall, Evreux Way, Rugby CV21 2RR ☎ 01788 533737 sean.lawson@rugby.gov.uk

Environmental / Technical Services: Mr Chris Worman, Parks & Open Spaces Team Leader, Town Hall, Evreux Way, Rugby CV21 2RR ☎ 01788 533706 chris.worman@rugby.gov.uk

Environmental Health: Mr Sean Lawson, Head of Environmental Services, Town Hall, Evreux Way, Rugby CV21 2RR ☎ 01788 533737 ✉ sean.lawson@rugby.gov.uk

Estates, Property & Valuation: Ms Anna Rose, Head of Planning & Culture, Town Hall, Evreux Way, Rugby CV21 2RR ☎ 01788 533737 ✉ anna.rose@rugby.gov.uk

Finance and Treasurer: Mr Adam Norburn, Head of Resources, Town Hall, Evreux Way, Rugby CV21 2RR ☎ 01788 533737 ✉ adam.norburn@rugby.gov.uk

Grounds Maintenance: Mr Chris Worman, Parks & Open Spaces Team Leader, Town Hall, Evreux Way, Rugby CV21 2RR ☎ 01788 533706 ✉ chris.worman@rugby.gov.uk

Health and Safety: Mr Sean Lawson, Head of Environmental Services, Town Hall, Evreux Way, Rugby CV21 2RR ☎ 01788 533737 ✉ sean.lawson@rugby.gov.uk

Housing: Mr Steve Shanahan, Head of Housing, Town Hall, Evreux Way, Rugby CV21 2RR ☎ 01788 533801 ✉ steve.shanahan@rugby.gov.uk

Housing Maintenance: Mr Steve Shanahan, Head of Housing, Town Hall, Evreux Way, Rugby CV21 2RR ☎ 01788 533801 ✉ steve.shanahan@rugby.gov.uk

Legal: Mr Mark Neale, Legal & Elections Manager, Town Hall, Evreux Way, Rugby CV21 2RR ☎ 01788 533510 ✉ mark.neale@rugby.gov.uk

Leisure and Cultural Services: Ms Anna Rose, Head of Planning & Culture, Town Hall, Evreux Way, Rugby CV21 2RR ☎ 01788 533737 ✉ anna.rose@rugby.gov.uk

Licensing: Mr Sean Lawson, Head of Environmental Services, Town Hall, Evreux Way, Rugby CV21 2RR ☎ 01788 533737 ✉ sean.lawson@rugby.gov.uk

Member Services: Mr Steve Garrison, Democratic Services Manager, Town Hall, Evreux Way, Rugby CV21 2RR ☎ 01788 533521 ✉ steve.garrison@rugby.gov.uk

Parking: Mr Jim Owen, Parking Services Team Leader, Town Hall, Evreux Way, Rugby CV21 2RR ☎ 01788 533729 ✉ jim.owen@rugby.gov.uk

Personnel / HR: Ms Suzanne Turner, Human Resources Manager, Town Hall, Evreux Way, Rugby CV21 2RR ☎ 01788 533570 ✉ suzanne.turner@rugby.gov.uk

Planning: Ms Anna Rose, Head of Planning & Culture, Town Hall, Evreux Way, Rugby CV21 2RR ☎ 01788 533737 ✉ anna.rose@rugby.gov.uk

Procurement: Mr Doug Jones, Head of Business Transformation, Town Hall, Evreux Way, Rugby CV21 2RR ☎ 01788 533668 ✉ doug.jones@rugby.gov.uk

Recycling & Waste Minimisation: Mr Sean Lawson, Head of Environmental Services, Town Hall, Evreux Way, Rugby CV21 2RR ☎ 01788 533737 ✉ sean.lawson@rugby.gov.uk

Regeneration: Mr Steve Shanahan, Head of Housing, Town Hall, Evreux Way, Rugby CV21 2RR ☎ 01788 533801 ✉ steve.shanahan@rugby.gov.uk

Staff Training: Ms Elaine McGladdery, Learning & Organisational Development Officer, Town Hall, Evreux Way, Rugby CV21 2RR ☎ 01788 533574 ✉ rozey.plowright@rugby.gov.uk

Street Scene: Mr Sean Lawson, Head of Environmental Services, Town Hall, Evreux Way, Rugby CV21 2RR ☎ 01788 533737 ✉ sean.lawson@rugby.gov.uk

Sustainable Communities: Mr Ian Davis, Deputy Chief Executive, PO Box 123, Town Hall, Evreux Way, Rugby CV21 2RR ☎ 01788 533700 🖷 01788 533778 ✉ ian.davis@rugby.gov.uk

Sustainable Development: Mr Doug Jones, Head of Business Transformation, Town Hall, Evreux Way, Rugby CV21 2RR ☎ 01788 533668 ✉ doug.jones@rugby.gov.uk

Tourism: Mrs Nikki Grange, Arts Heritage & Tourism Manager, Rugby Art Gallery & Museum, Little Elborow Street, Rugby CV21 3BZ ☎ 01788 533203 ✉ nikki.grange@rugby.gov.uk

Town Centre: Mr Robin Richter, Managing Director - Rugby Town Centre Company Ltd, Office Suite 20-21, 9 North Street, Rugby CV21 2AB ☎ 01788 572150 ✉ robin.richter@rugby.gov.uk

Transport: Mr Sean Lawson, Head of Environmental Services, Town Hall, Evreux Way, Rugby CV21 2RR ☎ 01788 533737 ✉ sean.lawson@rugby.gov.uk

Waste Collection and Disposal: Mr Sean Lawson, Head of Environmental Services, Town Hall, Evreux Way, Rugby CV21 2RR ☎ 01788 533737 ✉ sean.lawson@rugby.gov.uk

Waste Management: Mr Sean Lawson, Head of Environmental Services, Town Hall, Evreux Way, Rugby CV21 2RR ☎ 01788 533737 ✉ sean.lawson@rugby.gov.uk

MEMBERS OF THE COUNCIL (42)

***Mayor:* Lawrence**, Kathryn (CON - Hillmorton)
kathryn.lawrence@rugby.gov.uk

***Deputy Mayor:* Gillias**, Anthony (CON - Revel & Binley Woods)
anthony.gillias@rugby.gov.uk

***Leader of the Council:* Humphrey**, Craig (CON - Bilton)
craig.humphrey@rugby.gov.uk

***Deputy Leader of the Council:* Poole**, Derek (CON - Wolston & the Lawfords)
derek.poole@rugby.gov.uk

***Group Leader:* Roodhouse**, Jerry (LD - Paddox)
jerry.roodhouse@rugby.gov.uk

***Group Leader:* Shera**, Jim (LAB - Benn)
jim.shera@rugby.gov.uk

Allen, Nigel (CON - Hillmorton)
nigel.allen@rugby.gov.uk

Avis, Tina (LAB - New Bilton)
tina.avis@rugby.gov.uk

Avis, Howard (LAB - Rokeby & Overslade) bluesteel@fsmail.net

Bragg, Sally (CON - Wolston & the Lawfords)
sally.bragg@rugby.gov.uk

Butlin, Peter (CON - Admirals & Cawston)
peter.butlin@rugby.gov.uk
Coles, Andy (LAB - Newbold & Brownsover)
andy.coles@rugby.gov.uk
Cranham, David (CON - Coton & Boughton)
david.cranham:rugby.gov.uk
Dodd, Richard (LD - Paddox)
richard.dodd@rugby.gov.uk
Edwards, Claire (LAB - Newbold & Brownsover)
claire.edwards@rugby.gov.uk
Francis, Graham (CON - Dunsmore)
graham.francis@rugby.gov.uk
Francis, Matthew (CON - Rokeby & Overslade)
matthew.francis@rugby.gov.uk
Garcia, Belinda (CON - Revel & Binley Woods)
belindagb@aol.com
Hazelton, Robin (CON - Leam Valley)
robin.hazelton@grandborough.net
Hunt, Leigh (CON - Clifton, Newton & Churchover)
leigh.hunt@rugby.gov.uk
Kaur, Kam (CON - Rokeby & Overslade)
kamalkit.kaur@rugby.gov.uk
Keeling, Dale (LD - Eastlands)
dale.keeling@rugby.gov.uk
Lowe, Ian (CON - Dunsmore)
ianlowe@auxilium.freeserve.co.uk
Mahoney, Tom (LAB - Benn)
tom.mahoney@rugby.gov.uk
McNally, Robert (LAB - New Bilton)
rmcnar001@aol.com
Mistry, Ish (LAB - New Bilton)
ishmistry@hotmail.co.uk
New, Noreen (LD - Paddox)
noreen.new@rugby.gov.uk
O'Rourke, Maggie (LAB - Benn)
maggie.o'rourke@rugby.gov.uk
Pacey-Day, Chris (CON - Wolvey & Shilton)
chris@hi-tekdial.co.uk
Parker, Lisa (CON - Bilton)
lisa.parker@rugby.gov.uk
Robbins, Carolyn (CON - Coton & Boughton)
carolyn.robbins@rugby.gov.uk
Roberts, Howard (IND - Dunsmore)
howard.roberts@rugby.gov.uk
Roodhouse, Sue (LD - Eastlands)
sue.roodhouse@rugby.gov.uk
Sandison, Neil (LD - Eastlands)
neil.sandison@rugby.gov.uk
Sewell, Bill (CON - Hillmorton)
bill.sewell@rugby.gov.uk
Srivastava, Ramesh (LAB - Newbold & Brownover)
ramesh.srivastava@rugby.gov.uk
Stokes, Michael (CON - Admirals & Cawston)
michael.stokes@rugby.gov.uk
Timms, Heather (CON - Revel & Binley Woods)
heather.timms@rugby.gov.uk
Walton, Helen (CON - Coton & Boughton)
helen.walton@rugby.gov.uk
Watson, Claire (CON - Wolston & the Lawfords)
claire.watson@rugby.gov.uk
Williams, Mark (CON - Admirals & Cawston)
mark.williams@rugby.gov.uk
Wright, David (CON - Bilton)
david.wright@rugby.gov.uk

POLITICAL COMPOSITION
CON: 25, LAB: 10, LD: 6, IND: 1

CABINET
Leader: Mr Craig Humphreys
Deputy Leader: Mr Derek Poole
Economy, Development & Culture: Mrs Heather Timms
Resources & Corporate Governance: Mr David Cranham
Sustainable Environment: Dr Mark Williams
Sustainable Inclusive Communities: Ms Leigh Hunt

COMMITTEE CHAIRS
Appeals (Scrutiny): Mr Anthony Gillias
Audit (Scrutiny): Mr P Dudfield (External)
Corporate Performance (Scrutiny): Mr Ish Mistry
Crime & Disorder: Mr Michael Stokes
Customer & Partnerships (Scrutiny): Ms Claire Edwards
Licensing & Safety (Scrutiny): Mrs Lisa Parker
Overview & Scrutiny Management Board: Dr Jim Shera
Planning (Scrutiny): Mr Peter Butlin

RUNNYMEDE D

Runnymede Borough Council, Civic Offices, Station Road, Addlestone KT15 2AH ☎ 01932 838383 🖷 01932 838384 ✉ generalenquiries@runnymede.gov.uk 🖳 www.runnymede.gov.uk

FACTS & FIGURES
Police Authority: Surrey Police Authority
Health Authority: South East Coast Strategic Health Authority
Learning and Skills Council: South East
Parliamentary Constituencies: Runnymede and Weybridge
EU Constituencies: South East
Election Frequency: Elections are by thirds
Twinning: Bergisch-Gladbach (Germany); Herndon (USA); Joinville-le-Pont (France)

PRINCIPAL OFFICERS
Chief Executive: Mr Paul Turrell, Chief Executive, Civic Offices, Station Road, Addlestone KT15 2AH ☎ 01932 425500 🖷 01932 838384 ✉ paul.turrell@runnymede.gov.uk

Senior Management: Mrs Deborah Blowers, Director of Housing & Community Services, Civic Offices, Station Road, Addlestone KT15 2AH ☎ 01932 425800 🖷 01932 838384 ✉ deborah.blowers@runnymede.gov.uk

Senior Management: Mr Mario Leo, Head of Governance and Assets, Civic Offices, Station Road, Addlestone KT15 2AH ☎ 01932 425640 ✉ mario.leo@runnymede.gov.uk

Senior Management: Mr Peter Sims, Director of Technical Services, Civic Offices, Station Road, Addlestone KT15 2AH ☎ 01932 415100 🖷 01932 838384 ✉ peter.sims@runnymede.gov.uk

Architect, Building / Property Services: Mr Brian Mannian, Principal Building Services Manager, Civic Offices, Station Road, Addlestone KT15 2AH ☎ 01932 425170 🖷 01932 838384 ✉ brian.mannian@runnymede.gov.uk

Building Control: Mr David Jones, Building Control Manager,

Civic Offices, Station Road, Addlestone KT15 2AH ☎ 01932 425160 🖷 01932 838384 ✉ david.jones@runnymede.gov.uk

PR / Communications: Ms Kayo Rippingham, Communications Officer, Civic Offices, Station Road, Addlestone KT15 2AH ☎ 01932 425504 ✉ kayo.rippingham@runnymede.gov.uk

Community Safety: Mrs Wendy Roberts, Community Safety Officer, Civic Offices, Station Road, Addlestone KT15 2AH ☎ 01932 425065 ✉ wendy.roberts@runnymede.gov.uk

Computer Management: Mrs Helen Dunn, Information Systems Manager, Civic Offices, Station Road, Addlestone KT15 2AH ☎ 01784 446248 ✉ h.dunn@spelthorne.gov.uk

Contracts: Mr Hywel Jones, Head of Procurement, Civic Offices, Station Road, Addlestone KT15 2AH ☎ 01932 425772 🖷 01932 838384 ✉ hywel.jones@runnymede.gov.uk

Corporate Services: Mr Mario Leo, Head of Governance and Assets, Civic Offices, Station Road, Addlestone KT15 2AH ☎ 01932 425640 ✉ mario.leo@runnymede.gov.uk

Economic Development: Mr Paul Turrell, Chief Executive, Civic Offices, Station Road, Addlestone KT15 2AH ☎ 01932 425500 🖷 01932 838384 ✉ paul.turrell@runnymede.gov.uk

E-Government: Mrs Helen Dunn, Information Systems Manager, Civic Offices, Station Road, Addlestone KT15 2AH ☎ 01784 446248 ✉ h.dunn@spelthorne.gov.uk

Electoral Registration: Mr Rob Curtis, Elections Services Supervisor, Civic Offices, Station Road, Addlestone KT15 2AH ☎ 01932 425650 🖷 01932 838384 ✉ rob.curtis@runnymede.gov.uk

Emergency Planning: Mr Nicholas Moon, Emergency Planning Officer, Civic Offices, Station Road, Addlestone KT15 2AH ☎ 01932 425178 🖷 01932 838384 ✉ nicholas.moon@runnymede.gov.uk

Energy Management: Mr Brian Mannian, Principal Building Services Manager, Civic Offices, Station Road, Addlestone KT15 2AH ☎ 01932 425170 🖷 01932 838384 ✉ brian.mannian@runnymede.gov.uk

Environmental / Technical Services: Mr Peter Burke, Acting Environmental Health Manager, Civic Offices, Station Road, Addlestone KT15 2AH ☎ 01932 425734 🖷 01932 838384 ✉ peter.burke@runnymede.gov.uk

Environmental Health: Mr Peter Burke, Acting Environmental Health Manager, Civic Offices, Station Road, Addlestone KT15 2AH ☎ 01932 425734 🖷 01932 838384 ✉ peter.burke@runnymede.gov.uk

Estates, Property & Valuation: Mr Ian Gifford, Borough Valuer, Civic Offices, Station Road, Addlestone KT15 2AH ☎ 01932 425690 🖷 01932 838384 ✉ ian.gifford@runnymede.gov.uk

Facilities: Mr Brian Mannian, Principal Building Services Manager, Civic Offices, Station Road, Addlestone KT15 2AH ☎ 01932 425170 🖷 01932 838384 ✉ brian.mannian@runnymede.gov.uk

Finance and Treasurer: Mr Nigel Boyd, Head of Revenues, Civic Offices, Station Road, Addlestone KT15 2AH ☎ 01932 838383 🖷 01932 838384 ✉ nigel.boyd@runnymede.gov.uk

Fleet Management: Mr Alan Potter, Transport Officer, Chertsey Depot, Ford Road, Chertsey KT16 8HG ☎ 01932 425770 🖷 01932 425771 ✉ alan.potter@runnymede.gov.uk

Grounds Maintenance: Mr Peter Winfield, Parks and Amenities Manager, Civic Offices, Station Road, Addlestone KT15 2AH ☎ 01932 425673 🖷 01932 838384 ✉ peter.winfield@runnymede.gov.uk

Health and Safety: Mr Ed Keith, Safety Adviser/Technician, Civic Offices, Station Road, Addlestone KT15 2AH ☎ 01932 425724 🖷 01932 838384 ✉ ed.keith@runnymede.gov.uk

Highways: Mr Stephen Fuggles, Head of Engineering, Civic Offices, Station Road, Addlestone KT15 2AH ☎ 01932 425120 🖷 01932 838384 ✉ stephen.fuggles@runnymede.gov.uk

Home Energy Conservation: Mrs Verena Boxall, Energy Project Manager, Civic Offices, Station Road, Addlestone KT15 2AH ☎ 01932 425120 🖷 01932 838384 ✉ verena.boxall@runnymede.gov.uk

Housing: Mrs Deborah Blowers, Director of Housing & Community Services, Civic Offices, Station Road, Addlestone KT15 2AH ☎ 01932 425800 🖷 01932 838384 ✉ deborah.blowers@runnymede.gov.uk

Housing Maintenance: Mr Ian Blowers, Head of Tenant Services, Civic Offices, Station Road, Addlestone KT15 2AH ☎ 01932 425850 🖷 01932 425803 ✉ ian.blowers@runnymede.gov.uk

Legal: Mr Mario Leo, Head of Governance and Assets, Civic Offices, Station Road, Addlestone KT15 2AH ☎ 01932 425640 ✉ mario.leo@runnymede.gov.uk

Leisure and Cultural Services: Mr Chris Hunt, Head of Leisure Services, Civic Offices, Station Road, Addlestone KT15 2AH ☎ 01932 425670 🖷 01938 838384 ✉ chris.hunt@runnymede.gov.uk

Licensing: Mr Peter Burke, Acting Environmental Health Manager, Civic Offices, Station Road, Addlestone KT15 2AH ☎ 01932 425734 🖷 01932 838384 ✉ peter.burke@runnymede.gov.uk

Lighting: Mr Paul Sebego, Electrical Works Division, Chertsey Depot, Ford Road, KT16 8HG ☎ 01932 425773 🖷 01932 425771 ✉ paul.sebego@runnymede.gov.uk

Member Services: Mr Mario Leo, Head of Governance and Assets, Civic Offices, Station Road, Addlestone KT15 2AH ☎ 01932 425640 ✉ mario.leo@runnymede.gov.uk

Parking: Mr Stephen Fuggles, Head of Engineering, Civic Offices, Station Road, Addlestone KT15 2AH ☎ 01932 425120

🖷 01932 838384 ✉ stephen.fuggles@runnymede.gov.uk

Partnerships: Miss Suzanne Harrison, Community Partnership Officer, Civic Offices, Station Road, Addlestone KT15 2AH ☎ 01932 425869 🖷 01932 838384 ✉ suzanne.harrison@runnymede.gov.uk

Personnel / HR: Ms Jan Hunt, Head of HR, Civic Offices, Station Road, Addlestone KT15 2AH ☎ 01932 425510 ✉ jan.hunt@runnymede.gov.uk

Planning: Mr Peter Sims, Director of Technical Services, Civic Offices, Station Road, Addlestone KT15 2AH ☎ 01932 415100 🖷 01932 838384 ✉ peter.sims@runnymede.gov.uk

Procurement: Mr Hywel Jones, Head of Procurement, Civic Offices, Station Road, Addlestone KT15 2AH ☎ 01932 425772 🖷 01932 838384 ✉ hywel.jones@runnymede.gov.uk

Recycling & Waste Minimisation: Mr Peter Burke, Acting Environmental Health Manager, Civic Offices, Station Road, Addlestone KT15 2AH ☎ 01932 425734 🖷 01932 838384 ✉ peter.burke@runnymede.gov.uk

Regeneration: Mr Paul Turrell, Chief Executive, Civic Offices, Station Road, Addlestone KT15 2AH ☎ 01932 425500 🖷 01932 838384 ✉ paul.turrell@runnymede.gov.uk

Staff Training: Mrs Angela Brown, Assistant Personnel Officer, Civic Offices, Station Road, Addlestone KT15 2AH ☎ 01932 425513 🖷 01932 838384 ✉ angela.brown@runnymede.gov.uk

Street Scene: Mr Stephen Fuggles, Head of Engineering, Civic Offices, Station Road, Addlestone KT15 2AH ☎ 01932 425120 🖷 01932 838384 ✉ stephen.fuggles@runnymede.gov.uk

Sustainable Development: Mr Bob Etheridge, Policy & Implementation Manager, Civic Offices, Station Road, Addlestone KT15 2AH ☎ 01932 425270 🖷 01932 838384 ✉ bob.etheridge@runnymede.gov.uk

Tourism: Mr Chris Hunt, Head of Leisure Services, Civic Offices, Station Road, Addlestone KT15 2AH ☎ 01932 425670 🖷 01938 838384 ✉ chris.hunt@runnymede.gov.uk

Town Centre: Mr Stephen Fuggles, Head of Engineering, Civic Offices, Station Road, Addlestone KT15 2AH ☎ 01932 425120 🖷 01932 838384 ✉ stephen.fuggles@runnymede.gov.uk

Transport: Mr Alan Potter, Transport Officer, Chertsey Depot, Ford Road, Chertsey KT16 8HG ☎ 01932 425770 🖷 01932 425771 ✉ alan.potter@runnymede.gov.uk

Transport Planner: Mr Paul Turrell, Chief Executive, Civic Offices, Station Road, Addlestone KT15 2AH ☎ 01932 425500 🖷 01932 838384 ✉ paul.turrell@runnymede.gov.uk

Waste Collection and Disposal: Mr Dave Stedman, Director - Service Organisation Manager, Chertsey Depot, Ford Road, Chertsey KT16 8HG ☎ 01932 425760 🖷 01932 425771 ✉ dave.stedman@runnymede.gov.uk

Waste Management: Mr Paul Turrell, Chief Executive, Civic Offices, Station Road, Addlestone KT15 2AH ☎ 01932 425500 🖷 01932 838384 ✉ paul.turrell@runnymede.gov.uk

MEMBERS OF THE COUNCIL (42)

***Mayor:* Gillham**, Linda (R - Thorpe)
cllr.linda.gillham@runnymede.gov.uk
***Deputy Mayor:* Lay**, Yvonna (CON - Egham Hythe)
cllr.yvonna.lay@runnymede.gov.uk
***Leader of the Council:* Roberts**, Patrick (CON - Englefield Green East)
cllr.patrick.roberts@runnymede.gov.uk
***Deputy Leader of the Council:* Woodger**, Geoffrey (CON - Virginia Water)
cllr.geoffrey.woodger@runnymede.gov.uk
***Group Leader:* Alderson**, Alan (R - Egham Town)
cllr.alan.alderson@runnymede.gov.uk
Chertsey Meads: Vacant
Ashmore, John (R - Egham Town)
cllr.john.ashmore@runnymede.gov.uk
Barden, Frances (CON - Foxhills)
cllr.frances.barden@runnymede.gov.uk
Broadhead, Jim (CON - Addlestone North)
cllr.jim.broadhead@runnymede.gov.uk
Brown, Michael (CON - Woodham)
cllr.michael.brown@runnymede.gov.uk
Butterfield, Howard (CON - Foxhills)
cllr.howard.butterfield@runnymede.gov.uk
Chaudhri, Iftikhar (CON - Foxhills)
cllr.iftikhar.chaudhri@runnymede.gov.uk
Clarke, Dolsie (CON - Chertsey St Ann's)
cllr.dolsie.clarke@runnymede.gov.uk
Cotty, Derek (CON - Chertsey Meads)
cllr.derek.cotty@runnymede.gov.uk
Dicks, Terry (CON - Chertsey South and Rowtown)
cllr.terry.dicks@runnymede.gov.uk
Dunster, Valerie (CON - Woodham)
cllr.valerie.dunster@runnymede.gov.uk
Edis, Richard (CON - Chertsey St Ann's)
cllr.richard.edis@runnymede.gov.uk
Edwards, John (CON - Chertsey South and Rowtown)
cllr.john.edwards@runnymede.gov.uk
Furey, John (CON - Addlestone Bourneside)
cllr.john.furey@runnymede.gov.uk
Gill, Elaine (R - Thorpe)
cllr.elaine.gill@runnymede.gov.uk
Harnden, Margaret (R - Thorpe)
cllr.margaret.harnden@runnymede.gov.uk
Heath, Marisa (CON - Englefield Green East)
cllr.marisa.heath@runnymede.gov.uk
Kingerley, Gail (CON - Woodham)
cllr.gail.kingerley@runnymede.gov.uk
Knight, Christopher (CON - New Haw)
cllr.christopher.knight@runnymede.gov.uk
Knight, David (R - Egham Town)
cllr.david.knight@runnymede.gov.uk
Kusneraitis, Michael (CON - Englefield Green West)
cllr.michael.kusneraitis@runnymede.gov.uk
Mackay, Stewart (CON - Chertsey South and Rowtown)
cllr.stewart.mackay@runnymede.gov.uk
Meares, Hugh (CON - Englefield Green West)
cllr.hugh.meares@runnymede.gov.uk
Parr, David (CON - Addlestone North)
cllr.david.parr@runnymede.gov.uk

Prescot, Nick (CON - Englefield Green West)
cllr.nick.prescot@runnymede.gov.uk
Roberts, Margaret (CON - Virginia Water)
cllr.margaret.roberts@runnymede.gov.uk
Saise-Marshall, Shannon (CON - Chertsey St Ann's)
cllr.shannon.saise-marshall@runnymede.gov.uk
Simmons, Cherith (CON - Addlestone Bourneside)
cllr.cherith.simmons@runnymede.gov.uk
Sohi, Parshotam (CON - Virginia Water)
cllr.parshotam.sohi@runnymede.gov.uk
Sorgiovanni, Damian (CON - New Haw)
cllr.damian.sorgiovanni@runnymede.gov.uk
Taylor, Peter (CON - Englefield Green East)
cllr.peter.taylor@runnymede.gov.uk
Tollett, Adrian (CON - New Haw)
cllr.adrian.tollett@runnymede.gov.uk
Tuley, Paul (CON - Chertsey Meads)
cllr.paul.tuley@runnymede.gov.uk
Waddell, Peter (CON - Addlestone Bourneside)
cllr.peter.waddell@runnymede.gov.uk
Warner, Gill (CON - Egham Hythe)
cllr.gill.warner@runnymede.gov.uk
Wase-Rogers, Nick (CON - Addlestone North)
cllr.nick.wase-rogers@runnymede.gov.uk
Wilson, Jonathan (CON - Egham Hythe)
cllr.jonathan.wilson@runnymede.gov.uk

POLITICAL COMPOSITION

CON: 35, R: 6, Vacant: 1

COMMITTEE CHAIRS

Corporate Management: Mr Patrick Roberts
Crime & Disorder: Mr Paul Tuley
Housing & Community Services: Mr John Furey
Licensing: Mr David Parr
Overview (Scrutiny): Mr Paul Tuley
Planning: Mr Geoffrey Woodger
Regulatory: Mrs Frances Barden
Standards & Audit: Mr Stephen Tully (External)

RUSHCLIFFE D

Rushcliffe Borough Council, Civic Centre, Pavilion Road, West Bridgford NG2 5FE ☎ 0115 981 9911 🖷 0115 945 5882 🖱 customerservices@rushcliffe.gov.uk 🖥 www.rushcliffe.gov.uk

FACTS & FIGURES

Police Authority: Nottinghamshire Police Authority
Health Authority: East Midlands Strategic Health Authority
Learning and Skills Council: East Midlands
Parliamentary Constituencies: Rushcliffe
EU Constituencies: East Midlands
Election Frequency: Elections are of whole council
Twinning: Bingham: Wallenfels (Germany); Keyworth: Feignies (France)

PRINCIPAL OFFICERS

Chief Executive: Mr Allen Graham, Chief Executive, Civic Centre, Pavilion Road, West Bridgford NG2 5FE ☎ 0115 981 9911 🖷 0115 945 5882 🖱 agraham@rushcliffe.gov.uk

Deputy Chief Executive: Mr Colin Bullett, Deputy Chief Executive, Civic Centre, Pavilion Road, West Bridgford NG2 5FE ☎ 0115 981 9911 🖷 0115 945 5882 🖱 cbullett@rushcliffe.gov.uk

Deputy Chief Executive: Mr Paul Randle, Deputy Chief Executive, Civic Centre, Pavilion Road, West Bridgford NG2 5FE ☎ 0115 981 9911 🖷 0115 945 5882 🖱 prandle@rushcliffe.gov.uk

Architect, Building / Property Services: Mr Adrian Hutson, Construction & Energy Manager, Civic Centre, Pavilion Road, West Bridgford NG2 5FE ☎ 0115 914 8442 🖱 ahutson@rushcliffe.gov.uk

Building Control: Mr John Neal, Principal Building Control Officer, Civic Centre, Pavilion Road, West Bridgford NG2 5FE ☎ 0115 981 9911 🖷 0115 945 5882 🖱 jneal@rushcliffe.gov.uk

PR / Communications: Mrs Nicky Mee, Communications Manager, Civic Centre, Pavilion Road, West Bridgford NG2 5FE ☎ 0115 914 8555 🖷 0115 945 5882 🖱 nmee@rushcliffe.gov.uk

Community Planning: Mrs Charlotte McGraw, Head of Community Shaping, Civic Centre, Pavilion Road, West Bridgford NG2 5FE ☎ 0115 981 9911 Ext 351 🖷 0115 945 5882 🖱 cmcgraw@rushcliffe.gov.uk

Community Safety: Mr Derek Hayden, Community Partnership Manager, Civic Centre, Pavilion Road, West Bridgford NG2 5FE ☎ 0115 9148 270 🖷 0115 945 5882 🖱 dhayden@rushcliffe.gov.uk

Computer Management: Mr Kevin Hall, ICT Manager, Civic Centre, Pavilion Road, West Bridgford NG2 5FE ☎ 0115 914 8267 🖷 0115 945 5882 🖱 khall@rushcliffe.gov.uk

Contracts: Mr David Mitchell, Head of Partnerships & Performance, Civic Centre, Pavilion Road, West Bridgford NG2 5FE ☎ 0115 914 8267 🖷 0115 945 5882 🖱 dmitchell@rushcliffe.gov.uk

Corporate Services: Mr Dan Swaine, Head of Corporate Services, Civic Centre, Pavilion Road, West Bridgford NG2 5FE ☎ 0115 914 8343 🖷 0115 945 5882 🖱 dswaine@rushcliffe.gov.uk

Customer Service: Ms Shirley Woltman, Customer Services Manager, Civic Centre, Pavilion Road, West Bridgford NG2 5FE ☎ 0115 981 9911 🖷 0115 945 5882 🖱 swoltman@rushcliffe.gov.uk

E-Government: Mr David Mitchell, Head of Partnerships & Performance, Civic Centre, Pavilion Road, West Bridgford NG2 5FE ☎ 0115 914 8267 🖷 0115 945 5882 🖱 dmitchell@rushcliffe.gov.uk

Electoral Registration: Mr Jeff Saxby, Elections & Democratic Engagement Manager, Civic Centre, Pavilion Road, West Bridgford NG2 5FE ☎ 0115 981 9216 🖷 0115 945 5882 🖱 jsaxby@rushcliffe.gov.uk

Emergency Planning: Mr Ed Shaw, Emergencing Planning Officer, Civic Centre, Pavilion Road, West Bridgford NG2 5FE ☎ 0115 914 9439 🖷 0115 945 5882 🖱 eshaw@rushcliffe.gov.uk

Environmental Health: Mr David Banks, Head of Environment & Waste Management, Civic Centre, Pavilion Road, West Bridgford NG2 5FE ☎ 0115 981 9911 🖷 0115 945 5882

dbanks@rushcliffe.gov.uk

Estates, Property & Valuation: Ms Leanne Baines, Property Estates Manager, Civic Centre, Pavilion Road, West Bridgford NG2 5FE lbaines@rushcliffe.gov.uk

Events Manager: Miss Nicola Pearson, Arts & Events Officer, Civic Centre, Pavilion Road, West Bridgford NG2 5FE 0115 914 8320 0115 945 5882 npearson@rushcliffe.gov.uk

Finance and Treasurer: Mr Paul Sutton, Interim Head of Financial Services, Civic Centre, Pavilion Road, West Bridgford NG2 5FE 0115 981 9911 0115 945 5882 psutton@rushcliffe.gov.uk

Fleet Management: Mr David Banks, Head of Environment & Waste Management, Civic Centre, Pavilion Road, West Bridgford NG2 5FE 0115 981 9911 0115 945 5882 dbanks@rushcliffe.gov.uk

Grounds Maintenance: Mr David Banks, Head of Environment & Waste Management, Civic Centre, Pavilion Road, West Bridgford NG2 5FE 0115 981 9911 0115 945 5882 dbanks@rushcliffe.gov.uk

Health and Safety: Ms Joanne Wilkinson, Safety & Risk Management Officer, Civic Centre, Pavilion Road, West Bridgford NG2 5FE 0115 981 9911 0115 945 5882 jwilkinson@rushcliffe.gov.uk

Home Energy Conservation: Ms Sheila Hood, Community Energy Officer, Civic Centre, Pavillion Road, West Bridgford NG2 5FE 0115 981 9911 0115 945 5882 shood@rushcliffe.gov.uk

Housing: Ms Donna Dwyer, Housing Development & Strategy Manager, Civic Centre, Pavilion Road, West Bridgford NG2 5FE 0115 981 9911 Ext 351 0115 945 5882 ddwyer@rushcliffe.gov.uk

Legal: Mr Paul Cox, Borough Solicitor, Civic Centre, Pavilion Road, West Bridgford NG2 5FE 0115 981 9911 0115 945 5882 pcox@rushcliffe.gov.uk

Leisure and Cultural Services: Mr Craig Taylor, Cultural Services Manager, Civic Centre, Pavilion Road, West Bridgford NG2 5FE 0115 981 9911 0115 914 8452 ctaylor@rushcliffe.gov.uk

Licensing: Mr David Banks, Head of Environment & Waste Management, Civic Centre, Pavilion Road, West Bridgford NG2 5FE 0115 981 9911 0115 945 5882 dbanks@rushcliffe.gov.uk

Lottery Funding, Charity and Voluntary: Ms Kath Marriott, Community Engagement Manager, Civic Centre, Pavilion Road, West Bridgford NG2 5FE 0115 981 9911 0115 945 5882 kmarriott@rushcliffe.gov.uk

Member Services: Mrs Liz Reid-Jones, Democratic Services Manager, Civic Centre, Pavilion Road, West Bridgford NG2 5FE 0115 981 9911 0115 945 5882 lreid-jones@rushcliffe.gov.uk

Member Services: Mr Dan Swaine, Head of Corporate Services, Civic Centre, Pavilion Road, West Bridgford NG2 5FE 0115 914 8343 0115 945 5882 dswaine@rushcliffe.gov.uk

Partnerships: Mr David Mitchell, Head of Partnerships & Performance, Civic Centre, Pavilion Road, West Bridgford NG2 5FE 0115 914 8267 0115 945 5882 dmitchell@rushcliffe.gov.uk

Personnel / HR: Mrs Juli Hicks, Strategic Human Resources Manager, Civic Centre, Pavilion Road, West Bridgford NG2 5FE 0115 981 9911 jhicks@rushcliffe.gov.uk

Planning: Ms Susan Harley, Head of Planning & Place Shaping, Civic Centre, Pavilion Road, West Bridgford NG2 5FE 0115 981 9911 0115 914 8452 sharley@rushcliffe.gov.uk

Procurement: Mr David Hayes, Procurement Officer, Civic Centre, Pavilion Road, West Bridgford NG2 5FE dhayes@rushcliffe.gov.uk

Recycling & Waste Minimisation: Mr David Banks, Head of Environment & Waste Management, Civic Centre, Pavilion Road, West Bridgford NG2 5FE 0115 981 9911 0115 945 5882 dbanks@rushcliffe.gov.uk

Staff Training: Mrs Anne Cotterill, Learning & Development Officer, Civic Centre, Pavilion Road, West Bridgford NG2 5FE acotterill@rushcliffe.gov.uk

Sustainable Development: Mrs Charlotte McGraw, Head of Community Shaping, Civic Centre, Pavilion Road, West Bridgford NG2 5FE 0115 981 9911 Ext 351 0115 945 5882 cmcgraw@rushcliffe.gov.uk

Waste Collection and Disposal: Mr Robert Alderton, Streetwise Manager, Civic Centre, Pavilion Road, West Bridgford NG2 5FE ralderton@rushcliffe.gov.uk

Waste Management: Mr David Banks, Head of Environment & Waste Management, Civic Centre, Pavilion Road, West Bridgford NG2 5FE 0115 981 9911 0115 945 5882 dbanks@rushcliffe.gov.uk

MEMBERS OF THE COUNCIL (50)

***Mayor:* Korn**, Irving (CON - Lutterell)
cllr.ikorn@rushcliffe.gov.uk

***Deputy Mayor:* Buschman**, Brian (CON - Abbey)
cllr.bbuschman@rushcliffe.gov.uk

***Leader of the Council:* Clarke**, Neil (CON - Trent)
cllr.jclarke@rushcliffe.gov.uk

***Deputy Leader of the Council:* Cranswick**, John (CON - Thoroton)
cllr.jcranswick@rushcliffe.gov.uk

***Group Leader:* Davidson**, George (LD - Bingham East)
cllr.gdavidson@rushcliffe.gov.uk

***Group Leader:* MacInnes**, Alistair (LAB - Trent Bridge)
cllr.amacInnes@rushcliffe.gov.uk

***Group Leader:* Mallender**, Richard (GRN - Lady Bay)
cllr.rmallender@rushcliffe.gov.uk

Abbey, Linda (LD - South Keyworth)
cllr.labbey@rushcliffe.gov.uk

Adair, Reginald (CON - Stanford)

cllr.radair@rushcliffe.gov.uk
Bailey, Sarah (CON - Wiverton)
cllr.sbailey@rushcliffe.gov.uk
Bannister, John (LAB - Abbey)
cllr.jbannister@rushcliffe.gov.uk
Bell, David (CON - Melton)
cllr.dbell@rushcliffe.gov.uk
Boote, Samuel (LD - North Keyworth)
cllr.sboote@rushcliffe.gov.uk
Boote, Deborah (LD - South Keyworth)
cllr.dboote@rushcliffe.gov.uk
Boughton-Smith, Nigel (LAB - Ruddington)
cllr.nboughton-smith@rushcliffe.gov.uk
Brown, Andrew (CON - Soar Valley)
cllr.abrown@rushcliffe.gov.uk
Butler, Richard (CON - Cotgrave)
cllr.rlbutler@rushcliffe.gov.uk
Chewings, Hayley (LAB - Cotgrave)
hchewings@rushcliffe.gov.uk
Combellack, Christine (CON - Nevile)
cllr.tcombellack@rushcliffe.gov.uk
Cooper, Leslie (CON - Gamston)
cllr.lcooper@rushcliffe.gov.uk
Cottee, John (CON - South Keyworth)
cllr.jcottee@rushcliffe.gov.uk
Dale, Brian (CON - Leake)
cllr.bdale@rushcliffe.gov.uk
Dickinson, Angela (CON - Melton)
cllr.adickinson@rushcliffe.gov.uk
Fearon, James (CON - Manvers)
cllr.jfearon@rushcliffe.gov.uk
Greenwood, Jean (CON - Ruddington)
cllr.jgreenwood@rushcliffe.gov.uk
Hemsley, Michael (CON - Gamston)
cllr.mhemsley@rushcliffe.gov.uk
Hetherington, Ronald (CON - Leake)
cllr.rhetherington@rushcliffe.gov.uk
Jones, Rodney (LD - Musters)
cllr.rjones@rushcliffe.gov.uk
Khan, Karrar (LD - Musters)
cllr.kkhan@rushcliffe.gov.uk
Lawrence, Nigel (CON - Oak)
cllr.nlawrence@rushcliffe.gov.uk
Lungley, John (CON - Ruddington)
cllr.jlungley@rushcliffe.gov.uk
Males, Margaret (CON - Leake)
cllr.mmales@rushcliffe.gov.uk
Mallender, Susan (GRN - Lady Bay)
cllr.smallender@rushcliffe.gov.uk
Marshall, Jacqui (CON - Cranmer)
cllr.jmarshall@rushcliffe.gov.uk
Mason, Fiona (CON - Wolds)
Cllr.FMason@rushcliffe.gov.uk
Mason, Debbie (CON - Tollerton)
cllr.dmason@rushcliffe.gov.uk
Moore, Gordon (CON - Wiverton)
cllr.gmoore@rushcliffe.gov.uk
Nicholls, Basil (CON - Lutterell)
cllr.bnicholls@rushcliffe.gov.uk
Plant, Elizabeth (LAB - Trent Bridge)
cllr.eplant@rushcliffe.gov.uk
Purdue-Horan, Francis (CON - Bingham West)
cllr.fpurdue-Horan@rushcliffe.gov.uk
Robinson, Simon (CON - Edwalton Village)
cllr.srobinson@rushcliffe.gov.uk
Smith, Peter (CON - Edwalton Village)
cllr.psmith@rushcliffe.gov.uk
Smith, David (CON - Manvers)
cllr.dsmith@rushcliffe.gov.uk
Smith, Jean (CON - Trent)
cllr.jsmith@rushcliffe.gov.uk
Stockwood, Maureen (CON - Bingham East)
cllr.mstockwood@rushcliffe.gov.uk
Stockwood, John (CON - Bingham West)
cllr.jstockwood@rushcliffe.gov.uk
Tansley, Bryan (CON - Cotgrave)
cllr.btansley@rushcliffe.gov.uk
Tipton, Harry (CON - Compton Acres)
cllr.htipton@rushcliffe.gov.uk
Vennett-Smith, Trevor (IND - Gotham)
cllr.tvennett-smith@rushcliffe.gov.uk
Wheeler, Douglas (CON - Compton Acres)
cllr.dwheeler@rushcliffe.gov.uk

POLITICAL COMPOSITION
CON: 36, LD: 6, LAB: 5, GRN: 2, IND: 1

CABINET
Leader: Mr Neil Clarke
Deputy Leader; Resources: Mr John Cranswick
Community Protection: Mr James Fearon
Environment: Mrs Debbie Mason
Sustainability: Mr David Bell
Community Services: Mrs Jean Smith

COMMITTEE CHAIRS
Alchohol and Entertainment Licensing: Mr James Fearon
Community Development: Mr Nigel Lawrence
Corporate Governance: Mr Gordon Moore
Development Control: Mrs Maureen Stockwood
Employment Appeals: Mr Neil Clarke
Licensing: Mr James Fearon
Partnership Delivery: Mr Ronald Hetherington
Performance Management: Mr Douglas Wheeler

RUSHMOOR D
Rushmoor Borough Council, Council Offices, Farnborough Road, Farnborough GU14 7JU ☎ 01252 398399 🖷 01252 524017
💻 www.rushmoor.gov.uk

FACTS & FIGURES
Police Authority: Hampshire Police Authority
Health Authority: South Central Strategic Health Authority
Learning and Skills Council: South East
Parliamentary Constituencies: Aldershot
EU Constituencies: South East
Election Frequency: Elections are by thirds
Twinning: Meudon (France); Oberursel (Germany); Sulechow (Poland)

PRINCIPAL OFFICERS
Chief Executive: Mr Andrew Lloyd, Chief Executive, Council Offices, Farnborough Road, Farnborough GU14 7JU ☎ 01252 398396 🖷 01252 524017 ✉ andrew.lloyd@rushmoor.gov.uk
Deputy Chief Executive: Mr Peter Gardner, Director of

Resources & Audit, Council Offices, Farnborough Road, Farnborough GU14 7JU ☎ 01252 398401 🖷 01252 398094 ✉ peter.gardner@rushmoor.gov.uk

Senior Management: Mr David Quirk, Director of Community and Environment, Council Offices, Farnborough Road, Farnborough GU14 7JU ☎ 01252 398100 🖷 01252 524017 ✉ david.quirk@rushmoor.gov.uk

Access Officer / Social Services (Disability): Mr Tony Patterson, Access Officer, Council Offices, Farnborough Road, Farnborough GU14 7JU ☎ 01252 398513 🖷 01252 398726 ✉ tony.patterson@rushmoor.gov.uk

Architect, Building / Property Services: Mr John Curtis, Building Surveyor, Council Offices, Farnborough Road, Farnborough GU14 7JU ☎ 01252 398414 ✉ john.curtis@rushmoor.gov.uk

Best Value: Mrs Karen Edwards, Head of Strategy & Communications, Council Offices, Farnborough Road, Farnborough GU14 7JU ☎ 01252 398800 ✉ karen.edwards@rushmoor.gov.uk

Building Control: Mr Geoff Saker, Chief Building Control Officer, Council Offices, Farnborough Road, Farnborough GU14 7JU ☎ 01252 398720 🖷 01252 398726 ✉ geoff.saker@rushmoor.gov.uk

Children / Youth Services: Ms Debbie Wall, Leisure Development Officer, Council Offices, Farnborough Road, Farnborough GU14 7JU ☎ 01252 398745 🖷 01252 398765 ✉ debbie.wall@rushmoor.gov.uk

PR / Communications: Miss Gill Chisnall, Corporate Communications Manager, Council Offices, Farnborough Road, Farnborough GU14 7JU ☎ 01252 398744 🖷 01252 398806 ✉ gill.chisnall@rushmoor.gov.uk

Community Planning: Mrs Karen Edwards, Head of Strategy & Communications, Council Offices, Farnborough Road, Farnborough GU14 7JU ☎ 01252 398800 ✉ karen.edwards@rushmoor.gov.uk

Community Safety: Mr Peter Amies, Head of Community & Environment, Council Offices, Farnborough Road, Farnborough GU14 7JU ☎ 01252 398750 🖷 01252 398765 ✉ peter.amies@rushmoor.gov.uk

Computer Management: Mr Nick Harding, Head of Information Technology, Council Offices, Farnborough Road, Farnborough GU14 7JU ☎ 01252 398650 ✉ nick.harding@rushmoor.gov.uk

Contracts: Mr Peter Amies, Head of Community & Environment, Council Offices, Farnborough Road, Farnborough GU14 7JU ☎ 01252 398750 🖷 01252 398765 ✉ peter.amies@rushmoor.gov.uk

Corporate Services: Mr Peter Gardner, Director of Resources & Audit, Council Offices, Farnborough Road, Farnborough GU14 7JU ☎ 01252 398401 🖷 01252 398094 ✉ peter.gardner@rushmoor.gov.uk

Customer Service: Mr Ian Harrison, Head of Customer Services, Council Offices, Farnborough Road, Farnborough GU14 7JU ☎ 01252 398398 ✉ ian.harrison@rushmoor.gov.uk

Economic Development: Mr Keith Holland, Head of Planning Services, Council Offices, Farnborough Road, Farnborough GU14 7JU ☎ 01252 398790 🖷 01252 398668 ✉ keith.holland@rushmoor.gov.uk

E-Government: Mrs Karen Edwards, Head of Strategy & Communications, Council Offices, Farnborough Road, Farnborough GU14 7JU ☎ 01252 398800 ✉ karen.edwards@rushmoor.gov.uk

Electoral Registration: Mr Andrew Colver, Head of Democratic & Facilities Management, Council Offices, Farnborough Road, Farnborough GU14 7JU ☎ 01252 398820 🖷 01252 524017 ✉ andrew.colver@rushmoor.gov.uk

Emergency Planning: Mr Jon Rundle, Assistant Head of Strategy & Communications, Council Offices, Farnborough Road, Farnborough GU14 7JU ☎ 01252 398801 🖷 01252 398806 ✉ jon.rundle@rushmoor.gov.uk

Energy Management: Mr Les Murrell, Energy and Environment Manager, Council Offices, Farnborough Road, Farnborough GU14 7JU ☎ 01252 398538 ✉ les.murrell@rushmoor.gov.uk

Environmental / Technical Services: Miss Qamer Yasin, Head of Environmental Health and Housing, Council Offices, Farnborough Road, Farnborough GU14 7JU ☎ 01252 398640 🖷 01252 398552 ✉ qamer.yasin@rushmoor.gov.uk

Environmental Health: Miss Qamer Yasin, Head of Environmental Health and Housing, Council Offices, Farnborough Road, Farnborough GU14 7JU ☎ 01252 398640 🖷 01252 398552 ✉ qamer.yasin@rushmoor.gov.uk

Estates, Property & Valuation: Mrs Karen Limmer, Solicitor of the Council, Council Offices, Farnborough Road, Farnborough GU14 7JU ☎ 01252 398600 ✉ karen.limmer@rushmoor.gov.uk

European Liaison: Mr Peter Amies, Head of Community & Environment, Council Offices, Farnborough Road, Farnborough GU14 7JU ☎ 01252 398750 🖷 01252 398765 ✉ peter.amies@rushmoor.gov.uk

Events Manager: Miss Gill Chisnall, Corporate Communications Manager, Council Offices, Farnborough Road, Farnborough GU14 7JU ☎ 01252 398744 🖷 01252 398806 ✉ gill.chisnall@rushmoor.gov.uk

Facilities: Mr Andrew Colver, Head of Democratic & Facilities Management, Council Offices, Farnborough Road, Farnborough GU14 7JU ☎ 01252 398820 🖷 01252 524017 ✉ andrew.colver@rushmoor.gov.uk

Facilities: Mrs Sheila MacFarlane, Facilities Manager, Council Offices, Farnborough Road, Farnborough GU14 7JU ☎ 01252 398480 🖷 01252 524017 ✉ sheila.macfarlane@rushmoor.gov.uk

Finance and Treasurer: Mr David Taylor, Head of Financial

Services, Council Offices, Farnborough Road, Farnborough GU14 7JU ☎ 01252 398440 🖷 01252 524017 ✉ david.taylor@rushmoor.gov.uk

Grounds Maintenance: Mr Andy Ford, Parks Development Officer, Council Offices, Farnborough Road, Farnborough GU14 7JU ☎ 01252 398771 ✉ andy.ford@rushmoor.gov.uk

Health and Safety: Mr Roger Sanders, Health and Safety Officer, Council Offices, Farnborough Road, Farnborough GU14 7JU ☎ 01252 398160 ✉ roger.sanders@rushmoor.gov.uk

Home Energy Conservation: Mr Les Murrell, Energy and Environment Manager, Council Offices, Farnborough Road, Farnborough GU14 7JU ☎ 01252 398538 ✉ les.murrell@rushmoor.gov.uk

Housing: Miss Qamer Yasin, Head of Environmental Health and Housing, Council Offices, Farnborough Road, Farnborough GU14 7JU ☎ 01252 398640 🖷 01252 398552 ✉ qamer.yasin@rushmoor.gov.uk

Legal: Mrs Karen Limmer, Solicitor of the Council, Council Offices, Farnborough Road, Farnborough GU14 7JU ☎ 01252 398600 ✉ karen.limmer@rushmoor.gov.uk

Leisure and Cultural Services: Mr Peter Amies, Head of Community & Environment, Council Offices, Farnborough Road, Farnborough GU14 7JU ☎ 01252 398750 🖷 01252 398765 ✉ peter.amies@rushmoor.gov.uk

Licensing: Mr John McNab, Environmental Health Manager (Licensing), Council Offices, Farnborough Road, Farnborough GU14 7JU ☎ 01252 398886 ✉ john.mcnab@rushmoor.gov.uk

Lifelong Learning: Mrs Karen Edwards, Head of Strategy & Communications, Council Offices, Farnborough Road, Farnborough GU14 7JU ☎ 01252 398800 ✉ karen.edwards@rushmoor.gov.uk

Lottery Funding, Charity and Voluntary: Mr Peter Amies, Head of Community & Environment, Council Offices, Farnborough Road, Farnborough GU14 7JU ☎ 01252 398750 🖷 01252 398765 ✉ peter.amies@rushmoor.gov.uk

Member Services: Mr Andrew Colver, Head of Democratic & Facilities Management, Council Offices, Farnborough Road, Farnborough GU14 7JU ☎ 01252 398820 🖷 01252 524017 ✉ andrew.colver@rushmoor.gov.uk

Parking: Mr Mike Bamber, Parking Manager, Council Offices, Farnborough Road, Farnborough GU14 7JU ☎ 01252 398291 ✉ mike.bamber@rushmoor.gov.uk

Partnerships: Miss Annie Denton, Strategic Partnership Officer, Council Offices, Farnborough Road, Farnborough GU14 7JU ☎ 01252 398221 ✉ annie.denton@rushmoor.gov.uk

Personnel / HR: Mrs Nicola Orchard, Head of Personnel Services, Council Offices, Farnborough Road, Farnborough GU14 7JU ☎ 01252 398420 🖷 01252 398094 ✉ nicola.orchard@rushmoor.gov.uk

Planning: Mr Keith Holland, Head of Planning Services, Council Offices, Farnborough Road, Farnborough GU14 7JU ☎ 01252 398790 🖷 01252 398668 ✉ keith.holland@rushmoor.gov.uk

Procurement: Mrs Karen Edwards, Head of Strategy & Communications, Council Offices, Farnborough Road, Farnborough GU14 7JU ☎ 01252 398800 ✉ karen.edwards@rushmoor.gov.uk

Recycling & Waste Minimisation: Mr James Duggin, Contracts Manager, Council Offices, Farnborough Road, Farnborough GU14 7JU ☎ 01252 398167 ✉ james.duggin@rushmoor.gov.uk

Regeneration: Mrs Debbie Whitcombe, Regeneration Officer, Council Offices, Farnborough Road, Farnborough GU14 7JU ☎ 01252 398793 ✉ debbie.whitcombe@rushmoor.gov.uk

Staff Training: Mrs Nicola Orchard, Head of Personnel Services, Council Offices, Farnborough Road, Farnborough GU14 7JU ☎ 01252 398420 🖷 01252 398094 ✉ nicola.orchard@rushmoor.gov.uk

Street Scene: Ms Toni Lockwood, Traffic Management Officer, Council Offices, Farnborough Road, Farnborough GU14 7JU ☎ 01252 398377 ✉ toni.lockwood@rushmoor.gov.uk

Sustainable Communities: Mr Les Murrell, Energy and Environment Manager, Council Offices, Farnborough Road, Farnborough GU14 7JU ☎ 01252 398538 ✉ les.murrell@rushmoor.gov.uk

Sustainable Development: Mr Les Murrell, Energy and Environment Manager, Council Offices, Farnborough Road, Farnborough GU14 7JU ☎ 01252 398538 ✉ les.murrell@rushmoor.gov.uk

Tourism: Mr Peter Amies, Head of Community & Environment, Council Offices, Farnborough Road, Farnborough GU14 7JU ☎ 01252 398750 🖷 01252 398765 ✉ peter.amies@rushmoor.gov.uk

Town Centre: Mr Keith Holland, Head of Planning Services, Council Offices, Farnborough Road, Farnborough GU14 7JU ☎ 01252 398790 🖷 01252 398668 ✉ keith.holland@rushmoor.gov.uk

Traffic Management: Ms Toni Lockwood, Traffic Management Officer, Council Offices, Farnborough Road, Farnborough GU14 7JU ☎ 01252 398377 ✉ toni.lockwood@rushmoor.gov.uk

Waste Collection and Disposal: Mr James Duggin, Contracts Manager, Council Offices, Farnborough Road, Farnborough GU14 7JU ☎ 01252 398167 ✉ james.duggin@rushmoor.gov.uk

Waste Management: Mr James Duggin, Contracts Manager, Council Offices, Farnborough Road, Farnborough GU14 7JU

☎ 01252 398167 ✉ james.duggin@rushmoor.gov.uk

MEMBERS OF THE COUNCIL (39)

***Mayor:* Crerar**, Peter (CON - Manor Park)
peter_crerar@btinternet.com
***Deputy Mayor:* Bridgeman**, Terry (LAB - Aldershot Park)
bridgemanterry@yahoo.co.uk
***Leader of the Council:* Moyle**, Peter (CON - St. John's)
peter.moyle@rushmoor.gov.uk
***Deputy Leader of the Council:* Dibbs**, Roland (CON - Knellwood)
rlgdibbs@aol.com
***Group Leader:* Dibble**, Keith (LAB - North Town)
keith.dibble@rushmoor.gov.uk
Bedford, Diane (CON - St. Mark's)
diane.bedford@tiscali.co.uk
Cappelman, Don (LAB - Aldershot Park)
don.cappelman@rushmoor.gov.uk
Carter, Sue (CON - Cove and Southwood)
sue.carter@rushmoor.gov.uk
Chainey, Alan (CON - Cove and Southwood)
alan.chainey@rushmoor.gov.uk
Choudhary, Attika (CON - Wellington)
attika.choudhary@rushmoor.gov.uk
Choudhary, Sophia (CON - Rowhill)
sophia.choudhary@rushmoor.gov.uk
Choudhary, Charles (CON - Rowhill)
charles.choudhary@btinternet.com
Clifford, David (CON - Empress)
david.clifford@rushmoor.gov.uk
Cooper, Rod (CON - St. Mark's)
rod.cooper@rushmoor.gov.uk
Corps, Liz (CON - St. Mark's)
liz.corps@ntlworld.com
Crawford, Alex (LAB - Wellington)
alex.crawford06@btinternet.com
Dibble, Sue (LAB - North Town)
sue.dibble@rushmoor.gov.uk
Evans, Jennifer (LAB - Wellington)
evans.jenniferevans@gmail.com
Ferrier, Alan (CON - Fernhill)
alan.ferrier@rushmoor.gov.uk
Grattan, Clive (LAB - Cherrywood)
Hughes, Ron (CON - Manor Park)
rhandi@btinternet.com
Hurst, Barbara (CON - St. John's)
barbara.hurst@rushmoor.gov.uk
Jackman, Adam (CON - Knellwood)
adam@jackman.org.uk
Jones, Barry (LAB - Cherrywood)
barry.jones@rushmoor.gov.uk
Lyon, Gareth (CON - Empress)
gareth.lyon@rushmoor.gov.uk
Marsh, John (CON - Fernhill)
johnmarsh@ntlworld.com
Muschamp, Ken (CON - Fernhill)
ken@laulind.co.uk
Parker, Brian (CON - Empress)
brian.parker@rushmoor.gov.uk
Roberts, Mike (LAB - Aldershot Park)
mike.roberts@rushmoor.gov.uk
Rust, Frank (LAB - North Town)
frank.rust@rushmoor.gov.uk
Small, Malcolm (UKIP - West Heath)
smallm30@hotmail.co.uk
Smith, Steve (UKIP - Westheath)
steve.smith@rushmoor.gov.uk
Staplehurst, Mark (UKIP - Westheath)
ukip.westheath@virginmedia.com
Taylor, Les (LAB - Cherrywood)
les.taylor@rushmoor.gov.uk
Taylor, Paul (CON - Knellwood)
paul.taylor@rsuhmoor.gov.uk
Tennant, Martin (CON - Cove and Southwood)
martin.tennant@rushmoor.gov.uk
Thomas, Bruce (CON - Manor Park)
bruce.thomas@rushmoor.gov.uk
Vosper, Jacqui (CON - St. John's)
jacqui.vosper@rushmoor.gov.uk
Welch, David (CON - Rowhill) david.welch@rushmoor.gov.uk

POLITICAL COMPOSITION

CON: 25, LAB: 11, UKIP: 3

CABINET

Leader: Mr Peter Moyle
Deputy Leader, Environment: Mr Roland Dibbs
Concessions & Community Support: Mr Charles Choudhary
Corporate Services: Mr Paul Taylor
Health & Housing: Mr David Welch
Leisure & Youth: Ms Diane Bedford
Safety & Regulation: Mr Ken Muschamp

COMMITTEE CHAIRS

Development Control: Mr Adam Jackman
Licensing & General Purposes: Mr Martin Tennant
Standards & Audits: Mr John Marsh

RUTLAND U

Rutland County Council, Council Offices, Catmose, Oakham LE15 6HP ☎ 01572 722577 🖷 01572 758307
✉ enquiries@rutland.gov.uk 💻 www.rutland.gov.uk

FACTS & FIGURES

Police Authority: Leicestershire Police Authority
Health Authority: East Midlands Strategic Health Authority
Learning and Skills Council: East Midlands
Parliamentary Constituencies: Rutland and Melton
EU Constituencies: East Midlands
Election Frequency: Elections are of whole council
Twinning: Oakham: Barmstedt (Germany); Uppingham: Caudebec-en-Caux (France)

PRINCIPAL OFFICERS

Chief Executive: Mrs Helen Briggs, Chief Executive, Catmose, Oakham LE15 6HP ☎ 01572 758203 🖷 01572 758385
✉ hbriggs@rutland.gov.uk

Deputy Chief Executive: Ms Carol Chambers, Deputy Chief Executive & Strategic Director - People, Catmose, Oakham LE15 6HP ☎ ; 01572 758481 ✉ cchambers@rutland.gov.uk

Senior Management: Mr Aman Mehra, Strategic Director - Place, Council Offices, Catmose, Oakham LE15 6HP ☎ 01572 758315 ✉ amehra@rutland.gov.uk

Senior Management: Ms Debbie Mogg, Director of Resources, Council Offices, Catmose, Oakham LE15 6HP ☎ 01572 758358 ✉ dmuddimer@rutland.gov.uk

Senior Management: Mr Mark Naylor, Assistant Director - People, Council Offices, Catmose, Oakham LE15 6HP ☎ 01572 758340 ✉ mnaylor@rutland.gov.uk

Architect, Building / Property Services: Ms Victoria Brambini, Head of Asset Management, Council Offices, Catmose, Oakham LE15 6HP ☎ 01572 722577 🖷 01572 758377 ✉ vbrambini@rutland.gov.uk

Building Control: Ms Victoria Brambini, Head of Asset Management, Council Offices, Catmose, Oakham LE15 6HP ☎ 01572 722577 🖷 01572 758377 ✉ vbrambini@rutland.gov.uk

Children / Youth Services: Ms Jill Haigh, Assistant Director - Services to People, Council Offices, Catmose, Oakham LE15 6HP ☎ 01572 722577 🖷 01572 758307 ✉ jhaigh@rutland.gov.uk

Civil Registration: Ms Tricia Goodchild, Superintendent Registrar, Council Offices, Catmose, Oakham LE15 6HP ☎ 01572 722577 ✉ tgoodchild@rutland.gov.uk

PR / Communications: Mr Chris Jones, Communications Officer, Council Offices, Catmose, Oakham LE15 6HP ☎ 01572 758328 🖷 01572 758385 ✉ cjones@rutland.gov.uk

Community Safety: Ms Jennifer Thornton, Team Manager - Stronger Families, Council Offices, Catmose, Oakham LE15 6HP ☎ 01572 722577 ✉ jthornton@rutland.gov.uk

Computer Management: Ms Lisa Wakeford, Head of Business Support - Places, Council Offices, Catmose, Oakham LE15 6HP ☎ 01572 758226 ✉ lwakeford@rutland.gov.uk

Consumer Protection and Trading Standards: Mr Stephen Haigh, Public Protection Manager, Council Offices, Catmose, Oakham LE15 6HP ☎ 01572 722577 ✉ shaigh@rutland.gov.uk

Contracts: Mr James Frieland, Contracts & Support, Council Offices, Catmose, Oakham LE15 6HP ☎ 01572 758288 🖷 01572 758307 ✉ jfrieland@rutland.gov.uk

Corporate Services: Ms Debbie Mogg, Director of Resources, Council Offices, Catmose, Oakham LE15 6HP ☎ 01572 758358 ✉ dmuddimer@rutland.gov.uk

Customer Service: Ms Kay Mitchell, Team Manager - Duty & Assessment, Council Offices, Catmose, Oakham LE15 6HP ☎ 01572 758422 ✉ kmitchell@rutland.gov.uk

Economic Development: Ms Libby Kingsley, Senior Economic Development Manager, Council Offices, Catmose, Oakham LE15 6HP ☎ 01572 722577 ✉ lkingsley@rutland.gov.uk

Education: Ms Carol Chambers, Deputy Chief Executive & Strategic Director - People, Council Offices, Catmose, Oakham LE15 6HP ☎ ; 01572 758481 ✉ cchambers@rutland.gov.uk

Electoral Registration: Ms Theresa Stokes, Senior Committee Administrator, Catmose, Oakham LE15 6HP ☎ 01572 722577 🖷 01572 758203 ✉ tstokes@rutland.gov.uk

Energy Management: Ms Isabel Clark, Climate Change Co-ordinator, Council Offices, Catmose, Oakham LE15 6HP ☎ 01572 722577 🖷 01572 758307 ✉ iclark@rutland.gov.uk

Estates, Property & Valuation: Ms Victoria Brambini, Head of Asset Management, Council Offices, Catmose, Oakham LE15 6HP ☎ 01572 722577 🖷 01572 758377 ✉ vbrambini@rutland.gov.uk

Finance and Treasurer: Ms Andrea Grinney, Head of Revenues & Benefits, Council Offices, Catmose, Oakham LE15 6HP ☎ 01572 722577 ✉ agrinney@rutland.gov.uk

Finance and Treasurer: Ms Debbie Mogg, Director of Resources, Council Offices, Catmose, Oakham LE15 6HP ☎ 01572 758358 ✉ dmuddimer@rutland.gov.uk

Grounds Maintenance: Mr George Chase, Waste & Amenities Manager, Council Offices, Catmose, Oakham LE15 6HP ☎ 01572 758430 🖷 01572 758307 ✉ gchase@rutland.gov.uk

Health and Safety: Mr Iain Watt, Corporate Health & Safety Officer, Council Offices, Catmose, Oakham LE15 6HP ☎ 01572 722577 ✉ iwatt@rutland.gov.uk

Highways: Mr Dave Brown, Head of Operations, Council Offices, Catmose, Oakham LE15 6HP ☎ 01572 758461 🖷 01572 724378 ✉ dbrown@rutland.gov.uk

Home Energy Conservation: Ms Isabel Clark, Climate Change Co-ordinator, Council Offices, Catmose, Oakham LE15 6HP ☎ 01572 722577 🖷 01572 758307 ✉ iclark@rutland.gov.uk

Legal: Mr Geoff Pook, Head of Corporate Governance, Council Offices, Catmose, Oakham LE15 6HP ☎ 01572 758202 🖷 01572 758307 ✉ gpook@rutland.gov.uk

Leisure and Cultural Services: Mr Robert Clayton, Head of Culture & Leisure, Council Offices, Catmose, Oakham LE15 6HP ☎ 01572 758435 ✉ rclayton@rutland.gov.uk

Licensing: Mr John Dwyer, Licensing Officer, Council Offices, Catmose, Oakham LE15 6HP ✉ jdwyer@rutland.gov.uk

Lifelong Learning: Ms Sarah Bysouth, Head of Service - Lifelong Learning, Council Offices, Catmose, Oakham LE15 6HP

☎ 01572 722577 🖷 01572 758307 ✉ sbysouth@rutland.gov.uk

Lighting: Mr Dave Brown, Head of Operations, Highways Depot, 28-34 Station Approach, Oakham LE15 6QW ☎ 01572 758461 🖷 01572 724378 ✉ dbrown@rutland.gov.uk

Member Services: Mr Geoff Pook, Head of Corporate Governance, Council Offices, Catmose, Oakham LE15 6HP ☎ 01572 758202 🖷 01572 758307 ✉ gpook@rutland.gov.uk

Parking: Ms Joanna Fraser, Parking Officer, Council Offices, Catmose, Oakham LE15 6HP ☎ 01572 72277 ✉ jfraser@rutland.gov.uk

Partnerships: Ms Katy Lynch, Partnerships Officer, Council Offices, Catmose, Oakham LE15 6HP ✉ klynch@rutland.gov.uk

Personnel / HR: Ms Michelle Sharman, Senior HR Adviser, Council Offices, Catmose, Oakham LE15 6HP ☎ 01572 722577 🖷 01572 758307 ✉ msharman@rutland.gov.uk

Public Libraries: Mr Robert Clayton, Head of Culture & Leisure, Council Offices, Catmose, Oakham LE15 6HP ☎ 01572 758435 ✉ rclayton@rutland.gov.uk

Recycling & Waste Minimisation: Mr George Chase, Waste & Amenities Manager, Council Offices, Catmose, Oakham LE15 6HP ☎ 01572 758430 🖷 01572 758307 ✉ gchase@rutland.gov.uk

Regeneration: Ms Libbie Kingsley, Economic Development Officer, Council Offices, Catmose, Oakham LE15 6HP ✉ lkingsley@rutland.gov.uk

Road Safety: Mr Dave Brown, Head of Operations, Council Offices, Catmose, Oakham LE15 6HP ☎ 01572 758461 🖷 01572 724378 ✉ dbrown@rutland.gov.uk

Social Services: Ms Carol Chambers, Deputy Chief Executive & Strategic Director - People, Catmose, Oakham LE15 6HP ☎ 01572 758481 ✉ cchambers@rutland.gov.uk

Staff Training: Ms Amy Forster, Training Officer, Council Offices, Catmose, Oakham LE15 6HP ☎ 01572 722577 🖷 01572 758307 ✉ aforster@rutland.gov.uk

Sustainable Development: Ms Libbie Kingsley, Economic Development Officer, Council Offices, Catmose, Oakham LE15 6HP ✉ lkingsley@rutland.gov.uk

Tourism: Mrs Mary Copley, Tourism Development Officer, Council Offices, Catmose, Oakham LE15 6HP ☎ 01572 722577 🖷 01572 758307 ✉ mcopley@rutland.gov.uk

Town Centre: Mr Aman Mehra, Strategic Director - Place, Highways Depot, 28-34 Station Approach, Oakham LE15 6QW ☎ 01572 758315 ✉ amehra@rutland.gov.uk

Traffic Management: Mr Dave Brown, Head of Operations, Council Offices, Catmose, Oakham LE15 6HP ☎ 01572 758461 🖷 01572 724378 ✉ dbrown@rutland.gov.uk

Transport: Mr Andrew Harris, Group Manager - Transport & Accessibility, RCC Highways Depot, 28-34 Station Approach, Oakham LE15 6QW ☎ 01572 772390 ✉ aharris@rutland.gov.uk

Transport Planner: Mr Andrew Harris, Group Manager - Transport & Accessibility, RCC Highways Depot, 28-34 Station Approach, Oakham LE15 6QW ☎ 01572 772390 aharris@rutland.gov.uk

Waste Collection and Disposal: Mr George Chase, Waste & Amenities Manager, Council Offices, Catmose, Oakham LE15 6HP ☎ 01572 758430 🖷 01572 758307 ✉ gchase@rutland.gov.uk

Waste Management: Mr George Chase, Waste & Amenities Manager, Council Offices, Catmose, Oakham LE15 6HP ☎ 01572 758430 🖷 01572 758307 ✉ gchase@rutland.gov.uk

MEMBERS OF THE COUNCIL (26)

***Leader of the Council:* Begy**, Roger (CON - Greetham)
rbegy@rutland.gov.uk

***Deputy Leader of the Council:* King**, Terry (CON - Exton)
tking@rutland.gov.uk

Baines, Edward (CON - Martinsthorpe)
democratic@rutland.gov.uk

Bool, Kenneth (CON - Normanton)
kbool@rutland.gov.uk

Cartwright, Carolyn (CON - Uppingham)
cjcartwright@rutland.gov.uk

Cross, William (CON - Braunston and Belton)
wcross@rutland.gov.uk

Dale, Jeffrey (IND - Oakham North East)
jdale@rutland.gov.uk

Emmett, Christine (CON - Ketton)
cemmett@rutland.gov.uk

Figgis, Joanna (CON - Oakham South West)
democratic@rutland.gov.uk

Gale, R (IND - Oakham North West)
rgale@rutland.gov.uk

Hollis, David (CON - Cottesmore)
dhollis@rutland.gov.uk

Lammie, James (CON - Lyddington)
jlammie@rutland.gov.uk

Montgomery, Brian (IND - Whissendine)
bmontgomery@rutland.gov.uk

Munton, Jonathan (CON - Oakham South East)
jmunton@rutland.gov.uk

Oxley, Marc (LD - Uppingham)
moxley@rutland.gov.uk

Parsons, Chris (IND - Ryhall and Casterton)
cparsons@rutland.gov.uk

Plews, Gene (CON - Oakham South East)
gplews@rutland.gov.uk

Pocock, Martyn (CON - Cottesmore)
mpocock@rutland.gov.uk

Richardson, David (R - Oakham South West)
drichardson@rutland.gov.uk

Roper, Barry (CON - Ketton)

broper@rutland.gov.uk
Stephenson, Lucy (CON - Uppingham)
listephenson@rutland.gov.uk
Vernon, Charlotte (CON - Rhyall and Casterton)
cvernon@rutland.gov.uk
Wainwright, Nicholas (CON - Langham)
nwainwright@rutland.gov.uk
Waller, Gale (LD - Normanton)
gwaller@rutland.gov.uk
Walters, Alan (IND - Oakham North East)
awalters@rutland.gov.uk
Woodcock, Mark (IND - Oakham North West)
mwoodcock@rutland.gov.uk

POLITICAL COMPOSITION
CON: 17, IND: 6, LD: 2, R: 1

CABINET
Leader; Environmental Services, Culture and Housing: Mr Roger Begy
Deputy Leader; Finance and Asset Management: Mr Terry King
Education & Children's Services: Mr Kenneth Bool
Health & Social Care: Mrs Christine Emmett
Youth, Sport & Community Safety: Mr Gene Plews
Resources: Mr Martyn Pocock

COMMITTEE CHAIRS
Adult Social Services (Scrutiny): Mr Jeffrey Dale
Children & Young People's Services (Scrutiny): Miss Gale Waller
Development & Control: Mrs Charlotte Vernon
Employment & Appeals: Mr Martyn Pocock
Licensing: Mr Gene Plews

RYEDALE — D
Ryedale District Council, Ryedale House, Malton YO17 7HH
☎ 01653 600666 🖷 01653 696801 ✉ info@ryedale.gov.uk
💻 www.ryedale.gov.uk

FACTS & FIGURES
Police Authority: North Yorkshire Police Authority
Health Authority: NHS Yorkshire & the Humber
Learning and Skills Council: Yorkshire and the Humber
Parliamentary Constituencies: Thirsk & Malton
EU Constituencies: Yorkshire and the Humber
Election Frequency: Elections are of whole council

PRINCIPAL OFFICERS
Chief Executive: Ms Janet Waggott, Chief Executive, Ryedale House, Malton YO17 7HH ☎ 01653 600666 🖷 01653 600175 ✉ janet.waggott@ryedale.gov.uk

Architect, Building / Property Services: Mr Phil Long, Head of Streetscene and Environment, Ryedale House, Malton YO17 7HH ☎ 01653 600666 ✉ phil.long@ryedale.gov.uk

Best Value: Mrs Clare Slater, Head of Policy and Partnerships, Ryedale House, Malton YO17 7HH ☎ 01653 600666 🖷 01653 696801 ✉ clare.slater@ryedale.gov.uk

Building Control: Mr Les Chapman, Building Control Manager, The Suite 2, Coxwold House, Easingwold Business Park, Easingwold, York YO61 3FB ☎ 01904 720281 🖷 01904 720282 ✉ les.chapman@ryedale.gov.uk

Children / Youth Services: Rachael Fox-Evans, Children & Young People Development Officer, Ryedale House, Malton YO17 7HH ☎ 01653 600666 ✉ rachael.fox-evans@ryedale.gov.uk

PR / Communications: Ms Jill Baldwin, Media Relations Officer, Ryedale House, Malton YO17 7HH ☎ 01653 600666 🖷 01653 696801 ✉ jill.baldwin@ryedale.gov.uk

PR / Communications: Miss Louise Sandall, Head of Corporate and Business Support, Ryedale House, Malton YO17 7HH ☎ 01653 600666 🖷 01653 696801 ✉ louise.sandall@ryedale.gov.uk

Community Planning: Mrs Jos Holmes, Cultural Service Manager, Ryedale House, Malton YO17 7HH ☎ 01653 600666 🖷 01653 696801 ✉ jos.holmes@ryedale.gov.uk

Community Planning: Mrs Clare Slater, Head of Policy and Partnerships, Ryedale House, Malton YO17 7HH ☎ 01653 600666 🖷 01653 696801 ✉ clare.slater@ryedale.gov.uk

Community Safety: Ms Gail Snowden, Technical Support Officer, Ryedale House, Malton YO17 7HH ☎ 01653 600666 Ext 314 ✉ gail.snowden@ryedale.gov.uk

Computer Management: Miss Louise Sandall, Head of Corporate and Business Support, Ryedale House, Malton YO17 7HH ☎ 01653 600666 🖷 01653 696801

Corporate Services: Miss Louise Sandall, Head of Corporate and Business Support, Ryedale House, Malton YO17 7HH ☎ 01653 600666 🖷 01653 696801 ✉ louise.sandall@ryedale.gov.uk

Corporate Services: Ms Janet Waggott, Chief Executive, Ryedale House, Malton YO17 7HH ☎ 01653 600666 🖷 01653 600175 ✉ janet.waggott@ryedale.gov.uk

Customer Service: Angela Jones, Business Support Manager, Ryedale House, Malton YO17 7HH ☎ 01653 600666 🖷 01653 696801 ✉ angela.jones@ryedale.gov.uk

Customer Service: Miss Louise Sandall, Head of Corporate and Business Support, Ryedale House, Malton YO17 7HH ☎ 01653 600666 🖷 01653 696801 ✉ louise.sandall@ryedale.gov.uk

Economic Development: Mr Julian Rudd, Head of Economy & Infrastructure, Ryedale House, Malton YO17 7HH ☎ 01653 600666 🖷 01653 696801 ✉ julian.rudd@ryedale.gov.uk

E-Government: Miss Louise Sandall, Head of Corporate and Business Support, Ryedale House, Malton YO17 7HH ☎ 01653 600666 🖷 01653 696801 ✉ louise.sandall@ryedale.gov.uk

Electoral Registration: Mr Simon Copley, Democratic Services Manager, Ryedale House, Malton YO17 7HH ☎ 01653 600666 🖷 01653 696801 ✉ simon.copley@ryedale.gov.uk

Emergency Planning: Mr Phil Long, Head of Streetscene and Environment, Ryedale House, Malton YO17 7HH ☎ 01653 600666 ✉ phil.long@ryedale.gov.uk

Environmental / Technical Services: Mr Phil Long, Head of Environment, Ryedale House, Malton YO17 7HH ☎ 01653 600666 Extn 461 ✉ phil.long@ryedale.gov.uk

Environmental Health: Mr Steven Richmond, Environmental Health Manager, Ryedale House, Malton YO17 7HH ☎ 01653 600666 🖷 01653 600764 ✉ steve.richmond@ryedale.gov.uk

European Liaison: Mr Julian Rudd, Head of Economy & Infrastructure, Ryedale House, Malton YO17 7HH ☎ 01653 600666 🖷 01653 696801 ✉ julian.rudd@ryedale.gov.uk

Events Manager: Mrs Jos Holmes, Cultural Service Manager, Ryedale House, Malton YO17 7HH ☎ 01653 600666 🖷 01653 696801 ✉ jos.holmes@ryedale.gov.uk

Finance and Treasurer: Mr Paul Cresswell, Corporate Director (S151), Ryedale House, Malton YO17 7HH ☎ 01653 600666 Extn 214 🖷 01653 696801 ✉ paul.cresswell@ryedale.gov.uk

Fleet Management: Mrs Beckie Bennett, Streetscene Manager, Depot, Showfield Lane, Malton YO17 0BY ☎ 01653 600666 Extn 483 ✉ beckie.bennett@ryedale.gov.uk

Fleet Management: Mr Phil Long, Head of Environment, Ryedale House, Malton YO17 7HH ☎ 01653 600666 Extn 461 ✉ phil.long@ryedale.gov.uk

Grounds Maintenance: Mrs Beckie Bennett, Streetscene Manager, Ryedale House, Malton YO17 7HH ☎ 01653 600666 Extn 483 ✉ beckie.bennett@ryedale.gov.uk

Grounds Maintenance: Mr Phil Long, Head of Streetscene and Environment, Ryedale House, Malton YO17 7HH ☎ 01653 600666 ✉ phil.long@ryedale.gov.uk

Home Energy Conservation: Mr John Brown, Environmental & Recycling Officer, Central Depot, Showfield Lane Industrial Estate, Malton Y017 0BY ☎ 01653 600666 🖷 01653 690737 ✉ john.brown@ryedale.gov.uk

Housing: Mr Gary Housden, Head of Planning and Housing, Ryedale House, Malton YO17 7HH ☎ 01653 600666 🖷 01653 696801 ✉ gary.housden@ryedale.gov.uk

Housing: Ms Kim Robertshaw, Housing Services Manager, Ryedale House, Malton YO17 7HH ☎ 01653 600666 ✉ kim.robertshaw@ryedale.gov.uk

Legal: Mr Anthony Winship, Council Solicitor, Ryedale House, Malton YO17 7HH ☎ 01653 600666 🖷 01653 696801 ✉ anthony.winship@ryedale.gov.uk

Leisure and Cultural Services: Mr Steven Richmond, Environmental Health Manager, Ryedale House, Malton YO17 7HH ☎ 01653 600666 🖷 01653 600764 ✉ steve.richmond@ryedale.gov.uk

Licensing: Mr Steven Richmond, Environmental Health Manager, Ryedale House, Malton YO17 7HH ☎ 01653 600666 🖷 01653 600764 ✉ steve.richmond@ryedale.gov.uk

Lottery Funding, Charity and Voluntary: Mrs Jos Holmes, Cultural Service Manager, Ryedale House, Malton YO17 7HH ☎ 01653 600666 🖷 01653 696801 ✉ jos.holmes@ryedale.gov.uk

Lottery Funding, Charity and Voluntary: Ms Gail Snowden, Technical Support Officer, Ryedale House, Malton YO17 7HH ☎ 01653 600666 Ext 314 ✉ gail.snowden@ryedale.gov.uk

Member Services: Mr Simon Copley, Democratic Services Manager, Ryedale House, Malton YO17 7HH ☎ 01653 600666 🖷 01653 696801 ✉ simon.copley@ryedale.gov.uk

Member Services: Miss Louise Sandall, Head of Corporate and Business Support, Ryedale House, Malton YO17 7HH ☎ 01653 600666 🖷 01653 696801 ✉ louise.sandall@ryedale.gov.uk

Parking: Mr Phil Long, Head of Streetscene and Environment, Ryedale House, Malton YO17 7HH ☎ 01653 600666 ✉ phil.long@ryedale.gov.uk

Partnerships: Mrs Clare Slater, Head of Policy and Partnerships, Ryedale House, Malton YO17 7HH ☎ 01653 600666 🖷 01653 696801 ✉ clare.slater@ryedale.gov.uk

Personnel / HR: Miss Louise Sandall, Head of Corporate and Business Support, Ryedale House, Malton YO17 7HH ☎ 01653 600666 🖷 01653 696801 ✉ louise.sandall@ryedale.gov.uk

Planning: Mr Gary Housden, Head of Planning and Housing, Ryedale House, Malton YO17 7HH ☎ 01653 600666 🖷 01653 696801 ✉ gary.housden@ryedale.gov.uk

Procurement: Mrs Clare Slater, Head of Policy and Partnerships, Ryedale House, Malton YO17 7HH ☎ 01653 600666 🖷 01653 696801 ✉ clare.slater@ryedale.gov.uk

Recycling & Waste Minimisation: Mr John Brown, Environmental & Recycling Officer, Central Depot, Showfield Lane Industrial Estate, Malton Y017 0BY ☎ 01653 600666 🖷 01653 690737 ✉ john.brown@ryedale.gov.uk

Regeneration: Mr Julian Rudd, Head of Economy & Infrastructure, Ryedale House, Malton YO17 7HH ☎ 01653 600666 🖷 01653 696801 ✉ julian.rudd@ryedale.gov.uk

Staff Training: Miss Louise Sandall, Head of Corporate and Business Support, Ryedale House, Malton YO17 7HH ☎ 01653 600666 🖷 01653 696801

louise.sandall@ryedale.gov.uk

Street Scene: Mrs Beckie Bennett, Streetscene Manager, Ryedale House, Malton YO17 7HH ☎ 01653 600666 Extn 483 beckie.bennett@ryedale.gov.uk

Sustainable Communities: Mr Julian Rudd, Head of Economy & Infrastructure, Ryedale House, Malton YO17 7HH ☎ 01653 600666 Fax 01653 696801 julian.rudd@ryedale.gov.uk

Sustainable Development: Mr John Brown, Environmental & Recycling Officer, Central Depot, Showfield Lane Industrial Estate, Malton Y017 0BY ☎ 01653 600666 Fax 01653 690737 john.brown@ryedale.gov.uk

Tourism: Mrs Jos Holmes, Cultural Service Manager, Ryedale House, Malton YO17 7HH ☎ 01653 600666 Fax 01653 696801 jos.holmes@ryedale.gov.uk

Town Centre: Mr Julian Rudd, Head of Economy & Infrastructure, Ryedale House, Malton YO17 7HH ☎ 01653 600666 Fax 01653 696801 julian.rudd@ryedale.gov.uk

Transport: Mrs Beckie Bennett, Streetscene Manager, Depot, Showfield Lane, Malton YO17 0BY ☎ 01653 600666 Extn 483 beckie.bennett@ryedale.gov.uk

Waste Collection and Disposal: Mrs Beckie Bennett, Streetscene Manager, Depot, Showfield Lane, Malton YO17 0BY ☎ 01653 600666 Extn 483
beckie.bennett@ryedale.gov.uk

Waste Collection and Disposal: Mr Phil Long, Head of Streetscene and Environment, Ryedale House, Malton YO17 7HH ☎ 01653 600666 phil.long@ryedale.gov.uk

Waste Management: Mr Phil Long, Head of Streetscene and Environment, Ryedale House, Malton YO17 7HH ☎ 01653 600666 phil.long@ryedale.gov.uk

MEMBERS OF THE COUNCIL (30)

***Chair:* Hope**, Eric (CON - Sheriff Hutton)
cllr.eric.hope@ryedale.gov.uk
***Vice-Chair:* Frank**, Janet (CON - Dales)
cllr.janet.frank@ryedale.gov.uk
***Leader of the Council:* Knaggs**, Keith (CON - Ryedale South West)
cllr.keith.knaggs@ryedale.gov.uk
***Group Leader:* Clark**, John (LIB - Cropton)
cllr.john.clark@ryedale.gov.uk
***Group Leader:* Shields**, Elizabeth (LD - Norton East)
cllr.elizabeth.shields@ryedale.gov.uk
***Group Leader:* Wainwright**, Robert (IND - Hovingham)
cllr.robert.wainwright@ryedale.gov.uk
Acomb, Geoffrey (CON - Thornton Dale)
cllr.geoffrey.acomb@ryedale.gov.uk
Andrews, Paul (IND - Malton)
cllr.paul.andrews@ryedale.gov.uk
Arnold, Steve (CON - Helmsley)
cllr.stephen.arnold@ryedale.gov.uk
Bailey, James (CON - Ampleforth)
cllr.james.bailey@ryedale.gov.uk
Burr, Lindsay (LD - Malton)
cllr.lindsay.burr@ryedale.gov.uk
Cowling, Linda (CON - Pickering West)
cllr.linda.cowling@ryedale.gov.uk
Cussons, David (CON - Kirkbymoorside)
cllr.david.cussons@ryedale.gov.uk
Denniss, Judith (CON - Norton West)
cllr.judith.denniss@rydale.gov.uk
Fraser, James (CON - Derwent)
cllr.james.fraser@ryedale.gov.uk
Goodrick, Caroline (CON - Derwent)
cllr.caroline.goodrick@ryedale.gov.uk
Hawkins, George (CON - Helmsley)
cllr.george.hawkins@ryedale.gov.uk
Hicks, J (CON - Amotherby)
Hopkinson, Ann (CON - Malton)
cllr.ann.hopkinson@ryedale.gov.uk
Ives, Luke (CON - Norton West)
cllr.luke.ives@ryedale.gov.uk
Knaggs, Vivienne (CON - Pickering East)
cllr.vivienne.knaggs@ryedale.gov.uk
Legard, Edward (CON - Wolds)
cllr.edward.legard@ryedale.gov.uk
Maud, Brian (IND - Rillington)
cllr.brian.maud@ryedale.gov.uk
Raper, John (CON - Sherburn)
cllr.john.raper@ryedale.gov.uk
Richardson, Luke (LIB - Pickering West)
cllr.luke.richardson@ryedale.gov.uk
Sanderson, Janet (CON - Thornton Dale)
cllr.janet.sanderson@ryedale.gov.uk
Walker, Peter (IND - Norton East)
cllr.peter.walker@ryedale.gov.uk
Ward, Sarah (LIB - Kirkbymoorside)
cllr.sarah.ward@ryedale.gov.uk
Windress, John (CON - Sinnington)
cllr.john.windress@ryedale.gov.uk
Woodward, Thomas (LIB - Pickering East)
cllr.tommy.woodward@ryedale.gov.uk

POLITICAL COMPOSITION

CON: 20, IND: 4, LIB: 4, LD: 2

COMMITTEE CHAIRS

Commissioning Board: Mrs Linda Cowling
Overview & Scrutiny: Mr Robert Wainwright
Planning: Mr John Raper
Policy & Resources: Mr Geoffrey Acomb

SALFORD CITY M

Salford City Council, Town Hall, Chorley Road, Swinton, Salford M27 5FJ ☎ 0161 794 4711 🖷 0161 793 3043 🖳 www.salford.gov.uk

FACTS & FIGURES

Police Authority: Greater Manchester Police Authority
Health Authority: North West Strategic Health Authority
Learning and Skills Council: North West
Parliamentary Constituencies: Blackley and Broughton, Salford and Eccles, Worsley and Eccles South
EU Constituencies: North West
Election Frequency: Elections are by thirds
Twinning: Clermont-Ferrand (France); Lunen (Germany); Narbonne (France); St. Ouen (France)

PRINCIPAL OFFICERS

Chief Executive: Ms Barbara Spicer, Chief Executive, Town Hall, Chorley Road, Swinton, Salford M27 5FJ ☎ 0161 793 3400 🖷 0161 793 3435 ✉ barbara.spicer@salford.gov.uk

Senior Management: Mr Ben Dolan, Strategic Director - Environment & Community Safety, Turnpike House, 631 Eccles New Road, Salford M50 1SW ☎ 0161 925 1112 🖷 0161 920 8481 ✉ ben.dolan@salford.gov.uk

Senior Management: Ms Sue Lightup, Strategic Director - Community, Health & Social Care, Turnpike Road, 631 Eccles New Road, Salford M50 1SW ☎ 0161 793 2200 🖷 0161 793 3606 ✉ sue.lightup@salford.gov.uk

Senior Management: Mr Nick Page, Strategic Director - Children's Services, Unity House, Salford Civic Centre, Chorley Road, Swinton M27 5AW ☎ 0161 778 0130 🖷 0161 728 6068 ✉ nick.page@salford.gov.uk

Senior Management: Mr Martin Vickers, Strategic Director - Customer & Support Services, Salford Civic Centre, Chorley Road, Swinton M27 5AW ☎ 0161 793 3407 🖷 0161 793 3435 ✉ martin.vickers@salford.gov.uk

Architect, Building / Property Services: Mr Steve Gogarty, Associate Director - Architectural & Landscape Design, Urban Vision Partnership, Emerson House, Albert Street, Eccles M30 0TE ☎ 0161 799 6062 🖷 0161 779 6008 ✉ steve.gogarty@urbanvision.org.uk

Best Value: Mr Martin Vickers, Strategic Director - Customer & Support Services, Salford Civic Centre, Chorley Road, Swinton M27 5DA ☎ 0161 793 3407 🖷 0161 793 3435 ✉ martin.vickers@salford.gov.uk

Building Control: Mr Dave Jolley, Director - Planning & Building Control, Urban Vision Partnership Ltd, Emerson House, Albert Street, Eccles M30 0TE ☎ 0161 604 7784 🖷 0161 779 6002 ✉ dave.jolley@urbanvision.org.uk

Catering Services: Ms Sharon Smith, Principal Service Manager - Catering & Cleaning, Turnpike House, 631 Eccles New Road, Salford M50 1SW ☎ 0161 925 1068 🖷 0161 925 1330 ✉ sharon.smith@salford.gov.uk

Catering Services: Ms Ruth Steenson, Commercial Catering Manager, Buile Hill Park Hall, Eccles Old Road, Salford M6 8GL ☎ 0161 736 4870 🖷 0161 745 9973 ✉ ruth.steenson@salford.gov.uk

Children / Youth Services: Ms Eileen Buchan, Head - Integrated Youth Support Services, Salford Opportunity Centre, 2 Paddington Close, Churchill Way, Salford M6 5PL ☎ 0161 603 6834 🖷 0161 603 6840 ✉ eileen.buchan@salford.gov.uk

Civil Registration: Ms Rebecca Roberts, Superintendent Registrar, Town Hall, Chorley Road, Swinton M27 5FJ ☎ 0161 603 6880 🖷 0161 603 6892 ✉ rebecca.wardley@salford.gov.uk

PR / Communications: Ms Clare Hunter, Press & PR Manager, Town Hall, Chorley Road, Swinton, Salford M27 5FJ ☎ 0161 793 2478 ✉ clare.hunter@salford.gov.uk

Community Planning: Mr Tim Field, Deputy Director - Community, Health & Social Care, Turnpike House, 631 Eccles New Road, Swinton M50 1SW ☎ 0161 793 2817 🖷 0161 793 2849 ✉ tim.field@salford.gov.uk

Community Safety: Mr Don Brown, Assistant Director - Community Safety, Turnpike House, 631 Eccles New Road, Salford M50 1SW ☎ 0161 925 1001 ✉ don.brown@salford.gov.uk

Computer Management: Mr David Hunter, Assistant Director - Corporate ICT, Salford City Centre, Chorley Road, Salford M27 5DA ☎ 0161 793 3911 🖷 0161 794 5221 ✉ david.hunter@salford.gov.uk

Consumer Protection and Trading Standards: Mr Ron Pennington, Head of Service - Regulatory Services, Turnpike House, 631 Eccles New Road, Salford M50 1SW ☎ 0161 925 1051 🖷 0161 920 8481 ✉ ron.pennington@salford.gov.uk

Contracts: Mr Neil Thornton, Chief Financial Officer, Unity House, Salford Civic Centre, Chorley Road, Swinton M27 5AW ☎ 0161 686 6200 ✉ neil.thornton@salford.gov.uk

Corporate Services: Mr Martin Vickers, Strategic Director - Customer & Support Services, Salford Civiv Centre, Chorley Road, Swinton M27 5DA ☎ 0161 793 3407 🖷 0161 793 3435 ✉ martin.vickers@salford.gov.uk

Customer Service: Mr John Tanner, Assistant Director - Customer Services, Salford Civic Centre, Chorley Road, Swinton, Salford M27 5DA ☎ 0161 793 3364 🖷 0161 793 2029 ✉ john.tanner@salford.gov.uk

Economic Development: Mr Rob Pickering, Assistant Director - Economic Futures, Salford Civic Centre, Chorley Road, Swinton, Salford M27 5BY ☎ 0161 793 2818 🖷 0161 793 2477 ✉ rob.pickering@salford.gov.uk

Education: Mrs Julie Cunningham, Head - Inclusive Learning Services, Halton House, 36 Eccles Old Road, Salford M6 8RA ☎ 0161 607 1677 ✉ julie.cunningham@salford.gov.uk

Education: Mr Nick Page, Strategic Director - Children's Services, Unity House, Salford Civic Centre, Chorley Road,

Swinton M27 5AW ☎ 0161 778 0130 🖷 0161 728 6068
✉ nick.page@salford.gov.uk

E-Government: Mr David Hunter, Assistant Director - Corporate ICT, Salford Civic Centre, Chorley Road, Swinton, Salford M27 5DA ☎ 0161 793 3911 🖷 0161 794 5221
✉ david.hunter@salford.gov.uk

Electoral Registration: Ms Allison Lobley, Assistant Director - Administration, Unity House, Salford Civic Centre, Chorley Road, Swinton M27 5AW ☎ 0161 793 3003
✉ allison.lobley@salford.gov.uk

Emergency Planning: Mr David Hunter, Assistant Director - Corporate ICT, Salford Civic Centre, Chorley Road, Swinton, Salford M27 5DA ☎ 0161 793 3911 🖷 0161 794 5221
✉ david.hunter@salford.gov.uk

Energy Management: Mr Majid Maqbool, Energy Manager, Salford Civic Centre, Chorley Road, Swinton M27 5DA ☎ 0161 793 6987 🖷 0161 793 2666 ✉ majid.maqbool@salford.gov.uk

Environmental Health: Mr Ron Pennington, Head of Service - Regulatory Services, Turnpike House, 631 Eccles New Road, Salford M50 1SW ☎ 0161 925 1051 🖷 0161 920 8481
✉ ron.pennington@salford.gov.uk

Estates, Property & Valuation: Mr Richard Wynne, Director - Property & Development, Emerson House, Albert Street, Eccles M30 0TE ☎ 0161 779 6127 ✉ richard.wynne@urbanvision.org.uk

Events Manager: Mrs Lindsey Hebden, Tourism Marketing Manager, Salford Civic Centre, Chorley Road, Swinton M27 5DA ☎ 0161 793 2375 ✉ lindsey.hebden@salford.gov.uk

Facilities: Mr Danny Hoy, Facilities Manager, 5th Floor, Emerson House, Albert Street, Eccles M30 0TE ☎ 0161 779 4977 🖷 0161 779 6005 ✉ danny.hoy@urbanvision.org.uk

Finance and Treasurer: Mr Neil Thornton, Chief Financial Officer, Unity House, Salford Civic Centre, Chorley Road, Swinton M27 5AW ☎ 0161 686 6200 ✉ neil.thornton@salford.gov.uk

Fleet Management: Mr Terry Dixie, Head of Services - Transportation, Turnpike House, 631 Eccles New Road, Salford M50 1SW ☎ 0161 925 1046 ✉ terry.dixie@salford.gov.uk

Grounds Maintenance: Mr David Seager, Assistant Director - Operation & Commercial Services, Turnpike House, 631 Eccles New Road, Salford M50 1SW ☎ 0161 925 1115 🖷 0161 920 8481
✉ david.seager@salford.gov.uk

Health and Safety: Mr Ron Pennington, Head of Service - Regulatory Services, Turnpike House, 631 Eccles New Road, Salford M50 1SW ☎ 0161 925 1051 🖷 0161 920 8481
✉ ron.pennington@salford.gov.uk

Highways: Mr Richard Goodwin, Director - Technical, Emerson House, Albert Street, Eccles M30 0TE ☎ 0161 603 4019
✉ richard.goodwin@urbanvision.org.uk

Home Energy Conservation: Mr Leslie Laws, Principal Officer - Affordable Warmth, Salford Civic Centre, Chorley Road, Swinton, Salford M27 5BY ☎ 0161 793 2264 🖷 0161 793 3377
✉ leslie.laws@salford.gov.uk

Housing: Mr David Galvin, Assistant Director - Housing Futures, Salford Civic Centre, Chorley Road, Swinton, Salford M27 5BY ☎ 0161 793 2310 🖷 0161 793 2477 ✉ david.galvin@salford.gov.uk

Housing Maintenance: Mr Paul Lister, Maintenance Manager, Diamond House, 2 Peel Cross Road, Salford M5 4BT ☎ 0161 779 8899 🖷 0161 779 8977 ✉ paul.lister@salixhomes.org

Local Area Agreement: Mr Martin Vickers, Strategic Director - Customer & Support Services, Salford Civiv Centre, Chorley Road, Swinton M27 5DA ☎ 0161 793 3407 🖷 0161 793 3435
✉ martin.vickers@salford.gov.uk

Legal: Mr Martin Vickers, Strategic Director - Customer & Support Services, Salford Civic Centre, Chorley Road, Swinton M27 5DA ☎ 0161 793 3407 🖷 0161 793 3435
✉ martin.vickers@salford.gov.uk

Leisure and Cultural Services: Mr Andy Howitt, Assistant Director - Culture & Leisure, Turnpike House, 631 Eccles New Road, Salford M50 1SW ☎ 0161 793 2243 🖷 0161 793 3606
✉ andy.howitt@salford.gov.uk

Licensing: Mr Ron Pennington, Head of Service - Regulatory Services, Turnpike House, 631 Eccles New Road, Salford M50 1SW ☎ 0161 925 1051 🖷 0161 920 8481
✉ ron.pennington@salford.gov.uk

Lighting: Mr Ian Darlington, Lighting Manager, Emerson House, Albert Street, Eccles M30 0TE ☎ 07825 937395
✉ ian.darlington@urbanvision.org.uk

Lottery Funding, Charity and Voluntary: Ms Sue Ford, Funding & Development Manager, Salford Civic Centre, Chorley Road, Swinton M27 5BY ☎ 0161 793 3443 🖷 0161 793 2477
✉ sue.ford@salford.gov.uk

Member Services: Mr Vincent Joseph, Head - Democratic Services, Town Hall, Chorley Road, Swinton, Salford M27 5FJ ☎ 0161 793 3009 ✉ vin.joseph@salford.gov.uk

Parking: Mr Steven Lee, Director - Engineering, Emerson House, Albert Street, Eccles M30 0TE ☎ 0161 779 4871 🖷 0161 779 6003
✉ steven.lee@urbanvision.org.uk

Partnerships: Mr Martin Vickers, Strategic Director - Customer & Support Services, Salford Civiv Centre, Chorley Road, Swinton M27 5DA ☎ 0161 793 3407 🖷 0161 793 3435
✉ martin.vickers@salford.gov.uk

Personnel / HR: Ms Debbie Brown, Assistant Director - Human Resources, Salford Civic Centre, Chorley Road, Swinton M27 5DA ☎ 0161 607 8600 🖷 0161 794 2027
✉ debbie.brown@salford.gov.uk

Planning: Mr Christopher Findley, Assistant Director - Planning & Transport Futures, Salford Civic Centre, Chorley Road, Swinton, Salford M27 5BY ☎ 0161 793 3654 🖷 0161 793 2477

chris.findley@salford.gov.uk

Procurement: Ms Sharon Robson, Acting Head - Procurement, Unity House, Salford Civic Centre, Chorley Road, Swinton M27 5AW ☎ 0161 686 6226 sharon.robson@salford.gov.uk

Public Libraries: Ms Sarah Spence, Libraries & Information Services Manager, New Bridgewater House, 12 Bridgewater Street, Walkden, Salford M28 3JE ☎ 0161 778 0840 🖷 0161 745 9490 sarah.spence@salford.gov.uk

Recycling & Waste Minimisation: Mr David Seager, Assistant Director - Operation & Commercial Services, Turnpike House, 631 Eccles New Road, Salford M50 1SW ☎ 0161 925 1115 🖷 0161 920 8481 david.seager@salford.gov.uk

Regeneration: Ms Karen Hirst, Director - Development, Town Hall, Chorley Road, Swinton M27 5FJ ☎ 0161 686 7411 karen.hirst@salford.gov.uk

Road Safety: Mr Steven Lee, Director - Engineering, Emerson House, Albert Street, Eccles M30 0TE ☎ 0161 779 4871 🖷 0161 779 6003 steven.lee@urbanvision.org.uk

Social Services: Mr Mike Kelly, Head - Service & Family Placement, Unity House, Salford Civic Centre, Chorley Road, Swinton M27 5AW ☎ 0161 779 7914 mike.kelly@salford.gov.uk

Social Services (Adult): Mr David Entwhistle, Assistant Director - Adults & Personalisation, Turnpike House, 631 Eccles New Road, Salford M50 1SW ☎ 0161 793 2205 🖷 0161 793 3606 david.entwhistle@salford.gov.uk

Social Services (Children): Mr Nick Page, Strategic Director - Children's Services, Unity House, Salford Civic Centre, Chorley Road, Swinton M27 5AW ☎ 0161 778 0130 🖷 0161 728 6068 nick.page@salford.gov.uk

Staff Training: Ms Debbie Brown, Assistant Director - Human Resources, Salford Civic Centre, Chorley Road, Swinton M27 5DA ☎ 0161 607 8600 🖷 0161 794 2027 debbie.brown@salford.gov.uk

Street Scene: Mr Steven Lee, Director - Engineering, Emerson House, Albert Street, Eccles M30 0TE ☎ 0161 779 4871 🖷 0161 779 6003 steven.lee@urbanvision.org.uk

Sustainable Communities: Mr Ben Dolan, Strategic Director - Environment & Community Safety, Turnpike House, 631 Eccles New Road, Salford M50 1SW ☎ 0161 920 8400 🖷 0161 920 8481 ben.dolan@salford.gov.uk

Sustainable Development: Mr Christopher Findley, Assistant Director - Planning & Transport Futures, Salford Civic Centre, Chorley Road, Swinton, Salford M27 5BY ☎ 0161 793 3654 🖷 0161 793 2477 chris.findley@salford.gov.uk

Tourism: Mrs Lindsey Hebden, Tourism Marketing Manager, Salford Civic Centre, Chorley Road, Swinton M27 5DA ☎ 0161 793 2375 lindsey.hebden@salford.gov.uk

Town Centre: Ms Maura Carey, Group Leader - Regeneration Strategy & Co-ordination, Town Hall, Chorley Road, Swinton M27 5FJ ☎ 0161 793 2903 🖷 0161 793 2477 maura.carey@salford.gov.uk

Traffic Management: Mr Steven Lee, Director - Engineering, Emerson House, Albert Street, Eccles M30 0TE ☎ 0161 779 4871 🖷 0161 779 6003 steven.lee@urbanvision.org.uk

Transport: Mr Terry Dixie, Head of Services - Transportation, Turnpike House, 631 Eccles New Road, Salford M50 1SW ☎ 0161 925 1046 terry.dixie@salford.gov.uk

Transport Planner: Mr Darren Findley, Strategic Transportation Manager, Salford Civic Centre, Chorley Road, Swinton, Salford M27 5BY ☎ 0161 793 3849 🖷 0161 793 3848 darren.findley@salford.gov.uk

Total Place: Mr Martin Vickers, Strategic Director - Customer & Support Services, Salford Civiv Centre, Chorley Road, Swinton M27 5DA ☎ 0161 793 3407 🖷 0161 793 3435 martin.vickers@salford.gov.uk

Waste Collection and Disposal: Mr David Seager, Assistant Director - Operation & Commercial Services, Turnpike House, 631 Eccles New Road, Salford M50 1SW ☎ 0161 925 1115 🖷 0161 920 8481 david.seager@salford.gov.uk

Waste Management: Mr David Seager, Assistant Director - Operation & Commercial Services, Turnpike House, 631 Eccles New Road, Salford M50 1SW ☎ 0161 925 1115 🖷 0161 920 8481 david.seager@salford.gov.uk

MEMBERS OF THE COUNCIL (60)

***Ceremonial Mayor:* Lea**, Bernard (LAB - Pendlebury)
councillor.blea@salford.gov.uk

***Deputy Mayor:* Lancaster**, David (LAB - Winton)
councillor.lancaster@salford.gov.uk

***Group Leader:* Garrido**, Karen (CON - Worsley)
councillor.garrido@salford.gov.uk

***Group Leader:* Pugh**, Sue (LAB - Claremont)
councillor.pugh@salford.gov.uk

Antrobus, Derek (LAB - Swinton North)
councillor.antrobus@salford.gov.uk

Balkind, Howard (LAB - Swinton South)
councillor.balkind@salford.gov.uk

Boshell, Paula (LAB - Winton)
councillor.boshell@salford.gov.uk

Brocklehurst, Adrian (LAB - Walkden North)
councillor.brocklehurst@salford.gov.uk

Burgoyne, Val (LAB - Little Hulton)
councillor.vburgoyne@salford.gov.uk

Burgoyne, Eric (LAB - Little Hulton)
councillor.eburgoyne@salford.gov.uk

Cheetham, Andy (CON - Boothstown and Ellenbrook)
councillor.cheetham@salford.gov.uk

Clague, Alan (LAB - Ordsall)
councillor.clague@salford.gov.uk

Clarkson, Christopher (CON - Worsley)
councillor.clarkson@salford.gov.uk

Coen, Stephen (LAB - Irwell Riverside)
councillor.coen@salford.gov.uk

Collinson, Jillian (CON - Boothstown and Ellenbrook)
councillor.collinson@salford.gov.uk

Compton, Graham (CON - Worsley)
councillor.compton@salford.gov.uk
Connor, Peter (LAB - Kersal)
councillor.connor@salford.gov.uk
Critchley, Richard (LAB - Walkden South)
councillor.critchley@salford.gov.uk
Dawson, Jim (LAB - Swinton North)
councillor.dawson@salford.gov.uk
Dennett, Paul (LAB - Langworthy)
councillor.dennett@salford.gov.uk
Dirir, Sareda (LAB - Claremont)
councillor.dirir@salford.gov.uk
Dobbs, Peter (LAB - Ordsall)
councillor.dobbs@salford.gov.uk
Ferguson, John (LAB - Pendlebury)
councillor.ferguson@salford.gov.uk
Garrido, Robin (CON - Boothstown and Ellenbrook)
councillor.rgarrido@salford.gov.uk
Hinds, Bill (LAB - Swinton North)
councillor.hinds@salford.gov.uk
Hudson, Christine (LAB - Cadishead)
councillor.hudson@salford.gov.uk
Humphreys, Ann-Marie (LAB - Kersal)
councillor.humphreys@salford.gov.uk
Hunt, Jimmy (LAB - Cadishead)
councillor.hunt@salford.gov.uk
Jolley, David (LAB - Barton)
councillor.jolley@salford.gov.uk
Jones, Roger (LAB - Irlam)
councillor.jones@salford.gov.uk
Kean, Joe (LAB - Irlam)
councillor.kean@salford.gov.uk
Kelly, Tracy (LAB - Irlam)
councillor.kelly@salford.gov.uk
King, Jim (LAB - Broughton)
councillor.king@salford.gov.uk
Lindley, Iain (CON - Walkden South)
councillor.lindley@salford.gov.uk
Mashiter, Ray (LAB - Ordsall)
councillor.mashiter@salford.gov.uk
McIntyre, Charles (LAB - Broughton)
councillor.mcintyre@salford.gov.uk
Merrett, Gina (LAB - Swinton South)
councillor.merrett@salford.gov.uk
Merry, John (LAB - Broughton)
councillor.merry@salford.gov.uk
Mold, Matt (LAB - Irwell Riverside)
councillor.mold@salford.gov.uk
Morris, Margaret (LAB - Winton)
councillor.morris@salford.gov.uk
Mullen, John (LAB - Barton)
councillor.mullen@salford.gov.uk
Mullen, Michelle (LAB - Barton)
councillor.mmullen@salford.gov.uk
Murphy, Thomas (LAB - Weaste and Seedley)
councillor.tmurphy@salford.gov.uk
Murphy, Joe (LAB - Claremont)
councillor.jmurphy@salford.gov.uk
Ord, Stephen (LAB - Irwell Riverside)
councillor.ord@salford.gov.uk
Pennington, Bernard (LAB - Walkden North)
councillor.pennington@salford.gov.uk
Potter, Norbert (LAB - Swinton South)
councillor.potter@salford.gov.uk
Reynolds, Gina (LAB - Langworthy)
councillor.reynolds@salford.gov.uk
Rochford, Jan (LAB - Weaste and Seedley)
councillor.rochford@salford.gov.uk
Ryan, Patricia (LAB - Little Hulton)
councillor.ryan@salford.gov.uk
Ryan, Brendan (LAB - Walkden North)
councillor.bryan@salford.gov.uk
Stone, Lisa (LAB - Eccles)
councillor.stone@salford.gov.uk
Turner, Les (CON - Walkden South)
councillor.turner@salford.gov.uk
Walsh, John (LAB - Cadishead)
councillor.walsh@salford.gov.uk
Warmisham, John (LAB - Langworthy)
councillor.warmisham@salford.gov.uk
Warner, Barry (LAB - Pendlebury)
councillor.warner@salford.gov.uk
Wheeler, Michael (LAB - Eccles)
councillor.wheeler@salford.gov.uk
Wheeler, Peter (LAB - Eccles)
councillor.pwheeler@salford.gov.uk
Wilson, Ronnie (LAB - Weaste and Seedley)
councillor.rwilson@salford.gov.uk
Wilson, George (LAB - Kersal)
councillor.wilson@salford.gov.uk

POLITICAL COMPOSITION

LAB: 52, CON: 8

CABINET

Adult Services & Services for Older People: Mr Peter Connor
Services for Children & Young People: Mr John Merry
Communications & Community Engagement: Ms Lisa Stone
Culture: Ms Ann-Marie Humphreys
Finance & Support Services: Mr Bill Hinds
Health & Wellbeing: Ms Margaret Morris
Housing & Environment: Ms Gina Merrett
HR & Workplace Reform: Mr Paul Dennett
International Relations: Mr Stephen Coen
Learning Skills & Employment: Ms Paula Boshell
Transport & City Regions: Mr Roger Jones

COMMITTEE CHAIRS

Audit & Accounts: Mr Robin Garrido
Budget: Mr David Jolley
Children, Young People & Families: Mr Bernard Pennington
Corporate Issues: Mr Les Turner
Health, Wellbeing & Social Care: Mr Joe Kean
Licensing & Safety Regulatory: Mr John Warmisham
Planning & Transportation Regulatory: Mr Ray Mashiter
Sustainable Regeneration: Mr Jim Dawson

SANDWELL M

Sandwell Metropolitan Borough Council, Sandwell Council House, Oldbury B69 3DE ☎ 0121 569 2200 🖷 0121 569 3100 smbc@sandwell.gov.uk www.sandwell.gov.uk

FACTS & FIGURES

Police Authority: West Midlands Police Authority
Health Authority: NHS West Midlands
Learning and Skills Council: West Midlands
Parliamentary Constituencies: Halesowen and Rowley Regis,

Warley, West Bromwich East, West Bromwich West
EU Constituencies: West Midlands
Election Frequency: Elections are by thirds
Twinning: Amritsar (India); Blanc Mesnil (France)

PRINCIPAL OFFICERS

Chief Executive: Mr Jan Britton, Chief Executive, Sandwell Council House, Oldbury B69 3DE ☎ 0121 569 3501 ✉ jan_britton@sandwell.gov.uk

Senior Management: Mr Brian Aldridge, Service Director - Learning & Culture, Sandwell Council House, Oldbury B69 3DE ☎ 0121 569 8325 ✉ brian_aldridge@sandwell.gov.uk

Senior Management: Ms Kerry Bollister, Area Director - Homes & Communities for Tipton & Wednesbury, Sandwell Council House, Oldbury B69 3DE ☎ 0121 569 5060 ✉ kerry_bollister@sandwell.gov.uk

Senior Management: Mr Nick Bubalo, Area Director - Regeneration & Economy for West Bromwich & Smethwick, Sandwell Council House, Oldbury B69 3DE ☎ 0121 569 4253 ✉ nick_bubalo@sandwell.gov.uk

Senior Management: Ms Melanie Dudley, Corporate Director - Improvement & Efficiency, Sandwell Council House, Oldbury B69 3DE ☎ 0121 569 3548 ✉ melanie_dudley@sandwell.gov.uk

Senior Management: Mr John Garrett, Corporate Director - Place, Sandwell Council House, Oldbury B69 3DE ☎ 0121 569 4748 ✉ john_garrett@sandwell.gov.uk

Senior Management: Mr Steve Handley, Director - Street Scene, Sandwell Council House, Oldbury B69 3DE ☎ 0121 569 3718 🖷 0121 569 6840 ✉ steve_handley@sandwell.gov.uk

Senior Management: Mr Stuart Kellas, Director - Strategic Resources, Sandwell Council House, Oldbury B69 3DE ☎ 0121 569 3504 ✉ stuart_kellas@sandwell.gov.uk

Senior Management: Ms Barbara Peacock, Corporate Director - People, Sandwell Council House, Oldbury B69 3DE ☎ 0121 569 8204 ✉ barbara_peacock@sandwell.gov.uk

Senior Management: Mr Martin Samuels, Service Director - Commissioning Services, Sandwell Council House, Oldbury B69 3DE ☎ 0121 569 5730 ✉ martin_samuels@sandwell.gov.uk

Senior Management: Mrs Neeraj Sharma, Director - Legal & Governance Services, Sandwell Council House, PO Box 2374, Oldbury B69 3DE ☎ 0121 569 3172 ✉ neeraj_sharma@sandwell.gov.uk

Senior Management: Ms Helen Smith, Service Director - Children & Families, Sandwell Council House, Oldbury B69 3DE ☎ 0121 569 8378 ✉ helen_smith@sandwell.gov.uk

Senior Management: Mr Tony Zaman, Service Director - Adult Social Care, Sandwell Council House, Oldbury B69 3DE ☎ 0121 569 5887 ✉ tony_zaman@sandwell.gov.uk

Civil Registration: Mr Paul Sheldon, Registration Services Manager, Sandwell Register Office, Highfields, High Street, West Bromwich B70 8RJ ☎ 0121 569 2480 🖷 0121 569 2473 ✉ paul_sheldon@sandwell.gov.uk

PR / Communications: Mr Steve Harrison, Communications Officer, Sandwell Council House, Oldbury B69 3DE ☎ 0121 569 3033 ✉ steve_harrison@sandwell.gov.uk

Computer Management: Mr Andy Nicholls, ICT Strategy & Client Manager, Sandwell Council House, Oldbury B69 3DE ☎ 0121 569 3371 ✉ andy_nicholls@sandwell.gov.uk

Customer Service: Ms Emma Botfield, Head - BT Customer Services, Sandwell Council House, Oldbury B69 3DE ☎ 0121 569 6803 ✉ emma_botfield@sandwell.gov.uk

Electoral Registration: Mrs Paula Bayes, Joint Electoral Services Manager, PO Box 2374, Sandwell Council House, Oldbury B69 3DE ☎ 0121 569 3244 🖷 0121 569 3367 ✉ paula_bayes@sandwell.gov.uk

Electoral Registration: Mrs Rosemary Winning, Joint Electoral Services Manager, PO Box 2374, Sandwell Council House, Oldbury B69 3DE ☎ 0121 569 3242 🖷 0121 569 3367 ✉ rosemary_winning@sandwell.gov.uk

Emergency Planning: Mr Alan Boyd, Resilience Manager, Sandwell Council House, Oldbury B69 3DE ☎ 0121 569 3060 ✉ alan_boyd@sandwell.gov.uk

Events Manager: Mr Tony Potter, Events Manager, Environment House, Lombard Street, West Bromwich B70 8RU ☎ 0121 569 4703 🖷 0121 569 4704 ✉ tony_potter@sandwell.gov.uk

Facilities: Ms Christine Bailey, Facilities Services Team Manager, Sandwell Council House, Oldbury B69 3DE ☎ 0121 569 5887 🖷 0121 569 3938 ✉ christine_bailey@sandwell.gov.uk

Fleet Management: Ms Carole Bishop, Fleet Manager, Transport Depot, Waterfall Lane, Cradley Heath B64 6RL ☎ 0121 569 6855 🖷 0121 559 5819 ✉ carole_bishop@sandwell.gov.uk

Health and Safety: Mr Chris Williams, Health, Safety & Welfare Manager, PO Box 2374, Sandwell Council House, Oldbury B69 3DE ☎ 0121 569 8328 ✉ chris_williams@sandwell.gov.uk

Legal: Mrs Neeraj Sharma, Director - Legal & Governance Services, Sandwell Council House, PO Box 2374, Oldbury B69 3DE ☎ 0121 569 3172 ✉ neeraj_sharma@sandwell.gov.uk

Leisure and Cultural Services: Mr Paul Slater, Chief Executive - Sandwell Leisure Trust, PO Box 42, Lombard Street, West Bromwich B70 8RU ☎ 0121 521 4422 ✉ paul_slater@sandwell.gov.uk

Lottery Funding, Charity and Voluntary: Ms Heather Chinner, Policy Officer, Sandwell Council House, Oldbury B69 3DE ☎ 0845 352 3020 ✉ heather_chinner@sandwell.gov.uk

Member Services: Mr Rob Hevican, Member Services Manager, Sandwell Council House, Oldbury B69 3DE ☎ 0121 569 3043 ✉ robert_hevican@sandwell.gov.uk

MEMBERS OF THE COUNCIL (72)

***Leader of the Council:* Cooper**, Darren (LAB - Soho and Victoria)
darren_cooper@sandwell.gov.uk
***Deputy Leader of the Council:* Eling**, Steve (LAB - Abbey)
steve_eling@sandwell.gov.uk
***Deputy Leader of the Council:* Hussain**, Mahboob (LAB - Oldbury)
mahoob_hussain@sandwell.gov.uk
Ahmed, Zahoor (LAB - St Pauls)
zahoor_ahmed@sandwell.gov.uk
Allen, Peter (LAB - Great Bridge)
peter_allen@sandwell.gov.uk
Ashman, Lorraine (LAB - Tividale)
lorraine_ashman@sandwell.gov.uk
Badham, Robert (LAB - Greets Green and Lyng)
bob_badham@sandwell.gov.uk
Bawa, Babu (LAB - St Pauls)
Bridges, Malcolm (LAB - Blackheath)
malcolm@pammal.fslife.co.uk
Carmichael, Kerrie (LAB - Blackheath)
blackheathlabour@hotmail.co.uk
Cashmore, Lucy (LAB - Bristnall)
lucy_cashmore@sandwell.gov.uk
Cherrington, Bill (LAB - Princes End)
bill_cherrington@sandwell.gov.uk
Costigan, Elaine (LAB - Wednesbury North)
elaine.costigan@fsmail.net
Crompton, Maria (LAB - Tividale)
cromptonm@parliament.uk
Crumpton, Trevor (LAB - Old Warley)
t.crumpton@talktalk.net
Crumpton, Susan (LAB - Old Warley)
Davies, Yvonne (LAB - Langley)
ydavies16@btinternet.com
Davies, Patricia (LAB - Hateley Heath)
patdavies2006@yahoo.co.uk
Davies, Mick (IND - Langley)
mickdavies09@googlemail.com
Davies, Keith (LAB - Smethwick)
keithdavies2004@yahoo.co.uk
Davies, Sharon (LAB - Langley)
cllrsharon_davies@sandwell.gov.uk
Dhallu, Bawa (LAB - West Bromwich Central)
Downing, Susan (LAB - Oldbury)
Edis, Joy (LAB - Friar Park)
Edwards, John (LAB - Greets Green and Lyng)
john.e@pep.org.uk
Evans, Susan (LAB - Rowley)
susan_eaves@sandwell.gov.uk
Frazer, Kim (LAB - West Bromwich Central)
kimfrazer5225@yahoo.com
Frear, Steven (LAB - Bristnall)
steven.frear@btinternet.com
Giles, Elizabeth (LAB - Wednesbury South)
elizabeth.giles1@btinternet.com
Giles, Elaine (LAB - Oldbury)
elainegiles2000@yahoo.co.uk
Gill, Preet (LAB - St Pauls)
preet_kaurgill@sandwell.gov.uk
Hackett, Simon (LAB - Friar Park)
simon_hackett@sandwell.gov.uk
Hadley, Joanne (LAB - Great Bridge)
Haque, Ahmadul (LAB - Tipton Green)
Hartwell, Suzanne (LAB - Princes End)
Horton, Linda (LAB - Smethwick)
linda_horton@sandwell.gov.uk
Horton, Roger (LAB - Soho and Victoria)
councillor@lrhorton.freeserve.co.uk
Hosell, Shirley (LAB - Great Barr with Yew Tree)
shirley_hosell@sandwell.gov.uk
Hosell, David (LAB - Newton)
hoselld@blueyonder.co.uk
Hughes, Pam (LAB - Wednesbury South)
pam_hughes@sandwell.gov.uk
Hughes, Anne (CON - Charlemont with Grove Vale)
ahughes@smbc.fsnet.co.uk
Hughes, Mavis (CON - Wednesbury North)
mavishughes556@yahoo.co.uk
Hughes, Peter (LAB - Wednesbury North)
cllrpeter_hughes@sandwell.gov.uk
Jaron, Ann (LAB - Abbey)
ann_jaron@sandwell.gov.uk
Jarvis, Ann (LAB - Bristnall)
ann_jarvis@sandwell.gov.uk
Jones, Ian (LAB - Tipton Green)
ian_jones@sandwell.gov.uk
Jones, Stephen (LAB - Princes End)
cllrstephen_jones@sandwell.gov.uk
Jones, Olwen (LAB - Wednesbury South)
Khatun, Syeda (LAB - Tipton Green)
Lewis, Geoffrey (LAB - Friar Park)
geoffreyjlewis@fsmail.net
Melia, Steve (LAB - Great Barr with Yew Tree)
smelia5751@aol.com
Moore, Paul (LAB - Hateley Heath)
paul_moore@sandwell.gov.uk
Piper, Bob (LAB - Abbey)
bob.piper@gmail.com
Preece, Liam (LAB - Charlemont with Grove Vale)
liam_preece@sandwell.gov.uk
Price, Barbara (LAB - Rowley)
councillor-mrs@bprice31.freeserve.co.uk
Price, Robert (LAB - Blackheath)
councillor@bprice31.freeserve.co.uk
Rouf, Mohammed (LAB - Soho and Victoria)
Rowley, Derek (LAB - Great Bridge)
derek_rowley@sandwell.gov.uk
Sandars, Paul (LAB - Hateley Heath)
sandarspaul@hotmail.com
Shackleton, Ann (LAB - Cradley Heath and Old Hill)
ann_shackleton@sandwell.gov.uk
Sidhu, Gurcharan (LAB - Greets Green and Lyng)
Silvester, Victor (LAB - Smethwick)
vic.silvester@btinternet.com
Tagger, Mohinder (LAB - West Bromwich Central)
Tipper, John (LAB - Cradley Heath and Old Hill)
john_tipper@sandwell.gov.uk
Tranter, Chris (LAB - Rowley)
chris_tranter@sandwell.gov.uk
Trow, Steve (LAB - Old Warley)
stevetrow@blueyonder.co.uk
Underhill, Tony (LD - Newton)
joyceunderhill@btinternet.com
Underhill, Joyce (LD - Newton)
joyceunderhill@btinternet.com
Ward, Anthony (IND - Charlemont with Grove Vale)
arwward@blueyonder.co.uk

Webb, Julie (LAB - Cradley Heath and Old Hill)
juliewebb55@hotmail.com
Wilkinson, Jayne (LAB - Tividale)
tividale4u@hotmail.co.uk
Worsey, Christopher (LAB - Great Barr with Yew Tree)
chirs_worsey@sandwell.gov.uk

POLITICAL COMPOSITION

LAB: 66, LD: 2, CON: 2, IND: 2

CABINET

Leader: Mr Darren Cooper
Deputy Leader / Strategic Resources: Mr Steve Eling
Children & Families: Mr Robert Badham
Housing: Mr Simon Hackett
Improvement & Efficiency: Mr Mahboob Hussain
Safer Neighbourhoods: Mr Derek Rowley
Youth, Culture & Leisure: Mrs Linda Horton

SCARBOROUGH D

Scarborough Borough Council, Town Hall, St. Nicholas Street, Scarborough YO11 2HG ☎ 01723 232323
ce@scarborough.gov.uk www.scarborough.gov.uk

FACTS & FIGURES

Police Authority: North Yorkshire Police Authority
Health Authority: NHS Yorkshire & the Humber
Learning and Skills Council: Yorkshire and the Humber
Parliamentary Constituencies: Scarborough and Whitby
EU Constituencies: Yorkshire and the Humber
Election Frequency: Elections are of whole council
Twinning: Scarborough: Osterode Am Harz (Germany); Whitby: Anchorage (USA); Nuku Alofa (Tonga); Port Stanley (Falkland Isles); Whitby (Canada)

PRINCIPAL OFFICERS

Chief Executive: Mr Jim Dillon, Chief Executive, Town Hall, St. Nicholas Street, Scarborough YO11 2HG ☎ 01723 232300 jim.dillon@scarborough.gov.uk

Senior Management: Mr David Archer, Strategic Director, Town Hall, St. Nicholas Street, Scarborough YO11 2HG ☎ 01723 232420 david.archer@scarborough.gov.uk

Senior Management: Mrs Hilary Jones, Strategic Director, Town Hall, St. Nicholas Street, Scarborough YO11 2HG ☎ 01723 232342 hilary.jones@scarborough.gov.uk

Architect, Building / Property Services: Ms Pauline Elliott, Head of Regeneration & Planning, Town Hall, St. Nicholas Street, Scarborough YO11 2HG ☎ 01723 232323 🖷 08701 913997 pauline.elliott@scarborough.gov.uk

Architect, Building / Property Services: Mr Martin Pedley, Asset & Risk Manager, Town Hall, St. Nicholas Street, Scarborough YO11 2HG ☎ 01723 232359 martin.pedley@scarborough.gov.uk

Best Value: Mr Alan Layton, Corporate Performance Manager, Town Hall, St. Nicholas Street, Scarborough YO11 2HG ☎ 01723 232323 alan.layton@scarborough.gov.uk

Catering Services: Mr Nick King, Catering & Functions Manager, Spa Complex, Foreshore Road, Scarborough YO11 2HQ ☎ 01723 357851 nick.king@scarborough.gov.uk

PR / Communications: Ms Gabrielle Jandzio, Communications Officer, Town Hall, St. Nicholas Street, Scarborough YO11 2HG ☎ 01723 232306 gabrielle.jandzio@scarborough.gov.uk

Community Planning: Ms Pauline Elliott, Head of Regeneration & Planning, Town Hall, St. Nicholas Street, Scarborough YO11 2HG ☎ 01723 232323 🖷 08701 913997 pauline.elliott@scarborough.gov.uk

Community Safety: Ms Mandy Chance, Safer Communities Manager, Town Hall, St. Nicholas Street, Scarborough YO11 2HG ☎ 01723 383626 mandy.chance@scarborough.gov.uk

Computer Management: Mr Greg Harper, ICT Delivery Manager, Town Hall, St. Nicholas Street, Scarborough YO11 2HG ☎ 01723 232404 🖷 01723 400636 greg.harper@scarborough.gov.uj

Contracts: Mrs Lisa Dixon, Head of Legal & Support Services, Town Hall, St. Nicholas Street, Scarborough YO11 2HG ☎ 01723 232350 🖷 0870 238 4159 lisa.dixon@scarborough.gov.uk

Corporate Services: Mrs Hilary Jones, Strategic Director, Town Hall, St. Nicholas Street, Scarborough YO11 2HG ☎ 01723 232342 hilary.jones@scarborough.gov.uk

Customer Service: Miss Elaine Rhodes, Customer Services Delivery Manager, Town Hall, St. Nicholas Street, Scarborough YO11 2HG ☎ 01723 232570 elaine.rhodes@scarborough.gov.uk

Economic Development: Ms Pauline Elliott, Head of Regeneration & Planning, Town Hall, St. Nicholas Street, Scarborough YO11 2HG ☎ 01723 232323 🖷 08701 913997 pauline.elliott@scarborough.gov.uk

E-Government: Mr Greg Harper, ICT Delivery Manager, Town Hall, St. Nicholas Street, Scarborough YO11 2HG ☎ 01723 232404 🖷 01723 400636 greg.harper@scarborough.gov.uj

Electoral Registration: Mrs Susan Bedford, Team Leader of Elections & Regulation, Town Hall, St. Nicholas Street, Scarborough YO11 2HG ☎ 01723 232309 🖷 01723 354979 sue.bedford@scarborough.gov.uk

Emergency Planning: Mr Andy Skelton, Head of Environmental Services, Town Hall, St. Nicholas Street, Scarborough YO11 2HG ☎ 01723 232493 🖷 01723 365280 andy.skelton@scarborough.gov.uk

Energy Management: Mr Nick Edwards, Head of Finance & Asset Management, Town Hall, St. Nicholas Street, Scarborough YO11 2HG ☎ 01723 232323 nick.edwards@scarborough.gov.uk

Environmental / Technical Services: Mr Andy Skelton, Head of Environmental Services, Town Hall, St. Nicholas Street, Scarborough YO11 2HG ☎ 01723 232493 🖷 01723 365280

✉ andy.skelton@scarborough.gov.uk

Environmental Health: Mr Andy Skelton, Head of Environmental Services, Town Hall, St. Nicholas Street, Scarborough YO11 2HG ☎ 01723 232493 🖷 01723 365280 ✉ andy.skelton@scarborough.gov.uk

Estates, Property & Valuation: Mr Nick Edwards, Head of Finance & Asset Management, Town Hall, St. Nicholas Street, Scarborough YO11 2HG ☎ 01723 232323 ✉ nick.edwards@scarborough.gov.uk

Events Manager: Ms Rowena Marsden, Arts Development Officer, Town Hall, St. Nicholas Street, Scarborough YO11 2HG ☎ 01723 383615 ✉ rowena.marsden@scarborough.gov.uk

Finance and Treasurer: Mr Nick Edwards, Head of Finance & Asset Management, Town Hall, St. Nicholas Street, Scarborough YO11 2HG ☎ 01723 232323 ✉ nick.edwards@scarborough.gov.uk

Fleet Management: Mr Kevin Scholey, Transport & Vehicle Maintenance Manager, Dean Road Depot, Scarborough YO12 7QS ☎ 01723 232323 🖷 01723 364075 ✉ kevin.scholey@scarborough.gov.uk

Grounds Maintenance: Mr Paul Thompson, Operations Manager of Environmental Services, Dean Road Depot, Scarborough YO12 7QS ☎ 01723 383112 ✉ paul.thompson@scarborough.gov.uk

Health and Safety: Mr Robert Webster, Health & Safety Officer, Town Hall, St. Nicholas Street, Scarborough YO11 2HG ☎ 01723 232101 ✉ robert.webster@scarborough.gov.uk

Housing: Mr Andrew Rowe, Housing Manager, Town Hall, St. Nicholas Street, Scarborough YO11 2HG ☎ 01723 383598 ✉ andrew.rowe@scarborough.gov.uk

Legal: Mrs Lisa Dixon, Head of Legal & Support Services, Town Hall, St. Nicholas Street, Scarborough YO11 2HG ☎ 01723 232350 🖷 0870 238 4159 ✉ lisa.dixon@scarborough.gov.uk

Leisure and Cultural Services: Mr Brian Bennett, Head of Tourism & Culture Services, Town Hall, St. Nicholas Street, Scarborough YO11 2HG ☎ 01723 232566 🖷 01723 376941 ✉ brian.bennett@scarborough.gov.uk

Licensing: Ms Una Faithfull, Licensing Manager, Town Hall, St. Nicholas Street, Scarborough YO11 2HG ☎ 01723 232522 ✉ una.faithfull@scarborough.gov.uk

Lottery Funding, Charity and Voluntary: Ms Rowena Marsden, Arts Development Officer, Town Hall, St. Nicholas Street, Scarborough YO11 2HG ☎ 01723 383615 ✉ rowena.marsden@scarborough.gov.uk

Member Services: Mrs Gill Wilkinson, Democratic & Admin Services Manager, Town Hall, St. Nicholas Street, Scarborough YO11 2HG ☎ 01723 232303 🖷 0870 238 4159 ✉ gill.wilkinson@scarborough.gov.uk

Parking: Mr Stuart Clark, Parking & Venues Manager, Town Hall, St. Nicholas Street, Scarborough YO11 2HG ☎ 01723 383582 ✉ stuart.clark@scarborough.gov.uk

Partnerships: Ms Pauline Elliott, Head of Regeneration & Planning, Town Hall, St. Nicholas Street, Scarborough YO11 2HG ☎ 01723 232323 🖷 08701 913997 ✉ pauline.elliott@scarborough.gov.uk

Personnel / HR: Mr Roger Kaye, Head of Human Resources & Performance, Town Hall, St. Nicholas Street, Scarborough YO11 2HG ☎ 01723 232312 🖷 08701 911323 ✉ roger.kaye@scarborough.gov.uk

Planning: Ms Pauline Elliott, Head of Regeneration & Planning, Town Hall, St. Nicholas Street, Scarborough YO11 2HG ☎ 01723 232323 🖷 08701 913997 ✉ pauline.elliott@scarborough.gov.uk

Planning: Ms Jill Lowe, Planning Services Manager, Town Hall, St. Nicholas Street, Scarborough YO11 2HG ☎ 01723 232438 ✉ jill.lowe@scarborough.gov.uk

Procurement: Mr David Gomersall, Procurement Officer, Town Hall, St. Nicholas Street, Scarborough YO11 2HG ☎ 01723 232323 ✉ david.gomersall@scarborough.gov.uk

Recycling & Waste Minimisation: Mr Harry Briggs, Recycling & Waste Enforcement Manager, Town Hall, St. Nicholas Street, Scarborough YO11 2HG ☎ 01723 232323 ✉ harry.briggs@scarborough.gov.uk

Regeneration: Mr David Kelly, Economic Development Manager, Town Hall, St. Nicholas Street, Scarborough YO11 2HG ☎ 01723 232321 ✉ david.kelly@scarborough.gov.uk

Staff Training: Mr Roger Kaye, Head of Human Resources & Performance, Town Hall, St. Nicholas Street, Scarborough YO11 2HG ☎ 01723 232312 🖷 08701 911323 ✉ roger.kaye@scarborough.gov.uk

Sustainable Communities: Ms Pauline Elliott, Head of Regeneration & Planning, Town Hall, St. Nicholas Street, Scarborough YO11 2HG ☎ 01723 232323 🖷 08701 913997 ✉ pauline.elliott@scarborough.gov.uk

Sustainable Communities: Mr Andy Skelton, Head of Environmental Services, Town Hall, St. Nicholas Street, Scarborough YO11 2HG ☎ 01723 232493 🖷 01723 365280 ✉ andy.skelton@scarborough.gov.uk

Tourism: Mr Brian Bennett, Head of Tourism & Culture Services, Town Hall, St. Nicholas Street, Scarborough YO11 2HG ☎ 01723 232566 🖷 01723 376941 ✉ brian.bennett@scarborough.gov.uk

Town Centre: Mr Nick Taylor, Investment Manager, Town Hall, St. Nicholas Street, Scarborough YO11 2HG ☎ 01723 232440 ✉ nick.taylor@scarborough.gov.uk

Transport: Mr Kevin Scholey, Transport & Vehicle Maintenance Manager, Dean Road Depot, Scarborough YO12 7QS ☎ 01723 232323 🖷 01723 364075 ✉ kevin.scholey@scarborough.gov.uk

Transport Planner: Mr Kevin Scholey, Transport & Vehicle Maintenance Manager, Dean Road Depot, Scarborough YO12

7QS ☎ 01723 232323 🖷 01723 364075
✉ kevin.scholey@scarborough.gov.uk

Waste Collection and Disposal: Mr Paul Thompson, Operations Manager of Environmental Services, Dean Road Depot, Scarborough YO12 7QS ☎ 01723 383112
✉ paul.thompson@scarborough.gov.uk

Waste Management: Mr Paul Thompson, Operations Manager of Environmental Services, Dean Road Depot, Scarborough YO12 7QS ☎ 01723 383112 ✉ paul.thompson@scarborough.gov.uk

Children's Play Areas: Mr Andrew Williams, Leisure Manager, Town Hall, St. Nicholas Street, Scarborough YO11 2HG ☎ 01723 383610 ✉ andrew.williams@scarborough.gov.uk

MEMBERS OF THE COUNCIL (49)

Abbot, Alf (CON - Whitby West Cliff)
cllr.alf.abbott@scarborough.gov.uk
Allanson, Godfrey (CON - Hertford)
cllr.godgrey.allanson@scarborough.gov.uk
Armsby, John (IND - Mulgrave)
cllr.john.armsby@scarborough.gov.uk
Backhouse, Andrew G (CON - Lindhead)
cllr.andrew.backhouse@scarborough.gov.uk
Bairstow, Steve (LAB - Woodlands)
cllr.steve.bairstow@scarborough.gov.uk
Bastiman, Lynn (CON - Stepney)
cllr.lynn.bastiman@scarborough.gov.uk
Bastiman, Derek (CON - Scalby)
cllr.derek.bastiman@scarborough.gov.uk
Billing, David (LAB - Central)
cllr.david.billing@scarborough.gov.uk
Blackburn, John (CON - Cayton)
cllr.john.blackburn@scarborough.gov.uk
Broadbent, Eric (LAB - Central)
cllr.eric.broadbent@scarborough.gov.uk
Brown, Nick (CON - Ramshill)
cllr.nick.brown@scarborough.gov.uk
Challen, Colin (LAB - Castle)
Cllr.Colin.Challen@scarborough.gov.uk
Chance, David (CON - Mayfield)
clld.david.chance@scarborough.gov.uk
Chatt, William (IND - Woodlands)
cllr.bill.chatt@scarborough.gov.uk
Clegg, Dorothy (IND - Streonshalh)
cllr.dorothy.clegg@scarborough.gov.uk
Cluer, Dilys Vine (GRN - Stepney)
cllr.dilys.cluer@scarborough.gov.uk
Cockerill, Michael John (NP - Filey)
cllr.mike.cockerill@scarborough.gov.uk
Cooper, Mick (IND - Newby)
cllr.mick.cooper@scarborough.gov.uk
Cross, Sam (IND - Filey)
cllr.sam.cross@scarborough.gov.uk
Donohue-Moncrieff, Michelle (CON - Hertford)
cllr.michelle.donohue-moncrieff@scarborough.gov.uk
Evans, Geoffrey (LD - Eastfield)
cllr.geoffrey.evans@scarborough.gov.uk
Flinton, John (CON - Scalby)
cllr.john.flinton@scarborough.gov.uk
Fox, Thomas (CON - Weaponness)
cllr.tom.fox@scarborough.gov.uk
Green, Simon (IND - Cayton)
cllr.simon.green@scarborough.gov.uk
Haddington, Colin (CON - Filey)
cllr.colin.haddington@scarborough.gov.uk
Harland, Marie (CON - Mulgrave)
cllr.marie.harland@scarborough.gov.uk
Jay-Hanmer, Michael (IND - Derwent Valley)
cllr.michael.jay-hanmer@scarborough.gov.uk
Jeffels, David (CON - Derwent Valley)
cllr.david.jeffels@scarborough.gov.uk
Jefferson, Janet (IND - Castle)
cllr.janet.jefferson@scarborough.gov.uk
Jenkinson, Andrew (CON - Newby)
cllr.andrew.jenkinson@scarborough.gov.uk
Kenyon, Jane (CON - Mayfield)
cllr.jane.kenyon@scarborough.gov.uk
Lawn, Tim (CON - Esk Valley)
cllr.tim.lawn@scarborough.gov.uk
Mallory, Helen (CON - Seamer)
cllr.helen.mallory@scarborough.gov.uk
Marsburg, Patricia (NP - Falsgrave Park)
cllr.pat.marsburg@northyorks.gov.uk
Marsden, Penny (IND - Weaponness)
cllr.penny.marsden@scarborough.gov.uk
Mortimer, Jane (CON - Flyingdales)
cllr.jane.mortimer@scarborough.gov.uk
Murphy, Norman (IND - Northstead)
cllr.norman.murphy@scarborough.gov.uk
Murphy, Roxanne (IND - Seamer)
cllr.roxanne.murphy@scarborough.gov.uk
Plant, Joseph (CON - Whitby West Cliff)
cllr.joseph.plant@scarborough.gov.uk
Popple, Peter (IND - Northstead)
cllr.peter.popple@scarborough.gov.uk
Ritchie, John (LAB - Falsgrave Park)
cllr.john.ritchie@scarborough.gov.uk
Robinson, Amanda (IND - Ramshill)
cllr.amanda.robinson@scarborough.gov.uk
Sharma, Subash (LAB - North Bay)
cllr.subash.sharma@scarborough.gov.uk
Simpson, Brian (LD - Eastfield)
cllr.brian.simpson@scarborough.gov.uk
Smith, Martin (CON - North Bay)
cllr.martin.smith@scarborough.gov.uk
Tindall, Herbert (CON - Danby)
cllr.herbert.tindall@northyorks.gov.uk
Turner, Sandra (IND - Streonshalh)
cllr.sandra.turner@scarborough.gov.uk
Watson, Brian (IND - Newby)
cllr.brian.watson@scarborough.gov.uk
Zegstroo, Johan (LD - Eastfield)
cllr.johan.zegstroo@scarborough.gov.uk

POLITICAL COMPOSITION

CON: 22, IND: 15, LAB: 6, LD: 3, NP: 2, GRN: 1

CABINET

Leader / Transformational Management: Mr Thomas Fox
Finance, Procurement & Legal: Miss Jane Kenyon
Harbours, Assets, Coast & Flood Protection: Mr Michael John Cockerill
Human Resources, Performance Management & ICT: Ms Penny Marsden
Neighbourhood Renewal, Community Involvement & Partnerships, Democratic Services, Customer Services &

Safer Communities: Mr Brian Simpson
Public Health & Housing: Mr William Chatt
Strategic Planning & Regeneration: Mr Derek Bastiman
Tourism & Culture: Mr David Chance

COMMITTEE CHAIRS

Audit: Mr Andrew G Backhouse
Enviroment & Economy (Scrutiny): Mr Godfrey Allanson
Health & Wellbeing (Scrutiny): Mr David Jeffels
Licensing: Mr Brian Watson
Planning & Development: Mrs Jane Mortimer
Resources (Scrutiny): Mr Joseph Plant
Safer and Stronger Community (Scrutiny): Mr Colin Challen

SCOTTISH BORDERS S

Scottish Borders Council, Council Headquarters, Newtown St. Boswells, Melrose TD6 0SA ☎ 01835 824000 🖷 01835 825001 ✉ enquiries@scotborders.gov.uk 💻 www.scotborders.gov.uk

FACTS & FIGURES

Police Authority: Lothian & Borders Police Board
Health Authority: NHS Borders
Learning and Skills Council: Scotland
Parliamentary Constituencies: Berwickshire, Roxburgh and Selkirk, Dumfriesshire, Clydesdale and Tweedale
EU Constituencies: Scotland
Election Frequency: Elections are of whole council

PRINCIPAL OFFICERS

Chief Executive: Ms Tracey Logan, Chief Executive, Council Headquarters, Newtown St. Boswells, Melrose TD6 0SA ☎ 01835 825055 ✉ tracey.logan@scotborders.gov.uk

Assistant Chief Executive: Ms Jenny Wilkinson, Assistant Chief Executive / Clerk to the Council, Council Headquarters, Newtown St. Boswells, Melrose TD6 0SA ☎ 01835 825004 ✉ jjwilkinson@scotborder.gov.uk

Senior Management: Mr Rob Dickson, Director of Environment & Infrastructure, Council Headquarters, Newtown St. Boswells, Melrose TD6 0SA ☎ 01835 825075 🖷 01835 825158 ✉ rob.dickson@scotborders.gov.uk

Senior Management: Mr Andrew Lowe, Director of Social Work, Council Headquarters, Newtown St. Boswells, Melrose TD6 0SA ☎ 01835 825085 🖷 01835 825081 ✉ alowe@scotborders.gov.uk

Senior Management: Mr Glenn Rodger, Director of Education & Lifelong Learning, Council Headquarters, Newtown St. Boswells, Melrose TD6 0SA ☎ 01835 825095 🖷 01835 825091 ✉ grodger@scotborders.gov.uk

Architect, Building / Property Services: Mr Andrew Drummond-Hunt, Head of Properties & Facilities Management, Council Headquarters, Newtown St. Boswells, Melrose TD6 0SA ☎ 01835 826672 🖷 01835 825158 ✉ adrummond-hunt@scotborders.gov.uk

Building Control: Mr Brian Frater, Head of Planning & Regulatory Services, Council Headquarters, Newtown St. Boswells, Melrose TD6 0SA ☎ 01835 825067 🖷 01835 825158 ✉ bfrater@scotborders.gov.uk

Catering Services: Mr Alastair McIntyre, Catering & Building Cleaning Manager, Council Headquarters, Newtown St. Boswells, Melrose TD6 0SA ☎ 01835 826564 ✉ amcintyre@scotborders.gov.uk

Children / Youth Services: Ms Stella Everingham, Head of Integrated Children's Services, Council Headquarters, Newtown St. Boswells, Melrose TD6 0SA ☎ 01835 825083 ✉ severingham@scotborders.gov.uk

Children / Youth Services: Mr Andrew Lowe, Director of Social Work, Council Headquarters, Newtown St. Boswells, Melrose TD6 0SA ☎ 01835 825085 🖷 01835 825081 ✉ alowe@scotborders.gov.uk

Civil Registration: Ms Lisa Lauder, Chief Registrar, Council Headquarters, Newtown St. Boswells, Melrose TD6 0SA ☎ 01450 364710 🖷 01450 364711 ✉ llauder@scotborders.gov.uk

PR / Communications: Ms Tracey Graham, Corporate Communications Officer, Council Headquarters, Newtown St. Boswells, Melrose TD6 0SA ☎ 01835 826592 ✉ tgraham@scotborders.gov.uk

Community Planning: Ms Sue Glendinning, Community Planning Co-ordinator, Council Headquarters, Newtown St. Boswells, Melrose TD6 0SA ☎ 01835 824000 ✉ sglendinning@scotborders.gov.uk

Community Safety: Mrs Jan Pringle, Community Safety Manager, Council Headquarters, Newtown St. Boswells, Melrose TD6 0SA ☎ 01835 826541 ✉ jpringle@scotborders.gov.uk

Computer Management: Mr Henry Thompson, Head of Business Information Systems, Council Headquarters, Newtown St. Boswells, Melrose TD6 0SA ☎ 01835 825045 🖷 01835 825041 ✉ hthompson@scotborders.gov.uk

Consumer Protection and Trading Standards: Mr Brian Frater, Head of Planning & Regulatory Services, Council Headquarters, Newtown St. Boswells, Melrose TD6 0SA ☎ 01835 825067 🖷 01835 825158 ✉ bfrater@scotborders.gov.uk

Customer Service: Mrs Jenni Craig, Head of Customer Services, Council Headquarters, Newtown St. Boswells, Melrose TD6 0SA ☎ 01835 824000 ✉ jcraig@scotborders.gov.uk

Direct Labour: Mr Robert Young, Head of Engineering & Infrastructure, Council Headquarters, Newtown St. Boswells, Melrose TD6 0SA ☎ 01835 825075 🖷 01835 825158 ✉ ryoung@scotborders.gov.uk

Economic Development: Mr Bryan McGrath, Head of Economic Development & Environment, Council Headquarters, Newtown St. Boswells, Melrose TD6 0SA ☎ 01835 826525 ✉ bmcgrath@scotborders.gov.uk

Education: Ms Y McCracken, Head of School Services West, Council Headquarters, Newtown St. Boswells, Melrose TD6 0SA ☎ 01835 825455 ✉ ymccracken@scotborders.gov.uk

Education: Mr Glenn Rodger, Director of Education & Lifelong

Learning, Council Headquarters, Newtown St. Boswells, Melrose TD6 0SA ☎ 01835 825095 🖷 01835 825091 ✉ grodger@scotborders.gov.uk

Education: Mrs Jackie Swanston, School Services East, Council Headquarters, Newtown St. Boswells, Melrose TD6 0SA ☎ 01835 825092 ✉ jswanston@scotborders.gov.uk

Electoral Registration: Mr Mark Dickson, Assessor & Electoral Registration Officer, Council Headquarters, Newtown St. Boswells, Melrose TD6 0SA ☎ 01835 825100 ✉ mdickson@scotborders.gov.uk

Emergency Planning: Mr Jim Fraiser, Emergency Planning Officer, Council Headquarters, Newtown St. Boswells, Melrose TD6 0SA ☎ 01835 825056 ✉ jfraiser@scotborders.gov.uk

Energy Management: Mr Stuart Mawson, Building & Services Officer, Council Headquarters, Newtown St. Boswells, Melrose TD6 0SA ☎ 01835 826758 🖷 01835 822728 ✉ stuart.mawson@scotborders.gov.uk

Environmental / Technical Services: Mr Ray Beard, Head of Neighbourhood Services, Scott House, Sprouston Road, Newtown St. Boswells, Melrose TD6 0QD ☎ 01835 825115 🖷 01835 825158 ✉ rbeard@scotborders.gov.uk

Environmental / Technical Services: Mr Rob Dickson, Director of Environment & Infrastructure, Council Headquarters, Newtown St. Boswells, Melrose TD6 0SA ☎ 01835 825075 🖷 01835 825158 ✉ rob.dickson@scotborders.gov.uk

Environmental Health: Mr Brian Frater, Head of Planning & Regulatory Services, Council Headquarters, Newtown St. Boswells, Melrose TD6 0SA ☎ 01835 825067 🖷 01835 825158 ✉ bfrater@scotborders.gov.uk

Estates, Property & Valuation: Mr Andrew Drummond-Hunt, Head of Properties & Facilities Management, Council Headquarters, Newtown St. Boswells, Melrose TD6 0SA ☎ 01835 826672 🖷 01835 825158 ✉ adrummond-hunt@scotborders.gov.uk

European Liaison: Mr Douglas Scott, Senior Consultant, Council Headquarters, Newtown St. Boswells, Melrose TD6 0SA ☎ 01835 824000 ✉ dscott@scotborders.gov.uk

Events Manager: Ms Jane Warcup, Events Officer, Council Headquarters, Newtown St. Boswells, Melrose TD6 0SA ☎ 01835 825060 ✉ jwarcup@scotborders.gov.uk

Facilities: Mr Andrew Drummond-Hunt, Head of Properties & Facilities Management, Council Headquarters, Newtown St. Boswells, Melrose TD6 0SA ☎ 01835 826672 🖷 01835 825158 ✉ adrummond-hunt@scotborders.gov.uk

Finance and Treasurer: Mr David Robertson, Chief Financial Officer, Council Headquarters, Newtown St. Boswells, Melrose TD6 0SA ☎ 01835 825012 ✉ drobertson@scotborders.gov.uk

Fleet Management: Mr Robert Young, Head of Engineering & Infrastructure, Council Headquarters, Newtown St. Boswells, Melrose TD6 0SA ☎ 01835 825075 🖷 01835 825158 ✉ ryoung@scotborders.gov.uk

Grounds Maintenance: Mr Ray Beard, Head of Neighbourhood Services, Scott House, Sprouston Road, Newtown St. Boswells, Melrose TD6 0QD ☎ 01835 825115 🖷 01835 825158 ✉ rbeard@scotborders.gov.uk

Health and Safety: Ms Jill Stacey, Head of Wellbeing & Safety, Council Headquarters, Newtown St. Boswells, Melrose TD6 0SA ☎ 01835 824000 ✉ jstacey@scotborders.gov.uk

Home Energy Conservation: Ms Cathie Fancy, Group Manager - Housing Strategy & Services, Council Headquarters, Newtown St. Boswells, Melrose TD6 0SA ☎ 01835 825080 Ext: 5144 ✉ cfancy@scotborders.gov.uk

Housing: Mr David Cressey, Head of Housing & Criminal Justice, Council Headquarters, Newtown St. Boswells, Melrose TD6 0SA ☎ 01835 825082 ✉ dcressey@scotborders.gov.uk

Legal: Mr Ian Wilkie, Head of Legal & Democratic Services, Council Headquarters, Newtown St. Boswells, Melrose TD6 0SA ☎ 01835 825005 🖷 01835 825001 ✉ iwilkie@scotborders.gov.uk

Leisure and Cultural Services: Mr Glenn Rodger, Director of Education & Lifelong Learning, Council Headquarters, Newtown St. Boswells, Melrose TD6 0SA ☎ 01835 825095 🖷 01835 825091 ✉ grodger@scotborders.gov.uk

Licensing: Ms Ann Isles, Legal & Licensing Services Manager, Council Buildings, Albert Place, Galashiels TD1 3AW ☎ 01896 754751 ✉ aisles@scotborders.gov.uk

Lifelong Learning: Mr Glenn Rodger, Director of Education & Lifelong Learning, Council Headquarters, Newtown St. Boswells, Melrose TD6 0SA ☎ 01835 825095 🖷 01835 825091 ✉ grodger@scotborders.gov.uk

Lighting: Mr Alex Young, Roads Lighting Manager, Council Headquarters, Newtown St. Boswells, Melrose TD6 0SA ☎ 01835 825131 ✉ ayoung1@scotborders.gov.uk

Lottery Funding, Charity and Voluntary: Ms Jean Robertson, Lottery / External Funding Officer, Council Headquarters, Newtown St. Boswells, Melrose TD6 0SA ☎ 01835 824000 🖷 01835 825059 ✉ jarobertson@scotborders.gov.uk

Member Services: Ms Pauline Bolson, Member Support Officer (Corporate Services), Council Headquarters, Newtown St. Boswells, Melrose TD6 0SA ☎ 01835 826053 🖷 01835 825001 ✉ pbolson@scotborders.gov.uk

Parking: Mr Robert Young, Head of Engineering & Infrastructure, Council Headquarters, Newtown St. Boswells, Melrose TD6 0SA ☎ 01835 825075 🖷 01835 825158 ✉ ryoung@scotborders.gov.uk

Partnerships: Mr Douglas Scott, Senior Consultant, Council Headquarters, Newtown St. Boswells, Melrose TD6 0SA ☎ 01835 824000 ✉ dscott@scotborders.gov.uk

Personnel / HR: Ms Clair Hepburn, Acting Senior HR Adviser, Council Headquarters, Newtown St. Boswells, Melrose TD6 0SA

☎ 01835 824000

Planning: Mr Brian Frater, Head of Planning & Regulatory Services, Council Headquarters, Newtown St. Boswells, Melrose TD6 0SA ☎ 01835 825067 🖷 01835 825158 ✉ bfrater@scotborders.gov.uk

Public Libraries: Mr Iain Macaulay, Community Services Business Manager, Library Headquarters, St. Mary's Mill, Selkirk TD7 5EW ☎ 01750 20842 🖷 01750 22875 ✉ imacaulay@scotborders.gov.uk

Recycling & Waste Minimisation: Mr Ross Sharp-Dent, Waste Treatment Manager, Scott House, Sprouston Road, Newtown St. Boswells, Melrose TD6 0QD ☎ 01835 825111 🖷 01835 825112 ✉ rsharp-dent@scotborders.gov.uk

Regeneration: Mr Bryan McGrath, Head of Economic Development & Environment, Council Headquarters, Newtown St. Boswells, Melrose TD6 0SA ☎ 01835 826525 ✉ bmcgrath@scotborders.gov.uk

Road Safety: Mr Brian Young, Network Manager, Council Headquarters, Newtown St. Boswells, Melrose TD6 0SA ☎ 01835 825178 🖷 01835 825158 ✉ byoung@scotborders.gov.uk

Social Services: Mr Andrew Lowe, Director of Social Work, Council Headquarters, Newtown St. Boswells, Melrose TD6 0SA ☎ 01835 825085 🖷 01835 825081 ✉ alowe@scotborders.gov.uk

Social Services: Mrs Elaine Torrance, Head of Social Care & Health, Council Headquarters, Newtown St. Boswells, Melrose TD6 0SA ☎ 01835 825084 ✉ etorrance@scotborders.gov.uk

Social Services (Adult): Mrs Elaine Torrance, Head of Social Care & Health, Council Headquarters, Newtown St. Boswells, Melrose TD6 0SA ☎ 01835 825084 ✉ etorrance@scotborders.gov.uk

Social Services (Children): Ms Stella Everingham, Head of Integrated Children's Services, Council Headquarters, Newtown St. Boswells, Melrose TD6 0SA ☎ 01835 825083 ✉ severingham@scotborders.gov.uk

Staff Training: Ms Joanne Tolland, Organsiation Design & Development Manager, Council Headquarters, Newtown St. Boswells, Melrose TD6 0SA ☎ 01835 826754 ✉ joanne.tolland@scotborders.gov.uk

Street Scene: Mr Bryan McGrath, Head of Economic Development & Environment, Council Headquarters, Newtown St. Boswells, Melrose TD6 0SA ☎ 01835 826525 ✉ bmcgrath@scotborders.gov.uk

Sustainable Communities: Mr Glenn Rodger, Director of Education & Lifelong Learning, Council Headquarters, Newtown St. Boswells, Melrose TD6 0SA ☎ 01835 825095 🖷 01835 825091 ✉ grodger@scotborders.gov.uk

Sustainable Development: Mr Bryan McGrath, Head of Economic Development & Environment, Council Headquarters, Newtown St. Boswells, Melrose TD6 0SA ☎ 01835 826525 ✉ bmcgrath@scotborders.gov.uk

Tourism: Mr Bryan McGrath, Head of Economic Development & Environment, Council Headquarters, Newtown St. Boswells, Melrose TD6 0SA ☎ 01835 826525 ✉ bmcgrath@scotborders.gov.uk

Town Centre: Mr Bryan McGrath, Head of Economic Development & Environment, Council Headquarters, Newtown St. Boswells, Melrose TD6 0SA ☎ 01835 826525 ✉ bmcgrath@scotborders.gov.uk

Traffic Management: Mr Robbie Yates, Assistant Road User Manager for Traffic, Council Headquarters, Newtown St. Boswells, Melrose TD6 0SA ☎ 01835 825116 🖷 01835 825158 ✉ robbie.yates@scotborders.gov.uk

Transport: Mr Colin Douglas, Passenger Transport Manager, Council Headquarters, Newtown St. Boswells, Melrose TD6 0SA ☎ 01835 826586 ✉ cdouglas@scotborders.gov.uk

Transport Planner: Mr Graeme Johnstone, Principal Officer - Strategic Transport, Council Headquarters, Newtown St. Boswells, Melrose TD6 0SA ☎ 01835 825138 🖷 01835 825158 ✉ gjohnstone@scotborders.gov.uk

Waste Collection and Disposal: Mr Ross Sharp-Dent, Waste Treatment Manager, Scott House, Sprouston Road, Newtown St. Boswells, Melrose TD6 0QD ☎ 01835 825111 🖷 01835 825112 ✉ rsharp-dent@scotborders.gov.uk

Waste Management: Mr Ray Beard, Head of Neighbourhood Services, Scott House, Sprouston Road, Newtown St. Boswells, Melrose TD6 0QD ☎ 01835 825115 🖷 01835 825158 ✉ rbeard@scotborders.gov.uk

Children's Play Areas: Mr Ray Beard, Head of Neighbourhood Services, Scott House, Sprouston Road, Newtown St. Boswells, Melrose TD6 0QD ☎ 01835 825115 🖷 01835 825158 ✉ rbeard@scotborders.gov.uk

MEMBERS OF THE COUNCIL (34)

***Convener:* Garvie**, Graham (LD - Tweedale East)
ggarvie@scotsborders.gov.uk
***Leader of the Council:* Parker**, David (IND - Leaderdale and Melrose)
dparker@scotsborders.gov.uk
***Deputy Leader of the Council:* Mitchell**, John (SNP - Galashiels and District)
jmitchell@scotsborders.gov.uk
Aitchison, Sandy (O - Galashiels and District)
saitchison@scotborders.gov.uk
Archibald, Willie (SNP - Tweedale West)
warchibald@scotborders.gov.uk
Ballantyne, Michelle (CON - Selkirkshire)
Bell, Stuart (SNP - Tweedale East)
Bhatia, Catriona (LD - Tweedale West)
cbhatia@scotsborders.gov.uk
Brown, Jim (SNP - Jedburgh and District)
jbrown@scotborders.gov.uk
Buckingham, Nathaniel (CON - Tweedale West)
Campbell, Joan (SNP - East Berwickshire)

Cook, Michael (IND - East Berwickshire)
mcook@scotsborders.gov.uk
Cranston, Alastair (SNP - Hawick and Denholm)
Davidson, Vicky (LD - Selkirkshire)
vdavidson@scotsborders.gov.uk
Edgar, Gordon (IND - Selkirkshire)
Elliott, Zandra (O - Hawick and Denholm)
zelliot@scotborders.gov.uk
Fullarton, James (CON - East Berwickshire)
jfullarton@scotsborders.gov.uk
Greenwell, John (CON - Mid Berwickshire)
Herd, Bill (SNP - Galashiels and District)
Logan, Gavin (O - Tweedale East)
glogan@scotborders.gov.uk
Marshall, Stuart (IND - Hawick and Denholm)
smarshall@scotborders.gov.uk
Moffat, Donald (SNP - Mid Berwickshire)
dmoffat@scotborders.gov.uk
Mountford, Simon (CON - Kelso and District)
Nicol, Alexander (LD - Kelso and District)
anicol@scotsborders.gov.uk
Paterson, David (IND - Hawick and Hermitage)
dpaterson@scotsborders.gov.uk
Renton, Frances (LD - Mid Berwickshire)
frenton@scotborders.gov.uk
Scott, Sandy (CON - Jedburgh and District)
sandyscott@scotsborders.gov.uk
Smith, Ron (LD - Hawick and Hermitage)
rsmith@scotborders.gov.uk
Stewart, Rory (IND - Jedburgh and District)
Torrance, Jim (SNP - Leaderdale and Melrose)
Turnbull, George (O - Hawick and Hermitage)
gturnbull@scotborders.gov.uk
Watson, Nicholas (O - Leaderdale and Melrose)
nwatson@scotborders.gov.uk
Weatherston, Tom (IND - Kelso and District)
tweatherston@scotborders.gov.uk
White, Bill (IND - Galashiels and District)

POLITICAL COMPOSITION
SNP: 9, IND: 8, LD: 6, CON: 6, O: 5

CABINET
Leader: Mr David Parker
Deputy Leader / Finance: Mr John Mitchell

COMMITTEE CHAIRS
Audit: Ms Michelle Ballantyne
Planning & Building Standards: Mr Ron Smith
Scrutiny: Mr Gavin Logan
Standards: Mr Alexander Nicol

SEDGEMOOR D

Sedgemoor District Council, Bridgwater House, King Square, Bridgwater TA6 3AR ☎ 0845 408 2540 🖷 01278 446412
🖳 www.sedgemoor.gov.uk

FACTS & FIGURES
Police Authority: Avon & Somerset Police Authority
Learning and Skills Council: South West
Parliamentary Constituencies: Bridgwater and Somerset West, Wells
EU Constituencies: South West
Election Frequency: Elections are of whole council
Twinning: Axbridge: Houlgate (France); Bridgwater: La Ciotat (France), Uherske Hradiste (Czech Republic); Burnham on Sea: Cassis (France); Sedgemoor: Schwalen-Eder Kreis (Germany); Wedmore: St. Medard de Guigieres (France)

PRINCIPAL OFFICERS
Chief Executive: Mr Kerry Rickards, Chief Executive, Bridgwater House, King Square, Bridgwater TA6 3AR ☎ 01278 435423 🖷 01278 446412 ✉ kerry.rickards@sedgemoor.gov.uk

Senior Management: Mr Doug Bamsey, Corporate Director - Regeneration, Bridgwater House, King Square, Bridgwater TA6 3AR ☎ 01278 435219 🖷 01278 446412
✉ doug.bamsey@sedgemoor.gov.uk

Senior Management: Mr Bob Brown, Corporate Director - Corporate Services, Bridgwater House, King Square, Bridgwater TA6 3AR ☎ 01278 435327 🖷 01278 446412
✉ bob.brown@sedgemoor.gov.uk

Senior Management: Mrs Allison Griffin, Corporate Director - Customer & Community, Bridgwater House, King Square, Bridgwater TA6 3AR ☎ 01278 435741 🖷 01278 446411
✉ allison.griffin@sedgemoor.gov.uk

Architect, Building / Property Services: Mr Tim Mander, Estates, Property & Valuation Officer, Bridgwater House, King Square, Bridgwater TA6 3AR ☎ 01278 435331 🖷 01278 446412
✉ tim.mander@sedgemoor.gov.uk

Best Value: Mr Robin Starr, Information Officer, Bridgwater House, King Square, Bridgwater TA6 3AR ☎ 01278 435751
✉ robin.starr@sedgemoor.gov.uk

PR / Communications: Ms Claire Faun, Corporate Relations Manager, Bridgwater House, King Square, Bridgwater TA6 3AR ☎ 01278 435320 🖷 01278 446412
✉ pressoffice@sedgemoor.gov.uk

Community Planning: Mrs Claire Pearce, Group Manager - Strategy & Business Services, Bridgwater House, King Square, Bridgwater TA6 3AR ☎ 01278 435262 🖷 01278 444076
✉ claire.pearce@sedgemoor.gov.uk

Community Safety: Mrs Kristy Blackwell, Community Safety & Environmental Services Officer, Bridgwater House, King Square, Bridgwater TA6 3AR ☎ 01278 435216
✉ kristy.blackwell@sedgemoor.gov.uk

Computer Management: Mr Paul Davidson, Head of E-Government, Bridgwater House, King Square, Bridgwater TA6 3AR ☎ 01278 435448 🖷 01278 446411
✉ paul.davidson@sedgemoor.gov.uk

Contracts: Ms Melanie Wellman, Group Manager - Legal & Procurement, Bridgwater House, King Square, Bridgwater TA6 3AR ☎ 01278 435734 🖷 01278 446412
✉ melanie.wellman@sedgemoor.gov.uk

Corporate Services: Mr Bob Brown, Corporate Director -

Corporate Services, Bridgwater House, King Square, Bridgwater TA6 3AR ☎ 01278 435327 🖷 01278 446412 ✉ bob.brown@sedgemoor.gov.uk

Customer Service: Mrs Allison Griffin, Corporate Director - Customer & Community, Bridgwater House, King Square, Bridgwater TA6 3AR ☎ 01278 435741 🖷 01278 446411 ✉ allison.griffin@sedgemoor.gov.uk

Customer Service: Mrs Teresa Harvey, Group Manager - Health & Wellbeing, Bridgwater House, King Square, Bridgwater TA6 3AR ☎ 01278 435232 🖷 01278 444076 ✉ teresa.harvey@sedgemoor.gov.uk

Economic Development: Mrs Claire Pearce, Group Manager - Strategy & Business Services, Bridgwater House, King Square, Bridgwater TA6 3AR ☎ 01278 435262 🖷 01278 444076 ✉ claire.pearce@sedgemoor.gov.uk

E-Government: Mr Paul Davidson, Head of E-Government, Bridgwater House, King Square, Bridgwater TA6 3AR ☎ 01278 435448 🖷 01278 446411 ✉ paul.davidson@sedgemoor.gov.uk

Electoral Registration: Mrs Christine Facey, Electoral Services Officer, Bridgwater House, King Square, Bridgwater TA6 3AR ☎ 01278 435334 🖷 0870 400 3103 ✉ chris.facey@sedgemoor.gov.uk

Emergency Planning: Mr Malcolm Brooks, Senior Environmental Health Officer, Bridgwater House, King Square, Bridgwater TA6 3AR ☎ 01278 435398 ✉ malcolm.brooks@sedgemoor.gov.uk

Energy Management: Mr David Baxter, Street Housing Manager, Bridgwater House, King Square, Bridgwater TA6 3AR ☎ 01278 435496 🖷 01278 446410 ✉ david.baxter@sedgemoor.gov.uk

Environmental / Technical Services: Mr Adrian Gardner, Group Manager - Environmental Health, Bridgwater House, King Square, Bridgwater TA6 3AR ☎ 01278 435339 🖷 01278 446410 ✉ adrian.gardner@sedgemoor.gov.uk

Environmental Health: Mr Adrian Gardner, Group Manager - Environmental Health, Bridgwater House, King Square, Bridgwater TA6 3AR ☎ 01278 435339 🖷 01278 446410 ✉ adrian.gardner@sedgemoor.gov.uk

Estates, Property & Valuation: Mr Tim Mander, Estates, Property & Valuation Officer, Bridgwater House, King Square, Bridgwater TA6 3AR ☎ 01278 435331 🖷 01278 446412 ✉ tim.mander@sedgemoor.gov.uk

Facilities: Mr Bill Smith, Facilities Manager, Bridgwater House, King Square, Bridgwater TA6 3AR ☎ 01278 435240

Finance and Treasurer: Mrs Alison Turner, Group Finance & Section 151 Manager, Bridgwater House, King Square, Bridgwater TA6 3AR ☎ 01278 435426 🖷 01278 446411 ✉ alison.turner@sedgemoor.gov.uk

Fleet Management: Mr Bob Kondys, Transport Supervisor, Bridgwater House, King Square, Bridgwater TA6 3AR ☎ 0845 408 2543 ✉ bob.kondys@sedgemoor.gov.uk

Grounds Maintenance: Mr Richard Stokes, Interim Operations Manager - Clear Surroundings, Bridgwater House, King Square, Bridgwater TA6 3AR ☎ 01278 435301 🖷 01278 455260

Health and Safety: Mrs Derrick Cox, Corporate Health & Safety Officer, Bridgwater House, King Square, Bridgwater TA6 3AR ☎ 01278 435403 🖷 01278 446410 ✉ derrick.cox@sedgemoor.gov.uk

Home Energy Conservation: Mr David Baxter, Street Housing Manager, Bridgwater House, King Square, Bridgwater TA6 3AR ☎ 01278 435496 🖷 01278 446410 ✉ david.baxter@sedgemoor.gov.uk

Housing: Mr David Baxter, Street Housing Manager, Bridgwater House, King Square, Bridgwater TA6 3AR ☎ 01278 435496 🖷 01278 446410 ✉ david.baxter@sedgemoor.gov.uk

Housing: Mr Adrian Gardner, Group Manager - Environmental Health, Bridgwater House, King Square, Bridgwater TA6 3AR ☎ 01278 435339 🖷 01278 446410 ✉ adrian.gardner@sedgemoor.gov.uk

Housing Maintenance: Mr Stephen Bennett, Partnering Manager, Bridgwater House, King Square, Bridgwater TA6 3AR ☎ 0845 408 2540 ✉ stephen.bennett@sedgemoor.gov.uk

Legal: Ms Melanie Wellman, Group Manager - Legal & Procurement, Bridgwater House, King Square, Bridgwater TA6 3AR ☎ 01278 435734 🖷 01278 446412 ✉ melanie.wellman@sedgemoor.gov.uk

Leisure and Cultural Services: Mrs Teresa Harvey, Group Manager - Health & Wellbeing, Bridgwater House, King Square, Bridgwater TA6 3AR ☎ 01278 435232 🖷 01278 444076 ✉ teresa.harvey@sedgemoor.gov.uk

Licensing: Mr Tony Baker, Licensing Officer, Bridgwater House, King Square, Bridgwater TA6 3AR ☎ 01278 435314 🖷 01278 446410

Parking: Mrs Teresa Harvey, Group Manager - Health & Wellbeing, Bridgwater House, King Square, Bridgwater TA6 3AR ☎ 01278 435232 🖷 01278 444076 ✉ teresa.harvey@sedgemoor.gov.uk

Partnerships: Mr Stephen Bennett, Partnering Manager, Bridgwater House, King Square, Bridgwater TA6 3AR ☎ 0845 408 2540 ✉ stephen.bennett@sedgemoor.gov.uk

Personnel / HR: Mrs Clare Johnson, Personnel Manager, Bridgwater House, King Square, Bridgwater TA6 3AR ☎ 01278 435451 🖷 0870 4003105 ✉ clare.johnson@sedgemoor.gov.uk

Planning: Mr Steve Atkinson, Group Manager Development Management, Bridgwater House, King Square, Bridgwater TA6 3AR ☎ 01278 435246 🖷 01278 735076 ✉ steve.atkinson@sedgemoor.gov.uk

Planning: Mr Doug Bamsey, Corporate Director - Regeneration,

Bridgwater House, King Square, Bridgwater TA6 3AR ☎ 01278 435219 🖷 01278 446412 ⌨ doug.bamsey@sedgemoor.gov.uk

Procurement: Ms Melanie Wellman, Group Manager - Legal & Procurement, Bridgwater House, King Square, Bridgwater TA6 3AR ☎ 01278 435734 🖷 01278 446412 ⌨ melanie.wellman@sedgemoor.gov.uk

Recycling & Waste Minimisation: Mr Adrian Gardner, Group Manager - Environmental Health, Bridgwater House, King Square, Bridgwater TA6 3AR ☎ 01278 435339 🖷 01278 446410 ⌨ adrian.gardner@sedgemoor.gov.uk

Regeneration: Mr Doug Bamsey, Corporate Director - Regeneration, Bridgwater House, King Square, Bridgwater TA6 3AR ☎ 01278 435219 🖷 01278 446412 ⌨ doug.bamsey@sedgemoor.gov.uk

Regeneration: Mrs Teresa Harvey, Group Manager - Health & Wellbeing, Bridgwater House, King Square, Bridgwater TA6 3AR ☎ 01278 435232 🖷 01278 444076 ⌨ teresa.harvey@sedgemoor.gov.uk

Staff Training: Mrs Clare Johnson, Personnel Manager, Bridgwater House, King Square, Bridgwater TA6 3AR ☎ 01278 435451 🖷 0870 4003105 ⌨ clare.johnson@sedgemoor.gov.uk

Sustainable Communities: Mrs Teresa Harvey, Group Manager - Health & Wellbeing, Bridgwater House, King Square, Bridgwater TA6 3AR ☎ 01278 435232 🖷 01278 444076 ⌨ teresa.harvey@sedgemoor.gov.uk

Sustainable Development: Mrs Claire Pearce, Group Manager - Strategy & Business Services, Bridgwater House, King Square, Bridgwater TA6 3AR ☎ 01278 435262 🖷 01278 444076 ⌨ claire.pearce@sedgemoor.gov.uk

Tourism: Mrs Claire Pearce, Group Manager - Strategy & Business Services, Bridgwater House, King Square, Bridgwater TA6 3AR ☎ 01278 435262 🖷 01278 444076 ⌨ claire.pearce@sedgemoor.gov.uk

Transport: Mr Bob Kondys, Transport Supervisor, Bridgwater House, King Square, Bridgwater TA6 3AR ☎ 0845 408 2543 ⌨ bob.kondys@sedgemoor.gov.uk

Transport Planner: Mr Bob Kondys, Transport Supervisor, Bridgwater House, King Square, Bridgwater TA6 3AR ☎ 0845 408 2543 ⌨ bob.kondys@sedgemoor.gov.uk

Total Place: Mrs Claire Pearce, Group Manager - Strategy & Business Services, Bridgwater House, King Square, Bridgwater TA6 3AR ☎ 01278 435262 🖷 01278 444076 ⌨ claire.pearce@sedgemoor.gov.uk

Waste Collection and Disposal: Mr Adrian Gardner, Group Manager - Environmental Health, Bridgwater House, King Square, Bridgwater TA6 3AR ☎ 01278 435339 🖷 01278 446410 ⌨ adrian.gardner@sedgemoor.gov.uk

Waste Management: Mr Adrian Gardner, Group Manager - Environmental Health, Bridgwater House, King Square, Bridgwater TA6 3AR ☎ 01278 435339 🖷 01278 446410 ⌨ adrian.gardner@sedgemoor.gov.uk

Children's Play Areas: Mrs Teresa Harvey, Group Manager - Health & Wellbeing, Bridgwater House, King Square, Bridgwater TA6 3AR ☎ 01278 435232 🖷 01278 444076 ⌨ teresa.harvey@sedgemoor.gov.uk

MEMBERS OF THE COUNCIL (48)

***Chair:* Slocombe**, Gill (CON - Bridgwater Wyndham)
gill.slocombe@sedgemoor.gov.uk

***Vice-Chair:* Downing**, Peter (CON - Cheddar & Shipham)
peter.downing@sedgemoor.gov.uk

***Leader of the Council:* McGinty**, Duncan (CON - East Polden)
duncan.mcginty@sedgemoor.gov.uk

***Deputy Leader of the Council:* Hill**, Dawn (CON - Cheddar & Shipham)
dawn.hill@sedgemoor.gov.uk

Alder, Derek (CON - King's Isle)
derek.alder@sedgemoor.gov.uk

Austen, Steve (LAB - Bridgwater Hamp)
steve.austen@sedgemoor.gov.uk

Baker, David (CON - Bridgwater Wyndham)
david.baker@sedgemoor.gov.uk

Bayliss, Diana (CON - Wedmore & Mark)
diana.bayliss@sedgemoor.gov.uk

Bown, Ann (CON - Cannington & Wembdon)
ann.bown@sedgemoor.gov.uk

Bradford, Alan (CON - North Petherton)
alan.bradford@sedgemoor.gov.uk

Burden, Richard (CON - Wedmore & Mark)

Burridge-Clayton, Peter (CON - Burnham North)
peter.clayton@sedgemoor.gov.uk

Caswell, Michael (CON - Quantocks)
michael.caswell@sedgemoor.gov.uk

Clarke, Michael (CON - Burnham Central)
michael.clarke@sedgemoor.gov.uk

Davey, Dennis (CON - Burnham North)
dennis.davey@sedgemoor.gov.uk

Denbee, John (CON - Axevale)
john.denbee@sedgemoor.gov.uk

Dyer, Ian (CON - Cannington & Wembdon)
ian.dyer@sedgemoor.gov.uk

Filmer, Bob (CON - Knoll)
bob.filmer@sedgemoor.gov.uk

Fraser, Anne (CON - North Petherton)
anne.fraser@sedgemoor.gov.uk

Gilling, Andrew (CON - Knoll)
andrew.gilling@sedgemoor.gov.uk

Glassford, Alex (LAB - Bridgwater Fairfax)
alex.glassford@sedgemoor.gov.uk

Granter, Graham (LAB - Bridgwater Fairfax)
graham.granter@sedgemoor.gov.uk

Grimes, Tony (CON - Berrow)
tony.grimes@sedgemoor.gov.uk

Hamlin, Alison (CON - Puriton & Woolavington)
alison.hamlin@sedgemoor.gov.uk

Healey, Mark (CON - Puriton & Woolavington)
mark.healey@sedgemoor.gov.uk

Jones, Neville (CON - Burnham North)
neville.jones@sedgemoor.gov.uk

Kingham, Stuart (CON - West Polden)
stuart.kingham@sedgemoor.gov.uk

Lawson, Katie (LD - Burnham Central)

katie.lawson@sedgemoor.gov.uk
Leach, Joe (LD - Highbridge & Burnham Marine)
joe.leach@sedgemoor.gov.uk
Lerry, Mick (LAB - Bridgwater Victoria)
michael.lerry@sedgemoor.gov.uk
Loveridge, Dave (LAB - Bridgwater Eastover)
david.loveridge@sedgemoor.gov.uk
Mansfield, Mike (LD - Highbridge & Burnham Marine)
mike.mansfield@sedgemoor.gov.uk
Moore, Adrian (LAB - Bridgwater Hamp)
adrian.moore@sedgemoor.gov.uk
Moreton, Jane (CON - Huntspill & Pawlett)
jane.moreton@sedgemoor.gov.uk
Pay, Julie (CON - Quantocks)
julie.pay@sedgemoor.gov.uk
Pearce, Kathy (LAB - Bridgwater Westover)
kathy.pearce@sedgemoor.gov.uk
Redman, Leigh (LAB - Bridgwater Dunwear)
leigh.redman@sedgemoor.gov.uk
Richards, Ken (LAB - Bridgwater Victoria)
ken.richards@sedgemoor.gov.uk
Savage, Jeff (CON - Cheddar & Shipham)
jeff.savage@sedgemoor.gov.uk
Scott, Liz (CON - Axevale)
liz.scott@sedgemoor.gov.uk
Smedley, Brian (LAB - Bridgwater Westover)
brian.smedley@sedgemoor.gov.uk
Smout, Ken (CON - Burnham North)
ken.smout@sedgemoor.gov.uk
Swayne, John (CON - North Petherton)
john.swayne@sedgemoor.gov.uk
Taylor, Julian (LAB - Bridgwater Eastover)
julian.taylor@sedgemoor.gov.uk
Tucker, Ian (LAB - Bridgwater Dunwear)
ian.tucker@sedgemoor.gov.uk
Turner, Nobby (CON - King's Isle)
nobby.turner@sedgemoor.gov.uk
Williams, Chris (IND - Highbridge & Burnham Marine)
chris.williams@sedgemoor.gov.uk
Winslow, Reg
(LAB - Bridgwater Fairfax)
reginald.winslow@sedgemoor.gov.uk

POLITICAL COMPOSITION
CON: 31, LAB: 13, LD: 3, IND: 1

CABINET
Leader: Mr Duncan McGinty
Deputy Leader: Mrs Dawn Hill
Community & Scrutiny: Mr John Swayne
Corporate & Scrutiny: Mrs Ann Bown
Economic Strategy: Mrs Anne Fraser
Environment: Mr Richard Burden
Housing: Mr Andrew Gilling
Planning & Policy: Mr Stuart Kingham

COMMITTEE CHAIRS
Audit & Governance: Mr John Denbee
Community (Scrutiny): Mr Julian Taylor
Corporate (Scrutiny): Mr Brian Smedley
Development: Mr Bob Filmer
Licensing & General Purpose: Mr Jeff Savage

SEFTON — M

Sefton Metropolitan Borough Council, Town Hall, Southport PR8 1DA ☎ 01704 533133 🖷 0151 934 2293 🖳 www.sefton.gov.uk

FACTS & FIGURES
Police Authority: Merseyside Police Authority
Health Authority: North West Strategic Health Authority
Learning and Skills Council: North West
Parliamentary Constituencies: Bootle, Sefton Central, Southport
EU Constituencies: North West
Election Frequency: Elections are by thirds
Twinning: Fort Lauderdale (USA); Gdansk (Poland); Mons (Belgium);

PRINCIPAL OFFICERS
Chief Executive: Mrs Margaret Carney, Chief Executive, Town Hall, Southport PR8 1DA ☎ 0151 934 2057 🖷 0151 934 2268 ✉ margaret.carney@sefton.gov.uk

Senior Management: Mr Graham Bayliss, Director of Corporate Commissioning, 1st Floor, Bootle Town Hall, Oriel Road, Bootle L20 4AE ☎ 0151 934 2721 🖷 0151 934 4600 ✉ graham.bayliss@sefton.gov.uk

Senior Management: Mr Mike Fogg, Director of Corporate Services, 4th Floor, Magdalen House, 30 Trinity Road, Bootle L20 3NJ ☎ 0151 934 4081 🖷 0151 934 4560 ✉ mike.fogg@sefton.gov.uk

Senior Management: Mr Bill Millburn, Strategic Director of Place, 4th Floor, Magdalen House, 30 Trinity Road, Bootle L20 3NJ ☎ 0151 934 4190 🖷 0151 934 4560 ✉ bill.millburn@sefton.gov.uk

Architect, Building / Property Services: Mr David Kay, Client Services Group, Magdalen House, 30 Trinity Road, Bootle L20 3NJ ☎ 0151 934 4527 🖷 0151 934 4220 ✉ david.kay@sefton.gov.uk

Building Control: Mr Ian Berrington, Building Control Manager, Ground Floor, Magdalen House, 30 Trinity Road, Bootle L20 3NJ ☎ 0151 934 4626 🖷 0151 934 4627 ✉ ian.berrington@sefton.gov.uk

Catering Services: Mr Colin Upton, School Meals & Catering Services Manager, Hawthorne Road Depot, Hawthorne Road, Bootle L20 9PR ☎ 0151 934 3420 🖷 0151 934 3419 ✉ colin.upton@sefton.gov.uk

Children / Youth Services: Mr Peter Morgan, Strategic Director of People, 9th Floor Merton House, Stanley Road, Bootle L20 3JA ☎ 0151 934 3706 🖷 0151 934 3520 ✉ peter.morgan@sefton.gov.uk

Civil Registration: Ms Jane Gowing, Head of Planning Services, Ground Floor, Magdalen House, 30 Trinity Road, Bootle L20 3NJ ☎ 0151 934 3544 🖷 0151 934 4627 ✉ jane.gowing@sefton.gov.uk

Civil Registration: Mrs Diana Wright, Superintendent Registrar, Town Hall, Lord Street, Southport PR8 1DA ☎ 0115 934 2012

🖷 0115 934 2014 ✆ diana.wright@sefton.gov.uk

PR / Communications: Mr Richard Roscoe, Data Protection & Information Security Officer, 4th Floor Magdalen House, 30 Trinity Road, Bootle L20 3NJ ☎ 0151 934 4416 🖷 0151 934 3316 ✆ richard.roscoe@sefton.gov.uk

Community Safety: Ms Amanda Langan, Head of Investment Programmes & Infrastructure, 4th Floor, Magdalen House, 30 Trinity Road, Bootle L20 3NJ ☎ 0151 934 2171 🖷 0151 934 2270 ✆ amanda.langan@chief-executives.sefton.gov.uk

Computer Management: Ms Christine Finnigan, Customer & Transactional Service Manager, 4th Floor, Magdalen House, 30 Trinity Road, Bootle L20 3NJ ☎ 0151 934 4161 🖷 0151 934 4050 ✆ christine.finnigan@sefton.gov.uk

Consumer Protection and Trading Standards: Mr Dave Packard, Assistant Director of Environment Protection, Magdalen House, 30 Trinity Road, Bootle L20 3NJ ☎ 0151 934 2100 🖷 0151 934 4596 ✆ dave.packard@sefton.gov.uk

Contracts: Ms Jill Coule, Head of Corporate Legal Services, Ground Floor, Magdalen House, 30 Trinity Road, Bootle L20 3NJ ☎ 0151 934 2031 🖷 0151 934 2195 ✆ jill.coule@sefton.gov.uk

Corporate Services: Ms Christine Finnigan, Customer & Transactional Service Manager, 4th Floor, Magdalen House, 30 Trinity Road, Bootle L20 3NJ ☎ 0151 934 4161 🖷 0151 934 4050 ✆ christine.finnigan@sefton.gov.uk

Corporate Services: Mr Mike Fogg, Director of Corporate Services, 4th Floor, Magdalen House, 30 Trinity Road, Bootle L20 3NJ ☎ 0151 934 4081 🖷 0151 934 4560 ✆ mike.fogg@sefton.gov.uk

Customer Service: Ms Christine Finnigan, Customer & Transactional Service Manager, 4th Floor, Magdalen House, 30 Trinity Road, Bootle L20 3NJ ☎ 0151 934 4161 🖷 0151 934 4050 ✆ christine.finnigan@sefton.gov.uk

Economic Development: Ms Jane Gowing, Head of Planning Services, Ground Floor, Magdalen House, 30 Trinity Road, Bootle L20 3NJ ☎ 0151 934 3544 🖷 0151 934 4627 ✆ jane.gowing@sefton.gov.uk

Education: Mr Peter Morgan, Strategic Director of People, 9th Floor Merton House, Stanley Road, Bootle L20 3JA ☎ 0151 934 3706 🖷 0151 934 3520 ✆ peter.morgan@sefton.gov.uk

Electoral Registration: Ms Andrea Grant, Head of Governance & Civil Services, Bootle Town Hall, Oriel Road, Bootle L20 7AE ☎ 0151 934 2030 🖷 0151 934 2195 ✆ andrea.grant@sefton.gov.uk

Energy Management: Mr Alan Lunt, Director of Built Environment, Magdalen House, 30 Trinity Road, Bootle L20 3NJ ☎ 0151 934 4580 🖷 0151 934 4876 ✆ alan.lunt@sefton.gov.uk

Environmental / Technical Services: Mr Alan Lunt, Director of Built Environment, Magdalen House, 30 Trinity Road, Bootle L20 3NJ ☎ 0151 934 4580 🖷 0151 934 4876 ✆ alan.lunt@sefton.gov.uk

Environmental Health: Mr Alan Lunt, Director of Built Environment, Magdalen House, 30 Trinity Road, Bootle L20 3NJ ☎ 0151 934 4580 🖷 0151 934 4876 ✆ alan.lunt@sefton.gov.uk

Estates, Property & Valuation: Mr David Street, Property & Asset Manager, Magdalen House, 30 Trinity Road, Bootle L20 3NJ ☎ 0151 934 2751 🖷 0151 934 4220 ✆ david.street@sefton.gov.uk

European Liaison: Mr Mark Long, Assistant Director of Regeneration, Investment Centre, 375 Stanley Road, Bootle L20 5EF ☎ 0151 934 3471 🖷 0151 934 3449 ✆ mark.long@sefton.gov.uk

European Liaison: Mr James Sharples, Senior European Policy Officer, Merseyside Brussels Office, North West of England House, 21 Rue du Marteau, Brussels, B 1000 ☎ 0151 934 2725 ✆ james.sharples@merseyside-europe.org

Events Manager: Mr Tony Corfield, Head of Tourism, Town Hall, Southport PR8 1DA ☎ 0151 934 2315 🖷 0151 934 2326 ✆ tony.corfield@sefton.gov.uk

Facilities: Mr Alan Lunt, Director of Built Environment, Magdalen House, 30 Trinity Road, Bootle L20 3NJ ☎ 0151 934 4580 🖷 0151 934 4876 ✆ alan.lunt@sefton.gov.uk

Finance and Treasurer: Ms Margaret Rawding, Head of Corporate Finance & ICT Strategy, 4th Floor, Magdalen House, 30 Trinity Road, Bootle L20 3NJ ☎ 0151 934 4082 🖷 0151 934 4560 ✆ margaret.rawding@sefton.gov.uk

Fleet Management: Mr Jim Black, Director of Street Scene, Hawthorne Road Depot, Hawthorne Road, Bootle L20 9PR ☎ 0151 288 6133 🖷 0151 285 5217 ✆ jim.black@sefton.gov.uk

Health and Safety: Mr Steve Harper, Assistant Personnel Director, 2nd Floor, Magdalen House, 30 Trinity Road, Bootle L20 3NJ ☎ 0151 934 3397 🖷 0151 934 3651 ✆ steve.harper@sefton.gov.uk

Highways: Mr Jeremy McConkey, Network Manager, Magdalen House, 30 Trinity Road, Bootle L20 3NJ ☎ 0151 934 4222 🖷 0151 934 4801 ✆ jerry.mcconkey@sefton.gov.uk

Home Energy Conservation: Mr Ian Weller, Energy Manager, Magdalen House, 30 Trinity Road, Bootle L20 3NJ ☎ 0151 934 4221 🖷 0151 934 4559 ✆ ian.weller@sefton.gov.uk

Local Area Agreement: Mr Ian Willman, LAA Co-ordinator, Bootle Town Hall, Oriel Road, Bootle L20 7AE ☎ 0151 934 2015 🖷 0151 934 4600 ✆ ian.willman@sefton.gov.uk

Legal: Ms Jill Coule, Head of Corporate Legal Services, Ground Floor, Magdalen House, 30 Trinity Road, Bootle L20 3NJ ☎ 0151 934 2031 🖷 0151 934 2195 ✆ jill.coule@sefton.gov.uk

Leisure and Cultural Services: Mr Graham Bayliss, Director of Corporate Commissioning, 1st Floor, Bootle Town Hall, Oriel Road, Bootle L20 4AE ☎ 0151 934 2371 🖷 0151 934 4600 ✆ graham.bayliss@sefton.gov.uk

Leisure and Cultural Services: Mr Rajan Paul, Assistant Director of Strategic Development & Management, Magdalen House, 30 Trinity Road, Bootle L20 3NJ ☎ 0151 934 2382 🖷 0151 934 2370 ✉ rajan.paul@sefton.gov.uk

Licensing: Mr Alan Lunt, Director of Built Environment, Magdalen House, 30 Trinity Road, Bootle L20 3NJ ☎ 0151 934 4580 🖷 0151 934 4876 ✉ alan.lunt@sefton.gov.uk

Member Services: Ms Andrea Grant, Head of Governance & Civil Services, Bootle Town Hall, Oriel Road, Bootle L20 7AE ☎ 0151 934 2030 🖷 0151 934 2195 ✉ andrea.grant@sefton.gov.uk

Parking: Mr Dave Marrin, Traffic Services Manager, Magdalen House, 30 Trinity Road, Bootle L20 3NJ ☎ 0151 934 4295 🖷 0151 934 4532 ✉ dave.marrin@sefton.gov.uk

Personnel / HR: Mr Mark Dale, Interim Head of Corporate Personnel, 2nd Floor, Magdalen House, 30 Trinity Road, Bootle L20 3NJ ☎ 0151 934 3949 🖷 0151 934 3396 ✉ mark.dale@sefton.gov.uk

Planning: Ms Jane Gowing, Head of Planning Services, Ground Floor, Magdalen House, 30 Trinity Road, Bootle L20 3NJ ☎ 0151 934 3544 🖷 0151 934 4627 ✉ jane.gowing@sefton.gov.uk

Procurement: Mr Brian Gibson, Head of Procurement, Central Purchasing, Bootle Town Hall, Oriel Road, Bootle L20 7AE ☎ 0151 934 2505 🖷 0151 934 4579 ✉ brian.gobson@sefton.gov.uk

Public Libraries: Ms Christine Hall, Head of Libraries & Information Services, Magdalen House, 30 Trinity Road, Bootle L20 3NJ ☎ 0151 934 2376 🖷 0151 934 2370 ✉ christine.hall@sefton.gov.uk

Recycling & Waste Minimisation: Mr Jim Black, Director of Street Scene, Hawthorne Road Depot, Hawthorne Road, Bootle L20 9PR ☎ 0151 288 6133 🖷 0151 285 5217 ✉ jim.black@sefton.gov.uk

Regeneration: Ms Jane Gowing, Head of Planning Services, Ground Floor, Magdalen House, 30 Trinity Road, Bootle L20 3NJ ☎ 0151 934 3544 🖷 0151 934 4627 ✉ jane.gowing@sefton.gov.uk

Regeneration: Mr Mark Long, Assistant Director of Regeneration, Investment Centre, 375 Stanley Road, Bootle L20 5EF ☎ 0151 934 3471 🖷 0151 934 3449 ✉ mark.long@sefton.gov.uk

Regeneration: Mr Bill Millburn, Strategic Director of Place, 4th Floor, Magdalen House, 30 Trinity Road, Bootle L20 3NJ ☎ 0151 934 4190 🖷 0151 934 4560 ✉ bill.millburn@sefton.gov.uk

Road Safety: Mr Dave Marrin, Traffic Services Manager, Magdalen House, 30 Trinity Road, Bootle L20 3NJ ☎ 0151 934 4295 🖷 0151 934 4532 ✉ dave.marrin@sefton.gov.uk

Social Services (Adult): Ms Robina Critchley, Director of Older People, Merton House, Stanley Road, Bootle L20 3DL ☎ 0151 934 4900 🖷 0151 934 3697 ✉ robina.critchley@sefton.gov.uk

Social Services (Children): Mr Colin Pettigrew, Director of Young People & Families, 9th Floor Merton House, Stanley Road, Bootle L20 3JA ☎ 0151 934 3333 🖷 0151 934 3520 ✉ colin.pettigrew@sefton.gov.uk

Staff Training: Mr Mark Dale, Interim Head of Corporate Personnel, 2nd Floor, Magdalen House, 30 Trinity Road, Bootle L20 3NJ ☎ 0151 934 3949 🖷 0151 934 3396 ✉ mark.dale@sefton.gov.uk

Street Scene: Mr Jim Black, Director of Street Scene, Hawthorne Road Depot, Hawthorne Road, Bootle L20 9PR ☎ 0151 288 6133 🖷 0151 285 5217 ✉ jim.black@sefton.gov.uk

Sustainable Communities: Mr Alan Lunt, Director of Built Environment, Magdalen House, 30 Trinity Road, Bootle L20 3NJ ☎ 0151 934 4580 🖷 0151 934 4876 ✉ alan.lunt@sefton.gov.uk

Sustainable Development: Mr Dave Packard, Assistant Director of Environment Protection, Magdalen House, 30 Trinity Road, Bootle L20 3NJ ☎ 0151 934 2100 🖷 0151 934 4596 ✉ dave.packard@sefton.gov.uk

Tourism: Mr Tony Corfield, Head of Tourism, Town Hall, Southport PR8 1DA ☎ 0151 934 2315 🖷 0151 934 2326 ✉ tony.corfield@sefton.gov.uk

Town Centre: Mr Jim Breen, Southport Business Enterprise Partnership Manager, 74 Wayfarer's Arcade, Lord Street, Southport PR8 9PR ☎ 01704 512215 🖷 01704 512266

Traffic Management: Mr Dave Marrin, Traffic Services Manager, Magdalen House, 30 Trinity Road, Bootle L20 3NJ ☎ 0151 934 4295 🖷 0151 934 4532 ✉ dave.marrin@sefton.gov.uk

Transport: Mr Vin Donnelly, Transport Manager, Hawthorne Road Depot, Hawthorne Road, Bootle L20 9PR ☎ 0151 288 6158 🖷 0151 285 5225 ✉ vin.donnelly@sefton.gov.uk

Transport Planner: Mr Dave Marrin, Traffic Services Manager, Magdalen House, 30 Trinity Road, Bootle L20 3NJ ☎ 0151 934 4295 🖷 0151 934 4532 ✉ dave.marrin@sefton.gov.uk

Waste Collection and Disposal: Mr Jim Black, Director of Street Scene, Hawthorne Road Depot, Hawthorne Road, Bootle L20 9PR ☎ 0151 288 6133 🖷 0151 285 5217 ✉ jim.black@sefton.gov.uk

Waste Management: Mr Jim Black, Director of Street Scene, Hawthorne Road Depot, Hawthorne Road, Bootle L20 9PR ☎ 0151 288 6133 🖷 0151 285 5217 ✉ jim.black@sefton.gov.uk

Children's Play Areas: Mr Rajan Paul, Assistant Director of Strategic Development & Management, Magdalen House, 30 Trinity Road, Bootle L20 3NJ ☎ 0151 934 2382 🖷 0151 934 2370 ✉ rajan.paul@sefton.gov.uk

MEMBERS OF THE COUNCIL (66)

***Mayor:* Cluskey**, Kevin (LAB - Ford)
kevin.cluskey@councillors.sefton.gov.uk

***Deputy Chair:* Fearn**, Maureen (LD - Kew)
maureen.fearn@councillors.sefton.gov.uk

***Leader of the Council:* Dowd**, Peter (LAB - St. Oswald)
peter.dowd@councillors.sefton.gov.uk
***Deputy Leader of the Council:* Maher**, Ian (LAB - Netherton and Orrell)
ian.maher@councillors.sefton.gov.uk
***Group Leader:* Brodie-Browne**, Iain (LD - Birkdale)
iain.brodie.brown@councillors.sefton.gov.uk
***Group Leader:* Papworth**, Peter (CON - Blundellsands)
peter.papworth@sefton.gov.uk
Ashton, Nigel (LD - Meols)
nigel.ashton@councillors.sefton.gov.uk
Atkinson, Marion (LAB - Molyneux)
marion.atkinson@councillors.sefton.gov.uk
Ball, Pat (CON - Dukes)
pat.ball@councillors.sefton.gov.uk
Bennett, Veronica (LAB - Blundellsands)
veronica.bennett@councillors.sefton.gov.uk
Blackburn, Andrew (LD - Park)
libdems@sefton.gov.uk
Booth, Mike (LD - Kew)
mike.booth@councillors.sefton.gov.uk
Bradshaw, Susan (LAB - Netherton and Orrell)
susan.bradshaw@councillors.sefton.gov.uk
Brennan, Robert (LAB - Netherton and Orrell)
robert.brennan@councillors.sefton.gov.uk
Byrom, Leslie (LAB - Victoria)
les.byrom@councillors.sefton.gov.uk
Carr, Anthony (LAB - Molyneux)
anthony.carr@councillors.sefton.gov.uk
Cluskey, Linda (LAB - Derby)
linda.cluskey@councillors.sefton.gov.uk
Crabtree, Tony (CON - Cambridge)
tony.crabtreet@councillors.sefton.gov.uk
Cummins, Paul (LAB - Church)
paul.cummins@councillors.sefton.gov.uk
Cuthbertson, Gillian (CON - Harington)
gillian.cuthbertson@councillors.sefton.gov.uk
Dawson, Tony (LD - Dukes)
td@southportlibdems.com
Dodd, John (LD - Meols)
john.dodd@councillors.sefton.gov.uk
Dorgan, Sean (CON - Blundellsands)
sean.dorgan@councillors.sefton.gov.uk
Dowd, Mark (LAB - St. Oswald)
mark.dowd@councillors.sefton.gov.uk
Dutton, Denise (CON - Harington)
denise.dutton@councillors.sefton.gov.uk
Fairclough, John (LAB - Linacre)
john.fairclough@councillors.sefton.gov.uk
Fearn of Southport, Ronnie (LD - Norwood)
libdems@sefton.gov.uk
Friel, Gordon (LAB - Linacre)
gordon.friel@councillors.sefton.gov.uk
Gatherer, Lynn (LAB - Sudell)
lynn.gatherer@councillors.sefton.gov.uk
Gustafson, Carol (LAB - Derby)
carol.gustafson@councillors.sefton.gov.uk
Hands, Richard (LD - Birkdale)
richard.hands@councillors.sefton.gov.uk
Hardy, Patricia (LAB - Litherland)
patricia.hardy@councillors.sefton.gov.uk
Hartill, Ted (CON - Ainsdale)
ted.hartill@councillors.sefton.gov.uk
Hubbard, Bruce (LD - Sudell)
bruce.hubbard@councillors.sefton.gov.uk
Jones, Terry (CON - Ainsdale)
terry.jones@councillors.sefton.gov.uk
Keith, Pat (LD - Cambridge)
pat.keith@councillors.sefton.gov.uk
Kelly, John (LAB - Litherland)
john.kelly@councillors.sefton.gov.uk
Kelly, John (LAB - Manor)
john.joseph.kelly@councillors.sefton.gov.uk
Kermode, Stephen (LAB - Park)
stephen.kermode@councillors.sefton.gov.uk
Kerrigan, Doreen (LAB - Linacre)
doreen.kerrigan@councillors.sefton.gov.uk
Killen, Nina (LAB - Harington)
nina.killen@councillors.sefton.gov.uk
Lappin, Paulette (LAB - Ford)
paulette.lappin@councillors.sefton.gov.uk
Maguire, Peter (LAB - Ravenmeols)
peter.maguire@councillors.sefton.gov.uk
Mahon, James (LAB - St. Oswald)
james.mahon@councillors.sefton.gov.uk
McGinnity, Steve (LAB - Manor)
steve.mcginnity@councillors.sefton.gov.uk
McGuire, Sue (LD - Cambridge)
sue.mcguire@councillor.sefton.gov.uk
McIvor, David (CON - Ravenmeols)
david.mcivor@councillors.sefton.gov.uk
McKinley, Patrick (LAB - Sudell)
patrick.mckinley@councillors.sefton.gov.uk
Moncur, Ian (LAB - Ford)
ian.moncur@councillors.sefton.gov.uk
Murphy, Paula (LAB - Molyneux)
paula.murphy@councillors.sefton.gov.uk
Page, Catie (LAB - Ravenmeols)
catie.page@councillors.sefton.gov.uk
Preece, Haydn (LD - Ainsdale)
haydn.preece@councillors.sefton.gov.uk
Rimmer, David (LD - Meols)
david.rimmer@councillors.sefton.gov.uk
Roberts, Diane (LAB - Manor)
diane.roberts@councillors.sefton.gov.uk
Robertson, Tony (LD - Park)
t3robertson@tiscali.co.uk
Robinson, Dave (LAB - Derby)
dave.robinson@councillors.sefton.gov.uk
Roche, Michael (LAB - Victoria)
michael.roche@councillors.sefton.gov.uk
Shaw, Simon (LD - Birkdale)
simon.shaw@councillors.sefton.gov.uk
Sumner, David (LD - Norwood)
david.sumner@councillors.sefton.gov.uk
Tonkiss, Andrew (LD - Victoria)
andrew.tonkinss@councillors.sefton.gov.uk
Tweed, Paul (LAB - Litherland)
paul.tweed@councillors.sefton.gov.uk
Veidman, Daren (LAB - Church)
daren.veidman@councillors.sefton.gov.uk
Watson, Ron (CON - Dukes)
ron.watson@councillors.sefton.gov.uk
Weavers, Frederick (LD - Kew)
frederick.weavers@councillors.sefton.gov.uk
Webster, Veronica (LAB - Church)
veronica.webster@councillors.sefton.gov.uk
Welsh, Marianne (LD - Norwood)
marianne.welsh@councillors.sefton.gov.uk

POLITICAL COMPOSITION
LAB: 36, LD: 20, CON: 10

CABINET
Leader: Mr Peter Dowd
Deputy Leader / Regeneration & Tourism: Mr Ian Maher
Children, Schools, Families & Leisure: Mr Ian Moncur
Communities & Environment: Ms Patricia Hardy
Corporate Services & Performance: Mr Paul Tweed
Older People & Health: Mr Paul Cummins
Transportation: Mr John Fairclough

COMMITTEE CHAIRS
Audit & Governance: Mr Anthony Carr
Children's Services (Scrutiny): Mr Robert Brennen
Health & Social Care (Scrutiny): Ms Catie Page
Licensing & Regulatory: Ms Doreen Kerrigan
Overview & Scrutiny: Mr Steve McGinnity
Planning: Mr Daren Veidman
Regeneration & Environmental Services: Mr Patrick McKinley

SELBY D

Selby District Council, Civic Centre, Doncaster Road, Selby YO8 9FT ☏ 01757 705101 🖷 01757 292176 ✉ info@selby.gov.uk 🖳 www.selby.gov.uk

FACTS & FIGURES
Police Authority: North Yorkshire Police Authority
Health Authority: NHS Yorkshire & the Humber
Learning and Skills Council: Yorkshire and the Humber
Parliamentary Constituencies: Selby and Ainsty
EU Constituencies: Yorkshire and the Humber
Election Frequency: Elections are of whole council
Twinning: Selby: Carentan (France)
Selby: Filderstadt (Germany)

PRINCIPAL OFFICERS
Chief Executive: Mr Martin Connor, Chief Executive, Civic Centre, Portholme Road, Selby YO8 4SB ☏ 01757 292001 🖷 01757 292035 ✉ adavison@selby.gov.uk

Deputy Chief Executive: Mr Jonathan Lund, Deputy Chief Executive, Civic Centre, Portholme Road, Selby YO8 4SB ☏ 01757 292056 ✉ jlund@selby.gov.uk

Senior Management: Mrs Janette Barlow, Director - Business Services, Civic Centre, Doncaster Road, Selby YO8 9FT ☏ 01757 705101 🖷 01757 292229 ✉ jbarlow@selby.gov.uk

Senior Management: Mr Keith Dawson, Director - Community Services, Civic Centre, Doncaster Road, Selby YO8 9FT ☏ 01757 705101 🖷 01757 292229 ✉ kdawson@selby.gov.uk

Senior Management: Mrs Karen Iveson, Executive Director & s151 Officer, Civic Centre, Portholme Road, Selby YO8 4SB ☏ 01757 292056 🖷 01757 292035 ✉ kiveson@selby.gov.uk

Senior Management: Mrs Rose Norris, Executive Director, Civic Centre, Doncaster Road, Selby YO8 9FT ☏ 01757 705101 🖷 01757 292035 ✉ rnorris@selby.gov.uk

Senior Management: Mr Mark Steward, Managing Director - Access Selby, Civic Centre, Portholme Road, Selby YO8 4SB ☏ 01757 705101 🖷 01757 292229 ✉ msteward@selby.gov.uk

Architect, Building / Property Services: Mrs Eileen Scothern, Business Manager, Civic Centre, Doncaster Road, Selby YO8 9FT ☏ 01757 705101 🖷 01757 292229 ✉ escothern@selby.gov.uk

Building Control: Mr Les Chapman, Building Control Manager, Suite 2, North Yorkshire Building Control, Coxwold House, Easingwold Business Park, Easingwold, York YO16 3FB ☏ 01347 822703 ✉ lchapman@selby.gov.uk

Building Control: Mr Keith Dawson, Director - Community Services, Civic Centre, Doncaster Road, Selby YO8 9FT ☏ 01757 705101 🖷 01757 292229 ✉ kdawson@selby.gov.uk

PR / Communications: Mr Mike James, Lead Officer - Marketing & Communications, Civic Centre, Doncaster Road, Selby YO8 9FT ☏ 01757 705101 🖷 01757 292229 ✉ mjames@selby.gov.uk

Community Planning: Mrs Rose Norris, Executive Director, Civic Centre, Portholme Road, Selby YO8 4SB ☏ 01757 705101 🖷 01757 292035 ✉ rnorris@selby.gov.uk

Computer Management: Mr Graham Thistlewhaite, Head - IS, Civic Centre, Doncaster Road, Selby YO8 9FT ☏ 01757 705101; 01756 706313 🖷 01756 700657; 01757 292229 ✉ gthistlewhaite@cravendc.gov.uk

Contracts: Mrs Sarah Smith, Business Manager, Civic Centre, Portholme Road, Selby YO8 4SB ☏ 01757 705101 🖷 01757 292229 ✉ sesmith@selby.gov.uk

Customer Service: Mr Dean Richardson, Business Manager, Civic Centre, Doncaster Road, Selby YO8 9FT ☏ 01757 705101 🖷 01757 292229 ✉ drichardson@selby.gov.uk

Economic Development: Mrs Eileen Scothern, Business Manager, Civic Centre, Doncaster Road, Selby YO8 9FT ☏ 01757 705101 🖷 01757 292229 ✉ escothern@selby.gov.uk

Electoral Registration: Mrs Janice Senior, Business Support Supervisor, Civic Centre, Doncaster Road, Selby YO8 9FT ☏ 01757 705101 🖷 01757 292229 ✉ jsenior@selby.gov.uk

Emergency Planning: Mr Dean Richardson, Business Manager, Civic Centre, Doncaster Road, Selby YO8 9FT ☏ 01757 705101 🖷 01757 292229 ✉ drichardson@selby.gov.uk

Environmental / Technical Services: Mr Dean Richardson, Business Manager, Civic Centre, Doncaster Road, Selby YO8 9FT ☏ 01757 705101 🖷 01757 292229 ✉ drichardson@selby.gov.uk

Environmental Health: Mr Wayne Palmer, Lead Officer - Environmental Health & Housing, Civic Centre, Doncaster Road, Selby YO8 9FT ☏ 01757 705101 🖷 01757 292229 ✉ wpalmer@selby.gov.uk

Estates, Property & Valuation: Mrs Eileen Scothern, Business Manager, Civic Centre, Doncaster Road, Selby YO8 9FT ☏ 01757

705101 ☎ 01757 292229 ✉ escothern@selby.gov.uk

Finance and Treasurer: Mrs Karen Iveson, Executive Director & s151 Officer, Civic Centre, Portholme Road, Selby YO8 4SB ☎ 01757 292056 ☎ 01757 292035 ✉ kiveson@selby.gov.uk

Health and Safety: Mr Dean Richardson, Business Manager, Civic Centre, Doncaster Road, Selby YO8 9FT ☎ 01757 705101 ☎ 01757 292229 ✉ drichardson@selby.gov.uk

Housing: Mr Dean Richardson, Business Manager, Civic Centre, Doncaster Road, Selby YO8 9FT ☎ 01757 705101 ☎ 01757 292229 ✉ drichardson@selby.gov.uk

Housing Maintenance: Mrs Eileen Scothern, Business Manager, Civic Centre, Doncaster Road, Selby YO8 9FT ☎ 01757 705101 ☎ 01757 292229 ✉ escothern@selby.gov.uk

Legal: Mrs Michelle Sacks, Solicitor to the Council, Civic Centre, Doncaster Road, Selby YO8 9FT ☎ 01757 705101 ☎ 01757 292229 ✉ msacks@selby.gov.uk

Legal: Mrs Eileen Scothern, Business Manager, Civic Centre, Doncaster Road, Selby YO8 9FT ☎ 01757 705101 ☎ 01757 292229 ✉ escothern@selby.gov.uk

Leisure and Cultural Services: Mrs Sarah Smith, Business Manager, Civic Centre, Portholme Road, Selby YO8 4SB ☎ 01757 705101 ☎ 01757 292229 ✉ sesmith@selby.gov.uk

Licensing: Mr Dylan Jones, Business Manager, Civic Centre, Doncaster Road, Selby YO8 9FT ☎ 01757 705101 ☎ 01757 292229 ✉ djones@selby.gov.uk

Member Services: Mr Glenn Shelley, Democratic Services Manager, Civic Centre, Doncaster Road, Selby YO8 9FT ☎ 01757 292007 ☎ 01757 292035 ✉ gshelley@selby.gov.uk

Parking: Mrs Eileen Scothern, Business Manager, Civic Centre, Doncaster Road, Selby YO8 9FT ☎ 01757 705101 ☎ 01757 292229 ✉ escothern@selby.gov.uk

Partnerships: Mrs Sarah Smith, Business Manager, Civic Centre, Portholme Road, Selby YO8 4SB ☎ 01757 705101 ☎ 01757 292229 ✉ sesmith@selby.gov.uk

Personnel / HR: Mrs Sarah Smith, Business Manager, Civic Centre, Portholme Road, Selby YO8 4SB ☎ 01757 705101 ☎ 01757 292229 ✉ sesmith@selby.gov.uk

Planning: Mr Dylan Jones, Business Manager, Civic Centre, Doncaster Road, Selby YO8 9FT ☎ 01757 705101 ☎ 01757 292229 ✉ djones@selby.gov.uk

Procurement: Mrs Sarah Smith, Business Manager, Civic Centre, Portholme Road, Selby YO8 4SB ☎ 01757 705101 ☎ 01757 292229 ✉ sesmith@selby.gov.uk

Recycling & Waste Minimisation: Mrs Sarah Smith, Business Manager, Civic Centre, Portholme Road, Selby YO8 4SB ☎ 01757 705101 ☎ 01757 292229 ✉ sesmith@selby.gov.uk

Regeneration: Mrs Eileen Scothern, Business Manager, Civic Centre, Doncaster Road, Selby YO8 9FT ☎ 01757 705101 ☎ 01757 292229 ✉ escothern@selby.gov.uk

Staff Training: Mrs Sarah Smith, Business Manager, Civic Centre, Portholme Road, Selby YO8 4SB ☎ 01757 705101 ☎ 01757 292229 ✉ sesmith@selby.gov.uk

Street Scene: Mrs Sarah Smith, Business Manager, Civic Centre, Portholme Road, Selby YO8 4SB ☎ 01757 705101 ☎ 01757 292229 ✉ sesmith@selby.gov.uk

Sustainable Communities: Mrs Rose Norris, Head of Service - Partnerships & Commissioning, Civic Centre, Portholme Road, Selby YO8 4SB ☎ 01757 292254 ✉ rnorris@selby.gov.uk

Waste Collection and Disposal: Mrs Sarah Smith, Business Manager, Civic Centre, Portholme Road, Selby YO8 4SB ☎ 01757 705101 ☎ 01757 292229 ✉ sesmith@selby.gov.uk

Waste Management: Mrs Sarah Smith, Business Manager, Civic Centre, Portholme Road, Selby YO8 4SB ☎ 01757 705101 ☎ 01757 292229 ✉ sesmith@selby.gov.uk

MEMBERS OF THE COUNCIL (41)

***Chair:* Crawford**, Jack (LAB - Fairburn with Brotherton)
jcrawford@selby.gov.uk
***Vice-Chair:* Dyson**, Michael (CON - Selby West)
cllrmdyson@selby.gov.uk
***Leader of the Council:* Crane**, Mark (CON - Brayton)
mcrane@selby.gov.uk
***Deputy Leader of the Council:* Ivey**, Gillian (CON - Whitley)
givey@selby.gov.uk
Casling, Elizabeth (CON - Riccall with Escrick)
ecasling@selby.gov.uk
Cattanach, John (CON - Cawood with Wistow)
jcattanach@Selby.gov.uk
Chilvers, Ian (CON - Brayton)
ichilvers@selby.gov.uk
Davies, Doreen (LAB - Selby South)
ddavies@selby.gov.uk
Davis, Melanie (LAB - Selby North)
melaniedavis@selby.gov.uk
Deans, James Thomas (CON - Hemingbrough)
jdeans@selby.gov.uk
Duckett, Stephanie (LAB - Barlby)
sduckett@selby.gov.uk
Ellis, Keith (CON - Cawood with Wistow)
kellis@selby.gov.uk
Hobson, Mel (CON - Sherburn in Elmet)
cllrmhobson@selby.gov.uk
Inness, William (CON - North Duffield)
binness@selby.gov.uk
Jordan, Mike (CON - Sherburn in Elmet)
mjordan@selby.gov.uk
Lunn, Clifford (CON - Hambleton)
clunn@selby.gov.uk
Mackay, Donald (CON - Tadcaster West)
dbain-macay@selby.gov.uk
Mackay, Patricia Ann (CON - Tadcaster East)
pbainmackay@selby.gov.uk
Mackman, John (CON - Monk Fryston with South Milford)
jmackman@selby.gov.uk
Mackman, Carol (CON - Monk Fryston with South Milford)

cmackman@selby.gov.uk
Marshall, Brian (LAB - Barlby)
bmarshall@selby.gov.uk
McCartney, Mary (IND - Eggborough)
mmccartney@selby.gov.uk
McCartney, John (IND - Eggborough)
jmccartney@Selby.gov.uk
McSherry, Kathleen (CON - Hemingbrough)
kmcsherry@selby.gov.uk
Metcalfe, Christopher William (CON - Tadcaster West)
cmetcalfe@selby.gov.uk
Metcalfe, Eileen (CON - Saxton & Ulleskelf)
emetcalfe@selby.gov.uk
Musgrave, Richard (CON - Appleton Roebuck)
rmusgrave@selby.gov.uk
Nichols, Wendy (LAB - Selby South)
wnichols@selby.gov.uk
Nutt, Iain (CON - Brayton)
inutt@selby.gov.uk
Packham, Robert (LAB - Sherburn in Elmet)
cllrbpackham@selby.gov.uk
Pearson, Christopher (CON - Hambleton)
cpearson@selby.gov.uk
Peart, Dave (CON - Selby West)
dpeart@selby.gov.uk
Pound, Andrew (CON - Fairburn with Brotherton)
apound@selby.gov.uk
Price, Rod (LAB - Camblesforth)
cllrprice@selby.gov.uk
Reynolds, Ian (CON - Riccall with Escrick)
cllrireynolds@selby.gov.uk
Ryder, Susan (CON - Whitley)
suryder@selby.gov.uk
Sayner, Ruth (CON - Hambleton)
rsayer@selby.gov.uk
Shaw-Wright, Steve (LAB - Selby North)
cllr.s.shawwright@btinternet.com
Spetch, Ann (CON - Camblesforth)
aspetch@selby.gov.uk
Sweeting, Richard (CON - Tadcaster East)
rsweeting@selby.gov.uk
Thurlow, Anthony Jude (LAB - Selby North)

POLITICAL COMPOSITION
CON: 29, LAB: 10, IND: 2

CABINET
Leader: Mr Mark Crane
Deputy Leader / External Relations & Partnerships: Ms Gillian Ivey
Communities: Mr Christopher William Metcalfe
Finance & Resources: Mr Clifford Lunn
Place Shaping: Mr John Mackman

COMMITTEE CHAIRS
Audit (Scrutiny): Mrs Elizabeth Casling
Licensing: Mrs Ruth Sayner
Planning: Mr James Thomas Deans
Policy & Resources: Mr Mike Jordan

SEVENOAKS D

Sevenoaks District Council, Council Offices, Argyle Road, Sevenoaks TN13 1HG ☎ 01732 227000 🖷 01732 740693
✉ communications@sevenoaks.gov.uk 🖳 www.sevenoaks.gov.uk

FACTS & FIGURES
Police Authority: Kent Police Authority
Health Authority: South East Coast Strategic Health Authority
Learning and Skills Council: South East
Parliamentary Constituencies: Dartford, Sevenoaks, Tonbridge and Malling
EU Constituencies: South East
Election Frequency: Elections are of whole council
Twinning: Edenbridge: Mont St. Aignan (France); Sevenoaks Town: Pontoise (France); Swanley: Verriere-le-Buisson (France); Westerham: Bonneval (France)

PRINCIPAL OFFICERS
Chief Executive: Mr Robin Hales, Chief Executive, Council Offices, Argyle Road, Sevenoaks TN13 1HG ☎ 01732 227394 ✉ robin.hales@sevenoaks.gov.uk

Deputy Chief Executive: Ms Kristen Paterson, Deputy Chief Executive & Director of Community & Planning, Council Offices, Argyle Road, Sevenoaks TN13 1HG ☎ 01732 227268 ✉ kristen.paterson@sevenoaks.gov.uk

Deputy Chief Executive: Dr Pav Ramewal, Deputy Chief Executive & Director of Corporate Resources, Council Offices, Argyle Road, Sevenoaks TN13 1HG ☎ 01732 227298 ✉ pav.ramewal@sevenoaks.gov.uk

Architect, Building / Property Services: Mr Jim Latheron, Professional Services Manager, Council Offices, Argyle Road, Sevenoaks TN13 1HG ☎ 01732 227209 🖷 01732 227176 ✉ jim.latheron@sevenoaks.gov.uk

Building Control: Mr Kevin Tomsett, Building Control & Emergency Planning Manager, Council Offices, Argyle Road, Sevenoaks TN13 1HG ☎ 01732 227368 ✉ kevin.tomsett@sevenoaks.gov.uk

PR / Communications: Mr Daniel Whitmarsh, Communications & Consultation Manager, Council Offices, Argyle Road, Sevenoaks TN13 1HG ☎ 01732 227414 ✉ daniel.whitmarsh@sevenoaks.gov.uk

Community Planning: Mr Alan Whiting, Community Planning & Projects Officer, Council Offices, Argyle Road, Sevenoaks TN13 1HG ☎ 01732 227446 ✉ alan.whiting@sevenoaks.gov.uk

Community Safety: Ms Kelly Webb, Community Safety Co-ordinator, Council Offices, Argyle Road, Sevenoaks TN13 1HG ☎ 01732 227474 ✉ kelly.webb@sevenoaks.gov.uk

Computer Management: Mr Jim Carrington-West, Head of Information & Customer Services, Council Offices, Argyle Road, Sevenoaks TN13 1HG ☎ 01732 227266 🖷 01732 227151 ✉ jim.carrington-west@sevenoaks.gov.uk

Contracts: Ms Christine Nuttall, Head of Legal & Democratic Services, Council Offices, Argyle Road, Sevenoaks TN13 1HG ☎ 01732 227245 ✉ christine.nuttall@sevenoaks.gov.uk

Corporate Services: Dr Pav Ramewal, Deputy Chief Executive &

Director of Corporate Resources, Council Offices, Argyle Road, Sevenoaks TN13 1HG ☎ 01732 227298 ✉ pav.ramewal@sevenoaks.gov.uk

Direct Labour: Mr Richard Wilson, Head of Environmental & Operational Services, Council Offices, Argyle Road, Sevenoaks TN13 1HG ☎ 01732 227262 ✉ richard.wilson@sevenoaks.gov.uk

Economic Development: Mrs Lesley Bowles, Head of Community Development, Council Offices, Argyle Road, Sevenoaks TN13 1HG ☎ 01732 227335 ✉ lesley.bowles@sevenoaks.gov.uk

Electoral Registration: Mr Ian Bigwood, Electoral Services & Land Charges Manager, Council Offices, Argyle Road, Sevenoaks TN13 1HG ☎ 01732 227242 🖷 01732 227176 ✉ ian.bigwood@sevenoaks.gov.uk

Emergency Planning: Mr Kevin Tomsett, Building Control & Emergency Planning Manager, Council Offices, Argyle Road, Sevenoaks TN13 1HG ☎ 01732 227368 ✉ kevin.tomsett@sevenoaks.gov.uk

Environmental / Technical Services: Mr Richard Wilson, Head of Environmental & Operational Services, Council Offices, Argyle Road, Sevenoaks TN13 1HG ☎ 01732 227262 ✉ richard.wilson@sevenoaks.gov.uk

Environmental Health: Mrs Annie Sargent, Environmental Health Manager, Dartford Borough Council, Civic Centre, Home Gardens, Dartford DA1 1DR ✉ annie.sargent@dartford.gov.uk

Estates, Property & Valuation: Mr Jim Latheron, Professional Services Manager, Council Offices, Argyle Road, Sevenoaks TN13 1HG ☎ 01732 227209 🖷 01732 227176 ✉ jim.latheron@sevenoaks.gov.uk

Facilities: Mr William Bowen, Facilities Manager, Council Offices, Argyle Road, Sevenoaks TN13 1HG ☎ 01732 227304 ✉ william.bowen@sevenoaks.gov.uk

Finance and Treasurer: Mr Adrian Rowbotham, Group Manager for Financial Services, Council Offices, Argyle Road, Sevenoaks TN13 1HG ☎ 01732 227153 ✉ adrian.rowbotham@sevenoaks.gov.uk

Fleet Management: Mr Ian Finch, Operations Manager, Sevenoaks Direct Services, Dunbrik Depot, 2 Main Road, Sundridge, Sevenoaks TN14 6EP ☎ 01959 567352 ✉ ian.finch@sevenoaks.gov.uk

Grounds Maintenance: Mr David Boorman, Senior Parking & Amenities Officer, Council Offices, Argyle Road, Sevenoaks TN13 1HG ☎ 01732 227175 ✉ david.boorman@sevenoaks.gov.uk

Health and Safety: Mr Richard Wilson, Head of Environmental & Operational Services, Council Offices, Argyle Road, Sevenoaks TN13 1HG ☎ 01732 227262 ✉ richard.wilson@sevenoaks.gov.uk

Housing: Mrs Pat Smith, Head of Housing and Communications, Council Offices, Argyle Road, Sevenoaks TN13 1HG ☎ 01732 227355 🖷 01732 451332 ✉ pat.smith@sevenoaks.gov.uk

Local Area Agreement: Mrs Lesley Bowles, Head of Community Development, Council Offices, Argyle Road, Sevenoaks TN13 1HG ☎ 01732 227335 ✉ lesley.bowles@sevenoaks.gov.uk

Legal: Ms Christine Nuttall, Head of Legal & Democratic Services, Council Offices, Argyle Road, Sevenoaks TN13 1HG ☎ 01732 227245 ✉ christine.nuttall@sevenoaks.gov.uk

Leisure and Cultural Services: Mrs Hayley Baldock, Health & Leisure Manager, Council Offices, Argyle Road, Sevenoaks TN13 1HG ☎ 01732 227272 ✉ hayley.baldock@sevenoaks.gov.uk

Licensing: Mrs Claire Perry, Licensing Partnership Manager, Council Offices, Argyle Road, Sevenoaks TN13 1HG ☎ 01732 227325; 07970 731616 ✉ claire.perry@sevenoaks.gov.uk; claire.perry@tunbridgewells.gov.uk

Lottery Funding, Charity and Voluntary: Mrs Lesley Bowles, Head of Community Development, Council Offices, Argyle Road, Sevenoaks TN13 1HG ☎ 01732 227335 ✉ lesley.bowles@sevenoaks.gov.uk

Member Services: Miss Phillipa Stone, Democratic Services Manager, Council Offices, Argyle Road, Sevenoaks TN13 1HG ☎ 01732 227247 ✉ phillipa.stone@sevenoaks.gov.uk

Parking: Mr Gary Connor, Parking & Amenity Manager, Council Offices, Argyle Road, Sevenoaks TN13 1HG ☎ 01732 227310 ✉ gary.connor@sevenoaks.gov.uk

Personnel / HR: Miss Syreeta Gill, Human Resources Manager, Council Offices, Argyle Road, Sevenoaks TN13 1HG ☎ 01732 227403 ✉ syreeta.gill@sevenoaks.gov.uk

Planning: Mr Alan Dyer, Acting Planning Services Manager, Council Offices, Argyle Road, Sevenoaks TN13 1HG

Procurement: Mr Bami Cole, Audit, Risk & Anti-Fraud Manager, Dartford Borough Council, Civic Centre, Home Gardens, Dartford DA1 1DR ☎ 01322 343023 ✉ bami.cole@dartford.gov.uk

Recycling & Waste Minimisation: Mr Ian Finch, Operations Manager, Sevenoaks Direct Services, Dunbrik Depot, 2 Main Road, Sundridge, Sevenoaks TN14 6EP ☎ 01959 567352 ✉ ian.finch@sevenoaks.gov.uk

Staff Training: Mrs Hilary Holder, HR Officer, Council Offices, Argyle Road, Sevenoaks TN13 1HG ☎ 01732 227169 ✉ hilary.holder@sevenoaks.gov.uk

Street Scene: Mr Ian Finch, Operations Manager, Sevenoaks Direct Services, Dunbrik Depot, 2 Main Road, Sundridge, Sevenoaks TN14 6EP ☎ 01959 567352 ✉ ian.finch@sevenoaks.gov.uk

Tourism: Mrs Hayley Baldock, Health & Leisure Manager, Council Offices, Argyle Road, Sevenoaks TN13 1HG ☎ 01732 227272 ✉ hayley.baldock@sevenoaks.gov.uk

Transport: Mr Mike Holdsworth, Transport Manager, Sevenoaks Direct Services, Dunbrik Depot, 2 Main Road, Sundridge, Sevenoaks TN14 6EP ☎ 01959 567376

michael.holdsworth@sevenoaks.gov.uk

Waste Collection and Disposal: Mr Ian Finch, Operations Manager, Sevenoaks Direct Services, Dunbrik Depot, 2 Main Road, Sundridge, Sevenoaks TN14 6EP ☎ 01959 567352 ian.finch@sevenoaks.gov.uk

Waste Management: Mr Richard Wilson, Head of Environmental & Operational Services, Council Offices, Argyle Road, Sevenoaks TN13 1HG ☎ 01732 227262 richard.wilson@sevenoaks.gov.uk

Children's Play Areas: Mr David Boorman, Senior Parking & Amenities Officer, Council Offices, Argyle Road, Sevenoaks TN13 1HG ☎ 01732 227175 david.boorman@sevenoaks.gov.uk

MEMBERS OF THE COUNCIL (54)

***Chair:* Morris**, Dee (CON - Hextable)
cllr.morris@sevenoaks.gov.uk
***Leader of the Council:* Fleming**, Peter (CON - Sevenoaks Town and St. John's)
cllr.fleming@tory.co.uk
***Deputy Leader of the Council:* Davison**, Jill (CON - Edenbridge North and East)
cllr.j.davison@sevenoaks.gov.uk
***Group Leader:* Fittock**, Mark (LAB - Swanley St Mary's)
cllr.fittock@sevenoaks.gov.uk
***Group Leader:* Walshe**, Roger (LD - Sevenoaks Eastern)
cllr.walshe@sevenoaks.gov.uk
Abraham, Larry (CON - Hartley and Hodsoll Street)
cllr.abraham@sevenoaks.gov.uk
Ayres, Leslie (CON - Swanley Christchurch and Swanley Village)
cllr.l.ayres@sevenoaks.gov.uk
Ayres, Barbara (CON - Hextable)
cllr.b.ayres@sevenoaks.gov.uk
Ball, Laurence (CON - Swanley White Oak)
cllr.ball@sevenoaks.gov.uk
Bayley, Kim (CON - Dunton Green and Riverhead)
cllr.bayley@sevenoaks.oov.uk
Bosley, Ian (CON - Fawkham and West Kingsdown)
cllr.bosley@sevenoaks.gov.uk
Bosley, Pat (CON - Fawkham and West Kingsdown)
cllrp.bosley@sevenoaks.gov.uk
Bracken, Elaine (CON - Westerham and Crockham Hill)
cllr.bracken@sevenoaks.gov.uk
Brookbank, Robert (CON - Swanley Christchurch and Swanley Village)
cllr.brookbank@sevenoaks.gov.uk
Brown, Cameron (CON - Dunton Green and Riverhead)
cllr.brown@sevenoaks.gov.uk
Butler, Mark (CON - Kemsing)
cllr.butler@sevenoaks.gov.uk
Chetram, Ingrid (CON - Farningham, Horton Kirby and South Darenth)
cllr.chetram@sevenoaks.gov.uk
Clark, Cameron (CON - Ash)
cllr.c.clark@sevenoaks.gov.uk
Clark, Carol (CON - Ash)
cllr.clark@sevenoaks.gov.uk
Cook, Alison (CON - Leigh and Chiddingstone Causeway)
cllr.cook@sevenoaks.gov.uk
Cooke, Paddy (CON - Penshurst, Forcombe and Chiddingstone)
cllr.cooke@sevenoaks.gov.uk
Davison, Richard (CON - Edenbridge South and West)
cllrr.davison@sevenoaks.gov.uk
Dawson, Ann (CON - Sevenoaks Town and St. John's)
cllr.dawson@sevenoaks.gov.uk
Dibsdall, Jenny (LAB - Crockenhill and Well Hill)
cllr.j.dibsall@sevenoaks.gov.uk
Dickins, Matthew (CON - Sevenoaks Northern)
cllr.dickins@sevenoaks.gov.uk
Edwards-Winser, John (CON - Otford and Shoreham)
cllr.edwards-winser@sevenoaks.gov.uk
Eyre, Andrew (CON - Sevenoaks Kippington)
cllr.eyre@sevenoaks.gov.uk
Firth, Anna (CON - Brasted, Chevening and Sundridge)
cllr.firth@sevenoaks.gov.uk
Gaywood, James (CON - Hartley and Hodsoll Street)
cllr.gaywood@sevenoaks.gov.uk
George, Angela (LAB - Swanley White Oak)
cllr.george@sevenoaks.gov.uk
Grint, John (CON - Halstead, Knockholt and Badgers Mount)
cllr.grint@sevenoaks.gov.uk
Hogarth, Roderick (CON - Seal and Weald)
cllr.hogarth@sevenoaks.gov.uk
Horwood, Michael (CON - Eynsford)
cllr.horwood@sevenoaks.gov.uk
Hunter, Avril (CON - Sevenoaks Kippington)
cllr.hunter@sevenoaks.gov.uk
London, James (CON - Brasted, Chevening and Sundridge)
cllr.london@sevenoaks.gov.uk
Lowe, Michelle (CON - Otford and Shoreham)
cllr.lowe@sevenoaks.gov.uk
Maskell, Kevin (CON - Westerham and Crockham Hill)
cllr.maskell@sevenoaks.gov.uk
McGarvey, Philip (LD - Farningham, Horton Kirby and South Darenth)
cllr.mcgarvey@sevenoaks.gov.uk
Neal, Chris (CON - Cowden and Hever)
cllr.neal@sevenoaks.gov.uk
Orridge, Bob (CON - Edenbridge South and West)
cllr.orridge@sevenoaks.gov.uk
Parkin, Faye (CON - Fawkham and West Kingsdown)
cllr.parkin@sevenoaks.gov.uk
Pett, Alan (IND - Ash)
cllr.pett@sevenoaks.gov.uk
Piper, Robert (CON - Brasted, Chevening and Sundridge)
cllr.piper@sevenoaks.gov.uk
Purves, Elizabeth (LD - Sevenoaks Eastern)
cllr.purves@sevenoaks.gov.uk
Raikes, Simon (CON - Sevenoaks Town and St. John's)
cllr.raikes@sevenoaks.gov.uk
Ramsay, Brian (CON - Hartley and Hodsoll Street)
cllr.ramsay@sevenoaks.gov.uk
Sargeant, Janet (LAB - Swanley White Oak)
cllr.sargeant@sevenoaks.gov.uk
Scholey, John (CON - Edenbridge North and East)
cllr.scholey@sevenoaks.gov.uk
Searles, Tony (CON - Swanley Christchurch and Swanley Villlage)
cllr.searles@sevenoaks.gov.uk
Stack, Lorraine (CON - Kemsing)
cllr.stack@sevenoaks.gov.uk
Thornton, Julia (CON - Seal and Weald)
cllr.thornton@sevenoaks.gov.uk
Towell, Paul (CON - Sevenoaks Northern)
cllr.towell@sevenoaks.gov.uk
Underwood, John (LAB - Swanley St. Mary's)
cllr.underwood@sevenoaks.gov.uk

Williamson, Gary (CON - Halstead, Knockholt and Badgers Mount)
cllr.williamson@sevenoaks.gov.uk

POLITICAL COMPOSITION
CON: 45, LAB: 5, LD: 3, IND: 1

CABINET
Leader: Mr Peter Fleming
Deputy Leader / Planning and Improvement: Mrs Jill Davison
Community Wellbeing: Mrs Pat Bosley
Finance & Value for Money: Mr Brian Ramsay
Housing & Balanced Communities: Mrs Carol Clark
Safe Community: Mrs Elaine Bracken
The Cleaner & Greener Environment: Mrs Avril Hunter

COMMITTEE CHAIRS
Development Control: Mrs Ann Dawson
Environment Select: Mr Ian Bosley
Licensing: Mr Alan Pett
Performance and Governance: Mr Mark Fittock

SHEFFIELD CITY M
Sheffield City Council, 2-10 Carbrook Hall Road, Town Hall, Pinstone Street, Sheffield S1 2DB ☎ 0114 273 4567
🖳 www.sheffield.gov.uk

FACTS & FIGURES
Police Authority: South Yorkshire Police Authority
Health Authority: NHS Yorkshire & the Humber
Learning and Skills Council: Yorkshire and the Humber
Parliamentary Constituencies: Sheffield Brightside and Hillsborough, Sheffield South East, Sheffield, Central, Sheffield, Hallam, Sheffield, Heeley
EU Constituencies: Yorkshire and the Humber
Election Frequency: Elections are by thirds
Twinning: Anshan (China); Bochum (Germany); Donetsk (Ukraine)

PRINCIPAL OFFICERS
Chief Executive: Mr John Mothersole, Chief Executive, Room 126, Town Hall, Pinstone Street, Sheffield S1 2HH ☎ 0114 273 4002 🖷 0114 273 6644 ✉ john.mothersole@sheffield.gov.uk

Deputy Chief Executive: Mr Lee Adams, Deputy Chief Executive, Room 126, Town Hall, Pinstone Street, Sheffield S1 2HH ☎ 0114 273 6920 🖷 0114 273 4002
✉ lee.adams@sheffield.gov.uk

Access Officer / Social Services (Disability): Mr Brian Messider, Disability Access Officer, Howden House, Union Street, Sheffield S1 2SH ☎ 0114 273 4197
✉ brian.messider@sheffield.gov.uk

Architect, Building / Property Services: Mr Jim Breakley, Architect's Practice Manager, Carbrook Hall Road, Sheffield S9 2DB ☎ 0114 273 6021 ✉ jim.breakley@sheffield.gov.uk

Building Control: Mr Andrew Taylor, Chief Building Control Manager, Carbrook Hall Road, Sheffield S9 2DB ☎ 0114 273 4165
✉ andrew.taylor@sheffield.gov.uk

Catering Services: Mr Mark Cummins, Operations Manager, Town Hall, Pinstone Street, Sheffield S1 2HH ☎ 0114 205 3835
✉ mark.cummins@kier.gov.uk

Children / Youth Services: Dr Sonia Sharp, Executive Director of Children, Young People & Families, Floor 1, Town Hall, Pinstone Street, Sheffield S1 2HH ☎ 0114 273 5726
✉ sonia.sharpoffice@sheffield.gov.uk

Civil Registration: Mrs Samantha Williams, Register Office Manager, 2-10 Carbrook Hall Road, Town Hall, Pinstone Street, Sheffield S1 2DB ☎ 0114 203 9434 🖷 0114 275 9965
✉ samantha.williams@sheffield.gov.uk

PR / Communications: Mr Joe Fowler, Director of Performance & Communications, Level 3 Morfoot Building, Moorfoot, Sheffield S1 4PQ ☎ 0114 205 3126 🖷 0114 273 5033
✉ joe.fowler@sheffield.gov.uk

Community Planning: Mr Vince Roberts, Head of Locality Management, Floor 8, Redvers House, Union Street, Sheffield S1 2JQ ☎ 0114 273 6751 🖷 0114 273 6878
✉ vince.roberts@sheffield.gov.uk

Community Safety: Ms Sarah Banks, Head of Safer Communities, Sovereign House, Queen Street, Sheffield S1 2HH
☎ 0114 273 6605 🖷 0114 273 6878
✉ sarah.banks@sheffield.gov.uk

Computer Management: Mr Paul Green, Director of Information Services, Floor 4, Derwent House, 150 Arundel Gate, Sheffield S1 2JY ☎ 0114 205 3181 🖷 0114 273 5043
✉ paul.green2@sheffield.gov.uk

Consumer Protection and Trading Standards: Mr Philip Glaves, Principal Officer of Consumer Affairs, 2-10 Carbrook Hall Road, Town Hall, Pinstone Street, Sheffield S1 2DB ☎ 0114 273 6284 ✉ philip.glaves@sheffield.gov.uk

Contracts: Mr Barry Mellor, Director of Commercial Services, G41, Town Hall, Pinstone Street, Sheffield S1 2HH ☎ 0114 205 3928 🖷 0114 273 5015 ✉ barry.mellor@sheffield.gov.uk

Corporate Services: Ms Julie Bullen, Director of Customer Services, Howden House, Union Street, Sheffield S1 2SH ☎ 0114 273 6972 ✉ julie.bullen@sheffield.gov.uk

Corporate Services: Mr Neil Dawson, Head of Transport, Staniforth Road, Sheffield S9 3GZ ☎ 0114 203 7592
✉ neil.dawson@sheffield.gov.uk

Corporate Services: Mr Kevin Foster, Director of Transformation Services & Performance, Level 7 Morfoot Building, Moorfoot, Sheffield S1 4PQ ☎ 0114 205 3873
✉ kevin.foster@sheffield.gov.uk

Corporate Services: Mr Paul Green, Director of Information Services, Floor 4 Derwent House, 150 Arundel Gate, Sheffield S1 2JY ☎ 0114 205 3181 🖷 0114 273 5043
✉ paul.green2@sheffield.gov.uk

Corporate Services: Mr Nalin Seneviratne, Director of Property

& Facilities Management Services, Floor 11, Moorfoot Building, 1 Moorfoot, Sheffield S1 4PL ☎ 0114 273 4120 ✉ nalin.seneviratne@sheffield.gov.uk

Corporate Services: Mr Eugene Walker, Director of Finance, Level 7, Moorfoot Building, 1 Moorfoot, Sheffield S1 4PL ☎ 0114 273 5872 ✉ eugene.walker@sheffield.gov.uk

Customer Service: Ms Julie Bullen, Director of Customer Services, Howden House, Union Street, Sheffield S1 2SH ☎ 0114 273 6972 ✉ julie.bullen@sheffield.gov.uk

Customer Service: Ms Jo Hallam, Head of Customer First, Floor 2, Howden House, Union Street, Sheffield S1 2SH ☎ 0114 273 5077 ✉ jo.hallam@sheffield.gov.uk

Economic Development: Mr Edward Highfield, Director of Economy, Skills & Enterprise, Room 217, Town Hall, Pinstone Street, Sheffield S1 2HH ☎ 0114 205 3126 ✉ edward.highfield@sheffield.gov.uk

Education: Ms Maggie Williams, Deputy Executive Director of Children, Young People & Families, Town Hall, Pinstone Street, Sheffield S1 2SH ☎ 0114 293 0968 ✉ maggie.williams@sheffield.gov.uk

E-Government: Mr Paul Green, Director of Information Services, Floor 4, Derwent House, 150 Arundel Gate, Sheffield S1 2JY ☎ 0114 205 3181 🖷 0114 273 5043 ✉ paul.green2@sheffield.gov.uk

Electoral Registration: Mr John Tomlinson, Electoral Services Manager, Room LG42, Town Hall, Pinstone Street, Sheffield S1 2HH ☎ 0114 273 4091 🖷 0114 273 4092 ✉ john.tomlinson@sheffield.gov.uk

Emergency Planning: Mr Keith Bradley, Emergency Planning Officer, Bailey House, Rawmarsh Road, Rotherham S60 1TD ☎ 01709 255356 ✉ keith.bradley@sheffield.gov.uk

Energy Management: Ms Lynn Mapley, Acting Principal Engineer, Energy Unit, 2-10 Carbrook Hall Road, Town Hall, Pinstone Street, Sheffield S1 2DB ☎ 0114 273 5370 ✉ lynn.mapley@sheffield.gov.uk

Environmental / Technical Services: Mr Simon Green, Executive Director of Place, Room 212, Town Hall, Pinstone Street, Sheffield S1 2HH ☎ 0114 273 4201 ✉ simon.green@sheffield.gov.uk

Environmental Health: Mr Chris Green, Health Protection Manager, 2-10 Carbrook Hall Road, Sheffield S9 2DB ☎ 0114 205 3165 ✉ chris.green@sheffield.gov.uk

Estates, Property & Valuation: Mr Mohammed Mahroof, Strategic Asset Management Manager, 4th Floor, Cathedral Court, 1 Vicar Lane, Sheffield S1 1HD ☎ 0114 273 4510 ✉ mohammed.mahroof@kier.co.uk

European Liaison: Mr Vince Roberts, Head of Locality Management, Sovereign House, Queen Street, Sheffield S1 2HH ☎ 0114 273 6751 🖷 0114 273 6878 ✉ vince.roberts@sheffield.gov.uk

Events Manager: Ms Natasha Wagstaff, Events Manager, 2nd Floor, Yorkshire House, 66 Leopold Street, Sheffield S1 3RT ☎ 0114 273 6620 ✉ natasha.wagstaff@sheffield.gov.uk

Facilities: Mr Nalin Seneviratne, Director of Property & Facilities Management Services, Floor 11, Moorfoot Building, 1 Moorfoot, Sheffield S1 4PL ☎ 0114 273 4120 ✉ nalin.seneviratne@sheffield.gov.uk

Finance and Treasurer: Ms Laraine Manley, Executive Director of Resources, Corporate Finance, Town Hall, Pinstone Street, Sheffield S1 2HH ☎ 0114 273 4300 🖷 0114 273 5043 ✉ laraine.manley@sheffield.gov.uk

Fleet Management: Mr Neil Dawson, Head of Transport, Staniforth Road, Sheffield S9 3GZ ☎ 0114 203 7592 ✉ neil.dawson@sheffield.gov.uk

Grounds Maintenance: Mr Paul Billington, Director of Culture & Environment, Central Library, Surrey Street, Sheffield S1 1XZ ☎ 0114 273 4700 ✉ paul.billington@sheffield.gov.uk

Health and Safety: Mr Steve Clark, OD Manager of Safety & Employee Wellbeing, Room 209, Town Hall, Pinstone Street, Sheffield S1 2HH ☎ 0114 273 4796 ✉ steve.clark@sheffield.gov.uk

Highways: Mr John Charlton, Director of Street Force, Olive Grove Depot, Olive Grove Road, Sheffield S2 3GE ☎ 0114 273 6501 🖷 0114 273 6712 ✉ john.charlton@sheffield.gov.uk

Home Energy Conservation: Mr Robert Almond, Manager - SHAW Team, 2nd Floor, New Bank House, Sheffield S1 2XX ☎ 0114 273 4193 ✉ robert.almond@sheffield.gov.uk

Housing: Mr Derek Martin, Director of Housing, Enterprise & Regeneration, Howden House, 1 Union Street, Sheffield S1 2SH ☎ 0114 273 6639 ✉ derek.martin@sheffield.gov.uk

Housing: Ms Miranda Plowden, Director of Commissioning & Communities, New Bank House, Queen Street, Sheffield S1 2DW ☎ 0114 273 5396 ✉ miranda.plowden@sheffield.gov.uk

Housing Maintenance: Mr Neil Piper, Project Officer, New Bank House, Queen Street, Sheffield S1 2DW ☎ 0114 273 4617 🖷 0114 273 6010 ✉ neil.piper@sheffield.gov.uk

Local Area Agreement: Mr David Hewitt, Corporate Performance Officer, Level 3, West Wing, Morfoot Building, 1 Moorfoot, Sheffield S1 4PL ☎ 0114 273 5773 ✉ david.hewitt@sheffield.gov.uk

Legal: Ms Lynne Bird, Interim Director of Legal Services, Room G18, Town Hall, Pinstone Street, Sheffield S1 2HH ☎ 0114 273 4018 ✉ lynne.bird@sheffield.gov.uk

Leisure and Cultural Services: Mr Paul Billington, Director of Culture & Environment, Central Library, Surrey Street, Sheffield S1 1XZ ☎ 0114 273 4700 ✉ paul.billington@sheffield.gov.uk

Licensing: Mr Steve Lonnia, Chief Licensing Officer, Block C, Staniforth Road Depot, 609 Staniforth Road, Sheffield S9 3GZ

☎ 0114 205 3798 🖷 0114 273 5003 ✉ stephen.lonnia@sheffield.gov.uk

Lifelong Learning: Ms Jayne Hawley, Senior Manager, Learning, Skills & Employment, 145 Crookesmoor Road, Sheffield S6 3FP ☎ 0114 266 7503 🖷 0114 266 7092 ✉ jayne.hawley@sheffield.gov.uk

Lighting: Mr John Charlton, Director of Street Force, Olive Grove Depot, Olive Grove Road, Sheffield S2 3GE ☎ 0114 273 6501 🖷 0114 273 6712 ✉ john.charlton@sheffield.gov.uk

Lottery Funding, Charity and Voluntary: Mr Vince Roberts, Head of Locality Management, Floor 8 Redvers House, Union Street, Sheffield S1 2JQ ☎ 0114 273 6751 🖷 0114 273 6878 ✉ vince.roberts@sheffield.gov.uk

Member Services: Mr Jason Dietsch, Head of Democratic Services for Executive and Mayoral, G13, Town Hall, Pinstone Street, Sheffield S1 2HH ☎ 0114 273 4117 🖷 0114 273 6695 ✉ jason.dietsch@sheffield.gov.uk

Member Services: Mr Paul Robinson, Head of Democratic Services for Council and Members, G13, Town Hall, Pinstone Street, Sheffield S1 2HH ☎ 0114 273 4029 🖷 0114 273 6695 ✉ paul.robinson@sheffield.gov.uk

Parking: Mr John Bann, Head of Transport & Highways, Howden House, 1 Union Street, Sheffield S1 2SH ☎ 0114 273 6030 🖷 0114 273 6712 ✉ john.bann@sheffield.gov.uk

Partnerships: Mr Andy Howells, Assistant Commercial Director, Levil 3, East and West Wing, Moorfoot Building, 1 Moorfoot, Sheffield S1 4PL ☎ 0114 205 7303 ✉ andy.howells@sheffield.gov.uk

Personnel / HR: Ms Julie Toner, Director of Human Resources, Room 216C, Town Hall, Pinstone Street, Sheffield S1 2HH ☎ 0114 273 4081 🖷 0114 273 6657 ✉ julie.toner@sheffield.gov.uk

Planning: Mr David Caulfield, Head of Planning, Floor 5 Howden House, Union Street, Sheffield S1 2SH ☎ 0114 273 4188 ✉ david.caulfield@sheffield.gov.uk

Planning: Mr Simon Green, Executive Director of Place, Room 212, Town Hall, Pinstone Street, Sheffield S1 2HH ☎ 0114 273 4201 ✉ simon.green@sheffield.gov.uk

Procurement: Mr Barry Mellor, Director of Commercial Services, G41, Town Hall, Pinstone Street, Sheffield S1 2HH ☎ 0114 205 3928 🖷 0114 273 5015 ✉ barry.mellor@sheffield.gov.uk

Public Libraries: Mr Andrew Milroy, Acting Head of Libraries, Archives & Information, Central Library, Surrey Street, Sheffield S1 1XZ ☎ 0114 273 4751 🖷 0114 273 5009 ✉ andrew.milroy@sheffield.gov.uk

Recycling & Waste Minimisation: Ms Gillian Charters, Head of Waste Management, 2-10 Carbrook Hall Road, Town Hall, Pinstone Street, Sheffield S1 2DB ☎ 0114 203 7528 🖷 0114 273 7620 ✉ gillian.charters@sheffield.gov.uk

Regeneration: Mr Simon Ogden, Head of City Development Division, Floor 4, Howden House, 1 Union Street, Sheffield S1 2SH ☎ 0114 273 4189 🖷 0114 273 6204 ✉ simon.ogden@sheffield.gov.uk

Road Safety: Mr John Bann, Head of Transport & Highways, Howden House, 1 Union Street, Sheffield S1 2SH ☎ 0114 273 6030 🖷 0114 273 6712 ✉ john.bann@sheffield.gov.uk

Social Services: Mr Richard Webb, Executive Director of Communities, Room 208, Town Hall, Pinstone Street, Sheffield S1 2HH ☎ 0114 273 5167 ✉ richard.webb@sheffield.gov.uk

Social Services (Adult): Mr Robert Broadhead, Head of Service, Care & Support Management, Floor 8 Redvers House, Sheffield S1 2JQ ☎ 0114 273 5891 ✉ robert.broadhead@sheffield.gov.uk

Social Services (Children): Ms Jayne Ludlam, Deputy Executive Director of Children, Young People & Families, Room 140, Town Hall, Pinstone Street, Sheffield S1 2HH ☎ 0114 273 5116 🖷 0114 273 4981 ✉ jayne.ludlam@sheffield.gov.uk

Staff Training: Ms Julie Toner, Director of Human Resources, Room 216C, Town Hall, Pinstone Street, Sheffield S1 2HH ☎ 0114 273 4081 🖷 0114 273 6657 ✉ julie.toner@sheffield.gov.uk

Street Scene: Mr John Charlton, Director of Street Force, Olive Grove Depot, Olive Grove Road, Sheffield S2 3GE ☎ 0114 273 6501 🖷 0114 273 6712 ✉ john.charlton@sheffield.gov.uk

Sustainable Communities: Mr Richard Webb, Executive Director of Communities, Room 208, Town Hall, Pinstone Street, Sheffield S1 2HH ☎ 0114 273 5167 ✉ richard.webb@sheffield.gov.uk

Sustainable Development: Mr Andy Nolan, Director of Sustainable Development, 4th Floor Howden House, 1 Union Street, Sheffield S1 2SH ☎ 0114 273 6135 ✉ andy.nolan@sheffield.gov.uk

Tourism: Ms Jo Hallam, Head of Customer First, Floor 1, Howden House, Union Street, Sheffield S1 2SH ☎ 0114 273 5077 ✉ jo.hallam@sheffield.gov.uk

Town Centre: Mr Richard Eyre, Head of City Centre Management & Major Events, 2nd Floor, Yorkshire House, Leopold Street, Sheffield S1 2GY ☎ 0114 273 4704 ✉ richard.eyre@sheffield.gov.uk

Traffic Management: Mr John Bann, Head of Transport & Highways, Howden House, 1 Union Street, Sheffield S1 2SH ☎ 0114 273 6030 🖷 0114 273 6712 ✉ john.bann@sheffield.gov.uk

Transport: Mr Stephen Ash, Assistant Transport Services Managerof Fleet, Environment & Enforcement, Staniforth Road, Sheffield S9 3GZ ☎ 0114 203 7056 ✉ stephen.ash@sheffield.gov.uk

Transport Planner: Mr John Bann, Head of Transport & Highways, Howden House, 1 Union Street, Sheffield S1 2SH ☎ 0114 273 6030 🖷 0114 273 6712 ✉ john.bann@sheffield.gov.uk

Waste Collection and Disposal: Ms Gillian Charters, Head of Waste Management, 2-10 Carbrook Hall Road, Town Hall, Pinstone Street, Sheffield S1 2DB ☎ 0114 203 7528 🖷 0114 273 7620 ✉ gillian.charters@sheffield.gov.uk

Waste Management: Ms Gillian Charters, Head of Waste Management, 2-10 Carbrook Hall Road, Town Hall, Pinstone Street, Sheffield S1 2DB ☎ 0114 203 7528 🖷 0114 273 7620 ✉ gillian.charters@sheffield.gov.uk

Children's Play Areas: Mr Paul Billington, Director of Culture & Environment, Central Library, Surrey Street, Sheffield S1 1XZ ☎ 0114 273 4700 ✉ paul.billington@sheffield.gov.uk

MEMBERS OF THE COUNCIL (84)

***The Lord Mayor:* Campbell**, John (LAB - Richmond)
john.campbell@sheffield.gov.uk
***Deputy Lord Mayor:* Priestley**, Vickie (LD - Stannington)
vickie.priestley@sheffield.gov.uk
***Leader of the Council:* Dore**, Julie (LAB - Arbourthorne)
julie.dore@sheffield.gov.uk
***Deputy Leader of the Council:* Harpham**, Harry (LAB - Darnall)
harry.harpham@sheffield.gov.uk
Alston, Sue (LD - Fulwood)
sue.alston@sheffield.gov.uk
Anginotti, Sylvia (LD - Crookes)
sylvia.anginotti@sheffield.gov.uk
Armstrong, Jenny (LAB - Manor Castle)
jennifer.armstrong2@sheffield.gov.uk
Auckland, Ian (LD - Graves Park)
ian.auckland@sheffield.gov.uk
Bagshaw, Trevor (LD - West Ecclesfield)
trevor.bagshaw@sheffield.gov.uk
Baker, Penny (LD - Ecclesall)
penny.baker@sheffield.gov.uk
Baker, David (LD - Stannington)
david.baker@sheffield.gov.uk
Barker, David (LAB - Mosborough)
david.barker@sheffield.gov.uk
Bond, Nikki (LAB - Nether Edge)
nikki.bond@sheffield.gov.uk
Bowler, Isobel (LAB - Mosborough)
isobel.bowler@sheffield.gov.uk
Bragg, Janet (LAB - Hillsborough)
janet.bragg@sheffield.gov.uk
Bramall, Leigh (LAB - Southey)
leigh.bramall@sheffield.gov.uk
Brelsford, Alison (LD - Stocksbridge and Upper Don)
alison.brelsford@sheffield.gov.uk
Clement-Jones, Simon (LD - Beauchief and Greenhill)
simon.clement-jones@sheffield.gov.uk
Condliffe, Katie (LD - Stannington)
katie.condliffe@sheffield.gov.uk
Constance, Sheila (LAB - Firth Park)
sheila.constance@sheffield.gov.uk
Creasy, Jillian (GRN - Central)
jillian.creasy@sheffield.gov.uk
Crowther, Richard (LAB - Stocksbridge and Upper Don)
richard.crowther@sheffield.gov.uk
Curran, Ben (LAB - Walkley)
ben.curran@sheffield.gov.uk
Damms, Tony (LAB - Southey)
anthony.damms@sheffield.gov.uk
Davison, Roger (LD - Ecclesall)
roger.davison@sheffield.gov.uk
Downing, Tony (LAB - Mosborough)
tony.downing@sheffield.gov.uk
Drayton, Jackie (LAB - Burngreave)
jackie.drayton@sheffield.gov.uk
Dunn, Jayne (LAB - Broomhill)
jayne.dunn@sheffield.gov.uk
Fox, Denise (LAB - Birley)
denise.fox@sheffield.gov.uk
Fox, Terry (LAB - Manor Castle)
t.fox@sheffield.gov.uk
Frost, Rob (LD - Crookes)
rob.frost@sheffield.gov.uk
Furniss, Gillian (LAB - Southey)
gill.furniss@sheffield.gov.uk
Gibson, Neale (LAB - Walkley)
neale.gibson@sheffield.gov.uk
Hanson, Anders (LD - Nether Edge)
anders.hanson@sheffield.gov.uk
Hill, Keith (LD - Dore and Totley)
keith.hill@sheffield.gov.uk
Hurst, Adam (LAB - West Ecclesfield)
adam.hurst@sheffield.gov.uk
Hussain, Talib (LAB - Burngreave)
talib.hussain@sheffield.gov.uk
Hussain, Qurban (LAB - Nether Edge)
qurban.hussain@sheffield.gov.uk
Hussain, Ibrar (LAB - Burngreave)
ibrar.hussain@sheffield.gov.uk
Iqbal, Mazher (LAB - Darnall)
mazher.iqbal@sheffield.gov.uk
Johnson, Bob (LAB - Hillsborough)
robert.johnson2@sheffield.gov.uk
Jones, Steve (LAB - Gleadless Valley)
steve.jones@sheffield.gov.uk
Law, Alan (LAB - Firth Park)
alan.law@sheffield.gov.uk
Lawton, Martin (LAB - Richmond)
martin.lawton@sheffield.gov.uk
Lea, Mary (LAB - Darnall)
mary.lea@sheffield.gov.uk
Lindars-Hammond, George (LAB - Hillsborough)
george.lindars-hammond@sheffield.gov.uk
Lodge, Bryan (LAB - Birley)
bryan.lodge@sheffield.gov.uk
Maroof, Mohammed (LAB - Central)
mohammad.maroof@sheffield.gov.uk
McCann, Bob (LD - Graves Park)
bob.mccann@sheffield.gov.uk
McDonald, Cate (LAB - Gleadless Valley)
cate.mcdonald@sheffield.gov.uk
McGowen, Karen (LAB - Birley)
karen.mcgowan@sheffield.gov.uk
Meade, Alf (LAB - West Ecclesfield)
alf.meade@sheffield.gov.uk
Midgley, Pat (LAB - Manor Castle)
patricia.midgley@sheffield.gov.uk
Mirfin-Boukouris, Helen (LAB - Beighton)
helen.mirfin-boukouris@sheffield.gov.uk
Mohammed, Shaffaq (LD - Broomhill)
shaffaq.mohammed@sheffield.gov.uk
Munn, Roy (LAB - Beauchief and Greenhill)
roy.munn@sheffield.gov.uk
Murphy, Robert (GRN - Central)
robert.murphy@sheffield.gov.uk

Otten, Joe (LD - Dore and Totley)
joe.otten@sheffield.gov.uk
Price, Peter (LAB - Shiregreen and Brightside)
peter.price@sheffield.gov.uk
Reaney, Denise (LD - Graves Park)
denise.reaney@sheffield.gov.uk
Richards, Sioned-Mair (LAB - Shiregreen and Brightside)
sm.richards@sheffield.gov.uk
Rippon, Peter (LAB - Shiregreen and Brightside)
peter.rippon@sheffield.gov.uk
Rippon, Tim (LAB - Gleadless Valley)
tim.rippon@sheffield.gov.uk
Robson, John (LAB - Arbourthorne)
john.robson@sheffield.gov.uk
Rooney, Michael (LAB - Woodhouse)
michael.rooney@sheffield.gov.uk
Rooney, Lynn (LAB - Richmond)
lynn.rooney@sheffield.gov.uk
Rosling-Josephs, Chris (LAB - Beighton)
c.rosling-josephs@sheffield.gov.uk
Ross, Colin (LD - Dore and Totley)
colin.ross@sheffield.gov.uk
Sangar, Andrew (LD - Fulwood)
andrew.sangar@sheffield.gov.uk
Satur, Ray (LAB - Woodhouse)
raymond.satur@sheffield.gov.uk
Satur, Jackie (LAB - Woodhouse)
jackie.satur@sheffield.gov.uk
Saunders, Ian (LAB - Beighton)
ian.saunders@sheffield.gov.uk
Scott, Jack (LAB - Arbourthorne)
jack.scott@sheffield.gov.uk
Sharpe, Nikki (LAB - Walkley)
nikki.sharpe@sheffield.gov.uk
Sidebottom, Janice (LD - Fulwood)
janice.sidebottom@sheffield.gov.uk
Skelton, Clive (LD - Beauchief and Greenhill)
clive.skelton@sheffield.gov.uk
Smith, Geoff (LAB - Crookes)
geoff.smith@sheffield.gov.uk
Stimley, Diana (LD - Ecclesall)
diana.stimley@sheffield.gov.uk
Wattam, Stuart (LAB - Broomhill)
stuart.wattam@sheffield.gov.uk
Weatherall, Garry (LAB - East Ecclesfield)
garry.weatherall@sheffield.gov.uk
Weldon, Chris (LAB - Firth Park)
christopher.weldon@sheffield.gov.uk
Wilson, Steve (LAB - East Ecclesfield)
steven.wilson@sheffield.gov.uk
Wood, Philip (LAB - Stocksbridge and Upper Don)
philip.wood@sheffield.gov.uk
Wright, Joyce (LAB - East Ecclesfield)
joyce.wright@sheffield.gov.uk

POLITICAL COMPOSITION

LAB: 59, LD: 23, GRN: 2

CABINET

Leader: Ms Julie Dore
Deputy Leader / Homes & Neighbourhoods: Mr Harry Harpham
Business, Skills & Development: Mr Leigh Bramall
Children, Young People & Families: Ms Jackie Drayton
Communities & Inclusion: Mr Mazher Iqbal
Culture, Sport & Leisure: Ms Isobel Bowler
Environment, Waste & Streetscene: Mr Jack Scott
Finance & Resources: Mr Bryan Lodge
Health, Care & Independent Living: Ms Mary Lea

COMMITTEE CHAIRS

Audit: Mr Ray Satur
Licensing: Mr John Robson

SHEPWAY D

Shepway District Council, Civic Centre, Castle Hill Avenue, Folkestone CT20 2QY ☎ 01303 853000 🖷 01303 245978 ✉ sdc@shepway.gov.uk 💻 www.shepway.gov.uk

FACTS & FIGURES

Police Authority: Kent Police Authority
Health Authority: South East Coast Strategic Health Authority
Learning and Skills Council: South East
Parliamentary Constituencies: Folkestone and Hythe
EU Constituencies: South East
Election Frequency: Elections are of whole council
Twinning: Hythe: Berck-sur-Mer (France); Lydd: Etrechy (France); Poperinge (Belgium); Shepway: Boulogne-sur-Mer (France)

PRINCIPAL OFFICERS

Chief Executive: Mr Alistair Stewart, Chief Executive, Civic Centre, Castle Hill Avenue, Folkestone CT20 2QY ☎ 01303 853203 🖷 01303 245978 ✉ alistair.stewart@shepway.gov.uk

Deputy Chief Executive: Ms Kathryn Beldon, Corporate Director - Resources, Civic Centre, Castle Hill Avenue, Folkestone CT20 2QY ☎ 01303 853263 🖷 01303 853293 ✉ kathryn.beldon@shepway.gov.uk

Senior Management: Ms Kathryn Beldon, Corporate Director - Resources, Civic Centre, Castle Hill Avenue, Folkestone CT20 2QY ☎ 01303 853263 🖷 01303 853293 ✉ kathryn.beldon@shepway.gov.uk

Architect, Building / Property Services: Mr Paul Marshall, Property Manager, Civic Centre, Castle Hill Avenue, Folkestone CT20 2QY ☎ 01303 853439 🖷 01303 245978 ✉ paul.marshall@shepway.gov.uk

Building Control: Mr Nick Lewington, Principal Building Control Officer, Civic Centre, Castle Hill Avenue, Folkestone CT20 2QY ☎ 01303 853478 🖷 01303 258288 ✉ nick.lewington@shepway.gov.uk

Children / Youth Services: Mrs Tamasin Jarrett, Youth Development Officer, Civic Centre, Castle Hill Avenue, Folkestone CT20 2QY ☎ 01303 853277 🖷 01303 853502 ✉ tamasin.jarrett@shepway.gov.uk

PR / Communications: Mrs Sarah Smith, Media Officer, Civic Centre, Castle Hill Avenue, Folkestone CT20 2QY ☎ 01303 853461 🖷 01303 245978 ✉ sarah.smith@shepway.gov.uk

Community Planning: Mr Christopher Lewis, Head - Planning Services, Civic Centre, Castle Hill Avenue, Folkestone CT20 2QY ☎ 01303 853456 🖷 01303 858288 ✉ chris.lewis@shepway.gov.uk

Community Safety: Ms Jyotsna Leney, Crime Reduction Manager, Civic Centre, Castle Hill Avenue, Folkestone CT20 2QY ☎ 01303 853460 🖷 01303 853388 ✉ jyotsna.leney@shepway.gov.uk

Computer Management: Mr Steve Makin, Network Services Manager, Civic Centre, Castle Hill Avenue, Folkestone CT20 2QY ☎ 01303 853541 🖷 01303 853412 ✉ steve.makin@shepway.gov.uk

Consumer Protection and Trading Standards: Mr Steve Courts, Principal Environmental Health Officer, Civic Centre, Castle Hill Avenue, Folkestone CT20 2QY ☎ 01303 853295 ✉ steve.courts@shepway.gov.uk

Contracts: Mr Andy Rush, Contracts Manager, Civic Centre, Castle Hill Avenue, Folkestone CT20 2QY ☎ 01303 853271 🖷 01303 254978 ✉ andy.rush@shepway.gov.uk

Corporate Services: Mr Jeremy Chambers, Head - Strategic Projects, Civic Centre, Castle Hill Avenue, Folkestone CT20 2QY ☎ 01303 853248 🖷 01303 853388 ✉ jeremy.chambers@shepway.gov.uk

Customer Service: Mr Jason Couch, Head - Customer Contact, Civic Centre, Castle Hill Avenue, Folkestone CT20 2QY ☎ 01303 853389 🖷 01303 245978 ✉ jason.couch@shepway.gov.uk

Economic Development: Mr David Shore, Planning Policy & Economic Development Manager, Civic Centre, Castle Hill Avenue, Folkestone CT20 2QY ☎ 01303 853459 🖷 01303 853502 ✉ david.shore@shepway.gov.uk

E-Government: Mr Mark Coulthwaite, ICT Business Support Manager, Civic Centre, Castle Hill Avenue, Folkestone CT20 2QY ☎ 01303 853364 🖷 01303 853412 ✉ mark.coulthwaite@shepway.gov.uk

Electoral Registration: Mr Dylan Jeffrey, Democratic Services Manager, Civic Centre, Castle Hill Avenue, Folkestone CT20 2QY ☎ 01303 853283 🖷 01303 853388 ✉ dylan.jeffrey@shepway.gov.uk

Emergency Planning: Miss Amy Golder, Emergency Planning Officer, Civic Centre, Castle Hill Avenue, Folkestone CT20 2QY ☎ 01303 853254 🖷 01303 245978 ✉ amy.golder@shepway.gov.uk

Environmental / Technical Services: Mr Roger Walton, Head - Environmental Services, Civic Centre, Castle Hill Avenue, Folkestone CT20 2QY ☎ 01303 247385 🖷 01303 247385 ✉ roger.walton@shepway.gov.uk

Environmental Health: Mr Arthur Atkins, Principal Environmental Health Officer, Civic Centre, Castle Hill Avenue, Folkestone CT20 2QY ☎ 01303 853242 🖷 01303 852294 ✉ arthur.atkins@shepway.gov.uk

Estates, Property & Valuation: Mr Paul Marshall, Property Manager, Civic Centre, Castle Hill Avenue, Folkestone CT20 2QY ☎ 01303 853439 🖷 01303 245978 ✉ paul.marshall@shepway.gov.uk

Events Manager: Mrs Beverley Saunders, Events Officer, Civic Centre, Castle Hill Avenue, Folkestone CT20 2QY ☎ 01303 853264 🖷 01303 853548 ✉ beverley.saunders@shepway.gov.uk

Facilities: Mrs Sarah House, Senior Front Office Officer, Civic Centre, Castle Hill Avenue, Folkestone CT20 2QY ☎ 01303 853336 ✉ sarah.house@shepway.gov.uk

Finance and Treasurer: Ms Kathryn Beldon, Corporate Director - Resources, Civic Centre, Castle Hill Avenue, Folkestone CT20 2QY ☎ 01303 853263 🖷 01303 853293 ✉ kathryn.beldon@shepway.gov.uk

Grounds Maintenance: Mr Chris McCreedy, Contract Manager - Grounds, Ross Depot, Military Road, Folkestone CT20 3SP ☎ 01303 247370 🖷 01303 715250 ✉ chris.mccreedy@shepway.gov.uk

Health and Safety: Mr Arthur Atkins, Principal Environmental Health Officer, Civic Centre, Castle Hill Avenue, Folkestone CT20 2QY ☎ 01303 853242 🖷 01303 852294 ✉ arthur.atkins@shepway.gov.uk

Home Energy Conservation: Mr Mike Macdonald, Neighbourhood Renewal Officer, Civic Centre, Castle Hill Avenue, Folkestone CT20 2QY ☎ 01303 853280 🖷 01303 853502 ✉ mike.macdonald@shepway.gov.uk

Housing: Mr Bob Porter, Head - Communities, Civic Centre, Castle Hill Avenue, Folkestone CT20 2QY ☎ 01303 851750 🖷 01303 853774 ✉ bob.porter@shepway.gov.uk

Housing Maintenance: Ms Foronda Smith, Housing Manager, 3 / 5 Shorncliffe Road, Folkestone CT20 2SQ ☎ 01303 851719 🖷 01303 853775 ✉ foronda.smith@shepway.gov.uk

Legal: Ms Estelle Culligan, Principal Solicitor, Civic Centre, Castle Hill Avenue, Folkestone CT20 2QY ☎ 01303 853539 🖷 01303 853388 ✉ estelle.culligan@shepway.gov.uk

Licensing: Ms Sandra Francis, Licensing Manager, Civic Centre, Castle Hill Avenue, Folkestone CT20 2QY ☎ 01303 853421 🖷 01303 853294 ✉ sandra.francis@shepway.gov.uk

Member Services: Ms Lorraine Burley, Committee Services Manager, Civic Centre, Castle Hill Avenue, Folkestone CT20 2QY ☎ 01303 853411 🖷 01303 853388 ✉ lorraine.burley@shepway.gov.uk

Parking: Mr Fred Miller, Transportation Manager, Civic Centre, Castle Hill Avenue, Folkestone CT20 2QY ☎ 01303 853207 🖷 01303 853548 ✉ fred.miller@shepway.gov.uk

Partnerships: Mr David Shore, Planning Policy & Economic Development Manager, Civic Centre, Castle Hill Avenue, Folkestone CT20 2QY ☎ 01303 853459 🖷 01303 853502 ✉ david.shore@shepway.gov.uk

Personnel / HR: Mrs Andrina Smith, Strategic HR Manager, Civic Centre, Castle Hill Avenue, Folkestone CT20 2QY ☎ 01303 853405 🖷 01303 245978 ✉ andrina.smith@shepway.gov.uk

Planning: Mr Christopher Lewis, Head - Planning Services, Civic Centre, Castle Hill Avenue, Folkestone CT20 2QY ☎ 01303 853456 🖷 01303 858288 ✉ chris.lewis@shepway.gov.uk

Procurement: Mrs Margaret Creed, Procurement Manager, Civic Centre, Castle Hill Avenue, Folkestone CT20 2QY ☎ 01303 853377 🖷 01303 583293 ✉ margaret.creed@shepway.gov.uk

Recycling & Waste Minimisation: Mr Roger Walton, Head - Environmental Services, Civic Centre, Castle Hill Avenue, Folkestone CT20 2QY ☎ 01303 247385 🖷 01303 247385 ✉ roger.walton@shepway.gov.uk

Regeneration: Mr David Shore, Planning Policy & Economic Development Manager, Civic Centre, Castle Hill Avenue, Folkestone CT20 2QY ☎ 01303 853459 🖷 01303 853502 ✉ david.shore@shepway.gov.uk

Staff Training: Mrs Pat Holley, HR Business Partner - Organisational Development, Civic Centre, Castle Hill Avenue, Folkestone CT20 2QY ☎ 01303 853465 🖷 01303 245978 ✉ pat.holley@shepway.gov.uk

Town Centre: Mr John Barber, Town Centre Manager, The Management Suite, Bouverie West Shopping Centre, Folkestone CT20 1AU ☎ 01303 850522

Waste Collection and Disposal: Mr Roger Walton, Head - Environmental Services, Civic Centre, Castle Hill Avenue, Folkestone CT20 2QY ☎ 01303 247385 🖷 01303 247385 ✉ roger.walton@shepway.gov.uk

Waste Management: Mr Roger Walton, Head - Environmental Services, Civic Centre, Castle Hill Avenue, Folkestone CT20 2QY ☎ 01303 247385 🖷 01303 247385 ✉ roger.walton@shepway.gov.uk

MEMBERS OF THE COUNCIL (45)

***Chair:* Hollingsbee**, Jennifer (CON - North Downs West)
jennifer.hollingsbee@shepway.gov.uk
***Vice-Chair:* Carr**, Pamela (CON - Elham and Stelling Minnis)
pamela.carr@shepway.gov.uk
***Leader of the Council:* Bliss**, Robert (CON - Folkestone Sandgate)
robert.bliss@shepway.gov.uk
***Group Leader:* Copping**, Brian (O - Folkestone Foord)
brian.copping@shepway.gov.uk
Allen, Tristan (CON - Folkestone Park)
tristan.allen@shepway.gov.uk
Arnold, Emily (CON - Folkestone Harbour)
emily.arnold@shepway.gov.uk
Barker, Hugh (CON - Folkestone Harvey Central)
hugh.barker@shepway.gov.uk
Belcourt, Keren (CON - Hythe East)
keren.belcourt@shepway.gov.uk
Berry, Ann (CON - Folkestone Park)
annclr.berry@shepway.gov.uk
Bunting, George (CON - Folkestone Harvey West)
george.bunting@shepway.gov.uk
Carey, Susan (CON - Tolsford)
susan.carey@shepway.gov.uk
Clifton-Holt, Alan (CON - Romney Marsh)
alan.clifton-holt@shepway.gov.uk
Collier, John (CON - Folkestone Morehall)
john.collier@shepway.gov.uk
Dawson, Victoria (CON - Lydd)
victoria.dawson@shepway.gov.uk
Dearden, Malcolm (CON - Hythe Central)
malcolm.dearden@shepway.gov.uk
Dunning, Anthony (CON - Folkestone East)
anthony.dunning@shepway.gov.uk
Ewart-James, Alan (CON - Hythe Central)
alan.ewart-james@shepway.gov.uk
Goddard, Clive (CON - Lydd)
clive.goddard@shepway.gov.uk
Godfrey, David (CON - North Downs East)
david.godfrey@shepway.gov.uk
Grundy, Richard (CON - Folkestone Cheriton)
richard.grundy@shepway.gov.uk
Hayward, Stanley (CON - Hythe West)
stanley.hayward@shepway.gov.uk
Hills, Anthony (CON - Lydd)
anthony.hills@shepway.gov.uk
Holben, Janet (CON - Folkestone Sandgate)
janet.holben@shepway.gov.uk
Johnson, David (CON - Folkestone Harvey Central)
david.johnson@shepway.gov.uk
Lawrence, Shane (CON - New Romney Coast)
shane.lawrence@shepway.gov.uk
Love, Rory (CON - Folkestone Harvey West)
rory.love@shepway.gov.uk
Lyons, Michael (CON - Hythe Central)
michael.lyons@shepway.gov.uk
Marsh, Paul (O - Folkestone Foord)
paul.marsh@shepway.gov.uk
Martin, Phillip (CON - North Downs East)
phillip.martin@shepway.gov.uk
Monk, David (CON - North Downs West)
david.monk@shepway.gov.uk
Monk, Peter (CON - Folkestone Morehall)
peter.monk@shepway.gov.uk
Mullard, Terence (CON - Dymchurch and St Mary's Bay)
teremce.mullard@shepway.gov.uk
Newlands, Shirley (CON - Lympne and Stanford)
shirley.newlands@shepway.gov.uk
North, Alan (CON - Folkestone East)
alan.north@shepway.gov.uk
Owen, David (CON - Hythe East)
david.owen@shepway.gov.uk
Pascoe, Richard (CON - Folkestone Park)
richard.pascoe@shepway.gov.uk
Peacock, Paul (CON - Hythe West)
paul.peacock@shepway.gov.uk
Peall, Stuart (CON - North Downs East)
stuart.peall@shepway.gov.uk
Simmons, Peter (CON - New Romney Coast)
peter.simmons@shepway.gov.uk
Stephenson, David (CON - New Romney Town)
david.stephenson@shepway.gov.uk
Tillson, Russell (CON - Dymchurch and St Mary's Bay)
russell.tillson@shepway.gov.uk
Wallace, Susan (CON - Folkestone Harbour)
susan.wallace@shepway.gov.uk
West, Roger (CON - Folkestone Cheriton)

Wilkins, Roger (CON - Dymchurch and St. Mary's Bay)
roger.wilkins@shepway.gov.uk
Wimble, David (CON - New Romney Town)
william.wimble@shepway.gov.uk

POLITICAL COMPOSITION

CON: 43, O: 2

CABINET

Leader / Overall Strategy: Mr Robert Bliss
Communities: Mr Hugh Barker
Customer Contact: Mr Stuart Peall
Economic Development: Mr Alan Clifton-Holt
Environment: Mr Rory Love
Finance: Mr David Monk
Housing: Mrs Keren Belcourt
Localism: Mr Russell Tillson
Traffic Management & Parking: Mr Malcolm Dearden

COMMITTEE CHAIRS

Audit & Standards: Mr David Owen
Community Overview: Mr Paul Marsh
Development Control: Ms Janet Holben
Licensing: Mrs Shirley Newlands
Resources: Mr Peter Monk

SHETLAND S

Shetland Islands Council, Town Hall, Lerwick ZE1 0HB ☎ 01595 693535 🖷 01595 744509 ✉ info@shetland.gov.uk
💻 www.shetland.gov.uk

FACTS & FIGURES

Police Authority: Northern Joint Police Board
Health Authority: NHS Shetland
Learning and Skills Council: Scotland
Parliamentary Constituencies: Orkney and Shetland
EU Constituencies: Scotland
Election Frequency: Elections are of whole council
Twinning: Maloy (Norway)

PRINCIPAL OFFICERS

Chief Executive: Mr Alistair Buchan, Chief Executive, Office Headquarters, 8 North Ness, Lerwick ZE1 0LZ ☎ 01595 744500 ✉ chief.executive@shetland.gov.uk

Deputy Chief Executive: Ms Hazel Sutherland, Executive Director - Education & Social Care Department, Hayfield House, Hayfield Lane, Lerwick ZE1 0QD ☎ 01595 744001 🖷 01595 744010 ✉ hazel.sutherland@shetland.gov.uk

Architect, Building / Property Services: Mr Alan Rolfe, Team Leader Asset & Properties Manager, Office Headquarters, 8 North Ness Business park, Lerwick ZE1 0LZ ☎ 01595 744587 🖷 01595 744136 ✉ alan.rolfe@shetland.gov.uk

Architect, Building / Property Services: Mr Carl Symons, Acting Executive Manager - Building Services, Gremista, Lerwick ZE1 0PX ☎ 015959 744100 ✉ carl.symons@shetland.gov.uk

Best Value: Mr John Smith, Head of Service - Organisational Development, 32 Hillhead, Lerwick ZE1 0HB ☎ 01595 744513 ✉ john.r.smith@shetland.gov.uk

Building Control: Mr Iain McDiarmid, Executive Manager - Planning, Grantfield, Lerwick ZE1 0NT ☎ 01595 744813 🖷 01595 744804 ✉ planning@shetland.gov.uk

Catering Services: Mrs Valerie Hall, Catering & Cleaning Manager, Hayfield House, Hayfield Lane, Lerwick ZE1 0QD ☎ 01595 744129 🖷 01595 744010 ✉ val.hall@shetland.gov.uk

Civil Registration: Mrs Marilyn Williamson, Chief Registrar, County Buildings, Lerwick ZE1 0HB ☎ 01595 744562 🖷 01595 744585 ✉ registrar@shetland.gov.uk

Community Planning: Ms Emma Perring, Policy & Development Co-ordinator, 32 Hillhead, Lerwick ZE1 OEJ ☎ 01595 744537 🖷 01595 744514 ✉ emma.perring@shetland.gov.uk

Community Safety: Mrs Jenny Wylie, Community Safety Officer, Office Headquarters, 8 North Ness Buisness Park, Lerwick ZE1 0LZ ☎ 01595 744527 ✉ jenny.wylie@shetland.gov.uk

Computer Management: Mr Stuart Moncrieff, ICT Unit Manager, Garthspool, Lerwick ZE1 0NP ☎ 01595 744798 🖷 01595 744797 ✉ stuart.moncrieff@shetland.gov.uk

Consumer Protection and Trading Standards: Mr David Marsh, Service Manager - Trading Standards, Grantfield, Lerwick ZE1 0NT ☎ 01595 744862 🖷 01595 744804 ✉ trading.standards@shetland.gov.uk

Contracts: Mr Colin Black, Procurement Manager, Office Headquarters, 8 North Ness Business park, Lerwick ZE1 0LZ ☎ 01595 744595 🖷 01595 744136 ✉ colin.black@shetland.gov.uk

Direct Labour: Mr Carl Symons, Acting Executive Manager-Building Services, Gremista, Lerwick ZE1 0PX ☎ 01595 744100 ✉ carl.symons@shetland.gov.uk

Economic Development: Mr Neil Grant, Head - Development Services, Grantfield, Lerwick ZE1 0NT ☎ 01595 744968 🖷 01595 744961 ✉ mail.development@shetland.gov.uk

Education: Mrs Helen Budge, Director - Children Services, Hayfield House, Hayfield Lane, Lerwick ZE1 0QD ☎ 01595 744064 🖷 01595 744010 ✉ helen.budge@shetland.gov.uk

Electoral Registration: Mr Michael Forbes, Electoral Registration Officer, Charlotte House, Commercial Road, Lerwick, Shetland ZE1 0LX ☎ 01595 745700; 01595 745700 🖷 01595 745710; 01595 745710 ✉ ero@shetland.gov.uk

Electoral Registration: Mr Jan-Robert Riise, Executive Manager - Goverment & Law, Office Headquarters, 8 North Ness Business park, Lerwick ZE1 0LZ ☎ ; 01595 744551 🖷 01595 744585 ✉ legal.and.admin.services@shetland.gov.uk

Emergency Planning: Ms Ingrid Goll, Emergency Planning & Resilience Officer, 20 Commercial Road, Lerwick ZE2 0LX ☎ 01595 744740 ✉ emergency.planning@shetland.gov.uk

Energy Management: Mr John Simpson, Energy Manager, Grantfield, Lerwick ZE1 0NT ☎ 01595 744819 🖷 01595 744804 john.simpson@shetland.gov.uk

Environmental Health: Mrs Margaret Sandison, Executive Manager - Environmental Health & Trading Standards, Grantfield, Lerwick ZE1 0NT ☎ 01595 744841 margaret.sandison@shetland.gov.uk

Estates, Property & Valuation: Mr Alan Rolfe, Team Leader Asset & Properties Manager, Office Headquarters, 8 North Ness Business Park, Lerwick ZE1 0LZ ☎ 01595 744587 🖷 01595 744136 alan.rolfe@shetland.gov.uk

European Liaison: Miss Sally Spence, Project Manager, Solharus, 3 North Ness Business Centre, Lerwick ZE1 0LZ ☎ 01595 744915 🖷 01595 744961 sally.spence@shetland.gov.uk

Events Manager: Ms Nicola Halcrow, Events Co-ordinator, Solharus, 3 North Ness Business Park, Lerwick ZE1 0LZ ☎ 01595 744944 🖷 01595 744961 nicola.halcrow@shetland.gov.uk

Finance and Treasurer: Mr James Gray, Executive Manager - Finance, Town Hall, Lerwick ZE1 0HB ☎ 01595 744607

Fleet Management: Mr Michael Craigie, Executive Manager - Transport Planning, Office Headquarters, 8 North Ness Business park, Lerwick ZE1 0LZ ☎ 01595 744160 🖷 01595 744880 michael.craigie@shetland.gov.uk

Grounds Maintenance: Mr Jonathan Emptage, Team Leader - Cleansing Grounds & Burial Services, Grantfield, Lerwick ZE1 0NT ☎ 01595 744898 🖷 01595 744804 jonathan.emptage@shetland.gov.uk

Health and Safety: Mrs Fiona Johnson, Safety Manager, Office Headquarters, 8 North Ness Business park, Lerwick ZE1 0LZ ☎ 01595 744567 🖷 01595 744585 fiona.johnson@shetland.gov.uk

Highways: Mr Dave Coupe, Executive Manager - Roads, Gremista, Lerwick ZE1 0PX ☎ 01595 744104 dave.coupe@shetland.gov.uk

Home Energy Conservation: Mr John Simpson, Energy Manager, Grantfield, Lerwick ZE1 0NT ☎ 01595 744819 🖷 01595 744804 john.simpson@shetland.gov.uk

Housing: Mrs Anita Jamieson, Head - Housing, 6 North Ness Business Park, Lerwick ZE1 0LZ ☎ 01595 744360 🖷 01595 744395 housing@shetland.gov.uk

Housing Maintenance: Mrs Anita Jamieson, Head - Housing, 6 North Ness Business Park, Lerwick ZE1 0LZ ☎ 01595 744360 🖷 01595 744395 housing@shetland.gov.uk

Legal: Ms Susan Brunton, Team Leader - Legal, Office Headquarters, 8 North Ness Business park, Lerwick ZE1 0LZ ☎ 01595 744550 susan.brunton@shetland.gov.uk

Leisure and Cultural Services: Mr Neil Watt, Sport & Leisure Services Executive Manager, Hayfield House, Hayfield Lane, Lerwick ZE1 0QD ☎ 01595 744046 🖷 01595 744056 neil.watt@shetland.gov.uk

Licensing: Mr Jan-Robert Riise, Executive Manager - Goverment & Law, Office Headquarters, 8 North Ness Business Park, Lerwick ZE1 OLZ ☎ ; 01595 744551 🖷 01595 744585 legal.and.admin.services@shetland.gov.uk

Lifelong Learning: Ms Heather Moncrieff, Team Leader - Community, Town Hall, Lerwick ZE1 0HB ☎ 01595 693535 heather.moncrieff@shetland.gov.uk

Lighting: Mr Dave Coupe, Executive Manager - Roads, Gremista, Lerwick ZE1 OPX ☎ 01595 744104 dave.coupe@shetland.gov.uk

Member Services: Ms Leah Colyer, Administration Officer, Town Hall, Lerwick ZE1 0HB ☎ 01595 744511 leah.colyer@shetland.gov.uk

Parking: Mr Dave Coupe, Executive Manager - Roads, Gremista, Lerwick ZE1 0PX ☎ 01595 744104 dave.coupe@shetland.gov.uk

Personnel / HR: Ms Denise Bell, Human Resources Manager, 64 St Olaf Street, Lerwick ZE1 0EN ☎ 01595 744573 🖷 01595 743959 denise.bell@shetland.gov.uk

Planning: Mr Iain McDiarmid, Executive Manager - Planning, Grantfield, Lerwick ZE1 0NT ☎ ; 01595 744813 🖷 01595 744804 planning@shetland.gov.uk

Procurement: Mr Colin Black, Procurement Manager, Office Headquarters, 8 North Ness Business park, Lerwick ZE1 0LZ ☎ 01595 744595 🖷 01595 744136 colin.black@shetland.gov.uk

Public Libraries: Ms Karen Fraser, Library & Information Services Manager, Shetland Libary, Lower Hillhead, Lerwick ZE1 0EL ☎ 01595 743868 karen.fraser@shetland.gov.uk

Recycling & Waste Minimisation: Mrs Mary Lisk, Environmental Management Officer, Grantfield, Lerwick ZE1 0NT ☎ 01595 744818 🖷 ; 01595 744177 mary.lisk@shetland.gov.uk

Regeneration: Mr Neil Grant, Head - Development Services, Grantfield, Lerwick ZE1 ONT ☎ 01595 744968 🖷 01595 744961 mail.development@shetland.gov.uk

Road Safety: Mr Dave Coupe, Executive Manager - Roads, Gremista, Lerwick ZE1 0PX ☎ 01595 744104 dave.coupe@shetland.gov.uk

Social Services: Ms Hazel Sutherland, Executive Director - Education & Social Care Department, Hayfield House, Hayfield Lane, Lerwick ZE1 0QD ☎ 01595 744001 🖷 01595 744010 hazel.sutherland@shetland.gov.uk

Social Services (Adult): Ms Sally Shaw, Interim Director - Community Care, Kanterstead Office, Seafield House, Lerwick ZE1 0WZ ☎ 01595 744310 sally.shaw@shetland.gov.uk

Staff Training: Ms Fiona Stirling, Short Course Manager, North

Gremista Industrial Estate, Lerwick ZE1 0PX ☎ 01595 744 749 🖷 01595 744746 ✉ fiona.stirling@shetland.gov.uk

Sustainable Communities: Mr Douglas Irvine, Executive Manager - Economic Development, Solharus, 3 North Ness Business Park, Lerwick ZE1 0LZ ☎ 01595 744932 🖷 01595 744961 ✉ douglas.irvine@shetland.gov.uk

Sustainable Development: Mr Austin Taylor, Heritage Manager, Grantfield, Lerwick ZE1 0NT ☎ 01595 744833 ✉ john.taylor@shetland.gov.uk

Tourism: Mrs Linda Coutts, Project Manager, Solharus, 3 North Ness Business Manager, Lerwick ZE1 0LZ ☎ 01595 744943 🖷 01595 744961 ✉ linda.coutts@shetland.gov.uk

Town Centre: Mr Iain McDiarmid, Executive Manager - Planning, Grantfield, Lerwick ZE1 0NT ☎ 01595 744813 🖷 01595 744804 ✉ planning@shetland.gov.uk

Traffic Management: Mr Dave Coupe, Executive Manager - Roads, Gremista, Lerwick ZE1 0PX ☎ 01595 744104 ✉ dave.coupe@shetland.gov.uk

Transport: Mr Michael Craigie, Executive Manager - Transport Planning, Office Headquarters, 8 North Ness Buisness Park, Lerwick ZE1 0LZ ☎ 01595 744160 🖷 01595 744880 ✉ michael.craigie@shetland.gov.uk

Transport Planner: Mr Michael Craigie, Executive Manager - Transport Planning, Office Headquarters, 8 North Ness, Lerwick ZE1 0LZ ☎ 01595 744160 🖷 01595 744880 ✉ michael.craigie@shetland.gov.uk

MEMBERS OF THE COUNCIL (22)

Convener: **Bell**, Malcolm (NP - Lerwick North)
malcolm.bell@shetland.gov.uk
Burgess, Mark (IND - Shetland Central)
mark.burgess@shetland.gov.uk
Campbell, Peter (IND - Lerwick South)
peter.campbell@shetland.gov.uk
Cleaver, Gary (IND - North Isles)
gary.cleaver@shetland.gov.uk
Cooper, Alastair (IND - Shetland North)
alastair.cooper@shetland.gov.uk
Coutts, Steven (NP - North Isles)
steven.coutts@shetland.gov.uk
Duncan, Allison (IND - Shetland South)
allison.duncan@shetland.gov.uk
Fox, Billy (NP - Shetland South)
billy.fox@shetland.gov.uk
Henderson, Robert S (NP - North Isles)
robert.henderson@shetland.gov.uk
Manson, Andrea (NP - Shetland North)
andrea.manson@shetland.gov.uk
Ratter, Drew (NP - Shetland North)
drew.ratter@shetland.gov.uk
Robertson, Frank (IND - Shetland West)
frank.robertson@shetland.gov.uk
Robinson, Gary (IND - Shetland West)
gary.robinson@shetland.gov.uk
Sandison, Davie (NP - Shetland Central)
davie.sandison@shetland.gov.uk
Smith, George (NP - Shetland South)
george.smith@shetland.gov.uk
Smith, Theo (NP - Shetland West)
theo.smith@shetland.gov.uk
Smith, Cecil (IND - Lerwick South)
cecil.smith@shetland.gov.uk
Stout, Michael (NP - Lerwick North)
michael.stout@shetland.gov.uk
Westlake, Amanda (NP - Lerwick South)
amanda.westlake@shetland.gov.uk
Wills, Jonathan (IND - Lerwick South)
jonathan.wills@shetland.gov.uk
Wishart, Allan (IND - Lerwick North)
allan.wishart@shetland.gov.uk
Wishart, Vaila (NP - Shetland Central)
vaila.wishart@shetland.gov.uk

POLITICAL COMPOSITION

NP: 12, IND: 10

SHROPSHIRE UNITARY U

Shropshire Council, Shirehall, Abbey Foregate, Shrewsbury SY2 6ND ☎ 0345 678 9000 ✉ customer.service@shropshire.gov.uk 💻 www.shropshire.gov.uk

FACTS & FIGURES

Parliamentary Constituencies: Ludlow, Shrewsbury and Atcham, Shropshire North, Wrekin, The

PRINCIPAL OFFICERS

Chief Executive: Mrs Kim Ryley, Chief Executive, Shirehall, Abbey Foregate, Shrewsbury SY2 6ND ☎ 01743 252702 ✉ kim.ryley@shropshire.gov.uk

Assistant Chief Executive: Mr Michael Hyatt, Corporate Head of Strategic Planning, Shirehall, Abbey Foregate, Shrewsbury SY2 6ND ☎ 01743 252006 ✉ michael.hyatt@shropshire.gov.uk

Assistant Chief Executive: Ms Claire Porter, Corporate Head of Legal & Democratic Services Monitoring Officer, Shirehall, Abbey Foregate, Shrewsbury SY2 6ND ☎ 01743 252763 ✉ claire.porter@shropshire.gov.uk

Senior Management: Ms Jackie Kelly, Corporate Head of Organisational Development, Shirehall, Abbey Foregate, Shrewsbury SY2 6ND ☎ 01743 252804 ✉ jackie.kelly@shropshire.gov.uk

Senior Management: Ms Wendy Marston, Corporate Head of Business Improvement, Shirehall, Abbey Foregate, Shrewsbury SY2 6ND ☎ 01743 252004 ✉ wendy.marston@shropshire.gov.uk

Senior Management: Mr Tom McCabe, Corporate Director of Places, Shirehall, Abbey Foregate, Shrewsbury SY2 6ND ☎ 01743 255002 ✉ tom.mccabe@shropshire.gov.uk

Senior Management: Mr David Taylor, Corporate Director of People, Shirehall, Abbey Foregate, Shrewsbury SY2 6ND ☎ 01743 252402 ✉ david.taylor@shropshire.gov.uk

Access Officer / Social Services (Disability): Mr Stephen Chandler, Group Manager of Assessment & Eligibility, Shirehall,

Abbey Foregate, Shrewsbury SY2 6ND ☎ 01743 253704 ✆ stephen.chandler@shropshire.gov.uk

Architect, Building / Property Services: Mr Tim Smith, Group Manager of Facilities Management, Shirehall, Abbey Foregate, Shrewsbury SY2 6ND ☎ 01743 252411 ✆ tim.smith@shropshire.gov.uk

Best Value: Ms Wendy Marston, Corporate Head of Business Improvement, Shirehall, Abbey Foregate, Shrewsbury SY2 6ND ☎ 01743 252004 ✆ wendy.marston@shropshire.gov.uk

Building Control: Mr Ian Maddox, Building Control Manager, Shirehall, Abbey Foregate, Shrewsbury SY2 6ND ☎ 01743 255985 ✆ ian.maddox@shropshire.gov.uk

Children / Youth Services: Ms Karen Bradshaw, Group Manager of Learning & Skills, The Guildhall, Frankwell Quay, Shrewsbury SY3 8HQ ☎ 01743 254201 ✆ karen.bradshaw@shropshire.gov.uk

Children / Youth Services: Mr David Taylor, Corporate Director of People, Shirehall, Abbey Foregate, Shrewsbury SY2 6ND ☎ 01743 252402 ✆ david.taylor@shropshire.gov.uk

PR / Communications: Ms Nicki Beardmore, Communications Team Manager, Shirehall, Abbey Foregate, Shrewsbury SY2 6ND ☎ 01743 252134 ✆ nicki.beardmore@shropshire.gov.uk

Community Planning: Ms Steph Jackson, Group Manager of Customer Care & Involvement, Shirehall, Abbey Foregate, Shrewsbury SY2 6ND ☎ 01743 256127

Computer Management: Ms Wendy Marston, Corporate Head of Business Improvement, Shirehall, Abbey Foregate, Shrewsbury SY2 6ND ☎ 01743 252004 ✆ wendy.marston@shropshire.gov.uk

Contracts: Mr Mike Morris, Group Manager of Commissioning & Procurement, Shirehall, Abbey Foregate, Shrewsbury SY2 6ND ☎ 01743 253709 ✆ mike.morris@shropshire.gov.uk

Corporate Services: Ms Kathryn Edwards, Head of Safeguards, Shirehall, Abbey Foregate, Shrewsbury SY2 6ND ☎ 01743 254254 ✆ kath.edwards@shropshire.gov.uk

Corporate Services: Ms Helena Griffith, Head of Multi-Agency Teams, Shirehall, Abbey Foregate, Shrewsbury SY2 6ND ☎ 01743 254212 ✆ helena.griffith@shropshire.gov.uk

Corporate Services: Mr Phil Wilson, Head of Service Performance & Commercial Management, Shirehall, Abbey Foregate, Shrewsbury SY2 6ND ☎ 01743 282370 ✆ phil.wilson@shropshire.gov.uk

Customer Service: Ms Steph Jackson, Group Manager of Customer Care & Involvement, Shirehall, Abbey Foregate, Shrewsbury SY2 6ND ☎ 01743 256127

Customer Service: Ms Bobby Mulheir, Head of Customer Services, Shirehall, Abbey Foregate, Shrewsbury SY2 6ND ☎ 01743 252164 ✆ bobby.mulheir@shropshire.gov.uk

Economic Development: Mr Andy Evans, Entitlement & Resources Team Leader, Shirehall, Abbey Foregate, Shrewsbury SY2 6ND ☎ 01743 253033 ✆ andy.evans@shropshire.gov.uk

Education: Ms Jan Lane, Head of Behaviour Support & Inclusion, The Guildhall, Frankwell Quay, Shrewsbury SY3 8HQ ☎ 01743 254323 ✆ jan.lane@shropshire.gov.uk

Education: Mr David Taylor, Corporate Director of People, Shirehall, Abbey Foregate, Shrewsbury SY2 6ND ☎ 01743 252402 ✆ david.taylor@shropshire.gov.uk

Electoral Registration: Mrs Stacey Ijewsky, Elections Officer, Shirehall, Abbey Foregate, Shrewsbury SY2 6ND ☎ 01743 252334 ✆ stacey.ijewsky@shropshire.gov.uk

Electoral Registration: Ms Claire Porter, Corporate Head of Legal & Democratic Services Monitoring Officer, Shirehall, Abbey Foregate, Shrewsbury SY2 6ND ☎ 01743 252763 ✆ claire.porter@shropshire.gov.uk

Emergency Planning: Ms Angie Beechey, Risk & Insurance Manager, Shirehall, Abbey Foregate, Shrewsbury SY2 6ND ☎ 01743 252073 ✆ angela.beechey@shropshire.gov.uk

Environmental / Technical Services: Mr John Harrison, Head of Environment, Shirehall, Abbey Foregate, Shrewsbury SY2 6ND ☎ 01743 252565 ✆ john.harrison@shropshire.gov.uk

Environmental / Technical Services: Mr Tom McCabe, Corporate Director of Places, Shirehall, Abbey Foregate, Shrewsbury SY2 6ND ☎ 01743 255002 ✆ tom.mccabe@shropshire.gov.uk

Environmental Health: Mr Paul McGreary, Group Manager - Public Protection & Enforcement, Shirehall, Abbey Foregate, Shrewsbury SY2 6ND ☎ 01743 253868 ✆ paul.mcgreary@shropshire.gov.uk

Estates, Property & Valuation: Mr Tim Smith, Group Manager of Facilities Management, Shirehall, Abbey Foregate, Shrewsbury SY2 6ND ☎ 01743 252411 ✆ tim.smith@shropshire.gov.uk

Facilities: Mr Tim Smith, Group Manager of Facilities Management, Shirehall, Abbey Foregate, Shrewsbury SY2 6ND ☎ 01743 252411 ✆ tim.smith@shropshire.gov.uk

Finance and Treasurer: Ms Rachel Musson, Corporate Head of Finance & Governance, Shirehall, Abbey Foregate, Shrewsbury SY2 6ND ☎ 01743 252007 ✆ rachel.musson@shropshire.gov.uk

Highways: Mr Chris Edwards, Area Director - South, Shirehall, Abbey Foregate, Shrewsbury SY2 6ND ☎ 01746 255478 ✆ chris.edwards@shropshire.gov.uk

Local Area Agreement: Mr Michael Hyatt, Corporate Head of Strategic Planning, Shirehall, Abbey Foregate, Shrewsbury SY2 6ND ☎ 01743 252006 ✆ michael.hyatt@shropshire.gov.uk

Legal: Ms Claire Porter, Corporate Head of Legal & Democratic Services Monitoring Officer, Shirehall, Abbey Foregate, Shrewsbury SY2 6ND ☎ 01743 252763

claire.porter@shropshire.gov.uk

Leisure and Cultural Services: Mr George Candler, Assistant Director of Culture & Leisure, Shirehall, Abbey Foregate, Shrewsbury SY2 6ND ☎ 01743 255003 george.candler@shropshire.gov.uk

Licensing: Mrs Lynne Towers, Public Health & Safety Manager, Shirehall, Abbey Foregate, Shrewsbury SY2 6ND ☎ 01743 257492 lynne.towers@shropshire.gov.uk

Member Services: Ms Penny Chamberlain, Principal Committee Officer, Shirehall, Abbey Foregate, Shrewsbury SY2 6ND ☎ 01743 252729 penny.chamberlain@shropshire.gov.uk

Member Services: Ms Claire Porter, Corporate Head of Legal & Democratic Services Monitoring Officer, Shirehall, Abbey Foregate, Shrewsbury SY2 6ND ☎ 01743 252763 claire.porter@shropshire.gov.uk

Parking: Mr Hugh Dannatt, Group Manager of Traffic & Highway Engineering, Shirehall, Abbey Foregate, Shrewsbury SY2 6ND ☎ 01743 255469 hugh.dannatt@shropshire.gov.uk

Personnel / HR: Ms Jackie Kelly, Corporate Head of Organisational Development, Shirehall, Abbey Foregate, Shrewsbury SY2 6ND ☎ 01743 252804 jackie.kelly@shropshire.gov.uk

Planning: Mr Tom McCabe, Corporate Director of Places, Shirehall, Abbey Foregate, Shrewsbury SY2 6ND ☎ 01743 255002 tom.mccabe@shropshire.gov.uk

Procurement: Mr Mike Morris, Group Manager of Commissioning & Procurement, Shirehall, Abbey Foregate, Shrewsbury SY2 6ND ☎ 01743 253709 mike.morris@shropshire.gov.uk

Public Libraries: Mr George Candler, Assistant Director of Culture & Leisure, Shirehall, Abbey Foregate, Shrewsbury SY2 6ND ☎ 01743 255003 george.candler@shropshire.gov.uk

Social Services: Ms Kathryn Edwards, Head of Safeguards, The Guildhall, Frankwell Quay, Shrewsbury SY3 8HQ ☎ 01743 254254 kath.edwards@shropshire.gov.uk

Social Services (Adult): Mr Stephen Chandler, Group Manager of Assessment & Eligibility, Shirehall, Abbey Foregate, Shrewsbury SY2 6ND ☎ 01743 253704 stephen.chandler@shropshire.gov.uk

Social Services (Children): Ms Karen Bradshaw, Group Manager of Learning & Skills, The Guildhall, Frankwell Quay, Shrewsbury SY3 8HQ ☎ 01743 254201 karen.bradshaw@shropshire.gov.uk

Social Services (Children): Mr Chris Dennison, Service Manager, Shirehall, Abbey Foregate, Shrewsbury SY2 6ND ☎ 01743 250106 chris.dennison@shropshire.gov.uk

Social Services (Children): Ms Kathryn Edwards, Head of Safeguards, The Guildhall, Frankwell Quay, Shrewsbury SY3 8HQ ☎ 01743 254254 kath.edwards@shropshire.gov.uk

Social Services (Children): Mr Adam Scott, Service Manager, Shirehall, Abbey Foregate, Shrewsbury SY2 6ND ☎ 01743 250160 adam.scott@shropshire.gov.uk

Staff Training: Ms Jackie Kelly, Corporate Head of Organisational Development, Shirehall, Abbey Foregate, Shrewsbury SY2 6ND ☎ 01743 252804 jackie.kelly@shropshire.gov.uk

Street Scene: Mr George Candler, Assistant Director of Culture & Leisure, Shirehall, Abbey Foregate, Shrewsbury SY2 6ND ☎ 01743 255003 george.candler@shropshire.gov.uk

Traffic Management: Mr Tom McCabe, Corporate Director of Places, Shirehall, Abbey Foregate, Shrewsbury SY2 6ND ☎ 01743 255002 tom.mccabe@shropshire.gov.uk

Transport: Mr Ron Buzzacott, Highways & Transport Manager, Shirehall, Abbey Foregate, Shrewsbury SY2 6ND ☎ 01743 255469 ron.buzzacott@shropshire.gov.uk

Waste Management: Mr Larry Wolfe, Head of Waste Management, Shirehall, Abbey Foregate, Shrewsbury SY2 6ND ☎ 01743 255995 larry.wolfe@shropshire.gov.uk

MEMBERS OF THE COUNCIL (74)

***Leader of the Council:* Barrow**, Keith (CON - Oswestry South)
keith.barrow@shropshire.gov.uk

***Deputy Leader of the Council:* Hartley**, Ann (CON - Ellesmere Urban)
ann.hartley@shropshire.gov.uk

Church Stretton and Craven Arms: Vacant

Adams, Peter (CON - Bowbrook)
peter.m.adams@shropshire.gov.uk

Baker, Beverley (LD - Bagley)
beverly.baker@shropshire.gov.uk

Bannerman, Andrew (LD - Quarry and Coton Hill)
andrew.bannerman@shropshire.gov.uk

Barker, Timothy (CON - Burnell)
tim.baker@shropshire.gov.uk

Barnes, Charlotte (LD - Bishop's Castle)
charlotte.barnes@shropshire.gov.uk

Barrow, Joyce (CON - St Oswald)
joyce.barrow@shropshire.gov.uk

Bebb, Tudor (CON - Rea Valley)
tudor.bebb@shropshire.gov.uk

Bennett, Martin (CON - Oswestry East)
martin.bennett@shropshire.gov.uk

Benyon, William (CON - Oswestry East)
bill.benyon@shropshire.gov.uk

Biggins, Thomas (CON - Whitchurch North)
thomas.biggins@shropshire.gov.uk

Burgoyne, Karen (CON - Sundorne)
karen.burgoyne@shropshire.gov.uk

Bushell, Vernon (LAB - Harlescott)
vernon.bushell@shropshire.gov.uk

Butler, Gwilym (CON - Cleobury Mortimer)
gwilym.butler@shropshire.gov.uk

Caesar-Homden, Aggie (CON - Ruyton and Baschurch)
aggie.caesar-homden@shropshire.gov.uk

Calder, Karen (CON - Hodnet)
karen.calder@shropshire.gov.uk

Charmley, Stephen (CON - Whittington)

steve.charmley@shropshire.gov.uk
Chebsey, Anne (LD - Porthill)
anne.chebsey@shropshire.gov.uk
Clarke, Ted (LAB - Bayston Hill, Column and Sutton)
ted.clarke@shropshire.gov.uk
Dakin, Gerald (CON - Whitchurch South)
gerald.dakin@shropshire.gov.uk
Davenport, Steve (CON - St Martin's)
steve.davenport@shropshire.gov.uk
Davies, Andrew (CON - Cheswardine)
andrew.b.davies@shropshire.gov.uk
Davies, Trevor (LD - Gobowen, Selatty and Weston Rhyn)
trevor.davies@shropshire.gov.uk
Dee, Pauline (IND - Wem)
pauline.dee@shropshire.gov.uk
Durnell, Tony (CON - Monkmoor)
tony.durnell@shropshire.gov.uk
Evans, David (CON - Church Stretton and Craven Arms)
david.evans@shropshire.gov.uk
Evans, Roger (LD - Longden)
roger.evans@shropshire.gov.uk
Everall, John (CON - Tern)
john.everall@shropshire.gov.uk
Fraser, Hannah (LD - Abbey)
hannah.fraser@shropshire.gov.uk
Gillow, Brian (CON - Market Drayton East)
brian.gillow@shropshire.gov.uk
Hartin, Nigel (LD - Clun)
nigel.hartin@shropshire.gov.uk
Howe, Fiona (CON - Radbrook)
keith.roberts@shropshire.gov.uk
Huffer, Richard (LD - Clee)
richard.huffer@shropshire.gov.uk
Huffer, Tracey (LD - Ludlow East)
tracey.huffer@shropshire.gov.uk
Hughes, Roger (CON - Market Drayton West)
roger.hughes@shropshire.gov.uk
Hunt, Vincent (CON - Oswestry West)
vince.hunt@shropshire.gov.uk
Hurst-Knight, John (CON - Bridgnorth West and Tasley)
john.hurst-knight@shropshire.gov.uk
Jones, Jean (LAB - Broseley)
jean.e.jones@shropshire.gov.uk
Jones, Simon (CON - Shawbury)
simon.p.jones@shropshire.gov.uk
Kenny, Miles (LD - Underdale)
miles.kenny@shropshire.gov.uk
Kidd, Heather (LD - Chirbury and Worthen)
heather.kidd@shropshire.gov.uk
Lea, Christian (CON - Bridgnorth East and Astley Abbots)
christian.lea@shropshire.gov.uk
Lloyd, David (CON - Gobwen, Selattyn and Weston Rhyn)
david.lloyd@shropshire.gov.uk
Mellings, Christopher (LD - Wem)
chris.mellings@shropshire.gov.uk
Minnery, David (CON - Market Drayton West)
david.minnery@shropshire.gov.uk
Mosley, Alan (LAB - Castlefields and Ditherington)
alan.mosley@shropshire.gov.uk
Motley, Cecilia (CON - Corvedale)
cecilia.motley@shropshire.gov.uk
Mullock, Peggy (CON - Whitchurch North)
peggy.mullock@shropshire.gov.uk
Nicholls, Mary (LD - Highley)
mary.nicholls@shropshire.gov.uk
Nutting, Peter (CON - Copthorne)
peter.nutting@shropshire.gov.uk
Owen, Mike (CON - Meole)
mike.owen@shropshire.gov.uk
Parr, William (CON - Bridgnorth East and Astley Abbots)
william.parr@shropshire.gov.uk
Parsons, Elizabeth (LAB - Bayston Hill, Column and Sutton)
liz.parsons@shropshire.gov.uk
Pate, Malcolm (CON - Albrighton)
malcolm.pate@shropshire.gov.uk
Price, Malcolm (CON - Battlefield)
malcolm.price@shropshire.gov.uk
Roberts, David (CON - Loton)
david.roberts@shropshire.gov.uk
Shineton, Madge (IND - Cleobury Mortimer)
madge.shineton@shropshire.gov.uk
Tandy, Jon (LAB - Bayston Hill, Column and Sutton)
jon.tandy@shropshire.gov.uk
Taylor-Smith, Martin (CON - Ludlow South)
martin.taylor-smith@shropshire.gov.uk
Taylor-Smith, Rosanna (CON - Ludlow North)
rosanna.taylor-smith@shropshire.gov.uk
Tindall, Robert (CON - Brown Clee)
robert.tindal@shropshire.gov.uk
Tonkinson, Gordon (CON - Shifnal North)
gordon.tonkinson@shropshire.gov.uk
Walpole, Arthur (CON - Llanymynech)
arthur.walpole@shropshire.gov.uk
West, Stuart (CON - Shifnal South and Cosford)
stuart.west@shropshire.gov.uk
Whiteman, Milner (CON - Much Wenlock)
milner.whiteman@shropshire.gov.uk
Wild, Claire (CON - Severn Valley)
claire.wild@shropshire.gov.uk
Williams, Brian (CON - The Meres)
brian.williams@shropshire.gov.uk
Williams, Mansel (LAB - Belle Vue)
mansel.williams@shropshire.gov.uk
Winwood, Les (CON - Bridgnorth West and Tasley)
les.winwood@shropshire.gov.uk
Wood, Michael (CON - Worfield)
michael.wood@shropshire.gov.uk
Woodward, Tina (CON - Alveley and Claverley)
tina.woodward@shropshire.gov.uk
Wynn, Paul (CON - Prees)
paul.wynn@shropshire.gov.uk

POLITICAL COMPOSITION

CON: 50, LD: 14, LAB: 7, IND: 2, Vacant: 1

CABINET

Leader / Public Confidence: Mr Keith Barrow
Deputy Leader / Health & Wellbeing: Mrs Ann Hartley
Economic Growth & Prosperity: Mr Mike Owen
Education & Skills: Mr Simon Jones
Flourishing Shropshire Communities: Mr Gwilym Butler
Health & Wellbeing: Mr Stephen Charmley
Strategic Planning / Transport & Housing: Mr Malcolm Price

SLOUGH U

Slough Borough Council, St Martin's Place, Bath Road, Slough SL1 3UQ ☎ 01753 552288 🖷 01753 692499
💻 www.slough.gov.uk

LOCAL AUTHORITIES

FACTS & FIGURES

Police Authority: Thames Valley Police Authority
Health Authority: South Central Strategic Health Authority
Learning and Skills Council: South East
Parliamentary Constituencies: Slough, Windsor
EU Constituencies: South East
Election Frequency: Elections are by thirds
Twinning: Montreuil (France)

PRINCIPAL OFFICERS

Chief Executive: Ms Ruth Bagley, Chief Executive, St Martin's Place, Bath Road, Slough SL1 3UQ ☎ 01753 875000 🖷 01753 875058 ✉ ruth.bagley@slough.gov.uk

Senior Management: Ms Julie Evans, Strategic Director of Resources, Housing & Regeneration, St Martin's Place, Bath Road, Slough SL1 3UQ ☎ 01753 875301 🖷 01753 478657 ✉ julie.evans@slough.gov.uk

Senior Management: Mr Roger Parkin, Director of Customer & Transactional Services, Airways House, Langley Road, Slough SL3 7HF ☎ 01753 875207 ✉ roger.parkin@slough.gov.uk

Senior Management: Ms Jane Wood, Strategic Director of Community & Wellbeing, St Martin's Place, Bath Road, Slough SL1 3UF ☎ 01753 875751 ✉ jane.wood@slough.gov.uk

Architect, Building / Property Services: Mr Trevor Roffe, Director of Property Services, St Martin's Place, Bath Road, Slough SL1 3UQ ☎ 01753 787594 🖷 01753 875691 ✉ trevor.roffe@slough.gov.uk

Best Value: Mr Kevin Gordon, Assistant Director of Professional Services, St Martin's Place, Bath Road, Slough SL1 3UQ ☎ 01753 875213 🖷 01753 875659 ✉ kevin.gordon@slough.gov.uk

Building Control: Mr Sanjay Dhuna, Head of Building Control, Landmark Place, Windsor Road, Slough SL1 1HL ☎ 01753 875813 🖷 01753 875809 ✉ sanjay.dhuna@slough.gov.uk

Children / Youth Services: Ms Clair Pyper, Strategic Director of Education & Children's Services, St Martin's Place, Bath Road, Slough SL1 3UQ ☎ 01753 875704 🖷 01753 875012 ✉ clair.pyper@slough.gov.uk

Civil Registration: Ms Julie Evans, Strategic Director of Resources, Housing & Regeneration, St Martin's Place, Bath Road, Slough SL1 3UQ ☎ 01753 875301 🖷 01753 478657 ✉ julie.evans@slough.gov.uk

PR / Communications: Ms Kate Pratt, Communications Manager, St Martin's Place, Bath Road, Slough SL1 3UQ ☎ 01753 875088 ✉ kate.pratt@slough.gov.uk

Community Safety: Mr James Priestman, Head of Community Safety, St Martin's Place, Bath Road, Slough SL1 3UQ ☎ 01753 875556 🖷 01753 875419 ✉ james.priestman@slough.gov.uk

Computer Management: Mr Simon Pallett, Interim Head of Inofrmation Systems & Technology, St Martin's Place, Bath Road, Slough SL1 3UQ ☎ 01753 875095 🖷 01753 875897 ✉ simon.pallett@slough.gov.uk

Consumer Protection and Trading Standards: Mr Patrick Kelleher, Assistant Director of Public Protection, St Martin's Place, Bath Road, Slough SL1 3UQ ☎ 01753 875211 🖷 01753 875223 ✉ pat.kelleher@slough.gov.uk

Contracts: Ms Amardip Healy, Head of Legal Services, St Martin's Place, Bath Road, Slough SL1 3UQ ☎ 01753 875035 🖷 01753 875183 ✉ amardip.healy@slough.gov.uk

Corporate Services: Ms Julie Evans, Strategic Director of Resources, Housing & Regeneration, St Martin's Place, Bath Road, Slough SL1 3UQ ☎ 01753 875301 🖷 01753 478657 ✉ julie.evans@slough.gov.uk

Education: Mr Tony Browne, Head of School Services, St Martin's Place, Bath Road, Slough SL1 3UQ ☎ 01753 875717 ✉ tony.browne@slough.gov.uk

Education: Ms Clair Pyper, Strategic Director of Education & Children's Services, St Martin's Place, Bath Road, Slough SL1 3UQ ☎ 01753 875704 🖷 01753 875012 ✉ clair.pyper@slough.gov.uk

E-Government: Ms Julie Evans, Strategic Director of Resources, Housing & Regeneration, St Martin's Place, Bath Road, Slough SL1 3UQ ☎ 01753 875301 🖷 01753 478657 ✉ julie.evans@slough.gov.uk

Electoral Registration: Ms Melanie Dark-Gale, Election Services Manager, Town Hall, Bath Road, Slough SL1 3UQ ☎ 01753 477236 🖷 01753 875331 ✉ melanie.dark-gale@slough.gov.uk

Emergency Planning: Mr Dean Trussler, Emergency Planning Officer, St Martin's Place, Bath Road, Slough SL1 3UQ ☎ 01753 875131 🖷 01753 694515 ✉ dean.trussler@slough.gov.uk

Energy Management: Mr Martin Lower, Emergency Planning Officer, St Martin's Place, Bath Road, Slough SL1 3UQ ☎ 01753 474043 ✉ martin.lower@slough.gov.uk

Environmental Health: Mr Patrick Kelleher, Assistant Director of Public Protection, St Martin's Place, Bath Road, Slough SL1 3UQ ☎ 01753 875211 🖷 01753 875223 ✉ pat.kelleher@slough.gov.uk

Estates, Property & Valuation: Mr Trevor Roffe, Director of Property Services, St Martin's Place, Bath Road, Slough SL1 3UQ ☎ 01753 787594 🖷 01753 875691 ✉ trevor.roffe@slough.gov.uk

Events Manager: Ms Lynsey Hellewell, Communications Projects Officer, St Martin's Place, Bath Road, Slough SL1 3UQ ☎ 01753 875194 ✉ lynsey.hellewell@slough.gov.uk

Facilities: Ms Charan Dhillon, Head of Facilities Management, St Martin's Place, Bath Road, Slough SL1 3UF ☎ 01753 845945 🖷 01753 875691 ✉ charan.dhillon@slough.gov.uk

Finance and Treasurer: Ms Julie Evans, Strategic Director of Resources, Housing & Regeneration, St Martin's Place, Bath Road, Slough SL1 3UQ ☎ 01753 875301 🖷 01753 478657 ✉ julie.evans@slough.gov.uk

Health and Safety: Mr Robin Pringle, Health & Safety Manager, St Martin's Place, Bath Road, Slough SL1 3UQ ☎ 01753 875763 🖷 01753 478645 ✉ robin.pringle@slough.gov.uk

Highways: Ms Gillian Ralphs, Assistant Director of Transport & Planning, St Martin's Place, Bath Road, Slough SL1 3UQ ☎ 01753 575081 🖷 01753 875869 ✉ gillian.ralphs@slough.gov.uk

Housing: Mr Neil Aves, Assistant Director of Housing Services, The Centre, Farnham Road, Slough SL1 4UT ☎ 01753 875527 ✉ neil.aves@slough.gov.uk

Housing Maintenance: Mr Neil Aves, Assistant Director of Housing Services, The Centre, Farnham Road, Slough SL1 4UT ☎ 01753 875527 ✉ neil.aves@slough.gov.uk

Local Area Agreement: Ms Keren Bailey, Policy Officer, St Martin's Place, Bath Road, Slough SL1 3UQ ☎ 01753 875172 ✉ keren.bailey@slough.gov.uk

Legal: Ms Amardip Healy, Head of Legal Services, St Martin's Place, Bath Road, Slough SL1 3UQ ☎ 01753 875035 🖷 01753 875183 ✉ amardip.healy@slough.gov.uk

Leisure and Cultural Services: Mr Andrew Stevens, Assistant Director of Learning & Cultural Engagement, St Martin's Place, Bath Road, Slough SL1 3UQ ☎ 01753 875507 🖷 01753 875419 ✉ andrew.stevens@slough.gov.uk

Licensing: Ms Gillian Ralphs, Assistant Director of Transport & Planning, St Martin's Place, Bath Road, Slough SL1 3UQ ☎ 01753 575081 🖷 01753 875869 ✉ gillian.ralphs@slough.gov.uk

Lifelong Learning: Mr Philip Wright, Head of Lifelong Learning, St Martin's Place, Bath Road, Slough SL1 3UF ☎ 01753 875741 🖷 01753 875419 ✉ philip.wright@slough.gov.uk

Lighting: Mr Steve Brocklebank, Principal Engineer of Drainage & Lighting, St Martin's Place, Bath Road, Slough SL1 3UQ ☎ 01753 875625 🖷 01753 875660 ✉ steve.brocklebank@slough.gov.uk

Lottery Funding, Charity and Voluntary: Ms Surinder Jassal, Programme Manager of Voluntary Sector, St Martin's Place, Bath Road, Slough SL1 3UQ ☎ 01753 875597 🖷 01753 875419 ✉ surinder.jassal@slough.gov.uk

Parking: Mr Gary Sullivan, Team Leader of Traffic Development, St Martin's Place, Bath Road, Slough SL1 3UQ ☎ 01753 477337 ✉ gary.sullivan@slough.gov.uk

Partnerships: Ms Habibah Ibrahim, Programme Manager of Partnerships, St Martin's Place, Bath Road, Slough SL1 3UQ ☎ 01753 875538 🖷 01753 875419 ✉ habibah.ibrahim@slough.gov.uk

Personnel / HR: Mr Kevin Gordon, Assistant Director of Professional Services, St Martin's Place, Bath Road, Slough SL1 3UQ ☎ 01753 875213 🖷 01753 875659 ✉ kevin.gordon@slough.gov.uk

Planning: Mr Paul Stimpson, Head of Planning Policy & Projects, St Martin's Place, Bath Road, Slough SL1 3UQ ☎ 01753 875820 🖷 01753 875623 ✉ paul.stimpson@slough.gov.uk

Procurement: Ms Joanna Anderson, Assistant Director of Commissioning, Procurement & Shared Sevices, St Martin's Place, Bath Road, Slough SL1 3UF ☎ 01753 875285 🖷 01753 478645 ✉ joanna.head@slough.gov.uk

Public Libraries: Mr Geoff Elgar, Libraries Contracts Manager, St Martin's Place, Bath Road, Slough SL1 3UQ ☎ 01753 875578 ✉ geoff.elgar@essex.gov.uk

Recycling & Waste Minimisation: Ms Dympna Molloy, Head of Neighbourhood Enforcement, St Martin's Place, Bath Road, Slough SL1 3UQ ☎ 01753 875215 ✉ dympna.molloy@slough.gov.uk

Road Safety: Ms Caroline Beasley, Assistant Engineer of Road Safety, St Martin's Place, Bath Road, Slough SL1 3UF ☎ 01753 875641 ✉ caroline.beasley@slough.gov.uk

Social Services (Children): Ms Margaret Dennison, Assistant Director of Children & Families, St Martin's Place, Bath Road, Slough SL1 3UQ ☎ 01753 690901 ✉ margaret.dennison@slough.gov.uk

Staff Training: Ms Lisa Nuttall, Leadership Development Manager, St Martin's Place, Bath Road, Slough SL1 3UQ ☎ 01753 875198 🖷 01753 875764 ✉ lisa.nuttall@slough.gov.uk

Street Scene: Ms Julie Evans, Strategic Director of Resources, Housing & Regeneration, St Martin's Place, Bath Road, Slough SL1 3UQ ☎ 01753 875301 🖷 01753 478657 ✉ julie.evans@slough.gov.uk

Tourism: Ms Kate Pratt, Communications Manager, St Martin's Place, Bath Road, Slough SL1 3UQ ☎ 01753 875088 ✉ kate.pratt@slough.gov.uk

Traffic Management: Mr Alex Deans, Head of Highway Engineering, St Martin's Place, Bath Road, Slough SL1 3UQ ☎ 01753 575633 ✉ alex.deans@slough.gov.uk

Transport: Mr Joe Carter, Head of Transport, St Martin's Place, Bath Road, Slough SL1 3UQ ☎ 01753 575653 ✉ joe.carter@slough.gov.uk

Transport Planner: Ms Gillian Ralphs, Assistant Director of Transport & Planning, St Martin's Place, Bath Road, Slough SL1 3UQ ☎ 01753 575081 🖷 01753 875869 ✉ gillian.ralphs@slough.gov.uk

Waste Collection and Disposal: Ms Dympna Molloy, Head of Neighbourhood Enforcement, St Martin's Place, Bath Road, Slough SL1 3UQ ☎ 01753 875215 ✉ dympna.molloy@slough.gov.uk

Waste Management: Ms Dympna Molloy, Head of Neighbourhood Enforcement, St Martin's Place, Bath Road, Slough SL1 3UQ ☎ 01753 875215 ✉ dympna.molloy@slough.gov.uk

MEMBERS OF THE COUNCIL (41)

***Mayor:* Small**, Christine (LAB - Kedermister)
Christine.small@slough.gov.uk
***Deputy Mayor:* Bains**, Balvinder (LAB - Upton)
balvinder.bains@slough.gov.uk
***Leader of the Council:* Anderson**, Robert (LAB - Britwell)
rob.anderson@slough.gov.uk
***Deputy Leader of the Council:* Swindlehurst**, James (LAB - Cippenham Green)
james.swindlehurst@slough.gov.uk
***Group Leader:* Wright**, Anna (CON - Haymill)
anna.s.wright@hotmail.com
Abe, Frank (CON - Langley St. Mary's)
Abe14uk@hotmail.com
Aujla, Harpreet (LAB - Cippenham Meadows)
harps.aujla@googlemail.com
Bal, Joginder (LAB - Farnham)
joginder.bal@slough.gov.uk
Brooker, Preston (LAB - Haymill)
preston.brooker@slough.gov.uk
Carter, Martin (LAB - Britwell)
martin.carter@slough.gov.uk
Chaudhry, Shafiq (LAB - Central)
Shafiq.chaudhry@slough.gov.uk
Chohan, Nimrit (LAB - Cippenham Meadows)
nimritc@hotmail.com
Coad, Diana (CON - Langley St. Mary's)
Dianacoad@aol.com
Dar, Haqeeq (LAB - Wexham Lea)
haqeeq.dar@slough.gov.uk
Davis, Roger (LAB - Cippenham Green)
Roger_rebel40@hotmail.com
Dhaliwal, Sukhjit (LAB - Farnham)
cllr_sukhjitdhaliwal@hotmail.com
Dhaliwal, Arvind (LAB - Central)
Arvind.dhaliwal@slough.gov.uk
Dhillon, Antreev (LAB - Baylis and Stoke)
antreev.dhillon@slough.gov.uk
Grewal, Jagjit (LAB - Kederminster)
cllrjsgrewal@yahoo.co.uk
Hussain, Sabia (LAB - Chalvey)
sabiahussain786@gmail.com
Malik, Sandra (LAB - Wexham Lea)
sandymalik5@yahoo.co.uk
Mann, Mewa (LAB - Kederminster)
mewamann@yahoo.co.uk
Mann, Pavitar (LAB - Central)
pavy2@hotmail.com
Matloob, Fiza (LAB - Baylis and Stoke)
fizamatloob@yahoo.co.uk
Minhas, Harjinder (LAB - Upton)
harjinder.minhas@slough.gov.uk
Mittal, Bharat (LAB - Upton)
bbkdmittal@gmail.com
Munawar, Sohail (LAB - Farnham)
s_munawar@hotmail.co.uk
Nazir, Mohammed (LAB - Baylis and Stoke)
mohammed.nazir@slough.gov.uk
O'Connor, Patricia (LAB - Cippenham Green)
Patriciaoconnor_405@hotmail.co.uk
Pantelic, Natasa (LAB - Chalvey)
natasa.pantelic@slough.gov.uk
Parmar, Satpal (LAB - Cippenham Meadows)
Satpal.parmar@slough.gov.uk
Plenty, Ted (LAB - Foxborough)
ted.plenty@slough.gov.uk
Plimmer, Robert (LD - Foxborough)
plimmer_robert@hotmail.com
Rasib, Mohammed (LAB - Chalvey)
councillors@slough.gov.uk
Sandhu, Amrit (LAB - Langley St Mary's)
amrit_sl3@hotmail.co.uk
Shah, Ishrat (LAB - Foxborough)
ishrato8@hotmail.co.uk
Sharif, Mohamemd (LAB - Chalvey)
gbsharim@yahoo.co.uk
Smith, Dexter J. (CON - Colnbrook with Poyle)
dexter.j.smith@btinternet.com
Sohal, Paul (LAB - Wexham Lea)
Sohal51@aol.com
Strutton, Wayne (CON - Haymill)
w.strutton@sky.com
Walsh, James (LAB - Colnbrook with Poyle)
colnbrooklabour@hotmail.co.uk

POLITICAL COMPOSITION

LAB: 35, CON: 5, LD: 1

CABINET

Leader / Finance & Strategy: Mr Robert Anderson
Deputy Leader / Neighbourhoods & Renewal: Mr James Swindlehurst
Community & Leisure: Mr Sohail Munawar
Education & Children: Miss Natasa Pantelic
Environment & Open Spaces: Mr Satpal Parmar
Health & Wellbeing: Mr James Walsh
Opportunity & Skills: Ms Pavitar Mann
Performance & Accountability: Mr Shafiq Chaudhry

COMMITTEE CHAIRS

Educations & Children's Services: Mr Paul Sohal
Licensing: Mr Roger Davis
Overview & Scrutiny: Mr Mewa Mann
Planning: Mr Martin Carter

SOLIHULL — M

Solihull Metropolitan Borough Council, Solihull Metropolitan Borough Council, PO Box 18, Council House, Solihull B91 9QS
☎ 0121 704 6000 🖷 0121 704 6114 ✉ connectcc@solihull.gov.uk
🖳 www.solihull.gov.uk

FACTS & FIGURES

Police Authority: West Midlands Police Authority
Health Authority: NHS West Midlands
Learning and Skills Council: West Midlands
Parliamentary Constituencies: Meriden, Solihull
EU Constituencies: West Midlands
Election Frequency: Elections are by thirds
Twinning: Cholet (France); Main-Taunus Kreis (Germany)

PRINCIPAL OFFICERS

Chief Executive: Mr Mark Rogers, Chief Executive, Solihull Metropolitan Borough Council, Council House, Manor Square, Solihull B91 3QB ☎ 0121 704 6018 🖷 0121 704 8341
✉ mrogers@solihull.gov.uk

Architect, Building / Property Services: Mr Aiden Oakes, Corporate Facilities Manager, Solihull Metropolitan Borough Council, Council House, Manor Square, Solihull B91 3QB ☎ 0121 704 6805 ✉ aoakes@solihill.gov.uk

Best Value: Mr Ian Ash, Head of Corporate Performance, Policy & Information, Solihull Metropolitan Borough Council, Council House, Manor Square, Solihull B91 3QB ☎ 0121 704 6992 🖷 0121 704 8311 ✉ iash@solihull.gov.uk

Building Control: Mr Steve Elliott, Head of Building Control & Performance, Solihull Metropolitan Borough Council, Council House, Manor Square, Solihull B91 3QB ☎ 0121 704 6562 ✉ selliott@solihull.gov.uk

Catering Services: Ms Carrieanne Bishop, General Manager, Solihull Metropolitan Borough Council, Council House, Manor Square, Solihull B91 3QB ☎ 0121 704 6604 ✉ cabishop@solihull.gov.uk

Children / Youth Services: Ms Vanessa Bishop, Director for Children's Services, Solihull Metropolitan Borough Council, Council House, Manor Square, Solihull B91 3QB ☎ 0121 704 6734 ✉ vbishop@solihull.gov.uk

Civil Registration: Ms Emma Mayhew, Customer Services Manager, Solihull Metropolitan Borough Council, Council House, Manor Square, Solihull B91 3QB ☎ 0121 704 8667 ✉ emayhew@solihull.gov.uk

PR / Communications: Mrs Deborah Martin-Williams, Head of Communications, Solihull Metropolitan Borough Council, Council House, Manor Square, Solihull B91 3QB ☎ 0121 704 6772 🖷 0121 704 6008 ✉ dmartinwilliams@solihull.gov.uk

Community Planning: Mrs Lynda Hackwell, Head of Community & Economic Regeneration, Solihull Metropolitan Borough Council, Council House, Manor Square, Solihull B91 3QB ☎ 0121 704 8081 🖷 0121 704 8130 ✉ lhackwell@solihull.gov.uk

Community Safety: Ms Gillian Magee, Community Safety Manager, Solihull Metropolitan Borough Council, Council House, Manor Square, Solihull B91 3QB ☎ 0121 704 8093 ✉ gmagee@solihull.gov.uk

Computer Management: Mr Steve Halliday, Head of ICT, Solihull Metropolitan Borough Council, Council House, Manor Square, Solihull B91 3QB ☎ 0121 704 6196 ✉ shalliday@solihull.gov.uk

Consumer Protection and Trading Standards: Mr Jim Harte, Service Director for Transport, Highways & the Environment, Solihull Metropolitan Borough Council, Council House, Manor Square, Solihull B91 3QB ☎ 0121 704 6453 ✉ jharte@solihull.gov.uk

Contracts: Mrs Liz Welton, Corporate Procurement Manager, Solihull Metropolitan Borough Council, Council House, Manor Square, Solihull B91 3QB ☎ 0121 704 6088 🖷 0121 704 6081 ✉ lizwelton@solihull.gov.uk

Corporate Services: Ms A McGrory, Acting Head of Incomes & Awards, Solihull Metropolitan Borough Council, Council House, Manor Square, Solihull B91 3QB ☎ 0121 704 8110 ✉ amcgrory@solihull.gov.uk

Corporate Services: Mr Steve Sparkes, Head of Internal Audit Services, Solihull Metropolitan Borough Council, Council House, Manor Square, Solihull B91 3QB ☎ 0121 704 6282 ✉ ssparkes@solihull.gov.uk

Customer Service: Ms Emma Mayhew, Customer Services Manager, Solihull Metropolitan Borough Council, Council House, Manor Square, Solihull B91 3QB ☎ 0121 704 8667 ✉ emayhew@solihull.gov.uk

Economic Development: Mrs Lynda Hackwell, Head of Community & Economic Regeneration, Solihull Metropolitan Borough Council, Council House, Manor Square, Solihull B91 3QB ☎ 0121 704 8081 🖷 0121 704 8130 ✉ lhackwell@solihull.gov.uk

Education: Ms Vanessa Bishop, Director for Children's Services, Solihull Metropolitan Borough Council, Council House, Manor Square, Solihull B91 3QB ☎ 0121 704 6734 ✉ vbishop@solihull.gov.uk

E-Government: Ms Rebecca Jones, Website Manager, Solihull Metropolitan Borough Council, Council House, Manor Square, Solihull B91 3QB ✉ rjones@solihull.gov.uk

Electoral Registration: Mr Farooq Mirza, Elections Officer, Solihull Metropolitan Borough Council, Council House, Manor Square, Solihull B91 3QB ☎ 0121 704 6045 🖷 0121 704 6008 ✉ fmirza@solihull.gov.uk

Emergency Planning: Mr Michael Enderby, Emergency Planning Manager, Solihull Metropolitan Borough Council, Council House, Manor Square, Solihull B91 3QB ☎ 0121 704 8179 ✉ menderby@solihull.gov.uk

Environmental / Technical Services: Mr Jim Harte, Service Director for Transport, Highways & the Environment, Solihull Metropolitan Borough Council, Council House, Manor Square, Solihull B91 3QB ☎ 0121 704 6453 ✉ jharte@solihull.gov.uk

Environmental Health: Mr Jim Harte, Service Director for Transport, Highways & the Environment, Solihull Metropolitan Borough Council, Council House, Manor Square, Solihull B91 3QB ☎ 0121 704 6453 ✉ jharte@solihull.gov.uk

Estates, Property & Valuation: Mr Adrian Stringer, Senior Corporate Land & Property Manager, Solihull Metropolitan Borough Council, Council House, Manor Square, Solihull B91 3QB ☎ 0121 704 6132 ✉ adrian.stringer@solihull.gov.uk

European Liaison: Mrs Lynda Hackwell, Head of Community & Economic Regeneration, Solihull Metropolitan Borough Council, Council House, Manor Square, Solihull B91 3QB ☎ 0121 704 8081 🖷 0121 704 8130 ✉ lhackwell@solihull.gov.uk

Events Manager: Ms Becki Wood, Events & Marketing Manager, Solihull Metropolitan Borough Council, Council House, Manor Square, Solihull B91 3QB ☎ 0121 704 8752 ✉ bwood@solihull.gov.uk

Facilities: Mr Philip Mayhew, Director of Business Transformation, Solihull Metropolitan Borough Council, Council House, Manor Square, Solihull B91 3QB ☎ 0121 704 6652 🖷 0121 704 8129 ✉ pmayhew@solihull.gov.uk

Facilities: Mr Tony Richardson, Head of Facilities & Asset Management, Solihull Metropolitan Borough Council, Council House, Manor Square, Solihull B91 3QB ☎ 0121 704 6802 ✉ trichardson@solihull.gov.uk

Finance and Treasurer: Mr Paul Johnson, Director of Resources, Solihull Metropolitan Borough Council, Council House, Manor Square, Solihull B91 3QB ☎ 0121 704 6194 ✉ pjohnson@solihull.gov.uk

Health and Safety: Mrs Catherine Halford, Governance Services Manager, Solihull Metropolitan Borough Council, Council House, Manor Square, Solihull B91 3QB ☎ 0121 704 8396 🖷 0121 704 8311 ✉ chalford@solihull.gov.uk

Highways: Mr Jim Harte, Service Director for Transport, Highways & the Environment, Solihull Metropolitan Borough Council, Council House, Manor Square, Solihull B91 3QB ☎ 0121 704 6453 ✉ jharte@solihull.gov.uk

Home Energy Conservation: Mr Robin Dunlevy, Energy Conservation Officer, Solihull Metropolitan Borough Council, Council House, Manor Square, Solihull B91 3QB ☎ 0121 704 6450 🖷 0121 704 8738 ✉ rdunlevy@solihull.gov.uk

Housing: Mr Steve Boyd, Chief Executive for Solihull Community Housing, Endeavour House, Meriden Drive, Solihull B37 6BX ☎ 0121 779 8810 🖷 0121 779 8820 ✉ sboyd@solihullcommunityhousing.org.uk

Housing Maintenance: Mr Steve Boyd, Chief Executive for Solihull Community Housing, Endeavour House, Meriden Drive, Solihull B37 6BX ☎ 0121 779 8810 🖷 0121 779 8820 ✉ sboyd@solihullcommunityhousing.org.uk

Local Area Agreement: Ms Melanie Lockey, Solihull Partnership Commissiong Manager, Solihull Metropolitan Borough Council, Council House, Manor Square, Solihull B91 3QB ☎ 0121 704 8403 ✉ mlockey@solihull.gov.uk

Legal: Mr Philip Lloyd-Williams, Director for Governance, Solihull Metropolitan Borough Council, Council House, Manor Square, Solihull B91 3QB ☎ 0121 704 6721 🖷 0121 704 8341 ✉ plwilliams@solihull.gov.uk

Leisure and Cultural Services: Mr Nick Garnett, Leisure & Arts Services Manager, Central Library, Homer Road, Solihull B91 3RG ☎ 0121 704 6996 🖷 0121 704 6991 ✉ ngarnett@solihull.gov.uk

Licensing: Mr Jim Harte, Service Director for Transport, Highways & the Environment, Solihull Metropolitan Borough Council, Council House, Manor Square, Solihull B91 3QB ☎ 0121 704 6453 ✉ jharte@solihull.gov.uk

Lifelong Learning: Ms Tracey Cox, Head of Library & Information Services, Solihull Central Library, Homer Road, Solihull B91 3RG ☎ 0121 704 6945 ✉ tcox@solihull.gov.uk

Lighting: Ms Debbie Grindrod, Street Lighting Manager, Solihull Metropolitan Borough Council, Moat Lane Depot, Moat Lane, Solihull B91 2LW ✉ dgrindrod@solihull.gov.uk

Lottery Funding, Charity and Voluntary: Mrs Lynda Hackwell, Head of Community & Economic Regeneration, Solihull Metropolitan Borough Council, Council House, Manor Square, Solihull B91 3QB ☎ 0121 704 8081 🖷 0121 704 8130 ✉ lhackwell@solihull.gov.uk

Member Services: Ms Deborah Merry, Democratic Services Manager, Solihull Metropolitan Borough Council, Council House, Manor Square, Solihull B91 3QB ☎ 0121 704 6022 🖷 0121 704 6008 ✉ dmerry@solihull.gov.uk

Parking: Mr Toby Wilson, Parking Services Manager, Solihull Metropolitan Borough Council, Council House, Manor Square, Solihull B91 3QB ☎ 0121 704 6111 🖷 0121 704 6929 ✉ twilson@solihull.gov.uk

Partnerships: Ms Melanie Lockey, Solihull Partnership Commissiong Manager, Solihull Metropolitan Borough Council, Council House, Manor Square, Solihull B91 3QB ☎ 0121 704 8403 ✉ mlockey@solihull.gov.uk

Personnel / HR: Mr Adrian Cattell, Head of HR, Solihull Metropolitan Borough Council, Council House, Manor Square, Solihull B91 3QB ☎ 0121 704 6038 🖷 0121 704 6074 ✉ acattell@solihull.gov.uk

Planning: Mr Gary Palmer, Head of Design & Development, Solihull Central Library, Homer Road, Solihull B91 3RG ☎ 0121 704 6372 ✉ gpalmer@solihull.gov.uk

Procurement: Mrs Liz Welton, Corporate Procurement Manager, Solihull Metropolitan Borough Council, Council House, Manor Square, Solihull B91 3QB ☎ 0121 704 6088 🖷 0121 704 6081 ✉ lizwelton@solihull.gov.uk

Public Libraries: Ms Tracey Cox, Head of Library & Information Services, Solihull Central Library, Homer Road, Solihull B91 3RG ☎ 0121 704 6945 ✉ tcox@solihull.gov.uk

Recycling & Waste Minimisation: Mr Steve Hawkins, Senior Waste & Recycling Officer, Solihull Metropolitan Borough Council, Moat Lane Depot, Moat Lane, Solihull B91 2LW ☎ 0121 704 8520 ✉ shawkins@solihull.gov.uk

Regeneration: Ms Becke Ayres, Regeneration Manager, Endeavour House, Meriden Drive, Solihull B37 6BX ☎ 0121 704 8773

Road Safety: Ms Kathryn Hemmings, Neighbourhood Manager, Solihull Metropolitan Borough Council, Council House, Manor Square, Solihull B91 3QB ☎ 0121 704 6358 🖷 0121 704 6929 ✉ kathrynhemmings@solihull.gov.uk

Social Services (Adult): Mr Dave Martin, Interim Director for Adult Social Services, Solihull Metropolitan Borough Council, Council House, Manor Square, Solihull B91 3QB ☎ 0121 704 6124 ✉ dave.martin@solihull.gov.uk

Social Services (Children): Ms Vanessa Bishop, Director for Children's Services, Solihull Metropolitan Borough Council, Council House, Manor Square, Solihull B91 3QB ☎ 0121 704 6734 vbishop@solihull.gov.uk

Staff Training: Ms Sarah Blunt, Organisational Development Manager, Solihull Metropolitan Borough Council, Council House, Manor Square, Solihull B91 3QB ☎ 0121 704 6539 sblunt@solihull.gov.uk

Street Scene: Mr Alan Brown, Environmental Manager, Solihull Metropolitan Borough Council, Council House, Manor Square, Solihull B91 3QB ☎ 0121 704 8334 albrown@solihull.gov.uk

Sustainable Development: Mr David Biss, Environmental Co-ordinator, Solihull Metropolitan Borough Council, Council House, Manor Square, Solihull B91 3QB dbiss@solihull.gov.uk

Tourism: Ms Tracey Cox, Head of Library & Information Services, Solihull Central Library, Homer Road, Solihull B91 3RG ☎ 0121 704 6945 tcox@solihull.gov.uk

Town Centre: Ms Becki Wood, Events & Marketing Manager, Solihull Metropolitan Borough Council, Council House, Manor Square, Solihull B91 3QB ☎ 0121 704 8752 bwood@solihull.gov.uk

Traffic Management: Mr David Lechmere, Principal Engineer for Road Safety, Solihull Metropolitan Borough Council, Council House, Manor Square, Solihull B91 3QB ☎ 0121 704 6475 🖷 0121 704 6929 dlechmere@solihull.gov.uk

Transport: Mr David Strang, Transport Policy Manager, Solihull Metropolitan Borough Council, Council House, Manor Square, Solihull B91 3QB ☎ 0121 704 6678 dstrang@solihull.gov.uk

Transport Planner: Mr Danny Gouveia, Transport Planner & Engineer, Solihull Metropolitan Borough Council, Council House, Manor Square, Solihull B91 3QB ☎ 0121 704 6560 🖷 0121 704 6929 dgouveia@solihull.gov.uk

Waste Collection and Disposal: Mr Steve Hawkins, Senior Waste & Recycling Officer, Solihull Metropolitan Borough Council, Moat Lane Depot, Moat Lane, Solihull B91 3QB ☎ 0121 704 8520 shawkins@solihull.gov.uk

Waste Management: Mr Alan Brown, Environmental Manager, Solihull Metropolitan Borough Council, Moat Lane Depot, Moat Lane, Solihull B91 2LW ☎ 0121 704 8334 albrown@solihull.gov.uk

MEMBERS OF THE COUNCIL (50)

Mayor: **Hawkins**, Ken (CON - Blythe)
khawkins@solihull.gov.uk
Deputy Mayor: **Chamberlain**, Irene (LD - Lyndon)
ichamberlain@solihull.gov.uk
Leader of the Council: **Meeson**, Ken (CON - Dorridge and Hockley Heath)
kmeeson@solihull.gov.uk
Group Leader: **Hedley**, Ian (LD - Shirley East)
ihedley@solihull.gov.uk
Group Leader: **Jamieson**, David (LAB - Kingshurst and Fordbridge)
djamieson@solihull.gov.uk
Group Leader: **Macnaughton**, Karl (GRN - Chelmsley Wood)
kmacnaughton@solihull.gov.uk
Allen, Howard (GRN - Shirley West)
hallen@solihull.gov.uk
Allport, Gary (CON - Shirley South)
gallport@solihull.gov.uk
Allsopp, Ken (CON - Meriden)
kallsopp@solihull.gov.uk
Bell, David (CON - Meriden)
dbell@aolihull.gov.uk
Brown, Linda (R - Blythe)
linda.brown@solihull.gov.uk
Burgess, Brian (CON - Blythe)
bburgess@solihull.gov.uk
Cornock, Don (LAB - Smiths Wood)
dcornock@solihull.gov.uk
Courts, Ian (CON - Dorridge and Hockley Heath)
icourts@solihull.gov.uk
Davies, Norman (LD - Olton)
ndavies@solihull.gov.uk
Davis, Stuart (CON - St Alphege)
sdavis@solihull.gov.uk
Dicicco, Tony (CON - Meriden)
tony.dicicco@solihull.gov.uk
Doyle, Peter (CON - Shirley South)
pedoyle@solihull.gov.uk
Grinsell, Karen (CON - Shirley East)
karen.grinsall@solihull.gov.uk
Hamilton, Jean (LD - Elmdon)
jeanhamilton@solihull.gov.uk
Hewings, Martin (LD - Elmdon)
mhewings@solihull.gov.uk
Hodgson, Andrew (LD - Shirley South)
ahodgson@solihull.gov.uk
Hogarth, Peter (CON - Silhill)
phogarth@solihull.gov.uk
Holl-Allen, Diana (CON - Knowle)
dhollallen@solihull.gov.uk
Hulland, Robert (CON - Sihill)
rhulland@solihull.gov.uk
Mackiewicz, Andrew (CON - Dorridge and Hockley Heath)
amackiewicz@solihull.gov.uk
Martin, Alan (CON - Bickenhill)
amartin@solihull.gov.uk
Nash, Alan (LAB - Kingshurst and Fordbridge)
fnash@solihull.gov.uk
O'Kane, Claire Louise (LD - Olton)
claire.okane@solihull.gov.uk
Parker, Mark (CON - Shirley East)
mparker@solihull.gov.uk
Pittaway, Sheila (CON - Silhill)
spittaway@solihull.gov.uk
Potts, Jeffrey (CON - Knowle)
jpotts@solihull.gov.uk
Rebeiro, Alan (CON - Knowle)
arebeiro@solihull.gov.uk
Richards, Ted (CON - Castle Bromwich)
grichards@solihull.gov.uk
Robinson, Michael (CON - Castle Bromwich)
mrobinson@solihull.gov.uk
Rushen, Ken (LD - Lyndon)
krushen@solihull.gov.uk
Ryan, Jim (CON - Bickenhill)

jiryan@solihull.gov.uk
Sheridan, Michael (GRN - Smith's Wood)
msheridan@solihull.gov.uk
Slater, Glenis (LD - Elmdon)
gslater@solhihull.gov.uk
Slater, Simon (LAB - Shirley West)
sslater@solihull.gov.uk
Sleigh, Robert (CON - Bickenhill)
rsleigh@solihull.gov.uk
Sleigh, Gail (CON - Castle Bromwich)
gsleigh@solihull.gov.uk
Stephens, Nick (LAB - Chelmsey Wood)
nickstephens@solihull.gov.uk
Tedd, Teresa (LD - Lyndon)
ttedd@solihull.gov.uk
Tildesley, Joe (CON - St Alphege)
joetildesley@solihull.gov.uk
Tildesley, Hannah (CON - Shirley West)
hannahtildesley@solihull.gov.uk
Walters, Alison (GRN - Smiths Wood)
awalters@solihull.gov.uk
Wild, Kate (CON - St Alphege)
kwild@solihull.gov.uk
Williams, Chris (GRN - Chelmsley Wood)
chris.williams@solihull.gov.uk
Windmill, John (LD - Olton)
jwindmill@solihull.gov.uk

POLITICAL COMPOSITION
CON: 28, LD: 11, LAB: 5, GRN: 5, R: 1

CABINET
Leader: Mr Ken Meeson
Children & Young People: Mr Joe Tildesley
Community Services: Mrs Kate Wild
Economic Development & Regeneration: Mr Ian Courts
Health & Wellbeing: Mr Robert Sleigh
Safer Communities: Mrs Diana Holl-Allen
Transport & Highways: Mr Ted Richards

COMMITTEE CHAIRS
Economic Development & Regeneration: Mr Jim Ryan
Education, Children & Young People: Mr Alan Rebeiro
Healthier Communities: Mr Robert Hulland
Overview & Scrutiny: Mr Stuart Davis
Planning: Mr David Bell

SOMERSET C
Somerset County Council, County Hall, Taunton TA1 4DY
☎ 0845 345 9166 🖷 01823 355258 ✉ info@somerset.gov.uk
💻 www.somerset.gov.uk

FACTS & FIGURES
Police Authority: Avon & Somerset Police Authority
Health Authority: NHS South West
Learning and Skills Council: South West
Parliamentary Constituencies: Somerset North, Somerset North East
EU Constituencies: South West
Election Frequency: Elections are of whole council
Twinning: Orne (France)

PRINCIPAL OFFICERS
Chief Executive: Ms Sheila Wheeler, Chief Executive, County Hall, Taunton TA1 4DY ☎ 01823 355000 🖷 01823 355333 ✉ sheila.wheeler@somerset.gov.uk

Access Officer / Social Services (Disability): Mr David Dick, Head - Learning Disability Services, County Hall, Taunton TA1 4DY ☎ 01823 423127 ✉ ddick@somerset.gov.uk

Catering Services: Ms Julie Burnett, General Manager - SCS, Broughton House, Blackbrook Park Avenue, Taunton TA1 2PR ☎ 01823 446775 ✉ jburnett@somerset.gov.uk

Children / Youth Services: Mr John Kirby, Lead Commissioner - Children & Learning, County Hall, Taunton TA1 4DY ☎ 01823 355886 ✉ jkirby@somerset.gov.uk

Civil Registration: Mr Steve Brown, Business Developer - Resources Directorate, County Hall, Taunton TA1 4DY ☎ 01823 357978 ✉ sabrown@somerset.gov.uk

Civil Registration: Dr Michael Patrick, Head - Data Protection, Records & FOI, County Hall, Taunton TA1 4DY ☎ 01823 357156 ✉ mjpatrick@somerset.gov.uk

PR / Communications: Dr Michael Patrick, Head - Data Protection, Records & FOI, County Hall, Taunton TA1 4DY ☎ 01823 357156 ✉ mjpatrick@somerset.gov.uk

Computer Management: Mr Vic Freir, County Information & Communications Technology Officer, County Hall, Taunton TA1 4DY ☎ 01823 355260 🖷 01823 273995 ✉ vsfreir@somerset.gov.uk

Education: Mr John Kirby, Lead Commissioner - Children & Learning, County Hall, Taunton TA1 4DY ☎ 01823 355886 ✉ jkirby@somerset.gov.uk

E-Government: Mr Vic Freir, County Information & Communications Technology Officer, County Hall, Taunton TA1 4DY ☎ 01823 355260 🖷 01823 273995 ✉ vsfreir@somerset.gov.uk

Electoral Registration: Ms Sheila Wheeler, Chief Executive, County Hall, Taunton TA1 4DY ☎ 01823 355000 🖷 01823 355333 ✉ sheila.wheeler@somerset.gov.uk

Emergency Planning: Ms Nicola Dawson, Civil Contingencies Manager, County Hall, Taunton TA2 8LQ ☎ 01823 364612 ✉ ndawson@somerset.gov.uk

Energy Management: Mr Mike Fackrell, Sustainable Development Group Manager, County Hall, Taunton TA1 4DY ☎ 01823 355310 🖷 01823 356107 ✉ mikefackrell@somerset.gov.uk

Estates, Property & Valuation: Mr Andrew Tucker, Head of Service - Property, County Hall, Taunton TA1 4DY ☎ 01823 356236 🖷 01823 356107 ✉ agtucker@somerset.gov.uk

European Liaison: Mr Jamshid Ahmadi, Acting European Unit Manager, County Hall, Taunton TA1 4DY ☎ 01823 356131

jahmadi@somerset.gov.uk

Facilities: Ms Heidi Boyle, Facilities Manager, County Hall, Taunton TA1 4DY ☎ 01823 365524 hboyle@somerset.gov.uk

Finance and Treasurer: Mr Kevin Nacey, Finance & Performance Director, County Hall, Taunton TA1 4DY ☎ 01823 356908 kbnacey@somerset.gov.uk

Fleet Management: Mr Clive Kemp, Chief Fire Officer, County Hall, Taunton TA2 8LQ ☎ 01823 364500 cskemp@somerset.gov.uk

Fleet Management: Mr N Tomlinson, Managing Director - Fleet & Transport, Atkins Transport, Crown Industrial Estate, Priorswood, Taunton TA2 8QY ☎ 01823 285800 ntomlinson@somerset.gov.uk

Grounds Maintenance: Mr Andrew Tucker, Head of Service - Property, County Hall, Taunton TA1 4DY ☎ 01823 356236 🖷 01823 356107 agtucker@somerset.gov.uk

Health and Safety: Mr Brian Oldham, Operations Manager - Health & Safety, County Hall, Taunton TA1 4DY ☎ 01823 355089 🖷 01823 355521 boldham@somerset.gov.uk

Highways: Mr Ioan Rees, Head of Service - Highways, County Hall, Taunton TA1 4DY ☎ 01823 355094 irees@somerset.gov.uk

Legal: Mrs Honor Clarke, Deputy County Solicitor, County Hall, Taunton TA1 4DY ☎ 01823 355022 HCClarke@somerset.gov.uk

Lighting: Mr Trevor Gutteridge, Highway Lighting Engineer, Atmos Ltd. (WS Atkins), The Crescent, Taunton TA1 4XE ☎ 01823 423367 🖷 01823 353430 tjgutteridge@wsatkins.co.uk

Member Services: Mr Julian Gale, Group Manager - Community Governance, County Hall, Taunton TA1 4DY ☎ 01823 355025 🖷 01823 355258 jgale@somerset.gov.uk

Partnerships: Mr Trevor Gillham, Head - Partnerships & Community Development, County Hall, Taunton TA1 4DY ☎ 01823 355101 tgillham@somerset.gov.uk

Partnerships: Mr John Kirby, Lead Commissioner - Children & Learning, County Hall, Taunton TA1 4DY ☎ 01823 355886 jkirby@somerset.gov.uk

Personnel / HR: Mr Richard Crouch, HR & OD Director, County Hall, Taunton TA1 4DY ☎ 01823 355074 rmcrouch@somerset.gov.uk

Planning: Ms Paula Hewitt, Lead Commissioner - Economic & Community Infrastructure, County Hall, Taunton TA1 4DY ☎ 01823 356020 prhewitt@somerset.gov.uk

Public Libraries: Mr Rob Froud, County Librarian, Library Administration Centre, Mount Street, Bridgwater TA6 3ES ☎ 01278 451201 🖷 01278 452787 rnfroud@somerset.gov.uk

Regeneration: Mr Paul Hickson, Head of Service - Community Regeneration, County Hall, Taunton TA1 4DY ☎ 01823 358285 phickson@somerset.gov.uk

Social Services (Adult): Ms Clare Steel, Lead Commissioner - Adults & Health, County Hall, Taunton TA1 4DY ☎ 01823 355100 csteel@somerset.gov.uk

Social Services (Children): Mr John Kirby, Lead Commissioner - Children & Learning, County Hall, Taunton TA1 4DY ☎ 01823 355886 jkirby@somerset.gov.uk

Staff Training: Mr Chris Brawn, Group Manager - Training & Development, County Hall, Taunton TA1 4DY ☎ 01823 355340 🖷 01823 355521 cbrawn@somerset.gov.uk

Sustainable Communities: Mr Trevor Gillham, Head - Partnerships & Community Development, County Hall, Taunton TA1 4DY ☎ 01823 355101 tgillham@somerset.gov.uk

Transport: Ms Paula Hewitt, Lead Commissioner - Economic & Community Infrastructure, County Hall, Taunton TA1 4DY ☎ 01823 356020 prhewitt@somerset.gov.uk

Transport: Mr N Tomlinson, Managing Director - Fleet & Transport, Atkins Transport, Crown Industrial Estate, Priorswood, Taunton TA2 8QY ☎ 01823 285800 ntomlinson@somerset.gov.uk

MEMBERS OF THE COUNCIL (58)

***Chair:* Edney**, John (CON - Cannington)
jedney@somerset.gov.uk

***Leader of the Council:* Osman**, John (CON - Wells)
jdosman@somerset.gov.uk

***Deputy Leader of the Council:* Hall**, David (CON - Bridgwater East and Bawdrip)
dhall@somerset.gov.uk

Alder, Derek (CON - North Petherton)
dsalder@somerset.gov.uk

Bailey, John (LD - Martock)
jabailey@somerset.gov.uk

Bakewell, Catherine (LD - Coker)
cmbakewell@somerset.gov.uk

Bown, Ann (CON - Bridgwater West)
aebown@somerset.gov.uk

Brooks, Stephen (LD - Taunton East)
sabrooks@somerset.gov.uk

Burridge-Clayton, Peter (CON - Burnham on Sea North)
pburridgeclayton@somerset.gov.uk

Carroll, Tim (LD - Yeovil West)
tcarroll@somerset.gov.uk

Cawood, Gloria (LD - Mendip Central and East)
gmcawood@somerset.gov.uk

Crabb, Samuel (LD - Ilchester)
sdcrabb@somerset.gov.uk

Daniell, Maggy (LD - Frome Selwood)
mdaniell@somerset.gov.uk

Denbee, John (CON - Brent)
jdenbee@somerset.gov.uk

Dyke, John (LD - Crewkerne)
jdyke@somerset.gov.uk

Ellis, Matthew (CON - Mendip North East)
mjellis@somerset.gov.uk

Forrest, Ronald (CON - Mendip West)
rwforrest@somerset.gov.uk
Fothergill, David (CON - North Curry)
djafothergill@somerset.gov.uk
Gill, Steve (LD - Bridgwater South)
sjgill@somerset.gov.uk
Gloak, Alan (LD - Glastonbury)
afgloak@somerset.gov.uk
Gordon, Claire (LD - Taunton North)
cgordon@somerset.gov.uk
Govier, Andrew (LAB - Wellington)
ajgovier@somerset.gov.uk
Greene, David (LD - Yeovil South)
dagreene@somerset.gov.uk
Groskop, Anna (CON - Wincanton and Bruton)
amgroskop@somerset.gov.uk
Gubbins, Peter (LD - Yeovil North and Central)
pgubbins@somerset.gov.uk
Healey, Mark (CON - Huntspill)
mhealey@somerset.gov.uk
Henley, Ross (LD - Blackdown and Wellington East)
rlhenley@somerset.gov.uk
Hill, Dawn (CON - Cheddar)
dmhill@somerset.gov.uk
Horsfall, Alvin (LD - Frome South)
ajhorsfall@somerset.gov.uk
Huxtable, David (CON - King Alfred)
djhuxtable@somerset.gov.uk
John, Peter (CON - Frome North)
pfjohn@somerset.gov.uk
Kenton, Jenny (LD - Chard North)
jkenton@somerset.gov.uk
Lawrence, Christine (CON - Dunster)
cmlawrence@somerset.gov.uk
Little, Bob (CON - Castle Cary)
blittle@somerset.gov.uk
Lock, Tony (LD - Yeovil East)
tlock@somerset.gov.uk
Loveridge, David (LAB - Bridgwater North and Central)
dloveridge@somerset.gov.uk
Maddock, Kenneth (CON - Mendip South)
kmaddock@somerset.gov.uk
Maitland-Walker, Brenda (CON - Minehead)
bmaitlandwalker@somerset.gov.uk
Martin-Scott, Stephen (CON - Taunton and Trull)
shmartin-scott@somerset.gov.uk
Maxwell, Paul (LD - South Petherton)
pmmaxwell@somerset.gov.uk
McMahon, Tony (CON - Upper Tone)
tmcmahon@somerset.gov.uk
Napper, Terry (CON - Street)
twenapper@somerset.gov.uk
Nelson, Derek (CON - Curry Rivel)
dinelson@somerset.gov.uk
Nicholson, Frances (CON - Dulverton and Exmoor)
fmnicholson@somerset.gov.uk
Parham, John (CON - Shepton Mallet)
jparham@somerset.gov.uk
Paul, Alan (LD - Taunton West)
apaul@somerset.gov.uk
Prior-Sankey, Hazel (LD - Taunton South)
hrprior-sankey@somerset.gov.uk
Shortland, Jill (LD - Chard South)
jcshortland@somerset.gov.uk
Siggs, Harvey (CON - Mendip North West)
hsiggs@somerset.gov.uk
Trollope-Bellew, Anthony (CON - Watchet and Quantocks)
ahtrollope-bellew@somerset.gov.uk
Turner, Kim (LD - Ilminster)
ktturner@somerset.gov.uk
Wallace, William (CON - Blackmore Vale)
wwallace@somerset.gov.uk
Waymouth, Elaine (CON - Staplegrove)
ewaymouth@somerset.gov.uk
Wedderkopp, Danny (LD - Taunton Fairwater)

Wilkins, John (CON - Lydeard)
jewilkins@somerset.gov.uk
Woodman, John (CON - Highbridge and Burnham on Sea South)
jwoodman@somerset.gov.uk
Yeomans, Derek (CON - Langport)
dnyeomans@somerset.gov.uk
Zouche, Jimmy (CON - Somerton)
jzouche@somerset.gov.uk

POLITICAL COMPOSITION
CON: 33, LD: 23, LAB: 2

CABINET
Leader: Mr John Osman
Deputy Leader / Economic Development, Infrastructure & Innovation: Mr David Hall
Children & Families: Ms Frances Nicholson
Customers & Communities: Mr Bob Little
Health & Adult Social Care: Mrs Christine Lawrence
Resources: Mr David Huxtable
Transformation & Highways: Mr Harvey Siggs

COMMITTEE CHAIRS
Audit: Mr John Wilkins
Pensions: Mrs Dawn Hill
Regulation: Mr Derek Yeomans
Scrutiny: Mr Andrew Govier

SOUTH AYRSHIRE S
South Ayrshire Council, County Buildings, Wellington Square, Ayr KA7 1DR ☎ 0300 123 0900 🖷 01292 612143
💻 www.south-ayrshire.gov.uk

FACTS & FIGURES
Police Authority: Strathclyde Police Authority
Health Authority: NHS Ayrshire & Arran
Learning and Skills Council: Scotland
Parliamentary Constituencies: Ayr, Carrick and Cumnock, Ayrshire Central
EU Constituencies: Scotland
Election Frequency: Elections are of whole council
Twinning: Ayr: Girvan: Torcy (France); Saint-Germaine-en-Laye (France); Maybole: Beldeil (Belgium); Crosne (France); Schotten (Germany); Prestwick: Lichtenfels (Germany); Vandalia (USA); Troon: Villeneuve-sur-Lot (France)

PRINCIPAL OFFICERS
Chief Executive: Mr David Anderson, Chief Executive, County Buildings, Wellington Square, Ayr KA7 1DR ☎ 01292 612109

🖷 01292 612158 ✉ david.anderson@south-ayrshire.gov.uk

Senior Management: Mrs Lesley Bloomer, Executive Director of Development & Environment, County Buildings, Wellington Square, Ayr KA7 1DR ☎ 01290 612185 ✉ lesley.bloomer@south-ayrshire.gov.uk

Senior Management: Mr Harry Garland, Executive Director, County Buildings, Wellington Square, Ayr KA7 1DR ☎ 01292 612419 🖷 01292 612481 ✉ harry.garland@south-ayrshire.gov.uk

Senior Management: Mrs Eileen Howat, Executive Director, County Buildings, Wellington Square, Ayr KA7 1DR ☎ 01292 612612 ✉ eileen.howat@south-ayrshire.gov.uk

Architect, Building / Property Services: Mr Jim McQuillan, Head of Property & Neighbourhood Services, Burns House, Burns Statue Square, Ayr KA7 1UT ☎ 01292 616334 ✉ jim.mcquillan@south-ayrshire.gov.uk

Best Value: Ms Claire Monaghan, Head of Policy, Performance & Communication, County Buildings, Wellington Square, Ayr KA7 1DR ☎ 01292 612757 🖷 01292 612158 ✉ claire.monaghan@south-ayrshire.gov.uk

Building Control: Mr Mike Newall, Head of Planning & Enterprise, Burns House, Burns Statue Square, Ayr KA7 1UT ☎ 01292 616231 ✉ mike.newall@south-ayrshire.gov.uk

Catering Services: Ms Jennifer McGill, Facilities Manager, Burns House, Burns Statue Square, Ayr KA7 1UT ☎ 01292 616045 ✉ jennifer.mcgill@south-ayrshire.gov.uk

Children / Youth Services: Mr Hugh Carswell, Head of Children's Services, County Buildings, Wellington Square, Ayr KA7 1DR ☎ 01292 612244 ✉ hugh.carswell@south-ayrshire.gov.uk

Civil Registration: Mr Philip Ewing, Registration & Bereavement Manager, Masonhill Crematorium, Ayr KA6 6EN ☎ 01292 266051 🖷 01292 610096 ✉ philip.ewing@south-ayrshire.gov.uk

PR / Communications: Ms Claire Monaghan, Head of Policy, Performance & Communication, County Buildings, Wellington Square, Ayr KA7 1DR ☎ 01292 612757 🖷 01292 612158 ✉ claire.monaghan@south-ayrshire.gov.uk

Community Planning: Ms Claire Monaghan, Head of Policy, Performance & Communication, County Buildings, Wellington Square, Ayr KA7 1DR ☎ 01292 612757 🖷 01292 612158 ✉ claire.monaghan@south-ayrshire.gov.uk

Community Safety: Ms Louise Fyfe, Community Safety Manager, 1st Floor, John Pollock Centre, Ayr KA8 0QD ☎ 01292 616615 🖷 01292 616611 ✉ louise.fyfe@south-ayrshire.gov.uk

Computer Management: Mr Gordon Muir, ICT Strategy Officer, County Buildings, Wellington Square, Ayr KA7 1DR ☎ 01292 612731 🖷 01292 6121402 ✉ gordon.muir@south-ayrshire.gov.uk

Consumer Protection and Trading Standards: Mr David Thompson, Trading Standards & Environmental Health Manager, River Terrace, Ayr KA8 0BJ ☎ 01292 616055 ✉ david.thompson@south-ayrshire.gov.uk

Contracts: Mr David Alexander, Head of Corporate Resources, County Buildings, Wellington Square, Ayr KA7 1DR ☎ 01292 612777 ✉ david.alexander@south-ayrshire.gov.uk

Corporate Services: Mrs Eileen Howat, Executive Director, County Buildings, Wellington Square, Ayr KA7 1DR ☎ 01292 612612 ✉ eileen.howat@south-ayrshire.gov.uk

Customer Service: Ms Kate O'Hagan, Head of HR & Organisational Development, County Buildings, Wellington Square, Ayr KA7 1DR ☎ 01292 612696 ✉ kate.ohagan@south-ayrshire.gov.uk

Economic Development: Mr Mark Hastings, Enterprise Manager, Burns House, Burns Statue Square, Ayr KA7 1UT ☎ 01292 616347 ✉ mark.hastings@south-ayrshire.gov.uk

Education: Mr Harry Garland, Executive Director, County Buildings, Wellington Square, Ayr KA7 1DR ☎ 01292 612419 🖷 01292 612481 ✉ harry.garland@south-ayrshire.gov.uk

Education: Mr Brian McInroy, Head of Service & School Management, County Buildings, Wellington Square, Ayr KA7 1DR ☎ 01292 612234 🖷 01292 612258 ✉ brian.mcinroy@south-ayrshire.gov.uk

Education: Ms Margo Williamson, Head of Curriculum & Service Improvement, County Buildings, Wellington Square, Ayr KA7 1DR ☎ 01292 612240 🖷 01292 612258 ✉ margo.williamson@south-ayrshire.gov.uk

E-Government: Mrs Eileen Howat, Executive Director, County Buildings, Wellington Square, Ayr KA7 1DR ☎ 01292 612612 ✉ eileen.howat@south-ayrshire.gov.uk

Electoral Registration: Mr William Sommerville, Assessor & Electoral Registration Officer, 9 Wellington Square, Ayr KA7 1HL ☎ 01292 612538 🖷 01292 612673 ✉ william.sommerville@south-ayrshire.gov.uk

Emergency Planning: Mr David Whyte, Civil Contingencies Manager, Prestwick Airport, Building 372 Alpha Freight Area, Robertson Road, Prestwick KA9 2PL ☎ 01292 692180 🖷 01292 692184 ✉ david.whyte@south-ayrshire.gov.uk

Environmental / Technical Services: Mr Jim McQuillan, Head of Property & Neighbourhood Services, Burns House, Burns Statue Square, Ayr KA7 1UT ☎ 01292 616334 ✉ jim.mcquillan@south-ayrshire.gov.uk

Environmental Health: Mr David Thompson, Trading Standards & Environmental Health Manager, River Terrace, Ayr KA8 0BJ ☎ 01292 616055 ✉ david.thompson@south-ayrshire.gov.uk

Estates, Property & Valuation: Ms Audrey Greenwood, Estates Manager, Burns House, Burns Statue Square, Ayr KA7 1UT ☎ 01292 616213 🖷 01292 616263 ✉ audrey.greenwood@south-ayrshire.gov.uk

European Liaison: Ms Carole Coull, Senior Enterprise Project Development & Funding Officer, Burns House, Burns Statue Square, Ayr KA7 1UT ☎ 01292 616226 carole.coull@south-ayrshire.gov.uk

Events Manager: Mr Mark Hastings, Enterprise Manager, Burns House, Burns Statue Square, Ayr KA7 1UT ☎ 01292 616347 mark.hastings@south-ayrshire.gov.uk

Facilities: Ms Jennifer McGill, Facilities Manager, Burns House, Burns Statue Square, Ayr KA7 1UT ☎ 01292 616045 jennifer.mcgill@south-ayrshire.gov.uk

Finance and Treasurer: Mrs Eileen Howat, Executive Director, County Buildings, Wellington Square, Ayr KA7 1DR ☎ 01292 612612 eileen.howat@south-ayrshire.gov.uk

Fleet Management: Mr Robert Howe, Fleet Manager, Burns House, Burns Statue Square, Ayr KA7 1UT ☎ 01292 616266 🖷 01292 616171 robert.howe@south-ayrshire.gov.uk

Grounds Maintenance: Mr Kenny Dalrymple, Neighbourhood Services Manager, Burns House, Burns Statue Square, Ayr KA7 1UT ☎ 01292 612041 🖷 01292 616284 kenny.dalrymple@south-ayrshire.gov.uk

Health and Safety: Ms Kate O'Hagan, Head of HR & Organisational Development, County Buildings, Wellington Square, Ayr KA7 1DR ☎ 01292 612696 kate.ohagan@south-ayrshire.gov.uk

Highways: Mr Mike Newall, Head of Planning & Enterprise, Burns House, Burns Statue Square, Ayr KA7 1UT ☎ 01292 616231 mike.newall@south-ayrshire.gov.uk

Housing: Mr Kenny Leinster, Head of Community Care & Housing, County Buildings, Wellington Square, Ayr KA7 1DR ☎ 01292 612735 🖷 01292 612258 kenny.leinster@south-ayrshire.gov.uk

Housing Maintenance: Mr Kenny Leinster, Head of Community Care & Housing, County Buildings, Wellington Square, Ayr KA7 1DR ☎ 01292 612735 🖷 01292 612258 kenny.leinster@south-ayrshire.gov.uk

Local Area Agreement: Ms Claire Monaghan, Head of Policy, Performance & Communication, County Buildings, Wellington Square, Ayr KA7 1DR ☎ 01292 612757 🖷 01292 612158 claire.monaghan@south-ayrshire.gov.uk

Legal: Ms Valerie Andrews, Head of Legal & Administration, County Buildings, Wellington Square, Ayr KA7 1DR ☎ 01292 612466 🖷 01292 612455 valerie.andrews@south-ayrshire.gov.uk

Leisure and Cultural Services: Mrs Jill Cronin, Acting Head of Community Development, County Buildings, Wellington Square, Ayr KA7 1DR ☎ 01292 612473 🖷 01292 612261 jill.cronin@south-ayrshire.gov.uk

Licensing: Ms Valerie Andrews, Head of Legal & Administration, County Buildings, Wellington Square, Ayr KA7 1DR ☎ 01292 612466 🖷 01292 612455 valerie.andrews@south-ayrshire.gov.uk

Lifelong Learning: Mrs Jill Cronin, Acting Head of Community Development, County Buildings, Wellington Square, Ayr KA7 1DR ☎ 01292 612473 🖷 01292 612261 jill.cronin@south-ayrshire.gov.uk

Lottery Funding, Charity and Voluntary: Ms Carole Coull, Senior Enterprise Project Development & Funding Officer, Burns House, Burns Statue Square, Ayr KA7 1UT ☎ 01292 616226 carole.coull@south-ayrshire.gov.uk

Member Services: Ms Valerie Andrews, Head of Legal & Administration, County Buildings, Wellington Square, Ayr KA7 1DR ☎ 01292 612466 🖷 01292 612455 valerie.andrews@south-ayrshire.gov.uk

Parking: Mr Mike Newall, Head of Planning & Enterprise, Burns House, Burns Statue Square, Ayr KA7 1UT ☎ 01292 616231 mike.newall@south-ayrshire.gov.uk

Partnerships: Ms Claire Monaghan, Head of Policy, Performance & Communication, County Buildings, Wellington Square, Ayr KA7 1DR ☎ 01292 612757 🖷 01292 612158 claire.monaghan@south-ayrshire.gov.uk

Personnel / HR: Ms Kate O'Hagan, Head of HR & Organisational Development, County Buildings, Wellington Square, Ayr KA7 1DR ☎ 01292 612696 kate.ohagan@south-ayrshire.gov.uk

Planning: Ms Christina Cox, Planning Manager, Burns House, Burns Statue Square, Ayr KA7 1UT ☎ 01292 616234 christina.cox@south-ayrshire.gov.uk

Procurement: Mrs Jill Cronin, Acting Head of Community Development, County Buildings, Wellington Square, Ayr KA7 1DR ☎ 01292 612473 🖷 01292 612261 jill.cronin@south-ayrshire.gov.uk

Public Libraries: Mrs Jill Cronin, Acting Head of Community Development, County Buildings, Wellington Square, Ayr KA7 1DR ☎ 01292 612473 🖷 01292 612261 jill.cronin@south-ayrshire.gov.uk

Recycling & Waste Minimisation: Mr Kenny Dalrymple, Neighbourhood Services Manager, Burns House, Burns Statue Square, Ayr KA7 1UT ☎ 01292 612041 🖷 01292 616284 kenny.dalrymple@south-ayrshire.gov.uk

Regeneration: Mrs Jill Cronin, Acting Head of Community Development, County Buildings, Wellington Square, Ayr KA7 1DR ☎ 01292 612473 🖷 01292 612261 jill.cronin@south-ayrshire.gov.uk

Road Safety: Mr Mike Newall, Head of Planning & Enterprise, Burns House, Burns Statue Square, Ayr KA7 1UT ☎ 01292 616231 mike.newall@south-ayrshire.gov.uk

Social Services (Adult): Mr Kenny Leinster, Head of Community Care & Housing, County Buildings, Wellington Square, Ayr KA7 1DR ☎ 01292 612735 🖷 01292 612258 kenny.leinster@south-ayrshire.gov.uk

Social Services (Children): Mr Hugh Carswell, Head of Children's Services, County Buildings, Wellington Square, Ayr KA7 1DR ☎ 01292 612244 ✉ hugh.carswell@south-ayrshire.gov.uk

Staff Training: Ms Kate O'Hagan, Head of HR & Organisational Development, County Buildings, Wellington Square, Ayr KA7 1DR ☎ 01292 612696 ✉ kate.ohagan@south-ayrshire.gov.uk

Sustainable Communities: Ms Lorna Jarvie, Sustainable Development Policy Officer, County Buildings, Wellington Square, Ayr KA7 1DR ☎ 01292 612297 ✉ lorna.jarvie@south-ayrshire.gov.uk

Sustainable Development: Ms Lorna Jarvie, Sustainable Development Policy Officer, County Buildings, Wellington Square, Ayr KA7 1DR ☎ 01292 612297 ✉ lorna.jarvie@south-ayrshire.gov.uk

Tourism: Mr Mark Hastings, Enterprise Manager, Burns House, Burns Statue Square, Ayr KA7 1UT ☎ 01292 616347 ✉ mark.hastings@south-ayrshire.gov.uk

Town Centre: Mr David Bell, Managing Director of Ayr Renaissance, County Buildings, Wellington Square, Ayr KA7 1DR ☎ 01292 612477 ✉ david.bell@south-ayrshire.gov.uk

Transport: Mr Mike Newall, Head of Planning & Enterprise, Burns House, Burns Statue Square, Ayr KA7 1UT ☎ 01292 616231 ✉ mike.newall@south-ayrshire.gov.uk

Waste Collection and Disposal: Mr Kenny Dalrymple, Neighbourhood Services Manager, Burns House, Burns Statue Square, Ayr KA7 1UT ☎ 01292 612041 🖷 01292 616284 ✉ kenny.dalrymple@south-ayrshire.gov.uk

Waste Management: Mr Kenny Dalrymple, Neighbourhood Services Manager, Burns House, Burns Statue Square, Ayr KA7 1UT ☎ 01292 612041 🖷 01292 616284 ✉ kenny.dalrymple@south-ayrshire.gov.uk

MEMBERS OF THE COUNCIL (30)

***Provost:* Moonie**, Helen (LAB - Prestwick)
helen.moonie@south-ayrshire.gov.uk
***Deputy Provost:* Kilpatrick**, Mary (CON - Ayr East)
mary.kilpatrick@south-ayrshire.gov.uk
***Leader of the Council:* McIntosh**, Bill (CON - Troon)
bill.mcintosh@south-ayrshire.gov.uk
***Deputy Leader of the Council:* McDowall**, John (LAB - Girvan and South Carrick)
john.mcdowall@south-ayrshire.gov.uk
Allan, John (SNP - Kyle)
john.allan@south-ayrshire.gov.uk
Campbell, Andy (LAB - Kyle)
andy.campbell@south-ayrshire.gov.uk
Campbell, Douglas (IND - Ayr North)
douglas.campbell@south-ayrshire.gov.uk
Cavana, Ian (LAB - Ayr North)
ian.cavana@south-ayrshire.gov.uk
Clark, Alec (IND - Girvan and South Carrick)
alec.clark@south-ayrshire.gov.uk
Cochrane, Ian (SNP - Prestwick)
ian.cochrane@south-ayrshire.gov.uk
Connolly, Brian (IND - Maybole, North Carrick and Coylton)
brian.connolly@south-ayrshire.gov.uk
Convery, Peter (CON - Troon)
peter.convery@south-ayrshire.gov.uk
Darwent, Kirsty (LAB - Ayr West)
kirsty.darwent@south-ayrshire.gov.uk
Davies, Hywel (CON - Kyle)
hywel.davies@south-ayrshire.gov.uk
Dorans, Allan (SNP - Ayr West)
allan.dorans@south-ayrshire.gov.uk
Douglas, Ian (SNP - Ayr East)
ian.douglas@south-ayrshire.gov.uk
Galbraith, Ann (CON - Maybole, North Carrick and Coylton)
ann.galbraith@south-ayrshire.gov.uk
Goldie, Sandra (LAB - Maybole, North Carrick and Coylton)
sandra.goldie@south-ayrshire.gov.uk
Grant, Bill (CON - Ayr West)
bill.grant@south-ayrshire.gov.uk
Grant, William (SNP - Maybole, North Carrick and Coylton)
william.grant@south-ayrshire.gov.uk
Hampton, John (CON - Ayr North)
john.hampton@south-ayrshire.gov.uk
Hunter, Hugh (CON - Prestwick)
hugh.hunter@south-ayrshire.gov.uk
McFarlane, Nan (SNP - Troon)
nan.mcfarlane@south-ayrshire.gov.uk
McGinley, Brian (LAB - Ayr East)
brian.mcginley@south-ayrshire.gov.uk
Miller, Rita (LAB - Ayr North)
rita.miller@south-ayrshire.gov.uk
Oattes, Alec (SNP - Girvan and South Carrick)
alec.oattes@south-ayrshire.gov.uk
Reid, Robin (CON - Ayr West)
robin.reid@south-ayrshire.gov.uk
Saxton, Phil (LAB - Troon)
philip.saxton@south-ayrshire.gov.uk
Toner, Margaret (CON - Prestwick)
margaret.toner@south-ayrshire.gov.uk
Wilson, Corri (SNP - Ayr East)
corri.wilson@south-ayrshire.gov.uk

POLITICAL COMPOSITION

CON: 10, LAB: 9, SNP: 8, IND: 3

COMMITTEE CHAIRS

Community Services Standing Scrutiny Panel : Mr John Hampton
Corporate & Community Planning Standing Scrutiny Panel: Mr Brian Connolly
Development & Environment Standing Scrutiny Panel: Ms Kirsty Darwent
Regulatory: Mr Peter Convery
Scrutiny/Governance Panel: Mr Brian McGinley

SOUTH BUCKS D

South Bucks District Council, Council Offices, Capswood, Oxford Road, Denham UB9 4LH ☎ 01895 837200 🖷 01895 837277 ✉ sbdc@southbucks.gov.uk 🖳 www.southbucks.gov.uk

FACTS & FIGURES

Police Authority: Thames Valley Police Authority
Health Authority: South Central Strategic Health Authority
Learning and Skills Council: South East

Parliamentary Constituencies: Beaconsfield
EU Constituencies: South East
Election Frequency: Elections are of whole council

PRINCIPAL OFFICERS

Chief Executive: Mr Alan Goodrum, Chief Executive, Council Offices, King George V Road, Amersham HP6 5AW ☎ 01494 732001; 01494 732001 🖷 01494 586506; 01494 586506 ✉ agoodrum@chiltern.gov.uk; agoodrum@chiltern.gov.uk

Senior Management: Mr Jim Burness, Director of Resources, Council Offices, Capswood, Oxford Road, Denham UB9 4LH ☎ 01895 837367 ✉ jim.burness@southbucks.gov.uk

Senior Management: Mr Bob Smith, Director of Services, Council Offices, Capswood, Oxford Road, Denham UB9 4LH ☎ 01895 837367 ✉ bob.smith@southbucks.gov.uk

Architect, Building / Property Services: Mr Bob Smith, Director of Services, Council Offices, Capswood, Oxford Road, Denham UB9 4LH ☎ 01895 837367 ✉ bob.smith@southbucks.gov.uk

Building Control: Mr Bob Smith, Director of Services, Council Offices, Capswood, Oxford Road, Denham UB9 4LH ☎ 01895 837367 ✉ bob.smith@southbucks.gov.uk

Children / Youth Services: Mrs Rachael Winfield, Community & Partnerships Officer, Council Offices, Capswood, Oxford Road, Denham UB9 4LH ☎ 01895 837318 ✉ rachael.winfield@southbucks.gov.uk

PR / Communications: Mrs Rachael Winfield, Community & Partnerships Officer, Council Offices, Capswood, Oxford Road, Denham UB9 4LH ☎ 01895 837318 ✉ rachael.winfield@southbucks.gov.uk

Community Safety: Mr Bob Smith, Director of Services, Council Offices, Capswood, Oxford Road, Denham UB9 4LH ☎ 01895 837367 ✉ bob.smith@southbucks.gov.uk

Computer Management: Mr Jim Burness, Director of Resources, Council Offices, Capswood, Oxford Road, Denham UB9 4LH ☎ 01895 837367 ✉ jim.burness@southbucks.gov.uk

Computer Management: Mr Rodney Fincham, Head of Financial & ICT, Council Offices, Capswood, Oxford Road, Denham UB9 4LH ☎ 01895 837268 ✉ rodney.fincham@southbucks.gov.uk

Contracts: Mr Bob Smith, Director of Services, Council Offices, Capswood, Oxford Road, Denham UB9 4LH ☎ 01895 837367 ✉ bob.smith@southbucks.gov.uk

Corporate Services: Mr Jim Burness, Director of Resources, Council Offices, Capswood, Oxford Road, Denham UB9 4LH ☎ 01895 837367 ✉ jim.burness@southbucks.gov.uk

Economic Development: Mr Bob Smith, Director of Services, Council Offices, Capswood, Oxford Road, Denham UB9 4LH ☎ 01895 837367 ✉ bob.smith@southbucks.gov.uk

Electoral Registration: Mrs Kulvinder Tumber, Democratic & Electoral Services Manager, Council Offices, Capswood, Oxford Road, Denham UB9 4LH ☎ 01895 837225 ✉ kully.tumber@southbucks.gov.uk

Emergency Planning: Mr Dave Gilmour, Environmental Health Manager, Council Offices, Capswood, Oxford Road, Denham UB9 4LH ☎ 01895 837200 ✉ david.gilmour@southbucks.gov.uk

Energy Management: Mr Bob Smith, Director of Services, Council Offices, Capswood, Oxford Road, Denham UB9 4LH ☎ 01895 837367 ✉ bob.smith@southbucks.gov.uk

Environmental / Technical Services: Mr Peter Beckford, Head of Sustainable Development, Council Offices, Capswood, Oxford Road, Denham UB9 4LH ☎ 01895 837208 ✉ peter.beckford@southbucks.gov.uk

Environmental / Technical Services: Mr Chris Marchant, Head of Environment, Council Offices, Capswood, Oxford Road, Denham UB9 4LH ☎ 01895 837360 ✉ chris.marchant@southbucks.gov.uk

Environmental / Technical Services: Mr Bob Smith, Director of Services, Council Offices, Capswood, Oxford Road, Denham UB9 4LH ☎ 01895 837367 ✉ bob.smith@southbucks.gov.uk

Environmental Health: Mr Bob Smith, Director of Services, Council Offices, Capswood, Oxford Road, Denham UB9 4LH ☎ 01895 837367 ✉ bob.smith@southbucks.gov.uk

Estates, Property & Valuation: Mr Bob Smith, Director of Services, Council Offices, Capswood, Oxford Road, Denham UB9 4LH ☎ 01895 837367 ✉ bob.smith@southbucks.gov.uk

Facilities: Mr Andrew Crow, Facilities Manager, Council Offices, Capswood, Oxford Road, Denham UB9 4LH ☎ 01895 837200 ✉ andrew.crow@southbucks.gov.uk

Finance and Treasurer: Mr Jim Burness, Director of Resources, Council Offices, Capswood, Oxford Road, Denham UB9 4LH ☎ 01895 837367 ✉ jim.burness@southbucks.gov.uk

Finance and Treasurer: Mr Rodney Fincham, Head of Financial & ICT, Council Offices, Capswood, Oxford Road, Denham UB9 4LH ☎ 01895 837268 ✉ rodney.fincham@southbucks.gov.uk

Health and Safety: Mr Bob Smith, Director of Services, Council Offices, Capswood, Oxford Road, Denham UB9 4LH ☎ 01895 837367 ✉ bob.smith@southbucks.gov.uk

Housing: Mr Bob Smith, Director of Services, Council Offices, Capswood, Oxford Road, Denham UB9 4LH ☎ 01895 837367 ✉ bob.smith@southbucks.gov.uk

Legal: Miss Lynne Reardon, Head of Legal Services, Council Offices, Capswood, Oxford Road, Denham UB9 4LH ☎ 01895 837229 ✉ lynne.reardon@southbucks.gov.uk

Leisure and Cultural Services: Mr Bob Smith, Director of Services, Council Offices, Capswood, Oxford Road, Denham UB9 4LH ☎ 01895 837367 ✉ bob.smith@southbucks.gov.uk

Licensing: Mr Bob Smith, Director of Services, Council Offices,

Capswood, Oxford Road, Denham UB9 4LH ☎ 01895 837367 ✉ bob.smith@southbucks.gov.uk

Member Services: Mrs Kulvinder Tumber, Democratic & Electoral Services Manager, Council Offices, Capswood, Oxford Road, Denham UB9 4LH ☎ 01895 837225 ✉ kully.tumber@southbucks.gov.uk

Parking: Mr Christopher Jones, Car Parks Operations Manager, Council Offices, Capswood, Oxford Road, Denham UB9 4LH ☎ 01895 837359 ✉ christopher.jones@southbucks.gov.uk

Partnerships: Mrs Rachael Winfield, Community & Partnerships Officer, Council Offices, Capswood, Oxford Road, Denham UB9 4LH ☎ 01895 837318 ✉ rachael.winfield@southbucks.gov.uk

Personnel / HR: Ms Alex Roland, Policy & HR Manager, Council Offices, Capswood, Oxford Road, Denham UB9 4LH ☎ 01895 837334 ✉ alex.roland@southbucks.gov.uk

Planning: Mr Bob Smith, Director of Services, Council Offices, Capswood, Oxford Road, Denham UB9 4LH ☎ 01895 837367 ✉ bob.smith@southbucks.gov.uk

Recycling & Waste Minimisation: Mr Bob Smith, Director of Services, Council Offices, Capswood, Oxford Road, Denham UB9 4LH ☎ 01895 837367 ✉ bob.smith@southbucks.gov.uk

Sustainable Communities: Mrs Lynn Trigwell, Head of Community, Council Offices, Capswood, Oxford Road, Denham UB9 4LH ☎ 01895 837215 ✉ lynn.trigwell@southbucks.gov.uk

Sustainable Development: Mr Bob Smith, Director of Services, Council Offices, Capswood, Oxford Road, Denham UB9 4LH ☎ 01895 837367 ✉ bob.smith@southbucks.gov.uk

Waste Collection and Disposal: Mr Bob Smith, Director of Services, Council Offices, Capswood, Oxford Road, Denham UB9 4LH ☎ 01895 837367 ✉ bob.smith@southbucks.gov.uk

Waste Management: Mr Bob Smith, Director of Services, Council Offices, Capswood, Oxford Road, Denham UB9 4LH ☎ 01895 837367 ✉ bob.smith@southbucks.gov.uk

MEMBERS OF THE COUNCIL (40)

***Chair:* Walters**, Alan (CON - Beaconsfield North)
cllr.alan.walters@southbucks.gov.uk
***Vice-Chair:* Chhokar**, Santokh (CON - Gerrards Cross East and Denham South West)
cllr.santokh.chhokar@southbucks.gov.uk
***Leader of the Council:* Busby**, Adrian (CON - Beaconsfield North)
cllr.adrian.busby@southbucks.gov.uk
***Deputy Leader of the Council:* Reed**, Roger (CON - Denham North)
cllr.roger.reed@southbucks.gov.uk
Anthony, David (CON - Farnham Royal)
cllr.david.anthony@southbucks.gov.uk
Bagge, Robert (CON - Stoke Poges)
cllr.ralph.bagge@southbucks.gov.uk
Bradford, Malcolm (CON - Wexham and Iver West)
cllr.malcolm.bradford@southbucks.gov.uk
Brown, Ken (IND - Beaconsfield West)
cllr.ken.brown@southbucks.gov.uk
Burrows, Emma (CON - Iver Village and Richings Park)
cllr.emma.burrows@southbucks.gov.uk
Clark, Damon (CON - Iver Heath)
cllr.damon.clark@southbucks.gov.uk
Cranmer, Anita (CON - Hedgerley and Fulmer)
cllr.anita.cranmer@southbucks.gov.uk
Denyer, Matthew (CON - Beaconsfield West)
cllr.matt.denyer@southbucks.gov.uk
Dhillon, Dev (CON - Farnham Royal)
cllr.dev.dhillon@southbucks.gov.uk
Dhillon, Amandeep (CON - Dorney and Burnham South)
cllr.aman.dhillon@southbucks.gov.uk
Egleton, Trevor (CON - Stoke Poges)
cllr.trevor.egleton@southbucks.gov.uk
Harding, Barry (CON - Denham North)
cllr.barry.harding@southbucks.gov.uk
Hardy, Peter (CON - Gerrards Cross South)
cllr.peter.hardy@southbucks.gov.uk
Hazell, Lin (CON - Burnham Beeches)
cllr.lin.hazel@southbucks.gov.uk
Hollis, Guy (CON - Denham South)
cllr.guy.hollis@southbucks.gov.uk
Holloway, Deidre (CON - Gerrards Cross North)
cllr.deidre.holloway@southbucks.gov.uk
Jones, Steve (CON - Beaconsfield South)
cllr.steve.jones@southbucks.gov.uk
Kelly, Paul (CON - Burnham Church)
cllr.paul.kelly@southbucks.gov.uk
Lidgate, Bill (CON - Iver Heath)
cllr.bill.lidgate@southbucks.gov.uk
Lowen-Cooper, Jacquetta (CON - Beaconsfield South)
cllr.jacquetta.lowen-cooper@southbucks.gov.uk
Matthews, Wendy (CON - Iver Village and Richings Park)
cllr.wendy.matthews@southbucks.gov.uk
Naylor, Nicholas (CON - Burnham Lent Rise)
cllr.nick.naylor@southbucks.gov.uk
Oxley, Alan (LD - Iver Village and Richings Park)
cllr.alan.oxley@southbucks.gov.uk
Pepler, David (CON - Burnham Lent Rise)
cllr.david.pepler@southbucks.gov.uk
Plant, Penelope (CON - Burnham Church)
cllr.penny.plant@southbucks.gov.uk
Pope, Rachel (CON - Gerrards Cross North)
cllr.rachel.pope@southbucks.gov.uk
Royston, Maureen (CON - Farnham Royal)
cllr.maureen.royston@southbucks.gov.uk
Samson, Alan (CON - Burnham Church)
cllr.alan.samson@southbucks.gov.uk
Sandy, George (CON - Taplow)
cllr.george.sandy@southbucks.gov.uk
Simmonds, Janet (CON - Beaconsfield North)
cllr.janet.simmonds@southbucks.gov.uk
Smith, Duncan (CON - Stoke Poges)
cllr.duncan.smith@southbucks.gov.uk
Stockton, Alexander (CON - Denham South)
cllr.theearlof.stockton@southbucks.gov.uk
Sullivan, Luisa (CON - Iver Heath)
cllr.luisa.sullivan@southbucks.gov.uk
Vigor-Hedderly, Ruth (CON - Wexham and Iver West)
cllr.ruth.vigor-hedderly@southbucks.gov.uk
Wallis, Jane (CON - Burnham Lent Rise)
cllr.jane.wallis@southbucks.gov.uk
Woolveridge, Jennifer (CON - Gerrards Cross South)
cllr.jennifer.woolveridge@southbucks.gov.uk

POLITICAL COMPOSITION
CON: 38, IND: 1, LD: 1

CABINET
Leader: Mr Adrian Busby
Deputy Leader / Sustainable Development: Mr Roger Reed
Community: Mrs Anita Cranmer
Environment: Mr Bill Lidgate
Health & Housing: Mrs Jennifer Woolveridge
Resources: Mr Duncan Smith

COMMITTEE CHAIRS
Audit: Mr Guy Hollis
Licensing: Mr Peter Hardy
Overview & Scrutiny: Mr Alan Oxley
Personnel: Mr Barry Harding
Planning: Mrs Jacquetta Lowen-Cooper

SOUTH CAMBRIDGESHIRE D

South Cambridgeshire District Council, South Cambridgeshire Hall, Cambourne Business Park, Cambourne, Cambridge CB23 6EA ☎ 03450 450500 🖷 01954 713149 ✉ scdc@scambs.gov.uk 💻 www.scambs.gov.uk

FACTS & FIGURES
Police Authority: Cambridgeshire Police Authority
Health Authority: East of England Strategic Health Authority
Learning and Skills Council: Eastern
Parliamentary Constituencies: Cambridgeshire South, Cambridgeshire South East
EU Constituencies: Eastern
Election Frequency: Elections are by thirds
Twinning: Great & Little Shelford: Verneuil-en-Halatte (France); Sawston: Selsingen (Germany); Stapleford: Villedomer (France)

PRINCIPAL OFFICERS
Chief Executive: Mrs Jean Hunter, Chief Executive, South Cambridgeshire Hall, Cambourne Business Park, Cambourne, Cambridge CB23 6EA ☎ 01954 713081 ✉ jean.hunter@scambs.gov.uk

Deputy Chief Executive: Mr Alex Colyer, Executive Director of Corporate Services, South Cambridgeshire Hall, Cambourne Business Park, Cambourne, Cambridge CB23 6EA ☎ 01954 713023 ✉ alex.colyer@scambs.gov.uk

Best Value: Mr Paul Howes, Corporate Manager of Community & Customer Services, South Cambridgeshire Hall, Cambourne Business Park, Cambourne, Cambridge CB23 6EA ☎ 08450 450 500 ✉ paul.howes@scambs.gov.uk

Best Value: Mr Sean Missin, Procurement Officer, South Cambridgeshire Hall, Cambourne Business Park, Cambourne, Cambridge CB3 6EA ☎ 01954 713378 ✉ sean.missin@scambs.gov.uk

Building Control: Mr Andrew Beyer, Building Control Manager, South Cambridgeshire Hall, Cambourne Business Park, Cambourne, Cambridge CB23 6EA ☎ 08450 450 500 ✉ andrew.beyer@scambs.gov.uk

Catering Services: Mrs Eileen Simmons, Catering Manager, South Cambridgeshire Hall, Cambourne Business Park, Cambourne, Cambridge CB23 6EA ☎ 08450 450 500 ✉ eileen.simmons@scambs.gov.uk

PR / Communications: Mr Gareth Bell, Communications Manager, South Cambridgeshire Hall, Cambourne Business Park, Cambourne, Cambridge CB23 6EA ☎ 03450 450500 ✉ gareth.bell@scambs.gov.uk

Community Safety: Mr Phil Aldis, Community Safety Officer, South Cambridgeshire District Council, South Cambridgeshire Hall, Cambourne, Cambridge CB23 6EA ☎ 08450 450500 ✉ phil.aldis@scambs.gov.uk

Computer Management: Mr Stephen Rayment, Head of ICT, South Cambridgeshire Hall, Cambourne Business Park, Cambourne, Cambridge CB23 6EA ☎ 08450 450 500 🖷 01954 713234 ✉ steve.rayment@scambs.gov.uk

Contracts: Mr Paul Quigley, Environment Services Manager, South Cambridgeshire Hall, Cambourne Business Park, Cambourne, Cambridge CB23 6EA ☎ 08450 450 500 🖷 01954 713248 ✉ paul.quigley@scambs.gov.uk

Customer Service: Miss Rachael Fox, Customer Services Officer, South Cambridgeshire Hall, Cambourne Business Park, Cambourne, Cambridge CB23 6EA ☎ 03450 450500 ✉ rachael.fox@scambs.gov.uk

Customer Service: Mr Paul Howes, Corporate Manager of Community & Customer Services, South Cambridgeshire Hall, Cambourne Business Park, Cambourne, Cambridge CB23 6EA ☎ 08450 450 500 ✉ paul.howes@scambs.gov.uk

Direct Labour: Mr Stuart Harwood Clark, Environment Operations Manager, South Cambridgeshire Hall, Cambourne Business Park, Cambourne, Cambridge CB23 6EA ☎ 08450 450500 ✉ stuart.harwoodclark@scambs.gov.uk

Economic Development: Ms Nicole Kritzinger, Economic Development Officer, South Cambridgeshire Hall, Cambourne Business Park, Cambourne, Cambridge CB23 6EA ☎ 01954 713454 ✉ economicdevelopment@scambs.gov.uk

Economic Development: Mr Keith Miles, Planning Policy Manager, South Cambridgeshire Hall, Cambourne Business Park, Cambourne, Cambridge CB23 6EA ☎ 08450 450 500 🖷 01954 713152 ✉ keith.miles@scambs.gov.uk

E-Government: Mr Stephen Rayment, Head of ICT, South Cambridgeshire Hall, Cambourne Business Park, Cambourne, Cambridge CB23 6EA ☎ 08450 450 500 🖷 01954 713234 ✉ steve.rayment@scambs.gov.uk

Electoral Registration: Mr Andrew Francis, Electoral & Support Services Manager, South Cambridgeshire Hall, Cambourne Business Park, Cambourne, Cambridge CB23 6EA ☎ 03450 450 500 ✉ andrew.francis@scambs.gov.uk

Emergency Planning: Mr Lawrence Green, Health & Safety Advisor, South Cambridgeshire Hall, Cambourne Business Park,

Cambourne, Cambridge CB23 6EA ☏ 08450 450 500 🖷 01954 713248 ✉ lawrence.green@scambs.gov.uk

Energy Management: Mr Richard Hales, Strategic Sustainability Officer, South Cambridgeshire District Council, South Cambridgeshire Hall, Cambourne, Cambridge CB23 6EA ☏ 08450 450500 ✉ richard.hales@scambs.gov.uk

Environmental / Technical Services: Mr Paul Quigley, Environment Services Manager, South Cambridgeshire Hall, Cambourne Business Park, Cambourne, Cambridge CB23 6EA ☏ 08450 450 500 🖷 01954 713248 ✉ paul.quigley@scambs.gov.uk

Environmental Health: Mr Paul Quigley, Environment Services Manager, South Cambridgeshire Hall, Cambourne Business Park, Cambourne, Cambridge CB23 6EA ☏ 08450 450 500 🖷 01954 713248 ✉ paul.quigley@scambs.gov.uk

Estates, Property & Valuation: Mr Paul Howes, Corporate Manager of Community & Customer Services, South Cambridgeshire Hall, Cambourne Business Park, Cambourne, Cambridge CB23 6EA ☏ 08450 450 500 ✉ paul.howes@scambs.gov.uk

Events Manager: Mr Andy O'Hanlon, Arts Development Officer, South Cambridgeshire Hall, Cambourne Business Park, Cambourne, Cambridge CB23 6EA ☏ 01954 713343 ✉ andy.ohanlon@scambs.gov.uk

Facilities: Mr Sid Webb, Repairs Operations Manager, South Cambridgeshire Hall, Cambourne Business Park, Cambourne, Cambridge CB23 6EA ☏ 08450 450500

Finance and Treasurer: Mr Phil Bird, Head of Revenues, South Cambridgeshire Hall, Cambourne Business Park, Cambourne, Cambridge CB23 6EA ☏ 03450 450 500 ✉ phillip.bird@scambs.gov.uk

Finance and Treasurer: Mr R A Burns, Head of Accountancy, South Cambridgeshire Hall, Cambourne Business Park, Cambourne, Cambridge CB23 6EA ☏ 0845 045 0500

Finance and Treasurer: Mrs Jean Hunter, Chief Executive, South Cambridgeshire Hall, Cambourne Business Park, Cambourne, Cambridge CB23 6EA ☏ 01954 713081 ✉ jean.hunter@scambs.gov.uk

Health and Safety: Mr Lawrence Green, Health & Safety Advisor, South Cambridgeshire Hall, Cambourne Business Park, Cambourne, Cambridge CB23 6EA ☏ 08450 450 500 🖷 01954 713248 ✉ lawrence.green@scambs.gov.uk

Home Energy Conservation: Mr Paul Quigley, Environment Services Manager, South Cambridgeshire Hall, Cambourne Business Park, Cambourne, Cambridge CB23 6EA ☏ 08450 450 500 🖷 01954 713248 ✉ paul.quigley@scambs.gov.uk

Housing: Ms Anita Goddard, Housing Services Manager, South Cambridgeshire Hall, Cambourne Business Park, Cambourne, Cambridge CB23 6EA ☏ 08450 450 500 ✉ anita.goddard@scambs.gov.uk

Housing: Mr Stephen Hills, Corporate Manager for Affordable Housing, South Cambridgeshire Hall, Cambourne Business Park, Cambourne, Cambridge CB23 6EA ☏ 08450 450 500 ✉ stephen.hills@scambs.gov.uk

Housing Maintenance: Mr Mark Allan, Interim Property Services Manager, South Cambridgeshire Hall, Cambourne Business Park, Cambourne, Cambridge CB23 6EA ☏ 03450 450 500 ✉ mark.allan@scambs.gov.uk

Housing Maintenance: Mr Stephen Hills, Corporate Manager for Affordable Housing, South Cambridgeshire Hall, Cambourne Business Park, Cambourne, Cambridge CB23 6EA ☏ 08450 450 500 ✉ stephen.hills@scambs.gov.uk

Legal: Mrs Fiona McMillan, Principal Solicitor, South Cambridgeshire District Council, South Cambridgeshire Hall, Cambourne, Cambridge CB23 6EA ☏ 08450 450500 ✉ fiona.mcmillan@scambs.gov.uk

Licensing: Mr Myles Bebbington, Licensing Officer, South Cambridgeshire Hall, Cambourne Business Park, Cambourne, Cambridge CB23 6EA ☏ 08450 450 500 🖷 01954 713248 ✉ myles.bebbington@scambs.gov.uk

Lighting: Mr Paul Quigley, Environment Services Manager, South Cambridgeshire Hall, Cambourne Business Park, Cambourne, Cambridge CB23 6EA ☏ 08450 450 500 🖷 01954 713248 ✉ paul.quigley@scambs.gov.uk

Member Services: Mrs Holly Adams, Democratic Services Manager, South Cambridgeshire Hall, Cambourne Business Park, Cambourne, Cambridge CB23 6EA ☏ 03450 450 500 ✉ holly.adams@scambs.gov.uk

Partnerships: Mr Paul Howes, Corporate Manager of Community & Customer Services, South Cambridgeshire Hall, Cambourne Business Park, Cambourne, Cambridge CB23 6EA ☏ 08450 450 500 ✉ paul.howes@scambs.gov.uk

Personnel / HR: Ms Susan Gardner Craig, Human Resources Manager, South Cambridgeshire Hall, Cambourne Business Park, Cambourne, Cambridge CB3 6EA ☏ 08450 450 500 ✉ susan.gardnercraig@scambs.gov.uk

Planning: Mr Chris Collison, Interim Head of Planning & Sustainable Communities, South Cambridgeshire Hall, Cambourne Business Park, Cambourne, Cambridge CB23 6EA ☏ 03450 450 500 ✉ chris.collison@scambs.gov.uk

Planning: Mr Keith Miles, Planning Policy Manager, South Cambridgeshire Hall, Cambourne Business Park, Cambourne, Cambridge CB23 6EA ☏ 08450 450 500 🖷 01954 713152 ✉ keith.miles@scambs.gov.uk

Procurement: Mr Sean Missin, Procurement Officer, South Cambridgeshire Hall, Cambourne Business Park, Cambourne, Cambridge CB23 6EA ☏ 01954 713378 ✉ sean.missin@scambs.gov.uk

Recycling & Waste Minimisation: Mr Paul Quigley, Environment Services Manager, South Cambridgeshire Hall, Cambourne

Business Park, Cambourne, Cambridge CB23 6EA ☎ 08450 450 500 🖷 01954 713248 ✉ paul.quigley@scambs.gov.uk

Staff Training: Ms Susan Gardner Craig, Human Resources Manager, South Cambridgeshire Hall, Cambourne Business Park, Cambourne, Cambridge CB3 6EA ☎ 08450 450 500 ✉ susan.gardnercraig@scambs.gov.uk

Sustainable Communities: Mr Richard Hales, Strategic Sustainability Officer, South Cambridgeshire District Council, South Cambridgeshire Hall, Cambourne, Cambridge CB23 6EA ☎ 08450 450500 ✉ richard.hales@scambs.gov.uk

Sustainable Communities: Mr Paul Howes, Corporate Manager of Community & Customer Services, South Cambridgeshire Hall, Cambourne Business Park, Cambourne, Cambridge CB23 6EA ☎ 08450 450 500 ✉ paul.howes@scambs.gov.uk

Sustainable Development: Mr Chris Collison, Interim Head of Planning & Sustainable Communities, South Cambridgeshire Hall, Cambourne Business Park, Cambourne, Cambridge CB23 6EA ☎ 03450 450 500 ✉ chris.collison@scambs.gov.uk

Sustainable Development: Mr Richard Hales, Strategic Sustainability Officer, South Cambridgeshire District Council, South Cambridgeshire Hall, Cambourne, Cambridge CB23 6EA ☎ 08450 450500 ✉ richard.hales@scambs.gov.uk

Transport Planner: Mr Jonathan Dixon, Principal Planning Policy Officer of Transport, South Cambridgeshire Hall, Cambourne Business Park, Cambourne, Cambridge CB3 6EA ☎ 08450 450 500 ✉ jonathan.dixon@scambs.gov.uk

Waste Collection and Disposal: Mr Stuart Harwood Clark, Environment Operations Manager, South Cambridgeshire Hall, Cambourne Business Park, Cambourne, Cambridge CB23 6EA ☎ 08450 450500 ✉ stuart.harwoodclark@scambs.gov.uk

Waste Management: Mr Stuart Harwood Clark, Environment Operations Manager, South Cambridgeshire Hall, Cambourne Business Park, Cambourne, Cambridge CB23 6EA ☎ 08450 450500 ✉ stuart.harwoodclark@scambs.gov.uk

MEMBERS OF THE COUNCIL (57)

***Chair:* Orgee**, Tony (CON - The Abingtons)
cllr.orgee@scambs.gov.uk
***Vice-Chair:* Bard**, David (CON - Sawston)
cllr.bard@scambs.gov.uk
***Leader of the Council:* Manning**, Ray (CON - Willingham and Over)
cllr.manning@scambs.gov.uk
***Deputy Leader of the Council:* Edwards**, Simon (CON - Cottenham)
cllr.edwards@scambs.gov.uk
***Group Leader:* Kindersley**, Sebastian (LD - Gamlingay)
cllr.kindersley@scambs.gov.uk
Barrett, Richard (CON - Balsham)
cllr.barrettre@scambs.gov.uk
Barrett, Val (CON - Melbourn)
cllr.barrettvm@scambs.gov.uk
Bear, Trisha (LD - Linton)
cllr.bear@scambs.gov.uk
Burkitt, Francis (CON - Barton)
cllr.burkitt@scambs.gov.uk
Burling, Brian (CON - Willingham and Over)
cllr.burling@scambs.gov.uk
Bygott, Thomas (CON - Girton)
cllr.bygott@scambs.gov.uk
Cathcart, Nigel (LAB - Bassingbourn)
cllr.cathcart@scambs.gov.uk
Chatfield, Jonathan (LD - Histon and Impington)
cllr.chatfield@scambs.gov.uk
Corney, Pippa (CON - Willingham and Over)
cllr.corney@scambs.gov.uk
Davies, Neil (IND - Histon and Impington)
cllr.davies@scambs.gov.uk
De Lacey, Douglas (IND - Girton)
cllr.delacey@scambs.gov.uk
Elcox, Alison (CON - Bourn)
cllr.elcox@scambs.gov.uk
Ellington, Sue (CON - Swavesey)
cllr.ellington@scambs.gov.uk
Hales, Jose (LD - Melbourn)
cllr.hales@scambs.gov.uk
Hall, Roger (CON - Bar Hill)
cllr.hall@scambs.gov.uk
Harangozo, Stephen (LD - Comberton)
cllr.harangozo@scambs.gov.uk
Harford, Lynda (LD - Cottenham)
cllr.harford@scambs.gov.uk
Hatton, Sally (IND - Sawston)
cllr.hatton@scambs.gov.uk
Hawkins, Tumi (LD - Caldecote)
cllr.hawkins@scambs.gov.uk
Hersom, Mark (LD - Milton)
cllr.hersom@scambs.gov.uk
Hickford, Roger (CON - Linton)
cllr.hickford@scambs.gov.uk
Hockney, James (CON - Waterbeach)
cllr.hockney@scambs.gov.uk
Howell, Mark (CON - Papworth and Elsworth)
cllr.howell@scambs.gov.uk
Hudson, Clayton (CON - Bourn)
cllr.hudson@scambs@gov.uk
Hunt, Caroline (CON - Teversham)
cllr.hunt@scambs.gov.uk
Jarvis, Pauline (LD - Balsham)
cllr.jarvis@scambs.gov.uk
Johnson, Peter (CON - Waterbeach)
cllr.johnson@scambs.gov.uk
Lockwood, Janet (LD - Harston and Hauxton)
cllr.lockwood@scambs.gov.uk
Loynes, Mervyn (CON - Bourn)
Martin, Mick (CON - Duxford)
cllr.martin@scambs.gov.uk
Matthews, Raymond (CON - Sawston)
cllr.matthews@scambs.gov.uk
McCraith, David (CON - Bassingbourn)
cllr.mccraith@scambs.gov.uk
Murfitt, Cicely (IND - The Mordens)
cllr.murfitt@scambs.gov.uk
Nightingale, Charles (CON - The Shelfords and Stapleford)
cllr.nightingale@scambs.gov.uk
Page, Robin (IND - Haslingfield and the Eversdens)
cllr.page@scambs.gov.uk
Ridgway - Watt, Ted (CON - Orwell and Barrington)

cllr.ridgwaywatt@scamb.gov.uk
Riley, Alex (IND - Longstanton)
cllr.riley@scambs.gov.uk
Roberts, Deborah (IND - Fowlmere and Foxton)
cllr.roberts@scambs.gov.uk
Scarr, Neil (IND - Fulbourn)
cllr.scarr@scambs.gov.uk
Shelton, Ben (CON - The Shelfords and Stapleford)
cllr.shelton@scambs.gov.uk
Smith, Bridget (LD - Gamlingay)
cllr.smithbz@scambs.gov.uk
Smith, Hazel (LD - Milton)
cllr.smithhm@scambs.gov.uk
Soond, Surinder (LD - Meldreth)
cllr.soond@scambs.gov.uk
Stewart, Jim (LD - Hardwick)
cllr.stewart@scambs.gov.uk
Stonham, Edd (LD - Histon and Impington)
cllr.stonham@scambs.gov.uk
Topping, Peter (CON - Whittlesford)
cllr.topping@scambs.gov.uk
Turner, Robert (CON - The Wilbrahams)
cllr.turner@scambs.gov.uk
Waters, Bunty (CON - Bar Hill)
cllr.waters@scambs.gov.uk
Whiteman-Downes, David (CON - The Shelfords and Stapleford)
cllr.whiteman-downes@scambs.gov.uk
Williams, John G (LD - Fulbourn)
cllr.williamsjg@scambs.gov.uk
Wotherspoon, Tim (CON - Cottenham)
cllr.wotherspoon@scambs.gov.uk
Wright, Nick (CON - Papworth and Elsworth)
cllr.wright@scambs.gov.uk

POLITICAL COMPOSITION

CON: 32, LD: 16, IND: 8, LAB: 1

CABINET

Leader: Mr Ray Manning
Deputy Leader / Finance & Staffing: Mr Simon Edwards
Customer Services: Mr James Hockney
Environmental Services: Mrs Sue Ellington
Housing: Mr Mark Howell
Planning & Economic Development: Mr Tim Wotherspoon
Planning Policy & Localism: Mrs Pippa Corney

COMMITTEE CHAIRS

Employment: Mr David Whiteman-Downes
Licensing: Mr Roger Hall
Overview & Scrutiny: Mr Ben Shelton
Planning: Mr Robert Turner

SOUTH DERBYSHIRE D

South Derbyshire District Council, Civic Offices, Civic Way, Swadlincote DE11 0AH ☎ 01283 221000 🖷 01283 550128 ✉ civic.offices@south-derbys.gov.uk 💻 www.south-derbys.gov.uk

FACTS & FIGURES

Police Authority: Derbyshire Police Authority
Health Authority: East Midlands Strategic Health Authority
Learning and Skills Council: East Midlands
Parliamentary Constituencies: Derbyshire South
EU Constituencies: East Midlands
Election Frequency: Elections are of whole council

PRINCIPAL OFFICERS

Chief Executive: Mr Frank McArdle, Chief Executive, Civic Offices, Civic Way, Swadlincote DE11 0AH ☎ 01283 595702 🖷 01283 595854 ✉ frank.mcardle@south-derbys.gov.uk

Best Value: Mr Kevin Stackhouse, Head of Corporate Services, Civic Offices, Civic Way, Swadlincote DE11 0AH ☎ 01283 595811 🖷 01283 595854 ✉ kevin.stackhouse@south-derbys.gov.uk

Building Control: Mr Stuart Batchelor, Head of Community & Planning Services, Civic Offices, Civic Way, Swadlincote DE11 0AH ☎ 01283 595820 🖷 01283 595720 ✉ stuart.batchelor@south-derbys.gov.uk

PR / Communications: Mrs Carole Warburton, Public Relations Officer, Civic Offices, Civic Way, Swadlincote DE11 0AH ☎ 01283 595741 🖷 01283 595802 ✉ carole.warburton@south-derbys.gov.uk

Community Safety: Mr Stuart Batchelor, Head of Community & Planning Services, Civic Offices, Civic Way, Swadlincote DE11 0AH ☎ 01283 595820 🖷 01283 595720 ✉ stuart.batchelor@south-derbys.gov.uk

Computer Management: Mr Nigel Glossop, Head of IT Services, Civic Offices, Civic Way, Swadlincote DE11 0AH ☎ 01283 595703 🖷 01283 595720 ✉ nigel.glossop@south-derbys.gov.uk

Corporate Services: Mr Kevin Stackhouse, Head of Corporate Services, Civic Offices, Civic Way, Swadlincote DE11 0AH ☎ 01283 595811 🖷 01283 595854 ✉ kevin.stackhouse@south-derbys.gov.uk

Direct Labour: Mr Robert Ledger, Head of Housing & Environmental Services, Civic Offices, Civic Way, Swadlincote DE11 0AH ☎ 01283 595775 🖷 01283 595852 ✉ bob.ledger@south-derbys.gov.uk

Economic Development: Mr Stuart Batchelor, Head of Community & Planning Services, Civic Offices, Civic Way, Swadlincote DE11 0AH ☎ 01283 595820 🖷 01283 595720 ✉ stuart.batchelor@south-derbys.gov.uk

E-Government: Mr Nigel Glossop, Head of IT Services, Civic Offices, Civic Way, Swadlincote DE11 0AH ☎ 01283 595703 🖷 01283 595720 ✉ nigel.glossop@south-derbys.gov.uk

Electoral Registration: Ms Brenda Reed, Elections & Democratic Services Officer, Civic Offices, Civic Way, Swadlincote DE11 0AH ☎ 01283 595723 🖷 01283 595854 ✉ brenda.reed@south-derbys.gov.uk

Emergency Planning: Mr Mark Alflat, Director of Operations, Civic Offices, Civic Way, Swadlincote DE11 0AH ☎ 01283 595712 🖷 01283 595760 ✉ mark.alflat@south-derbys.gov.uk

Environmental / Technical Services: Mr Robert Ledger, Head of Housing & Environmental Services, Civic Offices, Civic Way, Swadlincote DE11 0AH ☎ 01283 595775 🖷 01283 595852

bob.ledger@south-derbys.gov.uk

Environmental Health: Mr Robert Ledger, Head of Housing & Environmental Services, Civic Offices, Civic Way, Swadlincote DE11 0AH ☎ 01283 595775 🖷 01283 595852 bob.ledger@south-derbys.gov.uk

Estates, Property & Valuation: Mr Kevin Stackhouse, Head of Corporate Services, Civic Offices, Civic Way, Swadlincote DE11 0AH ☎ 01283 595811 🖷 01283 595854 kevin.stackhouse@south-derbys.gov.uk

European Liaison: Mr Frank McArdle, Chief Executive, Civic Offices, Civic Way, Swadlincote DE11 0AH ☎ 01283 595702 🖷 01283 595854 frank.mcardle@south-derbys.gov.uk

Events Manager: Mr Stuart Batchelor, Head of Community & Planning Services, Civic Offices, Civic Way, Swadlincote DE11 0AH ☎ 01283 595820 🖷 01283 595720 stuart.batchelor@south-derbys.gov.uk

Finance and Treasurer: Mr Kevin Stackhouse, Head of Corporate Services, Civic Offices, Civic Way, Swadlincote DE11 0AH ☎ 01283 595811 🖷 01283 595854 kevin.stackhouse@south-derbys.gov.uk

Grounds Maintenance: Mr Robert Ledger, Head of Housing & Environmental Services, Civic Offices, Civic Way, Swadlincote DE11 0AH ☎ 01283 595775 🖷 01283 595852 bob.ledger@south-derbys.gov.uk

Health and Safety: Mr Mark Alflat, Director of Operations, Civic Offices, Civic Way, Swadlincote DE11 0AH ☎ 01283 595712 🖷 01283 595760 mark.alflat@south-derbys.gov.uk

Home Energy Conservation: Mr Robert Ledger, Head of Housing & Environmental Services, Civic Offices, Civic Way, Swadlincote DE11 0AH ☎ 01283 595775 🖷 01283 595852 bob.ledger@south-derbys.gov.uk

Housing: Mr Robert Ledger, Head of Housing & Environmental Services, Civic Offices, Civic Way, Swadlincote DE11 0AH ☎ 01283 595775 🖷 01283 595852 bob.ledger@south-derbys.gov.uk

Housing Maintenance: Mr Robert Ledger, Head of Housing & Environmental Services, Civic Offices, Civic Way, Swadlincote DE11 0AH ☎ 01283 595775 🖷 01283 595852 bob.ledger@south-derbys.gov.uk

Legal: Mr Kevin Stackhouse, Head of Corporate Services, Civic Offices, Civic Way, Swadlincote DE11 0AH ☎ 01283 595811 🖷 01283 595854 kevin.stackhouse@south-derbys.gov.uk

Leisure and Cultural Services: Mr Stuart Batchelor, Head of Community & Planning Services, Civic Offices, Civic Way, Swadlincote DE11 0AH ☎ 01283 595820 🖷 01283 595720 stuart.batchelor@south-derbys.gov.uk

Licensing: Mr Kevin Stackhouse, Head of Corporate Services, Civic Offices, Civic Way, Swadlincote DE11 0AH ☎ 01283 595811 🖷 01283 595854 kevin.stackhouse@south-derbys.gov.uk

Lottery Funding, Charity and Voluntary: Mr Stuart Batchelor, Head of Community & Planning Services, Civic Offices, Civic Way, Swadlincote DE11 0AH ☎ 01283 595820 🖷 01283 595720 stuart.batchelor@south-derbys.gov.uk

Member Services: Mr Kevin Stackhouse, Head of Corporate Services, Civic Offices, Civic Way, Swadlincote DE11 0AH ☎ 01283 595811 🖷 01283 595854 kevin.stackhouse@south-derbys.gov.uk

Partnerships: Mr Kevin Stackhouse, Head of Corporate Services, Civic Offices, Civic Way, Swadlincote DE11 0AH ☎ 01283 595811 🖷 01283 595854 kevin.stackhouse@south-derbys.gov.uk

Personnel / HR: Mr David Clamp, Head of Organisational Development, Civic Offices, Civic Way, Swadlincote DE11 0AH ☎ 01283 595729 🖷 01283 595854 david.clamp@south-derbys.gov.uk

Planning: Mr Stuart Batchelor, Head of Community & Planning Services, Civic Offices, Civic Way, Swadlincote DE11 0AH ☎ 01283 595820 🖷 01283 595720 stuart.batchelor@south-derbys.gov.uk

Procurement: Mr Kevin Stackhouse, Head of Corporate Services, Civic Offices, Civic Way, Swadlincote DE11 0AH ☎ 01283 595811 🖷 01283 595854 kevin.stackhouse@south-derbys.gov.uk

Recycling & Waste Minimisation: Mr Robert Ledger, Head of Housing & Environmental Services, Civic Offices, Civic Way, Swadlincote DE11 0AH ☎ 01283 595775 🖷 01283 595852 bob.ledger@south-derbys.gov.uk

Staff Training: Mr David Clamp, Head of Organisational Development, Civic Offices, Civic Way, Swadlincote DE11 0AH ☎ 01283 595729 🖷 01283 595854 david.clamp@south-derbys.gov.uk

Sustainable Development: Mr Stuart Batchelor, Head of Community & Planning Services, Civic Offices, Civic Way, Swadlincote DE11 0AH ☎ 01283 595820 🖷 01283 595720 stuart.batchelor@south-derbys.gov.uk

Tourism: Mr Stuart Batchelor, Head of Community & Planning Services, Civic Offices, Civic Way, Swadlincote DE11 0AH ☎ 01283 595820 🖷 01283 595720 stuart.batchelor@south-derbys.gov.uk

Waste Collection and Disposal: Mr Robert Ledger, Head of Housing & Environmental Services, Civic Offices, Civic Way, Swadlincote DE11 0AH ☎ 01283 595775 🖷 01283 595852 bob.ledger@south-derbys.gov.uk

Waste Management: Mr Robert Ledger, Head of Housing & Environmental Services, Civic Offices, Civic Way, Swadlincote DE11 0AH ☎ 01283 595775 🖷 01283 595852 bob.ledger@south-derbys.gov.uk

MEMBERS OF THE COUNCIL (36)

***Chair:* Bale**, Michael (CON - Hilton)
michael.bale@south-derby.gov.uk

Leader of the Council: **Wheeler**, Robert (CON - Linton)
bob.wheeler@south-derbys.gov.uk
Atkin, Neil (CON - Aston)
neil.atkin@south-derbys.gov.uk
Bambrick, Sean (LAB - Newhall and Stanton)
sean.bambrick@south-derbys.gov.uk
Bell, Roy (LAB - Woodville)
roy.bell@south-derbys.gov.uk
Brown, Lisa (CON - Etwall)
lisa.brown@south-derbys.gov.uk
Chahal, Manjit (LAB - Stenson)
manji.chahal@south-derbys.gov.uk
Dunn, Paul (LAB - Midway)
paul.dunn@south-derbys.gov.uk
Ford, Martyn (CON - Willington and Findern)
martyn.ford@south-derbys.gov.uk
Frost, Steven (LAB - Seales)
steve.frost@south-derbys.gov.uk
Hall, Margaret (CON - Seales)
margaret.hall@south-derbys.gov.uk
Harrison, John (CON - Melbourne)
john.harrison@south-derbys.gov.uk
Heath, Yvonne (LAB - Swadlincote)
yvonne.heath@south-derbys.gov.uk
Hewlett, Jim (CON - Melbourne)
jim.hewlett@south-derbys.gov.uk
Hood, Ann (CON - Willington and Findern)
ann.hood@south-derbys.gov.uk
Jones, Charles (CON - Linton)
charles.jones@south-derbys.gov.uk
Lemmon, John (CON - Etwall)
john.lemmon@south-derbys.gov.uk
Mead, Jean (LAB - Newhall and Stanton)
jean.mead@south-derbys.gov.uk
Mulgrew, Michael (LAB - Swadlincote)
mick.mulgrew@south-derbys.gov.uk
Murray, Patrick (CON - Woodville)
pat.murray@south-derbys.gov.uk
Patten, Julie (CON - Hilton)
julie.patten@south-derbys.gov.uk
Pearson, Robert (LAB - Midway)
rob.pearson@south-derbys.gov.uk
Plenderleith, Amy (CON - Hilton)
amy.plenderleith@south-derbys.gov.uk
Rhind, Gordon (LAB - Church Gresley)
gordon.rhind@south-derbys.gov.uk
Richards, Kevin (LAB - Newhall and Stanton)
kevin.richards@south-derbys.gov.uk
Roberts, Andy (CON - Hatton)
andy.roberts@south-derbys.gov.uk
Shepherd, David (LAB - Stenson)
david.shepherd@south-derbys.gov.uk
Smith, Peter (CON - Repton)
peterhenrysmith@hotmail.com
Southerd, Trevor (LAB - Church Gresley)
trevor.southerd@south-derbys.gov.uk
Stanton, Michael (CON - Repton)
michael.stanton@south-derbys.gov.uk
Stuart, Benjamin (LAB - Church Gresley)
ben.stuart@south-derbys.gov.uk
Taylor, Stephen (LAB - Woodville)
stephen.taylor@south-derbys.gov.uk
Tilley, Neil (LAB - Swadlincote)
neil.tilley@south-derbys.gov.uk
Watson, Peter (CON - Aston)
peter.watson@south-derbys.gov.uk
Watson, Ann (CON - Aston)
ann.watson@south-derbys.gov.uk
Wilkins, Peter (LAB - Midway)
peter.wilkins@south-derbys.gov.uk

POLITICAL COMPOSITION
CON: 19, LAB: 17

CABINET
Leader: Mr Robert Wheeler

COMMITTEE CHAIRS
Environmental & Development Services: Mr Peter Watson
Finance & Management: Mr Robert Wheeler
Housing & Community Services: Mr John Lemmon
Overview & Scrutiny: Mrs Amy Plenderleith
Planning: Mr Martyn Ford

SOUTH GLOUCESTERSHIRE U

South Gloucestershire Council, The Council Offices, Castle Street, Thornbury BS35 1HF ☎ 01454 868686 🖷 01454 863067 ✉ mailbox@southglos.gov.uk 💻 www.southglos.gov.uk

FACTS & FIGURES
Police Authority: Avon & Somerset Police Authority
Health Authority: NHS South West
Learning and Skills Council: South West
Parliamentary Constituencies: Bristol North West, Filton and Bradley Stoke, Kingswood, Thornbury and Yate
EU Constituencies: South West
Election Frequency: Elections are of whole council

PRINCIPAL OFFICERS
Chief Executive: Mrs Amanda Deeks, Chief Executive, The Council Offices, Castle Street, Thornbury BS35 3HF ☎ 01454 863851 🖷 01454 863855 ✉ amanda.deeks@southglos.gov.uk

Deputy Chief Executive: Mr David Perry, Director of Corporate Services, The Council Offices, Castle Street, Thornbury BS35 1HF ☎ 01454 865001 🖷 01454 863855 ✉ dave.perry@southglos.gov.uk

Access Officer / Social Services (Disability): Ms Alice Cleaveland, Access Officer, Badminton Road Offices, Badminton Road, Yate BS37 5AF ☎ 01454 863860 🖷 01454 868150 ✉ alice.cleaveland@southglos.gov.uk

Architect, Building / Property Services: Mr Zulfiquar Darr, Head of Corporate Finance & Technology, The Council Offices, Castle Street, Thornbury BS35 1HF ☎ 01454 864670 🖷 01454 865026 ✉ zulfiquar.darr@southglos.gov.uk

Best Value: Ms Sue Covello, Value for Money & Procurement Manager, The Council Offices, Castle Street, Thornbury BS35 1HF ☎ 01454 864703 ✉ sue.covello@southglos.gov.uk

Building Control: Mr Brian Glasson, Head of Strategic Planning, Badminton Road Offices, Badminton Road Offices, Yate BS37 5AF ☎ 01454 863535 🖷 01454 863737 ✉ brian.glasson@southglos.gov.uk

Catering Services: Ms Kay Knight, Head of Traded & Support Services, Badminton Road Offices, Badminton Road, Yate BS37 1HF ☎ 01454 863246 🖷 01454 863998 ✉ kay.knight@southglos.gov.uk

Children / Youth Services: Ms Geri Palfreeman, Service Manager of Preventative Services, Kingswood Locality Hub, High Street, Kingswood BS15 9TR ☎ 01454 863152 ✉ geri.palfreeman@southglos.gov.uk

Civil Registration: Ms Marilyn Heffer, Superintendent Registrar, Register Office, Poole Court, Poole Court Drive, Yate BS37 5PT ☎ 01454 863604 ✉ marilyn.heffer@southglos.gov.uk

PR / Communications: Mr Dominic Moody, Senior External Communications Officer, The Council Offices, Castle Street, Thornbury BS35 1HF ☎ 01454 863291 🖷 01454 863886 ✉ dominic.moody@southglos.gov.uk

Community Planning: Mrs Usha Kumar, Voluntary & Community Sector Support Co-ordinator, Badminton Road Offices, Badminton Road, Yate BS37 5AF ☎ 01454 865684 🖷 01454 868535 ✉ usha.kumar@southglos.gov.uk

Community Safety: Mr Robert Walsh, Head of Safe Strong Communities, Badminton Road Offices, Badminton Road, Yate BS37 5AF ☎ 01454 865818 ✉ robert.walsh@southglos.gov.uk

Computer Management: Mr Tim Peters, Head of ICT Business Support & E-Support, The Council Offices, Castle Street, Thornbury BS35 1HF ☎ 01454 865014 🖷 01454 865041 ✉ tim.peters@southglos.gov.uk

Contracts: Ms Sue Covello, Value for Money & Procurement Manager, The Council Offices, Castle Street, Thornbury BS35 1HF ☎ 01454 864703 ✉ sue.covello@southglos.gov.uk

Corporate Services: Mr Andrew Birch, Head of Business Management & Budget Strategy, St Lukes Close, Emersons Way, Emersons Green, BS16 7AL ☎ 01454 865985 ✉ andrew.birch@southglos.gov.uk

Corporate Services: Mr Zulfiquar Darr, Head of Corporate Finance & Technology, The Council Offices, Castle Street, Thornbury BS35 1HF ☎ 01454 864670 🖷 01454 865026 ✉ zulfiquar.darr@southglos.gov.uk

Corporate Services: Mr Martin Dear, Head of Strategy, Quality & Standards, Badminton Road Offices, Badminton Road, Yate BS37 5AF ☎ 01454 863197 ✉ martin.dear@southglos.gov.uk

Corporate Services: Ms Clare Medland, Head of Strategy Access & Planning, Badminton Road Offices, Badminton Road, Yate BS37 5AF ☎ 01454 863239 ✉ clare.medland@southglos.gov.uk

Corporate Services: Mr David Perry, Director of Corporate Services, The Council Offices, Castle Street, Thornbury BS35 1HF ☎ 01454 865001 🖷 01454 863855 ✉ dave.perry@southglos.gov.uk

Customer Service: Mr Nick Aslett, Service Manager of Preventative Services, Kingswood Hub, High Street, Kingswood BS15 9TR ☎ 01454 863338 ✉ nick.aslett@southglos.gov.uk

Customer Service: Ms Liz Crocker, Head of Integrated Locality Services for Severnvale, Badminton Road Offices, Badminton Road, Yate BS37 5AF ☎ 01454 865904 ✉ liz.crocker@southglos.gov.uk

Customer Service: Mr Mike Hayesman, Head of Customer & Transactional Services, Badminton Road Offices, Badminton Road, Yate BS37 5AF ☎ 01454 865290 ✉ mike.hayesman@southglos.gov.uk

Customer Service: Mr Mike Hennessey, Head of Strategic Support Services, St Lukes Close, Emerson Way, Emersons Green, BS16 7AL ☎ 01454 866325 ✉ mike.hennessey@southglos.gov.uk

Direct Labour: Mr Mark King, Head of Street Care, Broad Lane Offices, Engine Common Lane, Yate BS37 7PN ☎ 01454 863912 🖷 01454 865812 ✉ mark.king@southglos.gov.uk

Economic Development: Mr Steve Evans, Director of Environment & Community Services, The Council Offices, Castle Street, Thornbury BS35 1HF ☎ 01454 865811 🖷 01454 865812 ✉ steve.evans@southglos.gov.uk

Education: Ms Therese Gillespie, Director for Children & Young People, Badminton Road Offices, Badminton Road, Yate BS37 5AF ☎ 01454 863253 🖷 01454 863264 ✉ therese.gillespie@southglos.gov.uk

Education: Mr Richard Swan, Special Projects Adviser, Badminton Road Offices, Badminton Road, Yate BS37 5AF ☎ 01454 863942 ✉ richard.swan@southglos.gov.uk

E-Government: Mr Tim Peters, Head of ICT Business Support & E-Support, The Council Offices, Castle Street, Thornbury BS35 1HF ☎ 01454 865014 🖷 01454 865041 ✉ tim.peters@southglos.gov.uk

Electoral Registration: Mr Stuart Hook, Head of Democratic & Statutory Services, The Council Offices, Castle Street, Thornbury BS35 1HF ☎ 01454 863053 🖷 01454 864661 ✉ stuart.hook@southglos.gov.uk

Emergency Planning: Mr Simon Hailwood, Senior Emergency Planning Officer, The Council Offices, Castle Street, Thornbury BS35 1HF ☎ 01454 863869 ✉ simon.hailwood@southglos.gov.uk

Energy Management: Mr Sean Prior, Senior Energy Engineer, Badminton Road Offices, Badminton Road, Yate BS37 5AF ☎ 01454 865141 🖷 01454 865069 ✉ sean.prior@southglos.gov.uk

Environmental / Technical Services: Mr Gerald Madden, Health Manager, Badminton Road Offices, Badminton Road, Yate BS37 5AF ☎ 01454 863569 🖷 01454 863642 ✉ gerald.madden@southglos.gov.uk

Environmental Health: Mr Brian Glasson, Head of Strategic Planning, Badminton Road Offices, Badminton Road Offices, Yate BS37 5AF ☎ 01454 863535 🖷 01454 863737

brian.glasson@southglos.gov.uk

Environmental Health: Mr Chris Taylor, Environmental Protection Manager, Badminton Road Offices, Badminton Road, Yate BS37 5AF ☎ 01454 863474 🖷 01454 863484 chris.taylor@southglos.gov.uk

Estates, Property & Valuation: Mr Zulfiquar Darr, Head of Corporate Finance & Technology, The Council Offices, Badminton Road, Yate BS37 5AF ☎ 01454 864670 🖷 01454 865026 zulfiquar.darr@southglos.gov.uk

European Liaison: Mr George Kousouros, Community Project Manager, Badminton Road Offices, Badminton Road, Yate BS37 5AF ☎ 01454 868152 🖷 01454 868150 george.kousouros@southglos.gov.uk

Facilities: Mr Warren Attwell, Facilities Officer, Badminton Road Offices, Badminton Road, Yate BS37 5AF ☎ 01454 865058 warren.attwell@southglos.gov.uk

Finance and Treasurer: Mr Andy Brown, Head of Finance & Customer Services, Badminton Road Offices, Badminton Road, Yate BS37 5AF ☎ 01454 863410 🖷 01454 864473 andy.brown@southglos.gov.uk

Finance and Treasurer: Mr Zulfiquar Darr, Head of Corporate Finance & Technology, The Council Offices, Badminton Road, Yate BS37 5AF ☎ 01454 864670 🖷 01454 865026 zulfiquar.darr@southglos.gov.uk

Finance and Treasurer: Ms Janet Faire, Head of Operational Support, Badminton Road Offices, Badminton Road, Yate BS37 5AF ☎ 01454 865841 janet.faire@southglos.gov.uk

Finance and Treasurer: Mr David Perry, Director of Corporate Services, The Council Offices, Castle Street, Thornbury BS35 1HF ☎ 01454 865001 🖷 01454 863855 dave.perry@southglos.gov.uk

Fleet Management: Mr Colin Shepherd, Fleet Operations Manager for Transport, Broad Lane Offices, Engine Common Lane, Yate BS37 7PN ☎ 01454 863918 colin.shepherd@southglos.gov.uk

Grounds Maintenance: Mr Simon Spedding, Street Care Design & Operations Manager, Broad Lane Offices, Engine Common Lane, Yate BS37 7PN ☎ 01454 863971 🖷 01454 865819 simon.spedding@southglos.gov.uk

Health and Safety: Mr Tom Magnone, Health & Safety Manager, The Council Offices, Castle Street, Thornbury BS35 1HF ☎ 01454 863096 🖷 01454 863071 tom.magnone@southglos.gov.uk

Highways: Mr Steve Evans, Director of Environment & Community Services, Broad Lane Offices, Engine Common Lane, Yate BS37 7PN ☎ 01454 865811 🖷 01454 865812 steve.evans@southglos.gov.uk

Highways: Mr Chris Sane, Head of Transport & Strategic Projects, Badminton Road Offices, Badminton Road, Yate BS37 5AF ☎ 01454 863402 chris.sane@southglos.gov.uk

Home Energy Conservation: Ms Debby Paice, Home Energy Co-ordinator (Enabling), The Council Offices, High Street, Kingswood BS15 9TR ☎ 01454 865453 🖷 01454 865555 debby.paice@southglos.gov.uk

Housing: Mr Jon Shaw, Head of Strategy & Commissioning, St Lukes Close, Emersons Way, Emersons Green, BS16 7AL ☎ 01454 865547 jon.shaw@southglos.gov.uk

Local Area Agreement: Mrs Yvonne Davis, Strategic Partnerships & Planning Manager, The Council Offices, Castle Street, Thornbury BS35 1HF ☎ 01454 863865 yvonne.davis@southglos.gov.uk

Legal: Mr John McCormack, Head of Legal & Democratic Services & Monitoring, The Council Offices, Castle Street, Thornbury BS35 1HF ☎ 01454 865980 john.mccormack@southglos.gov.uk

Leisure and Cultural Services: Mr Steve Evans, Director of Environment & Community Services, The Council Offices, Badminton Road, Yate BS37 5AF ☎ 01454 865811 🖷 01454 865812 steve.evans@southglos.gov.uk

Lifelong Learning: Ms Elizabeth Mawson, Community Learning Interim Manager, Badminton Road Offices, Badminton Road, Yate SB37 5AF ☎ 01454 864633 🖷 01454 863330 elizabeth.mawson@southglos.gov.uk

Lighting: Mr Andrew Porter, Electrical & Building Maintenance Manager, Almondsnury Depot, Gloucester Road, Almondsbury BS32 4AG ☎ 01454 863982 🖷 01454 863999 andrew.porter@southglos.gov.uk

Lottery Funding, Charity and Voluntary: Mrs Usha Kumar, Voluntary & Community Sector Support Co-ordinator, Badminton Road Offices, Badminton Road, Yate BS37 5AF ☎ 01454 865684 🖷 01454 868535 usha.kumar@southglos.gov.uk

Member Services: Mr Stuart Hook, Head of Democratic & Statutory Services, The Council Offices, Castle Street, Thornbury BS35 1HF ☎ 01454 863053 🖷 01454 864661 stuart.hook@southglos.gov.uk

Parking: Mr Alan Garwood, Senior ECO, Broad Lane Offices, Engine Common Lane, Yate BS37 7PN ☎ 01454 868494 alan.garwood@southglos.gov.uk

Partnerships: Mrs Yvonne Davis, Strategic Partnerships & Planning Manager, The Council Offices, Castle Street, Thornbury BS35 1HF ☎ 01454 863865 yvonne.davis@southglos.gov.uk

Personnel / HR: Mrs Claire Kerswill, Head of HR & HRBP for Corporate Resources, The Council Offices, Castle Street, Thornbury BS35 1HF ☎ 01454 866348 claire.kerswill@southglos.gov.uk

Planning: Mr Steve Evans, Director of Environment & Community Services, The Council Offices, Badminton Road, Yate BS37 5AF ☎ 01454 865811 🖷 01454 865812 steve.evans@southglos.gov.uk

Planning: Mr Brian Glasson, Head of Strategic Planning,

Badminton Road Offices, Badminton Road Offices, Yate BS37 5AF ☎ 01454 863535 🖷 01454 863737 brian.glasson@southglos.gov.uk

Procurement: Mr Zulfiquar Darr, Head of Corporate Finance & Technology, The Council Offices, Badminton Road, Yate BS37 5AF ☎ 01454 864670 🖷 01454 865026 zulfiquar.darr@southglos.gov.uk

Public Libraries: Mr Martin Burton, Library, Arts & Information Manager, Badminton Road Offices, Badminton Road, Yate BS37 5AF ☎ 01454 865782 🖷 01454 868150 martin.burton@southglos.gov.uk

Recycling & Waste Minimisation: Ms Yvonne Pearce, Waste Management Manager, Badminton Road Offices, Badminton Road, Yate BS37 5AF ☎ 01454 863587 🖷 01454 863679 yvonne.pearce@southglos.gov.uk

Regeneration: Mr Mike Luton, Senior Principal Planning Officer for Policy, Badminton Road Offices, Badminton Road, Yate BS37 5AF ☎ 01454 863573 mike.luton@southglos.gov.uk

Road Safety: Ms Chris Studley, Capital Programme & Projects Manager, Badminton Road Offices, Badminton Road, Yate BS37 5AF ☎ 01454 863751 🖷 01454 863697 chris.studley@southglos.gov.uk

Social Services: Ms Tracy Allison, Head of Integrated Children & Young People's Services, Badminton Road Offices, Badminton Road, Yate BS37 5AF ☎ 01454 863254 tracy.allison@southglos.gov.uk

Social Services: Mr Peter Murphy, Director of Community Care & Housing, The Council Offices, Castle Street, Thornbury BS35 1HF ☎ 01454 865901 🖷 01454 865940 peter.murphy@southglos.gov.uk

Social Services (Adult): Mr Brian Clarke, Safeguarding Adults Manager, Vinney Green House, Emersons Green Lane, Mangotsfield BS16 7AT ☎ 01454 864325 🖷 01454 865940 brian.clarke@southglos.gov.uk

Social Services (Children): Ms Therese Gillespie, Director for Children & Young People, Badminton Road Offices, Badminton Road, Yate BS37 5AF ☎ 01454 863253 🖷 01454 863264 therese.gillespie@southglos.gov.uk

Staff Training: Mrs Alison McIver, HR Business Partner, The Council Offices, Castle Street, Thornbury BS35 1HF ☎ 01454 863093 🖷 01454 868654 alison.mciver@southglos.gov.uk

Street Scene: Mr Simon Spedding, Street Care Design & Operations Manager, Broad Lane Offices, Engine Common Lane, Yate BS37 7PN ☎ 01454 863971 🖷 01454 865819 simon.spedding@southglos.gov.uk

Sustainable Communities: Ms Karen Whitaker, Community Engagement Officer, Badminton Road Offices, Badminton Road, Yate BS37 5AF ☎ 01454 868127 🖷 01454 868150 karen.whitaker@southglos.gov.uk

Sustainable Development: Ms Jane Thompson, SHEP Team Manager, Badminton Road Offices, Badminton Road, Yate BS37 5AF ☎ 01454 863870 🖷 01454 863886 jane.thompson@southglos.gov.uk

Traffic Management: Ms Chris Studley, Capital Programme & Projects Manager, Badminton Road Offices, Badminton Road, Yate BS37 5AF ☎ 01454 863751 🖷 01454 863697 chris.studley@southglos.gov.uk

Transport: Mr Steve Evans, Director of Environment & Community Services, The Council Offices, Badminton Road, Yate BS37 5AF ☎ 01454 865811 🖷 01454 865812 steve.evans@southglos.gov.uk

Transport: Mr Chris Sane, Head of Transport & Strategic Projects, Badminton Road Offices, Badminton Road, Yate BS37 5AF ☎ 01454 863402 chris.sane@southglos.gov.uk

Transport Planner: Ms Emma Blackham, Transport Policy & Promotions Group Manager, Badminton Road Offices, Badminton Road, Yate BS37 5AF ☎ 01454 864115 🖷 01454 864473 emma.blackham@southglos.gov.uk

Waste Collection and Disposal: Ms Yvonne Pearce, Waste Management Manager, Badminton Road Offices, Badminton Road, Yate BS37 5AF ☎ 01454 863587 🖷 01454 863679 yvonne.pearce@southglos.gov.uk

Waste Management: Mr Steve Evans, Director of Environment & Community Services, Broad Lane Offices, Engine Common Lane, Yate BS37 7PN ☎ 01454 865811 🖷 01454 865812 steve.evans@southglos.gov.uk

MEMBERS OF THE COUNCIL (70)

Leader of the Council: **Calway**, John (CON - Longwell Green)
john.calway@southglos.gov.uk

Adams, Ian (CON - Siston)
ian.adams@southglos.gov.uk

Allinson, Jane (LD - Oldland Common)
jane.allinson@southglos.gov.uk

Allinson, Brian (CON - Stoke Gifford)
brian.allinson@southglos.gov.uk

Apps, Pat (LAB - King's Chase)
pat.apps@southglos.gov.uk

Ashe, John (CON - Bradley Stoke South)
john.ashe@southglos.gov.uk

Bamford, June (CON - Hanham)
june.bamford@southglos.gov.uk

Barrett, Nick (CON - Parkwall)
nick.barrett@southglos.gov.uk

Bell, Michael (LAB - Rodway)
michael.bell@southglos.gov.uk

Biggin, Janet (CON - Downend)
janet.biggin@southglos.gov.uk

Blair, Ian (LD - Yate North)
ian.blair@southglos.gov.uk

Boon, Linda (LD - Chipping Sodbury)
linda.boon@southglos.gov.uk

Boulton, Ian (LAB - Staple Hill)
ian.boulton@southglos.gov.uk

Bowles, Tim (CON - Winterbourne)
tim.bowles@southglos.gov.uk

Bowrey, Bill (LAB - King's Chase)
bill.bowrey@southglos.gov.uk
Cook, Sheila (CON - Almondsbury)
sheila.cook@southglos.gov.uk
Cranney, Keith (CON - Stoke Gifford)
keith.cranney@southglos.gov.uk
Davis, Ruth (LD - Yate Central)
ruth.davis@southglos.gov.uk
Drew, Mike (LD - Yate North)
mike.drew@southglos.gov.uk
Fardell, Clare (LD - Thornbury North)
clare.fardell@southglos.gov.uk
Gawler, Howard (LD - Ladden Brook)
howard.gawler@southglos.gov.uk
Goddard, Heather (CON - Hanham)
heather.goddard@southglos.gov.uk
Goddard, John (CON - Hanham)
john.goddard@southglos.gov.uk
Godwin, John (CON - Winterbourne)
john.godwin@southglos.gov.uk
Griffin, Robert (CON - Pilning and Severn Beach)
robert.griffin@southglos.gov.uk
Halsall, Neil (LD - Thornbury North)
neil.halsall@southglos.gov.uk
Hockey, Dave (LD - Frampton Cotterell)
dave.hockey@southglos.gov.uk
Hockey, Pat (LD - Frampton Cotterell)
pat.hockey@southglos.gov.uk
Holbrook, Dafydd (LD - Dodington)
dafydd.holbrook@southglos.gov.uk
Holloway, Shirley (LD - Thornbury South and Alveston)
shirley.holloway@southglos.gov.uk
Hope, Sue (LD - Cotswold Edge)
sue.hope@southglos.gov.uk
Hopkinson, Brian (CON - Bradley Stoke Central and Stoke Lodge)
brian.hopkinson@southglos.gov.uk
Howells, Justin (CON - Stoke Gifford)
justin.howells@southglos.gov.uk
Hunt, James (CON - Emersons Green)
james.hunt@southglos.gov.uk
Hunt, Colin (CON - Emersons Green)
colin.hunt@southglos.gov.uk
Hunt, Jon (CON - Downend)
jon.hunt@southglos.gov.uk
Hutchinson, Roger (LAB - Filton)
roger.hutchinson@southglos.gov.uk
Jones, Robert (CON - Bradley Stoke South)
robert.jones@southglos.gov.uk
Jones, Trevor (CON - Frenchay and Stoke Park)
trevor.jones@southglos.gov.uk
Kearns, Dave (CON - Emersons Green)
dave.kearns@southglos.gov.uk
Lawrance, Alan (LD - Dodington)
alan.lawrancee@southglos.gov.uk
Manson, Gary (LAB - Woodstock)
gareth.manson@southglos.gov.uk
McCarthy, Carol (CON - Rodway)
carol.mccarthy@southglos.gov.uk
Monk, Adam (LAB - Filton)
adam.monk@southglos.gov.uk
Morris, Katherine (CON - Downend)
katherine.morris@southglos.gov.uk
Olpin, Tony (CON - Parkwall)
tony.olpin@southglos.gov.uk
O'Neil, John (LD - Charfield)
john.o'neil@southglos.gov.uk
Opren, Eve (LAB - Patchway)
eve.opren@southglos.gov.uk
Perkins, Andy (LAB - Woodstock)
andy.perkins@southglos.gov.uk
Pomfret, Sarah (CON - Bradley Stoke Central and Stoke Lodge)
sarah.pomfret@southglos.gov.uk
Potts, Shirley (LAB - Staple Hill)
shirley.potts@southglos.gov.uk
Price, Christine (CON - Longwell Green)
christine.price@southglos.gov.uk
Pullin, Bob (CON - Frenchay and Stoke Park)
bob.pullin@southglos.gov.uk
Reade, Steve (CON - Boyd Valley)
stephen.reade.southglos.gov.uk
Riddle, Matthew (CON - Severn)
matthew.riddle@southglos.gov.uk
Robbins, Mike (LD - Yate North)
mike.robbins@southglos.gov.uk
Rooney, Pat (LAB - Woodstock)
pat.ronney@southglos.gov.uk
Rush, Adrian (LD - Chipping Sodbury)
adrian.rush@southglos.gov.uk
Scawen, Marc (LD - Oldland Common)
marc.scawen@southglos.gov.uk
Scott, Ian (LAB - Filton)
ian.scott@southglos.gov.uk
Scott, Sam (LAB - Patchway)
sam.scot@southglos.gov.uk
Seager, Kevin (CON - Rodway)
kevin.seager@southglos.gov.uk
Stokes, Benjamin (CON - Boyd Valley)
ben.stokes@southglos.gov.uk
Tyrrell, Maggie (LD - Thornbury South and Alveston)
maggie.tyrrell@southglos.gov.uk
Walker, Terry (LAB - King's Chase)
terry.walker@southglos.gov.uk
Walker, Ben (UKIP - Bradley Stoke North)
ben.walker@southglos.gov.uk
Walker, Sue (LD - Yate Central)
sue.walker@southglos.gov.uk
Walker, Keith (LAB - Patchway)
keith.walker@southglos.gov.uk
Williams, Erica (CON - Bitton)
erica.williams@southglos.gov.uk
Young, Claire (LD - Westerleigh)
claire.young@southglos.gov.uk

POLITICAL COMPOSITION

CON: 33, LD: 21, LAB: 15, UKIP: 1

COMMITTEE CHAIRS

Adults & Housing: Mr Matthew Riddle
Audit & Accounts: Mr Ian Boulton
Children & Young People: Mr Ian Blair
Communities: Ms Claire Young
Environment: Mr Dave Hockey
Licensing, Regulatory & General Purposes: Ms Shirley Potts
Planning, Transportation & Strategic Environment: Mr Brian Allinson
Public Health & Health Scrutiny: Mr Ian Scott

SOUTH HAMS D

South Hams District Council, Follaton House, Plymouth Road, Totnes TQ9 5NE ☎ 01803 861234 🖷 01803 866151
✉ customer.services@southhams.gov.uk
🖳 www.southhams.gov.uk

FACTS & FIGURES

Police Authority: Devon & Cornwall Police Authority
Health Authority: NHS South West
Learning and Skills Council: South West
Parliamentary Constituencies: Totnes
EU Constituencies: South West
Election Frequency: Elections are of whole council
Twinning: Dartmouth: Courseulles-sur-Mer (France); Dartmouth (Canada); Dartmouth (USA); Ermington: Clecy (France); Ivybridge: St. Pierre-sur-Dives (France); Kingsbridge: Isigny-sur-Mer (France); Salcombe: Cabourg (France); Scorriton: Fontaine Henry (France); South Brent: Chateauneuf-du-Faou (France); Totnes: Vire (France); South Hams: Pays des Abers-Cotes des Legendes (France); Modbury: Le Saou (France); Wembury: Locmaria-Plouzam (France);

PRINCIPAL OFFICERS

Chief Executive: Mr Richard Sheard, Chief Executive, Follaton House, Plymouth Road, Totnes TQ9 5NE ☎ 01822 813629 🖷 01822 813634 ✉ rsheard@southhams.gov.uk

Senior Management: Mr Alan Robinson, Strategic Director of Community, Follaton House, Plymouth Road, Totnes TQ9 5NE ☎ 01803 861234 🖷 01803 866151 ✉ alan.robinson@southhams.gov.uk

Senior Management: Ms Tracy Winser, Acting Head of Customer Services, Follaton House, Plymouth Road, Totnes TQ9 5NE ☎ 01803 861234 🖷 01803 866151 ✉ tracy.winser@southhams.gov.uk

Access Officer / Social Services (Disability): Mr David Bartlett, Building Control Officer, Follaton House, Plymouth Road, Totnes TQ9 5NE ☎ 01803 861234 🖷 01803 866151 ✉ david.bartlett@southhams.gov.uk

Architect, Building / Property Services: Mrs Kate Cassar, Head of Assets, Follaton House, Plymouth Road, Totnes TQ9 5NE ☎ 01803 861234 ✉ kate.cassar@swdevon.gov.uk

Building Control: Mr Andrew Carpenter, Head of Building Control Partnership, Forde House, Brunel Road, Newton Abbot TQ12 4XX ☎ 01626 215721 ✉ andrew.carpenter@teignbridge.gov.uk

PR / Communications: Mrs Alison Stoneham, Shared Communications Manager, Follaton House, Plymouth Road, Totnes TQ9 5NE ☎ 01803 861234 ✉ astoneham@westdevon.gov.uk

Community Planning: Mrs Marion Playle, Head of Service, Follaton House, Plymouth Road, Totnes TQ9 5NE ☎ 01803 861234

Community Safety: Mr Peter Dale, Community Safety & Emergency Planning Officer, Follaton House, Plymouth Road, Totnes TQ9 5NE ☎ 01803 861234 🖷 01803 866151 ✉ peter.dale@southhams.gov.uk

Computer Management: Mr Robin Barlow, ICT Manager, Follaton House, Plymouth Road, Totnes TQ9 5NE ☎ 01803 861234 ✉ robin.barlow@swdevon.gov.uk

Corporate Services: Miss Delyth Jenkins Evans, Head of Legal & Monitoring Officer, Follaton House, Plymouth Road, Totnes TQ9 5NE ☎ 01803 861234 ✉ delyth.jenkins-evans@southhams.gov.uk

Corporate Services: Mrs Jan Montague, Head of Personnel & Payroll, Follaton House, Plymouth Road, Totnes TQ9 5NE ☎ 01803 861234 🖷 01803 866151 ✉ jan.montague@southhams.gov.uk

Customer Service: Ms Kate Hamp, Customer Services Manager, Follaton House, Plymouth Road, Totnes TQ9 5NE ☎ 01803 861234 ✉ kate.hamp@swdevon.gov.uk

Customer Service: Ms Tracy Winser, Acting Head of Customer Services, Follaton House, Plymouth Road, Totnes TQ9 5NE ☎ 01803 861234 🖷 01803 866151 ✉ tracy.winser@southhams.gov.uk

Economic Development: Mrs Marion Playle, Head of Service, Follaton House, Plymouth Road, Totnes TQ9 5NE ☎ 01803 861234

Electoral Registration: Mrs Elizabeth Tucker, Electoral Administrator, Follaton House, Plymouth Road, Totnes TQ9 5NE ☎ 01803 861234 🖷 01803 866151 ✉ liz.tucker@southhams.gov.uk

Emergency Planning: Mr Peter Dale, Community Safety & Emergency Planning Officer, Follaton House, Plymouth Road, Totnes TQ9 5NE ☎ 01803 861234 🖷 01803 866151 ✉ peter.dale@southhams.gov.uk

Environmental / Technical Services: Mrs Helen Dobby, Head of Service, Follaton House, Plymouth Road, Totnes TQ9 5NE ☎ 01803 861234

Environmental Health: Mr Ian Bollans, Head of Environmental Health, Follaton House, Plymouth Road, Totnes TQ9 5NE ☎ 01803 861234 🖷 01803 866151 ✉ ian.bollans@southhams.gov.uk

Estates, Property & Valuation: Mr Stephen Forsey, Estates & Facilities Manager, Follaton House, Plymouth Road, Totnes TQ9 5NE ☎ 01803 861234 ✉ stephen.forsey@swdevon.gov.uk

Facilities: Mr Stephen Forsey, Estates & Facilities Manager, Follaton House, Plymouth Road, Totnes TQ9 5NE ☎ 01803 861234 ✉ stephen.forsey@swdevon.gov.uk

Finance and Treasurer: Mrs Lisa Buckle, Head of Service, Follaton House, Plymouth Road, Totnes TQ9 5NE ☎ 01803 861234

Grounds Maintenance: Mrs Helen Dobby, Head of Service, Follaton House, Plymouth Road, Totnes TQ9 5NE ☎ 01803 861234

Health and Safety: Mr Peter Osborne, Health & Safety Advisor, Follaton House, Plymouth Road, Totnes TQ9 5NE ☎ 01803 861234 🖷 01803 866151 ✉ pete.osborne@southhams.gov.uk

Housing: Mr Paul Eells, Housing Advice Manager, Follaton House, Plymouth Road, Totnes TQ9 5NE ☎ 01803 861234 🖷 01803 866151 ✉ paul.eells@southhams.gov.uk

Housing: Mr Liam Reading, Affordable Housing Manager, Follaton House, Plymouth Road, Totnes TQ9 5NE ☎ 01803 861234 🖷 01803 866151 ✉ liam.reading@southhams.gov.uk

Legal: Miss Delyth Jenkins Evans, Head of Legal & Monitoring Officer, Follaton House, Plymouth Road, Totnes TQ9 5NE ☎ 01803 861234 ✉ delyth.jenkins-evans@southhams.gov.uk

Leisure and Cultural Services: Mr Ross Kennerley, Landscape & Recreation Manager, Follaton House, Plymouth Road, Totnes TQ9 5NE ☎ 01803 861234 🖷 01803 861478 ✉ ross.kennerley@southhams.gov.uk

Licensing: Mr Graham Munson, Licensing Manager, Follaton House, Plymouth Road, Totnes TQ9 5NE ☎ 01803 861234 🖷 01803 861294 ✉ graham.munson@southhams.gov.uk

Member Services: Mr Darryl White, Member Services Manager, Follaton House, Plymouth Road, Totnes TQ9 5NE ☎ 01803 861234 🖷 01803 866669 ✉ darryl.white@southhams.gov.uk

Parking: Ms Cathy Aubertin, Street Scene Manager, Follaton House, Plymouth Road, Totnes TQ9 5NE ☎ 01803 861234 ✉ cathy.aubertin@swdevon.gov.uk

Personnel / HR: Mr Andy Wilson, HR Manager, Follaton House, Plymouth Road, Totnes TQ9 5NE ☎ 01803 861234 ✉ andy.wilson@swdevon.gov.uk

Planning: Mr Malcolm Elliot, Development Manager, Follaton House, Plymouth Road, Totnes TQ9 5NE ☎ 01803 861234 ✉ malcolm.elliott@swdevon.gov.uk

Recycling & Waste Minimisation: Miss Ruth Edwards, Waste Strategy & Policy Officer, Follaton House, Plymouth Road, Totnes TQ9 5NE ☎ 01803 861234 ✉ ruth.edwards@southhams.gov.uk

Regeneration: Mrs Marion Playle, Head of Service, Follaton House, Plymouth Road, Totnes TQ9 5NE ☎ 01803 861234

Staff Training: Mrs Jan Montague, Head of Personnel & Payroll, Follaton House, Plymouth Road, Totnes TQ9 5NE ☎ 01803 861234 🖷 01803 866151 ✉ jan.montague@southhams.gov.uk

Staff Training: Mr Andy Wilson, HR Manager, Follaton House, Plymouth Road, Totnes TQ9 5NE ☎ 01803 861234 ✉ andy.wilson@swdevon.gov.uk

Street Scene: Ms Cathy Aubertin, Street Scene Manager, Follaton House, Plymouth Road, Totnes TQ9 5NE ☎ 01803 861234 ✉ cathy.aubertin@swdevon.gov.uk

Sustainable Development: Mrs Marion Playle, Head of Service, Follaton House, Plymouth Road, Totnes TQ9 5NE ☎ 01803 861234

Transport Planner: Mr Graham Swiss, Forward Planning Manager, Follaton House, Plymouth Road, Totnes TQ9 5NE ☎ 01803 861234 🖷 01803 866151 ✉ graham.swiss@southhams.gov.uk

Waste Collection and Disposal: Mrs Helen Dobby, Head of Service, Follaton House, Plymouth Road, Totnes TQ9 5NE ☎ 01803 861234

Waste Management: Mrs Helen Dobby, Head of Service, Follaton House, Plymouth Road, Totnes TQ9 5NE ☎ 01803 861234

Waste Management: Mr Stuart Jellings, Logistics Manager, Follaton House, Plymouth Road, Totnes TQ9 5NE ☎ 01803 861256 ✉ stuart.jellings@southhams.gov.uk

MEMBERS OF THE COUNCIL (40)

***Chair:* Rowe**, Rosemary (CON - East Dart)
cllr.rowe@southhams.gov.uk

***Leader of the Council:* Tucker**, John (CON - West Dart)
cllr.tucker@southhams.gov.uk

***Deputy Leader of the Council:* Hicks**, Michael (CON - Allington and Loddiswell)
cllr.hicks@southhams.gov.uk

Baldry, Keith (LD - Yealmpton)
cllr.baldry@southhams.gov.uk

Barber, Tony (LD - Ivybridge Fillham)
cllr.barber@southhams.gov.uk

Bastone, Hilary (CON - Dartmouth and Kingswear)
cllr.bastone@southhams.gov.uk

Baverstock, John (LD - South Brent)
cllr.pannell@southhams.gov.uk

Baverstock, John (CON - Stokenham)
cllr.baverstock@southhams.gov.uk

Blackler, Ian (CON - Cornwood and Sparkwell)
cllr.blackler@southhams.gov.uk

Bramble, I (CON - Thurlestone)
cllr.bramble@southhams.gov.uk

Brazil, Julian (LD - Saltstone)
cllr.brazil@southhams.gov.uk

Bruce-Spencer, CG (CON - Bickleigh and Shaugh)
cllr.bruce-spencer@southhams.gov.uk

Cane, Basil (CON - Brixton and Wembury)
cllr.cane@southhams.gov.uk

Carson, Bryan (CON - Charterlands)
cllr.carson@southhams.gov.uk

Carter, John (CON - Salcombe and Malborough)
cllr.carter@southhams.gov.uk

Cooper, Suzie (CON - Newton and Noss)
cllr.cooper@southhams.gov.uk

Cooper, B S (LAB - Dartmouth Townstal)
cllr.bcooper@southhams.gov.uk

Coulson, Paul (CON - Salcombe and Malborough)
cllr.coulson@southhams.gov.uk

Cuthbert, P K (CON - Ivybridge Fillham)
cllr.cuthbert@southhams.gov.uk

Foss, R J (CON - Skerries)

cllr.foss@southhams.gov.uk
Gilbert, Rufus (CON - Kingsbridge North)
cllr.gilbert@southhams.gov.uk
Gorman, A S (GRN - Totnes Town)
cllr.gorman@southhams.gov.uk
Hannaford, Mike (LD - Totnes Bridgetown)
cllr.hannaford@southhams.gov.uk
Hawkins, Jonathan (CON - Dartmouth and Kingswear)
cllr.hawkins@southhams.gov.uk
Hitchins, Bill (CON - Bickleigh and Shaugh)
cllr.hitchins@southhams.gov.uk
Hodgson, J M (GRN - Dartington)
cllr.hodgson@southhams.gov.uk
Holway, T R (CON - Erme Valley)
cllr.holway@southhams.gov.uk
Jones, Louise (CON - Ivybridge Woodlands)
cllr.ljones@southhams.gov.uk
May, David (CON - Ivybridge Woodlands)
cllr.may@southhams.gov.uk
Pennington, Trevor (CON - Marldon)
cllr.pennington@southhams.gov.uk
Saltern, Michael (CON - Ivybridge Central)
cllr.saltern@southhams.gov.uk
Smerdon, P C (CON - Eastmoor)
cllr.smerdon@southhams.gov.uk
Squire, John (CON - Brixton and Wembury)
cllr.squire@southhams.gov.uk
Steer, Robert (CON - Avon and Harbourne)
cllr.steer@southhams.gov.uk
Stone, Melvyn (CON - Dartmouth and Kingswear)
cllr.stone@southhams.gov.uk
Vint, Robert (GRN - Totnes Town)
cllr.vint@southhams.gov.uk
Ward, L A (CON - Erme Valley)
cllr.lward@southhams.gov.uk
Westacott, Judy (IND - Totnes Bridgetown)
cllr.westacott@southhams.gov.uk
Wingate, K R (CON - Kingsbridge East)
cllr.wingate@southhams.gov.uk
Wright, S A (CON - Westville and Alvington)
cllr.wright@southhams.gov.uk

POLITICAL COMPOSITION
CON: 30, LD: 5, GRN: 3, IND: 1, LAB: 1

CABINET
Leader of the Council: Mr John Tucker
Deputy Leader / Finance & Audit: Mr Michael Hicks
Assets: Mr Bill Hitchins
Corporate Services: Mrs Suzie Cooper
Environment Services: Mr Jonathan Hawkins
Environmental Health & Housing: Mr Michael Saltern
ICT & Customer Services: Mr Hilary Bastone
Planning, Economy & Community: Mr John Carter

COMMITTEE CHAIRS
Audit: Mr Trevor Pennington
Community Life & Housing: Mr S A Wright
Corporate Performance & Resources: Mr John Baverstock
Development Control: Mr David May
Economy & Environment: Mr Paul Coulson
Licensing: Mr John Squire

SOUTH HOLLAND DISTRICT COUNCIL D

South Holland District Council, Council Offices, Priory Road, Spalding PE11 2XE ☎ 01775 761161 🖷 01775 711253 info@sholland.gov.uk www.sholland.gov.uk

FACTS & FIGURES
Police Authority: Lincolnshire Police Authority
Health Authority: East Midlands Strategic Health Authority
Learning and Skills Council: East Midlands
Parliamentary Constituencies: South Holland and The Deepings
EU Constituencies: East Midlands
Election Frequency: Elections are of whole council
Twinning: Holbeach: Sezanne (France); Spalding: Speyer (Germany)

PRINCIPAL OFFICERS
Chief Executive: Mr Terry Huggins, Chief Executive, Council Offices, Priory Road, Spalding PE11 2XE ☎ 01362 656870 chief.executive@breckland-sholland.gov.uk

Deputy Chief Executive: Mr Mark Stokes, Deputy Chief Executive, Elizabeth House, Walpole Loke, Dereham NR19 1EE ☎ 01362 656870 mark.stokes@breckland-sholland.gov.uk

Senior Management: Mr Mark Finch, Assistant Director - Finance, Elizabeth House, Walpole Loke, Dereham NR19 1EE ☎ 01362 656870 mark.finch@breckland-sholland.gov.uk

Senior Management: Ms Maxine O'Mahony, Director - Commissioning, Council Offices, Priory Road, Spalding PE11 2XE ☎ 01362 656870 maxine.omahony@breckland-sholland.gov.uk

Senior Management: Mrs Vicky Thomson, Assistant Director - Democratic Services, Elizabeth House, Walpole Loke, Dereham NR19 1EE ☎ 01362 656870 vicky.thomson@breckland-sholland.gov.uk

Senior Management: Mr Robert Walker, Assistant Director - Commissioning, Elizabeth House, Walpole Loke, Dereham NR19 1EE ☎ 01362 656870 robert.walker@breckland-sholland.gov.uk

Architect, Building / Property Services: Mr Stephen Udberg, Asset & Property Manager, Council Offices, Priory Road, Spalding PE11 2XE ☎ 01362 656870 steve.udberg@breckland-sholland.gov.uk

Best Value: Ms Vicky Thomson, Assistant Director - Democratic Services, Council Offices, Priory Road, Spalding PE11 2XE ☎ 01775 761161 🖷 01775 711253 vicky.thomson@breckland-sholland.gov.uk

Building Control: Mr Phil Adams, Building Control Manager, Council Offices, Priory Road, Spalding PE11 2XE ☎ 01362 656870 phillip.adams@breckland-sholland.gov.uk

PR / Communications: Ms Vicky Thomson, Assistant Director - Democratic Services, Council Offices, Priory Road, Spalding PE11 2XE ☎ 01775 761161 🖷 01775 711253 vicky.thomson@breckland-sholland.gov.uk

Community Planning: Mr Paul Jackson, Planning Manager, Council Offices, Priory Road, Spalding PE11 2XE ☎ 01775 761161 🖷 01775 710772 ✉ pjackson@sholland.gov.uk

Community Safety: Mr Rob Leigh, Community Development Manager, Council Offices, Priory Road, Spalding PE11 2XE ☎ 01775 761161 🖷 01775 711253 ✉ rleigh@sholland.gov.uk

Computer Management: Mr Marcus Coleman, Operations Director, Tedder Hall, Manby Park, Louth LN11 8UP ☎ 01507 613307 🖷 01507 329599 ✉ marcus.coleman@cpbs.com

Computer Management: Mr Kevin Rump, ICT & Customer Manager, Elizabeth House, Walpole Loke, Dereham NR19 1EE ☎ 01362 656870 ✉ kevin.rump@breckland.gov.uk

Corporate Services: Ms Vicky Thomson, Assistant Director - Democratic Services, Council Offices, Priory Road, Spalding PE11 2XE ☎ 01775 761161 🖷 01775 711253 ✉ vicky.thomson@breckland-sholland.gov.uk

Customer Service: Mr Kevin Rump, ICT & Customer Manager, Elizabeth House, Walpole Loke, Dereham NR19 1EE ☎ 01362 656870 ✉ kevin.rump@breckland.gov.uk

Direct Labour: Mr Steve Udberg, Asset & Property Manager, Council Offices, Priory Road, Spalding PE11 2XE ☎ 01775 761161 🖷 01775 711253 ✉ sudberg@sholland.gov.uk

Economic Development: Mr Mark Stanton, Economic Development Manager, Council Offices, Priory Road, Spalding PE11 2XE ☎ 01362 656870 🖷 01362 656360 ✉ mark.stanton@breckland-sholland.gov.uk

E-Government: Mr Kevin Rump, ICT & Customer Manager, Council Offices, Priory Road, Spalding PE11 2XE ☎ 01362 656870 ✉ kevin.rump@breckland.gov.uk

Electoral Registration: Ms Vicky Thomson, Assistant Director - Democratic Services, Council Offices, Priory Road, Spalding PE11 2XE ☎ 01775 761161 🖷 01775 711253 ✉ vicky.thomson@breckland-sholland.gov.uk

Emergency Planning: Mr Rob Leigh, Community Development Manager, Council Offices, Priory Road, Spalding PE11 2XE ☎ 01775 761161 🖷 01775 711253 ✉ rleigh@sholland.gov.uk

Environmental / Technical Services: Ms Sarah Bruton, Environmental Services Manager, Council Offices, Priory Road, Spalding PE11 2XE ☎ 01775 7611253 🖷 01775 711253 ✉ sbruton@sholland.gov.uk

Environmental Health: Ms Sarah Bruton, Environmental Services Manager, Council Offices, Priory Road, Spalding PE11 2XE ☎ 01775 7611253 🖷 01775 711253 ✉ sbruton@sholland.gov.uk

Estates, Property & Valuation: Mr Steve Udberg, Asset & Property Manager, Council Offices, Priory Road, Spalding PE11 2XE ☎ 01775 761161 🖷 01775 711253 ✉ sudberg@sholland.gov.uk

European Liaison: Mr Rob Leigh, Community Development Manager, Council Offices, Priory Road, Spalding PE11 2XE ☎ 01775 761161 🖷 01775 711253 ✉ rleigh@sholland.gov.uk

European Liaison: Mr Mark Stanton, Economic Development Manager, Elizabeth House, Walpole Loke, Dereham NR19 1EE ☎ 01362 656870 🖷 01362 656360 ✉ mark.stanton@breckland-sholland.gov.uk

Events Manager: Ms Sarah Bruton, Environmental Services Manager, Council Offices, Priory Road, Spalding PE11 2XE ☎ 01775 7611253 🖷 01775 711253 ✉ sbruton@sholland.gov.uk

Facilities: Mr Steve Udberg, Asset & Property Manager, Council Offices, Priory Road, Spalding PE11 2XE ☎ 01775 761161 🖷 01775 711253 ✉ sudberg@sholland.gov.uk

Finance and Treasurer: Mr Mark Finch, Assistant Director - Finance, Council Offices, Priory Road, Spalding PE11 2XE ☎ 01775 761161 🖷 01775 711253 ✉ mfinch@sholland.gov.uk

Fleet Management: Ms Sarah Bruton, Environmental Services Manager, Council Offices, Priory Road, Spalding PE11 2XE ☎ 01775 7611253 🖷 01775 711253 ✉ sbruton@sholland.gov.uk

Grounds Maintenance: Ms Sarah Bruton, Environmental Services Manager, Council Offices, Priory Road, Spalding PE11 2XE ☎ 01775 7611253 🖷 01775 711253 ✉ sbruton@sholland.gov.uk

Home Energy Conservation: Mr Phil Adams, Building Control & Environmental Health Manager, Council Offices, Priory Road, Spalding PE11 2XE ☎ 01775 761161 🖷 01775 711253 ✉ padams@sholland.gov.uk

Housing: Ms Anita Brennan, 01775 761161, Council Offices, Priory Road, Spalding PE11 2XE 🖷 info@sholland.gov.uk

Housing Maintenance: Mr Steve Udberg, Asset & Property Manager, Council Offices, Priory Road, Spalding PE11 2XE ☎ 01775 761161 🖷 01775 711253 ✉ sudberg@sholland.gov.uk

Leisure and Cultural Services: Mr Steve Udberg, Asset & Property Manager, Council Offices, Priory Road, Spalding PE11 2XE ☎ 01775 761161 🖷 01775 711253 ✉ sudberg@sholland.gov.uk

Lighting: Mr Phil Adams, Building Control & Environmental Health Manager, Council Offices, Priory Road, Spalding PE11 2XE ☎ 01775 761161 🖷 01775 711253 ✉ padams@sholland.gov.uk

Lottery Funding, Charity and Voluntary: Mr Rob Leigh, Community Development Manager, Council Offices, Priory Road, Spalding PE11 2XE ☎ 01775 761161 🖷 01775 711253 ✉ rleigh@sholland.gov.uk

Member Services: Mrs Vicky Thomson, Assistant Director - Democratic Services, Council Offices, Priory Road, Spalding PE11 2XE ☎ 01362 656870 ✉ vicky.thomson@breckland-sholland.gov.uk

Parking: Ms Sarah Bruton, Environmental Services Manager, Council Offices, Priory Road, Spalding PE11 2XE ☎ 01775 7611253 🖷 01775 711253 ✉ sbruton@sholland.gov.uk

Partnerships: Mr Rob Leigh, Community Development Manager, Council Offices, Priory Road, Spalding PE11 2XE ☎ 01775 761161 🖷 01775 711253 ✉ rleigh@sholland.gov.uk

Personnel / HR: Mrs Natalie King, HR Manager, Council Offices, Priory Road, Spalding PE11 2XE ☎ 01362 656870 ✉ natalie.king@breckland-sholland.gov.uk

Personnel / HR: Mr Tony Lascelles, Head - HR, Tedder Hall, Manby Park, Louth LN11 8UP ☎ 01507 613230 🖷 01507 600206 ✉ tony.lascelles@cpbs.com

Planning: Mr Paul Jackson, Planning Manager, Elizabeth House, Walpole Loke, Dereham NR19 1EE ☎ 01362 656870 ✉ paul.jackson@breckland-sholland.gov.uk

Procurement: Ms Vicky Thomson, Assistant Director - Democratic Services, Council Offices, Priory Road, Spalding PE11 2XE ☎ 01775 761161 🖷 01775 711253 ✉ vicky.thomson@breckland-sholland.gov.uk

Recycling & Waste Minimisation: Ms Sarah Bruton, Environmental Services Manager, Council Offices, Priory Road, Spalding PE11 2XE ☎ 01775 7611253 🖷 01775 711253 ✉ sbruton@sholland.gov.uk

Regeneration: Mr Mark Stanton, Economic Development Manager, Council Offices, Priory Road, Spalding PE11 2XE ☎ 01362 656870 🖷 01362 656360 ✉ mark.stanton@breckland-sholland.gov.uk

Staff Training: Ms Natalie King, Human Resources Manager, Council Offices, Priory Road, Spalding PE11 2XE ☎ 01775 761161 🖷 01775 711253 ✉ nking@sholland.gov.uk

Street Scene: Ms Sarah Bruton, Environmental Services Manager, Council Offices, Priory Road, Spalding PE11 2XE ☎ 01775 7611253 🖷 01775 711253 ✉ sbruton@sholland.gov.uk

Sustainable Communities: Mr Paul Jackson, Planning Manager, Council Offices, Priory Road, Spalding PE11 2XE ☎ 01775 761161 🖷 01775 710772 ✉ pjackson@sholland.gov.uk

Sustainable Communities: Mr Rob Leigh, Community Development Manager, Council Offices, Priory Road, Spalding PE11 2XE ☎ 01775 761161 🖷 01775 711253 ✉ rleigh@sholland.gov.uk

Sustainable Development: Mr Paul Jackson, Planning Manager, Council Offices, Priory Road, Spalding PE11 2XE ☎ 01775 761161 🖷 01775 710772 ✉ pjackson@sholland.gov.uk

Tourism: Mr Rob Leigh, Community Development Manager, Council Offices, Priory Road, Spalding PE11 2XE ☎ 01775 761161 🖷 01775 711253 ✉ rleigh@sholland.gov.uk

Town Centre: Mr Mark Stanton, Economic Development Manager, Council Offices, Priory Road, Spalding PE11 2XE ☎ 01775 761161 🖷 01775 711253 ✉ mstanton@sholland.gov.uk

Transport Planner: Mr Paul Jackson, Planning Manager, Council Offices, Priory Road, Spalding PE11 2XE ☎ 01775 761161 🖷 01775 710772 ✉ pjackson@sholland.gov.uk

Waste Collection and Disposal: Ms Sarah Bruton, Environmental Services Manager, Council Offices, Priory Road, Spalding PE11 2XE ☎ 01775 7611253 🖷 01775 711253 ✉ sbruton@sholland.gov.uk

Waste Management: Ms Sarah Bruton, Environmental Services Manager, Council Offices, Priory Road, Spalding PE11 2XE ☎ 01775 7611253 🖷 01775 711253 ✉ sbruton@sholland.gov.uk

MEMBERS OF THE COUNCIL (37)

***Leader of the Council:* Porter**, Gary (CON - Spalding St Mary's)
gporter@sholland.gov.uk

***Deputy Leader of the Council:* Przyszlak**, Paul (CON - Crowland and Deeping St Nicholas)
pprzyszlak@sholland.gov.uk

***Deputy Leader of the Council:* Worth**, Charles (CON - Holbeach Hurn)
nworth@sholland.gov.uk

Fleet: Vacant

Long Sutton: Vacant

Alcock, Bryan (IND - Crowland and Deeping St Nicholas)
balcock@sholland.gov.uk

Aley, George (CON - Spalding Monkshouse)
galey@sholland.gov.uk

Ashby, David (CON - Spalding St Paul's)
david.ashby@sholland.gov.uk

Avery, James (CON - Pinchbeck and Surfleet)
javery@sholland.gov.uk

Biggadike, Francis (CON - Holbeach Town)
fbiggadike@sholland.gov.uk

Booth, Michael (IND - Sutton Bridge)
mbooth@sholland.gov.uk

Booth, Simon (IND - Long Sutton)
sbooth@sholland.gov.uk

Brewis, Christopher (IND - Sutton Bridge)
cbrewis@sholland.gov.uk

Casson, Anthony (CON - Moulton, Weston and Cowbit)
acasson@sholland.gov.uk

Chandler, Malcolm (CON - Whaplode and Holbeach St Johns)
mchandler@sholland.gov.uk

Clark, Robert (CON - Donington, Quadring and Gosberton)
rclark@sholland.gov.uk

Creese, Robert (IND - Whaplode and Holbeach St John's)
rcreese@sholland.gov.uk

Dark, Graham (IND - Spalding St John's)
gdark@sholland.gov.uk

Gambba-Jones, Roger (CON - Spalding Wygate)
rgambba-jones@sholland.gov.uk

Grocock, Rodney (CON - Moulton, Weston and Cowbit)
rgrocock@sholland.gov.uk

Harrison, Angela (CON - Crowland and Deeping St Nicholas)
angelaharrison@sholland.gov.uk

Howard, Martin (IND - Holbeach Town)
martin.howard@sholland.gov.uk

Johnson, Howard (CON - Spalding St Mary's)
hjohnson@sholland.gov.uk

King, Jane (IND - Donington, Quadring and Gosberton)
janeking@sholland.gov.uk

Lawton, Christine (CON - Spalding Wygate)
clawton@sholland.gov.uk

Miller, Andrew (CON - Spalding St Paul's)
andrew.miller@sholland.gov.uk

Newton, Angela (IND - Spalding Monkshouse)
anewton@sholland.gov.uk
Perkins, Roger (IND - Spalding St John's)
roger.perkins@sholland.gov.uk
Puttick, Amanda (CON - Donington, Quadring and Gosberton)
aputtick@sholland.gov.uk
Rudkin, Rita (CON - Holbeach Town)
rrudkin@sholland.gov.uk
Seymour, Michael (CON - The Saints)
mseymour@sholland.gov.uk
Slade, Sally-Ann (CON - Pinchbeck and Surfleet)
sally-ann.slade@sholland.gov.uk
Sneath, Elizabeth (CON - Pinchbeck and Surfleet)
elizabeth.sneath@sholland.gov.uk
Taylor, Gary (CON - Spalding Castle)
gtaylor@sholland.gov.uk
Wilkinson, Sarah (IND - Gedney)
sara.wilkinson@sholland.gov.uk
Wilkinson, David (IND - Long Sutton)
dwilkinson@sholland.gov.uk
Woolf, Andrew (CON - Moulton, Weston and Cowbit)
awoolf@sholland.gov.uk

POLITICAL COMPOSITION

CON: 23, IND: 12, Vacant: 2

CABINET

Leader: Mr G Porter
Deputy Leader / Localism & Big Society: Mr Charles Worth
Deputy Leader / Strategic Finance & Democratic Services: Mr P Przyszlak
Economic Development, Commerical Assets & Strategic Planning: Mr H Johnson
Housing Landlord: Ms Christine Lawton
Internal Services, Performance & Business Development: Mr G Taylor
Regulatory Services: Mr Malcolm Chandler
Waste Management, Green Spaces & Operational Planning: Mr R Gambba-Jones

COMMITTEE CHAIRS

Audit and Governance: Mr George Aley
Licensing Committee: Mr Malcolm Chandler
Performance Monitoring: Mr Bryan Alcock
Planning: Mr Roger Gambba-Jones
Policy Development: Mrs Amanda Puttick

SOUTH KESTEVEN D

South Kesteven District Council, Council Offices, St. Peter's Hill, Grantham NG31 6PZ ☎ 01476 406080 🖷 01476 406000 frontdesk@southkesteven.gov.uk 💻 www.southkesteven.gov.uk

FACTS & FIGURES

Police Authority: Lincolnshire Police Authority
Health Authority: East Midlands Strategic Health Authority
Learning and Skills Council: East Midlands
Parliamentary Constituencies: Grantham and Stamford
EU Constituencies: East Midlands
Election Frequency: Elections are of whole council
Twinning: Bourne: Doudeville (France); Grantham: Sankt Augustin (Germany); Stamford: Vence (France); Partnership: South Kesteven and Przemysl (Poland)

PRINCIPAL OFFICERS

Chief Executive: Ms Beverly Agass, Chief Executive, Council Offices, St. Peter's Hill, Grantham NG31 6PZ ☎ 01476 406080 🖷 01476 406101 b.agass@southkesteven.gov.uk

Senior Management: Mrs Tracey Blackwell, Strategic Director, South Kesteven District Council, Council Offices, St. Peter's Hill, Grantham NG31 6PZ ☎ 01476 406080 🖷 01476 406000 t.blackwell@southkesteven.gov.uk

Senior Management: Mr Ian Richardson, Head of Housing & Neighbourhoods, Council Offices, St. Peter's Hill, Grantham NG31 6PZ ☎ 01476 406080 🖷 01476 406000 i.richardson@southkesteven.gov.uk

Senior Management: Mr Paul Stokes, Corporate Head of Assets, Council Offices, St. Peter's Hill, Grantham NG31 6PZ ☎ 01476 406080 🖷 01476 406000 p.stokes@southkesteven.gov.uk

Senior Management: Mr Richard Wyles, Corporate Head of Finance & Customer Services, Council Offices, St. Peter's Hill, Grantham NG31 6PZ ☎ 01476 406080 🖷 01476 406100 r.wyles@southkesteven.gov.uk

Senior Management: Mr Ian Yates, Strategic Director, Council Offices, St. Peter's Hill, Grantham NG31 6PZ ☎ 01476 406080 🖷 01476 406101 i.yates@southkesteven.gov.uk

Architect, Building / Property Services: Ms Liz Banner, Assets & Facilities Service Manager, Council Offices, St. Peter's Hill, Grantham NG31 6PZ ☎ 01476 406080 🖷 01476 406000 l.banner@southkesteven.gov.uk

PR / Communications: Mr Geoff O'Neil, Communications Officer, Council Offices, St. Peter's Hill, Grantham NG31 6PZ ☎ 01476 406080 🖷 01476 406000 pr@southkesteven.gov.uk

PR / Communications: Mr Sam Selby, Performance Management, Council Offices, St. Peter's Hill, Grantham NG31 6PZ ☎ 01476 406080 🖷 01476 406000 s.yates@southkesteven.gov.uk

Community Safety: Mr Mark Jones, Partnerships & Community Safety Service Manager, Council Offices, St. Peter's Hill, Grantham NG31 6PZ ☎ 01476 406080 🖷 01476 406000 m.jones@southkesteven.gov.uk

Community Safety: Mr Sandy Kavanagh, Community Safety Officer, Council Offices, St. Peter's Hill, Grantham NG31 6PZ ☎ 01476 406080 🖷 01476 406000 s.kavanagh@southkesteven.gov.uk

Computer Management: Mr Andy Nix, Business Transformation Management & Service Manager, Council Offices, St. Peter's Hill, Grantham NG31 6PZ ☎ 01476 406080 🖷 01476 406000 a.nix@southkesteven.gov.uk

Contracts: Ms Liz Banner, Assets & Facilities Service Manager, Council Offices, St. Peter's Hill, Grantham NG31 6PZ ☎ 01476 406080 🖷 01476 406000 l.banner@southkesteven.gov.uk

Corporate Services: Mr Paul Stokes, Corporate Head of Assets, Council Offices, St. Peter's Hill, Grantham NG31 6PZ ☎ 01476 406080 🖷 01476 406000 ✉ p.stokes@southkesteven.gov.uk

Customer Service: Mrs Hayley Kent-Simpson, Customer Services Manager, Council Offices, St. Peter's Hill, Grantham NG31 6PZ ☎ 01476 406080 ✉ h.kent-simpson@southkesteven.gov.uk

Direct Labour: Mr Pat Swinton, Waste & Recycling Service Manager, Council Offices, St. Peter's Hill, Grantham NG31 6PZ ☎ 01476 406080 🖷 01476 406000 ✉ p.swinton@southkesteven.gov.uk

Economic Development: Mr David Mather, Economic Development & Investment Service Manager, Council Offices, St. Peter's Hill, Grantham NG31 6PZ ☎ 01476 406080 🖷 01476 406000 ✉ d.mather@southkesteven.gov.uk

Emergency Planning: Mr Mark Jones, Partnerships & Community Safety Service Manager, Council Offices, St. Peter's Hill, Grantham NG31 6PZ ☎ 01476 406080 🖷 01476 406000 ✉ m.jones@southkesteven.gov.uk

Energy Management: Mr K Munford, Energy Officer, Council Offices, St. Peter's Hill, Grantham NG31 6PZ ☎ 01476 406080 🖷 01476 406000 ✉ k.munford@southkesteven.gov.uk

Environmental / Technical Services: Mr David Price, Environmental Health Manager (Commercial), Council Offices, St. Peter's Hill, Grantham NG31 6PZ ☎ 01476 406080 🖷 01476 406000 ✉ d.price@southkesteven.gov.uk

Environmental / Technical Services: Mr Mark Taylor, Head of Environment & Public Protection, Council Offices, St. Peter's Hill, Grantham NG31 6PZ ☎ 01529 414155; 01476 406080 🖷 01476 406000 ✉ mark_taylor@n-kesteven.gov.uk

Environmental Health: Mr David Price, Environmental Health Manager (Commercial), Council Offices, St. Peter's Hill, Grantham NG31 6PZ ☎ 01476 406080 🖷 01476 406000 ✉ d.price@southkesteven.gov.uk

Estates, Property & Valuation: Mr Paul Stokes, Head of Property Services, Council Offices, St. Peter's Hill, Grantham NG31 6PZ ☎ 01476 406080 🖷 01476 406000 ✉ p.stokes@southkesteven.gov.uk

Facilities: Ms Liz Banner, Assets & Facilities Service Manager, Council Offices, St. Peter's Hill, Grantham NG31 6PZ ☎ 01476 406080 🖷 01476 406000 ✉ l.banner@southkesteven.gov.uk

Finance and Treasurer: Mr Richard Wyles, Corporate Head of Finance & Customer Services, Council Offices, St. Peter's Hill, Grantham NG31 6PZ ☎ 01476 406080 🖷 01476 406000 ✉ r.wyles@southkesteven.gov.uk

Fleet Management: Ms Liz Banner, Assets & Facilities Service Manager, Council Offices, St. Peter's Hill, Grantham NG31 6PZ ☎ 01476 406080 🖷 01476 406000 ✉ l.banner@southkesteven.gov.uk

Grounds Maintenance: Ms Liz Banner, Assets & Facilities Service Manager, Council Offices, St. Peter's Hill, Grantham NG31 6PZ ☎ 01476 406080 🖷 01476 406000 ✉ l.banner@southkesteven.gov.uk

Health and Safety: Mr David Price, Healthy Communities Service Manager, Council Offices, St. Peter's Hill, Grantham NG31 6PZ ☎ 01476 406080 🖷 01476 406000 ✉ d.price@southkesteven.gov.uk

Home Energy Conservation: Mr K Munford, Energy Officer, Council Offices, St. Peter's Hill, Grantham NG31 6PZ ☎ 01476 406080 🖷 01476 406000 ✉ k.munford@southkesteven.gov.uk

Housing: Mr Ian Richardson, Head of Housing & Neighbourhoods, Council Offices, St. Peter's Hill, Grantham NG31 6PZ ☎ 01476 406080 🖷 01476 406000 ✉ i.richardson@southkesteven.gov.uk

Legal: Mrs Lucy Youles, Legal Services Manager, Council Offices, St. Peter's Hill, Grantham NG31 6PZ ☎ 01476 406080 🖷 01476 406000 ✉ l.youles@southkesteven.gov.uk

Leisure and Cultural Services: Ms Liz Banner, Assets & Facilities Service Manager, Council Offices, St. Peter's Hill, Grantham NG31 6PZ ☎ 01476 406080 🖷 01476 406000 ✉ l.banner@southkesteven.gov.uk

Licensing: Mr David Price, Environmental Health Manager (Commercial), Council Offices, St. Peter's Hill, Grantham NG31 6PZ ☎ 01476 406080 🖷 01476 406000 ✉ d.price@southkesteven.gov.uk

Member Services: Mrs Lucy Youles, Legal Services Manager, Council Offices, St. Peter's Hill, Grantham NG31 6PZ ☎ 01476 406080 🖷 01476 406000 ✉ l.youles@southkesteven.gov.uk

Parking: Mr Paul Stokes, Corporate Head of Assets, Council Offices, St. Peter's Hill, Grantham NG31 6PZ ☎ 01476 406080 🖷 01476 406000 ✉ p.stokes@southkesteven.gov.uk

Partnerships: Mr Mark Jones, Partnerships & Community Safety Service Manager, Council Offices, St. Peter's Hill, Grantham NG31 6PZ ☎ 01476 406080 🖷 01476 406000 ✉ m.jones@southkesteven.gov.uk

Personnel / HR: Mr Paul Stokes, Corporate Head of Assets, Council Offices, St. Peter's Hill, Grantham NG31 6PZ ☎ 01476 406080 🖷 01476 406000 ✉ p.stokes@southkesteven.gov.uk

Planning: Mr Ian Richardson, Head of Housing & Neighbourhoods, Council Offices, St. Peter's Hill, Grantham NG31 6PZ ☎ 01476 406080 🖷 01476 406000 ✉ i.richardson@southkesteven.gov.uk

Procurement: Ms Liz Banner, Assets & Facilities Service Manager, Council Offices, St. Peter's Hill, Grantham NG31 6PZ ☎ 01476 406080 🖷 01476 406000 ✉ l.banner@southkesteven.gov.uk

Recycling & Waste Minimisation: Mr Mark Taylor, Head of Environment & Public Protection, Council Offices, St. Peter's Hill, Grantham NG31 6PZ ☎ 01529 414155; 01476 406080 🖷 01476

406000 ✉ mark_taylor@n-kesteven.gov.uk; mark_taylor@n-kesteven.gov.uk

Staff Training: Mrs Joyce Slater, Human Resources & Organisational Development Service Manager, Council Offices, St. Peter's Hill, Grantham NG31 6PZ ☎ 01476 406080 🖷 01476 406000 ✉ joyce.slater@southkesteven.gov.uk

Street Scene: Mr Pat Swinton, Waste & Recycling Service Manager, Council Offices, St. Peter's Hill, Grantham NG31 6PZ ☎ 01476 406080 🖷 01476 406000 ✉ p.swinton@southkesteven.gov.uk

Sustainable Communities: Mr Ian Richardson, Head of Housing & Neighbourhoods, Council Offices, St. Peter's Hill, Grantham NG31 6PZ ☎ 01476 406080 🖷 01476 406000 ✉ i.richardson@southkesteven.gov.uk

Town Centre: Mr David Mather, Economic Development & Investment Service Manager, Council Offices, St. Peter's Hill, Grantham NG31 6PZ ☎ 01476 406080 🖷 01476 406000 ✉ d.mather@southkesteven.gov.uk

Transport Planner: Mr Pat Swinton, Waste & Recycling Service Manager, Council Offices, St. Peter's Hill, Grantham NG31 6PZ ☎ 01476 406080 🖷 01476 406000 ✉ p.swinton@southkesteven.gov.uk

Waste Collection and Disposal: Mr Pat Swinton, Waste & Recycling Service Manager, Council Offices, St. Peter's Hill, Grantham NG31 6PZ ☎ 01476 406080 🖷 01476 406000 ✉ p.swinton@southkesteven.gov.uk

Waste Management: Mr Pat Swinton, Waste & Recycling Service Manager, Council Offices, St. Peter's Hill, Grantham NG31 6PZ ☎ 01476 406080 🖷 01476 406000 ✉ p.swinton@southkesteven.gov.uk

MEMBERS OF THE COUNCIL (58)

***Chair:* Kaberry-Brown**, Rosemary (CON - Witham Valley)
r.kaberry-brown@southkesteven.gov.uk
***Leader of the Council:* Neal**, Linda (CON - Bourne West)
l.neal@southkesteven.gov.uk
***Deputy Leader of the Council:* Carpenter**, Paul (CON - Forest)
p.carpenter@southkesteven.gov.uk
Adams, Bob (CON - Issac Newton)
b.adams@southkesteven.gov.uk
Ashberry, Mark (LAB - Harrowby)
m.ashberry@southkesteven.gov.uk
Auger, Ray (CON - Deeping St. James)
r.auger@southkesteven.gov.uk
Bevan, Jean (CON - St. Mary's)
j.bevan@southkesteven.gov.uk
Bisnauthsing, Harrish (LD - St. Mary's)
h.bisnauthsing@southkesteven.gov.uk
Bosworth, Pam (CON - Barrowby)
p.bosworth@southkesteven.gov.uk
Broughton, Robert (IND - Market and West Deeping)
b.broughton@southkesteven.gov.uk
Bryant, Terl (CON - Stamford St. Johns)
t.bryant@southkesteven.gov.uk
Cartwright, Frances (CON - Ringstone)
f.cartright@southkesteven.gov.uk
Channell, Ibis (IND - Hillsides)
i.channell@southkesteven.gov.uk
Chivers, George (CON - Belmont)
g.chivers@southkesteven.gov.uk
Cook, Michael (CON - St. Annes)
m.cook@southkesteven.gov.uk
Cooke, Kelham (CON - Truesdale)
k.cooke@southkesteven.gov.uk
Cosham, Paul (CON - Market and West Deeping)
p.cosham@southkesteven.gov.uk
Craft, Nicholas (CON - Belmont)
n.craft@southkesteven.gov.uk
Davidson, Alan (LAB - Earlesfield)
alan.davidson5@ntlworld.com
Dilks, Phil (NP - Deeping St. James)
p.dilks@southkesteven.gov.uk
Griffin, Brenda (CON - All Saints)
b.griffin@southkesteven.gov.uk
Higgs, David (CON - Bourne East)
d.higgs@southkesteven.gov.uk
Howard, Reginald (IND - Market and West Deeping)
r.howard@southkesteven.gov.uk
Kerr, Jock (IND - Earlesfield)
j.kerr2@southkesteven.gov.uk
Kerr, Vic (IND - Loveden)
King, Michael (CON - Toller)
m.king@southkesteven.gov.uk
Morgan, Charmaine (LAB - St. Annes)
c.morgan@southkesteven.gov.uk
Nalson, David (CON - Stamford St. Johns)
d.nalson@southkesteven.gov.uk
Nicholson, John (CON - Thurlby)
j.nicholson@southkesteven.gov.uk
Parkin, Alan (CON - Green Hill)
a.parkin@southkesteven.gov.uk
Powell, Helen (IND - Bourne West)
h.powell@southkesteven.gov.uk
Robins, Nick (CON - Glen Eden)
n.robins@southkesteven.gov.uk
Rowlands, Graddon (CON - Stamford St. Johns)
g.rowlands@southkesteven.gov.uk
Russell, Bob (CON - Bourne East)
b.russell@southkesteven.gov.uk
Sampson, Bob (IND - Heath)
b.sampson@southkesteven.gov.uk
Sandall, Bob (IND - St. George's)
r.sandall@southkesteven.gov.uk
Sandall, Susan (IND - All Saints)
s.sandall@southkesteven.gov.uk
Scott, Trevor (CON - Ermine)
t.scott@southkesteven.gov.uk
Selby, Ian (LAB - Harrowby)
ian@ieselby.freeserve.co.uk
Shorrock, Rob (LAB - Earlesfield)
r.shorrock@southkesteven.gov.uk
Smith, Jacky (CON - St. Wulfram's)
j.smith@southkesteven.gov.uk
Smith, John (CON - Bourne West)
john.smith@southkesteven.gov.uk
Smith, Judy (CON - Bourne East)
judy.smith@southkesteven.gov.uk
Stephens, Peter (CON - Lincrest)
Stevens, Judy (IND - Deeping St. James)
j.stevens@southkesteven.gov.uk
Stokes, Adam (CON - Grantham St. Johns)

a.stokes@southkesteven.gov.uk
Stokes, Ian (CON - Greyfriars)
i.stokes@southkesteven.gov.uk
Sumner, Brenda (CON - St. George's)
brenda.sumner@southkesteven.gov.uk
Taylor, Jean (CON - Grantham St. Johns)
j.taylor@southkesteven.gov.uk
Taylor, Mike (CON - Greyfriars)
m.taylor@southkesteven.gov.uk
Thompson, Jeff (IND - Peascliffe)
jeff.thompson@southkesteven.gov.uk
Turner, Frank (CON - Green Hill)
f.turner@southkesteven.gov.uk
Wells, Bruce (LAB - Harrowby)
b.wells@southkesteven.gov.uk
Wilkins, Martin (CON - Morkery)
m.wilkins@southkesteven.gov.uk
Wood, Paul (IND - Saxonwell)
p.wood@southkesteven.gov.uk
Woolley, Rosemary (CON - Truesdale)
rh.woolley@southkesteven.gov.uk
Wootten, Raymond (CON - St. Wulfram's)
r.wootten@southkesteven.gov.uk
Wren, Debbie (CON - Aveland)
d.wren@southkesteven.gov.uk

POLITICAL COMPOSITION
CON: 38, IND: 12, LAB: 6, LD: 1, NP: 1

CABINET
Leader / Policy, Strategy & Strategic Partnerships: Mrs Linda Neal
Deputy Leader / Governance & Communication: Mr Paul Carpenter
Good Housing: Mr Terl Bryant
Green, Healthy & Arts: Mr John Smith
Grow the Economy & Economic Development: Mrs Frances Cartwright
Strategic Resources: Mr Mike Taylor

COMMITTEE CHAIRS
Alcohol and Entertainment Licensing: Ms Pam Bosworth
Communities Policy Development: Mr John Nicholson
Development Control: Mr Martin Wilkins
Governance and Audit: Mr Ian Stokes
Resources Policy Development: Mr Nicholas Craft
Scrutiny: Mr Reginald Howard

SOUTH LAKELAND D

South Lakeland District Council, South Lakeland House, Lowther Street, Kendal LA9 4UQ ☎ 01539 733333 🖷 01539 740300 ✉ info@southlakeland.gov.uk 🖳 www.southlakeland.gov.uk

FACTS & FIGURES
Police Authority: Cumbria Police Authority
Health Authority: North West Strategic Health Authority
Learning and Skills Council: North West
Parliamentary Constituencies: Westmorland and Lonsdale
EU Constituencies: North West
Election Frequency: Elections are by thirds
Twinning: Kendal: Rinteln (Germany); Ulverston: Albert (France)

PRINCIPAL OFFICERS
Chief Executive: Mr Lawrence Conway, Chief Executive, South Lakeland House, Lowther Street, Kendal LA9 4UD ☎ 0845 050 4434 🖷 01539 740300 ✉ l.conway@southlakeland.gov.uk

Senior Management: Ms Debbie Storr, Corporate Director - Policy & Resources (Monitoring Officer), South Lakeland House, Lowther Street, Kendal LA9 4UQ ☎ 0845 050 4434 🖷 01539 740300 ✉ d.storr@southlakeland.gov.uk

Building Control: Mr Mark Shipman, Development Management Group Manager, South Lakeland House, Lowther Street, Kendal LA9 4UQ ☎ 0845 050 4434 🖷 01539 740300 ✉ m.shipman@southlakeland.gov.uk

PR / Communications: Mr Mark McAdam, Communications Manager, South Lakeland House, Lowther Street, Kendal LA9 4UQ ☎ 0845 050 4434 🖷 01539 740300 ✉ m.mcadam@southlakeland.gov.uk

Community Planning: Ms Claire Gould, Change & Improvement Manager, South Lakeland House, Lowther Street, Kendal LA9 4UQ ☎ 0845 050 4434 🖷 01539 740300 ✉ c.gould@southlakeland.gov.uk

Community Safety: Ms Claire Gould, Change & Improvement Manager, South Lakeland House, Lowther Street, Kendal LA9 4UQ ☎ 0845 050 4434 🖷 01539 740300 ✉ c.gould@southlakeland.gov.uk

Computer Management: Mr Ben Wright, IT Manager, South Lakeland House, Lowther Street, Kendal LA9 4UQ ☎ 01768 212206; 0845 050 4434 🖷 01768 890470; 01539 740300 ✉ ben.wright@eden.gov.uk; b.wright@southlakeland.gov.uk

Contracts: Mr George Holme, Procurement Manager, South Lakeland House, Lowther Street, Kendal LA9 4UQ ☎ 0845 050 4434 🖷 01539 740300 ✉ g.holme@southlakeland.gov.uk

Corporate Services: Ms Debbie Storr, Corporate Director - Policy & Resources (Monitoring Officer), South Lakeland House, Lowther Street, Kendal LA9 4UQ ☎ 0845 050 4434 🖷 01539 740300 ✉ d.storr@southlakeland.gov.uk

Customer Service: Mr Keith Moore, Customer Services Manager, South Lakeland House, Lowther Street, Kendal LA9 4UQ ☎ 0845 050 4434 🖷 01539 740300 ✉ k.moore@southlakeland.gov.uk

Economic Development: Mr David Sykes, Assistant Director - Community Investment & Development, South Lakeland House, Lowther Street, Kendal LA9 4UQ ☎ 0845 050 4434 🖷 01539 740300 ✉ d.sykes@southlakeland.gov.uk

E-Government: Mr Simon Mcvey, Assistant Director - Customer Focus, South Lakeland House, Lowther Street, Kendal LA9 4UQ ☎ 0845 050 4434 🖷 01539 740300 ✉ s.mcvey@southlakeland.gov.uk

Electoral Registration: Ms Debbie Storr, Corporate Director - Policy & Resources (Monitoring Officer), South Lakeland House, Lowther Street, Kendal LA9 4UQ ☎ 0845 050 4434 🖷 01539

740300 ✉ d.storr@southlakeland.gov.uk

Emergency Planning: Mr Lawrence Conway, Chief Executive, South Lakeland House, Lowther Street, Kendal LA9 4UD ☎ 0845 050 4434 🖷 01539 740300 ✉ l.conway@southlakeland.gov.uk

Energy Management: Ms Claire Gould, Change & Improvement Manager, South Lakeland House, Lowther Street, Kendal LA9 4UQ ☎ 0845 050 4434 🖷 01539 740300 ✉ c.gould@southlakeland.gov.uk

Environmental / Technical Services: Mr Phil Greenup, Environment & Housing Manager, South Lakeland House, Lowther Street, Kendal LA9 4UQ ☎ 0845 050 4434 🖷 01539 740300 ✉ p.greenup@southlakeland.gov.uk

Environmental Health: Mr Simon Rowley, Assistant Director - Communities, South Lakeland House, Lowther Street, Kendal LA9 4UQ ☎ 0845 050 4434 🖷 01539 740300 ✉ s.rowley@southlakeland.gov.uk

Estates, Property & Valuation: Mr Michael Keane, Assistant Director - Social Enterprise, South Lakeland House, Lowther Street, Kendal LA9 4UQ ☎ 0845 050 4434 🖷 01539 740300 ✉ m.keane@southlakeland.gov.uk

Events Manager: Ms Imelda Winters-Lewis, Arts & Events Officer, South Lakeland House, Lowther Street, Kendal LA9 4UQ ☎ 0845 050 4434 🖷 01539 740300 ✉ l.winterslewis@southlakeland.gov.uk

Facilities: Mr Michael Keane, Assistant Director - Social Enterprise, South Lakeland House, Lowther Street, Kendal LA9 4UQ ☎ 0845 050 4434 🖷 01539 740300 ✉ m.keane@southlakeland.gov.uk

Finance and Treasurer: Ms Shelagh McGregor, Assistant Director - Resources, South Lakeland House, Lowther Street, Kendal LA9 4UQ ☎ 0845 050 4434 🖷 01539 740300 ✉ s.mcgregor@southlakeland.gov.uk

Fleet Management: Mr George Sierpinski, Fleet Manager, South Lakeland House, Lowther Street, Kendal LA9 4UQ ☎ 0845 050 4434 🖷 01539 740300 ✉ g.sierpinski@southlakeland.gov.uk

Grounds Maintenance: Mr Tony Naylor, Parks & Leisure Client Officer, South Lakeland House, Lowther Street, Kendal LA9 4UQ ☎ 0845 050 4434 🖷 01539 740300 ✉ t.naylor@southlakeland.gov.uk

Health and Safety: Ms Andrea Wilson, Human Resources Services Manager, South Lakeland House, Lowther Street, Kendal LA9 4UQ ☎ 0845 050 4434 🖷 01539 740300 ✉ a.wilson@southlakeland.gov.uk

Home Energy Conservation: Mr David Sykes, Assistant Director - Community Investment & Development, South Lakeland House, Lowther Street, Kendal LA9 4UQ ☎ 0845 050 4434 🖷 01539 740300 ✉ d.sykes@southlakeland.gov.uk

Housing: Mr David Sykes, Assistant Director - Community Investment & Development, South Lakeland House, Lowther Street, Kendal LA9 4UQ ☎ 0845 050 4434 🖷 01539 740300 ✉ d.sykes@southlakeland.gov.uk

Housing Maintenance: Mr Peter Thomas, Chief Executive - South Lakes Housing, Aynam Mills, Canal Head, Kendal LA9 4UQ ☎ 01539 717717 ✉ p.thomas@southlakeland.gov.uk

Local Area Agreement: Ms Claire Gould, Change & Improvement Manager, South Lakeland House, Lowther Street, Kendal LA9 4UQ ☎ 0845 050 4434 🖷 01539 740300 ✉ c.gould@southlakeland.gov.uk

Legal: Mr Matthew Neal, Solicitor to the Council, South Lakeland House, Lowther Street, Kendal LA9 4UQ ☎ 0845 050 4434 🖷 01539 740300 ✉ m.neal@southlakeland.gov.uk

Leisure and Cultural Services: Mr David Sykes, Assistant Director - Community Investment & Development, South Lakeland House, Lowther Street, Kendal LA9 4UQ ☎ 0845 050 4434 🖷 01539 740300 ✉ d.sykes@southlakeland.gov.uk

Licensing: Mr Simon Rowley, Assistant Director - Communities, South Lakeland House, Lowther Street, Kendal LA9 4UQ ☎ 0845 050 4434 🖷 01539 740300 ✉ s.rowley@southlakeland.gov.uk

Lighting: Mr Simon Rowley, Assistant Director - Communities, South Lakeland House, Lowther Street, Kendal LA9 4UQ ☎ 0845 050 4434 🖷 01539 740300 ✉ s.rowley@southlakeland.gov.uk

Lottery Funding, Charity and Voluntary: Mr Lawrence Conway, Chief Executive, South Lakeland House, Lowther Street, Kendal LA9 4UD ☎ 0845 050 4434 🖷 01539 740300 ✉ l.conway@southlakeland.gov.uk

Member Services: Ms Debbie Storr, Corporate Director - Policy & Resources (Monitoring Officer), South Lakeland House, Lowther Street, Kendal LA9 4UQ ☎ 0845 050 4434 🖷 01539 740300 ✉ d.storr@southlakeland.gov.uk

Parking: Mr Michael Keane, Assistant Director - Social Enterprise, South Lakeland House, Lowther Street, Kendal LA9 4UQ ☎ 0845 050 4434 🖷 01539 740300 ✉ m.keane@southlakeland.gov.uk

Partnerships: Ms Claire Gould, Change & Improvement Manager, South Lakeland House, Lowther Street, Kendal LA9 4UQ ☎ 0845 050 4434 🖷 01539 740300 ✉ c.gould@southlakeland.gov.uk

Personnel / HR: Ms Andrea Wilson, Human Resources Services Manager, South Lakeland House, Lowther Street, Kendal LA9 4UQ ☎ 0845 050 4434 🖷 01539 740300 ✉ a.wilson@southlakeland.gov.uk

Planning: Mr David Sykes, Assistant Director - Community Investment & Development, South Lakeland House, Lowther Street, Kendal LA9 4UQ ☎ 0845 050 4434 🖷 01539 740300 ✉ d.sykes@southlakeland.gov.uk

Procurement: Mr George Holme, Procurement Manager, South

Lakeland House, Lowther Street, Kendal LA9 4UQ ☎ 0845 050 4434 🖷 01539 740300 ✉ g.holme@southlakeland.gov.uk

Recycling & Waste Minimisation: Mr Lawrence Conway, Chief Executive, South Lakeland House, Lowther Street, Kendal LA9 4UD ☎ 0845 050 4434 🖷 01539 740300 ✉ l.conway@southlakeland.gov.uk

Regeneration: Mr David Sykes, Assistant Director - Community Investment & Development, South Lakeland House, Lowther Street, Kendal LA9 4UQ ☎ 0845 050 4434 🖷 01539 740300 ✉ d.sykes@southlakeland.gov.uk

Staff Training: Ms Andrea Wilson, Human Resources Services Manager, South Lakeland House, Lowther Street, Kendal LA9 4UQ ☎ 0845 050 4434 🖷 01539 740300 ✉ a.wilson@southlakeland.gov.uk

Street Scene: Mr Nick Pearson, Street Scene Manager, South Lakeland House, Lowther Street, Kendal LA9 4UQ ☎ 0845 050 4434 🖷 01539 740300 ✉ n.pearson@southlakeland.gov.uk

Sustainable Communities: Ms Claire Gould, Change & Improvement Manager, South Lakeland House, Lowther Street, Kendal LA9 4UQ ☎ 0845 050 4434 🖷 01539 740300 ✉ c.gould@southlakeland.gov.uk

Sustainable Development: Mr David Sykes, Assistant Director - Community Investment & Development, South Lakeland House, Lowther Street, Kendal LA9 4UQ ☎ 0845 050 4434 🖷 01539 740300 ✉ d.sykes@southlakeland.gov.uk

Tourism: Mr David Sykes, Assistant Director - Community Investment & Development, South Lakeland House, Lowther Street, Kendal LA9 4UQ ☎ 0845 050 4434 🖷 01539 740300 ✉ d.sykes@southlakeland.gov.uk

Town Centre: Mr David Sykes, Assistant Director - Community Investment & Development, South Lakeland House, Lowther Street, Kendal LA9 4UQ ☎ 0845 050 4434 🖷 01539 740300 ✉ d.sykes@southlakeland.gov.uk

Transport: Mr Simon Rowley, Assistant Director - Communities, South Lakeland House, Lowther Street, Kendal LA9 4UQ ☎ 0845 050 4434 🖷 01539 740300 ✉ s.rowley@southlakeland.gov.uk

Waste Collection and Disposal: Mr Simon Rowley, Assistant Director - Communities, South Lakeland House, Lowther Street, Kendal LA9 4UQ ☎ 0845 050 4434 🖷 01539 740300 ✉ s.rowley@southlakeland.gov.uk

Waste Management: Mr Simon Rowley, Assistant Director - Communities, South Lakeland House, Lowther Street, Kendal LA9 4UQ ☎ 0845 050 4434 🖷 01539 740300 ✉ s.rowley@southlakeland.gov.uk

MEMBERS OF THE COUNCIL (51)

***Chair:* Stephenson**, Jo (LD - Windermere Town)
***Vice-Chair:* Westwood**, Evelyn (LD - Sedbergh and Kirkby Lonsdale)
e.westwood@southlakeland.gov.uk
***Leader of the Council:* Thornton**, Peter (LD - Whinfell)
p.thornton@southlakeland.gov.uk
***Deputy Leader of the Council:* Feeney-Johnson**, Claire (LD - Kendal Nether)
c.feeneyjohnson@southlakeland.gov.uk
***Group Leader:* Airey**, James (CON - Low Furness)
j.airey@southlakeland.gov.uk
***Group Leader:* Wilson**, Mark (LAB - Ulverston East)
mark.wilson@southlakeland.gov.uk
Airey, Caroline (CON - Mid Furness)
c.airey@southlakeland.gov.uk
Archibald, Giles (LD - Kendal Fell)
g.archibald@southlakeland.gov.uk
Berry, Ben (CON - Windermere Applethwaite and Troutbeck)
b.berry@southlakeland.gov.uk
Bingham, Roger (CON - Burton and Holme)
r.bingham@southlakeland.gov.uk
Boden, Rob (LD - Kendal Underley)
r.boden@southlakeland.gov.uk
Brook, Jonathan (LD - Kendal Parks)
j.brook@southlakeland.gov.uk
Clough, John (LAB - Ulverston Town)
j.clough@southlakeland.gov.uk
Coleman, Stephen (LD - Kendal Strickland)
s.coleman@southlakeland.gov.uk
Collins, Stan (LD - Staveley-in-Westmorland)
s.collins@southlakeland.gov.uk
Cooper, Brian (CON - Burton and Holme)
b.cooper@southlakeland.gov.uk
Cotton, Nick (LD - Sedbergh and Kirkby Lonsdale)
n.cotton@southlakeland.gov.uk
Curwen, Joss (CON - Broughton)
j.curwen@southlakeland.gov.uk
Dawson, Julie (LD - Kendal Kirkland)
j.dawson@southlakeland.gov.uk
Dixon, Philip (LD - Kendal Highgate)
p.dixon@southlakeland.gov.uk
Eccles, Sheila (LD - Crooklands)
s.eccles@southlakeland.gov.uk
Emmott, Sylvia (LD - Kendal Stonecross)
s.emmott@southlakeland.gov.uk
Evans, David (LD - Kendal Mintsfleet)
d.evans@southlakeland.gov.uk
Fletcher, David (LIB - Hawkeshead)
d.fletcher@southlakeland.gov.uk
Gardiner, Gill (LD - Holker)
g.gardner@southlakeland.gov.uk
Gardiner, Andrew (CON - Grange North)
a.gardiner@southlakeland.gov.uk
Graham, Clive (LD - Kendal Far Cross)
clive.graham@southlakeland.gov.uk
Gray, Brenda (LD - Kendal Oxenholme and Natland)
b.gray@southlakeland.gov.uk
Hall, Anne (CON - Coniston and Crake Valley)
anne.hall@southlakeland.gov.uk
Halliday, Heidi (LD - Ambleside and Grasmere)
h.halliday@southlakeland.gov.uk
Harvey, Tom (CON - Grange South)
t.harvey@southlakeland.gov.uk
Holland, Chris (LD - Burneside)
c.holland@southlakeland.gov.uk
Holmes, John (CON - Lyth Valley)
j.holmes@southlakeland.gov.uk
Irving, Helen (CON - Ulverston North)

h.irving@southlakeland.gov.uk
Jenkinson, Janette (CON - Ulverston West)
j.jenkinson@southlakeland.gov.uk
Jupe, Prudence (LD - Arnside and Beetham)
p.jupe@southlakeland.gov.uk
Lawson, Sonia (LD - Kendal Castle)
sonia.lawson@southlakeland.gov.uk
McPherson, Ian (LD - Sedbergh and Kirkby Lonsdale)
i.mcpherson@southlakeland.gov.uk
Orr, Mary (LD - Levens)
m.orr@southlakeland.gov.uk
Rajan, Bharath (LAB - Ulverston Central)
b.rajan@southlakeland.gov.uk
Rees, Vivienne (LD - Ambleside and Grasmere)
v.rees@southlakeland.gov.uk
Rigg, Amanda (CON - Ulverston South)
a.rigg@southlakeland.gov.uk
Ryder, David (LD - Milnthorpe)
d.ryder@southlakeland.gov.uk
Sanderson, Sue (LD - Staveley-in-Cartmel)
s.sanderson@southlakeland.gov.uk
Shine, Andy (LD - Kendal Heron Hill)
andy.shine@southlakeland.gov.uk
Stephenson, Hilary (LD - Windermere Bowness North)
h.stephenson@southlakeland.gov.uk
Stewart, Ian (LD - Arnside and Beetham)
i.stewart@southlakeland.gov.uk
Vincent, Graham (LD - Kendal Romney)
g.vincent@southlakeland.gov.uk
Williams, David (CON - Windermere Bowness South)
d.williams@southlakeland.gov.uk
Willis, Janet (LD - Mid Furness)
j.willis@southlakeland.gov.uk
Wilson, Mary
(LD - Cartmel and Grange West)
m.wilson@southlakeland.gov.uk

POLITICAL COMPOSITION

LD: 33, CON: 14, LAB: 3, LIB: 1

CABINET

Leader / Promoting South Lakeland: Mr Peter Thornton
Deputy Leader / Environment & Sustainability: Ms Claire Feeney-Johnson
Central Services: Ms Janet Willis
Communities & Well Being: Mr Graham Vincent
Economy & Enterprise: Mr Ian Stewart
Housing & Development: Mr Jonathan Brook
Policy, Performance & Resources: Mr David Evans

COMMITTEE CHAIRS

Audit: Mr Stephen Coleman
Communities (Scrutiny): Mrs Mary Wilson
Human Resources: Ms Sylvia Emmott
Licensing: Mrs Sheila Eccles
Planning: Mr Ian McPherson
Resources & Partnerships (Scrutiny): Mr Andy Shine

SOUTH LANARKSHIRE S

South Lanarkshire Council, Council Offices, Almada Street, Hamilton ML3 0AA ☎ 01698 454444 🖷 01698 454275
💻 www.southlanarkshire.gov.uk

FACTS & FIGURES

Police Authority: Strathclyde Police Authority
Health Authority: NHS Lanarkshire
Learning and Skills Council: Scotland
Parliamentary Constituencies: Dumfriesshire, Clydesdale and Tweedale, East Kilbride, Strathaven and Lesmahagow, Lanark & Hamilton East, Rutherglen and Hamilton West
EU Constituencies: Scotland
Election Frequency: Elections are of whole council
Twinning: Bothwell: Jouy en Josas (France); Clydesdale: Yvetot (France); East Kilbride: Ballerup (Denmark); Hamilton: Chatellerault (France); Hemmingen (Germany); Larkhall: Seclin (France)

PRINCIPAL OFFICERS

Chief Executive: Mr Archibald Strang, Chief Executive & Interim Executive Director of Finance, Council Offices, Almada Street, Hamilton ML3 0AA ☎ 01698 454530 🖷 01698 454682
🖰 archie.strang@southlanarkshire.gov.uk

Senior Management: Mr Larry Forde, Executive Director of Education, Council Offices, Almada Street, Hamilton ML3 0AA
☎ 01698 454379 🖷 01698 454465
🖰 larry.forde@southlanarkshire.gov.uk

Senior Management: Mr Lindsay Freeland, Executive Director of Housing & Technical Resources, Council Offices, Almada Street, Hamilton ML3 0AL ☎ 01698 454405 🖷 01698 455616
🖰 lindsay.freeland@southlanarkshire.gov.uk

Senior Management: Mr Robert McIlwain, Executive Director of Corporate Resources, Corporate Resources, Council Offices, Almada Street, Hamilton ML3 0AA ☎ 01698 454660 🖷 01698 454275 🖰 robert.mcilwain@southlanarkshire.gov.uk

Senior Management: Mr Harry Stevenson, Executive Director of Social Work Resources, Council Offices, Almada Street, Hamilton ML3 0AA ☎ 01698 453700 🖷 01698 453784
🖰 harry.stevenson@southlanarkshire.gov.uk

Architect, Building / Property Services: Mr John Stobie, Head of Property Services, Housing & Technical Resources, Council Offices, Almada Street, Hamilton ML3 0AA ☎ 01698 455621
🖷 01698 455616 🖰 john.stobie@southlanarkshire.gov.uk

Best Value: Ms Helen Black, Improvement Manager, Finance & Information Technology Resources, Floor 4, Almada Street, Hamilton ML3 0AA ☎ 01698 454618 🖷 01698 454682
🖰 helen.black@southlanarkshire.gov.uk

Building Control: Mr Michael McGlynn, Head of Planning & Building Standards, Montrose House, 154 Montrose Crescent, Hamilton ML3 6LB ☎ 01698 455127 🖷 01698 455195
🖰 michael.mcglynn@southlanarkshire.gov.uk

Catering Services: Mr Norrie Anderson, Executive Director of Community Resources, Blantyre, Hamilton G72 0JP ☎ 01698 454849 🖰 norrie.anderson@southlanarkshire.gov.uk

Children / Youth Services: Ms Roz Gallagher, Youth Learning Services Manager, Council Offices, Almada Street, Hamilton ML3

0AA ☎ 01698 454466 ✉ roz.gallagher@southlanarkshire.gov.uk

Civil Registration: Ms Teresa Stone, Registration & Licensing Manager, Council Offices, Almada Street, Hamilton ML3 0AA ☎ 01698 454806 ✉ teresa.stone@southlanarkshire.gov.uk

PR / Communications: Mr Drew King, Head of Corporate Communications & Public Affairs, Council Offices, Almada Street, Hamilton ML3 0AA ☎ 01698 454904 🖷 01698 454949 ✉ drew.king@southlanarkshire.gov.uk

Community Planning: Mr Alistair McKinnon, Head of Community Support Services, Council Offices, Almada Street, Hamilton ML3 0AA ☎ 01698 454700 ✉ alistair.mckinnon@southlanarkshire.gov.uk

Community Safety: Mr Ian Murray, Policy Manager, Community Resources, Council Offices, Almada Street, Hamilton ML3 0AA ☎ 01698 455297 🖷 01698 454362 ✉ ian.murray@southlanarkshire.gov.uk

Computer Management: Mrs Kay Brown, Head of Information Technology Services, Council Offices, Beckford Street, Hamilton ML3 0AQ ☎ 01698 454344 🖷 01698 454753 ✉ kay.brown@southlanarkshire.gov.uk

Computer Management: Mr Alan Colthart, Head of Support Services, Montrose House, 154 Montrose Crescent, Hamilton ML3 6LL ☎ 01698 455600 ✉ alan.colthart@southlanarkshire.gov.uk

Corporate Services: Mr Tom Barrie, Head of Support Services & Social Work, Council Offices, Almada Street, Hamilton ML3 0AA ☎ 01698 454444 ✉ tom.barrie@southlanarkshire.gov.uk

Corporate Services: Mr Robert McIlwain, Executive Director of Corporate Resources, Corporate Resources, Council Offices, Almada Street, Hamilton ML3 0AA ☎ 01698 454660 🖷 01698 454275 ✉ robert.mcilwain@southlanarkshire.gov.uk

Corporate Services: Mr Douglas Wilson, Head of Administration, Council Offices, Almada Street, Hamilton ML3 0AA ☎ 01698 454461 ✉ douglas.wilson@southlanarkshire.gov.uk

Direct Labour: Mr Daniel Lowe, Head of Property Services, Council Offices, Almada Street, Hamilton ML3 0AA ☎ 01698 455621 ✉ daniel.lowe@southlanarkshire.gov.uk

Economic Development: Mr James McCaffer, Head of Regeneration Services, Montrose House, 154 Montrose Crescent, Hamilton ML3 6LB ☎ 01698 453813 🖷 01698 455195 ✉ jim.mccaffer@southlanarkshire.gov.uk

Education: Ms Sara Fellows, Head of Education of Resources, Council Offices, Almada Street, Hamilton ML3 0AA ☎ 01698 454408 ✉ sara.fellows@southlanarkshire.gov.uk

Education: Mr Larry Forde, Executive Director of Education, Council Offices, Almada Street, Hamilton ML3 0AA ☎ 01698 454379 🖷 01698 454465 ✉ larry.forde@southlanarkshire.gov.uk

Education: Mr Jim Gilhooly, Deputy Director of Education (Curriculum & Quality Improvement), Council Offices, Almada Street, Hamilton ML3 0AA ☎ 01698 454475 ✉ jim.gilhooly@southlanarkshire.gov.uk

E-Government: Mrs Kay Brown, Head of Information Technology Services, Council Offices, Beckford Street, Hamilton ML3 0AQ ☎ 01698 454344 🖷 01698 454753 ✉ kay.brown@southlanarkshire.gov.uk

Electoral Registration: Mr Robert McIlwain, Executive Director of Corporate Resources, Corporate Resources, Council Offices, Almada Street, Hamilton ML3 0AA ☎ 01698 454660 🖷 01698 454275 ✉ robert.mcilwain@southlanarkshire.gov.uk

Emergency Planning: Mr Kin Ratten, Contingency Planning Manager, Council Offices, Almada Street, Hamilton ML3 0AA ☎ 01698 454648 ✉ kin.ratten@southlanarkshire.gov.uk

Energy Management: Mr Ian Douglas, Operations Manager for Property Services, Council Offices, Almada Street, Hamilton ML3 0AA ☎ 01355 806818 ✉ ian.douglas@southlanarkshire.gov.uk

Estates, Property & Valuation: Ms Heather McNeil, Head of Audit & Improvement Services, Montrose House, 154 Montrose Crescent, Hamilton ML3 6LB ☎ 01698 455915 🖷 01698 454801 ✉ heather.mcneil@southlanarkshire.gov.uk

European Liaison: Mr Kenny Lean, Team Leader of Funding & Development, Council Offices, Almada Street, Hamilton ML3 0AA ☎ 01698 455129 ✉ kenny.lean@southlanarkshire.gov.uk

Events Manager: Mrs Angie Moakler, Design & Production Manager, Council Offices, Almada Street, Hamilton ML3 0AA ☎ 01698 453853 ✉ angie.moakler@southlanarkshire.gov.uk

Facilities: Mr Stephen Kelly, Head of Facilities & Grounds Services, Community Resources, Council Offices, Almada Street, Hamilton ML3 0AA ☎ 01698 454705 🖷 01698 454362 ✉ stephen.kelly@southlanarkshire.gov.uk

Finance and Treasurer: Mr Paul Manning, Head of Finance & IT, Council Offices, Almada Street, Hamilton ML3 0AA ☎ 01698 454532 ✉ paul.manning@southlanarkshire.gov.uk

Fleet Management: Ms Shirley Clelland, Waste & Enviromental Services, Blantyre, Hamilton G72 0JP ☎ 01698 717752 🖷 01698 717750 ✉ shirley.clelland@southlanarkshire.gov.uk

Grounds Maintenance: Ms Shirley Clelland, Waste & Enviromental Services, Blantyre, Hamilton G72 0JP ☎ 01698 717752 🖷 01698 717750 ✉ shirley.clelland@southlanarkshire.gov.uk

Health and Safety: Mr Kin Ratten, Contingency Planning Manager, Council Offices, Almada Street, Hamilton ML3 0AA ☎ 01698 454648 ✉ kin.ratten@southlanarkshire.gov.uk

Highways: Mr Gordon Mackay, Head of Roads & Transportation, Montrose House, 154 Montrose Crescent, Hamilton ML3 6LL ☎ 01698 454484 🖷 01698 454488 ✉ gordon.mackay@southlanarkshire.gov.uk

Home Energy Conservation: Mr Ian Douglas, Operations Manager for Property Services, Council Offices, Almada Street, Hamilton ML3 0AA ☎ 01355 806818

ian.douglas@southlanarkshire.gov.uk

Housing: Mr Patrick Murphy, Head Support Services for Housing & Tech Resources, Council Offices, Almada Street, Hamilton ML3 0AA ☎ 01698 454065 patrick.j.murphy@southlanarkshire.gov.uk

Housing Maintenance: Mr Lindsay Freeland, Executive Director of Housing & Technical Resources, Council Offices, Almada Street, Hamilton ML3 0AL ☎ 01698 454405 🖷 01698 455616 lindsay.freeland@southlanarkshire.gov.uk

Legal: Ms Geraldine McCann, Head of Legal Services, Montrose House, 154 Montrose Crescent, Hamilton ML3 6LL ☎ 01698 454516 geraldine.mccann@southlanarkshire.gov.uk

Leisure and Cultural Services: Mr Gerry Campbell, General Manager, South Lanarkshire Leisure Ltd, Floor 1, North Stand, Cadzow Avenue, Hamilton ML3 0LX ☎ 01698 476095 🖷 01698 476198 gerry.campbell@southlanarkshire.gov.uk

Licensing: Ms Geraldine McCann, Head of Legal Services, Montrose House, 154 Montrose Crescent, Hamilton ML3 6LL ☎ 01698 454516 geraldine.mccann@southlanarkshire.gov.uk

Lifelong Learning: Ms Andrea Batchelor, Head of Education (Inclusion), Council Offices, Almada Street, Hamilton ML3 0AE ☎ 01698 454475 🖷 01698 454465 andrea.batchelor@southlanarkshire.gov.uk

Lighting: Mr David Black, Lighting Engineer, Montrose House, 154 Montrose Crescent, Hamilton ML3 6LL ☎ 01698 452401 🖷 01698 453600 david.black@southlanarkshire.gov.uk

Lottery Funding, Charity and Voluntary: Mr Kenny Lean, Team Leader of Funding & Development, Council Offices, Almada Street, Hamilton ML3 0AA ☎ 01698 455129 kenny.lean@southlanarkshire.gov.uk

Member Services: Ms Linda Cunningham, Member Services Manager & PA to Leader, Council Offices, Almada Street, Hamilton ML3 0AA ☎ 01698 454027 🖷 01698 454345 linda.cunningham@southlanarkshire.gov.uk

Parking: Mr Donald Gibson, Parking Manager, Brandon Gate, 1 Leechlee Road, Hamilton ML3 0XB ☎ 01698 455359 🖷 01698 453535 donald.gibson@southlanarkshire.gov.uk

Personnel / HR: Mr Gerry Killin, Head of Personnel Services, Council Offices, Almada Street, Hamilton ML3 0AA ☎ 01698 454330 🖷 01698 454637 gerry.killin@southlanarkshire.gov.uk

Planning: Mr Michael McGlynn, Head of Planning & Building Standards, Montrose House, 154 Montrose Crescent, Hamilton ML3 6LB ☎ 01698 455127 🖷 01698 455195 michael.mcglynn@southlanarkshire.gov.uk

Procurement: Mr Peter Field, Procurement Manager, Council Offices, Almada Street, Hamilton ML3 0AA ☎ 01698 454707 peter.field@southlanarkshire.gov.uk

Public Libraries: Ms Diana Barr, Library & Museum Services Manager, Council Offices, Almada Street, Hamilton ML3 0AA ☎ 01698 454444 🖷 01698 454465 diana.barr@southlanarkshire.gov.uk

Recycling & Waste Minimisation: Mr Charlie Kelly, Waste Manager, Council Offices, Almada Street, Hamilton ML3 0AA ☎ 01698 717777 land.services@southlanarkshire.gov.uk

Regeneration: Mr James McCaffer, Head of Regeneration Services, Montrose House, 154 Montrose Crescent, Hamilton ML3 6LB ☎ 01698 453813 🖷 01698 455195 jim.mccaffer@southlanarkshire.gov.uk

Road Safety: Mr Gordon Mackay, Head of Roads & Transportation, Montrose House, 154 Montrose Crescent, Hamilton ML3 6LL ☎ 01698 454484 🖷 01698 454488 gordon.mackay@southlanarkshire.gov.uk

Social Services: Mr Harry Stevenson, Executive Director of Social Work Resources, Council Offices, Almada Street, Hamilton ML3 0AA ☎ 01698 453700 🖷 01698 453784 harry.stevenson@southlanarkshire.gov.uk

Social Services: Mr Jim Wilson, Head of Older People's Services, Council Offices, Almada Street, Hamilton ML3 0AA ☎ 01698 453783 jim.wilson@southlanarkshire.gov.uk

Social Services (Adult): Mr Jim Wilson, Head of Older People's Services, Council Offices, Almada Street, Hamilton ML3 0AA ☎ 01698 453783 jim.wilson@southlanarkshire.gov.uk

Social Services (Children): Mr Robert Swift, Head of Child & Family Services, Council Offices, Almada Street, Hamilton ML3 0AA ☎ 01698 454887 robert.swift@southlanarkshire.gov.uk

Staff Training: Mrs Gill Bhatti, Employee Development & Diversity Manager, Council Offices, Almada Street, Hamilton ML3 0AQ ☎ 01698 455604 🖷 01698 454637 gill.bhatti@southlanarkshire.gov.uk

Street Scene: Mr Steve Keating, Property Development Manager, Council Offices, Almada Street, Hamilton ML3 0AA ☎ 01698 455191 steve.keating@southlanarkshire.gov.uk

Sustainable Communities: Mr Simon Carey, Regeneration & Inclusion Manager, Enterprise Resources, 154 Montrose Crescent, Hamilton ML3 6LB ☎ 01698 453812 🖷 01698 453804 simon.carey@southlanarkshire.gov.uk

Sustainable Development: Mr Charlie Kelly, Waste Manager, Council Offices, Almada Street, Hamilton ML3 0AA ☎ 01698 717777 land.services@southlanarkshire.gov.uk

Traffic Management: Mr Gordon Mackay, Head of Roads & Transportation, Montrose House, 154 Montrose Crescent, Hamilton ML3 6LL ☎ 01698 454484 🖷 01698 454488 gordon.mackay@southlanarkshire.gov.uk

Waste Collection and Disposal: Ms Shirley Clelland, Waste & Enviromental Services, Blantyre, Hamilton G72 0JP ☎ 01698 717752 🖷 01698 717750 shirley.clelland@southlanarkshire.gov.uk

Waste Management: Ms Shirley Clelland, Waste & Enviromental Services, Blantyre, Hamilton G72 0JP ☎ 01698 717752 🖷 01698 717750 ✉ shirley.clelland@southlanarkshire.gov.uk

MEMBERS OF THE COUNCIL (67)

***Provost:* Logan**, Eileen (LAB - Clydesdale West)
eileen.logan@southlanarkshire.gsx.gov.uk
***Deputy Provost:* Clearie**, Pam (LAB - Cambuslang East)
pamela.clearie@southlanarkshire.gsx.gov.uk
***Leader of the Council:* McAvoy**, Edward (LAB - Rutherglen Central and North)
councillor.mcaboy@southlanarkshire.gsx.gov.uk
***Deputy Leader of the Council:* Burns**, Jackie (LAB - Larkhall)
jackie.burns@southlanarkshire.gsx.gov.uk
Adams, Lynn (SNP - Hamilton North and East)
lynn.adams@southlanarkshire.gsx.gov.uk
Anderson, John (SNP - East Kilbride Central South)
j.anderson@southlanarkshire.gsx.gov.uk
Archer, Ed (IND - Clydesdale North)
ed.archer@southlankarkshire.gsx.gov.uk
Barker, Ralph (LAB - Clydesdale East)
ralph.barker@southlanarkshire.gsx.gov.uk
Brogan, Walter (LAB - Cambuslang East)
walter.brogan@southlanarkshire.gsx.gov.uk
Brown, Robert (LD - Rutherglen South)
robert.brown@southlanarkshire.gsx.gov.uk
Buchanan, Archie (SNP - East Kilbride South)
archie.buchanan@southlanarkshire.gsx.gov.uk
Cairney, John (LAB - East Kilbride East)
john.cairney@southlanarkshire.gsx.gov.uk
Campbell, Graeme (CON - Avondale and Stonehouse)
graeme.campbell@southlanarkshire.gov.uk
Carmichael, Andy (LAB - Larkhall)
andy.carmichael@southlanarkshire.gsx.gov.uk
Clark, Gordon (SGP - Rutherglen Central and North)
gordon.clark@southlanarkshire.gsx.gov.uk
Clearie, Russell (LAB - Cambuslang West)
russell.clearie@southlanarkshire.gsx.gov.uk
Convery, Gerry (LAB - East Kilbride Central South)
gerry.convery@southlanarkshire.gsx.gov.uk
Cooper, Margaret (LAB - Avondale and Stonehouse)
margaret.cooper@southlanarkshire.gov.uk
Craig, Peter (SNP - Larkhall)
peter.craig@southlanarkshire.gsx.gov.uk
Crawley, Angela (SNP - Hamilton South)
angela.crawley@southlanarkshire.gsx.gov.uk
Deanie, Christine (SNP - Cambuslang East)
christine.deanie@southlanarkshire.gsx.gov.uk
Devlin, Maureen (LAB - Bothwell and Uddingston)
maureen.devlin@southlanarkshire.gsx.gov.uk
Docherty, James (LAB - East Kilbride South)
james.dockerty@southlanarkshire.gsx.gov.uk
Dorman, Isobel (SNP - Avondale and Stonehouse)
isobel.dorman@southlanarkshire.gov.uk
Dunsmuir, Hugh (LAB - Blantyre)
hugh.dunsmuir@southlanarkshire.gsx.gov.uk
Edwards, Douglas (SNP - East Kilbride South)
douglas.edwards@southlanarkshire.gsx.gov.uk
Falconer, Alan (LAB - Hamilton West and Earnock)
alan.falconer@southlanarkshire.gsx.gov.uk
Gauld, Bev (SNP - Clydesdale East)
beverly.gauld@southlanarkshire.gsx.gov.uk
Greenshields, George (LAB - Clydesdale South)
george.greenshields@southlanarkshire.gov.uk
Hamilton, Lynsey (LAB - Clydesdale West)
lynsey.hamilton@southlanarkshire.gsx.gov.uk
Handibode, Jim (LAB - Blantyre)
james.handibode@southlanarkshire.gsx.gov.uk
Higgins, Anne (SNP - Rutherglen South)
anne.higgins@southlanarkshire.gsx.gov.uk
Holman, Bill (SNP - Avondale and Stonehouse)
bill.holman@southlanarkshire.gov.uk
Horne, Graeme (SNP - Hamilton West and Earnock)
graeme.horne@southlanarkshire.gsx.gov.uk
Kegg, Anne (CON - Bothwell and Uddingston)
anne.kegg@southlanarkshire.gsx.gov.uk
Kerr, Susan (LAB - East Kilbride Central South)
susan.kerr2@southlanarkshire.gov.uk
Lawson, Bobby (SNP - Hamilton South)
bobby.lawson@southlanarkshire.gsx.gov.uk
Lee, Pat (SNP - Clydesdale West)
pat.lee@southlanarkshire.gsx.gov.uk
Lennon, Monica (LAB - Hamilton North and East)
monica.lennon@southlanarkshire.gsx.gov.uk
Lowe, Joe (LAB - Hamilton South)
joe.lowe@southlanarkshire.gsx.gov.uk
Maggs, Anne (SNP - East Kilbride Central North)
anne.maggs@southlanarkshire.gsx.gov.uk
Manson, Archie (SNP - Clydesdale South)
archibald.manson@southlanarkshire.gsx.gov.uk
McCaig, Brian (LAB - Hamilton South)
brian.mccaig@southlanarkshire.gsx.gov.uk
McClymont, Catherine (LAB - Clydesdale North)
catherine.mcclymont@southlanarkshire.gov.uk
McColl, Clare (SNP - Cambuslang West)
clare.mccoll@southlanarshire.gsx.gov.uk
McDonald, Lesley (SNP - Larkhall)
lesley.mcdonald@southlanarkshire.gsx.gov.uk
McGinaly, Janice (LAB - East Kilbride West)
janice.mcginlay@southlanarkshire.gsx.gov.uk
McGuigan, Jim (SNP - Bothwell and Uddingston)
jim.mcguigan@southlanarkshire.gsx.gov.uk
McInnes, Alex (LAB - Clydesdale South)
alex.mcinnes@southlanarkshire.gsx.gov.uk
McKenna, Denis (LAB - Rutherglen Central and North)
denis.mckenna@southlanarkshire.gsx.gov.uk
McKenna, Brian (LAB - Rutherglen South)
brian.mckenna@southlanarkshire.gsx.gov.uk
McKeown, Jean (LAB - Hamilton West and Earnock)
jean.mckeown@southlanarkshire.gsx.gov.uk
McLachlan, Davie (LAB - Hamilton North and East)
davie.mclachlan@southlanarkshire.gsx.gov.uk
McNamee, John (LAB - Blantyre)
john.mcnamee@southlanarkshire.gsx.gov.uk
Menzies, John (SNP - Hamilton West and Earnock)
john.menzies@southlanarkshire.gsx.gov.uk
Miller, Gladys (SNP - East Kilbride East)
gladys.miller@southlanarkshire.gsx.gov.uk
Mitchell, Alice-Marie (LAB - East Kilbride Central North)
alice.mitchell@southlanarkshire.gsx.gov.uk
Shaw, Vivienne (SNP - Clydesdale North)
vivienne.shaw@southlanarkshire.gov.uk
Shearer, David (SNP - Clydesdale West)
david.shearer@southlanarkshire.gsx.gov.uk
Simpson, Graham (CON - East Kilbride West)
graham.simpson@southlanarkshire.gsx.gov.uk
Stewart, Hamish (CON - Clydesdale East)
hamish.stewart@southlanarkshire.gsx.gov.uk
Thompson, Chris (LAB - East Kilbride Central North)

councillor.thompson@southlanarkshire.gsx.gov.uk
Thomson, Bert (SNP - Blantyre)
bert.thomson@southlanarkshire.gsx.gov.uk
Tullett, Richard (LAB - Cambuslang West)
richard.tullett@southlanarkshire.gsx.gov.uk
Wardhaugh, Jim (SNP - East Kilbride East)
james.wardhaugh@southlanarkshire.gsx.gov.uk
Wardhaugh, Sheena (SNP - East Kilbride Central North)
sheena.wardhaugh@southlanarkshire.gsx.gov.uk
Watson, David (SNP - East Kilbride West)
david.watson@southlanarkshire.gsx.gov.uk

POLITICAL COMPOSITION

LAB: 33, SNP: 27, CON: 4, IND: 1, LD: 1, SGP: 1

COMMITTEE CHAIRS

Community Services: Mr Hamish Stewart
Education Resources: Mr John Menzies
Enterprise Services: Mr Chris Thompson
Finance & Corporate Resources: Mr Gerry Convery
Housing & Technical: Mr Alex McInnes
Licensing: Ms Maureen Devlin
Planning: Mr Hugh Dunsmuir
Social Work: Mr Jim Handibode

SOUTH NORFOLK D

South Norfolk District Council, South Norfolk House, Swan Lane, Long Stratton NR15 2XE ☎ 01508 533633 🖷 01508 533695 ✉ reception@south-norfolk.gov.uk 💻 www.south-norfolk.gov.uk

FACTS & FIGURES

Police Authority: Norfolk Police Authority
Health Authority: East of England Strategic Health Authority
Learning and Skills Council: Eastern
Parliamentary Constituencies: Norfolk Mid, Norfolk South, Norwich South
EU Constituencies: Eastern
Election Frequency: Elections are of whole council

PRINCIPAL OFFICERS

Chief Executive: Ms Sandra Dinneen, Chief Executive, South Norfolk House, Swan Lane, Long Stratton NR15 2XE ☎ 01508 533942 ✉ sdinneen@s-norfolk.gov.uk

Deputy Chief Executive: Mr Andy Radford, Deputy Chief Executive, South Norfolk House, Swan Lane, Long Stratton NR15 2XE ☎ 01508 533857 🖷 01598 533616 ✉ aradford@s-norfolk.gov.uk

Senior Management: Mr David Ellis, Communities Director, South Norfolk House, Swan Lane, Long Stratton NR15 2XE ☎ 01508 533902 ✉ dellis@s-norfolk.gov.uk

Senior Management: Mr Andy Jarvis, Director of Development & Environment, South Norfolk House, Swan Lane, Long Stratton NR15 2XE ☎ 01508 533703 ✉ ajarvis@s-norfolk.gov.uk

Senior Management: Mr Andy Radford, Deputy Chief Executive, South Norfolk House, Swan Lane, Long Stratton NR15 2XE ☎ 01508 533857 🖷 01598 533616 ✉ aradford@s-norfolk.gov.uk

Architect, Building / Property Services: Mr Andy Radford, Deputy Chief Executive, South Norfolk House, SwanLane, Long Stratton NR15 2XE ☎ 01508 533857 🖷 01598 533616 ✉ aradford@s-norfolk.gov.uk

Best Value: Mr Paul Kearsey, Business Improvement Manager, South Norfolk Council, Swan Lane, Long Stratton NR15 2XE ☎ 01508 533983 ✉ pkearsey@s-norfolk.gov.uk

Best Value: Mr Mike Nott, Head of Partnerships & Performance, South Norfolk House, Swan Lane, Long Stratton NR15 2XE ☎ 01508 533982 🖷 01508 533619 ✉ mnott@s-norfolk.gov.uk

Building Control: Mr Andy Jarvis, Director of Development & Environment, South Norfolk House, Swan Lane, Long Stratton NR15 2XE ☎ 01508 533703 ✉ ajarvis@s-norfolk.gov.uk

Building Control: Mr Kevin Love, Director, CNC Building Control Consultancy, Thorpe Lodge, 1 Yarmouth Road, Thorpe St Andrew, Norwich NR7 0DU ☎ 01603 430541 ✉ kevinlove@ cncbuildingcontrol.gov.uk

Catering Services: Mr Andy Radford, Deputy Chief Executive, South Norfolk House, SwanLane, Long Stratton NR15 2XE ☎ 01508 533857 🖷 01598 533616 ✉ aradford@s-norfolk.gov.uk

PR / Communications: Mr David Peel, Communications Manager, South Norfolk House, Swan Lane, Long Stratton NR15 2XE ☎ 01508 533611 🖷 01508 533619 ✉ dpeel@s-norfolk.gov.uk

Community Planning: Ms Sandra Dinneen, Chief Executive, South Norfolk House, Swan Lane, Long Stratton NR15 2XE ☎ 01508 533942 ✉ sdinneen@s-norfolk.gov.uk

Community Planning: Mr David Ellis, Communities Director, South Norfolk House, Swan Lane, Long Stratton NR15 2XE ☎ 01508 533902 🖷 01508 533695 ✉ dellis@s-norfolk.gov.uk

Community Planning: Mr Mike Nott, Head of Partnerships & Performance, South Norfolk House, Swan Lane, Long Stratton NR15 2XE ☎ 01508 533982 🖷 01508 533619 ✉ mnott@s-norfolk.gov.uk

Community Safety: Mr Mark Bishop, Localities & Communities Manager, South Norfolk House, Swan Lane, Long Stratton NR15 2XE ☎ 01508 533934 ✉ mbishop@s-norfolk.gov.uk

Community Safety: Ms Sandra Dinneen, Chief Executive, South Norfolk House, Swan Lane, Long Stratton NR15 2XE ☎ 01508 533942 ✉ sdinneen@s-norfolk.gov.uk

Community Safety: Mr David Ellis, Communities Director, South Norfolk House, Swan Lane, Long Stratton NR15 2XE ☎ 01508 533902 🖷 01508 533695 ✉ dellis@s-norfolk.gov.uk

Community Safety: Mr Tim Horspole, Planning Policy Officer, South Norfolk House, Swan Lane, Long Stratton NR15 2XE ☎ 01508 533806 🖷 01508 533625 ✉ thorsepole@s-norfolk.gov.uk

Community Safety: Mr Michael Pursehouse, Communities Manager, South Norfolk House, Swan Lane, Long Stratton NR15 2XE ☎ 01508 533718 ✉ mpursehouse@s-norfolk.gov.uk

Computer Management: Mr Sean Green, IT Manager, South Norfolk House, Swan Lane, Long Stratton NR15 2XE ☎ 01508 533871 🖷 01508 533616 🖰 sgreen@s-norfolk.gov.uk

Corporate Services: Mrs S King, Head of Audit, South Norfolk House, Swan Lane, Long Stratton NR15 2XE ☎ 01508 533863 🖰 sking@s-norfolk.gov.uk

Corporate Services: Mr Andy Radford, Deputy Chief Executive, South Norfolk House, Swan Lane, Long Stratton NR15 2XE ☎ 01508 533857 🖷 01598 533616 🖰 aradford@s-norfolk.gov.uk

Customer Service: Mr Paul Kearsey, Business Improvement Manager, South Norfolk Council, Swan Lane, Long Stratton NR15 2XE ☎ 01508 533983 🖰 pkearsey@s-norfolk.gov.uk

Economic Development: Ms Sandra Dinneen, Chief Executive, South Norfolk House, Swan Lane, Long Stratton NR15 2XE ☎ 01508 533942 🖰 sdinneen@s-norfolk.gov.uk

Economic Development: Mr Tim Horspole, Planning Policy Officer, South Norfolk House, Swan Lane, Long Stratton NR15 2XE ☎ 01508 533806 🖷 01508 533625 🖰 thorsepole@s-norfolk.gov.uk

E-Government: Mr Sean Green, IT Manager, South Norfolk House, Swan Lane, Long Stratton NR15 2XE ☎ 01508 533871 🖷 01508 533616 🖰 sgreen@s-norfolk.gov.uk

Electoral Registration: Ms Sandra Dinneen, Chief Executive, South Norfolk House, Swan Lane, Long Stratton NR15 2XE ☎ 01508 533942 🖰 sdinneen@s-norfolk.gov.uk

Electoral Registration: Mr David Ellis, Communities Director, South Norfolk House, Swan Lane, Long Stratton NR15 2XE ☎ 01508 533902 🖷 01508 533695 🖰 dellis@s-norfolk.gov.uk

Electoral Registration: Mr Paul Kearsey, Business Improvement Manager, South Norfolk Council, Swan Lane, Long Stratton NR15 2XE ☎ 01508 533983 🖰 pkearsey@s-norfolk.gov.uk

Emergency Planning: Mr Andy Jarvis, Director of Development & Environment, South Norfolk House, Swan Lane, Long Stratton NR15 2XE ☎ 01508 533703 🖰 ajarvis@s-norfolk.gov.uk

Energy Management: Mr Tony Cooke, Renewal Manager, South Norfolk Council, Swan Lane, Long Stratton NR15 2XE ☎ 01508 533712 🖰 tcooke@s-norfolk.gov.uk

Environmental / Technical Services: Mr Andy Jarvis, Director of Development & Environment, South Norfolk House, Swan Lane, Long Stratton NR15 2XE ☎ 01508 533703 🖰 ajarvis@s-norfolk.gov.uk

Environmental / Technical Services: Mr Andy Jarvis, Director of Development & Environment, South Norfolk House, Swan Lane, Long Stratton NR15 2XE ☎ 01508 533703 🖷 01508 533626 🖰 ajarvis@s-norfolk.gov.uk

Environmental Health: Mr Andy Jarvis, Director of Development & Environment, South Norfolk House, Swan Lane, Long Stratton NR15 2XE ☎ 01508 533703 🖷 01508 533626 🖰 ajarvis@s-norfolk.gov.uk

Environmental Health: Mr Andy Jarvis, Director of Development & Environment, South Norfolk House, Swan Lane, Long Stratton NR15 2XE ☎ 01508 533703 🖰 ajarvis@s-norfolk.gov.uk

Estates, Property & Valuation: Mr Andy Radford, Deputy Chief Executive, South Norfolk House, Swan Lane, Long Stratton NR15 2XE ☎ 01508 533857 🖷 01598 533616 🖰 aradford@s-norfolk.gov.uk

Events Manager: Ms Sarah Bartlett, Corporate & Events Manager, South Norfolk House, Swan Lane, Long Stratton NR15 2XE 🖰 sbartlett@s-norfolk.gov.uk

Facilities: Mr Andy Radford, Deputy Chief Executive, South Norfolk House, Swan Lane, Long Stratton NR15 2XE ☎ 01508 533857 🖷 01598 533616 🖰 aradford@s-norfolk.gov.uk

Finance and Treasurer: Ms Debbie Lorimer, Financial Services Manager, South Norfolk House, Swan Lane, Long Stratton NR15 2XE ☎ 01508 533981 🖰 dlorimer@s-norfolk.gov.uk

Finance and Treasurer: Mr Andy Radford, Deputy Chief Executive, South Norfolk House, SwanLane, Long Stratton NR15 2XE ☎ 01508 533857 🖷 01598 533616 🖰 aradford@s-norfolk.gov.uk

Fleet Management: Mr David Renaut, Exchequer Manager, South Norfolk House, Swan Lane, Long Stratton NR15 2XE ☎ 01508 533869 🖷 01508 533616 🖰 drenaut@s-norfolk.gov.uk

Grounds Maintenance: Mr Andy Jarvis, Director of Development & Environment, South Norfolk House, Swan Lane, Long Stratton NR15 2XE ☎ 01508 533703 🖷 01508 533626 🖰 ajarvis@s-norfolk.gov.uk

Grounds Maintenance: Mr Andy Jarvis, Director of Development & Environment, South Norfolk House, Swan Lane, Long Stratton NR15 2XE ☎ 01508 533703 🖰 ajarvis@s-norfolk.gov.uk

Grounds Maintenance: Mr Kelly Lunness, Operations Manager, South Norfolk Council, Swan Lane, Long Stratton NR15 2XE ☎ 01508 533633 🖰 klunness@s-norfolk.gov.uk

Health and Safety: Mr Phil Rose, Health & Safety Advisor, South Norfolk House, Swan Lane, Long Stratton NR15 2XE ☎ 01508 533667 🖷 01508 533695 🖰 prose@s-norfolk.gov.uk

Home Energy Conservation: Mr Andy Jarvis, Director of Development & Environment, South Norfolk House, Swan Lane, Long Stratton NR15 2XE ☎ 01508 533703 🖰 ajarvis@s-norfolk.gov.uk

Housing: Mr Tony Cooke, Renewal Manager, South Norfolk Council, Swan Lane, Long Stratton NR15 2XE ☎ 01508 533712 🖰 tcooke@s-norfolk.gov.uk

Legal: Mr Andy Radford, Deputy Chief Executive, South Norfolk House, Swan Lane, Long Stratton NR15 2XE ☎ 01508 533857 🖷 01598 533616 🖰 aradford@s-norfolk.gov.uk

Legal: Mr Stuart Shortman, Solicitor to the Council, South Norfolk House, Swan Lane, Long Stratton NR15 2XE ☎ 01508 533671 🖷 01508 533695 ✉ sshortman@s-norfolk.gov.uk

Leisure and Cultural Services: Mr Rob Adams, Business & Operations Manager, South Norfolk House, Swan Lane, Long Stratton NR15 2XE ✉ radams@s-norfolk.gov.uk

Leisure and Cultural Services: Ms Sandra Dinneen, Chief Executive, South Norfolk House, Swan Lane, Long Stratton NR15 2XE ☎ 01508 533942 ✉ sdinneen@s-norfolk.gov.uk

Leisure and Cultural Services: Mr David Ellis, Communities Director, South Norfolk House, Swan Lane, Long Stratton NR15 2XE ☎ 01508 533902 ✉ dellis@s-norfolk.gov.uk

Licensing: Mr David Ellis, Communities Director, South Norfolk House, Swan Lane, Long Stratton NR15 2XE ☎ 01508 533902 ✉ dellis@s-norfolk.gov.uk

Licensing: Mr Andy Jarvis, Director of Development & Environment, South Norfolk House, Swan Lane, Long Stratton NR15 2XE ☎ 01508 533703 ✉ ajarvis@s-norfolk.gov.uk

Licensing: Mr Paul Kearsey, Business Improvement Manager, South Norfolk Council, Swan Lane, Long Stratton NR15 2XE ☎ 01508 533983 ✉ pkearsey@s-norfolk.gov.uk

Lottery Funding, Charity and Voluntary: Ms Sandra Dinneen, Chief Executive, South Norfolk House, Swan Lane, Long Stratton NR15 2XE ☎ 01508 533942 ✉ sdinneen@s-norfolk.gov.uk

Lottery Funding, Charity and Voluntary: Mr David Ellis, Communities Director, South Norfolk House, Swan Lane, Long Stratton NR15 2XE ☎ 01508 533902 🖷 01508 533695 ✉ dellis@s-norfolk.gov.uk

Member Services: Mr David Ellis, Communities Director, South Norfolk House, Swan Lane, Long Stratton NR15 2XE ☎ 01508 533902 ✉ dellis@s-norfolk.gov.uk

Member Services: Mr Paul Kearsey, Business Improvement Manager, South Norfolk Council, Swan Lane, Long Stratton NR15 2XE ☎ 01508 533983 ✉ pkearsey@s-norfolk.gov.uk

Parking: Mr Andy Jarvis, Director of Development & Environment, South Norfolk House, Swan Lane, Long Stratton NR15 2XE ☎ 01508 533703 ✉ ajarvis@s-norfolk.gov.uk

Partnerships: Mr David Ellis, Communities Director, South Norfolk House, Swan Lane, Long Stratton NR15 2XE ☎ 01508 533902 ✉ dellis@s-norfolk.gov.uk

Partnerships: Mr Mike Nott, Head of Partnerships & Performance, South Norfolk House, Swan Lane, Long Stratton NR15 2XE ☎ 01508 533982 🖷 01508 533619 ✉ mnott@s-norfolk.gov.uk

Personnel / HR: Mr Andy Radford, Deputy Chief Executive, South Norfolk House, Swan Lane, Long Stratton NR15 2XE ☎ 01508 533857 🖷 01598 533616 ✉ aradford@s-norfolk.gov.uk

Planning: Mr Andy Jarvis, Director of Development & Environment, South Norfolk House, Swan Lane, Long Stratton NR15 2XE ☎ 01508 533703 ✉ ajarvis@s-norfolk.gov.uk

Procurement: Ms Debbie Lorimer, Financial Services Manager, South Norfolk House, Swan Lane, Long Stratton NR15 2XE ☎ 01508 533981 ✉ dlorimer@s-norfolk.gov.uk

Procurement: Mr Andy Radford, Deputy Chief Executive, South Norfolk House, SwanLane, Long Stratton NR15 2XE ☎ 01508 533857 🖷 01598 533616 ✉ aradford@s-norfolk.gov.uk

Recycling & Waste Minimisation: Mr Andy Jarvis, Director of Development & Environment, South Norfolk House, Swan Lane, Long Stratton NR15 2XE ☎ 01508 533703 🖷 01508 533626 ✉ ajarvis@s-norfolk.gov.uk

Recycling & Waste Minimisation: Mr Andy Jarvis, Director of Development & Environment, South Norfolk House, Swan Lane, Long Stratton NR15 2XE ☎ 01508 533703 ✉ ajarvis@s-norfolk.gov.uk

Regeneration: Mr Tim Horspole, Planning Policy Officer, South Norfolk House, Swan Lane, Long Stratton NR15 2XE ☎ 01508 533806 🖷 01508 533625 ✉ thorsepole@s-norfolk.gov.uk

Staff Training: Mr Andy Radford, Deputy Chief Executive, South Norfolk House, Swan Lane, Long Stratton NR15 2XE ☎ 01508 533857 🖷 01598 533616 ✉ aradford@s-norfolk.gov.uk

Street Scene: Mr Andy Jarvis, Director of Development & Environment, South Norfolk House, Swan Lane, Long Stratton NR15 2XE ☎ 01508 533703 ✉ ajarvis@s-norfolk.gov.uk

Sustainable Development: Mr Tim Horspole, Planning Policy Officer, South Norfolk House, Swan Lane, Long Stratton NR15 2XE ☎ 01508 533806 🖷 01508 533625 ✉ thorsepole@s-norfolk.gov.uk

Tourism: Mrs Colette Davies, Tourism & Events Co-ordinator, South Norfolk House, Swan Lane, Long Stratton NR15 2XE ☎ 01508 533816 🖷 01508 533695 ✉ cdavies@s-norfolk.gov.uk

Tourism: Mr David Ellis, Communities Director, South Norfolk House, Swan Lane, Long Stratton NR15 2XE ☎ 01508 533902 ✉ dellis@s-norfolk.gov.uk

Tourism: Mr David Ellis, Communities Director, South Norfolk House, Swan Lane, Long Stratton NR15 2XE ☎ 01508 533902 🖷 01508 533695 ✉ dellis@s-norfolk.gov.uk

Waste Collection and Disposal: Mr Andy Jarvis, Director of Development & Environment, South Norfolk House, Swan Lane, Long Stratton NR15 2XE ☎ 01508 533703 ✉ ajarvis@s-norfolk.gov.uk

Waste Collection and Disposal: Mr Andy Jarvis, Director of Development & Environment, South Norfolk House, Swan Lane, Long Stratton NR15 2XE ☎ 01508 533703 🖷 01508 533626 ✉ ajarvis@s-norfolk.gov.uk

Waste Collection and Disposal: Mr Kelly Lunness, Operations

Manager, South Norfolk Council, Swan Lane, Long Stratton NR15 2XE ☎ 01508 533633 ✉ klunness@s-norfolk.gov.uk

Waste Management: Mr Andy Jarvis, Director of Development & Environment, South Norfolk House, Swan Lane, Long Stratton NR15 2XE ☎ 01508 533703 🖷 01508 533626 ✉ ajarvis@s-norfolk.gov.uk

MEMBERS OF THE COUNCIL (46)

***Chair:* McClenning**, Bob (LD - Forncett)
bmcclenning@s-norfolk.gov.uk
***Chair:* Thomson**, Sue (CON - Rockland)
sthomson@s-norfolk.gov.uk
***Leader of the Council:* Fuller**, John (CON - Brooke)
jfuller@s-norfolk.gov.uk
***Deputy Leader of the Council:* Wilby**, Martin (CON - Dickleburgh)
mwilby@s-norfolk.gov.uk
***Group Leader:* Gray**, Murray (LD - Earsham)
mgray@s-norfolk.gov.uk
Allen, Pauline (LD - Ditchingham and Broome)
pallen@s-norfolk.gov.uk
Bell, Vivienne (LD - Old Costessey)
vbell@s-norfolk.gov.uk
Bendle, Yvonne (CON - Hingham and Deopham)
Ybendle@s-norfolk.gov.uk
Billig, Kay (CON - Gillingham)
kbillig@s-norfolk.gov.uk
Bills, David (CON - Hethersett)
dbills@s-norfolk.gov.uk
Blake, Derek (CON - Chedgrave and Thurton)
dblake@s-norfolk.gov.uk
Blowfield, Terry (CON - Stratton)
tblowfield@s-norfolk.gov.uk
Dale, Leslie (CON - Hethersett)
ldale@s-norfolk.gov.uk
Dewsbury, Margaret (CON - Easton)
mdewsbury@s-norfolk.gov.uk
East, Tim (LD - Old Costessey)
teast@s-norfolk.gov.uk
Edney, Michael (CON - Wicklewood)
medney@s-norfolk.gov.uk
Ellis, Florence (CON - Tasburgh)
fellis@s-norfolk.gov.uk
Foulger, Colin (CON - Rustens)
cfoulger@s-norfolk.gov.uk
Goldson, David Roydon: Vacant
dgoldson@s-norfolk.gov.uk
Gould, Colin (CON - Loddon)
cgould@s-norfolk.gov.uk
Hardinge, Jan (LD - New Costessey)
jhardinge@s-norfolk.gov.uk
Herbert, Jon (CON - Mulbarton)
jherbert@s-norfolk.gov.uk
Hornby, Lee (CON - Town)
Lhornby@s-norfolk.gov.uk
Kemp, Christopher (CON - Cringleford)
ckemp@s-norfolk.gov.uk
Kemp, William (CON - Thurlton)
wkemp@s-norfolk.gov.uk
Kiddie, Keith (CON - Diss)
kkiddie@s-norfolk.gov.uk
Legg, Nigel (CON - Mulbarton)
nlegg@s-norfolk.gov.uk
Lewis, Trevor (LD - Stoke Holy Cross)
tlewis@s-norfolk.gov.uk
Mooney, Joseph (CON - Northfields)
jmooney@s-norfolk.gov.uk
Neal, Lisa (CON - Poringland with the Framinghams)
lneal@s-norfolk.gov.uk
Overton, John (CON - Poringland with the Framlinghams)
joverton@s-norfolk.gov.uk
Palmer, Tony (CON - Diss)
tpalmer@s-norfolk.gov.uk
Pond, Andrew (CON - Stratton)
apond@s-norfolk.gov.uk
Riches, Brian (CON - Harleston)
briches@s-norfolk.gov.uk
Savage, Jeremy (CON - Harleston)
jsavage@s-norfolk.gov.uk
Savage, Robert (CON - Abbey)
rsavage@s-norfolk.gov.uk
Spratt, Beverley (CON - Bunwell)
bspratt@s-norfolk.gov.uk
Tilcock, Keith (CON - Beck Vale)
ktilcock@s-norfolk.gov.uk
Walden, Glyn (CON - Diss)
gwalden@s-norfolk.gov.uk
Ward, Neil (CON - Cromwells)
nward@s-norfolk.gov.uk
Watt, Gerard (LD - New Costessey)
gwatt@s-norfolk.gov.uk
Webster, Laura (CON - Newton Flotman)
lwebster@s-norfolk.gov.uk
Weeks, Keith (CON - Bressingham and Burston)
kweeks@s-norfolk.gov.uk
Wheatley, Garry (CON - Cringleford)
gwheatley@s-norfolk.gov.uk
Wilby, Jenny (CON - Scole)
jwilby@s-norfolk.gov.uk
Windridge, Michael (CON - Hempnall)
michael.windridge@talk21.com

POLITICAL COMPOSITION

CON: 37, LD: 8, UKWN: 1

CABINET

Leader / External Affairs: Mr John Fuller
Deputy Leader / Communities & Localism: Mr Martin Wilby
Environment & Regulation: Mr Keith Kiddie
Finance & Resources: Mr Garry Wheatley
Housing & Public Health: Mrs Yvonne Bendle
Innovation & Efficiency: Mr David Bills

COMMITTEE CHAIRS

Development Management: Mr Joseph Mooney
Finance, Resources, Audit & Governance: Mr Michael Edney
Licensing and Appeals: Mr Robert Savage
Scrutiny: Ms Margaret Dewsbury

SOUTH NORTHAMPTONSHIRE D

South Northamptonshire Council, Council Offices, Springfields, Towcester NN12 6AE ☎ 0845 230 0226 🖷 01327 322074 ✉ info@southnorthants.gov.uk 💻 www.southnorthants.gov.uk

FACTS & FIGURES

Police Authority: Northamptonshire Police Authority

Health Authority: East Midlands Strategic Health Authority
Learning and Skills Council: East Midlands
Parliamentary Constituencies: Daventry, Northamptonshire South
EU Constituencies: East Midlands
Election Frequency: Elections are of whole council
Twinning: Brackley: Les Pavillons-sous-Bois (France); Montabaur (Germany)

PRINCIPAL OFFICERS

Chief Executive: Mrs Susan Smith, Chief Executive, Bodicote House, Bodicote, Banbury OX15 4AA ☎ 01295 221573 ✉ sue.smith@cherwellandsouthnorthants.gov.uk

Senior Management: Mr Calvin Bell, Director of Development, Council Offices, Springfields, Towcester NN12 6AE ☎ 0300 003 0103 🖷 01327 322310 ✉ calvin.bell@cherwellandsouthnorthants.gov.uk

Senior Management: Mr Ian Davies, Director of Environment & Community, Council Offices, Springfields, Towcester NN12 6AE ☎ 01327 322302 ✉ ian.davies@cherwellandsouthnorthants.gov.uk

Senior Management: Mr Martin Henry, Director of Resources, Council Offices, Springfields, Towcester NN12 6AE ☎ 0300 003 0102 🖷 01327 322310 ✉ martin.henry@cherwellandsouthnorthants.gov.uk

Architect, Building / Property Services: Mr Chris Stratford, Head of Regeneration & Housing, Council Offices, Springfields, Towcester NN12 6AE ☎ 01295 251871 ✉ chris.stratford@cherwellandsouthnorthants.gov.uk

Best Value: Ms Claire Taylor, Corporate Performance Manager, Council Offices, Springfields, Towcester NN12 6AE ☎ 01295 221563 ✉ claire.taylor@cherwellandsouthnorthants.gov.uk

Catering Services: Mr Steve Wright, Facilities Officer, Council Offices, Springfields, Towcester NN12 6AE ☎ 01327 322322 🖷 01327 322114 ✉ stephen.wright@southnorthants.gov.uk

PR / Communications: Ms Janet Ferris, Corporate Communications Manager, Council Offices, Springfields, Towcester NN12 6AE ☎ 01295 221870 🖷 01295 270028 ✉ janet.ferris@cherwellandsouthnorthants.gov.uk

Community Planning: Ms Claire Taylor, Corporate Performance Manager, Council Offices, Springfields, Towcester NN12 6AE ☎ 01295 221563 ✉ claire.taylor@cherwellandsouthnorthants.gov.uk

Community Safety: Mr Chris Rothwell, Head of Community Services, Council Offices, Springfields, Towcester NN12 6AE ☎ 01295 251774 ✉ chris.rothwell@cherwellandsouthnorthants.gov.uk

Computer Management: Mr Gareth Jones, Information Services Manager, Council Offices, Springfields, Towcester NN12 6AE ☎ 01295 753729 ✉ gareth.jones@cherwellandsouthnorthants.gov.uk

Computer Management: Ms Pat Simpson, Programme Manager, Council Offices, Springfields, Towcester NN12 6AE ☎ 01295 221575 ✉ pat.simpson@cherwellandsouthnorthants.gov.uk

Corporate Services: Mr Chris Rothwell, Head of Community Services, Council Offices, Springfields, Towcester NN12 6AE ☎ 01295 251774 ✉ chris.rothwell@cherwellandsouthnorthants.gov.uk

Customer Service: Ms Liz Crussell, Customer Contact Centre Manager, Council Offices, Springfields, Towcester NN12 6AE ☎ 01327 322120 ✉ liz.crussell@southnorthants.gov.uk

Economic Development: Mr Calvin Bell, Director of Development, Council Offices, Springfields, Towcester NN12 6AE ☎ 0300 003 0103 🖷 01327 322310 ✉ calvin.bell@cherwellandsouthnorthants.gov.uk

Economic Development: Mr Adrian Colwell, Head of Strategic Planning & the Economy, Council Offices, Springfields, Towcester NN12 6AE ☎ 0300 003 0110 ✉ adrian.colwell@cherwellandsouthnorthants.gov.uk

Electoral Registration: Mr James Doble, Democratic & Elections Manager, Council Offices, Springfields, Towcester NN12 6AE ☎ 01295 221587 ✉ james.doble@cherwellandsouthnorthants.gov.uk

Emergency Planning: Mr Gary Crook, Emergency Planning Officer, Council Offices, Springfields, Towcester NN12 6AE ☎ 01327 322293 ✉ gary.crook@southnorthants.gov.uk

Energy Management: Mr Alan Isaac, Senior Technical Officer of Public Health, Council Offices, Springfields, Towcester NN12 6AE ☎ 01327 322292 🖷 01327 322074 ✉ alan.isaac@southnorthants.gov.uk

Environmental / Technical Services: Mr Ian Davies, Director of Environment & Community, Bodicote House, Bodicote, Banbury OX15 4AA ☎ 01327 322302 ✉ ian.davies@cherwellandsouthnorthants.gov.uk

Environmental / Technical Services: Mr John Maynard, Environmental Services Officer, Council Offices, Springfields, Towcester NN12 6AE ☎ 01327 322348 ✉ john.maynard@southnorthants.gov.uk

Environmental / Technical Services: Mr Ed Potter, Head of Envrionmental Services, Council Offices, Springfields, Towcester NN12 6AE ☎ 01295 227023 ✉ ed.potter@cherwellandsouthnorthants.gov.uk

Environmental / Technical Services: Mr Andy Preston, Head of Public Protection & Development Management, Council Offices, Springfields, Towcester NN12 6AE ☎ 01327 322356 🖷 01327 322074 ✉ andy.preston@cherwellandsouthnorthants.gov.uk

Environmental Health: Mr Andy Preston, Head of Public Protection & Development Management, Council Offices, Springfields, Towcester NN12 6AE ☎ 01327 322356 🖷 01327 322074 ✉ andy.preston@cherwellandsouthnorthants.gov.uk

Estates, Property & Valuation: Mr Duncan Wigley, Estates Surveyor, Council Offices, Springfields, Towcester NN12 6AE

☎ 01327 322345 🖷 01327 322074
🖰 duncan.wigley@southnorthants.gov.uk

Facilities: Mr Steve Wright, Facilities Officer, Council Offices, Springfields, Towcester NN12 6AE ☎ 01327 322322 🖷 01327 322114 🖰 stephen.wright@southnorthants.gov.uk

Finance and Treasurer: Ms Karen Curtin, Head of Finance & Procurement, Bodicote House, Bodicote, Banbury OX15 4AA ☎ 01295 227936
🖰 karen.curtin@cherwellandsouthnorthants.gov.uk

Finance and Treasurer: Mr Martin Henry, Director of Resources, Council Offices, Springfields, Towcester NN12 6AE ☎ 0300 003 0102 🖷 01327 322310
🖰 martin.henry@cherwellandsouthnorthants.gov.uk

Health and Safety: Ms Jackie Fitzsimmons, Health Protection, Council Offices, Springfields, Towcester NN12 6AE ☎ 01327 322283 🖰 jackie.fitzsimmons@southnorthants.gov.uk

Home Energy Conservation: Mr Andy Preston, Head of Public Protection & Development Management, Council Offices, Springfields, Towcester NN12 6AE ☎ 01327 322356 🖷 01327 322074 🖰 andy.preston@cherwellandsouthnorthants.gov.uk

Housing: Ms Jo Harrison, Principal Strategic Housing Officer, Council Offices, Springfields, Towcester NN12 6AE ☎ 01327 322369 🖰 jo.harrison@southnorthants.gov.uk

Legal: Mr Kevin Lane, Head of Law & Governance, Council Offices, Springfields, Towcester NN12 6AE ☎ 01327 322127 🖷 01327 322114; 01327 322114
🖰 kevin.lane@cherwellandsouthnorthants.gov.uk

Leisure and Cultural Services: Mr Ashley Davey, Principal Leisure Officer, Council Offices, Springfields, Towcester NN12 6AE ☎ 01327 322338 🖰 ashley.davey@southnorthants.gov.uk

Licensing: Ms Jackie Fitzsimons, Environmental Manager Commercial, Council Offices, Springfields, Towcester NN12 6AE ☎ 01327 322283 🖰 jackie.fitzsimons@southnorthants.gov.uk

Licensing: Mr David Macey, Acting Senior Licensing Officer, Council Offices, Springfields, Towcester NN12 6AE
☎ 01327 322119 🖰 david.macey@southnorthants.gov.uk

Licensing: Mr Andy Preston, Head of Public Protection & Development Management, Council Offices, Springfields, Towcester NN12 6AE ☎ 01327 322356 🖷 01327 322074
🖰 andy.preston@cherwellandsouthnorthants.gov.uk

Lottery Funding, Charity and Voluntary: Mrs Pam Wood, Leisure & Community Support Officer, Council Offices, Springfields, Towcester NN12 6AE ☎ 01327 322336
🖰 pam.wood@southnorthants.gov.uk

Member Services: Mr James Doble, Democratic & Elections Manager, Council Offices, Springfields, Towcester NN12 6AE ☎ 01295 221587
🖰 james.doble@cherwellandsouthnorthants.gov.uk

Parking: Mr Andy Preston, Head of Public Protection & Development Management, Council Offices, Springfields, Towcester NN12 6AE ☎ 01327 322356 🖷 01327 322074
🖰 andy.preston@cherwellandsouthnorthants.gov.uk

Partnerships: Mr Chris Rothwell, Head of Community Services, Council Offices, Springfields, Towcester NN12 6AE ☎ 01295 251774 🖰 chris.rothwell@cherwellandsouthnorthants.gov.uk

Personnel / HR: Ms Jo Pitman, Head of Transformation, Council Offices, Springfields, Towcester NN12 6AE ☎ 01295 221758
🖰 jo.pitman@southnorthants.gov.uk

Personnel / HR: Mrs Gina Thomas, Manager of Human Resources, Council Offices, Springfields, Towcester NN12 6AE ☎ 01327 322328 🖷 01327 322325
🖰 gina.thomas@southnorthants.gov.uk

Planning: Mr Robert Fallon, Development & Implementation Manager, Council Offices, Springfields, Towcester NN12 6AE ☎ 01327 322047 🖰 robert.fallon@southnorthants.gov.uk

Procurement: Mr Richard Stirling, Procurement & Administration Manager, Council Offices, Springfields, Towcester NN12 6AE ☎ 01327 322113 🖷 01327 322144
🖰 richard.stirling@southnorthants.gov.uk

Recycling & Waste Minimisation: Mr Ed Potter, Head of Envrionmental Services, Council Offices, Springfields, Towcester NN12 6AE ☎ 01295 227023
🖰 ed.potter@cherwellandsouthnorthants.gov.uk

Staff Training: Ms Stephanie Cowell, Employee & Organisation Development Officer, Council Offices, Springfields, Towcester NN12 6AE ☎ 01327 322329
🖰 stephanie.cowell@southnorthants.gov.uk

Staff Training: Mrs Gina Thomas, Manager of Human Resources, Council Offices, Springfields, Towcester NN12 6AE ☎ 01327 322328 🖷 01327 322325 🖰 gina.thomas@southnorthants.gov.uk

Street Scene: Mr Andy Preston, Head of Public Protection & Development Management, Council Offices, Springfields, Towcester NN12 6AE ☎ 01327 322356 🖷 01327 322074
🖰 andy.preston@cherwellandsouthnorthants.gov.uk

Sustainable Communities: Mr Calvin Bell, Director of Development, Council Offices, Springfields, Towcester NN12 6AE ☎ 0300 003 0103 🖷 01327 322310
🖰 calvin.bell@cherwellandsouthnorthants.gov.uk

Sustainable Development: Mr Ed Potter, Head of Envrionmental Services, Council Offices, Springfields, Towcester NN12 6AE ☎ 01295 227023
🖰 ed.potter@cherwellandsouthnorthants.gov.uk

Tourism: Mr Adrian Colwell, Head of Strategic Planning & the Economy, Council Offices, Springfields, Towcester NN12 6AE ☎ 0300 003 0110
🖰 adrian.colwell@cherwellandsouthnorthants.gov.uk

Transport Planner: Mr David Allen, Lead Officer of Transport, Council Offices, Springfields, Towcester NN12 6AE ☎ 01327 322268 🖷 01327 322325 🖰 david.allen@southnorthants.gov.uk

Waste Collection and Disposal: Mr Ed Potter, Head of Envrionmental Services, Council Offices, Springfields, Towcester NN12 6AE ☎ 01295 227023
🖰 ed.potter@cherwellandsouthnorthants.gov.uk

Waste Management: Mr Ed Potter, Head of Envrionmental Services, Council Offices, Springfields, Towcester NN12 6AE
☎ 01295 227023 ✉ ed.potter@cherwellandsouthnorthants.gov.uk

MEMBERS OF THE COUNCIL (42)

Chair: **Townsend**, Sally (CON - Blisworth and Roade)
tumbledown@btinternet.com
Leader of the Council: **Clarke**, Mary (CON - Old Stratford)
mary.clarke@southnorthants.gov.uk
Deputy Leader of the Council: **Herring**, Rosie (CON - Danvers and Wardoun)
rosie.herring@southnorthants.gov.uk
Group Leader: **Johns**, Martin (LD - Towcester Brook)
martin.johns@southnorthants.gov.uk
Aaronson, David (IND - Deanshanger)
david.aaronson@southnorthants.gov.uk
Addison, Ann (CON - Harpole and Grange)
a_addison@btinternet.com
Atkinson, Robert (CON - Hackleton)
bob.atkinson@southnorthants.gov.uk
Bambridge, Dermot (CON - Silverstone)
dermot.bambridge@southnorthants.gov.uk
Barnes, Sandra (CON - Tove)
sandra.barnes@southnorthants.gov.uk
Baxter, Judith (CON - Middleton Cheney)
judith.baxter@southnorthants.gov.uk
Bignell, Phil (CON - Heyfords and Bugbrooke)
phil.bignell@southnorthants.gov.uk
Billingham, Caryl (IND - Brackley South)
caryl@billingham-brackley.com
Bonner-Dunham, Kath (CON - Brackley West)
kath.bonner-dunham@southnorthants.gov.uk
Breese, Rebecca (CON - Steane)
rebecca.breese@southnorthants.gov.uk
Cartmell, Christopher (IND - Brackley West)
Clarke, Roger (CON - Blakesley and Cote)
roger.clarke@southnorthants.gov.uk
Clarke, Carole (CON - Brafield and Yardley)
carole.clarke@southnorthants.gov.uk
Clarke, Stephen (CON - Blisworth and Roade)
stephen.clarke@southnorthants.gov.uk
Davidson, Mark (CON - Grange Park)
Davies, Peter (CON - Washington)
peter.davies@southnorthants.gov.uk
Digby, Robin (CON - Astwell)
diggers@whitfield345.fsnet.co.uk
Eliot, Janet (CON - Harpole and Grange)
eliot942@btinternet.com
Fordham, Rupert (CON - Whittlewood)
rupert.fordham@southnorthants.gov.uk
Grant, Andrew (CON - Towcester Mill)
andrew.grant@southnorthants.gov.uk
Harries, David (IND - Heyfords and Bugbrooke)
Hollowell, Steven (IND - Brafield and Yardley)
steven.hollowell@southnorthants.gov.uk
Jainu-Deen, Tharik (CON - Grange Park)
Kilminster, John (CON - Middleton Cheney)
Lofts, Christoper (LD - Towcester Brook)
chris.lofts@southnorthants.gov.uk
McCord, Ian (CON - Cosgrove and Grafton)
snc@ianmccord.com
Morris, Ian (CON - King's Sutton)
ian.morris@southnorthants.gov.uk
Rawlinson, Peter (CON - Brackley East)
peter.rawlinson@southnorthants.gov.uk
Samiotis, Lisa (LD - Towcester Brook)
lisa.samiotis@southnorthants.gov.uk
Sergison-Brooke, Mary-Anne (CON - Danvers and Wardoun)
Smallman, Sandi (CON - Blakesley and Cote)
sandi.smallman@southnorthants.gov.uk
Stimpson, Blake (IND - Brackley East)
blake.stimpson@o2.co.uk
Titchener, Paul (IND - Brackley South)
Townsend, John (CON - Little Brook)
john.townsend@southnorthants.gov.uk
Walker, Allen (CON - Deanshanger)
Wilby, Andrew (CON - Towcester Mill)
andrew.wilby@southnorthants.gov.uk
Wilkinson, Tony (CON - Kingthorn)
Wilson, Martin (CON - Salcey)
martin.wilson@southnorthants.gov.uk

POLITICAL COMPOSITION

CON: 32, IND: 7, LD: 3

CABINET

Leader / Partnership Working: Mrs Mary Clarke
Deputy Leader / Community Engagement & Wellbeing: Ms Rosie Herring
Economic Development & Regeneration: Mr Rupert Fordham
Environmental Services: Mr Dermot Bambridge
Planning & Environment: Mrs Rebecca Breese
Resources & Change Management: Mr Ian McCord

COMMITTEE CHAIRS

Appointments & Personnel: Mr Stephen Clarke
Audit: Mrs Sandra Barnes
Community & Resources Review & Development: Mr Allen Walker
Development Control: Mr Stephen Clarke

SOUTH OXFORDSHIRE D

South Oxfordshire District Council, Benson Lane, Crowmarsh Gifford, Wallingford OX10 8HQ ☎ 01491 823000 🖷 01491 823001
✉ info@southoxon.gov.uk 💻 www.southoxon.gov.uk

FACTS & FIGURES

Police Authority: Thames Valley Police Authority
Health Authority: South Central Strategic Health Authority
Learning and Skills Council: South East
Parliamentary Constituencies: Henley, Wantage
EU Constituencies: South East
Election Frequency: Elections are of whole council
Twinning: Didcot: Meylan (France); Goring: Bellerne (France); Henley-on-Thames: Borama (Somalia), Falaise (France), Leichlingen (Germany); Thame: Badulla (Sri Lanka), Nontron (France); Wallingford: Badwurzach (Germany), Luxeuil-les-Bains (France), Whitchurch: La Bouile (France)

PRINCIPAL OFFICERS

Chief Executive: Mr David Buckle, Chief Executive, Benson Lane, Crowmarsh Gifford, Wallingford OX10 8HQ ☎ 01491 823103 🖷 01491 823134 ✉ david.buckle@southandvale.gov.uk

Deputy Chief Executive: Mr Steve Bishop, Strategic Director, Benson Lane, Crowmarsh Gifford, Wallingford OX10 8HQ

☎ 01491 823702 🖷 01491 823134
✉ steve.bishop@southandvale.gov.uk

Deputy Chief Executive: Mr Matt Prosser, Strategic Director, Benson Lane, Crowmarsh Gifford, Wallingford OX10 8HQ
☎ 01491 823103 🖷 01491 823134
✉ matt.prosser@southandvale.gov.uk

Deputy Chief Executive: Mrs Anna Robinson, Strategic Director, Benson Lane, Crowmarsh Gifford, Wallingford OX10 8HQ
☎ 01491 823702 🖷 01491 823134
✉ anna.robinson@southandvale.gov.uk

Building Control: Mr Adrian Duffield, Shared Head of Planning, Benson Lane, Crowmarsh Gifford, Wallingford OX10 8NJ ☎ 01491 823729 🖷 01491 823746 ✉ adrian.duffield@southandvale.gov.uk

PR / Communications: Mrs Clare Kingston, Shared Head of Corporate Strategy, Benson Lane, Crowmarsh Gifford, Wallingford OX10 8NL ☎ 01491 823094 🖷 01491 823605
✉ clare.kingstonsouthandvale.gov.uk

Community Safety: Mrs Clare Kingston, Shared Head of Corporate Strategy, Benson Lane, Crowmarsh Gifford, Wallingford OX10 8NL ☎ 01491 823094 🖷 01491 823605
✉ clare.kingstonsouthandvale.gov.uk

Community Safety: Mrs Margaret Reed, Shared Head of Legal & Democratic Services, Benson Lane, Crowmarsh Gifford, Wallingford OX10 8QS ☎ 01491 823656 🖷 01491 823658
✉ margaret.reed@southandvale.gov.uk

Computer Management: Mr Andrew Down, Shared Head of HR, IT & Customer Services, Benson Lane, Crowmarsh Gifford, Wallingford OX10 8AZ ☎ 01491 823939 🖷 01491 823106
✉ andrew.down@southandvale.gov.uk

Contracts: Mrs Margaret Reed, Shared Head of Legal & Democratic Services, Benson Lane, Crowmarsh Gifford, Wallingford OX10 8QS ☎ 01491 823656 🖷 01491 823658
✉ margaret.reed@southandvale.gov.uk

Corporate Services: Mr Geoff Bushell, Performance, Projects & Customer Services Manager, Council Offices, Crowmarsh, Wallingford OX10 8AX ☎ 01491 823024
✉ geoff.bushell@southoxon.gov.uk

Economic Development: Mr Chris Tyson, Shared Head of Economy, Leisure & Property, Benson Lane, Crowmarsh Gifford, Wallingford OX10 8QX ☎ 01491 823125 🖷 01491 823015
✉ chris.tyson@southandvale.gov.uk

E-Government: Mr Andrew Down, Shared Head of HR, IT & Customer Services, Benson Lane, Crowmarsh Gifford, Wallingford OX10 8AZ ☎ 01491 823939 🖷 01491 823106
✉ andrew.down@southandvale.gov.uk

Electoral Registration: Mr David Buckle, Chief Executive, Benson Lane, Crowmarsh Gifford, Wallingford OX10 8HQ
☎ 01491 823103 🖷 01491 823134
✉ david.buckle@southandvale.gov.uk

Emergency Planning: Mr Chris Tyson, Shared Head of Economy, Leisure & Property, Benson Lane, Crowmarsh Gifford, Wallingford OX10 8QX ☎ 01491 823125 🖷 01491 823015
✉ chris.tyson@southandvale.gov.uk

Environmental Health: Mr Paul Staines, Shared Head of Housing & Health, Benson Lane, Crowmarsh Gifford, Wallingford OX10 8HQ ☎ 01491 823471 🖷 01491 823201
✉ paul.staines@southandvale.gov.uk

Estates, Property & Valuation: Mr Chris Tyson, Shared Head of Economy, Leisure & Property, Benson Lane, Crowmarsh Gifford, Wallingford OX10 8QX ☎ 01491 823125 🖷 01491 823015
✉ chris.tyson@southandvale.gov.uk

Facilities: Mr Chris Tyson, Shared Head of Economy, Leisure & Property, Benson Lane, Crowmarsh Gifford, Wallingford OX10 8QX ☎ 01491 823125 🖷 01491 823015
✉ chris.tyson@southandvale.gov.uk

Finance and Treasurer: Mr William Jacobs, Shared Head of Finance, Benson Lane, Crowmarsh Gifford, Wallingford OX10 8AU
☎ 01491 823326 🖷 01491 823547
✉ william.jacobs@southandvale.gov.uk

Grounds Maintenance: Mrs Clare Kingston, Shared Head of Corporate Strategy, Benson Lane, Crowmarsh Gifford, Wallingford OX10 8NL ☎ 01491 823094 🖷 01491 823605
✉ clare.kingstonsouthandvale.gov.uk

Health and Safety: Mr Andrew Down, Shared Head of HR, IT & Customer Services, Benson Lane, Crowmarsh Gifford, Wallingford OX10 8AZ ☎ 01491 823939 🖷 01491 823106
✉ andrew.down@southandvale.gov.uk

Home Energy Conservation: Mr Paul Staines, Shared Head of Housing & Health, Benson Lane, Crowmarsh Gifford, Wallingford OX10 8HQ ☎ 01491 823471 🖷 01491 823201
✉ paul.staines@southandvale.gov.uk

Housing: Mr Paul Staines, Shared Head of Housing & Health, Benson Lane, Crowmarsh Gifford, Wallingford OX10 8HQ
☎ 01491 823471 🖷 01491 823201
✉ paul.staines@southandvale.gov.uk

Legal: Mrs Margaret Reed, Shared Head of Legal & Democratic Services, Benson Lane, Crowmarsh Gifford, Wallingford OX10 8QS ☎ 01491 823656 🖷 01491 823658
✉ margaret.reed@southandvale.gov.uk

Leisure and Cultural Services: Mr Chris Tyson, Shared Head of Economy, Leisure & Property, Benson Lane, Crowmarsh Gifford, Wallingford OX10 8QX ☎ 01491 823125 🖷 01491 823015
✉ chris.tyson@southandvale.gov.uk

Licensing: Mrs Margaret Reed, Shared Head of Legal & Democratic Services, Benson Lane, Crowmarsh Gifford, Wallingford OX10 8QS ☎ 01491 823656 🖷 01491 823658
✉ margaret.reed@southandvale.gov.uk

Lottery Funding, Charity and Voluntary: Mrs Clare Kingston, Shared Head of Corporate Strategy, Benson Lane, Crowmarsh

Gifford, Wallingford OX10 8NL ☎ 01491 823094 🖷 01491 823605
✉ clare.kingstonsouthandvale.gov.uk

Member Services: Mrs Margaret Reed, Shared Head of Legal & Democratic Services, Benson Lane, Crowmarsh Gifford, Wallingford OX10 8QS ☎ 01491 823656 🖷 01491 823658
✉ margaret.reed@southandvale.gov.uk

Parking: Mr Chris Tyson, Shared Head of Economy, Leisure & Property, Benson Lane, Crowmarsh Gifford, Wallingford OX10 8QX ☎ 01491 823125 🖷 01491 823015
✉ chris.tyson@southandvale.gov.uk

Partnerships: Mrs Clare Kingston, Shared Head of Corporate Strategy, Benson Lane, Crowmarsh Gifford, Wallingford OX10 8NL ☎ 01491 823094 🖷 01491 823605
✉ clare.kingstonsouthandvale.gov.uk

Personnel / HR: Mr Andrew Down, Shared Head of HR, IT & Customer Services, Benson Lane, Crowmarsh Gifford, Wallingford OX10 8AZ ☎ 01491 823939 🖷 01491 823106
✉ andrew.down@southandvale.gov.uk

Planning: Mr Adrian Duffield, Shared Head of Planning, Benson Lane, Crowmarsh Gifford, Wallingford OX10 8NJ ☎ 01491 823729 🖷 01491 823746 ✉ ; adrian.duffield@southandvale.gov.uk

Recycling & Waste Minimisation: Mrs Clare Kingston, Shared Head of Corporate Strategy, Benson Lane, Crowmarsh Gifford, Wallingford OX10 8NL ☎ 01491 823094 🖷 01491 823605
✉ clare.kingstonsouthandvale.gov.uk

Staff Training: Mr Andrew Down, Shared Head of HR, IT & Customer Services, Benson Lane, Crowmarsh Gifford, Wallingford OX10 8AZ ☎ 01491 823939 🖷 01491 823106
✉ andrew.down@southandvale.gov.uk

Sustainable Communities: Mr Adrian Duffield, Shared Head of Planning, Benson Lane, Crowmarsh Gifford, Wallingford OX10 8NJ ☎ 01491 823729 🖷 01491 823746
✉ adrian.duffield@southandvale.gov.uk

Sustainable Development: Mrs Clare Kingston, Shared Head of Corporate Strategy, Benson Lane, Crowmarsh Gifford, Wallingford OX10 8NL ☎ 01491 823094 🖷 01491 823605
✉ clare.kingstonsouthandvale.gov.uk

Tourism: Mr Chris Tyson, Shared Head of Economy, Leisure & Property, Benson Lane, Crowmarsh Gifford, Wallingford OX10 8QX ☎ 01491 823125 🖷 01491 823015
✉ chris.tyson@southandvale.gov.uk

Waste Collection and Disposal: Mrs Clare Kingston, Shared Head of Corporate Strategy, Benson Lane, Crowmarsh Gifford, Wallingford OX10 8NL ☎ 01491 823094 🖷 01491 823605
✉ clare.kingstonsouthandvale.gov.uk

Waste Management: Mrs Clare Kingston, Shared Head of Corporate Strategy, Benson Lane, Crowmarsh Gifford, Wallingford OX10 8NL ☎ 01491 823094 🖷 01491 823605
✉ clare.kingstonsouthandvale.gov.uk

MEMBERS OF THE COUNCIL (48)

***Chair:* Carr**, Janet (CON - Wheatley)
janet.carr2@virgin.net

***Vice-Chair:* Brown**, Dorothy (CON - Aston Rowant)
dorothy.brown@southoxon.gov.uk

***Leader of the Council:* Ducker**, Ann (CON - Goring)
ann.ducker@southoxon.gov.uk

***Deputy Leader of the Council:* Paterson**, Angie (CON - Watlington)
angie.paterson@southoxon.gov.uk

Badcock, Anna (CON - Watlington)
annabadcock1@gmail.com

Bell, Roger (LD - Wheatley)
roger_bell@tiscali.co.uk

Bland, Joan (CON - Henley North)
joan@asquiths.com

Bloomfield, Felix (CON - Benson)
felixbloomfield@hotmail.com

Bretherton, David (LD - Thame North)
dw.bretherton@btinternet.com

Collett, Celia (IND - Brightwell)
celia.collett@southoxon.gov.uk

Connel, Steve (CON - Didcot Northbourne)
sconnel@hotmail.com

Cooper, Bernard (LAB - Didcot Northbourne)
bcooper@ntlworld.com

Cotton, John (CON - Sandford)
john.cotton@yourcouncillor.com

Crabbe, Kristina (CON - Crowmarsh)
kristinacrabbe@hotmail.com

Cross, Phillip (CON - Berinsfield)
philcross2006@googlemail.com

Davies, Margaret (LAB - Didcot Park)
mldaviesbb@btinternet.com

Dawe, Pat (CON - Chosley and Wallingford South)
pat.dawe@southoxon.gov.uk

Docherty, Leo (CON - Hagbourne)
leo.docherty@hotmail.co.uk

Dodds, David (CON - Thame South)
david.dodds@southoxon.gov.uk

Gillespie, Elizabeth (CON - Garsington)
elizabethgillespie@uk2.net

Gray, Mark (IND - Chosley and Wallingford South)
limasheepdog@yahoo.com

Hall, Will (CON - Henley South)
wahhall@gmail.com

Harbour, Tony (CON - Didcot Ladygrove)
tony.harbour@southoxon.gov.uk

Hards, Eleanor (LAB - Didcot Park)
eleanorhards@aol.com

Harris, Marcus (CON - Wallingford North)
marcus.harris2008@googlemail.com

Harris, Neville (INDNA - Didcot Ladygrove)
nevhar@aol.com

Harrison, Paul (CON - Sonning Common)
paul.harrison@suk.sas.com

Harrod, Stephen (CON - Great Milton)
stephen.harrod@southoxon.gov.uk

Hiles, Marc (IND - Berinsfield)
marc.hiles@btinternet.com

Hodgkin, Elizabeth (R - Henley North)
elizabeth.hodgkin@southoxon.gov.uk

Hood, Christopher (CON - Chinnor)
drchood@medmus.com

Joslin, Terry (LAB - Didcot All Saints)

terryjoslin@ntlworld.com
Leonard, Malcolm (CON - Shiplake)
mandeleonard@waitrose.com
Lloyd, Lynn (CON - Chinnor)
Lokhon, Imran (CON - Wallingford North)
imran@yourwallingford.co.uk
Midwinter, Ann (IND - Thame South)
ann.midwinter@southoxon.gov.uk
Nimmo-Smith, Judith (CON - Chiltern Woods)
councillorjns@btinternet.com
Purse, Anne (LD - Forest Hill and Holton)
anne.purse@oxfordshire.gov.uk
Quinton, Christopher (CON - Woodcote)
cjq1@quincorn.co.uk
Rooke, Alan (CON - Sonning Common)
alanrooke@orangehome.co.uk
Service, Bill (CON - Didcot Ladygrove)
bill.service@hotmail.co.uk
Simister, Robert (CON - Shiplake)
robsodc@live.co.uk
Slatter, Pearl (CON - Goring)
pearl.slatter@southoxon.gov.uk
Turner, David (LD - Chalgrove)
david.turner@southoxon.gov.uk
Turner, Margaret (CON - Didcot All Saints)
margaret.turner@southoxon.gov.uk
Wallis, Rachel (CON - Benson)
rachel.e.wallis@hotmail.com
Welply, Mike (CON - Thame North)
mike.welpy@gmail.com
Wood, Jennifer (R - Henley South)
jennifer.wood@southoxon.gov.uk

POLITICAL COMPOSITION

CON: 33, IND: 4, LAB: 4, LD: 4, R: 2, INDNA: 1

CABINET

Leader / HR, Customer Services & Legal & Democratic: Mrs Ann Ducker
Deputy Leader / Planning & IT: Rev Angie Paterson
Economic Development, Property & Technical Services: Mrs Judith Nimmo-Smith
Finance, Waste & Parks: Mr David Dodds
Health & Housing: Ms Anna Badcock
Leisure, Grants & Community Safety: Mr Bill Service

SOUTH RIBBLE D

South Ribble Borough Council, Civic Centre, West Paddock, Leyland PR25 1DH ☎ 01772 421491 🖷 01772 622287 ✉ info@southribble.gov.uk 🖳 www.southribble.gov.uk

FACTS & FIGURES

Police Authority: Lancashire Police Authority
Health Authority: North West Strategic Health Authority
Learning and Skills Council: North West
Parliamentary Constituencies: South Ribble
EU Constituencies: North West
Election Frequency: Elections are by thirds
Twinning: Kreis Schleswig-Flensburg (Germany)

PRINCIPAL OFFICERS

Chief Executive: Mr Mike Nuttall, Chief Executive, Civic Centre, West Paddock, Leyland PR25 1DH ☎ 01772 421491 🖷 01772 622287 ✉ mnuttall@southribble.gov.uk

Senior Management: Mr G Barclay, Head of Shared Assurance Services, Civic Centre, West Paddock, Leyland PR25 1DH ☎ 01772 421491 ✉ gbarclay@southribble.gov.uk

Senior Management: Mr John Dalton, Director of Planning & Housing, Civic Centre, West Paddock, Leyland PR25 1DH ☎ 01772 421491 Extn 5380 🖷 01772 622287 ✉ jdalton@southribble.gov.uk

Senior Management: Mr Mark Gaffney, Director of Neighbourhoods, Civic Centre, West Paddock, Leyland PR25 1DH ☎ 01772 625671 🖷 01772 622287 ✉ mgaffney@southribble.gov.uk

Senior Management: Mrs S Guinness, Head of Shared Financial Services, Civic Centre, West Paddock, Leyland PR25 1DH ☎ 01772 421491 ✉ sguinness@southribble.gov.uk

Senior Management: Ms Denise Johnson, Director of Regeneration & Healthy Communities, Civic Centre, West Paddock, Leyland PR25 1DH ☎ 01772 421491 🖷 01772 622287 ✉ djohnson@southribble.gov.uk

Senior Management: Mr Ian Parker, Director of Business Transformation, Civic Centre, West Paddock, Leyland PR25 1DH ☎ 01772 625426 ✉ iparker@southribble.gov.uk

Senior Management: Ms Maureen Wood, Director of Corporate Governance, Civic Centre, West Paddock, Leyland PR25 1DH ☎ 01772 625247 ✉ mwood@southribble.gov.uk

Architect, Building / Property Services: Mr Martin Fahy, Property Services Manager, Civic Centre, West Paddock, Leyland PR25 1DH ☎ 01772 421491 🖷 01772 622287 ✉ mfahy@southribble.gov.uk

PR / Communications: Mr Dave Pollard, Public Relations Officer, Civic Centre, West Paddock, Leyland PR25 1DH ☎ 01772 421491 🖷 01772 622287 ✉ dpollard@southribble.gov.uk

Community Planning: Ms Helen Hockenhull, Planning Manager, Civic Centre, West Paddock, Leyland PR25 1DH ☎ 01772 421491 🖷 01772 622287 ✉ hhockenhull@southribble.gov.uk

Community Safety: Mr Paul Lowe, Joint Community Safety Manager, Civic Centre, West Paddock, Leyland PR25 1DH ☎ 01772 421491 🖷 01772 622287 ✉ paul.lowe@chorley.gov.uk

Computer Management: Mr John Healey, ICT Manager, Civic Centre, West Paddock, Leyland PR25 1DH ☎ 01772 421491 ✉ jhealey@southribble.gov.uk

Corporate Services: Ms Maureen Wood, Director of Corporate Governance, Civic Centre, West Paddock, Leyland PR25 1DH ☎ 01772 625247 ✉ mwood@southribble.gov.uk

Customer Service: Mr Ian Parker, Director of Business Transformation, Civic Centre, West Paddock, Leyland PR25 1DH ☎ 01772 625426 ✉ iparker@southribble.gov.uk

Direct Labour: Mr Mark Gaffney, Director of Neighbourhoods, Civic Centre, West Paddock, Leyland PR25 1DH ☎ 01772 625671 🖷 01772 622287 ✉ mgaffney@southribble.gov.uk

Electoral Registration: Ms Kate Gascoigne, Principal Elections Officer, Civic Centre, West Paddock, Leyland PR25 1DH ☎ 01772 625390 ✉ kgascoigne@southribble.gov.uk

Emergency Planning: Mr Andy Armstrong, Risk Manager, Civic Centre, West Paddock, Leyland PR25 1DH ☎ 01772 625256

Energy Management: Mr Martin Fahy, Property Services Manager, Civic Centre, West Paddock, Leyland PR25 1DH ☎ 01772 421491 🖷 01772 622287 ✉ mfahy@southribble.gov.uk

Environmental Health: Ms Denise Johnson, Director of Regeneration & Healthy Communities, Civic Centre, West Paddock, Leyland PR25 1DH ☎ 01772 421491 🖷 01772 622287 ✉ djohnson@southribble.gov.uk

Environmental Health: Mrs Jennifer Mullin, Public Health Manager, Civic Centre, West Paddock, Leyland PR25 1DH ☎ 01772 625329

Estates, Property & Valuation: Mr Martin Fahy, Property Services Manager, Civic Centre, West Paddock, Leyland PR25 1DH ☎ 01772 421491 🖷 01772 622287 ✉ mfahy@southribble.gov.uk

Estates, Property & Valuation: Ms Jane Maguire, Housing Manager, Civic Centre, West Paddock, Leyland PR25 1DH ☎ 01772 421491 Extn 5361 🖷 01772 622287 ✉ jmaguire@southribble.gov.uk

Finance and Treasurer: Mrs S Guinness, Head of Shared Financial Services, Civic Centre, West Paddock, Leyland PR25 1DH ☎ 01772 421491 ✉ sguinness@southribble.gov.uk

Fleet Management: Mr Mark Gaffney, Director of Neighbourhoods, Civic Centre, West Paddock, Leyland PR25 1DH ☎ 01772 625671 🖷 01772 622287 ✉ mgaffney@southribble.gov.uk

Grounds Maintenance: Mr Roger Ashcroft, Waste, Transport & Neighbourhoods Manager, Civic Centre, West Paddock, Leyland PR25 1DH ☎ 01772 421491; 01772 421491

Grounds Maintenance: Mr Andrew Richardson, Parks & Neighbourhoods Manager, Civic Centre, West Paddock, Leyland PR25 1DH ☎ 01772 625674 ✉ arichardson@southribble.gov.uk

Health and Safety: Mr Jeff Lambert, Health & Safety Officer, Civic Centre, West Paddock, Leyland PR25 1DH ☎ 01772 625331 ✉ jlambertl@southribble.gov.uk

Home Energy Conservation: Mr Dave Bradley, Senior Environmental Health Officer, Civic Centre, West Paddock, Leyland PR25 1DH ☎ 01772 421491 🖷 01772 622287 ✉ dbradleyl@southribble.gov.uk

Housing: Ms Jane Maguire, Housing Manager, Civic Centre, West Paddock, Leyland PR25 1DH ☎ 01772 421491 Extn 5361 🖷 01772 622287 ✉ jmaguire@southribble.gov.uk

Legal: Mr David Whelan, Legal Services Manager, Civic Centre, West Paddock, Leyland PR25 1DH ☎ 01772 421491 🖷 01772 622287 ✉ dwhelan@southribble.gov.uk

Licensing: Mr David Whelan, Legal Services Manager, Civic Centre, West Paddock, Leyland PR25 1DH ☎ 01772 421491 🖷 01772 622287 ✉ dwhelan@southribble.gov.uk

Member Services: Mr Martin O'Loughlin, Democratic Services Manager, Civic Centre, West Paddock, Leyland PR25 1DH ☎ 01772 625307 🖷 01772 622287 ✉ moloughlin@southribble.gov.uk

Member Services: Ms Maureen Wood, Director of Corporate Governance, Civic Centre, West Paddock, Leyland PR25 1DH ☎ 01772 625247 ✉ mwood@southribble.gov.uk

Parking: Mr Andrew Richardson, Parks & Neighbourhoods Manager, Civic Centre, West Paddock, Leyland PR25 1DH ☎ 01772 625674 ✉ arichardson@southribble.gov.uk

Personnel / HR: Mr Steve Nugent, Interim HR Manager, Civic Centre, West Paddock, Leyland PR25 1DH ☎ 01772 421491 🖷 01772 622287 ✉ snugent@southribble.gov.uk

Planning: Ms Helen Hockenhull, Planning Manager, Civic Centre, West Paddock, Leyland PR25 1DH ☎ 01772 421491 🖷 01772 622287 ✉ hhockenhull@southribble.gov.uk

Procurement: Ms Janet Hinds, Procurement & Partnerships Manager, Civic Centre, West Paddock, Leyland PR25 1DH ☎ 01772 421491 🖷 01772 622287 ✉ janet.hinds@chorley.gov.uk

Recycling & Waste Minimisation: Ms Imogen Brettell, Recycling Officer, Civic Centre, West Paddock, Leyland PR25 1DH ☎ 01772 421491 🖷 01772 622287 ✉ ibrettell@southribble.gov.uk

Regeneration: Mr Howerd Booth, Regeneration Manager, Civic Centre, West Paddock, Leyland PR25 1DH ☎ 01772 421491 🖷 01772 622287 ✉ hbooth@southribble.gov.uk

Staff Training: Mr Steve Nugent, Interim HR Manager, Civic Centre, West Paddock, Leyland PR25 1DH ☎ 01772 421491 🖷 01772 622287 ✉ snugent@southribble.gov.uk

Street Scene: Mr Mark Gaffney, Director of Neighbourhoods, Civic Centre, West Paddock, Leyland PR25 1DH ☎ 01772 625671 🖷 01772 622287 ✉ mgaffney@southribble.gov.uk

Tourism: Miss Jennifer Clough, Principal Economic Development Officer, Civic Centre, West Paddock, Leyland PR25 1DH ☎ 01772 421491 🖷 01772 622287 ✉ jclough@southribble.gov.uk

Waste Collection and Disposal: Mr Roger Ashcroft, Waste, Transport & Neighbourhoods Manager, Civic Centre, West Paddock, Leyland PR25 1DH ☎ 01772 421491; 01772 421491

Waste Collection and Disposal: Mr Mark Gaffney, Director of Neighbourhoods, Civic Centre, West Paddock, Leyland PR25 1DH ☎ 01772 625671 🖷 01772 622287

✉ mgaffney@southribble.gov.uk

Waste Management: Mr Roger Ashcroft, Waste, Transport & Neighbourhoods Manager, Civic Centre, West Paddock, Leyland PR25 1DH ☎ 01772 421491; 01772 421491

Waste Management: Mr Mark Gaffney, Director of Neighbourhoods, Civic Centre, West Paddock, Leyland PR25 1DH ☎ 01772 625671 🖷 01772 622287
✉ mgaffney@southribble.gov.uk

MEMBERS OF THE COUNCIL (56)

***Mayor:* Clark**, Colin (CON - Longton and Hutton West)
cllr.cclark@southribble.gov.uk
***Mayor:* Marsh**, James (CON - Coupe Green and Gregson Lane)
cllr.jmarsh@southribble.gov.uk
***Deputy Mayor:* Gardner**, Dorothy (CON - Charnock)
cllr.dgardner@southribble.gov.uk
***Leader of the Council:* Smith**, Margaret (CON - New Longton and Hutton East)
cllr.msmith@southribble.gov.uk
***Deputy Leader of the Council:* Mullineaux**, Peter (CON - Samlesbury and Walton)
cllr.pmullineaux@southribble.gov.uk
Ball, Andrea (CON - Bamber Bridge North)
cllr.aball@southribble.gov.uk
Beattie, Kathleen (CON - Lostock Hall)
cllr.kbeattie@southribble.gov.uk
Bell, Jane (LAB - Earnshaw Bridge)
cllr.jbell@southribble.gov.uk
Bennett, Warren (CON - Coupe Green and Gregson Lane)
cllr.wgennett@southribble.gov.uk
Bennett, Stephen (LAB - Bamber Bridge North)
cllr.sbennett@southribble.gov.uk
Bradley, Mark (LAB - Farington East)
cllr.mbradley@southribble.gov.uk
Coulton, Colin (CON - Longton and Hutton West)
cllr.ccoulton@southribble.gov.uk
Crook, Cameron (LAB - Lostock Hall)
cllr.ccrook@southribble.gov.uk
Evans, William (LAB - Earnshaw Bridge)
cllr.wevans@southribble.gov.uk
Forrest, Derek (LAB - Leyland Central)
cllr.dforrest@southribble.gov.uk
Foster, Paul (LAB - Bamber Bridge West)
cllr.pfoster@southribble.gov.uk
Gardner, Melvyn (CON - Charnock)
cllr.mgardner@southribble.gov.uk
Green, Michael (CON - Moss Side)
cllr.michael.green@southribble.gov.uk
Green, Michael (CON - Moss Side)
cllr.michael.green@southribble.gov.uk
Green, Mary (CON - Moss Side)
cllr.mary.green@southribble.gov.uk
Hamman, Philip (CON - Leyland St Mary's)
cllr.phamman@southribble.gov.uk
Hanson, Tom (LAB - Bamber Bridge West)
cllr.thanson@southribble.gov.uk
Harrison, Donald (LAB - Seven Stars)
cllr.dharrison@southribble.gov.uk
Hesketh, Jon (CON - Longton and Hutton West)
cllr.jhesketh@southribble.gov.uk
Heyworth, Fred (LAB - Lowerhouse)
cllr.fheyworth@southribble.gov.uk
Higgins, Mick (LAB - Bamber Bridge East)
cllr.mhiggins@southribble.gov.uk
Hothersall, Jenny (CON - Middleforth)
cllr.jenny.hothersall@southribble.gov.uk
Hughes, Cliff (CON - Tardy Gate)
cllr.chughes@southribble.gov.uk
Jones, Susan (LAB - Leyland St Ambrose)
cllr.sjones@southribble.gov.uk
Kelly, Joseph (LAB - Lowerhouse)
cllr.tkelly@southribble.gov.uk
Martin, Keith (LAB - Kingsfold)
cllr.kmartin@southribble.gov.uk
McNulty, Michael (CON - Leyland St Mary's)
cllr.mmcnulty@southribble.gov.uk
Moon, Caroline (CON - Seven Stars)
cllr.cmoon@southribble.gov.uk
Mort, Jacqueline (CON - Tardy Gate)
cllr.jmort@southribble.gov.uk
Nelson, Michael (CON - Walton-le-Dale)
cllr.mnelson@southribble.gov.uk
Noblet, Rebecca (CON - Whitefield)
cllr.rnoblet@southribble.gov.uk
O'Hare, Graham (CON - Walton-le-Dale)
cllr.go'hare@southribble.gov.uk
Otter, Mike (CON - Farington East)
cllr.motter@southribble.gov.uk
Patten, James (LAB - Kingsfold)
cllr.jpatten@southribble.gov.uk
Pimblett, Anthony (LD - Whitefield)
cllr.tpimblett@southribble.gov.uk
Prynn, Susan (LAB - Middleforth)
cllr.sprynn@southribble.gov.uk
Rainsbury, John (CON - Farington West)
cllr.jrainsbury@southribble.gov.uk
Robinson, Stephen (CON - Howick and Priory)
cllr.srobinson@southribble.gov.uk
Robinson, Mary (CON - Howick and Priory)
cllr.mrobinson@southribble.gov.uk
Smith, Phil (CON - New Longton and Hutton East)
cllr.psmith@southribble.gov.uk
Stettner, Peter (CON - Little Hoole and Much Hoole)
cllr.pstettner@southribble.gov.uk
Suthers, David (CON - Little Hoole and Much Hoole)
cllr.dsuthers@southribble.gov.uk
Titherington, Michael (LAB - Golden Hill)
cllr.mtitherington@southribble.gov.uk
Tomlinson, Matthew (LAB - Golden Hill)
cllr.mtomlinson@southribble.gov.uk
Tomlinson, Caleb (LAB - Leyland Central)
cllr.ctomlinson@southribble.gov.uk
Tomlinson, Sarah (LAB - Leyland St Ambrose)
cllr.stomlinson@southribble.gov.uk
Walker, Frances (CON - Broad Oak)
Walton, Graham (CON - Farington West)
cllr.gwalton@southribble.gov.uk
Watts, David (LAB - Bamber Bridge East)
cllr.dwatts@southribble.gov.uk
Woollard, Linda (CON - Broad Oak)
cllr.lwoollard@southribble.gov.uk
Yates, Barrie (CON - Samlesbury and Walton)
cllr.byates@southribble.gov.uk

POLITICAL COMPOSITION

CON: 34, LAB: 21, LD: 1

CABINET

Leader: Mrs Margaret Rose Smith
Deputy Leader / Neighbourhoods & Street Scene: Mr Peter Mullineaux
Finance & Resources: Mr Stephen Robinson
Regeneration, Leisure & Healthy Communities: Mr Phil Smith
Shared Services & Corporate Support: Mr Philip Hamman
Strategic Planning & Housing: Mr Cliff Hughes

COMMITTEE CHAIRS

Governance: Mr Graham O'Hare
Licensing: Mr John Rainsbury
Planning: Mr Jon Hesketh
Scrutiny: Mr Michael Titherington

SOUTH SOMERSET D

South Somerset District Council, Council Offices, Brympton Way, Yeovil BA20 2HT ☎ 01935 462462 🖷 01935 462188
✉ ssdc@southsomerset.gov.uk 💻 www.southsomerset.gov.uk

FACTS & FIGURES

Police Authority: Avon & Somerset Police Authority
Learning and Skills Council: South West
Parliamentary Constituencies: Somerton and Frome, Yeovil
EU Constituencies: South West
Election Frequency: Elections are of whole council
Twinning: Ansford/Castle Cary: Remalard (France); Chard: Helmstedt (Germany); Crewkerne: Igny (France); Somerton: Sille-le-Guillaume (France); Wincanton: Rosiers and Gennes (France); Yeovil: Herblay (France); Taunusstein (Germany); Samarate (Italy)

PRINCIPAL OFFICERS

Chief Executive: Mr Mark Williams, Chief Executive, South Somerset & East Devon District Councils, Council Offices, Brympton Way, Yeovil BA20 2HT ☎ 01935 462462 🖷 01935 462503 ✉ mwilliams@southsomerset.gov.uk

Senior Management: Mr Ian Clarke, Assistant Director - Legal & Corporate Services, Council Offices, Brympton Way, Yeovil BA20 2HT ☎ 01935 462462 🖷 01935 462188
✉ ian.clarke@southsomerset.gov.uk

Senior Management: Mr Steve Joel, Assistant Director - Health & Wellbeing, Council Offices, Brympton Way, Yeovil BA20 2HT ☎ 01935 462462 ✉ steve.joel@southsomerset.gov.uk

Senior Management: Ms Donna Parham, Assistant Director - Financial & Corporate Services, Council Offices, Brympton Way, Yeovil BA20 2HT ☎ 01935 462462 🖷 01935 462188
✉ donna.parham@southsomerset.gov.uk

Senior Management: Mrs Helen Rutter, Assistant Director - Communities, Council Offices, Brympton Way, Yeovil BA20 2HT ☎ 01935 462462 🖷 01935 462503
✉ helen.rutter@southsomerset.gov.uk

Senior Management: Mrs Rina Singh, Strategic Director - Place & Performance, Council Offices, Brympton Way, Yeovil BA20 2HT ☎ 01935 462462 🖷 01935 462188
✉ rina.singh@southsomerset.gov.uk

Senior Management: Ms Vega Sturgess, Strategic Director - Operations & Customer Focus, Council Offices, Brympton Way, Yeovil BA20 2HT ☎ 01935 462462
✉ vega.sturgess@southsomerset.gov.uk

Senior Management: Mr Laurence Willis, Assistant Director - Environment, Council Offices, Brympton Way, Yeovil BA20 2HT ☎ 01935 462462 🖷 01935 412955
✉ laurence.willis@southsomerset.gov.uk

Senior Management: Mr Martin Woods, Assistant Director - Economy, Council Offices, Brympton Way, Yeovil BA20 2HT ☎ 01935 462462 🖷 01935 462503
✉ martin.woods@southsomerset.gov.uk

Architect, Building / Property Services: Mr Garry Green, Engineering & Property Services Manager, Council Offices, Brympton Way, Yeovil BA20 2HT ☎ 01935 462462
🖷 01935 462248 ✉ garry.green@southsomerset.gov.uk

Best Value: Mrs Rina Singh, Strategic Director - Place & Performance, Council Offices, Brympton Way, Yeovil BA20 2HT ☎ 01935 462462 🖷 01935 462188
✉ rina.singh@southsomerset.gov.uk

Building Control: Mr David Durrant, Building Control Manager, Houndstone Close, Abbey Manor Park, Taunton BA20 1AS ☎ 01935 462462 🖷 01935 412955
✉ david.durrant@southsomerset.gov.uk

PR / Communications: Mr Martin Hacker, Communications Officer, Council Offices, Brympton Way, Yeovil BA20 2HT ☎ 01935 462462 🖷 01935 462503
✉ martin.hacker@southsomerset.gov.uk

PR / Communications: Miss Dawn Haydon, Media & Communications Officer, Council Offices, Brympton Way, Yeovil BA20 2HT ☎ 01935 462462 🖷 01935 462188
✉ dawn.haydon@southsomerset.gov.uk

Community Planning: Mrs Helen Rutter, Assistant Director - Communities, Council Offices, Brympton Way, Yeovil BA20 2HT ☎ 01935 462462 🖷 01935 462503
✉ helen.rutter@southsomerset.gov.uk

Community Safety: Mr Steve Brewer, Community Safety Co-ordinator, Council Offices, Brympton Way, Yeovil BA20 2HT ☎ 01935 462462 🖷 01935 462503
✉ steve.brewer@southsomerset.gov.uk

Computer Management: Mr Roger Brown, ICT Manager, Council Offices, Brympton Way, Yeovil BA20 2HT ☎ 01935 462462 🖷 01935 462188 ✉ roger.brown@southsomerset.gov.uk

Corporate Services: Mr Ian Clarke, Assistant Director - Legal & Corporate Services, Council Offices, Brympton Way, Yeovil BA20 2HT ☎ 01935 462462 🖷 01935 462188
✉ ian.clarke@southsomerset.gov.uk

Customer Service: Mr Jason Toogood, Customer Services Manager, Council Offices, Brympton Way, Yeovil BA20 2HT ☎ 01935 462462 🖷 01935 462188

jason.toogood@southsomerset.gov.uk

Direct Labour: Mr Chris Cooper, Streetscene Manager, South Somerset Direct Services, 7 Artillery Road, Luton Trading Estate, Yeovil BA22 8RP ☎ 01935 462462 🖷 01935 477107 chris.cooper@southsomerset.gov.uk

Economic Development: Mr David Julian, Economic Development Manager, Council Offices, Brympton Way, Yeovil BA20 2HT ☎ 01935 462462 🖷 01935 462188 david.julian@southsomerset.gov.uk

Economic Development: Mr Martin Woods, Assistant Director - Economy, Council Offices, Brympton Way, Yeovil BA20 2HT ☎ 01935 462462 🖷 01935 462503 martin.woods@southsomerset.gov.uk

E-Government: Mr Bruce Soord, Spatial Systems Manager, Council Offices, Brympton Way, Yeovil BA20 2HT ☎ 01935 462462 🖷 01935 462188 bruce.soord@southsomerset.gov.uk

Electoral Registration: Mr Roger Quantock, Senior Democractic Services Officer, Council Offices, Brympton Way, Yeovil BA20 2HT ☎ 01935 462462 🖷 01935 462188 roger.quantock@southsomerset.gov.uk

Emergency Planning: Ms Pam Harvey, Civil Contingencies Manager, Council Offices, Brympton Way, Yeovil BA20 2HT ☎ 01935 462462 🖷 01935 462503 pam.harvey@southsomerset.gov.uk

Energy Management: Mr Keith Wheaton-Green, Environmental Performance Manager, Council Offices, Brympton Way, Yeovil BA20 2HT ☎ 01935 462462 🖷 01935 462503 keith.wheaton-green@southsomerset.gov.uk

Environmental Health: Mr Laurence Willis, Assistant Director - Environment, Council Offices, Brympton Way, Yeovil BA20 2HT ☎ 01935 462462 🖷 01935 412955 laurence.willis@southsomerset.gov.uk

Estates, Property & Valuation: Mr Garry Green, Engineering & Property Services Manager, Council Offices, Brympton Way, Yeovil BA20 2HT ☎ 01935 462462 🖷 01935 462248 garry.green@southsomerset.gov.uk

Facilities: Mr Garry Green, Engineering & Property Services Manager, Council Offices, Brympton Way, Yeovil BA20 2HT ☎ 01935 462462 🖷 01935 462248 garry.green@southsomerset.gov.uk

Finance and Treasurer: Ms Donna Parham, Assistant Director - Financial & Corporate Services, Council Offices, Brympton Way, Yeovil BA20 2HT ☎ 01935 462462 🖷 01935 462188 donna.parham@southsomerset.gov.uk

Fleet Management: Ms Niki Atkins, Fleet Service Supervisor, Lufton Depot, 7 Artillery Road, Yeovil BA22 8RP ☎ 01935 462462 🖷 01935 462188 niki.atkins@southsomerset.gov.uk

Grounds Maintenance: Mr Chris Cooper, Streetscene Manager, South Somerset Direct Services, 7 Artillery Road, Luton Trading Estate, Yeovil BA22 8RP ☎ 01935 462462 🖷 01935 477107 chris.cooper@southsomerset.gov.uk

Health and Safety: Ms Pam Harvey, Civil Contingencies Manager, Council Offices, Brympton Way, Yeovil BA20 2HT ☎ 01935 462462 🖷 01935 462503 pam.harvey@southsomerset.gov.uk

Home Energy Conservation: Mr Martin Chapman, Principal Housing Standards Officer, Unit 10 Bridge Barns, Long Sutton TA10 9PZ ☎ 01935 462462 martin.chapman@southsomerset.gov.uk

Housing: Mr Colin McDonald, Strategic Housing Manager, Council Offices, Brympton Way, Yeovil BA20 2HT ☎ 01935 462462 colin.mcdonald@southsomerset.gov.uk

Legal: Mr Ian Clarke, Assistant Director - Legal & Corporate Services, Council Offices, Brympton Way, Yeovil BA20 2HT ☎ 01935 462462 🖷 01935 462188 ian.clarke@southsomerset.gov.uk

Leisure and Cultural Services: Ms Lynda Pincombe, Community Health & Leisure Manager, Council Offices, Brympton Way, Yeovil BA20 2HT ☎ 01935 462462 lynda.pincombe@southsomerset.gov.uk

Licensing: Mr Nigel Marston, Licensing Manager, Council Offices, Brympton Way, Yeovil BA20 2HT ☎ 01935 462462 🖷 01935 462188 nigel.marston@southsomerset.gov.uk

Lottery Funding, Charity and Voluntary: Ms Alice Knight, Third Sector & Partnership Manager, Council Offices, Brympton Way, Yeovil BA20 2HT ☎ 01935 462462 🖷 01935 462188 alice.knight@southsomerset.gov.uk

Member Services: Ms Angela Cox, Democratic Services Manager, Council Offices, Brympton Way, Yeovil BA20 2HT ☎ 01935 462462 🖷 01935 462188 angela.cox@southsomerset.gov.uk

Parking: Mr Garry Green, Engineering & Property Services Manager, Council Offices, Brympton Way, Yeovil BA20 2HT ☎ 01935 462462 🖷 01935 462248 garry.green@southsomerset.gov.uk

Partnerships: Ms Alice Knight, Third Sector & Partnership Manager, Council Offices, Brympton Way, Yeovil BA20 2HT ☎ 01935 462462 🖷 01935 462188 alice.knight@southsomerset.gov.uk

Personnel / HR: Mr Mike Holliday, Human Resources & Performance Manager, Council Offices, Brympton Way, Yeovil BA20 2HT ☎ 01935 462462 🖷 01935 462188 mike.holliday@southsomerset.gov.uk

Planning: Mr David Norris, Development Control Manager, Council Offices, Brympton Way, Yeovil BA20 2HT ☎ 01935 462462 david.norris@southsomerset.gov.uk

Procurement: Mr Gary Russ, Procurement & Risk Manager, Council Offices, Brympton Way, Yeovil BA20 2HT ☎ 01935

462462 🖷 01935 462188 ✉ gary.russ@southsomerset.gov.uk

Recycling & Waste Minimisation: Mr Dave Mansell, Recycling Development Officer, Somerset County Council, County Hall, Taunton TA1 4DY ☎ 01823 356013 ✉ dgmansell@somerset.gov.uk

Regeneration: Mr David Julian, Economic Development Manager, Council Offices, Brympton Way, Yeovil BA20 2HT ☎ 01935 462462 🖷 01935 462188 ✉ david.julian@southsomerset.gov.uk

Staff Training: Mr Mike Holliday, Human Resources & Performance Manager, Council Offices, Brympton Way, Yeovil BA20 2HT ☎ 01935 462462 🖷 01935 462188 ✉ mike.holliday@southsomerset.gov.uk

Street Scene: Mr Chris Cooper, Streetscene Manager, South Somerset Direct Services, 7 Artillery Road, Luton Trading Estate, Yeovil BA22 8RP ☎ 01935 462462 🖷 01935 477107 ✉ chris.cooper@southsomerset.gov.uk

Sustainable Communities: Mr Andy Foyne, Spatial Policy Manager, Council Offices, Brympton Way, Yeovil BA20 2HT ☎ 01935 462462 ✉ andy.foyne@southsomerset.gov.uk

Tourism: Mr David Julian, Economic Development Manager, Council Offices, Brympton Way, Yeovil BA20 2HT ☎ 01935 462462 🖷 01935 462188 ✉ david.julian@southsomerset.gov.uk

Transport: Mr Nigel Collins, Transport Strategy Officer, Council Offices, Brympton Way, Yeovil BA20 2HT ☎ 01935 462462 🖷 01935 462188 ✉ nigel.collins@southsomerset.gov.uk

Transport Planner: Mr Nigel Collins, Transport Strategy Officer, Council Offices, Brympton Way, Yeovil BA20 2HT ☎ 01935 462462 🖷 01935 462188 ✉ nigel.collins@southsomerset.gov.uk

MEMBERS OF THE COUNCIL (60)

***Chair:* Best**, Mike (LD - Crewkerne)
mike.best@southsomerset.gov.uk
***Vice-Chair:* Mills**, Roy (LD - Langport and Huish)
roy.mills@southsomerset.gov.uk
***Leader of the Council:* Pallister**, Ric (LD - Parrett)
ric.pallister@southsomerset.gov.uk
***Deputy Leader of the Council:* Carroll**, Tim (LD - Wincanton)
tim.carroll@southsomerset.gov.uk
***Group Leader:* Palmer**, Patrick (IND - Martock)
patrick.palmer@southsomerset.gov.uk
***Group Leader:* Wale**, Martin (CON - Combe (Chard))
martin.wale@southsomerset.gov.uk
***Group Leader:* Winder**, Colin (CON - Wincanton)
colin.winder@southsomerset.gov.uk
Bakewell, Cathy (LD - Coker)
cathy.bakewell@southsomerset.gov.uk
Beech, Mike (CON - Tower)
mike.beech@southsomerset.gov.uk
Bulmer, Dave (IND - Jocelyn (Chard))
dave.bulmer@southsomerset.gov.uk
Calvert, John (CON - Northstone)
john.calvert@southsomerset.gov.uk
Capozzoli, Tony (IND - Ivelchester)
tony.capozzoli@southsomerset.gov.uk
Chainey, John (LD - Yeovil (Central))
jvincent.chainey@southsomerset.gov.uk
Clarke, Pauline (LD - Wessex)
pauline.clarke@southsomerset.gov.uk
Colbert, Nick (CON - Wincanton)
nick.colbert@southsomerset.gov.uk
Dyke, John (LD - Crewkerne Town)
john.dyke@southsomerset.gov.uk
Fife, Tony (LD - Yeovil (East))
tony.fife@southsomerset.gov.uk
Fysh, Marcus (CON - Yeovil (South))
marcus.fysh@southsomerset.gov.uk
Gage, Nigel (CON - Yeovil (South))
nigel.gage@southsomerset.gov.uk
Gleeson, Jon (LD - Yeovil Without)
jon.gleeson@southsomerset.gov.uk
Goodall, Carol (LD - Ilminster)
carol.goodall@southsomerset.gov.uk
Greene, Dave (LD - Yeovil (South))
dave.greene@southsomerset.gov.uk
Groskop, Anna (CON - Bruton)
anna.groskop@southsomerset.gov.uk
Gubbins, Peter (LD - Yeovil Central)
peter.gubbins@southsomerset.gov.uk
Halse, Brennie (CON - Holyrood (Chard))
brennie.halse@southsomerset.gov.uk
Hobhouse, Henry (LD - Cary)
henry.hobhouse@southsomerset.gov.uk
Inglefield, Tim (CON - Blackmoor Vale)
tim.inglefield@southsomerset.gov.uk
Kendall, Andy (LD - Yeovil (Central))
andy.kendall@southsomerset.gov.uk
Kenton, Jenny (LD - Crimchard (Chard))
jenny.kenton@southsomerset.gov.uk
Lewis, Mike (CON - Camelot)
michael.lewis@southsomerset.gov.uk
Lock, Pauline (LD - Yeovil Without)
pauline.lock@southsomerset.gov.uk
Lock, Tony (LD - Yeovil (East))
tony.lock@southsomerset.gov.uk
Martin, Ian (LD - Yeovil (West))
ian.martin@southsomerset.gov.uk
Maxwell, Paul (LD - Eggwood)
paul.maxwell@southsomerset.gov.uk
Mermagen, Nigel (LD - Avishayes (Chard))
nigel.mermagen@southsomerset.gov.uk
Middleton, Graham (CON - Martock)
graham.middleton@southsomerset.gov.uk
Mounter, Terry (IND - Curry Rivel)
terry.mounter@southsomerset.gov.uk
Norris, David (CON - Wessex)
david.norriscllr@southsomerset.gov.uk
Oakes, Graham (LD - Yeovil Without)
graham.oakes@southsomerset.gov.uk
Osborne, Sue (CON - Windwhistle)
sue.osborne@southsomerset.gov.uk
Pledger, Shane (CON - Turn Hill)
shane.pledger@southsomerset.gov.uk
Read, Wes (CON - Yeovil (West))
wes.read@southsomerset.gov.uk
Recardo, David (LD - Yeovil (East))
david.recardo@southsomerset.gov.uk
Richardson, John (LD - Brympton)
john.richardson@southsomerset.gov.uk
Roderigo, Ros (CON - Blackdown)

ros.roderigo@southsomerset.gov.uk
Roundell Greene, Jo (LD - St Michael's)
jo.roundellgreene@southsomerset.gov.uk
Seal, Sylvia (LD - Hamdon)
sylvia.seal@southsomerset.gov.uk
Seaton, Gina (CON - Coker)
gina.seaton@southsomerset.gov.uk
Seib, Peter (LD - Brympton)
peter.seib@southsomerset.gov.uk
Singleton, Angie (LD - Crewkerne Town)
angie.singleton@southsomerset.gov.uk
Steele, Sue (CON - Islemoor)
sue.steele@southsomerset.gov.uk
Thompson, Paul (CON - South Petherton)
paul.thompson@southsomerset.gov.uk
Turner, Kim (LD - Ilminster Town)
kim.turner@southsomerset.gov.uk
Turpin, Andrew (LD - Tatworth and Forton)
andrew.turpin@southsomerset.gov.uk
Vijeh, Linda (CON - Neroche)
linda.vijeh@southsomerset.gov.uk
Walker, Barry (CON - South Petherton)
barry.walker@southsomerset.gov.uk
Wallace, William (CON - Blackmoor Vale)
william.wallace@southsomerset.gov.uk
Wallace, Lucy (CON - Milborne Port)
lucy.wallace@southsomerset.gov.uk
Weeks, Nick (CON - Cary)
nick.weeks@southsomerset.gov.uk
Yeomans, Derek (CON - Burrow Hill)
derek.yeomans@southsomerset.gov.uk

POLITICAL COMPOSITION
LD: 30, CON: 26, IND: 4

CABINET
Leader: Mr Ric Pallister
Deputy Leader: Mr Tim Carroll
Environment & Economic Development: Mrs Jo Roundell Greene
Leisure & Culture: Mrs Sylvia Seal
Property & Climate Change: Mr Henry Hobhouse
Regulatory & Democratic Services: Mr Peter Seib

COMMITTEE CHAIRS
Audit: Mr Derek Yeomans
Licensing: Mr Nigel Mermagen
Regulation: Mr Peter Gubbins
Scrutiny: Mrs Sue Steele

SOUTH STAFFORDSHIRE D

South Staffordshire District Council, (South Staffordshire Council), Council Offices, Codsall WV8 1PX ☎ 01902 696000 🖷 01902 696800 ✉ info@sstaffs.gov.uk 💻 www.sstaffs.gov.uk

FACTS & FIGURES
Police Authority: Staffordshire Police Authority
Health Authority: NHS West Midlands
Learning and Skills Council: West Midlands
Parliamentary Constituencies: Staffordshire South
EU Constituencies: West Midlands
Election Frequency: Elections are of whole council

Twinning: Codsall and Bilbrook: St. Pryve-St. Mesmin (France); Kinver: Mer (France); City of Park Ridge, Illinois (USA); Penkridge: Ablon-sur-Seine (France); Trysull and Seisdon: Conde St. Libiare

PRINCIPAL OFFICERS
Chief Executive: Mr Steve Winterflood, Chief Executive, Council Offices, Codsall WV8 1PX ☎ 01902 696102 🖷 01902 696445 ✉ s.winterflood@sstaffs.gov.uk

Deputy Chief Executive: Mr Dave Heywood, Deputy Chief Executive, Council Offices, Codsall WV8 1PX ☎ 01902 696100 🖷 01902 696546 ✉ d.heywood@sstaffs.gov.uk

Senior Management: Ms Frankie Cartwright, Director of Revenue & Customer Services, Council Offices, Codsall WV8 1PX ☎ 01902 696640 ✉ f.cartwright@sstaffs.gov.uk

Senior Management: Mr Phil Cooper, Director of Finance, Council Offices, Codsall WV8 1PX ☎ 01902 696607 🖷 01902 696800 ✉ p.cooper@sstaffs.gov.uk

Senior Management: Mr Dave Heywood, Deputy Chief Executive, Council Offices, Codsall WV8 1PX ☎ 01902 696100 🖷 01902 696546 ✉ d.heywood@sstaffs.gov.uk

Senior Management: Mr Andrew Johnson, Director of Planning & Strategic Services, Council Offices, Codsall WV8 1PX ☎ 01902 696457 ✉ a.johnson@sstaffs.gov.uk

Senior Management: Mr David Pattison, Head of Legal & Licensing Services, Council Offices, Codsall WV8 1PX ☎ 01902 696132 🖷 01902 696448 ✉ d.pattison@sstaffs.gov.uk

Senior Management: Mr Steve Winterflood, Chief Executive, Council Offices, Codsall WV8 1PX ☎ 01902 696102 🖷 01902 696445 ✉ s.winterflood@sstaffs.gov.uk

Architect, Building / Property Services: Mr Hayden Baugh-Jones, Landscape Planning Manager, Council Offices, Codsall WV8 1PX ☎ 01902 696000 ✉ h.baugh-jones@sstaffs.gov.uk

Architect, Building / Property Services: Mr Howard Medlicott, Landscape Manager, Council Offices, Codsall WV8 1PX ☎ 01902 696000 ✉ h.medlicott@sstaffs.gov.uk

Architect, Building / Property Services: Mr John Round, Architect & Facilities Manager, Council Offices, Codsall WV8 1PX ☎ 01902 696510 ✉ j.round@sstaffs.gov.uk

Best Value: Ms Clodagh Peterson, Principal Corporate Policy Officer, Council Offices, Codsall WV8 1PX ☎ 01902 696424 ✉ c.peterson@sstaffs.gov.uk

Best Value: Mr Steve Winterflood, Chief Executive, Council Offices, Codsall WV8 1PX ☎ 01902 696102 🖷 01902 696445 ✉ s.winterflood@sstaffs.gov.uk

Building Control: Mrs Jackie Smith, Director of Environmental Services, Council Offices, Codsall WV8 1PX ☎ 01902 696601 🖷 01902 696222 ✉ j.smith@sstaffs.gov.uk

PR / Communications: Mr Steve Winterflood, Chief Executive, Council Offices, Codsall WV8 1PX ☎ 01902 696102 🖷 01902 696445 🖰 s.winterflood@sstaffs.gov.uk

Community Safety: Mrs Maggie Quinn, Community Safety Co-ordinator, Council Offices, Codsall WV8 1PX ☎ 01902 696530 🖷 01902 696800 🖰 m.quinn@sstaffs.gov.uk

Computer Management: Mr Leigh Brookes, Head of Information Technology Services, Council Offices, Codsall WV8 1PX ☎ 01902 696614 🖰 l.brookes@sstaffs.gov.uk

Corporate Services: Ms Clodagh Peterson, Principal Corporate Policy Officer, Council Offices, Codsall WV8 1PX ☎ 01902 696424 🖰 c.peterson@sstaffs.gov.uk

Customer Service: Ms Frankie Cartwright, Director of Revenue & Customer Services, Council Offices, Codsall WV8 1PX ☎ 01902 696640 🖰 f.cartwright@sstaffs.gov.uk

Customer Service: Mrs Karen Childs, Customer Services Manager, Council Offices, Codsall WV8 1PX ☎ 01902 696526 🖰 k.childs@sstaffs.gov.uk

Economic Development: Mr Andrew Johnson, Director of Planning & Strategic Services, Council Offices, Codsall WV8 1PX ☎ 01902 696457 🖰 a.johnson@sstaffs.gov.uk

Economic Development: Mr Grant Mitchell, Principal House Officer for Strategy, Council Offices, Codsall WV8 1PX ☎ 01902 696438 🖰 g.mitchell@sstaffs.gov.uk

E-Government: Mr Leigh Brookes, Head of Information Technology Services, Council Offices, Codsall WV8 1PX ☎ 01902 696614 🖰 l.brookes@sstaffs.gov.uk

Electoral Registration: Mr Philip Hardy, Head of Customer & Electoral Services, Council Offices, Codsall WV8 1PX ☎ 01902 696119 🖷 01902 696800 🖰 p.hardy@sstaffs.gov.uk

Emergency Planning: Mr Philip Hardy, Head of Customer & Electoral Services, Council Offices, Codsall WV8 1PX ☎ 01902 696119 🖷 01902 696800 🖰 p.hardy@sstaffs.gov.uk

Environmental Health: Mr Dave Heywood, Deputy Chief Executive, Council Offices, Codsall WV8 1PX ☎ 01902 696100 🖷 01902 696546 🖰 d.heywood@sstaffs.gov.uk

Environmental Health: Miss Jenny Rhodes, Environmental Health Manager (Commercial), Council Offices, Codsall WV8 1PX ☎ 01902 696205 🖰 j.rhodes@sstaffs.gov.uk

Finance and Treasurer: Mr Phil Cooper, Director of Finance, Council Offices, Codsall WV8 1PX ☎ 01902 696607 🖷 01902 696800 🖰 p.cooper@sstaffs.gov.uk

Grounds Maintenance: Mr Howard Medlicott, Landscape Manager, Council Offices, Codsall WV8 1PX ☎ 01902 696000 🖰 h.medlicott@sstaffs.gov.uk

Health and Safety: Mrs Wendy Bridgwater, Head of Human Resources, Council Offices, Codsall WV8 1PX ☎ 01902 696103 🖷 01902 696145 🖰 w.bridgwater@sstaffs.gov.uk

Housing: Mr Grant Mitchell, Principal House Officer for Strategy, Council Offices, Codsall WV8 1PX ☎ 01902 696438 🖰 g.mitchell@sstaffs.gov.uk

Legal: Mr David Pattison, Head of Legal & Licensing Services, Council Offices, Codsall WV8 1PX ☎ 01902 696132 🖷 01902 696448 🖰 d.pattison@sstaffs.gov.uk

Leisure and Cultural Services: Mr Dave Heywood, Deputy Chief Executive, Council Offices, Codsall WV8 1PX ☎ 01902 696100 🖷 01902 696546 🖰 d.heywood@sstaffs.gov.uk

Leisure and Cultural Services: Mrs Jackie Smith, Director of Environmental Services, Council Offices, Codsall WV8 1PX ☎ 01902 696601 🖷 01902 696222 🖰 j.smith@sstaffs.gov.uk

Licensing: Mr David Pattison, Head of Legal & Licensing Services, Council Offices, Codsall WV8 1PX ☎ 01902 696132 🖷 01902 696448 🖰 d.pattison@sstaffs.gov.uk

Lighting: Mr Steve Poyser, Head of Engineering Services, Council Offices, Codsall WV8 1PX ☎ 01902 696503 🖷 01902 696800 🖰 s.poyser@sstaffs.gov.uk

Lighting: Mrs Jackie Smith, Director of Environmental Services, Council Offices, Codsall WV8 1PX ☎ 01902 696601 🖷 01902 696222 🖰 j.smith@sstaffs.gov.uk

Parking: Mrs Jackie Smith, Director of Environmental Services, Council Offices, Codsall WV8 1PX ☎ 01902 696601 🖷 01902 696222 🖰 j.smith@sstaffs.gov.uk

Partnerships: Ms Clodagh Peterson, Principal Corporate Policy Officer, Council Offices, Codsall WV8 1PX ☎ 01902 696424 🖰 c.peterson@sstaffs.gov.uk

Personnel / HR: Mrs Wendy Bridgwater, Head of Human Resources, Council Offices, Codsall WV8 1PX ☎ 01902 696103 🖷 01902 696145 🖰 w.bridgwater@sstaffs.gov.uk

Planning: Mr Andrew Johnson, Director of Planning & Strategic Services, Council Offices, Codsall WV8 1PX ☎ 01902 696457 🖰 a.johnson@sstaffs.gov.uk

Planning: Mrs Sarah Poxon, Development Control Manager, Council Offices, Codsall WV8 1PX ☎ 01902 696413 🖷 01902 696800 🖰 s.poxon@sstaffs.gov.uk

Recycling & Waste Minimisation: Mrs Jackie Smith, Director of Environmental Services, Council Offices, Codsall WV8 1PX ☎ 01902 696601 🖷 01902 696222 🖰 j.smith@sstaffs.gov.uk

Regeneration: Mr Andrew Johnson, Director of Planning & Strategic Services, Council Offices, Codsall WV8 1PX ☎ 01902 696457 🖰 a.johnson@sstaffs.gov.uk

Regeneration: Mr Grant Mitchell, Principal House Officer for Strategy, Council Offices, Codsall WV8 1PX ☎ 01902 696438 🖰 g.mitchell@sstaffs.gov.uk

Staff Training: Mrs Wendy Bridgwater, Head of Human Resources, Council Offices, Codsall WV8 1PX ☎ 01902 696103 🖷 01902 696145 ✉ w.bridgwater@sstaffs.gov.uk

Staff Training: Mr David Coghill, Staff Training, Council Offices, Codsall WV8 1PX ☎ 01902 696704 ✉ d.coghill@sstaffs.gov.uk

Sustainable Communities: Mr Andrew Johnson, Director of Planning & Strategic Services, Council Offices, Codsall WV8 1PX ☎ 01902 696457 ✉ a.johnson@sstaffs.gov.uk

Tourism: Mr Dave Heywood, Deputy Chief Executive, Council Offices, Codsall WV8 1PX ☎ 01902 696100 🖷 01902 696546 ✉ d.heywood@sstaffs.gov.uk

Tourism: Mr Andrew Johnson, Director of Planning & Strategic Services, Council Offices, Codsall WV8 1PX ☎ 01902 696457 ✉ a.johnson@sstaffs.gov.uk

Tourism: Mr Grant Mitchell, Principal House Officer for Strategy, Council Offices, Codsall WV8 1PX ☎ 01902 696438 ✉ g.mitchell@sstaffs.gov.uk

MEMBERS OF THE COUNCIL (49)

***Leader of the Council:* Edwards**, Brian (CON - Kinver)
b.edwards@sstaffs.gov.uk
***Deputy Leader of the Council:* Billson**, David (CON - Perton East)
d.billson@sstaffs.gov.uk
Ashley, Jeff (LAB - Huntington and Hatherton)
j.ashley@sstaffs.gov.uk
Bates, Brian (CON - Great Wyrley Town)
b.bates@sstaffs.gov.uk
Bates, Leonard (CON - Penkridge North East and Acton Trussell)
l.bates@sstaffs.gov.uk
Beardsmore, Frank (IND - Featherstone and Shareshill)
f.beardsmore@sstaffs.gov.uk
Bond, Mary (CON - Wombourne South West)
m.bond@sstaffs.gov.uk
Boyle, Michael (IND - Cheslyn Hay North and Saredon)
m.boyle@sstaffs.gov.uk
Burton, Joan (CON - Pattingham and Patshull)
j.burton@sstaffs.gov.uk
Campbell, Patricia (CON - Codsall North)
p.campbell@sstaffs.gov.uk
Cartwright, Donald (CON - Penkridge West)
d.cartwright@sstaffs.gov.uk
Chapman, Val (CON - Bilbrook)
v.chapman@sstaffs.gov.uk
Clay, Ivor (CON - Brewood and Coven)
i.clay@sstaffs.gov.uk
Clifft, David (IND - Essington)
d.clifft@sstaffs.gov.uk
Cope, Robert (IND - Featherstone and Shareshill)
r.cope@sstaffs.gov.uk
Cox, Brian (CON - Wheaton Aston, Bishopswood and Lapley)
b.cox@sstaffs.gov.uk
Davies, Michael (CON - Wombourne South West)
m.davies@sstaffs.gov.uk
Ewart, Matthew (CON - Codsall North)
m.ewart@sstaffs.gov.uk
Fereday, David (CON - Perton Lakeside)
d.fereday@sstaffs.gov.uk
Ford, Isabel (CON - Penkridge North East and Acton Trussell)
i.ford@sstaffs.gov.uk
Granger, Jacqueline (CON - Wombourne South East)
j.granger@sstaffs.gov.uk
Hampson, Michael (CON - Brewood and Coven)
m.hampson@sstaffs.gov.uk
Harris, Mac (LAB - Cheslyn Hay North and Saredon)
m.harris@sstaffs.gov.uk
Heseltine, David (CON - Cheslyn Hay South)
d.heseltine@sstaffs.gov.uk
Heseltine, Rita (CON - Perton Lakeside)
r.heseltine@sstaffs.gov.uk
Hingley, Lin (CON - Kinver)
l.hingley@sstaffs.gov.uk
Hinton, Alan (CON - Wombourne North and Lower Penn)
a.hinton@sstaffs.gov.uk
Holmes, Diane (CON - Brewood and Coven)
d.holmes@sstaffs.gov.uk
James, Keith (CON - Perton Dippons)
k.james@sstaffs.gov.uk
Johnson, Janet (CON - Great Wyrley Town)
j.johnson@sstaffs.gov.uk
Lees, Roger (CON - Himley and Swindon)
r.lees@sstaffs.gov.uk
Marshall, Robert (CON - Codsall South)
r.marshall@sstaffs.gov.uk
McCardle, Robert (CON - Trysull and Seisdon)
r.mccardle@sstaffs.gov.uk
Michell, John (CON - Codsall South)
j.michell@sstaffs.gov.uk
Moreton, Roy (CON - Perton Lakeside)
r.moreton@sstaffs.gov.uk
Oatley, Sonja (CON - Bilbrook)
s.oatley@sstaffs.gov.uk
Perry, Raymond (CON - Great Wyrley Landywood)
r.perry@sstaffs.gov.uk
Perry, Kathleen (CON - Great Wyrley Town)
k.perry@sstaffs.gov.uk
Raven, John (CON - Penkridge South East)
j.raven@sstaffs.gov.uk
Raven, Christine (CON - Penkridge South East)
c.raven@sstaffs.gov.uk
Reade, Robert (CON - Wombourne North and Lower Penn)
r.reade@sstaffs.gov.uk
Whitehouse, Wayne (IND - Essington)
w.whitehouse@sstaffs.gov.uk
Williams, Bernard (CON - Cheslyn Hay South)
b.williams@sstaffs.gov.uk
Williams, Reginald (CON - Wombourne South East)
r.williams@sstaffs.gov.uk
Williams, Joan (CON - Wombourne North and Lower Penn)
j.williams@sstaffs.gov.uk
Williams, Kathleen (CON - Great Wyrley Landywood)
k.williams@sstaffs.gov.uk
Williams, David (CON - Huntington and Hatherton)
d.williams@sstaffs.gov.uk
Wooddisse, Paul (CON - Kinver)
p.wooddisse@sstaffs.gov.uk
Wright, Royston (CON - Wheaton Aston, Bishopswood and Lapley)
r.wright@sstaffs.gov.uk

POLITICAL COMPOSITION

CON: 42, IND: 5, LAB: 2

CABINET

Leader / Partnership Services: Mr Brian Edwards
Deputy Leader / Strategic Services: Mr David Billson
Direct Services: Mr Royston Wright
Environmental Services: Mrs Joan Williams
Public Health Protection Services: Mr Roger Lees
Support Services: Mr Robert Reade

COMMITTEE CHAIRS

Audit: Mr Robert McCardle
Licensing: Mrs Kathleen Perry
Overview & Scrutiny: Mrs Janet Johnson
Regulatory: Mr Brian Cox

SOUTH TYNESIDE M

South Tyneside Council, Town Hall and Civic Offices, Westoe Road, South Shields NE33 2RL ☎ 0191 427 1717 🖷 0191 455 0208
💻 www.southtyneside.info

FACTS & FIGURES

Police Authority: Northumbria Police Authority
Health Authority: North East Strategic Health Authority
Learning and Skills Council: North East
Parliamentary Constituencies: Jarrow, South Shields
EU Constituencies: North East
Election Frequency: Elections are by thirds
Twinning: Epinay-sur-Seine (France); Noisy-le-Sec (France); Wuppertal (Germany)

PRINCIPAL OFFICERS

Chief Executive: Mr Martin Swales, Chief Executive, Town Hall and Civic Offices, Westoe Road, South Shields NE33 2RL
🖱 martin.swales@southtyneside.gov.uk

Senior Management: Mr David Cramond, Corporate Director - Economic Regeneration, Town Hall and Civic Offices, Westoe Road, South Shields NE33 2RL ☎ 0191 424 7969
🖱 David.Cramond@southtyneside.gov.uk

Senior Management: Mr Patrick Melia, Corporate Director - Business & Area Management, South Tyneside Council, Town Hall & Civic Offices, Westoe Road, South Shields NE33 2RL ☎ 0191 424 7499 🖱 patrick.melia@southtyneside.gov.uk

Senior Management: Ms Helen Watson, Corporate Director - Children, Adults & Families, Town Hall and Civic Offices, Westoe Road, South Shields NE33 2RL ☎ 0191 424 7701 🖷 0191 427 0584 🖱 helen.watson@southtyneside.gov.uk

Architect, Building / Property Services: Mr Rick O'Farrell, Head of Regeneration, Town Hall and Civic Offices, Westoe Road, South Shields NE33 2RL ☎ 0191 424 7541
🖱 rick.o'farrell@southtyneside.gov.uk

Best Value: Mr Dan Patterson, Performance & Information Manager, Town Hall & Civic Offices, Westoe Road, South Shields NE33 2RL ☎ 0191 424 7495
🖱 dan.patterson@southtyneside.gov.uk

Building Control: Mr George Mansbridge, Head of Planning, Housing, Transport & Regulatory Services, Town Hall and Civic Offices, Westoe Road, South Shields NE33 2RL ☎ 0191 424 6599 🖷 0191 427 7171 🖱 george.mansbridge@southtyneside.gov.uk

Catering Services: Ms Elizabeth Luke, Catering Services Manager, Town Hall and Civic Offices, Westoe Road, South Shields NE33 2RL ☎ 0191 424 7739 🖷 0191 427 0584
🖱 elizabeth.luke@southtyneside.gov.uk

Children / Youth Services: Mr Mike Conlon, Head - Corporate & Commercial Services, Town Hall and Civic Offices, Westoe Road, South Shields NE33 2RL ☎ 0191 424 7765 🖷 0191 427 0584 🖱 mike.conlon@southtyneside.gov.uk

Children / Youth Services: Ms Helen Watson, Corporate Director - Children, Adults & Families, Town Hall and Civic Offices, Westoe Road, South Shields NE33 2RL ☎ 0191 424 7701 🖷 0191 427 0584 🖱 helen.watson@southtyneside.gov.uk

Civil Registration: Mrs Ann Best, Service Lead, Democratic Services, Town Hall & Civic Offices, Westoe Road, South Shields NE33 2RL ☎ 0191 424 7257 🖱 ann.best@southtyneside.gov.uk

Civil Registration: Mr Brian Scott, Head of Corporate Governance, Town Hall and Civic Offices, Westoe Road, South Shields NE33 2RL ☎ 0191 424 7200 🖷 0191 455 0208
🖱 brian.t.scott@southtyneside.gov.uk

PR / Communications: Mr Paul Robinson, Corporate Lead - Partnerships & Affairs, Town Hall & Civic Offices, Westoe Road, South Shields NE33 2RL ☎ 0191 424 7491
🖱 paul.robinson@southtyneside.gov.uk

Community Planning: Mr Mike Linsley, Community Engagement & Development Manager, Town Hall & Civic Offices, Westoe Road, South Shields NE33 2RL ☎ 0191 424 7574

Community Safety: Mr Dave Owen, Team Leader - Community Health & Safety, Town Hall and Civic Offices, Westoe Road, South Shields NE33 2RL ☎ 0191 424 7938
🖱 dave.owen@southtyneside.gov.uk

Consumer Protection and Trading Standards: Mr Stuart Wright, Trading Standards Manager, Town Hall and Civic Offices, Westoe Road, South Shields NE33 2RL ☎ 0191 424 6255
🖱 stuart.wright@southtyneside.gov.uk

Contracts: Mr Rick O'Farrell, Head of Regeneration, Town Hall and Civic Offices, Westoe Road, South Shields NE33 2RL ☎ 0191 424 7541 🖱 rick.o'farrell@southtyneside.gov.uk

Corporate Services: Mrs Ann Best, Service Lead - Democratic Services, Town Hall & Civic Offices, Westoe Road, South Shields NE33 2RL ☎ 0191 424 7257 🖱 ann.best@southtyneside.gov.uk

Corporate Services: Mr Mike Conlon, Head - Corporate & Commercial Services, Town Hall and Civic Offices, Westoe Road, South Shields NE33 2RL ☎ 0191 424 7765 🖷 0191 427 0584
🖱 mike.conlon@southtyneside.gov.uk

Corporate Services: Mr Gordon Ditchburn, IT Client Manager, Town Hall & Civic Offices, Westoe Road, South Shields NE33

2RL ☎ 0191 4271717

Corporate Services: Mrs Hayley Johnson, Corporate Lead - Strategy & Performance, Town Hall & Civic Offices, Westoe Road, South Shields NE33 2RL ☎ 0191 4271717 hayley.johnson@southtyneside.gov.uk

Corporate Services: Mr Paul Robinson, Corporate Lead - Partnerships & Affairs, Town Hall & Civic Offices, Westoe Road, South Shields NE33 2RL ☎ 0191 424 7491 paul.robinson@southtyneside.gov.uk

Economic Development: Mr David Cramond, Corporate Director - Economic Regeneration, Town Hall and Civic Offices, Westoe Road, South Shields NE33 2RL ☎ 0191 424 7969 David.Cramond@southtyneside.gov.uk

Economic Development: Mr Rick O'Farrell, Head of Regeneration, Town Hall and Civic Offices, Westoe Road, South Shields NE33 2RL ☎ 0191 424 7541 rick.o'farrell@southtyneside.gov.uk

Economic Development: Mr John Scott, Corporate Lead, Town Hall and Civic Offices, Westoe Road, South Shields NE33 2RL ☎ 0191 424 6250 john.scott@southtyneside.gov.uk

Education: Mr Mike Conlon, Head - Corporate & Commercial Services, Town Hall and Civic Offices, Westoe Road, South Shields NE33 2RL ☎ 0191 424 7765 🖷 0191 427 0584 mike.conlon@southtyneside.gov.uk

Education: Mr Peter Cutts, Head of Education, Learning & Skills, Town Hall and Civic Offices, Westoe Road, South Shields NE33 2RL ☎ 0191 424 7697 peter.cutts@southtyneside.gov.uk

Electoral Registration: Mrs Ann Best, Service Lead - Democratic Services, Town Hall & Civic Offices, Westoe Road, South Shields NE33 2RL ☎ 0191 424 7257 ann.best@southtyneside.gov.uk

Electoral Registration: Mr Brian Scott, Head of Corporate Governance, Town Hall and Civic Offices, Westoe Road, South Shields NE33 2RL ☎ 0191 424 7200 🖷 0191 455 0208 brian.t.scott@southtyneside.gov.uk

Emergency Planning: Mr George Mansbridge, Head of Planning, Housing, Transport & Regulatory Services, Town Hall and Civic Offices, Westoe Road, South Shields NE33 2RL ☎ 0191 424 6599 🖷 0191 427 7171 george.mansbridge@southtyneside.gov.uk

Energy Management: Mr Rick O'Farrell, Head of Regeneration, Town Hall and Civic Offices, Westoe Road, South Shields NE33 2RL ☎ 0191 424 7541 rick.o'farrell@southtyneside.gov.uk

Environmental / Technical Services: Mr George Mansbridge, Head of Planning, Housing, Transport & Regulatory Services, Town Hall and Civic Offices, Westoe Road, South Shields NE33 2RL ☎ 0191 424 6599 🖷 0191 427 7171 george.mansbridge@southtyneside.gov.uk

Environmental Health: Mr George Mansbridge, Head of Planning, Housing, Transport & Regulatory Services, Town Hall and Civic Offices, Westoe Road, South Shields NE33 2RL ☎ 0191 424 7566 george.mansbridge@southtyneside.gov.uk

Environmental Health: Mr George Mansbridge, Head of Planning, Housing, Transport & Regulatory Services, Town Hall and Civic Offices, Westoe Road, South Shields NE33 2RL ☎ 0191 424 6599 🖷 0191 427 7171 george.mansbridge@southtyneside.gov.uk

Estates, Property & Valuation: Mr Paul Scrafton, Interim Head of Asset Management, Town Hall and Civic Offices, Westoe Road, South Shields NE33 2RL ☎ 0191 427 1717 paul.scrafton@southtyneside.gov.uk

European Liaison: Mr Daniel Crawford, Regeneration Programmes Manager, Town Hall and Civic Offices, Westoe Road, South Shields NE33 2RL ☎ 0191 424 7672 🖷 0191 427 7171 daniel.crawford@southtyneside.gov.uk

Events Manager: Mr Ben Landon, Interim Marketing & Press Manager, Town Hall and Civic Offices, Westoe Road, South Shields NE33 2RL ☎ 0191 424 7463 ban.landon@southtyneside.gov.uk

Finance and Treasurer: Mr Stephen Moore, Head of Pensions, Hebburn Civic Centre, Campbell Park Road, Hebburn NE31 2SW ☎ 0191 424 4119 stephen.moore@southtyneside.gov.uk

Finance and Treasurer: Mr Stuart Reid, Head of Finance, South Tyneside Council, Town Hall & Civic Offices, Westoe Road, South Shields NE33 2RL ☎ 0191 424 7046 🖷 0191 424 7166 stuart.reid@southtyneside.gov.uk

Grounds Maintenance: Mr John Elsender, Greenspace Manager, Middlefields, South Shields NE34 0NT ☎ 0191 4247532

Grounds Maintenance: Mr Caine Spence, Acting Commercial Services Manager, Middlefields, South Shields NE34 0NT ☎ 0191 427 2599 caine.spence@southtyneside.gov.uk

Health and Safety: Mr Graham Fells, Corporate Manager - HR, Town Hall and Civic Offices, Westoe Road, South Shields NE33 2RL ☎ 0191 424 7323 graham.fells@southtyneside.gov.uk

Highways: Mr Dave Elliott, Highways & Transportation Design Manager, Town Hall and Civic Offices, Westoe Road, South Shields NE33 2RL ☎ 0191 427 7501 dave.elliott@southtyneside.gov.uk

Home Energy Conservation: Mr Rick O'Farrell, Head of Regeneration, Town Hall and Civic Offices, Westoe Road, South Shields NE33 2RL ☎ 0191 424 7541 rick.o'farrell@southtyneside.gov.uk

Housing: Mr Gary Kirsop, Head of Property Services, Middlefields, South Shields NE34 0NT ☎ 0191 4272557 Gary.kirsop@southtynesidehomes.org.uk

Legal: Mr Mike Harding, Head of Legal, Town Hall & Civic Offices, Westoe Road, South Shields NE33 2RL ☎ 0191 424 7009

Legal: Mr Brian Scott, Head of Corporate Governance, Town Hall and Civic Offices, Westoe Road, South Shields NE33 2RL ☎ 0191 424 7200 🖷 0191 455 0208 ✉ brian.t.scott@southtyneside.gov.uk

Licensing: Mr George Mansbridge, Head of Planning, Housing, Transport & Regulatory Services, Town Hall and Civic Offices, Westoe Road, South Shields NE33 2RL ☎ 0191 4247566 ✉ george.mansbridge@southtyneside.gov.uk

Lifelong Learning: Mr Mike Conlon, Head - Corporate & Commercial Services, Town Hall and Civic Offices, Westoe Road, South Shields NE33 2RL ☎ 0191 427 7765 🖷 0191 427 0584 ✉ mike.conlon@southtyneside.gov.uk

Lifelong Learning: Mr Peter Cutts, Head of Education, Learning & Skills, Town Hall and Civic Offices, Westoe Road, South Shields NE33 2RL ☎ 0191 424 7697 ✉ peter.cutts@southtyneside.gov.uk

Lighting: Mr Caine Spence, Acting Commercial Services Manager, Middlefields, South Shields NE34 0NT ☎ 0191 427 2599 ✉ caine.spence@southtyneside.gov.uk

Lottery Funding, Charity and Voluntary: Mr Daniel Crawford, Regeneration Programmes Manager, Town Hall and Civic Offices, Westoe Road, South Shields NE33 2RL ☎ 0191 424 7672 🖷 0191 427 7171 ✉ daniel.crawford@southtyneside.gov.uk

Member Services: Mrs Ann Best, Service Lead - Democratic Services, Town Hall & Civic Offices, Westoe Road, South Shields NE33 2RL ☎ 0191 424 7257 ✉ ann.best@southtyneside.gov.uk

Member Services: Mr Brian Scott, Head of Corporate Governance, Town Hall and Civic Offices, Westoe Road, South Shields NE33 2RL ☎ 0191 424 7200 🖷 0191 455 0208 ✉ brian.t.scott@southtyneside.gov.uk

Parking: Mr Dave Elliott, Highways & Transportation Design Manager, Town Hall and Civic Offices, Westoe Road, South Shields NE33 2RL ☎ 0191 427 7501 ✉ dave.elliott@southtyneside.gov.uk

Partnerships: Mr Paul Robinson, Corporate Lead - Partnerships & Affairs, Town Hall & Civic Offices, Westoe Road, South Shields NE33 2RL ☎ 0191 424 7491 ✉ paul.robinson@southtyneside.gov.uk

Personnel / HR: Mr Graham Fells, Corporate Manager - HR, Town Hall and Civic Offices, Westoe Road, South Shields NE33 2RL ☎ 0191 424 7323 ✉ graham.fells@southtyneside.gov.uk

Planning: Mr George Mansbridge, Head of Planning, Housing, Transport & Regulatory Services, Town Hall and Civic Offices, Westoe Road, South Shields NE33 2RL ☎ 0191 424 7566 ✉ george.mansbridge@southtyneside.gov.uk

Planning: Mr George Mansbridge, Head of Planning, Housing, Transport & Regulatory Services, Town Hall and Civic Offices, Westoe Road, South Shields NE33 2RL ☎ 0191 424 6599 🖷 0191 427 7171 ✉ george.mansbridge@southtyneside.gov.uk

Procurement: Mr Mike Conlon, Head - Corporate & Commercial Services, Town Hall and Civic Offices, Westoe Road, South Shields NE33 2RL ☎ 0191 424 7765 🖷 0191 427 0584 ✉ mike.conlon@southtyneside.gov.uk

Recycling & Waste Minimisation: Mr Bob Cummins, Waste & Recycling Team Leader, Town Hall and Civic Offices, Westoe Road, South Shields NE33 2RL ☎ 0191 427 2656 ✉ bob.cummins@southtyneside.gov.uk

Regeneration: Mr Rick O'Farrell, Head of Regeneration, Town Hall and Civic Offices, Westoe Road, South Shields NE33 2RL ☎ 0191 424 7541 ✉ rick.o'farrell@southtyneside.gov.uk

Road Safety: Mr Dave Elliott, Highways & Transportation Design Manager, Town Hall and Civic Offices, Westoe Road, South Shields NE33 2RL ☎ 0191 427 7501 ✉ dave.elliott@southtyneside.gov.uk

Social Services: Mr Richard Burrows, Interim Head of Early Intervention & Safeguarding, Town Hall and Civic Offices, Westoe Road, South Shields NE33 2RL ☎ 0191 4244749 ✉ richard.burrows@southtyneside.gov.uk

Social Services: Mr Peter Cutts, Head of Education, Learning & Skills, Town Hall and Civic Offices, Westoe Road, South Shields NE33 2RL ☎ 0191 424 7697 ✉ peter.cutts@southtyneside.gov.uk

Social Services (Adult): Ms Tanya Robertson, Head - Marketing & Communications, Town Hall and Civic Offices, Westoe Road, South Shields NE33 2RL ☎ 0191 424 7817 ✉ tanya.robertson@southtyneside.gov.uk

Social Services (Adult): Ms Jane Robinson, Head of Adult Services, Kelly House, Campbell Park Road, Hebburn NE31 2SR ☎ 0191 427 1717 ✉ jane.robinson@southtyneside.gov.uk

Social Services (Adult): Ms Helen Watson, Corporate Director - Children, Adults & Families, Town Hall and Civic Offices, Westoe Road, South Shields NE33 2RL ☎ 0191 424 7701 🖷 0191 427 0584 ✉ helen.watson@southtyneside.gov.uk

Social Services (Children): Ms Helen Watson, Corporate Director - Children, Adults & Families, Town Hall and Civic Offices, Westoe Road, South Shields NE33 2RL ☎ 0191 424 7701 🖷 0191 427 0584 ✉ helen.watson@southtyneside.gov.uk

Staff Training: Mr Graham Fells, Corporate Manager - HR, Town Hall and Civic Offices, Westoe Road, South Shields NE33 2RL ☎ 0191 424 7323 ✉ graham.fells@southtyneside.gov.uk

Street Scene: Mr Bob Cummins, Waste & Recycling Team Leader, Town Hall and Civic Offices, Westoe Road, South Shields NE33 2RL ☎ 0191 427 2656 ✉ bob.cummins@southtyneside.gov.uk

Street Scene: Mr Ron Weetman, Acting Head of Sustainable Communities, Town Hall and Civic Offices, Westoe Road, South Shields NE33 2RL ☎ 0191 427 2652 ✉ ron.weetman@southtyneside.gov.uk

Town Centre: Mr Rick O'Farrell, Head of Regeneration, Town Hall and Civic Offices, Westoe Road, South Shields NE33 2RL ☎ 0191 424 7541 ✉ rick.o'farrell@southtyneside.gov.uk

Traffic Management: Mr Dave Elliott, Highways & Transportation Design Manager, Town Hall and Civic Offices, Westoe Road, South Shields NE33 2RL ☎ 0191 427 7501
dave.elliott@southtyneside.gov.uk

Transport: Mr Dave Elliott, Highways & Transportation Design Manager, Town Hall and Civic Offices, Westoe Road, South Shields NE33 2RL ☎ 0191 427 7501
dave.elliott@southtyneside.gov.uk

Transport Planner: Mr Dave Elliott, Highways & Transportation Design Manager, Town Hall and Civic Offices, Westoe Road, South Shields NE33 2RL ☎ 0191 427 7501
dave.elliott@southtyneside.gov.uk

Waste Collection and Disposal: Mr Bob Cummins, Waste & Recycling Team Leader, Town Hall and Civic Offices, Westoe Road, South Shields NE33 2RL ☎ 0191 427 2656
bob.cummins@southtyneside.gov.uk

Waste Collection and Disposal: Mr Andrew Whittaker, Waste Service Manager, Middlefields Depot, Hudson Street, South Shields NE34 0AD ☎ 0191 427 2063 🖷 0191 427 2061
andrew.whittaker@southtyneside.gov.uk

Waste Management: Mr Andrew Whittaker, Waste Service Manager, Middlefields Depot, Hudson Street, South Shields NE34 0AD ☎ 0191 427 2063 🖷 0191 427 2061
andrew.whittaker@southtyneside.gov.uk

MEMBERS OF THE COUNCIL (54)

***Mayor:* Leask**, Eileen (LAB - Horsley Hill)
cllr.eileen.leask@southtyneside.co.uk
***Leader of the Council:* Malcolm**, Iain (LAB - Horsley Hill)
cllr.iain.malcolm@southtyneside.co.uk
***Deputy Leader of the Council:* Kerr**, Alan (LAB - Monkton)
cllr.alan.kerr@southtyneside.co.uk
Anglin, John (LAB - Beacon and Bents)
john.anglin@southtyneside.gov.uk
Atkinson, Joan (LAB - Cleadon and East Boldon)
joan.atkinson@southtyneside.gov.uk
Bell, Joanne (LAB - Boldon Colliery)
cllr.joan.bell@southtyneside.co.uk
Boyack, Peter (LAB - Whitburn and Marsden)
cllr.peter.boyack@southtyneside.gov.uk
Brady, Bill (LAB - Whiteleas)
cllr.bill.brady@southtyneside.co.uk
Branley, Jane (IND - Westoe)
server@janebranley.co.uk
Butler, Mary (LAB - Hebburn North)
mary.butler@southtyneside.gov.uk
Cartwright, Melanie (LAB - Monkton)
melanie.cartwright@southtyneside.gov.uk
Clare, Michael (LAB - Simonside and Rekendyke)
cllr.michael.clare@southtyneside.co.uk
Cunningham, Fay (LAB - Bede)
fay.cunningham@southtyneside.gov.uk
Dix, Robert (LAB - Harton)
cllr.rob.dix@southtyneside.gov.uk
Dixon, Tracey (LAB - Whitburn and Marsden)
cllr.tracey.dixon@southtyneside.co.uk
Donaldson, Alexander (LAB - Cleadon Park)
cllr.alex.donaldson@southtyneside.gov.uk
Elsom, George (IND - Cleadon Park)
cllr.george.elsom@southtyneside.co.uk
Foreman, Jim (LAB - Cleadon Park)
cllr.jim.foreman@southtyneside.co.uk
Gibson, Ernest (LAB - Whiteleas)
cllr.ernest.gibson@southtyneside.co.uk
Harkus, Ian (LAB - Hebburn North)
ian.harkus@southtyneside.gov.uk
Harrison, Steven (IND - Fellgate and Hedworth)
cllr.edith.battye@southtyneside.co.uk
Hay, Pat (LAB - Harton)
pat.hay@southtyneside.gov.uk
Hemmer, Linda (IND - Fellgate and Hedworth)
cllr.linda.hemmer@southtyneside.gov.uk
Hobson, Gladys (LAB - West Park)
gladys.hobson@southtyneside.gov.uk
Lewell-Buck, Emma (LAB - Primrose)
cllr.emma.lewell@southtyneside.co.uk
Malcolm, Edward (LAB - Simonside and Rekendyke)
cllr.ed.malcolm@southtyneside.co.uk
Maxwell, Neil (LAB - Harton)
cllr.neil.maxwell@southtyneside.gov.uk
Maxwell, Nancy (LAB - Hebburn South)
cllr.nancy.maxwell@southtyneside.co.uk
McAtominey, Eddie (LAB - Hebburn South)
cllr.eddie.mcatominey@southtyneside.co.uk
McCabe, John (LAB - Hebburn South)
cllr.john.mccabe@southtyneside.co.uk
McMillan, Audrey (LAB - Beacon and Bents)
cllr.audrey.mcmillan@southtyneside.co.uk
Meeks, Arthur (LAB - Bede)
cllr.arthur.meeks@southtyneside.co.uk
Milburn, Jeffrey (CON - Cleadon and East Boldon)
cllr.jeffrey.milburn@southtyneside.gov.uk
Murphy, Sherie (LAB - Boldon Colliery)
cllr.sherie.murphy@southtyneside.gov.uk
Peacock, Margaret (LAB - Bede)
margaret.peacock@southtyneside.gov.uk
Perry, Jim (LAB - Primrose)
cllr.jim.perry@southtyneside.co.uk
Pigott, Thomas (LAB - Biddick and All Saints)
cllr.tom.pigott@southtyneside.co.uk
Porthouse, Richard (LAB - Hebburn North)
cllr.richard.porthouse@southtyneside.gov.uk
Potts, David (UKIP - Cleadon and East Boldon)
cllr.david.potts@southtyneside.co.uk
Proudlock, Lynne (LAB - Simonside and Rekendyke)
lynne.proudlock@southtyneside.gov.uk
Punchion, Olive (LAB - Biddick and All Saints)
cllr.olive.punchion@southtyneside.gov.uk
Purvis, Doreen (LAB - Whiteleas)
doreen.purvis@southtyneside.gov.uk
Sewell, Jim (LAB - Monkton)
cllr.jim.sewell@southtyneside.co.uk
Smith, Alan (LAB - Fellgate and Hedworth)
alan.smith@southtyneside.gov.uk
Spraggon, Sylvia (LAB - Whitburn and Marsden)
cllr.sylvia.spraggon@southtyneside.co.uk
Stephenson, Sheila (LAB - Westoe)
sheila.stephenson@southtyneside.gov.uk
Stephenson, Ken (LAB - Primrose)
cllr.ken.stephenson@southtyneside.gov.uk
Strike, Alison (LAB - Boldon Colliery)
cllr.alison.strike@southtyneside.co.uk
Walsh, Mark (LAB - Horsley Hill)

mark.walsh@southtyneside.gov.uk
Walsh, Anne (LAB - Biddick and All Saints)
cllr.anne.walsh@southtyneside.gov.uk
Watters, Bob (LAB - West Park)
cllr.bob.watters@southtyneside.gov.uk
Welsh, Joyce (LAB - West Park)
joyce.welsh@southtyneside.gov.uk
West, Alan (LAB - Westoe)
cllr.allan.west@southtyneside.gov.uk
Wood, John (LAB - Beacon and Bents)
cllr.john.wood@southtyneside.gov.uk

POLITICAL COMPOSITION
LAB: 48, IND: 4, CON: 1, UKIP: 1

CABINET
Leader: Mr Iain Malcolm
Deputy Leader: Mr Alan Kerr
Adult Social Care & Support: Mrs Emma Lewell-Buck
Area Management & Community Safety: Ms Tracey Dixon
Children, Young People & Families: Ms Joan Atkinson
Health & Wellbeing: Cllr Alan West
Housing & Transport: Mr Jim Foreman
Regeneration & Economy: Mr Michael Clare
Resources & Innovation: Mr Edward Malcolm

COMMITTEE CHAIRS
Audit: Mr Jeffrey Milburn
General Purposes: Mr Iain Malcolm
Overview & Scrutiny Co-ordinating & Call-in (Scrutiny): Mr Robert Dix
Pensions: Mr Jim Perry
Planning: Mr John Wood
Regulatory: Mr Arthur Meeks

SOUTHAMPTON CITY U

Southampton City Council, Civic Centre, Southampton SO14 7LY
☎ 023 8022 3855 🖷 023 8083 2817
city.information@southampton.gov.uk
www.southampton.gov.uk

FACTS & FIGURES
Police Authority: Hampshire Police Authority
Health Authority: NHS South West
Learning and Skills Council: South East
Parliamentary Constituencies: Romsey and Southampton North, Southampton, Itchen, Southampton, Test
EU Constituencies: South East
Election Frequency: Elections are by thirds
Twinning: Le Havre (France); Rems-Murr-Kreis (Germany)

PRINCIPAL OFFICERS
Chief Executive: Mr Alistair Neil, Chief Executive Officer, Civic Centre, Southampton SO14 7LY
alistair.neil@southampton.gov.uk

Assistant Chief Executive: Ms Dawn Baxendale, Assistant Chief Executive (Economic Development), Civic Centre, Southampton SO14 7LY ☎ 02380 917713
dawn.baxendale@southampton.gov.uk

Senior Management: Ms Margaret Geary, Head of Adult Housing & Community Care, Civic Centre, Southampton SO14 7LY ☎ 023 8083 2602 margaret.geary@southampton.gov.uk

Senior Management: Ms Francis Martin, Deputy Director - Environment & Economy, Civic Centre, Southampton SO14 7LY ☎ 023 8083 2602 francis.martin@southampton.gov.uk

Senior Management: Mr John Spiers, Head of Property & Procurement, Southbrook Rise, 4-8 Millbrook Road East, Southampton SO15 1GY ☎ 023 8083 4146
john.spiers@southampton.gov.uk

Senior Management: Mr Clive Webster, Director - Children's Services & Learning, Civic Centre, Southampton SO14 7LY ☎ 023 8083 2602 🖷 023 8083 3221
clive.webster@southampton.gov.uk

Best Value: Mr Paul Mansbridge, Associate Director, 1 Guildhall Square, Southampton SO14 7FP ☎ 023 8083 2635
paul.mansbridge@southampton.gov.uk

Building Control: Mr Neil Ferris, Building Control Partnership Manager, Civic Centre, Southampton SO14 7LP ☎ 023 8083 2781 🖷 023 8083 3200 neil.ferris@southampton.gov.uk

Catering Services: Mr Stephen Price, Head of City Catering Services, Civic Centre, Southampton SO14 7LY ☎ 023 8083 3087
stephen.price@southampton.gov.uk

Children / Youth Services: Ms Felicity Budgen, Head of Service - Children's Services & Learning, Civic Centre, Southampton SO14 7LY ☎ 023 8083 3021
felicity.budgen@southampton.gov.uk

Children / Youth Services: Mr Clive Webster, Director of Children's Services & Learning, Civic Centre, Southampton SO14 7LY ☎ 023 8083 2011 🖷 023 8083 3221
clive.webster@southampton.gov.uk

PR / Communications: Mr Ben White, Communications Director, Civic Centre, Southampton SO14 7LY ☎ 023 8083 3040
ben.white@southampton.gov.uk

Computer Management: Mr Kevin Foley, Head of IT Solutions, Civic Centre, Southampton SO14 7LY ☎ 023 8022 3855
kevin.foley@southampton.gov.uk

Consumer Protection and Trading Standards: Ms Francis Martin, Deputy Director - Environment & Economy, Civic Centre, Southampton SO14 7LY ☎ 023 8083 2602
francis.martin@southampton.gov.uk

Contracts: Mr John Spiers, Head of Property & Procurement, Southbrook Rise, 4-8 Millbrook Road East, Southampton SO15 1GY ☎ 023 8083 4146 john.spiers@southampton.gov.uk

Corporate Services: Mr Michael Thomas, Waste Strategy & Disposal Manager, City Depot, First Avenue, Millbrook, Southampton SO15 0LJ ☎ 023 8083 2466
michael.thomas@southampton.gov.uk

Customer Service: Mr Paul Medland, Head of Partnerships & Customer Services, Civic Centre, Southampton SO14 7LY ☎ 023 8083 2836 ✉ paul.medland@southampton.gov.uk

Customer Service: Mr Ben White, Communications Director, Civic Centre, Southampton SO14 7LY ☎ 023 8083 3040 ✉ ben.white@southampton.gov.uk

Direct Labour: Ms Francis Martin, Deputy Director - Environment & Economy, Civic Centre, Southampton SO14 7LY ☎ 023 8083 2602 ✉ francis.martin@southampton.gov.uk

Economic Development: Ms Dawn Baxendale, Assistant Chief Executive (Economic Development), Civic Centre, Southampton SO14 7LY ☎ 02380 917713 ✉ dawn.baxendale@southampton.gov.uk

Economic Development: Mr Jeff Walters, Economic Development Manager, Civic Centre, Southampton SO14 7LY ☎ 023 8083 2256 🖷 023 8083 2962 ✉ jeff.walters@southampton.gov.uk

Education: Mr Karl Limbert, Head of Infrastructure, Civic Centre, Southampton SO14 7LY ☎ 023 8091 7503 ✉ karl.limbert@southampton.gov.uk

Education: Mr Clive Webster, Director of Children's Services & Learning, Civic Centre, Southampton SO14 7LY ☎ 023 8083 2011 🖷 023 8083 3221 ✉ clive.webster@southampton.gov.uk

Electoral Registration: Ms Marijke Elst, Electoral Registration Manager, Civic Centre, Southampton SO14 7LY ☎ 023 8083 2422 ✉ marijke.elst@southampton.gov.uk

Emergency Planning: Mr Mike Jukes, Emergency Planning & Business Continuity Manager, City Depot, First Avenue, Millbrook, Southampton SO15 0LJ ☎ 023 8083 2089 ✉ mike.jukes@southampton.gov.uk

Emergency Planning: Mr Graham Wyeth, Emergency Planning & Business Continuity Manager, City Depot, First Avenue, Millbrook, Southampton SO15 0JL ☎ 023 8083 2089 🖷 023 8033 0696 ✉ graham.wyeth@southampton.gov.uk

Energy Management: Mr Jason Taylor, Energy Manager, 45 Castle Way, Southampton SO14 2PD ☎ 023 8022 3855 ✉ jason.taylor@southampton.gov.uk

Environmental Health: Ms Francis Martin, Deputy Director - Environment & Economy, Civic Centre, Southampton SO14 7LY ☎ 023 8083 2602 ✉ francis.martin@southampton.gov.uk

Environmental Health: Mr Mitch Sanders, Regulatory Services Senior Manager, Floor 5, 1 Guildhall Square, Southampton SO14 7FP ☎ 023 8083 3613 ✉ mitch.sanders@southampton.gov.uk

Estates, Property & Valuation: Ms Margaret Geary, Head of Adult Housing & Community Care, Civic Centre, Southampton SO14 7LY ☎ 023 8083 2602 ✉ margaret.geary@southampton.gov.uk

Events Manager: Mr Nigel Greene, Business Support & Events Manager, Civic Centre, Southampton SO14 7LY ☎ 023 8083 3419 ✉ nigel.greene@southampton.gov.uk

Facilities: Mr Charles Stewart, Civic Buildings Manager, Civic Centre, Southampton SO14 7LY ☎ 023 8083 2877 ✉ chez.stewart@southampton.gov.uk

Finance and Treasurer: Mr Andrew Lowe, Head of Finance, Civic Centre, Civic Centre Road, Southampton SO14 7LY ☎ 023 8083 2049 🖷 023 8083 3432 ✉ andew.lowe@southampton.gov.uk

Grounds Maintenance: Ms Francis Martin, Deputy Director - Environment & Economy, Civic Centre, Southampton SO14 7LY ☎ 023 8083 2602 ✉ francis.martin@southampton.gov.uk

Health and Safety: Ms Margaret Geary, Head of Adult Housing & Community Care, Civic Centre, Southampton SO14 7LY ☎ 023 8083 2602 ✉ margaret.smith@southampton.gov.uk

Housing: Ms Barbara Compton, Senior Manager - Skills, Economy & Housing Renewal, Civic Centre, Southampton SO14 7LY ☎ 023 8083 2155 🖷 023 8083 2136 ✉ barbara.compton@southampton.gov.uk

Housing: Mr Nick Cross, Senior Manager - Housing Services, Civic Centre, Southampton SO14 7LY ☎ 023 8083 2241 ✉ nick.cross@southampton.gov.uk

Housing: Mr Jon Dyer-Slade, Senior Manager - Street Scene & Community Safety, 1 Guildhal Square, Southampton SO14 7FP ☎ 023 8083 2873 🖷 023 8023 1384 ✉ jon.dyer-slade@southampton.gov.uk

Housing: Mr Mike Harris, Senior Manager - Leisure & Culture, Civic Centre, Civic Centre Road, Southampton SO14 7LP ☎ 023 8083 2438 🖷 023 8083 3382 ✉ mike.harris@southampton.gov.uk

Housing: Ms Francis Martin, Deputy Director - Environment & Economy, Civic Centre, Southampton SO14 7LY ☎ 023 8083 2602 ✉ francis.martin@southampton.gov.uk

Housing: Mr Jon Wallace, Head of Policy & Performance, Civic Centre, Civic Centre Road, Southampton SO14 7LY ☎ 023 8083 2602 🖷 023 8083 2817 ✉ jon.wallace@southampton.gov.uk

Housing Maintenance: Mr Nick Cross, Senior Manager - Housing Services, Civic Centre, Southampton SO14 7LY ☎ 023 8083 2241 ✉ nick.cross@southampton.gov.uk

Legal: Mr Mark Heath, Director of Corporate Services, Civic Centre, Southampton SO14 7LY ☎ 023 8083 2371 🖷 023 8083 2308 ✉ mark.heath@southampton.gov.uk

Legal: Mr Richard Ivory, Head of Legal HR & Democratic Services, Civic Centre, Southampton SO14 7LY ☎ 023 8083 2371 ✉ richard.ivory@southampton.gov.uk

Leisure and Cultural Services: Mr Mike Harris, Senior Manager - Leisure & Culture, Civic Centre, Civic Centre Road, Southampton SO14 7LP ☎ 023 8083 2438 🖷 023 8083 3382 ✉ mike.harris@southampton.gov.uk

Licensing: Mr John Burke, Licensing Manager, Civic Centre, Southampton SO14 7LY ☎ 023 8083 2306 🖷 023 8083 4061 ✉ john.burke@southampton.gov.uk

Lighting: Mr Mike Adams, PFI Lighting Technical Manager, Castle Way, Flr 1, Southampton SO14 2PD ☎ 01489 771790 🖷 023 8033 7020 ✉ mike.adams@southampton.gov.uk

Lottery Funding, Charity and Voluntary: Ms Maureen Read, Senior Co-ordinator for Infrastructure, 1 Guildhall Square, Southampton SO14 7FP ☎ 023 8083 4698 ✉ maureen.read@southampton.gov.uk

Member Services: Mrs Sandra Coltman, Democratic Services Manager, Democratic Services, Civic Centre, Southampton SO14 7LY ☎ 023 8083 2718 ✉ sandra.coltman@southampton.gov.uk

Member Services: Mr Mark Heath, Director of Corporate Services, Civic Centre, Southampton SO14 7LY ☎ 023 8083 2371 🖷 023 8083 2308 ✉ mark.heath@southampton.gov.uk

Parking: Mr Ken Byng, Enforcement & Parking Services Manager, Wyndham Court, Southampton SO14 7LY ☎ 023 8083 4622 ✉ ken.byng@southampton.gov.uk

Partnerships: Mr Paul Medland, Head of Partnerships & Customer Services, Civic Centre, Southampton SO14 7LY ☎ 023 8083 2836 ✉ paul.medland@southampton.gov.uk

Planning: Mr Tim Levenson, Head of City Development, 3rd Floor Marland House, 17 Civic Centre Road, Southampton SO14 7LT ☎ 023 8083 2550 🖷 023 8083 2962 ✉ tim.levenson@southampton.gov.uk

Planning: Mr Chris Lyons, Development Control Manager, Civic Centre, Southampton SO14 7LY ☎ 023 8083 3901

Planning: Mr Paul Nichols, Senior Manager - Planning, Transport & Sustainability, Civic Centre, Southampton SO14 7LY ☎ 023 8083 2553 ✉ paul.nichols@southampton.gov.uk

Procurement: Mr John Spiers, Head of Property & Procurement, Southbrook Rise, 4-8 Millbrook Road East, Southampton SO15 1GY ☎ 023 8083 4146 ✉ john.spiers@southampton.gov.uk

Public Libraries: Mr David Baldwin, Libraries Manager, Civic Centre, Southampton SO14 7LY ☎ 023 8083 2219 🖷 023 8036 6305 ✉ david.baldwin@southampton.gov.uk

Recycling & Waste Minimisation: Mr Richard Williams, Waste & Recycling Manager, City Depot & Recycling Park, First Avenue, Millbrook, Southampton SO15 0LJ ☎ 023 8083 4334 ✉ richard.williams@southampton.gov.uk

Regeneration: Ms Sue Jones, Manager - Estates Regeneration Projects, Civic Centre, Southampton SO14 7LY ☎ 023 8083 3929 ✉ sue.jones@southampton.gov.uk

Regeneration: Ms Liz Smith, Regeneration Officer, Civic Centre, Southampton SO14 7LY ☎ 023 8083 2925 ✉ liz.smith@southampton.gov.uk

Social Services: Ms Margaret Geary, Head of Adult Housing & Community Care, Civic Centre, Southampton SO14 7LY ☎ 023 8083 2602 ✉ margaret.geary@southampton.gov.uk

Social Services (Adult): Ms Jane Brentor, Head of Care Provisions, Marlands House, Flr 1, Civic Centre Road, Southampton SO14 7PR ☎ 023 8083 3439 🖷 023 8083 4809 ✉ jane.brentor@southampton.gov.uk

Social Services (Adult): Ms Margaret Geary, Head of Adult Housing & Community Care, Civic Centre, Southampton SO14 7LY ☎ 023 8083 2602 ✉ margaret.geary@southampton.gov.uk

Social Services (Children): Ms Felicity Budgen, Head of Service - Children's Services & Learning, Marlands House, Civic Centre Road, Southampton SO14 7PR ☎ 023 8083 3021 ✉ felicity.budgen@southampton.gov.uk

Social Services (Children): Mr Karl Limbert, Head of Infrastructure, Civic Centre, Southampton SO14 7LY ☎ 023 8091 7503 ✉ karl.limbert@southampton.gov.uk

Street Scene: Ms Francis Martin, Deputy Director - Environment & Economy, Civic Centre, Southampton SO14 7LY ☎ 023 8083 2602 ✉ francis.martin@southampton.gov.uk

Sustainable Communities: Ms Suki Sitaram, Senior Manager - Customer & Business Improvements, Civic Centre, Southampton SO14 7LY ☎ 023 8083 2060 ✉ suki.sitaram@southampton.gov.uk

Tourism: Mr Mike Harris, Senior Manager - Leisure & Culture, Civic Centre, Civic Centre Road, Southampton SO14 7LP ☎ 023 8083 2438 🖷 023 8083 3382 ✉ mike.harris@southampton.gov.uk

Traffic Management: Mr John Harvey, Highways Manager, 1 Guild Hall Sqaure, Southampton SO14 7FP ☎ 02380 833927 ✉ john.harvery@southampton.gov.uk

Transport: Mr Richard Williams, Waste & Recycling Manager, City Depot & Recycling Park, First Avenue, Millbrook, Southampton SO15 0LJ ☎ 023 8083 4334 ✉ richard.williams@southampton.gov.uk

Transport Planner: Ms Francis Martin, Deputy Director - Environment & Economy, Civic Centre, Southampton SO14 7LY ☎ 023 8083 2602 ✉ francis.martin@southampton.gov.uk

Waste Collection and Disposal: Mr Jon Dyer-Slade, Senior Manager - Street Scene & Community Safety, 1 Guildhall Square, Southampton SO14 7FP ☎ 023 8083 2873 🖷 023 8023 1384 ✉ jon.dyer-slade@southampton.gov.uk

Waste Collection and Disposal: Mr Michael Thomas, Waste Strategy & Disposal Manager, Civic Centre, Southampton SO14 7LY ☎ 023 8083 2466 ✉ michael.thomas@southampton.gov.uk

Waste Management: Mr Michael Thomas, Waste Strategy & Disposal Manager, Civic Centre, Southampton SO14 7LY ☎ 023 8083 2466 ✉ michael.thomas@southampton.gov.uk

MEMBERS OF THE COUNCIL (48)

***Mayor:* Burke**, Derek (LAB - Bevois)
councillor.d.burke@southampton.gov.uk

Sheriff: **White**, Ivan (CON - Bitterne Park)
councillor.i.white@southampton.gov.uk
Leader of the Council: **Williams**, Richard (LAB - Woolston)
councillor.r.williams@southampton.gov.uk
Group Leader: **Smith**, Royston (CON - Harefield)
councillor.r.smith@southampton.gov.uk
Group Leader: **Vinson**, Adrian (LD - Portswood)
councillor.a.vinson@southampton.gov.uk
Baillie, Peter (CON - Bitterne Park)
councillor.p.baillie@southampton.gov.uk
Barnes-Andrews, Stephen (LAB - Bevois)
councillor.s.barnes-andrews@southampton.gov.uk
Blatchford, Susan (LAB - Sholing)
councillor.S.Blatchford@southampton.gov.uk
Bogle, Sarah (LAB - Bargate)
councillor.s.bogle@southampton.gov.uk
Chaloner, Mark (LAB - Shirley)
councillor.m.chaloner@southampton.gov.uk
Claisse, Matthew (CON - Portswood)
Councillor.M.Claisse@southampton.gov.uk
Cunio, Carol (LAB - Woolston)
councillor.c.cunio@southampton.gov.uk
Daunt, Edward (CON - Harefield)
councillor.e.daunt@southampton.gov.uk
Fitzhenry, Daniel (CON - Harefield)
councillor.d.fitzhenry@southampton.gov.uk
Furnell, David (LAB - Millbrook)
councillor.d.furnell@southampton.gov.uk
Hannides, John (CON - Bassett)
councillor.j.hannides@southampton.gov.uk
Harris, Les (CON - Bassett)
Councillor.L.Harris@southampton.gov.uk
Harris, Beryl (CON - Bassett)
councillor.b.harris@southampton.gov.uk
Inglis, John (CON - Bitterne Park)
councillor.j.inglis@southampton.gov.uk
Jeffery, Daniel (LAB - Sholing)
councillor.d.jeffery@southampton.gov.uk
Kaur, Satvir (LAB - Shirley)
Councillor.S.Kaur@southampton.gov.uk
Keogh, Eamonn (LAB - Peartree)
councillor.e.keogh@southampton.gov.uk
Kolker, Anthony (CON - Sholing)
councillor.a.kolker@southampton.gov.uk
Laming, Georgina (LAB - Millbrook)
councillor.g.laming@southampton.gov.uk
Letts, Simon (LAB - Bitterne)
councillor.s.letts@southampton.gov.uk
Lewzey, Paul (LAB - Peartree)
councillor.p.lewzey@southampton.gov.uk
Lloyd, Mary (LAB - Bitterne)
councillor.m.lloyd@southampton.gov.uk
McEwing, Catherine (LAB - Redbridge)
councillor.c.mcewing@southampton.gov.uk
Mead, Raymond (CON - Shirley)
councillor.r.mead@southampton.gov.uk
Mintoff, Sharon (LAB - Swaythling)
councillor.s.mintoff@southamptong.gov.uk
Morrell, Keith (LAB - Coxford)
councillor.k.morrell@southampton.gov.uk
Moulton, Jeremy (CON - Freemantle)
councillor.j.moulton@southampton.gov.uk
Noon, John (LAB - Bargate)
Councillor.J.Noon@southampton.gov.uk
Norris, Linda (CON - Portswood)
councillor.l.norris@southampton.gov.uk
Paffey, Darren (LAB - Peartree)
Councillor.D.Paffey@Southampton.gov.uk
Parnell, Brian (CON - Freemantle)
councillor.b.parnell@southampton.gov.uk
Payne, Warwick (LAB - Woolston)
councillor.w.payne@southampton.gov.uk
Pope, Andrew (LAB - Redbridge)
Councillor.A.Pope@southampton.gov.uk
Rayment, Jacqui (LAB - Bevois)
councillor.j.rayment@southampton.gov.uk
Shields, Dave (LAB - Freemantle)
councillor.d.shields@southampton.gov.uk
Spicer, Sally (LAB - Coxford)
councillor.s.spicer@southampton.gov.uk
Stevens, Matthew (LAB - Bitterne)
councillor.m.stevens@southampton.gov.uk
Thomas, Don (LAB - Coxford)
councillor.d.thomas@southampton.gov.uk
Thorpe, Asa (LAB - Millbrook)
Councillor.A.Thorpe@Southampton.gov.uk
Tucker, Matt (LAB - Bargate)
councillor.m.tucker@southampton.gov.uk
Turner, Maureen (LD - Swaythling)
councillor.m.turner@southampton.gov.uk
Vassiliou, Spiros (CON - Swaythling)
Councillor.S.Vassiliou@southampton.gov.uk
Whitbread, Lee (LAB - Redbridge)
councillor.l.whitbread@southampton.gov.uk

POLITICAL COMPOSITION
LAB: 30, CON: 16, LD: 2

CABINET
Leader: Dr Richard Williams
Adult Services: Mr Matthew Stevens
Children's Services: Ms Sarah Bogle
Communities: Ms Jacqui Rayment
Efficiency & Improvement: Mr John Noon
Environment & Transport: Mr Asa Thorpe
Housing & Leisure Services: Mr Warwick Payne
Resources: Mr Simon Letts

COMMITTEE CHAIRS
Health Overview & Scrutiny: Mr Andrew Pope
Licensing: Ms Carol Cunio
Overview & Scrutiny Management: Mr Jeremy Moulton

SOUTHEND-ON-SEA U

Southend-on-Sea Borough Council, Civic Centre, Southend-on-Sea SS2 6ER ☎ 01702 215000 🖷 01702 215110
💻 www.southend.gov.uk

FACTS & FIGURES
Police Authority: Essex Police Authority
Health Authority: East of England Strategic Health Authority
Learning and Skills Council: Eastern
Parliamentary Constituencies: Rochford and Southend East, Southend West
EU Constituencies: Eastern
Election Frequency: Elections are by thirds
Twinning: Sopot (Poland)

PRINCIPAL OFFICERS

Chief Executive: Mr Robert Tinlin, Chief Executive & Town Clerk, PO Box 6, Civic Centre, Victoria Avenue, Southend-on-Sea SS2 6ER ☎ 01702 215101 🖷 01702 215594 ✉ robtinlin@southend.gov.uk

Senior Management: Ms Shazia Ullah, Head of Policy & Improvement, PO Box 6, Civic Centre, Victoria Avenue, Southend-on-Sea SS2 6ER ☎ 01702 215194 ✉ shaziaullah@southend.gov.uk

Best Value: Mr Tim Cusack, Strategy & Performance Manager, Civic Centre, Southend-on-Sea SS2 6ER ☎ 01702 534369 ✉ timcusack@southend.gov.uk

Building Control: Dr Peter Geraghty, Group Manager for Development & Building Control, Civic Centre, Southend-on-Sea SS2 6ER ☎ 01702 215339 ✉ petergeraghty@southend.gov.uk

Children / Youth Services: Ms Sue Cook, Head of Specialist Children's Services, Civic Centre, Victoria Avenue, Southend-on-Sea SS2 6ER ☎ 01702 215000 ✉ suecook@southend.gov.uk

Children / Youth Services: Ms Sue Hadley, Head of Children's Commissioning, Civic Centre, Southend-on-Sea SS2 6ER ☎ 01702 215955 ✉ sue.hadley@southend.gov.uk

PR / Communications: Ms Kirsty Horseman, Media & Communications Manager, Civic Centre, Southend-on-Sea SS2 6ER ☎ 01702 215110 🖷 01702 215465 ✉ kirstyhorseman@southend.gov.uk

Community Planning: Ms Jacqui Lansley, Head of Community Strategy & Development, Civic Centre, Southend-on-Sea SS2 6ER ☎ 01702 534611 ✉ jacquilansley@southend.gov.uk

Community Safety: Mr Simon Ford, Community Safety Manager, Civic Centre, Victoria Avenue, Southend-on-Sea SS2 6ER ☎ 01702 215185 ✉ simonford@southend.gov.uk

Computer Management: Mr Laurence Cops, Group Manager - ICT, Civic Centre, Southend-on-Sea SS2 6ER ☎ 01702 534963 ✉ laurencecops@southend.gov.uk

Consumer Protection and Trading Standards: Mr Dipti Patel, Head of Public Protection, Civic Centre, Southend-on-Sea SS2 6ER ☎ 01702 215325 ✉ diptipatel@southend.gov.uk

Corporate Services: Ms Sally Holland, Corporate Director - Support Services, Civic Centre, Victoria Avenue, Southend-on-Sea SS2 6ER ☎ 01702 215000 ✉ sallyholland@southend.gov.uk

Customer Service: Mr Nick Corrigan, Head of Customer Services, Civic Centre, Victoria Avenue, Southend-on-Sea SS2 6ER ☎ 01702 215000 ✉ nickcorrigan@southend.gov.uk

Economic Development: Ms Anita Thornberry, Head of Enterprise, Tourism & Regeneration, Civic Centre, Southend-on-Sea SS2 6ER ☎ 01702 215648 ✉ anitathornberry@southend.gov.uk

Education: Mr Paul Greenhalgh, Corporate Director - Children & Learning, PO Box 6, Civic Centre, Victoria Avenue, Southend-on-Sea SS2 6ER ☎ 01702 215000 ✉ paulgreenhalgh@southend.gov.uk

Education: Ms Sue Hadley, Head of Children's Commissioning & Learning Infrastructure, Civic Centre, Southend-on-Sea SS2 6ER ☎ 01702 215000 ✉ suehadley@southend.gov.uk

Education: Ms Jane Theadom, Head of School Support & Preventative Services, Civic Centre, Victoria Avenue, Southend-on-Sea SS2 6ER ☎ 01702 215000 ✉ janetheadom@southend.gov.uk

Electoral Registration: Mr Colin Gamble, Group Manager - Democratic Services, Civic Centre, Southend-on-Sea SS2 6ER ☎ 01702 534820 🖷 01702 215107 ✉ colingamble@southend.gov.uk

Emergency Planning: Mr Keith Holden, Emergency Planning Officer, PO Box 6, Civic Centre, Victoria Avenue, Southend-on-Sea SS2 6ER ☎ 01702 215023 ✉ keithholden@southend.gov.uk

Energy Management: Mr Pete Harmsworth, Energy Officer, Civic Centre, Southend-on-Sea SS2 6ER ☎ 01702 215190 ✉ peteharmsworth@southend.gov.uk

Environmental / Technical Services: Mr Andy Lewis, Corporate Director - Enterprise, Tourism & the Environment, PO Box 6, Civic Centre, Victoria Avenue, Southend-on-Sea SS2 6ER ☎ 01702 215100 ✉ andrewlewis@southend.gov.uk

Environmental Health: Ms Dipti Patel, Head of Public Protection & Waste, Civic Centre, Victoria Avenue, Southend-on-Sea SS2 6ER ☎ 01702 215000 ✉ diptipatel@southend.gov.uk

European Liaison: Mr Mark Murphy, Regeneration Services Manager, Civic Centre, Southend-on-Sea SS2 6ER ☎ 01702 215429 🖷 01702 215707 ✉ markmurphy@southend.gov.uk

Events Manager: Ms Lisa Ferne, Tourism & Events Manager, Civic Centre, Southend-on-Sea SS2 6ER ☎ 01702 215119 ✉ lisaferne@southend.gov.uk

Facilities: Ms Karen Wright, Group Manager - Access to Services, Civic Centre, Victoria Avenue, Southend-on-Sea SS2 6ER ☎ 01702 215000 ✉ karenwright@southend.gov.uk

Finance and Treasurer: Mr Joe Chesterton, Head of Finance & Resources, Civic Centre, Victoria Avenue, Southend-on-Sea SS2 6ER ☎ 01702 215000 ✉ joechesterton@southend.gov.uk

Finance and Treasurer: Ms Linda Everard, Head of Internal Audit, Civic Centre, Southend-on-Sea SS2 6ER ☎ 01702 215215 ✉ lindaeverard@southend.gov.uk

Grounds Maintenance: Mr Graham Owen, Health & Safety Officer, Civic Centre, Southend-on-Sea SS2 6ER ☎ 01702 215350 ✉ grahamowen@southend.gov.uk

Health and Safety: Mr Lee Colby, Health & Safety Officer, Civic Centre, Southend-on-Sea SS2 6ER ☎ 01702 215000

leecolby@southend.gov.uk

Highways: Mr Mehmet Mazhar, Group Manager - Traffic & Highways, Civic Centre, Southend-on-Sea SS2 6ER ☎ 01702 215369 mehmetmazhar@southend.gov.uk

Local Area Agreement: Mr Ade Butteriss, Strategy & Performance Manager, Civic Centre, Victoria Avenue, Southend-on-Sea SS2 6ER ☎ 01702 215187 adebutteriss@southend.gov.uk

Legal: Mr John Williams, Head of Legal & Democratic Services, Civic Centre, Southend-on-Sea SS2 6ER ☎ 01702 215102 🖷 01702 215110 johnwilliams@southend.gov.uk

Leisure and Cultural Services: Mr Nick Harris, Head of Culture, Civic Centre, Victoria Avenue, Southend-on-Sea SS2 6ER ☎ 01702 215000 nickharris@southend.gov.uk

Licensing: Mr Carl Robinson, Group Manager - Regulatory Services, Civic Centre, Southend-on-Sea SS2 6ER ☎ 01702 215156 carlrobinson@southend.gov.uk

Lifelong Learning: Mr Paul Greenhalgh, Corporate Director - Children & Learning, PO Box 6, Civic Centre, Victoria Avenue, Southend-on-Sea SS2 6ER ☎ 01702 215000 paulgreenhalgh@southend.gov.uk

Lottery Funding, Charity and Voluntary: Ms Lysane Eddy, Partnerships Manager, Civic Centre, Southend-on-Sea SS2 6ER ☎ 01702 215111 lysanneeddy@southend.gov.uk

Member Services: Mr Colin Gamble, Group Manager - Democratic Services, Civic Centre, Southend-on-Sea SS2 6ER ☎ 01702 534820 🖷 01702 215107 colingamble@southend.gov.uk

Member Services: Mr John Williams, Head of Legal & Democratic Services, Civic Centre, Southend-on-Sea SS2 6ER ☎ 01702 215102 🖷 01702 215110 johnwilliams@southend.gov.uk

Parking: Mr Derek Kenyon, Parking Manager, Civic Centre, Southend-on-Sea SS2 6ER ☎ 01702 534960 derekkenyon@southend.gov.uk

Partnerships: Ms Lysane Eddy, Partnerships Manager, Civic Centre, Southend-on-Sea SS2 6ER ☎ 01702 215111 lysanneeddy@southend.gov.uk

Personnel / HR: Ms Joanna Ruffle, Interim Head of People & Change, Civic Centre, Southend-on-Sea SS2 6ER ☎ 01702 215393; 01708 432181 joannaruffle@southend.gov.uk; joanna.ruffle@havering.gov.uk

Planning: Mr Andrew Meddle, Head of Planning & Transport, Civic Centre, Southend-on-Sea SS2 6ER ☎ 01702 215332 andrewmeddle@southend.gov.uk

Public Libraries: Mr Simon May, Libraries Services Manager, Civic Centre, Southend-on-Sea SS2 6ER ☎ 01702 534101 simonmay@southend.gov.uk

Recycling & Waste Minimisation: Ms Dipti Patel, Head of Public Protection & Waste, Civic Centre, Victoria Avenue, Southend-on-Sea SS2 6ER ☎ 01702 215000 diptipatel@southend.gov.uk

Regeneration: Ms Anita Thornberry, Head of Enterprise, Tourism & Regeneration, Civic Centre, Victoria Avenue, Southend-on-Sea SS2 6ER ☎ 01702 215000 anitathornberry@southend.gov.uk

Social Services: Mr Simon Leftley, Corporate Director - Adult & Community Services, Civic Centre, Victoria Avenue, Southend-on-Sea SS2 6ER ☎ 01702 215000 simonleftley@southend.gov.uk

Social Services (Adult): Mr Mike Boyle, Head of Adult Commissioning, Civic Centre, Southend-on-Sea SS2 6ER ☎ 01702 215612 martinelliott@southend.gov.uk

Social Services (Children): Ms Sue Cook, Head of Specialist Children's Services, Civic Centre, Victoria Avenue, Southend-on-Sea SS2 6ER ☎ 01702 215000 suecook@southend.gov.uk

Staff Training: Ms Joanna Ruffle, Interim Head of People & Change, Civic Centre, Southend-on-Sea SS2 6ER ☎ 01702 215393; 01708 432181 joannaruffle@southend.gov.uk; joanna.ruffle@havering.gov.uk

Street Scene: Mrs Marzia Abel, Town Centre Manager, Civic Centre, Southend-on-Sea SS2 6ER ☎ 01702 215448 🖷 01702 215707 marziaabel@southend.gov.uk

Sustainable Communities: Mr Mark Murphy, Regeneration Services Manager, Civic Centre, Southend-on-Sea SS2 6ER ☎ 01702 215429 🖷 01702 215707 markmurphy@southend.gov.uk

Sustainable Development: Mr Chris Livemore, Sustainable Officer, Civic Centre, Southend-on-Sea SS2 6ER ☎ 01702 215429 chrislivemore@southend.gov.uk

Tourism: Ms Anita Thornberry, Head of Enterprise, Tourism & Regeneration, Civic Centre, Victoria Avenue, Southend-on-Sea SS2 6ER ☎ 01702 215000 anitathornberry@southend.gov.uk

Town Centre: Mrs Marzia Abel, Town Centre Manager, Civic Centre, Southend-on-Sea SS2 6ER ☎ 01702 215448 🖷 01702 215707 marziaabel@southend.gov.uk

Traffic Management: Mr Andrew Meddle, Head of Planning & Transport, Civic Centre, Southend-on-Sea SS2 6ER ☎ 01702 215332 andrewmeddle@southend.gov.uk

Transport: Mr Andrew Meddle, Head of Planning & Transport, Civic Centre, Southend-on-Sea SS2 6ER ☎ 01702 215332 andrewmeddle@southend.gov.uk

Transport Planner: Mr Andrew Meddle, Head of Planning & Transport, Civic Centre, Southend-on-Sea SS2 6ER ☎ 01702 215332 andrewmeddle@southend.gov.uk

Total Place: Ms Lysane Eddy, Partnerships Manager, Civic Centre, Southend-on-Sea SS2 6ER ☎ 01702 215111 lysanneeddy@southend.gov.uk

Waste Collection and Disposal: Ms Dipti Patel, Head of Public

Protection & Waste, Civic Centre, Victoria Avenue, Southend-on-Sea SS2 6ER ☎ 01702 215000 ✉ diptipatel@southend.gov.uk

Waste Management: Mr John Whiddon, Project Manager - Waste Solutions, Civic Centre, Southend-on-Sea SS2 6ER ☎ 01702 215710 🖷 01702 339607 ✉ johnwhiddon@southend.gov.uk

MEMBERS OF THE COUNCIL (52)

***Mayor:* Carr**, Sally (CON - St Luke's)
cllrcarr@southend.gov.uk
***Deputy Mayor:* Kelly**, Brian (CON - Southchurch)
cllrkelly@southend.gov.uk
***Leader of the Council:* Holdcroft**, Nigel (CON - West Leigh)
cllrholdcroft@southend.gov.uk
***Deputy Leader of the Council:* Lamb**, John (CON - West Leigh)
cllrlamb@southend.gov.uk
***Group Leader:* Gilbert**, Ian (LAB - Victoria)
cllrgilbert@southend.gov.uk
***Group Leader:* Terry**, Martin (IND - Westborough)
cllrterry@southend.gov.uk
Assenheim, Michael (IND - Shoeburyness)
cllrassenheim@southend.gov.uk
Aylen, Stephen (CON - Belfairs)
cllraylen@southend.gov.uk
Ayling, Brian (IND - St Luke's)
cllrayling@southend.gov.uk
Betson, Mary (LD - Prittlewell)
cllrbetson@southend.gov.uk
Borton, Margaret (LAB - Victoria)
cllrborton@southend.gov.uk
Brown, Richard (CON - Chalkwell)
cllrbrown@southend.gov.uk
Burdett, Louise (CON - Kursaal)
cllrburdett@southend.gov.uk
Byford, Trevor (CON - Eastwood Park)
cllrbyford@southend.gov.uk
Caunce, Maria (CON - Milton)
cllrcaunce@southend.gov.uk
Chalk, Anne (IND - Shoeburyness)
cllrchalk@southend.gov.uk
Collins, Paul (LD - Westborough)
cllrcollins@southend.gov.uk
Courtenay, James (CON - Blenheim Park)
cllrcourtenay@southend.gov.uk
Cox, Tony (CON - West Shoebury)
cllrcox@southend.gov.uk
Crystall, Alan (LD - Leigh)
cllrcrystall@southend.gov.uk
Day, Elizabeth (CON - West Shoebury)
cllreday@southend.gov.uk
Delaney, Tony (IND - Southchurch)
cllrdelaney@southend.gov.uk
Evans, Margaret (CON - Belfairs)
cllrevans@southend.gov.uk
Flewitt, Mark (CON - St Laurence)
cllrflewitt@southend.gov.uk
Garston, David (CON - Southchurch)
cllrdgarston@southend.gov.uk
Garston, Jonathan (CON - Milton)
cllrjgartson@southend.gov.uk
Godwin, Barry (LD - Leigh)
cllrgodwin@southend.gov.uk
Grimwade, Mike (LD - Prittlewell)
cllrgrimwade@southend.gov.uk
Habermel, Stephen (CON - Chalkwell)
cllrhabermel@southend.gov.uk
Hadley, Roger (CON - Shoeburyness)
cllrhadley@southend.gov.uk
Holland, Ann (CON - Southchurch)
cllrholland@southend.gov.uk
Horrigan, Gwendoline (CON - West Leigh)
cllrhorrigan@southend.gov.uk
Jarvis, Derek (CON - West Shoebury)
cllrjarvis@southend.gov.uk
Jones, Adam (CON - St Laurence)
cllrjones@southend.gov.uk
Jones, Anne (LAB - Kursaal)
cllrannejones@southend.gov.uk
Kaye, Alex (IND - Thorpe)
cllrkaye@southend.gov.uk
Lewin, George (LD - St Laurence)
cllrlewin@southend.gov.uk
Longley, Graham (LD - Blenheim Park)
cllrlongley@southend.gov.uk
McMahon, Judith (LAB - Kursaal)
CllrMcMahon@southend.gov.uk
Morgan, Ric (LD - Prittlewell)
cllrmorgan@southend.gov.uk
Moring, Andrew (CON - Eastwood Park)
cllrmoring@southend.gov.uk
Norman, David (LAB - Victoria)
cllrdnorman@southend.gov.uk
Robertson, Ian (CON - Chalkwell)
cllrirobertson@southend.gov.uk
Russell, Duncan (LD - Blenheim Park)
cllrrussell@southend.gov.uk
Salter, Lesley (CON - Belfairs)
cllrsalter@southend.gov.uk
Stafford, Mike (IND - Thorpe)
cllrstafford@southend.gov.uk
Van Looy, Paul (IND - St Luke's)
cllrvanlooy@southend.gov.uk
Velmurugan, Marimuthu (IND - Westborough)
cllrvelmurugan@southend.gov.uk
Walker, Christopher (CON - Eastwood Park)
cllrwalker@southend.gov.uk
Ware-Lane, Julian (LAB - Milton)
cllrware-lane@southend.gov.uk
Wexham, Peter (LD - Leigh)
cllrwexham@southend.gov.uk
Woodley, Ronald (IND - Thorpe)
cllrwoodley@southend.gov.uk

POLITICAL COMPOSITION

CON: 26, IND: 10, LD: 10, LAB: 6

CABINET

Leader / Policy & Finance: Mr Nigel Holdcroft
Deputy Leader: Mr John Lamb
Adult Social Care, Health & Housing: Mrs Lesley Salter
Children & Learning: Mr Mark Flewitt
Corporate Support Services: Mr Andrew Moring
Planning: Mr Jonathan Garston
Culture & Tourism: Mr Derek Jarvis
Public Protection, Waste & Transport: Mr Tony Cox

COMMITTEE CHAIRS

Audit: Mr Paul Collins
Community Services & Culture: Mrs Alex Kaye
Development Control: Mr David Norman
Economy & Environmental Scrutiny: Mr Ronald Woodley
General Purposes: Mr Christopher Walker
Licensing: Mrs Margaret Evans
Standards: Mrs Ann Holland

SOUTHWARK L

Southwark London Borough Council, 160 Tooley Street, London Bridge, London SE1 2TZ ☎ 020 7525 5000
www.southwark.gov.uk

FACTS & FIGURES

Police Authority: Metropolitan Police Authority
Health Authority: NHS London
Learning and Skills Council: London
Parliamentary Constituencies: Bermondsey and Old Southwark, Camberwell and Peckham, Dulwich and West Norwood
EU Constituencies: London
Election Frequency: Elections are of whole council
Twinning: Clichy (France); Langenhagen (Germany)

PRINCIPAL OFFICERS

Chief Executive: Mrs Eleanor Kelly, Acting Chief Executive, 160 Tooley Street, London Bridge, London SE1 2TZ ☎ 020 7525 7171
eleanor.kelly@southwark.gov.uk

Senior Management: Ms Romi Bowen, Strategic Director of Children's Services, Southwark Council, 2nd Floor, Tooley Street, London Bridge, London SE1 2QH ☎ 020 7525 0338
romi.bowen@southwark.gov.uk

Senior Management: Ms Deborah Collins, Strategic Director of Communities Law & Governance, Southwark Council, 2nd Floor, Tooley Street, London Bridge, London SE1 2QH ☎ 020 7525 7630 deborah.collins@southwark.gov.uk

Senior Management: Mr Stuart Robinson-Marshall, Head of Service Development, Southwark Council, 3rd Floor, HUB 42, 160 Tooley Street, London SE1 2QH ☎ 020 7525 0703

Senior Management: Ms Gerri Scott, Strategic Director of Housing, Southwark Council, 2nd Floor, Tooley Street, London Bridge, London SE1 2QH ☎ 020 7525 7464
gerri.scott@southwark.gov.uk

Senior Management: Ms Susanna White, Strategic Director of Health & Community Services, Southwark Council, 1st Floor, Tooley Street, London Bridge, London SE1 2QH ☎ 020 7525 3890 susanna.white@southwark.gov.uk

Senior Management: Mr Duncan Whitfield, Finance Director, Southwark Council, 2nd Floor, Tooley Street, London Bridge, London SE1 2QH ☎ 020 7525 7180
duncan.whitfield@southwark.gov.uk

Access Officer / Social Services (Disability): Mr Stephen Douglass, Head of Community Engagement, Southwark Council, 2nd Floor, Tooley Street, London Bridge, London SE1 2QH ☎ 020 7525 0886 stephen.douglass@southwark.gov.uk

Building Control: Mr Peter Card, Head of Building Control, Southwark Council, 5th Floor, Tooley Street, London SE1 2QH ☎ 020 7525 5588 peter.card@southwark.gov.uk

Civil Registration: Ms Marcia Mitchell, Senior Registration Officer, Registrar Section, 34 Peckham Road, London SE5 8UB ☎ 020 7525 7474 📠 020 7525 7652
marcia.mitchell@southwark.gov.uk

PR / Communications: Mr Robin Campbell, Head of Communications, Southwark Council, 2nd Floor, Tooley Street, London Bridge, London SE1 2QH ☎ 020 7525 7023
robin.campbell@southwark.gov.uk

Community Safety: Mr Jonathon Toy, Head of Community Safety & Enforcement, Southwark Council, 3rd Floor, Tooley Street, London Bridge, London SE1 2QH ☎ 020 7525 1479
jonathon.toy@southwark.gov.uk

Consumer Protection and Trading Standards: Mr Des Waters, Head of Public Realm, Southwark Council, 3rd Floor, Tooley Street, London Bridge, London SE1 2QH ☎ 020 7525 2080
des.waters@southwark.gov.uk

Contracts: Mr George Amery, Senior Systems & Processes Officer, Southwark Council, 1st Floor, Tooley Street, London Bridge, London SE1 2QH ☎ 020 7525 3436
george.amery@southwark.gov.uk

Corporate Services: Mr Graeme Gordon, Head of Corporate Strategy, Southwark Council, 2nd Floor, Tooley Street, London Bridge, London SE1 2QH ☎ 020 7525 7384

Customer Service: Mr Dominic Cain, Assistant Director - Revenues & Benefits, Southwark Council, 1st Floor, Tooley Street, London Bridge, London SE1 2QH ☎ 020 7525 0636
dominic.cain@southwark.gov.uk

Customer Service: Mr Robin Campbell, Head of Communications, Southwark Council, 2nd Floor, Tooley Street, London Bridge, London SE1 2QH ☎ 020 7525 7023
robin.campbell@southwark.gov.uk

Education: Ms Maggie Donnellan, Head of Primary Achievement, Southwark Council , 1st Floor, PCT, 160 Tooley Street, London SE1 2HZ ☎ 020 7525 5030
maggie.donnellan@southwark.gov.uk

Education: Mr Glenn Garcia, Head of Pupil Access, Southwark Council, 4th Floor, Tooley Street, London Bridge, London SE1 2QH ☎ 020 7525 2717 glenn.garcia@southwark.gov.uk

Education: Ms Sara Waller, Project Director of Aylesbury Regeneration, Southwark Council, 5th Floor, Tooley Street, London Bridge, London SE1 1QH ☎ 020 7525 5524
sara.waller@southwark.gov.uk

Electoral Registration: Ms Frances Biggs, Electoral Services & Land Charges Manager, Southwark Council, 2nd Floor, Tooley Street, London Bridge, London SE1 2QH ☎ 020 7525 7694
frances.biggs@southwark.gov.uk

Emergency Planning: Mr Ken Matthews, Emergency Planning Manager, Southwark Council, 5th Floor, Tooley Street, London Bridge, London SE1 2QH ☎ 020 7525 4959 ✉ ken.matthews@southwark.gov.uk

Energy Management: Mr Ian Smith, Acting Head of Sustainable Services, Southwark Council , Manor Place Depot, 30-34 Penrose Street, London SE17 3DW ☎ 020 7525 2484 📠 020 7525 3636 ✉ ian.smith@southwark.gov.uk

Environmental / Technical Services: Ms Gill Davies, Strategic Director of Environment, Southwark Council, 2nd Floor, Tooley Street, London Bridge, London SE1 2QH ☎ 020 7525 0899 ✉ gill.davies@southwark.gov.uk

Estates, Property & Valuation: Mr Stephen Platts, Director of Regeneration, Southwark Council, 5th Floor, Tooley Street, London Bridge, London SE1 2QH ☎ 020 7525 5640 ✉ stephen.platts@southwark.gov.uk

European Liaison: Ms Lisa Marie Bowles, European & Funding Officer, Southwark Council, 1st Floor, Tooley Street, London Bridge, London SE1 2QH ☎ 020 7525 1022 ✉ lisa-marie.bowles@southwark.gov.uk

Events Manager: Mr Paul Cowell, Events & Film Manager, Southwark Council, 2nd Floor, Tooley Street, London Bridge, London SE1 2QH ✉ paul.cowell@southwark.gov.uk

Facilities: Mr Joe Heming, Facilities Manager, Southwark Council, 2nd Floor, Tooley Street, London Bridge, London SE1 2QH ☎ 020 7525 7335 ✉ joe.heming@southwark.gov.uk

Finance and Treasurer: Mr Duncan Whitfield, Finance Director, Southwark Council, 2nd Floor, Tooley Street, London Bridge, London SE1 2QH ☎ 020 7525 7180 ✉ duncan.whitfield@southwark.gov.uk

Fleet Management: Mr Ian Smith, Acting Head of Sustainble Services, Manor Place Depot, 30-34 Penrose Street, London SE17 3DW ☎ 020 7525 2484 ✉ ian.smith@southwark.gov.uk

Health and Safety: Mr Chris Rackley, Health & Safety Strategy Manager, Southwark Council, 2nd Floor, Tooley Street, London Bridge, London SE1 2QH ☎ 020 7525 7001 ✉ chris.rackley@southwark.gov.uk

Housing: Mr Martin Green, Head of Home Ownership & Tenant Management, Southwark Council, 3rd Floor, Tooley Street, London Bridge, London SE1 2QH ☎ 020 7525 1418

Housing: Ms Miny Jansen, Housing Options Manager, Southwark Council, 25 - 27 Bournemouth Road, London SE15 4UJ ☎ 020 7525 4089 ✉ miny.jansen@southwark.gov.uk

Housing: Mr Jonathan Joseph, Head of Community Housing Services, 17 Bournemouth Road, Peckham, London SE15 4UJ ☎ 020 7525 0991 ✉ jonathan.joseph@southwark.gov.uk

Housing: Ms Gerri Scott, Strategic Director of Housing, Southwark Council, 2nd Floor, Tooley Street, London Bridge, London SE1 2QH ☎ 020 7525 7464 ✉ gerri.scott@southwark.gov.uk

Housing Maintenance: Ms Gill Davies, Strategic Director of Environment, Southwark Council, 2nd Floor, Tooley Street, London Bridge, London SE1 2QH ☎ 020 7525 0899 ✉ gill.davies@southwark.gov.uk

Legal: Ms Shelley Burke, Head of Overview & Scrutiny, Southwark Council, 2nd Floor, Tooley Street, London Bridge, London SE1 2QH ☎ 020 7525 7344 ✉ shelley.burke@southwark.gov.uk

Legal: Ms Deborah Collins, Strategic Director of Communities Law & Governance, Southwark Council, 2nd Floor, Tooley Street, London Bridge, London SE1 2QH ☎ 020 7525 7630 ✉ deborah.collins@southwark.gov.uk

Legal: Ms Doreen Forrester-Brown, Head of Legal Services, Southwark Council, 2nd Floor, Tooley Street, London Bridge, London SE1 2QH ☎ 020 7525 7502 ✉ doreen.forrester-brown@southwark.gov.uk

Leisure and Cultural Services: Ms Rebecca Towers, Parks & Open Spaces Manager, Southwark Council, 3rd Floor, Tooley Street, London Bridge, London SE1 2QH ☎ 020 7525 0771 ✉ rebecca.towers@southwark.gov.uk

Leisure and Cultural Services: Mr Adrian Whittle, Head of Culture, Libraries, Learning & Leisure, Southwark Council, 3rd Floor, Tooley Street, London Bridge, London SE1 2QH ☎ 020 7525 1577 ✉ adrian.whittle@southwark.gov.uk

Leisure and Cultural Services: Mr Jay Yeats, Head of Leisure & Wellbeing, Southwark Council, 3rd Floor, Tooley Street, London Bridge, London SE1 2QH ☎ 020 7525 0891 ✉ jay.yeats@southwark.gov.uk

Licensing: Mr Richard Parkins, Licensing Unit Manager, Southwark Council, 3rd Floor, Tooley Street, London Bridge, London SE1 2QH ☎ 020 7525 5767 ✉ richard.parkins@southwark.gov.uk

Lottery Funding, Charity and Voluntary: Ms Bonnie Royal, Commissioning & Voluntary Sector Support Manager, Southwark Council, 2nd Floor, Tooley Street, London Bridge, London SE1 2QH ☎ 020 7525 7389 ✉ bonnie.royal@southwark.gov.uk

Member Services: Mr Graham Love, Head of Democratic Services, Southwark Council, 2nd Floor, Tooley Street, London Bridge, London SE1 2QH ☎ 020 7525 0617 ✉ graham.love@southwark.gov.uk

Parking: Mr David Sole, Parking Service & Development Manager, Southwark Council, 3rd Floor, Tooley Street, London Bridge, London SE1 2QH ☎ 020 7525 2037 ✉ david.sole@southwark.gov.uk

Personnel / HR: Mr John Howard, Head of Organisational Development, Southwark Council, 2nd Floor, Tooley Street, London Bridge, London SE1 2QH ☎ 020 7525 1253 ✉ john.howard@southwark.gov.uk

Personnel / HR: Mr Bernard Nawrat, Head of Human Resources, Southwark Council, 2nd Floor, Tooley Street, London Bridge, London SE1 2QH ☎ 020 7525 7185 ✉ bernard.nawrat@southwark.gov.uk

Procurement: Mrs Jennifer Seeley, Deputy Finance Director, Southwark Council, 2nd Floor, Tooley Street, London Bridge, London SE1 2QH ☎ 020 7525 0695 ✉ jennifer.seeley@southwark.gov.uk

Public Libraries: Mr Adrian Whittle, Head of Culture, Libraries, Learning & Leisure, Southwark Council, 2nd Floor, Tooley Street, London Bridge, London SE1 2QH ☎ 020 7525 1577 ✉ adrian.whittle@southwark.gov.uk

Recycling & Waste Minimisation: Ms Gill Davies, Strategic Director of Environment, Southwark Council, 2nd Floor, Tooley Street, London Bridge, London SE1 2QH ☎ 020 7525 0899 ✉ gill.davies@southwark.gov.uk

Road Safety: Mr Eamon Doran, Group Manager - Sustainable Travel & Road Safety, Southwark Council, 5th Floor, Tooley Street, London Bridge, London SE1 2QH ☎ 020 7525 0513 ✉ eamon.doran@southwark.gov.uk

Social Services: Ms Sarah Desai, Director of Commissioning, Modernisation & Partners, Southwark Council , PCT, 1st Floor, PO Box 64529, London SE1P 5LX ☎ 020 7525 0446 ✉ sarah.desai@southwarkpct.nhs.uk

Social Services: Ms Gillian Holdsworth, Director of Public Health & Health Improvement, Southwark Council, 1st Floor, Tooley Street, London Bridge, London SE1 2QH ☎ 020 7525 0280

Social Services: Ms Lesley Humber, Director of Health & Social Care Provider Services, Southwark Council, 1st Floor, Tooley Street, London Bridge, London SE1 2QH ☎ 020 7525 0407

Social Services: Ms Susanna White, Strategic Director of Health & Community Services, Southwark Council, 2nd Floor, Tooley Street, London Bridge, London SE1 2QH ☎ 020 7525 3890 ✉ susanna.white@southwark.gov.uk

Social Services (Children): Ms Romi Bowen, Strategic Director of Children's Services, Southwark Council, 2nd Floor, Tooley Street, London Bridge, London SE1 2QH ☎ 020 7525 0338 ✉ romi.bowen@southwark.gov.uk

Street Scene: Mr Qassim Kazaz, Head of Street Scene & Transport, PO Box 64529, HUB 1, 3rd Floor, London SE1P 5LX ☎ 020 7525 2091 ✉ qassim.kazaz@southwark.gov.uk

Street Scene: Mr Des Waters, Head of Public Realm, Southwark Council, 3rd Floor, Tooley Street, London Bridge, London SE1 2QH ☎ 020 7525 2080 ✉ des.waters@southwark.gov.uk

Sustainable Communities: Ms Gill Davies, Strategic Director of Environment, Southwark Council, 2nd Floor, Tooley Street, London Bridge, London SE1 2QH ☎ 020 7525 0899 ✉ gill.davies@southwark.gov.uk

Tourism: Mr Jay Yeats, Head of Leisure & Wellbeing, Southwark Council, 3rd Floor, Tooley Street, London Bridge, London SE1 2QH ☎ 020 7525 0891 ✉ jay.yeats@southwark.gov.uk

Town Centre: Mr Jon Abbott, Project Director, Southwark Council, 5th Floor, Tooley Street, London Bridge, London SE1 2QH ☎ 020 7525 4902 ✉ jon.abbott@southwark.gov.uk

Town Centre: Mr David Strevens, Peckham Town Centre Manager, Peckham Partnership Project Team, Sumner House, Sumner Road, London SE15 5QS ☎ 020 7525 1001 🖷 020 7525 1020 ✉ david.strevens@southwark.gov.uk

Transport: Mr Ian Smith, Acting Head of Sustainble Services, Manor Place Depot, 30-34 Penrose Street, London SE17 3DW ☎ 020 7525 2484 ✉ ian.smith@southwark.gov.uk

Transport Planner: Mr Simon Bevan, Acting Director of Planning, Southwark Council, 5th Floor, Tooley Street, London Bridge, London SE1 2QH ☎ 020 7525 5655 ✉ simon.bevan@southwark.gov.uk

Children's Play Areas: Ms Rebecca Towers, Parks & Open Spaces Manager, Southwark Council, 3rd Floor, Tooley Street, London Bridge, London SE1 2QH ☎ 020 7525 0771 ✉ rebecca.towers@southwark.gov.uk

MEMBERS OF THE COUNCIL (63)

***Mayor:* Smith**, Althea (LAB - Nunhead)
althea.smith@southwark.gov.uk

***Deputy Mayor:* Mohamed**, Abdul (LAB - Faraday)
abdul.mohamed@southwark.gov.uk

***Leader of the Council:* John**, Peter (LAB - South Camberwell)
peter.john@southwark.gov.uk

***Deputy Leader of the Council:* Wingfield**, Ian (LAB - Brunswick Park)
ian.wingfield@southwark.gov.uk

***Group Leader:* Al-Samerai**, Anood (LD - Riverside)
anood.al-samerai@southwark.gov.uk

***Group Leader:* Robinson**, Lewis (CON - College)
lewis.robinson@southwark.gov.uk

Ahern, Kevin (LAB - Camberwell Green)
kevin.ahern@southwark.gov.uk

Barber, James (LD - East Dulwich)
james.barber@southwark.gov.uk

Blango, Columba (LD - Rotherhithe)
columba.blango@southwark.gov.uk

Bowman, Catherine (LD - Newington)
catherine.bowman@southwark.gov.uk

Brown, Chris (LAB - Peckham)
chris.brown@southwark.gov.uk

Bukola, Michael (LD - South Bermondsey)
michael.bukola@southwark.gov.uk

Capstick, Denise (LD - Grange)
denise.capstick@southwark.gov.uk

Chopra, Sunil (LAB - Nunhead)
sunil.chopra@southwark.gov.uk

Clark, Poddy (LD - Chaucer)
poddy.clark@southwark.gov.uk

Colley, Fiona (LAB - Nunhead)
fiona.colley@southwark.gov.uk

Coyle, Neil (LAB - Newington)
neil.coyle@southwark.gov.uk

Crookshank-Hilton, Robin (LD - Village)

robin.crookshank.hilton@southwark.gov.uk
Davis, Rowenna (LAB - The Lane)
rowenna.davis@southwark.gov.uk
Diamond, Patrick (LAB - Newington)
patrick.diamond@southwark.gov.uk
Dixon-Fyle, Dora (LAB - Camberwell Green)
dora.dixon-fyle@southwark.gov.uk
Dolezal, Nick (LAB - The Lane)
nick.dolezal@southwark.gov.uk
Eckersley, Toby (CON - Village)
toby.eckersley@southwark.gov.uk
Edwards, Gavin (LAB - Peckham Rye)
gavin.edwards@southwark.gov.uk
Garfield, Dan (LAB - Faraday)
dan.garfield@southwark.gov.uk
Gettleson, Mark (LD - Grange)
mark.gettleson@southwark.gov.uk
Gibbes, Norma (LAB - Brunswick Park)
norma.gibbes@southwark.gov.uk
Glover, Mark (LAB - The Lane)
mark.glover@southwark.gov.uk
Govier, Stephen (IND - South Camberwell)
stephen.govier@southwark.gov.uk
Hamvas, Renata (LAB - Peckham Rye)
renata.hamvas@southwark.gov.uk
Hargrove, Barrie (LAB - Peckham)
barrie.hargrove@southwark.gov.uk
Hayes, Helen (LAB - College)
helen.hayes@southwark.gov.uk
Hickson, Claire (LAB - Chaucer)
claire.hickson@southwark.gov.uk
Hook, Jeffrey (LD - Rotherhithe)
jeffrey.hook@southwark.gov.uk
Hubber, David (LD - Surrey Docks)
david.hubber@southwark.gov.uk
Kyriacou, Paul (LD - South Bermondsey)
paul.kyriacou@southwark.gov.uk
Lauder, Lorraine (LAB - Faraday)
lorraine.lauder@southwark.gov.uk
Livingstone, Richard (LAB - Livesey)
richard.livingstone@southwark.gov.uk
Manchester, Linda (LD - Grange)
linda.manchester@southwark.gov.uk
Mann, Eliza (LD - Riverside)
eliza.mann@southwark.gov.uk
McDonald, Catherine (LAB - Livesey)
catherine.mcdonald@southwark.gov.uk
McNally, Tim (LD - Chaucer)
tim.mcnally@southwark.gov.uk
Merrill, Darren (LAB - East Walworth)
darren.merrill@southwark.gov.uk
Mills, Victoria (LAB - Peckham Rye)
victoria.mills@southwark.gov.uk
Mitchell, Michael (CON - Village)
michael.mitchell@southwark.gov.uk
Mitchell, Jonathan (LD - East Dulwich)
jonathan.mitchell@southwark.gov.uk
Morris, Adele (LD - Cathedrals)
adele.morris@southwark.gov.uk
Morrissey, Helen (LAB - East Walworth)
helen.morrissey@southwark.gov.uk
Neale, Graham (LD - South Bermondsey)
graham.neale@southwark.gov.uk
Nelson, Wilma (LD - Rotherhithe)
wilma.nelson@southwark.gov.uk
Noakes, David (LD - Cathedrals)
david.noakes@southwark.gov.uk
Noblet, Paul (LD - Surrey Docks)
paul.noblet@southwark.gov.uk
Oyewole, Emmanuel (LAB - Camberwell Green)
emmanuel.oyewole@southwark.gov.uk
Rajan, Lisa (LD - Surrey Docks)
lisa.rajan@southwark.gov.uk
Seaton, Martin (LAB - East Walworth)
martin.seaton@southwark.gov.uk
Shimell, Rosie (LD - East Dulwich)
rosie.shimell@southwark.gov.uk
Simmons, Andy (LAB - College)
andy.simmons@southwark.gov.uk
Situ, Michael (LAB - Livesey)
michael.situ@southwark.gov.uk
Soanes, Cleo (LAB - Peckham)
cleo.soanes@southwark.gov.uk
Stanton, Nick (LD - Riverside)
nicholas.stanton@southwark.gov.uk
Thornton, Geoffrey (LD - Cathedrals)
geoffrey.thornton@southwark.gov.uk
Ward, Veronica (LAB - South Camberwell)
veronica.ward@southwark.gov.uk
Williams, Mark (LAB - Brunswick Park)
mark.williams@southwark.gov.uk

POLITICAL COMPOSITION
LAB: 34, LD: 25, CON: 3, IND: 1

CABINET
Leader: Mr Peter John
Deputy Leader / Housing Management: Mr Ian Wingfield
Children's Services: Ms Dora Dixon-Fyle
Communities & Economic Development: Ms Claire Hickson
Corporate Strategy: Ms Fiona Colley
Culture, Leisure, Sport & The Olympics: Ms Veronica Ward
Finance, Resources & Community Safety: Mr Richard Livingstone
Health & Adult Social Care: Ms Catherine McDonald
Transport, Environment & Recycling: Mr Barrie Hargrove

COMMITTEE CHAIRS
Audit & Governance: Mr Mark Glover
Licensing: Mr Sunil Chopra
Overview & Scrutiny: Ms Catherine Bowman
Planning: Mr Nick Dolezal
Standards: Ms Cleo Soanes

SPELTHORNE D

Spelthorne Borough Council, Council Offices, Knowle Green, Staines TW18 1XB ☎ 01784 451499; Minicom 01784 446423
🖷 01784 463356 ✉ customer.services@spelthorne.gov.uk
🖳 www.spelthorne.gov.uk

FACTS & FIGURES
Police Authority: Surrey Police Authority
Health Authority: South East Coast Strategic Health Authority
Learning and Skills Council: South East
Parliamentary Constituencies: Spelthorne
EU Constituencies: South East
Election Frequency: Elections are of whole council

Twinning: Melun (France)

PRINCIPAL OFFICERS

Chief Executive: Mr Roberto Tambini, Chief Executive, Council Offices , Knowle Green, Staines TW18 1XB ☎ 01784 446250 🖷 01784 446333 ✉ r.tambini@spelthorne.gov.uk

Deputy Chief Executive: Mr Nigel Lynn, Deputy Chief Executive, Council Offices, Knowle Green, Staines TW18 1XB ☎ 01784 446300 🖷 01784 446362 ✉ n.lynn@spelthorne.gov.uk

Assistant Chief Executive: Ms Liz Borthwick, Assistant Chief Executive, Council Offices, Knowle Green, Staines TW18 1XB ☎ 01784 446376 🖷 01784 463356 ✉ e.borthwick@spelthorne.gov.uk

Assistant Chief Executive: Mr Terry Collier, Assistant Chief Executive & Chief Finance Officer, Council Offices, Knowle Green, Staines TW18 1XB ☎ 01784 446296 ✉ terry.collier@spelthorne.gov.uk

Senior Management: Mr John Brooks, Deputy Head of Planning & Housing Strategy, Council Offices, Knowle Green, Staines TW18 1XB ☎ 01784 446346 ✉ j.brooks@spelthorne.gov.uk

Senior Management: Mr Michael Graham, Head of Corporate Governance & Monitoring Officer, Council Offices, Knowle Green, Staines TW18 1XB ☎ 01784 446227 🖷 01784 446333 ✉ m.graham@spelthorne.gov.uk

Senior Management: Mrs Jan Hunt, Head of Human Resources, Council Offices, Knowle Green, Staines TW18 1XB ☎ 01784 446264 🖷 01784 463356 ✉ j.hunt@spelthorne.gov.uk

Access Officer / Social Services (Disability): Mr Nigel Lynn, Deputy Chief Executive, Council Offices, Knowle Green, Staines TW18 1XB ☎ 01784 446300 🖷 01784 446362 ✉ n.lynn@spelthorne.gov.uk

Access Officer / Social Services (Disability): Mr Stuart Mann, Corporate Health & Safety Officer, Council Offices, Knowle Green, Staines TW18 1XB ☎ 01784 446270 ✉ s.mann@spelthorne.gov.uk

Architect, Building / Property Services: Mr Dave Phillips, Head of Asset Management, Council Offices, Knowle Green, Staines TW18 1XB ☎ 01784 446424 🖷 01784 463356 ✉ d.phillips@spelthorne.gov.uk

Best Value: Mr Terry Collier, Assistant Chief Executive & Chief Finance Officer, Council Offices, Knowle Green, Staines TW18 1XB ☎ 01784 446296 ✉ terry.collier@spelthorne.gov.uk

Best Value: Mr Lee O'Neil, Assistant Chief Executive, Council Offices, Knowle Green, Staines TW18 1XB ☎ 01784 446377 🖷 01784 446333 ✉ l.oneil@spelthorne.gov.uk

Building Control: Mr John Brooks, Deputy Head of Planning & Housing Strategy, Council Offices, Knowle Green, Staines TW18 1XB ☎ 01784 446346 ✉ j.brooks@spelthorne.gov.uk

Building Control: Mr Lee O'Neil, Assistant Chief Executive, Council Offices, Knowle Green, Staines TW18 1XB ☎ 01784 446377 🖷 01784 446333 ✉ l.oneil@spelthorne.gov.uk

Children / Youth Services: Ms Liz Borthwick, Assistant Chief Executive, Council Offices, Knowle Green, Staines TW18 1XB ☎ 01784 446376 🖷 01784 463356 ✉ e.borthwick@spelthorne.gov.uk

Civil Registration: Mr Michael Graham, Head of Corporate Governance & Monitoring Officer, Council Offices , Knowle Green, Staines TW18 1XB ☎ 01784 446227 🖷 01784 446333 ✉ m.graham@spelthorne.gov.uk

PR / Communications: Mr Nigel Lynn, Deputy Chief Executive, Council Offices, Knowle Green, Staines TW18 1XB ☎ 01784 446300 🖷 01784 446362 ✉ n.lynn@spelthorne.gov.uk

Community Planning: Ms Liz Borthwick, Assistant Chief Executive, Council Offices, Knowle Green, Staines TW18 1XB ☎ 01784 446376 🖷 01784 463356 ✉ e.borthwick@spelthorne.gov.uk

Community Planning: Mr Nigel Lynn, Deputy Chief Executive, Council Offices, Knowle Green, Staines TW18 1XB ☎ 01784 446300 🖷 01784 446362 ✉ n.lynn@spelthorne.gov.uk

Computer Management: Mr Terry Collier, Assistant Chief Executive & Chief Finance Officer, Council Offices, Knowle Green, Staines TW18 1XB ☎ 01784 446296 ✉ terry.collier@spelthorne.gov.uk

Computer Management: Mrs Helen Dunn, Information Systems Manager, Council Offices, Knowle Green, Staines TW18 1XB ☎ 01784 446248 ✉ h.dunn@spelthorne.gov.uk; helen.dunn@runnymede.gov.uk

Contracts: Mr Terry Collier, Assistant Chief Executive & Chief Finance Officer, Council Offices, Knowle Green, Staines TW18 1XB ☎ 01784 446296 ✉ terry.collier@spelthorne.gov.uk

Contracts: Mr Steve Connor, Neighbourhood Manager, Council Offices, Knowle Green, Staines TW18 1XB ☎ 01784 446339 🖷 01784 457879 ✉ s.connor@spelthorne.gov.uk

Contracts: Dr Sandy Muirhead, Head of Sustainability & Leisure Services, Council Offices, Knowle Green, Staines TW18 1XB ☎ 01784 446318 🖷 01784 463356 ✉ s.muirhead@spelthorne.gov.uk

Contracts: Mr Dave Phillips, Head of Asset Management, Council Offices, Knowle Green, Staines TW18 1XB ☎ 01784 446424 🖷 01784 463356 ✉ d.phillips@spelthorne.gov.uk

Contracts: Ms Jackie Taylor, Head of Street Scene, Central Depot, Kingston Road, Staines TW15 3SE ☎ 01784 446412 ✉ j.taylor@spelthorne.gov.uk

Corporate Services: Mr Terry Collier, Assistant Chief Executive & Chief Finance Officer, Council Offices, Knowle Green, Staines TW18 1XB ☎ 01784 446296 ✉ terry.collier@spelthorne.gov.uk

Corporate Services: Mr Michael Graham, Head of Corporate Governance & Monitoring Officer, Council Offices , Knowle Green, Staines TW18 1XB ☎ 01784 446227 🖷 01784 446333

m.graham@spelthorne.gov.uk

Corporate Services: Mrs Jan Hunt, Head of Human Resources, Council Offices, Knowle Green, Staines TW18 1XB ☎ 01784 446264 🖷 01784 463356 j.hunt@spelthorne.gov.uk

Corporate Services: Mr Nigel Lynn, Deputy Chief Executive, Council Offices, Knowle Green, Staines TW18 1XB ☎ 01784 446300 🖷 01784 446362 n.lynn@spelthorne.gov.uk

Corporate Services: Mrs Linda Norman, Head of Customer Services, Council Offices, Knowle Green, Staines TW18 1XB ☎ 01784 446375 l.norman@spelthorne.gov.uk

Customer Service: Mr Nigel Lynn, Deputy Chief Executive, Council Offices, Knowle Green, Staines TW18 1XB ☎ 01784 446300 🖷 01784 446362 n.lynn@spelthorne.gov.uk

Customer Service: Mrs Linda Norman, Head of Customer Services, Council Offices, Knowle Green, Staines TW18 1XB ☎ 01784 446375 l.norman@spelthorne.gov.uuk

Direct Labour: Mrs Jan Hunt, Head of Human Resources, Council Offices, Knowle Green, Staines TW18 1XB ☎ 01784 446264 🖷 01784 463356 j.hunt@spelthorne.gov.uk

Direct Labour: Mr Nigel Lynn, Deputy Chief Executive, Council Offices, Knowle Green, Staines TW18 1XB ☎ 01784 446300 🖷 01784 446362 n.lynn@spelthorne.gov.uk

Direct Labour: Ms Jackie Taylor, Head of Street Scene, Central Depot, Kingston Road, Staines TW15 3SE ☎ 01784 446412 j.taylor@spelthorne.gov.uk

E-Government: Mr Terry Collier, Assistant Chief Executive & Chief Finance Officer, Council Offices, Knowle Green, Staines TW18 1XB ☎ 01784 446296 terry.collier@spelthorne.gov.uk

E-Government: Mrs Helen Dunn, Information Systems Manager, Council Offices, Knowle Green, Staines TW18 1XB ☎ 01784 446248; 01932 425550 h.dunn@spelthorne.gov.uk; helen.dunn@runnymede.gov.uk

Electoral Registration: Ms Jayne McEwan, Electoral Services Officer, Council Offices, Knowle Green, Staines TW18 1XB ☎ 01784 446232 j.mcewan@spelthorne.gov.uk

Emergency Planning: Mr Nigel Lynn, Deputy Chief Executive, Council Offices, Knowle Green, Staines TW18 1XB ☎ 01784 446300 🖷 01784 446362 n.lynn@spelthorne.gov.uk

Emergency Planning: Mr Stuart Mann, Corporate Health & Safety Officer, Council Offices, Knowle Green, Staines TW18 1XB ☎ 01784 446270 s.mann@spelthorne.gov.uk

Emergency Planning: Mr Nicholas Moon, Emergency Planning Officer, Civic Offices, Station Road, Addlestone KT15 2AH ☎ 01932 425178; 01784 451499 🖷 01932 838384 nicholas.moon@runnymede.gov.uk

Emergency Planning: Dr Sandy Muirhead, Head of Sustainability & Leisure Services, Council Offices, Knowle Green, Staines TW18 1XB ☎ 01784 446318 🖷 01784 463356 s.muirhead@spelthorne.gov.uk

Energy Management: Dr Sandy Muirhead, Head of Sustainability & Leisure Services, Council Offices, Knowle Green, Staines TW18 1XB ☎ 01784 446318 🖷 01784 463356 s.muirhead@spelthorne.gov.uk

Environmental / Technical Services: Dr Sandy Muirhead, Head of Sustainability & Leisure Services, Council Offices, Knowle Green, Staines TW18 1XB ☎ 01784 446318 🖷 01784 463356 s.muirhead@spelthorne.gov.uk

Environmental Health: Ms Liz Borthwick, Assistant Chief Executive, Council Offices, Knowle Green, Staines TW18 1XB ☎ 01784 446376 🖷 01784 463356 e.borthwick@spelthorne.gov.uk

Environmental Health: Mr Lee O'Neil, Assistant Chief Executive, Council Offices, Knowle Green, Staines TW18 1XB ☎ 01784 446377 🖷 01784 446333 l.oneil@spelthorne.gov.uk

Estates, Property & Valuation: Mr Dave Phillips, Head of Asset Management, Council Offices, Knowle Green, Staines TW18 1XB ☎ 01784 446424 🖷 01784 463356 d.phillips@spelthorne.gov.uk

European Liaison: Ms Jayne McEwan, Electoral Services Officer, Council Offices, Knowle Green, Staines TW18 1XB ☎ 01784 446232 j.mcewan@spelthorne.gov.uk

Events Manager: Ms Lisa Stonehouse, Leisure Services Manager, Council Offices, Knowle Green, Staines TW18 1XB ☎ 01784 446431 🖷 01784 463356 l.stonehouse@spelthorne.gov.uk

Facilities: Mrs Linda Norman, Head of Customer Services, Council Offices, Knowle Green, Staines TW18 1XB ☎ 01784 446375 l.norman@spelthorne.gov.uk

Finance and Treasurer: Mr Terry Collier, Assistant Chief Executive & Chief Finance Officer, Council Offices, Knowle Green, Staines TW18 1XB ☎ 01784 446296 terry.collier@spelthorne.gov.uk

Finance and Treasurer: Ms Deanna Harris, Head of Audit Services, Council Offices, Knowle Green, Staines TW18 1XB ☎ 01784 446207 d.harris@spelthorne.gov.uk

Fleet Management: Ms Jackie Taylor, Head of Street Scene, Central Depot, Kingston Road, Staines TW15 3SE ☎ 01784 446412 j.taylor@spelthorne.gov.uk

Grounds Maintenance: Mr Nigel Lynn, Deputy Chief Executive, Council Offices, Knowle Green, Staines TW18 1XB ☎ 01784 446300 🖷 01784 446362 n.lynn@spelthorne.gov.uk

Grounds Maintenance: Ms Jackie Taylor, Head of Street Scene, Central Depot, Kingston Road, Staines TW15 3SE ☎ 01784 446412 j.taylor@spelthorne.gov.uk

Health and Safety: Ms Liz Borthwick, Assistant Chief Executive, Council Offices, Knowle Green, Staines TW18 1XB ☎ 01784 446376 🖷 01784 463356 e.borthwick@spelthorne.gov.uk

Health and Safety: Mr Stuart Mann, Corporate Health & Safety Officer, Council Offices, Knowle Green, Staines TW18 1XB ☎ 01784 446270 ✉ s.mann@spelthorne.gov.uk

Health and Safety: Mr Lee O'Neil, Assistant Chief Executive, Council Offices, Knowle Green, Staines TW18 1XB ☎ 01784 446377 🖷 01784 446333 ✉ l.oneil@spelthorne.gov.uk

Health and Safety: Ms Jackie Taylor, Head of Street Scene, Central Depot, Kingston Road, Staines TW15 3SE ☎ 01784 446412 ✉ j.taylor@spelthorne.gov.uk

Highways: Mr Nigel Lynn, Deputy Chief Executive, Council Offices, Knowle Green, Staines TW18 1XB ☎ 01784 446300 🖷 01784 446362 ✉ n.lynn@spelthorne.gov.uk

Highways: Ms Jackie Taylor, Head of Street Scene, Central Depot, Kingston Road, Staines TW15 3SE ☎ 01784 446412 ✉ j.taylor@spelthorne.gov.uk

Home Energy Conservation: Dr Sandy Muirhead, Head of Sustainability & Leisure Services, Council Offices, Knowle Green, Staines TW18 1XB ☎ 01784 446318 🖷 01784 463356 ✉ s.muirhead@spelthorne.gov.uk

Housing: Mrs Deborah Ashman, Joint Head of Housing & Independent Living, Council Offices, Knowle Green, Staines TW18 1XB ☎ 01784 446206 ✉ d.ashman@spelthorne.gov.uk

Housing: Ms Liz Borthwick, Assistant Chief Executive, Council Offices, Knowle Green, Staines TW18 1XB ☎ 01784 446376 🖷 01784 463356 ✉ e.borthwick@spelthorne.gov.uk

Housing: Ms Karen Sinclair, Joint Head of Housing Benefits & Independent Living, Council Offices, Knowle Green, Staines TW18 1XB ☎ 01784 446206 ✉ k.sinclair@spelthorne.gov.uk

Legal: Mr Michael Graham, Head of Corporate Governance & Monitoring Officer, Council Offices , Knowle Green, Staines TW18 1XB ☎ 01784 446227 🖷 01784 446333 ✉ m.graham@spelthorne.gov.uk

Leisure and Cultural Services: Ms Liz Borthwick, Assistant Chief Executive, Council Offices, Knowle Green, Staines TW18 1XB ☎ 01784 446376 🖷 01784 463356 ✉ e.borthwick@spelthorne.gov.uk

Leisure and Cultural Services: Ms Jackie Taylor, Head of Street Scene, Central Depot, Kingston Road, Staines TW15 3SE ☎ 01784 446412 ✉ j.taylor@spelthorne.gov.uk

Licensing: Mr Lee O'Neil, Assistant Chief Executive, Council Offices, Knowle Green, Staines TW18 1XB ☎ 01784 446377 🖷 01784 446333 ✉ l.oneil@spelthorne.gov.uk

Lifelong Learning: Mrs Jan Hunt, Head of Human Resources, Council Offices, Knowle Green, Staines TW18 1XB ☎ 01784 446264 🖷 01784 463356 ✉ j.hunt@spelthorne.gov.uk

Lottery Funding, Charity and Voluntary: Mr Terry Collier, Assistant Chief Executive & Chief Finance Officer, Council Offices, Knowle Green, Staines TW18 1XB ☎ 01784 446296 ✉ terry.collier@spelthorne.gov.uk

Member Services: Mr Michael Graham, Head of Corporate Governance & Monitoring Officer, Council Offices , Knowle Green, Staines TW18 1XB ☎ 01784 446227 🖷 01784 446333 ✉ m.graham@spelthorne.gov.uk

Member Services: Mr Gregg Halliwell, Principal Committee Manager, Council Offices, Knowle Green, Staines TW18 1XB ☎ 01784 446267 ✉ g.halliwell@spelthorne.gov.uk

Member Services: Mrs Linda Norman, Head of Customer Services, Council Offices, Knowle Green, Staines TW18 1XB ☎ 01784 446375 ✉ l.norma@spelthorne.gov.uk

Parking: Dr Sandy Muirhead, Head of Sustainability & Leisure Services, Council Offices, Knowle Green, Staines TW18 1XB ☎ 01784 446318 🖷 01784 463356 ✉ s.muirhead@spelthorne.gov.uk

Partnerships: Mr Roberto Tambini, Chief Executive, Council Offices , Knowle Green, Staines TW18 1XB ☎ 01784 446250 🖷 01784 446333 ✉ r.tambini@spelthorne.gov.uk

Personnel / HR: Mrs Jan Hunt, Head of Human Resources, Council Offices, Knowle Green, Staines TW18 1XB ☎ 01784 446264 🖷 01784 463356 ✉ j.hunt@spelthorne.gov.uk

Planning: Mr John Brooks, Deputy Head of Planning & Housing Strategy, Council Offices, Knowle Green, Staines TW18 1XB ☎ 01784 446346 ✉ j.brooks@spelthorne.gov.uk

Planning: Mr Nigel Lynn, Deputy Chief Executive, Council Offices, Knowle Green, Staines TW18 1XB ☎ 01784 446300 🖷 01784 446362 ✉ n.lynn@spelthorne.gov.uk

Planning: Ms Heather Morgan, Head of Planning & Housing Strategy, Council Offices, Knowle Green, Staines TW18 1XB ☎ 01784 446352 🖷 01784 463356 ✉ h.morgan@spelthorne.gov.uk

Procurement: Mr Terry Collier, Assistant Chief Executive & Chief Finance Officer, Council Offices, Knowle Green, Staines TW18 1XB ☎ 01784 446296 ✉ terry.collier@spelthorne.gov.uk

Procurement: Mr Michael Graham, Head of Corporate Governance & Monitoring Officer, Council Offices, Knowle Green, Staines TW18 1XB ☎ 01784 446227 🖷 01784 446333 ✉ m.graham@spelthorne.gov.uk

Recycling & Waste Minimisation: Mr Nigel Lynn, Deputy Chief Executive, Council Offices, Knowle Green, Staines TW18 1XB ☎ 01784 446300 🖷 01784 446362 ✉ n.lynn@spelthorne.gov.uk

Recycling & Waste Minimisation: Dr Sandy Muirhead, Head of Sustainability & Leisure Services, Council Offices, Knowle Green, Staines TW18 1XB ☎ 01784 446318 🖷 01784 463356 ✉ s.muirhead@spelthorne.gov.uk

Recycling & Waste Minimisation: Ms Jackie Taylor, Head of Street Scene, Central Depot, Kingston Road, Staines TW15 3SE ☎ 01784 446412 ✉ j.taylor@spelthorne.gov.uk

Regeneration: Mr Michael Graham, Head of Corporate Governance & Monitoring Officer, Council Offices, Knowle Green, Staines TW18 1XB ☎ 01784 446227 🖷 01784 446333 ✉ m.graham@spelthorne.gov.uk

Staff Training: Mrs Jan Hunt, Head of Human Resources, Council Offices, Knowle Green, Staines TW18 1XB ☎ 01784 446264 🖷 01784 463356 ✉ j.hunt@spelthorne.gov.uk

Staff Training: Mrs Linda Norman, Head of Customer Services, Council Offices, Knowle Green, Staines TW18 1XB ☎ 01784 446375 ✉ l.norman@spelthorne.gov.uk

Street Scene: Dr Sandy Muirhead, Head of Sustainability & Leisure Services, Council Offices, Knowle Green, Staines TW18 1XB ☎ 01784 446318 🖷 01784 463356 ✉ s.muirhead@spelthorne.gov.uk

Street Scene: Ms Jackie Taylor, Head of Street Scene, Central Depot, Kingston Road, Staines TW15 3SE ☎ 01784 446412 ✉ j.taylor@spelthorne.gov.uk

Sustainable Communities: Mr John Brooks, Deputy Head of Planning & Housing Strategy, Council Offices, Knowle Green, Staines TW18 1XB ☎ 01784 446346 ✉ j.brooks@spelthorne.gov.uk

Sustainable Communities: Mr Nigel Lynn, Deputy Chief Executive, Council Offices, Knowle Green, Staines TW18 1XB ☎ 01784 446300 🖷 01784 446362 ✉ n.lynn@spelthorne.gov.uk

Sustainable Communities: Ms Heather Morgan, Head of Planning & Housing Strategy, Council Offices, Knowle Green, Staines TW18 1XB ☎ 01784 446352 🖷 01784 463356 ✉ h.morgan@spelthorne.gov.uk

Sustainable Communities: Dr Sandy Muirhead, Head of Sustainability & Leisure Services, Council Offices, Knowle Green, Staines TW18 1XB ☎ 01784 446318 🖷 01784 463356 ✉ s.muirhead@spelthorne.gov.uk

Sustainable Development: Mr John Brooks, Deputy Head of Planning & Housing Strategy, Council Offices, Knowle Green, Staines TW18 1XB ☎ 01784 446346 ✉ j.brooks@spelthorne.gov.uk

Sustainable Development: Mr Nigel Lynn, Deputy Chief Executive, Council Offices, Knowle Green, Staines TW18 1XB ☎ 01784 446300 🖷 01784 446362 ✉ n.lynn@spelthorne.gov.uk

Sustainable Development: Ms Heather Morgan, Head of Planning & Housing Strategy, Council Offices, Knowle Green, Staines TW18 1XB ☎ 01784 446352 🖷 01784 463356 ✉ h.morgan@spelthorne.gov.uk

Sustainable Development: Dr Sandy Muirhead, Head of Sustainability & Leisure Services, Council Offices, Knowle Green, Staines TW18 1XB ☎ 01784 446318 🖷 01784 463356 ✉ s.muirhead@spelthorne.gov.uk

Tourism: Ms Liz Borthwick, Assistant Chief Executive, Council Offices, Knowle Green, Staines TW18 1XB ☎ 01784 446376 🖷 01784 463356 ✉ e.borthwick@spelthorne.gov.uk

Town Centre: Ms Heather Morgan, Head of Planning & Housing Strategy, Council Offices, Knowle Green, Staines TW18 1XB ☎ 01784 446352 🖷 01784 463356 ✉ h.morgan@spelthorne.gov.uk

Transport: Ms Jackie Taylor, Head of Street Scene, Central Depot, Kingston Road, Staines TW15 3SE ☎ 01784 446412 ✉ j.taylor@spelthorne.gov.uk

Transport Planner: Mr John Brooks, Deputy Head of Planning & Housing Strategy, Council Offices, Knowle Green, Staines TW18 1XB ☎ 01784 446346 ✉ j.brooks@spelthorne.gov.uk

Transport Planner: Ms Jackie Taylor, Head of Street Scene, Central Depot, Kingston Road, Staines TW15 3SE ☎ 01784 446412 ✉ j.taylor@spelthorne.gov.uk

Waste Collection and Disposal: Dr Sandy Muirhead, Head of Sustainability & Leisure Services, Council Offices, Knowle Green, Staines TW18 1XB ☎ 01784 446318 🖷 01784 463356 ✉ s.muirhead@spelthorne.gov.uk

Waste Collection and Disposal: Ms Jackie Taylor, Head of Street Scene, Central Depot, Kingston Road, Staines TW15 3SE ☎ 01784 446412 ✉ j.taylor@spelthorne.gov.uk

Waste Management: Dr Sandy Muirhead, Head of Sustainability & Leisure Services, Council Offices, Knowle Green, Staines TW18 1XB ☎ 01784 446318 🖷 01784 463356 ✉ s.muirhead@spelthorne.gov.uk

Waste Management: Ms Jackie Taylor, Head of Street Scene, Central Depot, Kingston Road, Staines TW15 3SE ☎ 01784 446412 ✉ j.taylor@spelthorne.gov.uk

MEMBERS OF THE COUNCIL (39)

***Mayor:* Sider**, Robin (CON - Shepperton Town)
cllr.sider@spelthorne.gov.uk

***Deputy Mayor:* Napper**, Isobel (CON - Riverside and Laleham)
cllr.napper@spelthorne.gov.uk

***Leader of the Council:* Ayers**, Frank (CON - Ashford Common)
cllr.ayers@spelthorne.gov.uk

***Deputy Leader of the Council:* Pinkerton**, Jean (CON - Staines South)
cllr.jeanpinkerton@spelthorne.gov.uk

Ayub, Asif (CON - Ashford East)
cllr.ayub@spelthorne.gov.uk

Bannister, Christine (CON - Staines)
cllr.bannister@spelthorne.gov.uk

Beardsmore, Ian (LD - Sunbury Common)
cllr.beardsmore@spelthorne.gov.uk

Broom, Philippa Ann (CON - Riverside and Laleham)
cllr.broom@spelthorne.gov.uk

Budd, Samuel (CON - Ashford North and Stanwell South)
cllr.budd@spelthorne.gov.uk

Bushnell, Marion (CON - Ashford Common)
cllr.bushnell@spelthorne.gov.uk

Colison-Crawford, Robbie (LD - Sunbury Common)
cllr.colisoncrawford@spelthorne.gov.uk

Dale, Judy (CON - Stanwell North)

cllr.dale@spelthorne.gov.uk
Davis, Colin (CON - Staines South)
cllr.davis@spelthorne.gov.uk
Dunn, Sandra (LD - Halliford and Sunbury West)
cllr.dunn@spelthorne.gov.uk
Dunn, Richard (LD - Laleham and Shepperton Green)
cllr.rdunn@spelthorne.gov.uk
Evans, Tim (CON - Halliford and Sunbury West)
cllr.evans@spelthorne.gov.uk
Forbes-Forsyth, Penny (CON - Staines South)
cllr.forbes-forsyth@spelthorne.gov.uk
Forsbrey, Gerald (CON - Ashford Town)
cllr.forsbrey@spelthorne.gov.uk
Francis, Mark (CON - Staines)
cllr.francis@spelthorne.gov.uk
Frazer, Chris (CON - Ashford East)
cllr.frazer@spelthorne.gov.uk
Friday, Alfred (CON - Sunbury East)
cllr.friday@spelthorne.gov.uk
Gething, Nick (CON - Ashford Common)
cllr.gething@spelthorne.gov.uk
Gohill, Dipak (CON - Stanwell North)
cllr.gohil@spelthorne.gov.uk
Grant, Denise (CON - Ashford Town)
cllr.grant@spelthorne.gov.uk
Harman, Tony (CON - Riverside and Laleham)
cllr.harman@spelthorne.gov.uk
Leighton, Vivienne (CON - Shepperton Town)
cllr.leighton@spelthorne.gov.uk
Madams, Mary (CON - Laleham and Shepperton Green)
cllr.madams@spelthorne.gov.uk
Mitchell, Tony (CON - Ashford East)
cllr.mitchell@spelthorne.gov.uk
Nichols, Caroline (LD - Sunbury East)
cllr.cnichols@spelthorne.gov.uk
Patel, Daxa (CON - Halliford and Sunbury West)
cllr.patel@spelthorne.gov.uk
Patterson, Alan (CON - Staines)
cllr.patterson@spelthorne.gov.uk
Rough, Marian (CON - Ashford North and Stanwell South)
cllr.rough@spelthorne.gov.uk
Sexton, Joanne (CON - Ashford North and Stanwell South)
cllr.sexton@spelthorne.gov.uk
Smith-Ainsley, Richard (CON - Laleham and Shepperton Green)
cllr.smith-ainsley@spelthorne.gov.uk
Spencer, Caroline (IND - Ashford Town)
cllr.spencer@spelthorne.gov.uk
Strong, Colin (LD - Sunbury Common)
cllr.strong@spelthorne.gov.uk
Taylor, Spencer (CON - Stanwell North)
cllr.taylor@spelthorne.gov.uk
Watts, Robert (CON - Shepperton Town)
cllr.watts@spelthorne.gov.uk
Webb, Suzy (CON - Sunbury East)
cllr.webb@spelthorne.gov.uk

POLITICAL COMPOSITION
CON: 32, LD: 6, IND: 1

CABINET
Leader/ Strategy & Staff: Mr Frank Ayers
Deputy Leader / Health, Wellbeing & Independent Living: Mrs Jean Pinkerton
Community Safety & Young People: Ms Penny Forbes-Forsyth
Corporate Governance, Communications & IT: Ms Christine Bannister
Economic Development: Mr Nick Gething
Environment: Mr Robert Watts
Finance & Resources: Mr Tim Evans
Parks & Assets: Mrs Denise Grant
Planning & Housing: Mr Gerald Forsbrey

COMMITTEE CHAIRS
Audit: Mr Dipak Gohill
Licensing: Mrs Marian Rough
Overview & Scrutiny: Ms Philippa Ann Broom
Planning: Mr Richard Smith-Ainsley

ST. ALBANS CITY D

St. Albans City & District Council, District Council Offices, St. Peter's Street, St. Albans AL1 3JE ☎ 01727 866100
feedback@stalbans.gov.uk www.stalbans.gov.uk

FACTS & FIGURES
Police Authority: Hertfordshire Police Authority
Health Authority: East of England Strategic Health Authority
Learning and Skills Council: Eastern
Parliamentary Constituencies: Hitchin and Harpenden, St. Albans
EU Constituencies: Eastern
Election Frequency: Elections are by thirds
Twinning: Nevers (France); Odense (Denmark); Worms-am-Rhein (Germany); Nyiregyhaza (Hungary); Colney Heath: Boissy-sous-St. Yon (France); Cosne-sur-Loire (France); Harpenden: Alzey (Germany); Friendship Link: Fane (Italy); Sylhet (Bangladesh)

PRINCIPAL OFFICERS
Chief Executive: Mr Daniel Goodwin, Chief Executive, District Council Offices, St. Peter's Street, St. Albans AL1 3JE ☎ 01727 819302 daniel.goodwin@stalbans.gov.uk

Senior Management: Mr James Blake, Chief Policy & Partnership Officer, District Council Offices, St. Peter's Street, St. Albans AL1 3JE ☎ 01727 819552 🖷 01727 819534 james.blake@stalbans.gov.uk

Best Value: Mr James Blake, Chief Policy & Partnership Officer, District Council Offices, St. Peter's Street, St. Albans AL1 3JE ☎ 01727 819552 🖷 01727 819534 james.blake@stalbans.gov.uk

Building Control: Ms Heather Cheesbrough, Head of Planning & Building Control, District Council Offices, St. Peter's Street, St. Albans AL1 3JE ☎ 01727 819343 🖷 01727 845658 heather.cheesbrough@stalbans.gov.uk

Children / Youth Services: Mr Richard Shwe, Head of Community Services, District Council Offices, St. Peter's Street, St. Albans AL1 3JE ☎ 01727 819365 🖷 01727 819478 richard.shwe@stalbans.gov.uk

PR / Communications: Ms Claire Wainwright, Principal Communications & Marketing Officer, District Council Offices, St. Peter's Street, St. Albans AL1 3JE ☎ 01727 819572 🖷 01727 819534 claire.wainwright@stalbans.gov.uk

Community Safety: Mr Neil Kieran, Principal Community Protection Officer, District Council Offices, St. Peter's Street, St. Albans AL1 3JE ☎ 01727 819416 ✉ neil.kieran@stalbans.gov.uk

Computer Management: Ms Amanda Foley, Head of Human Resources, Customer Services & IT, District Council Offices, St. Peter's Street, St. Albans AL1 3JE ☎ 01727 819308 ✉ amanda.foley@stalbans.gov.uk

Corporate Services: Mr Daniel Goodwin, Chief Executive, District Council Offices, St. Peter's Street, St. Albans AL1 3JE ☎ 01727 819302 ✉ daniel.goodwin@stalbans.gov.uk

Customer Service: Ms Amanda Foley, Head of Human Resources, Customer Services & IT, District Council Offices, St. Peter's Street, St. Albans AL1 3JE ☎ 01727 819308 ✉ amanda.foley@stalbans.gov.uk

Economic Development: Ms Maria Cutler, Sustainable Economic Development Officer, District Council Offices, St. Peter's Street, St. Albans AL1 3JE ☎ 01727 819243 ✉ maria.cutler@stalbans.gov.uk

Electoral Registration: Mr Mike Lovelady, Head of Legal, Democratic & Regulatory Services, District Council Offices, St. Peter's Street, St. Albans AL1 3JE ☎ 01727 819502 🖷 01727 819255 ✉ mike.lovelady@stalbans.gov.uk

Emergency Planning: Mr Ian Skelt, Emergency Planning & Community Resilience Officer, District Council Offices, St. Peter's Street, St. Albans AL1 3JE ☎ 01727 814612 🖷 01727 819534 ✉ ian.skelt@stalbans.gov.uk

Environmental Health: Ms Maria Stagg, Regulatory Services Manager, District Council Offices, St. Peter's Street, St. Albans AL1 3JE ☎ 01727 819424 🖷 01727 819433 ✉ maria.stagg@stalbans.gov.uk

Estates, Property & Valuation: Ms Debbie White, Property & Asset Transition Manager, District Council Offices, St. Peter's Street, St. Albans AL1 3JE ☎ 01727 819515 🖷 01727 819478 ✉ debbi.white@stalbans.gov.uk

Facilities: Ms Debbie White, Property & Asset Transition Manager, District Council Offices, St. Peter's Street, St. Albans AL1 3JE ☎ 01727 819515 🖷 01727 819478 ✉ debbi.white@stalbans.gov.uk

Finance and Treasurer: Mr Colm O'Callaghan, Chief Finance Officer, District Council Offices, St. Peter's Street, St. Albans AL1 3JE ☎ 01727 819200 🖷 01727 819467 ✉ colm.o'callaghan@stalbans.gov.uk

Grounds Maintenance: Mr Jon Green, Green Spaces Manager, District Council Offices, St. Peter's Street, St. Albans AL1 3JE ☎ 01727 819233 🖷 01727 819478 ✉ jon.green@stalbans.gov.uk

Health and Safety: Mr Karl Riahi, Business Compliance Officer, District Council Offices, St. Peter's Street, St. Albans AL1 3JE ☎ 01727 573023 🖷 01727 819433 ✉ karl.riahi@stalbans.gov.uk

Housing: Ms Karen Dragovic, Head of Housing, District Council Offices, St. Peter's Street, St. Albans AL1 3JE ☎ 01727 819400 ✉ karen.dragovic@stalbans.gov.uk

Housing Maintenance: Ms Karen Dragovic, Head of Housing, District Council Offices, St. Peter's Street, St. Albans AL1 3JE ☎ 01727 819400 ✉ karen.dragovic@stalbans.gov.uk

Legal: Mr Mike Lovelady, Head of Legal, Democratic & Regulatory Services, District Council Offices, St. Peter's Street, St. Albans AL1 3JE ☎ 01727 819502 🖷 01727 819255 ✉ mike.lovelady@stalbans.gov.uk

Leisure and Cultural Services: Mr Richard Shwe, Head of Community Services, District Council Offices, St. Peter's Street, St. Albans AL1 3JE ☎ 01727 819365 🖷 01727 819478 ✉ richard.shwe@stalbans.gov.uk

Licensing: Mrs Lesley Cameron, Business Compliance Manager, District Council Offices, St. Peter's Street, St. Albans AL1 3JE ☎ 01727 819454 🖷 01727 819433 ✉ lesley.cameron@stalbans.gov.uk

Lottery Funding, Charity and Voluntary: Mr Alan Partington, Financial Services Manager, District Council Offices, St. Peter's Street, St. Albans AL1 3JE ☎ 01727 819201 ✉ alan.partington@stalbans.gov.uk

Member Services: Mrs Jill Durham, Democratic Services Manager, District Council Offices, St. Peter's Street, St. Albans AL1 3JE ☎ 01727 819519 ✉ jill.durham@stalbans.gov.uk

Parking: Ms Maria Stagg, Regulatory Services Manager, District Council Offices, St. Peter's Street, St. Albans AL1 3JE ☎ 01727 819424 🖷 01727 819433 ✉ maria.stagg@stalbans.gov.uk

Partnerships: Mr James Blake, Chief Policy & Partnership Officer, District Council Offices, St. Peter's Street, St. Albans AL1 3JE ☎ 01727 819552 🖷 01727 819534 ✉ james.blake@stalbans.gov.uk

Personnel / HR: Ms Amanda Foley, Head of Human Resources, Customer Services & IT, District Council Offices, St. Peter's Street, St. Albans AL1 3JE ☎ 01727 819308 ✉ amanda.foley@stalbans.gov.uk

Planning: Ms Heather Cheesbrough, Head of Planning & Building Control, District Council Offices, St. Peter's Street, St. Albans AL1 3JE ☎ 01727 819343 🖷 01727 845658 ✉ heather.cheesbrough@stalbans.gov.uk

Procurement: Mr Richard Shwe, Head of Community Services, District Council Offices, St. Peter's Street, St. Albans AL1 3JE ☎ 01727 819365 🖷 01727 819478 ✉ richard.shwe@stalbans.gov.uk

Recycling & Waste Minimisation: Mr Richard Shwe, Head of Community Services, District Council Offices, St. Peter's Street, St. Albans AL1 3JE ☎ 01727 819365 🖷 01727 819478 ✉ richard.shwe@stalbans.gov.uk

Regeneration: Ms Maria Cutler, Sustainable Economic Development Officer, District Council Offices, St. Peter's Street, St. Albans AL1 3JE ☎ 01727 819243

maria.cutler@stalbans.gov.uk

Staff Training: Ms Amanda Foley, Head of Human Resources, Customer Services & IT, District Council Offices, St. Peter's Street, St. Albans AL1 3JE ☎ 01727 819308
amanda.foley@stalbans.gov.uk

Street Scene: Ms Heather Cheesbrough, Head of Planning & Building Control, District Council Offices, St. Peter's Street, St. Albans AL1 3JE ☎ 01727 819343 🖷 01727 845658
heather.cheesbrough@stalbans.gov.uk

Sustainable Communities: Mr James Blake, Chief Policy & Partnership Officer, District Council Offices, St. Peter's Street, St. Albans AL1 3JE ☎ 01727 819552 🖷 01727 819534
james.blake@stalbans.gov.uk

Sustainable Development: Ms Candice Luper, Sustainability Projects Officer, District Council Offices, St. Peter's Street, St. Albans AL1 3JE ☎ 01727 819466 🖷 01727 819534
candice.luper@stalbans.gov.uk

Tourism: Mr Charles Baker, Tourism & Cultural Hub Manager, District Council Offices, St. Peter's Street, St. Albans AL1 3JE ☎ 01727 819275 charles.baker@stalbans.gov.uk

Waste Collection and Disposal: Mr Richard Shwe, Head of Community Services, District Council Offices, St. Peter's Street, St. Albans AL1 3JE ☎ 01727 819365 🖷 01727 819478
richard.shwe@stalbans.gov.uk

Waste Management: Mr Richard Shwe, Head of Community Services, District Council Offices, St. Peter's Street, St. Albans AL1 3JE ☎ 01727 819365 🖷 01727 819478
richard.shwe@stalbans.gov.uk

MEMBERS OF THE COUNCIL (58)

***Mayor:* Harris**, Eileen (LAB - Sopwell)
cllr.e.harris@stalbans.gov.uk
***Deputy Mayor:* Bell**, Julie (CON - Harpenden North)
cllr.j.bell@stalbans.gov.uk
***Leader of the Council:* Daly**, Julian (CON - Harpenden West)
cllr.j.daly@stalbans.gov.uk
***Group Leader:* Grover**, Simon (GRN - St Peters)
cllr.s.grover@stalbans.gov.uk
Allen, Heidi (CON - Marshalswick South)
cllr.h.allen@stalbans.gov.uk
Altun, Dursun (CON - Verulam)
cllr.d.altun@stalbans.gov.uk
Bowes-Phipps, Steve (CON - Park Street)
cllr.s.bowes-phipps@stalbans.gov.uk
Brazier, Chris (LD - Colney Heath)
cllr.c.brazier@stalbans.gov.uk
Brewster, Annie (CON - Wheathampstead)
cllr.a.brewster@stalbans.gov.uk
Burton, Sheila (LD - Clarence)
cllr.s.burton@stalbans.gov.uk
Calder, Simon (CON - London Colney)
cllr.s.calder@stalbans.gov.uk
Campbell, Alec (CON - St Peters)
cllr.a.campbell@stalbans.gov.uk
Chichester-Miles, Daniel (CON - Harpenden West)
cllr.d.chichester-miles@stalbans.gov.uk
Churchard, Janet (LD - Marshalswick North)
cllr.j.churchard@stalbans.gov.uk
Churchard, Geoffrey (LD - Marshalswick North)
cllr.g.churchard@stalbans.gov.uk
Clark, Gillian (CON - Wheathampstead)
cllr.g.clark@stalbans.gov.uk
Clegg, Thomas (LD - Marshalswick North)
cllr.t.clegg@stalbans.gov.uk
Crawley, Maxine (CON - Redbourn)
cllr.m.crawley@stalbans.gov.uk
Day, Ian (LD - Colney Heath)
cllr.i.day@stalbans.gov.uk
Donald, Robert (LD - Cunningham)
cllr.r.donald@stalbans.gov.uk
Ellis, Brian (CON - Harpenden South)
cllr.b.ellis@stalbans.gov.uk
Farmer, Rosemary (CON - Harpenden East)
cllr.r.farmer@stalbans.gov.uk
Featherstone, Sue (CON - St Stephen)
cllr.s.featherstone@stalbans.gov.uk
Gaygusuz, Salih (CON - Marshalswick South)
cllr.m.salih@stalbans.gov.uk
Gibbard, Brian (CON - St Stephen)
cllr.b.gibbard@stalbans.gov.uk
Gordon, Dreda (LAB - London Colney)
cllr.d.gordon@stalbans.gov.uk
Gray, Roger (CON - Redbourn)
cllr.r.gray@stalbans.gov.uk
Green, Michael (LD - St Peters)
cllr.m.green@stalbans.gov.uk
Harrison, Geoffrey (LD - Cunningham)
cllr.g.harrison@stalbans.gov.uk
Heritage, Teresa (CON - Harpenden South)
cllr.t.heritage@stalbans.gov.uk
Heritage, David (CON - Harpenden South)
cllr.d.heritage@stalbans.gov.uk
Huddleston, Nigel (CON - Wheathampstead)
cllr..huddleston@stalbans.gov.uk
Leach, Martin (LAB - Batchwood)
cllr.m.leach@stalbans.gov.uk
Lee, Aislinn (LD - Park Street)
cllr.a.lee@stalbans.gov.uk
Leonard, Frances (CON - Sandbridge)
cllr.f.leonard@stalbans.gov.uk
Lusby, Joyce (LD - Clarence)
cllr.j.lusby@stalbans.gov.uk
Mills, Roma (LAB - Batchwood)
cllr.r.mills@stalbans.gov.uk
Myland, Gordon (CON - St Stephen)
cllr.g.myland@stalbans.gov.uk
Pakenham, Malachy (LAB - Batchwood)
cllr.m.pakenham@stalbans.gov.uk
Pawle, Bert (CON - Harpenden North)
cllr.a.pawle@stalbans.gov.uk
Perks, Rod (LD - Marshalswick South)
cllr.r.perks@stalbans.gov.uk
Poor, David (LD - Sopwell)
cllr.d.poor@stalbans.gov.uk
Prowse, Robert (LD - Cunningham)
cllr.r.prowse@stalbans.gov.uk
Quagliozzi, Jacob (LAB - London Colney)
cllr.j.quagliozzi@stalbans.gov.uk
Rahim, Momotaz (LAB - Ashley)
cllr.m.rahim@stalbans.gov.uk
Read, Beric (CON - Sandridge)

cllr.b.read@stalbans.gov.uk
Rowlands, Anthony (LD - Ashley)
cllr.a.rowlands@stalbans.gov.uk
Russell, Dean (CON - Harpenden East)
cllr.d.russell@stalbans.gov.uk
Smith, Janet (LAB - Sopwell)
cllr.j.smith@stalbans.gov.uk
Swendell, Tony (IND - Redbourn)
cllr.a.swendwell@stalbans.gov.uk
Turner, Geoffrey (CON - Harpenden North)
cllr.g.turner@stalbans.gov.uk
Wakely, Mike (CON - Harpenden East)
cllr.m.wakely@stalbans.gov.uk
Wartenberg, Fred (LD - Verulam)
cllr.f.wartenberg@stalbans.gov.uk
Weaver, Michael (CON - Harpenden West)
cllr.m.weaver@stalbans.gov.uk
White, Chris (LD - Clarence)
cllr.c.white@stalbans.gov.uk
Yates, David (LD - Park Street)
cllr.d.yates@stalbans.gov.uk
Young, Nat (CON - Verulam)
cllr.n.young@stalbans.gov.uk
Zia, Iqbal (LD - Ashley)
cllr.i.zia@stalbans.gov.uk

POLITICAL COMPOSITION

CON: 29, LD: 19, LAB: 8, GRN: 1, IND: 1

CABINET

Leader / Resources: Mr Julian Daly
Community Engagement & Localism: Mr Beric Read
Environment: Mr Daniel Chichester-Miles
Housing: Mr Brian Ellis
Planning & Conservation: Ms Teresa Heritage
Sports, Leisure & Heritage: Mr Mike Wakely

COMMITTEE CHAIRS

Audit: Mr Chris White
Licensing & Regulatory: Mr Gordon Myland
Planning: Mr Thomas Clegg

ST. EDMUNDSBURY D

St. Edmundsbury Borough Council, West Suffolk House, Western Way, Bury St. Edmunds IP33 3YB ☎ 01284 763233 ✉ stedmundsbury@stedsbc.gov.uk 💻 www.stedmundsbury.gov.uk

FACTS & FIGURES

Police Authority: Suffolk Police Authority
Health Authority: East of England Strategic Health Authority
Learning and Skills Council: Eastern
Parliamentary Constituencies: Bury St. Edmunds
EU Constituencies: Eastern
Election Frequency: Elections are of whole council
Twinning: Compiegne (France); Ehringshausen (Germany); Kevelaer (Germany); Pont St. Esprit (France)

PRINCIPAL OFFICERS

Chief Executive: Mr Ian Gallin, Joint Chief Executive, District Offices, College Heath Road, Mildenhall IP28 7EY ☎ 01638 719324 🖷 01638 719310 ✉ ian.gallin@forest-heath.gov.uk

Assistant Chief Executive: Mr Alex Wilson, Corporate Director - Community Services, West Suffolk House, Western Way, Bury St. Edmunds IP33 3YB ☎ 01284 757695 ✉ alex.wilson@stedsbc.gov.uk

Senior Management: Mrs Sandra Pell, Corporate Director - Economy & Environment, West Suffolk House, Western Way, Bury St. Edmunds IP33 3YU ☎ 01284 757301 🖷 01284 757378 ✉ sandra.pell@stedsbc.gov.uk

Architect, Building / Property Services: Mr Ivan Sams, Head of Property Services & Engineering, West Suffolk House, Western Way, Bury St. Edmunds IP33 3YU ☎ 01284 757304 🖷 01284 757378 ✉ ivan.sams@stedsbc.gov.uk

Best Value: Ms Cathy Manning, Head of Neighbourhood Management & Development, West Suffolk House, Western Way, Bury St. Edmunds IP33 3YB ☎ 01284 757002 🖷 01284 757137 ✉ cathy.manning@stedsbc.gov.uk

Building Control: Mr Tim Bartlett, Development & Building Control Manager, West Suffolk House, Western Way, Bury St. Edmunds IP33 3YU ☎ 01284 757384 🖷 01440 757391 ✉ tim.bartlett@stedsbc.gov.uk

Building Control: Mrs Sandra Pell, Corporate Director - Economy & Environment, West Suffolk House, Western Way, Bury St. Edmunds IP33 3YU ☎ 01284 757301 🖷 01284 757378 ✉ sandra.pell@stedsbc.gov.uk

Children / Youth Services: Ms Cathy Manning, Head of Neighbourhood Management & Development, West Suffolk House, Western Way, Bury St. Edmunds IP33 3YU ☎ 01284 757002 🖷 01284 757137 ✉ cathy.manning@stedsbc.gov.uk

PR / Communications: Ms Marianne Hulland, Communications Manager, West Suffolk House, Western Way, Bury St. Edmunds IP33 3YU ☎ 01284 757034; 01638 719361 🖷 01284 757032; 01638 716493 ✉ marianne.hulland@stedsbc.gov.uk; marianne.hulland@forest-heath.gov.uk

Community Planning: Ms Cathy Manning, Head of Neighbourhood Management & Development, West Suffolk House, Western Way, Bury St. Edmunds IP33 3YB ☎ 01284 757002 🖷 01284 757137 ✉ cathy.manning@stedsbc.gov.uk

Community Planning: Mr Alex Wilson, Corporate Director - Community Services, West Suffolk House, Western Way, Bury St. Edmunds IP33 3YB ☎ 01284 757695 ✉ alex.wilson@stedsbc.gov.uk

Community Safety: Mrs Carole Herries, Head of Environmental Health & Housing, West Suffolk House, Western Way, Bury St. Edmunds IP33 3YB ☎ 01284 757603 ✉ carole.herries@stedsbc.gov.uk

Computer Management: Mr Steve Newey, ICT Manager, PO Box 1, College Heath Road, Mildenhall IP28 7UZ ☎ 01638 719762 🖷 01638 716493 ✉ steve.newey@forest-heath.gov.uk

Computer Management: Mr Chris Woodhouse, ICT & E-Services Manager, West Suffolk House, Western Way, Bury St.

Edmunds IP33 3YU ☎ 01284 752230 🖷 01284 757378
✉ chris.woodhouse@stedsbc.gov.uk

Customer Service: Ms Louise Hammond, Head of Human Resources, West Suffolk House, Western Way, Bury St. Edmunds IP33 3YU ☎ 01284 757008 🖷 01284 769603
✉ louise.hammond@stedsbc.gov.uk

Direct Labour: Mr Mark Walsh, Head of Waste, Street Scene Services & Projects, West Suffolk House, Western Way, Bury St. Edmunds IP33 3YU ☎ 01284 757331 🖷 01284 757462
✉ mark.walsh@stedsbc.gov.uk

Economic Development: Mrs Andrea Mayley, Economic Development Manager, West Suffolk House, Western Way, Bury St. Edmunds IP33 3YU ☎ 01284 757343 🖷 01284 757215
✉ andrea.mayley@stedsbc.gov.uk

E-Government: Mr Chris Woodhouse, ICT & E-Services Manager, West Suffolk House, Western Way, Bury St. Edmunds IP33 3YB ☎ 01284 752230 🖷 01284 757378
✉ chris.woodhouse@stedsbc.gov.uk

Electoral Registration: Ms Fiona Osman, Electoral Services Manager, West Suffolk House, Western Way, Bury St. Edmunds IP33 3YU ☎ 01284 757105 ✉ fiona.osman@stedsbc.gov.uk

Emergency Planning: Mr Alan Points, Emergency Planning Officer, West Suffolk House, Western Way , Bury St. Edmunds IP33 1YU ☎ 01284 758461 🖷 01284 757039
✉ alan.points@stedsbc.gov.uk

Energy Management: Mr Ivan Sams, Head of Property Services & Engineering, West Suffolk House, Western Way, Bury St. Edmunds IP33 3YU ☎ 01284 757304 🖷 01284 757378
✉ ivan.sams@stedsbc.gov.uk

Environmental / Technical Services: Mrs Carole Herries, Head of Environmental Health & Housing, West Suffolk House, Western Way, Bury St. Edmunds IP33 3YU ☎ 01284 757603
✉ carole.herries@stedsbc.gov.uk

Environmental / Technical Services: Mr Alex Wilson, Corporate Director - Community Services, West Suffolk House, Western Way, Bury St. Edmunds IP33 3YB ☎ 01284 757695
✉ alex.wilson@stedsbc.gov.uk

Environmental Health: Mrs Carole Herries, Head of Environmental Health & Housing, West Suffolk House, Western Way, Bury St. Edmunds IP33 3YB ☎ 01284 757603
✉ carole.herries@stedsbc.gov.uk

Environmental Health: Mr Richard Whitehead, Principal Environmental Health Officer, West Suffolk House, Western Way , Bury St. Edmunds IP33 1XB ☎ 01284 757037 🖷 01284 763039
✉ richard.whitehead@stedsbc.gov.uk

Environmental Health: Mr Alex Wilson, Corporate Director - Community Services, West Suffolk House, Western Way, Bury St. Edmunds IP33 3YB ☎ 01284 757695
✉ alex.wilson@stedsbc.gov.uk

Estates, Property & Valuation: Mrs Betty Albon, Corporate Property Officer, West Suffolk House, Western Way, Bury St. Edmunds IP33 3YU ☎ 01284 757307 🖷 01284 757386
✉ betty.albon@stedsbc.gov.uk

European Liaison: Ms Cathy Manning, Head of Neighbourhood Management & Development, West Suffolk House, Western Way, Bury St. Edmunds IP33 3YB ☎ 01284 757002 🖷 01284 757137
✉ cathy.manning@stedsbc.gov.uk

Facilities: Mr Ivan Sams, Head of Property Services & Engineering, West Suffolk House, Western Way, Bury St. Edmunds IP33 3YU ☎ 01284 757304 🖷 01284 757378
✉ ivan.sams@stedsbc.gov.uk

Finance and Treasurer: Ms Liz Watts, Chief Finance Officer, West Suffolk House, Western Way, Bury St. Edmunds IP23 3YU ☎ 01284 757252 🖷 01284 757206 ✉ liz.watts@stedsbc.gov.uk

Fleet Management: Mr Philip Clifford, Fleet & Technical Manager, West Suffolk House, Western Way, Bury St. Edmunds IP33 3YU ☎ 01284 757459 🖷 01284 757473
✉ philip.clifford@stedsbc.gov.uk

Fleet Management: Mr Mark Walsh, Head of Waste, Street Scene Services & Projects, West Suffolk House, Western Way, Bury St. Edmunds IP33 3YU ☎ 01284 757331 🖷 01284 757462
✉ mark.walsh@stedsbc.gov.uk

Grounds Maintenance: Mr Damien Parker, Parks Manager, West Suffolk House, Western Way, Bury St. Edmunds IP33 3YU ☎ 01284 757090 🖷 01284 757066
✉ damien.parker@stedsbc.gov.uk

Health and Safety: Mr Martin Hosker, Health & Safety Manager, West Suffolk House, Western Way, Bury St. Edmunds IP33 3YU ☎ 01284 757010 🖷 01284 757014
✉ martin.hosker@stedsbc.gov.uk

Highways: Mr Ivan Sams, Head of Property Services & Engineering, West Suffolk House, Western Way, Bury St. Edmunds IP33 3YU ☎ 01284 757304 🖷 01284 757378
✉ ivan.sams@stedsbc.gov.uk

Home Energy Conservation: Mr Richard Whitehead, Principal Environmental Health Officer, West Suffolk House, Western Way , Bury St. Edmunds IP33 1XB ☎ 01284 757037 🖷 01284 763039
✉ richard.whitehead@stedsbc.gov.uk

Housing: Mrs Carole Herries, Head of Environmental Health & Housing, West Suffolk House, Western Way, Bury St. Edmunds IP33 3YB ☎ 01284 757603 ✉ carole.herries@stedsbc.gov.uk

Housing: Mr Alex Wilson, Corporate Director - Community Services, West Suffolk House, Western Way, Bury St. Edmunds IP33 3YB ☎ 01284 757695 ✉ alex.wilson@stedsbc.gov.uk

Legal: Miss Joy Bowes, Head of Legal & Democratic Services, West Suffolk House, Western Way, Bury St. Edmunds IP33 3YU ☎ 01284 757141 🖷 01284 757155 ✉ joy.bowes@stedsbc.gov.uk

Leisure and Cultural Services: Mr Neil Anthony, Head of

Leisure, West Suffolk House, Western Way, Bury St. Edmunds IP33 3YB ☎ 01284 757064 🖷 01284 757066 ✉ neil.anthony@stedsbc.gov.uk

Leisure and Cultural Services: Mr Alex Wilson, Corporate Director - Community Services, West Suffolk House, Western Way, Bury St. Edmunds IP33 3YB ☎ 01284 757695 ✉ alex.wilson@stedsbc.gov.uk

Licensing: Mrs Carole Herries, Head of Environmental Health & Housing, West Suffolk House, Western Way, Bury St. Edmunds IP33 3YB ☎ 01284 757603 ✉ carole.herries@stedsbc.gov.uk

Licensing: Mr Alex Wilson, Corporate Director - Community Services, West Suffolk House, Western Way, Bury St. Edmunds IP33 3YB ☎ 01284 757695 ✉ alex.wilson@stedsbc.gov.uk

Licensing: Mrs Hilary Workman, Licensing Services Manager, West Suffolk House, Western Way , Bury St. Edmunds IP33 1XB ☎ 01284 757113 🖷 01284 757110 ✉ hilary.workman@stedsbc.gov.uk

Member Services: Miss Joy Bowes, Head of Legal & Democratic Services, West Suffolk House, Western Way, Bury St. Edmunds IP33 3YU ☎ 01284 757141 🖷 01284 757155 ✉ joy.bowes@stedsbc.gov.uk

Parking: Mr Cameron Findlay, Markets & Car Parks Manager, West Suffolk House, Western Way, Bury St. Edmunds IP33 3YU ☎ 01284 757413 🖷 01284 763233 ✉ cameron.findlay@stedsbc.gov.uk

Parking: Mrs Sandra Pell, Corporate Director - Economy & Environment, West Suffolk House, Western Way, Bury St. Edmunds IP33 3YU ☎ 01284 757301 🖷 01284 757378 ✉ sandra.pell@stedsbc.gov.uk

Parking: Mr Ivan Sams, Head of Property Services & Engineering, West Suffolk House, Western Way, Bury St. Edmunds IP33 3YU ☎ 01284 757304 🖷 01284 757378 ✉ ivan.sams@stedsbc.gov.uk

Partnerships: Ms Cathy Manning, Head of Neighbourhood Management & Development, West Suffolk House, Western Way, Bury St. Edmunds IP33 3YU ☎ 01284 757002 🖷 01284 757137 ✉ cathy.manning@stedsbc.gov.uk

Personnel / HR: Ms Louise Hammond, Head of Human Resources, West Suffolk House, Western Way, Bury St. Edmunds IP33 3YU ☎ 01284 757008 🖷 01284 769603 ✉ louise.hammond@stedsbc.gov.uk

Planning: Ms Nicola Baker, Head of Planning Services, West Suffolk House, Western Way, Bury St. Edmunds IP33 3YU ☎ 01284 757306; 01638 719423 🖷 01284 757374; 01638 719493 ✉ nicola.baker@stedsbc.gov.uk; nicola.baker@forest-heath.gov.uk

Procurement: Mr Mark Walsh, Head of Waste, Street Scene Services & Projects, West Suffolk House, Western Way, Bury St. Edmunds IP33 3YU ☎ 01284 757331 🖷 01284 757462 ✉ mark.walsh@stedsbc.gov.uk

Recycling & Waste Minimisation: Mrs Sandra Pell, Corporate Director - Economy & Environment, West Suffolk House, Western Way, Bury St. Edmunds IP33 3YU ☎ 01284 757301 🖷 01284 757378 ✉ sandra.pell@stedsbc.gov.uk

Recycling & Waste Minimisation: Mr Mark Walsh, Head of Waste, Street Scene Services & Projects, West Suffolk House, Western Way, Bury St. Edmunds IP33 3YU ☎ 01284 757331 🖷 01284 757462 ✉ mark.walsh@stedsbc.gov.uk

Regeneration: Mrs Andrea Mayley, Economic Development Manager, West Suffolk House, Western Way, Bury St. Edmunds IP33 3YU ☎ 01284 757343 🖷 01284 757215 ✉ andrea.mayley@stedsbc.gov.uk

Road Safety: Mr Ivan Sams, Head of Property Services & Engineering, West Suffolk House, Western Way, Bury St. Edmunds IP33 3YU ☎ 01284 757323 🖷 01284 757304 ✉ ivan.sams@stedsbc.gov.uk

Street Scene: Mrs Sandra Pell, Corporate Director - Economy & Environment, West Suffolk House, Western Way, Bury St. Edmunds IP33 3YU ☎ 01284 757301 🖷 01284 757378 ✉ sandra.pell@stedsbc.gov.uk

Street Scene: Mr Mark Walsh, Head of Waste, Street Scene Services & Projects, West Suffolk House, Western Way, Bury St. Edmunds IP33 3YU ☎ 01284 757331 🖷 01284 757462 ✉ mark.walsh@stedsbc.gov.uk

Sustainable Communities: Ms Nicola Baker, Head of Planning Services, West Suffolk House, Western Way, Bury St. Edmunds IP33 3YU ☎ 01284 757306; 01638 719423 🖷 01284 757374; 01638 719493 ✉ nicola.baker@stedsbc.gov.uk; nicola.baker@forest-heath.gov.uk

Sustainable Communities: Ms Cathy Manning, Head of Neighbourhood Management & Development, West Suffolk House, Western Way, Bury St. Edmunds IP33 3YU ☎ 01284 757002 🖷 01284 757137 ✉ cathy.manning@stedsbc.gov.uk

Sustainable Communities: Mr Alex Wilson, Corporate Director - Community Services, West Suffolk House, Western Way, Bury St. Edmunds IP33 3YB ☎ 01284 757695 ✉ alex.wilson@stedsbc.gov.uk

Sustainable Development: Mrs Sandra Pell, Corporate Director - Economy & Environment, West Suffolk House, Western Way, Bury St. Edmunds IP33 3YU ☎ 01284 757301 🖷 01284 757378 ✉ sandra.pell@stedsbc.gov.uk

Tourism: Ms Sharon Fairweather, Tourist Information Centre Manager, Tourist Information Centre, 6 Angel Hill, Bury St. Edmunds IP33 1UZ ☎ 01284 757094 🖷 01284 757093 ✉ sharon.fairweather@stedsbc.gov.uk

Tourism: Mr Alex Wilson, Corporate Director - Community Services, West Suffolk House, Western Way, Bury St. Edmunds IP33 3YB ☎ 01284 757695 ✉ alex.wilson@stedsbc.gov.uk

Traffic Management: Mr Ivan Sams, Head of Property Services & Engineering, West Suffolk House, Western Way, Bury St. Edmunds IP33 3YU ☎ 01284 757323 🖷 01284 757304 ✉ ivan.sams@stedsbc.gov.uk

Traffic Management: Mr Ivan Sams, Head of Property Services & Engineering, West Suffolk House, Western Way, Bury St. Edmunds IP33 3YU ☎ 01284 757304 🖷 01284 757378 ✉ ivan.sams@stedsbc.gov.uk

Transport: Mrs Sandra Pell, Corporate Director - Economy & Environment, West Suffolk House, Western Way, Bury St. Edmunds IP33 3YU ☎ 01284 757301 🖷 01284 757378 ✉ sandra.pell@stedsbc.gov.uk

Transport Planner: Ms Nicola Baker, Head of Planning Services, West Suffolk House, Western Way, Bury St. Edmunds IP33 3YU ☎ 01284 757306; 01638 719423 🖷 01284 757374; 01638 719493 ✉ nicola.baker@stedsbc.gov.uk; nicola.baker@forest-heath.gov.uk

Waste Collection and Disposal: Mrs Sandra Pell, Corporate Director - Economy & Environment, West Suffolk House, Western Way, Bury St. Edmunds IP33 3YU ☎ 01284 757301 🖷 01284 757378 ✉ sandra.pell@stedsbc.gov.uk

Waste Collection and Disposal: Mr Mark Walsh, Head of Waste, Street Scene Services & Projects, West Suffolk House, Western Way, Bury St. Edmunds IP33 3YU ☎ 01284 757331 🖷 01284 757462 ✉ mark.walsh@stedsbc.gov.uk

Waste Management: Mrs Sandra Pell, Corporate Director - Economy & Environment, West Suffolk House, Western Way, Bury St. Edmunds IP33 3YU ☎ 01284 757301 🖷 01284 757378 ✉ sandra.pell@stedsbc.gov.uk

Waste Management: Mr Mark Walsh, Head of Waste, Street Scene Services & Projects, West Suffolk House, Western Way, Bury St. Edmunds IP33 3YU ☎ 01284 757331 🖷 01284 757462 ✉ mark.walsh@stedsbc.gov.uk

MEMBERS OF THE COUNCIL (45)

***Mayor:* Marks**, Tim (CON - Haverhill North)
tim.marks@suffolkcc.gov.uk

***Leader of the Council:* Griffiths**, John (CON - Ixworth)
john.griffiths@stedsbc.gov.uk

***Deputy Leader of the Council:* Mildmay-White**, Sara (CON - Rougham)
sara.mildmay-white@stedsbc.gov.uk

Ager, Les (CON - Haverhill East)
les.ager@stedsbc.gov.uk

Beckwith, Trevor (IND - Moreton Hall Ward)
trevor.beckwith@stedsbc.gov.uk

Broughton, Sarah (CON - Great Barton)
sarah.broughton@stedsbc.gov.uk

Buckle, Terry (CON - Moreton Hall)
terry.buckle@stedsbc.gov.uk

Byrne, Maureen (LAB - Haverhill South)
maureen.byrne@stedsbc.gov.uk

Chung, Patrick (CON - Southgate)
patrick.chung@stedsbc.gov.uk

Clements, Terry (CON - Horringer and Whelnetham)
terry.clements@stedsbc.gov.uk

Clifton-Brown, Robert (CON - Withersfield)
robert.clifton-brown@stedsbc.gov.uk

Cockle, Bob (LAB - St Olaves)
bob.cockle@stedsbc.gov.uk

Cox, Gordon (CON - Haverhill East)
gordon.cox@stedsbc.gov.uk

Everitt, Robert (CON - MInden)
robert.everitt@stedsbc.gov.uk

Farmer, Paul (CON - Abbeygate)
mail@paulfarmer.com

Farthing, Jeremy (CON - Haverhill West)
jeremy.farthing@stedsbc.gov.uk

French, Phillip (CON - Haverhill South)
phillip.french@stedsbc.gov.uk

Gower, Anne (CON - Haverhill North)
anne.gower@stedsbc.gov.uk

Hale, John (CON - Bardwell)
john.hale@stedsbc.gov.uk

Hind, Diane (LAB - Northgate)
diane.hind@stedsbc.gov.uk

Hopfensperger, Rebecca (CON - Fornham)
rebecca.hopfensperger@stedsbc.gov.uk

Hopfensperger, Paul (IND - St Olaves)
paul.hopfensperger@stedsbc.gov.uk

Hordern, Joshua (CON - Risbygate)
joshua.hordern@stedsbs.gov.uk

Houlder, Ian (CON - Barrow)
ian.houlder@stedsbc.gov.uk

Levack, Helen (CON - Risby)
helen.levack@stedsbc.gov.uk

McManus, Paul (CON - Haverhill North)
paul.mcmanus@stedsbc.gov.uk

Nettleton, David (IND - Risbygate)
david.nettleton@stedsbc.gov.uk

Oliver, Stefan (CON - Westgate)
stefan.oliver@stedsbc.gov.uk

Pugh, Alaric (CON - Clare)
alaric.pugh@stedsbc.gov.uk

Ray, David (CON - Barningham)
david.ray@stedsbc.gov.uk

Redhead, Derek (IND - Wickhambrook)
derek.redhead@stedsbc.gov.uk

Richardson, Karen Denise (CON - Haverhill East)
karen.richardson@stedsbc.gov.uk

Rout, Richard (CON - Abbeygate)
richard.rout@stedsbc.gov.uk

Rushbrook, Marion (CON - Kedington)
marion.rushbrook@stedsbc.gov.uk

Rushen, Angela (CON - Chedburgh)
angela.rushen@stedsbc.gov.uk

Simner, Paul (CON - Westgate)
paul.simner@stedsbc.gov.uk

Spicer, Christopher (CON - Pakenham)
christopher.spice@stedsbc.gov.uk

Springett, Clive (CON - Minden)
clive.springett@stedsbc.gov.uk

Stamp, Sarah (CON - Southgate)
sarah.stamp@stedsbc.gov.uk

Stevens, Peter (CON - Cavendish)
peter.stevens@stedsbc.gov.uk

Thorndyke, Jim (CON - Stanton)
jim.thorndyke@stedsbc.gov.uk

Warby, Frank (CON - Moreton Hall)
frank.warby@stedsbc.gov.uk

Warby, Patricia (CON - Eastgate)
patricia.warby@stedsbc.gov.uk

Whittaker, Adam (CON - Haverhill West)
adam.whittaker@stedsbc.gov.uk

Whittaker, Dorothy Ann (CON - Hundon)
dorothy.whittaker@stedsbc.gov.uk

POLITICAL COMPOSITION
CON: 38, IND: 4, LAB: 3

CABINET
Leader / Corporate & Rural Affairs: Mr John Griffiths
Deputy Leader / Culture & Sport: Mrs Sara Mildmay-White
Environment & Waste Management: Mr Peter Stevens
Housing, Licensing & Environmental Health: Mrs Anne Gower
Performance & Resources: Mr David Ray
Planning & Transport: Mr Terry Clements
Tourism & Community Services: Mr Robert Everitt

COMMITTEE CHAIRS
Development Control: Mr Jim Thorndyke
Licensing & Regulatory: Mr Frank Warby
Overview & Scrutiny: Mr David Nettleton
Performance & Audit: Mr John Hale

ST. HELENS M
St. Helens Metropolitan Borough Council, Town Hall, Victoria Square, Corporation Street, St. Helens WA10 1HP ☎ 01744 456789 🖷 01744 456895 🖳 www.sthelens.gov.uk

FACTS & FIGURES
Police Authority: Merseyside Police Authority
Health Authority: North West Strategic Health Authority
Learning and Skills Council: North West
Parliamentary Constituencies: St. Helens North, St. Helens South and Whiston
EU Constituencies: North West
Election Frequency: Elections are by thirds
Twinning: Chalon-sur-Saone (France); Stuttgart (Germany); Rainford: Verneuil-sur-Seine (France); Seneley Green: Nienhagen (Germany)

PRINCIPAL OFFICERS
Chief Executive: Mrs Carole Hudson, Chief Executive, Town Hall, Victoria Square, Corporation Street, St. Helens WA10 1HP ☎ 01744 456100 🖷 01744 456889 ✉ carolehudson@sthelens.gov.uk

Senior Management: Ms Angela Sanderson, Assistant Chief Executive - Legal & Administrative Services, Town Hall, Victoria Square, Corporation Street, St. Helens WA10 1HP ☎ 01744 673255 🖷 01744 676208 ✉ angelasanderson@sthelens.gov.uk

Architect, Building / Property Services: Mr Martin Farrell, Property Assets & Facilities Management, Wesley House, Corporation Street, St. Helens WA10 1HF ☎ 01744 676459 ✉ martinfarrell@sthelens.gov.uk

Architect, Building / Property Services: Mr Stuart Rainbow, Manager - Architectural Services, Wesley House, Corporation Street, St. Helens WA10 1HP ☎ 01744 456463 🖷 01744 454206 ✉ stuartrainbow@Sthelens.gov.uk

Building Control: Mr John Murdock, Principal Building Control Officer, Town Hall, Victoria Square, Corporation Street, St. Helens WA10 1HP ☎ 01744 456241 🖷 01744 676255 ✉ johnmurdock@sthelens.gov.uk

Catering Services: Mrs Lorraine Simpson, Strategic Events Manager, Hardshaw Brook Depot, Parr Street, St. Helens WA9 1JR ☎ 01744 455349 🖷 01744 456361 ✉ lorrainesimpson@sthelens.gov.uk

Children / Youth Services: Mrs Susan Richardson, Director of Children & Young People's Services, Atlas House, Corporation Street, St. Helens WA9 1LD ☎ 01744 671801 🖷 01744 671270 ✉ susanrichardson@sthelens.gov.uk

Civil Registration: Ms Anne Atherton, Registration Services Manager, Town Hall, Victoria Square, Corporation Street, St. Helens WA10 1HP ☎ 01744 677540 ✉ anneatherton@sthelens.gov.uk

PR / Communications: Mrs Chris Cahill, Press & Public Relations Manager, Town Hall, Victoria Square, Corporation Street, St. Helens WA10 1HP ☎ 01744 456166 🖷 01744 456168 ✉ chriscahill@sthelens.gov.uk

Community Safety: Mr Andy Dempsey, Head of Corporate & Community Safety, Atlas House, Corporation Street, St. Helens WA9 1LD ☎ 01744 455933 🖷 01744 455936 ✉ andydempsey@sthelens.gov.uk

Computer Management: Mr Steve Sharples, ICT Business Manager, Lincoln House, Corporation Street, St. Helens WA9 1LD ☎ 01744 676930 🖷 01744 456906 ✉ stesharples@sthelens.gov.uk

Consumer Protection and Trading Standards: Mr Darrell Wilson, Chief Trading Standards Officer, Wesley House, Corporation Street, St. Helens WA10 1HF ☎ 01744 456493 ✉ darrellwilson@sthelens.gov.uk

Corporate Services: Mr Peter Hughes, Head of Policy, Town Hall, Victoria Square, Corporation Street, St. Helens WA10 1HP ☎ 01744 673209 ✉ peterhughes@sthelens.gov.uk

Customer Service: Mrs Karen Gillis, Customer Relations Manager, Wesley House, Corporation Street, St. Helens WA10 1HF ☎ 01744 676917 ✉ karengillis@sthelens.gov.uk

Direct Labour: Mr Paul Sanderson, Director of Environmental Protection, Wesley House, Corporation Street, St. Helens WA10 1HF ☎ 01744 456383 🖷 01744 456895 ✉ paulsanderson@sthelens.gov.uk

Economic Development: Mr Steve Berlyne, Funding & Economic Intelligence Manager, Town Hall, Victoria Square, Corporation Street, St. Helens WA10 1HP ☎ 01744 671750 ✉ stevenberlyne@sthelens.gov.uk

Education: Mrs Susan Richardson, Director of Children & Young People's Services, Atlas House, Corporation Street, St. Helens WA9 1LD ☎ 01744 671801 🖷 01744 671270 ✉ susanrichardson@sthelens.gov.uk

Electoral Registration: Ms Beverley Hatton, Electoral Services Officer, Town Hall, Victoria Square, Corporation Street, St. Helens WA10 1HP ☎ 01744 456140 🖷 01744 677370 ✉ beverleyhatton@sthelens.gov.uk

Emergency Planning: Mr Iain Evans, Safety, Risk & Resilience Manager, Lincoln House, Corporation Street, St. Helens WA10 1UQ ☎ 01744 676206 🖷 01744 673404 ✉ iainevans@sthelens.gov.uk

Environmental / Technical Services: Mr Paul Sanderson, Director of Environmental Protection, Wesley House, Corporation Street, St. Helens WA10 1HF ☎ 01744 456383 🖷 01744 456895 ✉ paulsanderson@sthelens.gov.uk

Environmental Health: Mr Anthony Smith, Chief Environmental Health Officer, Wesley House, Corporation Street, St. Helens WA10 1HF ☎ 01744 676339 ✉ anthonysmith@sthelens.gov.uk

Estates, Property & Valuation: Mr Stephen Littler, Estates Manager, Town Hall, Victoria Square, Corporation Street, St. Helens WA10 1HP ☎ 01744 676138 🖷 01744 673407 ✉ stevelittler@sthelens.gov.uk

European Liaison: Mr Steve Berlyne, Funding & Economic Intelligence Manager, Town Hall, Vistoria Square, Corporation Street, St. Helens WA10 1HP ☎ 01744 671750 ✉ stevenberlyne@sthelens.gov.uk

Events Manager: Mrs Lorraine Simpson, Strategic Events Manager, Wesley House, Corporation Street, St. Helens WA10 1HF ☎ 01744 455349 🖷 01744 456361 ✉ lorrainesimpson@sthelens.gov.uk

Facilities: Mr Chris Dove, Public Buildings & Support Services Manager, Town Hall, Victoria Square, Corporation Street, St. Helens WA10 1HP ☎ 01744 456216 🖷 01744 456013 ✉ chrisdove@sthelens.gov.uk

Finance and Treasurer: Mr Ian Roberts, Assistant Chief Executive - Finance, Chief Executive's Department, Town Hall, Victoria Square, Corporation Street, St. Helens WA10 1HP ☎ 01744 673201 🖷 01744 733337 ✉ ianroberts@sthelens.gov.uk

Fleet Management: Mr Peter Mavers, Assistant Director - Environmental Protection, Hardshaw Brook Depot, Parr Street, St. Helens WA9 1JR ☎ 01744 456715 🖷 01744 28617 ✉ petermavers@sthelens.gov.uk

Grounds Maintenance: Mr Tim Jones, Civic Pride & Community Spaces Manager, Hardshaw Brook Depot, Parr Street, St. Helens WA9 1JR ☎ 01744 456761 🖷 01744 428617 ✉ timjones@sthelens.gov.uk

Health and Safety: Mr Iain Evans, Safety, Risk & Resilience Manager, Lincoln House, Corporation Street, St. Helens WA10 1UQ ☎ 01744 676206 🖷 01744 673404 ✉ iainevans@sthelens.gov.uk

Highways: Mr Rory Lingham, Assistant Director - Engineering, Wesley House, Corporation Street, St. Helens WA10 1HF ☎ 01744 456381 🖷 01744 453280 ✉ rorylingham@sthelens.gov.uk

Home Energy Conservation: Mr Jim Nixon, Energy Efficiency Officer, Wesley House, Corporation Street, St. Helens WA10 1HF ☎ 01744 456659 🖷 01744 456648 ✉ jimnixon@sthelens.gov.uk

Housing: Mr Stephen Tracey, Head of Housing & Neighbourhoods, Wesley House, Victoria Square, Corporation Street, St. Helens WA10 1HF ☎ 01744 456490 🖷 01744 456244 ✉ stephentracey@sthelens.gov.uk

Local Area Agreement: Mr Peter Hughes, Head of Policy, Town Hall, Victoria Square, Corporation Street, St. Helens WA10 1HP ☎ 01744 456048 🖷 01744 456073 ✉ peterhughes@sthelens.gov.uk

Legal: Ms Angela Sanderson, Assistant Chief Executive - Legal & Administrative Services, Town Hall, Victoria Square, Corporation Street, St. Helens WA10 1HP ☎ 01744 673255 🖷 01744 676208 ✉ angelasanderson@sthelens.gov.uk

Leisure and Cultural Services: Mr David Parry, Head of Public Affairs, Town Hall, Victoria Square, Corporation Street, St. Helens WA10 1HP ☎ 01744 456608 🖷 01744 456889 ✉ davidparry@sthelens.gov.uk

Licensing: Mr David Breeze, Licensing & Land Charges Officer, Wesley House, Corporation Street, St. Helens WA10 1HF ☎ 01744 456288 🖷 01744 456290 ✉ davidbreeze@sthelens.gov.uk

Lifelong Learning: Mrs Kathy Johnson, Head of the Library Service, Chester Lane Library, Four Acre Lane, St. Helens WA9 4DE ☎ 01744 677493 ✉ kathrynjohnson@sthelens.gov.uk

Lighting: Mr William May, Assistant Head of Asset Management, 4th Floor, Wesley House, Corporation Street, St. Helens WA10 1HP ☎ 01744 456650 ✉ williammay@sthelens.gov.uk

Lottery Funding, Charity and Voluntary: Mr Rod Anders, Assistant Treasurer - Accountancy & Payments, Town Hall, Victoria Square, Corporation Street, St. Helens WA10 1HP ☎ 01744 456009 🖷 01744 456180 ✉ rodanders@sthelens.gov.uk

Lottery Funding, Charity and Voluntary: Mr Peter Hughes, Head of Policy, Town Hall, Victoria Square, Corporation Street, St. Helens WA10 1HP ☎ 01744 673209 ✉ peterhughes@sthelens.gov.uk

Member Services: Mrs Joanne Griffiths, Democratic Services Manager, Town Hall, Victoria Square, Corporation Street, St. Helens WA10 1HP ☎ 01744 456065 🖷 01744 677370 ✉ joanne.griffiths@sthelens.gov.uk

Parking: Mr Robert McAllister, Parking Services Manager, Town Hall, Victoria Square, Corporation Street, St. Helens WA10 1HP ☎ 01744 676138 🖷 01744 673407 ✉ bobmcallister@sthelens.gov.uk

Partnerships: Mr Peter Hughes, Head of Policy, Town Hall, Victoria Square, Corporation Street, St. Helens WA10 1HP ☎ 01744 456048 🖷 01744 456073 ✉ peterhughes@sthelens.gov.uk

Personnel / HR: Mr Brendan Farrell, Head of Human Resources, Town Hall, Victoria Square, Corporation Street, St. Helens WA10 1HP ☎ 01744 456070 🖷 01744 456997 ✉ brendanfarrell@sthelens.gov.uk

Planning: Mr Stuart Barnes, Development Control Manager,

Town Hall, Victoria Square, Corporation Street, St. Helens WA10 1HP ☎ 01744 456115 ✉ stuartbarnes@sthelens.gov.uk

Procurement: Mr Phil Pokato, Corporate Procurement Manager, Wesley House, Corporation Street, St. Helens WA10 1HP ☎ 01744 676783 🖷 01744 676813 ✉ philpokato@sthelens.gov.uk

Public Libraries: Mrs Kathy Johnson, Head of the Library Service, Chester Lane Library, Four Acre Lane, St. Helens WA9 4DE ☎ 01744 677493 ✉ kathrynjohnson@sthelens.gov.uk

Recycling & Waste Minimisation: Mr Brian Malcolm, Environmental Care Manager, Hardshaw Brook Depot, Parr Street, St. Helens WA9 1JR ☎ 01744 456430 🖷 01744 456471 ✉ brianmalcolm@sthelens.gov.uk

Regeneration: Mr Mark Dickens, Head of Regeneration, Town Hall, Victoria Square, Corporation Street, St. Helens WA10 1HP ☎ 01744 676606 🖷 01744 676154 ✉ markdickens@sthelens.gov.uk

Road Safety: Mrs Gillian Roberts, Senior Road Safety Officer, Town Hall, Victoria Square, Corporation Street, St. Helens WA10 1HP ☎ 01744 673233 🖷 01744 673404 ✉ gillianroberts@sthelens.gov.uk

Social Services (Adult): Mr Mike Wyatt, Director of Adult Social Care & Health, Gamble Building, Victoria Square, Corporation Street, St. Helens WA10 1DY ☎ 01744 676309 🖷 01744 676551 ✉ mikewyatt@sthelens.gov.uk

Social Services (Children): Ms Christine Williams, Senior Assistant Director of Children & Families, Atlas House, Corporation Street, St. Helens WA9 1LD ☎ 01744 671803 🖷 01744 671270 ✉ christinewilliams@sthelens.gov.uk

Staff Training: Mr David Broster, Training & Development Manager, Chief Executive's Department, Gamble Building, Victoria Square, St. Helens WA10 1DY ☎ 01744 456084 🖷 01744 456848 ✉ davidbroster@sthelens.gov.uk

Town Centre: Mr Chris Dove, Public Buildings & Support Services Manager, Town Hall, Victoria Square, Corporation Street, St. Helens WA10 1HP ☎ 01744 456216 🖷 01744 456013 ✉ chrisdove@sthelens.gov.uk

Traffic Management: Mr George Houghton, Head of Traffic Engineering, Wesley House, Corporate Street, St. Helens WA10 1HF ☎ 01744 641616 ✉ georgehoughton@sthelens.gov.uk

Transport: Mr Peter Mavers, Assistant Director - Environmental Protection, Hardshaw Brook Depot, Parr Street, St. Helens WA9 1JR ☎ 01744 456715 🖷 01744 28617 ✉ petermavers@sthelens.gov.uk

Transport Planner: Mr Daniel Caffrey, Principal Transport Officer (Policy), Town Hall, Victoria Square, Corporation Street, St. Helens WA10 1HP ☎ 01744 641616 ✉ danielcaffrey@sthelens.gov.uk

Waste Collection and Disposal: Mr Brian Malcolm, Environmental Care Manager, Hardshaw Brook Depot, Parr Street, St. Helens WA9 1JR ☎ 01744 456430 🖷 01744 456471 ✉ brianmalcolm@sthelens.gov.uk

Waste Management: Mr Brian Malcolm, Environmental Care Manager, Hardshaw Brook Depot, Parr Street, St. Helens WA9 1JR ☎ 01744 456430 🖷 01744 456471 ✉ brianmalcolm@sthelens.gov.uk

MEMBERS OF THE COUNCIL (48)

***Mayor:* Almond**, Geoffrey (LAB - Town Centre)
cllrgalmond@sthelens.gov.uk

***Deputy Mayor:* Bowden**, Andy (LAB - Parr)
cllrabowden@sthelens.gov.uk

***Leader of the Council:* Rimmer**, Marie (LAB - West Park)
cllrMERimmer@sthelens.gov.uk

***Deputy Leader of the Council:* Grunewald**, Barrie (LAB - Rainhill)
cllrbgrunewald@sthelens.gov.uk

***Group Leader:* Monk**, David (CON - Rainford)
cllrdmonk@sthelens.gov.uk

***Group Leader:* Topping**, Stephanie (LD - Sutton)
cllrstephtopping@sthelens.gov.uk

Anderton, William (LAB - Haydock)
cllrbanderton@sthelens.gov.uk

Ayres, Robbie (LAB - West Park)
cllrrayres@sthelens.gov.uk

Bacon, Alison (LAB - Billinge and Seneley Green)
CllrAbacon@sthelens.gov.uk

Banks, Charles (LAB - Earlestown)
cllrcdbanks@sthelens.gov.uk

Banks, Jeanette (LAB - Haydock)
cllrjbanks@sthelens.gov.uk

Burns, Anthony (LAB - Haydock)
cllraburns@sthelens.gov.uk

Cross, Gareth (LAB - Bold)
cllrgcross@sthelens.gov.uk

Cunliffe, Alan (LAB - Blackbrook)
cllracunliffe@sthelens.gov.uk

Deakin, Keith (LAB - Earlestown)
cllrkdeakin@sthelens.gov.uk

De'Asha, Joe (LAB - Rainhill)
cllrde'asha@sthelens.gov.uk

Dyer, Sandra (LAB - Newton-le-Willows)
cllrsdyer@sthelens.gov.uk

Fletcher, Jeffrey (LAB - Moss Bank)
cllrjfletcher@sthelens.gov.uk

Fulham, John (LAB - Moss Bank)
cllrjfulham@sthelens.gov.uk

Gill, Carole Ann (LAB - Town Centre)
cllrcgill@sthelens.gov.uk

Glover, Stephen (LAB - Rainhill)
cllrsglover@sthelens.gov.uk

Glover, Lynn (LAB - Windle)
cllrlglover@sthelens.gov.uk

Gomez-Aspron, Steve (LAB - Newton-le-Willows)
cllrsgomez-aspron@sthelens.gov.uk

Hargreaves, Thomas (LAB - Bold)
cllrhargreaves@sthelens.gov.uk

Haw, Michael (LD - Eccleston)
cllrmhaw@sthelens.gov.uk

Ireland, Pat (LAB - Thatto Heath)
cllrpireland@sthelens.gov.uk

Jackson, Jimmy (LAB - Sutton)

Johnson, Anthony (LAB - Bold)

cllrajohnson@sthelens.gov.uk
Johnson, Janet (LAB - Sutton)
cllrjjohnson@sthelens.gov.uk
Jones, Allan (CON - Rainford)
cllrajones@sthelens.gov.uk
Lynch, Paul (LAB - Moss Bank)
Maloney, Linda (LAB - Blackbrook)
cllrlmaloney@sthelens.gov.uk
Martinez-Williams, Patricia (LAB - Windle)
cllrpmartinez-williams@sthelens.gov.uk
McCauley, Richard (LAB - Thatto Heath)
cllrrmcCauley@sthelens.gov.uk
McQuade, Paul (LAB - Blackbrook)
cllrpmcQuade@sthelens.gov.uk
Murphy, Susan (LAB - Billinge and Seneley Green)
cllrsmurphy@sthelens.gov.uk
Nichols, Rupert (CON - Rainford)
cllrrnichols@sthelens.gov.uk
Pearl, Geoff (LD - Eccleston)
cllrgpearl@sthelens.gov.uk
Pearson, Joe (LAB - Billinge and Seneley Green)
cllrjpearson@sthelens.gov.uk
Preston, Charlie (LAB - Earlestown)
cllrcpreston@sthelens.gov.uk
Quinn, Marlene (LAB - West Park)
cllrmquinn@sthelens.gov.uk
Roberts, Keith (LAB - Parr)
cllrkroberts@sthelens.gov.uk
Robinson, Sophie (LAB - Windle)
cllrsrobinson@sthelens.gov.uk
Seddon, Sheila (LAB - Thatto Heath)
cllrsseddon@sthelens.gov.uk
Shields, Terry (LAB - Parr)
cllrtshields@sthelens.gov.uk
Sims, Teresa (LD - Eccleston)
cllrsims@sthelens.gov.uk
Taylor, Neil (LD - Newton-le-Willows)
cllrntaylor@sthelens.gov.uk
Willmitt, Jo-Ann (LAB - Town Centre)
cllrjwillmitt@sthelens.gov.uk

POLITICAL COMPOSITION
LAB: 40, LD: 5, CON: 3

CABINET
Leader / Corporate Services, Governance & External Affairs: Ms Marie Rimmer
Deputy Leader / Urban Regeneration, Housing & Culture: Mr Barrie Grunewald
Adult Social Care & Health: Mr Joe Pearson
Children & Young People's Services: Mr Eric Smith
Environmental Protection & Safer Communities: Mr Richard McCauley
Public Health: Ms Susan Murphy
Service Audits, Quality Control & Enforcement: Mr Gareth Cross
Without Portfolio: Ms Marlene Quinn

COMMITTEE CHAIRS
Audit & Governance: Ms Marie Rimmer
Licensing & Environmental Protection: Mr Terry Shields
Planning: Mr Stephen Glover

STAFFORD — D

Stafford Borough Council, Civic Centre, Riverside, Stafford ST16 3AQ ☎ 01785 619000 🖷 01785 619119 🖳 www.staffordbc.gov.uk

FACTS & FIGURES
Police Authority: Staffordshire Police Authority
Health Authority: NHS West Midlands
Learning and Skills Council: West Midlands
Parliamentary Constituencies: Stafford, Stone
EU Constituencies: West Midlands
Election Frequency: Elections are of whole council

PRINCIPAL OFFICERS
Chief Executive: Mr Ian Thompson, Chief Executive, Civic Centre, Riverside, Stafford ST16 3AQ ☎ 01785 619200 🖷 01785 619119 ✉ ianthompson@staffordbc.gov.uk

Deputy Chief Executive: Mr Malcolm Vickers, Deputy Chief Executive, Civic Centre, Riverside, Stafford ST16 3AQ ☎ 01785 619203 🖷 01785 619119 ✉ mvickers@staffordbc.gov.uk

Architect, Building / Property Services: Mr Jim Davis, Property Services Manager, Civic Centre, Riverside, Stafford ST16 3AQ ☎ 01785 619395 🖷 01785 619688 ✉ jdavis@staffordbc.gov.uk

Best Value: Mr Norman Jones, Head of Policy & Improvement, Civic Centre, Riverside, Stafford ST16 3AQ ☎ 01785 619199 🖷 01785 619119 ✉ npjones@staffordbc.gov.uk

PR / Communications: Mr Will Conaghan, Press & Communications Manager, Civic Centre, Riverside, Stafford ST16 3AQ ☎ 01785 619230 🖷 01785 619230 ✉ wjconghan@staffordbc.gov.uk

Community Planning: Mr Norman Jones, Head of Policy & Improvement, Civic Centre, Riverside, Stafford ST16 3AQ ☎ 01785 619199 🖷 01785 619119 ✉ npjones@staffordbc.gov.uk

Community Safety: Mr Russ Cartlidge, Community Services Manager, Civic Centre, Riverside, Stafford ST16 3AQ ☎ 01785 619307 🖷 01785 619753 ✉ rcartlidge@staffordbc.gov.uk

Computer Management: Mr Peter Kendrick, Head of Technology, Civic Centre, Riverside, Stafford ST16 3AQ ☎ 01785 619274 🖷 01785 619219 ✉ pkendrick@staffordbc.gov.uk

Contracts: Mr Jim Davis, Property Services Manager, Civic Centre, Riverside, Stafford ST16 3AQ ☎ 01785 619395 🖷 01785 619688 ✉ jdavis@staffordbc.gov.uk

Customer Service: Mr Norman Jones, Head of Policy & Improvement, Civic Centre, Riverside, Stafford ST16 3AQ ☎ 01785 619199 🖷 01785 619119 ✉ npjones@staffordbc.gov.uk

Economic Development: Mr Ted Manders, Head of Regeneration, Civic Centre, Riverside, Stafford ST16 3AQ ☎ 01785 619583 🖷 01785 619753 ✉ tmanders@staffordbc.gov.uk

E-Government: Mr Peter Kendrick, Head of Technology, Civic Centre, Riverside, Stafford ST16 3AQ ☎ 01785 619274 🖷 01785 619219 ✉ pkendrick@staffordbc.gov.uk

Electoral Registration: Mrs Jane Peat, Electoral Services Manager, Civic Centre, Riverside, Stafford ST16 3AQ ☎ 01785 619424 🖷 01785 619119 ✉ jpeat@staffordbc.gov.uk

Emergency Planning: Mr Ian Thompson, Chief Executive, Civic Centre, Riverside, Stafford ST16 3AQ ☎ 01785 619200 🖷 01785 619119 ✉ ianthompson@staffordbc.gov.uk

Energy Management: Mr Ted Manders, Head of Regeneration, Civic Centre, Riverside, Stafford ST16 3AQ ☎ 01785 619583 🖷 01785 619753 ✉ tmanders@staffordbc.gov.uk

Environmental / Technical Services: Mr Howard Thomas, Head of Environment, Civic Centre, Riverside, Stafford ST16 3AQ ☎ 01785 619358 🖷 01785 619319 ✉ hthomas@staffordbc.gov.uk

Environmental Health: Mr Howard Thomas, Head of Environment, Civic Centre, Riverside, Stafford ST16 3AQ ☎ 01785 619358 🖷 01785 619319 ✉ hthomas@staffordbc.gov.uk

Estates, Property & Valuation: Mr Jim Davis, Property Services Manager, Civic Centre, Riverside, Stafford ST16 3AQ ☎ 01785 619395 🖷 01785 619688 ✉ jdavis@staffordbc.gov.uk

Events Manager: Ms Liz Hulse, Events Manager, Civic Centre, Riverside, Stafford ST16 3AQ ☎ 01785 619300 🖷 01785 619419 ✉ lhulse@staffordbc.gov.uk

Facilities: Mr Jim Davis, Property Services Manager, Civic Centre, Riverside, Stafford ST16 3AQ ☎ 01785 619395 🖷 01785 619688 ✉ jdavis@staffordbc.gov.uk

Finance and Treasurer: Mr Bryan Law, Head of Finance, Civic Centre, Riverside, Stafford ST16 3AQ ☎ 01785 619241 🖷 01785 619219 ✉ blaw@staffordbc.gov.uk

Grounds Maintenance: Mr Phil Gammon, Head of Operational Services, Civic Centre, Riverside, Stafford ST16 3AQ ☎ 01785 619108 ✉ pgammon@staffordbc.gov.uk

Health and Safety: Mr Neville Raby, Head of Human Resources, Civic Centre, Riverside, Stafford ST16 3AQ ☎ 01785 619205 🖷 01785 619450 ✉ nraby@staffordbc.gov.uk

Legal: Mr Alistair Welch, Head of Law & Administration, Civic Centre, Riverside, Stafford ST16 3AQ ☎ 01785 619204 🖷 01785 619119 ✉ awelch@staffordbc.gov.uk

Leisure and Cultural Services: Mr Adam Hill, Head of Leisure, Civic Centre, Riverside, Stafford ST16 3AQ ☎ 01785 619299 🖷 01785 619419 ✉ amhill@staffordbc.gov.uk

Lottery Funding, Charity and Voluntary: Mr Russ Cartlidge, Community Services Manager, Civic Centre, Riverside, Stafford ST16 3AQ ☎ 01785 619307 🖷 01785 619753 ✉ rcartlidge@staffordbc.gov.uk

Member Services: Mr Alistair Welch, Head of Law & Administration, Civic Centre, Riverside, Stafford ST16 3AQ ☎ 01785 619204 🖷 01785 619119 ✉ awelch@staffordbc.gov.uk

Parking: Mr Steve Allen, Car Parking Manager, Drummond Road, Stafford ST16 3HJ ☎ 01785 619071 🖷 01785 619613 ✉ sallen@staffordbc.gov.uk

Partnerships: Mr Norman Jones, Head of Policy & Improvement, Civic Centre, Riverside, Stafford ST16 3AQ ☎ 01785 619199 🖷 01785 619119 ✉ npjones@staffordbc.gov.uk

Personnel / HR: Mr Neville Raby, Head of Human Resources, Civic Centre, Riverside, Stafford ST16 3AQ ☎ 01785 619205 🖷 01785 619450 ✉ nraby@staffordbc.gov.uk

Planning: Mr John Holmes, Development Control Manager, Civic Centre, Riverside, Stafford ST16 3AQ ☎ 01785 619302 🖷 01785 619419 ✉ jholmes@staffordbc.gov.uk

Procurement: Mr Malcolm Vickers, Deputy Chief Executive, Civic Centre, Riverside, Stafford ST16 3AQ ☎ 01785 619203 🖷 01785 619119 ✉ mvickers@staffordbc.gov.uk

Recycling & Waste Minimisation: Mr Mark Street, Environmental Health Manager, Civic Centre, Riverside, Stafford ST16 3AQ ☎ 01785 619390 🖷 01785 619319 ✉ mstreet@staffordbc.gov.uk

Regeneration: Mr Ted Manders, Head of Regeneration, Civic Centre, Riverside, Stafford ST16 3AQ ☎ 01785 619583 🖷 01785 619753 ✉ tmanders@staffordbc.gov.uk

Staff Training: Mr Neville Raby, Head of Human Resources, Civic Centre, Riverside, Stafford ST16 3AQ ☎ 01785 619205 🖷 01785 619450 ✉ nraby@staffordbc.gov.uk

Street Scene: Mr Phil Gammon, Head of Operational Services, Civic Centre, Riverside, Stafford ST16 3AQ ☎ 01785 619108 ✉ pgammon@staffordbc.gov.uk

Sustainable Communities: Mr Ian Thompson, Chief Executive, Civic Centre, Riverside, Stafford ST16 3AQ ☎ 01785 619200 🖷 01785 619119 ✉ ianthompson@staffordbc.gov.uk

Sustainable Development: Ms Karen Davies, Climate Change & Sustainable Development Co-ordinator, Civic Centre, Riverside, Stafford ST16 3AQ ☎ 01785 619408 🖷 01785 619319 ✉ kdavies@staffordbc.gov.uk

Tourism: Ms Lisa Heaton, Tourism, Heritage & Visitor Services Manager, Civic Centre, Riverside, Stafford ST16 3AQ ☎ 01785 619348 🖷 01785 619319 ✉ lheaton@staffordbc.gov.uk

Town Centre: Mr Ted Manders, Head of Regeneration, Civic Centre, Riverside, Stafford ST16 3AQ ☎ 01785 619583 🖷 01785 619753 ✉ tmanders@staffordbc.gov.uk

Waste Collection and Disposal: Mr Mark Street, Environmental Health Manager, Civic Centre, Riverside, Stafford ST16 3AQ ☎ 01785 619390 🖷 01785 619319 ✉ mstreet@staffordbc.gov.uk

Waste Collection and Disposal: Mr Howard Thomas, Head of Environment, Civic Centre, Riverside, Stafford ST16 3AQ ☎ 01785 619358 🖷 01785 619319 ✉ hthomas@staffordbc.gov.uk

Waste Management: Mr Howard Thomas, Head of Environment, Civic Centre, Riverside, Stafford ST16 3AQ ☎ 01785 619358

☎ 01785 619319 ✉ hthomas@staffordbc.gov.uk

MEMBERS OF THE COUNCIL (59)

***Mayor:* Cross**, Bryan (CON - Holmcroft)
bcross@staffordbc.gov.uk
***Leader of the Council:* Heenan**, Michael Richard (CON - Weeping Cross)
mheenan@staffordbc.gov.uk
***Deputy Leader of the Council:* Smith**, Mike (CON - Gnosall and Woodseaves)
rmsmith@staffordbc.gov.uk
***Group Leader:* Kemp**, William John (LAB - Coton)
jkemp@staffordbc.gov.uk
***Group Leader:* Stamp**, Barry (LD - Church Eaton)
bstamp@staffordbc.gov.uk
Bakker-Collier, Lynne (CON - Barlaston and Oulton)
lbakker-collier@staffordbc.gov.uk
Baron, Christine (LD - Forebridge)
cabaron@staffordbc.gov.uk
Beatty, Frances (CON - Chartley)
fbeatty@staffordbc.gov.uk
Bhakhri, Ravi Rai (LAB - Holmcroft)
rbhakhri@staffordbc.gov.uk
Bowen, Maureen (LAB - Highfields and Western Downs)
mbowen@staffordbc.gov.uk
Chapman, Frank Arthur (CON - Eccleshall)
fchapman@staffordbc.gov.uk
Collier, Geoffrey (CON - St Michaels)
gcollier@staffordbc.gov.uk
Cooke, Ralph (LAB - Penkside)
rcooke@staffordbc.gov.uk
Dalgarno, Judith (CON - Weeping Cross)
jdalgarno@staffordbc.gov.uk
Davies, Isabella (CON - Tillington)
iedavies@staffordbc.gov.uk
Dodson, Michael (CON - Fulford)
mdodson@staffordbc.gov.uk
Draper, Rowan (LAB - Littleworth)
rdraper@staffordbc.gov.uk
Edgeller, Ann (CON - Baswich)
aedgeller@staffordbc.gov.uk
Farnham, Joyce (CON - Stonefield and Christchurch)
jfarnham@staffordbc.gov.uk
Farrington, Patrick (CON - Rowley)
pfarrington@staffordbc.gov.uk
Finlay, Francis (CON - Milford)
ffinlay@staffordbc.gov.uk
Francis, John (CON - Weeping Cross)
jfrancis@staffordbc.gov.uk
Godfrey, Aidan (LAB - Highfields and Western Downs)
agodfrey@staffordbc.gov.uk
Goodall, Margaret (CON - Walton)
mgoodall@staffordbc.gov.uk
Goodland, Peter (CON - Tillington)
pgoodland@staffordbc.gov.uk
Harp, Andrew (CON - Milwich)
aharp@staffordbc.gov.uk
Harris, Thomas (GRN - Forebridge)
trharris@staffordbc.gov.uk
Highfield, James (CON - Swynnerton)
jhighfield@staffordbc.gov.uk
Hobbs, Anne (O - Rowley)
ahobbs@staffordbc.gov.uk
Hollinshead, Ian (LAB - Littleworth)
ihollinshead@staffordbc.gov.uk
Holmes, Thomas (CON - Fulford)
tholmes@staffordbc.gov.uk
Hood, Jill (O - Walton)
jhood@staffordbc.gov.uk
James, Frank (LAB - Holmcroft)
fjames@staffordbc.gov.uk
Jones, Philip Ezra (CON - St Michaels)
pejones@staffordbc.gov.uk
Jones, Gareth (CON - Barlaston and Oulton)
ejones@staffordbc.gov.uk
Jones, Peter (CON - Eccleshall)
pjones@staffordbc.gov.uk
Kelly, Ann (CON - Gnosall and Woodseaves)
akelly@staffordbc.gov.uk
Leason, Philip (LD - Stonefield and Christchurch)
pleason@staffordbc.gov.uk
Loughran, Angela (LAB - Manor)
aloughran@staffordbc.gov.uk
Millichap, Malcolm (LAB - Penkside)
mmillichap@staffordbc.gov.uk
O'Connor, Stephen (LAB - Highfields and Western Downs)
soconnor@staffordbc.gov.uk
Perkins, Alan (CON - Haywood and Hixon)
aperkins@staffordbc.gov.uk
Pert, Jeremy (CON - Eccleshall)
jpert@staffordbc.gov.uk
Price, David (CON - Swynnerton)
dprice@staffordbc.gov.uk
Rowlands, Geoffrey (LAB - Manor)
growlands@staffordbc.gov.uk
Rowlands, Patricia (LAB - Manor)
prowlands@staffordbc.gov.uk
Roycroft, Peter (CON - Fulford)
proycroft@staffordbc.gov.uk
Simpson, William (LAB - Common)
wsimpson@staffordbc.gov.uk
Stafford Northcote, Amyas (CON - Haywood and Hixon)
anorthcote@staffordbc.gov.uk
Stephens, Robert (CON - Milford)
rstephens@staffordbc.gov.uk
Sutherland, Raymond (CON - Seighford)
rsutherland@staffordbc.gov.uk
Tabernor, Jean (CON - Haywood and Hixon)
jtabernor@staffordbc.gov.uk
Thorley, Julian (LAB - Common)
jthorley@staffordbc.gov.uk
Trainor, Paul (CON - Baswich)
ptrainor@staffordbc.gov.uk
Welch, Anthony (LAB - Coton)
ajwelch@staffordbc.gov.uk
Williamson, Michael (CON - Walton)
mwilliamson@staffordbc.gov.uk
Williamson, Kenneth (CON - Gnosall and Woodseaves)
kwilliamson@staffordbc.gov.uk
Winkle, Michael (LAB - Littleworth)
mwinkle@staffordbc.gov.uk
Winnington, Mark (CON - Seighford)
mwinnington@staffordbc.gov.uk

POLITICAL COMPOSITION

CON: 36, LAB: 17, LD: 3, O: 2, GRN: 1

CABINET

Leader: Mr Michael Richard Heenan

Deputy Leader / Leisure: Mr Mike Smith
Community: Mr Patrick Farrington
Environment & Health: Mr Francis Finlay
Planning & Regeneration: Ms Frances Beatty
Resources: Mr Kenneth Williamson

COMMITTEE CHAIRS

Audit & Accounts: Mr W R Simpson
Community Services Scrutiny (Scrutiny): Mr Ralph Cooke
Development Control: Mr Raymond Sutherland
Health Scrutiny: Mrs Patricia Rowlands
Licensing: Mr J S Francis
Planning: Mr Raymond Sutherland
Resources & Corporate Services: Mr Aidan Godfrey

STAFFORDSHIRE C

Staffordshire County Council, County Buildings, Martin Street, Stafford ST16 2LH ☎ 01785 223121 🖷 01785 276178 💻 www.staffordshire.gov.uk

FACTS & FIGURES

Police Authority: Staffordshire Police Authority
Health Authority: NHS West Midlands
Learning and Skills Council: West Midlands
Parliamentary Constituencies: Cannock Chase, Lichfield, Staffordshire South
EU Constituencies: West Midlands
Election Frequency: Elections are of whole council

PRINCIPAL OFFICERS

Chief Executive: Mr Nick Bell, Chief Executive, County Buildings, Martin Street, Stafford ST16 2LH ☎ 01785 277200 nick.bell@staffordshire.gov.uk

Deputy Chief Executive: Dr Catherine Raines, Director for Place (Deputy Chief Executive), Staffordshire Place, Tipping Street, Stafford ST16 2DH ☎ 01785 277200 catherine.raines@staffordshire.gov.uk

Assistant Chief Executive: Mrs Helen Riley, Director of Strategy & Transformation (Assistant Chief Executive), Staffordshire Place, Tipping Street, Stafford ST16 2DH ☎ 01785 278580 🖷 01785 276115 helen.riley@staffordshire.gov.uk

Architect, Building / Property Services: Mr Jamie MacDonald, Head of Strategic Property, Staffordshire Place, Tipping Street, Stafford ST16 2DH ☎ 01785 277508 jamie.macdonald@staffordshire.gov.uk

Best Value: Mrs Helen Riley, Director of Strategy & Transformation (Assistant Chief Executive), Staffordshire Place, Tipping Street, Stafford ST16 2DH ☎ 01785 278580 🖷 01785 276115 helen.riley@staffordshire.gov.uk

Catering Services: Ms Mary Buttler, Head of Catering Services, Wedgwood Building, Tipping Street, Stafford ST16 2DH ☎ 01785 276030 🖷 01785 278751 mary.buttler@staffordshire.gov.uk

Children / Youth Services: Mrs Anne Birch, Commissioner for Education & Skills, Children and Lifelong Learning Directorate, Tipping Street, Stafford ST16 2DH ☎ 01785 278602 🖷 01785 278619 anne.birch@staffordshire.gov.uk

PR / Communications: Ms Jacqui McKinlay, Director of Communications & Customer Services, Staffordshire Place, Tipping Street, Stafford ST16 2DH ☎ 01785 276188 🖷 01785 277347 jacqui.mckinlay@staffordshire.gov.uk

Computer Management: Mr Sander Kristel, Chief Information Officer & ICT, Staffordshire Place, Tipping Street, Stafford ST16 2DH ☎ 01785 278105 sander.kristel@staffordshire.gov.uk

Consumer Protection and Trading Standards: Mr Stephen Butterworth, Deputy Corporate Director of Health & Consumer Services Officer, Staffordshire Place, Tipping Street, Stafford ST16 2DH ☎ 01785 277801 🖷 01785 277127 stephen.butterworth@staffordshire.gov.uk

Contracts: Mr Ian Simpson, Head of Staffordshire Purchasing, Staffordshire Place 2, Tipping Street, Stafford ST16 2DH ☎ 01785 854640 🖷 01785 276390 ian.simpson@staffordshire.gov.uk

Economic Development: Mr Steve Burrows, Deputy Corporate Director, (Regeneration), Staffordshire Place, Tipping Street, Stafford ST16 2DH ☎ 01785 277204 🖷 01785 227213 steve.burrows@staffordshire.gov.uk

Education: Mrs Anne Birch, Commissioner for Education & Skills, Children and Lifelong Learning Directorate, Tipping Street, Stafford ST16 2DH ☎ 01785 278602 🖷 01785 278619 anne.birch@staffordshire.gov.uk

E-Government: Mr Sander Kristel, Chief Information Officer & ICT, Staffordshire Place, Tipping Street, Stafford ST16 2DH ☎ 01785 278105 sander.kristel@staffordshire.gov.uk

Emergency Planning: Mr Mike Slaney, County Emergency Planning Officer, Fire and Rescue Service Headquarters, Pirehill, Stone, Stafford ST15 0BS ☎ 01785 285121 🖷 01785 285208 mslaney@staffordshirefire.gov.uk

Estates, Property & Valuation: Mr Kevin Danks, Principal Valuer, Staffordshire Place, Tipping Street, Stafford ST16 2DH ☎ 01785 277702 🖷 01785 277712 kevin.danks@staffordshire.gov.uk

Finance and Treasurer: Mr Andrew Burns, Director of Finance, Staffordshire Place, Tipping Street, Stafford ST16 2DH ☎ 01785 276302 🖷 01785 276390 andrew.burns@staffordshire.gov.uk

Health and Safety: Mrs Becky Lee, Corporate Health & Safety Advisor, County Buildings, 12 Martin Street, Stafford ST16 2LH ☎ 01785 276846 becky.lee@staffordshire.gov.uk

Highways: Mr David Wilson, Commissioner for Physical Environment, Staffordshire Place, Tipping Street, Stafford ST16 2DH ☎ 01785 276695 🖷 01785 277213 david.wilson@staffordshire.gov.uk

Local Area Agreement: Mrs Helen Riley, Deputy Corporate Director (Policy & Performance), PO Box 11, County Buildings, 17 Eastgate Street, Stafford ST16 2LH ☎ 01785 278580 🖷 01785

276115 ✉ helen.riley@staffordshire.gov.uk

Legal: Mr John Tradewell, Director of Law & Democracy, Staffordshire Place, Tipping Street, Stafford ST16 2DH ☎ 01785 276102 🖷 01785 278355 ✉ john.tradewell@staffordshire.gov.uk

Lifelong Learning: Mrs Anne Birch, Commissioner for Education & Skills, Children and Lifelong Learning Directorate, Tipping Street, Stafford ST16 2DH ☎ 01785 278602 🖷 01785 278619 ✉ anne.birch@staffordshire.gov.uk

Lighting: Mr Glynn Hook, Principal Lighting Engineer, Staffordshire Place, Tipping Street, Stafford ST16 2DH ☎ 01785 276561 🖷 01785 211279 ✉ glynn.hook@staffordshire.gov.uk

Member Services: Ms Ann-Marie Davidson, Head of Member & Democratic Services, County Buildings, Martin Street, Stafford ST16 2LH ☎ 01785 276131 🖷 01785 276178 ✉ ann-marie.davidson@staffordshire.gov.uk

Personnel / HR: Ms Lisa Cartwright, Corporate Head of Human Resources and Organisational Development, Wedgwood Building, Tipping Street, Stafford ST16 2DH ☎ 01785 278800 🖷 01785 278859 ✉ jann.russell@staffordshire.gov.uk

Procurement: Mr Ian Simpson, Head of Staffordshire Purchasing, Staffordshire Place 2, Tipping Street, Stafford ST16 2DH ☎ 01785 854640 🖷 01785 276390 ✉ ian.simpson@staffordshire.gov.uk

Public Libraries: Mrs Janene Cox, Head of Culture & Library Services, Children & Lifelong Learning Directorate, Tipping Street, Stafford ST16 2DH ☎ 01785 278368 🖷 01785 278319 ✉ janene.cox@staffordshire.gov.uk

Recycling & Waste Minimisation: Mr Mark Parkinson, Group Manager Waste Management, Staffordshire Place 1, Tipping Street, Stafford ST16 2DH ☎ 01785 276807 🖷 01785 277695 ✉ mark.parkinson@staffordshire.gov.uk

Regeneration: Mr Steve Burrows, Deputy Corporate Director, (Regeneration), Staffordshire Place, Tipping Street, Stafford ST16 2DH ☎ 01785 277204 🖷 01785 227213 ✉ steve.burrows@staffordshire.gov.uk

Road Safety: Mr Nick Lloyd, Head of Road Safety & Sustainable Travel, Staffordshire Place, Tipping Street, Stafford ST16 2DH ☎ 01785 276610 🖷 01785 276613 ✉ nick.lloyd@staffordshire.gov.uk

Social Services: Mr Eric Robinson, Director for People (Deputy Chief Executive), Staffordshire Place, Tipping Street, Stafford ST16 2DH ☎ 01785 277000 🖷 01785 277127 ✉ eric.robinson@staffordshire.gov.uk

Staff Training: Ms Kim Davies, Management Development Manager, Kingston Centre, Fairway, Stafford ST16 3TW ☎ 01785 854134 ✉ kim.davies@staffordshire.gov.uk

Sustainable Development: Mr Andrew Christelow, Sustainability Officer, Staffordshire Place, Tipping Street, Stafford ST16 2DH ☎ 01785 276705 🖷 01785 211279 ✉ andy.christelow@staffordshire.gov.uk

Tourism: Mr Roger Bradshaw, Economic Development & Tourism Officer, Staffordshire Place, Tipping Street, Stafford ST16 2DH ☎ 01785 277335 🖷 01785 215286 ✉ roger.bradshaw@staffordshire.gov.uk

Traffic Management: Mr Nick Dawson, Transport Planning & Strategy, Staffordshire Place, Tipping Street, Stafford ST16 2DH ☎ 01785 276629 ✉ nick.dawson@staffordshire.gov.uk

Transport: Mr Charles Soutar, Head of Integrated Planning & Transport Policy, Staffordshire Place, Tipping Street, Stafford ST16 2DH ☎ 01785 276735 ✉ charles.soutar@staffordshire.gov.uk

Transport Planner: Mr Nick Dawson, Transport Planning & Strategy, Staffordshire Place, Tipping Street, Stafford ST16 2DH ☎ 01785 276629 ✉ nick.dawson@staffordshire.gov.uk

Waste Collection and Disposal: Mr Mark Parkinson, Group Manager Waste Management, Staffordshire Place 1, Tipping Street, Stafford ST16 2DH ☎ 01785 276807 🖷 01785 277695 ✉ mark.parkinson@staffordshire.gov.uk

Waste Management: Mr Ian Benson, Director of Staffordshire Municipal Waste Strategy, Staffordshire Place, Tipping Street, Stafford ST16 2DH ☎ 01785 276550 ✉ ian.benson@staffordshire.gov.uk

Waste Management: Mr Mark Parkinson, Group Manager Waste Management, Staffordshire Place 1, Tipping Street, Stafford ST16 2DH ☎ 01785 276807 🖷 01785 277695 ✉ mark.parkinson@staffordshire.gov.uk

MEMBERS OF THE COUNCIL (62)

***Chair:* Lewis**, Frank (CON - Lichfield - Lichfield Rural West)
frank.lewis@staffordshire.gov.uk

***Vice-Chair:* Fraser**, Bob (CON - East Staffordshire - Dove)
bob.fraser@staffordshire.gov.uk

***Leader of the Council:* Atkins**, Philip (CON - East Staffordshire - Uttoxeter Rural)
philip.atkins@staffordshire.gov.uk

***Deputy Leader of the Council:* Adams**, Ben (CON - Tamworth - Perrycrofts)
ben.adams@staffordshire.gov.uk

***Group Leader:* Davis**, Derek (LAB - Cannock Chase - Chadsmoor)
derek.davis@staffordshire.gov.uk

***Group Leader:* Huckfield**, Derrick (UKIP - Newcastle - Bradwell and Porthill)
derrick.huckfield@staffordshire.gov.uk

***Group Leader:* Jebb**, Christina (LD - Staffordshire Moorlands - Biddulph South and Endon)
christina.jebb@staffordshire.gov.uk

Atkins, Paul (IND - Lichfield - Burntwood South)
paul.atkins1@staffordshire.gov.uk

Barron, Ray (CON - Stafford - Stafford North)
ray.barron@staffordshire.gov.uk

Bates, Lee (CON - Tamworth - Watling South)
lee.bates@staffordshire.gov.uk

Bayliss, Erica (CON - Lichfield - Lichfield Rural South)
erica.bayliss@staffordshire.gov.uk

Beale, Brian (CON - Tamworth - Stoneydelph)
brian.beale@staffordshire.gov.uk
Bernard, John (CON - Cannock Chase - Hednesford and Rawnsley)
john.bernard@staffordshire.gov.uk
Billson, David (CON - South Staffordshire - Perton)
david.billson@staffordshire.gov.uk
Bloomer, Len (CON - Stafford - Stafford Trent Valley)
leonard.bloomer@staffordshire.gov.uk
Butter, Henry (CON - Stafford - Eccleshall)
henry.butter@staffordshire.gov.uk
Chapman, Frank (CON - Newcastle - Newcastle Rural)
frankachapman@btinternet.com
Clarke, Ron (LAB - East Staffordshire - Burton Town)
ron.clarke@staffordshire.gov.uk
Cooper, John (CON - Newcastle - Wolstanton)
john.cooper@staffordshire.gov.uk
Corbett, Tim (CON - East Staffordshire - Needwood Forest)
timothy.corbett@staffordshire.gov.uk
Corfield, Patrick (CON - Cannock Chase - Cannock Town Centre)
patrick.corfield@staffordshire.gov.uk
Cornes, Dylis (LD - Newcastle - Audley and Chesterton)
dylis.cornes@staffordshire.gov.uk
Davies, Peter (LAB - East Staffordshire - Burton Trent)
peter.davies@staffordshire.gov.uk
Day, William (IND - Staffordshire Moorlands - Caverswall)
william.day@staffordshire.gov.uk
Downes, Veronica (CON - South Staffordshire - Penkridge)
veronica.downes@staffordshire.gov.uk
Eagland, Janet (CON - Lichfield - Lichfield Rural North)
janet.eagland@staffordshire.gov.uk
Easton, Ray (LD - Cannock Chase - Brereton and Ravenhill)
raymond.easton@staffordshire.gov.uk
Edwards, Brian (CON - South Staffordshire - Kinver)
brian.edwards@staffordshire.gov.uk
Ellis, Matthew (CON - Lichfield - Lichfield Rural East)
matthew.ellis@staffordshire.gov.uk
Finn, Terry (CON - Lichfield - Lichfield City South)
terence.finn@staffordshire.gov.uk
Francis, John (CON - Stafford - Stafford South East)
john.francis@staffordshire.gov.uk
Heath, Gill (CON - Staffordshire Moorlands - Leek Rural)
gill.heath@staffordshire.gov.uk
Heenan, Mark (CON - Stafford - Stafford Central)
mark.heenan@staffordshire.gov.uk
Jennings, Ivan (CON - Stafford - Stafford West)
ivan.jennings@staffordshire.gov.uk
Jones, Philip (CON - Stafford - Stone Urban)
philip.e.jones@staffordshire.gov.uk
Jones, Phil (CON - Cannock Chase - Hednesford and Rawnsley)
phil.jones@staffordshire.gov.uk
Lamb, Kathy (CON - East Staffordshire - Burton Tower)
kathy.lamb@staffordshire.gov.uk
Lawrence, Mike (CON - South Staffordshire - Cheslyn Hay, Essington and Great Wyrley)
michael.lawrence@staffordshire.gov.uk
Lawson, Ian (CON - Staffordshire Moorlands - Biddulph North)
ian.lawson@staffordshire.gov.uk
Locke, Geoffrey (UKIP - Newcastle - Kidsgrove and Talke)
geoffrey.locke@staffordshire.gov.uk
Marshall, Robert (CON - South Staffordshire - Codsall)
robert.marshall@staffordshire.gov.uk
Martin, Geoffrey (CON - Cannock Chase - Etchinghill and Heath)
geoffrey.martin@staffordshire.gov.uk
Maryon, Michael (CON - Staffordshire Moorlands - Cheadle and Checkley)
mike.maryon@staffordshire.gov.uk
Maxfield, Mary (LD - Newcastle - Kidsgrove and Talke)
mary.maxfield@staffordshire.gov.uk
Morrison, Geoff (CON - East Staffordshire - Uttoxeter Town)
geoffrey.morrison@staffordshire.gov.uk
Nixon, David (UKIP - Newcastle - Cross Heath and Silverdale)
david.nixon@staffordshire.gov.uk
Oates, Michael (CON - Tamworth - Bolebridge)
michael.oates@staffordshire.gov.uk
Oates, Jeremy (CON - Tamworth - Amington)
jeremy.oates@staffordshire.gov.uk
Parry, Ian (CON - Stafford - Stone Rural)
ian.parry@staffordshire.gov.uk
Perry, Kath (CON - South Staffordshire - Cheslyn Hay, Essington and Great Wyrley)
kathleen.perry@staffordshire.gov.uk
Podmore, Neal (CON - Staffordshire Moorlands - Leek South)
neal.podmore@staffordshire.gov.uk
Reade, Robert (CON - South Staffordshire - Wombourne)
robert.reade@staffordshire.gov.uk
Roberts, Rex (CON - South Staffordshire - Brewood)
rex.roberts@staffordshire.gov.uk
Rowley, John (CON - Cannock Chase - Cannock Villages)
john.rowley@staffordshire.gov.uk
Staples, Liz (CON - East Staffordshire - Horninglow and Stretton)
liz.staples@staffordshire.gov.uk
Sweeney, Stephen (CON - Newcastle - Newcastle South)
stephen.sweeney@staffordshire.gov.uk
Tagg, Simon (CON - Newcastle - Keele and Westlands)
simon.tagg@staffordshire.gov.uk
Tranter, Steve (CON - Lichfield - Burntwood North)
steve.tranter@staffordshire.gov.uk
Wells, John (CON - Tamworth - Watling North)
john.wells@staffordshire.gov.uk
White, Alan (CON - Lichfield - Lichfield City North)
alan.white@staffordshire.gov.uk
Winnington, Mark (CON - Stafford - Gnosall and Doxey)
mark.winnington@staffordshire.gov.uk
Worthington, Mike (CON - Staffordshire Moorlands - Churnet Valley)
mike.worthington@staffordshire.gov.uk

POLITICAL COMPOSITION

CON: 50, LD: 4, UKIP: 3, LAB: 3, IND: 2

CABINET

Leader: Mr Philip Atkins
Deputy Leader / Economic Growth & Enterprise: Mr Ben Adams
Adults' Wellbeing: Mr Matthew Ellis
Children's Wellbeing: Mr Mike Lawrence
Culture & Communities: Mr Patrick Corfield
Education & Skills: Ms Liz Staples
Environment & Assets: Mr Mark Winnington
Finance & Transformation: Mr Ian Parry
Highways & Transport: Mr Michael Maryon
Public Health & Community Safety: Mr Robert Marshall

COMMITTEE CHAIRS

Audit & Standards: Mr Brian Edwards
Health (Scrutiny): Mrs Kath Perry
Pensions: Mr Stephen Sweeney
Planning: Mr Tim Corbett
Prosperity, Skills & Education: Mr Jeremy Oates

STAFFORDSHIRE MOORLANDS D

Staffordshire Moorlands District Council, Moorlands House, Stockwell Street, Leek ST13 6HQ ☎ 01538 395400 🖷 01538 395474 ✉ info@staffsmoorlands.gov.uk
💻 www.staffsmoorlands.gov.uk

FACTS & FIGURES

Police Authority: Staffordshire Police Authority
Health Authority: NHS West Midlands
Learning and Skills Council: West Midlands
Parliamentary Constituencies: Staffordshire Moorlands, Stoke-on-Trent North, Stone
EU Constituencies: West Midlands
Election Frequency: Elections are of whole council
Twinning: Leek is twinned with Este, in Italy. Biddulph is twinned with Fusignano, also Italy. Cheddleton is twinned with Mitterteich, Germany.

PRINCIPAL OFFICERS

Chief Executive: Mr Simon Baker, Chief Executive (Joint with High Peak BC), Moorlands House, Stockwell Street, Leek ST13 6HQ ☎ 01538 395400 🖷 01538 395474
✉ simon.baker@staffsmoorlands.gov.uk

Deputy Chief Executive: Mr Andrew Stokes, Executive Director & Chief Finance Officer, Moorlands House, Stockwell Street, Leek ST13 6HQ ☎ 01538 395622 🖷 01538 395474
✉ andrew.stokes@staffsmoorlands.gov.uk

Senior Management: Mr Mark Trillo, Executive Director & Monitoring Officer, Moorlands House, Stockwell Street, Leek ST13 6HQ ☎ 01538 395623 🖷 01538 395474
✉ mark.trillo@staffsmoorlands.gov.uk

Access Officer / Social Services (Disability): Mr Mike Green, Planning Applications Manager, Moorlands House, Stockwell Street, Leek ST13 6HQ ☎ 01538 395400 🖷 01538 395474
✉ mike.green@staffsmoorlands.gov.uk

Architect, Building / Property Services: Ms Joanne Higgins, Property Services Manager, Moorlands House, Stockwell Street, Leek ST13 6HQ ☎ 01538 395400 🖷 01538 395474
✉ joanne.higgins@staffsmoorlands.gov.uk

Best Value: Mr Chris Elliott, Transformation Manager, Moorlands House, Stockwell Street, Leek ST13 6HQ ☎ 01538 395400 🖷 01538 395474 ✉ chris.elliott@staffsmoorlands.gov.uk

Building Control: Mr Mike Green, Planning Applications Manager, Moorlands House, Stockwell Street, Leek ST13 6HQ ☎ 01538 395400 🖷 01538 395474
✉ mike.green@staffsmoorlands.gov.uk

Catering Services: Mr Terry Crawford, Head of Visitor Services, Pavilion Gardens, Buxton SK17 6BE ☎ 0845 129 7777
✉ terryc@highpeak.gov.uk

PR / Communications: Mr Charles Malkin, Media Relations Manager, Moorlands House, Stockwell Street, Leek ST13 6HQ ☎ 01538 395588 🖷 01538 395474
✉ charles.malkin@staffsmoorlands.gov.uk

Community Planning: Mr Mark Forrester, Communities & Cultural Services Manager, Moorlands House, Stockwell Street, Leek ST13 6HQ ☎ 01538 395768 🖷 01538 395474
✉ mark.forrester@staffsmoorlands.gov.uk

Community Planning: Ms Alison Gregory, Environmental Policy Officer, Moorlands House, Stockwell Street, Leek ST13 6HQ ☎ 0845 129 7777 🖷 01538 395474
✉ alison.gregory@staffsmoorlands.gov.uk

Community Safety: Mr Mark Forrester, Communities & Cultural Services Manager, Moorlands House, Stockwell Street, Leek ST13 6HQ ☎ 01538 395768 🖷 01538 395474
✉ mark.forrester@staffsmoorlands.gov.uk

Community Safety: Mr David Smith, Community Safety & Enforcement Manager, Moorlands House, Stockwell Street, Leek ST13 6HQ ☎ 01538 395692 🖷 01538 395474
✉ david.smith@staffsmoorlands.gov.uk

Computer Management: Mr Chris Elliott, Transformation Manager, Moorlands House, Stockwell Street, Leek ST13 6HQ ☎ 01538 395400 🖷 01538 395474
✉ chris.elliott@staffsmoorlands.gov.uk

Contracts: Mr Andrew Stokes, Executive Director & Chief Finance Officer, Moorlands House, Stockwell Street, Leek ST13 6HQ ☎ 01538 395622 🖷 01538 395474
✉ andrew.stokes@staffsmoorlands.gov.uk

Corporate Services: Mr Peter Dunkley, Customer Services Manager, Moorlands House, Stockwell Street, Leek ST13 6HQ ☎ 01538 395614 🖷 01538 395474
✉ peter.dunkley@staffsmoorlands.gov.uk

Customer Service: Mr Terry Crawford, Head of Visitor Services, Pavilion Gardens, Buxton SK17 6BE ☎ 0845 129 7777
✉ terryc@highpeak.gov.uk

Customer Service: Mr Peter Dunkley, Customer Services Manager, Moorlands House, Stockwell Street, Leek ST13 6HQ ☎ 01538 395614 🖷 01538 395474 ✉ peter.dunkley@staffsmoorlands.gov.uk

Customer Service: Ms Tammy Towers, Environmental Health Manager, Moorlands House, Stockwell Street, Leek ST13 6HQ ☎ 0845 129 7777 ✉ tammy.towers@staffsmoorlands.gov.uk

Economic Development: Mr Perry Wardle, Regeneration Manager, Moorlands House, Stockwell Street, Leek ST13 6HQ ☎ 01538 395582 🖷 01538 395474
✉ perry.wardle@staffsmoorlands.gov.uk

E-Government: Mr Chris Elliott, Transformation Manager,

Moorlands House, Stockwell Street, Leek ST13 6HQ ☎ 01538 395400 🖷 01538 395474 ✉ chris.elliott@staffsmoorlands.gov.uk

Electoral Registration: Ms Caroline Cooke, Electoral Administratrion Manager, Moorlands House, Stockwell Street, Leek ST13 6HQ ☎ 01538 395400 🖷 01538 395474 ✉ caroline.cooke@staffsmoorlands.gov.uk

Electoral Registration: Ms Jeanette Marsh, Legal Services Manager, Moorlands House, Stockwell Street, Leek ST13 6HQ ☎ 01538 395400 🖷 01538 395474 ✉ jeanette.marsh@staffsmoorlands.gov.uk

Emergency Planning: Mr David Owen, Emergency Planning, Health & Safety Advisor, Moorlands House, Stockwell Street, Leek ST13 6HQ ☎ 01538 395595 🖷 01538 395474 ✉ david.owen@staffsmoorlands.gov.uk

Emergency Planning: Mr David Owen, Emergency Planning, Health & Safety Advisor, Moorlands House, Stockwell Street, Leek ST13 6HQ ☎ 01538 395589 🖷 01538 395474 ✉ david.owen@staffsmoorlands.gov.uk

Energy Management: Ms Joanne Higgins, Property Services Manager, Moorlands House, Stockwell Street, Leek ST13 6HQ ☎ 01538 395400 🖷 01538 395474 ✉ joanne.higgins@staffsmoorlands.gov.uk

Environmental / Technical Services: Mr Shaun Hollinshead, Street Cleansing Manager, Fowlchurch Depot, Fowlchurch Road, Leek ST13 6BH ☎ 01538 395798 🖷 01538 388393 ✉ shaun.hollinshead@staffsmoorlands.gov.uk

Environmental / Technical Services: Mr John Tildesley, Environmental Health Services Manager, Fowlchurch Depot, Fowlchurch Road, Leek ST13 6BH ☎ 01538 395797 🖷 01538 388393 ✉ john.tildesley@staffsmoorlands.gov.uk

Environmental / Technical Services: Ms Tammy Towers, Environmental Health Manager, Moorlands House, Stockwell Street, Leek ST13 6HQ ☎ 0845 129 7777 ✉ tammy.towers@staffsmoorlands.gov.uk

Environmental Health: Ms Tammy Towers, Environmental Health Manager, Moorlands House, Stockwell Street, Leek ST13 6HQ ☎ 0845 129 7777 ✉ tammy.towers@staffsmoorlands.gov.uk

Estates, Property & Valuation: Ms Joanne Higgins, Property Services Manager, Moorlands House, Stockwell Street, Leek ST13 6HQ ☎ 01538 395400 🖷 01538 395474 ✉ joanne.higgins@staffsmoorlands.gov.uk

Facilities: Ms Joanne Higgins, Property Services Manager, Moorlands House, Stockwell Street, Leek ST13 6HQ ☎ 01538 395400 🖷 01538 395474 ✉ joanne.higgins@staffsmoorlands.gov.uk

Finance and Treasurer: Mr Chris Hartgrove, Finance & Performance Manager, Moorlands House, Stockwell Street, Leek ST13 6HQ ☎ 01538 395400 ✉ chris.hartgrove@staffsmoorlands.gov.uk

Finance and Treasurer: Mr Rob Jones, Revenue & Benefits Manager, Town Hall, Buxton SK17 6EL ☎ 0845 129 7777 ✉ rob.jones@highpeak.gov.uk

Finance and Treasurer: Mr Andrew Stokes, Executive Director & Chief Finance Officer, Moorlands House, Stockwell Street, Leek ST13 6HQ ☎ 01538 395622 🖷 01538 395474 ✉ andrew.stokes@staffsmoorlands.gov.uk

Fleet Management: Ms Joy Redfern, Street Scene Manager, Moorlands House, Stockwell Street, Leek ST13 6HQ ☎ 01298 28400 Ext 4411 ✉ joy.redfern@staffsmoorlands.gov.uk

Grounds Maintenance: Mr Tony Wheat, Leisure Services Manager, Town Hall, Market Place, Buxton SK17 6EL ☎ (01538) 395400 ✉ anthony.wheat@staffsmoorlands.gov.uk

Health and Safety: Mr David Owen, Emergency Planning, Health & Safety Advisor, Moorlands House, Stockwell Street, Leek ST13 6HQ ☎ 01538 395595 🖷 01538 395474 ✉ david.owen@staffsmoorlands.gov.uk

Home Energy Conservation: Mr Ian Young, Housing Strategy Manager, Moorlands House, Stockwell Street, Leek ST13 6HQ ☎ 01538 395426 🖷 01538 395474 ✉ ian.young@staffsmoorlands.gov.uk

Housing: Mr Ian Young, Housing Strategy Manager, Moorlands House, Stockwell Street, Leek ST13 6HQ ☎ 01538 395426 🖷 01538 395474 ✉ ian.young@staffsmoorlands.gov.uk

Legal: Ms Jeanette Marsh, Legal Services Manager, Moorlands House, Stockwell Street, Leek ST13 6HQ ☎ 01538 395400 🖷 01538 395474 ✉ jeanette.marsh@staffsmoorlands.gov.uk

Legal: Mr Mark Trillo, Executive Director & Monitoring Officer, Moorlands House, Stockwell Street, Leek ST13 6HQ ☎ 01538 395623 🖷 01538 395474 ✉ mark.trillo@staffsmoorlands.gov.uk

Leisure and Cultural Services: Ms Alison Gregory, Environmental Policy Officer, Moorlands House, Stockwell Street, Leek ST13 6HQ ☎ 0845 129 7777 🖷 01538 395474 ✉ alison.gregory@staffsmoorlands.gov.uk

Leisure and Cultural Services: Mr Tony Wheat, Leisure Services Manager, Moorlands House, Stockwell Street, Leek ST13 6HQ ☎ (01538) 395400 ✉ anthony.wheat@staffsmoorlands.gov.uk

Licensing: Mr Peter Dunkley, Customer Services Manager, Moorlands House, Stockwell Street, Leek ST13 6HQ ☎ 01538 395614 🖷 01538 395474 ✉ peter.dunkley@staffsmoorlands.gov.uk

Licensing: Ms Tammy Towers, Environmental Health Manager, Town Hall, Market Place, Buxton SK17 6EL ☎ 0845 129 7777 ✉ tammy.towers@staffsmoorlands.gov.uk

Lottery Funding, Charity and Voluntary: Mr Mark Forrester, Communities & Cultural Services Manager, Moorlands House, Stockwell Street, Leek ST13 6HQ ☎ 01538 395768 🖷 01538 395474 ✉ mark.forrester@staffsmoorlands.gov.uk

Member Services: Ms Jeanette Marsh, Legal Services Manager,

Moorlands House, Stockwell Street, Leek ST13 6HQ ☎ 01538 395400 🖷 01538 395474 ✉ jeanette.marsh@staffsmoorlands.gov.uk

Member Services: Mr Mark Trillo, Executive Director & Monitoring Officer, Moorlands House, Stockwell Street, Leek ST13 6HQ ☎ 01538 395623 🖷 01538 395474 ✉ mark.trillo@staffsmoorlands.gov.uk

Parking: Mr Mark Forrester, Communities & Cultural Services Manager, Moorlands House, Stockwell Street, Leek ST13 6HQ ☎ 01538 395768 🖷 01538 395474 ✉ mark.forrester@staffsmoorlands.gov.uk

Parking: Ms Joanne Higgins, Property Services Manager, Moorlands House, Stockwell Street, Leek ST13 6HQ ☎ 01538 395400 🖷 01538 395474 ✉ joanne.higgins@staffsmoorlands.gov.uk

Partnerships: Mr Mark Forrester, Communities & Cultural Services Manager, Moorlands House, Stockwell Street, Leek ST13 6HQ ☎ 01538 395768 🖷 01538 395474 ✉ mark.forrester@staffsmoorlands.gov.uk

Personnel / HR: Ms Julie Grime, Human Resources Manager, Moorlands House, Stockwell Street, Leek ST13 6HQ ☎ 01538 395690 🖷 01538 395474 ✉ julie.grime@staffsmoorlands.gov.uk

Personnel / HR: Mr Peter Hutt, Head of Human Resources, Moorlands House, Stockwell Street, Leek ST13 6HQ ☎ 0845 129 7777 🖷 01663 751042 ✉ peter.hutt@staffsmoorlands.gov.uk

Planning: Mr Mike Green, Planning Applications Manager, Moorlands House, Stockwell Street, Leek ST13 6HQ ☎ 01538 395400 🖷 01538 395474 ✉ mike.green@staffsmoorlands.gov.uk

Procurement: Mr Chris Elliott, Transformation Manager, Moorlands House, Stockwell Street, Leek ST13 6HQ ☎ 01538 395400 🖷 01538 395474 ✉ chris.elliott@staffsmoorlands.gov.uk

Recycling & Waste Minimisation: Ms Nicola Kemp, Waste Collection Manager, Fowlchurch Depot, Fowlchurch Road, Leek ST13 6BH ☎ 01538 395794 🖷 01538 388393 ✉ nicola.kemp@staffsmoorlands.gov.uk

Recycling & Waste Minimisation: Ms Joy Redfern, Street Scene Manager, Moorlands House, Stockwell Street, Leek ST13 6HQ ☎ 01298 28400 Ext 4411 ✉ joy.redfern@staffsmoorlands.gov.uk

Regeneration: Mr Perry Wardle, Regeneration Manager, Moorlands House, Stockwell Street, Leek ST13 6HQ ☎ 01538 395582 🖷 01538 395474 ✉ perry.wardle@staffsmoorlands.gov.uk

Social Services: Mr Rob Jones, Revenue & Benefits Manager, Town Hall, Market Place, Buxton SK17 6EL ☎ 0845 129 7777 ✉ rob.jones@highpeak.gov.uk

Staff Training: Ms Julie Grime, Human Resources Manager, Moorlands House, Stockwell Street, Leek ST13 6HQ ☎ 01538 395690 🖷 01538 395474 ✉ julie.grime@staffsmoorlands.gov.uk

Staff Training: Mr Peter Hutt, Interim Head of Organisational Development, Moorlands House, Stockwell Street, Leek ST13 6HQ ☎ 0845 129 7777 🖷 01663 751042 ✉ peterhutt@highpeak.gov.uk

Street Scene: Mr Shaun Hollinshead, Environment Manager (Operations), Fowlchurch Depot, Fowlchurch Road, Leek ST13 6BH ☎ 01538 395798 🖷 01538 388393 ✉ shaun.hollinshead@staffsmoorlands.gov.uk

Street Scene: Ms Joy Redfern, Street Scene Manager, Moorlands House, Stockwell Street, Leek ST13 6HQ ☎ 01298 28400 Ext 4411 ✉ joy.redfern@staffsmoorlands.gov.uk

Sustainable Communities: Mr Mark Forrester, Communities & Cultural Services Manager, Moorlands House, Stockwell Street, Leek ST13 6HQ ☎ 01538 395768 🖷 01538 395474 ✉ mark.forrester@staffsmoorlands.gov.uk

Sustainable Development: Ms Alison Gregory, Environmental Policy Officer, Moorlands House, Stockwell Street, Leek ST13 6HQ ☎ 0845 129 7777 🖷 01538 395474 ✉ alison.gregory@staffsmoorlands.gov.uk

Tourism: Mr Terry Crawford, Head of Visitor Services, Pavilion Gardens, Buxton SK17 6BE ☎ 0845 129 7777 ✉ terryc@highpeak.gov.uk

Tourism: Mr Perry Wardle, Regeneration Manager, Moorlands House, Stockwell Street, Leek ST13 6HQ ☎ 01538 395582 🖷 01538 395474 ✉ perry.wardle@staffsmoorlands.gov.uk

Town Centre: Mr Perry Wardle, Regeneration Manager, Moorlands House, Stockwell Street, Leek ST13 6HQ ☎ 01538 395582 🖷 01538 395474 ✉ perry.wardle@staffsmoorlands.gov.uk

Waste Collection and Disposal: Mr Shaun Hollinshead, Environment Manager (Operations), Fowlchurch Depot, Fowlchurch Road, Leek ST13 6BH ☎ 01538 395798 🖷 01538 388393 ✉ shaun.hollinshead@staffsmoorlands.gov.uk

Waste Management: Ms Nicola Kemp, Waste Collection Manager, Fowlchurch Depot, Fowlchurch Road, Leek ST13 6BH ☎ 01538 395794 🖷 01538 388393 ✉ nicola.kemp@staffsmoorlands.gov.uk

MEMBERS OF THE COUNCIL (56)

***Chair:* Hails**, Jason (CON - Manifold)
jason.hails@staffsmoorlands.gov.uk

***Vice-Chair:* Ellis**, Stephen (CON - Cheadle West)
stephen.ellis@staffsmoorlands.gov.uk

***Leader of the Council:* Ralphs**, Sybil (CON - Bagnall & Stanley)
sybil.ralphs@staffsmoorlands.gov.uk

Ahmood, Mahfooz (LAB - Cheddleton)
mahfooz.ahmad@staffsmoorlands.gov.uk

Aktins, Charlotte (LAB - Leek North)
charlotte.atkins@staffsmoorlands.gov.uk

Alcock, Richard (IND - Cheadle South East)
richard.alcock@staffsmoorlands.gov.uk

Baddeley, Elaine (IND - Biddulph West)
elaine.baddeley@staffsmoorlands.gov.uk

Banks, Alan (CON - Cheadle West)

alan.banks@staffsmoorlands.gov.uk
Bowen, Michael (CON - Cheddleton)
michael.bowen@staffsmoorlands.gov.uk
Bull, Julie (CON - Cheadle North East)
julie.bull@staffsmoorlands.gov.uk
Burton, Gillian (IND - Forsbrook)
gillian.burton@staffsmoorlands.gov.uk
Clowes, Josephine (CON - Churnet)
josephine.clowes@staffsmoorlands.gov.uk
Cooper, Sandra (LAB - Leek North)
sandra.cooper@staffsmoorlands.gov.uk
Cowie, Barry (INDNA - Leek East)
barry.cowie@staffsmoorlands.gov.uk
Davies, Jim (IND - Biddulph North)
jim.davies@staffsmoorlands.gov.uk
Day, May (IND - Cellarhead)
may.day@staffsmoorlands.gov.uk
Deaville, Mark (CON - Checkley)
mark.deaville@staffsmoorlands.gov.uk
Elkin, Peter (IND - Cheadle South East)
peter.elkin@staffsmoorlands.gov.uk
Emery, Ben (CON - Leek West)
ben.emery@staffsmoorlands.gov.uk
Fallows, Elsie (CON - Churnet)
elsie.fallows@staffsmoorlands.gov.uk
Fisher, John (LD - Leek West)
john.fisher@staffsmoorlands.gov.uk
Forrester, Arthur (CON - Alton)
arthur.forrester@staffsmoorlands.gov.uk
Hall, Tony (IND - Biddulph North)
tony.hall@staffsmoorlands.gov.uk
Harrison, Keith (R - Leek South)
keith.harrison@staffsmoorlands.gov.uk
Hart, Andrew (IND - Biddulph North)
andrew.hart@staffsmoorlands.gov.uk
Hawkins, Norma (CON - Horton)
norma.hawkins@staffsmoorlands.gov.uk
Heath, Gill (CON - Dane)
gill.heath@staffsmoorlands.gov.uk
Hopley, Frank (INDNA - Forsbrook)
frank.hopley@staffsmoorlands.gov.uk
Jackson, Kevin (LAB - Biddulph East)
kevin.jackson@staffsmoorlands.gov.uk
Jebb, Christina (LD - Brown Edge and Endon)
christina.jebb@staffsmoorlands.gov.uk
Jebb, Henry (LD - Brown Edge and Endon)
henry.jebb@staffsmoorlands.gov.uk
Johnson, Brian (CON - Leek East)
brian.johnson@staffsmoorlands.gov.uk
Jones, John (LD - Biddulph Moor)
john.jones@staffsmoorlands.gov.uk
Locker, Ron (INDNA - Cheadle West)
ron.locker@staffsmoorlands.gov.uk
Lovatt, Margaret (LAB - Leek North)
margaret.lovatt@staffsmoorlands.gov.uk
Lovatt, Madelaine (LAB - Biddulph East)
madelaine.lovatt@staffsmoorlands.gov.uk
Malyon, Linda (R - Ipstones)
linda.maylon@staffsmoorlands.gov.uk
Martin, Lisa (INDNA - Werrington)
lisa.martin@staffsmoorlands.gov.uk
McNicol, Tony (CON - Cellarhead)
tony.mcnicol@staffsmoorlands.gov.uk
Pearce, Collin (CON - Checkley)
colin.pearce@staffsmoorlands.gov.uk
Plant, Robert (CON - Leek West)
robert.plant@staffsmoorlands.gov.uk
Podmore, Neal (CON - Leek South)
neal.podmore@staffsmoorlands.gov.uk
Povey, John (CON - Leek South)
john.povey@staffsmoorlands.gov.uk
Redfern, John (LD - Biddulph South)
john.redfern@staffsmoorlands.gov.uk
Roberts, Paul (CON - Caverswall)
paul.roberts@staffsmoorlands.gov.uk
Shaw, David (CON - Werrington)
david.shaw@staffsmoorlands.gov.uk
Sheldon, Hilda (IND - Biddulph West)
hilda.sheldon@staffsmoorlands.gov.uk
Tigger, David (CON - Checkley)
david.trigger@staffsmoorlands.gov.uk
Wain, Edwin (CON - Hamps Valley)
Walley, Jeanette (LAB - Biddulph East)
jeanette.walley@staffsmoorlands.gov.uk
Whitehouse, Ian (LD - Cheadle North East)
ian.whitehouse@staffsmoorlands.gov.uk
Wilkinson, Abigail (CON - Forsbrook)
abigail.wilkinson@staffsmoorlands.gov.uk
Williams, Barney (CON - Brown Edge and Endon)
barney.williams@staffsmoorlands.gov.uk
Wood, Pamela (INDNA - Leek East)
pam.wood@staffsmoorlands.gov.uk
Wood, Christopher (LAB - Biddulph West)
chris.wood@staffsmoorlands.gov.uk
Worthington, Michael (CON - Cheddleton)
michael.worthington@staffsmoorlands.gov.uk

POLITICAL COMPOSITION

CON: 26, IND: 9, LAB: 8, LD: 6, INDNA: 5, R: 2

CABINET

Leader: Ms Sybil Ralphs
Communities: Ms Gillian Burton
Customer Services: Mr Tony Hall
Environment: Mr Arthur Forrester
Finance & Resources: Mrs Gill Heath
Housing & Regeneration: Mr Andrew Hart
Planning, Development & Property: Mr Edwin Wain
Sport, Parks & Countryside: Mr Mark Deaville

COMMITTEE CHAIRS

Appeals Board: Mr Michael Worthington
Community (Scrutiny): Mr Michael Bowen
Health (Scrutiny): Ms Barbara Hughes
Licensing & Regulatory: Mr Jason Hails
Standards: Mr Harry Mawdsley OBE JP DL (External)

STEVENAGE D

Stevenage Borough Council, Daneshill House, Danestrete, Stevenage SG1 1HN ☎ 01438 242242 🖷 01438 242566
csc@stevenage.gov.uk 💻 www.stevenage.gov.uk

FACTS & FIGURES

Police Authority: Hertfordshire Police Authority
Health Authority: East of England Strategic Health Authority
Learning and Skills Council: Eastern
Parliamentary Constituencies: Stevenage

EU Constituencies: Eastern
Election Frequency: Elections are by thirds
Twinning: Autun (France); Ingelheim-am-Rhein (Germany); Kadoma (Zimbabwe); Shimkent (Kazakstan)

PRINCIPAL OFFICERS

Chief Executive: Mr Nick Parry, Chief Executive, Daneshill House, Danestrete, Stevenage SG1 1HN ☎ 01438 242225 🖷 01438 242134 ✉ nick.parry@stevenage.gov.uk

Deputy Chief Executive: Mr Scott Crudgington, Strategic Director, Daneshill House, Danestrete, Stevenage SG1 1HN ☎ 01438 242185 🖷 01438 242344 ✉ scott.crudgington@stevenage.gov.uk

Senior Management: Mr Peter Bandy, Strategic Director, Daneshill House, Danestrete, Stevenage SG1 1HN ☎ 01438 242288 🖷 01438 242134 ✉ peter.bandy@stevenage.gov.uk

Senior Management: Mr Marcel Coiffait, Head of Environmental Services, Daneshill House, Danestrete, Stevenage SG1 1HN ☎ 01438 242456 🖷 01438 242434 ✉ marcel.coffait@stevenage.gov.uk

Senior Management: Mr Scott Crudgington, Strategic Director, Daneshill House, Danestrete, Stevenage SG1 1HN ☎ 01438 242185 🖷 01438 242344 ✉ scott.crudgington@stevenage.gov.uk

Architect, Building / Property Services: Mr Keith Brown, Head of Property & Estates, Daneshill House, Danestrete, Stevenage SG1 1HN ☎ 01438 242154 🖷 01438 242157 ✉ keith.brown@stevenage.gov.uk

Building Control: Mr Steve Polfreman, Building Control Manager, Daneshill House, Danestrete, Stevenage SG1 1HN ☎ 01438 242256 ✉ steve.polfreman@stevenage.gov.uk

Children / Youth Services: Mr Aidan Sanderson, Head of Leisure, Community & Children's Services, Daneshill House, Danesrete, Stevenage SG1 1HN ☎ 01438 242311 ✉ aidan.sanderson@stevenage.gov.uk

PR / Communications: Ms Lucy Culkin, Communications Team Leader, Daneshill House, Danestrete, Stevenage SG1 1HN ☎ 01438 242168 🖷 01438 242344 ✉ lucie.culkin@stevenage.gov.uk

Community Safety: Ms Iman Helfin-Scott, Partnerships Officer (Community Safety), Daneshill House, Danestrete, Stevenage SG1 1HN ☎ 01438 242581 ✉ iman.helfin-scott@stevenage.gov.uk

Computer Management: Mr Henry Lewis, Head of Customer Services & Business Improvement, Daneshill House, Danestrete, Stevenage SG1 1HN ☎ 01438 242496 ✉ henry.lewis@stevenage.gov.uk

Contracts: Mr Lee Myers, Head of Environmental Services, Cavendish Road, Stevenage SG1 2ES ☎ 01438 248710 🖷 01438 242434 ✉ lee.myers@stevenage.gov.uk

Customer Service: Mr Henry Lewis, Head of Customer Services & Business Improvement, Daneshill House, Danestrete, Stevenage SG1 1HN ☎ 01438 242496 ✉ henry.lewis@stevenage.gov.uk

Direct Labour: Mr Lee Myers, Head of Environmental Services, Cavendish Road, Stevenage SG1 2ES ☎ 01438 248710 🖷 01438 242434 ✉ lee.myers@stevenage.gov.uk

Economic Development: Ms Liz Dand, Economic Development Officer, Daneshill House, Danestrete, Stevenage SG1 1HN ☎ 01438 242177 🖷 01438 242134 ✉ liz.dand@stevenage.gov.uk

E-Government: Mr Henry Lewis, Head of Customer Services & Business Improvement, Daneshill House, Danestrete, Stevenage SG1 1HN ☎ 01438 242496 ✉ henry.lewis@stevenage.gov.uk

Electoral Registration: Ms Jacqui Edwards, Electoral Services Manager, Daneshill House, Danestrete, Stevenage SG1 1HN ☎ 01438 242174 ✉ jacqui.edwards@stevenage.gov.uk

Emergency Planning: Mr Scott Crudgington, Strategic Director, Daneshill House, Danestrete, Stevenage SG1 1HN ☎ 01438 242185 🖷 01438 242344 ✉ scott.crudgington@stevenage.gov.uk

European Liaison: Mrs Maureen Nicholson, Member Services Officer, Daneshill House, Danestrete, Stevenage SG1 1HN ☎ 01438 242278 🖷 01438 242228 ✉ maureen.nicholson@stevenage.gov.uk

Facilities: Mr Gavin Coombs, Facilities Manager, Daneshill House, Danestrete, Stevenage SG1 1HN ☎ 01438 242705 🖷 01438 242157 ✉ gavin.coombs@stevenage.gov.uk

Finance and Treasurer: Mr Scott Crudgington, Strategic Director, Daneshill House, Danestrete, Stevenage SG1 1HN ☎ 01438 242185 🖷 01438 242344 ✉ scott.crudgington@stevenage.gov.uk

Fleet Management: Mr Simon Martin, Contracts Manager, Cavendish Road, Stevenage SG1 2ES ☎ 01438 218800 🖷 01438 218702 ✉ simon.martin@stevenage.gov.uk

Grounds Maintenance: Mr Paul Seaby, Contracts Manager, Cavandish Road, Stevenage SG1 2ES ☎ 01438 242772 🖷 01438 242273 ✉ paul.seaby@stevenage.gov.uk

Health and Safety: Mr Tony Hughes, Corporate Health & Safety Advisor, Daneshill House, Danestrete, Stevenage SG1 1HN ☎ 01438 218033 ✉ tony.hughes@stevenage.gov.uk

Highways: Mr Peter Bandy, Strategic Director, Daneshill House, Danestrete, Stevenage SG1 1HN ☎ 01438 242288 🖷 01438 242134 ✉ peter.bandy@stevenage.gov.uk

Home Energy Conservation: Mr Jim Archibald, Acting Head of Environmental Health and Licensing, Daneshill House, Danestrete, Stevenage SG1 1HN ☎ 01438 242242 ✉ jim.archibald@stevenage.gov.uk

Legal: Mr Paul Froggatt, Borough Solicitor, Swingate House, Danestrete, Stevenage SG1 1HN ☎ 01438 242212 🖷 01438 242197 ✉ paul.froggatt@stevenage.gov.uk

Leisure and Cultural Services: Mr Aidan Sanderson, Head of

Leisure, Community & Children's Services, Daneshill House, Danesrete, Stevenage SG1 1HN ☎ 01438 242311 ✉ aidan.sanderson@stevenage.gov.uk

Licensing: Ms Heather Morris, Licensing Manager, Daneshill House, Danestrete, Stevenage SG1 1HN ☎ 01438 212175 ✉ heather.morris@stevenage.gov.uk

Member Services: Ms Jackie Cansick, Constitutional Services Manager, Daneshill House, Danestrete, Stevenage SG1 1HN ☎ 01438 242216 🖷 01438 242963 ✉ jackie.cansick@stevenage.gov.uk

Parking: Mr Keith Moore, Parking Services Manager, Daneshill House, Danestrete, Stevenage SG1 1HN ☎ 01438 242277 🖷 01438 242242 ✉ keith.moore@stevenage.gov.uk

Partnerships: Mr Richard Protheroe, Head of Housing, Performance & Communications, Daneshill House, Danestrete, Stevenage SG1 1HN ☎ 01438 242938 🖷 01483 242344 ✉ richard.protheroe@stevenage.gov.uk

Personnel / HR: Ms Cath Cashin, Head of Human Resources & Operational Development, Daneshill House, Danestrete, Stevenage SG1 1HN ☎ 01438 242164 🖷 01438 242112 ✉ cath.cashin@stevenage.gov.uk

Planning: Mr Viv Evans, Head of Development & Planning, Daneshill House, Danestrete, Stevenage SG1 1HN ☎ 01438 242457 🖷 01438 242134 ✉ viv.evans@stevenage.gov.uk

Procurement: Ms Lisa Baldock, Corporate Procurement Manager, Daneshill House, Danestrete, Stevenage SG1 1HN ☎ 01438 242083

Recycling & Waste Minimisation: Mr Lee Myers, Head of Environmental Services, Cavendish Road, Stevenage SG1 2ES ☎ 01438 248710 🖷 01438 242434 ✉ lee.myers@stevenage.gov.uk

Regeneration: Mr Neil Cuttell, Regeneration Manager, Daneshill House, Danestrete, Stevenage SG1 1HN ☎ 01438 242825 ✉ neil.cuttell@stevenage.gov.uk

Regeneration: Mr Viv Evans, Head of Development & Planning, Daneshill House, Danestrete, Stevenage SG1 1HN ☎ 01438 242457 🖷 01438 242134 ✉ viv.evans@stevenage.gov.uk

Staff Training: Ms Edith Gardner, Training & Development Manager, Daneshill House, Danestrete, Stevenage SG1 1HN ☎ 01438 242222 ✉ edith.gardner@stevenage.gov.uk

Street Scene: Ms Julia Knight, Green Spaces Policy & Development Manager, Daneshill House, Danestrete, Stevenage SG1 1HN ☎ 01438 242900 ✉ julia.knight@stevenage.gov.uk

Sustainable Communities: Mr Viv Evans, Head of Development & Planning, Daneshill House, Danestrete, Stevenage SG1 1HN ☎ 01438 242457 🖷 01438 242134 ✉ viv.evans@stevenage.gov.uk

Town Centre: Ms Tracey Parry, Town Centre Manager, Daneshill House, Danestrete, Stevenage SG1 1HN ☎ 01438 242242

Transport: Mr Rob Woodisse, Principal Engineer, Daneshill House, Danestrete, Stevenage SG1 1HN ☎ 01438 242272 🖷 01438 242134 ✉ rob.woodisse@stevenage.gov.uk

Waste Collection and Disposal: Mr Lee Myers, Head of Environmental Services, Cavendish Road, Stevenage SG1 2ES ☎ 01438 248710 🖷 01438 242434 ✉ lee.myers@stevenage.gov.uk

Waste Management: Mr Lee Myers, Head of Environmental Services, Cavendish Road, Stevenage SG1 2ES ☎ 01438 248710 🖷 01438 242434 ✉ lee.myers@stevenage.gov.uk

Children's Play Areas: Mr Aidan Sanderson, Head of Leisure, Community & Children's Services, Daneshill House, Danesrete, Stevenage SG1 1HN ☎ 01438 242311 ✉ aidan.sanderson@stevenage.gov.uk

MEMBERS OF THE COUNCIL (39)

***Mayor:* Lloyd**, John (LAB - Roebuck)
john.lloyd@stevenage.gov.uk

***Leader of the Council:* Taylor**, Sharon (LAB - Symonds Green)
sharon.taylor@stevenage.gov.uk

***Deputy Leader of the Council:* Gardner**, John (LAB - Roebuck)
john.gardner@stevenage.gov.uk

***Group Leader:* Clark**, Graham (CON - Woodfield)
graham.clark@stevenage.gov.uk

Batson, Sherma (LAB - Roebuck)
sherma.batson@stevenage.gov.uk

Bell, Lorraine (LAB - Longmeadow)
lorraine.bell@stevenage.gov.uk

Bibby, Philip (CON - Woodfield)
philip.bibby@stevenage.gov.uk

Brown, Jim (LAB - Old Town)
jim.brown@stevenage.gov.uk

Burrell, Howard (LAB - Chells)
howard.burrell@stevenage.gov.uk

Cherney-Craw, Monika (LAB - Longmeadow)
monika.cherneycraw@stevenage.gov.uk

Chester, Laurie (LAB - Symonds Green)
laurie.chester@stevenage.gov.uk

Clark, Bob (LAB - Shephall)

Cullen, David (LAB - Bedwell)
david.cullen@stevenage.gov.uk

Gardner, Michelle (LAB - Bandley Hill)
michelle.gardner@stevenage.gov.uk

Harrington, Liz (LAB - Bedwell)
liz.harrington@stevenage.gov.uk

Hearn, Michael (CON - Martins Wood)
michael.hearn@stevenage.gov.uk

Henry, Richard (LAB - St Nicholas)
richard.henry@stevenage.gov.uk

Hollywell, Jacqueline (LAB - Bandley Hill)
jacqueline.hollywell@stevenage.gov.uk

Hurst, Christine (CON - Longmeadow)
christine.hurst@stevenage.gov.uk

Kissane, Patrick (LAB - Symonds Green)
david.kissane@stevenage.gov.uk

Latif, Carol (LAB - St Nicholas)
carol.latif@stevenage.gov.uk

Lloyd, Joan (LAB - Bandley Hill)
joan.lloyd@stevenage.gov.uk

Martin-Haugh, Lin (LAB - Pin Green)
lin.martin-haugh@stevenage.gov.uk

McKay, Maureen (LAB - Martins Wood)

maureen.mckay@stevenage.gov.uk
Mead, John (LD - Manor)
john.mead@stevenage.gov.uk
Notley, Margaret (CON - Woodfield)
margaret.notley@stevenage.gov.uk
Parker, Robin (LD - Manor)
robin.parker@stevenage.gov.uk
Pickersgill, Jack (LAB - Shephall)
jack.pickersgill@stevenage.gov.uk
Raynor, Ralph (LAB - St Nicholas)
ralph.raynor@stevenage.gov.uk
Snell, Graham (LD - Manor)
graham.snell@stevenage.gov.uk
Speller, Simon (LAB - Pin Green)
simon.speller@stevenage.gov.uk
Stuart, Pam (LAB - Chells)
pam.stuart@stevenage.gov.uk
Tessier, Hugh (LAB - Old Town)
hugh.tessier@stevenage.gov.uk
Thomas, Jeanette (LAB - Pin Green)
jeannette.thomas@stevenage.gov.uk
Underwood, Brian (LAB - Bedwell)
brian.underwood@stevenage.gov.uk
Walker, Sarah (LAB - Martins Wood)
sarah.walker@stevenage.gov.uk
Warwick, Vickie (LAB - Chells)
vickie.warwick@stevenage.gov.uk
Webb, Ann (LAB - Shephall)
ann.webb@stevenage.gov.uk
Yarnold-Forrester, Marilyn (CON - Old Town)
marilyn.yarnold-forrester@stevenage.gov.uk

POLITICAL COMPOSITION
LAB: 30, CON: 6, LD: 3

CABINET
Leader: Ms Sharon Taylor
Deputy Leader / Environment & Regeneration: Mr John Gardner
Children & Young People, Culture, Sport & Leisure: Mr Howard Burrell
Community, Health & Older People: Ms Sherma Batson
Economy, Enterprise & Transport: Mr Ralph Raynor
Housing: Ms Ann Webb
Resources: Mrs Joan Lloyd
Safer & Stronger Communities: Mr Richard Henry

COMMITTEE CHAIRS
Appointments: Ms Sharon Taylor
Audit: Mrs Laurie Chester
Children, Young People, Culture, Sport & Leisure (Scrutiny): Mr Hugh Tessier
Community, Health & Older People (Scrutiny): Mrs Jacqueline Hollywell
Economy, Enterprise & Transport (Scrutiny): Ms Pam Stuart
Environment & Regeneration (Scrutiny): Ms Vickie Warwick
General Purposes: Mr Patrick Kissane
Housing (Scrutiny): Mrs Monika Cherney-Craw
Licensing: Mr Patrick Kissane
Planning & Development: Mr David Cullen
Resources (Scrutiny): Ms Jeanette Thomas
Safer & Stronger Communities (Scrutiny): Ms Liz Harrington
Standards: Mr Allen Holland (External)
Statement of Accounts: Mrs Joan Lloyd

STIRLING S

Stirling Council, Old Viewforth, Stirling FK8 2ET ☎ 0845 277 7000 ✉ info@stirling.gov.uk 💻 www.stirling.gov.uk

FACTS & FIGURES
Police Authority: Central Scotland Police Authority
Health Authority: NHS Forth Valley
Learning and Skills Council: Scotland
Parliamentary Constituencies: Stirling
EU Constituencies: Scotland
Election Frequency: Elections are of whole council
Twinning: Obuda (Hungary); Villeneuve d'Asq (France); Friendship links: Dunedin (Florida, USA); Summerside (Prince Edward Island, Canada)

PRINCIPAL OFFICERS
Chief Executive: Mr Bob Jack, Chief Executive, Old Viewforth, Stirling FK8 2ET ☎ 01786 443320 ✉ jackb@stirling.gov.uk

Assistant Chief Executive: Ms Janice Hewitt, Assistant Chief Executive, Old Viewforth, Stirling FK8 2ET ☎ 01786 442677 🖷 01786 443474 ✉ hewittj@stirling.gov.uk

Assistant Chief Executive: Ms Linda Kinney, Assistant Chief Executive, Old Viewforth, Stirling FK8 2ET ☎ 01786 442526 🖷 01786 443474 ✉ kinneyl@stirling.gov.uk

Assistant Chief Executive: Ms Rebecca Maxwell, Assistant Chief Executive, Old Viewforth, Stirling FK8 2ET ☎ 01786 443366 🖷 01786 443474 ✉ maxwellr@stirling.gov.uk

Senior Management: Mr Tony Cain, Head of Service: Housing & Customer Service, Old Viewforth, Stirling FK8 2ET ☎ 01786 443018 ✉ caint@stirling.gov.uk

Senior Management: Ms Deirdre Cilliers, Head of Joint Services / Chief Social Work Officer, Viewforth, Stirling FK8 2ET ☎ 01259 450000; 01786 442935 🖷 01259 452440; 01786 442782 ✉ dcilliers@clacks.gov.uk; dcilliers@clacks.gov.uk

Senior Management: Mr Des Friel, Head of Service: Employment, Communities & Youth, Old Viewforth, Stirling FK8 2ET ☎ 0845 443419 ✉ frield@stirling.gov.uk

Senior Management: Mr Bob Gil, Head of Service: Corporate Projects Implementation, Old Viewforth, Stirling FK8 2ET ☎ 01786 442643 ✉ gilr@stirling.gov.uk

Senior Management: Mr Les Goodfellow, Head of Environment Services, Old Viewforth, Stirling FK8 2ET ☎ 01786 443308 🖷 01786 443058 ✉ goodfellowl@stirling.gov.uk

Senior Management: Ms Belinda Greer, Head of Service: Education, Viewforth, Stirling FK8 2ET ☎ 01786 442680 ✉ greerb@stirling.gov.uk

Senior Management: Mr John Risk, Head of Service: Assets & Support, Old Viewforth, Stirling FK8 2ET ☎ 01786 443086

🖷 01786 442993 ✉ riskj@stirling.gov.uk

Senior Management: Mr Kevin Robertson, Head of Service: Planning, Regulation & Waste Services, Old Viewforth, Stirling FK8 2ET ☎ 01786 442872 🖷 01786 442451 ✉ robertsonk@stirling.gov.uk

Senior Management: Mr Willie Watson, Head of Governance & Resources, Old Viewforth, Stirling FK8 2ET ☎ 01786 442811 🖷 01786 442993 ✉ watsonw@stirling.gov.uk

Architect, Building / Property Services: Mr Drew Leslie, Landlord Services Manager, Viewforth, Pitt Terrace, Stirling FK8 2ET ☎ 01786 442465 🖷 01786 442471 ✉ leslied@stirling.gov.uk

Architect, Building / Property Services: Mrs Lesley Malkin, Strategic Asset Manager, Viewforth, Pitt Terrace, Stirling FK8 2ET ☎ 01786 442597 🖷 01786 442471 ✉ malkinl@stirling.gov.uk

Best Value: Mr Bill Scott, Manager, Old Viewforth, Stirling FK8 2ET ☎ 01786 443341 🖷 01786 442933 ✉ scottb@stirling.gov.uk

Building Control: Mrs Joyce Wighton, Service Manager / Building Standards & Licensing, Municipal Buildings, 8-10 Corn Exchange Road, Stirling FK8 2HU ☎ 01786 443418 🖷 01786 432203 ✉ wightonj@stirling.gov.uk

Catering Services: Ms Margaret Gilmour, FM Services Manager, Viewforth, Stirling FK8 2ET ☎ 01786 442474 ✉ gilmourm@stirling.gov.uk

Children / Youth Services: Mr Bill Miller, Service Manager (Youth Services), Viewforth, Stirling FK8 2ET ☎ 01786 443169 ✉ millerb@stirling.gov.uk

Civil Registration: Mr Alan Whisker, Customer Services Development Manager, Viewforth, Stirling FK8 2ET ☎ 01786 443258 ✉ whiskera@stirling.gov.uk

PR / Communications: Ms Katy Oliver, Team Leader: Communications & Marketing, Old Viewforth, Stirling FK8 2ET ☎ 01786 443362 🖷 01786 443395 ✉ oliverk@stirling.gov.uk

Community Planning: Ms Cath Sutherland, Team Leader: Strategic & Community Planning, Old Viewforth, Stirling FK8 2ET ☎ 01786 442963 🖷 01786 442933 ✉ sutherlandc@stirling.gov.uk

Community Safety: Ms Anne Allan, Service Manager: Safer Communities, Viewforth, Stirling FK8 2ET ☎ 01786 442475 ✉ allana@stirling.gov.uk

Computer Management: Mr Mark Tye, Business Transformation & Technology Manager, Old Viewforth, Stirling FK8 2ET ☎ 01786 443090 🖷 01786 443023 ✉ tyem@stirling.gov.uk

Consumer Protection and Trading Standards: Mr Leslie Fisher, Service Manager: Environmental Health & Trading Standards, Municipal Buildings, Stirling FK8 2QU ☎ 01786 432180 🖷 01786 432203 ✉ fisherl@stirling.gov.uk

Contracts: Ms Liz Duncan, Chief Governance Officer, Old Viewforth, Stirling FK8 2ET ☎ 01786 443352 🖷 01786 443078 ✉ duncanl@stirling.gov.uk

Direct Labour: Mr John MacMillan, Technical Services Manager, Springkerse Depot, Kerse Road, Stirling FK7 7TE ☎ 01786 443566 🖷 01786 446042 ✉ macmillanj@stirling.gov.uk

Direct Labour: Mr Jamie Wright, Roads Maintenance Manager, Springkerse Depot, Kerse Road, Stirling FK7 7SN ☎ 01786 443526 🖷 01786 442696 ✉ wrightj@stirling.gov.uk

Economic Development: Mrs Deborah Murray, Service Manager: Economic Development & Tourism, Viewforth, Stirling FK8 2ET ☎ 01786 442821 ✉ murrayd@stirling.gov.uk

Education: Mr Kevin Kelman, Assistant Head of Education, Viewforth, Stirling FK8 2ET ☎ 01786 442680; 01786 442680 ✉ kelmank@stirling.gov.uk; kelmank@stirling.gov.uk

Education: Mr Alan Millikin, Assistant Head of Education, Viewforth, Stirling FK8 2ET ☎ 01786 442945; 01786 442945 ✉ millikina@stirling.gov.uk; millikina@stirling.gov.uk

E-Government: Mr Mark Tye, Business Transformation & Technology Manager, Old Viewforth, Stirling FK8 2ET ☎ 01786 443090 🖷 01786 443023 ✉ tyem@stirling.gov.uk

Emergency Planning: Mr David Bright, Resilience & Risk Manager, Viewforth, Stirling FK8 2ET ☎ 01786 443186 🖷 01786 443474 ✉ brightd@stirling.gov.uk

Energy Management: Mr Pierre Boinot, Energy Officer, Viewforth, Stirling FK8 2ET ☎ 01786 442915 🖷 01786 442471 ✉ bionotp@stirling.gov.uk

Energy Management: Mrs Grace Conner, Energy Officer, Viewforth, Stirling FK8 2ET ☎ 01786 442478 🖷 01786 442471 ✉ connerg@stirling.gov.uk

Environmental Health: Mr Leslie Fisher, Service Manager: Environmental Health & Trading Standards, Municipal Buildings, Stirling FK8 2QU ☎ 01786 432180 🖷 01786 432203 ✉ fisherl@stirling.gov.uk

Estates, Property & Valuation: Mrs Lesley Malkin, Strategic Asset Manager, Viewforth, Pitt Terrace, Stirling FK8 2ET ☎ 01786 442597 🖷 01786 442471 ✉ malkinl@stirling.gov.uk

European Liaison: Ms Cath Sutherland, Team Leader: Strategic & Community Planning, Old Viewforth, Stirling FK8 2ET ☎ 01786 442963 🖷 01786 442933 ✉ sutherlandc@stirling.gov.uk

Facilities: Ms Margaret Gilmour, FM Services Manager, Viewforth, Stirling FK8 2ET ☎ 01786 442474 ✉ gilmourm@stirling.gov.uk

Facilities: Mr Jim McNeish, Office Facilities Manager, Old Viewforth, Stirling FK8 2ET ☎ 01786 443349 ✉ mcneishj@stirling.gov.uk

Fleet Management: Mr Gavin Hutton, Fleet Manager, Fleet Services, Springkerse Depot, Kerse Road, Stirling FK7 7TE ☎ 01786 443513 ✉ huttong@stirling.gov.uk

Grounds Maintenance: Ms Nicole Paterson, Land Services Manager, Streetscape Services, Springkerse Depot, Kerse Road, Stirling FK7 7TE ☎ 01786 443820 ✉ patersonn@stirling.gov.uk

Health and Safety: Mr Nick Sabo, Health & Safety Adviser, Viewforth, Stirling FK8 2ET ☎ 01786 442953 ✉ sabon@stirling.gov.uk

Highways: Mr Les Goodfellow, Head of Environment Services, Old Viewforth, Stirling FK8 2ET ☎ 01786 443308 🖷 01786 443058 ✉ goodfellowl@stirling.gov.uk

Home Energy Conservation: Mr Brian Cree, Energy Officer, Viewforth, Stirling FK8 2ET ☎ 01786 442887 ✉ creeb@stirling.gov.uk

Housing: Mr Tony Cain, Head of Service: Housing & Customer Service, Viewforth, Stirling FK8 2ET ☎ 01786 443018 ✉ caint@stirling.gov.uk

Housing: Ms Carol Hamilton, Homeless & Tenant Services Manager, Old Viewforth, Stirling FK8 2ET ☎ 01786 442624 ✉ hamiltonc@stirling.gov.uk

Housing Maintenance: Mr John MacMillan, Technical Services Manager, Springkerse Depot, Kerse Road, Stirling FK7 7TE ☎ 01786 443566 🖷 01786 446042 ✉ macmillanj@stirling.gov.uk

Legal: Ms Liz Duncan, Chief Governance Officer, Old Viewforth, Stirling FK8 2ET ☎ 01786 443352 🖷 01786 443078 ✉ duncanl@stirling.gov.uk

Licensing: Mrs Joyce Wighton, Service Manager / Building Standards & Licensing, Municipal Buildings, 8-10 Corn Exchange Road, Stirling FK8 2HU ☎ 01786 443418 🖷 01786 432203 ✉ wightonj@stirling.gov.uk

Lifelong Learning: Ms Lynne Gibbons, Service Manager: Culture & Adult Learning, Cowane Centre, Cowane Street, Stirling FK8 1JP ☎ 01786 432361 ✉ gibbonsla@stirling.gov.uk

Lighting: Mr Ian Young, Team Leader, Springkerse Depot, Kerse Road, Stirling FK7 7TS ☎ 01786 443941 ✉ youngi@stirling.gov.uk

Lottery Funding, Charity and Voluntary: Ms Jean Cowie, Funding Officer, One Stop Shop, 1 - 5 Port Street, Stirling FK8 2EJ ☎ 01786 442050 ✉ cowiej@stirling.gov.uk

Member Services: Ms Joyce Allen, Democratic Support Manager, Viewforth, Stirling FK8 2ET ☎ 01786 443370 🖷 01786 443078 ✉ allenj@stirling.gov.uk

Parking: Mr Alan Ogilvie, Team Leader: Traffic Management, Viewforth, Stirling FK8 2ET ☎ 01786 442487 ✉ ogilvieaf@stirling.gov.uk

Partnerships: Ms Lesley Gallagher, Community Planning Manager, Old Viewforth, Stirling FK8 2ET ☎ 01786 443184 ✉ gallagherl@stirling.gov.uk

Personnel / HR: Ms Kristine Johnson, Chief Officer, Viewforth, Stirling FK8 2ET ☎ 01786 442554 🖷 01786 443136 ✉ johnsonk@stirling.gov.uk

Planning: Mr Peter Morgan, Chief Planning Officer, Viewforth, Stirling FK8 2ET ☎ 01786 442683 ✉ morganp@stirling.gov.uk

Procurement: Mr Don MacMillan, Procurement Officer, Viewforth, Stirling FK8 2ET ☎ 01786 442770 ✉ macmilland@stirling.gov.uk

Recycling & Waste Minimisation: Mr David Hopper, Waste Services Manager, Lower Polmaise Waste Management Facility, Fallin, Stirling FK7 7LU ☎ 01786 443038 ✉ hopperd@stirling.gov.uk

Road Safety: Mr Stuart Geddes, Road Safety Engineer, Viewforth, Stirling FK8 2ET ☎ 01786 442442 ✉ geddess@stirling.gov.uk

Social Services: Ms Deirdre Cilliers, Head of Joint Services / Chief Social Work Officer, Viewforth, Stirling FK8 2ET ☎ 01259 450000; 01786 442935 🖷 01259 452440; 01786 442782 ✉ dcilliers@clacks.gov.uk; dcilliers@clacks.gov.uk

Staff Training: Ms Suzan Duffus, Organisational Development Manager, Viewforth, Stirling FK8 2ET ☎ 01786 443161 ✉ duffuss@stirling.gov.uk

Street Scene: Ms Nicole Paterson, Land Services Manager, Streetscape Services, Springkerse Depot, Kerse Road, Stirling FK7 7TE ☎ 01786 443820 ✉ patersonn@stirling.gov.uk

Sustainable Communities: Ms Angela Heaney, Policy Officer (Sustainability), Old Viewforth, Stirling FK8 2ET ☎ 01786 442996 ✉ heaneya@stirling.gov.uk

Tourism: Mrs Deborah Murray, Service Manager: Economic Development & Tourism, Viewforth, Stirling FK8 2ET ☎ 01786 442821 ✉ murrayd@stirling.gov.uk

Town Centre: Mr Andrew Kennedy, City Centre Manager, Regeneration Services, Viewforth, Stirling FK8 2ET ☎ 01786 442534 🖷 01786 443104

Traffic Management: Mr Alan Ogilvie, Team Leader: Traffic Management, Viewforth, Stirling FK8 2ET ☎ 01786 442487 ✉ ogilvieaf@stirling.gov.uk

Transport Planner: Mr Colin McNicol, Service Manager: Roads Support, Viewforth, Stirling FK8 2ET ☎ 01786 443556 🖷 01786 442451 ✉ mcnicolc@stirling.gov.uk

Waste Collection and Disposal: Mr David Hopper, Waste Services Manager, Viewforth, Stirling FK8 2ET ☎ 01786 443038 ✉ hopperd@stirling.gov.uk

Waste Management: Mr David Hopper, Waste Services Manager, Viewforth, Stirling FK8 2ET ☎ 01786 443038 ✉ hopperd@stirling.gov.uk

MEMBERS OF THE COUNCIL (22)

Leader of the Council: **McChord**, Corrie (LAB - Stirling East) mcchordc@stirling.gov.uk

Deputy Leader of the Council: **Berrill**, Alistair (CON - Forth and Endrick)
berrilla@stirling.gov.uk
Benny, Neil (CON - Stirling West)
bennyn@stirling.gov.uk
Boyd, Johanna (LAB - Castle)
boydj@stirling.gov.uk
Brisley, Margaret (LAB - BannockBurn)
brisleym@stirling.gov.uk
Campbell, Callum (CON - Dunblaine and Bridge of Allan)
campbellc@stirling.gov.uk
Earl, Martin (CON - Trossachs and Teith)
earlm@stirling.gov.uk
Farmer, Scott (SNP - Stirling West)
farmers@stirling.gov.uk
Gibson, Danny (LAB - Stirling East)
gibsond@stirling.gov.uk
Hayes, Alycia (SNP - Trossachs and Teith)
hayesa@stirling.gov.uk
Hendry, John (LAB - Castle)
hendryj@stirling.gov.uk
Houston, Graham (SNP - Dunblaine and Bridge of Allan)
houstong@stirling.gov.uk
Lambie, Graham (SNP - Forth and Endrick)
lambieg@stirling.gov.uk
MacPherson, Alasdair (SNP - BannockBurn)
macphersona@stirling.gov.uk
Muirhead, Ian (SNP - Forth and Endrick)
muirheadi@stirling.gov.uk
Paterson, Steven (SNP - Stirling East)
patersonst@stirling.gov.uk
Robbins, Mike (LAB - Dunblane and Bridge of Allan)
robbinsm@stirling.gov.uk
Ruskell, Mark (SGP - Dunblane and Bridge of Allan)
ruskellm@stirling.gov.uk
Simpson, Christine (LAB - Stirling West)
simpsonc@stirling.gov.uk
Thomson, Jim (SNP - Castle)
thomsonjo3@stirling.gov.uk
Weir, Violet (LAB - BannockBurn)
weirv@stirling.gov.uk
Wood, Fergus (SNP - Trossachs and Teith)
woodf@stirling.gov.uk

POLITICAL COMPOSITION
SNP: 9, LAB: 8, CON: 4, SGP: 1

CABINET
Leader / Community Planning: Mr Corrie McChord
Deputy Leader / Education: Mr Alistair Berrill
Environment, Transport & Public Land: Mr Danny Gibson
Finance, Economy & Culture: Mr Neil Benny
Housing & Regeneration: Ms Violet Weir
Policy & Performance: Ms Johanna Boyd
Social Care, Health & Sport: Ms Margaret Brisley

COMMITTEE CHAIRS
Education: Mr Alistair Berrill
Finance: Mr Neil Benny
Scrutiny & Audit: Mr Scott Farmer

STOCKPORT M

Stockport Metropolitan Borough Council, (Stockport Council), Town Hall, Edward Street, Stockport SK1 3XE ☎ 0161 480 4949 🖷 0161 477 9530 🖳 www.stockport.gov.uk

FACTS & FIGURES
Police Authority: Greater Manchester Police Authority
Health Authority: North West Strategic Health Authority
Learning and Skills Council: North West
Parliamentary Constituencies: Cheadle, Denton and Reddish, Hazel Grove, Stockport
EU Constituencies: North West
Election Frequency: Elections are by thirds
Twinning: Beziers (France); Heilbronn (Germany)

PRINCIPAL OFFICERS
Chief Executive: Mr Eamonn Boylan, Chief Executive, Town Hall, Edward Street, Stockport SK1 3XE ☎ 0161 474 3001 🖷 0161 480 6773 eamonn.boylan@stockport.gov.uk

Assistant Chief Executive: Mrs Laureen Donnan, Assistant Chief Executive (Strategy & Democracy), Town Hall, Edward Street, Stockport SK1 3XE ☎ 0161 474 3180 🖷 0161 474 3009 laureen.donnan@stockport.gov.uk

Assistant Chief Executive: Mrs Janine Watson, Assistant Chief Executive (Communications), Town Hall, Edward Street, Stockport SK1 3XE ☎ 0161 474 3060 🖷 0161 474 3099 janine.watson@stockport.gov.uk

Senior Management: Mr Steve Houston, Corporate Director, Stopford House, Piccadilly, Stockport SK1 3XE ☎ 0161 474 4000 🖷 0161 474 4006 steve.houston@stockport.gov.uk

Senior Management: Mr Andrew Webb, Corporate Director, Stopford House, Piccadilly, Stockport SK1 3XE ☎ 0161 474 3808 🖷 0161 480 3497 andrew.webb@stockport.gov.uk

Architect, Building / Property Services: Mr Nigel Lawford, Director of Design & Procurement, NPS Stockport Ltd, Atlas House, Hercules Office Park, Bird Hall Lane, Cheadle Heath, Stockport SK3 0UX ☎ 0161 495 6051 🖷 0161 474 6138 nigel.lawford@nps.co.uk

Best Value: Ms Andrea Stewart, Acting Head of Policy & Performance, Stopford House, Piccadilly, Stockport SK1 3XE ☎ 0161 474 3243 🖷 0161 474 3079 andrea.stewart@stockport.gov.uk

Building Control: Mr Ian O'Donnell, Head of Environmental Health & Trading Standards, Stopford House, Piccadilly, Stockport SK1 3XE ☎ 0161 474 4175 🖷 0161 474 4369 ian.odonnell@stockport.gov.uk

Catering Services: Ms Joyce Rowe, Venue Catering Operations Manager, Solutions SK Ltd, Venue Catering, Stopford House, Piccadilly, Stockport SK1 3XE ☎ 0161 474 4575 joyce.rowe@solutionssk.co.uk

Children / Youth Services: Ms Jacqui Belfield-Smith, Head of Service - Youth Offending, 1st Floor Owl House, 59-61 Great Underbank, Stockport SK1 1NE ☎ 0161 476 2876 jacqui.belfield-smith@stockport.gov.uk

Children / Youth Services: Mr Andrew Webb, Corporate Director, Stopford House, Piccadilly, Stockport SK1 3XE ☎ 0161 474 3808 🖷 0161 480 3497 ✉ andrew.webb@stockport.gov.uk

Civil Registration: Mr William Roberts, Superintendent Registrar, Town Hall, Edward Street, Stockport SK1 3XE ☎ 0161 474 3391 🖷 0161 474 3390 ✉ bill.roberts@stockport.gov.uk

PR / Communications: Mr John Pasiecznik, Media & Public Relations Manager, Town Hall, Edward Street, Stockport SK1 3XE ☎ 0161 474 3063 🖷 0161 474 3099 ✉ john.pasiecznik@stockport.gov.uk

Community Planning: Ms Andrea Stewart, Acting Head of Policy & Performance, Stopford House, Piccadilly, Stockport SK1 3XE ☎ 0161 474 3243 🖷 0161 474 3079 ✉ andrea.stewart@stockport.gov.uk

Community Safety: Mr Steve Brown, Head of Community Safety & Neighbourhoods, Fred Perry House, Edward Street, Stockport SK1 3AA ☎ 0161 474 3140 🖷 0161 474 3144 ✉ steve.brown@stockport.gov.uk

Computer Management: Mr Andrew Kirkham, Head of ICT, Stopford House, Piccadilly, Stockport SK1 3XE ☎ 0161 474 5401 🖷 0161 474 5403 ✉ andrew.kirkham@stockport.gov.uk

Consumer Protection and Trading Standards: Mr Stuart Jackson, Service Director for the Environment, Fred Perry House, Edward Street, Stockport SK1 3XE ☎ 0161 474 3504 ✉ stuart.jackson@stockport.gov.uk

Consumer Protection and Trading Standards: Mr Ian O'Donnell, Head of Environmental Health & Trading Standards, Stopford House, Piccadilly, Stockport SK1 3XE ☎ 0161 474 4175 🖷 0161 474 4369 ✉ ian.odonnell@stockport.gov.uk

Contracts: Mr Murray Carr, Head of Property & Procurement, Stopford House, Stockport SK1 3XE ☎ 0161 474 3649 🖷 0161 474 4119 ✉ murray.carr@stockport.gov.uk

Customer Service: Mr Adrian Moores, Head of Customer Services, Stopford House, Piccadilly, Stockport SK1 3XE ☎ 0161 474 5405 ✉ adrian.moores@stockport.gov.uk

Direct Labour: Mr Nic Cox, Managing Director, Solutions SK Ltd, Enterprise House, Birdhall Lane, Cheadle Heath, Stockport SK3 0XT ☎ 0161 474 5566 🖷 0161 474 5640 ✉ nic.cox@solutionssk.co.uk

Economic Development: Mr Sean Dillon, Funding Officer, Fred Perry House, Edward Street, Stockport SK1 3XE ☎ 0161 474 3752 🖷 0161 474 3701 ✉ sean.dillon@stockport.gov.uk

Economic Development: Ms Nicola Turner, Head of Economic Regeneration, Fred Perry House, Edward Street, Stockport SK1 3XE ☎ 0161 218 1635 ✉ nicola.turner@stockport.gov.uk

Education: Mr Richard Bates, Service Director - Learning & Achievement, Stopford House, Piccadilly, Stockport SK1 3XE ☎ 0161 474 3832 ✉ richard.bates@stockport.gov.uk

Education: Ms Pat Morgan, Head of School Support Services, Stopford House, Piccadilly, Stockport SK1 3XE ☎ 0161 474 3917 🖷 0161 953 0012 ✉ pat.morgan@stockport.gov.uk

Education: Mr Andrew Webb, Corporate Director, Stopford House, Piccadilly, Stockport SK1 3XE ☎ 0161 474 3808 🖷 0161 480 3497 ✉ andrew.webb@stockport.gov.uk

E-Government: Mr Andrew Kirkham, Head of ICT, Stopford House, Piccadilly, Stockport SK1 3XE ☎ 0161 474 5401 🖷 0161 474 5403 ✉ andrew.kirkham@stockport.gov.uk

Electoral Registration: Mr Steve Callender, Scrutiny Manager, Town Hall, Edward Street, Stockport SK1 3XE ☎ 0161 474 3184 🖷 0161 474 3259 ✉ steve.callender@stockport.gov.uk

Energy Management: Mr Nathaniel Stott, Energy Manager, NPS Stockport Ltd, Atlas House, Bird Hall Lane, Cheadle Heath, Stockport SK3 0UX ☎ 0161 495 6113 🖷 0161 495 6138 ✉ nat.stott@nps-stockport.co.uk

Environmental / Technical Services: Mr Ian O'Donnell, Head of Environmental Health & Trading Standards, Stopford House, Piccadilly, Stockport SK1 3XE ☎ 0161 474 4175 🖷 0161 474 4369 ✉ ian.odonnell@stockport.gov.uk

Environmental Health: Mr Ian O'Donnell, Head of Environmental Health & Trading Standards, Stopford House, Piccadilly, Stockport SK1 3XE ☎ 0161 474 4175 🖷 0161 474 4369 ✉ ian.odonnell@stockport.gov.uk

Estates, Property & Valuation: Mr Brian Ormerod, Director of Estates & Asset Management, NPS Stockport Ltd, Atlas House, Bird Hall Lane, Cheadle Heath, Stockport SK3 0UX ☎ 0161 495 6083 🖷 0161 495 6138 ✉ brian.ormerod@nps-stockport.co.uk

European Liaison: Mr Sean Dillon, Funding Officer, Stopford House, Piccadilly, Stockport SK1 3XE ☎ 0161 474 3752 🖷 0161 474 3701 ✉ sean.dillon@stockport.gov.uk

Events Manager: Ms Cheryl Garnett, Event Co-ordinator, Town Hall, Edward Street, Stockport SK1 3XE ☎ 0161 474 3452 🖷 0161 474 7698 ✉ cheryl.garnett@stockport.gov.uk

Events Manager: Ms Katherine Hilditch, Event Co-ordinator, Town Hall, Edward Street, Stockport SK1 3XE ☎ 0161 474 3458 🖷 0161 474 7698 ✉ katherine.hilditch@stockport.gov.uk

Events Manager: Ms Samantha Jones, Event Co-ordinator, Town Hall, Edward Street, Stockport SK1 3XE ☎ 0161 474 3457 🖷 0161 474 7698 ✉ samantha.jones@stockport.gov.uk

Events Manager: Ms Heidi LeBrun, Event Co-ordinator, Town Hall, Edward Street, Stockport SK1 3XE ☎ 0161 474 3452 🖷 0161 474 7698 ✉ heidi.lebrun@stockport.gov.uk

Facilities: Ms Joanne Chadwick, Team Manager, Venues & Functions (Town Hall Manager), Town Hall, Edward Street, Stockport SK1 3XE ☎ 0161 474 3450 🖷 0161 474 7698

Finance and Treasurer: Mr Steve Houston, Corporate Director, Stopford House, Piccadilly, Stockport SK1 3XE ☎ 0161 474 4000 🖷 0161 474 4006 ✉ steve.houston@stockport.gov.uk

Fleet Management: Mr Alan Lowe, Fleet Manager, Solutions SK Ltd, Enterprise House, Birdhall Lane, Cheadle Heath, Stockport SK3 0XS ☎ 0161 474 5527 📠 0161 474 5640 ✉ alan.lowe@solutionssk.co.uk

Grounds Maintenance: Mr David Brayshay, Head of Parks & Recreation, Fred Perry House, Edward Street, Stockport SK1 3XE ☎ 0161 474 4494 ✉ david.brayshay@stockport.gov.uk

Health and Safety: Mr Bob Youel, Senior Occupational Safety & Health Adviser, Stopford House, Piccadilly, Stockport SK1 3XE ☎ 0161 474 3056 📠 0161 474 3046 ✉ bob.youel@stockport.gov.uk

Home Energy Conservation: Ms Clare Redfern, Affordable Warmth Officer, Fred Perry House, Stockport SK1 3DA ☎ 0161 474 4397 📠 0161 474 4337 ✉ clare.redfern@stockport.gov.uk

Housing Maintenance: Mr Mark Hudson, Director of Technical Services, Stockport Homes, 2nd Floor, St Peter's Square, Stockport SK1 1NZ ☎ 0161 474 4508 📠 0161 474 4557 ✉ mark.hudson@stockporthomes.org

Local Area Agreement: Ms Andrea Stewart, Acting Head of Policy & Performance, Stopford House, Piccadilly, Stockport SK1 3XE ☎ 0161 474 3243 📠 0161 474 3079 ✉ andrea.stewart@stockport.gov.uk

Legal: Mr Barry Khan, Service Director / Council Solicitor, Town Hall, Edward Street, Stockport SK1 3XE ☎ 0161 474 3202 📠 0161 477 9835 ✉ barry.khan@stockport.gov.uk

Leisure and Cultural Services: Mr Peter Ashworth, Head of Culture, Tourism & Venues, Wellington Mill, Wellington Road South, Stockport SK3 0EU ☎ 0161 218 9473 ✉ peter.ashworth@stockport.gov.uk

Licensing: Mr Ian O'Donnell, Head of Environment & Trading Standards, Sopford House, Piccadilly, Stockport SK1 3XE ☎ 0161 474 4175 ✉ ian.odonnell@stockport.gov.uk

Lifelong Learning: Mr Richard Mortimer, Head of Stockport Continuing Education Service, Stopford House, Piccadilly, Stockport SK1 3XE ☎ 0161 474 3864 📠 0161 953 0012 ✉ richard.mortimer@stockport.gov.uk

Lighting: Mr Chris Yuille, Commercial Manager, Solutions SK Ltd, Enterprise House, Oakhurst Drive, off Bird Hall Lane, Cheadle Heath, Stockport SK3 0XS ☎ 0161 474 5623 📠 0161 491 0686 ✉ chris.yuille@stockport.gov.uk

Member Services: Mr Steve Callender, Scrutiny Manager, Town Hall, Edward Street, Stockport SK1 3XE ☎ 0161 474 3184 📠 0161 474 3259 ✉ steve.callender@stockport.gov.uk

Parking: Mr Stephen Thompson, Parking Manager, Fred Perry House, Edward Street, Stockport SK1 3XE ☎ 0161 474 4873 📠 0161 474 4833 ✉ s.thompson@stockport.gov.uk

Partnerships: Ms Andrea Stewart, Acting Head of Policy & Performance, Stopford House, Piccadilly, Stockport SK1 3XE ☎ 0161 474 3243 📠 0161 474 3079 ✉ andrea.stewart@stockport.gov.uk

Planning: Mr Steve Burns, Head of Service: Economic Regeneration, Stopford House, Piccadilly, Stockport SK1 3XE ☎ 0161 474 2648 📠 0161 474 2610 ✉ steve.burns@stockport.gov.uk

Procurement: Mr Murray Carr, Head of Property & Procurement, Stopford House, Stockport SK1 3XE ☎ 0161 474 3649 📠 0161 474 4119 ✉ murray.carr@stockport.gov.uk

Public Libraries: Ms Janet Wood, Head of Service: Libraries, Advice & Information, Fred Perry House, Edward Street, Stockport SK1 3XE ☎ 0161 474 4443 ✉ janet.wood@stockport.gov.uk

Recycling & Waste Minimisation: Mr Barry Brockbank, Group Business Manager, Enterprise House, Oakhurst Drive, Off Bird Hall Lane, Cheadle Heath, Stockport SK3 0XS ☎ 0161 474 5500 📠 0161 474 5640 ✉ barry.brockbank@stockport.gov.uk

Regeneration: Mr Sean Dillon, Funding Officer, Fred Perry House, Edward Street, Stockport SK1 3XE ☎ 0161 474 3752 📠 0161 474 3701 ✉ sean.dillon@stockport.gov.uk

Regeneration: Ms Nicola Turner, Head of Economic Regeneration, Fred Perry House, Edward Street, Stockport SK1 3XE ☎ 0161 218 1635 ✉ nicola.turner@stockport.gov.uk

Road Safety: Mr Richard Clark, Road Safety Manager, Fred Perry House, Edward Street, Stockport SK1 3XE ☎ 0161 474 4837 📠 0161 474 4833 ✉ richard.clark@stockport.gov.uk

Social Services: Ms Chris McLoughlin, Service Director - Social Care & Health, Stopford House, Piccadilly, Stockport SK1 3XE ☎ 0161 474 4624 📠 0161 480 3497 ✉ chris.mcloughlin@stockport.gov.uk

Social Services (Adult): Mr Terry Dafter, Director of Adult Social Care, Stopford House, Piccadilly, Stockport SK1 3XE ☎ 0161 218 1644 📠 0161 474 7895 ✉ terry.dafter@stockport.gov.uk

Social Services (Children): Mr Mike Walsh, Children & Young People Officer, Stopford House, Town Hall, Stockport SK1 3XE ☎ 0161 406 6931 📠 0161 953 0012 ✉ mike.walsh@stockport.gov.uk

Staff Training: Ms Kathy Heaton, Head of Transformation, Fred Perry House, Edward Street, Stockport SK1 3XE ☎ 0161 474 3667 ✉ kath.gresty@stockport.gov.uk

Sustainable Communities: Ms Andrea Stewart, Acting Head of Policy & Performance, Stopford House, Piccadilly, Stockport SK1 3XE ☎ 0161 474 3243 📠 0161 474 3079 ✉ andrea.stewart@stockport.gov.uk

Sustainable Development: Ms Nicola Turner, Head of Economic Regeneration, Fred Perry House, Edward Street, Stockport SK1 3XE ☎ 0161 218 1635 ✉ nicola.turner@stockport.gov.uk

Tourism: Ms Alison Farthing, Manager, Visitor Economy &

Tourism, Stopford House, Piccadilly, Stockport SK1 3XE ☎ 0161 474 4469 🖷 0161 474 2610 ✉ alison.farthing@stockport.gov.uk

Town Centre: Ms Nicola Turner, Head of Economic Regeneration, Fred Perry House, Edward Street, Stockport SK1 3XE ☎ 0161 218 1635 ✉ nicola.turner@stockport.gov.uk

Traffic Management: Mr Ian Thompson, Head of Traffic Services, Fred Perry House, Edward Street, Stockport SK1 3XE ☎ 0161 474 4804 🖷 0161 474 4833 ✉ ian.thompson@stockport.gov.uk

Transport: Mr Nic Cox, Managing Director, Solutions SK Ltd, Enterprise House, Birdhall Lane, Cheadle Heath, Stockport SK3 0XT ☎ 0161 474 5566 🖷 0161 474 5640 ✉ nic.cox@solutionssk.co.uk

Transport Planner: Mr Ian Thompson, Head of Traffic Services, Hygarth House, 103 Wellington Road South, Stockport SK1 3TT ☎ 0161 474 4804 🖷 0161 474 4833 ✉ ian.thompson@stockport.gov.uk

Waste Collection and Disposal: Mr Barry Brockbank, Group Business Manager, Enterprise House, Oakhurst Drive, Off Bird Hall Lane, Cheadle Heath, Stockport SK3 0XS ☎ 0161 474 5500 🖷 0161 474 5640 ✉ barry.brockbank@stockport.gov.uk

Waste Management: Mr Barry Brockbank, Group Business Manager, Enterprise House, Oakhurst Drive, Off Bird Hall Lane, Cheadle Heath, Stockport SK3 0XS ☎ 0161 474 5500 🖷 0161 474 5640 ✉ barry.brockbank@stockport.gov.uk

MEMBERS OF THE COUNCIL (63)

***Mayor:* Meikle**, Wendy (LD - Offerton)
cllr.wendy.meikle@stockport.gov.uk
***Deputy Mayor:* O'Neill**, Anthony (CON - Heatons North)
anthonyoneill@hotmail.com
***Leader of the Council:* Derbyshire**, Sue (LD - Manor)
leader@stockport.gov.uk
***Deputy Leader of the Council:* Candler**, Martin (LD - Marple North)
martin.candler@stockport.gov.uk
***Group Leader:* Lloyd**, Syd (CON - Bredbury Green and Romiley)
syd@sparkling-ice.com
Alexander, Ben (LD - Stepping Hill)
cllr.ben.alexander@stockport.gov.uk
Alexander, Shan (LD - Marple South)
cllr.shan.alexander@stockport.gov.uk
Bagnall, Brian (CON - Bramhall South)
brian.bagnall3@btinternet.com
Bailey, Sheila (LAB - Edgeley and Cheadle Heath)
bailey.harding@ntlworld.com
Bellis, Paul (CON - Bramhall South)
cllr.paul.bellis@stockport.gov.uk
Bispham, Andrew (LD - Marple North)
cllr.andrew.bispham@stockport.gov.uk
Bodsworth, Stuart (LD - Cheadle Hulme South)
cllr.stuart.bodsworth@stockport.gov.uk
Booth, Laura (LAB - Offerton)
cllr.laura.booth@stockport.gov.uk
Brett, Walter (LAB - Reddish South)
cllr.walter.brett@stockport.gov.uk
Burns, Peter (R - Heald Green)
peterind@aol.com
Butler, Kate (LAB - Reddish North)
cllr.kate.butler@stockport.gov.uk
Coaton, Richard (LAB - Edgeley and Cheadle Heath)
each.labour@ntlworld.com
Corris, Stuart (LD - Hazel Grove)
cllr.stuart.corris@stockport.gov.uk
Corris, Christine (LD - Bredbury and Woodley)
cllr.christine.corris@stockport.gov.uk
Dowling, Kevin (LD - Marple South)
cllr.kevin.dowling@stockport.gov.uk
Fitzpatrick, Dean (LAB - Heatons South)
cllr.d.fitzpatrick@stockport.gov.uk
Foster, Colin (LAB - Heatons South)
colfoster@colfoster.demon.co.uk
Ganotis, Alexander (LAB - Heatons North)
cllr.a.ganotis@stockport.gov.uk
Gordon, Chris (LD - Bredbury and Woodley)
cllr.chris.gordon@stockport.gov.uk
Grice, Lenny (LD - Cheadle Hulme South)
cllr.lenny.grice@stockport.gov.uk
Grundy, Tom (LAB - Reddish South)
cllr.tom.grundy@stockport.gov.uk
Harding, Philip (LAB - Edgeley and Cheadle Heath)
bailey.harding@ntlworld.com
Hawthorne, Daniel (LD - Manor)
cllr.d.hawthorne@stockport.gov.uk
Hendley, Brian (LAB - Davenport and Cale Green)
cllr.brian.hendley@stockport.gov.uk
Hogg, Kevin (LD - Hazel Grove)
cllr.kevin.hogg@stockport.gov.uk
Holloway, Keith (LD - Cheadle and Gatley)
cllr.keith.holloway@stockport.gov.uk
Holt, Linda (CON - Bramhall North)
cllr.linda.holt@stockport.gov.uk
Humphreys, Sylvia (R - Heald Green)
cllr.sylvia.humphreys@stockport.gov.uk
Ingham, Susan (LD - Marple South)
cllr.susan.ingham@stockport.gov.uk
King, Pam (LD - Cheadle and Gatley)
cllr.pamela.king@stockport.gov.uk
Kirkham, Mags (LD - Bredbury Green and Romiley)
cllr.m.kirkham@stockport.gov.uk
Leck OBE, Bryan (CON - Bramhall South)
cllr.bryan.leck@stockport.gov.uk
Lees, Hazel (LD - Bredbury Green and Romiley)
cllr.hazel.lees@stockport.gov.uk
McAuley, Patrick (IND - Manor)
cllr.patrick.mcauley@stockport.gov.uk
McGee, Tom (LAB - Heatons South)
tom.mcgee@btinternet.com
Moss, Paul (LAB - Reddish North)
cllr.paul.moss@stockport.gov.uk
Murphy, Christopher (LAB - Brinnington and Central)
chris.murf@btinternet.com
Nottingham, Adrian (R - Heald Green)
cllr.a.nottingham@stockport.gov.uk
Orrell, Wendy (LD - Stepping Hill)
cllr.wendy.orrell@stockport.gov.uk
Pantall, John (LD - Cheadle Hulme North)
cllr.john.pantall@stockport.gov.uk
Porgess, Paul (LD - Cheadle Hulme North)
cllr.paul.porgess@stockport.gov.uk
Roberts, Iain (LD - Cheadle and Gatley)
cllr.iain.roberts@stockport.gov.uk

Rowles, Maureen (LAB - Brinnington and Central)
cllr.maureen.rowles@stockport.gov.uk
Sedgwick, David (LAB - Heatons North)
cllr.david.sedgwick@stockport.gov.uk
Smith, John (CON - Offerton)
cllr.john.smith@stockport.gov.uk
Somekh, June (LD - Cheadle Hulme North)
cllr.june.somekh@stockport.gov.uk
Sorton, Andy (LAB - Brinnington and Central)
cllr.andy.sorton@stockport.gov.uk
Verdeille, Andrew (LAB - Reddish South)
cllr.a.verdeille@stockport.gov.uk
Vine, Alanna (CON - Bramhall North)
cllr.alanna.vine@stockport.gov.uk
Walker, Lisa (CON - Bramhall North)
cllr.lisa.walker@stockport.gov.uk
Weldon, Mark (LD - Stepping Hill)
cllr.mark.weldon@stockport.gov.uk
White, David (LD - Davenport and Cale Green)
cllr.david.white@stockport.gov.uk
Wild, Wendy (LAB - Davenport and Cale Green)
cllr.wendy.wild@stockport.gov.uk
Wilson, Michael (LD - Bredbury and Woodley)
cllr.mike.wilson@stockport.gov.uk
Wilson, David (LAB - Reddish North)
cllr.david.wilson@stockport.gov.uk
Wragg, William (CON - Hazel Grove)
cllr.william.wragg@stockport.gov.uk
Wright, Craig (LD - Marple North)
cllr.craig.wright@stockport.gov.uk
Wyatt, Suzanne (LD - Cheadle Hulme South)
cllr.suzanne.wyatt@stockport.gov.uk

POLITICAL COMPOSITION
LD: 29, LAB: 20, CON: 10, R: 3, IND: 1

CABINET
Leader / Policy Reform & Finance: Ms Sue Derbyshire
Deputy Leader / Governance & Corporate Services: Mr Martin Candler
Adults' Care Services: Mr Daniel Hawthorne
Children & Young People: Mr Kevin Dowling
Economic Development & Regeneration: Mr Iain Roberts
Health & Wellbeing: Mr John Pantall
Lifelong Learning & Achievement: Ms Shan Alexander
Public Realm: Mr Kevin Hogg
Supporting Communities: Mr Mark Weldon
Sustainable Future: Mr Stuart Bodsworth

COMMITTEE CHAIRS
Adults & Communities (Scrutiny): Ms Sheila Bailey
Audit: Mr Stuart Corris
Children & Young People (Scrutiny): Ms Linda Holt
Corporate, Resource Management & Governance Scrutiny: Mr Ben Alexander
Environment & Economy (Scrutiny): Ms Christine Corris
Health (Scrutiny): Mr Tom McGee
Licensing, Environment & Safety: Mr Christopher Gordon
Planning & Highways Regulation: Mr Lenny Grice

STOCKTON-ON-TEES U

Stockton-on-Tees Borough Council, (Stockton Borough Council), PO Box 11, Municipal Buildings, Church Road, Stockton-on-Tees TS18 1LD ☎ 01642 393939 🖷 01642 393092
✉ customercomments@stockton.gov.uk 💻 www.stockton.gov.uk

FACTS & FIGURES
Police Authority: Cleveland Police Authority
Health Authority: North East Strategic Health Authority
Learning and Skills Council: North East
Parliamentary Constituencies: Stockton North, Stockton South
EU Constituencies: North East
Election Frequency: Elections are of whole council

PRINCIPAL OFFICERS
Chief Executive: Mr Neil Schneider, Chief Executive, PO Box 34, Municipal Buildings, Church Road, Stockton-on-Tees TS18 1LD ☎ 01642 527000 🖷 01642 527002
✉ neil.schneider@stockton.gov.uk

Senior Management: Mrs Julie Danks, Corporate Director of Resources, Municipal Buildings, Church Road, Stockton-on-Tees TS18 1LD ☎ 01642 527007 🖷 01642 527009
✉ julie.danks@stockton.gov.uk

Senior Management: Ms Jane Humphreys, Corporate Director of Children, Education & Social Care, PO Box 228, Municipal Buildings, Stockton-on-Tees TS18 1XE ☎ 01642 527053 🖷 01642 527037 ✉ jane.humphreys@stockton.gov.uk

Architect, Building / Property Services: Mr Richard McGuckin, Head of Technical Services, PO Box 229, Kingsway House, West Precinct, Billingham TS23 2YS ☎ 01642 526765 🖷 01642 526713
✉ richard.mcguckin@stockton.gov.uk

Building Control: Mr Raymond Sullivan, Building Control Manager, Gloucester House, Church Road, Stockton-on-Tees TS18 1TW ☎ 01642 526040 🖷 01642 526048
✉ raymond.sullivan@stockton.gov.uk

Catering Services: Mr Jamie McCann, Head of Direct Services, Stirling House, Tedder Avenue, Thornaby, Thornbury TS17 9JP ☎ 01642 527071 🖷 01642 528885
✉ jamie.mccann@stockton.gov.uk

Children / Youth Services: Ms Jane Humphreys, Corporate Director of Children, Education & Social Care, PO Box 228, Municipal Buildings, Stockton-on-Tees TS18 1XE ☎ 01642 527053 🖷 01642 527037 ✉ jane.humphreys@stockton.gov.uk

Children / Youth Services: Mr Shaun McLurg, Head of Children & Young People (Operations), Municipal Buildings, Church Road, Stockton-on-Tees TS18 1LD ☎ 01642 527049
✉ shaun.mclurg@stockton.gov.uk

Children / Youth Services: Mr Peter Seller, Head of Children & Young People's Strategy, Municipal Buildings, Church Road, Stockton-on-Tees TS18 1LD ☎ 01642 527043
✉ peter.seller@stockton.gov.uk

Civil Registration: Ms Sue Daniels, Head of Performance & Business Services, Municipal Buildings, Church Road, Stockton-on-Tees TS18 1LE ☎ 01642 527296 🖷 01642 527070
✉ sue.daniels@stockton.gov.uk

Civil Registration: Ms Jayne Robins, Registration & Bereavement Services Manager, Nightingale House, Balaclava Street, Stockton-on-Tees TS18 2AL ☎ 01642 527724 🖷 01642 527725 ✉ jayne.robins@stockton.gov.uk

PR / Communications: Ms Beccy Brown, Head of Human Resources, Municipal Buildings, Church Road, Stockton-on-Tees TS18 1LD ☎ 01642 527016 🖷 01642 527003 ✉ beccy.brown@stockton.gov.uk

PR / Communications: Mr Vince Rutland, Communications Manager, PO Box 117, Municipal Buildings, Church Road, Stockton-on-Tees TS18 1YD ☎ 01642 526097 🖷 01642 526166 ✉ vince.rutland@stockton.gov.uk

Community Planning: Mr Gregory Archer, Community Planning Officer, PO Box 11, Municipal Buildings, Church Road, Stockton-on-Tees TS18 1LD ☎ 01642 526052 ✉ Gregory.Archer@stockton.gov.uk

Community Safety: Mr Mike Batty, Head of Community Protection, 16 Church Road, PO Box 323, Stockton-on-Tees TS18 1XD ☎ 01642 527074 🖷 01642 526583 ✉ mike.batty@stockton.gov.uk

Computer Management: Mr Ian Miles, Head of ICT, Design, Print, The Studio, Lingfield Point, Darlington DL2 1RT ☎ 01642 527012 🖷 01642 528245 ✉ ian.miles@xentrall.org.uk

Consumer Protection and Trading Standards: Mr David Kitching, Trading Standards & Licensing Manager, 16 Church Road, Stockton-on-Tees TS18 1XD ☎ 01642 526530 🖷 01642 526584 ✉ david.kitching@stockton.gov.uk

Contracts: Mr Jamie McCann, Head of Direct Services, Stirling House, Tedder Avenue, Thornaby, Thornbury TS17 9JP ☎ 01642 527071 🖷 01642 528885 ✉ jamie.mccann@stockton.gov.uk

Corporate Services: Mrs Julie Danks, Corporate Director of Resources, Municipal Buildings, Church Road, Stockton-on-Tees TS18 1LD ☎ 01642 527007 🖷 01642 527009 ✉ julie.danks@stockton.gov.uk

Corporate Services: Ms Lesley King, Head of Corporate Performance & Corporate Strategy, PO Box 11, Municipal Buildings, Church Road, Stockton-on-Tees TS18 1LD ☎ 01642 527003 ✉ lesley.king@stockton.gov.uk

Customer Service: Ms Kath Hornsey, Customer Services Manager, PO Box 11, Municipal Buildings, Church Road, Stockton-on-Tees TS18 1LD ☎ 01642 526283 ✉ kath.hornsey@stockton.gov.uk

Direct Labour: Mr Jamie McCann, Head of Direct Services, Stirling House, Tedder Avenue, Thornaby, Thornbury TS17 9JP ☎ 01642 527071 🖷 01642 528885 ✉ jamie.mccann@stockton.gov.uk

Economic Development: Mr Richard Poundford, Head of Regeneration & Economic Development, PO Box 34, Municipal Buildings, Church Road, Stockton-on-Tees TS18 1LE ☎ 01642 393939 ✉ richard.poundford@stockton.gov.uk

Economic Development: Mr Mark Rowell, Funding & Business Manager, PO Box 34, Municipal Buildings, Church Road, Stockton-on-Tees TS18 1LE ☎ 01642 526010 🖷 01642 527023 ✉ mark.rowell@stockton.gov.uk

Education: Ms Lynda Brown, Head of School Effectiveness, Municipal Buildings, Church Road, Stockton-on-Tees TS18 1LD ☎ 01642 527041 ✉ lynda.brown@stockton.gov.uk

Education: Ms Jane Humphreys, Corporate Director of Children, Education & Social Care, PO Box 228, Municipal Buildings, Stockton-on-Tees TS18 1XE ☎ 01642 527053 🖷 01642 527037 ✉ jane.humphreys@stockton.gov.uk

E-Government: Mr Ian Miles, Head of ICT, Design, Print, The Studio, Lingfield Point, Darlington DL2 1RT ☎ 01642 527012 🖷 01642 528245 ✉ ian.miles@xentrall.org.uk

Electoral Registration: Mrs Margaret Waggott, Head of Democratic Services, PO Box 11, Municipal Buildings, Church Road, Stockton-on-Tees TS18 1LD ☎ 01642 527064 🖷 01642 527062 ✉ margaret.waggott@stockton.gov.uk

Emergency Planning: Mr Stuart Marshall, Emergency Planning Officer, Stirling House, Teddar Avenue, Thornaby, Stockton-on-Tees TS19 9JP ☎ 01642 524694

Energy Management: Mr Ian Hodgson, Building & Engineering Services Manager, PO Box 319, Queensway House, Billingham TS23 2YQ ☎ 01642 526889 🖷 01642 528414 ✉ ian.hodgson@stockton.gov.uk

Environmental / Technical Services: Mr Mike Chicken, Built & Natural Environment Manager, Kingsway House, West Precinct, Billingham TS18 2YS ☎ 01642 528148 🖷 01642 528217 ✉ mike.chicken@stockton.gov.uk

Environmental / Technical Services: Mr Paul Dobson, Corporate Director of Development & Neighbourhood Services, Municipal Buildings, Church Road, Stockton-on-Tees TS18 1LD ☎ 01642 527068 ✉ paul.dobson@stockton.gov.uk

Environmental / Technical Services: Mr Neil Schneider, Chief Executive, PO Box 34, Municipal Buildings, Church Road, Stockton-on-Tees TS18 1LD ☎ 01642 527000 🖷 01642 527002 ✉ neil.schneider@stockton.gov.uk

Environmental Health: Mr Colin Snowdon, Environmental Health Manager, 16 Church Road, Stockton-on-Tees TS18 1XD ☎ 01642 526555 🖷 01642 526584 ✉ colin.snowdon@stockton.gov.uk

Estates, Property & Valuation: Mr Paul Hutchinson, Land & Property Manager, Queensway House, West Precinct, Billingham TS23 2YQ ☎ 01642 526898 ✉ paul.hutchinson@stockton.gov.uk

European Liaison: Mr Mark Rowell, Funding & Business Manager, PO Box 34, Municipal Buildings, Church Road, Stockton-on-Tees TS18 1LE ☎ 01642 526010 🖷 01642 527023 ✉ mark.rowell@stockton.gov.uk

Events Manager: Mr Graham Reeves, Events Manager, Environment Centre, 21 West Row, Stockton-on-Tees TS18 1BT ☎ 01642 527344 ✉ graham.reeves@stockton.gov.uk

Facilities: Mr Steve Chaytor, Managing Director, Tees Active Ltd, Redheugh House, Thornaby Place, Thornaby, Stockton-on-Tees TS17 6SG ☎ 01642 529322 🖷 01642 528541 ✉ steven.chaytor@teesactive.co.uk

Finance and Treasurer: Mrs Julie Danks, Corporate Director of Resources, Municipal Buildings, Church Road, Stockton-on-Tees TS18 1LD ☎ 01642 527007 🖷 01642 527009 ✉ julie.danks@stockton.gov.uk

Finance and Treasurer: Mrs Debbie Hurwood, Head of Taxation & Administration, Kingsway House, West Precinct, Billingham TS23 2YL ☎ 01642 527014 ✉ debbie.hurwood@stockton.gov.uk

Finance and Treasurer: Mr Paul Saunders, Head of Finance, Municipal Buildings, Church Road, Stockton-on-Tees TS18 1LD ☎ 01642 527010 🖷 01642 528244 ✉ paul.saunders@stockton.gov.uk

Fleet Management: Mr Jamie McCann, Head of Direct Services, Stirling House, Tedder Avenue, Thornaby, Thornbury TS17 9JP ☎ 01642 527071 🖷 01642 528885 ✉ jamie.mccann@stockton.gov.uk

Fleet Management: Mr Maurice Stephenson, Fleet Services Manager, Cowpen Depot, Billingham TS23 4DD ☎ 01642 528325 🖷 01642 527176 ✉ maurice.stephenson@stockton.gov.uk

Grounds Maintenance: Mr Richard Bradley, Care For Your Area Service Manager, Cowpen Lane Depot, Billingham, Stockton-on-Tees TS23 4DD ☎ 01642 527739 🖷 01642 527175 ✉ richard.bradley@stockton.gov.uk

Grounds Maintenance: Mr Jamie McCann, Head of Direct Services, Stirling House, Tedder Avenue, Thornaby, Thornbury TS17 9JP ☎ 01642 527071 🖷 01642 528885 ✉ jamie.mccann@stockton.gov.uk

Health and Safety: Mr Derek MacDonald, Health & Safety Manager, Queensway House, West Precinct, Billingham TS23 2YQ ☎ 01642 528205 ✉ derek.macdonald@stockton.gov.uk

Health and Safety: Mr Mick McLone, Head of Security Services, Surveillance Centre, The Square, Stockton-on-Tees TS18 1TE ☎ 01642 527607 ✉ doug.carhart@stockton.gov.uk

Highways: Mr Brian Buckley, Group Leader (Highway Network Management), PO Box 229, Kingsway House, West Precinct, Billingham TS23 2YL ☎ 01642 526703 🖷 01642 361690 ✉ brian.buckley@stockton.gov.uk

Home Energy Conservation: Mr Mike Chicken, Built & Natural Environment Manager, Gloucester House, 70 Church Road, Stockton-on-Tees TS18 1TW ☎ 01642 528148 🖷 01642 528217 ✉ mike.chicken@stockton.gov.uk

Housing: Mr Steve Boyd, Managing Director for Tristar Homes Ltd., Tristar House, Lockheed Court, Preston Farm Industrial Estate, Stockton-on-Tees TS18 3SH ☎ 01642 527080 🖷 01642 526614 ✉ steve.boyd@tristarhomes.co.uk

Housing: Ms Julie Nixon, Head of Housing, 16 Church Road, Stockton-on-Tees TS18 1TX ☎ 01642 527072 🖷 01642 528483 ✉ julie.nixon@stockton.gov.uk

Local Area Agreement: Ms Lesley King, Head of Corporate Performance & Corporate Strategy, PO Box 11, Municipal Buildings, Church Road, Stockton-on-Tees TS18 1LD ☎ 01642 527003 ✉ lesley.king@stockton.gov.uk

Legal: Mr David Bond, Director of Law & Democracy (Monitoring Officer), PO Box 11, Municipal Buildings, Church Road, Stockton-on-Tees TS18 1LD ☎ 01642 527060 🖷 01642 527062 ✉ david.bond@stockton.gov.uk

Legal: Mrs Julie Grant, Head of Legal Services, PO Box 11, Municipal Buildings, Church Road, Stockton-on-Tees TS18 1LD ☎ 01642 527063 🖷 01642 527062 ✉ julie.grant@stockton.gov.uk

Leisure and Cultural Services: Mr Steve Chaytor, Managing Director, Tees Active Ltd, Redheugh House, Thornaby Place, Thornaby, Stockton-on-Tees TS17 6SG ☎ 01642 529322 🖷 01642 528541 ✉ steven.chaytor@teesactive.co.uk

Leisure and Cultural Services: Mr Reuben Kench, Head of Culture, PO Box 228, Municipal Buildings, Church Road, Stockton-on-Tees TS18 1XE ☎ 01642 527039 🖷 01642 527037 ✉ reuben.kench@stockton.gov.uk

Leisure and Cultural Services: Mr Neil Russell, Leisure & Sports Development Manager, Kingsway House, Billingham Town Centre, Billingham TS23 2YS ☎ 01642 526699 🖷 01642 528369 ✉ neil.russell@stockton.gov.uk

Licensing: Mr David Kitching, Trading Standards & Licensing Manager, 16 Church Road, Stockton-on-Tees TS18 1XD ☎ 01642 526530 🖷 01642 526584 ✉ david.kitching@stockton.gov.uk

Lifelong Learning: Mr Reuben Kench, Head of Culture, PO Box 228, Municipal Buildings, Church Road, Stockton-on-Tees TS18 1LD ☎ 01642 527039 🖷 01642 527037 ✉ reuben.kench@stockton.gov.uk

Lighting: Mr Brian Buckley, Group Leader (Highway Network Management), PO Box 229, Kingsway House, West Precinct, Billingham TS23 2YL ☎ 01642 526703 🖷 01642 361690 ✉ brian.buckley@stockton.gov.uk

Lottery Funding, Charity and Voluntary: Ms Julie Nixon, Head of Housing, 16 Church Road, Stockton-on-Tees TS18 1TX ☎ 01642 527072 🖷 01642 528483 ✉ julie.nixon@stockton.gov.uk

Member Services: Mrs Margaret Waggott, Head of Democratic Services, PO Box 11, Municipal Buildings, Church Road, Stockton-on-Tees TS18 1LD ☎ 01642 527064 🖷 01642 527062 ✉ margaret.waggott@stockton.gov.uk

Parking: Mr Nigel Gibb, Car Park Manager, Parking Office, Gloucester House, 72 Church Road, Stockton-on-Tees TS18 1TW ☎ 01642 527347 🖷 01642 528204 ✉ nigel.gibb@stockton.gov.uk

Parking: Mr William Trewick, Transportation Engineer, PO Box

229, Kingsway House, West Precinct, Billingham TS23 2YL ☎ 01642 526716 🖷 01642 526713 ✉ bill.trewick@stockton.gov.uk

Partnerships: Ms Ruth Hill, Head of Adult Strategy, PO Box 228, Municipal Buildings, Church Road, Stockton-on-Tees TS18 1XE ☎ 01642 527055 🖷 01642 527037 ✉ ruth.hill@stockton.gov.uk

Personnel / HR: Ms Beccy Brown, Head of Human Resources, Municipal Buildings, Church Road, Stockton-on-Tees TS18 1LD ☎ 01642 527016 🖷 01642 527003 ✉ beccy.brown@stockton.gov.uk

Planning: Ms Carol Straughan, Head of Planning, Gloucester House, 70 Church Road, Stockton-on-Tees TS18 1TW ☎ 01642 527026 🖷 01642 528788 ✉ carol.straughan@stockton.gov.uk

Procurement: Mr Martin Skipsey, Procurement Manager, PO Box 11, Municipal Buildings, Church Road, Stockton-on-Tees TS18 1LD ☎ 01642 526364 🖷 01642 528244 ✉ martin.skipsey@stockton.gov.uk

Public Libraries: Mr Reuben Kench, Head of Culture, PO Box 228, Municipal Buildings, Church Road, Stockton-on-Tees TS18 1LD ☎ 01642 527039 🖷 01642 527037 ✉ reuben.kench@stockton.gov.uk

Recycling & Waste Minimisation: Mr Jamie McCann, Head of Direct Services, Stirling House, Tedder Avenue, Thornaby, Thornbury TS17 9JP ☎ 01642 527071 🖷 01642 528885 ✉ jamie.mccann@stockton.gov.uk

Recycling & Waste Minimisation: Mr Dale Rowbotham, Projects & Supports Officer, Stirling House, Tedder Avenue, Thornaby, Thornbury TS17 9JP ☎ 01642 527181 ✉ dale.rowbotham@stockton.gov.uk

Regeneration: Mr James Glancey, Regeneration Manager, PO Box 11, Municipal Buildings, Church Road, Stockton-on-Tees TS18 1LD ☎ 01642 526023 ✉ james.glancey@stockton.gov.uk

Regeneration: Mr Richard Poundford, Head of Regeneration & Economic Development, PO Box 34, Municipal Buildings, Church Road, Stockton-on-Tees TS18 1LE ☎ 01642 393939 ✉ richard.poundford@stockton.gov.uk

Road Safety: Mr Neil Ellison, Sustainability Manager, PO Box 229, Kingsway House, West Precinct, Billingham TS23 2YL ☎ 01642 526736 🖷 01642 526740 ✉ neil.ellison@stockton.gov.uk

Road Safety: Mr Simon Milner, Group Leader, Traffic Management, PO Box 229, Kingsway House, West Precinct, Billingham TS23 2YS ☎ 01642 526728 🖷 01642 526713 ✉ david.lynch@stockton.gov.uk

Road Safety: Mr William Trewick, Transportation Engineer, PO Box 229, Kingsway House, West Precinct, Billingham TS23 2YL ☎ 01642 526716 🖷 01642 526713 ✉ bill.trewick@stockton.gov.uk

Social Services: Mr Tony Beckwith, Head of Support Services, PO Box 228, Municipal Buildings, Church Road, Stockton-on-Tees TS18 1XE ☎ 01642 527052 🖷 01642 527037 ✉ tony.beckwith@stockton.gov.uk

Social Services: Ms Jane Humphreys, Corporate Director of Children, Education & Social Care, PO Box 228, Municipal Buildings, Stockton-on-Tees TS18 1XE ☎ 01642 527053 🖷 01642 527037 ✉ jane.humphreys@stockton.gov.uk

Social Services (Adult): Ms Ruth Hill, Head of Adult Strategy, PO Box 228, Municipal Buildings, Church Road, Stockton-on-Tees TS18 1XE ☎ 01642 527055 🖷 01642 527037 ✉ ruth.hill@stockton.gov.uk

Social Services (Adult): Mr Sean McEneany, Head of Adults Operational Services, Municipal Buildings, Church Road, Stockton-on-Tees TS18 1LD ☎ 01642 527045 ✉ sean.mceneany@stockton.gov.uk

Staff Training: Ms Angie Blaylock, Training & Organisational Development Manager, Wynyard House, Town Centre, Billingham TS23 2LN ☎ 01642 528401 🖷 01642 528328 ✉ angie.blaylock@stockton.gov.uk

Street Scene: Mr Jamie McCann, Head of Direct Services, Stirling House, Tedder Avenue, Thornaby, Thornbury TS17 9JP ☎ 01642 527071 🖷 01642 528885 ✉ jamie.mccann@stockton.gov.uk

Sustainable Communities: Mr Paul Dobson, Corporate Director of Development & Neighbourhood Services, Municipal Buildings, Church Road, Stockton-on-Tees TS18 1LD ☎ 01642 527068 ✉ paul.dobson@stockton.gov.uk

Sustainable Communities: Mr Neil Ellison, Sustainability Manager, Kingsway House, West Precinct, Billingham TS23 2YL ☎ 01642 526736 🖷 01642 526740 ✉ neil.ellison@stockton.gov.uk

Sustainable Communities: Mr Neil Schneider, Chief Executive, PO Box 34, Municipal Buildings, Church Road, Stockton-on-Tees TS18 1LD ☎ 01642 527000 🖷 01642 527002 ✉ neil.schneider@stockton.gov.uk

Sustainable Development: Mr Mike Chicken, Built & Natural Environment Manager, Gloucester House, 70 Church Road, Stockton-on-Tees TS18 1TW ☎ 01642 528148 🖷 01642 528217 ✉ mike.chicken@stockton.gov.uk

Sustainable Development: Mr Neil Ellison, Sustainability Manager, Kingsway House, Billingham Town Centre, Billingham TS23 2YS ☎ 01642 526736 🖷 01642 526740 ✉ neil.ellison@stockton.gov.uk

Tourism: Mr Richard Poundford, Head of Regeneration & Economic Development, PO Box 34, Municipal Buildings, Church Road, Stockton-on-Tees TS18 1LE ☎ 01642 393939 ✉ richard.poundford@stockton.gov.uk

Town Centre: Mr James Glancey, Regeneration Manager, PO Box 11, Municipal Buildings, Church Road, Stockton-on-Tees TS18 1LD ☎ 01642 526023 ✉ james.glancey@stockton.gov.uk

Traffic Management: Mr Richard McGuckin, Head of Technical Services, PO Box 229, Kingsway House, West Precinct, Billingham TS23 2YS ☎ 01642 526765 🖷 01642 526713 ✉ richard.mcguckin@stockton.gov.uk

Traffic Management: Mr Simon Milner, Group Leader, Traffic Management, PO Box 229, Kingsway House, West Precinct, Billingham TS23 2YS ☎ 01642 526728 🖷 01642 526713 david.lynch@stockton.gov.uk

Transport: Mr Richard McGuckin, Head of Technical Services, PO Box 229, Kingsway House, West Precinct, Billingham TS23 2YS ☎ 01642 526765 🖷 01642 526713 richard.mcguckin@stockton.gov.uk

Transport Planner: Mr Richard McGuckin, Head of Technical Services, PO Box 229, Kingsway House, West Precinct, Billingham TS23 2YS ☎ 01642 526765 🖷 01642 526713 richard.mcguckin@stockton.gov.uk

Transport Planner: Mr William Trewick, Transportation Engineer, PO Box 229, Kingsway House, West Precinct, Billingham TS23 2YL ☎ 01642 526716 🖷 01642 526713 bill.trewick@stockton.gov.uk

Waste Collection and Disposal: Mr Richard Bradley, Care For Your Area Service Manager, Cowpen Lane Depot, Billingham, Stockton-on-Tees TS23 4DD ☎ 01642 527739 🖷 01642 527175 richard.bradley@stockton.gov.uk

Waste Collection and Disposal: Mr Jamie McCann, Head of Direct Services, Stirling House, Tedder Avenue, Thornaby, Thornbury TS17 9JP ☎ 01642 527071 🖷 01642 528885 jamie.mccann@stockton.gov.uk

Waste Management: Mr Jamie McCann, Head of Direct Services, Stirling House, Tedder Avenue, Thornaby, Thornbury TS17 9JP ☎ 01642 527071 🖷 01642 528885 jamie.mccann@stockton.gov.uk

MEMBERS OF THE COUNCIL (56)

***Mayor:* Apedaile**, Lynne (INDNA - Billingham North)
lynne.apedaile@stockton.gov.uk

***Deputy Mayor:* Nelson**, Kath (LAB - Norton North)
kathryn.nelson@stockton.gov.uk

***Leader of the Council:* Cook**, Robert (LAB - Norton South)
robert.cook@stockton.gov.uk

***Deputy Leader of the Council:* Beall**, Jim (LAB - Roseworth)
jim.beall@stockton.gov.uk

***Group Leader:* Lupton**, Kenneth (CON - Hartburn)
kenneth.lupton@stockton.gov.uk

Baker, Paul (LAB - Newtown)
paul.baker@stockton.gov.uk

Brown, Derrick (LAB - Stainsby Hill)
derrick.brown@stockton.gov.uk

Chatburn, Mark (CON - Yarm)
mark.chatburn@stockton.gov.uk

Cherrett, Julia (LD - Bishopsgarth and Elm Tree)
julia.roberts@stockton.gov.uk

Clark, Carol (LAB - Grangefield)
carol.clark@stockton.gov.uk

Clark, Michael (LAB - Grangefield)
michael.clark@stockton.gov.uk

Coleman, David (LAB - Stockton Town Centre)
david.coleman@stockton.gov.uk

Cooke, Nigel (LAB - Hardwick)
nigel.cooke@stockton.gov.uk

Corr, Gillian (IND - Ingleby Barwick East)
gillian.corr@stockton.gov.uk

Cunningham, Evaline (LAB - Billingham East)
evaline.cunningham@stockton.gov.uk

Dalgarno, Ian (INDNA - Village)
ian.dalgarno@stockton.gov.uk

Dennis, Phillip (CON - Eaglescliffe)
phil.dennis@stockton.gov.uk

Dixon, Kenneth (INDNA - Ingleby Barwick West)
kenneth.dixon@stockton.gov.uk

Eddy, Mick (INDNA - Village)
mick.eddy@stockton.gov.uk

Faulks, Kevin (INDNA - Ingleby Barwick East)
kevin.faulks@stockton.gov.uk

Gardner, John (CON - Northern Parishes)
john.gardner@stockton.gov.uk

Gibson, Robert (LAB - Newtown)
robert.gibson@stockton.gov.uk

Harrington, David (IND - Ingleby Barwick West)
david.harrington@stockton.gov.uk

Houchen, Ben (CON - Yarm)
ben.houchen@stockton.gov.uk

Inman, Barbara (LAB - Roseworth)
barbara.inman@stockton.gov.uk

Javed, Mohammed (LAB - Parkfield and Oxbridge)
mohammed.javed@stockton.gov.uk

Johnson, Eileen (LAB - Norton South)
eileen.johnson@stockton.gov.uk

Kennedy, Elliot (LD - Bishopsgarth and Elm Tree)
elliot.kennedy@stockton.gov.uk

Kirby, Jean (IND - Ingleby Barwick East)
jean.kirby@stockton.gov.uk

Kirton, Paul (LAB - Stockton Town Centre)
paul.kirton@stockton.gov.uk

Laing, Terry (CON - Hartburn)
terry.laing@stockton.gov.uk

Large, Tina (INDNA - Mandale and Victoria)
tina.large@stockton.gov.uk

Leckonby, Colin (INDNA - Billingham North)
colin.leckonby@stockton.gov.uk

Lewis, Alan (LD - Eaglescliffe)
alan.lewis@stockton.gov.uk

McCall, Ray (LAB - Billingham North)
ray.mccall@stockton.gov.uk

McCoy, Ann (LAB - Billingham Central)
ann.mccoy@stockton.gov.uk

Nelson, Steve (LAB - Norton North)
steve.nelson@stockton.gov.uk

O'Donnell, Jean (LAB - Billingham South)
jean.odonnell@stockton.gov.uk

Patterson, Ross (INDNA - Ingleby Barwick West)
ross.patterson@stockton.gov.uk

Perry, Maurice (CON - Fairfield)
maurice.perry@stockton.gov.uk

Rigg, Maureen (LD - Eaglescliffe)
maureen.rigg@stockton.gov.uk

Rose, David (LAB - Parkfield and Oxbridge)
david.rose@stockton.gov.uk

Sherris, Andrew (CON - Yarm)
andrew.sherris@stockton.gov.uk

Smith, Michael (LAB - Billingham South)
michael.smith@stockton.gov.uk

Stephenson, Norma (LAB - Hardwick)
norma.stephenson@stockton.gov.uk

Stephenson, Andrew (CON - Western Parishes)
afsegg@hotmail.co.uk

Stoker, Mick (LAB - Billingham East)
mick.stoker@stockton.gov.uk
Stott, Tracey (LAB - Mandale and Victoria)
tracey.stott@stockton.gov.uk
Walmsley, Sylvia (INDNA - Stainsby Hill)
sylvia.walmsley@stockton.gov.uk
Walmsley, Stephen (INDNA - Mandale and Victoria)
steve.walmsley@stockton.gov.uk
Wilburn, Norma (LAB - Norton West)
norma.wilburn@stockton.gov.uk
Wilburn, David (LAB - Norton West)
david.wilburn@stockton.gov.uk
Womphrey, Mick (CON - Billingham West)
michael.womphrey@stockton.gov.uk
Womphrey, Mary (CON - Billingham West)
mary.womphrey@stockton.gov.uk
Woodhead, Bill (CON - Fairfield)
william.woodhead@stockton.gov.uk
Woodhouse, Barry (LAB - Billingham Central)
barry.woodhouse@stockton.gov.uk

POLITICAL COMPOSITION
LAB: 27, CON: 12, INDNA: 10, LD: 4, IND: 3

CABINET
Leader: Mr Robert Cook
Deputy Leader / Adult Services & Health: Mr Jim Beall
Access & Communities: Mr David Coleman
Arts, Leisure & Culture: Mr Kenneth Dixon
Children & Young People: Mrs Ann McCoy
Corporate Management & Finance: Mr David Harrington
Housing & Community Safety: Mr Steve Nelson
Environment: Mr David Rose
Housing & Community Safety: Mr Steve Nelson
Regeneration & Transport: Mr Michael Smith

COMMITTEE CHAIRS
Audit: Mr Barry Woodhouse
Children & Young People: Miss Barbara Inman
Education Support: Miss Barbara Inman
Environment: Mr Nigel Cooke
Health: Mr Mohammed Javed
Housing & Community Safety: Mrs Julia Cherrett
Licensing: Mr Paul Kirton
Planning: Mr Robert Gibson
Regeneration & Transport: Mr Maurice Perry

STOKE-ON-TRENT CITY U
Stoke-on-Trent City Council, Civic Centre, Glebe Street, Stoke-on-Trent ST4 1RN ☎ 01782 234567 🖷 01782 232603
🖳 www.stoke.gov.uk

FACTS & FIGURES
Police Authority: Staffordshire Police Authority
Health Authority: NHS West Midlands
Learning and Skills Council: West Midlands
Parliamentary Constituencies: Stoke-on-Trent Central, Stoke-on-Trent North, Stoke-on-Trent South
EU Constituencies: West Midlands
Election Frequency: Elections are by thirds
Twinning: Erlangen (Germany)

PRINCIPAL OFFICERS
Chief Executive: Mr John van de Laarschot, Chief Executive & Council Manager, Civic Centre, Glebe Street, Stoke-on-Trent ST4 1RN ☎ 01782 232602 ✉ chief.execadmin@stoke.gov.uk

Architect, Building / Property Services: Ms Julie Griffin, Strategic Manager - Landlord Services, Civic Centre, Glebe Street, Stoke-on-Trent ST4 1RN ☎ 01782 236365 ✉ julie.griffin@stoke.gov.uk

Children / Youth Services: Mr Geoff Caterall, Strategic Manager - Inclusion, Civic Centre, Glebe Street, Stoke-on-Trent ST4 1RN ☎ 01782 238812 ✉ geoff.caterall@stoke.gov.uk

Children / Youth Services: Mr Paul Gerrard, Strategic Manager - School Support, Civic Centre, Glebe Street, Stoke-on-Trent ST4 1RN ☎ 01782 236860 ✉ paul.gerrard@stoke.gov.uk

Children / Youth Services: Mr Mark Kenyon, HRA Finance Team Leader, Civic Centre, Glebe Street, Stoke-on-Trent ST4 1RN ☎ 01782 235960 ✉ mark.kenyon@stoke.gov.uk

Children / Youth Services: Ms Diane Mason, Strategic Manager - School Improvement, Civic Centre, Glebe Street, Stoke-on-Trent ST4 1RN ☎ 01782 236855 ✉ diane.mason@stoke.gov.uk

Computer Management: Mr Mick Bailey, Strategic Development Manager - IT, Civic Centre, Glebe Street, Stoke-on-Trent ST4 1RN ☎ 01782 236021 ✉ mick.bailey@stoke.gov.uk

Computer Management: Mr John Bowler, Client Manager IT, Civic Centre, Glebe Street, Stoke-on-Trent ST4 1RN ☎ 01782 232553 ✉ john.bowler@stoke.gov.uk

Corporate Services: Mr Paul Bicknell, Corporate Fraud Manager, Civic Centre, Glebe Street, Stoke-on-Trent ST4 1RN ☎ 01782 232828 ✉ paul.bicknell@stoke.gov.uk

Corporate Services: Ms Kerry Cartlidge, Corporate Services Financial & Commercial Manager, Civic Centre, Glebe Street, Stoke-on-Trent ST4 1RN ☎ 01782 232704 ✉ kerry.cartlidge@stoke.gov.uk

Corporate Services: Ms Helen Dos Santos, Business Administration Manager, Civic Centre, Glebe Street, Stoke-on-Trent ST4 1RN ☎ 01782 232655 ✉ helen.dossantos@stoke.gov.uk

Corporate Services: Mr Neil Mason, Client Infrastructure Manager, Civic Centre, Glebe Street, Stoke-on-Trent ST4 1RN ☎ 01782 232877 ✉ neil.mason@stoke.gov.uk

Corporate Services: Ms Jan Preece, Core Infrastructure Manager, Civic Centre, Glebe Street, Stoke-on-Trent ST4 1RN ☎ 01782 232899 ✉ jan.preece@stoke.gov.uk

Customer Service: Ms Emma Mottram, Customer Feedback & Information Rights Team Leader, Civic Centre, Glebe Street, Stoke-on-Trent ST4 1RN ☎ 01782 233019 ✉ emma.mottram@stoke.gov.uk

Finance and Treasurer: Mr Neil Harvey, Team Manager -

Exchequer Services, Civic Centre, Glebe Street, Stoke-on-Trent ST4 1RN ☎ 01782 232651 ✉ neil.harvey@stoke.gov.uk

Finance and Treasurer: Mr Mark Kenyon, HRA Finance Team Leader, Civic Centre, Glebe Street, Stoke-on-Trent ST4 1RN ☎ 01782 235960 ✉ mark.kenyon@stoke.gov.uk

Finance and Treasurer: Ms Debbie Middleton, City Renewal Finance & Commercial Manager, Civic Centre, Glebe Street, Stoke-on-Trent ST4 1RN ☎ 01782 235931 ✉ debbie.middleton@stoke.gov.uk

Finance and Treasurer: Ms Lesley Orton, Audit Manager, Civic Centre, Glebe Street, Stoke-on-Trent ST4 1RN ☎ 01782 232871 ✉ lesley.orton@stoke.gov.uk

Finance and Treasurer: Ms Adele Ovenden, Team Manager - Benefits, Civic Centre, Glebe Street, Stoke-on-Trent ST4 1RN ☎ 01782 236805 ✉ adele.ovenden@stoke.gov.uk

Finance and Treasurer: Ms Teresa Powell, Team Manager - Revenues, Civic Centre, Glebe Street, Stoke-on-Trent ST4 1RN ☎ 01782 232186 ✉ teresa.powell@stoke.gov.uk

Finance and Treasurer: Mr David Whiteman, Audit Manager, Civic Centre, Glebe Street, Stoke-on-Trent ST4 1RN ☎ 01782 232696 ✉ david.whiteman@stoke.gov.uk

Finance and Treasurer: Ms Sue Woodall, Audit Services Manager, Civic Centre, Glebe Street, Stoke-on-Trent ST4 1RN ☎ 01782 232689 ✉ sue.woodall@stoke.gov.uk

Housing: Ms Carmen Muir, Strategic Manager - Housing Standards Manager, Civic Centre, Glebe Street, Stoke-on-Trent ST4 1RN ☎ 01782 232090 ✉ carmen.muir@stoke.gov.uk

Member Services: Ms Helen Barr, Democratic Services Lead, Civic Centre, Glebe Street, Stoke-on-Trent ST4 1RN ☎ 01782 232784 ✉ helen.barr@stoke.gov.uk

Member Services: Mr Neil Chadwick, Governance Manager, Civic Centre, Glebe Street, Stoke-on-Trent ST4 1RN ☎ 01782 233386 ✉ neil.chadwick@stoke.gov.uk

Member Services: Ms Suzanne Hackley, Team Leader - Cabinet & Committee Support, Civic Centre, Glebe Street, Stoke-on-Trent ST4 1RN ☎ 01782 232622 ✉ suzanne.hackley@stoke.gov.uk

Member Services: Ms Julie Harvey, Democratic Services Lead, Civic Centre, Glebe Street, Stoke-on-Trent ST4 1RN ☎ 01782 232617 ✉ julie.harvey@stoke.gov.uk

Member Services: Ms Michaleen Hilton, Council & Civil Support Team Leader, Civic Centre, Glebe Street, Stoke-on-Trent ST4 1RN ☎ 01782 232638 ✉ michaleen.hilton@stoke.gov.uk

Member Services: Mr John Ross, Overview & Scrutiny Team Leader, Civic Centre, Glebe Street, Stoke-on-Trent ST4 1RN ☎ 01782 232956 ✉ john.ross@stoke.gov.uk

Partnerships: Ms Sue Barnes, Strategic Manager - Partnerships & Planning, Civic Centre, Glebe Street, Stoke-on-Trent ST4 1RN ☎ 01782 236894 ✉ sue.barnes@stoke.gov.uk

Partnerships: Mr Mark Warr, Strategic Manager - Integrated Specialist Services, Civic Centre, Glebe Street, Stoke-on-Trent ST4 1RN ☎ 01782 231971 ✉ mark.warr@stoke.gov.uk

Planning: Ms Sue Barnes, Strategic Manager - Partnerships & Planning, Civic Centre, Glebe Street, Stoke-on-Trent ST4 1RN ☎ 01782 236894 ✉ sue.barnes@stoke.gov.uk

Procurement: Ms Carolyn Colduck, Specialist Commissioning Manager, Civic Centre, Glebe Street, Stoke-on-Trent ST4 1RN ☎ 01782 237791 ✉ carolyn.colduck@stoke.gov.uk

Procurement: Mr Darren Pearce, Corporate Procurement Manager, Civic Centre, Glebe Street, Stoke-on-Trent ST4 1RN ☎ 01782 232841 ✉ darren.pearce@stoke.gov.uk

Regeneration: Ms Debbie Middleton, City Renewal Finance & Commercial Manager, Civic Centre, Glebe Street, Stoke-on-Trent ST4 1RN ☎ 01782 235931 ✉ debbie.middleton@stoke.gov.uk

Social Services (Children): Ms Sue Hammersley, Strategic Manager - Children in Care Lead, Civic Centre, Glebe Street, Stoke-on-Trent ST4 1RN ☎ 01782 231873 ✉ sue.hammersley@stoke.gov.uk

MEMBERS OF THE COUNCIL (44)

***The Lord Mayor:* Crowe**, Terry (LAB - Eaton Park)
terry.crowe@stoke.gov.uk

***Deputy Lord Mayor:* Pitt**, Sheila (LAB - Bentilee and Ubberley)
sheila.pitt@stoke.gov.uk

***Leader of the Council:* Pervez**, Mohammed (LAB - Moorcroft)
mohammed.pervez@stoke.gov.uk

***Deputy Leader of the Council:* Shotton**, Paul (LAB - Fenton East)
paul.shotton@stoke.gov.uk

***Group Leader:* Brown**, Abi (CON - Meir Park)
abi.brown@stoke.gov.uk

***Group Leader:* Conway**, David (IND - Little Chell and Stanfield)
david.conway@stoke.gov.uk

Ali, Bagh (LAB - Lightwood North and Normacot)
bagh.ali@stoke.gov.uk

Aumir, Muhammad (LAB - Meir Hay)
muhammad.aumir@stoke.gov.uk

Banks, Kath (LAB - Hollybush and Longton West)
kath.banks@stoke.gov.uk

Barnes, Jackie (IND - Springfields and Trent Vale)
jackie.barnes@stoke.gov.uk

Breeze, Paul (INDNA - Birches Head and Central Forest Park)
alison.wedgwood@stoke.gov.uk

Brereton, Jack (CON - Baddeley, Milton and Norton)
jack.brereton@stoke.gov.uk

Bridges, Janine (LAB - Great Chell and Packmoor)
janine.bridges@stoke.gov.uk

Clarke, Karen (LAB - Fenton West and Mount Pleasant)
karen.clarke@stoke.gov.uk

Conteh, Randolph (IND - Penkhull and Stoke)
randolph.conteh@stoke.gov.uk

Day, Neil (LAB - Blurton West and Newstead)
neil.day@stoke.gov.uk

Dutton, Alan (LAB - Burslem Central)
alan.dutton@stoke.gov.uk

Follows, Terence (IND - Hanford and Trentham)

terence.follows@stoke.gov.uk
Fry, Matthew (LAB - Weston Coyney)
matthew.fry@stoke.gov.uk
Garner, Martin (LAB - Goldenhill and Sandyford)
martin.garner@stoke.gov.uk
Garner, Joy (LAB - Burslem Park)
joy.garner@stoke.gov.uk
Gratton, Debra (LAB - Sneyd Green)
debra.gratton@stoke.gov.uk
Hamer, Olwen (LAB - Sandford Hill)
olwen.hamer@stoke.gov.uk
Hassall, Gwen (LAB - Abbey Hulton and Townsend)
gwen.hassall@stoke.gov.uk
Hayward, Peter (IND - Hanford and Trentham)
peter.hayward@stoke.gov.uk
Hussain, Shazad (LAB - Dresden and Florence)
shazad.hussain@stoke.gov.uk
James, Ann (IND - Great Chell and Packmoor)
ann.james@stoke.gov.uk
Kallar, Gurmeet Singh (LAB - Bradeley and Chell Heath)
gurmeetsingh.kallar@stoke.gov.uk
Khan, Majid (LAB - Etruria and Hanley)
majid.khan@stoke.gov.uk
Knapper, Adrian (LAB - Abbey Hulton and Townsend)
adrian.knapper@stoke.gov.uk
Lilley, Andy (LAB - Baddeley, Milton and Norton)
andy.lilley@stoke.gov.uk
Meredith, Mark (LAB - Birches Head and Central Forest Park)
mark.meredith@stoke.gov.uk
Pender, Shaun (LAB - Hartshill and Basford)
shaun.pender@stoke.gov.uk
Platt, Andy (LAB - Boothen and Oakhill)
andy.platt@stoke.gov.uk
Reynolds, Tom (LAB - Broadway and Longton East)
tom.reynolds@stoke.gov.uk
Rosenau, Ruth (LAB - Meir North)
ruth.rosenau@stoke.gov.uk
Wagner, Lee (IND - Tunstall)
lee.wanger@stoke.gov.uk
Walker, Duncan (LAB - Baddeley, Milton and Norton)
duncan.walker@stoke.gov.uk
Ward, Glenys (IND - Blurton East)
glenys.ward@stoke.gov.uk
Watson, Alastair (LAB - Joiners Square)
alastair.watson@stoke.gov.uk
Wazir, Amjid (LAB - Hanley Park and Shelton)
amjid.wazir@stoke.gov.uk
Wedgwood, Alison (LAB - Bentilee and Ubberley)
alison.wedgwood@stoke.gov.uk
Wheeldon, Debbie (LAB - Meir South)
debbie.wheeldon@stoke.gov.uk
Wilcox, Matt (LAB - Ford Green and Smallthorne)
matt.wilcox@stoke.gov.uk

POLITICAL COMPOSITION
LAB: 33, IND: 8, CON: 2, INDNA: 1

CABINET
Leader: Mr Mohammed Pervez
Deputy Leader / Finance, Procurement & Commissioning: Mr Paul Shotton
Economic Development, Culture & Sport: Mr Mark Meredith
Education: Mr Alan Dutton
Green Enterprises & Clean City: Mr Andy Platt
Housing, Neighbourhoods & Community Safety: Ms Janine Bridges
Public Health & Health: Mr Adrian Knapper
Social Care: Ms Gwen Hassall
Regeneration, Planning & Housing: Ms Ruth Rosenau
Transformation & Resources: Ms Olwen Hamer

COMMITTEE CHAIRS
Adults & Neighbourhoods Overview and Scrutiny: Mr Bagh Ali
Audit: Mr Shaun Pender
Children & Young People's Overview & Scrutiny: Mr David Conway
Development Management: Mr Tom Reynolds
Licensing & General Purposes: Mr Duncan Walker
Licensing & Registration: Mr Neil Day

STRABANE — N
Strabane District Council, 47 Derry Road, Strabane BT82 8DY
☎ 028 7138 2204 🖷 028 7138 1348 ✉ admin@strabanedc.com
💻 www.strabanedc.com

FACTS & FIGURES
Police Authority: Northern Ireland Policing Board
Health Authority: Western Local Commissioning Group
Learning and Skills Council: Northern Ireland
Parliamentary Constituencies: Tyrone West
EU Constituencies: Northern Ireland
Election Frequency: Elections are of whole council

PRINCIPAL OFFICERS
Chief Executive: Mr Daniel McSorley, Interim Clerk & Chief Executive, Council Offices, The Grange, Mountjoy Road, Omagh BT79 7BL ☎ 028 8225 6206; 028 7138 2204 🖷 028 8225 2380 ✉ daniel.mcsorley@omagh.gov.uk; dmcsorley@strabanedc.com

Access Officer / Social Services (Disability): Mr John Stewart, Chief Building Control Officer, District Council Offices, 47 Derry Road, Strabane BT82 8DY ☎ 028 7138 2204 🖷 028 7138 1348 ✉ jstewart@strabanedc.com

Architect, Building / Property Services: Mr John Stewart, Chief Building Control Officer, District Council Offices, 47 Derry Road, Strabane BT82 8DY ☎ 028 7138 2204 🖷 028 7138 1348 ✉ jstewart@strabanedc.com

Building Control: Mr John Stewart, Chief Building Control Officer, District Council Offices, 47 Derry Road, Strabane BT82 8DY ☎ 028 7138 2204 🖷 028 7138 1348 ✉ jstewart@strabanedc.com

Children / Youth Services: Mrs Karen McFarland, Head of Culture, Arts & Leisure, District Council Offices, 47 Derry Road, Strabane BT82 8DY ☎ 028 7138 2204 🖷 028 7138 1348 ✉ kmcfarland@strabanedc.com

PR / Communications: Ms Rachelle Craig, Corporate Policy Officer, 47 Derry Road, Strabane BT82 8DY ☎ 028 7138 2204 🖷 028 7138 1349 ✉ rcraig@strabanedc.com

Community Safety: Mr Ryan Tracey, Community Safety Officer, 47 Derry Road, Strabane BT82 8DY ☎ 028 7138 2204 🖷 028 7138 1348 ✉ rtracey@strabanedc.com

Computer Management: Ms Charlotte Connelley, Information Technology Manager, 47 Derry Road, Strabane BT82 8DY ☎ 028 7138 2204 ✉ cmconnelley@strabanedc.com

Consumer Protection and Trading Standards: Mr Patrick Cosgrove, Chief Environmental Health Officer, District Council Offices, 47 Derry Road, Strabane BT82 8DY ☎ 028 7138 2204 🖷 028 7138 1347 ✉ pcosgrove@strabanedc.com

Contracts: Mr Malcolm Scott, Chief Technical Services Officer, District Council Offices, 47 Derry Road, Strabane BT82 8DY ☎ 028 7138 2204 🖷 028 7138 1348 ✉ mscott@strabanedc.com

Direct Labour: Mr Liam Donnelly, Technical Services Officer, District Council Offices, 47 Derry Road, Strabane BT82 8DY ☎ 028 7138 2204 🖷 028 7138 1348 ✉ ldonnelly@strabanedc.com

Economic Development: Ms Geraldine Stafford, Economic Development Manager, District Council Offices, 47 Derry Road, Strabane BT82 8DY ☎ 028 7138 1303 🖷 028 7138 1348 ✉ gstafford@strabanedc.com

Electoral Registration: Mrs Sharon Maxwell, Business Manager, District Council Offices, 47 Derry Road, Strabane BT82 8DY ☎ 028 7138 1304 🖷 028 7138 1348 ✉ samaxwell@strabanedc.com

Emergency Planning: Mr Patrick Cosgrove, Chief Environmental Health Officer, District Council Offices, 47 Derry Road, Strabane BT82 8DY ☎ 028 7138 2204 🖷 028 7138 1347 ✉ pcosgrove@strabanedc.com

Energy Management: Mr John Stewart, Chief Building Control Officer, District Council Offices, 47 Derry Road, Strabane BT82 8DY ☎ 028 7138 2204 🖷 028 7138 1348 ✉ jstewart@strabanedc.com

Environmental / Technical Services: Mr Malcolm Scott, Chief Technical Services Officer, District Council Offices, 47 Derry Road, Strabane BT82 8DY ☎ 028 7138 2204 🖷 028 7138 1348 ✉ mscott@strabanedc.com

Environmental Health: Mr Patrick Cosgrove, Chief Environmental Health Officer, District Council Offices, 47 Derry Road, Strabane BT82 8DY ☎ 028 7138 2204 🖷 028 7138 1347 ✉ pcosgrove@strabanedc.com

Estates, Property & Valuation: Mr John Stewart, Chief Building Control Officer, District Council Offices, 47 Derry Road, Strabane BT82 8DY ☎ 028 7138 2204 🖷 028 7138 1348 ✉ jstewart@strabanedc.com

Facilities: Mr Malcolm Scott, Chief Technical Services Officer, District Council Offices, 47 Derry Road, Strabane BT82 8DY ☎ 028 7138 2204 🖷 028 7138 1348 ✉ mscott@strabanedc.com

Finance and Treasurer: Mrs Maureen Henebery, Head of Finance, District Council Offices, 47 Derry Road, Strabane BT82 8DY ☎ 028 7138 2204 🖷 028 7138 1348 ✉ mhenebery@strabanedc.com

Fleet Management: Mr Malcolm Scott, Chief Technical Services Officer, District Council Offices, 47 Derry Road, Strabane BT82 8DY ☎ 028 7138 2204 🖷 028 7138 1348 ✉ mscott@strabanedc.com

Grounds Maintenance: Mr Malcolm Scott, Chief Technical Services Officer, District Council Offices, 47 Derry Road, Strabane BT82 8DY ☎ 028 7138 2204 🖷 028 7138 1348 ✉ mscott@strabanedc.com

Health and Safety: Mr Patrick Cosgrove, Chief Environmental Health Officer, District Council Offices, 47 Derry Road, Strabane BT82 8DY ☎ 028 7138 2204 🖷 028 7138 1347 ✉ pcosgrove@strabanedc.com

Leisure and Cultural Services: Mrs Karen McFarland, Head of Culture, Arts & Leisure, District Council Offices, 47 Derry Road, Strabane BT82 8DY ☎ 028 7138 2204 🖷 028 7138 1348 ✉ kmcfarland@strabanedc.com

Licensing: Mr David Turner, Technical Services Licensing Officer, District Council Offices, 47 Derry Road, Strabane BT82 8DY ☎ 028 7138 2204 🖷 028 7138 1349 ✉ dturner@strabanedc.com

Lottery Funding, Charity and Voluntary: Mrs Karen McFarland, Head of Culture, Arts & Leisure, District Council Offices, 47 Derry Road, Strabane BT82 8DY ☎ 028 7138 2204 🖷 028 7138 1348 ✉ kmcfarland@strabanedc.com

Member Services: Mrs Sharon Maxwell, Business Manager, District Council Offices, 47 Derry Road, Strabane BT82 8DY ☎ 028 7138 1304 🖷 028 7138 1348 ✉ samaxwell@strabanedc.com

Personnel / HR: Ms Paula Donnelly, Human Resources Manager, District Council Offices, 47 Derry Road, Strabane BT82 8DY ☎ 028 7138 2204 🖷 028 7138 1348 ✉ pdonnelly@strabanedc.com

Recycling & Waste Minimisation: Mr Malcolm Scott, Chief Technical Services Officer, District Council Offices, 47 Derry Road, Strabane BT82 8DY ☎ 028 7138 2204 🖷 028 7138 1348 ✉ mscott@strabanedc.com

Staff Training: Ms Paula Donnelly, Human Resources Manager, District Council Offices, 47 Derry Road, Strabane BT82 8DY ☎ 028 7138 2204 🖷 028 7138 1348 ✉ pdonnelly@strabanedc.com

Sustainable Development: Mr Patrick Cosgrove, Chief Environmental Health Officer, District Council Offices, 47 Derry Road, Strabane BT82 8DY ☎ 028 7138 2204 🖷 028 7138 1347 ✉ pcosgrove@strabanedc.com

Tourism: Mr Philip McShane, Tourist Information Officer, 47 Derry Road, Strabane BT82 8DY ☎ 028 7138 2400 🖷 020 7138 1348 ✉ pmcshane@strabanedc.com

Town Centre: Mrs Heather Torrens, Project Officer - Strabane 2000, District Council Offices, 47 Derry Road, Strabane BT82 8DY ☎ 028 7138 1302 🖷 028 7138 1349 ✉ htorrens@strabanedc.com

Waste Collection and Disposal: Mr Malcolm Scott, Chief

Technical Services Officer, District Council Offices, 47 Derry Road, Strabane BT82 8DY ☎ 028 7138 2204 🖷 028 7138 1348 ✉ mscott@strabanedc.com

Waste Management: Mr Malcolm Scott, Chief Technical Services Officer, District Council Offices, 47 Derry Road, Strabane BT82 8DY ☎ 028 7138 2204 🖷 028 7138 1348 ✉ mscott@strabanedc.com

MEMBERS OF THE COUNCIL (16)

***Chair:* Kerrigan**, Thomas (DUP - Derg)
tkerrigan@strabanedc.com
***Vice-Chair:* Kelly**, Dan (SF - Glenelly)
dkelly@strabanedc.com
Bresland, Allan (DUP - Glenelly)
a.bresland@btconnect.com
Carlin, Karina (SF - Mourne)
kcarlin@strabanedc.com
Donnell, John (DUP - Glenelly)
jdonnell@strabanedc.com
Hamilton, Rhonda (DUP - Glenelly)
rhamilton@strabanedc.com
Hussey, Derek (UUP - Derg)
drhussey@strabanedc.com
Kelly, Patsy (SDLP - Mourne)
pkelly@strabanedc.com
McCauley, Jay (SF - Mourne)
jmccauley@strabanedc.com
McGuire, Kieran (SF - Derg)
kmcguire@strabanedc.com
McHugh, Maoliosa (SF - Derg)
mmchugh@strabanedc.com
McHugh, Ruairi (SF - Derg)
rmchugh@strabanedc.com
McMackin, Michelle (SF - Glenelly)
mmcmackin@strabanedc.com
McMahon, Brian (SF - Mourne)
bmcmahon@strabanedc.com
McMenamin, Eugene (SDLP - Mourne)
eugenemcm@hotmail.com
O'Kane, James (IND - Mourne)
jokane@strabanedc.com

POLITICAL COMPOSITION

SF: 8, DUP: 4, SDLP: 2, UUP: 1, IND: 1

COMMITTEE CHAIRS

Corporate & Regulatory Services: Ms Michelle McMackin
Culture, Arts & Leisure: Ms Karina Carlin
Economic Development: Mr Brian McMahon
Environment: Mr John Donnell

STRATFORD-UPON-AVON D

Stratford-upon-Avon District Council, Elizabeth House, Church Street, Stratford-upon-Avon CV37 6HX ☎ 01789 267575 🖷 01789 260007 ✉ info@stratford-dc.gov.uk 🖳 www.stratford.gov.uk

FACTS & FIGURES

Police Authority: Warwickshire Police Authority
Health Authority: NHS West Midlands
Learning and Skills Council: West Midlands
Parliamentary Constituencies: Stratford-on-Avon
EU Constituencies: West Midlands
Election Frequency: Elections are by thirds
Twinning: Alcester: Vallet (France); Bidford-on-Avon: Ebsdorfergrund (Germany); Long Compton: Guirey-en-Vexin (France)

PRINCIPAL OFFICERS

Chief Executive: Mr Paul Lankester, Chief Executive, Elizabeth House, Church Street, Stratford-upon-Avon CV37 6HX ☎ 01789 260100 🖷 01789 260007 ✉ paul.lankester@stratford-dc.gov.uk

Assistant Chief Executive: Mr David Buckland, Assistant Chief Executive, Elizabeth House, Church Street, Stratford-upon-Avon CV37 6HX ☎ 01789 260425 🖷 01789 260909 ✉ david.buckland@stratford-dc.gov.uk

Access Officer / Social Services (Disability): Mr Dave Webb, Head of Business, Housing & Revenues, Elizabeth House, Church Street, Stratford-upon-Avon CV37 6HX ☎ 01789 260900 🖷 01789 260444 ✉ dave.webb@stratford-dc.gov.uk

Architect, Building / Property Services: Mr Robert Weeks, Head of Environment & Planning, Elizabeth House, Church Street, Stratford-upon-Avon CV37 6HX ☎ 01789 260810 🖷 01789 260860 ✉ robert.weeks@stratford-dc.gov.uk

Best Value: Ms Balvinder Heran, Head of Customer Access, Elizabeth House, Church Street, Stratford-upon-Avon CV37 6HX ☎ 01789 260470 🖷 01789 260777 ✉ balvinder.heran@stratford-dc.gov.uk

Building Control: Mr Tony Perks, Head of Technical Services, Elizabeth House, Church Street, Stratford-upon-Avon CV37 6HX ☎ 01789 260620 ✉ tony.perks@stratford-dc.gov.uk

PR / Communications: Ms Beverley Hemming, Corporate Communications Manager, Elizabeth House, Church Street, Stratford-upon-Avon CV37 6HX ☎ 01789 260105 🖷 01789 260007 ✉ beverley.hemming@stratford-dc.gov.uk

Computer Management: Ms Balvinder Heran, Head of Customer Access, Elizabeth House, Church Street, Stratford-upon-Avon CV37 6HX ☎ 01789 260470 🖷 01789 260777 ✉ balvinder.heran@stratford-dc.gov.uk

Contracts: Mr Liam Nevin, Head of Corporate Support, Elizabeth House, Church Street, Stratford-upon-Avon CV37 6HX ☎ 01789 260400 ✉ liam.nevin@stratford-dc.gov.uk

Corporate Services: Mr Liam Nevin, Head of Corporate Support, Elizabeth House, Church Street, Stratford-upon-Avon CV37 6HX ☎ 01789 260400 ✉ liam.nevin@stratford-dc.gov.uk

Customer Service: Ms Balvinder Heran, Head of Customer Access, Elizabeth House, Church Street, Stratford-upon-Avon CV37 6HX ☎ 01789 260470 🖷 01789 260777 ✉ balvinder.heran@stratford-dc.gov.uk

Economic Development: Mr Liam Nevin, Head of Corporate Support, Elizabeth House, Church Street, Stratford-upon-Avon CV37 6HX ☎ 01789 260400 ✉ liam.nevin@stratford-dc.gov.uk

E-Government: Ms Balvinder Heran, Head of Customer Access, Elizabeth House, Church Street, Stratford-upon-Avon CV37 6HX ☎ 01789 260470 🖷 01789 260777 ✉ balvinder.heran@stratford-dc.gov.uk

Electoral Registration: Mr Liam Nevin, Head of Corporate Support, Elizabeth House, Church Street, Stratford-upon-Avon CV37 6HX ☎ 01789 260400 ✉ liam.nevin@stratford-dc.gov.uk

Emergency Planning: Mr Robert Weeks, Head of Environment & Planning, Elizabeth House, Church Street, Stratford-upon-Avon CV37 6HX ☎ 01789 260810 🖷 01789 260860 ✉ robert.weeks@stratford-dc.gov.uk

Energy Management: Mr Paul Chapman, Policy Officer, Elizabeth House, Church Street, Stratford-upon-Avon CV37 6HX ☎ 01789 267125 🖷 01789 260909 ✉ paul.chapman@stratford-dc.gov.uk

Environmental / Technical Services: Mr Robert Weeks, Head of Environment & Planning, Elizabeth House, Church Street, Stratford-upon-Avon CV37 6HX ☎ 01789 260810 🖷 01789 260860 ✉ robert.weeks@stratford-dc.gov.uk

Environmental Health: Mr Robert Weeks, Head of Environment & Planning, Elizabeth House, Church Street, Stratford-upon-Avon CV37 6HX ☎ 01789 260810 🖷 01789 260860 ✉ robert.weeks@stratford-dc.gov.uk

Estates, Property & Valuation: Mr Tony Perks, Head of Technical Services, Elizabeth House, Church Street, Stratford-upon-Avon CV37 6HX ☎ 01789 260620 ✉ tony.perks@stratford-dc.gov.uk

Finance and Treasurer: Mr David Buckland, Assistant Chief Executive, Elizabeth House, Church Street, Stratford-upon-Avon CV37 6HX ☎ 01789 260425 🖷 01789 260909 ✉ david.buckland@stratford-dc.gov.uk

Grounds Maintenance: Mr Tony Perks, Head of Technical Services, Elizabeth House, Church Street, Stratford-upon-Avon CV37 6HX ☎ 01789 260620 ✉ tony.perks@stratford-dc.gov.uk

Health and Safety: Mr Mark Sainsbury, Premises & Safety Manager, Elizabeth House, Church Street, Stratford-upon-Avon CV37 6HX ☎ 01789 260708 ✉ mark.sainsbury@stratford-dc.gov.uk

Home Energy Conservation: Mr Dave Webb, Head of Business, Housing & Revenues, Elizabeth House, Church Street, Stratford-upon-Avon CV37 6HX ☎ 01789 260900 🖷 01789 260444 ✉ dave.webb@stratford-dc.gov.uk

Housing: Mr Dave Webb, Head of Business, Housing & Revenues, Elizabeth House, Church Street, Stratford-upon-Avon CV37 6HX ☎ 01789 260900 🖷 01789 260444 ✉ dave.webb@stratford-dc.gov.uk

Legal: Mr Liam Nevin, Head of Corporate Support, Elizabeth House, Church Street, Stratford-upon-Avon CV37 6HX ☎ 01789 260400 ✉ liam.nevin@stratford-dc.gov.uk

Leisure and Cultural Services: Mr Tony Perks, Head of Technical Services, Elizabeth House, Church Street, Stratford-upon-Avon CV37 6HX ☎ 01789 260620 ✉ tony.perks@stratford-dc.gov.uk

Licensing: Mr Robert Weeks, Head of Environment & Planning, Elizabeth House, Church Street, Stratford-upon-Avon CV37 6HX ☎ 01789 260810 🖷 01789 260860 ✉ robert.weeks@stratford-dc.gov.uk

Member Services: Mr Liam Nevin, Head of Corporate Support, Elizabeth House, Church Street, Stratford-upon-Avon CV37 6HX ☎ 01789 260400 ✉ liam.nevin@stratford-dc.gov.uk

Parking: Mr Tony Perks, Head of Technical Services, Elizabeth House, Church Street, Stratford-upon-Avon CV37 6HX ☎ 01789 260620 ✉ tony.perks@stratford-dc.gov.uk

Partnerships: Ms Balvinder Heran, Head of Customer Access, Elizabeth House, Church Street, Stratford-upon-Avon CV37 6HX ☎ 01789 260470 🖷 01789 260777 ✉ balvinder.heran@stratford-dc.gov.uk

Personnel / HR: Mr David Buckland, Assistant Chief Executive, Elizabeth House, Church Street, Stratford-upon-Avon CV37 6HX ☎ 01789 260425 🖷 01789 260909 ✉ david.buckland@stratford-dc.gov.uk

Planning: Mr Robert Weeks, Head of Environment & Planning, Elizabeth House, Church Street, Stratford-upon-Avon CV37 6HX ☎ 01789 260810 🖷 01789 260860 ✉ robert.weeks@stratford-dc.gov.uk

Recycling & Waste Minimisation: Mr Tony Perks, Head of Technical Services, Elizabeth House, Church Street, Stratford-upon-Avon CV37 6HX ☎ 01789 260620 ✉ tony.perks@stratford-dc.gov.uk

Staff Training: Mr David Buckland, Assistant Chief Executive, Elizabeth House, Church Street, Stratford-upon-Avon CV37 6HX ☎ 01789 260425 🖷 01789 260909 ✉ david.buckland@stratford-dc.gov.uk

Street Scene: Mr Robert Weeks, Head of Environment & Planning, Elizabeth House, Church Street, Stratford-upon-Avon CV37 6HX ☎ 01789 260810 🖷 01789 260860 ✉ robert.weeks@stratford-dc.gov.uk

Sustainable Communities: Mr Dave Webb, Head of Business, Housing & Revenues, Elizabeth House, Church Street, Stratford-upon-Avon CV37 6HX ☎ 01789 260900 🖷 01789 260444 ✉ dave.webb@stratford-dc.gov.uk

Sustainable Development: Mr Dave Webb, Head of Business, Housing & Revenues, Elizabeth House, Church Street, Stratford-upon-Avon CV37 6HX ☎ 01789 260900 🖷 01789 260444 ✉ dave.webb@stratford-dc.gov.uk

Tourism: Mr Dave Webb, Head of Business, Housing & Revenues, Elizabeth House, Church Street, Stratford-upon-Avon CV37 6HX ☎ 01789 260900 🖷 01789 260444 ✉ dave.webb@stratford-dc.gov.uk

Transport Planner: Mr Robert Weeks, Head of Environment & Planning, Elizabeth House, Church Street, Stratford-upon-Avon CV37 6HX ☎ 01789 260810 🖷 01789 260860 robert.weeks@stratford-dc.gov.uk

Waste Collection and Disposal: Mr Tony Perks, Head of Technical Services, Elizabeth House, Church Street, Stratford-upon-Avon CV37 6HX ☎ 01789 260620 tony.perks@stratford-dc.gov.uk

Waste Management: Mr Tony Perks, Head of Technical Services, Elizabeth House, Church Street, Stratford-upon-Avon CV37 6HX ☎ 01789 260620 tony.perks@stratford-dc.gov.uk

MEMBERS OF THE COUNCIL (53)

***Chair:* Beamer**, Neville (CON - Stratford Guild and Hathaway)
neville.beamer@stratford-dc.gov.uk
***Deputy Chair:* Mills**, Christopher (CON - Kineton)
christopher.mills@stratford-dc.gov.uk
***Leader of the Council:* Saint**, Christopher (CON - Tredington)
chris.saint@stratford-dc.gov.uk
***Deputy Leader of the Council:* Thirlwell**, Stephen (CON - Henley)
stephen.thirlwell@stratford-dc.gov.uk
***Group Leader:* Cheney**, Richard (LD - Shipston)
richard.cheney@stratford-dc.gov.uk
***Group Leader:* Short**, Julie (IND - Stratford Avenue and New Town)
Adams, Susan (CON - Alcester)
susan.adams@stratford-dc.gov.uk
Atkinson, George (CON - Tanworth)
george.atkinson@stratford-dc.gov.uk
Barnes, Peter (LD - Welford)
peter.barnes@stratford-dc.gov.uk
Beaman, Paul (LD - Studley)
paul.beaman@stratford-dc.gov.uk
Brain, Mike (CON - Quinton)
mike.brain@stratford-dc.gov.uk
Crump, Andrew (CON - Southam)
andrew.crump@stratford-dc.gov.uk
Dowling, William (LD - Stratford Guild and Hathaway)
william.dowling@stratford-dc.gov.uk
Ellard, Jennie (CON - Southam)
jennie.ellard@stratford-dc.gov.uk
Fradgley, Jennifer (LD - Stratford Guild and Hathaway)
jenny.fradgley@stratford-dc.gov.uk
Fradgley, Ian (LD - Stratford Alveston)
ian.fradgley@stratford-dc.gov.uk
Gittus, Mike (CON - Kinwarton)
mike.gittus@stratford-dc.gov.uk
Gray, Stephen (CON - Long Compton)
stephen.gray@stratford-dc.gov.uk
Gullis, Jonathan (CON - Shipston)
jonathan.gullis@stratford-dc.gov.uk
Hamburger, Richard (CON - Harbury)
richard.hamburger@stratford-dc.gov.uk
Hayter, Helen (CON - Snitterfield)
helen.hayter@stratford-dc.gov.uk
Holder, Eric (LD - Studley)
eric.holder@stratford-dc.gov.uk
Horner, John (CON - Claverdon)
john.horner@stratford-dc.gov.uk
Howse, Maurice (CON - Bidford and Salford)
maurice.howse@stratford-dc.gov.uk
Jackson, Simon (CON - Burton Dassett)
simon.jackson@stratford-dc.gov.uk
Johnston, David (LD - Wellesbourne)
david.johnston@stratford-dc.gov.uk
Juned, Susan (LD - Alcester)
susan.juned@stratford-dc.gov.uk
Kendall, Danny (CON - Wellesbourne)
danny.kendall@stratford-dc.gov.uk
Kerridge, Justin (CON - Sambourne)
justin.kerridge@stratford-dc.gov.uk
Kittendorf, Steven (LD - Stockton and Napton)
steven.kittendorf@stratford-dc.gov.uk
Lawrence, William (CON - Aston Cantlow)
sirwilliam.lawrence@stratford-dc.gov.uk
Lloyd, Keith (IND - Stratford Avenue and New Town)
keith.lloyd@stratford-dc.gov.uk
Mann, Beverley (LD - Harbury)
beverley.mann@stratford-dc.gov.uk
Matheou, George (CON - Henley)
george.matheou@stratford-dc.gov.uk
Moorse, Peter (LD - Stratford Mount Pleasant)
peter.moorse@stratford-dc.gov.uk
Oakley, Peter (CON - Tanworth)
peter.oakley@stratford-dc.gov.uk
Organ, Lynda (CON - Stratford Alveston)
lynda.organ@stratford-dc.gov.uk
Payne, Eric (CON - Alcester)
eric.payne@stratford-dc.gov.uk
Pemberton, Daren (LD - Bidford and Salford)
daren.pemberton@stratford-dc.gov.uk
Roache, Gillian (CON - Vale of Red Horse)
gillian.roache@stratford-dc.gov.uk
Rolfe, Kate (LD - Stratford Alveston)
kate.rolfe@stratford-dc.gov.uk
Scorer, Alan (CON - Kineton)
alan.scorer@stratford-dc.gov.uk
Seccombe, Isobel (CON - Ettington)
isobel.seccombe@stratford-dc.gov.uk
Seccombe, Philip (CON - Brailes)
philip.seccombe@stratford-dc.gov.uk
Spence, Jonathan (CON - Bidford and Salford)
jonathan.spence@stratford-dc.gov.uk
Spencer, Chris (CON - Long Itchington)
chris.spencer@stratford-dc.gov.uk
Taylor, Joyce (LD - Stratford Mount Pleasant)
joyce.taylor@stratford-dc.gov.uk
Thomas, Clive (LD - Stratford Avenue and New Town)
clive.thomas@stratford-dc.gov.uk
Vaudry, Robert (CON - Bardon)
robert.vaudry@stratford-dc.gov.uk
Williams, Chris (CON - Fenny Compton)
chris.williams@stratford-dc.gov.uk
Wise, David (CON - Southam)
david.wise@stratford-dc.gov.uk
Wright, Roger (IND - Wellesbourne)
roger.wright@stratford-dc.gov.uk
Wright, Hazel (LD - Studley)
hazel.wright@stratford-dc.gov.uk

POLITICAL COMPOSITION

CON: 33, LD: 17, IND: 3

CABINET

Leader / Leadership & Governance: Mr Christopher Saint

Deputy Leader / Partnerships: Mr Stephen Thirlwell
Corporate Support: Ms Gillian Roache
Customer Access: Mr Mike Brain
Enterprise, Housing & Revenues: Mr Maurice Howse
Environment & Planning: Mr Mike Gittus
Finance & Business Administration: Ms Jennie Ellard
Technical Services: Ms Lynda Organ

COMMITTEE CHAIRS

Audit: Mr Philip Seccombe
Licensing: Ms Susan Adams
Overview & Scruinty: Mr Stephen Gray
Regulatory: Mr Chris Williams

STROUD D

Stroud District Council, Council Offices, Ebley Mill, Westward Road, Stroud GL5 4UB ☎ 01453 766321 🖷 01453 750932 ✉ information@stroud.gov.uk 💻 www.stroud.gov.uk

FACTS & FIGURES

Police Authority: Gloucestershire Police Authority
Health Authority: NHS South West
Learning and Skills Council: South West
Parliamentary Constituencies: Cotswold, Stroud
EU Constituencies: South West
Election Frequency: Elections are by thirds
Twinning: Landkreis Gottingen (Germany)

PRINCIPAL OFFICERS

Chief Executive: Mr David Hagg, Chief Executive, Council Offices, Ebley Mill, Westward Road, Stroud GL5 4UB ☎ 01453 754290 🖷 01453 754934 ✉ david.hagg@stroud.gov.uk

Architect, Building / Property Services: Ms Alison Fisk, Head of Asset Management, Council Offices, Ebley Mill, Westward Road, Stroud GL5 4UB ☎ 01453 754430 🖷 01453 754309 ✉ alison.fisk@stroud.gov.uk

Building Control: Mr Phil Skill, Head of Planning, Council Offices, Ebley Mill, Westward Road, Stroud GL5 4UB ☎ 01453 754345 🖷 01453 754222 ✉ phil.skill@stroud.gov.uk

Children / Youth Services: Mrs Joanne Jordan, Strategic Head of Customer Services, Council Offices, Ebley Mill, Westward Road, Stroud GL5 4UB ☎ 01453 754005 🖷 01453 754933 ✉ joanne.jordan@stroud.gov.uk

PR / Communications: Mr Nick Watkins, Head of Communications, Council Offices, Ebley Mill, Westward Road, Stroud GL5 4UB ☎ 01453 754250 🖷 01453 750932 ✉ nick.watkins@stroud.gov.uk

Community Planning: Mr Barry Wyatt, Strategic Head of Development Service, Council Offices, Ebley Mill, Westward Road, Stroud GL5 4UB ☎ 01453 754210 ✉ barry.wyatt@stroud.gov.uk

Community Safety: Mr Philip Sullivan, Head of Community Safety, Council Offices, Ebley Mill, Westward Road, Stroud GL5 4UB ☎ 01453 754280 🖷 01453 754947 ✉ philip.sullivan@stroud.gov.uk

Computer Management: Mr Nick Watkins, Head of Communications, Council Offices, Ebley Mill, Westward Road, Stroud GL5 4UB ☎ 01453 754250 🖷 01453 750932 ✉ nick.watkins@stroud.gov.uk

Corporate Services: Miss Allison Sharpe, Head of Corporate Resources, Council Offices, Ebley Mill, Westward Road, Stroud GL5 4UB ☎ 01453 754272 🖷 01453 750932 ✉ allison.sharpe@stroud.gov.uk

Customer Service: Mrs Joanne Jordan, Strategic Head of Customer Services, Council Offices, Ebley Mill, Westward Road, Stroud GL5 4UB ☎ 01453 754005 🖷 01453 754933 ✉ joanne.jordan@stroud.gov.uk

Economic Development: Mr Phil Skill, Head of Planning, Council Offices, Ebley Mill, Westward Road, Stroud GL5 4UB ☎ 01453 754345 🖷 01453 754222 ✉ phil.skill@stroud.gov.uk

E-Government: Mr Nick Watkins, Head of Communications, Council Offices, Ebley Mill, Westward Road, Stroud GL5 4UB ☎ 01453 754250 🖷 01453 750932 ✉ nick.watkins@stroud.gov.uk

Electoral Registration: Miss Allison Sharpe, Head of Corporate Resources, Council Offices, Ebley Mill, Westward Road, Stroud GL5 4UB ☎ 01453 754272 🖷 01453 750932 ✉ allison.sharpe@stroud.gov.uk

Emergency Planning: Mr Mike Hammond, Facilities Manager / Civil Contingencies Manager, Council Offices, Ebley Mill, Westward Road, Stroud GL5 4UB ☎ 01453 754447 🖷 01453 754947 ✉ mike.hammond@stroud.gov.uk

Energy Management: Mr Jon Beckett, Head of Environmental Health, Council Offices, Ebley Mill, Westward Road, Stroud GL5 4UB ☎ 01453 754443 🖷 01453 754963 ✉ jon.beckett@stroud.gov.uk

Environmental / Technical Services: Mr Jon Beckett, Head of Environmental Health, Council Offices, Ebley Mill, Westward Road, Stroud GL5 4UB ☎ 01453 754443 🖷 01453 754963 ✉ jon.beckett@stroud.gov.uk

Environmental Health: Mr Jon Beckett, Head of Environmental Health, Council Offices, Ebley Mill, Westward Road, Stroud GL5 4UB ☎ 01453 754443 🖷 01453 754963 ✉ jon.beckett@stroud.gov.uk

Estates, Property & Valuation: Ms Jill Fallows, Property Investment Manager, Council Offices, Ebley Mill, Westward Road, Stroud GL5 4UB ☎ 01453 754433 ✉ jill.fallows@stroud.gov.uk

Facilities: Mr Mike Hammond, Facilities Manager / Civil Contingencies Manager, Council Offices, Ebley Mill, Westward Road, Stroud GL5 4UB ☎ 01453 754447 🖷 01453 754947 ✉ mike.hammond@stroud.gov.uk

Finance and Treasurer: Mrs Sandra Cowley, Head of Finance & Section 151 Officer, Council Offices, Ebley Mill, Westward Road, Stroud GL5 4UB ☎ 01453 754340 ✉ sandra.cowley@stroud.gov.uk

Grounds Maintenance: Mr Carlos Novoth, Public Spaces Manager, Council Offices, Ebley Mill, Westward Road, Stroud GL5 4UB ☎ 01453 754412 ✉ carlos.novoth@stroud.gov.uk

Health and Safety: Mr Phil Park, Commercial Services Manager, Council Offices, Ebley Mill, Westward Road, Stroud GL5 4UB ☎ 01453 754471 🖷 01453 754963 ✉ phil.park@stroud.gov.uk

Home Energy Conservation: Mr Jon Beckett, Head of Environmental Health, Council Offices, Ebley Mill, Westward Road, Stroud GL5 4UB ☎ 01453 754443 🖷 01453 754963 ✉ jon.beckett@stroud.gov.uk

Housing: Mr Carl Brazier, Strategic Head of Tenant Services, Council Offices, Ebley Mill, Westward Road, Stroud GL5 4UB ☎ 01453 754150 ✉ carl.brazier@stroud.gov.uk

Housing Maintenance: Mr Carl Brazier, Strategic Head of Tenant Services, Council Offices, Ebley Mill, Westward Road, Stroud GL5 4UB ☎ 01453 754150 ✉ carl.brazier@stroud.gov.uk

Legal: Mr Peter Woodcock, Legal Services Manager & Monitoring Officer, Council Offices, Ebley Mill, Westward Road, Stroud GL5 4UB ☎ 01453 754396 ✉ peter.woodcock@stroud.gov.uk

Leisure and Cultural Services: Mr Ray Figg, Head of Cultural Services, Council Offices, Ebley Mill, Westward Road, Stroud GL5 4UB ☎ 01453 754407 🖷 01453 754309 ✉ ray.figg@stroud.gov.uk

Licensing: Mr Jon Beckett, Head of Environmental Health, Council Offices, Ebley Mill, Westward Road, Stroud GL5 4UB ☎ 01453 754443 🖷 01453 754963 ✉ jon.beckett@stroud.gov.uk

Lottery Funding, Charity and Voluntary: Mr Ray Figg, Head of Cultural Services, Council Offices, Ebley Mill, Westward Road, Stroud GL5 4UB ☎ 01453 754407 🖷 01453 754309 ✉ ray.figg@stroud.gov.uk

Member Services: Mr Nick Watkins, Head of Communications, Council Offices, Ebley Mill, Westward Road, Stroud GL5 4UB ☎ 01453 754250 🖷 01453 750932 ✉ nick.watkins@stroud.gov.uk

Personnel / HR: Miss Allison Sharpe, Head of Corporate Resources, Council Offices, Ebley Mill, Westward Road, Stroud GL5 4UB ☎ 01453 754272 🖷 01453 750932 ✉ allison.sharpe@stroud.gov.uk

Planning: Mr Phil Skill, Head of Planning, Council Offices, Ebley Mill, Westward Road, Stroud GL5 4UB ☎ 01453 754345 🖷 01453 754222 ✉ phil.skill@stroud.gov.uk

Procurement: Miss Sarah Turner, Business Efficiency Officer, Council Offices, Ebley Mill, Westward Road, Stroud GL5 4UB ☎ 01453 754346 ✉ sarah.turner@stroud.gov.uk

Recycling & Waste Minimisation: Mr Carlos Novoth, Public Spaces Manager, Council Offices, Ebley Mill, Westward Road, Stroud GL5 4UB ☎ 01453 754412 ✉ carlos.novoth@stroud.gov.uk

Regeneration: Mr Phil Skill, Head of Planning, Council Offices, Ebley Mill, Westward Road, Stroud GL5 4UB ☎ 01453 754345 🖷 01453 754222 ✉ phil.skill@stroud.gov.uk

Staff Training: Miss Allison Sharpe, Head of Corporate Resources, Council Offices, Ebley Mill, Westward Road, Stroud GL5 4UB ☎ 01453 754272 🖷 01453 750932 ✉ allison.sharpe@stroud.gov.uk

Street Scene: Mr Carlos Novoth, Public Spaces Manager, Council Offices, Ebley Mill, Westward Road, Stroud GL5 4UB ☎ 01453 754412 ✉ carlos.novoth@stroud.gov.uk

Sustainable Communities: Mr Barry Wyatt, Strategic Head of Development Service, Council Offices, Ebley Mill, Westward Road, Stroud GL5 4UB ☎ 01453 754210 ✉ barry.wyatt@stroud.gov.uk

Sustainable Development: Mr Barry Wyatt, Strategic Head of Development Service, Council Offices, Ebley Mill, Westward Road, Stroud GL5 4UB ☎ 01453 754210 ✉ barry.wyatt@stroud.gov.uk

Tourism: Mr Ray Figg, Head of Cultural Services, Council Offices, Ebley Mill, Westward Road, Stroud GL5 4UB ☎ 01453 754407 🖷 01453 754309 ✉ ray.figg@stroud.gov.uk

Total Place: Mrs Joanne Jordan, Strategic Head of Customer Services, Council Offices, Ebley Mill, Westward Road, Stroud GL5 4UB ☎ 01453 754005 🖷 01453 754933 ✉ joanne.jordan@stroud.gov.uk

Waste Collection and Disposal: Mr Carlos Novoth, Public Spaces Manager, Council Offices, Ebley Mill, Westward Road, Stroud GL5 4UB ☎ 01453 754412 ✉ carlos.novoth@stroud.gov.uk

Waste Management: Mr Carlos Novoth, Public Spaces Manager, Council Offices, Ebley Mill, Westward Road, Stroud GL5 4UB ☎ 01453 754412 ✉ carlos.novoth@stroud.gov.uk

Children's Play Areas: Mr Ray Figg, Head of Cultural Services, Council Offices, Ebley Mill, Westward Road, Stroud GL5 4UB ☎ 01453 754407 🖷 01453 754309 ✉ ray.figg@stroud.gov.uk

MEMBERS OF THE COUNCIL (51)

***Chair:* Hudson**, John (CON - Cam East)
cllr.john.hudson@stroud.gov.uk

***Vice-Chair:* Rees**, Mark (LAB - Cainscross)
cllr.mark.rees@stroud.gov.uk

***Leader of the Council:* Wheeler**, Geoff (LAB - Dursley)
cllr.geoff.wheeler@stroud.gov.uk

Andrewartha, Dennis (LD - Cam West)
cllr.dennis.andrewartha@stroud.gov.uk

Ashton, Liz (LAB - Berkeley)
cllr.liz.ashton@stroud.gov.uk

Binns, Dorcas (CON - Minchinhampton)
cllr.dorcas.binns@stroud.gov.uk

Blackwell, Roland (CON - Nailsworth)
cllr.rowland.blackwell@stroud.gov.uk

Booth, Philip (GRN - Randwick, Whiteshill and Ruscombe)
cllr.philip.booth@stroud.gov.uk

Boxall, Tim (CON - Coaley and Uley)
cllr.tim.boxall@stround.gov.uk

Brine, Chris (LAB - Stonehouse)
cllr.chris.brine@stroud.gov.uk

Carter, Paul (CON - Nailsworth)
cllr.paul.carter@stroud.gov.uk

Cato, Molly (GRN - Valley)
cllr.molly.scott.cato@stroud.gov.uk
Cooper, Nigel (CON - Painswick)
cllr.nigel.cooper@stroud.gov.uk
Cordwell, June (LD - Wootton-under-Edge)
cllr.june.cordwell@stroud.gov.uk
Cornell, Doina (LAB - Dursley)
cllr.doina.cornell@stroud.gov.uk
Craig, Gordon (CON - Berkeley)
cllr.gordon.craig@stroud.gov.uk
Cross, Karon (LAB - Cainscross)
cll.karon.cross@stroud.gov.uk
Denney, Paul (LAB - Cam West)
cllr.paul.denney@stroud.gov.uk
Drew, David (LAB - Farmhill and Paganhill)
cllr.david.drew@stroud.gov.uk
Fellows, Chas (CON - Chalford)
cllr.chas.fellows@stroud.gov.uk
Hemming, Paul (LD - Kingswood)
cllr.paul.hemming@stroud.gov.uk
Hurst, Nick (CON - Minchinhampton)
cllr.nick.hurst@stroud.gov.uk
Jones, John (CON - Severn)
cllr.john.jones@stroud.gov.uk
Jones, Haydn (CON - Severn)
cllr.haydn.jones@stroud.gov.uk
Le Fleming, Daniel (CON - Bisley)
cllr.daniel.lefleming@stroud.gov.uk
Littleton, Graham (CON - Hardwicke)
cllr.graham.littleton@stroud.gov.uk
Lydon, Stephen (LAB - The Stanleys)
cllr.stephen.lydon@stroud.gov.uk
Marjoram, John (GRN - Trinity)
cllr.john.marjoram@stroud.gov.uk
Marsh, Brian (LD - Dursley)
cllr.brian.marsh@stroud.gov.uk
Miles, Russell (CON - Hardwicke)
cllr.russell.miles@stroud.gov.uk
Moore, Stephen (LAB - Rodborough)
cllr.stephen.moore@stroud.gov.uk
O'Connor, Alan (LD - Wootton-under-Edge)
cllr.alan.oconnor@stroud.gov.uk
Pearson, Keith (CON - Upton St Leonards)
cllr.keith.pearson@stroud.gov.uk
Peters, Elizabeth (CON - Chalford)
cllr.elizabeth.peters@stroud.gov.uk
Pickering, Simon (GRN - Slade)
cllr.simon.pickering@stroud.gov.uk
Powell, Gary (LAB - Stonehouse)
cllr.gary.powell@stroud.gov.uk
Prenter, Nigel (LAB - Rodborough)
cllr.nigel.prenter@stroud.gov.uk
Read, Andy (IND - Central)
cllr.andy.read@stroud.gov.uk
Roden, Frances (CON - Painswick)
cllr.frances.roden@stroud.gov.uk
Ross, Mattie (LAB - Stonehouse)
cllr.mattie.ross@stroud.gov.uk
Sanders, Roger (LAB - Uplands)
cllr.roger.sanders@stroud.gov.uk
Sims, Emma (CON - Nailsworth)
cllr.emma.sims@stroud.gov.uk
Smith, Paul (LD - Wootton-under-Edge)
cllr.paul.smith@stroud.gov.uk
Stephens, Ken (LAB - Eastington and Standish)
cllr.ken.stephens@stroud.gov.uk
Studdert-Kennedy, Nigel (IND - The Stanleys)
cllr.nigel.studdert-kennedy@stroud.gov.uk
Tipper, Brain (CON - Cam East)
cllr.brian.tipper@stroud.gov.uk
Whiteside, Martin (GRN - Thrupp)
cllr.martin.whiteside@stroud.gov.uk
Wigzell, Rhiannon (CON - Amberley and Woodchester)
cllr.rhiannon.wigzell@stroud.gov.uk
Williams, Tom (LAB - Cainscross)
cllr.tom.williams@stroud.gov.uk
Wride, Penelope (CON - Vale)
cllr.penelope.wride@stroud.gov.uk
Young, Debbie (CON - Chalford)
cllr.debbie.young@stroud.gov.uk

POLITICAL COMPOSITION
CON: 22, LAB: 16, LD: 6, GRN: 5, IND: 2

CABINET
Leader: Mr Geoff Wheeler
Community Services: Ms June Cordwell
Environment: Mr Simon Pickering
Finance: Mr Tom Williams
Health & Wellbeing: Ms Karon Cross
Housing: Ms Mattie Ross
Planning: Mr Dennis Andrewartha
Regeneration: Mr Roger Sanders

COMMITTEE CHAIRS
Audit (Scrutiny): Mr Paul Smith
Development Control: Mr Ken Stephens
Housing Management: Mr Chris Brine
Licensing & Regulation: Mr Gary Powell
Performance Overview & Scrutiny: Mr Keith Pearson
Strategic Overview & Scrutiny: Ms Debbie Young

SUFFOLK C

Suffolk County Council, Endeavour House, 8 Russell Road, Ipswich IP1 2BX ☎ 01473 583000 🖷 01473 214549
💻 www.suffolk.gov.uk

FACTS & FIGURES
Police Authority: Suffolk Police Authority
Health Authority: East of England Strategic Health Authority
Learning and Skills Council: Eastern
Parliamentary Constituencies: Suffolk Central and Ipswich North, Suffolk South, Suffolk West
EU Constituencies: Eastern
Election Frequency: Elections are of whole council

PRINCIPAL OFFICERS
Chief Executive: Ms Deborah Cadman, Chief Executive, Endeavour House, 8 Russell Road, Ipswich IP1 2BX
☎ 01473 216843 ✉ deborah.cadman@suffolkcc.gov.uk

Senior Management: Ms Lucy Robinson, Director - Economy, Skills & Environment, Endeavour House, 8 Russell Road, Ipswich IP1 2BX ☎ 01473 264384 🖷 01473 216843
✉ lucy.robinson@et.suffolkcc.gov.uk

Architect, Building / Property Services: Mr Duncan Johnson, Interim Corporate Property Director, Endeavour House, 8 Russell

Road, Ipswich IP1 2BX ☎ 01473 264180

Architect, Building / Property Services: Mr Matthew Self, Development Manager, Endeavour House, 8 Russell Road, Ipswich IP1 2BX ☎ 01473 264158 ✉ Matthew.self@suffolk.gov.uk

Best Value: Ms Sue Roper, Assistant Director - Economic Development & Greenest County, Endeavour House, 8 Russell Road, Ipswich IP1 2BX ☎ 01473 265301 ✉ sue.roper@sufolk.gov.uk

Children / Youth Services: Mr Stephen Toye, Head of Youth Offending & Integrated Youth Sport, Endeavour House, 8 Russell Road, Ipswich IP1 2BX ☎ 0845 606 6067 ✉ stephen.toye@suffolk.gov.uk

Children / Youth Services: Mr Simon White, Director - Children & Young People, Endeavour House, 8 Russell Road, Ipswich IP1 2BX ☎ 01473 265353 ✉ simon.white@suffolk.gov.uk

PR / Communications: Mr Simon Higgins, Head of Communications, Endeavour House, 8 Russell Road, Ipswich IP1 2BX ☎ 01473 264391 ✉ simon.higgins@suffolk.gov.uk

Community Planning: Ms Alison Wheeler, Head of Service Development, St Andrew House, County Hall, Ipswich IP4 1LJ ☎ 01473 264611 ✉ alison.wheeler@libher.suffolkcc.gov.uk

Community Safety: Ms Julia Stephens-Row, Assistant Director - Social Inclusion & Diversity, Endeavour House, 8 Russell Road, Ipswich IP1 2BX ☎ 01473 265151 ✉ julia.stephens-row@socinc.suffolkcc.gov.uk

Computer Management: Mr Craig Anderson, Chief Operating Officer, Endeavour House, 8 Russell Road, Ipswich IP1 2BX ☎ 01473 265895 ✉ craig.anderson@suffolk.gov.uk

Consumer Protection and Trading Standards: Mr Steve Greenfield, County Trading Standards Officer, Endeavour House, 8 Russell Road, Ipswich IP1 2BX ☎ 01473 264866 🖷 01473 216850 ✉ steve.greenfield@tradstan.suffolkcc.gov.uk

Customer Service: Mr Simon Higgins, Head of Communications, Endeavour House, 8 Russell Road, Ipswich IP1 2BX ☎ 01473 264391 ✉ simon.higgins@suffolk.gov.uk

Economic Development: Ms Judith Mobbs, Assistant Director - Skills, Endeavour House, 8 Russell Road, Ipswich IP1 2BX ☎ 01473 264830 ✉ judith.mobbs@suffolk.gov.uk

Education: Mr Simon White, Director - Children & Young People, Endeavour House, 8 Russell Road, Ipswich IP1 2BX ☎ 01473 265353 ✉ simon.white@suffolk.gov.uk

Electoral Registration: Ms Sue Morgan, Head of Democratic Services, Endeavour House, 8 Russell Road, Ipswich IP1 2BX ☎ 01473 264512 ✉ sue.morgan@suffolk.gov.uk

Emergency Planning: Mr Andrew Osman, Head of Emergency Planning, Suffolk Joint Emergency Planning Unit, GFB3 Endeavour House, 8 Russell Road, Ipswich IP1 2BX ☎ 01473 265332 🖷 01473 216826 ✉ andrew.osman@fire.suffolkcc.gov.uk

Energy Management: Ms Lucy Robinson, Director - Economy, Skills & Environment, Endeavour House, 8 Russell Road, Ipswich IP1 2BX ☎ 01473 264384 🖷 01473 216843 ✉ lucy.robinson@et.suffolkcc.gov.uk

European Liaison: Mr Iain Dunnett, Low Carbon Development Manager, Economic Development, Endeavour House, 8 Russell Road, Ipswich IP1 2BX ☎ 01473 264829 ✉ iain.dunnett@econdev.suffolkcc.gov.uk

Events Manager: Mr Simon Higgins, Head of Communications, Endeavour House, 8 Russell Road, Ipswich IP1 2BX ☎ 01473 264391 ✉ simon.higgins@suffolk.gov.uk

Facilities: Mr James Carrick, Corporate Facilities Co-ordinator, Endeavour House, 8 Russell Road, Ipswich IP1 2BX ☎ 01473 264321 ✉ james.carrick@socserv.suffolkcc.gov.uk

Finance and Treasurer: Mr Geoff Dobson, Head of Strategic Finance, Endeavour House, 8 Russell Road, Ipswich IP1 2BX ☎ 01473 264347 ✉ geoff.dobson@accy.suffolkcc.gov.uk

Finance and Treasurer: Mr Tim Ryder, Interim Head of Scrutiny & Monitoring, Endeavour House, 8 Russell Road, Ipswich IP1 2BX ☎ 01473 264210 ✉ tim.ryder@suffolk.gov.uk

Health and Safety: Mr Nick Wilding, Health & Safety Manager - Education, Endeavour House, 8 Russell Road, Ipswich IP1 2BX ☎ 01473 264587 ✉ nick.wilding@pers.suffolkcc.gov.uk

Local Area Agreement: Ms Clair Harvey, Business Development Specialist, Endeavour House, 8 Russell Road, Ipswich IP1 2BX ☎ 01473 265304 ✉ clair.harvey@suffolk.gov.uk

Legal: Mr Tim Earl, Interim Head of Legal Services, Endeavour House, 8 Russell Road, Ipswich IP1 2BX ☎ 01473 260860 ✉ tim.earl@suffolk.gov.uk

Legal: Mr Tim Ryder, Interim Head of Scrutiny & Monitoring, Endeavour House, 8 Russell Road, Ipswich IP1 2BX ☎ 01473 264210 ✉ tim.ryder@suffolk.gov.uk

Lifelong Learning: Ms Sally Butcher, Head of Service - Adult & Community Service Learning & Development, Endeavour House, 8 Russell Road, Ipswich IP1 2BX ☎ 01473 264611 ✉ sally.butcher@suffolk.gov.uk

Member Services: Ms Sue Morgan, Head of Democratic Services, Endeavour House, 8 Russell Road, Ipswich IP1 2BX ☎ 01473264512 ✉ sue.morgan@suffolk.gov.uk

Personnel / HR: Ms Sally Marlow, Head of Human Resources, Endeavour House, 8 Russell Road, Ipswich IP1 2BX ☎ 0845 606 6067 ✉ sally.marlow@suffolk.gov.uk

Planning: Ms Lucy Robinson, Director - Economy, Skills & Environment, Endeavour House, 8 Russell Road, Ipswich IP1 2BX ☎ 01473 264384 🖷 01473 216843 ✉ lucy.robinson@et.suffolkcc.gov.uk

Recycling & Waste Minimisation: Mr Steve Palfrey, Head - Waste, Endeavour House, 8 Russell Road, Ipswich IP1 2BX

☎ 01473 264787 ✉ steve.palfrey@suffolk.gov.uk

Road Safety: Mr Mike Motteram, Road Safety Manager, Endeavour House, 8 Russell Road, Ipswich IP1 2BX ☎ 01743 264996 ✉ mike.motteram@suffolk.gov.uk

Social Services (Children): Mr John Gregg, Service Director - Specialist Services, Endeavour House, 8 Russell Road, Ipswich IP1 2BX ☎ 01473 264785 ✉ john.gregg@cyp.suffolkcc.gov.uk

Sustainable Communities: Ms Judith Mobbs, Assistant Director - Skills, Endeavour House, 8 Russell Road, Ipswich IP1 2BX ☎ 01473 264830 ✉ judith.mobbs@suffolk.gov.uk

Transport Planner: Ms Lucy Robinson, Director - Economy, Skills & Environment, Endeavour House, 8 Russell Road, Ipswich IP1 2BX ☎ 01473 264384 🖷 01473 216843 ✉ lucy.robinson@et.suffolkcc.gov.uk

Waste Collection and Disposal: Mr Steve Palfrey, Head - Waste, Endeavour House, 8 Russell Road, Ipswich IP1 2BX ☎ 01473 264787 ✉ steve.palfrey@suffolk.gov.uk

Waste Management: Mr Steve Palfrey, Head - Waste, Endeavour House, 8 Russell Road, Ipswich IP1 2BX ☎ 01473 264787 ✉ steve.palfrey@suffolk.gov.uk

MEMBERS OF THE COUNCIL (75)

***Chair:* Pembroke**, Jeremy (CON - Cosford)
jeremy.pembroke@suffolk.gov.uk
***Vice-Chair:* Whybrow**, Anne (CON - Stowmarket South)
anne.whybrow@suffolk.gov.uk
***Leader of the Council:* Bee**, Mark (CON - Beccles)
mark.bee@suffolk.gov.uk
***Deputy Leader of the Council:* Storey**, Jane (CON - Thedwastre North)
jane.storey@suffolk.gov.uk
***Group Leader:* Ereira**, Mark (GRN - Tower)
mark.ereira@suffolk.gov.uk
***Group Leader:* Martin**, Sandy (LAB - St John's)
sandy.martin@suffolk.gov.uk
***Group Leader:* Wood**, David (LD - Peninsula)
david.wood@suffolk.gov.uk
Alcock, Eddy (CON - Thredling)
eddy.alcock@suffolk.gov.uk
Barber, Nick (CON - Felixstowe Coastal)
nick.barber@suffolk.gov.uk
Barnard, Mike (CON - Oulton)
mike.barnard@suffolk.gov.uk
Beckwith, Trevor (IND - Eastgate and Moreton Hall)
trevor.beckwith@suffolk.gov.uk
Beer, Peter (CON - Great Cornard)
peter.beer@suffolk.gov.uk
Bellfield, Peter (CON - Carlford)
peter.bellfield@suffolk.gov.uk
Bishop, Bill (CON - Brandon)
bill.bishop@suffolk.gov.uk
Bond, Michael (CON - Wickham)
michael.bond@suffolk.gov.uk
Cann, Andrew (LD - St Margaret's and Westgate)
andrew.cann@suffolk.gov.uk
Chambers, Jane (LD - St Helen's)
jane.chambers@suffolk.gov.uk
Chambers, Lisa (CON - Newmarket and Red Lodge)
lisa.chambers@suffolk.gov.uk
Clements, Terry (CON - Thingoe South)
terry.clements@suffolk.gov.uk
Dearden-Phillips, Craig (LD - Hardwick)
craig.dearden-phillips@suffolk.gov.uk
Debman, Carol (CON - Gainsborough)
carol.debman@suffolk.gov.uk
Field, John (LD - Gipping Valley)
john.field@suffolk.gov.uk
Finch, James (CON - Stour Valley)
james.finch@suffolk.gov.uk
French, Phillip (CON - Haverhill Cangle)
phillip.french@suffolk.gov.uk
Frost, Stephen (CON - Mildenhall)
stephen.frost@suffolk.gov.uk
Gardiner, Peter (LAB - Chantry)
peter.gardiner@suffolk.gov.uk
Goldsmith, John (CON - Kessingland and Southwold)
john.goldsmith@suffolk.gov.uk
Goldson, Tony (CON - Halesworth)
tony.goldson@suffolk.gov.uk
Goodwin, John (CON - Felixstowe North and Trimley)
john.goodwin@suffolk.gov.uk
Gosling, Kathy (CON - Pakefield)
kathy.gosling@suffolk.gov.uk
Gower, Anne (CON - Haverhill East and Kedington)
anne.gower@suffolk.gov.uk
Green, Gary (CON - Stowmarket North and Stowupland)
gary.green@suffolk.gov.uk
Grutchfield, David (LD - Hadleigh)
david.grutchfield@suffolk.gov.uk
Hart, Colin (CON - Framlingham)
colin.hart@suffolk.gov.uk
Hopfensperger, Rebecca (CON - Thingoe North)
rebecca.hopfensperger@suffolk.gov.uk
Hudson, Christopher (CON - Kesgrave and Rushmere St Andrew)
christopher.hudson@suffolk.gov.uk
Hudson, Steven (CON - Kesgrave and Rushmere St Andrew)
steven.hudson@suffolk.gov.uk
Kemp, Richard (IND - Melford)
richard.kemp@suffolk.gov.uk
Law, Colin (CON - Oulton)
colin.law@suffolk.gov.uk
Law, Deanna (CON - Lowestoft South)
deanna.law@suffolk.gov.uk
Leighton, Rae (CON - Blything)
rae.leighton@suffolk.gov.uk
Lockington, Inga (LD - St Margaret's and Westgate)
inga.lockington@suffolk.gov.uk
Maguire, Susan (LAB - Priory Heath)
susan.maguire@suffolk.gov.uk
Marks, Tim (CON - Haverhill Cangle)
tim.marks@suffolk.gov.uk
McGregor, Guy (CON - Hoxne and Eye)
guy.mcgregor@suffolk.gov.uk
Michell, Charles (CON - Hartismere)
charles.michell@suffolk.gov.uk
Midwood, Jane (CON - Clare)
jane.midwood@suffolk.gov.uk
Mountford, Bill (UKIP - Lowestoft South)
bill.mountford@suffolk.gov.uk
Murray, Alan (CON - Bixley)
alan.murray@suffolk.gov.uk
Newman, Graham (CON - Felixstowe Coastal)

graham.newman@suffolk.gov.uk
Noble, Colin (CON - Row Heath)
colin.noble@suffolk.gov.uk
O'Brien, Patricia (CON - Martlesham)
patricia.obrien@suffolk.gov.uk
Oliver, Stefan (CON - Tower)
stefan.oliver@suffolk.gov.uk
Otton, Penny (LD - Thedwastre South)
penny.otton@.suffolk.gov.uk
Page, Caroline (LD - Woodbridge)
caroline.page@suffolk.gov.uk
Pollard, Kathy (LD - Belstead Brook)
kathy.pollard@suffolk.gov.uk
Provan, Bruce (CON - Gunton)
bruce.provan@suffolk.gov.uk
Punt, Chris (CON - Beccles)
chris.punt@suffolk.gov.uk
Reid, Andrew (CON - Wilford)
andrew.reid@suffolk.gov.uk
Ritchie, David (CON - Bungay)
david.ritchie@suffolk.gov.uk
Rudd, Mary (CON - Gunton)
mary.rudd@suffolk.gov.uk
Rudkin, Bryony (LAB - Bridge)
bryony.rudkin@suffolkcc.gov.uk
Sadler, Bill (CON - Exning and Newmarket)
bill.sadler@suffolk.gov.uk
Sale, Ken (CON - Pakefield)
ken.sale@suffolk.gov.uk
Sayers, John (CON - Sudbury)
john.sayers@suffolk.gov.uk
Smith, Richard (CON - Aldeburgh and Leiston)
richard.smith@suffolk.gov.uk
Spence, Colin (CON - Sudbury East and Waldingfield)
colin.spence@suffolk.gov.uk
Spicer, Joanna (CON - Blackbourn)
joanna.spicer@suffolk.gov.uk
Stringer, Andrew (GRN - Upper Gipping)
andrew.stringer@suffolk.gov.uk
Terry, Judy (CON - Rushmere)
judy.terry@suffolk.gov.uk
Truelove, Julia (LD - Bosmere)
julia.truelove@suffolk.gov.uk
Vickery, Robin (CON - Whitehouse and Whitton)
robin.vickery@suffolk.gov.uk
West, Paul (CON - Chantry)
paul.west@suffolk.gov.uk
Yorke-Edwards, David (CON - Samford)
david.yorke-edwards@suffolk.gov.uk
Young, Mary (CON - Whitehouse and Whitton)
mary.young@suffolk.gov.uk

POLITICAL COMPOSITION
CON: 55, LD: 11, LAB: 4, GRN: 2, IND: 2, UKIP: 1

CABINET
Leader / Communications: Mr Mark Bee
Deputy Leader / Finance: Ms Jane Storey
Economic Development: Ms Judy Terry
Education & Young People: Mr Graham Newman
Environment & Property Management: Ms Lisa Chambers
Health & Adult Care: Mr Colin Noble
Public Protection: Mr Colin Spence
Roads & Transport: Mr Guy McGregor

COMMITTEE CHAIRS
Audit: Mr Richard Smith
Development Control: Mr Charles Michell
Health (Scrutiny): Ms Kathy Gosling
Pension Fund: Mr Peter Bellfield
Scrutiny (Scrutiny): Mr Colin Hart

SUFFOLK COASTAL — D
Suffolk Coastal District Council, Council Offices, Melton Hill, Woodbridge IP12 1AU ☎ 01394 383789 🖷 01394 385100
💻 www.suffolkcoastal.gov.uk

FACTS & FIGURES
Police Authority: Suffolk Police Authority
Health Authority: East of England Strategic Health Authority
Learning and Skills Council: Eastern
Parliamentary Constituencies: Suffolk Coastal
EU Constituencies: Eastern
Election Frequency: Elections are of whole council
Twinning: Felixstowe: Wesel (Germany); Framlingham: Coucy-le-Chateau (France); Sutton: St. Laurent-des-Hommes (France); Woodbridge: Mussidan (France)

PRINCIPAL OFFICERS
Chief Executive: Mr Stephen Baker, Chief Executive, Council Offices, Melton Hill, Woodbridge IP12 1AU ☎ 01394 444348 🖷 01394 385100 ✉ stephen.baker@suffolkcoastal.gov.uk

Assistant Chief Executive: Mr Arthur Charvonia, Assistant Chief Executive, Council Offices, Melton Hill, Woodbridge IP12 1AU ☎ 01502 523606 🖷 01502 523500 ✉ Arthur.charvonia@waveney.gov.uk

Senior Management: Mr Alan McFarlane, Director of Resources, Council Offices, Melton Hill, Woodbridge IP12 1AU ☎ 01502 523330 🖷 01502 523500 ✉ alan.mcfarlane@suffolkcoastal.gov.uk

Senior Management: Mr Tony Osmanski, Strategic Director, Council Offices, Melton Hill, Woodbridge IP12 1AU ☎ 01394 444323 🖷 01394 385100 ✉ tony.osmanski@suffolkcoastal.gov.uk

Architect, Building / Property Services: Mr Richard Vest, Property Services Manager, Council Offices, Melton Hill, Woodbridge IP12 1AU ☎ 01394 444244 🖷 01394 385100 ✉ richard.vest@suffolkcoastal.gov.uk

Building Control: Mr Philip Ridley, Head of Planning Services, Council Offices, Melton Hill, Woodbridge IP12 1AU ☎ 01394 444432 🖷 01394 385100 ✉ philip.ridley@suffolkcoastal.gov.uk

PR / Communications: Mr Viv Hotten, Head of Press & Promotions, Council Offices, Melton Hill, Woodbridge IP12 1AU ☎ 01394 444361 🖷 01394 385100 ✉ viv.hotten@suffolkcoastal.gov.uk

Computer Management: Mr Pete Kalinowski, ICT Manager, Council Offices, Melton Hill, Woodbridge IP12 1AU ☎ 01394 444574 ✉ pete.kalinowski@suffolkcoastal.gov.uk

Contracts: Mr Ian Purdom, Principal Service Manager for Procurement, Council Offices, Melton Hill, Woodbridge IP12 1AU ☎ 01502 562111 ✉ ian.purdom@waveney.gov.uk

Corporate Services: Mrs Bev Herring, Head of Transformation & Customer Services, Council Offices, Melton Hill, Woodbridge IP12 1AU ☎ 01502 523215 ✉ bev.herring@suffolkcoastal.gov.uk

Customer Service: Mr David Gallagher, Head of Commercial Partnerships & Strategic Commissioning, Council Offices, Melton Hill, Woodbridge IP12 1AU ☎ 01502 523007 🖷 01502 523500 ✉ david.gallagher@waveney.gov.uk

Direct Labour: Mr Dennis Ball, Managing Director, Suffolk Coastal Services Ltd, Council Offices, Melton Hill, Woodbridge IP12 1AU ☎ 01394 444374 🖷 01394 385100 ✉ dennis.ball@suffolkcoastal.gov.uk

Economic Development: Mr Andy Wright, Head of Community & Economic Services, Council Offices, Melton Hill, Woodbridge IP12 1AU ☎ 01394 444249 ✉ andy.wright@suffolkcoastal.gov.uk

Electoral Registration: Mrs Ingrid Askew, Electoral Registration Officer, Council Offices, Melton Hill, Woodbridge IP12 1AU ☎ 01394 444329 🖷 01394 385100 ✉ ingrid.askew@suffolkcoastal.gov.uk

Emergency Planning: Mr Robin Buncombe, District Emergency Plans Officer, Council Offices, Melton Hill, Woodbridge IP12 1AU ☎ 01394 444453 🖷 01394 385100 ✉ robin.buncombe@suffolkcoastal.gov.uk

Energy Management: Mr Chris Walker, Building Services Engineer, Council Offices, Melton Hill, Woodbridge IP12 1AU ☎ 01394 444719 🖷 01394 385100

Environmental Health: Mr Phil Gore, Head of Environmental Services & Port Health, Council Offices, Melton Hill, Woodbridge IP12 1AU ☎ 01394 444286 🖷 01394 385100 ✉ phil.gore@suffolkcoastal.gov.uk

Estates, Property & Valuation: Mr Gary Lowe, Estates Office (Client), Council Offices, Melton Hill, Woodbridge IP12 1AU ☎ 01394 444717 🖷 01394 385100 ✉ gary.lowe@suffolkcoastal.gov.uk

Facilities: Mr Gary Lowe, Estates Office (Client), Council Offices, Melton Hill, Woodbridge IP12 1AU ☎ 01394 444717 🖷 01394 385100 ✉ gary.lowe@suffolkcoastal.gov.uk

Finance and Treasurer: Mr Andrew Cook, Finance Manager, Council Offices, Melton Hill, Woodbridge IP12 1AU ☎ 01502 523660 ✉ andrew.cook@waveney.gov.uk

Grounds Maintenance: Mr Tim Collard, Assistant Contracts Manager (Amenities), Ufford Park, Yarmouth Road, Ufford, Woodbridge IP13 6ET ☎ 01394 444003 🖷 01394 385698 ✉ tim.collard@suffolkcoastal.gov.uk

Health and Safety: Mr Phil Gore, Head of Environmental Services & Port Health, Council Offices, Melton Hill, Woodbridge IP12 1AU ☎ 01394 444286 🖷 01394 385100 ✉ phil.gore@suffolkcoastal.gov.uk

Health and Safety: Mr Mark Sims, Principal Environmental Health Officer, Council Offices, Melton Hill, Woodbridge IP12 1AU ☎ 01394 444356 🖷 01394 385100 ✉ mark.sims@suffolkcoastal.gov.uk

Home Energy Conservation: Mrs Teresa Howarth, Environmental Health Officer, Council Offices, Melton Hill, Woodbridge IP12 1AU ☎ 01394 444206 🖷 01394 385100 ✉ teresa.howarth@suffolkcoastal.gov.uk

Housing: Mr Robert Prince, Head of Strategic Housing, Council Offices, Melton Hill, Woodbridge IP12 1AU ☎ 01502 523144 🖷 01502 523500 ✉ Robert.prince@waveney.gov.uk

Legal: Mrs Hilary Slater, Head of Legal & Democratic Services, Council Offices, Melton Hill, Woodbridge IP12 1AU ☎ 01394 444336 🖷 01394 385100 ✉ hilary.slater@suffolkcoastal.gov.uk

Leisure and Cultural Services: Mr Tony Osmanski, Strategic Director, Council Offices, Melton Hill, Woodbridge IP12 1AU ☎ 01394 444323 🖷 01394 385100 ✉ tony.osmanski@suffolkcoastal.gov.uk

Licensing: Mrs Ingrid Askew, Electoral Registration Officer, Council Offices, Melton Hill, Woodbridge IP12 1AU ☎ 01394 444329 🖷 01394 385100 ✉ ingrid.askew@suffolkcoastal.gov.uk

Lifelong Learning: Mrs Heather Shilling, Human Resources Officer, Council Offices, Melton Hill, Woodbridge IP12 1AU ☎ 01502 562611 ✉ heather.shilling@waveney.gov.uk

Lottery Funding, Charity and Voluntary: Mrs Ingrid Askew, Electoral Registration Officer, Melton Hill, Woodbridge IP12 1AU ☎ 01394 444329 🖷 01394 385100 ✉ ingrid.askew@suffolkcoastal.gov.uk

Member Services: Mrs Karen Cook, Cabinet Business Manager, Council Offices, Melton Hill, Woodbridge IP12 1AU ☎ 01394 444326 🖷 01394 385100 ✉ Karen.cook@suffolkcoastal.gov.uk

Partnerships: Mrs Bev Herring, Head of Transformation & Customer Services, Council Offices, Melton Hill, Woodbridge IP12 1AU ☎ 01502 523215 ✉ bev.herring@suffolkcoastal.gov.uk

Personnel / HR: Mrs Carol Lower, HR Manager, Council Offices, Melton Hill, Woodbridge IP12 1AU ☎ 01502 532611 ✉ carol.lower@waveney.gov.uk

Planning: Mr Philip Ridley, Head of Planning Services, Council Offices, Melton Hill, Woodbridge IP12 1AU ☎ 01394 444432 🖷 01394 385100 ✉ philip.ridley@suffolkcoastal.gov.uk

Procurement: Mr Ian Purdom, Principal Service Manager for Procurement, Council Offices, Melton Hill, Woodbridge IP12 1AU ☎ 01502 562111 ✉ ian.purdom@waveney.gov.uk

Recycling & Waste Minimisation: Mr Malcolm Duesbury, Waste Management Services Manager, Ufford Park, Yarmouth Road, Ufford, Woodbridge IP13 6ET ☎ 01394 444044 🖷 01394 444354 ✉ malcolm.duesbury@suffolkcoastal.gov.uk

Regeneration: Mr Andy Wright, Head of Community & Economic Services, Council Offices, Melton Hill, Woodbridge IP12 1AU ☎ 01394 444249 ✉ andy.wright@suffolkcoastal.gov.uk

Staff Training: Mrs Heather Shilling, Human Resources Officer, Council Offices, Melton Hill, Woodbridge IP12 1AU ☎ 01502 562611 ✉ heather.shilling@waveney.gov.uk

Sustainable Development: Mr Phil Gore, Head of Environmental Services & Port Health, Council Offices, Melton Hill, Woodbridge IP12 1AU ☎ 01394 444286 🖷 01394 385100 ✉ phil.gore@suffolkcoastal.gov.uk

Tourism: Mr Andy Wright, Head of Community & Economic Services, Council Offices, Melton Hill, Woodbridge IP12 1AU ☎ 01394 444249 ✉ andy.wright@suffolkcoastal.gov.uk

Waste Collection and Disposal: Mr Dennis Ball, Managing Director, Suffolk Coastal Services Ltd, Council Offices, Melton Hill, Woodbridge IP12 1AU ☎ 01394 444374 🖷 01394 385100 ✉ dennis.ball@suffolkcoastal.gov.uk

Waste Management: Mr Malcolm Duesbury, Waste Management Services Manager, Ufford Park, Yarmouth Road, Ufford, Woodbridge IP13 6ET ☎ 01394 444044 🖷 01394 444354 ✉ malcolm.duesbury@suffolkcoastal.gov.uk

MEMBERS OF THE COUNCIL (55)

***Chair:* Kerry**, Richard (CON - Trimleys with Kirton)
richard.kerry@suffolkcoastal.gov.uk
***Vice-Chair:* Bellfield**, Peter (CON - Otley)
peter.bellfield@suffolkcoastal.gov.uk
***Leader of the Council:* Herring**, Ray (CON - Orford and Tunstall)
ray.herring@suffolkcoastal.gov.uk
***Deputy Leader of the Council:* Smith**, Andy (CON - Felixstowe South East)
andy.smith@suffolkcoastal.gov.uk
***Group Leader:* Deacon**, Mike (LAB - Felixstowe North)
michael.deacon@suffolkcoastal.gov.uk
Andrews, Marian (LD - Saxmundham)
marian.andrews@suffolkcoastal.gov.uk
Ball, Diana (LD - Woodbridge Farlingaye)
diana.ball@suffolkcoastal.gov.uk
Batho, Peter (CON - Saxmundham)
peter.batho@suffolkcoastal.gov.uk
Bidwell, James (CON - Melton and Ufford)
james.bidwell@suffolkcoastal.gov.uk
Binns, Les (CON - Woodbridge Kyson)
edward.binns@suffolkcoastal.gov.uk
Bird, Stuart (CON - Felixstowe West)
stuart.bird@suffolkcoastal.gov.uk
Block, Christine (LD - Sutton)
christine.block@suffolkcoastal.gov.uk
Blundell, Chris (CON - Martlesham)
chris.blundell@suffolkcoastal.gov.uk
Bond, Michael (CON - Melton and Ufford)
michael.bond@suffolkcoastal.gov.uk
Burroughes, Stephen (CON - Peasenhall)
stephen.burroughes@suffolkcoastal.gov.uk
Coleman, Peter
(CON - Felixstowe South)
peter.coleman@suffolkcoastal.gov.uk
Cooper, Tony (INDNA - Leiston)
tony.cooper@suffolkcoastal.gov.uk
Dunnett, Phillip (CON - Snape)
phillip.dunnett@suffolkcoastal.gov.uk
Eastman, Terry (CON - Rendlesham)
terry.eastman@suffolkcoastal.gov.uk
Falconer, Veronica (CON - Nacton)
veronica.falconer@suffolkcoastal.gov.uk
Fellowes, Marianne (CON - Aldeburgh)
marianne.fellowes@suffolkcoastal.gov.uk
Fryatt, Tony (CON - Grundisburgh)
tony.fryatt@suffolkcoastal.gov.uk
Garfield, Jan (CON - Felixstowe South East)
cllr.robertstrachan@lichfielddc.gov.uk
Gower, Michael (CON - Walberswick and Wenhaston)
michael.gower@suffolkcoastal.gov.uk
Grimwood, Martin (CON - Kesgrave West)
robert.grimwood@suffolkcoastal.gov.uk
Hall, Bryan (LD - Wickham Market)
bryan.hall@suffolkcoastal.gov.uk
Harding, Graham (CON - Trimleys with Kirton)
graham.harding@suffolkcoastal.gov.uk
Harvey, Susan (CON - Trimleys with Kirton)
susan.harvey@suffolkcoastal.gov.uk
Hawkins, Trevor (CON - Leiston)
trevor.hawkins@suffolkcoastal.gov.uk
Haworth, Terry-Jill (CON - Aldeburgh)
terry-jill.haworth@suffolkcoastal.gov.uk
Holdcroft, Geoff (CON - Woodbridge Riverside)
geoff.holdcroft@suffolkcoastal.gov.uk
Hudson, Steven (CON - Witnesham)
Hudson, Christopher (CON - Framlingham)
christopher.hudson@suffolkcoastal.gov.uk
Kelso, John (LD - Martlesham)
john.kelso@suffolkcoastal.gov.uk
Lynch, Geoff (CON - Kesgrave East)
geoff.lynch@suffolkcoastal.gov.uk
Marson, Jane (CON - Hollesley with Eyke)
jane.marson@suffolkcoastal.gov.uk
McCallum, Debbie (CON - Kesgrave West)
debbie.mccallum@suffolkcoastal.gov.uk
Morris, Margaret (LAB - Felixstowe West)
margaret.morris@suffolkcoastal.gov.uk
Neale, Mary (CON - Kesgrave East)
mary.neale@suffolkcoastal.gov.uk
Newton, Mark (CON - Rushmere St. Andrew)
mark.newton@suffolkcoastal.gov.uk
Nunn, Andrew (CON - Leiston)
andrew.nunn@suffolkcoastal.gov.uk
O'Brien, Patricia (CON - Nacton)
patricia.obrien@suffolkcoastal.gov.uk
Ogden, Sally (CON - Kesgrave East)
sally.ogden@suffolkcoastal.gov.uk
Peck, Graham (CON - Hacheston)
graham.peck@suffolkcoastal.gov.uk
Savage, Doreen (CON - Felixstowe East)
doreen.savage@suffolkcoastal.gov.uk
Sayles, Josh (CON - Woodbridge Seckford)
josh.sayles@suffolkcoastal.gov.uk
Sennington, Joan (CON - Felixstowe South)
joan.sennington@suffolkcoastal.gov.uk
Sharman, Michael (LAB - Felixstowe West)
Slater, Barry (LD - Yoxford)
barry.slater@suffolkcoastal.gov.uk
Slemmings, Chris (CON - Felixstowe East)
chris.slemmings@suffolkcoastal.gov.uk
Snell, Bob (CON - Earl Soham)

bob.snell@suffolkcoastal.gov.uk
Walker, Colin (CON - Framlingham)
colin.walker@suffolkcoastal.gov.uk
Whiting, Robert (CON - Rushmere St. Andrew)
robert.whiting@suffolkcoastal.gov.uk
Williams, Kimberley (LAB - Felixstowe North)
kimberley.williams@suffolkcoastal.gov.uk
Withey, John (CON - Rushmere St. Andrew)
john.withey@suffolkcoastal.gov.uk

POLITICAL COMPOSITION
CON: 44, LD: 6, LAB: 4, INDNA: 1

CABINET
Leader: Mr Ray Herring
Deputy Leader / Planning: Mr Andy Smith
Customers & Communities: Mrs Doreen Savage
Green Environment: Mr Andrew Nunn
Housing: Ms Terry-Jill Haworth
Leisure & Economic Development: Mr Geoff Holdcroft
Fiscal & Democratic: Mr Robert Whiting

COMMITTEE CHAIRS
Audit & Governance: Mr Michael Bond
Development Control: Mr Bob Snell
Scrutiny: Mr Phillip Dunnett

SUNDERLAND M
Sunderland City Council, Civic Centre, Sunderland SR2 7DN
☎ 0191 520 5555 🖷 0191 553 1020
enquiries@sunderland.gov.uk 💻 www.sunderland.gov.uk

FACTS & FIGURES
Police Authority: Northumbria Police Authority
Health Authority: North East Strategic Health Authority
Learning and Skills Council: North East
Parliamentary Constituencies: Houghton and Sunderland South, Sunderland Central, Washington and Sunderland West
EU Constituencies: North East
Election Frequency: Elections are by thirds
Twinning: Essen (Germany); St. Nazaire (France)

PRINCIPAL OFFICERS
Chief Executive: Mr Dave Smith, Chief Executive, Civic Centre, Sunderland SR2 7DN ☎ 0191 561 1112 dave.smith@sunderland.gov.uk

Deputy Chief Executive: Ms Janet Johnson, Deputy Chief Executive, Civic Centre, Sunderland SR2 7DN ☎ 0191 561 1134 janet.johnson@sunderland.gov.uk

Assistant Chief Executive: Ms Sarah Reed, Assistant Chief Executive, Civic Centre, Sunderland SR2 7DN ☎ 0191 561 1114 or 1134 sarah.reed@sunderland.gov.uk

Senior Management: Mr Ron Odunaiya, Executive Director of City Services, Jack Crawford House, Commercial Road, Sunderland SR2 8QR ☎ 0191 561 7556 ron.odunaiya@sunderland.gov.uk

Senior Management: Mr Stephen Pickering, Deputy Executive Director, Civic Centre, Sunderland SR2 7DN ☎ 0191 561 7572 stephen.pickering@sunderland.gov.uk

Access Officer / Social Services (Disability): Mr Neil Revely, Executive Director of Health, Housing & Adult Services, Leechmere Training Centre, Leechmere Industrial Estate, Carrmere Road, Sunderland SR2 9TQ ☎ 0191 566 1882 🖷 0191 553 6114 neil.revely@sunderland.gov.uk

Architect, Building / Property Services: Mr Colin Clark, Head of Land & Property, Civic Centre, Sunderland SR2 7DN ☎ 0191 561 7849 colin.clark@sunderland.gov.uk

Best Value: Ms Sarah Reed, Assistant Chief Executive, Civic Centre, Sunderland SR2 7DN ☎ 0191 561 1114 or 1134 sarah.reed@sunderland.gov.uk

Building Control: Mr Keith Lowes, Head of Planning & Environment, Civic Centre, Sunderland SR2 7DN ☎ 0191 561 1564 keith.lowes@sunderland.gov.uk

Catering Services: Mr Colin Ranson, Catering Services Manager, Civic Centre, Sunderland SR2 7DN ☎ 0191 561 4642 colin.ranson@sunderland.gov.uk

Children / Youth Services: Ms Meg Boustead, Head of Safeguarding, Civic Centre, Sunderland SR2 7DN ☎ 0191 561 1349 meg.boustead@sunderland.gov.uk

Children / Youth Services: Ms Judith Hay, Head of Positive Contribution & Economic Wellbeing, Civic Centre, Sunderland SR2 7DN ☎ 0191 561 1972 judith.hay@sunderland.gov.uk

Children / Youth Services: Dr Helen Paterson, Executive Director of Children's Services, Civic Centre, Sunderland SR2 7DN ☎ 0191 561 1351 helen.paterson@sunderland.gov.uk

Civil Registration: Mr Martin Lancaster, Support Services Co-ordinator, Civic Centre, Sunderland SR2 7DN ☎ 0191 561 7925 🖷 0191 553 1762 martin.lancaster@sunderland.gov.uk

PR / Communications: Ms Deborah Lewin, Director of Communications & Marketing, Civic Centre, Sunderland SR2 7DN ☎ 0191 561 1135 🖷 0191 553 1138 deborah.lewin@sunderland.gov.uk

Community Planning: Ms Janet Johnson, Deputy Chief Executive, Civic Centre, Sunderland SR2 7DN ☎ 0191 561 1134 janet.johnson@sunderland.gov.uk

Community Planning: Mr Mike Poulter, Head of Project & Service Development, Jack Crawford House, Sunderland SR2 8QR ☎ 0191 561 7549 mike.poulter@sunderland.gov.uk

Community Planning: Mr Andrew Seekings, Head of Programme & Project Office, Civic Centre, Sunderland SR2 7DN ☎ 0191 561 2349 andrew.seekings@sunderland.gov.uk

Community Safety: Ms Meg Boustead, Head of Safeguarding, Civic Centre, Sunderland SR2 7DN ☎ 0191 561 1349 meg.boustead@sunderland.gov.uk

Community Safety: Ms Janet Johnson, Deputy Chief Executive,

Civic Centre, Sunderland SR2 7DN ☎ 0191 561 1134 ✉ janet.johnson@sunderland.gov.uk

Computer Management: Mr Tom Baker, Head of ICT, 7 Camberwell Way, Moorside Park, Sunderland SR3 3XN ☎ 0191 561 4201 🖷 0191 553 4200 ✉ tom.baker@sunderland.gov.uk

Consumer Protection and Trading Standards: Mr Thomas Terrett, Trading Standards & Licensing Manager, Civic Centre, Sunderland SR2 7DN ☎ 0191 561 1715 🖷 0191 553 1658 ✉ tom.terrett@sunderland.gov.uk

Contracts: Mr Robert Rayner, Chief Solicitor, Civic Centre, Sunderland SR2 7DN ☎ 0191 561 1003 🖷 0191 553 1033 ✉ bob.rayner@sunderland.gov.uk

Corporate Services: Ms Charlotte Burnham, Head of Overview & Scrutiny, Civic Centre, Sunderland SR2 7DN ☎ 0191 561 1147 ✉ charlotte.burnham@sunderland.gov.uk

Corporate Services: Ms Rhiannon Hood, Assistant Chief Solicitor, Civic Centre, Sunderland SR2 7DN ☎ 0191 561 1005 ✉ rhiannon.hood@sunderland.gov.uk

Corporate Services: Mr Malcolm Page, Executive Director of Commercial & Corporate Services, PO Box 100, Civic Centre, Sunderland SR2 7DN ✉ malcolm.page@sunderland.gov.uk

Corporate Services: Mr Phil Spooner, Community Leadership Programmes, Civic Centre, Sunderland SR2 7DN ☎ 0191 561 1146 🖷 0191 553 1461 ✉ phil.spooner@sunderland.gov.uk

Corporate Services: Ms Sue Stanhope, Director of Human Resources & Organisational Development, Civic Centre, Sunderland SR2 7DN ☎ 0191 561 1722 ✉ sue.stanhope@sunderland.gov.uk

Customer Service: Ms Lynda Brown, Head of Standards, Civic Centre, Sunderland SR2 7DN ☎ 0191 561 1410 ✉ lynda.brown@sunderland.gov.uk

Customer Service: Ms Margaret Douglas, Customer Services Manager, Civic Centre, Sunderland SR2 7DN ☎ 0191 561 1065 🖷 0191 553 1020 ✉ margaret.douglas@sunderland.gov.uk

Customer Service: Ms Judith Hay, Head of Positive Contribution & Economic Wellbeing, Civic Centre, Sunderland SR2 7DN ☎ 0191 561 1972 ✉ judith.hay@sunderland.gov.uk

Customer Service: Ms Hilary Phillips, Head of Resources, Civic Centre, Sunderland SR2 7DN ☎ 0191 561 1505 ✉ hilary.phillips@sunderland.gov.uk

Customer Service: Ms Liz St Louis, Head of Customer Service & Development, Civic Centre, Sunderland SR2 7DN ☎ 0191 561 4902 ✉ liz.stlouis@sunderland.gov.uk

Direct Labour: Mr Ray Telfer, Assistant Head of Environmental Services, Civic Centre, Sunderland SR2 7DN ☎ 0191 561 5155 ✉ ray.telfer@sunderland.gov.uk

Economic Development: Mr Taylor Vince, Head of Strategic Economic Development, Civic Centre, Sunderland SR2 7DN ☎ 0191 561 1113 ✉ vince.taylor@sunderland.gov.uk

Education: Dr Helen Paterson, Executive Director of Children's Services, Civic Centre, Sunderland SR2 7DN ☎ 0191 561 1351 ✉ helen.paterson@sunderland.gov.uk

E-Government: Ms Debbie Ross, E-Neighbourhood Programme Manager, Moorside, Sunderland SR3 3XN ☎ 0191 561 4216 ✉ debbie.ross@sunderland.gov.uk

Electoral Registration: Mr Bill Crawford, Head of Electoral Services, Civic Centre, Sunderland SR2 7DN ☎ 0191 561 1144 ✉ bill.crawford@sunderland.gov.uk

Emergency Planning: Mr Barry Frost, Security & Emergency Planning Manager, Civic Centre, Sunderland SR2 7DN ☎ 0191 561 2643 🖷 0191 553 1461 ✉ barry.frost@sunderland.gov.uk

Energy Management: Mr Keith Lowes, Head of Planning & Environment, Civic Centre, Sunderland SR2 7DN ☎ 0191 561 1564 ✉ keith.lowes@sunderland.gov.uk

Environmental / Technical Services: Mr Jim Alprovich, Assistant Head of Environmental Services, Civic Centre, Sunderland SR2 7DN ☎ 0191 561 4525 ✉ james.alprovich@sunderland.gov.uk

Environmental / Technical Services: Mr Ray Telfer, Assistant Head of Environmental Services, Civic Centre, Sunderland SR2 7DN ☎ 0191 561 5155 ✉ ray.telfer@sunderland.gov.uk

Environmental Health: Mr Peter High, Project Director - Strategic Waste, Jack Crawford House, Commercial Road, Sunderland SR2 8QR ☎ 0191 561 4550 ✉ peter.high@sunderland.gov.uk

Environmental Health: Ms Norma Johnston, Assistant Head of Environmental Services, PO Box 100, Civic Centre, Sunderland SR2 7DN ☎ 0191 561 1657 🖷 0191 553 1658 ✉ norma.johnston@sunderland.gov.uk

Estates, Property & Valuation: Mr Keith Lowes, Head of Planning & Environment, Civic Centre, Sunderland SR2 7DN ☎ 0191 561 1564 ✉ keith.lowes@sunderland.gov.uk

European Liaison: Mr Gordon Bell, Strategic Programmes & Europe Team Manager, Civic Centre, Sunderland SR2 7DN ☎ 0191 561 1155 🖷 0191 553 1159 ✉ gordon.bell@sunderland.gov.uk

Events Manager: Mr Chris Alexander, Head of Culture & Tourism, City Library, Sunderland SR1 1RE ☎ 0191 561 8420 🖷 0191 514 8428 ✉ chris.alexander@sunderland.gov.uk

Facilities: Mr Trevor Stavers, Civic Centre Manager, Civic Centre, Sunderland SR2 7DN ☎ 0191 561 1101 ✉ trevor.stavers@sunderland.gov.uk

Finance and Treasurer: Mr Malcolm Page, Executive Director of Commercial & Corporate Services, PO Box 100, Civic Centre, Sunderland SR2 7DN ✉ malcolm.page@sunderland.gov.uk

Fleet Management: Mr Ron Odunaiya, Executive Director of City Services, Jack Crawford House, Commercial Road, Sunderland SR2 8QR ☎ 0191 561 7556 ✉ ron.odunaiya@sunderland.gov.uk

Grounds Maintenance: Mr Peter High, Project Director - Strategic Waste, South Hylton House, Hylton Bank, Sunderland SR4 0JL ☎ 0191 561 4550 ✉ peter.high@sunderland.gov.uk

Health and Safety: Ms Sue Stanhope, Director of Human Resources & Organisational Development, Civic Centre, Sunderland SR2 7DN ☎ 0191 561 1722 ✉ sue.stanhope@sunderland.gov.uk

Highways: Mr Allan Calvert, Traffic Manager, Civic Centre, Sunderland SR2 7DN ☎ 0191 561 1520 ✉ allan.calvert@sunderland.gov.uk

Home Energy Conservation: Mr Mike Lowe, Principal Planner, Civic Centre, Sunderland SR2 7DN ☎ 0191 561 2546 ✉ mike.lowe@sunderland.gov.uk

Housing: Mr Alan Caddick, Head of Housing, Leechmere Centre, Leechmere Industrial Estate, Carrmere Road, Sunderland SR2 9TQ ☎ 0191 566 1711 ✉ alan.caddick@sunderland.gov.uk

Local Area Agreement: Mr Lee Cranston, Assistant Head of Corporate Policy, Civic Centre, Sunderland SR2 7DN ☎ 0191 561 1160 ✉ lee.cranston@sunderland.gov.uk

Legal: Mr Robert Rayner, Chief Solicitor, Civic Centre, Sunderland SR2 7DN ☎ 0191 561 1003 🖷 0191 553 1033 ✉ bob.rayner@sunderland.gov.uk

Legal: Mrs Elaine Waugh, Head of Law & Governance, PO Box 100, Civic Centre, Sunderland SR2 7DN ☎ 0191 561 1053 ✉ elaine.waugh@sunderland.gov.uk

Leisure and Cultural Services: Mrs Julie Gray, Head of Community Services, Jack Crawford House, Sunderland SR2 8QR ☎ 0191 561 7574 🖷 0191 553 7564 ✉ julie.d.gray@sunderland.gov.uk

Licensing: Ms Norma Johnston, Assistant Head of Environmental Services, PO Box 100, Civic Centre, Sunderland SR2 7DN ☎ 0191 561 1657 🖷 0191 553 1658 ✉ norma.johnston@sunderland.gov.uk

Lifelong Learning: Ms Sandra Kenny, Children, Adult & Community Manager, Civic Centre, Sunderland SR2 7DN ☎ 0191 561 2618 ✉ sandra.kenny@sunderland.govu.uk

Lighting: Mr Colin Clark, Head of Land & Property, Civic Centre, Sunderland SR2 7DN ☎ 0191 561 7849 ✉ colin.clark@sunderland.gov.uk

Lottery Funding, Charity and Voluntary: Ms Janet Johnson, Deputy Chief Executive, Civic Centre, Sunderland SR2 7DN ☎ 0191 561 1134 ✉ janet.johnson@sunderland.gov.uk

Member Services: Mr Robert Rayner, Chief Solicitor, Civic Centre, Sunderland SR2 7DN ☎ 0191 561 1003 🖷 0191 553 1033 ✉ bob.rayner@sunderland.gov.uk

Parking: Mr Earl Belshaw, Parking Services Manager, Civic Centre, Sunderland SR2 7DN ☎ 0191 561 1575 ✉ earl.belshaw@sunderland.gov.uk

Partnerships: Ms Jessica May, Partnership Manager, Civic Centre, Sunderland SR2 7DN ☎ 0191 561 1476 🖷 0191 553 1153 ✉ jessica.may@sunderland.gov.uk

Personnel / HR: Ms Sue Stanhope, Director of Human Resources & Organisational Development, Civic Centre, Sunderland SR2 7DN ☎ 0191 561 1722 ✉ sue.stanhope@sunderland.gov.uk

Planning: Mr Keith Lowes, Head of Planning & Environment, Civic Centre, Sunderland SR2 7DN ☎ 0191 561 1564 ✉ keith.lowes@sunderland.gov.uk

Procurement: Mr Paul Davies, Assistant City Treasurer (Audit & Procurement), Corporate Services, PO Box 100, Civic Centre, Sunderland SR2 7DN ☎ 0191 561 2825 ✉ paul.davies@sunderland.gov.uk

Public Libraries: Mr Chris Alexander, Head of Culture & Tourism, City Library, Sunderland SR1 1RE ☎ 0191 561 8420 🖷 0191 514 8428 ✉ chris.alexander@sunderland.gov.uk

Recycling & Waste Minimisation: Mr Jim Alprovich, Assistant Head of Environmental Services, Civic Centre, Sunderland SR2 7DN ☎ 0191 561 4525 ✉ james.alprovich@sunderland.gov.uk

Recycling & Waste Minimisation: Mr Peter High, Project Director - Strategic Waste, Jack Crawford House, Commercial Road, Sunderland SR2 8QR ☎ 0191 561 4550 ✉ peter.high@sunderland.gov.uk

Regeneration: Ms Janet Johnson, Deputy Chief Executive, Civic Centre, Sunderland SR2 7DN ☎ 0191 561 1134 ✉ janet.johnson@sunderland.gov.uk

Road Safety: Mr Allan Calvert, Traffic Manager, Civic Centre, Sunderland SR2 7DN ☎ 0191 561 1520 ✉ allan.calvert@sunderland.gov.uk

Social Services: Mr Neil Revely, Executive Director of Health, Housing & Adult Services, 50 Fawcett Street, Sunderland SR1 1RF ☎ 0191 566 1882 🖷 0191 553 6114 ✉ neil.revely@sunderland.gov.uk

Social Services: Ms Janette Sherratt, Head of Health Improvement, Civic Centre, Sunderland SR2 7DN ☎ 0191 561 1493 ✉ janette.sherratt@sunderland.gov.uk

Social Services (Adult): Ms Jean Carter, Deputy Director, 50 Fawcett Street, Sunderland SR1 1RF ☎ 0191 566 2684 ✉ jean.carter@sunderland.gov.uk

Social Services (Adult): Mr John Fisher, Head of Adult Services, Carrmere Road, Leechmere, Sunderland SR2 9TQ ☎ 0191 566 1876 ✉ john.fisher@sunderland.gov.uk

Social Services (Children): Mr Keith Moore, Deputy Director of Children's Services, Civic Centre, Sunderland SR2 7DN

☏ 0191 561 1397 ✉ keith.moore@sunderland.gov.uk

Staff Training: Ms Sue Stanhope, Director of Human Resources & Organisational Development, Civic Centre, Sunderland SR2 7DN ☏ 0191 561 1722 ✉ sue.stanhope@sunderland.gov.uk

Street Scene: Mr Les Clark, Head of Street Scene, Civic Centre, Sunderland SR2 7DN ☏ 0191 561 4501 ✉ les.clark@sunderland.gov.uk

Street Scene: Mr Peter High, Project Director - Strategic Waste, Jack Crawford House, Commercial Road, Sunderland SR2 8QR ☏ 0191 561 4550 ✉ peter.high@sunderland.gov.uk

Sustainable Communities: Ms Janet Johnson, Deputy Chief Executive, Civic Centre, Sunderland SR2 7DN ☏ 0191 561 1134 ✉ janet.johnson@sunderland.gov.uk

Sustainable Development: Ms Janet Johnson, Deputy Chief Executive, Civic Centre, Sunderland SR2 7DN ☏ 0191 561 1134 ✉ janet.johnson@sunderland.gov.uk

Tourism: Mr Chris Alexander, Head of Culture & Tourism, City Library, Sunderland SR1 1RE ☏ 0191 561 8420 🖷 0191 514 8428 ✉ chris.alexander@sunderland.gov.uk

Town Centre: Ms Louise Hardy, City Centre Manager, West Sunniside, Sunderland SR1 2BG ☏ 0191 565 3806 ✉ louise.hardy@sunderland.gov.uk

Traffic Management: Mr Allan Calvert, Traffic Manager, Civic Centre, Sunderland SR2 7DN ☏ 0191 561 1520 ✉ allan.calvert@sunderland.gov.uk

Transport: Mr Keith Atkinson, Deputy Manager, Civic Centre, Sunderland SR2 7DN ☏ 0191 561 1562 ✉ keith.atkinson@sunderland.gov.uk

Transport: Mr Allan Calvert, Traffic Manager, Civic Centre, Sunderland SR2 7DN ☏ 0191 561 1520 ✉ allan.calvert@sunderland.gov.uk

Transport Planner: Mr Keith Lowes, Head of Planning & Environment, Civic Centre, Sunderland SR2 7DN ☏ 0191 561 1564 ✉ keith.lowes@sunderland.gov.uk

Waste Collection and Disposal: Mr Peter High, Project Director - Strategic Waste, Jack Crawford House, Commercial Road, Sunderland SR2 8QR ☏ 0191 561 4550 ✉ peter.high@sunderland.gov.uk

Waste Management: Mr Jim Alprovich, Assistant Head of Environmental Services, Civic Centre, Sunderland SR2 7DN ☏ 0191 561 4525 ✉ james.alprovich@sunderland.gov.uk

Waste Management: Ms Norma Johnston, Assistant Head of Environmental Services, PO Box 100, Civic Centre, Sunderland SR2 7DN ☏ 0191 561 1657 🖷 0191 553 1658 ✉ norma.johnston@sunderland.gov.uk

MEMBERS OF THE COUNCIL (75)

***Mayor:* Martin**, Thomas (LAB - Hendon)
cllr.thomas.martin@sunderland.gov.uk

***Leader of the Council:* Watson**, Paul (LAB - Pallion)
cllr.paul.watson@sunderland.gov.uk

***Deputy Leader of the Council:* Trueman**, Henry (LAB - Washington West)
cllr.henry.trueman@sunderland.gov.uk

***Group Leader:* Oliver**, Robert (CON - St. Chad's)
cllr.robert.oliver@sunderland.gov.uk

Allan, David (LAB - Sandhill)
cllr.dave.allan@sunderland.gov.uk

Anderson, Florence (LAB - Hetton)
cllr.florence.anderson@sunderland.gov.uk

Atkinson, Rebecca (LAB - Barnes)
cllr.rebecca.atkinson@sunderland.gov.uk

Ball, Ellen (LAB - Ryhope)
cllr.ellen.ball@sunderland.gov.uk

Bell, Richard (LAB - Redhill)
cllr.richard.bell@sunderland.gov.uk

Blackburn, James (LAB - Hetton)
cllr.james.blackburn@sunderland.gov.uk

Bonallie, Stephen (LAB - St. Peter's)
cllr.stephen.bonallie@sunderland.gov.uk

Copeland, Rosalind (LAB - Southwick)
cllr.rosalind.copeland@sunderland.gov.uk

Curran, Barry (LAB - St. Peter's)
cllr.barry.curran@sunderland.gov.uk

Davison, Ronny (LAB - Redhill)
cllr.ronny.davison@sunderland.gov.uk

Dixon, Darryl (LAB - St. Chad's)
cllr.darryl.dixon@sunderland.gov.uk

Ellis, Sheila (IND - Houghton)
cllr.sheila.ellis@sunderland.gov.uk

Emmerson, Alan (LAB - Ryhope)
cllr.alan.emerson@sunderland.gov.uk

Errington, David (LAB - Doxford)
cllr.david.g.errington@sunderland.gov.uk

Essl, Michael (LAB - Barnes)
cllr.michael.essl@sunderland.gov.uk

Farr, Anthony (LAB - Ryhope)
cllr.anthony.farr@sunderland.gov.uk

Farthing, Louise (LAB - Washington South)
cllr.louise.farthing@sunderland.gov.uk

Fletcher, Jill (LAB - Washington North)
cllr.jill.fletcher@sunderland.gov.uk

Forbes, Margaret (CON - St. Michael's)
cllr.margaret.forbes@sunderland.gov.uk

Foster, Stephen (LAB - Castle)
cllr.stephen.foster@sunderland.gov.uk

Francis, Bob (CON - Fulwell)
cllr.bob.francis@sunderland.gov.uk

Gibson, Peter (LAB - Silksworth)
cllr.peter.gibson@sunderland.gov.uk

Gibson, Elizabeth (LAB - Doxford)
cllr.elizabeth.gibson@sunderland.gov.uk

Gofton, Cecilia (LAB - Pallion)
cllr.cecilia.gofton@sunderland.gov.uk

Heron, Robert (LAB - Copt Hill)
cllr.robert.heron@sunderland.gov.uk

Howe, George (CON - Fulwell)
cllr.george.howe@sunderland.gov.uk

Jackson, Julia (LAB - St. Peter's)
cllr.julia.jackson@sunderland.gov.uk

Kay, Ian (LAB - Millfield)
cllr.iain.kay@sunderland.gov.uk

Kelly, John (LAB - Washington North)

cllr.john.kelly@sunderland.gov.uk
Lauchlan, Len (LAB - Washington Central)
cllr.len.lauchlan@sunderland.gov.uk
Lawson, Anne (LAB - Shiney Row)
cllr.anne.lawson@sunderland.gov.uk
MacKnight, Doris (LAB - Castle)
cllr.doris.macknight@sunderland.gov.uk
Maddison, Paul (CON - St. Michael's)
cllr.paul.maddison@sunderland.gov.uk
Marshall, Christine (LAB - Doxford)
cllr.christine.marshall@sunderland.gov.uk
Martin, Lee (CON - Barnes)
cllr.lee.martin@sunderland.gov.uk
McClennan, Barbara (LAB - Hendon)
cllr.barbara.mcclennan@sunderland.gov.uk
Miller, Fiona (LAB - Washington East)
cllr.fiona.miller@sunderland.gov.uk
Miller, Graeme (LAB - Washington South)
cllr.graeme.miller@sunderland.gov.uk
Mordey, Michael (LAB - Hendon)
cllr.michael.mordey@sunderland.gov.uk
Padgett, Neville (LAB - Washington East)
cllr.neville.padgett@sunderland.gov.uk
Porthouse, Stuart (LAB - St. Chad's)
cllr.stuart.porthouse@sunderland.gov.uk
Price, Bob (LAB - Millfield)
cllr.bob.price@sunderland.gov.uk
Richardson, Dennis (LAB - Houghton)
cllr.dennis.richardson@sunderland.gov.uk
Rolph, Kathryn (LAB - Houghton)
cllr.kathryn.rolph@sunderland.gov.uk
Scanlan, Lynda (LAB - Millfield)
cllr.lynda.scanlan@sunderland.gov.uk
Scaplehorn, Bernard (LAB - Washington West)
cllr.bernard.scaplehorn@sunderland.gov.uk
Scott, John (LAB - Shiney Row)
cllr.john.scott@sunderland.gov.uk
Shattock, Christine (LAB - Southwick)
cllr.christine.shattock@sunderland.gov.uk
Smiles, Lisa (LAB - St. Anne's)
cllr.lisa.smiles@sunderland.gov.uk
Smith, Derrick (IND - Copt Hill)
cllr.derrick.smith@sunderland.gov.uk
Smith, Patricia (LAB - Silksworth)
cllr.patricia.smith@sunderland.gov.uk
Snowdon, Dianne (LAB - Washington Central)
cllr.derrick.snowdon@sunderland.gov.uk
Snowdon, David (LAB - Washington East)
cllr.david.snowdon@sunderland.gov.uk
Speding, Melville (LAB - Shiney Row)
cllr.melville.speding@sunderland.gov.uk
Stewart, Paul (LAB - Redhill)
cllr.paul.stewart@sunderland.gov.uk
Tate, Richard (LAB - Hetton)
cllr.richard.tate@sunderland.gov.uk
Thompson, George (LAB - Washington South)
cllr.george.thompson@sunderland.gov.uk
Trueman, Dorothy (LAB - Washington West)
cllr.dorothy.trueman@sunderland.gov.uk
Turton, Mary (LAB - Sandhill)
cllr.mary.turton@sunderland.gov.uk
Tye, Philip (LAB - Silksworth)
cllr.philip.tye@sunderland.gov.uk
Wakefield, Colin (IND - Copt Hill)
cllr.colin.wakefield@sunderland.gov.uk
Walker, Peter (LAB - Washington North)
cllr.peter.walker@sunderland.gov.uk
Waller, Debra (LAB - Sandhill)
cllr.debra.waller@sunderland.gov.uk
Watson, Susan (LAB - St. Anne's)
cllr.thomas.wright@sunderland.gov.uk
Williams, Linda (LAB - Washington Central)
cllr.linda.williams@sunderland.gov.uk
Wilson, Amy (LAB - Pallion)
cllr.amy.wilson@sunderland.gov.uk
Wilson, Denny (LAB - Castle)
cllr.denny.wilson@sunderland.gov.uk
Wiper, John (CON - Fulwell)
cllr.john.wiper@sunderland.gov.uk
Wood, Peter (CON - St. Michael's)
cllr.peter.wood@sunderland.gov.uk
Wright, Thomas (LAB - St. Anne's)
cllr.thomas.wright@sunderland.gov.uk
Wright, Norma (LAB - Southwick)
cllr.norma.wright@sunderland.gov.uk

POLITICAL COMPOSITION
LAB: 64, CON: 8, IND: 3

CABINET
Leader: Mr Paul Watson
Deputy Leader: Mr Henry Trueman
Attractive & Inclusive City: Mr James Blackburn
Cabinet Secretary: Mr Melville Speding
Children & Learning Services: Ms Patricia Smith
Responsive Services & Customer Care: Ms Cecilia Gofton
Safer City & Culture: Mr John Kelly

COMMITTEE CHAIRS
Children, Young People & Learning: Mr Paul Stewart
Community & Safer City: Ms Florence Anderson
Health & Wellbeing: Mr Peter Walker
Licensing: Ms Doris MacKnight
Personnel: Mr David Errington
Planning & Highways: Mr Philip Tye
Prosperity & Economic Development: Mr Michael Mordey
Regulatory: Ms Amy Wilson
Sustainable Communities: Ms Susan Watson

SURREY C

Surrey County Council, County Hall, Penrhyn Road, Kingston upon Thames KT1 2DN ☎ 0845 600 9009 🖷 020 8541 9004 ✉ contact.centre@surreycc.gov.uk 🖳 www.surreycc.gov.uk

FACTS & FIGURES
Police Authority: Surrey Police Authority
Health Authority: South East Coast Strategic Health Authority
Learning and Skills Council: South East
Parliamentary Constituencies: Surrey East
EU Constituencies: South East
Election Frequency: Elections are of whole council

PRINCIPAL OFFICERS
Chief Executive: Mr David McNulty, Chief Executive, County Hall, Penrhyn Road, Kingston upon Thames KT1 2DN ☎ 020 8541 9008 ✉ david.mcnulty@surreycc.gov.uk

Assistant Chief Executive: Ms Susie Kemp, Assistant Chief Executive, County Hall, Penrhyn Road, Kingston upon Thames KT1 2DN ☎ 020 8541 9008 ✉ susie.kemp@surreycc.gov.uk

Senior Management: Mrs Julie Fisher, Strategic Director for Change & Efficiency, County Hall, Penrhyn Road, Kingston upon Thames KT1 2DN ☎ 020 8541 9550 🖷 020 8541 8968 ✉ julie.fisher@surreycc.gov.uk

Senior Management: Ms Sarah Mitchell, Strategic Director for Adult Social Care, County Hall, Penrhyn Road, Kingston upon Thames KT1 2DN ☎ 020 8541 9020 ✉ sarah.mitchell@surreycc.gov.uk

Senior Management: Mr Trevor Pugh, Strategic Director for Environment & Infrastructure, County Hall, Penrhyn Road, Kingston upon Thames KT1 2DN ☎ 020 8541 9628 ✉ trevor.pugh@surreycc.gov.uk

Senior Management: Ms Yvonne Rees, Strategic Director for Customers & Communities, County Hall, Penrhyn Road, Kingston upon Thames KT1 2DN ☎ 020 8541 7045 🖷 01372 371704 ✉ yvonne.rees@surreycc.gov.uk

Senior Management: Mr Nick Wilson, Strategic Director for Children, Schools & Families, County Hall, Penrhyn Road, Kingston upon Thames KT1 2DN ☎ 020 8541 9502 ✉ nick.wilson@surreycc.gov.uk

Access Officer / Social Services (Disability): Mr David Sargeant, Assistant Director for Personal Care & Support, South West Area Office, Grosvenor House, AO3, London Road, Guildford GU1 1FA ☎ 01483 518455 ✉ david.sargeant@surreycc.gov.uk

Architect, Building / Property Services: Mr John Stebbings, Chief Property Officer, County Hall, Penrhyn Road, Kingston upon Thames KT1 2DN ☎ 020 8213 2554 ✉ john.stebbings@surreycc.gov.uk

Building Control: Mr Pelham Walker, Asset Strategy Manager, County Hall, Penrhyn Road, Kingston upon Thames KT1 2DN ✉ pelham.walker@surreycc.gov.uk

Catering Services: Ms Beverley Baker, Head of Commercial Services, Epsom Local Office, The Parade, Epsom KT18 5BY ☎ 01372 832370 ✉ beverley.baker@surreycc.gov.uk

Children / Youth Services: Ms Caroline Budden, Assistant Director for Children's Services & Safeguarding, Fairmont House, Bull Hill, Leatherhead KT22 7AH ☎ 01372 833400 ✉ caroline.budden@surreycc.gov.uk

Children / Youth Services: Mr Garath Symonds, Assistant Director for Young People, County Hall, Penrhyn Road, Kingston upon Thames KT1 2DN ☎ 01372 833543 ✉ garath.symonds@surreycc.gov.uk

Children / Youth Services: Mr Nick Wilson, Strategic Director for Children, Schools & Families, County Hall, Penrhyn Road, Kingston upon Thames KT1 2DN ☎ 020 8541 9502 ✉ nick.wilson@surreycc.gov.uk

Civil Registration: Mrs Linda Aboe, Registration & Nationality Service Member, Rylston, 81 Oatlands Drive, Weybridge KT13 9LN ☎ 01932 794704 ✉ linda.aboe@surreycc.gov.uk

PR / Communications: Ms Louise Footner, Head of Communications, County Hall, Room G29, Penrhyn Road, Kingston upon Thames KT1 2DN ☎ 020 8541 9624 🖷 020 8541 8004 ✉ louise.footner@surreycc.gov.uk

Community Safety: Mr Gordon Falconer, Community Safety Unit Senior Manager, County Hall, Penrhyn Road, Kingston upon Thames KT1 2DN ☎ 020 8541 7296 ✉ gordon.falconer@surreycc.gov.uk

Computer Management: Mr Paul Brocklehurst, Head of Information Management & Technology, County Hall, Penrhyn Road, Kingston upon Thames KT1 2DN ☎ 020 8541 7210 ✉ paul.brocklehurst@surreycc.gov.uk

Consumer Protection and Trading Standards: Mr Peter Denard, Head of Trading Standards, A02 Lebourne Road, Reigate RH2 7JP ☎ 01372 371710 🖷 01372 371703 ✉ peter.denard@surreycc.gov.uk

Contracts: Mr Andrew Forzani, Head of Procurement & Commissioning, County Hall, Penrhyn Road, Kingston upon Thames KT1 2DN ☎ 0208 541 9233 ✉ andrew.forzani@surreycc.gov.uk

Customer Service: Mr Simon Pollock, Head of Customer Services, Conquest House, Wood Street, Kingston upon Thames KT1 1AB ☎ 020 8541 7848 ✉ simon.pollock@surreycc.gov.uk

Emergency Planning: Mr Ian Good, Head of Emergency Management, Room 194, County Hall, Penrhyn Road, Kingston upon Thames KT1 2DN ☎ 020 8541 9168 🖷 020 8541 9162 ✉ ian.good@surreycc.gov.uk

Environmental Health: Mr Ian Boast, Head of Waste & Sustainability, County Hall, Penrhyn Road, Kingston upon Thames KT1 2DN ☎ 020 8541 9479 ✉ ian.boast@surreycc.gov.uk

Estates, Property & Valuation: Mr Keith Brown, Planning & Management - Technical & Contracts Development Manager, County Hall, Penrhyn Road, Kingston upon Thames KT1 2DN ☎ 020 8541 8651 🖷 020 8541 9311 ✉ keith.brown@surreycc.gov.uk

Facilities: Mr Ian Creswell, Area Delivery Manager, County Hall, Penrhyn Road, Kingston upon Thames KT1 2DN ☎ 020 8541 9301 🖷 020 8541 9997 ✉ icresswell@surreycc.gov.uk

Finance and Treasurer: Ms Sheila Little, Deputy Head of Finance, County Hall, Penrhyn Road, Kingston upon Thames KT1 2DN ☎ 020 8541 7012 ✉ sheila.little@surreycc.gov.uk

Fleet Management: Mr Chris Butler, Transport Co-ordination Centre Manager, County Hall, Penrhyn Road, Kingston upon Thames KT1 2DN ☎ 020 8541 9592 🖷 020 8541 9389 ✉ christopher.butler@surreycc.gov.uk

Grounds Maintenance: Mr Edwin O'Donnell, East Area

Maintenance & Facilities Manager, Room 407, County Hall, Penrhyn Road, Kingston upon Thames KT1 2DN ☎ 020 8541 9863

Health and Safety: Mr Dave Blane, Senior Health & Safety Manager, County Hall, Penrhyn Road, Kingston upon Thames KT1 2DN ☎ 020 8541 8736 ✉ dave.blane@surreycc.gov.uk

Highways: Mr Jason Russell, Assistant Director of Highways, Merrow Complex, Merrow Lane, Merrow, Guildford GU4 7BQ ☎ 020 8541 7102 ✉ jason.russell@surreycc.gov.uk

Legal: Mrs Ann Charlton, Head of Legal & Democratic Services, County Hall, Room 129, Penrhyn Road, Kingston upon Thames KT1 2DN ☎ 020 8541 9001 🖷 020 8541 9392 ✉ ann.charlton@surreycc.gov.uk

Leisure and Cultural Services: Mr Peter Milton, Head of Cultural Services, Room 353, County Hall, Penrhyn Road, Kingston upon Thames KT1 2DN ☎ 020 8541 7679 ✉ peter.milton@surreycc.gov.uk

Lottery Funding, Charity and Voluntary: Mrs Mary Burguieres, Policy & Strategy Partnership Lead Manager, Room 318, County Hall, Penrhyn Road, Kingston upon Thames KT1 2DN

Member Services: Ms Rachel Crossley, Democratic Services Lead Manager, County Hall, Penrhyn Road, Kingston upon Thames KT1 2DN ☎ 020 8541 9993 🖷 020 8541 8968 ✉ rachel.crossley@surreycc.gov.uk

Partnerships: Mr James Painter, Community Partnership Manager, East Surrey Area Office A02, Lesbourne Road, Reigate RH2 7JP ✉ james.painter@surreycc.gov.uk

Personnel / HR: Mrs Carmel Millar, Head of HR & Organisational Development, County Hall, Penrhyn Road, Kingston upon Thames KT1 2DN ☎ 020 8541 9824 ✉ carmel.millar@surreycc.gov.uk

Planning: Mr Dominic Forbes, Planning & Development Group Manager, County Hall, Penrhyn Road, Kingston upon Thames KT1 2DN ☎ 020 8541 9312 🖷 020 8541 9335 ✉ dominic.forbes@surreycc.gov.uk

Procurement: Mr Andrew Forzani, Head of Procurement & Commissioning, County Hall, Penrhyn Road, Kingston upon Thames KT1 2DN ☎ 0208 541 9233 ✉ andrew.forzani@surreycc.gov.uk

Public Libraries: Mrs Rose Wilson, Library Operations Manager, Cultural Services, Runnymede Centre, Chertsey Road, Addlestone KT15 2EP ☎ ; 01932 794178 ✉ rose.wilson@surreycc.gov.uk

Recycling & Waste Minimisation: Mr Ian Boast, Head of Waste & Sustainability, County Hall, Penrhyn Road, Kingston upon Thames KT1 2DN ☎ 020 8541 9479 ✉ ian.boast@surreycc.gov.uk

Regeneration: Mr Tony Samuels, Cabinet Member for Assets & Regeneration Programmes, County Hall, Penrhyn Road, Kingston upon Thames KT1 2DN ✉ tony.samuels@surreycc.gov.uk

Road Safety: Mr Duncan Knox, Road Safety Team Manager, Surrey Safety Camera Partnership, PO Box 930, Guildford GU4 8WU ☎ 020 8541 7443 ✉ duncan.knox@surreycc.gov.uk

Social Services: Ms Sarah Mitchell, Strategic Director for Adult Social Care, County Hall, Penrhyn Road, Kingston upon Thames KT1 2DN ☎ 020 8541 9020 ✉ sarah.mitchell@surreycc.gov.uk

Social Services (Children): Mr Garath Symonds, Assistant Director for Young People, County Hall, Penrhyn Road, Kingston upon Thames KT1 2DN ☎ 01372 833543 ✉ garath.symonds@surreycc.gov.uk

Staff Training: Mrs Carmel Millar, Head of HR & Organisational Development, County Hall, Penrhyn Road, Kingston upon Thames KT1 2DN ☎ 020 8541 9824 ✉ carmel.millar@surreycc.gov.uk

Traffic Management: Mr Iain Reeve, Assistant Director for Strategy Transport & Planning, County Hall, Penrhyn Road, Kingston upon Thames KT1 2DN ☎ 0845 600 9009 🖷 020 8541 9004 ✉ iain.reeve@surreycc.gov.uk

Transport: Mr Iain Reeve, Assistant Director for Strategy Transport & Planning, County Hall, Penrhyn Road, Kingston upon Thames KT1 2DN ☎ 0845 600 9009 🖷 020 8541 9004 ✉ iain.reeve@surreycc.gov.uk

Transport Planner: Mr Iain Reeve, Assistant Director for Strategy Transport & Planning, County Hall, Penrhyn Road, Kingston upon Thames KT1 2DN ☎ 0845 600 9009 🖷 020 8541 9004 ✉ iain.reeve@surreycc.gov.uk

Waste Management: Mr Ian Boast, Head of Waste & Sustainability, County Hall, Penrhyn Road, Kingston upon Thames KT1 2DN ☎ 020 8541 9479 ✉ ian.boast@surreycc.gov.uk

MEMBERS OF THE COUNCIL (80)

***Vice-Chair:* Munro**, David (CON - Farnham South)
d.munro@surreycc.gov.uk

***Leader of the Council:* Hodge**, David (CON - Warlingham)
david.hodge@surreycc.gov.uk

***Deputy Leader of the Council:* Martin**, Peter (CON - Godalming South, Milford and Witley)
peterj.martin@surreycc.gov.uk

Agarwal, Victor (LAB - Stanwell and Stanwell Moor)
victor.agarwal@surreycc.gov.uk

Amin, Mohammed (LD - Woking Central)
mohammed.amin@surreycc.gov.uk

Angell, Mary (CON - Woodham and New Haw)
mary.angell@surreycc.gov.uk

Barker, William (CON - Horsleys)
b.barker@surreycc.gov.uk

Beardsmore, Ian (LD - Sunbury Common and Ashford Common)
ian.beardsmore@btinternet.com

Bennison, Mike (CON - Hinchley Wood Claygate and Oxshott)
michael.bennison@surreycc.gov.uk

Bowes, Liz (CON - Pyrford)
liz.bowes@surreycc.gov.uk

Brett-Warburton, Mark (CON - Guildford South East)
mark.brett-warburton@surreycc.gov.uk

Butcher, John (CON - Cobham)
jvcbutcher@btinternet.com

Carasco, Ben (CON - Horsell)

ben.carasco@surreycc.gov.uk
Chapman, Bill (CON - Camberley East)
bill.chapman@surreycc.gov.uk
Clack, Helyn (CON - Dorking Rural)
helyn.clack@surreycc.gov.uk
Coleman, Carol (CON - Ashford)
carol.coleman@surreycc.gov.uk
Cooksey, Stephen (LD - Dorking and the Holmwoods)
stephen.cooksey@surreycc.gov.uk
Cooper, Nigel (R - East Molesey and Esher)
nigel@thecooperfamily.org.uk
Cosser, Steve (CON - Godalming North)
steve.cosser@surreycc.gov.uk
Curran, Clare (CON - Bookham and Fetcham West)
clare.curran@surreycc.gov.uk
Elias, Tony (CON - Godstone)
tony.elias@surreycc.gov.uk
Ellwood, Graham (CON - Guildford East)
graham.ellwood@surreycc.gov.uk
Few, Mel (CON - Foxhills and Virginia Water)
mel.few@surreycc.gov.uk
Forster, Will (LD - Woking South)
will.forster@surreycc.gov.uk
Fraser, Angela (CON - Banstead East)
angela.fraser@surreycc.gov.uk
Frost, Chris (R - Epsom and Ewell South East)
c.frost@surreycc.gov.uk
Frost, Pat (CON - Farnham Central)
pat.frost@surreycc.gov.uk
Fuller, Denis (CON - Camberley West)
denis.fuller@surreycc.gov.uk
Furey, John (CON - Addlestone)
john.furey@surreycc.gov.uk
Gimson, Simon (CON - Shalford)
simongimson8@gmail.com
Goodwin, David (LD - Guildford South West)
goodwind@guildford.gov.uk
Gosling, Michael (CON - Banstead South)
michael.gosling@surreycc.gov.uk
Grant-Duff, Zully (CON - Merstham and Reigate Hill)
zully.grantduff@surreycc.gov.uk
Hack, Lynne (CON - Redhill)
lynne.hack@surreycc.gov.uk
Hall, Tim (CON - Leatherhead and Fetcham East)
tim.hall@surreycc.gov.uk
Hammond, Kay (CON - Horley West)
k.hammond@surreycc.gov.uk
Harmer, David (CON - Waverley Western Villages)
david.harmer@surreycc.gov.uk
Harrison, Nick (R - Banstead West)
nicholas.harrison@surreycc.gov.uk
Heath, Marisa (CON - Englefield Green)
marisa.heath@surreycc.gov.uk
Hickman, Peter (R - The Dittons)
peter.hickman@surreycc.gov.uk
Hicks, Margaret (CON - Hersham)
margaret.hicks@surreycc.gov.uk
Ivison, David (CON - Heatherside and Parkside)
david.ivison@surreycc.gov.uk
Kemeny, Linda (CON - St Johns and Brookwood)
linda.kemeny@surreycc.co.uk
King, Frances (CON - Earlswood and Reigate South)
frances.king@surreycc.gov.uk
Kington, Eber (R - Epsom and Ewell North)
ekington@epsom-ewell.gov.uk
Lake, Ian (CON - Weybridge)
i.lake@surreycc.gov.uk
Lambell, Peter (LD - Reigate Central)
peter.lambell@surreycc.gov.uk
Lay, Yvonna (CON - Egham Hythe and Thorpe)
yvonna.lay@surreycc.gov.uk
Le Gal, Denise (CON - Farnham North)
denise.legal@surreycc.gov.uk
MacLeod, Stuart (CON - Windlesham)
stuart.macleod@surreycc.gov.uk
Mallett, Ernest (R - West Molesey)
ernest.mallett@surreycc.gov.uk
Marks, Sally (CON - Caterham Valley)
sally.marks@surreycc.gov.uk
Marlow, Geoff (CON - The Byfleets)
geoff.marlow@surreycc.gov.uk
Mason, Jan (R - Epsom and Ewell West)
jmason@epsom-ewell.gov.uk
Moseley, Marsha (CON - Ash)
marsha.moseley@guildford.gov.uk
Nichols, Caroline (LD - Lower Sunbury and Halliford)
cllr.cnichols@spelthorne.gov.uk
Norman, Chris (CON - Chertsey)
chris.norman@surreycc.gov.uk
Orrick, John (LD - Caterham Hill)
john.orrick@surreycc.gov.uk
Phelps-Penry, Tom (R - Walton)
tom.phelpspenry@surreycc.gov.uk
Pitt, Chris (CON - Frimley Green and Mytchett)
chris.pitt@surreycc.gov.uk
Povey, Andrew (CON - Waverley Eastern Villages)
poveya@btconnect.com
Renshaw, Steve (CON - Haslemere)
steve.renshaw@surreycc.gov.uk
Ross-Tomlin, Dorothy (CON - Horley East)
dorothy.rosstomlin@surreycc.gov.uk
Saliagopoulos, Denise (CON - Staines)
denise.saliagopoulos@surreycc.gov.uk
Samuels, Tony (CON - Walton South and Oatlands)
tony.samuels@surreycc.gov.uk
Sealy, Lavinia (CON - Bisley, Cobham and West End)
l.sealy@surreycc.gov.uk
Searle, Pauline (LD - Guildford North)
pauline.searle@surreycc.gov.uk
Skellett, Nick (CON - Oxted)
n.skellett@surreycc.gov.uk
Smith, Diana (LD - Knaphill)
diana.smith@surreycc.gov.uk
Sydney, Michael (CON - Lingfield)
michael.sydney@surreycc.gov.uk
Taylor, Keith (CON - Shere)
keith.taylor@surreycc.gov.uk
Taylor, Colin (LD - Epsom and Ewell South West)
colin.taylor@surreycc.gov.uk
Townsend, Chris (IND - Ashtead)
cllr.townsend@molevalley.gov.uk
Turner-Stewart, Denise (CON - Staines South and Ashford West)
denise.turner@surreycc.gov.uk
Walsh, Richard (CON - Laleham and Shepperton)
richard.walsh@surreycc.gov.uk
Watson, Hazel (LD - Dorking Hills)
h.watson@surreycc.gov.uk
White, Fiona (LD - Guildford West)

fiona.white@surreycc.gov.uk
Witham, Keith (CON - Worplesdon)
keithwitham1@hotmail.co.uk
Wood, David (R - Epsom and Ewell North East)
david.wood@surreycc.gov.uk
Young, Alan (CON - Cranleigh and Ewhurst)
ayoung500@yahoo.co.uk

POLITICAL COMPOSITION

CON: 56, LD: 13, R: 9, IND: 1, LAB: 1

CABINET

Leader: Mr David Hodge
Deputy Leader: Mr Peter Martin
Adult Social Care: Mr Michael Gosling
Assets & Regeneration: Mr Tony Samuels
Change & Efficiency: Ms Denise Le Gal
Children & Families: Mrs Mary Angell
Children & Learning: Mrs Linda Kemeny
Community Safety: Mrs Kay Hammond
Community Services & the 2012 Games: Mrs Helyn Clack
Transport & Environment: Mr John Furey

COMMITTEE CHAIRS

Adult Social Care: Mrs Sally Marks
Audit & Governance: Mr Nick Harrison
Children & Families: Mrs Clare Curran
Communities: Mr Steve Cosser
Education: Mrs Denise Turner-Stewart
Environment & Transport: Mr Steve Renshaw
Health (Scrutiny): Mr Nick Skellett
Overview & Scrutiny (Scrutiny): Mr Mel Few
Planning & Regulatory: Miss Marisa Heath

SURREY HEATH D

Surrey Heath Borough Council, Surrey Heath House, Knoll Road, Camberley GU15 3HD ☎ 01276 707100 🖷 01276 707177 ✉ enquiries@surreyheath.gov.uk 🖳 www.surreyheath.gov.uk

FACTS & FIGURES

Police Authority: Surrey Police Authority
Health Authority: South East Coast Strategic Health Authority
Learning and Skills Council: South East
Parliamentary Constituencies: Surrey Heath
EU Constituencies: South East
Election Frequency: Elections are of whole council
Twinning: Bietigheim Bissingen (Germany); Sucy-en-Brie (France)

PRINCIPAL OFFICERS

Chief Executive: Mrs Karen Whelan, Chief Executive, Surrey Heath House, Knoll Road, Camberley GU15 3HD ☎ 01276 707100 ✉ karen.whelan@surreyheath.gov.uk

Deputy Chief Executive: Mr Chas Bradfield, Deputy Chief Executive, Surrey Heath House, Knoll Road, Camberley GU15 3HD ☎ 01276 707100 ✉ chas.bradfield@surreyheath.gov.uk

Best Value: Mr Kelvin Menon, Head of Corporate Finance, Surrey Heath House, Knoll Road, Camberley GU15 3HD ☎ 01276 707100 ✉ kelvin.menon@surreyheath.gov.uk

Building Control: Mr Brian Townley, Head of Planning, Development & Homes, Surrey Heath House, Knoll Road, Camberley GU15 3HD ☎ 01276 707100 ✉ brian.townley@surreyheath.gov.uk

PR / Communications: Mr Daniel Harrison, Media & Marketing Manager, Surrey Heath House, Knoll Road, Camberley GU15 3HD ☎ 01276 707100 ✉ daniel.harrison@surreyheath.gov.uk

PR / Communications: Mr Ian Macey, Media & Marketing Officer, Surrey Heath House, Knoll Road, Camberley GU15 3HD ☎ 01276 707100 ✉ ian.macey@surreyheath.gov.uk

Community Safety: Mr Kevin Cantlon, Business & Community Development Manager, Surrey Heath House, Knoll Road, Camberley GU15 3HD ☎ 01276 707100 ✉ kevin.cantlon@surreyheath.gov.uk

Computer Management: Mrs Rita Hall, Head of Corporate Resources, Surrey Heath House, Knoll Road, Camberley GU15 3HD ☎ 01276 707100 ✉ rita.hall@surreyheath.gov.uk

Corporate Services: Mrs Rita Hall, Head of Corporate Resources, Surrey Heath House, Knoll Road, Camberley GU15 3HD ☎ 01276 707100 ✉ rita.hall@surreyheath.gov.uk

Customer Service: Mr Richard Payne, Head of Customer Relations, Surrey Heath House, Knoll Road, Camberley GU15 3HD ☎ 01276 707100 ✉ richard.payne@surreyheath.gov.uk

Economic Development: Mr Kevin Cantlon, Business & Community Development Manager, Surrey Heath House, Knoll Road, Camberley GU15 3HD ☎ 01276 707100 ✉ kevin.cantlon@surreyheath.gov.uk

E-Government: Mrs Rita Hall, Head of Corporate Resources, Surrey Heath House, Knoll Road, Camberley GU15 3HD ☎ 01276 707100 ✉ rita.hall@surreyheath.gov.uk

Electoral Registration: Ms Nicola Vooght, Elections Manager, Surrey Heath House, Knoll Road, Camberley GU15 3HD ☎ 01276 707100 ✉ nicola.vooght@surreyheath.gov.uk

Emergency Planning: Mr Daniel Harrison, Media & Marketing Manager, Surrey Heath House, Knoll Road, Camberley GU15 3HD ☎ 01276 707100 ✉ daniel.harrison@surreyheath.gov.uk

Environmental / Technical Services: Mr Tim Pashen, Head of Neighbourhood Services, Surrey Heath House, Knoll Road, Camberley GU15 3HD ☎ 01276 707100 ✉ tim.pashen@surreyheath.gov.uk

Environmental Health: Mr Tim Pashen, Head of Neighbourhood Services, Surrey Heath House, Knoll Road, Camberley GU15 3HD ☎ 01276 707100 ✉ tim.pashen@surreyheath.gov.uk

Facilities: Ms Debbie Pompei, Facilities & Maintenance Manager, Surrey Heath House, Knoll Road, Camberley GU15 3HD ☎ 01276 707100 ✉ deborah.pompei@surreyheath.gov.uk

Finance and Treasurer: Mr Kelvin Menon, Head of Corporate Finance, Surrey Heath House, Knoll Road, Camberley GU15 3HD

☏ 01276 707100 ✉ kelvin.menon@surreyheath.gov.uk

Fleet Management: Ms Debbie Pompei, Facilities & Maintenance Manager, Surrey Heath House, Knoll Road, Camberley GU15 3HD ☏ 01276 707100 ✉ deborah.pompei@surreyheath.gov.uk

Grounds Maintenance: Mr Leigh Thornton, Commercial Services Manager, Surrey Heath House, Knoll Road, Camberley GU15 3HD ☏ 01276 707100 ✉ leigh.thornton@surreyheath.gov.uk

Health and Safety: Mr Tim Pashen, Head of Neighbourhood Services, Surrey Heath House, Knoll Road, Camberley GU15 3HD ☏ 01276 707100 ✉ tim.pashen@surreyheath.gov.uk

Housing: Mr Clive Jinman, Housing Services Manager, Surrey Heath House, Knoll Road, Camberley GU15 3HD ☏ 01276 707100 ✉ clive.jinman@surreyheath.gov.uk

Licensing: Ms Jessica Harris, Licensing Officer, Surrey Heath House, Knoll Road, Camberley GU15 3HD ☏ 01276 707100 ✉ jessica.harris@surreyheath.gov.uk

Member Services: Mrs Jane Sherman, Democratic Services Manager, Surrey Heath House, Knoll Road, Camberley GU15 3HD ☏ 01276 707100 ✉ jane.sherman@surreyheath.gov.uk

Parking: Mr Kash Dhadwar, Parking Services Manager, Surrey Heath House, Knoll Road, Camberley GU15 3HD ☏ 01276 707100 ✉ kash.dhadwar@surreyheath.gov.uk

Partnerships: Mr Jerry Fisher, Partnership Organisational Development Officer, Surrey Heath House, Knoll Road, Camberley GU15 3HD ☏ 01276 707100 ✉ jerry.fisher@surreyheath.gov.uk

Personnel / HR: Mrs Louise Livingstone, HR Manager, Surrey Heath House, Knoll Road, Camberley GU15 3HD ☏ 01276 707100 ✉ louise.livingstone@surreyheath.gov.uk

Planning: Mr Brian Townley, Head of Planning, Development & Homes, Surrey Heath House, Knoll Road, Camberley GU15 3HD ☏ 01276 707100 ✉ brian.townley@surreyheath.gov.uk

Procurement: Mr Hywel Jones, Head of Procurement, Civic Offices, Station Road, Addlestone KT15 2AH ☏ 01932 425772 🖷 01932 838384 ✉ hywel.jones@runnymede.gov.uk

Procurement: Mr Kelvin Menon, Head of Corporate Finance, Surrey Heath House, Knoll Road, Camberley GU15 3HD ☏ 01276 707100 ✉ kelvin.menon@surreyheath.gov.uk

Recycling & Waste Minimisation: Mr Tim Pashen, Head of Neighbourhood Services, Surrey Heath House, Knoll Road, Camberley GU15 3HD ☏ 01276 707100 ✉ tim.pashen@surreyheath.gov.uk

Regeneration: Mr Chas Bradfield, Deputy Chief Executive, Surrey Heath House, Knoll Road, Camberley GU15 3HD ☏ 01276 707100 ✉ chas.bradfield@surreyheath.gov.uk

Staff Training: Ms Melody Port, Senior HR Advisor, Surrey Heath House, Knoll Road, Camberley GU15 3HD ☏ 01276 707100 ✉ melody.port@surreyheath.gov.uk

Sustainable Development: Mrs Jenny Rickard, Planning Policy & Support Manager, Surrey Heath House, Knoll Road, Camberley GU15 3HD ☏ 01276 707100 ✉ jenny.rickard@surreyheath.gov.uk

Town Centre: Mr Chas Bradfield, Deputy Chief Executive, Surrey Heath House, Knoll Road, Camberley GU15 3HD ☏ 01276 707100 ✉ chas.bradfield@surreyheath.gov.uk

Waste Collection and Disposal: Mr Tim Pashen, Head of Neighbourhood Services, Surrey Heath House, Knoll Road, Camberley GU15 3HD ☏ 01276 707100 ✉ tim.pashen@surreyheath.gov.uk

Waste Management: Mr Tim Pashen, Head of Neighbourhood Services, Surrey Heath House, Knoll Road, Camberley GU15 3HD ☏ 01276 707100 ✉ tim.pashen@surreyheath.gov.uk

Children's Play Areas: Mr Leigh Thornton, Commercial Services Manager, Surrey Heath House, Knoll Road, Camberley GU15 3HD ☏ 01276 707100 ✉ leigh.thornton@surreyheath.gov.uk

MEMBERS OF THE COUNCIL (40)

***Mayor:* Mansell**, Bruce (CON - Frimley)
bruce.mansell@surreyheath.gov..uk

***Deputy Mayor:* Harding**, Beverley (CON - Parkside)
beverley.harding@surreyheath.gov.uk

***Leader of the Council:* Gibson**, Moira (CON - Windlesham)
moira.gibson@surreyheath.gov..uk

***Deputy Leader of the Council:* Brooks**, Richard (CON - Town)
richard.brooks@surreyheath.gov..uk

Allen, David (CON - Frimley Green)
David.Allen@surreyheath.gov.uk

Bates, Rodney (LAB - Old Dean)
rodney.bates@surreyheath.gov..uk

Bush, Keith (CON - West End)
keith.bush@surreyheath.gov.uk

Carpenter, Glyn (CON - Bagshot)
Glyn.Carpenter@surreyheath.gov.uk

Chapman, Bill (CON - St. Pauls)
bill.chapman@surreyheath.gov..uk

Chapman, Vivienne (CON - St. Pauls)
vivienne.chapman@surreyheath.gov..uk

Cullen, Ian (CON - Heatherside)
ian.cullen@surreyheath.gov.uk

Deach, Paul (CON - Mytchett and Deepcut)
Paul.Deach@surreyheath.gov.uk

Dodds, Timothy (CON - Lightwater)
tim.dodds@surreyheath.gov.uk

Dougan, Colin (CON - St. Michaels)
colin.dougan@surreyheath.gov..uk

Fennell, Craig (CON - Mytchett and Deepcut)
craig.fennell@surreyheath.gov.uk

Gandhum, Surinder (CON - Lightwater)
surinder.gandhum@surreyheath.gov.uk

Gibson, Liane (CON - Windlesham)
liane.gibson@surreyheath.gov.uk

Graham, Alastair (CON - Bagshot)
alastair.graham@surreyheath.gov.uk

Hamiliton, David (CON - Frimley)
david.hamiliton@surreyheath.gov..uk
Hawkins, Josephine (CON - Parkside)
josephine.hawkins@surreyheath.gov..uk
Hawkins, Edward (CON - Parkside)
edward.hawkins@surreyheath.gov..uk
Ilnicki, Paul (CON - Heatherside)
paul.ilnicki@surreyheath.gov..uk
Kemp, Lexi (CON - Heatherside)
Lexie.Kemp@surreyheath.gov.uk
Mansfield, David (CON - Bisley)
David.Mansfield@surreyheath.gov.uk
May, John (CON - Watchetts)
john.may@surreyheath.gov.uk
Moher, Margeret (LAB - Old Dean)
margeret.moher@surreyheath.gov..uk
Morley, Charlotte (CON - Watchetts)
Charlotte.Morley@surreyheath.gov.uk
Page, Adrian (CON - West End)
Adrian.Page@surreyheath.gov.uk
Patton, David (CON - St. Michaels)
Bob.Paton@surreyheath.gov.uk
Pedder, Ken (CON - Town)
ken.pedder@surreyheath.gov..uk
Pitt, Chris (CON - Frimley Green)
chris.pitt@surreyheath.gov.uk
Potter, Joanne (CON - Mytchett and Deepcut)
Joanne.Potter@surreyheath.gov.uk
Price, Wynne (CON - Bisley)
wynne.price@surreyheath.gov..uk
Roxburgh, Audrey (CON - St. Pauls)
audrey.roxburgh@surreyheath.gov..uk
Sams, Ian (CON - Frimley)
ian.sams@surreyheath.gov.uk
Tedder, Pat (IND - Chobham)
Pat.Tedder@surreyheath.gov.uk
Trow, Judith (IND - Chobham)
judith.trow@surreyheath.gov..uk
White, Valerie (CON - Bagshot)
valerie.white@surreyheath.gov.uk
Whittart, Alan (LD - Frimley Green)
alan.whittart@surreyheath.gov..uk
Winterton, John (CON - Lightwater)
John.Winterton@surreyheath.gov.uk

POLITICAL COMPOSITION
CON: 35, IND: 2, LAB: 2, LD: 1

CABINET
Leader: Miss Moira Gibson
Deputy Leader / Finance: Mr Richard Brooks
Arts & Leisure: Mr Craig Fennell
Built Environment: Ms Liane Gibson
Community: Mrs Vivienne Chapman
Corporate: Mr Colin Dougan
Organisational Development: Mr Keith Bush

COMMITTEE CHAIRS
Appointments: Miss Moira Gibson
Community (Scrutiny): Mrs Audrey Roxburgh
External Partnerships (Scrutiny): Mrs Josephine Hawkins
Leisure & Environment (Scrutiny): Mr Ian Sams
Licensing: Mr Bruce Mansell
Planning Applications: Mr Paul Ilnicki
Policy & Audit (Scrutiny): Mr Edward Hawkins
Selection: Miss Moira Gibson

SUTTON L

Sutton London Borough Council, Civic Offices, St. Nicholas Way, Sutton SM1 1EA ☎ 020 8770 5000 🖷 020 8770 5404 contactcentre@sutton.gov.uk www.sutton.gov.uk

FACTS & FIGURES
Police Authority: Metropolitan Police Authority
Health Authority: NHS London
Learning and Skills Council: London
Parliamentary Constituencies: Carshalton and Wallington, Sutton and Cheam
EU Constituencies: London
Election Frequency: Elections are of whole council
Twinning: Gagny (France); Gladsaxe (Denmark); Minden and Charllotenburg-Wilmersdorf (Germany)

PRINCIPAL OFFICERS
Chief Executive: Mr Niall Bolger, Chief Executive, Civic Offices, St. Nicholas Way, Sutton SM1 1EA ☎ 020 8770 5203 naill.bolger@sutton.gov.uk

Access Officer / Social Services (Disability): Mr Simon Latham, Executive Head of Community Living & Strategic Commissioning, Civic Offices, Sutton SM1 1EA ☎ 020 8770 4005 🖷 020 8770 5214 simon.latham@sutton.gov.uk

Architect, Building / Property Services: Mr Ade Adebayo, Executive Head of Construction & Property, Environment and Leisure, 24 Denmark Road, Carshalton SM1 2JG ☎ 020 8770 6109 🖷 020 8770 6234 ade.adebayo@sutton.gov.uk

Architect, Building / Property Services: Mr Alex Fitzgerald, Head of Asset Management, 24 Denmark Road, Carshalton SM5 2JG ☎ 020 8770 6154 alex.fitxgerald@sutton.gov.uk

Children / Youth Services: Ms Ann Goldsmith, Interim Executive Head - Safegaurding Child Protection & Corporate Parenting, Civic Offices, St. Nicholas Way, Sutton SM1 1EA ☎ 020 8770 4502 ann.goldsmith@sutton.gov.uk

Civil Registration: Mr Colin Beech, Executive Head of Leisure & Libraries, 24 Denmark Road, Carshalton SM5 2JG ☎ 020 8770 4642 🖷 020 8770 6234 colin.beech@sutton.gov.uk

PR / Communications: Ms Gill Bull, Executive Head of Policy & Customer Services, Civic Offices, St. Nicholas Way, Sutton SM1 1EA ☎ 020 8770 5000 gill.bull@sutton.gov.uk

Community Safety: - Warren Shadbolt, Executive Head of Community Safety & Youth Services, Sutton Police Station, 6 Carshalton Road, Sutton SM1 4RF ☎ 020 8649 0601 🖷 020 8649 0609 warren.shadbolt@met.pnn.police.uk

Computer Management: Ms Nicky Wilkins, Head of ICT Stragey Manager And Buisness Lead, Civic Offices, St. Nicholas Way, Sutton SM1 1EA ☎ 020 8770 5070

Consumer Protection and Trading Standards: Ms Sara Shackleton, Inspection & Enforcement Manager, Civic Offices, St.

Nicholas Way, Sutton SM1 1EA ☎ 020 8770 5595 🖰 sara.shackleton@sutton.gov.uk

Contracts: Mr Mark Brewer, Head of Procurement, Civic Offices, St. Nicholas Way, Sutton SM1 1EA ☎ 020 8770 5300 🖷 020 8770 5318 🖰 mark.brewer@sutton.gov.uk

Customer Service: Ms Janette Garlick, Head of Customer Service, Civic Offices, St. Nicholas Way, Sutton SM1 1EA ☎ 020 8770 5317 🖷 020 8770 5209 🖰 janette.garlick@sutton.gov.uk

Economic Development: Ms Mandy Cherrington, Head of Economic Renewal & Business Environment, Sutton Council, Sutton SM1 1EA ☎ 020 8770 5530 🖷 020 8770 5633 🖰 amanda.cherrington@sutton.gov.uk

Education: Ms Sharman Lawson, Executive Head of Planning & Commissioning, The Grove, Carshalton SM5 3AL ☎ 020 8770 6513 🖰 sharman.lawson@sutton.gov.uk

Electoral Registration: Mr Richard Shortman, Democratic Services & Electorial Service Manager, Civic Offices, St. Nicholas Way, Sutton SM1 1EA ☎ 020 8770 5120 🖷 020 8770 5404 🖰 richard.shortman@sutton.gov.uk

Emergency Planning: Mr Ian Kershaw, Head of Planning & Performance, Old Police Station, 6 Carshalton Road, SM1 4LE ☎ 020 8649 0684 🖷 020 8649 0606 🖰 ian.kershaw@sutton.gov.uk

Environmental / Technical Services: Ms Karen Fossett, Head of Development Services, 24 Denmark Road, Carshalton SM5 2JG ☎ 020 8770 6217 🖰 karen.fossett@sutton.gov.uk

Environmental / Technical Services: Mr Daniel Ratchford, Strategic Director of Environment & Leisure, 24 Denmark Road, Carshalton SM5 2JG ☎ 020 8770 6402 🖷 020 8770 6234 🖰 daniel.ratchford@sutton.gov.uk

Estates, Property & Valuation: Mr Ade Adebayo, Executive Head of Construction & Property, Environment and Leisure, 24 Denmark Road, Carshalton SM1 2JG ☎ 020 8770 6109 🖷 020 8770 6234 🖰 ade.adebayo@sutton.gov.uk

Facilities: Ms Pauline Easton, Corporate Facilities Manager, Civic Offices, St. Nicholas Way, Sutton SM1 1EA ☎ 020 8770 5000 🖰 pauline.easton@sutton.gov.uk

Finance and Treasurer: Mr Gerald Almeroth, Strategic Director - Resources, Civic Offices, St. Nicholas Way, Sutton SM1 1EA ☎ 020 8770 5501 🖷 020 8770 5340 🖰 gerald.almeroth@sutton.gov.uk

Grounds Maintenance: Mr Mark Dalzell, Head of Parks and Highways, 24 Denmark Road, Carshalton SM5 2JG ☎ 020 8770 4695 🖷 020 8770 4101 🖰 mark.dalzell@sutton.gov.uk

Health and Safety: Mr David Garioch, Corporate Health & Safety Manager, Civic Offices, St. Nicholas Way, Sutton SM1 1EA ☎ 020 8770 5070 🖰 david.garioch@surreycc.gov.uk

Health and Safety: Ms Sara Shackleton, Inspection & Enforcement Manager, Civic Offices, St. Nicholas Way, Sutton SM1 1EA ☎ 020 8770 5070 🖰 sara.shackleton@surreycc.gov.uk

Highways: Mr Mark Dalzell, Head of Parks and Highways, 24 Denmark Road, Carshalton SM5 2JG ☎ 020 8770 4695 🖷 020 8770 4101 🖰 mark.dalzell@sutton.gov.uk

Home Energy Conservation: Mrs Jan Gransden, Head of Environmental Control, Environment and Leisure, 24 Denmark Road, Carshalton SM5 2JG ☎ 020 8770 5550 🖷 020 8770 5540 🖰 jan.gransden@sutton.gov.uk

Legal: Mr Sanjay Prashar, Executive Head of Legal & Democratic Services, Sutton Council, Sutton SM1 1EA ☎ 020 8770 5073 🖷 020 8770 5059 🖰 sanjay.prashar@sutton.gov.uk

Leisure and Cultural Services: Mr Colin Beech, Executive Head of Leisure & Libraries, 24 Denmark Road, Carshalton SM5 2JG ☎ 020 8770 4642 🖷 020 8770 6234 🖰 colin.beech@sutton.gov.uk

Lighting: Mr Steve Shew, Head of Smarter Travel Sutton, Environment and Leisure, 24 Denmark Road, Carshalton SM5 2JG ☎ 020 8770 6423 🖷 020 8770 6410 🖰 steve.shew@sutton.gov.uk

Member Services: Mr Richard Shortman, Democratic Services & Electorial Service Manager, Civic Offices, St. Nicholas Way, Sutton SM1 1EA ☎ 020 8770 5120 🖷 020 8770 5404 🖰 richard.shortman@sutton.gov.uk

Parking: Mr Ransford Stewart, Executive Head of Planning, Transportation & Highways, Civic Offices, St. Nicholas Way, Sutton SM1 1EA ☎ 020 8770 6105 🖰 ransford.stewart@sutton.gov.uk

Personnel / HR: Mr Dean Shoesmith, Executive Head of Human Resources, Civic Offices, St. Nicholas Way, Sutton SM1 1EA ☎ 020 8770 5211 🖰 dean.shoesmith@sutton.gov.uk

Planning: Mr Ransford Stewart, Executive Head of Planning, Transportation & Highways, Civic Offices, St. Nicholas Way, Sutton SM1 1EA ☎ 020 8770 6105 🖰 ransford.stewart@sutton.gov.uk

Procurement: Mr Mark Brewer, Head of Procurement, Civic Offices, St. Nicholas Way, Sutton SM1 1EA ☎ 020 8770 5300 🖷 020 8770 5318 🖰 mark.brewer@sutton.gov.uk

Public Libraries: Mr Colin Beech, Executive Head of Leisure & Libraries, 24 Denmark Road, Carshalton SM5 2JG ☎ 020 8770 4642 🖷 020 8770 6234 🖰 colin.beech@sutton.gov.uk

Public Libraries: Ms Angela Fletcher, Head of Libraries & Heritage, Central Library, St Nicholas Way, Sutton SM1 1EA ☎ 020 8770 4755 🖰 angela.fletcher@sutton.gov.uk

Recycling & Waste Minimisation: Mr Peter O'Connell, Executive Head of Street Scene Services, 24 Denmark Road, Carshalton SM5 2JG ☎ 020 8770 6402 🖰 peter.o'connell@sutton.gov.uk

Social Services: Dr Adi Cooper, Strategic Director of Adult Social Services & Housing, Civic Offices, St. Nicholas Way,

Sutton SM1 1EA ☎ 020 8770 4500 🖷 020 8770 5214
🖱 adi.cooper@sutton.gov.uk

Social Services: Mr Shaun O'Leary, Executive Head of Adults & Safeguarding, Civic Offices, St Nicholas Way, Sutton SM1 1EA ☎ 020 8770 4505 🖱 shaun.o'leary@sutton.gov.uk

Social Services (Adult): Dr Adi Cooper, Strategic Director of Adult Social Services & Housing, Civic Offices, St. Nicholas Way, Sutton SM1 1EA ☎ 020 8770 4500 🖷 020 8770 5214
🖱 adi.cooper@sutton.gov.uk

Social Services (Children): Ms Ann Goldsmith, Interim Executive Head - Safegaurding Child Protection & Corporate Parenting, Civic Offices, St. Nicholas Way, Sutton SM1 1EA ☎ 020 8770 4502 🖱 ann.goldsmith@sutton.gov.uk

Social Services (Children): Mr Tolis Vouyioukas, Strategic Director - Children, Young People & Learning Directorate, Civic Offices, St. Nicholas Way, Sutton SM1 1EA ☎ 020 8770 4502
🖱 tolis.vouyiokas@sutton.gov.uk

Staff Training: Ms Kim Brown, Joint Head - HR & Policy Development, Sutton Council, Sutton SM1 1EA ☎ 020 8770 5025
🖱 kim.brown@sutton.gov.uk

Street Scene: Mr Peter O'Connell, Executive Head of Street Scene Services, 24 Denmark Road, Carshalton SM5 2JG ☎ 020 8770 6402 🖱 peter.o'connell@sutton.gov.uk

Sustainable Development: Mr Daniel Ratchford, Strategic Director of Environment & Leisure, 24 Denmark Road, Carshalton SM5 2JG ☎ 020 8770 6402 🖷 020 8770 6234
🖱 daniel.ratchford@sutton.gov.uk

Tourism: Mr Colin Beech, Executive Head of Leisure & Libraries, 24 Denmark Road, Carshalton SM5 2JG ☎ 020 8770 4642
🖷 020 8770 6234 🖱 colin.beech@sutton.gov.uk

Town Centre: Mr Martin Furtauer-Hayes, Town Centre Manager, Civic Offices, St. Nicholas Way, Sutton SM1 1EA ☎ 020 8770 5125 🖱 martin.furtauer-hayes@sutton.gov.uk

Traffic Management: Mr Steve Shew, Head of Smarter Travel Sutton, Environment and Leisure, 24 Denmark Road, Carshalton SM5 2JG ☎ 020 8770 6423 🖷 020 8770 6410
🖱 steve.shew@sutton.gov.uk

Transport: Mr Steve Shew, Head of Smarter Travel Sutton, Environment and Leisure, 24 Denmark Road, Carshalton SM5 2JG ☎ 020 8770 6423 🖷 020 8770 6410
🖱 steve.shew@sutton.gov.uk

Transport Planner: Mr Steve Shew, Head of Smarter Travel Sutton, Environment and Leisure, 24 Denmark Road, Carshalton SM5 2JG ☎ 020 8770 6423 🖷 020 8770 6410
🖱 steve.shew@sutton.gov.uk

Waste Collection and Disposal: Mr Peter O'Connell, Executive Head of Street Scene Services, 24 Denmark Road, Carshalton SM5 2JG ☎ 020 8770 6402 🖱 peter.o'connell@sutton.gov.uk

Waste Management: Mr Peter O'Connell, Executive Head of Street Scene Services, 24 Denmark Road, Carshalton SM5 2JG
☎ 020 8770 6402 🖱 peter.o'connell@sutton.gov.uk

MEMBERS OF THE COUNCIL (54)

***Mayor:* Brennan**, Sean (LD - Sutton Central)
sean.brennan@sutton.gov.uk
***Deputy Mayor:* Melican**, Joyce (LD - Beddington South)
joyce.melican@sutton.gov.uk
***Leader of the Council:* Dombey**, Ruth (LD - Sutton North)
ruth.dombey@sutton.gov.uk
***Deputy Leader of the Council:* Hall**, Colin (LD - Wallington South)
colin.hall@sutton.gov.uk
***Group Leader:* Whitham**, Graham (CON - Cheam)
graham.whitham@sutton.gov.uk
Ali, Pathumal (LD - Beddington North)
pathumal.ali@sutton.gov.uk
Allen, Eric (CON - Nonsuch)
Andrews, Sheila (LD - St Helier)
sheila.andrews@sutton.gov.uk
Brown, Malcolm (CON - Beddington South)
malcolm.brown@sutton.gov.uk
Burstow, Mary (LD - Cheam)
mary.burstow@sutton.gov.uk
Butt, Moira (CON - Carshalton South and Clockhouse)
moira.butt@sutton.gov.uk
Callaghan, Dave (LD - St Helier)
david.callaghan@sutton.gov.uk
Callaghan, Anisha (LD - St Helier)
anisha.callaghan@sutton.gov.uk
Clifton, Richard (LD - Sutton South)
richard.clifton@sutton.gov.uk
Coleman, Monica (LD - Wallington South)
monica.coleman@sutton.gov.uk
Court, Margaret (LD - Wandle Valley)
mpcourt@hotmail.com
Crowley, Tim (CON - Carshalton South and Clockhouse)
timcrowley@blueyonder.co.uk
Davey, Adrian (LD - Stonecot)
adrian.davey@sutton.gov.uk
Drage, John (LD - Wandle Valley)
john.drage@sutton.gov.uk
Fenwick, Stephen (LD - Worcester Park)
stephen.fenwick@sutton.gov.uk
Fosdike, Peter (LD - Carshalton South and Clockhouse)
peter.fosdike@sutton.gov.uk
Geiringer, Peter (CON - Belmont)
Glithero, Bruce (LD - Wallington North)
bruce.glithero@sutton.gov.uk
Gordon, Sunita (LD - Wallington North)
sunita.gordon@sutton.gov.uk
Gordon-Bullock, Stuart (CON - Worcester Park)
sgb2006@hotmail.co.uk
Heron, Marlene (LD - Sutton North)
marlene.heron@sutton.gov.uk
Hicks, David (CON - Belmont)
david.hicks@sutton.gov.uk
Holloway, Lester (LD - Sutton North)
lester.holloway@sutton.gov.uk
Honour, Heather (LD - Sutton South)
heather.honour@sutton.gov.uk
Hudson, Brendan (LD - Stonecot)
brendan.hudson@sutton.gov.uk

Javelot, Miquel (LD - Stonecot)
miquel.javelot@sutton.gov.uk
Jerome, Kirsty (LD - Nonsuch)
kirsty.jerome@sutton.gov.uk
Jerome, Gerry (LD - Nonsuch)
gerry.jerome@sutton.gov.uk
Joyce, Edward (LD - Beddington South)
edward.joyce@sutton.gov.uk
Kane, Paddy (LD - Wandle Valley)
Keys, John (LD - Beddington North)
john.keys@sutton.gov.uk
Leach, John (LD - Beddington North)
john.leach@sutton.gov.uk
Lowne, Janet (LD - Sutton Central)
Mathys, Wendy (LD - Sutton West)
wendy.mathys@sutton.gov.uk
McCoy, Jayne (LD - Wallington South)
jayne.mccoy@sutton.gov.uk
Picknett, Pamela (CON - Belmont)
Pollock, Hamish (LD - Carshalton Central)
hamish.pollock@sutton.gov.uk
Pritchard, Jonathan (CON - Cheam)
jonathan@cheamlive.com
Roberts, Roger (LD - Worcester Park)
roger.roberts@sutton.gov.uk
Salter, Alan (LD - Carshalton Central)
alan.salter@sutton.gov.uk
Shields, Tony (CON - Sutton South)
tony.shields@sutton.gov.uk
Stears, Colin (LD - The Wrythe)
colin.stears@sutton.gov.uk
Stears, Sue (LD - The Wrythe)
Theed, Stan (LD - Wallington North)
stan.theed@sutton.gov.uk
Thistle, Roger (LD - The Wrythe)
roger.thistle@sutton.gov.uk
Tope, Graham (LD - Sutton Central)
graham.tope@sutton.gov.uk
Wales, Simon (LD - Sutton West)
simon.wales@sutton.gov.uk
Wallace, Myfanwy (LD - Sutton West)
myfanwy.wallace@sutton.gov.uk
Whitehead, Jill (LD - Carshalton Central)
jill.whitehead@sutton.gov.uk

POLITICAL COMPOSITION

LD: 43, CON: 11

CABINET

Leader: Ms Ruth Dombey
Deputy Leader: Mr Colin Hall
Adult Social Services & Health: Mr Colin Stears
Children, Families & Youth Services: Mr Dave Callaghan
Communities, Transport & Voluntary Sector: Mr Simon Wales
Community Safety, Leisure & Libraries: Mr Graham Tope
Environment & Climate Change: Mr Colin Hall
Education & Schools: Mrs Kirsty Jerome
Planning, Economic Development & Housing: Ms Jayne McCoy

COMMITTEE CHAIRS

Appeals: Mr Miquel Javelot
Audit (Scrutiny): Mr Tim Crowley
Children & Young People (Scrutiny): Ms Wendy Mathys
Development Control: Mr John Leach
Health & Well Being (Scrutiny): Ms Mary Burstow
Licensing: Mrs Sue Stears
Scrutiny Overview: Ms Joyce Melican
Sustainable Communities (Scrutiny): Mr Paddy Kane

SWALE D

Swale Borough Council, Swale House, East Street, Sittingbourne ME10 3HT ☎ 01795 417850 🖷 01795 417217 ✉ csc@swale.gov.uk
💻 www.swale.gov.uk

FACTS & FIGURES

Police Authority: Kent Police Authority
Health Authority: South East Coast Strategic Health Authority
Learning and Skills Council: South East
Parliamentary Constituencies: Faversham & Mid Kent, Sittingbourne and Sheppey
EU Constituencies: South East
Election Frequency: Elections are by thirds
Twinning: Faversham: Hazebrouck (France); Swale Borough: Ypres (Belgium);

PRINCIPAL OFFICERS

Chief Executive: Mr Abdool Kara, Chief Executive, Swale House, East Street, Sittingbourne ME10 3HT ☎ 01795 424341
✉ abdoolkara@swale.gov.uk

Senior Management: Ms Louise Matthews, Head of Policy & Performance, Swale House, East Street, Sittingbourne ME10 3HT
☎ 01795 417533 🖷 01795 417384
✉ louisematthews@swale.gov.uk

Senior Management: Mr Mark Radford, Director of Corporate Services, Swale House, East Street, Sittingbourne ME10 3HT
☎ 01795 417269 🖷 01795 417217 ✉ markradford@swale.gov.uk

Architect, Building / Property Services: Mr James Freeman, Head of Development, Swale House, East Street, Sittingbourne ME10 3HT ☎ 01795 417309 🖷 01795 417217
✉ jamesfreeman@swale.gov.uk

Best Value: Ms Louise Matthews, Head of Policy & Performance, Swale House, East Street, Sittingbourne ME10 3HT ☎ 01795 417533 🖷 01795 417384 ✉ louisematthews@swale.gov.uk

Building Control: Mr James Freeman, Head of Development, Swale House, East Street, Sittingbourne ME10 3HT ☎ 01795 417309 🖷 01795 417217 ✉ jamesfreeman@swale.gov.uk

PR / Communications: Mr Mark James, Media Officer, Swale House, East Street, Sittingbourne ME10 3HT ☎ 01795 417153
🖷 01795 417141 ✉ markjames@swale.gov.uk

Community Planning: Ms Emma Wiggins, Head of Economic Development & Cultural Services, Swale House, East Street, Sittingbourne ME10 3HT ☎ 01795 417396
✉ emmawiggins@swale.gov.uk

Community Safety: Ms Emma Wiggins, Head of Economic Development & Cultural Services, Swale House, East Street, Sittingbourne ME10 3HT ☎ 01795 417396

⌂ emmawiggins@swale.gov.uk

Computer Management: Mr Tony Bullock, ICT Services Manager, Swale House, East Street, Sittingbourne ME10 3HT ☎ 01795 417264 🖷 01795 417141 ⌂ tonybullock@swale.gov.uk

Contracts: Mr Dave Thomas, Head of ICT & Customer Service, Swale House, East Street, Sittingbourne ME10 3HT ☎ 01795 417263 ⌂ davethomas@swale.gov.uk

Contracts: Mr Dave Thomas, Contracts Officer, Swale House, East Street, Sittingbourne ME10 3HT ☎ 01795 41 7263 ⌂ davethomas@swale.gov.uk

Corporate Services: Mr Mark Radford, Director of Corporate Services, Swale House, East Street, Sittingbourne ME10 3HT ☎ 01795 417269 🖷 01795 417217 ⌂ markradford@swale.gov.uk

Customer Service: Mrs Carol Sargeant, Customer Services Manager, Swale House, East Street, Sittingbourne ME10 3HT ☎ 01795 417055 🖷 01795 417217 ⌂ carolsargeant@swale.gov.uk

Customer Service: Mr Dave Thomas, Head of ICT & Customer Service, Swale House, East Street, Sittingbourne ME10 3HT ☎ 01795 417263 ⌂ davethomas@swale.gov.uk

Economic Development: Mr Kieren Mansfield, Economic Development Officer, Swale House, East Street, Sittingbourne ME10 3HT ☎ 01795 417262 🖷 01795 417141 ⌂ kierenmansfield@swale.gov.uk

Economic Development: Ms Emma Wiggins, Head of Economic Development & Cultural Services, Swale House, East Street, Sittingbourne ME10 3HT ☎ 01795 417396 ⌂ emmawiggins@swale.gov.uk

Electoral Registration: Ms Katherine Bescoby, Democratic & Electoral Services Officer, Swale House, East Street, Sittingbourne ME10 3HT ☎ 01795 417330 🖷 01795 417217 ⌂ katherinebescoby@swale.gov.uk

Electoral Registration: Mrs Bev Olds, Electoral Services Officer, Swale House, East Street, Sittingbourne ME10 3HJ ☎ 01795 417316 🖷 01795 417217 ⌂ bevolds@swale.gov.uk

Emergency Planning: Ms Della Fackrell, Emergency Planning Officer, Swale House, East Street, Sittingbourne ME10 3HT ☎ 01795 417430 🖷 01795 417217 ⌂ dellafackrell@swale.gov.uk

Energy Management: Mr Phil Garland, Lead Officer for the Home Energy Conservation Act, Swale House, East Street, Sittingbourne ME10 3HT ☎ 01795 417231 🖷 01795 417478 ⌂ philgarland@swale.gov.uk

Energy Management: Ms Janet Hill, Energy Efficiency Officer, Swale House, East Street, Sittingbourne ME10 3HT ☎ 01795 417296 ⌂ janethill@swale.gov.uk

Environmental / Technical Services: Mr Brian Planner, Head of Service Delivery, Swale House, East Street, Sittingbourne ME10 3HT ☎ 01795 417357 🖷 01795 417217 ⌂ brianplanner@swale.gov.uk

Environmental Health: Mr Phil Garland, Lead Officer for the Home Energy Conservation Act, Swale House, East Street, Sittingbourne ME10 3HT ☎ 01795 417231 🖷 01795 417478 ⌂ philgarland@swale.gov.uk

Estates, Property & Valuation: Mr Kent Parker, Estates Surveyor, Swale House, East Street, Sittingbourne ME10 3HT ☎ 01795 417349 🖷 01795 417217 ⌂ kentparker@swale.gov.uk

Events Manager: Ms Emma Wiggins, Head of Economic Development & Cultural Services, Swale House, East Street, Sittingbourne ME10 3HT ☎ 01795 417396 ⌂ emmawiggins@swale.gov.uk

Facilities: Mrs Anne Adams, Head of Swale / Ashford Property Partnership, Swale House, East Street, Sittingbourne ME10 3HT ☎ 01795 417311 ⌂ anneadams@swale.gov.uk

Finance and Treasurer: Mr Nick Vickers, Head of Finance, Swale House, East Street, Sittingbourne ME10 3HT ☎ 01795 417396 ⌂ nickvickers@swale.gov.uk

Grounds Maintenance: Mr Graeme Tuff, Landscape Officer, Swale House, East Street, Sittingbourne ME10 3HT ☎ 01795 417127 ⌂ graemetuff@swale.gov.uk

Health and Safety: Ms Emma Moore, Health & Safety & Risk Officer, Swale House, East Street, Sittingbourne ME10 3HT ☎ 01795 417078 🖷 01794 417141

Home Energy Conservation: Mr Phil Garland, Lead Officer for the Home Energy Conservation Act, Swale House, East Street, Sittingbourne ME10 3HT ☎ 01795 417231 🖷 01795 417478 ⌂ philgarland@swale.gov.uk

Housing: Ms Amber Christou, Head of Housing Services, Swale House, East Street, Sittingbourne ME10 3HT ☎ 01795 417237 🖷 01795 417141 ⌂ amberchristou@swale.gov.uk

Legal: Ms Monica Blades Chase, Head of Legal, Swale House, East Street, Sittingbourne ME10 3HT ☎ 01795 417324 ⌂ monicabladeschase@swale.gov.uk

Leisure and Cultural Services: Ms Emma Wiggins, Head of Economic Development & Cultural Services, Swale House, East Street, Sittingbourne ME10 3HT ☎ 01795 417396 ⌂ emmawiggins@swale.gov.uk

Licensing: Ms Samantha Potts, Licensing Officer, Swale House, East Street, Sittingbourne ME10 3HT ☎ 01795 417364 ⌂ samanthapotts@swale.gov.uk

Lottery Funding, Charity and Voluntary: Mr Kieren Mansfield, Economic Development Officer, Swale House, East Street, Sittingbourne ME10 3HT ☎ 01795 417262 🖷 01795 417141 ⌂ kierenmansfield@swale.gov.uk

Member Services: Ms Katherine Bescoby, Democratic & Electoral Services Officer, Swale House, East Street, Sittingbourne ME10 3HT ☎ 01795 417330 🖷 01795 417217 ⌂ katherinebescoby@swale.gov.uk

Parking: Mr Brian Planner, Head of Service Delivery, Swale House, East Street, Sittingbourne ME10 3HT ☎ 01795 417357 🖷 01795 417217 ✉ brianplanner@swale.gov.uk

Partnerships: Ms Louise Matthews, Head of Policy & Performance, Swale House, East Street, Sittingbourne ME10 3HT ☎ 01795 417533 🖷 01795 417384 ✉ louisematthews@swale.gov.uk

Personnel / HR: Ms Dena Smart, Personnel Officer, Swale House, East Street, Sittingbourne ME10 3HT ☎ 01795 417391 ✉ denasmart@swale.gov.uk

Planning: Mr James Freeman, Head of Development, Swale House, East Street, Sittingbourne ME10 3HT ☎ 01795 417309 🖷 01795 417217 ✉ jamesfreeman@swale.gov.uk

Procurement: Mr Dave Thomas, Head of ICT & Customer Service, Swale House, East Street, Sittingbourne ME10 3HT ☎ 01795 417263 ✉ davethomas@swale.gov.uk

Recycling & Waste Minimisation: Mr Brian Planner, Head of Amenities & Environmental Services, Swale House, East Street, Sittingbourne ME10 3HT ☎ 01795 417357 🖷 01795 417217 ✉ brianplanner@swale.gov.uk

Recycling & Waste Minimisation: Mr Alan Turner, Principal Cleansing Officer, Swale House, East Street, Sittingbourne ME10 3HT ☎ 01795 417285 🖷 01795 417418 ✉ alanturner@swale.gov.uk

Regeneration: Mr Pete Raine, Director of Regeneration, Swale House, East Street, Sittingbourne ME10 3HT ☎ 01795 417321 ✉ peteraine@swale.gov.uk

Regeneration: Ms Emma Wiggins, Head of Economic Development & Cultural Services, Swale House, East Street, Sittingbourne ME10 3HT ☎ 01795 417396 ✉ emmawiggins@swale.gov.uk

Staff Training: Mrs Catherine Harrison, Training & Development Manager, Swale House, East Street, Sittingbourne ME10 3HT ☎ 01795 417381 ✉ catherineharrison@swale.gov.uk

Street Scene: Mr Brian Planner, Head of Amenities & Environmental Services, Swale House, East Street, Sittingbourne ME10 3HT ☎ 01795 417357 🖷 01795 417217 ✉ brianplanner@swale.gov.uk

Sustainable Communities: Ms Katherine Bescoby, Democratic & Electoral Services Officer, Swale House, East Street, Sittingbourne ME10 3HT ☎ 01795 417330 🖷 01795 417217 ✉ katherinebescoby@swale.gov.uk

Tourism: Ms Lyn Newton, Tourism Development Officer, Swale House, East Street, Sittingbourne ME10 3HT ☎ 01795 417420 🖷 01795 417477 ✉ lynnewton@swale.gov.uk

Tourism: Ms Emma Wiggins, Head of Economic Development & Cultural Services, Swale House, East Street, Sittingbourne ME10 3HT ☎ 01795 417396 ✉ emmawiggins@swale.gov.uk

Total Place: Mr Abdool Kara, Chief Executive, Swale House, East Street, Sittingbourne ME10 3HT ☎ 01795 424341 ✉ abdoolkara@swale.gov.uk

Waste Collection and Disposal: Mr Alan Turner, Principal Cleansing Officer, Swale House, East Street, Sittingbourne ME10 3HT ☎ 01795 417285 🖷 01795 417418 ✉ alanturner@swale.gov.uk

Waste Management: Mr Dave Thomas, Head of ICT & Customer Service, Swale House, East Street, Sittingbourne ME10 3HT ☎ 01795 417263 ✉ davethomas@swale.gov.uk

Waste Management: Mr Alan Turner, Principal Cleansing Officer, Swale House, East Street, Sittingbourne ME10 3HT ☎ 01795 417285 🖷 01795 417418 ✉ alanturner@swale.gov.uk

Children's Play Areas: Mr Graeme Tuff, Landscape Officer, Swale House, East Street, Sittingbourne ME10 3HT ☎ 01795 417127 ✉ graemetuff@swale.gov.uk

MEMBERS OF THE COUNCIL (47)

Leader of the Council: **Bowles**, Andrew (CON - Boughton and Courtenay)
leader@swale.gov.uk

Deputy Leader of the Council: **Lewin**, Gerry (CON - Hartlip, Newington and Upchurch)
cllrlewin@swale.gov.uk

Group Leader: **Henderson**, Mike (LD - Davington Priory)
mr.michaelhenderson@virgin.net

Group Leader: **Truelove**, Roger (LAB - Chalkwell)
labourleader@swale.gov.uk

Barnicott, Richard (CON - Teynham and Lynsted)
rickbarnicott@swale.gov.uk

Bennett, Sylvia (CON - St Michael's)

Bobbin, George (CON - Boughton and Courtenay)
george.bobbin@btinternet.com

Bonney, Monique (IND - West Downs)
montybon1@aol.com

Booth, Andy (CON - Minster Cliffs)
andybooth@swale.gov.uk

Bowen, Lloyd (CON - Teynham and Lynsted)
councillor_l_bowen@hotmail.com

Constable, Jackie (LAB - Queenborough and Halfway)

Constable, Mick (LAB - Queenborough and Halfway)

Conway, Derek (CON - St Michael's)
derekconway@swale.gov.uk

Cosgrove, Mike (CON - St Ann's)
cllrcosgrove@swale.gov.uk

Coulter, John (CON - St Ann's)
johncoulter@swale.gov.uk

Crowther, Adrian (CON - Minster Cliffs)
adrian.crowther@kent.gov.uk

Dewar-Whalley, Duncan (CON - Grove)
duncandewar-whalley@swale.gov.uk

Ellen, Mark (LAB - Sheerness East)
cllr.markellen@yahoo.co.uk

Garrard, June (CON - Sheppey Central)
jvgarrad@aol.com

Gent, Sue (CON - Kemsley)
gentmiss@blueyonder.co.uk

Gent, Ed (CON - Murston)
e.gent@sky.com

Hampshire, Nicholas (CON - Borden)
nicholashampshire@hotmail.com
Harrison, Angela (LAB - Sheerness West)
angelaharrison@swale.gov.uk
Haywood, Mike (LAB - Roman)
haywoodm@sky.com
Ingham, Lesley (CON - Sheppey Central)
inghamg89@btinternet.com
Marchington, Peter (CON - Queenborough and Halfway)
petermarchington@hotmail.co.uk
McCusker, Martin (LAB - Roman)
martinmccusker@swale.gov.uk
Morris, John (CON - Sheppey Central)
johnmorris@swale.gov.uk
Mulhern, Bryan (CON - Abbey)
bryanmulhern@btinternet.com
Prescott, Colin (CON - East Downs)
colinprescott@swale.gov.uk
Pugh, Kenneth (CON - Minster Cliffs)
ken.pugh@kent.gov.uk
Randall, Gareth (CON - Grove)
gareth.randall@virgin.net
Sandle, Patricia (CON - Leysdown and Warden)
patriciasandle@aol.com
Sargent, David (LAB - Sheerness East)
david.sargent@14cavour.freeserve.co.uk
Simmons, David (CON - Watling)
davidsimmons@swale.gov.uk
Stokes, Ben (CON - Iwade and Lower Halstow)
Tolhurst, Adam (LAB - Milton Regis)
adamtolhurst@swale.gov.uk
Walker, Anita (CON - Abbey)
anitajwalker@yahoo.co.uk
Whelan, Ghlin (LAB - Chalkwell)
ghlinwhelan@blueyonder.co.uk
Whiting, Mike (CON - Kemsley)
mikewhiting@swale.gov.uk
Wilcox, Ted (CON - Watling)
ted.wilcox@btinternet.com
Williams, Nick (LAB - Murston)
nick_p_williams@yahoo.co.uk
Willicombe, Alan (CON - Woodstock)
alan188@aol.com
Willicombe, Jean (CON - Woodstock)
jeanwillicombe@aol.com
Winckless, Tony (LAB - Milton Regis)
tonywinckless@swale.gov.uk
Worrall, Stephen (LAB - Sheerness West)

Wright, John (CON - Hartlip, Newington and Upchurch)
johnwright@swale.gov.uk

POLITICAL COMPOSITION

CON: 32, LAB: 13, LD: 1, IND: 1

CABINET

Leader: Mr Andrew Bowles
Deputy Leader / Planning: Mr Gerry Lewin
Community Safety & Health: Ms Lesley Ingham
Environment & Rural Affairs: Mr David Simmons
Finance: Mr Duncan Dewar-Whalley
Housing: Mr Derek Conway
Localism: Mr Mike Cosgrove
Performance: Mr Ted Wilcox
Regeneration & Economy: Mr John Wright

COMMITTEE CHAIRS

Audit: Mr Nicholas Hampshire
Emergency Committee: Mr Andrew Bowles
General Licensing: Ms Lesley Ingham
General Purposes Committee: Mrs Patricia Sandle
Planning: Mr Richard Barnicott
Scrutiny: Ms Angela Harrison

SWANSEA, CITY OF — W

City and County of Swansea Council, Civic Centre, Oystermouth Road, Swansea SA1 3SN ☎ 01792 636000 🖷 01792 636340 ✉ chiefexecutive@swansea.gov.uk 💻 www.swansea.gov.uk

FACTS & FIGURES

Police Authority: South Wales Police Authority
Learning and Skills Council: Wales
Parliamentary Constituencies: Gower, Swansea East, Swansea West
EU Constituencies: Wales
Election Frequency: Elections are of whole council
Twinning: Arhus (Denmark); Cork (Ireland); Ferrara (Italy); Mannheim (Germany); Pau (France)

PRINCIPAL OFFICERS

Chief Executive: Mr Jack Straw, Chief Executive, Civic Centre, Oystermouth Road, Swansea SA1 3SN ☎ 01792 636000 🖷 01792 636700 ✉ jack.straw@swansea.gov.uk

Senior Management: Mrs Reena Owen, Corporate Director - Environment, Civic Centre, Oystermouth Road, Swansea SA1 3SN ☎ 01792 637520 🖷 01792 646700 ✉ reena.owen@swansea.gov.uk

Senior Management: Mr Richard Parry, Corporate Director - Education, Civic Centre, Oystermouth Road, Swansea SA1 3SN ☎ 01792 637515 🖷 01792 636700 ✉ richard.parry@swansea.gov.uk

Senior Management: Mr Phil Roberts, Corporate Director - Regeneration & Housing, Civic Centre, Oystermouth Road, Swansea SA1 3SN ☎ 01792 637525 🖷 01792 636700 ✉ phil.roberts@swansea.gov.uk

Senior Management: Mr Mike Trubey, Head of Finance, Civic Centre, Oystermouth Road, Swansea SA1 3SN ☎ 01792 636391 🖷 01792 636700 ✉ mike.trubey@swansea.gov.uk

Architect, Building / Property Services: Mr Martin Nicholls, Head of Corporate Property & Building Services, Heol y gors, Cwmbwrla, Swansea SA5 8LD ☎ 01792 511002 🖷 01792 511068 ✉ martin.nicholls@swansea.gov.uk

Building Control: Mr Peter Richards, Divisional Officer, Civic Centre, Oystermouth Road, Swansea SA1 3SN ☎ 01792 635622 🖷 01792 648079 ✉ peter.richards@swansea.gov.uk

Catering Services: Ms Bet Jenkins, Catering & Cleaning Facilities Manager, Catering & Cleaning Facilities Manager, 5th Floor Oldway Centre, Swansea SA1 5LD ☎ 01792 773473

☏ 01792 773534 ✉ bet.jenkins@swansea.gov.uk

Children / Youth Services: Mr David Howes, Head of Children & Family Services, Oldway Centre, High Street, Swansea SA1 1LT ☎ 01792 636248 ☏ 01792 637221 ✉ david.howes@swansea.gov.uk

Civil Registration: Mr Noel Evans, Registration & Bereavement Services Manager, Civic Centre, Oystermouth Road, Swansea SA1 3SN ☎ 01792 636275 ✉ noel.evans@swansea.gov.uk

PR / Communications: Mr Lee Wenham, Head of Communications, Marketing, Overview & Scrutiny, Civic Centre, Oystermouth Road, Swansea SA1 3SN ☎ 01792 637158 ☏ 01792 636038 ✉ lee.wenham@swansea.gov.uk

Community Safety: Mr Jeff Davison, Community Safety Co-ordinator, Cockett Police Station, John Street, Cockett, Swansea SA2 0FR ☎ 01792 635570 ☏ 01792 648079 ✉ jeff.davison@swansea.gov.uk

Consumer Protection and Trading Standards: Mr Martin Saville, Head of Public Protection, Civic Centre, Oystermouth Road, Swansea SA1 3SN ☎ 01792 635602 ✉ martin.saville@swansea.gov.uk

Direct Labour: Mr Martin Nicholls, Head of Corporate Property & Building Services, Heol y gors, Cwmbwrla, Swansea SA5 8LD ☎ 01792 511002 ☏ 01792 511068 ✉ martin.nicholls@swansea.gov.uk

Economic Development: Mr Phillip Holmes, Head of Economic Regeneration & Planning, Civic Centre, Oystermouth Road, Swansea SA1 3SN ☎ 01792 636979 ☏ 01792 636700 ✉ phillip.holmes@swansea.gov.uk

Education: Mr Robin Brown, Head of Education Inclusion, Civic Centre, Oystermouth Road, Swansea SA1 3SN ☎ 01792 636000 ✉ robin.brown@swansea.gov.uk

Education: Mr Ian James, Head of Education Effectiveness, Civic Centre, Oystermouth Road, Swansea SA1 3SN ☎ 01792 562668 ✉ ian.james@swansea.gov.uk

Education: Mr Richard Parry, Corporate Director - Education, Civic Centre, Oystermouth Road, Swansea SA1 3SN ☎ 01792 637515 ☏ 01792 636700 ✉ richard.parry@swansea.gov.uk

Education: Mr Brian Roles, Head of Planning & Resources, Oldway Centre, 36 Orchard Street, Swansea SA1 5AQ ☎ 01792 636357 ✉ brian.roles@swansea.gov.uk

Electoral Registration: Mr Patrick Arran, Head of Legal, Democratic Services & Procurement, Civic Centre, Oystermouth Road, Swansea SA1 3SN ☎ 01792 636699 ☏ 01792 637261 ✉ patrick.arran@swansea.gov.uk

Emergency Planning: Mr Jeremy Stephens, Head of Performance & Strategic Projects, Civic Centre, Oystermouth Road, Swansea SA1 3SN ☎ 01792 636849 ✉ jeremy.stephens@swansea.gov.uk

Energy Management: Mr John Llewellyn, Energy Manager, Civic Centre, Oystermouth Road, Swansea SA1 3SN ☎ 01792 636359 ✉ john.llewellyn@swansea.gov.uk

Environmental / Technical Services: Mr Martin Saville, Head of Public Protection, Civic Centre, Oystermouth Road, Swansea SA1 3SN ☎ 01792 635602 ✉ martin.saville@swansea.gov.uk

Environmental Health: Mrs Reena Owen, Corporate Director - Environment, Civic Centre, Oystermouth Road, Swansea SA1 3SN ☎ 01792 637520 ☏ 01792 646700 ✉ reena.owen@swansea.gov.uk

Environmental Health: Mr Martin Saville, Head of Public Protection, Civic Centre, Oystermouth Road, Swansea SA1 3SN ☎ 01792 635602 ✉ martin.saville@swansea.gov.uk

Estates, Property & Valuation: Mr Martin Nicholls, Head of Corporate Property & Building Services, Heol y gors, Cwmbwrla, Swansea SA5 8LD ☎ 01792 511002 ☏ 01792 511068 ✉ martin.nicholls@swansea.gov.uk

European Liaison: Mr David Horne, European Officer, Civic Centre, Oystermouth Road, Swansea SA1 3SN ☎ 01792 363858 ✉ david.horne@swansea.gov.uk

European Liaison: Mr Paul Relf, European Officer, Civic Centre, Oystermouth Road, Swansea SA1 3SN ☎ 01792 636858 ✉ paul.relf@swansea.gov.uk

Events Manager: Mr Nigel Jones, Special Events Manager, Penllergaer Offices, Swansea SA4 9GJ ☎ 01792 635413 ☏ 01792 635447 ✉ nigel.jones@swansea.gov.uk

Facilities: Ms Amanda Davies, Facilities Manager, Civic Centre, Swansea SA1 3SN ☎ 01792 636030 ☏ 01792 637161 ✉ amanda.davies@swansea.gov.uk

Finance and Treasurer: Mr Mike Trubey, Head of Finance, Civic Centre, Oystermouth Road, Swansea SA1 3SN ☎ 01792 636391 ☏ 01792 636700 ✉ mike.trubey@swansea.gov.uk

Fleet Management: Mr Mark Barrow, Fleet Manager, The Central Transport Unit, Morfa Road, Swansea SA1 2EN ☎ 01792 511909 ✉ mark.barrow@swansea.gov.uk

Health and Safety: Ms Heather Swinnerton, Health, Safety & Wellbeing Manager, Guildhall, Swansea SA1 4PE ☎ 01792 636620 ✉ heather.swinnerton@swansea.gov.uk

Highways: Mr Carlton Humphrey, Head of Streetscene, City and County of Swansea, Environment Department, Clydach Depot, Clydach, Swansea SA1 5BJ ☎ 01792 841602 ✉ carlton.humphrey@swansea.gov.uk

Housing: Mr Lee Morgan, Head of Housing & Community Regeneration, Guildhall, Swansea SA1 4PE ☎ 01792 635017 ✉ lee.morgan@swansea.gov.uk

Housing Maintenance: Mr Den Thomas, Housing Maintenance Manager, Guildhall, Swansea SA1 3SN ☎ 01792 635771 ☏ 01792 635020 ✉ den.thomas@swansea.gov.uk

Legal: Mr Patrick Arran, Head of Legal, Democratic Services & Procurement, Civic Centre, Oystermouth Road, Swansea SA1 3SN ☎ 01792 636699 🖷 01792 637261 ✉ patrick.arran@swansea.gov.uk

Leisure and Cultural Services: Mr Iwan Davies, Head of Culture & Tourism, Guildhall, Swansea SA1 4PE ☎ 01792 635403 🖷 01792 635408 ✉ iwan.davies@swansea.gov.uk

Leisure and Cultural Services: Mr Steve Hardman, Library & Service Manager, Civic Centre, Oystermouth Road, Swansea SA1 3SN ☎ 01792 636610 ✉ steve.hardman@swansea.gov.uk

Licensing: Mrs Lynda Anthony, Divisional Officer, Civic Centre, Oystermouth Road, Swansea SA1 3SN ☎ 01792 635600 🖷 01792 648079 ✉ lynda.anthony@swansea.gov.uk

Lifelong Learning: Mr Mike Hughes, Lifelong Learning Services Manager, Dynevor Information Centre, Dynevor Place, Swansea SA1 3ET ☎ 01792 648081 ✉ mike.hughes@swansea.gov.uk

Lighting: Mr Jonathan Hurley, Principal Lighting Manager (Design), Civic Centre, Oystermouth Road, Swansea SA1 3SN ☎ 01792 841666 ✉ jonathan.hurley@swansea.gov.uk

Lighting: Mr Steve Searle, Principal Lighting Manager (Operations), Highways Department, Clydach, Swansea SA6 5BJ ☎ 01792 841677 🖷 01792 841600 ✉ steve.searle@swansea.gov.uk

Lottery Funding, Charity and Voluntary: Mr Spencer Martin, Voluntary Sector Relationship Co-ordinator, Civic Centre, Oystermouth Road, Swansea SA1 3SN ☎ 01792 636734 🖷 01792 637206 ✉ spencer.martin@swansea.gov.uk

Member Services: Mr Patrick Arran, Head of Legal, Democratic Services & Procurement, Civic Centre, Oystermouth Road, Swansea SA1 3SN ☎ 01792 636699 🖷 01792 637261 ✉ patrick.arran@swansea.gov.uk

Member Services: Mr Huw Evans, Democratic Services & Complaints Manager, Civic Centre, Oystermouth Road, Swansea SA1 3SN ☎ 01792 637347 ✉ huw.evans@swansea.gov.uk

Parking: Mr Philip Davies, Parking Manager, Guildhall, Swansea SA1 3SN ☎ 01792 635987 ✉ philip.davies2@swansea.gov.uk

Partnerships: Mr Jeremy Stephens, Head of Performance & Strategic Projects, Civic Centre, Oystermouth Road, Swansea SA1 3SN ☎ 01792 636849 ✉ jeremy.stephens@swansea.gov.uk

Personnel / HR: Mr Steve Rees, Head of Human Resources, Guildhall, Swansea SA1 4PE ☎ 01792 636067 ✉ steve.rees@swansea.gov.uk

Planning: Mr Phillip Holmes, Head of Economic Regeneration & Planning, Civic Centre, Oystermouth Road, Swansea SA1 3SN ☎ 01792 636979 🖷 01792 636700 ✉ phillip.holmes@swansea.gov.uk

Procurement: Mr Simon Griffiths, Head of Legal, Democratic Services & Procurement, Civic Centre, Oystermouth Road, Swansea SA1 3SN ☎ 01792 636699 🖷 01792 637261 ✉ simon.griffiths@swansea.gov.uk

Public Libraries: Mr Steve Hardman, Library & Service Manager, Civic Centre, Oystermouth Road, Swansea SA1 3SN ☎ 01792 636610 ✉ steve.hardman@swansea.gov.uk

Recycling & Waste Minimisation: Ms Trish Flint, Recycling Leader, Pipehouse Wharf, Off Morta Road, Swansea SA1 2EN ☎ 01792 511924 🖷 01792 648079 ✉ trish.flint@swansea.gov.uk

Regeneration: Mr Phil Roberts, Corporate Director - Regeneration & Housing, Civic Centre, Oystermouth Road, Swansea SA1 3SN ☎ 01792 637525 🖷 01792 636700 ✉ phil.roberts@swansea.gov.uk

Road Safety: Mr Mark Thomas, Team Leader - Traffic Management, Penllergaer Offices, Swansea SA4 9GJ ☎ 01792 636233 🖷 01792 652712 ✉ mark.thomas@swansea.gov.uk

Social Services: Mr Phil Hodgson, Corporate Director, Social Services, Civic Centre, Oystermouth Road, Swansea SA1 3SN ☎ 01792 636245 ✉ phil.hodgson@swansea.gov.uk

Social Services (Adult): Ms Deborah Driffield, Head of Adult Services, Oldway Centre, High Street, Swansea SA1 1LT ☎ 01792 636249 ✉ deborah.driffield@swansea.gov.uk

Social Services (Children): Mr David Howes, Head of Children & Family Services, Oldway Centre, High Street, Swansea SA1 1LT ☎ 01792 636248 🖷 01792 637221 ✉ david.howes@swansea.gov.uk

Staff Training: Mr Khan Prince, Senior Organisational Development Officer, Guildhall, Swansea SA1 4PE ☎ 01792 636742 ✉ khan.prince@swansea.gov.uk

Street Scene: Mr Martin Saville, Head of Public Protection, Civic Centre, Oystermouth Road, Swansea SA1 3SN ☎ 01792 635602 ✉ martin.saville@swansea.gov.uk

Sustainable Development: Ms Tanya Nash, Sustainable Development Manager, Civic Centre, Oystermouth Road, Swansea SA1 3SN ☎ 01792 635198 ✉ tanya.nash@swansea.gov.uk

Tourism: Mrs Frances Jenkins, Strategic Manager, Tourism, Marketing & Events, Penllergaer Offices, Swansea SA4 9GJ ☎ 01792 635201 🖷 01792 635216 ✉ frances.jenkins@swansea.gov.uk

Town Centre: Ms Lisa Wells, City Centre Manager, Civic Centre, Oystermouth Road, Swansea SA1 3SN ☎ 01792 476370 🖷 01792 476368 ✉ lisa.wells@swansea.gov.uk

Traffic Management: Mr Mark Thomas, Team Leader - Traffic Management, Penllergaer Offices, Swansea SA4 9GJ ☎ 01792 636233 🖷 01792 652712 ✉ mark.thomas@swansea.gov.uk

Transport: Mr Mark Thomas, Team Leader - Traffic Management, Penllergaer Offices, Swansea SA4 9GJ ☎ 01792 636233 🖷 01792 652712 ✉ mark.thomas@swansea.gov.uk

Waste Collection and Disposal: Mr Ian Whettleton, Divisional Officer - Waste Management, Guildhall, Swansea SA1 4PE ☎ 01792 635600 🖷 01792 648079 ✉ ian.whettleton@swansea.gov.uk

Waste Management: Mr Ian Whettleton, Divisional Officer - Waste Management, Guildhall, Swansea SA1 4PE ☎ 01792 635600 🖷 01792 648079 ✉ ian.whettleton@swansea.gov.uk

MEMBERS OF THE COUNCIL (72)

***Chair:* Thomas**, Des (LAB - West Cross)
des.thomas@swansea.gov.uk
***Leader of the Council:* Phillips**, David (LAB - Castle)
david.philips@swansea.gov.uk
***Deputy Leader of the Council:* Richards**, Christine (LAB - Lower Loughor)
christine.richards@swansea.gov.uk
***Group Leader:* Sullivan**, Gareth (IND - Llangyfelach)
gareth.sullivan@swansea.gov.uk
Bayliss, John (LAB - Uplands)
john.bayliss@swansea.gov.uk
Black, Peter (LD - Cwmbwrla)
peter.black@swansea.gov.uk
Bradley, Nicholas (LAB - Townhill)
nicholas.bradley@swansea.gov.uk
Burtonshaw, June (LAB - Penderry)
june.burtonshaw@swansea.gov.uk
Child, Mark (LAB - West Cross)
mark.child@swansea.gov.uk
Clay, Uta (LAB - Llansamlet)
uta.clay@swansea.gov.uk
Colburn, Anthony (CON - Oystermouth)
tony.colburn@swansea.gov.uk
Cole, David (LAB - Penyrheol)
david.cole@swansea.gov.uk
Cook, Ann (LAB - Cockett)
ann.cook@swansea.gov.uk
Crouch, Sybil (LAB - Castle)
sybil.crouch@swansea.gov.uk
Curtice, Jan (LAB - Penyrheol)
jan.curtice@swansea.gov.uk
Davies, Nick (LAB - Uplands)
nick.davies2@swansea.gov.uk
Davies, John (LAB - Morriston)
john.davies@swansea.gov.uk
Day, Mike (LD - Sketty)
mike.day@swansea.gov.uk
Downing, Philip (LAB - Pontarddulais)
philip.downing@swansea.gov.uk
Doyle, Ryland (LAB - Llansamlet)
ryland.doyle@swansea.gov.uk
Evans, William (LAB - Kingsbridge)
william.evans@swansea.gov.uk
Evans, Mandy (LAB - Bonymaen)
mandy.evans2@swansea.gov.uk
Fitzgerald, Wendy (IND - Penllergaer)
wendy.fitzgerald@swansea.gov.uk
Francis-Davies, Robert (LAB - Morriston)
robert.davies@swansea.gov.uk
Gordon, Fiona (LAB - Castle)
fiona.gordon@swansea.gov.uk
Hale, Joe (LAB - St Thomas)
joe.hale@swansea.gov.uk
Harrington, Andrea (LAB - Morriston)
andrea.harrington@swansea.gov.uk
Harris, Jane (LAB - Pontarddulais)
jane.harris@swansea.gov.uk
Hennegan, Terry (LAB - Penderry)
terry.hennegan@swansea.gov.uk
Holley, Chris (LD - Cwmbwrla)
chris.holley@swansea.gov.uk
Hood-Williams, Paxton (CON - Fairwood)
paxton.hood-williams@swansea.gov.uk
Hopkins, Beverley (LAB - Landore)
beverley.hopkins@swansea.gov.uk
Hopkins, David (LAB - Townhill)
david.hopkins@swansea.gov.uk
James, Dennis (LAB - Llansamlet)
dennis.james@swansea.gov.uk
James, Lynda (IND - Pennard)
lynda.james@swansea.gov.uk
Jardine, Yvonne (LAB - Morriston)
yvonne.jardine@swansea.gov.uk
Jones, Mary (LD - Killay North)
mary.jones@swansea.gov.uk
Jones, Susan (IND - Gowerton)
susan.jones3@swansea.gov.uk
Jones, Andrew (LAB - Cockett)
andrew.jones@swansea.gov.uk
Jones, Jeffrey (LD - Killay South)
jeff.w.jones@swansea.gov.uk
Kirchner, Erika (LAB - Castle)
erika.kirchner@swansea.gov.uk
Lewis, Richard (LD - Gower)
richard.lewis@swansea.gov.uk
Lewis, David (LAB - Gorseinon)
david.lewis2@swansea.gov.uk
Lloyd, Paul (LAB - Bonymaen)
paul.lloyd@swansea.gov.uk
Lloyd, Clive (LAB - St Thomas)
clive.lloyd@swansea.gov.uk
Marsh, Keith (IND - Bishopston)
keith.marsh@swansea.gov.uk
Matthews, Penny (LAB - Llansamlet)
penny.matthews@swansea.gov.uk
Meara, Paul (LD - Sketty)
paul.meara@swansea.gov.uk
Morris, Hazel (LAB - Penderry)
hazel.morris@swansea.gov.uk
Newbury, John (LD - Dunvant)
john.newbury@swansea.gov.uk
Owen, Byron (LAB - Mynyddbach)
byron.g.owen@swansea.gov.uk
Owens, Geraint (LAB - Cockett)
geraint.owens@swansea.gov.uk
Philpott, Cheryl (LD - Sketty)
cheryl.philpott@swansea.gov.uk
Raynor, Jennifer (LAB - Dunvant)
jennifer.raynor@swansea.gov.uk
Rees, Huw (LD - Sketty)
huw.rees2@swansea.gov.uk
Richard, Ioan (O - Mawr)
ioan.richard@swansea.gov.uk
Ronconi-Woollard, Neil (LAB - Uplands)
neil.ronconi-woollard@swansea.gov.uk
Sangha, Pearleen (LAB - Uplands)
pearleen.sangha@swansea.gov.uk
Smith, Robert (LAB - Upper Loughor)
robert.smith@swansea.gov.uk

Smith, Paulette (LAB - Clydach)
paulette.smith@swansea.gov.uk
Stanton, June (LD - Sketty)
june.stanton@swansea.gov.uk
Stewart, Rob (LAB - Morriston)
rob.stewart@swansea.gov.uk
Tanner, Gloria (LAB - Mynyddbach)
gloria.tanner@swansea.gov.uk
Theaker, Michael (LAB - Cockett)
mitchell.theaker@swansea.gov.uk
Thomas, Mark (LAB - Penclawdd)
mark.thomas2@swansea.gov.uk
Thomas, Ceinwen (LAB - Mynyddbach)
ceinwen.thomas@swansea.gov.uk
Thomas, Graham (LD - Cwmbwrla)
graham.thomas@swansea.gov.uk
Thomas, Miles (CON - Newton)
miles.thomas2@swansea.gov.uk
Tyler-Lloyd, Linda (CON - Mayals)
linda.tyler-lloyd@swansea.gov.uk
Walker, Gordon (IND - Clydach)
gordon.walker@swansea.gov.uk
Walton, Lesley (LAB - Townhill)
lesley.walton@swansea.gov.uk
White, Mike (LAB - Landore)
mike.white@swansea.gov.uk

POLITICAL COMPOSITION

LAB: 49, LD: 12, IND: 6, CON: 4, O: 1

CABINET

Leader / Anti-Poverty: Mr David Phillips
Deputy Leader / Citizen & Community Engagement & Democracy: Ms Christine Richards
Finance & Resources: Mr Rob Stewart
Learning & Skills: Mr William Evans
Opportunities for Children & Young People: Mr Michael Theaker
Place: Mrs June Burtonshaw
Regeneration: Mr Nicholas Bradley
Sustainability: Ms Sybil Crouch
Target Areas: Mr Ryland Doyle
Wellbeing: Mr Mark Child

COMMITTEE CHAIRS

Democratic Services: Mrs Mary Jones
Licensing: Mrs Penny Matthews
People Overview & Scrutiny: Mr Mike Day
Performance & Delivery (Scrutiny): Mr Des Thomas
Place Overview & Scrutiny: Mr John Newbury
Safer & Stronger Communities: Ms Uta Clay

SWINDON U

Swindon Borough Council, Civic Offices, Euclid Street, Swindon SN1 2JH ☎ 01793 463000 🖷 01793 463930
✉ swindon-council@swindon.gov.uk 💻 www.swindon.gov.uk

FACTS & FIGURES

Police Authority: Wiltshire Police Authority
Health Authority: NHS South West
Learning and Skills Council: South West
EU Constituencies: South West
Election Frequency: Elections are by thirds
Twinning: Ocotal (Nicaragua); Salzgitter (Germany)

PRINCIPAL OFFICERS

Chief Executive: Mr Gavin Jones, Chief Executive, Civic Offices, Euclid Street, Swindon SN1 2JH ☎ 01793 463008
✉ gjones@swindon.gov.uk

Senior Management: Mr Bernie Brannan, Board Director - Service Delivery, Civic Offices, Euclid Street, Swindon SN1 2JH
☎ 01793 464376 🖷 01793 463306 ✉ bbrannan@swindon.gov.uk

Senior Management: Mr John Gilbert, Board Director - Commissioning, Swanford House, Swindon SN1 2JH
☎ 01793 463068 ✉ jgilbert@swindon.gov.uk

Senior Management: Mr Matt Gott, Board Director - Localities, Civic Offices, Euclid Street, Swindon SN1 2JH ☎ 01793 463097
🖷 01793 463248 ✉ mgott@swindon.gov.uk

Senior Management: Mr Stuart McKellar, Board Director - Finance, Revenues, Benefits & Property, Wat Tyler House West, Beckhampton Street, Swindon SN1 2JG ☎ 01793 463300
✉ smckellar@swindon.gov.uk

Senior Management: Mr Hitesh Patel, Board Director - Business Transformation & Strategic Projects, Wat Tyler House West, Beckhampton Street, Swindon SN1 2JG ☎ 01793 463000
✉ hpatel@swindon.gov.uk

Access Officer / Social Services (Disability): Ms Sue Wald, Lead Commissioner - Vulnerable People, Sandford House, Sandford Street, Swindon SN1 1QH ☎ 01793 463169
✉ swald@swindon.gov.uk

Architect, Building / Property Services: Mr Nic Newland, Head of Design, Construction & Health & Safety, Wat Tyler West House, Beckhampton Street, Swindon SN1 1JG ☎ 01793 463620
✉ nnewland@swindon.gov.uk

Architect, Building / Property Services: Mr Rob Richards, Head of Property Services, Wat Tyler House West, Beckhampton Street, Swindon SN1 2JG ☎ 01793 463520
✉ rrichards@swindon.gov.uk

Civil Registration: Ms Karen Knapton, Superintendent Registrar, Civic Offices, Euclid Street, Swindon SN1 2JH ☎ 01793 521734
✉ karen.knapton@swindon.gov.uk

PR / Communications: Mr Galvin Calthrop, Head of Communications & Insight, Civic Offices, Euclid Street, Swindon SN1 2JH ☎ 01793 463176 ✉ gcalthrop@swindon.gov.uk

PR / Communications: Mrs Sue Mendham, Head of Commercial Services, Wat Tyler House West, Beckhampton Street, Swindon SN1 1JG ✉ smendham@swindon.gov.uk

Community Planning: Mr Matt Gott, Board Director - Localities, Civic Offices, Euclid Street, Swindon SN1 2JH ☎ 01793 463097
🖷 01793 463248 ✉ mgott@swindon.gov.uk

Community Safety: Mr Phil Thomas, Lead - Public Protection & StreetSmart, Wat Tyler West, Beckhampton Street, Swindon SN1

2JG ☎ 01793 466146 ✉ pthomas@swindon.gov.uk

Community Safety: Mr Chris Wilson, Lead Finance Manager - Helping People & Safety, Wat Tyler House West, Beckhampton Street, Swindon SN1 2JG ☎ 01793 463072 ✉ cwilson@swindon.gov.uk

Computer Management: Mr Dave Titcombe, Head of Core Process, Information & Technology, Wat Tyler House West, Beckhampton Street, Swindon SN1 2LG ☎ 01793 465848 ✉ dtitcombe@swindon.gov.uk

Corporate Services: Ms Kirsty Cole, Head of Corporate Finance, Wat Tyler House West, Beckhampton Street, Swindon SN1 2JG ☎ 01793 464610 ✉ kcole@swindon.gov.uk

Corporate Services: Mr James Griffin, Head of Strategy & Innovation, Civic Offices, Euclid Street, Swindon SN1 2JH ☎ 01793 463648 ✉ jgriffin@swindon.gov.uk

Corporate Services: Mrs Karen McMahon, Head of Business Services & Support, Wat Tyler West, Beckhampton Street, Swindon SN1 1JG ☎ 01793 464935 ✉ kmcmahon@swindon.gov.uk

Corporate Services: Mr Hitesh Patel, Board Director - Business Transformation & Strategic Projects, Wat Tyler House West, Beckhampton Street, Swindon SN1 2JG ☎ 01793 463000 ✉ hpatel@swindon.gov.uk

Direct Labour: Mr Bill Fisher, Managing Director of Swindon Commercial Services, Waterside, Derby Close, Swindon SN1 1TZ ☎ 01793 464596 ✉ wfisher@swindon.gov.uk

Economic Development: Mr Paddy Bradley, Lead Commissioner - Economic Attainment, Sandford House, Sandford Street, Swindon SN1 1QH ☎ 01793 463201 ✉ pbradley@swindon.gov.uk

Education: Mr Steve Haley, Lead Finance Manager - Education & Innovation, Wat Tyler House West, Beckhampton Street, Swindon SN1 2LG ☎ 01793 465794 ✉ shaley@swindon.gov.uk

Electoral Registration: Mr Stephen Taylor, Director of Law & Democratic Services, Civic Offices, Euclid Street, Swindon SN1 2JH ☎ 01793 463012 ✉ staylor@swindon.gov.uk

Facilities: Ms Marion Ward, Facilities Manager, Clarence House, Euclid Street, Swindon SN1 2JH ☎ 01793 469952 ✉ mward@swindon.gov.uk

Finance and Treasurer: Mr Adrian Arnold, Lead Finance Manager - General Housing & Place, Wat Tyler House West, Beckhampton Street, Swindon SN1 2JG ☎ 01793 466217 ✉ aarnold@swindon.gov.uk

Finance and Treasurer: Mr Steve Haley, Lead Finance Manager - Education & Innovation, Wat Tyler House West, Beckhampton Street, Swindon SN1 2LG ☎ 01793 465794 ✉ shaley@swindon.gov.uk

Finance and Treasurer: Mr Nick Hobbs, Head of Internal Audit, Wat Tyler East, Beckhampton Street, Swindon SN1 2JG ☎ 01793 463940 ✉ nhobbs@swindon.gov.uk

Finance and Treasurer: Mr Stuart McKellar, Board Director - Finance, Revenues, Benefits & Property, Wat Tyler House West, Beckhampton Street, Swindon SN1 2JG ☎ 01793 463300 ✉ smckellar@swindon.gov.uk

Finance and Treasurer: Mr Paul Smith, Lead Finance Manager - Treasury & Growth, Wat Tyler House West, Beckhampton Street, Swindon SN1 2JG ☎ 01793 463976 ✉ psmith@swindon.gov.uk

Finance and Treasurer: Mr Andy Stevens, Head of Revenues & Benefits, Civic Offices, Euclid Street, Swindon SN1 2JH ☎ 01793 464661 ✉ astevens@swindon.gov.uk

Finance and Treasurer: Mr Chris Wilson, Lead Finance Manager - Helping People & Safety, Wat Tyler House West, Beckhampton Street, Swindon SN1 2JG ☎ 01793 463072 ✉ cwilson@swindon.gov.uk

Fleet Management: Mr Steve Kemble, Fleet Manager, Waterside, Derby Close, Swindon SN1 1TZ ☎ 01793 464596 ✉ skemble@swindon.gov.uk

Health and Safety: Mr Nic Newland, Head of Design, Construction & Health & Safety, Wat Tyler West House, Beckhampton Street, Swindon SN1 1JG ☎ 01793 463620 ✉ nnewland@swindon.gov.uk

Health and Safety: Dr Jose Ortega, Director of Public Health, David Murray John Tower, Swindon SN1 1LH ☎ 01793 444673 ✉ moira.shields@swindon-pct.nhs.uk

Highways: Mr Gwilliam Lloyd, Head of Highway Maintenance, Wat Tyler West, Beckhampton Street, Swindon SN1 2JG ☎ 01793 463541 ✉ glloyd@swindon.gov.uk

Housing: Mr Adrian Arnold, Lead Finance Manager - General Housing & Place, Wat Tyler House West, Beckhampton Street, Swindon SN1 2JG ☎ 01793 466217 ✉ aarnold@swindon.gov.uk

Housing: Mr Mike Ash, SD Lead - Housing Services, Wat Tyler East, Beckhampton Street, Swindon SN2 2JG ☎ 01793 466146 ✉ mash@swindon.gov.uk

Legal: Mr Stephen Taylor, Director of Law & Democratic Services, Civic Offices, Euclid Street, Swindon SN1 2JH ☎ 01793 463012 ✉ staylor@swindon.gov.uk

Leisure and Cultural Services: Mr Ian Bickerton, Lead - Leisure, Libraries & Culture, Sandford House, Swindon SN1 2JH ☎ 01793 465724 ✉ ibickerton@swindon.gov.uk

Member Services: Mr Ian Willcox, Committee & Members Services Manager, Civic Offices, Euclid Street, Swindon SN1 2JH ☎ 01793 463601 🖷 01793 490420 ✉ iwillcox@swindon.gov.uk

Parking: Ms Dawn Woollard, Head of Parking, Wat Tyler West, Beckhampton Street, Swindon SN1 2JG ✉ dwoollard@swindon.gov.uk

Partnerships: Mrs Alison Chamberlain, Partnership Development Officer, Civic Offices, Euclid Street, Swindon SN1 2JH ☎ 01793

466301 ✉ achamberlain@swindon.gov.uk

Personnel / HR: Ms Nicola Houwayek, Head of People & Change, Civic Offices, Euclid Street, Swindon SN1 2JH ☎ 01793 463000 ✉ nhouwayek@swindon.gov.uk

Planning: Mr Richard Bell, Lead - Planning, Wat Tyler West, Beckhampton Street, Swindon SN1 2JG ☎ 01793 466706 ✉ rbell@swindon.gov.uk

Planning: Mr Matt Gott, Board Director - Localities, Civic Offices, Euclid Street, Swindon SN1 2JH ☎ 01793 463097 🖷 01793 463248 ✉ mgott@swindon.gov.uk

Public Libraries: Mr Ian Bickerton, Lead - Leisure, Libraries & Culture, Sandford House, Swindon SN1 2JH ☎ 01793 465724 ✉ ibickerton@swindon.gov.uk

Regeneration: Mr Nazakat Ali, Locality Lead - East, Civic Offices, Euclid Street, Swindon SN1 2JH ☎ 01793 464498 ✉ nali@swindon.gov.uk

Regeneration: Ms Andrea Barratt, Locality Lead - North East (Job Share), Civic Offices, Euclid Street, Swindon SN1 2JH ☎ 01793 463387 ✉ abarratt@swindon.gov.uk

Regeneration: Mr Matt Gott, Board Director - Localities, Civic Offices, Euclid Street, Swindon SN1 2JH ☎ 01793 463097 🖷 01793 463248 ✉ mgott@swindon.gov.uk

Regeneration: Ms Pam Gough, Locality Lead - North East (Job Share), Civic Offices, Euclid Street, Swindon SN1 2JH ☎ 01793 463140 ✉ pgough@swindon.gov.uk

Regeneration: Ms Paula Harrison, Locality Lead - West, Civic Offices, Euclid Street, Swindon SN1 2JH ☎ 01793 466418 ✉ pharrison@swindon.gov.uk

Regeneration: Ms Jackie Moyles, Locality Lead - South, Civic Offices, Euclid Street, Swindon SN1 2JH ☎ 01793 446418 ✉ jmoyles@swindon.gov.uk

Regeneration: Mr Andy Reeves, Locality Lead - Central North, Civic Offices, Euclid Street, Swindon SN1 2JH ☎ 01793 466499 ✉ areeves@swindon.gov.uk

Regeneration: Ms Helena Robinson, Locality Lead - North, Civic Offices, Euclid Street, Swindon SN1 2JH ☎ 01793 466210 ✉ hrobinson@swindon.gov.uk

Regeneration: Mr Mark Walker, Locality Lead - Central, Civic Offices, Euclid Street, Swindon SN1 2JH ☎ 01793 464605 ✉ mwalker@swindon.gov.uk

Road Safety: Ms Margaret Tester, Road Safety Officer, Wat Tyler West, Beckhampton Street, Swindon SN1 2JG ☎ 01793 466399 ✉ mtester@swindon.gov.uk

Social Services: Ms Sue Wald, Lead Commissioner - Vulnerable People, Sandford House, Sandford Street, Swindon SN1 1QH ☎ 01793 463169 ✉ swald@swindon.gov.uk

Social Services (Children): Ms S Tough, Service Delivery Lead - Helping People & Families, Sandford House, Sandford Street, Swindon SN1 1QH ☎ 01793 463067 ✉ stough@swindon.gov.uk

Street Scene: Mr Phil Thomas, Lead - Public Protection & StreetSmart, Wat Tyler West, Beckhampton Street, Swindon SN1 2JG ☎ 01793 466146 ✉ pthomas@swindon.gov.uk

Transport: Mr Gwilliam Lloyd, Head of Highway Maintenance, Wat Tyler West, Beckhampton Street, Swindon SN1 2JG ☎ 01793 463541 ✉ glloyd@swindon.gov.uk

Transport Planner: Mr Gwilliam Lloyd, Head of Highway Maintenance, Wat Tyler West, Beckhampton Street, Swindon SN1 2JG ☎ 01793 463541 ✉ glloyd@swindon.gov.uk

MEMBERS OF THE COUNCIL (57)

***Mayor:* Bray**, Michael (CON - Lydiard and Freshbrook)
brmicha454@aol.com
***Deputy Mayor:* Martin**, Nick (CON - Shaw)
nmartin@swindon.gov.uk
***Leader of the Council:* Bluh**, Roderick (CON - Old Town)
rbluh@swindon.gov.uk
***Deputy Leader of the Council:* Renard**, David (CON - Haydon Wick)
drenard@swindon.gov.uk
***Group Leader:* Grant**, James (LAB - Rodbourne Cheney)
grant4gt@btinternet.com
***Group Leader:* Pajak**, Stan (LD - Eastcott)
stanpajak@ymail.com
Ali, Junab (LAB - Central)
junab@hotmail.co.uk
Allsopp, Steve (LAB - Walcot and Park North)
jean.norris1@ntlworld.com
Amin, Abdul (LAB - Walcot and Park North)
abdulamin22@gmail.com
Baker, Paul (LAB - Penhill and Upper Stratton)
pauljbaker@ntlworld.com
Ballman, John (LAB - Gorse Hill and Pinehurst)
jbswin@yahoo.co.uk
Ballman, Ray (LAB - Gorse Hill and Pinehurst)
jbswin@yahoo.co.uk
Barnett, Rex (CON - Haydon Wick)
rexbarnett@hotmail.com
Bawden, Mike (CON - Chiseldon and Lawn)
mbawden@swindon.gov.uk
Bennett, Andrew (CON - Ridgeway)
abennett@ndirect.co.uk
Bishop, Alan (CON - Blunsdon and Highworth)
alanandjulie@live.com
Crabbe, Wayne (CON - Wroughton and Wichelstowe)
Dart, Doreen (CON - Blunsdon and Highworth)
ddart@swindon.gov.uk
Dempsey, Mark (LAB - Walcot and Park North)
mark@markdempsey.org.uk
Dickinson, Michael (CON - Lydiard and Freshbrook)
mdickinson@swindon.gov.uk
Edwards, Mark (CON - Priory Vale)
markaedwards@yahoo.co.uk
Elliott, Toby (CON - Priory Vale)
toby@tobyelliott.com
Ellis, Claire (CON - Haydon Wick)
claireellis@hotmail.co.uk

Faramarzi, Emma (CON - Priory Vale)
efaramarzi@swindon.gov.uk
Foley, Fionuala (CON - Chiseldon and Lawn)
ffoley@swindon.gov.uk
Ford, Brian (CON - Wroughton and Wichelstowe)
brian.ford@absolutely-independent.co.uk
Friend, Mary (CON - St Andrews)
Haines, John (CON - St Margaret and South Marston)
Heaton-Jones, Peter (CON - St Andrews)
peter@swindonconservatives.com
Heavens, Neil (LAB - Liden, Eldene and Park South)
neil@nheavens.wanadoo.co.uk
Heenan, Dale (CON - Covingham and Dorcan)
dale@covinghamandnytheintouch.com
Holland, Russell (CON - St. Margaret and South Marston)
rholland@swindon.gov.uk
Howard, Fay (LAB - Liden, Eldene and Park South)
fayhoward@live.co.uk
Hurley, Richard (CON - Covingham and Dorcan)
rhurley@swindon.gov.uk
Lovell, Colin (CON - St Margaret and South Marston)
colin.lovell2@ntlworld.com
Matthews, Cindy (LAB - Lydiard and Freshbrook)
cindy.matthews@virgin.net
Mattock, Brian (CON - Old Town)
brian.mattock@ntlworld.com
Moffatt, Des (LAB - Rodbourne Cheney)
fendessy@yahoo.co.uk
Montaut, Derique (LAB - Liden, Eldene and Park South)
derique.montaut@ntlworld.com
Page, Teresa (LAB - Penhill and Upper Stratton)
teresapageswindon@yahoo.co.uk
Penny, Maureen (CON - Blunsdon and Highworth)
Perkins, Garry (CON - Shaw)
ecp@swindon1.fsnet.co.uk
Price, Julian (LAB - Covingham and Dorcan)
jcp490806@hotmail.co.uk
Richards, Ann (LD - Wroughton and Wichelstowe)
ann.richards@live.com
Robbins, James (LAB - Mannington and Western)
Russell, Rochelle (LAB - Gorsehill and Pinehurst)
russellrochelle15@gmail.com
Sewell, Nicky (LD - Eastcott)
nicky@swindonlibdems.org
Small, Kevin (LAB - Mannington and Western)
kevinsmall@hotmail.com
Tomlinson, Vera (CON - St Andrews)
vtomlinson@swindon.gov.uk
Tray, Joe (LAB - Penhill and Upper Stratton)
j.tray@ntlworld.com
Wakefield, Steve (IND - Mannington and Western)
steve4labour@yahoo.com
Watts, Nadine (LAB - Old Town)
nadine.watts@live.co.uk
Watts, Peter (LAB - Rodbourne Cheney)
peterwattsrodbournecheney@live.co.uk
Williams, Keith (CON - Shaw)
krwilliams@swindon.gov.uk
Wood, David (LD - Eastcott)
dave@swindonlibdems.org
Wright, Robert (LAB - Central)
bob.wright.gov@ntlworld.com
Wright, Julie (LAB - Central)
juliecaseworker@hotmail.co.uk

POLITICAL COMPOSITION
CON: 29, LAB: 23, LD: 4, IND: 1

CABINET
Leader: Mr Roderick Bluh
Deputy Leader / Children's Services: Mr David Renard
A Safer, Stronger Borough: Mrs Vera Tomlinson
Finance: Mr Mark Edwards
Health & Adult Social Care: Mr Brian Mattock
Leisure & Strategic Transport: Mr Keith Williams
One Swindon, Localities & Housing: Mr Russell Holland
Regeneration & Culture: Mr Garry Perkins
Strategic Planning & Sustainability: Mr Dale Heenan
Streetsmart & Corporate Services: Ms Fionuala Foley

COMMITTEE CHAIRS
Audit: Mr Michael Dickinson
Children & Young People (Scrutiny): Mr David Wood
Economic, Environmental & Sustainability (Scrutiny): Mr Peter Heaton-Jones
Health (Scrutiny): Ms Claire Ellis
Licensing: Mr Richard Hurley
Planning: Mr Colin Lovell
Safer & Stronger Communities (Scrutiny): Mr Brian Ford
Scrutiny (Scrutiny): Mr Kevin Small
Standards: Mr David Wood

TAMESIDE M

Tameside Metropolitan Borough Council, Council Offices, Wellington Road, Ashton-under-Lyne OL6 6DL ☎ 0161 342 8355 🖷 0161 342 3070 ✉ general@tameside.gov.uk 🖳 www.tameside.gov.uk

FACTS & FIGURES
Police Authority: Greater Manchester Police Authority
Health Authority: North West Strategic Health Authority
Learning and Skills Council: North West
Parliamentary Constituencies: Ashton under Lyne, Denton and Reddish, Stalybridge and Hyde
EU Constituencies: North West
Election Frequency: Elections are by thirds
Twinning: Chaumont (France); Droylsden: Villemomble (France); Dukinfield: Champagnole (France); ; Denton: Montigny-le-Bretonneaux (France); Bengbu (China); Co. Mayo (Ireland); Hyde: Colmar (France); Longdendale: Ruppichteroth (Germany); Mossley: Hem (France); Stalybridge: Armentieres (France)

PRINCIPAL OFFICERS
Chief Executive: Mr Steven Pleasant, Chief Executive, Council Offices, Wellington Road, Ashton-under-Lyne OL6 6DL ☎ 0161 342 3500 🖷 0161 342 3543 ✉ steven.pleasant@tameside.gov.uk

Assistant Chief Executive: Ms Megan Nurse, Assistant Chief Executive - Performance & Change, Council Offices, Wellington Road, Ashton-under-Lyne OL6 6DL ☎ 0161 342 2852 ✉ megan.nurse@tameside.gov.uk

Assistant Chief Executive: Mr Tim Rainey, Assistant Chief Executive - Media, Marketing & Communications, Council Offices, Wellington Road, Ashton-under-Lyne OL6 6DL ☎ 0161 342 3299

🖷 0161 342 2836 🖰 tim.rainey@tameside.gov.uk

Access Officer / Social Services (Disability): Mr Martin Garnett, Assistant Executive Director - Adult Services, Council Offices, Wellington Road, Ashton-under-Lyne OL6 6DL ☎ 0161 342 3466 🖰 martin.garnett@tameside.gov.uk

Architect, Building / Property Services: Mr Robin Monk, Assistant Executive Director - Economy & Environment, Council Offices, Wellington Road, Ashton-under-Lyne OL6 6DL ☎ 0161 342 3340 🖰 robin.monk@tameside.gov.uk

Best Value: Ms Megan Nurse, Assistant Chief Executive - Performance & Change, Council Offices, Wellington Road, Ashton-under-Lyne OL6 6DL ☎ 0161 342 2852 🖰 megan.nurse@tameside.gov.uk

Children / Youth Services: Ms Claire Bibby, Assistant Executive Director - Schools, Youth & Community Services, Council Offices, Wellington Road, Ashton-under-Lyne OL6 6DL ☎ 0161 342 3725 🖰 claire.bibby@tameside.gov.uk

Civil Registration: Ms Sandra Stewart, Assistant Chief Executive - Borough Solicitor, Council Offices, Wellington Road, Ashton-under-Lyne OL6 6DL ☎ 0161 342 3028 🖰 sandra.stewart@tameside.gov.uk

PR / Communications: Mr Tim Rainey, Assistant Chief Executive - Media, Marketing & Communications, Council Offices, Wellington Road, Ashton-under-Lyne OL6 6DL ☎ 0161 342 3299 🖷 0161 342 2836 🖰 tim.rainey@tameside.gov.uk

PR / Communications: Ms Nicola Smith, Head of Communications, Council Offices, Wellington Road, Ashton-under-Lyne OL6 6DL ☎ 0161 342 3548 🖷 0161 342 3779 🖰 nicola.smith@tameside.gov.uk

Community Planning: Mr Mike Round, Assistant Executive Director - District Assemblies, Council Offices, Wellington Road, Ashton-under-Lyne OL6 6DL ☎ 0161 342 3725 🖰 mike.round@tameside.gov.uk

Community Safety: Mr Mike Round, Assistant Executive Director - District Assemblies, Council Offices, Wellington Road, Ashton-under-Lyne OL6 6DL ☎ 0161 342 3725 🖰 mike.round@tameside.gov.uk

Computer Management: Mr Norman Crawford, Head of ICT, Council Offices, Wellington Road, Ashton-under-Lyne OL6 6DL ☎ 0161 342 2197 🖰 norman.crawford@tameside.gov.uk

Consumer Protection and Trading Standards: Mr Ian Saxon, Head of Environmental Enforcement, Council Offices, Wellington Road, Ashton-under-Lyne OL6 6DL ☎ 0161 342 3470 🖰 ian.saxon@tameside.gov.uk

Contracts: Ms Pam Williams, Assistant Chief Executive - Borough Treasurer, Council Offices, Wellington Road, Ashton-under-Lyne OL6 6DL ☎ 0161 342 3863 🖰 pam.williams@tameside.gov.uk

Customer Service: Mr Adam Allen, Assistant Executive Director - Culture, Tourism & Customer Services, Council Offices, Wellington Road, Ashton-under-Lyne OL6 6DL ☎ 0161 342 3304 🖰 adam.allen@tameside.gov.uk

Direct Labour: Mr Paul Jennings, Head of Technical Services, Council Offices, Wellington Road, Ashton-under-Lyne OL6 6DL ☎ 0161 342 2760 🖰 paul.jennings@tameside.gov.uk

Economic Development: Mr Colin Woodrow, Economic Development Officer, Council Offices, Wellington Road, Ashton-under-Lyne OL6 6DL ☎ 0161 342 2741 🖰 colin.woodrow@tameside.gov.uk

E-Government: Ms Nicola Smith, Head of Communications, Council Offices, Wellington Road, Ashton-under-Lyne OL6 6DL ☎ 0161 342 3548 🖷 0161 342 3779 🖰 nicola.smith@tameside.gov.uk

Emergency Planning: Mr Dean Hall, Emergency Planning Manager, Council Offices, Wellington Road, Ashton-under-Lyne OL6 6DL 🖰 dean.hall@tameside.gov.uk

Energy Management: Ms B Revathi, Energy Manager, Council Offices, Wellington Road, Ashton-under-Lyne OL6 6DL ☎ 0161 342 2557 🖷 0161 342 2382 🖰 ; revathi.b@tameside.gov.uk

Environmental Health: Mr Ian Saxon, Head of Environmental Enforcement, Council Offices, Wellington Road, Ashton-under-Lyne OL6 6DL ☎ 0161 342 3470 🖰 ian.saxon@tameside.gov.uk

Estates, Property & Valuation: Mr Robin Monk, Assistant Executive Director - Economy & Environment, Council Offices, Wellington Road, Ashton-under-Lyne OL6 6DL ☎ 0161 342 3340 🖰 robin.monk@tameside.gov.uk

Events Manager: Ms Leanne Feeley, Events Manager, Council Offices, Wellington Road, Ashton-under-Lyne OL6 6DL ☎ 0161 342 3385 🖰 leanne.feeley@tameside.gov.uk

Facilities: Ms Helen Smith, Facilities Management, Council Offices, Wellington Road, Ashton-under-Lyne OL6 6DL ☎ 0161 342 4083 🖰 helen.smith@tameside.gov.uk

Finance and Treasurer: Mr Ben Jay, Assistant Executive Director of Finance, Council Offices, Wellington Road, Ashton-under-Lyne OL6 6DL ☎ 0161 342 3864 🖰 ben.jay@tameside.gov.uk

Finance and Treasurer: Ms Pam Williams, Assistant Chief Executive - Borough Treasurer, Council Offices, Wellington Road, Ashton-under-Lyne OL6 6DL ☎ 0161 342 3863 🖰 pam.williams@tameside.gov.uk

Health and Safety: Ms Debbie Bishop, Head of Health & Safety & Wellbeing, Council Offices, Wellington Road, Ashton-under-Lyne OL6 6DL ☎ 0161 342 8355 🖰 debbie.bishop@tameside.gov.uk

Highways: Mr Robin Monk, Assistant Executive Director - Economy & Environment, Council Offices, Wellington Road, Ashton-under-Lyne OL6 6DL ☎ 0161 342 3340 🖰 robin.monk@tameside.gov.uk

Home Energy Conservation: Ms B Revathi, Energy Manager, Council Offices, Wellington Road, Ashton-under-Lyne OL6 6DL ☎ 0161 342 2557 🖷 0161 342 2382 ✉ revathi.b@tameside.gov.uk

Local Area Agreement: Mr Simon Brunet, Performance Advisor, Council Offices, Wellington Road, Ashton-under-Lyne OL6 6DL ☎ 0161 342 3542 ✉ simon.brunet@tameside.gov.uk

Legal: Ms Sandra Stewart, Assistant Chief Executive - Borough Solicitor, Council Offices, Wellington Road, Ashton-under-Lyne OL6 6DL ☎ 0161 342 3028 ✉ sandra.stewart@tameside.gov.uk

Legal: Mr Paul Turner, Deputy Borough Solicitor, Council Offices, Wellington Road, Ashton-under-Lyne OL6 6DL ☎ 0161 342 2924 ✉ paul.turner@tameside.gov.uk

Leisure and Cultural Services: Mr Adam Allen, Assistant Executive Director - Culture, Tourism & Customer Services, Council Offices, Wellington Road, Ashton-under-Lyne OL6 6DL ☎ 0161 342 3304 ✉ adam.allen@tameside.gov.uk

Licensing: Mr Ian Saxon, Head of Environmental Enforcement, Council Offices, Wellington Road, Ashton-under-Lyne OL6 6DL ☎ 0161 342 3470 ✉ ian.saxon@tameside.gov.uk

Lighting: Mr Paul Jennings, Head of Technical Services, Council Offices, Wellington Road, Ashton-under-Lyne OL6 6DL ☎ 0161 342 2760 ✉ paul.jennings@tameside.gov.uk

Lottery Funding, Charity and Voluntary: Mr Colin Woodrow, Economic Development Officer, Council Offices, Wellington Road, Ashton-under-Lyne OL6 6DL ☎ 0161 342 2741 ✉ colin.woodrow@tameside.gov.uk

Member Services: Ms Joanne Green, Member Services Officer, Council Offices, Wellington Road, Ashton-under-Lyne OL6 6DL ✉ joanne.green@tameside.gov.uk

Member Services: Mr Robert Landon, Head of Democratic Services, Council Offices, Wellington Road, Ashton-under-Lyne OL6 6DL ☎ 0161 342 8355 ✉ robert.landon@tameside.gov.uk

Parking: Mr Mike Thompson, Executive Director - Economy & Environment, Council Offices, Wellington Road, Ashton-under-Lyne OL6 6DL ☎ 0161 342 2722 ✉ mike.thompson@tameside.gov.uk

Partnerships: Ms Megan Nurse, Assistant Chief Executive - Performance & Change, Council Offices, Wellington Road, Ashton-under-Lyne OL6 6DL ☎ 0161 342 2852 ✉ megan.nurse@tameside.gov.uk

Personnel / HR: Ms Tracy Brennand, Assistant Executive Director - People & Performance, Council Offices, Wellington Road, Ashton-under-Lyne OL6 6DL ☎ 0161 342 3279 ✉ tracy.brennand@tameside.gov.uk

Procurement: Ms Suzanne McCormack, Strategic Procurement Officer, Council Offices, Wellington Road, Ashton-under-Lyne OL6 6DL ☎ 0161 342 4429 ✉ suzanne.mccormack@tameside.gov.uk

Public Libraries: Ms Mandy Kinder, Service Unit Manager (Customer Services & Libraries), Council Offices, Wellington Road, Ashton-under-Lyne OL6 6DL ☎ 0161 342 2061 ✉ mandy.kinder@tameside.gov.uk

Recycling & Waste Minimisation: Mr Robin Monk, Assistant Executive Director - Economy & Environment, Council Offices, Wellington Road, Ashton-under-Lyne OL6 6DL ☎ 0161 342 3340 ✉ robin.monk@tameside.gov.uk

Road Safety: Mr Stephen Dickinson, Road Safety Officer, Council Offices, Wellington Road, Ashton-under-Lyne OL6 6DL ☎ 0161 342 3821 🖷 0161 342 3924 ✉ stephen.dickinson@tameside.gov.uk

Social Services (Adult): Mr Martin Garnett, Assistant Executive Director - Adult Services, Council Offices, Wellington Road, Ashton-under-Lyne OL6 6DL ☎ 0161 342 3466 ✉ martin.garnett@tameside.gov.uk

Social Services (Children): Ms Claire Bibby, Assistant Executive Director - Schools, Youth & Community Services, Council Offices, Wellington Road, Ashton-under-Lyne OL6 6DL ☎ 0161 342 3725 ✉ claire.bibby@tameside.gov.uk

Staff Training: Mr Martin Collett, Head of Organisational Development, Council Offices, Wellington Road, Ashton-under-Lyne OL6 6DL ☎ 0161 342 3156 🖷 0161 342 3739 ✉ martin.collett@tameside.gov.uk

Tourism: Mr Roger Platt, Head of Tourism, Council Offices, Wellington Road, Ashton-under-Lyne OL6 6DL ☎ 0161 342 2181 🖷 0161 342 3779 ✉ roger.platt@tameside.gov.uk

Town Centre: Mr Mike Round, Assistant Executive Director - District Assemblies, Council Offices, Wellington Road, Ashton-under-Lyne OL6 6DL ☎ 0161 342 3725 ✉ mike.round@tameside.gov.uk

Traffic Management: Mr John Lyssejko, Principal Engineer, Council Offices, Wellington Road, Ashton-under-Lyne OL6 6LD ☎ 0161 342 2497 🖷 0161 342 3924 ✉ john.lyssejko@tameside.gov.uk

Transport Planner: Mr Mike Thompson, Executive Director - Economy & Environment, Council Offices, Wellington Road, Ashton-under-Lyne OL6 6DL ☎ 0161 342 2722 ✉ mike.thompson@tameside.gov.uk

Waste Collection and Disposal: Mr Robin Monk, Assistant Executive Director - Economy & Environment, Council Offices, Wellington Road, Ashton-under-Lyne OL6 6DL ☎ 0161 342 3340 ✉ robin.monk@tameside.gov.uk

MEMBERS OF THE COUNCIL (57)

Mayor: **Warrington**, Brenda (LAB - Denton West)
Deputy Mayor: **Ricci**, Vincent (LAB - Denton North East)
Leader of the Council: **Quinn**, Kieran (LAB - Droylsden East)
Deputy Leader of the Council: **Taylor**, John (LAB - Dukinfield)
Bailey, Maria (LAB - Audenshaw)
Beeley, Basil (CON - Stalybridge South)

Bell, John (CON - Hyde Werneth)
Bowden, Helen (LAB - Hyde Newton)
Bowerman, Joyce (LAB - St. Peters)
Bray, Warren (LAB - St. Peters)
Buckley, David (CON - Stalybridge South)
Cartey, Yvonne (LAB - St Michaels)
Cooney, Gerald (LAB - Droylsden West)
Cooper, Janet (LAB - Longdendale)
Dickinson, Doreen (CON - Stalybridge South)
Downs, Margaret (LAB - Denton South)
Dowthwaite, Paul (LAB - Mossley)
Drennan, Leigh (LAB - Ashton Hurst)
Fairfoull, Bill (LAB - St Michaels)
Fitzpatrick, Jim (LAB - Hyde Godley)
Fitzpatrick, Philip (LAB - Hyde Newton)
Fowler, Mike (LAB - Denton South)
Francis, Claire (LAB - Denton South)
Gwynne, Allison (LAB - Denton North East)
Harrison, Pauline (LAB - Ashton Hurst)
Holland, Barrie (LAB - Droylsden West)
Holland, Ann (LAB - Droylsden West)
Jackson, Jan (LAB - Stalybridge North)
Kitchen, Joseph (LAB - Hyde Godley)
Lane, Jacqueline (LAB - Dukinfield)
Lane, Dawson (LAB - Denton West)
McNally, David (LAB - St. Peters)
Miah, Raja (LAB - Hyde Werneth)
Miah, Idu (LAB - Mossley)
Middleton, Jim (LAB - Droylsden East)
Peet, Gillian (LAB - Longdendale)
Piddington, Catherine (LAB - Ashton Waterloo)
Quinn, Susan (LAB - Droylsden East)
Reynolds, Claire (LAB - Dukinfield and Stalybridge)
Roberts, George (LAB - Stalybridge North)
Robinson, Peter (LAB - Hyde Newton)
Shember-Critchley, Ellie (LAB - Mossley)
Shorrock, Eileen (LAB - Dukinfield and Stalybridge)
Sidebottom, Margaret (LAB - St Michaels)
Smith, Teresa (LAB - Audenshaw)
Smith, Michael (LAB - Denton West)
Sullivan, John (LAB - Hyde Godley)
Sweeton, David (LAB - Dukinfield and Stalybridge)
Travis, Lynn (LAB - Ashton Waterloo)
Ward, Denise (LAB - Denton North East)
Welsh, Kevin (LAB - Stalybridge North)
Welsh, Ruth (CON - Hyde Werneth)
White, Colin (LAB - Audenshaw)
White, Alan (LAB - Longdendale)
Whitehead, Alan (LAB - Ashton Hurst)
Whitley, Michael (LAB - Ashton Waterloo)
Wild, Brian (LAB - Dukinfield)

POLITICAL COMPOSITION
LAB: 52, CON: 5

CABINET
Leader: Mr Kieran Quinn
Deputy Leader: Mr John Taylor
Adults' Services: Ms Lynn Travis
Business & Community Development: Mr David Sweeton
Children & Families: Mrs Allison Gwynne
Environmental Services: Mrs Catherine Piddington
Learning & Achievement: Mr Gerald Cooney
Neighbourhoods: Mr Kevin Welsh
Transport & Development: Mr Peter Robinson

COMMITTEE CHAIRS
Audit: Mr Vincent Ricci
Licensing: Mr Colin White
Planning: Mr Warren Bray

TAMWORTH D
Tamworth Borough Council, Marmion House, Lichfield Street, Tamworth B79 7BZ ☎ 01827 709709 🖷 01827 709271 ✉ enquiries@tamworth.gov.uk 🖳 www.tamworth.gov.uk

FACTS & FIGURES
Police Authority: Staffordshire Police Authority
Health Authority: NHS West Midlands
Learning and Skills Council: West Midlands
Parliamentary Constituencies: Tamworth
EU Constituencies: West Midlands
Election Frequency: Elections are by thirds
Twinning: Bad Laasphe (Germany); Vaujours (France)

PRINCIPAL OFFICERS
Chief Executive: Mr Anthony Goodwin, Chief Executive, Marmion House, Lichfield Street, Tamworth B79 7BZ ☎ 01827 709212 🖷 01827 709271 ✉ tony-goodwin@tamworth.gov.uk

Deputy Chief Executive: Mr John Wheatley, Executive Director - Corporate Services, Marmion House, Lichfield Street, Tamworth B79 7BZ ☎ 01827 709252 🖷 01827 709271 ✉ john-wheatley@tamworth.gov.uk

Assistant Chief Executive: Ms Anica Goodwin, Director - Transformation & Corporate Performance, Marmion House, Lichfield Street, Tamworth B79 7BZ ☎ 01827 709225 🖷 01827 709271 ✉ anica-goodwin@tamworth.gov.uk

Architect, Building / Property Services: Mr Paul Weston, Head of Asset Management, Marmion House, Lichfield Street, Tamworth B79 7BZ ☎ 01827 709377 🖷 01827 709271 ✉ paul-weston@tamworth.gov.uk

PR / Communications: Ms Jane Eason, Corporate Communications & PR Manager, Marmion House, Lichfield Street, Tamworth B79 7BZ ☎ 01827 709571 🖷 01827 709271 ✉ jane-eason@tamworth.gov.uk

Community Planning: Mr Robert Mitchell, Director - Communities, Planning & Partnerships, Marmion House, Lichfield Street, Tamworth B79 7BZ ☎ 01827 709616 🖷 01827 709310 ✉ robert-mitchell@tamworth.gov.uk

Community Safety: Mr Dave Fern, Head of Community Safety, Marmion House, Lichfield Street, Tamworth B79 7BZ ☎ 01785 234647 🖷 01827 709271 ✉ david-fern@tamworth.gov.uk

Computer Management: Mrs Nicki Burton, Director - Technology & Corporate Programmes, Marmion House, Lichfield Street, Tamworth B79 7BZ ☎ 01827 709420 🖷 01827 709271

nicki-burton@tamworth.gov.uk

Contracts: Mr David Onion, Corporate Procurement Officer, Marmion House, Lichfield Street, Tamworth B79 7BZ ☎ 01827 709371 🖷 01827 709271 david-onion@tamworth.gov.uk

Customer Service: Mrs Tracey Yeomans, Head of Customer Services, Marmion House, Lichfield Street, Tamworth B79 7BZ ☎ 01827 709427 🖷 01827 709271 tracey-yeomans@tamworth.gov.uk

Economic Development: Mr James Roberts, Economic Development & Enterprise Manager, Marmion House, Lichfield Street, Tamworth B79 7BZ ☎ 01827 709204 🖷 01827 709271 james-roberts@tamworth.gov.uk

E-Government: Mrs Nicki Burton, Director - Technology & Corporate Programmes, Marmion House, Lichfield Street, Tamworth B79 7BZ ☎ 01827 709420 🖷 01827 709271 nicki-burton@tamworth.gov.uk

Electoral Registration: Mr John Wheatley, Executive Director - Corporate Services, Marmion House, Lichfield Street, Tamworth B79 7BZ ☎ 01827 709252 🖷 01827 709271 john-wheatley@tamworth.gov.uk

Emergency Planning: Mr Derek Bolton, Corporate Information Security Manager, Marmion House, Lichfield Street, Tamworth B79 7BZ ☎ 01827 709587 🖷 01827 709271 derek-bolton@tamworth.gov.uk

Energy Management: Mr Paul Weston, Head of Asset Management, Marmion House, Lichfield Street, Tamworth B79 7BZ ☎ 01827 709377 🖷 01827 709271 paul-weston@tamworth.gov.uk

Environmental Health: Mr Stephen Lewis, Head of Environmental Health, Marmion House, Lichfield Street, Tamworth B79 7BZ ☎ 01827 709428 🖷 01827 709271 stephen-lewis@tamworth.gov.uk

Estates, Property & Valuation: Mr Paul Weston, Head of Asset Management, Marmion House, Lichfield Street, Tamworth B79 7BZ ☎ 01827 709377 🖷 01827 709271 paul-weston@tamworth.gov.uk

Finance and Treasurer: Mr Stefan Garner, Director of Finance, Marmion House, Lichfield Street, Tamworth B79 7BZ ☎ 01827 709242 🖷 01827 709271 stefan-garner@tamworth.gov.uk

Grounds Maintenance: Mrs Sarah McGrandle, Head of Environmental Management, Marmion House, Lichfield Street, Tamworth B79 7BZ ☎ 01827 709349 🖷 01827 709271 sarah-mcgrandle@tamworth.gov.uk

Health and Safety: Mr Steve Langston, Health & Safety Manager, Marmion House, Lichfield Street, Tamworth B79 7BZ ☎ 01543 308107; 01827 709224 🖷 01543 308103; 01827 709271 steven.langston@lichfielddc.gov.uk

Housing: Mr Rob Barnes, Director - Housing & Health, Marmion House, Lichfield Street, Tamworth B79 7BZ ☎ 01827 709447 🖷 01827 709271 robert-barnes@tamworth.gov.uk

Housing Maintenance: Mr John Murden, Repairs Manager, Marmion House, Lichfield Street, Tamworth B79 7BZ ☎ 01827 709406 john-murden@tamworth.gov.uk

Legal: Mrs Jane Hackett, Solicitor to the Council & Monitoring Officer, Marmion House, Lichfield Street, Tamworth B79 7BZ ☎ 01827 709258 🖷 01827 709271 jane-hackett@tamworth.gov.uk

Leisure and Cultural Services: Mr Robert Mitchell, Director - Communities, Planning & Partnerships, Marmion House, Lichfield Street, Tamworth B79 7BZ ☎ 01827 709616 🖷 01827 709310 robert-mitchell@tamworth.gov.uk

Lottery Funding, Charity and Voluntary: Mr Robert Mitchell, Director - Communities, Planning & Partnerships, Marmion House, Lichfield Street, Tamworth B79 7BZ ☎ 01827 709616 🖷 01827 709310 robert-mitchell@tamworth.gov.uk

Member Services: Mrs Jane Hackett, Solicitor to the Council & Monitoring Officer, Marmion House, Lichfield Street, Tamworth B79 7BZ ☎ 01827 709258 🖷 01827 709271 jane-hackett@tamworth.gov.uk

Parking: Mr Andrew Barratt, Director - Assets & Environment, Marmion House, Lichfield Street, Tamworth B79 7BZ ☎ 01827 709453 🖷 01872 709271 andrew-barratt@tamworth.gov.uk

Personnel / HR: Mrs Christie Tims, Head of Organisational Development, Marmion House, Lichfield Street, Tamworth B79 7BZ ☎ 01827 709215 🖷 01827 709271 christie-tims@tamworth.gov.uk

Planning: Mr Matthew Bowers, Head of Planning & Regeneration, Marmion House, Lichfield Street, Tamworth B79 7BZ ☎ 01827 709276 🖷 01827 709271 matthew-bowers@tamworth.gov.uk

Procurement: Mr David Onion, Corporate Procurement Officer, Marmion House, Lichfield Street, Tamworth B79 7BZ ☎ 01827 709371 🖷 01827 709271 david-onion@tamworth.gov.uk

Recycling & Waste Minimisation: Mr Andrew Barratt, Director - Assets & Environment, Marmion House, Lichfield Street, Tamworth B79 7BZ ☎ 01827 709453 🖷 01872 709271 andrew-barratt@tamworth.gov.uk

Regeneration: Mr Robert Mitchell, Director - Communities, Planning & Partnerships, Marmion House, Lichfield Street, Tamworth B79 7BZ ☎ 01827 709616 🖷 01827 709310 robert-mitchell@tamworth.gov.uk

Staff Training: Ms Zoe-Louise Blake, Human Resources Advisor/Training, Marmion House, Lichfield Street, Tamworth B79 7BZ ☎ 01827 709223 🖷 01827 709271 zoe-blake@tamworth.gov.uk

Street Scene: Mrs Sarah McGrandle, Head of Environmental Management, Marmion House, Lichfield Street, Tamworth B79 7BZ ☎ 01827 709349 🖷 01827 709271 ✉ sarah-mcgrandle@tamworth.gov.uk

Tourism: Ms Stacy Birt, Tourism & Town Centre Development Manager, Marmion House, Lichfield Street, Tamworth B79 7BZ ☎ 01827 709583 🖷 01827 709271 ✉ stacy-birt@tamworth.gov.uk

Town Centre: Mrs Joanne Sands, Neighbourhood Services Manager, Sandy Way Depot, Amington, Tamworth B77 4ED ☎ 01827 709585 ✉ joanne-sands@tamworth.gov.uk

Total Place: Mr Robert Mitchell, Director - Communities, Planning & Partnerships, Marmion House, Lichfield Street, Tamworth B79 7BZ ☎ 01827 709616 🖷 01827 709310 ✉ robert-mitchell@tamworth.gov.uk

Waste Collection and Disposal: Mr Andrew Barratt, Director - Assets & Environment, Marmion House, Lichfield Street, Tamworth B79 7BZ ☎ 01827 709453 🖷 01872 709271 ✉ andrew-barratt@tamworth.gov.uk

Waste Management: Mr Andrew Barratt, Director - Assets & Environment, Marmion House, Lichfield Street, Tamworth B79 7BZ ☎ 01827 709453 🖷 01872 709271 ✉ andrew-barratt@tamworth.gov.uk

MEMBERS OF THE COUNCIL (30)

***Mayor:* Clements**, Tina (CON - Wilnecote)
tina-clements@tamworth.gov.uk
***Deputy Mayor:* Garner**, John (CON - Amington)
john-garner@tamworth.gov.uk
***Leader of the Council:* Cool**, Daniel (CON - Trinity)
daniel-cook@tamworh.gov.uk
***Deputy Leader of the Council:* Pritchard**, Robert (CON - Spital)
robert-pritchard@tamworth.gov.uk
Bates, Lee (CON - Trinity)
lee-bates@tamworth.gov.uk
Beale, Brian (CON - Wilnecote)
micheal-greatorex@tamworth.gov.uk
Clarke, Margaret (LAB - Stonydelph)
margaret-clarke@tamworth.gov.uk
Claymore, Steven (CON - Castle)
steven-claymore@tamworth.gov.uk
Cooke, Chris (IND - Glascote)
pdg@eurothruth.fsnet.gov.uk
Couchman, Marion (LAB - Belgrave)
marion-couchman@tamworth.gov.uk
Doyle, Stephen (CON - Stonydelph)
stephen-doyle@tamworth.gov.uk
Faulkner, John (LAB - Bolehall)
john-faulkner@tamworth.gov.uk
Foster, David (LAB - Belgrave)
david-foster@tamworth.govuk
Gant, Maureen (CON - Spital)
maureen-gant@tamworth.gov.uk
Gant, Ken (CON - Spital)
kenneth-grant@tamworth.gov.uk
Greatorex, Michael (CON - Mercian)
michael-greatorex@tamworth.gov.uk
Hirons, Garry (LAB - Glascote)
garry-hirons@tamworth.gov.uk
James, Andrew (CON - Mercian)
andrew-james@tamworth.gov.uk
Kingstone, Richard (CON - Mercian)
Richard-Kingstone@tamworth.gov.uk
Lunn, Allan (CON - Castle)
allan-lunn@tamworth.gov.uk
McDermid, Richard (LAB - Belgrave)
richard-mcdermid@tamworth.gov.uk
McDermid, Matthew (LAB - Castle)
Matthew-McDermid@tamworth.gov.uk
Norchi, Ken (LAB - Bolehall)
kenneth-norchi@tamworth.gov.uk
Oates, Jeremy (CON - Trinity)
jeremy-oates@tamworth.gov.uk
Peaple, Simon (LAB - Glascote)
simon.peaple@tamworth.gov.uk
Pritchard, Steven (CON - Stonydelph)
steven-pritchard@tamworth.gov.uk
Rowe, Evelyn (CON - Amington)
evelyn-rowe@tamworth.gov.uk
Seekings, Peter (LAB - Bolehall)
peter-seekings@tamworth.gov.uk
Standen, Patrick (LAB - Wilnecote)
Patrick-Standen@tamworth.gov.uk
Thurgood, Michelle (CON - Amington)
michelle-thurgood@tamworth.gov.uk

POLITICAL COMPOSITION

CON: 18, LAB: 11, IND: 1

CABINET

Leader: Mr Daniel Cook
Deputy Leader / Corporate Services & Assets: Mr Robert Pritchard
Community Development: Mr Jeremy Oates
Environment & Waste Management: Mr Stephen Doyle
Economic Development & Enterprise: Mr Steven Claymore
Housing: Mr Michael Greatorex
Reputation & Engagement: Mr Lee Bates

COMMITTEE CHAIRS

Appointments & Staffing: Mr Daniel Cook
Audit & Governance: Mrs Maureen Gant
Licensing: Mr Brian Beale
Planning: Mrs Evelyn Rowe

TANDRIDGE D

Tandridge District Council, Council Offices, Station Road East, Oxted RH8 0BT ☎ 01883 722000 🖷 01883 722015 ✉ the.council@tandridge.gov.uk 🖳 www.tandridge.gov.uk

FACTS & FIGURES

Police Authority: Surrey Police Authority
Health Authority: South East Coast Strategic Health Authority
Learning and Skills Council: South East
EU Constituencies: South East
Election Frequency: Elections are by thirds
Twinning: Lingfield: Plaisance-du-Touch (France); Tatsfield: Vern d'Anjou (France)

PRINCIPAL OFFICERS

Chief Executive: Mr Stephen Weigel, Chief Executive, Council

Offices, Station Road East, Oxted RH8 0BT ☎ 01883 732999 🖷 01883 715004 ✉ sweigel@tandridge.gov.uk

Assistant Chief Executive: Mr Clive Moore, Assistant Chief Executive - Legal, Council Offices, Station Road East, Oxted RH8 0BT ☎ 01883 732740 🖷 01883 722015 ✉ cmoore@tandridge.gov.uk

Assistant Chief Executive: Mr Keith Price, Assistant Chief Executive, Council Offices, Station Road East, Oxted RH8 0BT ☎ 01883 732709 🖷 01883 723743 ✉ kprice@tandridge.gov.uk

Building Control: Mr Chris Ap Simon, Head of Building Control, Council Offices, Station Road East, Oxted RH8 0BT ☎ 01883 732872 🖷 01883 722015 ✉ capsimon@tandridge.gov.uk

Children / Youth Services: Mr Richard Woodward, Director of Community Services, Council Offices, Station Road East, Oxted RH8 0BT ☎ 01883 732800 🖷 01883 722015 ✉ rwoodward@tandridge.gov.uk

PR / Communications: Ms Giuseppina Valenza, Communications Manager, Council Offices, Station Road East, Oxted RH8 0BT ☎ 01883 732704 🖷 01883 723743 ✉ gvalenza@tandridge.gov.uk

Community Safety: Ms Hilary New, Community Safety Manager, Council Offices, Station Road East, Oxted RH8 0BT ☎ 01883 732703 🖷 01883 723743 ✉ hnew@tandridge.gov.uk

Computer Management: Mr Stuart Mitchenall, Head of Business Support Services, Council Offices, Station Road East, Oxted RH8 0BT ☎ 01883 732724 🖷 01883 722015 ✉ smitchenall@tandridge.gov.uk

Contracts: Mr Keith Masters, Contracts Manager - Refuse & Recycling, Council Offices, Station Road East, Oxted RH8 0BT ☎ 01883 732955 ✉ kmasters@tandridge.gov.uk

Customer Service: Ms Jane Hermanowski, Customer Service Team Leader, Council Offices, Station Road East, Oxted RH8 0BT ☎ 01883 732721 🖷 01883 722015 ✉ jhermanowski@tandridge.gov.uk

Direct Labour: Mr Denis Winter, Direct Works Manager, Council Offices, Station Road East, Oxted RH8 0BT ☎ 01883 732758 🖷 01883 714368

E-Government: Mr Stuart Mitchenall, Head of Business Support Services, Council Offices, Station Road East, Oxted RH8 0BT ☎ 01883 732724 🖷 01883 722015 ✉ smitchenall@tandridge.gov.uk

Electoral Registration: Ms Hazel Oakley, Electoral Services Manager, Council Offices, Station Road East, Oxted RH8 0BT ☎ 01883 732976 ✉ hoakley@tandridge.gov.uk

Emergency Planning: Mr Richard Woodward, Director of Community Services, Council Offices, Station Road East, Oxted RH8 0BT ☎ 01883 732800 🖷 01883 722015 ✉ rwoodward@tandridge.gov.uk

Environmental Health: Mr Paul Barton, Deputy Director of Community Services, Council Offices, Station Road East, Oxted RH8 0BT ☎ 01883 732840 🖷 01883 722015 ✉ pbarton@tandridge.gov.uk

Facilities: Ms Linda Barnett, Facilities Manager & Health & Safety Officer, Council Offices, Station Road East, Oxted RH8 0BT ☎ 01883 732899 ✉ lbarnett@tandridge.gov.uk

Finance and Treasurer: Mr Alistair Montgomery, Chief Finance Officer, Council Offices, Station Road East, Oxted RH8 0BT ☎ 01883 732902 🖷 01883 722015 ✉ amontgomery@tandridge.gov.uk

Health and Safety: Ms Linda Barnett, Facilities Manager & Health & Safety Officer, Council Offices, Station Road East, Oxted RH8 0BT ☎ 01883 732899 ✉ lbarnett@tandridge.gov.uk

Home Energy Conservation: Mr Clifford Darby, Private Sector Housing Manager, Council Offices, Station Road East, Oxted RH8 0BT ☎ 01883 732838 ✉ cdarby@tandridge.gov.uk

Housing: Mr Richard Woodward, Director of Community Services, Council Offices, Station Road East, Oxted RH8 0BT ☎ 01883 732800 🖷 01883 722015 ✉ rwoodward@tandridge.gov.uk

Housing Maintenance: Mr Stephen Blount, Technical Manager, Council Offices, Station Road East, Oxted RH8 0BT ☎ 01883 732830 🖷 01883 722015 ✉ sblount@tandridge.gov.uk

Legal: Mr Clive Moore, Assistant Chief Executive - Legal, Council Offices, Station Road East, Oxted RH8 0BT ☎ 01883 732740 🖷 01883 722015 ✉ cmoore@tandridge.gov.uk

Licensing: Mr Paul Barton, Deputy Director of Community Services, Council Offices, Station Road East, Oxted RH8 0BT ☎ 01883 732840 🖷 01883 722015 ✉ pbarton@tandridge.gov.uk

Lottery Funding, Charity and Voluntary: Mr Richard Woodward, Director of Community Services, Council Offices, Station Road East, Oxted RH8 0BT ☎ 01883 732800 🖷 01883 722015 ✉ rwoodward@tandridge.gov.uk

Member Services: Mr Vince Sharp, Committee Services Manager, Council Offices, Station Road East, Oxted RH8 0BT ☎ 01883 732776 ✉ vsharp@tandridge.gov.uk

Parking: Mr Richard Woodward, Director of Community Services, Council Offices, Station Road East, Oxted RH8 0BT ☎ 01883 732800 🖷 01883 722015 ✉ rwoodward@tandridge.gov.uk

Personnel / HR: Miss Seanne Giddy, Head of Personnel & Training Services, Council Offices, Station Road East, Oxted RH8 0BT ☎ 01883 732979 🖷 01883 722015 ✉ sgiddy@tandridge.gov.uk

Planning: Mr Piers Mason, Chief Planning Officer, Council Offices, Station Road East, Oxted RH8 0BT ☎ 01883 732893 ✉ pmason@tandridge.gov.uk

Planning: Mr Paul Newdick, Head of Planning Policy, Council Offices, Station Road East, Oxted RH8 0BT ☎ 01883 732860

pnewdick@tandridge.gov.uk

Procurement: Mr Alistair Montgomery, Chief Finance Officer, Council Offices, Station Road East, Oxted RH8 0BT ☎ 01883 732902 📠 01883 722015 amontgomery@tandridge.gov.uk

Recycling & Waste Minimisation: Mr Paul Barton, Deputy Director of Community Services, Council Offices, Station Road East, Oxted RH8 0BT ☎ 01883 732840 📠 01883 722015 pbarton@tandridge.gov.uk

Staff Training: Miss Seanne Giddy, Head of Personnel & Training Services, Council Offices, Station Road East, Oxted RH8 0BT ☎ 01883 732979 📠 01883 722015 sgiddy@tandridge.gov.uk

Street Scene: Mr Paul Barton, Deputy Director of Community Services, Council Offices, Station Road East, Oxted RH8 0BT ☎ 01883 732840 📠 01883 722015 pbarton@tandridge.gov.uk

Sustainable Development: Mr Matt Chapman, Planning Policy Officer, Council Offices, Station Road East, Oxted RH8 0BT ☎ 01883 732764 📠 01883 722015 mchapman@tandridge.gov.uk

Transport: Mr John Phillips, Transport & Policy Officer, Council Offices, Station Road East, Oxted RH8 0BT ☎ 01883 732867 📠 01883 722015 jphillips@tandridge.gov.uk

Transport Planner: Mr John Phillips, Transport & Policy Officer, Council Offices, Station Road East, Oxted RH8 0BT ☎ 01883 732867 📠 01883 722015 jphillips@tandridge.gov.uk

Waste Collection and Disposal: Mr Paul Barton, Deputy Director of Community Services, Council Offices, Station Road East, Oxted RH8 0BT ☎ 01883 732840 📠 01883 722015 pbarton@tandridge.gov.uk

Waste Management: Mr Paul Barton, Deputy Director of Community Services, Council Offices, Station Road East, Oxted RH8 0BT ☎ 01883 732840 📠 01883 722015 pbarton@tandridge.gov.uk

Children's Play Areas: Mr Richard Woodward, Director of Community Services, Council Offices, Station Road East, Oxted RH8 0BT ☎ 01883 732800 📠 01883 722015 rwoodward@tandridge.gov.uk

MEMBERS OF THE COUNCIL (45)

Chair: **Bradbury**, Sakina (CON - Whyteleafe)
cllr.sakina.bradbury@tandridgedc.gov.uk
Leader of the Council: **Keymer**, Gordon (CON - Oxted North and Tandridge)
cllr.gordon.keymer@tandridgedc.gov.uk
Ainsworth, Simon (CON - Oxted South)
cllr.simon.ainsworth@tandridgedc.gov.uk
Bangs, Lisa (IND - Lingfield and Crowhurst)
cllr.lisa.bangs@tandridgedc.gov.uk
Black, Gill (CON - Bletchingley and Nutfield)
cllr.gill.black@tandridgedc.gov.uk
Bond, Peter (CON - Burstow, Horne and Outwood)
cllr.peter.bond@tandridgedc.gov.uk
Botten, Chris (LD - Portley)
cllr.chris.botten@tandridgedc.gov.uk
Butcher, Richard (CON - Woldingham)
cllr.richard.butcher@tandridgedc.gov.uk
Camden, Chris (CON - Warlingham East and Chelsham and Farleigh)
cllr.chris.camden@tandridgedc.gov.uk
Cannon, Patrick (CON - Chaldon)
cllr.patrick.cannon@tandridgedc.gov.uk
Caudle, Alexandra (LD - Valley)
cllr.jill.caudle@tandridgedc.gov.uk
Childs, Nick (CON - Godstone)
cllr.nick.childs@tandridgedc.gov.uk
Compton, Barry (CON - Oxted South)
cllr.barry.compton@tandridgedc.gov.uk
Compton, Barry (CON - Warlingham West)
cllr.glynis.whittle@tandridgedc.gov.uk
Connolly, Beverley (CON - Harestone)
cllr.beverley.connolly@tandridgedc.gov.uk
Cooley, David (CON - Warlingham West)
cllr.david.cooley@tandridgedc.gov.uk
Cooper, Michael (CON - Harestone)
cllr.michael.cooper@tandridgedc.gov.uk
David, Robert (IND - Bletchingley)
cllr.robert.david@tandridgedc.gov.uk
Dempsey, Tom (CON - Whyteleafe)
cllr.tom.dempsey@tandridgedc.gov.uk
Duck, Geoffrey (CON - Queens Park)
cllr.geoffrey.duck@tandridgedc.gov.uk
Dunbar, Lindsey (CON - Limpsfield)
cllr.lindsey.dunbar@tandridgedc.gov.uk
Elias, Tony (CON - Bletchingley and Nutfield)
cllr.tony.elias@tandridgedc.gov.uk
Fisher, Martin (CON - Oxted North and Tandridge)
cllr.martin.fisher@tandridgedc.gov.uk
Gascoigne, Jules (CON - Godstone)
cllr.jules.gascoigne@tandridgedc.gov.uk
Gosling, David (LD - Westway)
cllr.david.gosling@tandridgedc.gov.uk
Harwood, Ken (CON - Felbridge)
cllr.ken.harwood@tandridgedc.gov.uk
Ingham, Jane (CON - Valley)
cllr.jane.ingham@tandridgedc.gov.uk
Jones, Alan (CON - Burstoe, Horne and Outwood)
cllr.alan.jones@tandridgedc.gov.uk
Keenan, Michael (CON - Burstow, Horne and Outwood)
cllr.michael.keenan@tandridgedc.gov.uk
Lee, David (LD - Whyteleafe)
cllr.david.lee@tandridgedc.gov.uk
Marks, Sally (CON - Woldingham)
cllr.sally.marks@tandridgedc.gov.uk
Morrow, Simon (LD - Warlingham East, Chelsham and Farleigh)
cllr.simon.morrow@tandridgedc.gov.uk
Pannett, John (CON - Limpsfield)
cllr.john.pannett@tandridgedc.gov.uk
Parker, Elizabeth (CON - Oxted South)
cllr.elizabeth.parker@tandridgedc.gov.uk
Perkins, Brian (CON - Lingfield and Crowhurst)
cllr.brian.perkins@tandridgedc.gov.uk
Pursehouse, Jeremy (LD - Warlingham East & Chelsham & Farleigh)
cllr.j.pursehouse@tandridgedc.gov.uk
Stead, Rod (CON - Queens Park)
cllr.rod.stead@tandridgedc.gov.uk
Steeds, Lesley (CON - Dormansland & Felcourt)
cllr.lesley.steeds@tandridgedc.gov.uk

Sydney, Michael (CON - Dormansland and Felcourt)
cllr.michael.sydney@tandridgedc.gov.uk
Thorn, Rosemary (CON - Godstone)
cllr.rosemary.thorn@tandridgedc.gov.uk
Turner, Hilary (LD - Portley)
cllr.hilary.turner@tandridgedc.gov.uk
Vickers, Debbie (CON - Bletchingley & Nutfield)
cllr.debbie.vickers@tandridgedc.gov.uk
Wall, Mike (CON - Warlingham East & Chelsham & Farleigh)
cllr.mike.wall@tandridgedc.gov.uk
Webster, Eithne (CON - Westway)
cllr.eithne.webster@tandridgedc.gov.uk
Weightman, David (CON - Oxted North and Tandridge)
cllr.david.weightman@tandridgedc.gov.uk

POLITICAL COMPOSITION
CON: 36, LD: 7, IND: 2

CABINET
Leader: Mr Gordon Keymer

COMMITTEE CHAIRS
Community Services: Mr Tony Elias
Housing: Mrs Elizabeth Parker
Licensing: Ms Rosemary Thorn
Overview & Scrutiny: Mr Barry Compton
Planning Policy: Mr David Weightman
Planning: Mrs Gill Black
Resources: Mr Martin Fisher

TAUNTON DEANE D

Taunton Deane Borough Council, The Deane House, Belvedere Road, Taunton TA1 1HE ☎ 01823 356356 🖷 01823 356329
enquiries@tauntondeane.gov.uk www.tauntondeane.gov.uk

FACTS & FIGURES
Police Authority: Avon & Somerset Police Authority
Health Authority: NHS South West
Learning and Skills Council: South West
Parliamentary Constituencies: Taunton Deane
EU Constituencies: South West
Election Frequency: Elections are of whole council
Twinning: Lisieux (France); Taunton (USA); Königslutter (Germany); Milverton: Longny-au-Perche (France); North Curry: Les Sept Villages du Vexin (France); Wellington: Lillebonne (France); Immenstadt (Germany); Wiveliscombe: Le Lion D'Angers (France

PRINCIPAL OFFICERS
Chief Executive: Mrs Penny James, Chief Executive, The Deane House, Belvedere Road, Taunton TA1 1HE ☎ 01823 356356 🖷 01823 356329 p.james@tauntondeane.gov.uk

Access Officer / Social Services (Disability): Mr Edwin Norton, Principal Building Control Surveyor & Access Officer, The Deane House, Belvedere Road, Taunton TA1 1HE ☎ 01823 356476 🖷 01823 356478 e.norton@tauntondeane.gov.uk

Architect, Building / Property Services: Mr Adrian Priest, Assets Holding Manager, The Deane House, Belvedere Road, Taunton TA1 1HE ☎ 01823 356509 🖷 01823 356526 a.priest@tauntondeane.gov.uk

Building Control: Mr Darren Rowbottom, Building Control Manager, The Deane House, Belvedere Road, Taunton TA1 1HE ☎ 01823 356473 🖷 01823 356478 d.rowbottom@tauntondeane.gov.uk

PR / Communications: Mrs Debbie Rundle, Media & PR Officer, The Deane House, Belvedere Road, Taunton TA1 1HE ☎ 01823 356407 🖷 01823 356329 d.rundle@tauntondeane.gov.uk

Community Planning: Mr Tim Burton, Growth & Development Manager, The Deane House, Belvedere Road, Taunton TA1 1HE ☎ 01823 358403 🖷 01823 356329 t.burton@tauntondeane.gov.uk

Community Safety: Mr Scott Weetch, Community Development Lead, The Deane House, Belvedere Road, Taunton TA1 1HE ☎ 01823 356317 🖷 01823 356329 s.weetch@tauntondeane.gov.uk

Computer Management: Ms Fiona Kirkham, Information Systems Manager, The Deane House, Belvedere Road, Taunton TA1 1HE ☎ 01823 356396 🖷 01823 356329 f.kirkham@tauntondeane.gov.uk

Customer Service: Ms Claire Bramley, Head of Customer Contact, The Deane House, Belvedere Road, Taunton TA1 1HE ☎ 01823 356356 🖷 01823 356429 c.bramley@tauntondeane.gov.uk

Direct Labour: Mr Brendon Cleere, Strategic Director - Operations, The Deane House, Belvedere Road, Taunton TA1 1HE ☎ 01823 356406 🖷 01823 356329 b.cleere@tauntondeane.gov.uk

Economic Development: Mr David Evans, Economic Development Manager, The Deane House, Belvedere Road, Taunton TA1 1HE ☎ 01823 356534 🖷 01823 356545 d.evans@tauntondeane.gov.uk

E-Government: Mrs Tonya Meers, Legal & Democratic Services Manager, The Deane House, Belvedere Road, Taunton TA1 1HE ☎ 01823 356403 🖷 01823 356329 t.meers@tauntondeane.gov.uk

Electoral Registration: Mr Craig Morse, Electoral Services Officer, The Deane House, Belvedere Road, Taunton TA1 1HE ☎ 01823 356316 🖷 01823 356303 c.morse@tauntondeane.gov.uk

Emergency Planning: Mr John Lewis, Parking & Civil Contingencies Manager, The Deane House, Belvedere Road, Taunton TA1 1HE ☎ 01823 356501 🖷 01823 356329 j.lewis@tauntondeane.gov.uk

Energy Management: Mr Torsten Daniel, Strategy Officer - Climate Change, The Deane House, Belvedere Road, Taunton TA1 1HE ☎ 01823 356592 t.daniels@tauntondeane.gov.uk

Estates, Property & Valuation: Mr Adrian Priest, Assets Holding Manager, The Deane House, Belvedere Road, Taunton TA1 1HE

☎ 01823 356509 🖷 01823 356526
✉ a.priest@tauntondeane.gov.uk

Facilities: Ms Angela Hill, Facilities & Corporate Administration Manager, The Deane House, Belvedere Road, Taunton TA1 1HE ☎ 01823 356597 ✉ a.hill@tauntondeane.gov.uk

Finance and Treasurer: Ms Shirlene Adam, Strategic Manager & S151 Officer / Deputy Chief Executive, The Deane House, Belvedere Road, Taunton TA1 1HE ☎ 01823 356310
✉ s.adam@tauntondeane.gov.uk

Grounds Maintenance: Mr Chris Hall, Depot Manager, Priory Depot, Priory Way, Taunton TA7 2BB ☎ 01823 356370
✉ c.hall@tauntondeane.gov.uk

Health and Safety: Mr David Woodbury, Health & Safety Advisor, The Deane House, Belvedere Road, Taunton TA1 1HE ☎ 01823 356578 ✉ d.woodbury@tauntondeane.gov.uk

Home Energy Conservation: Ms Barbara Wells, Energy Efficiency Officer, Sedgemoor Council, Bridgwater House, King's Square, Bridgwater TA6 3AR ☎ 01278 436426
✉ b.wells@sedgemoor.gov.uk

Housing: Mr S Boland, Housing Services Lead, The Deane House, Belvedere Road, Taunton TA1 1HE ☎ 01823 356332 🖷 01823 356446 ✉ s.boland@tauntondeane.gov.uk

Housing Maintenance: Mr Phil Webb, Housing Manager, The Deane House, Belvedere Road, Taunton TA1 1HE
☎ 01823 356505 ✉ p.webb@tauntondeane.gov.uk

Legal: Mrs Tonya Meers, Legal & Democratic Services Manager, The Deane House, Belvedere Road, Taunton TA1 1HE ☎ 01823 356403 🖷 01823 356329 ✉ t.meers@tauntondeane.gov.uk

Licensing: Mr Ian Carter, Licensing Manager, The Deane House, Belvedere Road, Taunton TA1 1HE ☎ 01823 356343
✉ i.carter@tauntondeane.gov.uk

Member Services: Mrs Tonya Meers, Legal & Democratic Services Manager, The Deane House, Belvedere Road, Taunton TA1 1HE ☎ 01823 356403 🖷 01823 356329
✉ t.meers@tauntondeane.gov.uk

Parking: Mr Jon Pallett, Parking Services Manager, The Deane House, Belvedere Road, Taunton TA1 1HE ☎ 01823 356508 🖷 01823 356329 ✉ j.pallett@tauntondeane.gov.uk

Personnel / HR: Ms Fiona Wills, Human Resources Manager, The Deane House, Belvedere Road, Taunton TA1 1HE ☎ 01823 356450 🖷 01823 356329 ✉ f.wills@tauntondeane.gov.uk

Planning: Mr Tim Burton, Growth & Development Manager, The Deane House, Belvedere Road, Taunton TA1 1HE ☎ 01823 358403 🖷 01823 356329 ✉ t.burton@tauntondeane.gov.uk

Procurement: Mr Jon Batstone, Procurement Officer, The Deane House, Belvedere Road, Taunton TA1 1HE ☎ 01823 358286
✉ j.batstone@tauntondeane.gov.uk

Sustainable Communities: Mr Mark Leeman, Strategy Lead, The Deane House, Belvedere Road, Taunton TA1 1HE ☎ 01823 356350 🖷 01823 356411 ✉ m.leeman@tauntondeane.gov.uk

Town Centre: Mr Graham Love, Town Centre Manager, The Deane House, Belvedere Road, Taunton TA1 1HE ☎ 01823 354299 ✉ info@tauntontowncentre.co.uk

MEMBERS OF THE COUNCIL (56)

Leader of the Council: **Williams**, John (CON - Neroche)
cllr.j.williams@tauntondeane.gov.uk
Adkins, Jean (CON - Norton Fitzwarren)
cllr.j.adkins@tauntondeane.gov.uk
Allgrove, Jean (CON - Manor and Wilton)
cllr.j.allgrove@tauntondeane.gov.uk
Baker, Justine (LD - Bishops Hull)
cllr.j.baker@tauntondeane.gov.uk
Beaven, Anthony (CON - Bishops Lydeard)
cllr.a.beaven@tauntondeane.gov.uk
Bishop, Clifford (CON - Bradford on Tone)
cllr.c.bishop@tauntondeane.gov.uk
Bowrah, Robert (CON - Wellington, Rockwell Green and West)
cllr.r.bowrah@tauntondeane.gov.uk
Brooks, Steve (LD - Halcon)
cllr.s.brooks@tauntondeane.gov.uk
Cavill, Norman (CON - West Monkton)
cllr.n.cavill@tauntondeane.gov.uk
Coles, Simon (LD - Eastgate)
cllr.s.coles@tauntondeane.gov.uk
Denington, Bryan (CON - Killams and Mountfield)
cllr.b.denington@tauntondeane.gov.uk
Durdan, David (CON - Ruishton & Creech)
cllr.d.durdan@tauntondeane.gov.uk
Durdan, Kelly (CON - Ruishton & Creech)
cllr.k.durdan@tauntondeane.gov.uk
Edwards, Mark (CON - Trull)
cllr.m.edwards@tauntondeane.gov.uk
Farbahi, Habib (LD - Comeytrowe)
cllr.h.farbahi@tauntondeane.gov.uk
Floyd, Mollie (LD - Comeytrowe)
cllr.m.floyd@tauntondeane.gov.uk
Gaines, Edward (IND - Wiveliscombe and West Deane)
cllr.e.gaines@tauntondeane.gov.uk
Govier, Andrew (LAB - Wellington North)
cllr.a.govier@tauntondeane.gov.uk
Govier, Jackie (LAB - Wellington North)
cllr.j.govier@tauntondeane.gov.uk
Hall, Terence (CON - Manor and Wilton)
cllr.t.hall@tauntondeane.gov.uk
Hayward, Kenneth (CON - Norton Fitzwarren)
cllr.k.hayward@tauntondeane.gov.uk
Henley, Ross (LD - Wellington East)
cllr.r.henley@tauntondeane.gov.uk
Herbert, Catherine (CON - Killams and Mountfield)
cllr.c.herbert@tauntondeane.gov.uk
Hill, Chris (CON - Monument)
cllr.c.hill@tauntondeane.gov.uk
Hill, Marcia (LD - Pyrland and Rowbarton)
cllr.m.hill@tauntondeane.gov.uk
Horsley, Jefferson (LD - Fairwater)
cllr.j.horsley@tauntondeane.gov.uk
Hunt, James (CON - Wellington East)
cllr.j.hunt@tauntondeane.gov.uk
James, Louise (LD - Pyrland and Rowbarton)

cllr.l.james@tauntondeane.gov.uk
Lees, Sue (LD - Fairwater)
cllr.s.lees@tauntondeane.gov.uk
Lees, Richard (LD - Eastgate)
cllr.r.lees@tauntondeane.gov.uk
Lisgo, Libby (LAB - Lyngford)
cllr.l.lisgo@tauntondeane.gov.uk
Meikle, John (CON - Manor and Wilton)
cllr.j.meikle@tauntondeane.gov.uk
Messenger, Nicci (LD - Lyngford)
cllr.n.messenger@tauntondeane.gov.uk
Morrell, Ian (IND - Bishops Hull)
cllr.i.morrell@tauntondeane.gov.uk
Mullins, Melvyn (LD - Halcon)
cllr.m.mullins@tauntondeane.gov.uk
Nottrodt, Bruce (CON - Staplegrove)
cllr.b.nottrodt@tauntondeane.gov.uk
Palmer, Umi (CON - West Monkton)
cllr.u.palmer@tauntondeane.gov.uk
Priory-Sankey, Hazel (LD - Blackbrook and Holway)
cllr.h.prior-sankey@tauntondeane.gov.uk
Reed, David (CON - Blackdown)
cllr.d.reed@tauntondeane.gov.uk
Reed, Janet (CON - Wellington, Rockwell Green and West)
cllr.j.reed@tauntondeane.gov.uk
Ross, Steve (IND - Wiveliscombs and West Deane)
cllr.s.ross@tauntondeane.gov.uk
Slattery, Gill (LD - North Curry & Stoke St Gregory)
cllr.g.slattery@tauntondeane.gov.uk
Slattery, Timothy (LD - Halcon)
cllr.t.slattery@tauntondeane.gov.uk
Smith, Peter (LD - Blackbrook and Holway)
cllr.p.smith@tauntondeane.gov.uk
Smith, Francesca (LD - Blackbrook and Holway)
cllr.f.smith@tauntondeane.gov.uk
Stock-Williams, Vivienne (IND - Wellington, Rockwell Green and West)
cllr.v.stock-williams@tauntondeane.gov.uk
Stone, Philip (LD - North Curry & Stoke St Gregory)
cllr.p.stone@tauntondeane.gov.uk
Swaine, Ben (LD - Lyngford)
cllr.b.swaine@tauntondeane.gov.uk
Tooze, Paul (LD - Pyrland and Rowbarton)
cllr.p.tooze@tauntondeane.gov.uk
Warmington, Jane (CON - Bishops Lydeard)
cllr.j.warmington@tauntondeane.gov.uk
Watson, Peter (CON - Bishops Lydeard)
cllr.p.watson@tauntondeane.gov.uk
Waymouth, Elaine (CON - Staplegrove)
cllr.e.waymouth@tauntondeane.gov.uk
Webber, Denise (CON - West Monkton)
cllr.d.webber@tauntondeane.gov.uk
Wedderkopp, Danny (LD - Fairwater)
cllr.d.wedderkopp@tauntondeane.gov.uk
Wedderkopp, Alan (LD - Comeytrowe)
cllr.a.wedderkopp@tauntondeane.gov.uk
Wren, Gwilyn (CON - Milverton and North Deane)
cllr.g.wren@tauntondeane.gov.uk

POLITICAL COMPOSITION

CON: 26, LD: 23, IND: 4, LAB: 3

CABINET

Leader: Mr John Williams
Community Leadership: Ms Jane Warmington
Corporate Resources: Mrs Vivienne Stock-Williams
Economic Development, Asset Management, Arts & Tourism: Mr Norman Cavill
Environmental Services: Mr Kenneth Hayward
Housing Services: Mrs Jean Adkins
Planning & Transportation / Communications: Mr Mark Edwards
Sports, Parks & Leisure: Ms Catherine Herbert

COMMITTEE CHAIRS

Community (Scrutiny): Ms Hazel Priory-Sankey
Corporate Governance: Mr Bryan Denington
Corporate Scrutiny: Mr Ross Henley
Planning: Mr Bruce Nottrodt

TEIGNBRIDGE D

Teignbridge District Council, Forde House, Brunel Road, Newton Abbot TQ12 4XX ☏ 01626 361101 ✉ info@teignbridge.gov.uk
🖳 www.teignbridge.gov.uk

FACTS & FIGURES

Police Authority: Devon & Cornwall Police Authority
Health Authority: NHS South West
Learning and Skills Council: South West
EU Constituencies: South West
Election Frequency: Elections are of whole council
Twinning: Abbotskerswell: Le Pre D-Auge (France); Les Monceaux (France); Ashburton: Ashburton (New Zealand); Cleder (France); Bishopsteignton: La Roche Maurice (France); Bovey Tracey: Le Molay-Littry (France); Bridford: St. Vaast-sur-Seulles (France); Combeinteignhead: Osmanville (France); Chudleigh: Troarn (France); Dawlish: Carhaix-Plouguer (France); Exminster: Sannerville (France); Ide: Canteloup-Cleville (France); Ilsington: Brasparts (France); Ipplepen: Soliers (France); Kenton: St. Lambert Du Latley

PRINCIPAL OFFICERS

Chief Executive: Ms Nicola Bulbeck, Chief Executive, Forde House, Brunel Road, Newton Abbot TQ12 4XX ☏ 01626 361101 🖷 01626 215169 ✉ nicola.bulbeck@teignbridge.gov.uk

Deputy Chief Executive: Mr Phil Shears, Deputy Chief Executive, Forde House, Brunel Road, Newton Abbot TQ12 4XX ☏ 01626 361101 🖷 01626 215169 ✉ phil.shears@teignbridge.gov.uk

Senior Management: Mr Simon Barnes, Director, Forde House, Brunel Road, Newton Abbot TQ12 4XX ☏ 01626 215117 🖷 01626 215169 ✉ simon.barnes@teignbridge.gov.uk

Senior Management: Mr John Cocker, Director, Forde House, Brunel Road, Newton Abbot TQ12 4XX ☏ 01262 215800 🖷 01626 215169 ✉ john.cocker@teignbridge.gov.uk

Architect, Building / Property Services: Mr Neil Baglow, Service Manager - Property & Design, Forde House, Brunel Road, Newton Abbot TQ12 4XX ☏ 01626 215830 🖷 01626 215483 ✉ neil.baglow@teignbridge.gov.uk

Best Value: Ms Adrienne Steatham, Service Lead - Customer

Excellence and Improvement, Forde House, Brunel Road, Newton Abbot TQ12 4XX ☎ 01626 215200 🖷 01626 215169 ✉ adrienne.steatham@teignbridge.gov.uk

Building Control: Mr Andy Carpenter, Head of Building Control Partnership, Forde House, Brunel Road, Newton Abbot TQ12 4XX ☎ 01626 215721 🖷 01626 215761 ✉ andrew.carpenter@teignbridge.gov.uk

PR / Communications: Mr Tim Borrett, Communications Officer, Forde House, Brunel Road, Newton Abbot TQ12 4XX ☎ 01626 215135 🖷 01626 215169 ✉ tim.borrett@teignbridge.gov.uk

Community Planning: Ms Adrienne Steatham, Service Lead - Customer Excellence & Improvement, Forde House, Brunel Road, Newton Abbot TQ12 4XX ☎ 01626 215200 🖷 01626 215169 ✉ adrienne.steatham@teignbridge.gov.uk

Community Safety: Mr Ben Hosford, Service Lead - Environment & Safety, Forde House, Brunel Road, Newton Abbot TQ12 4XX ☎ 01626 215400 🖷 01626 215436 ✉ ben.hosford@teignbridge.gov.uk

Computer Management: Mr Julian Niles, Service Manager - Information & Communication Technology, Forde House, Brunel Road, Newton Abbot TQ12 4XX ☎ 01626 215209 🖷 01626 215538

Contracts: Mr John Cocker, Director, Forde House, Brunel Road, Newton Abbot TQ12 4XX ☎ 01262 215800 🖷 01626 215169 ✉ john.cocker@teignbridge.gov.uk

Customer Service: Ms Adrienne Steatham, Service Lead - Customer Excellence & Improvement, Forde House, Brunel Road, Newton Abbot TQ12 4XX ☎ 01626 215200 🖷 01626 215169 ✉ adrienne.steatham@teignbridge.gov.uk

Economic Development: Mrs Allie Clark, Economic Development Officer, Forde House, Brunel Road, Newton Abbot TQ12 4XX ☎ 01626 215478 🖷 01626 215483 ✉ allie.clark@teignbridge.gov.uk

Electoral Registration: Mrs Cathy Ruelens, Electoral Services Co-ordinator, Forde House, Brunel Road, Newton Abbot TQ12 4XX ☎ 01626 215103 🖷 01626 215169 ✉ cathy.ruelens@teignbridge.gov.uk

Emergency Planning: Mr Ian Flood Page, Emergency Planning Officer, Forde House, Brunel Road, Newton Abbot TQ12 4XX ☎ 01626 361101 🖷 01626 215857 ✉ iflood@teignbridge.gov.uk

Energy Management: Mr John Cocker, Director, Forde House, Brunel Road, Newton Abbot TQ12 4XX ☎ 01262 215800 🖷 01626 215169 ✉ john.cocker@teignbridge.gov.uk

Energy Management: Mr Ben Hosford, Service Lead - Environment & Safety, Forde House, Brunel Road, Newton Abbot TQ12 4XX ☎ 01626 215400 🖷 01626 215436 ✉ ben.hosford@teignbridge.gov.uk

Environmental Health: Mr Ben Hosford, Service Lead - Environment & Safety, Forde House, Brunel Road, Newton Abbot TQ12 4XX ☎ 01626 215400 🖷 01626 215436 ✉ ben.hosford@teignbridge.gov.uk

Estates, Property & Valuation: Mr Neil Baglow, Service Manager - Property & Design, Forde House, Brunel Road, Newton Abbot TQ12 4XX ☎ 01626 215830 🖷 01626 215483 ✉ neil.baglow@teignbridge.gov.uk

European Liaison: Mrs Allie Clark, Economic Development Officer, Forde House, Brunel Road, Newton Abbot TQ12 4XX ☎ 01626 215478 🖷 01626 215483 ✉ allie.clark@teignbridge.gov.uk

Facilities: Mr Neil Baglow, Service Manager - Property & Design, Forde House, Brunel Road, Newton Abbot TQ12 4XX ☎ 01626 215830 🖷 01626 215483 ✉ neil.baglow@teignbridge.gov.uk

Finance and Treasurer: Mrs Lesley Tucker, Service Lead - Financial Services (Section 151 Officer), Forde House, Brunel Road, Newton Abbot TQ12 4XX ☎ 01626 215203 🖷 01626 215169 ✉ lesley.tucker@teignbridge.gov.uk

Grounds Maintenance: Ms Lorraine Montgomery, Service Manager - Green Spaces & Active Leisure, Forde House, Brunel Road, Newton Abbot TQ12 4XX ☎ 01626 215852 🖷 01626 215613

Health and Safety: Mr Peter Wilson, Health & Safety Officer, Forde House, Brunel Road, Newton Abbot TQ12 4XX ☎ 01626 215155 🖷 01626 215436 ✉ peter.wilson@teignbridge.gov.uk

Home Energy Conservation: Ms Zoe Farmer, Affordable Warmth & Home Energy Officer, Forde House, Brunel Road, Newton Abbot TQ12 4XX ☎ 01626 215764 🖷 01626 215316

Home Energy Conservation: Mr Ben Hosford, Service Lead - Environment & Safety, Forde House, Brunel Road, Newton Abbot TQ12 4XX ☎ 01626 215400 🖷 01626 215436 ✉ ben.hosford@teignbridge.gov.uk

Housing: Ms Amanda Downie, Service Lead for Housing, Forde House, Newton Abbot TQ12 4XX ☎ 01626 215301 🖷 01626 215316 ✉ amanda.downie@teignbridge.gov.uk

Legal: Mrs Sue Aggett, Service Lead - Legal & Democratic Services, Forde House, Brunel Road, Newton Abbot TQ12 4XX ☎ 01626 215163 🖷 01626 215169 ✉ saggett@teignbridge.gov.uk

Leisure and Cultural Services: Mrs Tracey Higgs, Service Manager - Leisure Facilities & Resorts, Forde House, Brunel Road, Newton Abbot TQ12 4XX ☎ 01626 215601 🖷 01626 215613

Leisure and Cultural Services: Ms Adrienne Steatham, Service Lead - Customer Excellence & Improvement, Forde House, Brunel Road, Newton Abbot TQ12 4XX ☎ 01626 215200 🖷 01626 215169 ✉ adrienne.steatham@teignbridge.gov.uk

Licensing: Mrs Andrea Furness, Licensing Officer, Forde House, Brunel Road, Newton Abbot TQ12 4XX ☎ 01626 215108 🖷 01626 215169 ✉ afurness@teignbridge.gov.uk

Member Services: Mr Neil Aggett, Democratic Services Manager, Forde House, Brunel Road, Newton Abbot TQ12 4XX ☎ 01626 215113 🖷 01626 215169 ✉ naggett@teignbridge.gov.uk

LOCAL AUTHORITIES

Parking: Miss Sue Edwards, Service Lead - Environment & Safety, Forde House, Brunel Road, Newton Abbot TQ12 4XX ☎ 01626 215870 🖷 01626 215807 ✉ sue.edwards@teignbridge.gov.uk

Partnerships: Ms Adrienne Steatham, Service Lead - Customer Excellence and Improvement, Forde House, Brunel Road, Newton Abbot TQ12 4XX ☎ 01626 215200 🖷 01626 215169 ✉ adrienne.steatham@teignbridge.gov.uk

Personnel / HR: Mr Steve Penford, Service Manager - Human Resources, Forde House, Brunel Road, Newton Abbot TQ12 4XX ☎ 01626 215162 🖷 01626 215191

Planning: Mr Nick Davies, Service Manager - Development Manager, Forde House, Brunel Road, Newton Abbot TQ12 4XX ☎ 01626 215745 🖷 01626 215770 ✉ nick.davies@teignbridge.gov.uk

Procurement: Ms Melanie Staton, Corporate Procurement Officer, Forde House, Brunel Road, Newton Abbot TQ12 4XX ☎ 01626 215472 🖷 01626 215169 ✉ mel.staton@teignbridge.gov.uk

Recycling & Waste Minimisation: Mr Chris Braines, Waste Management Officer, Forde House, Brunel Road, Newton Abbot TQ12 4XX ☎ 01626 215841 🖷 01626 334882 ✉ cbraines@teignbridge.gov.uk

Staff Training: Mrs Debbie Hutchings, Training & Development Manager, Forde House, Brunel Road, Newton Abbot TQ12 4XX ☎ 01626 215138 🖷 01626 215191

Sustainable Communities: Ms Adrienne Steatham, Service Lead - Customer Excellence and Improvement, Forde House, Brunel Road, Newton Abbot TQ12 4XX ☎ 01626 215200 🖷 01626 215169 ✉ adrienne.steatham@teignbridge.gov.uk

Tourism: Mrs Michelle Taylor, Tourism & Marketing Officer, Forde House, Brunel Road, Newton Abbot TQ12 4XX ☎ 01626 215614 ✉ michelle.taylor@teignbridge.gov.uk

Town Centre: Mr Tony Watson, Service Manager for Economy and Regeneration, Forde House, Brunel Road, Newton Abbot TQ12 4XX ☎ 01626 215828 🖷 01626 215483 ✉ tony.watson@teignbridge.gov.uk

Waste Collection and Disposal: Mr Chris Braines, Waste Management Officer, Forde House, Brunel Road, Newton Abbot TQ12 4XX ☎ 01626 215841 🖷 01626 334882 ✉ cbraines@teignbridge.gov.uk

Waste Management: Mr Chris Braines, Waste Management Officer, Forde House, Brunel Road, Newton Abbot TQ12 4XX ☎ 01626 215841 🖷 01626 334882 ✉ cbraines@teignbridge.gov.uk

MEMBERS OF THE COUNCIL (46)

***Chair:* Clarance**, Chris (CON - Shaldon and Stokeinteignhead)
Christopher.Clarence@teignbridge.gov.uk

***Vice-Chair:* Bromell**, Peter (IND - Teignbridge North)
Peter.Bromell@teignbridge.gov.uk

***Leader of the Council:* Christophers**, Jeremy (CON - Haytor)
Jeremy.Christophers@teignbridge.gov.uk

***Deputy Leader of the Council:* Barker**, Stuart (CON - Ashburton and Buckfastleigh)
stuart.barker@teignbridge.gov.uk

Austen, Beryl (IND - Kingsteignton East)
beryl.austen@teignbridge.gov.uk

Ballinger, Anthony (CON - Kerswell with Combe)
anthony.ballimger@teignbridge.gov.uk

Brodie, Jackie (LD - Bushell)
jackie.brodie@teignbridge.gov.uk

Bunday, Carol (LD - College)
Carol.Bunday@teignbridge.gov.uk

Clemens, Humphrey (CON - Dawlish South West)
Humphrey.Clemens@teignbridge.gov.uk

Colclough, Mary (IND - Ambrook)
Mary.Colclough@teignbridge.gov.uk

Connett, Alan (LD - Kenton with Starcross)
Alan.Connett@teignbridge.gov.uk

Corney-Walker, David (LD - Buckland and Milber)
David.Corney-walker@teignbridge.gov.uk

Cox, David (LD - Teignmouth West)
David.Cox@teignbridge.gov.uk

Dennis, Charlie (CON - Ashburton and Buckfastleigh)
charlie.dennis@teignbridge.gov.uk

Dewhurst, Alistair (LD - Ipplepen)
alistair.dewhirst@teignbridge.gov.uk

Evans, Lorraine (CON - Chudleigh)
Lorraine.Evans@teignbridge.gov.uk

Falcao, Terry (LD - Teignmouth Central)
Terry.Falcao@teignbridge.gov.uk

Fry, Anne (LD - Bradley)
Anne.Fry@teignbridge.gov.uk

Fusco, Vince (CON - Teignmouth East)
vince.fusco@teignbridge.gov.uk

Goodey, John (CON - Kenn Valley)
john.goodey@teignbridge.gov.uk

Gribble, George (CON - Bovey)
george.gribble@teignbridge.gov.uk

Haines, Mike (IND - Kerswell with Combe)
Mike.Haines@teignbridge.gov.uk

Hockin, Ted (CON - Dawlish Central and North East)
Edward.Hockin@teignbridge.gov.uk

Hocking, Michael (LD - Bradley)
Michael.Hocking@teignbridge.gov.uk

Holmes, Fernley (IND - Bovey)
Fernley.Holmes@teignbridge.gov.uk

Hook, Gordon (LD - Buckland and Milber)
Gordon.Hook@teignbridge.gov.uk

Jefferey, Mike (CON - Moorland)
Mike.Jefferey@teignbridge.gov.uk

Kelling, Richard (IND - Chudleigh)
richard.keeling@teignbridge.gov.uk

Klinkenberg, Anna (CON - Bovey)
Anna.Klinkenberg@teignbridge.gov.uk

Lake, Kevin (CON - Kenn Valley)
Kevin.Lake@teignbridge.gov.uk

Lambert, Joan (CON - Kingsteignton West)
Joan.Lambert@teignbridge.gov.uk

Lewis, Ken (CON - Bushell)
Ken.Lewis@teignbridge.gov.uk

Lonsdale, Anne (LD - Kingsteignton West)
Anne.Lonsdale@teignbridge.gov.uk

Matthews, Dave (CON - Teignmouth West)

dave.matthews@teignbridge.gov.uk
McMurray, James (CON - Teignmouth Central)
james.mcmurray@teignbridge.gov.uk
Parker, Colin (LD - Buckland and Milber)
colin.parker@teignbridge.gov.uk
Petherick, John (IND - Dawlish Central and North East)
john.petherick@teignbridge.gov.uk
Price, Graham (CON - Dawlish Central and North East)
Graham.Price@teignbridge.gov.uk
Prowse, Rosalind (CON - Dawlish South West)
Rosalind.Prowse@teignbridge.gov.uk
Purser, Stephen (IND - Teign Valley)
Stephen.Purser@teignbridge.gov.uk
Russell, Sylvia (CON - Teignmouth East)
Sylvia.Russell@teignbridge.gov.uk
Shantry, Kelvyn (CON - College)
kelvyn.shantry@teignbridge.gov.uk
Smith, Dennis (CON - Ambrook)
Dennis.Smith@teignbridge.gov.uk
Vogel, Philip (CON - Ashburton and Buckfastleigh)
philip.vogel@teignbridge.gov.uk
Walters, Mike (CON - Kingsteignton East)
Mike.Walters@teignbridge.gov.uk
Williams, Alun (LD - Bishopsteignton)
Alun.Williams@teignbridge.gov.uk

POLITICAL COMPOSITION
CON: 25, LD: 13, IND: 8

CABINET
Leader / Economy, Strategic Direction & PR / Media: Mr Jeremy Christophers
Deputy Leader / Assets & Resources: Mr Ray Frost
Economic Development: Mr David Corney-Walker
Environmental Services: Mr Kevin Lake
Housing & Planning: Mr Philip Vogel
Recreation & Leisure: Ms Anne Fry

COMMITTEE CHAIRS
Development Control: Mr Howard Milton
Licensing & Appeals: Mr Ted Hockin
Licensing (Scrutiny): Mr Ted Hockin
Overview & Scrutiny: Mr Jeremy Christophers
Planning: Mr Humphrey Clemens
Regulatory & Appeals: Mr Alan Connet

TELFORD & WREKIN U

Telford & Wrekin Council, Civic Offices, Telford TF3 4LD ☎ 01952 380000 🖷 01952 290820 ✉ telford@telford.gov.uk 🖳 www.telford.gov.uk

FACTS & FIGURES
Police Authority: West Mercia Police Authority
Health Authority: NHS West Midlands
Learning and Skills Council: West Midlands
Parliamentary Constituencies: Telford, Wrekin, The
EU Constituencies: West Midlands
Election Frequency: Elections are of whole council

PRINCIPAL OFFICERS
Chief Executive: Mr Richard Partington, Managing Director, PO Box 213, Civic Offices, Telford TF3 4LD ☎ 01952 380130 🖷 01952 380104 ✉ richard.partington@telford.gov.uk

Deputy Chief Executive: Mr Richard Partington, Managing Director, PO Box 213, Civic Offices, Telford TF3 4LD ☎ 01952 380130 🖷 01952 380104 ✉ richard.partington@telford.gov.uk

Assistant Chief Executive: Mr Richard Partington, Managing Director, PO Box 213, Civic Offices, Telford TF3 4LD ☎ 01952 380130 🖷 01952 380104 ✉ richard.partington@telford.gov.uk

Senior Management: Mr Paul Clifford, Corporate Director, Civic Offices, Coach Central, Telford TF3 4HD ☎ 01952 383700 🖷 01952 380104 ✉ paul.clifford@telford.gov.uk

Architect, Building / Property Services: Mr Dave Sidaway, Assistant Director - Business & Housing, Civic Offices, Coach Central, Telford TF3 4HD ☎ 01952 384300 ✉ dave.sidaway@telford.gov.uk

Best Value: Mr Richard Partington, Managing Director, Civic Offices, Coach Central, Telford TF3 4LD ☎ 01952 380130 🖷 01952 380104 ✉ richard.partington@telford.gov.uk

Catering Services: Ms Kate Sumner, Commercial Schools & Catering Service Delivery Manager, Civic Offices, Coach Central, Telford TF3 4LD ☎ 01952 380917 ✉ kate.sumner@telford.gov.uk

Civil Registration: Ms Kerry Caitlin, Superintendent Registrar / Registration Services Manager, Telford & Wrekin Register Office, The Beeches, 29 Vineyard Road, Wellington, Telford TF1 1HB ☎ 01952 382444 🖷 01952 382452 ✉ kerry.caitlin@telford.gov.uk

PR / Communications: Mr Nigel Newman, Corporate Communications Manager, Civic Offices, Coach Central, Telford TF3 4LD ☎ 01952 382403 ✉ nigel.newman@telford.gov.uk

Community Safety: Mr Jas Bedesha, Safer Communities Strategic Manager, Civic Offices, Coach Central, Telford TF3 4HD ☎ 01952 382101 ✉ jas.bedesha@telford.gov.uk

Computer Management: Mr Dave Sidaway, Assistant Director - Business & Housing, PO Box 212, Darby House, Telford TF3 4LD ☎ 01952 384300 ✉ dave.sidaway@telford.gov.uk

Consumer Protection and Trading Standards: Mr Ian Mercer, Public Protection Manager, Darby House, Lawn Central, Telford TF3 4LB ☎ 01952 381805 🖷 01952 384254 ✉ ian.mercer@telford.gov.uk

Contracts: Mr Ken Clarke, Assistant Director - Finance, Audit & Information Governance, Civic Offices, Coach Central, Telford TF3 4HD ☎ 01952 202455 🖷 01952 291003 ✉ ken.clarke@telford.gov.uk

Customer Service: Ms Angie Astley, Head of Customer & People Services, Civic Offices, Coach Central, Telford TF3 4HD ☎ 01952 382400 ✉ angie.astley@telford.gov.uk

Education: Mr Jim Collins, Assistant Director - Education Culture & Skills, Civic Offices, Coach Central, Telford TF3 4HD ☎ 01952 380800 ✉ jim.collins@telford.gov.uk

Electoral Registration: Mr Phil Griffiths, Democratic Services Officer, Civic Offices, Coach Central, Telford TF3 4HD ☎ 01952 383210 🖷 01952 383253 ✉ phil.griffiths@telford.gov.uk

Emergency Planning: Ms Heather Gumsley, Resiliance Team Leader, Pergo House, Wellington Road, Telford TF2 8AB ☎ 01952 381957 🖷 01952 381010 ✉ heather.gumsley@telford.gov.uk

Energy Management: Mr Michael Barker, Planning Specialist, Civic Offices, Coach Central, Telford TF3 4HD ☎ 01952 384100 🖷 01952 384020 ✉ michael.barker@telford.gov.uk

Environmental Health: Mr Ian Mercer, Public Protection Manager, Darby House, Lawn Central, Telford TF3 4LB ☎ 01952 381805 🖷 01952 384254 ✉ ian.mercer@telford.gov.uk

Estates, Property & Valuation: Mr Dave Sidaway, Assistant Director - Business & Housing, Civic Offices, Coach Central, Telford TF3 4HD ☎ 01952 384300 ✉ dave.sidaway@telford.gov.uk

Facilities: Mr Clive Barton, Facilities Mangement Group Manager, Civic Offices, Telford TF3 4LD ☎ 01952 380000 ✉ clive.barton@telford.gov.uk

Fleet Management: Mr Ray Faulkner, Fleet Service Manager, St George's Road, Donnington Wood, Telford TF2 7RA ☎ 01952 384825 🖷 01952 384836 ✉ ray.faulkner@telford.gov.uk

Grounds Maintenance: Mr Danny Chetwood, Service & Contract Development Group Manager, Granville House, Telford TF3 4LL ☎ 01952 384384 🖷 01952 384701 ✉ danny.chetwood@telford.gov.uk

Health and Safety: Ms Jo Revell, Health & Safety Manager, Civic Offices, Coach Central, Telford TF3 4HD ☎ 01952 383625 🖷 01952 383634 ✉ jo.revell@telford.gov.uk

Housing: Mr Michael Barker, Planning Specialist, Civic Offices, Coach Central, Telford TF3 4HD ☎ 01952 384100 🖷 01952 384020 ✉ michael.barker@telford.gov.uk

Housing Maintenance: Mr Michael Barker, Planning Specialist, Civic Offices, Coach Central, Telford TF3 4HD ☎ 01952 384100 🖷 01952 384020 ✉ michael.barker@telford.gov.uk

Local Area Agreement: Mr Jon Power, Delivery & Planning Manager, Civic Offices, Telford TF3 4LD ☎ 01952 380141 ✉ john.power@telford.gov.uk

Legal: Mr Jonathan Eatough, Assistant Director - Education, Democracy & Public Protection, Civic Offices, Coach Central, Telford TF3 4HD ☎ 01952 383200 🖷 01352 383005 ✉ jonathon.eatough@telford.gov.uk

Leisure and Cultural Services: Ms Angie Astley, Head of Customer & People Services, Civic Offices, Coach Central, Telford TF3 4HD ☎ 01952 382400 ✉ angie.astley@telford.gov.uk

Licensing: Mr Michael Barker, Planning Specialist, Civic Offices, Coach Central, Telford TF3 4HD ☎ 01952 384100 🖷 01952 384020 ✉ michael.barker@telford.gov.uk

Lifelong Learning: Mr Richard Probert, Lifelong Learning Manager, Civic Offices, Coach Central, Telford TF3 4HD ☎ 01952 382880 🖷 01952 382327 ✉ richard.probert@telford.gov.uk

Member Services: Miss Emma Price, Senior Member Services Officer, Civic Offices, Coach Central, Telford TF3 4HD ☎ 01952 380110 ✉ emma.price@telford.gov.uk

Parking: Mr Stuart Freeman, Highways & Transport Manager, Civic Offices, Coach Central, Telford TF3 4HD ☎ 01952 384601 ✉ stuart.freeman@telford.gov.uk

Partnerships: Mr Richard Partington, Managing Director, Civic Offices, Coach Central, Telford TF3 4HD ☎ 01952 380130 🖷 01952 380104 ✉ richard.partington@telford.gov.uk

Personnel / HR: Mr John Harris, Human Resources Manager, Civic Offices, Coach Central, Telford TF3 4HD ☎ 01952 383520 ✉ john.harris@telford.gov.uk

Planning: Mr Michael Barker, Planning Specialist, Civic Offices, Coach Central, Telford TF3 4HD ☎ 01952 384100 🖷 01952 384020 ✉ michael.barker@telford.gov.uk

Procurement: Ms Sarah Bass, Strategic Procurement Service Delivery Specalist, Civic Offices, Telford TF3 4LD ☎ 01952 383726 ✉ sarah.bass@telford.gov.uk

Public Libraries: Ms Sharon Smith, Service Delivery Manager Libaries, Civic Offices, Coach Central, Telford TF3 4HD ☎ 01952 382881 🖷 01952 382327 ✉ sharon.smith@telford.gov.uk

Recycling & Waste Minimisation: Ms Katherine Kynaston, Development Plans & Sustainability Manager, PO Box 212, Darby House, Lawn Central, Telford TF3 4LB ☎ 01952 384201 🖷 01952 384254 ✉ katherine.kynaston@telford.gov.uk

Regeneration: Mr Clive Jones, Assistant Director - Family & Cohesion Services, Civic Offices, Coach Central, Telford TF3 4HD ☎ 01952 385100 ✉ clive.jones@telford.gov.uk

Road Safety: Ms Amanda Roberts, Team Leader - Road Safety, PO Box 212, Darby House, Lawn Central, Telford TF3 4LB ☎ 01952 384631 🖷 01952 384634 ✉ amanda.roberts@telford.gov.uk

Social Services: Ms Karen Kalinowski, Head of Care & Support, Civic Offices, Coach Central, Telford TF3 4HD ☎ 01952 381011 ✉ karen.kalinowski@telford.gov.uk

Social Services (Adult): Ms Karen Kalinowski, Head of Care & Support, Civic Offices, Coach Central, Telford TF3 4HD ☎ 01952 381011 ✉ karen.kalinowski@telford.gov.uk

Social Services (Children): Mrs Laura Johnston, Director of Children & Family Services, Civic Offices, Coach Central, Telford TF3 4HD ☎ 01952 385100 ✉ laura.johnston@telford.gov.uk

Street Scene: Mr Stuart Freeman, Highways & Transport Manager, Civic Offices, Coach Central, Telford TF3 4HD ☎ 01952

384601 ✉ stuart.freeman@telford.gov.uk

Sustainable Communities: Ms Katherine Kynaston, Development Plans & Sustainability Manager, PO Box 212, Darby House, Lawn Central, Telford TF3 4LB ☎ 01952 384201 🖷 01952 384254 ✉ katherine.kynaston@telford.gov.uk

Sustainable Development: Ms Katherine Kynaston, Development Plans & Sustainability Manager, PO Box 212, Darby House, Lawn Central, Telford TF3 4LB ☎ 01952 384201 🖷 01952 384254 ✉ katherine.kynaston@telford.gov.uk

Town Centre: Mr Dave Sidaway, Assistant Director - Business & Housing, Civic Offices, Coach Central, Telford TF3 4HD ☎ 01952 384300 ✉ dave.sidaway@telford.gov.uk

Transport: Mr Stuart Freeman, Highways & Transport Manager, Civic Offices, Coach Central, Telford TF3 4HD ☎ 01952 384601 ✉ stuart.freeman@telford.gov.uk

Transport Planner: Mr Stuart Freeman, Highways & Transport Manager, Civic Offices, Coach Central, Telford TF3 4HD ☎ 01952 384601 ✉ stuart.freeman@telford.gov.uk

Waste Collection and Disposal: Ms Katherine Kynaston, Development Plans & Sustainability Manager, PO Box 212, Darby House, Lawn Central, Telford TF3 4LB ☎ 01952 384201 🖷 01952 384254 ✉ katherine.kynaston@telford.gov.uk

Waste Management: Ms Katherine Kynaston, Development Plans & Sustainability Manager, PO Box 212, Darby House, Lawn Central, Telford TF3 4LB ☎ 01952 384201 🖷 01952 384254 ✉ katherine.kynaston@telford.gov.uk

MEMBERS OF THE COUNCIL (54)

***Mayor:* Guy**, Kevin (LAB - Woodside)
kevin.guy@telford.gov.uk
***Deputy Mayor:* Murray**, Leon (LAB - Hadley and Leegomery)
leon.murray@telford.gov.uk
***Leader of the Council:* Sahota**, Kuldip Singh (LAB - Malinslee)
kuldip.sahota@telford.gov.uk
***Deputy Leader of the Council:* Overton**, Richard (LAB - St Georges)
richard.overton@telford.gov.uk
Austin, Keith (LAB - Hadley and Leegomery)
keith.austin@telford.gov.uk
Bentley, Stephen (CON - Ercall Magna)
stephen.bentley@telford.gov.uk
Blundell, Karen (LD - Apley Castle)
karen.blundell@telford.gov.uk
Bould, Frances (LAB - Dawley Magna)
frances.bould@telford.gov.uk
Burrell, Stephen (CON - Edgmond)
stephen.burrell@telford.gov.uk
Carter, Eric (CON - Newport East)
eric.carter@telford.gov.uk
Clare, Elizabeth (LAB - Donnington)
elizabeth.clare@telford.gov.uk
Davies, Shaun (LAB - Malinslee)
shaun.davies@telford.go.uk
Duce, Brian (LAB - Dawley Magna)
brian.duce@telford.gov.uk
Dugmore, Nigel (CON - Muxton)
nigel.dugmore@telford.gov.uk
Eade, Andrew (CON - Church Aston and Lilleshall)
andrew.eade@telford.gov.uk
Elliott, Clive (LAB - Dawley Magna)
clive.elliott@telford.gov.uk
England, Arnold (LAB - Brookside)
arnold.england@telford.gov.uk
England, Nathan (LAB - The Nedge)
nathan.england@telford.gov.uk
Evans, Gillian Green (LAB - Woodside)
rae.evans@telford.gov.uk
Fletcher, Ian (CON - Priorslee)
ian.fletcher@telford.gov.uk
Fletcher, Veronica (CON - Priorslee)
veronica.fletcher@telford.gov.uk
Green, Gillian (LD - Madeley)
gillian.green@telford.gov.uk
Greenway, Jane (CON - Lawley and Overdale)
jayne.greenway@telford.gov.uk
Hope, Tracy (CON - Horsehay and Lightmoor)
tracy.hope@telford.gov.uk
Hosken, Miles (CON - Ercall)
miles.hosken@telford.gov.uk
Ion, Michael (LAB - College)
mike.ion@telford.gov.uk
Jhawar, Amrik Singh (LAB - Ketley and Oakengates)
amrik.jhawar@telford.gov.uk
Kiernan, Terry (CON - Wrockwardine)
terry.kiernan@telford.gov.uk
Lawrence, Adrian (CON - Muxton)
adrian.lawrence@telford.gov.uk
Loveridge, Jackie (LAB - Brookside)
jackie.loveridge@telford.gov.uk
MacKenzie, Alan (LAB - Cuckoo Oak)
alan.mackenzie@telford.gov.uk
Mason, Clive (LAB - Donnington)
clive.mason@telford.gov.uk
McClements, Bill (LAB - The Nedge)
bill.mcclements@telford.gov.uk
McClements, Angela (LAB - Arleston)
angela.mcclements@telford.gov.uk
Meredith, Adrian (CON - Newport South)
adrian.meredith@telford.gov.uk
Minor, John (LAB - St Georges)
john.minor@telford.gov.uk
Mollet, Clive (CON - Hosehay and Lightmoor)
clive.mollet@telford.gov.uk
Picken, Roy (LAB - Lawley and Overdale)
roy.picken@telford.gov.uk
Reynolds, Gillian (LAB - Kettley and Oakengates)
gilly.reynolds@telford.gov.uk
Reynolds, Shirley (LAB - Wrockwardine Wood and Trench)
shirley.reynolds@telford.gov.uk
Rhodes, Hilda (LAB - Ketley and Oakengates)
hilda.rhodes@telford.gov.uk
Scammell, Roy (CON - Newport North)
roy.scammell@telford.gov.uk
Seymour, Jacqui (CON - Wrockwardine)
jacqui.seymour@telford.gov.uk
Sloan, Robert (LAB - Haygate)
rob.sloan@telford.gov.uk
Sloan, Robert (LAB - Ironbridge Gorge)
david.davies@telford
Smith, Charles (LAB - Wrockwardine Wood and Trench)
charles.smith@telford.gov.uk

Smith, Malcolm (LAB - Hadley and Leegomery)
malcolm.smith@telford.gov.uk
Stanton, Adam (CON - Newport West)
adam.stanton@telford.gov.uk
Thompson, John (LAB - Park)
john.thompson@telford.go.uk
Tomlinson, Bill (LD - Shawbirch)
bill.tomlinson@telford.gov.uk
Tomlinson, Karen (LD - Dothill)
karen.tomlinson@telford.gov.uk
Turley, Chris (LAB - The Nedge)
chris.turley@telford.gov.uk
Watling, Paul (LAB - Madeley)
paul.watling@telford.gov.uk
White, Derek (LAB - Cuckoo Oak)
derek.white@telford.gov.uk

POLITICAL COMPOSITION
LAB: 33, CON: 17, LD: 4

CABINET
Leader: Mr Kuldip Singh Sahota
Deputy Leader: Mr Richard Overton
Adult & Social Care: Ms Elizabeth Clare
Children, Young People & Families: Mr Paul Watling
Housing Regeneration & Economic Development: Mr Charles Smith
Leisure & Well-being: Mr Arnold England
Neighbourhood Services & Co-operative Council: Mr Shaun Davies
Resources & Service Delivery: Mr Bill McClements

COMMITTEE CHAIRS
Appeals: Ms Gillian Green Evans
Audit: Mr Robert Sloan
Health & Wellbeing: Mr Richard Overton
Licensing: Mr Neil Mason
Personnel: Mr Kuldip Singh Sahota
Plans Board: Mr John Minor

TENDRING D

Tendring District Council, Town Hall, Station Road, Clacton-on-Sea CO15 1SE ☎ 01255 686868 🖳 www.tendringdc.gov.uk

FACTS & FIGURES
Police Authority: Essex Police Authority
Health Authority: East of England Strategic Health Authority
Learning and Skills Council: Eastern
Parliamentary Constituencies: Clacton, Harwich and Essex North
EU Constituencies: Eastern
Election Frequency: Elections are of whole council
Twinning: Biberach (Germany); Swidnica (Poland); Valence-sur-Rhone (France)

PRINCIPAL OFFICERS
Chief Executive: Mr Ian Davidson, Chief Executive, Town Hall, Station Road, Clacton-on-Sea CO15 1SE ☎ 01255 686007 🖷 01255 686414 ✉ idavidson@tendringdc.gov.uk

Senior Management: Mr David Appleby, Strategic Director, Town Hall, Station Road, Clacton-on-Sea CO15 1SE ☎ 01255 686740 🖷 01225 686414 ✉ dappleby@tendringdc.gov.uk

Senior Management: Mr Martyn Knappett, Head of Corporate Services, Town Hall, Station Road, Clacton-on-Sea CO15 1SE ☎ 01255 686501 🖷 01225 686414 ✉ mknappett@tendringdc.gov.uk

Building Control: Mr Alan Corbyn, Building Control Manager, Council Offices, Thorpe Road, Weeley, Clacton-on-Sea CO16 9AJ ☎ 01255 686160 🖷 01255 686425 ✉ acorbyn@tendringdc.gov.uk

PR / Communications: Mr Nigel Brown, Communications Manager, Town Hall, Station Road, Clacton-on-Sea CO15 1SE ☎ 01255 686338 🖷 01225 686414 ✉ nbrown@tendringdc.gov.uk

Community Safety: Miss Leanne Thornton, Community Safety Manager, Council Offices, Thorpe Road, Weeley, Clacton-on-Sea CO16 9AJ ☎ 01225 686353 🖷 01225 686417 ✉ lthornton@tendringdc.gov.uk

Contracts: Mr Tim Clarke, Pollution & Environment Manager, Council Offices, Thorpe Road, Weeley, Clacton-on-Sea CO16 9AJ ☎ 01255 686742 🖷 01255 686404 ✉ tclarke@tendringdc.gov.uk

Contracts: Mr David Hall, Horticultural & Bereavement Services Manager, Town Hall, Station Road, Clacton-on-Sea CO15 1SE ☎ 01255 686661 🖷 01255 686411 ✉ dhall@tendringdc.gov.uk

Corporate Services: Mr Martyn Knappett, Head of Corporate Services, Town Hall, Station Road, Clacton-on-Sea CO15 1SE ☎ 01255 686501 🖷 01225 686414 ✉ mknappett@tendringdc.gov.uk

Customer Service: Mrs Anastasia Simpson, HR Manager, Town Hall, Station Road, Clacton-on-Sea CO15 1SE ☎ 01255 686324 ✉ asimpson@tendringdc.gov.uk

E-Government: Miss Karen Neath, Head of Resource Management, Town Hall, Station Road, Clacton-on-Sea CO15 1SE ☎ 01255 686520 ✉ kneath@tendringdc.gov.uk

Electoral Registration: Ms Judith Raison, Electoral Registration, Westleigh House, Carnarvon Road, Clacton-on-Sea CO15 6QF ☎ 01255 686586 ✉ jraison@tendringdc.gov.uk

Emergency Planning: Mr Damian Williams, Facilities Manager, Town Hall, Station Road, Clacton-on-Sea CO15 1SE ☎ 01255 686319 ✉ dwilliams@tendringdc.gov.uk

Environmental Health: Mrs June Clare, Head of Public Experience, Council Offices, Thorpe Road, Weeley, Clacton-on-Sea CO16 9AJ ☎ 01255 686741 ✉ jclare@tendringdc.gov.uk

Estates, Property & Valuation: Mr Andrew White, Assets Manager, Town Hall, Station Road, Clacton-on-Sea CO15 1SE ☎ 01255 686933 ✉ awhite@tendringdc.gov.uk

Events Manager: Mr Michael Carran, Life Opportunities, Town Hall, Station Road, Clacton-on-Sea CO15 1SE ☎ 01255 686689 🖷 01255 686411 ✉ mcarran@tendringdc.gov.uk

Facilities: Mr Damian Williams, Facilities Manager, Town Hall, Station Road, Clacton-on-Sea CO15 1SE ☎ 01255 686319

dwilliams@tendringdc.gov.uk

Finance and Treasurer: Miss Karen Neath, Head of Resource Management, Town Hall, Station Road, Clacton-on-Sea CO15 1SE ☎ 01255 686520 kneath@tendringdc.gov.uk

Fleet Management: Mr Trevor Mills, Horticultural Services Manager, Northbourne Depot, Vista Road, Clacton-on-Sea CO15 6AY ☎ 01255 686643 🖷 01255 479739 tmills@tendringdc.gov.uk

Grounds Maintenance: Mr Trevor Mills, Horticultural Services Manager, Northbourne Depot, Vista Road, Clacton-on-Sea CO15 6AY ☎ 01255 686643 🖷 01255 479739 tmills@tendringdc.gov.uk

Health and Safety: Mr John Fox, Food & Health & Safety Manager, Council Offices, Thorpe Road, Weeley, Clacton-on-Sea CO16 9AJ ☎ 01255 686746 🖷 01255 686404 jfox@tendringdc.gov.uk

Highways: Mr Mike Badger, Engineering Services Manager, Town Hall, Station Road, Clacton-on-Sea CO15 1SE ☎ 01255 686975 mbadger@tendringdc.gov.uk

Home Energy Conservation: Mr Tim Clarke, Pollution & Environment Manager, Council Offices, Thorpe Road, Weeley, Clacton-on-Sea CO16 9AJ ☎ 01255 686742 🖷 01255 686404 tclarke@tendringdc.gov.uk

Housing: Mr Paul Price, Head of Life Opportunities, Town Hall, Station Road, Clacton-on-Sea CO15 1SE ☎ 01255 686430 🖷 01255 686407 pprice@tendringcc.gov.uk

Housing Maintenance: Mr Frank Stilwell, Life Opportunities, Town Hall, Station Road, Clacton-on-Sea CO15 1SE ☎ 01255 686945 🖷 01255 222813 fstilwell@tendringdc.gov.uk

Legal: Mr Michael Gibson-Davies, Legal Services Manager, Town Hall, Station Road, Clacton-on-Sea CO15 1SE ☎ 01255 686564 mgibson-davies@tendringdc.gov.uk

Leisure and Cultural Services: Mr Michael Carran, Life Opportunities, Town Hall, Station Road, Clacton-on-Sea CO15 1SE ☎ 01255 686689 🖷 01255 686411 mcarran@tendringdc.gov.uk

Licensing: Mr Ian Taylor, Streets & Seafronts Manager, Westleigh House, Carnarvon Road, Clacton-on-Sea CO15 6QF ☎ 01255 686982 itaylor@tendring.gov.uk

Lifelong Learning: Mr Stuart Brian, Workforce Development Manager, Town Hall, Station Road, Clacton-on-Sea CO15 1SE ☎ 01255 686308 sbrian@tendringdc.gov.uk

Lighting: Mr Mike Badger, Engineering Services Manager, Town Hall, Station Road, Clacton-on-Sea CO15 1SE ☎ 01255 686975 mbadger@tendringdc.gov.uk

Member Services: Mrs Jenifer Eames, Personal Secretary to the Leader of the Council, Town Hall, Station Road, Clacton-on-Sea CO15 1SE ☎ 01255 686583 jeames@tendringdc.gov.uk

Parking: Mr Ian Taylor, Streets & Seafronts Manager, Westleigh House, Carnarvon Road, Clacton-on-Sea CO15 6QF ☎ 01255 686982 itaylor@tendring.gov.uk

Personnel / HR: Mrs Anastasia Simpson, HR Manager, Town Hall, Station Road, Clacton-on-Sea CO15 1SE ☎ 01255 686324 asimpson@tendringdc.gov.uk

Planning: Mrs Sarah Stevens, Temporary Head of Planning, Council Offices, Thorpe Road, Weeley, Clacton-on-Sea CO16 9AJ ☎ 01255 686101 🖷 01255 686417 sstevens@tendringdc.gov.uk

Procurement: Mrs Jane Taylor, Procurement Officer, Town Hall, Station Road, Clacton-on-Sea CO15 1SE ☎ 01255 686955 jtaylor@tendringdc.gov.uk

Recycling & Waste Minimisation: Mr William Smith, Senior Waste & Recycling Officer, Council Offices, Thorpe Road, Weeley, Clacton-on-Sea CO16 9AJ ☎ 01255 686765 🖷 01255 686404 wsmith@tendringdc.gov.uk

Staff Training: Mr Stuart Brian, Workforce Development Manager, Town Hall, Station Road, Clacton-on-Sea CO15 1SE ☎ 01255 686308 sbrian@tendringdc.gov.uk

Street Scene: Mr Mike Badger, Engineering Services Manager, Town Hall, Station Road, Clacton-on-Sea CO15 1SE ☎ 01255 686975 mbadger@tendringdc.gov.uk

Sustainable Development: Mr Tim Clarke, Pollution & Environment Manager, Council Offices, Thorpe Road, Weeley, Clacton-on-Sea CO16 9AJ ☎ 01255 686742 🖷 01255 686404 tclarke@tendringdc.gov.uk

Tourism: Mr Michael Carran, Life Opportunities, Town Hall, Station Road, Clacton-on-Sea CO15 1SE ☎ 01255 686689 🖷 01255 686411 mcarran@tendringdc.gov.uk

Town Centre: Mrs Rachel Fryer, Town Centre Co-ordinator, Council Offices, Thorpe Road, Weeley, Clacton-on-Sea CO16 9AJ ☎ 01255 686149 🖷 01255 831291 rfryer@tendringdc.gov.uk

Total Place: Mr Martyn Knappett, Head of Corporate Services, Town Hall, Station Road, Clacton-on-Sea CO15 1SE ☎ 01255 686501 🖷 01225 686414 mknappett@tendringdc.gov.uk

Waste Collection and Disposal: Mr Tim Clarke, Pollution & Environment Manager, Council Offices, Thorpe Road, Weeley, Clacton-on-Sea CO16 9AJ ☎ 01255 686742 🖷 01255 686404 tclarke@tendringdc.gov.uk

Waste Management: Mrs June Clare, Head of Public Experience, Council Offices, Thorpe Road, Weeley, Clacton-on-Sea CO16 9AJ ☎ 01255 686741 jclare@tendringdc.gov.uk

Children's Play Areas: Mr David Hall, Horticultural & Bereavement Services Manager, Town Hall, Station Road, Clacton-on-Sea CO15 1SE ☎ 01255 686661 🖷 01255 686411 dhall@tendringdc.gov.uk

MEMBERS OF THE COUNCIL (59)

Chair: **Mayzes**, Danny (CON - Rush Green)

cllr.dmayzes@tendringdc.gov.uk
***Vice-Chair:* Honeywood**, Susan (CON - Pier)
cllr.shoneywood@tendringdc.gov.uk
***Leader of the Council:* Stock**, Neil (CON - Ardleigh and Little Bromley)
cllr.nstock@tendringdc.gov.uk
Aldis, Delia (LAB - Alton Park)
cllr.daldis@tendringdc.gov.uk
Amos, Chris (CON - St Johns)
cllr.camos@tendringdc.gov.uk
Broderick, Joy (IND - Haven)
cllr.jbroderick@tendringdc.gov.uk
Brown, Nick (LAB - Golf Green)
cllr.nbrown@tendringdc.gov.uk
Caines, Graham (LAB - Alton Park)
cllr.gcaines@tendringdc.gov.uk
Callender, Ricky (CON - Harwich West)
cllr.rcallender@tendringdc.gov.uk
Callender, Claire (CON - Harwich West Central)
cllr.ccallender@tendringdc.gov.uk
Calver, Garry (LAB - Harwich East Central)
cllr.gcalver@tendringdc.gov.uk
Candy, Sarah (CON - Manningtree, Mistley, Little Bentley and Tendring)
cllr.scandy@tendringdc.gov.uk
Casey, Daniel (LAB - Golf Green)
cllr.dcasey@tendringdc.gov.uk
Challinor, Siggy (CON - Bockings Elm)
cllr.schallinor@tendringdc.gov.uk
Chapman, Jayne (IND - Brightlingsea)
cllr.jchapman@tendringdc.gov.uk
Colbourne, Anthony (CON - Ramsey and Parkeston)
cllr.acolbourne@tendringdc.gov.uk
Cossens, Mark (O - Holland and Kirby)
cllr.mcossens@tendringdc.gov.uk
De-Vaux Balbirnie, Peter (O - Little Clacton and Weeley)
cllr.pbalbirnie@tendringdc.gov.uk
Double, Leslie (LAB - Harwich West)
cllr.les.double@essex.gov.uk
Downing, Gill (CON - St James)
cllr.gdowning@tendringdc.gov.uk
Fawcett, Tony (CON - St Marys)
cllr.tfawcett@tendringdc.gov.uk
Goggin, Alan (CON - Brightlingsea)
cllr.agoggin@tendringdc.gov.uk
Griffiths, Christopher (CON - St James)
cllr.cgriffiths@tendringdc.gov.uk
Guglielmi, Carlo (CON - Manningtree, Mistley, Little Bentley and Tendring)
cllr.gguglielmi@tendringdc.gov.uk
Guglielmi, Valerie (CON - Lawford)
cllr.vguglielmi@tendringdc.gov.uk
Halliday, Peter (CON - St Johns)
cllr.phalliday@tendringdc.gov.uk
Heaney, Rosemary (CON - Thorrington, Frating, Elmstead and Great Bromley)
cllr.rheaney@tendringdc.gov.uk
Henderson, Jo (LAB - Harwich West Central)
cllr.jhenderson@tendringdc.gov.uk
Henderson, Ivan (LAB - Harwich East)
cllr.ihenderson@tendringdc.gov.uk
Honeywood, Paul (CON - Pier)
cllr.phoneywood@tendringdc.gov.uk
Howard, Tom (IND - Great and Little Oakley)
cllr.thoward@tendringdc.gov.uk
Johnson, Iris (O - Hamford)
cllr.ijohnson@tendringdc.gov.uk
King, Kanagsasund- Ram (O - St Bartholomews)
cllr.kking@tendringdc.gov.uk
Mayzes, Stephen (CON - Rush Green)
cllr.smayzes@tendringdc.gov.uk
McLeod, David (LAB - Harwich East Central)
cllr.dmcleod@tendringdc.gov.uk
McWilliams, Lynda (CON - Great Bentley)
cllr.lmcwilliams@tendringdc.gov.uk
Miles, Delyth (CON - Walton)
cllr.dmiles@tendringdc.gov.uk
Mitchell, Mitch (CON - Peter Bruff)
cllr.mmitchell@tendringdc.gov.uk
Mitchell, Gwen (CON - Peter Bruff)
cllr.gmitchell@tendringdc.gov.uk
Nicholls, Fred (CON - Thorrington, Frating, Elmstead and Great Bromley)
cllr.fnicholls@tendringdc.gov.uk
Oxley, David (O - St Pauls)
cllr.doxley@tendringdc.gov.uk
Oxley, Pierre (O - St Pauls)
cllr.oxley@tendringdc.gov.uk
Page, Mick (CON - Homelands)
cllr.mpage@tendringdc.gov.uk
Patten, Matthew (CON - Bradfield, Wrabness and Wix)
cllr.mpatten@tendringdc.gov.uk
Platt, Mark (CON - Hamford)
cllr.mplatt@tendringdc.gov.uk
Powell, Jose (IND - Beaumont and Thorpe)
cllr.jpowell@tendringdc.gov.uk
Pugh, Antony (CON - Walton)
cllr.apugh@endringdc.gov.uk
Sambridge, Pamela (CON - Burrsville)
cllr.psambridge@tendringdc.gov.uk
Scott, Gary (LD - Alresford)
cllr.gscott@tendringdc.gov.uk
Shearing, Harry (LD - Bockings Elm)
cllr.hshearing@tendringdc.gov.uk
Simons, Keith (CON - Lawford)
cllr.ksimons@tendringdc.gov.uk
Skeels, Dawn (CON - Little Clacton and Weeley)
cllr.dskeels@tendringdc.gov.uk
Steady, Graham (IND - Brightlingsea)
cllr.gsteady@tendringdc.gov.uk
Steady, Graham (O - Holland and Kirby)
cllr.rbuckle@tendringdc.gov.uk
Talbot, Michael (IND - St Osyth and Point Clear)
cllr.mtalbot@tendringdc.gov.uk
Tracey, Irene (O - St Marys)
cllr.itracey@tendringdc.gov.uk
Turner, Nicholas (CON - Frinton)
cllr.nturner@tendringdc.gov.uk
Watling, Giles (CON - Frinton)
cllr.gwatling@tendringdc.gov.uk
White, John (IND - St Osyth and Point Clear)
cllr.jwhite@tendringdc.gov.uk

POLITICAL COMPOSITION

CON: 33, LAB: 9, O: 8, IND: 7, LD: 2

CABINET

Leader: Mr Neil Stock

Benefits & Revenues: Mr Giles Watling
Customer & Central Services: Mrs Lynda McWilliams
Environment: Mr Nicholas Turner
Finance: Mr Peter Halliday
Housing: Mr Paul Honeywood
Planning: Mr Carlo Guglielmi
Regeneration: Ms Sarah Candy
Technical Services: Mrs Pamela Sambridge
Tourism & Community Life: Mr Stephen Mayzes

COMMITTEE CHAIRS

Audit: Mr Mick Page
Community Leadership & Partnerships: Ms Delyth Miles
Corporate Management: Mr Graham Steady
Council Tax: Mr Peter Halliday
Human Resources: Mr Mitch Mitchell
Licensing: Mr Tony Fawcett
Planning: Mrs Rosemary Heaney
Regulatory: Mrs Susan Honeywood
Service Development & Delivery: Mr Christopher Griffiths
Standards: Mr Jim Addison (External)

TEST VALLEY D

Test Valley Borough Council, Beech Hurst, Weyhill Road, Andover SP10 3AJ ☎ 01264 368000 🖳 www.testvalley.gov.uk

FACTS & FIGURES

Police Authority: Hampshire Police Authority
Health Authority: South Central Strategic Health Authority
Learning and Skills Council: South East
Parliamentary Constituencies: Hampshire North West, Romsey and Southampton North
EU Constituencies: South East
Election Frequency: Elections are of whole council
Twinning: Andover: Goch (Germany); Redon (France); Massachusetts (USA); Braishfield: Crouay (France); Romsey: Paimpol (France), Battenberg (Germany); Broughton: Sauve (France); Nursling and Rownhams: Percy (France); Michelmersh and Timsbury: Ryes (France); Kings Somborne: St. Paul du Vernay (France); North Baddesley: Authie and Carpiquet (France); Wellow: Couffe (France)

PRINCIPAL OFFICERS

Chief Executive: Mr Roger Tetstall, Chief Executive, Beech Hurst, Weyhill Road, Andover SP10 3AJ ☎ 01264 368102 🖱 rtetstall@testvalley.gov.uk

Deputy Chief Executive: Mrs Carol Moore, Corporate Director, Beech Hurst, Weyhill Road, Andover SP10 3AJ ☎ 01264 368113 🖱 cmoore@testvalley.gov.uk

Senior Management: Mr Paul Wykes, Head of Environmental Services, Portway Depot, Macadam Way, West Portway, Andover SP10 3XW ☎ 01264 368000 🖷 01264 369568 🖱 pwykes@testvalley.gov.uk

Access Officer / Social Services (Disability): Mr Graham Murrell, Building Control Manager, Council Offices, Duttons Road, Romsey SO51 8XG ☎ 01794 527875 🖷 01264 368799 🖱 gmurrell@testvalley.gov.uk

Architect, Building / Property Services: Mr Mark Lambert, Property Services Manager, Beech Hurst, Weyhill Road, Andover SP10 3AJ ☎ 01264 368701 🖷 01264 368799 🖱 mlambert@testvalley.gov.uk

Building Control: Mr Graham Murrell, Building Control Manager, Council Offices, Duttons Road, Romsey SO51 8XG ☎ 01794 527875 🖷 01264 368799 🖱 gmurrell@testvalley.gov.uk

PR / Communications: Mr Keith Kerslake, Communications Manager, Beech Hurst, Weyhill Road, Andover SP10 3AJ ☎ 01264 368108 🖷 01264 368149 🖱 kkerslake@testvalley.gov.uk

Community Planning: Mr Andrew Ferrier, Corporate Director, Beech Hurst, Weyhill Road, Andover SP10 3AJ ☎ 01264 368000 🖱 aferrier@testvalley.gov.uk

Community Safety: Ms Verna Brown, Communities Manager, Beech Hurst, Weyhill Road, Andover SP10 3AJ ☎ 01264 368606 🖱 vbrown@testvalley.gov.uk

Computer Management: Mr Tony Fawcett, Head of IT Services, Beech Hurst, Weyhill Road, Andover SP10 3AJ ☎ 01264 368901 🖷 01264 368999 🖱 tfawcett@testvalley.gov.uk

Contracts: Mr Mark Lambert, Property Services Manager, Beech Hurst, Weyhill Road, Andover SP10 3AJ ☎ 01264 368701 🖷 01264 368799 🖱 mlambert@testvalley.gov.uk

Corporate Services: Mrs Carol Moore, Corporate Director, Beech Hurst, Weyhill Road, Andover SP10 3AJ ☎ 01264 368113 🖱 cmoore@testvalley.gov.uk

Customer Service: Mrs Paula Staff, Customer Relationship Manager, Beech Hurst, Weyhill Road, Andover SP10 3AJ ☎ 01264 368938 🖱 pstaff@testvalley.gov.uk

Economic Development: Mr David Gleave, Economic Development Officer, Beech Hurst, Weyhill Road, Andover SP10 3AJ ☎ 01264 368309 🖷 01264 368349 🖱 dgleave@testvalley.gov.uk

E-Government: Mr Tony Fawcett, Head of IT Services, Beech Hurst, Weyhill Road, Andover SP10 3AJ ☎ 01264 368901 🖷 01264 368999 🖱 tfawcett@testvalley.gov.uk

Electoral Registration: Mrs Sue Gamalatge, Electoral Services Manager, Beech Hurst, Weyhill Road, Andover SP10 3AJ ☎ 01264 368020 🖷 01264 368099 🖱 sgamalatge@testvalley.gov.uk

Emergency Planning: Mr Tom Van Der Hoven, Head of Administration, Beech Hurst, Weyhill Road, Andover SP10 3AJ ☎ 01264 368001 🖷 01264 368099 🖱 tvanderhoven@testvalley.gov.uk

Energy Management: Mr Mark Lambert, Property Services Manager, Beech Hurst, Weyhill Road, Andover SP10 3AJ ☎ 01264 368701 🖷 01264 368799 🖱 mlambert@testvalley.gov.uk

Environmental / Technical Services: Mr Paul Wykes, Head of Environmental Services, Portway Depot, Macadam Way, West

Portway, Andover SP10 3XW ☎ 01264 368000 🖷 01264 369568 ✉ pwykes@testvalley.gov.uk

Environmental Health: Ms Carol Ruddle, Environmental Health Manager, Beech Hurst, Weyhill Road, Andover SP10 3AJ ☎ 01264 368000 ✉ cruddle@testvalley.gov.uk

Estates, Property & Valuation: Mr Simon Ellis, Head of Estates & Economic Development Services, Beech Hurst, Weyhill Road, Andover SP10 3AJ ☎ 01264 368301 ✉ sellis@testvalley.gov.uk

Facilities: Mr Mark Lambert, Property Services Manager, Beech Hurst, Weyhill Road, Andover SP10 3AJ ☎ 01264 368701 🖷 01264 368799 ✉ mlambert@testvalley.gov.uk

Finance and Treasurer: Ms Gill Cranswick, Head of Revenues & Benefits, Beech Hurst, Weyhill Road, Andover SP10 3AJ ☎ 01962 840190 ✉ gcranswick@winchester.gov.uk; gcranswick@testvalley.gov.uk

Finance and Treasurer: Mr William Fullbrook, Head of Finance, Beech Hurst, Weyhill Road, Andover SP10 3AJ ☎ 01264 368201 ✉ wfullbrook@testvalley.gov.uk

Fleet Management: Mr Paul Wykes, Head of Environmental Services, Portway Depot, Macadam Way, West Portway, Andover SP10 3XW ☎ 01264 368000 🖷 01264 369568 ✉ pwykes@testvalley.gov.uk

Grounds Maintenance: Mr Paul Wykes, Head of Environmental Services, Portway Depot, Macadam Way, West Portway, Andover SP10 3XW ☎ 01264 368000 🖷 01264 369568 ✉ pwykes@testvalley.gov.uk

Health and Safety: Ms Pauline Thrush, Health & Safety Officer, Beech Hurst, Weyhill Road, Andover SP10 3AJ ☎ 01264 368000 🖷 01264 368099 ✉ pthrush@testvalley.gov.uk

Housing: Mr Brian Cowcher, Head of Housing & Community Services, Beech Hurst, Weyhill Road, Andover SP10 3AJ ☎ 01264 368601 🖷 01264 368649 ✉ bcowcher@testvalley.gov.uk

Legal: Ms Susan Tovey, Head of Legal Services, Beech Hurst, Weyhill Road, Andover SP10 3AJ ☎ 01264 368401 🖷 01264 368449 ✉ stovey@testvalley.gov.uk

Leisure and Cultural Services: Mr David Tasker, Head of Community & Leisure Services, Beech Hurst, Weyhill Road, Andover SP10 3AJ ☎ 01264 368801 🖷 01264 368899 ✉ dtasker@testvalley.gov.uk

Licensing: Mr Michael White, Licensing Manager, Beech Hurst, Weyhill Road, Andover SP10 3AJ ☎ 01264 368013 🖷 01264 368099 ✉ mwhite@testvalley.gov.uk

Lottery Funding, Charity and Voluntary: Ms Verna Brown, Communities Manager, Beech Hurst, Weyhill Road, Andover SP10 3AJ ☎ 01264 368606 ✉ vbrown@testvalley.gov.uk

Member Services: Mr Tom Van Der Hoven, Head of Administration, Beech Hurst, Weyhill Road, Andover SP10 3AJ ☎ 01264 368001 🖷 01264 368099 ✉ tvanderhoven@testvalley.gov.uk

Parking: Mr Steve Lees, Property Services Manager, Council Offices, Duttons Road, Romsey SO51 3AJ ☎ 01794 527700 🖷 01794 527723 ✉ slees@testvalley.gov.uk

Personnel / HR: Ms Jessie Bell, Strategic HR Manager, Beech Hurst, Weyhill Road, Andover SP10 3AJ ☎ 01264 368251 🖷 01264 368099 ✉ jbell@testvalley.gov.uk

Planning: Mr Paul Jackson, Head of Planning & Building Services, Council Offices, Duttons Road, Romsey SO51 8XG ☎ 01794 527801 🖷 01794 527874 ✉ pjackson@testvalley.gov.uk

Procurement: Mr Mark Lambert, Property Services Manager, Beech Hurst, Weyhill Road, Andover SP10 3AJ ☎ 01264 368701 🖷 01264 368799 ✉ mlambert@testvalley.gov.uk

Recycling & Waste Minimisation: Mr Paul Wykes, Head of Environmental Services, Portway Depot, Macadam Way, West Portway, Andover SP10 3XW ☎ 01264 368000 🖷 01264 369568 ✉ pwykes@testvalley.gov.uk

Regeneration: Mr Simon Ellis, Head of Estates & Economic Development Services, Beech Hurst, Weyhill Road, Andover SP10 3AJ ☎ 01264 368301 ✉ sellis@testvalley.gov.uk

Staff Training: Ms Jessie Bell, Strategic HR Manager, Beech Hurst, Weyhill Road, Andover SP10 3AJ ☎ 01264 368251 🖷 01264 368099 ✉ jbell@testvalley.gov.uk

Sustainable Communities: Mr Brian Cowcher, Head of Housing & Community Services, Beech Hurst, Weyhill Road, Andover SP10 3AJ ☎ 01264 368601 🖷 01264 368649 ✉ bcowcher@testvalley.gov.uk

Sustainable Communities: Mr David Tasker, Head of Community & Leisure Services, Beech Hurst, Weyhill Road, Andover SP10 3AJ ☎ 01264 368801 🖷 01264 368899 ✉ dtasker@testvalley.gov.uk

Sustainable Development: Mr Paul Wykes, Head of Environmental Services, Portway Depot, Macadam Way, West Portway, Andover SP10 3XW ☎ 01264 368000 🖷 01264 369568 ✉ pwykes@testvalley.gov.uk

Tourism: Mr David Gleave, Economic Development Officer, Beech Hurst, Weyhill Road, Andover SP10 3AJ ☎ 01264 368309 🖷 01264 368349 ✉ dgleave@testvalley.gov.uk

Town Centre: Mr Simon Ellis, Head of Estates & Economic Development Services, Beech Hurst, Weyhill Road, Andover SP10 3AJ ☎ 01264 368301 ✉ sellis@testvalley.gov.uk

Traffic Management: Mr Steve Lees, Property Services Manager, Council Offices, Duttons Road, Romsey SO51 3AJ ☎ 01794 527700 🖷 01794 527723 ✉ slees@testvalley.gov.uk

Transport: Mr Steve Lees, Property Services Manager, Council Offices, Duttons Road, Romsey SO51 3AJ ☎ 01794 527700 🖷 01794 527723 ✉ slees@testvalley.gov.uk

Transport Planner: Ms Vivien Messenger, Transport Planner, Council Offices, Duttons Road, Romsey SO51 8XG ☎ 01794

527811 🖷 01794 527874 ✉ vmessenger@testvalley.gov.uk

Transport Planner: Mrs Anne Tomlinson, Transport Planner, Council Offices, Duttons Road, Romsey SO51 8XG ☎ 01794 527811 🖷 01794 527874 ✉ atomlinson@testvalley.gov.uk

Waste Collection and Disposal: Mr Paul Wykes, Head of Environmental Services, Portway Depot, Macadam Way, West Portway, Andover SP10 3XW ☎ 01264 368000 🖷 01264 369568 ✉ pwykes@testvalley.gov.uk

Waste Management: Mr Paul Wykes, Head of Environmental Services, Portway Depot, Macadam Way, West Portway, Andover SP10 3XW ☎ 01264 368000 🖷 01264 369568 ✉ pwykes@testvalley.gov.uk

MEMBERS OF THE COUNCIL (48)

Leader of the Council: **Carr**, Ian (CON - Charlton)
cllricarr@testvalley.gov.uk
Deputy Leader of the Council: **Hatley**, Martin (CON - Ampfield and Braishfield)
cllrmhatley@testvalley.gov.uk
Anderdon, Nigel (CON - Chilworth, Nursling and Rownhams)
cllrnanderdon@testvalley.gov.uk
Andersen, Iris (CON - Andover - St Mary's)
cllriandersen@testvalley.gov.uk
Bailey, Gordon (CON - Blackwater)
cllrgbailey@testvalley.gov.uk
Baverstock, Dorothy (LD - Romsey - Cupernham)
cllrdbaverstock@testvalley.gov.uk
Beesley, Andrew (LD - Valley Park)
cllrabeesley@testvalley.gov.uk
Bird, Katherine (LD - Andover - St. Mary's)
cllrkbird@testvalley.gov.uk
Borg-Neal, Carl (CON - Andover - Harroway)
cllrcborg-neal@testvalley.gov.uk
Boulton, Peter (CON - Broughton and Stockbridge)
cllrpboulton@testvalley.gov.uk
Brook, Alexander (CON - Andover - Alamein)
CllrABrook@testvalley.gov.uk
Brookes, Zilliah (CON - Andover - Millway)
cllrzbrooks@testvalley.gov.uk
Budzynski, Jan (CON - Andover - Winton)
cllrjbudzynski@testvalley.gov.uk
Bundy, Philip (CON - Chilworth, Nursling and Rownhams)
cllrpbundy@testvalley.gov.uk
Busk, Daniel (CON - Broughton and Stockbridge)
cllrdbusk@testvalley.gov.uk
Charnley, Ellie (CON - Penton Bellinger)
cllrecharnley@testvalley.gov.uk
Collier, Clive (CON - Romsey - Abbey)
cllrccollier@testvalley.gov.uk
Cooper, Mark (LD - Romsey - Tadburn)
cllrmcooper@testvalley.gov.uk
Cosier, Stephen (LD - North Baddesley)
cllrscosier@testvalley.gov.uk
Dowden, Alan (LD - Valley Park)
cllradowden@testvalley.gov.uk
Dowden, Celia (LD - North Baddesley)
cllrcdowden@testvalley.gov.uk
Dunleavey, Karen (LD - Romsey - Cupernham)
cllrkdunleavey@testvalley.gov.uk
Few Brown, Benjamin (CON - Amport)
cllrbfewbrown@testvalley.gov.uk
Finlay, Alison (CON - Chilworth, Nursling and Rownhams)
cllrafinlay@testvalley.gov.uk
Flood, Maureen (CON - Anna)
cllrmflood@testvalley.gov.uk
Gentle, Anthony (CON - Blackwater)
cllragentle@testvalley.gov.uk
Giddings, Peter (CON - Bourne Valley)
cllrpgiddings@testvalley.gov.uk
Hamilton, Karen (CON - Andover - Harroway)
cllrkhamilton@testvalley.gov.uk
Hawke, Sandra (CON - Andover - Millway)
cllrshawke@testvalley.gov.uk
Hibberd, Ian (CON - Romsey Extra)
cllrihibberd@testvalley.gov.uk
Hope, Anthony (CON - Over Wallop)
cllrahope@testvalley.gov.uk
Hurst, Peter (LD - Romsey - Tadburn)
cllrphurst@testvalley.gov.uk
Johnston, Alison (CON - Romsey Extra)
cllrajohnston@testvalley.gov.uk
Lashbrook, Philip (CON - Penton Bellinger)
cllrplashbrook@testvalley.gov.uk
Long, Nigel (LD - Andover - St. Mary's)
cllrnlong@testvalley.gov.uk
Lovell, Jan (CON - Andover - Winton)
cllrjlovell@testvalley.gov.uk
Lynn, Christopher (CON - Andover - Winton)
cllrclynn@testvalley.gov.uk
Neal, Jim (CON - Harewood)
cllrjneal@testvalley.gov.uk
North, Phil (CON - Andover - Alamein)
cllrpnorth@testvalley.gov.uk
Page, Brian (CON - Andover - Harroway)
cllrbpage@testvalley.gov.uk
Richards, Ian (CON - Romsey - Abbey)
cllririchards@testvalley.gov.uk
Robin, Ian (CON - Andover - Millway)
cllrirobin@testvalley.gov.uk
Stallard, Graham (CON - Anna)
cllrgstallard@testvalley.gov.uk
Tilling, Katherine (LD - Valley Park)
cllrktilling@testvalley.gov.uk
Tupper, Ann (LD - North Baddesley)
cllratupper@testvalley.gov.uk
Ward, Anthony (CON - King's Somborne and Michelmersh)
cllrtward@testvalley.gov.uk
Whiteley, Janet (CON - Andover - Alamein)
cllrjwhiteley@testvalley.gov.uk
Whiteley, Neville (CON - Dun Valley)
cllrnwhiteley@testvalley.gov.uk

POLITICAL COMPOSITION

CON: 36, LD: 12

CABINET

Leader: Mr Ian Carr
Deputy Leader / Planning & Transport: Mr Martin Hatley
Corporate Services: Mr Daniel Busk
Economic: Mr Peter Giddings
Environment & Health: Mr Peter Boulton
Housing & Community Services: Ms Sandra Hawke
Leisure & Culture: Mr Anthony Ward

COMMITTEE CHAIRS

General Purposes: Mr Martin Hatley
Licensing: Mr Anthony Hope
Overview & Scrutiny: Mr Graham Stallard
Planning Control: Mr Clive Collier
Standards: Mrs V Hughes (External)

TEWKESBURY D

Tewkesbury Borough Council, Council Offices, Gloucester Road, Tewkesbury GL20 5TT ☎ 01684 295010 🖷 01684 272040
democraticservices@tewkesbury.gov.uk
www.tewkesbury.gov.uk

FACTS & FIGURES

Police Authority: Gloucestershire Police Authority
Health Authority: NHS South West
Learning and Skills Council: South West
Parliamentary Constituencies: Tewkesbury
EU Constituencies: South West
Election Frequency: Elections are of whole council
Twinning: Miesbach (Germany)

PRINCIPAL OFFICERS

Chief Executive: Mr Mike Dawson, Chief Executive, Council Offices, Gloucester Road, Tewkesbury GL20 5TT ☎ 01684 272001 chiefexecutive@tewkesbury.gov.uk

Senior Management: Ms Sara Freckleton, Borough Solicitor & Monitoring Officer, Council Offices, Gloucester Road, Tewkesbury GL20 5TT ☎ 01684 272010 sara.freckleton@tewkesbury.gov.uk

Senior Management: Mrs Verna Green, Director of Community, Council Offices, Gloucester Road, Tewkesbury GL20 5TT ☎ 01684 272198 verna.green@tewkesbury.gov.uk

Senior Management: Mr George Hill, Director of Resources, Council Offices, Gloucester Road, Tewkesbury GL20 5TT ☎ 01684 272111 george.hill@tewkesbury.gov.uk

Senior Management: Ms Mella McMahon, Director of Development, Council Offices, Gloucester Road, Tewkesbury GL20 5TT ☎ 01684 272051 mella.mcmahon@tewkesbury.gov.uk

Best Value: Mr Graeme Simpson, Performance & Audit Manager, Council Offices, Gloucester Road, Tewkesbury GL20 5TT ☎ 01684 272002 graeme.simpson@tewkesbury

Building Control: Mr Iain Houston, Building Control Manager, Municipal Offices, The Promenade, Cheltenham GL50 9SA ☎ 01242 264293 🖷 01242 227323 iain.houston@cheltenham.gov.uk

Children / Youth Services: Mr Andy Sanders, Leisure & Culture Manager, Council Offices, Gloucester Road, Tewkesbury GL20 5TT ☎ 01684 272094 andy.sanders@tewkesbury.gov.uk

PR / Communications: Ms Clare Davies, Communications Officer, Council Offices, Gloucester Road, Tewkesbury GL20 5TT ☎ 01684 272291 clare.davies@tewkesbury.gov.uk

Community Planning: Ms Lesa West, Community Planning & Partnerships Officer, Council Offices, Gloucester Road, Tewkesbury GL20 5TT ☎ 01684 272058 lesa.west@tewkesbury.gov.uk

Community Safety: Mrs Val Garside, Housing Options & Community Safety Manager, Council Offices, Gloucester Road, Tewkesbury GL20 5TT ☎ 01684 272259 val.garside@tewkesbury.gov.uk

Computer Management: Ms Tina Nicholls, Customer Services & ICT Manager, Council Offices, Gloucester Road, Tewkesbury GL20 5TT ☎ 01684 272117 tina.nicholls@tewkesbury.gov.uk

Contracts: Mrs Shirin Wotherspoon, Principal Solicitor, Tewkesbury Borough Council, Council Offices, Gloucester Road, Tewkesbury GL20 5TT ☎ 01684 272017 shirin.wotherspoon@tewkesbury.gov.uk

Customer Service: Ms Tina Nicholls, Customer Services & ICT Manager, Council Offices, Gloucester Road, Tewkesbury GL20 5TT ☎ 01684 272117 tina.nicholls@tewkesbury.gov.uk

Direct Labour: Mr Nick Firkins, Assistant Direct Services Officer, Swindon Road Depot, Cheltenham GL51 9JZ ☎ 01684 272199 nick.firkins@tewkesbury.gov.uk

Economic Development: Mrs Julie Wood, Economic Development & Tourism Manager, Council Offices, Gloucester Road, Tewkesbury GL20 5TT ☎ 01684 272095 julie.wood@tewkesbury.gov.uk

E-Government: Ms Tina Nicholls, Customer Services & ICT Manager, Council Offices, Gloucester Road, Tewkesbury GL20 5TT ☎ 01684 272117 tina.nicholls@tewkesbury.gov.uk

Electoral Registration: Mrs Lin O'Brien, Democratic Services Manager, Council Offices, Gloucester Road, Tewkesbury GL20 5TT ☎ 01684 272020 lin.o'brien@tewkesbury.gov.uk

Emergency Planning: Mrs Verna Green, Director of Community, Council Offices, Gloucester Road, Tewkesbury GL20 5TT ☎ 01684 272198 verna.green@tewkesbury.gov.uk

Energy Management: Mr Chris Bosley, Strategic Waste Policy Officer, Council Offices, Gloucester Road, Tewkesbury GL20 5TT ☎ 01684 272181 chris.bosley@tewkesbury.gov.uk

Environmental Health: Ms Sonia Bagshaw, Commercial Services Manager, Council Offices, Gloucester Road, Tewkesbury GL20 5TT ☎ 01684 272173 sonia.bagshaw@tewkesbury.gov.uk

Estates, Property & Valuation: Mr Chris Johns, Land & Property Manager, Council Offices, Gloucester Road, Tewkesbury GL20 5TT ☎ 01684 272274 chris.johns@tewkesbury.gov.uk

Facilities: Mr Chris Johns, Land & Property Manager, Council Offices, Gloucester Road, Tewkesbury GL20 5TT ☎ 01684 272274; 01594 810000 chris.johns@tewkesbury.gov.uk

Finance and Treasurer: Mr George Hill, Director of Resources, Council Offices, Gloucester Road, Tewkesbury GL20 5TT ☎ 01684 272111 george.hill@tewkesbury.gov.uk

Fleet Management: Mr Nick Firkins, Assistant Direct Services Officer, Swindon Road Depot, Cheltenham GL51 9JZ ☎ 01684 272199 ✉ nick.firkins@tewkesbury.gov.uk

Grounds Maintenance: Mr Rob Hainsworth, Contract Agency Officer, Council Offices, Gloucester Road, Tewkesbury GL20 5TT ☎ 01684 272182 ✉ rob.hainsworth@tewkesbury.gov.uk

Health and Safety: Ms Sonia Bagshaw, Commercial Services Manager, Council Offices, Gloucester Road, Tewkesbury GL20 5TT ☎ 01684 272173 ✉ sonia.bagshaw@tewkesbury.gov.uk

Home Energy Conservation: Mr Chris Bosley, Strategic Waste Policy Officer, Council Offices, Gloucester Road, Tewkesbury GL20 5TT ☎ 01684 272181 ✉ chris.bosley@tewkesbury.gov.uk

Housing: Mrs Val Garside, Housing Options & Community Safety Manager, Council Offices, Gloucester Road, Tewkesbury GL20 5TT ☎ 01684 272259 ✉ val.garside@tewkesbury.gov.uk

Legal: Mr Peter Lewis, Shared Head of ONE Legal, Council Offices, Gloucester Road, Tewkesbury GL20 5TT ☎ 01684 272012 ✉ peter.lewis@tewkesbury.gov.uk

Leisure and Cultural Services: Mr Andy Sanders, Leisure & Culture Manager, Council Offices, Gloucester Road, Tewkesbury GL20 5TT ☎ 01684 272094 ✉ andy.sanders@tewkesbury.gov.uk

Licensing: Mr David Steels, Residential Services Manager, Council Offices, Gloucester Road, Tewkesbury GL20 5TT ☎ 01684 272172 ✉ david.steels@tewkesbury.gov.uk

Lottery Funding, Charity and Voluntary: Mrs Julie Wood, Economic Development & Tourism Manager, Council Offices, Gloucester Road, Tewkesbury GL20 5TT ☎ 01684 272095 ✉ julie.wood@tewkesbury.gov.uk

Member Services: Mrs Lin O'Brien, Democratic Services Manager, Council Offices, Gloucester Road, Tewkesbury GL20 5TT ☎ 01684 272020 ✉ lin.o'brien@tewkesbury.gov.uk

Parking: Mr John Horsey, Car Parking & Transport Manager, Council Offices, Gloucester Road, Tewkesbury GL20 5TT ☎ 01684 272063 ✉ john.horsey@tewkesbury.gov.uk

Partnerships: Ms Lesa West, Community Planning & Partnerships Officer, Council Offices, Gloucester Road, Tewkesbury GL20 5TT ☎ 01684 272058 ✉ lesa.west@tewkesbury.gov.uk

Personnel / HR: Ms Janet Martin, HR Advisor, Council Offices, Gloucester Road, Tewkesbury GL20 5TT ☎ 01684 272057 ✉ janet.martin@tewkesbury.gov.uk

Planning: Mr Paul Skelton, Development Control Manager, Council Offices, Gloucester Road, Tewkesbury GL20 5TT ☎ 01684 272102 ✉ paul.skelton@tewkesbury.gov.uk

Recycling & Waste Minimisation: Mrs Verna Green, Director of Community, Council Offices, Gloucester Road, Tewkesbury GL20 5TT ☎ 01684 272198 ✉ verna.green@tewkesbury.gov.uk

Regeneration: Mrs Julie Wood, Economic Development & Tourism Manager, Council Offices, Gloucester Road, Tewkesbury GL20 5TT ☎ 01684 272095 ✉ julie.wood@tewkesbury.gov.uk

Staff Training: Ms Janet Martin, HR Advisor, Council Offices, Gloucester Road, Tewkesbury GL20 5TT ☎ 01684 272057 ✉ janet.martin@tewkesbury.gov.uk

Sustainable Development: Mr Chris Bosley, Strategic Waste Policy Officer, Council Offices, Gloucester Road, Tewkesbury GL20 5TT ☎ 01684 272181 ✉ chris.bosley@tewkesbury.gov.uk

Tourism: Mrs Julie Wood, Economic Development & Tourism Manager, Council Offices, Gloucester Road, Tewkesbury GL20 5TT ☎ 01684 272095 ✉ julie.wood@tewkesbury.gov.uk

Waste Collection and Disposal: Mrs Verna Green, Director of Community, Council Offices, Gloucester Road, Tewkesbury GL20 5TT ☎ 01684 272198 ✉ verna.green@tewkesbury.gov.uk

Waste Management: Mrs Verna Green, Director of Community, Council Offices, Gloucester Road, Tewkesbury GL20 5TT ☎ 01684 272198 ✉ verna.green@tewkesbury.gov.uk

MEMBERS OF THE COUNCIL (38)

***Mayor:* Surman**, Philip (CON - Shurdington)
councillor.surman@tewkesbury.gov.uk

***Deputy Mayor:* Wright**, Claire (CON - Tewkesbury Prior's Park)
councillor.wright@tewkesbury.gov.uk

***Leader of the Council:* Vines**, Robert (CON - Badgeworth)
councillor.vines@tewkesbury.gov.uk

***Deputy Leader of the Council:* Keyte**, Allen (CON - Oxenton Hill)
councillor.keyte@tewkesbury.gov.uk

***Group Leader:* Hillier-Richardson**, Sue (LD - Cleeve Grange)
councillor.hillier-richardson@tewkesbury.gov.uk

***Group Leader:* Sztymiak**, Mike (IND - Tewkesbury Town with Mitton)
councillor.sztymiak@tewkesbury.gov.uk

Allen, Ron (CON - Winchcombe)
councillor.allen@tewkesbury.gov.uk

Awford, Philip (CON - Highnam with Hawbridge)
councillor.awford@tewkesbury.gov.uk

Berry, Kay (LD - Churchdown St John's)
councillor.berry@tewkesbury.gov.uk

Bird, Robert (CON - Cleeve West)
councillor.bird@tewkesbury.gov.uk

Blackwell, Gillian (LD - Churchdown Brookfield)
councillor.blackwell@tewkesbury.gov.uk

Calway, Brian (CON - Tewkesbury Prior's Park)
councillor.bcalway@tewkesbury.gov.uk

Carter, Adele (CON - Northway)
councillor.carter@tewkesbury.gov.uk

Davies, Derek (CON - Highnam with Hawbridge)
councillor.davies@tewkesbury.gov.uk

Day, Janet (CON - Winchcombe)
councillor.day@tewkesbury.gov.uk

Dean, Mike (CON - Cleeve Hill)
councillor.dean@tewkesbury.gov.uk

East, Bob (CON - Cleeve St Michael's)
councillor.east@tewkesbury.gov.uk
Evetts, John (CON - Isbourne)
councillor.evetts@tewkesbury.gov,uk
Healy, Hannah (LD - Cleeve St Michael's)
councillor.healy@twekesbury.gov.uk
Hesketh, John (CON - Ashchurch with Walton Cardiff)
councillor.hesketh@tewkesbury.gov.uk
Jones, Brian (IND - Churchdown Brookfield)
councillor.jones@tewkesbury.gov.uk
Mackinnon, Anthony (LD - Cleeve West)
councillor.mackinnon@tewkesbury.gov.uk
Mactienan, Elaine (CON - Northway)
councillor.mactiernan@tewkesbury.gov.uk
Mason, Jim (CON - Winchcombe)
councillor.mason@tewkesbury.gov.uk
Ogden, Margaret (CON - Cleeve Hill)
councillor.ogden@tewkesbury.gov.uk
Perez, Jude (LD - Brockworth)
councillor.perez@tewkesbury.gov.uk
Perez, Vince (LD - Brockworth)
councillor.perezv@tewkesbury.gov.uk
Ricks, Audrey (LD - Churchdown St John's)
councillor.ricks@tewkesbury.gov.uk
Rowcliffe-Quarry, Maureen (LD - Brockworth)
councillor.rowcliffe-quarry@tewkesbury.gov.uk
Shurmer, Gordon (CON - Twyning)
councillor.shurmer@tewkesbury.gov.uk
Silverthorn, Marc (CON - Hucclecote)
councillor.silverthorn@tewkesbury.gov.uk
Smith, Vernon (CON - Tewkesbury Newtown)
councillor.smithv@tewkesbury.gov.uk
Stokes, Pearl (LD - Churchdown St John's)
councillor.stokes@tewkesbury.gov.uk
Tugwell, Adam (CON - Ashchurch with Walton Cardiff)
councillor.tugwell@tewkesbury.gov.uk
Tugwell, Adam (LD - Innsworth with Down Hatherley)
councillor.whelan@tewkesbury.gov.uk
Waters, David (CON - Coombe Hill)
councillor.waters@tewkesbury.gov.uk
Williams, Mark (CON - Coombe Hill)
councillor.williams@tewkesbury.gov.uk
Workman, Philip (IND - Tewkesbury Town With Mitton)
councillor.workman@tewkesbury.gov.uk

POLITICAL COMPOSITION

CON: 24, LD: 11, IND: 3

CABINET

Leader: Mr Robert Vines
Deputy Leader / Finance & Asset Management: Mr Allen Keyte
Built Environment: Mr Derek Davies
Clean & Green Environment: Mr Jim Mason
Community Development: Mrs Sue Hillier-Richardson
Corporate Governance: Mrs Jude Perez
Economic Development & Promotion: Mr David Waters
Organisational Development: Ms Audrey Ricks
Safer, Stronger & Healthier Communities: Mrs Claire Wright

COMMITTEE CHAIRS

Audit: Mr Anthony Mackinnon
Executive: Mr Robert Vines
Licensing: Mr Adam Tugwell
Overview & Scrutiny: Mr Brian Calway
Planning: Mr John Evetts

THANET D

Thanet District Council, Thanet Council Offices, Cecil Street, Margate CT9 1XZ ☎ 01843 577000 🖷 01843 290906
✉ customer.services@thanet.gov.uk 💻 www.thanet.gov.uk

FACTS & FIGURES

Police Authority: Kent Police Authority
Health Authority: South East Coast Strategic Health Authority
Learning and Skills Council: South East
EU Constituencies: South East
Election Frequency: Elections are biennial
Twinning: Broadstairs and St. Peters: Nettetal (Germany); Wattignies (France); Margate: Les Mureaux (France); Idar Oberstein (Germany); Yalta (Ukraine); Ramsgate: Conflans-Ste-Honorine (France); Frederiksund (Denmark)

PRINCIPAL OFFICERS

Chief Executive: Dr Sue McGonnigal, Chief Executive & S.151 Officer, Thanet Council Offices, Cecil Street, Margate CT9 1XZ ☎ 01843 577001 🖷 01843 290906
✉ sue.mcgonnigal@thanet.gov.uk

Senior Management: Ms Sarah Carroll, Business Services Manager, Thanet Council Offices, Cecil Street, Margate CT9 1XZ ☎ 01843 577188 🖷 01843 290906 ✉ sarah.carroll@thanet.gov.uk

Senior Management: Ms Madeline Homer, Community Services Manager, Thanet Council Offices, Cecil Street, Margate CT9 1XZ ☎ 01843 577123 🖷 01843 290906
✉ madeline.homer@thanet.gov.uk

Senior Management: Ms Sarah Martin, Financial Services Manager and Deputy S.151 Officer, Thanet Council Offices, Cecil Street, Margate CT9 1XZ ☎ 01843 577617
✉ sarah.martin@thanet.gov.uk

Senior Management: Mr Harvey Patterson, Corporate & Regulatory Services Manager, Thanet District Council, Environmental Services, Council Offices, PO Box 9, Margate CT9 1XZ ☎ 01843 577005 🖷 01843 290906
✉ harvey.patterson@thanet.gov.uk

Senior Management: Mr Mark Seed, Commercial Services Manager, Council Offices, Cecil Street, Margate CT9 1XZ ☎ 01843 577742 🖷 01843 577686 ✉ mark.seed@thanet.gov.uk

Architect, Building / Property Services: Mrs Paul Verrall, Landscape & Building Services Manager, Council Offices, Cecil Street, Margate CT9 1XZ ☎ 01843 577960 🖷 01843 577686
✉ paul.verrall@thanet.gov.uk

Best Value: Ms Sarah Carroll, Business Services Manager, Thanet Council Offices, Cecil Street, Margate CT9 1XZ ☎ 01843 577188 🖷 01843 290906 ✉ sarah.carroll@thanet.gov.uk

Building Control: Mr Geoff Musk, Building Control Manager, Council Offices, Cecil Street, Margate CT9 1XZ ☎ 01843 577156

🖷 01843 231755 ✉ geoff.musk@thanet.gov.uk

PR / Communications: Mrs Justine Wingate, Corporate Information Manager, Thanet Council Offices, Cecil Street, Margate CT9 1XZ ☎ 01843 577908 🖷 01843 290906 ✉ justine.wingate@thanet.gov.uk

Community Planning: Ms Madeline Homer, Community Services Manager, Thanet Council Offices, Cecil Street, Margate CT9 1XZ ☎ 01843 577123 🖷 01843 290906 ✉ madeline.homer@thanet.gov.uk

Community Safety: Mr Martyn Cassell, Community Safety Manager, Thanet Council Offices, Cecil Street, Margate CT9 1XZ ☎ 01843 577367 ✉ martyn.cassell@thanet.gov.uk

Computer Management: Mrs Angela Waite, Head of ICT, EK Services, Military Road, Canterbury CT1 1YW ☎ 01227 862028 🖷 01227 862208 ✉ angela.waite@canterbury.gov.uk

Contracts: Ms Karen Paton, Procurement & Contracts Manager, Council Offices, Cecil Street, Margate CT9 1XZ ☎ 01843 577111 🖷 01843 290906 ✉ karen.paton@thanet.gov.uk

Corporate Services: Mr Harvey Patterson, Corporate & Regulatory Services Manager, Thanet District Council, Cecil Street, Margate CT9 1XZ ☎ 01843 577005 🖷 01843 290906 ✉ harvey.patterson@thanet.gov.uk

Customer Service: Ms Donna Reed, Shared Services Director, EK Services, Military Road, Canterbury CT1 1YW ☎ 01227 862073 ✉ donna.reed@ekservices.org

Economic Development: Mr Rob Hetherington, Economic Development & Regeneration Manager, Thanet Council Offices, Cecil Street, Margate CT9 1XZ ☎ 01843 577153 🖷 01843 290906 ✉ rob.hetherington@thanet.gov.uk

E-Government: Mrs Roz Edridge, Business Systems Manager, East Kent Services, Council Offices, Cecil Street, Margate CT9 1XZ ☎ 01843 577033; 01843 577033; 01843 577033 ✉ roz.edridge@thanet.gov.uk

Electoral Registration: Dr Glenn Back, Democratic Services & Scrutiny Manager, Thanet Council Offices, Cecil Street, Margate CT9 1XZ ☎ 01843 577187 ✉ glenn.back@thanet.gov.uk

Emergency Planning: Mr Mike Humber, District Engineer, Thanet Council Offices, Cecil Street, Margate CT9 1XZ ☎ 01843 577083 ✉ mike.humber@thanet.gov.uk

Environmental / Technical Services: Ms Madeline Homer, Community Services Manager, Thanet Council Offices, Cecil Street, Margate CT9 1XZ ☎ 01843 577123 🖷 01843 290906 ✉ madeline.homer@thanet.gov.uk

Environmental Health: Ms Penny Button, Environmental Health Manager, Thanet Council Offices, Cecil Street, Margate CT9 1XZ ☎ 01843 577425 🖷 01843 290906 ✉ penny.button@thanet.gov.uk

Events Manager: Ms Janice Watson, Community Development Manager, Thanet Council Offices, Cecil Street, Margate CT9 1XZ ☎ 01843 5577792 ✉ janice.watson@thanet.gov.uk

Facilities: Mrs Paul Verrall, Landscape & Building Services Manager, Council Offices, Cecil Street, Margate CT9 1XZ ☎ 01843 577960 🖷 01843 577686 ✉ paul.verrall@thanet.gov.uk

Finance and Treasurer: Ms Sarah Martin, Financial Services Manager and Deputy S.151 Officer, Thanet Council Offices, Cecil Street, Margate CT9 1XZ ☎ 01843 577617 ✉ sarah.martin@thanet.gov.uk

Fleet Management: Mr Mark Seed, Commercial Services Manager, Council Offices, Cecil Street, Margate CT9 1XZ ☎ 01843 577742 🖷 01843 577686 ✉ mark.seed@thanet.gov.uk

Grounds Maintenance: Mrs Paul Verrall, Landscape & Building Services Manager, Council Offices, Cecil Street, Margate CT9 1XZ ☎ 01843 577960 🖷 01843 577686 ✉ paul.verrall@thanet.gov.uk

Health and Safety: Ms Penny Button, Environmental Health Manager, Thanet Council Offices, Cecil Street, Margate CT9 1XZ ☎ 01843 577425 🖷 01843 290906 ✉ penny.button@thanet.gov.uk

Home Energy Conservation: Miss Tanya Wenham, Housing Regeneration Manager, Thanet Council Offices, Cecil Street, Margate CT9 1XZ ☎ 01843 577006 🖷 01843 290606 ✉ tanya.wenham@thanet.gov.uk

Housing: Mr Craig George, Housing Services Manager, Thanet Council Offices, Cecil Street, Margate CT9 1XZ ☎ 01843 577220 🖷 01843 290906 ✉ craig.george@thanet.gov.uk

Housing Maintenance: Mr Elliot Austin, Housing Maintenance Manager, East Kent Housing Ltd, c/o Council Offices, Cecil Street, Margate CT9 1XZ ☎ 01843 577085; 01843 577085 🖷 01843 290906 ✉ elliot.austin@thanet.gov.uk

Legal: Mr Gary Cordes, Legal Services Manager, Thanet Council Offices, Cecil Street, Margate CT9 1XZ ☎ 01843 577906 🖷 01843 577606

Leisure and Cultural Services: Ms Janice Watson, Community Development Manager, Thanet Council Offices, Cecil Street, Margate CT9 1XZ ☎ 01843 5577792 ✉ janice.watson@thanet.gov.uk

Licensing: Mr Philip Bensted, Regulatory Services Manager, Council Offices, Cecil Street, Margate CT9 1XZ ☎ 01843 577630 🖷 01843 290906 ✉ philip.bensted@thanet.gov.uk

Lottery Funding, Charity and Voluntary: Ms Janice Watson, Community Development Manager, Thanet Council Offices, Cecil Street, Margate CT9 1XZ ☎ 01843 5577792 ✉ janice.watson@thanet.gov.uk

Member Services: Dr Glenn Back, Democratic Services & Scrutiny Manager, Thanet Council Offices, Cecil Street, Margate CT9 1XZ ☎ 01843 577187 ✉ glenn.back@thanet.gov.uk

Parking: Mr Robin Chantrill-Smith, Civil Enforcement Manager, Thanet Council Offices, Cecil Street, Margate CT9 1XZ ☎ 01843

577472 robin.chantrill-smith@thanet.gov.uk

Partnerships: Ms Janice Watson, Community Development Manager, Thanet Council Offices, Cecil Street, Margate CT9 1XZ ☎ 01843 5577792 janice.watson@thanet.gov.uk

Personnel / HR: Ms Juli Oliver-Smith, Head of EK Human Resources, East Kent HR Partnership, Dover District Council, White Cliffs Business Park, Whitfield, Dover CT16 3PJ ☎ 07917 473616 hrpartnership@dover.gov.uk

Planning: Mr Simon Thomas, Planning Manager, Thanet Council Offices, Cecil Street, Margate CT9 1XZ ☎ 01843 577752 01843 290906 simon.thomas@thanet.gov.uk

Procurement: Ms Karen Paton, Procurement & Contracts Manager, Council Offices, Cecil Street, Margate CT9 1XZ ☎ 01843 577111 01843 290906 karen.paton@thanet.gov.uk

Recycling & Waste Minimisation: Mr Mark Seed, Commercial Services Manager, Council Offices, Cecil Street, Margate CT9 1XZ ☎ 01843 577742 01843 577686 mark.seed@thanet.gov.uk

Regeneration: Mr Rob Hetherington, Economic Development & Regeneration Manager, Thanet Council Offices, Cecil Street, Margate CT9 1XZ ☎ 01843 577153 01843 290906 rob.hetherington@thanet.gov.uk

Staff Training: Ms Sonia Godfrey, HR Manager - Business Services, East Kent HR Partnership, Dover District Council, White Cliffs Business Park, Whitfield, Dover CT16 3PJ ☎ 07854 763690 hrpartnership@dover.gov.uk

Street Scene: Mr Phil Snook, Street Scene Enforcement Manager, Thanet Council Offices, Cecil Street, Margate CT9 1XZ ☎ 01843 577658 phil.snook@thanet.gov.uk

Sustainable Communities: Ms Janice Watson, Community Development Manager, Thanet Council Offices, Cecil Street, Margate CT9 1XZ ☎ 01843 5577792 janice.watson@thanet.gov.uk

Tourism: Mrs Paula Harbidge, Tourism Manager, Thanet Council Offices, Cecil Street, Margate CT9 1XZ ☎ 01843 577644 01843 290906 paula.harbidge

Waste Collection and Disposal: Mr Mark Seed, Commercial Services Manager, Council Offices, Cecil Street, Margate CT9 1XZ ☎ 01843 577742 01843 577686 mark.seed@thanet.gov.uk

Waste Management: Mr Mark Seed, Commercial Services Manager, Council Offices, Cecil Street, Margate CT9 1XZ ☎ 01843 577742 01843 577686 mark.seed@thanet.gov.uk

Children's Play Areas: Mr Martyn Cassell, Community Safety Manager, Thanet Council Offices, Cecil Street, Margate CT9 1XZ ☎ 01843 577367 martyn.cassell@thanet.gov.uk

MEMBERS OF THE COUNCIL (57)

***Chair:* Clark**, Douglas (LAB - Cliftonville West)
cllr-doug.clark@thanet.gov.uk
***Vice-Chair:* Dark**, Kay (LAB - Northwood)
cllr-kay.dark@thanet.gov.uk
***Mayor:* Nicholson**, Richard (CON - Westbrook)
cllr-mick.tomlinson@thanet.gov.uk
***Leader of the Council:* Hart**, Clive (LAB - Cliftonville West)
cllr-clive.hart@thanet.gov.uk
***Group Leader:* Bayford**, Robert (CON - Kingsgate)
cllr-robert.bayford@thanet.gov.uk
***Group Leader:* King**, Thomas (IND - Westgate-on-Sea)
cllr-thomas.king@thanet.gov.uk
Aldred, Linda (LAB - Cliftonville West)
cllr-linda.aldred@thanet.gov.uk
Alexandrou, Steve (LAB - Nethercourt)
cllr-steve.alexandrou@thanet.gov
Binks, Rosalind (CON - Beacon Road)
cllr-rosalind.binks@thanet.gov.uk
Bruce, Alasdair (CON - Birchington South)
cllr-alasdair.bruce@thanet.gov.uk
Campbell, Peter (LAB - Central Harbour)
cllr-peter.campbell@thanet.gov.uk
Cohen, Jack (IND - Birchington South)
cllr-Jack.cohen@thanet.gov.uk
Coleman-Cooke, Keith (CON - Birchington North)
cllr-jennifer.matterface@thanet.gov.uk
Day, Simon (CON - Birchington North)
cllr-simon.day@thanet.gov.uk
Driver, Ian (LAB - Newington)
cllr-mike.harrison@thanet.gov.uk
Driver, Ian (LAB - Northwood)
cllr-ian.driver@thanet.gov.uk
Dwyer, Mary (LAB - Central Harbour)
cllr-mary.dwyer@thanet.gov.uk
Edwards, John (LAB - Dane Valley)
cllr-john.edwards@thanet.gov.uk
Everitt, Rick (LAB - Eastcliff)
cllr-richard.everitt@thanet.gov.uk
Ezekiel, Sandy (CON - Cliftonville East)
cllr-sandy.ezekiel@thanet.gov.uk
Fenner, Michelle (LAB - Sir Moses Montefiore)
cllr-michelle.fenner@thanet.gov.uk
Gibson, Kim (LAB - Nethercourt)
cllr-kim.gibson@thanet.gov.uk
Gideon, Joanna (CON - Cliffsend and Pegwell)
cllr-jo.gideon@thanet.gov.uk
Goodwin, Brian (CON - Westgate-on-Sea)
cllr-brian.goodwin@thanet.gov.uk
Green, David (LAB - Eastcliff)
cllr-david.green@thanet.gov.uk
Green, Elizabeth (LAB - Northwood)
cllr-elizabeth.green@thanet.gov.uk
Gregory, Ken (CON - Garlinge)
cllr-ken.gregory@thanet.gov.uk
Gregory, Ian (CON - St Peters)
cllr-ian.gregory@thanet.gov.uk
Grove, Bob (IND - Thanet Villages)
cllr-bob.grove@thanet.gov.uk
Hart, Sandra (LAB - Dane Valley)
cllr-sandra.hart@thanet.gov.uk
Hayton, William (CON - Bradstowe)
cllr-bill.hayton@thanet.gov.uk
Hibbert, Jodie (LAB - Westgate-on-sea)
Hornus, Neil (CON - Westbrook)

cllr-neil.hornus@thanet.gov.uk
Huxley, Corinna (LAB - Central Harbour)
cllr-corinna.huxley@thanet.gov.uk
Johnston, Iris (LAB - Margate Central)
cllr-iris.johnston@thanet.gov.uk
Kirby, John (CON - Cliffsend and Pegwell)
cllr-john.kirby@thanet.gov.uk
Lodge-Pritchard, Ela (LAB - Salmestone)
cllr-ela.lodge-pritchard@thanet.gov.uk
Marson, Julie (CON - Viking)
cllr-julie.marson@thanet.gov.uk
Matterface, Jennifer (LAB - Beacon Road)
cllr-jennifer.matterface@thanet.gov.uk
Moore, Pat (LAB - Eastcliff)
cllr-richard.everitt@thanet.gov.uk
Moores, Simon (CON - Westgate-on-Sea)
cllr-simon.moores@thanet.gov.uk
Nicholson, Richard (LAB - Newington)
cllr-richard.nicholson@thanet.gov.uk
Poole, Alan (LAB - Sir Moses Montefiore)
cllr-alan.poole@thanet.gov.uk
Roberts, Michael (CON - Thanet Villages)
cllr-michael.roberts@thanet.gov.uk
Saunders, David (CON - Bradstowe)
cllr-david.saunders@thanet.gov.uk
Saunders, Mave (CON - Viking)
cllr-mave.saunders@thanet.gov.uk
Scobie, William (LAB - Dane Valley)
cllr-William.Scobie@thanet.gov.uk
Scobie, Harry (LAB - Salmestone)
cllr-harry.scobie@thanet.gov.uk
Sullivan, Brian (CON - Cliftonville East)
cllr-brian.sullivan@thanet.gov.uk
Tomlinson, Shirley (CON - Garlinge)
cllr-shirley.tomlinson@thanet.gov.uk
Watkins, John (LAB - Margate Central)
cllr-john.watkins@thanet.gov.uk
Wells, Christopher (CON - Viking)
cllr-chris.wells@thanet.gov.uk
Wiltshire, Zita (CON - St Peters)
cllr-zita.wiltshire@thanet.gov.uk
Wise, Martin (CON - Cliftonville East)
cllr-martin.wise@thanet.gov.uk
Worrow, John (CON - Birchington South)
cllr-John.Worrow@thanet.gov.uk
Worrow, John (CON - St Peters)
cllr-jason.savage@thanet.gov.uk
Wright, Linda
(CON - Thanet Villages)
cllr-Linda.Wright@thanet.gov.uk

POLITICAL COMPOSITION

CON: 27, LAB: 27, IND: 3

CABINET

Leader / Corporate Regulatory & Strategic Economic Development: Mr Clive Hart
Deputy Leader / Commercial Services: Mr Alan Poole
Business Services: Mrs Michelle Fenner
Community Services: Mrs Iris Johnston
Financial Services: Mr Rick Everitt
Housing & Planning: Mr David Green

COMMITTEE CHAIRS

Governance & Audit: Mr John Worrow
Joint Transportation: Mr John Kirby
Licensing Board: Mr Richard Nicholson
Overview & Scrutiny Panel: Mr Ian Driver
Planning: Mr Jack Cohen
Standards: Mr Robin Hills (External)

THREE RIVERS D

Three Rivers District Council, Three Rivers House, Northway, Rickmansworth WD3 1RL ☎ 01923 776611 🖷 01923 896119
enquiries@threerivers.gov.uk www.threerivers.gov.uk

FACTS & FIGURES

Police Authority: Hertfordshire Police Authority
Health Authority: East of England Strategic Health Authority
Learning and Skills Council: Eastern
Parliamentary Constituencies: South West Hertfordshire, St. Albans, Watford
EU Constituencies: Eastern
Election Frequency: Elections are by thirds

PRINCIPAL OFFICERS

Chief Executive: Dr Steven Halls, Chief Executive, Three Rivers House, Northway, Rickmansworth WD3 1RL ☎ 01923 727281 🖷 01923 727282 steven.halls@threerivers.gov.uk

Senior Management: Mr Peter Brooker, Director of Community & Environmental Services, Three Rivers House, Northway, Rickmansworth WD3 1RL ☎ 01923 776611 🖷 01923 896119 peter.brooker@threerivers.gov.uk

Senior Management: Mr David Gardner, Director of Corporate Resources & Governance, Three Rivers House, Northway, Rickmansworth WD3 1RL ☎ 01923 776611 🖷 01923 896119 david.gardner@threerivers.gov.uk

Architect, Building / Property Services: Mr Nick Dimbleby, Head of Sustainability, Three Rivers House, Northway, Rickmansworth WD3 1RL ☎ 01923 776611 🖷 01923 896119 nick.dimbleby@threerivers.gov.uk

Building Control: Mr Clive Fuller, Chief Building Control Officer, Three Rivers House, Northway, Rickmansworth WD3 1RL ☎ 01923 776611 🖷 01923 727137 clive.fuller@threerivers.gov.uk

Building Control: Mr James White, Principal Building Control Surveyor, Three Rivers House, Northway, Rickmansworth WD3 1RL ☎ 01923 776611 james.white@threerivers.gov.uk

PR / Communications: Mr Kevin Snow, Communications Manager, Three Rivers House, Northway, Rickmansworth WD3 1RL ☎ 01923 776611 🖷 01923 727258 kevin.snow@threerivers.gov.uk

Community Planning: Mr Renato Messere, Head of Local Development Plans, Three Rivers House, Northway, Rickmansworth WD3 1RL ☎ 01923 776611 🖷 01923 896119 renato.messere@threerivers.gov.uk

Community Safety: Mr Andy Stovold, Community Partnerships Manager, Three Rivers House, Northway, Rickmansworth WD3

1RL ☎ 01923 776611 🖷 01923 896119 ✉ andy.stovold@threerivers.gov.uk

Computer Management: Mrs Avni Patel, Head of ICT, Three Rivers House, Northway, Rickmansworth WD3 1RL ☎ 01923 776611 🖷 01923 896119 ✉ avni.patel@threerivers.gov.uk

Customer Service: Mr William Hall, Customer Services Manager, Three Rivers House, Northway, Rickmansworth WD3 1RL ☎ 01923 776611 🖷 01923 896119 ✉ billy.hall@threerivers.gov.uk

Economic Development: Mr Renato Messere, Head of Local Development Plans, Three Rivers House, Northway, Rickmansworth WD3 1RL ☎ 01923 776611 🖷 01923 896119 ✉ renato.messere@threerivers.gov.uk

E-Government: Mrs Avni Patel, Head of ICT, Three Rivers House, Northway, Rickmansworth WD3 1RL ☎ 01923 776611 🖷 01923 896119 ✉ avni.patel@threerivers.gov.uk

Electoral Registration: Mr Elwyn Wilson, Democratic Services Manager, Three Rivers House, Northway, Rickmansworth WD3 1RL ☎ 01923 776611 🖷 01923 896119 ✉ elwyn.wilson@threerivers.gov.uk

Emergency Planning: Mr Phil King, Emergency Planning & Risk Management Manager, Three Rivers House, Northway, Rickmansworth WD3 1RL ☎ 01923 776611 🖷 01923 896119 ✉ phil.king@threerivers.gov.uk

Energy Management: Mr Nick Dimbleby, Head of Sustainability, Three Rivers House, Northway, Rickmansworth WD3 1RL ☎ 01923 776611 🖷 01923 896119 ✉ nick.dimbleby@threerivers.gov.uk

Environmental / Technical Services: Mr Malcolm Clarke, Services Manager, Batchwood Depot, Harefield Road, Rickmansworth WD3 1RL ☎ 01923 776611 ✉ malcolm.clarke@threerivers.gov.uk

Environmental Health: Mr Geof Muggeridge, Head of Development Management and Environmental Health, Three Rivers House, Northway, Rickmansworth WD3 1RL ☎ 01923 776611 🖷 01923 896119 ✉ geof.muggeridge@threerivers.gov.uk

Estates, Property & Valuation: Mr Nick Dimbleby, Head of Sustainability, Three Rivers House, Northway, Rickmansworth WD3 1RL ☎ 01923 776611 🖷 01923 896119 ✉ nick.dimbleby@threerivers.gov.uk

Facilities: Ms Yvonne Petagine, Services Manager, Three Rivers House, Northway, Rickmansworth WD3 1RL ☎ 01923 776611 🖷 01923 896119 ✉ yvonne.petagine@threerivers.gov.uk

Finance and Treasurer: Mr David Gardner, Director of Corporate Resources & Governance, Three Rivers House, Northway, Rickmansworth WD3 1RL ☎ 01923 776611 🖷 01923 896119 ✉ david.gardner@threerivers.gov.uk

Grounds Maintenance: Mr Malcolm Clarke, Services Manager, Batchwood Depot, Harefield Road, Rickmansworth WD3 1RL ☎ 01923 776611 ✉ malcolm.clarke@threerivers.gov.uk

Health and Safety: Mr Darren Williams, Corporate Health & Safety Advisor, Three Rivers House, Northway, Rickmansworth WD3 1RL ☎ 01923 776611 ✉ darren.williams@threerivers.gov.uk

Housing: Ms Patsy Gilbert, Housing Strategy & Development Officer, Three Rivers House, Northway, Rickmansworth WD3 1RL ☎ 01923 776611 ✉ patsy.gilbert@threerivers.gov.uk

Housing: Mr Nyack Semelo-Shaw, Head of Housing, Three Rivers House, Northway, Rickmansworth WD3 1RL ☎ 01923 776611 ✉ nyack.semelo-shaw@threerivers.gov.uk

Legal: Mrs Anne Morgan, Solicitor to the Council, Three Rivers House, Northway, Rickmansworth WD3 1RL ☎ 01923 776611 🖷 01923 727213 ✉ anne.morgan@threerivers.gov.uk

Leisure and Cultural Services: Mr Chris Hope, Head of Leisure & Community Services, Three Rivers House, Northway, Rickmansworth WD3 1RL ☎ 01923 776611 🖷 01923 727150 ✉ chris.hope@threerivers.gov.uk

Licensing: Mr David Shorto, Licensing Officer, Three Rivers House, Northway, Rickmansworth WD3 1RL ☎ 01923 776611 🖷 01923 896119 ✉ david.shorto@threerivers.gov.uk

Lottery Funding, Charity and Voluntary: Mr Karl Stonebank, Voluntary Sector Officer, Three Rivers House, Northway, Rickmansworth WD3 1RL ☎ 01923 776611 ✉ karl.stonebank@threerivers.gov.uk

Member Services: Mr Elwyn Wilson, Democratic Services Manager, Three Rivers House, Northway, Rickmansworth WD3 1RL ☎ 01923 776611 🖷 01923 896119 ✉ elwyn.wilson@threerivers.gov.uk

Parking: Mr Peter Kerr, Principal Projects Manager, Three Rivers House, Northway, Rickmansworth WD3 1RL ☎ 01923 776611 🖷 01923 896119 ✉ peter.kerr@threerivers.gov.uk

Partnerships: Mr Andy Stovold, Community Partnerships Manager, Three Rivers House, Northway, Rickmansworth WD3 1RL ☎ 01923 776611 🖷 01923 896119 ✉ andy.stovold@threerivers.gov.uk

Personnel / HR: Mr Terry Baldwin, Head of HR, Three Rivers House, Northway, Rickmansworth WD3 1RL ☎ 01923 776611 ✉ terry.baldwin@threerivers.gov.uk

Planning: Mr Geof Muggeridge, Head of Development Management and Environmental Health, Three Rivers House, Northway, Rickmansworth WD3 1RL ☎ 01923 776611 🖷 01923 896119 ✉ geof.muggeridge@threerivers.gov.uk

Recycling & Waste Minimisation: Mrs Alison Page, Head of Environmental Protection, Three Rivers House, Northway, Rickmansworth WD3 1RL ☎ 01923 776611 🖷 01923 727037 ✉ alison.page@threerivers.gov.uk

Staff Training: Ms Marj Setters, Organisational Development Manager, Three Rivers House, Northway, Rickmansworth WD3

1RL ☏ 01923 776611 ✉ marj.setters@threerivers.gov.uk

Street Scene: Mr Peter Kerr, Principal Projects Manager, Three Rivers House, Northway, Rickmansworth WD3 1RL ☏ 01923 776611 🖷 01923 896119 ✉ peter.kerr@threerivers.gov.uk

Sustainable Communities: Dr Steven Halls, Chief Executive, Three Rivers House, Northway, Rickmansworth WD3 1RL ☏ 01923 727281 🖷 01923 727282 ✉ steven.halls@threerivers.gov.uk

Sustainable Development: Mr Renato Messere, Head of Local Development Plans, Three Rivers House, Northway, Rickmansworth WD3 1RL ☏ 01923 776611 🖷 01923 896119 ✉ renato.messere@threerivers.gov.uk

Tourism: Mr Peter Kerr, Principal Projects Manager, Three Rivers House, Northway, Rickmansworth WD3 1RL ☏ 01923 776611 🖷 01923 896119 ✉ peter.kerr@threerivers.gov.uk

Town Centre: Mr Peter Kerr, Principal Projects Manager, Three Rivers House, Northway, Rickmansworth WD3 1RL ☏ 01923 776611 🖷 01923 896119 ✉ peter.kerr@threerivers.gov.uk

Transport Planner: Mr Renato Messere, Head of Local Development Plans, Three Rivers House, Northway, Rickmansworth WD3 1RL ☏ 01923 776611 🖷 01923 896119 ✉ renato.messere@threerivers.gov.uk

Waste Collection and Disposal: Mr Malcolm Clarke, Services Manager, Batchwood Depot, Harefield Road, Rickmansworth WD3 1RL ☏ 01923 776611 ✉ malcolm.clarke@threerivers.gov.uk

Waste Management: Mr Malcolm Clarke, Services Manager, Batchwood Depot, Harefield Road, Rickmansworth WD3 1RL ☏ 01923 776611 ✉ malcolm.clarke@threerivers.gov.uk

Children's Play Areas: Mr Chris Hope, Head of Leisure & Community Services, Three Rivers House, Northway, Rickmansworth WD3 1RL ☏ 01923 776611 🖷 01923 727150 ✉ chris.hope@threerivers.gov.uk

MEMBERS OF THE COUNCIL (48)

***Chair:* Butt**, Kemal (CON - Moor Park and Eastbury)
cllr.kbutt@gmail.com
***Vice-Chair:* Mead**, Les (LD - Penn)
les.mead@threerivers.gov.uk
***Leader of the Council:* Shaw**, Ann (LD - Maple Cross and Mill End)
ann.shaw@threerivers.gov.uk
Ayrton, Chris (LD - Langleybury)
chris.ayrton@threerivers.gov.uk
Bakshi, Ana (LAB - Northwick)
ana.bakashi@threerivers.gov.uk
Barton, Tony (CON - Sarratt)
tony.barton@threerivers.gov.uk
Bedford, Sara (LD - Abbots Langley)
sara.bedford@threerivers.gov.uk
Bedford, Matthew (LD - Abbots Langley)
matthew.bedford@threerivers.gov.uk
Bishop, Eric (CON - Carpenders Park)
eric.bishop@threerivers.gov.uk
Brading, Phil (LD - Croxley Green South)
phil.brading@threerivers.gov.uk
Cox, Stephen (LAB - Hayling)
stephen.cox@threerivers.gov.uk
Dann, Leighton (LD - Croxley Green)
leighton.dann@threerivers.gov.uk
Davis, Guy (CON - Chorleywood East)
guy.davis@threerivers.gov.uk
Drury, Steve (LD - Croxley Green North)
steve.drury@threerivers.gov.uk
Giles-Medhurst, Stephen (LD - Leavesden)
sgm@cix.co.uk
Goggins, Paul (LD - Langleybury)
paul.goggins@hertscc.gov.uk
Gordon, Paul (LAB - Ashridge)
paul.gordon@threerivers.gov.uk
Hames, Pam (LD - Carpenders Park)
pam.hames@threerivers.gov.uk
Harris, Ty (CON - Northwick)
ty.harris@threerivers.gov.uk
Hayward, Chris (CON - Chorleywood East)
chris.hayward@threerivers.gov.uk
Hiscocks, Paula (CON - Rickmansworth)
paula.hiscocks@threerivers.gov.uk
King, Stephen (LAB - Hayling)
cllr.stephenking@yahoo.co.uk
Lamb, Barbara (CON - Rickmansworth West)
barbara.lamb@threerivers.gov.uk
Lehrle, Helen (LD - Bedmond and Primrose Hill)
helen.lehrle@threerivers.gov.uk
Lloyd, Chris (LD - Croxley Green North)
chris.lloyd@threerivers.gov.uk
Lucas, Chris (LD - Maple Cross and Mill End)
chris.lucas@threerivers.gov.uk
Major, David (LD - Abbots Langley)
david.major@threerivers.gov.uk
Mann, Joy (LD - Bedmond and Primrose Hill)
joy.mann@threerivers.gov.uk
May, James (CON - Chorleywood West)
Mediratta, Amrit (CON - Moor Park and Eastbury)
amrit.mediratta@threerivers.gov.uk
Nelmes, Sarah (LD - Penn)
sarah.nelmes@threerivers.gov.uk
Nolan, Marie-Louise (LAB - Ashridge)
marie-louise.nolan@threerivers.gov.uk
Norman, Brian (LD - Croxley Green)
brian.norman@threerivers.gov.uk
Ramos, Terry (CON - Carpenders Park)
terry.dosramos@threerivers.gov.uk
Ray, Peter (LD - Oxhey Hall)
peter.ray@threerivers.gov.uk
Sangster, Ralph (CON - Moor Park and Eastbury)
ralph.sangster@threerivers.gov.uk
Sansom, David (CON - Rickmansworth)
david.sansom@threerivers.gov.uk
Scarth, Alison (LD - Oxhey Hall)
alison.scarth@threerivers.gov.uk
Seabourne, Roger (LD - Croxley Green)
roger.seabourne@threerivers.gov.uk
Smith, Russell (CON - Rickmansworth West)
russell.smith@threerivers.gov.uk
Stibbs, Sue (LD - Chorleywood West)
sue.stibbs@threerivers.gov.uk
Tippen, Len (LAB - Northwick)
len.tippen@threerivers.gov.uk
Trevett, Martin (LD - Chorleywood West)

martin.trevett@threerivers.gov.uk
Turner, Kate (LD - Leavesden)
kate.turner@threerivers.gov.uk
Wakeling, Peter (LD - Maple Cross and Mill End)
peter.wakeling@threerivers.gov.uk
Whately-Smith, Chris (LD - Langleybury)
chris.whately-smith@threerivers.gov.uk
White, Brian (LD - Croxley Green South)
brian.white@threerivers.gov.uk
Williams, Keith (LD - Leavesden)
keith.williams@threerivers.gov.uk

POLITICAL COMPOSITION
LD: 28, CON: 14, LAB: 6

CABINET
Leader: Ms Ann Shaw
Community Safety: Mr Roger Seabourne
Environment: Mr Martin Trevett
Leisure & Community: Mr Keith Williams
Public Services & Health: Mr Phil Brading
Sustainability: Mrs Sara Bedford
Resources: Mr Matthew Bedford

COMMITTEE CHAIRS
Audit: Ms Sarah Nelmes
Leisure & Community Safety (Scrutiny): Mr Steve Drury
Licensing: Ms Pam Hames
Planning: Mr Chris Whately-Smith
Public Services & Health (Scrutiny): Mr Stephen Giles-Medhurst
Regulatory Services: Ms Pam Hames
Resources Policy (Scrutiny): Ms Sarah Nelmes
Sustainable Environment Policy (Scrutiny): Ms Alison Scarth

THURROCK U

Thurrock Borough Council, Civic Offices, New Road, Grays RM17 6SL ☎ 01375 390000 or 01375 652652 🖷 01375 652359 ✉ initialsurname@thurrock.gov.uk 💻 www.thurrock.gov.uk

FACTS & FIGURES
Police Authority: Essex Police Authority
Health Authority: East of England Strategic Health Authority
Learning and Skills Council: Eastern
Parliamentary Constituencies: Thurrock
EU Constituencies: Eastern
Election Frequency: Elections are by thirds
Twinning: Monchengladbach (Germany)

PRINCIPAL OFFICERS
Chief Executive: Mr Graham Farrant, Chief Executive, Civic Offices, New Road, Grays RM17 6SL ☎ 01375 652652 ✉ gfarrant@thurrock.gov.uk

Assistant Chief Executive: Mr Steve Cox, Assistant Chief Executive, Civic Offices, New Road, Grays RM17 6SL ☎ 01375 652105 ✉ scox@thurrock.gov.uk

Best Value: Mr Chris Stephenson, Corporate Performance Improvement Manager, Civic Offices, New Road, Grays RM17 6SL ☎ 01375 652707 ✉ cstephenson@thurrock.gov.uk

Building Control: Mr Alex Neilson, Building Control Manager, Civic Offices, New Road, Grays RM17 6SL ☎ 01375 652098 🖷 01375 652359 ✉ aneilson@thurrock.gov.uk

Children / Youth Services: Ms Jo Olsson, Director of People Services, Civic Offices, New Road, Grays RM17 6SL ☎ 01375 652587 🖷 01375 652359 ✉ jolsson@thurrock.gov.uk

Civil Registration: Ms Lynn Whipps, Superintendent Registrar, Civic Offices, New Road, Grays RM17 6SL ☎ 01375 375245 ✉ lwhipps@thurrock.gov.uk

PR / Communications: Mr Phil McCusker, Communications Manager, Civic Offices, New Road, Grays RM17 6SL ☎ 01375 652062 ✉ pmccusker@thurrock.gov.uk

Community Safety: Ms Natalie Warren, Community Development Manager, Civic Offices, New Road, Grays RM17 6SL ☎ 01375 652186 ✉ nwarren@thurrock.gov.uk

Computer Management: Mr Steve Abbott, Head of ICT, Civic Offices, New Road, Grays RM17 6SL ☎ 01375 652951 🖷 01375 652359 ✉ sabbott@thurrock.gov.uk

Consumer Protection and Trading Standards: Mr Terry Everett, Senior Trading Standards Officer, Civic Offices, New Road, Grays RM17 6SL ☎ 01375 652483 ✉ teverett@thurrock.gov.uk

Customer Service: Ms Tracie Heiser, Head of Customer Services & Business Administration, Vertex, Civic Offices, New Road, Grays RM17 6SL ☎ 01375 366243 ✉ tracie.heiser@vertex.co.uk

Economic Development: Mr Andrew Millard, Head of Planning & Transportation, Civic Offices, New Road, Grays RM17 6SL ☎ 01375 652710 🖷 01375 652359 ✉ amillard@thurrock.gov.uk

Education: Ms Jo Olsson, Director of People Services, Civic Offices, New Road, Grays RM17 6SL ☎ 01375 652587 🖷 01375 652359 ✉ jolsson@thurrock.gov.uk

E-Government: Mr Steve Rigden, Web Manager, Civic Offices, New Road, Grays RM17 6SL ☎ 01375 652038 ✉ srigden@thurrock.gov.uk

Electoral Registration: Ms Elaine Sheridan, Electoral Services Manager, Civic Offices, New Road, Grays RM17 6SL ☎ 01375 652580 ✉ esheridan@thurrock.gov.uk

Emergency Planning: Ms Lucy Magill, Head of Public Protection, Civic Offices, New Road, Grays RM17 6SL ☎ 01375 652513 ✉ lmagill@thurrock.gov.uk

Environmental / Technical Services: Mr Andrew Murphy, Head of Environment, Thurrock Council, Curzon Drive, Grays RM17 6BQ ☎ 01375 413768 🖷 01375 652359 ✉ amurphy@thurrock.gov.uk

Environmental Health: Ms Lucy Magill, Head of Public Protection, Civic Offices, New Road, Grays RM17 6SL ☎ 01375 652513 ✉ lmagill@thurrock.gov.uk

Events Manager: Ms Helen Saward, Publicity & Events Officer,

Civic Offices, New Road, Grays RM17 6SL ☎ 01375 652476 ✉ hsaward@thurrock.gov.uk

Facilities: Ms Jan Hughes, Business & Strategic Development Manager, Civic Offices, New Road, Grays RM17 6SL ☎ 01375 652775 🖷 01375 652794 ✉ jhughes@thurrock.gov.uk

Finance and Treasurer: Mr Sean Clark, Head of Corporate Finance, Civic Offices, New Road, Grays RM17 6SL ☎ 01375 652010 ✉ sclark@thurrock.gov.uk

Finance and Treasurer: Mr Martin Hone, Director of Finance & Corporate Governance, Civic Offices, Civic Centre Road, Havant PO9 2AX ☎ 01375 652152 🖷 01375 652359 ✉ mhone@thurrock.gov.uk

Grounds Maintenance: Mr Andrew Murphy, Head of Environment, Civic Offices, New Road, Grays RM17 6SL ☎ 01375 413768 🖷 01375 652359 ✉ amurphy@thurrock.gov.uk

Health and Safety: Ms Lucy Magill, Head of Public Protection, Civic Offices, New Road, Grays RM17 6SL ☎ 01375 652513 ✉ lmagill@thurrock.gov.uk

Highways: Mr Les Burns, Chief Highways Engineer, Civic Offices, New Road, Grays RM17 6SL ☎ 01375 413842 🖷 01375 652359 ✉ lburns@thurrock.gov.uk

Housing: Ms Barbara Brownlee, Director of Housing, Civic Offices, New Road, Grays RM17 6SL ☎ 01375 652230 🖷 01375 652033 ✉ bbrownlee@thurrock.gov.uk

Housing Maintenance: Mr Darren McLoughlin, Client Contract Manager, Civic Offices, New Road, Grays RM17 6SL ☎ 01375 652847 🖷 01375 652033 ✉ dmcloughlin@thurrock.gov.uk

Local Area Agreement: Ms Laura Last, Performance & Communications Manager, Civic Offices, New Road, Grays RM17 6SL ☎ 01375 652560 ✉ llast@thurrock.gov.uk

Legal: Ms Tasnim Shawkat, Head of Legal & Democratic Services, Civic Offices, New Road, Grays RM17 6SL ☎ 01375 652442 ✉ tshawkat@thurrock.gov.uk

Leisure and Cultural Services: Mr Grant Greatrex, Sport, Leisure & Policy Development Manager, Civic Offices, New Road, Grays RM17 6SL ☎ 01375 413940 ✉ ggreatrex@thurrock.gov.uk

Licensing: Mr Paul Adams, Principal Licensing Officer, Civic Offices, New Road, Grays RM17 6SL ☎ 01375 652104 ✉ padams@thurrock.gov.uk

Lifelong Learning: Ms Carmel Littleton, Interim Head of Learning & Universal Outcomes, Civic Offices, New Road, Grays RM17 6SL ☎ 01375 652208 ✉ clittleton@thurrock.gov.uk

Lighting: Mr Dave Parish, Street Lighting Engineer, Crown House, Crown Road, Grays RM17 6JH ☎ 01375 387430 ✉ dparish@thurrock.gov.uk

Parking: Mr Andrew Millard, Head of Planning & Transportation, Civic Offices, New Road, Grays RM17 6SL ☎ 01375 652710 🖷 01375 652359 ✉ amillard@thurrock.gov.uk

Partnerships: Mr Richard Waterhouse, Director of Transformation, Civic Offices, New Road, Grays RM17 6SL ☎ 01375 652070 ✉ jhinchliffe@thurrock.gov.uk

Personnel / HR: Ms Jackie Hinchliffe, Interim Head of Human Resources & Organisational Development and Customer Strategy, Civic Offices, New Road, Grays RM17 6SL ☎ 01375 652016 ✉ jhinchliffe@thurrock.gov.uk

Planning: Mr Andrew Millard, Head of Planning & Transportation, Civic Offices, New Road, Grays RM17 6SL ☎ 01375 652710 🖷 01375 652359 ✉ amillard@thurrock.gov.uk

Procurement: Mr Peter Stone, Head of Procurement, Civic Offices, New Road, Grays RM17 6SL ☎ 01375 652652 ✉ pstone@thurrock.gov.uk

Public Libraries: Ms Jenny Meads, Operations & Data Manager, Thameside Theatre Complex, Orsett Road, Grays RM17 5DX ☎ 01375 652294 ✉ jmeads@thurrock.gov.uk

Recycling & Waste Minimisation: Mr John Gilford, Waste & Recycling Manager, Thurrock Council, Curzon Drive, Grays RM17 6BQ ☎ 01708 862851 🖷 01375 652780 ✉ jgilford@thurrock.gov.uk

Regeneration: Mr Steve Cox, Assistant Chief Executive, Civic Offices, New Road, Grays RM17 6SL ☎ 01375 652105 ✉ scox@thurrock.gov.uk

Road Safety: Ms Denise Langan, Road Safety Manager, Crown House, Crown Road, Grays RM17 6JH ☎ 01375 413386 🖷 01375 653385 ✉ dlandgan@thurrock.gov.uk

Social Services: Ms Jo Olsson, Director of People Services, Civic Offices, New Road, Grays RM17 6SL ☎ 01375 652587 🖷 01375 652359 ✉ jolsson@thurrock.gov.uk

Social Services (Adult): Ms Jo Olsson, Director of People Services, Civic Offices, New Road, Grays RM17 6SL ☎ 01375 652587 🖷 01375 652359 ✉ jolsson@thurrock.gov.uk

Social Services (Children): Ms Jo Olsson, Director of People Services, Civic Offices, New Road, Grays RM17 6SL ☎ 01375 652587 🖷 01375 652359 ✉ jolsson@thurrock.gov.uk

Street Scene: Mr Andrew Murphy, Head of Environment, Thurrock Council, Curzon Drive, Grays RM17 6BQ ☎ 01375 413768 🖷 01375 652359 ✉ amurphy@thurrock.gov.uk

Sustainable Development: Ms Clare Lambert, Regeneration & Sustainability Manager, Civic Offices, New Road, Grays RM17 6SL ☎ 01375 652962 ✉ clambert@thurrock.gov.uk

Traffic Management: Mr David Freestone, Transportation Manager, Civic Offices, New Road, Grays RM17 6SL ☎ 01375 652091 ✉ dfreestone@thurrock.gov.uk

Transport: Mr David Freestone, Transportation Manager, Civic Offices, New Road, Grays RM17 6SL ☎ 01375 652091

dfreestone@thurrock.gov.uk

Transport Planner: Mr David Freestone, Transportation Manager, Civic Offices, New Road, Grays RM17 6SL ☎ 01375 652091
dfreestone@thurrock.gov.uk

Waste Collection and Disposal: Mr John Gilford, Waste & Recycling Manager, Thurrock Council, Curzon Drive, Grays RM17 6BQ ☎ 01708 862851 🖷 01375 652780
jgilford@thurrock.gov.uk

Waste Management: Mr John Gilford, Waste & Recycling Manager, Thurrock Council, Curzon Drive, Grays RM17 6BQ ☎ 01708 862851 🖷 01375 652780 jgilford@thurrock.gov.uk

MEMBERS OF THE COUNCIL (49)

***Mayor:* Gupta**, Yash (LAB - Grays Thurrock)
ygupta@thurrock.gov.uk
***Deputy Mayor:* Fish**, Anthony (LAB - Chadwell St Mary)
tfish@thurrock.gov.uk
***Deputy Leader of the Council:* Morris-Cook**, Val (LAB - Grays Riverside)
vmorriscook@thurrock.gov.uk
***Group Leader:* Palmer**, Barry (IND - East Tilbury)
bpalmer@thurrock.gov.uk
Anderson, Phil (CON - Stanford East and Corringham Town)
panderson@thurrock.gov.uk
Baldwin, Clare (LAB - Tilbury Riverside and Thurrock Park)
cbaldwin@thurrock.gov.uk
Carr, Lynn (CON - Ockendon)
lcarr@thurrock.gov.uk
Coxshall, Mark (CON - Corringham and Fobbing)
mcoxshall@thurrock.gov.uk
Curtis, Charles (LAB - Belhus)
mayors.office@thurrock.gov.uk
Curtis, Wendy (LAB - Belhus)
wcurtis@thurrock.gov.uk
Gaywood, Angie (LAB - Stifford Clays)
agaywood@thurrock.gov.uk
Gerrish, Oliver (LAB - West Thurrock and South Stifford)
ogerrish@thurrock.gov.uk
Gledhill, Robert (CON - Little Thurrock Rectory)
rgledhill@thurrock.gov.uk
Gray, Sue (LAB - Belhus)
sgray@thurrock.gov.uk
Hague, Garry (CON - Chafford and North Stifford)
ghague@thurrock.gov.uk
Halden, James (CON - The Homesteads)
jhalden@thurrock.gov.uk
Hale, Diana (LAB - Stifford Clays)
dehale@thurrock.gov.uk
Healy, Martin (LAB - Grays Riverside)
mhealy@thurrock.gov.uk
Hebb, Shane (CON - Stanford-le-Hope West)
shebb@thurrock.gov.uk
Herd, Wendy (CON - Aveley and Uplands)
wherd@thurrock.gov.uk
Hipsey, Terence (LAB - Stanford-le-Hope West)
thipsey@thurrock.gov.uk
Holloway, Victoria (LAB - West Thurrock and South Stifford)
vholloway@thurrock.gov.uk
Johnson, Barry (CON - Ockendon)
bjohnson@thurrock.gov.uk
Kelly, Tom (CON - Little Thurrock Rectory)
tkelly@thurrock.gov.uk
Kent, John (LAB - Grays Riverside)
jkent@thurrock.gov.uk
Kent, Catherine (LAB - Grays Thurrock)
ckent@thurrock.gov.uk
Key, Charlie (CON - South Chafford)
ckey@thurrock.gov.uk
Kiely, Aaron (LAB - Ockendon)
akiely@thurrock.gov.uk
Liddiard, Steve (LAB - Tilbury St Chads)
sliddiard@thurrock.gov.uk
Little, Susan (CON - Orsett)
slittle@thurrock.gov.uk
MacPherson, Suzanne (CON - The Homesteads)
smacpherson@thurrock.gov.uk
Maney, Benjamin (CON - Little Thurrock Blackshots)
bmaney@thurrock.gov.uk
Ojetola, Tunde (CON - South Chafford)
tojetola@thurrock.gov.uk
Okunade, Bukky (LAB - Tilbury Riverside and Thurrock Park)
bokunade@thurrock.gov.uk
Pearce, Maureen (CON - Aveley and Uplands)
mpearce@thurrock.gov.uk
Purkiss, John (IND - East Tilbury)
jpurkiss@thurrock.gov.uk
Ray, Robert (UKIP - Aveley and Uplands)
rray@thurrock.gov.uk
Redsell, Joycelyn (CON - Little Thurrock Blackshots)
jredsell@thurrock.gov.uk
Revell, Michael (CON - Orsett)
mrevell@thurrock.gov.uk
Rice, Barbara (LAB - Chadwell St Mary)
brice@thurrock.gov.uk
Rice, Gerard (LAB - Chadwell St. Mary)
grice@thurrock.gov.uk
Roast, Andrew (CON - Corringham and Fobbing)
aroast@thurrock.gov.uk
Smith, Andrew (LAB - West Thurrock and South Stifford)
ajsmith@thurrock.gov.uk
Smith, Philip (LAB - Standford East and Corringham Town)
pgsmith@thurrock.gov.uk
Speight, Richard (LAB - Stanford East and Corringham Town)
rspeight@thurrock.gov.uk
Stone, Michael (LAB - Grays Thurrock)
mstone@thurrock.gov.uk
Tolson, Pauline (CON - The Homesteads)
ptolson@thurrock.gov.uk
Wootton, Simon (CON - Chafford and North Stifford)
swootton@thurrock.gov.uk
Worrall, Lynn (LAB - Tidbury St Chads)
lworrall@thurrock.gov.uk

POLITICAL COMPOSITION

LAB: 25, CON: 21, IND: 2, UKIP: 1

CABINET

Leader / Finance: Mr John Kent
Deputy Leader / Housing: Ms Val Morris-Cook
Adult Social Care & Health: Mrs Barbara Rice
Central Services: Mr Philip Smith
Education & Children's Social Care: Mr Oliver Gerrish
Environment: Ms Victoria Holloway
Public Protection: Ms Angie Gaywood
Regeneration, Highways & Transportation: Mr Andrew Smith

Transformation & Community: Ms Lynn Worrall

COMMITTEE CHAIRS

Audit: Mr Trunde Revell
Children's Services Overview & Scrutiny: Ms Diana Hale
General Services: Mr John Kent
Health & Wellbeing Overview & Scrutiny: Ms Wendy Herd
Licensing: Mr Michael Stone
Planning: Mr Terence Hipsey

TONBRIDGE & MALLING D

Tonbridge & Malling Borough Council, Gibson Building, Gibson Drive, Kings Hill, West Malling ME19 4LZ ☎ 01732 844522 🖷 01732 842170 ✉ adminservices@tmbc.gov.uk 💻 www.tmbc.gov.uk

FACTS & FIGURES

Police Authority: Kent Police Authority
Health Authority: South East Coast Strategic Health Authority
Learning and Skills Council: South East
Parliamentary Constituencies: Tonbridge and Malling
EU Constituencies: South East
Election Frequency: Elections are of whole council
Twinning: Heusenstamm (Germany); Le Puy (France)

PRINCIPAL OFFICERS

Chief Executive: Mr David Hughes, Chief Executive, Gibson Building, Gibson Drive , Kings Hill, West Malling ME19 4LZ ☎ 01732 876003 🖷 01732 876231 ✉ david.hughes@tmbc.gov.uk

Architect, Building / Property Services: Mr John DeKnop, Building & Facilities Manager, Gibson Building, Gibson Drive, Kings Hill, West Malling ME19 4LZ ☎ 01732 876028 🖷 01732 842170 ✉ property.services@tmbc.gov.uk

Best Value: Miss Julie Beilby, Central Services Director, Gibson Building, Gibson Drive, Kings Hill, West Malling ME19 4LZ ☎ 01732 876382 ✉ central.services@tmbc.gov.uk

Building Control: Mr Mike Ingram, Chief Building Control Officer, Gibson Building, Gibson Drive , Kings Hill, West Malling ME19 4LZ ☎ 01732 876251 🖷 01732 876363 ✉ mike.ingram@tmbc.gov.uk

Building Control: Mr Kevin Tomsett, Building Control & Emergency Planning Manager, Council Offices, Argyle Road, Sevenoaks TN13 1HG ☎ 01732 227368 ✉ kevin.tomsett@sevenoaks.gov.uk

Children / Youth Services: Ms Jeni Ashmore, Youth & Play Development Officer, Leisure Services, Gibson Building, Gibson Drive, Kings Hill, West Malling ME19 4LZ ☎ 01732 876169 ✉ jeni.ashmore@tmbc.gov.uk

PR / Communications: Mrs Linda Moreau, Media & Communications Manager, Gibson Building, Gibson Drive, Kings Hill, West Malling ME19 4LZ ☎ 01732 876009 🖷 01732 876004 ✉ linda.moreau@tmbc.gov.uk

Community Planning: Mr Mark Raymond, Corporate Services Manager, Gibson Building, Gibson Drive, Kings Hill, West Malling ME19 4LZ ☎ 01732 876267 🖷 01732 876231 ✉ mark.raymond@tmbc.gov.uk

Community Safety: Mr David Hughes, Chief Executive, Gibson Building, Gibson Drive , Kings Hill, West Malling ME19 4LZ ☎ 01732 876003 🖷 01732 876231 ✉ david.hughes@tmbc.gov.uk

Community Safety: Mr Mark Raymond, Corporate Services Manager, Gibson Building, Gibson Drive, Kings Hill, West Malling ME19 4LZ ☎ 01732 876267 🖷 01732 876231 ✉ mark.raymond@tmbc.gov.uk

Computer Management: Mr Alan Burch, Information Technology Manager, Gibson Building, Gibson Drive, Kings Hill, West Malling ME19 4LZ ☎ 01732 876117 🖷 01732 876137 ✉ alan.burch@tmbc.gov.uk

Contracts: Mr Trevor Bowen, Principal Legal Officer, Gibson Building, Gibson Drive, Kings Hill, West Malling ME19 4LZ ☎ 01732 876039 🖷 01732 842170 ✉ trevor.bowen@tmbc.gov.uk

Corporate Services: Mr Mark Raymond, Corporate Services Manager, Gibson Building, Gibson Drive, Kings Hill, West Malling ME19 4LZ ☎ 01732 876267 🖷 01732 876231 ✉ mark.raymond@tmbc.gov.uk

Customer Service: Miss Julie Beilby, Central Services Director, Gibson Building, Gibson Drive, Kings Hill, West Malling ME19 4LZ ☎ 01732 876382 ✉ central.services@tmbc.gov.uk

Economic Development: Mr Mark Raymond, Corporate Services Manager, Gibson Building, Gibson Drive, Kings Hill, West Malling ME19 4LZ ☎ 01732 876267 🖷 01732 876231 ✉ mark.raymond@tmbc.gov.uk

E-Government: Mr Alan Burch, Information Technology Manager, Gibson Building, Gibson Drive, Kings Hill, West Malling ME19 4LZ ☎ 01732 876117 🖷 01732 876137 ✉ alan.burch@tmbc.gov.uk

Electoral Registration: Mr Richard Beesley, Principal Administrator, Gibson Building, Gibson Drive, Kings Hill, West Malling ME19 4LZ ☎ 01732 876229 🖷 01732 842170 ✉ paul.fowler@tmbc.gov.uk

Electoral Registration: Mr David Hughes, Chief Executive, Gibson Building, Gibson Drive , Kings Hill, West Malling ME19 4LZ ☎ 01732 876003 🖷 01732 876231 ✉ david.hughes@tmbc.gov.uk

Emergency Planning: Mr Mike O'Brien, Principal Engineer, Gibson Building, Gibson Drive, Kings Hill, West Malling ME19 4LZ ☎ 01732 876288 🖷 01732 876363 ✉ mike.o'brien@tmbc.gov.uk

Energy Management: Mr John DeKnop, Building & Facilities Manager, Gibson Building, Gibson Drive, Kings Hill, West Malling ME19 4LZ ☎ 01732 876028 🖷 01732 842170 ✉ property.services@tmbc.gov.uk

Environmental Health: Mr John Batty, Director of Health & Housing, Gibson Building, Gibson Drive, Kings Hill, West Malling ME19 4LZ ☎ 01732 876200 🖷 01732 841421 ✉ john.batty@tmbc.gov.uk

Estates, Property & Valuation: Ms Katie Iggulden, Estates Officer, Gibson Building, Gibson Drive, Kings Hill, West Malling ME19 4LZ ☎ 01732 876364 🖷 01732 842170 ✉ property.services@tmbc.gov.uk

Events Manager: Ms Lyndsey Bennett, Leisure Services Officer, Gibson Building, Gibson Drive, Kings Hill, West Malling ME19 4LZ ☎ 01732 876333 🖱 lyndsey.bennett@tmbc.gov.uk

Events Manager: Mr Robert Styles, Chief Leisure Officer, Gibson Building, Gibson Drive, Kings Hill, West Malling ME19 4LZ ☎ 01732 876166 🖱 robert.styles@tmbc.gov.uk

Facilities: Miss Julie Beilby, Central Services Director, Gibson Building, Gibson Drive, Kings Hill, West Malling ME19 4LZ ☎ 01732 876382 🖱 central.services@tmbc.gov.uk

Finance and Treasurer: Mrs Sharon Shelton, Finance Director, Gibson Building, Gibson Drive, Kings Hill, West Malling ME19 4LZ ☎ 01732 876092 🖷 01732 873530 🖱 sharon.shelton@tmbc.gov.uk

Grounds Maintenance: Mr John DeKnop, Building & Facilities Manager, Gibson Building, Gibson Drive, Kings Hill, West Malling ME19 4LZ ☎ 01732 876028 🖷 01732 842170 🖱 property.services@tmbc.gov.uk

Health and Safety: Mr John Batty, Director of Health & Housing, Gibson Building, Gibson Drive, Kings Hill, West Malling ME19 4LZ ☎ 01732 876200 🖷 01732 841421 🖱 john.batty@tmbc.gov.uk

Highways: Mr Steve Humphrey, Director of Planning, Transport & Leisure, Gibson Building, Gibson Drive, Kings Hill, West Malling ME19 4LZ ☎ 01732 876256 🖷 01732 846312 🖱 steve.humphrey@tmbc.gov.uk

Home Energy Conservation: Mr John Batty, Director of Health & Housing, Gibson Building, Gibson Drive, Kings Hill, West Malling ME19 4LZ ☎ 01732 876200 🖷 01732 841421 🖱 john.batty@tmbc.gov.uk

Housing: Mr John Batty, Director of Health & Housing, Gibson Building, Gibson Drive, Kings Hill, West Malling ME19 4LZ ☎ 01732 876200 🖷 01732 841421 🖱 john.batty@tmbc.gov.uk

Housing: Ms Janet Walton, Chief Housing Officer, Gibson Building, Gibson Drive, Kings Hill, West Malling ME19 4LZ ☎ 01732 844522 🖱 janet.walton@tmbc.gov.uk

Legal: Mr Adrian Stanfield, Chief Solicitor & Monitoring Officer, Gibson Building, Gibson Drive, Kings Hill, West Malling ME19 4LZ ☎ 01732 876346 🖷 01732 842170 🖱 legal.services@tmbc.gov.uk

Leisure and Cultural Services: Ms Jeni Ashmore, Youth & Play Development Officer, Leisure Services, Gibson Building, Gibson Drive, Kings Hill, West Malling ME19 4LZ ☎ 01732 876169 🖱 jeni.ashmore@tmbc.gov.uk

Leisure and Cultural Services: Ms Lyndsey Bennett, Leisure Services Officer, Gibson Building, Gibson Drive, Kings Hill, West Malling ME19 4LZ ☎ 01732 876333 🖱 lyndsey.bennett@tmbc.gov.uk

Leisure and Cultural Services: Mr Steve Humphrey, Director of Planning, Transport & Leisure, Gibson Building, Gibson Drive, Kings Hill, West Malling ME19 4LZ ☎ 01732 876256 🖷 01732 846312 🖱 steve.humphrey@tmbc.gov.uk

Licensing: Mr Adrian Stanfield, Chief Solicitor & Monitoring Officer, Gibson Building, Gibson Drive, Kings Hill, West Malling ME19 4LZ ☎ 01732 876346 🖷 01732 842170 🖱 legal.services@tmbc.gov.uk

Lighting: Mr Steve Humphrey, Director of Planning, Transport & Leisure, Gibson Building, Gibson Drive, Kings Hill, West Malling ME19 4LZ ☎ 01732 876256 🖷 01732 846312 🖱 steve.humphrey@tmbc.gov.uk

Lottery Funding, Charity and Voluntary: Mr Mark Raymond, Corporate Services Manager, Gibson Building, Gibson Drive, Kings Hill, West Malling ME19 4LZ ☎ 01732 876267 🖷 01732 876231 🖱 mark.raymond@tmbc.gov.uk

Member Services: Miss Claire Fox, Principal Administrator, Gibson Building, Gibson Drive, Kings Hill, West Malling ME19 4LZ ☎ 01732 876045 🖷 01732 842170 🖱 committee.services@tmbc.gov.uk

Parking: Mr Steve Humphrey, Director of Planning, Transport & Leisure, Gibson Building, Gibson Drive, Kings Hill, West Malling ME19 4LZ ☎ 01732 876256 🖷 01732 846312 🖱 steve.humphrey@tmbc.gov.uk

Partnerships: Mr Mark Raymond, Corporate Services Manager, Gibson Building, Gibson Drive, Kings Hill, West Malling ME19 4LZ ☎ 01732 876267 🖷 01732 876231 🖱 mark.raymond@tmbc.gov.uk

Personnel / HR: Miss Julie Beilby, Central Services Director, Gibson Building, Gibson Drive, Kings Hill, West Malling ME19 4LZ ☎ 01732 876382 🖱 central.services@tmbc.gov.uk

Personnel / HR: Mr Charlie Steel, Personnel & Customer Services Manager, Gibson Building, Gibson Drive, Kings Hill, West Malling ME19 4LZ ☎ 01732 876015 🖱 personnel.services@tmbc.gov.uk

Planning: Mr Steve Humphrey, Director of Planning, Transport & Leisure, Gibson Building, Gibson Drive, Kings Hill, West Malling ME19 4LZ ☎ 01732 876256 🖷 01732 846312 🖱 steve.humphrey@tmbc.gov.uk

Procurement: Mr John DeKnop, Building & Facilities Manager, Gibson Building, Gibson Drive, Kings Hill, West Malling ME19 4LZ ☎ 01732 876028 🖷 01732 842170 🖱 property.services@tmbc.gov.uk

Recycling & Waste Minimisation: Mr John Batty, Director of Health & Housing, Gibson Building, Gibson Drive, Kings Hill, West Malling ME19 4LZ ☎ 01732 876200 🖷 01732 841421 🖱 john.batty@tmbc.gov.uk

Staff Training: Ms Delia Gordon, Personnel & Development Manager, Gibson Building, Gibson Drive, Kings Hill, West Malling ME19 4LZ ☎ 01732 876019 🖱 personnel.services@tmbc.gov.uk

Street Scene: Mr Steve Humphrey, Director of Planning, Transport & Leisure, Gibson Building, Gibson Drive, Kings Hill, West Malling ME19 4LZ ☎ 01732 876256 🖷 01732 846312 🖱 steve.humphrey@tmbc.gov.uk

Sustainable Communities: Mr Mark Raymond, Corporate

Services Manager, Gibson Building, Gibson Drive, Kings Hill, West Malling ME19 4LZ ☎ 01732 876267 🖷 01732 876231 mark.raymond@tmbc.gov.uk

Sustainable Development: Mr John Batty, Director of Health & Housing, Gibson Building, Gibson Drive, Kings Hill, West Malling ME19 4LZ ☎ 01732 876200 🖷 01732 841421 john.batty@tmbc.gov.uk

Tourism: Miss Julie Beilby, Central Services Director, Gibson Building, Gibson Drive, Kings Hill, West Malling ME19 4LZ ☎ 01732 876382 central.services@tmbc.gov.uk

Waste Collection and Disposal: Mr John Batty, Director of Health & Housing, Gibson Building, Gibson Drive, Kings Hill, West Malling ME19 4LZ ☎ 01732 876200 🖷 01732 841421 john.batty@tmbc.gov.uk

Waste Management: Mr John Batty, Director of Health & Housing, Gibson Building, Gibson Drive, Kings Hill, West Malling ME19 4LZ ☎ 01732 876200 🖷 01732 841421 john.batty@tmbc.gov.uk

MEMBERS OF THE COUNCIL (53)

***Mayor:* Davis**, David Anthony Stuart (CON - Burham, Eccles and Wouldham)
dave.davis@tmbc.gov.uk
***Deputy Mayor:* Kemp**, Frances (CON - East Peckham and Golden Green)
howard.rogers@tmbc.gov.uk
***Leader of the Council:* Heslop**, Nicolas (CON - Cage Green, Tonbridge)
nicolas.heslop@tmbc.gov.uk
***Group Leader:* Simpson**, Elizabeth (LD - East Malling)
liz.simpson@tmbc.gov.uk
Allison, Andy (CON - Higham, Tonbridge)
andy.allison@tmbc.gov.uk
Anderson, Jill (CON - Hadlow, Mereworth and West Peckham)
jill.anderson@tmbc.gov.uk
Atkins, Julian (LAB - Snodland East)
julian.atkins@tmbc.gov.uk
Atkinson, Jean Audrey (CON - Trench, Tonbridge)
jean.atkinson@tmbc.gov.uk
Balcombe, John Albert Leonard (CON - Aylesford)
john.balcombe@tmbc.gov.uk
Baldock, Owen (CON - Castle, Tonbridge)
owen.baldock@tmbc.gov.uk
Balfour, Matthew (CON - Downs)
matthew.balfour@tmbc.gov.uk
Bates, Pam (CON - Trench, Tonbridge)
pam.bates@tmbc.gov.uk
Bellamy, Jeannett (CON - Ditton)
jeannett.bellamy@tmbc.gov.uk
Bishop, Timothy (LD - Larkfield South)
timothy.bishop@tmbc.gov.uk
Bolt, Peter (CON - Judd, Tonbridge)
peter.bolt@tmbc.gov.uk
Branson, Vivian (CON - Castle, Tonbridge)
vivian.branson@tmbc.gov.uk
Branson, Vivian (CON - Kings Hill)
christopher.brown@tmbc.gov.uk
Brown, Barbara Ann (CON - Snodland West)
barbara.brown@tmbc.gov.uk
Brown, Christopher (CON - Hadlow, Mereworth and West Peckham)
janet.sergison@tmbc.gov.uk
Chartres, Rodney (CON - Ightham)
rodney.chartres@tmbc.gov.uk
Coffin, Martin (CON - Wrotham)
martin.coffin@tmbc.gov.uk
Cure, David (CON - Judd, Tonbridge)
david.cure@tmbc.gov.uk
Dalton, Roger (CON - Burham, Eccles and Wouldham)
roger.dalton@tmbc.gov.uk
Davis, Mark Osmond (CON - Cage Green, Tonbridge)
mark.davis@tmbc.gov.uk
Davis, Mark (CON - Hildenborough)
mark.rhodes@tmbc.gov.uk
Edmondston-Low, Tom (CON - Higham, Tonbridge)
tom.edmondston-low@tmbc.gov.uk
Elks, Jessica (CON - Medway, Tonbridge)
jessica.elks@tmbc.gov.uk
Evans, David (CON - Borough Green and Long Mill)
david.evans@tmbc.gov.uk
Gale, Carol (CON - Ditton)
carol.gale@tmbc.gov.uk
Heslop, Maria (CON - Vauxhall, Tonbridge)
maria.heslop@tmbc.gov.uk
Holland, Elizabeth (CON - East Peckham and Golden Green)
elizabeth.holland@tmbc.gov.uk
Homewood, Peter (CON - Blue Bell Hill and Walderslade)
peter.homewood@tmbc.gov.uk
Jessel, Simon (CON - Wateringbury)
simon.jessel@tmbc.gov.uk
Keeley, David (CON - Snodland East)
david.keeley@tmbc.gov.uk
Kemp, Ann (CON - Downs)
ann.kemp@tmbc.gov.uk
King, Steven (CON - Snodland East)
steven.king@tmbc.gov.uk
Lancaster, Russell (CON - Medway, Tonbridge)
russell.lancaster@tmbc.gov.uk
Luck, Sasha (CON - West Malling and Leybourne)
sasha.luck@tmbc.gov.uk
Moloney, Anne (CON - Snodland West)
anne.moloney@tmbc.gov.uk
Murray, Sue (CON - Borough Green and Long Mill)
sue.murray@tmbc.gov.uk
Oakley, Anita (LD - Larkfield South)
anita.oakley@tmbc.gov.uk
Parry-Waller, Mike (CON - Larkfield North)
mike.parry-waller@tmbc.gov.uk
Robins, Trevor (CON - Kings Hill)
trevor.robins@tmbc.gov.uk
Rodgers, Howard (CON - West Malling and Leybourne)
brian.luker@tmbc.gov.uk
Sayer, Anthony (CON - Borough Green and Long Mill)
tony.sayer@tmbc.gov.uk
Shrubsole, Sophie (CON - West Malling and Leybourne)
sophie.shrubsole@tmbc.gov.uk
Smith, David (CON - Aylesford)
david.smith@tmbc.gov.uk
Smith, Christopher (CON - Higham, Tonbridge)
christopher.smith@tmbc.gov.uk
Spence, Sarah (CON - Vauxhall, Tonbridge)
sarah.spence@tmbc.gov.uk
Sullivan, Allan (CON - Blue Bell Hill and Walderslade)
allan.sullivan@tmbc.gov.uk

Taylor, Russ (CON - Larkfield North)
russ.taylor@tmbc.gov.uk
Trice, David (CON - Higham, Tonbridge)
david.trice@tmbc.gov.uk
Woodger, Christine (LD - East Malling)
christine.woodger@tmbc.gov.uk

POLITICAL COMPOSITION
CON: 48, LD: 4, LAB: 1

CABINET
Leader: Mr Nicolas Heslop
Communities: Mr Howard Rodgers
Community Safety: Mr Mark Davis
Environmental Services: Mrs Frances Kemp
Finance: Mr Martin Coffin
Health: Mr Howard Rodgers
Housing: Mrs Jill Anderson
Innovation & Service Delivery: Mr Matthew Balfour
Leisure, Youth & Arts: Mrs Maria Heslop
Planning & Transportation: Mrs Sue Murray

COMMITTEE CHAIRS
Audit: Mr Mark Davis
General Purposes: Mr Howard Rodgers
Licensing & Appeals: Mr Christopher Brown
Overview & Scrutiny: Miss Anne Moloney
Planning & Transportation Advisory: Ms Vivian Branson
Public Transport Panel: Mr Matthew Balfour
Standards: Mr D S Ashton (External)
Strategic Housing Advisory Board: Ms Jean Audrey Atkinson

TORBAY U
Torbay Council, Town Hall, Castle Circus, Torquay TQ1 3DR
☎ 01803 201201 🖷 01803 292866 ✉ fss@torbay.gov.uk
💻 www.torbay.gov.uk

FACTS & FIGURES
Police Authority: Devon & Cornwall Police Authority
Health Authority: NHS South West
Learning and Skills Council: South West
Parliamentary Constituencies: Torbay
EU Constituencies: South West
Election Frequency: Elections are of whole council
Twinning: Borough: Hamelin (Germany); Hellevoetsluis (Holland); Livermead-with-Cockington: Venvix (France)

PRINCIPAL OFFICERS
Chief Executive: Ms Elizabeth Raikes, Chief Executive, Town Hall, Castle Circus, Torquay TQ1 3DR ☎ 01803 201201 ✉ elizabeth.raikes@torbay.gov.uk

Deputy Chief Executive: Ms Caroline Taylor, Director of Adult Services & Resources, Town Hall, Castle Circus, Torquay TQ1 3DR ☎ 01803 207116 ✉ caroline.taylor@torbay.gov.uk

Architect, Building / Property Services: Mr Robert Mason, Property Records & Estates Assistant, Tor Hill House, Union Street, Torquay TQ2 5QW ☎ 01803 207925 ✉ robert.mason@torbay.gov.uk

Best Value: Ms Zoe Williamson, Corporate Policy Officer, Town Hall, Castle Circus, Torquay TQ1 3DR ☎ 01803 207019 🖷 01803 207225 ✉ zoe.williamson@torbay.gov.uk

Building Control: Mr Colin Edgecombe, Senior Service Manager, Roebuck House, Abbey Road, Torquay TQ2 5TF ☎ 01803 208085 🖷 01803 208858 ✉ colin.edgecombe@torbay.gov.uk

Children / Youth Services: Mr Richard Williams, Director of Children's Services, Tor Hill House, Union Street, Torquay TQ2 5QW ☎ 01803 208401 ✉ richard.williams@torbay.gov.uk

Civil Registration: Mr Stephen Lemming, Superintendent Registrar, Oldway Mansion, Paignton, Torquay TQ3 2TE ☎ 01803 207130 🖷 01803 525388 ✉ stephen.lemming@torbay.gov.uk

PR / Communications: Ms Claire Barrow, Head of Communications, Tor Hill House, Union Street, Torquay TQ2 5QW ☎ 01803 208832 ✉ claire.barrow@torbay.gov.uk

Community Planning: Ms Tracey Cabache, Community Partnership Manager, Pearl Assurance House, Union Street, Torquay TQ1 3DW ☎ 01803 208831 🖷 01803 208348 ✉ tracey.cabache@torbay.gov.uk

Community Safety: Ms Kirsty Passmore, Community Safety Manager, Paignton, Safer Communities Torbay, 2nd Floor, Paignton TQ4 7QR ☎ 01803 841274 ✉ kirsty.mooney@torbay.gov.uk

Computer Management: Mr Bob Clark, Executive Head of Information Services, Town Hall, Castle Circus, Torquay TQ1 3DR ☎ 01803 207420 🖷 01803 207355 ✉ bob.clark@torbay.gov.uk

Consumer Protection and Trading Standards: Ms Frances Hughes, Executive Head of Community Safety, Roebuck House, Abbey Road, Torquay TQ2 5TF ☎ 01803 208002 ✉ frances.hughes@torbay.gov.uk

Contracts: Mr Robert Love, Corporate Procurement Manager, Town Hall, Castle Circus, Torquay TQ1 3DR ☎ 01803 207953 ✉ robert.love@torbay.gov.uk

Customer Service: Ms Patsy Mellor, Customer First Service Manager, Town Hall, Castle Circus, Torquay TQ1 3DR ☎ 01803 207221 ✉ patsy.mellor@torbay.gov.uk

Economic Development: Mr Steve Parrock, Chief Executive - Torbay Development Agency, Tor Hill House, Union Street, Torquay TQ2 5QW ☎ 01803 208970 🖷 01803 208976 ✉ steve.parrock@torbay.gov.uk

Electoral Registration: Ms Melissa Tucker, Electoral Services Manager, Town Hall, Castle Circus, Torquay TQ1 3DR ☎ 01803 207076 🖷 01803 207112 ✉ melissa.tucker@torbay.gov.uk

Emergency Planning: Mr Chris Packer, Emergency Planning Officer, Town Hall, Castle Circus, Torquay TQ1 3DR ☎ 01803 207045 🖷 01803 207112 ✉ chris.packer@torbay.gov.uk

Energy Management: Mr Andrew Pedrick, Corporate Energy Manager, Tor Hill House, Union Street, Torquay TQ2 5QW ☎ 01803 208966 ✉ andrew.pedrick@torbay.gov.uk

Environmental / Technical Services: Mr Charles Uzzell, Director of Place & Resources, Town Hall, Castle Circus, Torquay TQ1 3DR ☎ 01803 207701 ✉ charles.uzzell@torbay.gov.uk

Environmental Health: Ms Frances Hughes, Executive Head of Community Safety, Roebuck House, Abbey Road, Torquay TQ2 5TF ☎ 01803 208002 ✉ frances.hughes@torbay.gov.uk

Estates, Property & Valuation: Mr Chris Bouchard, Principal Valuer, Tor Hill House, Union Street, Torquay TQ2 5QW ☎ 01803 207920 ✉ chris.bouchard@torbay.gov.uk

European Liaison: Mr Alan Denby, Director for Economic Strategy, Tor Hill House, Torquay TQ2 5QW ☎ 01803 208671 ✉ alan.denby@torbay.gov.uk

Events Manager: Mr Conway Hoare, Senior Events Officer, Roebuck House, Abbey Road, Torquay TQ2 5TF ☎ 01803 208862 ✉ conway.hoare@torbay.gov.uk

Facilities: Mr Stuart Left, Facilities Management Officer, Tor Hill House, Union Street, Torquay TQ2 5QW ☎ 01803 208979 🖷 01803 208976 ✉ stuart.left@torbay.gov.uk

Finance and Treasurer: Mr Paul Looby, Executive Head of Finance, Town Hall, Castle Circus, Torquay TQ1 3DR ☎ 01803 207283 ✉ paul.looby@torbay.gov.uk

Fleet Management: Mr Rob Jackson, Fleet Manager, Tor2, Aspen Way, Paignton, Torquay TQ4 7QR ☎ 01803 402952 ✉ rjackson@tor2.co.uk

Grounds Maintenance: Mr Richard Taylor, Leisure & Community Development Officer, Roebuck House, Abbey Road, Torquay TQ2 5TF ☎ 01803 207969 ✉ richard.taylor@torbay.gov.uk

Health and Safety: Mr Colin de Jongh, Health & Safety Manager, Town Hall, Castle Circus, Torquay TQ1 3DR ☎ 01803 207161 🖷 01803 207042 ✉ colin.dejongh@torbay.gov.uk

Highways: Mr Patrick Carney, Service Manager - Highways, 4th Floor, Roebuck House, Abbey Road, Torquay TQ2 5TF ☎ 01803 207710 ✉ patrick.carney@torbay.gov.uk

Home Energy Conservation: Mr John Pullen, Environmental Health Officer, Roebuck House, Abbey Road, Torquay TQ2 5TF ☎ 01803 208069 ✉ john.pullen@torbay.gov.uk

Housing: Ms Julie Sharland, Strategic Housing Manager, Pearl Assurance House, Union Street, Torquay TQ1 3DW ☎ 01803 208065 ✉ julie.sharland@torbay.gov.uk

Local Area Agreement: Mr Bernard Page, Service Manager - Policy & Partnership, Town Hall, Castle Circus, Torquay TQ1 3DR ☎ 01803 207021 ✉ bernard.page@torbay.gov.uk

Legal: Ms Anne-Marie Bond, Head of Legal Services, Town Hall, Castle Circus, Torquay TQ1 3DR ☎ 01803 207160 🖷 01803 207153 ✉ anne-marie.bond@torbay.gov.uk

Leisure and Cultural Services: Ms Sue Cheriton, Executive Head of Residents & Visitor Services, Roebuck House, Abbey Road, Torquay TQ2 5TF ☎ 01803 207972 ✉ sue.cheriton@torbay.gov.uk

Leisure and Cultural Services: Ms Anna Gilroy, Arts Development Officer, Roebuck House, Abbey Road, Torquay TW2 5TF ☎ 01803 207981 ✉ anna.gilroy@torbay.gov.uk

Leisure and Cultural Services: Ms Catherine Williams, Community & Sports Officer, Roebuck House, Abbey Road, Torquay TW2 5TF ☎ 01803 207976 ✉ catherine.williams@torbay.gov.uk

Licensing: Mr Steve Cox, Principal Safety & Licensing Officer, Roebuck House, Abbey Road, Torquay TQ2 5TF ☎ 01803 208034 ✉ steve.cox@torbay.gov.uk

Lifelong Learning: Dr Carol Tozer, Commissioner for Children, Schools & Families, Town Hall, Castle Circus, Torquay TQ1 3DR ☎ 01803 207991 ✉ carol.tozer@torbay.gov.uk

Lighting: Mr Dave Simmons, Street Lighting Engineer, Roebuck House, Abbey Road, Torquay TQ2 5TF ☎ 01803 207718 ✉ dave.simmons@torbay.gov.uk

Member Services: Mrs June Gurry, Democratic Services Manager, Town Hall, Castle Circus, Torquay TQ1 3DR ☎ 01803 207012 ✉ june.gurry@torbay.gov.uk

Parking: Mr Steve Hurley, Service Manager for Town Services, Pearl Assurance House, Union Street, Torquay TQ1 3DW ☎ 01803 207680 ✉ steve.hurley@torbay.gov.uk

Partnerships: Ms Tracey Cabache, Community Partnership Manager, Pearl Assurance House, Union Street, Torquay TQ1 3DW ☎ 01803 208831 🖷 01803 208348 ✉ tracey.cabache@torbay.gov.uk

Personnel / HR: Mr Mark Bennett, Executive Head of Business Services, Town Hall, Castle Circus, Torquay TQ1 3DR ☎ 01803 207360 ✉ mark.bennett@torbay.gov.uk

Planning: Mr Les Crump, Executive Head of Spatial Planning, Roebuck House, Abbey Road, Torquay TQ2 5TF ☎ 01803 207656 ✉ les.crump@torbay.gov.uk

Procurement: Mr Robert Love, Corporate Procurement Manager, Town Hall, Castle Circus, Torquay TQ1 3DR ☎ 01803 207953 ✉ robert.love@torbay.gov.uk

Recycling & Waste Minimisation: Ms Carol Arthur, Recycling Officer, Roebuck House, Abbey Road, Torquay TQ2 5TF ☎ 01803 207744 ✉ carol.arthur@torbay.gov.uk

Regeneration: Mr Alan Denby, Director for Economic Strategy, Tor Hill House, Torquay TQ2 5QW ☎ 01803 208671 ✉ alan.denby@torbay.gov.uk

Road Safety: Ms Bev Hannah, Road Safety Officer, Roebuck House, Abbey Road, Torquay TQ2 5TF ☎ 01803 207677 ✉ beverley.hannah@torbay.gov.uk

Social Services (Children): Mr John Skinner, Executive Head of Safeguarding & Wellbeing, Union House, Torquay TQ1 3YA ☎ 01803 208949

Staff Training: Mr Mark Bennett, Executive Head of Business Services, Town Hall, Castle Circus, Torquay TQ1 3DR ☎ 01803 207360 ✉ mark.bennett@torbay.gov.uk

Street Scene: Mr Steve Hurley, Service Manager for Town Services, Pearl Assurance House, Union Street, Torquay TQ1 3DW ☎ 01803 207680 ✉ steve.hurley@torbay.gov.uk

Sustainable Communities: Ms Frances Hughes, Executive Head of Community Safety, Roebuck House, Abbey Road, Torquay TQ2 5TF ☎ 01803 208002 ✉ frances.hughes@torbay.gov.uk

Tourism: Ms Carolyn Custerton, Chief Executive Officer, 5 Vaughan Parade, Torquay TQ2 5JG ☎ 01803 296296 ✉ carolyn.custer@englishriviera.co.uk

Town Centre: Mr Steve Hurley, Service Manager for Town Services, Pearl Assurance House, Union Street, Torquay TQ1 3DW ☎ 01803 207680 ✉ steve.hurley@torbay.gov.uk

Traffic Management: Mr Patrick Carney, Service Manager - Highways, 4th Floor, Roebuck House, Abbey Road, Torquay TQ2 5TF ☎ 01803 207710 ✉ patrick.carney@torbay.gov.uk

Transport: Ms Sue Cheriton, Executive Head of Residents & Visitor Services, Roebuck House, Abbey Road, Torquay TQ2 5TF ☎ 01803 207972 ✉ sue.cheriton@torbay.gov.uk

Transport Planner: Mr Les Crump, Executive Head of Spatial Planning, Roebuck House, Abbey Road, Torquay TQ2 5TF ☎ 01803 207656 ✉ les.crump@torbay.gov.uk

Waste Collection and Disposal: Mr Gareth Bourton, Strategic Development Director - TOR2, Aspen Way, Paignton, Torquay TQ4 7QR ☎ 01803 402957 ✉ gbourton@tor2.co.uk

Waste Management: Mr Gareth Bourton, Strategic Development Director - TOR2, Aspen Way, Paignton, Torquay TQ4 7QR ☎ 01803 402957 ✉ gbourton@tor2.co.uk

Children's Play Areas: Mr Ian Williams, Facilities & Operations Manager, Roebuck House, Abbey Road, Torquay TW2 5TF ☎ 01803 207954 ✉ ian.williams@torbay.gov.uk

MEMBERS OF THE COUNCIL (37)

***Chair:* Stringer**, Roger (LD - Watcombe)
roger.stringer@torbay.gov.uk
***Deputy Mayor:* Thomas**, David (CON - Blatchcombe)
david.thomas@torbay.gov.uk
***Leader of the Council:* Oliver**, Gordon (CON - No Ward)
Mayor@torbay.gov.uk
***Group Leader:* Darling**, Steve (LD - Watcombe)
steve.darling@torbay.gov.uk
Addis, Pete (CON - St Marychurch)
pete.addis@torbay.gov.uk
Amil, Nicole (CON - Cockington with Chelston)
Nicole.Amil@torbay.gov.uk
Baldrey, Andrew (LD - St Marys with Summercombe)
andrew.baldrey@torbay.gov.uk
Barnby, Jane (CON - Goodrington with Roselands)
jane.barnby@torbay.gov.uk
Bent, Neil (CON - Wellswood)
neil.bent@torbay.gov.uk
Brooksbank, Stephen (CON - Roundham with Hyde)
stephen.brooksbank@torbay.gov.uk
Butt, Dave (CON - Preston)
dave.butt@torbay.gov.uk
Cowell, Darren (LAB - Tormohun)
darren.cowell@torbay.gov.uk
Davies, Bobbie (LD - Roundham with Hyde)
bobbie.davies@torbay.gov.uk
Doggett, Ian (LD - Clifton with Maidenway)
ian.doggett@torbay.gov.uk
Ellery, Vic (IND - Berry Head with Furzeham)
vic.ellery@torbay.gov.uk
Excell, Robert (CON - Tormohun)
Robert.Excell@torbay.gov.uk
Faulkner, Alan (LD - St Marychurch)
alan.faulkner@torbay.gov.uk
Faulkner, Jenny (LD - Tormohun)
jenny.faulkner@torbay.gov.uk
Hernandez, Alison (CON - Shipay with the Willows)
alison.hernandez@torbay.gov.uk
Hill, Ray (CON - St Marychurch)
Hytche, Michael (CON - Cockington with Chelston)
michael.hytche@torbay.gov.uk
James, Matthew (CON - St Marys with Summercombe)
matthew.james@torbay.gov.uk
Kingscote, Mark (CON - Shiphay with The Willows)
mark.kingscote@torbay.gov.uk
Lewis, Chris (CON - Preston)
chris.lewis@torbay.gov.uk
McPhail, Beryl (CON - Wellswood)
beryl.mcphail@torbay.gov.uk
Mills, Derek (CON - Churston with Galmpton)
derek.mills@torbay.gov.uk
Morey, Mike (IND - Berry Head with Furzeham)
mike.morey@torbay.gov.uk
Parrott, Julien (UKIP - Ellacombe)
julien.parrott@torbay.gov.uk
Pentney, Ruth (LD - Clifton with Maidenway)
ruth.pentney@torbay.gov.uk
Pountney, Mark (LD - Cockington With Chelston)
Pritchard, Ken (CON - Churston with Galmpton)
ken.pritchard@torbay.gov.uk
Richards, Jeanette (CON - Blatchcome)
jeanette.richards@torbay.gov.uk
Scouler, Christine (CON - Preston)
christine.scouler@torbay.gov.uk
Stockman, Jackie (IND - Berry Head with Furzeham)
jackie.stockman@torbay.gov.uk
Stocks, Cindy (LD - Ellacombe)
cindy.stocks@torbay.gov.uk
Thomas, John (CON - Blatchcombe)
john.thomas@torbay.gov.uk
Tyerman, Alan (CON - Goodrington with Roselands)
alan.tyerman@torbay.gov.uk

POLITICAL COMPOSITION

CON: 22, LD: 10, IND: 3, LAB: 1, UKIP: 1

CABINET

Leader / Mayor, Employment & Regeneration: Mr Godron Oliver
Deputy Leader / Mayor, Strategic Planning, Housing & Energy: Mr Pete Addis
Adult Social Care & Older People: Ms Christine Scouler
Business Planning & Governance: Mr Ken Pritchard
Children, Schools & Famillies: Mr Chris Lewis
Finance & Audit: Mr Alan Tyerman

Involved & Healthy Communities: Ms Alison Hernandez
Safer Communities & Transport: Mr Robert Excell
Tourism & Environment: Ms Jeanette Richards

COMMITTEE CHAIRS

Audit: Mr Ray Hill
Employment: Mr Ken Pritchard
Health & Scrutiny: Ms Jane Barnby
Licensing: Mr Pete Addis
Overview & Scrutiny: Mr John Thomas

TORFAEN W

Torfaen County Borough Council, (Cyngor Bwrdeistref Sirol Torfaen), Civic Centre, Pontypool NP4 6YB ☎ 01495 762200 🖷 01495 755513 💻 www.torfaen.gov.uk

FACTS & FIGURES

Police Authority: Gwent Police Authority
Learning and Skills Council: Wales
Parliamentary Constituencies: Torfaen
EU Constituencies: Wales
Election Frequency: Elections are of whole council
Twinning: Karlsruhe (Germany)

PRINCIPAL OFFICERS

Chief Executive: Ms Alison Ward, Chief Executive, Civic Centre, Pontypool NP4 6YB ☎ 01495 742603 🖷 01495 750797 ✉ alison.ward@torfaen.gov.uk

Deputy Chief Executive: Mr Peter Durkin, Deputy Chief Executive, Civic Centre, Pontypool NP4 6YB ☎ 01495 742608 ✉ peter.durkin@torfaen.gov.uk

Assistant Chief Executive: Mr Nigel Aurelius, Assisant Chief Executive - Resources, Civic Centre, Pontypool NP4 6YB ☎ 01495 742623 ✉ nigel.aurelius@torfaen.gov.uk

Assistant Chief Executive: Mr Dave Congreve, Assistant Chief Executive - Communities, Civic Centre, Pontypool NP4 6YB ☎ 01495 742606 ✉ david.congreve@torfaen.gov.uk

Senior Management: Ms Sue Evans, Chief Officer - Social Care & Housing, County Hall, Cwmbran NP44 2WN ☎ 01633 648617 ✉ sue.evans@torfaen.gov.uk

Access Officer / Social Services (Disability): Ms Sue Evans, Chief Officer - Social Care & Housing, County Hall, Cwmbran NP44 2WN ☎ 01633 648617 ✉ sue.evans@torfaen.gov.uk

Architect, Building / Property Services: Mr Mike Wright, Property Management Group Leader, Civic Centre, Pontypool NP4 6YB ☎ 01495 766820 🖷 01495 766762 ✉ mike.wright@torfaen.gov.uk

Best Value: Mrs Lynne Williams, Head of Improvement, Civic Centre, Pontypool NP4 6YB ☎ 01495 742158 🖷 01495 766059 ✉ lynne.williams@torfaen.gov.uk

Building Control: Mr Dean Harris, Premises Manager, Civic Centre, Pontypool NP4 6YB ☎ 01495 764219 ✉ dean.harris@torfaen.gov.uk

Catering Services: Ms Toni Edwards, Catering & Cleaning Manager, Torfaen Council, County Hall, Cwmbran NP44 2WN ☎ 01633 647712 ✉ toni.edwards@torfaen.gov.uk

Children / Youth Services: Mr Keith Rutherford, Head of Children's Services, County Hall, Cwmbran NP44 2WN ☎ 01495 762200 ✉ keith.rutherford@torfaen.gov.uk

Civil Registration: Ms Lisa Dando-Ellis, Head of Customer Care Services, Civic Centre, Pontypool NP4 6YB ☎ 01495 742135 ✉ lisa.dando-ellis@torfaen.gov.uk

PR / Communications: Mr Neil Jones, Head of Communications, Civic Centre, Pontypool NP4 6YB ☎ 01495 742151 🖷 01495 766059 ✉ neil.jones@torfaen.gov.uk

Community Planning: Mr Mark Sharwood, Public Services Development Manager, Civic Centre, Pontypool NP4 6YB ☎ 01495 742157 ✉ mark.sharwood@torfaen.gov.uk

Community Safety: Ms Michele Chesterman, Policy & Performance Manager - Community Safety, Civic Centre, Pontypool NP4 6YB ☎ 01495 762200 ✉ michele.chesterman@torfaen gov.uk

Computer Management: Mr Stephen Jeynes, Service & Technical Manager, Civic Centre, Pontypool NP4 6YB ☎ 01495 747433 ✉ stephen.jeynes@torfaen.gov.uk

Consumer Protection and Trading Standards: Mr Stephen Whitehouse, Head of Trading Standards, County Hall, Cwmbran NP44 2WN ☎ 01495 747269 ✉ steve.whitehouse@torfaen.gov.uk

Contracts: Mr Mark Saunders, SEWIC Project Officer, Civic Centre, Pontypool NP4 6YB ☎ 01633 648598 ✉ mark.saunders@torfaen.gov.uk

Corporate Services: Mr Richard Gwinnell, Lead Officer - Council & Member Support, Civic Centre, Pontypool NP4 6YB ☎ 01495 742163 🖷 01495 766079 ✉ richard.gwinnell@torfaen.gov.uk

Corporate Services: Ms Christina Harrhy, Chief Officer - Neighbourhood Services, Central Depot, New Inn, Pontypool NP4 0LS ☎ 01495 766707 ✉ christina.harrhy@torfaen.gov.uk

Customer Service: Ms Lisa Dando-Ellis, Head of Customer Care Services, Civic Centre, Pontypool NP4 6YB ☎ 01495 742135 ✉ lisa.dando-ellis@torfaen.gov.uk

Customer Service: Ms Christina Harrhy, Chief Officer - Neighbourhood Services, Central Depot, New Inn, Pontypool NP4 0LS ☎ 01495 766707 ✉ christina.harrhy@torfaen.gov.uk

Customer Service: Ms Linda King, Customer Services Manager, Civic Centre, Pontypool NP4 6YB ☎ 01495 766363 ✉ linda.king@torfaen.gov.uk

Direct Labour: Ms Christina Harrhy, Chief Officer - Neighbourhood Services, Central Depot, New Inn, Pontypool NP4 0LS ☎ 01495 766707 ✉ christina.harrhy@torfaen.gov.uk

Economic Development: Ms Katie Gates, Informal Recreation Project Manager, County Hall, Cwmbran NP44 2WN ☎ 01633 648329 🖷 01633 648088 ✉ david.ludlow@torfaen.gov.uk

Education: Mr Dermot McChrystal, Head of Inclusion, Pearl

House, Hanbury Road, Pontypool NP4 6JL ☎ 01495 762200 ✉ dermot.mcchrystal@torfaen.gov.uk

Education: Mr Mark Provis, Chief Education Officer, Pearl House, Hanbury Road, Pontypool NP4 6JL ☎ 01495 762200 ✉ mark.provis@torfaen.gov.uk

E-Government: Mr Farooq Dastgir, Director of Technology Led Transformation, Civic Centre, Pontypool NP4 6YB ☎ 01495 762200

Electoral Registration: Ms Lyn Pask, Senior Corporate Services Officer (Elections), Civic Centre, Pontypool NP4 6YB ☎ 01495 766077 🖷 01495 766059 ✉ lyn.pask@torfaen.gov.uk

Emergency Planning: Mr Bob Crimp, Head of Emergency Management, Civic Centre, Pontypool NP4 6YB ☎ 01495 766071 🖷 01495 766071 ✉ bob.crimp@torfaen.gov.uk

Energy Management: Mr Allan Jones, Energy Manager, Civic Centre, Pontypool NP4 6YB ☎ 01495 742898 ✉ allan.jones@torfaen.gov.uk

Environmental / Technical Services: Ms Christina Harrhy, Chief Officer - Neighbourhood Services, Central Depot, New Inn, Pontypool NP4 0LS ☎ 01495 766707 ✉ christina.harrhy@torfaen.gov.uk

Environmental Health: Ms Kim Pugh, Head of Public Protection, Pearl House, Hanbury Road, Pontypool NP4 6JL ☎ 01495 747627 ✉ kim.pugh@torfaen.gov.uk

Estates, Property & Valuation: Mr Robert Flower, Team Leader (Valuation Services), Pearl House, Hanbury Road, Pontypool NP4 6JL ☎ 01495 742897 ✉ robert.flower@torfaen.gov.uk

European Liaison: Mr Rob Wellington, Head of European Policy & West, Civic Centre, Pontypool NP4 6YB ☎ 01495 742143 ✉ rob.wellington@tofaen.gov.uk

Events Manager: Ms Verity Hiscocks, Marketing & Events Manager, County Hall, Cwmbran NP44 2WN ☎ 01633 648968 ✉ verity.hiscocks@torfaen.gov.uk

Finance and Treasurer: Mr Nigel Aurelius, Assisant Chief Executive - Resources, Civic Centre, Pontypool NP4 6YB ☎ 01495 742623 ✉ nigel.aurelius@torfaen.gov.uk

Fleet Management: Mr Rico Cottrell, Transport & Depot Manager, Torfaen Council, Panteg Way, New Inn, Pontypool NP4 0LS ☎ 01495 766798 🖷 01495 766801 ✉ rico.cottrell@torfaen.gov.uk

Grounds Maintenance: Mr Steve Horseman, Head of Grounds Maintenance, Civic Centre, Pontypool NP4 6YB ☎ 01495 762200 ✉ steve.horseman@torfaen.gov.uk

Health and Safety: Ms Claire Burt, Health & Safety Officer, Civic Centre, Pontypool NP4 6YB ☎ 01495 762569 ✉ claire.burt@torfaen.gov.uk

Highways: Mr Kevin Mulcahy, Group Leader - Transportation, County Hall, Cwmbran NP44 2WN ☎ 01495 742426 ✉ kevin.mulcahy@torfaen.gov.uk

Home Energy Conservation: Mr Allan Jones, Energy Manager, County Hall, Cwmbran NP44 2WN ☎ 01495 742898 ✉ allan.jones@torfaen.gov.uk

Housing: Ms Sue Evans, Chief Officer - Social Care & Housing, County Hall, Cwmbran NP44 2WN ☎ 01633 648617 ✉ sue.evans@torfaen.gov.uk

Housing Maintenance: Ms Gloria Evans, Head of Customer Services, Civic Centre, Pontypool NP4 6YB ☎ 01495 766289 ✉ gloria.evans@torfaen.gov.uk

Legal: Ms Lynda Willis, County Borough Solicitor & Monitoring Officer, Civic Centre, Pontypool NP4 6YB ☎ 01495 766373 ✉ lynda.willis@torfaen.gov.uk

Leisure and Cultural Services: Ms Sally Church, Head of Leisure & Community Services, Civic Centre, Pontypool NP4 6YB ☎ 01633 628980 ✉ sally.church@torfaen.gov.uk

Licensing: Mr Steve Bendell, Team Leader - Licensing, Civic Centre, Pontypool NP4 6YB ☎ 01495 747279 ✉ steve.bendell@torfaen.gov.uk

Lifelong Learning: Ms Anne Brain, Adult Education Officer, County Hall, Cwmbran NP44 2WN ☎ 01633 648154 ✉ ann.brain@torfaen.gov.uk

Lighting: Mr Kevin Main, Streetscene Manager, Torfaen Council, Panteg Way, New Inn, Pontypool NP4 0LS ☎ 01495 762200 ✉ kevin.main@torfaen.gov.uk

Lottery Funding, Charity and Voluntary: Mr Rob Wellington, Head of European Policy & West, Civic Centre, Pontypool NP4 6YB ☎ 01495 742143 ✉ rob.wellington@tofaen.gov.uk

Member Services: Mr Richard Gwinnell, Lead Officer - Council & Member Support, Civic Centre, Pontypool NP4 6YB ☎ 01495 742163 🖷 01495 766079 ✉ richard.gwinnell@torfaen.gov.uk

Parking: Mr Kevin Main, Streetscene Manager, Torfaen Council, Panteg Way, New Inn, Pontypool NP4 0LS ☎ 01495 762200 ✉ kevin.main@torfaen.gov.uk

Personnel / HR: Mr Peter Durkin, Deputy Chief Executive, Civic Centre, Pontypool NP4 6YB ☎ 01495 742608 ✉ peter.durkin@torfaen.gov.uk

Planning: Mr Duncan Smith, Chief Officer - Planning & Public Protection, Torfaen Council, County Hall, Cwmbran NP44 2WN ☎ 01633 648021 ✉ duncan.smith@torfaen.gov.uk

Procurement: Mr Andrew Maisey, Head of Procurement, Civic Centre, Pontypool NP4 6YB ☎ 01495 742380 ✉ andrew.maisey@torfaen.gov.uk

Recycling & Waste Minimisation: Mr Cynon Edwards, Group Leader - Waste, Torfaen Council, Panteg Way, New Inn, Pontypool NP4 0LS ☎ 01495 766789 🖷 01495 766811 ✉ cynon.edwards@torfaen.gov.uk

Regeneration: Ms Cath Thomas, Co-ordinator Head of the Valleys Capital Projects, Civic Centre, Pontypool NP4 6YB cath.thomas@torfaen.gov.uk

Road Safety: Mr Pat Bates, Road Safety Strategy Officer, County Hall, Cwmbran NP44 2WN ☎ 01633 648803 patrick.bates@torfaen.gov.uk

Social Services: Ms Sue Evans, Chief Officer - Social Care & Housing, County Hall, Cwmbran NP44 2WN ☎ 01633 648617 sue.evans@torfaen.gov.uk

Social Services (Adult): Ms Sue Evans, Chief Officer - Social Care & Housing, County Hall, Cwmbran NP44 2WN ☎ 01633 648617 sue.evans@torfaen.gov.uk

Social Services (Children): Ms Sue Evans, Chief Officer - Social Care & Housing, County Hall, Cwmbran NP44 2WN ☎ 01633 648617 sue.evans@torfaen.gov.uk

Staff Training: Mr Peter Durkin, Deputy Chief Executive, Civic Centre, Pontypool NP4 6YB ☎ 01495 742608 peter.durkin@torfaen.gov.uk

Street Scene: Mr Kevin Main, Streetscene Manager, Torfaen Council, Panteg Way, New Inn, Pontypool NP4 0LS ☎ 01495 762200 kevin.main@torfaen.gov.uk

Sustainable Communities: Ms Rachael O'Shaughnessy, Environmental Co-ordinator, Civic Centre, Pontypool NP4 6YB ☎ 01633 648018 rachael.o'shaughnessy@torfaen.gov.uk

Sustainable Development: Ms Rachael O'Shaughnessy, Environmental Co-ordinator, Civic Centre, Pontypool NP4 6YB ☎ 01633 648018 rachael.o'shaughnessy@torfaen.gov.uk

Tourism: Ms Katie Gates, Informal Recreation Project Manager, County Hall, Cwmbran NP44 2WN ☎ 01633 648329 🖷 01633 648088 david.ludlow@torfaen.gov.uk

Town Centre: Mr David Evans, Lead Officer - Pontypool Regeneration, Pearl House, Hanbury Road, Pontypool NP4 6JL ☎ 01495 766029 david.evans@torfaen.gov.uk

Traffic Management: Mr Kevin Mulcahy, Group Leader - Transportation, County Hall, Cwmbran NP44 2WN ☎ 01495 742426 kevin.mulcahy@torfaen.gov.uk

Transport: Mr Kevin Mulcahy, Group Leader - Transportation, County Hall, Cwmbran NP44 2WN ☎ 01495 742426 kevin.mulcahy@torfaen.gov.uk

Transport Planner: Mr Kevin Mulcahy, Group Leader - Transportation, County Hall, Cwmbran NP44 2WN ☎ 01495 742426 kevin.mulcahy@torfaen.gov.uk

Waste Collection and Disposal: Mr Cynon Edwards, Group Leader - Waste, Torfaen Council, Panteg Way, New Inn, Pontypool NP4 0LS ☎ 01495 766789 🖷 01495 766811 cynon.edwards@torfaen.gov.uk

Waste Management: Mr Cynon Edwards, Group Leader - Waste, Torfaen Council, Panteg Way, New Inn, Pontypool NP4 0LS ☎ 01495 766789 🖷 01495 766811 cynon.edwards@torfaen.gov.uk

MEMBERS OF THE COUNCIL (44)

***Leader of the Council:* Wellington**, Robert (LAB - Greenmeadow)
leader@torfaen.gov.uk

***Deputy Leader of the Council:* Jones**, Lewis (LAB - Trevethin)
deputyleader@torfaen.gov.uk

Ashley, Stuart (LAB - Pontnewydd)
stuart.ashley@torfaen.gov.uk

Barnett, Mary (LAB - Upper Cwmbran)
mary.barnett@torfaen.gov.uk

Bevan, Huw (CON - Llanyravon South)
huw.beavan@torfaen.gov.uk

Beynon, Cynthia (LAB - Croesyceiliog North)
cynthia.beynon@torfaen.gov.uk

Brooks, Stephen (LAB - St. Dials)
stephen.brooks@torfaen.gov.uk

Burnett, Ronald (IND - Two Locks and Henllys)
ronald.burnett@torfaen.gov.uk

Cameron, Pamela (LAB - Two Locks and Henllys)
pamela.cameron@torfaen.gov.uk

Caron, Glyn (LAB - Llanyravon North)
glyn.caron@torfaen.gov.uk

Clark, Gwyneira (LAB - Abersychan)
gwyneira.clark@torfaen.gov.uk

Clark, Richard (LAB - Croesyceiliog North)
richard.clark@torfaen.gov.uk

Constance, Leonard (LAB - Brynwern)
leonard.constance@torfaen.gov.uk

Crick, Veronica (LAB - Croesyceiliog South)
veronica.crick@torfaen.gov.uk

Cross, Fiona (PC - Coed Eva)
fiona.cross@torfaen.gov.uk

Cunningham, B John (LAB - Upper Cwmbran)
john.cunningham@torfaen.gov.uk

Daniels, David (LAB - Llantarnam)
david.daniels@torfaen.gov.uk

Davies, Giles (LAB - Abersychan)
giles.davies@torfaen.gov.uk

Evans, Stuart (IND - Blaenavon)
stuart.evans@torfaen.gov.uk

Furzer, Alun (LAB - Blaenavon)
alun.furzer@torfaen.gov.uk

Graham, Maria (IND - Llantarnam)
pcllantarnam1@googlemail.com

Harnett, Kelvin (IND - Pontnewynydd)
kelvin.harnett@torfaen.gov.uk

Harris, Michael (IND - Pontypool)
michael.harris@torfaen.gov.uk

Haynes, Elizabeth (IND - St Dials)
elizabeth.haynes@torfaen.gov.uk

Hunt, Anthony (LAB - Panteg)
anthony.hunt@torfaen.gov.uk

James, David (CON - New Inn)
davidkeith.james@torfaen.gov.uk

Jeremiah, Mike (IND - Wainfelin)
mike.jeremiah@torfaen.gov.uk

Jones, Alan (LAB - Blaenavon)
alan.s.jones@torfaen.gov.uk

Kemp, Robert (IND - Upper Cwmbran)
robert.kemp@torfaen.gov.uk

Mason, Neil (LAB - St Cadocs/Penygarn)
neil.mason@torfaen.gov.uk

Mawby, Brian (LAB - Pontnewydd)

brian.mawby@torfaen.gov.uk
Mawby, Brian (LAB - Trevethin)
john.marshall@torfaen.gov.uk
Mills, Raymond (CON - New Inn)
raymond.mills@torfaen.gov.uk
Owen, Amanda (LAB - Greenmeadow)
amanda.owen@torfaen.gov.uk
Parrish, Norma (LAB - Panteg)
norma.parrish@torfaen.gov.uk
Powell, Jessica (LAB - Pontnewydd)
jessica.powell@torfaen.gov.uk
Rees, Jeff (PC - Fairwater)
pcfairwater@googlemail.com
Seabourne, Philip (LAB - Fairwater)
phil.seabourne@torfaen.gov.uk
Smith, Graham (CON - New Inn)
graham.smith@torfaen.gov.uk
Taylor, Barry (LAB - Snatchwood)
barry.taylor@torfaen.gov.uk
Thomas, Colette (LAB - Two Locks and Henllys)
colette.thomas@torfaen.gov.uk
Tomlinson, Wayne (IND - Abersychan)
wayne.tomlinson@torfaen.gov.uk
Waite, Neil (LAB - Cwmynyscoy)
neil.waite@torfaen.gov.uk
Yeowell, David (LAB - Panteg)
david.yeowell@torfaen.gov.uk

POLITICAL COMPOSITION
LAB: 29, IND: 9, CON: 4, PC: 2

CABINET
Leader: Mr Robert Wellington
Deputy Leader: Mr Lewis Jones
Children & Young People: Ms Mary Barnett
Corporate Governance & Community Safety: Mr Richard Clark
Equalities & Community Safety: Mrs Cynthia Beynon
Health, Social Care & Well Being: Ms Cynthia Beynon
Neighbourhood Services: Mr B John Cunningham
Planning, Public Protection & Housing: Ms Gwyneira Clark
Resources: Mr Anthony Hunt

COMMITTEE CHAIRS
Cleaner Communities & Scrutiny: Mr Alan Jones
Democratic Services: Mrs Elizabeth Haynes
Licensing: Mrs Norma Parish
Planning: Mr Brian Mawby

TORRIDGE D

Torridge District Council, Riverbank House, Bideford EX39 2QG
☎ 01237 428700 🖷 01237 479164
customer.services@torridge.gov.uk 💻 www.torridge.gov.uk

FACTS & FIGURES
Police Authority: Devon & Cornwall Police Authority
Health Authority: NHS South West
Learning and Skills Council: South West
Parliamentary Constituencies: Devon West and Torridge
EU Constituencies: South West
Election Frequency: Elections are of whole council
Twinning: Bideford: Landivisiau (France); Clovelly: Cesny Bois Halbout (France); Dolton: Amfreville (France); Great Torrington: Roscoff (France); Holsworthy: Aunay-sur-Odon (France); Northam: Mondeville (France); Buddenstedt (Germany); Shebbear: Balleroy (France); Woolsery: Brauvron-en-Cuige (France)

PRINCIPAL OFFICERS
Chief Executive: Mrs Jenny Wallace, Head of Paid Service, Riverbank House, Bideford EX39 2QG ☎ 01237 428700 jenny.wallace@torridge.gov.uk

Senior Management: Mrs Jenny Wallace, Head of Paid Service, Riverbank House, Bideford EX39 2QG ☎ 01237 428700 jenny.wallace@torridge.gov.uk

Access Officer / Social Services (Disability): Mr Ray Webster, Head of Environmental Health, Planning & Public Protection, Riverbank House, Bideford EX39 2QG ☎ 01237 428700 🖷 01237 424971 ray.webster@torridge.gov.uk

PR / Communications: Ms Kathy McCormack, PR, Communications & Consultation Manager, Riverbank House, Bideford EX39 2QG ☎ 01237 428772 kathy.mccormack@torridge.gov.uk

Community Safety: Ms Ruth Staddon, Emergency Planning Officer, Town Hall, Bridge Street, Bideford EX39 2HS ☎ 01237 428806 ruth.staddon@torridge.gov.uk

Computer Management: Mr Roger Bonaparte, ICT Manager, Bridge Buildings, Bideford EX39 2HT ☎ 01237 428942 roger.bonaparte@torridge.gov.uk

Contracts: Mr Doug Jenkin, Contracts Manager, Riverbank House, Bideford EX39 2QG ☎ 01237 428739 🖷 01237 428849 doug.jenkin@torridge.gov.uk

Contracts: Mr Andrew Waite, Corporate Property Manager, Riverbank House, Bideford EX39 2QG ☎ 01237 428752 🖷 01237 428849 andrew.waite@torridge.gov.uk

Corporate Services: Mr Ken Miles, Solicitor, Riverbank House, Bideford EX39 2QG ☎ 01237 428700 🖷 01237 478849 ken.miles@torridge.gov.uk

Customer Service: Mr Doug Claydon, Customer Services Manager, Riverbank House, Bideford EX39 2QG ☎ 01237 428700 doug.claydon@torridge.gov.uk

Direct Labour: Mr Ricky McCormack, Head of Operational Services, Westcombe Depot, Westcombe, Bideford EX39 3JQ ☎ 01237 428892 🖷 01237 423481 ricky.mccormack@torridge.gov.uk

Economic Development: Mrs Vanessa Saunders, Special Projects Manager, Riverbank House, Bideford EX39 2QG ☎ 01237 428700 vanessa.saunders@torridge.gov.uk

E-Government: Mr Steven Burgess, Senior E-Government Project Officer, Riverbank House, Bideford EX39 2QG ☎ 01237 428910 🖷 01237 478849 steve.burgess@torridge.gov.uk

Electoral Registration: Mrs Paula Hunter, Elections Officer, Riverbank House, Bideford EX39 2QG ☎ 01237 428702 🖷 01237 425972 paula.hunter@torridge.gov.uk

Emergency Planning: Mrs Ruth Staddon, Emergency Planning

Officer, Riverbank House, Bideford EX39 2QG ☎ 01237 428751 ✉ ruth.staddon@torridge.gov.uk

Energy Management: Mr Doug Jenkin, Contracts Manager, Riverbank House, Bideford EX39 2QG ☎ 01237 428739 🖷 01237 428849 ✉ doug.jenkin@torridge.gov.uk

Environmental / Technical Services: Mr Ray Webster, Head of Environmental Health, Planning & Public Protection, Riverbank House, Bideford EX39 2QG ☎ 01237 428700 🖷 01237 424971 ✉ ray.webster@torridge.gov.uk

Environmental Health: Mr Ray Webster, Head of Environmental Health, Planning & Public Protection, Riverbank House, Bideford EX39 2QG ☎ 01237 428700 🖷 01237 424971 ✉ ray.webster@torridge.gov.uk

Estates, Property & Valuation: Mr Andrew Waite, Corporate Property Manager, Riverbank House, Bideford EX39 2QG ☎ 01237 428752 🖷 01237 428849 ✉ andrew.waite@torridge.gov.uk

Health and Safety: Mr Christopher Parkhouse, Corporate Health & Safety Advisor, Town Hall, Bideford EX39 2HS ☎ 01237 428820 🖷 01237 474407 ✉ christopher.parkhouse@torridge.gov.uk

Housing: Mrs Liz Steele, Housing Strategy Manager, Riverbank House, Bideford EX39 2QG ☎ 01237 428700 ✉ liz.steele@torridge.gov.uk

Legal: Mr Ken Miles, Solicitor, Riverbank House, Bideford EX39 2QG ☎ 01237 428700 🖷 01237 478849 ✉ ken.miles@torridge.gov.uk

Leisure and Cultural Services: Mrs Vikki Braddick, Culture & Leisure Services Manager, Riverbank House, Bideford EX39 2QG ☎ 01237 428736 🖷 01237 424971 ✉ vikki.braddick@torridge.gov.uk

Licensing: Mr Tony Nicholls, Licensing Manager, Town Hall, Bideford EX39 2HS ☎ 01237 428991 🖷 01237 474407 ✉ tony.nicholls@torridge.gov.uk

Parking: Mr Simon Toon, Car Parks Officer, Westcombe Depot, Westcombe, Bideford EX39 3JQ ☎ 01237 428980 🖷 01237 423481 ✉ simon.toon@torridge.gov.uk

Personnel / HR: Mr John Edwards, Head of Human Resources, Riverbank House, Bideford EX39 2QG ☎ 01237 428700 🖷 01237 428799 ✉ john.edwards@torridge.gov.uk

Planning: Mr David Green, Development Manager, Riverbank House, Bideford EX39 2QG ☎ 01237 428721 ✉ david.green@torridge.gov.uk

Planning: Ms Kate Little, Joint Head of Strategic Development & Planning, Civic Centre, North Walk, Barnstaple EX31 1EA ☎ 01271 388297 🖷 01271 343968 ✉ kate.little@northdevon.gov.uk

Procurement: Mr Doug Jenkin, Contracts Manager, Riverbank House, Bideford EX39 2QG ☎ 01237 428739 🖷 01237 428849 ✉ doug.jenkin@torridge.gov.uk

Recycling & Waste Minimisation: Mr Ricky McCormack, Head of Operational Services, Westcombe Depot, Westcombe, Bideford EX39 3JQ ☎ 01237 428892 🖷 01237 423481 ✉ ricky.mccormack@torridge.gov.uk

Regeneration: Mrs Vanessa Saunders, Special Projects Manager, Riverbank House, Bideford EX39 2QG ☎ 01237 428700 ✉ vanessa.saunders@torridge.gov.uk

Staff Training: Mr John Edwards, Head of Human Resources, Riverbank House, Bideford EX39 2QG ☎ 01237 428700 🖷 01237 428799 ✉ john.edwards@torridge.gov.uk

Street Scene: Mr Ricky McCormack, Head of Operational Services, Westcombe Depot, Westcombe, Bideford EX39 3JQ ☎ 01237 428892 🖷 01237 423481 ✉ ricky.mccormack@torridge.gov.uk

Waste Collection and Disposal: Mr Ricky McCormack, Head of Operational Services, Westcombe Depot, Westcombe, Bideford EX39 3JQ ☎ 01237 428892 🖷 01237 423481 ✉ ricky.mccormack@torridge.gov.uk

Waste Management: Mr Ricky McCormack, Head of Operational Services, Westcombe Depot, Westcombe, Bideford EX39 3JQ ☎ 01237 428892 🖷 01237 423481 ✉ ricky.mccormack@torridge.gov.uk

MEMBERS OF THE COUNCIL (36)

***Chair:* Brown**, Margaret (IND - Torrington)
councillor.brown@torridge.gov.uk

***Chair:* Eastman**, Andrew (CON - Appledore)
councillor.eastman@torridge.gov.uk

***Vice-Chair:* Inch**, Anthony (CON - Bideford South)
councillor.tonyinch@torridge.gov.uk

***Leader of the Council:* Parsons**, Barry (CON - Forest)
councillor.parsons@torridge.gov.uk

***Deputy Leader of the Council:* Johnson**, Roger (CON - Northam)
councillor.johnson@torridge.gov.uk

Boyd, Andy (CON - Torrington)
councillor.boyd@torridge.gov.uk

Brenton, David (LAB - Bideford South)
councillor.brenton@torridge.gov.uk

Christie, Peter (O - Bideford North)
councillor.christie@torridge.gov.uk

Clarke, Stephen (INDNA - Bideford East)
councillor.clarke@torridge.gov.uk

Collins, Philiip (IND - Clinton)
councillor.collins@torridge.gov.uk

Dart, Anna (LD - Hartland and Bradworthy)
councillor.dart@torridge.gov.uk

Davies, Pauline (CON - Bideford East)
councillor.davies@torridge.gov.uk

Edwards, Barry (IND - Appledore)
councillor.edwards@torridge.gov.uk

Footitt, Michael (CON - Holsworthy)
councillor.footitt@torridge.gov.uk

Fulford, David (CON - Bideford North)
councillor.fulford@torridge.gov.uk

Hicks, Robert (IND - Waldon)
councillor.hicks@torridge.gov.uk

Himan, John (CON - Northam)
councillor.himan@torridge.gov.uk

Inch, Simon (CON - Bideford South)

councillor.simoninch@torridge.gov.uk
James, Kenneth (IND - Tamarside)
councillor.james@torridge.gov.uk
Johns, Trevor (NP - Bideford North)
councillor.tjohns@orridge.gov.uk
Langmead, Mervyn (CON - Bideford East)
councillor.langmead@torridge.gov.uk
Lausen, David (O - Winkleigh)
councillor.lausen@torridge.gov.uk
Leather, Chris (IND - Orchard Hill)
councillor.leather@torridge.gov.uk
Lee, Geoff (LD - Torrington)
councillor.lee@torridge.gov.uk
Lewis, John (CON - Shebbear and Langtree)
councillor.lewis@torridge.gov.uk
Lock, Rosemary (CON - Three Moors)
councillor.lock@torridge.gov.uk
Martin, Harold (CON - Two Rivers)
councillor.martin@torridge.gov.uk
Murdock, Kathy (CON - Kenwith)
councillor.murdock@torridge.gov.uk
Pennington, Philip (IND - Monkleigh and Littleham)
councillor.pennington@torridge.gov.uk
Ratledge, Howard (LD - Holsworthy)
councillor.ratledge@torridge.gov.uk
Redwood, Brian (LD - Hartland and Bradworthy)
councillor.redwood@torridge.gov.uk
Symons, Adam (LD - Clovelly Bay)
councillor.symons@torridge.gov.uk
Tabor, Gaye (CON - Coham Bridge)
councillor.tabor@torridge.gov.uk
Tisdale, Roger (IND - Westward Ho!)
councillor.tisdale@torridge.gov.uk
Watson, Peter (CON - Broadheath)
councillor.watson@torridge.gov.uk
Whittaker, Jane (NP - Northam)
councillor.whittaker@torridge.gov.uk

POLITICAL COMPOSITION

CON: 17, IND: 8, LD: 5, NP: 2, O: 2, INDNA: 1, LAB: 1

COMMITTEE CHAIRS

Audit & Governance (Scrutiny): Mr Geoff Lee
Community & Resources: Mr Barry Parsons
Licensing: Mr Andy Boyd
Overview & Scrutiny External: Mr Philip Pennington
Overview & Scrutiny Internal: Mr Philip Collins
Plans: Mrs Rosemary Lock
Standards: Mr B Ormerod (External)

TOWER HAMLETS — L

Tower Hamlets London Borough Council, Town Hall, Mulberry Place, 5 Clove Crescent, London E14 2BG ☎ 020 7364 5000 🖷 020 7364 4296 ✉ forename.surname@towerhamlets.gov.uk 🖳 www.towerhamlets.gov.uk

FACTS & FIGURES

Police Authority: Metropolitan Police Authority
Health Authority: NHS London
Learning and Skills Council: London
Parliamentary Constituencies: Bethnal Green and Bow, Poplar and Limehouse
EU Constituencies: London
Election Frequency: Elections are of whole council

PRINCIPAL OFFICERS

Assistant Chief Executive: Ms Isabella Freeman, Assistant Chief Executive - Legal Services, Town Hall, Mulberry Place, 5 Clove Crescent, London E14 2BG ☎ 020 7364 4801 🖷 020 7364 4804 ✉ isabella.freeman@towerhamlets.gov.uk

Architect, Building / Property Services: Mr Martin Stevens, Interim Head - Corporate Property Services, Mulberry Place, 5 Clove Crescent, London E14 2BG ☎ 020 7364 5000 ✉ martin.stevens@towerhamlets.gov.uk

Architect, Building / Property Services: Ms Ann Sutcliffe, Service Head - Building Schools for the Future, Anchorage House, 2 Clove Crescent, London E14 2BE ☎ 020 7364 4077 🖷 020 7364 4828 ✉ ann.sutcliffe@towerhamlets.gov.uk

Building Control: Mr Peter Hamilton, Head - Building Control, 41-47 Bow Road, London E3 2BS ☎ 020 7364 5254 🖷 020 7364 5358 ✉ peter.hamilton@towerhamlets.gov.uk

Children / Youth Services: Ms Isobel Cattermole, Acting Corporate Director, Mulberry Place, 5 Clove Crescent, London E14 2BG ☎ 020 7364 4953 ✉ isobel.cattermole@towerhamlets.gov.uk

Civil Registration: Ms Catherine Sutton, Chief Superintendent Registrar, Bromley Public Hall, Bow Road, London E3 3AA ☎ 020 7364 7983 🖷 020 7364 7885 ✉ catherine.sutton@towerhamlets.gov.uk

PR / Communications: Mr Takki Sulaiman, Head - Communications, Town Hall, Mulberry Place, 5 Clove Crescent, London E14 2BG ☎ 020 7364 4396 🖷 020 7364 4917 ✉ takki.sulaiman@towerhamlets.gov.uk

Community Planning: Ms Shazia Hussain, Interim Director Tower Hamlets Partnership, Town Hall, Mulberry Place, 5 Clove Crescent, London E14 2BG ☎ 020 7364 4470 🖷 020 7364 4676 ✉ shazia.hussain@towerhamlets.gov.uk

Community Safety: Mr Andy Bamber, Service Head - Safer Communities, Town Hall, Mulberry Place, 5 Clove Crescent, London E14 2BG ☎ 020 7364 0764 ✉ andy.bamber@towerhamlets.gov.uk

Computer Management: Ms Claire Symonds, Service Head - Customer Services, Town Hall, Mulberry Place, 5 Clove Crescent, London E14 2BG ☎ 020 7364 0839 🖷 020 7364 3121 ✉ claire.symonds@towerhamlets.gov.uk

Consumer Protection and Trading Standards: Mr Colin Perrins, Head - Trading Standards & Environmental Health Commercial, Town Hall, Mulberry Place (AH), PO Box 55739, London E14 1BY ☎ 020 7364 6872 🖷 020 7364 6901 ✉ colin.perrins@towerhamlets.gov.uk

Contracts: Mr Michael Hales, Head - Contracts Services, Toby Lane Depot, 1st Floor, Harford Street, London E1 4DN ☎ 020 7364 5153 🖷 020 7364 5161 ✉ michael.hales@towerhamlets.gov.uk

Contracts: Mr Peter Hayday, Service Head - Procurement & Corporate Programme, Town Hall, Mulberry Place, 5 Clove

Crescent, London E14 2BG ☎ 020 7364 4915 🖷 020 7364 4973 🖰 richard.parsons@towehamlets.gov.uk

Corporate Services: Ms Isobel Cattermole, Acting Corporate Director, Mulberry Place, 5 Clove Crescent, London E14 2BG ☎ 020 7364 4953 🖰 isobel.cattermole@towerhamlets.gov.uk

Corporate Services: Mr Martin Stevens, Interim Head - Corporate Property Services, Mulberry Place, 5 Clove Crescent, London E14 2BG ☎ 020 7364 5000 🖰 martin.stevens@towerhamlets.gov.uk

Customer Service: Ms Claire Symonds, Service Head - Customer Services, Town Hall, Mulberry Place, 5 Clove Crescent, London E14 2BG ☎ 020 7364 0839 🖷 020 7364 3121 🖰 claire.symonds@towerhamlets.gov.uk

Economic Development: Mr Aman Dalvi, Chief Executive, Anchorage House, 5 Clove Crescent, London E14 1BY ☎ 020 7634 4247 🖷 020 7364 4400 🖰 aman.dalvi@towerhamlets.gov.uk

Education: Ms Isobel Cattermole, Acting Corporate Director, Mulberry Place, 5 Clove Crescent, London E14 2BG ☎ 020 7364 4953 🖰 isobel.cattermole@towerhamlets.gov.uk

Electoral Registration: Ms Isabella Freeman, Assistant Chief Executive - Legal Services, Town Hall, Mulberry Place, 5 Clove Crescent, London E14 2BG ☎ 020 7364 4801 🖷 020 7364 4804 🖰 isabella.freeman@towerhamlets.gov.uk

Emergency Planning: Mr Steve Crawley, Civil Protection & Business Continuity Co-ordinator, 3rd Floor, Mulberry Place, 5 Clove Crescent, London E14 2BE ☎ 020 7364 4181 🖰 steve.crawley@towerhamlets.gov.uk

Energy Management: Ms Sian Pipe, Energy Manner, Energy Efficiency Unit, Gladstone Place, Roman Road, London E3 5ES ☎ 020 7364 2523 🖷 020 7364 2512 🖰 sian.pipe@towerhamlets.gov.uk

Environmental / Technical Services: Mr Andy Bamber, Service Head - Safer Communities, Town Hall, Mulberry Place, 5 Clove Crescent, London E14 2BG ☎ 020 7364 0764 🖰 andy.bamber@towerhamlets.gov.uk

Environmental / Technical Services: Mr Andrew Weaver, Head - Environmental Health & Environmental Protection, Town Hall, Mulberry Place, 5 Clove Crescent, London E14 2BG ☎ 020 7364 6896 🖰 andrew.weaver@towerhamlets.gov.uk

Environmental Health: Mr Andrew Weaver, Head - Environmental Health & Environmental Protection, Town Hall, Mulberry Place, 5 Clove Crescent, London E14 2BG ☎ 020 7364 6896 🖰 andrew.weaver@towerhamlets.gov.uk

Estates, Property & Valuation: Ms Ann Sutcliffe, Service Head - Building Schools for the Future, Anchorage House, 2 Clove Crescent, London E14 2BE ☎ 020 7364 4077 🖷 020 7364 4828 🖰 ann.sutcliffe@towerhamlets.gov.uk

Events Manager: Mr Steve Murray, Head - Arts, Town Hall, Mulberry Place, 5 Clove Crescent, London E14 2BG ☎ 020 7364 7910 🖰 stephen.murray@towerhamlets.gov.uk

Facilities: Ms Ann Sutcliffe, Service Head - Building Schools for the Future, Anchorage House, 2 Clove Crescent, London E14 2BE ☎ 020 7364 4077 🖷 020 7364 4828 🖰 ann.sutcliffe@towerhamlets.gov.uk

Finance and Treasurer: Mr Chris Naylor, Director - Resources, Mulberry Place, 5 Clove Crescent, London E14 2BG ☎ 020 7364 4262 🖷 020 7364 4536 🖰 chris.naylor@towerhamlets.gov.uk

Fleet Management: Mr John Stevens, Transport Contracts Manager, 1 Silvocea Way, Blackwall, London E14 0JJ ☎ 020 7364 1071 🖷 020 7364 1070 🖰 john.e.stevens@towerhamlets.gov.uk

Grounds Maintenance: Ms Ann Sutcliffe, Service Head - Building Schools for the Future, Anchorage House, 2 Clove Crescent, London E14 2BE ☎ 020 7364 4077 🖷 020 7364 4828 🖰 ann.sutcliffe@towerhamlets.gov.uk

Health and Safety: Mr Dave Tolley, Health & Safety Manager, 4th Floor, Mulberry Place, 5 Clove Crescent, London E14 2BE ☎ 020 7364 6724 🖷 020 7364 6901 🖰 dave.tolley@towerhamlets.gov.uk

Highways: Ms Ruth Seager, Planning Group Manager, Town Hall, Mulberry Place (AH), PO Box 55739, 5 Clove Crescent, London E14 1BY ☎ 020 7364 6588 🖷 020 7364 6753 🖰 ruth.seager@towerhamlets.gov.uk

Home Energy Conservation: Ms Sian Pipe, Energy Manner, Energy Efficiency Unit, Gladstone Place, Roman Road, London E3 5ES ☎ 020 7364 2523 🖷 020 7364 2512 🖰 sian.pipe@towerhamlets.gov.uk

Housing: Mr Gavin Cansfield, Chief Executive - Tower Hamlets Homes, 1st Floor, 2 Lawn House Close, London E14 9YQ ☎ 0207 364 7134 🖰 gavin.cansfield@towerhamlets.gov.uk

Local Area Agreement: Mr Kevin Kewin, Policy Manager, Town Hall, Mulberry Place, 5 Clove Crescent, London E14 2BG ☎ 020 7296 6880 🖰 kevin.kewin@towerhamlets.gov.uk

Legal: Ms Isabella Freeman, Assistant Chief Executive - Legal Services, Town Hall, Mulberry Place, 5 Clove Crescent, London E14 2BG ☎ 020 7364 4801 🖷 020 7364 4804 🖰 isabella.freeman@towerhamlets.gov.uk

Leisure and Cultural Services: Ms Heather Bonfield, Interim Service Head - Culture Services, Anchorage House, 4th Floor, 5 Clove Crescent, London E14 2BE ☎ 020 7364 1667 🖷 020 7364 3286 🖰 heather.bonfield@towerhamlets.gov.uk

Licensing: Mr Colin Perrins, Head - Trading Standards & Environmental Health Commercial, Town Hall, Mulberry Place (AH), PO Box 55739, London E14 1BY ☎ 020 7364 6872 🖷 020 7364 6901 🖰 colin.perrins@towerhamlets.gov.uk

Lifelong Learning: Ms Mary Durkin, Service Head - Youth & Community Learning, Town Hall, Mulberry Place, 5 Clove Crescent, London E14 2BG ☎ 020 7364 4373 🖰 mary.durkin@towerhamlets.gov.uk

Lighting: Mr Stanley Perpie, Street Lighting Engineer, Anchorage House, 4th Floor, 5 Clove Crescent, London E14 2BE

☎ 020 7364 6802 🖷 020 7364 6867
✉ stanley.perpie@towerhamlets.gov.uk

Lottery Funding, Charity and Voluntary: Mr Everett Haughton, Head - External Funding, Mulberry Place, Anchorage House, 2 Clove Crescent, London E14 2BG ☎ 020 7364 5000
✉ everett.haughton@towerhamlets.gov.uk

Lottery Funding, Charity and Voluntary: Ms Louise Russell, Service Head - Scrutiny & Equalities, Town Hall, Mulberry Place, 5 Clove Crescent, London E14 2BG ☎ 020 7364 3267
✉ louise.russell@towerhamlets.gov.uk

Member Services: Mr John Williams, Service Head - Democratic Services, Town Hall, Mulberry Place (AH), PO Box 55739, 5 Clove Crescent, London E14 1BY ☎ 020 7364 4204 🖷 020 7364 3232
✉ john.williams@towerhamlets.gov.uk

Parking: Mr John Chilton, Head - Parking Services, 4th Floor, Mulberry Place, 5 Clove Crescent, London E14 2BE ☎ 020 7364 6999 🖷 020 7364 6921 ✉ john.chilton@towerhamlets.gov.uk

Partnerships: Ms Shazia Hussain, Service Head - Localisation, 4th Floor, Mulberry Place, 5 Clove Crescent, London E14 2BE
☎ 020 7364 4470 ✉ shazia.hussain@towerhamlets.gov.uk

Personnel / HR: Mr Simon Kilbey, Service Head - HR & Work Force Development, Mulberry Place, 5 Clove Crescent, London E14 2BG ☎ 020 7364 4922

Planning: Mr Owen Whalley, Service Head - Development Control & Building Control, Anchorage House, 2 Clove Crescent, London E14 2BE ☎ 020 7364 5314 🖷 020 7364 5412
✉ owen.whalley@towerhamlets.gov.uk

Procurement: Mr Peter Hayday, Service Head - Procurement & Corporate Programme, Town Hall, Mulberry Place, 5 Clove Crescent, London E14 2BG ☎ 020 7364 4915 🖷 020 7364 4973
✉ richard.parsons@towehamlets.gov.uk

Public Libraries: Ms Judith St John, Head - Libraries, 3rd Floor, 1 Gladstone Place, London E3 5EG ☎ 020 7364 5630
✉ judith.stjohn@towerhamlets.gov.uk

Recycling & Waste Minimisation: Mr Simon Baxter, Head - Clean & Green, Anchorage House, 5 Clove Crescent, London E14 2BE ☎ 020 7364 4422 ✉ simon.baxter@towerhamlets.gov.uk

Regeneration: Ms Jackie Odunoye, Service Head - Strategy, Innovation & Sustainability, Anchorage House, 5 Clove Crescent, London E14 1BY ☎ 020 7364 4247
✉ jackie.odunoye@towerhamlets.gov.uk

Road Safety: Ms Margaret Cooper, Senior Road Safety Officer, Anchorage House, 5 Clove Crescent, London E14 2BE
☎ 020 7364 6851 ✉ margaret.cooper@towerhamlets.gov.uk

Social Services (Adult): Ms Katherinw Marks, Interim Service Head - Adult Social Care, Anchorage House, 5 Clove Crescent, London E14 2BE ☎ 020 7364 2127
✉ katherine.marks@towerhamlets.gov.uk

Social Services (Children): Ms Isobel Cattermole, Acting Corporate Director, Mulberry Place, 5 Clove Crescent, London E14 2BG ☎ 020 7364 4953
✉ isobel.cattermole@towerhamlets.gov.uk

Social Services (Children): Mr Steve Liddicott, Interim Service Head - Children's Social Care, Town Hall, Mulberry Place, 5 Clove Crescent, London E14 2BG ☎ 020 7364 4953
✉ steve.liddicott@towerhamlets.gov.uk

Staff Training: Mr Simon Kilbey, Service Head - HR & Work Force Development, Mulberry Place, 5 Clove Crescent, London E14 2BG ☎ 020 7364 4922

Street Scene: Mr Jamie Blake, Service Head - Public Realm, Anchorage House, 5 Clove Crescent, London E14 1BY
☎ 020 7364 6769 ✉ jamie.blake@towerhamlets.gov.uk

Sustainable Communities: Ms Jackie Odunoye, Service Head - Strategy, Innovation & Sustainability, Town Hall, Mulberry Place, 5 Clove Crescent, London E14 2BG ☎ 020 7364 4247
✉ jackie.odunoye@towerhamlets.gov.uk

Sustainable Development: Ms Jackie Odunoye, Service Head - Strategy, Innovation & Sustainability, Town Hall, Mulberry Place, 5 Clove Crescent, London E14 2BG ☎ 020 7364 4247
✉ jackie.odunoye@towerhamlets.gov.uk

Tourism: Ms Patricia Holmes, Investment & Business Officer, Town Hall, Mulberry Place, 5 Clove Crescent, London E14 2BG
☎ 020 7364 4368 🖷 020 7364 4267
✉ patricia.holmes@towerhamlets.gov.uk

Traffic Management: Ms Margaret Cooper, Senior Road Safety Officer, Anchorage House, 4th Floor, 5 Clove Crescent, London E14 2BE ☎ 020 7364 6851
✉ margaret.cooper@towerhamlets.gov.uk

Transport: Mr John Stevens, Transport Contracts Manager, 1 Silvocea Way, Blackwall, London E14 0JJ ☎ 020 7364 1071
🖷 020 7364 1070 ✉ john.e.stevens@towerhamlets.gov.uk

Transport Planner: Mr John Stevens, Transport Contracts Manager, 1 Silvocea Way, Blackwall, London E14 0JJ ☎ 020 7364 1071 🖷 020 7364 1070 ✉ john.e.stevens@towerhamlets.gov.uk

Waste Collection and Disposal: Mr Simon Baxter, Head - Clean & Green, Anchorage House, 5 Clove Crescent, London E14 2BE
☎ 020 7364 4422 ✉ simon.baxter@towerhamlets.gov.uk

Waste Management: Mr Simon Baxter, Head - Clean & Green, Anchorage House, 5 Clove Crescent, London E14 2BE ☎ 020 7364 4422 ✉ simon.baxter@towerhamlets.gov.uk

MEMBERS OF THE COUNCIL (52)

Directly Elected Mayor: **Rahman**, Lutfur (O - Mayors Ward)
mayor@towerhamlets.gov.uk
Chair: **Ahmed**, Rajib (LAB - East India and Lansbury)
cllr.rajib.ahmed@towerhamlets.gov.uk
Deputy Mayor: **Ahmed**, A M Ohid (IND - East India and Lansbury)
cllr.ohid.ahmed@towerhamlets.gov.uk
Group Leader: **Golds**, Peter (CON - Blackwall and Cubitt Town)
cllrpetergolds@aol.com
Group Leader: **Peck**, Joshua (LAB - Bow West)
cllr.joshua.peck@towerhamlets.gov.uk

Abbas, Helal (LAB - Spitalfields and Banglatown)
cllr.helal.abbas@towerhamlets.gov.uk
Ahmed, Rofique (LAB - Mile End and Globe Town)
cllr.rofique.ahmed@towerhamlets.gov.uk
Ahmed, Kabir (IND - Weavers)
cllr.kabir.ahmedx@towerhamlets.gov.uk
Ahmed, Khales (LAB - Bromley-by-Bow)
cllr.khales.ahmed@towerhamlets.gov.uk
Ali, Shahed (LAB - Whitechapel)
cllr.shahed.ali@towerhamlets.gov.uk
Archer, Timothy (CON - Blackwall and Cubitt Town)
tim@tarcher.fsbusiness.co.uk
Asad, Abdul (LAB - Whitechapel)
cllr.abdul.asad@towerhamlets.gov.uk
Aston, Craig (CON - Limehouse)
cllrcraigaston@gmaill.com
Begum, Lutfa (IND - Limehouse)
cllr.lutfa.begum@towerhamlets.gov.uk
Chaudhury, Mizanur (LAB - Bethnal Green South)
cllr.mizanur.chaudhury@towerhamlets.gov.uk
Choudhury, Alibor (IND - Shadwell)
cllr.alibor.choudhury@towerhamlets.gov.uk
Davies, Zara (CON - Millwall)
cllrzaradavis@gmail.com
Eaton, Stephanie (LD - Bethnal Green North)
cllr.stephanie.eaton@towerhamlets.gov.uk
Edgar, David (LAB - Limehouse)
cllr.david.edgar@towerhamlets.gov.uk
Francis, Marc (LAB - Bow East)
cllr.marc.francis@towerhamlets.gov.uk
Gardner, Judith (LAB - St Dunstan's and Stepney Green)
cllr.judith.gardner@towerhamlets.gov.uk
Gibbs, Carlo (LAB - Bethnal Green North)
cllr.carlo.gibbs@towerhamlets.gov.uk
Haque, Shafiqul (LAB - St. Katherine's and Wapping)
cllr.shafiqul.haque@towerhamlets.gov.uk
Harper-Penman, Carli (LAB - Bow East)
cllr.carli.harper-penman@towerhamlets.gov.uk
Islam, Sirajul (LAB - Bethnal Green South)
cllr.sirajul.islam@towerhamlets.gov.uk
Jackson, Ann (LAB - Bow West)
cllr.ann.jackson@towerhamlets.gov.uk
Jones, Emma (CON - St. Katharine's and Wapping)
cllr.emma.jones@towerhamlets.gov.uk
Jones, Denise (LAB - St Katherine's and Wapping)
cllr.denise.jones@towerhamlets.gov.uk
Khan, Rania (IND - Bromley-by-Bow)
cllr.rania.khan@towerhamlets.gov.uk
Khan, Anwar (LAB - Bow West)
cllr.anwar.khan@towerhamlets.gov.uk
Khan, Aminur (IND - Whitechapel)
cllr.aminur.khan@towerhamlets.gov.uk
Khan, Rabina (IND - Shadwell)
rabina.khan@towerhamlets.gov.uk
Khatun, Shiria (LAB - East India and Lansbury)
cllr.sharia.khatun@towerhamlets.gov.uk
Miah, Fozol (RSP - Spitalfields and Banglatown)
cllr.fozol.miah@towerhamlets.gov.uk
Miah, Harun (RSP - Shadwell)
harun.miah@towerhamlets.gov.uk
Miah, Maium (CON - Millwall)
mdmaium@gmail.com
Mukit, Abdul (LAB - Weavers)
AbdulC.Mukit@towerhamlets.gov.uk
Omer, Ahmed (LAB - Bow East)
cllr.ahmed.omer@towerhamlets.gov.uk
Pavitt, Lesley (LAB - Bethnal Green South)
cllr.lesley.pavitt@towerhamlets.gov.uk
Pierce, John (LAB - Weavers)
cllr.john.pierce@towerhamlets.gov.uk
Rahman, Oliur (IND - St Dunstan's and Stepney Green)
cllroliur.rahman@yahoo.co.uk
Rahman, Zenith (LAB - Bethnal Green North)
cllr.zenith.rahman@towerhamlets.gov.uk
Robbani, Gulam (IND - Spitalfields and Bangaltown)
cllr.gulam.robbani@towerhamlets.gov.uk
Saunders, Rachael (LAB - Mile End East)
cllr.rachael.saunders@towerhamlets.gov.uk
Snowden, David (CON - Millwall)
david.snowden@towerhamlets.gov.uk
Thienel, Gloria (CON - Blackwall and Cubitt Town)
gloriathienel@aol.com
Turner, Bill (LAB - Mile End and Globe Town)
cllr.bill.turner@towerhamlets.gov.uk
Uddin, Kosru (LAB - Mile End East)
cllr.kosru.uddin@towerhamlets.gov.uk
Uddin, Helal (LAB - Bromley-by-Bow)
cllr.helal.uddin@towerhamlets.gov.uk
Ullah, Abdal (LAB - St Dunstan's and Stepney Green)
cllr.abdal.ullah@towerhamlets.gov.uk
Uz-Zaman, Motin (LAB - Mile End East)
cllr.motin.uz-zaman@towerhamlets.gov.uk
Whitelock, Amy (LAB - Mile End and Globe Town)
cllr.amy.whitelock@towerhamlets.gov.uk

POLITICAL COMPOSITION
LAB: 31, IND: 9, CON: 8, RSP: 2, LD: 1, O: 1

CABINET
Mayor: Mr Lutfur Rahman
Deputy Mayor: Mr A M Ohid Ahmed
Children's Services: Mr Oliur Rahman
Culture: Ms Rania Khan
Environment: Mr Shahed Ali
Health & Wellbeing: Mr Abdul Asad
Housing: Ms Rabina Khan
Jobs & Skills: Mr Shafiqul Haque
Resources: Mr Alibor Choudhury
Regeneration: Mr Rofique Ahmed

COMMITTEE CHAIRS
Appeals: Mr Bill Turner
Audit: Mr Carlo Gibbs
Development: Mr Helal Abbas
General Purposes: Ms Shiria Khatun
Health & Scrutiny: Ms Rachael Saunders
Human Resources: Mr Abdul Mukit
Licensing: Ms Carli Harper-Penman
Overview & Scrutiny: Ms Ann Jackson
Pensions: Mr Zenith Rahman

TRAFFORD M

Trafford Metropolitan Borough Council, Trafford Council, Talbot Road, Stretford, Manchester M32 0TH ☎ 0161 912 2000
🖷 0161 912 1354
💻 www.trafford.gov.uk

FACTS & FIGURES

Police Authority: Greater Manchester Police Authority
Health Authority: North West Strategic Health Authority
Learning and Skills Council: North West
Parliamentary Constituencies: Altrincham and Sale West, Stretford and Urmston, Wythenshawe and Sale East
EU Constituencies: North West
Election Frequency: Elections are by thirds

PRINCIPAL OFFICERS

Chief Executive: Ms Theresa Grant, Chief Executive, Quay West, Trafford Wharf Road, Trafford Park, Manchester M17 1HH ☎ 0161 912 1900 ✉ theresa.grant@trafford.gov.uk

Senior Management: Ms Deborah Brownlee, Corporate Director for Children & Young People's Services, Quay West, Trafford Wharf Road, Trafford Park, Manchester M17 1HH ☎ 0161 912 1901 ✉ deborah.brownlee@trafford.gov.uk

Senior Management: Mr Ian Duncan, Acting Corporate Director for Transformation & Resources, Quay West, Trafford Wharf Road, Trafford Park, Manchester M17 1HH ☎ 0161 912 4238 🖷 0161 912 1250 ✉ ian.duncan@trafford.gov.uk

Senior Management: Mr Nick Gerrard, Corporate Director for Economic Growth & Prosperity, Quay West, Trafford Wharf Road, Trafford Park, Manchester M17 1HH ☎ 0161 912 1915 ✉ nick.gerrard@trafford.gov.uk

Senior Management: Ms Anne Higgins, Corporate Director for Communities & Wellbeing, Quay West, Trafford Wharf Road, Trafford Park, Manchester M17 1HH ☎ 0161 912 4009 🖷 0161 912 4199 ✉ anne.higgins@trafford.gov.uk

Senior Management: Mr Peter Molyneux, Corporate Director for Environment, Transport & Operations, Quay West, Trafford Wharf Road, Trafford Park, Manchester M17 1HH ☎ 0161 912 1902 ✉ peter.molyneux@trafford.gov.uk

Architect, Building / Property Services: Mr Jeremy Valentine, Head of Asset Management, Waterside House, Sale Waterside, Sale M33 7ZF ☎ 0161 912 4264 🖷 0161 912 1652 ✉ jeremy.valentine@trafford.gov.uk

Building Control: Mr Stuart Beesley, Building Control Business Manager, Waterside House, Sales Waterside, Sale M33 6FZ ☎ 0161 912 3116 ✉ stuart.beesley@trafford.gov.uk

Catering Services: Ms Christine Holden, Catering Operations Manager, Trafford Council, Talbot Road, Stretford, Manchester M32 0TH ☎ 0161 912 4195 ✉ christine.holden@trafford.gov.uk

Children / Youth Services: Ms Deborah Brownlee, Corporate Director for Children & Young People's Services, Quay West, Trafford Wharf Road, Trafford Park, Manchester M17 1HH ☎ 0161 912 1901 ✉ deborah.brownlee@trafford.gov.uk

Children / Youth Services: Mr John Pearce, Director of Commissioning, Performance & Strategy, Quay West, Trafford Wharf Road, Trafford Park, Manchester M17 1HH ☎ 0161 912 5100 ✉ john.pearce@trafford.gov.uk

Civil Registration: Ms Jane Lefevre, Acting Director of Legal & Democratic Services, Quay West, Trafford Wharf Road, Trafford Park, Manchester M17 1HH ☎ 0161 912 4215 ✉ jane.lefevre@trafford.gov.uk

PR / Communications: Mr James Blandy, Communications Manager, Quay West, Trafford Wharf Road, Trafford Park, Manchester M17 1HH ☎ 0161 912 3289 ✉ james.blandy@trafford.gov.uk

Community Planning: Mrs Sonia Cubrilo, Strategic Manager for Neighbourhood, Community & Enterprise, Quay West, Trafford Wharf Road, Trafford Park, Manchester M17 1HH ☎ 0161 912 4245 ✉ sonia.cubrillo@trafford.gov.uk

Community Safety: Ms Helen McFarlane, Director of Safe, Strong Communities, Waterside House, Sale Waterside, Sale M33 7ZF ☎ 0161 912 3437 🖷 0161 912 3444 ✉ helen.mcfarlane@trafford.gov.uk

Computer Management: Ms Sharon Richardson, Acting Head of Business Change & ICT, Friars Court, Sibson Road, Sale M33 7SF ☎ 0161 912 4602 ✉ sharon.richardson@trafford.gov.uk

Consumer Protection and Trading Standards: Mr Iain Veitch, Head of Public Protection, Quay West, Trafford Wharf Road, Trafford Park, Manchester M17 1HH ☎ 0161 912 4174 🖷 0161 912 4917 ✉ iain.veitch@trafford.gov.uk

Contracts: Mr Carl Brennan, Head of Procurement, Quay West, Trafford Wharf Road, Trafford Park, Manchester M17 1HH ☎ 0161 912 1209 🖷 0161 912 4272 ✉ carl.brennan@trafford.gov.uk

Customer Service: Mr Mike Lewis, Director of Customer Service, Waterside House, Sale Waterside, Sale M33 7ZF ☎ 0121 912 2003 ✉ mike.lewis@trafford.gov.uk

Customer Service: Ms Jayne Stephenson, Head of Partnerships & Performance, Quay West, Trafford Wharf Road, Trafford Park, Manchester M17 1HH ☎ 0161 912 1231 ✉ jayne.stephenson@trafford.gov.uk

Economic Development: Mr Nick Gerrard, Corporate Director for Economic Growth & Prosperity, Quay West, Trafford Wharf Road, Trafford Park, Manchester M17 1HH ☎ 0161 912 1915 ✉ nick.gerrard@trafford.gov.uk

Economic Development: Ms Suzanne Hilton, Head of Regeneration & Economic Development, Waterside House, Sale Waterside, Sale M33 7ZF ☎ 0161 912 4230 🖷 0161 912 4490 ✉ suzanne.hilton@trafford.gov.uk

Education: Ms Deborah Brownlee, Corporate Director for Children & Young People's Services, Quay West, Trafford Wharf Road, Trafford Park, Manchester M17 1HH ☎ 0161 912 1901 ✉ deborah.brownlee@trafford.gov.uk

Education: Mr George Herbert, Deputy Director of Education & Early Years Services, Quay West, Trafford Wharf Road, Trafford Park, Manchester M17 1HH ☎ 0161 911 8607 ✉ george.herbert@trafford.gov.uk

E-Government: Ms Sharon Richardson, Acting Head of Business Change & ICT, Friars Court, Sibson Road, Sale M33 7SF ☎ 0161 912 4602 ✉ sharon.richardson@trafford.gov.uk

Electoral Registration: Ms Jane Lefevre, Acting Director of

Legal & Democratic Services, Quay West, Trafford Wharf Road, Trafford Park, Manchester M17 1HH ☎ 0161 912 4215 ✉ jane.lefevre@trafford.gov.uk

Emergency Planning: Mr David Hooley, Emergency Planning Manager, 7th Floor Quay West, Trafford Wharf Road, Trafford, Manchester M17 1HH ☎ 0161 912 3425 🖷 0161 912 3444 ✉ david.hooley@trafford.gov.uk

Energy Management: Mr Andrew Hunt, Sustainability Manager, Waterside House, Sale Waterside, Sale M33 7ZF ☎ 0161 912 4691 ✉ andrew.hunt@trafford.gov.uk

Environmental Health: Mr Iain Veitch, Head of Public Protection, Quay West, Trafford Wharf Road, Trafford Park, Manchester M17 1HH ☎ 0161 912 4174 🖷 0161 912 4917 ✉ iain.veitch@trafford.gov.uk

Estates, Property & Valuation: Mr David Challis, Manager of Estates & Valuations, Waterside House, Sale Waterside, Sale M33 7ZF ☎ 0161 912 4227 🖷 0161 912 1652 ✉ david.challis@trafford.gov.uk

European Liaison: Ms Suzanne Hilton, Head of Regeneration & Economic Development, Waterside House, Sale Waterside, Sale M33 7ZF ☎ 0161 912 4230 🖷 0161 912 4490 ✉ suzanne.hilton@trafford.gov.uk

Events Manager: Mrs Sonia Cubrilo, Strategic Manager for Neighbourhood, Community & Enterprise, Quay West, Trafford Wharf Road, Trafford Park, Manchester M17 1HH ☎ 0161 912 4245 ✉ sonia.cubrillo@trafford.gov.uk

Facilities: Mr Jeremy Valentine, Head of Asset Management, Waterside House, Sale Waterside, Sale M33 7ZF ☎ 0161 912 4264 🖷 0161 912 1652 ✉ jeremy.valentine@trafford.gov.uk

Finance and Treasurer: Mr Ian Duncan, Acting Corporate Director for Transformation & Resources, Quay West, Trafford Wharf Road, Trafford Park, Manchester M17 1HH ☎ 0161 912 4238 🖷 0161 912 1250 ✉ ian.duncan@trafford.gov.uk

Fleet Management: Mr Colin Maycroft, Service Operations Manager, Moss View Centre, Moss View Road, Partington, Manchester M31 4DX ☎ 0161 912 5061 ✉ colin.maycroft@trafford.gov.uk

Health and Safety: Mr Iain Veitch, Head of Public Protection, Quay West, Trafford Wharf Road, Trafford Park, Manchester M17 1HH ☎ 0161 912 4174 🖷 0161 912 4917 ✉ iain.veitch@trafford.gov.uk

Highways: Mr Aidan Flynn, Head of Highways, Structures, Transportation, Green Spaces & Sustainability, Waterside House, Sale Waterside, Sale M33 7ZF 🖷 0161 912 1113 ✉ aidan.flynn@trafford.gov.uk

Home Energy Conservation: Mr Andrew Hunt, Sustainability Manager, Waterside House, Sale Waterside, Sale M33 7ZF ☎ 0161 912 4691 ✉ andrew.hunt@trafford.gov.uk

Housing: Mr Richard Roe, Housing Strategy Manager, Waterside House, Sale Waterside, Sale M33 7ZF ☎ 0161 912 4265 ✉ richard.roe@trafford.gov.uk

Housing Maintenance: Mr Rob Haslam, Head of Strategic Planning, Waterside House, Sale Waterside, Sale M33 7ZF ☎ 0161 912 4788 ✉ rob.haslam@trafford.gov.uk

Local Area Agreement: Ms Suzanne Hilton, Head of Regeneration & Economic Development, Waterside House, Sale Waterside, Sale M33 7ZF ☎ 0161 912 4230 🖷 0161 912 4490 ✉ suzanne.hilton@trafford.gov.uk

Legal: Ms Jane Lefevre, Acting Director of Legal & Democratic Services, Quay West, Trafford Wharf Road, Trafford Park, Manchester M17 1HH ☎ 0161 912 4215 ✉ jane.lefevre@trafford.gov.uk

Leisure and Cultural Services: Ms Debbie Cowley, Principal Commissioner for Culture & Sport, Waterside House, Sale Waterside, Sale M33 7ZF ☎ 0161 912 3110 ✉ debbie.cowley@trafford.gov.uk

Licensing: Mr Iain Veitch, Head of Public Protection, Quay West, Trafford Wharf Road, Trafford Park, Manchester M17 1HH ☎ 0161 912 4174 🖷 0161 912 4917 ✉ iain.veitch@trafford.gov.uk

Lifelong Learning: Ms Deborah Brownlee, Corporate Director for Children & Young People's Services, Quay West, Trafford Wharf Road, Trafford Park, Manchester M17 1HH ☎ 0161 912 1901 ✉ deborah.brownlee@trafford.gov.uk

Lottery Funding, Charity and Voluntary: Mr Melvyn Dawson, Regeneration & Funding Officer, Waterside House, Sale Waterside, Sale M33 7ZF ☎ 0161 912 4167 🖷 0161 912 4490 ✉ melvyn.dawson@trafford.gov.uk

Member Services: Mr James McLaughlin, Democratic Services Manager, Quay West, Trafford Wharf Road, Trafford Park, Manchester M17 1HH ☎ 0161 912 1815 ✉ james.mclaughlin@trafford.gov.uk

Parking: Ms Nicola Henry, Parking Services Manager, Waterside House, Sale Waterside, Sale M33 7ZF ☎ 0161 912 4046 ✉ nicola.henry@trafford.gov.uk

Partnerships: Ms Jayne Stephenson, Head of Partnerships & Performance, Quay West, Trafford Wharf Road, Trafford Park, Manchester M17 1HH ☎ 0161 912 1231 ✉ jayne.stephenson@trafford.gov.uk

Personnel / HR: Ms Joanne Hyde, Director of Human Resources, Quay West, Trafford Wharf Road, Trafford Park, Manchester M17 1HH ☎ 0161 912 1586 🖷 0161 912 4171 ✉ joanne.hyde@trafford.gov.uk

Planning: Mr Simon Castle, Chief Planning Officer, Waterside House, Sale Waterside, Sale M33 6FZ ☎ 0161 912 3111 🖷 0161 912 3128 ✉ simon.castle@trafford.gov.uk

Planning: Mr Rob Haslam, Head of Strategic Planning, Waterside House, Sale Waterside, Sale M33 7ZF ☎ 0161 912 4788 ✉ rob.haslam@trafford.gov.uk

Procurement: Mr Carl Brennan, Head of Procurement, Quay West, Trafford Wharf Road, Trafford Park, Manchester M17 1HH ☎ 0161 912 1209 🖷 0161 912 4272 ✉ carl.brennan@trafford.gov.uk

Public Libraries: Mr Mike Lewis, Director of Customer Service, Waterside House, Sale Waterside, Sale M33 7ZF ☎ 0121 912 2003 ✉ mike.lewis@trafford.gov.uk

Recycling & Waste Minimisation: Mr Gary Taylor, Waste Manager, Carrington Depot, Carrington, Manchester M31 4WS ☎ 0161 912 4912 🖷 0161 912 5705 ✉ gary.taylor@trafford.gov.uk

Regeneration: Ms Suzanne Hilton, Head of Regeneration & Economic Development, Waterside House, Sale Waterside, Sale M33 7ZF ☎ 0161 912 4230 🖷 0161 912 4490 ✉ suzanne.hilton@trafford.gov.uk

Social Services: Ms Anne Higgins, Corporate Director for Communities & Wellbeing, Quay West, Trafford Wharf Road, Trafford Park, Manchester M17 1HH ☎ 0161 912 4009 🖷 0161 912 4199 ✉ anne.higgins@trafford.gov.uk

Social Services (Adult): Mr David Hanley, Deputy Director of Communities & Wellbeing, Quay West, Trafford Wharf Road, Trafford Park, Manchester M17 1HH ☎ 0161 912 4107 ✉ david.hanley@trafford.gov.uk

Social Services (Children): Ms Charlotte Ramsden, Director of Services for Children, Young People & Families, Quay West, Trafford Wharf Road, Trafford Park, Manchester M17 1HH ☎ 0161 911 8650 ✉ charlotte.ramsden@trafford.gov.uk

Street Scene: Mr Paul Harvey, Senior Director of Environment, Quay West, Trafford Wharf Road, Trafford Park, Manchester M17 1HH ☎ 0161 912 4694 🖷 0161 912 1113 ✉ paul.harvey@trafford.gov.uk

Sustainable Communities: Mr Andrew Hunt, Sustainability Manager, Waterside House, Sale Waterside, Sale M33 7ZF ☎ 0161 912 4691 ✉ andrew.hunt@trafford.gov.uk

Sustainable Development: Ms Suzanne Hilton, Head of Regeneration & Economic Development, Waterside House, Sale Waterside, Sale M33 7ZF ☎ 0161 912 4230 🖷 0161 912 4490 ✉ suzanne.hilton@trafford.gov.uk

Tourism: Ms Kay Harwood, Tourism Officer, Quay West, Trafford Wharf Road, Trafford Park, Manchester M17 1HH ☎ 0161 912 4502 🖷 0161 912 4490 ✉ kay.harwood@trafford.gov.uk

Town Centre: Mrs Sonia Cubrilo, Strategic Manager for Neighbourhood, Community & Enterprise, Quay West, Trafford Wharf Road, Trafford Park, Manchester M17 1HH ☎ 0161 912 4245 ✉ sonia.cubrillo@trafford.gov.uk

Traffic Management: Mr Paul Harvey, Senior Director of Environment, Quay West, Trafford Wharf Road, Trafford Park, Manchester M17 1HH ☎ 0161 912 4694 🖷 0161 912 1113 ✉ paul.harvey@trafford.gov.uk

Transport: Mr Colin Maycroft, Service Operations Manager, Moss View Centre, Moss View Road, Partington, Manchester M31 4DX ☎ 0161 912 2926 🖷 0161 912 2931 ✉ colin.maycroft@trafford.gov.uk

Waste Collection and Disposal: Mr Gary Taylor, Waste Manager, Carrington Depot, Carrington, Manchester M31 4WS ☎ 0161 912 4912 🖷 0161 912 5705 ✉ gary.taylor@trafford.gov.uk

Waste Management: Mr Gary Taylor, Waste Manager, Carrington Depot, Carrington, Manchester M31 4WS ☎ 0161 912 4912 🖷 0161 912 5705 ✉ gary.taylor@trafford.gov.uk

MEMBERS OF THE COUNCIL (63)

***Mayor:* Young**, Patricia (CON - Hale Central)
patricia.young@trafford.gov.uk

***Deputy Mayor:* Butt**, Dylan (CON - Hale Barns)
dylan.butt@trafford.gov.uk

***Leader of the Council:* Colledge**, Matthew (CON - Altrincham)
matthew.colledge@trafford.gov.uk

***Deputy Leader of the Council:* Williams**, Alex (CON - Altrincham)
alex.williams@trafford.gov.uk

***Group Leader:* Acton**, David (LAB - Gorse Hill)
david.acton@trafford.gov.uk

***Group Leader:* Bowker**, Ray (LD - Village)
ray.bowker@trafford.gov.uk

Adshead, Stephen (LAB - Stretford)
stephen.adshead@trafford.gov.uk

Anstee, Sean (CON - Bowdon)
sean.anstee@trafford.gov.uk

Barclay, Karen (CON - Bowdon)
karen.barclay@trafford.gov.uk

Baugh, Jane (LAB - Priory)
jane.baugh@trafford.gov.uk

Bennett, Joanne (LAB - Sale Moor)
joanne.bennett@trafford.gov.uk

Blackburn, Linda (CON - Davyhulme East)
linda.blackburn@trafford.gov.uk

Boyes, Chris (CON - Brooklands)
chris.boyes@trafford.gov.uk

Brophy, Jane (LD - Timperley)
jane.brophy@trafford.gov.uk

Brotherton, Barry (LAB - Priory)
barry.brotherton@trafford.gov.uk

Bruer-Morris, Angela (CON - Timperley)
angela.bruer-morris@trafford.gov.uk

Bunting, Daniel (CON - St. Mary's)
dan.bunting@trafford.gov.uk

Candish, Chris (CON - Hale Central)
chris.candish@trafford.gov.uk

Chilton, Rob (CON - St. Mary's)
robert.chilton@trafford.gov.uk

Cooke, Lisa (CON - Davyhulme East)
lisa.cooke@trafford.gov.uk

Cordingley, Mike (LAB - Gorse Hill)
michael.cordingley@trafford.gov.uk

Cornes, Michael (CON - Davyhulme East)
michael.cornes@trafford.gov.uk

Coupe, Jonathan (CON - Flixton)
jonathan.coupe@trafford.gov.uk

Dixon, Pamela (CON - Brooklands)
pamela.dixon@trafford.gov.uk

Duffield, Anne (LAB - Longford)
anne.duffield@trafford.gov.uk

Evans, Laura (CON - Village)
laura.evans@trafford.gov.uk

Fishwick, Tony (LD - Village)
tony.fishwick@trafford.gov.uk

Freeman, Mike (LAB - Sale Moor)
mike.freeman@trafford.gov.uk

Gratix, Philip (LAB - Sale Moor)
philip.gratix@trafford.gov.uk
Harding, Joanne (LAB - Urmston)
joanne.harding@trafford.gov.uk
Higgins, David (CON - Brooklands)
david.higgins@trafford.gov.uk
Holden, John (CON - St. Mary's)
john.holden@trafford.gov.uk
Hyman, Michael (CON - Bowdon)
michael.hyman@trafford.gov.uk
Hynes, Catherine (LAB - Urmston)
catherine.hynes@trafford.gov.uk
Jarman, David (LAB - Longford)
david.jarman@trafford.gov.uk
Lally, Paul (CON - Flixton)
paul.lally@trafford.gov.uk
Lamb, John (CON - Ashton on Mersey)
john.lamb@trafford.gov.uk
Lloyd, Judith (LAB - Longford)
judith.lloyd@trafford.gov.uk
Malik, Ejaz (LAB - Clifford)
ejaz.malik@trafford.gov.uk
Mitchell, Alan (CON - Hale Central)
alan.mitchell@trafford.gov.uk
Myers, Patrick (CON - Hale Barns)
patrick.myers@trafford.gov.uk
O'Sullivan, Dolores (LAB - Stretford)
dolores.osullivan@trafford.gov.uk
Platt, Ian (LAB - Bucklow St. Martins)
ian.platt@trafford.gov.uk
Procter, Kevin (LAB - Urmston)
kevin.procter@trafford.gov.uk
Quayle, Dave (LAB - Bucklow St. Martins)
dave.quayle@trafford.gov.uk
Reilly, June (CON - Davyhulme West)
june.reilly@trafford.gov.uk
Reilly, John (CON - Davyhulme West)
john.reilly@trafford.gov.uk
Ross, Tom (LAB - Stretford)
tom.ross@trafford.gov.uk
Sharp, Bernard (CON - Hale Barns)
bernard.sharp@trafford.gov.uk
Shaw, Brian (CON - Davyhulme West)
brian.shaw@trafford.gov.uk
Smith, John (LAB - Bucklow St. Martins)
john.smith@trafford.gov.uk
Stennett, Whit (LAB - Clifford)
whit.stennett@trafford.gov.uk
Taylor, Sophie (LAB - Clifford)
sophie.taylor@trafford.gov.uk
Taylor, Neil (LD - Timperley)
neil.taylor@trafford.gov.uk
Walsh, Laurence (LAB - Gorse Hill)
laurence.walsh@trafford.gov.uk
Ward, Vivienne (CON - Flixton)
viv.ward@trafford.gov.uk
Western, Denise (LAB - Broadheath)
denise.western@trafford.gov.uk
Western, Andrew (LAB - Priory)
andrew.western@trafford.gov.uk
Weston, Kenneth (CON - Broadheath)
kenneth.weston@trafford.gov.uk
Whetton, Michael (CON - Ashton on Mersey)
brian.rigby@trafford.gov.uk
Whetton, Michael (CON - Ashton on Mersey)
michael.whetton@trafford.gov.uk
Wilkinson, Jacki (CON - Broadheath)
jacki.wilkinson@trafford.gov.uk
Young, Michael (CON - Altrincham)
michael.young@trafford.gov.uk

POLITICAL COMPOSITION

CON: 34, LAB: 25, LD: 4

CABINET

Leader: Mr Matthew Colledge
Deputy Leader / Transformation & Resources: Mr Alex Williams
Adult Care, Health & Wellbeing: Mr Michael Young
Education: Mr Michael Cornes
Environmental Services: Mr John Reilly
Finance: Mr Sean Anstee
Economic Growth & Prosperity: Mr Michael Hyman
Highways & Transportation: Mr Alan Mitchell
Safe, Strong Communities: Mr Jonathan Coupe
Supporting Children & Families: Miss Linda Blackburn

COMMITTEE CHAIRS

Accounts & Audit: Mr Michael Whetton
Community Wellbeing Select: Mr Michael Hyman
Employment: Mr Michael Whetton
Health & Wellbeing Select: Ms Judith Lloyd
Licensing: Mr Chris Candish
Overview & Scrutiny Core: Mr Brian Shaw
Planning Development Control: Mrs Vivienne Ward
Standards: Mr D Goodman (External)

TUNBRIDGE WELLS D

Tunbridge Wells Borough Council, Town Hall, Tunbridge Wells TN1 1RS ☎ 01892 526121 🖷 01892 534227
✉ info@tunbridgewells.gov.uk 💻 www.tunbridgewells.gov.uk

FACTS & FIGURES

Police Authority: Kent Police Authority
Health Authority: South East Coast Strategic Health Authority
Learning and Skills Council: South East
Parliamentary Constituencies: Tunbridge Wells
EU Constituencies: South East
Election Frequency: Elections are by thirds
Twinning: Wiesbaden (Germany)

PRINCIPAL OFFICERS

Chief Executive: Mr William Benson, Chief Executive, Town Hall, Tunbridge Wells TN1 1RS ☎ 01892 526121
✉ william.benson@tunbridgewells.gov.uk

Senior Management: Mr Jonathan MacDonald, Director of Regeneration & Sustainability, Town Hall, Tunbridge Wells TN1 1RS ☎ 01892 526121
✉ jonathan.macdonald@tunbridgewells.gov.uk

Senior Management: Mr Paul Taylor, Director of Change & Communities, Town Hall, Tunbridge Wells TN1 1RS ☎ 01892 526121 ✉ paul.taylor@tunbridgewells.gov.uk

Building Control: Mr Patrick Arthur, Building Control Team Leader, Town Hall, Tunbridge Wells TN1 1RS ☎ 01892 554116 🖷 01892 534227 ✉ patrick.arthur@tunbridgewells.gov.uk

Catering Services: Mr Matthew Eyre, Refreshments Assistant, Town Hall, Tunbridge Wells TN1 1RS ☎ 01892 526121

PR / Communications: Ms Lizzie Goodwin, Communications and Engagement Team Leader, Town Hall, Tunbridge Wells TN1 1RS ☎ 01892 554273 🖷 01892 534227 lizzie.goodwin@tunbridgewells.gov.uk

Community Planning: Ms Nazeya Hussain, Head of Policy & Partnerships, Town Hall, Tunbridge Wells TN1 1RS ☎ 01892 554158 nazeya.hussain@tunbridgewells.gov.uk

Community Safety: Mrs Frances Taylor, Community Safety Co-ordinator, Town Hall, Tunbridge Wells TN1 1RS ☎ 01892 554273 🖷 01892 534227 frances.taylor@tunbridgewells.gov.uk

Computer Management: Mr Andrew Cole, Head of Customer Access, Transformation & Delivery, Town Hall, Tunbridge Wells TN1 1RS ☎ 01892 526121 🖷 01892 534227 andrew.cole@tunbridgewells.gov.uk

Contracts: Mr Mel Henley, Contracts Manager, Town Hall, Tunbridge Wells TN1 1RS ☎ 01892 554109 mel.henley@tunbridgewells.gov.uk

Customer Service: Mr Andrew Cole, Head of Customer Access, Transformation & Delivery, Town Hall, Tunbridge Wells TN1 1RS ☎ 01892 526121 🖷 01892 534227 andrew.cole@tunbridgewells.gov.uk

Customer Service: Mrs Denise Shortall, Customer Service & Gateway Manager, Town Hall, Tunbridge Wells TN1 1RS ☎ 01892 554218 denise.shortall@tunbridgewells.gov.uk

Customer Service: Ms Ingrid Weatherup, Customer Care Manager, Town Hall, Tunbridge Wells TN1 1RS ☎ 01895 554077 🖷 01892 554204 ingrid.weatherup@tunbridgewells.gov.uk

Economic Development: Ms Hilary Smith, Economic Development Manager, Town Hall, Tunbridge Wells TN1 1RS ☎ 01454 554433 🖷 01454 554023 hilary.smith@tunbridgewells.gov.uk

E-Government: Mr Andrew Cole, Head of Customer Access, Transformation & Delivery, Town Hall, Tunbridge Wells TN1 1RS ☎ 01892 526121 🖷 01892 534227 andrew.cole@tunbridgewells.gov.uk

Electoral Registration: Mrs Nicola Timms, Electoral Services Manager, Town Hall, Tunbridge Wells TN1 1RS ☎ 01892 554106 🖷 01892 554255 nicola.timms@tunbridgewells.gov.uk

Energy Management: Ms Kathy Alcock, Housing Policy & Initiatives Officer, Town Hall, Tunbridge Wells TN1 1RS ☎ 01892 554275 🖷 01892 534227 kathy.alcock@tunbridgewells.gov.uk

Environmental / Technical Services: Mr Gary Stevenson, Head of Environment & Street Scene, Town Hall, Tunbridge Wells TN1 1RS ☎ 01892 554014 gary.stevenson@tunbridgewells.gov.uk

Environmental Health: Mr Gary Stevenson, Head of Environment & Street Scene, Town Hall, Tunbridge Wells TN1 1RS ☎ 01892 554014 gary.stevenson@tunbridgewells.gov.uk

Estates, Property & Valuation: Mrs Diana Brady, Property & Development Manager, Town Hall, Tunbridge Wells TN1 1RS ☎ 01892 526121 diana.brady@tunbridgewells.gov.uk

Estates, Property & Valuation: Ms Karen Downs, Facilities Officer, Town Hall, Tunbridge Wells TN1 1RS ☎ 01892 526121 karen.downs@tunbridgewells.gov.uk

Events Manager: Ms Sue Latham, Events Manager, Town Hall, Tunbridge Wells TN1 1RS ☎ 01892 526121 sue.latham@tunbridgewells.gov.uk

Facilities: Ms Karen Downs, Facilities Officer, Town Hall, Tunbridge Wells TN1 1RS ☎ 01892 526121 karen.downs@tunbridgewells.gov.uk

Finance and Treasurer: Mr Lee Colyer, Head of Finance & Governance, Town Hall, Tunbridge Wells TN1 1RS ☎ 01892 554132 lee.colyer@tunbridgewells.gov.uk

Grounds Maintenance: Mr Mel Henley, Contracts Manager, Town Hall, Tunbridge Wells TN1 1RS ☎ 01892 554109 mel.henley@tunbridgewells.gov.uk

Highways: Mrs Lene Beynon, Borough Engineering Officer, Town Hall, Tunbridge Wells TN1 1RS ☎ 01892 526121 lene.beynon@tunbridgewells.gov.uk

Home Energy Conservation: Ms Kathy Alcock, Housing Policy & Initiatives Officer, Town Hall, Tunbridge Wells TN1 1RS ☎ 01892 554275 🖷 01892 534227 kathy.alcock@tunbridgewells.gov.uk

Housing: Mr Kevin Hetherington, Head of Housing & Wellbeing, Town Hall, Tunbridge Wells TN1 1RS ☎ 01892 526121 kevin.hetherington@tunbridgewells.gov.uk

Legal: Mr Paul Cummins, Head of Legal Services, Town Hall, Tunbridge Wells TN1 1RS ☎ 01892 554257 🖷 01892 554207 paul.cummins@tunbridgewells.gov.uk

Leisure and Cultural Services: Mr Kevin Hetherington, Head of Housing & Wellbeing, Town Hall, Tunbridge Wells TN1 1RS ☎ 01892 526121 kevin.hetherington@tunbridgewells.gov.uk

Licensing: Mrs Claire Perry, Licensing Partnership Manager, Council Offices, Argyle Road, Sevenoaks TN13 1HG ☎ 01732 227325; 07970 731616 claire.perry@sevenoaks.gov.uk; claire.perry@tunbridgewells.gov.uk

Lighting: Mrs Lene Beynon, Borough Engineering Officer, Town Hall, Tunbridge Wells TN1 1RS ☎ 01892 526121 lene.beynon@tunbridgewells.gov.uk

Member Services: Ms Jane Clarke, Local Democracy Officer, Town Hall, Tunbridge Wells TN1 1RS ☎ 01892 554179 jane.clarke@tunbridgewells.gov.uk

Parking: Mrs Emma Pell, Parking Manager, Town Hall, Tunbridge Wells TN1 1RS ☎ 01892 554082 emma.pell@tunbridgewells.gov.uk

Partnerships: Ms Estelle Hudson, Democratic & Community

Engagement Manager, Town Hall, Tunbridge Wells TN1 1RS ☎ 01892 554064 🖷 01892 554255 ✉ estelle.hudson@tunbridgewells.gov.uk

Personnel / HR: Ms Val Green, Organisational Development & HR Manager, Town Hall, Tunbridge Wells TN1 1RS ☎ 01892 554064 🖷 01892 534227 ✉ val.green@tunbridgewells.gov.uk

Planning: Mr Jim Kehoe, Head of Planning Services, Town Hall, Tunbridge Wells TN1 1RS ☎ 01892 526121 🖷 01892 554076 ✉ jim.kehoe@tunbridgwells.gov.uk

Recycling & Waste Minimisation: Mr Mel Henley, Contracts Manager, Town Hall, Tunbridge Wells TN1 1RS ☎ 01892 554109 ✉ mel.henley@tunbridgewells.gov.uk

Regeneration: Mr David Candlin, Head of Economic Development, Town Hall, Tunbridge Wells TN1 1RS ☎ 01892 554038 🖷 01892 554023 ✉ david.candlin@tunbridgewells.gov.uk

Street Scene: Mr Gary Stevenson, Head of Environment & Street Scene, Town Hall, Tunbridge Wells TN1 1RS ☎ 01892 554014 ✉ gary.stevenson@tunbridgewells.gov.uk

Sustainable Development: Ms Karin Grey, Sustainability Manager, Town Hall, Tunbridge Wells TN1 1RS ☎ 01892 554240 🖷 01892 554118 ✉ karin.grey@tunbridgewells.gov.uk

Traffic Management: Mrs Lene Beynon, Borough Engineering Officer, Town Hall, Tunbridge Wells TN1 1RS ☎ 01892 526121 ✉ lene.beynon@tunbridgewells.gov.uk

Transport: Mrs Lene Beynon, Borough Engineering Officer, Town Hall, Tunbridge Wells TN1 1RS ☎ 01892 526121 ✉ lene.beynon@tunbridgewells.gov.uk

Waste Collection and Disposal: Mr Mel Henley, Contracts Manager, Town Hall, Tunbridge Wells TN1 1RS ☎ 01892 554109 ✉ mel.henley@tunbridgewells.gov.uk

Waste Management: Mr Mel Henley, Contracts Manager, Town Hall, Tunbridge Wells TN1 1RS ☎ 01892 554109 ✉ mel.henley@tunbridgewells.gov.uk

MEMBERS OF THE COUNCIL (48)

***Mayor:* Smith**, John (CON - Frittenden and Sissingham)
john.smith@tunbridgewells.gov.uk
***Deputy Mayor:* Basu**, Ronen (CON - Culverden)
ronen.basu@tunbridgewells.gov.uk
***Leader of the Council:* Jukes**, David (CON - Speldhurst and Bidborough)
david.jukes@tunbridgewells.gov.uk
Backhouse, Bob (CON - Sherwood)
bob.backhouse@tunbridgewells.gov.uk
Barrington-King, Paul (CON - Pembury)
paul.barrington-king@tunbridgewells.gov.uk
Bothwell, Colin (CON - Southborough and High Brooms)
colin.bothwell@tunbridgewells.gov.uk
Bulman, Peter (CON - Park)
peter.bulman@tunbridgewells.gov.uk
Chapelard, Ben (LD - St James')
ben.chapelard@tunbridgewells.gov.uk
Cobbold, Barbara (CON - Broadwater)
barbara.cobbold@tunbridgewells.gov.uk
Crowhurst, June (CON - Pembury)
june.crowhurst@tunbridgewells.gov.uk
Cunningham, John (CON - Hawkhurst and Sandhurst)
john.cunningham@tunbridgewells.gov.uk
Derrick, Caroline (CON - St John's)
caroline.derrick@tunbridgewells.gov.uk
Elliot, David (CON - Southborough North)
david.elliott@tunbridgewells.gov.uk
Hall, Linda (CON - Benenden and Cranbrook)
linda.hall@tunbridgewels.gov.uk
Hall, Glenn (CON - Pantiles and St Mark's)
glenn.hall@tunbridgewells.gov.uk
Hastie, Edmund (CON - Goudhurst and Lamberhurst)
edmund.hastie@tunbridgewells.gov.uk
Hill, Dianne (LAB - Southborough and High Brooms)
dianne.hill@tunbridgewells.gov.uk
Hills, Bill (CON - Paddock Wood (East))
bill.hills@tunbridgewells.gov.uk
Holden, Sean (CON - Benenden and Cranbrook)
seanholden@aol.com
Horwood, Len (CON - Pantiles and St Mark's)
len.horwood@tunbridgewells.gov.uk
Lewis, Alan (LAB - Southborough and High Brooms)
alan.lewis@tunbridgewells.gov.uk
Lockhart, Sean (CON - Park)
sean.lockhart@tunbridgewells.gov.uk
Marsh, Jane (CON - Brenchley and Horsmonden)
jane.march@tunbridgewells.gov.uk
Mayhew, Catherine (CON - Park)
catherine.mayhew@tunbridgewells.gov.uk
McDermott, Alan (CON - Brenchley and Horsmonden)
alan.mcdermott@tunbridgewells.gov.uk
Neve, David (LD - St James')
david.neve@tunbridgewells.gov.uk
Noakes, Barry (CON - Goudhurst and Lamberhurst)
barry.noakes@tunbridgewells.gov.uk
Palmer, Beverley (CON - Hawkhurst and Sandhurst)
beverley.palmer@tunbridgewells.gov.uk
Patterson, Hugh (LD - Capel)
hugh.patterson@tunbridgewells.gov.uk
Poile, Trevor (LD - St John's)
trevor.poile@tunbridgewells.gov.uk
Price, Len (CON - Culverden)
len.price@tunbridgewells.gov.uk
Rogers, Nicholas (CON - Culverden)
nicholas.rogers@tunbridgewells.gov.uk
Rook, Francis (LD - Benenden and Cranbrook)
francis.rook@tunbridgewells.gov.uk
Rusbridge, Michael (CON - Southborough North)
michael.rusbridge@tunbridgewells.gov.uk
Scholes, James (CON - Pantiles and St Mark's)
james.scholes@tunbridgewells.gov.uk
Scott, David (CON - St John's)
david.scott@tunbridgewells.gov.uk
Soyke, Julia (CON - Speldhurst and Bidborough)
julia.soyke@tunbridgewells.gov.uk
Stanyer, Julian (CON - Speldhurst and Bidborough)
julian.stanyer@tunbridgewells.gov.uk
Thomas, Elizabeth (CON - Paddock Wood (West))
elizabeth.thomas@tunbridgewells.gov.uk
Tompsett, Mike (IND - Pembury)
mike.tompsett@tunbridewells.gov.uk
Waldock, Peter (CON - Paddock Wood (East))
peter.waldcock@tunbridgewells.gov.uk

Ward, Stanley (CON - Paddock Wood (West))
stanley.ward@tunbridgewells.gov.uk
Wauchope, Piers (UKIP - Rusthall)
piers.wauchope@tunbridgewells.gov.uk
Weatherly, Lynne (CON - Sherwood)
Webb, Victor (UKIP - Rusthall)
victor.webb@tunbridgewells.gov.uk
Weeden, Ron (CON - Hawkhurst and Sandhurst)
ron.weeden@tunbridgewells.gov.uk
Williams, Frank (CON - Sherwood)
frank.williams@tunbridgewells.gov.uk
Woodward, Chris (CON - Broadwater)
chris.woodward@tunbridgewells.gov.uk

POLITICAL COMPOSITION
CON: 38, LD: 5, UKIP: 2, LAB: 2, IND: 1

CABINET
Leader: Mr David Jukes
Finance & Governance: Mr James Scholes
Housing, Health, Wellbeing & Rural Communities: Mr John Cunningham
Planning & Transportation: Mr Alan McDermott
Tourism, Leisure & Economic Development: Mrs Jane Marsh
Sustainability: Mr Paul Barrington-King

COMMITTEE CHAIRS
General Purposes: Mr Edmund Hastie
Joint Transportation: Mr Nicholas Rogers
Licensing: Mrs Barbara Cobbold
Overview and Scrutiny: Mrs Catherine Mayhew

UTTLESFORD D

Uttlesford District Council, Council Offices, London Road, Saffron Walden CB11 4ER ☎ 01799 510510 🖷 01799 510550 postroom@uttlesford.gov.uk www.uttlesford.gov.uk

FACTS & FIGURES
Police Authority: Essex Police Authority
Health Authority: East of England Strategic Health Authority
Learning and Skills Council: Eastern
Parliamentary Constituencies: Saffron Walden
EU Constituencies: Eastern
Election Frequency: Elections are of whole council

PRINCIPAL OFFICERS
Chief Executive: Mr John Mitchell, Chief Executive, Council Offices, London Road, Saffron Walden CB11 4ER ☎ 01799 510510 🖷 01799 510550 jmitchell@uttlesford.gov.uk

Assistant Chief Executive: Mr Stephen Joyce, Assistant Chief Executive - Finance, Council Offices, London Road, Saffron Walden CB11 4ER ☎ 01799 510628 🖷 01799 510550 sjoyce@uttlesford.gov.uk

Assistant Chief Executive: Mr Michael Perry, Assistant Chief Executive - Legal, Council Offices, London Road, Saffron Walden CB11 4ER ☎ 01799 510416 🖷 01799 510550 mperry@uttlesford.gov.uk

Senior Management: Mr Roger Harborough, Director of Public Services, Council Offices, London Road, Saffron Walden CB11 4ER ☎ 01799 510457 🖷 01799 510550 rharborough@uttlesford.gov.uk

Senior Management: Mr Stephen Joyce, Assistant Chief Executive - Finance, Council Offices, London Road, Saffron Walden CB11 4ER ☎ 01799 510628 🖷 01799 510550 sjoyce@uttlesford.gov.uk

Senior Management: Mr Adrian Webb, Director of Central Services, Council Offices, London Road, Saffron Walden CB11 4ER ☎ 01799 510421 🖷 01799 510550 awebb@uttlesford.gov.uk

Access Officer / Social Services (Disability): Ms Sue Locke, Projects Officer, Council Offices, London Road, Saffron Walden CB11 4ER ☎ 01799 510537 🖷 01799 510534 slocke@uttlesford.gov.uk

Building Control: Mr Keith Osborne, Head of Building Surveying, Council Offices, London Road, Saffron Walden CB11 4ER ☎ 01799 510530 🖷 01799 510534 kosborne@uttlesford.gov.uk

Building Control: Mr Andrew Taylor, Head of Planning & Building Surveying, Council Offices, London Road, Saffron Walden CB11 4ER ☎ 01799 510510 🖷 01799 510550 ataylor@uttlesford.gov.uk

Children / Youth Services: Ms Gaynor Bradley, Community Partnerships Manager, Council Offices, London Road, Saffron Walden CB11 4ER ☎ 01799 510348 🖷 01799 510550 gbradley@uttlesford.gov.uk

PR / Communications: Mr Richard Auty, Assistant Director - Public Services, Council Offices, London Road, Saffron Walden CB11 4ER ☎ 01799 510500 🖷 01799 510550 rauty@uttlesford.gov.uk

Community Safety: Ms Gaynor Bradley, Community Partnerships Manager, Council Offices, London Road, Saffron Walden CB11 4ER ☎ 01799 510348 🖷 01799 510550 gbradley@uttlesford.gov.uk

Computer Management: Mr Adrian Webb, Director of Central Services, Council Offices, London Road, Saffron Walden CB11 4ER ☎ 01799 510421 🖷 01799 510550 awebb@uttlesford.gov.uk

Computer Management: Mr N Wittman, Head of IT Information, Council Offices, London Road, Saffron Walden CB11 4ER ☎ 01799 510413 nwittman@uttlesford.gov.uk

Corporate Services: Mr Simon Martin, Head of Customer Support Services, Council Offices, London Road, Saffron Walden CB11 4ER ☎ 01799 510422 🖷 01799 510550 smartin@uttlesford.gov.uk

Corporate Services: Mr Adrian Webb, Director of Central Services, Council Offices, London Road, Saffron Walden CB11 4ER ☎ 01799 510421 🖷 01799 510550 awebb@uttlesford.gov.uk

Customer Service: Mr Simon Martin, Head of Customer Support Services, Council Offices, London Road, Saffron Walden CB11 4ER ☎ 01799 510422 🖷 01799 510550 smartin@uttlesford.gov.uk

Economic Development: Mr Roger Harborough, Director of Public Services, Council Offices, London Road, Saffron Walden CB11 4ER ☎ 01799 510457 🖷 01799 510550 rharborough@uttlesford.gov.uk

E-Government: Mr Adrian Webb, Director of Central Services, Council Offices, London Road, Saffron Walden CB11 4ER ☎ 01799 510421 🖷 01799 510550 awebb@uttlesford.gov.uk

Electoral Registration: Mr Peter Snow, Democratic & Electoral Services Manager, Council Offices, London Road, Saffron Walden CB11 4ER ☎ 01799 510431 🖷 01799 510550 psnow@uttlesford.gov.uk

Emergency Planning: Mrs Lisa Lipscombe, Emergency Planning Officer, Council Offices, London Road, Saffron Walden CB11 4ER ☎ 01799 510624 🖷 01799 510550 llipscombe@uttlesford.gov.uk

Environmental / Technical Services: Mr Roger Harborough, Director of Public Services, Council Offices, London Road, Saffron Walden CB11 4ER ☎ 01799 510457 🖷 01799 510550 rharborough@uttlesford.gov.uk

Environmental / Technical Services: Mr Geoff Smith, Head of Environmental Health, Council Offices, London Road, Saffron Walden CB11 4ER ☎ 01799 510582 🖷 01799 510550 gsmith@uttlesford.gov.uk

Environmental Health: Mr Roger Harborough, Director of Public Services, Council Offices, London Road, Saffron Walden CB11 4ER ☎ 01799 510457 🖷 01799 510550 rharborough@uttlesford.gov.uk

Environmental Health: Mrs Roz Millership, Head of Housing & Environmental Services, Council Offices, London Road, Saffron Walden CB11 4ER ☎ 01799 510516 🖷 01799 510550 rmillership@uttlesford.gov.uk

Environmental Health: Mr Geoff Smith, Head of Environmental Health, Council Offices, London Road, Saffron Walden CB11 4ER ☎ 01799 510582 🖷 01799 510550 gsmith@uttlesford.gov.uk

European Liaison: Mr Michael Perry, Assistant Chief Executive - Legal, Council Offices, London Road, Saffron Walden CB11 4ER ☎ 01799 510416 🖷 01799 510550 mperry@uttlesford.gov.uk

Facilities: Mr Simon Martin, Head of Customer Support Services, Council Offices, London Road, Saffron Walden CB11 4ER ☎ 01799 510422 🖷 01799 510550 smartin@uttlesford.gov.uk

Finance and Treasurer: Mr Stephen Joyce, Assistant Chief Executive - Finance, Council Offices, London Road, Saffron Walden CB11 4ER ☎ 01799 510628 🖷 01799 510550 sjoyce@uttlesford.gov.uk

Finance and Treasurer: Mr Adrian Webb, Director of Central Services, Council Offices, London Road, Saffron Walden CB11 4ER ☎ 01799 510421 🖷 01799 510550 awebb@uttlesford.gov.uk

Fleet Management: Mr Ron Pridham, Head of Street Services, Council Offices, London Road, Saffron Walden CB11 4ER ☎ 01799 510597 🖷 01799 510550 rpridham@uttlesford.gov.uk

Health and Safety: Mr Geoff Smith, Head of Environmental Health, Council Offices, London Road, Saffron Walden CB11 4ER ☎ 01799 510582 🖷 01799 510550 gsmith@uttlesford.gov.uk

Housing: Mrs Roz Millership, Head of Housing & Environmental Services, Council Offices, London Road, Saffron Walden CB11 4ER ☎ 01799 510516 🖷 01799 510550 rmillership@uttlesford.gov.uk

Housing Maintenance: Mrs Roz Millership, Head of Housing & Environmental Services, Council Offices, London Road, Saffron Walden CB11 4ER ☎ 01799 510516 🖷 01799 510550 rmillership@uttlesford.gov.uk

Legal: Mr Michael Perry, Assistant Chief Executive - Legal, Council Offices, London Road, Saffron Walden CB11 4ER ☎ 01799 510416 🖷 01799 510550 mperry@uttlesford.gov.uk

Leisure and Cultural Services: Ms Gaynor Bradley, Community Partnerships Manager, Council Offices, London Road, Saffron Walden CB11 4ER ☎ 01799 510348 🖷 01799 510550 gbradley@uttlesford.gov.uk

Licensing: Mr Murray Hardy, Licensing Officer, Council Offices, London Road, Saffron Walden CB11 4ER ☎ 01799 510598 🖷 01799 510550 mhardy@uttlesford.gov.uk

Lottery Funding, Charity and Voluntary: Ms Gaynor Bradley, Community Partnerships Manager, Council Offices, London Road, Saffron Walden CB11 4ER ☎ 01799 510348 🖷 01799 510550 gbradley@uttlesford.gov.uk

Member Services: Mr Peter Snow, Democratic & Electoral Services Manager, Council Offices, London Road, Saffron Walden CB11 4ER ☎ 01799 510431 🖷 01799 510550 psnow@uttlesford.gov.uk

Parking: Mr Ron Pridham, Head of Street Services, Council Offices, London Road, Saffron Walden CB11 4ER ☎ 01799 510597 🖷 01799 510550 rpridham@uttlesford.gov.uk

Personnel / HR: Mr Simon Martin, Head of Customer Support Services, Council Offices, London Road, Saffron Walden CB11 4ER ☎ 01799 510422 🖷 01799 510550 smartin@uttlesford.gov.uk

Personnel / HR: Mr Adrian Webb, Director of Central Services, Council Offices, London Road, Saffron Walden CB11 4ER ☎ 01799 510421 🖷 01799 510550 awebb@uttlesford.gov.uk

Planning: Mr Nigel Brown, Head of Development Control, Council Offices, London Road, Saffron Walden CB11 4ER ☎ 01799 510486 nbrown@uttlesford.gov.uk

Planning: Mr Roger Harborough, Director of Public Services, Council Offices, London Road, Saffron Walden CB11 4ER ☎ 01799 510457 🖷 01799 510550 rharborough@uttlesford.gov.uk

Planning: Mr Andrew Taylor, Head of Planning & Building Surveying, Council Offices, London Road, Saffron Walden CB11 4ER ☎ 01799 510510 🖷 01799 510550 ataylor@uttlesford.gov.uk

Procurement: Mr Michael Perry, Assistant Chief Executive - Legal, Council Offices, London Road, Saffron Walden CB11 4ER ☎ 01799 510416 🖷 01799 510550 mperry@uttlesford.gov.uk

Recycling & Waste Minimisation: Mr Ron Pridham, Head of Street Services, Council Offices, London Road, Saffron Walden CB11 4ER ☎ 01799 510597 🖷 01799 510550 rpridham@uttlesford.gov.uk

Street Scene: Mr Ron Pridham, Head of Street Services, Council Offices, London Road, Saffron Walden CB11 4ER ☎ 01799 510597 🖷 01799 510550 rpridham@uttlesford.gov.uk

Sustainable Communities: Mr Roger Harborough, Director of Public Services, Council Offices, London Road, Saffron Walden CB11 4ER ☎ 01799 510457 🖷 01799 510550 rharborough@uttlesford.gov.uk

Sustainable Development: Mr Roger Harborough, Director of Public Services, Council Offices, London Road, Saffron Walden CB11 4ER ☎ 01799 510457 🖷 01799 510550 rharborough@uttlesford.gov.uk

Waste Collection and Disposal: Mr Ron Pridham, Head of Street Services, Council Offices, London Road, Saffron Walden CB11 4ER ☎ 01799 510597 🖷 01799 510550 rpridham@uttlesford.gov.uk

Waste Management: Mr Ron Pridham, Head of Street Services, Council Offices, London Road, Saffron Walden CB11 4ER ☎ 01799 510597 🖷 01799 510550 rpridham@uttlesford.gov.uk

MEMBERS OF THE COUNCIL (44)

***Chair:* Cant**, Christina (LD - Stebbing)
cllrcant@uttlesford.gov.uk
***Leader of the Council:* Ketteridge**, Jim (CON - Saffron Walden Shire)
cllrketteridge@uttlesford.gov.uk
Artus, Keith (CON - Broad Oak and the Hallingburys)
cllrartus@uttesford.gov.uk
Asker, Heather (CON - Saffron Walden Castle)
cllrasker@uttlesford.gov.uk
Barker, Graham (CON - Great Dunmow South)
cllrgbarker@uttlesford.gov.uk
Barker, Susan (CON - The Rodings)
cllrbarker@uttlesford.gov.uk
Chambers, Robert (CON - Wenden Lofts)
cllrchambers@uttlesford.gov.uk
Cheetham, Jackie (CON - Takeley and The Cranfields)
cllrcheetham@uttlesford.gov.uk
Crome, David (CON - Felsted)
cllrcrome@uttlesford.gov.uk
Davey, John (CON - Great Dunmow North)
cllrdavey@uttlesford.gov.uk
Davies, Paul (CON - Great Dunmow North)
cllrdavies@uttlesford.gov.uk
Dean, Alan (LD - Stansted South)
cllrdean@uttlesford.gov.uk
Eastham, Bob (CON - Saffron Walden Castle)
cllreastham@uttlesford.gov.uk
Eden, Keith (CON - Saffron Walden Shire)
cllreden@uttlesford.gov.uk
Evans, Iris (LD - Stansted South)
cllrevans@uttlesford.gov.uk
Foley, Martin (LD - Thaxted)
cllrfoley@uttersford.gov.uk
Freeman, John (CON - Thaxted)
cllrfreeman@uttersford.gov.uk
Godwin, Elizabeth (IND - Birchanger)
cllrgodwin@uttlesford.gov.uk
Harris, Stephanie (CON - Felsted)
cllrfavell@uttlesford.gov.uk
Hicks, Eric (CON - Barnston and High Easter)
cllrhicks@uttlesford.gov.uk
Howell, Simon (CON - Saffron Walden Audley)
cllrhowell@uttlesford.gov.uk
Jones, Derek (CON - Takeley and The Canfields)
cllrjones@uttlesford.gov.uk
Ketteridge, Andrew (CON - Ashdon)
cllrjketteridge@uttlesford.gov.uk
Knight, Tina (CON - Wimbish)
cllrknight@uttlesford.gov.uk
Lemon, Mark (IND - Hatfield Heath)
cllrlemon@uttersford.gov.uk
Loughlin, Janice (LD - Stort Valley)
cllrloughlin@uttlesford.gov.uk
Mackman, Keith (CON - Great Dunmow South)
cllrmackman@uttlesford.gov.uk
Menell, Jan (CON - Littlebury)
cllrmenell@uttlesford.gov.uk
Morson, David (LD - Elsenham and Henham)
cllrmorson@uttlesford.gov.uk
Oliver, Edward (CON - Clavering)
cllroliver@uttlesford.gov.uk
Parr, Elizabeth (LD - Elsenham and Henham)
cllrparr@uttlesford.gov.uk
Perry, Doug (CON - Saffron Walden Audley)
cllrperry@uttlesford.gov.uk
Ranger, Vic (CON - Great Dunmow South)
cllrranger@uttlesford.gov.uk
Redfern, Julie (CON - The Chesterfords)
cllrredfern@uttersford.gov.uk
Rich, Joe (CON - Stansted North)
cllrrich@uttlesford.gov.uk
Rolfe, Howard (CON - Saffron Walden Shire)
cllrrolfe@uttlesford.gov.uk
Rose, Jeremy (CON - Newport)
cllrrose@uttersford.gov.uk
Sadler, David (CON - Saffron Walden Castle)
cllrsadler@uttlesford.gov.uk
Salmon, John (CON - Stansted North)
cllrsalmon@uttlesford.gov.uk
Smith, Lawrence (CON - The Eastons)
cllrlsmith@uttersford.gov.uk
Walters, Alastair (CON - Saffron Walden Audley)
cllrwalters@uttlesford.gov.uk
Watson, David (CON - Saffron Walden Audley)
cllrwatson@uttersford.gov.uk
Wells, Lesley (CON - Broad Oak and the Hallingburys)
cllrwells@uttlesford.gov.uk
Wilcock, Peter (LD - Newport)
cllrwilcock@uttlesford.gov.uk

POLITICAL COMPOSITION

CON: 34, LD: 8, IND: 2

VALE OF GLAMORGAN W

Vale of Glamorgan Council, Civic Offices, Holton Road, Barry CF63 4RU ☎ 01446 700111 🖷 01446 745566 ✉ enquiries@valeofglamorgan.gov.uk 🖳 www.valeofglamorgan.gov.uk

FACTS & FIGURES

Police Authority: South Wales Police Authority
Learning and Skills Council: Wales
Parliamentary Constituencies: Cardiff South and Penarth, Vale of Glamorgan
EU Constituencies: Wales
Election Frequency: Elections are of whole council
Twinning: Fecamp (France); Mouscron (Belgium); Rheinfelden (Germany)

PRINCIPAL OFFICERS

Chief Executive: Mr John Maitland Evans, Chief Executive, Civic Offices, Holton Road, Barry CF63 4RU ☎ 01446 709303 🖷 01446 421479 ✉ JMaitlandEvans@valeofglamorgan.gov.uk

Senior Management: Mrs Sian Davies, Director of Finance, ICT & Property, Civic Offices, Holton Road, Barry CF63 4RU ☎ 01446 709202 🖷 01446 709201 ✉ sdavies@valeofglamorgan.gov.uk

Senior Management: Mr Phil Evans, Director of Social Services, Dock Offices, Subway Road, Barry CF63 4RT ☎ 01446 704676 🖷 01446 704839 ✉ pjevans@valeofglamorgan.gov.uk

Senior Management: Mr Peter Evans, Director of Legal, Public Protection & Housing Services, Civic Offices, Holton Road, Barry CF63 4RU ☎ 01446 709401 🖷 01446 701189 ✉ phevans@valeofglamorgan.gov.uk

Senior Management: Mr Rob Quick, Director of Environmental & Economic Regeneration, Dock Office, Subway Road, Barry CF63 4RT ☎ 01446 704610 🖷 01446 704612 ✉ rjquick@valeofglamorgan.gov.uk

Access Officer / Social Services (Disability): Mrs Linda Brown, Joint Corporate Equality Officer, Civic Offices, Holton Road, Barry CF63 4RU ☎ 01446 709362 ✉ librown@valeofglamorgan.gov.uk

Access Officer / Social Services (Disability): Ms Nicola Hinton, Joint Corporate Equality Officer, Civic Offices, Holton Road, Barry CF63 4RU ☎ 01446 709362 ✉ equalities@valeofglamorgan.gov.uk

Architect, Building / Property Services: Ms Jane Wade, Operational Manager - Property Services, Civic Buildings, Holton Road, Barry CF63 4RU ☎ 01446 709270 ✉ jlwade@valeofglamorgan.gov.uk

Best Value: Ms Beverly Noon, Operational Manager - Corporate Policy & Communications, Civic Offices, Holton Road, Barry CF63 4RU ☎ 01446 709760 🖷 01446 421479 ✉ banoon@valeofglamorgan.gov.uk

Building Control: Mr Marcus Goldworthy, Operational Manager - Development & Building Control, Dock Office, Barry Docks, Barry CF63 4RT ☎ 01446 700111 🖷 01446 704843 ✉ buildingcontrol@valeofglamorgan.gov.uk

Catering Services: Mrs Carole Tyley, Catering Manager, Civic Offices, Holton Road, Barry CF63 4RU ☎ 029 2067 3037 ✉ ctyley@valeofglamorgan.gov.uk

Children / Youth Services: Mr Gareth Jenkins, Head of Children & Young People Services, Dock Offices, Subway Road, Barry CF63 4RT ☎ 01446 700111 ✉ gajenkins@valeofglamorgan.gov.uk

Civil Registration: Mrs Tania Carter, Superintendent Registrar, Civic Offices, Holton Road, Barry CF63 4RU ☎ 01446 709166 🖷 01446 709502 ✉ tcarter@valeofglamorgan.gov.uk

PR / Communications: Mrs Alison Cummins, Communications Manager, Civic Offices, Holton Road, Barry CF63 4RU ☎ 01446 709825 🖷 01446 421485 ✉ acummins@valeofglamorgan.gov.uk

Community Planning: Mr Huw Isaac, Head of Performance & Development, Civic Offices, Holton Road, Barry CF63 4RU ☎ 01446 709760 🖷 01446 421479 ✉ hisaac@valeofglamorgan.gov.uk

Community Safety: Mr Alun Billinghurst, Head of Public Protection, Civic Offices, Holton Road, Barry CF63 4RU ☎ 01446 709720 ✉ arbillinghurst@valeofglamorgan.gov.uk

Computer Management: Mr David Vining, Head of Strategic ICT, Civic Offices, Holton Road, Barry CF63 4RU ☎ 01446 709382 🖷 01446 722036 ✉ divining@valeofglamorgan.gov.uk

Consumer Protection and Trading Standards: Ms Christina Roberts-Kinsey, Principal Trading Standards Officer, Civic Offices, Holton Road, Barry CF63 4RU ☎ 01446 709344 🖷 01446 709768 ✉ croberts-kinsey@valeofglamorgan.gov.uk

Contracts: Mrs Gill Howells, Operational Manager - Finance & Systems, Civic Offices, Holton Road, Barry CF63 4RU ☎ 01446 709524 ✉ ghowells@valeofglamorgan.gov.uk

Customer Service: Mr Tony Curliss, Operational Manager - Customer Relations, Civic Offices, Holton Road, Barry CF63 4RU ☎ 01446 709521 🖷 01446 421479 ✉ tcurliss@valeofglamorgan.gov.uk

Direct Labour: Mr Miles Punter, Head of Visible Services, The Alps, Quarry Road, Wenvoe CF5 6AA ☎ 029 2067 3101 🖷 029 2067 3102 ✉ mepunter@valeofglamorgan.gov.uk

Economic Development: Mr Rob Quick, Director of Environmental & Economic Regeneration, Dock Office, Subway Road, Barry CF63 4RT ☎ 01446 704610 🖷 01446 704612 ✉ rjquick@valeofglamorgan.gov.uk

E-Government: Mr Huw Isaac, Head of Performance & Development, Civic Offices, Holton Road, Barry CF63 4RU ☎ 01446 709760 🖷 01446 421479 ✉ hisaac@valeofglamorgan.gov.uk

Electoral Registration: Miss Rebecca Light, Electoral Services Officer, Civic Offices, Holton Road, Barry CF63 4RU ☎ 01446

709304 🖷 01446 421623 ✉ blight@valeofglamorgan.gov.uk

Emergency Planning: Mr Peter Evans, Director of Legal, Public Protection & Housing Services, Civic Offices, Holton Road, Barry CF63 4RU ☎ 01446 709401 🖷 01446 701189 ✉ phevans@valeofglamorgan.gov.uk

Energy Management: Mr David Powell, Energy Manager, Civic Offices, Holton Road, Barry CF63 4RU ☎ 01446 709576 ✉ dpowell@valeofglamorgan.gov.uk

Environmental / Technical Services: Mr Rob Quick, Director of Environmental & Economic Regeneration, Dock Office, Subway Road, Barry CF63 4RT ☎ 01446 704610 🖷 01446 704612 ✉ rjquick@valeofglamorgan.gov.uk

Estates, Property & Valuation: Ms Jane Wade, Operational Manager - Property Services, Civic Buildings, Holton Road, Barry CF63 4RU ☎ 01446 709270 ✉ jlwade@valeofglamorgan.gov.uk

Events Manager: Ms Sarah Jones, Events Officer, Dock Office, Subway Road, Barry CF63 4RT ☎ 01446 704737 🖷 01446 704892 ✉ sejones@valeofglamorgan.gov.uk

Facilities: Mr Patrick Carroll, Facilities Manager, Civic Offices, Holton Road, Barry CF63 4RU ☎ 01446 709243 ✉ pjcarroll@valeofglamorgan.gov.uk

Finance and Treasurer: Mrs Sian Davies, Director of Finance, ICT & Property, Civic Offices, Holton Road, Barry CF63 4RU ☎ 01446 709202 🖷 01446 709201 ✉ sdavies@valeofglamorgan.gov.uk

Fleet Management: Mr Miles Punter, Head of Visible Services, The Alps, Quarry Road, Wenvoe CF5 6AA ☎ 029 2067 3101 🖷 029 2067 3102 ✉ mepunter@valeofglamorgan.gov.uk

Grounds Maintenance: Mr Phil Beaman, Operational Manager - Parks & Grounds Maintenance, Court Road Depot, Barry CF63 1ST ☎ 01446 709543 🖷 01446 420863 ✉ pbeaman@valeofglamorgan.gov.uk

Health and Safety: Ms Andrea Davies, Principal Corporate Health & Safety Officer, Provincial House, Kendrick Road, Barry CF62 8BF ☎ 01446 709361 🖷 01446 709792 ✉ ardavies@valeofglamorgan.gov.uk

Highways: Mr Andrew Loosemore, Operational Manager - Highways & Engineering, The Alps Depot, Quarry Road, Wenvoe CF5 6AA ☎ 029 2067 3200 🖷 029 2067 3019 ✉ aloosemore@valeofglamorgan.gov.uk

Home Energy Conservation: Mr David Powell, Energy Manager, Civic Offices, Holton Road, Barry CF63 4RU ☎ 01446 709576 ✉ dpowell@valeofglamorgan.gov.uk

Housing: Mr Tony Jaques, Head of Housing, 2-8 Haltow Road, Barry CF63 4HD ☎ 01446 709488 🖷 01446 709481 ✉ tjaques@valeofglamorgan.gov.uk

Housing Maintenance: Mr Steve Morris, Head of Building Services, The Alps, Quarry Road, Wenvoe CF5 6AA ☎ 029 2067 3124 🖷 029 2067 3049 ✉ smmorris@valeofglamorgan.gov.uk

Legal: Mr Peter Evans, Director of Legal, Public Protection & Housing Services, Civic Offices, Holton Road, Barry CF63 4RU ☎ 01446 709401 🖷 01446 701189 ✉ phevans@valeofglamorgan.gov.uk

Legal: Ms Debbie Marles, Head of Legal Services, Civic Offices, Holton Road, Barry CF63 4RU ☎ 01446 709402 🖷 01446 701189 ✉ dmarles@valeofglamorgan.gov.uk

Leisure and Cultural Services: Mr David Knevett, Operational Manager - Leisure & Tourism, Dock Offices, Barry Dock, Barry CF63 4RU ☎ 01446 704817 🖷 01446 704892 ✉ dpknevett@valeofglamorgan.gov.uk

Licensing: Mrs Kate Thompson, Principal Regulatory Services Officer, Civic Offices, Holton Road, Barry CF63 4RU ☎ 01446 709356 🖷 01446 709449 ✉ kathompson@valeofglamorgan.gov.uk

Lighting: Mr Andrew Loosemore, Operational Manager - Highways & Engineering, The Alps Depot, Quarry Road, Wenvoe CF5 6AA ☎ 029 2067 3200 🖷 029 2067 3019 ✉ aloosemore@valeofglamorgan.gov.uk

Lottery Funding, Charity and Voluntary: Mrs Sian Davies, Director of Finance, ICT & Property, Civic Offices, Holton Road, Barry CF63 4RU ☎ 01446 709202 🖷 01446 709201 ✉ sdavies@valeofglamorgan.gov.uk

Member Services: Miss Rebecca Light, Electoral Services Officer, Civic Offices, Holton Road, Barry CF63 4RU ☎ 01446 709304 🖷 01446 421623 ✉ blight@valeofglamorgan.gov.uk

Parking: Mr Andrew Loosemore, Operational Manager - Highways & Engineering, The Alps Depot, Quarry Road, Wenvoe CF5 6AA ☎ 029 2067 3200 🖷 029 2067 3019 ✉ aloosemore@valeofglamorgan.gov.uk

Personnel / HR: Mr Reuben Bergman, Head of Human Resources, Provincial House, Kendrick Road, Barry CF62 8BF ☎ 01446 709357 ✉ rbergman@valeofglamorgan.gov.uk

Planning: Mr Rob Thomas, Head of Planning & Transportation, Dock Office, Subway Road, Barry CF63 4RT ☎ 01446 704630 🖷 01446 704622 ✉ drthomas@valeofglamorgan.gov.uk

Procurement: Mr Alan Jenkins, Head of Accountancy & Resource Management, Civic Offices, Holton Road, Barry CF63 4RU ☎ 01446 709254 ✉ ajenkins@valeofglamorgan.gov.uk

Public Libraries: Mrs Sian Jones, Chief Librarian, Civic Offices, Holton Road, Barry CF63 4RU ☎ 01446 709381 🖷 01446 709448 ✉ sjones@valeofglamorgan.gov.uk

Recycling & Waste Minimisation: Mr Clifford Parrish, Operational Manager - Waste Management & Cleansing, The Alps, Quarry Road, Wenvoe CF5 6AA ☎ 029 2067 3220 🖷 029 2067 3221 ✉ csparish@valeofglamorgan.gov.uk

Regeneration: Mr Rob Quick, Director of Environmental & Economic Regeneration, Dock Office, Subway Road, Barry CF63

4RT ☎ 01446 704610 🖷 01446 704612
rjquick@valeofglamorgan.gov.uk

Road Safety: Ms Clare Cameron, Principal Transport & Road Safety Officer, Dock Office, Barry Docks, Barry CF63 4RT
☎ 01446 704768
ccameron@valeofglamorgan.gov.uk

Social Services: Mr Phil Evans, Director of Social Services, Dock Offices, Subway Road, Barry CF63 4RT ☎ 01446 704676
🖷 01446 704839
pjevans@valeofglamorgan.gov.uk

Social Services (Adult): Mr Lance Carver, Head of Adult Services & Locality Manager, Dock Offices, Subway Road, Barry CF63 4RT ☎ 01446 704678 🖷 01446 704839
lcarver@valeofglamorgan.gov.uk

Social Services (Children): Mr Gareth Jenkins, Head of Children & Young People Services, Dock Office, Subway Road, Barry CF63 4RT ☎ 01446 704864 🖷 01446 704839
gajenkins@valeofglamorgan.gov.uk

Staff Training: Mr Allan Williams, Corporate Training & Development Manager, Dock Offices, Subway Road, Barry CF63 4RT ☎ 01446 709762
apwilliams@valeofglamorgan.gov.uk

Street Scene: Mr Miles Punter, Head of Visible Services, The Alps, Quarry Road, Wenvoe CF5 6AA ☎ 029 2067 3101
🖷 029 2067 3102
mepunter@valeofglamorgan.gov.uk

Sustainable Communities: Mr Rob Quick, Director of Environmental & Economic Regeneration, Dock Office, Subway Road, Barry CF63 4RT ☎ 01446 704610 🖷 01446 704612
rjquick@valeofglamorgan.gov.uk

Tourism: Mrs Claire Evans, Tourism Marketing Manager, Dock Offices, Barry Docks, Barry CF63 4RT ☎ 01446 704868 🖷 01446 704612
chevans@valeofglamorgan.gov.uk

Town Centre: Miss Emma Smith, Town Centre Manager, Dock Office, Subway Road, Barry CF63 4RT ☎ 01446 704731 🖷 01446 704892 esmith@valeofglamorgan.gov.uk

Traffic Management: Mr Andrew Loosemore, Operational Manager - Highways & Engineering, The Alps Depot, Quarry Road, Wenvoe CF5 6AA ☎ 029 2067 3200 🖷 029 2067 3019
aloosemore@valeofglamorgan.gov.uk

Transport: Mr Rob Thomas, Head of Planning & Transportation, Dock Office, Subway Road, Barry CF63 4RT ☎ 01446 704630
🖷 01446 704622
drthomas@valeofglamorgan.gov.uk

Transport Planner: Mr Rob Thomas, Head of Planning & Transportation, Dock Office, Subway Road, Barry CF63 4RT
☎ 01446 704630 🖷 01446 704622
drthomas@valeofglamorgan.gov.uk

Waste Collection and Disposal: Mr Clifford Parrish, Operational Manager - Waste Management & Cleansing, The Alps, Quarry Road, Wenvoe CF5 6AA ☎ 029 2067 3220 🖷 029 2067 3221
csparish@valeofglamorgan.gov.uk

Waste Management: Mr Clifford Parrish, Operational Manager - Waste Management & Cleansing, The Alps, Quarry Road, Wenvoe CF5 6AA ☎ 029 2067 3220 🖷 029 2067 3221
csparish@valeofglamorgan.gov.uk

MEMBERS OF THE COUNCIL (47)

***Mayor:* Geary**, Keith (IND - Llantwit Major)
kjgeary@valeofglamorgan.gov.uk
***Deputy Mayor:* Birch**, Janice (LAB - Stanwell)
jbirch@valeofglamorgan.gov.uk
***Leader of the Council:* Moore**, Neil (LAB - Cadoc)
nmoore@valeofglamorgan.gov.uk
***Deputy Leader of the Council:* Egan**, Stuart (LAB - Buttrills)
scegan@valeofglamorgan.gov.uk
Buttrills: Vacant
Bertin, Richard (IND - Court)
rjbertin@valeofglamorgan.gov.uk
Birch, Rhiannon (LAB - Cornerswell)
rbirch@valeofglamorgan.gov.uk
Bird, Jonathan (CON - Wenvoe)
jbird@valeofglamorgan.gov.uk
Brooks, Bronwen (LAB - Court)
bbrooks@valeofglamorgan.gov.uk
Burnett, Lis (LAB - St. Augustines)
lburnett@valeofglamorgan.gov.uk
Clarke, Philip (IND - Rhoose)
pjclarke@valeofglamorgan.gov.uk
Cox, Geoffrey (CON - Cowbridge)
gacox@valeofglamorgan.gov.uk
Curtis, Robert (LAB - Gibbonsdown)
rfcurtis@valeofglamorgan.gov.uk
Curtis, Claire (LAB - Dyfan)
ccurtis@valeofglamorgan.gov.uk
Drake, Pamela (LAB - Castleland)
pdrake@valeofglamorgan.gov.uk
Drysdale, John (LAB - Illtyd)
jdrysdale@valeofglamorgan.gov.uk
Edmunds, Kate (LAB - Llandough)
kedmunds@valeofglamorgan.gov.uk
Elmore, Christopher (LAB - Castleland)
celmore@valeofglamorgan.gov.uk
Franks, Christopher (PC - Dinas Powys)
familyfranks@btinternet.com
Hacker, Eric (IND - Llantwit Major)
ehacker@valeofglamorgan.gov.uk
Hamilton, Howard (LAB - Illtyd)
hhamilton@valeofglamorgan.gov.uk
Hartrey, Val (PC - Dinas Powys)
vmhartrey@valeofglamorgan.gov.uk
Hatton, Keith (PC - Dinas Powys)
khatton@valeofglamorgan.gov.uk
Hodges, Nic (PC - Baruc)
nphodges@valeofglamorgan.gov.uk
James, Jeff (CON - Rhoose)
hjwjames@valeofglamorgan.gov.uk
Jarvie, Hunter (CON - Cowbridge)
hjarvie@valeofglamorgan.gov.uk
John, Gwyn (IND - Llantwit Major)
gjohn@valeofglamorgan.gov.uk

Johnson, Frederick (LAB - Cadoc)
ftjohnson@valeofglamorgan.gov.uk
Kelly Owen, Maureen (CON - Plymouth)
mkellyowen@valeofglamorgan.gov.uk
King, Peter (LAB - Cornerswell)
pking@valeofglamorgan.gov.uk
Mahoney, Kevin (UKIP - Sully)
kpmahoney@valeofglamorgan.gov.uk
Moore, Anne (LAB - Cadoc)
ajmoore@valeofglamorgan.gov.uk
Parker, Andrew (CON - Cowbridge)
aparker@valeofglamorgan.gov.uk
Penrose, Bob (IND - Sully)
bpenrose@valeofglamorgan.gov.uk
Powell, Anthony (LAB - Dyfan)
agpowell@valeofglamorgan.gov.uk
Preston, Audrey (CON - St. Brides Major)
ajpreston@valeofglamorgan.gov.uk
Probert, Rhona (LAB - Illtyd)
rprobert@valeofglamorgan.gov.uk
Roberts, Gwyn (LAB - St. Augustines)
groberts@valeofglamorgan.gov.uk
Thomas, John (CON - St. Athan)
jwthomas@valeofglamorgan.gov.uk
Thomas, Raymond (CON - Llandow / Ewenny)
rathomas@valeofglamorgan.gov.uk
Traherne, Rhodri (CON - Peterston-Super-Ely)
rtraherne@valeofglamorgan.gov.uk
Wiliam, Steffan (PC - Baruc)
stwiliam@valeofglamorgan.gov.uk
Wilkinson, Margaret (LAB - Gibbonsdown)
mrwilkinson@valeofglamorgan.gov.uk
Williams, A Clive (CON - Plymouth)
cwilliams@valeofglamorgan.gov.uk
Williams, Christopher (PC - Dinas Powys)
cjwilliams@valeofglamorgan.gov.uk
Williams, Edward (IND - Llantwit Major)
edwilliams@valeofglamorgan.gov.uk
Wilson, Mark (LAB - Stanwell)
mrwilson@valeofglamorgan.gov.uk

POLITICAL COMPOSITION

LAB: 21, CON: 11, IND: 7, PC: 6, UKIP: 1, Vacant: 1

CABINET

Leader: Mr Neil Moore
Deputy Leader: Mr Stuart Egan
Business Innovation, Regeneration, Economic Development, Planning & Transportation: Mrs Lis Burnett
Environment & Visible Services: Mr Robert Curtis
Housing, Building Maintenance & Community Safety: Ms Bronwen Brooks
Leisure, Park, Culture & Sports Development: Mr Gwyn John
Social Care, Health & Schools: Mr Christopher Elmore

COMMITTEE CHAIRS

Appeals: Mr Gwyn Roberts
Corporate Resources Scrutiny: Mr Mark Wilson
Democratic Services: Mr Christopher Franks
Economy & Environment Scrutiny: Mr Rhodri Traherne
Housing & Public Protection Scrutiny: Mrs Margaret Wilkinson
Licensing: Mr Anthony Powell
Planning: Mr Frederick Johnson
Scrutiny: Mr Nic Hodges
Social Care & Health Scrutiny: Mr Richard Bertin

VALE OF WHITE HORSE D

Vale of White Horse District Council, Abbey House, Abbey Close, Abingdon OX14 3JE ☎ 01235 520202 🖷 01235 554960 💻 www.whitehorsedc.gov.uk

FACTS & FIGURES

Police Authority: Thames Valley Police Authority
Health Authority: South Central Strategic Health Authority
Learning and Skills Council: South East
Parliamentary Constituencies: Oxford West and Abingdon, Wantage
EU Constituencies: South East
Election Frequency: Elections are of whole council

PRINCIPAL OFFICERS

Chief Executive: Mr David Buckle, Chief Executive, Abbey House, Abbey Close, Abingdon OX14 3JE ☎ 01235 520202 🖷 01235 522684 ✉ david.buckle@southandvale.gov.uk

Senior Management: Mr Steve Bishop, Strategic Director, Abbey House, Abbey Close, Abingdon OX14 3JE ☎ 01235 520202 ✉ steve.bishop@southandvale.gov.uk

Senior Management: Mr Andrew Down, Head of HR, IT & Customer Services, Abbey House, Abbey Close, Abingdon OX14 3JE ☎ 01235 520202 ✉ andrew.down@southandvale.gov.uk

Senior Management: Mr Adrian Duffield, Head of Planning, Abbey House, Abbey Close, Abingdon OX14 3JE ☎ 01235 520202 🖷 01235 554960 ✉ adrian.duffield@southandvale.gov.uk

Senior Management: Mr William Jacobs, Head of Finance, Abbey House, Abbey Close, Abingdon OX14 3JE ☎ 01235 520202 ✉ william.jacobs@southandvale.gov.uk

Senior Management: Ms Clare Kingston, Head of Corporate Strategy, Abbey House, Abbey Close, Abingdon OX14 3JE ☎ 01235 520202 🖷 01235 540395 ✉ clare.kingston@southandvale.gov.uk

Senior Management: Mr Matt Prosser, Strategic Director, Abbey House, Abbey Close, Abingdon OX14 3JE ☎ 01235 520202 ✉ matt.prosser@southandvale.gov.uk

Senior Management: Ms Margaret Reed, Head of Legal & Democratic Services, Abbey House, Abbey Close, Abingdon OX14 3JE ☎ 01235 520202 ✉ margaret.reed@southandvale.gov.uk

Senior Management: Mrs Anna Robinson, Strategic Director, Abbey House, Abbey Close, Abingdon OX14 3JE ☎ 01235 520202 ✉ anna.robinson@southandvale.gov.uk

Senior Management: Mr Paul Staines, Head of Health & Housing, Abbey House, Abbey Close, Abingdon OX14 3JE ☎ 01235 520202 🖷 01235 547629 ✉ paul.staines@southandvale.gov.uk

Senior Management: Mr Chris Tyson, Head of Economy,

Leisure & Property, Abbey House, Abbey Close, Abingdon OX14 3JE ☎ 01235 520202 ✉ chris.tyson@southandvale.gov.uk

Access Officer / Social Services (Disability): Ms Cheryl Reeves, Equalities Officer, Abbey House, Abbey Close, Abingdon OX14 3JE ☎ 01235 520202 ✉ cheryl.reeves@southandvale.gov.uk

Architect, Building / Property Services: Mr Graham Hawkins, Strategic Property Officer, Abbey House, Abbey Close, Abingdon OX14 3JE ☎ 01235 520202 🖷 01235 540336 ✉ graham.hawkins@southandvale.gov.uk

Best Value: Mr Geoff Bushell, Performance, Projects & Customer Services Manager, Abbey House, Abbey Close, Abingdon OX14 3JE ☎ 01235 520202 ✉ geoff.bushell@southandvale.gov.uk

Building Control: Mr Richard Beel, Building Control Manager, Abbey House, Abbey Close, Abingdon OX14 3JE ☎ 01235 520202 🖷 01235 554960 ✉ richard.beel@southandvale.gov.uk

Building Control: Mr Adrian Duffield, Head of Planning, Abbey House, Abbey Close, Abingdon OX14 3JE ☎ 01235 520202 🖷 01235 554960 ✉ adrian.duffield@southandvale.gov.uk

PR / Communications: Ms Clare Kingston, Head of Corporate Strategy, Abbey House, Abbey Close, Abingdon OX14 3JE ☎ 01235 520202 🖷 01235 540395 ✉ clare.kingston@southandvale.gov.uk

Community Planning: Ms Clare Kingston, Head of Corporate Strategy, Abbey House, Abbey Close, Abingdon OX14 3JE ☎ 01235 520202 🖷 01235 540395 ✉ clare.kingston@southandvale.gov.uk

Community Safety: Mrs Liz Hayden, Legal, Licensing & Community Safety Manager, Abbey House, Abbey Close, Abingdon OX14 3JE ☎ 01235 520202 🖷 01235 547612 ✉ liz.hayden@southandvale.gov.uk

Computer Management: Mr Simon Turner, IT Operations Manager, Abbey House, Abbey Close, Abingdon OX14 3JE ☎ 01235 520202 ✉ simon.turner@southandvale.gov.uk

Corporate Services: Ms Clare Kingston, Head of Corporate Strategy, Abbey House, Abbey Close, Abingdon OX14 3JE ☎ 01235 520202 🖷 01235 540395 ✉ clare.kingston@southandvale.gov.uk

Customer Service: Mr Geoff Bushell, Performance, Projects & Customer Services Manager, Abbey House, Abbey Close, Abingdon OX14 3JE ☎ 01235 520202 ✉ geoff.bushell@southandvale.gov.uk

Customer Service: Mr Andrew Down, Head of HR, IT & Customer Services, Abbey House, Abbey Close, Abingdon OX14 3JE ☎ 01235 520202 ✉ andrew.down@southandvale.gov.uk

E-Government: Mr Simon Turner, IT Operations Manager, Abbey House, Abbey Close, Abingdon OX14 3JE ☎ 01235 520202 ✉ simon.turner@southandvale.gov.uk

Electoral Registration: Ms Marcia Beviere, Electoral Services Manager, Abbey House, Abbey Close, Abingdon OX14 3JE ☎ 01235 520202 ✉ marcia.beviere@whitehorsedc.gov.uk

Emergency Planning: Mr John Backley, Head of Commercial Services, Abbey House, Abbey Close, Abingdon OX14 3JE ☎ 01235 520202 🖷 01235 554960 ✉ john.backley@southandvale.gov.uk

Energy Management: Mrs Heather Saunders, Climate Change Officer, Abbey House, Abbey Close, Abingdon OX14 3JE ☎ 01235 520202 🖷 01235 547629 ✉ heather.saunders@southandvale.gov.uk

Environmental / Technical Services: Mr John Backley, Head of Commercial Services, Abbey House, Abbey Close, Abingdon OX14 3JE ☎ ; 01235 520202 🖷 01235 554960 ✉ john.backley@southandvale.gov.uk

Environmental Health: Mr Paul Staines, Head of Health & Housing, Abbey House, Abbey Close, Abingdon OX14 3JE ☎ 01235 520202 🖷 01235 547629 ✉ paul.staines@southandvale.gov.uk

Estates, Property & Valuation: Mr Graham Hawkins, Strategic Property Officer, Abbey House, Abbey Close, Abingdon OX14 3JE ☎ 01235 520202 🖷 01235 540336 ✉ graham.hawkins@southandvale.gov.uk

Facilities: Mr Graham Hawkins, Strategic Property Officer, Abbey House, Abbey Close, Abingdon OX14 3JE ☎ 01235 520202 🖷 01235 540336 ✉ graham.hawkins@southandvale.gov.uk

Finance and Treasurer: Mr Steve Bishop, Strategic Director, Abbey House, Abbey Close, Abingdon OX14 3JE ☎ 01235 520202 ✉ steve.bishop@southandvale.gov.uk

Finance and Treasurer: Mr William Jacobs, Head of Finance, Abbey House, Abbey Close, Abingdon OX14 3JE ☎ 01235 520202 ✉ william.jacobs@southandvale.gov.uk

Grounds Maintenance: Ms Clare Kingston, Head of Corporate Strategy, Abbey House, Abbey Close, Abingdon OX14 3JE ☎ 01235 520202 🖷 01235 540395 ✉ clare.kingston@southandvale.gov.uk

Grounds Maintenance: Mr Ian Matten, Waste & Parks Manager, Abbey House, Abbey Close, Abingdon OX14 3JE ☎ 01235 520202 🖷 01235 554960 ✉ ian.matten@southandvale.gov.uk

Health and Safety: Ms Clare Kingston, Head of Corporate Strategy, Abbey House, Abbey Close, Abingdon OX14 3JE ☎ 01235 520202 🖷 01235 540395 ✉ clare.kingston@southandvale.gov.uk

Health and Safety: Ms Sarah Minns, Health & Safety Adviser, Abbey House, Abbey Close, Abingdon OX14 3JE ☎ 01235 520202 ✉ sarah.minns@southandvale.gov.uk

Home Energy Conservation: Mrs Heather Saunders, Climate Change Officer, Abbey House, Abbey Close, Abingdon OX14 3JE ☎ 01235 520202 🖷 01235 547629

✉ heather.saunders@southandvale.gov.uk

Housing: Mr Paul Staines, Head of Health & Housing, Abbey House, Abbey Close, Abingdon OX14 3JE ☎ 01235 520202 🖷 01235 547629 ✉ paul.staines@southandvale.gov.uk

Legal: Mrs Liz Hayden, Legal, Licensing & Community Safety Manager, Abbey House, Abbey Close, Abingdon OX14 3JE ☎ 01235 520202 🖷 01235 547612 ✉ liz.hayden@southandvale.gov.uk

Licensing: Mr Robert Draper, Licensing Team Leader, Abbey House, Abbey Close, Abingdon OX14 3JE ☎ 01235 520202 ✉ robert.draper@southandvale.gov.uk

Licensing: Mr Robert Draper, Licensing Team Leader, Abbey House, Abbey Close, Abingdon OX14 3JE ☎ 01235 520202 ✉ nigel.haverson@southandvale.gov.uk

Licensing: Mrs Liz Hayden, Legal, Licensing & Community Safety Manager, Abbey House, Abbey Close, Abingdon OX14 3JE ☎ 01235 520202 🖷 01235 547612 ✉ liz.hayden@southandvale.gov.uk

Member Services: Mr Steven Corrigan, Democratic Services Manager, Abbey House, Abbey Close, Abingdon OX14 3JE ☎ 01235 520202 🖷 01235 547609 ✉ steven.corrigan@southandvale.gov.uk

Parking: Mrs Beverly Mizen, Car Park Manager, Abbey House, Abbey Close, Abingdon OX14 3JE ☎ 01235 520202 🖷 01235 554960 ✉ beverley.mizen@whitehorsedc.gov.uk

Personnel / HR: Mrs Helen Hall, Human Resouces Manager, Abbey House, Abbey Close, Abingdon OX14 3JE ☎ 01235 520202 🖷 01235 554960 ✉ helen.hall@southandvale.gov.uk

Planning: Mr Adrian Duffield, Head of Planning, Abbey House, Abbey Close, Abingdon OX14 3JE ☎ 01235 520202 🖷 01235 554960 ✉ adrian.duffield@southandvale.gov.uk

Procurement: Mr Geoff Bushell, Performance, Projects & Customer Services Manager, Abbey House, Abbey Close, Abingdon OX14 3JE ☎ 01235 520202 ✉ geoff.bushell@southandvale.gov.uk

Recycling & Waste Minimisation: Ms Clare Kingston, Head of Corporate Strategy, Abbey House, Abbey Close, Abingdon OX14 3JE ☎ 01235 520202 🖷 01235 540395 ✉ clare.kingston@southandvale.gov.uk

Recycling & Waste Minimisation: Mr Ian Matten, Waste & Parks Manager, Abbey House, Abbey Close, Abingdon OX14 3JE ☎ 01235 520202 🖷 01235 554960 ✉ ian.matten@southandvale.gov.uk

Staff Training: Ms Lynn Barden, Corporate Learning & Development Manager, Abbey House, Abbey Close, Abingdon OX14 3JE ☎ 01235 520202 🖷 01235 554960 ✉ lynn.barden@southandvale.gov.uk

Street Scene: Ms Clare Kingston, Head of Corporate Strategy, Abbey House, Abbey Close, Abingdon OX14 3JE ☎ 01235 520202 🖷 01235 540395 ✉ clare.kingston@southandvale.gov.uk

Waste Collection and Disposal: Ms Clare Kingston, Head of Corporate Strategy, Abbey House, Abbey Close, Abingdon OX14 3JE ☎ 01235 520202 🖷 01235 540395 ✉ clare.kingston@southandvale.gov.uk

Waste Collection and Disposal: Mr Ian Matten, Waste & Parks Manager, Abbey House, Abbey Close, Abingdon OX14 3JE ☎ 01235 520202 🖷 01235 554960 ✉ ian.matten@southandvale.gov.uk

Waste Management: Ms Clare Kingston, Head of Corporate Strategy, Abbey House, Abbey Close, Abingdon OX14 3JE ☎ 01235 520202 🖷 01235 540395 ✉ clare.kingston@southandvale.gov.uk

Waste Management: Mr Ian Matten, Waste & Parks Manager, Abbey House, Abbey Close, Abingdon OX14 3JE ☎ 01235 520202 🖷 01235 554960 ✉ ian.matten@southandvale.gov.uk

Children's Play Areas: Mr Ian Matten, Waste & Parks Manager, Abbey House, Abbey Close, Abingdon OX14 3JE ☎ 01235 520202 🖷 01235 554960 ✉ ian.matten@southandvale.gov.uk

MEMBERS OF THE COUNCIL (51)

***Chair:* Thomson**, Alison (CON - Faringdon and the Coxwells)
amthomson5491@yahoo.co.uk

***Vice-Chair:* Badcock**, Mike (CON - Abingdon Ock Meadow)
michael.badcock@oxfordshire.gov.uk

***Leader of the Council:* Barber**, Matthew (CON - Hanneys)
matthew.barber@whitehorsedc.gov.uk

***Deputy Leader of the Council:* Cox**, Roger (CON - Faringdon and the Coxwells)
roger.cox@whitehorsedc.gov.uk

Amys, John (CON - Grove)
johnamys@aol.com

Badcock, Marilyn (CON - Abingdon Ock Meadow)
marilyn.badcock@oxfordshire.gov.uk

Batts, Eric (CON - North Hinksey and Wytham)
cllrericbatts@gmail.com

Bricknell, Julia (LD - Abingdon Dunmore)
julia.bricknell@whitehorsedc.gov.uk

Constance, Yvonne (CON - Craven)
yvonne.constance@whitehorsedc.gov.uk

Crawford, Andrew (LD - Greendown)
cllr.andrew.crawford@gmail.com

Crossley, Jane (CON - Sunningwell and Wootton)
jane.crossley@whitehorsedc.gov.uk

De Vere, Tony (LD - Abingdon Abbey and Barton)
tony.devere@whitehorsedc.gov.uk

Dickson, Charlotte (CON - Wantage Charlton)
charlotte@leahouse.com

Duffield, Gervase (CON - Sutton Courtenay and Appleford)
gervase.duffield@whitehorsedc.gov.uk

Fiddaman, Jason (CON - Abingdon Caldecott)
jasfid@ntlworld.com

Foggin, Timothy (CON - Sunningwell and Wootton)

Hallett, Debby (LD - North Hinksey and Wytham)
debby.hallett@gmail.com

Halliday, Jim (LD - Abingdon Fitzharris)
jim.halliday@whitehorsedc.gov.uk

Hanna, Jane (LD - Marcham and Shippon)
jane.hanna@epilepsybereaved.org.uk

Hannaby, Jenny (LD - Wantage Segsbury)
jenny@yeomanryhouse.co.uk
Hayward, Anthony (CON - Longworth)
anthony.hayward@whitehorsedc.gov.uk
Hoddinott, Dudley (LD - Appleton and Cumnor)
dudley.hoddinott@whitehorsedc.gov.uk
Holman, Holly (CON - Abingdon Fitzharris)
holly.holman@whitehorsedc.gov.uk
Howell, Simon (CON - Shrivenham)
simon.p.howell@btinternet.com
Johnston, Bob (LD - Radley)
bob.johnston@whitehorsedc.gov.uk
Jones, Bill (CON - Hendreds)
felicity@tudorwalk.co.uk
Jones, Peter (CON - Abingdon Peachcroft)
Kainth, Mohinder (CON - Faringdon and the Coxwells)
mohinder.kainth@gmail.com
Lawrence, Angela (IND - Abingdon Northcourt)
angela.lawrence@whitehorsedc.gov.uk
Lonergan, Pat (LD - Abingdon Peachcroft)
pat.lonergan@whitehorsedc.gov.uk
Lovatt, Sandy (CON - Abingdon Dunmore)
alovatt@alexanderlovatt.co.uk
Mansfield, Ron (LD - Kennington and South Hinksey)
enquiries.rjm@gmail.com
Marchant, Sue (LD - Grove)
sue.marchant@whitehorsedc.gov.uk
Mayhew-Archer, Julie (LD - Abingdon Abbey and Barton)
Melville, Aidan (LAB - Abingdon Caldecott)
melville.aidan@gmail.com
Morgan, John (CON - Wantage Charlton)
john.morgan@whitehorsedc.gov.uk
Morgan, Gill (CON - Wantage Segbury)
down.pl@btinternet.com
Murray, Mike (CON - Hendreds)
michael.murray@whitehorsedc.gov.uk
Patterson, Jerry (LD - Kennington and South Hinksey)
jerry.patterson@whitehorsedc.gov.uk
Pighills, Helen (LD - Abingdon Northcourt)
helen.pighills@whitehorsedc.gov.uk
Precious, Kate (CON - Grove)
Roberts, Judy (LD - Appleton and Cumnor)
judy.roberts@whitehorsedc.gov.uk
Roper, Fiona (CON - Wantage Charlton)
fiona@widcombehouse.co.uk
Sharp, Robert (CON - Stanford)
robert.sharp@whitehorsedc.gov.uk
Shelley, Janet (CON - Blewbury and Upton)
janet.shelley@whitehorsedc.gov.uk
Tilley, Melinda (CON - Kingston Bagpuize with Southmoor)
melinda.tilley@oxfordshire.gov.uk
Turner, Margaret (CON - Harwell)
margaret.turner@whitehorsedc.gov.uk
Waite, Reg (CON - Harwell)
reg.waite@whitehorsedc.gov.uk
Ware, Elaine (CON - Shrivenham)
elaine.ware@whitehorsedc.gov.uk
Webber, Richard (LD - Drayton)
richard.webber@whitehorsedc.gov.uk
Woodford, John (LD - Appleton and Cumnor)
john.woodford@whitehorsedc.gov.uk

POLITICAL COMPOSITION

CON: 31, LD: 18, IND: 1, LAB: 1

CABINET

Leader / Corporate Strategy & Finance: Mr Matthew Barber
Deputy Leader / Planning & Housing: Mr Roger Cox
Commercial Services: Mr Reg Waite
Economy & Leisure: Ms Elaine Ware
Legal, Democratic & Customer Services: Ms Yvonne Constance

COMMITTEE CHAIRS

Audit & Governance: Mr Mike Murray
General Licensing: Ms Melinda Tilley
Planning: Mr Robert Sharp
Scrutiny: Mr Jim Halliday

WAKEFIELD CITY — M

Wakefield City Council, (City of Wakefield Metropolitan District Council), Town Hall, Wood Street, Wakefield WF1 2HQ
☎ 0845 8506 506; 01924 306090 🖳 www.wakefield.gov.uk

FACTS & FIGURES

Police Authority: West Yorkshire Police Authority
Health Authority: NHS Yorkshire & the Humber
Learning and Skills Council: Yorkshire and the Humber
Parliamentary Constituencies: Hemsworth, Morley and Outwood, Normanton, Pontefract and Castleford, Wakefield
EU Constituencies: Yorkshire and the Humber
Election Frequency: Elections are by thirds
Twinning: Alfeld / Leine (Germany); Belgorod (Russia); Castrop-Rauxel (Germany); Castres (France); Girona (Spain); Herne (Germany); Henin-Beaumont (France); Konin (Poland)

PRINCIPAL OFFICERS

Chief Executive: Ms Joanne Roney, Chief Executive, Town Hall, Wakefield WF1 2HQ ☎ 01924 305101 ✉ jroney@wakefield.gov.uk

Access Officer / Social Services (Disability): Mr Stuart Bolton, Community Cohesion Officer, Town Hall, Wood Street, Wakefield WF1 2HQ ☎ 01924 305174 🖷 01924 305164 ✉ sbolton@wakefield.gov.uk

Architect, Building / Property Services: Ms Judith Badger, Service Director - Finance, County Hall, Bond Street, Wakefield WF1 2QW ☎ 01924 305388 ✉ jbadger@wakefield.gov.uk

Children / Youth Services: Mr Stephen Crofts, Youth & Support Service Development, Manygates Education Centre, Manygates Lane, Sandal, Wakefield WF2 7DQ ☎ 01924 304155 ✉ scrofts@wakefield.gov.uk

Children / Youth Services: Mrs Elaine McHale, Corporate Director - Family Services, County Hall, Bond Street, Wakefield WF1 2QL ☎ 01924 307728 🖷 01924 307768 ✉ emchale@wakefield.gov.uk

Civil Registration: Ms Bernadette Livesey, Service Director - Legal & Democratic Services, County Hall, Bond Street, Wakefield WF1 2QW ☎ 01924 305177 🖷 01924 305195 ✉ blivesey@wakefield.gov.uk

PR / Communications: Mr Simon Hope, Head of Communications, Town Hall, Wood Street, Wakefield WF1 2HQ

☎ 01924 305107 ⌖ shope@wakefield.gov.uk

Community Planning: Mr Andrew Balchin, Corporate Director - Communities, Leeds Road, Newton Bar, Wakefield WF1 2TX ☎ 01924 306576 ⌖ abalchin@wakefield.gov.uk

Community Safety: Mr Andrew Balchin, Corporate Director - Communities, Leeds Road, Newton Bar, Wakefield WF1 2TX ☎ 01924 306576 ⌖ abalchin@wakefield.gov.uk

Computer Management: Mr Alan Kirkham, Service Director - Strategic Procurement & IT, Municipal Buildings, Pontefract WF8 1BE ☎ 01924 306780 ⌖ akirkham@wakefield.gov.uk

Customer Service: Mr Simon Hope, Head of Communications, Town Hall, Wood Street, Wakefield WF1 2HQ ☎ 01924 305107 ⌖ shope@wakefield.gov.uk

Electoral Registration: Ms Sandra Hardy, Electoral Services Manager, Town Hall, Wood Street, Wakefield WF1 2HQ ☎ 01924 605020 🖷 01924 605722 ⌖ shardy@wakefield.gov.uk

Emergency Planning: Ms Margaret Saunders, EP Manager, County Hall, Bond Street, Wakefield WF1 2QW ☎ 01294 305048 🖷 01924 305214 ⌖ msaunders@wakefield.gov.uk

Environmental / Technical Services: Mr Glynn Humphries, Service Director - Environment, Lower Building, Leeds Road, Newton Bar, Wakefield WF1 2TX ☎ 01924 306518 ⌖ ghumphries@wakefield.gov.uk

Events Manager: Ms Karen Baker, Service Manager for Library & Museums, Town Hall, Wood Street, Wakefield WF1 2HQ ☎ 01924 305183 ⌖ kbaker@wakefield.gov.uk

Finance and Treasurer: Ms Judith Badger, Service Director - Finance, County Hall, Bond Street, Wakefield WF1 2QW ☎ 01924 305388 ⌖ jbadger@wakefield.gov.uk

Highways: Mr Ian Thomson, Service Director - Planning, Newton Bar, Leeds Road, Wakefield WF1 2TX ☎ 01924 305858 🖷 01924 306629 ⌖ ithomson@wakefield.gov.uk

Housing: Ms Sarah Pearson, Service Director - Strategic Housing, Top Building, Newton Bar, Wakefield WF1 2TX ☎ 01924 305802 ⌖ spearson@wakefield.gov.uk

Legal: Ms Bernadette Livesey, Service Director - Legal & Democratic Services, County Hall, Bond Street, Wakefield WF1 2QW ☎ 01924 305177 🖷 01924 305195 ⌖ blivesey@wakefield.gov.uk

Leisure and Cultural Services: Ms Lisa Dodd, Service Director - Sport & Culture, Town Hall, Wood Street, Wakefield WF1 2HQ ☎ 01924 306931 ⌖ ldodd@wakefield.gov.uk

Licensing: Ms Pam Taylor, Licensing Officer, Town Hall, Wood Street, Wakefield WF1 2HQ ☎ 01924 306090 ⌖ ptaylor@wakefield.gov.uk

Lifelong Learning: Ms Sue Johnson, Service Director - Schools & Lifelong Learning, County Hall, Bond Street, Wakefield WF1 2QW ☎ 01924 305501 ⌖ sjohnson@wakefield.gov.uk

Lifelong Learning: Mrs Elaine McHale, Corporate Director - Family Services, County Hall, Bond Street, Wakefield WF1 2QL ☎ 01924 307728 🖷 01924 307768 ⌖ emchale@wakefield.gov.uk

Member Services: Ms Bernadette Livesey, Service Director - Legal & Democratic Services, County Hall, Bond Street, Wakefield WF1 2QW ☎ 01924 305177 🖷 01924 305195 ⌖ blivesey@wakefield.gov.uk

Parking: Mr Keith Bloomfield, Transport - Strategy Development Manager, Newton Bar, Wakefield WF1 2TX ☎ 01924 306069 🖷 01924 306074 ⌖ kbloomfield@wakefield.gov.uk

Personnel / HR: Ms Helen Grantham, Service Director - People & Customers, County Hall, Bond Street, Wakefield WF1 2QW ☎ 01924 306700 🖷 01924 305214 ⌖ hgrantham@wakefield.gov.uk

Planning: Mr Ian Thomson, Service Director - Planning, Newton Bar, Leeds Road, Wakefield WF1 2TX ☎ 01924 305858 🖷 01924 306629 ⌖ ithomson@wakefield.gov.uk

Procurement: Mr Alan Kirkham, Service Director - Strategic Procurement & E-Services, Municipal Offices, Headlands Road, Pontefract WF8 1BE ☎ 01924 306780 ⌖ akirkham@wakefield.gov.uk

Public Libraries: Ms Lisa Dodd, Service Director - Sport & Culture, Town Hall, Wood Street, Wakefield WF1 2HQ ☎ 01924 306931 ⌖ ldodd@wakefield.gov.uk

Recycling & Waste Minimisation: Mr Jay Smith, Recycling Manager, Lower Building, Leeds Road, Newton Bar, Wakefield WF1 2TX ☎ 01924 306367 ⌖ jaysmith@wakefield.gov.uk

Regeneration: Mr Andrew Wallhead, Corporate Director - Regeneration, Culture & Sport, Town Hall, Wakefield WF1 2QW ☎ 01924 306950 ⌖ awallhead@wakefield.gov.uk

Road Safety: Mr Paul Stevenson, Transport - Strategy Development Manager, Newton Bar, Wakefield WF1 2TX ☎ 01924 306069 🖷 01924 306074 ⌖ pstevenson@wakefield.gov.uk

Social Services: Mrs C Hobson, Service Director - Commissioning, Town Hall, Wood Street, Wakefield WF1 2HQ ☎ 01924 307779 ⌖ chobson@wakefield.gov.uk

Social Services: Mrs Elaine McHale, Corporate Director - Family Services, County Hall, Bond Street, Wakefield WF1 2QL ☎ 01924 307728 🖷 01924 307768 ⌖ emchale@wakefield.gov.uk

Social Services (Adult): Mr R Hurren, Service Director - Older People, Town Hall, Wood Street, Wakefield WF1 2HQ ☎ 01924 307760 ⌖ rhurren@wakefield.gov.uk

Social Services (Adult): Mrs Elaine McHale, Corporate Director - Family Services, County Hall, Bond Street, Wakefield WF1 2QL ☎ 01924 307728 🖷 01924 307768 ⌖ emchale@wakefield.gov.uk

Social Services (Adult): Mr Sam Pratheepan, Service Director - Adults, County Hall, Wood Street, Wakefield WF1 2QW ☎ 01924

306791 ✉ spratheepan@wakefield.gov.uk

Social Services (Children): Ms Lyn Burns, Interim Service Director - Safeguarding & Family Support, County Hall, Bond Street, Wakefield WF1 2QW ☎ 01924 307734 ✉ lburns@wakefield.gov.uk

Social Services (Children): Mrs Elaine McHale, Corporate Director - Family Services, County Hall, Bond Street, Wakefield WF1 2QL ☎ 01924 307728 🖷 01924 307768 ✉ emchale@wakefield.gov.uk

Staff Training: Mr John Ward, Corporate Learning & Development Advisor, County Hall, Bond Street, Wakefield WF1 2QW ☎ 01924 305893 ✉ jward@wakefield.gov.uk

Tourism: Mr Graham Riding, Culture Manager, Town Hall, Wakefield WF1 2HQ ☎ 01924 305146 ✉ griding@wakefield.gov.uk

Traffic Management: Mr Keith Bloomfield, Transport - Strategy Development Manager, Newton Bar, Wakefield WF1 2TX ☎ 01924 306069 🖷 01924 306074 ✉ kbloomfield@wakefield.gov.uk

Waste Collection and Disposal: Mr Glynn Humphries, Service Director - Environment, Lower Building, Leeds Road, Newton Bar, Wakefield WF1 2TX ☎ 01924 306518 ✉ ghumphries@wakefield.gov.uk

Waste Management: Mr Glynn Humphries, Service Director - Environment, Lower Building, Leeds Road, Newton Bar, Wakefield WF1 2TX ☎ 01924 306518 ✉ ghumphries@wakefield.gov.uk

MEMBERS OF THE COUNCIL (63)

***Mayor:* Blezard**, Elaine (LAB - Normanton)
eblezard@wakefield.gov.uk

***Deputy Mayor:* Holmes**, Brian (LAB - Horbury and South Ossett)
bholmes@wakefield.gov.uk

***Leader of the Council:* Box**, Peter (LAB - Altofts and Whitwood)
pbox@wakefield.gov.uk

***Deputy Leader of the Council:* Jeffery**, Denise (LAB - Castleford Central and Glasshoughton)
djeffery@wakefield.gov.uk

Ahmed, Nadeem (CON - Wakefield South)
cllrnahmed@wakefield.gov.uk

Askew, Jean (LAB - Ackworth, North Elmsall and Upton)
jeanaskew@wakefield.gov.uk

Austin, Tracey (LAB - Wakefield North)
taustin@wakefield.gov.uk

Broom, Linda (LAB - Airedale and Ferry Fryston)
lbroom@wakefield.gov.uk

Bunney, Ian (CON - Ossett)
ibunney@wakefield.gov.uk

Burns-Williamson, Mark (LAB - Castleford Central and Glasshoughton)
mburns-williamson@wakefield.gov.uk

Burton, Glenn (LAB - Knottingley)
gburton@wakefield.gov.uk

Collins, Michelle (LAB - South Emsall and South Kirkby)
michellecollins@wakefield.gov.uk

Crewe, Yvonne (LAB - Airedale and Ferry Fryston)
ycrewe@wakefield.gov.uk

Cummings, Maureen (LAB - Crofton, Ryhill and Walton)
mcummings@wakefield.gov.uk

Cunliffe, June (LAB - Featherstone)
jcunliffe@wakefield.gov.uk

Dagger, David (LAB - Normanton)
ddagger@wakefield.gov.uk

Dean, Tony (LAB - Pontefract South)
tonydean@wakefield.gov.uk

Drysdale, June (CON - Wakefield Rural)
jdrysdale@wakefield.gov.uk

Ellis, Harry (LAB - Knottingley)
hellis@wakefield.gov.uk

Garbutt, Patricia (LAB - Pontefract North)
pgarbutt@wakefield.gov.uk

Garbutt, Alan (LAB - Ackworth, North Elmsall and Upton)
agarbutt@wakefield.gov.uk

Graham, Monica (CON - Wakefield South)
mgraham@wakefield.gov.uk

Halliday, Ronald (LAB - Wakefield East)
rhalliday@wakefield.gov.uk

Harrison, Laurie (LAB - South Elmsall and South Kirkby)
lharrison@wakefield.gov.uk

Hemingway, Jack (LAB - Horbury and South Ossett)
jackhemingway@wakefield.gov.uk

Heptinstall, Faith (LAB - Crofton, Ryhill and Walton)
fheptinstall@wakefield.gov.uk

Hodson, Shaun (LAB - Hemsworth)
shodson@wakefield.gov.uk

Holmes, Janet (LAB - Horbury and South Ossett)
jholmes@wakefield.gov.uk

Hopkins, David (CON - Wakefield South)
dhopkins@wakefield.gov.uk

Hudson, Clive (LAB - Stanley and Outwood East)
chudson@wakefield.gov.uk

Hudson, Heather (LAB - Altofts and Whitwood)
hhudson@wakefield.gov.uk

Isherwood, Graham (LAB - Featherstone)
gisherwood@wakefield.gov.uk

Isherwood, Margaret (LAB - Wakefield North)
margaretisherwood@wakefield.gov.uk

Johnson, Martyn (LAB - Wrenthorpe and Outwood West)
martynjohnson@wakefield.gov.uk

Keith, Charlie (LAB - Wrenthorpe and Outwood West)
ckeith@wakefield.gov.uk

Kirkpatrick, Lawrence (LAB - Wakefield Rural)
lkirkpatrick@wakefield.gov.uk

Liles, Betty (CON - Wrenthorpe and Outwood West)
bliles@wakefield.gov.uk

Lloyd, Glyn (LAB - Hemsworth)
glynlloyd@wakefield.gov.uk

Loughran, Celia (LAB - Pontefract South)
cloughran@wakefield.gov.uk

Lund, Ros (LAB - Wakefield East)
rlund@wakefield.gov.uk

Manifield, Albert (LAB - Crofton, Ryhill and Walton)
amanifield@wakefield.gov.uk

Mitchell, Hilary (LAB - Wakefield West)
hilarymitchell@wakefield.gov.uk

Morley, Matthew (LAB - Stanley and Outwood East)
mmorley@wakefield.gov.uk

Pickin, Sandra (LAB - Hemsworth)
spickin@wakefield.gov.uk

Rhodes, Elizabeth (LAB - Wakefield North)
brhodes@wakefield.gov.uk

Richardson, Tony (LAB - Ossett)

tonyrichardson@wakefield.gov.uk
Rowley, Olivia (LAB - Wakefield East)
orowley@wakefield.gov.uk
Sanders, Ian (CON - Wakefield Rural)
isanders@wakefield.gov.uk
Sanders, Wiliam (CON - Wakefield West)
wsanders@wakefield.gov.uk
Shaw, Les (LAB - Airedale and Ferry Fryston)
lesshaw@wakefield.gov.uk
Sherriff, Paula (LAB - Pontefract North)
psherriff@wakefield.gov.uk
Stokes, Graham (LAB - Knottingley)
gstokes@wakefield.gov.uk
Stone, John (CON - Wakefield West)
johnstone@wakefield.gov.uk
Taylor, Angela (CON - Ossett)
actaylor@wakefield.gov.uk
Taylor, Richard (LAB - Featherstone)
dicktaylor@wakefield.gov.uk
Tennant, Clive (LAB - Pontefract North)
clivetennant@wakefield.gov.uk
Travis, Darran (LAB - Altofts and Whitwood)
dtravis@wakefield.gov.uk
Tulley, Steve (LAB - South Elmsall and South Kirkby)
stulley@wakefield.gov.uk
Wallis, Anthony (LAB - Castleford Central and Glasshoughton)
awallis@wakefield.gov.uk
Walsh, Geoff (CON - Pontefract South)
gwalsh@wakefield.gov.uk
Ward, Martyn (LAB - Ackworth, North Elmsall and Upton)
martynward@wakefield.gov.uk
Wassell, Alan (LAB - Normanton)
alanwassel@wakefield.gov.uk
Williams, Jacqueline (LAB - Stanley and Outwood East)
jacquelinewilliams@wakefield.gov.uk

POLITICAL COMPOSITION
LAB: 52, CON: 11

CABINET
Leader: Mr Peter Box
Deputy Leader / Regeneration & Economic Growth: Mrs Denise Jeffery
Adults & Health: Mrs Patricia Garbutt
Children & Young People: Mrs Olivia Rowley
Corporate Performance: Mr Graham Stokes
Culture, Sport & Libraries: Mr David Dagger
Environment & Communities: Mrs Maureen Cummings

COMMITTEE CHAIRS
Crime & Community Safety: Mr Laurie Harrison
Licensing & Regulatory: Mr Glyn Lloyd
Lifelong Learning (Scrutiny): Mrs Ros Lund
Planning & Highways: Mr Alan Garbutt
Skills, Enterprise & Work (Scrutiny): Mr Albert Manifield
Social Care & Health (Scrutiny): Mrs Elizabeth Rhodes
Standards: Mr Emeritus Nairn-Briggs (External)

WALSALL M
Walsall Metropolitan Borough Council, Civic Centre, Darwall Street, Walsall WS1 1TP ☎ 01922 650000 🖷 01922 720885
💻 www.walsall.gov.uk

FACTS & FIGURES
Police Authority: West Midlands Police Authority
Health Authority: NHS West Midlands
Learning and Skills Council: West Midlands
Parliamentary Constituencies: Aldridge-Brownhills, Walsall North, Walsall South
EU Constituencies: West Midlands
Election Frequency: Elections are by thirds
Twinning: Mulhouse (France); Aldridge-Brownhills: Montelimar (France); Willenhall: Drancy (France)

PRINCIPAL OFFICERS
Chief Executive: Mr Paul Sheehan, Chief Executive, Civic Centre, Darwall Street, Walsall WS1 1TP ☎ 01922 652006 🖷 01922 614210 ✉ sheehanp@walsall.gov.uk

Senior Management: Mr Rory Borealis, Executive Director, Civic Centre, Darwall Street, Walsall WS1 1TP ☎ 01992 652910 🖷 01922 614210 ✉ borealisr@walsall.gov.uk

Senior Management: Mr Tim Johnson, Executive Director, Civic Centre, Darwall Street, Walsall WS1 1TP ☎ 01922 652431 🖷 01922 614210 ✉ johnsont@walsall.gov.uk

Senior Management: Ms Pauline Pilkington, Executive Director for Children's Services, Civic Centre, Darwall Street, Walsall WS1 1TP ☎ 01922 652035 🖷 01922 614210 ✉ pilkingtonp@walsall.gov.uk

Access Officer / Social Services (Disability): Ms Sue Fox, Access Officer - Policy Unit, Civic Centre, Dawall Street, Walsall WS1 1TP ☎ 01922 652010 🖷 01922 653302 ✉ foxs@walsall.gov.uk

Architect, Building / Property Services: Mr Keith Stone, Assistant Director of the Built Environment, Civic Centre, Darwall Street, Walsall WS1 1TP ☎ 01922 652100 🖷 01922 623234 ✉ stonek@walsall.gov.uk

Building Control: Mr David Elsworthy, Head of Planning & Building Control, Civic Centre, Darwall Street, Walsall WS1 1TP ☎ 01922 652409 🖷 01922 623234 ✉ elsworthyd@walsall.gov.uk

Catering Services: Ms Elaine Birch, Catering Manager, Catering Public Service Enterprise, Norfolk Place, Walsall WS2 7BA ☎ 01922 653120 ✉ birche@walsall.gov.uk

Civil Registration: Ms Lorraine Cotton, Superintendent Registrar, Civic Centre, Darwall Street, Walsall WS1 1TP ☎ 01922 652260 🖷 01922 652262 ✉ cottonl@walsall.gov.uk

PR / Communications: Mr Darren Caveney, Head of Communications & Marketing, The Council House, PO Box 23, Lichfield Street, Walsall WS1 1TW ☎ 01922 652007 🖷 01922 648066 ✉ caveneyd@walsall.gov.uk

Community Planning: Ms Carol Mason, Head of Community Development, Norwich Union House, 17 Lichfield Street, Darwall Street, Walsall WS1 1TU ☎ 01922 650444 ✉ masonc@walsall.gov.uk

Community Planning: Mr Clive Wright, Partnership Director, Civic Centre, Darwall Street, Walsall WS1 1TP ☎ 01922 654707 🖷 01922 653373 🖰 wrightclive@walsall.gov.uk

Community Safety: Ms Lynne Hughes, Area Manager Community Safety, 191a Broadway, The Delves, Walsall WS1 3HD ☎ 01922 709189 🖷 01922 709190 🖰 hughesl@walsall.gov.uk

Computer Management: Mr Paul Milmore, Head of Business Solutions, 3rd Floor, Civic Centre, Darwall Street, Walsall WS1 1TP ☎ 01922 655550 🖰 milmorep@walsall.gov.uk

Computer Management: Mr Martin Sadler, Head of Shared Services & Procurement, Civic Centre, Darwall Street, Walsall WS1 1TP ☎ 01922 654882 🖷 01922 652535 🖰 sadlerm@walsall.gov.uk

Consumer Protection and Trading Standards: Mr John Beavon, Trading Standards Manager - Environmental Health & Consumer Services, Challenge Building, Hatherton Road, Walsall WS1 1YG ☎ 01922 652214 🖷 01922 630697 🖰 beavonj@walsall.gov.uk

Contracts: Mr Lawrence Brazier, Head of Procurement, Civic Centre, Darwall Street, Walsall WS1 1TP ☎ 01922 653471 🖷 01922 653534 🖰 brazierl@walsall.gov.uk

Corporate Services: Mr Rory Borealis, Executive Director, 2910 Darwall Street, Walsall WA1 1TP ☎ 01992 652910 🖷 01922 614210 🖰 borealisr@walsall.gov.uk

Customer Service: Ms Helen Dudson, Acting Head of Performance, Civic Centre, Darwall Street, Walsall WS1 1TP ☎ 01922 650000

Customer Service: Mr Jez Holding, Customer Contact Manager, Civic Centre, Darwall Street, Walsall WS1 1TP ☎ 01922 652526 🖷 01922 652813 🖰 holdingj@walsall.gov.uk

Economic Development: Mr Tim Johnson, Executive Director, Civic Centre, Darwall Street, Walsall WS1 1TP ☎ 01922 652431 🖷 01922 614210 🖰 johnsont@walsall.gov.uk

Education: Ms Pauline Pilkington, Executive Director for Children's Services, Civic Centre, Darwall Street, Walsall WS1 1TP ☎ 01922 652035 🖷 01922 614210 🖰 pilkingtonp@walsall.gov.uk

E-Government: Mr Martin Sadler, Head of Shared Services & Procurement, Civic Centre, Darwall Street, Walsall WS1 1TP ☎ 01922 654882 🖷 01922 652535 🖰 sadlerm@walsall.gov.uk

Electoral Registration: Mr Peter Allsop, Chief Electoral Registrations & Elections Officer, Civic Centre, Darwall Street, Walsall WS1 1TH ☎ 01922 652012 🖷 01922 652040 🖰 allsopp@walsall.gov.uk

Emergency Planning: Mr Alan Boyd, Resilience Manager, Sandwell Council House, Oldbury B69 3DE ☎ 0121 569 3060; 0121 569 3983 🖰 alan_boyd@sandwell.gov.uk

Energy Management: Mr Kwame Alex-Eyitene, Energy Manager, Walsall Property Services, 28 New Forest Road, Walsall WS3 1TR ☎ 01922 471257 🖷 01922 616759 🖰 alex-eyitenek@walsall.gov.uk

Environmental / Technical Services: Mr Keith Stone, Assistant Director of the Built Environment, Civic Centre, Darwall Street, Walsall WS1 1TP ☎ 01922 652100 🖷 01922 623234 🖰 stonek@walsall.gov.uk

Estates, Property & Valuation: Mr Steve Law, Estates Manager, Civic Centre, Darwall Street, Walsall WS1 1TP ☎ 01922 652075 🖷 01922 636150 🖰 laws@walsall.gov.uk

European Liaison: Mr Clive Wright, Partnership Director, Civic Centre, Darwall Street, Walsall WS1 1TP ☎ 01922 654707 🖷 01922 653373 🖰 wrightclive@walsall.gov.uk

Events Manager: Ms Antonia Pompa, Events Manager, Civic Centre, Darwall Street, Walsall WS1 1TP ☎ 01922 650311 🖰 pompaa@walsall.gov.uk

Facilities: Mr Kevin Kendall, Head of Property Services, Civic Centre, Darwall Street, Walsall WS1 1TP ☎ 01922 642801 🖷 01922 616759 🖰 kendallk@walsall.gov.uk

Finance and Treasurer: Mr James Walsh, Chief Finance Officer, Civic Centre, Darwall Street, Walsall WS1 1TP ☎ 01922 653554 🖷 01922 722868 🖰 walshj@walsall.gov.uk

Fleet Management: Mr Steve Johnson, Head of Fleet Management, Norfolk Place, North Walsall Depot, Bloxwich Road, Walsall WS2 ☎ 01922 653719 🖷 01922 653709 🖰 johnsons@walsall.gov.uk

Grounds Maintenance: Mr Andy Ody, Service Manager - Grounds, Street Pride, Civic Centre, Darwall Street, Walsall WS1 1TP ☎ 01922 653715 🖷 01922 641853 🖰 odya@walsall.gov.uk

Health and Safety: Mr David Kempson, Senior Safety Advisor, Challenge Building, Hatherton Street, Walsall WS1 1YG ☎ 01922 652086 🖷 01922 616387 🖰 kempsond@walsall.gov.uk

Highways: Mr Glyn Oliver, Traffic & Transportation Service Manager, Civic Centre, Darwall Street, Walsall WS1 1TP ☎ 01922 652503 🖷 01922 623234 🖰 oliverg@walsall.gov.uk

Housing: Ms Andrea Potts, Head of Housing, Civic Centre, Darwall Street, Walsall WS1 1TP ☎ 01922 653460 🖷 01922 646350 🖰 pottsandrea@walsall.gov.uk

Local Area Agreement: Mr Clive Wright, Partnership Director, Civic Centre, Darwall Street, Walsall WS1 1TP ☎ 01922 654707 🖷 01922 653373 🖰 wrightclive@walsall.gov.uk

Legal: Mr Tony Cox, Acting Assistant Director Legal & Constitutional Services, The Council House, Lichfield Street, Walsall WS1 1JX ☎ 01992 654820 🖷 01992 638267 🖰 tcox@walsall.gov.uk

Leisure and Cultural Services: Mr Chris Holliday, Head of Leisure & Culture, 12th Floor, Tameway Tower, 48 Bridge Street, Walsall WS1 1JZ ☎ 01922 650339 🖷 01922 634093 🖰 hollidayc@walsall.gov.uk

Licensing: Mr Dave Brookhouse, Licensing Officer, Civic Centre, Darwall Street, Walsall WS1 1TP ☎ 01922 653583 🖷 01922 630697

Lighting: Mr Steve Pretty, Divisional Manager - Transportation Services, Civic Centre, Darwall Street, Walsall WS1 1TP ☎ 01922 652598 🖷 01922 623234 🖰 prettys@walsall.gov.uk

Lottery Funding, Charity and Voluntary: Mr Mike Gaffney, Planning & Development Manager - Service Improvements, Civic Centre, Darwall Street, Walsall WS1 1TZ ☎ 01922 653151 🖰 gaffneym@walsall.gov.uk

Member Services: Mr Bhupinder Gill, Assistant Director - Legal & Constitutional Services, The Council House, Lichfield Street, Walsall WS1 1JZ ☎ 01922 654820 🖷 01922 638267 🖰 gillb@walsall.gov.uk

Parking: Ms Glynnis Jeavons, Car Park Manager, Civic Centre, Darwall Street, Walsall WS1 1TP ☎ 01922 652493 🖷 01922 612608 🖰 jeavonsg@walsall.gov.uk

Partnerships: Mr Clive Wright, Partnership Director, Civic Centre, Darwall Street, Walsall WS1 1TP ☎ 01922 654707 🖷 01922 653373 🖰 wrightclive@walsall.gov.uk

Personnel / HR: Mr Rory Borealis, Executive Director, Civic Centre, Darwall Street, Walsall WS1 1TP ☎ 01992 652910 🖷 01922 614210 🖰 borealisr@walsall.gov.uk

Planning: Mr David Elsworthy, Head of Planning & Building Control, Civic Centre, Darwall Street, Walsall WS1 1TP ☎ 01922 652409 🖷 01922 623234 🖰 elsworthyd@walsall.gov.uk

Procurement: Mr Lawrence Brazier, Head of Procurement, Civic Centre, Darwall Street, Walsall WS1 1TP ☎ 01922 653471 🖷 01922 653534 🖰 brazierl@walsall.gov.uk

Public Libraries: Ms Sue Grainger, Group Co-ordinator / Lifelong Learning & Community, 12th Floor, Tameway Tower, 48 Bridge Street, Walsall WS1 1JZ ☎ 01922 650338 🖷 01922 634093 🖰 graingers@walsall.gov.uk

Recycling & Waste Minimisation: Mr David Roberts, Service Manager - Waste Management - Built Environment, Norfolk Place, Bloxwich Road, Walsall WS2 7BA ☎ 01922 653957 🖷 01922 644310 🖰 robertsd@walsall.gov.uk

Regeneration: Mr Tim Johnson, Executive Director, Civic Centre, Darwall Street, Walsall WS1 1TP ☎ 01922 652431 🖷 01922 614210 🖰 johnsont@walsall.gov.uk

Regeneration: Mr Mark Lavender, Head of Strategic Regeneration, Civic Centre, Darwall Street, Walsall WS1 1TP ☎ 01922 652522 🖰 lavenderm@walsall.gov.uk

Road Safety: Mr Mark Rickard, Group Leader - Transportation Forward Planning, Civic Centre, Darwall Street, Walsall WS1 1TP ☎ 01922 652508 🖷 01922 623234 🖰 rickardm@walsall.gov.uk

Social Services: Mr Paul Davies, Executive Director - Social Care & Inclusion, Civic Centre, Darwall Street, Walsall WS1 1TP ☎ 01922 652700 🖷 01922 646350 🖰 daviesapaul@walsall.gov.uk

Social Services (Children): Mr D Bovell, Head of Adoption & Fostering, 10th Floor Tameway Tower, Bridge Street, Walsall WS1 1JZ ☎ 01922 658363 🖰 bovelld@walsall.gov.uk

Social Services (Children): Ms Pauline Pilkington, Executive Director for Children's Services, Civic Centre, Darwall Street, Walsall WS1 1TP ☎ 01922 652035 🖷 01922 614210 🖰 pilkingtonp@walsall.gov.uk

Street Scene: Mr Andy Ody, Service Manager - Grounds, Street Pride, Civic Centre, Darwall Street, Walsall WS1 1TP ☎ 01922 653715 🖷 01922 641853 🖰 odya@walsall.gov.uk

Sustainable Communities: Mr Clive Wright, Partnership Director, Civic Centre, Darwall Street, Walsall WS1 1TP ☎ 01922 654707 🖷 01922 653373 🖰 wrightclive@walsall.gov.uk

Tourism: Ms Louise Oakley, Marketing Development Manager, Civic Centre, Darwall Street, Walsall WS1 1TP ☎ 01922 650320 🖷 01922 721682 🖰 oakleyl@walsall.gov.uk

Town Centre: Mr Chris Gregory, Town Centre Manager, Civic Centre, Darwall Street, Walsall WS1 1TP ☎ 01922 652095 🖰 gregoryc@walsall.gov.uk

Traffic Management: Mr Glyn Oliver, Traffic & Transportation Service Manager, Civic Centre, Darwall Street, Walsall WS1 1TP ☎ 01922 652503 🖷 01922 623234 🖰 oliverg@walsall.gov.uk

Transport: Mr Glyn Oliver, Traffic & Transportation Service Manager, Civic Centre, Darwall Street, Walsall WS1 1TP ☎ 01922 652503 🖷 01922 623234 🖰 oliverg@walsall.gov.uk

Transport Planner: Mr Mark Clough, Strategic Transport Manager - Urban Regeneration, Civic Centre, Darwall Street, Walsall WS1 1TP ☎ 01922 653266 🖷 01922 652535 🖰 mclough@walsall.gov.uk

Waste Collection and Disposal: Mr David Roberts, Service Manager - Waste Management - Built Environment, Norfolk Place, Bloxwich Road, Walsall WS2 7BA ☎ 01922 653957 🖷 01922 644310 🖰 robertsd@walsall.gov.uk

Waste Management: Mr David Roberts, Service Manager - Waste Management - Built Environment, Norfolk Place, Bloxwich Road, Walsall WS2 7BA ☎ 01922 653957 🖷 01922 644310 🖰 robertsd@walsall.gov.uk

Children's Play Areas: Mr Graham Hood, Head of Green Spaces, 12th Floor, Tameway Tower, 48 Bridge Street, Walsall WS1 1JZ ☎ 01922 650340 🖰 hoodg@walsall.gov.uk

MEMBERS OF THE COUNCIL (60)

Mayor: **Anson**, Dennis (LAB - Pleck)
ansond@walsall.gov.uk

Deputy Mayor: **Nazir**, Mohammed (LAB - Palfrey)
nazirm@walsall.gov.uk

Leader of the Council: **Bird**, Mike (CON - Pheasey Park Farm)

birdmike@walsall.gov.uk
***Deputy Leader of the Council:* Andrew**, Adrian (CON - Pheasey Park Farm)
andrewa@walsall.gov.uk
***Group Leader:* Oliver**, Tim (LAB - Birchills Leamore)
olivert@walsall.gov.uk
***Group Leader:* Shires**, Ian (LD - Willenhall North)
shiresi@walsall.gov.uk
Ali, Zahid (CON - Paddock)
aliz@walsall.gov.uk
Andrew, Rachel (CON - Rushall Shelfield)
andrewr@walsall.gov.uk
Ansell, Tom (CON - Aldridge Central and South)
ansellt@walsall.gov.uk
Arif, Mohammed (CON - St. Matthew's)
arifm@walsall.gov.uk
Azam, Imran (CON - St. Matthew's)
azami@walsall.gov.uk
Barker, Daniel (LD - Short Heath)
barkerdaniel@walsall.gov.uk
Bennett, Oliver (CON - Pelsall)
bennetto@walsall.gov.uk
Bott, Chris (IND - Darlaston South)
bottc@walsall.gov.uk
Bott, Paul (IND - Darlaston South)
bottp@walsall.gov.uk
Burley, Rose (LAB - Bentley and Darlaston North)
burleyr@walsall.gov.uk
Cassidy, Barbara (LAB - Brownhills)
cassidyb@walsall.gov.uk
Chambers, Keith (LAB - Bentley and Darlaston North)
chambersk@walsall.gov.uk
Clarke, Gary (CON - Streetly)
clarkeg@walsall.gov.uk
Cook, John (LD - Short Heath)
cookjr@walsall.gov.uk
Coughlan, Diane (LAB - Willenhall South)
coughland@walsall.gov.uk
Coughlan, Sean (LAB - Willenhall South)
coughland@walsall.gov.uk
Creaney, Carl (LAB - Willenhall South)
creaneyc@walsall.gov.uk
Ditta, Allah (LAB - Palfrey)
dittaa@walsall.gov.uk
Douglas-Maul, Brian (CON - Streetly)
douglas-maulb@walsall.gov.uk
Fitzpatrick, Shaun Francis (LAB - Bloxwich East)
fitzpatricks@walsall.gov.uk
Fitzpatrick, Julie (LAB - Bloxwich East)
fitzpatrickj@walsall.gov.uk
Fletcher-Hall, Sue Ann (LAB - Bloxwich West)
fletcher-halls@walsall.gov.uk
Flower, Michael (CON - Aldridge North and Walsall Wood)
flowermd@walsall.gov.uk
Harris, Anthony (CON - Aldridge North and Walsall Wood)
harrisanthony@walsall.gov.uk
Harrison, Louise (CON - Bloxwich West)
harrisonl@walsall.gov.uk
Hughes, Eddie (CON - Streetly)
hughese@walsall.gov.uk
Hussain, Khizar (LAB - Pleck)
hussainkhizar@walsall.gov.uk
Illmann-Walker, Gareth (LAB - Willenhall North)
gareth@walsall-labour.org.uk
James, Douglas (LAB - Darlaston South)
jamesdouglas@walsall.gov.uk
Jeavons, Lee (LAB - Birchills Leamore)
jeavonsl@walsall.gov.uk
Jukes, Tina (LAB - Birchills Leamore)
Longhi, Marco (CON - Pelsall)
longhim@walsall.gov.uk
Martin, Rose (CON - Paddock)
martinr@walsall.gov.uk
McCracken, Barbara (CON - Paddock)
mccrackenb@walsall.gov.uk
Murray, John (CON - Aldridge Central and South)
murrayjohn@walsall.gov.uk
Perry, Garry (CON - Pelsall)
perryg@walsall.gov.uk
Phillips, Kath (LAB - Bloxwich East)
phillipskath@walsall.gov.uk
Rattigan, Lorna (CON - Rushall Shelfield)
rattiganl@walsall.gov.uk
Rochelle, John (CON - Aldridge Central and South)
rochellejohn@walsall.gov.uk
Russell, Eileen (LAB - St. Mathew's)
russelle@walsall.gov.uk
Sarohi, Harbans (LAB - Pleck)
sarohih@walsall.gov.uk
Sears, Keith (CON - Aldridge North and Walsall Wood)
searsk@walsall.gov.uk
Shires, Doreen (LD - Short Heath)
shiresd@walsall.gov.uk
Smith, Pete (LAB - Blakenall)
smithpe@walsall.gov.uk
Thomas, Bob (LAB - Blakenall)
thomasbob@walsall.gov.uk
Towe, Christopher (CON - Pheasey Park Farm)
towec@walsall.gov.uk
Turner, David (CON - Brownhills)
turnerd@walsall.gov.uk
Underhill, Angela (LAB - Bentley and Darlaston North)
underhilla@walsall.gov.uk
Wade, Stephen (LAB - Brownhills)
wades@walsall.gov.uk
Westley, Fred (LAB - Bloxwich West)
westleyfj@walsall.gov.uk
Whyte, Victoria (LAB - Palfrey)
whytev@walsall.gov.uk
Woodruff, Val (LD - Willenhall North)
woodruffv@walsall.gov.uk
Worrall, Richard (LAB - Rushall-Shelfield)
worrallrv@walsall.gov.uk
Young, Ann (LAB - Blakenall)
youngann@walsall.gov.uk

POLITICAL COMPOSITION

LAB: 29, CON: 24, LD: 5, IND: 2

CABINET

Business Support Services: Mr Mohammed Arif
Children's Services: Ms Rachel Andrew
Community Engagement & Voluntary Sector: Mr Ian Shires
Finance & Personnel: Mr Christopher Towe
Leisure & Culture: Mr Anthony Harris
Public Protection: Mr Zahid Ali
Regeneration: Mr Adrian Andrew
Social Care & Health: Ms Barbara McCracken

COMMITTEE CHAIRS

Audit: Mr Eddie Hughes
Children & Young People (Scrutiny): Ms Barbara Cassidy
Health (Scrutiny): Mr Marco Longhi
Licensing & Safety: Mr Keith Sears
Planning: Mr Garry Perry

WALTHAM FOREST L

Waltham Forest London Borough Council, (London Borough of Waltham Forest), Town Hall, Forest Road, London E17 4JF ☎ 020 8496 3000 🖷 020 8527 8313 wfdirect@walthamforest.gov.uk www.walthamforest.gov.uk

FACTS & FIGURES

Police Authority: Metropolitan Police Authority
Health Authority: NHS London
Learning and Skills Council: London
Parliamentary Constituencies: Chingford and Woodford, Leyton and Wanstead, Walthamstow
EU Constituencies: London
Election Frequency: Elections are of whole council
Twinning: Antigua-Barbuda and Dominica (Caribbean); Wandsbek (Germany)

PRINCIPAL OFFICERS

Chief Executive: Mr Martin Esom, Chief Executive, Town Hall, Forest Road, London E17 4JF ☎ 020 8496 3000 🖷 020 8496 6244 martin.esom@walthamforest.gov.uk

Senior Management: Ms Moira Bishop, Assistant Director of Property & Major Projects, Town Hall, Forest Road, London E17 4JF ☎ 020 8496 3535 moira.bishop@walthamforest.gov.uk

Senior Management: Mr Paul Langford, Director of Housing and Safe & Strong Communities, Cedar Wood House, Forest Road, London E17 4GG ☎ 020 8496 5400 🖷 020 8496 5554 paul.langford@walthamforest.gov.uk

Senior Management: Ms Althea Loderick, Director of Human Resources & Organisational Development, Town Hall, Forest Road, London E17 4JF ☎ 020 8496 4202 althea.loderick@walthamforest.gov.uk

Senior Management: Ms Michele Moloney, Assistant Direc tor of Residents First, Town Hall, Forest Road, London E17 4JF ☎ 020 8496 4720 🖷 020 8496 4504 michele.moloney@walthamforest.gov.uk

Senior Management: Ms Shifa Mustafa, Executive Director of Environment & Regeneration, Sycamore House, Waltham Forest Town Hall, Forest Road, London E17 4JF ☎ 020 8496 6825 🖷 020 8496 6901 shifa.mustafa@walthamforest.gov.uk

Access Officer / Social Services (Disability): Ms Sheenagh Burgess, Head of Learning Disability Partnership, 47 Gainsford Road, London E17 6QB ☎ 020 8496 1832 sheenagh.burgess@walthamforest.gov.uk

Architect, Building / Property Services: Mr Paul Humphreys, Head of Corporate Asset Management, Town Hall, Forest Road, London E17 4JF ☎ 020 8496 8079 paul.humphreys@walthamforest.gov.uk

Building Control: Mr Julian Ruaux, Head of Building Control, Sycamore House, Waltham Forest Town Hall, Forest Road, London E17 4JF ☎ 020 8496 6770 🖷 020 8496 6122 julian.ruaux@walthamforest.gov.uk

Catering Services: Ms Linda Woods, Head of Catering Services, Silver Birch House, Blackhorse Lane, London E17 5SD ☎ 020 8496 8271 🖷 020 8496 4412

Children / Youth Services: Ms Denise Humphrey, Group Manager - Youth Support Service, Outset Centre, 1a Grange Road, London E17 8AH ☎ 020 8496 1530 🖷 020 8496 1536 denise.humphrey@walthamforest.gov.uk

Community Safety: Mr Paul Langford, Director of Housing and Safe & Strong Communities, Sycamore House, Waltham Forest Town Hall, Forest Road, London E17 4JF ☎ 020 8496 5400 🖷 020 8496 5554 paul.langford@walthamforest.gov.uk

Computer Management: Mr Graham Bell, Head of ICT, Silver Birch House, Blackhorse Lane, London E17 5SN ☎ 020 8496 3629 🖷 020 8496 4657 graham.bell@walthamforest.gov.uk

Consumer Protection and Trading Standards: Mr Keith Hanshaw, Director of Public Realm, Low Hall Depot, Argall Avenue, London E10 7AS ☎ 020 8496 2510 🖷 020 8496 2512 keith.hanshaw@walthamforest.gov.uk

Contracts: Mr David Levy, Assistant Director - Procurement & Commissioning, Town Hall, Forest Road, London E17 4JF ☎ 020 8496 4413 🖷 020 8257 8313 david.levy@walthamforest.gov.uk

Customer Service: Ms Sally Hodgson, Customer Services Manager, Town Hall, Forest Road, London E17 4JF ☎ 020 8496 3305 sally.hogdson@walthamforest.gov.uk

Customer Service: Ms Michele Moloney, Assistant Direc tor of Residents First, Town Hall, Forest Road, London E17 4JF ☎ 020 8496 4720 🖷 020 8496 4504 michele.moloney@walthamforest.gov.uk

E-Government: Mr Graham Bell, Head of ICT, Silver Birch House, Blackhorse Lane, London E17 5SN ☎ 020 8496 3629 🖷 020 8496 4657 graham.bell@walthamforest.gov.uk

Electoral Registration: Mr Peter Bailey, Head of Democratic Services, Town Hall, Forest Road, London E17 4JF ☎ 020 8496 4204 🖷 020 8523 5377 peter.bailey@walthamforest.gov.uk

Emergency Planning: Mr Ron Presswell, Urban Design Programme Manager, Sycamore House, Waltham Forest Town Hall Complex, Forest Road, London E17 4JF ☎ 020 8496 6736 ron.presswell@walthamforest.gov.uk

Energy Management: Mr Alan King, Energy Manager, Town Hall, Forest Road, London E17 4JF ☎ 020 8496 4803 alan.king@walthamforest.gov.uk

Environmental / Technical Services: Mr Keith Hanshaw, Director of Public Realm, Sycamore House, Uplands Business

Park, Blackhorse Lane, London E17 4JF ☎ 020 8496 2510 🖷 020 8496 2512 ✉ keith.hanshaw@walthamforest.gov.uk

Environmental / Technical Services: Ms Shifa Mustafa, Executive Director of Environment & Regeneration, Sycamore House, Waltham Forest Town Hall, Forest Road, London E17 4JF ☎ 020 8496 6825 🖷 020 8496 6901 ✉ shifa.mustafa@walthamforest.gov.uk

Environmental Health: Mr Keith Hanshaw, Director of Public Realm, Sycamore House, Uplands Business Park, Blackhorse Lane, London E17 4JF ☎ 020 8496 2510 🖷 020 8496 2512 ✉ keith.hanshaw@walthamforest.gov.uk

Estates, Property & Valuation: Ms Moira Bishop, Assistant Director of Property & Major Projects, Town Hall, Forest Road, London E17 4JF ☎ 020 8496 3535 ✉ moira.bishop@walthamforest.gov.uk

Events Manager: Mr Glen Watson, Principal Festivals Officer, Silver Birch House, Blackhorse Lane, London E17 5SN ☎ 020 8496 3586 ✉ glen.watson@walthamforest.gov.uk

Facilities: Ms Moira Bishop, Assistant Director of Property & Major Projects, Town Hall, Forest Road, London E17 4JF ☎ 020 8496 3535 ✉ moira.bishop@walthamforest.gov.uk

Finance and Treasurer: Mr John Turnball, Director of Finance, Town Hall, Forest Road, London E17 4JF ☎ 020 8496 4260 ✉ john.turnball@walthamforest.gov.uk

Fleet Management: Mr Keith Hanshaw, Director of Public Realm, Sycamore House, Uplands Business Park, Blackhorse Lane, London E17 4JF ☎ 020 8496 2510 🖷 020 8496 2512 ✉ keith.hanshaw@walthamforest.gov.uk

Grounds Maintenance: Mr Chris Moran, Service Development Manager, Low Hall Manor Business Centre, 30 South Access Road, London E17 8BS ☎ 020 8496 2633 ✉ chris.moran@walthamforest.gov.uk

Health and Safety: Mrs Shila Agnew, Health & Safety Manager, Silver Birch House, Blackhorse Lane, London E17 5SD ☎ 020 8496 3413 🖷 020 8496 4640 ✉ shila.agnew@walthamforest.gov.uk

Highways: Mr Keith Hanshaw, Director of Public Realm, Sycamore House, Uplands Business Park, Blackhorse Lane, London E17 4JF ☎ 020 8496 2510 🖷 020 8496 2512 ✉ keith.hanshaw@walthamforest.gov.uk

Highways: Mr Kathiraval Valavan, Head of Highways, Low Hall, Argall Avenue, London E10 7AS ☎ 020 8496 2525 ✉ velu.valavan@walthamforest.gov.uk

Home Energy Conservation: Mr Alan King, Energy Manager, Municipal Offices, 16 The Ridgeway, Chingford, London E4 6PS ☎ 020 8496 4803 ✉ alan.king@walthamforest.gov.uk

Housing: Mr Paul Langford, Director of Housing and Safe & Strong Communities, Cedar Wood House, Forest Road, London E17 4GG ☎ 020 8496 5400 🖷 020 8496 5554 ✉ paul.langford@walthamforest.gov.uk

Housing Maintenance: Mr Paul Langford, Director of Housing and Safe & Strong Communities, Cedar Wood House, Forest Road, London E17 4GG ☎ 020 8496 5400 🖷 020 8496 5554 ✉ paul.langford@walthamforest.gov.uk

Licensing: Mr Gavin Douglas, Head of Environmental Health & Trading Standards, Sycamore House, Waltham Forest Town Hall Complex, Forest Road, London E17 4JF ☎ 020 8496 2201 🖷 020 8496 6904 ✉ paul.langford@walthamforest.gov.uk

Lifelong Learning: Mr Harry Clibbens, Head of Community & Mental Health Commissioning, Silver Birch House, Upplands Business Park, Black Horse Lane, Waltham Forest, London E17 5SD ☎ 020 8496 3430 🖷 020 8496 3665 ✉ harry.clibbens@walthamforest.gov.uk

Lighting: Mr Keith Hanshaw, Director of Public Realm, Sycamore House, Uplands Business Park, Blackhorse Lane, London E17 4JF ☎ 020 8496 2510 🖷 020 8496 2512 ✉ keith.hanshaw@walthamforest.gov.uk

Lighting: Mr Chris Warner, Planned Maintenance & Public Lighting Manager, Low Hall, Argall Avenue, London E10 7AS ☎ 020 8496 2515 🖷 020 8496 2513 ✉ chris.warner@walthamforest.gov.uk

Lottery Funding, Charity and Voluntary: Ms Claire Witney, Community Engagement Manager, Town Hall, Forest Road, London E17 4JF ☎ 020 8496 4613 ✉ Claire.Witney@walthamforest.gov.uk

Member Services: Mr Peter Bailey, Head of Democratic Services, Town Hall, Forest Road, London E17 4JF ☎ 020 8496 4204 🖷 020 8523 5377 ✉ peter.bailey@walthamforest.gov.uk

Parking: Ms Karen Naylor, Parking Services Manager, Low Hall Depot, Argall Avenue, London E10 7AS ✉ Karen.naylor@walthamforest.gov.uk

Partnerships: Mr Paul Langford, Director of Housing and Safe & Strong Communities, Sycamore House, Waltham Forest Town Hall, Forest Road, London E17 4JF ☎ 020 8496 5400 🖷 020 8496 5554 ✉ paul.langford@walthamforest.gov.uk

Partnerships: Mr Alastair Macorkindale, Head of Community Safety, Cedar Wood House, Fulbourne Road, Walthamstow, London E17 4GG ☎ 020 8496 6827 ✉ alastair.macorkindale@walthamforest.gov.uk

Personnel / HR: Mr Stuart Petrie, Senior HR Business Partner, Silver Birch House, Uplands Business Park, Blackhorse Lane, Walthamstow, London E17 5SD ☎ 020 8496 3405 ✉ stuart.petrie@walthamforest.gov.uk

Planning: Ms Shifa Mustafa, Executive Director of Environment & Regeneration, Sycamore House, Waltham Forest Town Hall, Forest Road, London E17 4JF ☎ 020 8496 6825 🖷 020 8496 6901 ✉ shifa.mustafa@walthamforest.gov.uk

Procurement: Mr David Levy, Assistant Director - Procurement & Commissioning, Town Hall, Forest Road, London E17 4JF ☎ 020 8496 4413 🖷 020 8257 8313

david.levy@walthamforest.gov.uk

Public Libraries: Ms Lorna Lee, Head of Residents First Development Unit, Silverbirch House, Uplands Business Park, Blackhorse Lane, Walthamstow, London E17 5SN ☎ 020 8496 3203 lorna.lee@walthamforest.gov.uk

Recycling & Waste Minimisation: Mr Keith Hanshaw, Director of Public Realm, Sycamore House, Uplands Business Park, Blackhorse Lane, London E17 4JF ☎ 020 8496 2510 🖷 020 8496 2512 keith.hanshaw@walthamforest.gov.uk

Regeneration: Ms Shifa Mustafa, Executive Director of Environment & Regeneration, Sycamore House, Waltham Forest Town Hall, Forest Road, London E17 4JF ☎ 020 8496 6825 🖷 020 8496 6901 shifa.mustafa@walthamforest.gov.uk

Road Safety: Ms Safiah Ishfaq, Road Safety Section Manager, Low Hall Depot, Argall Avenue, London E10 7AS ☎ 020 8496 2599 safiah.ishfaq@walthamforest.gov.uk

Social Services: Mr Alan Adams, Interim Executive Director - CYPS, Silver Birch House, Blackhorse Lane, London E17 5SN ☎ 020 8496 3503 🖷 020 8496 3656 alan.adams@walthamforest.gov.uk

Social Services: Ms Linda Cointepas, Deputy Director of Children & Young People Services, Silver Birch House, Blakhorse Lane, Walthamstow, London E17 5SN ☎ 020 8496 3206 linda.cointepas@walthamforest.gov.uk

Social Services (Adult): Ms Claudia Thompson, Head of Assessment & Care, Silver Birch House, Blackhorse Lane, London E17 5SD ☎ 020 8496 3460 claudia.thompson@walthamforest.gov.uk

Social Services (Children): Ms Denise Humphrey, Group Manager - Youth Support Service, Town Hall, Forest Road, London E17 4JF ☎ 020 8496 1530 🖷 020 8496 1536 denise.humphrey@walthamforest.gov.uk

Staff Training: Mr Graeme Rawlings, Learning & Development Manager, Town Hall, Forest Road, London E17 4JF ☎ 020 8496 4419 graeme.rawlings@walthamforest.gov.uk

Street Scene: Mr Keith Hanshaw, Director of Public Realm, Sycamore House, Uplands Business Park, Blackhorse Lane, London E17 4JF ☎ 020 8496 2510 🖷 020 8496 2512 keith.hanshaw@walthamforest.gov.uk

Sustainable Communities: Mr Paul Langford, Director of Housing and Safe & Strong Communities, Sycamore House, Waltham Forest Town Hall, Forest Road, London E17 4JF ☎ 020 8496 5400 🖷 020 8496 5554 paul.langford@walthamforest.gov.uk

Tourism: Mr Eamonn O'Machail, Arts & Tourism Group Manager, Silver Birch House, Uplands Business Park, Blackhorse Lane, Walthamstow, London E17 5SN ☎ 020 8496 3582 🖷 020 8496 4640 eamonn.omachail@walthamforest.gov.uk

Traffic Management: Mr Keith Hanshaw, Director of Public Realm, Sycamore House, Uplands Business Park, Blackhorse Lane, London E17 4JF ☎ 020 8496 2510 🖷 020 8496 2512 keith.hanshaw@walthamforest.gov.uk

Transport: Mr Kathiraval Valavan, Head of Highways, Low Hall, Argall Avenue, London E10 7AS ☎ 020 8496 2525 velu.valavan@walthamforest.gov.uk

Transport Planner: Mr Neil Bullen, Programme Manager Transport Planning, Sycamore House, Town Hall, Forest Road, London E17 4JF ☎ 020 8496 6779 neil.bullen@walthamforest.gov.uk

Waste Collection and Disposal: Mr Keith Hanshaw, Director of Public Realm, Sycamore House, Uplands Business Park, Blackhorse Lane, London E17 4JF ☎ 020 8496 2510 🖷 020 8496 2512 keith.hanshaw@walthamforest.gov.uk

Waste Management: Mr Keith Hanshaw, Director of Public Realm, Sycamore House, Uplands Business Park, Blackhorse Lane, London E17 4JF ☎ 020 8496 2510 🖷 020 8496 2512 keith.hanshaw@walthamforest.gov.uk

Children's Play Areas: Ms Margaret Burke, Group Manager Extended Services, Silver Birch House, Uplands Business Park, Blackhorse Lane, Walthamstow, London E17 5SD ☎ 020 8496 3557 🖷 020 8496 3599 Margaret.burke@walthamforest.gov.uk

MEMBERS OF THE COUNCIL (60)

***Mayor:* Sweden**, Richard (LAB - Wood Street)
cllr.richard.sweden@walthamforest.gov.uk

***Deputy Mayor:* Ali**, Nadeem (LAB - William Morris)
cllr.nadeem.ali@walthamforest.gov.uk

***Leader of the Council:* Robbins**, Chris (LAB - Grove Green)
leader@walthamforest.gov.uk

***Deputy Leader of the Council:* Loakes**, Clyde (LAB - Leytonstone)
cllr.clyde.loakes@walthamforest.gov.uk

***Group Leader:* Davis**, Matt (CON - Endlebury)
cllr.matt.davies@walthamforest.gov.uk

***Group Leader:* Sullivan**, Robert (LD - Leyton)
cllr.bob.sullivan@walthamforest.gov.uk

Ahmad, Masood (LAB - Lea Bridge)
cllr.masood.ahmad@walthamforest.gov.uk

Akram, Afzal (LAB - Lea Bridge)
cllr.afzal.akram@walthamforest.gov.uk

Ali, Liaquat (LAB - High Street)
cllr.liaquat.ali@walthamforest.gov.uk

Anwar, Raja (LAB - William Morris)
cllr.raja.anwar@walthamforest.gov.uk

Asghar, Naheed (LAB - Cathall)
cllr.naheed.asghar@walthamforest.gov.uk

Asghar, Mohammad (LAB - Markhouse)
cllr.mohammad.asghar@walthamforest.gov.uk

Barnett, Peter (LAB - Wood Street)
cllr.peter.barnett@walthamforest.gov.uk

Bean, Angie (LAB - Wood Street)
cllr.angie.bean@walthamforest.gov.uk

Bellamy, Karen (LAB - Higham Hill)
cllr.karen.bellamy@walthamforest.gov.uk

Berg, Roy (CON - Endlebury)
cllr.roy.berg@walthamforest.gov.uk

Braham, Laurie (CON - Hatch Lane)
zc42@btconnect.com

Braham, Paul (CON - Hale End and Highams Park)
cllr.paul.braham@walthamforest.gov.uk
Buckmaster, Nick (CON - Larkswood)
cllr.nick.buckmaster@walthamforest.gov.uk
Coghill, Clare (LAB - High Street)
cllr.clare.coghill@walthamforest.gov.uk
Davies, Tunde (LAB - Cann Hall)
cllr.tunde.davies@walthamforest.gov.uk
Davies, Elisabeth (LAB - Lea Bridge)
cllr.elisabeth.davies@walthamforest.gov.uk
Douglas, Paul (LAB - Chapel End)
cllr.paul.douglas@walthamforest.gov.uk
Falconer, Kieran (LAB - Chapel End)
cllr.kieran.falconer@walthamforest.gov.uk
Fitzgerald, Marion (CON - Hatch Lane)
cllr.marion.fitzgerald@walthamforest.gov.uk
Goddard, Thom (CON - Chingford Green)
cllr.thom.goddard@walthamforest.gov.uk
Gray, Jenny (LAB - Leytonstone)
cllr.jenny.gray@walthamforest.gov.uk
Hammond, Geoff (LAB - Higham Hill)
cllr.geoff.hammond@walthamforest.gov.uk
Hemsted, Andy (CON - Chingford Green)
Andyhemsted1066@gmail.com
Hemsted, Jemma (CON - Valley)
cllr.jemma.hemsted@walthamforest.gov.uk
Herrington, Peter (CON - Endlebury)
cllr.peter.herrington@walthamforest.gov.uk
Highfield, Shameem (LAB - Cathall)
cllr.shameen.highfield@walthamforest.gov.uk
Hussain, Mahmood (LD - High Street)
cllr.mahmood.hussain@walthamforest.gov.uk
Khan, Ahsan (LAB - Hoe Street)
cllr.ahsan.khan@walthamforest.gov.uk
Khan, Haroon (LAB - Higham Hill)
cllr.haroon.khan@walthamforest.gov.uk
Lewis, Michael (CON - Chingford Green)
cllr.michael.lewis@walthamforest.gov.uk
Limbajee, Khevyn (LAB - Grove Green)
cllr.khevyn.limbajee@walthamforest.gov.uk
Lyons, Gerry (LAB - Forest)
cllr.gerry.lyons@walthamforest.gov.uk
Mahmood, Asim (LAB - Markhouse)
cllr.asim.mahmood@walthamforest.gov.uk
Mahmud, Saima (LAB - Hoe Street)
cllr.saima.mahmud@walthamforest.gov.uk
Mbachu, Anna (LAB - Grove Green)
cllr.anna.mbachu@walthamforest.gov.uk
Mill, Bernadette (CON - Larkswood)
cllr.bernadette.mill@walthamforest.gov.uk
Moss, John (CON - Larkswood)
cllr.john.jc.moss@walthamforest.gov.uk
Phillips, Elizabeth (LD - Cann Hall)
cllr.liz.phillips@walthamforest.gov.uk
Pye, Marie (LAB - Leytonstone)
cllr.marie.pye@walthamforest.gov.uk
Qadir, Shabana (LAB - Forest)
cllr.shabana.qadir@walthamforest.gov.uk
Qureshi, Farooq (LD - Forest)
cllr.farooq.qureshi@walthamforest.gov.uk
Qureshi, Naheed (LD - Leyton)
cllr.naheed.qureshi@walthamforest.gov.uk
Rackham, Sheree (CON - Hale End and Highams Park)
cllr.sheree.rackham@walthamforest.gov.uk
Reardon, Geraldine (LAB - William Morris)
cllr.geraldine.reardon@walthamforest.gov.uk
Rusling, Mark (LAB - Hoe Street)
cllr.mark.rusling@walthamforest.gov.uk
Russell, Nicholas (LAB - Cann Hall)
cllr.nicholas.russell@walthamforest.gov.uk
Samih, Abu (LAB - Chapel End)
cllr.abu.samih@walthamforest.gov.uk
Siggers, Alan (CON - Valley)
Smith, Winnifred (LD - Leyton)
cllr.winnie.smith@walthamforest.gov.uk
Sunger, Darshan (CON - Hale End and Highams Park)
Cllr.Sunger@instantemail.t-mobile.co.uk
Vincent, Ebony (LAB - Markhouse)
ebonyav@hotmail.com
Walker, Geoffrey (CON - Hatch Lane)
cllr.geoff.walker@ntlworld.com
Wedderburn, Laurance (CON - Valley)
cllr.laurance.wedderburn@walthamforest.gov.uk
Wheeler, Terry (LAB - Cathall)
cllr.terry.wheeler@walthamforest.gov.uk

POLITICAL COMPOSITION

LAB: 36, CON: 18, LD: 6

CABINET

Leader: Mr Chris Robbins
Adult Services: Ms Angie Bean
Children & Young People: Ms Clare Coghill
Community Safety & Cohesion: Mr Liaquat Ali
Corporate Resources & Economic Development: Mr Mark Rusling
Environment: Mr Clyde Loakes
Health & Wellbeing: Mr Ahsan Khan
Housing: Ms Marie Pye

COMMITTEE CHAIRS

Audit & Governance: Mr Paul Douglas
Licensing: Mr Kieran Falconer
Overview & Scrutiny Management: Mr Peter Herrington
Pension Fund: Mr Nick Buckmaster
Planning Committee: Mr Peter Barnett

WANDSWORTH L

Wandsworth London Borough Council, Town Hall, Wandsworth High Street, London SW18 2PU ☎ 020 8871 6000
🖳 www.wandsworth.gov.uk

FACTS & FIGURES

Police Authority: Metropolitan Police Authority
Health Authority: NHS London
Learning and Skills Council: London
Parliamentary Constituencies: Battersea, Putney, Tooting
EU Constituencies: London
Election Frequency: Elections are of whole council

PRINCIPAL OFFICERS

Chief Executive: Mr Paul Martin, Chief Executive & Director of Administration, Town Hall, Wandsworth High Street, London SW18 2PU ☎ 020 8871 6001 🖷 020 8871 8181
pmartin@wandsworth.gov.uk

Deputy Chief Executive: Mr Chris Buss, Director of Finance &

Deputy Chief Executive, Town Hall, Wandsworth High Street, London SW18 2PU ☎ 020 8871 8300 🖷 020 8877 1915 🖰 cbuss@wandsworth.gov.uk

Access Officer / Social Services (Disability): Toni Symonds, Access Team Manager, 2nd Floor, Bridas House, Putney Bridge Road, London SW18 1HR ☎ 020 8871 8811 🖷 020 8871 6949 🖰 tsymonds@wandsworth.gov.uk

Architect, Building / Property Services: Mr John Cornish, Head of Design Service, Reed House, Frogmore Complex, Dormay Street, London SW18 1EY ☎ 020 8871 6564 🖷 020 8871 7563 🖰 jcornish@wandsworth.gov.uk

Best Value: Mr Jon Evans, Interim Head of Policy, Town Hall, Wandsworth High Street, London SW18 2PU ☎ 020 8871 7815 🖷 020 8871 8181 🖰 jevans@wandsworth.gov.uk

Building Control: Mr Robert Foulgar, Head of Building Control (Acting), Town Hall, Wandsworth High Street, London SW18 2PU ☎ 020 8871 7616 🖷 020 8871 6003 🖰 rfoulgar@wandsworth.gov.uk

Building Control: Mr B Glocking, Head of Building & Development, Town Hall, Wandsworth High Street, London SW18 2PU ☎ 020 8871 8311 🖰 bglocking@wandsworth.gov.uk

Catering Services: Mr John Dutton, Head of Facilities Management, Room 33, Wandsworth Town Hall, Wandsworth High Street, London SW18 2PU ☎ 020 8871 7645 🖷 020 8871 7798 🖰 jdutton@wandsworth.gov.uk

Children / Youth Services: Mr Paul Robinson, Director of Children's Services, Town Hall, Wandsworth High Street, London SW18 2PU ☎ 020 8871 7890 🖷 020 8871 6609 🖰 probinson@wandsworth.gov.uk

Civil Registration: Mr Patrick Watson, Assistant Director of Administration, Town Hall, Wandsworth High Street, London SW18 2PU ☎ 020 8871 6026 🖷 020 8871 8181 🖰 pwatson@wandsworth.gov.uk

PR / Communications: Mr Simon Jones, Head of Communications, Town Hall, Wandsworth High Street, London SW18 2PU ☎ 020 8871 5289 🖷 020 8871 8444 🖰 sjones@wandworth.gov.uk

Community Planning: Mr Jon Evans, Interim Head of Policy, Town Hall, Wandsworth High Street, London SW18 2PU ☎ 020 8871 7815 🖷 020 8871 8181 🖰 jevans@wandsworth.gov.uk

Community Safety: Mr Stewart Low, Head of Community Safety, Tadmore House, Frogmore Complex, Dormay Street, London SW18 1EY ☎ 020 8871 6588 🖷 020 8871 6537 🖰 slow@wandsworth.gov.uk

Computer Management: Mr D Tidey, Head of IT & Business Communications, Town Hall, Wandsworth High Street, London SW18 2PU ☎ 020 8871 6080 🖷 020 8871 8650 🖰 dtidey@wandsworth.gov.uk

Consumer Protection and Trading Standards: Mr Chris Roe, Chief Trading Standards Officer, Tadmore House, Frogmore Complex, Dormay Street, London SW18 1EY ☎ 020 8871 6177 🖷 020 8871 6965 🖰 croe@wandsworth.gov.uk

Contracts: Mr Mark Glaister, Head of Procurement, Town Hall, Wandsworth High Street, London SW18 2PU ☎ 020 8871 5828 🖷 020 8871 6777 🖰 mglaister@wandsworth.gov.uk

Corporate Services: Mr S Mayner, Assistant Director of Administration, Town Hall, Wandsworth High Street, London SW18 2PU ☎ 020 8871 7524 🖰 smayner@wandsworth.gov.uk

Corporate Services: Mr Patrick Watson, Assistant Director of Administration, Town Hall, Wandsworth High Street, London SW18 2PU ☎ 020 8871 6026 🖷 020 8871 8181 🖰 pwatson@wandsworth.gov.uk

Customer Service: Mr D Tidey, Head of IT & Business Communications, Town Hall, Wandsworth High Street, London SW18 2PU ☎ 020 8871 6080 🖷 020 8871 8650 🖰 dtidey@wandsworth.gov.uk

Direct Labour: Mr Kevin Power, Assistant Director of Operational Services, Town Hall, Wandsworth High Street, London SW18 2PU ☎ 020 8871 6704 🖷 020 8871 7562 🖰 kpower@wandsworth.gov.uk

Economic Development: Mr Nick Smales, Economic Development Officer, Town Hall, Wandsworth High Street, London SW18 2PU ☎ 020 8871 6202 🖷 020 8871 8200 🖰 nsmales@wandsworth.gov.uk

Education: Mr Mike Benaim, Assistant Director of Children's Specialist Services, Town Hall, Wandsworth High Street, London SW18 2PU ☎ 020 8871 8177 🖷 020 8871 6609 🖰 mbenaim@wandsworth.gov.uk

Education: Mr John Johnson, Assistant Director of Standards & Schools, Town Hall, Wandsworth High Street, London SW18 2PU ☎ 020 8871 7891 🖷 020 8871 6609 🖰 jjohnson@wandsworth.gov.uk

E-Government: Mr D Tidey, Head of IT & Business Communications, Town Hall, Wandsworth High Street, London SW18 2PU ☎ 020 8871 6080 🖷 020 8871 8650 🖰 dtidey@wandsworth.gov.uk

Electoral Registration: Mr Patrick Watson, Assistant Director of Administration, Town Hall, Wandsworth High Street, London SW18 2PU ☎ 020 8871 6026 🖷 020 8871 8181 🖰 pwatson@wandsworth.gov.uk

Emergency Planning: Mr Ed Checkley, Emergency Planning Manager, 1st Floor, Frogmore House, Dormay Street, Wandsworth, London SW18 1HA ☎ 020 8871 5737 🖷 020 8871 5799 🖰 echeckley@wandsworth.gov.uk

Energy Management: Mr John Cornish, Head of Design Service, Reed House, Frogmore Complex, Dormay Street, London SW18 1EY ☎ 020 8871 6564 🖷 020 8871 7563 🖰 jcornish@wandsworth.gov.uk

Environmental / Technical Services: Mr Tony McDonald, Director of Environment & Community Services, Town Hall, Wandsworth High Street, London SW18 2PU ☎ 020 8871 6353 🖷 020 8871 8349 ✉ amcdonald@wandsworth.gov.uk

Environmental Health: Ms Seema Manchanda, Assistant Director of Planning & Environment Services, Town Hall Extension, Wandsworth High Street, London SW18 2PU ☎ 020 8871 6626 🖷 020 8871 7809 ✉ smanchanda@wandsworth.gov.uk

Estates, Property & Valuation: Mr Geoff Clark, Borough Valuer, Town Hall, Wandsworth High Street, London SW18 2PU ☎ 020 8871 6074 🖷 020 8871 6185 ✉ gclark@wandsworth.gov.uk

European Liaison: Mr Nick Smales, Economic Development Officer, Town Hall, Wandsworth High Street, London SW18 2PU ☎ 020 8871 6202 🖷 020 8871 8200 ✉ nsmales@wandsworth.gov.uk

Events Manager: Mr Jack Adam, Security, Arts, Events, Filming, Public Halls & Community Centres, Battersea Park, London SW11 4NJ ☎ 020 8871 7636 🖷 020 7223 7919 ✉ jadam@wandsworth.gov.uk

Facilities: Mr John Dutton, Head of Facilities Management, Town Hall, Wandsworth High Street, London SW18 2PU ☎ 020 8871 7645 🖷 020 8871 7798 ✉ jdutton@wandsworth.gov.uk

Finance and Treasurer: Mr Chris Buss, Director of Finance & Deputy Chief Executive, Town Hall, Wandsworth High Street, London SW18 2PU ☎ 020 8871 8300 🖷 020 8877 1915 ✉ cbuss@wandsworth.gov.uk

Fleet Management: Mr Ricky Cousins, Contract Transport & Mechanical Workshops, Mechanical Workshops, Frogmore Complex, Dormay Street, London SW18 1EY ☎ 020 8871 6762 🖷 020 8871 8656 ✉ rcousins@wandsworth.gov.uk

Grounds Maintenance: Mr Simon Cooper-Grundy, Head of Parks, Town Hall, Wandsworth High Street, London SW18 2PU ☎ 020 8871 8117 🖷 020 8871 7533 ✉ scooper-grundy@wandsworth.gov.uk

Health and Safety: Mr Shervin Nejand, Health & Safety Manager, Town Hall, Wandsworth High Street, London SW18 2PU ☎ 020 8871 8501 🖷 020 8871 8502 ✉ snejand@wandsworth.gov.uk

Highways: Mr Robert Langridge, Assistant Director of Engineering & Design Services, Town Hall Extension, Wandsworth High Street, London SW18 2PU ☎ 020 8871 6970 🖷 020 8871 7809 ✉ rlangridge@wandsworth.gov.uk

Housing: Mr Roy Evans, Director of Housing, 17/27 Garratt Lane, London SW18 4AE ☎ 020 8871 6780 🖷 020 8871 6778 ✉ housingdirectorate@wandsworth.gov.uk

Housing: Mr Brian Reilly, Deputy Director of Housing, Housing Department, 17-27 Garratt Lane, London SW18 4AE ☎ 020 8871 6591 🖷 020 8871 6778 ✉ housingdirectorate@wandsworth.gov.uk

Local Area Agreement: Mr Jon Evans, Interim Head of Policy, Town Hall, Wandsworth High Street, London SW18 2PU ☎ 020 8871 7815 🖷 020 8871 8181 ✉ jevans@wandsworth.gov.uk

Legal: Mr Martin Walker, Borough Solicitor, Town Hall, Wandsworth High Street, London SW18 2PU ☎ 020 8871 6110 🖷 020 8871 7506 ✉ mwalker@wandsworth.gov.uk

Licensing: Mrs Marie Whitbread, Assistant Head of Environmental Services, Reed House, Frogmore Complex, Dormay Street, London SW18 1EY ☎ 020 8871 6145 🖷 020 8871 6964 ✉ mwhitbread@wandsworth.gov.uk

Lifelong Learning: Mr Santino Fragola, Head of Lifelong Learning, Professional Centre, Franciscan Road, Tooting, London SW17 8HE ☎ 020 8871 8491 ✉ sfragola@wandsworth.gov.uk

Lighting: Mr Steve Kempster, Assistant Head of Operational Services, Frogmore Complex, Dormay Street, London SW18 1HA ☎ 020 8871 6704 🖷 020 8871 7562 ✉ skempster@wandsworth.gov.uk

Lottery Funding, Charity and Voluntary: Mr Nick Smales, Economic Development Officer, Town Hall, Wandsworth High Street, London SW18 2PU ☎ 020 8871 6202 🖷 020 8871 8200 ✉ nsmales@wandsworth.gov.uk

Member Services: Mr Patrick Watson, Assistant Director of Administration, Town Hall, Wandsworth High Street, London SW18 2PU ☎ 020 8871 6026 🖷 020 8871 8181 ✉ pwatson@wandsworth.gov.uk

Parking: Mr Robert Langridge, Assistant Director of Engineering & Design Services, Town Hall Extension, Wandsworth High Street, London SW18 2PU ☎ 020 8871 6970 🖷 020 8871 7809 ✉ rlangridge@wandsworth.gov.uk

Partnerships: Mr Jon Evans, Interim Head of Policy, Town Hall, Wandsworth High Street, London SW18 2PU ☎ 020 8871 7815 🖷 020 8871 8181 ✉ jevans@wandsworth.gov.uk

Personnel / HR: Mr Graeme Lennon, Head of Corporate HR, Town Hall, Wandsworth High Street, London SW18 2PU ☎ 020 8871 6190 🖷 020 8871 6185 ✉ glennon@wandsworth.gov.uk

Planning: Ms Seema Manchanda, Assistant Director of Planning & Environment Services, Town Hall Extension, Wandsworth High Street, London SW18 2PU ☎ 020 8871 6626 🖷 020 8871 7809 ✉ smanchanda@wandsworth.gov.uk

Procurement: Mr Mark Glaister, Head of Procurement, Town Hall, Wandsworth High Street, London SW18 2PU ☎ 020 8871 5828 🖷 020 8871 6777 ✉ mglaister@wandsworth.gov.uk

Public Libraries: Mr Andrew Green, Head of Library & Heritage Services, Town Hall, Wandsworth High Street, London SW18 2PU ☎ 020 8871 6364 🖷 020 8871 7630 ✉ agreen@wandsworth.gov.uk

Recycling & Waste Minimisation: Mr Shaun Morley, Head of Waste Management, Town Hall, Wandsworth High Street, London SW18 2PU ☎ 020 8871 6938 🖷 020 8871 6383 ✉ smorley@wandsworth.gov.uk

Regeneration: Ms Seema Manchanda, Assistant Director of Planning & Environment Services, Town Hall Extension, Wandsworth High Street, London SW18 2PU ☎ 020 8871 6626 🖷 020 8871 7809 ✉ smanchanda@wandsworth.gov.uk

Road Safety: Mr Robert Langridge, Assistant Director of Engineering & Design Services, Town Hall Extension, Wandsworth High Street, London SW18 2PU ☎ 020 8871 6970 🖷 020 8871 7809 ✉ rlangridge@wandsworth.gov.uk

Social Services: Ms Dawn Warwick, Director of Adult Social Services, 90 Putney Bridge Road, Wandsworth, London SW18 1HR ☎ 020 8871 6291 🖷 020 8871 7995 ✉ dwarwick@wandsworth.gov.uk

Social Services (Adult): Mr Rob Persey, Assistant Director of Commissioning, Partnerships & Procurement, 90 Putney Bridge Road, Wandsworth, London SW18 1HR ☎ 020 8871 6215 🖷 020 8871 7995 ✉ rpersey@wandsworth.gov.uk

Social Services (Adult): Mr Alistair Rush, Assistant Director of Business Resources, 90 Putney Bridge Road, Wandsworth, London SW18 1HR ☎ 020 8871 6216 🖷 020 8871 7995 ✉ arush@wandsworth.gov.uk

Social Services (Adult): Mr Kerry Stevens, Assistant Director of Operations, 90 Putney Bridge Road, Wandsworth, London SW18 1HR ☎ 020 8871 8423 🖷 020 8871 7995 ✉ kstevens1@wandsworth.gov.uk

Social Services (Children): Ms Linda Webber, Practice Development Manager, Welbeck House, 43-51 Wandsworth High Street, Wandsworth, London SW18 2PU ☎ 020 8871 8610 ✉ lwebber@wandsworth.gov.uk

Social Services (Children): Mr R Wright, Adoption Manager, Wellbeck House, 43-51 Wandsworth High Street, Wandsworth, London SW18 2PU ☎ 020 8871 7252 ✉ rwright2@wandsworth.gov.uk

Staff Training: Mrs Caroline Dempsey, Recruitment & Training Manager, Town Hall, Wandsworth High Street, London SW18 2PU ☎ 020 8871 6197 🖷 020 8871 7498 ✉ cdempsey@wandsworth.gov.uk

Street Scene: Mr Robert Langridge, Assistant Director of Engineering & Design Services, Town Hall Extension, Wandsworth High Street, London SW18 2PU ☎ 020 8871 6970 🖷 020 8871 7809 ✉ rlangridge@wandsworth.gov.uk

Sustainable Communities: Mr Jon Evans, Interim Head of Policy, Town Hall, Wandsworth High Street, London SW18 2PU ☎ 020 8871 7815 🖷 020 8871 8181 ✉ jevans@wandsworth.gov.uk

Sustainable Development: Mr Jon Evans, Interim Head of Policy, Town Hall, Wandsworth High Street, London SW18 2PU ☎ 020 8871 7815 🖷 020 8871 8181 ✉ jevans@wandsworth.gov.uk

Tourism: Mr Paul McCue, Assistant Director of Leisure & Culture, Town Hall, Wandsworth High Street, London SW18 2PU ☎ 020 8871 6868 🖷 020 8871 8349 ✉ pmccue@wandsworth.gov.uk

Town Centre: Mr Nick Smales, Economic Development Officer, Town Hall, Wandsworth High Street, London SW18 2PU ☎ 020 8871 6202 🖷 020 8871 8200 ✉ nsmales@wandsworth.gov.uk

Traffic Management: Mr Robert Langridge, Assistant Director of Engineering & Design Services, Town Hall Extension, Wandsworth High Street, London SW18 2PU ☎ 020 8871 6970 🖷 020 8871 7809 ✉ rlangridge@wandsworth.gov.uk

Transport: Mr Ricky Cousins, Contract Transport & Mechanical Workshops, Mechanical Workshops, Frogmore Complex, Dormay Street, London SW18 1EY ☎ 020 8871 6762 🖷 020 8871 8656 ✉ rcousins@wandsworth.gov.uk

Transport Planner: Mr John Stone, Head of Forward Planning & Transportation, Town Hall Extension, Wandsworth High Street, London SW18 2PU ☎ 020 8871 6628 🖷 020 8871 6003 ✉ jstone@wandsworth.gov.uk

Waste Collection and Disposal: Mr Shaun Morley, Head of Waste Management, Town Hall, Wandsworth High Street, London SW18 2PU ☎ 020 8871 6938 🖷 020 8871 6383 ✉ smorley@wandsworth.gov.uk

Waste Management: Mr Shaun Morley, Head of Waste Management, Town Hall, Wandsworth High Street, London SW18 2PU ☎ 020 8871 6938 🖷 020 8871 6383 ✉ smorley@wandsworth.gov.uk

MEMBERS OF THE COUNCIL (60)

***Mayor:* Knowles**, Adrian (CON - Roehampton and Putney Heath)
aknowles@wandsworth.gov.uk

***Deputy Mayor:* Nardelli**, Nicola (CON - Queenstown)
nnardelli@wandsworth.gov.uk

***Leader of the Council:* Govindia**, Ravi (CON - East Putney)
rgovindia@wandsworth.gov.uk

***Deputy Leader of the Council:* Cook**, Jonathan (CON - Shaftesbury)
jonathancook@wandsworth.gov.uk

Belton, Tony (LAB - Latchmere)
tbelton@wandsworth.gov.uk

Boswell, Sheila (LAB - Tooting)
sboswell@wandsworth.gov.uk

Browne, Jenny (CON - Northcote)
jennybrowne@wandsworth.gov.uk

Caddy, Kim (CON - Southfields)
kcaddy@wandsworth.gov.uk

Carpenter, Peter (LAB - Roehampton and Putney Heath)
pcarpenter@wandsworth.gov.uk

Clay, Claire (CON - Wandsworth Common)
cclay@wandsworth.gov.uk

Cooper, Leonie (LAB - Furzedown)
leoniecooper@wandsworth.gov.uk

Cooper, Jane (CON - West Putney)
janecooper@wandsworth.gov.uk

Cousins, James (CON - Shaftesbury)
jcousins@wandsworth.gov.uk

Cuff, Nick (CON - West Hill)
ncuff@wandsworth.gov.uk

Daley, James (LAB - Tooting)
jamesdaley@wandsworth.gov.uk

Davies, Mark (CON - St Mary's Park)
mdavies@wandsworth.gov.uk

Dawson, Peter (CON - Northcote)
pdawson@wandsworth.gov.uk
Dunn, Antonia (CON - Bedford)
adunn@wandsworth.gov.uk
Ellis, Paul (CON - Balham)
pellis@wandsworth.gov.uk
Farebrother, John (LAB - Furzedown)
jfarebrother@wandsworth.gov.uk
Gibbons, Andy (LAB - Graveney)
agibbons@wandsworth.gov.uk
Graham, Vanessa (CON - Fairfield)
vgraham@wandsworth.gov.uk
Graham, Angela (CON - Earlsfield)
agraham@wandsworth.gov.uk
Grimston, Malcolm (CON - West Hill)
mgrimston@wandsworth.gov.uk
Hallmark, John (CON - St Mary's Park)
jhallmark@wandsworth.gov.uk
Hart, Ian (CON - Nightingale)
ihart@wandsworth.gov.uk
Heaster, Maurice (CON - Wandsworth Common)
mheaster@wandsworth.gov.uk
Hogg, Simon (LAB - Latchmere)
shogg@wandsworth.gov.uk
Howlett, Elizabeth (CON - West Hill)
ehowlett@wandsworth.gov.uk
Humphries, Guy (CON - Southfields)
ghumphries@wandsworth.gov.uk
Jacob, Alex (CON - Bedford)
ajacob@wandsworth.gov.uk
Johnson, Martin (CON - Northcote)
martinjohnson@wandsworth.gov.uk
Johnson, Benjamin (LAB - Tooting)
bjohnson@wandsworth.gov.uk
King, Russell (CON - Balham)
rking@wandsworth.gov.uk
Locker, John (CON - Bedford)
jlocker@wandsworth.gov.uk
Maddan, James (CON - Thamesfield)
jmaddan@wandsworth.gov.uk
McCausland, Piers (CON - Fairfield)
pmccausland@wandsworth.gov.uk
McDermott, Sarah (CON - Nightingale)
smcdermott@wandsworth.gov.uk
McDonnell, Leslie (CON - East Putney)
lmcdonnell@wandsworth.gov.uk
McNaught-Davis, Charles (CON - Earlsfield)
cmcnaughtdavis@wandsworth.gov.uk
Morritt, Robert (CON - East Putney)
rmorritt@wandsworth.gov.uk
Nadler, Jo-Anne (CON - Queenstown)
jnadler@wandsworth.gov.uk
Nickels, Jenny (CON - Roehampton and Putney Heath)
jnickels@wandsworth.gov.uk
Osborn, Rex (LAB - Graveney)
rosborn@wandsworth.gov.uk
Randall, Billi (LAB - Graveney)
brandall@wandsworth.gov.uk
Raubitschek, Alexander (CON - Queenstown)
araubitschek@wandsworth.gov.uk
Ryder, Michael (CON - Thamesfield)
mryder@wandsworth.gov.uk
Scott, Matthew Maxwell (CON - Earlsfield)
mmaxwellscott@wandsworth.gov.uk
Senior, Guy (CON - Shaftesbury)
gsenior@wandsworth.gov.uk
Speck, Wendy (LAB - Latchmere)
wspeck@wandsworth.gov.uk
Stokes, Liz (CON - West Putney)
lizstokes@wandsworth.gov.uk
Strickland, Tessa (CON - St Mary's Park)
tstrickland@wandsworth.gov.uk
Sutters, Steffi (CON - West Putney)
ssutters@wandsworth.gov.uk
Thom, Stuart (CON - Fairfield)
sthom@wandsworth.gov.uk
Thomas, Mark (LAB - Furzedown)
markthomas@wandsworth.gov.uk
Torrington, Rosemary (CON - Thamesfield)
rtorrington@wandsworth.gov.uk
Tracey, Kathy (CON - Wandsworth Common)
ktracey@wandworth.gov.uk
Usher, Caroline (CON - Balham)
cusher@wandsworth.gov.uk
Walsh, Terence (CON - Southfields)
twalsh@wandsworth.gov.uk
Wilkie, Sheldon (CON - Nightingale)
swilkie@wandsworth.gov.uk

POLITICAL COMPOSITION

CON: 47, LAB: 13

CABINET

Leader: Mr Ravi Govindia
Adult Care & Health: Mr James Maddan
Communications & Co-ordination: Mr Alex Jacob
Economic Development & Business Partnerships: Mr James Cousins
Education & Children's Services: Mrs Kathy Tracey
Environment, Culture & Community Safety: Mr Jonathan Cook
Finance & Corporate Resources: Mr Guy Senior
Housing: Mr Paul Ellis
Strategic Planning & Transportation: Mr Russell King

COMMITTEE CHAIRS

Adult Health (Scrutiny): Mrs Caroline Usher
Audit: Mr Maurice Heaster
Education & Children's Services (Scrutiny): Mr Peter Dawson
Environment, Culture & Community Safety (Scrutiny): Mrs Claire Clay
Finance & Corporate Resources (Scrutiny): Mr Leslie McDonnell
General Purposes: Mr Matthew Maxwell Scott
Housing (Scrutiny): Mr Stuart Thom
Licensing: Mr Martin Johnson
Pensions: Mr Maurice Heaster
Planning Applications: Mr Nick Cuff
Regulatory Licensing: Mr Martin Johnson
Standards: Prof Elizabeth Howlett
Strategic Planning & Transportation (Scrutiny): Mr John Locker

WARRINGTON U

Warrington Borough Council, Town Hall, Sankey Street, Warrington WA1 1UH ☎ 01925 443322 🖷 01925 442138
💻 www.warrington.gov.uk

FACTS & FIGURES

Police Authority: Cheshire Police Authority
Health Authority: North West Strategic Health Authority
Learning and Skills Council: North West
Parliamentary Constituencies: Warrington North, Warrington South
EU Constituencies: North West
Election Frequency: Elections are by thirds
Twinning: Culcheth: St. Leu-la-Foret (France); Warrington Borough: Hilden (Germany), Nachod (Czech Rep); Lymm: Meung-sur-Loire (France)

PRINCIPAL OFFICERS

Chief Executive: Mr Steven Broomhead, Interim Chief Executive, Town Hall, Sankey Street, Warrington WA1 1UH ☎ 01925 442101 🖷 01925 442138 🖰 sbroomhead@warrington.gov.uk

Assistant Chief Executive: Ms Katherine Fairclough, Assistant Chief Executive, 5th Floor, Quattro, Buttermarket Street, Warrington WA1 1NJ ☎ 01925 442311 🖷 01925 442312 🖰 kfairclough@warrington.gov.uk

Senior Management: Mr Joe Blott, Executive Director - Neighbourhood & Community Services, 1st Floor, New Town House, Warrington WA1 1NJ ☎ 01925 442419 🖷 01925 444037 🖰 jblott@warrington.gov.uk

Senior Management: Ms Katherine Fairclough, Assistant Chief Executive, 5th Floor, Quattro, Buttermarket Street, Warrington WA1 1NJ ☎ 01925 442311 🖷 01925 442312 🖰 kfairclough@warrington.gov.uk

Senior Management: Mr Andy Farrall, Executive Director - Environment & Regeneration, 3rd Floor, New Town House, Buttermarket Street, Warrington WA1 1NJ ☎ 01925 442701 🖷 01925 442704 🖰 afarrall@warrington.gov.uk

Senior Management: Mrs Kath O'Dwyer, Executive Director - Children & Young People's Services, 2nd Floor, New Town House, Buttermarket Street, Warrington WA1 2NJ ☎ 01925 442900 🖷 01925 442929 🖰 kodwyer@warrington.gov.uk

Access Officer / Social Services (Disability): Mr Steve Reddy, Assistant Director - Adult Social Care, 1st Floor, New Town House, Buttermarket Street, Warrington WA1 2NJ ☎ 01925 444251 🖰 sreddy@warrington.gov.uk

Architect, Building / Property Services: Ms Elwyn Rowlands, Architecture & Building Maintenance Manager, 3rd Floor, Quattro, Buttermarket Street, Warrington WA1 1NJ ☎ 01925 442633 🖰 erowlands@warrington.gov.uk

Building Control: Mr John Groves, Development Services Manager, Ground Floor, New Town House, Buttermarket Street, Warrington WA1 2NJ ☎ 01925 442805 🖰 jgroves@warrington.gov.uk

Catering Services: Ms Anne Warren, Facilities Manager, New Town House, Buttermarket Street, Warrington WA1 2NJ 🖰 awarren@warrington.gov.uk

Children / Youth Services: Mrs Kath O'Dwyer, Executive Director - Children & Young People's Services, New Town House, Buttermarket Street, Warrington WA1 2NJ ☎ 01925 442900 🖷 01925 442929 🖰 kodwyer@warrington.gov.uk

Children / Youth Services: Ms Fiona Waddington, Assistant Director - Targeted Services, 2nd Floor, New Town House, Buttermarket Street, Warrington WA1 1NJ ☎ 01925 443900 🖰 fwaddington@warrington.gov.uk

Civil Registration: Ms Jane Briscall, Superintendant Registrar, Register Office, Museum Street, Warrington WA1 1JX ☎ 01925 442762 🖷 01925 442739

Community Safety: Mr Doug Ryan, Crime & Disorder Reduction Partnership Co-ordinator, Charles Stewart House, 55 Museum Street, Warrington WA1 1NE ☎ 01244 614871 🖷 01925 442138 🖰 Douglas.Ryan@cheshire.pnn.police.uk

Computer Management: Mr Steve Park, Chief Customer & Technology Officer, 3rd Floor, Quattro, Buttermarket Street, Warrington WA1 2NH ☎ 01925 443940 🖰 spark@warrington.gov.uk

Consumer Protection and Trading Standards: Mr Peter Astley, Public Protection Services Manager, New Town House, Buttermarket Street, Warrington WA1 1NJ ☎ 01925 442672 🖷 01925 442655 🖰 pastley@warrington.gov.uk

Corporate Services: Ms Katherine Fairclough, Assistant Chief Executive, 5th Floor, Quattro, Buttermarket Street, Warrington WA1 1NJ ☎ 01925 442311 🖷 01925 442312 🖰 kfairclough@warrington.gov.uk

Customer Service: Ms Alex Grundy, Customer Services Manager, New Town House, Buttermarket Street, Warrington WA1 2NJ ☎ 01925 442418 🖰 agrundy@warrington.gov.uk

Direct Labour: Mr John Rowson, Acting Assistant Director - Environment & Public Protection, Hawthorne Avenue, Woolston, Warrington WA1 4AL ☎ 01925 442750 🖷 01925 443594 🖰 jrowson@warrington.gov.uk

Economic Development: Mr Andy Farrall, Executive Director - Environment & Regeneration, 3rd Floor, New Town House, Buttermarket Street, Warrington WA1 2NJ ☎ 01925 442700 🖷 01925 442704 🖰 afarrall@warrington.gov.uk

Education: Mr Pinaki Ghoshal, Assistant Director - Universal Services, New Town House, Buttermarket Street, Warrington WA1 2NJ ☎ 01925 442906 🖰 pghoshal@warrington.gov.uk

Education: Mrs Kath O'Dwyer, Executive Director - Children & Young People's Services, New Town House, Buttermarket Street, Warrington WA1 2NJ ☎ 01925 442900 🖷 01925 442929 🖰 kodwyer@warrington.gov.uk

E-Government: Mr Steve Park, Chief Customer & Technology Officer, 3rd Floor, Quattro, Buttermarket Street, Warrington WA1 2NH ☎ 01925 443940 🖰 spark@warrington.gov.uk

Electoral Registration: Mr Bryan Magan, Head - Democratic &

Member Services, Town Hall, Sankey Street, Warrington WA1 1UH ☎ 01925 442112 🖷 01925 442044 🖰 bmagan@warrington.gov.uk

Emergency Planning: Mrs Theresa Whitfield, Risk & Resilience Manager, 4th Floor, Quattro, Buttermarket Street, Warrington WA1 1NJ ☎ 01925 442657 🖷 01925 442825 🖰 twhitfield@warrington.gov.uk

Energy Management: Mr Mark McGiveron, Energy Officer, 3rd Floor, New Town House, Buttermarket Street, Warrington WA1 1NJ ☎ 01925 442572 🖰 mmcgiveron@warrington.gov.uk

Environmental / Technical Services: Mr Andy Farrall, Executive Director - Environment & Regeneration, New Town House, Buttermarket Street, Warrington WA1 2NJ ☎ 01925 442701 🖷 01925 442704 🖰 afarrall@warrington.gov.uk

Environmental Health: Mr Peter Astley, Public Protection Services Manager, New Town House, Buttermarket Street, Warrington WA1 1NJ ☎ 01925 442672 🖷 01925 442655 🖰 pastley@warrington.gov.uk

Estates, Property & Valuation: Mr Stewart Brown, Property & Estates Service Manager, 3rd Floor, Quattro, Buttermarket Street, Warrington WA1 1NJ ☎ 01925 442850 🖰 s_brown@warrington.gov.uk

Finance and Treasurer: Ms Katherine Fairclough, Assistant Chief Executive, 5th Floor, Quattro, Buttermarket Street, Warrington WA1 1NJ ☎ 01925 442311 🖷 01925 442312 🖰 kfairclough@warrington.gov.uk

Finance and Treasurer: Mr Lynton Green, Head - Finance & s151 Officer, Quattro Building, Buttermarket Street, Warrington WA1 1BN ☎ 01925 442237 🖰 lgreen@warrington.gov.uk

Grounds Maintenance: Mr John Rowson, Acting Assistant Director - Environment & Public Protection, Hawthorne Avenue, Woolston, Warrington WA1 4AL ☎ 01925 442750 🖷 01925 443594 🖰 jrowson@warrington.gov.uk

Health and Safety: Mrs Theresa Whitfield, Risk & Resilience Manager, 4th Floor, Quattro, Buttermarket Street, Warrington WA1 1NJ ☎ 01925 442657 🖷 01925 442825 🖰 twhitfield@warrington.gov.uk

Highways: Mr David Boyer, Head - Sustainable Transport, New Town House, Buttermarket Street, Warrington WA1 1NJ ☎ 01925 442530 🖰 dboyer@warrington.gov.uk

Home Energy Conservation: Mr Kevin Normansell, Energy Efficiency Officer, The Gateway, 85-89 Sankey Street, Warrington WA1 1SR ☎ 01925 815481 🖷 01925 815481 🖰 knormansell@warrington.gov.uk

Housing Maintenance: Mr Peter Mercer, Director - Golden Gates Housing (ALMO), The Gateway, 85-89 Sankey Street, Warrington WA1 1SR ☎ 01925 442403 🖷 01925 442488 🖰 pmercer@warrington.gov.uk

Local Area Agreement: Mrs Kathryn Griffiths, Assistant Director - Partnerships & Performance, 4th Floor, Quattro, Buttermarket Street, Warrington WA1 1NJ ☎ 01925 442797 🖷 01925 442138 🖰 kgriffiths@warrington.gov.uk

Legal: Mr Tim Date, Solicitor to the Council & Head - Corporate Governance, 5th Floor, Quattro, Buttermarket Street, Warrington WA1 2NH ☎ 01925 442150 🖰 tdate@warrington.gov.uk

Licensing: Mr Peter Astley, Public Protection Services Manager, New Town House, Buttermarket Street, Warrington WA1 1NJ ☎ 01925 442672 🖷 01925 442655 🖰 pastley@warrington.gov.uk

Lifelong Learning: Mrs Penny Owen, Head - Learning & Skills, Professional Development Centre, Irwell Road, Warrington WA4 6QR ☎ 01925 458114 🖷 01925 458103 🖰 powen@warrington.gov.uk

Lighting: Mr Barry Hughes, Street Lighting Officer, Hawthorne Avenue, Woolston, Warrington WA1 4AL ☎ 01925 443074 🖰 bhughes@warrington.gov.uk

Member Services: Mr Bryan Magan, Head - Democratic & Member Services, Town Hall, Sankey Street, Warrington WA1 1UH ☎ 01925 442112 🖷 01925 442044 🖰 bmagan@warrington.gov.uk

Parking: Mr David Boyer, Head - Sustainable Transport, New Town House, Buttermarket Street, Warrington WA1 1NJ ☎ 01925 442530 🖰 dboyer@warrington.gov.uk

Partnerships: Mr David Boyer, Head - Sustainable Transport, New Town House, Buttermarket Street, Warrington WA1 1NJ ☎ 01925 442530 🖰 dboyer@warrington.gov.uk

Partnerships: Mrs Kathryn Griffiths, Assistant Director - Partnerships & Performance, 4th Floor, Quattro, Buttermarket Street, Warrington WA1 1NJ ☎ 01925 442797 🖷 01925 442138 🖰 kgriffiths@warrington.gov.uk

Personnel / HR: Mr John Hambling, Head - People & Organisational Development, Quattro Building, Buttermarket Street, Warrington WA1 2NH ☎ 01925 442117 🖰 jhambling@warrington.gov.uk

Planning: Mr Peter Taylor, Head - Service, Regeneration & Development, New Town House, Buttermarket Street, Warrington WA1 2NH ☎ 01925 442790 🖷 01925 242759 🖰 ptaylor@warrington.gov.uk

Procurement: Mr Chris Luke, Commissioning & Procurement Manager, Quattro Building, Buttermarket Street, Warrington WA1 1NJ ☎ 01925 442879 🖷 01925 443449 🖰 cluke@warrington.gov.uk

Recycling & Waste Minimisation: Mr John Rowson, Acting Assistant Director - Environment & Public Protection, Hawthorne Avenue, Woolston, Warrington WA1 4AL ☎ 01925 442750 🖷 01925 443594 🖰 jrowson@warrington.gov.uk

Regeneration: Mr Andy Farrall, Executive Director - Environment & Regeneration, 2nd Floor, New Town House, Buttermarket Street, Warrington WA1 1NJ ☎ 01925 442701 🖷 01925 442704 🖰 afarrall@warrington.gov.uk

Road Safety: Mr Mark Tune, Road Safety Officer, New Town House, Buttermarket Street, Warrington WA1 1NJ ✉ mtune@warrington.gov.uk

Social Services: Mr Joe Blott, Executive Director - Neighbourhood & Community Services, 1st Floor, New Town House, Warrington WA1 1NJ ☎ 01925 442419 🖷 01925 444037 ✉ jblott@warrington.gov.uk

Social Services: Mr Simon Kenton, Assistant Director - Integrated Health & Social Care Commissioning, 1st Floor, New Town House, Warrington WA1 1NJ ☎ 01925 444231 ✉ skenton@warrington.gov.uk

Social Services (Adult): Mr Joe Blott, Executive Director - Neighbourhood & Community Services, 1st Floor, New Town House, Warrington WA1 1NJ ☎ 01925 442419 🖷 01925 444037 ✉ jblott@warrington.gov.uk

Social Services (Adult): Mr Steve Reddy, Assistant Director - Adult Social Care, 1st Floor, New Town House, Warrington WA1 1NJ ☎ 01925 444251 ✉ sreddy@warrington.gov.uk

Social Services (Children): Mrs Kath O'Dwyer, Executive Director - Children & Young People's Services, New Town House, Buttermarket Street, Warrington WA1 2NJ ☎ 01925 442900 🖷 01925 442929 ✉ kodwyer@warrington.gov.uk

Social Services (Children): Ms Fiona Waddington, Assistant Director - Targeted Services, 2nd Floor, New Town House, Buttermarket Street, Warrington WA1 1NJ ☎ 01925 443900 ✉ fwaddington@warrington.gov.uk

Staff Training: Mrs Penny Owen, Head - Learning & Skills, Professional Development Centre, Irwell Road, Warrington WA4 6QR ☎ 01925 458114 🖷 01925 458103 ✉ powen@warrington.gov.uk

Street Scene: Mr John Rowson, Acting Assistant Director - Environment & Public Protection, Hawthorne Avenue, Woolston, Warrington WA1 4AL ☎ 01925 442750 🖷 01925 443594 ✉ jrowson@warrington.gov.uk

Sustainable Communities: Mr Joe Blott, Executive Director - Neighbourhood & Community Services, 1st Floor, New Town House, Warrington WA1 1NJ ☎ 01925 442419 🖷 01925 444037 ✉ jblott@warrington.gov.uk

Sustainable Communities: Mrs Kathryn Griffiths, Assistant Director - Partnerships & Performance, 4th Floor, Quattro, Buttermarket Street, Warrington WA1 1NJ ☎ 01925 442797 🖷 01925 442138 ✉ kgriffiths@warrington.gov.uk

Town Centre: Mr Neil Roberts, Acting Town Centre Manager, New Town House, Buttermarket Street, Warrington WA1 1NJ ☎ 01925 458016 ✉ nroberts@warrington.gov.uk

Traffic Management: Mr David Boyer, Head - Sustainable Transport, New Town House, Buttermarket Street, Warrington WA1 1NJ ☎ 01925 442530 ✉ dboyer@warrington.gov.uk

Transport: Mr David Boyer, Head - Sustainable Transport, New Town House, Buttermarket Street, Warrington WA1 1NJ ☎ 01925 442530 ✉ dboyer@warrington.gov.uk

Transport Planner: Mr David Boyer, Head - Sustainable Transport, New Town House, Buttermarket Street, Warrington WA1 1NJ ☎ 01925 442530 ✉ dboyer@warrington.gov.uk

Waste Collection and Disposal: Mr John Rowson, Acting Assistant Director - Environment & Public Protection, Hawthorne Avenue, Woolston, Warrington WA1 4AL ☎ 01925 442750 🖷 01925 443594 ✉ jrowson@warrington.gov.uk

Waste Management: Mr John Rowson, Acting Assistant Director - Environment & Public Protection, Hawthorne Avenue, Woolston, Warrington WA1 4AL ☎ 01925 442750 🖷 01925 443594 ✉ jrowson@warrington.gov.uk

Children's Play Areas: Mr John Rowson, Acting Assistant Director - Environment & Public Protection, Hawthorne Avenue, Woolston, Warrington WA1 4AL ☎ 01925 442750 🖷 01925 443594 ✉ jrowson@warrington.gov.uk

MEMBERS OF THE COUNCIL (57)

***Mayor:* Wright**, Steve (LAB - Latchford East)
stevewright@warrington.gov.uk

***Deputy Mayor:* Carey**, Peter (LAB - Fairfield and Howley)
petercarey@warrington.gov.uk

***Leader of the Council:* O'Neill**, Terry (LAB - Burtonwood and Winwick)
toneill@warrington.gov.uk

***Deputy Leader of the Council:* Hannon**, Mike (LAB - Orford)
mhannon@warrington.gov.uk

Axcell, Brian (LD - Appleton)
baxcell@warrington.gov.uk

Barr, Bob (LD - Lymm)
bbarr@warrington.gov.uk

Bennett, Kevin (LAB - Fairfield and Howley)
kbennett@warrington.gov.uk

Biggin, Mike (LD - Grappenhall and Thelwall)
mbiggin@warrington.gov.uk

Bland, Sue (CON - Culcheth, Glazebury and Croft)
sbland@warrington.gov.uk

Bowden, Russ (LAB - Birchwood)
rbowden@warrington.gov.uk

Bretherton, Paul (LAB - Rixton and Woolston)
pbretherton@warrington.gov.uk

Brinksman, Bill (LAB - Rixton and Woolston)
bbrinksman@warrington.gov.uk

Carter, Jean (LAB - Great Sankey South)
jcarter1@warrington.gov.uk

Davidson, Jan (LAB - Westbrook)
jdavidson@warrington.gov.uk

Dirir, Linda (LAB - Penketh and Cuerdley)
ldirir@warrington.gov.uk

Dirir, Allin (LAB - Penketh and Cuerdley)
adirir@warrington.gov.uk

Finnegan, Ted (LD - Grappenhall and Thelwall)
efinnegan@warrington.gov.uk

Fitzsimmons, Chris (LAB - Birchwood)
cfitzsimmons@warrington.gov.uk

Friend, Graham (LAB - Poulton North)
gfriend@warrington.gov.uk

Froggatt, Colin (LAB - Poulton South)

cfroggatt@warrington.gov.uk
Gleave, Keith (LD - Whittle Hall)
kgleave@warrington.gov.uk
Guthrie, Judith (LAB - Westbrook)
jgurthrie@warrington.gov.uk
Hannon, Kate (LAB - Orford)
khannon@warrington.gov.uk
Higgins, Tony (LAB - Fairfield and Howley)
thiggins@warrington.gov.uk
Hoyle, Les (CON - Culcheth, Glazebury and Croft)
tlhoyle@warrington.gov.uk
Hughes, Will (LAB - Whittle Hall)
whughes@warrington.gov.uk
Johnson, Wendy (LD - Grappenhall and Thelwall)
wjohnson@warrington.gov.uk
Jordan, Celia (LD - Stockton Heath)
cjordon@warrington.gov.uk
Joyce, John (LAB - Burtonwood and Winwick)
jjoyce@warrington.gov.uk
Keane, David (LAB - Penketh and Cuerdley)
dkeane@warrington.gov.uk
Kennedy, Paul (CON - Hatton, Stretton and Walton)
pzkennedy@warrington.gov.uk
Kerr-Brown, John (LAB - Poplars and Hulme)
jkerrbrown@warrington.gov.uk
Ladbury, Lottie (LAB - Poulton South)
lladbury@warrington.gov.uk
Lines-Rowland, Billy (LAB - Poulton North)
blinesrowland@warrington.gov.uk
Maher, Brian (LAB - Poplars and Hulme)
bmaher@warrington.gov.uk
Marks, Ian (LD - Lymm)
imarks@warrington.gov.uk
McCarthy, Tony (LAB - Rixton and Woolston)
tmccarthy@warrington.gov.uk
McLaughlin, Maureen (LAB - Latchford West)
mmclaughlin@warrington.gov.uk
Mundry, Hans (LAB - Latchford East)
hmundry@warrington.gov.uk
Murphy, Laurence (LAB - Stockton Heath)
lmurphy1@warrington.gov.uk
Nelson, Pauline (LAB - Birchwood)
pnelson@warrington.gov.uk
Parish, Steve (LAB - Bewsey and Whitecross)
sparish@warrington.gov.uk
Patel, Hitesh (LAB - Great Sankey South)
hpatel@warrington.gov.uk
Price, Dan (LAB - Great Sankey North)
dprice1@warrington.gov.uk
Rashid, Faisal (LAB - Whittle Hall)
frashid@warrington.gov.uk
Richards, Jeff (LAB - Bewsey and Whitecross)
jrichards@warrington.gov.uk
Roberts, Steve (LAB - Poplars and Hulme)
steveroberts@warrington.gov.uk
Settle, Geoff (LAB - Poulton North)
gsettle@warrington.gov.uk
Simcock, Kelly (LAB - Orford)
ksmicock@warrington.gov.uk
Vobe, Chris (LAB - Culcheth, Glazebury and Croft)
chrisvobe@googlemail.com
Walker, Peter (LD - Appleton)
pwalker1@warrington.gov.uk
Walker, Judith (LD - Appleton)
jwalker@warrington.gov.uk
Welborn, Graham (LD - Latchford West)
gwelborn@warrington.gov.uk
Williams, Tony (LAB - Great Sankey South)
twilliams2@warrington.gov.uk
Wood, Trudi (LD - Great Sankey North)
twood@warrington.gov.uk
Woodyatt, Sheila (CON - Lymm)
swoodyatt@warrington.gov.uk
Wright, Pat (LAB - Bewsey and Whitecross)
pwright@warrington.gov.uk

POLITICAL COMPOSITION
LAB: 41, LD: 12, CON: 4

CABINET
Leader: Mr Terry O'Neill
Deputy Leader: Mr Mike Hannon
Children & Young People's Services: Mr Colin Froggatt
Corporate Assignments: Mr Russ Bowden
Environment & Public Protection: Mr David Keane
Health & Wellbeing / Adult Services: Mrs Pat Wright
Highways, Transportation & Climate Change: Mrs Linda Dirir
Leisure, Community & Culture: Mrs Kate Hannon
Personnel & Communications: Mr Hitesh Patel

COMMITTEE CHAIRS
Appeals: Mrs Pauline Nelson
Audit & Corporate Governance: Mr Chris Fitzsimmons
Licensing: Mr Brian Maher
Traffic: Mr Bill Brinksman

WARWICK D

Warwick District Council, Riverside House, Milverton Hill, Leamington Spa CV32 5HZ ☎ 01926 450000 ✉ contactus@warwickdc.gov.uk 💻 www.warwickdc.gov.uk

FACTS & FIGURES
Police Authority: Warwickshire Police Authority
Health Authority: NHS West Midlands
Learning and Skills Council: West Midlands
Parliamentary Constituencies: Kenilworth and Southam, Warwick and Leamington
EU Constituencies: West Midlands
Election Frequency: Elections are of whole council
Twinning: Kenilworth: Bourg-la-Reine (France), Eppstein (Germany); Royal Leamington Spa: Bruhl (Germany); Heemstede (Netherlands); Sceaux (France); Warwick: Saumur (France), Verden (Germany); Warwick (Australia); Warwick (USA); Whitnash: Villebon-sur-Yvette (France); Weillerswist (Germany)

PRINCIPAL OFFICERS
Chief Executive: Mr Chris Elliott, Chief Executive, Riverside House, Milverton Hill, Leamington Spa CV32 5HZ ☎ 01926 456000 🖷 01926 456026 ✉ chris.elliott@warwickdc.gov.uk

Deputy Chief Executive: Mr Bill Hunt, Deputy Chief Executive, Riverside House, Milverton Hill, Leamington Spa CV32 5HZ ☎ 01926 456014 🖷 01926 456121 ✉ bill.hunt@warwickdc.gov.uk

Deputy Chief Executive: Mr Andrew Jones, Deputy Chief Executive, Riverside House, Milverton Hill, Leamington Spa CV32

5HZ ☎ 01926 456830 🖷 01926 456121
✉ andrew.jones@warwickdc.gov.uk

Senior Management: Mr Ian Coker, Head of Neighbourhood Services, Riverside House, Milverton Hill, Leamington Spa CV32 5HZ ☎ 01926 456227 🖷 01926 456210
✉ ian.coker@warwickdc.gov.uk

Senior Management: Ms Tracy Darke, Head of Development Services, PO Box 2178, Riverside House, Milverton Hill, Leamington Spa CV32 5QH ☎ 01926 456016 🖷 01926 456542
✉ tracy.darke@warwickdc.gov.uk

Senior Management: Mrs Susie Drummond, Head of Corporate & Community Services, Riverside House, Milverton Hill, Leamington Spa CV32 5HZ ☎ 01926 456081 🖷 01926 456121
✉ susie.drummond@warwickdc.gov.uk

Senior Management: Mr Richard Hall, Head of Environmental Services, PO Box 2176, Riverside House, Milverton Hill, Leamington Spa CV32 5QH ☎ 01926 456700 🖷 01926 456754
✉ richard.hall@warwickdc.gov.uk

Senior Management: Mr Roger Jewsbury, Head of Community Protection, Riverside House, Milverton Hill, Leamington Spa CV32 5HZ ☎ 01926 456320 🖷 01926 456345
✉ roger.jewsbury@warwickdc.gov.uk

Senior Management: Mr Jameel Malik, Head of Housing & Property Services, PO Box 2175, Riverside House, Milverton Hill, Leamington Spa CV32 5HZ ☎ 01926 456403 🖷 01926 456449
✉ jameel.malik@warwickdc.gov.uk

Senior Management: Mr Mike Snow, Head of Finance, PO Box 2180, Riverside House, Milverton Hill, Leamington Spa CV32 5QW ☎ 01926 456800 🖷 01926 456841 ✉ mike.snow@warwickdc.gov.uk

Senior Management: Ms Rose Winship, Head of Cultural Services, PO Box 2177, Riverside House, Milverton Hill, Leamington Spa CV32 5QG ☎ 01926 456223 🖷 01926 456210
✉ rose.winship@warwickdc.gov.uk

Access Officer / Social Services (Disability): Mr Dennis Maddy, Chief Buliding Control Officer, PO Box 2178, Riverside House, Milverton Hill, Leamington Spa CV32 5QH ☎ 01926 456511 🖷 01926 456542 ✉ dennis.maddy@warwickdc.gov.uk

Architect, Building / Property Services: Mr Anthony White, Property Manager, PO Box 1710, Riverside House, Milverton Hill, Leamington Spa CV32 5RQ ☎ 01926 456047 🖷 01926 456049
✉ anthony.white@warwickdc.gov.uk

Building Control: Mr Dennis Maddy, Chief Buliding Control Officer, PO Box 2178, Riverside House, Milverton Hill, Leamington Spa CV32 5QH ☎ 01926 456511 🖷 01926 456542
✉ dennis.maddy@warwickdc.gov.uk

PR / Communications: Miss Rachael Carpenter, Communications & Marketing Officer, Riverside House, Milverton Hill, Leamington Spa CV32 5HZ ☎ 01926 456069
✉ rachael.carpenter@warwickdc.gov.uk

Community Planning: Ms Alison Williams, Manager - Joint Community Partnership, Riverside House, Milverton Hill, Leamington Spa CV32 5HZ ☎ 01926 456019 🖷 01926 456121
✉ alisonwilliams@warwickshire.gov.uk

Community Safety: Mr Peter Cutts, Community Safety Manager, Riverside House, Milverton Hill, Leamington Spa CV32 5HZ
☎ 01926 456021 🖷 01926 456324 ✉ pete.cutts@warwickdc.gov.uk

Computer Management: Mr Ty Walter, Systems Development Manager, Riverside House, Milverton Hill, Leamington Spa CV32 5HZ ☎ 01926 456651 🖷 01926 456663
✉ ty.walters@warwickdc.gov.uk

Corporate Services: Mr Chris Elliott, Chief Executive, Riverside House, Milverton Hill, Leamington Spa CV32 5HZ ☎ 01926 456000 🖷 01926 456026 ✉ chris.elliott@warwickdc.gov.uk

Customer Service: Mrs Susie Drummond, Head of Corporate & Community Services, Riverside House, Milverton Hill, Leamington Spa CV32 5HZ ☎ 01926 456081 🖷 01926 456121
✉ susie.drummond@warwickdc.gov.uk

Economic Development: Mr Joe Bacconet, Economic Development & Regeneration Manager, PO Box 2178, Riverside House, Milverton Hill, Leamington Spa CV32 5QG ☎ 01926 456011 🖷 01926 456542 ✉ joseph.bacconet@warwickdc.gov.uk

Electoral Registration: Mrs Gillian Friar, Electoral / Administration Officer, Deputy Chief Executive's Office, Riverside House, Milverton Hill, Leamington Spa CV32 5HZ ☎ 01926 456111 🖷 01926 456121 ✉ gillian.friar@warwickdc.gov.uk

Emergency Planning: Mr Roger Jewsbury, Head of Community Protection, Riverside House, Milverton Hill, Leamington Spa CV32 5HZ ☎ 01926 456320 🖷 01926 456345
✉ roger.jewsbury@warwickdc.gov.uk

Energy Management: Mr Mark Perkins, Energy Manager, PO Box 1710, Riverside House, Milverton Hill, Leamington Spa CV32 5RQ ☎ 01926 456037 🖷 01926 456049
✉ mark.perkins@warwickdc.gov.uk

Environmental Health: Mr Richard Hall, Head of Environmental Services, PO Box 2176, Riverside House, Milverton Hill, Leamington Spa CV32 5QH ☎ 01926 456700 🖷 01926 456754
✉ richard.hall@warwickdc.gov.uk

Estates, Property & Valuation: Mr Chris Makasis, Estates Manager, Riverside House, Milverton Hill, Leamington Spa CV32 5HZ ☎ 01926 546040 ✉ chris.makasis@warwickdc.gov.uk

Facilities: Mr Roger Jewsbury, Head of Community Protection, Riverside House, Milverton Hill, Leamington Spa CV32 5HZ
☎ 01926 456320 🖷 01926 456345
✉ roger.jewsbury@warwickdc.gov.uk

Finance and Treasurer: Mr Mike Snow, Head of Finance, PO Box 2180, Riverside House, Milverton Hill, Leamington Spa CV32 5QW ☎ 01926 456800 🖷 01926 456841
✉ mike.snow@warwickdc.gov.uk

Grounds Maintenance: Mr Ian Coker, Head of Neighbourhood Services, Riverside House, Milverton Hill, Leamington Spa CV32 5HZ ☎ 01926 456227 🖷 01926 456210 ✉ ian.coker@warwickdc.gov.uk

Health and Safety: Mr Grahame Helm, Environmental Protection Manager, PO Box 2176, Riverside House, Milverton Hill, Leamington Spa CV32 5QF ☎ 01926 456714 🖷 01926 456746 ✉ grahame.helme@warwickdc.gov.uk

Home Energy Conservation: Mr Mark Perkins, Energy Manager, PO Box 1710, Riverside House, Milverton Hill, Leamington Spa CV32 5RQ ☎ 01926 456037 🖷 01926 456049 ✉ mark.perkins@warwickdc.gov.uk

Housing: Mr Jameel Malik, Head of Housing & Property Services, PO Box 2175, Riverside House, Milverton Hill, Leamington Spa CV32 5HZ ☎ 01926 456403 🖷 01926 456449 ✉ jameel.malik@warwickdc.gov.uk

Housing Maintenance: Mr Jameel Malik, Head of Housing & Property Services, PO Box 2175, Riverside House, Milverton Hill, Leamington Spa CV32 5HZ ☎ 01926 456403 🖷 01926 456449 ✉ jameel.malik@warwickdc.gov.uk

Leisure and Cultural Services: Ms Rose Winship, Head of Cultural Services, PO Box 2177, Riverside House, Milverton Hill, Leamington Spa CV32 5QG ☎ 01926 456223 🖷 01926 456210 ✉ rose.winship@warwickdc.gov.uk

Licensing: Mr David Davies, Licensing Services Manager, Riverside House, Milverton Hill, Leamington Spa CV32 5HZ ☎ 01926 456107 🖷 01926 456121 ✉ david.davies@warwickdc.gov.uk

Member Services: Mr Graham Leach, Senior Committee Services Officer, Deputy Chief Executive's Office, Riverside House, Milverton Hill, Leamington Spa CV32 5HZ ☎ 01926 456114 🖷 01926 456121 ✉ graham.leach@warwickdc.gov.uk

Parking: Mr Gary Charlton, Car Parks Manager, PO Box 2179, Riverside House, Milverton Hill, Leamington Spa CV32 5HZ ☎ 01926 456315 ✉ gary.charlton@warwickdc.gov.uk

Personnel / HR: Mrs Karen Warren, HR Manager, Riverside House, Milverton Hill, Leamington Spa CV32 5HZ ☎ 01926 456307 🖷 01926 456027 ✉ karen.warren@warwickdc.gov.uk

Planning: Ms Tracy Darke, Head of Development Services, PO Box 2178, Riverside House, Milverton Hill, Leamington Spa CV32 5QH ☎ 01926 456016 🖷 01926 456542 ✉ tracy.darke@warwickdc.gov.uk

Procurement: Ms Melanie Gillman, Procurement Manager, PO Box 2180, Riverside House, Milverton Hill, Leamington Spa CV32 5HZ ☎ 01926 456201 🖷 01926 456481 ✉ melanie.gillman@warwickdc.gov.uk

Recycling & Waste Minimisation: Mr Ian Coker, Head of Neighbourhood Services, Riverside House, Milverton Hill, Leamington Spa CV32 5HZ ☎ 01926 456227 🖷 01926 456210 ✉ ian.coker@warwickdc.gov.uk

Regeneration: Mr Joe Bacconet, Economic Development & Regeneration Manager, PO Box 2178, Riverside House, Milverton Hill, Leamington Spa CV32 5QG ☎ 01926 456011 🖷 01926 456542 ✉ joseph.bacconet@warwickdc.gov.uk

Staff Training: Ms Tracy Dolphin, Learning & Development Officer, Riverside House, Milverton Hill, Leamington Spa CV32 5HZ ☎ 01926 456350 🖷 01926 456027 ✉ tracy.dolphin@warwickdc.gov.uk

Street Scene: Mr Ian Coker, Head of Neighbourhood Services, Riverside House, Milverton Hill, Leamington Spa CV32 5HZ ☎ 01926 456227 🖷 01926 456210 ✉ ian.coker@warwickdc.gov.uk

Town Centre: Mr David Butler, Town Centre Development Officer, PO Box 2178, Riverside House, Milverton Hill, Leamington Spa CV32 5QG ☎ 01926 456012 🖷 01926 456542 ✉ david.butler@warwickdc.gov.uk

Town Centre: Ms Pamela Dunsdon, Town Centre Business Development Manager - Leamington Sea, Riverside House, Milverton Hill, Leamington Spa CV32 5HZ ☎ 01926 456017 🖷 01926 456542 ✉ pamela.dunsdon@warwickdc.gov.uk

Town Centre: Mr Ian Kirkwood, Town Centre Development Officer, Riverside House, Milverton Hill, Leamington Spa CV32 5HZ ☎ 01926 410815 🖷 01926 456542 ✉ ian.kirkwood@warwickdc.gov.uk

Waste Collection and Disposal: Mr Ian Coker, Head of Neighbourhood Services, Riverside House, Milverton Hill, Leamington Spa CV32 5HZ ☎ 01926 456227 🖷 01926 456210 ✉ ian.coker@warwickdc.gov.uk

Waste Management: Mr Ian Coker, Head of Neighbourhood Services, Riverside House, Milverton Hill, Leamington Spa CV32 5HZ ☎ 01926 456227 🖷 01926 456210 ✉ ian.coker@warwickdc.gov.uk

MEMBERS OF THE COUNCIL (46)

***Chair:* Kinson**, Michael (CON - Warwick West)
michael.kinson@warwickdc.gov.uk

***Deputy Chair:* Davies**, Richard (CON - Kenilworth St John's)
richard.davies@warwickdc.gov.uk

***Leader of the Council:* Doody**, Michael (CON - Radford Semele)
michael.doody@warwickdc.gov.uk

***Deputy Leader of the Council:* Caborn**, Les (CON - Lapworth)
les.caborn@warwickdc.gov.uk

***Group Leader:* Barrott**, John (LAB - Leamington Wiles)
john.barrott@warwickdc.gov.uk

***Group Leader:* Boad**, Alan (LD - Leamington Crown)
alan.boad@warwickdc.gov.uk

***Group Leader:* Kirton**, Bernard (IND - Whitnash)
bernard.kirton@warwickdc.gov.uk

Blacklock, Ann (LD - Kenilworth Abbey)
ann.blacklock@warwickdc.gov.uk

Bromley, Linda (CON - Warwick South)
linda.bromley@warwickdc.gov.uk

Brookes, Richard (CON - Bishop's Tachbrook)
richard.brookes@warwickdc.gov.uk

Bunker, Felicity (CON - Kenilworth Park Hill)
felicity.bunker@warwickdc.gov.uk

Coker, Michael (CON - Kenilworth Abbey)

michael.coker@warwickdc.gov.uk
Copping, Roger (LD - Leamington Manor)
roger.copping@warwickdc.gov.uk
Cross, Stephen (CON - Warwick North)
stephen.cross@warwickdc.gov.uk
Dagg, John (CON - Kenilworth St John's)
john.dagg@warwickdc.gov.uk
Dean, Janice (LAB - Leamington Clarendon)
janice.dean@warwickdc.gov.uk
De-Lara-Bond, Cymone (LD - Leamington Manor)
cymone.delarabond@warwickdc.gov.uk
Dhillon, Prabhjiet (CON - Warwick West)
bob.dhillon@warwickdc.gov.uk
Edwards, Richards (LAB - Leamington Wiles)
richard.edwards@warwickdc.gov.uk
Falp, Judith (IND - Whitnash)
judith.falp@warwickdc.gov.uk
Gallagher, Sue (CON - Leek Wooton)
susan.gallagher@warwickdc.gov.uk
Gifford, Bill (LD - Leamington Milverton)
bill.gifford@warwickdc.gov.uk
Gill, Balvinder (LAB - Leamington Brunswick)
balvinder.gill@warwickdc.gov.uk
Goode, Eithne (LD - Leamington Manor)
eithne.goode@warwickdc.gov.uk
Grainger, Moira-Ann (CON - Warwick North)
moira-ann.grainger@warwickdc.gov.uk
Guest, Gerald (CON - Warwick South)
gerry.guest@warwickdc.gov.uk
Hammon, John (CON - Cubbington)
john.hammon@warwickdc.gov.uk
Heath, Tony (IND - Whitnash)
tony.heath@warwickdc.gov.uk
Higgins, Elizabeth (CON - Warwick West)
elizabeth.higgins@warwickdc.gov.uk
Illingworth, George (CON - Kenilworth Abbey)
george.illingworth@warwickdc.gov.uk
Knight, Jane (LAB - Leamington Brunswick)
jane.knight@warwickdc.gov.uk
Mackay, Bertie (IND - Stoneleigh)
bertie.mackay@warwickdc.gov.uk
Mellor, Anne (CON - Warwick South)
anne.mellor@warwickdc.gov.uk
Mobbs, Andrew (CON - Kenilworth Park Hill)
andrew.mobbs@warwickdc.gov.uk
Pittarello, Nick (LD - Leamington Milverton)
nick.pittarello@warwickdc.gov.uk
Pratt, Norman (CON - Cubbington)
norman.pratt@warwickdc.gov.uk
Rhead, Alan (CON - Budbrooke)
alan.rhead@warwickdc.gov.uk
Sawdon, Clare (CON - Budbrooke)
clare.sawdon@warwickdc.gov.uk
Shilton, David (CON - Kenilworth Park Hill)
david.shilton@warwickdc.gov.uk
Syson, Sidney (LD - Leamington Milverton)
sidney.syson@warwickdc.gov.uk
Vincett, Norman (CON - Kenilworth St John's)
norman.vincett@warwickdc.gov.uk
Weber, Jerry (LAB - Leamington Clarendon)
jerry.weber@warwickdc.gov.uk
Weed, Barbara (LAB - Leamington Willes)
barbara.weed@warwickdc.gov.uk
Wilkinson, Alan (LAB - Leamington Brunswick)
alan.wilkinson@warwickdc.gov.uk
Williams, Glenn (CON - Warwick North)
glenn.williams@warwickdc.gov.uk
Wreford-Bush, David (LD - Leamington Crown)
dave.wreford-bush@warwickdc.gov.uk

POLITICAL COMPOSITION

CON: 25, LD: 9, LAB: 8, IND: 4

CABINET

Leader / Strategic Leadership: Mr Michael Doody
Deputy Leader: Mr Les Caborn
Corporate & Community Services: Mrs Moira-Ann Grainger
Culture: TBA
Development Services: Mr John Hammon
Environment & Community Protection: Mr Michael Coker
Finance: Mr Andrew Mobbs
Housing & Property: Mr Norman Vincett
Neighbourhood Services: Mr Dave Shilton

COMMITTEE CHAIRS

Employment: Mrs Felicity Bunker
Overview (Scrutiny): Mr Bill Gifford
Planning: Mr George Illingworth
Regulatory: Mrs Eithne Goode
Standards: Mr Christopher Purser (External)

WARWICKSHIRE C

Warwickshire County Council, PO Box 9, Shire Hall, Warwick CV34 4RR ☎ 01926 410410 💻 www.warwickshire.gov.uk

FACTS & FIGURES

Police Authority: Warwickshire Police Authority
Health Authority: NHS West Midlands
Learning and Skills Council: West Midlands
Parliamentary Constituencies: Nuneaton, Stratford-on-Avon, Warwick and Leamington, Warwickshire North
EU Constituencies: West Midlands
Election Frequency: Elections are by thirds

PRINCIPAL OFFICERS

Chief Executive: Mr Jim Graham, Chief Executive, PO Box 9, Shire Hall, Warwick CV34 4RR ☎ 01926 410410 ✉ jimgraham@warwickshire.gov.uk

Senior Management: Mr David Carter, Strategic Director for Resources Group, PO Box 9, Shire Hall, Warwick CV34 4RR ☎ 01926 412564 ✉ davidcarter@warwickshire.gov.uk

Senior Management: Ms Wendy Fabbro, Strategic Director for People, PO Box 9, Shire Hall, Warwick CV34 4RR ☎ 01926 742665 ✉ wendyfabbro@warwickshire.gov.uk

Senior Management: Ms Monica Fogarty, Strategic Director for Communities, PO Box 9, Shire Hall, Warwick CV34 4RR ☎ 01926 412514 📠 01926 476881 ✉ monicafogarty@warwickshire.gov.uk

Senior Management: Mr Graeme Smith, Chief Fire Officer, Warwick Street, Leamington Spa CV32 5LH ☎ 01926 423231 ✉ graemesmith@warwickshire.gov.uk

Access Officer / Social Services (Disability): Ms Lynne Barton,

Head of Integrated Disability Service, Saltisford Office Park, Ansell Way, Warwick CV34 4UL ☎ 01926 742977 ✉ lynnebarton@warwickshire.gov.uk

Architect, Building / Property Services: Mr Steve Smith, Head of Physical Assets, PO Box 3, Shire Hall, Warwick CV34 4RH ☎ 01926 412352 ✉ stevesmith@warwickshire.gov.uk

Catering Services: Ms Sandra Russell, Head of Catering, PO Box 9, Shire Hall, Warwick CV34 4RR ☎ 01926 412789 ✉ sandrarussell@warwickshire.gov.uk

Children / Youth Services: Mr Hugh Disley, Head of Service for Early Intervention, Saltisford Office Park, Ansell Way, Warwick CV34 4UL ☎ 01926 742589 ✉ hughdisley@warwickshire.gov.uk

Civil Registration: Mrs Alison John, Communications Manager, PO Box 9, Shire Hall, Warwick CV34 4RR ☎ 01926 412482 ✉ alison.john@warwickshire.gov.uk

PR / Communications: Mrs Anne Goodey, Communications (Press & PR), PO Box 9, Shire Hall, Warwick CV34 4RR ☎ 01926 412757 🖷 01926 412759 ✉ annegoodey@warwickshire.gov.uk

Community Safety: Mr Mark Ryder, Head of Localities & Community Safety, PO Box 43, Barrack Street, Warwick CV34 4SX ☎ 01926 412811 ✉ markryder@warwickshire.gov.uk

Computer Management: Mr Tonino Ciuffini, Head of ICT, PO Box 2, Shire Hall, Warwick CV34 4UB ☎ 01926 412879 ✉ toninociuffini@warwickshire.gov.uk

Consumer Protection and Trading Standards: Mr Mark Ryder, Head of Localities & Community Safety, PO Box 43, Barrack Street, Warwick CV34 4SX ☎ 01926 412811 ✉ markryder@warwickshire.gov.uk

Customer Service: Ms Kushal Birla, Head of Customer Service & Communications, PO Box 9, Shire Hall, Warwick CV34 4RR ☎ 01926 412013 ✉ kushalbirla@warwickshire.gov.uk

Economic Development: Ms Louise Wall, Head of Sustainable Communities, PO Box 43, Barrack Street, Warwick CV34 4SX ☎ 01926 412422 ✉ louisewall@warwickshire.gov.uk

Education: Mr Mark Gore, Head of Learning & Achievement, Saltisford Office Park, Ansell Way, Warwick CV34 4UL ☎ 01926 742588 ✉ markgore@warwickshire.gov.uk

E-Government: Mr Tonino Ciuffini, Head of ICT, PO Box 2, Shire Hall, Warwick CV34 4UB ☎ 01926 412879 ✉ toninociuffini@warwickshire.gov.uk

Estates, Property & Valuation: Mr David Soanes, Group Manager - Strategic Assets, Shire Hall, Warwick CV34 4SA ☎ 01926 736128 ✉ davidsoanes@warwickshire.gov.uk

Events Manager: Mrs Alison John, Communications Manager, PO Box 9, Shire Hall, Warwick CV34 4RR ☎ 01926 412482 ✉ alison.john@warwickshire.gov.uk

Facilities: Mr John Findlay, Property Support Group Manager, PO Box 9, Shire Hall, Warwick CV34 4RR ☎ 01926 418642 ✉ johnfindlay@warwickshire.gov.uk

Finance and Treasurer: Mr John Betts, Head of Corporate Finance, PO Box 9, Shire Hall, Warwick CV34 4RR ☎ 01926 412441 ✉ johnbetts@warwickshire.gov.uk

Fleet Management: Mr Stephen Trout, Fleet Service Manager, PO Box 43, Barrack Street, Warwick CV34 4SX ☎ 01926 412885 ✉ stephentrout@warwickshire.gov.uk

Health and Safety: Ms Ruth Pickering, County Health, Safety & Wellbeing Manager, PO Box 9, Shire Hall, Warwick CV34 4RR ☎ 01926 412316 ✉ ruthpickering@warwickshire.gov.uk

Highways: Mr Graeme Fitton, Head of Transport & Highways, PO Box 43, Barrack Street, Warwick CV34 4SX ☎ 01926 412046 ✉ graemefitton@warwickshire.gov.uk

Local Area Agreement: Mr Bill Basra, Partnerships Delivery Manager, PO Box 9, Shire Hall, Warwick CV34 4RR ☎ 01926 412127 ✉ billbasra@warwickshire.gov.uk

Legal: Mrs Greta Needham, Head of Law & Governance, PO Box 9, Shire Hall, Warwick CV34 4RR ☎ 01926 412319 ✉ gretaneedham@warwickshire.gov.uk

Lighting: Mr Mike Cunningham, Principal Lighting Engineer, Budbrooke Depot, Old Budbrooke Road, Warwick CV35 7DP ☎ 01926 736548 ✉ mikecunningham@warwickshire.gov.uk

Member Services: Mrs Jane Pollard, Democratic Services Manager, PO Box 9, Shire Hall, Warwick CV34 4RR ☎ 01926 412565 ✉ janepollard@warwickshire.gov.uk

Partnerships: Mr Nick Gower-Johnson, Localities Manager, PO Box 9, Shire Hall, Warwick CV34 4RR ☎ 01926 417053 ✉ nickgowerjohnson@warwickshire.gov.uk

Personnel / HR: Mrs Sue Evans, Head of HR & OD, PO Box 9, Shire Hall, Warwick CV34 4RR ☎ 01926 412314 ✉ sueevans@warwickshire.gov.uk

Planning: Ms Eva Neale, Planning Officer, PO Box 9, Shire Hall, Warwick CV34 4RR ☎ 01926 412907 ✉ evaneale@warwickshire.gov.uk

Procurement: Mr Paul White, County Procurement Manager, PO Box 9, Shire Hall, Warwick CV34 4RR ☎ 01926 736146 🖷 01926 412326 ✉ paulwhite@warwickshire.gov.uk

Public Libraries: Mr Ayub Khan, Head of Libraries - Strategy, Barrack Street, Warwick CV34 4TH ☎ 01926 412657 ✉ ayubkhan@warwickshire.gov.uk

Recycling & Waste Minimisation: Mr Glenn Fleet, Waste Management Manager, PO Box 43, Barrack Street, Warwick CV34 4SX ☎ 01926 418106 ✉ glennfleet@warwickshire.gov.uk

Regeneration: Ms Mandy Walker, Group Manager - Regeneration Projects & Funding, PO Box 43, Barrack Street, Warwick CV34 4SX ☎ 01926 412843

mandywalker@warwickshire.gov.uk

Road Safety: Mr Estyn Williams, Group Manager - Road Safety Unit, PO Box 43, Barrack Street, Warwick CV34 4SX ☎ 01926 412712 estynwilliams@warwickshire.gov.uk

Social Services (Adult): Ms Wendy Fabbro, Strategic Director for People, PO Box 9, Shire Hall, Warwick CV34 4RR ☎ 01926 742665 wendyfabbro@warwickshire.gov.uk

Social Services (Children): Ms Wendy Fabbro, Strategic Director for People, PO Box 9, Shire Hall, Warwick CV34 4RR ☎ 01926 742665 wendyfabbro@warwickshire.gov.uk

Staff Training: Mrs Sue Evans, Head of HR & OD, PO Box 9, Shire Hall, Warwick CV34 4RR ☎ 01926 412314 sueevans@warwickshire.gov.uk

Sustainable Communities: Ms Louise Wall, Head of Sustainable Communities, PO Box 43, Barrack Street, Warwick CV34 4SX ☎ 01926 412422 louisewall@warwickshire.gov.uk

Sustainable Development: Ms Louise Wall, Head of Sustainable Communities, PO Box 43, Barrack Street, Warwick CV34 4SX ☎ 01926 412422 louisewall@warwickshire.gov.uk

Tourism: Ms Caroline Sampson, Heritage & Cultural Service Manager, PO Box 43, Barrack Street, Warwick CV34 4SX ☎ 01926 738950 carolinesampson@warwickshire.gov.uk

Town Centre: Ms Mandy Walker, Group Manager - Regeneration Projects & Funding, PO Box 43, Barrack Street, Warwick CV34 4SX ☎ 01926 412843 mandywalker@warwickshire.gov.uk

Traffic Management: Mr Graeme Fitton, Head of Transport & Highways, PO Box 43, Shire Hall, Warwick CV34 4SX ☎ 01926 765675 🖷 01926 735662 graemefitton@warwickshire.gov.uk

Transport: Mr Kevin McGovern, Group Manager, PO Box 43, Barrack Street, Warwick CV34 4SX ☎ 01926 412930 kevinmcgovern@warwickshire.gov.uk

Transport Planner: Mr Roger Newham, County Transport Planner, PO Box 43, Barrack Street, Warwick CV34 4SX ☎ 01926 412203 rogernewham@warwickshire.gov.uk

Waste Collection and Disposal: Mr Christopher Moreton, Operation Manager - Waste Management, PO Box 43, Barrack Street, Warwick CV34 4SX ☎ 01926 412103 christophermoreton@warwickshire.gov.uk

Waste Management: Mr Glenn Fleet, Waste Management Manager, PO Box 43, Barrack Street, Warwick CV34 4SX ☎ 01926 418106 glennfleet@warwickshire.gov.uk

MEMBERS OF THE COUNCIL (62)

***Chair:* Doody**, Michael (CON - Cubbington)
cllrdoody@warwickshire.gov.uk

***Vice-Chair:* Shilton**, Dave (CON - Kenilworth Park Hill)
cllrshilton@warwickshire.gov.uk

***Leader of the Council:* Farnell**, Alan (CON - Nuneaton Weddington)
cllrfarnell@warwickshire.gov.uk

***Deputy Leader of the Council:* Stevens**, Bob (CON - Feldon)
cllrstevens@warwickshire.gov.uk

***Group Leader:* Roodhouse**, Jeremy (LD - Eastlands and Hillmorton)
cllrroodhouse@warwickshire.gov.uk

***Group Leader:* Tandy**, June (LAB - Nuneaton Wem Brook)
cllrtandy@warwickshire.gov.uk

Appleton, John (CON - Southam)
cllrappleton@warwickshire.gov.uk

Ashford, Martyn (CON - Warwick North)
cllrashford@warwickshire.gov.uk

Balaam, Peter (LD - Stratford Avenue & New Town)
cllrbalaam@warwickshire.gov.uk

Barnes, Peter (LD - Bidford-on-Avon)
cllrbarnes@warwickshire.gov.uk

Boad, Sarah (LD - Leamington North)
cllrboad@warwickshire.gov.uk

Bould, Penny (LAB - Leamington Brunswick)
cllrbould@warwickshire.gov.uk

Butlin, Peter (CON - Admirals)
cllrbutlin@warwickshire.gov.uk

Caborn, Les (CON - Bishops Tachbrook)
cllrcaborn@warwickshire.gov.uk

Chattaway, Richard (LAB - Bede)
cllrchattaway@warwickshire.gov.uk

Clarke, Jeff (CON - Nuneaton St. Nicholas)
cllrclarke@warwickshire.gov.uk

Cockburn, Alan (CON - Kenilworth St. Johns)
cllrcockburn@warwickshire.gov.uk

Cockings, Ron (CON - Stratford South)
cllrcockings@warwickshire.gov.uk

Compton, Jose (CON - Leek Wootton)
cllrcompton@warwickshire.gov.uk

Davis, Chris (LD - Leamington Milverton)
cllrdavis@warwickshire.gov.uk

Dodd, Richard (LD - Eastlands and Hillmorton)
cllrdodd@warwickshire.gov.uk

Foster, Jim (CON - Nuneaton Galley Common)
cllrfoster@warwickshire.gov.uk

Fowler, Peter (CON - Coleshill)
cllrfowler@warwickshire.gov.uk

Fox, Carol (CON - Hartshill)
cllrfox@warwickshire.gov.uk

Gittus, Mike (CON - Alcester)
cllrgittus@warwickshire.gov.uk

Goode, Eithne (LD - Leamington North)
cllrgoode@warwickshire.gov.uk

Hayfield, Colin (CON - Arley)
cllrhayfield@warwickshire.gov.uk

Hazleton, Robin (CON - Dunchurch)
cllrhazelton@warwickshire.gov.uk

Heatley, Martin (CON - Nuneaton Whitestone)
cllrheatley@warwickshire.gov.uk

Hicks, Bob (LAB - Nuneaton Abbey)
cllrhicks@warwickshire.gov.uk

Hobbs, Richard (CON - Aston Cantlow)
cllrhobbs@warwickshire.gov.uk

Hopkinson, Clare (CON - Warwick West)
cllrhopkinson@warwickshire.gov.uk

Jackson, Julie (LAB - Poplar)
cllrjackson@warwickshire.gov.uk

Johnston, David (LD - Wellesbourne)
cllrjohnston@warwickshire.gov.uk

Kirton, Bernard (IND - Whitnash)

cllrkirton@warwickshire.gov.uk
Lea, Joan (CON - Water Orton)
cllrmrslea@warwickshire.gov.uk
Lobbett, Barry (CON - Bedworth North)
cllrlobbett@warwickshire.gov.uk
Longden, Barry (LAB - Arbury & Stockingford)
cllrlongden@warwickshire.gov.uk
May, Tilly (CON - Polesworth)
cllrmay@warwickshire.gov.uk
McCarney, Frank (LAB - Bedworth West)
cllrmccarney@warwickshire.gov.uk
Morris-Jones, Phillip (CON - Fosse)
cllrmorris-jones@warwickshire.gov.uk
Moss, Brian (LAB - Kingsbury)
cllrmoss@warwickshire.gov.uk
Naylor, Tim (LAB - Leamington Willes)
cllrnaylor@warwickshire.gov.uk
Perry, Mike (CON - Henley-in-Arden)
cllrperry@warwickshire.gov.uk
Rickhards, Clive (LD - Studley)
cllrrickhards@warwickshire.gov.uk
Robbins, Carolyn (CON - Brownsover)
cllrrobbins@warwickshire.gov.uk
Rolfe, Kate (LD - Stratford South)
cllrrolfe@warwickshire.gov.uk
Ross, John (CON - Bulkington)
cllrross@warwickshire.gov.uk
Saint, Chris (CON - Shipston-on-Stour)
cllrsaint@warwickshire.gov.uk
Seccombe, Izzi (CON - Stour and the Vale)
cllrmrsseccombe@warwickshire.gov.uk
Shaw, Martin (CON - Atherstone)
cllrshaw@warwickshire.gov.uk
Sweet, Ray (LAB - Baddesley Ensor)
cllrsweet@warwickshire.gov.uk
Timms, Heather (CON - Earl Craven)
cllrtimms@warwickshire.gov.uk
Tooth, Sid (LAB - Nuneaton Camp Hill)
cllrtooth@warwickshire.gov.uk
Vereker, John (CON - Caldecott)
cllrvereker@warwickshire.gov.uk
Walton, Helen (CON - Brownsover)
cllrwalton@warwickshire.gov.uk
Warner, Angela (CON - Warwick South)
cllrwarner@warwickshire.gov.uk
Watson, Claire (CON - Lawford & New Bilton)
cllrwatson@warwickshire.gov.uk
Whitehouse, John (LD - Kenilworth Abbey)
cllrwhitehouse@warwickshire.gov.uk
Williams, Chris (CON - Kineton)
cllrwilliams@warwickshire.gov.uk
Wilson, Sonja (CON - Arbury & Stockingford)
cllrmrswilson@warwickshire.gov.uk
Wright, David (CON - Caldecott)
cllrwright@warwickshire.gov.uk

POLITICAL COMPOSITION

CON: 39, LAB: 11, LD: 11, IND: 1

CABINET

Leader: Mr Alan Farnell
Deputy Leader: Mr Bob Stevens
Adult Social Care: Mrs Izzi Seccombe
Children & Schools: Ms Heather Timms
Community Safety: Mr Richard Hobbs
Customers, Access & Physical Assets: Mr Colin Hayfield
Finance, Governance & IT: Mr David Wright
Sustainable Communities: Mr Alan Cockburn
Transport & Highways: Mr Peter Butlin
Workforce & Governance: Mr Martin Heatley

COMMITTEE CHAIRS

Adult & Community Services (Scrutiny): Mr Les Caborn
Audit & Standards: Mr John Bridgeman (External)
Children, Young People & Families (Scrutiny): Ms Julie Jackson

WATFORD D

Watford Borough Council, Town Hall, Watford WD17 3EX
☎ 01923 226400 🖷 01923 278100 ✉ enquiries@watford.gov.uk
🖳 www.watford.gov.uk

FACTS & FIGURES

Police Authority: Hertfordshire Police Authority
Health Authority: East of England Strategic Health Authority
Learning and Skills Council: Eastern
Parliamentary Constituencies: Watford
EU Constituencies: Eastern
Election Frequency: Elections are by thirds
Twinning: Nanterre (France); Mainz (Germany); Novgorod (Russia); Wilmington (Delaware, USA); Pesaro (Italy)

PRINCIPAL OFFICERS

Chief Executive: Mr Manny Lewis, Managing Director, Town Hall, Watford WD17 3EX ☎ 01923 278128 ✉ manny.lewis@watford.gov.uk

Architect, Building / Property Services: Mr Alistair Burg, Interim Property Section Head, Town Hall, Watford WD17 3EX ☎ 01923 278221; 01923 278221 ✉ alistair.burg@watford.gov.uk; alistair.burg@watford.gov.uk

Building Control: Mr Clive Fuller, Building Control Manager, Town Hall, Watford WD17 3EX ☎ 01923 278331 🖷 01923 278273 ✉ clive.fuller@watford.gov.uk

Children / Youth Services: Mr Gary Oliver, Section Head, Town Hall, Watford WD17 3EX ☎ 01923 278251 ✉ gary.oliver@watford.gov.uk

PR / Communications: Mr Mark Jeffery, Communications Manager, Town Hall, Watford WD17 3EX ☎ 01923 278392 🖷 01923 220635 ✉ mark.jeffery@watford.gov.uk

Community Safety: Ms Jane Taylor, Community Safety Manager, Town Hall, Watford WD17 3EX ☎ 01923 278455 ✉ jane.taylor@watford.gov.uk

Computer Management: Mrs Avni Patel, Head of Shared Services ICT, Town Hall, Watford WD17 3EX ☎ 01923 727441 ✉ avni.patel@watford.gov.uk

Customer Service: Ms Danielle Negrello, Customer Service Section Head, Town Hall, Watford WD17 3EX ☎ 01923 278927 ✉ danielle.negrello@watford.gov.uk

Economic Development: Mr Andrew Gibson, Economic Development Officer, Town Hall, Watford WD17 3EX ☎ 01923 278286 🖱 andrew.gibson@watford.gov.uk

Electoral Registration: Mr Gordon Amos, Elections Manager, Town Hall, Watford WD17 3EX ☎ 01923 278339 🖱 gordon.amos@watford.gov.uk

Emergency Planning: Mrs Carol Chen, Head of Legal & Property Services, Town Hall, Watford WD17 3EX ☎ 01923 278350 📠 01923 278366 🖱 carol.chen@watford.gov.uk

Energy Management: Mr Neil Walker, Energy & Renewal Surveyor, Town Hall, Watford WD17 3EX ☎ 01923 278149 🖱 neil.walker@watford.gov.uk

Environmental / Technical Services: Mr Alan Gough, Head of Environmental Services, Town Hall, Watford WD17 3EX ☎ 01923 278600 🖱 alan.gough@watford.gov.uk

Environmental Health: Ms Justine Hoy, Environmental Health & Licensing Section Head, Town Hall, Watford WD17 3EX ☎ 01923 278449 🖱 justine.hoy@watford.gov.uk

Estates, Property & Valuation: Mr Alistair Burg, Interim Property Section Head, Town Hall, Watford WD17 3EX ☎ 01923 278221; 01923 278221 🖱 alistair.burg@watford.gov.uk; alistair.burg@watford.gov.uk

Facilities: Mr Clive Goodchild, Facilities Manager, Town Hall, Watford WD17 3EX ☎ 01923 278378 🖱 clive.goodchild@watford.gov.uk

Finance and Treasurer: Mr Bernard Clarke, Head of Strategic Finance, Town Hall, Watford WD17 3EX ☎ 01923 278189 🖱 bernard.clarke@watford.gov.uk

Grounds Maintenance: Mr Paul Rabbitts, Parks & Open Spaces, Town Hall, Watford WD17 3EX ☎ 01923 278250 🖱 paul.rabbitts@watford.gov.uk

Health and Safety: Mr Darren Williams, Health & Safety Adviser, Town Hall, Watford WD17 3EX ☎ 07767 851209 🖱 darren.williams@watford.gov.uk

Home Energy Conservation: Mr Neil Walker, Energy & Renewal Surveyor, Town Hall, Watford WD17 3EX ☎ 01923 278149 🖱 neil.walker@watford.gov.uk

Housing: Ms Rachel Dawson, Housing Section Head, Town Hall, Watford WD17 3EX ☎ 01923 278902; 01923 278902 🖱 rachel.dawson@watford.gov.uk; rachel.dawson@watford.gov.uk

Legal: Mrs Carol Chen, Head of Legal & Property Services, Town Hall, Watford WD17 3EX ☎ 01923 278350 📠 01923 278366 🖱 carol.chen@watford.gov.uk

Leisure and Cultural Services: Ms Lesley Palumbo, Head of Community Services, Town Hall, Watford WD17 3EX ☎ 01923 278561 🖱 lesley.palumbo@watford.gov.uk

Licensing: Mr Jeffrey Leib, Licensing Manager, Town Hall, Watford WD17 3EX ☎ 01923 278503 🖱 jeffrey.leib@watford.gov.uk

Member Services: Ms Caroline Harris, Members & Civic Events Officer, Town Hall, Watford WD17 3EX ☎ 01923 278374 🖱 caroline.harris@watford.gov.uk

Parking: Ms Jane Custance, Head of Planning & Development, Town Hall, Watford WD17 3EX ☎ 01923 278044 🖱 jane.custance@watford.gov.uk

Partnerships: Mrs Kathryn Robson, Partnerships & Performance Section Head, Town Hall, Watford WD17 3EX ☎ 01923 278077 🖱 kathryn.robson@watford.gov.uk

Personnel / HR: Mr Terry Baldwin, Head of Shared Services Human Resources, Town Hall, Watford WD17 3EX ☎ 01923 278133 🖱 terry.baldwin@watford.gov.uk

Planning: Ms Jane Custance, Head of Planning & Development, Town Hall, Watford WD17 3EX ☎ 01923 278044 🖱 jane.custance@watford.gov.uk

Recycling & Waste Minimisation: Ms Beverley Beri, Waste & Recycling Section Head, Wiggenhall Depot, Wiggenhall Road, Watford WD18 0FB ☎ 01923 278461 📠 01923 239588 🖱 beverley.beri@watford.gov.uk

Regeneration: Ms Jane Custance, Head of Planning & Development, Town Hall, Watford WD17 3EX ☎ 01923 278044 🖱 jane.custance@watford.gov.uk

Staff Training: Ms Marj Setters, Organisational Development Manager, Town Hall, Watford WD17 3EX ☎ 01923 278048 🖱 marj.setters@watford.gov.uk

Street Scene: Mr Alan Gough, Head of Environmental Services, Town Hall, Watford WD17 3EX ☎ 01923 278600 🖱 alan.gough@watford.gov.uk

Sustainable Communities: Ms Cate Hall, Executive Director, Town Hall, Watford WD17 3EX ☎ 01923 278195 📠 01923 220635 🖱 cate.hall@watford.gov.uk

Waste Collection and Disposal: Mr Brandon Begley, Operations Manager - Waste Services, Wiggenhall Depot, Wiggenhall Road, Watford WD18 0FB ☎ 01923 278612 📠 01923 239588 🖱 brandon.begley@watford.gov.uk

Waste Management: Mr Brandon Begley, Operations Manager - Waste Services, Wiggenhall Depot, Wiggenhall Road, Watford WD18 0FB ☎ 01923 278612 📠 01923 239588 🖱 brandon.begley@watford.gov.uk

Children's Play Areas: Mr Paul Rabbitts, Parks & Open Spaces, Town Hall, Watford WD17 3EX ☎ 01923 278250 🖱 paul.rabbitts@watford.gov.uk

MEMBERS OF THE COUNCIL (37)

Directly Elected Mayor: **Thornhill**, Dorothy (LD -)
themayor@watford.gov.uk
Chair: **Counter**, Shirena (LD - Oxhey)

shirena.counter@watford.gov.uk
***Vice-Chair:* Rackett**, Steve (GRN - Callowland)
steve.rackett@watford.gov.uk
***Deputy Mayor:* Scudder**, Derek (LD - Stanborough)
derek.scudder@watford.gov.uk
***Group Leader:* Bell**, Nigel (LAB - Holywell)
nigel.bell@watford.gov.uk
***Group Leader:* Sharpe**, Iain (LD - Oxhey)
iain.sharpe@watford.gov.uk
Aron, Jeanette (LD - Nascot)
jeanette.aron@watford.gov.uk
Brandon, Ian (GRN - Callowland)
ian.brandon@watford.gov.uk
Brown, Ian (LD - Woodside)
ian.brown@watford.gov.uk
Brown, Jan (LD - Meriden)
jan.brown@watford.gov.uk
Burtenshaw, Alan (LD - Woodside)
alan.burtenshaw@watford.gov.uk
Collett, Karen (LD - Woodside)
karen.collett@watford.gov.uk
Connal, Jackie (LAB - Holywell)
jackie.connal@watford.gov.uk
Crout, Keith (LD - Stanborough)
keith.crout@watford.gov.uk
Derbyshire, George (LD - Park)
george.derbyshire@watford.gov.uk
Dhindsa, Jagtar Singh (LAB - Vicarage)
jagtar.dhindsa@watford.gov.uk
Greenslade, Sue (LD - Meriden)
sue.greenslade@watford.gov.uk
Hastrick, Kareen (LD - Meriden)
kareen.hastrick@watford.gov.uk
Hofman, Mark (LD - Nascot)
mark.hofman@watford.gov.uk
Jeffree, Peter (LD - Park)
Peter.jeffree@watford.gov.uk
Johnson, Stephen (CON - Leggatts)
stephen.johnson@watford.gov.uk
Joynes, Anne (LAB - Leggatts)
anne.joynes@watford.gov.uk
Khan, Asif (LAB - Leggatts)
asif.khan@watford.gov.uk
Leslie, Chris (LD - Central)
chris.leslie@watford.gov.uk
Lovejoy, Ann (GRN - Callowland)
ann.lovejoy@watford.gov.uk
Lynch, Helen (LD - Central)
helen.lynch@watford.gov.uk
Martins, Rabi (LD - Central)
rabi.martins@watford.gov.uk
McLeod, Kelly (LD - Tudor)
kelly.mcleod@watford.gov.uk
Meerabux, Malcolm (IND - Park)
malcolm.meerabux@watford.gov.uk
Mills, Mo (LAB - Vicarage)
mo.mills@watford.gov.uk
Scudder, Lindsay (LD - Tudor)
lindsey.scudder@watford.gov.uk
Shah, Nasreen (LAB - Vicarage)
nasreen.shah@watford.gov.uk
Taylor, Peter (LD - Oxhey)
peter.taylor@watford.gov.uk
Turmaine, Matt (LAB - Holywell)
matt.turmaine@watford.gov.uk
Walford, Darren (LD - Tudor)
darren.walford@watford.gov.uk
Watkin, Mark (LD - Nascot)
mark.watkin@watford.gov.uk
Williams, Tim (LD - Stanborough)
tim.williams@watford.gov.uk

POLITICAL COMPOSITION
LD: 24, LAB: 8, GRN: 3, CON: 1, IND: 1

CABINET
Directly Elected Mayor, Community Services: Mrs Dorothy Thornhill
Environmental Services: Mr Derek Scudder
Finance & Shared Services: Mr Mark Watkin
Planning & Development, Legal & Property Services: Mr Iain Sharpe

COMMITTEE CHAIRS
Audit: Mr Ian Brown
Budget Panel: Mr Jagtar Singh Dhindsa
Development Control: Mr Rabi Martins
Licensing: Mrs Jan Brown
Policy Development (Scrutiny): Ms Kelly McLeod

WAVENEY — D
Waveney District Council, Town Hall, High Street, Lowestoft NR32 1HS ☎ 01502 562111 🖷 01502 589327 ✉ chiefexecutive@waveney.gov.uk 💻 www.waveney.gov.uk

FACTS & FIGURES
Police Authority: Suffolk Police Authority
Health Authority: East of England Strategic Health Authority
Learning and Skills Council: Eastern
Parliamentary Constituencies: Suffolk Coastal, Waveney
EU Constituencies: Eastern
Election Frequency: Elections are by thirds
Twinning: Beccles: Petit Couronne (France); Halesworth: Bouchain (France)and Eitorf (Suffolk); Lowestoft: Plaisir (France);

PRINCIPAL OFFICERS
Chief Executive: Mr Stephen Baker, Strategic Director, Town Hall, High Street, Lowestoft NR32 1HS ☎ 01502 562111 🖷 01502 589327 ✉ stephen.baker@waveney.gov.uk

Assistant Chief Executive: Mr Arthur Charvonia, Assistant Chief Executive, Town Hall, High Street, Lowestoft NR32 1HS ☎ 01502 562111 🖷 01502 589327 ✉ arthur.charvonia@waveney.gov.uk

Senior Management: Mr Alan McFarlane, Director of Resources, Town Hall, High Street, Lowestoft NR32 1HS ☎ 01502 562111 🖷 01502 589327 ✉ alan.mcfarlane@waveney.gov.uk

Senior Management: Mr Tony Osmanski, Strategic Director, Town Hall, High Street, Lowestoft NR32 1HS ☎ 01502 562111 🖷 01502 589327 ✉ tony.osmanski@suffolkcoastal.gov.uk

Architect, Building / Property Services: Mrs Gayle Hart, Manager, Town Hall, High Street, Lowestoft NR32 1HS ☎ 01502 562111 🖷 01502 523478 ✉ gayle.hart@nps.co.uk

Best Value: Mr Richard Best, Policy Manager, Town Hall, High Street, Lowestoft NR32 1HS ☎ 01502 562111 🖷 01502 589327 🖱 richard.best@waveney.gov.uk

Building Control: Mr Barry Reid, Principal Service Manager (Planning & Building Control), Town Hall, High Street, Lowestoft NR32 1HS ☎ 01502 562111 🖷 01502 589327 🖱 barry.reid@waveney.gov.uk

PR / Communications: Mr Phil Harris, Communications Officer, Town Hall, High Street, Lowestoft NR32 1HS ☎ 01502 523637 🖷 01502 589327 🖱 phil.harris@waveney.gov.uk

Community Safety: Ms Karen Hubbard, Community Safety Officer, Town Hall, High Street, Lowestoft NR32 1HS ☎ 01502 562111 🖷 01502 598327 🖱 karen.hubbard@waveney.gov.uk

Computer Management: Mr Peter Kalinowski, ICT Officer, Town Hall, High Street, Lowestoft NR32 1HS ☎ 01502 562111 🖱 peter.kalinowski@suffolkcoastal.gov.uk

Contracts: Mr Ian Purdom, Senior Procurement Officer, Town Hall, High Street, Lowestoft NR32 1HS ☎ 01502 562111 🖷 01502 589327 🖱 ian.purdom@waveney.gov.uk

Customer Service: Mr Scott Luxton, Principal Service Manager (Customer Services), Town Hall, High Street, Lowestoft NR32 1HS 🖱 scott.luxton@waveney.gov.uk

Economic Development: Mr Paul Moss, Principal Service Manager (Economic Regeneration), Town Hall, High Street, Lowestoft NR32 1HS ☎ 01502 523394 🖷 01502 589327 🖱 paul.moss@waveney.gov.uk

Electoral Registration: Mrs Sharon Shand, Service Manager (Electoral Services), Town Hall, High Street, Lowestoft NR32 1HS ☎ 01502 523253 🖷 01502 589327 🖱 sharon.shand@waveney.gov.uk

Emergency Planning: Mr Robin Buncombe, District Emergency Planning Officer, Town Hall, High Street, Lowestoft NR32 1HS ☎ 01502 562111 🖷 01502 589327 🖱 robin.buncombe@waveney.gov.uk

Environmental / Technical Services: Mr Phil Gore, Head of Health, Town Hall, High Street, Lowestoft NR32 1HS ☎ 01502 562111 🖷 01502 589327 🖱 phil.gore@suffolkcoastal.gov.uk

Environmental Health: Mr Phil Gore, Head of Health, Town Hall, High Street, Lowestoft NR32 1HS ☎ 01502 562111 🖷 01502 589327 🖱 phil.gore@suffolkcoastal.gov.uk

Estates, Property & Valuation: Mrs Gayle Hart, Manager, Town Hall, High Street, Lowestoft NR32 1HS ☎ 01502 562111 🖷 01502 523478 🖱 gayle.hart@nps.co.uk

Events Manager: Mr Darren Newman, Tourism Officer, Town Hall, High Street, Lowestoft NR32 1HS ☎ 01502 523385 🖷 01502 589327 🖱 darren.newman@waveney.gov.uk

Facilities: Mr John Brown, Principal Service Manager (Building & Housing), Town Hall, High Street, Lowestoft NR32 1HS ☎ 01502 562111 🖷 ; 01502 589327 🖱 john.brown@waveney.gov.uk

Finance and Treasurer: Mr Alan McFarlane, Director of Resources, Town Hall, High Street, Lowestoft NR32 1HS ☎ 01502 562111 🖷 01502 589327 🖱 alan.mcfarlane@waveney.gov.uk

Grounds Maintenance: Mr David Gallagher, Head of Service (Customer Services & Commercial Contracts), Town Hall, High Street, Lowestoft NR32 1HS ☎ 01502 523007 🖷 01502 589327 🖱 david.gallagher@waveney.gov.uk

Health and Safety: Ms Sheila Warnes, Health & Safety Advisor, Town Hall, High Street, Lowestoft NR32 1HS ☎ 01502 562111 🖷 01502 589327 🖱 sheila.warnes@waveney.gov.uk

Housing: Mr Robert Prince, Head of Strategic Housing, Town Hall, High Street, Lowestoft NR32 1HS ☎ 01502 562111 🖷 01502 589327 🖱 robert.prince@waveney.gov.uk

Housing Maintenance: Mr John Brown, Principal Service Manager (Building & Housing), Town Hall, High Street, Lowestoft NR32 1HS ☎ 01502 562111 🖷 01502 589327 🖱 john.brown@waveney.gov.uk

Legal: Mrs Hilary Slater, Head of Legal & Democratic Services, Town Hall, High Street, Lowestoft NR32 1HS ☎ 01502 562111 🖷 01502 589327 🖱 hilary.slater@suffolkcoatal.gov.uk

Leisure and Cultural Services: Mr Asa Morrison, Principal Service Manager (Tourism, Culture & Sports Development), Town Hall, High Street, Lowestoft NR32 1HS ☎ 01502 562111 🖷 01502 514617 🖱 asa.morrison@waveney.gov.uk

Licensing: Mr Dick Woodrow, Senior Licensing Officer, Town Hall, High Street, Lowestoft NR32 1HS ☎ 01502 589327 🖷 01502 589327 🖱 dick.woodrow@waveney.gov.uk

Lifelong Learning: Mrs Heather Shilling, HR Officer (Learning & Development), Town Hall, High Street, Lowestoft NR32 1HS ☎ 01502 523221 🖷 01502 589327 🖱 heather.shilling@waveney.gov.uk

Lottery Funding, Charity and Voluntary: Mrs Kathleen Scott, Grants Co-ordinator, Town Hall, High Street, Lowestoft NR32 1HS ☎ 01502 562111 🖷 01502 598327 🖱 kathleen.scott@waveney.gov.uk

Member Services: Mrs Donna Offord, Principal Service Manager (Democratic Services), Town Hall, High Street, Lowestoft NR32 1HS ☎ 01502 562111 🖷 01502 589327 🖱 donna.offord@waveney.gov.uk

Personnel / HR: Mrs Carol Lower, Principal Service Manager (Human Resources), Town Hall, High Street, Lowestoft NR32 1HS ☎ 01502 562111 🖷 01502 589327 🖱 carol.lower@waveney.gov.uk

Planning: Mr Philip Ridley, Head of Planning Services, Town Hall, High Street, Lowestoft NR32 1HS ☎ 01502 562111 🖷 01502 589327 🖱 philip.ridley@waveney.gov.uk

Procurement: Mr Ian Purdom, Senior Procurement Officer, Town Hall, High Street, Lowestoft NR32 1HS ☎ 01502 562111 🖷 01502 589327 🖱 ian.purdom@waveney.gov.uk

Recycling & Waste Minimisation: Mr Alan McFarlane, Director of Resources, Town Hall, High Street, Lowestoft NR32 1HS ☎ 01502 562111 🖷 01502 589327 ✉ alan.mcfarlane@waveney.gov.uk

Regeneration: Mr Stephen Baker, Strategic Director, Town Hall, High Street, Lowestoft NR32 1HS ☎ 01502 562111 🖷 01502 589327 ✉ stephen.baker@waveney.gov.uk

Staff Training: Mrs Heather Shilling, HR Officer (Learning & Development), Town Hall, High Street, Lowestoft NR32 1HS ☎ 01502 523221 🖷 01502 589327 ✉ heather.shilling@waveney.gov.uk

Sustainable Communities: Mr Philip Ridley, Head of Planning Services, Town Hall, High Street, Lowestoft NR32 1HS ☎ 01502 562111 🖷 01502 589327 ✉ philip.ridley@waveney.gov.uk

Sustainable Development: Mr Philip Ridley, Head of Planning Services, Town Hall, High Street, Lowestoft NR32 1HS ☎ 01502 562111 🖷 01502 589327 ✉ philip.ridley@waveney.gov.uk

Tourism: Mr Asa Morrison, Principal Service Manager (Tourism, Culture & Sports Development), Town Hall, High Street, Lowestoft NR32 1HS ☎ 01502 562111 🖷 01502 514617 ✉ asa.morrison@waveney.gov.uk

Waste Management: Mr David Gallagher, Head of Service (Operations & Facilities), Town Hall, High Street, Lowestoft NR32 1HS ☎ 01502 562111 ✉ david.gallagher@waveney.gov.uk

MEMBERS OF THE COUNCIL (48)

***Mayor:* Webb**, Nick (LAB - Whitton)
nick.webb@waveney.gov.uk
***Deputy Mayor:* Ford**, June (LAB - Kirkley)
june.ford@waveney.gov.uk
***Leader of the Council:* Law**, Colin (CON - Oulton Broad)
colin.law@waveney.gov.uk
***Deputy Leader of the Council:* Ardley**, Stephen (CON - Carlton)
steve.ardley@waveney.gov.uk
***Group Leader:* Sullivan**, Tod (LAB - Whitton)
tod.sullivan@waveney.gov.uk
Allen, Sue (CON - Southwold and Reydon)
sue.allen@waveney.gov.uk
Ashdown, Paul (CON - Lothingland)
paul.ashdown@waveney.gov.uk
Bamonde, Jose (LAB - Carlton Colville)
jose.bamonde@waveney.gov.uk
Barker, Sonia (LAB - Pakefield)
sonia.barker@waveney.gov.uk
Barnard, Mike (CON - Oulton Broad)
mike.barnard@waveney.gov.uk
Barron, Allyson (LAB - St. Margarets)
allyson.barron@waveney.gov.uk
Bee, Mark (CON - Worlingham)
mark.bee@waveney.gov.uk
Bellham, Roger (LAB - St. Margarets)
roger.bellham@waveney.gov.uk
Brooks, Norman (CON - Worlingham)
norman.brooks@waveney.gov.uk
Brown, Alan (LAB - Kessingland)
alan.brown@waveney.gov.uk
Byatt, Peter (LAB - Pakefield)
peter.byatt@waveney.gov.uk
Cackett, Alison (CON - Blything)
alison.cackett@waveney.gov.uk
Cherry, Yvonne (LAB - Kirkley)
yvonne.cherry@waveney.gov.uk
Cherry, Malcolm (LAB - St Margaret's)
malcolm.cherry@waveney.gov.uk
Coghill, Peter (LAB - Normanston)
peter.coghill@waveney.gov.uk
Collecott, Peter (IND - Oulton)
pete.collecott@waveney.gov.uk
Coulam, David (CON - Gunton and Corton)
david.coulam@waveney.gov.uk
Douce, Gareth (LAB - Kirkley)
gareth.douce@waveney.gov.uk
Elliott, Graham (GRN - Beccles North)
graham.elliott@waveney.gov.uk
Flegg, Patricia (CON - Halesworth)
paddy.flegg@waveney.gov.uk
Gandy, Tess (LAB - Harbour)
tess.gandy@waveney.gov.uk
Goldson, Tony (CON - Halesworth)
tony.goldson@waveney.gov.uk
Graham, Ian (LAB - Harbour)
ian.graham@waveney.gov.uk
Grant, Kathleen (CON - Carlton Colville)
kathleen.grant@waveney.gov.uk
Groom, John (CON - Bungay)
john.groom@waveney.gov.uk
Ives-Keeler, Mike (LAB - Oulton)
mike.ives-keeler@waveney.gov.uk
Jenkins, Keith (LAB - Beccles South)
keith.jenkins@waveney.gov.uk
Ladd, Michael (CON - Southwold and Reydon)
michael.ladd@waveney.gov.uk
Light, Paul (CON - Carlton Colville)
paul.light@waveney.gov.uk
Mortimer, Frank (CON - Carlton)
frank.mortimer@waveney.gov.uk
Parsons, Martin (CON - Wrentham)
martin.parsons@waveney.gov.uk
Patience, Keith (LAB - Normanston)
keith.patience@waveney.gov.uk
Pitchers, Malcolm (LAB - Pakefield)
malcolm.pitchers@waveney.gov.uk
Provan, Bruce (CON - Kessingland)
bruce.provan@waveney.gov.uk
Punt, Chris (CON - Beccles North)
chris.punt@waveney.gov.uk
Ritchie, David (CON - The Saints)
david.ritchie@waveney.gov.uk
Rudd, Mary (CON - Gunton and Corton)
mary.rudd@waveney.gov.uk
Springall, Kevin (CON - Wainford)
kevin.springall@waveney.gov.uk
Swainson, Julian (LAB - Harbour)
julian.swainson@waveney.gov.uk
Thwaites, Alan (LAB - Beccles South)
alan.thwaites@waveney.gov.uk
Webb, Sarah (LAB - Whitton)
sarah.webb@waveney.gov.uk
Wheatley, Jacki (LAB - Normanston)
jacki.wheatley@waveney.gov.uk

Woods, Simon (CON - Bungay)
simon.woods@waveney.gov.uk

POLITICAL COMPOSITION

CON: 23, LAB: 23, GRN: 1, IND: 1

CABINET

Leader: Mr Colin Law
Deputy Leader: Mr Stephen Ardley
Community Health & Information Technology: Mrs Mary Rudd
Customers & Communities: Mr Frank Mortimer
Green Environment & Operational Partnerships: Mr Stephen Ardley
Housing: Mrs Sue Allen
Leisure, Tourism & Economic Development: Mr Bruce Provan
Planning & Coastal Management: Mr David Ritchie
Resources: Mr Mike Barnard

COMMITTEE CHAIRS

Audit & Risk Management: Mr Simon Woods
Community Safety, Health & Wellbeing: Mr Frank Mortimer
Development Control: Mr John Groom
Licensing: Mrs Kathleen Grant
Overview & Scrutiny: Mr Tod Sullivan

WAVERLEY D

Waverley Borough Council, Council Offices, The Burys, Godalming GU7 1HR ☎ 01483 523333 🖷 01483 426337 enquiries@waverley.gov.uk www.waverley.gov.uk

FACTS & FIGURES

Police Authority: Surrey Police Authority
Health Authority: South East Coast Strategic Health Authority
Learning and Skills Council: South East
Parliamentary Constituencies: South West Surrey
EU Constituencies: South East
Election Frequency: Elections are of whole council
Twinning: Bramley: Rhens-am-Rhein (Germany); Cranleigh: Vallendar (Germany); Farnham: Andernach (Germany); Mayen-Koblenz (Germany); Godalming: Mayen (Germany); Joigny (France); Haslemere: Bernay (France); Horb am Nekar (Germany);

PRINCIPAL OFFICERS

Chief Executive: Mrs Mary Orton, Chief Executive, Council Offices, The Burys, Godalming GU7 1HR ☎ 01483 523208 mary.orton@waverley.gov.uk

Deputy Chief Executive: Mr Paul Wenham, Deputy Chief Executive / Strategic Director (Resources), Council Offices, The Burys, Godalming GU7 1HR ☎ 01483 523238 🖷 01483 523245 paul.wenham@waverley.gov.uk

Senior Management: Mr Damian Roberts, Strategic Director, Council Offices, The Burys, Godalming GU7 1HR ☎ 01483 523398 🖷 01483 523175 damian.roberts@waverley.gov.uk

Senior Management: Mrs Angela Smithers, Head of Housing, Council Offices, The Burys, Godalming GU7 1HR ☎ 01483 523375 🖷 01483 523050 angela.smithers@waverley.gov.uk

Building Control: Mr Paul Frame, Building Control Manager, Council Offices, The Burys, Godalming GU7 1HR ☎ 01483 523322 🖷 01483 523118 paul.frame@waverley.gov.uk

Catering Services: Mr Roger Standing, Head of Customer, IT & Office Services, Council Offices, The Burys, Godalming GU7 1HR ☎ 01483 523221 🖷 01483 523475 roger.standing@waverley.gov.uk

Children / Youth Services: Ms Katie Webb, Community Services Manager, Council Offices, The Burys, Godalming GU7 1HR ☎ 01483 523340 katie.webb@waverley.gov.uk

PR / Communications: Mrs Julie Jackson, Communications Manager, Council Offices, The Burys, Godalming GU7 1HR ☎ 01483 523204 🖷 01483 523200 julie.jackson@waverley.gov.uk

Community Safety: Mr Ian Grist, Community Safety Co-ordinator, Council Offices, The Burys, Godalming GU7 1HR ☎ 01483 523386 🖷 01483 523200 ian.grist@waverley.gov.uk

Community Safety: Mr Kelvin Mills, Head of Community Services, Council Offices, The Burys, Godalming GU7 1HR ☎ 01483 523432 kelvin.mills@waverley.gov.uk

Customer Service: Mr Roger Standing, Head of Customer, IT & Office Services, Council Offices, The Burys, Godalming GU7 1HR ☎ 01483 523221 🖷 01483 523475 roger.standing@waverley.gov.uk

Economic Development: Mr Kelvin Mills, Head of Community Services, Council Offices, The Burys, Godalming GU7 1HR ☎ 01483 523432 kelvin.mills@waverley.gov.uk

E-Government: Mr Roger Standing, Head of Customer, IT & Office Services, Council Offices, The Burys, Godalming GU7 1HR ☎ 01483 523221 🖷 01483 523475 roger.standing@waverley.gov.uk

Electoral Registration: Mrs Tracey Stanbridge, Senior Manager - Elections, Council Offices, The Burys, Godalming GU7 1HR ☎ 01483 523413 🖷 01483 523475 tracey.stanbridge@waverley.gov.uk

Emergency Planning: Mr Aaron Carter, Safety & Emergency Planning Adviser, Council Offices, The Burys, Godalming GU7 1HR ☎ 01483 523480 🖷 01483 523381 aaron.carter@waverley.gov.uk

Energy Management: Ms Fotini Kallipoliti, Sustainability Manager, Council Offices, The Burys, Godalming GU7 1HR ☎ 01483 523448 fotini.kallipoliti@waverley.gov.uk

Environmental / Technical Services: Mr Robert Anderton, Head of Environmental Services, Council Offices, The Burys, Godalming GU7 1HR ☎ 01483 523411 rob.anderton@waverley.gov.uk

Environmental Health: Miss Victoria Buckroyd, Environmental Health Manager, Council Offices, The Burys, Godalming GU7 1HR ☎ 01483 523436 🖷 01483 523175 victoria.buckroyd@waverley.gov.uk

Estates, Property & Valuation: Mrs Ailsa Woodruff, Estates & Valuation Manager, Council Offices, The Burys, Godalming GU7 1HR ☎ 01483 523459 🖷 01483 523118 ✉ ailsa.woodruff@waverley.gov.uk

Facilities: Mr Roger Standing, Head of Customer, IT & Office Services, Council Offices, The Burys, Godalming GU7 1HR ☎ 01483 523221 🖷 01483 523475 ✉ roger.standing@waverley.gov.uk

Finance and Treasurer: Mr Paul Wenham, Deputy Chief Executive / Strategic Director (Resources), Council Offices, The Burys, Godalming GU7 1HR ☎ 01483 523238 🖷 01483 523245 ✉ paul.wenham@waverley.gov.uk

Grounds Maintenance: Mr Kelvin Mills, Head of Community Services, Council Offices, The Burys, Godalming GU7 1HR ☎ 01483 523432 ✉ kelvin.mills@waverley.gov.uk

Health and Safety: Mr Aaron Carter, Safety & Emergency Planning Adviser, Council Offices, The Burys, Godalming GU7 1HR ☎ 01483 523480 🖷 01483 523381 ✉ aaron.carter@waverley.gov.uk

Home Energy Conservation: Ms Fotini Kallipoliti, Sustainability Manager, Council Offices, The Burys, Godalming GU7 1HR ☎ 01483 523448 ✉ fotini.kallipoliti@waverley.gov.uk

Housing: Mrs Angela Smithers, Head of Housing, Council Offices, The Burys, Godalming GU7 1HR ☎ 01483 523375 🖷 01483 523050 ✉ angela.smithers@waverley.gov.uk

Housing Maintenance: Mrs Angela Smithers, Head of Housing, Council Offices, The Burys, Godalming GU7 1HR ☎ 01483 523375 🖷 01483 523050 ✉ angela.smithers@waverley.gov.uk

Legal: Mr Robin Pellow, Head of Democratic & Legal Services, Council Offices, The Burys, Godalming GU7 1HR ☎ 01483 523222 🖷 01483 523475 ✉ robin.pellow@waverley.gov.uk

Leisure and Cultural Services: Mr Kelvin Mills, Head of Community Services, Council Offices, The Burys, Godalming GU7 1HR ☎ 01483 523432 ✉ kelvin.mills@waverley.gov.uk

Licensing: Mr Robin Pellow, Head of Democratic & Legal Services, Council Offices, The Burys, Godalming GU7 1HR ☎ 01483 523222 🖷 01483 523475 ✉ robin.pellow@waverley.gov.uk

Member Services: Mr Robin Pellow, Head of Democratic & Legal Services, Council Offices, The Burys, Godalming GU7 1HR ☎ 01483 523222 🖷 01483 523475 ✉ robin.pellow@waverley.gov.uk

Parking: Mr Robert Anderton, Head of Environmental Services, Council Offices, The Burys, Godalming GU7 1HR ☎ 01483 523411 ✉ rob.anderton@waverley.gov.uk

Personnel / HR: Mr Matthew Baker, HR Consultant, Council Offices, The Burys, Godalming GU7 1HR ☎ 01483 523345 ✉ matthew.baker@waverley.gov.uk

Planning: Mr Matthew Evans, Head of Planning, Council Offices, The Burys, Godalming GU7 1HR ☎ 01483 523298 🖷 01483 523118 ✉ matthew.evans@waverley.gov.uk

Recycling & Waste Minimisation: Mr Robert Anderton, Head of Environmental Services, Council Offices, The Burys, Godalming GU7 1HR ☎ 01483 523411 ✉ rob.anderton@waverley.gov.uk

Staff Training: Ms Julie Vickers, Training & Systems Adviser, Council Offices, The Burys, Godalming GU7 1HR ☎ 01483 523167 ✉ julie.vickers@waverly.gov.uk

Sustainable Development: Ms Fotini Kallipoliti, Sustainability Manager, Council Offices, The Burys, Godalming GU7 1HR ☎ 01483 523448 ✉ fotini.kallipoliti@waverley.gov.uk

Waste Collection and Disposal: Mr Robert Anderton, Head of Environmental Services, Council Offices, The Burys, Godalming GU7 1HR ☎ 01483 523411 ✉ rob.anderton@waverley.gov.uk

Waste Management: Mr Robert Anderton, Head of Environmental Services, Council Offices, The Burys, Godalming GU7 1HR ☎ 01483 523411 ✉ rob.anderton@waverley.gov.uk

Children's Play Areas: Mr Matt Lank, Parks Manager, Council Offices, The Burys, Godalming GU7 1HR ☎ 01483 523190 ✉ matt.lank@waverley.gov.uk

MEMBERS OF THE COUNCIL (57)

***Mayor:* Gordon-Smith**, Tony (CON - Godalming Charterhouse)
tony.gordon-smith@waverley.gov.uk

***Deputy Mayor:* Ellis**, Patricia (CON - Cranleigh West)
patricia.ellis@waverley.gov.uk

***Leader of the Council:* Knowles**, Robert (CON - Haslemere East and Grayswood)
robert.knowles@waverley.gov.uk

***Deputy Leader of the Council:* Band**, Mike (CON - Shamley Green and Cranleigh North)
mike.band@waverley.gov.uk

Adams, Brian (CON - Frensham Dockenfield and Tilford)
brian.adams@waverley.gov.uk

Andersen-Payne, Stella (CON - Frensham, Dockenfield and Tilford)
stella.andersen-payne@waverley.gov.uk

Beel, Gillian (CON - Farnham Weybourne and Badshot Lea)
gillian.beel@waverley.gov.uk

Blagden, Patrick (CON - Farnham Castle)
patrick.blagden@waverley.gov.uk

Byham, Maurice (CON - Bramley, Busbridge and Hascombe)
maurice.byham@waverley.gov.uk

Cable, Elizabeth (CON - Witley and Hambledon)
elizabeth.cable@waverley.gov.uk

Cockburn, Carole (CON - Farnham Bourne)
carole.cockburn@waverley.gov.uk

Edwards, Jim (CON - Haslemere Critchmere and Shottermill)
james.edwards@waverley.gov.uk

Ellis, Brian (CON - Cranleigh West)
brian.ellis@waverley.gov.uk

Else, Jenny (CON - Elstead and Thursley)
jenny.else@waverley.gov.uk

Foryszewski, Mary (CON - Alfold, Cranleigh Rural and Ellens Green)
mary.foryszewski@waverley.gov.uk

Frost, Pat (CON - Farnham Wrecclesham and Rowledge)

pat.frost@waverley.gov.uk
Gates, Richard (CON - Bramley, Busbridge and Hascombe)
richard.gates@waverley.gov.uk
Goodridge, Michael (CON - Blackheath and Wonersh)
michael.goodridge@waverley.gov.uk
Graffham, Lynn (CON - Milford)
lynn.graffham@waverley.gov.uk
Hargreaves, Jill (CON - Farnham Firgrove)
jill.hargreaves@waverley.gov.uk
Hesse, Christiaan (CON - Hindhead)
christiaan.hesse@waverley.gov.uk
Hill, Stephen (CON - Farnham Moor Park)
stephen.hill@waverley.gov.uk
Holder, Nicholas (CON - Chiddingfold and Dunsfold)
nicholas.holder@waverley.gov.uk
Inchbald, Simon (CON - Chiddingfold and Dunsfold)
simon.inchbald@waverley.gov.uk
Isherwood, Peter (CON - Hindhead)
peter.isherwood@waverley.gov.uk
James, Diane (IND - Ewhurst)
diane.james@waverley.gov.uk
King, Carole (CON - Haslemere Critchmere and Shottermill)
carole.king@waverley.gov.uk
Lear, Martin (CON - Farnham Bourne)
martin.lear@waverley.gov.uk
Lee, Nicky (CON - Haslemere East and Grayswood)
nicky.lee@waverley.gov.uk
Leigh, Denis (CON - Milford)
denis.leigh@waverley.gov.uk
Martin, Tom (CON - Godalming Holloway)
tom.martin@waverley.gov.uk
Martin, Peter (CON - Godalming Holloway)
peter.martin@waverley.gov.uk
Morgan, Bryn (CON - Elstead and Thursley)
bryn.morgan@waverley.gov.uk
Mulliner, Stephen (CON - Haslemere Critchmere and Shottermill)
stephen.mulliner@waverley.gov.uk
Munro, David (CON - Farnham Shortheath and Boundstone)
david.munro@waverley.gov.uk
Nichols, Elliot (CON - Farnham Firgrove)
elliot.nichols@waverley.gov.uk
O'Grady, Stephen (CON - Farnham Hale and Heath End)
stephen.ogrady@waverley.gov.uk
O'Grady, Jennifer (CON - Farnham Hale and Heath End)
jennifer.ogrady@waverley.gov.uk
O'Neill, Donal (CON - Farnham Upper Hale)
donal.oneill@waverley.gov.uk
Potts, Julia (CON - Farnham Upper Hale)
julia.potts@waverley.gov.uk
Reynolds, Stefan (CON - Godalming Charterhouse)
stefan.reynolds@waverley.gov.uk
Sampson, Ian (CON - Farnham Castle)
ian.sampson@waverley.gov.uk
Somerville, Janet (CON - Cranleigh East)
janet.somerville@waverley.gov.uk
Steel, Roger (CON - Farnham Moor Park)
roger.steel@waverley.gov.uk
Stennett, Stewart (CON - Cranleigh East)
stewart.stennett@waverley.gov.uk
Storey, Christopher (CON - Farnham Weybourne and Badshot Lea)
christopher.storey@waverley.gov.uk
Taylor-Smith, Adam (CON - Witley and Hambledon)
adam.taylor-smith@waverley.gov.uk
Thomson, Jane (CON - Godalming Central and Ockford)
jane.thomson@waverley.gov.uk
Thornton, Simon (CON - Godalming Central and Ockford)
simon.thornton@waverley.gov.uk
Vorley, Brett (CON - Cranleigh East)
brett.vorley@waverley.gov.uk
Ward, John (CON - Farnham Shortheath and Boundstone)
john.ward@waverley.gov.uk
Warner-O'Neill, Nerissa (CON - Farnham Wrecclesham and Rowledge)
nerissa.warner-oneill@waverley.gov.uk
Webster, Keith (CON - Haslemere East and Grayswood)
keith.webster@waverley.gov.uk
Welland, Ross (CON - Godalming Farncombe and Catteshall)
ross.welland@waverley.gov.uk
Wheatley, Liz (CON - Godalming Binscombe)
liz.wheatley@waverley.gov.uk
Williams, Nick (CON - Godalming Farncombe and Catteshall)
nick.williams@waverley.gov.uk
Wilson, Andrew (CON - Godalming Binscombe)
andrew.wilson@waverley.gov.uk

POLITICAL COMPOSITION
CON: 56, IND: 1

CABINET
Leader: Mr Robert Knowles
Deputy Leader / Finance: Mr Mike Band
Communications & Customer Services: Mr Stefan Reynolds
Economic Development & Community: Mr David Munro
Housing: Mr Keith Webster
IT & Green Spaces: Mr Stephen O'Grady
Leisure & Culture: Ms Julia Potts
Major Projects & Economic Development: Mr Adam Taylor-Smith
Parking & Community Safety: Mrs Carole King
Planning: Mr Bryn Morgan
Waste & Recycling: Mr Brian Adams

COMMITTEE CHAIRS
Audit: Mr Tom Martin
Community (Scrutiny): Mr Jim Edwards
Corporate (Scrutiny): Mr Michael Goodridge
Environment & Leisure (Scrutiny): Mrs Diane James
Joint Planning Management: Mr Brian Ellis
Licensing & Regulatory: Mrs Elizabeth Cable

WEALDEN D

Wealden District Council, Council Offices, Vicarage Lane, Hailsham BN27 2AX ☎ 01323 443322 info@wealden.gov.uk
www.wealden.gov.uk

FACTS & FIGURES
Police Authority: Sussex Police Authority
Health Authority: South East Coast Strategic Health Authority
Learning and Skills Council: South East
Parliamentary Constituencies: Wealden
EU Constituencies: South East
Election Frequency: Elections are of whole council
Twinning: Crowborough: Montargis (France); Polegate: Appen (Germany); Saintry-sur-Seine (France); Rotherfield: St. Cheron (France); Forest Row: Milly-la-Foret (France); Uckfield: Quickborn

(Germany); Chiddingly: Lachelle (France); East Hoathly/Halland: Juziers (France); Herstmonceux: Varengeville-sur-Mer (France); Heathfield: Forges-les-Eaux (France)

PRINCIPAL OFFICERS

Chief Executive: Mr Charles Lant, Chief Executive, Council Offices, Pine Grove, Crowborough TN6 1DH ☎ 01892 653311 🖷 01892 602222 🖱 chiefexec@wealden.gov.uk

Architect, Building / Property Services: Mr Terry Crone, Head of Corporate Assets, Council Offices, Vicarage Lane, Hailsham BN27 2AX ☎ 01323 443354 🖷 01323 443349 🖱 terry.crone@wealden.gov.uk

Best Value: Mr Malcolm Harris, Policy Officer, Council Offices, Pine Grove, Crowborough TN6 1DH ☎ 01323 443744 🖱 malcolm.harris@wealden.gov.uk

Building Control: Mr Kelvin Williams, Head of Planning & Business Control, Council Offices, Pine Grove, Crowborough TN6 1DH ☎ 01892 602484 🖷 01892 602777 🖱 kelvin.williams@wealden.gov.uk

PR / Communications: Mr Jim Van den Bos, Communications Officer, Council Offices, Vicarage Lane, Hailsham BN27 2AX ☎ 01892 602745 🖷 01892 602220 🖱 jim.vandenbos@wealden.gov.uk

Community Planning: Ms Mary Clare Deane, Director of Community Services, Council Offices, Vicarage Lane, Hailsham BN27 2AX ☎ 01323 443360 🖷 01323 443320 🖱 mcdeane@wealden.gov.uk

Computer Management: Mrs Helen Standen, Head of Customer Services & Systems, Vicarage Lane, Hailsham BN27 2AX ☎ 01323 443210 🖱 helen.standen@wealden.gov.uk

Contracts: Mr Nigel Hannam, Director of Corporate Services, Council Offices, Vicarage Lane, Hailsham BN27 2AX ☎ 01892 653311 🖷 01892 602222 🖱 nigel.hannam@wealden.gov.uk

Contracts: Mr Gerry Palmer, Corporate Procurement Manager, Council Offices, Vicarage Lane, Hailsham BN27 2AX ☎ 01323 443350 🖷 01323 443351 🖱 gerry.palmer@wealden.gov.uk

Corporate Services: Mr Nigel Hannam, Director of Corporate Services, Council Offices, Vicarage Lane, Hailsham BN27 2AX ☎ 01892 653311 🖷 01892 602222 🖱 nigel.hannam@wealden.gov.uk

Customer Service: Mr Nigel Hannam, Director of Corporate Services, Council Offices, Vicarage Lane, Hailsham BN27 2AX ☎ 01892 653311 🖷 01892 602222 🖱 nigel.hannam@wealden.gov.uk

Customer Service: Mrs Helen Standen, Head of Customer Services & Systems, Vicarage Lane, Hailsham BN27 2AX ☎ 01323 443210 🖱 helen.standen@wealden.gov.uk

Direct Labour: Mr Mike Pashler, Head of Waste & Commercial Services, Amberstone Depot, Bexhill Road, Hailsham BN27 1PE ☎ 01323 443420 🖷 01323 443425 🖱 mike.pashler@wealden.gov.uk

Economic Development: Mr Peter Griggs, Head of Public Health & Community Development, Council Offices, Vicarage Lane, Hailsham BN27 2AX ☎ 01323 443307 🖷 01323 443320 🖱 peter.griggs@wealden.gov.uk

E-Government: Mr Nigel Hannam, Director of Corporate Services, Council Offices, Vicarage Lane, Hailsham BN27 2AX ☎ 01892 653311 🖷 01892 602222 🖱 nigel.hannam@wealden.gov.uk

E-Government: Mrs Helen Standen, Head of Customer Services & Systems, Vicarage Lane, Hailsham BN27 2AX ☎ 01323 443210 🖱 helen.standen@wealden.gov.uk

Electoral Registration: Mr Terry Crone, Head of Corporate Assets, Council Offices, Vicarage Lane, Hailsham BN27 2AX ☎ 01323 443354 🖷 01323 443349 🖱 terry.crone@wealden.gov.uk

Electoral Registration: Mr Trevor Scott, Chief Legal Officer, Council Offices, Pine Grove, Crowborough TN6 1DH ☎ 01892 602524 🖱 trevor.scott@wealden.gov.uk

Emergency Planning: Mr Jim Foster, Emergency Planning Officer, Council Offices, Vicarage Lane, Hailsham BN27 2AX ☎ 01892 653311 🖱 jim.foster@wealden.gov.uk

Energy Management: Mr Terry Crone, Head of Corporate Assets, Council Offices, Vicarage Lane, Hailsham BN27 2AX ☎ 01323 443354 🖷 01323 443349 🖱 terry.crone@wealden.gov.uk

Environmental / Technical Services: Mr Mike Fleming, Director of Environmental Services, Council Offices, Pine Grove, Crowborough TN6 1DH ☎ 01892 602402 🖷 01892 602220 🖱 mike.fleming@wealden.gov.uk

Environmental Health: Ms Mary Clare Deane, Director of Community Services, Council Offices, Vicarage Lane, Hailsham BN27 2AX ☎ 01323 443360 🖷 01323 443320 🖱 mcdeane@wealden.gov.uk

Environmental Health: Mr Peter Griggs, Head of Public Health & Community Development, Council Offices, Vicarage Lane, Hailsham BN27 2AX ☎ 01323 443307 🖷 01323 443320 🖱 peter.griggs@wealden.gov.uk

Estates, Property & Valuation: Mr Terry Crone, Head of Corporate Assets, Council Offices, Vicarage Lane, Hailsham BN27 2AX ☎ 01323 443354 🖷 01323 443349 🖱 terry.crone@wealden.gov.uk

Facilities: Mr Terry Crone, Head of Corporate Assets, Council Offices, Vicarage Lane, Hailsham BN27 2AX ☎ 01323 443354 🖷 01323 443349 🖱 terry.crone@wealden.gov.uk

Finance and Treasurer: Mr Nigel Hannam, Director of Corporate Services, Council Offices, Vicarage Lane, Hailsham BN27 2AX ☎ 01892 653311 🖷 01892 602222 🖱 nigel.hannam@wealden.gov.uk

Finance and Treasurer: Mr Steve Linnett, Chief Finance Officer, Council Offices, Vicarage Lane, Hailsham BN27 2AX ☎ 01323

443234 🖷 01323 443245 🖰 steve.linnett@wealden.gov.uk

Fleet Management: Mr Kevin Donovan, Operations Manager, Amberstone Depot, Bexhill Road, Hailsham BN27 1PE ☎ 01323 443421 🖷 01323 443449 🖰 kevin.donovan@wealden.gov.uk

Grounds Maintenance: Mr Mike Pashler, Head of Waste & Commercial Services, Amberstone Depot, Bexhill Road, Hailsham BN27 1PE ☎ 01323 443420 🖷 01323 443425 🖰 mike.pashler@wealden.gov.uk

Health and Safety: Mr Peter Griggs, Head of Public Health & Community Development, Council Offices, Vicarage Lane, Hailsham BN27 2AX ☎ 01323 443307 🖷 01323 443320 🖰 peter.griggs@wealden.gov.uk

Home Energy Conservation: Mrs Julie Wilkins, Property Services Manager, Council Offices, Vicarage Lane, Hailsham BN27 2AX ☎ 01323 443312 🖷 01323 443320 🖰 julie.wilkins@wealden.gov.uk

Housing: Ms Mary Clare Deane, Director of Community Services, Council Offices, Vicarage Lane, Hailsham BN27 2AX ☎ 01323 443360 🖷 01323 443320 🖰 mcdeane@wealden.gov.uk

Housing: Ms Amanda Hodge, Head of Housing, Council Offices, Vicarage Lane, Hailsham BN27 2AX ☎ 01323 443364 🖰 amanda.hodge@wealden.gov.uk

Housing Maintenance: Mr Terry Crone, Head of Corporate Assets, Council Offices, Vicarage Lane, Hailsham BN27 2AX ☎ 01323 443354 🖷 01323 443349 🖰 terry.crone@wealden.gov.uk

Legal: Mr Trevor Scott, Chief Legal Officer, Council Offices, Pine Grove, Crowborough TN6 1DH ☎ 01892 602524 🖰 trevor.scott@wealden.gov.uk

Leisure and Cultural Services: Mr Peter Griggs, Head of Public Health & Community Development, Council Offices, Vicarage Lane, Hailsham BN27 2AX ☎ 01323 443307 🖷 01323 443320 🖰 peter.griggs@wealden.gov.uk

Licensing: Mr Peter Griggs, Head of Public Health & Community Development, Council Offices, Vicarage Lane, Hailsham BN27 2AX ☎ 01323 443307 🖷 01323 443320 🖰 peter.griggs@wealden.gov.uk

Member Services: Mrs Gabriella Paterson-Griggs, Democratic Services Manager, Council Offices, Vicarage Lane, Hailsham BN27 2AX ☎ 01892 602433 🖷 01892 602222 🖰 gabriella.paterson@wealden.gov.uk

Member Services: Mr Trevor Scott, Chief Legal Officer, Council Offices, Pine Grove, Crowborough TN6 1DH ☎ 01892 602524 🖰 trevor.scott@wealden.gov.uk

Parking: Mr Nigel Hannam, Director of Corporate Services, Council Offices, Vicarage Lane, Hailsham BN27 2AX ☎ 01892 653311 🖷 01892 602222 🖰 nigel.hannam@wealden.gov.uk

Partnerships: Mr Nigel Hannam, Director of Corporate Services, Council Offices, Vicarage Lane, Hailsham BN27 2AX ☎ 01892 653311 🖷 01892 602222 🖰 nigel.hannam@wealden.gov.uk

Personnel / HR: Mrs Isabel Garden, Head of Human Resources, Council Offices, Pine Grove, Crowborough TN6 1DH ☎ 01892 602404 🖷 01892 602220 🖰 isabel.garden@wealden.gov.uk

Planning: Mr Mike Fleming, Director of Environmental Services, Council Offices, Pine Grove, Crowborough TN6 1DH ☎ 01892 602402 🖷 01892 602220 🖰 mike.fleming@wealden.gov.uk

Planning: Mr David Phillips, Head of Enforcement, Conservation & Design, Council Offices, Pine Grove, Crowborough TN6 1DH ☎ 01892 653311 🖰 david.phillips@wealden.gov.uk

Planning: Mr Kelvin Williams, Head of Planning & Building Control, Council Offices, Vicarage Lane, Hailsham BN27 2AX ☎ 01892 602484 🖷 01892 602777 🖰 kelvin.williams@wealden.gov.uk

Procurement: Mr Nigel Hannam, Director of Corporate Services, Council Offices, Vicarage Lane, Hailsham BN27 2AX ☎ 01892 653311 🖷 01892 602222 🖰 nigel.hannam@wealden.gov.uk

Procurement: Mr Gerry Palmer, Corporate Procurement Manager, Council Offices, Vicarage Lane, Hailsham BN27 2AX ☎ 01323 443350 🖷 01323 443351 🖰 gerry.palmer@wealden.gov.uk

Recycling & Waste Minimisation: Mr Terry Crone, Head of Corporate Assets, Council Offices, Vicarage Lane, Hailsham BN27 2AX ☎ 01323 443354 🖷 01323 443349 🖰 terry.crone@wealden.gov.uk

Regeneration: Ms Mary Clare Deane, Director of Community Services, Council Offices, Vicarage Lane, Hailsham BN27 2AX ☎ 01323 443360 🖷 01323 443320 🖰 mcdeane@wealden.gov.uk

Regeneration: Mr Peter Griggs, Head of Public Health & Community Development, Council Offices, Vicarage Lane, Hailsham BN27 2AX ☎ 01323 443307 🖷 01323 443320 🖰 peter.griggs@wealden.gov.uk

Staff Training: Mr Leslie Newell, Learning & Development Manager, Council Offices, Pine Grove, Crowborough TN6 1DH ☎ 01892 602537 🖷 01892 602220 🖰 leslie.newell@wealden.gov.uk

Sustainable Communities: Mr David Phillips, Head of Enforcement, Conservation & Design, Council Offices, Pine Grove, Crowborough TN6 1DH ☎ 01892 653311 🖰 david.phillips@wealden.gov.uk

Sustainable Development: Mr David Phillips, Head of Enforcement, Conservation & Design, Council Offices, Pine Grove, Crowborough TN6 1DH ☎ 01892 653311 🖰 david.phillips@wealden.gov.uk

Tourism: Mr Peter Griggs, Head of Public Health & Community Development, Council Offices, Vicarage Lane, Hailsham BN27 2AX ☎ 01323 443307 🖷 01323 443320 🖰 peter.griggs@wealden.gov.uk

Transport: Mr Kevin Donovan, Operations Manager, Amberstone Depot, Bexhill Road, Hailsham BN27 1PE ☎ 01323 443421 🖷 01323 443449 🖰 kevin.donovan@wealden.gov.uk

Waste Collection and Disposal: Mr Mike Fleming, Director of Environmental Services, Council Offices, Pine Grove, Crowborough TN6 1DH ☎ 01892 602402
🖷 01892 602220
mike.fleming@wealden.gov.uk

Waste Management: Mr Mike Fleming, Director of Environmental Services, Council Offices, Pine Grove, Crowborough TN6 1DH ☎ 01892 602402
🖷 01892 602220
mike.fleming@wealden.gov.uk

Waste Management: Mr Mike Pashler, Head of Waste & Commercial Services, Amberstone Depot, Bexhill Road, Hailsham BN27 1PE ☎ 01323 443420 🖷 01323 443425
mike.pashler@wealden.gov.uk

MEMBERS OF THE COUNCIL (54)

***Chair:* Fox**, Jonica (CON - Cross-in-Hand/Five Ashes)
cllr.jonica.fox@wealden.gov.uk
***Vice-Chair:* Redman**, Brian (CON - Mayfield)
cllr.brian.redman@wealden.gov.uk
***Leader of the Council:* Standley**, Robert (CON - Wadhurst)
cllr.robert.standley@wealden.gov.uk
***Deputy Leader of the Council:* Dowling**, Claire (CON - Uckfield Central)
cllr.claire.dowling@wealden.gov.uk
***Group Leader:* Blake**, John (LD - Hellingly (including Arlington & Upper Horsebridge))
cllr.john.blake@wealden.gov.uk
***Group Leader:* Shing**, Stephen (IND - Willingdon)
cllr.stephen.shing@wealden.gov.uk
Angel, Dick (CON - Heathfield North and Central)
cllr.dick.angel@wealden.gov.uk
Bentley, Jo (CON - Hailsham South and West)
cllr.jo.bentley@wealden.gov.uk
Buck, Norman (CON - Buxted and Maresfield)
cllr.norman.buck@wealden.gov.uk
Carvey, John (CON - Uckfield Ridgewood)
cllr.john.carvey@wealden.gov.uk
Clark, Lin (CON - Pevensey and Westham)
cllr.lin.mckeever@wealden.gov.uk
Collinson, Nicholas (CON - Hailsham Central and North)
cllr.nicholas.collinson@wealden.gov.uk
Coltman, Nigel (CON - Hailsham South and West)
cllr.Nigel.coltman@wealden.gov.uk
Cussons, Ronald (CON - Willingdon)
cllr.ron.cussons@wealden.gov.uk
Dashwood-Morris, Barby (CON - Chiddingly and East Hoathly)
cllr.barby.dashwood-morris@wealden.gov.uk
Dear, Dianne (CON - Pevensey and Westham)
cllr.dianne.dear@wealden.gov.uk
Doodes, Pam (CON - Ninfield and Hooe with Wartling)
cllr.pam.doodes@wealden.gov.uk
Dunk, Jan (CON - Heathfield North and Central)
cllr.jan.dunk@wealden.gov.uk
Eastwood, Lousie (CON - Uckfield North)
cllr.louise.eastwood@wealden.gov.uk
Firth, Helen (CON - Uckfield New Town)
cllr.helen.firth@wealden.gov.uk
Galley, Roy (CON - Danehill / Fletching / Nutley)
cllr.roy.galley@wealden.gov.uk
Hardy, Chris (CON - Hartfield)
cllr.chris.hardy@wealden.gov.uk
Harms, Steve (CON - Alfriston)
cllr.steve.harms@wealden.gov.uk
Hollins, Jim (CON - Crowborough St Johns)
cllr.jim.hollins@wealden.gov.uk
Holloway, Peter (CON - Forest Row)
cllr.peter.holloway@wealden.gov.uk
Howell, Johanna (CON - Frant / Withyham)
cllr.johanna.howell@wealden.gov.uk
Isted, Stephen (NP - Crowborough Jarvis Brook)
cllr.stephen.isted@wealden.gov.uk
Larkhin, David (CON - Crowborough East)
cllr.david.larkhin@wealden.gov.uk
Long, Andy (CON - Herstmonceux)
Lunn, Michael (CON - Uckfield North)
cllr.michael.lunn@wealden.gov.uk
Marlowe, Barry (CON - Hailsham Central and North)
cllr.barry.marlowe@wealden.gov.uk
McKeenman, Nigel (CON - Heathfield East)
cllr.nigel.mckeeman@wealden.gov.uk
Merriman, Huw (CON - Rotherfield)
cllr.huw.merriman@wealden.gov.uk
Moore, Rowena (CON - Forest Row)
cllr.rowena.moore@wealden.gov.uk
Newnham, Peter (CON - Heathfield North and Central)
cllr.peter.newnham@wealden.gov.uk
Newton, Ann (CON - Framfield)
cllr.ann.newton@wealden.gov.uk
Ogden, Ken (CON - Buxted and Maresfield)
cllr.ken.ogden@wealden.gov.uk
Peck, Charles (CON - East Dean)
cllr.charles.peck@wealden.gov.uk
Phillips, Diane (CON - Crowborough West)
cllr.diane.phillips@wealden.gov.uk
Quin, Antony (CON - Crowborough West)
cllr.antony.quin@wealden.gov.uk
Reynolds, Carol (CON - Crowborough East)
cllr.carol.reynolds@wealden.gov.uk
Roundell, Peter (CON - Danehill/Fletching/Nutley)
cllr.peter.roundell@wealden.gov.uk
Rutherford, William (CON - Frant/Withyham)
william.rutherford@wealden.gov.uk
Shing, Daniel (IND - Polegate South)
daniel.shing@wealden.gov.uk
Shing, Raymond (IND - Willingdon)
cllr.raymond.shing@wealden.gov.uk
Shing, Oi Lin (IND - Polegate North)
cllr.oilin.shing@wealden.gov.uk
Stedman, Susan (CON - Horam)
cllr.susan.stedman@wealden.gov.uk
Tooley, Bill (CON - Pevensey and Westham)
cllr.bill.tooley@wealden.gov.uk
Towner, Stuart (CON - Hailsham East)
cllr.stuart.towner@wealden.gov.uk
Triandafyllou, Chriss (CON - Halisham South and West)
cllr.chriss.triandafyllou@wealden.gov.uk
Waller, Neil (CON - Crowborough North)
cllr.neil.waller@wealden.gov.uk
Weaver, Mark (CON - Crowborough North)
cllr.mark.weaver@wealden.gov.uk
Wells, Graham (CON - Wadhurst)
cllr.graham.wells@wealden.gov.uk
White, David (LD - Hellingly (including Arlington & Upper Horsebridge))
cllr.david.white@wealden.gov.uk

POLITICAL COMPOSITION
CON: 47, IND: 4, LD: 2, NP: 1

CABINET
Leader: Mr Robert Standley
Deputy Leader / Corporate Services: Mrs Claire Dowling
Affordable Housing: Mr Graham Wells
Community & Voluntary Sector: Mrs Johanna Howell
Corporate Assets: Ms Jan Dunk
Planning & Development: Mr Roy Galley
Waste Management: Ms Rowena Moore

COMMITTEE CHAIRS
Community & Environment (Scrutiny): Mr Charles Peck
Internal & Audit (Scrutiny): Mr Huw Merriman
Licensing: Mrs Susan Stedman
Personnel (Scrutiny): Mrs Claire Dowling
Planning North (Scrutiny): Mrs Ann Newton
Planning South (Scrutiny): Ms Barby Dashwood-Hall
Standards (Scrutiny): Mrs Lin Clark

WELLINGBOROUGH D
Wellingborough Borough Council, Council Offices, Swanspool House, Wellingborough NN8 1BP ☎ 01933 229777
🖷 01933 231543; 01933 231540
✉ customerservices@wellingborough.gov.uk
💻 www.wellingborough.gov.uk

FACTS & FIGURES
Police Authority: Northamptonshire Police Authority
Health Authority: East Midlands Strategic Health Authority
Learning and Skills Council: East Midlands
Parliamentary Constituencies: Wellingborough
EU Constituencies: East Midlands
Election Frequency: Elections are of whole council
Twinning: Niort (France); Wittlich (Germany)

PRINCIPAL OFFICERS
Chief Executive: Mr John Campbell, Chief Executive, Council Offices, Swanspool House, Wellingborough NN8 1BP ☎ 01933 231500 🖷 01933 231542 ✉ jcampbell@wellingborough.gov.uk

Deputy Chief Executive: Mr Joe Hubbard, Deputy Chief Executive, Council Offices, Swanspool House, Wellingborough NN8 1BP ☎ 01933 231505 🖷 01933 231542
✉ jhubbard@wellingborough.gov.uk

Senior Management: Mr Richard Micklewright, Director - Resources, Council Offices, Swanspool House, Wellingborough NN8 1BP ☎ 01933 231539 🖷 01933 231542
✉ rmicklewright@wellingborough.gov.uk

Senior Management: Mr Terry Wright, Director - Services, Council Offices, Swanspool House, Wellingborough NN8 1BP ☎ 01933 231581 🖷 01933 231542 ✉ twright@wellingborough.gov.uk

Architect, Building / Property Services: Mrs Bridget Lawrence, Head - Resources, Council Offices, Swanspool House, Wellingborough NN8 1BP ☎ 01933 231512 🖷 01933 231542
✉ blawrence@wellingborough.gov.uk

Building Control: Mr Steven Wood, Head - Planning & Local Development, Council Offices, Swanspool House, Wellingborough NN8 1BP ☎ 01933 231924 🖷 01933 231542
✉ swood@wellingborough.gov.uk

Children / Youth Services: Ms Gill Chapman, Principal Community Support Manager, Council Offices, Swanspool House, Wellingborough NN8 1BP ☎ 01933 231839 🖷 01933 231542
✉ gchapman@wellingborough.gov.uk

PR / Communications: Mrs Bridget Lawrence, Head - Resources, Council Offices, Swanspool House, Wellingborough NN8 1BP ☎ 01933 231512 🖷 01933 231542
✉ blawrence@wellingborough.gov.uk

Community Planning: Mr Chris Pittman, Head - Community, Council Offices, Swanspool House, Wellingborough NN8 1BP ☎ 01933 231710 🖷 01933 231542 ✉ cpittman@wellingborough.gov.uk

Community Safety: Mr Chris Pittman, Head - Community, Council Offices, Swanspool House, Wellingborough NN8 1BP ☎ 01933 231710 🖷 01933 231542
✉ cpittman@wellingborough.gov.uk

Computer Management: Mr Gareth Jones, Head - IT Department, East Northamptonshire Council, Cedar Drive, Thrapston NN14 4LZ ☎ 01832 742076 🖷 01933 231540
✉ gjones@east_northamptonshire.gov.uk

Contracts: Mr Chris Pittman, Head - Community, Council Offices, Swanspool House, Wellingborough NN8 1BP ☎ 01933 231710 🖷 01933 231542 ✉ cpittman@wellingborough.gov.uk

Customer Service: Mrs Bridget Lawrence, Head - Resources, Council Offices, Swanspool House, Wellingborough NN8 1BP ☎ 01933 231512 🖷 01933 231542
✉ blawrence@wellingborough.gov.uk

Economic Development: Mr Steven Wood, Head - Planning & Local Development, Council Offices, Swanspool House, Wellingborough NN8 1BP ☎ 01933 231924 🖷 01933 231542
✉ swood@wellingborough.gov.uk

Electoral Registration: Mrs Bridget Lawrence, Head - Resources, Council Offices, Swanspool House, Wellingborough NN8 1BP ☎ 01933 231512 🖷 01933 231542
✉ blawrence@wellingborough.gov.uk

Emergency Planning: Mr Chris Pittman, Head - Community, Council Offices, Swanspool House, Wellingborough NN8 1BP ☎ 01933 231710 🖷 01933 231542
✉ cpittman@wellingborough.gov.uk

Energy Management: Mrs Bridget Lawrence, Head - Resources, Council Offices, Swanspool House, Wellingborough NN8 1BP ☎ 01933 231512 🖷 01933 231542
✉ blawrence@wellingborough.gov.uk

Environmental / Technical Services: Mr John Casserly, Head - Environmental Services, Wellinborough Norse, Trafalgar House, Sanders Park, Sanders Road, Finedon Road Industrial Estate, Wellingborough NN8 4FR ☎ 01933 234523

john.casserly@ncsgrp.co.uk

Environmental Health: Mr Chris Pittman, Head - Community, Council Offices, Swanspool House, Wellingborough NN8 1BP ☎ 01933 231710 🖷 01933 231542 cpittman@wellingborough.gov.uk

Estates, Property & Valuation: Mrs Bridget Lawrence, Head - Resources, Council Offices, Swanspool House, Wellingborough NN8 1BP ☎ 01933 231512 🖷 01933 231542 blawrence@wellingborough.gov.uk

Events Manager: Mr Chris Pittman, Head - Community, Council Offices, Swanspool House, Wellingborough NN8 1BP ☎ 01933 231710 🖷 01933 231542 cpittman@wellingborough.gov.uk

Facilities: Mrs Bridget Lawrence, Head - Resources, Council Offices, Swanspool House, Wellingborough NN8 1BP ☎ 01933 231512 🖷 01933 231542 blawrence@wellingborough.gov.uk

Finance and Treasurer: Mr Richard Micklewright, Director - Resources, Council Offices, Swanspool House, Wellingborough NN8 1BP ☎ 01933 231539 🖷 01933 231542 rmicklewright@wellingborough.gov.uk

Fleet Management: Mr John Casserly, Head - Environmental Services, Wellingborough Norse, Trafalgar House, Sanders Park, Sanders Road, Finedon Road Industrial Park, Wellingborough NN8 4FR ☎ 01933 234523 john.casserly@ncsgrp.co.uk

Grounds Maintenance: Mr John Casserly, Head - Environmental Services, Wellingborough Norse, Trafalgar House, Sanders Park, Sanders Road, Finedon Road Industrial Park, Wellingborough NN8 4FR ☎ 01933 234523 john.casserly@ncsgrp.co.uk

Health and Safety: Mr R Sullivan, Senior Health & Safety Officer, Council Offices, Swanspool House, Wellingborough NN8 1BP ☎ 01933 231955 🖷 01933 231542 rsullivan@wellingborough.gov.uk

Home Energy Conservation: Mr Steven Wood, Head - Planning & Local Development, Council Offices, Swanspool House, Wellingborough NN8 1BP ☎ 01933 231924 🖷 01933 231542 swood@wellingborough.gov.uk

Housing: Mr Steven Wood, Head - Planning & Local Development, Council Offices, Swanspool House, Wellingborough NN8 1BP ☎ 01933 231924 🖷 01933 231542 swood@wellingborough.gov.uk

Legal: Ms Sue Lyons, Head - Democratic & Legal Services, Council Offices, Swanspool House, Wellingborough NN8 1BP ☎ 01536 534209 🖷 01933 231542 suelyons@kettering.gov.uk

Leisure and Cultural Services: Mr Chris Pittman, Head - Community, Council Offices, Swanspool House, Wellingborough NN8 1BP ☎ 01933 231710 🖷 01933 231542 cpittman@wellingborough.gov.uk

Licensing: Mr Chris Pittman, Head - Community, Council Offices, Swanspool House, Wellingborough NN8 1BP ☎ 01933 231710 🖷 01933 231542 cpittman@wellingborough.gov.uk

Member Services: Mrs Bridget Lawrence, Head - Resources, Council Offices, Swanspool House, Wellingborough NN8 1BP ☎ 01933 231512 🖷 01933 231542 blawrence@wellingborough.gov.uk

Personnel / HR: Mrs Bridget Lawrence, Head - Resources, Council Offices, Swanspool House, Wellingborough NN8 1BP ☎ 01933 231512 🖷 01933 231542 blawrence@wellingborough.gov.uk

Planning: Mr Steven Wood, Head - Planning & Local Development, Council Offices, Swanspool House, Wellingborough NN8 1BP ☎ 01933 231924 🖷 01933 231542 swood@wellingborough.gov.uk

Recycling & Waste Minimisation: Mr John Casserly, Head - Environmental Services, Wellingborough Norse, Trafalgar House, Sanders Park, Sanders Road, Finedon Road Industrial Park, Wellingborough NN8 4FR ☎ 01933 234523 john.casserly@ncsgrp.co.uk

Regeneration: Mr Steven Wood, Head - Planning & Local Development, Council Offices, Swanspool House, Wellingborough NN8 1BP ☎ 01933 231924 🖷 01933 231542 swood@wellingborough.gov.uk

Staff Training: Mrs Bridget Lawrence, Head - Resources, Council Offices, Swanspool House, Wellingborough NN8 1BP ☎ 01933 231512 🖷 01933 231542 blawrence@wellingborough.gov.uk

Street Scene: Mr John Casserly, Head - Environmental Services, Wellingborough Norse, Trafalgar House, Sanders Park, Sanders Road, Finedon Road Industrial Park, Wellingborough NN8 4FR ☎ 01933 234523 john.casserly@ncsgrp.co.uk

Sustainable Communities: Mr Steven Wood, Head - Planning & Local Development, Council Offices, Swanspool House, Wellingborough NN8 1BP ☎ 01933 231924 🖷 01933 231542 swood@wellingborough.gov.uk

Sustainable Development: Mr Steven Wood, Head - Planning & Local Development, Council Offices, Swanspool House, Wellingborough NN8 1BP ☎ 01933 231924 🖷 01933 231542 swood@wellingborough.gov.uk

Town Centre: Mr John Cable, Business Improvement District Manager, c/o The Management Suite, 18 Spring Lane, Wellingborough NN8 1EY ☎ 01933 270795 manager@wellingboroughtowncentre.co.uk

Waste Collection and Disposal: Mr John Casserly, Head - Environmental Services, Wellingborough Norse, Trafalgar House, Sanders Park, Sanders Road, Finedon Road Industrial Park, Wellingborough NN8 4FR ☎ 01933 234523 john.casserly@ncsgrp.co.uk

Waste Management: Mr John Casserly, Head - Environmental Services, Wellingborough Norse, Trafalgar House, Sanders Park, Sanders Road, Finedon Road Industrial Park, Wellingborough NN8 4FR ☎ 01933 234523 john.casserly@ncsgrp.co.uk

MEMBERS OF THE COUNCIL (36)

***Mayor:* Harrington**, Ken (CON - Redwell East)
Lord_Harrington@hotmail.com
***Deputy Mayor:* Patel**, Bhupendra (CON - Hemmingwell)
***Leader of the Council:* Bell**, Paul (CON - Swanspool)
Paul.bell@wellingborough.gov.uk
***Deputy Leader of the Council:* Graves**, Barry (CON - Great Doddington and Wilby)
Barry.graves@virgin.net
Ainge, Barbara (CON - Swanspool)
Barbara.ainge@ntlworld.com
Allebone, Timothy (CON - Brickhill)
tim.allebone@virgin.net
Bailey, John (CON - Finedon)
johnlhbailey1@btopenworld.com
Bass, Jim (CON - West)
Jim.bass@Sky.com
Beirne, Jo (CON - Wollaston)
Jbeirne@wellingborough.gov.uk
Blackwell, George (LAB - Earls Barton)
gblackwell@northamptonshire.gov.uk
Carr, Jon-Paul (CON - Irchester)
jpcarr@wellingborough.gov.uk
Dholakia, Shashi (LAB - Castle)
shashid_us@yahoo.co.uk
Elliott, Richard (LAB - Irchester)
Relio3@yahoo.com
Emerson, Brian (LAB - Castle)
Griffiths, Martin (CON - Croyland)
Cllr.martin.griffiths@btinternet.com
Hawkes, Robert (CON - Swanspool)
Cllr.robert.hawkes@gmail.com
Henley, Adam (LAB - Queensway)
Adamhenley2@hotmail.com
Higgins, Eileen (CON - Wollaston)
eileenwollaston@yahoo.co.uk
Hollyman, Mark (CON - Croyland)
Lawman, Graham (CON - Hemmingwell)
Graham.lawman@btinternet.com
Lawman, Lora (CON - Brickhill)
Lora.lawman@btopenworld.com
Maguire, Timothy (LAB - Irchester)
Tmaguire1@btinternet.com
Morrall, Peter (CON - Earls Barton)
peter.morrall@tinyworld.co.uk
Partridge-Underwood, Tom (CON - South)
p.u@btinternet.com
Patel, Mahendra (CON - Castle)
Pursglove, Thomas (CON - Croyland)
tpursglove@wellingborough.gov.uk
Raymond, John (CON - Redwell West)
Jraymond@wellingborough.gov.uk
Raymond, Patricia (CON - Redwell West)
patriciaraymond@onetel.com
Scarborough, Andrew (LAB - Queensway)
Andrew@scarborough11.fsnet.co.uk
Simmons, Geoffrey (CON - Brickhill)
gsimmons@wellingborough.gov.uk
Timms, Geoff (CON - North)
g.timms@tesco.net
Ward, Malcolm (CON - Finedon)
malcolmward1@btinternet.com
Warwick, Alan (CON - Redwell East)
Waters, Malcolm (CON - Hemmingwell)
malcolmwaters@yahoo.co.uk
Watts, Andrea (LAB - Queensway)
Andreawatts39@yahoo.co.uk
Wright, Peter (LAB - Earls Barton)
peter.wright@wellingborough.gov.uk

POLITICAL COMPOSITION

CON: 27, LAB: 9

CABINET

Leader: Mr Paul Bell
Deputy Leader: Mr Barry Graves
Care For The Environment: Mr Timothy Allebone
Community: Mr Peter Morrall
Heritage: Mr John Bailey
Reducing Crime & Disorder: Mrs Patricia Raymond
Regulation: Mr Malcolm Ward
Sport: Mr Mark Hollyman
Young People: Mr Thomas Pursglove

COMMITTEE CHAIRS

Appointment: Mr John Bailey
Audit: Mr Graham Lawman
Community: Mr Peter Morrall
Development: Mr Timothy Allebone
Licensing: Mr Robert Hawkes
Overview & Scrutiny: Mr Thomas Pursglove
Planning: Mr Malcolm Ward
Resources: Mr Paul Bell

WELWYN HATFIELD — D

Welwyn Hatfield Borough Council, Council Offices, The Campus, Welwyn Garden City AL8 6AE ☎ 01707 357000 🖷 01707 357257 ✉ contact-whc@welhat.gov.uk 💻 www.welhat.gov.uk

FACTS & FIGURES

Police Authority: Hertfordshire Police Authority
Health Authority: East of England Strategic Health Authority
Learning and Skills Council: Eastern
Parliamentary Constituencies: Broxbourne, Welwyn Hatfield
EU Constituencies: Eastern
Election Frequency: Elections are by thirds
Twinning: Hatfield: Zierikzee (Netherlands); Welwyn: Champagne-sur-Oise (France)

PRINCIPAL OFFICERS

Chief Executive: Mr Michel Saminaden, Chief Executive, Council Offices, The Campus, Welwyn Garden City AL8 6AE ☎ 01707 357327 ✉ m.saminaden@welhat.gov.uk

Architect, Building / Property Services: Mr Mike Storey, Corporate Property Manager, Council Offices, The Campus, Welwyn Garden City AL8 6AE ☎ 01707 357457 ✉ m.storey@welhat.gov.uk

Best Value: Mr Paul Underwood, Head of Policy & Culture, Council Offices, The Campus, Welwyn Garden City AL8 6AE ☎ 01707 357220 ✉ p.underwood@welhat.gov.uk

Building Control: Mrs Tracy Harvey, Head of Planning, Council Offices, The Campus, Welwyn Garden City AL8 6AE ☎ 01707

357239 ✉ t.harvey@welhat.gov.uk

Children / Youth Services: Mr Paul Underwood, Head of Policy & Culture, Council Offices, The Campus, Welwyn Garden City AL8 6AE ☎ 01707 357220 ✉ p.underwood@welhat.gov.uk

PR / Communications: Mr Chris Conway, Director of Strategy & Development, Council Offices, The Campus, Welwyn Garden City AL8 6AE ☎ 01707 357346 🖷 01707 357330 ✉ c.conway@welhat.gov.uk

PR / Communications: Ms Nancy Sardari-Kermani, Policy & Communications Manager, Council Offices, The Campus, Welwyn Garden City AL8 6AE ☎ 01707 357271 ✉ n.sardari-kermani@welhat.gov.uk

Community Planning: Mr Chris Conway, Director of Strategy & Development, Council Offices, The Campus, Welwyn Garden City AL8 6AE ☎ 01707 357346 🖷 01707 357330 ✉ c.conway@welhat.gov.uk

Community Safety: Mr Tim Beyer, Partnerships & Community Safety Manager, Council Offices, The Campus, Welwyn Garden City AL8 6AE ☎ 01707 357184 🖷 01707 357185 ✉ t.beyer@welhat.gov.uk

Computer Management: Mr Warwick Turnbull, ICT Client Manager, Council Offices, The Campus, Welwyn Garden City AL8 6AE ☎ 01707 357260 ✉ w.turnbull@welhat.gov.uk

Contracts: Mr Andrew Harper, Procurement Manager, Council Offices, The Campus, Welwyn Garden City AL8 6AE ☎ 020 8207 2277 🖷 020 8207 7441 ✉ a.harper@welhat.gov.uk

Customer Service: Ms Nancy Sardari-Kermani, Policy & Communications Manager, Council Offices, The Campus, Welwyn Garden City AL8 6AE ☎ 01707 357271 ✉ n.sardari-kermani@welhat.gov.uk

Economic Development: Mr Chris Conway, Director of Strategy & Development, Council Offices, The Campus, Welwyn Garden City AL8 6AE ☎ 01707 357346 🖷 01707 357330 ✉ c.conway@welhat.gov.uk

E-Government: Mrs Pam Kettle, Head of Resources, Council Offices, The Campus, Welwyn Garden City AL8 6AE ☎ 01707 357275 ✉ p.kettle@welhat.gov.uk

Electoral Registration: Mr Neil Ellis, Electoral Services Manager, Council Offices, The Campus, Welwyn Garden City AL8 6AE ☎ 01707 357354 ✉ n.ellis@welhat.gov.uk

Emergency Planning: Mr Andy Cremer, Head of Governance, Council Offices, The Campus, Welwyn Garden City AL8 6AE ☎ 01707 357169 ✉ a.cremer@welhat.gov.uk

Energy Management: Mr Vin Appasawmy, Energy Efficiency Officer, Council Offices, The Campus, Welwyn Garden City AL8 6AE ☎ 01707 357399 ✉ v.appasawmy@welhat.gov.uk

Environmental / Technical Services: Mrs Pam Kettle, Head of Resources, Council Offices, The Campus, Welwyn Garden City AL8 6AE ☎ 01707 357275 ✉ p.kettle@welhat.gov.uk

Environmental / Technical Services: Mr Durk Reyner, Head of Environment, Council Offices, The Campus, Welwyn Garden City AL8 6AE ☎ 01707 357160 ✉ d.reyner@welhat.gov.uk

Environmental Health: Mr Nick Long, Head of Public Health & Protection, Council Offices, The Campus, Welwyn Garden City AL8 6AE ☎ 01707 357401 🖷 01707 375464 ✉ n.long@welhat.gov.uk

Estates, Property & Valuation: Mr Mike Storey, Corporate Property Manager, Council Offices, The Campus, Welwyn Garden City AL8 6AE ☎ 01707 357457 ✉ m.storey@welhat.gov.uk

Finance and Treasurer: Mrs Pam Kettle, Head of Resources, Council Offices, The Campus, Welwyn Garden City AL8 6AE ☎ 01707 357275 ✉ p.kettle@welhat.gov.uk

Grounds Maintenance: Mr Durk Reyner, Head of Environment, Council Offices, The Campus, Welwyn Garden City AL8 6AE ☎ 01707 357160 ✉ d.reyner@welhat.gov.uk

Health and Safety: Ms Claire Hall, Risk & Resilience Officer, Council Offices, The Campus, Welwyn Garden City AL8 6AE ☎ 01707 357176 ✉ c.hall2@welhat.gov.uk

Home Energy Conservation: Mr Vin Appasawmy, Energy Efficiency Officer, Council Offices, The Campus, Welwyn Garden City AL8 6AE ☎ 01707 357399 ✉ v.appasawmy@welhat.gov.uk

Housing: Mrs Sian Chambers, Head of Housing & Community, Council Offices, The Campus, Welwyn Garden City AL8 6AE ☎ 01707 357640 ✉ s.chambers@welhat.gov.uk

Housing Maintenance: Mr John Briggs, Chief Executive, Welwyn Hatfield Community Housing Trust, 51 Bridge Road East, Welwyn Garden City AL8 1JR ☎ 01707 357742 ✉ j.briggs@welhat.gov.uk

Legal: Ms Nicola Swan, Legal Services Manager, Council Offices, The Campus, Welwyn Garden City AL8 6AE ☎ 01707 357575 ✉ n.swan@welhat.gov.uk

Leisure and Cultural Services: Mr Paul Underwood, Head of Policy & Culture, Council Offices, The Campus, Welwyn Garden City AL8 6AE ☎ 01707 357220 ✉ p.underwood@welhat.gov.uk

Licensing: Mr Nick Long, Head of Public Health & Protection, Council Offices, The Campus, Welwyn Garden City AL8 6AE ☎ 01707 357401 🖷 01707 375464 ✉ n.long@welhat.gov.uk

Member Services: Mr Graham Seal, Governance Services Manager, Council Offices, The Campus, Welwyn Garden City AL8 6AE ☎ 01707 357444 ✉ g.seal@welhat.gov.uk

Parking: Ms Vikki Hatfield, Parking Services Team Leader, Council Offices, The Campus, Welwyn Garden City AL8 6AE ☎ 01707 357555 ✉ v.hatfield@welhat.gov.uk

Partnerships: Mr Chris Conway, Director of Strategy & Development, Council Offices, The Campus, Welwyn Garden City

AL8 6AE ☎ 01707 357346 🖷 01707 357330
✉ c.conway@welhat.gov.uk

Personnel / HR: Ms Kamini Patel, Human Resources Manager, Council Offices, The Campus, Welwyn Garden City AL8 6AE ☎ 01707 357294 ✉ k.patel@welhat.gov.uk

Planning: Mrs Tracy Harvey, Head of Planning, Council Offices, The Campus, Welwyn Garden City AL8 6AE ☎ 01707 357239 ✉ t.harvey@welhat.gov.uk

Procurement: Mr Andrew Harper, Procurement Manager, Council Offices, The Campus, Welwyn Garden City AL8 6AE ☎ 020 8207 2277 🖷 020 8207 7441 ✉ a.harper@welhat.gov.uk

Recycling & Waste Minimisation: Mr Durk Reyner, Head of Environment, Council Offices, The Campus, Welwyn Garden City AL8 6AE ☎ 01707 357160 ✉ d.reyner@welhat.gov.uk

Regeneration: Mrs Tracy Harvey, Head of Planning, Council Offices, The Campus, Welwyn Garden City AL8 6AE ☎ 01707 357239 ✉ t.harvey@welhat.gov.uk

Staff Training: Ms Kamini Patel, Human Resources Manager, Council Offices, The Campus, Welwyn Garden City AL8 6AE ☎ 01707 357294 ✉ k.patel@welhat.gov.uk

Street Scene: Mr Durk Reyner, Head of Environment, Council Offices, The Campus, Welwyn Garden City AL8 6AE ☎ 01707 357160 ✉ d.reyner@welhat.gov.uk

Sustainable Communities: Mrs Tracy Harvey, Head of Planning, Council Offices, The Campus, Welwyn Garden City AL8 6AE ☎ 01707 357239 ✉ t.harvey@welhat.gov.uk

Town Centre: Mrs Nicola Wolff, Town Centre Manager, Council Offices, The Campus, Welwyn Garden City AL8 6AE ☎ 01707 357565 ✉ n.wolff@welhat.gov.uk

Transport: Mr John Lynch, Transportation Officer, Council Offices, The Campus, Welwyn Garden City AL8 6AE ☎ 01707 357124 ✉ j.lynch@welhat.gov.uk

Waste Collection and Disposal: Mr Durk Reyner, Head of Environment, Council Offices, The Campus, Welwyn Garden City AL8 6AE ☎ 01707 357160 ✉ d.reyner@welhat.gov.uk

Waste Management: Mr Durk Reyner, Head of Environment, Council Offices, The Campus, Welwyn Garden City AL8 6AE ☎ 01707 357160 ✉ d.reyner@welhat.gov.uk

Children's Play Areas: Mr Durk Reyner, Head of Environment, Council Offices, The Campus, Welwyn Garden City AL8 6AE ☎ 01707 357160 ✉ d.reyner@welhat.gov.uk

MEMBERS OF THE COUNCIL (48)

***Mayor:* Bromley**, Helen (CON - Handside)
helen.bromley@welhat.gov.uk
***Deputy Mayor:* Morgan**, Howard (CON - Hatfield Villages)
howard.morgan@welhat.gov.uk
***Leader of the Council:* Dean**, John (CON - Brookmans Park and Little Heath)
john.dean@welhat.gov.uk
***Deputy Leader of the Council:* Franey**, Alan (CON - Sherrards)
alan.franey@welhat.gov.uk
***Group Leader:* Skottowe**, Tony (LD - Handside)
tony.skottowe@welhat.gov.uk
***Group Leader:* Thorpe**, Kieran (LAB - Hatfield South)
kieran.thorpe@welhat.gov.uk
Beckerman, Jon (CON - Sherrards)
jon.beckerman@welhat.gov.uk
Bell, Duncan (CON - Hatfield Villages)
duncan.bell@welhat.gov.uk
Bennett, Darren (CON - Panshanger)
darren.bennett@welhat.gov.uk
Birleson, Margaret (LAB - Hollybush)
margaret.birleson@welhat.gov.uk
Boulton, Stephen (CON - Brookmans Park and Little Heath)
stephen.boulton@welhat.gov.uk
Chesterman, Lynn (LAB - Hollybush)
lynn.chesterman@welhat.gov.uk
Chesterman, Alan (LAB - Howlands)
alan.chesterman@welhat.gov.uk
Cook, Maureen (LAB - Hatfield Central)
maureen.cook@welhat.gov.uk
Couch, Colin (CON - Northaw and Cuffley)
colin.couch@welhat.gov.uk
Cowan, Malcolm (LD - Peartree)
malcolm.cowen@welhat.gov.uk
Cox, Dom (CON - Peartree)
dom.cox@welhat.gov.uk
Cragg, Julie (CON - Welwyn East)
julie.cragg@welhat.gov.uk
Croft, Colin (LAB - Hatfield Central)
colin.croft@welhat.gov.uk
Dean, Irene (CON - Brookmans Park and Little Heath)
irene.dean@welhat.gov.uk
Hughes, David (CON - Howlands)
david.hughes@welhat.gov.uk
Johnston, Sara (CON - Panshangar)
sara.johnston@welhat.gov.uk
Juggins, Caron (CON - Hatfield West)
caron.juggins@welhat.gov.uk
Kingsbury, Tony (CON - Hatfield East)
tony.kingsbury@welhat.gov.uk
Kyriakides, Sandra (IND - Welwyn West)
sandra.kyriakides@welhat.gov.uk
Langley, Kim (CON - Hatfield West)
kim.langley@welhat.gov.uk
Larkins, Mike (LAB - Haldens)
mike.larkins@welhat.gov.uk
Levitt, Martyn (CON - Haldens)
martyn.levitt@welhat.gov.uk
Long, Michael (CON - Hatfield East)
michael.long@welhat.gov.uk
Mabbott, Patricia (CON - Sherrards)
patricia.mabbott@welhat.gov.uk
Markiewicz, Steven (CON - Welwyn East)
steven.markiewicz@welhat.gov.uk
Mendez, Linda (LAB - Hatfield South)
linda.mendez@welhat.gov.uk
Michaelides, George (CON - Howlands)
george.michaelides@welhat.gov.uk
Nicholls, John (CON - Northaw and Cuffley)
john.nicholls@welhat.gov.uk
Olawoyin, Bukky (CON - Hatfield Central)
bukky.olawoyin@welhat.gov.uk

Pace, Nick (CON - Hollybush)
nick.pace@welhat.gov.uk
Page, Les (CON - Welham Green)
les.page@welhat.gov.uk
Perkins, Mandy (CON - Welwyn West)
mandy.perkins@welhat.gov.uk
Pieri, Keith (CON - Welham Green)
keith.pieri@welhat.gov.uk
Prest, Adrian (CON - Northaw and Cuffley)
adrian.prest@welhat.gov.uk
Roberts, Steve (LAB - Peartree)
steve.roberts@welhat.gov.uk
Sarson, Bernard (CON - Hatfield East)
bernard.sarson@welhat.gov.uk
Sparks, Lynne (CON - Hatfield Villages)
lynne.sparks@welhat.gov.uk
Storer, Carl (CON - Welwyn East)
carl.storer@welhat.gov.uk
Thomson, Fiona (CON - Handside)
fiona.thomson@welhat.gov.uk
Trigg, Roger (CON - Panshanger)
roger.trigg@welhat.gov.uk
Watson, Cathy (LAB - Hatfield West)
cathy.watson@welhat.gov.uk
Yetts, Benjamin (LAB - Haldens)
benjamin.yetts@welhat.gov.uk

POLITICAL COMPOSITION

CON: 34, LAB: 11, LD: 2, IND: 1

CABINET

Leader / Local Strategic Partnerships: Mr John Dean
Deputy Leader / Resources: Mr Alan Franey
Children & Young People: Mrs Irene Dean
Environment & Communications: Mr Colin Couch
Housing & Community: Mr Roger Trigg
Planning & Business: Ms Mandy Perkins

COMMITTEE CHAIRS

Appeals: Mr Keith Pieri
Audit: Mr Nick Pace
Licensing & Regulated Entertainment: Mr Les Page
Planning Control: Mr Stephen Boulton
Resources (Scrutiny): Mr George Michaelides
Standards: Mr John Dean

WEST BERKSHIRE U

West Berkshire Council, Council Offices, Market Street, Newbury RG14 5LD ☎ 01635 42400 🖷 01635 519431
info@westberks.gov.uk 💻 www.westberks.gov.uk

FACTS & FIGURES

Police Authority: Thames Valley Police Authority
Health Authority: South Central Strategic Health Authority
Learning and Skills Council: South East
Parliamentary Constituencies: Newbury, Reading West, Wokingham
EU Constituencies: South East
Election Frequency: Elections are of whole council
Twinning: Braunfels (Germany); Eeklo (Belgium); Hungerford: Ligueil (France); Newbury: Bagnols-sur-Ceze (France); Thatcham: Nideggen (Germany)

PRINCIPAL OFFICERS

Chief Executive: Mr Nick Carter, Chief Executive, Council Offices, Market Street, Newbury RG14 5LD ☎ 01635 519104 🖷 01635 519547 ncarter@westberks.gov.uk

Senior Management: Mr John Ashworth, Corporate Director of Environment, Council Offices, Faraday Road, Newbury RG14 2AF ☎ 01635 519587 🖷 01635 519872 jashworth@westberks.gov.uk

Senior Management: Ms Margaret Goldie, Director of Communities, West Street House, West Street, Newbury RG14 1BD ☎ 01635 519723 mgoldie@westberks.gov.uk

Access Officer / Social Services (Disability): Ms Valerie Witton, Access Officer, Council Offices, Market Street, Newbury RG14 5LD ☎ 01635 42400 🖷 01635 519408 vwitton@westberks.gov.uk

Children / Youth Services: Mr Mark Evans, Head of Children's Services, Council Offices, Market Street, Newbury RG14 5LD ☎ 01635 519735 mevans@westberks.gov.uk

Children / Youth Services: Ms Margaret Goldie, Director of Communities, West Street House, West Street, Newbury RG14 1BD ☎ 01635 519723 mgoldie@westberks.gov.uk

Civil Registration: Mr David Holling, Head of Legal Services, Council Offices, Market Street, Newbury RG14 5LD ☎ 01635 519422 🖷 01635 519431 dholling@westberks.gov.uk

PR / Communications: Mr Keith Ulyatt, Public Relations Manager, Council Offices, Market Street, Newbury RG14 5LD ☎ 01635 519125 🖷 01635 519613 kulyatt@westberks.gov.uk

Community Safety: Mrs Susan Powell, Safer Communities Partnership Team Manager, 20 Mill Lane, Newbury RG14 5LE ☎ 01635 264703 spowell@westberks.gov.uk

Computer Management: Mr Kevin Griffin, Head of ICT, Council Offices, Market Street, Newbury RG14 5LD ☎ 01635 519292 🖷 01635 519392 kgriffin@westberks.gov.uk

Consumer Protection and Trading Standards: Mr Sean Murphy, Trading Standards & Licensing Manager - Public Protection, Council Offices, Market Street, Newbury RG14 5LD ☎ 01635 519840 🖷 01635 519172 smurphy@westberks.gov.uk

Customer Service: Mr Sean Anderson, Head of Customer Services, Council Offices, Market Street, Newbury RG14 5LD ☎ 01635 519149 🖷 01635 519431 sanderson@westberks.gov.uk

Education: Mr Ian Pearson, Head of Education, West Street House, West Street, Newbury RG14 1BD ☎ 01635 519729 🖷 01635 519048 ipearson@westberks.gov.uk

E-Government: Mr David Lowe, Information Manager, Council Offices, Market Street, Newbury RG14 5LD ☎ 01635 42400 🖷 01635 519431 dlowe@westberks.gov.uk

Electoral Registration: Mr Phil Runacres, Elections & Registration Manager, Council Offices, Market Street, Newbury RG14 5LD ☎ 01635 519463 🖷 01635 519431

prunacres@westberks.gov.uk

Emergency Planning: Mrs Carolyn Richardson, Emergency Planning Officer, Council Offices, Market Street, Newbury RG14 5LD ☎ 01635 42400 cmurison@westberks.gov.uk

Energy Management: Mr Adrian Slaughter, Building Energy Officer, Council Offices, Faraday Road, Newbury RG14 2AF ☎ 01635 50325 aslaughter@westberks.gov.uk

Environmental / Technical Services: Mr Paul Hendry, Countryside Manager, Council Offices, Faraday Road, Newbury RG14 2AF ☎ 01635 519156 🖷 01635 519325 phendry@westberks.gov.uk

Environmental Health: Mr Paul Hendry, Countryside Manager, Council Offices, Faraday Road, Newbury RG14 2AF ☎ 01635 519156 🖷 01635 519325 phendry@westberks.gov.uk

Estates, Property & Valuation: Mr Stephen Broughton, Head of Property, Council Offices, Market Street, Newbury RG14 5LD ☎ 01635 519837 🖷 01635 519408 slbroughton@westberks.gov.uk

Facilities: Mr Stephen Broughton, Head of Property, Council Offices, Market Street, Newbury RG14 5LD ☎ 01635 519837 🖷 01635 519408 slbroughton@westberks.gov.uk

Finance and Treasurer: Mr Andy Walker, Head of Finance, Council Offices, Faraday Road, Newbury RG14 2AF ☎ 01635 519433 🖷 01635 519872 awalker@westberks.gov.uk

Fleet Management: Mrs Jacquie Chambers, Benefit & Expenses Assistant, Council Offices, Market Street, Newbury RG14 5LD ☎ 01635 519272 🖷 01635 519351 jchambers@westberks.gov.uk

Health and Safety: Mr Spencer Scott, Risk & Safety Manager, Council Offices, Farady Road, Newbury RG14 2AF ☎ 01635 519230 🖷 01635 519310 sscott@westberks.gov.uk

Highways: Mr Mark Edwards, Head of Highways & Transport, Council Offices, Market Street, Newbury RG14 5LD ☎ 01635 519208 🖷 01635 519865 medwards@westberks.gov.uk

Housing: Mrs June Graves, Head - Care Commissioning, West Street House, West Street, Newbury RG14 1BD ☎ 01635 519733 🖷 01635 519939 jgraves@westberks.gov.uk

Legal: Mr David Holling, Head of Legal Services, Council Offices, Market Street, Newbury RG14 5LD ☎ 01635 519422 🖷 01635 519431 dholling@westberks.gov.uk

Licensing: Mr Paul Anstey, Environmental Health & Licensing Manager, Public Protection, Faraday Road, Newbury RG14 2AF ☎ 01635 519002 🖷 01635 519172 panstey@westberks.gov.uk

Lifelong Learning: Mrs Sara Hanson, Lifelong Learning Officer, West Street House, West Street, Newbury RG14 1BD ☎ 01635 519792 🖷 01635 519048 shanson@westberks.gov.uk

Lighting: Mr Mark Edwards, Head of Highways & Transport, Council Offices, Faraday Road, Newbury RG14 2AF ☎ 01635 519208 🖷 01635 519865 medwards@westberks.gov.uk

Member Services: Mrs Jo Watt, Members' Services Officer, Council Offices, Market Street, Newbury RG14 5LD ☎ 01635 519242 🖷 01635 519613 jwatt@westberks.gov.uk

Parking: Mr Mark Edwards, Head of Highways & Transport, Council Offices, Faraday Road, Newbury RG14 2AF ☎ 01635 519208 🖷 01635 519865 medwards@westberks.gov.uk

Personnel / HR: Mr Rob O'Reilly, Head of Human Resources, Council Offices, Market Street, Newbury RG14 5LD ☎ 01635 519575 roreilly@westberks.gov.uk

Planning: Mr Gary Lugg, Head of Planning & Countryside, Council Offices, Market Street, Newbury RG14 5LD ☎ 01635 519511 🖷 01635 519408 glugg@westberks.gov.uk

Procurement: Mr David Holling, Head of Legal Services, Council Offices, Market Street, Newbury RG14 5LD ☎ 01635 519422 🖷 01635 519431 dholling@westberks.gov.uk

Recycling & Waste Minimisation: Mr Paul Hendry, Countryside Manager, Council Offices, Faraday Road, Newbury RG14 2AF ☎ 01635 519156 🖷 01635 519325 phendry@westberks.gov.uk

Road Safety: Mr Mark Edwards, Head of Highways & Transport, Council Offices, Faraday Road, Newbury RG14 2AF ☎ 01635 519208 🖷 01635 519865 medwards@westberks.gov.uk

Social Services (Adult): Ms Jan Evans, Head of Adult Social Care, West Street House, West Street, Newbury RG14 1BD ☎ 01635 519736 🖷 01635 519740 jevans@westberks.gov.uk

Social Services (Children): Ms Margaret Goldie, Director of Communities, West Street House, West Street, Newbury RG14 1BD ☎ 01635 519723 mgoldie@westberks.gov.uk

Staff Training: Mr Rob O'Reilly, Head of Human Resources, Council Offices, Market Street, Newbury RG14 5LD ☎ 01635 519575 roreilly@westberks.gov.uk

Street Scene: Mr Mark Edwards, Head of Highways & Transport, Council Offices, Faraday Road, Newbury RG14 2AF ☎ 01635 519208 🖷 01635 519865 medwards@westberks.gov.uk

Traffic Management: Mr Mark Edwards, Head of Highways & Transport, Council Offices, Faraday Road, Newbury RG14 2AF ☎ 01635 519208 🖷 01635 519865 medwards@westberks.gov.uk

Transport: Mr Mark Edwards, Head of Highways & Transport, Council Offices, Faraday Road, Newbury RG14 2AF ☎ 01635 519208 🖷 01635 519865 medwards@westberks.gov.uk

Transport Planner: Mr Gary Lugg, Head of Planning & Countryside, Council Offices, Market Street, Newbury RG14 5LD ☎ 01635 519511 🖷 01635 519408 glugg@westberks.gov.uk

Waste Collection and Disposal: Mr Andrew Deacon, Waste Services Manager, Council Offices, Faraday Road, Newbury RG14 2AF ☎ 01635 519312 🖷 01635 519453 adeacon@westberks.gov.uk

Waste Collection and Disposal: Mr Paul Hendry, Countryside

Manager, Council Offices, Faraday Road, Newbury RG14 2AF ☎ 01635 519156 🖷 01635 519325 ✉ phendry@westberks.gov.uk

Waste Management: Mr Paul Hendry, Countryside Manager, Council Offices, Faraday Road, Newbury RG14 2AF ☎ 01635 519156 🖷 01635 519325 ✉ phendry@westberks.gov.uk

MEMBERS OF THE COUNCIL (52)

***Chair:* Edwards**, Adrian (CON - Falkland)
adrian.edwards@westberks.gov.uk
***Vice-Chair:* Jackson-Doerge**, Carol (CON - Burghfield)
cjacksondoerge@westberks.gov.uk
***Leader of the Council:* Jones**, Graham (CON - Lambourn Valley)
gjones@westberks.gov.uk
***Group Leader:* Brooks**, Jeffrey (LD - Thatcham West)
jbrooks@westberks.gov.uk
Allen, David (LD - Victoria)
dallen@westberks.gov.uk
Argyle, Peter (CON - Calcot)
pargyle@westberks.gov.uk
Bairstow, Howard (CON - Falkland)
hbairstow@westberks.gov.uk
Bale, Pamela (CON - Pangbourne)
pbale@westberks.gov.uk
Beck, Jeff (CON - Clay Hill)
jbeck@westberks.gov.uk
Bedwell, Brian (CON - Calcot)
bbedwell@westberks.gov.uk
Betts, David (CON - Purley on Thames)
dbetts@westberks.gov.uk
Boeck, Dominic (CON - Thatcham South and Crookham)
dboeck@westberks.gov.uk
Bryant, Paul (CON - Speen)
pbryant@westberks.gov.uk
Chandler, George (CON - Downlands)
gchandler@westberks.gov.uk
Chopping, Keith (CON - Sulhamstead)
kchopping@westberks.gov.uk
Cole, Hilary (CON - Chieveley)
hcole@westberks.gov.uk
Croft, Roger (CON - Thatcham South and Crookham)
rcroft@westberks.gov.uk
Crumly, Richard (CON - Thatcham Central)
rcrumly@westberks.gov.uk
Drummond, Billy (LD - Greenham)
bdrummond@westberks.gov.uk
Ellison, Sheila (CON - Thatcham North)
sellison@westberks.gov.uk
Franks, Marcus (CON - Speen)
mfranks@westberks.gov.uk
Goff, Dave (CON - Clay Hill)
dgoff@westberks.gov.uk
Gopal, Manohar (CON - Calcot)
mgopal@westberks.gov.uk
Hewer, Paul (CON - Hungerford)
phewer@westberks.gov.uk
Holtby, David (CON - Hungerford)
dholtby@westberks.gov.uk
Horton, John (CON - Thatcham North)
jhorton@westberks.gov.uk
Hunneman, Roger (LD - Victoria)
rhunneman@westberks.gov.uk
Johnston, Mike (CON - St John's)
mjohnston@westberks.gov.uk
Law, Alan (CON - Basildon)
alaw@westberks.gov.uk
Linden, Tony (CON - Birch Copse)
tlinden@westberks.gov.uk
Lock, Mollie (LD - Mortimer)
mlock@westberks.gov.uk
Longton, Royce (LD - Burghfield)
rlongton@westberks.gov.uk
Lundie, Gordon (CON - Lambourn Valley)
glundie@westberks.gov.uk
Macro, Alan (LD - Theale)
amacro@westberks.gov.uk
Mason, Gwen (LD - Northcroft)
gmason@westberks.gov.uk
Mayes, Geoff (LD - Mortimer)
gmayes@westberks.gov.uk
Metcalfe, Tim (CON - Purley on Thames)
tmetcalfe@westberks.gov.uk
Mooney, Joe (CON - Birch Copse)
jmooney@westberks.gov.uk
Neill, Irene (CON - Aldermaston)
ineill@westberks.gov.uk
Pask, Graham (CON - Bucklebury)
gpask@westberks.gov.uk
Rendel, David (LD - Thatcham Central)
drendel@westberks.gov.uk
Rowles, Andrew (CON - Kintbury)
arowles@westberks.gov.uk
Simpson, Garth (CON - Cold Ash)
gsimpson@westberks.gov.uk
Stansfeld, Anthony (CON - Kintbury)
astansfeld@westberks.gov.uk
Swift-Hook, Julian (LD - Greenham)
Tuck, Ieuan (CON - St Johns)
ituck@westberks.gov.uk
Vickers, Tony (LD - Northcroft)
tvickers@westberks.gov.uk
von Celsing, Virginia (CON - Compton)
vvoncelsing@westberks.gov.uk
Webb, Quentin (CON - Bucklebury)
qwebb@westberks.gov.uk
Webster, Emma (CON - Birch Copse)
ewebster@westberks.gov.uk
Woodhams, Keith (LD - Thatcham West)
kwoodhams@westberks.gov.uk
Zverko, Laszlo (CON - Westwood)
lzverko@westberks.gov.uk

POLITICAL COMPOSITION

CON: 39, LD: 13

CABINET

Leader: Mr Graham Jones
Children & Young People, Youth Service & Education: Mrs Irene Neill
Community Care, Insurance: Mr Joe Mooney
Countryside, Environmental Protection, 'Cleaner & Greener', Culture: Ms Hilary Cole
Finance, Economic Development, Health & Safety, Pensions: Mr Alan Law
Highways & Transport (Operational), ICT, Corporate Services & Customer Services: Mr David Betts
Partnerships, Equality & The Visions: Mrs Pamela Bale
Performance, Strategic Support, Emergency Planning,

Community Safety: Mr Anthony Stansfeld
Planning, Transport Policy & Property: Mr Keith Chopping
Strategy, Council Plan, Housing: Mr Roger Croft

COMMITTEE CHAIRS

District Planning: Mr Keith Chopping
Governance & Audit: Mr Jeff Beck
Health (Scrutiny): Mr Quentin Webb
Licensing: Mr Jeff Beck
Overview & Scrutiny: Mr Brian Bedwell
Personnel: Mr Quentin Webb
Standards: Mr Dominic Boeck
Stronger Communities Select: Mrs Irene Neill

WEST DEVON D

West Devon Borough Council, Kilworthy Park, Drake Road, Tavistock PL19 0BZ ☎ 01822 813600 🖷 01822 813634 ✉ postcentre@westdevon.gov.uk 💻 www.westdevon.gov.uk

FACTS & FIGURES

Police Authority: Devon & Cornwall Police Authority
Health Authority: NHS South West
Learning and Skills Council: South West
Parliamentary Constituencies: Devon Central, Devon West and Torridge
EU Constituencies: South West
Election Frequency: Elections are of whole council

PRINCIPAL OFFICERS

Chief Executive: Mr Richard Sheard, Chief Executive, Kilworthy Park, Drake Road, Tavistock PL19 0BZ ☎ 01822 813629 🖷 01822 813634 ✉ richard.sheard@swdevon.gov.uk

Senior Management: Mr Alan Robinson, Corporate Director, Kilworthy Park, Drake Road, Tavistock PL19 0BZ ☎ 01822 813642 ✉ alan.robinson@swdevon.gov.uk

Senior Management: Ms Tracy Winser, Corporate Director, Kilworthy Park, Drake Road, Tavistock PL19 0BZ ☎ 01822 813697 ✉ tracy.winser@swdevon.gov.uk

Building Control: Ms Kate Cassar, Head of Assets, Kilworthy Park, Drake Road, Tavistock PL19 0BZ ☎ 01822 813600 🖷 01822 813634 ✉ kate.cassar@westdevon.gov.uk

Children / Youth Services: Mrs Marion Playle, Head of Planning & Community Delivery, Kilworthy Park, Drake Road, Tavistock PL19 0BZ ☎ 01822 813647 🖷 01822 813634 ✉ marion.playle@swdevon.gov.uk

PR / Communications: Mrs Alison Stoneham, Communications Manager, Kilworthy Park, Drake Road, Tavistock PL19 0BZ ☎ 01822 813648 🖷 01822 813634 ✉ astoneham@westdevon.gov.uk

Community Planning: Mrs Marion Playle, Head of Planning & Community Delivery, Kilworthy Park, Drake Road, Tavistock PL19 0BZ ☎ 01822 813647 🖷 01822 813634 ✉ marion.playle@swdevon.gov.uk

Community Safety: Ms Louisa Wall, Community Safety Officer, Kilworthy Park, Drake Road, Tavistock PL19 0BZ ☎ 01822 813624 🖷 01822 813634 ✉ lwall@westdevon.gov.uk

Computer Management: Mr Darren Cole, Head of ICT & Customer Services, Kilworthy Park, Drake Road, Tavistock PL19 0BZ ☎ 01822 813601 🖷 01822 813634 ✉ darren.cole@swdevon.gov.uk

Contracts: Mrs Catherine Aubertin, Car Parking & Contracts Performance Manager, Kilworthy Park, Drake Road, Tavistock PL19 0BZ ☎ 01822 813650 🖷 01822 813634 ✉ caubertin@westdevon.gov.uk

Contracts: Mrs Helen Dobby, Head of Environmental Services, Kilworthy Park, Drake Road, Tavistock PL19 0BZ ☎ 01822 813522 🖷 01822 813634 ✉ helen.dobby@swdevon.gov.uk

Corporate Services: Mr Alan Robinson, Corporate Director, Kilworthy Park, Drake Road, Tavistock PL19 0BZ ☎ 01822 813629

Corporate Services: Mr Darryl White, Democratic Services Manager, Kilworthy Park, Drake Road, Tavistock PL19 0BZ ☎ 01822 813662 🖷 01822 813634 ✉ darryl.white@swdevon.gov.uk

Customer Service: Mr Darren Cole, Head of ICT & Customer Services, Kilworthy Park, Drake Road, Tavistock PL19 0BZ ☎ 01822 813601 🖷 01822 813634 ✉ darren.cole@swdevon.gov.uk

Economic Development: Mrs Marion Playle, Head of Planning & Community Delivery, Kilworthy Park, Drake Road, Tavistock PL19 0BZ ☎ 01822 813647 🖷 01822 813634 ✉ marion.playle@swdevon.gov.uk

Electoral Registration: Mrs Carissa Allen, Electoral Services Officer, Kilworthy Park, Drake Road, Tavistock PL19 0BZ ☎ 01822 813664 🖷 01822 813634 ✉ callen@westdevon.gov.uk

Emergency Planning: Mr Ian Bollans, Head of Environmental Health, Kilworthy Park, Drake Road, Tavistock PL19 0BZ ☎ 01822 813600 🖷 01822 813634 ✉ ian.bollans@swdevon.gov.uk

Energy Management: Mr John Illes, Facilities Manager, Kilworthy Park, Drake Road, Tavistock PL19 0BZ ☎ 01822 813633 🖷 01822 813634 ✉ jilles@westdevon.gov.uk

Environmental / Technical Services: Mr Ian Bollans, Head of Environmental Health, Kilworthy Park, Drake Road, Tavistock PL19 0BZ ☎ 01822 813600 🖷 01822 813634 ✉ ian.bollans@swdevon.gov.uk

Environmental Health: Mr Ian Bollans, Head of Environmental Health, Kilworthy Park, Drake Road, Tavistock PL19 0BZ ☎ 01822 813600 🖷 01822 813634 ✉ ian.bollans@swdevon.gov.uk

Environmental Health: Mr I Luscombe, Principal Environmental Health Officer, Kilworthy Park, Drake Road, Tavistock PL19 0BZ ☎ 01822 813711 🖷 01822 813634 ✉ iluscombe@westdevon.gov.uk

Facilities: Mr John Illes, Facilities Manager, Kilworthy Park, Drake Road, Tavistock PL19 0BZ ☎ 01822 813633 🖷 01822 813634 ✉ jilles@westdevon.gov.uk

Finance and Treasurer: Miss Lisa Buckle, Head of Finance &

Audit, Kilworthy Park, Drake Road, Tavistock PL19 0BZ ☎ 01822 813644 🖷 01822 813634 ✉ lisa.buckle@westdevon.gov.uk

Grounds Maintenance: Mrs Jill Skelton, Grounds Maintenance Officer, Kilworthy Park, Drake Road, Tavistock PL19 0BZ ☎ 01822 813654 🖷 01822 813634 ✉ jill.skelton@swdevon.gov.uk

Health and Safety: Mr Ian Bollans, Head of Environmental Health, Kilworthy Park, Drake Road, Tavistock PL19 0BZ ☎ 01822 813600 🖷 01822 813634 ✉ ian.bollans@swdevon.gov.uk

Home Energy Conservation: Mr Ian Bollans, Head of Environmental Health, Kilworthy Park, Drake Road, Tavistock PL19 0BZ ☎ 01822 813600 🖷 01822 813634 ✉ ian.bollans@swdevon.gov.uk

Housing: Mr Ian Bollans, Head of Environmental Health, Kilworthy Park, Drake Road, Tavistock PL19 0BZ ☎ 01822 813600 🖷 01822 813634 ✉ ian.bollans@swdevon.gov.uk

Legal: Mrs Catherine Bowen, Borough Solicitor, Kilworthy Park, Drake Road, Tavistock PL19 0BZ ☎ 01822 813666 🖷 01822 813634 ✉ cbowen@westdevon.gov.uk

Leisure and Cultural Services: Mr Jon Parkinson, Leisure & Recreation Officer, Kilworthy Park, Drake Road, Tavistock PL19 0BZ ☎ 01822 813698 🖷 01822 813634 ✉ jon.parkinson@southhams.gov.uk

Licensing: Miss Sarah Clarke, Licensing Administrator, Kilworthy Park, Drake Road, Tavistock PL19 0BZ ☎ 01822 813548 🖷 01822 813634 ✉ sclarke@westdevon.gov.uk

Lottery Funding, Charity and Voluntary: Mrs Marion Playle, Head of Planning & Community Delivery, Kilworthy Park, Drake Road, Tavistock PL19 0BZ ☎ 01822 813647 🖷 01822 813634 ✉ marion.playle@swdevon.gov.uk

Member Services: Mr Darryl White, Democratic Services Manager, Kilworthy Park, Drake Road, Tavistock PL19 0BZ ☎ 01822 813662 🖷 01822 813634 ✉ darryl.white@swdevon.gov.uk

Parking: Mrs Catherine Aubertin, Car Parking & Contracts Performance Manager, Kilworthy Park, Drake Road, Tavistock PL19 0BZ ☎ 01822 813650 🖷 01822 813634 ✉ caubertin@westdevon.gov.uk

Partnerships: Mrs Catherine Aubertin, Car Parking & Contracts Performance Manager, Kilworthy Park, Drake Road, Tavistock PL19 0BZ ☎ 01822 813650 🖷 01822 813634 ✉ caubertin@westdevon.gov.uk

Personnel / HR: Mrs Jan Montague, Head of HR, Kilworthy Park, Drake Road, Tavistock PL19 0BZ ☎ 01822 813671 🖷 01822 813634 ✉ jan.montague@swdevon.gov.uk

Planning: Mrs Marion Playle, Head of Planning & Community Delivery, Kilworthy Park, Drake Road, Tavistock PL19 0BZ ☎ 01822 813647 🖷 01822 813634 ✉ marion.playle@swdevon.gov.uk

Procurement: Mr John Illes, Facilities Manager, Kilworthy Park, Drake Road, Tavistock PL19 0BZ ☎ 01822 813633 🖷 01822 813634 ✉ jilles@westdevon.gov.uk

Recycling & Waste Minimisation: Mrs Jane Savage, Waste Reduction & Recycling Officer, Kilworthy Park, Drake Road, Tavistock PL19 0BZ ☎ 01822 813655 🖷 01822 813634 ✉ jsavage@westdevon.gov.uk

Regeneration: Mrs Marion Playle, Head of Planning & Community Delivery, Kilworthy Park, Drake Road, Tavistock PL19 0BZ ☎ 01822 813647 🖷 01822 813634 ✉ marion.playle@swdevon.gov.uk

Staff Training: Mrs Jan Montague, Head of HR, Kilworthy Park, Drake Road, Tavistock PL19 0BZ ☎ 01822 813671 🖷 01822 813634 ✉ jan.montague@swdevon.gov.uk

Street Scene: Mrs Jill Skelton, Grounds Maintenance Officer, Kilworthy Park, Drake Road, Tavistock PL19 0BZ ☎ 01822 813654 🖷 01822 813634 ✉ jill.skelton@swdevon.gov.uk

Sustainable Communities: Mrs Marion Playle, Head of Planning & Community Delivery, Kilworthy Park, Drake Road, Tavistock PL19 0BZ ☎ 01822 813647 🖷 01822 813634 ✉ marion.playle@swdevon.gov.uk

Sustainable Development: Mrs Marion Playle, Head of Planning & Community Delivery, Kilworthy Park, Drake Road, Tavistock PL19 0BZ ☎ 01822 813647 🖷 01822 813634 ✉ marion.playle@swdevon.gov.uk

Tourism: Ms Nadine Trout, Tourism Officer, Kilworthy Park, Drake Road, Tavistock PL19 0BZ ☎ 01822 813700 🖷 01822 813634 ✉ ntrout@westdevon.gov.uk

Waste Collection and Disposal: Mrs Jane Savage, Waste Reduction & Recycling Officer, Kilworthy Park, Drake Road, Tavistock PL19 0BZ ☎ 01822 813655 🖷 01822 813634 ✉ jsavage@westdevon.gov.uk

Waste Management: Mrs Helen Dobby, Head of Environmental Services, Kilworthy Park, Drake Road, Tavistock PL19 0BZ ☎ 01822 813522 🖷 01822 813634 ✉ helen.dobby@swdevon.gov.uk

MEMBERS OF THE COUNCIL (31)

***Mayor:* Musgrave**, Robin (LD - Bere Ferrers)
cllr.robin.musgrave@westdevon.gov.uk

***Deputy Mayor:* Cann**, William (IND - South Tawton)
cllr.william.cann@westdevon.gov.uk

***Leader of the Council:* Sanders**, Philip (CON - Buckland Manochorum)
cllr.philip.sanders@westdevon.gov.uk

***Deputy Leader of the Council:* Baldwin**, Bob (CON - Milton Ford)
clr.bob.baldwin@westdevon.gov.uk

Bailey, Sue (CON - Tavistock North)
cllr.sue.bailey@westdevon.gov.uk

Ball, Kevin (CON - Okehampton East)
cllr.kevin.ball@westdevon.gov.uk

Benson, Mike (CON - Bere Ferrers)
cllr.mike.benson@westdevon.gov.uk

Clish-Green, Alison (LD - Tavistock South West)
cllr.alison.cg@westdevon.gov.uk

Cloke, David (IND - Walkham)
cllr.david.cloke@westdevon.gov.uk

Ewings, Mandy (CON - Tavistock South)
cllr.mandy.govier@westdevon.gov.uk
Hall, Christine (CON - Hatherleigh)
cllr.christine.hall@westdevon.gov.uk
Hill, Trevor (IND - Exbourne)
cllr.trevor.hill@westdevon.gov.uk
Hockridge, John (IND - Bridestowe)
cllr.john.hockridge@westdevon.gov.uk
Horn, Donald (CON - Thrushel)
cllr.donald.horn@westdevon.gov.uk
Leech, Tony (IND - Okehampton East)
cllr.tony.leech@westdevon.gov.uk
Marsh, Christine (CON - Okehampton West)
christine.marsh@devon.gov.uk
McInnes, James (CON - Lew Valley)
cllr.james.mcinnes@westdevon.gov.uk
Moody, Jeffrey (IND - Tavistock North)
Cllr.Jeffrey.Moody@westdevon.gov.uk
Morgan, Nick (IND - North Tawton)
cllr.nick.morgan@westdevon.gov.uk
Morse, Mike (CON - Okehampton West)
cllr.mike.morse@westdevon.gov.uk
Moyse, Diana (CON - Burrator)
cllr.diana.moyse@westdevon.gov.uk
Oxborough, Robert (CON - Tavistock South)
cllr.robert.oxborough@westdevon.gov.uk
Pearce, Terry (IND - Mary Tavy)
cllr.terry.pearce@westdevon.gov.uk
Ridgers, Paul (CON - Drewsteignton)
cllr.paul.ridgers@westdevon.gov.uk
Rose, Lynne (CON - Lydford)
cllr.lynne.rose@westdevon.gov.uk
Sampson, Robert (IND - Chagford)
cllr.robert.sampson@westdevon.gov.uk
Sellis, Deborah (CON - Walkham)
cllr.debo.sellis@westdevon.gov.uk
Sheldon, John (CON - Tavistock North)
cllr.john.sheldon@westdevon.gov.uk
Sherrell, Edward (IND - Tavistock South)
services@westdevon.gov.uk
Wilde, David (LD - Buckland Monachorum)
cllr.david.wilde@westdevon.gov.uk
Witcomb, David (CON - Tamarside)
cllr.david.whitcomb@westdevon.gov.uk

POLITICAL COMPOSITION
CON: 18, IND: 10, LD: 3

COMMITTEE CHAIRS
Audit: Mrs Deborah Sellis
Community Services: Mr Robert Oxborough
Overview & Scrutiny: Mr David Cloke
Planning & Licensing: Mrs Christine Marsh
Resources: Mr Philip Saunders
Standards: Mrs Victoria Spence (External)

WEST DORSET — D

West Dorset District Council, Stratton House, 58-60 High West Street, Dorchester DT1 1UZ ☎ 01305 251010 🖷 01305 251481
🖳 www.dorsetforyou.com

FACTS & FIGURES
Police Authority: Dorset Police Authority
Health Authority: NHS South West
Learning and Skills Council: South West
Parliamentary Constituencies: Dorset West
EU Constituencies: South West
Election Frequency: Elections are of whole council
Twinning: Beaminster: St. James (France); Bridport: St. Vaast-la-Hougue (France); Dorchester: Bayeux (France); Lubbecke (Germany); Holbaeck (Denmark); Sherborne: Granville (France)

PRINCIPAL OFFICERS
Chief Executive: Mr David Clarke, Chief Executive, Stratton House, 58-60 High West Street, Dorchester DT1 1UZ ☎ 01305 251010; 01305 252202 ✉ d.clarke@westdorset-dc.gov.uk

Senior Management: Mr David Evans, Director of Environment, Stratton House, 58-60 High West Street, Dorchester DT1 1UZ ☎ 01305 252232; 01305 251010
✉ davidevans2@weymouth.gov.uk;
d.evans@westdorset-weymouth.gov.uk

Senior Management: Ms Kate Hindson, Director of Communities, West Dorset District Council, 58/60 High West Street, Dorchester DT1 1UZ ☎ 01305 838037; 01305 251010
🖷 01305 838438 ✉ katehindson@weymouth.gov.uk;
k.hindson@westdorset-weymouth.gov.uk

Senior Management: Mr Adrian Stuart, Director of Corporate Services, Stratton House, 58-60 High West Street, Dorchester DT1 1UZ ☎ 01305 252315; 01305 251010
✉ adrianstuart2@weymouth.gov.uk;
a.stuart@westdorset-weymouth.gov.uk

Senior Management: Mr Jason Vaughan, Director of Resources, West Dorset District Council, 58/60 High West Street, Dorchester DT1 1UZ ☎ 01305 838233; 01305 251010
✉ jasonvaughan@weymouth.gov.uk;
j.vaughan@westdorset-weymouth.gov.uk

Architect, Building / Property Services: Ms Rosie Darkin, Property & Facilities Manager, Stratton House, 58-60 High West Street, Dorchester DT1 1UZ ☎ 01305 252292; 01305 251010
✉ rosiedarkin@weymouth.gov.uk;
r.darkin@westdorset-weymouth.gov.uk

Best Value: Mr Chris Churchill, Head of Performance Management, Stratton House, 58-60 High West Street, Dorchester DT1 1UZ ☎ 01305 251010
✉ c.churchill@westdorset-weymouth.gov.uk

Building Control: Mr John Greenslade, Development Services Manager, Stratton House, 58-60 High West Street, Dorchester DT1 1UZ ☎ 01305 252230; 01305 251010
✉ johngreenslade@weymouth.gov.uk;
j.greenslade@westdorset-weymouth.gov.uk

PR / Communications: Mr Bob Hanton, Customer & Communications Manager, Stratton House, 58-60 High West Street, Dorchester DT1 1UZ ☎ 01305 252210
✉ bobhanton@weymouth.gov.uk;
r.hanton@westdorset-weymouth.gov.uk

PR / Communications: Mr Adrian Stuart, Director of Corporate Services, Stratton House, 58-60 High West Street, Dorchester DT1 1UZ ☎ 01305 252315; 01305 251010 ✉ adrianstuart2@weymouth.gov.uk; a.stuart@westdorset-weymouth.gov.uk

PR / Communications: Mr Colin Wood, Head of Communications & Dorsetforyou, Stratton House, 58-60 High West Street, Dorchester DT1 1UZ ☎ 01305 251010 ✉ c.wood@westdorset-weymouth.gov.uk

Community Planning: Ms Hilary Jordan, Spatial & Community Planning Manager, Stratton House, 58-60 High West Street, Dorchester DT1 1UZ ☎ 01305 251010 ✉ h.jordan@westdorset-weymouth.gov.uk

Community Safety: Mr Graham Duggan, Community Protection Manager, Stratton House, 58-60 High West Street, Dorchester DT1 1UZ ☎ 01305 252285; 01305 251010 ✉ grahamduggan@weymouth.gov.uk; g.duggan@westdorset-weymouth.gov.uk

Computer Management: Mr A Crouch, Head of IT Development, Stratton House, 58-60 High West Street, Dorchester DT1 1UZ ☎ 01305 252422 ✉ a.crouch@westdorset-weymouth.gov.uk

Computer Management: Mr Adrian Stuart, Director of Corporate Services, Stratton House, 58-60 High West Street, Dorchester DT1 1UZ ☎ 01305 252315; 01305 251010 ✉ adrianstuart2@weymouth.gov.uk; a.stuart@westdorset-weymouth.gov.uk

Contracts: Mr David Clarke, Chief Executive, Stratton House, 58-60 High West Street, Dorchester DT1 1UZ ☎ 01305 251010; 01305 252202 ✉ d.clarke@westdorset-dc.gov.uk; d.clarke@westdorset-dc.gov.uk

Corporate Services: Mr Adrian Stuart, Director of Corporate Services, Stratton House, 58-60 High West Street, Dorchester DT1 1UZ ☎ 01305 252315; 01305 251010 ✉ adrianstuart2@weymouth.gov.uk; a.stuart@westdorset-weymouth.gov.uk

Customer Service: Mr Bob Hanton, Customer & Communications Manager, Stratton House, 58-60 High West Street, Dorchester DT1 1UZ ☎ 01305 252210 ✉ bobhanton@weymouth.gov.uk; r.hanton@westdorset-weymouth.gov.uk

Economic Development: Mr Ian Doyle, Economic Regeneration Manager, Stratton House, 58-60 High West Street, Dorchester DT1 1UZ ☎ 01305 252617; 01305 251010 ✉ iandoyle@weymouth.gov.uk; i.doyle@westdorset-weymouth.gov.uk

E-Government: Mr Mark Chivers, Strategic IT Manager, Stratton House, 58-60 High West Street, Dorchester DT1 1UZ ☎ 01305 252266; 01305 251010 ✉ markchivers@weymouth.gov.uk; m.chivers@westdorset-weymouth.gov.uk

E-Government: Mr Adrian Stuart, Director of Corporate Services, Stratton House, 58-60 High West Street, Dorchester DT1 1UZ ☎ 01305 252315; 01305 251010 ✉ adrianstuart2@weymouth.gov.uk; a.stuart@westdorset-weymouth.gov.uk

Electoral Registration: Mr Mike Hickman, Elections Team Leader, Stratton House, 58-60 High West Street, Dorchester DT1 1UZ ☎ 01305 251010 ✉ m.hickman@westdorset-weymouth.gov.uk

Emergency Planning: Mr Steve Woollard, Technical Services Manager, Stratton House, 58-60 High West Street, Dorchester DT1 1UZ ☎ 01305 252297; 01305 251010 ✉ stevewoollard@weymouth.gov.uk; s.woollard@westdorset-weymouth.gov.uk

Energy Management: Mr Steve Woollard, Technical Services Manager, Stratton House, 58-60 High West Street, Dorchester DT1 1UZ ☎ 01305 252297; 01305 251010 ✉ stevewoollard@weymouth.gov.uk; s.woollard@westdorset-weymouth.gov.uk

Environmental / Technical Services: Mr Steve Woollard, Technical Services Manager, Stratton House, 58-60 High West Street, Dorchester DT1 1UZ ☎ 01305 252297; 01305 251010 ✉ stevewoollard@weymouth.gov.uk; s.woollard@westdorset-weymouth.gov.uk

Environmental Health: Mr Graham Duggan, Community Protection Manager, Stratton House, 58-60 High West Street, Dorchester DT1 1UZ ☎ 01305 252285; 01305 251010 ✉ grahamduggan@weymouth.gov.uk; g.duggan@westdorset-weymouth.gov.uk

Environmental Health: Ms Kate Hindson, Director of Communities, West Dorset District Council, 58/60 High West Street, Dorchester DT1 1UZ ☎ 01305 838037; 01305 251010 🖷 01305 838438 ✉ katehindson@weymouth.gov.uk; k.hindson@westdorset-weymouth.gov.uk

Environmental Health: Ms Sarah Ward, Housing Manager, Stratton House, 58-60 High West Street, Dorchester DT1 1UZ ☎ 01305 252313; 01305 251010 ✉ sarahward@weymouth.gov.uk; s.ward@westdorset-weymouth.gov.uk

Estates, Property & Valuation: Ms Rosie Darkin, Property & Facilities Manager, Stratton House, 58-60 High West Street, Dorchester DT1 1UZ ☎ 01305 252292; 01305 251010 ✉ rosiedarkin@weymouth.gov.uk; r.darkin@westdorset-weymouth.gov.uk

Events Manager: Mr Nick Thornley, Leisure & Tourism Manager, Stratton House, 58-60 High West Street, Dorchester DT1 1UZ ☎ 01305 252474; 01305 251010 ✉ nickthornley@weymouth.gov.uk; n.thornley@westdorset-weymouth.gov.uk

Facilities: Ms Rosie Darkin, Property & Facilities Manager, Stratton House, 58-60 High West Street, Dorchester DT1 1UZ ☎ 01305 252292; 01305 251010 ✉ rosiedarkin@weymouth.gov.uk; r.darkin@westdorset-weymouth.gov.uk

Facilities: Mr Steve Woollard, Technical Services Manager, Stratton House, 58-60 High West Street, Dorchester DT1 1UZ

☎ 01305 252297; 01305 251010
✉ stevewoollard@weymouth.gov.uk;
s.woollard@westdorset-weymouth.gov.uk

Finance and Treasurer: Ms Julie Strange, Financial Services Manager, West Dorset District Council, 58/60 High West Street, Dorchester DT1 1UZ ☎ 01305 838252; 01305 251010
✉ juliestrange@weymouth.gov.uk;
j.strange@westdorset-weymouth.gov.uk

Finance and Treasurer: Mr Jason Vaughan, Director of Resources, West Dorset District Council, 58/60 High West Street, Dorchester DT1 1UZ ☎ 01305 838233; 01305 251010
✉ jasonvaughan@weymouth.gov.uk;
j.vaughan@westdorset-weymouth.gov.uk

Health and Safety: Ms Melanie Earnshaw, Human Resources Manager, West Dorset District Council, 58/60 High West Street, Dorchester DT1 1UZ ☎ 01305 838212
✉ melanieearnshaw@weymouth.gov.uk;
m.earnshaw@westdorset-weymouth.gov.uk

Home Energy Conservation: Ms Sarah Ward, Housing Manager, Stratton House, 58-60 High West Street, Dorchester DT1 1UZ ☎ 01305 252313; 01305 251010 ✉ sarahward@weymouth.gov.uk;
s.ward@westdorset-weymouth.gov.uk

Housing: Ms Kate Hindson, Director of Communities, West Dorset District Council, 58/60 High West Street, Dorchester DT1 1UZ ☎ 01305 838037; 01305 251010 🖷 01305 838438
✉ katehindson@weymouth.gov.uk;
k.hindson@westdorset-weymouth.gov.uk

Housing: Ms Sarah Ward, Housing Manager, Stratton House, 58-60 High West Street, Dorchester DT1 1UZ ☎ 01305 252313; 01305 251010 ✉ sarahward@weymouth.gov.uk;
s.ward@westdorset-weymouth.gov.uk

Housing Maintenance: Ms Sarah Ward, Housing Manager, Stratton House, 58-60 High West Street, Dorchester DT1 1UZ ☎ 01305 252313; 01305 251010 ✉ sarahward@weymouth.gov.uk;
s.ward@westdorset-weymouth.gov.uk

Legal: Mr Glen Harding, Legal & Democratic Manager, West Dorset District Council, 58/60 High West Street, Dorchester DT1 1UZ ☎ 01305 252244; 01305 251010
✉ glenharding@weymouth.gov.uk;
g.harding@westdorset-weymouth.gov.uk

Legal: Mr Jason Vaughan, Director of Resources, West Dorset District Council, 58/60 High West Street, Dorchester DT1 1UZ ☎ 01305 838233; 01305 251010
✉ jasonvaughan@weymouth.gov.uk;
j.vaughan@westdorset-weymouth.gov.uk

Leisure and Cultural Services: Ms Kate Hindson, Director of Communities, West Dorset District Council, 58/60 High West Street, Dorchester DT1 1UZ ☎ 01305 838037; 01305 251010 🖷 01305 838438 ✉ katehindson@weymouth.gov.uk;
k.hindson@westdorset-weymouth.gov.uk

Leisure and Cultural Services: Mr Nick Thornley, Leisure & Tourism Manager, Stratton House, 58-60 High West Street, Dorchester DT1 1UZ ☎ 01305 252474; 01305 251010
✉ nickthornley@weymouth.gov.uk;
n.thornley@westdorset-weymouth.gov.uk

Licensing: Mr Graham Duggan, Community Protection Manager, Stratton House, 58-60 High West Street, Dorchester DT1 1UZ ☎ 01305 252285; 01305 251010
✉ grahamduggan@weymouth.gov.uk;
g.duggan@westdorset-weymouth.gov.uk

Lottery Funding, Charity and Voluntary: Mr Nick Thornley, Leisure & Tourism Manager, Stratton House, 58-60 High West Street, Dorchester DT1 1UZ ☎ 01305 252474; 01305 251010
✉ nickthornley@weymouth.gov.uk;
n.thornley@westdorset-weymouth.gov.uk

Member Services: Ms Sue Bonham-Lovett, Head of Elector & Member Services, West Dorset District Council, 58/60 High West Street, Dorchester DT1 1UZ ☎ 01305 838477; 01305 251010 🖷 01305 838289 ✉ suebonhamlovett@weymouth.gov.uk;
s.bonham-lovett@westdorset-weymouth.gov.uk

Member Services: Mr Glen Harding, Legal & Democratic Manager, West Dorset District Council, 58/60 High West Street, Dorchester DT1 1UZ ☎ 01305 252244; 01305 251010
✉ glenharding@weymouth.gov.uk;
g.harding@westdorset-weymouth.gov.uk

Parking: Mr Steve Woollard, Technical Services Manager, Stratton House, 58-60 High West Street, Dorchester DT1 1UZ ☎ 01305 252297; 01305 251010
✉ stevewoollard@weymouth.gov.uk;
s.woollard@westdorset-weymouth.gov.uk

Personnel / HR: Ms Melanie Earnshaw, Human Resources Manager, West Dorset District Council, 58/60 High Street, Dorchester DT1 1UZ ☎ 01305 838212
✉ melanieearnshaw@weymouth.gov.uk;
m.earnshaw@westdorset-weymouth.gov.uk

Personnel / HR: Mr Adrian Stuart, Director of Corporate Services, Stratton House, 58-60 High West Street, Dorchester DT1 1UZ ☎ 01305 252315; 01305 251010
✉ adrianstuart2@weymouth.gov.uk;
a.stuart@westdorset-weymouth.gov.uk

Planning: Mr David Evans, Director of Environment, Stratton House, 58-60 High West Street, Dorchester DT1 1UZ ☎ 01305 252232; 01305 251010 ✉ davidevans2@weymouth.gov.uk;
d.evans@westdorset-weymouth.gov.uk

Planning: Mr John Greenslade, Development Services Manager, Stratton House, 58-60 High West Street, Dorchester DT1 1UZ ☎ 01305 252230; 01305 251010
✉ johngreenslade@weymouth.gov.uk;
j.greenslade@westdorset-weymouth.gov.uk

Procurement: Ms Julie Strange, Financial Services Manager, West Dorset District Council, 58/60 High West Street, Dorchester DT1 1UZ ☎ 01305 838252; 01305 251010 juliestrange@weymouth.gov.uk; j.strange@westdorset-weymouth.gov.uk

Recycling & Waste Minimisation: Ms Karyn Punchard, Street Scene Manager, West Dorset District Council, 58/60 High West Street, Dorchester DT1 1UZ ☎ 01305 838226; 01305 251010 karynpunchard@weymouth.gov.uk; k.punchard@westdorset-weymouth.gov.uk

Staff Training: Ms Melanie Earnshaw, Human Resources Manager, West Dorset District Council, 58/60 High West Street, Dorchester DT1 1UZ ☎ 01305 838212 melanieearnshaw@weymouth.gov.uk; m.earnshaw@westdorset-weymouth.gov.uk

Street Scene: Ms Kate Hindson, Director of Communities, West Dorset District Council, 58/60 High West Street, Dorchester DT1 1UZ ☎ 01305 838037; 01305 251010 🖷 01305 838438 katehindson@weymouth.gov.uk; k.hindson@westdorset-weymouth.gov.uk

Street Scene: Ms Karyn Punchard, Street Scene Manager, West Dorset District Council, 58/60 High West Street, Dorchester DT1 1UZ ☎ 01305 838226; 01305 251010 karynpunchard@weymouth.gov.uk; k.punchard@westdorset-weymouth.gov.uk

Sustainable Communities: Ms Hilary Jordan, Spatial & Community Planning Manager, Stratton House, 58-60 High West Street, Dorchester DT1 1UZ ☎ 01305 251010 h.jordan@westdorset-weymouth.gov.uk

Sustainable Development: Ms Hilary Jordan, Spatial & Community Planning Manager, Stratton House, 58-60 High West Street, Dorchester DT1 1UZ ☎ 01305 251010 h.jordan@westdorset-weymouth.gov.uk

Tourism: Mr Nick Thornley, Leisure & Tourism Manager, Stratton House, 58-60 High West Street, Dorchester DT1 1UZ ☎ 01305 252474; 01305 251010 nickthornley@weymouth.gov.uk; n.thornley@westdorset-weymouth.gov.uk

Waste Collection and Disposal: Ms Karyn Punchard, Street Scene Manager, West Dorset District Council, 58/60 High West Street, Dorchester DT1 1UZ ☎ 01305 838226; 01305 251010 karynpunchard@weymouth.gov.uk; k.punchard@westdorset-weymouth.gov.uk

Waste Management: Ms Karyn Punchard, Street Scene Manager, West Dorset District Council, 58/60 High West Street, Dorchester DT1 1UZ ☎ 01305 838226; 01305 251010 karynpunchard@weymouth.gov.uk; k.punchard@westdorset-weymouth.gov.uk

MEMBERS OF THE COUNCIL (48)

***Chair:* Summers**, Gillian (CON - Chideock and Symondsbury)
cllrg.summers@westdorset-dc.gov.uk

***Vice-Chair:* Seall**, Teresa (CON - Owermoigne)
cllrt.seall@westdorset-dc.gov.uk

***Leader of the Council:* Gould**, Robert (CON - Queen Thorne)
cllrr.gould@westdorset-dc.gov.uk

***Group Leader:* Barrett**, David (IND - Dorchester West)
cllrd.barrett@westdorset-dc.gov.uk

***Group Leader:* Jones**, Stella (LD - Dorchester East)
stella@sywardcottage.co.uk

Alford, Anthony (CON - Netherbury)
cllra.alford@westdorset-dc.gov.uk

Bartlett, Thomas (CON - Chesil Bank)
cllrt.bartlett@westdorset-dc.gov.uk

Bremner, Jane (CON - Charmouth Ward)
cllrj.bremner@westdorset-dc.gov.uk

Brown, Sandra (CON - Bridport South and Bothenhampton)
cllrs.brown@westdorset-dc.gov.uk

Canning, Andy (LD - Dorchester North)
cllra.canning@westdorset-dc.gov.uk

Chisholm, Alistair (IND - Charminster and Cerne Valley)
cllra.chisholm@westdorset-dc.gov.uk

Coatsworth, Ronald (CON - Bradpole)
cllrr.coatsworth@westdorset-dc.gov.uk

Cooke, Patrick (CON - Puddletown)
cllrp.cooke@westdorset-dc.gov.uk

Cuff, Jacqui (CON - Piddle Valley)
cllrj.cuff@westdorset-dc.gov.uk

Day, Keith (CON - Bridport North)
KeithADay@aol.com

Dunseith, Jean (CON - Chickerell)
cllrj.dunseith@westdorset-dc.gov.uk

East, Sarah (CON - Charminster and Cerne Valley)
cllrs.east@westdorset-dc.gov.uk

Elliott, Dominic (CON - Sherborne East)
cllrd.elliott@westdorset-dc.gov.uk

Farmer, Terry (CON - Sherborne East)
cllrt.farmer@westdorset-dc.gov.uk

Frost, Tony (IND - Halstock)
cllrt.frost@westdorset-dc.gov.uk

Gardner, Ian (CON - Chickerell)
Ian_C_Gardner@talk21.com

Harries, Tim (LD - Dorchester East)

Haynes, Jill (CON - Maiden Newton)
Jill.Haynes@dorsetcc.gov.uk

Hosford, Susie (LD - Dorchester North)
shosford@btinernet.com

Jones, Trevor (LD - Dorchester West)
trevor@sywardcottage.co.uk

Jungius, Richard (CON - Cam Vale)
cllrr.jungius@westdorset-dc.gov.uk

Kayes, Ros (LD - Bridport North)
roskayes@gmail.com

Lawrence, Margaret (CON - Yetminster)
cllrm.lawrence@westdorset-dc.gov.uk

Legg, Robin (LD - Bradford Abbas)
robin.legg@btinternet.com

McKenzie, Frances (CON - Bridport South and Bothenhampton)
fmfkmckenzie28@gmail.com

Page, Janet (LD - Beaminster)
cllrj.page@westdorset-dc.gov.uk

Payne, Caroline (LD - Beaminster)
cllrc.payne@westdorset-dc.gov.uk

Penfold, Mary (CON - Frome Valley)
cllrm.penfold@westdorset-dc.gov.uk

Potter, Robin (LD - Dorchester South)
cllrr.potter@westdorset-dc.gov.uk

Rennie, Molly (LD - Dorchester South)
mollymadgerennie@hotmail.co.uk

Roberts, Mark (CON - Loders)
lucullas.luccas@virgin.net

Robinson, Michael (CON - Marshwood Vale)
cllrm.robinson@westdorset-dc.gov.uk
Russell, John (CON - Burton Bradstock)
cllrj.russell@westdorset-dc.gov.uk
Sewell, Jacqui (CON - Broadwindsor)
cllrj.sewell@westdorset-dc.gov.uk
Shorland, Peter (CON - Sherborne West)
cllrp.shorland@westdorset-dc.gov.uk
Slade, Stephen (IND - Winterborne St Martin)
Snowden, Marjorie (CON - Sherborne West)
cllrm.snowden@westdorset-dc.gov.uk
Stein, Peter (CON - Owermoigne)
cllrp.stein@westdorset-dc.gov.uk
Symonds, George (CON - Lyme Regis)
cllrg.symonds@westdorset-dc.gov.uk
Tett, David (IND - Bridport South and Bothenhampton)
cllrd.tett@westdorset-dc.gov.uk
Thacker, Alan (CON - Broadmayne)
cllra.thacker@westdorset-dc.gov.uk
Turner, Daryl (CON - Lyme Regis)
cllrd.turner@westdorset-dc.gov.uk
Whyte, Elaine (CON - Chickerell)
cllre.whyte@westdorset-dc.gov.uk

POLITICAL COMPOSITION
CON: 32, LD: 11, IND: 5

COMMITTEE CHAIRS
Audit & Governance: Mrs Janet Page
Development Control: Mr Ian Gardner
Efficiency (Scrutiny): Mr Michael Robinson
Licensing & Appeals: Mr Ronald Coatsworth
Policy (Scrutiny): Mr Peter Shorland

WEST DUNBARTONSHIRE S

West Dunbartonshire Council, Council Offices, Garshake Road, Dumbarton G82 3PU ☎ 01389 737000 🖷 01389 737700
💻 www.west-dunbarton.gov.uk

FACTS & FIGURES
Police Authority: Strathclyde Police Authority
Health Authority: NHS Greater Glasgow & Clyde Health Board
Learning and Skills Council: Scotland
Parliamentary Constituencies: Dunbartonshire West
EU Constituencies: Scotland
Election Frequency: Elections are of whole council
Twinning: Argenteuil (France)

PRINCIPAL OFFICERS
Chief Executive: Mr David McMillan, Chief Executive, Council Offices, Garshake Road, Dumbarton G82 3PU ☎ 01389 737667 🖷 01389 737669 ✉ david.mcmillan@west-dunbarton.gov.uk

Senior Management: Mr Terry Lanagan, Executive Director of Educational Services, Council Offices, Garshake Road, Dumbarton G82 3PU ☎ 01389 737000 ✉ terry.lanagan@west-dunbarton.gov.uk

Senior Management: Ms Elaine Melrose, Executive Director of Housing, Environment & Economic Development, Council Offices, Garshake Road, Dumbarton G82 3PU ☎ 01389 737000 ✉ elaine.melrose@west-dunbarton.gov.uk

Senior Management: Mr Keith Redpath, Director of Community Health & Care Partnership, Council Offices, Garshake Road, Dumbarton G82 3PU ☎ 01389 737526 ✉ keith.redpath@west-dunbarton.gov.uk

Senior Management: Mrs Angela Wilson, Executive Director of Corporate Services, Council Offices, Garshake Road, Dumbarton G82 3PU ☎ 01389 737606 ✉ am.wilson@west-dunbarton.gov.uk

Access Officer / Social Services (Disability): Mr Lewis Morrison, Policy Officer (Disability & Accessibility), Council Offices, Garshake Road, Dumbarton G82 3PU ☎ 01389 737201 🖷 01389 737223 ✉ lewis.morrison@west-dunbarton.gov.uk

Architect, Building / Property Services: Mr Jim McAloon, Head of Regeneration & Economic Development, Council Offices, Garshake Road, Dumbarton G82 3PU ☎ 01389 737000 ✉ jim.mcaloon@west-dunbarton.gov.uk

Best Value: Mrs Joyce White, Executive Director of Corporate Services, Council Offices, Garshake Road, Dumbarton G82 3PU ☎ 01389 737000 ✉ joyce.white@west-dunbarton.gov.uk

Building Control: Ms Pamela Clifford, Planning & Building Standards Manager, Council Offices, Garshake Road, Dumbarton G82 3PU ☎ 01389 738656 ✉ pamela.clifford@west-dunbarton.gov.uk

Catering Services: Mrs Lynda McLaughlin, Leisure & Facilities Manager, Elm Road, Dumbarton G82 1NR ☎ 01389 602097 ✉ lynda.mclaughlin@west-dunbarton.gov.uk

Children / Youth Services: Mr Terry Lanagan, Executive Director of Educational Services, Council Offices, Garshake Road, Dumbarton G82 3PU ☎ 01389 737000 ✉ terry.lanagan@west-dunbarton.gov.uk

Children / Youth Services: Mr Jim Watson, Section Head - Child Care, 6 - 14 Bridge Street, Dumbarton G82 1LG ☎ 01389 772170 ✉ jim.watson@west-dunbarton.gov.uk

Civil Registration: Mr George Hawthorn, Section Head - Democratic Services, Council Offices, Garshake Road, Dumbarton G82 3PU ☎ 01389 737204 ✉ george.hawthorn@west-dunbarton.gov.uk

PR / Communications: Mr Malcolm Bennie, Manager of Community Planning, Council Offices, Garshake Road, Dumbarton G82 3PU ☎ 01389 737187 ✉ malcolm.bennie@west-dunbarton.gov.uk

Community Planning: Mr Peter Barry, Manager of Community Planning, Council Offices, Garshake Road, Dumbarton G82 3PU ☎ 01389 737573 ✉ peter.barry@west-dunbarton.gov.uk

Community Safety: Ms Janice Winder, Partnership Officer, Levenvalley Enterprise Centre, Castlehill Road, Dumbarton G82 5BN ☎ 01389 772127 ✉ janice.winder@west-dunbarton.gov.uk

Computer Management: Mr Stephen West, Head of Finance & Resources, Council Offices, Garshake Road, Dumbarton G82 3PU ☎ 01389 737000 ✉ stephen.west@west-dunbarton.gov.uk

Consumer Protection and Trading Standards: Mr David McCulloch, Section Head - Trading Standards, Council Offices, Rosebery Place, Clydebank G81 1TG ☎ 01389 738286 🖷 01389 738674 ✉ david.mcculloch@west-dunbarton.gov.uk

Consumer Protection and Trading Standards: Mr Graham Pollock, Manager of Regulatory Services, Council Offices, Rosebery Place, Clydebank G81 1TG ☎ 01389 738593 🖷 01389 738283 ✉ graham.pollock@west-dunbarton.gov.uk

Corporate Services: Mrs Angela Wilson, Executive Director of Corporate Services, Council Offices, Garshake Road, Dumbarton G82 3PU ☎ 01389 737606 ✉ am.wilson@west-dunbarton.gov.uk

Customer Service: Mr Colin McDougall, Manager of Risk & Performance, Council Offices, Garshake Road, Dumbarton G82 3PU ☎ 01389 737436 ✉ colin.mcdougall@west-dunbarton.gov.uk

Direct Labour: Mr Stephen McGonagle, Maintenance & Repairs Manager, Overburn Road, Dumbarton G82 3LG ☎ 01389 608338 ✉ stephen.mcgonagle@west-dunbarton.gov.uk

Economic Development: Mr Michael McGuinness, Economic Development Manager, Council Offices, Garshake Road, Dumbarton G82 3PU ☎ 01389 737415 ✉ michael.mcguinness@west-dunbarton.gov.uk

Education: Mr Terry Lanagan, Executive Director of Educational Services, Council Offices, Garshake Road, Dumbarton G82 3PU ☎ 01389 737000 ✉ terry.lanagan@west-dunbarton.gov.uk

Electoral Registration: Mr David Thomson, Assessor & Electoral Registration Officer, 235 Dumbarton Road, Clydebank G81 4XJ ☎ 0141 562 1200 🖷 0141 562 1220

Emergency Planning: Mr John Duffy, Section Head - Risk, Council Offices, Garshake Road, Dumbarton G82 3PU ☎ 01389 737897 ✉ john.duffy2@west-dunbarton.gov.uk

Environmental / Technical Services: Mr Graham Pollock, Manager of Regulatory Services, Council Offices, Rosebery Place, Clydebank G81 1TG ☎ 01389 738593 🖷 01389 738283 ✉ graham.pollock@west-dunbarton.gov.uk

Environmental Health: Mr Graham Pollock, Manager of Regulatory Services, Council Offices, Rosebery Place, Clydebank G81 1TG ☎ 01389 738593 🖷 01389 738283 ✉ graham.pollock@west-dunbarton.gov.uk

Estates, Property & Valuation: Mr Stuart Gibson, Assets Co-ordinator (Acting), Council Offices, Garshake Road, Dumbarton G82 3PU ☎ 01389 737157 ✉ stuart.gibson@west-dunbarton.gov.uk

European Liaison: Mr Michael McGuinness, Economic Development Manager, Council Offices, Garshake Road, Dumbarton G82 3PU ☎ 01389 737415 ✉ michael.mcguinness@west-dunbarton.gov.uk

Events Manager: Mrs Lynda McLaughlin, Leisure & Facilities Manager, Elm Road, Dumbarton G82 1NR ☎ 01389 602097 ✉ lynda.mclaughlin@west-dunbarton.gov.uk

Facilities: Mrs Lynda McLaughlin, Leisure & Facilities Manager, Elm Road, Dumbarton G82 1NR ☎ 01389 602097 ✉ lynda.mclaughlin@west-dunbarton.gov.uk

Finance and Treasurer: Mr Stephen West, Head of Finance & Resources, Council Offices, Garshake Road, Dumbarton G82 3PU ☎ 01389 737000 ✉ stephen.west@west-dunbarton.gov.uk

Fleet Management: Mr Ronald Dinnie, Head of Neighbourhood Services, Council Offices, Garshake Road, Dumbarton G82 3PU ☎ 01389 737601 🖷 01389 737637 ✉ ronald.dinnie@west-dunbarton.gov.uk

Grounds Maintenance: Mr Ronald Dinnie, Head of Neighbourhood Services, Council Offices, Garshake Road, Dumbarton G82 3PU ☎ 01389 737601 🖷 01389 737637 ✉ ronald.dinnie@west-dunbarton.gov.uk

Health and Safety: Mr John Duffy, Section Head - Risk, Council Offices, Garshake Road, Dumbarton G82 3PU ☎ 01389 737897 ✉ john.duffy2@west-dunbarton.gov.uk

Highways: Mr Ronald Dinnie, Head of Neighbourhood Services, Council Offices, Garshake Road, Dumbarton G82 3PU ☎ 01389 737601 🖷 01389 737637 ✉ ronald.dinnie@west-dunbarton.gov.uk

Housing: Ms Helen Turley, Head of Housing & Community Safety, Council Offices, Garshake Road, Dumbarton G82 3PU ☎ 01389 737598 ✉ helen.turley@west-dunbarton.gov.uk

Housing Maintenance: Ms Helen Turley, Head of Housing & Community Safety, Council Offices, Garshake Road, Dumbarton G82 3PU ☎ 01389 737598 ✉ helen.turley@west-dunbarton.gov.uk

Legal: Mr Andrew Fraser, Head of Legal, Administrative & Regulatory Services, Council Offices, Garshake Road, Dumbarton G82 3PU ☎ 01389 737800 🖷 01389 737870 ✉ andrew.fraser@west-dunbarton.gov.uk

Leisure and Cultural Services: Mrs Lynda McLaughlin, Leisure & Facilities Manager, Elm Road, Dumbarton G82 1NR ☎ 01389 602097 ✉ lynda.mclaughlin@west-dunbarton.gov.uk

Leisure and Cultural Services: Mrs Lynda McLaughlin, Leisure & Facilities Manager, Elm Road, Dumbarton G82 1NR ☎ 01389 602097 ✉ lynda.mclaughlin@west-dunbarton.gov.uk

Licensing: Mr Andrew Fraser, Head of Legal, Administrative & Regulatory Services, Council Offices, Garshake Road, Dumbarton G82 3PU ☎ 01389 737800 🖷 01389 737870 ✉ andrew.fraser@west-dunbarton.gov.uk

Lifelong Learning: Mr Terry Lanagan, Executive Director of Educational Services, Council Offices, Garshake Road, Dumbarton G82 3PU ☎ 01389 737000 ✉ terry.lanagan@west-dunbarton.gov.uk

Lighting: Mr Ronald Dinnie, Head of Neighbourhood Services, Council Offices, Garshake Road, Dumbarton G82 3PU ☎ 01389 737601 🖷 01389 737637 ✉ ronald.dinnie@west-dunbarton.gov.uk

Member Services: Mr George Hawthorn, Section Head - Democratic Services, Council Offices, Garshake Road, Dumbarton G82 3PU ☎ 01389 737204 george.hawthorn@west-dunbarton.gov.uk

Personnel / HR: Ms Tricia O'Neill, Head of Human Resources & Organisational Development, Council Offices, Garshake Road, Dumbarton G82 3PU ☎ 01389 737584 📠 01389 737534 tricia.oneill@west-dunbarton.gov.uk

Planning: Ms Pamela Clifford, Planning & Building Standards Manager, Council Offices, Garshake Road, Dumbarton G82 3PU ☎ 01389 738656 pamela.clifford@west-dunbarton.gov.uk

Procurement: Mr Ian Hutchison, E-Procurement Officer, Council Offices, Garshake Road, Dumbarton G82 3PU ☎ 01389 737664 📠 01389 737870 ian.hutchison@west-dunbarton.gov.uk

Public Libraries: Mr Richard Aird, Section Head - Libraries, 19 Poplar Road, Dumbarton G82 2RJ ☎ 01389 608040 richard.aird@west-dunbarton.gov.uk

Recycling & Waste Minimisation: Mr Graham Pollock, Manager of Regulatory Services, Council Offices, Rosebery Place, Clydebank G81 1TG ☎ 01389 738593 📠 01389 738283 graham.pollock@west-dunbarton.gov.uk

Regeneration: Mr Jim McAloon, Head of Regeneration & Economic Development, Council Offices, Garshake Road, Dumbarton G82 3PU ☎ 01389 737000 jim.mcaloon@west-dunbarton.gov.uk

Road Safety: Mr Ronald Dinnie, Head of Neighbourhood Services, Council Offices, Garshake Road, Dumbarton G82 3PU ☎ 01389 737601 📠 01389 737637 ronald.dinnie@west-dunbarton.gov.uk

Social Services: Mr Keith Redpath, Director of Community Health & Care Partnership, Council Offices, Garshake Road, Dumbarton G82 3PU ☎ 01389 737526 keith.redpath@west-dunbarton.gov.uk

Social Services (Adult): Mr David Elliott, General Manager, Beardmore Business Centre, Dalmuir, Clydebank G81 4HA ☎ 0141 562 2332 david.elliott@west-dunbarton.gov.uk

Social Services (Children): Mr Jim Watson, Section Head - Child Care, 7 Bruce Street, Clydebank G81 1TT ☎ 01389 772170 jim.watson@west-dunbarton.gov.uk

Staff Training: Ms Tricia O'Neill, Head of Human Resources & Organisational Development, Council Offices, Garshake Road, Dumbarton G82 3PU ☎ 01389 737584 📠 01389 737534 tricia.oneill@west-dunbarton.gov.uk

Traffic Management: Mr Ronald Dinnie, Head of Neighbourhood Services, Council Offices, Garshake Road, Dumbarton G82 3PU ☎ 01389 737601 📠 01389 737637 ronald.dinnie@west-dunbarton.gov.uk

Transport: Mr Ronald Dinnie, Head of Neighbourhood Services, Council Offices, Garshake Road, Dumbarton G82 3PU ☎ 01389 737601 📠 01389 737637 ronald.dinnie@west-dunbarton.gov.uk

Transport Planner: Mr Ronald Dinnie, Head of Neighbourhood Services, Council Offices, Garshake Road, Dumbarton G82 3PU ☎ 01389 737601 📠 01389 737637 ronald.dinnie@west-dunbarton.gov.uk

Waste Collection and Disposal: Mr Ronald Dinnie, Head of Neighbourhood Services, Council Offices, Garshake Road, Dumbarton G82 3PU ☎ 01389 737601 📠 01389 737637 ronald.dinnie@west-dunbarton.gov.uk

Waste Management: Mr Ronald Dinnie, Head of Neighbourhood Services, Council Offices, Garshake Road, Dumbarton G82 3PU ☎ 01389 737601 📠 01389 737637 ronald.dinnie@west-dunbarton.gov.uk

MEMBERS OF THE COUNCIL (22)

***Provost:* O'Neill**, Lawrence (SNP - Kilpatrick)
jim.finn@west-dunbarton.gov.uk
***Deputy Provost:* Millar**, John (LAB - Leven)
john.millar@west-dunbarton.gov.uk
***Leader of the Council:* Rooney**, Martin (LAB - Lomond)
martin.rooney@west-dunbarton.gov.uk
Agnew, Denis (IND - Clydebank Central)
Black, George (IND - Dumbarton)
george.black@west-dunbarton.gov.uk
Bollan, James (SSP - Leven)
james.bollan@west-dunbarton.gov.uk
Brown, Jim (SNP - Clydebank Central)
jim.brown@west-dunbarton.gov.uk
Casey, Gail (LAB - Clydebank Waterfront)
gail.casey@west-dunbarton.gov.uk
McAllister, Douglas (LAB - Kilpatrick)
douglas.mcallister@west-dunbarton.gov.uk
Mcbride, David (SNP - Clydebank Waterfront)
william.hendrie@west-dunbarton.gov.uk
McBride, David (LAB - Dumbarton)
david.mcbride@west-dunbarton.gov.uk
McGlinchey, Patrick (LAB - Clydebank Central)
patrick.mcglinchey@west-dunbarton.gov.uk
McNair, Marie (IND - Clydebank Waterfront)
marie.mcnair@west-dunbarton.gov.uk
Mooney, John (LAB - Clydebank Central)
john.mooney@west-dunbarton.gov.uk
Murray, Ian (SNP - Dumbarton)
ian.murray@west-dunbarton.gov.uk
O'Neill, Lawrence (LAB - Kilpatrick)
lawrence.oneill@west-dunbarton.gov.uk
Rainey, Tommy (LAB - Dumbarton)
thomas.rainey@west-dunbarton.gov.uk
Robertson, Gail (SNP - Leven)
gail.robertson@west-dunbarton.gov.uk
Rooney, Martin (SNP - Lomond)
ronnie.mccoll@west-dunbarton.gov.uk
Ryall, Kath (LAB - Clydebank Waterfront)
kath.ryall@west-dunbarton.gov.uk
Sorrell, Hazel (LAB - Lomond)
hazel.sorrell@west-dunbarton.gov.uk
Stewart, Michelle (LAB - Leven)
michelle.stewart@west-dunbarton.gov.uk

POLITICAL COMPOSITION
LAB: 12, SNP: 6, IND: 3, SSP: 1

COMMITTEE CHAIRS
Appeals: Mr Tommy Rainey
Corporate & Efficient Governance: Ms Kath Ryall
Education & Lifelong Learning: Mr Patrick Mcglinchey
Housing, Environment & Economic Development: Mr David Mcbride
Licensing: Mr Lawrence O'neill
Planning: Mr Lawrence O'Neill

WEST LANCASHIRE D
West Lancashire Borough Council, 52 Derby Street, Ormskirk L39 2DF ☎ 01695 577177 🖷 01695 585082
💻 www.westlancs.gov.uk

FACTS & FIGURES
Police Authority: Lancashire Police Authority
Health Authority: North West Strategic Health Authority
Learning and Skills Council: North West
Parliamentary Constituencies: Lancashire West
EU Constituencies: North West
Election Frequency: Elections are by thirds
Twinning: Cergy Pontoise (France); Erkrath (Germany)

PRINCIPAL OFFICERS
Senior Management: Ms Gill Rowe, Managing Director - People & Places, 52 Derby Street, Ormskirk L39 2DF ☎ 01695 585004 🖷 01695 585082 🖱 gill.rowe@westlancs.gov.uk

Senior Management: Ms Kim Webber, Managing Director - Transformation, 52 Derby Street, Ormskirk L39 2DF ☎ 01695 585005 🖷 01695 585229 🖱 kim.webber@westlancs.gov.uk

Architect, Building / Property Services: Mr Phil Holland, Property Services Manager, Sandy Lane Centre, 61 Westgate, Skelmersdale WN8 8LP ☎ 01695 585226 🖷 01695 556544 🖱 phil.holland@westlancs.gov.uk

Best Value: Ms Alison Grimes, Performance Officer, 52 Derby Street, Ormskirk L39 2DF ☎ 01695 585409 🖷 01695 585229 🖱 alison.grimes@westlancs.gov.uk

Best Value: Ms Kim Webber, Managing Director - Transformation, 52 Derby Street, Ormskirk L39 2DF ☎ 01695 585005 🖷 01695 585229 🖱 kim.webber@westlancs.gov.uk

Building Control: Mr John Harrison, Borough Planner, 52 Derby Street, Ormskirk L39 2DF ☎ 01695 585132 🖷 01695 585113 🖱 john.harrison@westlancs.gov.uk

Children / Youth Services: Mr John Nelson, Head of Leisure & Cultural Services, 52 Derby Street, Ormskirk L39 2DF ☎ 01695 585157 🖷 01695 585156 🖱 john.nelson@westlancs.gov.uk

PR / Communications: Ms Edwina Leigh, Consultation & Communications Manager, 52 Derby Street, Ormskirk L39 2DF ☎ 01695 577177 Extn 5433 🖷 01695 585082 🖱 edwina.leigh@westlancs.gov.uk

Community Planning: Mr John Harrison, Borough Planner, 52 Derby Street, Ormskirk L39 2DF ☎ 01695 585132 🖷 01695 585113 🖱 john.harrison@westlancs.gov.uk

Community Safety: Mr Andrew Hill, Environmental Protection & Community Safety Manager, Robert Hodge Centre, Stanley Industrial Estate, Stanley Way, Skelmersdale WN8 8EE ☎ 01695 585243 (585242) 🖷 01695 585082 (585126) 🖱 andrew.hill@westlancs.gov.uk

Computer Management: Mr Shaun Walsh, Transformation Manager, 52 Derby Street, Ormskirk L39 2DF ☎ 01695 585262 🖷 01695 585340 🖱 shaun.walsh@westlancs.gov.uk

Contracts: Mr Phil Holland, Property Services Manager, Sandy Lane Centre, 61 Westgate, Skelmersdale WN8 8LP ☎ 01695 585226 🖷 01695 556544 🖱 phil.holland@westlancs.gov.uk

Contracts: Mr John Ryding, Procurement & Projects Manager, 52 Derby Street, Ormskirk L39 2DF ☎ 01695 585022 🖷 01695 585021 🖱 john.ryding@westlancsdc.gov.uk

Customer Service: Mr Shaun Walsh, Transformation Manager, 52 Derby Street, Ormskirk L39 2DF ☎ 01695 585262 🖷 01695 585340 🖱 shaun.walsh@westlancs.gov.uk

Economic Development: Mrs Paula Huber, Economic Regeneration Manager, West Lancashire Investment Centre, Maple View, White Moss Business Park, Skelmersdale WN8 9TG ☎ 01695 585359 🖷 01695 712620 🖱 paula.huber@westlancs.gov.uk

E-Government: Mr Shaun Walsh, Transformation Manager, 52 Derby Street, Ormskirk L39 2DF ☎ 01695 585262 🖷 01695 585340 🖱 shaun.walsh@westlancs.gov.uk

Electoral Registration: Mrs Jane Smith, Administration & Electoral Services Manager, 52 Derby Street, Ormskirk L39 2DF ☎ 01695 585013 🖷 01695 585050 🖱 jane.smith@westlancs.gov.uk

Emergency Planning: Mr David Tilleray, Assistant Director - Community Services, Robert Hodge Centre, Stanley Industrial Estate, Stanley Way, Skelmersdale WN8 8EE ☎ 01695 585202 🖷 01695 585126 🖱 david.tilleray@westlancs.gov.uk

Energy Management: Mr Phil Holland, Property Services Manager, Sandy Lane Centre, 61 Westgate, Skelmersdale WN8 8LP ☎ 01695 585226 🖷 01695 556544 🖱 phil.holland@westlancs.gov.uk

Environmental Health: Mr Paul Charlson, Commercial Safety & Licensing Manager, Robert Hodge Centre, Stanley Industrial Estate, Stanley Way, Skelmersdale WN8 8EE ☎ 01695 585246 🖷 01695 585126 🖱 paul.charlson@westlancs.gov.uk

Environmental Health: Mr Andrew Hill, Environmental Protection & Community Safety Manager, Robert Hodge Centre, Stanley Industrial Estate, Stanley Way, Skelmersdale WN8 8EE ☎ 01695 585243 (585242) 🖷 01695 585082 (585126) 🖱 andrew.hill@westlancs.gov.uk

Environmental Health: Mr David Tilleray, Assistant Director - Community Services, Robert Hodge Centre, Stanley Industrial

Estate, Stanley Way, Skelmersdale WN8 8EE ☎ 01695 585202 🖷 01695 585126 ✉ david.tilleray@westlancs.gov.uk

Estates, Property & Valuation: Mrs Rachel Kneale, Estates & Valuations Manager, West Lancashire Investment Centre, Maple View, White Moss Business Park, Skelmersdale WN8 9TG ☎ 01695 712611 🖷 01695 716260 ✉ rachel.kneale@westlancs.gov.uk

European Liaison: Ms Gill Rowe, Managing Director - People & Places, 52 Derby Street, Ormskirk L39 2DF ☎ 01695 585004 🖷 01695 585082 ✉ gill.rowe@westlancs.gov.uk

Facilities: Ms Gill Rowe, Managing Director - People & Places, 52 Derby Street, Ormskirk L39 2DF ☎ 01695 585004 🖷 01695 585082 ✉ gill.rowe@westlancs.gov.uk

Finance and Treasurer: Mr Marc Taylor, Borough Treasurer, 52 Derby Street, Ormskirk L39 2DF ☎ 01695 585092 🖷 01695 585366 ✉ marc.taylor@westlancs.gov.uk

Fleet Management: Mr Jimmy Cummins, Fleet Maintenance Manager, Robert Hodge Centre, Stanley Industrial Estate, Stanley Way, Skelmersdale WN8 8EE ☎ 01695 577177 Extn: 5448 🖷 01695 50373 ✉ jimmy.cummins@westlancs.gov.uk

Grounds Maintenance: Mr Graham Concannon, Assistant Director - Street Scene, Robert Hodge Centre, Stanley Industrial Estate, Stanley Way, Skelmersdale WN8 8EE ☎ 01695 577177 ✉ graham.concannon@westlancs.gov.uk

Health and Safety: Mr Paul Adamson, Health & Safety Manager, 52 Derby Street, Ormskirk L39 2DF ☎ 01695 585241 🖷 01695 585021 ✉ paul.adamson@westlancs.gov.uk

Housing: Mr Bob Livermore, Assistant Director - Housing & Regeneration, 49 Westgate, Sandy Lane Centre, Skelmersdale WN8 8LP ☎ 01695 585200 🖷 01695 572331 ✉ bob.livermore@westlancs.gov.uk

Housing Maintenance: Mr Phil Holland, Property Services Manager, Sandy Lane Centre, 61 Westgate, Skelmersdale WN8 8LP ☎ 01695 585226 🖷 01695 556544 ✉ phil.holland@westlancs.gov.uk

Legal: Mr Terry Broderick, Acting Borough Solicitor, 52 Derby Street, Ormskirk L39 2DF ☎ 01695 585001 🖷 01695 585082 ✉ terry.broderick@westlancs.gov.uk

Leisure and Cultural Services: Mr John Nelson, Head of Leisure & Cultural Services, 52 Derby Street, Ormskirk L39 2DF ☎ 01695 585157 🖷 01695 585156 ✉ john.nelson@westlancs.gov.uk

Licensing: Mr Paul Charlson, Commercial Safety & Licensing Manager, Robert Hodge Centre, Stanley Industrial Estate, Stanley Way, Skelmersdale WN8 8EE ☎ 01695 585246 🖷 01695 585126 ✉ paul.charlson@westlancs.gov.uk

Lottery Funding, Charity and Voluntary: Ms Kim Webber, Managing Director - Transformation, 52 Derby Street, Ormskirk L39 2DF ☎ 01695 585005 🖷 01695 585229 ✉ kim.webber@westlancs.gov.uk

Member Services: Mr Mathew Jones, Legal & Member Services Manager, 52 Derby Street, Ormskirk L39 2DF ☎ 01695 585025 🖷 01695 585082 ✉ mathew.jones@westlancs.gov.uk

Parking: Mr Ken Knowles, Markets & Parking Officer, 52 Derby Street, Ormskirk L39 2DF ☎ 01695 585105 🖷 01695 585156 ✉ ken.knowles@westlancs.gov.uk

Personnel / HR: Mr Shaun Walsh, Transformation Manager, 52 Derby Street, Ormskirk L39 2DF ☎ 01695 585262 🖷 01695 585340 ✉ shaun.walsh@westlancs.gov.uk

Planning: Mr Ian Gill, Deputy Borough Planner, 52 Derby Street, Ormskirk L39 2DF ☎ 01695 585192 🖷 01695 585132 ✉ ian.gill@westlancs.gov.uk

Planning: Mr John Harrison, Borough Planner, 52 Derby Street, Ormskirk L39 2DF ☎ 01695 585132 🖷 01695 585113 ✉ john.harrison@westlancs.gov.uk

Procurement: Mr Stephen Tinsley, Purchasing & Land Charges Manager, 52 Derby Street, Ormskirk L39 2DF ☎ 01695 577177 Extn: 5426 🖷 01695 585082 ✉ stephen.tinsley@westlancs.gov.uk

Recycling & Waste Minimisation: Mr Graham Concannon, Assistant Director - Street Scene, Robert Hodge Centre, Stanley Industrial Estate, Stanley Way, Skelmersdale WN8 8EE ☎ 01695 577177 ✉ graham.concannon@westlancs.gov.uk

Regeneration: Mr Bob Livermore, Assistant Director - Housing & Regeneration, 49 Westgate, Sandy Lane Centre, Skelmersdale WN8 8LP ☎ 01695 585200 🖷 01695 572331 ✉ bob.livermore@westlancs.gov.uk

Staff Training: Mr Shaun Walsh, Transformation Manager, 52 Derby Street, Ormskirk L39 2DF ☎ 01695 585262 🖷 01695 585340 ✉ shaun.walsh@westlancs.gov.uk

Street Scene: Mr Graham Concannon, Assistant Director - Street Scene, Robert Hodge Centre, Stanley Industrial Estate, Stanley Way, Skelmersdale WN8 8EE ☎ 01695 577177 ✉ graham.concannon@westlancs.gov.uk

Sustainable Communities: Ms Kim Webber, Managing Director - Transformation, 52 Derby Street, Ormskirk L39 2DF ☎ 01695 585005 🖷 01695 585229 ✉ kim.webber@westlancs.gov.uk

Sustainable Development: Ms Christina Iball, Environmental Strategy Officer, Robert Hodge Centre, Stanley Industrial Estate, Stanley Way, Skelmersdale WN8 8EE ☎ 01695 585197 🖷 01695 585113 ✉ tina.iball@westlancs.gov.uk

Tourism: Mrs Paula Huber, Economic Regeneration Manager, West Lancashire Investment Centre, Maple View, White Moss Business Park, Skelmersdale WN8 9TG ☎ 01695 585359 🖷 01695 712620 ✉ paula.huber@westlancs.gov.uk

Town Centre: Mr Colin Brady, Technical Services Manager, 52 Derby Street, Ormskirk L39 2DF ☎ 01695 585125 🖷 01695 585113 ✉ colin.brady@westlancs.gov.uk

Waste Collection and Disposal: Mr Graham Concannon,

Assistant Director - Street Scene, Robert Hodge Centre, Stanley Industrial Estate, Stanley Way, Skelmersdale WN8 8EE ☎ 01695 577177 graham.concannon@westlancs.gov.uk

Waste Management: Mr Graham Concannon, Assistant Director - Street Scene, Robert Hodge Centre, Stanley Industrial Estate, Stanley Way, Skelmersdale WN8 8EE ☎ 01695 577177 graham.concannon@westlancs.gov.uk

MEMBERS OF THE COUNCIL (54)

***Mayor:* Greenall**, Paul (CON - Derby)
cllr.greenall@westlancs.gov.uk
***Deputy Mayor:* Ashcroft**, Iain (CON - Hesketh-with-Becconsall)
cllr.ashcroft@westlancs.gov.uk
***Leader of the Council:* Grant**, Ian (CON - Aughton Park)
cllr.grant@westlancs.gov.uk
***Deputy Leader of the Council:* Owens**, Adrian (CON - Derby)
cllr.owens@westlancs.gov.uk
Aldridge, Terry (LAB - Moorside)
cllr.aldridge@westlancs.gov.uk
Atherley, Una (CON - Aughton and Downholland)
cllr.atherley@westlancs.gov.uk
Bailey, Rob (CON - Knowsley)
cllr.bailey@westlancs.gov.uk
Baldock, John (CON - North Meols)
cllr.baldock@westlancs.gov.uk
Baybutt, Pam (CON - Wrightington)
cllr.baybutt@westlancs.gov.uk
Bell, Roger (LAB - Burscough East)
cllr.bell@westlancs.gov.uk
Blake, May (CON - Parbold)
cllr.blake@westlancs.gov.uk
Blane, Paul (CON - North Meols)
cllr.blane@westlancs.gov.uk
Cheetham, Andrew (CON - Tarleton)
cllr.cheetham@westlancs.gov.uk
Coyle, Jackie (LAB - Digmoor)
cllr.coyle@westlancs.gov.uk
Cropper, William (CON - Scarisbrick)
cllr.cropper@westlancs.gov.uk
Davis, John (LAB - Burscough West)
cllr.davis@westlancs.gov.uk
Delaney, Noel (LAB - Scott)
cllr.delaney@westlancs.gov.uk
Dereli, Cynthia (LAB - Burscough West)
cllr.dereli@westlancs.gov.uk
Evans, Rosemary (CON - Tarleton)
cllr.revans@westlancs.gov.uk
Evans, Carolyn (CON - Wrightington)
cllr.cevans@westlancs.gov.uk
Fillis, John (LAB - Up Holland)
Cllr.Fillis@westlancs.gov.uk
Forshaw, Martin (CON - Hesketh-with-Becconsall)
cllr.forshaw@westlancs.gov.uk
Fowler, Andrew (CON - Scarisbrick)
cllr.fowler@westlancs.gov.uk
Furey, Neil Stuart (LAB - Skelmersdale North)
cllr.furey@westlancs.gov.uk
Gagen, Yvonne (LAB - Ashurst)
cllr.gagen@westlancs.gov.uk
Gibson, Julie (LAB - Moorside)
cllr.gibson@westlancs.gov.uk
Griffiths, David (CON - Bickerstaffe)
cllr.griffiths@westlancs.gov.uk
Hennessy, Nikki (LAB - Tanhouse)
cllr.hennessy@westlancs.gov.uk
Hodson, Lucy (LAB - Birch Green)
cllr.lhodson@westlancs.gov.uk
Hodson, Gail (LAB - Ashurst)
cllr.ghodson@westlancs.gov.uk
Hodson, John (LAB - Scott)
cllr.hodson@westlancs.gov.uk
Hopley, Val (CON - Knowsley)
cllr.hopley@westlancs.gov.uk
Houlgrave, Jane (CON - Rufford)
cllr.houlgrave@westlancs.gov.uk
Jones, Graham Rhys (CON - Aughton Park)
cllr.gjones@westlancs.gov.uk
Kay, James (CON - Tarleton)
cllr.kay@westlancs.gov.uk
Kean, Barbara (CON - Parbold)
cllr.kean@westlancs.gov.uk
McKay, David (LAB - Skelmersdale South)
cllr.mckay@westlancs.gov.uk
Melling, Ruth (CON - Burscough East)
cllr.melling@westlancs.gov.uk
Moran, Ian (LAB - Up Holland)
Cllr.Moran@westlancs.gov.uk
Nolan, Barry (LAB - Skelmersdale North)
cllr.nolan@westlancs.gov.uk
Oliver, George (LAB - Knowsley)
cllr.oliver@westlancs.gov.uk
O'Toole, David (CON - Aughton and Downholland)
cllr.otoole@westlancs.gov.uk
Owen, Gaynar (LAB - Up Holland)
cllr.owen@westlancs.gov.uk
Pendleton, Robert (LAB - Tanhouse)
cllr.bpendleton@westlancs.gov.uk
Pope, Edward (CON - Newburgh)
cllr.pope@westlancs.gov.uk
Pryce-Roberts, Nicola (LAB - Skelmersdale South)
Cllr.Pryce-Roberts@westlancs.gov.uk
Pye, Neil (LAB - Birch Green)
cllr.pye@westlancs.gov.uk
Savage, Liz (LAB - Ashurst)
cllr.savage@westlancs.gov.uk
Stephenson, Doreen (CON - Halsall)
cllr.stephenson@westlancs.gov.uk
Sudworth, David (CON - Derby)
cllr.sudworth@westlancs.gov.uk
West, Donna (LAB - Skelmersdale South)
Westley, David (CON - Aughton and Downholland)
cllr.westley@westlancs.gov.uk
Wilkie, Kevin (LAB - Digmoor)
cllr.wilkie@westlancs.gov.uk
Wright, Kevin (LAB - Scott)
cllr.wright@westlancs.gov.uk

POLITICAL COMPOSITION

CON: 28, LAB: 26

CABINET

Leader: Mr Ian Grant
Deputy Leader / Housing (Finance), Regeneration & Estates: Mr Adrian Owens
Health, Leisure & Community Safety: Mr David Sudworth
Landlord Services & Human Resources: Mrs Val Hopley
Planning & Development: Mr Martin Forshaw

Public Realm: Mr Andrew Fowler
Resources & Transformation: Mr David Westley

COMMITTEE CHAIRS

Affordable Housing: Mrs Val Hopley
Audit & Governance: Mr Edward Pope
Corporate & Environment Overview & Scrutiny: Mr Rob Bailey
Environment Overview & Scutiny: Mrs May Blake
Licensing & Gambling: Mr James Kay
Planning: Mr Edward Pope
Standards: Mr Ian Grant

WEST LINDSEY D

West Lindsey District Council, The Guildhall, Marshall's Yard, Gainsborough DN21 2NA ☎ 01427 676676 🖷 01427 810622
💻 www.west-lindsey.gov.uk

FACTS & FIGURES

Police Authority: Lincolnshire Police Authority
Health Authority: East Midlands Strategic Health Authority
Learning and Skills Council: Eastern
Parliamentary Constituencies: Gainsborough
EU Constituencies: Eastern
Election Frequency: Elections are by thirds
Twinning: Neunkirchen (Germany); Market Rasen: Bouenkarspel (Netherlands); Mamers (France); Nettleham: Mulsanne (France); Welton: Monce-en-Belin (France); Cherry Willingham: Le Grand Luce (France); Grasby: St. Remy de Sille (France); Bardney: La Bazoga (France); Saxilby: Haarlemmerliede en Spaarnwoude (Holland); Caistor: Savigne-L'Eveque (France); Keelby: Maisdon-sur-Suvre (France), Willingham by Stow: Moyenneville (France)

PRINCIPAL OFFICERS

Chief Executive: Mrs Manjeet Gill, Chief Executive, The Guildhall, Marshall's Yard, Gainsborough DN21 2NA ☎ 01427 676676
🖰 manjeet.gill@west-lindsey.gov.uk

Deputy Chief Executive: Mr Adrian McCormick, Director of Resources & Deputy Chief Executive, The Guildhall, Marshalls Yard, Gainsborough DN21 2NA ☎ 01427 676524 🖷 01427 675170
🖰 adrian.mccormick@west-lindsey.gov.uk

PR / Communications: Mr Adrian McCormick, Director of Resources & Deputy Chief Executive, The Guildhall, Marshalls Yard, Gainsborough DN21 2NA ☎ 01427 676524 🖷 01427 675170
🖰 adrian.mccormick@west-lindsey.gov.uk

PR / Communications: Ms Rachel North, Director of Strategy & Regeneration, The Guildhall, Marshalls Yard, Gainsborough DN21 2NA ☎ 01427 676535 🖰 rachel.north@west-lindsey.gov.uk

Community Safety: Mr Chris Allen, Public Protection Services Manager, The Guildhall, Marshall's Yard, Gainsborough DN21 2NA ☎ 01427 675133 🖰 chris.allen@west-lindsey.gov.uk

Community Safety: Mr Grant Lockett, Housing & Renewal Services Manager, The Guildhall, Marshall's Yard, Gainsborough DN21 2NA ☎ 01427 676190 🖰 grant.lockett@west-lindsey.gov.uk

Computer Management: Mr Adrian McCormick, Director of Resources & Deputy Chief Executive, The Guildhall, Marshalls Yard, Gainsborough DN21 2NA ☎ 01427 676524 🖷 01427 675170
🖰 adrian.mccormick@west-lindsey.gov.uk

Customer Service: Ms Lyn Marlow, Customer Relations Manager, The Guildhall, Marshalls Yard, Gainsborough DN21 2NA ☎ 01427 676684 🖷 01427 675170
🖰 lyn.marlow@west-lindsey.gov.uk

Customer Service: Mr Alan Robinson, Revenues, Benefits & Customer Services Manager, The Guildhall, Marshall's Yard, Gainsborough DN21 2NA ☎ 01427 676676
🖰 alan.robinson@wwest-lindsey.gov.uk

Economic Development: Ms Suzanne Fysh, Regeneration Services Manager, The Guildhall, Marshalls Yard, Gainsborough DN21 2NA ☎ 01427 676632 🖷 01427 675170
🖰 suzanne.fysh@west-lindsey.gov.uk

E-Government: Mr Matthew Clarke, Business Transformation Services Manager, The Guildhall, Marshall's Yard, Gainsborough DN21 2NA ☎ 01427 676676
🖰 matthew.clarke@west-lindsey.gov.uk

E-Government: Mr Adrian McCormick, Director of Resources & Deputy Chief Executive, The Guildhall, Marshalls Yard, Gainsborough DN21 2NA ☎ 01427 676524 🖷 01427 675170
🖰 adrian.mccormick@west-lindsey.gov.uk

Electoral Registration: Mr Graham Spicksley, Assistant Electoral Registration Officer, The Guildhall, Marshalls Yard, Gainsborough DN21 2NA ☎ 01427 676576 🖷 01427 616466
🖰 graham.spicksley@west-lindsey.gov.uk

Emergency Planning: Mr Chris Allen, Public Protection Services Manager, The Guildhall, Marshall's Yard, Gainsborough DN21 2NA ☎ 01427 675133 🖰 chris.allen@west-lindsey.gov.uk

Emergency Planning: Mrs Joanna Riddell, Community Health Services Manager, The Guildhall, Marshalls Yard, Gainsborough DN21 2NA ☎ 01427 676113 🖰 joanna.riddell@west-lindsey.gov.uk

Energy Management: Mr Grant Lockett, Housing & Renewal Services Manager, The Guildhall, Marshall's Yard, Gainsborough DN21 2NA ☎ 01427 676190 🖰 grant.lockett@west-lindsey.gov.uk

Environmental / Technical Services: Mr James Nicholson, Director of Neighbourhoods & Health, The Guildhall, Marshalls Yard, Gainsborough DN21 2NA ☎ 01427 676105
🖰 jim.nicholson@west-lindsey.gov.uk

Environmental Health: Mr James Nicholson, Director of Neighbourhoods & Health, The Guildhall, Marshalls Yard, Gainsborough DN21 2NA ☎ 01427 676105
🖰 jim.nicholson@west-lindsey.gov.uk

Estates, Property & Valuation: Mr Grant Lockett, Housing & Renewal Services Manager, The Guildhall, Marshall's Yard, Gainsborough DN21 2NA ☎ 01427 676190 🖰 grant.lockett@west-lindsey.gov.uk

Events Manager: Ms Suzanne Fysh, Regeneration Services Manager, The Guildhall, Marshall's Yard, Gainsborough DN21 2NA

☎ 01427 676632 🖷 01427 675170
✉ suzanne.fysh@west-lindsey.gov.uk

Events Manager: Miss Nicola Turnbull, EPA to the Chief Executive & Chairman's Officer, The Guildhall, Marshall's Yard, Gainsborough DN21 2NA ☎ 01427 676501
✉ nicola.turnbull@west-lindsey.gov.uk

Facilities: Mr Adrian McCormick, Director of Resources & Deputy Chief Executive, The Guildhall, Marshalls Yard, Gainsborough DN21 2NA ☎ 01427 676524 🖷 01427 675170
✉ adrian.mccormick@west-lindsey.gov.uk

Finance and Treasurer: Mr Adrian McCormick, Director of Resources & Deputy Chief Executive, The Guildhall, Marshalls Yard, Gainsborough DN21 2NA ☎ 01427 676524 🖷 01427 675170
✉ adrian.mccormick@west-lindsey.gov.uk

Finance and Treasurer: Mr Russell Stone, Acting Financial Services Manager, The Guildhall, Marshall's Yard, Gainsborough DN21 2NA ☎ 01427 676676 ✉ russell.stone@west-lindsey.gov.uk

Fleet Management: Mr Glyn Pilkington, Waste Management Services Manager, North Warren Street Depot, Gainsborough DN21 2TT ☎ 01427 676676
✉ glyn.pilkington@west-lindsey.gov.uk

Health and Safety: Mr Chris Allen, Public Protection Services Manager, The Guildhall, Marshall's Yard, Gainsborough DN21 2NA ☎ 01427 675133 ✉ chris.allen@west-lindsey.gov.uk

Health and Safety: Mrs Joanna Riddell, Community Health Services Manager, The Guildhall, Marshalls Yard, Gainsborough DN21 2NA ☎ 01427 676113 ✉ joanna.riddell@west-lindsey.gov.uk

Home Energy Conservation: Ms Karen Lond, Energy & Efficiency Adviser, The Guildhall, Marshall's Tard, Gainsborough DN24 2NA ☎ 01427 676618 🖷 01427 675170
✉ karen.lond@west-lindsey.gov.uk

Housing: Mr Grant Lockett, Housing & Renewal Services Manager, The Guildhall, Marshall's Yard, Gainsborough DN21 2NA ☎ 01427 676190 ✉ grant.lockett@west-lindsey.gov.uk

Housing: Mr Grant Lockett, Housing & Renewal Services Manager, The Guildhall, Marshall's Yard, Gainsborough DN21 2NA ☎ 01427 676190 ✉ grant.lockett@west-lindsey.gov.uk

Housing Maintenance: Mr Grant Lockett, Housing & Renewal Services Manager, The Guildhall, Marshall's Yard, Gainsborough DN21 2NA ☎ 01427 676190 ✉ grant.lockett@west-lindsey.gov.uk

Legal: Ms Rachel North, Director of Strategy & Regeneration, The Guildhall, Marshalls Yard, Gainsborough DN21 2NA ☎ 01427 676535 ✉ rachel.north@west-lindsey.gov.uk

Leisure and Cultural Services: Mr Chris Allen, Public Protection Services Manager, The Guildhall, Marshall's Yard, Gainsborough DN21 2NA ☎ 01427 675133 ✉ chris.allen@west-lindsey.gov.uk

Lighting: Mr Chris Allen, Public Protection Services Manager, The Guildhall, Marshall's Yard, Gainsborough DN21 2NA ☎ 01427 675133 ✉ chris.allen@west-lindsey.gov.uk

Lottery Funding, Charity and Voluntary: Mr Chris Allen, Public Protection Services Manager, The Guildhall, Marshall's Yard, Gainsborough DN21 2NA ☎ 01427 675133
✉ chris.allen@west-lindsey.gov.uk

Lottery Funding, Charity and Voluntary: Ms Suzanne Fysh, Regeneration Services Manager, The Guildhall, Marshalls Yard, Gainsborough DN21 2NA ☎ 01427 676632 🖷 01427 675170
✉ suzanne.fysh@west-lindsey.gov.uk

Member Services: Mr Chris Allen, Public Protection Services Manager, The Guildhall, Marshall's Yard, Gainsborough DN21 2NA ☎ 01427 675133 ✉ chris.allen@west-lindsey.gov.uk

Parking: Mrs Joanna Riddell, Community Health Services Manager, The Guildhall, Marshalls Yard, Gainsborough DN21 2NA ☎ 01427 676113 ✉ joanna.riddell@west-lindsey.gov.uk

Partnerships: Ms Rachel North, Director of Strategy & Regeneration, The Guildhall, Marshalls Yard, Gainsborough DN21 2NA ☎ 01427 676535 ✉ rachel.north@west-lindsey.gov.uk

Personnel / HR: Ms Elaine Pepper, HR Manager, The Guildhall, Marshalls Yard, Gainsborough DN21 2NA ☎ 01427 676577 🖷 01427 675159 ✉ elaine.pepper@west-lindsey.gov.uk

Planning: Mr Adrian McCormick, Director of Resources & Deputy Chief Executive, The Guildhall, Marshalls Yard, Gainsborough DN21 2NA ☎ 01427 676524 🖷 01427 675170
✉ adrian.mccormick@west-lindsey.gov.uk

Recycling & Waste Minimisation: Mr Glyn Pilkington, Waste Management Services Manager, North Warren Street Depot, Gainsborough DN21 2TT ☎ 01427 676676
✉ glyn.pilkington@west-lindsey.gov.uk

Regeneration: Ms Rachel North, Director of Strategy & Regeneration, The Guildhall, Marshalls Yard, Gainsborough DN21 2NA ☎ 01427 676535 ✉ rachel.north@west-lindsey.gov.uk

Staff Training: Ms Elaine Pepper, HR Manager, The Guildhall, Marshalls Yard, Gainsborough DN21 2NA ☎ 01427 676577 🖷 01427 675159 ✉ elaine.pepper@west-lindsey.gov.uk

Street Scene: Mr James Nicholson, Director of Neighbourhoods & Health, The Guildhall, Marshalls Yard, Gainsborough DN21 2NA ☎ 01427 676105 ✉ jim.nicholson@west-lindsey.gov.uk

Sustainable Communities: Ms Suzanne Fysh, Regeneration Services Manager, The Guildhall, Marshalls Yard, Gainsborough DN21 2NA ☎ 01427 676632 🖷 01427 675170
✉ suzanne.fysh@west-lindsey.gov.uk

Sustainable Development: Ms Suzanne Fysh, Regeneration Services Manager, The Guildhall, Marshalls Yard, Gainsborough DN21 2NA ☎ 01427 676632 🖷 01427 675170
✉ suzanne.fysh@west-lindsey.gov.uk

Tourism: Ms Suzanne Fysh, Regeneration Services Manager, The Guildhall, Marshall's Yard, Gainsborough DN21 2NA ☎ 01427

676632 🖷 01427 675170 ✉ suzanne.fysh@west-lindsey.gov.uk

Tourism: Ms Marion Thomas, Arts & Tourism Manager, The Guildhall, Marshall's Yard, Gainsborough DN21 2NA ☎ 01427 675162 ✉ marion.thomas@west-lindsey.gov.uk

Town Centre: Ms Suzanne Fysh, Regeneration Services Manager, The Guildhall, Marshalls Yard, Gainsborough DN21 2NA ☎ 01427 676632 🖷 01427 675170 ✉ suzanne.fysh@west-lindsey.gov.uk

Waste Collection and Disposal: Mr Glyn Pilkington, Waste Management Services Manager, North Warren Street Depot, Gainsborough DN21 2TT ☎ 01427 676676 ✉ glyn.pilkington@west-lindsey.gov.uk

Waste Management: Mr Glyn Pilkington, Waste Management Services Manager, North Warren Street Depot, Gainsborough DN21 2TT ☎ 01427 676676 ✉ glyn.pilkington@west-lindsey.gov.uk

MEMBERS OF THE COUNCIL (36)

***Chair:* Milne**, Jessie (CON - Lea)
jessie.milne393@btinternet.com
***Vice-Chair:* Parish**, Malcolm (CON - Welton)
cllr.parish@btinernet.com
***Leader of the Council:* Keimach**, Burt (CON - Market Rasen)
burbette123@yahoo.com
Bardsley, Gillian (CON - Gainsborough North)
cllr.g.bardsley@west-lindsey.gov.uk
Bierley, Owen (CON - Yarborough)
owen@bierley.com
Bowler, Nigel (LAB - Gainsborough North)
nigelbowler@tiscali.co.uk
Bridger, Ken (LD - Market Rasen)
ken@waveneycottage.co.uk
Brockway, Jackie (CON - Saxilby)
jackiebrockway@gmail.com
Caine, Alan (IND - Caistor)
alncn100@gmail.com
Cotton, David (LD - Saxilby)
david.cotton500@ntlworld.com
Curtis, Stuart (CON - Sudbrooke)
stuartlyncurtis@aol.com
Darcel, Christopher (IND - Fiskerton)
chris@darcel.entadsl.com
Dobbie, David (LD - Gainsborough North)
dobbiedave@hotmail.com
Doran, Richy (LAB - Gainsborough East)
richy.doran@gmail.com
Fleetwood, Ian (CON - Bardney)
ifleet@barlings.demon.co.uk
Howitt-Cowan, Paul (CON - Hemswell)
kenmare01@hotmail.com
Kinch, Stuart (CON - Torksey)
stuart@thejohnkinchgroup.co.uk
Lawrence, Angela (CON - Caistor)
atlcaistor@gmail.com
Leaning, Malcolm (LD - Nettleham)
cllr.m.leaning@west-lindsey.gov.uk
Parrott, Irmgard (CON - Cherry Willingham)
irmgard@norwegianblue.com
Parry, William (CON - Scotter)
wsparry@hotmail.com
Patterson, Roger (CON - Scampton)
rogermpatterson@aol.com
Rainsforth, Judy (LD - Gainsborough South-West)
judyrainsforth@talktalk.net
Rawlins, Sue (CON - Dunholme)
sue.rawlins@virgin.net
Regis, Thomas (CON - Wold View)
tom@tomregis.com
Rodgers, Diana (IND - Welton)
cllr.D.Rodgers@west-lindsey.gov.uk
Rollings, Lesley (LD - Thonock)
cllr.l.rollings@west-lindsey.gov.uk
Shore, Reg (LD - Stow)
regshore@mac.com
Starkey, Mel (LD - Gainsborough East)
mel_starkey@yahoo.co.uk
Strange, Lewis (CON - Kelsey)
Cllrc.strange@lincolnshire.gov.uk
Summers, Jeff (CON - Waddingham and Spital)
jjscllr@btinternet.com
Tinker, M (LD - Gainsborough East)
cllrm.timker@lincolnshire.gov.uk
Underwood-Frost, Chris (CON - Scotter)
cllrc.underwoodfrost@lincolnshire.gov.uk
Welburn, Anne (CON - Cherry Willingham)
anne.welburn@btinernet.com
Wiseman, Geoff (CON - Middle Rasen)
geoff09@btinernet.com
Young, Trevor (LD - Gainsborough South-West)
t.young91@btinternet.com

POLITICAL COMPOSITION

CON: 21, LD: 10, IND: 3, LAB: 2

COMMITTEE CHAIRS

Governance & Audit: Mrs Sue Rawlins
Licensing & Regulatory: Mrs Irmgard Parrott
Planning: Mr Chris Underwood-Frost
Policy & Resources: Mr Thomas Regis
Prosperous Communities: Mr Malcolm Parish

WEST LOTHIAN S

West Lothian Council, West Lothian Civic Centre, Howden South Road, Livingston EH54 6FF ☎ 01506 775000 🖷 01506 777249 ✉ customer.service@westlothian.gov.uk 💻 www.westlothian.gov.uk

FACTS & FIGURES

Police Authority: Lothian & Borders Police Board
Health Authority: NHS Lothian
Learning and Skills Council: Scotland
Parliamentary Constituencies: Linlithgow and Falkirk East, Livingston
EU Constituencies: Scotland
Election Frequency: Elections are of whole council
Twinning: Guyancourt (France); Hochsauerland (Germany); Grapevine (Texas, US)

PRINCIPAL OFFICERS

Chief Executive: Mr Graham Hope, Chief Executive, West Lothian Civic Centre, Howden South Road, Livingston EH54 6FF ☎ 01506 281679 ✉ graham.hope@westlothian.gov.uk

Deputy Chief Executive: Mr Jim Forrest, Depute Chief Executive - Community Health & Care, West Lothian Civic Centre, Howden South Road, Livingston EH54 6FF ☎ 01506 281679 ✉ jim.forrest@westlothian.gov.uk

Deputy Chief Executive: Mr John Hill, Depute Chief Executive - Corporate, Operational & Housing Services, West Lothian Civic Centre, Howden South Road, Livingston EH54 6FF ☎ 01506 281679 ✉ john.hill@westlothian.gov.uk

Deputy Chief Executive: Ms Moira Niven, Depute Chief Executive - Education, Planning & Area Services, West Lothian Civic Centre, Howden South Road, Livingston EH54 6FF ☎ 01506 281679 ✉ moira.niven@westlothian.gov.uk

Access Officer / Social Services (Disability): Ms Jennifer Scott, Head of Social Policy, West Lothian Civic Centre, Howden South Road, Livingston EH54 6FF ☎ 01506 281925 ✉ jennifer.scott@westlothian.gov.uk

Best Value: Mr Graeme Struthers, Head of Corporate Services, West Lothian Civic Centre, Howden South Road, Livingston EH54 6FF ☎ 01506 281679 ✉ graeme.struthers@westlothian.gov.uk

Building Control: Mr Jim McGinley, Building Standards Manager, County Buildings, High Street, Linlithgow EH49 7EZ ☎ 01506 282395 ✉ jim.mcginley@westlothian.gov.uk

Catering Services: Mrs Liz Wark, Service Manager, Carmondean House, Carmondean Road South, Carmondean, Livingston EH54 8PT ☎ 01506 777544 ✉ liz.wark@westlothian.gov.uk

Children / Youth Services: Ms Jane Kellock, Manager - Children & Families / Health Improvement (Interim), Stratbrock Partnership Centre, 189a West Main Street, Broxburn EH25 5LH ☎ 01506 281920 ✉ jane.kellock@westlothian.gov.uk

Civil Registration: Mr James Lambert, Chief Registrar, Bathgate Partnership Centre, South Bridge Street, Bathgate EH48 1TS ☎ 01506 282916 ✉ jim.lambert@westlothian.gov.uk

PR / Communications: Mrs Evelyn Cargill, Corporate Communications Manager, West Lothian Civic Centre, Howden South Road, Livingston EH54 6FF ☎ 01506 282003 ✉ evelyn.cargill@westlothian.gov.uk

Community Planning: Ms Lorraine Gillis, Community Planning Manager, West Lothian Civic Centre, Howden South Road, Livingston EH54 6FF ☎ 01506 281690 ✉ lorraine.gillies@westlothian.gov.uk

Community Safety: Mr Ian Hepburn, Community Regeneration Manager, West Lothian Civic Centre, Howden South Road, Livingston EH54 6FF ☎ 01506 281089 ✉ ian.hepburn@westlothian.gov.uk

Computer Management: Ms Jennifer Milne, IT Manager, West Lothian Civic Centre, Howden South Road, Livingston EH54 6FF ☎ 01506 281521 ✉ jennifer.milne@westlothian.gov.uk

Consumer Protection and Trading Standards: Mr Andrew Blake, Environmental Health & Trading Standards Manager, County Buildings, High Street, Linlithgow EH49 7EZ ☎ 01506 775346 ✉ andrew.blake@westlothian.gov.uk

Corporate Services: Mr Graeme Struthers, Head of Corporate Services, West Lothian Civic Centre, Howden South Road, Livingston EH54 6FF ☎ 01506 281679 ✉ graeme.struthers@westlothian.gov.uk

Customer Service: Mr Alistair Shaw, Head of Area Services, West Lothian Civic Centre, Howden South Road, Livingston EH54 6FF ☎ 01506 281754 ✉ alistair.shaw@westlothian.gov.uk

Direct Labour: Mr John Hill, Depute Chief Executive - Corporate, Operational & Housing Services, West Lothian Civic Centre, Howden South Road, Livingston EH54 6FF ☎ 01506 281679 ✉ john.hill@westlothian.gov.uk

Economic Development: Mr Steve Field, Head of Planning & Economic Development, County Buildings, High Street, Linlithgow EH49 7EZ ☎ 01506 282386 ✉ steve.field@westlothian.gov.uk

Education: Ms Elaine Cook, Head of Service for Education, West Lothian Civic Centre, Howden South Road, Livingston EH54 6FF ☎ 01506 283050 ✉ elaine.cook@westlothian.gov.uk

Education: Ms Moira Niven, Depute Chief Executive - Education, Planning & Area Services, West Lothian Civic Centre, Howden South Road, Livingston EH54 6FF ☎ 01506 281679 ✉ moira.niven@westlothian.gov.uk

Electoral Registration: Mr Gordon Blair, Chief Legal Officer, West Lothian Civic Centre, Howden South Road, Livingston EH54 6FF ☎ 01506 281695 ✉ gordon.blair@westlothian.gov.uk

Emergency Planning: Ms Caroline Burton, Emergency Planning Officer, West Lothian Civic Centre, Howden South Road, Livingston EH54 6FF ☎ 01506 281651 ✉ caroline.burton@westlothian.gov.uk

Energy Management: Ms Rona Gold, Climate Change Policy Officer, County Buildings, High Street, Linlithgow EH49 7EZ ☎ 01506 281288 ✉ rona.gold@westlothian.gov.uk

Environmental Health: Mr Andrew Blake, Environmental Health & Trading Standards Manager, County Buildings, High Street, Linlithgow EH49 7EZ ☎ 01506 775346 ✉ andrew.blake@westlothian.gov.uk

Estates, Property & Valuation: Mr Donald Forrest, Head of Finance & Estates, West Lothian Civic Centre, Howden South Road, Livingston EH54 6FF ☎ 01506 281679 ✉ donald.forrest@westlothian.gov.uk

European Liaison: Mr David Greaves, Policy Manager, West Lothian Civic Centre, Howden South Road, Livingston EH54 6FF ☎ 01506 283097 ✉ david.greaves@westlothian.gov.uk

Finance and Treasurer: Mr Donald Forrest, Head of Finance & Estates, West Lothian Civic Centre, Howden South Road, Livingston EH54 6FF ☎ 01506 281679 ✉ donald.forrest@westlothian.gov.uk

Fleet Management: Mr Joe Drew, Fleet Co-ordinator, Fleet & Cleansing Depot, Nairn Road, Deans Industrial Estate, Livingston EH54 8AY ☎ 01506 777822 ✉ joe.drew@westlothian.gov.uk

Grounds Maintenance: Mr Jim Jack, Head of Operational Services, Whitehill House, Whitehill Industrial Estate, Bathgate EH48 2HA ☎ 01506 776601 ✉ jim.jack@westlothian.gov.uk

Health and Safety: Ms Marion Johnstone, Health & Safety Manager, West Lothian Civic Centre, Howden South Road, Livingston EH54 6FF ☎ 01506 281418 ✉ marion.johnstone@westlothian.gov.uk

Highways: Mr Jim Jack, Head of Operational Services, Whitehill House, Whitehill Industrial Estate, Bathgate EH48 2HA ☎ 01506 776601 ✉ jim.jack@westlothian.gov.uk

Local Area Agreement: Mr Alistair Shaw, Head of Area Services, West Lothian Civic Centre, Howden South Road, Livingston EH54 6FF ☎ 01506 281754 ✉ alistair.shaw@westlothian.gov.uk

Legal: Mrs Julie Whitelaw, Chief Solicitor, West Lothian Civic Centre, Howden South Road, Livingston EH54 6FF ☎ 01506 281626 ✉ julie.whitelaw@westlothian.gov.uk

Leisure and Cultural Services: Mr Keir Stevenson, Sport & Outdoor Education Team Leader, West Lothian Civic Centre, Howden South Road, Livingston EH54 6FF ☎ 01506 282775 ✉ keir.stevenson@westlothian.gov.uk

Licensing: Legal Services, West Lothian Civic Centre, Howden South Road, Livingston EH54 6FF ☎ 01506 281632 ✉ licensingservices@westlothian.gov.uk

Lifelong Learning: Mr Alistair Shaw, Head of Area Services, West Lothian Civic Centre, Howden South Road, Livingston EH54 6FF ☎ 01506 281754 ✉ alistair.shaw@westlothian.gov.uk

Lighting: Mr David Wilson, Manager, West Lothian Civic Centre, Howden South Road, Livingston EH54 6FF ☎ 01506 776651 ✉ david.wilson@westlothian.gov.uk

Lottery Funding, Charity and Voluntary: Mr Ian Hepburn, Community Regeneration Manager, West Lothian Civic Centre, Howden South Road, Livingston EH54 6FF ☎ 01506 281089 ✉ ian.hepburn@westlothian.gov.uk

Member Services: Mr Graeme Struthers, Head of Corporate Services, West Lothian Civic Centre, Howden South Road, Livingston EH54 6FF ☎ 01506 281679 ✉ graeme.struthers@westlothian.gov.uk

Partnerships: Mr Alistair Shaw, Head of Area Services, West Lothian Civic Centre, Howden South Road, Livingston EH54 6FF ☎ 01506 281754 ✉ alistair.shaw@westlothian.gov.uk

Personnel / HR: Mr Derek Stark, HR Services Manager, West Lothian Civic Centre, Howden South Road, Livingston EH54 6FF ☎ 01506 281452 ✉ derek.stark@westlothian.gov.uk

Planning: Mr Graeme Malcolm, Transportation Manager, County Buildings, High Street, Linlithgow EH49 7EZ ☎ 01506 775296 ✉ graeme.malcolm@westlothian.gov.uk

Planning: Mr Craig McCorriston, Planning Services Manager, County Buildings, High Street, Linlithgow EH49 7EZ ☎ 01506 282443 ✉ craig.mccorriston@westlothian.gov.uk

Planning: Mr Chris Norman, Development Control Manager, County Buildings, High Street, Linlithgow EH49 7EZ ☎ 01506 282412 ✉ chris.norman@westlothian.gov.uk

Procurement: Mr Tom Henderson, Procurement Manager, West Lothian Civic Centre, Howden South Road, Livingston EH54 6FF ☎ 01506 281805 ✉ tom.henderson@westlothian.gov.uk

Public Libraries: Ms Jeanette Castle, Library Services Manager, West Lothian Civic Centre, Howden South Road, Livingston EH54 6FF ☎ 01506 281273 ✉ jeanette.castle@westlothian.gov.uk

Regeneration: Mr David Greaves, Policy Manager, West Lothian Civic Centre, Howden South Road, Livingston EH54 6FF ☎ 01506 283097 ✉ david.greaves@westlothian.gov.uk

Road Safety: Mr Kevin Hamilton, Team Leader, County Buildings, High Street, Linlithgow EH49 7EZ ☎ 01506 282341 ✉ kevin.hamilton@westlothian.gov.uk

Social Services: Ms Jennifer Scott, Head of Social Policy, West Lothian Civic Centre, Howden South Road, Livingston EH54 6FF ☎ 01506 281925 ✉ jennifer.scott@westlothian.gov.uk

Social Services (Adult): Ms Jennifer Scott, Head of Social Policy, West Lothian Civic Centre, Howden South Road, Livingston EH54 6FF ☎ 01506 281925 ✉ jennifer.scott@westlothian.gov.uk

Social Services (Children): Ms Jennifer Scott, Head of Social Policy, West Lothian Civic Centre, Howden South Road, Livingston EH54 6FF ☎ 01506 281925 ✉ jennifer.scott@westlothian.gov.uk

Staff Training: Mr Derek Stark, HR Services Manager, West Lothian Civic Centre, Howden South Road, Livingston EH54 6FF ☎ 01506 281452 ✉ derek.stark@westlothian.gov.uk

Sustainable Communities: Mr Ian Hepburn, Community Regeneration Manager, West Lothian Civic Centre, Howden South Road, Livingston EH54 6FF ☎ 01506 281089 ✉ ian.hepburn@westlothian.gov.uk

Sustainable Development: Mr Steve Field, Head of Planning & Economic Development, County Buildings, High Street, Linlithgow EH49 7EZ ☎ 01506 282386 ✉ steve.field@westlothian.gov.uk

Tourism: Ms Anna Young, Tourism Executive, West Lothian Civic Centre, Howden South Road, Livingston EH54 6FF ☎ 01506 283093 ✉ anna.young@westlothian.gov.uk

Town Centre: Mr Alistair Shaw, Head of Area Services, West Lothian Civic Centre, Howden South Road, Livingston EH54 6FF ☎ 01506 281754 ✉ alistair.shaw@westlothian.gov.uk

Traffic Management: Mr Kevin Hamilton, Team Leader, County

Buildings, High Street, Linlithgow EH49 7EZ ☎ 01506 282341 ✉ kevin.hamilton@westlothian.gov.uk

Transport: Mr Ian Forbes, Public Transport Manager, County Buildings, High Street, Linlithgow EH49 7EZ ☎ 01506 282317 ✉ ian.forbes@westlothian.gov.uk

Children's Play Areas: Mr Colin Bell, Principal Officer, 7 Whitestone Place, Whitehill Industrial Estate, Bathgate EH48 2HA ☎ 01506 77629 ✉ colin.bell@westlothian.gov.uk

MEMBERS OF THE COUNCIL (33)

***Provost:* Kerr**, Tom (CON - Linlithgow)
tom.kerr@westlothian.gov.uk
***Leader of the Council:* McGinty**, John (LAB - Bathgate)
john.mcginty@westlothian.gov.uk
***Deputy Leader of the Council:* Muldoon**, Cathy (LAB - Fauldhouse and the Briech Valley)
cathy.muldoon@westlothian.gov.uk
Anderson, Frank (SNP - East Livingston and East Calder)
frank.anderson@westlothian.gov.uk
Borrowman, Stuart (IND - Armdale and Blackridge)
stuart.borrowman@westlothian.gov.uk
Boyle, William (SNP - Bathgate)
william.boyle@westlothian.gov.uk
Boyle, Tony (LAB - Broxburn, Uphall and Winchburgh)
tony.boyle@westlothian.gov.uk
Calder, Diane (SNP - Broxburn, Uphall and Winchburgh)
diane.calder@westlothian.gov.uk
Campbell, Janet (SNP - Broxburn, Uphall and Winchburgh)
janet.campbell@westlothian.gov.uk
Cartmill, Harry (LAB - Bathgate)
harry.cartmill@westlothian.gov.uk
Conn, Tom (LAB - Linlithgow)
tom.conn@westlothian.gov.uk
Davidson, Alex (LAB - Broxburn, Uphall and Winchburgh)
alex.davidson@westlothian.gov.uk
Day, Martyn (SNP - Linlithgow)
martyn.day@westlothian.gov.uk
De Bold, Robert (SNP - Livingston North)
robert.debold@westlothian.gov.uk
Dickson, Jim (SNP - Whitburn and Blackburn)
jim.dickson3@westlothian.gov.uk
Dickson, Mary (SNP - Whitburn and Blackburn)
mary.dickson@westlothian.gov.uk
Dixon, Jim (LAB - Armadale and Blackridge)
jim.dixon@westlothian.gov.uk
Dodds, David (LAB - Fauldhouse and The Breich Valley)
david.dodds@westlothian.gov.uk
Fitzpatrick, Lawrence (LAB - Livingston South)
lawrence.fitzpatrick@westlothian.gov.uk
Hutton, Isabel (SNP - Armadale and Blackbridge)
isabel.hutton@westlothian.gov.uk
John, Carl (SNP - East Livingston and East Calder)
carl.john@westlothian.gov.uk
Johnston, Peter (SNP - Livingston South)
peter.johnston@westlothian.gov.uk
King, Dave (LAB - East Livingston and East Calder)
dave.king@westlothian.gov.uk
Logue, Danny (LAB - Livingston South)
danny.logue@westlothian.gov.uk
McCarra, Greg (SNP - Fauldhouse and the Briech Valley)
greg.mccarra@westlothian.gov.uk
McMillan, Anne (LAB - Livingston North)
anne.mcmillan@westlothian.gov.uk
Miller, Andrew (SNP - Livingston North)
andrew.miller@westlothian.gov.uk
Moohan, Angela (LAB - Livingston North)
angela.moohan@westlothian.gov.uk
Muir, John (SNP - Livingston South)
john.muir@westlothian.gov.uk
Paul, George (LAB - Whitburn and Blackburn)
george.paul@westlothian.gov.uk
Robertson, Barry (LAB - Whitburn and Blackburn)
barry.robertson@westlothian.gov.uk
Toner, Frank (LAB - East Livingstone and East Calder)
frank.toner@westlothian.gov.uk
Walker, Jim (SNP - Bathgate)
jim.walker@westlothian.gov.uk

POLITICAL COMPOSITION

LAB: 16, SNP: 15, CON: 1, IND: 1

CABINET

Leader / Policy & Resources: Mr John McGinty
Culture & Leisure: Mr Dave King
Development & Transport: Ms Cathy Muldoon
Education: Mr Lawrence Fitzpatrick
Environment: Mr Tom Conn
Health & Care: Ms Anne McMillan
Services for the Community: Mr George Paul
Social Policy: Mr Danny Logue
Voluntary Organisations: Mr Jim Dixon

COMMITTEE CHAIRS

Audit: Mr Carl John
Development Control: Mr Jim Dickson
Environment Policy Development (Scrutiny): Mr Tom Conn
Licensing: Mr Tony Boyle
Social Policy Development & Scrutiny (Scrutiny): Mr Danny Logue

WEST OXFORDSHIRE — D

West Oxfordshire District Council, Council Offices, Woodgreen, Witney OX28 1NB ☎ 01993 861000 🖷 01993 861050 ✉ enquiries@westoxon.gov.uk 💻 www.westoxon.gov.uk

FACTS & FIGURES

Police Authority: Thames Valley Police Authority
Health Authority: South Central Strategic Health Authority
Learning and Skills Council: South East
Parliamentary Constituencies: Witney
EU Constituencies: South East
Election Frequency: Elections are by thirds
Twinning: Chipping Norton: Magny-en-Vexin (France); Witney: Le Touquet (France); Unterhaching (Germany)

PRINCIPAL OFFICERS

Chief Executive: Mr David Neudegg, Chief Executive, Council Offices, Woodgreen, Witney OX28 1NB ☎ 01993 861613 🖷 01993 861453 ✉ david.neudegg@westoxon.gov.uk

Senior Management: Mr David Neudegg, Chief Executive, Council Offices, Woodgreen, Witney OX28 1NB ☎ 01993 861613 🖷 01993 861453 ✉ david.neudegg@westoxon.gov.uk

Senior Management: Mr Andrew Tucker, Strategic Director, Council Offices, Woodgreen, Witney OX28 1NB ☎ 01993 861721 🖷 01993 861453 ✉ andrew.tucker@westoxon.gov.uk

Senior Management: Mr Frank Wilson, Strategic Director, Council Offices, Woodgreen, Witney OX28 1NB ☎ 01993 861291 🖷 01993 861453 ✉ frank.wilson@westoxon.gov.uk

Building Control: Mr John Hill, Building Control Manager, Council Offices, Elmfield, New Yatt Road, Witney OX28 1PB ☎ 01993 861668 ✉ john.hill@westoxon.gov.uk

PR / Communications: Ms Carys Davis, Publicity & Information Officer, Council Offices, Woodgreen, Witney OX28 1NB ☎ 01993 861615 🖷 01993 861450 ✉ communications@westoxon.gov.uk

Community Safety: Mr Bill Oddy, Head of Community Safety, Council Offices, Elmfield, New Yatt Road, Witney OX28 1PB ☎ 01993 861631 ✉ bill.oddy@westoxon.gov.uk

Computer Management: Mr John Chorlton, ICT Operations Manager, Council Offices, Woodgreen, Witney OX28 1NB ☎ 01993 861144 🖷 01993 861450 ✉ john.chorlton@westoxon.gov.uk

Contracts: Mr Frank Wilson, Strategic Director, Council Offices, Woodgreen, Witney OX28 1NB ☎ 01993 861291 🖷 01993 861453 ✉ frank.wilson@westoxon.gov.uk

Corporate Services: Mr Phil Martin, Head of Business Improvement, Council Offices, Woodgreen, Witney OX28 1NB ☎ 01993 861201 ✉ phil.martin@westoxon.gov.uk

Corporate Services: Mr Paul Stuart, Head of Corporate Resources, Council Offices, Woodgreen, Witney OX28 1NB ☎ 01993 861171 ✉ paul.stuart@westoxon.gov.uk

Customer Service: - Clare Martin, Customer Services Manager, 3 Welch Way, Witney OX28 6JH ☎ 01993 861000 🖷 01993 861050

Customer Service: - Clare Martin, Customer Services Manager, 3 Welch Way, Witney OX28 6JH ☎ 01993 861000 🖷 01993 861050 ✉ clare.martin@westoxon.gov.uk

Economic Development: Mr Dene Robson, Head of Rural Development, Council Offices, Woodgreen, Witney OX28 1NB ☎ 01993 861481 ✉ dene.robson@westoxon.gov.uk

E-Government: Mr John Chorlton, ICT Operations Manager, Council Offices, Woodgreen, Witney OX28 1NB ☎ 01993 861144 🖷 01993 861450 ✉ john.chorlton@westoxon.gov.uk

Electoral Registration: Mr David Bloomfield, Electoral Services & Committee Officer, Council Offices, Woodgreen, Witney OX28 1NB ☎ 01993 861522 🖷 01993 861450 ✉ dave.bloomfield@westoxon.gov.uk

Emergency Planning: Mr Bill Oddy, Head of Community Safety, Council Offices, Elmfield, New Yatt Road, Witney OX28 1PB ☎ 01993 861631 ✉ bill.oddy@westoxon.gov.uk

Energy Management: Ms Deborah Haines, Energy Management Officer, Council Offices, Woodgreen, Witney OX28 1NB ☎ 01993 861000 ✉ deborah.haines@westoxon.gov.uk

Environmental Health: Mr Bill Oddy, Head of Community Safety, Council Offices, Elmfield, New Yatt Road, Witney OX28 1PB ☎ 01993 861631 ✉ bill.oddy@westoxon.gov.uk

Estates, Property & Valuation: Mr David Thurlow, Estates Manager, Council Offices, Woodgreen, Witney OX28 1NB ☎ 01993 861583 ✉ david.thurlow@westoxon.gov.uk

Facilities: - Alison Leask, Facilities Manager, Council Offices, Elmfield, New Yatt Road, Witney OX28 1PB ☎ 01993861000 🖷 01993861450 ✉ alison.leask@westoxon.gov.uk

Health and Safety: Mrs Pauline Smith, Safety Adviser, Council Offices, Woodgreen, Witney OX28 1NB ☎ 01993 861740 🖷 01993 861053 ✉ pauline.smith@westoxon.gov.uk

Housing: Ms Lesley Sherratt, Head of Housing, Council Offices, Elmfield, New Yatt Road, Witney OX28 1PB ☎ 01993 861151 ✉ lesley.sherratt@westoxon.gov.uk

Legal: Mr Keith Butler, Head of Legal & Democratic Services, Council Offices, Woodgreen, Witney OX28 1NB ☎ 01993 861521 🖷 01993 861450 ✉ keith.butler@westoxon.gov.uk

Leisure and Cultural Services: Ms Diane Shelton, Head of Leisure & Tourism, Council Offices, Woodgreen, Witney OX28 1NB ☎ 01993 861551 🖷 01993 861450 ✉ diane.shelton@westoxon.gov.uk

Licensing: Mr Bill Oddy, Head of Community Safety, Council Offices, Elmfield, New Yatt Road, Witney OX28 1PB ☎ 01993 861631 ✉ bill.oddy@westoxon.gov.uk

Member Services: Mr Keith Butler, Head of Legal & Democratic Services, Council Offices, Woodgreen, Witney OX28 1NB ☎ 01993 861521 🖷 01993 861450 ✉ keith.butler@westoxon.gov.uk

Parking: Mr Bill Oddy, Head of Community Safety, Council Offices, Elmfield, New Yatt Road, Witney OX28 1PB ☎ 01993 861631 ✉ bill.oddy@westoxon.gov.uk

Personnel / HR: Ms Sara Mullen, Joint HR Manager of West Oxon & Cotswold DC, Council Offices, Woodgreen, Witney OX28 1NB ☎ 01993 861505 🖷 01993 861455

Planning: Mr Ian Morrow, Head of Planning & Sustainable Communities, Council Offices, Elmfield, New Yatt Road, Witney OX28 1PB ☎ 01993 861651 ✉ ian.morrow@westoxon.gov.uk

Street Scene: Mr Trevor Askew, Head of Environmemt & Commercial Services, Council Offices, Woodgreen, Witney OX28 1NB ☎ 01993 861344 ✉ trevor.askew@westoxon.gov.uk

Sustainable Communities: Mr Ian Morrow, Head of Planning & Sustainable Communities, Council Offices, Elmfield, New Yatt Road, Witney OX28 1PB ☎ 01993 861651 ✉ ian.morrow@westoxon.gov.uk

Tourism: Ms Diane Shelton, Head of Leisure & Tourism, Council Offices, Woodgreen, Witney OX28 1NB ☎ 01993 861551 📠 01993 861450 ✉ diane.shelton@westoxon.gov.uk

MEMBERS OF THE COUNCIL (49)

***Vice-Chair:* Chapman**, Louise (CON - Witney West)
louise.chapman@westoxon.gov.uk
***Leader of the Council:* Norton**, Barry (CON - North Leigh)
barry.norton@westoxon.gov.uk
***Deputy Leader of the Council:* Booty**, Mark (CON - Bampton and Clanfield)
mark.booty@westoxon.gov.uk
***Group Leader:* Coles**, Eve (LAB - Chipping Norton)
eve.coles@westoxon.gov.uk
Adams, Alvin (CON - Witney South)
alvin.adams@westoxon.gov.uk
Barrett, Martin (CON - Bampton and Clanfield)
martin.barrett@westoxon.gov.uk
Beaney, Andrew (CON - Kingham, Rollright and Enstone)
andrew.beaney@westoxon.gov.uk
Biles, Hilary (CON - Ascott and Shipton)
hilary.biles@westoxon.gov.uk
Brennan, Mick (CON - Carterton South)
michael.brennan@westoxon.gov.uk
Coles, Andrew (LAB - Witney Central)
andrew.coles@westoxon.gov.uk
Colston, Nigel (CON - Kingham, Rollright and Enstone)
nigel.colston@westoxon.gov.uk
Cooper, Julian (LD - Woodstock and Bladon)
julian.cooper@westoxon.gov.uk
Cotterill, Derek (CON - Burford)
derek.cotterill@westoxon.gov.uk
Cottrell-Dormer, Charles (CON - Stonesfield and Tackley)
charles.cottrell-dormer@westoxon.gov.uk
Crossland, Maxine (CON - Carterton North West)
maxine.crossland@westoxon.gov.uk
Davies, Sian (CON - Witney East)
sian.davies@westoxon.gov.uk
Davies, Hywel (CON - Charlbury and Finstock)
hywel.davies@westoxon.gov.uk
Dingwall, Colin (CON - Freeland and Hanborough)
colin.dingwall@westoxon.gov.uk
Dorward, Pete (CON - Witney Central)
pete.dorward@westoxon.gov.uk
Doughty, Jane (CON - Witney South)
jane.doughty@westoxon.gov.uk
Eaglestone, Harry (CON - Witney West)
harry.eaglestone@westoxon.gov.uk
Enright, Duncan (LAB - Witney East)
duncan.enright@westoxon.gov.uk
Evans, Rob (LAB - Chipping Norton)
rob.evans@westoxon.gov.uk
Fenton, Hilary (CON - Standlake, Aston and Stanton Harcourt)
hilary.fenton@westoxon.gov.uk
Goffe, Arthur (CON - The Bartons)
arthur.goffe@westoxon.gov.uk
Good, Steve (CON - Standlake, Aston and Stanton Harcourt)
steve.good@westoxon.gov.uk
Haine, Jeff (CON - Milton under Wychwood)
jeff.haine@westoxon.gov.uk
Handley, Peter (CON - Carterton North West)
peter.handley@westoxon.gov.uk
Harvey, David (CON - Witney South)
david.harvey@westoxon.gov.uk
Hayward, Steve (CON - Ducklington)
steve.hayward@westoxon.gov.uk
Hoare, Simon (CON - Hailey, Minster Lovell and Leafield)
simon.hoare@westoxon.gov.uk
Howard, Henry (CON - Carterton North East)
henry.howard@westoxon.gov.uk
Hunt, Verena (CON - Brize Norton and Shilton)
verena.hunt@westoxon.gov.uk
James, Edward (CON - Eynsham and Cassington)
edward.james@westoxon.gov.uk
Kelland, Peter (CON - Eynsham and Cassington)
peter.kelland@westoxon.gov.uk
Langridge, Richard (CON - Witney North)
richard.langridge@westoxon.gov.uk
Leffman, Liz (LD - Charlbury and Finstock)
liz.leffman@westoxon.gov.uk
MacRae, Norman (CON - Carterton North East)
norman.macrae@westoxon.gov.uk
McFarlane, David (CON - Alvescot and Filkins)
david.mcfarlane@westoxon.gov.uk
Millard, Derrick (CON - Stonesfield and Tackley)
derrick.millard@westoxon.gov.uk
Mills, James (CON - Witney East)
james.mills@westoxon.gov.uk
Morris, Toby (CON - Freeland and Hanborough)
toby.morris@westoxon.gov.uk
Owen, Neil (CON - Chadlington and Churchill)
neil.owen@westoxon.gov.uk
Poole, Larry (LD - Eynsham and Cassington)
larry.poole@westoxon.gov.uk
Poskitt, Elizabeth (LD - Woodstock and Bladon)
elizabeth.poskitt@westoxon.gov.uk
Robinson, Warwick (CON - Hailey, Minster Lovell and Leafield)
warwick.robinson@westoxon.gov.uk
Roy-Barker, Annie (CON - Chipping Norton)
annie.roy-barker@westoxon.gov.uk
Snow, David (CON - Witney North)
david.snow@westoxon.gov.uk
Walcott, Joe (CON - Carterton South)
joe.walcott@westoxon.gov.uk

POLITICAL COMPOSITION

CON: 41, LAB: 4, LD: 4

CABINET

Leader: Mr Barry Norton
Deputy Leader / Innovation, Health & Community Safety: Mr Mark Booty
Environment: Mr David Harvey
Local Economy & Communities: Mr Richard Langridge
Resources: Mr Simon Hoare
Strategic Planning & Housing: Mr Warwick Robinson

COMMITTEE CHAIRS

Audit & General Purposes: Mr Alvin Adams
Development Control: Mr Jeff Haine
Economic & Social (Scrutiny): Mr Peter Handley
Environment (Scrutiny): Mr Steve Hayward
Finance & Management (Scrutiny): Mr Colin Dingwall

Human Resources: Mr Simon Hoare
Licensing: Mr Norman Macrae
Standards: Mr Stuart Harrison (External)

WEST SOMERSET D

West Somerset District Council, West Somerset House, Killick Way, Williton, Taunton TA4 4QA ☎ 01643 703704 🖷 01984 633022 ✉ westsomersetdc@westsomerset.gov.uk
💻 www.westsomersetonline.gov.uk

FACTS & FIGURES

Police Authority: Avon & Somerset Police Authority
Health Authority: NHS South West
Learning and Skills Council: South West
Parliamentary Constituencies: Bridgwater and Somerset West
EU Constituencies: South West
Election Frequency: Elections are of whole council
Twinning: Minehead: St. Berthevin (France); Watchet: St. Renan (France); Williton: Neung-sur-Beuvron (France)

PRINCIPAL OFFICERS

Chief Executive: Mr Adrian Dyer, Chief Executive, West Somerset House, Killick Way, Williton, Taunton TA4 4QA ☎ 01984 635212 🖷 01984 633022 ✉ adyer@westsomerset.gov.uk

Senior Management: Mr Bruce Lang, Corporate Director, West Somerset House, Killick Way, Williton, Taunton TA4 4QA ☎ 01984 635200 🖷 01984 633022 ✉ bdlang@westsomerset.gov.uk

Best Value: Miss Sam Rawle, Scrutiny Performance Officer, West Somerset House, Killick Way, Williton, Taunton TA4 4QA ☎ 01984 635223 🖷 01984 635365 ✉ srawle@westsomerset.gov.uk

Building Control: Mrs Jayne Hall, Building Control Manager, West Somerset House, Killick Way, Williton, Taunton TA4 4QA ☎ 01984 635364 🖷 01984 635268 ✉ jhall@westsomerset.gov.uk

PR / Communications: Miss Stacey Beaumont, Media, PR & Communications Officer, West Somerset House, Killick Way, Williton, Taunton TA4 4QA ☎ 01984 635285 ✉ sbeaumont@westsomerset.gov.uk

Community Safety: Mr Peter Hughes, Community Safety Officer, West Somerset House, Killick Way, Williton, Taunton TA4 4QA ☎ 01984 635302 ✉ phughes@westsomerset.gov.uk

Consumer Protection and Trading Standards: Mr Ian Timms, Housing & Community Group Manager, West Somerset House, Killick Way, Williton, Taunton TA4 4QA ☎ 01984 635271 🖷 01984 633022 ✉ itimms@westsomerset.gov.uk

Contracts: Mr Steve Watts, Group Manager - Environment & Services, West Somerset House, Killick Way, Williton, Taunton TA4 4QA ☎ 01984 635261 🖷 01984 633022 ✉ swatts@westsomerset.gov.uk

Corporate Services: Mr Bruce Lang, Corporate Director, West Somerset House, Killick Way, Williton, Taunton TA4 4QA ☎ 01984 635200 🖷 01984 633022 ✉ bdlang@westsomerset.gov.uk

Customer Service: Mr Graham Carne, Group Manager - Resources & Central Support, West Somerset House, Killick Way, Williton, Taunton TA4 4QA ☎ 01984 635253 🖷 01984 633022 ✉ gcarne@westsomerset.gov.uk

Economic Development: Ms Corinne Matthews, Economic Regeneration Manager, West Somerset House, Killick Way, Williton, Taunton TA4 4QA ☎ 01984 635287 🖷 01984 633022 ✉ cmatthews@westsomerset.gov.uk

E-Government: Ms Kim Batchelor, Improvement & Performance Manager, West Somerset House, Killick Way, Williton, Taunton TA4 4QA ☎ 01984 635264 ✉ kbatchelor@westsomerset.gov.uk

Electoral Registration: Mrs Elisa Day, Electoral Services Officer, West Somerset House, Killick Way, Williton, Taunton TA4 4QA ☎ 01984 635272 🖷 01984 633022 ✉ eday@westsomerset.gov.uk

Emergency Planning: Mr Ian Timms, Housing & Community Group Manager, West Somerset House, Killick Way, Williton, Taunton TA4 4QA ☎ 01984 635271 🖷 01984 633022 ✉ itimms@westsomerset.gov.uk

Environmental Health: Mr Ian Timms, Housing & Community Group Manager, West Somerset House, Killick Way, Williton, Taunton TA4 4QA ☎ 01984 635271 🖷 01984 633022 ✉ itimms@westsomerset.gov.uk

Facilities: Mr Steve Watts, Group Manager - Environment & Services, West Somerset House, Killick Way, Williton, Taunton TA4 4QA ☎ 01984 635261 🖷 01984 633022 ✉ swatts@westsomerset.gov.uk

Finance and Treasurer: Mr Graham Carne, Group Manager - Resources & Central Support, West Somerset House, Killick Way, Williton, Taunton TA4 4QA ☎ 01984 635253 🖷 01984 633022 ✉ gcarne@westsomerset.gov.uk

Grounds Maintenance: Mr Adrian Turner, Grounds Maintenance Officer, West Somerset House, Killick Way, Williton, Taunton TA4 4QA ☎ 07739 956436 ✉ aturner@westsomerset.gov.uk

Housing: Mr Ian Timms, Housing & Community Group Manager, West Somerset House, Killick Way, Williton, Taunton TA4 4QA ☎ 01984 635271 🖷 01984 633022 ✉ itimms@westsomerset.gov.uk

Licensing: Mrs Kay O'Sullivan, Licensing Officer, West Somerset House, Killick Way, Williton, Taunton TA4 4QA ☎ 01984 635282 🖷 01984 633022 ✉ kosullivan@westsomerset.gov.uk

Lottery Funding, Charity and Voluntary: Mrs Kay O'Sullivan, Licensing Officer, West Somerset House, Killick Way, Williton, Taunton TA4 4QA ☎ 01984 635282 🖷 01984 633022 ✉ kosullivan@westsomerset.gov.uk

Member Services: Miss Claire Richards, Member Services Officer, West Somerset House, Killick Way, Williton, Taunton TA4 4QA ☎ 01984 635307 ✉ clrichards@westsomerset.gov.uk

Parking: Mr Mike Lewis, Car Parks Officer, West Somerset House, Killick Way, Williton, Taunton TA4 4QA ☎ 01984 635290 ✉ mlewis@westsomerset.gov.uk

Personnel / HR: Mrs Alex Groves, Human Resources Officer, West Somerset House, Killick Way, Williton, Taunton TA4 4QA
☎ 01984 635327 🖷 01984 633022
agroves@westsomerset.gov.uk

Planning: Mr Andrew Goodchild, Planning Manager, West Somerset House, Killick Way, Williton, Taunton TA4 4QA
☎ 01984 635245 🖷 01984 633022
agoodchild@westsomerset.gov.uk

Procurement: Mr Steve Watts, Group Manager - Environment & Services, West Somerset House, Killick Way, Williton, Taunton TA4 4QA ☎ 01984 635261 🖷 01984 633022
swatts@westsomerset.gov.uk

Regeneration: Ms Corinne Matthews, Economic Regeneration Manager, West Somerset House, Killick Way, Williton, Taunton TA4 4QA ☎ 01984 635287 🖷 01984 633022
cmatthews@westsomerset.gov.uk

Staff Training: Mrs Alex Groves, Human Resources Officer, West Somerset House, Killick Way, Williton, Taunton TA4 4QA
☎ 01984 635327 🖷 01984 633022
agroves@westsomerset.gov.uk

Street Scene: Mr Steve Watts, Group Manager - Environment & Services, West Somerset House, Killick Way, Williton, Taunton TA4 4QA ☎ 01984 635261 🖷 01984 633022
swatts@westsomerset.gov.uk

Tourism: Ms Corinne Matthews, Economic Regeneration Manager, West Somerset House, Killick Way, Williton, Taunton TA4 4QA ☎ 01984 635287 🖷 01984 633022
cmatthews@westsomerset.gov.uk

Waste Collection and Disposal: Mr Steve Watts, Group Manager - Environment & Services, West Somerset House, Killick Way, Williton, Taunton TA4 4QA ☎ 01984 635261
🖷 01984 633022 swatts@westsomerset.gov.uk

MEMBERS OF THE COUNCIL (28)

***Chair:* Ross**, Doug (IND - Minehead North)
dross@westsomerset.gov.uk
***Vice-Chair:* Dowding**, Stuart (CON - West Quantock)
sdowding@westsomerset.gov.uk
***Leader of the Council:* Taylor**, Tim (CON - Carhampton and Withycombe)
ttaylor@westsomerset.gov.uk
***Deputy Leader of the Council:* Morgan**, Chris (IND - Quantock Vale)
cmorgan@westsomerset.gov.uk
Chick, Alec (CON - Dunster and Timberscombe)
achick@westsomerset.gov.uk
Chilcott, Mandy (CON - Minehead Central)
mchilcott@westsomerset.gov.uk
Davies, Hugh (IND - Williton)
hdavies@westsomerset.gov.uk
Dewdney, Martin (CON - Old Cleeve)
mdewdney@westsomerset.gov.uk
Freeman, Jon (IND - Porlock and District)
jfreeman@westsomerset.gov.uk
Goss, Susan (CON - Quantock Vale)
sgoss@westsomerset.gov.uk
Grierson, Paul (CON - Alcombe)
pgrierson@westsomerset.gov.uk
Hadley, Andrew (IND - Minehead Central)
ahadley@westsomerset.gov.uk
Heywood, Bruce (CON - Dulverton and Brushford)
bheywood@westsomerset.gov.uk
Knight, Anthony (CON - Watchet)
afknight@westsomerset.gov.uk
Kravis, Kate (IND - Old Cleeve)
kvkravis@westsomerset.gov.uk
Lillis, Richard (CON - Minehead Central)
rlillis@westsomerset.gov.uk
May, Edwin (IND - Williton)
emay@westsomerset.gov.uk
Melhuish, Ian (IND - Alcombe)
imelhuish@westsomerset.gov.uk
Mills, Karen (CON - Porlock and District)
kmills@westsomerset.gov.uk
Murphy, Peter (LAB - Watchet)
pmurphy@westsomerset.gov.uk
Pugsley, Steven (CON - Greater Exmoor)
sjpugsley@westsomerset.gov.uk
Ross, Keith (IND - Dulverton and Brushford)
kjross@westsomerset.gov.uk
Sanders, David (CON - Minehead North)
dsanders@westsomerset.gov.uk
Smith, Maureen (LAB - Minehead South)
msmith@westsomerset.gov.uk
Smith, Leslie (CON - Minehead South)
lsmith@westsomerset.gov.uk
Trollope-Bellew, Anthony (CON - Crowcombe and Stogumber)
atrollope-bellew@westsomerset.gov.uk
Turner, Keith (CON - Brendon Hills)
kturner@westsomerset.gov.uk
Westcott, David (CON - Watchet)
dwestcott@westsomerset.gov.uk

POLITICAL COMPOSITION

CON: 17, IND: 9, LAB: 2

CABINET

Leader / Performance & Corporate Support: Mr Tim Taylor
Deputy Leader: Mr Chris Morgan
Community & Customer: Mr David Westcott
Environment: Mr Chris Morgan
Executive Support & Democracy: Mr Steven Pugsley
Housing, Environmental Health & Licensing: Mr Keith Turner
Regeneration & Economic Growth: Mr David Sanders
Resources & Central Support: Mrs Kate Kravis

COMMITTEE CHAIRS

Audit: Mr Anthony Trollope-Bellew
Licensing: Mr Hugh Davies
Local Development Panel: Mr Keith Turner
Planning: Mr Anthony Knight
Scrutiny: Mr Keith Ross
Standards: Mr T Evans (External)

WEST SUSSEX C

West Sussex County Council, County Hall, Chichester PO19 1RQ
☎ 01243 777100 🖷 01243 530439
webmaster@westsussex.gov.uk www.westsussex.gov.uk

FACTS & FIGURES

Police Authority: Sussex Police Authority
Health Authority: South East Coast Strategic Health Authority
Learning and Skills Council: South East
Parliamentary Constituencies: Arundel and South Downs, Bognor Regis and Littlehampton, Chichester, Crawley, Horsham, Sussex Mid, Worthing East and Shoreham, Worthing West
EU Constituencies: South East
Election Frequency: Elections are of whole council

PRINCIPAL OFFICERS

Chief Executive: Mr Kieran Stigant, Chief Executive, County Hall, Chichester PO19 1RQ ☎ 01243 382676 ✉ kieran.stigant@westsussex.gov.uk

Senior Management: Mrs Amanda Aviss, Head of Communications & Marketing, County Hall, Chichester PO19 1RQ ☎ 01243 777055 🖷 01243 777266 ✉ amanda.aviss@westsussex.gov.uk

Senior Management: Ms Sue Cart, Head of Safeguarding, County Hall, Chichester PO19 1QT ☎ 01243 382694 ✉ sue.cart@westsussex.gov.uk

Senior Management: Mr Stuart Gallimore, Director of Children's Services, County Hall, Chichester PO19 1RQ ☎ 01243 382666 🖷 01243 777421 ✉ stuart.gallimore@westsussex.gov.uk

Senior Management: Mrs Susan Hawker, Director of Business Change, County Hall, Chichester PO19 1RQ ☎ 01243 382663 🖷 01243 756714 ✉ susan.hawker@westsussex.gov.uk

Senior Management: Mr Derek Irvine, Director of Commercial Services, County Hall, Chichester PO19 1RQ ☎ 01243 777103 ✉ derek.irvine@westsussex.gov.uk

Senior Management: Mr Colin James, Head of Capital & Asset Management, County Hall, Chichester PO19 1RQ ☎ 01243 382682 ✉ colin.james@westsussex.gov.uk

Senior Management: Mr Tony Kershaw, Head of Legal & Democratic Services, County Hall, Chichester PO19 1RQ ☎ 01243 777922 ✉ tony.kershaw@westsussex.gov.uk

Senior Management: Mr Mike Link, Head of Planning & Partnerships, 1st Floor, Durban House, Bognor Regis PO22 9RE ☎ 01243 382697 ✉ mike.link@westsussex.gov.uk

Senior Management: Ms Amanda Rogers, Director of Adults' Services, County Hall, Chichester PO19 1RQ ☎ 01243 382693

Senior Management: Mr Kieran Stigant, Chief Executive, County Hall, Chichester PO19 1RQ ☎ 01243 382676 ✉ kieran.stigant@westsussex.gov.uk

Senior Management: Mr David Sword, Director of Learning, County Hall, Chichester PO19 1RQ ☎ 01243 382695 🖷 01243 777421 ✉ david.sword@westsussex.gov.uk

Senior Management: Mr Tony Toynton, Director of Communities & Infrastructure, County Hall, Chichester PO19 1RG ☎ 01243 382688 ✉ tony.toynton@westsussex.gov.uk

Senior Management: Mr Mark Warner, Head of Human Resources, County Hall, Chichester PO19 1RQ ☎ 01243 382685 ✉ mark.warner@westsussex.gov.uk

Architect, Building / Property Services: Mr Colin James, Head of Capital & Asset Management, County Hall, Chichester PO19 1RQ ☎ 01243 382682 ✉ colin.james@westsussex.gov.uk

Best Value: Mr Andy Hammond, Performance Manager, County Hall, Chichester PO19 1RQ ☎ 01243 777582 🖷 01243 777099 ✉ andy.hammond@westsussex.gov.uk

Children / Youth Services: Mr Stuart Gallimore, Director of Children's Services, County Hall, Chichester PO19 1RQ ☎ 01243 382666 🖷 01243 777421 ✉ stuart.gallimore@westsussex.gov.uk

Civil Registration: Mrs Susan Hawker, Director of Business Change, County Hall, Chichester PO19 1RQ ☎ 01243 382663 🖷 01243 756714 ✉ susan.hawker@westsussex.gov.uk

Civil Registration: Mr Graeme MacPherson, Head of Waste Management & Regulatory Services, Centenary House, Durrington Lane, Worthing BN13 2QB ☎ 01903 839733 ✉ graeme.macpherson@westsussex.gov.uk

Civil Registration: Mr Tony Toynton, Director of Communities & Infrastructure, County Hall, Chichester PO19 1RG ☎ 01243 382688 ✉ tony.toynton@westsussex.gov.uk

PR / Communications: Mrs Amanda Aviss, Head of Communications & Marketing, County Hall, Chichester PO19 1RQ ☎ 01243 777055 🖷 01243 777266 ✉ amanda.aviss@westsussex.gov.uk

Community Safety: Mrs Emily King, Better Communities Manager, County Hall, Chichester PO19 1RQ ☎ 01243 382612 ✉ emily.king@westsussex.gov.uk

Computer Management: Mr Derek Irvine, Director of Commercial Services, County Hall, Chichester PO19 1RQ ☎ 01243 777103 ✉ derek.irvine@westsussex.gov.uk

Consumer Protection and Trading Standards: Mrs Susan Hawker, Director of Business Change, County Hall, Chichester PO19 1RQ ☎ 01243 382663 🖷 01243 756714 ✉ susan.hawker@westsussex.gov.uk

Consumer Protection and Trading Standards: Mr Graeme MacPherson, Head of Waste Management & Regulatory Services, Centenary House, Durrington Lane, Worthing BN13 2QB ☎ 01903 839733 ✉ graeme.macpherson@westsussex.gov.uk

Consumer Protection and Trading Standards: Mr Kieran Stigant, Chief Executive, County Hall, Chichester PO19 1RQ ☎ 01243 382676 ✉ kieran.stigant@westsussex.gov.uk

Consumer Protection and Trading Standards: Mr Tony Toynton, Director of Communities & Infrastructure, County Hall, Chichester PO19 1RG ☎ 01243 382688 ✉ tony.toynton@westsussex.gov.uk

Consumer Protection and Trading Standards: Mr Tony

Toynton, Director of Communities and Infrastructure, City Gates, 2-4 Southgate, Chichester PO19 1RQ ☎ 01243 382950 ✉ tony.toynton@westsussex.gov.uk

Contracts: Mrs Kim Medhurst, Procurement Strategy Manager, County Hall, Chichester PO19 1QT ☎ 01243 382168 ✉ kim.medhurst@westsussex.gov.uk

Corporate Services: Mr Derek Irvine, Director of Commercial Services, County Hall, Chichester PO19 1RQ ☎ 01243 777103 ✉ derek.irvine@westsussex.gov.uk

Corporate Services: Mr Tony Toynton, Director of Communities & Infrastructure, County Hall, Chichester PO19 1RG ☎ 01243 382688 ✉ tony.toynton@westsussex.gov.uk

Customer Service: Mrs Diane Ashby, Executive Director of Customers & Change, County Hall, Chichester PO19 1QT ☎ 01243 382687 ✉ diane.ashby@westsussex.gov.uk

Customer Service: Mrs Susan Hawker, Director of Business Change, County Hall, Chichester PO19 1RQ ☎ 01243 382663 🖷 01243 756714 ✉ susan.hawker@westsussex.gov.uk

Economic Development: Mrs Sarah Hardman, Economic Development Team Manager, Communities and Infrastructure, West Sussex County Council, The Grange, Chichester PO19 1RH ☎ 01243 753515 ✉ sarah.hardman@westsussex.gov.uk

Education: Mr David Sword, Director of Learning, County Hall, Chichester PO19 1RQ ☎ 01243 382695 🖷 01243 777421 ✉ david.sword@westsussex.gov.uk

Electoral Registration: Mr Tony Kershaw, Head of Legal & Democratic Services, County Hall, Chichester PO19 1RQ ☎ 01243 777922 ✉ tony.kershaw@westsussex.gov.uk

Emergency Planning: Mr Alan Jones, Head of Emergency Management, 23b Orchard Street, Chichester PO19 1DD ☎ 01243 382133 ✉ alan.jones@westsussex.gov.uk

Energy Management: Mr Vic Bass, Maintenance Manager, The Tannery, Westgate, Chichester PO19 3RJ ☎ 01243 752315 ✉ vic.bass@westsussex.gov.uk

Estates, Property & Valuation: Mr Colin James, Head of Capital & Asset Management, County Hall, Chichester PO19 1RQ ☎ 01243 382682 ✉ colin.james@westsussex.gov.uk

Facilities: Mr Derek Irvine, Director of Commercial Services, County Hall, Chichester PO19 1RQ ☎ 01243 777103 ✉ derek.irvine@westsussex.gov.uk

Finance and Treasurer: Mr Richard Hornby, Executive Director of Finance & Performance, County Hall, Chichester PO19 1RQ ☎ 01243 382677 ✉ richard.hornby@westsussex.gov.uk

Fleet Management: Ms Sue Dyer, County Cars Manager, Minerva Accord, County Hall, Chichester PO19 1RB ☎ 01243 777590 🖷 01243 777586 ✉ sue.dyer@westsussex.gov.uk

Health and Safety: Mr David Ramsbottom, Senior Health & Safety Officer, County Hall, Chichester PO19 1RQ ☎ 01243 756854 ✉ david.ramsbottom@westsussex.gov.uk

Highways: Mr Kieran Stigant, Chief Executive, County Hall, Chichester PO19 1RQ ☎ 01243 382676 ✉ kieran.stigant@westsussex.gov.uk

Highways: Mr Tony Toynton, Director of Communities & Infrastructure, County Hall, Chichester PO19 1RG ☎ 01243 382688 ✉ tony.toynton@westsussex.gov.uk

Legal: Mr Tony Kershaw, Head of Legal & Democratic Services, County Hall, Chichester PO19 1RQ ☎ 01243 777922 ✉ tony.kershaw@westsussex.gov.uk

Lifelong Learning: Mr David Sword, Director of Learning, County Hall, Chichester PO19 1RQ ☎ 01243 382695 🖷 01243 777421 ✉ david.sword@westsussex.gov.uk

Member Services: Mrs Debbie Allman, Service Manager - Non-Executive Support, Democratic Services Unit, County Hall, Chichester PO19 1RQ ☎ 01243 752719 ✉ debbie.allman@westsussex.gov.uk

Member Services: Mr Tony Kershaw, Head of Legal & Democratic Services, County Hall, Chichester PO19 1RQ ☎ 01243 777922 ✉ tony.kershaw@westsussex.gov.uk

Parking: Mr Mike Link, Head of Planning & Partnerships, 1st Floor, Durban House, Bognor Regis PO22 9RE ☎ 01243 382697 ✉ mike.link@westsussex.gov.uk

Partnerships: Mr Mike Link, Head of Planning & Partnerships, 1st Floor, Durban House, Bognor Regis PO22 9RE ☎ 01243 382697 ✉ mike.link@westsussex.gov.uk

Personnel / HR: Mr Mark Warner, Head of Human Resources, County Hall, Chichester PO19 1RQ ☎ 01243 382685 ✉ mark.warner@westsussex.gov.uk

Planning: Mr Kieran Stigant, Chief Executive, County Hall, Chichester PO19 1RQ ☎ 01243 382676 ✉ kieran.stigant@westsussex.gov.uk

Planning: Mr Tony Toynton, Director of Communities & Infrastructure, County Hall, Chichester PO19 1RG ☎ 01243 382688 ✉ tony.toynton@westsussex.gov.uk

Procurement: Mrs Kim Medhurst, Procurement Strategy Manager, County Hall, Chichester PO19 1QT ☎ 01243 382168 ✉ kim.medhurst@westsussex.gov.uk

Public Libraries: Mrs Susan Hawker, Director of Business Change, County Hall, Chichester PO19 1RQ ☎ 01243 382663 🖷 01243 756714 ✉ susan.hawker@westsussex.gov.uk

Public Libraries: Mrs Lesley Sim, Service Manager - Libraries, Willow Park, 4B Terminus Road, Chichester PO19 8EG ☎ 01243 816731 ✉ lesley.sim@westsussex.gov.uk

Public Libraries: Mr Kieran Stigant, Chief Executive, County Hall, Chichester PO19 1RQ ☎ 01243 382676

✉ kieran.stigant@westsussex.gov.uk

Road Safety: Mr Ron Paterson, Team Leader - Road Safety Education, County Hall, Chichester PO19 1RQ ☎ 01243 777581 🖷 01243 777257 ✉ ron.paterson@westsussex.gov.uk

Social Services: Ms Sue Cart, Head of Safeguarding, County Hall, Chichester PO19 1QT ☎ 01243 382694 ✉ sue.cart@westsussex.gov.uk

Social Services (Adult): Mr Mike Link, Head of Planning & Partnerships, 1st Floor, Durban House, Bognor Regis PO22 9RE ☎ 01243 382697 ✉ mike.link@westsussex.gov.uk

Social Services (Adult): Ms Amanda Rogers, Director of Adults' Services, County Hall, Chichester PO19 1RQ ☎ 01243 382693

Social Services (Children): Mr Mike Link, Head of Planning & Partnerships, 1st Floor, Durban House, Bognor Regis PO22 9RE ☎ 01243 382697 ✉ mike.link@westsussex.gov.uk

Staff Training: Ms Julie Ferroni, Learning & Development Operations Manager, County Hall, Chichester PO19 1RQ ☎ 01243 752096 ✉ julie.ferroni@westsussex.gov.uk

Sustainable Communities: Mr Kieran Stigant, Chief Executive, County Hall, Chichester PO19 1RQ ☎ 01243 382676 ✉ kieran.stigant@westsussex.gov.uk

Sustainable Development: Mrs Susan Hawker, Director of Business Change, County Hall, Chichester PO19 1RQ ☎ 01243 382663 🖷 01243 756714 ✉ susan.hawker@westsussex.gov.uk

Sustainable Development: Mr Tony Toynton, Director of Communities & Infrastructure, Room 108, The Grange, County Hall, Chichester PO19 1RH ☎ 01243 382688 ✉ tony.toynton@westsussex.gov.uk

Sustainable Development: Mrs Siobhan Walker, Sustainability Team Manager, Communities and Infrastructure, West Sussex County Council, The Grange, Chichester PO19 1RH ☎ 01243 382018 ✉ siobhan.walker@westsussex.gov.uk

Traffic Management: Mr Peter Bradley, Service Manager - Safety & Traffic Management, County Hall, Chichester PO19 1RQ ☎ 01243 777877 ✉ peter.bradley@westsussex.gov.uk

Transport: Mr Ian Patrick, Team Leader - Safer to School & Travelwise, Northleigh, Tower Street, Chichester PO19 1RH ☎ 01243 777161 🖷 01243 777257 ✉ ian.patrick@westsussex.gov.uk

Transport: Mr Kieran Stigant, Chief Executive, County Hall, Chichester PO19 1RQ ☎ 01243 382676 ✉ kieran.stigant@westsussex.gov.uk

Transport: Mr Tony Toynton, Director of Communities & Infrastructure, County Hall, Chichester PO19 1RG ☎ 01243 382688 ✉ tony.toynton@westsussex.gov.uk

Transport Planner: Mr Ian Patrick, Team Leader - Safer to School & Travelwise, Northleigh, Tower Street, Chichester PO19 1RH ☎ 01243 777161 🖷 01243 777257 ✉ ian.patrick@westsussex.gov.uk

Waste Collection and Disposal: Mr Peter Robinson, Recycling & Waste Handling Contract Manager, County Hall, Chichester PO19 1RQ ☎ 01243 753571 ✉ peter.robinson@westsussex.gov.uk

Waste Management: Mr Graeme MacPherson, Head of Waste Management & Regulatory Services, Centenary House, Durrington Lane, Worthing BN13 2QB ☎ 01903 839733 ✉ graeme.macpherson@westsussex.gov.uk

Waste Management: Mr Kieran Stigant, Chief Executive, County Hall, Chichester PO19 1RQ ☎ 01243 382676 ✉ kieran.stigant@westsussex.gov.uk

MEMBERS OF THE COUNCIL (71)

***Chair:* Coleman**, Mike (CON - Nyetimber)
mike.coleman@westsussex.gov.uk
***Vice-Chair:* Hodgson**, Mick (CON - Warnham and Rusper)
michael.hodgson@westsussex.gov.uk
***Leader of the Council:* Goldsmith**, Louise (CON - Chichester West)
louise.goldsmith@westsussex.gov.uk
***Deputy Leader of the Council:* Barnard**, Lionel (CON - Henfield)
lionel.barnard@westsussex.gov.uk
Acraman, Bill (CON - Worth Forest)
bill.acraman@westsussex.gov.uk
Arculus, Patricia (CON - Pulborough)
patricia.arculus@westsussex.gov.uk
Bennett, Liz (CON - East Grinstead Meridian)
liz.bennett@westsussex.gov.uk
Blake, Keith (CON - Gossops Green & Ifield East)
keith.blake@westsussex.gov.uk
Blampied, George (CON - Felpham)
george.blampied@westsussex.gov.uk
Bloom, Howard (CON - Southgate & Crawley Central)
howard.bloom@westsussex.gov.uk
Bradbury, Peter (CON - Cuckfield and Lucastes)
peter.bradbury@westsussex.gov.uk
Britton, David (CON - Littlehampton Town)
david.britton@westsussex.gov.uk
Brown, Michael (CON - Fernhurst)
michael.brown@westsussex.gov.uk
Brunsdon, Heidi (CON - Imberdown)
heidi.brunsdon@westsussex.gov.uk
Burgess, Bob (CON - Northgate and Three Bridges)
bob.burgess@westsussex.gov.uk
Burrett, Richard (CON - Pound Hill & Worth)
richard.burrett@westsussex.gov.uk
Catchpole, Peter (CON - Holbrook)
peter.catchpole@westsussex.gov.uk
Coleman, Christina (CON - Middleton)
christina.freeman@westsussex.gov.uk
Coomber, Brian (CON - Shoreham)
brian.coomber@westsussex.gov.uk
Crow, Duncan (CON - Tilgate and Furnace Green)
duncan.crow@westsussex.gov.uk
Deedman, Derek (LD - Bramber Castle)
derek.deedman@westsussex.gov.uk
Dennis, Nigel (LD - Horsham Hurst)
nigel.dennis@westsussex.gov.uk

Doyle, James (IND - Worthing Pier)
james.doyle@westsussex.gov.uk
Duncton, Chris (CON - Petworth)
chris.duncton@westsussex.gov.uk
Dunn, Mark (CON - Bourne)
mark.dunn@westsussex.gov.uk
Dunn, Robert (CON - Saltings)
robert.dunn@westsussex.gov.uk
Evans, Peter (CON - East Preston and Ferring)
peter.evans@westsussex.gov.uk
Field, Christine (CON - Lindfield and High Weald)
christine.field@westsussex.gov.uk
Graysmark, Paul (CON - Kingston Buci)
paul.graysmark@westsussex.gov.uk
Griffiths, Peter (CON - Hurstpierpoint & Bolney)
peter.griffiths@westsussex.gov.uk
Hall, Michael (CON - Chichester North)
michael.hall@westsussex.gov.uk
Hall, Anne (LD - Haywards Heath East)
anne.hall@westsussex.gov.uk
Hall, Brian (IND - Haywards Heath Town)
brian.hall@westsussex.gov.uk
Hellawell, Warwick (LD - Roffey)
warwick.hellawell@westsussex.gov.uk
Hendon, Nola (CON - Midhurst)
nola.hendon@westsussex.gov.uk
Jones, Peter (CON - Selsey)
peter.jones@westsussex.gov.uk
Jupp, Amanda (CON - Billingshurst)
amanda.jupp@westsussex.gov.uk
Knight, Susan (LD - Burgess Hill East)
susan.knight@westsussex.gov.uk
Lanzer, Robert (CON - Maidenbower)
bob.lanzer@westsussex.gov.uk
Livermore, John (CON - Worthing West)
john.livermore@westsussex.gov.uk
McDougall, Simon (LD - Bersted)
simon.mcdougall@westsussex.gov.uk
Mills, Angie (CON - Lancing)
angie.mills@westsussex.gov.uk
Millson, Morwen (LD - Horsham Riverside)
morwen.millson@westsussex.gov.uk
Mockridge, Janet (CON - Southwick)
janet.mockridge@westsussex.gov.uk
Montyn, Pieter (CON - The Witterings)
pieter.montyn@westsussex.gov.uk
O'Brien, John (CON - East Grinstead South & Ashurst)
Oppler, Francis (LD - Bognor Regis East)
francis.oppler@westsussex.gov.uk
Oxlade, Chris (LAB - Bewbush & Ifield West)
chris.oxlade@westsussex.gov.uk
Peters, Nigel (CON - Arundel & Wick)
nigel.peters@westsussex.gov.uk
Quirk, Alan (CON - Broadfield)
alan.quirk@westsussex.gov.uk
Rice, Alan (LD - Broadwater)
alan.rice@westsussex.gov.uk
Richards, Irene (LD - Worthing East)
irene.richards@westsussex.gov.uk
Rogers, Robin (LD - Northbrook)
robin.rogers@westsussex.gov.uk
Ross, Heather (LD - Burgess Hill Town)
heather.ross@westsussex.gov.uk
Sheldon, David (LD - Horsham Tanbridge & Broadbridge Heath)
david.sheldon@westsussex.gov.uk
Simmons, David (CON - Sompting & North Lancing)
david.simmons@westsussex.gov.uk
Smith, Brenda (LAB - Langley Green & West Green)
brenda.smith@westsussex.gov.uk
Smith, Andrew (LD - Chichester East)
andrew.smith@westsussex.gov.uk
Smytherman, Bob (LD - Tarring)
bob.smytherman@westsussex.gov.uk
Stevens, Clem (CON - Cissbury)
clem.stevens@westsussex.gov.uk
Tyler, Graham (CON - Rustington)
graham.tyler@westsussex.gov.uk
Urquhart, Deborah (CON - Angmering and Findon)
deborah.urquhart@westsussex.gov.uk
Waight, Nicola (CON - Durrington & Salvington)
nicola.waight@westsussex.gov.uk
Waight, Steve (CON - Goring)
steve.waight@westsussex.gov.uk
Walsh, James (LD - Littlehampton East)
james.walsh@westsussex.gov.uk
Watson, Brad (CON - Southwater and Nuthurst)
brad.watson@westsussex.gov.uk
Wells, Paul (LD - Bognor Regis West & Aldwick)
paul.wells@westsussex.gov.uk
Whitehead, Margaret (CON - Chichester South)
margaret.whitehead@westsussex.gov.uk
Whittington, Derek (CON - Fontwell)
derek.whittington@westsussex.gov.uk
Wilkinson, Frank (CON - Storrington)
frank.wilkinson@westsussex.gov.uk
Wilsdon, Colin (LD - Hassocks and Victoria)
colin.wilsdon@westsussex.gov.uk

POLITICAL COMPOSITION

CON: 49, LD: 18, IND: 2, LAB: 2

CABINET

Leader: Ms Louise Goldsmith
Deputy Leader / Communities, Environment & Enterprise: Mr Lionel Barnard
Children & Families: Mr Peter Evans
Education & Schools: Mr Peter Griffiths
Finance & Resources: Mr Michael Brown
Health & Adults' Services: Mr Peter Catchpole
Highways & Transport: Mr Pieter Montyn
Public Protection: Mrs Christine Field

COMMITTEE CHAIRS

Children & Young People's Services Select Committee (Scrutiny): Mr Richard Burrett
Environmental & Community Services Select Committee (Scrutiny): Mr Duncan Crow
Governance: Mr Mike Coleman
Health & Adult Social Care Select Committee (Scrutiny): Mrs Margaret Whitehead
Pensions Pannel: Mr Michael Brown
Planning: Mr Derek Whittington
Policy & Resources Select Committee (Scrutiny): Mr David Britton
Regulation, Audit & Accounts: Mr Derek Deedman
Standards: Mr Mike Coleman (External)

WESTERN ISLES S

Western Isles Council, (Comhairle nan Eilean Siar), Council Offices, Sandwick Road, Stornoway HS1 2BW ☎ 01851 703773 🖷 01851 705349 💻 www.cne-siar.gov.uk

FACTS & FIGURES

Police Authority: Northern Joint Police Board
Health Authority: NHS Western Isles
Learning and Skills Council: Scotland
Parliamentary Constituencies: Na h-Eileanan an Iar
EU Constituencies: Scotland
Election Frequency: Elections are of whole council
Twinning: County Clare County Council; Newry and Mourne District Council & Pendleton, South Carolina

PRINCIPAL OFFICERS

Chief Executive: Mr Malcolm Burr, Chief Executive, Council Offices, Sandwick Road, Stornoway HS1 2BW ☎ 0845 600 7090 🖱 m.burr@cne-siar.gov.uk

Architect, Building / Property Services: Mr Iain Mackinnon, Director of Technical Services, Council Offices, Sandwick Road, Stornoway HS1 2BW ☎ 01851 822656 🖱 iain.mackinnon@cne-siar.gov.uk

Best Value: Ms Norma Morrison, Organisational Development, Council Offices, Sandwick Road, Stornoway HS1 2BW ☎ 01851 822614 🖱 norma.morrison@cne-siar.gov.uk

Building Control: Mr Keith Bray, Head of Development Services, Council Offices, Sandwick Road, Stornoway HS1 2BW ☎ 01851 822686 🖱 kbray@cne-siar.gov.uk

Catering Services: Ms Joan MacKinnon, Director of Education & Children's Services, Council Offices, Sandwick Road, Stornoway HS1 2BW ☎ 01851 822727 🖱 joanmackinnon@cne-siar.gov.uk

Children / Youth Services: Ms Joan MacKinnon, Director of Education & Children's Services, Council Offices, Sandwick Road, Stornoway HS1 2BW ☎ 01851 822727 🖱 joanmackinnon@cne-siar.gov.uk

PR / Communications: Mr Nigel Scott, Communications Officer, Council Offices, Sandwick Road, Stornoway HS1 2BW 🖷 01851 822622 🖱 nscott@cne-siar.gov.uk

Community Planning: Ms Gayle Findlay, Community Planning Co-ordinator, Council Offices, Sandwick Road, Stornoway HS1 2BW ☎ 01851 822617

Computer Management: Mr Angus Macarthur, Head of IT, Council Offices, Sandwick Road, Stornoway HS1 2BW ☎ 01851 709573 🖷 ; 01851 822635; 01851 822635 🖱 amacarthur@cne-siar.gov.uk

Consumer Protection and Trading Standards: Ms Marina MacSween, Trading Standards Officer, Council Offices, Sandwick Road, Stornoway HS1 2BW ☎ 01851 822694 🖱 mmacsween@cne-siar.gov.uk

Customer Service: Mr Robert Emmott, Director of Finance & Corporate Resources, Council Offices, Sandwick Road, Stornoway HS1 2BW ☎ ; 01851 822628 🖱 remmott@cne-siar.gov.uk

Direct Labour: Mr Marten James, Principal Maintenance Officer, Council Offices, Sandwick Road, Stornoway HS1 2BW ☎ 01851 822668 🖷 01851 706022 🖱 mjames@cne-siar.gov.uk

Economic Development: Mr Calum Iain Maciver, Director of Development, Council Offices, Sandwick Road, Stornoway HS1 2BW ☎ ; 01851 822685 🖷 ; 01851 705349 🖱 calum.maciver@cne-siar.gov.uk

Education: Ms Joan MacKinnon, Director of Education & Children's Services, Council Offices, Sandwick Road, Stornoway HS1 2BW ☎ 01851 822727 🖱 joanmackinnon@cne-siar.gov.uk

E-Government: Mr Robert Emmott, Director of Finance & Corporate Resources, Council Offices, Sandwick Road, Stornoway HS1 2BW ☎ ; 01851 822628 🖱 remmott@cne-siar.gov.uk

Electoral Registration: Mr Derek Mackay, Head Democractic Services, Council Offices, Sandwick Road, Stornoway HS1 2BW ☎ ; 01851 822613 🖷 01852 705349 🖱 dmackay@cne-siar.gov.uk

Emergency Planning: Mr Andy MacDonald, Risk & Emergency Planning Manager, Council Offices, Sandwick Road, Stornoway HS1 2BW ☎ 01851 822612 🖷 01851 706935 🖱 andy-macdonald@cne-siar.gov.uk

Energy Management: Mr Donald Macsween, Energy & Building Services Manager, Council Offices, Sandwick Road, Stornoway HS1 2BW ☎ 01851 822668 🖱 djmacsween@cne-siar.gov.uk

Environmental / Technical Services: Mr Iain Mackinnon, Director of Technical Services, Council Offices, Sandwick Road, Stornoway HS1 2BW ☎ 01851 822656 🖱 iain.mackinnon@cne-siar.gov.uk

Environmental Health: Mr Colm Fraser, Consumer & Environmental Health Services Manager, Council Offices, Sandwick Road, Stornoway HS1 2BW ☎ 01851 822688 🖱 cfraser@cne-siar.gov.uk

Estates, Property & Valuation: Mr Calum MacKenzie, Head of Estates, Council Offices, Sandwick Road, Stornoway HS1 2BW ☎ 01851 822659 🖷 01851 705349 🖱 calum.mackenzie@cne-siar.gov.uk

European Liaison: Miss Lesley McDonald, Head of Executive Office, Council Offices, Sandwick Road, Stornoway HS1 2BW ☎ 01851 822604 🖷 01851 705349 🖱 lmcdonald@cne-siar.gov.uk

Events Manager: Miss Lesley McDonald, Head of Executive Office, Council Offices, Sandwick Road, Stornoway HS1 2BW ☎ 01851 822604 🖷 01851 705349 🖱 lmcdonald@cne-siar.gov.uk

Finance and Treasurer: Mr Robert Emmott, Director of Finance & Corporate Resources, Council Offices, Sandwick Road, Stornoway HS1 2BW ☎ 01851 822628 🖱 remmott@cne-siar.gov.uk

Grounds Maintenance: Mr Iain Mackinnon, Director of Technical

Services, Council Offices, Sandwick Road, Stornoway HS1 2BW ☎ 01851 822656 ✉ iain.mackinnon@cne-siar.gov.uk

Health and Safety: Mr Andy MacDonald, Risk & Emergency Planning Manager, Council Offices, Sandwick Road, Stornoway HS1 2BW ☎ 01851 822612 🖷 01851 706935 ✉ andy-macdonald@cne-siar.gov.uk

Highways: Mr Iain Mackinnon, Director of Technical Services, Council Offices, Sandwick Road, Stornoway HS1 2BW ☎ 01851 822656 ✉ iain.mackinnon@cne-siar.gov.uk

Home Energy Conservation: Mr M Bruce, Housing Strategy Officer, Council Offices, Sandwick Road, Stornoway HS1 2BW ☎ 01851 822656 🖷 01851 709346 ✉ mbruce@cne-siar.gov.uk

Legal: Miss Lesley McDonald, Head of Executive Office, Council Offices, Sandwick Road, Stornoway HS1 2BW ☎ 01851 822604 🖷 01851 705349 ✉ lmcdonald@cne-siar.gov.uk

Leisure and Cultural Services: Ms Emma MacSween, Head of Social & Partnership Services, Council Offices, Sandwick Road, Stornoway HS1 2BW ☎ 01851 822706 🖷 01851 705349 ✉ emacsween@cne-siar.gov.uk

Licensing: Miss Lesley McDonald, Head of Executive Office, Council Offices, Sandwick Road, Stornoway HS1 2BW ☎ 01851 822604 🖷 01851 705349 ✉ lmcdonald@cne-siar.gov.uk

Member Services: Miss Lesley McDonald, Head of Executive Office, Council Offices, Sandwick Road, Stornoway HS1 2BW ☎ 01851 822604 🖷 01851 705349 ✉ lmcdonald@cne-siar.gov.uk

Parking: Mr Iain Mackinnon, Director of Technical Services, Council Offices, Sandwick Road, Stornoway HS1 2BW ☎ 01851 822656 ✉ iain.mackinnon@cne-siar.gov.uk

Personnel / HR: Mrs Katherine MacKinnon, Head of Human Resources, Council Offices, Sandwick Road, Stornoway HS1 2BW ☎ 01851 822605 🖷 01851 706935 ✉ kmackinnon@cne-siar.gov.uk

Planning: Mr Keith Bray, Head of Development Services, Council Offices, Sandwick Road, Stornoway HS1 2BW ☎ 01851 822686 ✉ kbray@cne-siar.gov.uk

Planning: Mr John Cunningham, Policy Development Officer, Council Offices, Sandwick Road, Stornoway HS1 2BW ☎ 01851 822693 🖷 01851 705349 ✉ jcunningham@cne-siar.gov.uk

Procurement: Mr Ian Cockburn, Procurement Manager, Council Offices, Sandwick Road, Stornoway HS1 2BW ☎ 01851 822639 🖷 01851 706686 ✉ icockburn@cne-siar.gov.uk

Public Libraries: Ms Trish Campbell-Botten, Manager - Culture & Information Services, Council Offices, Sandwick Road, Stornoway HS1 2BW ☎ 01851 822746 🖷 01851 705657 ✉ trish.campbell-botten@cne-siar.gov.uk

Recycling & Waste Minimisation: Mr David Macleod, Recycling Officer, Council Offices, Sandwick Road, Stornoway HS1 2BW ☎ ; 01851 822663 🖷 01851 705349 ✉ david-macleod@cne-siar.gov.uk

Social Services: Mr Iain MacAulay, Director of Social & Community Services, Council Offices, Sandwick Road, Stornoway HS1 2BW ☎ 01851 822706 🖷 01851 701381 ✉ imacaulay@cne-siar.gov.uk

Staff Training: Mrs Katherine MacKinnon, Head of Human Resources, Council Offices, Sandwick Road, Stornoway HS1 2BW ☎ 01851 822605 🖷 01851 706935 ✉ kmackinnon@cne-siar.gov.uk

Staff Training: Miss Marina Macleod, Personnel Officer (Training), Council Offices, Sandwick Road, Stornoway HS1 2BW ☎ 01851 822607 🖷 01851 706935 ✉ marina.macleod@cne-siar.gov.uk

Sustainable Communities: Mr Calum Iain Maciver, Director of Development, Council Offices, Sandwick Road, Stornoway HS1 2BW ☎ 01851 822685 🖷 01851 705349 ✉ calum.maciver@cne-siar.gov.uk

Sustainable Development: Mr Calum Iain Maciver, Director of Development, Council Offices, Sandwick Road, Stornoway HS1 2BW ☎ 01851 822685 🖷 01851 705349 ✉ calum.maciver@cne-siar.gov.uk

Tourism: Mr Calum Iain Maciver, Director of Development, Council Offices, Sandwick Road, Stornoway HS1 2BW ☎ 01851 822685 🖷 01851 705349 ✉ calum.maciver@cne-siar.gov.uk

Traffic Management: Mr Iain Mackinnon, Director of Technical Services, Council Offices, Sandwick Road, Stornoway HS1 2BW ☎ 01851 822656 ✉ iain.mackinnon@cne-siar.gov.uk

Transport: Mr Iain Mackinnon, Director of Technical Services, Council Offices, Sandwick Road, Stornoway HS1 2BW ☎ 01851 822656 ✉ iain.mackinnon@cne-siar.gov.uk

Transport Planner: Mr Iain Mackinnon, Director of Technical Services, Council Offices, Sandwick Road, Stornoway HS1 2BW ☎ 01851 822656 ✉ iain.mackinnon@cne-siar.gov.uk

Waste Collection and Disposal: Mr Kenny John MacLeod, Head of Community Services, Council Offices, Sandwick Road, Stornoway HS1 2BW ☎ 01851 822663 ✉ kjmacleod@cne-siar.gov.uk

Waste Management: Mr Kenny John MacLeod, Head of Community Services, Council Offices, Sandwick Road, Stornoway HS1 2BW ☎ 01851 822663 ✉ kjmacleod@cne-siar.gov.uk

MEMBERS OF THE COUNCIL (31)

***Convener:* Macdonald**, Norman (LAB - Sgir' Uige Agus Ceann A Tuath Nan Loch)
namacdonald@cne-siar.gov.uk

***Leader of the Council:* Campbell**, Angus (IND - Steornabhagh a Deas)
angus.campbell@cne-siar.gov.uk

Blaney, David (IND - Barraigh, Bhatersaigh, Eiriosgeigh agus Uibhist a Deas)

d.blaney@cne-siar.gov.uk
Campbell, Archie (LAB - Beinn na Faoghla Agus Uibhist A Tuath)
akcampbell@cne-siar.gov.uk
Crichton, Donald (IND - Loch A Tuath)
donald.crichton@cne-siar.gov.uk
Houston, Bill (SNP - Sgir' Uige Agus Ceann A Tuath Nan Loch)
bill.houston@cne-siar.gov.uk
Macdonald, Catherine (IND - Na Hearadh agus Ceann a Deas nan Loch)
c.macdonald@cne-siar.gov.uk
MacDonald Beaton, Neil (IND - Beinn na Faoghla Agus Uibhist A Tuath)
neil.beaton@cne-siar.gov.uk
Maciver, John (IND - Loch a Tuath)
johna.maciver@cne-siar.gov.uk
Mackay, John (O - An Taobh Siar agus Nis)
john.mackay@cne-siar.gov.uk
Mackay, Roddie (IND - Steornabhagh a Tuath)
roddie.mackay@cne-siar.gov.uk
Mackenzie, Iain (IND - Steornabhagh a Tuath)
iain.mackenzie@cne-siar.gov.uk
MacKenzie, Rae (SNP - Steornabhagh A Deas)
rae.mackenzie@cne-siar.gov.uk
MacKinnon, Ronald (LAB - Barraigh, Bhatersaigh, Eiriosgeigh agus Uibhist a Deas)
ronald.mackinnon@cne-siar.gov.uk
MacLean MacAulay, Iain (IND - Steornabhagh a Tuath)
iainm.macaulay@cne-siar.gov.uk
MacLeod, Alasdair (IND - Sgire An Rubha)
alasdair.macleod@cne-siar.gov.uk
MacLeod, Cudig (IND - Sgir' Uige Agus Ceann A Tuath Nan Loch)
cudig.macleod@cne-siar.gov.uk
Macleod, Norman (IND - Sgire an Rubha)
nmmacleod@cne-siar.gov.uk
MacLeod, Kenneth (SNP - An Taobh Siar agus Nis)
kennethmacleod@cne-siar.gov.uk
MacRae, Donald (LAB - Na Hearadh Agus Ceann A Deas Nan Loch)
djmacrae@cne-siar.gov.uk
Manford, Donald (SNP - Barraigh, Bhatersaigh, Eiriosgeigh agus Uibhist a Deas)
dmanford@cne-siar.gov.uk
Mccormack, Angus (IND - Steornabhagh a Deas)
a.mccormack@cne-siar.gov.uk
Mclean, Philip (SNP - Na Hearadh agus Ceann a Deas nan Loch)
p.mclean@cne-siar.gov.uk
Morrison, Iain (IND - An Taobh Siar agus Nis)
imorrison@cne-siar.gov.uk
Murray, Kenneth (IND - An Taobh Siar agus Nis)
kmmurray@cne-siar.gov.uk
Murray, Gordon (SNP - Steornabhagh a Tuath)
gordon.murray@cne-siar.gov.uk
Nicolson, Charlie (IND - Steornabhagh a Deas)
charlie.nicolson@cne-siar.gov.uk
Robertson, Uisdean (IND - Beinn na Faoghla Agus Uibhist A Tuath)
u.robertson@cne-siar.gov.uk
Steele, Donnie (IND - Barraigh, Bhatarsaigh, Eiriosgaigh agus Uibhist a Deas)
donnie.steele@cne-siar.gov.uk
Stewart, Zena (IND - Sgire An Rubha)
zena.stewart@cne-siar.gov.uk
Stewart, Catriona (IND - Loch a Tuath)
catriona.stewart@cne-siar.gov.uk

POLITICAL COMPOSITION
IND: 20, SNP: 6, LAB: 4, O: 1

COMMITTEE CHAIRS
Audit & Scrutiny: Mr Angus Mccormack
Environmental & Protective Services: Mr Norman Macdonald
Policy & Resources: Mr Angus Campbell
Sustainable Development: Mr Archie Campbell
Transportation & Infrastructure: Mr John Mackay

WESTMINSTER CITY L

Westminster City Council, Westminster City Hall, 64 Victoria Street, London SW1E 6QP ☎ 020 7641 6000
💻 www.westminster.gov.uk

FACTS & FIGURES
Police Authority: Metropolitan Police Authority
Health Authority: NHS London
Learning and Skills Council: London
Parliamentary Constituencies: Cities of London and Westminster, Westminster North
EU Constituencies: London
Election Frequency: Elections are of whole council

PRINCIPAL OFFICERS
Chief Executive: Mr Mike More, Chief Executive, Westminster City Hall, 64 Victoria Street, London SW1E 6QP ☎ 020 7641 2358 🖷 020 7641 3438 ✉ mmore@westminster.gov.uk

Assistant Chief Executive: Ms Robyn Fairman, Assistant Chief Executive, Westminster City Hall, 64 Victoria Street, London SW1E 6QP ☎ 020 7641 2361 🖷 020 641 3438 ✉ rfairman@westminster.gov.uk

Senior Management: Mr Andrew Webster, Executive Director of Adult Social Care, Westminster Council, London SW1E 6QP ☎ 020 8753 5000 ✉ awebster@westminster.gov.uk; andrew.webster@lbhf.gov.uk

Access Officer / Social Services (Disability): Ms Karen Clark, Older People / Physical Disabilities Service Manager, Westminster City Hall, 64 Victoria Street, London SW1E 6QP ☎ 020 7641 3952 ✉ kclark@westminster.gov.uk

Access Officer / Social Services (Disability): Mr Bill Davis, Older People / Physical Disabilities Service Manager, Westminster City Hall, 64 Victoria Street, London SW1E 6QP ☎ 020 7641 1628 ✉ bdavis@westminster.gov.uk

Access Officer / Social Services (Disability): Ms June Simson, Head of Special Educational & Additional Needs, Westminster City Hall, 64 Victoria Street, London SW1E 6QP ☎ 020 7641 5356 ✉ jsimson@westminster.gov.uk

Architect, Building / Property Services: Mr Steve Harrison, Operational Director - Premises Management, Westminster City Hall, 64 Victoria Street, London SW1E 6QP ☎ 020 7641 8505

✉ sharrison@westminster.gov.uk

Best Value: Mr Ben Goward, Head of Service Delivery, Westminster City Hall, 64 Victoria Street, London SW1E 6QP ☎ 020 7641 5504 ✉ bgoward@westminster.gov.uk

Best Value: Mr Paul Kinnon, Head of Corporate Delivery, Westminster City Hall, 64 Victoria Street, London SW1E 6QP ☎ 020 7641 2742 ✉ pkinnon@westminster.gov.uk

Building Control: Mr Tony Fenton, District Surveyor, Westminster City Hall, 64 Victoria Street, London SW1E 6QP ☎ 020 7641 7048 🖷 020 7641 7115 ✉ tfenton@westminster.gov.uk

Building Control: Mr Steve Harrison, Operational Director - Premises Management, Westminster City Hall, 64 Victoria Street, London SW1E 6QP ☎ 020 7641 8505 ✉ sharrison@westminster.gov.uk

Building Control: Mr Graham King, Head of Strategic Planning & Transport, Westminster City Hall, 64 Victoria Street, London SW1E 6QP ☎ 020 7641 2749 ✉ gking@westminster.gov.uk

Building Control: Mr Richard Platt, Head of Corporate Property, Westminster City Hall, 64 Victoria Street, London SW1E 6QP ☎ 020 7641 2898 ✉ rplatt@westminster.gov.uk

Building Control: Mr John Walker, Operational Director - Development Planning, Westminster City Hall, 64 Victoria Street, London SW1E 6QP ☎ 020 7641 2519 ✉ jwalker@westminster.gov.uk

Building Control: Mr Glenn Woodhead, Head of Building Operations, Westminster City Hall, 64 Victoria Street, London SW1E 6QP ☎ 020 7641 6270 ✉ gwoodhead@westminster.gov.uk

Children / Youth Services: Mr Eamon Brennan, Head of Young People's Services, Westminster City Hall, 64 Victoria Street, London SW1E 6QP ☎ 020 7641 6047 ✉ ebrennan@westminster.gov.uk

Children / Youth Services: Mr Andrew Christie, Tri-Borough Director of Children's Services, Westminster City Hall, 64 Victoria Street, London SW1E 6QP ☎ 020 8753 5002 🖷 020 7361 3300 ✉ andrew.christie@lbhf.gov.uk; andrew.christie@rbkc.gov.uk

Children / Youth Services: Mr Chris Pickles, Head of Building Schools for the Future, Westminster City Hall, 64 Victoria Street, London SW1E 6QP ☎ 020 7641 3457 ✉ cpickles@westminster.gov.uk

Children / Youth Services: Ms Christine Reeves, Assistant Director - Joint Commissioning - Children & Families (Joint with NHS), Westminster City Hall, 64 Victoria Street, London SW1E 6QP ☎ 020 7641 3176 ✉ creeves@westminster.gov.uk

Children / Youth Services: Mr Geoff Skinner, Operational Director of Children, Young People & Families, Westminster City Hall, 64 Victoria Street, London SW1E 6QP ☎ 020 7641 2253 ✉ gskinner@westminster.gov.uk

PR / Communications: Mr Alex Aiken, Director of Communications & Strategy, Westminster City Hall, 64 Victoria Street, London SW1E 6QP ☎ 020 7641 8088 ✉ aaiken@westminster.gov.uk

PR / Communications: Mr Fergus Sheppard, Media Relations Manager, Westminster City Hall, 64 Victoria Street, London SW1E 6QP ☎ 020 7641 3995 ✉ fsheppard@westminster.gov.uk

Community Planning: Ms Jackie Gibson, Joint Head of Commissioning, Westminster City Hall, 64 Victoria Street, London SW1E 6QP ☎ 020 7641 3091 🖷 020 7641 2621 ✉ jgibson@westminster.gov.uk

Community Planning: Mr Kevin Goad, Joint Head of Commissioning, Westminster City Hall, 64 Victoria Street, London SW1E 6QP ☎ 020 7641 1903 🖷 020 7641 3481 ✉ kgoad@westminster.gov.uk

Community Planning: Mr Robert McAlister, City Co-ordination Manager, Westminster City Hall, 64 Victoria Street, London SW1E 6QP ☎ 020 7641 2576 ✉ rmcalister@westminster.gov.uk

Community Planning: Mrs Lisa O'Donnell, Spatial Planning Manager, Westminster City Hall, 64 Victoria Street, London SW1E 6QP ☎ 020 7641 4240 ✉ lodonnell@westminster.gov.uk

Community Planning: Mr Stuart Reilly, Head of Commissioning, Westminster City Hall, 64 Victoria Street, London SW1E 6QP ☎ 020 7641 5949 ✉ sreilly@westminster.gov.uk

Community Planning: Mr Barry Smith, Operational Director - City Planning, Westminster City Hall, 64 Victoria Street, London SW1E 6QP ☎ 020 7641 2923 🖷 020 7641 3050 ✉ bsmith@westminster.gov.uk

Community Planning: Mr Martin Whittles, Head of Public Realm, Westminster City Hall, 64 Victoria Street, London SW1E 6QP ☎ 020 7641 3040 ✉ mwhittles@westminster.gov.uk

Community Safety: Ms Laura Cavanagh, Head of Neighbourhood Crime Reduction, Westminster City Hall, 64 Victoria Street, London SW1E 6QP ☎ 020 7641 1738 ✉ lcavanagh@westminster.gov.uk

Community Safety: Mr Dean Ingledew, Operational Director - Street Management, Westminster City Hall, 64 Victoria Street, London SW1E 6QP ☎ 020 7641 6042 ✉ dingledew@westminster.gov.uk

Computer Management: Mr Ben Goward, Head of Service Delivery, Westminster City Hall, 64 Victoria Street, London SW1E 6QP ☎ 020 7641 5504 ✉ bgoward@westminster.gov.uk

Computer Management: Ms Barbara Moorhouse, Chief Operating Officer, Westminster City Hall, 64 Victoria Street, London SW1E 6QP ☎ 020 7641 2904 ✉ bmoorhouse@westminster.gov.uk

Computer Management: Ms Deborah Wisdom, Head of IS Strategy, Westminster City Hall, 64 Victoria Street, London SW1E 6QP ☎ 020 7641 6255 ✉ dwisdom@westminster.gov.uk

Computer Management: Ms Fatima Zohra, Corporate Information Manager, Westminster City Hall, 64 Victoria Street, London SW1E 6QP ☎ 020 7641 8578 ✉ fzohra@westminster.gov.uk

Consumer Protection and Trading Standards: Ms Sue Jones, Service Manager - Trading Standards, Westminster City Hall, 64 Victoria Street, London SW1E 6QP ☎ 020 7641 2721 📠 020 7641 1213 ✉ sjones@westminster.gov.uk

Contracts: Ms Barbara Moorhouse, Chief Operating Officer, Westminster City Hall, 64 Victoria Street, London SW1E 6QP ☎ 020 7641 2904 ✉ bmoorhouse@westminster.gov.uk

Corporate Services: Ms Twila Midgley, Business Manager, Westminster City Hall, 64 Victoria Street, London SW1E 6QP ☎ 020 7641 2939 ✉ tmidgley@westminster.gov.uk

Corporate Services: Mr Fergus Sheppard, Media Relations Manager, Westminster City Hall, 64 Victoria Street, London SW1E 6QP ☎ 020 7641 3995 ✉ fsheppard@westminster.gov.uk

Customer Service: Ms Sue Howell, Complaints Manager, Westminster City Hall, 64 Victoria Street, London SW1E 6QP ☎ 020 7641 8013 ✉ showell@westminster.gov.uk

Economic Development: Mr David Apps, Group Resources Manager, Westminster City Hall, 64 Victoria Street, London SW1E 6QP ☎ 020 7641 1949 ✉ dapps@westminster.gov.uk

Economic Development: Mr Mike Fairmaner, Economic Policy & Area Programmes Manager, Westminster City Hall, 64 Victoria Street, London SW1E 6QP ☎ 020 7641 3172 ✉ mfairmaner@westminster.gov.uk

Economic Development: Mrs Lisa O'Donnell, Spatial Planning Manager, Westminster City Hall, 64 Victoria Street, London SW1E 6QP ☎ 020 7641 4240 ✉ lodonnell@westminster.gov.uk

Economic Development: Mr Stuart Reilly, Head of Commissioning, Westminster City Hall, 64 Victoria Street, London SW1E 6QP ☎ 020 7641 5949 ✉ sreilly@westminster.gov.uk

Economic Development: Mr Barry Smith, Operational Director - City Planning, Westminster City Hall, 64 Victoria Street, London SW1E 6QP ☎ 020 7641 2923 📠 020 7641 3050 ✉ bsmith@westminster.gov.uk

Education: Mr Ian Heggs, Director of Schools Quality & Standards, Town Hall, Hornton Street, London W8 7NX ☎ 020 8753 2880 ✉ ian.heggs@lbhf.gov.uk; ian.heggs@rbkc.gov.uk

Education: Mr Chris Pickles, Head of Building Schools for the Future, Westminster City Hall, 64 Victoria Street, London SW1E 6QP ☎ 020 7641 3457 ✉ cpickles@westminster.gov.uk

Education: Ms June Simson, Head of Special Educational & Additional Needs, Westminster City Hall, 64 Victoria Street, London SW1E 6QP ☎ 020 7641 5356 ✉ jsimson@westminster.gov.uk

Education: Mr James Thomas, Operational Director of Children's Services, Westminster City Hall, 64 Victoria Street, London SW1E 6QP ☎ 020 7641 1620 ✉ jthomas@westminster.gov.uk

Education: Ms Daria Wignall, Head of Schools & Learning, Westminster City Hall, 64 Victoria Street, London SW1E 6QP ☎ 020 7641 3032 ✉ dwignall@westminster.gov.uk

Electoral Registration: Mr Martin Pyroyiannos, Electoral Services, Local Land Charges - Legal Secretariat & Business Support, Westminster City Hall, 64 Victoria Street, London SW1E 6QP ☎ 020 7641 2732 ✉ mpyroyiannos@westminster.gov.uk

Emergency Planning: Mr Robert McAlister, City Co-ordination Manager, Westminster City Hall, 64 Victoria Street, London SW1E 6QP ☎ 020 7641 2576 ✉ rmcalister@westminster.gov.uk

Environmental Health: Dr Leith Penny, Strategic Director for City Management, Westminster City Hall, Victoria Street, London SW1E 6QP ☎ 020 7641 7940 📠 020 7641 3091 ✉ lpenny@westminster.gov.uk

Environmental Health: Mr Andrew Ralph, Service Manager - Noise & Licensing Enforcement, Westminster City Hall, 64 Victoria Street, London SW1E 6QP ☎ 020 7641 2706 ✉ aralph@westminster.gov.uk

Environmental Health: Mr Garry Sheppard, Business Unit Manager - Pest Control, Lisson Grove Depot, 101 Orchardson Street, London NW8 8EA ☎ 020 7641 6844 📠 020 7641 1525 ✉ gsheppard@westminster.gov.uk

Events Manager: Ms Levana Deutschman, Commissioning Manager - Events, Filming & Contingencies, Westminster City Hall, 64 Victoria Street, London SW1E 6QP ☎ 020 7641 5967 ✉ ldeutschman@westminster.gov.uk

Events Manager: Mr Tim Owen, Commissioner - Events, Filming & Contingencies, Westminster City Hall, 64 Victoria Street, London SW1E 6QP ☎ 020 7641 5929 ✉ towen@westminster.gov.uk

Finance and Treasurer: Mr Peter Carpenter, Deputy Director of Finance (Corporate Finance), Westminster City Hall, 64 Victoria Street, London SW1E 6QP ☎ 020 7641 2832 ✉ pcarpenter@westminster.gov.uk

Finance and Treasurer: Mr Jonathan Hunt, Deputy Director for Finance, Westminster City Hall, 64 Victoria Street, London SW1E 6QP ☎ 020 7641 2297 ✉ jhunt@westminster.gov.uk

Finance and Treasurer: Ms Barbara Moorhouse, Chief Operating Officer, Westminster City Hall, 64 Victoria Street, London SW1E 6QP ☎ 020 7641 2904 ✉ bmoorhouse@westminster.gov.uk

Finance and Treasurer: Mr Chris Undrell, Head of Finance - Children's, Westminster City Hall, 64 Victoria Street, London SW1E 6QP ☎ 020 7641 2824 ✉ cundrell@westminster.gov.uk

Health and Safety: Mr Richard Block, Service Manager: Food, Health & Safety, Westminster City Hall, 64 Victoria Street, London SW1E 6QP ☎ 020 7641 2774 ✉ rblock@westminster.gov.uk

Highways: Mr Sean Dwyer, Highways Planning Manager, Westminster City Hall, 64 Victoria Street, London SW1E 6QP ☎ 020 7641 3326 ✉ sdwyer@westminster.gov.uk

Highways: Ms Sally Keiller, Group SRM, Highways and Roads, Westminster City Hall, 64 Victoria Street, London SW1E 6QP ☎ 020 7641 2677 ✉ skeiller@westminster.gov.uk

Housing: Mr Fergus Coleman, Housing Supply Commissioning Manager, Westminster City Hall, 64 Victoria Street, London SW1E 6QP ☎ 020 7641 3211 ✉ fcoleman@westminster.gov.uk

Housing: Mr Ben Denton, Director of Housing, Regeneration & Property, Westminster City Hall, 64 Victoria Street, London SW1E 6QP ☎ 020 7641 3025 🖷 020 7641 217 ✉ bdenton@westminster.gov.uk

Housing: Ms Janet Haddington, Head of Rough Sleeping Commissioning, Westminster City Hall, 64 Victoria Street, London SW1E 6QP ☎ 020 7641 3469 ✉ jhaddington@westminster.gov.uk

Housing: Mr Jonathan Hunt, Deputy Director for Finance, Westminster City Hall, 64 Victoria Street, London SW1E 6QP ☎ 020 7641 2297 ✉ jhunt@westminster.gov.uk

Housing: Ms Victoria Midwinter, Head of Housing Needs, Westminster City Hall, 64 Victoria Street, London SW1E 6QP ☎ 020 7641 2029 ✉ vmidwinter@westminster.gov.uk

Housing: Mr Gregory Roberts, Head of Supporting People & Homelessness Commissioning, Westminster City Hall, 64 Victoria Street, London SW1E 6QP ☎ 020 7641 2834 ✉ groberts@westminster.gov.uk

Housing: Mr Kevin Williamson, Housing with Care Services Manager, Westminster City Hall, 64 Victoria Street, London SW1E 6QP ☎ 020 7641 1663 ✉ kwilliamson@westminster.gov.uk

Legal: Mr Gary Blackwell, Head of Litigation, Westminster City Hall, 64 Victoria Street, London SW1E 6QP ☎ 020 7641 2718 ✉ gblackwell@westminster.gov.uk

Legal: Ms Rhian Davies, Corporate Lawyer, Westminster City Hall, 64 Victoria Street, London SW1E 6QP ☎ 020 7641 2729 ✉ rdavies@westminster.gov.uk

Legal: Mr Peter Large, Head of Legal Services, Westminster City Hall, 64 Victoria Street, London SW1E 6QP ☎ 020 7641 2711 ✉ plarge@westminster.gov.uk

Legal: Ms Patricia Narebor, Legal Services - Planning & Property, Westminster City Hall, 64 Victoria Street, London SW1E 6QP ☎ 020 7641 2734 ✉ pnarebor@westminster.gov.uk

Legal: Mr Peter Nixon, Corporate Lawyer, Westminster City Hall, 64 Victoria Street, London SW1E 6QP ☎ 020 7641 2715 ✉ pnixon@westminster.gov.uk

Legal: Mr Barry Panto, Advocacy & Advice, Westminster City Hall, 64 Victoria Street, London SW1E 6QP ☎ 020 7641 2712 ✉ bpanto@westminster.gov.uk

Leisure and Cultural Services: Mr Richard Barker, Operational Director - Sport & Leisure, Westminster City Hall, 64 Victoria Street, London SW1E 6QP ☎ 020 7641 2693 ✉ rbarker@westminster.gov.uk

Leisure and Cultural Services: Mr Andrew Durrant, Head of Westminster Sports Unit, Westminster City Hall, 64 Victoria Street, London SW1E 6QP ☎ 020 7641 5885 ✉ adurrant@westminster.gov.uk

Leisure and Cultural Services: Mr David Kerrigan, Head of Commissioning - Sport, Leisure & Wellbeing, Westminster City Hall, 64 Victoria Street, London SW1E 6QP ☎ 020 7641 2696 🖷 020 7641 2959 ✉ dkerrigan1@westminster.gov.uk

Licensing: Ms Dierdre Hayes, Services Manager EH Consultation & Licensing, Westminster City Hall, 64 Victoria Street, London SW1E 6QP ☎ 020 7641 3189 ✉ dhayes@westminster.gov.uk

Licensing: Mr Andrew Ralph, Service Manager - Noise & Licensing Enforcement, Westminster City Hall, 64 Victoria Street, London SW1E 6QP ☎ 020 7641 2706 ✉ aralph@westminster.gov.uk

Licensing: Mr Chris Wroe, Licensing Policy & Strategy Manager, Westminster City Hall, 64 Victoria Street, London SW1E 6QP ☎ 020 7641 5903 ✉ cwroe@westminster.gov.uk

Member Services: Mr Simon Gartshore, Members' Services Manager, Westminster City Hall, 64 Victoria Street, London SW1E 6QP ☎ 020 7641 2799 ✉ sgartshore@westminster.gov.uk

Partnerships: Ms Taryn Dilly, Senior Policy Officer, Westminster City Hall, 64 Victoria Street, London SW1E 6QP ☎ 020 7641 2894 ✉ tdilly@westminster.gov.uk

Partnerships: Ms Jane Little, Head of Change Liaison & Support, Westminster City Hall, 64 Victoria Street, London SW1E 6QP ☎ 020 7641 3459 ✉ jlittle@westminster.gov.uk

Personnel / HR: Ms Carolyn Beech, Head of HR, Westminster City Hall, 64 Victoria Street, London SW1E 6QP ☎ 020 7641 3221 ✉ cbeech@westminster.gov.uk

Personnel / HR: Mr Philip Berechree, Head of Quality & Training, Westminster City Hall, 64 Victoria Street, London SW1E 6QP ☎ 020 7641 2048 ✉ pberechree@westminster.gov.uk

Personnel / HR: Ms Julie Marks, Senior HR Manager, Westminster City Hall, 64 Victoria Street, London SW1E 6QP ☎ 020 7641 2786 ✉ mlow@westminster.gov.uk

Personnel / HR: Mr Trevor Webster, Senior HR Manager, Westminster City Hall, 64 Victoria Street, London SW1E 6QP ☎ 020 7641 2803 ✉ twebster@westminster.gov.uk

Planning: Mr Graham King, Head of Strategic Planning & Transport, Westminster City Hall, 64 Victoria Street, London SW1E 6QP ☎ 020 7641 2749 ✉ gking@westminster.gov.uk

Planning: Mrs Rosemary MacQueen, Strategic Director, Westminster City Hall, 64 Victoria Street, London SW1E 6QP

☎ 020 7641 5949 ✉ rmacqueen@westminster.gov.uk

Planning: Mr Daniel McCarthy, Head of Housing Strategy & Neighbourhoods Commissioning, Westminster City Hall, 64 Victoria Street, London SW1E 6QP ☎ 020 7641 1913 ✉ dmccarthy@westminster.gov.uk

Planning: Mr Giles Roca, Head of Strategy, Westminster City Hall, 64 Victoria Street, London SW1E 6QP ☎ 020 7641 2412 ✉ groca@westminster.gov.uk

Procurement: Mr Sagar Barua, Supplier Relationship Officer, Westminster City Hall, 64 Victoria Street, London SW1E 6QP ☎ 020 7641 2962 ✉ sbarua@westminster.gov.uk

Procurement: Mr Anthony Oliver, Chief Procurement Officer, Westminster City Hall, 64 Victoria Street, London SW1E 6QP ☎ 020 7641 2608 ✉ aoliver@westminster.gov.uk

Procurement: Mr Sean Stewart, Supplier Relationship Officer, Westminster City Hall, 64 Victoria Street, London SW1E 6QP ☎ 020 7641 1846 ✉ sstewart@westminster.gov.uk

Procurement: Ms Melissa Thorpe, Group Procurement Manager, Westminster City Hall, 64 Victoria Street, London SW1E 6QP ☎ 020 7641 1939 ✉ dloseby@westminster.gov.uk

Public Libraries: Mr David Ruse, Tri-Borough Director of Libraries & Archives, Westminster City Hall, 64 Victoria Street, London SW1E 6QP ☎ 020 7641 2496 🖷 020 7641 3406 ✉ druse@westminster.gov.ukdruse@westminster@gov.uk

Recycling & Waste Minimisation: Mr Mark Banks, Head of Waste Strategy, 3rd Floor, Westminster City Hall, Victoria Street, London SW1E 6QP ☎ 020 7641 3369 🖷 020 7641 7964 ✉ mbanks@westminster.gov.uk

Regeneration: Mr Ben Denton, Director of Housing, Regeneration & Property, Westminster City Hall, 64 Victoria Street, London SW1E 6QP ☎ 020 7641 3025 🖷 020 7641 217 ✉ bdenton@westminster.gov.uk

Social Services: Ms Stella Baillie, Director of Adult Social Care, Provided Services & Mental Health Partnerships, Town Hall, Hornton Street, London W8 7NX ☎ 020 7361 2401 ✉ stella.baillie@rbkc.gov.uk

Social Services: Ms Natasha Bishopp, Head of Family Recovery, Westminster City Hall, 64 Victoria Street, London SW1E 6QP ☎ 020 7641 4578 ✉ nbishopp@westminster.gov.uk

Social Services: Ms Monique Carayol, Joint Commissioning Manager - Sexual Health (NHS Post), Westminster City Hall, 64 Victoria Street, London SW1E 6QP ☎ 020 7150 8011 ✉ monique.carayo@westminster-pct.nhs.uk

Social Services: Ms Christine Reeves, Assistant Director - Joint Commissioning - Children & Families (Joint with NHS), Westminster City Hall, 64 Victoria Street, London SW1E 6QP ☎ 020 7641 3176 ✉ creeves@westminster.gov.uk

Social Services (Adult): Ms Helen Banham, Service Manager - Safeguarding Adults, Westminster City Hall, 64 Victoria Street, London SW1E 6QP ☎ 020 7641 4196 ✉ hbanham@westminster.gov.uk

Social Services (Adult): Mr Eamon Brennan, Head of Young People's Services, Westminster City Hall, 64 Victoria Street, London SW1E 6QP ☎ 020 7641 6047 ✉ ebrennan@westminster.gov.uk

Social Services (Adult): Mr Hugh Cole, Head of Joint Commissioning - Personalisation, Westminster City Hall, 64 Victoria Street, London SW1E 6QP ☎ 020 7641 5523 ✉ hcole@westminster.gov.uk

Social Services (Adult): Ms Mary Dalton, Head of Joint Commissioning - LD, Carers & Transition, Westminster City Hall, 64 Victoria Street, London SW1E 6QP ☎ 020 7641 6615 ✉ mdalton@westminster.gov.uk

Social Services (Adult): Ms Zena Deayton, Director of Adult Social Care Operations, Westminster City Hall, 64 Victoria Street, London SW1E 6QP ☎ 020 7641 2262 ✉ zdeayton@westminster.gov.uk; zena.deayton@lbhf.gov.uk

Social Services (Adult): Ms Selina Douglas, Head of Joint Commissioning - DAAT & Homeless Health, Westminster City Hall, 64 Victoria Street, London SW1E 6QP ☎ 020 7641 3467 ✉ sdouglas@westminster.gov.uk

Social Services (Adult): Mr John Higgins, Head of Joint Commissioning - OPPD, Westminster City Hall, 64 Victoria Street, London SW1E 6QP ☎ 020 7641 7404 ✉ jhiggins@westminster.gov.uk

Social Services (Adult): Mrs Janet Lang, Learning Disabilities Partnership Service Manager, Westminster City Hall, 64 Victoria Street, London SW1E 6QP ☎ 020 7641 7400 ✉ jlang@westminster.gov.uk

Social Services (Adult): Ms Sue Lipscombe, Substance Misuse Team & Joint Homelessness Team Manager, Westminster City Hall, 64 Victoria Street, London SW1E 6QP ☎ 020 7641 6704 ✉ kclark@westminster.gov.uk

Social Services (Adult): Mr Sarah Rushton, Head of Joint Commissioning - Mental Health, Westminster City Hall, 64 Victoria Street, London SW1E 6QP ☎ 020 7150 8010 ✉ sarah.rushton@westminster-pct.nhs.uk

Social Services (Adult): Mr Andrew Webster, Executive Director of Adult Social Care, Westminster Council, London SW1E 6QP ☎ 020 8753 5000 ✉ awebster@westminster.gov.uk andrew.webster@lbhf.gov.uk

Social Services (Children): Ms Carla Acket, Head of Safeguarding & Quality, Westminster City Hall, 64 Victoria Street, London SW1E 6QP ☎ 020 7641 7665 ✉ cacket@westminster.gov.uk

Social Services (Children): Ms Pauline Bastick, Head of Social Inclusion, Westminster City Hall, 64 Victoria Street, London SW1E 6QP ☎ 020 7641 2377 ✉ pbastick@westminster.gov.uk

Social Services (Children): Mr Andrew Christie, Tri-Borough Director of Children's Services, Town Hall, Hornton Street, London W8 7NX ☎ 020 8753 5002 🖷 020 7361 3300 ✉ andrew.christie@lbhf.gov.uk; andrew.christie@rbkc.gov.uk

Social Services (Children): Mr Trevor Moores, Head of Child Specialist Services, Westminster City Hall, 64 Victoria Street, London SW1E 6QP ☎ 020 7641 5687 ✉ tmoores@westminster.gov.uk

Social Services (Children): Mr Mike Potter, Head of Early Years, Extended Services & Play, Westminster City Hall, 64 Victoria Street, London SW1E 6QP ☎ 020 7641 2165 ✉ mpotter@westminster.gov.uk

Social Services (Children): Ms Janine Rowe, Head of Looked After Children & Resources, Westminster City Hall, 64 Victoria Street, London SW1E 6QP ☎ 020 7641 6710 ✉ jrowe@westminster.gov.uk

Social Services (Children): Mr Geoff Skinner, Operational Director of Children, Young People & Families, Westminster City Hall, 64 Victoria Street, London SW1E 6QP ☎ 020 7641 2253 ✉ gskinner@westminster.gov.uk

Social Services (Children): Mr John Thomas, Head of Assessment, Localities & Early Intervention, Westminster City Hall, 64 Victoria Street, London SW1E 6QP ☎ 020 7641 1620 ✉ jthomas@westminster.gov.uk

Staff Training: Ms Carolyn Beech, Head of HR, Westminster City Hall, 64 Victoria Street, London SW1E 6QP ☎ 020 7641 3221 ✉ cbeech@westminster.gov.uk

Staff Training: Mr Philip Berechree, Head of Quality & Training, Westminster City Hall, 64 Victoria Street, London SW1E 6QP ☎ 020 7641 2048 ✉ pberechree@westminster.gov.uk

Street Scene: Mr Paul Reid, Head of City Operations, Westminster City Hall, 64 Victoria Street, London SW1E 6QP ☎ 020 7641 3057 ✉ preid@westminster.gov.uk

Sustainable Communities: Dr Leith Penny, Strategic Director for City Management, Westminster City Hall, Victoria Street, London SW1E 6QP ☎ 020 7641 7940 🖷 020 7641 3091 ✉ lpenny@westminster.gov.uk

Sustainable Development: Mrs Rosemary MacQueen, Strategic Director, Westminster City Hall, 64 Victoria Street, London SW1E 6QP ☎ 020 7641 5949 ✉ rmacqueen@westminster.gov.uk

Town Centre: Ms Jackie Gibson, Joint Head of Commissioning, Westminster City Hall, 64 Victoria Street, London SW1E 6QP ☎ 020 7641 3091 🖷 020 7641 2621 ✉ jgibson@westminster.gov.uk

Town Centre: Mr Kevin Goad, Joint Head of Commissioning, Westminster City Hall, Victoria Street, London SW1E 6QP ☎ 020 7641 1903 🖷 020 7641 3481 ✉ kgoad@westminster.gov.uk

Town Centre: Dr Leith Penny, Strategic Director for City Management, Westminster City Hall, Victoria Street, London SW1E 6QP ☎ 020 7641 7940 🖷 020 7641 3091 ✉ lpenny@westminster.gov.uk

Traffic Management: Mr Martin Low, City Commissioner of Transportation, Westminster City Hall, Victoria Street, London SW1E 6QP ☎ 020 7641 1981 ✉ mlow@westminster.gov.uk

Transport: Mr Martin Low, City Commissioner of Transportation, Westminster City Hall, Victoria Street, London SW1E 6QP ☎ 020 7641 1981 ✉ mlow@westminster.gov.uk

Transport: Mr John Taylor, Service Manager - Transportation Projects, Westminster City Hall, 64 Victoria Street, London SW1E 6QP ☎ 020 7641 2943 ✉ jtaylor@westminster.gov.uk

Transport: Mr David Yeoell, Assistant City Commissioner of Transportation, Westminster City Hall, 64 Victoria Street, London SW1E 6QP ☎ 020 7641 2622 ✉ dyeoell@westminster.gov.uk

Transport Planner: Mr Graham King, Head of Strategic Planning & Transport, Westminster City Hall, 64 Victoria Street, London SW1E 6QP ☎ 020 7641 2749 ✉ gking@westminster.gov.uk

Transport Planner: Mr Martin Low, City Commissioner of Transportation, Westminster City Hall, Victoria Street, London SW1E 6QP ☎ 020 7641 1981 ✉ mlow@westminster.gov.uk

Transport Planner: Mr David Yeoell, Assistant City Commissioner of Transportation, Westminster City Hall, 64 Victoria Street, London SW1E 6QP ☎ 020 7641 2622 ✉ dyeoell@westminster.gov.uk

Waste Collection and Disposal: Dr Leith Penny, Strategic Director for City Management, Westminster City Hall, Victoria Street, London SW1E 6QP ☎ 020 7641 7940 🖷 020 7641 3091 ✉ lpenny@westminster.gov.uk

Waste Management: Dr Leith Penny, Strategic Director for City Management, Westminster City Hall, Victoria Street, London SW1E 6QP ☎ 020 7641 7940 🖷 020 7641 3091 ✉ lpenny@westminster.gov.uk

MEMBERS OF THE COUNCIL (60)

***Mayor:* Burbridge**, Susie (CON - Lancaster Gate)
sburbridge@westminster.gov.uk

***Leader of the Council:* Roe**, Philippa (CON - Knightsbridge and Belgravia)

***Deputy Leader of the Council:* Davis**, Robert (CON - Lancaster Gate)

Abdel-Hamid, Ahmed (LAB - Church Street)
ahamid@westminster.gov.uk

Acton, Heather (CON - Hyde Park)
hacton@westminster.gov.uk

Adams, Ian (CON - Little Venice)
iadams@westminster.gov.uk

Aitken, Nicola (CON - Warwick)

Argar, Edward (CON - Warwick)

Astaire, Daniel (CON - Regent's Park)

Baxter, Edward (CON - Marylebone High Street)
ebaxter@westminster.gov.uk

Beddoe, Richard (CON - Bryanston and Dorset Square)
rbeddoe@westminster.gov.uk

Boothroyd, David (LAB - Westbourne)
dboothroyd@westminster.gov.uk

Bradley, Alan (CON - Tachbrook)
abradley@westminster.gov.uk
Brahams, Michael (CON - Bayswater)
mbrahams@westminster.gov.uk
Bush, Ruth (LAB - Harrow Road)
rbush@westminster.gov.uk
Caplan, Melvyn (CON - Little Venice)
Chalkley, Danny (CON - Vincent Square)
dchalkley@westminster.gov.uk
Connell, Brian (CON - Bayswater)
bconnell@westminster.gov.uk
Connell, Brian (CON - Tachbrook)
angelaharvey@westminster.gov.uk
Cox, Antonia (CON - Hyde Park)
Devenish, Antony (CON - Knightsbridge and Belgravia)
tdevenish@westminster.gov.uk
Dimoldenberg, Paul (LAB - Queens Park)
Doyle, Margaret (CON - Little Venice)
mdoyle@westminster.gov.uk
D'Souza, Sheila (CON - Bryanston and Dorset Square)
sdsouza@westminster.gov.uk
Evans, Nicholas (CON - Tachbrook)
nevans@westminster.gov.uk
Flight, Christabel (CON - Warwick)
cflight@westminster.gov.uk
Floru, Jean-Paul (CON - Hyde Park)
jfloru@westminster.gov.uk
Glanz, Jonathan (CON - West End)
Grahame, Barbara (LAB - Church Street)
bgrahame@westminster.gov.uk
Hall, Lindsey (CON - Abbey Road)
lhall@westminster.gov.uk
Hampson, Gwyneth (CON - Regent's Park)
ghampson@westminster.gov.uk
Harvey, David (CON - Vincent Square)
davidharvey@westminster.gov.uk
Havery, Andrew (CON - Churchill)
andrewhavery@westminster.gov.uk
Havery, Andrew (CON - Bryanston and Dorset Square)
alewis@westminster.gov.uk
Hug, Adam (LAB - Westbourne)
ahug@westminster.gov.uk
Hyams, Louise (CON - St James's)
lhyams@westminster.gov.uk
Marshall, Harvey (CON - Marylebone High Street)
hmarshall@westminster.gov.uk
McAllister, Patricia (LAB - Queen's Park)
pmcallister@westminster.gov.uk
McKie, Guthrie (LAB - Harrow Road)
gmckie@westminster.gov.uk
Mitchell, Tim (CON - St James's)
tmitchell@westminster.gov.uk
Moss, Alastair (CON - Maida Vale)
amoss@westminster.gov.uk
Mukerji, Nilavra (LAB - Harrow Road)
nmukerji@westminster.gov.uk
Nemeth, Cyril (CON - Abbey Road)
cnemeth@westminster.gov.uk
Prendergast, Jan (CON - Maida Vale)
jprendergast@westminster.gov.uk
Qureshi, Papya (LAB - Westbourne)
pqureshi1@westminster.gov.uk
Rahuja, Suhail (CON - Bayswater)
srahuja@westminster.gov.uk
Richardson, Sarah (CON - Churchill)
srichardson2@westminster.gov.uk
Rigby, Robert (CON - Regent's Park)
rrigby@westminster.gov.uk
Robathan, Rachael (CON - Knightsbridge and Belgravia)
rrobathan@westminster.gov.uk
Roberts, Glenys (CON - West End)
groberts@westminster.gov.uk
Rowley, Ian (CON - Marylebone High Street)
irowley@westminster.gov.uk
Rowley, Lee (CON - Maida Vale)
Smith, Andrew (CON - Lancaster Gate)
asmith@westminster.gov.uk
Summers, Steven (CON - Vincent Square)
stevesummers@westminster.gov.uk
Taylor, Barrie (LAB - Queen's Park)
btaylor@westminster.gov.uk
Thomson, Cameron (CON - St James's)
cthomson@westminster.gov.uk
Toki, Aziz (LAB - Church Street)
atoki@westminster.gov.uk
Tombolis, Frixos (CON - West End)
ftombolis1@westminster.gov.uk
Warner, Judith (CON - Abbey Road)
judithwarner@westminster.gov.uk
Yarker, Nicholas (CON - Churchill)
nyarker@westminster.gov.uk

POLITICAL COMPOSITION

CON: 48, LAB: 12

CABINET

Leader: Ms Philippa Roe
Deputy Leader / Built Environment: Mr Robert Davis
Adults: Ms Rachael Robathan
Business: Mr Daniel Astaire
Children, Young People & Community Protection: Mrs Nicola Aitken
City Management: Mr Edward Argar
Community Services: Mr Lee Rowley
Finance & Customer Services: Mr Melvyn Caplan
Housing & Property: Mr Jonathan Glanz
Strategic Finance: Ms Philippa Roe

COMMITTEE CHAIRS

Audit & Performance: Mr Tim Mitchell
Children & Young People Policy & Scrutiny: Mr Ian Adams
Environment Policy & Scrutiny: Mr Brian Connell
General Purposes: Mr Melvyn Caplan
Housing & Community Services Policy & Scrutiny: Mr Andrew Havery
Licensing: Mr Alan Bradley
Planning & City Development: Mr Alastair Moss
Standards: Mr Tim Mitchell (External)
Superannuation: Mr Suhail Rahuja

WEYMOUTH & PORTLAND D

Weymouth & Portland Borough Council, Council Offices, North Quay, Weymouth DT4 8TA ☎ 01305 838000 🖷 01305 760971
chiefexecutive@weymouth.gov.uk
www.weymouth.gov.uk

FACTS & FIGURES

Police Authority: Dorset Police Authority
Health Authority: NHS South West
Learning and Skills Council: South East
Parliamentary Constituencies: Dorset South
EU Constituencies: South East
Election Frequency: Elections are by thirds
Twinning: Holzwickede (Germany); Louviers (France)

PRINCIPAL OFFICERS

Chief Executive: Mr David Clarke, Chief Executive, Council Offices, North Quay, Weymouth DT4 8TA ☎ 01305 251010; 01305 252202 ✉ d.clarke@westdorset-dc.gov.uk

Senior Management: Mr David Evans, Director of Environment, Council Offices, North Quay, Weymouth DT4 8TA ☎ 01305 252232; 01305 251010 ✉ davidevans2@weymouth.gov.uk; d.evans@westdorset-weymouth.gov.uk

Senior Management: Ms Kate Hindson, Director of Communities, Council Offices, North Quay, Weymouth DT4 8TA ☎ 01305 838037; 01305 251010 🖷 01305 838438 ✉ katehindson@weymouth.gov.uk; k.hindson@westdorset-weymouth.gov.uk

Senior Management: Mr Adrian Stuart, Director of Corporate Services, Council Offices, North Quay, Weymouth DT4 8TA ☎ 01305 252315; 01305 251010 ✉ adrianstuart2@weymouth.gov.uk; a.stuart@westdorset-weymouth.gov.uk

Senior Management: Mr Jason Vaughan, Director of Resources, Council Offices, North Quay, Weymouth DT4 8TA ☎ 01305 838233; 01305 251010 ✉ jasonvaughan@weymouth.gov.uk; j.vaughan@westdorset-weymouth.gov.uk

Senior Management: Mr Simon Williams, Head of 2012 Operations, Council Offices, North Quay, Weymouth DT4 8TA ☎ 01305 838483 🖷 01305 838600 ✉ simonwilliams@weymouth.gov.uk

Architect, Building / Property Services: Ms Rosie Darkin, Property & Facilities Manager, Council Offices, North Quay, Weymouth DT4 8TA ☎ 01305 252292; 01305 251010 ✉ rosiedarkin@weymouth.gov.uk; r.darkin@westdorset-weymouth.gov.uk

Best Value: Mr Chris Churchill, Head of Performance Management, Stratton House, 58-60 High West Street, Dorchester DT1 1UZ ☎ 01305 251010 ✉ c.churchill@westdorset-weymouth.gov.uk

PR / Communications: Mr Bob Hanton, Customer & Communications Manager, Council Offices, North Quay, Weymouth DT4 8TA ☎ 01305 252210; 01305 251010 ✉ bobhanton@weymouth.gov.uk; r.hanton@westdorset-weymouth.gov.uk

Community Planning: Ms Kate Hindson, Director of Communities, Council Offices, North Quay, Weymouth DT4 8TA ☎ 01305 838037; 01305 251010 🖷 01305 838438 ✉ katehindson@weymouth.gov.uk; k.hindson@westdorset-weymouth.gov.uk

Community Safety: Mr Graham Duggan, Community Protection Manager, Council Offices, North Quay, Weymouth DT4 8TA ☎ 01305 252285; 01305 251010 ✉ grahamduggan@weymouth.gov.uk; g.duggan@westdorset-weymouth.gov.uk

Computer Management: Mr Mark Chivers, Strategic IT Manager, Council Offices, North Quay, Weymouth DT4 8TA ☎ 01305 252266; 01305 251010 ✉ markchivers@weymouth.gov.uk; m.chivers@westdorset-weymouth.gov.uk

Corporate Services: Mr Adrian Stuart, Director of Corporate Services, Council Offices, North Quay, Weymouth DT4 8TA ☎ 01305 252315; 01305 251010 ✉ adrianstuart2@weymouth.gov.uk; a.stuart@westdorset-weymouth.gov.uk

Customer Service: Mr Bob Hanton, Customer & Communications Manager, Council Offices, North Quay, Weymouth DT4 8TA ☎ 01305 252210 ✉ bobhanton@weymouth.gov.uk; r.hanton@westdorset-weymouth.gov.uk

Economic Development: Mr Ian Doyle, Economic Regeneration Manager, Council Offices, North Quay, Weymouth DT4 8TA ☎ 01305 252617; 01305 251010 ✉ iandoyle@weymouth.gov.uk; i.doyle@westdorset-weymouth.gov.uk

Electoral Registration: Ms Sue Bonham-Lovett, Head of Elector & Member Services, Council Offices, North Quay, Weymouth DT4 8TA ☎ 01305 838477; 01305 251010 🖷 01305 838289 ✉ suebonhamlovett@weymouth.gov.uk; s.bonham-lovett@westdorset-weymouth.gov.uk

Emergency Planning: Mr Steve Woollard, Technical Services Manager, Council Offices, North Quay, Weymouth DT4 8TA ☎ 01305 252297; 01305 251010 ✉ stevewoollard@weymouth.gov.uk; s.woollard@westdorset-weymouth.gov.uk

Energy Management: Mr Bob Savage, Technician Engineer, Council Offices, North Quay, Weymouth DT4 8TA ☎ 01305 838318 🖷 01305 838469 ✉ bobsavage@weymouth.gov.uk

Environmental / Technical Services: Mr Steve Woollard, Technical Services Manager, Council Offices, North Quay, Weymouth DT4 8TA ☎ 01305 252297; 01305 251010 ✉ stevewoollard@weymouth.gov.uk; s.woollard@westdorset-weymouth.gov.uk

Environmental Health: Mr Graham Duggan, Community Protection Manager, Council Offices, North Quay, Weymouth DT4 8TA ☎ 01305 252285; 01305 251010 ✉ grahamduggan@weymouth.gov.uk; g.duggan@westdorset-weymouth.gov.uk

Estates, Property & Valuation: Ms Rosie Darkin, Property &

Facilities Manager, Council Offices, North Quay, Weymouth DT4 8TA ☎ 01305 252292; 01305 251010 rosiedarkin@weymouth.gov.uk; r.darkin@westdorset-weymouth.gov.uk

Events Manager: Mr Nick Thornley, Leisure & Tourism Manager, Council Offices, North Quay, Weymouth DT4 8TA ☎ 01305 252474; 01305 251010 nickthornley@weymouth.gov.uk; n.thornley@westdorset-weymouth.gov.uk

Facilities: Ms Rosie Darkin, Property & Facilities Manager, Council Offices, North Quay, Weymouth DT4 8TA ☎ 01305 252292; 01305 251010 rosiedarkin@weymouth.gov.uk; r.darkin@westdorset-weymouth.gov.uk

Finance and Treasurer: Mr Jason Vaughan, Director of Resources, Council Offices, North Quay, Weymouth DT4 8TA ☎ 01305 838233; 01305 251010 jasonvaughan@weymouth.gov.uk; j.vaughan@westdorset-weymouth.gov.uk

Grounds Maintenance: Ms Karyn Punchard, Street Scene Manager, Council Offices, North Quay, Weymouth DT4 8TA ☎ 01305 838226; 01305 251010 karynpunchard@weymouth.gov.uk; k.punchard@westdorset-weymouth.gov.uk

Health and Safety: Mr Grant Armfield, Emergency Planning Officer, Council Offices, North Quay, Weymouth DT4 8TA ☎ 01305 838213 🖷 01305 838317 grantarmfield@weymouth.gov.uk

Home Energy Conservation: Ms Sarah Ward, Housing Manager, Council Offices, North Quay, Weymouth DT4 8TA ☎ 01305 252313; 01305 251010 sarahward@weymouth.gov.uk; s.ward@westdorset-weymouth.gov.uk

Housing: Ms Sarah Ward, Housing Manager, Council Offices, North Quay, Weymouth DT4 8TA ☎ 01305 252313; 01305 251010 sarahward@weymouth.gov.uk; s.ward@westdorset-weymouth.gov.uk

Legal: Mr Glen Harding, Legal & Democratic Manager, Council Offices, North Quay, Weymouth DT4 8TA ☎ 01305 252244; 01305 251010 glenharding@weymouth.gov.uk; g.harding@westdorset-weymouth.gov.uk

Leisure and Cultural Services: Mr Nick Thornley, Leisure & Tourism Manager, Council Offices, North Quay, Weymouth DT4 8TA ☎ 01305 252474; 01305 251010 nickthornley@weymouth.gov.uk; n.thornley@westdorset-weymouth.gov.uk

Licensing: Mr Graham Duggan, Community Protection Manager, Council Offices, North Quay, Weymouth DT4 8TA ☎ 01305 252285; 01305 251010 grahamduggan@weymouth.gov.uk; g.duggan@westdorset-weymouth.gov.uk

Lottery Funding, Charity and Voluntary: Ms Julie Strange, Financial Services Manager, Council Offices, North Quay, Weymouth DT4 8TA ☎ 01305 838252; 01305 251010 juliestrange@weymouth.gov.uk; j.strange@westdorset-weymouth.gov.uk

Member Services: Mr Glen Harding, Legal & Democratic Manager, Council Offices, North Quay, Weymouth DT4 8TA ☎ 01305 252244; 01305 251010 glenharding@weymouth.gov.uk; g.harding@westdorset-weymouth.gov.uk

Parking: Mr Steve Woollard, Technical Services Manager, Council Offices, North Quay, Weymouth DT4 8TA ☎ 01305 252297; 01305 251010 stevewoollard@weymouth.gov.uk; s.woollard@westdorset-weymouth.gov.uk

Partnerships: Ms Louise Stewart, Partnership Manager, Council Offices, North Quay, Weymouth DT4 8TA ☎ 01305 838364 louisestewart@weymouth.gov.uk

Personnel / HR: Ms Melanie Earnshaw, Human Resources Manager, Council Offices, North Quay, Weymouth DT4 8TA ☎ 01305 838212 melanieearnshaw@weymouth.gov.uk; m.earnshaw@westdorset-weymouth.gov.uk

Planning: Mr John Greenslade, Development Services Manager, Council Offices, North Quay, Weymouth DT4 8TA ☎ 01305 252230; 01305 251010 johngreenslade@weymouth.gov.uk; j.greenslade@westdorset-weymouth.gov.uk

Procurement: Ms Julia Long, Procurement Co-ordinator, Council Offices, North Quay, Weymouth DT4 8TA ☎ 01305 838543 julialong@weymouth.gov.uk

Recycling & Waste Minimisation: Ms Karyn Punchard, Street Scene Manager, Council Offices, North Quay, Weymouth DT4 8TA ☎ 01305 838226; 01305 251010 karynpunchard@weymouth.gov.uk; k.punchard@westdorset-weymouth.gov.uk

Regeneration: Mr Ian Doyle, Economic Regeneration Manager, Council Offices, North Quay, Weymouth DT4 8TA ☎ 01305 252617; 01305 251010 iandoyle@weymouth.gov.uk; i.doyle@westdorset-weymouth.gov.uk

Staff Training: Ms Melanie Earnshaw, Human Resources Manager, Council Offices, North Quay, Weymouth DT4 8TA ☎ 01305 838212 melanieearnshaw@weymouth.gov.uk; m.earnshaw@westdorset-weymouth.gov.uk

Street Scene: Ms Karyn Punchard, Street Scene Manager, Council Offices, North Quay, Weymouth DT4 8TA ☎ 01305 838226; 01305 251010 karynpunchard@weymouth.gov.uk; k.punchard@westdorset-weymouth.gov.uk

Sustainable Development: Mr John Greenslade, Development Services Manager, Council Offices, North Quay, Weymouth DT4 8TA ☎ 01305 252230; 01305 251010 johngreenslade@weymouth.gov.uk; j.greenslade@westdorset-weymouth.gov.uk

Tourism: Mr Nick Thornley, Leisure & Tourism Manager, Council Offices, North Quay, Weymouth DT4 8TA ☎ 01305 252474; 01305 251010 nickthornley@weymouth.gov.uk;

n.thornley@westdorset-weymouth.gov.uk

Waste Collection and Disposal: Ms Karyn Punchard, Street Scene Manager, Council Offices, North Quay, Weymouth DT4 8TA ☎ 01305 838226; 01305 251010 ✉ karynpunchard@weymouth.gov.uk; k.punchard@westdorset-weymouth.gov.uk

Waste Management: Ms Karyn Punchard, Street Scene Manager, Council Offices, North Quay, Weymouth DT4 8TA ☎ 01305 838226; 01305 251010 ✉ karynpunchard@weymouth.gov.uk; k.punchard@westdorset-weymouth.gov.uk

Children's Play Areas: Ms Karyn Punchard, Street Scene Manager, Council Offices, North Quay, Weymouth DT4 8TA ☎ 01305 838226; 01305 251010 ✉ karynpunchard@weymouth.gov.uk; k.punchard@westdorset-weymouth.gov.uk

MEMBERS OF THE COUNCIL (36)

***Mayor:* Leicester**, Margaret (IND - Tophill East)
***Deputy Mayor:* Banham**, Ray (LD - Melcombe Regis)
Birtwistle, John (LD - Weymouth East)
Blackwood, Andy (LAB - Westham North)
Bruce, Hazel (CON - Preston)
Bruce, Ian (CON - Preston)
Byatt, Mike (LAB - Westham East)
Chapman, Peter (CON - Preston)
Dunster, Robbie (CON - Upwey and Broadwey)
Farrell, Peter (CON - Melcombe Regis)
Goodman, Michael (CON - Upwey and Broadwey)
Hall, Jane (CON - Weymouth East)
Hamilton, Lucy (LAB - Westham West)
Hawkins, David (IND - Tophill East)
Hodder, Kevin (CON - Wey Valley)
Hope, Ryan (LD - Westham North)
Huckle, Colin (LAB - Weymouth West)
James, Ian (CON - Westham East)
James, Christine (LD - Westham North)
Kenwood, Anne (LAB - Wyke Regis)
Kimber, Paul (LAB - Underhill)
Kosior, Richard (CON - Weymouth West)
Lonsdale, Dominic (CON - Weymouth West)
Munro, Amanda (CON - Tophill West)
Munro-Price, Ian (CON - Tophill West)
Nixon, Pamela (CON - Wey Valley)
Nowark, Ray (LAB - Tophill West)
Petherick, Geoff (IND - Wyke Regis)
Roebuck, Ian (LD - Radipole)
Rogers, Rachel (LAB - Littlemoor)
Stanley, Joy (LD - Melcombe Regis)
Taylor, Gill (LD - Westham West)
Tewkesbury, Mark (LAB - Littlemoor)
West, Sandy (LAB - Underhill)
Wheller, Kate (LAB - Wyke Regis)
White, Bill (LD - Radipole)

POLITICAL COMPOSITION

CON: 14, LAB: 11, LD: 8, IND: 3

CABINET

Community & Facilites: Mr Andy Blackwood
Community Safety: Mr Geoff Petherick
Corporate Affairs & Continuous Improvement: Mr Michael Goodman
Economic Development: Mr Ian Munro-Price
Environment & Sustainability: Mr Ian Roebuck
Finance & Assets: Mr Peter Chapman
Housing: Mr Ray Nowark
Social Inclusion: Mrs Kate Wheller
Tourism & Culture: Mr Ian Bruce
Transport & Infrastructure: Ms Christine James

COMMITTEE CHAIRS

Appeals: Ms Pamela Nixon
Audit: Mr Colin Huckle
Licensing: Mr Robbie Dunster
Management: Mr Michael Goodman
Planning & Traffic: Mr Mark Tewkesbury
Scrutiny: Ms Lucy Hamilton

WIGAN M

Wigan Metropolitan Borough Council, Town Hall, Library Street, Wigan WN1 1YN ☎ 01942 244991 🖷 01942 827451 ✉ pr@wigan.gov.uk 💻 www.wigan.gov.uk

FACTS & FIGURES

Police Authority: Greater Manchester Police Authority
Health Authority: North West Strategic Health Authority
Learning and Skills Council: North West
Parliamentary Constituencies: Leigh, Makerfield, Wigan
EU Constituencies: North West
Election Frequency: Elections are by thirds
Twinning: Angers (France)

PRINCIPAL OFFICERS

Chief Executive: Ms Donna Hall, Chief Executive, Town Hall, Library Street, Wigan WN1 1YN ☎ 01942 827148 🖷 01942 828174 ✉ donna.hall@wigan.gov.uk

Chief Executive: Mr Stuart Murray, Chief Executive WLCT, The Indoor Sports Complex, Loire Drive, Robin Park, Wigan WN5 0UL ☎ 01942 828500 🖷 01942 828540 ✉ s.murray2@wigan.gov.uk

Senior Management: Ms Gillian Bishop, Corporate Director of Places - Economy, Waste & Infrastructure, Town Hall, Library Street, Wigan WN1 1YN ✉ g.bishop@wigan.gov.uk

Senior Management: Mr Nick Hudson, Corporate Director of People - Children, Adults & Families, Town Hall, Library Street, Wigan WN1 1YN ☎ 01942 486000 ✉ n.hudson@wigan.gov.uk

Senior Management: Mr Stephen Normington, Director of Economy, Wigan Life Centre, Library Street, Wigan WN1 1YN ☎ 01942 404303 ✉ stephen.normington@wigan.gov.uk

Senior Management: Mr Stuart Smith, Director of Education & Children's Services, 2nd Floor, Millennium House, 60 Victoria Street, Liverpool L1 6JF ☎ 0151 233 2799 🖷 0151 233 8200 ✉ stuart.smith@liverpool.gov.uk

Architect, Building / Property Services: Mr Derek Gee, Director of Architecture, Waterside House, Waterside Drive, Wigan WN3 5AZ ☎ 01942 898486 🖷 01942 823891 ✉ derek.gee@nps-nw.co.uk

Architect, Building / Property Services: Mrs Andrea Yates, Leigh Building Services Manager, Town Hall, Library Street, Wigan WN1 1YN ☎ 01942 828333 ✉ andrea.yates@wigan.gov.uk

Catering Services: Ms Debbie Clarke, Strategic Manager of Catering, Town Hall, Library Street, Wigan WN1 1YN ☎ 01942 705071 ✉ d.clarke@wigan.gov.uk

Children / Youth Services: Mrs Sharon Bond, Youth Offending Team, 93 Victoria Road, Platt Bridge, Wigan WN2 5DN ☎ 01942 776886 ✉ yot@wiganmbc.gov.uk

Children / Youth Services: Ms Anne Goldsmith, Director of Specialist & Targeted, Progress House, Westwood Park Drive, Wigan WN3 4HH ☎ 01942 244991 ✉ anne.goldsmith@wigan.gov.uk

Children / Youth Services: Mrs Kirston Nelson, Head of Service - Education, Civic Centre, Millgate, Wigan WN1 1YD ☎ 01942 486238 ✉ kirston.nelson@wigan.gov.uk

Children / Youth Services: Ms Andrea Smith, Youth Development Officer, Elizabeth House, The Pier, Wallgate, Wigan WN3 4BD ☎ 01942 486923

Civil Registration: Mr Melvyn Jones, Superintendent Registrar, Town Hall, Library Street, Wigan WN1 1YN ☎ 01942 705014 🖷 01942 705013 ✉ m.jones2@wigan.gov.uk

PR / Communications: Ms Susan Roberts, Media & Communications Manager, Town Hall, Library Street, Wigan WN1 1YN ☎ 01942 827446 🖷 01942 827365 ✉ susan.roberts@wigan.gov.uk

Community Planning: Mr Alan Blundell, Head of Regulatory Services, Town Hall, Library Street, Wigan WN1 1YN ☎ 01942 244991 ✉ alan.blundell@wigan.gov.uk

Community Planning: Mr Simon Dale, Policy & Planning Manager, Town Hall, Library Street, Wigan WN1 1YN ☎ 01942 827320 🖷 01942 776175 ✉ s.dale@wigan.gov.uk

Community Safety: Ms Joyce Swift, Projects Manager, Unity House, Westwood Park Drive, Wigan WN3 4HE ☎ 01942 828111 🖷 01942 828013

Corporate Services: Mr Paul McKevitt, Director of Corporate Services, Town Hall, Library Street, Wigan WN1 1YN ☎ 01942 827235 ✉ p.mckevitt@wigan.gov.uk

Customer Service: Ms Alison McKenzie-Folan, Director of Policy & Customer, Town Hall, Library Street, Wigan WN1 1YN ☎ 01942 827784 ✉ a.mckenzie-folan@wigan.gov.uk

Customer Service: Ms Sharon Weetman, Head of Customer Services, Town Hall, Library Street, Wigan WN1 1YN ☎ 01942 488312 ✉ s.weetman@wigan.gov.uk

Direct Labour: Mr Mark Tilley, Head of Service - Infrastructure, Civic Buildings, New Market Street, Wigan WN1 1RP ☎ 01942 404341 🖷 01942 404210 ✉ m.tilley@wigan.gov.uk

Economic Development: Ms Ann-Marie Edwards, Regeneration Officer, Town Hall, Library Street, Wigan WN1 1YN ☎ 01942 828985 ✉ a.edwards@wigan.gov.uk

Economic Development: Ms Susan Gambles, Head of Service - Economic Development, Economic Regeneration Office, Gateway House, Standishgate, Wigan WN1 1AE ☎ 01942 828934 🖷 01942 828938 ✉ s.gambles@wigan.gov.uk

Education: Mr Nick Hudson, Corporate Director of People - Children, Adults & Families, Progress House, Westwood Park Drive, Wigan WN3 4HH ☎ 01942 486000 ✉ n.hudson@wigan.gov.uk

Electoral Registration: Ms Anne Loftus, Principal Electoral Services Officer, Town Hall, Library Street, Wigan WN1 1YN ☎ 01942 827170 🖷 01942 488383 ✉ a.loftus@wigan.gov.uk

Emergency Planning: Mr Stuart Cowley, Head of Personalisation & Partnerships (People Directorate), Town Hall, Library Street, Wigan WN1 1YN ☎ 01942 244991 ✉ stuart.cowley@wigan.gov.uk

Emergency Planning: Ms Tina Smith, Civil Contingencies Manager, Ashton Town Hall, Bryn Street, Ashton, Wigan WN4 9AY ☎ 01942 404904 ✉ t.smith@wigan.gov.uk

Energy Management: Ms Sally Wolstencroft, Head of Service - Safer, Cleaner, Greener, Town Hall, Library Street, Wigan WN1 1YN ☎ 01942 705102 ✉ sally.wolstencroft@wigan.gov.uk

Environmental / Technical Services: Ms Penny McGinty, Head of Service - Leisure & Community, Town Hall, Library Street, Wigan WN1 1YN ☎ 01942 488275 ✉ penny.mcginty@wigan.gov.uk

Environmental / Technical Services: Ms Sally Wolstencroft, Head of Service - Safer, Cleaner, Greener, Town Hall, Library Street, Wigan WN1 1YN ☎ 01942 705102 ✉ sally.wolstencroft@wigan.gov.uk

European Liaison: Ms Patricia Evans, Service Manager - European Programmes, Gateway House, Standishgate, Wigan WN1 1AE ☎ 01942 828948 🖷 01942 828938 ✉ p.evans@wigan.gov.uk

Events Manager: Mrs Glynis Harrison, Catering & Events Manager, Town Hall, Library Street, Wigan WN1 1YN ☎ 01942 828096 🖷 01942 827451 ✉ glynis.harrison@wigan.gov.uk

Finance and Treasurer: Mr Paul McKevitt, Director of Corporate Services, Town Hall, Library Street, Wigan WN1 1YN ☎ 01942 827235 ✉ p.mckevitt@wigan.gov.uk

Fleet Management: Mr Keith Simpson, Transport DSO Manager, Transport DSO, Hindley Towns Yard, Wigan Road, Hindley, Wigan WN2 3BQ ☎ 01942 705103 🖷 01942 705108 ✉ k.simpson@wigan.gov.uk

Grounds Maintenance: Mr Stuart Murray, Chief Executive WLCT, The Indoor Sports Complex, Loire Drive, Robin Park, Wigan WN5 0UL ☎ 01942 828500 🖷 01942 828540 ✉ s.murray2@wigan.gov.uk

Health and Safety: Mr Paul McKevitt, Director of Corporate Services, Civic Centre, Millgate, Wigan WN1 1YD ☎ 01942 827235 ✉ p.mckevitt@wigan.gov.uk

Highways: Mr Mark Tilley, Head of Service - Infrastructure, Civic Buildings, New Market Street, Wigan WN1 1RP ☎ 01942 404341 🖷 01942 404210 ✉ m.tilley@wigan.gov.uk

Housing: Mr Ashley Crumbley, Chief Executive, Wigan & Leigh Housing, Unity House, Westwood Park Drive, Wigan WN3 4HE ☎ 01942 486507 🖷 01942 827079 ✉ a.crumbley@wigan.gov.uk

Housing: Mr Peter Layland, Head of Housing & Community Regeneration, Gateway House, Standishgate, Wigan WN1 1AE ☎ 01942 244991 ✉ peter.layland@wigan.gov.uk

Housing Maintenance: Mr Mike Sterlicchi, Director of Asset Management & Development, CT3 Building, Investment Centre, Waterside Drive, Wigan WN3 5BA ☎ 01942 705846 ✉ m.sterlicchi@wigan.gov.uk

Local Area Agreement: Mrs Katherine Fairclough, Service Director - Business Transformation, Town Hall, Library Street, Wigan WN1 1YN ☎ 01942 827095 🖷 01942 827297 ✉ k.fairclough@wigan.gov.uk

Legal: John Mitchell, Head of Service - Legal & Risk (Monitoring Officer), Town Hall, Library Street, Wigan WN1 1YN ☎ 01942 827023

Leisure and Cultural Services: Mr Stuart Murray, Chief Executive WLCT, The Indoor Sports Complex, Loire Drive, Robin Park, Wigan WN5 0UL ☎ 01942 828500 🖷 01942 828540 ✉ s.murray2@wigan.gov.uk

Licensing: Mr Steve Wearing, Licensing Manager, Town Hall, Library Street, Wigan WN1 1YN ☎ 01942 827114 ✉ s.wearing@wigan.gov.uk

Lifelong Learning: Mr Nick Hudson, Corporate Director of People - Children, Adults & Families, Progress House, Westwood Park Drive, Wigan WN3 4HH ☎ 01942 486000 ✉ n.hudson@wigan.gov.uk

Lighting: Mr Keith Benson, Street Scene & Lighting Manager, Wigan Life Centre, Library Street, Wigan WN1 1YN ☎ 01942 488025 🖷 01942 404210 ✉ k.benson@wigan.gov.uk

Lottery Funding, Charity and Voluntary: Ms Susan Gambles, Head of Service - Economic Development, Economic Regeneration Office, Gateway House, Standishgate, Wigan WN1 1AE ☎ 01942 828934 🖷 01942 828938 ✉ s.gambles@wigan.gov.uk

Member Services: Ms Christine Charnock-Jones, Principal Democratic Services Officer, Town Hall, Library Street, Wigan WN1 1YN ☎ 01942 827156 🖷 01942 488383 ✉ c.charnock@wigan.gov.uk

Parking: Ms Sharon Brightcliffe, Car Parks Officer, Civic Centre, Millgate, Wigan WN1 1AZ ☎ 01942 827057 ✉ s.brightcliffe@wigan.gov.uk

Personnel / HR: Ms Sharon Adams, Interim Head of HR & OD, Town Hall, Library Street, Wigan WN1 1YN ☎ 01942 827132 ✉ s.adams@wigan.gov.uk

Personnel / HR: Mrs L Jackson, Head of Corporate Personnel, Town Hall, Library Street, Wigan WN1 1YN ☎ 01942 827129

Planning: Mr Mike Worden, Head of Planning & Transport, Wigan Life Centre, Library Street, Wigan WN1 1YN ☎ 01942 404357 ✉ mike.worden@wigan.gov.uk

Procurement: Mr J Cliff, Corporate Procurement Manager, Town Hall, Library Street, Wigan WN1 1YN ☎ 01942 827671 🖷 01942 827454 ✉ j.cliff@wigan.gov.uk

Public Libraries: Mr Pete Gasgoine, Executive Director (Culture) WLCT, Wigan Leisure & Culture Trust, Robin Park Indoor Leisure Centre, Loire Drive, Wigan WN5 0UL ☎ 01942 828503 🖷 01942 828540 ✉ p.gasgoine@wlct.org

Recycling & Waste Minimisation: Ms Gail Robinson, Waste Disposal & Recycling Manager, Hindley Towns Yard, Wigan Road, Hindley, Wigan WN2 3BQ ☎ 01942 705131 🖷 01942 404210 ✉ gail.robinson@wigan.gov.uk

Regeneration: Mr Peter Layland, Head of Housing & Community Regeneration, Gateway House, Standishgate, Wigan WN1 1AE ☎ 01942 244991 ✉ peter.layland@wigan.gov.uk

Road Safety: Ms Carmel Foster-Devine, Transport Plan & Road Safety Manager, Wigan Life Centre, Library Street, Wigan WN1 1NY ☎ 01942 404687 🖷 01942 404210 ✉ c.foster-devine@wigan.gov.uk

Social Services (Children): Ms Trish Anderson, Service Director of Strategy & Commissioning, Progress House, Westwood Park Drive, Wigan WN3 4HH ☎ 01942 486005 🖷 01942 404796 ✉ trish.anderson@wigan.gov.uk

Staff Training: Ms Sharon Adams, Interim Head of HR & OD, Hindley Professional Development Centre, Park Road, Hindley, Wigan WN2 3RY ☎ 01942 827132 ✉ s.adams@wigan.gov.uk

Street Scene: Mr Damian Jenkinson, Wigan Borough in Bloom Co-ordinator, Wigan Life Centre, Library Street, Wigan WN1 1YN ☎ 01942 488299 ✉ d.jenkinson@wigan.gov.uk

Sustainable Communities: Mr Nick Burdekin, CSG Environment & Education Co-ordinator, Development Division, Civic Buildings, New Market Street, Wigan WN1 1RP ☎ 01942 488222 ✉ n.burdekin@wigan.gov.uk

Sustainable Communities: Mr Ian Harris, Head of Sustainable Communities, Town Hall, Library Street, Wigan WN1 1YN ☎ 01942 244991 ✉ ian.harrison@wigan.gov.uk

Sustainable Development: Ms Janet Withington, Sustainability Officer, Civic Buildings, New Market Street, Wigan WN1 1RP ☎ 01942 404236 🖷 01942 404222 ✉ j.withington@wigan.gov.uk

Tourism: Mr Keith Bergman, Hospitality & Events Manager, Elizabeth House, The Pier, Wallgate, Wigan WN3 4BD ☎ 01942 486951 🖷 01942 776467 ✉ k.bergman@wigan.gov.uk

Town Centre: Mr Michael Matthews, Town Centre Manager, Economic Regeneration Office, Gateway House, Standishgate, Wigan WN1 1AE ☎ 01942 828890 🖷 01942 828938 ✉ m.matthews@wmbc.gov.uk

Traffic Management: Mr Mark Tilley, Head of Service - Infrastructure, Wigan Life Centre, Library Street, Wigan WN1 1YN ☎ 01942 404341 🖷 01942 404210 ✉ m.tilley@wigan.gov.uk

Transport: Mr Keith Simpson, Transport DSO Manager, Transport DSO, Hindley Towns Yard, Wigan Road, Hindley, Wigan WN2 3BQ ☎ 01942 705103 🖷 01942 705108 ✉ k.simpson@wigan.gov.uk

Transport Planner: Ms Carmel Foster-Devine, Transport Plan & Road Safety Manager, Wigan Life Centre, Library Street, Wigan WN1 1YN ☎ 01942 404687 🖷 01942 404210 ✉ c.foster-devine@wigan.gov.uk

Transport Planner: Mr Mike Worden, Head of Planning & Transport, Wigan Life Centre, Library Street, Wigan WN1 1YN ☎ 01942 404357 ✉ mike.worden@wigan.gov.uk

Waste Collection and Disposal: Ms Sally Wolstencroft, Head of Service - Safer, Cleaner, Greener, Town Hall, Library Street, Wigan WN1 1YN ☎ 01942 705102 ✉ sally.wolstencroft@wigan.gov.uk

Waste Management: Ms Gail Robinson, Waste Disposal & Recycling Manager, Hindley Towns Yard, Wigan Road, Hindley, Wigan WN2 3BQ ☎ 01942 705131 🖷 01942 404210 ✉ gail.robinson@wigan.gov.uk

MEMBERS OF THE COUNCIL (75)

***Mayor:* Whiteside**, Myra (LAB - Leigh West)
m.whiteside@wigan.gov.uk
***Deputy Mayor:* Rotherham**, William (LAB - Worsley Mesnes)
w.rotherham@wigan.gov.uk
***Leader of the Council:* Smith**, Peter (LAB - Leigh West)
leader@wigan.gov.uk
***Deputy Leader of the Council:* Molyneux**, David (LAB - Ince)
d.molyneux@wigan.gov.uk
Aldred, Mark (LAB - Atherleigh)
m.aldred@wigan.gov.uk
Aldred, Karen (LAB - Atherton)
k.aldred@wigan.gov.uk
Anderson, Kevin (LAB - Leigh South)
k.anderson@wigan.gov.uk
Arrowsmith, David (LAB - Orrell)
D.Arrowsmith@wigan.gov.uk
Ash, Nigel (LAB - Ashton)
N.Ash@wigan.gov.uk
Birch, Joy (LAB - Douglas)
j.birch@wigan.gov.uk
Bleakley, Robert (LD - Tyldesley)
r.bleakley@wigan.gov.uk
Bourne, Barbara (LAB - Pemberton)
b.bourne@wigan.gov.uk
Bowen, Brendan (LAB - Astley Mosley Common)
b.bowen@wigan.gov.uk
Bradbury, Norman (IND - Atherton)
n.bradbury@wigan.gov.uk
Bretherton, Gerard (LAB - Golborne and Lowton West)
g.bretherton@wigan.gov.uk
Brierley, Robert (IND - Hindley Green)
r.brierley@wigan.gov.uk
Carmichael, Francis (IND - Hindley Green)
F.Carmichael@wigan.gov.uk
Churton, James (LAB - Hindley)
j.eccles-churton@wigan.gov.uk
Clarke, Bill (LAB - Ashton)
b.clarke@wigan.gov.uk
Collins, Paul (LAB - Shevington with Lower Ground)
paul.collins@wigan.gov.uk
Conway, Ronald (LAB - Aspull New Springs Whelley)
R.Conway@wigan.gov.uk
Cowley, James (LAB - Lowton East)
J.Cowley@wigan.gov.uk
Crosby, Michael (LAB - Shevington with Lower Ground)
M.Crosby@wigan.gov.uk
Cullen, Phyll (LAB - Wigan West)
p.cullen@wigan.gov.uk
Cunliffe, Keith (LAB - Leigh East)
k.cunliffe@wigan.gov.uk
Davies, George (LAB - Wigan Central)
george.davies@wigan.gov.uk
Dawber, Stephen (LAB - Wigan West)
steve.dawber@wigan.gov.uk
Dewhurst, Shirley (LAB - Douglas)
shirley.dewhurst@wigan.gov.uk
Dewhurst, Michael (LAB - Douglas)
m.dewhurst@wigan.gov.uk
Edwardson, Damian (LAB - Shevington with Lower Ground)
d.edwardson@wigan.gov.uk
Ellis, Jim (IND - Hindley)
james.ellis@wigan.gov.uk
Fairhurst, Gareth (IND - Standish with Langtree)
gareth.fairhurst@wigan.gov.uk
Fairhurst, George (IND - Standish with Langtree)
george.fairhurst@wigan.gov.uk
Gillgan, Pamela (LAB - Lowton East)
P.Gillgan@wigan.gov.uk
Greensmith, Susan (LAB - Leigh West)
s.greensmith@wigan.gov.uk
Grundy, James (CON - Lowton East)
james.grundy@wigan.gov.uk
Haddley, Joel (LAB - Ashton)
J.Haddley
Halliwell, Terence (LAB - Wigan West)
t.halliwell@wigan.gov.uk
Hellier, John (LAB - Tyldesley)
s.hellier@wigan.gov.uk
Hilton, John (LAB - Aspull New Springs Whelley)
j.hilton@wigan.gov.uk
Hodgkinson, Jamie (IND - Atherton)
jamie.hodgkinson@wigan.gov.uk
Hodgkinson, John (IND - Bryn)
don.hodgkinson@wigan.gov.uk
Holland, Patricia (LAB - Worsley Mesnes)
p.holland@wigan.gov.uk

Hunt, Lawrence (LAB - Wigan Central)
l.Hunt@wigan.gov.uk
Keane, Stuart (LAB - Golborne and Lowton West)
s.keane@wigan.gov.uk
Kelly, Phil (LAB - Worsley Mesnes)
p.kelly@wigan.gov.uk
Klieve, Yvonne (LAB - Golborne and Lowton West)
y.klieve@wigan.gov.uk
Loudon, Susan (LAB - Atherleigh)
s.loudon@wigan.gov.uk
McGurrin, Emma (LAB - Standish with Langtree)
E.McGurrin@wigan.gov.uk
McLoughin, Michael (LAB - Wigan Central)
m.mcloughin@wigan.gov.uk
Moodie, James (LAB - Ince)
j.moodie@wigan.gov.uk
Morgan, Clive (LAB - Winstanley)
clive.morgan@wigan.gov.uk
Murphy, Stephen (LAB - Orrell)
stephen.murphy@wigan.gov.uk
O'Brien, John (LAB - Leigh South)
j.o'brien@wigan.gov.uk
Platt, Joanne (LAB - Astley Mosley Common)
joanne.platt@wigan.gov.uk
Prescott, Paul (LAB - Pemberton)
paul.prescott@wigan.gov.uk
Prescott, Jeanette (LAB - Pemberton)
j.prescott@wigan.gov.uk
Rampling, Margaret (LAB - Bryn)
A.Rampling@wigan.gov.uk
Ready, Christopher (LAB - Aspull New Springs Whelley)
c.ready@wigan.gov.uk
Ready, Kelly (LAB - Orrell)
kelly.ready@wigan.gov.uk
Rigby, Charles (LAB - Leigh South)
c.rigby@wigan.gov.uk
Sharratt, Janice (LAB - Ince)
J.Sharratt@wigan.gov.uk
Smethurst, Martyn (LAB - Abram)
m.smethurst@wigan.gov.uk
Smethurst, Eunice (LAB - Abram)
e.smethurst@wigan.gov.uk
Stewart, Pamela (LAB - Atherleigh)
p.stewart@wigan.gov.uk
Stitt, David (LAB - Hindley Green)
K.Stitt@wigan.gov.uk
Sweeney, Carl (LAB - Abram)
c.sweeney@wigan.gov.uk
Talbot, James (LAB - Hindley)
j.talbot@wigan.gov.uk
Taylor, Barry (LAB - Astley Mosley Common)
Barry.Taylor@wigan.gov.uk
Terence, Paul (LAB - Winstanley)
p.kenny@wigan.gov.uk
Thorpe, Anita (LAB - Leigh East)
A.Thorpe@wigan.gov.uk
Valentine, Paul (LD - Tyldesley)
p.valentine@wigan.gov.uk
Walker, Frederick (LAB - Leigh East)
f.walker@wigan.gov.uk
Wilkes, Gary (IND - Bryn)
g.wilkes@wigan.gov.uk
Winkworth, Rona (LAB - Winstanley)
r.winkworth@wigan.gov.uk

POLITICAL COMPOSITION
LAB: 63, IND: 9, LD: 2, CON: 1

CABINET
Leader: Lord Peter Smith
Deputy Leader / Regeneration: Mr David Molyneux
Adults & Social Care: Mr Keith Cunliffe
Children & Young People: Mrs Susan Loudon
Environment: Mr Kevin Anderson
Housing, Leisure Client Communications: Mr Christopher Ready

COMMITTEE CHAIRS
Audit Governance & Improvement: Mr Joel Haddley
Licensing: Mr Paul Prescott
Pay & Reward: Lord Peter Smith
Planning: Mr Paul Prescott
Regulation: Mr Paul Prescott

WILTSHIRE UNITARY U
Wiltshire Council, County Hall, Trowbridge BA14 8JN
☎ 0300 456 0100 🖳 www.wiltshire.gov.uk

FACTS & FIGURES
Parliamentary Constituencies: Chippenham, Devizes, Salisbury, Wiltshire North, Wiltshire South West
E

PRINCIPAL OFFICERS
Senior Management: Ms Laurie Bell, Director - Communications, County Hall, Trowbridge BA14 8JN ☎ 0300 456 0100 🖷 01225 456 0100 ✉ laurie.bell@wiltshire.gov.uk

Senior Management: Ms Mandy Bradley, Service Director - Public Protection, County Hall, Trowbridge BA14 8JN ☎ 0300 456 0100 ✉ mandy.bradley@wiltshire.gov.uk

Senior Management: Mr James Cawley, Service Director - Strategy & Commissioning, County Hall, Trowbridge BA14 8JN ☎ 0300 456 0100 ✉ james.cawley@wiltshire.gov.uk

Senior Management: Mr Brad Fleet, Service Director - Development Services, County Hall, Trowbridge BA14 8JN ☎ 0300 456 0100 ✉ brad.fleet@wiltshire.gov.uk

Senior Management: Mr Graham Hogg, Service Director - Housing, County Hall, Trowbridge BA14 8JN ☎ 0300 456 0100 ✉ graham.hogg@wiltshire.gov.uk

Best Value: Ms Sharon Britton, Service Director - Policy, Performance & Partnership, County Hall, Trowbridge BA14 8JF ☎ 01225 713170 🖷 01225 713400 ✉ sharon.britton@wiltshire.gov.uk

Children / Youth Services: Ms Julia Cramp, Service Director - Commissioning & Performance, County Hall, Trowbridge BA14 8JN ☎ 01225 718221 ✉ julia.cramp@wiltshire.gov.uk

Children / Youth Services: Mrs Carolyn Godfrey, Corporate Director, County Hall, Bythesea Road, Trowbridge BA14 8JN ☎ 01225 713750 🖷 01225 713982 ✉ carolyn.godfrey@wiltshire.gov.uk

PR / Communications: Ms Laurie Bell, Director - Communications, County Hall, Trowbridge BA14 8JN ☎ 0300 456 0100 🖷 01225 456 0100 ✉ laurie.bell@wiltshire.gov.uk

Community Planning: Dr Carlton Brand, Corporate Director, County Hall, Trowbridge BA14 8JN ☎ 01225 713001 🖷 01225 713161 ✉ carltonbrand@wiltshire.gov.uk

Community Safety: Ms Mandy Bradley, Service Director - Public Protection, Court Mills Centre, Polebarn Road, Trowbridge BA14 7EG ☎ 0300 456 0100 ✉ mandy.bradley@wiltshire.gov.uk

Consumer Protection and Trading Standards: Ms Yvonne Bennett, Consumer Protection Manager, County Hall, Trowbridge BA14 8JN ☎ 0300 456 0100 ✉ yvonne.bennett@wiltshire.gov.uk

Contracts: Mr Michael Swabey, Strategy Manager, County Hall, Trowbridge BA14 8JD ☎ 01225 718662 ✉ mikeswabey@wiltshire.gov.uk

Contracts: Mr Arthur Williams, Principal Contracts Officer, County Hall, Trowbridge BA14 8JN ☎ 01225 713252 ✉ arthur.williams@wiltshire.gov.uk

Corporate Services: Dr Carlton Brand, Corporate Director, County Hall, Trowbridge BA14 8JN ☎ 01225 713001 🖷 01225 713161 ✉ carltonbrand@wiltshire.gov.uk

Customer Service: Mrs Jacqui White, Service Director - Business Services, County Hall, Trowbridge BA14 8JN ☎ 01225 713013 ✉ jacquiwhite@wiltshire.gov.uk

Economic Development: Mr Alistair Cunningham, Director - Economy & Regeneration, County Hall, Bythesea Road, Trowbridge BA14 8JN ☎ 01225 713203 🖷 01225 713400 ✉ alistair.cunningham@wiltshire.gov.uk

Education: Ms Julia Cramp, Service Director - Commissioning & Performance, County Hall, Trowbridge BA14 8JN ☎ 01225 718221 ✉ julia.cramp@wiltshire.gov.uk

Education: Mrs Stephanie Denovan, Service Director - Schools & Learning, County Hall, Bythesea Road, Trowbridge BA14 8JN ☎ 01225 713838 ✉ stephanie.denovan@wiltshire.gov.uk

Education: Ms Carolyn Godfrey, Corporate Director, County Hall, Trowbridge BA14 8JB ☎ 01225 713750 🖷 01225 713982 ✉ carolyn.godfrey@wiltshire.gov.uk

E-Government: Mr Ian Gibbons, Director - Legal & Democratic Services, County Hall, Bythesea Road, Trowbridge BA14 8JN ☎ 01225 713052 🖷 01225 713998 ✉ ian.gibbons@wiltshire.gov.uk

Environmental / Technical Services: Ms Tracy Carter, Director - Waste Management Services, County Hall, Trowbridge BA14 8JN ☎ 01225 713258 🖷 01225 713200 ✉ tracy.carter@wiltshire.gov.uk

Environmental / Technical Services: Mr Parvis Khansari, Service Director - Highways & Transport, County Hall, Bythesea Road, Trowbridge BA14 8JN ☎ 01225 713340 ✉ parvis.khansari@wiltshire.gov.uk

Events Manager: Ms Barbara Gray, Events & Sponsorship Manager, County Hall, Trowbridge BA14 8JN ☎ 0300 456 0100

Facilities: Mr Mark Smith, Service Director - Neighbourhood Services, County Hall, Trowbridge BA14 8JN ☎ 01225 734789 ✉ mark.smith@wiltshire.gov.uk

Finance and Treasurer: Mr Michael Hudson, Director - Finance, County Hall, Trowbridge BA14 8JN ☎ 01225 713600 🖷 01225 713697 ✉ michael.hudson@wiltshire.gov.uk

Grounds Maintenance: Mr Mark Smith, Service Director - Neighbourhood Services, County Hall, Trowbridge BA14 8JN ☎ 01225 734789 ✉ mark.smith@wiltshire.gov.uk

Health and Safety: Mr Paul Collyer, Head of Occupational Health & Safety, County Hall, Trowbridge BA14 8JN ☎ 01225 713119 🖷 01225 713177 ✉ paulcollyer@wiltshire.gov.uk

Highways: Mr Parvis Khansari, Service Director - Highways & Transport, County Hall, Bythesea Road, Trowbridge BA14 8JN ☎ 01225 713340 ✉ parvis.khansari@wiltshire.gov.uk

Housing: Mr Graham Hogg, Service Director - Housing, County Hall, Trowbridge BA14 8JN ☎ 0300 456 0100 ✉ graham.hogg@wiltshire.gov.uk

Local Area Agreement: Ms Sharon Britton, Director - Policy, Performance & Partnership, County Hall, Trowbridge BA14 8JF ☎ 01225 713170 🖷 01225 713400 ✉ sharon.britton@wiltshire.gov.uk

Legal: Mr Ian Gibbons, Director - Legal & Democratic Services, County Hall, Bythesea Road, Trowbridge BA14 8JN ☎ 01225 713052 🖷 01225 713998 ✉ ian.gibbons@wiltshire.gov.uk

Leisure and Cultural Services: Mr Mark Smith, Service Director - Neighbourhood Services, County Hall, Trowbridge BA14 8JN ☎ 01225 734789 ✉ mark.smith@wiltshire.gov.uk

Lifelong Learning: Mr Helen Mehring, Head of Service - Organisational, Learning & Development, County Hall, Trowbridge BA14 8JN ☎ 01225 713194 ✉ helen.mehring@wiltshire.gov.uk

Lottery Funding, Charity and Voluntary: Ms Sandie Lewis, Head of Community Strategy & Voluntary Sector Support, County Hall, Trowbridge BA14 8JN ☎ 01225 713150 🖷 01225 713515 ✉ sandie.lewis@wiltshire.gov.uk

Member Services: Mr Ian Gibbons, Director - Legal & Democratic Services, County Hall, Bythesea Road, Trowbridge BA14 8JN ☎ 01225 713052 🖷 01225 713998 ✉ ian.gibbons@wiltshire.gov.uk

Member Services: Mr John Quinton, Head of Democratic & Member Services & Cabinet Secretary, County Hall, Trowbridge BA14 8JN ☎ 01225 713054 🖷 01225 713099 ✉ johnquinton@wiltshire.gov.uk

Partnerships: Mrs Maggie Rae, Director - Public Health, County Hall, Bythesea Road, Trowbridge BA14 8JN ☎ 01225 718338 ✉ maggie.rae@wiltshire.gov.uk

Personnel / HR: Mr Barry Pirie, Director - Human Resources & Organisational Development, County Hall, Bythesea Road, Trowbridge BA14 8JN ☎ 01225 718226 barrie.pirie@wiltshire.gov.uk

Planning: Mr Brad Fleet, Service Director - Development Services, County Hall, Trowbridge BA14 8JN ☎ 0300 456 0100 brad.fleet@wiltshire.gov.uk

Procurement: Mr Tony Brett, Head of Procurement, County Hall, Trowbridge BA14 8JN ☎ 0125 718581 tony.brett@wiltshire.gov.uk

Public Libraries: Ms Niki Lewis, Service Director - Community, Libraries, Heritage & Arts, County Hall, Bythesea Road, Trowbridge BA14 8JN ☎ 01225 713180 niki.lewis@wiltshire.gov.uk

Social Services: Ms Sharon Davies, Service Director - Children & Families, County Hall, Trowbridge BA14 8JN ☎ 0300 456 0100 sharon.davies@wiltshire.gov.uk

Social Services: Ms Sue Geary, Head of Performance, Health and Workforce, County Hall, Trowbridge BA14 8JN ☎ 01225 713922 sue.geary@wiltshire.gov.uk

Social Services: Ms Sue Redmond, Corporate Director, County Hall, Trowbridge BA14 8JG ☎ 01225 713901 🖷 01225 713983 sue.redmond@wiltshire.gov.uk

Social Services (Adult): Mr James Cawley, Service Director - Strategy & Commissioning, County Hall, Trowbridge BA14 8JN ☎ 0300 456 0100 james.cawley@wiltshire.gov.uk

Social Services (Adult): Ms Sue Redmond, Corporate Director, County Hall, Bythesea Road, Trowbridge BA14 8JN ☎ 01225 713901 🖷 01225 713983 sue.redmond@wiltshire.gov.uk

Social Services (Children): Ms Sharon Davies, Service Director - Children & Families, County Hall, Trowbridge BA14 8JN ☎ 0300 456 0100 sharon.davies@wiltshire.gov.uk

Staff Training: Ms Niki Lewis, Service Director - Community, Libraries, Heritage & Arts, County Hall, Trowbridge BA14 8JN ☎ 01225 713180 niki.lewis@wiltshire.gov.uk

Staff Training: Mr Barry Pirie, Director - Human Resources & Organisational Development, County Hall, Bythesea Road, Trowbridge BA14 8JN ☎ 01225 718226 barry.pirie@wiltshire.gov.uk

Sustainable Communities: Ms Niki Lewis, Service Director - Community, Libraries, Heritage & Arts, County Hall, Bythesea Road, Trowbridge BA14 8JN ☎ 01225 713180 niki.lewis@wiltshire.gov.uk

Transport: Mr Parvis Khansari, Service Director - Highways & Transport, County Hall, Bythesea Road, Trowbridge BA14 8JN ☎ 01225 713340 parvis.khansari@wiltshire.gov.uk

Waste Collection and Disposal: Ms Tracy Carter, Director - Waste Management Services, County Hall, Trowbridge BA14 8JN ☎ 01225 713258 🖷 01225 713200 tracy.carter@wiltshire.gov.uk

Waste Management: Mr Michael Wood, Contracts & Waste Manager, County Hall, Trowbridge BA14 8JD ☎ 01225 713373 🖷 01225 713400 mikewood@wiltshire.gov.uk

MEMBERS OF THE COUNCIL (98)

***Chair:* Crisp**, Christine (CON - Calne Rural)
christine.crisp@wiltshire.gov.uk

***Vice-Chair:* While**, Roy (CON - Melksham Without South)
roy.while@wiltshire.gov.uk

***Leader of the Council:* Scott**, Jane (CON - By Brook)
jane.scott@wiltshire.gov.uk

Allen, Desna (LD - Chippenham Queens and Sheldon)
desna.allen@wiltshire.gov.uk

Beattie, Richard (CON - Wilton and Lower Wylye Valley)
richard.beattie@wiltshire.gov.uk

Berry, Chuck (CON - Calne North)
chuck.berry@wiltshire.gov.uk

Brady, John (CON - Salisbury St Martins and Cathedral)
john.brady@wiltshire.gov.uk

Britton, Richard (CON - Alderbury and Whiteparish)
richard.britton@wiltshire.gov.uk

Brown, Rosemary (LD - Bradford-on-Avon North)
rosemary.brown@wiltshire.gov.uk

Bryant, Liz (CON - Bromham, Rowde and Potterne)
liz.bryant@wiltshire.gov.uk

Bucknell, Allison (CON - Lyneham)
allison.bucknell@wiltshire.gov.uk

Burton, Jane (O - Devizes East)
jane.burton@wiltshire.gov.uk

Carbin, Trevor (LD - Holt and Staverton)
trevor.carbin@wiltshire.gov.uk

Carter, Nigel (O - Devizes North)
nigel.carter@wiltshire.gov.uk

Caswill, Chris (LD - Chippenham Monkton)
chris.caswill@wiltshire.gov.uk

Clark, Ernie (IND - Hilperton)
ernie.clark@wiltshire.gov.uk

Clewer, Richard (CON - Salisbury St Pauls)
richard.clewer@wiltshire.gov.uk

Cochrane, Christopher (CON - Salisbury Fisherton and Bemerton)
chris.cochrane@wiltshire.gov.uk

Colmer, Peter (LD - Cricklade and Latton)
peter.colmer@wiltshire.gov.uk

Conley, Linda (CON - Winsley and Westwood)
linda.conley@wiltshire.gov.uk

Connolly, Mark (CON - Tidworth)
mark.connolly@wiltshire.gov.uk

Cuthbert-Murray, Michael (IND - Westbury East)
michael.cuthbert-murray@wiltshire.gov.uk

Dalton, Brian (LD - Salisbury Harnham)
brian.dalton@wiltshire.gov.uk

Darby, Paul (LD - Chippenham Hardenhuish)
paul.darby@wiltshire.gov.uk

Davis, Andrew (CON - Warminster East)
andrew.davis@wiltshire.gov.uk

Davis, Peter (CON - Corsham Town)
peter.davis@wiltshire.gov.uk

Deane, Tony (CON - Tisbury)
tony.deane@wiltshire.gov.uk

Devine, Christopher (CON - Winterslow)
christopher.devine@wiltshire.gov.uk

Douglas, Bill (LD - Chippenham Hardens and England)
bill.douglas@wiltshire.gov.uk
Douglas, Mary (CON - Salisbury St Francis and Stratford)
mary.douglas@wiltshire.gov.uk
Dow, Peggy (LD - Marlborough East)
peggy.dow@wiltshire.gov.uk
Doyle, Peter (CON - Wootton Bassett South)
peter.doyle@wiltshire.gov.uk
Eaton, Rod (CON - Melksham North)
rod.eaton@wiltshire.gov.uk
Fogg, Nick (IND - Marlborough West)
nick.fogg@wiltshire.gov.uk
Fuller, Peter (CON - Trowbridge Park)
peter.fuller@wiltshire.gov.uk
Gamble, Richard (CON - The Lavingtons and Erlestoke)
richard.gamble@wiltshire.gov.uk
Green, Jose (CON - Fovant & Chalke Valley)
jose.green@wiltshire.gov.uk
Greenman, Howard (CON - Kington)
howard.greenman@wiltshire.gov.uk
Griffiths, Mark (CON - Melksham Without North)
mark.griffiths@wiltshire.gov.uk
Groom, Mollie (CON - Wootton Bassett East)
mollie.groom@wiltshire.gov.uk
Grundy, Lionel (CON - Urchfont and The Cannings)
lionel.grundy@wiltshire.gov.uk
Hall, Robert (CON - Pewsey Vale)
robert.hall@wiltshire.gov.uk
Hawker, Russell (IND - Westbury West)
russell.hawker@wiltshire.gov.uk
Hewitt, Mike (CON - Bourne and Woodford Valley)
mike.hewitt@wiltshire.gov.uk
Hewson, Malcolm (LD - Bradford-on-Avon South)
malcolm.hewson@wiltshire.gov.uk
Hill, Alan (CON - Calne South and Cherhill)
alan.hill@wiltshire.gov.uk
Howard, Charles (CON - The Collingbournes and Netheravon)
charles.howard@wiltshire.gov.uk
Hubbard, Jon (LD - Melksham South)
jon.hubbard@wiltshire.gov.uk
Humphries, Chris (CON - Aldbourne and Ramsbury)
chris.humphries@wiltshire.gov.uk
Humphries, Keith (CON - Warminster Broadway)
keith.humphries@wiltshire.gov.uk
Hutton, Peter (CON - Chippenham Cepen Park and Derriads)
peter.hutton@wiltshire.gov.uk
James, Tom (IND - Trowbridge Adcroft)
thomas.james@wiltshire.gov.uk
Jeans, George (IND - Mere)
george.jeans@wiltshire.gov.uk
Jenkins, David (LD - Westbury North)
david.jenkins2@wiltshire.gov.uk
Johnson, Julian (CON - Downton and Ebble Valley)
julian.johnson@wiltshire.gov.uk
Killane, Simon (LD - Malmesbury)
simon.killane@wiltshire.gov.uk
Knight, John (LD - Trowbridge Central)
john.knight@wiltshire.gov.uk
Kunkler, Jerry (CON - Pewsey)
jerry.kunkler@wiltshire.gov.uk
Lay, Jacqui (CON - Purton)
jacqui.lay@wiltshire.gov.uk
Macrae, Alan (CON - Corsham Pickwick)
alan.macrae@wiltshire.gov.uk
Marshall, Howard (LD - Calne Central)
howard.marshall@wiltshire.gov.uk
Mayes, Laura (CON - Roundway)
laura.mayes@wiltshire.gov.uk
McLennan, Ian (LAB - Laverstock, Ford and Old Sarum)
ian.mclennan@wiltshire.gov.uk
Milton, Jemima (CON - West Selkley)
jemima.milton@wiltshire.gov.uk
Morland, Francis (IND - Southwick)
Moss, Bill (CON - Salisbury St Marks and Bishopdown)
bill.moss@wiltshire.gov.uk
Newbury, Christopher (IND - Warminster Copheap and Wylye)
christopher.newbury@wiltshire.gov.uk
Noeken, John (CON - Amesbury East)
john.noeken@wiltshire.gov.uk
Ody, Jeffrey (O - Devizes and Roundway South)
jeff.ody@wiltshire.gov.uk
Oldrieve, Stephen (LD - Trowbridge Paxcroft)
steve.oldrieve@wiltshire.gov.uk
Osborn, Jeff (LD - Trowbridge Grove)
jeff.osborn@wiltshire.gov.uk
Osborn, Helen (LD - Trowbridge Lambrok)
helen.osborn@wiltshire.gov.uk
Packard, Mark (LD - Chippenham Pewsham)
mark.packard@wiltshire.gov.uk
Parker, Sheila (CON - Box and Colerne)
sheila.parker@wiltshire.gov.uk
Payne, Graham (CON - Trowbridge Drynham)
graham.payne@wiltshire.gov.uk
Petty, Stephen (LD - Melksham Central)
stephen.petty@wiltshire.gov.uk
Phillips, Nina (CON - Chippenham Cepen Park and Redlands)
nina.phillips@wiltshire.gov.uk
Randall, Leo (CON - Redlynch and Landford)
leo.randall@wiltshire.gov.uk
Rhe-Philipe, Fleur de (CON - Warminster Without)
fleur.derhephilipe@wiltshire.gov.uk
Ridout, Pip (CON - Warminster West)
pip.ridout@wiltshire.gov.uk
Roberts, William (CON - Wootton Bassett North)
bill.roberts@wiltshire.gov.uk
Rogers, Ricky (LAB - Salisbury Bemerton)
ricky.rogers@wiltshire.gov.uk
Rooke, Judy (LD - Chippenham Lowden and Rowden)
judy.rooke@wiltshire.gov.uk
Sample, Paul (LD - Salisbury St Edmund and Milford)
Seed, Jonathon (CON - Summerham and Seend)
jonathon.seed@wiltshire.gov.uk
Smale, John (CON - Bulford, Allington and Figheldean)
johnf.smale@wiltshire.gov.uk
Soden, Carole (CON - Minety)
carole.soden@wiltshire.gov.uk
Sturgis, Toby (CON - Brinkworth)
toby.sturgis@wiltshire.gov.uk
Swabey, Julie (CON - Ethandune)
julie.swabey@wiltshire.gov.uk
Thomson, John (CON - Sherston)
john.thomson@wiltshire.gov.uk
Tonge, Dick (CON - Corsham Without and Box Hill)
richard.tonge@wiltshire.gov.uk
Trotman, Anthony (CON - Calne Chilvester and Abberd)
tony.trotman@wiltshire.gov.uk
Wayman, Bridget (CON - Nadder and East Knoyle)
bridget.wayman@wiltshire.gov.uk
West, Ian (LD - Till and Wylye Valley)

ian.west@wiltshire.gov.uk
Westmoreland, Fred (CON - Amesbury West)
fred.westmoreland@wiltshire.gov.uk
Wheeler, Stuart (CON - Burbage and The Bedwyns)
stuart.wheeler@wiltshire.gov.uk
Williams, Christopher (CON - Ludgershall and Perham Down)
christopher.williams@wiltshire.gov.uk
Wright, Graham (LD - Durrington and Larkhill)
graham.wright@wiltshire.gov.uk

POLITICAL COMPOSITION
CON: 61, LD: 24, IND: 8, O: 3, LAB: 2

CABINET
Leader: Ms Jane Scott
Deputy Leader / Adult Care, Communities & Housing: Mr John Thomson
Children's Services: Mr Lionel Grundy
Economic Development & Strategic Planning: Ms Fleur de Rhe-Philipe
Finance Performance & Risk: Mr John Brady
Highways & Transport: Mr Dick Tonge
Public Health & Protection Services: Mr Keith Humphries
Resources: Mr John Noeken
Transformation, Culture, Leisure & Libraries: Mr Stuart Wheeler
Waste, Property, Environment & Development Control Services: Mr Toby Sturgis

COMMITTEE CHAIRS
Audit: Mr Roy While
Children's Select: Ms Carole Soden
Corporate Parenting Panel: Ms Sheila Parker
Environment Select: Mr Jon Hubbard
Licensing: Mr Jonathon Seed
Management Overview & Scrutiny: Mr Trevor Carbin
Procurement & Commissioning Panel: Mr Peter Hutton
Standards: Mr Julian Johnson
Strategic Planning: Mr Andrew Davis
Wiltshire Pension Fund: Mr Tony Deane

WINCHESTER CITY D

Winchester City Council, City Offices, Colebrook Street, Winchester SO23 9LJ ☎ 01962 840222 🖷 01962 841365 ✉ info@winchester.gov.uk 🖳 www.winchester.gov.uk

FACTS & FIGURES
Police Authority: Hampshire Police Authority
Health Authority: South Central Strategic Health Authority
Learning and Skills Council: South East
Parliamentary Constituencies: Winchester
EU Constituencies: South East
Election Frequency: Elections are by thirds

PRINCIPAL OFFICERS
Chief Executive: Mr Simon Eden, Chief Executive, City Offices, Colebrook Street, Winchester SO23 9LJ ☎ 01962 848230 🖷 01962 848208 ✉ seden@winchester.gov.uk

Architect, Building / Property Services: Mr Andrew Kingston, Property Services Manager, City Offices, Colebrook Street, Winchester SO23 9LJ ☎ 01962 848240 🖷 01962 841365 ✉ akingston@winchester.gov.uk

Architect, Building / Property Services: Mr Kevin Warren, Head of Estates, City Offices, Colebrook Street, Winchester SO23 9LJ ☎ 01962 848528 ✉ kwarren@winchester.gov.uk

Best Value: Ms Alexis Garlick, Head of Finance, City Offices, Colebrook Street, Winchester SO23 9LJ ☎ 01962 848224 ✉ agarlick@winchester.gov.uk

Building Control: Mr Chris Griffith-Jones, Head of Building Control, City Offices, Colebrook Street, Winchester SO23 9LJ ☎ 01962 840222 🖷 01962 849101 ✉ cgriffith-jones@winchester.gov.uk

Children / Youth Services: Ms Jen Anderson, Assistant Director - Active Communities, City Offices, Colebrook Street, Winchester SO23 9LJ ☎ 01962 848592 🖷 01962 840586 ✉ janderson@winchester.gov.uk

PR / Communications: Mrs Eleanor Davies, Corporate Communications Manager, City Offices, Colebrook Street, Winchester SO23 9LJ ☎ 01962 848504 🖷 01962 848208 ✉ edavies@winchester.gov.uk

Community Planning: Mrs Lorraine Ronan, Community Wellbeing Manager, City Offices, Colebrook Street, Winchester SO23 9LJ ☎ 01962 848369 🖷 01962 841365 ✉ lronan@winchester.gov.uk

Community Safety: Ms Sandra Tuddenham, Community Safety Officer, City Offices, Colebrook Street, Winchester SO23 9LJ ☎ 01962 848132 ✉ studdenham@winchester.gov.uk

Computer Management: Mr Stephen Whetnall, Corporate Director - Governance, City Offices, Colebrook Street, Winchester SO23 9LJ ☎ 01962 840222 🖷 01962 848555 ✉ swhetnall@winchester.gov.uk

Contracts: Mr Andrew Kingston, Property Services Manager, City Offices, Colebrook Street, Winchester SO23 9LJ ☎ 01962 848240 🖷 01962 841365 ✉ akingston@winchester.gov.uk

Customer Service: Mr Paul Wood, Head of Customer Services, City Offices, Colebrook Street, Winchester SO23 9LJ ☎ 01962 848437 ✉ pwood@winchester.gov.uk

Economic Development: Mrs Kate Cloud, Head of Economy & Arts, City Offices, Colebrook Street, Winchester SO23 9LJ ☎ 01962 848563 🖷 01962 848101 ✉ kcloud@winchester.gov.uk

E-Government: Mr Stephen Whetnall, Corporate Director - Governance, City Offices, Colebrook Street, Winchester SO23 9LJ ☎ 01962 840222 🖷 01962 848555 ✉ swhetnall@winchester.gov.uk

Electoral Registration: Mrs Frances Cleland, Electoral Services Manager, City Offices, Colebrook Street, Winchester SO23 9LJ ☎ 01962 848125 🖷 01962 848472 ✉ fcleland@winchester.gov.uk

Emergency Planning: Mr Dave Shaw, Principal Democratic Services Officer, City Offices, Colebrook Street, Winchester SO23 9LJ ☎ 01962 848221 🖷 01962 848555 ✉ dshaw@winchester.gov.uk

Energy Management: Mr Robert Heathcock, Assistant Director - High Quality Environment, City Offices, Colebrook Street, Winchester SO23 9LJ ☎ 01962 848476 🖷 01962 840586 ✉ rheathcock@winchester.gov.uk

Environmental / Technical Services: Mr Robert Heathcock, Assistant Director - High Quality Environment, City Offices, Colebrook Street, Winchester SO23 9LJ ☎ 01962 848476 🖷 01962 840586 ✉ rheathcock@winchester.gov.uk

Environmental Health: Mr Robert Heathcock, Assistant Director - High Quality Environment, City Offices, Colebrook Street, Winchester SO23 9LJ ☎ 01962 848476 🖷 01962 840586 ✉ rheathcock@winchester.gov.uk

Estates, Property & Valuation: Mr Kevin Warren, Head of Estates, City Offices, Colebrook Street, Winchester SO23 9LJ ☎ 01962 848528 ✉ kwarren@winchester.gov.uk

European Liaison: Ms Nancy Graham, Senior Democratic Services Officer, City Offices, Colebrook Street, Winchester SO23 9LJ ☎ 01962 848221 🖷 01962 848555 ✉ ngraham@winchester.gov.uk

Facilities: Ms Wendy Steele, Facilities Manager, City Offices, Colebrook Street, Winchester SO23 9LJ ☎ 01962 848397 ✉ wsteele@winchester.gov.uk

Finance and Treasurer: Ms Gill Cranswick, Head of Revenues & Benefits, City Offices, Colebrook Street, Winchester SO23 9LJ ☎ 01962 840190 ✉ gcranswick@winchester.gov.uk; gcranswick@testvalley.gov.uk

Finance and Treasurer: Ms Alexis Garlick, Head of Finance, City Offices, Colebrook Street, Winchester SO23 9LJ ☎ 01962 848224 ✉ agarlick@winchester.gov.uk

Fleet Management: Mr Dave Howarth, Exchequer Services Manager, City Offices, Colebrook Street, Winchester SO23 9LJ ☎ 01962 848157 🖷 01962 841365 ✉ dhowarth@winchester.gov.uk

Grounds Maintenance: Ms Amanda Ford, Head of Sports & Physical Activity, City Offices, Colebrook Street, Winchester SO23 9LJ ☎ 01962 840274 🖷 01962 841365 ✉ aford@winchester.gov.uk

Health and Safety: Mr Robert Cole, Health & Safety Officer, City Offices, Colebrook Street, Winchester SO23 9LJ ☎ 01962 848164 🖷 01962 840586 ✉ bcole@winchester.gov.uk

Housing: Mr Olu Fajuyitan, Senior Housing Needs Officer, City Offices, Colebrook Street, Winchester SO23 9LJ ☎ 01962 840222 ✉ ofajuyitan@winchester.gov.uk

Housing: Mr Andy Palmer, Head of Strategic Housing, City Offices, Colebrook Street, Winchester SO23 9LJ ☎ 01962 840152 ✉ apalmer@winchester.gov.uk

Housing Maintenance: Mr Andrew Kingston, Property Services Manager, City Offices, Colebrook Street, Winchester SO23 9LJ ☎ 01962 848240 🖷 01962 841365 ✉ akingston@winchester.gov.uk

Legal: Mr Howard Bone, Head of Legal Services, City Offices, Colebrook Street, Winchester SO23 9LJ ☎ 01962 848310 ✉ hbone@winchester.gov.uk

Legal: Mr Stephen Whetnall, Corporate Director - Governance, City Offices, Colebrook Street, Winchester SO23 9LJ ☎ 01962 840222 🖷 01962 848555 ✉ swhetnall@winchester.gov.uk

Leisure and Cultural Services: Ms Eloise Appleby, Assistant Director - Economic Prosperity, City Offices, Colebrook Street, Winchester SO23 9LJ ☎ 01962 848181 🖷 01962 848101 ✉ eappleby@winchester.gov.uk

Licensing: Mr John Myall, Licensing & Registration Officer, City Offices, Colebrook Street, Winchester SO23 9LJ ☎ 01962 848188 ✉ jmyall@winchester.gov.uk

Lifelong Learning: Mrs Marian Ives, Training & Development Advisor, City Offices, Colebrook Street, Winchester SO23 9LJ ☎ 01962 840222 🖷 01962 841365 ✉ mives@winchester.gov.uk

Lighting: Mr Neville Crisp, Assistant Engineer (Traffic), City Offices, Colebrook Street, Winchester SO23 9LJ ☎ 01962 848484 ✉ ncrisp@winchester.gov.uk

Lottery Funding, Charity and Voluntary: Mrs Lorraine Ronan, Community Wellbeing Manager, City Offices, Colebrook Street, Winchester SO23 9LJ ☎ 01962 848369 🖷 01962 841365 ✉ lronan@winchester.gov.uk

Member Services: Mr Christopher Ashcroft, Head of Democratic Services, City Offices, Colebrook Street, Winchester SO23 9LJ ☎ 01962 848284 🖷 01962 848555 ✉ cashcroft@winchester.gov.uk

Parking: Mr Richard Hein, Parking Manager, City Offices, Colebrook Street, Winchester SO23 9LJ ☎ 01962 848346 ✉ rhein@winchester.gov.uk

Partnerships: Ms Jen Anderson, Assistant Director - Active Communities, City Offices, Colebrook Street, Winchester SO23 9LJ ☎ 01962 848592 🖷 01962 840586 ✉ janderson@winchester.gov.uk

Personnel / HR: Ms Alison Gavin, Head of Organisational Development, City Offices, Colebrook Street, Winchester SO23 9LJ ☎ 01962 840222 🖷 01962 841365 ✉ agavin@winchester.gov.uk

Planning: Mr Simon Finch, Head of Planning Control, City Offices, Colebrook Street, Winchester SO23 9LJ ☎ 01962 840551 ✉ sfinch@winchester.gov.uk

Planning: Mr Steve Opacic, Head of Strategic Planning, City Offices, Colebrook Street, Winchester SO23 9LJ ☎ 01962 848101 ✉ sopacic@winchester.gov.uk

Planning: Mr Steve Tilbury, Corporate Director - Operations, City

Offices, Colebrook Street, Winchester SO23 9LJ ☎ 01962 848256 🖷 01962 848101 ✉ stilbury@winchester.gov.uk

Procurement: Mr Nigel Green, Procurement Officer, City Offices, Colebrook Street, Winchester SO23 9LJ ☎ 01962 848356 🖷 01962 848208 ✉ nigel.green@winchester.gov.uk

Recycling & Waste Minimisation: Mr Martin Taylor, Waste Management / Street Scene Team Leader, City Offices, Colebrook Street, Winchester SO23 9LJ ☎ 01962 848540 🖷 01962 848272 ✉ mtaylor@winchester.gov.uk

Regeneration: Ms Jen Anderson, Assistant Director - Active Communities, City Offices, Colebrook Street, Winchester SO23 9LJ ☎ 01962 848592 🖷 01962 840586 ✉ janderson@winchester.gov.uk

Staff Training: Ms Alison Gavin, Head of Organisational Development, City Offices, Colebrook Street, Winchester SO23 9LJ ☎ 01962 840222 🖷 01962 841365 ✉ agavin@winchester.gov.uk

Street Scene: Mr Andy Hickman, Head of Access & Infrastructure, City Offices, Colebrook Street, Winchester SO23 9LJ ☎ 01962 840222 🖷 01962 848232 ✉ ahickman@winchester.gov.uk

Sustainable Communities: Ms Jen Anderson, Assistant Director - Active Communities, City Offices, Colebrook Street, Winchester SO23 9LJ ☎ 01962 848592 🖷 01962 840586 ✉ janderson@winchester.gov.uk

Tourism: Ms Ellen Simpson, Head of Tourism, City Offices, Colebrook Street, Winchester SO23 9LJ ☎ 01962 848219 🖷 01962 848101 ✉ esimpson@winchester.gov.uk

Town Centre: Mr Keith Wilson, Town Centre Manager, City Offices, Colebrook Street, Winchester SO23 9LJ ☎ 01962 841000 ✉ keith.wilson@wincity.uk.com

Traffic Management: Mr Andy Hickman, Head of Access & Infrastructure, City Offices, Colebrook Street, Winchester SO23 9LJ ☎ 01962 840222 🖷 01962 848232 ✉ ahickman@winchester.gov.uk

Transport: Mr Andy Hickman, Head of Access & Infrastructure, City Offices, Colebrook Street, Winchester SO23 9LJ ☎ 01962 840222 🖷 01962 848232 ✉ ahickman@winchester.gov.uk

Transport: Mr Dave Howarth, Exchequer Services Manager, City Offices, Colebrook Street, Winchester SO23 9LJ ☎ 01962 848157 🖷 01962 841365 ✉ dhowarth@winchester.gov.uk

Transport Planner: Mr Andy Hickman, Head of Access & Infrastructure, City Offices, Colebrook Street, Winchester SO23 9LJ ☎ 01962 840222 🖷 01962 848232 ✉ ahickman@winchester.gov.uk

Waste Collection and Disposal: Mr Brian Turner, Environmental Services Manager - Contracts, Penns Place, Petersfield GU31 4EX ☎ 01730 234283; 01730 234383 ✉ brian.turner@easthants.gov.uk

Waste Management: Mr Brian Turner, Environmental Services Manager - Contracts, Penns Place, Petersfield GU31 4EX ☎ 01730 234283; 01730 234383 ✉ brian.turner@easthants.gov.uk

MEMBERS OF THE COUNCIL (57)

***Group Leader:* Clear**, Angela (LD - Wickham)
aclear@winchester.gov.uk

***Group Leader:* Gemmell**, Linda (CON - Shedfield)
lgemmell@winchester.gov.uk

Achwal, Vivian (LD - Whiteley)
vachwal@winchester.gov.uk

Banister, Lynda (LD - Olivers Battery and Badger Farm)
lbanister@winchester.gov.uk

Berry, Eileen (CON - St Barnabas)
eberry@winchester.gov.uk

Berry, Janet (LAB - St John and All Saints)
jberry@winchester.gov.uk

Bodtger, Norma (CON - Upper Meon Valley)
nbodtger@winchester.gov.uk

Byrnes, James (CON - Littleton and Harestock)
jbyrnes@winchester.gov.uk

Chamberlain, Colin (IND - Bishops Waltham)
cchamberlain@winchester.gov.uk

Coates, Tony (CON - Droxford, Soberton and Hambledon)
tcoates@winchester.gov.uk

Collin, Brian (LD - St John and All Saints)
bcollin@winchester.gov.uk

Cook, Simon (LD - The Alresfords)
scook@winchester.gov.uk

Cutler, Neil (LD - Boarhunt and Southwick)
ncutler@winchester.gov.uk

Evans, Therese (LD - Wickham)
tevans@winchester.gov.uk

Godfrey, Stephen (CON - Wonston and Milcheldever)
sgodfrey@winchester.gov.uk

Gottlieb, Kim (CON - Itchen Valley)
kgottlieb@winchester.gov.uk

Green, Derek (CON - St Luke)
dgreen@winchester.gov.uk

Henry, Daryl (LD - Colden Common and Twyford)
dhenry@winchester.gov.uk

Hiscock, Dominic (LD - St Bartholomew)
dhiscock@winchester.gov.uk

Humby, Robert (CON - Owslebury and Curdridge)
rhumby@winchester.gov.uk

Hutchison, Robert (LD - St Paul)
rhutchison@winchester.gov.uk

Huxstep, Roger (CON - Shedfield)
rhuxstep@winchester.gov.uk

Izard, Richard (LD - Colden Common and Twyford)
rizard@winchester.gov.uk

Jeffs, Ernest (CON - The Alresfords)
ejeffs@winchester.gov.uk

Johnston, Robert (LD - Kings Worthy)
rjohnston@winchester.gov.uk

Laming, Brian (LD - Olivers Battery and Badger Farm)
blaming@winchester.gov.uk

Learney, Kelsie (LD - Littleton and Harestock)
klearney@winchester.gov.uk

Lipscomb, Barry (CON - Wonston and Micheldever)
blipscomb@winchester.gov.uk

Mason, Peter (LD - Colden Common and Tywford)
pmason@winchester.gov.uk

Mather, Fiona (CON - St Michael)
fmather@winchester.gov.uk

Maynard, James (LD - St Batholomew)
jmaynard@winchester.gov.uk
McLean, David (CON - Bishops Waltham)
dmclean@winchester.gov.uk
Miller, Steve (CON - Bishops Waltham)
smiller@winchester.gov.uk
Nelmes, Sue (LD - St Bartholomew)
snelmes@winchester.gov.uk
Newman-McKie, Sam (LD - Whiteley)
snewmanmckie@winchester.gov.uk
Pearce, Raymond (LD - St Paul)
rpearce@winchester.gov.uk
Pearson, Frank (CON - Swanmore and Newtown)
fpearson@winchester.gov.uk
Phillips, Kirk (CON - Denmead)
kphillips@winchester.gov.uk
Pines, Chris (LAB - St John and All Saints)
cpines@winchester.gov.uk
Power, Margot (LD - The Alresfords)
mpower@winchester.gov.uk
Prowse, Rose (LD - St Luke)
rprowse@winchester.gov.uk
Read, Michael (CON - Denmead)
mread@winchester.gov.uk
Ruffell, Laurence (CON - Owlesbury and Culdridge)
lruffell@winchester.gov.uk
Rutter, Jane (LD - Kings Worthy)
jrutter@winchester.gov.uk
Sanders, Robert (CON - St Michael)
rsanders@winchester.gov.uk
Scott, Jamie (CON - St Luke)
jscott@winchester.gov.uk
Southgate, Mike (CON - Compton and Otterbourne)
msouthgate@winchester.gov.uk
Stallard, Patricia (CON - Denmead)
pstallard@winchester.gov.uk
Tait, Ian (CON - St Michael)
itait@winchester.gov.uk
Tod, Martin (LD - St Paul)
mtod@winchester.gov.uk
Verney, Harry (CON - Cheriton and Bishops Sutton)
hverney@winchester.gov.uk
Warwick, Jan (CON - Compton and Otterbourne)
jwarwick@winchester.gov.uk
Weir, Anne (LD - St Barnabas)
aweir@winchester.gov.uk
Weston, Victoria (CON - Swanmore and Newtown)
vweston@winchester.gov.uk
Witt, Susan (LD - St Barnabas)
switt@winchester.gov.uk
Wood, Keith (CON - Sparsholt)
kwood@winchester.gov.uk
Wright, Malcolm (CON - Wonston and Micheldever)
mwright@winchester.gov.uk

POLITICAL COMPOSITION
CON: 29, LD: 25, LAB: 2, IND: 1

CABINET
Leader: Mr Keith Wood
Deputy Leader / Strategic Planning & Economic Development: Mr Robert Humby
Communities, Culture & Sport: Mrs Patricia Stallard
Environment: Mr Roger Huxstep
Finance & Administration: Mr Stephen Godfrey
Housing: Mr Tony Coates
New Homes Delivery: Mr Ian Tait
Planning & Transport: Mrs Victoria Weston

COMMITTEE CHAIRS
Audit: Ms Lynda Banister
Licensing & Regulation: Mrs Fiona Mather
Overview & Scrutiny: Mr Chris Pines
Personnel: Mr Barry Lipscomb
Planning & Development Control: Mr Ernest Jeffs
Standards: Mr Michael Read

WINDSOR & MAIDENHEAD U

The Royal Borough of Windsor & Maidenhead, Town Hall, St. Ives Road, Maidenhead SL6 1RF ☎ 01628 798888 🖷 01628 796408 🖳 www.rbwm.gov.uk

FACTS & FIGURES
Police Authority: Thames Valley Police Authority
Health Authority: South Central Strategic Health Authority
Learning and Skills Council: South East
Parliamentary Constituencies: Maidenhead, Windsor
EU Constituencies: South East
Election Frequency: Elections are of whole council
Twinning: Bonn-Bad Godesberg (Germany); Frascati (Italy); Goslar (Germany); Kortrijk (Belgium); Nueilly-sur-Seine (France); Saint-Cloud (France)

PRINCIPAL OFFICERS
Chief Executive: Mr David Oram, Chief Executive, Town Hall, St. Ives Road, Maidenhead SL6 1RF ☎ 01628 796016 🖷 01628 796016 ✉ david.oram@rbwm.gov.uk

Senior Management: Mr Mike McGaughrin, Chief Operating Officer, Town Hall, St. Ives Road, Maidenhead SL6 1RF ☎ 01628 796484 🖷 01628 685805 ✉ mike.mcgaughrin@rbwm.gov.uk

Senior Management: Ms Christabel Shawcross, Strategic Director of Adult & Community Services, Town Hall, St. Ives Road, Maidenhead SL6 1RF ☎ 01628 796159 🖷 01628 683700 ✉ christabel.shawcross@rbwm.gov.uk

Senior Management: Mr Cliff Turner, Strategic Director of Children's Services, Town Hall, St. Ives Road, Maidenhead SL6 1RF ☎ 01628 796367 🖷 01628 683700 ✉ cliff.turner@rbwm.gov.uk

Access Officer / Social Services (Disability): Mr Andrew Small, Safeguarding Manager, York House, Sheet Street, Windsor SL4 4LR ☎ 01628 683710 ✉ access.services@rbwm.gov.uk

Access Officer / Social Services (Disability): Mrs Debbie Verity, Learning Difficulties & Disabilities Service Manager, York House, Sheet Street, Windsor SL4 1DD ☎ 01628 683680 ✉ debbie.verity@rbwm.gov.uk

Architect, Building / Property Services: Mr Rob Packham, Building Services Manager, Town Hall, St. Ives Road, Maidenhead SL6 1RF ☎ 01628 796773 ✉ rob.packham@rbwm.gov.uk

Best Value: Mr Andrew Elkington, Head of Policy & Performance, Town Hall, St. Ives Road, Maidenhead SL6 1RF ☎ 01628 796025 ✉ andrew.elkington@rbwm.gov.uk

Building Control: Mr Jason White, Building Control Consultancy Manager, Town Hall, St. Ives Road, Maidenhead SL6 1RF ☎ 01628 796880 ✉ jason.white@rbwm.gov.uk

Children / Youth Services: Mr David Scott, Head of Services for Families & Young People, Town Hall, St. Ives Road, Maidenhead SL6 1RF ☎ 01628 796748 ✉ david.scott@rbwm.gov.uk

Civil Registration: Ms Clair Williams, Superintendent Registrar, Town Hall, St. Ives Road, Maidenhead SL6 1RF ☎ 01628 796101 ✉ clair.williams@rbwm.gov.uk

PR / Communications: Mrs Anne Dackombe, Senior Press / Public Relations Officer, Town Hall, St. Ives Road, Maidenhead SL6 1RF ☎ 01628 796410 ✉ anne.dackombe@rbwm.gov.uk

Community Planning: Mr Simon Hurrell, Head of Planning & Development, Town Hall, St. Ives Road, Maidenhead SL6 1RF ☎ 01628 685712 ✉ simon.hurrell@rbwm.gov.uk

Community Safety: Mr Brian Martin, Community Safety Manager, Town Hall, St Ives Road, Maidenhead SL6 1RF ☎ 01628 796337 ✉ brian.martin@rbwm.gov.uk

Computer Management: Mr Kevin Griffiths, Commercial Manager & Head of ICT, Town Hall, St. Ives Road, Maidenhead SL6 1RF ☎ 01628 796527 ✉ kevin.griffiths@rbwm.gov.uk

Consumer Protection and Trading Standards: Mr Steve Johnson, Trading Standards Manager, York House, Sheet Street, Windsor SL4 1DD ☎ 01628 683555 🖷 01628 683594 ✉ steve.johnson@rbwm.gov.uk

Contracts: Ms Sarah Rayner, Group Procurement & Commissioning Manager, Town Hall, St. Ives Road, Maidenhead SL6 1RF ☎ 01628 796527 ✉ sarah.rayner@rbwm.gov.uk

Customer Service: Ms Alison Anthony, Central Services Manager, Town Hall, St. Ives Road, Maidenhead SL6 1RF ☎ 01628 796000 ✉ alison.anthony@rbwm.gov.uk

Economic Development: Mr Harjit Hunjan, Community & Business Partnerships Manager, Town Hall, St. Ives Road, Maidenhead SL6 1RF ☎ 01628 796947 ✉ harjit.hunjan@rbwm.gov.uk

Education: Ms Christabel Shawcross, Strategic Director of Adult & Community Services, Town Hall, St. Ives Road, Maidenhead SL6 1RF ☎ 01628 796159 🖷 01628 683700 ✉ christabel.shawcross@rbwm.gov.uk

Education: Mr Cliff Turner, Strategic Director of Children's Services, St Ives House, St Ives Road, Maidenhead SL6 1RF ☎ 01628 796367 🖷 01628 683700 ✉ cliff.turner@rbwm.gov.uk

E-Government: Mr Kevin Griffiths, Commercial Manager & Head of ICT, Town Hall, St. Ives Road, Maidenhead SL6 1RF ☎ 01628 796527 ✉ kevin.griffiths@rbwm.gov.uk

Electoral Registration: Mrs Wendy Allum, Electoral Administrator, Town Hall, St. Ives Road, Maidenhead SL6 1RF ☎ 01628 685717 ✉ wendy.allum@rbwm.gov.uk

Emergency Planning: Mr Darren Firth, Control Room Services Manager, Tinkers Lane Depot, Tinkers Lane, Windsor SL4 4LR ☎ 01628 796865 🖷 01628 796861 ✉ Darren.firth@rbwm.gov.uk

Energy Management: Mr Martin Fitzpatrick, Energy Awareness Officer, York House, Sheet Street, Windsor SL4 1DD ☎ 01628 683634 ✉ martin.fitzpartick@rbwm.gov.uk

Environmental / Technical Services: Mr Terry Gould, Head of Public Protection, York House, Sheet Street, Windsor SL4 1DD ☎ 01628 683501 ✉ terry.gould@rbwm.gov.uk

Environmental Health: Mr Terry Gould, Head of Public Protection, York House, Sheet Street, Windsor SL4 1DD ☎ 01628 683501 ✉ terry.gould@rbwm.gov.uk

Estates, Property & Valuation: Mr Ralph Brown, Principal Valuer, Town Hall, St. Ives Road, Maidenhead SL6 1RF ☎ 01628 796065 ✉ ralph.brown@rbwm.gov.uk

Facilities: Mr Dean Graham, Front of House Team Leader, Town Hall, St. Ives Road, Maidenhead SL6 1RF ☎ 01628 796409 ✉ dean.graham@rbwm.gov.uk

Finance and Treasurer: Mr Andrew Brooker, Head of Strategic Finance, Town Hall, St. Ives Road, Maidenhead SL6 1RF ☎ 01628 796341 🖷 01628 796224 ✉ andrew.brooker@rbwm.gov.uk

Fleet Management: Mr Mark Green, Fleet Management Officer, York House, Sheet Street, Windsor SL4 1DD ☎ 01628 796821 ✉ mark.green@rbwm.gov.uk

Grounds Maintenance: Mr Stephen Anderson, Outdoor Facilities Manager, York Stream House, St. Ives Road, Maidenhead SL6 1RF ☎ 01628 796279 ✉ stephen.anderson@rbwm.gov.uk

Health and Safety: Mr Phil West, Health & Safety Advisor, Town Hall, St. Ives Road, Maidenhead SL6 1RF ☎ 01628 796000 ✉ phil.west@rbwm.gov.uk

Highways: Mr Stephen Brown, Head of Highways & Engineering Services, St. Ives House, St. Ives Road, Maidenhead SL6 1RF ☎ 01628 796770 ✉ stephen.brown@rbwm.gov.uk

Home Energy Conservation: Mr Martyn Clemence, Housing Project Officer, York House, Sheet Street, Windsor SL4 1DD ☎ 01628 683596 ✉ martyn.clemence@rbwm.gov.uk

Housing: Mr Keith Skerman, Head of Adult Services, York House, Sheet Street, Windsor SL4 1DD ☎ 01628 683701 ✉ keith.skerman@rbwm.gov.uk

Housing Maintenance: Mr Keith Skerman, Head of Adult Services, York House, Sheet Street, Windsor SL4 1DD ☎ 01628 683701 ✉ keith.skerman@rbwm.gov.uk

Local Area Agreement: Mr Andrew Brooker, Head of Strategic Finance, Town Hall, St. Ives Road, Maidenhead SL6 1RF ☎ 01628

796341 🖷 01628 796224 🖱 andrew.brooker@rbwm.gov.uk

Legal: Ms Maria Lucas, Head of Strategic Legal Services, Town Hall, St. Ives Road, Maidenhead SL6 1RF ☎ 01628 796014 🖱 maria.lucas@rbwm.gov.uk

Leisure and Cultural Services: Mr Kevin Mist, Head of Leisure Services, York Stream House, St. Ives Road, Maidenhead SL6 1RF ☎ 01628 796443 🖱 kevin.mist@rbwm.gov.uk

Licensing: Mr Alan Barwise, Licensing Manager, Town Hall, St. Ives Road, Maidenhead SL6 1RF ☎ 01628 685608 🖱 alan.barwise@rwbm.gov.uk

Lifelong Learning: Ms Zena Chittenden, Family & Community Learning Manager, Town Hall, St. Ives Road, Maidenhead SL6 1RF ☎ 01628 686709 🖱 zena.chittenden@rbwm.gov.uk

Lighting: Mr Stephen Brown, Head of Highways & Engineering Services, St. Ives House, St. Ives Road, Maidenhead SL6 1RF ☎ 01628 796770 🖱 stephen.brown@rbwm.gov.uk

Lottery Funding, Charity and Voluntary: Mr Jonathan Adams, Business Manager - Development & Funding, Town Hall, St. Ives Road, Maidenhead SL6 1RF ☎ 01628 682945 🖱 jonathan.adams@rbwm.gov.uk

Member Services: Mr Ian Hunt, Democratic Services Manager, Town Hall, St. Ives Road, Maidenhead SL6 1RF ☎ 01628 796186 🖱 ian.hunt@rbwm.gov.uk

Parking: Mr Neil Walter, Parking Manager, Town Hall, St. Ives Road, Maidenhead SL6 1RF ☎ 01628 796485 🖱 neil.walter@rbwm.gov.uk

Partnerships: Mr Harjit Hunjan, Community & Business Partnerships Manager, Town Hall, St. Ives Road, Maidenhead SL6 1RF ☎ 01628 796947 🖱 harjit.hunjan@rbwm.gov.uk

Personnel / HR: Ms Carol Naismith, Head of Human Resources, Town Hall, St. Ives Road, Maidenhead SL6 1RF ☎ 01628 796992 🖱 carol.naismith@rbwm.gov.uk

Planning: Mr Simon Hurrell, Head of Planning & Development, Town Hall, St. Ives Road, Maidenhead SL6 1RF ☎ 01628 685712 🖱 simon.hurrell@rbwm.gov.uk

Procurement: Ms Sarah Rayner, Group Procurement & Commissioning Manager, Town Hall, St. Ives Road, Maidenhead SL6 1RF ☎ 01628 796527 🖱 sarah.rayner@rbwm.gov.uk

Public Libraries: Mr Mark Taylor, Head of Library, Information Heritage & Arts Service, Maidenhead Library, St. Ives Road, Maidenhead SL6 1RF ☎ 01628 796989 🖱 mark.taylor@rbwm.gov.uk

Recycling & Waste Minimisation: Mr Rowan Ralley, Service Development Officer, Town Hall, St. Ives Road, Maidenhead SL6 1RF ☎ 01628 683556 🖱 rowan.ralley@rbwm.gov.uk

Regeneration: Mr Simon Hurrell, Head of Planning & Development, Town Hall, St. Ives Road, Maidenhead SL6 1RF ☎ 01628 685712 🖱 simon.hurrell@rbwm.gov.uk

Road Safety: Mr Stephen Brown, Head of Highways & Engineering Services, St. Ives House, St. Ives Road, Maidenhead SL6 1RF ☎ 01628 796770 🖱 stephen.brown@rbwm.gov.uk

Social Services: Mr Cliff Turner, Strategic Director of Children's Services, Town Hall, St. Ives Road, Maidenhead SL6 1RF ☎ 01628 796367 🖷 01628 683700 🖱 cliff.turner@rbwm.gov.uk

Social Services (Adult): Ms Christabel Shawcross, Strategic Director of Adult & Community Services, Town Hall, St. Ives Road, Maidenhead SL6 1RF ☎ 01628 796159 🖷 01628 683700 🖱 christabel.shawcross@rbwm.gov.uk

Social Services (Adult): Mr Keith Skerman, Head of Adult Services, York House, Sheet Street, Windsor SL4 1DD ☎ 01628 683701 🖱 keith.skerman@rbwm.gov.uk

Social Services (Children): Ms Heather Andrews, Head of Safeguarding & Specialist Services, St Ives House, St Ives Road, Maidenhead SL6 1RP ☎ 01628 683177 🖱 heather.andrews@rbwm.gov.uk

Staff Training: Ms Alison Anthony, Central Services Manager, Town Hall, St. Ives Road, Maidenhead SL6 1RF ☎ 01628 796000 🖱 alison.anthony@rbwm.gov.uk

Street Scene: Mr David Perkins, Head of Streetcare & Operations, Tinkers Lane Depot, Windsor SL6 1RF ☎ 01628 796860 🖱 david.perkins@rbwm.gov.uk

Sustainable Communities: Mr Terry Gould, Head of Public Protection, York House, Sheet Street, Windsor SL4 1DD ☎ 01628 683501 🖱 terry.gould@rbwm.gov.uk

Sustainable Development: Mr Terry Gould, Head of Public Protection, York House, Sheet Street, Windsor SL4 1DD ☎ 01628 683501 🖱 terry.gould@rbwm.gov.uk

Tourism: Ms Barbara Hunt, Accommodation & Information Manager, York House, Sheet Street, Windsor SL4 1DD ☎ 01628 583909 🖱 barbara.hunt@rbwm.gov.uk

Town Centre: Ms Steph James, Maidenhead Town Manager, Town Hall, St. Ives Road, Maidenhead SL6 1RF ☎ 01628 796128 🖱 steph.james@rbwm.gov.uk

Town Centre: Mr Paul Roach, Windsor Town Manager, York House, Sheet Street, Windsor SL4 1DD ☎ 01753 743921 🖱 paul.roach@rbwm.gov.uk

Traffic Management: Mr Anthony Carr, Traffic & Road Safety Manager, York Stream House, St. Ives Road, Maidenhead SL6 1RF ☎ 01628 796405 🖱 tony.carr@rbwm.gov.uk

Transport: Ms Gail Kenyon, Planning Infrastructure & Transport Policy Manager, York Stream House, St. Ives Road, Maidenhead SL6 1QS ☎ 01628 796157 🖱 gail.kenyon@rbwm.gov.uk

Transport Planner: Ms Gail Kenyon, Planning Infrastructure & Transport Policy Manager, York Stream House, St. Ives Road,

Maidenhead SL6 1QS ☎ 01628 796157
✉ gail.kenyon@rbwm.gov.uk

Total Place: Ms Heather Andrews, Head of Safeguarding & Specialist Services, St. Ives House, St. Ives Road, Maidenhead SL6 1RP ☎ 01628 683177 ✉ heather.andrews@rbwm.gov.uk

Waste Collection and Disposal: Mr Craig Miller, Waste & Environmental Protection Manager, York House, Sheet Street, Windsor SL4 1DD ☎ 01628 683598 ✉ craig.miller@rbwm.gov.uk

Waste Management: Mr Craig Miller, Waste & Environmental Protection Manager, York House, Sheet Street, Windsor SL4 1DD ☎ 01628 683598 ✉ craig.miller@rbwm.gov.uk

Children's Play Areas: Mr Stephen Anderson, Outdoor Facilities Manager, York Stream House, St. Ives Road, Maidenhead SL6 1RF ☎ 01628 796279 ✉ stephen.anderson@rbwm.gov.uk

MEMBERS OF THE COUNCIL (57)

Leader of the Council: **Burbage**, David (CON - Bray)
cllr.burbage@rbwm.gov.uk
Deputy Leader of the Council: **Dudley**, Simon (CON - Maidenhead Riverside)
cllr.dudley@rbwm.gov.uk
Airey, Natasha (CON - Park)
cllr.airey@rbwm.gov.uk
Archer, Sinead (CON - Belmont)
cllr.archer@rbwm.gov.uk
Bateson, Christine (CON - Sunningdale)
cllr.bateson@rbwm.gov.uk
Bathurst, George (CON - Castle Without)
cllr.bathurst@rbwm.gov.uk
Beer, Malcolm (IND - Old Windsor)
cllr.beer@rbwm.gov.uk
Bicknell, Phillip (CON - Park)
cllr.bicknell@rbwm.gov.uk
Brimacombe, Paul (CON - Cox Green)
cllr.brimacombe@rbwm.gov.uk
Bullock, Clive (CON - Cox Green)
cllr.bullock@rbwm.gov.uk
Bursnall, Tom (UKIP - Clewer East)
cllr.bursnall@rbwm.gov.uk
Bursnall, Catherine (UKIP - Castle Without)
cllr.c.bursnall@rbwm.gov.uk
Comber, Peter (CON - Sunninghill and South Ascot)
cllr.comber@rbwm.gov.uk
Coppinger, David (CON - Bray)
cllr.coppinger@rbwm.gov.uk
Cox, Carwyn (CON - Hurley and Walthams)
cllr.cox@rbwm.gov.uk
Endacott, Cynthia (R - Clewer North)
cllr.endacott@rbwm.gov.uk
Evans, David (CON - Hurley and Walthams)
cllr.d.evans@rbwm.gov.uk
Evans, James (CON - Clewer South)
cllr.j.evans@rbwm.gov.uk
Evans, Sue (CON - Castle Without)
cllr.s.evans@rbwm.gov.uk
Fido, John (R - Clewer North)
cllr.fido@rbwm.gov.uk
Fussey, George (LD - Eton and Castle)
cllr.fussey@rbwm.gov.uk
Grey, Jesse (CON - Datchet)
cllr.grey@rbwm.gov.uk
Harris, Christian (CON - Boyn Hill)
cllr.harris@rbwm.gov.uk
Hendry, Wilson (CON - Pinkneys Green)
cllr.hendry@rbwm.gov.uk
Hill, Geoffrey (CON - Oldfield)
cllr.hill@rbwm.gov.uk
Hilton, David (CON - Ascot and Cheapside)
cllr.hilton@rbwm.gov.uk
Hollingsworth, Charles (CON - Pinkneys Green)
cllr.hollingsworth@rbwm.gov.uk
Hunt, Maureen (CON - Hurley and Walthams)
cllr.hunt@rbwm.gov.uk
Ilyas, Mohammed (CON - Furze Platt)
cllr.ilyas@rbwm.gov.uk
Jenner, Andrew (CON - Maidenhead Riverside)
cllr.jenner@rbwm.gov.uk
Jones, Lynne (R - Old Windsor)
cllr.jones@rbwm.gov.uk
Kellaway, Richard (CON - Bisham and Cookham)
cllr.kellaway@rbwm.gov.uk
Lawless, Peter (CON - Eton Wick)
cllr.lawless@rbwm.gov.uk
Lenton, John (CON - Horton and Wraysbury)
cllr.lenton@rbwm.gov.uk
Lion, Paul (CON - Boyn Hill)
cllr.lion@rbwm.gov.uk
Love, Philip (CON - Belmont)
cllr.love@rbwm.gov.uk
Luxton, Sayonara (CON - Sunningdale)
cllr.luxton@rbwm.gov.uk
Majeed, Ashgar (CON - Oldfield)
cllr.majeed@rbwm.gov.uk
McBride, Duncan (CON - Ascot and Cheapside)
cllr.mcbride@rbwm.gov.uk
Meadowcroft, Simon (CON - Clewer South)
cllr.meadowcroft@rbwm.gov.uk
Mellins, Alan (CON - Cox Green)
cllr.mellins@rbwm.gov.uk
Mills, Marion (CON - Belmont)
cllr.mills@rbwm.gov.uk
Muir, Gary (CON - Datchet)
cllr.muir@rbwm.gov.uk
Newbound, Kathy (LD - Pinkneys Green)
cllr.newbound@rbwm.gov.uk
Penfold, John (R - Clewer North)
cllr.penfold@rbwm.gov.uk
Quick, Eileen (CON - Clewer East)
cllr.quick@rbwm.gov.uk
Rayner, Colin (CON - Horton and Wraysbury)
cllr.rayner@rbwm.gov.uk
Saunders, MJ (CON - Bisham and Cookham)
cllr.saunders@rbwm.gov.uk
Sharma, Hari (CON - Furze Platt)
cllr.sharma@rbwm.gov.uk
Sharp, Derek (CON - Furze Platt)
cllr.sharp@rbwm.gov.uk
Smith, Adam (CON - Maidenhead Riverside)
cllr.smith@rbwm.gov.uk
Story, John (CON - Sunninghill and South Ascot)
cllr.story@rbwm.gov.uk
Stretton, John (CON - Bisham and Cookham)
cllr.stretton@rbwm.gov.uk
Stretton, Claire (CON - Boyn Hill)
cllr.claire.stretton@rbwm.gov.uk

Walters, Leo (CON - Bray)
cllr.walters@rbwm.gov.uk
Wilson, Derek (CON - Oldfield)
cllr.d.wilson@rbwm.gov.uk
Yong, Lynda (CON - Sunninghill and South Ascot)
cllr.yong@rbwm.gov.uk

POLITICAL COMPOSITION
CON: 48, R: 4, UKIP: 2, LD: 2, IND: 1

CABINET
Leader: Mr David Burbage
Deputy Leader / Adult & Community Services: Mr Simon Dudley
Children's Services: Mrs Eileen Quick
Finance: Mr Richard Kellaway
Highways, Transport & Environment: Mr Phillip Bicknell
Planning & Partnerships: Ms Christine Bateson
Policy & Performance: Mr MJ Saunders

COMMITTEE CHAIRS
Audit & Performance Review: Mr Duncan McBride
Berkshire Pension Fund: Mr John Lenton
Children's Services Overview & Scrutiny: Mr James Evans
Corporate Services: Mr Christian Harris
Employement: Mr David Burbage
Licensing: Mr Andrew Jenner
Maidenhead Development Control: Mr Derek Wilson
Sustainability: Mr David Coppinger
Windsor Rural Development Control: Ms Christine Bateson
Windsor Urban Development Control: Mrs Eileen Quick

WIRRAL M

Wirral Metropolitan Borough Council, (Wirrall Council), Wallasey Town Hall, Brighton Street, Wallasey, Wirral CH44 8ED ☎ 0151 606 2000 🖷 0151 691 8468 ✉ comments@wirral.gov.uk
💻 www.wirral.gov.uk

FACTS & FIGURES
Police Authority: Merseyside Police Authority
Health Authority: North West Strategic Health Authority
Learning and Skills Council: North West
Parliamentary Constituencies: Birkenhead, Wallasey, Wirral South, Wirral West
EU Constituencies: North West
Election Frequency: Elections are by thirds
Twinning: Gennevilliers (France); Latina (Italy); Lorient (France)

PRINCIPAL OFFICERS
Chief Executive: Mr Graham Burgess, Chief Executive, Wallasey Town Hall, Brighton Street, Wallasey, Wirral CH44 8ED ☎ 0151 6918589 🖷 0151 691 8273 ✉ grahamburgess@wirral.gov.uk

Deputy Chief Executive: Mr Ian Coleman, Director of Finance & Deputy Chief Executive, PO Box 2, Treasury Building, Cleveland Street, Birkenhead, Wirral CH41 6BU ☎ 0151 666 3056 🖷 0151 666 3058 ✉ iancoleman@wirral.gov.uk

Senior Management: Mr Ian Coleman, Director of Finance & Deputy Chief Executive, PO Box 2, Treasury Building, Cleveland Street, Birkenhead, Wirral CH41 6BU ☎ 0151 666 3056 🖷 0151 666 3058 ✉ iancoleman@wirral.gov.uk

Senior Management: Mr Michael Peet, Service Manager - Traffic and Transport Division (Client Design), Cheshire Lines, Canning Street, Birkenhead CH41 0ND ☎ 0151 606 2000 ✉ michaelpeet@wirral.gov.uk

Access Officer / Social Services (Disability): Mr Ged Smyth, NRAC Auditor, Wallasey Town Hall, Brighton Street, Wallasey, Wirral CH44 8ED ☎ 0151 691 8217 🖷 0151 691 8468 ✉ gerardsmyth@wirral.gov.uk

Architect, Building / Property Services: Mr David Green, Director of Technical Services, Cheshire Lines Building, Canning Street, Birkenhead CH41 1ND ☎ 0151 606 2104 ✉ davidgreen@wirral.gov.uk

Best Value: Mr Jim Wilkie, Chief Executive, Town Hall, Brighton Street, Wallasey CH44 8ED ☎ 0151 691 8183 🖷 0151 691 8273 ✉ jimwilkie@wirral.gov.uk

Building Control: Mr Paul Grey, Assistant Director, Cheshire Lines Building, Canning Street, Birkenhead CH41 1ND ☎ 0151 606 2128 🖷 0151 691 8468 ✉ paulgrey@wirral.gov.uk

Children / Youth Services: Mr David Armstrong, Interim Director of Children's Services, Hamilton Buildings, Conway Street, Birkenhead CH41 4FD ☎ 0151 666 4288 🖷 0151 666 4207 ✉ davidarmstrong@wirral.gov.uk

Civil Registration: Ms Suzanne Johnston, Superintendent Registrar, Town Hall, Brighton Street, Wallasey CH44 8ED ☎ 0151 666 3679 🖷 0151 691 8468 ✉ suzannejohnston@wirral.gov.uk

PR / Communications: Ms Emma Degg, Interim Head of Planning, Engagement & Communications, Wallasey Town Hall, Brighton Street, Wallasey, Wirral CH44 8ED ☎ 0151 691 8688 🖷 0151 691 8361 ✉ emmadegg@wirral.gov.uk

Community Planning: Mr Jim Wilkie, Chief Executive, Town Hall, Brighton Street, Wallasey CH44 8ED ☎ 0151 691 8183 🖷 0151 691 8273 ✉ jimwilkie@wirral.gov.uk

Community Safety: Mr Ian Lowrie, Volume Property Crime Manager, Westminster House, Hamilton Street, Birkenhead, Wirral CH41 5FW ☎ 0151 606 5493 🖷 0151 666 5004 ✉ ianlowrie@wirral.gov.uk

Computer Management: Mr Ian Coleman, Director of Finance & Deputy Chief Executive, PO Box 2, Treasury Building, Cleveland Street, Birkenhead, Wirral CH41 6BU ☎ 0151 666 3056 🖷 0151 666 3058 ✉ iancoleman@wirral.gov.uk

Consumer Protection and Trading Standards: Mr Derek Payet, Trading Standards Strategic Manager, Wallasey Town Hall, Brighton Street, Wallasey, Wirral CH44 8ED ☎ 0151 691 8640 🖷 0151 691 8098 ✉ derekpayet@wirral.gov.uk

Contracts: Mr Ian Coleman, Director of Finance & Deputy Chief Executive, Treasury Building, Cleveland Street, Birkenhead CH41 4FD ☎ 0151 666 3056 🖷 0151 666 3058

🖰 iancoleman@wirral.gov.uk

Corporate Services: Mr Jim Wilkie, Chief Executive, Town Hall, Brighton Street, Wallasey CH44 8ED ☏ 0151 691 8183 🖷 0151 691 8273 🖰 jimwilkie@wirral.gov.uk

Customer Service: Mr Ian Coleman, Director of Finance & Deputy Chief Executive, PO Box 2, Treasury Building, Cleveland Street, Birkenhead, Wirral CH41 6BU ☏ 0151 666 3056 🖷 0151 666 3058 🖰 iancoleman@wirral.gov.uk

Customer Service: Mr Malcolm Flanagan, Head of Service, Revenues, Benefits & Customer Services, PO Box 2, Treasury Building, Cleveland Street, Birkenhead CH41 6BU ☏ 0151 606 2000 🖷 0151 666 3379 🖰 malcolmflanagan@wirral.gov.uk

Direct Labour: Mr David Green, Director of Technical Services, Cheshire Lines Building, Canning Street, Birkenhead CH41 1ND ☏ 0151 606 2104 🖰 davidgreen@wirral.gov.uk

Economic Development: Mr Jim Wilkie, Chief Executive, Town Hall, Brighton Street, Wallasey CH44 8ED ☏ 0151 691 8183 🖷 0151 691 8273 🖰 jimwilkie@wirral.gov.uk

Education: Mr David Armstrong, Interim Director of Children's Services, Hamilton Buildings, Conway Street, Birkenhead CH41 4FD ☏ 0151 666 4288 🖷 0151 666 4207 🖰 davidarmstrong@wirral.gov.uk

E-Government: Mr Ian Coleman, Director of Finance & Deputy Chief Executive, PO Box 2, Treasury Building, Cleveland Street, Birkenhead, Wirral CH41 6BU ☏ 0151 666 3056 🖷 0151 666 3058 🖰 iancoleman@wirral.gov.uk

Electoral Registration: Mr Bill Norman, Director of Law, HR & Asset Management, Wallasey Town Hall, Brighton Street, Wallasey, Wirral CH44 8ED ☏ 0151 691 8498 🖷 0151 691 8583 🖰 billnorman@wirral.gov.uk

Emergency Planning: Mr Mark Camborne, Health, Safety & Resilience Manager, Town Hall, Brighton Street, Wallasey, Wirral CH44 8ED ☏ 0151 606 2071 🖰 markcamborne@wirral.gov.uk

Energy Management: Mr Tony Dodd, Energy Manager, Town Hall, South Annexe, Brighton Street, Wallasey CH44 8ED ☏ 0151 606 2354 🖷 0151 691 8354 🖰 tonydodd@wirral.gov.uk

Environmental / Technical Services: Mr David Green, Director of Technical Services, Cheshire Lines Building, Canning Street, Birkenhead CH41 1ND ☏ 0151 606 2104 🖰 davidgreen@wirral.gov.uk

Environmental Health: Mr Robert Beresford, Head of Regulation, Town Hall, Brighton Street, Wallasey CH44 8ED ☏ 0151 691 8208 🖷 0151 666 5215 🖰 robertberesford@wirral.gov.uk

Estates, Property & Valuation: Mr Jim Wilkie, Chief Executive, Town Hall, Brighton Street, Wallasey CH44 8ED ☏ 0151 691 8183 🖷 0151 691 8273 🖰 jimwilkie@wirral.gov.uk

European Liaison: Mr Neil Mitchell, Project Manager, Town Hall, Brighton Street, Wallasey CH44 8ED ☏ 0151 691 8423 🖰 neilmitchell@wirral.gov.uk

Events Manager: Ms Emma Degg, Interim Head of Planning, Engagement & Communications, Town Hall (North Annexe), Brighton Street, Wallasey, Wirral CH44 8ED ☏ 0151 691 8688 🖷 0151 691 8361 🖰 emmadegg@wirral.gov.uk

Facilities: Mr David Green, Director of Technical Services, Cheshire Lines Building, Canning Street, Birkenhead CH41 1ND ☏ 0151 606 2104 🖰 davidgreen@wirral.gov.uk

Finance and Treasurer: Mr Ian Coleman, Director of Finance & Deputy Chief Executive, PO Box 2, Treasury Building, Cleveland Street, Birkenhead, Wirral CH41 6BU ☏ 0151 666 3056 🖷 0151 666 3058 🖰 iancoleman@wirral.gov.uk

Grounds Maintenance: Mr Roger Calvert, Principal Officer - Parks & Countryside, Cheshire Lines Building, Canning Street, Birkenhead CH41 1ND ☏ 0151 666 4701 🖷 0151 606 2418 🖰 rogercalvert@wirral.gov.uk

Health and Safety: Mr Andy McMillan, Principal Corporate Health & Safety Officer, Cheshire Lines Building, Canning Street, Birkenhead CH41 1ND ☏ 0151 606 2364 🖷 0151 606 2188 🖰 andymcmillan@wirral.gov.uk

Highways: Mr Mark Smith, Head of Service - Streetscene & Waste, Cheshire Lines Building, Canning Street, Birkenhead CH41 8ED ☏ 0151 606 2103 🖰 marksmith@wirral.gov.uk

Home Energy Conservation: Mr Tony Dodd, Energy Manager, Town Hall, South Annexe, Brighton Street, Wallasey CH44 8ED ☏ 0151 606 2354 🖷 0151 691 8354 🖰 tonydodd@wirral.gov.uk

Housing: Mr David Ball, Interim Head of Strategic Development & Regeneration, Town Hall, Brighton Street, Wallasey CH44 8ED ☏ 0151 691 8395 🖰 davidball@wirral.gov.uk

Local Area Agreement: Ms Lucy Beed, Corporate Performance Manager, Wallasey Town Hall, Brighton Street, Wallasey, Wirral CH44 8ED ☏ 0151 691 8006 🖰 lucybeed@wirral.gov.uk

Legal: Mr Bill Norman, Director of Law, HR & Asset Management, Wallasey Town Hall, Brighton Street, Wallasey, Wirral CH44 8ED ☏ 0151 691 8498 🖷 0151 691 8583 🖰 billnorman@wirral.gov.uk

Leisure and Cultural Services: Mr Jim Lester, Head of Cultural Services, Cheshire Lines Building, Canning Street, Birkenhead CH41 1ND ☏ ; 0151 666 2082 🖰 jimlester@wirral.gov.uk

Licensing: Mrs Margaret O'Donnell, Licensing Manager, Town Hall, Brighton Street, Wallasey CH44 8ED ☏ 0151 691 8606 🖷 0151 691 8468 🖰 margaretodonnell@wirral.gov.uk

Lifelong Learning: Mr David Armstrong, Interim Director of Children's Services, Hamilton Buildings, Conway Street, Birkenhead CH41 4FD ☏ 0151 666 4288 🖷 0151 666 4207 🖰 davidarmstrong@wirral.gov.uk

Lighting: Mr David Green, Director of Technical Services, Cheshire Lines Building, Canning Street, Birkenhead CH41 1ND

☎ 0151 606 2104 ✉ davidgreen@wirral.gov.uk

Lottery Funding, Charity and Voluntary: Mr Jim Wilkie, Chief Executive, Town Hall, Brighton Street, Wallasey CH44 8ED ☎ 0151 691 8183 🖷 0151 691 8273 ✉ jimwilkie@wirral.gov.uk

Member Services: Mr Surjit Tour, Head of Legal & Democratic Services, Wallasey Town Hall, Brighton Street, Wallasey, Wirral CH44 8ED ☎ 0151 691 8569 🖷 0151 691 8468 ✉ surjittour@wirral.gov.uk

Parking: Mr David Green, Director of Technical Services, Cheshire Lines Building, Canning Street, Birkenhead CH41 1ND ☎ 0151 606 2104 ✉ davidgreen@wirral.gov.uk

Personnel / HR: Ms Chris Hyams, Head of Human Resources & Organisational Development, Wallasey Town Hall, Brighton Street, Wallasey, Wirral CH44 8ED ☎ 0151 691 8590 ✉ chrishyams@wirral.gov.uk

Planning: Mr Kevin Adderley, Acting Director of Regeneration, Housing and Planning, Wallasey Town Hall, Brighton Street, Wallasey, Wirral CH44 8ED ☎ 0151 691 8187 ✉ kevinadderley@wirral.gov.uk

Procurement: Mr Ray Williams, Corporate Procurement Manager, Town Hall, Brighton Street, Wallasey, Wirral CH44 8ED ☎ 0151 666 3377 ✉ raywilliams@wirral.gov.uk

Public Libraries: Mr Ian Coleman, Director of Finance & Deputy Chief Executive, PO Box 2, Treasury Building, Cleveland Street, Birkenhead, Wirral CH41 6BU ☎ 0151 666 3056 🖷 0151 666 3058 ✉ iancoleman@wirral.gov.uk

Recycling & Waste Minimisation: Mr David Green, Director of Technical Services, Cheshire Lines Building, Canning Street, Birkenhead CH41 1ND ☎ 0151 606 2104 ✉ davidgreen@wirral.gov.uk

Regeneration: Mr Jim Wilkie, Chief Executive, Town Hall, Brighton Street, Wallasey CH44 8ED ☎ 0151 691 8183 🖷 0151 691 8273 ✉ jimwilkie@wirral.gov.uk

Road Safety: Mr David Green, Director of Technical Services, Cheshire Lines Building, Canning Street, Birkenhead CH41 1ND ☎ 0151 606 2104 ✉ davidgreen@wirral.gov.uk

Social Services: Mr Graham Hodkinson, Director of Adult Social Services, PO Box 351, Social Services Headquarters, Birkenhead CH25 9EF ☎ 0151 666 3632 🖷 0151 666 3531 ✉ grahamhodkinson@wirral.gov.uk

Social Services (Adult): Mr Graham Hodkinson, Director of Adult Social Services, PO Box 351, Social Services Headquarters, Birkenhead CH25 9EF ☎ 0151 666 3632 🖷 0151 666 3531 ✉ grahamhodkinson@wirral.gov.uk

Social Services (Adult): Mr Graham Hodkinson, Director of Adult Social Services, PO Box 351, Social Services Headquarters, Birkenhead CH25 9EF ☎ 0151 666 3632 🖷 0151 666 3531 ✉ grahamhodkinson@wirral.gov.uk

Social Services (Children): Ms Julia Hassall, Head of Branch (Children's Social Care), Social Services Headquarters, Westminster House, Hamilton Street, Birkenhead CH41 5FN ☎ 0151 666 4293 🖷 0151 666 3531 ✉ juliahassall@wirral.gov.uk

Staff Training: Ms Chris Hyams, Head of Human Resources & Organisational Development, Wallasey Town Hall, Brighton Street, Wallasey, Wirral CH44 8ED ☎ 0151 691 8590 ✉ chrishyams@wirral.gov.uk

Street Scene: Mr David Green, Director of Technical Services, Cheshire Lines Building, Canning Street, Birkenhead CH41 1ND ☎ 0151 606 2104 ✉ davidgreen@wirral.gov.uk

Sustainable Communities: Mr Jim Wilkie, Chief Executive, Town Hall, Brighton Street, Wallasey CH44 8ED ☎ 0151 691 8183 🖷 0151 691 8273 ✉ jimwilkie@wirral.gov.uk

Sustainable Development: Mr David Green, Director of Technical Services, Cheshire Lines Building, Canning Street, Birkenhead CH41 1ND ☎ 0151 606 2104 ✉ davidgreen@wirral.gov.uk

Tourism: Ms Emma Degg, Interim Head of Planning, Engagement & Communications, Town Hall (North Annexe), Brighton Street, Wallasey, Wirral CH44 8ED ☎ 0151 691 8688 🖷 0151 691 8361 ✉ emmadegg@wirral.gov.uk

Traffic Management: Mr David Green, Director of Technical Services, Cheshire Lines Building, Canning Street, Birkenhead CH41 1ND ☎ 0151 606 2104 ✉ davidgreen@wirral.gov.uk

Transport: Mr David Green, Director of Technical Services, Cheshire Lines Building, Canning Street, Birkenhead CH41 1ND ☎ 0151 606 2104 ✉ davidgreen@wirral.gov.uk

Transport Planner: Mr David Green, Director of Technical Services, Cheshire Lines Building, Canning Street, Birkenhead CH41 1ND ☎ 0151 606 2104 ✉ ; davidgreen@wirral.gov.uk

Waste Collection and Disposal: Mr David Green, Director of Technical Services, Cheshire Lines Building, Canning Street, Birkenhead CH41 1ND ☎ 0151 606 2104 ✉ davidgreen@wirral.gov.uk

Waste Management: Mr David Green, Director of Technical Services, Cheshire Lines Building, Canning Street, Birkenhead CH41 1ND ☎ 0151 606 2104 ✉ davidgreen@wirral.gov.uk

MEMBERS OF THE COUNCIL (66)

***Mayor:* Ellis**, Gerry (CON - Hoylake and Meols)
gerryellis@wirral.gov.uk

***Deputy Mayor:* Mitchell**, Dave (LD - Eastham)
davemitchell@wirral.gov.uk

***Leader of the Council:* Davies**, Phil (LAB - Birkenhead and Tranmere)
phildavies@wirral.gov.uk

***Group Leader:* Green**, Jeff (CON - West Kirby and Thurstaston)
jeffgreen@wirral.gov.uk

***Group Leader:* Harney**, Tom (LD - Eastham)
tomharney@wirral.gov.uk

Abbey, Ron (LAB - Leasowe and Moreton East)
ronabbey@wirral.gov.uk

Blakeley, Chris (CON - Moreton West and Saughall Massie)
chrisblakeley@wirral.gov.uk
Boult, Eddie (CON - Hoylake and Meols)
Eddieboult@wirral.gov.uk
Brighouse, Alan (LD - Oxton)
alanbrighouse@wirral.gov.uk
Clements, Wendy (CON - Greasby, Frankby and Irby)
Wendyclements@wirral.gov.uk
Cox, Tony (CON - Greasby, Frankby and Irby)
tonycox@wirral.gov.uk
Crabtree, Jim (LAB - Bidston and St James)
jimcrabtree@wirral.gov.uk
Davies, Bill (LAB - Rock Ferry)
billdavies@wirral.gov.uk
Davies, George (LAB - Claughton)
georgedavies@wirral.gov.uk
Dodd, Darren (LAB - Liscard)
darrengdodd@wirral.gov.uk
Doughty, Paul (LAB - Prenton)
pauldoughty@wirral.gov.uk
Elderton, David (CON - West Kirby and Thurstaston)
davidelderton@wirral.gov.uk
Foulkes, Steve (LAB - Claughton)
stevefoulkes@wirral.gov.uk
Fraser, Leah (CON - Wallasey)
leahfraser@wirral.gov.uk
Gilchrist, Phil (LD - Eastham)
philgilchrist@wirral.gov.uk
Glasman, Patricia (LAB - New Brighton)
patriciaglasman@wirral.gov.uk
Gregson, Robert (LAB - New Brighton)
robgregson@wirral.gov.uk
Hackett, Pat (LAB - New Brighton)
pathackett@wirral.gov
Hale, John (CON - Hoylake and Meols)
johnhale@wirral.gov.uk
Hayes, Paul (CON - Wallasey)
paulhayes@wirral.gov.uk
Hodrien, Sylvia (LAB - Upton)
sylviahodrien@wirral.gov.uk
Hodson, Andrew (CON - Heswall)
andrewhodson@wirral.gov.uk
Hornby, Mike (CON - Greasby, Frankby and Irby)
mikehornby@wirral.gov.uk
Johnson, Peter (CON - Heswall)
peterjohnson@wirral.gov.uk
Johnston, Mark (LD - Pensby and Thingwall)
markjohnston@wirral.gov.uk
Jones, Adrian (LAB - Seacombe)
adrianjones@wirral.gov.uk
Jones, Chris (LAB - Seacombe)
christinejones@wirral.gov.uk
Kearney, Peter (CON - Clatterbridge)
peterkearney@wirral.gov.uk
Kelly, Stuart (LD - Oxton)
stuartkelly@wirral.gov.uk
Kenny, Brian (LAB - Birkenhead and Tranmere)
briankenny@wirral.gov.uk
Leech, Anita (LAB - Leasowe & Moreton East Ward)
anitaleech@wirral.gov.uk
McArdle, Anne (LAB - Leasowe and Moreton East)
annemcardle@wirral.gov.uk
McCubbin, Don (CON - Pensby and Thingwall)
donmccubbin@wirral.gov.uk
McLachlan, Ann (LAB - Bidston and St James)
annmclachlan@wirral.gov.uk
McLaughlin, Moira (LAB - Rock Ferry)
moiramclaughlin@wirral.gov.uk
Meaden, Chris (LAB - Rock Ferry)
chrismeaden@wirral.gov.uk
Mooney, Bernie (LAB - Liscard)
berniemooney@wirral.gov.uk
Mountney, Simon (CON - Moreton West and Saughall Massie)
simonmountney@wirral.gov.uk
Muspratt, Christina (LAB - Bebington)
christinamuspratt@wirral.gov.uk
Niblock, Steve (LAB - Bromborough)
steveniblock@wirral.gov.uk
Norbury, Tony (LAB - Prenton)
tonynorbury@wirral.gov.uk
Povall, Cherry (CON - Clatterbridge)
cherrypovall@wirral.gov.uk
Realey, Denise (LAB - Prenton)
deniserealey@wirral.gov.uk
Rennie, Lesley (CON - Wallasey)
lesleyrennie@wirral.gov.uk
Roberts, Denise (LAB - Claughton)
deniseroberts@wirral.gov.uk
Rowlands, Les (CON - Heswall)
lesrowlands@wirral.gov.uk
Salter, John (LAB - Seacombe)
johnsalter@wirral.gov.uk
Smith, Harry (LAB - Bidston and St James)
harrysmith@wirral.gov.uk
Smith, Walter (LAB - Bebington)
waltersmith@wirral.gov.uk
Smith, Tony (LAB - Upton)
tonysmith@wirral.gov.uk
Stapleton, Jean (LAB - Birkenhead and Tranmere)
jeanstapleton@wirral.gov.uk
Sullivan, Michael (LAB - Pensby & Thingwall)
mikesullivan@wirral.gov.uk
Sykes, Adam (CON - Clatterbridge)
adamsykes@wirral.gov.uk
Walsh, Joe (LAB - Bromborough)
joewalsh@wirral.gov.uk
Watt, Geoffrey (CON - West Kirby and Thurstaston)
geoffreywatt@wirral.gov.uk
Whittingham, Stuart (LAB - Upton)
stuartw@labour4wirral.gov.uk
Williams, Jerry (LAB - Bebington)
jerrywilliams@wirral.gov.uk
Williams, Patricia (LD - Oxton)
patwilliams@wirral.gov.uk
Williams, Steve (CON - Moreton West and Saughall Massie)
stevewilliams@wirral.gov.uk
Williams, Irene (LAB - Bromborough)
irenewilliams@wirral.gov.uk
Williamson, Janette (LAB - Liscard)
janettewilliamson@wirral.gov.uk

POLITICAL COMPOSITION

LAB: 37, CON: 22, LD: 7

CABINET

Leader / Finance: Mr Phil Davies
Deputy Leader / Improvement & Governance: Ms Ann McLachlan
Adult Social Care & Public Health: Ms Anne McArdle

Children's Services & Lifelong Learning: Mr Tony Smith
Corporate Resources: Mr Adrian Jones
Culture, Tourism & Leisure: Mrs Chris Meaden
Environment: Mr Brian Kenny
Housing & Community Safety: Mr George Davies
Regeneration & Planning Strategy: Mr Pat Hackett
Streetscene & Transport Services: Mr Harry Smith

COMMITTEE CHAIRS

Audit & Risk Management: Mr Jim Crabtree
Children & Young People Overview & Scrutiny: Ms Wendy Clements
Economy & Regeneration Overview & Scrutiny: Mr Mark Johnston
Employment & Appointments: Mr Paul Doughty
Health & Wellbeing Overview & Scrutiny: Mr Simon Mountney
Highway & Traffic: Mr John Hale
Licensing, Health & Safety & General Purposes: Mr Bill Davies
Pensions: Ms Patricia Glasman
Planning: Ms Bernie Mooney
Scrutiny Programme: Mr Andrew Hodson
Standards: Mr Bill Davies
Sustainable Communities Overview & Scrutiny: Mr David Elderton

WOKING D

Woking Borough Council, Civic Offices, Gloucester Square, Woking GU21 6YL ☎ 01483 755855 🖷 01483 768746 ✉ wokbc@woking.gov.uk 🖳 www.woking.gov.uk

FACTS & FIGURES

Police Authority: Surrey Police Authority
Health Authority: South East Coast Strategic Health Authority
Learning and Skills Council: South East
Parliamentary Constituencies: Woking
EU Constituencies: South East
Election Frequency: Elections are by thirds
Twinning: Amstelveen (Netherlands); Le Plessis-Robinson (France); Rastatt (Germany)

PRINCIPAL OFFICERS

Chief Executive: Mr Ray Morgan, Chief Executive, Civic Offices, Gloucester Square, Woking GU21 6YL ☎ 01483 743051 🖷 01483 768746 ✉ ray.morgan@woking.gov.uk

Deputy Chief Executive: Mr Douglas Spinks, Deputy Chief Executive, Civic Offices, Gloucester Square, Woking GU21 6YL ☎ 01483 743783 🖷 01483 768746 ✉ douglas.spinks@woking.gov.uk

Senior Management: Ms Sue Barham, Strategic Director, Civic Offices, Gloucester Square, Woking GU21 6YL ☎ 01483 743810 🖷 01483 725318 ✉ sue.barham@woking.gov.uk

Senior Management: Mr Steve Bonsor, Strategic Director, Civic Offices, Gloucester Square, Woking GU21 6YL ☎ 01483 743221 🖷 01483 724032 ✉ steve.bonsor@woking.gov.uk

Senior Management: Mr Mark Rolt, Strategic Director, Civic Offices, Gloucester Square, Woking GU21 6YL ☎ 01483 743050 🖷 01483 768746 ✉ mark.rolt@woking.gov.uk

Access Officer / Social Services (Disability): Ms Rafeia Zaman, Senior Policy Officer (Equality & Diversity), Civic Offices, Gloucester Square, Woking GU21 6YL ☎ 01483 743479 🖷 01483 756842 ✉ rafeia.zaman@woking.gov.uk

Architect, Building / Property Services: Ms Diane Spencer, Asset Manager, Civic Offices, Gloucester Square, Woking GU21 6YL ☎ 01483 743552 🖷 01483 723580 ✉ diane.spencer@woking.gov.uk

Best Value: Mr David Johnson, Corporate Strategy Manager, Civic Offices, Gloucester Square, Woking GU21 6YL ☎ 01483 743060 🖷 01483 756842 ✉ david.johnson@woking.gov.uk

Building Control: Mr David Edwards, Chief Building Control Surveyor, Civic Offices, Gloucester Square, Woking GU21 6YL ☎ 01483 743430 🖷 01483 776298 ✉ david.edwards@woking.gov.uk

Children / Youth Services: Ms Sue Barham, Strategic Director, Civic Offices, Gloucester Square, Woking GU21 6YL ☎ 01483 743810 🖷 01483 725318 ✉ sue.barham@woking.gov.uk

PR / Communications: Mr Andy Denner, Acting Marketing Communications Manager, Civic Offices, Gloucester Square, Woking GU21 6YL ☎ 01483 743024 🖷 01483 743055 ✉ andy.denner@woking.gov.uk

Community Planning: Ms Sue Barham, Strategic Director, Civic Offices, Gloucester Square, Woking GU21 6YL ☎ 01483 743810 🖷 01483 725318 ✉ sue.barham@woking.gov.uk

Community Safety: Mrs Camilla Edmiston, Community Safety Officer, Civic Offices, Gloucester Square, Woking GU21 6YL ☎ 01483 743080 🖷 01483 743055 ✉ camilla.edmiston@woking.gov.uk

Computer Management: Mrs Adele Devon, ICT Manager, Civic Offices, Gloucester Square, Woking GU21 6YL ☎ 01483 743279 🖷 01483 768746 ✉ adele.devon@woking.gov.uk

Corporate Services: Mr David Johnson, Corporate Strategy Manager, Civic Offices, Gloucester Square, Woking GU21 6YL ☎ 01483 743060 🖷 01483 756842 ✉ david.johnson@woking.gov.uk

Customer Service: Mr David Ripley, Revenue & Benefits Manager, Civic Offices, Gloucester Square, Woking GU21 6YL ☎ 01483 743630 ✉ david.ripley@woking.gov.uk

Economic Development: Mr David Johnson, Corporate Strategy Manager, Civic Offices, Gloucester Square, Woking GU21 6YL ☎ 01483 743060 🖷 01483 756842 ✉ david.johnson@woking.gov.uk

E-Government: Ms Adele Devon, IT Manager, Civic Offices, Gloucester Square, Woking GU21 6YL ☎ 01483 743279 🖷 01483 768746 ✉ adele.devon@woking.gov.uk

Electoral Registration: Mrs Charlotte Griffiths, Electoral &

Information Services Manager, Civic Offices, Gloucester Square, Woking GU21 6YL ☎ 01483 743215 📠 01483 768746 🖱 charlotte.griffiths@woking.gov.uk

Emergency Planning: Mr Geoff McManus, Environmental Manager, Civic Offices, Gloucester Square, Woking GU21 6YL ☎ 01483 743707 📠 01483 776335 🖱 geoff.mcmanus@woking.gov.uk

Environmental / Technical Services: Mr Geoff McManus, Environmental Manager, Civic Offices, Gloucester Square, Woking GU21 6YL ☎ 01483 743707 📠 01483 776335 🖱 geoff.mcmanus@woking.gov.uk

Environmental Health: Ms Emma Doherty, Environmental Health Manager, Civic Offices, Gloucester Square, Woking GU21 6YL ☎ 01483 743654 📠 01483 768746 🖱 emma.doherty@woking.gov.uk

Estates, Property & Valuation: Ms Diane Spencer, Asset Manager, Civic Offices, Gloucester Square, Woking GU21 6YL ☎ 01483 743552 📠 01483 723580 🖱 diane.spencer@woking.gov.uk

European Liaison: Mr Peter Bryant, Head of Legal Services, Civic Offices, Gloucester Square, Woking GU21 6YL ☎ 01483 743030 📠 01483 768746 🖱 peter.bryant@woking.gov.uk

Events Manager: Mr Andy Denner, Acting Marketing Communications Manager, Civic Offices, Gloucester Square, Woking GU21 6YL ☎ 01483 743024 📠 01483 743055 🖱 andy.denner@woking.gov.uk

Facilities: Mr Daniel Ogle, Temp Facilities Contract Management & Procurement Team Leader, Civic Offices, Gloucester Square, Woking GU21 6YL ☎ 01483 743407 📠 01483 768746 🖱 daniel.ogle@woking.gov.uk

Finance and Treasurer: Mrs Leigh Clarke, Financial Services Manager, Civic Offices, Gloucester Square, Woking GU21 6YL ☎ 01483 743277 📠 01483 724032 🖱 leigh.clarke@woking.gov.uk

Grounds Maintenance: Mr Geoff McManus, Environmental Manager, Civic Offices, Gloucester Square, Woking GU21 6YL ☎ 01483 743707 📠 01483 776335 🖱 geoff.mcmanus@woking.gov.uk

Health and Safety: Ms Lisa Harrington, Safety & Insurance Officer, Civic Offices, Gloucester Square, Woking GU21 6YL ☎ 01483 743213 📠 01483 724032 🖱 lisa.harrington@woking.gov.uk

Housing Maintenance: Mr Barry Montgomery, Director - New Vision Homes, Civic Offices, Gloucester Square, Woking GU21 6YL ☎ 01483 743743 🖱 barry.montgomery@woking.gov.uk

Legal: Mr Peter Bryant, Head of Legal Services, Civic Offices, Gloucester Square, Woking GU21 6YL ☎ 01483 743030 📠 01483 768746 🖱 peter.bryant@woking.gov.uk

Leisure and Cultural Services: Ms Sue Barham, Strategic Director, Civic Offices, Gloucester Square, Woking GU21 6YL ☎ 01483 743810 📠 01483 725318 🖱 sue.barham@woking.gov.uk

Licensing: Mr Russell Ellis, Licensing Manager, Civic Offices, Gloucester Square, Woking GU21 6YL ☎ 01483 743732 📠 01483 768746 🖱 russell.ellis@woking.gov.uk

Lottery Funding, Charity and Voluntary: Mr Frank Jeffrey, Principal Member Services Officer, Civic Offices, Gloucester Square, Woking GU21 6YL ☎ 01483 743012 📠 01483 768746 🖱 frank.jeffrey@woking.gov.uk

Member Services: Mr Frank Jeffrey, Principal Member Services Officer, Civic Offices, Gloucester Square, Woking GU21 6YL ☎ 01483 743012 📠 01483 768746 🖱 frank.jeffrey@woking.gov.uk

Parking: Ms Tracy Baker, Senior Parking Manager, Civic Offices, Gloucester Square, Woking GU21 6YL ☎ 01483 743468 📠 01483 768746 🖱 tracy.baker@woking.gov.uk

Partnerships: Mr David Johnson, Corporate Strategy Manager, Civic Offices, Gloucester Square, Woking GU21 6YL ☎ 01483 743060 📠 01483 756842 🖱 david.johnson@woking.gov.uk

Personnel / HR: Mrs Amanda Jeffrey, HR Manager, Civic Offices, Gloucester Square, Woking GU21 6YL ☎ 01483 743904 📠 01483 725318 🖱 amanda.jeffrey@woking.gov.uk

Planning: Mr Douglas Spinks, Deputy Chief Executive, Civic Offices, Gloucester Square, Woking GU21 6YL ☎ 01483 743783 📠 01483 768746 🖱 douglas.spinks@woking.gov.uk

Procurement: Mr David Johnson, Corporate Strategy Manager, Civic Offices, Gloucester Square, Woking GU21 6YL ☎ 01483 743060 📠 01483 756842 🖱 david.johnson@woking.gov.uk

Recycling & Waste Minimisation: Mr Geoff McManus, Environmental Manager, Civic Offices, Gloucester Square, Woking GU21 6YL ☎ 01483 743707 📠 01483 776335 🖱 geoff.mcmanus@woking.gov.uk

Staff Training: Mrs Amanda Jeffrey, HR Manager, Civic Offices, Gloucester Square, Woking GU21 6YL ☎ 01483 743904 📠 01483 725318 🖱 amanda.jeffrey@woking.gov.uk

Sustainable Communities: Mr Tim Lowe, Senior Policy Officer (Sustainability), Civic Offices, Gloucester Square, Woking GU21 6YL ☎ 01483 743413 📠 01483 768746 🖱 tim.lowe@woking.gov.uk

Sustainable Development: Mr Tim Lowe, Senior Policy Officer (Sustainability), Civic Offices, Gloucester Square, Woking GU21 6YL ☎ 01483 743413 📠 01483 768746 🖱 tim.lowe@woking.gov.uk

Tourism: Mr Andy Denner, Acting Marketing Communications Manager, Civic Offices, Gloucester Square, Woking GU21 6YL ☎ 01483 743024 📠 01483 743055 🖱 andy.denner@woking.gov.uk

Town Centre: Ms Joanne Walker, Town Centre Manager, Civic Offices, Gloucester Square, Woking GU21 6YL ☎ 01483 743487 📠 01483 743055 🖱 joanne.walker@woking.gov.uk

Waste Collection and Disposal: Mr Geoff McManus, Environmental Manager, Civic Offices, Gloucester Square, Woking

GU21 6YL ☎ 01483 743707 🖷 01483 776335 geoff.mcmanus@woking.gov.uk

Children's Play Areas: Mr Geoff Ward, Cultural & Community Development Manager, Civic Offices, Gloucester Square, Woking GU21 6YL ☎ 01483 743802 geoff.ward@woking.gov.uk

MEMBERS OF THE COUNCIL (36)

***Mayor:* Smith**, Michael (CON - Horsell East and Woodham)
cllrmichael.smith@woking.gov.uk
***Leader of the Council:* Kingsbury**, John (CON - St Johns and Hook Heath)
cllrjohn.kingsbury@woking.gov.uk
***Deputy Leader of the Council:* Bittleston**, David (CON - Mount Hermon East)
cllrdavid.bittleston@woking.gov.uk
***Group Leader:* Coulson**, Denzil (LD - Goldsworth West)
cllrdenzil.coulson@woking.gov.uk
Addison, Hilary (CON - Goldsworth East)
cllrhilary.addison@woking.gov.uk
Ali, Mazaffar (CON - Maybury and Sheerwater)
cllrmazaffar.ali@woking.gov.uk
Barker, Ann-Marie (LD - Horswell West)
cllrann-marie.barker@woking.gov.uk
Bashir, Mohammed (LD - Maybury and Sheerwater)
cllrmohammed.bashir@woking.gov.uk
Bellord, Simon (CON - Mayford and Sutton Green)
cllrsimon.bellord@woking.gov.uk
Bowes, Ashley (CON - Pyrford)
cllrashley.bowes@woking.gov.uk
Branagan, Tony (CON - Horsell West)
cllrtony.branagan@woking.gov.uk
Chrystie, Graham (CON - Pyrford)
cllrgraham.chrystie@woking.gov.uk
Coulson, Amanda (LD - Goldsworth East)
cllramanda.coulson@woking.gov.uk
Cross, Bryan (LD - Goldsworth East)
cllrbryan.cross@woking.gov.uk
Cundy, Graham (CON - St Johns and Hook Heath)
cllrgraham.cundy@woking.gov.uk
Davis, Kevin (CON - Brookwood)
cllrkevin.davis@woking.gov.uk
Eastwood, Ian (LD - Goldsworth West)
cllrian.eastwood@woking.gov.uk
Elson, Gary (CON - West Byfleet)
cllrgary.elson@woking.gov.uk
Farrant, Dorothy (CON - Byfleet)
cllrdorothy.farrant@woking.gov.uk
Forster, Will (LD - Kingfield and Westfield)
cllrwill.forster@woking.gov.uk
Howard, Ken (LD - Hermitage and Knaphill South)
cllrken.howard@woking.gov.uk
Hunwicks, Beryl (CON - Horsell West)
cllrberyl.hunwicks@woking.gov.uk
Hussain, Saj (CON - Knaphill)
cllrsaj.hussain@woking.gov.uk
Iqbal, Mohammed (CON - Maybury and Sheerwater)
cllrmohammed.iqbal@woking.gov.uk
Johnson, Ian (LD - Mount Hermon West)
cllrian.johnson@woking.gov.uk
Liddington, Tina (LD - Hermitage and Knaphill South)
cllrtina.liddington@woking.gov.uk
Lyons, Liam (LD - Mount Hermon West)
cllrliam.lyons@woking.gov.uk
McCrum, Derek (LD - Kingfield and Westfield)
cllrderek.mccrum@woking.gov.uk
Morales, Louise (LD - Old Woking)
cllrlouise.morales@woking.gov.uk
Murray, Anne (CON - Horsell East and Woodham)
cllranne.murray@woking.gov.uk
Roberts, Anne (LD - Byfleet)
cllranne.roberts@woking.gov.uk
Sharp, Richard (LD - Knaphill)
cllrrichard.sharp@woking.gov.uk
Thomson, Carl (CON - Mount Hermon East)
cllrcarl.thomson@woking.gov.uk
Watson Green, Esther (CON - Byfleet)
cllresther.watsongreen@woking.gov.uk
Whitehand, Melanie (CON - Knaphill)
cllrmelanie.whitehand@woking.gov.uk
Wilson, Richard (CON - West Byfleet)
cllrrichard.wilson@woking.gov.uk

POLITICAL COMPOSITION

CON: 21, LD: 15

CABINET

Leader / Asset Management: Mr John Kingsbury
Deputy Leader: Mr David Bittleston
Accessibility: Ms Melanie Whitehand
Centres for the Community: Ms Melanie Whitehand
Climate Change / Strategy: Mrs Beryl Hunwicks
Community Safety: Mrs Beryl Hunwicks
Corporate Financial Planning & Policy: Mr John Kingsbury
Corporate Management & Members' Services: Mr John Kingsbury
Corporate Planning & Policy: Mr John Kingsbury
Environmental Control: Mrs Beryl Hunwicks
Environment & Sustainability: Mr Graham Cundy
General Community Service Functions: Mr David Bittleston
Health & Wellbeing: Mr David Bittleston
Information Technology: Mr Gary Elson
Leisure Centre & Pool in the Park: Mr David Bittleston
Planning Policy: Mr Graham Cundy
Promoting the Local Economy: Mr Gary Elson
Revenue Collection: Mr John Kingsbury
Waste & Recycling: Mrs Beryl Hunwicks

COMMITTEE CHAIRS

Appeals: Mr Ashley Bowes
Licensing: Mr Carl Thomson
Overview & Scrutiny: Mr Liam Lyons
Planning: Mr Ashley Bowes

WOKINGHAM U

Wokingham Borough Council, Wokingham Borough Council, Shute End, Wokingham RG40 1BN ☎ 0118 974 6000 🖷 0118 978 9078 wokinghambc@wokingham.gov.uk
www.wokingham.gov.uk

FACTS & FIGURES

Police Authority: Thames Valley Police Authority
Health Authority: South Central Strategic Health Authority
Learning and Skills Council: South East
Parliamentary Constituencies: Bracknell, Maidenhead, Reading

East, Wokingham
EU Constituencies: South East
Election Frequency: Elections are by thirds

PRINCIPAL OFFICERS

Chief Executive: Mr Andy Couldrick, Chief Executive, Wokingham Borough Council, Shute End, Wokingham RG40 1BN ☎ 0118 974 6247 🖷 0118 978 9078 ✉ andy.couldrick@wokingham.gov.uk

Architect, Building / Property Services: Mr Bernard Pich, Head - Strategic Assets & Capital Resources, PO Box 151, Council Offices, Shute End, Wokingham RG40 1WH ☎ 0118 974 6700 🖷 0118 974 6724 ✉ bernie.pich@wokingham.gov.uk

Building Control: Mr Neil Badley, Head - Infrastructure Implementation, Civic Offices, Wokingham RG40 1WQ ☎ 0118 974 6366 🖷 0118 974 6385 ✉ neil.badley@wokingham.gov.uk

Children / Youth Services: Mr Andy Couldrick, Chief Executive, Wokingham Borough Council, Shute End, Wokingham RG40 1BN ☎ 0118 974 6247 🖷 0118 978 9078 ✉ andy.couldrick@wokingham.gov.uk

Children / Youth Services: Ms Judith Ramsden, Head - Safeguarding & Social Care, PO Box 156, Civic Offices, 2nd Floor, Shute End, Wokingham RG40 1BN ☎ 0118 974 6203 ✉ judith.ramsden@wokingham.gov.uk

Children / Youth Services: Mr Richard Stanley, Head - Learning & Achievement, Wokingham Borough Council, Shute End, Wokingham RG40 1BN ☎ 0118 974 6121 🖷 0118 974 6135 ✉ richard.stanley@wokingham.gov.uk

Children / Youth Services: Ms Rachael Wardell, Assistant Director - Early Intervention & Community, PO Box 156, Civic Offices, 2nd Floor, Shute End, Wokingham RG40 1BN ☎ 0118 974615 ✉ rachael.wardell@wokingham.gov.uk

Civil Registration: Ms Liz Lepere, Superintendent Registrar, Council Offices, Shute End, Wokingham RG40 1BN ☎ 0118 974 6554 🖷 0118 978 2813 ✉ liz.lepere@wokingham.gov.uk

PR / Communications: Miss Andrea Jenkins, Strategic Communications Lead, PO Box 150, Council Offices, Shute End, Wokingham RG40 1WQ ☎ 0118 974 6010 🖷 0118 978 5053 ✉ andrea.jenkins@wokingham.gov.uk

Community Planning: Ms Sarah Hollamby, Head - Corporate Strategy & Performance, Wokingham Borough Council, Shute End, Wokingham RG40 1BN ☎ 0118 974 6817 🖷 0118 979 0877 ✉ sarah.hollamby@wokingham.gov.uk

Community Planning: Mr Mark Moon, Strategic Director - Neighbourhood Services, Council Offices, Shute End, Wokingham RG40 1BN ☎ 0118 974 6315 🖷 0118 974 6313 ✉ mark.moon@wokingham.gov.uk

Community Safety: Mr Stuart Rowbotham, Strategic Director - Health & Wellbeing, Council Offices, Shute End, Wokingham RG40 1BN ☎ 0118 974 6762 🖷 0118 974 6770 ✉ stuart.rowbotham@wokingham.gov.uk

Computer Management: Mr Mike Ibbitson, Head - Operational IMT, Wokingham Borough Council, Shute End, Wokingham RG40 1BN ☎ 0118 974 6962 ✉ mike.ibbitson@wokingham.gov.uk

Consumer Protection and Trading Standards: Mr Steve Richardson, Environmental Health Manager - Health & Safety / Licensing, Civic Offices, Wokingham RG40 1WQ ☎ 0118 974 6378 🖷 0118 974 6401 ✉ steve.richardson@wokingham.gov.uk

Contracts: Mr Graham Ebers, Strategic Director - Resources, PO Box 152, Council Offices, Shute End, Wokingham RG40 1WJ ☎ 0118 974 6557 🖷 0118 974 6574 ✉ graham.ebers@wokingham.gov.uk

Corporate Services: Mr Neil Badley, Head - Infrastructure Implementation, Civic Offices, Wokingham RG40 1WQ ☎ 0118 974 6366 🖷 0118 974 6385 ✉ neil.badley@wokingham.gov.uk

Corporate Services: Mr Rob Stubbs, Head - Corporate Finance, PO Box 154, Civic Offices, 2nd Floor, Shute End, Wokingham RG40 1WN ☎ 0118 974 6973 ✉ rob.stubbs@wokingham.gov.uk

Customer Service: Ms Marion Wood, Senior Complaints Officer, Wokingham Borough Council, Shute End, Wokingham RG40 1BN ☎ 0118 974 6026 ✉ marion.wood@wokingham.gov.uk

Economic Development: Mr Andrew Nicholls, Economic Development Officer, PO Box 157, Council Offices, Shute End, Wokingham RG40 1WR ☎ 0118 974 6398 🖷 0118 974 6401 ✉ andrew.nicholls@wokingham.gov.uk

Education: Mr Andy Couldrick, Chief Executive, Wokingham Borough Council, Shute End, Wokingham RG40 1BN ☎ 0118 974 6247 🖷 0118 978 9078 ✉ andy.couldrick@wokingham.gov.uk

E-Government: Mr Andrew Moulton, Director - Transformation, Wokingham Borough Council, Shute End, Wokingham RG40 1BN ☎ 0118 974 6677 ✉ andrew.moulton@wokingham.gov.uk

Electoral Registration: Ms Alison Wood, Electoral Services Manager, Council Offices, Shute End, Wokingham RG40 1WQ ☎ 0118 974 6521 🖷 0118 974 6542 ✉ alison.wood@wokingham.gov.uk

Emergency Planning: Mr Peter Stuart, Community Resilience Manager, PO Box 152, Council Offices, Shute End, Wokingham RG40 1WJ ☎ 0118 974 6347 🖷 0118 974 6313 ✉ peter.stuart@wokingham.gov.uk

Energy Management: Ms Gabriell Berry, Energy Manager, Wokingham Borough Council, Shute End, Wokingham RG40 1BN ☎ 0118 974 6711 ✉ gabriell.berry@wokingham.gov.uk

Environmental / Technical Services: Mr Matt Davey, Head - Technical Services, PO Box 155, Civic Offices, Shute End, Wokingham RG40 1WW ☎ 0118 974 6000 ✉ matt.davey@wokingham.gov.uk

Environmental / Technical Services: Mr Mark Moon, Strategic Director - Neighbourhood Services, Council Offices, Shute End, Wokingham RG40 1BN ☎ 0118 974 6315 🖷 0118 974 6313 ✉ mark.moon@wokingham.gov.uk

Environmental Health: Mr Steve Richardson, Environmental Health Manager - Health & Safety / Licensing, Civic Offices, Wokingham RG40 1WQ ☎ 0118 974 6378 🖷 0118 974 6401 ✉ steve.richardson@wokingham.gov.uk

Estates, Property & Valuation: Mr Bernard Pich, Head - Strategic Assets & Capital Resources, PO Box 151, Council Offices, Shute End, Wokingham RG40 1WH ☎ 0118 974 6700 🖷 0118 974 6724 ✉ bernie.pich@wokingham.gov.uk

European Liaison: Mrs Sue Roberts, Partnership Development Manager, Council Offices, Shute End, Wokingham RG40 1BN ☎ 0118 974 6016 🖷 0118 979 0877 ✉ sue.roberts@wokingham.gov.uk

Facilities: Mrs Jenny Birks, Interim Facilities Manager, Wokingham Borough Council, Shute End, Wokingham RG40 1BN ☎ 0118 974 6593 🖷 0118 978 9078 ✉ jenny.birks@wokingham.gov.uk

Grounds Maintenance: Mrs Julia Woodbridge, Senior Parks Officer, Civic Offices, Shute End, Wokingham RG40 1BR ☎ 0118 974 6273 🖷 0118 974 6312 ✉ julia.woodbridge@wokingham.gov.uk

Highways: Mr Mark Moon, Strategic Director - Neighbourhood Services, Council Offices, Shute End, Wokingham RG40 1BN ☎ 0118 974 6315 🖷 0118 974 6313 ✉ mark.moon@wokingham.gov.uk

Housing: Mr Stuart Rowbotham, Strategic Director - Health & Wellbeing, Council Offices, Shute End, Wokingham RG40 1BN ☎ 0118 974 6762 🖷 0118 974 6770 ✉ stuart.rowbotham@wokingham.gov.uk

Housing: Ms Jude Whyte, Head - Housing Needs, Wokingham Borough Council, Shute End, Wokingham RG40 1BN ☎ 0118 974 6755 ✉ jude.whyte@wokingham.gov.uk

Housing Maintenance: Mr Simon Price, Head - Tenant Services, Waterford House, Erfstadt Court, Wokingham RG40 2YF ☎ 0118 974 3775 🖷 0118 974 3788 ✉ simon.price@wokingham.gov.uk

Local Area Agreement: Mr Mark Redfearn, Policy Manager - Community Safety, Wokingham Borough Council, Shute End, Wokingham RG40 1BN ☎ 0118 974 6012 ✉ mark.redfearn@wokingham.gov.uk

Legal: Mrs Susanne Nelson-Wehrmeyer, Director - Legal & Electoral Services, PO Box 151, Council Offices, Shute End, Wokingham RG40 1WH ☎ 0118 974 6520 🖷 0118 974 6723 ✉ susanne.nelson-wehrmeyer@wokingham.gov.uk

Licensing: Mr Steve Richardson, Environmental Health Manager - Health & Safety / Licensing, Civic Offices, Wokingham RG40 1WQ ☎ 0118 974 6378 🖷 0118 974 6401 ✉ steve.richardson@wokingham.gov.uk

Lottery Funding, Charity and Voluntary: Mrs Sue Roberts, Partnership Development Manager, Council Offices, Shute End, Wokingham RG40 1BN ☎ 0118 974 6016 🖷 0118 979 0877 ✉ sue.roberts@wokingham.gov.uk

Member Services: Ms Anne Hunter, Democratic Services Manager, PO Box 150, Council Offices, Shute End, Wokingham RG40 1WQ ☎ 0118 974 6051 🖷 0118 974 6057 ✉ anne.hunter@wokingham.gov.uk

Parking: Mr Mark Moon, Strategic Director - Neighbourhood Services, Council Offices, Shute End, Wokingham RG40 1BN ☎ 0118 974 6315 🖷 0118 974 6313 ✉ mark.moon@wokingham.gov.uk

Partnerships: Ms Josie Wragg, Head - Community Sustainability, Wokingham Borough Council, Shute End, Wokingham RG40 1BN ☎ 0118 974 6002 🖷 0118 978 9078 ✉ josie.wragg@wokingham.gov.uk

Personnel / HR: Ms Jan Hale, Interim Human Resources Manager, Wokingham Borough Council, Shute End, Wokingham RG40 1BN ☎ 0118 974 6087 ✉ jan.hale@wokingham.gov.uk

Planning: Mr Mark Cupit, Head - Development Management, Wokingham Borough Council, Shute End, Wokingham RG40 1BN ☎ 0118 974 6487 🖷 0118 978 9078 ✉ mark.culpit@wokingham.gov.uk

Public Libraries: Mr Neil Carr, Head - Neighbourhoods, Wokingham Borough Council, Shute End, Wokingham RG40 1BN ☎ 0118 974 6349 🖷 0118 979 0877 ✉ neil.carr@wokingham.gov.uk

Recycling & Waste Minimisation: Mr Peter Baveystock, Waste & Recycling Manager, Civic Centre, Shute End, Wokingham RG40 1NL ☎ 0118 974 6338 🖷 0118 974 6312 ✉ peter.baveystock@wokingham.gov.uk

Regeneration: Ms Heather Thwaites, Stragecic Director - Development & Regeneration, Wokingham Borough Council, Shute End, Wokingham RG40 1BN ☎ 0118 974 6425 🖷 0118 974 6385 ✉ heather.thwaites@wokingham.gov.uk

Road Safety: Mr Mark Moon, Strategic Director - Neighbourhood Services, Council Offices, Shute End, Wokingham RG40 1BN ☎ 0118 974 6315 🖷 0118 974 6313 ✉ mark.moon@wokingham.gov.uk

Social Services: Ms Karen Jackson, Head - Older People Stratergy & Functions, PO Box 154, Civic Offices, 2nd Floor, Shute End, Wokingham RG40 1WN ☎ 0118 974 6833 ✉ karen.jackson@wokingham.gov.uk

Social Services: Mr Stuart Rowbotham, Strategic Director - Health & Wellbeing, Wokingham Borough Council, Shute End, Wokingham RG40 1BN ☎ 0118 974 6762 🖷 0118 974 6770 ✉ stuart.rowbotham@wokingham.gov.uk

Social Services (Adult): Mr Stuart Rowbotham, Strategic Director - Health & Wellbeing, Wokingham Borough Council, Shute End, Wokingham RG40 1BN ☎ 0118 974 6762 🖷 0118 974 6770 ✉ stuart.rowbotham@wokingham.gov.uk

Social Services (Children): Mr Andy Couldrick, Chief Executive, Wokingham Borough Council, Shute End, Wokingham RG40 1BN ☎ 0118 974 6247 🖷 0118 978 9078 ~

andy.couldrick@wokingham.gov.uk

Staff Training: Mr Geoffrey Munday, Personnel Strategy & Organisation Development Manager, PO Box 150, Council Offices, Shute End, Wokingham RG40 1WQ ☎ 0118 974 6037 🖷 0118 974 6092 geoff.munday@wokingham.gov.uk

Street Scene: Mr Neil Carr, Head - Neighbourhoods, Wokingham Borough Council, Shute End, Wokingham RG40 1BN ☎ 0118 974 6349 🖷 0118 979 0877 neil.carr@wokingham.gov.uk

Town Centre: Mr Bernard Pich, Head - Strategic Assets & Capital Resources, Wokingham Borough Council, Shute End, Wokingham RG40 1BN ☎ 0118 974 6700 🖷 0118 974 6724 bernie.pich@wokingham.gov.uk

Traffic Management: Mr Mark Moon, Strategic Director - Neighbourhood Services, Council Offices, Shute End, Wokingham RG40 1BN ☎ 0118 974 6315 🖷 0118 974 6313 mark.moon@wokingham.gov.uk

Waste Collection and Disposal: Mr Peter Baveystock, Waste & Recycling Manager, Civic Centre, Shute End, Wokingham RG40 1NL ☎ 0118 974 6338 🖷 0118 974 6312 peter.baveystock@wokingham.gov.uk

Waste Management: Mr Peter Baveystock, Waste & Recycling Manager, Civic Centre, Shute End, Wokingham RG40 1NL ☎ 0118 974 6338 🖷 0118 974 6312 peter.baveystock@wokingham.gov.uk

MEMBERS OF THE COUNCIL (54)

Auty, Alistair (CON - Norreys)
alistair.auty@wokingham.gov.uk
Baker, Keith (CON - Coronation)
keith.baker@wokingham.gov.uk
Batth, Parry (CON - Shinfield North)
Parry.batth@wokingham.gov.uk
Bowring, Chris (CON - Evendons)
chris.bowring@wokingham.gov.uk
Bradley, Andrew (CON - Hillside)
andrew.bradley@wokingham.gov.uk
Bray, Prue (LD - Winnersh)
prue.bray@wokingham.gov.uk
Chopping, David (CON - Maiden Erlegh)
david.chopping@wokingham.gov.uk
Clark, UllaKarin (CON - Emmbrook)
ullakarin.clark@wokingham.gov.uk
Corrie, Alistair (CON - Evendons)
alistair.corrie@wokingham.gov.uk
Cowan, Gary (CON - Arborfield)
gary.cowan@wokingham.gov.uk
Ferris, Lindsay (LD - Twyford)
lindsay.ferris@wokingham.gov.uk
Firmager, Michael (CON - Hawkedon)
michael.firmager@wokingham.gov.uk
Gilder, Kay (LD - South Lake)
kay.gilder@wokingham.gov.uk
Gore, Mike (CON - Finchampstead North)
mike.gore@wokingham.gov.uk
Grandison, Guy (CON - Hawkedon)
guy.grandison@wokingham.gov.uk
Haines, Mike (CON - Sonning)
mike.haines@wokingham.gov.uk
Haines, Kate (CON - Coronation)
kate.haines@wokingham.gov.uk
Haitham Taylor, Charlotte (CON - Shinfield South)
charlotte.haithamtaylor@wokingham.gov.uk
Halsall, John (CON - Remenham Wargrave and Ruscombe)
john.halsall@wokingham.gov.uk
Hayward, Lesley (LD - Bulmershe and Whitegates)
lesley.hayward@wokingham.gov.uk
Helliar-Symons, Pauline (CON - Wokingham Without)
pauline.helliar-symons@wokingham.gov.uk
Holton, Tim (CON - Hawkedon)
tim.holton@wokinghaam.gov.uk
Houldsworth, Philip (CON - Winnersh)
philip.houldsworth@wokingham.gov.uk
Jorgensen, Pauline (CON - Hillside)
pauline.jorgensen@wokingham.gov.uk
Jorgensen, Norman (CON - Hillside)
norman.jorgensen@wokingham.gov.uk
Kaiser, John (CON - Barkham)
john.kaiser@wokingham.gov.uk
King, Dianne (CON - Evendons)
dianne.king@wokingham.gov.uk
Lee, David (CON - Norreys)
david.lee@wokingham.gov.uk
Loyes, Abdul (CON - Loddon)
abdul.loyes@wokingham.gov.uk
McCann, Tom (LD - Loddon)
McGhee- Sumner, Julian (CON - Wescott)
julian.mcghee-sumner@wokingham.gov.uk
Miall, Ken (CON - Maiden Erlegh)
ken.miall@wokingham.gov.uk
Mirfin, Philip (CON - Emmbrook)
philip.mirfin@wokingham.gov.uk
Munro, Stuart (CON - Swallowfield)
stuart.munro@wokingham.gov.uk
Patman, Barrie (CON - Shinfield South)
barrie.patman@wokingham.gov.uk
Pittock, Ian (CON - Finchampstead South)
ian.pittock@wokingham.gov.uk
Pitts, Bob (CON - Remenham Wargrave & Ruscombe)
bob.pitts@wokingham.gov.uk
Pollock, Anthony (CON - Shinfield)
anthonyp@anthonypollock.co.uk
Rahmouni, Sam (LD - Bulmershe and Whitegates)
sam.rahmouni@wokingham.gov.uk
Ray, Nick (IND - Charvil)
nick.ray@wokingham.gov.uk
Richards, Malcolm (CON - Norreys)
malcolm.richards@wokingham.gov.uk
Ross, Angus (CON - Wokingham Without)
angus.ross@wokingham.gov.uk
Rowland, Beth (LD - South Lake)
beth.rowland@wokingham.gov.uk
Shepher-DuBey, Rachelle (LD - Winnersh)
rachelle.shepherd-dubey@wokingham.gov.uk
Singleton, Chris (CON - Emmbrook)
chris.singleton@wokingham.gov.uk
Sleight, David (CON - Wokingham Without)
david.sleight@wokingham.gov.uk
Smith, Wayne (CON - Hurst)
wayne.smith@wokingham.gov.uk
Smith, Sue (IND - Loddon)
sue.smith@wokingham.gov.uk
Stanton, Rob (CON - Finchampstead North)

rob.stanton@wokingham.gov.uk
Swaddle, Paul (CON - Maiden Erlegh)
paul.swaddle@wokingham.gov.uk
Tomlin, Dee (LD - Twyford and Ruscombe)
dee@deetomlin.org.uk
Weeks, Simon (CON - Finchampstead South)
simon.weeks@wokingham.gov.uk
Wyatt, Bob (CON - Wescott)
r.wyatt325@btinternet.com
Younis, Shahid (CON - Bulmershe & Whitegates)
shahid.younis@wokingham.gov.uk

POLITICAL COMPOSITION
CON: 43, LD: 9, IND: 2

CABINET
Leader: Mr David Lee
Deputy Leader: Mr Rob Stanton
Children's Services: Ms Charlotte Haitham Taylor
Environment: Mr Angus Ross
Finance: Mr Anthony Pollock
Health & Wellbeing: Mr Julian McGhee- Sumner
Highways & Planning: Mr Keith Baker
Internal Services: Ms Pauline Jorgensen
Regeneration & Affordable Housing: Mr Alistair Corrie

COMMITTEE CHAIRS
Audit: Mr Philip Mirfin
Health Overview & Scrutiny: Mr Tim Holton
Licensing & Appeals: Mr Barrie Patman
Overview & Scrutiny Management: Mr Norman Jorgensen
Overview & Scrutiny: Mrs Pauline Helliar-Symons
Personnel: Mr Stuart Munro
Planning: Mr Simon Weeks
Standards: Mr David Comben (External)

WOLVERHAMPTON M

Wolverhampton City Council, Civic Centre, St. Peter's Square, Wolverhampton WV1 1SH ☎ 01902 556556 🖷 01902 554030 ✉ citydirect@wolverhampton.gov.uk 💻 www.wolverhampton.gov.uk

FACTS & FIGURES
Police Authority: West Midlands Police Authority
Health Authority: NHS West Midlands
Learning and Skills Council: West Midlands
Parliamentary Constituencies: Wolverhampton North East, Wolverhampton South East, Wolverhampton South West
EU Constituencies: West Midlands
Election Frequency: Elections are by thirds

PRINCIPAL OFFICERS
Chief Executive: Mr Simon Warren, Chief Executive, Civic Centre, St. Peter's Square, Wolverhampton WV1 1SH ☎ 01902 554000 🖷 01902 554006 ✉ simon.warren@wolverhampton.gov.uk

Assistant Chief Executive: Ms Joanne Lancaster, Assistant Chief Executive, Civic Centre, St. Peter's Square, Wolverhampton WV1 1SH ☎ 01902 554002 🖷 01902 554006 ✉ joanne.lancaster@wolverhampton.gov.uk

Senior Management: Mr Charles Green, Strategic Director - Education and Enterprise, Civic Centre, St. Peter's Square, Wolverhampton WV1 1SH ☎ 01902 555400 ✉ charles.green@wolverhampton.gov.uk

Senior Management: Ms Sarah Norman, Strategic Director - Community, Civic Centre, St Peter's Square, Wolverhampton WV1 1RT ☎ 01902 555300 ✉ sarah.norman@wolverhampton.gov.uk

Senior Management: Mr Tom Rennie, Strategic Director - Delivery, Civic Centre, St. Peter's Square, Wolverhampton WV1 1SH ☎ 01902 554500 ✉ tom.rennie@wolverhampton.gov.uk

Access Officer / Social Services (Disability): Ms Clare Peterson, Equality and Diversity - CYP Manager, Civic Centre, St. Peter's Square, Wolverhampton WV1 1SH ☎ 01902 555230 ✉ clare.peterson@wolverhampton.gov.uk

Architect, Building / Property Services: Mr Kevin Moore, Property Manager, Civic Centre, St. Peter's Square, Wolverhampton WV1 1SH ☎ 01902 555570 ✉ kevin.moore@wolverhampton.gov.uk

Architect, Building / Property Services: Ms Sue Samways, Performance and Support Services - Property, Civic Centre, St. Peter's Square, Wolverhampton WV1 1SH ☎ 01902 555763 ✉ sue.samways@wolverhampton.gov.uk

Architect, Building / Property Services: Mr Richard Wassell, Strategic Planning, Housing Policy and Sustainability Housing Strategy Officer, Civic Centre, St. Peter's Square, Wolverhampton WV1 1SH ☎ 01902 554007 ✉ richard.wassell@wolverhampton.gov.uk

Building Control: Mr Stephen Alexander, Development and Building Control Manager, Civic Centre, St. Peter's Square, Wolverhampton WV1 1SH ☎ 01902 555610 ✉ stephen.alexander@wolverhampton.gov.uk

Catering Services: Mr Chris East, Catering and Cleaning Services Officer, Civic Centre, St. Peter's Square, Wolverhampton WV1 1SH ☎ 01902 555227 ✉ chris.east@wolverhampton.gov.uk

Children / Youth Services: Mr Robin Morris, Youth Services, Civic Centre, St. Peter's Square, Wolverhampton WV1 1SH ☎ 01902 555117 ✉ robin.morris@wolverhampton.gov.uk

Children / Youth Services: Ms Lois Stewart, Learning and Development Officer, Civic Centre, St. Peter's Square, Wolverhampton WV1 1SH ☎ 01902 554085 ✉ lois.stewart@wolverhampton.gov.uk

Civil Registration: Mr Steve Wright, Chief Registrar, Civic Centre, St. Peter's Square, Wolverhampton WV1 1SH ☎ 01902 554998 ✉ steve.wright@wolverhampton.gov.uk

PR / Communications: Ms Mel Whyatt, Marketing Communications Manager, Civic Centre, St. Peter's Square, Wolverhampton WV1 1SH ☎ 01902 551254 ✉ mel.whyatt@wolverhampton.gov.uk

Community Planning: Ms Sheila Collett, Head - Local Neighbourhood Partnerships Service, Civic Centre, St. Peter's

Square, Wolverhampton WV1 1SH ☎ 01902 556043 ✉ Sheila@wton-partnership.org.uk

Community Planning: Ms Karen Cross, Community Initiatives Officer, Civic Centre, St. Peter's Square, Wolverhampton WV1 1SH ☎ 01902 554034 ✉ karen.cross@wolverhampton.gov.uk

Community Planning: Mr Richard Welch, Community Recreation Manager, Civic Centre, St. Peter's Square, Wolverhampton WV1 1SH ☎ 01902 552162 ✉ richard.welch@wolverhampton.gov.uk

Community Safety: Ms Karen Samuels, Community Safety Manager, Civic Centre, St. Peter's Square, Wolverhampton WV1 1SH ☎ 01902 551341 ✉ karen.samuels@wolverhampton.gov.uk

Computer Management: Mr Steve Adams, Information Management Officer, Civic Centre, St. Peter's Square, Wolverhampton WV1 1SH ☎ 01902 555320 ✉ steve.adams@wolverhampton.gov.uk

Computer Management: Mr Paul Dunlavey, Technical Operations Manager, Civic Centre, St. Peter's Square, Wolverhampton WV1 1SH ☎ 01902 551436 ✉ paul.dunlavey@wolverhampton.gov.uk

Consumer Protection and Trading Standards: Mr Peter Calvert, Trading Standards Manager, Civic Centre, St. Peter's Square, Wolverhampton WV1 1SH ☎ 01902 556052 ✉ peter.calvert@wolverhampton.gov.uk

Consumer Protection and Trading Standards: Mr Andy Jervis, Environmental Health, Trading Standards and Licensing Officer, Civic Centre, St. Peter's Square, Wolverhampton WV1 1SH ☎ 01902 551261 ✉ andy.jervis@wolverhampton.gov.uk

Consumer Protection and Trading Standards: Mr Oliver Wassell, Food and Environmental Safety Officer, Civic Centre, St. Peter's Square, Wolverhampton WV1 1SH ☎ 01902 554351 ✉ oliver.wassell@wolverhampton.gov.uk

Corporate Services: Ms Sarah Bidwell, Senior Policy and Equality Officer, Civic Centre, St. Peter's Square, Wolverhampton WV1 1SH ☎ 01902 554080 🖷 01902 554443 ✉ sarah.bidwell@wolverhampton.gov.uk

Corporate Services: Mr Ian Gladwin, Corporate Asset Manager, Civic Centre, St. Peter's Square, Wolverhampton WV1 1SH ☎ 01902 555472 ✉ ian.gladwin@wolverhampton.gov.uk

Corporate Services: Mr Andy Hoare, Business Support Manager, Civic Centre, St. Peter's Square, Wolverhampton WV1 1SH ☎ 01902 554563 ✉ andy.hoare@wolverhampton.gov.uk

Corporate Services: Mr David Johnston, Risk Management and Insurance, Civic Centre, St. Peter's Square, Wolverhampton WV1 1SH ☎ 01902 554565 ✉ david.johnston@wolverhampton.gov.uk

Corporate Services: Ms Susan Kembrey, Assistant Director - Solicitor to the Council, Civic Centre, St. Peter's Square, Wolverhampton WV1 1SH ☎ 01902 554910 ✉ susan.kembrey@wolverhampton.gov.uk

Corporate Services: Ms Pat Main, Assistant Director - Corporate Services, Civic Centre, St. Peter's Square, Wolverhampton WV1 1SH ☎ 01902 554410 ✉ pat.main@wolverhampton.gov.uk

Corporate Services: Ms Penelope Mell, Corporate Policy, Programmes and Projects Manager, Civic Centre, St. Peter's Square, Wolverhampton WV1 1SH ☎ 01902 554240 ✉ penelope.mell@wolverhampton.gov.uk

Corporate Services: Mr David Sheldon, Corporate Procurement Officer, Civic Centre, St. Peter's Square, Wolverhampton WV1 1SH ☎ 01902 555066 ✉ david.sheldon@wolverhampton.gov.uk

Corporate Services: Mr Michael Webb, Corporate and Commercial Services - Legal Manager, Civic Centre, St. Peter's Square, Wolverhampton WV1 1SH ☎ 01902 554931 ✉ michael.webb@wolverhampton.gov.uk

Economic Development: Mr Jay Patel, Business and Economic Partnerships Manager, Civic Centre, St. Peter's Square, Wolverhampton WV1 1SH ☎ 01902 554955 ✉ jay.patel@wolverhampton.gov.uk

Education: Ms Chris Parsons, Adult Education Officer, Civic Centre, St. Peter's Square, Wolverhampton WV1 1SH ☎ 01902 558158 ✉ christine.parsons@aes.wolverhampton.gov.uk

Education: Mr Tim Westwood, Assistant Director - Schools, Skills and Learning, Civic Centre, St. Peter's Square, Wolverhampton WV1 1SH ☎ 01902 554225 ✉ tim.westwood@wolverhampton.gov.uk

E-Government: Ms Julie Nomicas, E-Services Manager, Civic Centre, St. Peter's Square, Wolverhampton WV1 1SH ☎ 01902 555107 ✉ julie.nomicas@wolverhampton.gov.uk

E-Government: Mr James Plant, E-Services Manager, Civic Centre, St. Peter's Square, Wolverhampton WV1 1SH ☎ 01902 551456 ✉ james.plant@wolverhampton.gov.uk

Emergency Planning: Mr Charlie Hickman, Business Continuity and Emergency Planning Officer, Civic Centre, St. Peter's Square, Wolverhampton WV1 1SH ☎ 01902 554070 ✉ charlie.hickman@wolverhampton.gov.uk

Environmental Health: Mr Andy Jervis, Environmental Health, Trading Standards and Licensing Officer, Civic Centre, St. Peter's Square, Wolverhampton WV1 1SH ☎ 01902 551261 ✉ andy.jervis@wolverhampton.gov.uk

Events Manager: Mr Mark Blackstock, Civic Halls and Outdoor Events Manager, Civic Centre, St. Peter's Square, Wolverhampton WV1 1SH ☎ 01902 556245 ✉ mark.blackstock@wolverhampton.gov.uk

Facilities: Mr Gary Newberry, Facilities Manager, Civic Centre, St. Peter's Square, Wolverhampton WV1 1SH ☎ 01902 550132 ✉ gary.newberry@wolverhampton.gov.uk

Finance and Treasurer: Mr Brian Burgess, Internal Audit Officer, Civic Centre, St. Peter's Square, Wolverhampton WV1 1SH ☎ 01902 554460 ✉ brian.burgess@wolverhampton.gov.uk

Finance and Treasurer: Mr Simon Lunn, Operational Finance Director, Civic Centre, St. Peter's Square, Wolverhampton WV1 1SH ☎ 01902 554664 ✉ simon.lunn@wolverhampton.gov.uk

Finance and Treasurer: Ms Sue Martin, Revenues and Benefits, Civic Centre, St. Peter's Square, Wolverhampton WV1 1SH ☎ 01902 554772 ✉ sue.martin@wolverhampton.gov.uk

Finance and Treasurer: Mr Mark Taylor, Financial Controller and Deputy Section 151 Officer, Civic Centre, St. Peter's Square, Wolverhampton WV1 1SH ☎ 01902 556609 ✉ mark.taylor@wolverhampton.gov.uk

Fleet Management: Mr Graham Bloxsome, Fleet Services Manager, Civic Centre, St. Peter's Square, Wolverhampton WV1 1SH ☎ 01902 554866 ✉ graham.bloxsome@wolverhampton.gov.uk

Health and Safety: Ms Dawn Phillips, Health and Saftey Officer, Civic Centre, St. Peter's Square, Wolverhampton WV1 1SH ☎ 01902 554035 ✉ dawn.phillips@wolverhampton.gov.uk

Highways: Mr Steve Woodward, Head - Street Scene, Civic Centre, St. Peter's Square, Wolverhampton WV1 1SH ☎ 01902 554260 ✉ steve.woodward@wolverhampton.gov.uk

Housing: Ms Fiona Gough, Head - Commissioning - Housing Support and Social Inclusion, Civic Centre, St. Peter's Square, Wolverhampton WV1 1SH ☎ 01902 555815 ✉ fiona.gough@wolverhampton.gov.uk

Housing: Mr Anthony Ivko, Assistant Director - Adult Social Care and Housing Support, Civic Centre, St. Peter's Square, Wolverhampton WV1 1SH ☎ 01902 555310 ✉ anthony.ivko@wolverhampton.gov.uk

Housing: Ms Linda Smith, Housing Support Manager, Civic Centre, St. Peter's Square, Wolverhampton WV1 1SH ☎ 01902 554740 ✉ linda.smith@wolverhampton.gov.uk

Legal: Ms Susan Kembrey, Assistant Director - Solicitor to the Council, Civic Centre, St. Peter's Square, Wolverhampton WV1 1SH ☎ 01902 554910 ✉ susan.kembrey@wolverhampton.gov.uk

Leisure and Cultural Services: Ms Tina Clark, Sport and Recreation Officer, Civic Centre, St. Peter's Square, Wolverhampton WV1 1SH ☎ 01902 555736 ✉ tina.clark@wolverhampton.gov.uk

Leisure and Cultural Services: Ms Corinne Miller, Arts and Museums Officer, Civic Centre, St. Peter's Square, Wolverhampton WV1 1SH ☎ 01902 552050 ✉ corinne.miller@wolverhampton.gov.uk

Leisure and Cultural Services: Mr Richard Welch, Community Recreation Manager, Civic Centre, St. Peter's Square, Wolverhampton WV1 1SH ☎ 01902 552162 ✉ richard.welch@wolverhampton.gov.uk

Leisure and Cultural Services: Mr Rob Willoughby, Assistant Director, Civic Centre, St. Peter's Square, Wolverhampton WV1 1SH ☎ 01902 551215 ✉ rob.willoughby@wolverhampton.gov.uk

Licensing: Mr Andy Jervis, Environmental Health, Trading Standards and Licensing Officer, Civic Centre, St. Peter's Square, Wolverhampton WV1 1SH ☎ 01902 551261 ✉ andy.jervis@wolverhampton.gov.uk

Licensing: Mr Colin Parr, Licensing Officer, Civic Centre, St. Peter's Square, Wolverhampton WV1 1SH ☎ 01902 550105 ✉ colin.parr@wolverhampton.gov.uk

Member Services: Mr Paul Tedstone, Democratic Services Manager, Civic Centre, St. Peter's Square, Wolverhampton WV1 1SH ☎ 01902 555043 ✉ paul.tedstone@wolverhampton.gov.uk

Parking: Mr Steve Woodward, Head - Street Scene, Civic Centre, St. Peter's Square, Wolverhampton WV1 1SH ☎ 01902 554260 ✉ steve.woodward@wolverhampton.gov.uk

Partnerships: Ms Heather Ernstsons, Local Strategic Partnerships Officer, Civic Centre, St. Peter's Square, Wolverhampton WV1 1SH ☎ 01902 551998 ✉ heather.ernstsons

Partnerships: Ms Keren Jones, Assistant Director - Promotions and Partnerships, Civic Centre, St. Peter's Square, Wolverhampton WV1 1SH ☎ 01902 555410 ✉ keren.jones@wolverhampton.gov.uk

Partnerships: Mr Jay Patel, Business and Economic Partnerships Manager, Civic Centre, St. Peter's Square, Wolverhampton WV1 1SH ☎ 01902 554955 ✉ jay.patel@wolverhampton.gov.uk

Personnel / HR: Ms Sue Davies, Head - Human Resources and Organisational Development Strategy, Civic Centre, St. Peter's Square, Wolverhampton WV1 1SH ☎ 01902 554056 ✉ sue.davies@wolverhampton.gov.uk

Personnel / HR: Ms Janet Lowe, Head - Human Resources Operations, Civic Centre, St. Peter's Square, Wolverhampton WV1 1SH ☎ 01902 551411 ✉ janet.lowe@wolverhampton.gov.uk

Procurement: Mr David Sheldon, Corporate Procurement Officer, Civic Centre, St. Peter's Square, Wolverhampton WV1 1SH ☎ 01902 555066 ✉ david.sheldon@wolverhampton.gov.uk

Public Libraries: Ms Karen Lees, Libraries Officer, Civic Centre, St. Peter's Square, Wolverhampton WV1 1SH ☎ 01902 552010 ✉ karen.lees@wolverhampton.gov.uk

Regeneration: Mr John Brothers, Regeneration Officer, Civic Centre, St. Peter's Square, Wolverhampton WV1 1SH ☎ 01902 554823 ✉ john.brothers@wolverhampton.gov.uk

Regeneration: Mr Nick Edwards, Assistant Director - Prosperity, Civic Centre, St. Peter's Square, Wolverhampton WV1 1SH ☎ 01902 554310 ✉ nick.edwards@wolverhampton.gov.uk

Regeneration: Mr Alistair Merrick, Assistant Director - City Services, Civic Centre, St. Peter's Square, Wolverhampton WV1 1SH ☎ 01902 555216 ✉ alistair.merrick@wolverhampton.gov.uk

Social Services: Ms Anita Bowden, Learning Disabilities Manager, Civic Centre, St. Peter's Square, Wolverhampton WV1

1SH ☎ 01902 552572 ✆ anita.bowden@wolverhampton.gov.uk

Social Services: Mr Steve Brotherton, Joint Head of Commissioning - Older People, Civic Centre, St. Peter's Square, Wolverhampton WV1 1SH ☎ 01902 555318 ✆ steve.brotherton@wolverhampton.gov.uk

Social Services: Mr Gurdip Cheema, Joint Head of Commissioning - Mental Health, Civic Centre, St. Peter's Square, Wolverhampton WV1 1SH ☎ 01902 555304 ✆ gurdip.cheema@wovlerhampton.gov.uk

Social Services: Ms Vivienne Griffin, Assistant Director - Health and Wellbeing, Civic Centre, St. Peter's Square, Wolverhampton WV1 1SH ☎ 01902 555370 ✆ vivienne.griffin@wolverhampton.gov.uk

Social Services: Mr Allan Reynolds, Head - Commissioning - Children, Civic Centre, St. Peter's Square, Wolverhampton WV1 1SH ☎ 01902 553099 ✆ allan.reynolds@wolverhampton.gov.uk

Social Services: Ms Kathy Roper, Joint Head of Commissioning - Disabilities, Civic Centre, St. Peter's Square, Wolverhampton WV1 1SH ☎ 01902 550975 ✆ kathy.roper@wolverhampton.gov.uk

Social Services (Adult): Ms Chrissie Clark, Older People Assesment and Care Manager, Civic Centre, St. Peter's Square, Wolverhampton WV1 1SH ☎ 01902 551241 ✆ chrissie.clark@wolverhampton.gov.uk

Social Services (Adult): Ms Penny Darlington, Head - Adult Safeguarding, Civic Centre, St. Peter's Square, Wolverhampton WV1 1SH ☎ 01902 553258 ✆ penny.darlington@wolverhampton.gov.uk

Social Services (Adult): Mr Anthony Ivko, Assistant Director - Adult Social Care and Housing Support, Civic Centre, St. Peter's Square, Wolverhampton WV1 1SH ☎ 01902 555310 ✆ anthony.ivko@wolverhampton.gov.uk

Social Services (Adult): Ms Jeanette Mason, Older People Provision Officer, Civic Centre, St. Peter's Square, Wolverhampton WV1 1SH ☎ 01902 551238 ✆ jeanette.mason@wolverhampton.gov.uk

Social Services (Adult): Ms June Pickersgill, Community Mental Health Services Officer, Civic Centre, St. Peter's Square, Wolverhampton WV1 1SH ☎ 01902 555802 ✆ june.pickersgill@wolverhampton.gov.uk

Social Services (Children): Ms Emma Bennett, Head - Looked After Children, Civic Centre, St. Peter's Square, Wolverhampton WV1 1SH ☎ 01902 553035 ✆ emma.bennett@wolverhampton.gov.uk

Social Services (Children): Ms Viv East, SEN and Disabilities Officer, Civic Centre, St. Peter's Square, Wolverhampton WV1 1SH ☎ 01902 555874 ✆ viv.east@wolverhampton.gov.uk

Social Services (Children): Ms Gren Knight, Social Inclusion - CYP Officer, Civic Centre, St. Peter's Square, Wolverhampton WV1 1SH ☎ 01902 555953 ✆ gren.knight@wolverhampton.gov.uk

Social Services (Children): Ms Sally Nash, Youth Offending Service Officer, Civic Centre, St. Peter's Square, Wolverhampton WV1 1SH ☎ 01902 553722 ✆ sally.nash@wolverhampton.gov.uk

Social Services (Children): Ms Adele Penfold, Children in Need and Child Protection, Civic Centre, St. Peter's Square, Wolverhampton WV1 1SH ☎ 01902 553034 ✆ adele.penfold@wolverhampton.gov.uk

Social Services (Children): Ms Janet Toplis, Head - Children's Safeguarding, Civic Centre, St. Peter's Square, Wolverhampton WV1 1SH ☎ 01902 550655 ✆ janet.toplis@wolverhampton.gov.uk

Social Services (Children): Mr John Welsby, Assistant Director - Children and Family Support, Civic Centre, St. Peter's Square, Wolverhampton WV1 1SH ☎ 01902 551449 ✆ john.wesley@wolverhampton.gov.uk

Street Scene: Mr Steve Woodward, Head - Street Scene, Civic Centre, St. Peter's Square, Wolverhampton WV1 1SH ☎ 01902 554260 ✆ steve.woodward@wolverhampton.gov.uk

Transport: Mr David Orton, Transportation Strategy and Development Manager, Civic Centre, St. Peter's Square, Wolverhampton WV1 1SH ☎ 01902 555685 ✆ david.orton@wolverhampton.gov.uk

Waste Management: Mr Chris Huddart, Waste Management Officer, Civic Centre, St. Peter's Square, Wolverhampton WV1 1SH ☎ 01902 552052 ✆ chris.huddart@wolverhampton.gov.uk

Children's Play Areas: Mr Pete Rawlinson, Play Manager, Civic Centre, St. Peter's Square, Wolverhampton WV1 1SH ☎ 01902 552174 ✆ pete.rawlinson@wolverhampton.gov.uk

MEMBERS OF THE COUNCIL (59)

Leader of the Council: **Lawrence**, Roger (LAB - St.Peter's)
Labourleadersoffice@wolverhampton.gov.uk

Deputy Leader of the Council: **Bilson**, Peter (LAB - Bushbury South and Low Hill)
peter.bilson@wolverhampton.gov.uk

Angus, Ian (LAB - Bushbury North)
ian.angus@wolverhampton.gov.uk

Banger, Harman (LAB - East Park)
harman.banger@wolverhampton.gov.uk

Bateman, Philip (LAB - Wednesfield North)
phil.bateman@wolverhampton.gov.uk

Bedi, Payal (LAB - East Park)
payal.bedi@wolverhampton.gov.uk

Brookfield, Paula (LAB - Wednesfield South)
paula.brookfield@wolverhampton.gov.uk

Brookfield, Ian (LAB - Fallings Park)
ian.brookfield@wolverhampton.gov.uk

Clarke, Neil (CON - Wednesfield North)
councillorneil.clarke@wolverhampton.gov.uk

Claymore, Ian (LAB - Oxley)
ian.claymore@wolverhampton.gov.uk

Constable, Susan (LAB - Bilston North)
susan.constable@wolverhampton.gov.uk

Darke, Claire (LAB - Park)
claire.darke@wolverhampton.gov.uk

Dass, Bishan (LAB - Ettingshall)
bishan.dass@wolverhampton.gov.uk

David, Alan (LAB - Merry Hill)

alan.bolshaw@wolverhampton.gov.uk
Dehar, Jasbinder (LAB - Bushbury North)
jas.dehar@wolverhampton.gov.uk
Evans, Mark (CON - Tettenhall Regis)
cllrmark.evans@wolverhampton.gov.uk
Evans, Steven (LAB - Fallings Park)
steve.evans4@wolverhampton.gov.uk
Evans, Valerie (LAB - Fallings Park)
valerie.evans@wolverhampton.gov.uk
Findlay, Barry (CON - Tettenhall Regis)
barry.findlay@wolverhampton.gov.uk
Gakhal, Bhupinder (LAB - Wednesfield South)
bhupinder.gakhal@wolverhampton.gov.uk
Gibson, Val (LAB - Bilston East)
val.gibson@wolverhampton.gov.uk
Gwinnett, Malcolm (LD - Spring Vale)
malcolm.gwinnett@wolverhampton.gov.uk
Hardacre, Mike (LAB - Park)
mike.hardacre@wolverhampton.gov.uk
Haynes, Christopher (CON - Merry Hill)
christopher.haynes@wolverhampton.gov.uk
Heap, Michael (LD - Spring Vale)
michael.heap@wolverhampton.gov.uk
Hodgkiss, Julie (LAB - Oxley)
julie.hodgkiss@wolverhampton.gov.uk
Holdcroft, Matthew (CON - Wednesfield South)
matthew.holdcroft@wolverhampton.gov.uk
Inston, Keith (LAB - East Park)
keith.inston@wolverhampton.gov.uk
Jaspal, Milkinderpal (LAB - Heath Town)
milkinder.jaspal@wolverhampton.gov.uk
Jaspal, Jasbir (LAB - Heath Town)
jasbir.jaspal@wolverhampton.gov.uk
Johnson, Andrew (LAB - Ettingshall)
cllra.johnson@wolverhampton.gov.uk
Jones, Bob (LAB - Blakenhall)
bob.jones@wolverhampton.gov.uk
Leach, Linda (LAB - Bilston North)
linda.leach@wolverhampton.gov.uk
Mattu, Elias (LAB - Graiseley)
councillorelias.mattu@wolverhampton.gov.uk
McGregor, Lorna (LAB - Oxley)
lorna.mcgregor@wolverhampton.gov.uk
Mills, Christine (CON - Merry Hill)
councillor.mills@wolverhampton.gov.uk
O'Neill, Peter (LAB - Bushbury South and Low Hill)
peter.o'neill@wolverhampton.gov.uk
Page, Phillip (LAB - Bilston North)
phillip.page@wolverhampton.gov.uk
Patten, Patricia (CON - Penn)
patricia.patten@wolverhampton.gov.uk
Patten, Neville (CON - Bushbury North)
neville.pattern@wolverhampton.gov.uk
Photay, Arun (CON - Tettenhall Wightwick)
arun.photay@wolverhampton.gov.uk
Potter, Rita (LAB - Wednesfield North)
rita.potter@wolverhampton.gov.uk
Reynolds, John (LAB - Graiseley)
john.reynolds@wolverhampton.gov.uk
Rowley, Judith (LAB - Blakenhall)
judith.rowley@wolverhampton.gov.uk
Rowley, John (LAB - Blakenhall)
john.rowley@wolverhampton.gov.uk
Samuels, Sandra (LAB - Ettingshall)
sandra.samuels@wolverhampton.gov.uk
Sarkiewicz, Caroline (LAB - Heath Town)
caroline.siarkiewicz@wolverhampton.gov.uk
Shah, Zahid (LAB - St. Peter's)
zahid.shah@wolverhampton.gov.uk
Simkins, Stephen (LAB - Bilston East)
stephen.simkins@wolverhampton.gov.uk
Singh, Paul (CON - Penn)
paul.singh@wolverhampton.gov.uk
Singh, Tersaim (LAB - St. Peter's)
tersaim.singh@wolverhampton.gov.uk
Sweet, Paul (LAB - Bushbury South and Low Hill)
paul.sweet@wolverhampton.gov.uk
Sweetman, Jacqueline (LAB - Graiseley)
cllrsweetman@wolverhampton.gov.uk
Thompson, Wendy (CON - Tettenhall Wightwick)
wendy.thompson@wolverhampton.gov.uk
Turner, Thomas (LAB - Bilston East)
thomas.turner@wolverhamtpon.gov.uk
Waite, Martin (LAB - Penn)
martin.waite@wolverhampton.gov.uk
Whitehouse, Richard (LD - Spring Vale)
richard.whitehouse@wolverhampton.gov.uk
Wynne, Andrew (CON - Tettenhall Wightwick)
andrew.wynne@wolverhampton.gov.uk
Yardley, Johnathan (CON - Tettenhall Regis)
jonathan.yardley@wolverhampton.gov.uk

POLITICAL COMPOSITION

LAB: 43, CON: 13, LD: 3

CABINET

Leader: Mr Roger Lawrence
Deputy Leader/ Economic Regeneration & Prosperity: Mr Peter Bilson
Adult Services: Mr Steven Evans
Children & Families: Ms Susan Constable
City Services: Mr John Reynolds
Governance & Performance: Mr Paul Sweet
Health & Wellbeing: Ms Sandra Samuels
Leisure & Communities: Mr Elias Mattu
Resources: Mr Andrew Johnson
Schools, Skills & Learning: Mr Phillip Page

COMMITTEE CHAIRS

Adults & Community Scrutiny: Ms Val Gibson
Audit: Mr Keith Inston
Children & Young People Scrutiny: Mrs Julie Hodgkiss
Health Scrutiny: Ms Claire Darke
Licensing: Mr Bishan Dass
Pensions: Mr Tersaim Singh
Planning: Mrs Judith Rowley
Scrutiny: Mr Peter O'Neill
Sustainable Communities: Mr John Rowley

WORCESTER CITY — D

Worcester City Council, Orchard House Complex, Farrier Street, Worcester WR1 3BB ☎ 01905 722233 🖷 01905 722059; 01905 722028 💻 www.worcester.gov.uk

FACTS & FIGURES

Police Authority: West Mercia Police Authority
Health Authority: NHS West Midlands

Learning and Skills Council: West Midlands
Parliamentary Constituencies: Worcester
EU Constituencies: West Midlands
Election Frequency: Elections are by thirds

PRINCIPAL OFFICERS

Chief Executive: Mr Duncan Sharkey, Managing Director, Orchard House, Worcester WR1 3BB ☎ 01905 722233 🖷 01905 722028 ✉ duncan.sharkey@worcester.gov.uk

Senior Management: Ms Carol Brown, Corporate Director for Commissioning, Customer Services and Communication, Orchard House, Farrier Street, Worcester WR1 3BB ☎ 01905 722233 🖷 01905 722028 ✉ carol.brown@worcester.gov.uk

Senior Management: Mrs Ruth Mullen, Corporate Director for Service Delivery, Orhcard House Complex, Farrier Street, Worcester WR1 3BB ☎ 01905 722233 🖷 01905 722028 ✉ ruth.mullen@worcester.gov.uk

Building Control: Mr Reza Saneie, Building Control Partnership Manager, Council House, Avenue Road, Malvern WR14 3AF ☎ 01684 862146; 01905 722233 ✉ reza.saneie@malvernhills.gov.uk; mail@southworcestershirebuildingcontrol.gov.uk

PR / Communications: Mr Rob Byrne, Communications and PR Team Manager, Orchard House Complex, Farrier Street, Worcester WR1 3BB ☎ 01905 722233 🖷 01905 722350 ✉ rob.byrne@worcester.gov.uk

Community Safety: Mr Chris Hill, Service Manager, Orchard House Complex, Farrier Street, Worcester WR1 3BB ☎ 01905 722233 🖷 01905 722350 ✉ chris.hill@worcester.gov.uk

Computer Management: Mr Mac Chivers, Information Technology Manager, Copenhagen Street, Worcester WR1 3EY ☎ 01905 722121 ✉ SW2.ServiceDesk@worcester.gov.uk

Corporate Services: Miss Doreen Porter, Service Manager, Orchard House Complex, Farrier Street, Worcester WR1 3BB ☎ 01905 722233 🖷 01905 772028 ✉ doreen.porter@worcester.gov.uk

Customer Service: Ms Carol Brown, Corporate Director for Commissioning, Customer Services and Communication, Orchard House, Farrier Street, Worcester WR1 3BB ☎ 01905 722233 🖷 01905 722028 ✉ carol.brown@worcester.gov.uk

Economic Development: Mrs Anne Bonsor, Service Manager, Orchard House Complex, Farrier Street, Worcester WR1 3BB ☎ 01905 722233 🖷 01905 722370 ✉ anne.bonsor@worcester.gov.uk

E-Government: Mrs Julie Slatter, Service Manager, Orchard House Complex, Farrier Street, Worcester WR1 3BB ☎ 01905 722233 🖷 01905 722350 ✉ julie.slatter@worcester.gov.uk

Electoral Registration: Mrs Diane Thomas, Elections Officer, Guildhall, High Street, Worcester WR1 2EY ☎ 01905 722027 🖷 01905 722028 ✉ d.thomas@worcester.gov.uk

Emergency Planning: Ms Nina Warrington, Strategic Housing Services Manager, Orchard House Complex, Farrier Street, Worcester WR1 3BB ☎ 01905 722233 🖷 01905 722211 ✉ nina.warrington@worcester.gov.uk

Energy Management: Mrs Julie Slatter, Service Manager, Orchard House Complex, Farrier Street, Worcester WR1 3BB ☎ 01905 722233 🖷 01905 722350 ✉ julie.slatter@worcester.gov.uk

Environmental / Technical Services: Mr David Sutton, Service Manager, Orchard House Complex, Worcester WR1 3BB ☎ 01905 722233 🖷 01905 722350 ✉ david.sutton@worcester.gov.uk

Environmental Health: Mrs Anita Fletcher, Business Compliance Manager, Wyatt House, Farrier Street, Worcester WR1 3BH ☎ 01905 822799 ✉ wrsenquiries@worcsregservices.gov.uk

Events Manager: Ms Nadja Von Dahlen, Events Co-ordinator, 2-4 Copenhagen Street, Worcester WR1 2EY ☎ 01905 722320 🖷 01905 721149 ✉ nadja.vondahlen@visitworcester.gov.uk

Finance and Treasurer: Mr Andy Bromage, Acting Internal Audit Manager, Orchard House Complex, Farrier Street, Worcester WR1 3BB ☎ 01905 722233 🖷 01905 722168 ✉ andy.bromage@worcester.gov.uk

Finance and Treasurer: Mrs Lesley Meagher, Service Manager for Section 151 Responsbilities, Orchard House Complex, Farrier Street, Worcester WR1 3BB ☎ 01905 722233 🖷 01905 722190 ✉ lesley.meagher@worcester.gov.uk

Grounds Maintenance: Mr David Sutton, Service Manager, Orchard House Complex, Worcester WR1 3BB ☎ 01905 722233 🖷 01905 722350 ✉ david.sutton@worcester.gov.uk

Health and Safety: Mr Mike Mountford, Safety Officer, Orchard House, Farrier Street, Worcester WR1 3BZ ☎ 01905 722048 🖷 01905 722034 ✉ michael.mountford@worcester.gov.uk

Housing: Ms Nina Warrington, Strategic Housing Services Manager, Orchard House Complex, Farrier Street, Worcester WR1 3BB ☎ 01905 722233 🖷 01905 722211 ✉ nina.warrington@worcester.gov.uk

Local Area Agreement: Mrs Julie Slatter, Service Manager, Orchard House Complex, Farrier Street, Worcester WR1 3BB ☎ 01905 722233 🖷 01905 722350 ✉ julie.slatter@worcester.gov.uk

Legal: Miss Doreen Porter, Service Manager, Orchard House Complex, Farrier Street, Worcester WR1 3BB ☎ 01905 722233 🖷 01905 772028 ✉ doreen.porter@worcester.gov.uk

Leisure and Cultural Services: Mr Chris Hill, Service Manager, Orchard House Complex, Farrier Street, Worcester WR1 3BB ☎ 01905 722233 🖷 01905 722350 ✉ chris.hill@worcester.gov.uk

Licensing: Mr Niall McMenamin, Senior Practitioner, Wyatt House, Farrier Street, Worcester WR1 3BH ☎ 01905 822799 ✉ wrsenquiries@worcsregservices.gov.uk

Member Services: Miss Claire Chaplin, Democratic Services

Team Leader, Guildhall, Worcester WR1 2EY ☎ 01905 722233 🖷 01905 722028 ✉ claire.chaplin@worcester.gov.uk

Member Services: Mrs Margaret Johnson, Committee Administrator, Guild Hall, Worcester WR1 2EY ☎ 01905 722233 🖷 01905 721120 ✉ margaret.johnson@worcester.gov.uk

Member Services: Mr Julian Pugh, Democratic Services Administrator, Guildhall, Worcester WR1 2EY ☎ 01905 722233 🖷 01905 721120 ✉ julian.pugh@worcester.gov.uk

Parking: Mr David Sutton, Service Manager, Orchard House Complex, Worcester WR1 3BB ☎ 01905 722233 🖷 01905 722350 ✉ david.sutton@worcester.gov.uk

Personnel / HR: Mrs Gail Hatfield, Service Manager, Orchard House Complex, Farrier Street, Worcester WR1 3BB ☎ 01905 722233 🖷 01905 722304 ✉ gail.hatfield@worcester.gov.uk

Planning: Mr Paul O'Conner, Service Manager, Orchard House, Farrier Street, Worcester WR1 3BB ☎ 01905 722233 🖷 01905 722565 ✉ paul.o'conner@worcester.gov.uk

Procurement: Mr Darrell Pulver, Procurement Officer, Orhcard House, Farrier Street, Worcester WR1 3BB ☎ 01905 722233 🖷 01905 722190 ✉ darrell.pulver@worcester.gov.uk

Recycling & Waste Minimisation: Mr David Sutton, Service Manager, Orchard House Complex, Worcester WR1 3BB ☎ 01905 722233 🖷 01905 722350 ✉ david.sutton@worcester.gov.uk

Regeneration: Mrs Anne Bonsor, Service Manager, Orchard House Complex, Farrier Street, Worcester WR1 3BB ☎ 01905 722233 🖷 01905 722370 ✉ anne.bonsor@worcester.gov.uk

Staff Training: Mrs Gail Hatfield, Service Manager, Orchard House Complex, Farrier Street, Worcester WR1 3BB ☎ 01905 722233 🖷 01905 722304 ✉ gail.hatfield@worcester.gov.uk

Street Scene: Mr David Sutton, Service Manager, Orchard House Complex, Worcester WR1 3BB ☎ 01905 722233 🖷 01905 722350 ✉ david.sutton@worcester.gov.uk

Sustainable Communities: Mrs Anne Bonsor, Service Manager, Orchard House Complex, Farrier Street, Worcester WR1 3BB ☎ 01905 722233 🖷 01905 722370 ✉ anne.bonsor@worcester.gov.uk

Sustainable Development: Mrs Anne Bonsor, Service Manager, Orchard House Complex, Farrier Street, Worcester WR1 3BB ☎ 01905 722233 🖷 01905 722370 ✉ anne.bonsor@worcester.gov.uk

Tourism: Ms Amanda Millichip, Tourism and Marketing Officer, 2-4 Copenhagen Street, Worcester WR1 3ES ☎ 01905 721148 🖷 01905 721149 ✉ amanda.millichip@visitworcester.gov.uk

Town Centre: Ms Georgia Smith, Head of Visit Worcester, 2-4 Copenhagan Street, Worcester WR1 3ES ☎ 01905 722561 🖷 01905 721149 ✉ georgia.smith@visitworcester.gov.uk

Total Place: Mr Duncan Sharkey, Managing Director, Orchard House Complex, Farrier Street, Worcester WR1 3BB ☎ 01905 722233 🖷 01905 722028 ✉ duncan.sharkey@worcester.gov.uk

Waste Collection and Disposal: Mr David Sutton, Service Manager, Orchard House Complex, Worcester WR1 3BB ☎ 01905 722233 🖷 01905 722350 ✉ david.sutton@worcester.gov.uk

Children's Play Areas: Mr David Sutton, Service Manager, Orchard House Complex, Worcester WR1 3BB ☎ 01905 722233 🖷 01905 722350 ✉ david.sutton@worcester.gov.uk

MEMBERS OF THE COUNCIL (35)

***Mayor:* Berry**, Roger (LAB - Gorse Hill)
roger.berry@worcester.gov.uk

***Mayor:* Roberts**, Andrew (CON - Warndon Parish South)
andrew.roberts@worcester.gov.uk

***Mayor:* Tibbutt**, David (CON - Battenhall)
david.tibbutt@worcester.gov.uk

***Deputy Leader of the Council:* Bayliss**, Marc (CON - Bedwardine)
mbayliss@worcester.gov.uk

Agar, Patricia (LAB - Nunnery)
pat.agar@worcester.gov.uk

Amos, Alan (LAB - Warndon)
alan.amos@worcester.gov.uk

Boorn, Richard (LAB - Nunnery)
richard.boorn@worcester.gov.uk

Carpenter, Kenneth (LD - Claines)
kenneth.carpenter@worcester.gov.uk

Cawthorne, Chris (LAB - St. John)
christine.cawthorne@worcester.gov.uk

Cronin, Simon (LAB - Nunnery)
simon.cronin@worcester.gov.uk

Denham, Lynn (LAB - Cathedral)
lynn.denham@worcester.gov.uk

Denham, Paul (LAB - Rainbow Hill)
paul.denham@worcester.gov.uk

Ditta, Allah (CON - Cathedral)
aditta@worcester.gov.uk

Geraghty, Simon (CON - St. Clement)
simon.geraghty@worcester.gov.uk

Gregson, Adrian (LAB - Rainbow Hill)
adrian.gregson@worcester.gov.uk

Hodges, Jo (LAB - Warndon)
jo.hodges@worcester.gov.uk

Hodgson, Lucy (CON - Warndon Parish South)
lucy.hodgson@worcester.gov.uk

Hodgson, Stephen (CON - Warndon Parish North)
stephen.hodgson@worcester.gov.uk

Jones, Gareth (CON - St. Stephen)
gareth.jones@worcester.gov.uk

Knight, Roger (CON - St. Peter's Parish)
rogerdknight@tiscali.co.uk

Lamb, Matthew (LAB - St. John)
matthew.lamb@worcester.gov.uk

Laurenson, Neil (GRN - St. Stephen)
neil.laurenson@worcester.gov.uk

Mitchell, Chris (CON - St. Clement)
chris.mitchell@lmco.com

Prodger, Derek (CON - Bedwardine)
derek.prodger@worcester.gov.uk

Riaz, Jabba (CON - Cathedral)
jabba.riaz@worcester.gov.uk

Rowden, Robert (CON - Battenhall)

robert.rowden@worcester.gov.uk
Smith, Liz (LD - Claines)
esmith@worcester.gov.uk
Squires, Joy (LAB - Arboretum)
joy.squires@worcester.gov.uk
Squires, George (LAB - Arboretum)
george.squires@worcester.gov.uk
Tarbuck, Aubrey (CON - St. Peter's Parish)
aubrey.tarbuck@worcester.gov.uk
Udall, Richard (LAB - St. John)
richard.udall@worcester.gov.uk
Whitehouse, Mike (CON - Claines)
mike.whitehouse@worcester.gov.uk
Wilkinson, Douglas (CON - Warndon Parish North)
douglas.wilkinson@worcester.gov.uk
Wilkinson, David (CON - Bedwardine)
david.wilkinson@worcester.gov.uk
Williams, Geoffrey (LAB - Gorse Hill)
geoff.williams@worcester.gov.uk

POLITICAL COMPOSITION
CON: 17, LAB: 15, LD: 2, GRN: 1

CABINET
Leader: Mr Simon Geraghty
Deputy Leader / Economic Responsibility: Mr Marc Bayliss
Cleaner & Greener City: Mr Roger Knight
Customer Service & Communications: Mrs Lucy Hodgson
Delivering Value for Money: Mr Andrew Roberts
Safer & Stronger Communities: Mr Jabba Riaz

COMMITTEE CHAIRS
Accounts: Mr Gareth Jones
Accounts: Mr Simon Geraghty
Audit: Mrs Liz Smith
Licensing: Mr Paul Denham
Performance Management & Budgets: Mr Stephen Hodgson
Personnel & General Purposes: Mr Simon Geraghty
Planning: Mr Geoffrey Williams
Scrutiny: Mrs Joy Squires

WORCESTERSHIRE C

Worcestershire County Council, County Hall, Spetchley Road, Worcester WR5 2NP ☎ 01905 763763 🖷 01905 763000
💻 www.worcestershire.gov.uk

FACTS & FIGURES
Police Authority: West Mercia Police Authority
Health Authority: NHS West Midlands
Learning and Skills Council: West Midlands
Parliamentary Constituencies: Bromsgrove, Redditch, Worcester, Worcestershire Mid, Worcestershire West, Wyre Forest
EU Constituencies: West Midlands
Election Frequency: Elections are of whole council

PRINCIPAL OFFICERS
Chief Executive: Mrs Trish Haines, Chief Executive, County Hall, Spetchley Road, Worcester WR5 2NP ☎ 01905 766101
🖰 thaines@worcestershire.gov.uk

Senior Management: Mr Patrick Birch, Director of Resources, County Hall, Spetchley Road, Worcester WR5 2NP ☎ 01905 766200 🖷 01905 766644 🖰 pbirch@worcestershire

Senior Management: Mr John Hobbs, Director of Environmental Services, County Hall, Spetchley Road, Worcester WR5 2NP ☎ 01905 766700 🖷 01905 766899
🖰 jhobbs@worcestershire.gov.uk

Architect, Building / Property Services: Mr Peter Parkes, Head of Property Services, County Hall, Spetchley Road, Worcester WR5 2NP ☎ 01905 766400 🖷 01905 766498
🖰 pparkes@worcestershire.gov.uk

Best Value: Mr Patrick Birch, Director of Resources, County Hall, Spetchley Road, Worcester WR5 2NP ☎ 01905 766200 🖷 01905 766644 🖰 pbirch@worcestershire

Children / Youth Services: Mr Paul Finnemore, Operational Manager of Youth Support, County Hall, Spetchley Road, Worcester WR5 2NP ☎ 01905 765628 🖷 01905 765306
🖰 pfinnemore@worcestershire.gov.uk

Children / Youth Services: Mrs Gail Quinton, Director of Children's Services, County Hall, Spetchley Road, Worcester WR5 2NP ☎ 01905 766686 🖷 01905 766156
🖰 gquinton@worcestershire.gov.uk

Civil Registration: Ms Sharon Duggan, Registration & Coroner's Service Manager, County Hall, Spetchley Road, Worcester WR5 2NP ☎ 01905 728754 🖰 sduggan@worcestershire.gov.uk

PR / Communications: Mrs Katharine Clough, Marketing & Communications Manager, County Hall, Spetchley Road, Worcester WR5 2NP ☎ 01905 728831
🖰 kclough@worcestershire.gov.uk

Community Planning: Mr Simon Adams, Head of Community Leadership, County Hall, Spetchley Road, Worcester WR5 2NP ☎ 01905 766102 🖰 simonadams@worcestershire.gov.uk

Community Planning: Mr Neil Anderson, Head of Culture & Community, County Hall, Spetchley Road, Worcester WR5 2NP ☎ 01905 766104 🖷 01905 766498
🖰 dtilley@worcestershire.gov.uk

Community Safety: Ms Catherine Driscoll, Head of Adult Social Care, County Hall, Spetchley Road, Worcester WR5 2NP ☎ 01905 766580 🖰 cdriscoll@worcestershire.gov.uk

Computer Management: Mr Peter Bishop, Head of Technology, Systems & Customer Access, County Hall, Spetchley Road, Worcester WR5 2NP ☎ 01905 766020 🖷 01905 766199
🖰 pbishop@worcestershire.gov.uk

Contracts: Mr Nick Yarwood, Highways Contracts & Programme Manager, County Hall, Spetchley Road, Worcester WR5 2NP ☎ 01905 728648 🖷 01905 766839
🖰 nyarwood@worcestershire.gov.uk

Corporate Services: Mrs Clare Mitchell, Head of Change, County Hall, Spetchley Road, Worcester WR5 2NP ☎ 01905 763763 🖰 cmitchell@worcestershire.gov.uk

Customer Service: Ms Rachel Hill, Head of Customer Services, County Hall, Spetchley Road, Worcester WR5 2NP ☎ 01905 768711 🖱 rhill@worcestershire.gov.uk

Customer Service: Ms Annette Stock, Policy & Review Officer, County Hall, Spetchley Road, Worcester WR5 2NP ☎ 01905 766640 🖷 01905 766109 🖱 astock@worcestershire.gov.uk

Economic Development: Mr Ahmed Goga, Head of Economic Development & Planning, County Hall, Spetchley Road, Worcester WR5 2NP ☎ 01905 766387 🖱 agoga@worcestershire.gov.uk

Economic Development: Mr Glyn West, Head of Economic Development & Sustainability, County Hall, Spetchley Road, Worcester WR5 2NP ☎ 01905 766720 🖱 gwest@worcestershire.gov.uk

Education: Mr Paul Finnemore, Youth Service Senior Manager, County Hall, Spetchley Road, Worcester WR5 2NP ☎ 01905 765628 🖱 pfinnemore@worcestershire.gov.uk

E-Government: Mr Patrick Birch, Director of Resources, County Hall, Spetchley Road, Worcester WR5 2NP ☎ 01905 766200 🖷 01905 766644 🖱 pbirch@worcestershire

Electoral Registration: Mr Simon Mallinson, Head of Legal & Democratic Services, County Hall, Spetchley Road, Worcester WR5 2NP ☎ 01905 766670 🖷 01905 766677 🖱 smallinson@worcestershire.gov.uk

Emergency Planning: Mr Nick Riding, Emergency Planning Manager, County Hall, Spetchley Road, Worcester WR5 2NP ☎ 01905 728515 🖱 nriding@worcestershire.gov.uk

Energy Management: Mr Phil Harris, Chief Engineer, County Hall, Spetchley Road, Worcester WR5 2NP ☎ 01905 766406 🖷 01905 766498 🖱 pharris@worcestershire.gov.uk

Environmental / Technical Services: Mr John Hobbs, Director of Environmental Services, County Hall, Spetchley Road, Worcester WR5 2NP ☎ 01905 766700 🖷 01905 766899 🖱 jhobbs@worcestershire.gov.uk

Estates, Property & Valuation: Mr Mike Williams, Group Leader of Estates, County Hall, Spetchley Road, Worcester WR5 2NP ☎ 01905 766463 🖷 01905 766498 🖱 mjwilliams@worcestershire.gov.uk

European Liaison: Mr Aamir Kayani, Enterprise Employment & Skills Manager, County Hall, Spetchley Road, Worcester WR5 2NP ☎ 01905 766816 🖷 01905 766377 🖱 akayani@worcestershire.gov.uk

Facilities: Mr David Harrison, Facilities Manager, County Hall, Spetchley Road, Worcester WR5 2NP ☎ 01905 766301 🖷 01905 766498 🖱 dharrison2@worcestershire.gov.uk

Finance and Treasurer: Mrs Sue Alexander, Head of Finance & Business Support, County Hall, Spetchley Road, Worcester WR5 2NP ☎ 01905 766984 🖱 salexander@worcestershire.gov.uk

Finance and Treasurer: Mr Patrick Birch, Director of Resources, County Hall, Spetchley Road, Worcester WR5 2NP ☎ 01905 766200 🖷 01905 766644 🖱 pbirch@worcestershire

Finance and Treasurer: Mr Martin Finch, Head of Financial Practice & Standards, County Hall, Spetchley Road, Worcester WR5 2NP ☎ 01905 766510 🖱 mfinch@worcestershire.gov.uk

Fleet Management: Mr Stuart Payton, Access Manager, County Hall, Spetchley Road, Worcester WR5 2NP ☎ 01905 766889 🖱 spayton@worcestershire.gov.uk

Health and Safety: Dr Clive Werrett, Corporate Health & Safety Manager, County Hall, Spetchley Road, Worcester WR5 2NP ☎ 01905 766219 🖷 01905 766221 🖱 cwerrett@worcestershire.gov.uk

Highways: Mr Ian Bamforth, Countryside Manager, County Hall, Spetchley Road, Worcester WR5 2NP ☎ 01905 768210 🖷 01905 766839 🖱 ibamforth@worcestershire.gov.uk

Local Area Agreement: Mr Glyn West, Head of Economic Development & Sustainability, County Hall, Spetchley Road, Worcester WR5 2NP ☎ 01905 766720 🖱 gwest@worcestershire.gov.uk

Legal: Mr Simon Mallinson, Head of Legal & Democratic Services, County Hall, Spetchley Road, Worcester WR5 2NP ☎ 01905 766670 🖷 01905 766677 🖱 smallinson@worcestershire.gov.uk

Lifelong Learning: Ms Kathy Kirk, Strategic Libraries & Lifelong Learning Manager, County Hall, Spetchley Road, Worcester WR5 2NP ☎ 01905 766264 🖷 01905 766190 🖱 kkirk@worcestershire.gov.uk

Member Services: Ms Sian Clark, Democratic Services Manager, County Hall, Spetchley Road, Worcester WR5 2NP ☎ 01905 728753 🖷 01905 766644 🖱 sclark@worcestershire.gov.uk

Partnerships: Mrs Debbie Birch, Heritage Partnership Manager, County Hall, Spetchley Road, Worcester WR5 2NP ☎ 01905 766230 🖷 01905 766244 🖱 dbirch@worcestershire.gov.uk

Partnerships: Ms Catherine Driscoll, Head of Adult Social Care, County Hall, Spetchley Road, Worcester WR5 2NP ☎ 01905 766580 🖱 cdriscoll@worcestershire.gov.uk

Partnerships: Mr Nick Yarwood, Highways Contracts & Programme Manager, County Hall, Spetchley Road, Worcester WR5 2NP ☎ 01905 728648 🖷 01905 766839 🖱 nyarwood@worcestershire.gov.uk

Personnel / HR: Mr Kenny Brown, Head of Human Resources, County Hall, Spetchley Road, Worcester WR5 2NP ☎ 01905 766216 🖷 01905 766221 🖱 kbrown@worcestershire.gov.uk

Planning: Mr Ahmed Goga, Head of Economic Development & Planning, County Hall, Spetchley Road, Worcester WR5 2NP ☎ 01905 766387 🖱 agoga@worcestershire.gov.uk

Procurement: Mr Michael Howard, Strategic Procurement Officer, County Hall, Spetchley Road, Worcester WR5 2NP

☎ 01905 766507 🖷 01905 766578 ✉ mhoward@worcestershire.gov.uk

Public Libraries: Ms Catherine Driscoll, Head of Adult Social Care, County Hall, Spetchley Road, Worcester WR5 2NP ☎ 01905 766580 ✉ cdriscoll@worcestershire.gov.uk

Public Libraries: Ms Kathy Kirk, Strategic Libraries & Lifelong Learning Manager, County Hall, Spetchley Road, Worcester WR5 2NP ☎ 01905 766264 🖷 01905 766190 ✉ kkirk@worcestershire.gov.uk

Recycling & Waste Minimisation: Mr Richard Woodward, Waste Services Manager, County Hall, Spetchley Road, Worcester WR5 2NP ☎ 01905 768262 ✉ rwoodward@worcestershire.gov.uk

Road Safety: Mr Ed Dursley, Sustainable Schemes Manager, County Hall, Spetchley Road, Worcester WR5 2NP ☎ 01905 763763

Social Services: Mr Eddie Clarke, Director of Adult & Community Services, County Hall, Spetchley Road, Worcester WR5 2NP ☎ 01905 766900 🖷 01905 766930 ✉ eclarke@worcestershire.gov.uk

Social Services (Adult): Mr Eddie Clarke, Director of Adult & Community Services, County Hall, Spetchley Road, Worcester WR5 2NP ☎ 01905 766900 🖷 01905 766930 ✉ eclarke@worcestershire.gov.uk

Social Services (Adult): Ms Catherine Driscoll, Head of Adult Social Care, County Hall, Spetchley Road, Worcester WR5 2NP ☎ 01905 766580 ✉ cdriscoll@worcestershire.gov.uk

Social Services (Children): Ms Siobhan Williams, Head of Safeguarding & Services to Children & Young People, County Hall, Spetchley Road, Worcester WR5 2NP ☎ 01905 766894 🖷 01905 766930 ✉ sawiliams2@worcestershire.gov.uk

Staff Training: Mrs Elaine McCarthy, People Development, Well Being & Diversity Manager, County Hall, Spetchley Road, Worcester WR5 2NP ☎ 01905 766218 🖷 01905 763000 ✉ emccarthy@worcestershire.gov.uk

Sustainable Communities: Ms Liz Alston, Sustainability Officer, County Hall, Spetchley Road, Worcester WR5 2NP ☎ 01905 766745 🖷 01905 766899 ✉ lalston@worcestershire.gov.uk

Sustainable Development: Ms Liz Alston, Sustainability Officer, County Hall, Spetchley Road, Worcester WR5 2NP ☎ 01905 766745 🖷 01905 766899 ✉ lalston@worcestershire.gov.uk

Traffic Management: Mr Peter Blake, Head of Integrated Transportation, County Hall, Spetchley Road, Worcester WR5 2NP ☎ 01905 766844 🖷 01905 766899 ✉ pblake@worcestershire.gov.uk

Transport: Mr Andy Baker, Integrated Passenger Transport Manager, County Hall, Spetchley Road, Worcester WR5 2NP ☎ 01905 822071 ✉ acbaker@worcestershire.gov.uk

Transport: Mr Peter Blake, Head of Integrated Transportation, County Hall, Spetchley Road, Worcester WR5 2NP ☎ 01905 766844 🖷 01905 766899 ✉ pblake@worcestershire.gov.uk

Transport Planner: Mr Peter Blake, Head of Integrated Transportation, County Hall, Spetchley Road, Worcester WR5 2NP ☎ 01905 766844 🖷 01905 766899 ✉ pblake@worcestershire.gov.uk

Total Place: Mr Patrick Birch, Director of Resources, County Hall, Spetchley Road, Worcester WR5 2NP ☎ 01905 766200 🖷 01905 766644 ✉ pbirch@worcestershire

Waste Collection and Disposal: Mr Richard Woodward, Waste Services Manager, County Hall, Spetchley Road, Worcester WR5 2NP ☎ 01905 768262 ✉ rwoodward@worcestershire.gov.uk

Waste Management: Mr Richard Woodward, Waste Services Manager, County Hall, Spetchley Road, Worcester WR5 2NP ☎ 01905 768262 ✉ rwoodward@worcestershire.gov.uk

MEMBERS OF THE COUNCIL (58)

***Chair:* Adams**, Rob (CON - Upton Snodsbury)
radams@worcestershire.gov.uk

***Leader of the Council:* Hardman**, Adrian (CON - Bredon)
aihardman@worcestershire.gov.uk

***Group Leader:* Tucker**, Liz (LD - Pershore)
ltucker@worcestershire.gov.uk

Ahmed, Mumshad (LAB - Kidderminster - St Georges and St Oswalds)
mumshad@hotmail.co.uk

Amos, Alan (LAB - Gorse Hill & Warndon)
alan.amos@worcester.gov.uk

Askin, Susan (LD - Claines)
saskin@worcestershire.gov.uk

Banks, Robert (CON - Evesham South)
rbanks@btconnect.com

Bean, Tom (LD - Littletons)
tbean@worcestershire.gov.uk

Blagg, Sheila (CON - Woodvale)
sblagg@worcestershire.gov.uk

Blagg, Anthony (CON - Bromsgrove Central)
a.blagg@worcestershire.gov.uk

Broomfield, Maurice (CON - Ombersley)
mbroomfield2@worcestershire.gov.uk

Brown, Steve (LD - Malvern Chase)
steve4chase2009@hotmail.co.uk

Brunner, Juliet (CON - Arrow Valley East)
juliet.brunner@redditchbc.gov.uk

Bullock, Robert (CON - Croome)

Bunker, Maddy (CON - Bromsgrove South)
mbunker@worcestershire.gov.uk

Cairns, John (CON - Worcester - St Peter)
jcairns@worcestershire.gov.uk

Campion, John (CON - Bewdley)
jcampion@worcestershire.gov.uk

Clayton, Brandon (CON - Arrow Valley West)
brandon.clayton@redditchbc.gov.uk

Clee, Stephen (CON - Chaddesley)
sjclee@worcestershire.gov.uk

Davey, Pamela (CON - Droitwich East)
pdavey@worcestershire.gov.uk

Davies, Alwyn (CON - Hallow)
aedavies@worcestershire.gov.uk

Desmond, Nathan (CON - St Mary's)

nathan.desmond@wyreforestdc.gov.uk
Ditta, Allah (CON - Rainbow Hill)
aditta@worchester.gov.uk
Drinkwater, Mary (CON - Worcester - St Stephen)
mdrinkwater@worcestershire.gov.uk
Duffy, Lynne (CON - Droitwich West)
lduffy@worcestershire.gov.uk
Eyre, Liz (CON - Broadway)
eeyre@worcestershire.gov.uk
Gandy, Barry (CON - Redditch South)
bgandy@worcestershire.gov.uk
Geraghty, Simon (CON - Worcester Riverside)
sgeraghty@worcestershire.gov.uk
Gretton, Philip (CON - Redditch South)
pgretton@worcestershire.gov.uk
Griffiths, June (CON - Alvechurch)
j.griffiths@bromsgrove.gov.uk
Hart, Marcus (CON - Kidderminster St Johns)
marcushart78@yahoo.co.uk
Hingley, Anne (CON - St Barnabas)
anne.hingley@wyreforestdc.gov.uk
Hodgson, Lucy (CON - Nunnery)
lucy.hodgson@btinternet.com
Holt, Clive (CON - Harvington)
cholt@worcestershire.gov.uk
Hopkins, Gay (CON - Arrow Valley East)
gay.hopkins@redditchbc.gov.uk
McDonald, Peter (LAB - Beacon)
pmcdonald2@worcestershire.gov.uk
Miller, Tony (CON - Bowbrook)
a.miller88o@btinternet.com
Moffett, Emma (CON - Bromsgrove East)
emma.@emmamoffett.co.uk
Moore, Ed (CON - Clent Hill)
emoore@worcestershire.gov.uk
Morgan, Penelope (LD - Malvern Langland)
pmorgan@worcestershire.gov.uk
Nielsen, Beverley (LD - Malvern Trinity)
beverley.nielsen@bcu.ac.uk
Oborski, Fran (LIB - Kidderminster St Chads)
franoborski@btinternet.com
Parish, Jim (INDNA - Stourport on Severn)
jparish@worcestershire.gov.uk
Peters, Stephen (INDNA - Wythall)
speters@worcestershire.gov.uk
Pollock, Ken (CON - Tenbury)
kpollock2@worcestershire.gov.uk
Potter, Jane (CON - Arrow Valley West)
janeapotter@talktalk.net
Prodger, Derek (CON - Worcester - Bedwardine)
dprodger@worcestershire.gov.uk
Prodger, Derek (CON - Bedwardine)
dprodger@worcestershire.gov.uk
Roberts, Andrew (CON - Warndon)
acroberts@worchester.gov.uk
Smith, John (CON - Evesham North West)
jhsmith@worcestershire.gov.uk
Smith, Clive (LD - Malvern Link)
Spencer, Terry (CON - Redditch North)
TA6ospencer@aol.com
Taylor, Kit (CON - Bromsgrove West)
ktaylor3@worcestershire.gov.uk
Thain, David (CON - Redditch North)
davethain@gmail.com
Thomas, John (INDNA - Stourport on Severn)
jthomas2@worcestershire.gov.uk
Udall, Richard (LAB - Worcester - St John)
rudall2@worcestershire.gov.uk
Wells, Tom (LD - Powick)
talwells@btinternet.com
Yarranton, Gordon (CON - Cookley, Wolveryley and Wribbenhall)
gyarranton@worcestershire.gov.uk

POLITICAL COMPOSITION
CON: 42, LD: 8, LAB: 4, INDNA: 3, LIB: 1

CABINET
Leader / Finance: Mr Adrian Hardman
Deputy Leader / Economy & Infrastructure: Mr Simon Geraghty
Adult Social Care: Mr Philip Gretton
Children & Young Peoples Social Change: Mrs Liz Eyre
Education & Skills: Mrs Jane Potter
Environment & Waste Management: Mr Anthony Blagg
Health & Wellbeing: Mr Marcus Hart
Highways & Transport: Mr John Smith
Localism & Communities: Mr John Campion
Transformation & Change: Mr David Thain

COMMITTEE CHAIRS
Adult Care & Wellbeing Overview & Scrutiny: Mrs Maddy Bunker
Audit & Governance: Mr Clive Holt
Children & Young People Overview & Scrutiny: Mrs Juliet Brunner
Environment & Economy Overview & Scrutiny: Dr Ken Pollock
Health Overview & Scrutiny: Mr Andrew Roberts
Overview & Scrutiny Performance: Mr Tom Wells
Planning & Regulatory: Mr Alwyn Davies
Resources Overview & Scrutiny: Mr Robert Banks

WORTHING D
Worthing Borough Council, Worthing Town Hall, Chapel Road, Worthing BN11 1HA ☎ 01903 239999 🖷 01903 236552
enquiries@worthing.gov.uk 💻 www.worthing.gov.uk

FACTS & FIGURES
Police Authority: Sussex Police Authority
Health Authority: South East Coast Strategic Health Authority
Learning and Skills Council: South East
Parliamentary Constituencies: Worthing West
EU Constituencies: South East
Election Frequency: Elections are by thirds

PRINCIPAL OFFICERS
Chief Executive: Mr Peter Latham, Chief Executive, Worthing Town Hall, Chapel Road, Worthing BN11 1HA ☎ 01903 221001
peter.latham@adur-worthing.gov.uk

Senior Management: Mr Andrew Gardiner, Strategic Director, Worthing Town Hall, Chapel Road, Worthing BN11 1HA
☎ 01903 221301 andrew.gardiner@adur-worthing.gov.uk

Senior Management: Mrs Sarah Gobey, Executive Head of Financial Services, Worthing Town Hall, Chapel Road, Worthing BN11 1HA ☎ 01903 221221 sarah.gobey@adur-worthing.gov.uk

Senior Management: Mr Cliff Harrison, Executive Head of Technical Services, Portland House, Richmond Road, Worthing BN11 1HS ☎ 01903 221370 ✉ cliff.harrison@adur-worthing.gov.uk

Senior Management: Mr John Mitchell, Strategic Director, Adur Civic Centre, Ham Road, Shoreham-by-Sea BN43 6PR ☎ 01273 263312 ✉ john.mitchell@adur-worthing.gov.uk

Access Officer / Social Services (Disability): Mr Cliff Harrison, Executive Head of Technical Services, Portland House, Richmond Road, Worthing BN11 1HS ☎ 01903 221370 ✉ cliff.harrison@adur-worthing.gov.uk

Architect, Building / Property Services: Mr Cliff Harrison, Executive Head of Technical Services, Portland House, Richmond Road, Worthing BN11 1HS ☎ 01903 221370 ✉ cliff.harrison@adur-worthing.gov.uk

Best Value: Mr Bill Parsons, Performance, Scrutiny & Communications, Worthing Town Hall, Chapel Road, Worthing BN11 1HA ☎ 01903 221005 ✉ bill.parsons@adur-worthing.gov.uk

Best Value: Mrs Carol Stephenson, Adur & Worthing Partnership Programme Manager, Civic Centre, Ham Road, Shoreham-by-Sea BN43 6PR ☎ 01273 263205 ✉ carol.stephenson@adur-worthing.gov.uk

Building Control: Mr James Appleton, Executive Head of Planning, Regeneration & Wellbeing, Portland House, Richmond Road, Worthing BN11 1HS ☎ 01903 221333 ✉ james.appleton@adur-worthing.gov.uk

PR / Communications: Mrs Wendy Knight, Communications Manager, Worthing Town Hall, Chapel Road, Worthing BN11 1HA ☎ 01903 221017 ✉ wendy.knight@adur-worthing.gov.uk

Community Planning: Mr Paul Pennicott, Development Control Manager, Worthing Town Hall, Chapel Road, Worthing BN11 1HA ☎ 01903 221347 ✉ paul.pennicott@adur-worthing.gov.uk

Community Safety: Mrs Jacqui Cooke, Safer Communities Manager, Worthing Town Hall, Chapel Road, Worthing BN11 1HA ☎ 08456 070999 ✉ jacqui.cooke@adur-worthing.gov.uk

Computer Management: Mr Mark Gawley, Head of IT Contract Services, Worthing Town Hall, Chapel Road, Worthing BN11 1HA ☎ 01903 221477 ✉ mark.gawley@adur-worthing.gov.uk

Contracts: Mr Cliff Harrison, Executive Head of Technical Services, Portland House, Richmond Road, Worthing BN11 1HS ☎ 01903 221370 ✉ cliff.harrison@adur-worthing.gov.uk

Contracts: Mr Steve Spinner, Business Services Manager, Portland House, Richmond Road, Worthing BN11 1LF ☎ 01903 221019 ✉ steve.spinner@adur-worthing.gov.uk

Customer Service: Mr Kevin Masters, Executive Head of Customer Services, Worthing Town Hall, Chapel Road, Worthing BN11 1HA ☎ 01903 221243; 01903 221243 ✉ kevin.masters@adur-worthing.gov.uk; kevin.masters@adur-worthing.gov.uk

Direct Labour: Mr John Mitchell, Strategic Director, Adur Civic Centre, Ham Road, Shoreham-by-Sea BN43 6PR ☎ 01273 263312 ✉ john.mitchell@adur-worthing.gov.uk

Economic Development: Ms Tina Barker, Economic Development Officer, Commerce Way, Lancing BN15 8TA ☎ 01273 263147 ✉ tina.barker@adur-worthing.gov.uk

E-Government: Mr John Mitchell, Strategic Director, Adur Civic Centre, Ham Road, Shoreham-by-Sea BN43 6PR ☎ 01273 263312; 01273 263312 ✉ john.mitchell@adur-worthing.gov.uk

Electoral Registration: Ms Teresa Bryant, Electoral Services Manager, Worthing Town Hall, Chapel Road, Worthing BH11 1HA ☎ 01903 221474; 01903 221474 ✉ teresa.bryant@adur-worthing.gov.uk

Emergency Planning: Mr Tony Lucas, Emergency Planning Officer, Worthing Town Hall, Chapel Road, Worthing BH11 1HA ☎ 01903 221025 ✉ tony.lucas@adur-worthing.gov.uk

Energy Management: Mr Cliff Harrison, Executive Head of Technical Services, Portland House, Richmond Road, Worthing BN11 1HS ☎ 01903 221370 ✉ cliff.harrison@adur-worthing.gov.uk

Environmental / Technical Services: Mr Cliff Harrison, Executive Head of Technical Services, Portland House, Richmond Road, Worthing BN11 1HS ☎ 01903 221370 ✉ cliff.harrison@adur-worthing.gov.uk

Environmental Health: Mr James Elliot, Senior Environmental Health Officer, Adur Civic Centre, Ham Road, Shoreham-by-Sea BN43 6PR ☎ 01273 263032 ✉ james.elliot@adur-worthing.gov.uk

Estates, Property & Valuation: Mr Andrew Gardiner, Strategic Director, Worthing Town Hall, Chapel Road, Worthing BN11 1HA ☎ 01903 221301 ✉ andrew.gardiner@adur-worthing.gov.uk

Estates, Property & Valuation: Mr Cliff Harrison, Executive Head of Technical Services, Portland House, Richmond Road, Worthing BN11 1HS ☎ 01903 221370 ✉ cliff.harrison@adur-worthing.gov.uk

Facilities: Mr Cliff Harrison, Executive Head of Technical Services, Portland House, Richmond Road, Worthing BN11 1HS ☎ 01903 221370 ✉ cliff.harrison@adur-worthing.gov.uk

Finance and Treasurer: Mrs Sarah Gobey, Executive Head of Financial Services, Worthing Town Hall, Chapel Road, Worthing BN11 1HA ☎ 01903 221221 ✉ sarah.gobey@adur-worthing.gov.uk

Grounds Maintenance: Mr Chris Bradley, Park Manager, Commerce Way, Lancing BN15 8TA ☎ 01273 263134 ✉ chris.bradley@adur-worthing.gov.uk

Health and Safety: Mr Lesley Dexter, Senior Corporate Safety Officer, Portland House, Richmond Road, Worthing BN11 1LF ☎ 01903 221357 ✉ lesley.dexter@adur-worthing.gov.uk

Housing: Mr David Pannell, Executive Head of Adur Homes, Civic Centre, Ham Road, Shoreham-by-Sea BN43 6PR ☎ 01273 263358 ✉ david.pannell@adur-worthing.gov.uk

Housing: Mr Paul Spedding, Executive Head of Housing, Health & Community Services, Civic Centre, Ham Road, Shoreham-by-Sea BN43 6PR ☎ 01273 263363 ✉ paul.spedding@adur-worthing.gov.uk

Housing Maintenance: Mr David Pannell, Executive Head of Adur Homes, Civic Centre, Ham Road, Shoreham-by-Sea BN43 6PR ☎ 01273 263358 ✉ david.pannell@adur-worthing.gov.uk

Legal: Mr Jeremy Cook, Executive Head of Corporate & Cultural Services, Worthing Town Hall, Chapel Road, Worthing BN11 1HA ☎ 01903 221028 ✉ jeremy.cook@adur-worthing.gov.uk

Leisure and Cultural Services: Mr Jeremy Cook, Executive Head of Corporate & Cultural Services, Worthing Town Hall, Chapel Road, Worthing BN11 1HA ☎ 01903 221028 ✉ jeremy.cook@adur-worthing.gov.uk

Licensing: Ms Theresa Cuerva, Licensing Officer, Adur Civic Centre, Ham Road, Shoreham-by-Sea BN43 6PR ☎ 01273 263193 ✉ theresa.cuerva@adur-worthing.gov.uk

Lottery Funding, Charity and Voluntary: Ms Katie Neal, External Funding Officer, Worthing Town Hall, Chapel Road, Worthing BN11 1HA ☎ 01903 221283 ✉ katie.neal@worthing.gov.uk

Member Services: Mrs Julia Smith, Democratic Services Manager, Worthing Town Hall, Chapel Road, Worthing BN11 1HA ☎ 01903 221150 ✉ julia.smith@adur-worthing.gov.uk

Parking: Ms Mandy Ainsworth, Parking Enforcement Officer, Worthing Town Hall, Chapel Road, Worthing BH11 1HA ☎ 01903 221089 ✉ mandy.ainsworth@adur-worthing.gov.uk

Partnerships: Mr Peter Latham, Chief Executive, Civic Centre, Ham Road, Shoreham-by-Sea BN43 6PR ☎ 01903 221001 ✉ peter.latham@adur-worthing.gov.uk

Personnel / HR: Mrs Tracy Darey, Human Resources Manager, Civic Centre, Ham Road, Shoreham-by-Sea BN43 6PR ☎ 01273 263063 ✉ tracy.darey@adur-worthing.gov.uk

Planning: Mr James Appleton, Executive Head of Planning, Regeneration & Wellbeing, Portland House, Richmond Road, Worthing BN11 1HS ☎ 01903 221333 ✉ james.appleton@adur-worthing.gov.uk

Procurement: Mr Cliff Harrison, Executive Head of Technical Services, Portland House, Richmond Road, Worthing BN11 1HS ☎ 01903 221370 ✉ cliff.harrison@adur-worthing.gov.uk

Procurement: Mr Steve Spinner, Business Services Manager, Portland House, Richmond Road, Worthing BN11 1LF ☎ 01903 239999 🖷 01903 236552 ✉ steve.spinner@adur-worthing.gov.uk

Procurement: Mr Bill Williamson, Procurement Officer, Portland House, Richmond Road, Worthing BN11 1HS ☎ 01903 221056 ✉ bill.williamson@adur-worthing.gov.uk

Recycling & Waste Minimisation: Mr Kevin Masters, Executive Head of Customer Services, Worthing Town Hall, Chapel Road, Worthing BN11 1HA ☎ 01903 221243 ✉ kevin.masters@adur-worthing.gov.uk

Regeneration: Mr James Appleton, Executive Head of Planning, Regeneration & Wellbeing, Portland House, Richmond Road, Worthing BN11 1HS ☎ 01903 221333 ✉ james.appleton@adur-worthing.gov.uk

Staff Training: Ms Mo Belcher, Learning & Development Co-ordinator, Worthing Town Hall, Chapel Road, Worthing BN11 1HA ☎ 01903 221043 ✉ mo.belcher@adur-worthing.gov.uk

Street Scene: Mr David Steadman, Adur Town Centre & Street Scene Co-ordinator, Civic Centre, Ham Road, Shoreham-by-Sea BN43 6PR ☎ 01273 263152 ✉ david.steadman@adur-worthing.gov.uk

Sustainable Communities: Ms Colette Blackett, Planning Policy Manager, Civic Centre, Ham Road, Shoreham-by-Sea BN43 6PR ☎ 01273 263242 ✉ colette.blackett@adur-worthing.gov.uk

Sustainable Development: Mr James Appleton, Executive Head of Planning, Regeneration & Wellbeing, Portland House, Richmond Road, Worthing BN11 1HS ☎ 01903 221333 ✉ james.appleton@adur-worthing.gov.uk

Tourism: Ms Eileen Suchodolski, Tourist Information Centres Manager, Worthing Town Hall, Chapel Road, Worthing BN11 1HA ☎ 01903 239868 ✉ eileen.suchodolski@adur-worthing.gov.uk

Town Centre: Mr James Appleton, Executive Head of Planning, Regeneration & Wellbeing, Portland House, Richmond Road, Worthing BN11 1HS ☎ 01903 221333 ✉ james.appleton@adur-worthing.gov.uk

Town Centre: Ms Sharon Clarke, Town Centre Manager, 7 Richmond Road, Worthing BN11 1PN ☎ 01903 203252 🖷 01903 820753 ✉ sharonclarke@wtci.fsnet.co.uk

Waste Collection and Disposal: Mr Kevin Masters, Executive Head of Customer Services, Worthing Town Hall, Chapel Road, Worthing BN11 1HA ☎ 01903 221243 ✉ kevin.masters@adur-worthing.gov.uk

Waste Management: Mr Kevin Masters, Executive Head of Customer Services, Worthing Town Hall, Chapel Road, Worthing BN11 1HA ☎ 01903 221243 ✉ kevin.masters@adur-worthing.gov.uk

MEMBERS OF THE COUNCIL (37)

***Leader of the Council:* Yallop**, Paul (CON - Marine)
paul.yallop@worthing.gov.uk

***Group Leader:* Rice**, Alan (LD - Gaisford)
alan.rice@worthing.gov.uk

Atkins, Noel (CON - Salvington)
noel.atkins@worthing.gov.uk

Barraclough, Roy (CON - Goring)
roy.barraclough@worthing.gov.uk

Bradley, Joan (CON - Marine)
joan.bradley@worthing.gov.uk

Brickers, Keith (CON - Selden)
keith.brickers@worthing.gov.uk

Brown, Christine (LD - Selden)
christine.brown@worthing.gov.uk
Chapman, David (LD - Central)
david.chapman@worthing.gov.uk
Cloake, Michael (CON - Salvington)
michael.cloake@worthing.gov.uk
Donin, Michael (LD - Durrington)
michael.donin@worthing.gov.uk
England, Trevor (LD - Castle)
trevor.england@worthing.gov.uk
Fabes, Graham (IND - Offington)
graham.fabes@worthing.gov.uk
Fisher, Norah (LD - Tarring)
norah.fisher@worthing.gov.uk
High, Paul (CON - Heene)
paul.high@worthing.gov.uk
Howard, Paul (CON - Heene)
paul.howard@worthing.gov.uk
Humphreys, Daniel (CON - Castle)
daniel.humphreys@worthing.gov.uk
James, Charles (CON - Durrington)
charles.james@worthing.gov.uk
Jones, Diane (LD - Northbrook)
diane.jones@worthing.gov.uk
Lermitte, Mary (CON - Goring)
mary.lermitte@worthing.gov.uk
Molineaux, Carol (CON - Heene)
carol.molineaux@worthing.gov.uk
Oakley, Roger (CON - Selden)
roger.oakley@worthing.gov.uk
Potter, David (LD - Castle)
david.potter@worthing.gov.uk
Roberts, Clive (CON - Central)
clive.roberts@worthing.gov.uk
Rogers, John (CON - Offington)
john.roger@worthing.gov.uk
Smytherman, Robert (LD - Tarring)
robert.smytherman@worthing.gov.uk
Sparkes, Elizabeth (CON - Offington)
elizabeth.sparkes@worthing.gov.uk
Sunderland, Keith (LD - Northbrook)
keith.sunderland@worthing.gov.uk
Taylor, Victoria (LD - Broadwater)
victoria.taylor@worthing.gov.uk
Thorpe, Hazel (LD - Tarring)
hazel.thorpe@worthing.gov.uk
Turner, Valerie (CON - Gaisford)
val.turner@worthing.gov.uk
Turner, Bryan (CON - Gaisford)
bryan.turner@worthing.gov.uk
Vaughan, Vicky (CON - Broadwater)
vicky.vaughan@worthing.gov.uk
Vinojan, Vino (CON - Central)
vino.vinojan@worthing.gov.uk
Waight, Nicky (CON - Salvington)
nicky.waight@worthing.gov.uk
Waight, Steven (CON - Goring)
steve.waight@worthing.gov.uk
Walker, Vic (CON - Broadwater)
vic.walker@worthing.gov.uk
Wye, Tom (CON - Marine)
tom.wye@worthing.gov.uk

POLITICAL COMPOSITION
CON: 24, LD: 12, IND: 1

CABINET
Leader: Mr Paul Yallop
Customer Services: Ms Mary Lermitte
Environment: Mr Clive Roberts
Health & Wellbeing: Mr Tom Wye
Regeneration: Mr Bryan Turner
Resources: Mr Steven Waight

COMMITTEE CHAIRS
Audit & Governance: Mr Noel Atkins
Licensing: Mr John Rogers
Member Appointment: Mr Michael Cloake
Overview & Scrutiny: Mr Paul High
Planning: Ms Joan Bradley
Standards: Mr Dave Watson (External)

WREXHAM — W

Wrexham County Borough Council, (Cyngor Bwrdeistref Sirol Wrecsam), The Guildhall, Wrexham LL11 1AY ☎ 01978 292000 🖷 01978 292106 💻 www.wrexham.gov.uk

FACTS & FIGURES
Police Authority: North Wales Police Authority
Learning and Skills Council: Wales
Parliamentary Constituencies: Clwyd South, Wrexham
EU Constituencies: Wales
Election Frequency: Elections are of whole council
Twinning: Markischer Kreis (Germany); Raciburz (Poland)

PRINCIPAL OFFICERS
Chief Executive: Dr Helen Paterson, Chief Executive, The Guildhall, Wrexham LL11 1AY ☎ 01978 292100 🖷 01978 292106 ✉ helen.paterson@wrexham.gov.uk

Senior Management: Ms Clare Field, Strategic & Performance Director, The Guildhall, Wrexham LL11 1AY ☎ 01978 297421 🖷 01978 297422 ✉ clare.field@wrexham.gov.uk

Senior Management: Mr Lee Robinson, Strategic & Performance Director, The Guildhall, Wrexham LL11 1AY ☎ 01978 297420 🖷 01978 292445 ✉ lee.robinson@wrexham.gov.uk

Senior Management: Mr Philip Walton, Strategic & Performance Director, The Guildhall, Wrexham LL11 1AY ☎ 01978 297001 🖷 01978 297004 ✉ philip.walton@wrexham.gov.uk

Access Officer / Social Services (Disability): Mr Andrew Figiel, Head of Adult Social Care, 2nd Floor, Crown Buildings, 31 Chester Street, Wrexham LL13 8BG ☎ 01978 298010 🖷 01978 298029 ✉ andrew.figiel@wrexham.gov.uk

Architect, Building / Property Services: Mr Barry Hellen, Property Design Services Manager, Crown Buildings, 31 Chester Street, Wrexham LL13 8BG ☎ 01978 297180 🖷 01978 297202 ✉ barry.hellen@wrexham.gov.uk

Best Value: Mr Mark Owen, Head of Finance, Lambpit Street, Wrexham LL11 1AR ☎ 01978 292704 🖷 01978 292702 ✉ mark.owen@wrexham.gov.uk

Building Control: Mr Dave Sharp, Principal Building Control

Surveyor, Building Control Section, 2nd Floor, Crown Buildings, 31 Chester Street, Wrexham LL13 8BG ☎ 01978 298876 🖷 01978 292502 ✉ dave.sharp@wrexham.gov.uk

Catering Services: Mr Steve Jones, Support Services Manager, 2nd Floor, Crown Buildings, 31 Chester Street, Wrexham LL13 8BG ☎ 01978 298735 ✉ steve.jones@wrexham.gov.uk

Children / Youth Services: Ms Susan Evans, Head of Children & Young People, Crown Buildings, 31 Chester Street, Wrexham LL13 8BG ☎ 01978 298017 🖷 01978 297452 ✉ susan1.evans@wrexham.gov.uk

Civil Registration: Mrs Ruth Cooke, Superintendent Registrar, Ty Dewi Sant, Rhosddu Road, Wrexham LL11 1NF ☎ 01978 292670 🖷 01978 292676 ✉ ruth.cooke@wrexham.gov.uk

PR / Communications: Ms Sue Wyn Jones, Communications & Social Media Manager, Lambpit Street, Wrexham LL11 1AR ☎ 01978 292275 🖷 01978 292252 ✉ sue.wynjones@wrexham.gov.uk

Community Planning: Ms Gillian Grainger, Community Cohesion Officer, 16 Lord Street, Wrexham LL11 1LG ☎ 01978 298736 ✉ gillian.grainger@wrexham.gov.uk

Community Safety: Mrs Gillian Cowan, Partnerships & Health, Social Care & Wellbeing Manager, Lambpit Street, Wrexham LL11 1AR ☎ 01978 667215 ✉ gillian.cowan@wrexham.gov.uk

Computer Management: Mr Dave Coates, Business Service Manager, Old Library, Queens Square, Wrexham LL11 1AU ☎ 01978 292310 🖷 01978 292345 ✉ dave.coates@wrexham.gov.uk

Consumer Protection and Trading Standards: Ms Toni Slater, Public Protection Service Manager, Public Protection Services, Ruthin Road, Wrexham LL13 7TU ☎ 01978 315710 🖷 01978 315701 ✉ toni.slater@wrexham.gov.uk

Contracts: Mr John Bradbury, Head of Environment, The Guildhall, Wrexham LL11 1AY ☎ 01978 297060 ✉ john.bradbury@wrexham.gov.uk

Corporate Services: Mr Trevor Coxon, Head of Corporate & Customer Services, The Guildhall, Wrexham LL11 1AY ☎ 01978 292209 🖷 01978 292207 ✉ trevor.coxon@wrexham.gov.uk

Customer Service: Mrs Helen Gerrard, Customer Access Project Manager, 16 Lord Street, Wrexham LL11 1LG ☎ 01978 298951 🖷 01978 298950 ✉ helen.gerrard@wrexham.gov.uk

Direct Labour: Mr Andy Lewis, Head of Housing & Public Protection, The Guildhall, Wrexham LL11 1AY ☎ 01978 297005 ✉ andy.lewis@wrexham.gov.uk

Economic Development: Mr Stephen Bayley, Head of Assets & Economic Development, Crown Buildings, 31 Chester Street, Wrexham LL13 8BG ☎ 01978 292440 🖷 01978 292445 ✉ steve.bayley@wrexham.gov.uk

Education: Mr John Davies, Head of Lifelong Learning, Lambpit Street, Wrexham LL11 1AR ☎ 01978 295400 ✉ john.davies@wrexham.gov.uk

E-Government: Mrs Helen Gerrard, Customer Access Project Manager, 16 Lord Street, Wrexham LL11 1LG ☎ 01978 298951 🖷 01978 298950 ✉ helen.gerrard@wrexham.gov.uk

Electoral Registration: Ms Gaynor Coventry, Electoral & Regeneration Services Manager, Ty Dewi Sant, Rhosddu Road, Wrexham LL11 1AY ☎ 01978 292290 🖷 01978 292293 ✉ gaynor.coventry@wrexham.gov.uk

Emergency Planning: Mr Phil Harrison, Emergency Planning Manager, 16 Lord Street, Wrexham LL11 1LG ☎ 01978 292264 ✉ phil.harrison@wrexham.gov.uk

Energy Management: Mr Geraint Wyn Jones, Energy Efficiency Officer, Crown Buildings, 31 Chester Street, Wrexham LL13 8BG ☎ 01978 315363 🖷 01978 397199 ✉ geraint.wynjones@wrexham.gov.uk

Environmental / Technical Services: Mr Alan Guest, Service Manager for Environment, Abbey Road South, Industrial Estate, Wrexham LL13 9PW ☎ 01978 729610 ✉ alan.guest@wrexham.gov.uk

Environmental Health: Ms Toni Slater, Public Protection Service Manager, Ruthin Road, Wrexham LL13 7TU ☎ 01978 315710 🖷 01978 315701 ✉ toni.slater@wrexham.gov.uk

Estates, Property & Valuation: Mrs Denise Garland, Strategic Assets Manager, Crown Buildings, 31 Chester Street, Wrexham LL13 8BG ☎ 01978 297214 ✉ denise.garland@wrexham.gov.uk

European Liaison: Mr Allan Forrest, Regeneration Project Manager, 3rd Floor, Crown Buildings, 31 Chester Street, Wrexham LL13 8BG ☎ 01978 292446 🖷 01978 292445 ✉ allan.forrest@wrexham.gov.uk

Events Manager: Ms Kay Rickard, Events Co-ordinator, 3rd Floor, Crown Buildings, 31 Chester Street, Wrexham LL13 8BG ☎ 01978 292536 ✉ kay.rickard@wrexham.gov.uk

Facilities: Mr Simon Roberts, Facilities Management Manager, 3rd Floor, Crown Buildings, 31 Chester Street, Wrexham LL13 8BG ☎ 01978 297207 🖷 01978 292207 ✉ simon.roberts@wrexham.gov.uk

Finance and Treasurer: Mr Mark Owen, Head of Finance, Lambpit Street, Wrexham LL11 1AR ☎ 01978 292704 🖷 01978 292702 ✉ mark.owen@wrexham.gov.uk

Fleet Management: Mr Lee Roberts, Integrated Transport Unit Manager, Abbey Road South, Wrexham Industrial Estate, Wrexham LL13 9PW ☎ 01978 729752 🖷 01978 729600 ✉ lee.roberts@wrexham.gov.uk

Grounds Maintenance: Mr Alan Guest, Service Manager for Environment, Abbey Road South, Industrial Estate, Wrexham LL13 9PW ☎ 01978 729610 ✉ alan.guest@wrexham.gov.uk

Health and Safety: Mr Nigel Lawrence, Principal Health & Safety Officer, Ruthin Road, Wrexham LL13 7TU ☎ 01978 292135

🖷 01978 292132 ✉ nigel.lawrence@wrexham.gov.uk

Highways: Mr Alan Guest, Service Manager for Environment, Abbey Road South, Industrial Estate, Wrexham LL13 9PW ☎ 01978 729610 ✉ alan.guest@wrexham.gov.uk

Home Energy Conservation: Mr Geraint Wyn Jones, Energy Efficiency Officer, Ruthin Road, Wrexham LL13 7TU ☎ 01978 315363 🖷 01978 397199 ✉ geraint.wynjones@wrexham.gov.uk

Housing: Mr Fred Czulowski, Landlord Services Manager, Ruthin Road, Wrexham LL13 7TU ☎ 01978 315401 🖷 01978 315320 ✉ fred.czulowski@wrexham.gov.uk

Housing Maintenance: Mr Fred Czulowski, Landlord Services Manager, Ruthin Road, Wrexham LL13 7TU ☎ 01978 315401 🖷 01978 315320 ✉ fred.czulowski@wrexham.gov.uk

Legal: Mr Trevor Coxon, Head of Corporate & Customer Services, The Guildhall, Wrexham LL11 1AY ☎ 01978 292209 🖷 01978 292207 ✉ trevor.coxon@wrexham.gov.uk

Leisure and Cultural Services: Mr Lawrence Isted, Head of Community Well-being & Development, Lambpit Street, Wrexham LL1 1AR ☎ 01978 292500 🖷 01978 292502 ✉ lawrence.isted@wrexham.gov.uk

Licensing: Mr Andy Lewis, Head of Housing & Public Protection, The Guildhall, Wrexham LL11 1AY ☎ 01978 297005 ✉ andy.lewis@wrexham.gov.uk

Lifelong Learning: Mr John Davies, Head of Lifelong Learning, Lambpit Street, Wrexham LL11 1AR ☎ 01978 295400 ✉ john.davies@wrexham.gov.uk

Lighting: Mr Darren Williams, Network & Infrastructure Manager, Abbey Road South, Industrial Estate, Wrexham LL13 9PW ☎ 01978 729629 🖷 01978 667155 ✉ darren.williams@wrexham.gov.uk

Lottery Funding, Charity and Voluntary: Mr Chris Girvan, Partnership Liaison Officer, 2nd Floor, Crown Buildings, 31 Chester Street, Wrexham LL13 8BG ☎ 01978 298672 🖷 01978 298277 ✉ chris.girvan@wrexham.gov.uk

Member Services: Mr Peter Mullen, Committee & Member Services Manager, The Guildhall, Wrexham LL11 1AY ☎ 01978 292235 🖷 01978 292203 ✉ peter.mullen@wrexham.gov.uk

Parking: Ms Joanne Rodgers, Parking Services Co-ordinator, Abbey Road South, Industrial Estate, Wrexham LL13 9PW ☎ 01978 729697 ✉ joanne.rodgers@wrexham.gov.uk

Personnel / HR: Mr Trevor Coxon, Head of Corporate & Customer Services, The Guildhall, Wrexham LL11 1AY ☎ 01978 292209 🖷 01978 292207 ✉ trevor.coxon@wrexham.gov.uk

Planning: Mr Lawrence Isted, Head of Community Well-being & Development, Lambpit Street, Wrexham LL1 1AR ☎ 01978 292500 🖷 01978 292502 ✉ lawrence.isted@wrexham.gov.uk

Procurement: Mr Roger Barnett, Procurement Officer, Lambpit Street, Wrexham LL11 1AR ☎ 01978 292798 🖷 01978 292702 ✉ roger.barnett@wrexham.gov.uk

Public Libraries: Mr Dylan Hughes, Libraries Officer, Lambpit Street, Wrexham LL11 1AR ☎ 01978 297442 ✉ dylan.hughes@wrexham.gov.uk

Recycling & Waste Minimisation: Mrs Sarah Barton, Waste Strategy Manager, Abbey Road South, Wrexham Industrial Estate, Wrexham LL13 8BG ☎ 01978 729685 🖷 01978 729601 ✉ sarah.barton@wrexham.gov.uk

Regeneration: Ms Isobel Watson, Urban Development & Town Centre Manager, Lambpit Street, Wrexham LL11 1AR ☎ 01978 292457 🖷 01978 292445 ✉ isobel.watson@wrexham.gov.uk

Road Safety: Ms Wendy Davies-Williams, Road Safety Co-ordinator, Abbey Road South, Industrial Estate, Wrexham LL13 9PW ☎ 01978 729605 ✉ wendy.davieswilliams@wrexham.gov.uk

Social Services: Mr Andrew Figiel, Head of Adult Social Care, 2nd Floor, Crown Buildings, 31 Chester Street, Wrexham LL13 8BG ☎ 01978 298010 🖷 01978 298029 ✉ andrew.figiel@wrexham.gov.uk

Social Services (Adult): Mr Andrew Figiel, Head of Adult Social Care, 2nd Floor, Crown Buildings, 31 Chester Street, Wrexham LL13 8BG ☎ 01978 298010 🖷 01978 298029 ✉ andrew.figiel@wrexham.gov.uk

Social Services (Children): Ms Susan Evans, Head of Children & Young People, Lambpit Street, Wrexham LL11 1AR ☎ 01978 298017 🖷 01978 297452 ✉ susan1.evans@wrexham.gov.uk

Staff Training: Ms Susan Ratomski, Training Manager, The Learning Centre, Wrexham LL11 1AY ☎ 10978 292147 ✉ susan.ratomski@wrexham.gov.uk

Street Scene: Mr Alan Guest, Service Manager for Environment, Abbey Road South, Industrial Estate, Wrexham LL13 9PW ☎ 01978 729610 ✉ alan.guest@wrexham.gov.uk

Sustainable Communities: Mr Philip Walton, Strategic & Performance Director, The Guildhall, Wrexham LL11 1AY ☎ 01978 297001 🖷 01978 297004 ✉ philip.walton@wrexham.gov.uk

Sustainable Development: Mr Lawrence Isted, Head of Community Well-being & Development, Lambpit Street, Wrexham LL1 1AR ☎ 01978 292500 🖷 01978 292502 ✉ lawrence.isted@wrexham.gov.uk

Tourism: Mr Peter Scott, Investment & Business Development Manager, 3rd Floor, Crown Buildings, 31 Chester Street, Wrexham LL13 8BG ☎ 01978 292405 ✉ peter.scott@wrexham.gov.uk

Town Centre: Ms Isobel Watson, Urban Development & Town Centre Manager, Lambpit Street, Wrexham LL11 1AR ☎ 01978 292457 ✉ isobel.watson@wrexham.gov.uk

Traffic Management: Mr Darren Williams, Network & Infrastructure Manager, Abbey Road South, Industrial Estate, Wrexham LL13 9PW ☎ 01978 729629 🖷 01978 667155

darren.williams@wrexham.gov.uk

Transport: Mr Alan Guest, Service Manager for Environment, Abbey Road South, Industrial Estate, Wrexham LL13 9PW ☎ 01978 729610 alan.guest@wrexham.gov.uk

Transport Planner: Mr Darren Williams, Network & Infrastructure Manager, Abbey Road South, Industrial Estate, Wrexham LL13 9PW ☎ 01978 729629 🖷 01978 667155 darren.williams@wrexham.gov.uk

Waste Collection and Disposal: Mr Alan Guest, Service Manager for Environment, Abbey Road South, Industrial Estate, Wrexham LL13 9PW ☎ 01978 729610 alan.guest@wrexham.gov.uk

Waste Management: Mrs Sarah Barton, Waste Strategy Manager, Abbey Road South, Wrexham Industrial Estate, Wrexham LL13 8BG ☎ 01978 729685 🖷 01978 729601 sarah.barton@wrexham.gov.uk

Waste Management: Mr Philip Walton, Strategic & Performance Director, The Guildhall, Wrexham LL11 1AY ☎ 01978 297001 🖷 01978 297004 philip.walton@wrexham.gov.uk

Children's Play Areas: Mr Martin Howarth, Parks, Countryside & Public Rights of Way Manager, Abbey Road South, Industrial Estate, Wrexham LL13 9PW ☎ 01978 729630 martin.howarth@wrexham.gov.uk

MEMBERS OF THE COUNCIL (52)

***Mayor:* Roberts**, Ian (IND - Chirk North)
ian1.roberts@wrexham.gov.uk
***Deputy Mayor:* Bithell**, David (LAB - Stansty)
idavid.bithell@wrexham.gov.uk
***Leader of the Council:* Rogers**, Neil (LAB - Gwenfro)
neil.rogers@wrexham.gov.uk
***Deputy Leader of the Council:* Pritchard**, Mark (IND - Esclusham)
mark.pritchard@wrexham.gov.uk
***Group Leader:* Bithell**, David A (IND - Johnstown)
davida.bithell@wrexham.gov.uk
***Group Leader:* O'Toole**, Carole (LD - Maesydre)
carole.otoole@wrexham.gov.uk
***Group Leader:* Skelland**, Rodney (CON - Bronington)
rodney.skelland@wrexham.gov.uk
Bailey, Andrew (LAB - Gresford East and West)
andrew.bailey@wrexham.gov.uk
Baldwin, William (IND - Little Acton)
william.baldwin@wrexham.gov.uk
Blackwell, Paul (LAB - Plas Madoc)
paul.blackwell@wrexham.gov.uk
Boland, Terry (LAB - Llay)
terry.boland@wrexham.gov.uk
Cameron, Brian (LAB - Whitegate)
brian.cameron@wrexham.gov.uk
Childs, Krista (LAB - Coedpoeth)
krista.childs@wrexham.gov.uk
Davies, Dana (LAB - Ruabon)
dana.davies@wrexhams.gov.uk
Dutton, Robert (IND - Erddig)
bob.dutton@wrexham.gov.uk
Edwards, Terence Alan (IND - New Broughton)
talan.edwards@wrexham.gov.uk
Edwards, Michael (LD - Marford and Hoseley)
michael.edwards@wrexham.gov.uk
Evans, Anne (LAB - Rhosnesni)
anne.evans@wrexham.gov.uk
Evans, Terry (IND - Chirk South)
terry.evans@wrexham.gov.uk
Gregory, A Keith (IND - Smithfield)
keith.gregory@wrexham.gov.uk
Griffiths, David (LAB - Gwersyllt East and South)
david.griffiths@wrexham.gov.uk
Griffiths, Gareth (LAB - Coedpoeth)
gareth.wyngriffiths@wrexham.gov.uk
Hughes, Kevin (LAB - Ponciau)
kevin1.hughes@wrexham.gov.uk
Jeffares, Pat (O - Llan Rural)
pat.jeffares@wrexham.gov.uk
Jenkins, R Alun (LD - Offa)
alun.jenkins@wrexham.gov.uk
Jones, Hugh (CON - Rossett)
hugh.jones@wrexham.gov.uk
Jones, O Arfon (PC - Gwersyllt West)
arfon.jones@wrexham.gov.uk
Kelly, David (IND - Minera)
david.kelly@wrexham.gov.uk
Kelly, James (LD - Borras Park)
james.kelly@wrexham.gov.uk
Kenyon, Lloyd (CON - Overton)
lloyd.kenyon@wrexham.gov.uk
King, Malcolm (LAB - Wynnstay)
malcolm.king@wrexham.gov.uk
Lowe, Joan (IND - Penycae and Ruabon South)
joan.lowe@wrexham.gov.uk
Lowe, Geoffrey (LAB - Acton)
webmaster@wrexham.gov.uk
McCann, Bernie (LAB - Gwersyllt East and South)
bernard.mccann@wrexham.gov.uk
Morris, Michael (CON - Holt)
michael.morris@wrexham.gov.uk
Owens, Mark (IND - Pant)
marka.owens@wrexham.gov.uk
Pemberton, Paul (LD - Ponciau)
paul.pemberton@wrexham.gov.uk
Phillips, John (IND - Pen y Cae)
johnc.phillips@wrexham.gov.uk
Powell, Colin (LAB - Queensway)
colin.powell@wrexham.gov.uk
Prince, Ron (IND - Cartrefle)
ron.prince@wrexham.gov.uk
Pritchard, John (IND - Marchwiel)
john.pritchard@wrexham.gov.uk
Roberts, J M Barbara (IND - Dyffryn Ceiriog / Ceiriog Valley)
barbara.roberts@wrexham.gov.uk
Rogers, Paul (CON - Brymbo)
paul2.rogers@wrexham.gov.uk
Rogers, Graham (LAB - Hermitage)
graham1.rogers@wrexham.gov.uk
Roxburgh, Barbara (LAB - Bryn Cefn)
barbara.roxburgh@wrexham.gov.uk
Taylor, David (IND - Cefn)
david.taylor@wrexham.gov.uk
Williams, Michael (LAB - Gwersyllt North)
michael.williams@wrexham.gov.uk
Williams, Malcolm (IND - Llay)
malcolm.williams@wrexham.gov.uk

Williams, Andy (LAB - Garden Village)
andy.williams@wrexham.gov.uk
Wilson, Steve (LAB - Grosvenor)
steve.wilson@wrexham.gov.uk
Wright, Derek (LAB - Cefn)
derek.wright@wrexham.gov.uk
Wynn, Phil (IND - Brynyffynnon)
phil.wynn@wrexham.gov.uk

POLITICAL COMPOSITION

LAB: 22, IND: 18, CON: 5, LD: 5, O: 1, PC: 1

CABINET

Leader / Economic Development & Regeneration: Mr Neil Rogers
Deputy Leader / Housing & Planning: Mr Mark Pritchard
Children's Services & Education: Mr Malcolm Williams
Communities, Partnerships & Collaboration: Mr Hugh Jones
Environment: Mr Robert Dutton
Health & Adult Social Care: Mr David Griffiths
Policy, Finance, Performance & Governance: Mr Malcolm King
No Portfolio: Mr David Bithell
No Portfolio: Mrs Joan Lowe
No Portfolio: Mrs Carole O'Toole

COMMITTEE CHAIRS

Customer, Performance & Resource Scrutiny: Mr Steve Wilson
Democratic Services Scrutiny: Mr O Arfon Jones
Education Safeguarding & Wellbeing: Mr Andrew Bailey
Employment, Business & Investment Scrutiny: Mr Rodney Skelland
Houses, Environment & Communities Scrutiny: Mr David Kelly
Licensing: Mr Terence Alan Edwards
Partnership & Collaboration: Mr Ron Prince
Planning: Mr Michael Morris

WYCHAVON D

Wychavon District Council, Civic Centre, Queen Elizabeth Drive, Pershore WR10 1PT ☎ 01386 565000 🖷 01386 561091
servicecentre@wychavon.gov.uk www.wychavon.gov.uk

FACTS & FIGURES

Police Authority: West Mercia Police Authority
Health Authority: NHS West Midlands
Learning and Skills Council: West Midlands
Parliamentary Constituencies: Redditch
EU Constituencies: West Midlands
Election Frequency: Elections are of whole council
Twinning: Evesham: Dreux (France); Melsungen (Germany); Evesham (NJ USA); Droitwich: Bad Ems (Germany); Gyula (Hungary); Pershore: Bad Neustadt (Germany); Plouay (France)

PRINCIPAL OFFICERS

Chief Executive: Mr Jack Hegarty, Managing Director, Civic Centre, Queen Elizabeth Drive, Pershore WR10 1PT ☎ 01386 565401 🖷 01386 561091 jack.hegarty@wychavon.gov.uk

Deputy Chief Executive: Mr Vic Allison, Deputy Managing Director, Civic Centre, Queen Elizabeth Drive, Pershore WR10 1PT ☎ ; 01386 656401 🖷 01386 561091 vic.allison@wychavon.gov.uk

Senior Management: Mr Vic Allison, Deputy Managing Director, Civic Centre, Queen Elizabeth Drive, Pershore WR10 1PT ☎ 01386 656401 🖷 01386 561091 vic.allison@wychavon.gov.uk

Senior Management: Mr Giorgio Framalicco, Head of Housing & Planning Services, Civic Centre, Queen Elizabeth Drive, Pershore WR10 1PT ☎ 01386 656401 🖷 01386 561092 giorgio.framalicco@wychavon.gov.uk

Senior Management: Mr Ian Marshall, Head of Legal & Support Services, Civic Centre, Queen Elizabeth Drive, Pershore WR10 1PT ☎ 01386 565470 🖷 01386 561089 ian.marshall@wychavon.gov.uk

Senior Management: Mr Philip Merrick, Head of Community Services, Civic Centre, Queen Elizabeth Drive, Pershore WR10 1PT ☎ 01386 565588 🖷 01386 561634 phil.merrick@wychavon.gov.uk

Senior Management: Mrs Fiona Narburgh, Head of Strategy & Communications, Civic Centre, Queen Elizabeth Drive, Pershore WR10 1PT ☎ 01386 565101 🖷 01386 561091 fiona.narbugh@wychavon.gov.uk

Architect, Building / Property Services: Mr Giorgio Framalicco, Head of Housing & Planning Services, Civic Centre, Queen Elizabeth Drive, Pershore WR10 1PT ☎ 01386 656401 🖷 01386 561092 giorgio.framalicco@wychavon.gov.uk

Architect, Building / Property Services: Ms Kirsty May-Jones, Housing Development Officer, Civic Centre, Queen Elizabeth Drive, Pershore WR10 1PT ☎ 01386 565352 🖷 01386 554416 kirsty.may-jones@wychavon.gov.uk

Best Value: Mr Zach Butcher, Performance & Consultation Officer, Civic Centre, Queen Elizabeth Drive, Pershore WR10 1PT ☎ 01386 565333 🖷 01386 561091 zach.butcher@wychavon.gov.uk

PR / Communications: Mrs Fiona Narburgh, Head of Strategy & Communications, Civic Centre, Queen Elizabeth Drive, Pershore WR10 1PT ☎ 01386 565101 🖷 01386 561091 fiona.narbugh@wychavon.gov.uk

PR / Communications: Ms Emma Wild, Communications Officer, Civic Centre, Queen Elizabeth Drive, Pershore WR10 1PT ☎ 01386 565102 🖷 01386 561091 emma.wild@wychavon.gov.uk

Community Planning: Ms Cherrie Mansfield, Strategy & Review Manager, Civic Centre, Queen Elizabeth Drive, Pershore WR10 1PT ☎ 01386 565508 🖷 01386 561091 cherrie.mansfield@wychavon.gov.uk

Community Safety: Mr David Hemming, Community Safety Manager, Civic Centre, Queen Elizabeth Drive, Pershore WR10 1PT ☎ 01386 565301 🖷 01386 561091 david.hemming@wychavon.gov.uk

Computer Management: Mr Mac Chivers, IT Services Manager, Civic Centre, Queen Elizabeth Drive, Pershore WR10 1PT ☎ 01386 565212 🖷 01386 561091 mac.chivers@wychavon.gov.uk

Contracts: Mr Alex Haslam, Procurement Officer, The Council House, Burcot Lane, Bromsgrove B60 1AA ☎ 01527 64252 ext. 3010 🖷 01527 881414 🖰 a.haslam@bromsgroveandredditch.gov.uk

Contracts: Mr Philip Merrick, Head of Community Services, Civic Centre, Queen Elizabeth Drive, Pershore WR10 1PT ☎ 01386 565588 🖷 01386 561634 🖰 phil.merrick@wychavon.gov.uk

Customer Service: Mrs Kath Smith, Customer Services Manager, Civic Centre, Queen Elizabeth Drive, Pershore WR10 1PT ☎ 01386 565484 🖷 01386 564091 🖰 kath.smith@wychavon.gov.uk

Economic Development: Mr Philip Merrick, Head of Community Services, Civic Centre, Queen Elizabeth Drive, Pershore WR10 1PT ☎ 01386 565588 🖷 01386 561634 🖰 phil.merrick@wychavon.gov.uk

Electoral Registration: Mrs Elaine Dicks, Electoral Services Officer, Civic Centre, Queen Elizabeth Drive, Pershore WR10 1PT ☎ 01386 565162 🖷 01386 565290 🖰 elaine.dicks@wychavon.gov.uk

Emergency Planning: Mr Philip Merrick, Head of Community Services, Civic Centre, Queen Elizabeth Drive, Pershore WR10 1PT ☎ 01386 565588 🖷 01386 561634 🖰 phil.merrick@wychavon.gov.uk

Environmental Health: Mr Steven Jorden, Head of Worcestershire Regulatory Services, Wyatt House, Farrier Street, Worcester WR1 3BH ☎ 01905 822799 🖷 01905 617132 🖰 s.jorden@worcsregservices.gov.uk

Estates, Property & Valuation: Mr Vic Allison, Deputy Managing Director, Civic Centre, Queen Elizabeth Drive, Pershore WR10 1PT ☎ ; 01386 656401 🖷 01386 561091 🖰 vic.allison@wychavon.gov.uk

Events Manager: Ms Emma Wild, Communications Officer, Civic Centre, Queen Elizabeth Drive, Pershore WR10 1PT ☎ 01386 565102 🖷 01386 561091 🖰 emma.wild@wychavon.gov.uk

Facilities: Mr Vic Allison, Deputy Managing Director, Civic Centre, Queen Elizabeth Drive, Pershore WR10 1PT ☎ 01386 656401 🖷 01386 561091 🖰 vic.allison@wychavon.gov.uk

Finance and Treasurer: Mr Vic Allison, Deputy Managing Director, Civic Centre, Queen Elizabeth Drive, Pershore WR10 1PT ☎ ; 01386 656401 🖷 01386 561091 🖰 vic.allison@wychavon.gov.uk

Fleet Management: Mr Vic Allison, Deputy Managing Director, Civic Centre, Queen Elizabeth Drive, Pershore WR10 1PT ☎ 01386 656401 🖷 01386 561091 🖰 vic.allison@wychavon.gov.uk

Grounds Maintenance: Ms Lynn Stevens, Parks Officer, Civic Centre, Queen Elizabeth Drive, Pershore WR10 1PT ☎ 01386 565407 🖷 01386 561634 🖰 lynn.stevens@wychavon.gov.uk

Health and Safety: Mr Carl Wibberley, Safety Officer & Building Manager, Civic Centre, Queen Elizabeth Drive, Pershore WR10 1PT ☎ 01386 565493 🖷 01386 561617 🖰 carl.wibberley@wychavon.gov.uk

Housing: Ms Liza Handley, Senior Housing Needs Officer, Civic Centre, Queen Elizabeth Drive, Pershore WR10 1PT ☎ 01386 565000 🖷 01386 554416 🖰 liza.handley@wychavon.gov.uk

Housing: Ms Mary Unwin, Senior Housing Needs Officer, Civic Centre, Queen Elizabeth Drive, Pershore WR10 1PT ☎ 01386 565000 🖷 01386 554416 🖰 mary.unwin@wychavon.gov.uk

Legal: Mr Ian Marshall, Head of Legal & Support Services, Civic Centre, Queen Elizabeth Drive, Pershore WR10 1PT ☎ 01386 565470 🖷 01386 561089 🖰 ian.marshall@wychavon.gov.uk

Leisure and Cultural Services: Mr Jem Teal, Community Development Manager, Civic Centre, Queen Elizabeth Drive, Pershore WR10 1PT ☎ 01386 565235 🖷 01386 561634 🖰 jem.teal@wychavon.gov.uk

Licensing: Mr Steven Jorden, Head of Worcestershire Regulatory Services, Wyatt House, Farrier Street, Worcester WR1 3BH ☎ 01905 822799 🖷 01905 617132 🖰 s.jorden@worcsregservices.gov.uk

Lottery Funding, Charity and Voluntary: Mr Jem Teal, Community Development Manager, Civic Centre, Queen Elizabeth Drive, Pershore WR10 1PT ☎ 01386 565235 🖷 01386 561634 🖰 jem.teal@wychavon.gov.uk

Member Services: Ms Sheena Jones, Support Services Manager, Civic Centre, Queen Elizabeth Drive, Pershore WR10 1PT ☎ 01386 565428 🖷 01386 561091 🖰 sheena.jones@wychavon.gov.uk

Parking: Mrs Christine Baxter, Parking Services Officer, Civic Centre, Queen Elizabeth Drive, Pershore WR10 1PT ☎ 01386 565226 🖷 01386 565119 🖰 christine.baxter@wychavon.gov.uk

Partnerships: Mr Chris Brooks, Regeneration Manager, Civic Centre, Queen Elizabeth Drive, Pershore WR10 1PT ☎ 01386 565343 🖷 01386 561634 🖰 chris.brooks@wychavon.gov.uk

Partnerships: Ms Cherrie Mansfield, Strategy & Review Manager, Civic Centre, Queen Elizabeth Drive, Pershore WR10 1PT ☎ 01386 565508 🖷 01386 561091 🖰 cherrie.mansfield@wychavon.gov.uk

Personnel / HR: Mrs Kim Stallard, Personnel, Payroll & Development Officer, Civic Centre, Queen Elizabeth Drive, Pershore WR10 1PT ☎ 01386 565380 🖷 01386 565300 🖰 kim.stallard@wychavon.gov.uk

Planning: Mr Giorgio Framalicco, Head of Housing & Planning Services, Civic Centre, Queen Elizabeth Drive, Pershore WR10 1PT ☎ 01386 656401 🖷 01386 561092 🖰 giorgio.framalicco@wychavon.gov.uk

Procurement: Mr Vic Allison, Deputy Managing Director, Civic Centre, Queen Elizabeth Drive, Pershore WR10 1PT ☎ 01386 656401 🖷 01386 561091 🖰 vic.allison@wychavon.gov.uk

Recycling & Waste Minimisation: Mr Mark Edwards, Waste Management Officer, Civic Centre, Queen Elizabeth Drive, Pershore WR10 1PT ☎ 01386 565245 🖷 01386 561634 🖰 mark.edwards@wychavon.gov.uk

Regeneration: Mr Chris Brooks, Regeneration Manager, Civic Centre, Queen Elizabeth Drive, Pershore WR10 1PT ☎ 01386

565343 🖷 01386 561634 ✉ chris.brooks@wychavon.gov.uk

Staff Training: Mrs Kim Stallard, Personnel, Payroll & Development Officer, Civic Centre, Queen Elizabeth Drive, Pershore WR10 1PT ☎ 01386 565380 🖷 01386 565300 ✉ kim.stallard@wychavon.gov.uk

Sustainable Communities: Ms Cherrie Mansfield, Strategy & Review Manager, Civic Centre, Queen Elizabeth Drive, Pershore WR10 1PT ☎ 01386 565508 🖷 01386 561091 ✉ cherrie.mansfield@wychavon.gov.uk

Tourism: Ms Angela Tidmarsh, Tourism Officer, Civic Centre, Queen Elizabeth Drive, Pershore WR10 1PT ☎ 01386 565373 🖷 01386 561634 ✉ angela.tidmarsh@wychavon.gov.uk

Town Centre: Mr Chris Brooks, Regeneration Manager, Civic Centre, Queen Elizabeth Drive, Pershore WR10 1PT ☎ 01386 565343 🖷 01386 561634 ✉ chris.brooks@wychavon.gov.uk

Transport Planner: Mr Fred Davies, Policy Manager, Civic Centre, Queen Elizabeth Drive, Pershore WR10 1PT ☎ 01386 565367 🖷 01386 561092 ✉ fred.davies@wychavon.gov.uk

Waste Collection and Disposal: Ms Sharon Casswell, Client Services Manager, Civic Centre, Queen Elizabeth Drive, Pershore WR10 1PT ☎ 01386 565000 🖷 01386 561634 ✉ sharon.casswell@wychavon.gov.uk

Waste Management: Mr Mark Edwards, Waste Management Officer, Civic Centre, Queen Elizabeth Drive, Pershore WR10 1PT ☎ 01386 565245 🖷 01386 561634 ✉ mark.edwards@wychavon.gov.uk

MEMBERS OF THE COUNCIL (45)

***Chair:* Morris**, Richard (CON - Droitwich Spa South East)
richard.morris@wychavon.gov.uk

***Leader of the Council:* Middlebrough**, Paul (CON - Drakes Broughton)
paul.middlebrough@wychavon.gov.uk

***Deputy Leader of the Council:* Pearce**, Judy (CON - Dodderhill)
judy.pearce@wychavon.gov.uk

***Group Leader:* Rowley**, Margaret (LD - Bowbrook)
margaret.rowley@wychavon.gov.uk

Adams, Alastair (CON - Honeybourne and Pebworth)
Alastair.adams@wychavon.gov.uk

Adams, Robert (CON - Norton and Whttington)
robert.adams@wychavon.gov.uk

Banks, Robert (CON - Evesham South)
robert.banks@wychavon.gov.uk

Barratt, M (CON - Droitwich Spa East)

Beale, Graham (CON - Droitwich Spa South West)
graham.beale@wychavon.gov.uk

Brookes, Bob (CON - Droitwich Spa East)
bob.brookes@wychavon.gov.uk

Brotheridge, David (CON - Pershore)
David.brotheridge@wychavon.gov.uk

Bulman, James (CON - Bengeworth)
james.bulman@wychavon.gov.uk

Darby, Adrian (LD - South Bredon Hill)
adrian.darby@wychavon.gov.uk

Davis, Ron (CON - Eckington)
ronald.davis@wychavon.gov.uk

Dowty, Nigel (CON - Hartlebury)
nigel.dowty@wychavon.gov.uk

Duffy, Lynne (CON - Droitwich Spa West)
lynne.duffy@wychavon.gov.uk

Dyke, Andrew (CON - Little Hampton)
andrew.dyke@wychavon.gov.uk

Dyke, Wendy (CON - Little Hampton)
wendy.dyke@wychavon.gov.uk

Eyre, Elizabeth (CON - Broadway and Wickhamford)
elizabeth.eyre@wychavon.gov.uk

Fisher, Alan (CON - Lovett and North Claines)
tony.miller@wychavon.gov.uk

Hardman, Adrian (CON - Bredon)
adrian.hardman@wychavon.gov.uk

Homer, Charles (CON - Harvington and Norton)
charles.homer@wychavon.gov.uk

Jakeman, Reg (CON - Badsey)
reg.jakeman@wychavon.gov.uk

Jennings, K (CON - Droitwich Spa South East)

Kirke, Roma (CON - Elmley Castle and Somerville)
roma.kirke@wychavon.gov.uk

Lasota, Richard (CON - The Littletons)
richard.lasota@wychavon.gov.uk

Lee, David (CON - Inkberrow)
david.lee@wychavon.gov.uk

McDonald, Thomas (CON - Fladbury)
thomas.mcdonald@wychavon.gov.uk

Miller, Tony (CON - Lovett and North Claines)
tony.miller@wychavon.gov.uk

Noyes, Glenise (CON - Droitwich Spa Central)
glenise.noyes@wychavon.gov.uk

Noyes, Thomas (CON - Droitwich Spa South West)
tom.noyes@wychavon.gov.uk

O'Donnell, Gerry (CON - Evesham South)
gerry.o'donnell@wychavon.gov.uk

Parmenter, Barrie (CON - Broadway and Wickhamford)
barrie.parmenter@wychavon.gov.uk

Pinfield, Peter (LAB - Droitwich Spa West)
peter.pinfield@wychavon.gov.uk

Robinson, Linda (CON - Upton Snodsbury)
linda.robinson@wychavon.gov.uk

Sandalls, Josephine (CON - Evesham North)
josephine.sandalls@wychavon.gov.uk

Smith, Frances (CON - Evesham North)
frances.smith@wychavon.gov.uk

Smith, John (CON - Great Hampton)
john.smith@wychavon.gov.uk

Steel, Audrey (CON - Inkberrow)
audrey.steel@wychavon.gov.uk

Stokes, Emma (CON - Bengeworth)
emma.stokes@wychavon.gov.uk

Tomlinson, Peter (CON - Ombersley)
peter.tomlinson@wychavon.gov.uk

Tucker, Elizabeth (LD - Pinvin)
elizabeth.tucker@wychavon.gov.uk

Tucker, Charles (LD - Pershore)
charles.tucker@wychavon.gov.uk

Wood, Val (CON - Pershore)
val.wood@wychavon.gov.uk

Wright, Keith (LD - Bretforton and Offenhan)
keith.wright@wychavon.gov.uk

POLITICAL COMPOSITION

CON: 39, LD: 5, LAB: 1

CABINET

Leader: Mr Paul Middlebrough
Deputy Leader / Planning, Infrastructure & Housing: Mrs Judy Pearce
Community & Personal Health Welfare: Mr Ron Davis
Economic Development, Skills & Transport: Mr Thomas McDonald
Engagement & Rural Affairs: Mrs Audrey Steel
Environment & Contracted Services: Mrs Emma Stokes
Resources: Mr Robert Banks

COMMITTEE CHAIRS

Development Control: Mr Ron Davis
Licensing: Mr Gerry O'Donnell
Overview & Scrutiny: Mr Andrew Dyke
Planning: Mrs Linda Robinson

WYCOMBE D

Wycombe District Council, District Council Offices, Queen Victoria Road, High Wycombe HP11 1BB ☎ 01494 461000 🖷 01494 461292 💻 www.wycombe.gov.uk

FACTS & FIGURES

Police Authority: Thames Valley Police Authority
Health Authority: South Central Strategic Health Authority
Learning and Skills Council: South East
Parliamentary Constituencies: Aylesbury, Beaconsfield, Chesham and Amersham, Wycombe
EU Constituencies: South East
Election Frequency: Elections are of whole council
Twinning: Lacey Green: Hambye (France); High Wycombe: Kelkheim (Germany); Marlow: Marly-le-Roi (France); Radnage: Raderac (France);

PRINCIPAL OFFICERS

Chief Executive: Ms Karen Satterford, Chief Executive, Council Offices, Queen Victoria Road, High Wycombe HP11 1BB ☎ 01494 421101 🖷 01494 421109 🖰 karen_satterford@wycombe.gov.uk

Senior Management: Mr Charles Meakings, Head of Democratic, Policy & Legal Services & Research, Council Offices, Queen Victoria Road, High Wycombe HP11 1BB ☎ 01494 421980 🖷 01494 421109 🖰 charles_meakings@wycombe.gov.uk

Senior Management: Mr Ian Westgate, Corporate Director, Council Offices, Queen Victoria Road, High Wycombe HP11 1BB ☎ 01494 421400 🖷 01494 421464 🖰 ian_westgate@wycombe.gov.uk

Access Officer / Social Services (Disability): Mr Alan Switalski, Access Officer, Council Offices, Queen Victoria Road, High Wycombe HP11 1BB ☎ 01494 421438 🖷 01494 421439 🖰 alan_switalski@wycombe.gov.uk

Architect, Building / Property Services: Mr Charles Brocklehurst, Major Projects & Property Executive, Council Offices, Queen Victoria Road, High Wycombe HP11 1BB ☎ 01494 421280 🖷 01494 421285 🖰 charles_brocklehurst@wycombe.gov.uk

Best Value: Miss Jacqueline Ford, Corporate Policy Team Leader, Council Offices, Queen Victoria Road, High Wycombe HP11 1BB ☎ 01494 421983 🖷 01494 421109 🖰 jacqueline_l_ford@wycombe.gov.uk

Best Value: Mr Charles Meakings, Head of Democratic, Policy & Legal Services & Research, Council Offices, Queen Victoria Road, High Wycombe HP11 1BB ☎ 01494 421980 🖷 01494 421109 🖰 charles_meakings@wycombe.gov.uk

Building Control: Ms Alison Pipes, Building Control Manager, District Council Offices, Queen Victoria Road, High Wycombe HP11 1BB ☎ 01494 421425 🖷 01494 421439 🖰 alison_pipes@wycombe.gov.uk

PR / Communications: Mr Charles Meakings, Head of Democratic, Policy & Legal Services & Research, Council Offices, Queen Victoria Road, High Wycombe HP11 1BB ☎ 01494 421980 🖷 01494 421109 🖰 charles_meakings@wycombe.gov.uk

PR / Communications: Ms Catherine Spalton, Communications Team Leader, District Council Offices, Queen Victoria Road, High Wycombe HP11 1BB 🖷 01494 421230 🖰 catherine_spalton@wycombe.gov.uk

Community Planning: Mr Charles Meakings, Head of Democratic, Policy & Legal Services & Research, Council Offices, Queen Victoria Road, High Wycombe HP11 1BB ☎ 01494 421980 🖷 01494 421109 🖰 charles_meakings@wycombe.gov.uk

Community Safety: Ms Gillian Stimpson, Community Safety Manager, Council Offices, Queen Victoria Road, High Wycombe HP11 1BB ☎ 01494 421404 🖷 01494 421808 🖰 gillian_stimpson@wycombe.gov.uk

Computer Management: Mr Steve Bramhill, Corporate Manager, ICT & Customer Services, Council Offices, Queen Victoria Road, High Wycombe HP11 1BB ☎ 01494 421161 🖷 01494 421293 🖰 steve_bramhill@wycombe.gov.uk

Computer Management: Ms Mary Humphris, ICT Manager of Infrastructure, District Council Offices, Queen Victoria Road, High Wycombe HP11 1BB ☎ 01494 421179 🖰 mary_humphris@wycombe.gov.uk

Computer Management: Mr Mark Lansbury, Business Systems Manager, District Council Offices, Queen Victoria Road, High Wycombe HP11 1BB ☎ 01494 421168 🖰 mark_lansbury@wycombe.gov.uk

Computer Management: Mr John McMillan, Head of HR & Internal Shared Services, Council Offices, Queen Victoria Road, High Wycombe HP11 1BB ☎ 01494 421127 🖷 01494 421125 🖰 john_mcmillan@wycombe.gov.uk

Customer Service: Ms Dawny Davis, Customer Service Centre Manager, Council Offices, Queen Victoria Road, High Wycombe HP11 1BB ☎ 01494 421801 🖷 01494 461292 🖰 dawny_davis@wycombe.gov.uk

Customer Service: Mr John McMillan, Head of HR & Internal Shared Services, Council Offices, Queen Victoria Road, High

Wycombe HP11 1BB ☎ 01494 421127 🖷 01494 421125 ✉ john_mcmillan@wycombe.gov.uk

Economic Development: Mr Warren Ralls, Economic Development Advisor, District Council Offices, Queen Victoria Road, High Wycombe HP11 1BB ☎ 07411 009659 ✉ office@warrenralls.come

E-Government: Mr John McMillan, Head of HR & Internal Shared Services, Council Offices, Queen Victoria Road, High Wycombe HP11 1BB ☎ 01494 421127 🖷 01494 421125 ✉ john_mcmillan@wycombe.gov.uk

Electoral Registration: Miss Julie Mills, Statutory Services Manager, Council Offices, Queen Victoria Road, High Wycombe HP11 1BB ☎ 01494 421242 🖷 01494 461292 ✉ julie_mills@wycombe.gov.uk

Emergency Planning: Mr Charles Meakings, Head of Democratic, Policy & Legal Services & Research, Council Offices, Queen Victoria Road, High Wycombe HP11 1BB ☎ 01494 421980 🖷 01494 421109 ✉ charles_meakings@wycombe.gov.uk

Emergency Planning: Mr Brian Rodgers, Emergency Planning Liaison Officer, District Council Offices, Queen Victoria Road, High Wycombe HP11 1BB ☎ 01494 421890 🖷 01494 421285 ✉ brian_rodgers@wycombe.gov.uk

Energy Management: Mrs Lesley Stoner, Environmental Co-ordinator, Council Offices, Queen Victoria Road, High Wycombe HP11 1BB ☎ 01494 421744 🖷 01494 421791 ✉ lesley_stoner@wycombe.gov.uk

Energy Management: Mr Graham Weston, Energy Officer, Council Offices, Queen Victoria Road, High Wycombe HP11 1BB ☎ 01494 421565 🖷 01494 421285 ✉ graham_weston@wycombe.gov.uk

Environmental / Technical Services: Ms Caroline Hughes, Head of Environment, Council Offices, Queen Victoria Road, High Wycombe HP11 1BB ☎ 01494 421701 🖷 01494 421791 ✉ caroline_hughes@wycombe.gov.uk

Environmental / Technical Services: Mr Ian Westgate, Corporate Director, Council Offices, Queen Victoria Road, High Wycombe HP11 1BB ☎ 01494 421400 🖷 01494 421464 ✉ ian_westgate@wycombe.gov.uk

Environmental Health: Mr Neil Stannett, Environmental Health Officer, District Council Offices, Queen Victoria Road, High Wycombe HP11 1BB ☎ 01494 421092 🖷 01494 421971 ✉ neil_stannett@wycombe.gov.uk

Environmental Health: Mr Ian Westgate, Corporate Director, Council Offices, Queen Victoria Road, High Wycombe HP11 1BB ☎ 01494 421400 🖷 01494 421464 ✉ ian_westgate@wycombe.gov.uk

Estates, Property & Valuation: Mr Charles Brocklehurst, Major Projects & Property Executive, Council Offices, Queen Victoria Road, High Wycombe HP11 1BB ☎ 01494 421280 🖷 01494 421285 ✉ charles_brocklehurst@wycombe.gov.uk

Estates, Property & Valuation: Ms Monika Gibilaro, Senior Surveyor, District Council Offices, Queen Victoria Road, High Wycombe HP11 1BB ✉ monica_gibilaro@wycombe.gov.uk

Facilities: Mr John McMillan, Head of HR & Internal Shared Services, Council Offices, Queen Victoria Road, High Wycombe HP11 1BB ☎ 01494 421127 🖷 01494 421125 ✉ john_mcmillan@wycombe.gov.uk

Finance and Treasurer: Mr Steve Richardson, Head of Financial & Commercial Services, District Council Offices, Queen Victoria Road, High Wycombe HP11 1BB ☎ 01494 421322 ✉ steve_richardson@wycombe.gov.uk

Health and Safety: Mr John McMillan, Head of HR & Internal Shared Services, Council Offices, Queen Victoria Road, High Wycombe HP11 1BB ☎ 01494 421127 🖷 01494 421125 ✉ john_mcmillan@wycombe.gov.uk

Home Energy Conservation: Mrs Lesley Stoner, Environmental Co-ordinator, Council Offices, Queen Victoria Road, High Wycombe HP11 1BB ☎ 01494 421744 🖷 01494 421791 ✉ lesley_stoner@wycombe.gov.uk

Housing: Ms Caroline Hughes, Head of Environment, Council Offices, Queen Victoria Road, High Wycombe HP11 1BB ☎ 01494 421701 🖷 01494 421791 ✉ caroline_hughes@wycombe.gov.uk

Housing: Mr Ian Westgate, Corporate Director, Council Offices, Queen Victoria Road, High Wycombe HP11 1BB ☎ 01494 421400 🖷 01494 421464 ✉ ian_westgate@wycombe.gov.uk

Legal: Mr Charles Meakings, Head of Democratic, Policy & Legal Services & Research, Council Offices, Queen Victoria Road, High Wycombe HP11 1BB ☎ 01494 421980 🖷 01494 421109 ✉ charles_meakings@wycombe.gov.uk

Leisure and Cultural Services: Ms Sarah Randall, Cohesion & Leisure Manager, District Council Offices, Queen Victoria Road, High Wycombe HP11 1BB ☎ 01494 421888 ✉ sarah_randall@wycombe.gov.uk

Licensing: Ms Caroline Steven, Licensing Team Leader, District Council Offices, Queen Victoria Road, High Wycombe HP11 1BB ☎ 01494 421222 🖷 01494 421791 ✉ caroline_steven@wycombe.gov.uk

Lifelong Learning: Ms Elaine Jewell, Head of Community Services, District Council Offices, Queen Victoria Road, High Wycombe HP11 1BB ☎ 01494 421800 ✉ elaine_jewell@wycombe.gov.uk

Lighting: Mr Ben Eales, Engineering Project Manager, Council Offices, Queen Victoria Road, High Wycombe HP11 1BB ☎ 01494 421453 🖷 01494 421285 ✉ ben_eales@wycombe.gov.uk

Lottery Funding, Charity and Voluntary: Ms Elaine Jewell, Head of Community Services, District Council Offices, Queen Victoria Road, High Wycombe HP11 1BB ☎ 01494 421800 ✉ elaine_jewell@wycombe.gov.uk

Member Services: Mr Charles Meakings, Head of Democratic,

Policy & Legal Services & Research, Council Offices, Queen Victoria Road, High Wycombe HP11 1BB ☎ 01494 421980 🖷 01494 421109 ✉ charles_meakings@wycombe.gov.uk

Parking: Mr Robin Evans, Parking Services Manager, District Council Offices, Queen Victoria Road, High Wycombe HP11 1BB ☎ 01494 421471 🖷 01494 421474 ✉ robin_evans@wycombe.gov.uk

Partnerships: Mr Charles Meakings, Head of Democratic, Policy & Legal Services & Research, Council Offices, Queen Victoria Road, High Wycombe HP11 1BB ☎ 01494 421980 🖷 01494 421109 ✉ charles_meakings@wycombe.gov.uk

Personnel / HR: Mr John McMillan, Head of HR & Internal Shared Services, Council Offices, Queen Victoria Road, High Wycombe HP11 1BB ☎ 01494 421127 🖷 01494 421125 ✉ john_mcmillan@wycombe.gov.uk

Planning: Mr Alastair Nicholson, Development Manager, District Council Offices, Queen Victoria Road, High Wycombe HP11 1BB ☎ 01494 421510 🖷 01494 421464 ✉ alastair_nicholson@wycombe.gov.uk

Planning: Mr Jerry Unsworth, Head of Planning & Sustainability, Council Offices, Queen Victoria Road, High Wycombe HP11 1BB ☎ 01494 421519 🖷 01494 421181 ✉ jerry_unsworth@wycombe.gov.uk

Procurement: Mr Steve Middleton, Procurement Manager, District Council Offices, Queen Victoria Road, High Wycombe HP11 1BB ☎ 01494 421315 🖷 01494 421660 ✉ steve_middleton@wycombe.gov.uk

Procurement: Mr Steve Richardson, Head of Financial & Commercial Services, District Council Offices, Queen Victoria Road, High Wycombe HP11 1BB ☎ 01494 421322 ✉ steve_richardson@wycombe.gov.uk

Recycling & Waste Minimisation: Ms Sally Gordon, Waste & Recycling Services Manager, Council Offices, Queen Victoria Road, High Wycombe HP11 1BB ☎ 01494 421170 🖷 01494 421118 ✉ sally_gordon@wycombe.gov.uk

Recycling & Waste Minimisation: Mr Terry Hill, Contracts Services Manager, Council Offices, Queen Victoria Road, High Wycombe HP11 1BB ☎ 01494 421446 🖷 01494 421118 ✉ terry_hill@wycombe.gov.uk

Recycling & Waste Minimisation: Ms Caroline Hughes, Head of Environment, Council Offices, Queen Victoria Road, High Wycombe HP11 1BB ☎ 01494 421701 🖷 01494 421791 ✉ caroline_hughes@wycombe.gov.uk

Regeneration: Mrs Mayuri Naker, Economic Development Service Manager, District Council Offices, Queen Victoria Road, High Wycombe HP11 1BB ☎ 01494 421124 🖷 01494 421285 ✉ mayuri_naker@wycombe.gov.uk

Regeneration: Ms Satbir West, Regeneration & Tourism Manager, District Council Offices, Queen Victoria Road, High Wycombe HP11 1BB ☎ 01494 421290 ✉ satbir_west@wycombe.gov.uk

Staff Training: Mr John McMillan, Head of HR & Internal Shared Services, Council Offices, Queen Victoria Road, High Wycombe HP11 1BB ☎ 01494 421127 🖷 01494 421125 ✉ john_mcmillan@wycombe.gov.uk

Staff Training: Ms Sarah Taylor, Training & Development Officer, Council Offices, Queen Victoria Road, High Wycombe HP11 1BB ☎ 01494 421139 🖷 01494 421125 ✉ sarah_taylor@wycombe.gov.uk

Street Scene: Ms Caroline Hughes, Head of Environment, Council Offices, Queen Victoria Road, High Wycombe HP11 1BB ☎ 01494 421701 🖷 01494 421791 ✉ caroline_hughes@wycombe.gov.uk

Sustainable Communities: Ms Elaine Jewell, Head of Community Services, District Council Offices, Queen Victoria Road, High Wycombe HP11 1BB ☎ 01494 421800 ✉ elaine_jewell@wycombe.gov.uk

Sustainable Communities: Mr Ian Westgate, Corporate Director, Council Offices, Queen Victoria Road, High Wycombe HP11 1BB ☎ 01494 421400 🖷 01494 421464 ✉ ian_westgate@wycombe.gov.uk

Sustainable Development: Mrs Lesley Stoner, Environmental Co-ordinator, Council Offices, Queen Victoria Road, High Wycombe HP11 1BB ☎ 01494 421744 🖷 01494 421791 ✉ lesley_stoner@wycombe.gov.uk

Sustainable Development: Mr Jerry Unsworth, Head of Planning & Sustainability, Council Offices, Queen Victoria Road, High Wycombe HP11 1BB ☎ 01494 421519 🖷 01494 421181 ✉ jerry_unsworth@wycombe.gov.uk

Sustainable Development: Mr Ian Westgate, Corporate Director, Council Offices, Queen Victoria Road, High Wycombe HP11 1BB ☎ 01494 421400 🖷 01494 421464 ✉ ian_westgate@wycombe.gov.uk

Tourism: Ms Elaine Jewell, Head of Community Services, District Council Offices, Queen Victoria Road, High Wycombe HP11 1BB ☎ 01494 421800 ✉ elaine_jewell@wycombe.gov.uk

Tourism: Ms Jo Kane, Tourist Information Centre Manager, District Council Offices, Queen Victoria Road, High Wycombe HP11 1DJ ☎ 01494 421815 ✉ jo_kane@wycombe.gov.uk

Tourism: Ms Satbir West, Regeneration & Tourism Manager, District Council Offices, Queen Victoria Road, High Wycombe HP11 1BB ☎ 01494 421290 ✉ satbir_west@wycombe.gov.uk

Town Centre: Ms Melanie Williams, Town Centre Manager, District Council Offices, Queen Victoria Road, High Wycombe HP11 1BB ☎ 01494 452705 ✉ melanie.williams@hwtcp.co.uk

Total Place: Mr Charles Meakings, Head of Democratic, Policy & Legal Services & Research, Council Offices, Queen Victoria Road, High Wycombe HP11 1BB ☎ 01494 421980 🖷 01494 421109 ✉ charles_meakings@wycombe.gov.uk

Waste Collection and Disposal: Ms Sally Gordon, Waste & Recycling Services Manager, Council Offices, Queen Victoria Road, High Wycombe HP11 1BB ☎ 01494 421170 🖷 01494 421118 sally_gordon@wycombe.gov.uk

Waste Collection and Disposal: Mr Terry Hill, Contracts Services Manager, Council Offices, Queen Victoria Road, High Wycombe HP11 1BB ☎ 01494 421446 🖷 01494 421118 terry_hill@wycombe.gov.uk

Waste Collection and Disposal: Ms Caroline Hughes, Head of Environment, Council Offices, Queen Victoria Road, High Wycombe HP11 1BB ☎ 01494 421701 🖷 01494 421791 caroline_hughes@wycombe.gov.uk

Waste Management: Mr Terry Hill, Contracts Services Manager, Council Offices, Queen Victoria Road, High Wycombe HP11 1BB ☎ 01494 421446 🖷 01494 421118 terry_hill@wycombe.gov.uk

Waste Management: Ms Caroline Hughes, Head of Environment, Council Offices, Queen Victoria Road, High Wycombe HP11 1BB ☎ 01494 421701 🖷 01494 421791 caroline_hughes@wycombe.gov.uk

Waste Management: Mr Ian Westgate, Corporate Director, Council Offices, Queen Victoria Road, High Wycombe HP11 1BB ☎ 01494 421400 🖷 01494 421464 ian_westgate@wycombe.gov.uk

MEMBERS OF THE COUNCIL (60)

***Leader of the Council:* Collingwood**, Alex (CON - Marlow North and West)
alex_collingwood@wycombe.gov.uk

***Deputy Leader of the Council:* Carroll**, David (CON - Great Hughenden)
david_carroll@wycombe.gov.uk

***Deputy Leader of the Council:* Hussain**, Arif (CON - Terriers and Amersham Hill)
arif_hussain@wycombe.gov.uk

***Group Leader:* Groulef**, Victoria (LAB - Disraeli)
victoria.groulef@wycombe.gov.uk

***Group Leader:* Snaith**, Trevor (LD - Ryemead)
trevor_snaith@wycombe.gov.uk

***Group Leader:* Turner**, Alan (IND - The Risborough)
alan_turner@wycombe.gov.uk

Adey, Julia (CON - The Wooburns)
julia_adey@wycombe.gov.uk

Ahmed, Zia (CON - Sands)
zia.ahmed@wycombe.gov.uk

Ahmed, Khalil (LAB - Disraeli)
khalil_ahmed@wycombe.gov.uk

Angell, Marcus (CON - Bledlow and Bradenham)
marcus_angell@wycombe.gov.uk

Anson, Douglas (CON - Marlow South East)
douglas_anson@wycombe.gov.uk

Appleyard, Mike (CON - Bourne End cum Hedsor)
michael_appleyard@wycombe.gov.uk

Barnes, Dominic (CON - Greater Marlow)
dominic_barnes@wycombe.gov.uk

Bates, Ian (LAB - Totteridge)
ian_bates@wycombe.gov.uk

Bendyshe-Brown, William (CON - The Risboroughs)
william_bendyshe-brown@wycombe.gov.uk

Chair, Wendy (CON - Downley and Plomer Hill)
wendy_mallen@wycombe.gov.uk

Clarke, Lesley (CON - Abbey)
lesley_clarke@wycombe.gov.uk

Colomb, Roger (CON - Terriers and Amersham Hill)
roger_colomb@wycombe.gov.uk

Ditta, Chaudhary (LD - Bowerdean)
chaudhary_ditta@wycombe.gov.uk

Emmett, Roger (CON - Hambleden Valley)
roger_emmett@wycombe.gov.uk

Farmer, Ray (LD - Ryemead)
ray_farmer@wycombe.gov.uk

Foster, Mel (CON - Lacey Green, Speen and The Hampdens)
mel_foster@wycombe.gov.uk

Gaffney, Ron (CON - Hazlemere North)
ron_gaffney@wycombe.gov.uk

Gibbs, John (CON - Stokenchurch and Radnage)
john_gibbs@wycombe.gov.uk

Graham, Sebert (LAB - Oakridge and Castlefield)
sebert_graham@wycombe.gov.uk

Green, Tony (CON - Terriers and Amersham Hill)
tony_green@wycombe.gov.uk

Hall, Gary (IND - The Risboroughs)
gary_hall@wycombe.gov.uk

Hanif, Mohammed (LAB - Oakridge and Castlefield)
mohammed_hanif@wycombe.gov.uk

Harriss, Clive (CON - Tylers Green and Loudwater)
clive_harriss@wycombe.gov.uk

Hill, Alan (CON - Abbey)
alan_hill@wycombe.gov.uk

Hussain, Mahboob (CON - Abbey)
mahboob_hussain@wycombe.gov.uk

Johncock, David (CON - Flackwell Heath and Little Marlow)
david_johncock@wycombe.gov.uk

Jones, Audrey (CON - Greater Hughenden)
audrey_jones@wycombe.gov.uk

Knight, Matt (LD - Micklefield)
matt_knight@wycombe.gov.uk

Knight, Rachel (LAB - Oakridge and Castlefield)
rachel.knight@wycombe.gov.uk

Lacey, Steve (CON - Icknield)
steve.lacey@wycombe.gov.uk

Langley, Julia (CON - The Wooburns)
julia_langley@wycombe.gov.uk

Lee, Paula (LD - Micklefield)
paula_lee@wycombe.gov.uk

Malliff, James (CON - Hazlemere South)
james_malliff@wycombe.gov.uk

Manir, Sanna (CON - Sands)
sanna_manir@wycombe.gov.uk

Marshall, Neil (CON - Marlow North and West)
neil_marshall@wycombe.gov.uk

McCarthy, Hugh (CON - Hazlemere North)
hugh_mccarthy@wycombe.gov.uk

McEnnis, Ian (CON - Chiltern Rise)
ian_mcennis@wycombe.gov.uk

Morgan, Dory (CON - Greater Hughenden)
dory_morgan@wycombe.gov.uk

Neudecker, Michelle (CON - Stokenchurch and Radnage)
michelle_neudecker@wycombe.gov.uk

Parker, Simon (LD - Booker and Cressex)
simon_parker@wycombe.gov.uk

Pearce, Brian (UKIP - Booker and Cressex)
brian_pearce@wycombe.gov.uk

Pollock, Brian (LD - Bourne End-cum-Hedsor)

brian_pollock@wycombe.gov.uk
Richards, John (CON - Greater Marlow)
john_richards@wycombe.gov.uk
Savage, John (CON - Flackwell Heath and Little Marlow)
john_savage@wycombe.gov.uk
Scott, Richard (CON - Marlow South East)
richard_scott@wycombe.gov.uk
Shafique, Chauhdry (LAB - Totteridge)
chauhdry_shafique@wycombe.gov.uk
Shakespeare, David (CON - Tylers Green and Loudwater)
david_shakespeare@wycombe.gov.uk
Slater, Alex (LD - Hazlemere South)
alex.slater@wycombe.gov.uk
Teesdale, Jean (CON - Chiltern Rise)
jean_teesdale@wycombe.gov.uk
Turner, Paul (CON - Downley and Plomer Hill)
paul_turner@wycombe.gov.uk
Wassell, Julia (LD - Bowerdean)
julia_wassell@wycombe.gov.uk
Watson, David (CON - Flackwell Heath and Little Marlow)
david_watson@wycombe.gov.uk
Wilson, Roger (CON - Marlow North and West)
roger_wilson@wycombe.gov.uk
Wood, Katrina (CON - Tylers Green and Loudwater)
katrina_wood@wycombe.gov.uk

POLITICAL COMPOSITION
CON: 41, LD: 9, LAB: 7, IND: 2, UKIP: 1

CABINET
Leader: Mr Alex Collingwood
First Deputy Leader / Housing & External Partnerships: Mr David Carroll
Second Deputy Leader / Property & Economic Development: Mr Arif Hussain
Big Society & Localism: Mr David Shakespeare
Community: Ms Katrina Wood
Democratic, Legal & Policy Services: Mrs Jean Teesdale
Environment: Mrs Audrey Jones
Finance: Mr Roger Wilson
HR, ICT & Customer Services: Mr Dominic Barnes
Planning & Sustainability: Mr Hugh McCarthy

COMMITTEE CHAIRS
Audit: Mr Mike Appleyard
Licensing: Mr Alan Hill
Personnel & Development: Mr John Gibbs
Regulatory & Appeals: Mr John Savage

WYRE D
Wyre Borough Council, Civic Centre, Breck Road, Poulton-le-Fylde FY6 7PU ☎ 01253 891000 🖷 01253 899000 ✉ mailroom@wyrebc.gov.uk 🖳 www.wyrebc.gov.uk

FACTS & FIGURES
Police Authority: Lancashire Police Authority
Health Authority: North West Strategic Health Authority
Learning and Skills Council: North West
Parliamentary Constituencies: Wyre and Preston North
EU Constituencies: North West
Election Frequency: Elections are of whole council

PRINCIPAL OFFICERS
Chief Executive: Mr Garry Payne, Director of Regeneration, Civic Centre, Breck Road, Poulton-le-Fylde FY6 7PU ☎ 01253 891000 🖷 01253 899000 ✉ gpayne@wyrebc.gov.uk

Building Control: Mr Adrian Wyre, Principle Building Control Surveyor, The Council House, Burcot Lane, Bromsgrove B60 1AA ☎ 01527 881350 🖷 01527 881313 ✉ a.wyre@bromsgrove.gov.uk

Community Safety: Ms Jane Murray, Community Officer, Civic Centre, Breck Road, Poulton-le-Fylde FY6 7PU ☎ 01253 891000 🖷 01253 899000 ✉ jmurray@wyrebc.gov.uk

Customer Service: Ms Philippa Davies, Director of Resources, Civic Centre, Breck Road, Poulton-le-Fylde FY6 7PU ☎ 01253 891000 🖷 01253 899000 ✉ pdavies@wyrebc.gov.uk

Economic Development: Mr Peter Michael, Economic Development Officer, The Council House, Burcot Lane, Bromsgrove B60 1AA ☎ 01527 881327 🖷 01527 881313 ✉ p.michael@bromsgrove.gov.uk

E-Government: Ms Joanne Billington, Head of Governance, Civic Centre, Breck Road, Poulton-le-Fylde FY6 7PU ☎ 01253 887372; 01253 891000 🖷 01253 899000 ✉ joanne.billington@wyre.gov.uk

Electoral Registration: Ms Joanne Porter, Governance Manager, Civic Centre, Breck Road, Poulton-le-Fylde FY6 7PU ☎ 01253 891000 🖷 01253 899000 ✉ jporter@wyrebc.gov.uk

Emergency Planning: Mr John Blundell, Emergency Planning Officer, Civic Centre, Breck Road, Poulton-le-Fylde FY6 7PU ☎ 01253 891000 🖷 01253 899000 ✉ jblundell@wyrebc.gov.uk

Energy Management: Mr Mark Broadhurst, Head of Housing Services, Civic Centre, Breck Road, Poulton-le-Fylde FY6 7PU ☎ 01253 891000 🖷 01253 899000 ✉ mbroadhurst@wyrebc.gov.uk

Environmental Health: Mrs Corinne Mason, Senior Environmental Health Officer, Civic Centre, Breck Road, Poulton-le-Fylde FY6 7PU ☎ 01253 891000; 01253 891000 ✉ corinne.mason@wyre.gov.uk

European Liaison: Mrs Karen Stringer, Project Co-ordinator, Civic Centre, Breck Road, Poulton-le-Fylde FY6 7PU ☎ 01253 891000 🖷 01253 899000 ✉ kstringer@wyrebc.gov.uk

Finance and Treasurer: Ms Philippa Davies, Director of Resources, Civic Centre, Breck Road, Poulton-le-Fylde FY6 7PU ☎ 01253 891000 🖷 01253 899000 ✉ pdavies@wyrebc.gov.uk

Grounds Maintenance: Mr Mark Billington, Head of Operations, Civic Centre, Breck Road, Poulton-le-Fylde FY6 7PU ☎ 01253 891000🖷 01253 899000✉ philippa.davies@wyre.gov.uk

Health and Safety: Mrs Liesl Hadgraft, Head of Business Support, Civic Centre, Breck Road, Poulton-le-Fylde FY6 7PU ☎ 01253 891000 🖷 01253 899000 ✉ lhadgraft@wyrebc.gov.uk

Home Energy Conservation: Mr Mark Broadhurst, Head of Housing Services, Civic Centre, Breck Road, Poulton-le-Fylde

FY6 7PU ☎ 01253 891000 🖷 01253 899000
🖱 mbroadhurst@wyrebc.gov.uk

Housing: Mr Mark Broadhurst, Head of Housing Services, Civic Centre, Breck Road, Poulton-le-Fylde FY6 7PU ☎ 01253 891000 🖷 01253 899000 🖱 mbroadhurst@wyrebc.gov.uk

Legal: Ms Mary Grimshaw, Senior Solicitor, Civic Centre, Breck Road, Poulton-le-Fylde FY6 7PU ☎ 01253 891000; 01253 891000 🖷 01253 899000; 01253 899000 🖱 mary.grimshaw@wyre.gov.uk; mary.grimshaw@wyre.gov.uk

Leisure and Cultural Services: Mr Ian Munro, Head of Culture, Leisure & Tourism, Civic Centre, Breck Road, Poulton-le-Fylde FY6 7PU ☎ 01253 887208; 01253 887208 🖷 01253 889499; 01253 887499 🖱 ian.munro@wyre.gov.uk; ian.munro@wyre.gov.uk

Licensing: Ms Christa Ferguson, Licensing Manager, Civic Centre, Breck Road, Poulton-le-Fylde FY6 7PU ☎ 01253 891000 🖷 01253 899000 🖱 cferguson@wyre.gov.uk

Member Services: Ms Joanne Billington, Head of Governance, Civic Centre, Breck Road, Poulton-le-Fylde FY6 7PU ☎ 01253 887372; 01253 891000 🖷 01253 899000; 01253 899000 🖱 joanne.billington@wyre.gov.uk

Partnerships: Mrs Marianne Hesketh, Head of Transformation, Civic Centre, Breck Road, Poulton-le-Fylde FY6 7PU ☎ 01253 887350; 01253 887350 🖱 marianne.hesketh@wyre.gov.uk

Personnel / HR: Mrs Liesl Hadgraft, Head of Business Support, Civic Centre, Breck Road, Poulton-le-Fylde FY6 7PU ☎ 01253 891000 🖷 01253 899000 🖱 lhadgraft@wyrebc.gov.uk

Planning: Mr David Thow, Head of Planning Services, Civic Centre, Breck Road, Poulton-le-Fylde FY6 7PU ☎ 01253 891000; 01253 891000 🖷 01253 899000; 01253 899000 🖱 david.thow@wyre.gov.uk; david.thow@wyre.gov.uk

Procurement: Mr Allan Williams, Procurement Officer, Civic Centre, Breck Road, Poulton-le-Fylde FY6 7PU ☎ 01253 891000 🖷 01253 899000 🖱 awilliams@wyrebc.gov.uk

Recycling & Waste Minimisation: Ms Ruth Hunter, Street Scene Projects Officer, Civic Centre, Breck Road, Poulton-le-Fylde FY6 7PU ☎ 01253 891000; 01253 891000 🖷 01253 899000 🖱 ruth.hunter@wyre.gov.uk

Waste Collection and Disposal: Mr Michael Ryan, Director of People and Places, Civic Centre, Breck Road, Poulton-le-Fylde FY6 7PU ☎ 01253 887605 🖷 01253 887499 🖱 mryan@wyrebc.gov.uk

Waste Management: Mr Michael Ryan, Director of People and Places, Civic Centre, Breck Road, Poulton-le-Fylde FY6 7PU ☎ 01253 887605 🖷 01253 887499 🖱 mryan@wyrebc.gov.uk

Waste Management: Mr Michael Ryan, Director of People and Places, Civic Centre, Breck Road, Poulton-le-Fylde FY6 7PU ☎ 01253 887605 🖷 01253 887499 🖱 mryan@wyrebc.gov.uk

MEMBERS OF THE COUNCIL (55)

***Mayor:* Lawrenson**, Donald (CON - Pilling)
don.lawrenson@wyre.gov.uk

***Deputy Mayor:* Perkin**, Ian (CON - Staina)
ian.perkin@wyre.gov.uk

***Leader of the Council:* Gibson**, Peter (CON - Breck)
peter.gibson@wyre.gov.uk

***Deputy Leader of the Council:* Vincent**, Alan (CON - Victoria)
alanvincent@vslaw.co.uk

Amos, Rita (CON - Cleveleys Park)
rita.amos@wyre.gov.uk

Anderson, Julia (CON - Staina)
julie.anderson@wyre.gov.uk

Anderton, Emma (LAB - Warren)
emma.anderton@wyre.gov.uk

Anderton, Marge (LAB - Warren)
marge.anderton@wyre.gov.uk

Atkins, Dulcie (CON - Garstang)
datkins@wyrebc.gov.uk

Balmain, Tom (CON - Garstang)
tom.balmain@wyre.gov.uk

Bannister, David (CON - Tithebarn)
david.bannister@wyre.gov.uk

Beavers, Lorraine (LAB - Pharos)
cllrlorrainebeavers@hotmail.co.uk

Berry, Roger (CON - Highcross)
roger.berry@wyre.gov.uk

Birch, Barry (CON - Highcross)
barry.birch@wyre.gov.uk

Bowen, Lynne (CON - Hambleton and Stalmine-with-Staynall)
lynne.bowen@wyre.gov.uk

Bridge, Simon (CON - Hardhorn)
simon.bridge@wyre.gov.uk

Brooks, Roger (CON - Cabus)
roger.brooks@wyre.gov.uk

Catterall, Susan (CON - Great Eccleston)
sue.catterall@wyre.gov.uk

Cocker, Graeme (CON - Hardhorn)
graeme.cocker@wyre.gov.uk

Collinson, Alice (CON - Garstang)
alice.collinson@wyre.gov.uk

Duffy, Ruth (LAB - Mount)
ruthduffy111@btinternet.com

Duffy, Ian (LAB - Mount)

Gandhi, May (CON - Carleton)
may.gandhi@wyre.gov.uk

Gandhi, Ramesh (CON - Staina)
ramesh.gandhi@wyre.gov.uk

Greenhough, Ron (CON - Norcross)
ron.greenhough@wyre.gov.uk

Grunshaw, Julie (LAB - Park)
julie.grunshaw@wyre.gov.uk

Grunshaw, Clive (LAB - Pharos)
clive.grunshaw@wyre.gov.uk

Hargreaves, James (CON - Carleton)
james.hargreaves@wyre.gov.uk

Henderson, David (CON - Breck)
david.henderson@wyre.gov.uk

Hewitt, Rita (LAB - Rossall)
rita.hewitt@wyre.gov.uk

Hodgkinson, John (CON - Jubilee)
john.hodgkinson@wyre.gov.uk

Kay, Andrea (CON - Cleveleys Park)
andrea.kay@wyre.gov.uk

Lees, Terry (LAB - Bourne)

terry.lees@wyre.gov.uk
MacNaughton, Don (CON - Bourne)
don.macnaughton@wyre.gov.uk
Martin, Penny (LAB - Cleveleys Park)
penny.martin@wyre.gov.uk
McCann, Gordon (CON - Preesall)
gordon.mcann@wyre.gov.uk
McKay, Lesley (CON - Tithebarn)
lesley.mckay@wyre.gov.uk
Moon, Paul (CON - Preesall)
paul.moon@wyre.gov.uk
Murphy, Peter (CON - Brock)
pete.murphy@wyre.gov.uk
Newsham, Julie (CON - Bourne)
julie.newsham@wyre.gov.uk
Ormrod, Patsy (CON - Victoria)
patsy.ormrod@wyre.gov.uk
Pimbley, Susan (CON - Great Eccleston)
sue.pimbley@wyre.gov.uk
Robinson, Julie (CON - Hambleton and Stalmine-with-Staynall)
julie.robinson@wyre.gov.uk
Rogers, Terry (LAB - Rossall)
terry.rogers@wyre.gov.uk
Shewan, Ronald (LAB - Pharos)
ron.shewan@wyre.gov.uk
Smith, Christine (LAB - Park)
christine.smith@wyre.gov.uk
Swift, Dave (CON - Catterall)
dave.swift@wyre.gov.uk
Taylor, Vivien (CON - Preesall)
vivien.taylor@wyre.gov.uk
Taylor, Ted (LAB - Rossall)
ted.taylor@wyre.gov.uk
Treece - Birch, Paul (LAB - Warren)
paul.treece-birch@wyre.gov.uk
Turner, Ann (CON - Norcross)
a.m.turner13@btinternet.com
Vincent, Michael (CON - Victoria)
michael.vincent@wyre.gov.uk
Walmsley, David (CON - Jubilee)
david.walmsley@wyre.gov.uk
Williams, David (CON - Calder)
david.williams@wyre.gov.uk
Wilson, Val (CON - Wyresdale)
val.wilson@wyre.gov.uk

POLITICAL COMPOSITION
CON: 40, LAB: 15

CABINET
Leader: Mr Peter Gibson
Deputy Leader / Resources: Mr Alan Vincent
Economy: Mr Gordon McCann
Leisure & Culture: Mrs Lynne Bowen
Neighbourhood Services: Mr Roger Berry
Street Scene: Mr Peter Murphy

COMMITTEE CHAIRS
Audit: Mr Tom Balmain
Licensing: Mr Michael Vincent
Overview & Scrutiny: Ms May Gandhi
Planning Policy: Mr David Henderson
Planning: Mr David Henderson

WYRE FOREST — D

Wyre Forest District Council, Civic Centre, New Street, Stourport-on-Severn DY13 8UJ ☎ 01562 732928 🖷 01562 67673
communications@wyreforestdc.gov.uk
www.wyreforestdc.gov.uk

FACTS & FIGURES
Police Authority: West Mercia Police Authority
Health Authority: NHS West Midlands
Learning and Skills Council: West Midlands
Parliamentary Constituencies: Wyre Forest
EU Constituencies: West Midlands
Election Frequency: Elections are by thirds
Twinning: Bewdley: Fort-Mahon-Plage (France); Vellmar (Germany); Kidderminster: Husum (Germany); Stourport-on-Severn: Villeneuve-le-Roi (France)

PRINCIPAL OFFICERS
Chief Executive: Mr Ian Miller, Chief Executive, Civic Centre, New Street, Stourport-on-Severn DY13 8UJ ☎ 01562 732700 ian.miller@wyreforestdc.gov.uk

Building Control: Mr Paul Wright, Senior Building Control Officer, Duke House, Clensmore Street, Kidderminster DY10 2JX ☎ 01562 732928 paul.wright@wyreforestdc.gov.uk

PR / Communications: Mrs Jane Doyle, Media and Marketing Officer - Job Share, Green Street, Kidderminster DY10 1HA ☎ 01562 732928 jane.doyle@wyreforestdc.gov.uk

PR / Communications: Mrs Suzanne Johnston-Hubbold, Media and Marketing Officer - Job Share, Green Street, Kidderminster DY10 1HA ☎ 01562 732982 suzanne.johnston-hubbold@wyreforestdc.gov.uk

Community Planning: Ms Alison Braithwaite, Wyre Forest Forward Manager, Civic Centre, New Street, Stourport-on-Severn DY13 8UJ ☎ 01562 732781 🖷 01299 879688 alison.braithwaite@wyreforestdc.gov.uk

Community Safety: Mrs Kathryn Washington, Community Safety and Partnerships Officer, Green Street, Kidderminster DY10 1HA ☎ 01562 732956 🖷 01562 879688 kathryn.washington@wyreforestdc.gov.uk

Computer Management: Mr Dave Johnson, ICT Manager, Duke House, Clensmore Street, Kidderminster DY10 2JX ☎ 01562 732138 dave.johnson@wyreforestdc.gov.uk

Contracts: Mrs Sally Tallon, Contracts and Freedom of Information Solicitor, Civic Centre, New Street, Stourport-on-Severn DY13 8UJ ☎ 01562 732928 🖷 01562 732775 sally.tallon@wyreforestdc.gov.uk

Corporate Services: Mrs Caroline Newlands, Director of Community Asset and Localism, Civic Centre, New Street, Stourport-on-Severn DY13 8UJ ☎ 01562 732738 🖷 01299 879688 caroline.newlands@wyreforestdc.gov.uk

Customer Service: Mrs Lucy Wright, Customer Services Manager, Town Hall, Vicar Street, Kidderminster DY10 1DA

☎ 01562 732948 🖰 lucy.wright@wyreforestdc.gov.uk

Economic Development: Mr Steve Singleton, Economic Development and Tourism Manager, Duke House, Clensmore Street, Kidderminster DY10 2JX ☎ 01562 732928 🖷 01562 732168 🖰 steve.singleton@wyreforestdc.gov.uk

Electoral Registration: Ms Penelope Williams, Democratic Services Manager, Civic Centre, New Street, Stourport-on-Severn DY13 8UJ ☎ 01562 732728 🖷 01299 879688 🖰 penolope.williams@wyreforestdc.gov.uk

Emergency Planning: Mr Richard Davis-Leech, North Worcestershire Civil Contingencies Resilience Manager, Civic Centre, New Street, Stourport-on-Severn DY13 8UJ ☎ 01562 732711 🖰 richard.davis-leech@wyreforestdc.gov.uk

Environmental Health: Mr Mike Parker, Director of Economic Prosperity and Place, Duke House, Clensmore Street, Kidderminster DY10 2JX ☎ 01562 732928 🖷 01562 732500 🖰 mike.parker@wyreforestdc.gov.uk

Estates, Property & Valuation: Mrs Caroline Newlands, Director of Community Asset and Localism, Civic Centre, New Street, Stourport-on-Severn DY13 8UJ ☎ 01562 732738 🖷 01299 879688 🖰 caroline.newlands@wyreforestdc.gov.uk

Facilities: Mrs Elaine Brookes, Facilities Manager, Civic Centre, New Street, Stourport-on-Severn DY13 8UJ ☎ 01562 732797 🖷 01299 879688 🖰 elaine.brookes@wyreforestdc.gov.uk

Finance and Treasurer: Ms Joanne Wagstaffe, Director of Resources, Duke House, Clensmore Street, Kidderminster DY10 2JX ☎ 01562 732100 🖷 01562 732104 🖰 joanne.wagstaffe@wyreforestdc.gov.uk

Grounds Maintenance: Mr Joe Scully, Parks and Green Spaces Manager, Green Street, Kidderminster DY10 1HA ☎ 01562 732928 🖷 01562 732981 🖰 joe.scully@wyreforestdc.gov.uk

Health and Safety: Mr Steve Brant, Environmental Services Manager, Green Street, Kidderminster DY10 1HA ☎ 01562 732922 🖷 01562 732905 🖰 steve.brant@wyreforestdc.gov.uk

Home Energy Conservation: Ms Jenny Moreton, Principal Health and Sustainability Officer, Duke House, Clensmore Street, Kidderminster DY10 2JX ☎ 01562 732569 🖰 jennifer.moreton@wyreforestdc.gov.uk

Housing: Mrs Kate Bailey, Strategic Housing Services Manager, Duke House, Clensmore Street, Kidderminster DY10 2JX ☎ 01562 732560 🖷 01562 732556 🖰 kate.bailey@wyreforestdc.gov.uk

Legal: Mrs Caroline Newlands, Director of Community Asset and Localism, Civic Centre, New Street, Stourport-on-Severn DY13 8UJ ☎ 01562 732738 🖷 01299 879688 🖰 caroline.newlands@wyreforestdc.gov.uk

Leisure and Cultural Services: Ms Linda Collis, Director of Community Well-being and Environment, Civic Centre, New Street, Stourport-on-Severn DY13 8UJ ☎ 01562 732900 🖷 01299 879688 🖰 linda.collis@wyreforestdc.gov.uk

Leisure and Cultural Services: Ms Kay Higman, Cultural Services Manager, Green Street, Kidderminster DY10 1HA ☎ 01562 732902 🖷 01562 732938 🖰 kay.higman@wyreforestdc.gov.uk

Licensing: Mr Mike Parker, Director of Economic Prosperity and Place, Duke House, Clensmore Street, Kidderminster DY10 2JX ☎ 01562 732928 🖷 01562 732500 🖰 mike.parker@wyreforestdc.gov.uk

Lottery Funding, Charity and Voluntary: Mrs Lesley Fox, Community Development Manager, Green Street, Kidderminster DY10 1HA ☎ 01562 732976 🖷 01562 732905 🖰 lesley.fox@wyreforestdc.gov.uk

Member Services: Ms Penelope Williams, Democratic Services Manager, Civic Centre, New Street, Stourport-on-Severn DY13 8UJ ☎ 01562 732728 🖷 01299 879688 🖰 penolope.williams@wyreforestdc.gov.uk

Parking: Ms Susan Winmill, Environmental Maintenance Manager, Green Street, Kidderminster DY10 1HA ☎ 01562 732962 🖰 susan.winmill@wyreforestdc.gov.uk

Partnerships: Ms Lucy Bennett, Wyre Forest Matters Partnerships Manager, Green Street, Kidderminster DY10 1HA ☎ 01562 732909 🖰 lucy.bennett@wyreforestdc.gov.uk

Personnel / HR: Ms Ann-Marie Lockley, Human Resources Manager, Civic Centre, New Street, Stourport-on-Severn DY13 8UJ ☎ 01562 732773 🖷 01562 732790 🖰 ann-marie.lockley@wyreforestdc.gov.uk

Planning: Mr John Baggot, Development Manager, Duke House, Clensmore Street, Kidderminster DY10 2JX ☎ 01562 732515 🖷 01562 732556 🖰 john.baggot@wyreforestdc.gov.uk

Procurement: Mr David Tirebuck, Procurement Officer, Duke House, Clensmore Street, Kidderminster DY10 2JX ☎ 01562 732102 🖷 01562 732104 🖰 david.tirebuck@wyreforest.gov.uk

Recycling & Waste Minimisation: Mr Steve Brant, Environmental Services Manager, Green Street, Kidderminster DY10 1HA ☎ 01562 732922 🖷 01562 732905 🖰 steve.brant@wyreforestdc.gov.uk

Regeneration: Mr Ken Harrison, Head of Economic Development and Regeneration, Duke House, Clensmore Street, Kidderminster DY10 2JX ☎ 01562 732928 🖷 01562 732557 🖰 ken.harrison@wyreforestdc.gov.uk

Street Scene: Ms Susan Winmill, Environmental Maintenance Manager, Green Street, Kidderminster DY10 1HA ☎ 01562 732962 🖰 susan.winmill@wyreforestdc.gov.uk

Sustainable Communities: Mr Mike Parker, Director of Economic Prosperity and Place, Duke House, Clensmore Street, Kidderminster DY10 2JX ☎ 01562 732928 🖷 01562 732500 🖰 mike.parker@wyreforestdc.gov.uk

Sustainable Development: Mr Mike Parker, Director of Economic Prosperity and Place, Duke House, Clensmore Street, Kidderminster DY10 2JX ☎ 01562 732928 🖷 01562 732500 ✉ mike.parker@wyreforestdc.gov.uk

Tourism: Mr Ken Harrison, Head of Economic Development and Regeneration, Duke House, Clensmore Street, Kidderminster DY10 2JX ☎ 01562 732928 🖷 01562 732557 ✉ ken.harrison@wyreforestdc.gov.uk

Town Centre: Ms Jackie Roberts, Town Centre Manager, Weavers Wharf Shopping Centre, Unit 13, Lower Mill Street, Kidderminster DY11 6UU ☎ 01562 732928 ✉ jackie.roberts@wyreforestdc.gov.uk

Waste Management: Mr Steve Brant, Environmental Services Manager, Green Street, Kidderminster DY10 1HA ☎ 01562 732922 🖷 01562 732905 ✉ steve.brant@wyreforestdc.gov.uk

MEMBERS OF THE COUNCIL (42)

Aston, John (CON - Aggborough and Spennells)
john.aston@wyreforestdc.gov.uk
Ballinger, Graham (O - Greenhill)
graham.ballinger@wyreforestdc.gov.uk
Bishop, Rose (CON - Offmore and Comberton)
rose.bishop@wyreforestdc.gov.uk
Brewer, Cliff (O - Mitton)
cliff.brewer@wyreforestdc.gov.uk
Campion, John-Paul (CON - Sutton Park)
john.campion@wyreforestdc.gov.uk
Clee, Stephen (CON - Bewdley and Arley)
sjclee@tinyonline.co.uk
Davies, Liz (O - Wribbenhall)
liz.davies@wyreforestdc.gov.uk
Desmond, Nathan (CON - Oldington and Foley Park)
nathan.desmond@wyreforestdc.gov.uk
Dyke, Helen (IND - Aggborough and Spennells)
helen.dyke@wyreforestdc.gov.uk
Dyke, Peter (IND - Aggborough and Spennells)
peter.dyke@wyreforestdc.gov.uk
Gale, Nicky (CON - Oldington and Foley Park)
nicky.gale@wyreforestdc.gov.uk
Glass, Brian (O - Lickhill)
brian.glass@wyreforestdc.gov.uk
Godwin, Douglas (CON - Rock)
douglas.godwin@wyreforestdc.gov.uk
Greener, Jenny (CON - Bewdley and Arley)
jennifer.greener@wyreforestdc.gov.uk
Hardiman, Ian (CON - Habberley and Blakebrook)
ian.hardiman@wyreforestdc.gov.uk
Harrison, Paul (CON - Greenhill)
paul.harrison@wyreforestdc.gov.uk
Hart, Marcus (CON - Sutton Park)
marcus.hart@wyreforestdc.gov.uk
Hart, John (CON - Wolverley)
john.hart@wyreforestdc.gov.uk
Hayward, Pauline (CON - Blakedown and Chaddesley)
pauline.hayward@wyreforestdc.gov.uk
Higgs, Vi (LAB - Areley Kings)
Hingley, Anne (CON - Franche)
anne.hingley@wyreforestdc.gov.uk
Ingham, Tim (LIB - Greenhill)
tim@tsmingham.co.uk
Kelly, Michael (LAB - Habberley and Blakebrook)
mike.kelly@wyreforestdc.gov.uk
Knowles, Nigel (LAB - Franche)
nigel.knowles@wyreforestdc.gov.uk
Martin, Howard (IND - Broadwaters)
hmartinhc@blueyonder.co.uk
McCann, Daniel (CON - Franche)
daniel.mccann@wyreforestdc.gov.uk
McFarland, Barry (LAB - Habberley and Blakebrook)
barry.mcfarland@wyreforestdc.gov.uk
Nicholls, Christopher (LAB - Cookley)
christopher.nicholls@wyreforestdc.gov.uk
Oborski, Fran (LIB - Offmore and Comberton)
fran.oborski@wyreforestdc.gov.uk
Onslow, Tracey (CON - Sutton Park)
tracey.onslow@wyreforestdc.gov.uk
Parish, Jim (O - Lickhill)
jparish@wyreforestdc.gov.uk
Phillips, Julian (CON - Bewdley and Arley)
julian.phillips@wyreforestdc.gov.uk
Price, Mike (LIB - Offmore and Comberton)
michael.price@wyreforestdc.gov.uk
Rayner, Mary (O - Broadwaters)
mary.rayner@wyreforestdc.gov.uk
Rogers, Chris (CON - Mitton)
Salter, Michael (CON - Mitton)
mike.salter@wyreforestdc.gov.uk
Sewell, Adrian (LAB - Broadwaters)
adrian.sewell@wyreforestdc.gov.uk
Shaw, James (LAB - Areley Kings)
cllrjshaw@hotmail.com
Sheppard, Dixon (O - Lickhill)
dixon.sheppard@wyreforestdc.gov.uk
Thomas, Nigel (O - Areley Kings)
nigel.thomas@wyreforestdc.gov.uk
Williams, Steven (CON - Blakedown and Chaddesley)
stephen.williams@wyreforestdc.gov.uk
Yarranton, Gordon (CON - Wribbenhall)
gordon.yarranton@wyreforestdc.gov.uk

POLITICAL COMPOSITION

CON: 21, O: 8, LAB: 7, LIB: 3, IND: 3

CABINET

Leader / Economic Prosperity: Mr John-Paul Campion
Deputy Leader / Environmental Services: Mr Marcus Hart
Community Wellbeing: Mr Ian Hardiman
Place Shaping: Mr Julian Phillips
Resources & Transformation: Mr Nathan Desmond

COMMITTEE CHAIRS

Audit: Mr Daniel McCann
Ethics & Standards: Mr Graham Ballinger
Licensing & Environment: Mr Paul Harrison
Planning Overview & Scrutiny: Mr Steven Williams

YORK, CITY OF U

City of York Council, City of York Council, The Guildhall, York YO1 9QN ☎ 01904 551550 🖷 01904 553560 💻 www.york.gov.uk

FACTS & FIGURES

Police Authority: North Yorkshire Police Authority
Health Authority: NHS Yorkshire & the Humber

Learning and Skills Council: Yorkshire and the Humber
Parliamentary Constituencies: York Central, York Outer
EU Constituencies: Yorkshire and the Humber
Election Frequency: Elections are of whole council
Twinning: Munster (Germany); Dijon (France)

PRINCIPAL OFFICERS

Chief Executive: Ms Kersten England, Chief Executive, City of York Council, Library Square, York YO1 7DU ☎ 01904 552000 🖱 kersten.england@york.gov.uk

Deputy Chief Executive: Mr Bill Woolley, Deputy Chief Executive & Director of City & Environmental Services, 9 St. Leonard's Place, York YO1 7ET ☎ 01904 551330 🖷 01904 551390 🖱 bill.wooley@york.gov.uk

Senior Management: Mr Pete Dwyer, Director of Adults, Children & Education, Mill House, North Street, York YO1 6JD ☎ 01904 554200 🖷 01904 554293 🖱 pete.dwyer@york.gov.uk

Senior Management: Mr Ian Floyd, Director of Customer & Business Support Services, City Finance Centre, Library Square, York YO1 7DW ☎ 01904 551100 🖷 01904 551190 🖱 ian.floyd@york.gov.uk

Senior Management: Mr Kevin Hall, Assistant Director of Facilities Management, School & Children's Strategy & Planning, Mill House, North Street, York YO1 6JD ☎ 01904 554207 🖱 kevin.hall@york.gov.uk

Access Officer / Social Services (Disability): Mr Graham Terry, Assistant Director of Adult Commissioning, Modernisation & Provision, 10-12 George Hudson Street, York YO1 6ZE ☎ 01904 554004 🖱 graham.terry@york.gov.uk

Architect, Building / Property Services: Ms Tracey Carter, Assistant Director of Finance, Asset Management & Procurement, 2 St Leonards Place, York YO1 7DU ☎ 01904 551127 🖱 tracey.carter@york.gov.uk

Building Control: Mr John Fowler, Head of Building Control & Property Information, 9 St. Leonard's Place, York YO1 7ET ☎ 01904 551380 🖷 01904 551390 🖱 john.fowler@york.gov.uk

Children / Youth Services: Mr Simon Page, Head of Integrated Youth Support Services, 10-12 George Hudson Street, York YO1 6LP ☎ 01904 554565 🖱 simon.page@york.gov.uk

Children / Youth Services: Mr Eoin Rush, Assistant Director of Children's Specialist Services, 10 - 12 George Hudson Street, York YO1 6LP ☎ 01904 551071 🖱 eoin.rush@york.gov.uk

Civil Registration: Mr Robert Livesey, Registration Service Manager, Register Office, 50 Bootham, York YO30 7DA ☎ 01904 553194 🖷 01904 638090 🖱 robert.livesey@york.gov.uk

PR / Communications: Mr Stewart Halliday, Head of Strategy, Partnerships & Communication, City of York Council, The Guildhall, York YO1 9QN ☎ 01904 553042 🖷 01904 552525 🖱 stewart.halliday@york.gov.uk

Community Planning: Ms Kate Bowers, Head of Neighbourhood Management Unit, 18 Back Swinegate, York YO1 8ZD ☎ 01904 551817 🖷 01904 551059 🖱 kate.bowers@york.gov.uk

Community Planning: Mr Charlie Croft, Assistant Director of Culture, Leisure & Public Realm, 18 Back Swinegate Court, York YO1 8DZ ☎ 01904 553371 🖱 charlie.croft@york.gov.uk

Community Safety: Ms Jane Mowat, Director of Safer York Partnership, York Centre for Safer Communities, Lower Friargate, York YO10 9SE ☎ 01904 669520 🖷 01904 669077 🖱 jane.mowat@york.gov.uk

Computer Management: Mr Roy Grant, Head of Information Technology, 4 Museum Street, York YO1 7FD ☎ 01904 551030 🖷 01904 551190 🖱 roy.grant@york.gov.uk

Consumer Protection and Trading Standards: Mr Colin Rumford, Head of Public Protection, 20 George Hudson Street, York YO1 6WR ☎ 01904 551502 🖷 01904 551590 🖱 colin.rumford@york.gov.uk

Consumer Protection and Trading Standards: Mr Steve Waddington, Assistant Director of Housing & Public Protection, 10 - 12 George Hudson Street, York YO1 6LP ☎ 01904 554016 🖱 steve.waddington@york.gov.uk

Contracts: Mr David Walker, Head of Financial Procedures, 2 St Leonard's Place, York YO1 7DU ☎ 01904 552261 🖱 david.walker@york.gov.uk

Customer Service: Ms Pauline Stuchfield, Assistant Director of Customers & Employees, 2 St Leonards Place, York YO1 7DU ☎ 01904 551190 🖱 pauline.stuchfield@york.gov.uk

Direct Labour: Ms Sally Burns, Director of Communities & Neighbourhoods, City of York Council, The Guildhall, York YO1 9QN ☎ 01904 552003 🖱 sally.burns@york.gov.uk

Economic Development: Ms Katie Stewart, Head of Economic Development, City of York Council, The Guildhall, York YO1 9QN ☎ 01904 554418 🖱 katie.stewart@york.gov.uk

Education: Ms Jill Hodges, Assistant Director of Education, Mill House, North Street, York YO1 6JD ☎ 01904 554207 🖱 jill.hodges@york.gov.uk

E-Government: Mr Ian Graham, Head of Performance & Innovation, 18 Back Swinegate, York YO1 8ZD ☎ 01904 553046 🖱 ian.graham@york.gov.uk

Electoral Registration: Mr Andrew Flecknor, Electoral Services Manager, City of York Council, The Guildhall, York YO1 9QN ☎ 01904 552032 🖷 01904 551052 🖱 andrew.flecknor@york.gov.uk

Emergency Planning: Mr Jim Breen, Emergency Planning Co-ordinator, 13 Swinegate Court West, York YO1 8AB ☎ 01904 551003 🖷 01224 551001 🖱 jim.breen@york.gov.uk

Energy Management: Mr David Warburton, Head of Design Conservation & Sustainable Development, 5 - 9 St Leonards Place, York YO1 7ET ☎ 01904 551312

🖱 david.warburton@york.gov.uk

Environmental / Technical Services: Mr Mike Slater, Assistant Director of City Development & Sustainability, 9 St. Leonard's Place, York YO1 2ET ☎ 01904 551300 🖱 mike.slater@york.gov.uk

Environmental Health: Mr Colin Rumford, Head of Public Protection, 20 George Hudson Street, York YO1 6WR ☎ 01904 551502 🖷 01904 551590 🖱 colin.rumford@york.gov.uk

Estates, Property & Valuation: Mr Philip Callow, Head of Asset & Property Management, 18 Back Swinegate, York YO1 8ZD ☎ 01904 553360 🖷 01904 553314 🖱 philip.callow@york.gov.uk

European Liaison: Ms Katie Stewart, Head of Economic Development, City of York Council, The Guildhall, York YO1 9QN ☎ 01904 554418 🖱 katie.stewart@york.gov.uk

Events Manager: Ms Gill Cooper, Head of Arts & Culture, 18 Back Swinegate, York YO1 8ZD ☎ 01904 554671 🖱 gill.cooper@york.gov.uk

Facilities: Mr Ian Asher, Head of Design Construction & Facilities Management, 18 Swinegate, York YO1 8ZT ☎ 01904 553379 🖱 ian.asher@york.gov.uk

Finance and Treasurer: Ms Tracey Carter, Assistant Director of Finance, Asset Management & Procurement, 2 St Leonards Place, York YO1 7DU ☎ 01904 551127 🖱 tracey.carter@york.gov.uk

Fleet Management: Mr Roger Ranson, Assistant Director of Highways, Fleet & Waste, 9 St Leonard's Place, York YO1 7ET ☎ 01904 551614 🖱 roger.ranson@york.gov.uk

Grounds Maintenance: Mr Dave Meigh, Parks & Open Spaces Officer, 18 Back Swinegate, York YO1 8ZT ☎ 01904 553386 🖷 01904 553378 🖱 dave.meigh@york.gov.uk

Health and Safety: Mr Johnathan Grainger, Health & Safety Manager, City of York Council, The Guildhall, York YO1 9QN ☎ 01904 554522 🖱 johnathan.grainger@york.gov.uk

Highways: Mr Andy Binner, Head of Highway Infrastructure, Hazel Court, James Street, York YO10 3DS ☎ 01904 613231 🖱 andy.binner@york.gov.uk

Highways: Mr Dave Carter, Head of Network Management, 9 St. Leonard's Place, York YO1 7ET ☎ 01904 551414 🖱 highway.regulation@york.gov.uk

Home Energy Conservation: Mr David Warburton, Head of Design Conservation & Sustainable Development, 5 - 9 St Leonards Place, York YO1 7ET ☎ 01904 551312 🖱 david.warburton@york.gov.uk

Housing: Mr Steve Waddington, Assistant Director of Housing & Public Protection, 10 - 12 George Hudson Street, York YO1 6LP ☎ 01904 554016 🖱 steve.waddington@york.gov.uk

Housing Maintenance: Mr Tom Brittain, Head of Housing Services, Hazel Court, James Street, York YO10 3DS ☎ 01904 551262 🖱 tom.brittain@york.gov.uk

Local Area Agreement: Mr Stewart Halliday, Head of Strategy, Partnerships & Communication, City of York Council, The Guildhall, York YO1 9QN ☎ 01904 553042 🖷 01904 552525 🖱 stewart.halliday@york.gov.uk

Legal: Mr Andrew Docherty, Assistant Director of Legal, Civic, Democratic & IT, City of York Council, The Guildhall, York YO1 9QN ☎ 01904 551127 🖱 andrew.docherty@york.gov.uk

Legal: Ms Melanie Perara, Deputy Head of Legal Services, City of York Council, The Guildhall, York YO1 9QN ☎ 01904 551087 🖱 melanie.perara@york.gov.uk

Leisure and Cultural Services: Mr Charlie Croft, Assistant Director of Culture, Leisure & Public Realm, 18 Back Swinegate Court, York YO1 8DZ ☎ 01904 553371 🖱 charlie.croft@york.gov.uk

Licensing: Mr Colin Rumford, Head of Public Protection, 20 George Hudson Street, York YO1 6WR ☎ 01904 551502 🖷 01904 551590 🖱 colin.rumford@york.gov.uk

Lifelong Learning: Mr Charlie Croft, Assistant Director of Culture, Leisure & Public Realm, 18 Back Swinegate Court, York YO1 8DZ ☎ 01904 553371 🖱 charlie.croft@york.gov.uk

Lighting: Mr Andy Binner, Head of Highway Infrastructure, Hazel Court, James Street, York YO10 3DS ☎ 01904 613231 🖱 andy.binner@york.gov.uk

Lottery Funding, Charity and Voluntary: Mr Adam Gray, Senior Partnership Support Officer, City of York Council, The Guildhall, York YO1 9QN ☎ 01904 551053 🖱 adam.gray@york.gov.uk

Member Services: Ms Dawn Steel, Head of Civic & Democratic Services, City of York Council, The Guildhall, York YO1 9QN ☎ 01904 551030 🖱 dawn.steel@york.gov.uk

Parking: Ms Liz Levett, Head of Environmental Enforcement & Parking Services, Hazel Court, James Street, York YO10 3DS ☎ 01904 553101 🖱 elizabeth.levett@york.gov.uk

Partnerships: Mr Stewart Halliday, Head of Strategy, Partnerships & Communication, City of York Council, The Guildhall, York YO1 9QN ☎ 01904 553042 🖷 01904 552525 🖱 stewart.halliday@york.gov.uk

Personnel / HR: Ms Pauline Stuchfield, Assistant Director of Customers & Employees, 2 St Leonards Place, York YO1 7DU ☎ 01904 551190 🖱 pauline.stuchfield@york.gov.uk

Planning: Mr Jonathan Carr, Head of Development Management, 9 St Leonards Place, York YO1 2ET ☎ 01904 551303 🖱 jonathan.carr@york.gov.uk

Planning: Mr Mike Slater, Assistant Director of City Development & Sustainability, 9 St. Leonard's Place, York YO1 2ET ☎ 01904 551300 🖱 mike.slater@york.gov.uk

Procurement: Mrs Zara Carter, Head of Procurement, 2 - 4 St

Leonards Place, York YO1 7EY ☎ 01904 552930
✉ zara.carter@york.gov.uk

Public Libraries: Ms Fiona Williams, Head of Libraries & Heritage, 18 Back Swinegate, York YO1 8ZD ☎ 01904 555631
✉ fiona.williams@york.gov.uk

Recycling & Waste Minimisation: Mr Russell Stone, Head of Neighbourhood Pride Services, Hazel Court, James Street, York YO10 3DS ☎ 01904 553108 ✉ russell.stone@york.gov.uk

Regeneration: Mr Mike Slater, Assistant Director of City Development & Sustainability, 9 St. Leonard's Place, York YO1 2ET ☎ 01904 551300 ✉ mike.slater@york.gov.uk

Road Safety: Mr Andrew Bradley, Sustainable Transport Operations Manager, 9 St Leonards Place, York YO1 7ET
☎ 01904 551404 ✉ andrew.bradley@york.gov.uk

Social Services (Adult): Mr Graham Terry, Assistant Director of Adult Commissioning, Modernisation & Provision, 10-12 George Hudson Street, York YO1 6ZE ☎ 01904 554004
✉ graham.terry@york.gov.uk

Social Services (Children): Mr Eoin Rush, Assistant Director of Children's Specialist Services, 10 - 12 George Hudson Street, York YO1 6LP ☎ 01904 551071 ✉ eoin.rush@york.gov.uk

Staff Training: Ms Tracy Walters, Head of Strategic Workforce Development, 20 George Hudson Street, York YO1 6WR ☎ 01904 551071 ✉ eoin.rush@york.gov.uk

Street Scene: Mr Russell Stone, Head of Neighbourhood Pride Services, Eco Depot, Hazel Court, James Street, York YO10 3DS
☎ 01904 553108 ✉ russell.stone@york.gov.uk

Sustainable Communities: Mr Mike Slater, Assistant Director of City Development & Sustainability, 9 St. Leonard's Place, York YO1 2ET ☎ 01904 551300 ✉ mike.slater@york.gov.uk

Sustainable Development: Ms Jacqui Warren, Sustainability Officer, 9 St. Leonard's Place, York YO1 7ET ☎ 01904 551666
🖷 01904 551390 ✉ jacqueline.warren@york.gov.uk

Tourism: Mr Charlie Croft, Assistant Director of Culture, Leisure & Public Realm, 18 Back Swinegate Court, York YO1 8DZ
☎ 01904 553371 ✉ charlie.croft@york.gov.uk

Town Centre: Mr Paul Barrett, City Centre Operations Manager, City Centre Office, Parliament Street, York YO1 8RH ☎ 01904 552272 🖷 01904 551677 ✉ paul.barrett@york.gov.uk

Traffic Management: Mr Dave Carter, Head of Network Management, 9 St. Leonard's Place, York YO1 7ET
☎ 01904 551414 ✉ highway.regulation@york.gov.uk

Transport: Mr Andrew Bradley, Sustainable Transport Operations Manager, 9 St Leonards Place, York YO1 7ET ☎ 01904 551404
✉ andrew.bradley@york.gov.uk

Transport: Ms Ruth Stephenson, Head of Sustainable Transport Service, 9 St Leonards Place, York YO1 2ET ☎ 01904 551372
✉ ruth.stephenson@york.gov.uk

Transport: Mr Richard Wood, Assistant Director of Strategic Planning & Transport, 9 St Leonards Place, York YO1 2ET
☎ 01904 551448 ✉ richard.wood@york.gov.uk

Transport Planner: Ms Ruth Stephenson, Head of Sustainable Transport Service, 9 St Leonards Place, York YO1 2ET ☎ 01904 551372 ✉ ruth.stephenson@york.gov.uk

Waste Collection and Disposal: Mr Roger Ranson, Assistant Director of Highways, Fleet & Waste, 9 St Leonard's Place, York YO1 7ET ☎ 01904 551614 ✉ roger.ranson@york.gov.uk

Waste Management: Mr Geoff Derham, Head of Waste, Cleaning & Fleet Services, Hazel Court, James Street, York YO10 3DS ☎ 01904 553111 ✉ geoff.derham@york.gov.uk

Waste Management: Mr Roger Ranson, Assistant Director of Highways, Fleet & Waste, 9 St Leonard's Place, York YO1 7ET
☎ 01904 551614 ✉ roger.ranson@york.gov.uk

Children's Play Areas: Mr Dave Meigh, Parks & Open Spaces Officer, 18 Back Swinegate, York YO1 8ZT ☎ 01904 553386
🖷 01904 553378 ✉ dave.meigh@york.gov.uk

MEMBERS OF THE COUNCIL (47)

***Leader of the Council:* Alexander**, James (LAB - Holgate)
cllr.jalexander@york.gov.uk

***Deputy Leader of the Council:* Simpson-Laing**, Tracy (LAB - Acomb)
cllr.tsimpson-laing@york.gov.uk

***Group Leader:* D'Agorne**, Andrew (GRN - Fishergate)
cllr.adagorne@york.gov.uk

***Group Leader:* Gillies**, Ian (CON - Rural West York)
cllr.igillies@york.gov.uk

***Group Leader:* Runciman**, Carol (LD - Huntington and New Earswick)
cllr.crunciman@york.gov.uk

Aspden, Keith (LD - Fulford)
cllr.kaspden@york.gov.uk

Ayre, Nigel (LD - Heworth Without)
cllr.nayre@york.gov.uk

Barnes, Neil (LAB - Hull Road)
cllr.nbarnes@york.gov.uk

Barton, George (CON - Wheldrake)
cllr.gbarton@york.gov.uk

Boyce, Barbara (LAB - Heworth)
cllr.bboyce@york.gov.uk

Brooks, Jenny (CON - Derwent)
cllr.jbrooks@york.gov.uk

Burton, Stephen (LAB - Westfield)
cllr.sburton@york.gov.uk

Crisp, Sonja (LAB - Holgate)
cllr.scrisp@york.gov.uk

Cunningham-Cross, Linsay (LAB - Skelton, Rawcliffe and Clifton Without)
cllr.lcunningham-cross@york.gov.uk

Cuthbertson, Ian (LD - Haxby and Wigginton)
cllr.icuthbertson@york.gov.uk

Doughty, Paul (CON - Strensall)
cllr.pdoughty@york.gov.uk

Douglas, Helen (LAB - Clifton)
cllr.hdouglas@york.gov.uk

Firth, Paul (LD - Haxby and Wigginton)
cllr.pfirth@york.gov.uk
Fitzpatrick, Fiona (LAB - Hull Road)
cllr.ffitzpatrick@york.gov.uk
Fraser, Sandy (LAB - Micklegate)
cllr.sfraser@york.gov.uk
Funnell, Christina (LAB - Heworth)
cllr.cfunnell@york.gov.uk
Galvin, John (CON - Bishopthorpe)
cllr.jgalvin@york.gov.uk
Gunnell, Julie (LAB - Micklegate)
cllr.jgunnell@york.gov.uk
Healey, Paul (CON - Rural West York)
cllr.phealey@york.gov.uk
Hodgson, Gerard (LAB - Dringhouses and Woodthorpe)
cllr.ghodgson@york.gov.uk
Horton, David (LAB - Acomb)
cllr.dhorton@york.gov.uk
Hyman, Keith (LD - Huntington and New Earswick)
cllr.khyman@york.gov.uk
Jeffries, Lynn (LAB - Westfield)
cllr.ljeffries@york.gov.uk
King, Kenneth (LAB - Clifton)
cllr.kking@york.gov.uk
Levene, David (LAB - Heslington)
cllr.dlevene@york.gov.uk
Looker, Janet (LAB - Guildhall)
cllr.jlooker@york.gov.uk
McIlveen, Neil (LAB - Skelton, Rawcliffe and Clifton Without)
cllr.nmcilveen@york.gov.uk
Merrett, David (LAB - Micklegate)
cllr.dmerrett@york.gov.uk
Orrell, Keith (LD - Huntingdon and New Earswick)
cllr.korrell@york.gov.uk
Potter, Ruth (LAB - Heworth)
cllr.rpotter@york.gov.uk
Reid, Ann (LD - Dringhouses and Woodthorpe)
cllr.areid@york.gov.uk
Richardson, Tony (CON - Haxby and Wigginton)
cllr.trichardson@york.gov.uk
Riches, Joseph (LAB - Holgate)
cllr.jriches@york.gov.uk
Scott, David (LAB - Clifton)
cllr.dscott@york.gov.uk
Semlyen, Anna (LAB - Dringhouses and Woodthorpe)
cllr.asemlyen@york.gov.uk
Steward, Chris (CON - Rural West York)
cllr.csteward@york.gov.uk
Taylor, Dave (GRN - Fishergate)
cllr.dtaylor@york.gov.uk
Warters, Mark (IND - Osbaldwick)
cllr.mwarters@york.gov.uk
Watson, Brian (LAB - Guildhall)
cllr.brianwatson@york.gov.uk
Watt, Joe (CON - Skelton, Rawcliffe and Clifton Without)
cllr.jwatt@york.gov.uk
Williams, Dafydd (LAB - Westfield)
cllr.dwilliams@york.gov.uk
Wiseman, Sian (CON - Strensall)
cllr.swiseman@york.gov.uk

POLITICAL COMPOSITION

LAB: 26, CON: 10, LD: 8, GRN: 2, IND: 1

CABINET

Leader: Mr James Alexander
Deputy Leader / Health, Housing & Adult Social Services: Ms Tracy Simpson-Laing
Corporate Services: Ms Julie Gunnell
Crime & Stronger Communities: Mr Dafydd Williams
Education, Children & Young People's Services: Ms Janet Looker
Environmental Services: Mr David Levene
Leisure, Culture & Tourism: Ms Sonja Crisp
Transport, Planning & Sustainability: Mr David Merrett

COMMITTEE CHAIRS

Audit & Governance: Ms Linsay Cunningham-Cross
Corporate & Scrutiny Management: Ms Sian Wiseman
Economic & City Development Overview & Scrutiny: Mr David Levene
Gambling, Licensing & Regulatory: Ms Barbara Boyce
Health Overview & Scrutiny: Ms Christina Funnell
Learning & Culture Overview & Scrutiny: Ms Ann Reid
Planning: Mr David Horton

County

District

LOCAL AUTHORITIES

London

Metropolitan

Unitary

Scottish Unitary

Welsh Unitary

Northern Ireland District